Wolniej proszę.	Slow down.
Wracaj!	Get back!
Wracaj.	Come back.
Wyjdź stąd!	Get out of here!
Zabłądziłem.	I'm lost.
Zaczekaj!	Wait!
Zamknij się!	Shut up!
Zatrzymać tego człowieka!	Stop that man!
Zatrzymaj wóz!	Pull over!
Zejdź mi z drogi!	Get out of the way!
Zostań tutaj.	Stay here.
Zostaw mnie w spokoju!	Leave me alone!

Regiony Polski / Regions of Poland

Administrative	Geographical	Location
Województwo dol…		…a and the South-Western …ower Silesia)
Województwo kuj…		…nd Toruń area …ntral)
Województwo lub…		…East)
Województwo lub…		…and Gorzów Wielkopolski …t)
Województwo łód…		…outh-Central)
Województwo ma…		…(South and the Tatra …)
Województwo ma…		…(Mazovia)
Województwo opo…		…outh)
Województwo pod…		…and the South-Eastern
Województwo pod…		…Suwałki area and …Eastern corner
Województwo pon…		…and the Northernmost tip (Pomerania)
Województwo śląskie	Śląsk	Katowice and Częstochowa area (Silesia)
Województwo świętokrzyskie	Świętokrzyskie	Kielce area (South)
Województwo warmińsko-mazurskie	Warmia-Mazury	Olsztyn area (Mazurian Lake District)
Województwo wielkopolskie	Wielkopolska	Poznań area (West-Central)
Województwo zachodniopomorskie	Pomorze Zachodnie	Szczecin and Koszalin area and the South-Western corner (West Pomerania)

POLISH-ENGLISH

POLSKO-ANGIELSKI

THE NEW KOSCIUSZKO FOUNDATION DICTIONARY

POLISH-ENGLISH

EDITOR-IN-CHIEF

JACEK FISIAK

VOLUME EDITORS

PIOTR GĄSIOROWSKI

MARCIN FEDER

MACIEJ MACHNIEWSKI

MARIUSZ IDZIKOWSKI

THE KOSCIUSZKO FOUNDATION, Inc.

15 East 65th Street

New York, N. Y. 10021

With Appreciation to
Foundation for Polish Science/
Fundacja na Rzecz Nauki Polskiej
Warsaw, Poland

First Edition

Printing House Towarzystwo Autorów i Wydawców Prac Naukowych UNIVERSITAS,
30-063 Kraków, al. 3 Maja 7
tel./fax (012) 634 51 07, 634 37 85, 423 47 69
e-mail box@universitas.com.pl
www.universitas.com.pl

ISBN 0-917004-27-2
ISBN 83-242-0007-X

POL/Ref
PG
6640
.N69
2003
v. 2

Production Editor
Wanda Lohman

Layout (cover and book jacket)
Ewa Gray

Photo on the book jacket
Christopher Gore

Composition and imposition
„QUAD"

Printed and binded
Białostockie Zakłady Graficzne S.A.

CONTENTS

PREFACE

In 1959 the Kosciuszko Foundation, an "American Center for Polish Culture" published an English-Polish dictionary followed in 1961 with a Polish-English volume. Authored by Professors Kazimierz Bulas, Francis J. Whitfield and Lawrence L. Thomas, the bilingual dictionary served as an overt example of the Foundation's long-standing mission of promoting and strengthening cultural, historical and scholarly understanding and friendship between the peoples of Poland and the United States. In many circles it became the Foundation's most widely known and recognized "calling card".

For more than four decades these two volumes filled the gap among serious bilingual dictionaries available for other languages in the United States serving generations of general readers, students, academics and translators on both sides of the Atlantic. During these years it was reprinted as many as thirteen times. It was not until 1998 that a project to publish a completely new dictionary was undertaken. The decision to produce a completely new bilingual dictionary was determined when it became evident that an update of the existing two-volume dictionary was neither feasible nor frankly practicable after a span of over forty years since their first publication. The world has changed rapidly during the last half of the twentieth century and the proliferation of new words and new meanings to existing words dictated the need for a totally new dictionary.

All of the lexicographic work was done in Poznań under the direction of Professor Jacek Fisiak, Head of the School of English of the Adam Mickiewicz University, who served as the project's Editor-in-Chief supervising the team of experienced, professional lexicographers and consultants. Mr Michał Jankowski, Head of Computer Center, School of English, Adam Mickiewicz University, served as Deputy Editor-in-Chief. Editor of the Polish-English volume was Professor Arleta Adamska-Sałaciak, Head of Department of Lexicography and Lexicology, School of English, Adam Mickiewicz University. Mr Mariusz Idzikowski was Editor of the Polish-English volume until his resignation in May, 2000 being replaced by Professor Piotr Gąsiorowski, Professor at the School of English of the Adam Mickiewicz University, who was assisted by Dr. Marcin Feder and Mr. Maciej Machniewski since June 2002. Assisting the Polish team of lexicographers for current American usage was a U.S. Advisory Committee consisting of Professor Michael J. Mikoś, University of Wisconsin-Milwaukee; Professor Robert A. Rothstein, University of Massachusetts at Amherst; Professor Oscar E. Swan, University of Pittsburgh and Professor Charles E. Townsend, Princeton University.

While the five year project was financed principally from the "Stanislaw Chylinski Endowment Fund" established at the Kosciuszko Foundation in 1974, the project's financing was assisted by a number of institutions and individuals whom we gratefully acknowledge.

A major grant provided by the "Fundacja na Rzecz Nauki Polskiej" ("Foundation for Polish Science") (FNP) of Warsaw, Poland was of great importance to the initiation of this project. We extend our gratitude to FNP's Board of Directors and its Officers for their support. In addition, we are most grateful to FNP's President, Professor Maciej W. Grabski, for his encouragement and belief in the project from the outset.

Significant corporate support in the United States was provided by the Polish National Alliance of Brooklyn, USA, the Polish-Slavic Federal Credit Union, Brooklyn, New York and the Rockefeller Foundation.

Financial assistance also was provided by the New England Chapter of the Kosciuszko Foundation; the Western New York Chapter of the Kosciuszko Foundation; the United Poles Federal Credit Union of Perth Amboy, New Jersey; Association of the Sons of Poland, Carlstadt, New Jersey; Śląska Wytwórnia Wódek Gatunkowych *Polmos* S.A. of Bielsko-Biała, Poland; the Central Council of Polish Organizations, Pittsburgh and the Polish Falcons Alliance of America, Pittsburgh, Pennsylvania.

Significant individual support was received from Joseph E. Gore, Esq. (Trustee of the Kosciuszko Foundation) and Eugenia F. Gore of Clifton, New Jersey; Dr. Irene S. Pyszkowski, Ph.D. (Trustee of the Kosciuszko Foundation) of Sparkill, New York; Mr. Witold S. Sulimirski (Chairman of the Board) of Bronxville, New York in memory of Professor Tadeusz Sulimirski and Janet F. and John Skibski of Northampton, Massachusetts. Also Mr. John Czaplinski of Brooklyn, New York; Tom and Kathy Podl, Sammamish, Washington; Mrs. Mildred H. Tyszka and Miss Helen Mary M. Tyszka of Garden City, New York individually and in memory of George S. Tyszka and Stanley J. & Helen Sleziak; Mr. Philip W. Cadieux, Farmingdale, New York and Mr. & Mrs. John and Elizabeth Chludzinski of Longwood, Florida contributed to the Project.

A special word of appreciation and gratitude for all the legal services and advice provided pro bono by the attorneys at White and Case W. Danilowicz, W. Jurcewicz i Wspólnicy – Kancelaria Prawna sp. k., Warsaw, Poland with respect to this project. Their unstinting assistance was provided always professionally and courteously.

All proceeds from the sale of the dictionary will be used to further the Kosciuszko Foundation's educational and cultural programs and activities.

August, 2003   Joseph E. Gore, Esq.
New York, New York   President and Executive
                                                                    Director

INTRODUCTION

The New Kosciuszko Foundation Dictionary came into being at the School of English, A. Mickiewicz University, Poznań, Poland between 1998 and 2002. Originally it was to be a corrected and updated version of *The Kosciuszko Foundation Dictionary* by Kazimierz Bulas, Francis J. Whitfield and Lawrence L. Thomas published in 1959–1961 and reprinted thirteen times until 1995. Shortly after the work on the new dictionary started it turned out that for a variety of reasons this idea had to be abandoned and an entirely new dictionary, 60 percent larger than the original one, would have to be produced. Numerous new lexical items, which have entered the language, would have to be added and many of the already existing meanings would have to be removed entirely as obsolete or replaced by new ones. It is worth pointing out that the old *Kosciuszko Foundation Dictionary* had slightly over 90,000 head-words. It was written between 1940 and 1945 and was originally based on *The Concise Oxford Dictionary* from 1938 and later updated on the basis of the 1951 edition of that dictionary and two American dictionaries from the forties of the last century.

The present dictionary contains over 140,000 head-words, 400,000 meanings and 100,000 idioms and fixed phrases. It is one of the largest English-Polish, Polish-English dictionaries ever published. The dictionary is primarily addressed to native speakers of Polish but it can also be successfully used by speakers whose native language is English. The richness of lexical information including not only everyday usage but also technical terminology, literary language, archaic words and expressions, etc. makes the dictionary an indispensable tool in the hands of the translator, the university student of English and the intermediate and advanced learner of the language.

The New Kosciuszko Foundation Dictionary is basically an American English dictionary although specific British usage as well as forms typical of other varieties of English have also been noted.

The framework of the English-Polish part of the dictionary was expanded and updated on the basis of numerous monolingual dictionaries and available databases including among others *Webster's Third New International Dictionary* (1993), *Longman Advanced American English Dictionary* (2000), *NTC's American English Learner's Dictionary* (1998), *Random House Webster's Dictionary of American English* (1997), *Cambridge Dictionary of American English* (2000), and *The Shorter Oxford Dictionary* (1993). Numerous English and English-Polish technical dictionaries have also been consulted.

The Polish framework has been prepared by a team of Polish lexicographers (Dr. Tomasz Lisowski, Dr. Jolanta Migdał, Dr. Grzegorz Skommer and Dr. Małgorzata Witaszek-Samborska) under the supervision of Mariusz Idzikowski, who have consulted the lexical databases for Polish available in Poznań as well as major dictionaries of the Polish language, including H. Zgółkowa *Praktyczny słownik współczesnej polszczyzny* (in progress), B. Dunaj *Słownik współczesnego języka polskiego* (1996), M. Szymczak *Słownik języka polskiego* (1978-1992) in addition to numerous Polish-English technical dictionaries.

Throughout the period of the preparation of the dictionary we have used the services of a number of consultants on both sides of the Atlantic whose names have been singled out on the front page of the present dictionary. They have either read parts or the whole of the dictionary. We owe them deep gratitude for their precious remarks concerning both details as well as more general issues.

Below we include some useful information on how to use *The New Kosciuszko Foundation Dictionary*.

USING THE DICTIONARY

Entries

An entry in the Polish-English volume of the dictionary consists of the headword, a grammatical indicator, one or more stylistic indicators, one or more English translations with semantic indicators (included in round brackets), phrases and idioms, e.g.,

afekt *mi* **1.** *psych.* affect **2.** (= *silne wzruszenie*) emotion, passion; **zbrodnia w afekcie** crime in passion.

Sometimes irregular grammatical forms of nouns or verbs are listed after the grammatical indicator, e.g.,

abordaż *mi Gen. pl.* **-y** *l.* **-ów** *hist. żegl. wojsk.* boarding.

Not all the elements listed above have to appear in each entry.

Headwords

The headword is the first element of a dictionary entry. It is the word you look up in a dictionary. Headwords are arranged alphabetically and are printed in **bold type,** e.g., **afekt** or **abordaż** above.

Stylistic indicators

Stylistic indicators appear in the entry after grammatical indicators. They serve to distinguish those meanings and uses of words which depart from the neutral style, e.g., *arch.* = archaic, *sl.* = slang or *pot.* = colloquial.

Phrases and idioms

Phrases and idioms are listed in various places in the entry.

Abbreviations, acronyms and proper names

Abbreviations, acronyms and proper names are all treated as headwords and listed alphabetically.

GRAMMATICAL INFORMATION IN THE POLISH-ENGLISH DICTIONARY

A simplified guide to Polish grammar with tables of Polish irregular verbs appears below after numbers.

Grammatical information appears after the part of speech and refers to the whole entry, i.e., all the senses as in **akademia** *f. Gen.* **-ii.** Inflections limited to one sense only may be placed in the middle of the entry.

Nouns

Only irregular forms have been listed in dictionary entries, e.g., vowel alternations as in **stół** *mi* **-o-** or irregular endings, e.g., **afisz** *mi Gen.* **-a** *Gen.pl.* **-ów** *l.* **-y.** Regular forms can be found in tables included in the guide to Polish grammar.

Adjectives

Adjectives are given in the form of the nominative singular masculine. Irregular comparative forms are provided after the headword and the grammatical indicators, as in **wysoki** *a. comp.* **wyższy**.

Verbs

A large number of Polish verbs occur in aspectual pairs. The imperfective form, however, is treated as basic and translated in such cases. If perfective forms have a specific meaning they are listed separately.

Only irregular forms are given in dictionary entries.

ABBREVIATIONS

przymiotnik	*a.*	adjective
skrót	*abbr.*	abbreviation
biernik	*Acc.*	accusative
strona czynna	*act.*	active voice
administracyjny	*admin.*	administrative
przysłówek	*adv.*	adverb
algebra	*alg.*	algebra
anatomia	*anat.*	anatomy
anglo-indyjskie	*Anglo-Ind.*	Anglo-Indian
antropologia	*antrop.*	anthropology
archeologia	*archeol.*	archeology
rodzajnik	*art.*	article
astrologia	*astrol.*	astrology
astronomia	*astron.*	astronomy
przydawka	*attr.*	attribute
australijskie	*Austr.*	Australian
Biblia	*Bibl.*	Bible
bibliotekarstwo	*bibl.*	library
biochemia	*biochem.*	biochemistry
biologia	*biol.*	biology
botanika	*bot.*	botany
brytyjskie	*Br.*	British
budownictwo	*bud.*	architecture
kanadyjskie	*Can.*	Canadian
chemia	*chem.*	chemistry
chirurgia	*chir.*	surgery
stopień wyższy	*comp.*	comparative
spójnik	*conj.*	conjunction
policzalny	*count.*	countable
czasem	*czas.*	sometimes
celownik	*Dat.*	dative
określony	*def.*	definite
stomatologia	*dent.*	dentistry
gwarowe	*dial.*	dialectal
zdrobnienie	*dimin.*	diminutive
dosłowne	*dosł.*	literal
drukarstwo	*druk.*	printing

dziecinne	*dziec.*	nursery
dziennikarstwo	*dzienn.*	journalism
ekologia	*ekol.*	environment
ekonomia	*ekon.*	economy
elektronika, elektrotechnika	*el.*	electronics, electricity
emfatyczne	*emf.*	emphatic
entomologia	*ent.*	entomology
eufemistyczne	*euf.*	euphemistic
żeński	*f.*	feminine
filozofia	*fil.*	philosophy
finanse	*fin.*	finance
fizyka	*fiz.*	physics
fizjologia	*fizj.*	physiology
fonetyka	*fon.*	phonetics
formalne	*form.*	formal
fotografia	*fot.*	photography
francuskie	*Fr.*	French
dopełniacz	*Gen.*	genitive
geologia	*geol.*	geology
geografia	*geogr.*	geography
geometria	*geom.*	geometry
głównie	*gł.*	mainly
górnictwo	*górn.*	mining
gramatyka	*gram.*	grammar
greckie	*Gr.*	Greek
handel	*handl.*	commerce
heraldyka	*her.*	heraldry
historia	*hist.*	history
hydrologia	*hydrol.*	hydrology
ichtiologia	*icht.*	ichtiology
narzędnik	*Ins.*	instrumental
tryb rozkazujący	*imp.*	imperative
indyjskie	*Ind.*	Indian
nieokreślony	*indef.*	indefinite
bezokolicznik	*inf.*	infinitive
wykrzyknik	*int.*	interjection
introligatorstwo	*introl.*	bookbinding
czasownik niedokonany	*ipf.*	imperfective verb
irlandzkie	*Ir.*	Irish
ironiczne	*iron.*	ironic
włoskie	*It.*	Italian
jeździectwo	*jeźdz.*	horse-riding
językoznawstwo	*jęz.*	linguistics
jak wyżej	*jw.*	ditto
kartografia	*kartogr.*	cartography
kolejnictwo	*kol.*	railroads
komputery	*komp.*	computers
kościół	*kośc.*	church
krystalografia	*krystal.*	crystallography
kulinarne	*kulin.*	culinary
kynologia	*kynol.*	cynology
lub	*l.*	or
łacińskie	*Lat.*	Latin

leśnictwo	*leśn.*	forestry
literackie	*lit.*	literary
miejscownik	*Loc.*	locative
logika	*log.*	logic
lotnictwo	*lotn.*	aviation
męski	*m.*	masculine
rzeczownik męski ożywiony	*ma*	masculine animate noun
malarstwo	*mal.*	painting
matematyka	*mat.*	mathematics
mechanika	*mech.*	mechanics
medycyna	*med.*	medicine
metafizyka	*metafiz.*	metaphysics
metalurgia	*metal.*	metallurgy
meteorologia	*meteor.*	meteorology
rzeczownik męski nieożywiony	*mi*	masculine inanimate noun
miernictwo	*miern.*	surveying
mineralogia	*min.*	mineralogy
mitologia	*mit.*	mythology
motoryzacja	*mot.*	motorization, automobiles
rodzaj męski osobowy	*mp*	masculine personal noun
muzyka	*muz.*	music
myślistwo	*myśl.*	hunting
rzeczownik nijaki	*n.*	neuter noun
przeczenie	*neg.*	negative
rodzaj nijaki	*neut.*	neuter
nieosobowy	*nieos.*	impersonal
mianownik	*Nom.*	nominative
liczebnik	*num.*	numeral
obelżywe	*obelż.*	abusive
obsceniczne	*obsc.*	obscene
ogrodnictwo	*ogr.*	gardening
onomatopeiczne	*onomat.*	onomatopoeic
optyka	*opt.*	optics
ornitologia	*orn.*	ornithology
osoba	*os.*	person
się	*o.s.*	oneself
paleontologia	*paleont.*	paleontology
parlament	*parl.*	parliament
imiesłów	*part.*	participle
strona bierna	*pass.*	passive
patologia	*pat.*	pathology
czasownik dokonany	*pf.*	perfective verb
liczba mnoga	*pl.*	plural
południe	*płd.*	south
północ	*płn.*	north
poetyckie	*poet.*	poetic
pogardliwe	*pog.*	contemptuous
polityka	*polit.*	politics
porównaj	*por.*	compare
potoczne	*pot.*	colloquial
imiesłów bierny	*pp.*	past participle
prawo	*prawn.*	law
orzecznikowy	*pred.*	predicative

prefiks	*pref.*	prefix
przyimek	*prep.*	preposition
czas przeszły	*pret.*	preterite
zaimek	*pron.*	pronoun
przenośne	*przen.*	metaphorical
psychologia	*psych.*	psychology
pytające	*pyt.*	interrogative
religia	*rel.*	religion
retoryka	*ret.*	rhetoric
rolnictwo	*roln.*	agriculture
rybołówstwo, wędkarstwo	*ryb.*	fishing, angling
rzymskokatolicki	*rz.-kat.*	Roman Catholic
południowoafrykańskie	*S.Afr.*	South African
ktoś	*sb*	somebody
szkockie	*Scot.*	Scottish
liczba pojedyncza	*sing.*	singular
slang	*sl.*	slang
socjologia	*socjol.*	sociology
hiszpańskie	*Sp.*	Spanish
statystyka	*stat.*	statistics
coś	*sth*	something
stolarstwo	*stol.*	woodwork
stopień najwyższy	*sup.*	superlative
szermierka	*szerm.*	fencing
szkolny	*szkoln.*	school
także	*t.*	also
technika	*techn.*	technology
telekomunikacja	*tel.*	telecommunications
telewizja	*telew.*	television
teologia	*teol.*	theology
teoria	*teor.*	theory
tkactwo, tkaniny	*tk.*	weaving, fabrics
ubezpieczenia	*ubezp.*	insurance
ujemne	*uj.*	pejorative
uniwersytet	*uniw.*	university
amerykańskie	*US*	American
czasownik	*v.*	verb
wołacz	*Voc.*	vocative
w złożeniach	*w złoż.*	in compounds
wersyfikacja	*wers.*	versification
weterynaria	*wet.*	veterinary medicine
wojskowość	*wojsk.*	military (system, affairs)
wulgarne	*wulg.*	vulgar
wyjątek	*wyj.*	exception
zobacz	*zob.*	see
zoologia	*zool.*	zoology
zwykle	*zw.*	usually
zwłaszcza	*zwł.*	especially
żartobliwe	*żart.*	jocular
żegluga	*żegl.*	sailing

POLISH PRONUNCIATION

Vowels

Vowels are inherently short in Polish unlike in English where some vowels are long (e.g., heat) and some are short (e.g., hit). However, when stressed Polish vowels tend to be longer.

Polish has two nasal vowels, i.e., [õ] and [ẽ], as in kląć and kęs. In informal speech ą is pronounced as [õ] before [s z ʃ ʒ ç ʑ f v x], as in wąs, brązowy, ukąszenie, wiążesz, siąść, wąziutki, wziąwszy, wąwóz, wąchać. [õ] is pronounced [on] in front of [t d ts dz tʃ dʒ], e.g., kąt, mądry, chcąc, żądza, mączka. ą is pronounced [oŋ] in front of [k g], as in mąka and ciągi. [õ] changes into [om] before [p b], e.g., stąpać, rąbać. [ẽ] is pronounced in informal speech in front of [s z ʃ ʒ ç ʑ x], e.g., mięso, więzy, węszyć, węże, gęś, więźba, węch. [ẽ] is pronounced [en] before [t d ts dz tʃ], as in pręt, będę, ręce, nędza, męczyć. [ẽ] changes into [eŋ] in front of [k g], e.g., ręka, węgorz. ę is pronounced [em] in front of [p b], e.g., kępa, bęben. In word-final position [ẽ] is pronounced [e], e.g., robię.

There are no diphthongs in Polish. Two consecutive vowels belong to two different syllables.

Consonants

Polish has both palatal and palatalized consonants. [ɲ], as in skroń is a palatal consonant. 'Hard' consonants [p b k g m l f v x] have palatalized ('soft') counterparts which in spelling are marked by the 'softening' vowel letter i, as in piasek, bieda, kielich, Giewont, mienie, liana, fiasko, wiać, hierarcha. The palatalized consonants are articulated approximately like their 'hard' counterparts with simultaneous [j].

In Polish there are ten pairs of voiced and voiceless consonants:

voiced: [b d g v z ʒ ʑ dz dʒ dʑ],
voiceless: [p t k f s ʃ ç ts tʃ tç].

In the word-final position voiced consonants change into voiceless, e.g., Gen.pl. wód [vut] (cf. Nom.sg. woda [voda]).

A voiced consonant before a voiceless one becomes voiceless, e.g., wódka [vutka] vs. wóda [vuda].

Polish consonants [p t k] are unaspirated before stressed vowels, i.e., they are pronounced without a slight puff of air unlike as in English, as in pop, tak, koń.

The pronunciation of vowels

Symbol	Spelling	Polish example	English example/explanation
[i]	i	kit	Keats
[ɪ]	y	byt	bit
[e]	e	netto	net
[a]	a	mat	pronounced like the beginning of the diphthong in 'my' [mai]
[o]	o	kot	taught (but shorter)
[u]	u, ó	but, lód	boot, loot (but shorter)
[ẽ]	ę	kęs	see above **vowels**
[õ]	ą	wąż	see above **vowels**

The pronunciation of consonants

Symbol	Spelling	Polish example	English example/explanation
[b]	b	byt	bit
[b']	bi	biały	*see above* **consonants**
[p]	p, b	pył, łeb	pill, hip
[p']	pi	piana	*see above* **consonants**
[d]	d	daj	die
[t]	t, d	ten, nad	ten, art
[g]	g	gaj	gay
[g']	gi	Giewont	*see above* **consonants**
[k]	k, g	kat, Bug	cat, Luke
[k']	ki	kieł	*see above* **consonants**
[v]	w	wół	veal
[v']	wi	wiek	*see above* **consonants**
[f]	f, w	fala, chlew	fall
[f']	fi	fiasko	*see above* **consonants**
[s]	s, z	set, bez	set
[z]	z	za	zealot
[ʃ]	sz, ż, rz	szata, aż, malarz	shake
[ʒ]	ż, rz	żaba, rzeka	measure
[ɕ]	si, ś, ź	siano, śmiech, więź	pronounced 'softer' than [ʃ] in *she*
[ʑ]	zi, ź	zioło, bluźnić	pronounced 'softer' than [ʒ] in *measure*
[ts]	c, dz	cena, widz	tsetse
[dz]	dz	dzwon	adze
[tʃ]	cz, dż	czek, gwiżdż	check, catch
[dʒ]	dż	dżem	gem
[tɕ]	ci, ć, dź	cień, pić, wejdź	pronounced 'softer' than [tʃ] in *cheap*
[dʑ]	dzi, dź	dzięki, wiedźma	pronounced 'softer' than [dʒ] in *jam*
[r]	r	rak, chór	pronounced like the rolled Scots 'r' in all positions in the word
[l]	l	las	like
[l']	li	lipa	leap
[m]	m	maj	mine
[m']	mi	mieć	mean
[n]	n	nad	north
[ɲ]	ni, ń	nie, cień	'soft' [n]
[w]	ł	łup	wood
[j]	j	jak	yet
[x]	h, ch	hołd, cham	hard
[x']	hi, chi	hipis, chimera	*see above* **consonants**

NUMBERS

LICZEBNIKI GŁÓWNE		CARDINAL NUMBERS
jeden	1	one
dwa	2	two
trzy	3	three
cztery	4	four
pięć	5	five
sześć	6	six
siedem	7	seven
osiem	8	eight
dziewięć	9	nine
dziesięć	10	ten

jedenaście	11	eleven
dwanaście	12	twelve
trzynaście	13	thirteen
czternaście	14	fourteen
piętnaście	15	fifteen
szesnaście	16	sixteen
siedemnaście	17	seventeen
osiemnaście	18	eighteen
dziewiętnaście	19	nineteen
dwadzieścia	20	twenty
dwadzieścia jeden	21	twenty-one
dwadzieścia dwa	22	twenty-two
trzydzieści	30	thirty
czterdzieści	40	forty
pięćdziesiąt	50	fifty
sześćdziesiąt	60	sixty
siedemdziesiąt	70	seventy
osiemdziesiąt	80	eighty
dziewięćdziesiąt	90	ninety
sto	100	one hundred
sto jeden	101	one hundred and one
dwieście	200	two hundred
trzysta	300	three hundred
czterysta	400	four hundred
pięćset	500	five hundred
tysiąc	1,000	one thousand
milion	1,000,000	one million
miliard	1,000,000,000	one billion

LICZEBNIKI ZBIOROWE   COLLECTIVE NUMERALS

dwoje	2	two
troje	3	three
czworo	4	four
pięcioro	5	five
sześcioro	6	six
siedmioro	7	seven

LICZEBNIKI PORZĄDKOWE   ORDINAL NUMBERS

1.	pierwszy	1st	first
2.	drugi	2nd	second
3.	trzeci	3rd	third
4.	czwarty	4th	fourth
5.	piąty	5th	fifth
6.	szósty	6th	sixth
7.	siódmy	7th	seventh
8.	ósmy	8th	eighth
9.	dziewiąty	9th	ninth
10.	dziesiąty	10th	tenth
11.	jedenasty	11th	eleventh
12.	dwunasty	12th	twelfth
13.	trzynasty	13th	thirteenth

14.	czternasty	14th	fourteenth
15.	piętnasty	15th	fifteenth
16.	szesnasty	16th	sixteenth
17.	siedemnasty	17th	seventeenth
18.	osiemnasty	18th	eighteenth
19.	dziewiętnasty	19th	nineteenth
20.	dwudziesty	20th	twentieth
21.	dwudziesty pierwszy	21st	twenty-first
30.	trzydziesty	30th	thirtieth
40.	czterdziesty	40th	fortieth
50.	pięćdziesiąty	50th	fiftieth
60.	sześćdziesiąty	60th	sixtieth
70.	siedemdziesiąty	70th	seventieth
80.	osiemdziesiąty	80th	eightieth
90.	dziewięćdziesiąty	90th	ninetieth
100.	setny	100th	one hundredth
101.	sto pierwszy	101st	one hundred-and-first
1000.	tysiączny	1,000th	one thousandth
1 000 000.	milionowy	1,000,000th	one millionth
1 000 000 000.	miliardowy	1,000,000,000th	one billionth

UŁAMKI

pół, połowa	1/2
jedna trzecia	1/3
jedna czwarta	1/4
jedna piąta	1/5
trzy czwarte	3/4
dwie trzecie	2/3
półtora	1 1/2
pięć dziesiątych	0,5
trzy przecinek cztery	3,4
sześć przecinek osiemdziesiąt dziewięć	6,89
dziesięć procent	10%
sto procent	100%

FRACTIONS

one half	1/2
one third	1/3
one quarter	1/4
one fifth	1/5
three quarters	3/4
two thirds	2/3
one and a half	1 1/2
zero point five	0.5
three point four	3.4
six point eight nine	6.89
ten percent	10%
one hundred percent	100%

GUIDE TO POLISH GRAMMAR WITH TABLES
OF POLISH IRREGULAR FORMS
by Mariusz Idzikowski (revised by Piotr Gąsiorowski)

NOUNS

Gender
A Polish noun has one of three genders: masculine, feminine, or neuter. In most cases the gender of a noun is determinable by its ending:
- masculine: a consonant (e.g. **człowiek** 'man', **dom** 'house', **wilk** 'wolf')
- feminine: **-a, -i** (e.g. **kobieta** 'woman', **pani** 'Mrs')
- neuter: **-o, -e, -ę, -um** (e.g. **dziecko** 'child', **zdanie** 'sentence', **cielę** 'calf', **muzeum** 'museum')

Exceptions to this rule include masculine nouns ending in **-a** (e.g. **artysta** 'artist') or **-o** (e.g. **dziadzio** 'grandpa'), as well as feminine nouns ending in a consonant (e.g. **noc** 'night', **twarz** 'face').

The gender of a particular noun is significant since it determines, among other things, the ending of a qualifying adjective:

duży dom 'a large house'
duża suma 'a large amount'
duże krzesło 'a large chair'.

Declension

There are seven cases (nominative, genitive, dative, accusative, instrumental, locative and vocative) and two numbers (singular and plural) in the declension of Polish nouns. Since most endings are quite regular for each gender, they are not shown in this dictionary.

Irregular forms are given in smaller print before the gender information or, when limited to a specific sense of the word, inside the entry:

kot *ma Dat.sg.* **-u** ...

The following tables show noun endings assumed by default to be regular for each gender.

MASCULINE

Case	Singular		Plural	
	ma	*mi*	*mp*	*others*
Nom.	*always shown in noun entry*		**-i, -y, -owie**	**-y, -i**
Gen.	**-a**	**-u**	**-ów**	
Dat.	**-ow**		**-om**	
Acc.	*= Gen.sg.*	*= Nom.sg.*	*= Gen.pl.*	*= Nom.pl.*
Ins.	**-em**		**-ami**	
Loc.	**-ie, -u**		**-ach**	
Voc.	*= Loc.sg.*		*= Nom.pl.*	

Masculine animate nouns (*ma*) are those designating living persons or animals, masculine inanimate nouns (*mi*) those representing objects, plants and abstract ideas. Masculine personal nouns (*mp*) are those representing male human beings.

FEMININE

Case	Singular		Plural	
	Nom.sg. in **-a**	*Nom.sg. in a consonant*	*Nom.sg. in* **-a**	*Nom.sg. in a consonant*
Nom.	*always shown in noun entry*		**-y, -i**	
Gen.	**-y, -i**		*no ending*	*= Gen.sg.*

Dat.		**-ie, -i**	**-om**
Acc.	**-ę**	*no ending*	*= Nom.pl.*
Ins.		**-ą**	**-ami**
Loc.		*= Dat.sg.*	**-ach**
Voc.	**-o**	*= Gen.sg.*	*= Nom.pl.*

NEUTER

Case	Singular	Plural
Nom.	*always shown in noun entry*	**-a**
Gen.	**-a**	*no ending*
Dat.	**-u**	**-om**
Acc.	*= Nom.sg.*	*= Nom.pl.*
Ins.	**-em**	**-ami**
Loc.	**-u**	**-ach**
Voc.	*= Nom.sg.*	*= Nom.pl.*

ADJECTIVES

Adjective endings do not present major problems. They are declined according to the following pattern:

Case	Singular			Plural
	m.	*n.*	*f.*	
Nom.	**-y, -i**	**-e**	**-a**	**-e** (*mp* **-i, -y**)
Gen.	**-ego**		**-ej**	**-ich, -ych**
Dat.	**-emu**		**-ej**	**-im, -ym**
Acc.	*mi = Nom.sg.* *ma = Gen.pl.*	**-e**	**-ą**	*= Nom.pl.* (*mp = Gen.pl.*)
Ins.	**-im**	**-ym**		**-ą**
Loc.	*= Ins.sg.*		**-ej**	**-ich, -ych**
Voc.	*= Nom.sg.*		**-a**	*= Nom.pl.*

VERBS

Aspect

The majority of Polish verbs have two aspects, the imperfective for conveying the frequency of an action or describing a process, and the perfective for emphasis on a single action or a result. It follows that the perfective can only be used in the past and future, while the imperfective can also be used in the present tense.

Aspectual pairs can be differentiated either by the presence of a prefix in the perfective aspect, e.g., *pf.* **zrobić** 'do' (*ipf.* **robić**), by the presence of an infix in the imperfective aspect, e.g., *ipf.* **pokazywać** 'show' (*pf.* **pokazać**), or by a change in conjugation, e.g., *ipf.* **zaczynać** 'begin' (*pf.* **zacząć**).

It should be noted, though, that some aspectual pairs do not follow this pattern, for instance those that derive from different roots, e.g., **brać** 'take' (*pf.* **wziąć**). There are also a number of verbs, which exist in one aspect only, e.g., **pracować** 'work' (imperfective only), and some verbs which incorporate the two aspects in one form, e.g., **abdykować** 'abdicate'.

Aspect also determines the use of the imperative mood where, generally speaking, the perfective aspect is used in positive commands, while the imperfective is used in prohibitions, with the imperative form preceded by **nie**.

Conjugation

A Polish verb is conjugated according to one of four conjugation patterns. These are best described by the 1st and 2nd person singular present tense endings, which are always shown in verb entries in the dictionary (with the exception of 3rd-person-only verbs).

Conjugation	*1st p. sg.*	*2nd p. sg.*
I	**-ę**	**-esz**
II	**-ę**	**-isz/-ysz**
III	**-am**	**-asz**
IV	**-em**	**-esz**

The following tables show verb endings assumed by default to be regular and, as such, not shown in the dictionary:

NON-PAST (PRESENT OR FUTURE)

Person	*Singular*	*Plural*	
		Conjugations I and II	Conjugations III and IV
1st	*shown in verb entry*	= *3rd p. sg.* + **-my**	
2nd	*shown in verb entry*	= *3rd p. sg.* + **-cie**	
3rd	= *2nd p. sg.* (*without* **-sz**)	= *1st p. sg.* (*without* **-ę**) + **-ą**	= *1st p. sg.* (*without* **-m**) + **-ją**

IMPERATIVE (2nd person)

Group	Singular	Plural
-ę, -esz	= 2nd p. sg. non-past (without **-esz**)	= sg. + **-cie**
-ę, -isz	= 2nd p. sg. non-past (without **-isz**)	= sg. + **-cie**
-ę, -ysz	= 2nd p. sg. non-past (without **-ysz**)	= sg. + **-cie**
-am, -asz, -em, -esz	= 3rd p. sg. non-past (without **-ą**)	= sg. + **-cie**

PAST

Infinitive	3rd p. sg.			3rd p. pl.	
	m.	f.	n.	mp	others
-ać	**-ał**	**-ała**	**-ało**	**-ali**	**-ały**
-eć	**-ał**	**-ała**	**-ało**	**-eli**	**-ały**
-ić	**-ił**	**-iła**	**-iło**	**-ili**	**-iły**
-yć	**-ył**	**-yła**	**-yło**	**-yli**	**-yły**
-uć	**-uł**	**-uła**	**-uło**	**-uli**	**-uły**
-ąć	**-ął**	**-ęła**	**-ęło**	**-ęli**	**-ęły**
others	always shown in verb entries				

The 1st and 2nd person forms are formed by the addition of the following endings to the respective 3rd person forms:

Person	Singular		Plural
	m.	f.	
1st	**-em**	**-m**	**-śmy**
2nd	**-eś**	**-ś**	**-ście**

TABLES OF POLISH IRREGULAR FORMS

PRONOUNS

Table 1 (Personal pronouns, singular)

Nom.	ja	ty	on	ona	ono
Gen.	mnie	ciebie, cię	jego, niego, go	jej	niej
Dat.	mnie, mi	tobie, ci	jemu, niemu, mu	jej, niej	jemu, niemu, mu
Acc.	mnie	ciebie, cię	jego, niego, go	ją, nią	je
Ins.	mną	tobą	nim	nią	nim
Loc.	mnie	tobie	nim	niej	nim

Table 2 (Personal pronouns, plural)

Nom.	my	wy	oni	one
Gen.	nas	was	ich, nich	ich, nich
Dat.	nam	wam	im, nim	im, nim
Acc.	nas	was	ich, nich	je, nie
Ins.	nami	wami	nimi	nimi
Loc.	nas	was	nich	nich

Table 3 (Reflexive pronouns)

Nom.	–
Gen.	siebie, się
Dat.	sobie
Acc.	siebie, się
Ins.	sobą
Loc.	sobie

Table 4 (Interrogative/relative personal pronouns)

Nom.	kto	co
Gen.	kogo	czego

Dat.	komu	czemu
Acc.	kogo	co
Ins.	kim	czym
Loc.	kim	czym

(NB. Similarly with **nikt, nic, ktokolwiek, cokolwiek**, etc.)

Table 5 (Pronominal numerals)

Nom.	ile
Gen.	ilu
Dat.	ilu
Acc.	ile, ilu
Ins.	iloma
Loc.	ilu

(NB. Similarly with **wiele, niewiele, parę, kilka**, etc.)

Table 6 (Possessive interrogative pronouns)

	m.	f.	n.	pl. (mp)	pl. (others)
Nom.	czyj	czyja	czyje	czyi	czyje
Gen.	czyjego	czyjej	czyjego	czyich	czyich
Dat.	czyjemu	czyjej	czyjemu	czyim	czyim
Acc.	czyj, czyjego	czyją	czyje	czyich	czyje
Ins.	czyim	czyją	czyim	czyimi	czyimi
Loc.	czyim	czyją	czyim	czyich	czyich

(NB. Similarly with **niczyj, czyjś**)

Table 7 (Possessive pronouns, singular)

	m.	f.	n.	pl. (mp)	pl. (others)
Nom.	mój	moja	moje	moi	moje
Gen.	mojego	mojej	mojego	moich	moich
Dat.	mojemu	mojej	mojemu	moim	moim
Acc.	mój, mojego	moją	moje	moich	moje
Ins.	moim	moją	moim	moim	moim
Loc.	moim	mojej	moim	moich	moich

(NB. **twój** and the reflexive possessive pronoun **swój** are declined like **mój**)

Table 8 (Possessive pronouns, plural)

	m.	*f.*	*n.*	*pl. (mp)*	*pl. (others)*
Nom.	nasz	nasza	nasze	nasi	nasze
Gen.	naszego	naszej	naszego	naszych	naszych
Dat.	naszemu	naszej	naszemu	naszym	naszym
Acc.	nasz, naszego	naszą	nasze	naszych	nasze
Ins.	naszym	naszą	naszym	naszymi	naszymi
Loc.	naszym	naszej	naszym	naszych	naszych

(NB. **wasz** declines like **nasz**. The possessive forms **jego**, **jej**, **ich** are invariable)

Table 9 (Demonstrative pronouns)

	m.	*f.*	*n.*	*pl. (mp)*	*pl. (others)*
Nom.	ten	ta	to	ci	te
Gen.	tego	tej	tego	tych	tych
Dat.	temu	tej	temu	tym	tym
Acc.	ten, tego	tę	to	tych	te
Ins.	tym	tą	tym	tymi	tymi
Loc.	tym	tej	tym	tych	tych

(NB. Similarly with **tamten**, **tamta**, **tamto**, etc.)

Table 10 (Demonstrative pronouns implying distance)

	m.	*f.*	*n.*	*pl. (mp)*	*pl. (others)*
Nom.	ów	owa	owo	owi	owe
Gen.	owego	owej	owego	owych	owych
Dat.	owemu	owej	owemu	owym	owym
Acc.	ów (*ma* owego)	ową	owo	owych	owe
Ins.	owym	ową	owym	owymi	owymi
Loc.	owym	owej	owym	owych	owych

Table 11 (Indefinite pronouns)

Nom.	**ktoś**	**coś**
Gen.	**kogoś**	**czegoś**
Dat.	**komuś**	**czemuś**
Acc.	**kogoś**	**czegoś**
Ins.	**kimś**	**czymś**
Loc.	**kimś**	**czymś**

CARDINAL NUMERALS

Table 12

	m.	*f.*	*n.*	*pl. (mp)*	*pl. (others)*
Nom.	**jeden**	**jedna**	**jedno**	**jedni**	**jedne**
Gen.	**jednego**	**jednej**	**jednego**	**jednych**	**jednych**
Dat.	**jednemu**	**jednej**	**jednemu**	**jednym**	**jednym**
Acc.	**jeden** (*ma* **jednego**)	**jedną**	**jedno**	**jednych**	**jedne**
Ins.	**jednym**	**jedną**	**jednym**	**jednymi**	**jednymi**
Loc.	**jednym**	**jednej**	**jednym**	**jednych**	**jednych**

(NB. Similarly with **niejeden**)

Table 13a

	mp	*n., other m.*	*f.*
Nom.	**dwaj**	**dwa**	**dwie**
Gen.	**dwóch**	**dwóch, dwu**	**dwóch, dwu**
Dat.	**dwóm, dwom, dwu**	**dwóm, dwom, dwu**	**dwóm, dwom, dwu**
Acc.	**dwóch**	**dwa**	**dwie**
Instr.	**dwoma**	**dwoma**	**dwoma, dwiema**
Loc.	**dwóch, dwu**	**dwóch, dwu**	**dwóch, dwu**

(NB. Similarly with **obydwa**, etc.)

Table 13b

	mp	*n., other m.*	*f.*
Nom.	obaj	oba	obie
Gen.	obu	obu	obu
Dat.	obu	obu	obu
Acc.	obu	oba	obie
Ins.	oboma, obu	oboma, obu	oboma, obiema, obu
Loc.	obu	obu	obu

Table 14

	mp	*others*
Nom.	trzej	trzy
Gen.	trzech	trzech
Dat.	trzem	trzem
Acc.	trzech	trzy
Ins.	trzema	trzema
Loc.	trzech	trzech

(NB. Similarly with **cztery, czterej**)

Table 15

	mp	*others*
Nom.	pięciu	pięć
Gen.	pięciu	pięciu
Dat.	pięciu	pięciu
Acc.	pięciu	pięć
Ins.	pięcioma	pięcioma
Loc.	pięciu	pięciu

(NB. Similarly with **sześć, siedem, osiem, dziewięć**)

Table 16

	mp	*others*
Nom.	dziesięciu	dziesięć
Gen.	dziesięciu	dziesięciu
Dat.	dziesięciu	dziesięciu
Acc.	dziesięciu	dziesięć
Ins.	dziesięcioma	dziesięcioma
Loc.	dziesięciu	dziesięciu

(NB. Similarly with **pięćdziesiąt, sześćdziesiąt, siedemdziesiąt, osiemdziesiąt, dziewięćdziesiąt**)

Table 17

	mp	*others*
Nom.	jedenastu	jedenaście
Gen.	jedenastu	jedenastu
Dat.	jedenastu	jedenastu
Acc.	jedenastu	jedenaście
Ins.	jedenastoma	jedenastoma
Loc.	jedenastu	jedenastu

(NB. Similarly with **dwanaście, trzynaście, czternaście, piętnaście, szesnaście, siedemnaście, osiemnaście, dziewiętnaście, dwieście [dwustu]**)

Table 18

	mp	*others*
Nom.	dwudziestu	dwadzieścia
Gen.	dwudziestu	dwudziestu
Dat.	dwudziestu	dwudziestu
Acc.	dwudziestu	dwadzieścia
Ins.	dwudziestoma	dwudziestoma
Loc.	dwudziestu	dwudziestu

(NB. Similarly with **trzydzieści, czterdzieści, sto, trzysta, czterysta**)

Table 19

	mp	*others*
Nom.	pięciuset	pięćset
Gen.	pięciuset	pięciuset
Dat.	pięciuset	pięciuset
Acc.	pięciuset	pięćset
Ins.	pięciuset	pięciuset
Loc.	pięciuset	pięciuset

(NB. Similarly with **sześćset, siedemset, osiemset, dziewięćset**)

COLLECTIVE NUMERALS

Table 20

Nom.	dwoje
Gen.	dwojga
Dat.	dwojgu
Acc.	dwoje
Ins.	dwojgiem
Loc.	dwojgu

(NB. Similarly with **troje, oboje, obydwoje**)

Table 21

Nom.	czworo
Gen.	czworga
Dat.	czworgu
Acc.	czworo
Ins.	czworgiem
Loc.	czworgu

(NB. Similarly with **kilkoro, pięcioro**)

A

A, a *n. indecl.* **1.** (*litera*) A, a; **A jak Anna** A is for Alpha; A as in Alpha; **od a do z** from A to Z; **jeśli się powiedziało a, trzeba powiedzieć b** in for a penny, in for a pound *l.* in for a dollar. **2.** (*głoska*) a.

A¹ *n. indecl. muz.* A; **A-dur** A major; **a-moll** A minor.

A² *abbr.* (*fiz.*) A, amp; *zob.* **amper.**

a *conj.* **1.** (*łączy zdania wyrażające przeciwstawione sobie, ale związane ze sobą fakty*) and; while, whereas; **w kubku był sok, a w kieliszku wino** there was some juice in the mug, and some wine in the glass; **ja lubię ciebie, a ty mnie** I like you and you like me; **ty dyktujesz, a ja piszę** you dictate, and I'll write it down; **ty jesteś wesoły, a on smutny** you are merry, while *l.* whereas he is sad. **2.** (*wprowadza dodatkowe okoliczności lub dopowiedzenia*) **przeszliśmy przez ulicę, a pies szedł za nami** we crossed the street, and the dog was following us; **spał zdrowo, a jego dłonie mocno zaciskały się na poduszce** he was sound asleep, his hands clutching the pillow tightly; **spóźnisz się, a to jest źle widziane** you'll be late, and they don't like it; **statek poszedł na dno, a cała załoga wraz z nim** the ship foundered, and the whole crew with her. **3.** (*wyraża zaskoczenie lub zdziwienie*) **stary, a głupi** he's so old, and yet so foolish; **tylu was było, a (jednak) nikt mi nie pomógł** there were so many of you and *l.* but nobody helped me; **wyjechała, a (przecież) powinna była zostać** she left when she should have stayed; **uważa, że jest ważny, a (przecież) wcale tak nie jest** he thinks he's important, which is not so at all. **4.** (*charakteryzuje konsekwencje tego, o czym mówiono wcześniej*) **krzyknąłem, a on usłyszał i odwrócił się** I shouted, and he heard me and turned back; **przyjdź, a sam się przekonasz** come and you'll see for yourself. **5.** (*wyraża przeciwstawienie lub porównanie*) **ja pracuję, a on się bawi** I work and he plays *l.* while he plays; **ludzie a zwierzęta** humans and animals; humans versus animals; **zrób raczej mniej, a dokładniej** you'd better do less but more accurately. **6.** *arch. l. lit.* (= *i*) and; **dwa a dwa jest cztery** two and two makes four; **tak pewne, jak dwa a dwa cztery** (as) sure as eggs; **młoda a urocza** young and charming. **7. a nie** (*int.*) **pójdziemy do lekarza dzisiaj, a nie jutro** we'll see the doctor today, (and) not tomorrow; **to jest osioł, a nie koń** this is a donkey, (and) not a horse. **8. między** *l.* **pomiędzy... a...** between... and... **9.** (*poprzedza człony wyliczenia*) **a to... a to...** now... now...; **bę-**

dą pytać: a co, a gdzie, a jak? they will ask, what? where? how? **10.** (*w pytaniach*) **a ty?** and you?; how about you?; what about you?; **ja to widzę, a ty?** I can see it, can you?; **nie znam go, a ty?** I don't know him, do you? **11.** (*łączy wyrazy powtórzone dla wyrażenia nacisku*) **nic a nic** nothing at all; **nic a nic się nie boję/martwię** I'm not scared/worried in the least; **przykłady można by mnożyć a mnożyć** examples could be multiplied (ad infinitum); **wcale a wcale** not at all. **12.** (*łączy zaimki wskazujące, powtórzone dla wyrażenia nieokreśloności*) **taki a taki** such and such; **w tym a tym miejscu** at such and such a place; **nazywał się tak a tak** he was called so and so. **13.** (*w połączeniach z przysłówkami i spójnikami*) **a jednak** and yet; **a mianowicie** namely; **a mimo to** still, nevertheless, none the less; **a raczej** or rather; **a więc** (and) so, therefore; **a zwłaszcza** and in particular; **a co dopiero...** let alone..., not to mention...; **a już na pewno nie...** least of all...; **Bogiem a prawdą** truth to tell; **raz a dobrze** once for all. – *part.* **a bo co?** why (are you asking)?; **a bo ja wiem?** how (the hell) should I know?; **a cóż to takiego?** hey, what's that supposed to be?; **a jak sądzisz?** what do *you* think?; **a masz!** that's for you!; **a nie mówiłem?** didn't I tell you?; what did I tell you?; **a niech to!** shoot!, drat it!; **a niech to wszyscy diabli wezmą!** damn it!; **a to cudownie!** that's great!; wonderful!; brilliant!; **a to dopiero!** well, well, well!; **a to łajdak!** what a scoundrel!; **a to ci niespodzianka!** surprise, surprise!; **a to pech!** (that's) too bad!; **a niech tam!** what the heck!; **a dlaczegóżby nie?** why (ever) not?; **a widzisz?** see? (I was right); **a żeby cię!** damn you!; aha! – *int.* **1.** ah!, oh!, wow!, well!; **a, tu jesteście!** ah! here you are!; **a, wreszcie koniec pracy!** well, we've finished at last! **2.** (*w utartych wyrażeniach*) **a fe!** shame (on you)!; *żart. l. arch.* fie!; **a kuku!** peekaboo!; **a kysz!** *żart.* go away!; **a psik!** a(h)choo!; **a sio!** *pot.* go away!

abak *mi hist.* abacus.

abaka *f. techn.* Manila, Manila hemp.

abakus *mi Gen.* **-a** = **abak.**

abażur *mi Gen.* **-u** *l.* **-a** lampshade.

ABC, abc *n indecl.* (= *podstawy*) the ABCs *l.* ABC's; **ABC żeglarstwa** the ABCs of sailing.

abdominalny *a. anat., zool.* abdominal.

abdykacja *f.* abdication.

abdykacyjny *a.* (of) abdication; **akt abdykacyjny** *l.* **pismo abdykacyjne** the deed of abdication.

abdykować *ipf. l. pf.* **1.** abdicate; renounce *l.* relinquish the throne (*na czyjąś rzecz* to sb). **2.**

abdykować z urzędu *form.* resign from *l.* relinquish an office.

abecadło *n. Gen.* **-deł** *pot.* (= *alfabet*) **1.** alphabet. **2.** (= *podstawy*) the ABCs *l.* ABC's; **abecadło dobrego wychowania** the ABCs of good manners.

aberracja *f. form.* aberration; **aberracja myślowa** *form.* mental aberration; **aberracja chromosomów** *biol.* chromosomal aberration; **aberracja chromatyczna/sferyczna** *opt., astron.* chromatic/spherical aberration; **aberracja światła** *astron.* aberration of light.

aberracyjny *a. astron.* aberrational; **ruch aberracyjny** apparent motion.

abiogeneza *f. biol.* abiogenesis.

abiogenny *a. biol.* abiogenic.

abisal *mi geogr.* abyss.

abisalny *a. hydrol. i ekol.* abyssal; **strefa/fauna abisalna** abyssal zone/fauna.

Abisyńczyk *mp*, **Abisynka** *f. Gen.pl.* **-ek** *mp* Abyssinian.

abisyński *a.* Abyssinian; **kot abisyński** Abyssinian (cat).

abiturient *mp*, **abiturientka** *f. Gen.pl.* **-ek** graduate.

ablacja *f. med., techn., geol.* ablation.

ablatiwus *mi Gen.* **-wu** *jęz.* ablative.

ablaut *mi jęz.* ablaut, vowel gradation.

ablucja *f.* ablution; **dokonać ablucji** perform one's ablutions.

abnegacja *f.* **1.** *form.* (= *wyrzeczenie*) abnegation. **2.** (= *brak dbałości o siebie*) self-abnegation, self-denial. **3.** *pot.* (= *niechlujstwo*) slovenliness, negligence.

abnegat *mp*, **abnegatka** *f. Gen.pl.* **-ek** *form.* **1.** abnegator. **2.** *pot.* (= *niechluj*) sloven.

abolicja *f. prawn.* abolition.

abolicjonista *mp*, **abolicjonistka** *f. Gen.pl.* **-ek** *prawn., hist.* abolitionist.

abolicjonizm *mi prawn.* abolitionism.

abominacja *f. lit.* abomination.

abonament *mi* subscription (*na coś* to sth); **abonament telewizyjny** service fee; **abonament telefoniczny** standing charges; **abonament filatelistyczny** philatelic standing order.

abonamentowy *a.* subscription.

abonent *mp*, **abonentka** *f. Gen.pl.* **-ek** subscriber; **rozmowa na koszt abonenta** collect call.

abonować *ipf.* subscribe (*coś* to sth).

aborcja *f. med.* abortion; **aborcja sztuczna** *pat.* induced abortion; **aborcja samoistna** *pat.* spontaneous abortion; miscarriage.

aborcyjny *a.* abortion; **klinika aborcyjna** *med.* abortion clinic; **prawo aborcyjne** *prawn.* abortion laws.

abordaż *mi Gen.pl.* **-y** *l.* **-ów** *hist., żegl., wojsk.* boarding; **atakować abordażem** *l.* **przez abordaż** board; **podchodzić do abordażu** lay the ship aboard.

abordażowy *a.* **oddział abordażowy** *wojsk.* boarding unit.

aborygen *mp*, **aborygenka** *f. Gen.pl.* **-ek** aborigine, aboriginal, autochthon; **Aborygen** (=

rdzenny mieszkaniec Australii) Aboriginal, native Australian, Aborigine.

aborygeński *a.* aboriginal; (= *dotyczący Aborygenów*) Aboriginal.

abradować *ipf. geol.* abrade.

Abraham *mp t. Bibl.* Abraham; **na łonie Abrahama** *żart.* (= *w niebie*) in Abraham's bosom.

abrakadabra *f.* **1.** (*zaklęcie*) abracadabra. **2.** *uj.* (= *coś mętnego, niezrozumiałego*) abracadabra, gibberish, mumbo jumbo.

abrazja *f. geol.* abrasion.

abrazyjny *a. geol.* abrasive.

abrewiacja *f. form.* abbreviation.

abrewiatura *f.* abbreviations.

abrogacja *f. prawn.* abrogation.

abrogować *ipf. prawn.* abrogate.

ABS *abbr.* (= *urządzenie antypoślizgowe*) ABS, antilock braking system.

absces *mi med.* abscess.

absencja *f.* absence; **absencja chorobowa** sick leave; **notoryczna absencja** absenteeism.

absolucja *f. prawn., rel.* absolution; **dostać/uzyskać absolucję** be given/granted absolution; **udzielić komuś absolucji** give absolution to sb, absolve sb.

absolut *mi fil.* the absolute.

absolutnie *adv.* **1.** (= *zupełnie*) absolutely, perfectly, completely, totally; **absolutnie (nie)** (*stanowczy zakaz*) absolutely not; it's out of the question; **miasto absolutnie mi nieznane** a town perfectly unknown to me, a town I am totally unfamiliar with; **twierdzenie absolutnie nieprawdziwe** a completely false claim. **2.** (= *niepodzielnie*) arbitrarily, in an absolute way, with unrestricted authority.

absolutność *f.* absoluteness.

absolutny *a.* **1.** (= *całkowity*) absolute, complete, total, utter; **absolutna bzdura** utter nonsense; **absolutne kłamstwo** absolute lie; **cisza absolutna** deadly silence; **absolutny rekord** absolute record; **mieć absolutne zaufanie do kogoś** trust sb absolutely; **masz absolutną rację** you're absolutely right; **absolutna większość** *prawn.* absolute majority. **2.** *fil.* (= *ostateczny*) ultimate, absolute; **prawda absolutna** the ultimate truth; **byt absolutny** the absolute (being/reality). **3.** *nauk., techn.* (= *bezwzględny*) absolute; **jasność absolutna** *astron.* absolute magnitude; **temperatura/wilgotność absolutna** *fiz.* absolute temperature/humidity; **słuch absolutny** *muz.* absolute pitch; **wygłos absolutny** *jęz.* absolute final position; **zero absolutne** *fiz.* absolute zero. **4.** *chem.* (= *bezwodny*) **alkohol/eter absolutny** absolute ether/alcohol. **5.** (= *nieograniczony*) absolute, unlimited, autarchic; **monarchia absolutna** absolute monarchy; **rządy absolutne** absolute rule; **władza absolutna** absolute power.

absolutorium *n. indecl. in sing. pl.* **-ria** *Gen.* **-riów 1.** *prawn., polit.* vote of approval. **2.** *uniw.* certificate of completion.

absolutysta *ma*, **absolutystka** *f. Gen.pl.* **-ek** *polit., fil.* absolutist.

absolutystyczny *a. polit., fil.* absolutist; **państwo absolutystyczne** absolute state.

absolutyzm *mi* **1.** *polit.* absolutism, despotism; **absolutyzm oświecony** enlightened despotism. **2.** *fil.* absolutism.

absolwent *mp* graduate, leaver, alumnus.

absolwentka *f. Gen.pl.* **-ek** graduate, leaver, alumna.

absorbent *mi chem.* absorbent.

absorber *mi Gen.* **-a** *chem.* absorber.

absorbować *ipf. form.* (= *pochłaniać*) absorb; **praca całkowicie mnie absorbowała** I was completely absorbed in my work, my work absorbed me completely; **absorbujące studia** absorbing studies; **absorbować energię** *fiz.* absorb energy; **gaz absorbowany** *chem.* absorbed gas.

absorpcja *f. chem., fiz.* absorption.

absorpcyjny *a. chem., fiz.* absorptive; **aparat absorpcyjny** absorber; **widmo absorpcyjne** absorption spectrum.

abstrahować *ipf.* **1.** disregard, ignore (*od czegoś* sth); **abstrahując od czegoś** aside *l.* apart from sth. **2.** *fil.* abstract.

abstrakcja *f. fil., sztuka t. pot.* (= *coś nierealnego*) abstraction.

abstrakcjonista *mp*, **abstrakcjonistka** *f. Gen.pl.* **-ek** *sztuka* abstractionist.

abstrakcjonistyczny *a. sztuka* abstract; **sztuka abstrakcjonistyczna** abstract art.

abstrakcjonizm *mi sztuka* abstractionism.

abstrakcyjnie *adv.* abstractly, in the abstract; **myśleć abstrakcyjnie** think in abstract terms.

abstrakcyjność *f.* abstractness.

abstrakcyjny *a.* abstract; **abstrakcyjny pomysł** (= *mrzonka*) abstract idea; **myślenie abstrakcyjne** abstract thinking; **pojęcie abstrakcyjne** abstract notion; **sztuka abstrakcyjna** *sztuka* abstract art.

abstrakt *mi form. l. fil.* abstract.

abstynencja *f.* abstinence; **żyć w abstynencji** live a life of abstinence; **abstynencja od wódki** abstinence, teetotalism; **abstynencja seksualna** celibacy; **zachowywać abstynencję** abstain, refrain (*od czegoś* from sth).

abstynent *mp*, **abstynentka** *f. Gen.pl.* **-ek** abstainer, teetotaler.

absurd *mi* absurdity; (= *nonsens, bzdura*) nonsense, rubbish; **doprowadzić do absurdu** reduce (sth) to absurdity; **coś sprowadza się do absurdu** sth reduces *l.* is reduced to absurdity; **teatr absurdu** the theater of the absurd; **to absurd!** that's absurd!

absurdalnie *adv.* absurdly.

absurdalność *f.* absurdness, absurdity.

absurdalny *a.* absurd.

absyda *f.* **1.** *bud.* apse. **2.** *astron.* apsis.

absydalny *a. astron., bud.* apsidal.

absynt *mi* absinthe.

absztyfikant *mp żart.* wooer.

abulia *f. Gen.* **-ii** *pat.* aboulia.

aby *conj. form.* in order to, to, so that; **aby nie...** lest..., not to..., in order to avoid...; **wycofał się z interesu, aby uratować resztę pieniędzy** he withdrew from the business to save the rest of his money; **kupił dom nad jeziorem, aby spędzać tam wakacje** he bought a cottage at the lake to

spend his holidays there; **jemy, aby żyć** we eat (in order) to live; **powiedz jej, aby przyszła** tell her to come here; **niemożliwe, aby tam był** it's impossible for him to be there; **mówił bardzo cicho, aby go nikt nie usłyszał** he spoke in a very soft voice so that nobody would hear him *l.* lest anybody (should) hear him *l.* in order not to be heard; **zatrzymał się, aby znów po chwili jechać** he stopped only to move on a moment later; **pójdę na spacer, aby tylko była pogoda** I'll go for a walk, weather permitting. – *part.* **1.** (*wyraża niepewność*) **czy aby Kasia poszła spać?** has Kate really gone to bed?; **czy to aby prawda?** is it really true? **2.** (= *byle tylko*) **aby do jutra** if we only make it till tomorrow.

aby-aby *adv.* so-so; **robić coś na aby-aby** do a mediocre job.

AC *abbr.* BC (= *before Christ*).

a capella *adv. muz.* a cappella, unaccompanied.

acefaliczny *a. med., biol.* acephalous.

acetal *mi chem.* acetal.

acetaldehyd *mi chem.* acetaldehyde.

acetamid *mi chem.* acetamid.

acetometr *mi chem.* acetometer.

aceton *mi chem.* acetone, propanone.

acetonowy *a.* (of) acetone; **ciała acetonowe** *biochem.* ketone bodies.

acetyl *mi chem.* acetyl.

acetylen *mi* acetylene, ethyne.

acetylenowy *a.* acetylene; **palnik acetylenowy** acetylene burner.

acetylosalicylowy *a. chem.* acetylsalicylic.

ach *int.* oh!, wow!; **ach, jaka jesteś piękna!** oh, how beautiful you are!; **ach, jak się cieszę!** oh, I'm so glad!; **ach, co za niespodzianka!** wow, what a surprise! – *mi* **achy i ochy** ah's and oh's.

Achilles *mp* **1.** *mit.* Achilles. **2.** *anat.* **ścięgno Achillesa** Achilles tendon.

achillesowy *a.* Achillean; **pięta achillesowa** Achilles *l.* Achilles' heel.

achondryt *mi astron.* achondrite, stony meteorite.

achromat *mi opt.* achromat.

achromatyczność *f. opt.* achromaticity.

achromatyczny *a. opt.* achromatic; **szkło achromatyczne** achromatic lens; **układ achromatyczny** achromatic lens combination.

achromatyzm *mi opt.* achromatism.

achterdek *mi żegl.* afterdeck.

achterluk *mi żegl.* aft hatch.

achterpik *mi żegl.* aft pick, aft hold.

achtersztag *mi żegl.* backstay.

acydofilny *a biol. i bot.* acidophilic, acidophilous; **mleko acydofilne** acidophilus milk.

acydymetria *f. Gen.* **-ii** acidimetry.

acz, aczkolwiek *conj. form.* albeit, although; **szedł dalej, aczkolwiek był już bardzo zmęczony** he went on, although he was exhausted *l.* exhausted as he was; **pociąg odjedzie, aczkolwiek z dużym opóźnieniem** the train will leave, albeit much delayed; **podpisała, acz(kolwiek) niechętnie, tę umowę** reluctant as she was, she eventually signed the agreement; she signed the agreement, albeit reluctantly.

ad acta *adv.* odłożyć **ad acta** (*sprawę, problem, dokument*) shelve, put aside, postpone (from consideration).

adamaszek *mi* **-szk-** damask.

adamaszkowy *a.* damask.

adamita *mp*, **adamitka** *f. Gen.pl.* **-ek** *rel.* Adamite.

adamowy *a.* **w stroju adamowym** stark naked; *pot.* (as) naked as a jaybird; *żart.* in one's birthday suit.

adaptacja *f.* **1.** *t. biol.* (= *przystosowanie*) adaptation; **filmowa adaptacja powieści** film adaptation of a novel; **adaptacja budynku na szkołę** adaptation of a building for a school; **zdolność adaptacji** *biol.* adaptability. **2.** *psych.* adaptability; **proces adaptacji** adaptation.

adaptacyjny *a.* **1. prace adaptacyjne** adaptation (works). **2.** *biol., psych.* adaptive; **zdolności adaptacyjne** adaptability.

adaptator *mp*, **adaptatorka** *f. Gen.pl.* **-ek** adapter, adaptor.

adapter *mi Gen.* **-a** *l.* **-u** *el.* pickup; (*pot.* = *gramofon*) record player.

adaptować *ipf. l. pf.* adapt; **adaptować budynek na szpital** adapt a building for a hospital; **adaptować powieść na utwór sceniczny/na film** adapt a novel for the stage/for a movie.

adaptować się *ipf. l. pf.* adapt (*do czegoś* to sth).

addenda *pl. Gen.* **-ów** *form.* addendum, appendix.

addukcja *f. anat.* adduction.

adduktor *mi anat.* adductor (muscle).

adekwatność *f.* adequacy, sufficiency.

adekwatny *a.* adequate, sufficient, appropriate (*do czegoś* to *l.* for sth); (= *proporcjonalny, współmierny*) commensurate (*do czegoś* with sth).

adenina *f. chem.* adenine.

adenozyna *f. chem.* adenosine.

adept *mp*, **adeptka** *f. Gen.pl.* **-ek** **1.** (= *uczeń, początkujący specjalista*) student, pupil, apprentice. **2.** (= *zwolennik*) adherent.

adherent *mi form.* adherent, follower.

adhezja *f. chem. i fiz.* adhesion.

adhezyjny *a. chem. i fiz.* adhesive; **woda adhezyjna** *geol.* film water, pellicular water.

ad hoc *adv.* ad hoc; **decyzja podjęta ad hoc** an ad hoc decision.

adiabata *f. fiz.* adiabatic curve.

adiabatyczny *a. fiz.* adiabatic; **przemiana adiabatyczna** adiabatic process.

adiantum *n. pl.* **-a** *Gen.pl.* **-ów** *bot.* maidenhair (*Adianthum*).

adidas *mi Gen.* **-a** *zw. pl. pot.* (= *but sportowy*) sneaker, trainer; *pl.* tennies.

adiektywizacja *f. gram.* adjectivisation.

adiunkt *mp uniw.* (university) lecturer (*in Poland*).

adiunktura *f. uniw.* lectureship.

adiustacja *f.* editing, editorial revision.

adiustacyjny *a.* editorial.

adiustator *mp*, **adiustatorka** *f. Gen.pl.* **-ek** editor, reviser.

adiustować *ipf.* edit.

adiutancki *a.* (of) an aide-de-camp; **powinności adiutanckie** aide-de-camp's duties; **służba adiutancka** adjutancy.

adiutant *mp*, **adiutantka** *f. Gen.pl.* **-ek** *wojsk.* aide-de-camp, ADC.

administracja *f.* **1.** (= *zarządzanie*) administration, management; **zajmować się administracją przedsiębiorstwem** *l.* **przedsiębiorstwa** run a business. **2.** (= *zespół zarządzający*) management, board of directors; **pracownik/urzędnik administracji** administrative worker/officer. **3.** *polit.* (= *rząd, władza wykonawcza państwa*) administration, the authorities; **administracja Busha** the Bush administration.

administracyjny *a. polit.* administrative; **kara administracyjna** administrative penalty; **podział administracyjny kraju** the administrative division of a country; **prawo administracyjne** administrative law; **uprawnienia administracyjne** administrative prerogatives; **urzędnik administracyjny** administrative officer.

administrator *mp*, **administratorka** *f. Gen.pl.* **-ek** administrator, manager; **administrator domu mieszkalnego** housekeeper.

administratorski *a.* administrative.

administrować *ipf.* administer, manage.

admiracja *f.* admiration (*dla kogoś, czegoś* of *l.* for sb, sth).

admiralicja *f.* **1.** (= *dowództwo marynarki wojennej*) the Admiralty. **2.** (= *admirałowie*) the admirals.

admiralski *a. żegl., wojsk.* admiral('s); **admiralski okręt** flag ship; **flaga admiralska** admiral flag; **ranga admiralska** admiralship; **sąd admiralski** admiralty court.

admirał *mp pl.* **-owie** *żegl., wojsk.* admiral. – *ma pl.* **-y** (*motyl*) red admiral (*Vanessa atalanta*).

admirować *ipf.* admire.

adnominalny *a. gram.* adnominal.

adnotacja *f.* (= *uwaga w książce*) note, annotation; (*na dokumencie*) endorsement; **opatrywać adnotacjami** annotate.

adonis *mp pl.* **-i, -owie** *l.* **-y** *żart.* Adonis.

adopcja *f. prawn.* adoption; **oddać dziecko do adopcji** give a child up for adoption.

adopcyjny *a.* adoptive; **rodzina adopcyjna** adopted family.

adoptować *ipf. l. pf.* adopt; **adoptować sierotę** adopt *l.* foster an orphan; **dziecko adoptowane** adopted child, adoptee.

adoracja *f.* **1.** (= *uwielbienie*) admiration; **towarzystwo wzajemnej adoracji** *iron.* mutual admiration society. **2.** *rel.* adoration; **adoracja Najświętszego Sakramentu** *rz.-kat.* adoration of the Host.

adorator *mp*, **adoratorka** *f. Gen.pl.* **-ek** admirer, adorer; (*płci przeciwnej*) follower.

adorować *ipf. t. rel.* (= *uwielbiać*) adore; **adorować piękne kobiety** adore beautiful women.

adrenalina *f. biochem.* adrenalin.

adres *mi* **1.** (= *miejsce zamieszkania*) address; **adres stały/tymczasowy** permanent/temporary address; **adres do korespondencji** accommodation address; **iść pod wskazany adres** go to the indicated address; **adres pomocniczy** postal form (*which goes with a parcel*); **adres zwrotny** return address; **adres elektroniczny** e-mail address; **adres internetowy** *komp.* URL (= *uniform resource locator*); **mówić coś pod czyimś adresem** refer to sb; **skierować uwagę pod właściwym adresem** aim one's remarks at the right person; **trafić pod zły adres** *pot.* come to the wrong place. **2.** *przest.* (= *list, nota, pismo zbiorowe*) letter, address; **wystosować adres** send *l.* submit a note; **adres dziękczynny** letter of thanks.

adresat *mp*, **adresatka** *f. Gen.pl.* **-ek 1.** (*o odbiorcy przesyłki, listu*) addressee; **adresat nieznany** addressee unknown; **przesyłka na koszt adresata** freepost. **2.** (*o odbiorcy jakiejś wypowiedzi*) recipient, audience; **pisać z myślą o młodzieżowym adresacie** write for a teenager audience.

adresować *ipf.* (= *zaopatrywać w adres*) **1.** address. **2.** (= *wysyłać*) send, post (*do kogoś* to sb's address); **list adresowany do mamy** a letter for Mother. **3.** (= *kierować*) address (*do kogoś* to sb); **wykład adresowany do studentów matematyki** lecture for students of mathematics.

adresowy *a.* address; **biuro adresowe** address register; **księga adresowa** directory, address book.

adsorbat *mi chem.* adsorbate.

adsorbent *mi chem.* adsorbent.

adsorber *mi Gen.* **-a** *chem.* adsorber.

adsorbować *ipf. chem. i fiz.* adsorb.

adsorpcja *f. chem. i fiz.* adsorption.

adsorpcyjny *a. chem. i fiz.* adsorptive; **zdolność adsorpcyjna** adsorptive capacity, adsorptivity.

advocatus diaboli *mp indecl.* devil's advocate.

adwekcja *f. meteor.* advection.

adwekcyjny *a. meteor.* advective.

adwent *mi rel.* Advent.

adwentowy *a. rel.* **pieśni adwentowe** Advent hymns; **kalendarz adwentowy** Advent calendar.

adwentysta *mp*, **adwentystka** *f. Gen.pl.* **-ek** *rel.* Adventist; **adwentysta Dnia Siódmego** Seventh-Day Adventist.

adwerbalny *a. gram.* adverbal.

adwerbialny *a. gram.* adverbial.

adwersarz *mp* adversary, opponent.

adwokacina *mp decl. like f. pog.* pettifogger.

adwokacki *a. prawn.* attorney's, solicitor's, barrister's; **kancelaria adwokacka** barrister's office; **porada adwokacka** legal advice; **praktyka adwokacka** law practice; **zespół adwokacki** barristers' offices; **aplikacja adwokacka** articles.

adwokat[1] *mp* **1.** *prawn.* attorney, counselor, counselor-at-law, lawyer; *Br.* solicitor. **2.** (= *rzecznik, obrońca*) *iron.* advocate, champion; **adwokat diabła** devil's advocate; **odgrywać rolę adwokata diabła** play devil's advocate; **adwokat słusznej sprawy** advocate of a just cause.

adwokat[2] *mi Gen.* **-a** (*likier*) advocaat.

adwokatka *f. Gen.pl.* **-ek** *zob.* **adwokat**[1].

adwokatura *f.* **1.** (= *czynności adwokata*) attorneyship. **2.** (= *ogół adwokatów*) the Bar.

adyton *mi hist.* adytum.

adzuki *a. indecl.* **fasola adzuki** adzuki bean (*Phaseolum angularis*).

aeracja *f. techn.* aeration.

aerenchyma *f. bot.* aerenchyma.

aerob *ma biol.* aerobe.

aerobik *mi* aerobics.

aerobus *mi Gen.* **-a** *lotn.* (= *airbus*) airbus.

aerodrom *mi lotn.* airdrome; *Br.* aerodrome.

aerodyna *f. lotn.* aerodyne, heavier-than-air aircraft.

aerodynamiczny *a. fiz.* aerodynamic; **kształt aerodynamiczny** streamlined shape; **siła aerodynamiczna** aerodynamic force; **tunel aerodynamiczny** aerodynamic tunnel; **hamowanie aerodynamiczne** aerodynamic braking; **hamulec aerodynamiczny** airbrake.

aerodynamika *f. fiz.* aerodynamics.

aeroenergetyka *f. techn.* aeroenergetics.

aerofobia *f. Gen.* **-ii** *med., pat.* aerophobia.

aerofon *mi muz.* aerophone.

aeroklub *mi lotn.* flying club.

aerolit *mi astron.* aerolite.

aerologia *f. Gen.* **-ii** *nauk.* aerology.

aeronauta *mp*, **aeronautka** *f. Gen.pl.* **-ek** *lotn. przest.* aeronaut.

aeronautyka *f. lotn.* aeronautics, air navigation.

aeronawigacja *f. lotn.* air navigation.

aeroplankton *mi biol.* aeroplankton.

aeroponiczny *a. roln.* aeroponic.

aerostatyka *f. fiz.* aerostatics.

aerozol *mi* aerosol; **krople do nosa w aerozolu** aerosol nose drops.

aerozolować *ipf.* spray.

aerozolowy *a.* aerosol; **pojemnik/rozpylacz aerozolowy** aerosol container/dispenser.

afatyczny *a. pat.* aphasic.

afatyk *mp*, **afatyczka** *f. Gen.pl.* **-ek** *med.* aphasiac, aphasic.

afazja *f. pat.* aphasia.

afekt *mi* **1.** *psych.* affect. **2.** (= *silne wzruszenie*) emotion, passion; **zbrodnia w afekcie** crime of passion.

afektacja *f. form.* affectation, campiness, airs and graces; **mówić z afektacją** mince (one's words).

afektowany *a. form.* afected, artificial; (*o stylu kobiety*) actressy; (*o aktorze*) campy; **afektowany sposób mówienia** preciosity; **w afektowany sposób** in an affected manner, preciously.

afektywny *a. psych.* affective.

afera *f.* **1.** (= *skandal*) scandal; **afera łapówkarska** bribery scandal; **wykryć aferę** expose a scandal; **wplątać się w aferę** become entangled *l.* embroiled in a scandal. **2.** (= *ekscytujące wydarzenie*) affair; *pot.* (= *publiczna sensacja*) fuss, commotion, hullabaloo; **niezła afera z tym ślubem** (that was) quite a mess with the wedding; **ale afera!** what a fuss!; **zrobić aferę** kick up a fuss; make a fuss (*z czegoś l. o coś* about sth *l.* over sth).

aferzysta *mp*, **aferzystka** *f. Gen.pl.* **-ek** swindler.

afgan *mi Gen.* **-a** *kynol.* (= *chart afgański*) Afghan (hound).

Afganistan *mi geogr.* Afghanistan.

Afgańczyk *mp*, **Afganka** *f. Gen.pl.* **-ek** Afghan.

afgański *a.* Afghan.

afiks *mi gram.* affix.

afiksacja *f. gram.* affixation.

afiliacja *f.* affiliation.

afiliować *ipf.* affiliate (*kogoś/coś przy czymś* sb/sth to *l.* with sth).

afirmacja *f. form.* affirmation.

afirmatywny *a. form.* affirmative, positive; **mieć afirmatywny stosunek do rzeczywistości** have an affirmative attitude to reality, be positive about reality; **akcja afirmatywna** *polit.* affirmative action.

afirmować *ipf. form.* affirm.

afisz *mi Gen.* **-a** *Gen.pl.* **-ów** *l.* **-y** poster, bill; **afisz teatralny** playbill; **wejść na afisz** (*o sztuce*) be staged, be put on the stage; (*o utworze muzycznym*) be performed; **nie schodzić z afisza** be on; **zdjąć coś z afisza** take sth off the bill; **pchać się na afisz** *pot.* sell o.s., market o.s.

afiszować *ipf.* flaunt, show *sth* off. **~ się** *ipf.* flaunt o.s.; **afiszować się z czymś** flaunt *l.* parade sth.

afiszowy *a.* poster, placard; **papier afiszowy** poster paper, board.

aforysta *mp*, **aforystka** *f. Gen.pl.* **-ek** aphorist.

aforystyczny *a.* aphoristic.

aforystyka *f. teor.lit.* aphorisms.

aforyzm *mi teor.lit.* aphorism.

aforyzmowy *a.* aphoristic.

afrikaans *a. i mi indecl.* **(język) afrikaans** Afrikaans.

afro *a. i n. indecl.* (*fryzura*) Afro.

Afroamerykanin *mp pl.* **-anie** *pl.* **-anów**, **Afroamerykanka** *f. Gen.pl.* **-ek** African American, Afro-American.

afroamerykański *a.* African American, Afro-American.

afrocentryczny *a.* Afrocentric.

afrocentryzm *mi* Afrocentrism.

Afrodyta *f. mit.* Aphrodite.

afrodyzjak *mi* aphrodisiac.

afront *mi* affront; **robić komuś afront** affront sb; **spotkał kogoś afront** sb was affronted.

Afryka *f. geogr.* Africa.

afrykaner *ma*, **afrykanerka** *f. Gen.pl.* **-ek** Afrikaner.

Afrykanin *mp pl.* **-anie** *Gen.* **-ów** African.

afrykanista *mp*, **afrykanistka** *f. Gen.pl.* **-ek** Africanist.

afrykanistyczny *a.* Africanist; **studia afrykanistyczne** African studies.

afrykanistyka *f.* African studies.

Afrykanka *f. Gen.pl.* **-ek** *zob.* **Afrykanin**.

Afrykańczyk *mp* = **Afrykanin**.

afrykański *a.* African.

afrykata *f. fon.* affricate.

afta *f. Gen.pl.* **-t** *pat.* aphtha; *pot.* canker sore.

agape *f. indecl. rel., fil.* agape.

agar *mi* agar.

agat *mi min.* agate.

agatowy *a.* agate; **pierścionek z agatowym oczkiem** agate ring.

agawa *f. bot.* agave; **agawa amerykańska** century plant (*Agave americana*).

agencja *f.* **1.** (= *przedstawicielstwo*) office, agents; **agencja handlowa** commercial agents; **agencja pocztowa** post office outlet; **agencja konsularna** consular office; **oddać w agencję** franchise (*coś komuś* sth to sb). **2.** (= *placówka*) agency; **agencja nieruchomości** real estate agency; **agencja towarzyska** escort service; **agencja matrymonialna** dating service. **3.** (= *instytucja zbierająca informacje*) agency; **agencja prasowa** news agency; **agencja fotograficzna** photography *l.* photo agency.

agencyjny *a.* **1.** (*o przedstawicielstwie*) agent; **umowa agencyjna** agency agreement. **2.** (*o instytucji zbierającej informacje*) agency; **wiadomości agencyjne** news from a news agency.

agenda *f.* **1.** (*instytucji*) branch, office; (*urzędu*) agency, office; **agenda rządowa** government agency. **2.** (*terminarz*) notebook, (day *l.* personal) planner; (*w sądzie*) docket.

agens *mp pl.* **-y** *gram.* agent.

agent *mp*, **agentka** *f. Gen.pl.* **-ek** **1.** (= *przedstawiciel*) agent, representative; **agent handlowy** sales rep *l.* representative, commercial agent; **agent ubezpieczeniowy** insurance agent. **2.** (= *detektyw*) (police) agent. **3.** (= *szpieg*) agent, spy; **podwójny agent** double agent.

agentura *f.* **1.** (= *grupa szpiegów*) agents, spy ring; **działalność wrogiej agentury** the work of enemy agents. **2.** (= *agencja*) office, branch.

agenturalny *a.* spy; **sieć agenturalna** spy ring.

agitacja *f.* **1.** (= *propagowanie ideologii, haseł*) (political) agitation. **2.** (= *zjednywanie zwolenników, wyborców*) campaigning; (*przez osobiste spotkania z wyborcami*) canvass; (*na wiarę, przekonanie*) proselytize; **agitacja przedwyborcza** pre-election campaigning; **agitacja wyborcza** election campaigning, electioneering.

agitacyjny *a.* campaigning, rallying; **literatura agitacyjna** propaganda (literature); **przemówienie agitacyjne** rallying speech; (*na wiarę, przekonanie*) proselytizing.

agitator *mp pl.* **-rzy** (= *ten, kto agituje*) agitator; (*na rzecz polityki, ideologii*) campaigner, activist; (*na rzecz wiary, przekonania*) proselytizer. **– mi pl.** **-ry** *chem.* agitator.

agitatorka *f. Gen.pl.* **-ek** (= *kobieta agitator*) *zob.* **agitator**.

agitatorski *a.* campaigning, activist; **wiec agitatorski** campaign rally.

agitka *f. Gen.pl.* **-ek** *zw. uj.* propaganda leaflet.

agitować *ipf.* campaign, canvass, proselytize, agitate (*za czymś* for sth, *na rzecz czegoś* on behalf of sth).

aglomeracja *f.* **1.** (= *wielkie miasto*) urban agglomeration, metropolitan area. **2.** (= *skupisko*) agglomeration. **3.** *techn.* agglomeration.

aglomeracyjny *a. techn.* agglomerating, sintering; **piec aglomeracyjny** sintering oven.

aglomerat *mi* **1.** (= *zlepek*) agglomerate. **2.** *geol.* agglomerate. **3.** *techn.* agglomerate.

aglomerować *ipf.* agglomerate; *techn.* sinter.

aglutynacja *f. jęz., biol.* agglutination; **aglutynacja krwinek** *fizj.* agglutination of blood cells.

aglutynacyjny *a.* **1.** *jęz.* agglutinative; **języki aglutynacyjne** agglutinating *l.* agglutinative language; **końcówka aglutynacyjna** agglutinative *l.* agglutinated ending. **2.** *biol.* agglutinating; **właściwości aglutynacyjne krwi** *fizj.* agglutinating properties of blood.

aglutynować *ipf. biol.* agglutinate. ~ **się** *ipf. biol.* agglutinate, undergo agglutination.

agnostycyzm *mi fil.* agnosticism.

agnostyczny *a. fil.* agnostic; **pogląd agnostyczny** agnostic views; **krytycyzm agnostyczny** agnostic criticism.

agnostyk *mp fil.* agnostic.

agogiczny *a. muz.* agogic; **akcent agogiczny** agogic accent.

agogika *f. muz.* agogics.

agonalny *a.* of agony; **stan agonalny** state of agony.

agonia *f.* Gen. **-ii** agony, dying, death throes; **leżeć w agonii** lie in agony; **być w agonii** be dying.

agora *f. hist.* agora.

agorafobia *f.* Gen. **-ii** *pat.* agoraphobia.

agrafia *f.* Gen. **-ii** *pat.* agraphia.

agrafka *f.* Gen.pl. **-ek** safety pin; **spinać agrafką** fasten *l.* closed with a safety pin; **spódnica zapięta na agrafkę** skirt fastened with a safety pin.

agramatyczny *a. psych.* non-grammatical; **wypowiedź agramatyczna** non-grammatical response.

agramatyzm *mi psych.* agrammatism.

agrarny *a.* **1.** (= *dotyczący rolnictwa*) agrarian; **polityka agrarna** agrarian policy. **2.** (= *rolniczy, rolny*) agricultural; **system agrarny państwa** a country's agricultural system.

agrarysta *mp*, **agrarystka** *f.* Gen.pl. **-ek** *polit.* agrarianist.

agraryzm *mi polit.* agrarianism.

agregat *mi* **1.** *techn.* unit, assembly; **agregat prądotwórczy** power generating unit; **agregat chłodniczy** cooling unit. **2.** *log.* aggregate. **3.** *chem. l. fiz.* aggregate; **agregat krystaliczny** crystal aggregate. **4.** *form.* (*o całości, która powstała z niejednorodnych części*) aggregate, collective.

agregatownia *f.* Gen.pl. **-i** *techn.* aggregation.

agregatowy *a. techn.* aggregate; **wskaźnik agregatowy** aggregate index.

agresja *f.* **1.** (= *atak*) aggression; **zbrojna agresja** armed aggression; **akt agresji** act of aggression. **2.** *psych.* aggression; **agresja fizyczna** physical violence; **agresja słowna** verbal abuse; **napad agresji** fit of violence *l.* anger.

agresor *mp* aggressor.

agrest *mi* **1.** (*owoc l. krzew*) gooseberry; **krzak agrestu** gooseberry plant *l.* bush. **2.** *bot.* **agrest (pospolity)** (*także* **porzeczka agrest**) (European)

gooseberry (*Ribes grossularia*); **agrest amerykański** American gooseberry (*R. hirtellum*).

agrestowy *a.* gooseberry; **dżem agrestowy** gooseberry jam; **krzaki agrestowe** gooseberry bushes; **mszyca agrestowa** *ent.* gooseberry aphid (*Aphis grossulariae*).

agresywnie *adv.* aggressively; **zachowywać się agresywnie** behave aggressively; **odzywać się agresywnie** reply nastily *l.* belligerently.

agresywność *f.* **1.** (*w polityce*) militancy *l.* militance, belligerence *l.* belligerency; **agresywność polityki** political militancy. **2.** (*w psychologii*) aggressiveness; **agresywność charakteru** bellicosity. **3.** (= *właściwości niszczycielskie*) (*roślin*) invasiveness; (*wody, środków chemicznych*) corrosive power.

agresywny *a.* **1.** (*w polityce*) militant, belligerent; **państwo agresywne** belligerent state; **agresywna akcja** belligerent act. **2.** *psych.* aggressive, bellicose; **agresywne zachowanie** aggressive behavior; **agresywny charakter** aggressive *l.* violent nature. **3.** (= *niszczycielski*) corrosive; **agresywny gaz** corrosive; **agresywne środki chemiczne** corrosive chemical agent; (*rośliny*) invasive.

agrobiolog *mp pl.* **-dzy** *l.* **-owie** agrobiologist.

agrobiologia *f.* Gen. **-ii** agrobiology.

agrobiologiczny *a.* agrobiological; **badania agrobiologiczne** agrobiological study.

agrochemia *f.* Gen. **-ii** agrochemistry.

agrochemiczny *a.* agrochemical *l.* agrichemical; **instytut agrochemiczny** agrochemical institute.

agrochemik *mp* agrochemist.

agroekologia *f.* Gen. **-ii** agroenvironmental *l.* agrienvironmental.

agrominimum *n. sg. indecl. pl.* **-nima** Gen. **-nimów** *ekon.* minimum requirements for effective agricultural production.

agronom *mp pl.* **-owie** agronomist.

agronomia *f.* Gen. **-ii** agronomy.

agronomiczny *a.* agronomic; **wydział agronomiczny** department of agronomy.

agronomka *f.* Gen.pl. **-ek** *pot.* (= *kobieta agronom*) agronomist.

agrotechniczny *a.* agrotechnical *l.* agritechnical; **zabiegi agrotechniczne** agrotechnical procedures.

agrotechnik *mp* agricultural engineer.

agrotechnika *f.* agricultural science *l.* engineering.

aha *int.* aha; (= *jasne!*) I see, yeah, yup; **aha, już wiem** aha, now I've got it; **aha! nareszcie cię przyłapałem!** aha! I've caught you at last!

ahistoryczność *f.* ahistoricity.

ahistoryczny *a.* ahistorical.

ahoj *int. żegl.* ahoy.

AIDS *abbr. i n.* Gen. *i* Acc. **AIDS-a** AIDS.

aintelektualizm *mi sztuka* anti-intellectualism.

aintelektualny *a. sztuka* anti-intellectual; **malarstwo aintelektualne** anti-intellectual painting.

aj *int.* **1.** (*wyrażający ból*) ouch, ow; **aj, uważaj,**

to boli! ouch! be careful, that hurt's! **2.** (*wyrażający przestrach*) hey, oh.

ajatollah *mp rel.* ayatollah.

ajencja *f.* (= *dzierżawienie czegoś*) franchise; **brać coś w ajencję** obtain *l.* be granted a franchise on sth.

ajencyjny *a.* franchise; **sklep ajencyjny** franchise (store).

ajent *mp* franchisee.

ajerkoniak *mi* eggnog.

akacja *f.* **1.** *bot.* acacia, wattle. **2.** (= *grochodrzew*) locust.

akacjowy *a.* **1.** acacia; **gałęzie akacjowe** acacia branch. **2.** (*o grochodrzewie*) locust; **robinia akacjowa** *bot.* locust.

akademia *f. Gen.* **-ii 1.** (*gremium złożone z wybitnych naukowców, artystów*) academia *l.* academe. **2.** (*uczelnia wyższa*) academy, school; **akademia ekonomiczna** School of Economics; **akademia wychowania fizycznego** School of Physical Education; **akademia muzyczna** Academy of Music; **akademia sztuk pięknych** Art School; Academy of Art; **akademia medyczna** Medical School; **akademia wojskowa** Military Academy. **3.** (= *uroczystość z częścią artystyczną*) celebration (*dla uczczenia czegoś* to mark sth).

akademicki *a.* **1.** *uniw.* (= *dotyczący uczelni l. studentów*) academic, university; **chór akademicki** students' choir; **dom akademicki** dormitory, residence hall; **młodzież akademicka** college students; **kwadrans akademicki** fifteen minutes students are expected to wait for their instructor before class is cancelled (*in Poland*); **nauczyciel akademicki** university teacher; **placówka akademicka** academic institution, institution of higher learning; **rok akademicki** academic year. **2.** (*pozbawiony związku z rzeczywistością*) academic, pedantic, (excessively) abstract; **to czysto akademicka dyskusja** this discussion is (merely) academic. **3.** *sztuka* academic; **malarstwo akademickie** academic painting.

akademik *mp pl.* **-cy 1.** (= *wybitny uczony, artysta – członek akademii*) academic. **2.** (= *student*) student. **– mi Gen. -a pl. -i** *pot.* (= *dom studencki*) dorm; **mieszkać w akademiku** live in a dorm.

akademizm *mi sztuka* academicism *l.* academism.

akant *mi bot.* **1.** acanthus (*Acanthus*). **2.** *sztuka* acanthus; **liście akantu** (*motyw dekoracyjny*) acanthus leaves.

akantowy *a.* **1.** (*o roślinie*) acanthus; **krzew akantowy** acanthus shrub. **2.** (*sztuka*) acanthus, acanthine; **motyw akantowy** acanthus motif.

akapit *mi* **1.** (= *wcięcie pierwszego wiersza tekstu*) indentation, indention, indent. **2.** (= *wydzielony graficznie fragment tekstu*) paragraph.

akapitowy *a.* wcięcie akapitowe indentation (of the first line of a paragraph).

akceleracja *f. form.* acceleration; **akceleracja rozwoju technicznego** acceleration of technological progress *l.* advancement.

akcelerator *mi Gen.* **-a 1.** *fiz.* accelerator. **2.** *techn.* accelerator.

akcent *mi* **1.** stress, accent; **akcent główny/poboczny** primary/secondary stress; **akcent ruchomy** mobile stress; **akcent stały/swobodny** fixed/free stress; **akcent na sylabie początkowej/przedostatniej** initial/penultimate stress; **akcent zdaniowy** sentence stress; **akcent metryczny** ictus; **kłaść akcent na coś** put *l.* place accent on sth; **akcent spoczywa na czymś** accent falls on sth. **2.** (*znak graficzny nad literą*) accent (mark). **3.** (*zabarwienie emocjonalne wypowiedzi*) tone, note; **akcent szczerości** tone of honesty; **akcent prawdy** tone *l.* note of honesty *l.* truthfulness. **4.** (*szczegół decydujący o charakterze czegoś*) accent, feature; **szara suknia z czerwonymi akcentami** a gray dress with red accents. **5.** *pot.* (*sposób artykulacji*) accent; **mówić z akcentem** *pot.* speak with an accent; **mieć cudzoziemski akcent** have a foreign accent. **6.** *muz.* emphasis.

akcentować *ipf.* **1.** (*o artykulacji*) stress, accentuate, accent; **źle akcentować wyrazy rosyjskie** place the accent *l.* stress in Russian phrases improperly. **2.** (= *uwydatniać w wypowiedzi*) stress, emphasize; **akcentować potrzebę reformy szkolnictwa** stress the need for educational reform. **3.** *muz.* emphasis.

akcentowy *a.* (of) accentuation, (of) stress; **system akcentowy języka rosyjskiego** the Russian accentuation system.

akcentuacja *f. jęz.* accentuation.

akcentuacyjny *a. jęz.* accentual, (of) accentuation; **zmiany akcentuacyjne** accentuation changes.

akcept *mi* **1.** *ekon.* acceptance; **akcept bankowy** bank acceptance. **2.** *przest.* (= *akceptacja*) acceptance.

akceptacja *f.* **1.** (= *zgoda, aprobata*) approval, acceptance; **uzyskać akceptację władz miasta** receive approval from city authorities; **dać akceptację** give acceptance. **2.** *ekon.* acceptance.

akceptant *mp ekon.* acceptor.

akceptor *mi Gen.* **-a** *chem., fiz.* acceptor.

akceptować *ipf.* **1.** (= *aprobować*) accept, approve (*coś, kogoś* of sth, sb); (*niemoralne zachowanie, przemoc*) condone; **nie akceptować czyjegoś zachowania** not condone *l.* approve of sb's behavior. **2.** (= *zatwierdzać*) approve, accept; **akceptować budżet, plan** approve a budget, plan; **akceptować zmiany** accept changes; (= *przyjmować*) accept, agree (*coś* to sth); **akceptować warunki kapitulacji** agree to *l.* accept the terms *l.* conditions of surrender; **akceptować weksel** *ekon.* accept a bill of exchange.

akceptowany *a.* (= *przyjmowany, aprobowany*) accepted, approved; (= *do przyjęcia*) acceptable, approved (of); **akceptowany społecznie** socially acceptable.

akces *mi form.* accession; **przystąpić** *l.* **zgłosić akces** accede (*do czegoś* to sth).

akcesoria *pl. Gen.* **-ów** accessories; **akcesoria samochodowe** automobile accessories.

akcesoryczny *a. geol.* accessory; **minerały akcesoryczne** accessory minerals.

akcesyjny *a.* **1.** *prawn.* accession, accessional; **deklaracja akcesyjna** declaration of accession *l.* accession declaration; **umowa akcesyjna** accession contract. **2.** *bibl.* circulation; **sygnatura akcesyjna** call number.

akcja *f.* **1.** (= *zorganizowane działanie*) campaign, (cooperative *l.* organised) effort, action; **akcja wyborcza** political campaign; **akcja charytatywna** charitable effort; **akcja ratowania** rescue efforts; **akcja społeczna** social welfare efforts; **podjąć akcję** start *l.* initiate a campaign; **prowadzić akcję** carry out *l.* be engaged in a campaign; **przystąpić do akcji** join a campaign; **brać udział w akcji** take part in a campaign; **akcja bezpośrednia** direct action; **zasada akcji i reakcji** *fiz.* law *l.* principle of action and reaction. **2.** *wojsk.* (= *działania wojenne*) action, operation; **akcja zbrojna** military action; **akcja bojowa** combat *l.* battle; **akcja dywersyjna** diversion; **wprowadzać czołgi do akcji** lead the tanks into action *l.* battle. **3.** *film* **film akcji** action film *l.* movie; **kino akcji** (*gatunek*) action movies. **4.** *sl.* (= *sensacja, zamieszanie*) affair, fuss. **5.** (*fabuła*) story, plot, action; **miejsce akcji** scene of the action; **akcja się rozwija** plot *l.* story unfolds; **akcja się rozgrywa** action *l.* story takes place. **6.** *ekon.* share; **pakiet akcji** interest; **wartość akcji** share value; **wypuścić akcje** issue stocks *l.* shares; **kurs akcji** stock *l.* share price; **akcje zwyżkują** stocks *l.* shares are rising; **akcje spadają** stocks *l.* shares are falling; **czyjeś akcje idą w górę** *przen.* sb's star is on the rise. **7.** *sport* effort; **brawurowa akcja na bramkę przeciwnika** daring effort at the opponent's goal.

akcjonariusz *mp*, **akcjonariuszka** *f. Gen.pl.* **-ek** shareholder; **zebranie akcjonariuszy** shareholder's meeting.

akcydens *mi* **1.** *druk.* job; **akcydensy** jobbing. **2.** *fil.* accident.

akcydensowy *a. druk.* job; **druk akcydensowy** job printing.

akcyjność *f.* (*o wspólnym działaniu*) cooperation, collectivity.

akcyjny *a.* **1.** (*o wspólnym działaniu*) cooperative, collective; **turbina akcyjna** *techn.* impulse turbine. **2.** (= *o akcji jednorazowej, doraźnej*) campaign. **3.** *ekon.* stock; **spółka akcyjna** *US* public corporation; *Br.* joint stock company; **kapitał akcyjny** capital stock.

akcyza *f. ekon.* excise (tax); **nałożyć na coś akcyzę** levy an excise tax on sth.

akcyzowy *a. ekon.* excise; **podatek akcyzowy** excise tax.

aklamacja *f.* acclamation; **wybrać kogoś przez aklamację** choose sb by acclamation; **uchwalić coś przez aklamację** pass sth by acclamation.

aklimatyzacja *f.* **1.** *fizj.* acclimation; **aklimatyzacja roślin** acclimation of plants; **proces aklimatyzacji** acclimation process. **2.** *przen.* acclimation, acclimatization, getting accustomed.

aklimatyzacyjny *a. fizj.* acclimation; **proces aklimatyzacyjny** acclimation process.

aklimatyzować *ipf.* acclimate. ~ **się** *ipf.* **1.** *fizj.* acclimate. **2.** *przen.* become acclimated *l.* acclimatized; get accustomed.

akolada *f. muz.* accolade.

akolita *mp*, **akolitka** *f. Gen.pl.* **-ek** *form. l. rel.* acolyte.

akomodacja *f. fizj.* accommodation.

akomodacyjny *a. fizj.* accommodative; **siła akomodacyjna** accommodative power.

akomodować się *ipf. fizj.* accommodate.

akompaniament *mi* accompaniment; **śpiewać przy akompaniamencie** *l.* **z akompaniamentem akordeonu** sing accompanied by *l.* backed by an accordion.

akompaniator *mp*, **akompaniatorka** *f. Gen.pl.* **-ek** accompanist.

akompaniować *ipf.* accompany, back (*na czymś* on sth).

akonit *mi bot.* aconite, monkshood, wolfsbane (*Aconitum*).

akonto *n.* deposit, advance payment; **płacić akonto** pay *l.* make a deposit; **brać akonto** get an advance (on one's salary).

akord *mi* **1.** *muz.* chord; **akord harmoniczny** harmonic chord; **akord melodyczny** melodic chord. **2.** *ekon.* (*na czas*) job work; (*na sztukę*) piecework; **pracować na akord** work by the job, do piecework.

akordeon *mi* accordion.

akordeonista *mp*, **akordeonistka** *f. Gen.pl.* **-ek** accordionist.

akordowy *a.* **1.** *muz.* chordal. **2.** *ekon.* piecework, job work; **system akordowy** jobbing, piecework system; **pracownik akordowy** jobber, pieceworker; **praca akordowa** job work, piecework.

akowiec *mp* **-wc-** *pl.* **-y** *hist.* Polish Home Army soldier (*during World War II*).

akowski *a. hist.* Polish Home Army; **oddział akowski** Polish Home Army unit.

akr *mi Gen.* **-a** *miern.* acre.

akredytacja *f.* accreditation; **akredytacja przy rządzie** accreditation to a government.

akredytacyjny *a.* accreditation; **karta akredytacyjna** card of accreditation.

akredytować *ipf.* accredit (*przy czymś* to sth); **dziennikarz akredytowany przy Radzie Europy** journalist accredited to the European Council.

akrobacja *f.* **1.** (*ćwiczenie*) acrobatic exercise *l.* number; **wykonywać akrobacje** perform acrobatics; **akrobacja lotnicza** aerobatics, aerial stunts. **2.** (= *akrobatyka*) acrobatics.

akrobacyjny *a.* (*o ćwiczeniach*) acrobatic; **samolot akrobacyjny** stunt plane.

akrobata *mp*, **akrobatka** *f. Gen.pl.* **-ek** acrobat; (*zwł. na trapezie*) aerialist.

akrobatyczny *a.* (*o ćwiczeniach*) acrobatic; **popisy akrobatyczne** acrobatic act, acrobatics.

akrobatyka *f. sport* acrobatics.

akrofobia *f. Gen.* **-ii** *pat.* acrophobia.

akronim *mi.* acronym.

akropol *mi Gen.pl.* **-i** *l.* **-ów** *hist.* acropolis; **Akropol** (*w Atenach*) the Acropolis.

akrostych *mi* acrostic.

akryl *mi chem.* acrylic.

akrylan *mi chem.* acrylate.

akrylowy *a. chem.* acrylic; **farba akrylowa**

acrylic paint; **żywice akrylowe** acrylic resin; **kwas akrylowy** acrylic acid.

aksamit *mi* velvet; **gładki/miękki jak aksamit** (as) soft/smooth as velvet; velvety.

aksamitka *f. Gen.pl.* **-ek** 1. (*wstążka*) velvet ribbon. 2. *bot.* marigold (*Tagetes*). 3. *bot.* (*grzyb*) golden false pholiota (*Phaeololepiota aurea*).

aksamitność *f.* 1. (= *miękkość*) velvetiness. 2. (= *gładkość*) silkiness; **aksamitność czyjejś cery** velvety softness *l.* silky smoothness of sb's complexion.

aksamitny *a.* 1. (*z aksamitu*) velvet; **aksamitna suknia** velvet dress. 2. (*jak aksamit*) velvety; **aksamitny głos** velvety *l.* silky voice.

aksjologia *f. Gen.* **-ii** *fil.* axiology.

aksjologiczny *a. fil.* axiological.

aksjomat *mi log., mat.* (= *pewnik*) axiom; (= *postulat*) postulate.

aksjomatyczny *a. log.* axiomatic.

aksjomatyka *f. log.* axiomatics.

aksjomatyzacja *f. log.* axiomatization.

akt *mi* 1. *form.* (= *czyn*) act, deed; **akt agresji** act of aggression; **akt rozpaczy** act of desperation; desperate deed; **akt płciowy** sexual intercourse, sexual act, coitus; **akt stworzenia** *rel.* act of creation. 2. (= *uroczysta deklaracja l. wyznanie*) **akt łaski** amnesty, act of grace; **akt wiary/skruchy** act of faith/contrition. 3. (= *ceremonia, czynność formalna*) act, ceremony; **akt koronacyjny** act of coronation; **dokonać aktu dekoracji** decorate sb. 4. *teatr* act; **opera w trzech aktach** an opera in three acts; **pierwszy akt komedii** first act of a comedy. 5. *sztuka* (= *wyobrażenie nagiego ciała*) nude; **akt kobiecy** female nude; **pozować do aktu** pose for a nude. 6. *prawn.* (= *dokument*) certificate, deed, act, contract; **akt darowizny** deed of gift *l.* donation; **akt kupna-sprzedaży** bill of sale; sale contract; **akt kupna** deed of purchase; **akt prawny** legal act; **akt ślubu** marriage certificate; **akt urodzenia** birth certificate; **akt oskarżenia** arraignment, indictment; **sporządzić akt oskarżenia** draw up an indictment.

akta *pl. Gen.* **akt** (= *zbiór dokumentów*) files, records; **akta sprawy sądowej** *prawn.* records of the proceedings; **dołączyć do akt** file (in), add to the files *l.* records; **wpisać do akt** enter into the records; **akta stanu cywilnego** marriage records; **akta ziemskie** *hist.* land registry.

aktor *mp* actor; **aktor filmowy** movie actor; **aktor charakterystyczny** character actor; **aktor komediowy** comedian; **teatr jednego aktora** one-man theater.

aktoreczka *f. Gen.pl.* **-ek** *pog.* bad actress.

aktorka *f. Gen.pl.* **-ek** actor, actress.

aktorski *a.* acting; **sztuka aktorska** the art of acting; **zdolności aktorskie** talent for acting; **szkoła aktorska** acting school.

aktorstwo *n.* 1. (*sztuka aktorska*) acting. 2. (*sposób bycia*) acting.

aktorzyna *mp pl.* **-y** *pog.* bad actor.

aktówka *f.* folder, portfolio.

aktualia *pl. Gen.* **-ów** *lit.* current events; **aktualia kulturalne** current events in culture.

aktualizacja *f.* 1. (= *czynienie aktualnym*) update, bringing up to date; **aktualizacja danych** data update. 2. *fil.* actualization.

aktualizm *mi* 1. *fil.* actualism. 2. *geol.* uniformitarianism; **zasada aktualizmu** the uniformitarian principle.

aktualizować *ipf.* (= *czynić aktualnym*) update, bring up to date; **aktualizować dane** update data. **~ się** *ipf.* 1. (*stawać się aktualnym*) get up to date, become updated. 2. *fil.* become real.

aktualnie *adv.* currently, at the (present) moment.

aktualności *pl. Gen.* **-i** current events *l.* affairs; **aktualności kulturalne** current cultural events.

aktualność *f.* timeliness, relevance (to today *l.* the times), currency; **aktualność satyry** timeliness of satire; **tracić na aktualności** lose timeliness *l.* relevance.

aktualny *a.* 1. (= *obecny*) current, timely; **aktualne wyniki badań** recent research findings; **aktualny temat** subject of current interest; **coś już nie jest aktualne** sth is no longer timely *l.* topical. 2. (= *ważny*) open, good; **zaproszenie jest (wciąż) aktualne** invitation is (still) open; **oferta jest aktualna do piątku** offer is good until Friday. 3. *fil.* actual.

aktyn *mi chem.* actinium.

aktynowiec *mi* **-wc-** *chem.* actinide.

aktynowy *a. chem.* actinic; **szereg aktynowy** the actinide series.

aktyw *mi polit.* hard core; **aktyw partyjny** party's hard core.

aktywa *pl. Gen.* **-ów** *ekon.* assets; **aktywa spółki** company assets.

aktywacja *f. tel., chem., fiz.* activation; **telefon komórkowy z aktywacją** cell phone with activation; **energia aktywacji** *fiz.* activation energy.

aktywacyjny *a.* activation; **opłata aktywacyjna** *tel.* activation charge; **analiza aktywacyjna** *fiz.* activation analysis.

aktywator *mi Gen.* **-a** *chem.* activator; **aktywator enzymatyczny** enzyme activator.

aktywista *mp*, **aktywistka** *f. Gen.pl.* **-ek** *polit.* activist; **aktywista partyjny/związkowy** party/union activist.

aktywizacja *f.* activation.

aktywizator *mp polit.* organizer.

aktywizm *mi* activism.

aktywizować *ipf.* activate, motivate, stimulate (the activity of); (*jednostkę, społeczeństwo*) energize; **czynniki aktywizujące** motivating factors. **~ się** *ipf.* become active.

aktywnie *adv.* actively; **wypoczywać aktywnie** spend one's free time actively.

aktywność *f.* 1. (*czynne uczestniczenie*) activity, activeness; **aktywność uczniów** the diligence of students; **wykazywać aktywność** show activity. 2. *nauk.* activity; **aktywność promieniotwórcza** *fiz.* radioactivity; **aktywność tlenu** *chem.* activity of oxygen; **aktywność optyczna** *chem.* optical activity; **aktywność Słońca** *astron.* solar activity; **aktywność wzbudzona** *fiz.* induced activity.

aktywny *a.* active, busy; **aktywny uczeń** diligent student; **aktywny stosunek do życia** active lifestyle; **aktywny zawodowo** sb professionally active; **aktywny biologicznie** *biol.* biologically active; **aktywny chemicznie** *chem.* chemically active, reactive; **węgiel aktywny** *chem.* activated charcoal.

aktywować *ipf.* activate; **węgiel aktywowany** *chem.* activated charcoal.

akulturacja *f.* acculturation.

akumulacja *f.* (= *nagromadzenie*) accumulation; **akumulacja energii** *fiz.* accumulation of energy; **akumulacja kapitału/kosztów** *ekon.* capital/cost accumulation.

akumulacyjny *a.* 1. *techn.* accumulative; **piec akumulacyjny** clay-tile stove. 2. *roln.* accumulation; **akumulacyjny poziom glebowy** soil accumulation level.

akumulator *mi Gen.* **-a** 1. *el.* (storage) battery, rechargeable battery, secondary cell, accumulator; **akumulator kwasowo-ołowiowy** lead-acid battery; **akumulator zasadowy** alkaline battery; **akumulator samochodowy** *mot.* car battery; **naładowany/rozładowany akumulator** charged/discharged battery. 2. *techn.* (= *urządzenie magazynujące energię*) accumulator; **akumulator hydrauliczny** hydraulic accumulator. 3. *komp.* accumulator, storage register.

akumulatorowy *a. techn.* battery-powered; **wózek akumulatorowy** electric cart.

akumulować *ipf.* accumulate, amass; **akumulować kapitał** accumulate capital. **~ się** *ipf.* accumulate, amass.

akupresura *f. med.* acupressure.

akupunktura *f. med.* acupuncture; **leczyć akupunkturą** treat with acupuncture.

akurat *part.* 1. (= *dokładnie*) just, only just, exactly; **mam akurat tyle pieniędzy, ile potrzeba na bilet** I have just enough money to buy a ticket; **akurat tyle, ile potrzeba** just enough; **tak się akurat składa, że...** it just so happens that...; (*dzień, czas*) particular; **dlaczego akurat tego dnia?** why on that particular day? 2. (= *właśnie w danym czasie*) at that (very) moment, (just) then; **akurat wtedy byłem za granicą** I happened to be abroad then; **akurat przyjechała jego matka** at that very moment his mother arrived. 3. (*zaprzeczenie*) fat chance!, like hell!, my foot! 4. (*niedowierzanie, sprzeciw*) of all...!; **czemu akurat ona?** why she *l.* her of all people?; **dlaczego akurat tutaj?** why here of all places?

akustyczność *f.* acoustics; **akustyczność pomieszczenia** the acoustics of the room.

akustyczny *a.* 1. acoustic; (= *dotyczący dźwięku*) sound; **efekty akustyczne** *film* sound effects; **fale akustyczne** *fiz.* sound waves; **gitara akustyczna** *muz.* acoustic guitar; **radiometr akustyczny** *techn.* acoustic radiometer. 2. (= *dobrze propagujący dźwięk*) having good acoustics; **akustyczna sala koncertowa** concert hall with good acoustics; **akustyczne mieszkanie** *pot.* apartment with (paper) thin walls.

akustyk *mp* acoustician.

akustyka *f. fiz., bud.* acoustics; **sala o dobrej akustyce** hall with good acoustics.

akuszer *mp przest.* (= *położnik*) obstetrician.

akuszerka *f. Gen.pl.* **-ek** midwife.

akuzatyw *mi jęz.* accusative.

akwaforta *f. sztuka* etching.

akwanauta *mp* aquanaut; (= *nurek*) diver.

akwanautyka *f.* aquanautics.

akwarela *f.* (*farba*) watercolor; (*technika, obraz*) watercolor (painting), aquarelle; **uprawiać akwarelę** paint in *l.* with watercolors; **malować akwarele** paint watercolors.

akwarelowy *a.* watercolor, aquarelle; **farby akwarelowe** watercolor paints; **malarstwo akwarelowe** watercolor painting.

akwariowy *a.* aquarium; **rośliny akwariowe** aquarium plants; **rybki akwariowe** aquarium fish *l.* fishes.

akwarium *n. indecl. in sing. pl.* **-ria** *Gen.* **-riów** aquarium, fish tank; **akwarium morskie** marine aquarium.

akwarysta *mp*, **akwarystka** *f. Gen.pl.* **-ek** aquariast, aquarist, aquaria *l.* aquarium hobbyist.

akwarystyczny *a.* aquarium; (*o zainteresowaniach*) aquariast; **akcesoria akwarystyczne** aquarium accessories; **sklep akwarystyczny** aquarium shop.

akwarystyka *f.* aquaria, aquaristics, fish keeping.

akwatinta *f.* aquatint; (*odbitka*) aquatint print; **uprawiać akwatintę** be an aquatint printmaker; **wykonywać akwatinty** make aquatints.

akwedukt *mi bud.* aquaduct.

akwen *mi* body of water.

akwizycja *f.* 1. *handl.* soliciting, sales; **pracować w akwizycji** work as a sales agent. 2. *jęz.* acquisition; **akwizycja mowy** speech acquisition.

akwizytor *mp*, **akwizytorka** *f. Gen.pl.* **-ek** sales rep *l.* representative, (sales) agent.

Alabama *f. geogr.* Alabama.

alabaster *mi* **-tr-** alabaster.

alabastrowy *a.* alabaster; **alabastrowa cera** alabaster complexion; **szkło alabastrowe** alabaster glass; **wazon alabastrowy** alabaster vase.

alalia *f. Gen.* **-ii** *pat.* aphonia.

alarm *mi* 1. (= *sygnał ostrzegawczy*) alarm, alert; **alarm powodziowy/pożarowy** flood/fire alert; **alarm przeciwlotniczy** air-raid alert; **alarm bojowy** battle alert; **alarm ćwiczebny** drill; **próbny alarm** test alert; **fałszywy alarm** false alarm; **ogłosić alarm** sound *l.* raise an alarm; **odwoływać alarm** give *l.* sound the all clear; **bić na alarm** raise a clamor. 2. (= *stan zagrożenia*) warning, alert; **na całym terenie obowiązuje alarm powodziowy** a flood alert is in effect for the entire area.

alarmistyczny *a.* alarmist; **alarmistyczny komunikat/prognoza** alarmist report/forecast.

alarmować *ipf.* 1. (= *sygnalizować niebezpieczeństwo*) alert; **alarmować straż pożarną** alert the fire department. 2. (= *wywoływać niepokój*) cause alarm.

alarmowy *a.* alarm; **sygnał/system alarmowy**

alarm signal/system; **plac alarmowy** *wojsk.* drill ground.

Alaska *f. geogr.* Alaska.

alaskański *a.* Alaskan.

alba¹ *f. rel.* alb.

alba² *f. hist.lit.* alba.

Albania *f. Gen.* -ii Albania.

Albańczyk *mp*, **Albanka** *f. Gen.pl.* -ek Albanian.

albański *a.* Albanian.

albatros *ma orn.* albatross, gooney (*Diomedea*); **albatros wędrowny** wandering albatross (*D. exulans*).

albertyn *mp rz.-kat.* Albertine monk (*monk of the order founded by Adam Chmielowski [brother Albert]*).

albertyński *mp rz.-kat.* Albertine.

albigens *mp rel. zw. pl.* Albigense.

albinizm *mi biol., pat.* albinism.

albinos *mp pl.* -i (= *człowiek dotknięty albinizmem*) albino. – *ma pl.* -y *biol.* albino.

albinoska *f. Gen.pl.* -ek (= *kobieta albinos*) albino.

albinotyczny *a. biol., pat.* albinotic, albino.

albo *conj.* or; **albo... albo...** either... or...; **kup sok pomarańczowy albo wiśniowy** buy (either) orange juice or cherry juice; **wyjadę albo wieczorem, albo w nocy** I'll either leave in the evening or at night; **teraz albo nigdy** (it's) now or never; **albo jeden, albo drugi** either one (or the other); **może być albo jeden, albo drugi** either (one) will do. – *part.* (*w retorycznych pytaniach wyrażających wątpliwość*) **albo ja wiem?** how should I know?; **albo (to) mu źle?** does he have any reason to complain?

albo-albo *int.* it's either this or that; **postawa/sytuacja typu albo-albo** either-or attitude/situation.

albowiem *conj. lit.* for, as, because.

alboż *part.* = **albo**.

album *mi* **1.** (*na zdjęcia, znaczki*) album; **rodzinny album** family (photo) album. **2.** *druk.* art book, illustrated book; **album malarstwa renesansowego** book of Renaissance art. **3.** (*płytowy*) (record) album. **4.** (*księga w dziekanacie*) student register; **indeks z numerem albumu** student grade book with a registration number. **5.** *przest.* (= *szkicownik*) sketchbook.

albumik *mi Gen.* -a *l.* -u (*na zdjęcia, znaczki*) album.

albumina *Gen.* -n *biochem.* albumin.

albuminowy *a. biochem.* albumin; **klej albuminowy** albumin binder.

albumowy *a. druk.* (= *w formie albumu*) art-book; **wydanie albumowe** art-book edition.

alchemia *f. Gen.* -ii alchemy.

alchemiczny *a.* alchemic, alchemical; **doświadczenie alchemiczne** alchemic experiment.

alchemik *mp* alchemist.

aldehyd *mi chem.* aldehyde.

aldehydowy *a. chem.* aldehydic; **grupa aldehydowa** aldehyde group.

ale *conj.* but; **ale jednak** and yet; **nie pierwszy raz, ale ostatni** it's not the first time, but it's the last; **ale z drugiej strony** but then (again); **może się mylę, ale...** correct me if I'm wrong, but... – *part.* **1.** what!, how!; **ale zabawa!** what fun!; **ale numer!** holy cow!; **ale pomysł!** what an idea!; **ale fajnie!** wow, that's cool; **ale był wściekły!** was he ever mad!; **ale jestem głupi!** how stupid of me! **2.** **ale, ale** *pot.* hold on, wait a minute; **ale, ale!** chciałem ci coś dać hold on, I want to give you sth. **3.** **ale (gdzież tam)!** *iron.* right!, sure! – *n. indecl.* (= *wada, wątpliwość*) weak point, flaw; **każde rozwiązanie ma swoje ale** every solution has its flaws; **zawsze są jakieś ale** there are always ifs and buts.

aleatoryczny *a. muz.* aleatory, aleatoric; **muzyka aleatoryczna** aleatory *l.* chance music.

aleatoryzm *mi muz.* aleatoric music.

alegoria *f. Gen.* -ii *sztuka* allegory.

alegoryczność *f. sztuka* allegoricalness, allegorical nature.

alegoryczny *a. sztuka* allegorical; **rzeźba alegoryczna** allegorical sculpture; **malowidło alegoryczne** allegorical painting.

alegoryka *f. sztuka* allegory.

alegoryzm *mi sztuka* allegorism.

alegoryzować *ipf. sztuka* allegorize.

aleja *f. Gen.* -ei *Gen.pl.* -ej *l.* -ei *często pl.* (= *szeroka ulica*) avenue, boulevard; (*w parku, ogrodzie*) lane, path.

alejka *f.* lane, path; **alejka ogrodowa** garden path.

aleksandryjski *a.* Alexandrian; *sztuka, fil.* Alexandrine; **sztuka/szkoła aleksandryjska** Alexandrine art/school; **wiersz aleksandryjski** *teor.lit.* Alexandrine verse.

aleksandryn *mi teor.lit.* Alexandrine (verse).

aleksja *f. pat.* alexia.

aleksykalizm *mi pat.* alexicalism.

alergen *mi fizj., pat.* allergen.

alergenny *a. pat.* allergenic; **substancja alergenna** allergenic substance.

alergia *f. Gen.* -ii *pat.* allergy.

alergiczka *f. Gen.pl.* -ek *zob.* **alergik**.

alergiczny *a. pat.* allergic; **reakcja alergiczna** allergic reaction; **astma pochodzenia alergicznego** allergic asthma; **wstrząs alergiczny** allergic *l.* anaphilactic shock.

alergik *mp* person with an allergy.

alergolog *mp pl.* -dzy *l.* -owie allergist.

alergologia *f. Gen.* -ii allergology.

alergologiczny *a.* allergology; **klinika alergologiczna** allergy clinic; **laboratorium alergologiczne** allergy laboratory.

alert *mi* alert.

aleucki *a.* Aleutian.

aleukemia *f. Gen.* -ii *pat.* aleukemic leukemia.

Aleuta *mp*, **Aleutka** *f. Gen.pl.* -ek Aleut.

Aleuty *pl. Gen.* -ów the Aleutian Islands.

ależ *part.* but, why; **ależ oczywiście** why, certainly!; (*zaproszenie, zachęta*) be my guest; by all means. – *int.* why; **ależ to niedopuszczalne!** but it's unacceptable!; why, that's unacceptable!; **ależ skąd!** of course not!; not at all!

alfa¹ *f.* (*litera*) **1.** alpha; **być alfą i omegą** be the alpha and the omega. **2.** *astron.* Alpha; **alfa Per-**

seusza Alpha Persei. – *a. indecl. nauk.* alpha; **cząstka/promieniowanie alfa** *fiz.* alpha particle/ radiation; **helisa alfa** *biochem.* alpha helix; **rytm alfa** *fizj.* alpha rhythm.

alfa² *f. bot.* esparto (grass) (*Stipa tenacissima*).

alfabet *mi* alphabet; **alfabet Braille'a** Braille alphabet; **alfabet Morse'a** Morse code; **alfabet głuchoniemych** manual alphabet, fingerspelling system; **alfabet muzyczny** alphabetical notation.

alfabetyczny *a.* alphabetic, alphabetical; **lista alfabetyczna** alphabetical list; **porządek/układ alfabetyczny** alphabetical order/arrangement; **pismo alfabetyczne** alphabetic writing (system).

alfanumeryczny *a. komp.* alphanumeric.

alfons *mp pl.* **-i** *l.* **-y** *pog.* (= *stręczyciel*) pimp.

alga *f. zw. pl. bot.* alga.

algebra *f. mat.* algebra.

algebraiczny *a. mat.* algebraic; **działanie/wyrażenie algebraiczne** algebraic operation/expression; **wzór algebraiczny** algebraic formula.

algebraik *mp* algebraist.

Algier *mi geogr.* Algiers.

Algierczyk *mp* Algerian.

Algieria *f. Gen.* **-ii** *geogr.* Algeria.

Algierka *f. zob.* **Algierczyk.**

algierski *a.* Algerian.

algolog *mp pl.* **-dzy** *l.* **-owie** *bot.* phycologist.

algologia *f. Gen.* **-ii** *bot.* phycology, algology.

algologiczny *a. bot.* phycological.

algorytm *mi mat., komp.* algorithm.

algorytmiczny *a.* algorithmic; **animacja algorytmiczna** *komp.* algorithmic animation; **złożoność algorytmiczna** *mat.* algorithmic complexity.

alianci *pl. Gen.* **-ów** *hist.* the Allies.

aliancki *a.* allied; **wojska alianckie** allied armies.

alians *mi pl.* **-e** *lit.* alliance.

aliant *mp* **1.** (= *sprzymierzeniec*) ally. **2.** *pl. zob.* **alianci.**

aliantka *f. Gen.pl.* **-ek** *zob.* **aliant 1.**

alibi *n. indecl.* alibi; **mieć alibi** have an alibi.

alienacja *f.* alienation (*skądś l. z czegoś* from sth); **alienacja majątku** *prawn.* alienation of property.

alienacyjny *a. prawn.* alienation.

alienować *ipf. gł. prawn.* alienate.

aligator *ma zool.* alligator (*Alligator*); **aligator z Missisipi** American alligator (*A. mississipiensis*).

alikwoty *pl. Gen.* **-ów** *muz.* harmonics.

alimentacja *f. prawn.* payment of alimony.

alimentacyjny *a. prawn.* alimony; **obowiązek alimentacyjny** obligation to pay alimony.

alimentator *mp prawn.* person required to alimony.

alimentować *ipf. prawn.* support; **alimentować dziecko** pay child support.

alimenty *pl. Gen.* **-ów** *prawn.* alimony; **wysokość alimentów** amount of alimony; **płacić alimenty** pay alimony; **wystąpić o alimenty** seek alimony.

aliteracja *f. teor.lit.* alliteration.

aliteracyjny *a. teor.lit.* alliterative.

alka *f. zool.* auk (*Alca*); **alka olbrzymia** great auk, garefowl (*Pinguinus impennis*).

alkalia *pl. Gen.* **-ów** *chem.* alkalies.

alkaliczność *f. chem.* alkalinity.

alkaliczny *a. chem.* alkaline; **metale alkaliczne** alkaline metals; **roztwór alkaliczny** alkaline solution; **metale ziem alkalicznych** alkaline earth metals.

alkalizować *ipf. chem.* alkalize.

alkaloidy *pl. Gen.* **-ów** *chem.* alkaloids.

alkohol *mi Gen.pl.* **-i** *l.* **-ów** **1.** (*napój*) alcohol, liquor; **być pod wpływem alkoholu** be under the influence of alcohol. **2.** *chem.* alcohol; **alkohol etylowy/metylowy/butylowy** ethyl/methyl/butyl alcohol; **alkohol absolutny** absolute alcohol; **zawartość alkoholu** alcoholic content.

alkoholiczka *f. Gen.pl.* **-ek** *zob.* **alkoholik.**

alkoholiczny *a.* alcoholic; **rodzina alkoholiczna** alcoholic family.

alkoholik *mp* alcoholic; **anonimowi alkoholicy** Alcoholics Anonymous.

alkoholizm *mi* alcohol abuse; *pat.* alcoholism.

alkoholizować *ipf.* (= *nasycać alkoholem*) alcoholize, soak *l.* steep in alcohol; **wino alkoholizowane** fortified wine.

alkoholometr *mi* breathalyzer.

alkoholowy *a.* alcoholic; **napój alkoholowy** alcoholic beverage; **upojenie alkoholowe** intoxication, inebriation; **zatrucie alkoholowe** alcohol poisoning; **fermentacja alkoholowa** *chem.* alcoholic fermentation.

alkowa *f. bud.* **1.** alcove. **2.** *przest.* (= *sypialnia*) bedroom; **sekrety alkowy** bedroom secrets.

Allach, Allah *mp rel.* Allah.

allegro *adv. i n. indecl. muz.* allegro.

alleluja *int. i n. indecl. rel.* hallelujah, alleluia; **radosnego alleluja!** glory hallelujah!

almanach *mi* almanac.

alniko *n. metal.* alnico.

alochtoniczny *a. geol., biol.* allochthonous.

alodialny *a. hist.* alodial, allodial.

alodium *n. indecl. in sing. pl.* **-ia** *Gen.* **-iów** *hist.* alodium, allodium.

aloes *mi bot.* aloe, Aloë.

aloesowy *a. bot.* aloe; **wyciąg aloesowy** aloe extract.

alofon *mi jęz.* allophone.

alogiczność *f. form.* illogicality.

alogiczny *a. form.* illogical.

alogizm *mi form.* illogicality.

alokacja *f.* allocation, alotment; **alokacja środków finansowych** *ekon.* allocation of funds; **alokacja pamięci** *komp.* memory allocation.

alomorf *mi jęz.* allomorph.

alopata *mp med.* allopath.

alopatia *f. Gen.* **-ii** *med.* allopathy.

alopatyczny *a. med.* allopathic; **leczenie alopatyczne** allopathic care; **metody alopatyczne** allopathic methods.

alotropia *f. Gen.* **-ii** *chem.* allotropy.

alotropowy *a. chem.* allotropic; **przemiana alotropowa** allotropic change; **odmiany alotropowe** allotropic forms.

alpaga *f.* **1.** *sl.* cheep wine. **2.** *tk.* = alpaka 2.

alpaka *f.* **1.** *zool.* alpaca (*Llama pacos*). **2.** *tk.* alpaca. **3.** *metal.* alpaca, German silver, nickel silver.

alpakowy *a.* alpaca; **marynarka alpakowa** alpaca jacket; **wełna alpakowa** alpaca (wool).

alpejczyk *mp*, **alpejka** *f. Gen.pl.* **-ek 1.** (= *narciarz alpejski*) Alpine skier. **2.** (= *mieszkaniec Alp*) inhabitant of the Alps.

alpejski *a.* **1.** (= *dotyczący Alp*) Alpine; **kraje alpejskie** Alpine countries; **fauna alpejska** (= *zamieszkująca Alpy*) Alpine fauna; **orogeneza alpejska** *geol.* Alpine orogenesis. **2.** *sport* konkurencje **alpejskie** Alpine events; **narciarstwo alpejskie** Alpine skiing. **3.** (= *wysokogórski*) alpine; **ogród alpejski** *ogr.* alpine garden, rock garden; **rośliny alpejskie** (= *wysokogórskie*) alpine plants. **4. fiołek alpejski** *bot.* cyclamen (*Cyclamen*).

alpinarium *n. indecl. in sing. pl.* **-ria** *Gen.* **-riów** alpine garden.

alpinista *mp*, **alpinistka** *f. Gen.pl.* **-ek** *sport* alpinist, mountaineer, mountain climber.

alpinistyczny *a.* *sport* climbing, mountaineering; **sprzęt alpinistyczny** (mountain-)climbing equipment; **wyprawa alpinistyczna** climbing expedition; **klub alpinistyczny** mountaineering club.

alpinistyka *f.*, **alpinizm** *mi* *sport* alpine climbing, mountain climbing, mountaineering.

Alpy *pl. Gen.* **Alp** the Alps.

alt *mi Gen.* **-u 1.** (*niski głos kobiecy*) alto. **2.** (*głos w partyturze*) alto part. **3.** (*instrument*) alto. – *mp Gen.* **-a** *pl.* **-y** (*śpiewak, śpiewaczka*) alto.

altana *f.* bower, arbor.

altanka *f.* arbor.

altazymut *mi astron.* altazimuth.

alteracja *f. muz.* alteration.

alternacja *f. t. bud., jęz.* alternation.

alternacyjny *a. jęz.* alternating.

alternant *mi jęz.* alternant.

alternator *mi Gen.* **-a 1.** *el.* alternator. **2.** *komp.* OR element.

alternatywa *f.* **1.** (= *wybór*) alternative, choice; **stanąć przed alternatywą** *l.* **wobec alternatywy** face an alternative *l.* a choice. **2.** (= *jedna z dwu możliwości*) option, alternative (possibility). **3.** *log.* alternative.

alternatywnie *adv.* alternatively; as an option; as an alternative.

alternatywny *a.* alternative; **medycyna/sztuka alternatywna** (= *niekonwencjonalna*) alternative medicine/art.

alternować *ipf. jęz.* alternate.

alterować *ipf. muz.* inflect.

altocumulus *mi Gen.* **-a** *meteor.* altocumulus.

altostratus *mi Gen.* **-a** *meteor.* altostratus.

altowiolista *mp*, **altowiolistka** *f. Gen.pl.* **-ek** violist.

altowy *a. muz.* alto; **głos altowy** alto; **partia altowa** alto part; **flet/saksofon altowy** alto flute/saxophone.

altówka *f. muz.* viola; **altówka miłosna** viola d'amore.

altruista *mp*, **altruistka** *f. Gen.pl.* **-ek** altruist.

altruistyczny *a.* altruistic; **postawa altruistyczna** altruism, altruistic stance.

altruizm *mi* altruism.

aluminiować *ipf. techn.* (= *traktować aluminium*) aluminize; (= *powlekać aluminium*) coat with aluminum.

aluminiowy *a.* aluminum; **folia aluminiowa** aluminum foil; **garnek aluminiowy** aluminum pot; **ruda aluminiowa** aluminum ore.

aluminium *n. sg. indecl. chem.* aluminum; *Br.* aluminium.

aluminotermia *f. techn.* aluminothermy.

alumn *mp pl.* **-i** *l.* **-owie 1.** *rz.-kat.* seminarian, seminarist. **2.** (*absolwent w krajach anglosaskich*) alumnus, alum.

aluwia *pl. Gen.* **-ów 1.** *geol.* alluviums, alluvia. **2.** *geol.* (= *holocen*) *przest.* Recent, the Recent Epoch, Holocene.

aluwialny *a. geol.* alluvial; **gleba aluwialna** alluvial (soil).

aluzja *f.* allusion, hint; **czynić** *l.* **robić aluzje do czegoś** allude to sth; make an allusion to sth; hint at sth; **aluzja do kogoś/czegoś** allusion to sb/sth.

aluzyjność *f.* allusiveness.

aluzyjny *a.* allusive; **sztuka aluzyjna** *sztuka* allusive art; **mówić w aluzyjny sposób** speak in an allusive way.

alweolarny *a. jęz.* alveolar; **głoska/spółgłoska alweolarna** alveolar sound/consonant.

Alzacja *f. geogr.* Alsace.

alzacki *a.* Alsatian; **owczarek alzacki** *kynol.* German shepherd, Alsatian.

Alzheimer *mp* **choroba Alzheimera** *pat.* Alzheimer's disease.

ałun *mi chem.* alum.

ałunit *mi min.* alunite.

ałycza *f. Gen.pl.* **-y** *bot.* cherry plum, myrobalan (*Prunus cerasifera var. divaricata*).

amalgamacja *f.* **1.** *techn.* (*otrzymywanie metalu*) amalgamation. **2.** *techn.* (*tworzenie się warstewki*) amalgamation.

amalgamat *mi* **1.** *chem.* amalgam. **2.** *przen.* amalgam, blend; **amalgamat kultur** blend of cultures.

amant *mp* **1.** *żart.* (= *kochanek*) beau, lover. **2.** *teatr* (*aktor*) lover; **amant filmowy** *film* screen lover.

amantka *f. Gen.pl.* **-ek** *zob.* **amant** 2.

amarant *mi* **1.** (*kolor*) amaranth. **2.** *bot.* amaranth (*Amaranthus*).

amarantowaty *a. bot.* (= *z rodziny Amaranthaceae*) amaranthaceous.

amarantowy *a.* amaranthine.

amarylis *ma bot.* amaryllis, belladonna lily, naked lady (*Amaryllis beladonna*).

amarylkowaty *a. bot.* (= *z rodziny Amaryllidaceae*) amaryllidaceous.

amator *mp*, **amatorka** *f. Gen.pl.* **-ek 1.** (= *miłośnik*) lover, amateur; **amator kwaśnych jabłek** *pot.* oddball, crackpot. **2.** (= *dyletant*) amateur, layman, dilettante, dabbler; **muzyk amator** amateur musician; **zupełny amator** rank amateur. **3.** (*ten, kto ma na coś ochotę*) lover; **amator na używany samochód** prospective buyer of a used car. **4.** *sport* (*nieprofesjonalista w sporcie*) amateur; **mistrzostwa amatorów** amateur championship; **kolarz amator** amateur cyclist.

amatorski *a.* **1.** (= *nieprofesjonalny*) amateur; **teatr/chór/film amatorski** amateur theatre/choir/movie; **po amatorsku** amateurishly. **2.** *sport* amateur; **regaty amatorskie** amateur regatta; **wyścig amatorski** amateur race.

amatorstwo *n.* **1.** (= *upodobanie*) love, fondness. **2.** (= *dyletantyzm*) amateurishness, dilettantism. **3.** *sport* amateurism.

amatorszczyzna *f. uj.* ineptness, amateurishness; amateurish execution, lack of professional finish.

Amazonia *f. Gen.* **-ii** *geogr.* the Amazon basin.

amazonka[1] *f. Gen.pl.* **-ek 1. Amazonka** *geogr.* the Amazon (River); *mit. t. przen.* (= *kobieta po amputacji piersi*) Amazon. **2.** (= *kobieta jeździec*) horsewoman, equestrian, rider. **3.** (*strój*) riding habit.

amazonka[2] *f. Gen.pl.* **-ek** *orn.* (*papuga*) Amazon (*Amazona*).

amazoński *a.* Amazonian; **amazoński las tropikalny** Amazon rainforest.

ambasada *f.* embassy.

ambasador *mp* **1.** (*przedstawiciel państwa*) ambassador; **mianować ambasadora** appoint an ambassador; **odwołać ambasadora** (= *pozbawić stanowiska*) dismiss an ambassador; (= *wezwać do powrotu z placówki*) recall an ambassador. **2.** *przen.* (= *głosiciel*) champion, advocate.

ambasadorka *f. Gen.pl.* **-ek 1.** *pot.* (= *kobieta ambasador*) ambassador; *rzad.* ambassadress. **2.** *zob.* **ambasador** 2.

ambasadorostwo *n.* ambassador and his wife.

ambasadorowa *f. Gen.* **-ej 1.** *pot.* ambassadress. **2.** ambassador's wife.

ambasadorski *a.* ambassadorial; **urząd ambasadorski** ambassadorship, office of an ambassador, embassy.

ambasadorstwo *n.* ambassadorship; **objąć ambasadorstwo** take office of an ambassador.

ambicja *f.* (= *honor, duma*) **1.** dignity, pride, self-esteem, self-respect; **być bez ambicji** have no self-respect; **nie mieć krztyny ambicji** be deprived of self-respect; **urazić czyjąś ambicję** hurt/injure sb's pride; wound sb's ambition; **unieść się ambicją** not deign to do sth. **2.** (= *chęć wybicia się*) ambition; **wygórowane ambicje** vaulting/overweening ambitions; **mieć ambicje polityczne** have an ambition to become a politician; **podsycać czyjeś ambicje** fan/spur/stir/whet sb's ambition.

ambicjonalny *a.* ambitious, caused/dictated by ambition; **spory ambicjonalne** conflict/contest of vanities/ambitions; **względy ambicjonalne** honor.

ambit *mi* **1.** *bud.* ambulatory. **2.** *arch.* dignity, self-respect; **wziąć na ambit** make sth a point of honor.

ambitnie *adv.* ambitiously; **walczyć ambitnie** fight ambitiously.

ambitny *a.* ambitious; **ambitny student** ambitious student; **ambitne plany** ambitious plans.

ambiwalencja *f.* **1.** *form.* ambivalence, ambivalency. **2.** *jęz.* ambivalence. **3.** *psych.* ambivalence.

ambiwalentny *a. form.* ambivalent; **ambiwalentny stosunek do czegoś** ambivalent attitude to sth.

ambona *f.* **1.** *kośc.* pulpit; **spaść z ambony** *żart.* have one's banns called/published. **2.** *geogr., żegl.* pulpit. **3.** *myśl.* look-out.

ambra *f.* **1.** *chem.* ambergris. **2.** *bot.* = **ambrowiec**.

ambrowiec *mi* **-wc-** *Gen.* **-a** *bot.* liquidambar (*Liquidambar*).

ambrozja *f.* **1.** *mit. i przen.* ambrosia. **2.** *bot.* ambrosia (*Ambrosia*).

ambrozjański *a. muz.* Ambrosian; **śpiew ambrozjański** Ambrosian chant, Milanese chant.

ambulans *mi pl.* **-e** *l.* **-y** ambulance; **ambulans pocztowy** mail; **ambulans bankowy** (bank) armored car.

ambulatorium *n. sg. indecl. pl.* **-ria** *Gen.* **-riów** out-patients' clinic.

ambulatoryjny *a.* **leczenie ambulatoryjne** out-patients' clinic treatment.

ameba *f. biol.* ameba, amoeba.

ameboza *f. pat.* amebiasis, amoebiasis, amebic dysentery.

amen *int. i n. indecl.* amen; **jak amen w pacierzu** (as) sure as death (and taxes); **na amen** for good.

amencja *f. pat.* amentia.

ameryk *mi chem.* americium.

Ameryka *f. geogr.* America; **Ameryka Łacińska** Latin America; **Ameryka Północna/Południowa/Środkowa** North/South/Central America.

Amerykaniec *mp* **-ńc-** *Voc.* **-cze** *l.* **-cu** *Nom.pl.* **-y** *l.* **-e** *pog., iron.* Yankee.

Amerykanin *mp pl.* **-anie** *Gen.* **-anów** American.

amerykanista *mp,* **amerykanistka** *f. Gen.pl.* **-ek** Americanist.

amerykanistyka *f.* American studies.

amerykanizacja *f.* Americanization, American influence.

amerykanizm *mi* Americanism.

amerykanizować *ipf.* Americanize. **~ się** *ipf.* Americanize, become Americanized.

Amerykanka *f. Gen.pl.* **-ek** American (woman).

amerykanka *f.* **1.** (*kanapa*) sofa bed. **2.** *ekon.* double-entry bookkeeping, double entry. **3.** *sport* catch-as-catch-can wrestling, catch-can wrestling; (= *wolnoamerykanka*) *t. przen.* catch-as-catch-can, catch-can.

amerykański *a.* American; **amerykański sposób życia** the American way of life; **sosna amerykańska** *bot.* white pine (*Pinus strobus*); **księgowość amerykańska** *ekon.* double-entry bookkeeping.

amerykańskość *f.* Americanness.

ametyst *mi min.* amethyst.

ametystowy a. (= *fioletowy l. wykonany z ametystu*) amethyst.

amfa f. (*sl.* = *tabletka amfetaminy*) benny, speed.

amfetamina f. *chem., med.* amphetamine.

amfibia f. *Gen.* **-ii 1.** *wojsk.* amphibious vehicle *l.* airplane, amphibian. **2.** *biol. przest.* (= *płaz*) amphibian.

amfibiotyczny a. *biol.* amphibiotic.

amfibol *mi min.* amphibole.

amfibrach *mi lit.* amphibrach.

amfilada f. rooms en suite.

amfiladowy a. en suite; **układ amfiladowy** en suite arrangement.

amfiploid *ma biol.* amphiploid.

amfiteatr *mi* amphitheater.

amfiteatralny a. amphitheatric, amphitheatrical; **układ amfiteatralny widowni** amphitheatric arrangement of seats.

amfolit *mi chem.* ampholyte, amphoteric electrolyte.

amfora f. amphora.

amfoteryczny a. *chem.* amphoteric.

amid *mi chem.* amide.

amina f. *chem.* amine.

aminokwas *mi chem.* amino acid.

amnestia f. *Gen.* **-ii** amnesty; **powszechna amnestia** general amnesty; **ogłosić amnestię** declare amnesty.

amnestyjny a. **ustawa amnestyjna** *prawn.* amnesty act.

amnezja f. *psych.* amnesia.

amok *mi* amuck, amok; **wpaść w amok** go *l.* run amuck; *pred.* **opętany amokiem** amuck.

amon *mi chem.* ammonium; **węglan/azotan amonu** ammonium carbonate/nitrate.

amoniak *mi chem.* ammonia.

amoniakalny a. *chem.* ammoniac, ammoniacal; **woda amoniakalna** ammonia water, ammonium hydroxide; **roślinność amoniakalna** *bot.* nitrophilous plants.

amoniakować *ipf.* **1.** *chem.* ammoniate. **2.** *roln.* ammonify.

amonowy a. *chem.* ammonium; **grupa amonowa** ammonium; **saletra amonowa** *roln.* ammonium nitrate.

Amor *mp mit.* Cupid; **ugodzony strzałą Amora** *przest. l. lit.* shot with Cupid's dart.

amoralista *mp fil.* amoralist.

amoralizm *mi fil.* amoralism.

amoralność f. amorality.

amoralny a. amoral, immoral; **amoralna powieść** amoral novel; **amoralny związek** amoral relationship.

amorek *mp* **-rk-** *pl.* **-i** *sztuka* cupid, amoretto, amorino.

amorficzność f. amorphousness.

amorficzny a. amorphous; **ciało amorficzne** *chem., fiz.* amorphous body.

amorfizm *mi* amorphism.

amortyzacja f. **1.** *ekon.* depreciation; **stopa amortyzacji** depreciation rate. **2.** *techn.* shock absorption.

amortyzacyjny a. **1.** *ekon.* depreciative, depre-

ciatory; **stawka amortyzacyjna** depreciation rate. **2.** *techn.* shock-absorbing; **system amortyzacyjny** shock-absorbing system.

amortyzator *mi Gen.* **-a** *techn.* shock absorber; **amortyzator kołysania** *żegl.* stabilizer.

amortyzować *ipf.* **1.** *ekon.* depreciate. **2.** *techn.* absorb shocks. **~ się** *ipf. ekon.* depreciate, become depreciated.

amper *mi fiz.* ampere.

amperogodzina f. *fiz.* ampere-hour.

amperomierz *mi Gen.* **-a** *fiz.* ammeter.

ampicylina f. *med.* ampicillin.

amplituda f. *fiz., mat.* amplitude; **modulacja amplitudy** *el.* amplitude modulation, AM.

ampułka f. *Gen.pl.* **-ek 1.** *med.* ampule, ampoule. **2.** *rz.-kat.* ampulla.

amputacja f. *chir.* amputation; **amputacja nogi** leg amputation; **amputacja piersi** breast amputation, mastectomy.

amputacyjny a. *chir.* amputative; **zabieg amputacyjny** amputation procedure, amputation; **narzędzia amputacyjne** amputation instruments.

amputować *ipf. l. pf. med.* amputate.

amulet *mi* charm, amulet, talisman; **amulet przeciw czarom** charm to ward off evil.

amunicja f. ammunition; **amunicja artyleryjska/ćwiczebna/myśliwska** artillery/practice/hunting ammunition; **amunicja do broni ręcznej** small-arms ammunition; **ślepa amunicja** blank ammunition, dummy ammunition, blanks.

amunicyjny a. **magazyn amunicyjny** ammunition depot, magazine, dump. — *mp wojsk.* loader.

amur *ma zool.* grass carp (*Ctenopharyngodon idella*).

amurski a. Amur; **korkowiec amurski** *bot.* Amur cork tree (*Phellodendron amurense*).

amylaza f. *biochem.* amylase.

anabaptysta *mp*, **anabaptystka** f. *Gen.pl.* **-ek** *rel.* Anabaptist.

anabaptyzm *mi rel.* Anabaptism.

anabioza f. *biol.* anabiosis.

anaboliczny a. *biol.* anabolic; **leki/sterydy anaboliczne** *med.* anabolic drugs/steroids.

anabolizm *mi biol.* anabolism.

anachroniczność f. anachronic character.

anachroniczny a. **1.** (= *niezgodny z realiami danego czasu, z innej epoki*) anachronistic. **2.** (= *przestarzały*) outdated, outmoded, old-fashioned, dated; **anachroniczne poglądy** outmoded/old-fashioned ideas; **anachroniczne rozwiązania techniczne** outdated technical solutions.

anachronizm *mi* (*błąd chronologiczny l. coś, co jest już przestarzałe*) anachronism.

anaerob *ma biol.* anaerobe.

anafilaksja f. *med.* anaphylaxis.

anafilaktyczny a. *med.* anaphylactic; **wstrząs anafilaktyczny** anaphylactic shock.

anafora f. *teor.lit.* anaphora.

anaforeza f. *fiz.* anaphoresis.

anaforyczny a. *jęz.* anaphoric; **zaimek anaforyczny** anaphoric pronoun.

anagram *mi* anagram.

anakolut *mi jęz.* anacoluthon.

anakolutyczny a. **zdanie anakolutyczne** jęz. anacoluthon.

anakonda f. zool. anaconda (Eunectes murinus).

anakreontyk mi teor.lit. Anacreontic.

analeptyk mi med. analeptic.

analfabeta mp, **analfabetka** f. Gen.pl. -ek **1.** (= nieumiejąc-y/a czytać i pisać) illiterate. **2.** (= ignorant/ka) ignoramus.

analfabetyzm mi illiteracy.

analgetyczny a. med. analgesic.

analgezja f. med. analgesia.

analityczka f. Gen.pl. -ek zob. **analityk.**

analityczność f. analytic character.

analityczny a. analytic, analytical; **umysł analityczny** analytical brain; **metoda analityczna** analytic method; **chemia analityczna** chem. analytical chemistry; **zdanie analityczne** fil. analytic sentence; log. analytic proposition; **język analityczny** jęz. analytic language; **geometria analityczna** mat. analytic geometry.

analityk mp analyst.

analityka f. analythics; **analityka medyczna** medical testing.

analiza f. **1.** (= dociekania intelektualne, naukowe) analysis; **wnikliwa analiza** thorough/in-depth analysis; **analiza dzieła literackiego** analysis of a literary work; **przeprowadzić analizę** carry out/make an analysis; **poddać analizie** analyze; **analiza logiczna** logical analysis; **analiza matematyczna** mathematical analysis, calculus; **analiza funkcjonalna** mat. functional analysis. **2.** chem. analysis; **analiza ilościowo-jakościowa** quantitative-qualitative analysis; **analiza elementarna** elemental analysis, elementary analysis; **analiza aktywacyjna** activation analysis; **analiza widmowa** spectroanalysis, spectroscopic analysis.

analizator mi Gen. -a pl. -y **1.** chem., fiz., mat. analyzer. **2.** fizj. neural basis of conditioned reflex in Pavlov's theory. – mp pl. -rzy analyzer.

analizować ipf. **1.** (dociekać intelektualnie, naukowo) analyze. **2.** (badać skład czegoś) analyze, assay; **analizować skład zanieczyszczonego powietrza** analyze composition of polluted air; **lampa analizująca** telew. camera tube, pickup tube.

analny a. anat. anal; **seks analny** anal sex.

analog mi pl. -i **1.** (= odpowiednik) analogue. **2.** chem. analogue. **3.** komp. analog model. – mp pl. -dzy l. -owie analog-machine specialist.

analogia f. Gen. -ii **1.** (= odpowiedniość) t. jęz., prawn. analogy; **rozumowanie przez analogię** log. analogy, reasoning by analogy; **utworzony przez analogię** jęz. analogically created; **wykazać analogie między A a B** demonstrate analogies between A and B. **2.** (= odpowiednik) parallel, analogous case.

analogiczny a. **1.** analogous, parallel; **analogiczna sytuacja** similar situation; **analogiczna forma językowa** corresponding linguistic form; **analogiczny okres roku ubiegłego** corresponding period of last year; **narządy analogiczne** biol. analogous organs. **2.** jęz. analogic, analogical.

analogizm mi log. analogism.

analogowy a. komp., el. analogue, analog; **maszyna/płyta analogowa** analog machine/record; **model analogowy** analog model.

ananas mi bot. (roślina l. owoc) pineapple (Ananas comosus). – mp pl. -y pot. (= gagatek) scamp.

ananasowaty a. bot. (= z rodziny Bromeliaceae) bromeliaceous.

ananasowy a. **plantacja ananasowa** pinery, pineapple plantation; **sok ananasowy** pineapple juice.

anarchia f. Gen. -ii anarchy; **wydobyć kraj z anarchii** lift the country out of anarchy.

anarchiczny a. anarchic, anarchistic; **działalność anarchiczna** anarchist activity.

anarchista mp, **anarchistka** f. Gen.pl. -ek anarchist.

anarchistyczny a. anarchist; **ruch anarchistyczny** anarchist movement.

anarchizm mi polit. anarchism.

anarchizować ipf. **1.** (= zajmować się anarchią) be an anarchist. **2.** (= dezorganizować) throw into anarchy.

anatema f. rz.-kat. l. przen. anathema; **rzucić na kogoś anatemę** anathematize sb; pronounce anathema against sb.

anatolijski a. Anatolian; **języki anatolijskie** jęz. Anatolian languages; **koń anatolijski** hodowla Turk.

anatom mp pl. -owie anatomist.

anatomia f. Gen. -ii anatomy; **anatomia człowieka** human anatomy; **anatomia funkcjonalna/opisowa/patologiczna** functional/descriptive/pathologic anatomy; **anatomia mózgu** brain anatomy.

anatomiczny a. anatomical, anatomic; **budowa anatomiczna** anatomy; **opis anatomiczny** anatomical description.

anatomopatolog mp pl. -dzy l. -owie anatomicopathologist.

anatomopatologia f. anatomical pathology.

anatomopatologiczny a. anatomicopathological; **pracownia anatomopatologiczna** anathomicopathological laboratory.

ancestralny a. ancestral.

anchois n. indecl. canned anchovy.

ancymonek mp -nk- pl. -i przest., żart. slyboots.

andante n. indecl. muz. andante.

Andora f. geogr. Andorra.

Andorczyk mp, **Andorka** f. Gen.pl. -ek Andorran.

androfobia f. Gen. -ii psych. misandry.

androgen mi fizj. androgen.

androgenny a. fizj. androgenic; **ciała androgenne** androgenic bodies.

android mi Gen. -a android.

andrologia f. Gen. -ii andrology.

andrologiczny a. andrologic; **poradnia andrologiczna** andrologic clinic.

androny pl. Gen. -ów pot. poppycock.

andrut mi Gen. -a wafer.

andrzejki pl. Gen. -jek (tradycja polska) St. Andrew's Day party.

andrzejkowy *a.* zabawa andrzejkowa St. Andrew's Day party; wróżby andrzejkowe St. Andrew's Day fortunes.

Andy *pl. Gen.* -ów *geogr.* the Andes.

andyjski *a.* 1. Andean. 2. kondor andyjski *orn.* Andean condor (*Vultur gryphus*).

anegdota *f.* 1. (= *dowcip*) anecdote. 2. (*treść dzieła literackiego*) subject matter.

anegdotyczny *a.* anecdotal; anegdotyczne ujęcie tematu anecdotal depiction, anecdotalism; forma anegdotyczna anecdotal form.

anegdotyzm *mi* anecdotalism.

aneks *mi* (= *załącznik*) appendix, schedule, addendum; *t. bud.* annex; aneks kuchenny kitchenette; budynek z aneksem building with an annex.

aneksja *f.* annexation.

aneksyjny *a.* annexionist; polityka aneksyjna annexionist policy.

anektować *ipf.* annex.

anemia *f. Gen.* -ii *pat.* anemia, anaemia; anemia złośliwa pernicious anemia.

anemiczka *f. Gen.pl.* -ek *med. zob.* anemik.

anemiczny *a.* (= *niedokrwisty*) anemic, anaemic; *przen.* (= *rachityczny, słaby*) weak, listless, limpid; anemiczna cera pale complexion; anemiczne dziecko anemic child; anemiczna roślinność sparse vegetation; anemiczne słońce pale *l.* watery sun; anemiczne uczucia pent-up feelings.

anemik *mp med.* person suffering from anemia.

anemon *mi bot.* anemone (*Anemone*).

anergia *f. Gen.* -ii *med. i psych.* anergy.

anestetyczny *a. med.* anesthetic, anaesthetic; środki anestetyczne anesthetics.

anestetyk *mi med.* anesthetic, anaesthetic.

anestezja *f. med.* anesthesia.

anestezjolog *mp pl.* -dzy *l.* -owie anesthesiologist.

anestezjologia *f. Gen.* -ii *med.* anesthesiology.

anestezjologiczny *a. med.* anesthetic; przygotowanie anestezjologiczne pacjenta anasthetization.

angażować *ipf.* 1. (= *zatrudniać*) employ, hire. 2. (= *wikłać, wciągać*) engage, involve. ~ się *ipf.* 1. (= *zatrudniać się*) take up a job. 2. (= *dać się pochłonąć*) become involved.

angelologia *f. Gen.* -ii *teol.* angelology.

Angielka *f.* Englishwoman.

angielski *a.* English; język angielski English, the English language; angielska flegma *często iron.* English phlegm; angielska pogoda *iron.* English weather; haft angielski English embroidery *l.* work; konie angielskie *hodowla* English breeds; park angielski landscape garden; pszenica angielska *roln.* rivet wheat; rożek angielski *muz.* English horn; sól angielska *chem.* Epsom salt *l.* salts; walc angielski hesitation waltz; ziele angielskie *bot., kulin.* pimento, allspice (*Triticum turgidum*).

angielszczyć *ipf.* Anglicize.

angielszczyzna *f.* English, the English language.

angina *f. pat.* strep throat; angina ropna quinsy.

anglezować *v. jeźdz.* post.

Anglia *f. Gen.* -ii England; Nowa Anglia *geogr.* New England.

anglicyzm *mi jęz.* Anglicism, Englishism.

Anglik *mp* Englishman.

anglikanin *mp pl.* -anie *Gen.* -anów *rel.* Anglican.

anglikanizm *mi rel.* Anglicanism.

anglikanka *f. Gen.pl.* -ek *zob.* anglikanin.

anglikański *a. rel.* Anglican; Kościół Anglikański the Church of England.

anglista *mp*, anglistka *f. Gen.pl.* -ek Anglicist; teacher *l.* student of English.

anglistyka *f.* (*dziedzina*) English studies, English philology; (*wydział uczelni*) school of English, English department.

anglo-amerykański *a.* Anglo-American.

angloarab *mp jeźdz.* Anglo-Arab.

anglofil *mp* Anglophile, Anglophil.

anglofilia *f. Gen.* -ii Anglophilia.

anglofob *mp* Anglophobe.

anglofobia *f. Gen.* -ii Anglophobia.

anglojęzyczny *a.* English-speaking.

Anglosas *mp pl.* -i Anglo-Saxon.

anglosaski *a.* Anglo-Saxon.

Angol *mp pog.* (= *Anglik*) Brit, Pommy.

Angola *a. geogr.* Angola.

Angola *f. geogr.* Angola.

Angolczyk *mp*, Angolka *f. Gen.pl.* -ek Angolan.

angolski *a.* Angolan.

angora *f. l. ma decl. like f. Gen.pl.* -r *l.* -rów *hodowla* (*kot*) Angora (cat); (*koza*) Angora (goat); (*królik*) Angora (rabbit). – *f.* (*wełna*) Angora (wool).

angorski *a.* Angora.

angstrem *mi miern.* angstrom.

ani *conj.* (*łączy części zdania w zdaniu zaprzeczonym lub zdania zaprzeczone*) ani... ani... (*bez wyrazu przeczącego*) neither... nor...; (*po wyrazie przeczącym*) either... or...; nie mogę ruszyć ani ręką, ani nogą I can't move a muscle; ani widu, ani słychu not a trace; neither hide nor hair; ani be, ani me *pot.* not a single word; ani mnie to ziębi, ani parzy *pot.* I don't care; it leaves me cold. – *part.* (*wzmocniona partykuła przecząca*) (*bez wyrazu przeczącego*) not a; (*z wyrazem przeczącym*) a; ani ani in no circumstances; ani cienia dowodu not a shred of evidence; ani cienia nadziei/zainteresowania not a glimmer of hope/interest; ani krzty not a bit; ani mowy o czymś sth is out of the question; ani mru mru not a word; keep your mouth shut; ani myśleć o czymś not even think about sth; ani mu/mi to w głowie he/I won't even think about it; ani mu/mi się śni never in his/my life; not on your life; ani na jotę not one iota; not one jot; not one whit; (pieniędzy) ani na lekarstwo no (money) at all; ani pary z ust/z gęby nie puścić not say a word; keep one's mouth shut; ani pisnąć keep one's mouth shut; (bez tego) ani rusz we can't *l.* won't do without it; ani się spostrzeże(sz)/obejrzy(sz) in no time; ani słowa not a word; ani słowa! button your lip; ani

trochę not a bit; **ani w ząb nie rozumiem** I don't understand at all; **ani za grosz** not a bit; **ani znaku/śladu czegoś** neither hide nor hair; **ani żywej duszy/żywego ducha** not a soul; **ani chybi** *pot.* for sure; most certainly; without fail; **ani się umywa do czegoś** *pot.* it isn't anywhere near as good as sth.

aniele *mp zob.* **anioł.**

anielski *a.* angelic, angelical; **anielski uśmiech** *przen.* angelic smile; **pozdrowienie anielskie** (= *modlitwa*) Hail Mary, Ave Maria; **włosy anielskie** (= *ozdoba choinkowa*) angel hair.

anielskość *f.* angelicalness.

anihilacja *f. fiz.* annihilation.

anihilacyjny *a. fiz.* annihilative, annihilatory.

anilana *f. tk.* Polish synthetic textile made of polyacrylonitrile.

anilina *f. chem.* aniline.

animacja *f.* (*t.* = *ożywienie, inspiracja*) animation.

animacyjny *a. film*, *teatr* related to animation.

animator *mp*, **animatorka** *f. Gen.pl.* **-ek** animator, animater; *teatr* animation artist; *film* cartoonist.

animista *mp*, **animistka** *f. Gen.pl.* **-ek** *rel.* animist.

animistyczny *a. rel.* animist, animistic.

animizacja *f. teor.lit.* animatism.

animizm *mi rel., psych.* animism.

animować *ipf.* animate.

animowany *a.* animated; **film animowany** *film* animated cartoon, cartoon.

animozja *f.* animosity (*do kogoś* against, to *l.* towards sb).

animusz *mi* spirit, mettle, courage; **dodawać komuś animuszu** give sb's spirits a lift; animate sb, enliven sb, perk sb up; **nie tracić animuszu** keep one's spirit.

anioł *mp Loc. i Voc.* **-ele** *pl.* **-owie** *l.* **-y** *lit. l. arch.* **-eli** **1.** *rel.* angel; **Anioł Pański** Angelus; **anioł stróż** guardian angel; *żart.* (= *tajniak, policjant*) tail, shadow; **dzwon na Anioł Pański** Angelus bell; **anioł pokoju/śmierci/burzy** angel of peace/death/storm; **upadły anioł** fallen angel; **spać jak anioł** sleep like a baby; **to anioł nie człowiek** he is a saint. **2. anioł morski** *ma pl.* **-y** *icht.* angel shark (*Squatina squatina*).

aniołek *mp* **-łk-** *pl.* **-i** **1.** cherub; **powiększyć grono aniołków** *euf.* (= *umrzeć*) pass away. **2.** *przen.* (= *kochanie*) darling, angel; **aniołek z różkami** wolf in sheep's clothing; **spać jak aniołek** sleep like a baby.

anion *mi chem.* anion.

anionowy *a. chem.* anionic.

anizotropia *f. min.* anisotropy.

aniżeli *conj. lit.* than.

ankieta *f.* **1.** (= *kwestionariusz*) questionnaire; **ankieta personalna** personal data form. **2.** (= *zbieranie informacji*) poll, survey.

ankieter *mp*, **ankieterka** *f. Gen.pl.* **-ek** poller.

ankietować *ipf.* poll.

ankietowany *mp* pollee.

annalistyka *f.* = **annały.**

annały *pl. Gen.* **-ów** annals.

ano *part.* well; **ano pójdę już** well, I should be going; **ano prawda** well, it's true.

anoda *f. fiz., el.* anode.

anodować *ipf. techn.* anodize.

anodowy *a. fiz. el.* anodic; **bateria anodowa** anode battery; **szlam anodowy** anode slime.

anodyzacja *f. techn.* anodization.

anomalia *f. Gen.* **-ii** anomaly; **anomalia optyczna** *min.* optical anomaly; **anomalia magnetyczna/termiczna** magnetic/thermal anomaly.

anonim *mi Gen.* **-u** *Nom.pl.* **-y** anonymous letter. – *mp Gen.* **-a** *Nom.pl.* **-owie** anonym, anonymity, anonymous person.

anonimowość *f.* anonymity.

anonimowy *a.* anonymous.

anons *mi pl.* **-y** *l.* **-e** **1.** (*ogłoszenie*) (classified) advertisement, announcement. **2.** (*zwiastun*) preview, trailer.

anonsować *ipf.* **1.** (*zapowiadać, ogłaszać*) advertise, announce. **2.** (*prezentować, przedstawiać, meldować*) announce. **~ się** *ipf.* proclaim one's presence.

anoreksja *f. pat.* anorexia.

anorektyczka *f. Gen.pl.* **-ek, anorektyk** *mp* anorectic, anorexic.

anormalność *f.* abnormality.

anormalny *a.* abnormal; **człowiek anormalny** *med.* insane person.

anszlus *mi hist.* the Anschluss.

antagonista *mp* antagonist. – *mi sg. anat.* (*mięsień lub ząb*) antagonist.

antagonistka *f. Gen.pl.* **-ek** *zob.* **antagonista.**

antagonistyczny *a.* antagonistic.

antagonizm *mi* antagonism.

antałek *mi* **-łk-** *Gen.* **-a** *przest.* (= *beczułka*) hogshead, keg, cask.

antarktyczny *a.* Antarctic.

Antarktyda *f. geogr.* Antarctica.

Antarktyka *f. geogr.* the Antarctic.

antena *f. radio* aerial, antenna; **antena satelitarna** satellite dish; **antena zbiorcza** community aerial; **wejść na antenę, być na antenie** be on the air.

antenat *mp form.* ancestor, forefather.

antenatka *f. Gen.pl.* **-ek** (female) ancestor, ancestress, foremother.

antenowy *a.* **1.** *el.* antennal. **2. czas antenowy** *radio, telew.* air time.

antidotum *n. sg. indecl. pl.* **-ta** *Gen.* **-tów** *med. l. przen.* antidote (*na coś* against sth).

Antiochia *f. Gen.* **-ii** *geogr., hist.* Antioch.

antologia *f. Gen.* **-ii** anthology.

antonim *mi jęz.* antonym.

antonimia *f. Gen.* **-ii** *jęz.* antonymy.

antonimiczny *a. jęz.* antonymous, antonymic.

antracyt *mi geol.* anthracite.

antracytowy *a. geol.* anthracitic, anthracitous.

antraks *mi wet.* anthrax.

antrakt *mi* **1.** (= *przerwa w teatrze*) intermission. **2.** *muz.* entr'acte.

antresola *f. Gen.pl.* **-i** *l.* **-l** *bud.* entresol, mezzanine.

antropocentryczny *a.* anthropocentric.

antropocentryzm *mi* anthropocentrism.

antropofag *ma przest.* antropophage, cannibal.

antropolog *mp pl.* **-dzy** *l.* **-owie** anthropologist; **antropolog kultury** cultural anthropologist.

antropologia *f. Gen.* **-ii** anthropology; **antropologia filogenetyczna/ontogenetyczna** *biol.* phylogenetic/ontogenetic anthropology; **antropologia kulturowa** cultural anthropology.

antropologiczny *a.* (*związany z antropologią*) anthropological, anthropologic; **typy antropologiczne** anthropological types.

antropometria *f. Gen.* **-ii** anthropometry.

antropometryczny *a.* anthropometric, anthropometrical.

antropomorficzny *a.* anthropomorphic, anthropomorphous.

antropomorfizacja *f.* anthropomorphization.

antropomorfizm *mi biol., rel. i sztuka* anthropomorphism.

antropomorfizować *ipf.* anthropomorphize.

antroponimia *f. Gen.* **-ii** *jęz.* anthroponymy.

antrykot *mi kulin.* entrecôte, steak.

anturium *n. bot.* anthurium (*Anthurium*).

antyaborcyjny *a.* anti-abortion.

antyalkoholowy *a.* anti-alcoholic.

antyamerykański *a.* anti-American.

antyatomowy *a.* **1.** (= *dotyczący sprzeciwu wobec broni atomowej*) antinuclear, antinuke. **2.** (= *chroniący przed bronią atomową*) **schron antyatomowy** fallout shelter.

antybakteryjny *a.* antibacterial.

antybiotyk *mi med.* antibiotic.

antybiotykowy *a. biol., farm.* antibiotic.

antybioza *f. biol.* antibiosis.

antybohater *mp pl.* **-rzy** *l.* **-owie** antihero.

antycentrum *n. geol.* anticenter.

antychryst *mp pl.* **-y** **1.** *rel.* Antichrist. **2.** (= *szatan, diabeł*) Satan. **3.** *przen. pot.* hellhound.

antycyklon *mi meteor.* anticyclone.

antycypacja *f.* anticipation.

antycypować *ipf.* anticipate.

antycząstka *f. fiz.* antiparticle.

antyczny *a.* **1.** (= *dotyczący starożytności*) ancient. **2.** (= *zabytkowy*) antique; *często pog.* (= *staroświecki*) outdated, old-fashioned.

antydatować *ipf.* predate, antedate, backdate.

antydemokratyczny *a.* antidemocratic, antidemocratical.

antydepresyjny *a.* antidepressant, antidepressive; **lek antydepresyjny** antidepressant, antidepressant drug.

antydiuretyna *f. biochem.* antidiuretic hormone, vasopressin.

antydopingowy *a. sport* drug-testing.

antyenzym *mi biochem.* antienzyme.

antyfaszysta *mp*, **antyfaszystka** *f. Gen.pl.* **-ek** *polit.* anti-Nazi.

antyfaszystowski *a. polit.* anti-Nazi.

antyfeminista *mp* antifeminist.

antyfeministyczny *a.* antifeminist, antifeministic.

antyfeminizm *mi* antifeminism.

antyferromagnetyczny *a. fiz.* antiferromagnetic.

antyferromagnetyk *mi fiz.* antiferromagnet.

antyferromagnetyzm *mi fiz.* antiferromagnetism.

antyfeudalny *a.* antifeudal, antifeudalistic.

antyfona *f. rel., muz.* antiphon.

antyfrykcyjny *a.* antifriction, antifrictional.

antygen *mi biol.* antigen.

antygenowy *a. biol.* antigenic; **determinant antygenowy** antigenic determinant.

antygrypowy *a.* anti-flu, against flu.

antyhałasowy *a.* anti-noise.

antyhumanistyczny *a.* antihumanist.

antyhumanitarny *a.* antihumanitarian.

antyimperialistyczny *a. polit.* anti-imperialist.

antyimperializm *mi polit.* anti-imperialism.

antyimportowy *a. handl.* anti-import.

antyinflacyjny *a. ekon.* anti-inflationary.

antyintelektualny *a.* anti-intellectual.

antyk *mi* **1.** (= *świat starożytny*) antiquity. **2.** (= *zabytek, staroć*) antique.

antykapitalistyczny *a. polit.* anticapitalist, anticapitalistic.

antykatoda *f. fiz.* anticathode.

antykatolicki *a. rel.* anti-Catholic.

antyklerykalizm *mi* anticlericalism.

antyklerykalny *a.* anticlerical.

antyklerykał *mp pl.* **-owie** anticlericalist.

antykolonializm *mi polit.* anticolonialism.

antykolonialny *a. polit.* anticolonial.

antykomunista *mp*, **antykomunistka** *f. Gen.pl.* **-ek** *polit.* anti-Communist.

antykomunistyczny *a. polit.* anti-Communist, anticommunist.

antykomunizm *mi polit.* anticommunism, anti-Communism.

antykoncepcja *f. med.* contraception.

antykoncepcyjny *a. med.* **(środek) antykoncepcyjny** contraceptive.

antykorozyjny *a. techn.* **(środek) antykorozyjny** anticorrosive.

antykwa *f. druk.* Roman (typeface).

antykwariat *mi* **1.** (= *księgarnia ze starymi książkami*) antiquarian bookstore, second-hand bookstore. **2.** (= *sklep z antykami*) antique shop.

antykwariusz *mp Gen.pl.* **-y** *l.* **-ów** antiquarian; (= *bukinista, księgarz*) bibliopole, bibliopolist; (= *handlarz antykami*) antiquary.

antykwaryczny *a.* antiquarian.

Antyle *pl. Gen.* **-i** *geogr.* the Antilles; **Wielkie Antyle** the Greater Antilles; **Małe Antyle** *geogr.* the Lesser Antilles, the Caribees; **Antyle Holenderskie** the Netherlands Antilles.

antyliberalizm *mi polit.* antiliberalism.

antylogarytm *mi mat.* antilogarithm.

antylopa *f. zool.* antelope.

antymagnetyczny *a. techn.* antimagnetic.

antymateria *f. Gen.* **-ii** *fiz.* antimatter.

antymetabolit *mi biochem.* antimetabolite.

antymilitarystyczny *a.* antimilitaristic.

antymilitaryzm *mi* antimilitarism.

antymon *mi chem.* antimony.

antymonarchistyczny *a. polit.* antimonarchist, antimonarchistic.

antymonek *mi* **-nk-** *chem.* antimonide.

antymonian *mi chem.* antimonate.
antymonit *mi min.* antimonite.
antymonopolowy *a.* **ustawa antymonopolowa** (*prawn.*) antitrust law, antimonopoly act; **Urząd Antymonopolowy** (*admin.*) the Antimonopoly Office.
antynarkotykowy *a.* antidrug.
antynarodowy *a.* antinational.
antynaturalistyczny *a.* antinaturalist.
antynaturalizm *mi* antinaturalism.
antynaukowy *a.* antiscientific.
antyneutrino *n. fiz.* antineutrino.
antyneutron *mi fiz.* antineutron.
antynikotynowy *a.* anti-smoking.
antynomia *f. Gen.* **-ii** (= *sprzeczność, paradoks*) antinomy.
antynomiczny *a. log.* antinomic, antynomical.
antypaństwowy *a. polit.* antistate.
antypapieski *a. rel., polit.* antipapal.
antypapież *mp hist.kośc.* antipope.
antypasat *ma meteor.* antitrade.
antypatia *f. Gen.* **-ii** antipathy (*do kogoś/czegoś* to/towards sb/sth, *między A a B* between A and B).
antypatyczny *a.* antipathetic, antipathetical.
antyperystaltyka *f. fizj.* antiperistalsis.
antypka *f. bot.* mahaleb, mahaleb cherry, St. Lucie cherry (*Cerasus mahaleb*).
antypody *pl. Gen.* **-ów** *geogr.* antipodes.
antypolski *a.* anti-Polish.
antypowieść *f. teor.lit.* antinovel.
antyproton *mi fiz.* antiproton.
antyrepublikański *a. polit.* (= *o przeciwniku republiki l. republikanizmu*) anti-republican; (= *o przeciwniku Partii Republikańskiej*) anti-Republican.
antyreumatyczny *a.* antirheumatic.
antyrewolucyjny *a.* antirevolutionary.
antyreżimowy *a. polit.* antiregime.
antyrządowy *a. polit.* antigovernmental.
antysemicki *a.* anti-Semitic.
antysemita *mp*, **antysemitka** *f. Gen.pl.* **-ek** anti-Semite.
antysemityzm *mi* anti-Semitism.
antyseptyczny *a.* **(środek) antyseptyczny** *med.* antiseptic.
antyseptyk *mi med.* antiseptic (agent).
antyseptyka *f. med.* antisepsis.
antysocjalistyczny *a. polit.* anti-Socialist, antisocialist, antisocialistic.
antyspołeczny *a.* antisocial.
antytalent *mi* **1.** (= *brak talentu*) lack of ability, aptitude *l.* talent. **2.** (= *człowiek pozbawiony talentu*) person lacking ability, aptitude *l.* talent.
antytetyczny *a. log.* antithetic, antithetical.
antyteza *f. log., fil., teor.lit.* antithesis.
antytoksyczny *a. med.* antitoxic.
antytoksyna *f. med.* antitoxin.
antytrynitariusz *mp rel.* anti-Trinitarian.
antytrynitarski *a. rel.* anti-Trinitarian.
antytrynitaryzm *mi rel.* anti-Trinitarianism.
antyutleniacz *mi chem.* antioxidant.
antywitamina *f. biochem.* antivitamin.

antywojenny *a.* antiwar.
anulować *ipf. l. pf.* (*małżeństwo, umowę*) annul; (*traktat*) abrogate; (*czek, plany*) cancel; (*przepis prawny*) defeat, (make) void.
anyż *mi Gen.pl.* **-ów**, **anyżek** *mi* **-żk-** *bot., kulin.* anise (*Pimpinella anisum*); (*przyprawa, nasiona*) aniseed.
anyżkowy, anyżowy *a.* aniseed, anise.
anyżówka *f. Gen.pl.* **-ek** (= *wódka zaprawiona anyżem*) anisette.
aorta *f. anat.* aorta.
aoryst *mi jęz.* aorist (tense).
aorystyczny *a. jęz.* aorist, aoristic.
apanaże *pl. Gen.* **-y** *l.* **-ów** maintenance, livelihood.
aparat[1] *mi* apparatus, appliance, device, machine, set; **aparat fotograficzny** camera; **aparat ortodontyczny** brace, orthodontic; **aparat państwowy/partyjny** *przen.* state/party apparatus *l.* machinery; **aparat radiowy** radio (set); **aparat rentgenowski** radio (set); **aparat słuchowy** hearing aid; **aparat telefoniczny** telephone; **aparat telewizyjny** television *l.* TV set; **aparat tlenowy** oxygen respirator; **aparat trawienny** *anat.* digestive apparatus.
aparat[2] *mp pot.* (= *figlarz, numerant, model*) character; **niezły z niego aparat** he's quite a character.
aparatka *f. Gen.pl.* **-ek** *pot. zob.* **aparat**[2].
aparatura *f.* apparatus, equipment.
apartament *mi* (= *luksusowe mieszkanie*) luxury apartment; (*w hotelu*) suite.
apartheid *mi polit.* apartheid.
aparycja *f.* **1.** (= *wygląd*) looks, appearance. **2.** (= *prezencja*) presence, demeanor.
apaszka *f.* neckerchief, scarf; (*męska*) ascot.
apatia *f. Gen.* **-ii** **1.** *psych.* (= *obojętność, brak zainteresowań*) apathy, indifference; **popaść w apatię** become indifferent *l.* apathetic. **2.** (= *odrętwienie*) listlessness, dullness.
apatyczność *f. psych.* apathetic nature.
apatyczny *a.* **1.** (= *obojętny*) apathetic, indifferent. **2.** (= *otępiały*) listless, dull.
apatyt *mi min.* apatite.
apel *mi Gen.pl.* **-i** *l.* **-ów** **1.** (= *zbiórka*) assembly, roll; (*żołnierzy, więźniów*) roll call; **apel szkolny** school assembly; **apel poległych** reading of the roll of the dead; **stanąć do apelu** fall in (for roll call); **wzywać na apel** muster. **2.** (= *wezwanie, odezwa*) appeal (*do kogoś/czegoś* to sb/sth); **zwrócić się z apelem o coś do społeczeństwa** make a public appeal *l.* plea for sth.
apelacja *f. prawn.* appeal; **wnieść apelację** appeal *l.* launch an appeal; **odrzucić apelację** turn down an appeal; **prawo apelacji** right of appeal.
apelacyjny *a. prawn.* appeals; **sąd apelacyjny** appellate court; (*federalny w Stanach Zjednoczonych*) court of appeals.
apelant *mp prawn.* appellant.
apelatywny *a. jęz.* appellative.
apelować *ipf.* **1.** (= *nawoływać, wzywać, prosić*) appeal, make a plea (*do kogoś/czegoś* to sb/sth) (*o coś* for sth). **2.** *prawn.* appeal (*od czegoś* for sth).

apelowy *a.* appeals.

apendyks *mi* (= *dodatek, załącznik*) appendix.

Apeniny *pl. Gen.* -n *geogr.* the Apennines.

apercepcja *f. psych.* apperception.

aperitif *mi* apéritif.

apetyczny *a.* appetizing, mouth-watering.

apetyt *mi* 1. (= *chęć do jedzenia*) appetite, hunger (*na kogoś / coś* for sb/sth); jeść z apetytem eat heartily *l.* with relish; mieć wilczy apetyt have a voracious appetite; to be ravenous; zaostrzyć apetyt to whet one's appetite; popsuć, odebrać komuś apetyt spoil sb's appetite. 2. (= *chęć spożycia określonej potrawy*) taste. 3. (= *chętka*) eye, hankering, craving (*na kogoś / coś* for sb/sth).

aplanat *mi fot.* aplanatic lens.

aplauz *mi* 1. (= *poklask*) applause. 2. (= *uznanie*) acclaim.

aplikacja *f.* 1. (= *wzór, ozdoba*) appliqué (work). 2. *prawn.* (*sądowa, sędziowska, prokuratorska, radcowska, adwokacka*) legal training *l.* internship. 3. *komp.* application.

aplikacyjny *a.* 1. (*dotyczący wzoru*) appliqué. 2. (*związany z przygotowaniem*) training, internship; ćwiczenia aplikacyjne *wojsk.* training exercises.

aplikant *mp* 1. *prawn.* legal intern. 2. (*stopień w policji*) recruit.

aplikantura *f. prawn.* legal internship.

aplikować *ipf.* 1. (= *stosować, zalecać, podawać*) apply. 2. *prawn.* train, intern, do one's internship. 3. (*nakładać wzór, zdobić*) appliqué.

apodyktyczny *a.* domineering, bossy, imperious, overbearing; sąd apodyktyczny *log.* apodictic judgement.

apofonia *f. Gen.* -ii *jęz.* apophony, ablaut, vowel gradation.

apofoniczny *a. jęz.* apophonic.

apoftegmat *mi pl.* -y *l.* -a *teor.lit.* aphorism, maxim.

apogeum *n. indecl. in sing. pl.* -ea *Gen.* -eów 1. (= *szczyt, najwyższy punkt*) apogee, peak, apex, pinnacle; (= *najwyższy stopień*) height, summit; (*w rozwoju*) culmination; (*w serii akcji*) climax. 2. *astron.* apogee.

apokalipsa *f.* 1. *teor.lit.* (*rodzaj utworu*) apocalyptic story *l.* tale. 2. (= *kataklizm, katastrofa*) apocalypse, doom. 3. Apokalipsa *Bibl.* the Apocalypse, the Book of Revelations; Czterech jeźdźców Apokalipsy *Bibl.* Four Horsemen of the Apocalypse.

apokaliptyczny *a.* apocalyptic.

apokopa *f. jęz.* apocope.

apokryf *mi* 1. *pl. Bibl.* (= *utwory biblijne nieumieszczone w kanonie biblijnym*) Apocrypha. 2. *teor.lit.* (*utwór rzekomo odnaleziony i ogłoszony jako autentyczny dokument*) apocryphal text *l.* writing; *pl.* (*zbiorowo*) apocrypha.

apokryficzny *a. teor.lit.* apocryphal.

apolityczny *a.* 1. (= *obojętny wobec polityki*) apolitical. 2. (= *niebiorący udziału w życiu politycznym*) nonpolitical.

apollo *mp pl.* -owie *Gen.* -ów 1. *sg.* Apollo *mit.* Apollo. 2. (= *przystojny mężczyzna*) apollo. – ma *pl.* -e *Gen.* -ów (niepylak) apollo *ent.* apollo (butterfly), parnassian butterfly (*Parnassius apollo*).

apologeta *mp*, apologetka *f. Gen.pl.* -ek (= *głosiciel, obrońca*) apologist.

apologetyczny *a. t. rel.* apologetic.

apologetyk *mi Gen.* -u *pl.* -i *teor.lit.* apologetic. – *mp Gen.* -a *pl.* -cy (= *obrońca, apologeta*) apologist.

apologetyka *f.* 1. (= *obrona, pochwała*) apologetics, defense, justification. 2. *teor.lit., rel.* (*twórczość pisarska apologetów*) apologetics. 3. *rel.* (*dział teologii*) apologetics.

apologia *f. Gen.* -ii 1. (= *obrona, zachwyt, uwielbienie*) apologia, apology. 2. *teor.lit.* apologia, apology, vindication, defense.

apopleksja *f. pat.* (apoplectic) stroke, apoplexy; doznać apopleksji suffer a stroke.

apoplektyk *mp med.* apoplectic.

aport *int.* (*komenda wydana psu*) fetch! – *mi* 1. *myśl.* retrieving. 2. (*w okultyzmie*) apport.

aportować *ipf. myśl.* retrieve (*o psie*).

apostata *mp* (= *odszczepieniec, odstępca*) apostate.

apostazja *f.* (= *odszczepieństwo, odstępstwo*) (*wiara*) apostasy; (*zasady, przekonanie*) abandonment.

a posteriori *adv.* a posteriori, after the fact.

aposterioryczny *a.* a posteriori.

aposterioryzm *mi fil.* aposteriorism.

apostolat *mi* 1. *kośc.* (= *godność biskupa*) bishopric. 2. (*rel.*) (= *apostolstwo, nawracanie*) apostleship, mission; apostolat świeckich *rel.* lay apostolate *l.* ministry.

apostolski *a.* 1. *rel.* apostolic; Listy Apostolskie *rel., Bibl.* the Epistles; Dzieje Apostolskie *rel., Bibl.* Acts of the Apostles. 2. (*dotyczący papieża*) *rel., kośc.* apostolic; Skład Apostolski the Apostles' Creed; Stolica Apostolska Apostolic See. 3. *przen.* (= *misyjny*) missionary.

apostolstwo *n.* 1. *rel.* (*krzewienie wiary*) apostleship, mission. 2. *przen.* (*krzewienie jakiejś idei*) preaching, proselytizing.

apostoł *mp pl.* -owie 1. *rel.* apostle. 2. (= *krzewiciel, propagator*) apostle, advocate.

apostołować *ipf.* 1. (*głosić wiarę chrześcijańską*) evangelize, preach (the Gospel). 2. (= *propagować, szerzyć*) preach, advocate.

apostrof *mi* apostrophe.

apostrofa *f. teor.lit.* apostrophe.

apostroficzny *a. teor.lit.* apostrophic.

apoteoza *f.* 1. (= *gloryfikacja, ubóstwienie*) apotheosis. 2. *rel.* (= *deifikacja*) deification.

apoteozować *ipf.* 1. (= *uwielbiać, gloryfikować*) apotheosize, glorify. 2. (= *uznanie człowieka za bóstwo*) *hist.* deify.

apozycja *f. jęz.* apposition.

apozycyjny *a. jęz.* appositive.

Appalachy *pl. Gen.* -ów *geogr.* the Appalachians.

apraksja *f. pat.* apraxia.

apretura *f.* 1. *techn.* (*ostateczne wykańczanie materiałów*) finishing. 2. *techn.* (*substancja do apreturowania*) finish.

apreturować *ipf. techn.* finish.
a priori *adv.* a priori, in advance.
aprioryczność *f. fil., log.* apriority.
aprioryczny *a.* a priori.
aprioryzm *mi fil.* apriorism.
aprobata *f.* **1.** (= *uznanie, pochwała*) approbation, favor. **2.** (= *zgoda, akceptacja*) approval, endorsement, go-ahead; **wyrazić swoją aprobatę** to give one's approval; **uzyskać aprobatę** win approval; **spotkać się z aprobatą** to meet with approval.
aprobować *ipf.* endorse, approve (of).
aprobująco *adv.* approvingly, with approval.
aproksymacja *f. mat.* approximation.
aproksymować *ipf. mat.* approximate.
à propos *prep.* + *Gen.* apropos of, concerning, re, with regard to; **à propos tego twojego pytania** about that question of yours. − *adv. l. a. indecl.* apropos, to the point; **nie à propos** beside the point. − *int.* by the way; while we're at it.
aprowizacja *f.* **1.** (= *zaopatrzenie, wyżywienie*) supplying *l.* providing food. **2.** *pot.* (= *żywność*) provisions, food supplies.
aprowizacyjny *a.* of provision(s), food.
aprowizator *mp* (= *zaopatrzeniowiec*) purveyor.
a psik *int.* achoo!, ah-choo!
apsyda *f.* **1.** *bud.* apse. **2.** *astron.* apsis.
apsydowy *a. bud.* apsidal.
apteczka *f.* **1.** (= *szafka na lekarstwa*) medicine cabinet *l.* chest. **2.** (= *zestaw pierwszej pomocy*) first-aid kit.
apteczny *a.* pharmaceutical; **punkt apteczny** drugstore; (*przy szpitalu, zakładzie pracy*) infirmary.
apteka *f.* pharmacy, drug store; *Br.* chemist's (shop).
aptekarka *f. Gen.pl.* **-ek** *zob.* **aptekarz.**
aptekarski *a.* pharmacist's; **waga aptekarska** pharmaceutical scale.
aptekarstwo *n.* pharmacy, pharmaceutics.
aptekarz *mp* pharmacist, druggist; *Br.* chemist.
aptekarzowa *f. Gen.* **-ej** pharmacist's wife.
ar *mi Gen.* **-a** *miern.* are.
ara *f. orn.* (= *papuga z rodziny Psittacidae*) macaw; **ara błękitna** blue-and-yellow macaw (*Ara ararauna*); **ara czerwona** scarlet macaw (*A. macao*).
Arab *mp pl.* **-owie** Arab.
arab *ma* (= *koń arabski*) Arabian, Arab.
arabeska *f. Gen.pl.* **-ek** *muz., bud., sztuka* arabesque.
arabeskowy *a.* arabesque.
Arabia *f. Gen.* **-ii** *geogr.* Arabia; **Arabia Saudyjska** Saudi Arabia.
arabista *mp,* **arabistka** *f. Gen.pl.* **-ek** Arabist.
arabistyczny *a.* (*o studiach, badaniach*) Arabic.
arabistyka *f.* Arabic studies.
arabizm *mi jęz.* Arabism.
arabizować *ipf.* Arabize.
Arabka *f. Gen.pl.* **-ek** Arab (woman).
arabski *a.* **1.** Arab; (*o języku, piśmie*) Arabic;

cyfry arabskie Arabic numerals; **kraje arabskie** Arab countries; **guma arabska** gum arabic; **koń arabski** Arabian (horse), Arab. **2.** *geogr.* Arabian; **Półwysep Arabski** the Arabian Peninsula; **Morze Arabskie** the Arabian Sea; **Pustynia Arabska** the Arabian Desert, the Eastern Desert.
arabszczyzna *f.* **1.** *jęz.* Arabic, the Arabic language. **2.** (= *kultura i obyczaje arabskie*) Arabic culture.
arachid *mi bot., kulin.* peanut (*Arachis hypogaea*).
arachidowy *a. bot.* peanut; **olej arachidowy** peanut oil; **orzeszki arachidowe** peanuts.
aragonit *mi min.* aragonite.
arak *mi* arrack.
arakowy *a.* (*o zapachu, olejku*) arrack.
aralia *f. bot.* aralia (*Aralia*); **aralia amerykańska** devil's walking stick (*A. spinosa*).
aramejski *a.* Aramaic; **język aramejski** Aramaic, the Aramaic language.
aranż *mi muz. pot. zob.* **aranżacja.**
aranżacja *f. muz.* arrangement.
aranżer *mp pl.* **-owie,** **aranżerka** *f. Gen.pl.* **-ek** **1.** (*ktoś organizujący coś*) organizer. **2.** *muz.* arranger.
aranżować *ipf.* **1.** (= *urządzać, organizować*) organize, plan, arrange. **2.** *muz.* arrange.
araukaria *f. bot.* araucaria, monkeypuzzle, Chile pine (*Araucaria*).
arbiter *mp* **-tr-** *pl.* **-rzy** *l.* **-owie** **1.** (= *autorytet, wyrocznia*) arbiter. **2.** (= *osoba rozstrzygająca spory*) arbitrator, mediator, umpire. **3.** *sport* (*sędzia główny w futbolu, boksie itd.*) referee; (*w tenisie, baseballu, krykiecie*) umpire; **sędzia liniowy** line judge.
arbitralnie *adv.* **1.** (= *apodyktycznie, kategorycznie*) despotically, autocratically. **2.** (= *dowolnie, według własnego uznania*) arbitrarily, at will.
arbitralny *a.* **1.** (= *apodyktyczny, bezkompromisowy*) dictatorial, autocratic. **2.** (= *dowolny*) arbitrary.
arbitraż *mi Gen.* **-y** *l.* **-ów** *prawn.* arbitration, mediation; **arbitraż międzynarodowy** international arbitration; **arbitraż walutowy** *ekon.* foreign exchange arbitrage.
arbitrażowy *a. prawn.* arbitration.
arboretum *n. indecl. in sing. pl.* **-ta** *Gen.* **-tów** *ogr.* arboretum.
arbuz *mi Gen.* **-a** **1.** *bot.* watermelon. **2.** *bot.* (*o owocu*) watermelon; **dostać arbuza** *przest.* (= *dostać kosza*) get turned down; **dać komuś arbuza** *przest.* turn sb down; reject sb's advances. **3.** *żart.* (= *głowa*) noggin.
archaiczność *f.* **1.** (= *dawność, antyczność*) archaism. **2.** *przen.* (= *anachroniczność*) anachronism.
archaiczny *a.* **1.** (= *dawny, pradawny, antyczny*) archaic; **era archaiczna** *geol.* the Archaean (eon). **2.** *przen.* (= *nienowoczesny, anachroniczny*) archaic, anachronistic.
archaik *mi geol.* the Archaean.
archaizm *mi jęz.* archaism.
archaizować *ipf.* archaize.

archanioł *mp Loc. i Voc.* **-ele** *pl.* **-owie** *l.* **-y** *lit. l. arch.* **-eli** *rel.* archangel.

archeolog *mp pl.* **-dzy** *l.* **-owie** archeologist.

archeologia *f. Gen.* **-ii** archeology.

archeologiczny *a.* archeological; **kultura archeologiczna** archeological culture; **stanowisko/znalezisko archeologiczne** archeological site/find.

archeopteryks *ma paleont.* archaeopteryx (*Archaeopteryx*).

archeozoik *mi geol.* = **archaik**.

archetyp *mi psych. l. form.* archetype.

archetypiczny, archetypowy *a.* archetypal.

archidiakon *mp pl.* **-owie** *l.* **-i** *kośc.* archdeacon.

archidiakonat *mi* **1.** *kośc.* (*stanowisko*) archdeaconship. **2.** (*część diecezji*) *kośc.* archdeaconry.

archidiecezja *f. kośc.* archdiocese.

archidiecezjalny *a. kośc.* archdiocesan.

archikatedra *f. kośc.* archsee, archiepiscopal see.

archikatedralny *a. kośc.* archiepiscopal.

archipelag *mi geogr.* archipelago.

architekt *mp* **1.** architect; **architekt wnętrz** interior designer. **2.** *przen.* (= *twórca, autor*) architect (*czegoś* of sth).

architektka *f. Gen.pl.* **-ek** *pot. zob.* **architekt**.

architektoniczny *a.* architectural.

architektonika *f.* architectonics.

architektura *f.* **1.** (= *sztuka wznoszenia budowli l. styl budownictwa*) architecture; **mała architektura** decorative structures; **architektura wnętrz** interior design; **architektura ogrodnicza** landscaping. **2.** (= *forma konstrukcyjna, struktura*) construction, structure.

archiwalia *pl. Gen.* **-ów** archives.

archiwalny *a.* archival.

archiwista *mp* archivist.

archiwistyka *f.* archivist.

archiwum *n. indecl. in sing. pl.* **-wa** *Gen.* **-wów** **1.** (*zbiór dokumentów lub budynek, gdzie one się znajdują*) archive; **archiwum filmowe** film archive. **2.** (*instytucja*) archives.

arcybiskup *mp kośc.* archbishop.

arcybiskupi *a. kośc.* archiepiscopal.

arcybiskupstwo *n.* **1.** *kośc.* (*urząd*) archdiocese, archiepiscopate. **2.** (*prowincja kościelna*) archdiocese, archbishopric.

arcydzieło *n.* masterpiece; **małe arcydzieło** *przen.* little gem.

arcydzięgiel *mi* **-gl-** *Gen.* **-a** *l.* **-u** *Gen.pl.* **-i** *l.* **-ów** *bot.* angelica, archangel (*Angelica archangelica*).

arcykapłan *mp rel.* archpriest, high priest.

arcykapłański *a.* archpriestly.

arcykapłaństwo *n.* archpriesthood.

arcyksiążę *mp pl.* **-książ-** *Dat.* **-u** *pl.* **-ążęta** *Gen.* **-ąt** archduke.

arcyksiążęcy *a.* archduke's, archducal.

arcyksięstwo *n.* **1.** (*godność lub posiadłość*) archduchy. **2.** (*arcyksiążę z żoną*) archducal couple.

arcyksiężna *f. Gen.* **-ej** *l.* **-y** *Dat. i Loc.* **-ej** *l.* **-ie** *Acc.* **-ą** *l.* **-ę** *Voc.* **-o** *pl.* **-e** *Gen.* **-ych** *Dat.* **-ym** *l.* **-om** archduchess.

arcyksiężniczka *f.* archduchess.

arcymistrz *mp pl.* **-owie** *l.* **-e** great master; *szachy* grandmaster.

arcypasterz *mp kośc.* archprelate.

areał *mi roln., biol.* acreage, land area.

arena *f.* **1.** (*cyrkowa*) ring. **2.** *hist. l. przen.* arena; **wchodzić, wkraczać na arenę** enter the scene.

areszt *mi* **1.** (= *aresztowanie*) arrest, custody, detention; **nałożyć, kłaść areszt na kogoś** arrest *sb l.* place sb under arrest, take sb into custody; **nakaz aresztu** arrest warrant, warrant for sb's arrest. **2.** (= *pozbawienie wolności*) confinement, imprisonment, detention; **areszt śledczy** detention in police custody (*before being formally charged*); **areszt domowy** house arrest; **być w areszcie** be in jail, be incarcerated, be locked up. **3.** (*miejsce*) jail, prison. **4.** *prawn.* seizure, confiscation; **areszt statku** seizure of a ship; **areszt rzeczowy** seizure of assets.

aresztant *mp* prisoner, person arrested *l.* under arrest.

aresztować *ipf. l. pf.* **1.** (= *pozbawić wolności*) arrest *l.* place under arrest; take into custody. **2.** (= *uwięzić*) jail *l.* put in jail; incarcerate; lock up. **3.** *prawn.* seize, confiscate.

aresztowanie *n.* **1.** (= *pozbawienie wolności*) arrest, custody, detention; **nakaz aresztowania** arrest warrant. **2.** (= *uwięzienie*) confinement, imprisonment, detention. **3.** *prawn.* seizure, confiscation.

aresztowany *mp* (= *aresztant*) prisoner, person arrested *l.* under arrest.

Argentyna *f. geogr.* Argentina.

Argentyńczyk *mp*, **Argentynka** *f. Gen.pl.* **-ek** Argentinian.

argentyński *a.* Argentinian, Argentine.

argon *mi chem.* argon.

argot *mi jęz.* argot, cant.

argument *mi* **1.** (= *uzasadnienie*) argument, justification; **niezbity argument** irrefutable argument; (= *powód*) reason; **argument przetargowy** *przen.* trump card. **2.** *log., mat., jęz.* argument.

argumentacja *f.* **1.** (= *przekonywanie za pomocą argumentów*) argumentation, reasoning. **2.** (= *dowód*) argument.

argumentacyjny *a.* argumentative.

argumentować *ipf.* argue, reason (*za czymś* for sth *l.* in favour of sth) (*przeciwko czemuś* against sth).

aria *f. Gen.* **-ii** *muz.* (*utwór wokalny*) aria.

arianin *mp pl.* **-anie** *Gen.* **-an** *rel.* (= *wyznawca arianizmu, t. polskiego*) Arian; (= *antytrynitariusz*) Antitrinitarian.

arianizm *mi rel.* (*t. ruch religijny w Polsce XVI/XVII w.*) Arianism.

arianka *f.* (*wyznawczyni polskiego arianizmu*) Arian.

ariański *a. rel.* Arian.

ariergarda *f. wojsk.* rearguard.

Arizona *f. geogr.* Arizona.

arka *f. Gen.pl.* **-ek** **1.** *Bibl.* (*skrzynia z tablicami dziesięciorga przykazań*) the Ark; **Arka Przy-**

mierza the Ark of the Covenant; **arka przymierza między przeszłością a współczesnością** *lit. przen.* bridge between the past and the present. **2.** *lit. l. arch.* (= *statek*) ark; **arka Noego** *Bibl.* Noah's Ark.

arkada *f. bud.* arcade.

Arkadia *f. Gen.* -**ii** *geogr.* (*kraina w Grecji*) Arcadia.

arkadia *f. Gen.* -**ii** *przen.* (= *raj, eldorado*) arcadia.

arkadowy *a. bud.* arcaded.

arkadyjski *a.* **1.** *geogr.* (= *dotyczący Arkadii*) Arcadian. **2.** *przen.* (= *beztroski, sielankowy*) arcadian.

arkan *mi* lariat; **schwytać kogoś/coś na arkan** lasso sb/sth.

arkana *pl. Gen.* -**ów** (= *sekrety, wiedza tajemna*) **1.** arcana, secret wisdom. **2. arkana większe/mniejsze** *tarot* major/minor arcana.

Arkansas *f. geogr.* Arkansas.

arktyczny *a.* (= *związany z północnym biegunem Ziemi*) Arctic; (= *występujący na północy*) arctic; **roślinność/fauna arktyczna** *biol.* arctic flora/fauna.

Arktyka *f. geogr.* the Arctic.

arkusz *mi* sheet; **arkusz rozliczeniowy** balance sheet; **arkusz ocen** *szkoln.* grade sheet; **arkusz kalkulacyjny** *komp.* spread sheet; **arkusz drukarski** *druk.* printed sheet; **arkusz autorski/wydawniczy** *druk.* author's/publisher's sheet (*Polish unit of text length = 40,000 chars with spaces or 700 lines of verse*).

arkuszowy *a.* sheet.

arlekin *mp pl.* -**y** *l.* -**i** *teatr* harlequin. – *ma pl.* -**y** *kynol.* harlequin Great Dane.

armata *f. wojsk.* cannon, gun, (piece of) ordinance; **armata polowa** field gun; **wytoczyć (ciężkie) armaty** *przen.* bring out the big guns.

armatka *f. wojsk.* light gun, small-caliber gun; **armatka wodna** *techn.* water cannon, monitor.

armatni *a. wojsk.* cannon, gun; **kula armatnia** cannonball; **mięso armatnie** *przen.* cannon fodder.

armator *mp żegl.* (= *przewoźnik*) carrier; (= *właściciel statku*) shipowner; (= *użytkownik statku*) charterer.

armatorski *a. żegl.* shipping.

armatura *f.* **1.** *bud., techn.* (= *pomocnicze wyposażenie, osprzęt*) fittings, fixtures; **armatura urządzeń sanitarnych** pipe fittings. **2.** *sztuka* (= *rusztowanie rzeźby*) armature.

Armenia *f. Gen.* -**ii** *geogr.* Armenia.

armeński *a.* Armenian; **kościół armeński** *rel.* Armenian church.

armia *f. Gen.* -**ii** **1.** *wojsk.* (= *siły zbrojne, związek operacyjny*) army; (= *część sił zbrojnych*) force. **2.** *przen.* (= *tłum, gromada*) host.

armijny *a.* army.

arnika *f. bot., med.* arnica (*Arnica montana*).

arnikowy *a. med.* arnica.

arogancja *f.* **1.** (= *buta, zuchwalstwo*) arrogance, insolence, audacity. **2.** (= *pewność siebie, pycha*) cockiness, conceit, egotism.

arogancki *a.* **1.** (= *butny*) arrogant, insolent, audacious. **2.** (= *pewny siebie*) cocky, conceited, egotistical, full of o.s.

arogant *mp*, **arogantka** *f. Gen.pl.* -**ek** arrogant person.

aromat *mi* **1.** (*zapach, woń*) aroma, fragrance. **2.** (*substancja aromatyczna*) flavoring. **3.** *chem.* aroma.

aromatyczny *a.* aromatic, odoriferous; **rośliny aromatyczne** *bot.* aromatic plants, fragrant plants, oil(-bearing) plants; **związki aromatyczne** *chem.* aromatic compounds, aromatics; **rodniki aromatyczne** *chem.* aryls.

aromatyzować *ipf.* aromatize; (*o produktach spożywczych*) flavor.

aromatyzowany *a.* aromatized; flavored.

aronia *f. Gen.* -**ii** *bot.* chokeberry (*Aronia*).

arpeggio *n. muz.* arpeggio.

arras *mi* arras.

arrasowy *a.* arras.

arsen *mi chem.* arsenic; **tlenki arsenu** *chem.* arsenic oxides; **siarczki arsenu** *min.* arsenic sulfides.

arsenał *mi* arsenal, armory; **arsenał argumentów** *przen.* arsenal of arguments.

arsenawy *a. chem.* arsenious, arsenous.

arsenek *mi chem.* arsenide.

arsenian *mi chem.* arsenate.

arsenin *mi chem.* arsenite.

arsenit *mi chem.* arsenite.

arsenopiryt *mi min.* arsenopyrite.

arsenowodór *mi chem.* arsine.

arszenik *mi chem.* arsenic trioxide, arsenic.

arszenikowy *a. chem.* arsenic.

artefakt *mi* artifact.

arteria *f. Gen.* -**ii** **1.** *anat.* (= *tętnica, aorta*) artery. **2.** (= *droga, trasa*) artery, thoroughfare, highway; **główna arteria** major artery, major highway, major road; **arteria przelotowa** thoroughfare.

arterioskleroza *f. med.* (= *miażdżyca, skleroza*) arteriosclerosis.

artezyjski *a. geol.* artesian; **niecka/studnia artezyjska** artesian basin/well; **wody artezyjskie** artesian water; **źródło artezyjskie** artesian spring.

artretyczny *a. med.* arthritic.

artretyzm *mi med.* arthritis.

artrologia *f. Gen.* -**ii** *med.* arthrology.

artroskopia *f. Gen.* -**ii** *med.* arthroscopy.

artycha *mp sl.* **1.** (= *artysta*) artist. **2.** (= *ktoś, kto lubi się popisywać, numerant*) showman.

artykulacja *f.* **1.** *fon.* articulation; **miejsce/sposób artykulacji** place/manner of articulation. **2.** *form.* (= *wypowiadanie, formułowanie*) articulation, expression, formulation. **3.** *dent.* (= *zgryz*) articulation. **4.** *muz.* (= *sposób wykonania dźwięków*) performance. **5.** *muz.* (= *realizacja*) articulation.

artykulacyjny *a.* **1.** *fon.* articulatory; **system artykulacyjny** articulatory system; **narządy artykulacyjne** articulators; **cechy artykulacyjne** articulatory features. **2.** *dent.* articulatory. **3.** *muz.* (*dotyczący sposobu wykonania*) performance. **4.** *muz.* (*dotyczący realizacji dźwięków*) articulatory.

artykuł *mi* **1.** (= *tekst dziennikarski*) article; **artykuł wstępny** *dzienn.* editorial; **artykuł hasłowy** (*w leksykografii*) entry. **2.** (= *produkt, wyrób, towar*) (*spożywczy, konsumpcyjny, przemysłowy, papierniczy, chemiczny, gospodarstwa domowego*) article, commodity, item; **artykuły pierwszej potrzeby** necessities; (*o żywności*) staples; **artykuły spożywcze** groceries. **3.** *prawn.* (*część ustawy lub umowy*) article; **artykuł 5 kodeksu karnego** article 5 of the Penal Code. **4.** **artykuł wiary** *rel.* article of faith, article of belief, credendum.

artykułować *ipf.* **1.** *jęz.* articulate. **2.** *muz.* (= *wykonywać*) perform. **3.** *form.* (= *formułować, wyrażać*) articulate, express, formulate.

artykułowany *a.* (= *wypowiedziany zrozumiale*) articulated; **mowa artykułowana** articulated speech.

artyleria *f. Gen.* -ii *wojsk.* artillery, ordnance; **artyleria dalekiego zasięgu** long-range artillery; **artyleria konna/polowa** horse/field artillery; **artyleria przeciwlotnicza** antiaircraft artillery; **artyleria przeciwpancerna** antitank artillery, antiarmor artillery; **artyleria morska/przybrzeżna** naval/coast artillery; **lekka artyleria** light artillery; **ciężka artyleria** heavy artillery; *przen.* (= *miażdżące argumenty*) the big guns; *żart.* (= *ktoś nieruchawy l. ociężały umysłowo*) dawdler, laggard; **słychać artylerię niebieską** *przen. żart.* (*o grzmotach*) the gods *l.* angels are bowling, the angels *l.* gods are rearranging their furniture.

artyleryjski *a. wojsk.* artillery; **ostrzał, ogień artyleryjski** gunfire, artillery fire; **przygotowanie artyleryjskie** artillery preparation.

artylerzysta *mp,* **artylerzystka** *f. Gen.pl.* -ek *wojsk.* artilleryman, artillerist, gunner.

artysta *mp,* **artystka** *f. Gen.pl.* -ek **1.** (= *twórca lub odtwórca dzieła artystycznego*) artist; **artysta ludowy** *sztuka* folk artist, primitivist; **artysta słowa** wordsmith; writer who has a way with words. **2.** (= *mistrz, znakomitość*) master, celebrity. **3.** *pot.* (= *ktoś zręczny l. sprytny*) artist (*od czegoś* in sth). **4.** *pot.* (= *aktor*) actor, artist, artiste; **artystka** actor, actress; **artyści scen polskich** Polish actors.

artystyczny *a.* **1.** (*związany ze sztuką*) artistic; **język artystyczny** *teor.lit.* literary language; **nagroda artystyczna** art prize, prize in arts; **salon artystyczny** art exhibition (*wystawa*), salon (*zebranie towarzyskie z udziałem artystów*); **kierownik artystyczny** artistic director; **akademia artystyczna** Academy of Arts. **2.** (= *piękny, estetyczny*) beautiful, esthetic, aesthetic; **rzemiosło artystyczne** arts and crafts; **artystyczny nieład** creative mess; **artystyczna dusza** artistic soul.

artyzm *mi* artistry.

Aryjczyk *mp,* **Aryjka** *f. Gen.pl.* -ek **1.** *rzad.* (= *członek któregoś z ludów indoirańskich*) Arya, Aryan. **2.** (*w rasistowskiej terminologii hitlerowskiej*) Aryan.

aryjski *a.* **1.** (*o ludach, językach*) (= *indoirański*) Aryan; **języki aryjskie** Aryan languages; **lu-**

dy aryjskie the Aryas, the Aryans, the Aryan peoples. **2.** (*w terminologii rasistowskiej*) Aryan; **rasa aryjska** the Aryan race.

arystokracja *f.* **1.** (*warstwa, klasa społeczna*) aristocracy, nobility, peerage; **arystokracja rodowa** hereditary nobility. **2.** *przen.* (= *elita*) aristocracy, elite, élite; **arystokracja kupiecka** trade barons; **arystokracja przemysłowa** captains of industry; industry barons *l.* moguls; **arystokracja polityczna** political elite; **arystokracja umysłowa** intellectual elite; **arystokracja finansowa** plutocracy. **3.** *hist.* (*forma rządów w państwach starożytnych*) aristocracy.

arystokrata *mp* **1.** (*członek arystokracji*) aristocrat, noble, nobleman, peer. **2.** *przen.* aristocrat, member of the elite.

arystokratka *f.* **1.** aristocrat, noble, noblewoman, peeress. **2.** *przen. zob.* **arystokrata** 2.

arystokratyczny *a.* aristocratic, upper-class; **obóz arystokratyczny** *polit.* aristocratic party *l.* camp; **ustrój arystokratyczny** *hist.* aristocracy.

arystokratyzm *mi* **1.** (= *przynależność do arystokracji*) aristocratic birth *l.* descent. **2.** (= *elitarność, wyższość*) elitism.

arystotelik *ma fil.* Aristotelian, follower of Aristotle.

arystotelizm *mi fil.* Aristotelianism.

arystotelowski *a. fil.* Aristotelian, Aristotelean.

arytmetycznie *adv. mat.* (= *za pomocą liczb i działań*) arithmetically, numerically.

arytmetyczny *a. mat.* arithmetic, arithmetical; **działanie arytmetyczne** arithmetic operation; **postęp/szereg arytmetyczny** arithmetic progression/series; **średnia arytmetyczna** arithmetic mean.

arytmetyk *mp* arithmetician.

arytmetyka *f. mat.* arithmetic; **arytmetyka stosowana** applied arithmetic; **arytmetyka teoretyczna** theoretical arithmetic, higher arithmetic; **arytmetyka dwójkowa** *l.* **binarna** *komp.* binary arithmetic.

arytmia *f. Gen.* -ii **1.** *form.* (= *brak rytmu*) lack of rhythm, irregularity. **2.** *med.* arrhythmia.

arytmiczny *a. form.* (= *nierytmiczny*) lacking rhythm, irregular.

as[1] *mi Gen.* -a **1.** *karty* ace; **as trefl/karo/kier/pik** ace of clubs/diamonds/hearts/spades; **mieć asa w rękawie** have an ace up one's sleeve; **wyciągnąć asa z rękawa** pull an ace out of one's sleeve. **2.** *sport* ace, service ace. – *mp pl.* -y (= *mistrz, znakomitość*) ace; **as lotnictwa** ace (pilot); **as piłkarski** ace footballer.

as[2] *n. indecl. muz.* (*nazwa dźwięku*) A flat; **tonacja As-dur** key of A flat major; **tonacja as-moll** key of A flat minor.

asceta *mp,* **ascetka** *f. Gen.pl.* -ek ascetic.

ascetyczny *a.* ascetic, ascetical.

ascetyzm *mi* asceticism.

asceza *f.* **1.** (= *wstrzemięźliwość*) abstinence, temperance. **2.** *rel.* (= *umartwianie się*) (*chrześcijańska, katolicka, całkowita*) ascesis, askesis.

asejsmiczny *a. geol.* aseismic; **budownictwo asejsmiczne** *bud.* aseismic construction.

aseksualny *a.* asexual; (= *pozbawiony płci*) sexless; **rozmnażanie aseksualne** *biol.* asexual reproduction.

asekuracja *f.* **1.** (= *zabezpieczenie*) security measure, safety measure, safeguard. **2.** *sport* spotting; (*we wspinaczce*) belaying. **3.** *przest.* (= *ubezpieczenie*) insurance; **wykupić/wypłacić asekurację** take out/pay an insurance.

asekuracyjny *a.* **1.** (= *zabezpieczający*) security, safety, safeguarding, protective. **2.** (= *ubezpieczeniowy*) insurance; **składka asekuracyjna** premium; **polisa asekuracyjna** insurance policy; **towarzystwo asekuracyjne** insurance company; **agent asekuracyjny** insurance agent.

asekurancki *a. uj.* (= *ostrożny, bojaźliwy*) on the fence; unwilling to take risk; overcautious.

asekuranctwo *n. uj.* sitting on the fence; riding the fence; extreme caution.

asekurant *mp* **1.** *uj.* (= *osoba unikająca ryzyka*) person sitting on the fence *l.* riding the fence; person unwilling to take risk; coward. **2.** *sport* spotter. **3.** (= *osoba ubezpieczająca finansowo*) insurance broker, insurance agent, underwriter.

asekurantka *f. Gen.pl.* **-ek** *uj.* zob. **asekurant** 1.

asekurować *ipf.* **1.** (= *zapewniać bezpieczeństwo, ochronę*) protect, safeguard, secure. **2.** *sport* spot. **3.** *przest.* (= *ubezpieczać finansowo*) insure. ~ **się** *ipf.* **1.** (*chronić się przed czymś groźnym, niebezpiecznym, niemiłym*) play safe, cover o.s. **2.** *sport* spot o.s. **3.** (= *ubezpieczać się finansowo*) insure o.s.

asemantyczny *a. jęz.* asemantic.

asenizacja *f. form. l. techn.* sewage disposal, sanitation.

asenizacyjny *a.* **1.** *techn.* regarding sewage disposal. **2. dół asenizacyjny** *bud.* cesspool.

aseptyczny *a. med.* aseptic; **rana aseptyczna** aseptic wound; **aseptyczny opatrunek** aseptic dressing; **pomieszczenie aseptyczne** aseptic room.

aseptyka *f. med.* asepsis.

asesor *mp* **1.** *prawn.* (= *prawnik po odbyciu aplikacji, ale bez nominacji*) candidate to the bar. **2.** *prawn.* (= *członek kolegium sądowego*) assessor, assistant judge, associate judge, master. **3.** *hist.* (*dawny urząd*) assessor.

asesorski *a. prawn., hist.* assessorial.

asesura *f. prawn.* assessorship.

asfalt *mi* **1.** (*nawierzchnia drogi*) (road) asphalt. **2.** *geol.* (*skała osadowa*) asphalt, mineral pitch. **3.** *techn.* (*produkt destylacji ropy lub rafinacji olejów*) asphalt.

asfaltować *ipf. bud., techn.* asphalt; **papier asfaltowany** asphalt paper.

asfaltowy *a.* asphalt; *geol.* (*o złożu*) asphalt, mineral pitch; **lakier asfaltowy** *chem.* bituminous lacquer, asphalt paint, japan.

asocjacja *f. psych.* (= *skojarzenie*) *nauk.* (= *zbiór, zbiorowisko*) association; **asocjacja gwiazd** *astron.* stellar association, association of stars; **asocjacja roślinna** *bot.* (plant) association.

asocjacyjny *a.* **1.** associative. **2.** *psych.* associationistic; **psychologia asocjacyjna** associationism.

asocjować *ipf. psych.* associate.

asonans *mi pl.* **-e** *teor.lit.* (= *rym samogłoskowy*) assonance, vowel rhyme.

asonansowy *a. teor.lit.* assonant, assonantal, assonantic.

asortyment *mi handl.* assortment, range, line; **asortyment wyrobów** product line; **duży** *l.* **szeroki asortyment** wide choice *l.* selection; wide range.

asparagus *mi Gen.* **-a** *bot.* asparagus (*Asparagus*).

aspargina *f. chem.* asparagine.

aspekt *mi* **1.** (= *punkt widzenia*) angle, aspect, facet, side; **mieć inny aspekt** have a different side; **w różnych aspektach** from different points of view; from different sides *l.* angles. **2.** *jęz.* aspect; **aspekt dokonany/niedokonany** perfective/imperfective aspect. **3.** *astrol.* aspect.

aspektowy *a. jęz.* aspectual.

aspiracja *f.* **1.** (= *pragnienie, ambicja*) ambition, aspiration; **mieć wysokie aspiracje** aim high, fly high, have high *l.* lofty aspirations; **zaspokoić swoje aspiracje** fulfil *l.* satisfy one's aspirations, succeed in one's aspirations. **2.** *fon., med.* aspiration. **3.** *techn.* venting, drawing out by suction.

aspirant *mp pl.* **-ci** **1.** (= *pretendent, kandydat*) aspirant (*do czegoś* for *l.* to sth). **2.** (*stopień w policji i w pożarnictwie*) warrant officer, noncommissioned officer. – *mi pl.* **-y** *leśn.* candidate.

aspirantka *f. Gen.pl.* **-ek** zob. **aspirant** 1.

aspirantura *f. hist.* (*dawna forma kształcenia kadr naukowych*) post-graduate studies, doctoral studies (*especially in the former USSR*).

aspirata *f. fon.* (= *przydech*) aspirate; (= *głoska aspirowana*) aspirated sound.

aspirator *mi Gen.* **-a** *med.* **1.** aspirator. **2.** *techn.* aspirator, suction apparatus.

aspirować *ipf.* (= *pretendować, kandydować, ubiegać się*) **1.** aspire (*do czegoś* to *l.* after sth). **2.** *fon.* aspirate; **spółgłoska aspirowana** aspirate, aspirate(d) consonant.

aspiryna *f. med.* aspirin; **wziąć** *l.* **zażyć aspirynę** take (an) aspirin.

aspołeczny *a.* asocial.

astat *mi chem.* astatine.

astatyczny *a. fiz.* astatic.

astenia *f. Gen.* **-ii** *med.* asthenia.

aster *mi* **-tr-** *Gen.* **-a** *bot.* aster (*Aster*).

asteroida *f. astron.* asteroid, planetoid.

astma *f. pat.* (bronchial) asthma.

astmatyczka *f. Gen.pl.* **-ek** zob. **astmatyk**.

astmatyczny *a. pat.* asthmatic; **oddech astmatyczny** asthmatic respiration.

astmatyk *mp* asthmatic.

astralny *a.* **1.** *astron.* astral, stellar. **2.** *astrol.* (*w okultyzmie*) astral; **ciało astralne** astral body.

astrobiologia *f. Gen.* **-ii** *astron.* exobiology, astrobiology.

astrochemia *f. Gen.* **-ii** *astron.* astrochemistry.

astrofizyczny *a. astron.* astrophysical.

astrofizyk *mp astron.* astrophysicist.
astrofizyka *f. astron.* astrophysics.
astrolog *mp pl.* -dzy *l.* -owie astrologer, astrologist.
astrologia *f. Gen.* -ii astrology.
astrologiczny *a.* astrologic, astrological.
astronauta *mp*, **astronautka** *f. Gen.pl.* -ek astronaut; (*tylko o mężczyźnie*) spaceman.
astronautyczny *a.* astronautic, astronautical.
astronautyka *f.* astronautics; (= *podróże kosmiczne*) space travel.
astronawigacja *f. lotn., żegl.* astronavigation, celestial navigation.
astronawigacyjny *a. lotn., żegl.* astronavigational.
astronom *mp pl.* -owie astronomer.
astronomia *f. Gen.* -ii astronomy; **astronomia pozycyjna** astrometry, positional astronomy.
astronomiczny *a.* **1.** (*związany z astronomią*) astronomical; **wiosna/jesień astronomiczna** astronomical spring/autumn; **obserwatorium astronomiczne** astronomical observatory; **jednostka astronomiczna** *astron.* astronomical unit. **2.** *przen.* (= *wielki, ogromny*) astronomical, exorbitant, immense; **astronomiczne sumy** astronomical *l.* exorbitant amounts (of money).
astygmatyczny *a.* astigmatic.
astygmatyzm *mi* **1.** *med.* astigmatism, astigmia. **2.** *fiz.* astigmatism.
asygnata *f. handl.* (= *dowód kasowy*) (cash *l.* pay) voucher.
asygnować *ipf.* **1.** (*przeznaczyć pewną sumę pieniędzy na jakiś cel*) allot, appropriate. **2.** (*wystawiać przekaz, czek*) issue (*a payment order*), issue, make out, write out (*a check*).
asymetria *f. Gen.* -ii **1.** (= *brak symetrii*) asymmetry, dissymmetry. **2.** *log.* asymmetry.
asymetryczność *f.* asymmetry, dissymmetry.
asymetryczny *a.* asymmetrical.
asymilacja *f.* (= *upodobnienie się, dostosowanie, przyswojenie*) assimilation; **asymilacja wsteczna/postępowa** *fon.* regressive/progressive assimilation.
asymilacyjny *a.* assimilative, assimilatory; **polityka asymilacyjna** *polit.* assimilationism.
asymilować *ipf.* assimilate. ~ **się** *ipf.* assimilate, undergo assimilation (*do czegoś* to sth).
asymptota *f. mat.* asymptote.
asymptotyczny *a. mat.* asymptotic, asymptotical.
Asyria *f. Gen.* -ii *hist.* Assyria.
Asyryjczyk, **Asyryjka** *f. Gen.pl.* -ek *mp hist.* Assyrian.
asyryjski *a. hist.* Assyrian.
asysta *f.* **1.** (= *orszak, eskorta, straż, towarzystwo*) escort, company, suite, retinue, train; **w czyjejś asyście** accompanied by sb. **2.** (*obecność przy kimś*) assistance. **3.** *sport* assist.
asystencki *a.* assistant's; **staż asystencki** assistant's internship; **hotel asystencki** assistant's hall.
asystent *mp*, **asystentka** *f. Gen.pl.* -ek **1.** (= *pomocnik, współpracownik*) assistant, aide,

helper. **2.** *uniw.* (= *młodszy pracownik naukowy*) assistant.
asystentura *f. uniw.* post of an assistant.
asystować *ipf.* + *Dat.* **1.** (= *towarzyszyć*) accompany. **2.** (= *pomagać, współdziałać, współpracować*) assist; **asystować przy operacji** assist at an operation. **3.** *przest.* (= *nadskakiwać, adorować*) fawn.
atak *mi* **1.** *wojsk.* (= *natarcie*) attack, raid, assault; **atak bombowy** bomb raid, blitz; **atak lotniczy** air raid; **ruszyć do ataku** launch an attack; **odeprzeć atak** fend off an attack, ward off an attack, repel an attack, repulse an attack; **do ataku!** attack!; **przypuścić atak** make an attack; **być celem głównego ataku** come under a major attack, be subjected to a direct *l.* major attack, stand in the breach; **najskuteczniejszą obroną jest atak** attack is the best form of defense. **2.** *przen.* (= *napaść, nagonka, krytyka*) attack (*na kogoś* against *l.* on sb); **wystąpić z gwałtownym atakiem przeciw komuś** attack sb violently, launch a violent attack against sb, make a blistering attack on sb; **ataki prasy/mediów** press/media attacks; **być przedmiotem ataków z czyjejś strony** be subjected to attacks from sb, come under attack from sb. **3.** (*mocne niszczące uderzenie*) onslaught; **atak wichury** onslaught of a gale. **4.** *med.* (*nagłe wystąpienie objawów choroby lub przejaw stanu psychicznego*) attack, fit, bout; **atak gorączki** fit of fever; **atak malarii** attack of malaria; **atak złości/melancholii/wściekłości** fit of anger/melancholy/fury; **atak nerwowy** nervous fit, attack of nerves; **dostać ataku nerwowego** throw a fit; **dostać ataku szału** go berserk, be seized with a fit of rage; **atak serca** heart attack. **5.** *sport* (*akcja wobec przeciwnika*) attack; **atak bez piłki** off the ball (play *l.* attack); **atak ciałem** *hokej* bodycheck; **atak przy siatce** slam. **6.** *sport* (*zawodnicy grający w ofensywie*) forwards; **być** *l.* **grać w ataku** be a forward.
atakować *ipf.* **1.** (= *nacierać, uderzać na nieprzyjaciela*) attack. **2.** *przen.* (= *napadać na kogoś*) attack. **3.** *przen.* (= *domagać się*) bother, pester (*o coś* about *l.* for sth). **4.** *przen.* (*o czynnikach fizykochemicznych*) damage, destroy. **5.** *med.* (*o chorobie*) attack. **6.** *sport* attack; **atakować poprzeczkę** attempt the bar; **atakować bramkę** drive (and shoot); **atakować ciałem** *hokej* bodycheck, set a pick; **atakować rekord** go for the record, try to break a record.
ataksja *f. pat.* ataxia.
ataman *mp hist.* ataman, hetman (*of the cossacks*).
atamański *a. hist.* ataman.
ataszat *mi* **1.** (*stanowisko, urząd*) post *l.* office of an attaché. **2.** (*biuro*) attaché's office.
atawistyczny *a.* atavistic.
atawizm *mi* atavism.
ateista *mp*, **ateistka** *f. Gen.pl.* -ek atheist.
ateistyczny *a.* atheistic, atheistical.
ateizm *mi* atheism.
atelier *n. indecl.* **1.** (= *pracownia artysty*) ate-

lier, studio. **2.** *film* (= *studio filmowe*) (film) studio.

atencja *f. lit.* deference, respect.

Ateny *pl. Gen.* **-n** *geogr.* Athens.

Ateńczyk *mp hist.* Athenian.

ateński *a.* Athenian.

atest *mi techn., handl., prawn.* certificate.

atestować *ipf.* certify.

atlant *mi Gen.* **-a** *bud.* atlas, telamon.

atlantycki *a.* Atlantic; **Ocean Atlantycki** *geogr.* the Atlantic, the Atlantic Ocean.

Atlantyda *f. mit.* Atlantis.

Atlantyk *mi* the Atlantic.

atlas *mi* **1.** (= *zbiór map*) atlas; **atlas geograficzny/historyczny** geographical/historical atlas; **atlas samochodowy** road atlas; **atlas lingwistyczny** linguistic atlas; **atlas morski** marine *l.* sea *l.* maritime atlas; **atlas nieba** *astron.* atlas of the sky, sky atlas. **2.** (*zbiór ilustracji z opisami*) **atlas anatomiczny** anatomical atlas, atlas of anatomy; **atlas grzybów** mushroom atlas; **atlas ptaków/ryb** bird/fish atlas, book of birds/fishes. **3.** *anat.* atlas. **4.** *bud.* atlas, telamon. **5.** *sport* (*przyrząd do ćwiczeń siłowych*) weight trainer.

atleta *mp Gen.pl.* **-ów 1.** (= *siłacz, mocarz*) strongman. **2.** *sport, lit.* (= *zapaśnik*) wrestler; (= *ciężarowiec*) weightlifter; (= *kulturysta*) bodybuilder.

atletka *f. Gen.pl.* **-ek** *zob.* atleta 2.

atletycznie *adv.* athletically.

atletyczny *a.* **1.** (= *silny, dobrze zbudowany*) athletic, muscular. **2.** *sport* (= *dotyczący dyscyplin siłowych*) athletic.

atletyka *f. sport* athletics; **lekka atletyka** track and field sports; **ciężka atletyka** (= *zapasy*) wrestling; (= *podnoszenie ciężarów*) weight lifting; **atletyka terenowa** cross-country sports.

atłas *mi* satin; **szkoda czasu i atłasu** (*porzekadło*) it isn't worth the trouble; it's a waste of time.

atłasek *mi* **-sk- 1.** (= *nici bawełniane do haftu*) floss (silk). **2.** (= *haft wypukły*) raised embroidery.

atłasowy *a.* **1.** (*zrobiony z atłasu*) satin. **2.** *przen.* (= *gładki, aksamitny*) satin, smooth.

atmosfera *f.* **1.** (= *powietrze ziemskie*) the air, the atmosphere. **2.** *astron., chem.* atmosphere. **3.** (= *nastrój*) atmosphere, climate, mood; **atmosfera podejrzliwości** climate of suspicion; **napięta atmosfera** atmosphere of tension. **4.** *fiz.* (*jednostka ciśnienia*) atmosphere; **atmosfera fizyczna** atmosphere, standard atmosphere; **atmosfera techniczna** technical atmosphere.

atmosferyczny *a. meteor., astron.* atmospheric, atmospherical; **ciśnienie atmosferyczne** atmospheric pressure, barometric pressure; **zjawiska atmosferyczne** atmospheric phenomena; **front atmosferyczny** front; **opady atmosferyczne** precipitation.

atol *mi Gen.pl.* **-i** *l.* **-ów** *geogr.* atoll.

atom *mi* **1.** *fiz., chem.* atom. **2.** *przen.* (= *drobina*) atom, speck, mote, crumb.

atomistyczny *a.* **1.** *fil.* atomistic, atomistical. **2.** *psych.* atomistic.

atomistyka *f.* **1.** *fiz.* (= *fizyka atomowa*) atomics. **2.** *fil.* atomism.

atomizacja *f.* (= *rozdrabnianie, rozpylanie*) atomization.

atomizator *mi Gen.* **-a 1.** *roln.* atomizer, blower sprayer. **2.** (= *rozpylacz*) = **atomizer.**

atomizer *mi Gen.* **-a** atomizer.

atomizm *mi* **1.** *fil.* scientific atomism, modern atomism. **2.** *psych.* atomism.

atomizować *ipf.* **1.** (= *rozdrabniać, rozdzielać*) atomize. **2.** *techn.* (*rozpylać ciecz*) atomize.

atomowy *a. fiz., chem.* atomic; (= *dotyczący reakcji nuklearnych*) nuclear; **fizyka atomowa** atomics; **elektrownia atomowa** nuclear power plant; **reaktor atomowy** atomic reactor, nuclear reactor; **bomba atomowa** atomic bomb, atom bomb, A-bomb, nuclear bomb; **broń atomowa** nuclear *l.* atomic weapons; **energia atomowa** nuclear energy *l.* power; atomic energy; **jądro atomowe** atomic nucleus; **jednostka masy atomowej** atomic mass unit, dalton; **liczba atomowa** atomic number, proton number; **tlen/wodór atomowy** atomic oxygen/hydrogen; **masa atomowa** *l.* **ciężar atomowy** atomic mass; **zegar atomowy** atomic clock.

atonalność *f. muz.* atonality.

atonia *f. pat.* atony.

atoniczny[1] *a. fon.* atonic; **wyraz atoniczny** atonic.

atoniczny[2] *a. med.* atonic.

atrakcja *f.* attraction; **atrakcje turystyczne** sights, tourist attractions; **być atrakcją wieczoru** (*o osobie*) be the highlight *l.* headlight of the evening; **główna atrakcja** highlight, main feature.

atrakcyjny *a.* attractive; **atrakcyjna cena** attractive price.

atrament *mi* ink; **atrament sympatyczny** sympathetic ink, invisible ink.

atramentowy *a.* **1.** (= *dotyczący atramentu*) ink; **atramentowy ołówek** indelible pencil; **atramentowe pióro** fountain pen; **drukarka atramentowa** *komp.* ink-jet printer; **plama od atramentu** ink stain. **2.** *przen.* (= *czarny, bardzo ciemny*) pitch-black, pitch-dark, inky; **atramentowa noc** pitch-dark night, inky black night.

atrapa *f.* **1.** (= *imitacja, substytut*) dummy. **2.** *techn.* (*osłona chłodnicy*) grille.

atrofia *f. Gen.* **-ii** *pat.* atrophy.

atropina *f. chem., farm.* atropine.

atrybut *mi* **1.** attribute; **podstawowy atrybut** main attribute; **atrybut danych** *komp.* data attribute. **2.** *gram.* (= *przydawka*) attribute, attributive.

atrybutywny *a. jęz.* attributive.

attaché *mp indecl. dyplomacja* attaché; **attaché handlowy/kulturalny/wojskowy** commercial/cultural/military attaché.

attycki *a. hist.* (= *dotyczący Attyki*) Attic; **sól attycka** *lit.* (= *cięty dowcip*) attic salt, attic wit.

Attyka *f. hist.* Attica.

attyka *f. bud.* attic.

atu *n. indecl. karty* trump; **licytować/grać bez atu** bid/play no trump.

atut *mi* **1.** *karty* trump; **mieć atuty** have trumps. **2.** *przen.* (= *szansa, okazja*) trump card; **mieć atuty w ręce** have trumps in one's hand; **wykorzystać atut** play one's trump.

atutowy *a. karty* trump; **karta atutowa** trump card, winning card.

audiencja *f.* audience; **audiencja prywatna** private audience; **udzielić audiencji** give *l.* grant an audience; **być przyjętym na audiencji** receive an audience.

audiencyjny *a.* audience.

audio *a. indecl. techn.* audio; **sprzęt audio** audio equipment.

audiowizualny *a.* audiovisual; **środki audiowizualne** *szkoln.* audiovisuals, audiovisual aids.

audycja *f.* **1.** (= *program w radiu lub w telewizji*) broadcast, program; **audycja radiowa** radio broadcast; **audycja telewizyjna** television *l.* TV broadcast. **2.** *muz.* school concert.

audytorium *n. indecl. in sing. pl.* **-ria** *Gen.* **-riów 1.** (*ogół słuchaczy wykładu, koncertu*) audience. **2.** (= *sala wykładowa, aula*) auditorium, hall.

audytoryjny *a.* (*dotyczący sali wykładowej*) auditorium; **sala audytoryjna** auditorium, hall; **budynek audytoryjny** auditorium, hall.

augmentatyw *mi gram.* augmentative.

augmentatywny *a. gram.* augmentative.

augsburski *a.* Lutheran; **wyznanie augsburskie** *rel.* the Augsburg *l.* Augustan Confession; **ewangelik augsburski** *rel.* Lutheran.

augustianin *mp pl.* **-anie** *Gen.* **-anów** (*zakonnik*) Augustinian.

aukcja *f. handl.* (= *licytacja, sprzedaż*) auction, public sale; **aukcja dzieł sztuki** art auction; **aukcja na cele dobroczynne** charity auction; **prowadzić aukcję** hold an auction.

aukcyjny *a. handl.* auctionary; **dom/salon aukcyjny** auction house/room.

aula *f. Gen.pl.* **-i** *uniw.* (assembly) hall, auditorium.

aura *f.* **1.** (= *pogoda*) weather; **sprzyjająca aura** favourable weather conditions. **2.** *przen.* (= *nastrój, atmosfera*) aura, atmosphere; **aura tajemniczości** aura of mystery. **3.** *med.* aura.

aureola *f. Gen.pl.* **-i 1.** *sztuka* (= *krąg wokół głowy świętych*) halo, nimbus, aureole, aureola, gloriole; **otaczać aureolą** halo, surround with a halo. **2.** *przen.* (= *splendor, chwała, gloria*) glory. **3.** *fiz.* aureole, halo. **4.** *górn.* blue tip of the flame (*in a safety lamp*), (pale) blue flame.

auspicje *pl. Gen.* **-ów** (= *opieka, patronat*) auspices; **pod dobrymi auspicjami** auspiciously; **pod złymi auspicjami** inauspiciously, under a bad sign; **pod auspicjami rządu** under the auspices of the government.

Australia *f. Gen.* **-ii** *geogr.* Australia.

Australijczyk *mp*, **Australijka** *f. Gen.pl.* **-ek** Australian.

australijski *a. geogr.* Australian.

australoidalny *a. antrop.* Australoid; **osobnik typu australoidalnego** Australoid.

australopitek *ma paleont.* australopithecine, australopithecus.

Austria *f. Gen.* **-ii** *geogr.* Austria.

austriacki *a.* Austrian; **austriackie gadanie** *żart.* a lot of hot air, balderdash.

Austriak *mp*, **Austriaczka** *f. Gen.pl.* **-ek** Austrian.

aut *mi sport* out; **rzut z autu** *sport* throw-in; **posłać piłkę na aut** *sport* hit the ball out of bounds; **aut bramkowy** *sport* out of bounds on the goal side; **aut boczny (lewy/prawy)** *sport* out of bounds on the (left/right) side.

autarcha *mp pl.* **-owie** autarch.

autarchia *f. Gen.* **-ii** (= *absolutyzm, despotyzm*) autarchy.

autarkia *f. Gen.* **-ii** *ekon.* autarky.

autarkiczny *a. ekon.* autarkic, autarkical.

autentycznie *adv.* **1.** (= *prawdziwie, niefałszywie*) authentically, genuinely. **2.** *pot.* (= *naprawdę*) really.

autentyczność *f.* authenticity.

autentyczny *a.* **1.** (= *prawdziwy, niepodrobiony*) authentic, genuine. **2.** *pot.* (= *prawdziwy*) real, true.

autentyk *mi* original, authentic *l.* genuine object.

autentyzm *mi* conformity with the facts; authenticity, genuineness.

auto *n. pot.* (= *samochód*) auto, car.

autoalarm[1] *mi żegl.* distress receiver.

autoalarm[2] *mi mot.* car alarm.

autobiograf *mi teor.lit.* autobiographer.

autobiografia *f. Gen.* **-ii** *teor.lit.* autobiography.

autobiograficzny *a.* autobiographical, autobiographic; **film autobiograficzny** *film* autobiographical movie; **powieść autobiograficzna** *teor.lit.* autobiographical novel.

autobus *mi* coach, bus, motor coach, motorbus; **autobus wycieczkowy** *l.* turystyczny (package-tour) coach, sightseeing bus; **autobus miejski** bus, local bus; **autobus podmiejski** commuter bus; **autobus dalekobieżny** long-distance bus, coach; **autobus pośpieszny** limited bus *l.* coach; **autobus przegubowy** articulated bus; **autobus szkolny** school bus; **autobus zakładowy** company bus; **autobus piętrowy** double-decker (bus); **jechać autobusem** ride a bus *l.* coach; **wsiąść** *l.* **załadować do autobusu** board a bus *l.* coach, get on a bus *l.* coach.

autobusowy *a.* bus; **przystanek autobusowy** bus stop; **komunikacja autobusowa** bus transport; **dworzec autobusowy** coach station, bus station.

autocasco *n. indecl.* (*ubezpieczenie*) comprehensive and collision (insurance), (fully) comprehensive (insurance).

autocenzura *f.* self-censorship.

autocharakterystyka *f.* self-characterization.

autochton *mp pl.* **-i** (= *tubylec*) autochthon, aborigine, native. – *mi pl.* **-y 1.** *biol.* autochthon, native. **2.** *geol.* autochthon.

autochtoniczny *a.* **1.** *biol.* (*o człowieku, o zwierzęciu, o roślinie*) autochthonous, aboriginal, indigenous, native; **organizmy autochtoniczne** *biol.* native organisms. **2.** *geol.* autochtonous; **skały autochtoniczne** *geol.* autochtonous rocks.

autochtonka *f. Gen.pl.* **-ek** (= *kobieta autochton*) *zob.* **autochton**.

autodestrukcja *f.* self-destruction.

autogamia *f. biol.* autogamy, self-fertilization.

autograf *mi* **1.** (= *podpis*) autograph; **łowca autografów** autograph hunter. **2.** *teor.lit.* (= *rękopis*) manuscript, autograph. **3.** *techn.* plotter.

autoironia *f. Gen.* **-ii** self-irony.

autoironiczny *a.* self-ironic.

autokar *mi* coach, motor coach; **wsiąść do autokaru** board a coach, get on a coach; **podróżować autokarem** travel by coach; **klimatyzowany autokar** air-conditioned coach.

autokarowy *a.* coach; **wycieczka autokarowa** coach trip.

autokataliza *f. chem.* autocathalysis.

autokefalia *f. Gen.* **-ii** *kośc.* autocephaly.

autokefaliczny *a. rel., kośc.* autocephalous; **kościół autokefaliczny** *kośc.* autocephalous church.

autoklaw *mi med., chem.* autoclave.

autokontrola *f.* self-control.

autokracja *f. polit.* autocracy.

autokratyczny *a.* autocratic, autocratical.

autokratyzm *mi* **1.** (= *autokracja*) autocracy. **2.** (*cecha charakteru*) autocratic character.

automat *mi* **1.** *techn.* (*maszyna*) machine, automaton, automatic (machine); **automat (do sprzedaży)** vending machine; **automat pożarowy** automatic fire alarm. **2.** *mat.* automaton; **automat skończony** finite automaton. **3.** *pot.* (= *automat telefoniczny*) pay phone, public telephone. **4.** *pot.* (= *pralka automatyczna*) washing machine. **5.** *pot.* (= *pistolet maszynowy*) automatic (gun *l.* rifle). **6.** (= *robot*) robot, automaton.

automatycznie *adv.* **1.** *techn.* automatically. **2.** *pot.* (= *bezmyślnie, odruchowo*) automatically.

automatyczny *a.* **1.** *techn.* automatic; **broń automatyczna** automatic weapon; **ołówek automatyczny** propelling pencil; **automatyczna sekretarka** answering machine; **automatyczna skrzynia biegów** *mot.* automatic transmission, automatic gears; **pilot automatyczny** *lotn., żegl.* automatic pilot. **2.** (= *odruchowy, bezwiedny, machinalny*) automatic.

automatyka *f. techn.* automatics.

automatyzacja *f. techn.* automation.

automatyzm *mi* automatism.

automatyzować *ipf. techn.* automate. **~ się** *ipf. techn.* automate, become automated.

automyjnia *f. Gen.pl.* **-i** car wash.

autonaprawa *f. pot.* garage.

autonomia *f. Gen.* **-ii**, **autonomiczność** *f.* autonomy.

autonomiczny *a.* **1.** (= *niezależny, niepodległy, odrębny*) autonomous; **autonomiczne państwo** autonomous state. **2.** *anat.* autonomic; **autonomiczny układ nerwowy** autonomic nervous system.

autopilot *mi lotn., żegl.* autopilot, automatic pilot.

autoplastyka *f. med.* autoplasty.

autoportret *mi sztuka* self-portrait.

autopsja *f.* **1.** (= *ogląd*) inspection; **znać coś z autopsji** know sth from experience. **2.** *med.* (= *sekcja zwłok*) autopsy, post-mortem examination.

autor *mp* **1.** (= *twórca*) author; **autor powieści** novelist, writer, author of a novel; **autor wiersza** poet, author of a poem; **autor notatki** *l.* **artykułu** author of an article; **autor obrazu** painter; **autor rzeźby** sculptor; **słowo od autora** *teor.lit.* preface. **2.** (= *sprawca, inicjator*) author, originator, creator.

autoradiografia *f. fiz.* autoradiography, radioautography.

autoradiogram *mi fiz.* autoradiograph, autoradiogram.

autoreklama *f.* self-advertisement.

autorka *f. Gen.pl.* **-ek** author, authoress; *zob.* **autor**.

autorski *a.* author's; **komentarz autorski** author's commentary; **egzemplarz autorski** presentation copy; **prawa autorskie** *prawn.* copyright; **honorarium autorskie** royalty; **wieczór autorski** evening with the author, reading; **film autorski** *film* auteur film.

autorstwo *n.* authorship.

autorytaryzm *mi* authoritarianism.

autorytatywność *f.* authoritativeness.

autorytatywny *a.* authoritative; reliable.

autorytet *mi* **1.** (= *szacunek, poważanie*) prestige, esteem; **mieć autorytet** have prestige, enjoy prestige *l.* esteem; **zdobyć autorytet** gain *l.* achieve prestige; **utrzymać** *l.* **zachować autorytet** maintain prestige, keep up prestige, retain esteem; **cieszyć się autorytetem** enjoy prestige, bask in esteem; **powołać się na czyjś autorytet** defer to sb. **2.** (*ekspert, znawca*) authority; **być autorytetem** be an authority (*w dziedzinie czegoś* on sth).

autoryzacja *f.* authorization.

autoryzować *ipf.* authorize.

autoryzowany *a.* authorized; **przekład/wywiad autoryzowany** authorized translation/interview; **autoryzowana stacja obsługi samochodów** *mot.* authorized service center; **autoryzowany dealer firmy** *handl.* authorized dealer *l.* agent.

autoserwis *mi* **1.** *mot.* (= *techniczna obsługa pojazdów*) automobile service; (= *stacja obsługi*) service center, service station. **2.** *pot.* (= *warsztat samochodowy*) garage.

autosom *mi biol.* autosome, euchromosome.

autostop *mi* hitch-hiking; **podróżować autostopem** hitch-hike.

autostopowicz *mp Gen.pl.* **-ów**, **autostopowiczka** *f. Gen.pl.* **-ek** hitch-hiker; **podwozić autostopowiczów** give a ride to hitch-hikers; **zabierać autostopowiczów** take *l.* pick up hitch-hikers.

autostrada *f.* freeway, expressway; *Br.* motorway.

autosugestia *f. Gen.* **-ii** *psych.* autosuggestion.

autoszczepionka *f. med.* autovaccine.

autotrof *ma biol.* autotroph.

autotypia *f. fot.* autotype.

autowy *a. sport* out; **linia autowa** side-line *l.* end line; **sędzia autowy** line judge, linesman; **piłka autowa** out.

autsajder *mp*, **autsajderka** *f. Gen.pl.* **-ek** outsider.

autystyczny *a. psych.* autistic.

autyzm *mi pat.* autism.

awangarda *f.* **1.** (= *czołówka*) avant-garde, vanguard; **iść** *l.* **kroczyć w awangardzie** *przen.* be in the forefront *l.* vanguard; **awangarda filmowa** *film* film avant-garde. **2.** *wojsk.* advance guard.

awangardowość *f.* avant-gardism.

awangardowy *a.* **1.** (= *przodujący, nowatorski*) in the forefront *l.* vanguard, innovative. **2.** *sztuka* avant-garde; **awangardowa sztuka** avant-garde art; **awangardowa poezja** avant-garde poetry.

awangardysta *mp sztuka* avant-gardist.

awangardyzm *mi sztuka* avant-gardism.

awanport *mi żegl.* road, roads, roadstead.

awans *mi pl.* **-e** *l.* **-y** **1.** (= *kariera, promocja*) promotion; advancement; **awans społeczny** social advancement; **dać awans** promote; **zasłużyć na awans** deserve a promotion, earn a promotion; **uzyskać awans** get a promotion, get promoted; **przedstawić kogoś do awansu** put sb in for promotion, recommend sb for promotion; **starać się o awans** strive for promotion. **2.** (= *zaliczka, przedpłata*) *przest.* advance payment.

awanse *pl. Gen.* **-ów** *przest.* advances; **robić** *l.* **czynić komuś awanse** make advances to sb.

awansować *ipf. l. pf.* **1.** (*przesunąć na wyższe stanowisko*) promote (*z kogoś / czegoś* from sb/sth) (*na kogoś / coś* to sb/sth). **2.** (*objąć wyższe stanowisko*) be promoted; **awansować na stanowisko** be promoted to a post; **awansować do finału/do kolejnej rundy** *sport* advance to the finals/to the next round.

awansowy *a.* promotional.

awantura *f.* **1.** (= *kłótnia*) commotion, brawl, broil, fuss, hassle, kick-up (*z kimś* with sb) (*o kogoś / coś* about *l.* over sb/sth); **robić** *l.* **wszczynać awanturę** kick up a fuss; **o co ta cała awantura?** what's all the fuss?; **zrobić komuś awanturę** give sb a hard time; get into it with sb (*o coś* over sth). **2.** (= *przygoda*) *przest.* adventure; **arabska awantura** *żart.* strange incident, unusual experience; **wplątać się w awanturę** meet an adventure; **przeżyć awanturę** have an adventure. **3.** (= *afera, ryzykowne przedsięwzięcie*) *przest.* venture, risky undertaking.

awanturnica *f.* **1.** (= *kobieta kłótliwa*) zob. **awanturnik. 2.** *przest.* (= *kobieta ekstrawagancka*) adventuress.

awanturnictwo *n.* **1.** (= *kłótliwość*) rowdiness, quarrelsomeness. **2.** (= *ryzykanctwo, nieprzemyślana działalność*) adventurism; **awanturnictwo polityczne** political adventurism.

awanturniczy *a.* full of adventure.

awanturnik *mp* **1.** (= *osoba skłonna do kłótni*) rowdy, trouble-maker. **2.** *przest.* (= *poszukiwacz przygód*) adventurer.

awanturować się *ipf.* make a fuss, cause trouble, pick a fight (*z kimś* with sth, *o coś* about *l.* over sth); **awanturować się o byle co** *l.* **z byle powodu** make a fuss for no reason.

awaria *f. Gen.* **-ii** **1.** (= *usterka, zepsucie się*) breakdown, failure; **awaria silnika** engine failure; **awaria prądu** black-out, power cut; **awaria systemu** *komp.* system crash; **spowodować awarię czegoś** break sth down; **usunąć awarię** repair a failure. **2.** *żegl.* average.

awaryjność *f. techn.* failure frequency.

awaryjny *a.* emergency; stand-by; **światła awaryjne** *mot.* hazard lights; **wyjście awaryjne** emergency exit.

awers *mi* obverse; face.

awersja *f.* aversion, dislike, distaste, repugnance; **budzić w kimś awersję** repel sb; **czuć** *l.* **mieć awersję** have *l.* take an aversion (*do kogoś / czegoś* to sb/sth).

awionetka *f. lotn.* light plane, sports plane.

awista *a. indecl. ekon.* at sight; **konto awista** checking account, current account; **płatny awista** payable at sight.

awitaminoza *f. pat.* avitaminosis, vitamin deficiency.

awizo[1] *n. Gen.pl.* **-ów** **1.** (= *zawiadomienie*) advice (note), letter of advice, notice, notification; **pocztowe awizo** receipt. **2.** *ekon.* advice note; **awizo bankowe** bank advice note.

awizo[2] *n. Gen.pl.* **-ów** *żegl.* aviso, dispatch boat.

awizować *ipf.* **1.** (= *wypisywać, wysyłać awizo*) notify. **2.** *form.* (= *informować*) advise (*o czymś* of sth).

awokado *n. indecl. bot., kulin.* avocado (*Persea americana*).

azalia *f. Gen.* **-ii** *bot.* azalea (*Azalea*).

azbest *mi miner.* asbestos.

azbestowy *a.* asbestine, asbestous.

Azer *mp*, **Azerka** *f. Gen.pl.* **-ek** Azeri, Azerbaijani.

Azerbejdżan *mi geogr.* Azerbaijan.

azerbejdżański *a.* Azerbaijani, Azerbaijanian.

Azja *f. geogr.* Asia; **Azja Mniejsza** Asia Minor.

Azjata *mp*, **Azjatka** *f. Gen.pl.* **-ek** Asian.

azjatycki *a.* Asian, Asiatic.

azot *mi chem.* nitrogen.

azotan *mi chem.* nitrate.

azotek *mi chem.* nitride.

azotowy *a. chem.* nitric; **kwas azotowy** nitric acid; **nawóz azotowy** nitrogenous fertilizer.

azotyn *mi chem.* nitrite.

aztecki *a.* Aztec.

Aztek *mp pl.* **-owie** *l.* **-cy**, **Azteczka** *f. Gen.pl.* **-ek** Aztec.

azyl *mi Gen.pl.* **-ów** **1.** (= *prawo do nietykalności*) asylum; **azyl dyplomatyczny/polityczny** *polit.* diplomatic/political immunity; **prawo azylu** right to asylum; **prosić o azyl** ask for asylum; **szukać/udzielać azylu** grant asylum. **2.** *przen.* (= *zacisze, schronienie, przystań*) haven, harbor, refuge, asylum; **znaleźć azyl** find refuge.

azylant *mp*, **azylantka** *f. Gen.pl.* **-ek** refugee.

azymut *mi* (*kąt*) **1.** azimuth, bearing; **wyznaczać azymut** take a bearing (*czegoś* on sth); **kierować się na azymut** plot *l.* set one' course, follow the course, set (one's) sights on; **azymut astronomiczny** *astron.* astronomical azimuth; **azymut geograficzny/magnetyczny** *geogr.* geographical/

magnetic azimuth; **azymut anteny** *radio* antenna azimuth. **2.** *lit.* (= *kierunek działalności*) course, line.

aż *conj.* till, until; **poczekaj, aż przyjdę** wait till I come. – *part.* **1.** (*wzmacnia, uwydatnia, poprzedzając wyrażenia z przyimkami*) as... as..., as far as, as many as, as much as; till, until; all the way; **dojechać aż do granicy** go *l.* drive as far as the border, go *l.* drive all the way to the border; **pracować od świtu aż do nocy** work all day long, work from dawn till dusk; **przywieźć coś aż z Los Angeles** bring sth all the way from Los Angeles; **posunąć się aż do kradzieży** go so far as to steal; **nie budzić aż do ostatniej chwili** not wake up until the very last moment. **2.** (*uwydatnia znaczenie, poprzedzając poszczególne części mowy*) **pochodzić aż z czasów rzymskich** date as far back as the Roman times; **wypić aż pięć piw** drink as many as five beers. **3.** (*w utartych połączeniach*) **aż miło posłuchać** it's a pleasure to listen; **aż strach pomyśleć** one shudders to think; **aż do końca** until the end; to the bitter end; **aż do** till, until, up to, as late as, as far back as.

ażeby *conj.* (= *żeby, aby*) in order to, so that. – *part.* (= *oby, niech*) may, let; **ażeby go diabli wzięli** may he go to hell.

ażur *mi* **1.** (= *wzór składający się z otworów*) openwork. **2.** *tk.* (*cienka tkanina*) gossamer. **3.** *tk.* (= *haft*) openwork, tracery. **4.** (= *ażurowy przedmiot*) openwork object, filigree.

ażurowy *a.* openwork; **ażurowa konstrukcja** openwork structure; **ażurowa serweta/narzuta/tkanina** openwork tablecloth/bedspread/fabric.

B

B, b *n.* (*litera*) B, b; **B jak Barbara** B is for Bravo; B as in Bravo.

B *n. indecl. muz.* (*dźwięk*) B flat; **b-moll** *muz.* B flat minor; **B-dur** *muz.* B flat major.

b. *abbr.* **1.** (= *były*) ex-. **2.** (= *bardzo*) v. (= *very*); **b. dobry** v. good.

ba *int.* **1.** (*wyraża bezradność l. powątpiewanie*) well, sure, true; **ba, ale co mamy zrobić?** true, but what shall we do? **2.** (= *wyraża rezygnację*) oh well; **ba, nic na to nie poradzę** oh well, there's nothing I can do about it; **ba, sam bym chciał wiedzieć** true, but what shall we do? **3.** *lit.* (= *co ja mówię!*) nay; **sądzę, ba! jestem pewien...** I suppose, nay, I am sure...

baba[1] *f.* **1.** *pot. pog. l. żart.* woman; **stara baba** old woman, old bag; **latać za babami** chase skirt; womanize; **baba z wozu, koniom lżej** good riddance to bad rubbish; **masz babo placek** here's a pretty kettle of fish. **2.** (*w złożeniach*) **herod-baba** battle-axe, virago; **baba-chłop** mannish woman, manly woman; **baba-jaga** witch, hag. **3.** *przen.* (*tchórzliwy mężczyzna*) old woman; **zachowywać się jak baba** act like an old woman. **4.** (*ciasto*) baba cake (*Polish type of cake baked in a fluted tube pan*); **baba wielkanocna** Easter baba. **5.** *bud.* pile-driver head, monkey. **6.** *przest.* (= *staruszka*) old crone.

baba[2] *f. archeol.* stone baba (*female figure erected by the nomads of the Eurasian steppes*).

babcia *f. Voc.* **-u** *Gen.pl.* **-ć** *l.* **1.** (= *matka ojca lub matki*) grandmother, grandmom, grandma, granny; **jak babcię kocham** *żart.* honest Indian; (I swear) on my mother's grave. **2.** (= *staruszka*) old woman, granny; **babcia klozetowa** *pot.* restroom attendant.

babciny *a.* grandmother's.

babeczka *f.* **1.** *kulin.* cup cake, brioche. **2.** *pot.* (= *atrakcyjna kobieta l. dziewczyna*) babe, chick.

Babel *indecl.* **wieża Babel** *Bibl. l. przen.* the tower of Babel.

babi *a.* **1.** *pot.* woman's, women's. **2. babie lato** (= *pogodna jesień*) Indian summer; (= *pajęczyna unoszona przez wiatr*) gossamer.

babiarz *mp pot. uj.* womanizer.

babieć *ipf.* **1.** *pog.* (*o kobiecie*) (= *starzeć się*) become an old woman. **2.** *pog.* (= *niewieścieć*) turn into an old woman.

Babilon *mi hist.* Babylon.

babiloński *a. hist.* Babylonian; **niewola babilońska** Babylonian captivity.

babimór *mi* **-o-** *bot.* (= *widłak goździsty*) club moss (*Lycopodium clavatum*).

babina *f.* (*z politowaniem*) old biddy, old woman.

babiniec *mi* **-ńc-** *Gen.* **-a** *żart.* bevy (of women).

babka *f.* **1.** (= *matka ojca lub matki*) grandmother. **2.** (= *ciasto*) type of sponge cake; **babka piaskowa** sponge cake made from very fine flour; **babka kartoflana** potato cake; **babka drożdżowa** sponge cake with yeast in the mix. **3. babka z piasku** sand castle, sand pie. **4.** *pot.* (*o starszej kobiecie*) old woman. **5. ślepa babka** (= *ciuciubabka*) blind man's bluff *l.* buff. **6.** *pot.* (*o młodej, atrakcyjnej kobiecie*) babe, chick. **7.** *bot.* plantain (*Plantago*). **8. koźlarz babka** *bot.* birch bolete (*Leccinum scabrum*). **9.** *zool.* (= *ryba z rodziny Gobiidae*) goby.

babrać *ipf.* **-rzę -rzesz, -rz** *l.* **-ram -rasz, -raj** *pot.* **1.** (= *brudzić*) dirty, muddy. **2.** (= *mazać, smarować*) smudge, smear (*sth*) (*czymś* with sth). ~ **się** *ipf. pot.* **1.** (= *brudzić się*) get dirty. **2. babrać się w czymś** (= *grzebać, dłubać*) tinker with sth. **3. babrać się z czymś** (= *guzdrać się*) be stuck with sth *l.* in sth.

babranina *f. pot.* dirty work.

babski *a. pot.* girls'; **babskie zebranie** girls' get-together; **babska ciekawość** female nosiness.

babsztyl *mp Gen.pl.* **-i** *l.* **-ów** *pog.* cow, bitch.

babuleńka *f. Gen.pl.* **-niek** *żart.* old biddy.

babunia *f. Voc.* **-u** (*pieszczotliwie o babci*) gran, granny.

baca *mp pl.* **-owie** head shepherd (*in the Carpathians*).

bach *int.* **1.** smack, bang. **2.** *dziec.* **zrobić bach** (= *przewrócić się*) go boom.

bachanalia *pl. Gen.* **-ów** *hist. l. przen.* bacchanalia.

bachantka *f. Gen.pl.* **-ek** *hist. l. przen.* bacchante.

bachiczny *a. hist., teor.lit. l. przen.* Bacchic.

bachmat *ma arch.* Tartar horse.

bachnąć *pf.* **-ij** *pot.* (= *uderzyć*) smack, thump, punch; (= *cisnąć*) fling, hurl.

bachor *mp pl.* **-y** *pot.* brat; **rozpuszczony bachor** spoiled brat; **zrobić komuś bachora** *pot. pog.* put sb up the spout.

bacik *mi Gen.* **-a** (small) whip.

bacowski *a.* shepherd's.

bacówka *f. Gen.pl.* **-ek** shepherd's hut (*in the Carpathians*).

baczenie *n.* **mieć baczenie na kogoś/coś** keep a close eye on sb/sth.

baczki *pl. Gen.* **-ów** sideburns; *Br.* sideboards.

bacznie *adv.* (= *z uwagą*) attentively; (= *dokładnie, starannie*) carefully, closely.

baczność *f.* **1.** (= *postawa gotowości*) attention; **stać na baczność** stand at attention; **baczność!** *wojsk.* attention! **2. mieć się na baczności** be on one's guard (*przed kimś/czymś* against sb/sth).

baczny *a. lit.* attentive, vigilant; **mieć baczne oko na kogoś/coś** keep a close eye on sb/sth.

baczyć *ipf.* heed (*na kogoś/coś* sb/sh); pay heed (*na kogoś/coś* to sb/sh); **nie baczyć na kogoś/coś** take no heed of sb/sth.

bać się *ipf.* **boję boisz, bój 1.** (*doznawać strachu*) be afraid *l.* frightened (*kogoś/czegoś* of sb/sth); **bać się własnego cienia** be afraid of one's own shadow; **bać się czegoś jak ognia** be scared stiff of sth; **bój się Boga!** for God's sake! **2.** (= *niepokoić się, obawiać się*) fear, be afraid (*o kogoś/coś* for sb/sth); **bać się o zdrowie** fear for one's health; **bać się o swoją skórę** *l.* **o swoje życie** fear for one's life; be in fear of one's life; **boję się, że to prawda** I'm afraid it's true. **3.** (*nie ważyć się na coś*) fear (*robić coś* to do sth); be afraid (*robić coś* to do sth *l.* of doing sth). **4. nie bać się czegoś** *przen.* (= *znosić, wytrzymywać coś*) endure sth.

badacz *mp*, **badaczka** *f. Gen.pl.* **-ek** investigator, student, researcher.

badać *ipf.* **1.** (= *analizować, studiować*) investigate, examine, research. **2.** *med.* examine, test; **badać chorego** examine a patient; **badać serce/zęby pacjenta** examine a patient's heart/teeth; **badać czyjś puls/ciśnienie krwi** take sb's pulse/blood pressure. **3.** (= *sprawdzać, przeglądać*) check (up), examine, scrutinize; **badać grunt pod nogami** *przen.* take one's bearings. **4.** (= *przesłuchiwać*) interrogate, question. **~ się** *ipf.* **1.** (= *poddawać się badaniom*) be examined, have a checkup. **2. badać się (wzajemnie) wzrokiem** size each other up.

badanie *n.* **1.** (= *analiza, obserwacja, prace badawcze*) research, examination, scrutiny; **szczegółowe, wnikliwe badanie** detailed, thorough examination. **2.** *med.* examination, checkup, test; **badanie krwi/moczu** blood/urine test; **badanie cytologiczne/elektrokardiograficzne** cytological/ECG test; **badanie rentgenologiczne klatki piersiowej** chest X-ray; **badanie antydopingowe** drug testing. **3.** (= *sprawdzanie, przegląd*) check, checking, examination. **4.** (= *przesłuchiwanie*) interrogation, questioning.

badawczo *adv.* penetratingly, searchingly.

badawczy *a.* **1.** *nauk.* research; **prace badawcze** research; **instytut badawczy** research institute; **metody badawcze** research methods; **pracownik naukowo-badawczy** scientific research worker. **2.** (= *przenikliwy, uważny*) analytical; **badawczym okiem** with an analytical eye.

badminton *mi Gen. i Acc.* **-a** *sport* badminton.

badmintonista *mp*, **badmintonistka** *f. Gen.pl.* **-ek** *sport* badminton player.

badyl *mi Gen.* **-a** *Gen.pl.* **-i** *l.* **-ów 1.** (= *patyk*) stick; (= *łodyga*) stem, stalk. **2.** *pog.* (*o roślinie*) weed.

badylarka *f. Gen.pl.* **-ek** *zool.* (European) harvest mouse (*Micromys minutus*).

badylarz *mp pot.* gardener.

bagatela *f. Gen.pl.* **-i 1.** (= *drobnostka*) bagatelle, trifle. **2.** *muz.* bagatelle.

bagatelizować *ipf.* disregard, belittle, underestimate.

bagaż *mi Gen.pl.* **-y** *l.* **-ów 1.** baggage; *Br.* luggage; **przechowalnia bagażu** left baggage; **bagaż podręczny** hand baggage; **nadawać bagaż** check one's baggage; **przeszukanie bagażu** baggage search. **2.** *przen.* (= *brzemię, ciężar*) baggage, burden; **bagaż wspomnień** emotional baggage.

bagażnik *mi Gen.* **-a 1.** *mot.* trunk; *Br.* boot. **2.** (= *półka bagażowa*) baggage rack; (*na dachu pojazdu*) roof rack.

bagażowy *a.* baggage; *Br.* luggage; **kwit bagażowy** baggage check; **komora bagażowa** *lotn.* baggage compartment; **wózek bagażowy** baggage trolley; dolly. – *mp decl. like a.* porter.

bagażówka *f. pot.* delivery truck.

Bagdad *mi geogr.* Baghdad.

bagienko *n. Gen.pl.* **-nek** bog.

bagienny *a.* **1.** (= *charakterystyczny dla bagien*) bog, marsh, palustrine; **flora bagienna** marsh flora. **2.** (= *będący bagnem*) boggy, marshy, swampy.

bagietka *f. Gen.pl.* **-ek** (= *długa bułka*) **1.** baguette. **2.** *chem.* glass rod.

bagnet *mi broń, techn.* bayonet; **atak na bagnety** bayonet charge; **kłuć bagnetem** bayonet; **bagnet na broń!** *wojsk.* fix bayonets!; **opierać władzę na bagnetach** *przen.* rule by force.

bagnisko *n.* bog, marsh, wetland.

bagnisty *a.* boggy, swampy.

bagno *n. Gen.pl.* **-gien 1.** (= *trzęsawisko, mokradło*) bog, marsh, morass, swamp, wetland. **2.** *przen. uj.* quagmire, mire; **bagno moralne** moral quagmire. **3.** *bot.* marsh tea, swamp tea, wild rosemary, muskeegobug (*Ledum*).

bagrować *ipf. techn.* dredge.

bagrownica *f. techn.* dredger.

bahaizm *mi rel.* Baha'iism.

Bahrajn *mi geogr.* Bahrain.

baj *mp Gen.pl.* **-ów** *przest.* storyteller.

baja[1] *f. Gen.* **bai** *Gen.pl.* **baj 1.** (= *baśń, bajka*) tale, fairytale. **2.** *zw. lp. pot.* (= *bujda, androny*) baloney, bunkum, boatload.

baja[2] *f. Gen.* **bai** *tk.* baize.

bajać *ipf.* **-ę -esz** *l.* **-am -asz 1.** *lit.* (= *opowiadać bajki*) tell tales. **2.** *pot.* (= *bredzić, zmyślać*) tell stories.

bajadera *f.* **1.** (*hinduska tancerka*) Hindu temple dancer, bayadere. **2.** *tk.* bayadere.

bajarz *mp* fabler, fabulist, storyteller.

bajda *f.* **1.** *pot.* (= *bzdura, wymysł*) balderdash, baloney, bunkum, fairy story. **2.** *przest.* (= *bajka, baśń*) fairytale.

bajdurzyć *ipf. pot.* tell stories, talk nonsense.

bajecznie *adv.* fabulously; **bajecznie bogaty** fabulously rich; **bajecznie tani** fabulously cheap.

bajeczny *a.* fabulous, fantastic, fairytale.

bajer *mi* **1.** *pot.* (= *nieszczere słowa*) glib speech, smooth talk; (= *nieprawda*) tale, yarn;

brać kogoś na bajer spin sb a yarn; take sb in; **wciskać komuś bajery** feed sb baloney. **2.** *sl.* (= *efektowny przedmiot*) gadget, fancy thing.

bajerancki *a. pot.* fancy.

bajerant *mp*, **bajerantka** *f. Gen.pl.* **-ek** *pot.* smooth talker.

bajerować *ipf. pot.* **1.** (= *koloryzować, przesadzać*) cook up a story. **2.** (= *nabierać*) take (*sb*) in. **3.** (= *podrywać*) flirt with (*sb*).

bajka *f. Gen.pl.* **-ek 1.** (= *baśń*) fairytale, tale; **jak w bajce** like in a fairytale; **jak z bajki** out of a fairytale; **w każdej bajce jest trochę prawdy** in every fairytale there is a grain of truth. **2.** *lit.* fable; **bajka ezopowa** Aesop's fable. **3.** *pot.* (= *bzdura, zmyślenie, wymysł*) cock-and-bull story, fiction; **włożyć coś między bajki** write sth off as fiction.

bajkopisarstwo *n.* fairytale writing.

bajkopisarz *mp* fabler, fairytale writer.

bajkowy *a.* = **bajeczny**.

bajoński *a.* **bajońskie sumy** enormous sums.

bajorko *Gen.pl.* **-rek**, **bajoro** *n.* swampy pool; bog.

bajroniczny *a. lit.* Byronic.

bajronizm *mi lit.* Byronism.

bajt *mi Gen.* **-a** *komp.* byte.

bajtlować *ipf. pot.* (= *paplać*) blather, prattle.

bajzel *mi* **-zl-** (= *bałagan*) **1.** pigsty, mess. **2.** (= *dom publiczny, burdel*) brothel.

bak¹ *mi Gen.* **-u 1.** (= *zbiornik paliwa*) (fuel) tank. **2.** *żegl.* (= *górny pokład dziobowy*) forecastle, foredeck.

bak² *mi zob.* **baki**.

bak³ *mi Gen i Acc.* **-a** *karty, przest.* baccarat.

bakalarstwo *n. przest., żart.* teaching.

bakalaureat *mi hist., uniw.* baccalaureate.

bakalie *pl. Gen.* **-ii** mixed dried fruit and nuts.

bakaliowy *a.* fruit and nut.

bakałarz *mp hist. l. przest., żart.* schoolmaster, teacher.

bakarat¹ *mi Gen. i Acc.* **-a** *karty* baccarat.

bakarat² *mi Gen.* **-u** (*szkło kryształowe*) Baccarat crystal.

bakcyl *mi Gen.* **-a** *Gen.pl.* **-i** *l.* **-ów** *przest.* bug, germ, microbe; **połknąć bakcyla czegoś** *pot.* get the bug for sth.

bakelit *mi techn.* bakelite.

bakelitowy *a. techn.* bakelite.

baki *pl. Gen.* **-ów** sideburns; *Br.* sideboards.

bakier *mi indecl.* **1. na bakier** (= *krzywo*) askew, at an angle; **włożyć/nosić coś na bakier** put sth on/wear sth askew. **2.** *przen.* **być z kimś na bakier** be cross with sb; be at odds with sb; **być na bakier z prawem** fall foul of the law; **wszystko idzie na bakier** it's all going pear-shaped.

bakłażan *mi Gen.* **-a** *l.* **-u** *bot., kulin.* eggplant, aubergine (*Solanum melongena*).

bakonizm *mi fil.* Baconism.

baksztag *mi żegl.* backstay.

bakszysz *mi Gen.pl.* **-y** *l.* **-ów** baksheesh.

bakteria *f. Gen.* **-ii** *biol.* bacterium.

bakteriobójczy *a. biochem., med.* bactericidal; **środek bakteriobójczy** bactericide.

bakteriofag *mi Gen.* **-u** *l.* **-a** *biol.* bacteriophage.

bakteriolog *mp pl.* **-dzy** *l.* **-owie** bacteriologist.

bakteriologia *f. Gen.* **-ii** *biol.* bacteriology.

bakteriologiczny *a. nauk.* **1.** bacteriologic, bacteriological. **2.** *wojsk.* biological, bacteriological, germ; **broń/wojna bakteriologiczna** biological weapon/warfare.

bakteriostatyczny *a. biochem.* bacteriostatic; **środek bakteriostatyczny** *med.* bacteriostatic.

bakteryjny *a. biol.* bacterial; **choroba bakteryjna** bacterial disease; **zakażenie bakteryjne** bacterial infection; **jad bakteryjny** bacterial toxin.

baktrian *ma zool.* Bactrian camel (*Camelus bactrianus*).

bal¹ *mi Gen.* **-u** *Gen.pl.* **-ów** (= *zabawa taneczna*) **1.** ball; **bal karnawałowy/sylwestrowy** carnival/New Year's Eve ball; **bawić się/tańczyć na balu** have fun/dance at a ball; **bal kostiumowy/ maskowy** costume ball/masked ball; **bal przebierańców** masquerade, fancy-dress party; **bal dobroczynny** charitative ball; **bal maturalny** high-school prom; **urządzić sobie bal** have (o.s.) a ball. **2.** *przen. pot.* **sprawić komuś bal** give sb a thrashing; **ładny bal!** what a pretty kettle of fish!

bal² *mi Gen.* **-a** *Gen.pl.* **-i** *l.* **-ów** (= *pień, kłoda*) beam, log; *bud.* balk.

balanga *f. pot.* revel, noisy party.

balangować *ipf. pot.* revel (*z kimś* with sb).

balangowicz *mp Gen.pl.* **-ów**, **balangowiczka** *f. Gen.pl.* **-ek** *pot.* reveller, party-goer.

balans¹ *mi pl.* **-e 1.** (= *równowaga*) balance, equilibrium. **2.** (*drąg linoskoczka*) balancing pole. **3.** *sport* beam. **4.** *mech.* (*w zegarku*) balance wheel, flywheel.

balans² *int.* **kurde balans!** *pot.* holy cow!, holy ravioli.

balansjer *mi Gen.* **-a** *techn.* (= *wahacz*) crossbeam, rocker arm, balance lever.

balansować *ipf.* **1.** + *Ins.* balance; **balansować piłką na czubku nosa** balance a ball on the tip of one's nose. **2.** (= *utrzymywać równowagę*) balance, keep one's balance; **balansować na jednej nodze** balance on one foot; **balansować na linie** *t. przen.* walk a tightrope. **3.** *przen.* **balansować nad przepaścią** *przen.* be on the edge of the precipice; **balansować na granicy prawa** act half-legally; **balansować między prawdą a kłamstwem** walk a fine line between truth and lies.

balas *mi Gen.* **-a**, **balasek** *mi* **-sk-** *Gen.* **-a** *bud.* banister.

balast *mi t. przen.* ballast; **obciążać coś balastem** weigh sth down with ballast; ballast sth; **pozbywać się balastu** get rid of the ballast.

balastować *ipf. techn.* (= *obciążać*) ballast (*czymś* with sth).

baldach *mi* **1.** *bot.* umbel. **2.** *tk.* baldachin, baldaquin.

baldachim *mi* canopy; **łoże z baldachimem** canopy bed, four-poster bed; **nieść nad kimś/ czymś baldachim** carry a canopy over sb/sth; **pod baldachimem** beneath a canopy.

baldaszek *mi* **-szk-** *Gen.* **-a** *bot.* umbellule.

baldaszkowate *pl. Gen.* **-ych** *bot.* umbellifers, parsley family (*Apiaceae*).

balejaż *mi* (*technika fryzjerska*) baliage, balayage.

balerina *f.* **1.** *balet* (prima) ballerina. **2.** (*pantofel*) ballet slipper.

baleron *mi kulin.* ham sausage.

balet *mi taniec* (*widowisko, zespół*) ballet; **balet na lodzie** ice spectacular, skating spectacular.

baletka *f.* (*obuwie*) ballet slippers.

baletmistrz *mp taniec* ballet master, choreographer.

baletmistrzowski *a.* choreographic.

baletmistrzyni *f. taniec* ballet mistress, choreographer.

baletnica *f.* (= *tancerka w balecie*) ballet dancer.

baletowy *a.* ballet; **szkoła baletowa** ballet school; **wieczór baletowy** evening of ballet; **film baletowy** ballet film; **zespół baletowy** ballet troupe.

balety *pl. Gen.* **-ów** *pot.* (= *impreza taneczna, zabawa*) dancing (party).

balia *f. Gen.* **-ii** washtub.

balistyczny *a. wojsk., lotn.* ballistic; **pocisk/lot balistyczny** ballistic missile/flight; **krzywa balistyczna** ballistic curve.

balistyka *f.* ballistics.

balkon *mi* **1.** *bud.* balcony; **pokój z balkonem** room with a balcony. **2.** (*teatr, kino*) the circle; **pierwszy/drugi balkon** the lower/upper circle.

balkonowy *a.* **1.** *bud.* balcony; **okno/drzwi balkonowe** balcony window/door. **2.** *teatr* **miejsca balkonowe** seats in the circle.

ballada *f.* ballad; **ballada podwórzowa** street ballad.

balladowy *a. form.* balladic.

balladzista *mp*, **balladzistka** *f. Gen.pl.* **-ek** balladeer, ballad singer.

balneoklimatyczny *a. med.* balneoclimatic.

balneolog *mp pl.* **-dzy** *l.* **-owie** *med.* balneologist.

balneologia *f. Gen.* **-ii** *med.* balneology.

balneoterapeutyczny *a. med.* balneological; **zabiegi balneoterapeutyczne** balneological therapy *l.* treatment.

balneoterapia *f. Gen.* **-ii** *med.* balneological therapy.

balon *mi* **1.** balloon; **balon wolny/na uwięzi** *lotn.* free/captive balloon; **balon na gorące powietrze** *lotn.* hot-air balloon; **wzbijać się balonem** soar in a balloon; **lot balonem** balloon flight; **balon zaporowy** *wojsk.* barrage balloon. **2.** *techn.* (*naczynie*) flask, balloon. **3.** *mot.* (*typ opony*) balloon tire. **4.** *żegl.* balloon sail.

baloniarka *f. Gen.pl.* **-ek** *zob.* **baloniarz.**

baloniarski *a. sport* ballooning; **zawody baloniarskie** ballooning competition.

baloniarstwo *n. sport* ballooning.

baloniarz *mp sport* balloonist.

balonik *mi Gen.* **-a** **1.** (*zabawka*) balloon. **2.** *pot.* (*przyrząd do wykrywania alkoholu w orga-*

nizmie kierowcy) breathalyser; **dmuchać w balonik** blow into a breathalyser.

balonkliwer *mi* **-wr-** *Gen.* **-a** *żegl.* balloon jib, ballooner.

balonowy *a.* **1.** balloon, balloon-like; **pilot balonowy** balloon pilot; **lot balonowy** balloon flight; **sport balonowy** ballooning. **2.** *mot.* **opona balonowa** balloon tire. **3.** **guma (do żucia) balonowa** bubble gum.

balot *mi handl.* bale.

balotaż *mi* (*forma głosowania*) ballot.

balotować *ipf.* ballot.

balować *ipf. pot.* party; **balować całą noc** party all night (*z kimś* with sb).

balowicz *mp Gen.pl.* **-ów**, **balowiczka** *f. Gen.pl.* **-ek** *pot.* party-goer.

balowy *a.* ball; **suknia balowa** ball gown; **sala balowa** ballroom.

balsa *f. bot.* **1.** balsa. **2.** *stol.* balsa (wood), corkwood. **3.** *żegl.* balsa raft.

balsam *mi* **1.** *chem.* balsam; **balsam kanadyjski** Canada balsam; **balsam peruwiański** balsam of Peru. **2.** *bot.* balm. **3.** (= *aromatyczna maść lub olejek*) *przen.* (= *ukojenie, pociecha*) balm, balsam; **być balsamem na czyjeś rany** be a balm on sb's wounds. **4.** *hist.* (*w starożytnym Egipcie*) balm.

balsamiczny *a.* **1.** (*pachnący żywicą, aromatyczny*) balmy, fragrant; **balsamiczne powietrze** balmy breeze. **2.** *chem.* balsamic. **3.** (= *kojący*) balmy, soothing.

balsamować *ipf.* **1.** (= *utrwalać za pomocą balsamu*) embalm; **balsamować zwłoki** embalm a corpse. **2.** (= *aromatyzować*) perfume.

baltolog *mp pl.* **-dzy** *l.* **-owie** Baltologist.

baltologia *f. nauk.* Baltic studies.

balustrada *f.*, **balustradka** *f. Gen.pl.* **-ek** balustrade.

balzakowski *a.* **w wieku balzakowskim** *pot.* (*o kobiecie*) in her 30s.

bałagan *mi* (= *nieporządek*) mess, disorder; **piekielny bałagan** a hell *l.* one hell of a mess; **narobić bałaganu** make a mess; **mieć bałagan w głowie** be confused; be unable to think straight.

bałaganiara *f. pot. zob.* **bałaganiarz.**

bałaganiarski *a.* slovenly.

bałaganiarstwo *n.* slovenliness.

bałaganiarz *mp* sloven.

bałaganić *ipf.* make a mess.

bałałajka *f. muz.* balalaika.

bałamucić *ipf.* **1.** *żart. l. przest.* (= *uwodzić*) seduce. **2.** (= *zwodzić*) lead (*sb*) astray, mislead. **3.** *przest.* (= *próżnować, marnować czas*) waste time, idle (about).

bałamut *mp pl.* **-y** *l. rzad.* (= *krętacz, matacz*) schemer, snake in the grass. **2.** (= *podrywacz, uwodziciel*) seducer.

bałamutka *f. Gen.pl.* **-ek** *przest.* (= *kokietka*) coquette.

bałamutnie *adv.* confusingly, deceptively, disingenuously.

bałamutny *a.* **1.** (= *mylący, zwodniczy*) confusing, bamboozling, deceptive, misleading. **2.** (= *zalotny*) seductive, flirtatious, coquettish.

Bałkany *pl. Gen.* **-ów** *geogr.* the Balkans.

bałkański *a.* Balkan; **Półwysep Bałkański** *geogr.* the Balkan Peninsula; **kraje bałkańskie** *geogr.* the Balkan countries.

Bałt *mp* Balt.

bałtolog *mp pl.* **-dzy** *l.* **-owie** = baltolog.

bałtologia *f. Gen.* **-ii** *nauk.* = baltologia.

Bałtosłowianin *mp pl.* **-anie** *Gen.* **-an** *hist., jęz.* Balt-Slav, Balto-Slav.

bałtosłowiański *a. hist., jęz.* Balto-Slavic, Balto-Slavonic.

bałtycki *a.* Baltic; **Morze Bałtyckie** *geogr.* the Baltic (Sea).

Bałtyjka *f. Gen.pl.* **-ek** *zob.* **Balt.**

bałtyjski *a.* Baltic.

Bałtyk *mi geogr.* the Baltic (Sea).

bałwan *mi Gen.* **-a** **1.** (*figura ze śniegu*) snowman; **lepić bałwana** build a snowman. **2.** *hist.* (= *bożek*) idol. – *mp Gen.* **-a** *pl.* **-y** (= *tuman, głupiec*) moron, dimwit, geek. – *mi Gen.* **-a** *l.* **-u** (= *fala*) roller, comber.

bałwanek *mi* **-nk-** *Gen.* **-a** *dziec.* snowman.

bałwanieć *ipf.* become stupid.

bałwański *a.* silly, moronic.

bałwian *mi bot.* ailanthus (*Ailanthus*).

bałwochwalca *mp rel.* **1.** idolater. **2.** *przen.* idolater, idolizer.

bałwochwalczy *a.* idolatrous.

bałwochwalstwo *n. rel.* **1.** idolatry. **2.** *przen.* idolatry, idolization.

bam *int. dziec.* oops-a-daisy!

bamber *mp* **-br-** **1.** German farmer settled in or near Poznań. **2.** *uj.* (= *prostak*) simpleton, bumpkin, hick.

bambetle *pl. Gen.* **-i** **1.** *pot.* (= *manatki, toboły*) bundles. **2.** *pot.* (= *rupiecie, starocie*) trash, lumber.

bambosz *mi Gen.* **-a** *Gen.pl.* **-y** *l.* **-ów** carpet slipper.

bambus *mi Gen.* **-u** *l.* **-a** *bot., kulin., stol.* bamboo (*Bambusa*).

bambusowy *a.* bamboo; **kiełki bambusowe** *kulin.* bamboo shoots.

banalizacja *f.* trivialization.

banalizować *ipf.* trivialize.

banalnie *adv.* banally.

banalność *f.* (= *szablonowość*) **1.** triviality. **2.** (= *frazes, ogólnik, banał*) banality.

banalny *a.* **1.** (= *szablonowy, zwyczajny, pospolity*) banal, commonplace, unoriginal, clichéd; **banalna rozmowa** small talk, platitudinous chat. **2.** (= *błahy, nieistotny*) trivial; **banalne sprawy** commonplace matters.

banał *mi* banality, platitude, cliché.

banan *mi Gen.* **-a** *l.* **-u** *bot.* (*roślina*) **1.** banana (plant) (*Musa*). **2.** *Gen.* **-a** (*owoc*) banana; **kiść bananów** bunch of bananas; **poślizgnąć się, poślizgnąć się na skórce od banana** slip on a banana peel.

bananowiec *mi* **-wc-** *Gen.* **-a** *bot.* banana plant (*Musa sapientum*); plantain (*M. paradisica*).

bananowy *a.* **1.** *bot.* banana. **2.** (*kolor*) reddish-yellow. **3.** **republika bananowa** *iron.* banana republic.

banda *f.* (*grupa ludzi*) **1.** band, gang, pack; **tworzyć bandę** gang; **chodzić całą bandą** go about as a pack. **2.** (= *ogrodzenie, bariera*) board, headrail.

bandana *f.* bandanna.

bandaż *mi Gen.* **-a** *l.* **-u** **1.** (= *opatrunek, gaza*) bandage; **bandaż elastyczny** elastic bandage; **założyć bandaż** bandage. **2.** *techn.* flange. **3.** *żegl.* parcelling.

bandażować *ipf.* **1.** (= *opatrywać*) bandage; **bandażować rękę/nogę** bandage a hand/leg. **2.** *techn.* flange.

bandera *f.* **1.** *żegl.* (= *flaga*) banner, flag, colors; **podnieść banderę** hoist a flag, raise *l.* make the colors; **opuszczać banderę** lower the colors; **pływać pod włoską banderą** sail under the Italian flag. **2.** *przen.* (= *statek, okręt*) ship.

banderia *f. Gen.* **-ii** *hist.* (*oddział konny*) escort of horsemen.

banderilla *f. korrida* banderilla.

banderola *f. Gen.pl.* **-li** *l.* **-l** **1.** (= *opaska*) excise band. **2.** *sztuka* banderol, banderole.

banderolować *ipf.* band.

banderowy *a.* (= *flagowy*) flag.

bandolet *mi broń* shoulder belt.

bandolier *mi Gen.* **-a** *broń* bandolier, bandoleer.

bandoneon *mi muz.* bandoneon.

bandura *f. muz.* pandora, bandora.

bandycki *a.* criminal; **bandycki napad** mugging.

bandyta *mp* **1.** bandit, gangster; (= *brutalny rabuś*) mugger, robber; **uzbrojony bandyta** gunman. **2.** **jednoręki bandyta** (*automat do gry*) one-armed bandit, slot machine.

bandytyzm *mi* banditry, brigandage.

bandzior *mp pl.* **-y** *pog.* criminal, ruffian, mugger, thug.

bandżo *n. indecl. muz.* banjo.

Bangkok *mi geogr.* Bangkok.

Bangladesz *mi geogr.* Bangladesh.

bania *f. Gen.pl.* **-ni** *l.* **-ń** **1.** (*pękaty, kulisty przedmiot*) bulb; **rozbiła się bania z gośćmi** guests arrived in their dozens; **jest do bani** *pot.* it sucks; **być do bani** be no use; **do bani z kimś/czymś** *pot.* hell with sb/sth; **być na bani** *pot.* be stoned. **2.** (= *pojemnik, naczynie*) flagon; **bania do mleka** *l.* **na mleko** milk can. **3.** *pot.* (= *dynia*) pumpkin.

baniak *mi Gen.* **-a** (= *naczynie*) can.

banialuki *pl. Gen.* **-k** baloney, hokum, piffle; **opowiadać, prawić banialuki** talk nonsense.

banian *mi Gen.* **-u** *l.* **-a** *bot.* banyan, banian (*Ficus benghalensis*).

baniasty *a.* (= *pękaty, kulisty, brzuchaty*) bulbous.

banicja *f.* exile, proscription; **wyrok banicji** banishment; **skazać na banicję** outlaw, banish.

banita *mp* outlaw.

bank *mi* **1.** (*przedsiębiorstwo, które zajmuje się operacjami pieniężnymi*) bank; **mieć konto** *l.* **rachunek w banku** have an account with a bank; **bank handlowy** commercial *l.* business bank; **bank państwowy** national *l.* government *l.* state bank; **bank akcyjny** incorporated bank; **bank komercyjny** credit *l.* commercial bank; **bank depozytowy** deposit bank; **bank hipoteczny** mortgage *l.* land bank; **bank centralny** banker's *l.* central bank; **bank spółdzielczy** co-operative bank; **bank inwestycyjny** investment bank; **bank emisyjny** issuing bank, bank of issue; **obrabować bank** rob a bank; **Narodowy Bank Polski** Polish National Bank; **Bank Światowy** World Bank; **coś jest u kogoś, gdzieś jak w banku; masz to jak w banku** *pot.* you can bank on it; you can take that to the bank. **2.** (*miejsce, gdzie się gromadzi informacje, materiały*) bank; **bank pomysłów** idea bank; **bank danych** *komp.* data bank. **3.** *med.* bank; **bank krwi/narządów** blood/organ bank. **4.** (*w grze*) bank, pool; **trzymać bank** bank, hold the bank; **rozbić bank** break the bank.

bankier *mp* (= *bankowiec*) **1.** banker. **2.** (*w grze*) banker.

bankierski *a.* banker('s); **czek bankierski** cashier's check.

bankiet *mi* (= *przyjęcie*) banquet; **wydać bankiet na czyjąś cześć** give *l.* hold a banquet in sb's honour; **uczestniczyć w bankiecie** take part in a banquet.

bankietować *ipf. żart.* banquet (*z kimś* with sb, *u kogoś* at sb's).

bankietowicz *mp Gen.pl.* **-ów** *żart.* banqueter.

bankietowy *a.* banquet; **sala bankietowa** banqueting hall; **strój bankietowy** evening dress.

banknot *mi* banknote; **paczka banknotów** bankroll.

bankomat *mi techn.* ATM, cashpoint, cash machine; **pobrać pieniądze z bankomatu** withdraw cash from a cashpoint.

bankowiec *mp* **-wc-** *pl.* **-y** banker.

bankowość *f. ekon.* banking.

bankowy *a.* bank; **konto bankowe** bank account; **rachunek bankowy** bank account; **nadzór bankowy** bank audit; **prowizja bankowa** bank brokerage *l.* commission; **przekaz bankowy** bank order; **przelew bankowy** bank transfer *l.* draft; **dom bankowy** bank house; **gwarancja bankowa** bank guarantee.

bankructwo *n.* (= *upadłość*) **1.** bankruptcy; **ogłosić bankructwo** be declared bankrupt, declare oneself bankrupt; **doprowadzić kogoś do bankructwa** bankrupt sb. **2.** (= *przegrana, klęska, utrata znaczenia*) bankruptcy; **bankructwo moralne** moral bankruptcy.

bankrut *mp* (*po stracie majątku*) **1.** bankrupt. **2.** *przen.* (= *przegrany*) loser, bankrupt; **polityczny bankrut** political bankrupt.

bankrutować *ipf.* (= *plajtować, upadać*) **1.** go bankrupt. **2.** *przen.* (= *przegrywać*) lose.

bant *mi Gen.* **-u** *l.* **-a** *żegl.* **1.** king-posted beam. **2.** (*w rzemiośle*) band, clip.

bantuski *a.* Bantu.

bantustan *mi* Bantustan.

bańka *f. Dat.* **-c-** **1.** (*pojemnik*) can; (*szklana*) flagon; **bańka do mleka, na mleko, z mlekiem** milk-can, churn. **2.** *med.* cupping glass; **stawiać komuś bańki** cup sb. **3.** (= *pęcherzyk, bąbelek*) bubble; **bańka powietrza** air bubble; **bańki myd-**

lane soap bubbles; **puszczać bańki** blow soap-bubbles; **bańki na wodzie** water bubbles. **4.** (*kulisty przedmiot*) bulb; **być na bańce** *pot.* be stoned, be illuminated.

baobab *mi bot.* baobab (*Adansonia digitata*).

baon *mi wojsk.* battalion.

baptysta *mp rel.* Baptist; **kościół baptystów** the Baptist Church.

baptysterium *n. sg. indecl. pl.* **-ria** *Gen.* **-riów** *bud.* **1.** baptistry, baptistery. **2.** *rel.* baptismal font.

baptystyczny *a. rel.* baptismal.

bar[1] *mi* (*lokal*) **1.** bar; **bar mleczny** restaurant serving very cheap meals, milk bar; **bar przekąskowy** snack-bar; **bar kawowy** coffee bar; **bar szybkiej obsługi** fast-food restaurant; **bar samoobsługowy** self-service bar; **bar nocny** night club; **drink bar** cocktail lounge. **2.** (= *bufet*) cafeteria; **siedzieć przy barze** sit at the bar; **stać za barem** work at the counter. **3.** (= *blat, stół*) counter, bar; **siedzieć, jeść przy barze** sit/eat at the bar.

bar[2] *mi chem.* (*pierwiastek*) **1.** barium; **siarczan baru** barium meal; **(wodoro)tlenek baru** baryta. **2.** *fiz.* (*jednostka ciśnienia*) bar.

bara-bara *n. indecl.* (= *seks*) hanky-panky.

barachło *n. pot.* (= *rupiecie, graty*) **1.** trash. **2.** *pot.* (= *hołota, hałastra*) hoi polloi, rabble, riffraff.

barak *mi* barrack, bull pen; **drewniany barak** (wooden) hut.

barakowóz *mi* **-o-** caboose.

barakuda *f. zool.* barracuda (*Sphyraena*).

baran *ma zool.* **1.** ram; **uparty jak baran** (as) stubborn as a mule; **jak stado baranów** like a herd of sheep; **nosić kogoś na barana** give sb a piggyback ride; **(jazda) na barana** piggyback; **liczyć barany** count sheep. **2.** *pot.* (= *baranica*) sheepskin. **3.** *astron., astrol.* Aries, the Ram; **urodzić się pod znakiem Barana** be born an Aries/a Ram; **być typowym Baranem** *pot.* be a typical Aries. – *mp pl.* **-y** *pot., obelż., przen.* (= *głupek*) idiot, dimwit, dick.

baranek *ma* **-nk-** **1.** *zool.* lamb; **łagodny jak baranek** (as) meek as a lamb. **2.** *rel.* **Baranek Boży** the Lamb of God, Agnus Dei; **baranek wielkanocny** Easter lamb. **3.** *pot.* (*futro, skóra*) sheepskin. **4.** *bot.* chaste tree (*Vitex agnus-castus*). **5.** *przen.* (= *chmurka*) fleecy cloud; **baranki** mackerel sky. **6.** *przen.* (= *fala*) roller. – *mp* **-nk-** *pl.* **-i** *przen.* (*o osobie łagodnej, pokornej*) gentle lamb.

barani *a.* **1.** mutton; **baranie mięso** mutton, lamb; **barani łeb** *przen.* thick-head; **barani wzrok** dumb look. **2.** (*z mięsa lub z futra barana*) **baranie kotlety** mutton chops; **barani kożuch** sheepskin.

baranica *f.* (*skóra do okrywania nóg*) **1.** sheepskin. **2.** (*kożuch*) sheepskin coat. **3.** (*czapka*) fur cap.

baranina *f.* mutton.

baraszkować *ipf.* frolic.

baraż *mi Gen.pl.* **-y** *l.* **-ów** *sport* play-off; **walczyć w barażach** play off.

barażowy *a. sport* play-off.

Barbados *mi geogr.* Barbados.

barbakan *mi bud.* barbican.

barbaria *f. Gen.* **-ii 1.** (= *dzikość*) savagery. **2.** (*dzicy ludzie*) barbarians. **3.** *pog.* (*dzicz, pierwotny kraj*) barbarous land.

barbaryzm *mi jęz.* barbarism

barbarzyńca *mp* (= *prymityw, dzikus, prostak*) **1.** barbarian. **2.** (= *okrutnik, sadysta*) barbarian. **3.** (*człowiek pierwotny*) savage. **4.** *hist.* barbarian.

barbarzyński *a.* **1.** (= *prymitywny, prostacki*) barbarous. **2.** (= *okrutny, zły*) barbaric. **3.** (= *pierwotny*) savage, uncivilized. **4.** *hist.* barbarian, vandalic.

barbarzyństwo *n.* (= *prymitywizm, dzikość, okrucieństwo*) **1.** barbarity, savagery, vandalism. **2.** *antrop.* barbarous age..

barbecue *n. indecl.* **1.** (*zabawa ogrodowa w USA*) barbecue. **2.** (*pieczone na rożnie mięso*) barbecue. **3.** (= *grill*) barbecue.

barbet *mi kość.* barb.

barbituran *mi chem., farm.* barbiturate.

barbiturowy *a. chem.* barbituric acid.

Barbórka *f. górn.* Miners' Day (*in Poland = St. Barbara's Day, December 4*).

barbórkowy *a. górn.* of Miners' Day.

Barcelona *f. geogr.* Barcelona.

barchan *mi* (*tkanina*) fustian.

barchanowy *a.* fustian.

barchany *pl. Gen.* **-ów** (*ubranie, bielizna*) fustian cloths.

barciak *ma zool.* **barciak woszczywiaczek** waxmoth (*Galeria mellonella*).

barczatka *f. zool.* egger (*Lasiocampa*).

barczysty *a.* broad-shouldered.

barć *f. pl.* **-e** *l.* **-i** a beehive in a hole in a log or tree.

bard *mp pl.* **-owie** *hist.* **1.** Druid. **2.** *przen.* (= *poeta, wieszcz*) bard, poet.

bardo *n.* (= *grzebień tkacki*) weaver's reed.

bardotka *f. pot.* (= *biustonosz*) low-cut under wire bra (*usually strapless*).

bardziej *adv.* more; **bardziej niż** more than; **tym bardziej** the more so, especially as; **tym bardziej że...** the more so because; **im bardziej..., tym...** the more..., the...; **im bardziej próbuję, tym więcej się męczę** the more I try, the more tired I get; **im bardziej dojrzały, tym mądrzejszy** the more mature the wiser; **coraz bardziej** more and more.

bardzo *adv.* (*z przymiotnikiem, przysłówkiem*) very; **bardzo duży/mały/szczęśliwy/chory/dobry/ zły** very big/small/happy/ill/good/bad; **bardzo mało/dużo/dobrze/źle** very little/much/well/badly; (*z imiesłowem*) greatly, deeply; **bardzo zadowolony** greatly pleased; **bardzo wzruszony** deeply moved; (*z czasownikiem*) very much, a lot; **bardzo pomagać** help very much *l.* a lot; **bardzo za kimś tęsknić** miss sb very much; **bardzo cię kocham** I love you very much *l.* dearly; **bardzo dobrze** very well; **bardzo dobrze wiedzieć** know very well; **nie bardzo** not much, not really, not quite; **nie bardzo wypada tam iść** we shouldn't go there; **nie bardzo mógł** he hardly could; **nie bardzo go lubią** they don't really like him; **jak**

bardzo how much; **tak bardzo** so/that much; **za bardzo** too much; **za bardzo mu zaufałam** I trusted him too much; **bardzo być może** only maybe; **nie za bardzo** *pot.* not really.

barek *mi* **-rk-** (*mały lokal*) **1.** small bar. **2.** (= *bufet, miejsce na alkohole*) drinks cabinet, liquor cabinet; **dobrze zaopatrzony barek** well-stocked liquor cabinet. **3.** (*podręczny stolik na kółkach*) trolley.

barelief *mi sztuka* bas-relief.

baretka *f. wojsk.* ribbon.

baribal *ma* American black bear (*Ursus americanus*).

bariera *f.* **1.** (= *przeszkoda, szlaban, zapora*) barrier, bar. **2.** (*naturalna przeszkoda*) barrier, bar; **bariera ochronna** crash bar, guardrail. **3.** (= *granica, ograniczenie*) barrier; **usuwać bariery** open the floodgates; **bariera cieplna** heat barrier; **bariera dźwięku** sound barrier; **bariera językowa** language barrier; **bariera handlowa** trade barrier; **bariera społeczna** social barrier.

barierka *f.* barrier.

barierowy *a.* barrier.

barion *mi fiz.* baryon.

barionowy *a. fiz.* baryonic; **liczba barionowa** baryon number.

bark[1] *mi* **1.** *anat.* shoulder; **wziąć odpowiedzialność na swoje barki** take the responsibility on one's shoulders; **spoczywać na czyichś barkach** rest on sb's shoulders. **2.** *anat.* (*kości*) scapular bones.

bark[2] *mi żegl.* bark.

barka *f. żegl.* barge; (*rzeczna*) river boat, ark; **barka mieszkalna** houseboat.

barkarola *f. Gen.pl.* **-li** *l.* **-l** *muz.* barcarolle.

barkarz *mp* bargeman.

barkentyna *f. żegl.* barkentine.

barkowy *a. anat.* brachial; **staw barkowy** shoulder joint.

barłożyć *ipf. pot.* make a mess.

barłóg *mi* **-o-** (*nędzne posłanie*) **1.** pallet. **2.** *myśl.* bear's den.

barman *mp* bartender, barkeeper, barman.

barmanka *f.* barmaid, barkeeper.

barograf *mi meteor.* barograph.

barogram *mi meteor.* barogram.

barok *mi sztuka* baroque; **wczesny/późny barok** early/late baroque.

barokowy *a.* **1.** *sztuka* baroque. **2.** (= *ozdobny, kwiecisty*) ornate.

barometr *mi* **1.** *meteor.* barometer; **barometr spada** the glass is falling; **barometr podnosi się, idzie do góry** the glass is rising. **2.** *przen.* (= *wskaźnik, znak, symptom*) barometer.

barometryczny *a. meteor.* barometric.

baron *mp pl.* **-owie** (*tytuł szlachecki*) *przen.* (= *potentat*) baron; **baron węglowy** coal baron.

baronat *mi* baronage.

baronet *mp* baronet.

baronowa *f. Gen.* **-ej** baroness.

baronowski *a.* baronial.

baroreceptor *mi fizj.* baroreceptor.

baroskop *mi fiz.* baroscope.

barostat *mi fiz.* barostat.

barotropizm *mi bot.* barotripism.

barowy[1] *a.* (*dotyczący baru - lokalu*) bar; **stołek barowy** bar stool; **danie barowe** buffet meal, snack.

barowy[2] *a. chem.* baric; **biel barowa** permanent white.

barszcz *mi Gen.pl.* **-ów** *l.* **-y 1.** (*zupa*) beetroot soup; **barszcz biały** borsch; **barszcz czerwony** beetroot soup; **barszcz ukraiński** borsch; **tani jak barszcz** dirt-cheap; **dwa grzyby w barszcz** too much of a good thing. **2.** *bot.* hogweed (*Heracleum*).

barszczyk *mi pot.* beetroot soup.

barta *f. broń, hist.* battle axe.

barter *mi ekon.* barter.

barterowy *a. ekon.* barter; **wymiana barterowa** barter exchange; **handel barterowy** barter trade.

bartnictwo *n.* beekeeping.

bartnik *mp* (= *pszczelarz*) beekeeper.

barwa *f.* **1.** (= *kolor*) color, hue; **barwy podstawowe** primary colors; **barwy pochodne** secondary colors; **barwy dopełniające** complementary colors; **barwy ochronne** natural camouflage; **widzieć coś w różowych, w jasnych barwach** see sth through rose-colored spectacles; **widzieć coś w czarnych barwach** see the dark side of sth; **przedstawiać coś w jaskrawych barwach** paint sth in bright colors; **malować coś jasnymi/ciemnymi barwami** paint sth in bright/dark colors. **2.** (*sztandar, godło*) colors; **barwy klubowe** team colors; **barwy narodowe** national colors; **reprezentować czyjeś barwy** represent sb/sth. **3.** *myśl.* blood. **4.** *muz.* (*brzmienie głosu*) timbre; **barwa głosu** timbre; **barwa samogłoski** *jęz.* vowel quality *l.* timbre.

barwena *f. zool.* goatfish (*Mullus surmuletus*).

barwiarka[1] *f.* (*maszyna włókiennicza*) dye tank.

barwiarka[2] *f.* (*pracownica farbująca tkaniny*) dyer.

barwiarski *a.* **1.** (*związany z barwiarstwem*) dyer's, dyeing. **2.** (*służący do barwienia*) tinctorial.

barwiarstwo *n.* (= *farbiarstwo*) dyeing.

barwiarz *mp* (*robotnik farbujący tkaniny*) dyer.

barwić *ipf.* (= *nadawać kolor*) dye.

barwić się *ipf.* **1.** (= *nabierać koloru*) color, take on a color; **barwić się na czerwono/zielono/żółto** take on red/green/yellow. **2.** (= *mienić się*) sparkle.

barwierski *a. bot.* **marzanna barwierska** madder (*Rubia tinctorum*); **janowiec barwierski** dyer's weed, greenweed (*Genista tinctoria*); **porost barwierski** cudbear (*Roccella*); **urzet barwierski** dyer's weed, pastel (*Isatis tinctoria*).

barwinek *mi* **-nk-** *Gen.* **-a** *bot.* periwinkle (*Vinca*).

barwnie *adv.* **1.** (= *kolorowo, tęczowo*) colorfully. **2.** (= *interesująco, żywo, zachwycająco*) vividly.

barwnik *mi Gen.* **-a** dye, dyestuff; **barwniki naturalne** natural dyes; **barwniki syntetyczne** arti-

ficial dyes; **barwniki spożywcze** food coloring dye.

barwnikarstwo *n.* dyestuff industry.

barwnikowy *a.* dyeing, tinctorial, pigmental, pigmentary; **komórki barwnikowe** *zool., bot.* pigmentary cells.

barwny *a.* **1.** (= *różnobarwny, tęczowy*) colorful. **2.** (*nie tylko biały i czarny*) color; **barwny film** color film; **barwna fotografia** color photograph; **barwny druk** chromatic/color print.

barwoczuły *a. fot.* panchromatic.

bary *pl. Gen.* **-ów** *pot.* shoulders; **szeroki w barach** broad-shouldered; **brać się z kimś za bary** wrestle with sb.

baryczny *a. meteor.* baric; **niż baryczny** depression; **wyż baryczny** anticyclon.

barykada *f.* barricade; **wznosić barykady** raise barricades; **stać** *l.* **znajdować się po drugiej stronie barykady** *przen.* belong to the opposing camp.

barykadować *ipf.* barricade; (= *przegradzać, blokować*) bar, block. **~ się** *ipf.* barricade oneself (*przed kimś / czymś* from sb/sth).

baryła *f.* **1.** (= *beczka*) barrel, cask. **2.** *przen.* (= *grubas*) pot-belly.

baryłka *f.* keg, small cask; (*t. jednostka objętości*) barrel; **baryłka ropy** barrel of oil.

barysfera *f.* barysphere.

baryt *mi min.* barite, baryte, barytes.

baryton *mi Gen.* **-u** **1.** *muz.* (*głos męski*) baritone; **śpiewać barytonem** sing in a baritone voice. **2.** *muz.* (*instrument*) baritone. – *mp Gen.* **-a** *pl.* **-y** *muz.* (*śpiewak*) baritone.

barytoniczny *a. gram.* barytonic.

barytonowy *a. muz.* baritone.

barytowy *a. chem.* barytic; **glinka barytowa** heavy earth; **woda barytowa** baryta water.

bas *mi Gen.* **-u** **1.** *muz.* (*głos męski*) bass; **śpiewać basem** sing in a bass voice. **2.** *muz.* (*niski dźwięk*) bass; **bas cyfrowany** thorough bass; **bas podstawowy** ground bass; **bas figuralny** figured bass. **3.** *muz.* (*najniższy rejestr w instrumentach*) bass. – *mp Gen.* **-a** *pl.* **-y** *muz.* (*śpiewak*) bass.

basałyk *mp przest., żart.* (*swawolne dziecko*) brat. – *mi Gen.* **-a** *przest.* (= *bicz*) whip, lash.

baseball *mi sport* baseball.

baseballista *mp sport* ballplayer.

baseballowy *a. sport* baseball; **kij baseballowy** baseball bat; **piłka baseballowa** baseball.

basen *mi* **1.** (= *pływalnia*) swimming pool; **kryty basen** indoor swimming pool. **2.** *geogr., geol.* (*zespół dorzeczy*) basin; **basen Morza Bałtyckiego** the Baltic Sea basin. **3.** *geol.* (*zagłębienie w dnie morskim lub pod ziemią*) basin. **4.** *żegl.* basin, dock; **basen węglowy** coal dock; **basen jachtowy** yacht port; **basen rybacki** fishery. **5.** (*med.* = *naczynie do załatwiania potrzeb fizjologicznych*) bedpan.

basetla *f. Gen.pl.* **-i** *muz.* double-bass.

basetowy *a. muz.* **rożek basetowy** basset horn.

basista *mp muz.* bassist.

Bask *mp pl.* **-owie** Basque.

basket *mi sport* basketball.

Baskijka *f.* Basque.

baskijski *a.* Basque.

baskina *f.* 1. basque. 2. (= *spódnica hiszpań-ska*) basquina.

basklarnet *mi muz.* bass-clarinet.

basowy *a. muz.* bass; **klucz basowy** bass clef.

basset *ma kynol.* basset, basset-hound.

bassethorn *mi muz.* basset horn.

basso continuo *n. indecl. muz.* basso contin-uo, thorough bass.

basta *int.* enough!

bastard *mp pl.* **-y** (*nieślubne dziecko*) bastard, illegitimate child. – *ma zool.* bastard, hybrid.

bastion *mi* 1. *bud.* bastion; **bastion obronny** rampart. 2. *przen.* (= *ostoja*) mainstay, stronghold; **stanowić bastion czegoś** be the mainstay of sth.

basza *mp pl.* **-owie** *hist.* pasha, pacha; **roz-siąść się jak basza** sit back like a lord; **żyć jak basza** live like a lord.

baszta *f. bud.* donjon, keep, tower; **uwięzić, zamknąć w baszcie** imprison in a tower.

baśniowo *adv.* fabulously, fantastically.

baśniowy *a.* fabulous, fairylike.

baśń *f. pl.* **-ie** *l.* **-i** *lit.* fairy-tale; **baśń ludowa** folk tale; **baśń muzyczna** musical tale; **baśnie z tysiąca i jednej nocy** the Arabian Nights; the Thousand and One Nights; **świat baśni** fairy-land.

bat[1] *mi Gen.* **-a** 1. (= *bicz, batog*) whip; **bić, okładać batem** whip; **trzymać kogoś pod batem** have sb under one's thumb; **trzaskać, strzelać z bata** crack the whip; **pracować pod batem** work under the lash. 2. *zob.* **baty.**

bat[2] *mi Gen.* **-u** *żegl.* flatboat.

batalia *f. Gen.* **-ii** 1. *wojsk.* campaign; **roze-grać, stoczyć batalię** fight a campaign. 2. *przen.* (= *walka o stanowiska, spór*) struggle; **wygrać batalię** win the battle.

batalion *mi Gen.* **-u** *wojsk.* battalion; **batalion szturmowy** assault squad. – *ma Gen.* **-a** *orn.* (*ga-tunek i samiec*) ruff; (*samica*) reeve (*Philoma-chus pugnax*).

batalionowy *a. wojsk.* battalion.

batalistyczny *a. sztuka* battle.

batalistyka *f. sztuka* battle-piece painting.

batat *mi bot.* sweet potato (*Ipomoea batatas*).

bateria *f. Gen.* **-ii** 1. *el., chem., wojsk.* battery; (*el. = ogniwo suche*) dry-cell battery; **bateria aku-mulatorowa** storage battery, accumulator; **bate-ria słoneczna** solar battery. 2. *techn.* = zespół bench, bank, row; **bateria kotłów** bank of boilers. 3. *pot. przen.* set, collection; **bateria butelek** row of bottles.

bateriowy *a. fiz., chem.* battery.

bateryjka *f. pot.* battery; **bateryjka do latarki** flashlight battery.

batial *mi geogr.* bathyal.

batik *mi tk.* (*technika barwienia l. tkanina*) batik.

batikować *ipf. techn.* batik.

batog *mi Gen.* **-a** (= *bat*) whip.

batolit *mi geol.* batolith.

batometr *mi techn.* bathometer.

batometria *f. Gen.* **-ii** bathometry.

baton *mi Gen.* **-u** *l.* **-a**, **batonik** *mi Gen.* **-a** bar, candy bar; **baton czekoladowy** chocolate bar.

batut *mi sport, akrobatyka* trampoline.

batuta *f. muz.* baton; **pod czyjąś batutą** con-ducted by sb.

baty *pl. Gen.* **-ów** beating, whipping; **tęgie baty** good hiding; **dać** *l.* **spuścić komuś baty** give sb a good hiding; **oberwać, dostać** *l.* **wziąć baty** get a good hiding.

batybental *mi geogr.* bathybenthic.

batymetria *f. Gen.* **-ii** (*dział hydrometrii*) bathymetry.

batymetryczny *a. geogr.* bathymetric.

batypelagial *mi geogr.* bathypelagic, bathy-pelagian.

batysfera *f. techn.* bathysphere.

batyskaf *mi techn.* bathyscaphe.

batyst *mi* batiste.

Bawaria *f. Gen.* **-ii** *geogr.* Bavaria.

bawarka *f.* tea with milk.

bawarski *a. geogr.* Bavarian.

bawełna *f.* 1. *bot.* (*roślina*) cotton plant (*Gos-sypium*); **uprawiać bawełnę** grow cotton; **planta-cja bawełny** cotton plantation. 2. *bot.* (*włókno*) cotton; **zbierać bawełnę** pick cotton; **król bawełny** *przen.* cotton baron *l.* magnate. 3. (*nici i przę-dza*) cotton yarn; **owijać w bawełnę** *przen.* beat about the bush; **bez owijania w bawełnę** *przen.* straight from the shoulder. 4. (*tkanina, mate-riał*) cotton; **suknia/bluzka z bawełny** cotton dress/blouse. 5. *chem.* (*materiał wybuchowy*) **bawełna strzelnicza** gun-cotton.

bawełniany *a.* cotton; **krzewy bawełniane** cot-ton plants; **olej bawełniany** cotton oil; **przemysł bawełniany** cotton industry; **bawełniana bielizna** cotton underwear.

bawełniczka *f.* (*przędza, nić*) cotton yarn.

bawialnia *f. Gen.pl.* **-i** parlor, drawing-room.

bawialny *a.* **pokój bawialny** parlor, drawing-room.

bawić *ipf.* 1. (= *zajmować, umilać czas*) enter-tain; **bawić dzieci** play with children; **bawić to-warzystwo rozmową** entertain the company with conversation. 2. (= *podobać się, zachwy-cać*) amuse; **to mnie już nie bawi** it isn't funny anymore; **bawić oko** please the eye. 3. *lit.* (= *by-wać, przebywać*) stay (*u kogoś* at sb's); **bawić u przyjaciół z wizytą** be at one's friends'; **bawić na wsi u rodziny** stay with one's family in the coun-try; **bawić tydzień w górach** be on holiday in the mountains for a week. **~ się** *ipf.* 1. (*spędzać czas na grze l. zabawie*) play (*w coś* (at) sth) (*z kimś* with sb); **bawić się z przyjaciółmi** play with friends; **bawić się lalkami/samochodzikami/piłką** play with dolls/toy cars/a ball; **bawić się w pira-tów/w dom/w chowanego** play pirates/a family/hide-and-seek. 2. (= *uczestniczyć w zabawie to-warzyskiej*) **dobrze się bawić** have a good time; have fun; enjoy o.s.; **nieszczególnie** *l.* **źle się ba-wić** have a bad time; **bawić się na przyjęciu** enjoy a party; **bawić się do białego rana** have fun all night long; **bawić się do upadłego** have a night on the tiles; paint the town red. 3. (= *doświad-*

cząć uciechy l. rozrywki) have fun; **bawić się czymś kosztem** have fun at sb's expense; **bawić się z kimś jak kot z myszą** play cat and mouse with sb. **4.** (= *zajmować się czymś niedbale*) toy, mess, fool around (*kimś/czymś* with sb/sth); **nie ma się z tym co bawić** there's no point in fooling around with it.

bawidamek *mp* -mk- *pl.* -i *żart.* gallant.

bawoli *a.* buffalo; **bawola skóra** buff.

bawolica *f. zool.* buffalo cow.

bawół *ma* -o- *Gen.* -u **1.** buffalo, ox; **bawół azjatycki** Asian buffalo, water buffalo (*Bos bubalus*); **bawół afrykański** African buffalo, cape buffalo (*Syncerus caffer*). **2.** *pog.* moron, dummy.

baza *f.* **1.** (= *podstawa, fundament, niezbędny składnik*) base, basis, foundation; **baza materiałowa** material base; **na bazie czegoś** on the basis of sth; **baza surowcowa** *techn.* raw materials base; **baza materialno-techniczna** *ekon.* material-technical base. **2.** *ekon.* base. **3.** *bud.* (= *podstawa kolumny*) base. **4.** **baza danych** *komp.* database. **5.** (= *centrum, centrala, ośrodek dyspozycyjny*) headquarters, base; **baza transportowa/remontowa** transport/maintenance base *l.* (*Br.*) depot. **6.** *wojsk.* base; **baza wojskowa** military base; **baza morska/lotnicza** naval/air base.

bazalt *mi min.* basalt.

bazaltowy *a. min.* basalt, basaltic; **skały bazaltowe** basalt rocks.

bazar *mi* bazaar, market; **kupować warzywa na bazarze** buy vegetables at the market; **iść po zakupy na bazar** go shopping in *l.* at the market.

bazarowy *a.* bazaar.

bazgrać *ipf.* -rzę -rzesz (= *gryzmolić*) **bazgrać (jak kura pazurem)** scribble, scrawl (*na czymś* on sth, *po czymś* all over sth).

bazgranina *f. pot.* **1.** (= *gryzmoły*) scribbling. **2.** (= *bohomaz*) daub.

bazgrolić *ipf. pot.* = **bazgrać**.

bazgroły *pl. Gen.* -ów *pot.* scrawls.

bazia *f. Gen.pl.* -i catkin.

bazować *ipf.* **1.** (= *stacjonować, przebywać*) be stationed. **2.** (= *na czymś się opierać*) be based (*na czymś* on sth).

bazowy *a.* (= *podstawowy, główny*) **1.** basic, base, fundamental. **2.** (= *dotyczący bazy*) basal.

Bazylea *f. Gen.* -ei *geogr.* Basle, Basel.

bazylia *f. Gen.* -ii *bot.* basil (*Ocimum basilicum*).

bazylianin *mp pl.* -anie *Gen.* -anów *kośc.* Basilian monk.

bazyliański *a. kośc.* Basilian.

bazylika *f.* **1.** *bud.* basilica. **2.** *rel., kośc.* (*tytuł nadawany kościołowi przez papieża*) Basilica; **Bazylika Mniejsza** Minor Basilica; **Bazylika Większa** Major Basilica.

bazyliszek *ma* -szk- **1.** *zool.* (*jaszczurka*) basilisk (*Basiliscus*). **2.** (*legendarny stwór*) basilisk, cockatrice; **wzrok bazyliszka** basilisk('s) gaze.

bazyliszkowaty, bazyliszkowy *a.* basilisk.

bażanci *a.* pheasant('s).

bażant *ma zool.* pheasant (*Phasianus*).

bażantarnia *f. Gen.pl.* -i *l.* -ń pheasantry.

bażyna *f. bot.* crowberry (*Empetrum*).

bąbel *mi* -bl- *Gen.* -a **1.** (*pęcherzyk z gazu w cieczy lub w ciele stałym*) bubble. **2.** *med.* blister, swelling; **pokrywać się bąblami** blister; **powodować powstawanie bąbli** blister (*na czymś* sth); **bąbel od ukąszenia komara** swelling from a mosquito bite.

bąbelek *mi* -lk- *Gen.* -a **1.** (*mały pęcherzyk z gazu*) bubble; **woda z bąbelkami** carbonated water. **2.** *med.* blister.

bąblowica *f. pat.* echinococcosis.

bąblowiec *ma* -wc- *zool.* echinococcus tapeworm (*Echinococcus*).

bączek *ma* -czk- **1.** *orn.* little bittern (*Ixobrychus minutas*). **2.** *zool. pot.* (= *owad*) gadfly. – *mi* -czk- *Gen. i Acc.* -a **1.** (*zabawka*) spinning top. **2.** *żegl.* dinghy. – *mp* -czk- *pl.* -i *żart.* (*o małym dziecku*) tot.

bądź¹ *ipf. zob.* **być**.

bądź² *conj.* (= *lub, albo*) or; **bądź (to)..., bądź (to)...** either... or...

bądź³ *part.* (= *-kolwiek*) **co bądź** anything; **kto bądź** anybody; **jak bądź** anyhow; **gdzie bądź** *l.* dokąd bądź anywhere; **jaki bądź** any; **bądź co bądź** after all; at any rate.

bąk *ma* **1.** *pot.* (= *trzmiel*) bumblebee; **opić się czymś jak bąk** drink one's fill; **zbijać bąki** fiddlefaddle. **2.** *pot.* (= *puszczenie wiatru*) fart; **puścić bąka** fart; let out *l.* let fly a fart; pass wind *l.* gas. **3.** *ent.* (= *giez*) horsefly (*Tabanus bovinus*). **4.** *orn.* bittern (*Botaurus stellaris*); **krzyczeć jak bąk** bump. – *mi Gen. i Acc.* -a **1.** (*zabawka*) (peg) top, hummingtop; **puszczać, nakręcać bąka** spin a top; **kręcić się jak bąk** spin around. **2.** *żegl.* dinghy. – *mp pl.* -i *żart.* (*o małym dziecku*) tot.

bąkać *ipf.*, **bąknąć** *pf.* -ij **1.** (= *mówić niewyraźnie*) mutter, mumble; **bąkać coś pod nosem** mutter sth under one's breath. **2.** (= *szeptać o czymś*) hint, remark. **3.** *myśl.* (*o ptakach*) hum.

bąkojad *ma orn.* oxpecker (*Buphagus*).

b-cia *abbr. tylko w nazwach firm* (= *bracia*) Bros; *zob.* **brat**.

bdb *abbr. indecl. szkoln.* (= *ocena bardzo dobra*) A; **postawić bdb** give (an) A; **dostać, otrzymać bdb** get (an) A (*z czegoś* in sth, *za coś* for sth).

B-dur *n. muz.* B flat major.

be¹ *int. pot.* (*o kimś głupim*) **ani be, ani me (ani kukuryku)** dumb, stupid.

be² *a. indecl. dziec.* bad; **jesteś be** you're bad; **nie bierz tego, to jest be!** leave it, it's bad.

beatyfikacja *f. rel., kośc.* beatification.

beatyfikacyjny *a. rel., kośc.* beatific; **proces beatyfikacyjny** beatification process.

beatyfikować *ipf. rel., kośc.* beatify.

bebechy *pl. Gen.* -ów **1.** *pot.* (= *wnętrzności*) guts, bowels. **2.** *przen.* **dobry/zacny z bebechami** thoroughly good/decent; **wyprówać z siebie bebechy** sweat blood; **wypuścić z kogoś bebechy** gut sb; lay sb open; **bebechy się od tego skręcają** *l.* przewracają it's enough to make one's belly ache. **3.** *pot.* (= *wnętrze*) core.

bebeszyć *ipf. pot.* gut, disembowel; (*rybę*) clean.

bebop *mi muz.* bebop.

becik *mi Gen.* -u *l.* -a (*dla niemowląt*) baby wrap.

beczeć *ipf.* -ę -ysz **1.** (*o zwierzęciu*) bleat, baa, go baa. **2.** *pot.* (= *płakać*) boohoo; **przestań beczeć** stop crying. **3.** *pot.* (*o śpiewie*) (= *fałszować*) bellow. **4.** *muz.* (*o okarynie, kobzie, dudach*) moan.

beczka *f. Gen.pl.* -ek **1.** (*naczynie*) barrel, cask, keg; **beczka wina** cask of wine; **piwo z beczki** beer on draft; **beczka kapusty/ogórków** barrel of cabbage/cucumbers; **gruby jak beczka** *pot.* (as) fat as a barrel; roly-poly. **2.** *przen.* **beczka śmiechu** barrel of fun *l.* laughs; **beczka bez dna** bottomless pit; black hole; (*o człowieku*) spendthrift; **tłoczyć się jak śledzie w beczce** be packed like sardines; **prosto z beczki** straight from the shoulder; bluntly, frankly; **zacząć z innej beczki** change the subject; **a teraz coś z zupełnie innej beczki** and now for something completely different; **zjedliśmy razem beczkę soli** we've been through a lot together; **do stu tysięcy beczek solonych śledzi!** *żart.* drat it! **3.** *lotn.* barrel roll. **4.** *bud.* barrel vault.

beczkowaty *a.* barrel-like, bulgy; **sklepienie beczkowate** *bud.* barrel vault.

beczkowóz *mi* -o- water-cart.

beczkowy *a.* **1.** (*o części beczki*) barrel. **2.** (*przechowywany w beczce*) barrel; **piwo beczkowe** draft beer. **3.** (*o kształcie beczki*) barrel-like, bulgy; **sklepienie beczkowe** *bud.* barrel vault.

beczułka *f. Gen.pl.* -ek keg, small barrel.

bedeker *mi Gen.* -a (= *przewodnik*) tourist guide, guidebook.

bedłka *f. Gen.pl.* -ek *bot.* agaric, mushroom; (*także* **betka**) *pot.* (= *coś łatwego*) child's play, breeze.

bednarski *a.* cooper's; **warsztat bednarski** coopery.

bednarstwo *n.* cooperage.

bednarz *mp* cooper.

Beduin *mp*, **Beduinka** *f. Gen.pl.* -ek Bedouin.

beduiński *a.* Bedouin.

befsztyk *mi Gen.* -a *l.* -u beefsteak, steak; **krwisty befsztyk** rare *l.* bloody steak; **befsztyk tatarski** steak tartar.

begonia *f. Gen.* -ii *bot.* begonia (*Begonia*).

behapowiec *mp* -wc- *pl.* -y *pot.* safety inspector.

behawiorysta *mp*, **behawiorystka** *f. Gen.pl.* -ek *nauk.* behaviorist.

behawiorystyczny *a. psych.* behavioristic.

behawioryzm *mi* behaviorism.

bej *mp pl.* -owie *hist.* bey.

bejca *f.* **1.** *roln.* dressing. **2.** *techn.* (= *zaprawa farbiarska*) mordant.

bejcować *ipf.* **1.** *roln.* dress. **2.** (= *marynować*) pickle. **3.** *techn.* (= *pokrywać bejcą*) stain. **4.** *rymarstwo* (= *oczyszczać*) bate.

Bejrut *mi geogr.* Beirut.

bek[1] *mi Gen.* -u **1.** *tylko sing.* (*głos zwierzęcia*) bleeting, baa. **2.** *pot.* (= *płacz*) boohoo; **a ona w bek** and she burst out crying. **3.** *pot.* (= *fałsz*) (*o śpiewie*) bellowing. **4.** *myśl.* humming.

bek[2] *mp Gen.* -a *pl.* -owie piłka nożna back.

bekać *ipf.* **1.** *pot.* (= *odbijać się*) belch, burp. **2.** *myśl.* (*o bekasach*) squall.

bekas *ma orn.* snipe (*Gallinago*); **bekas kszyk** common snipe (*Gallinago gallinago*).

bekhend *mi sport* backhand, backhander; **odbicie z bekhendu** backhand return; **uderzać z bekhendu** *l.* bekhendem backhand.

beknąć[1] *pf.* -ij **1.** (*o owcy, kozie, cielęciu*) bleat, baa. **2.** *myśl.* squall.

beknąć[2] *pf.* -ij **1.** *zob.* **bekać. 2.** *pot.* (= *ponieść konsekwencje*) pay the bill (*za coś* for sth).

bekon *mi kulin.* bacon; **jajka na bekonie** bacon and eggs.

beksa *f. l. mp Gen.pl. f.* -s *mp* -sów *pot.* **beksa (-lala)** cry-baby.

bela *f. Gen.pl.* -l *l.* -li **1.** (*zwój papieru lub tkaniny*) bale. **2.** *techn.* (*sprasowany i opakowany prostopadłościan jakiegoś materiału*) pack; **bele bawełny** cotton bales. **3.** (*jednostka ciężaru*) bale. **4.** (*miara ilości papieru*) ream. **5.** (*duża, drewniana belka*) beam, log; **pijany/spity jak bela** *pot.* dead drunk; **zwalić się (na łóżko) jak bela** crash out; be asleep before one's head hits the pillow.

beleczka *f.* **1.** (*kawałek drewna*) little beam. **2.** *pot. żart.* (*o naszywce na mundurze*) bar. **3.** *anat.* trabecula.

beletrystyczny *a. lit.* fiction.

beletrystyka *f. lit.* fiction.

beletryzować *ipf. lit.* fictionalize.

Belfast *mi geogr.* Belfast.

belfer *mp* -fr- *pl.* -owie *l.* -rzy *rzad.* -ry *pot. żart. l. pog.* (= *nauczyciel*) teacher.

belferka *f.* -ek *pot. żart. l. pog.* (= *nauczycielka*) **1.** schoolmarm. **2.** *tylko sg. pot., pog.* = **belferstwo**.

belferski *a. pot. żart. l. pog.* teacher.

belferstwo *n. pot. żart. l. pog.* teaching.

Belg *mp pl.* -owie Belgian.

belg *ma hodowla* (*koń*) Belgian.

Belgia *f. Gen.* -ii *geogr.* Belgium.

Belgijka *f. Gen.pl.* -ek *zob.* **Belg**.

belgijski *a.* Belgian; **koń belgijski** a horse of Belgian breed; **bluza belgijska** hooded sweatshirt; **frank belgijski** Belgian franc.

Belgrad *mi geogr.* Belgrade.

belka *f. Gen.pl.* -ek **1.** (*obrobiony kawałek drewna lub przedmiot z betonu, żelaza*) beam; **drewniana belka** beam; **żelazna/betonowa belka** iron/concrete beam; **belki stropowe** joists. **2.** *pot.* (*naszywka na mundurze - oznaka rangi*) bar.

belkować *ipf. bud.* joist.

belkowanie *n.* **1.** *bud.* (*układ belek*) flooring. **2.** *bud.* (*górna część muru w budowlach antycznych*) entablature.

belkowy *a.* beam.

belladona *f. bot., med.* belladonna (*Atropa belladonna*).

belona *f. zool.* garfish (*Belone belone*).

belweder *mi bud.* belvedere.

Belzebub *mp rel.* Beelzebub.

bełkot *mi Gen.* -u (= *niewyraźna mowa*) **1.** mumble. **2.** (= *niezrozumiały tekst*) gobbledygook; **pseudonaukowy bełkot** pseudo-scholarly jabber.

bełkotać *ipf.* -**czę** -**czesz** *l.* -**cę** -**cesz**, -**cz** **1.** (= *niewyraźnie mówić*) mumble, gabble; **bełkotać bez związku** mutter, gibber; **bełkotać w zdenerwowaniu** mutter nervously. **2.** (*o cieczy*) (= *bulgotać, gulgotać*) gurgle.

bełkotliwie *adv.* **1.** (= *niewyraźnie*) mumblingly, indistinctly. **2.** *przen.* (= *zawile, niezrozumiale*) gibberishly.

bełkotliwy *a.* (= *niewyraźny*) mumbling, indistinct.

bełt[1] *mi* **1.** *broń, hist.* (= *strzała do kuszy*) bolt. **2.** *pot.* (= *kiepskie wino*) vino.

bełt[2] *mi geogr.* (= *jedna z cieśnin duńskich*) **Mały/Wielki Bełt** the Little/Great Belt.

bełtać *ipf.* stir.

bemol *mi Gen.* -**a** *Gen.pl.* -**i** *l.* -**ów** *muz.* flat.

benedyktyn *mp pl.* -**i** *rel.* Benedictine monk. – *mi pl.* -**y** (*likier korzenno-ziołowy*) Benedictine.

benedyktynka *f.* **1.** *rel.* Benedictine nun. **2.** (*likier korzenno-ziołowy*) Benedictine.

benedyktyński *a.* **1.** *rel.* Benedictine. **2.** *przen.* painstaking, meticulous; **benedyktyńska cierpliwość** limitless patience.

beneficjent *mp hist., prawn.* beneficiary.

beneficjum *n. indecl. in sg. pl.* -**ja** *Gen.* -**jów** *kośc., hist.* benefice.

benefis *mi* benefit.

benefisant *mp*, **benefisantka** *f. Gen.pl.* -**ek** actor for whose benefit a performance is held.

benefisowy *a. sztuka* benefit.

Beneluks *mi geogr.* Benelux.

Bengal *mi geogr.* Bengal.

bengalski *a. geogr.* Bengal; **Zatoka Bengalska** *geogr.* the Bay of Bengal; **tygrys bengalski** *zool.* Bengal tiger (*Panthera tigris bengalicus*); **ognie bengalskie** Bengal lights.

beniaminek *mp* -**nk-** *pl.* -**i** *l.* -**owie** **1.** (= *faworyt, pieszczoszek*) *t. sport* favorite. **2.** (= *rozpieszczane najmłodsze dziecko*) Benjamin.

benzen *mi chem.* benzene.

benzoes *mi chem.* (gum of) benzoin.

benzoesowy *a. chem.* benzoic; **kwas benzoesowy** benzoic acid.

benzoil *mi chem.* benzoyl.

benzol *mi chem.* benzol.

benzyna *f. chem.* gas, gasoline; *Br.* petrol; **benzyna bezołowiowa/wysokooktanowa** unleaded/high-octane gasoline; **benzyna lekka** benzine.

benzynowy *a.* gas, gasoline; **silnik benzynowy** gasoline engine; **stacja benzynowa** gas station, filling station.

Beocja *f. geogr.* Boeotia.

beocki *a.* Boeotian.

bera *f.* (*odmiana gruszki*) butter pear.

berbeć *mp Gen.pl.* -**i** *l.* -**ów** *pot.* moppet.

Berber *mp pl.* -**rzy** *l.* -**owie**, **Berberyjka** *f. Gen.pl.* -**ek** Berber.

berberyjski *a.* Berber; *hist.* (= *północnoafrykański*) Barbary; **koń berberyjski** *zool.* barb, Barbary horse.

berberys *mi bot.* barberry (*Berberis*).

berdysz *mi Gen.pl.* -**y** *l.* -**ów** *broń, hist.* battle axe.

berek *mi tylko sing.* -**rk-** *Gen. i Acc.* -**a** (*zabawa*) tag; **grać, bawić się w berka** play tag. – *mp* -**rk-** *pl.* -**i** (*osoba goniąca*) tag.

beret *mi* **1.** (*płaskie, okrągłe nakrycie głowy*) beret, cloth cap; **czerwone berety** *wojsk., pot.* parachute troops, paras. **2.** (= *biret*) academic hat.

bergamota *f.*, **bergamotka** *f. Gen.pl.* -**ek** **1.** (*odmiana gruszki*) bergamot (pear). **2.** *bot.* bergamot (orange).

Berlin *mi Gen.* -**a** *geogr.* Berlin.

berliński *a.* Berlin; **mur berliński** the Berlin Wall.

berło *n. Gen.pl.* -**eł** **1.** (*ozdobna laska, symbol władzy*) scepter, wand; **berło królewskie** royal scepter; **berło rektorskie** *uniw.* verge; **dzierżyć berło** hold the scepter; **sięgać po berło** reach for the scepter. **2.** *bot.* lousewort (*Pedicularis*).

Bermudy *pl. Gen.* -**ów** *geogr.* Bermuda, the Bermudas, the Bermuda Islands.

bermudy *pl. Gen.* -**ów** (= *szorty*) Bermuda shorts, Bermudas.

bermudzki *a. geogr.* Bermudian, Bermudan; **ożaglowanie bermudzkie** *żegl.* Bermudian rigging; **trójkąt bermudzki** *geogr.* the Bermuda Triangle.

bernardyn *mp pl.* -**i** *rel.* Bernardine (monk). – *ma pl.* -**y** *zool.* St. Bernard dog.

bernardynek *mi* -**nk-** *Gen.* -**a** *bot.* blessed thistle (*Cnicus benedictus*).

bernardyński *a.* Bernardine.

Berno *n. geogr.* Berne.

beryl *mi tylko sing. chem.* (*pierwiastek*) beryllium. – *mi pl.* -**e** *min.* beryl.

berylek *mi* -**lk-** *chem.* beryllide.

berylowce *pl. Gen.* -**ów** *chem.* the alkali earth metals.

Besarabia *f. Gen.* -**ii** *geogr., hist.* Bessarabia.

besarabski *a. geogr., hist.* Bessarabian.

besemerowski *a. techn.* (*o stali*) Bessemer.

Beskidy *pl. Gen.* -**ów** *geogr.* the Beskids (*a range of the Carpathians*).

beskidzki *a.* Beskid.

bessa *f. ekon.* fall; **bessa na giełdzie** stockmarket fall; **przeżywać bessę** *pot.* be down on one's luck.

bestia *f. Gen.* -**ii** **1.** (= *drapieżne zwierzę*) beast; **dzika bestia** wild beast. **2.** *przen.* (= *okrutnik, sadysta*) brute. **3.** *pot.* (*o kimś lub o czymś z podziwem, z zazdrością, ze złością, z pogardą*) devil, fiend; **ale bestia z niego!** what a devil he is!

bestialski *a.* bestial, brutal, savage.

bestialstwo *n.* brutality, savagery.

bestseller *mi Gen.* -**u** *l.* -**a** bestseller.

bestsellerowy *a. lit.* best-selling.

bestwić się *ipf.* -**ij** torment, torture, savage (*nad kimś/czymś* sb/sth).

beszamel *mi kulin.* béchamel (sauce).

beszamelowy *a.* **sos beszamelowy** béchamel sauce.

besztać *ipf.* scold, rebuke, castigate, keelhaul (*kogoś za coś* sb for sth).

beta *f.* **1.** (*druga litera greckiego alfabetu*) beta; **rozpad beta** *fiz.* beta decay. **2.** *astron.* (= *druga co do jasności gwiazda w konstelacji*) Beta; **beta Perseusza** Beta Persei.

betel *mi* **1.** *bot.* betel (*Piper betle*). **2.** (*używka do żucia*) pan, betel nut; **żuć betel** chew pan/betel.

betka *f. tylko sg. zob.* **bedłka**.

Betlejem *mi indecl.* Bethlehem.

betlejemski *a. geogr.* Bethlehem; **stajenka betlejemska** Bethlehem barn, nativity barn; **gwiazda betlejemska** the Star of Bethlehem; *bot.* poinsettia (*Euphorbia pulcherrima*).

beton *mi pl.* **-y** *techn.* concrete; **beton komórkowy** cellular concrete; **beton sprężony/zbrojony** prestressed/reinforced concrete. – *mp tylko sg. polit., pog.* (= *twardogłowi*) (party) hardliners.

betoniarka *f. techn.* concrete mixer.

betoniarnia *f. Gen.pl.* **-i** *techn.* concrete plant.

betoniarski *a. techn.* concreter's.

betoniarz *mp techn.* concreter.

betonować *ipf. techn.* concrete.

betonowy *a. techn.* concrete; **betonowa dżungla** *przen.* concrete jungle.

bety *pl. Gen.* **-ów** **1.** *pot.* (= *pościel*) bedding; **leżeć w betach** be in bed. **2.** *pot.* (*osobiste drobiazgi, rzeczy*) small belongings.

bez[1] *mi* **bz-** *bot.* lilac (*Syringa vulgaris*); **czarny bez** *bot.* elder (*Sambucus nigra*); **gałązka bzu** lilac twig.

bez[2] *prep.* + *Gen.* without; **bez narażania się na niebezpieczeństwo** without risk; **i bez tego trwonisz dosyć pieniędzy** you're wasting lots of money anyway; **niebo bez chmur** cloudless sky; **bez bajerów** (*o sprzęcie*) no-frills; **bez ceregieli** (*walczyć, dyskutować*) with the gloves off; **być bez grosza** be broke, be penniless; **bez końca** endlessly; **bez mała** almost, (very) nearly; **bez cienia wątpliwości** without a shadow of a doubt; **pozostawać bez echa** meet no response; **robić coś bez głowy** do sth thoughtlessly; **bez przyszłości** with no future; finished; **bez ładu i składu** without rhyme or reason; **bez miary, bez granic** without restraint, knowing no limits; **mówić bez ogródek** be explicit (*o czymś* about sth); **mówiąc bez ogródek** to put it bluntly; **być bez pamięci zakochanym** be head over heels in love; **bez perspektyw** dead-end; **bez płaczu** without tears; **bez porównania lepszy** certainly better; **bez precedensu** without precedent; **bez przerwy** continuously, without a break; **bez reszty** utterly; hook, line and sinker; **bez różnicy** no difference; **bez słowa** without a word; **bez śladu** without a trace; **tylko bez świntuszenia** keep it clean; **bez tchu** breathless; **bez urazy** no hard feelings; **bez ustanku** without cease, ceaselessly; **bez wyjątku** bar none, without exception; **bez wyjścia** (*o sytuacji*) inextricable; **bez wysiłku** effortlessly; **bez wytchnienia** without a pause; **bez zająknienia** glibly; **bez zarzutu** irreproachable, flawless; **bez znaczenia** of no/little account; **bez zwłoki** promptly; **bez żadnych ale** no buts; **ujść bez kary** get away; **nie ma dymu bez ognia** there's no smoke without fire; **bez pracy nie ma kołaczy** no pain, no gain; **nie ma róży bez kolców** there's no rose without a thorn; **wejść bez pukania** enter without knocking; **bez pożegnania** without saying goodbye; **zrobić/wziąć coś bez pytania** do/take sth without asking; **bez wątpienia** undoubtedly, doubtless, no doubt; **nie bez kozery** not without a reason, with a good reason; **bez paniki** don't panic; take it easy; **tylko bez kawałów, głupich niespodzianek** no tricks, don't try anything funny; **herbata, kawa bez cukru** tea, coffee without sugar.

beza *f.* (*ciastko*) meringue.

bezadresowy *a.* **druki, przesyłki bezadresowe** direct mail.

bezakcentowy *a. jęz.* unaccented, unstressed, atonic; **wyraz bezakcentowy** atonic word.

bezalkoholowy *a.* alcohol-free; **napoje, drinki bezalkoholowe** soft drinks; **bezalkoholowe piwo** non-alcoholic beer; **tonik bezalkoholowy** (*w kosmetyce*) alcohol-free lotion.

bezan *mi żegl.* **1.** (*żagiel*) mizzensail, driver. **2.** = **bezanmaszt**.

bezanmaszt *mi żegl.* mizzenmast.

bezapelacyjny *a.* undisputed, inappellable; **bezapelacyjny wyrok** final *l.* irrevocable verdict; **bezapelacyjne zwycięstwo** undisputed victory.

bezawaryjny *a.* unfailing.

bezbarwnie *adv.* **1.** (= *bez koloru*) colorlessly; **ubierać się bezbarwnie** dress colorlessly. **2.** *przen.* (= *nijako, nieciekawie*) dully; **bezbarwnie opowiadać** relate insipidly; **bezbarwnie wyglądać** look dull.

bezbarwny *a.* **1.** (= *bez koloru*) colorless; **bezbarwny lakier** enamel. **2.** *przen.* colorless, dull; (*o twarzy*) (= *blady*) pallid; (*o twarzy, uśmiechu*) (= *bez wyrazu*) blank, expressionless; (*o stylu*) insipid, dull; (*o głosie, dźwięku*) dull; **bezbarwny tłum** colorless crowd; **bezbarwne życie** dull life.

bezbłędnie *adv.* **1.** (= *poprawnie*) correctly; **bezbłędnie odpowiadać** answer correctly; **bezbłędnie rozwiązać test** solve the test correctly. **2.** *pot.* (= *wspaniale, rewelacyjnie*) perfectly.

bezbłędny *a.* **1.** (*bez błędu, poprawny*) correct, faultless, error-free; **bezbłędna odpowiedź** correct answer. **2.** *pot.* (= *wspaniały, rewelacyjny*) perfect; **być w czymś bezbłędny** be excellent at sth.

bezbolesny *a.* **1.** (*niesprawiający bólu*) painless; **bezbolesny poród** *med.* painless delivery; **bezbolesny zabieg** painless operation. **2.** (*niewywołujący smutku*) painless.

bezboleśnie *adv.* **1.** (*nie sprawiając bólu*) painlessly. **2.** (*nie wywołując smutku*) painlessly. **3.** *pot.* (= *łatwo, przyjemnie, swobodnie*) painlessly.

bezbożnik *mp* godless person.

bezbożny *a.* godless.

bezbramkowy *a. sport* goalless.

bezbronny *a.* **1.** (= *bezradny, bezsilny*) defenceless, helpless. **2.** (= *bez broni*) unarmed.

bezbrzeżny *a.* (*bez brzegów, bez granic*) boundless, limitless.

bezcelowy a. aimless, pointless.

bezcen mi indecl. nothing; **kupić/sprzedać coś za bezcen** buy/sell sth for nothing.

bezcenny a. priceless.

bezceremonialny a. unceremonious.

bezchmurny a. 1. (o pogodzie) cloudless. 2. przen. (= spokojny, bezproblemowy) calm, serene.

bezcielesność f. incorporeality.

bezcielesny a. incorporeal.

bezcłowy a. ekon., handl. duty-free; **strefa bezcłowa** duty-free zone; **bezcłowy import/eksport** duty-free import/export.

bezczaszkowiec ma -wc- zool. acraniate.

bezczelnie adv. insolently.

bezczelność f. insolence, cheek, gall; **szczyt bezczelności** the height of insolence; **niesłychana bezczelność** unheard-of insolence; **bezczelność z czyjejś strony** insolence on sb's part.

bezczelny a. insolent, arrogant, cheeky.

bezcześcić ipf. -szczę -ścisz defile, besmirch.

bezczynnie adv. idly.

bezczynność f. idleness; **słodka bezczynność** sweet idleness.

bezczynny a. idle, inactive.

bezdech mi pat. apnea, apnoea; **bezdech senny** sleep apnea.

bezdennie adv. unfathomably; **bezdennie głupi** pot. unfathomably stupid.

bezdenny a. 1. (= głęboki, bez dna) bottomless, fathomless. 2. (= ogromny, bezkresny) unfathomable.

bezdeszczowy a. rainless.

bezdętkowy a. mot. (o oponie) tubeless.

bezdomność f. homelessness.

bezdomny a. i mp homeless.

bezdroże n. Gen.pl. -y lit. wilderness; **zejść na bezdroża** przen. go astray.

bezdrzewny a. treeless; **papier bezdrzewny** techn. wood-free paper.

bezduszny a. heartless.

bezdymny a. smoke-free.

bezdyskusyjny a. unarguable.

bezdzietny a. childless.

bezdźwięczny a. 1. (= cichy, przytłumiony) noiseless. 2. jęz. (wygłos, artykulacja, wymowa) voiceless; **bezdźwięczne spółgłoski** voiceless consonants.

beze prep. zob. **bez²**.

bezeceństwo n. infamy.

bezecny a. lit. infamous; (= budzący odrazę) abominable, disgusting.

bezglutenowy a. (o żywności) gluten-free.

bezgłośny a. noiseless, mute.

bezgłowy a. headless.

bezgorączkowy a. med. feverless.

bezgotówkowy a. ekon. non-cash.

bezgranicznie adv. boundlessly.

bezgraniczny a. boundless, limitless, immeasurable.

bezgrzeszny a. sinless.

bezguście n. 1. (= brak gustu) tastelessness. 2. pot. (= tandeta) tat.

bezgwiezdny a. starless.

bezhołowie n. anarchy, disorder.

bezideowiec mp -wc- Voc. -cze l. -cu pl. -y person without an ideology.

bezideowy a. without an ideology.

bezik mi Gen. i Acc. -a karty bezique.

bezimiennie adv. anonymously, namelessly.

bezimienny a. (o osobie) nameless, anonymous; (o dziele, uczynku) anonymous.

bezinteresownie adv. disinterestedly.

bezinteresowny a. disinterested, unbiased, impartial.

bezkaloryczny a. calorie-free.

bezkarnie adv. with impunity; **uszło mu to bezkarnie** he got away with it (scot free); **działać/robić coś bezkarnie** act/do sth with impunity.

bezkarność f. impunity.

bezkarny a. unpunished.

bezkastowy a. casteless.

bezklasowy a. classless.

bezkofeinowy a. caffeine-free, decaffeinated; **kawa bezkofeinowa** decaffeinated coffee.

bezkolizyjny a. mot. (o skrzyżowaniu) two-level; (o ruchu, jeździe) safe.

bezkompromisowy a. uncompromising.

bezkonfliktowy a. peaceable, peaceful, complaisant.

bezkonkurencyjny a. unbeatable, unmatched; **ceny bezkonkurencyjne** handl. unbeatable prices.

bezkostny a. zool. soft-bodied.

bezkres mi poet. immensity, vastness.

bezkresny a. immense, vast, boundless, limitless.

bezkręgowiec ma -wc- zool. invertebrate.

bezkręgowy a. zool. invertebrate.

bezkrólewie n. Gen.pl. -i polit., hist. interregnum.

bezkrwawo adv. bloodlessly, without bloodshed.

bezkrwawy a. bloodless; **bezkrwawe zabiegi chirurgiczne** med. non-invasive surgery.

bezkrwisty a. 1. (= blady, anemiczny) bloodless, anemic, pale. 2. (= bez życia, bez wyrazistości) bloodless, lifeless, dull.

bezkrytyczny a. uncritical, gullible.

bezksiężycowy a. moonless.

bezkształtny a. 1. (= nieforemny, nieregularny) shapeless. 2. (= niejasny, niewyraźny) vague, indistinct. 3. (= bezpostaciowy, amorficzny) formless, amorphous.

bezleśny a. treeless.

bezlik mi form. plenty, great number.

bezlistny a. leafless.

bezlitosny a. merciless, pitiless, ruthless.

bezludny a. uninhabited, deserted, unpopulated; **bezludna wyspa** desert island.

bezludzie n. Gen.pl. -i backwoods, wilderness.

bezład mi disorder, chaos; **w zupełnym bezładzie** in complete disorder.

bezładnie adv. in disorder, chaotically.

bezładny a. disordered, disorderly, chaotic.

bezmiar mi lit. vastness, boundlessness, infinity; **bezmiar miłości/nienawiści** immeasurable love/hatred.

bezmierny *a. lit.* immeasurable, vast, boundless, infinite.

bezmięsny *a.* meat-free, vegetarian.

bezmózgi *a.* brainless.

bezmózgowiec *mp* -wc- *Voc.* -cze *l.* -cu, *pog.* moron.

bezmyślny *a.* **1.** (= *niemądry, niefrasobliwy*) thoughtless, reckless, rash. **2.** (= *automatyczny, mechaniczny*) mindless.

beznadzieja *f. Gen.* -ei, **beznadziejność** *f.* (= *rezygnacja, zwątpienie*) hopelessness.

beznadziejny *a.* hopeless.

beznamiętny *a.* impassive, indifferent.

beznikotynowy *a.* nicotine-free.

beznogi *a.* legless.

bezoar *n. zool., anat.* bezoar.

bezobjawowy *a. pat.* symptomless.

bezodpływowy *a. geogr.* (*o obszarze, jeziorze*) landlocked.

bezogoniasty, bezogonowy *a.* tailless.

bezokolicznik *mi Gen.* -a *gram.* infinitive.

bezokolicznikowy *a. gram.* infinitival.

bezolejowy *a.* oil-free.

bezołowiowy *a.* lead-free.

bezoperacyjny *a. med.* non-invasive.

bezosobowy *a.* impersonal.

bezowocnie *adv.* fruitlessly, to no effect, to no avail, without avail, in vain.

bezowocny *a.* fruitless, of no effect.

bezpański *a.* (*o zwierzęciu*) stray; (*o terenie*) unowned.

bezpaństwowy *a. prawn.* stateless.

bezpardonowo *adv.* to the bitter end, to the last, uncompromisingly.

bezpardonowy *a.* **1.** uncompromising. **2.** (= *zaciekły, zawzięty*) bitter.

bezpartyjny *a. polit.* nonparty, independent.

bezpestkowy *a.* seedless, stoneless, pipless.

bezpieczeństwo *n.* **1.** (= *brak zagrożenia*) safety, security; **gwarancje bezpieczeństwa** safe passage; **bezpieczeństwo publiczne** public order; **bezpieczeństwo zbiorowe** *polit.* collective security; **bezpieczeństwo i higiena pracy** health and safety at work; **kaftan bezpieczeństwa** *med.* straitjacket; **klapa, zawór bezpieczeństwa** *techn.* safety valve; **pas bezpieczeństwa** *techn.* safety belt; **współczynnik bezpieczeństwa** *techn.* safety quotient; **hamulec bezpieczeństwa** *techn.* emergency brake. **2.** *pot.* = **bezpieka**.

bezpiecznie *adv.* safely, securely.

bezpiecznik *mi Gen.* -a **1.** *el.* fuse. **2.** *broń* safety catch.

bezpieczny *a.* **1.** (= *niezagrożony*) safe, secure, out of harm's way. **2.** (= *niezagrażający*) safe; **bezpieczna odległość** safe distance; **bezpieczny seks** safe sex.

bezpieka *f. pot.* the secret police, the security service.

bezplanowy *a.* unplanned, haphazard, desultory.

bezpłatnie *adv.* free (of charge), gratuitously.

bezpłatny *a.* **1.** (= *darmowy*) free (of charge), gratuitous. **2.** (= *nieopłacany*) unpaid, gratuitous.

bezpłciowy *a.* **1.** *biol.* asexual. **2.** *pog.* (= *nijaki, bezbarwny*) insipid, lifeless, dull.

bezpłodność *f.* **1.** *pat.* infertility, sterility. **2.** (= *jałowość, nierodzajność*) barrenness. **3.** (= *daremność, bezskuteczność*) fruitlessness, futility, ineffectiveness.

bezpłodny *a.* **1.** *med.* infertile, infecund, sterile. **2.** (= *jałowy, nierodzajny*) barren, waste. **3.** (= *daremny, bezskuteczny*) fruitless, futile, ineffective, impotent.

bezpodmiotowy *a. gram.* subjectless.

bezpodstawnie *adv.* groundlessly, baselessly.

bezpodstawny *a.* groundless, unfounded, baseless, unjustified.

bezpostaciowy *a.* amorphous.

bezpośredni *a.* **1.** direct, immediate, straightforward; **głosowanie bezpośrednie** *polit.* direct elections; **bezpośrednie połączenie** *tel.* direct connection. **2.** (*o człowieku, manierach*) (= *naturalny, szczery*) direct, candid.

bezpośrednio *adv.* directly, immediately, straightforwardly, straight out.

bezpośredniość *f.* **1.** directness, immediacy, straightforwardness. **2.** (= *naturalność, szczerość*) directness, candidness.

bezpotomnie *adv.* childlessly; **umrzeć bezpotomnie** die childless.

bezpotomny *a.* childless, without issue, without descendants.

bezpowrotnie *adv.* irretrievably, irrevocably, forever.

bezpowrotny *a.* **1.** (= *miniony raz na zawsze*) irretrievable, irrevocable. **2.** (= *niepowetowany*) irreparable.

bezprawie *n.* lawlessness.

bezprawnie *adv. prawn.* unlawfully.

bezprawny *a. prawn.* unlawful.

bezprecedensowy *a.* unprecedented, without precedent.

bezpretensjonalny *a.* unpretentious, unaffected.

bezproblemowy *a.* (*niepowodujący problemów*) unproblematic, trouble-free; *pot.* (= *nieskomplikowany, nietrudny*) easy, uncomplicated.

bezprocentowy *a.* **1.** *ekon.* (*nieprzynoszący procentu*) interest-free. **2.** *pot.* (= *bezalkoholowy*) soft, alcohol-free.

bezproduktywny *a.* unproductive, ineffective, ineffectual, futile.

bezpruderyjny *a.* uninhibited, bold.

bezprzedmiotowy *a.* **1.** pointless. **2.** **sztuka bezprzedmiotowa** abstract art.

bezprzewodowy *a. el.* cordless.

bezprzyczynowy *a.* causeless.

bezprzykładny *a.* unparalleled, unprecedented.

bezradnie *adv.* helplessly.

bezradny *a.* helpless, lost, at a loss.

bezrefleksyjny *a.* unreflective, thoughtless, unthinking.

bezrękawnik *mi Gen.* -a sleeveless garment.

bezrobocie *n.* **1.** unemployment, joblessness;

ukryte bezrobocie *ekon.* hidden unemployment. **2. być na bezrobociu** *pot.* live on the dole.

bezrobotny *a.* unemployed, jobless, without a job. – *mp* unemployed *l.* jobless person; **zasiłek dla bezrobotnych** unemployment benefit; *pot.* the dole.

bezrozumny *a.* mindless, brainless; (*o zwierzęciu*) dumb.

bezrtęciowy *a.* mercury-free.

bezruch *mi* **1.** (= *brak ruchu*) stillness, motionlessness. **2.** (= *brak aktywności*) idleness.

bezrybie *n.* absence of fish; **na bezrybiu i rak ryba** *pot.* any port in a storm.

bezrybny *a.* fishless, fished out.

bezrymowy *a. lit.* unrhymed.

bezsennie *adv.* sleeplessly, dreamlessly.

bezsenność *f. pat.* insomnia, sleeplessness.

bezsenny *a.* sleepless.

bezsens *mi* **1.** (= *absurd*) absurdity, nonsens. **2.** (= *bezcelowość*) senselessness.

bezsensowny *a.* **1.** (= *niemający sensu*) meaningless. **2.** (= *absurdalny*) absurd, nonsensical. **3.** (= *bezcelowy, nieskuteczny*) pointless, senseless.

bezsilnikowy *a. techn.* motorless, unpowered; **statek bezsilnikowy** motorless boat.

bezsilność *f.* powerlessness, helplessness, impotence.

bezsilny *a.* powerless, helpless, impotent.

bezsiła *f.* = **bezsilność**.

bezskrzydły *a.* wingless; **owady bezskrzydłe** *ent.* wingless insects, apterygial insects.

bezskutecznie *adv.* ineffectively, without effect, to no avail, in vain.

bezskuteczny *a.* ineffective, ineffectual.

bezsłoneczny *a.* sunless.

bezsporny *a.* indisputable, unquestionable.

bezspójnikowy *a. gram.* asyndetic.

bezsprzeczny *a.* unquestionable, indisputable.

bezstresowy *a. psych.* stress-free.

bezstronność *f.* impartiality, fairness.

bezstronny *a.* impartial, unbiased, fair.

bezstylowy *a.* styleless.

bezszelestny *a.* noiseless, soft.

bezszmerowy *a.* silent, noiseless.

bezszwowy *a.* seamless.

bezszynowy *a. techn.* trackless.

bezśnieżny *a.* snowless.

beztalencie *n. pog.* (= *brak talentu*) lack of talent. – *mp Gen.pl.* -**i** *pog.* (*osoba bez talentu*) nohoper.

bezterminowy *a.* open-ended.

beztlenowiec *ma* -**wc**- *biol.* anaerobe.

beztlenowy *a.* **1.** *biol.* anaerobic. **2.** *chem.* oxygen-free.

beztłuszczowy *a.* fat-free.

beztroska *f.* **1.** (= *brak kłopotów*) carefreeness, freedom from care. **2.** (= *niefrasobliwość*) carelessness, lightheartedness.

beztroski *a.* **1.** (= *bez trosk*) carefree, cheerful, jaunty. **2.** (= *niefrasobliwy*) unconcerned, careless, footloose, lighthearted.

beztrosko *adv.* **1.** (= *bez kłopotów*) cheerfully, jauntily. **2.** (= *nieodpowiedzialnie, lekkomyślnie*) unconcernedly, carelessly, lightheartedly.

bezustanny *a.* unceasing, ceaseless, continuous, incessant.

bezusterkowy *a.* faultless.

bezustnikowy *a.* (*o papierosie*) plain, filterless, non-filter, untipped.

bezużyteczny *a.* useless.

bezwartościowy *a.* valueless.

bezwarunkowo *adv.* unconditionally, absolutely.

bezwarunkowy *a.* unconditional; **odruch bezwarunkowy** *biol.* unconditioned reflex.

bezwąsy *a.* having no moustache, moustacheless.

bezwiedny *a.* unwitting, involuntary, mechanical, automatic.

bezwietrzny *a.* windless.

bezwizowy *a.* without a visa.

bezwład *mi* **1.** (= *apatia, inercja*) listlessness, lethargy, inertness, inertia. **2.** *pat.* paralysis.

bezwładnie *adv.* listlessly.

bezwładnościowy *a. fiz.* inertial.

bezwładność *f.* **1.** *fiz.* inertia; **siła bezwładności** the force of inertia. **2.** = **bezwład** 1.

bezwładny *a.* **1.** (= *niemający sił lub ochoty działać*) listless, inert. **2.** *fiz.* inert. **3.** (= *niemogący się poruszać*) paralyzed.

bezwłasnowolny *a. prawn.* legally incapable.

bezwłosy *a.* hairless; (= *nie pokryty futrem*) furless.

bezwodny *a.* **1.** = *pozbawiony wody* waterless. **2.** *techn.* (= *działający bez wody*) water-free. **3.** *chem.* (= *niezawierający wody*) anhydrous.

bezwolny *a.* weak-willed, listless.

bezwonny *a.* odorless.

bezwstydnica *f.*, **bezwstydnik** *mp uj.* shameless *l.* impudent person.

bezwstydny *a. uj.* shameless, brazen, impudent; (*o człowieku*) brazen-faced.

bezwyjątkowo *adv.* without exception, exceptionlessly.

bezwyjątkowy *a.* exceptionless, absolute.

bezwyznaniowiec *mp* -**wc**- *Voc.* -**cze** *l.* -**cu** *pl.* -**y** person of no religious denomination.

bezwyznaniowy *a.* non-denominational.

bezwzględnie *adv.* **1.** (= *stanowczo*) absolutely. **2.** (= *surowo, bez litości*) ruthlessly, pitilessly, severely. **3.** (= *bezwarunkowo, mimo wszystko*) regardless, regardlessly, unconditionally.

bezwzględność *f.* **1.** (= *niezależność, niezmienność*) absoluteness. **2.** (= *surowość*) ruthlessness, pitilessness, severity. **3.** (= *obligatoryjność, bezwarunkowość*) finality.

bezwzględny *a.* **1.** (= *niezmienny, niezależny*) absolute; **wartości bezwzględne** absolute values; **prawda bezwzględna** *fil.* absolute truth; **czas bezwzględny** *fiz.* absolute time; **temperatura/wysokość bezwzględna** absolute temperature/altitude; **zero bezwzględne** absolute zero; **wartość bezwzględna** *mat.* absolute value. **2.** (= *surowy, nieprzejednany*) ruthless, pitiless, severe. **3.** (= *całkowity, bezwarunkowy*) final, unconditional.

bezzałogowy *a.* unmanned.

bezzapachowy *a.* odorless.

bezzasadny *a.* baseless, groundless, unjustified, unfounded.

bezzębny *a.* toothless.

bezzwłocznie *adv.* immediately, with no delay, at once, directly.

bezzwłoczny *a.* immediate.

bezzwrotny *a.* non-returnable, non-repayable.

bez żenady *adv.* blatantly, unceremoniously.

bezżenność *f.* bachelorhood.

bezżenny *a.* (*o mężczyźnie*) single, unmarried; **stan bezżenny** unmarried state, bachelorhood.

beż *mi Gen.pl.* -**żów** beige.

beżowy *a.* beige.

bęben *mi* -**bn**- *Gen.* -**a 1.** *muz.* drum. **2.** *techn.* drum, barrel. **3.** *techn.* (= *szpula*) reel. **4.** *bud.* (= *tambur*) tambour. **5.** *bud.* (*część kolumny*) drum. – *mp* -**bn**- *pl.* -**y** (*o małym dziecku*) tot.

bębenek *mi* -**nk**- *Gen.* -**a 1.** (small) drum; **bębenek baskijski** *muz.* tambourine. **2. podbijać komuś bębenka** *przen.* bang the drum for sb. **3.** *anat.* (= *błona bębenkowa*) eardrum; **bębenki komuś pękają od hałasu** sb's eardrums are bursting from the noise. **4.** (*do połowu ryb*) hoop net. **5.** *techn.* (= *element w kształcie walca*) drum, barrel; (= *szpulka*) reel, spool.

bębenkowy *a.* **1.** *med.* tympanic; **błona bębenkowa** tympanic membrane, eardrum. **2.** (*o sieci*) hoop. **3.** *techn.* = bębnowy.

bębnić *ipf.* -**ij 1.** drum; (= *stukać*) tap, rap; (= *walić*) bang; **bębnić palcami po stole** drum one's fingers on the table; **bębnić pięściami w drzwi** bang one's fists on the door; **bębnić na fortepianie** plonk away on the piano; **bębnić na maszynie do pisania** bang away on a typewriter; **deszcz bębni po szybach** *l.* **o szyby** the rain is drumming on the window-panes. **2.** *pot.* (= *recytować mechanicznie*) rattle off. **3. bębnić komuś do ucha/nad głową** bang away by sb's ear/over sb's head. **4.** *myśl.* (*o ptakach*) drum.

bębnowy *a.* *techn.* drum, reel, barrel; (*obrotowy*) revolving.

bęc *int.* bash, bang.

bęcnąć *pf.* -**ij** *pot.* bash, bang.

bęcwał *mp pl.* -**y** *pog.* moron, idiot.

będę, będzie *itd.* *ipf.* *zob.* **być**.

bękart *mp pl.* -**y 1.** (*o nieślubnym dziecku*) bastard. **2.** *obelż.* (*o niegrzecznym dziecku*) brat. **3.** *druk.* widow.

BHP *abbr.* (= *bezpieczeństwo i higiena pracy*) health and safety at work; **przepisy BHP** safety regulations.

biadać *ipf.* wail (*nad kimś/czymś* over sb/sth).

biadolić *ipf.* *pot.* **1.** complain (*na kogoś/coś* about sb/sth). **2.** = biadać.

białaczka *f.* *pat.* leukemia, leukaemia.

białawy *a.* whitish, off-white.

białko *n.* *Gen.pl.* -**łek 1.** (*część jajka*) white of an egg. **2.** (*część oka*) white of an eye; **łypać, przewracać białkami** to show the whites of one's eyes. **3.** *biochem.* protein.

białkować *ipf.* *techn.* whitewash.

białkowy *a.* *biochem.* proteinous.

białkówka *f.* *anat.* cornea.

biało-czerwony *a.* red and white. – *mp pot.* (*o sportowcach polskich*) the red-and-whites.

białogłowa *f.* *Gen.pl.* -**łów** *arch.* lady.

Białorusin *mp*, **Białorusinka** *f.* *Gen.pl.* -**ek** Belarusian.

białoruski *a.* Belarusian.

Białoruś *f.* *geogr.* Belarus.

biały *a.* **bielszy 1.** (*liczne znaczenia przenośne i idiomatyczne*) white; **biały jak śnieg** (as) white as (fresh-driven) snow; **biały człowiek** white man, Caucasian; **do białego rana** till the break of day; **białe noce** white nights (*in northern countries*); **białe mięso** white meat; **białe pieczywo** *l.* **biały chleb** white bread; **biały ryż** white rice; **białe wino** white wine; **biała kawa** white coffee; **biały mróz** hoarfrost; **biała flaga** white flag; **Orzeł Biały** (*w polskim godle narodowym*) the White Eagle; **Biały Dom** the White House; **biała substancja** *anat.* white matter; **biała krwinka** *l.* **ciałko krwi** *fizj.* white blood cell, leukocyte; **biała rasa** *antrop.* the Caucasian race; **biała flota** *żegl.* river craft; **biały karzeł** *astron.* white dwarf; **topola biała** *bot.* white poplar (*Populus alba*); **biały niedźwiedź** *zool.* polar bear (*Ursus maritimus*); **wal biały** *zool.* white whale, beluga (*Delphinapterus leucas*); **biała gorączka** *pot.* white fever; **białe szaleństwo** *żart.* (= *sporty zimowe*) white madness; **biały taniec** dance where the women ask the men; **biały kruk** *przen.* rara avis, rarity, curio; **biały murzyn** *iron.* white slave; **biała plama na mapie** unchartered territory; **w biały dzień** in broad daylight; **czarno na białym** black on white. **2.** (= *czysty*) clean, blank; **biała karta** blank sheet. **3. biała broń** *wojsk.* hand weapon; (*zbiorowo*) hand weapons. **4. biały wiersz** *lit.* blank verse. **5.** *kość.* **biały tydzień** Whitsun; **biała niedziela** Whitsunday. – *mp* (*o człowieku zaliczanym do rasy białej*) white, Caucasian. – *mi pl.* szachy, warcaby (= *gracz grający białymi bierkami*) White.

biatlon *mi* *sport* biathlon.

biatlonista *mp*, **biatlonistka** *f.* *Gen.pl.* -**ek** *sport* biathlete.

biba *f.* *pot.* drinking party, piss-up.

bibelot *mi* knick-knack, nick-nack.

bibka *f.* *Gen.pl.* -**ek** = biba.

biblia, Biblia *f.* *Gen.* -**ii 1.** the Bible; **przysięgać na Biblię** swear on the Bible. **2.** *przen.* bible.

biblijny *a.* Biblical; **papier biblijny** *druk.* bible paper.

bibliofil *mp Gen.pl.* -**ów** *l.* -**i** bibliophile.

bibliofilski *a.* bibliophilic.

bibliograf *mp pl.* -**owie** bibliographer.

bibliografia *f.* *Gen.* -**ii** bibliography.

bibliograficzny *a.* bibliographical, bibliographic.

bibliologia *f.* *Gen.* -**ii** bibliology.

biblioteczka *f.* **1.** *pot.* (= *księgozbiór*) library, book collection. **2.** (*mebel*) bookcase.

biblioteczny *a.* library; **karta biblioteczna** library card.

biblioteka *f.* **1.** (*instytucja*) library. **2.** (= *księgozbiór*) library, book collection; **chodząca biblioteka** *żart.* walking library. **3.** (*mebel*) library, bookcase. **4.** (= *seria wydawnicza*) series (of books).

bibliotekarka *f. Gen.pl.* **-ek** *zob.* **bibliotekarz**.

bibliotekarski *a.* librarian's.

bibliotekarstwo *n.* librarianship.

bibliotekarz *mp* librarian.

bibliotekoznawca *mp* librarianship expert.

bibliotekoznawczy *a.* librarianship.

bibliotekoznawstwo *n.* librarianship.

biblista *mp*, **biblistka** *f. Gen.pl.* **-ek** Biblist.

biblistyka *f.* **1.** (*dział teologii*) hermeneutics. **2.** (= *nauka o Biblii*) bible studies.

bibosz *mp Gen.pl.* **-y** *l.* **-ów** *przest.* soak, drinker.

bibuła *f.* **1.** (= *papier wchłaniający wodę*) blotting paper; **bibuła filtracyjna** *techn.* filter paper. **2.** (= *cienki papier do ozdób*) tissue paper. **3. bibuła przebitkowa** carbon paper. **4.** *pot.* (= *nielegalna literatura*) underground publications.

bibułka *f.* (= *cienki papier*) tissue paper; **bibułka przebitkowa** carbon paper; **owijać w bibułkę** *przen.* beat about the bush; **nie owijając w (różową) bibułkę** frankly speaking; not beating about the bush.

biceps *mi Gen.* **-a** *anat.* biceps.

bicie *n.* **1.** (*uderzanie, aby sprawić ból*) beating; **chłopiec do bicia** whipping-boy; **przyznać się bez bicia** confess freely. **2.** (= *uderzanie, łomotanie*) banging, beating; (*o sercu, mechanizmie*) beating, beat, pulse; **bicie serca** heartbeat. **3.** (*o dzwonach, zegarach*) beating, ringing, peal. **4.** (*czynność licznika*) clocking up, running. **5. bicie rekordu** beating *l.* breaking a record. **6.** (*w grze*) beating; (*karty*) beating; (*pionka, figury*) taking, capture. **7.** (= *zabijanie zwierząt*) slaughter. **8.** (= *tłoczenie, odciskanie, drukowanie*) coining, minting. **9.** (= *ubijanie*) beating, whisking, churning.

bicykl *mi Gen.* **-a** *Gen.pl.* **-i** *l.* **-ów** *przest.* velocipede, bicycle.

bicz *mi Gen.pl.* **-y** *l.* **-ów** whip; *lit.* scourge; **bicze wodne** hydromassage; **rozpuścić kogoś jak dziadowski bicz** spoil sb rotten; **kręcić bicze z piasku** try to make something out of nothing; **ukręcić bicz na samego siebie/na kogoś** make a rod for one's own/sb else's back; **bicz boży** the scourge of God; **bicz satyry** a satirist's barbs.

biczować *ipf.* whip, flog, scourge.

biczyk *mi Gen.* a small whip.

bić *ipf.* **biję bijesz 1.** (*uderzać, aby sprawić ból*) beat (*w coś* sth, *po czymś* on/about sth); **bić kogoś po twarzy/łapach/tyłku** beat sb about the face/on the hands/on the behind; **bij zabij!** at them! **2.** *przen.* **nie w ciemię bity** not thick in the head; **bić w oczy** *przen.* be blindingly obvious. **3.** (= *uderzać, łomotać*) to bang; **bić pięścią w stół** bang one's fist on the table; **bić oklaski** *l.* **brawo** clap loudly; **bić w bęben** bang a drum; **bić w dzwon** ring a bell; **bić na alarm** sound *l.* raise the alarm; **bić skrzydłami** (*o ptakach*) beat one's wings; **bić czołem** *l.* **bić pokłony** bow and scrape; **bić głową w mur** to bang one's head against a brick wall. **4.** (*o sercu, pulsie*) beat; **z bijącym sercem** with beating heart; **moje serce bije dla**

ciebie my heart beats for you. **5.** (*o dzwonach*) beat, peal; (*o zegarze*) strike. **6.** (*o liczniku*) clock up, run. **7.** (*o broni palnej*) (= *strzelać, grzmieć*) fire, bang, boom; (= *trafiać*) hit; **niech cię kule biją** I hope a bullet hits you; damn you!; go to hell! **8.** (= *wydobywać się, tryskać*) spring; **biły na mnie siódme poty** I broke into a cold sweat. **9.** (= *zwyciężać, pokonywać*) to beat. **10. bić rekord** break a record. **11.** (*w grze*) (= *pokonywać*) beat, win; (= *zdobywać*) take, win, capture, seize; **bić kartę** beat a card; **bić kartę atutem** trump a card; **bić piona/figurę** take *l.* capture a pawn/a piece; **bić kogoś na głowę** beat sb into the ground. **12.** (= *zabijać*) kill, slaughter. **13.** (= *tłoczyć, odciskać, drukować*) coin, mint. **14.** (= *ubijać, trzepać*) (*jaja*) beat, whisk; (*śmietanę*) whip; (*masło*) churn; **bić pianę** *iron.* go through the motions. **~ się** *ipf.* **1.** (*zadawać sobie wzajemnie ciosy*) fight. **2.** (*uderzać siebie samego*) hit o.s. (*po czymś* about sth, *w coś* on sth); **bić się w piersi** *przen.* to beat one's chest; **bić się w cudze piersi** put the blame on someone else. **3.** (= *walczyć, spierać się*) fight, battle (*o kogoś/coś* about *l.* over sb/sth, *z kimś/czymś* with *l.* against sb/sth, *za kogoś/coś* for sb/sth). **4. bić się z myślami** *przen.* fight with one's thoughts. **5.** (= *pojedynkować się*) duel (*o kogoś/coś* over sb/sth).

bidet *mi* bidet.

bidon *mi* water bottle.

biec *ipf.* = **biegnąć**.

bieda *f.* **1.** (= *niedostatek, nędza*) poverty; **bieda z nędzą** *l.* **bieda aż piszczy** abject poverty; **klepać, cierpieć biedę** live from hand to mouth. **2.** (= *nieszczęście, kłopot*) trouble, problem; **napytać** *l.* **narobić sobie/komuś biedy** make trouble for o.s./sb; **pół biedy** (only) half the problem; **od biedy** with difficulty; **z wielką biedą** with great difficulty. **3.** *pot.* (= *biedota*) the poor, paupers.

biedactwo *n.* poor thing, poor devil, poor beggar.

biedaczek *mp* **-czk-** *pl.* **-i** *l.* **-owie**, **biedaczysko** *n. Gen.pl.* **-ów** *zob.* **biedak** 2.

biedaczka *f. Gen.pl.* **-ek 1.** (*ze współczuciem o kobiecie lub dziewczynce*) *zob.* **biedactwo**. **2.** (= *uboga kobieta*) poor woman; (= *żebraczka*) beggar (woman).

biedak *mp pl.* **-cy** *l.* **-ki 1.** (= *ubogi mężczyzna*) poor man, pauper. **2.** (*ze współczuciem o mężczyźnie*) poor devil, poor beggar, poor fellow.

biedermeier *mi* (*styl w meblarstwie i dekoracji wnętrz*) **1.** Biedermeier. **2.** *Gen.* **-a** *pot.* (*przedmiot w tym stylu*) Biedermeier.

biedermeierowski *a.* Biedermeier.

biednie *adv.* poorly.

biednieć *ipf.* **1.** (= *ubożeć*) become *l.* grow poorer. **2.** (= *mizernieć, pogarszać się*) decline, deteriorate.

biedny *a.* **1.** (= *ubogi, niezamożny*) poor; **biedny jak mysz kościelna** (as) poor as a church mouse. **2.** (= *nieszczęśliwy*) poor, unlucky, hapless. **3.** (*o przedmiotach*) (= *skromny, zniszczony*) poor, shabby. – *mp* poor person; **biednemu zawsze wiatr w oczy** it never rains but it pours.

biedota *f.* **1.** (*ogół ludzi biednych*) the poor. **2.** *pot.* (*współczująco o kimś biednym l. nieszczęśliwym*) poor thing.

biedować *ipf.* rough it; live in poverty.

biedronka *f. ent.* ladybug; *zwł. Br.* ladybird (*Coccinella, Adalia*).

biedulka *f. Gen.pl.* **-ek** *zob.* **biedactwo**.

biedzić się *ipf.* worry (*nad czymś* over sth); toil, labor (*nad czymś* at sth); waste one's time (*z czymś* with sth).

bieg *mi* **1.** (= *szybkie posuwanie się naprzód*) run, running; **biegiem** at a run; running; **biegiem marsz!** *wojsk.* quick march! **2.** *sport* (running) race, run; **bieg krótkodystansowy** sprint; **bieg średniodystansowy/długodystansowy** middle-distance/long-distant race *l.* run; **bieg maratoński** marathon; **bieg sztafetowy** relay race; **bieg przez płotki** hurdle race; **bieg przełajowy** cross-country race; **biegi narciarskie** cross-country skiing. **3.** *jeźdz.* race, horserace. **4.** *kolarstwo* **bieg drużynowy** team pursuit; **bieg torowy** velodrome race. **5.** (= *ruch*) running, movement, motion; **bieg jałowy** *techn.* idling, ticking over. **6.** (= *prąd rzeczny*) current; **z biegiem rzeki** downstream. **7.** (= *trasa*) course; **dolny/górny bieg rzeki** the lower/upper course of a river. **8.** (= *dzianie się*) **bieg historii/wydarzeń/spraw** the course of history/events/things; **z biegiem lat/czasu** with the passing of years/time; **nadać czemuś bieg** set sth in motion. **9.** *mot., techn.* gear; **zmieniać biegi** change gear; **pierwszy/drugi/trzeci bieg** the first/second/third gear; **wsteczny bieg** the reverse gear; **skrzynia biegów** gearbox; **automatyczna skrzynia biegów** automatic transmission. **10.** *bud.* (*odcinek schodów*) flight.

biegacz *mp Gen.pl.* **-y** *l.* **-ów** *sport* runner; **biegacz krótkodystansowy** sprinter; **biegacz długodystansowy** long-distance runner. – *ma Gen.pl.* **-y** *ent.* (= *chrząszcz z rodziny Carabidae*) ground beetle. – *mi Gen.* **-a** *pl.* **-y** *tk.* (*element przędzarki*) shuttle, traveler.

biegaczka *f. Gen.pl.* **-ek** *sport* runner.

biegać *ipf.* (*poruszać się biegiem*) run; **biegać po sklepach** run round the shops; **biegać z wywieszonym językiem** to run with one's tongue hanging out; **biegać za czymś** chase sth up; **biegać za interesami** chase up business; **o co biega?** *sl.* what's up?

bieganina *f.* running (to and fro).

biegiem *adv.* at a run, running.

biegle *adv.* fluently.

biegłość *f.* fluency.

biegły *a.* fluent (*w czymś* in *l.* at sth). – *mp* (= *specjalista*) expert; **biegły sądowy** *prawn.* legal expert.

biegnąć, biec *ipf.* biegnę, -niesz, -nij; biegł **1.** (= *mknąć, pędzić*) run; **biec w podskokach** hop along; **biec na wyścigi** run a race; **biec bez tchu** run like the wind; **biec co sił w nogach** run as fast as one's legs will carry one. **2.** (= *spieszyć się, mknąć pośpiesznie*) speed (on *l.* along), hasten. **3.** *fiz.* (*o fali głosowej, promieniowaniu*) travel. **4.** (= *rozciągać się, ciągnąć się*) extend, carry on, run; **ścieżka biegnie przez ogród** the

path crosses the garden. **5.** (*o czasie*) pass. **6.** *przen.* **biec utartym trybem** run over the same old ground; **biec myślą ku czemuś** turn one's thoughts to sth.

biegowy *a.* **1.** **narty biegowe** *sport* race skis. **2.** **koło biegowe** *mot.* road wheel.

biegówka *f. Gen.pl.* **-ek** *sport* race ski.

biegun *mi Gen.* **-a 1.** *geogr.* pole; **biegun północny/południowy** the North/South Pole; **biegun magnetyczny** magnetic pole; **na przeciwnym biegunie** *przen.* on the opposite pole *l.* end. **2.** (*fiz.*) pole, end, terminal; **bieguny różnoimienne** opposite poles; **biegun baterii** battery terminal; **biegun ujemny/dodatni** positive/negative pole. **3.** (= *wygięta płoza*) rocker; **fotel/koń na biegunach** rocking chair/horse.

biegunka *f. Gen.pl.* **-ek** *pat.* diarrhea.

biegunowo *adv.* (= *krańcowo*) extremely, diametrically.

biegunowy *a. geogr.,fiz., mat.* polar; **równanie/współrzędne biegunowe** *mat.* polar equation/coordinates; **biegunowe przeciwieństwa** *przen.* polar opposites.

biel *f.* **1.** (= *biały kolor*) white; **w bieli** in white. **2.** *chem., techn.* (*pigment*) white; **biel barytowa** permanent white; **biel cynkowa** Chinese white; **biel ołowiowa** white lead; **biel mleczna** milk white; **biel tytanowa** titanium white.

bielactwo *n. biol., pat.* albinism.

bielak *ma zool.* mountain hare, arctic hare (*Lepus timidus*).

bieleć *ipf.* **-eję, -ejesz 1.** (= *stawać się białym*) whiten. **2.** (= *wydawać się białym, jasnym*) appear white.

bielić *ipf.* **1.** (= *malować na biało*) paint white; (*ścianę, sufit*) whitewash; **bielić drzewa** *ogr.* paint trees with lime. **2.** *techn.* (= *wybielać, pobielać*) bleach; (= *pokrywać cyną*) tin-plate. ~ **się** *ipf.* appear white.

bielidło *n. Gen.pl.* **-deł** (= *substancja bieląca*) whiting, whitening; *przest.* (*kosmetyk*) whiteface powder.

bielik *ma zool.* sea eagle (*Haliaeetus*); **bielik amerykański** bald eagle (*Haliaeetus leucocephalus*); **bielik europejski** European *l.* white-tailed sea eagle; erne (*Haliaeetus albicilla*).

bielizna *f.* **1.** (= *spodnia odzież*) underwear, lingerie; **w samej bieliźnie** in one's underwear. **2.** (*pościelowa, stołowa*) linen.

bieliźniany *a.* linen.

bieliźniarka *f. Gen.pl.* **-ek 1.** (*szafa*) chest of drawers. **2.** (*kobieta szyjąca bieliznę*) seamstress.

bieliźniarstwo *n.* lingerie making.

bielmo *n.* **1.** *pat.* leucoma; **mieć bielmo na oczach** *przen.* not see straight; **zdjąć komuś bielmo z oczu** *przen.* take the scales from sb's eyes. **2.** *bot.* endosperm.

bielszy *a. zob.* **biały**.

bieluń *mi Gen.* **-a** *Gen.pl.* **-ów** *bot.* jimsonweed, thorn apple (*Datura*).

biennale *n. indecl.* **sztuka** biennale.

bierka *f.* (= *figura l. pionek*) piece; (*w grze w bierki*) stick.

bierki *pl. Gen.* **-ek** (*gra*) pick-up-sticks.
biernie *adv.* passively, inactively.
biernik *mi Gen.* **-a** *gram.* accusative.
bierność *f.* **1.** (= *obojętność*) passivity, inactivity, inertia. **2.** *chem.* inertness.
bierny *a.* **1.** (= *obojętny*) passive, inactive; **bierna postawa** passive attitude; **bierny opór** passive resistance; **bierne prawo wyborcze** *polit.* the right to stand for election. **2.** *chem.* inert. **3.** *gram.* passive; **imiesłów bierny** past participle; **strona bierna** passive (voice).
bierwiono *n.* log, beam.
bierzmować *ipf. rz.-kat.* confirm.
bierzmowanie *n. rz.-kat.* confirmation.
bies *ma przest.* demon, devil, fiend; **bies go opętał** *l.* **bies w niego wstąpił** *żart.* something's got into him.
biesiada *f. lit.* feast, banquet.
biesiadniczka *f. Gen.pl.* **-ek, biesiadnik** *mp lit.* reveller.
biesiadny *a. form.* banqueting; **biesiadny stół** banquet table; **piosenka biesiadna** party song.
biesiadować *ipf. form.* revel, banquet, make merry.
bieżąco *adv.* currently, in progress; **być z czymś na bieżąco** be up to date with sth; **robić coś na bieżąco** do sth in the normal course.
bieżący *a.* **1.** (= *teraźniejszy*) current, present, this; **rok bieżący** the current year; **bieżący numer tygodnika** the current issue of the paper. **2.** (= *mierzony jednym ciągiem*) **metr bieżący** (one) meter length. **3.** (= *płynący*) running; **bieżąca woda** running water.
bieżnia *f. Gen.pl.* **-i** *sport* **1.** track; **bieżnia tartanowa** tartan track. **2. bieżnia łożyska** *techn.* bearing track *l.* race.
bieżnik *mi Gen.* **-a 1.** (*serweta*) runner. **2.** *mot.* tread.
bieżnikować *ipf. mot.* retread.
bigamia *f. Gen.* **-ii** bigamy; **popełnić bigamię** commit bigamy.
bigamiczny *a.* bigamous.
bigamista *mp,* **bigamistka** *f. Gen.pl.* **-ek** bigamist.
big-band *mi muz.* big band.
big-beat *mi muz.* = **bigbit.**
big-beatowiec *mp* **-wc-** *muz.* = **bigbitowiec.**
big-beatowy *a. muz.* = **bigbitowy.**
bigbit *mi muz., pot.* rock (*in Poland, especially in the 1960s*).
bigbitowiec *mp* **-wc-** *muz.* rock player *l.* singer (*in Poland*).
bigbitowy *a. muz., pot.* rock (*in Poland*); **zespół bigbitowy** rock group.
bigos *mi* **1.** bigos (*Polish dish of stewed sauerkraut and meat*). **2.** *pot.* (= *bałagan*) mess; **narobić bigosu** make a mess; **ładny bigos** fine mess; pretty kettle of fish.
bigot *mp* bigot.
bigoteria *f. Gen.* **-ii** bigotry.
bigotka *f. Gen.pl.* **-ek** *zob.* **bigot.**
bijać *ipf.* beat from time to time, beat regularly.

bijak *mi Gen.* **-a** *techn.* beater; (*do lnu l. część cepa*) swingle.
bijatyka *f.* fight, brawl, squabble, scuffle, tussle; **brać udział w bijatyce** be involved in a brawl.
bikini *n. indecl.* bikini.
bila *f. Gen.pl.* **-i** *l.* **bil** *bilard* ball.
bilans *mi pl.* **-e** (= *stosunek, zestawienie*) balance; (*dokument*) balance sheet; **bilans finansowy/księgowy/roczny** *fin.* financial/accounting/annual balance; **bilans płatniczy/handlowy** *ekon.* balance of payments/trade; **bilans ujemny/dodatni** negative/positive balance; **bilans próbny** test balance; **bilans cieplny** *fiz.* heat balance; **bilans energetyczny** *fiz.* energy balance; **bilans wodny** *hydrol.* water balance; **bilans sił** balance of power.
bilansować *ipf.* balance (out); **bilansując** (= *podsumowując*) on balance.
bilansowy *a. fin., ekon.* balance; **metoda bilansowa** balance-sheet method.
bilard *mi* **1.** (*gra*) billiards; **bilard amerykański** pool. **2.** (= *stół bilardowy*) billiard table, pool table.
bilardowy *a.* billiard, pool; **stół bilardowy** billiard table, pool table; **kij bilardowy** cue; **kula/sala bilardowa** billiard *l.* pool ball/hall.
bilardzista *mp,* **bilardzistka** *f. Gen.pl.* **-ek** billiard player, pool player.
bilateralny *a. form.* bilateral; **stosunki bilateralne** *polit.* bilateral relations; **umowa bilateralna** bilateral agreement.
bilet *mi* **1.** (= *dowód opłaty za wstęp l. podróż*) ticket; **bilet kolejowy/autobusowy** train/bus ticket; **bilet miesięczny/okresowy** monthly/season ticket; **bilet powrotny** return ticket; **bilet w jedną stronę** one-way ticket; *Br.* single ticket; **bilet zniżkowy** reduced fare ticket; **bilet do kina/teatru** movie/theater ticket. **2. bilet skarbowy** *ekon.* treasury bill. **3.** *przest.* (= *wizytówka*) visiting card. **4. wilczy bilet** negative reference (*given to sb expelled from school or fired*).
bileter *mp* usher.
bileterka *f. Gen.pl.* **-ek** usher, usherette.
biletowy *a.* ticket; **kasa biletowa** ticket office; (*w kinie l. teatrze*) box office.
bilion *mi Gen.* **-a** trillion.
bilionowy *a.* trillionth.
billboard *mi* billboard.
billing *mi* itemized bill.
bilon *mi* (small) change.
bimbać *ipf. pot.* not give two hoots, not give a damn (*na kogoś/coś l. z kogoś/czegoś* about sb/sth).
bimber *mi* **-br-** *pot.* moonshine, hooch.
bimbrownia *f. Gen.pl.* **-i** *pot.* illegal still.
bimbrownictwo *n. pot.* moonshine making.
bimbrownik *mp pot.* moonshiner.
bimetal *mi el.* bimetallic strip.
binarny *a. mat.* binary.
bingo *n. indecl. hazard* bingo.
binokle *pl. Gen.* **-i** pince-nez.
bioaktywny *a. biochem.* bioactive.
biocenoza *f. biol.* biocenosis.
biochemia *f. Gen.* **-ii** biochemistry.

biochemiczny *a.* biochemical.
biochemik *mp* biochemist.
biodegradacja *f.* biodegradation.
biodro *n. Gen.pl.* **-der** hip; **wąskie/szerokie biodra** narrow/broad hips.
biodrowy *a. anat.* pelvic; **staw biodrowy** pelvic joint; **obręcz biodrowa** pelvic arch *l.* girdle.
biodrówka *f. (mięso)* chump.
biodrówki *pl. Gen.* **-ek** *(spodnie)* hipsters.
biodrzasty *a. pot.* big-hipped, broad-hipped.
bioelektryczność *f. fizj.* bioelectricity.
bioelektryczny *a.* bioelectric.
bioenergia *f. Gen.* **-ii** bioenergy.
bioenergoterapeuta *mp,* **bioenergoterapeutka** *f. Gen.pl.* **-ek** energy healer.
bioenergoterapeutyczny *a.* energy-healing.
bioenergoterapia *f. Gen.* **-ii** energy healing.
biofizyczny *a.* biophysical.
biofizyk *mp* biophysicist.
biofizyka *f.* biophysics.
biograf *mp pl.* **-owie** biographer.
biografia *f. Gen.* **-ii** biography; *pot.* bio.
biograficzny *a.* biographic, biographical; **film biograficzny** biographic movie, biopic; **słownik biograficzny** biographic dictionary.
biogram *mi* biographic entry *l.* article.
bioinżynieria *f. Gen.* **-ii** bioengineering.
biokatalizator *mi Gen.* **-a** *biochem.* biocatalyst.
bioklimatologia *f.* bioclimatology.
biolog *mp pl.* **-dzy** *l.* **-owie** biologist.
biologia *f. Gen.* **-ii** biology; **biologia molekularna** molecular biology.
biologiczny *a.* biological; **nauki biologiczne** biological sciences; **jednostka biologiczna** biological unit; **stacja biologiczna** biological field site; **substancja biologiczna** biological substance; **środowisko biologiczne** biological environment; **procesy biologiczne** biological processes; **rytm biologiczny** biological rhythm, biorhythm.
biomedycyna *f.* biomedicine.
biomedyczny *a.* biomedicinal.
biometeorolog *mp pl.* **-dzy** *l.* **-owie** biometeorologist.
biometeorologia *f. Gen.* **-ii** biometeorology.
biometeorologiczny *a.* biometeorological; **warunki biometeorologiczne** biometeorological conditions; **prognoza biometeorologiczna** biometeorological forecast.
biometria *f. Gen.* **-ii** **1.** *(nauka)* biometry. **2.** *(technika pomiarowa)* biostatistics.
bionik *mp* bionics expert.
bionika *f.* bionics.
biopierwiastek *mi Gen.* **-a** bioelement.
biopole *n. Gen.pl.* **-pól** biofield.
biopolimer *mi biochem.* biopolymer.
biopotencjał *mi fizj.* biopotential.
bioprąd *mi fizj.* biocurrent.
bioprotetyczny *f. med.* bioprosthetic.
bioproteza *f. med.* bioprosthesis.
biopsja *f. chir.* biopsy.
biorca *mp chir.* recipient.
biorolnictwo *n.* organic farming.
biorolnik *mp* organic farmer.
biorytm *mi* biorhythm.

biosfera *f.* biosphere; **biosfera Ziemi** the Earth's biosphere.
biosynteza *f.* biosynthesis.
biotechnologia *f. Gen.* **-ii** biotechnology.
bioterapeuta *mp,* **bioterapeutka** *f. Gen.pl.* **-ek** energy healer.
bioterapia *f. Gen.* **-ii** energy healing.
biotop *mi* biotope.
biotyp *mi biol.* biotype.
birbant *mp,* **birbantka** *f. Gen.pl.* **-ek** *przest.* idler.
biret *mi uniw.* academic hat; *kośc.* biretta.
Birma *f. geogr.* Burma, Mayanmar.
Birmanka *f. Gen.pl.* **-ek,** **Birmańczyk** *mp* Burmese.
birmański *a.* Burmese.
bis *mi* encore; **nie puścili go bez bisów** they didn't let him go without an encore; **śpiewać na bis** sing an encore. – *n. muz.* bis (*= second time*). – *a. indecl.* **1.** special; **tramwaj 15 bis** tram number 15 special. **2.** (*= powtórzony*) revisited. – *int.* encore!, play it again!
biseks *mp pl.* **-y** *pot.* bi.
biseksualista *mp,* **biseksualistka** *f. Gen.pl.* **-ek** bisexual.
biseksualizm *mi* bisexuality.
biseksualny *a.* bisexual; **zachowania/skłonności biseksualne** bisexual behavior/tendencies.
bisior *mi biol., tk.* byssus.
biskajski *a. geogr.* **Zatoka Biskajska** the Bay of Biscay.
biskup *mp kośc.* bishop; **konsekrować biskupa** ordain *l.* consecrate a bishop; **biskup Rzymu** the Bishop of Rome; **konferencja biskupów** episcopal conference; **biskup polowy** army bishop; **biskup ordynariusz** ordinary bishop; **biskup tytularny** titular bishop; **biskup pomocniczy** assistant bishop; **biskup sufragan** suffragan bishop; (bishop) suffragan; **podobny jak zając do biskupa** *pot.* as like as chalk and cheese.
biskupi *a. kośc.* bishop's, episcopal; **stolica biskupia** episcopal see; **insygnia biskupie** bishop's insignia; **sakra biskupia** episcopal sacrament; **kuria biskupia** episcopal curia; **synod biskupi** episcopal synod; **purpura biskupia** bishop's purple.
biskupstwo *n. kośc.* bishopric, episcopate; **objąć biskupstwo** assume an episcopate.
bisować *ipf.* play *l.* sing an encore.
bistro *n.* bistro.
biszkopt *mi* **1.** *Gen.* **-u** *kulin.* (*ciasto*) sponge cake. **2.** *Gen.* **-a** (*herbatnik*) biscuit.
biszkoptowy *a. kulin.* **ciasto biszkoptowe** sponge cake mix.
bit[1] *mi komp.* bit.
bit[2] *mi muz.* = **bigbit**.
bitewny *a. lit.* battle('s); **zapał bitewny** the fury of the battle; **wrzawa bitewna** the battle's roar.
bitka *f. Gen.pl.* **-ek** **1.** *pot.* (*= bijatyka*) brawl, fight, squabble. **2.** *kulin.* cutlet. **3.** *karty* (*= lewa*) trick.
bitnik *mp przest.* beatnik.
bitność *f.* military prowess.

bitny *a.* (*o żołnierzu, wojsku*) tough, hardened, soldierly.

bitowiec *mp* -wc- = bigbitowiec.

bitowy[1] *a. inform.* byte; **układ bitowy.**

bitowy[2] *a. muz.* = bigbitowy.

bitwa *f. Gen.pl.* **bitew** *l.* **bitw 1.** (*starcie wojsk*) battle; **krwawa bitwa** bloody battle; **decydująca** *l.* **walna bitwa** decisive battle; **bitwa morska** sea battle; **pole bitwy** battlefield; **stoczyć bitwę** fight a battle. **2.** *pot.* (= *awantura*) fight, row, squabble.

bity *a.* **1.** beaten; **droga bita** beaten track. **2.** (= *cały, pełny*) **bita godzina/mila** full hour/mile; **bitych pięćdziesiąt stron** fifty whole pages; **sto bitych kilometrów** a hundred kilometers on the clock.

biuletyn *mi* bulletin.

biuralista *mp* office clerk.

biurko *n. Gen.pl.* -ek desk, bureau.

biuro *n.* (*urząd*) office, bureau; (*instytucja usługowa*) agency, bureau; **biuro obsługi klientów** customer service department; **biuro podróży** travel agency *l.* bureau; **biuro pośrednictwa pracy** employment agency; **biuro informacyjne** information point *l.* bureau; **biuro polityczne** *polit., przest.* politbureau (*in Communist countries*).

biurokracja *f.* **1.** (*system*) bureaucracy. **2.** *pot.* (= *biurokratyzm*) bureaucracy, red tape; **bezduszna biurokracja** heartless bureaucracy.

biurokrata *mp*, **biurokratka** *f. Gen.pl.* -ek bureaucrat.

biurokratyczny *a.* bureaucratic; *pot.* (= *bezduszny*) officious.

biurokratyzacja *f.* bureaucratization.

biurokratyzm *mi* bureaucracy; *pot.* red tape.

biurokratyzować *ipf.* bureaucratize.

biurowiec *mi* -wc- *Gen.* -a *bud.* office block.

biurowy *a.* office; **meble/sprzęty biurowe** office furniture/equipment; **pomieszczenie biurowe** office space; **personel biurowy** office workers; **wykwalifikowana siła biurowa** qualified office staff.

biust *mi* (= *popiersie*) **1.** bust. **2.** (= *piersi*) breasts.

biustonosz *mi Gen.* -a bra, brassiere.

biwak *mi* bivouac, camp.

biwakować *ipf.* bivouac, camp.

biwakowicz *mp Gen.pl.* -ów, **biwakowiczka** *f. Gen.pl.* -ek camper.

biwakowy *a.* camping; **śpiewy biwakowe** camping songs; **sprzęt biwakowy** camping equipment.

Bizancjum *n. indecl.* Byzantium.

bizantyjski *a.* Byzantine; **sztuka bizantyjska** Byzantine art; **cesarstwo bizantyjskie** the Byzantine Empire; **styl bizantyjski** Byzantine style.

bizantynizm *mi* Byzantinism.

bizmut *mi chem.* bismuth.

biznes *mi* business.

biznesmen *mp* businessman.

biznesmenka *f.* businesswoman.

biznesowy *a.* business; **spotkanie biznesowe** business meeting; **lunch biznesowy** business lunch.

biznesplan *mi* business plan.

bizneswoman *f. indecl.* businesswoman.

bizon *ma zool.* buffalo, (American) bison (*Bison bison*).

biżuteria *f. Gen.* -ii jewelry; **sztuczna biżuteria** fake jewelry.

blacha *f.* **1.** (*materiał*) sheet, sheeting; (*gruba*) plate; **blacha cynkowa/miedziana/metalowa** sheet zinc/copper/metal; **blacha stalowa** steel sheet *l.* plate. **2.** *przen.* **wykuć coś na blachę** *pot.* learn sth by heart. **3.** (*do pieczenia*) baking sheet, baking tray; **piec coś na płaskiej blasze** bake sth on a shallow tray. **4.** (*płyta pieca kuchennego*) top plate, griddle, kitchen range; **rozpalić ogień pod blachą** light the range. **5.** *muz. pot.* brass.

blacharka *f.* = blacharstwo.

blacharnia *f. Gen.pl.* -i *l.* -ń sheet-metal shop.

blacharski *a. techn.* sheet-metal; **roboty blacharskie** sheet-metal work.

blacharstwo *n.* sheet-metal work.

blacharz *mp* sheet-metal worker.

blachowkręt *mi* metal sheet screw.

blachownia *f. Gen.pl.* -i plate shop.

bladawy *a.* palish, wan.

blado *adv.* **bladziej** *l.* **bledziej 1.** palely; (= *słabo*) weakly; (= *marnie*) poorly; **twarz wyglądająca blado** pale-looking face. **2. słońce świecące blado** palely shining sun; **uśmiechać się blado** smile weakly; manage a weak smile.

bladolicy *a. lit.* palefaced.

bladość *f.* paleness, pallor.

blady *a.* **bledszy 1.** pale, pallid; **trupio blady** (as) pale as a ghost; **blady jak ściana** (as) pale as a sheet; **blady ze złości** white with anger; **blady strach padł na kogoś** a blind panic descended on sb; **krętek blady** *biol.* syphilis spirochete (*Treponema pallidus*). **2.** (= *nieintensywny*) weak, pale; **blada herbata** weak tea; **blada zieleń** pale tea; **blade światło lampy** weak *l.* pale lamplight; **blady świt** pale dawn; **blady cień** pale shadow.

blaga *f.* tall story, confabulation, fib.

blagier *mp*, **blagierka** *f. Gen.pl.* -ek confabulator.

blagierstwo *n.* confabulating.

blagować *ipf. pot.* tell tall stories, confabulate; (= *koloryzować, fantazjować*) lay it on thick; lay it on with a trowel.

blaknąć *ipf.* -ij -kł *l.* -knął -kła -kli (= *płowieć*) fade; (= *tracić intensywność*) fade away; **blakną wspomnienia** *przen.* memories fade away *l.* fade from one's mind.

blamaż *mi Gen.pl.* -ów humiliation.

blamować się *ipf. pot.* compromise o.s.

blank *mi* **1.** *bud.* crenel; **blanki** crenelation; **mur/wieża z blankami** crenelated wall/tower. **2.** (*skóra*) white leather.

blankiet *mi* form; **blankiet urzędowy** an official form.

blankować *ipf. bud.* crenelate.

blanszować *ipf. kulin.* blanch.

blask *mi* light, shine, glare; **blask lampy** lamplight; **blask słońca** sunlight, sunshine; **blask księżyca** moonlight, moonshine; **blask gwiazd**

starlight; **odbity blask** reflected light; **blaski i cienie** light and shade; **oślepiający blask** blinding light *l.* glare; **otoczony blaskiem** bathed in light; **przydawać blasku czemuś** add luster to sth.

blaszanka *f. Gen.pl.* **-ek** tin pot, tin can.

blaszany *a.* tin; **wiadro blaszane** tin bucket; **instrumenty blaszane** *muz.* brass (instruments).

blaszka *f.* **1.** (*kawałek blachy, płaski element*) plate. **2.** (*mała forma do pieczenia*) small baking tray. **3.** *bot.* (*część liścia*) lamina. **4.** *anat.* lamella; **blaszki grzybów** lamellae, gills.

blaszkodziobe *pl. orn.* (*rząd ptaków*) anseriform (*Anseriformes*).

blaszkowaty *a. anat., bot.* lamellate.

blat *mi* table top, desktop; **blat kuchenny** kitchen countertop.

blednąć *ipf.* **-ij**; **bladł** *l.* **blednął, bladła** *l.* **bledła, bledli 1.** (= *tracić rumieńce l. kolor*) pale; grow *l.* turn pale; **zasłony blednąć od słońca** the curtains are turning white from the sun. **2.** (= *tracić intensywność*) fade (away).

bledszy *a. zob.* **blady.**

bledziej *adv. zob.* **blado.**

blef *mi* bluff.

blefować *ipf.* bluff (*w czym* at sth).

blejtram *mi mal.* stretcher.

blekot *mi bot.* fool's parsley (*Aethusa cynapium*); **bredzi, jakby się objadł blekotu** he's babbling like a fool.

blenda *f.* **1.** *bud.* blind window. **2.** *min.* blende.

blezer *mi Gen.* **-a** blazer.

blichtr *mi zw. iron.* luster, glitter.

blin *mi Gen.* **-a** *kulin. pl.* blini, blinis.

bliski *a.* **bliższy 1.** (= *nieodległy od danego stanu l. miejsca; podobny, zbliżony*) close (*czegoś* to sth); near (*czegoś* sth *l.* to sth); **bliski płaczu/załamania nerwowego** close *l.* near to tears/to a nervous breakdown; **bliski odkrycia prawdy** close *l.* near to discovering the truth; **to, co mówisz, jest bliskie prawdy** what you're saying is close to the truth; **bliższy oryginału** closer to the original, nearer the original; **czuć się bliskim śmierci** feal close *l.* near to death; **bliska odległość** short distance, nearness, closeness; **bliskie spotkanie** close encounter. **2.** *sup.* (= *położony tuż obok, następny*) next; **najbliższy sąsiad** one's next-door neighbour; **w najbliższym roku** next year; in the coming year. **3.** (= *blisko spokrewniony*) close, near; **bliski krewny/kuzyn** close *l.* near relative/cousin. **4.** (= *mający się wkrótce zdarzyć*) near, approaching, imminent; *lit.* nigh; **w najbliższej przyszłości** *l.* **w najbliższym czasie** in the nearest future; **koniec jest już bliski** the end is near *l.* nigh; **bliskie niebezpieczeństwo** imminent danger. **5.** (= *niedawno miniony*) recent. **6.** (= *drogi, serdeczny, darzony uczuciem*) close, dear; **być bliskim czyjemuś sercu** be close to sb's heart; **ona jest mi bardzo bliska** she's very dear to me; **bliska przyjaźń** close *l.* intimate friendship; **nawiązać z kimś bliższe stosunki** become closely acquainted with sb; **moi najbliżsi** *żart.* my nearest and dearest; **bliższa koszula ciału, niż sukmana**

przen. near is my shirt but nearer is my skin. **7.** *comp.* (= *dokładniejszy*) more accurate, more precise, more detailed; **bliższe dane/informacje** more accurate data/information. **8.** *gram.* **dopełnienie bliższe** direct object. – *mp* (= *bliski krewny*) close *l.* near relative.

blisko *adv.* **bliżej 1.** (= *niedaleko*) close (*czegoś* to sth); near (by); **blisko rzeki** close to the river; **rzeka jest dość blisko** the river is quite near (by); **mam blisko do szkoły** I live close to school; **osoba bliżej ciebie** the person closer to you *l.* nearer you. **2.** (= *tuż obok, w sąsiedztwie*) next door, in the vicinity. **3.** **z bliska** (= *z małej odległości*) from close range, at close quarters; **strzelać do kogoś z bliska** fire point-blank at sb; (= *szczegółowo*) closely, in a detailed manner. **4.** (= *w bliskiej przyszłości*) not long, close; **jest blisko do Wielkanocy** it's not long to Easter; **Wielkanoc jest już blisko** Easter's approaching. **5.** (*o pokrewieństwie l. przyjaźni*) closely; **blisko spokrewniony** closely related (*z kimś/czymś* to sb/sth); **oni są ze sobą bardzo blisko** they're very close friends. **6.** *comp.* (= *dokładniej*) more accurately, in more detail; **czy możesz go bliżej opisać?** can you describe him in more detail?; **człowiek bliżej mi nieznany** man unknown to me. **7.** (*z liczebnikami l. jednostkami miar*) (= *prawie, niemal*) almost, nearly, close on; **czekam na ciebie blisko godzinę** I've been waiting for you almost an hour; **ma blisko 60 lat** he's close on 60 years old; **to blisko kilometr stąd** it's almost a kilometer from here.

bliskość *f.* **1.** (= *mała odległość w czasie l. przestrzeni*) nearness, closeness; *form.* proximity; **bliskość jeziora** the nearness *l.* proximity of the lake. **2.** (= *serdeczność*) closeness, intimacy; **uczucie bliskości między matką a córką** the feelings of closeness between a mother and daughter. **3.** *arch.* (= *sąsiedztwo, pobliże*) vicinity, neighborhood; **w bliskości** near by; in the vicinity.

bliskowschodni *a. geogr.* Near Eastern; Middle Eastern.

bliskoznacznik *mi Gen.* **-a** *jęz.* synonym.

bliskoznaczność *f. jęz.* synonymity.

bliskoznaczny *a. jęz.* synonymous; **wyraz bliskoznaczny** synonym.

bliziutko *adv. emf.* really close.

blizna *f.* **1.** scar; *pat.* cicatrix; **blizna po ranie** scar from a wound; **blizna od oparzenia** burn mark; **blizna na brzuchu/twarzy** scar on the stomach/face; **blizna pooperacyjna** *chir.* operation scar; **pozostawić bliznę na kimś/czymś** *t. przen.* leave a scar on sb/sth. **2.** *bot.* cicatrix. **3.** *techn.* defect.

bliznowacieć *ipf.* form a scar.

bliznowaty *a.* scar; *form.* cicatricial; **tkanka bliznowata** scar tissue, cicatrix.

bliźni *mp* fellow human being; *zwł. rel.* neighbor; **kochaj bliźniego swego** love thy neighbor.

bliźniaczka *f. Gen.pl.* **-ek** twin sister.

bliźniaczo *adv.* identically.

bliźniaczy *a.* **1.** (= *występujący w parze l. komplecie*) twin; **miasta bliźniacze** twin towns; **bliź-**

niacze liczby pierwsze *mat.* twin primes. **2.** (= *bardzo podobny*) twin-like, identical; **bliźniacze podobieństwo** twin-like resemblance. **3.** *biol.* geminate.

bliźniak *mp pl.* -ki *l.* -cy twin. – *mi Gen.* -a *pl.* -i **1.** *bud.* semi-detached villa, semi. **2.** *odzież* twin-set. **3.** *krystalografia* twin.

bliźnię *n.* -ęci- *pl.* -ęt- *Gen.* -ąt **1.** twin; **bliźnięta jednojajowe** identical twins; **bliźnięta dwujajowe** non-identical twins. **2. Bliźnięta** *astron.* Gemini; *pot.* the Twins; **Bliźnię** (*astrol.* = *osoba spod znaku Bliźniąt*) Gemini (*sg.*).

bliżej *adv. zob.* **blisko.**

bliższy *a. zob.* **bliski.**

bloczek *mi* -czk- *Gen.* -a **1.** (*do notowania*) pad, notepad. **2.** *pot.* (= *kupon*) coupon. **3.** *mech.* pulley.

blok *mi* **1.** (= *bryła, odłam*) block; **blok granitu** block of granite; **blok skalny** rock fragment. **2.** *techn.* (= *zespół urządzeń*) unit. **3.** *bud.* block; **blok mieszkalny** apartment house; *Br.* block of flats. **4.** (= *barak więzienny*) (prison) block. **5.** (*do rysunków l. pisania*) pad, block; **blok rysunkowy** sketch pad. **6.** *polit.* bloc, pact; **blok wyborczy** election bloc. **7.** (*zgrupowanie tematyczne, zwł. audycji radiowych l. TV*) block; **blok sportowy** sports block; **blok reklam** commercial pod; block of commercials. **8.** *druk.* die, (printing) block. **9.** *techn.* (= *urządzenie blokujące*) *fizj., psych., sport* (= *zablokowanie, zatrzymanie*) block; **blok serca** *pat.* heart block. **10.** *mech.* (= *krążek lub układ krążków wraz z obudową*) block, pulley; (= *wielokrążek*) block and tackle; compound pulley. **11.** *sport* **blok startowy** starting block.

blokada *f.* **1.** blockade; **blokada ekonomiczna** *polit.* economic blockade; **blokada morska/powietrzna** *polit., wojsk.* sea/air blockade; **blokada pokojowa** pacific blockade; **blokada policyjna/wojskowa** police/military blockade; **ustanowić/zastosować blokadę** declare/put up a blockade; **znieść** *l.* **uchylić blokadę** lift *l.* raise a blockade; **przełamać blokadę** *zwł. żegl.* run *l.* break a blockade; **blokada dróg** road block. **2.** *techn., sport* (= *zapobieżenie czemuś*) block; **blokada połączeń wychodzących** *telefon* dial block. **3.** *el.* interlock. **4.** *kol.* blocking system. **5.** *mot., techn.* (= *zablokowanie się mechanizmu*) lock. **6.** *mot.* (*zabezpieczenie samochodu*) immobilizer; **blokada kierownicy** steering-wheel lock. **7.** *mot.* (*unieruchomienie samochodu*) **blokada kół** wheel clamp; **założyć blokadę na koło** clamp a wheel. **8.** *pat.* blockage. **9.** *chir.* **blokada nerwu** nerve block.

bloker *mi biochem., med.* blocker.

blokers *mp sl.* downtown kid.

blokować *ipf.* **1.** (= *tarasować, zatrzymywać*) block (up); **blokować drogę** block a road. **2.** *polit., wojsk.* (= *obejmować blokadą*) blockage.

blokowisko *n. emf. uj.* bleak apartment houses.

blokowy *a.* **1.** (= *dotyczący bloku mieszkalnego*) apartment-house. **2.** *techn.* block; **schemat/układ blokowy** block diagram/arrangement. –

mp hist. (= *więzień zarządzający blokiem w obozie*) block overseer.

blond *a. indecl.* blond; **włosy blond** blond hair.

blondas *mp pl.* -y *żart.* blondie.

blondyn *mp* blond; **jasny/ciemny blondyn** light/dark blond; **świński blondyn** *pot. uj.* albino.

blondynka *f. Gen.pl.* -ek blonde; **jasna/ciemna blondynka** light blonde; **platynowa blondynka** platinum blonde.

blotka *f. Gen.pl.* -ek *karty* small card.

blues *mi Gen.* -a *muz.* blues.

bluesowy *a. muz.* blues; **kapela bluesowa** blues band.

bluszcz *mi Gen.pl.* -y *l.* -ów *bot.* ivy.

bluszczowaty *a.* **1.** (= *podobny do bluszczu*) ivy-like. **2.** *przen. uj.* (= *niesamodzielny*) dependent; (= *chwiejny*) pliable.

bluza *f.* tunic, shirt, jacket, blouse; **bluza harcerska** scout shirt; **bluza marynarska** sailor's smock; **bluza robocza** work shirt.

bluzeczka *f. Gen.pl.* -ek top.

bluzgać *ipf.*, **bluzgnąć** *pf.* -ij **1.** + *Ins. emf.* (= *tryskać*) spurt, gush, spew (*sth*); **bluzgać jadem** *przen.* spit venom (*na kogoś* at sb). **2.** *pot.* (= *kląć*) cuss, swear, spit out curses.

bluzka *f. Gen.pl.* -ek blouse, tunic, top; **bluzka z krótkimi rękawami** short-sleeved top; **bluzka bez rękawów** sleeveless blouse.

bluznąć *pf.* -znę -zniesz, -znij = bluzgnąć; *zob.* **bluzgać.**

bluźnić *ipf.* -ij **1.** *rel.* blaspheme (*przeciwko komuś/czemuś* against sb/sth). **2.** *pot.* (= *kląć*) blaspheme, swear (*na kogoś/coś* at sb/sth).

bluźnierca *mp* blasphemer.

bluźnierczy *a.* blasphemous.

bluźnierczyni *f. zob.* **bluźnierca.**

bluźnierstwo *n.* blasphemy; **bluźnierstwo przeciwko Bogu** blasphemy against God; **miotać bluźnierstwa** hurl blasphemies (*na kogoś/coś* at sb/sth).

błagać *ipf.* beg, beseech, implore, entreat (*sb*) (*o coś* for sth); **błagam cię, żebyś mnie wysłuchał** I beg you to hear me out; **błagam!** please!; **błagać (od) kogoś zmiłowania** *arch.* beg mercy of sb.

błagalnie *adv.* imploringly.

błagalny *a.* imploring; *rel.* propitiatory.

błahostka *f.* trifle.

błahy *a.* trivial, trifling; **błaha sprawa** trivial matter; **z błahej przyczyny** for no reason.

błam *mi* **1.** (= *podszycie futrzane*) fur lining; (*ze skór owczych*) fleece lining. **2.** (= *skórka zwierzęcia futerkowego*) skin.

bławatek *mi* -tk- *Gen.* -a (= *chaber*) cornflower (*Centaurea cyanus*).

błazen *mp* -zn- *Loc. i Voc.* -źnie *pl.* -zny *l.* -źni **1.** (= *klown*) clown; **błazen cyrkowy** circus clown. **2.** (= *głupiec*) fool. **3.** *hist.* jester, fool; **błazen dworski** court jester.

błazenada *f.* tomfoolery.

błazeński *a.* clownish; **błazeńska mina** clownish expression; **błazeński śmiech** clownish laugh; **strój błazeński** motley.

błaznować *ipf.* clown (about *l.* around), play the goat.

błaźnić się *ipf.* **-ij** make a fool of o.s. (*wobec kogoś* in front of sb).

błąd *mi* **-ę-** mistake, error; **popełnić błąd** make a mistake; commit an error; **błąd ortograficzny** misspelling, spelling mistake *l.* error; **błąd wymowy** mispronunciation; **błąd w obliczeniach** miscalculation; **błąd ludzki** human error; **błąd komputera** computer error; **błąd drukarski** printer's error, misprint; **błąd maszynowy** typo, mistyping; **robić błędy gramatyczne** make grammatical mistakes; **być w błędzie** be mistaken; be in error; **wprowadzić kogoś w błąd** mislead sb; **wyprowadzić kogoś z błędu** set sb straight; **popełnić gruby błąd** make a big mistake; **błędy młodości** mistakes of youth; **niewybaczalny błąd** unforgivable mistake; **zdać sobie sprawę ze swoich błędów** see the error of one's ways; **wytykać komuś błędy** point out sb's mistakes.

błądzić *ipf.* **1.** (= *gubić drogę*) lose one's way; **kto pyta, nie błądzi** it's better to ask first. **2.** (= *chodzić bez celu*) wander, roam, rove, walk at random; **błądzić (gdzieś) myślami** be lost in thought. **3.** *lit.* (= *czynić źle, mylić się*) go astray, err; **błądzić jest rzeczą ludzką** to err is human.

błąkać się *ipf.* drift, roam, wander about *l.* around; **błąkać się po mieście** wander around town.

błędnie *adv.* **1.** (= *niepoprawnie, niewłaściwie*) erroneously, incorrectly, wrongly; **błędnie interpretować dane** misinterpret the data; **napisać wyraz błędnie** misspell a word; spell a word incorrectly. **2.** (= *nieprzytomnie, obłąkanie*) blindly, wildly.

błędnik *mi* Gen. **-a** *anat.* labyrinth.

błędny *a.* **1.** (= *nieprawdziwy*) untrue, false; (= *niepoprawny*) wrong, incorrect, erroneous; **błędne obliczenia** miscalculation; **błędne założenie** false assumption; **błędne rozumowanie** incorrect reasoning; **błędne użycie przyimka** wrong use of a pronoun; **błędne koło** *log.* vicious circle. **2.** (= *nieprzytomny, obłąkany*) blind, wild; **błędny wzrok** blind look. **3.** *arch.* (= *zagubiony, błądzący*) lost, wandering; **chodzić jak błędna owca** wander like a lost sheep; **błędny rycerz** knight errant; **błędny ognik** *t. przen.* will o'the wisp; **nerw błędny** *anat.* vagus (nerve).

błędu *itp. mi zob.* **błąd.**

błękit *mi* **1.** (*kolor*) azure, (sky) blue; **błękit nieba** the sky's blue; **błękit czyichś oczu** the blue of sb's eyes. **2.** *przen.* (= *niebo*) the blue sky. **3.** *chem.* blue (pigment); **błękit pruski/paryski** Prussian/Parisian blue; **błękit indygowy** (synthetic) indigo.

błękitnooki *a.* blue-eyed.

błękitny *a.* blue, sky-blue; **błękitna krew** *przen.* blue blood.

błocić *ipf.* track mud; **błocić w domu** make the house muddy; **błocić sobie buty** get one's shoes muddy. **~ się** *ipf.* get muddy.

błocko *n emf.* mud, muck; **ugrzęznąć w błocku** get stuck in the mud.

błogi *a.* blissful, blessed; **błogi nastrój** blissful mood, bliss; **błogi spokój** blessed peace *l.* calm;

błogie ciepło blessed warmth; **błogi uśmiech** blissful smile.

błogo *adv.* blissfully; **jest mi błogo na duszy/sercu** it does my soul/heart good.

błogosławić *ipf.* **1.** *rel.* (= *udzielać błogosławieństwa*) bless; **błogosławić wiernych w kościele** bless the faithful in church; **niech ci Bóg błogosławi!** God bless you! **2.** (= *wspominać z wdzięcznością*) bless; **błogosławię chwilę, w której...** I bless the moment when...; **błogosławię los za ten dzień** I bless fate for that day.

błogosławieństwo *n.* **1.** *rel.* blessing, benediction; **udzielać komuś błogosławieństwa** give the benediction to sb; **ojcowskie błogosławieństwo** father's blessing; **obsypać błogosławieństwami** cover sb in blessings; **błogosławieństwa na górze** *Bibl.* the beatitudes. **2.** (= *dobrodziejstwo*) blessing; **być dla kogoś (prawdziwym) błogosławieństwem** be a (real) blessing to sb; **błogosławieństwo losu** blessed by fate.

błogosławiony *a.* **-eni** blessed; **niech będzie błogosławiona chwila, w której...** blessed be the moment when...; **być w błogosławionym stanie** *euf.* be expecting (a child). **– *mp rz.-kat.*** blessed; **błogosławione i błogosławieni Kościoła** the blessed of the Church; **uznany za błogosławionego** beatified.

błogostan *mi* (state *l.* feeling of) bliss; **zapaść w błogostan** fall into a state of bliss.

błogość *f.* bliss; **ogarnia mnie błogość** a feeling of bliss comes over me; **doznać błogości** experience bliss; **czuć błogość duszy** feel the soul's bliss.

błona *f.* **1.** *anat.* membrane; **błona komórkowa** cell membrane; **błona śluzowa** mucous membrane; **błony płodowe** embryonic membranes; **błona bębenkowa** tympanic membrane; **błona dziewicza** hymen, maidenhead; **błona półprzepuszczalna** *biochem.* semipermeable membrane; **błona skrzydeł** *zool.* wing membrane, patagium; **błona pławna** *zool.* webbing, web. **2.** (= *cienka warstwa*) film. **3.** *fot.* (photographic) film; **błona czarno-biała/kolorowa** black-and-white/color film.

błoniasty *a.* membranous; **błoniaste skrzydła** membranous wings.

błonica *f.* **1.** *pat.* diphtheria. **2.** *bot.* sea lettuce (*Ulva*).

błonie *n.* Gen.pl. **-ń** common, green; grassland.

błonka *f.* Gen.pl. **-ek** *anat.* **1.** membrane. **2.** (= *warstewka*) film.

błonkoskrzydłe *pl. decl. like a.*, **błonkówki** *pl.* Gen. **-ek** *ent.* hymenopterans (*Hymenoptera*).

błonnik *mi* Gen. **-a** *chem.* cellulose.

błotniak *ma orn.* harrier (*Circus*).

błotniarka *f.* Gen.pl. **-ek** *zool.* pond snail (*Lymnaea*).

błotnik *mi* Gen. **-a** mudguard.

błotnisty *a.* muddy, sludgy.

błotny *a.* *biol.* marsh; **rośliny błotne** marsh plants, helophytes; **ptactwo błotne** marsh birds; **gaz błotny** marsh gas.

błoto *n.* **1.** mud, sludge; **ugrzęznąć w błocie**

get stuck in the mud; **ubrudzić sobie błotem buty** get mud on one's shoes; **błoto lecznicze** *med.* mudpack. **2.** *przen.* **wyrzucać pieniądze w błoto** throw one's money away; **mieszać kogoś z błotem** drag sb *l.* sb's name through the mud; **obrzucać kogoś błotem** throw *l.* fling mud at sb. **3.** *pl.* marsh, bog, swamp.

błysk *mi* flash, flicker, gleam.

błyskać *ipf.* **1.** + *Ins.* (= *migotać, świecić*) flash (*sth*); **błyskać zębami** flash one's teeth. **2.** (= *jaśnieć, zapalać się*) flash. **3.** *przen.* (= *olśniewać*) sparkle; **błyskać dowcipem/talentem** sparkle with wit/talent. **4.** *przen.* (= *uzewnętrzniać się*) sparkle, flicker; **radość błyskała z jej oczu** happiness sparkled in her eyes. **~ się** *ipf.* (*o błyskawicy*) flash; **błyska się** lightning is flashing.

błyskawica *f.* (flash *l.* streak of) lightning; **szybki jak błyskawica** as fast as lightning; **lotem błyskawicy** at lightning speed; **ciskał błyskawice z oczu** lightning flashed from his eyes.

błyskawicznie *adv.* like lightning, instantly, immediately.

błyskawiczny *a.* (*szybki*) lightning, instant; **błyskawiczna reakcja** instant reaction; **wojna błyskawiczna** *wojsk.* blitzkrieg; **zamek błyskawiczny** zip; **zupa błyskawiczna** instant soup.

błyskotka *f. Gen.pl.* **-ek** bauble, tinsel.

błyskotliwie *adv.* brilliantly.

błyskotliwy *a.* **1.** (= *olśniewający*) brilliant; **błyskotliwa odpowiedź** brilliant answer; **błyskotliwy umysł/pomysł** brilliant mind/idea. **2.** *rzad.* (= *mieniący się*) glittering, shining.

błyskowy *a. fot.* flash; **lampa błyskowa** flash bulb.

błysnąć *pf.* **-snę -śniesz, -ij;** **-snął snęła** *l.* **-sła 1.** *zob.* **błyskać. 2.** (= *pojawić się niespodziewanie*) flash; **błysnął mi pewien pomysł** an idea flashed into my mind.

błystka *f. wędkarswo* lure.

błyszcz *mi Gen.pl.* **-y** *l.* **-ów 1.** = **błystka. 2.** *min.* glance; **błyszcz antymonu/bizmutu** antimony/bismuth glance.

błyszczący *a.* sparkling, shining, glittering, glossy.

błyszczeć *ipf.* **-ę -ysz 1.** (= *lśnić*) shine, glitter, glisten. **2.** (= *olśniewać*) = **błyskać 3. ~ się** *ipf.* = **błyszczeć 1.**

błyszczyk *mi Gen.* **-a 1.** *wędkarstwo* = **błystka. 2.** (= *pomadka*) lip gloss. **3.** *min.* (= *mika*) mica.

bm. *abbr.* (= *bieżącego miesiąca*) of the current month; this month.

bniec *mi* **bieńc-** *Gen.* **-a** *bot.* catchfly (*Silene*).

bo *conj.* **1.** (= *ponieważ*) because, for; **nie pójdę do kina, bo jestem zajęty** I'm not going to the movies because I'm busy. **2.** (= *w przeciwnym razie*) or; **bądź grzeczny, bo nie dostaniesz deseru** be good or you'll get no dessert. **3.** (*w funkcji dopowiedzenia, wyjaśnienia*) because, as, for; **te buty są niewygodne, bo za ciasne** these shoes are uncomfortable because they're too tight; **sekretarz, bo o niego chodziło, w tej sprawie milczał** the secretary, for it was he who was involved, said nothing about it. – *part.* **1.** (*wzmacnia przeciwstawienie*) **przystojny, bo przystojny, ale kompletnie głupi** handsome to be sure, but utterly stupid. **2.** (*wzmacnia przeczenie albo powątpiewanie*) **a bo ja wiem?** how should I know?; **a bo to prawda?** I doubt if it's true.

boa *ma indecl. zool.* (= *wąż z rodziny Boidae*) boa; **boa dusiciel** boa constrictor (*Boa constrictor*). – *n. indecl.* (*szal*) (feather) boa.

boazeria *f. Gen.* **-ii** wood panelling, wainscot.

bobak *ma zool.* bobac (*Marmota bobac*).

bobas *ma*, **bobasek** *ma* **-sk-** *emf.* (little) baby; **rozkoszny/śliczny bobas** gorgeous/cute little baby.

bobek *mi* **-bk-** *Gen.* **-a** piece of droppings; **sarnie/królicze bobki** roedeer/rabbit droppings.

bobem *itd. mi zob.* **bób.**

bobkowy *a. bot.* **drzewo bobkowe** (= *wawrzyn*) (true) laurel, bay tree (*Laurus nobilis*); **liść bobkowy** *kulin.* bay leaf.

bobo *n. indecl. dziec.* baby.

bobra *itd. ma zob.* **bóbr.**

bobrować *ipf.* **1.** *pot.* (= *szperać*) rummage, ferret about. **2.** *myśl.* wade.

bobrowy *a.* beaver('s); **tama bobrowa** beaver dam.

bobry *pl. Gen.* **-ów** (*futro*) beaver fur.

bobsleista *mp*, **bobsleistka** *f. Gen.pl.* **-ek** *sport* bobsledder; *Br.* bobsleigher.

bobslej *mi Gen.* **-a** *l.* **-u** *Gen.pl.* **-ów** *l.* **-ei** *sport* bobsled; *Br.* bobsleigh.

bochen *mi* **-chn-** *Gen.* **-a** (large) loaf; **bochen chleba** loaf of bread.

bochenek *mi* **-nk-** *Gen.* **-a** loaf.

bocian *ma* **1.** *zool.* stork (*Ciconia*); **sejm bocianów** mustering of storks; **klekot bociana** the clacking of a stork; **bocian biały** (common) white stork (*C. ciconia*); **bocian czarny** black stork (*C. nigra*). **2.** *techn.* (*nóż tokarski*) bar-and-knee turning tool.

bociani *a.* stork's; **bocianie gniazdo** stork's nest; *przen. żegl.* crow's nest.

bociek *ma* **-ćk-** *Gen.* **-a** *dziec.* = **bocian.**

boczek *mi* **-czk-** **1.** *kulin.* (streaky) bacon; **jajka na boczku** bacon and eggs; **boczek wędzony** smoked bacon. **2.** *emf.* (= *bok*) side; **na boczku** *pot.* on the side. **3.** *druk.* side heading.

boczkiem *adv.* sideways; **wymknąć się boczkiem** sidle out.

boczniak *mi Gen.* **-a** *bot., kulin.* oyster mushroom, oyster fungus (*Pleurotus*).

bocznica *f.* **1.** *kol.* siding; **na bocznicy** in the sidings. **2.** *rzad.* (= *boczna ulica*) side street.

bocznik *mi Gen.* **-a 1.** *el.* shunt. **2.** *techn.* side rabbet plane.

bocznikować *v. el.* shunt.

boczny *a.* side; **boczna ulica** side street; **boczne wejście** side entrance; **boczny tor** siding; **kieszeń boczna** hip pocket; **boczna linia kolejowa** branch line; **boczne światło** side light; **boczna kaplica** side chapel; **chodzić bocznymi drogami** *przen.* take the backroads; **boczna ścieżka** byway.

boczyć się *ipf.* (= *dąsać się*) bridle (*na kogoś / coś* at sb/sth); (= *być naburmuszonym*) sulk.

boćwina, boćwinka *f. zob.* **botwina.**

bodaj *int. przest. (wzmacnia życzenie)* (I) would that...; **bodajś tu nigdy więcej nie wrócił** would that you never returned; **bodajby każdy urzędnik był tak miły jak pan** would that every official was as nice as you; **bodajbym się nigdy nie urodził!** would that I had never been born. – *adv. (osłabia treść)* I think; **było to bodaj w maju** it was in May, I think; **miała bodaj jakieś kłopoty ze zdrowiem** I think she had some health problems; **daj mi czas bodaj do jutra** at least give me until tomorrow; **to bodaj dobra książka** it's a good book, I think.

bodajbym, bodajbyś *itd. int. zob.* **bodaj.**

bodajże *adv.* = **bodaj.**

bodę, bodzie *itd. ipf. zob.* **bóść.**

bodnąć *pf.* **-ij** *zob.* **bóść.**

body *n. indecl.* strój body.

bodziec *mi* **-dźc-** *Gen.* **-a 1.** *nauk.* (= *czynnik wywołujący reakcję*) stimulus; **bodziec chemiczny/wzrokowy** chemical/visual stimulus; **bodziec progowy** threshold stimulus; **bodziec negatywny** aversive stimulus; **bodziec-reakcja** stimulus and response. **2.** (= *zachęta do działania*) stimulus, incentive, goad; **bodziec do pracy** work incentive; **bodziec do dyskusji** stimulus for the conversation; **dostarczać komuś bodźców (do działania)** give sb incentives (to work); spur sb on; **bodźce ekonomiczne** economic stimuli. **3.** *przest.* (= *ostry kij do popędzania bydła*) goad; (= *ostroga*) spur.

bodziszek *mi* **-szk-** *Gen.* **-a** *bot.* geranium, cranesbill (*Geranium*); **bodziszek cuchnący** herb Robert (*G. robertianum*).

bodźcowy *a.* **1.** *fizj., med.* stimulus, stimulation; **terapia bodźcowa** stimulation therapy. **2.** (= *dotyczący zachęty*) incentive; **system bodźcowy** incentive system.

boga *itd. mp zob.* **bóg.**

bogacić *ipf.* **1.** (= *przysparzać majątku*) enrich. **2.** (= *doskonalić, urozmaicać*) enrich, enhance; **bogacić swoje życie duchowe** enrich one's spiritual life. **~ się** *ipf.* **1.** (= *stawać się zamożniejszym*) get rich *l.* richer (*czymś kosztem* off sb) (*na czymś* from sth); **jeden traci, drugi się bogaci** the rich get richer, the poor get poorer. **2.** (= *doskonalić się*) become enriched *l.* enhanced.

bogactwo *n.* **1.** (= *majątek*) wealth, fortune, riches, plenty; **gardzić bogactwem** despise riches; **zdobyć bogactwo** acquire wealth; make *l.* amass a fortune. **2.** *zw. pl.* (= *zasób*) resource, riches; **bogactwa mineralne/naturalne** *ekon.* mineral/natural resources. **3.** (= *obfitość, rozmaitość*) richness, wealth, abundance; **bogactwo dźwięków/barw** richness of sound/color.

bogacz *mp* rich man; *Bibl., lit.* Dives.

bogaczka *f. Gen.pl.* **-ek** rich woman.

Bogarodzica *f. arch., rz.-kat.* Mother of God.

bogatka *f. Gen.pl.* **-ek** *orn.* great tit (*Parus maior*).

bogato *adv.* **1.** (= *różnorodnie, obficie*) richly, copiously, abundantly; **bogato ilustrowany** richly illustrated. **2.** (= *zamożnie*) wealthily; **bogato się ożenić** marry money.

bogaty *a.* **1.** (= *zamożny*) rich, wealthy, well-off, well-to-do. **2.** (= *zasobny*) rich, well-stocked; abounding (*w coś* in sth); **bogate zbiory** rich collection; **kraj bogaty w ropę naftową** oil-rich country; country abounding in oil. **3.** (= *różnorodny*) rich; **bogata osobowość/twórczość** rich personality/creativity. **4.** (= *obficie zdobiony*) rich, copious; **bogaty wystrój** rich decoration. – *mp decl. like a.* (*bogacz*) rich man; *pl.* the rich.

bogdanka *f. Gen.pl.* **-ek** *arch. l. żart.* one' beloved, lady-love.

bogini *f.* **1.** goddess. **2. bogini piękności/seksu** *przen.* goddess of beauty/sex.

boginka *f. Gen.pl.* **-ek** *mit. l. przen.* nymph.

bogobojnie *adv.* piously.

bogobojność *f.* fear of God, piousness.

bogobojny *a.* God-fearing.

bogoojczyźniany *a. iron.* jingoistic.

bohater *mp pl.* **-owie** *l.* **-rzy 1.** (= *człowiek wyjątkowej odwagi*) hero; **bohater powstania** hero of an uprising; **cichy bohater** silent hero; **zginąć jak bohater** die a hero('s) death. **2.** (*w literaturze, filmie*) hero; **bohater literacki** literary hero; **główny bohater** the hero, the chief character. **3.** (= *ktoś chwilowo ważny*) hero, celebrity; **bohater mistrzostw** the hero of the championships; **bohater dnia** the hero of the day *l.* hour; **powitać kogoś jako bohatera** give sb a hero's welcome. **4.** *mit.* (= *heros*) hero.

bohaterka *f. Gen.pl.* **-ek** heroine; **(główna) bohaterka powieści** the heroine of the novel; **bohaterka wieczoru** the heroine of the evening.

bohaterski *a.* (*dzielny*) **1.** heroic; **bohaterski czyn** heroic act; **bohaterska śmierć** heroic *l.* hero's death. **2.** (*w sztuce, muzyce, literaturze*) **tenor bohaterski** *muz.* heroic tenor; **strofa bohaterska** *teor.lit.* heroic stanza.

bohatersko *adv.* heroically; **zginąć bohatersko** *l.* **po bohatersku** die heroically, die a hero('s) death.

bohaterstwo *n.* heroism.

bohema *f. lit.* (= *cyganeria artystyczna*) bohemians.

Bohemia *f. Gen.* **-ii** *geogr., hist.* Bohemia.

bohemistka *f. Gen.pl.* **-ek**, **bohemista** *mp* expert in Czech studies.

bohemistyczny *a.* (*o studiach itp.*) Czech.

bohemistyka *f.* Czech studies.

bohemizm *mi* Czechism.

bohomaz *mi uj.* daub, kitschy painting.

boi *itd. ipf. zob.* **bać się.**

boi *itd. f. zob.* **boja.**

boisko *n.* **1.** *sport* playing field, field of play; **boisko piłkarskie/baseballowe** soccer/baseball pitch. **2.** *przest.* (= *klepisko*) threshing floor.

boja *f. Gen. sg. i pl.* **boi** *żegl.* buoy; **boja świetlna** (floating) beacon; **boja dźwiękowa** sound buoy.

bojar *mp pl.* **-rzy** *l.* **-owie** *hist.* boyar.

bojarski *a. hist.* boyar('s).

bojarzyn *mp pl.* **-owie** *arch.* = **bojar.**

bojaźliwy *a.* timorous, timid, anxious, apprehensive.

bojaźń *f. lit.* fear, dread (*czegoś l. przed czymś*

of sth); **bojaźń Boża** fear of God; **bojaźń śmierci** fear of death; **okazywać bojaźń** show fear *l.* dread.

bojer *mi Gen.* **-a** *sport* iceboat; **regaty bojerów** iceboat regatta.

bojerowiec *mp* **-wc-** *pl.* **-y** *sport* iceboat racer.

bojerowy *a. sport* iceboat.

boję *itd. ipf. zob.* **bać się**.

bojkot *mi* boycott; **zastosować bojkot** stage a boycott.

bojkotować *ipf.* boycott.

bojler *mi Gen.* **-a** *techn.* boiler.

bojować *ipf. przest.* war, wage war.

bojowniczka *f. Gen.pl.* **-ek** *zob.* **bojownik** *mp.*

bojownik *mp pl.* **-cy** warrior, champion, fighter; **nieugięty bojownik** indomitable warrior; **bojnicy o wolność** freedom fighters. – *ma* **1.** *orn.* (= *batalion*) (*gatunek i samiec*) ruff; (*samica*) reeve (*Philomachus pugnax*). **2.** *icht.* **bojownik syjamski** betta, Siamese fighting fish (*Betta splendens*).

bojowo *adv.* militantly, aggressively.

bojowość *f.* **1.** (= *waleczność*) valiancy, combativeness; **bojowość oddziałów frontowych** the combativeness of the front divisions. **2.** (= *bezkompromisowość, agresywność*) militancy, aggressiveness.

bojowy *a.* **1.** (= *waleczny*) valiant, warlike. **2.** (= *wojenny*) military, combat, operational; **akcja bojowa** military action, combat; **oddziały/siły bojowe** combat troops/forces; **wóz bojowy** fighting vehicle, combat vehicle; **lotnictwo bojowe** combat aircraft; **bojowy gaz** *l.* **środek trujący** military gas; chemical warfare agent; **gotowość bojowa** operational readiness; **szyk bojowy** military formation; **lot bojowy** military flight; **w stanie bojowym** battle-ready; **okrzyk bojowy** battlecry; **rozkaz bojowy** military order; **rozpoznanie bojowe** military reconnaissance; **chrzest bojowy** *przen.* baptism of fire; **organizacja bojowa** *polit.* militia; paramilitary organisation. **3.** (= *bezkompromisowy, agresywny*) militant, aggressive, combative.

bojówka *f. Gen.pl.* **-ek** militia, armed group; *uj.* gang of henchmen *l.* thugs.

bojówkarski *a.* militia, paramilitary.

bojówkarz *mp* militiaman; *uj.* thug, henchman.

boju *itd. mi zob.* **bój**.

bok *mi* **1.** (= *boczna powierzchnia* *l.* *strona*) side, flank; **leżeć na prawym/lewym boku** lie on the right/left side; **z lewego/prawego boku** from the left/right (side); **przewracać się z boku na bok** turn from side to side; **wziąć się pod boki** stand with arms akimbo; **coś jest pod bokiem** sth is under one's nose; **mieć kogoś/coś u boku** have sb/sth at *l.* by one's side; **zrywać boki ze śmiechu** split one's sides with laughter; **odłożyć coś na bok** put sth to one side; *przen.* (= *odłożyć na później, zaoszczędzić, zignorować*) put sth aside; **na bok!** out of the way!; stand aside!; **żarty na bok** joking aside; **zostawić coś na boku** leave sth aside; **pozostawać** *l.* **trzymać się na boku** (= *nie angażować się*) keep out of the way; stay clear;

dorabiać sobie na boku earn on the side; **podejść z boku** approach from the side; **mieć kogoś na boku** *pot.* have a bit on the side; **robić bokami** *pot.* cope with difficulty; **jeszcze ci to wyjdzie bokiem** *pot.* you'll regret it yet. **2.** (= *krawędź powierzchni*) side; **dłuższe boki stołu** the longer sides of the table; **boki trójkąta** *geom.* the sides of a triangle.

bokiem *adv.* (= *jednym bokiem naprzód*) sideways, edgeways; (= *poboczem*) on *l.* along one side.

bokobrody *pl. Gen.* **-ów** sideburns, whiskers; *Br.* sideboards.

boks[1] *mi Gen.* **-u** *tylko sg. sport* boxing; **uprawiać boks** box; **boks amatorski** amateur boxing; **boks zawodowy** professional boxing, prizefighting.

boks[2] *mi Gen.* **-u** *pl.* **-y** (*pomieszczenie*) box, compartment.

bokser *mp sport* boxer, fighter; **bokser wagi ciężkiej/średniej/lekkiej** heavyweight/middleweight/lightweight (fighter *l.* boxer); **bokser wagi koguciej/piórkowej/muszej** bantamweight/featherweight/flyweight (fighter *l.* boxer); **bokser zawodowy** prizefighter. – *ma pl.* **-ry** (*pies*) boxer. – *mi Gen.* **-a** *pl.* **-y** *techn.* opposed-cylinder engine.

bokserki *pl. Gen.pl.* **-ek** (*spodenki*) boxers, boxer shorts.

bokserski *a. sport* boxing; **mistrz bokserski** boxing champion; **rękawice bokserskie** boxing gloves; **pojedynek bokserski** bout; **walka bokserska** (boxing) fight; **mecz bokserski** boxing match.

boksować *ipf.* hit *l.* strike (repeatedly) with one's fists, punch. **~ się** *ipf.* box (*z kimś* with *l.* against sb).

boksowy *a.* **1.** (= *podzielony na boksy*) divided into boxes. **2.** (*o rodzaju skóry*) box-calf; **skóra boksowa** box calf.

boksyt *mi min.* bauxite.

bola *f.*, **bolas** *mi broń* bola, bolas.

bolączka *f. Gen.pl.* **-ek** problem, difficulty, complaint; **wysłuchiwać czyichś bolączek** listen to sb's complaints; **bolączki społeczne** society's ills, social problems.

bolec *mi* **-lc-** *Gen.* **-a** pin, dowel; (*z gwintem*) bolt; **połączyć coś bolcami** bolt sth together.

boleć[1] *ipf.* **-i** **1.** (*o bólu fizycznym*) hurt; (*tępo, nieustannie*) ache; **boli mnie głowa** my head aches; **bolący palec** sore finger; **bolące plecy** aching back; **wszystko mnie boli** I hurt *l.* I ache all over; **bolą mnie stare kości** my old bones are aching; **co cię boli?** where does it hurt?; **boli jak cholera** it hurts like hell. **2.** (*o bólu psychicznym*) hurt, pain; **boli mnie twoja niesprawiedliwość** I am hurt *l.* pained by your unfairness; **tu cię boli!** I touched a sore spot *l.* a tender spot; **niech cię o to głowa nie boli** don't let that worry you; don't worry about that; never mind about that; **boli mnie serce, kiedy widzę, że...** my heart bleeds when I see that...; **od przybytku głowa nie boli** you can never have too much of a good thing.

boleć² *ipf.* (= *smucić się*) mourn, deplore (*nad kimś/czymś* sb/sth); **boleję nad waszym smutnym losem** I mourn your sad fate; **bolejące spojrzenie** mournful look.

bolerko *n. Gen.pl.* **-ek** = **bolero** 2.

bolero *n.* **1.** (*taniec*) bolero. **2.** (*kamizelka*) bolero. **3.** (*kapelusz*) bolero hat.

bolesność *f.* painfulness.

bolesny *a.* **-śniejszy** **1.** (= *sprawiający ból*) painful; **bolesne skaleczenie** painful injury; **bolesna kolka** painful colic; **dusznica bolesna** *pat.* angina pectoris. **2.** (= *bolący*) sore, aching; **bolesne miejsce** sore spot. **3.** (= *przykry*) painful, hurtful, sad; **bolesna wiadomość** sad news; **bolesne wspomnienia** painful memories; **bolesne słowa** hurtful words. **4.** (= *żałosny*) mournful, sorrowful; **bolesne spojrzenie/westchnienie** mournful look/sigh.

boleściwy *a. lit.* mournful, sorrowful; **boleściwe spojrzenie** mournful look; **Matka Boska Boleściwa** *rz.-kat.* Our Lady of Sorrows.

boleść *f. Gen.* **-i** **1.** *zw. pl.* (= *ból*) pain, ache; **silne boleści** strong pain; **mieć boleści** have (aches and) pains; **skarżyć się na boleści** complain of (aches and) pains; **łoże boleści** *lit.* bed of suffering; **od siedmiu boleści** *żart.* poor, paltry. **2.** *lit.* (= *żal*) sorrow, mourning; **słowa pełne boleści** words full of sorrow; **ulżyć czyjejś boleści** ease sb's sorrows.

boleśnie *adv.* **1.** (= *sprawiając ból*) painfully. **2.** (*raniąc uczucia*) cruelly; **dotknąć kogoś boleśnie** cause sb pain (*czymś* with sth). **3.** (= *żałośnie*) mournfully, sorrowfully; **łkać boleśnie** sob mournfully.

bolid *mi astron.* bolide, fireball.

Boliwia *f. Gen.* **-ii** Bolivia.

Boliwijczyk *mp*, **Boliwijka** *f. Gen.pl.* **-ek** Bolivian.

boliwijski *a.* Bolivian.

bolszewicki *a.* Bolshevik; **partia bolszewicka** the Bolshevik party.

bolszewik *mp* Bolshevik.

bolszewizm *mi* Bolshevism.

bom *mi żegl.* (= *gik l. żuraw*) boom; **bom przedni** foreboom.

bomba *f.* **1.** *broń, wojsk.* bomb; **bomba atomowa** atom *l.* nuclear bomb; *euf.* the bomb; **bomba neutronowa** neutron bomb; **bomba rozpryskowa** cluster bomb; **bomba wodorowa** hydrogen bomb; **bomba głębinowa** depth charge; **bomba lotnicza** aerial bomb; **bomba zapalająca** incendiary bomb, firebomb; **bomba zegarowa** time bomb; **bomba-pułapka** booby trap; **uzbrojona bomba** live bomb; **podłożyć bombę** plant a bomb; **wpaść jak bomba** *przen.* come bursting in. **2.** **bomba kobaltowa** *fiz.* cobalt bomb. **3.** (*sensacyjna wiadomość*) sensation; **bomba pękła** a bombshell was dropped; **bomba sezonu** (this) season's blockbuster; **(dla mnie) bomba!** *l.* **ale bomba!** that's awesome! **4.** (= *duży kulisty przedmiot*) ball; **bomba czekoladowa** chocolate ball. **5.** *żart.* (= *kufel*) mug. **6.** *sport* (= *silne odbicie*) whack; (*w siatkówce*) spike; (*w tenisie*) smash. **7.** *szkoln.* (= *najniższa ocena*) F; **dać komuś bombę** give sb an F; **dostałem bombę z egzaminu** I bombed on the test.

bombarda *f. broń, hist.* bombard.

bombardier *mp pl.* **-rzy** *lotn., wojsk., hist.* bombardier. **– ma** *pl.* **-ry** *zool.* (= *chrząszcz z rodziny Carabidae*) bombardier beetle.

bombardować *ipf.* **1.** *wojsk.* (= *zrzucać bomby*) bomb; (*z ciężkiej artylerii*) bombard, shell. **2.** *przen.* (= *obrzucać*) pelt (*czymś* with sth); (= *natarczywie niepokoić*) bombard; **bombardować kogoś telefonami/pytaniami** bombard sb with telephone calls/questions. **3.** *fiz.* bombard.

bombardowanie *n.* *wojsk.* bombardment, bombing; **bombardowanie precyzyjne** precision bombing.

bombastyczność *f. uj.* bombast, stiltedness, pomposity.

bombastyczny *a. uj.* bombastic, stilted, pompous; **bombastyczne przemówienie** bombastic speech; **bombastyczny styl** bombastic *l.* inflated style.

bombaż *mi techn.* (= *wzdęcie puszki*) swollen can (defect).

bombiasty *a.* spherical, domed; **bombiasta sukienka** farthingale.

bombka *f.* **1.** (= *coś kulistego*) ball; **bombka choinkowa** glass ball ornament; **bombka czekoladowa** chocolate ball. **2.** (= *koniakówka*) brandy glass. **3.** *żart.* (= *kufel*) mug.

bomblować *ipf. żart.* (= *hulać*) carouse, paint the town red, be (out) on a toot.

bomboniera *f.*, **bombonierka** *f. Gen.pl.* **-ek** box of chocolates.

bombowiec *mi* **-wc-** *Gen.* **-a** bomber; **bombowiec nurkujący** dive bomber.

bombowo *adv. pot.* awesomely, sensationally.

bombowy *a.* **1.** (= *dotyczący bomb l. bombardowania*) bombing; **nalot bombowy** bombing raid; **zamach bombowy** bombing. **2.** *pot.* (= *efektowny, szałowy*) awesome, sensational, cool; **bombowy film** awesome film; **bombowa fryzura** cool hairstyle; **bombowa wiadomość** sensational news.

bon *mi* **1.** (= *kupon, talon*) coupon, voucher; **bon towarowy** gift certificate; **bon stołówkowy** meal voucher. **2.** *fin.* (*papier wartościowy*) bond; **wypuścić bony** issue bonds.

bona *f. przest.* nursemaid.

bonapartysta *ma*, **bonapartystka** *f. Gen.pl.* **-ek** *hist.* Bonapartist.

bonifikata *f.* **1.** (= *rabat*) discount; (*od producenta*) rebate; **udzielić bonifikaty** offer discounts; **sprzedaż z bonifikatą** discount. **2.** *sport* bonus.

bonifrater *mp* **-tr-** *rz.-kat.* member of the Order of St. John of God.

bon mot *mi Gen.* **bon motu** *Fr.* bon mot.

bonsai *n. indecl. ogr.* bonsai.

bon ton *mi Gen.* **bon tonu** *Fr.* bon ton, polite manners.

bonus *mi indecl. ekon.* bonus.

bonza *mp pl.* **-owie** **1.** (*rel.*) Bhuddhist priest, bonze. **2.** *pot. uj.* (= *ważniak*) fat cat.

bonżurka *f. Gen.pl.* **-ek** smoking jacket.

boogie-woogie *n. indecl. muz.* boogie-woogie.

boom *mi ekon.* boom, prosperity; **boom gospodarczy** economic boom; **boom inwestycyjny** investment boom.

bor *mi chem.* boron; **węglik boru** boron carbide.

bora *f. meteor.* bora.

boracyt *mi min.* boracite.

boraks *mi chem.* **1.** borax. **2.** *min.* borax (ore), tincal.

boran *mi chem.* borate.

bordiura *f.* (= *pas dekoracyjny*) border.

bordo *n. indecl.* (*wino*) claret, Bordeaux. – *a. i n. indecl.* (*kolor*) maroon; **sukienka bordo** maroon dress; **przemalować na bordo** paint sth maroon.

bordowy *a.* = **bordo**.

borealny *a. geogr.* boreal; **las borealny** boreal forest.

Boreasz *mp mit.* Boreas.

borek *mi* -rk- *chem.* boride.

borelioza *f. pat.* Lyme disease.

bornit *mi min.* bornite.

borny *a. chem.* boric; **kwas borny** boric acid.

borować *ipf.* drill; (*zwł. w skale*) bore; **borować ząb** drill a tooth; **borować otwór w skale** bore *l.* drill a hole in (a) rock.

borowce *pl. Gen.* -ów *chem.* the boron group.

borowiec *ma* -wc- *zool.* noctule bat (*Nyctalus*).

borowik *mi Gen.* -a bolete, boletus (*Boletus*); **borowik szlachetny** king bolete, cep, penny bun (*B. edulis*); **borowik szatański** satan's bolete (*B. satanas*).

borowina *f.* **1.** (*zarośla*) huckleberry bushes. **2.** *med.* therapeutic peat; **kąpiel w borowinie** peat bath; **okład z borowiny** peat compress.

borowinowy *a. med.* peat.

borowodór *mi chem.* borane.

borówka *f.* **1.** *bot.* blueberry, whortleberry (*Vaccinium*); **borówka brusznica** cowberry, foxberry, mountain cranberry (*V. vitis-idaea*); **borówka czernica** bilberry, European blueberry (*V. myrtillus*); **borówka wysoka** *l.* **amerykańska** highbush blueberry (*V. corymbosum*). **2.** (*owoc*) blueberry.

borsalino *n.* borsalino hat.

borsuczy *a.* badger('s); **skóra borsucza** badger skin; **nora borsucza** sett.

borsuk *ma zool.* badger; **borsuk europejski** European badger (*Meles meles*); **borsuk amerykański** American badger (*Taxidea taxus*).

boru *itd. mi zob.* **bór**.

borykać się *ipf.* wrestle, grapple (*z czym* with sth); **muszę się z tym borykać** I have to cope with that.

borze *mi zob.* **bór**.

bosak[1] *mi Gen.* -a pike pole; (*strażacki*) fire hook; *żegl.* boat hook, grappling iron.

bosak[2] *adv.* **na bosaka** barefoot.

Bosfor *mi geogr.* the Bosporus *l.* Bosphorus.

boski *a.* **1.** (= *dotyczący Boga*) God's *l.* of God; (= *dotyczący jakiegokolwiek boga*) divine; **wola boska** God's will *l.* the will of God; **na litość boską!** for God's *l.* Christ's *l.* heaven's sake!; **niech ręka boska broni** God forbid; **skaranie boskie** *l.*

kara boska *pot.* pest, nuisance; **rany boskie!** *pot.* Jesus (Christ)!, Jeez!; **zostawić kogoś/coś na łasce boskiej** leave sb/sth in God's hands. **2.** *pot.* (= *wspaniały*) super (super), terrific, divine.

bosko *adv. pot.* super, great; **wyglądać/czuć się bosko** look/feel super.

boskość *f.* divinity.

bosman *mp* **1.** *żegl.* boatswain; *pot.* bosun. **2.** *wojsk.* (*stopień w marynarce*) chief petty officer.

bosmanat *mi żegl.* local port authority.

bosmanmat *mp wojsk.* petty officer.

bosmański *a. żegl.* boatswain's, bosun's; *wojsk.* petty officer's.

boso *adv.* barefoot, barefooted; **chodzić boso** go barefoot.

bosonogi *a.* barefoot, barefooted.

boss *mp pl.* -owie boss; **boss przemysłu filmowego** movie mogul; **boss narkotykowy** drug lord.

bossa nova *f. Gen.* **bossa novy** *muz., taniec* bossa nova.

boston[1] *mi Gen. i Acc.* -a *taniec* **1.** boston (waltz). **2.** *karty* boston.

boston[2] *mi Gen.* -u *tk.* twill-weave worsted.

bosy *a.* **1.** barefoot, barefooted; **bose nogi** bare feet. **2.** *kośc.* (*o zakonach*) discalced.

Bośnia *f. geogr.* Bosnia; **Bośnia i Hercegowina** Bosnia and Herzegovina.

bośniacki *a.* Bosnian; **Serbowie/Chorwaci bośniaccy** Bosnian Serbs/Croats.

Bośniaczka *f. Gen.pl.* -ek, **Bośniak** *mp* Bosnian.

botaniczka *f. Gen.pl.* -ek *zob.* **botanik**.

botaniczny *a.* botanical; **klasyfikacja botaniczna** botanical classification; **ogród botaniczny** botanic *l.* botanical garden.

botanik *mp* botanist.

botanika *f.* botany.

botek *mi* -tk- *Gen.* -a (*damski l. dziecięcy*) bootee.

Botswana *f.* Botswana.

botulizm *mi med.* botulism.

botwina *f.* **1.** *kulin.* young beet, chard; (*zupa*) young beet soup. **2.** *bot.* (Swiss) chard, leaf beet (*Beta vulgaris cicla*).

botwinka *f.* = **botwina** 1.

bouclé *a. indecl.* bouclé; **płaszcz bouclé** bouclé (wool) coat.

bowiem *conj. lit.* for, as, since, because; **spotkała mnie miła niespodzianka, bowiem śniadanie było wyśmienite** I was pleasantly surprised, for the breakfast was delicious; **regularnie chodził na koncerty, lubił bowiem muzykę klasyczną** since he liked classical music, he went to concerts regularly.

boy *mp Gen.pl.* -ów bellboy; *gł. Br.* page.

boże *mp zob.* **bóg**.

bożek *ma* -żk- lesser god, deity, idol.

bożnica *f.* = **bóżnica**.

bożodrzew *mi bot.* ailanthus (*Ailanthus*).

bożonarodzeniowy *a.* Christmas, Xmas; **pieśni bożonarodzeniowe** Christmas carols; **msza bożonarodzeniowa** Christmas Mass; **szopka bożonarodzeniowa** Nativity scene; crèche.

boży *a. rel.* **1.** God's, of God, divine; **opatrz-**

ność boża divine providence; **dary boże** God's gifts; **iskra boża** God-given talent; **palec boży** (= *dzieło opatrzności*) the hand of God; **słowo boże** the word of God; **zaczynajmy, w imię boże** let us begin, in the name of God; **wola boża** the will of God; **poczuć wolę bożą** *żart.* feel nature's call; **z bożej łaski** by the grace of God; **specjalista z bożej łaski** *iron.* jack of all trades, master of none; **Boże Narodzenie** Christmas, Xmas; **Boże Ciało** *rz.-kat.* Corpus Christi; **dom boży** *kośc.* the house of God; **pokój boży** *hist.* the truce of God, treuga Dei; **sąd boży** *hist.* ordeal; **żyć po bożemu** *przest. l. żart.* live honestly; stick to the straight and narrow. 2. **boże drzewko** *bot.* southernwood (*Artemisia abrotanum*); **boża krówka** *orn.* (= *biedronka*) ladybug; *Br.* ladybird.

bożyszcze *n. Gen.pl.* -y *l.* -cz 1. (= *bożek*) (lesser) god, deity; **pogańskie bożyszcze** pagan god *l.* deity. 2. (= *idol, bohater*) idol; **bożyszcze mas/tłumów** idol of the masses/crowds.

bób *mi* -o- *bot., kulin.* broad bean, horsebean (*Vicia faba*); **dać** *l.* **zadać komuś bobu** *przen.* teach sb a lesson.

bóbr *ma* -o- *zool.* 1. beaver (*Castor fiber*); **bóbr kanadyjski** North American beaver (*C. canadensis*); **płakać jak bóbr** *przen.* cry one's eyes out. 2. *zob.* **bobry**.

bóg *mp* -o- *Dat.* -u *Voc.* -że *pl.* -owie *arch.* -i 1. **Bóg** *rel.* God; **wierzyć w Boga** believe in God; **Pan Bóg** the Lord (God); **Bóg Ojciec** God the Father; **Bóg wszechmogący** almighty God; **mieć się jak u Pana Boga za piecem** be (as) snug as a bug in a rug; **pożal się Boże!** *l.* **Boże odpuść!** Lord have mercy!; God help us!; **Bóg zapłać!** God will repay you!; may God repay you!; **robić coś za Bóg zapłać** do sth out of the kindness of one's heart; **Bóg mi świadkiem** as God is my witness; I swear by (almighty) God; I swear to God; **jak Boga kocham!** honest to God!; **niech mnie Bóg skarze!** as God is my witness!; **tak mi dopomóż Bóg** so help me God; **szczęść Boże!** (may) God bless you!; **idź z Bogiem** go with God; **Bóg z tobą** *l.* **zostań z Bogiem** may God be with you; **na Boga!** for God's *l.* heaven's sake!; good God!; good heavens!; **dzięki Bogu** *l.* **chwała Bogu** *l.* **chwalić Boga** thank God; thank heavens; **niech Bóg broni!** *l.* **broń Boże** *l.* **nie daj Bóg!** *l.* **uchowaj Boże!** God *l.* heaven forbid!; **o, Boże!** *l.* **mój Boże!** oh, my God!; goodness gracious!; **kogo Bóg prowadzi?** *przest.* who is there?; **niech cię Bóg ma w swojej opiece** God help you; **miej Boga w sercu** *l.* **bój się Boga!** have a heart; **żyć jak Pan Bóg przykazał** stick to the straight and narrow; **Bóg wie co** (only) God knows; **Bóg jeden wie, gdzie ona jest** Lord knows where she is; **co to było, na miły Bóg?** what in God's name was that?; **zapomniany przez Boga (i ludzi)** God-forsaken; **(nagi) jak go Pan Bóg stworzył** *pot.* naked as a jaybird; *żart.* in his birthday suit; **Bogu ducha winien** (as) innocent as a lamb; **Bogiem a prawdą** to tell the truth; **Panu Bogu świeczkę i diabłu ogarek** run with the hare and hunt with the hounds; **Pan Bóg nierychliwy, ale sprawiedliwy** God's mills grind slow but sure; God comes with leaden feet but strikes with

iron hands; **kto rano wstaje, temu Pan Bóg daje** the early bird catches the worm; **gość w dom, Bóg w dom** a guest is a blessing to the home; **strzeżonego Pan Bóg strzeże** forewarned is forearmed; **jak Kuba Bogu, tak Bóg Kubie** like for like; you get what you give; what comes around goes around; **człowiek strzela, Pan Bóg kule nosi** man proposes, God disposes. 2. *mit.* god; **bóg wojny** god of war; war god; **bogowie greccy/rzymscy/germańscy** Greek/Roman/Germanic gods; **składać ofiarę bogom** make an offering *l.* a sacrifice to the gods.

bój¹ *mi* -o- 1. (= *bitwa, walka*) combat, battle, fight; **ciężki bój** heavy combat; **krwawy bój** carnage; **iść do boju** go into battle; **stanąć do boju** make a stand (*o coś* for sth); **bój na śmierć i życie** fight to the death; **toczyć bój** *l.* **boje** fight (*o coś* for sth, *z kimś/czymś* against sb/sth). 2. *sport* competition.

bój² *ipf. zob.* **bać się**.

bójka *f. Gen.pl.* -ek fight, brawl, squabble, scuffle, tussle; **wszcząć bójkę** start a fight.

ból *mi Gen.pl.* -ów 1. (*fizyczny*) pain, ache; **ostry ból** sharp *l.* acute pain; **dotkliwy ból** severe pain; **przejmujący ból** piercing pain; **ból zęba** toothache; **ból gardła** sore throat; **ból żołądka** stomach-ache; **ból głowy** headache; **ból w kolanie** pain in one's knee, sore knee; **ból w łokciu** sore elbow; **cierpieć na bóle w stawach** suffer from aching joints; **jęczeć z bólu** groan with pain; **odczuwać ból** feel (a) pain; **uśmierzyć ból** relieve *l.* soothe pain. 2. (*psychiczny*) grief, suffering, pain; **sprawić komuś ból** cause sb grief; **ból po stracie matki** the pain of losing one's mother; **z bólem serca** with a heavy heart; **dzielić z kimś ból** share sb's grief *l.* suffering; **sprawia mi ból, gdy słyszę, że...** it pains me to hear that...; **serce mi pęka z bólu** it's breaking my heart.

bór *mi* -o- (conifer) forest *l.* woods; **bór sosnowy** pine forest; **nieprzebyty bór** impenetrable forest; **zabłądzić w borze** get lost in the woods; **za borami, za lasami** over the hills and far away.

bóstwo *n.* 1. (= *bożek*) deity, god; **bóstwo wojny** god of war; **wyglądać jak bóstwo** *przen.* look divine. 2. (= *idol*) idol. 3. *rel.* (= *boskość*) divinity; **bóstwo Jezusa Chrystusa** the divinity of Jesus Christ.

bóść *ipf.* **bodę bodziesz, bódź, bódł bodła** 1. hit with the head; (*o baranie, kozie*) butt; (*o byku, krowie*) gore. 2. (*ostrogą*) prick, spur.

bóżnica *f. rel.* synagogue.

br. *abbr.* (= *bieżącego roku*) this year, of the current year.

braciszek *mp* -szk- *pl.* -owie *emf.* 1. (= *brat*) little *l.* younger brother. 2. (= *zakonnik*) brother, friar.

bractwo *n.* 1. *żart.* (= *towarzystwo*) company, fellowship. 2. *rz.-kat.* brotherhood, fraternity; **bractwo różańcowe** rosary fraternity; **bractwo miłosierdzia** the Brotherhood of Mercy. 3. *hist.* guild; **bractwo kurkowe** shooting society (*active since the Middle Ages in Poland*).

brać¹ *ipf.* **biorę bierzesz** 1. (= *chwytać*) take, pick up; **brać coś od kogoś** take sth from sb; **brać**

coś palcami/widelcem pick sth up with one's fingers/with a fork; **brać kogoś za rękę** take sb by the hand; **brać kogoś w ramiona** take sb in one's arms; embrace sb; **brać kogoś/coś na kolana** place sb/sth on one's lap; **weź dwa jajka i cztery łyżki cukru** take two eggs and four spoonfuls of sugar; **brać coś garściami** take handfuls of sth; **brać coś po kawałku** take sth bit by bit; **brać coś do kieszeni** put sth in one's pocket; **biorę cię za słowo** I'll take you at your word; I'll hold you to your promise; **brać coś na warsztat** *pot.* start working on sth. **2.** (= *zabierać z sobą*) take (out); **brać kogoś na obiad** take sb out for dinner; **brać psa na spacer** take the dog for a walk. **3.** (= *przyjmować na siebie*) take (on), assume, accept; **brać na siebie odpowiedzialność** take *l.* assume responsibility (*za kogoś/coś* for sb/sth); **brać coś na swoje barki** *l.* **ramiona** *przen.* take sth on one's shoulders; **brać coś na swoje sumienie** feel responsible for sth. **4.** (= *podejmować*) take up, accept; **brać pracę w supermarkecie** take up a job in a supermarket. **5.** (= *przyjmować, dostawać*) take, receive, get; **brać łapówki** take bribes; **brać pensję** receive a salary; **ile bierzesz miesięcznie?** how much do you get a month? **6.** (= *nabywać*) purchase, buy; **brać coś na kredyt/na raty** buy sth on credit/on an installment plan; **biorę tę książkę** I'll take this book. **7.** (= *wynajmować*) take; **brać w dzierżawę** rent, lease; **brać taksówkę** take a taxi; **brać pokój z widokiem na morze** take a room with a view of the sea. **8.** (= *zdobywać siłą*) take, capture, seize; **brać zakładników/jeńców** take hostages/prisoners; **brać kogoś do niewoli** take sb into captivity; take sb prisoner; **brać kogoś w karby** bring sb under control; **brać kogoś w dwa ognie** take sb from two sides; **brać miasto siłą** capture *l.* seize a town; **brać kogoś na lep** *l.* **na plewy** take sb for a ride. **9.** (= *kochać się z*) make love to (*sb*); take (*sb*); **brał ją podczas przechadzek** he took her during walks; **brać kogoś siłą** rape sb. **10.** (= *ogarniać*) **bierze mnie ciekawość** I'm getting curious; **strach mnie bierze** I'm getting scared; **bierze mnie znużenie** I'm getting tired; **litość bierze, kiedy się na to patrzy** it's a pitiful sight. **11.** (= *wykorzystywać jako źródło*) take; **brać przykład** *l.* **wzór z kogoś/czegoś** take sb/sth as an example; **brać pomysł z głowy** come up with an idea; **brać źródło** *l.* **początek** originate. **12.** (= *zatrudniać, przyjmować*) take (on), hire; **brać gosposię** hire a housekeeper; **brać sobie pomocnika** take an assistant; **brać kogoś za żonę/męża** take sb for one's (wedded) wife/husband. **13.** (= *przezwyciężać, pokonywać*) take; **brać zakręt zbyt ostro** take a corner too fast; **brać biegacza na ostatniej prostej** overtake a runner on the final staightaway; **koń bezbłędnie bierze przeszkody** the horse takes fences faultlessly. **14.** (= *stosować dla zdrowia* l. *higieny*) take; **brać środki przeciwbólowe** take painkillers; **brać kąpiel/prysznic** take a bath/a shower. **15.** (*uderzenie, atak*) take, get, receive; **brać baty/lanie** get a whipping/a spanking; **brać w skórę** take a licking *l.* beating; **brać za swoje** be rewarded according to one's deserts;

moje plany biorą w łeb my plans are coming to nothing. **16.** (= *uważać, poczytywać*) take; **brać coś za żart** take sth as a joke; **brać coś dosłownie/poważnie** take sth literally/seriously; **brać coś za punkt honoru** take sth as a point of honor; **brać coś do siebie** take sth personally; **za kogo mnie bierzesz?** what do you take me for?; **brać coś za dobrą monetę** take sth at face value; **biorą mnie często za mojego brata** I'm often mistaken for my brother. **17.** (*o rybie*) bite, take (the bait). **18.** (*w różnych utartych zwrotach*) **brać kurs na Nowy Jork** set a course for New York; **brać miarę** take measurements; **brać górę** get the upper hand (*nad kimś* over sb); **brać rozpęd** gain speed; **brać odwet** take revenge (*na kimś/czymś* on *l.* upon sb/sth); **brać czyjąś stronę** take sb's side; **brać udział** take part; be involved; participate (*w czymś* in sth); **brać ślub** get married; **brać coś na rozum** *pot.* think sth through; **brać pod uwagę** *l.* **pod rozwagę** *l.* **w rachubę** take sth into consideration; **brać coś do serca** take sth to heart; **brać nogi za pas** take to one's heels; **mróz bierze** it's beginning to freeze; **brać kogoś do galopu** *pot.* spur sb on; get sb into (high) gear; **diabli mnie biorą** *pot.* it burns me up.

brać² *f.* brotherhood, fellowship; **brać myśliwska/aktorska** fellow hunters/actors; **brać szlachecka** *hist.* gentry.

brać się *ipf.* **biorę bierzesz 1.** (= *chwytać, ściskać rękami*) **brać się za głowę** take one's head in one's hands; **brać się w garść** collect o.s. *l.* one's wits; **brać się za ręce** hold each other's hand; **brać się pod ręce** link arms; **brać się w ramiona** lock each other in their arms; **brać się z czymś/kimś za bary** wrestle with sth/sb; **brać się za łby** *pot.* start a fight. **2.** (= *zabierać się do* (*sth*)); start, begin; **brać się do jedzenia** start eating; **brać się do pracy** *l.* **roboty** get to work; **brać się do pióra** take pen to paper. **3.** (= *zdobywać się na coś*) **brać się na sposób** find a way; **brać się na odwagę** muster up one's courage. **4.** (= *pochodzić*) come from (*sth*); **skąd się biorą dzieci?** where do babies come from?; **skąd się biorą trzęsienia ziemi?** what causes earthquakes?; **skąd się u ciebie biorą takie myśli?** where do you get such ideas?

brajl *mi Gen. i Acc.* **-a** braille; **pisać/drukować brajlem** write/print in braille.

brajlowski *a.* braille; **alfabet/system brajlowski** the braille alphabet/system.

brak *mi* **1.** (= *niedostatek*) lack, shortage; **chroniczny/zupełny brak czasu** chronic/total shortage *l.* lack of time; **dotkliwy brak pieniędzy** severe shortage of money; **brak zainteresowania/apetytu** lack of interest/appetite. **2.** (= *nieobecność*) absence; **zauważyłem brak niektórych studentów** I noticed (that) some students were absent. **3.** (= *niedociągnięcie, luka*) deficiency, gap; **uzupełnij braki** fill in the gaps (*w czymś* in sth). **4.** *handl.* defective product. – *v.* (*nieodmienny predykatyw*) **1.** (*niedostatek, uczucie tęsknoty*) **brak mi słów** I don't know what to say; I'm at a loss for words; **będzie mi ciebie brak** I'll miss you. **2.** (*z przeczeniem: dostateczna ilość,* *obfitość*) **nie brak mu nigdy pomysłów** he never lacks ideas; **nie brak czasu** there's plenty of time; **nie brak mi było niczego** I had all I needed; *form.* I wanted for nothing.

brakarz *mp przemysł* sorter.

braknąć *ipf.* **-kło** run out, be in short supply; **brakło wszystkiego** there was a shortage of everything; **niczego mi nie braknie** I have everything I need; *zob.* **brakowało.**

brakorób *mp* -rob- *pl.* -y *pot.* bungler, botcher, spoiler.

brakoróbstwo *n. pot.* botchery.

brakować *ipf.* **1.** (= *nie wystarczać*) not be enough, not suffice, run short, be in short supply; **brakowało nam czasu** we were short of time; **brakuje mu odwagi, żeby...** he hasn't got the courage to..., he lacks courage to...; **tylko tego brakowało!** *iron.* that's just what I need!; **niewiele brakowało** that was close; that was a close call *l.* shave; **brakuje ropy** oil is in short supply; **brakuje mi pieniędzy/gotówki** I'm short of money/ cash; **brakuje mi słów** I can't find the words; words fail me; **brakuje mi pomysłów** I'm at a loss for ideas; **brakowało mu pół metra do wygrania** he was half a meter short *l.* shy of winning; **dużo brakuje nam do końca** we're nowhere near the end. **2.** (*z zaprzeczeniem*) (= *nie brak*) **nie brakowało nam pieniędzy** we had enough money; **nie brakuje ci tupetu** you have plenty of cheek. **3.** (*o odczuwaniu braku l. tęsknoty*) **brakuje mi ciebie** I miss you; **brakowało mi książek i muzyki** I yearned for books and music; **nie będzie go nikomu brakowało** he won't be missed. **4.** *przemysł* (= *odrzucać*) reject, sort out.

brama *f.* gate, gateway; **żelazna brama** iron gate; **kuta brama** wrought-iron gate; **przejechać przez bramę** drive through a gate; **klucz do bram miasta** key to the city gates; **nie tarasuj bramy** don't block the gateway.

bramin *mp Ind.* Brahman, Brahmin.

braminizm *mi rel.* Brahmanism, Brahminism.

Braminka *f. Gen.pl.* -ek *Ind.* Brahmani, Brahmini.

bramiński *a.* Brahmanical, Brahminical.

bramka *f. Gen.pl.* -ek **1.** (= *furtka*) gate, wicket, door. **2.** *sport* (*w piłce nożnej*) goal; *w krykiecie* wicket; (*w kajakarstwie, narciarstwie*) gate; **strzelić** *l.* **zdobyć bramkę** score a goal; **strzał na bramkę** goal shot. **3.** *el.* gate; **bramka logiczna** logical gate.

bramkarz *mp* **1.** *piłka nożna* goalie, goalkeeper, goaltender. **2.** (= *człowiek pilnujący wejścia*) doorman, bouncer.

bramkostrzelny *a.* piłka nożna high-scoring.

bramować *ipf.* border.

bramkowy *a. sport* goal; **linia bramkowa** goal line; **pole bramkowe** goal area.

bramkować *v. el.* gate.

bramowanie *n.* border, borderwork, edgework, edging; (*z nitek*) fringe; **futrzane bramowanie** fur border.

brandy *f. indecl.* brandy.

branka *f. Gen.pl.* -ek **1.** (= *kobieta jeniec*) captive woman. **2.** *hist.* forced conscription.

bransoleta *f.*, **bransoletka** *f. Gen.pl.* -ek bracelet.

branża *f. ekon.* (branch of) industry, (line of) business; **branża elektroniczna/metalowa** electronics/metals industry.

branżowiec *mp* -wc- *pl.* -y expert, specialist (*in l. from a given line of business*); **zebranie branżowców od bankowości** meeting of people from the banking industry.

branżowy *a.* industry, branch; **branżowe związki zawodowe** industrial union.

branżysta *mp* expert (*in an industry*).

bras *mi żegl.* brace.

brat *mp Dat.* -u *pl.* -cia *Gen.* -ci *Ins.* -ćmi **1.** (*członek rodziny*) brother; **młodszy brat** younger *l.* little brother; **starszy brat** elder *l.* older *l.* big brother; **brat przyrodni** stepbrother, half-brother; **brat cioteczny, stryjeczny** (first) cousin; **brat mleczny** foster brother; **bracia syjamscy** siamese twins; **mnie on ni brat, ni swat** *przen.* he doesn't mean anything to me. **2.** (= *osoba obdarzana życzliwością*) fellow, brother; **bracia Polacy!** fellow Poles!; **bracia żołnierze** brothers in arms; **bracia i siostry!** *rel.* brothers and sisters!; **brat łata** good guy; **być z kimś za pan brat** be on familiar terms with sb; **bracie!** brother! **3.** (*zakonnik*) (lay) brother, monk, friar. **4.** (= *członek bractwa*) brother; **bracia polscy** the Polish Brethren; **bracia czescy** the Unity of Brethren.

bratać *ipf.* unite (in brotherhood); **nieszczęście brata ludzi** misfortune unites people. **~ się** *ipf.* fraternize (*z kimś* with sb).

bratanek *mp* -nk- *pl.* -owie *l.* -i nephew.

bratanica *f.* niece.

bratek *mi* -tk- *Gen.* -a *pl.* -i *ogr.* pansy; *med.* violet; **bratek ogrodowy** *bot.* garden pansy (*Viola vittrockiana*). — *mp* -tk- *pl. rzad.* -owie *żart.* buddy, pal, man, dude; **słuchaj bratku!** listen buddy!

braterski *a.* fraternal, brotherly; **braterski uścisk dłoni** fraternal handshake; **braterskie zaufanie** fraternal trust; **po bratersku** fraternally.

braterstwo *n.* **1.** *Loc.* -ie brotherhood, brotherliness, fellowship; **braterstwo narodów** fellowship of nations; **braterstwo broni** brotherhood in arms. **2.** *Loc.* -u (= *brat z żoną*) brother and his wife.

bratni *a.* fraternal, allied, kindred; **podać bratnią dłoń** lend a helping hand; **bratni naród** allied nation; **bratnia partia** allied party; **bratnia dusza** kindred spirit.

bratobójca *mp* fratricide.

bratobójczy *a.* fratricidal.

bratobójczyni *f. zob.* **bratobójca.**

bratobójstwo *n.* fratricide; **popełnić bratobójstwo** commit fratricide.

bratowa *f. Gen.* -ej brother's wife, sister-in-law.

brauning *mi Gen.* -a Browning (automatic).

brawo *n.* applause; (*głośno z okrzykami*) cheers; **bić komuś brawo** applaud *l.* cheer sb; **powitać kogoś/coś brawami** welcome sb/sth with applause; **dostać szalone brawa** receive a wild round of applause. — *int.* bravo!; (*wyrażenie uznania dla mówcy*) hear! hear!

brawura *f.* **1.** (= *werwa*) bravura. **2.** (= *ryzy-*

kanctwo) bravado; **prowadzić z brawurą** (*o kierowcy*) drive like a daredevil; **przyczyną wypadku była brawura kierowcy** the cause of the accident was the bravado of the driver.

brawurowo *adv.* with bravura *l.* bravado.

brawurowy *a.* **1.** (= *szaleńczy*) bravado, daredevil; **brawurowa jazda** daredevil ride. **2.** (= *błyskotliwy*) bravura, brilliant; **brawurowe wykonanie** bravura performance.

Brazylia *f. Gen.* **-ii** *geogr.* Brazil.

Brazylijczyk *mp*, **Brazylijka** *f. Gen.pl.* **-ek** Brazilian.

brazylijski *a.* Brazilian.

brąz *mi* **1.** (*metal*) bronze; **wyrób z brązu** bronze artefact; **epoka brązu** the Bronze Age. **2.** (*kolor*) brown; **malować coś na brąz** paint sth brown. **3.** *zob.* **brązy.**

brązować *ipf.* **1.** *techn.* bronze, coat with bronze. **2.** *przen. lit.* (= *idealizować*) glorify, idealize.

brązowić *ipf.* (*barwić na brązowo*) paint brown; (= *opalać na brąz*) tan. **~ się** *v.* be *l.* appear brown.

brązowieć *ipf.* (= *barwić się na brązowo*) turn brown.

brązownictwo *n.* **1.** *metal.* bronzing. **2.** *iron.* glorification, idealization.

brązownik *mp* **1.** (*rzemieślnik*) brazier. **2.** *przen.* (= *chwalca*) glorifier.

brązowy *a.* (= *z brązu*) **1.** bronze; **brązowy medal** bronze medal; **brązowy świecznik** bronze candlestick. **2.** (= *koloru brązu*) brown; **malować/farbować coś na brązowo** paint/dye sth brown.

brązy *pl. Gen.* **-ów** (*wyroby l. ozdoby z brązu*) bronzework, bronzes.

brednie *pl. Gen.* **-i** nonsense, baloney; **mówić brednie** talk nonsense; **opowiadać brednie** tell *l.* give *l.* feed sb a bunch of baloney.

bredzić *ipf.* **1.** (= *majaczyć*) rave; **bredzić przez sen** rave in one's sleep; **bredzić w gorączce** rave feverishly. **2.** (= *mówić głupstwa*) talk nonsense *l.* gibberish, babble; **bredzić od rzeczy** *l.* **trzy po trzy** talk a load of nonsense.

breja *f. Gen.* **-ei** muck, glop.

breloczek *mi* **-czk-** *Gen.* **-a** (= *wisiorek*) pendant; (*na kółku do kluczy*) fob; (*razem z kółkiem do kluczy*) key ring.

brelok *mi Gen.* **-a** pendant.

Brema *f. geogr.* Bremen.

Bretania *f. Gen.* **-ii** *geogr.* Brittany.

bretnal *mi Gen.* **-a** *przest.* floor nail.

Bretonka *f. Gen.pl.* **-ek**, **Bretończyk** *mp* Breton.

brew *f.* **-rwi-** eyebrow, brow; **zmarszczyć brwi** knit one's brows; **gęste/krzaczaste brwi** thick/ bushy eyebrows.

brewerie *pl. Gen.* **-ii** uproar, tumult, commotion; **urządzać** *l.* **wyprawiać (dzikie) brewerie** raise *l.* cause a ruckus; make a (wild) commotion.

brewiarz *mi Gen.* **-a** *rz.-kat.* breviary.

brezent *mi tk., żegl.* canvas; **brezent impregnowany** tarpaulin.

brezentowy *a.* canvas; **plandeka brezentowa** canvas tarpaulin.

briefing *mi* briefing; **przeprowadzić briefing** hold a briefing.

brnąć *ipf.* **-ij** wade; make *l.* fight *l.* plod one's way (*przez coś* through *l.* across sth); **brnąć w śniegu/błocie** *l.* **przez śnieg/błoto** wade through snow/mud; **brnąć przez nudną książkę** *przen.* wade through a boring book; **brnąć w długi** *przen.* run into debt.

broczyć *ipf.* (*zw. o krwi*) flow (from a wound); **broczyć krwią** (*o człowieku, zwierzęciu l. ranie*) bleed.

broda *f. Gen.pl.* **bród 1.** (= *podbródek*) chin; **zawiązać chustkę pod brodą** tie a scarf under one's chin. **2.** (*zarost*) beard; **długa/gęsta broda** long/thick beard; **golić brodę** shave one's beard; **zapuścić brodę** grow a beard; **nosić brodę** wear a beard; **pluć sobie w brodę** *przen., żart.* feel like kicking o.s. **3.** (*u zwierząt*) beard.

brodacz *mp* bearded man, man with a beard. **– ma** *kynol.* **brodacz monachijski** giant schnauzer.

brodaty *a.* bearded; **orłosęp brodaty** *orn.* lammergeier, bearded vulture (*Gypaetus barbatus*).

brodawka *f.* **1.** *anat.* (*część sutka*) nipple; (*u zwierzęcia*) teat; **brodawka sutkowa** mamilla. **2.** *anat.* (*językowa*) papilla; *bot.* papilla, pustule. **3.** *pat., zool.* wart; **usuwać brodawki** remove warts.

brodawkowy *a. zool.* **świnia brodawkowa** warthog (*Phacochoerus aethiopicus*).

brodzić *ipf.* wade (*w czymś* in sth, *przez coś* across sth); **brodzić w rzece** wade (in) the river.

brodziec *ma* **-dźc- 1.** *orn.* sandpiper, redshank. **2. brodziec krwawodzioby** common redshank (*Tringa totanus*).

brodzik *mi Gen.* **-a 1.** (*mały basen*) wading pool. **2.** (*w kabinie prysznicowej*) basin.

broić *ipf.* **broję broisz, brój 1.** (*płatać figle*) frolic, romp. **2.** (*czynić coś złego*) cause mischief.

brojler *ma hodowla* broiler.

brojlernia *f. Gen.pl.* **-i** broiler house, battery farm.

brokat *mi* brocade.

brokatowy *a.* (= *z brokatu*) brocade; (= *ozdobiony brokatem*) brocaded.

broker *mp fin., ubezp.* broker.

brokerski *a.* brokerage; **firma brokerska** brokerage; **usługi brokerskie** brokerage services.

brokuły *pl. Gen.* **-ów** *ogr., kulin.* broccoli.

brom *mi chem., med.* bromine.

bromatologia *f. Gen.* **-ii** bromatology.

bromek *mi* **-mk-** *chem.* bromide; **bromek srebra** silver bromide.

bromelia *f. Gen.* **-ii** bromelia (*Bromelia*).

bromian *mi chem.* bromate.

bromowodorowy *a. chem.* **kwas bromowodorowy** hydrobromic acid.

bromowodór *mi* **-or-** *chem.* hydrogen bromide.

bromowy *a.* bromide; **kwas bromowy** *chem.* bromic acid; **papier bromowy** *fot.* bromide paper.

brona *f.* **1.** *roln.* harrow; **brona zębata** spike-tooth harrow; **brona talerzowa** disk harrow. **2.** *bud., hist.* portcullis.

bronchit *mi pat.* bronchitis.

bronchoskop *mi med.* bronchoscope.

bronchoskopia *f. Gen.* **-ii** bronchoscopy.

bronić *ipf.* **1.** + *Gen.* defend (*sb l. sth*) (*przed czymś/kimś* against sb/sth); **bronić kraju przed wrogiem** fight in defense of one's country; **bronić miasta** defend a city; **bronić domu przed napastnikami** defend one's home against aggressors. **2.** + *Gen. l. Acc.* (= *strzec, chronić*) protect, shield; **bronić przed niebezpieczeństwem** protect from *l.* against harm; **wały broniące miasta przed powodzią** embankments protecting the town against flooding; **bronić pokoju** keep the peace; **bronić swoich interesów** protect *l.* look after one's interests; **broń Boże!** *l.* **niech Bóg broni!** *l.* **niech ręka boska broni!** God *l.* heaven forbid! **3.** + *Gen.* (= *odpierać zarzuty wobec*) defend; (*sprawy, idei*) champion; **bronić swojego stanowiska** defend one's position; stick to one's guns; **bronić swoich praw** stand up for one's rights; **bronić przyjaciół** stand up *l.* stick up for one's friends; **bronić doktoratu** defend one's dissertation. **4.** + *Acc. prawn.* defend, plead the case of (*sb*). **5.** (= *zabraniać*) forbid (*komuś robienia czegoś* sb doing sth *l.* to do sth); prohibit (*komuś* (*robienia*) *czegoś* sb from (doing) sth); **bronić komuś łowić ryby** forbid sb fishing *l.* to fish; **bronić komuś wstępu do swojego domu** refuse sb entrance into one's house. **6.** *sport* defend; **bronić bramki** keep goal. **~ się** *ipf.* **1.** (= *odpierać atak*) defend o.s.; **bronić się dzielnie** put up a good fight; **bronić się do upadłego** fight to one's last *l.* to one's dying breath; **bronić się do ostatka** fight to the last *l.* to the bitter end. **2.** (= *odpierać zarzuty*) defend o.s.; **bronić się przed oskarżeniami** defend o.s. against accusations; **bronić się w sądzie** defend o.s. in court. **3.** (= *strzec się*) protect o.s., shield o.s. (*przed kimś/czymś* from *l.* against sb/sth); **bronić się przed złymi myślami** *l.* **od złych myśli** suppress bad thoughts; **bronić się przed ciekawością sąsiadów** shield o.s. against the prying of one's neighbors; **bronić się przed napływającymi łzami** fight back tears.

bronować *ipf.* harrow.

broń *f.* **1.** (= *narzędzie walki*) weapon; (= *często* = *broń palna*) gun, firearm; (*zbiorowo*) weapons, weaponry, arms; **broń myśliwska** hunting rifle *l.* rifles; **broń przeciwpancerna** anti-tank weapon *l.* gun; **broń przeciwlotnicza** anti-aircraft weapon *l.* gun; **broń ręczna** handgun; **broń artyleryjska** artillery piece, field gun, cannon; **broń małokalibrowa** small-caliber weapon; **broń obosieczna** double-edged sword; **chwytać za broń** take up arms; **nosić broń** carry arms; **złożyć broń** lay down (one's) arms; **naładować broń** load a gun; **kaliber broni** the caliber of a gun; **wystąpić z bronią w ręku** offer armed resistance; **broń biała** hand weapons; **broń sieczna** cutting weapon; **broń palna** firearm(s); **broń automatyczna** automatic weapon; **broń krótka** handgun; **broń konwencjonalna** conventional weapon; **broń masowej zagłady** weapon of mass

destruction; **broń biologiczna** biological weapon; **broń chemiczna** chemical weapon; **broń jądrowa** *l.* **nuklearna** *l.* **atomowa** atomic *l.* nuclear weapon; **broń termojądrowa** thermonuclear weapon; **zawieszenie broni** armistice, truce; **do nogi broń!** order arms!; **prezentuj broń!** present arms!; **bagnet na broń!** fix bayonets!; **towarzysze broni** brothers in arms; **wezwanie do broni** call to arms; **być pod bronią** be mobilised; **bez broni** unarmed; **prowadzić/trzymać kogoś pod bronią** lead/keep sb at gunpoint; **dać komuś broń do ręki** *przen.* play into sb's hands; **wytrącić komuś broń z ręki** *przen.* take the wind out of sb's sails; **pobić** *l.* **pokonać kogoś jego własną bronią** *przen.* beat sb at his own game. **2.** (= *rodzaj sił zbrojnych*) arm; **broń lotnicza** the air arm; **generał broni** lieutenant general.

broszka *f. Gen.pl.* **-ek** brooch.

broszura *f.*, **broszurka** *f. Gen.pl.* **-ek** brochure, pamphlet; **broszura reklamowa/propagandowa/informacyjna** advertising/propaganda/informational brochure.

broszurowy *a.* brochure; **wydanie broszurowe** cheap paperback edition.

browar *mi* **1.** brewery. **2.** *pot.* (= *piwo*) brew, brewski.

browarnictwo *n.* brewing, beermaking.

browarniczy *a.* beer-making; **urządzenia browarnicze** beer-making equipment; **przemysł browarniczy** beer industry.

browarnik *mp* brewer.

browarny *a.* brewer's, brewing; **jęczmień/chmiel browarny** brewer's barley/hops.

browning *mi Gen.* **-a broń** = brauning.

bród *mi* **-o- 1.** ford; **bród na rzece/przez rzekę** ford on a river/in a river; **przejść rzekę w bród** ford a river. **2. w bród** (= *pod dostatkiem*) galore, aplenty, in abundance; **mamy jedzenia i picia w bród** we have food and drink galore.

bródka *f. Gen.pl.* **-ek 1.** *emf.* (= *podbródek*) chin. **2.** (*zarost*) small beard; **hiszpańska** *l.* **kozia bródka** goatee. **3.** *bot.* tuft.

bróg *mi* **-o- 1.** (= *wiata na siano l. zboże*) Dutch barn. **2.** (= *stóg siana*) haystack.

brr *int.* **brr, ale zimno!** brr, its cold!; **brr, ale ohyda!** ugh! that's disgusting!

brud *mi* **1.** (= *zanieczyszczenie*) dirt, filth; **gruba warstwa brudu** thick layer of dirt; **brud na rękach** dirt on one's hands; **smugi brudu na szybie** smudges of dirt on a window pane; **czarny od brudu** black with dirt; **oczyścić coś z brudu** clean the dirt from sth; **zmyć brud** wash away dirt. **2.** *zob.* **brudy**.

brudas *mp pl.* **-y** slob.

bruderszaft *mi* toast of friendship (*between two people, after which they will be on a first-name terms*); **pić bruderszaft** drink a toast to a new friendship; **zaproponować bruderszaft** propose a toast of friendship; **nie piliśmy (ze sobą) bruderszaftu** we're not on first-name terms yet.

brudno *adv.* **1.** dirty, filthy; **ale tu brudno!** how filthy!; what a pigsty! **2. na brudno** in the rough; **pisać na brudno** write a rough draft.

brudnopis *mi* first *l.* rough draft.

brudny *a.* **1.** (= *nieczysty*) dirty, filthy; (= *za-nieczyszczony, pobrudzony*) soiled, polluted; **brudna koszula** dirty shirt; **brudne ręce** soiled hands; **brudne naczynia** dirty *l.* unwashed dishes; **brudna robota** messy work; **spodnie brudne od błota** pants dirty with mud. **2.** (= *szarawy*) dingy, dirty; **brudna zieleń** dingy green. **3.** (= *niemoralny*) dirty, filthy, foul, unclean; **brudne myśli** unclean *l.* impure thoughts; **brudne interesy** dirty *l.* foul business; **ktoś ma brudne ręce** someone's hand are dirty.

brudy *pl.* *Gen.* -ów **1.** (= *nieczystości*) filth; **brudy płynące w ściekach** filth flowing in the sewers; **kubeł z brudami** bucket (full) of filth; **sprzątać po kimś brudy** clean up sb's filth. **2.** (= *garderoba do prania*) dirty laundry *l.* clothes; **oddać brudy do prania** send one's dirty laundry to the cleaners. **3.** *przen.* (= *wstydliwe sekrety*) dirty linen *l.* laundry; **brudy rodzinne** the family's dirty linen; **prać swoje brudy publicznie** wash one's dirty linen in public.

brudzić *ipf.* get (*sth*) dirty, soil; **brudzić ubranie** get one's clothes dirty; **brudzić podłogę** get the floor dirty; **brudzić coś błotem** get sth muddy; **brudzić sobie ręce** get one's hands dirty; **on nie lubi sobie brudzić rączek** *iron.* he refuses to soil his hands. **~ się** *ipf.* get dirty *l.* soiled.

Brugia *f.* *Gen.* -ii Bruges.

bruk *mi* **1.** (stone) pavement; **wyboisty bruk** bumpy pavement; **układać bruk** lay (a) pavement; **pieniądze leżą na bruku** *przen.* money grows on trees. **2.** *przen.* **wyrzucić kogoś na bruk** (*z pracy*) give sb the ax; (*z domu*) throw sb out onto the street; **znaleźć się na bruku** (= *stracić pracę*) get the ax; (= *stracić dach nad głową*) find o.s. on the street; **szlifować bruki** wander *l.* walk the streets.

brukać *ipf.* **1.** *lit.* dirty, soil (*sth*) (*czymś* with sth); **brukać biel koszuli** soil a white shirt. **2.** *przen.* tarnish, stain, blemish; **brukać swój honor/swoje dobre imię** tarnish one's honor/one's good name; **brukać czyjąś reputację** tarnish sb's reputation; **brukać swoją duszę** stain one's soul. **~ się** *ipf.* *lit.* dirty o.s. (*czymś* with sth); *przen.* tarnish one's reputation.

brukiew *f.* -kwi- *pl.* -e *bot.*, *kulin.* rutabaga, Swedish turnip; *Br.* swede (*Brassica napus napobrassica*).

brukować *ipf.* pave; **brukowana droga** paved road.

brukowiec *mi* -wc- *Gen.* -a **1.** (*kamień*) paving stone; (*okrągły*) cobblestone. **2.** *uj.* tabloid; *pog.* (gutter) rag; **wiadomości z brukowca** tabloid news.

brukowy *a.* **1.** (*o nawierzchni*) stone-paved; **nawierzchnia brukowa** stone-paved surface; **kamień brukowy** paving stone, cobblestone. **2.** *uj.* (= *niewybredny*) vulgar; **brukowe plotki** vulgar rumors; **gazeta brukowa** tabloid, rag; **prasa brukowa** tabloid press, gutter press.

Bruksela *f.* *geogr.* Brussels.

brukselka *f.* *Gen.pl.* -ek *bot.*, *kulin.* Brussels sprouts (*Brassica oleracea gemmifera*).

brulion *mi* **1.** (= *zeszyt*) notebook. **2.** (= *brudnopis*) rough *l.* first draft.

brunatnieć *ipf.* **1.** (= *stawać się brunatnym, ciemnieć*) turn brown, darken; **skóra brunatnieje od słońca** skin darkens from the sun. **2.** (= *być brunatnym*) appear brown *l.* dark.

brunatny *a.* **1.** brown; **węgiel brunatny** brown coal, lignite; **gleba brunatna** *roln.* brown soil; **niedźwiedź brunatny** *zool.* brown bear (*Ursus arctos*); **zgnilizna brunatna** *ogr.*, *pat.* brown rot. **2.** *przen.* *polit.* (= *nazistowski*) (neo-)Nazi; **brunatne koszule** *hist.* the Brown Shirts.

brunet *mp* dark-haired man.

brunetka *f.* *Gen.pl.* -ek brunette.

brusznica *f.* **1.** *bot.* cowberry, foxberry, mountain cranberry (*Vaccinium vitis-idaea*). **2.** *kulin.* (*owoc*) cranberry.

brutal *mp* *Gen.pl.* -i *l.* -ów **1.** (= *bezwzględny człowiek*) beast. **2.** (= *grubianin*) brute, boor.

brutalizacja *f.* brutalization; **brutalizacja życia** brutalization of life; **brutalizacja języka** butchering the language.

brutalizm *mi* brutality.

brutalizować *ipf.* brutalize. **~ się** *ipf.* grow brutal.

brutalnie *adv.* brutally, harshly; **obejść się z kimś brutalnie** mistreat *l.* abuse sb.

brutalność *f.* brutality, harshness; **brutalność policji** police brutality; **traktować kogoś z wyjątkową brutalnością** treat sb with extreme brutality; **ofiara brutalności męża** victim of her husband's brutality.

brutalny *a.* brutal, harsh; **brutalny mąż** brutal husband; **brutalna napaść** brutal assault; **brutalne słowa** harsh words; **potraktować kogoś w brutalny sposób** treat sb harshly.

brutto *a.* *indecl.* gross; **waga brutto** gross weight; **cena brutto** price including *l.* with tax; **zysk brutto** *fin.* gross profit; **produkt krajowy/narodowy brutto** *ekon.* gross domestic/national product.

bruzda *f.* **1.** (*rowek w ziemi*) furrow. **2.** (= *zmarszczka*) wrinkle, line; (*na czole*) furrow; **twarz pokryta bruzdami** face covered in wrinkles. **3.** (= *zagłębienie*) rut, groove; **bruzdy na stoku narciarskim** ruts on the ski run. **4. bruzda niskiego ciśnienia** *meteor.* low-pressure trough; **bruzda gwintu** *techn.* the groove of a thread; **bruzda lufy** *broń* rifle.

bruzdka *f.* *Gen.pl.* -ek wrinkle, shallow groove *l.* furrow.

bruzdkowanie *n.* *biol.* cleavage.

bruzdowany *a.* grooved; **lufa bruzdowana** *broń* rifled barrel; *bot.* (*np. o łodydze*) sulcate.

bruździć *ipf.* -żdżę -ździsz **1.** mark with wrinkles *l.* furrows. **2.** (= *ryć*) root; **dziki brużdżą pole** boars root in the fields. **3.** *pot.* (= *utrudniać, szkodzić*) thwart, sabotage; **ktoś mi bruździ w moich poczynaniach** sb has thrown a monkey-wrench into my plans.

brwi *itd.* *f.* *zob.* **brew.**

brwiowy *a.* eyebrow, superciliary; **łuk brwiowy** *anat.* eyebrow ridge, superciliary ridge; **rozcięty łuk brwiowy** cut eyebrow.

bryczesy *pl. Gen.* **-ów** riding breeches.

bryczka *f. Gen.pl.* **-ek** chaise.

brydż *mi Gen. i Acc.* **-a** bridge; **brydż sportowy** duplicate *l.* tournament bridge; **brydż towarzyski** rubber bridge.

brydżowy *a.* bridge; **rozgrywki brydżowe** bridge games; **licytacja brydżowa** bridge bidding.

brydżysta *mp*, **brydżystka** *f. Gen.pl.* **-ek** bridge player.

bryg *mi żegl.* brig.

brygada *f.* 1. (= *ekipa*) crew; **brygada robocza** work crew. 2. *wojsk.* brigade; **generał brygady** brigadier general.

brygadier *mp* 1. (= *brygadzista*) foreman. 2. *wojsk.* brigadier.

brygadowy *a.* (*o ekipie*) 1. crew. 2. **system brygadowy** crew system.

brygadzista *mp*, **brygadzistka** *f. Gen.pl.* **-ek** foreworker; (*tylko o mężczyźnie*) foreman.

bryja *f. Gen.* **-yi** *emf.* = **breja**.

bryk *mi Gen.* **-a** *szkoln.* (= *skrypt, ściąga*) set of cribnotes.

bryka *f.* 1. *pot.* (= *samochód*) (set of) wheels. 2. *arch.* (= *powóz*) coach, carriage.

brykać *ipf.* (*o dorosłym koniu, byku*) buck; (*o dziecku, młodym zwierzęciu*) romp, frolic; **źrebaki brykają** the ponies are frolicking.

brykiet *mi* briquet, briquette.

bryknąć *pf.* **-ij** 1. *zob.* **brykać**. 2. *pot.* (= *uciec*) take off (running), take to one's heels; **złodziej bryknął** the thief took off (running).

brylant *mi* 1. (*kamień szlachetny*) (cut) diamond; **pierścionek z brylantem** diamond ring. 2. (*szlif*) brilliant (cut). 3. *przen.* gem; **brylant, nie dziewczyna** she' a real gem. 4. *druk.* brilliant.

brylantowy *a.* diamond; (*o połysku*) adamantine.

brylantyna *f.* hair gel *l.* grease, brilliantine, Brylcreem.

brylować *ipf.* shine; **brylować w towarzystwie** shine in society; **brylować wśród aktorów** shine among actors.

bryła *f.* 1. (*kawał czegoś*) lump, clump; **bezkształtna bryła** shapeless lump; **bryła węgla** lump of coal; **bryła ziemi** clod *l.* clump of earth; **bryła lodu** cake of ice. 2. *fiz.* solid body. 3. *mat.* solid figure. 4. *sztuka* form.

bryłka *f. Gen.pl.* **-ek** clod; **bryłka złota** gold nugget; **bryłka korzeniowa** *roln.* root ball.

bryłowaty *a.* 1. (*kształt*) lumpy. 2. (= *zbity*) clumped; **bryłowata gleba** clumped earth.

bryłowy *a.* **kąt bryłowy** *mat.* solid angle.

bryndza *f.* 1. (*ser*) ewe's cheese. 2. *pot.* hard times.

brystol *mi* Bristol board, bristol, construction paper.

Bryt *mp pl.* **-owie** *hist.* Brit.

bryt *mi* gore.

brytan *ma* mastiff; *pot.* large watchdog.

brytfanka *f. Gen.pl.* **-ek** small (baking) pan.

brytfanna *f.* (baking) pan; **piec indyka w brytfannie** roast a turkey in a baking pan.

Brytyjczyk *mp*, **Brytyjka** *f. Gen.pl.* **-ek** Briton, Britisher; **Brytyjczycy** the British.

brytyjski *a.* British; **akcent brytyjski** British accent; **brytyjska odmiana angielskiego** British English; **Wyspy Brytyjskie** *geogr.* the British Isles; **Brytyjska Wspólnota Narodów** *polit.* the British Commonwealth.

bryza *f.* sea breeze, ocean breeze; **bryza nocna** night breeze.

bryzg *mi* splash; **bryzgi deszczu** spatters of rain; **bryzgi fali** spray from the waves; **bryzgi chromosferyczne** *astron.* chromospheric faculae.

bryzgać *ipf.*, **bryzgnąć** *pf.* **-ij**, **bryznąć** *pf.* **-znę -źniesz, -źnij** 1. (= *rozpryskiwać się*) splash; **błoto bryzga spod kół** mud splashes from under the wheels. 2. (= *rozpryskiwać*) splash, spray; **bryzgać pianą** spray foam.

bryzol *mi Gen.pl.* **-i** *l.* **-ów** beef cutlet.

brzana *f. icht.* barbel, Barbus barbus.

brzanka *f. Gen.pl.* **-ek** *icht.* (*różne gatunki z rodzaju Barbus*) barb.

brzask *mi* 1. (= *świt*) dawn, daybreak. 2. (= *poświata*) reflection (of light).

brzdąkać *ipf.*, **brzdąknąć** *pf.* **-ij** 1. **brzdąkać na gitarze** strum on the guitar. 2. **brzdąkać na banjo** plink on the banjo; **brzdąkać na pianinie** *żart.* tickle the ivories. 3. (= *dźwięczeć*) clank; (*o metalowych przedmiotach*) jangle; (*o szkle*) clink; **w bagażniku brzdąkały butelki** the bottles clinked in the trunk.

brzdęk *mi* clank, clink, jangle. – *int.* bang; **butelka poturlała się i brzdęk! o podłogę** the bottle rolled over and hit the floor with a bang.

brzdęknąć *pf.* **-ij** 1. = **brzdąknąć**; *zob.* **brzdąkać**. 2. fall with a bang.

brzechwa *f. broń* (= *stateczniki pocisku*) stabilizing fins; (= *trzon strzały*) shaft.

brzeczka *f.* wort; **brzeczka garbarska** *techn.* tanning liquor.

brzeg *mi* 1. waterside; (*między lądem a wodą*) shore; (*rzeki*) bank; (*morza*) coast; (= *plaża*) beach; **piaszczysty brzeg** sandy shore; **niski/wysoki brzeg** low/high bank; **urwisty brzeg** precipitous bank; **lewy/prawy brzeg rzeki** the left/right bank of a river; **brzeg rzeki** riverbank; **brzeg jeziora** lakeshore; **brzeg morza** seacoast, seashore; **cicha woda brzegi rwie** *przen.* still waters run deep; **na brzeg** ashore, to the shore; **na brzegu** on the bank *l.* shore; **wyrzucony na brzeg** washed ashore; **statek osiadł na brzegu** *żegl.* the ship was driven ashore. 2. *Gen.* **-u** *rzad.* **-a** (*kraniec, krawędź*) edge, brim, rim; **brzeg stołu** the edge of a table; **brzeg kapelusza** the brim of a hat; **książka ze złoconymi brzegami** book with gilt edging; **brzeg lasu/łąki** the edge of a forest/meadow; **leżeć z brzegu łóżka** lie on the edge of the bed; **może być pierwszy z brzegu** *l.* **z brzega** any (old) one will do; **wino przelewa się przez brzegi kieliszka** wine is poured along the rim of the glass; **pełny po brzegi** full to the brim; **wypełnić widownię po brzegi** fill the house.

brzegowy *a.* coastal, waterside; (*morza*)

oceanside; (*rzeki*) riverside; (*jeziora*) lakeside; **linia brzegowa** shoreline.

brzemienny *a.* **1.** (*o kobiecie*) pregnant. **2.** *lit.* loaded, laden, burdened (*czymś* with sth); **wozy brzemienne zbożem** wagons loaded with grain; **chmura brzemienna deszczem** cloud heavy with rain; **epoka brzemienna w niebezpieczeństwa** era fraught with danger; **zdarzenie brzemienne w skutki** event with far-reaching consequences; **rok brzemienny w wypadki** eventful year.

brzemię *n.* -mieni- *pl.* -mion- **1.** *lit.* (= *ciężar*) burden, weight; **brzemię klęski** burden of defeat; **brzemię trosk/winy** weight of concern/guilt. **2.** *przest.* (= *ładunek*) load.

brzeszczot *mi techn., broń* blade.

Brześć *mi geogr.* Brest.

brzezina *f.*, **brzezinka** *f. Gen.pl.* -ek birch grove.

brzeżek *mi* -żk- *Gen.* -a *l.* -u edge; **brzeżek serwetki** edge of a napkin; **siedzieć na brzeżku krzesła** sit on the edge of a chair.

brzęczeć *ipf.* -ę -ysz clang, clank, clatter, tinkle; (*o łańcuchu, rozbitym szkle*) rattle; (*o kluczach, monetach*) jingle, jangle; (*o kieliszkach, butelkach*) clink; (*o owadach*) buzz, hum; (*o strunach*) twang, plink, plunk; **brzęcząca moneta** jingling change.

brzęczek *mi* -czk- *Gen.* -a, **brzęczyk** *mi Gen.* -a *techn.* buzzer; **brzęczek telefonu** telephone ringer.

brzęczyk *mi Gen.* -a *techn. zob.* **brzęczek.**

brzęk *mi* clank, clang; **brzęk kluczy** the jingle *l.* jangle of keys; **brzęk monet** the jingle of change; **brzęk tłuczonego szkła** the tinkle of broken glass; **brzęk pszczół** the buzzing of bees; *zob.* **brzęczeć.**

brzękadło *n. Gen.pl.* -deł clanging *l.* jangling thing.

brzękliwy *a.* clanging, clanking, jingling, rattling, clattering; *zob.* **brzęczeć.**

brzęknąć *pf.* -ij **1.** *zob.* **brzęczeć. 2.** *rzad.* (= *puchnąć*) swell.

brzmieć *ipf.* -ię -isz, -ij **1.** (= *dźwięczeć*) sound, resound, be heard; (*o dzwonach, echu*) ring; (*o trąbce*) blare; **śpiew brzmiał w oddali** the song could be heard from a distance; **organy brzmiały** the organs resounded. **2.** (= *wydawać dźwięk*) sound; **pianino bardzo ładnie brzmi** the piano sounds very nice. **3.** (= *znaczyć*) sound; **wiem, że to głupio brzmi, ale kocham cię** I know it sounds stupid, but I love you; **jak brzmi rozkaz?** what is the order?

brzmienie *n.* **1.** (*o głosie, barwie dźwięku*) sound, voice, tone; **brzmienie piosenki** the sound of a song; **doskonałe brzmienie kwartetu** the perfect harmony of the quartet; **zaskakujące brzmienie śpiewaczki** the amazing voice of the singer; **brzmienie skrzypiec** the voice of the violin; **brzmienie starych organów** the sound of the old organ. **2.** (= *dosłowne znaczenie, zawartość*) content; **brzmienie dokumentu/umowy** the letter of the document/agreement.

brzmieniowy *a. muz.* sound; **struktura brzmieniowa** sound structure; **efekty brzmieniowe** sound effects.

brzoskwinia *f. bot.* peach tree (*Prunus persica*); (*owoc*) peach; **soczysta brzoskwinia** juicy peach.

brzoskwiniowy *a.* peach; **nektar brzoskwiniowy** peach nectar; **kolor brzoskwiniowy** peach (color); **cera brzoskwiniowa** peach-colored complexion.

brzost *mi bot.* (= *wiąz górski*) wych elm (*Ulmus glabra*).

brzoza *f. Gen.pl.* -óz birch(-tree) (*Betula*).

brzozowy *a.* birch; **las brzozowy** birch wood; **miotła brzozowa** birch broom.

brzózka *f. Gen.pl.* -ek *emf. zob.* **brzoza.**

brzuch *mi Gen.* -a stomach, belly; **pusty brzuch** empty stomach; **wielki brzuch** big belly; *pot. żart.* spare tire; **wciągać brzuch** suck in *l.* pull in one's gut; **leżeć do góry brzuchem** laze around; **wiercić dziurę w brzuchu** to make a nuisance of oneself; **brzuch mi spadł** I've lost my belly.

brzuchacz *mp żart.* chubby, fatso.

brzuchaty *a.* **1.** (= *z dużym brzuchem*) potbellied. **2.** (= *wypukły*) fat, (wide-)bellied.

brzuchomówca *mp* ventriloquist.

brzuchomówstwo *n.* ventriloquism.

brzusiec *mi* -śc- *Gen.* -a (*kciuka*) ball; (*noża*) blade; (*naczynia*) belly.

brzuszek *mi* -szk- *Gen.* -a *emf.* belly, paunch, gut; *dziec.* tummy; **mieć brzuszek** have a belly *l.* gut; **mężczyzna z brzuszkiem** man with a gut; **boli mnie brzuszek** *dziec.* my tummy hurts; **rośnie mi brzuszek** I'm getting a belly; **pozbyć się brzuszka** lose one's belly.

brzuszny *a. anat.* abdominal; **jama brzuszna** abdominal cavity; **dur brzuszny** *pat.* typhoid fever.

brzydactwo *n.* **1.** (*o czymś brzydkim*) eyesore, monstrosity. **2.** (*o kimś brzydkim*) ugly thing.

brzydal *mp Gen.pl.* -i *l.* -ów ugly man.

brzydki *a.* -dszy **1.** (= *nieładny*) ugly; **brzydka dziewczyna** ugly girl; **brzydki dom** ugly house; **brzydka pogoda** bad weather; **brzydki dzień** cloudy *l.* rainy day; **brzydki jak grzech śmiertelny** *l.* **jak noc** (as) ugly as sin; **płeć brzydka** *żart.* the unfair sex. **2.** (= *zły, niedobry*) bad, naughty; **brzydkie postępowanie** naughty behaviour. **3.** (= *nieprzyzwoity*) dirty, bad; **brzydkie myśli** dirty thoughts; **brzydkie wyrazy** dirty *l.* bad words.

brzydko *adv.* -dziej **1.** (= *nieładnie*) in an ugly way; **brzydko pisać** have ugly handwriting; **jest dzisiaj brzydko** the weather is terrible today. **2.** (= *źle*) badly; **brzydko się zachowałeś** you behaved badly. **3.** (= *nieprzyzwoicie*) in a dirty way; **mówić brzydko** talk dirty.

brzydnąć *ipf.* -ij; -dł *l.* -dnął -dła **1.** (= *stawać się nieładnym*) get *l.* grow ugly; **starzała się i brzydła** she got old and grew ugly. **2.** (= *nużyć*) **życie mi brzydnie** I'm sick and tired of life; **codzienne obowiązki brzydną mi** I'm sick of the daily grind.

brzydota *f.* **1.** (= *brak piękna*) ugliness; **uderzająca brzydota** striking ugliness; **brzydota dzielnicy przemysłowej** the ugliness of the industrial area. **2.** (= *ktoś brzydki*) fright, ugly thing. **3.** (= *coś brzydkiego*) eyesore, monstrosity; **tandetna brzydota** cheap monstrosity.

brzydula *f. żart.* plain Jane, bow-wow; **ależ brzydula!** what a dog!

brzydzić *ipf.* disgust, sicken. ~ **się** *ipf. + Ins.* detest, loathe, find (*sb l. sth*) repulsive *l.* disgusting; **brzydzę się kłamstwem** I detest lies; **brzydzę się jeść surową rybę** I detest eating raw fish; **brzydzę się taką muzyką** I find such music disgusting; **brzydzę się tym oszustem** that cheater makes me sick.

brzytwa *f. Gen.pl.* **-tew** (straight) razor; **ostrzyć brzytwę** sharpen a razor; **ostry jak brzytwa** (as) sharp as a razor; **tonący brzytwy się chwyta** a drowning man will clutch at a straw.

bubek *mp* **-bk-** *pl.* **-i** *pot. pog.* fancy-pants, poser; **nadęty bubek** conceited poser.

bubel *mi* **-bl-** *Gen.* **-a** *pot.* trash, garbage, junk, crap; (*samochód*) lemon.

bubkowaty *a. pot. pog.* fancy-pants, la-di-da; **bubkowaty facet** Mr. Fancy-Pants.

bublowaty *a. pot.* lousy, crappy, crummy, cruddy; **bublowate towary** lousy merchandise; **bublowata pamiątka** crummy souvenir; **bublowaty produkt** crappy product.

buc *mp pot. pog.* stuffed shirt, big-head.

bucefał *ma żart.* (= *rumak*) steed.

buch *int.* bang, thump, wham, whack.

buchać *ipf.* burst; (*o ogniu*) flare; (*o dymie*) belch (out); (*o cieczy*) gush; **ogień buchał z pieca** flames flared from the stove; **krew buchnęła z rany** blood gushed from the wound.

buchalter *mp przest.* bookkeeper.

buchalteria *f. Gen.* **-ii** *przest.* bookkeeping.

buchalteryjny *a. przest.* book-keeping.

buchnąć *pf.* **-ij** **1.** (= *uderzyć*) smack, whack; **buchnąć kogoś w łeb** smack sb in the head; **buchnąć w rękę** *przest., żart.* kiss sb's hand. **2.** (= *ukraść*) *pot.* rip off, swipe; **buchnąć pieniądze** make off with cash; **buchnąć samochód** rip off a car.

bucie *mi zob.* **but.**

bucik *mi Gen.* **-a** *emf.* shoe; **niezłe buciki** nice pair of shoes; **mamo, bucik mi się rozwiązał** *dziec.* mommy, my shoe came untied.

bucior *mi emf.* clodhopper; **wojskowe buciory** combat boots; **gdzie z tymi brudnymi buciorami!** where are you going with those dirty clodhoppers!

buczeć *ipf.* **-ę -ysz 1.** (*o owadzie, silniku*) buzz; (*o świetlówce*) hum; (*o pszczole*) drone; (*o syrenie, klaksonie*) hoot. **2.** *pot.* (= *płakać*) boohoo; **czego buczysz, dziewczyno?** what are you boo-hooing about, girl?

buczek *mi* **-czk-** *Gen.* **-a 1.** (*sygnalizator*) (steam) whistle, horn; **sygnał buczka** sygnal whistle; **buczek okrętu** ship's horn. **2.** (= *młody buk*) beech (sapling).

buczyna *f.* **1.** (*las*) beech forest. **2.** (*drewno*) beech (wood). **3.** (*owoce*) beechmast.

buda *f.* **1.** shed; (*dla psa*) house; **psia buda** doghouse, kennel; **do budy!** go away!; **to wszystko psu na budę** it's all worthless *l.* useless. **2.** (*stragan*) booth, stand, stall; **jarmarczne budy** fair stands. **3.** (*zadaszenie pojazdu*) cab;

brezentowa buda canvas cab; **ciężarówka z budą** truck with a cab. **4.** *szkoln.* (= *szkoła*) school.

Budapeszt *mi geogr.* Budapest.

Budda *mp hist., rel.* Buddha.

buddyjski *a. rel.* Buddhist; **mnich buddyjski** Buddhist monk; **religia/świątynia buddyjska** Buddhist religion/temple.

buddysta *mp*, **buddystka** *f. Gen.pl.* **-ek** Buddhist.

buddyzm *mi rel.* Buddhism.

budka *f. Gen.pl.* **-ek 1.** (*dla ptaków*) shelter. **2.** (*pomieszczenie*) booth; **budka telefoniczna** telephone booth; **budka strażnika** guard's shelter; **budka suflera** prompter's box; shell. **3.** (*kiosk*) stand; **budka z lodami** ice-cream stand; **budka z gazetami** newsstand.

budowa *f. Gen.pl.* **-dów 1.** (*czynność*) building, construction; **budowa domu nie trwała długo** building the house did not take long; **materiały do budowy domu** materials for building a house; **pracować przy budowie domu** work building a house; **budowa posuwa się wolno** construction is moving ahead slowly. **2.** (*o miejscu*) construction site; **wstęp na teren budowy zabroniony** no entry allowed on the construction site; **pracować na budowie** work on a construction site. **3.** (*struktura*) structure; **budowa kryształu** the structure of a crystal; **budowa wyrazu** word structure; **być atletycznej budowy** have an athletic build.

budować *ipf.* **1.** (= *wznosić*) build; **budować dom/most/drogę** build a house/bridge/road; **budować linię kolejową** lay a rail line; **budować z cegły** build with brick; **budować na piasku** *przen.* build on sand; **budować wzajemne zaufanie** *przen.* build mutual trust. **2.** (= *konstruować*) build, construct; **budować silniki okrętowe** build ship engines. **3.** (= *kreślić*) construct; **budować czworokąt** construct a square. **4.** (= *wzmacniać czyjeś morale*) edify, inspire; **Adam buduje mnie swoim przykładem** Adam is an inspiring example. ~ **się** *ipf.* **1.** (= *wznosić się*) be built; **w pobliżu buduje się pięć nowych domów** five homes are being built in the vicinity. **2.** (= *stawiać swój dom*) be (in the course of) building one's house. **3.** (= *wzmacniać się moralnie*) be inspired *l.* edified (*czymś* by sth).

budowla *f. Gen.pl.* **-i** structure; (= *budynek*) building, edifice; **monumentalna budowla** monumental structure; **budowla podziemna/naziemna** underground/above-ground structure; **budowla ziemna** earthen structure; **budowla inżynierska** engineered structure.

budowlaniec *mp* **-ńc-** *pl.* **-y** construction worker; *pot.* hard hat.

budowlany *a.* building, construction; **elementy budowlane** building elements; **roboty budowlane** construction work; **robotnicy budowlani** construction workers; **przedsiębiorca budowlany** (building) contractor; **przepisy budowlane** the building code. – *mp* (*robotnik*) construction worker, builder.

budownictwo *n.* **1.** (= *dział gospodarki*) construction (industry), building trade; **budownic-**

two społeczne public works construction; **budownictwo lądowe** civil engineering; **budownictwo mieszkaniowe/przemysłowe** housing/industrial construction. **2.** *pot.* (= *architektura*) architecture; **budownictwo indyjskie** Indian architecture; **zabytek budownictwa rzymskiego** a monument of Roman architecture.

budowniczy *mp* builder; **budowniczy mostu** bridge builder; **budowniczy osiedla mieszkaniowego** housing development builder.

budrys *mp dial., żart.* Lithuanian.

budrysówka *f.* (*kurtka*) duffle coat.

buduar *mi przest.* boudoir.

budujący *a.* edifying, inspiring; **budująca opowieść** edifying tale; **budujący przykład** inspiring example; **budujące postępowanie** exemplary behavior.

budulcowy *a.* lumber; **drewno budulcowe** lumber.

budulec *mi* -lc- *Gen.* -a building material; (*drewno*) lumber; **zgromadzić potrzebny budulec na budowę** gather necessary building materials at the construction site; **jako budulec wykorzystano granit** granite was used as a building material.

budynek *mi* -nk- building, edifice; **budynek drewniany** wooden building; **budynek murowany** brick building; **budynek mieszkalny** living quarters; **budynek komunalny** housing project; **budynek fabryczny** factory building; **budynek administracji** administration building; **wysoki budynek** high-rise building.

budyniowy *a.* pudding; **krem budyniowy** custard.

budyń *mi Gen.pl.* -i *l.* -ów *kulin.* pudding; **budyń waniliowy** vanilla pudding; **budyń czekoladowy** chocolate pudding; **budyń z sokiem malinowym** pudding with raspberry sauce.

budzenie *n.* waking up; **budzenie telefoniczne** wake-up call; **zamówić budzenie na szóstą** order *l.* request a wake-up call for six.

budzić *ipf.* **1.** (*ze snu*) wake (up), waken; **budzić kogoś na śniadanie/do szkoły** waken sb for breakfast/for school; **budzić kogoś z głębokiego snu** waken sb from a deep sleep; **nie budź licha (póki śpi)** let sleeping dogs lie; **budzić coś do życia** *przen.* waken sth back to life. **2.** (*o uczuciach*) invoke, evoke; (*ciekawość, namiętność, podejrzenia*) arouse; (*zaufanie, strach*) inspire; (*myśl*) prompt; **twoje zachowanie budzi we mnie odrazę** your behavior disgusts me; **nic dziwnego, że to zdarzenie budziło naszą czujność** it's no wonder that the event aroused our vigilance.

budzić się *ipf.* **1.** (*ze snu*) wake up, awaken; **budzę się niewyspany** wake up tired; **budzę się z bólem głowy** wake up with a headache; **budzić się z głębokiego snu** awaken from a deep sleep. **2.** (*o uczuciach*) arise; **budzi się nadzieja** hope is aroused; **w sercu budzi się tęsknota** a longing arises in one's heart.

budzik *mi Gen.* -a alarm (clock); **nastawić budzik na szóstą** set the alarm for six; **budzik dzwonił o piątej** the alarm clock rang at five.

budżet *mi* budget; **budżet państwa** national

budget; **budżet roczny** annual budget; **budżet na rok 2000** budget for (the year) 2000; **uchwalić budżet** pass a budget; **przekroczyć budżet** exceed a budget; **sporządzić projekt budżetu** draft a budget; **wydatki z budżetu** budgeted expenses; **cięcia w budżecie** cuts in the budget *l.* budget cuts; **pozycja budżetu** budget item.

budżetowy *a.* budget, budgetary; **komisja budżetowa** budget committee; **posiedzenie budżetowe** budget meeting; **cięcia budżetowe** budget cuts; **deficyt budżetowy** budget deficit; **dyscyplina/polityka budżetowa** budgetary discipline/policy; **ustawa budżetowa** budgetary proposal; **rezerwy budżetowe** budgetary reserves; **prawo budżetowe** budgetary law; **rok budżetowy** fiscal year; **subwencja budżetowa** budget subsidy; **debata budżetowa** budget debate.

bufa *f. strój* puff.

bufet *mi* **1.** (= *lokal gastronomiczny*) snack bar; **bufet dworcowy** railway station snack bar; **bufet w wagonie** dining car. **2.** (= *kontuar*) counter; **usiąść przy bufecie** take a seat at the counter; **wypić kawę przy bufecie** drink coffee at the counter. **3.** (= *stół z przekąskami*) buffet; **zimny bufet** cold buffet; **bufet z kanapkami** sandwich bar. **4.** (*mebel kuchenny*) buffet, sideboard.

bufetowa *f.*, **bufetowy** *mp decl. like a.* counter help.

bufiasty *a.* puffed out, bouffant; **bufiaste rękawy** leg-of-mutton sleeves; **bufiaste spodnie** baggy pants.

bufon *mp pl.* -i *l.* -y buffoon.

bufonada *f.* buffoonery.

bufor *mi Gen.* -u *l.* -a **1.** *kol.* buffer plate. **2.** *chem.* buffer. **3.** *komp.* buffer (memory); **bufor nakładkowy** overlay buffer; **bufor wejścia/wyjścia** input/output buffer; **bufor szybkiego dostępu** quick access buffer; **bufor klawiatury** keyboard buffer; **bufor łączenia** connection buffer.

buforować *ipf. komp.* buffer.

buforowy *a.* **1.** buffer; **strefa buforowa** buffer zone; **państwo buforowe** *polit.* buffer state. **2.** *kol.* buffer; **talerze buforowe** buffer plates. **3.** *chem.* buffer; **roztwór buforowy** buffer solution.

buhaj *ma Gen.pl.* -ów *hodowla* breeding bull.

bujać *ipf.* **1.** (= *latać*) soar, glide; **bujać w obłokach** have one's head in the clouds. **2.** (= *być niczym nieskrępowanym*) roam; **bujać po łąkach** roam the meadows. **3.** (= *krzewić się*) grow luxuriantly *l.* lushly; **trawa buja** grass grows lushly. **4.** (= *huśtać*) rock; **fale bujają łódź** the waves are rocking the boat. **5.** *pot.* (= *kłamać*) fib *l.* tell fibs; **nie bujaj!** don't tell fibs!; no kidding! ~ **się** *ipf.* **1.** (= *huśtać się*) rock; **bujać się w fotelu** rock (o.s.) in a chair. **2. bujać się w kimś** *pot.* (= *podkochiwać się*) be infatuated with sb.

bujak *mi Gen.* -a rocking chair.

bujany *a.* rocking; **fotel bujany** rocking-chair; **bujany konik** rocking-horse.

bujda *f. pot.* fib; **opowiadać bujdy** tell fibs; **bujda na resorach** baloney.

bujnąć *pf.* -ij rock. ~ **się** *pf.* rock (o.s.).

bujnie *adv.* lushly, luxuriantly; **rozkrzewić się bujnie** grow lushly.

bujny *a.* lush, luxuriant; **bujna trawa** lush grass; **bujne włosy** luxuriant hair; **bujna wyobraźnia** vivid *l.* active imagination; **bujne życie** *przen.* eventful life.

buk *mi* **1.** *Gen.* -a *l.* -u *bot.* beech(-tree) (*Fagus, Notofagus*). **2.** *Gen.* -u *stol.* beech (wood).

Bukareszt *mi geogr.* Bucharest.

bukat *ma Gen.* -a (*zwierzę*) veal calf. – *mi Gen.* -u (*skóra*) calf skin.

bukieciarka *f. Gen.pl.* -ek *zob.* **bukieciarz.**

bukieciarstwo *n.* flower arrangement.

bukieciarz *mp* flower arranger.

bukiecik *mi D* -a *l.* -u *emf.* small bouquet; (*przypinany do sukni*) corsage; (*w butonierce*) boutonniere.

bukiet *mi* **1.** (= *wiązanka*) bouquet; **bukiet róż** bouquet of roses; **bukiet z jarzyn** *kulin.* mixed vegetables. **2.** (*aromat*) bouquet. **3.** *myśl.* doe's tail.

bukiew *f.* -kwi- beechmast.

bukinista *mp* second-hand bookseller.

bukłak *mi Gen.* -a *przest.* wine skin.

bukmacher *mp* bookmaker *l.* bookie.

bukoliczny *a.* pastoral, bucolic; **poezja bukoliczna** pastoral poetry.

bukolika *f.* pastoral, bucolic.

bukować[1] *ipf.* book, reserve; **bukować bilet** book a ticket.

bukować[2] *ipf. myśl.* (*o zwierzętach*) mate.

bukowy *a.* **1.** (*o drzewie*) beech; **las bukowy** beech forest. **2.** (*o drewnie*) beech, beechwood; **meble bukowe** beech furniture.

buksować *ipf.* **1.** spin. **2.** *żegl.* tow.

bukszpan *mi* **1.** *bot.* box (*Buxus sempervirens*). **2.** *stol.* boxwood.

bukszpanowy *mi* **1.** *o żywopłocie itp.* box. **2.** *stol.* boxwood.

bukszpryt *mi żegl.* bowsprit.

bulaj *mi Gen.* -a *l.* -u *Gen.pl.* -ów *l.* -ai *żegl.* bull's-eye.

buldog *ma* bulldog.

buldożer *mi Gen.* -a bulldozer.

bulgot *mi* gurgle, guggle, bubbling sound.

bulgotać *ipf.* -czę -czesz *l.* -cę -cesz, -cz **1.** (*o płynie*) gurgle, guggle, bubble. **2.** (*o indyku*) gobble.

bulić *ipf. pot.* shell out, fork out, cough up.

bulimia *f. Gen.* -ii *med.* bulimia.

bulion *mi* bouillon; **filiżanka bulionu** cup of bouillon.

bulionowy *a.* bouillon; **przyprawa/kostka bulionowa** bouillon powder/cube.

bulla *f. Gen.pl.* -i *kośc.* papal bull.

bulterier *ma* bullterrier.

bulwa *f.* **1.** *bot.* (*łodyga*) tuber; (*cebuli, czosnku, kwiatu*) bulb; **bulwy ziemniaków** potato tubers. **2.** *przen.* protuberance. **3.** *bot., kulin.* Jerusalem artichoke (*Helianthus tuberosus*).

bulwar *mi* **1.** (*ulica*) boulevard, avenue. **2.** (*nabrzeże*) embankment; (*nad morzem*) breakwater, seawall; **bulwar portowy** harbor breakwater. **3.** *hist.* (= *bastion*) bulwark, bastion.

bulwarowy *a.* **1.** boulevard; **teatr bulwarowy** boulevard theater. **2.** (= *brukowy*) street, gutter; **prasa bulwarowa** tabloid press.

bulwersować *ipf. lit.* disturb, shock; **bulwersująca wiadomość** shocking news.

bulwiasty *a.* **1.** (*w kształcie bulwy*) bulbous; **bulwiasta narośl** bulbous growth; **bulwiasty nos** bulbous nose. **2.** *bot.* (= *mający bulwy*) tuberous, bulbous; **rośliny bulwiaste** tuberous *l.* bulbous plant; **korzeń bulwiasty** corm.

bulwowy *a.* = **bulwiasty** 2.

buła *f.* **1.** *emf.* (= *bułka*) large roll; **policzki jak buły** apple cheeks. **2.** *pog.* (*o człowieku*) oaf. **3.** (*o bryle*) lump; *geol.* nodule.

bułanek *ma* -nk- dun(-colored) (horse).

bułany *a.* dun; **bułana klacz** dun mare; **bułany ogier** dun stallion. – *ma* (*koń*) dun; **dosiąść bułanego** mount a dun.

buława *f.* **1.** (*insygnium*) mace, baton; **buława marszałkowska** field-marshal's baton. **2.** (*godność*) mantle; **objąć buławę marszałkowską** assume the mantle of field marshal. **3.** *hist., broń* mace.

bułeczka *f. Gen.pl.* -ek *emf.* roll, bun.

Bułgar *mp* Bulgarian.

Bułgaria *f. Gen.* -ii Bulgaria.

Bułgarka *f. Gen.pl.* -ek *zob.* **Bułgar.**

bułgarski *a.* Bulgarian; **po bułgarsku** in Bulgarian.

bułgarysta *mp* specialist in Bulgarian studies.

bułgarystyczny *a.* **studia/publikacje bułgarystyczne** Bulgarian studies program/publications.

bułgarystyka *f.* Bulgarian studies.

bułka *f. Gen.pl.* -ek roll, bun; **świeża bułka** fresh roll; **czerstwa bułka** stale roll; **chrupiąca bułka** crispy roll; **sucha bułka** dry roll; **bułka paryska** French roll; **bułka tarta** bread crumbs *l.* breadcrumb; **bułka z masłem** *przen.* (= *łatwizna*) piece of cake; **dla mnie to bułka z masłem** it's easy as pie for me.

bum[1] *int.* boom, bang; **a moje serce bum, bum** and my heart went boom, boom; **z oddali słychać jak bębny bum, bum, bum** from a distance you could hear the drums going boom, boom, boom.

bum[2] *mi zob.* **bom.**

bumelanctwo *n.* **1.** (= *nieobecność*) *pot.* absenteeism. **2.** (= *marnowanie czasu*) *pot.* slacking *l.* goofing off, shirking.

bumelant *mp pot.* slacker, goof off.

bumelka *f. Gen.pl.* -ek *pot.* skipped day of work.

bumelować *ipf. pot.* slack *l.* goof off, shirk.

bumerang *mi Gen.* -u *l.* -a boomerang.

bungalow *mi* bungalow.

bunkier *mi* -kr- *Gen.* -a **1.** (*schron*) bunker. **2.** *hist.* underground prison cell (*in Nazi concentration camps*). **3.** *żegl.* (*magazyn paliwa*) bunker. **4.** *żegl.* (*woda i paliwo*) ship's water and fuel supply. **5.** *techn.* (*zbiornik*) (storage) bunker.

bunkrować *ipf. żegl.* bunker, fuel.

bunkrowiec *mi* -wc- *Gen.* -a *żegl.* bunker ship.

bunkrowy *a.* bunker; **stacja bunkrowa** *żegl.*

bunker station; **węgiel bunkrowy** *górn.* bunker coal.

bunt *mi* **1.** (= *wystąpienie przeciw władzy*) rebellion, revolt; (*marynarzy, żołnierzy*) mutiny; **zarzewie buntu** firebrand; **podnieść bunt** rise up (in revolt); **stłumić bunt** put down rebellion; **wzywać do buntu** incite to revolt; **bunt się szerzy** rebellion spread; **wybuchł bunt** rebellion broke out. **2.** (= *sprzeciw wewnętrzny*) defiance, protest, revolt; **bunt młodzieńczy** youth revolt.

buntować *ipf.* incite to rebel, stir up (*przeciw komuś, czemuś* against sb, sth). ~ **się** *ipf.* (= *wzniecać bunt*) rebel, revolt (*przeciw komuś / czemuś* against sb/sth); (= *działać na przekór nakazom*) defy; **buntować się przeciw nakazom ojca** defy one's father's orders; **buntować się przeciw monotonii życia** rebel against the monotony of life.

buntowniczka *f. Gen.pl.* **-ek** *zob.* **buntownik** 1.

buntowniczo *adv.* rebelliously, defiantly; **być buntowniczo usposobionym do czegoś** have a defiant attitude towards sth.

buntowniczy *a.* rebellious, defiant; **buntownicza postawa** defiant stance; **buntowniczy charakter** rebellious character.

buntownik *mp* **1.** rebel. **2.** (*marynarz, żołnierz*) mutineer.

buńczucznie *adv.* swaggeringly, cockily, with panache.

buńczuczny *a.* (= *zawadiacki*) cocky, swaggering; **buńczuczny charakter** swaggering character; **buńczuczna mina** cocky look; **buńczuczna odpowiedź** blustering reply.

buńczuk *mi Gen.* **-a 1.** *hist.* (*insygnium*) horsetail ensign. **2.** *hist.* (*ozdobny pęk włosia*) panache.

bura *f. pot.* dressing down, talking to; **dostać burę** get a dressing down; **dać komuś burę** give sb a dressing down.

buraczany *a.* beet; (*kolor*) beet-red; **sok buraczany** beet juice; **pole buraczane** beet fields.

buraczek *mi* **-czk-** *Gen.* **-a** (= *mały burak*) small beet.

buraczki *pl. Gen.* **-ów** *kulin.* beets.

buraczkowy *a.* (*o kolorze*) beet-red, claret (-colored); **buraczkowe wypieki** deep blush.

burak *mi Gen.* **-a 1.** *bot., roln.* beet (*Beta vulgaris*); **burak ćwikłowy** (red) beet; **burak cukrowy** sugar beet. **2.** (*warzywo*) beetroot, beet; **buraki na barszcz** beets for borshch; **czerwony jak burak** (as) red as a beet.

buraki *pl. Gen.* **-ów** *kulin.* beets; **zając z burakami** rabbit with beets.

burakowy *a. zob.* **buraczkowy.**

burczeć *ipf.* **-ę -ysz 1.** (*o brzuchu*) rumble *l.* grumble, growl; **burczy mi w brzuchu** my stomach is growling. **2.** *pot.* (= *zrzędzić*) grumble, gripe, bitch, belly-ache; **burczeć coś pod nosem** grumble under one's breath; **burczeć na męża** gripe at one's husband.

burczymucha *f. l. mp decl. like f. Gen.pl.* **-ch** *l.* **-ów** *żart.* griper, grumbler.

burda *f.* brawl, fracas; **wszczynać burdy** start a brawl.

burdel *mi* **1.** *pot.* (= *dom publiczny*) brothel, whorehouse. **2.** *pot.* (= *bałagan*) mess, pigsty; **ale tu burdel!** what a pigsty!; **zrobić u siebie burdel** turn one's place into a pigsty; **burdel na kółkach** a complete *l.* total mess.

burdelowy *a.* brothel; *pot. uj.* (= *w niestosownym guście*) risqué, racy.

burek *ma* **-rk- 1.** *pot.* (*pies*) mutt, mongrel. **2.** *pog.* (= *prostak*) hick, redneck, good ol' boy.

burgrabia *mp Gen.* **-ego** *l.* **-i** *Dat.* **-emu** *l.* **-i** *Acc.* **-ego** *l.* **-ę** *Ins.* **-ą** *Loc.* **-i** *l.* **-im** *Voc.* **-o** *pl.* **-owie** *Gen.* **-ów** *hist.* burgrave.

burgund *mi Gen.* **-a** burgundy (wine).

Burgundia *f. Gen.* **-ii** *geogr., hist.* Burgundy.

burkliwy *a.* surly, gruff; **burkliwa odpowiedź** surly *l.* curt reply; **burkliwy ton** gruff tone; **burkliwe dziecko** surly child.

burknąć *pf.* **-ij** snarl, growl; **burknąć coś ze złością** snarl sth angrily; **burknąć coś niewyraźnie** growl sth under one's breath.

burleska *f. Gen.pl.* **-ek** *lit., muz.* burlesque.

burmistrz *mp pl.* **-owie** *l.* **-e** mayor.

burmistrzowski *a.* mayor's, of the mayor.

burmistrzyni *f. zob.* **mayor;** (= *żona burmistrza*) mayor's wife; *gł. Br.* mayoress.

burnus *mi Gen.* **-a 1.** (*okrycie arabskie*) burnous *l.* burnoose. **2.** *przest.* (*płaszcz damski*) woman's overcoat.

buro *adv.* **na dworze jest buro** it's cloudy outside.

bursa *f. uniw.* dormitory.

burski *a.* Boer; **wojny burskie** *hist.* Boer wars.

bursztyn *mi* **1.** (*żywica*) amber. **2.** (*biżuteria*) amber jewelry.

bursztyniarstwo *n.* amber working.

bursztynowy *a.* **1.** (*z bursztynu*) amber; **bursztynowa broszka** amber broach; **bursztynowy trakt** *hist.* the Amber Trail; **bursztynowa komnata** *hist.* the Amber Room; **kwas bursztynowy** *chem.* succinic acid. **2.** (*o kolorze*) amber(-colored); **bursztynowy pukiel włosów** amber curl.

burta *f.* **1.** (*łodzi, statku*) board, side; **burta w burtę** aboard; **człowiek za burtą!** man overboard!; **lewa burta** port (side); **prawa burta** starboard (side); **burta zawietrzna** lee (side); **wolna burta** freeboard. **2.** (*samolotu*) board. **3.** (*kanału*) edge, brim. **4.** *bud.* border.

burtowy *a.* hull; **numer burtowy** hull number; **poszycie burtowe** hull sheathing.

bury *a.* **1.** dark dun, (dark) gray; (*o niebie*) cloudy, dark, overcast; **bury koń** dark dun(-colored) horse. **2. bure oczy** dark gray eyes; **w nocy wszystkie koty bure** in the dark *l.* night all cats are gray.

burza *f.* **1.** (*zjawisko przyrody*) storm; **burza śnieżna** snowstorm; **burza gradowa** hailstorm; **burza z piorunami** electrical storm; **zanosi się na burzę** a storm is brewing; **rozpętała się burza** a storm broke out; **burza przechodzi bokiem** a storm is passing by; **burza frontowa** *meteor.* line squall; **burza magnetyczna** *meteor.* magnetic storm; **burza piaskowa** *meteor.* sandstorm; **wpadać jak burza** storm in; **lecieć jak burza** fly like greased lighting; **kto wiatr sieje, burzę zbiera** sow the wind and reap the whirlwind. **2.** *przen.* storm, burst; **burza oklasków** burst of applause; **burza śmiechu** burst of laughter; **burza protestów** firestorm of protest; **rozpętać burzę uczuć** stir up a storm of emotions; **burza zieleni** burst of greenery; **burza włosów** shock of hair; **burza w szklance wody** tempest in a teacup; **burza mózgów** brainstorm.

burzliwie *adv.* stormily, wildly; **moje życie toczy się burzliwie** I have led a stormy life; **burzliwie dyskutować** discuss boisterously; **burzliwie się kochać** make love wildly.

burzliwy *a.* **1.** (*o burzy*) stormy; **burzliwe lato** stormy summer; **burzliwa pogoda** stormy weather; **burzliwe morze** rough sea. **2.** *przen.* stormy; **burzliwe wydarzenia** tumultuous events; **burzliwe czasy** turbulent times; **burzliwa młodość** wild youth; **burzliwe życie** checkered life; **burzliwe wody** turbulent *l.* rough waters; **czyjaś burzliwa natura** sb's tempestuous nature; **burzliwa dyskusja** boisterous discussion; **burzliwa miłość** tempestuous love.

burzowiec *mi* -wc- *Gen.* -a *bud.* storm sewer.

burzowy *a.* storm; **pogoda burzowa** stormy weather; **chmura burzowa** *meteor.* storm cloud; **kanał burzowy** *bud.* storm sewer; **nawałnik burzowy** *zool.* storm petrel.

burzyciel *mp*, **burzycielka** *f. Gen.pl.* -ek *lit.* destroyer, iconoclast; **burzyciel starego porządku** destroyer of the old order.

burzycielski *a.* destructive; **burzycielska teoria** subversive theory; **burzycielski charakter** destructive nature.

burzyć *ipf.* **1.** (= *niszczyć*) demolish, destroy; (*budynek*) tear down; (*plany*) upset; (*spokój*) shatter; **burzyć stare magazyny** demolish an old warehouse; **bomba burząca** *wojsk.* blockbuster. **2.** (= *wichrzyć*) stir up; (*włosy*) ruffle; **cała ta sprawa burzy we mnie krew** the whole business gets my blood boiling. ~ **się** *ipf.* **1.** (= *falować*) surge, churn, billow; **morze się burzy** the sea is churning. **2.** (= *denerwować się*) seethe (with anger); **burzyć się na myśl o czymś** seethe with anger at the thought of sth. **3.** (= *buntować się*) rebel, revolt. **4.** (= *fermentować*) ferment; **wino się burzy** wine ferments.

burżazja *f.* bourgeoisie.

burżuazyjny *a.* bourgeois; **demokracja burżuazyjna** bourgeois democracy; **społeczeństwo burżuazyjne** bourgeois society.

burżuj *mp Gen.pl.* -ów, **burżujka** *f. Gen.pl.* -ek *pog.* bourgeois; **burżuje** (*zbiorowo*) the bourgeoisie.

burżujski *a. pog.* bourgeois.

busola *f. żegl., lotn.* compass.

busz *mi* the bush; **przedzierać się przez busz** make one's way through the bush.

buszel *mi miern.* bushel.

Buszmen *mp*, **Buszmenka** *f. Gen.pl.* -ek Bushman.

buszmeński *a.* Bushman.

buszować *ipf.* scour (*po czymś* sth); **buszować po lesie** scour the forest; **buszować po mieście** scour the town; **buszować po szufladach** rummage through the drawers.

but *mi Gen.* -a **1.** (*na nodze*) shoe; (*wysoki*) boot; **damskie/męskie/dziecięce buty** women's/men's/children's shoes; **buty narciarskie** ski boots; **ciasne buty** tight(-fitting) shoes; **wygodne buty** comfortable shoes; **wysokie buty** high boots; **niskie buty** low boots; **buty na wysokich obcasach** high-heeled shoes *l.* boots; **włożyć buty** put on one's shoes; **zdjąć** *l.* **zzuć buty** take off one's shoes; **zawiązać buty** tie one's shoes; **pastować buty** polish shoes; **łyżka do butów** shoehorn; **takie buty!** well, well!; **nie kiwnąć palcem w bucie** not lift *l.* raise a finger; **umarł w butach!** tough luck!, so much for that; **głupi jak but** (as) dumb as an ox; **szewc bez butów chodzi** none worse shod than the shoemaker's wife. **2.** *techn.* (*okucie*) shoe; **but stępora** stamp head.

buta *f.* arrogance, haughtiness; **pełen buty** full of arrogance.

butadien *mi chem.* butadiene.

butan *mi chem.* butane.

butanol *mi chem.* butanol, butyl alcohol.

buteleczka *f. Gen.pl.* -ek small bottle, ampule.

butelka *f. Gen.pl.* -ek **1.** bottle; **pić z butelki** drink from the bottle; **zaglądać do butelki** be fond of the bottle; **wysuszyć butelkę** down a bottle; **nabić kogoś w butelkę** *pot. przen.* take sb in. **2. butelka lejdejska** *fiz.* Leyden jar.

butelkować *ipf.* bottle.

butelkowy *a.* bottled, in bottles; **piwo butelkowe** bottled beer; **zieleń butelkowa** (*kolor*) bottle green.

butik *mi* boutique.

butikowy *a.* boutique.

butla *f. Gen.pl.* -i **1.** (*na gaz*) cylinder, tank, container; **butla oplatana** carboy. **2.** *emf.* (= *gąsior*) demijohn.

butnie *adv.* arrogantly, haughtily; **zachowywać się butnie** behave arrogantly.

butny *a.* arrogant, haughty, overbearing.

butonierka *f.* buttonhole; **goździk w butonierce** carnation in one's buttonhole.

butwieć *ipf.* rot *l.* moulder (away).

buu *int.* (*okrzyk dezaprobaty*) boo; (*płacz*) boohoo.

buzdygan *mi Gen.* -a *l.* -u *broń, hist.* mace.

buzia *f. Gen.pl.* -i *l.* buź *emf.* **1.** (= *usta*) mouth. **2.** (= *całus*) **dać/dostać buzi** give/get a kiss. **3.** (= *twarz*) face; **ładna buzia** pretty face; **dostać po buzi** get one in the kisser; **trzymać kogoś za buzię** *przen.* keep sb on a leash.

buziak *mi Gen.* -a *emf.* = **buzia** 2, 3.

buzować *ipf.* (*o ogniu*) blaze.

buźka *f. Gen.pl.* -ek *emf.* = **buzia**; **duża buźka** big kiss.

by *partykuła trybu przypuszczającego* **bym byś byśmy byście** (*pisana łącznie z osobowymi formami czasownika i spójnikami*) **kiedy by można was odwiedzić?** when could we visit you?; **ty byś tego nie powiedział** you wouldn't say that; **trzeba by spróbować** one ought to try; **gdybyś przyszedł wcześniej, spotkalibyśmy się** if you had come earlier, we would have met. – *conj.* (in order) to; **poszedł do banku, by podjąć pieniądze** he went to the bank to get some money; **on jest za głupi, by to zrozumieć** he's too stupid to understand it; **wyszedł z domu, by po chwili wrócić** he left the house, only to return a moment later; **mówiłem mu, by tam nie szedł** I told him not to go there; **by tak rzec** so to speak.

bycie *n.* being; **sposób bycia** manner.

byczek *ma -czk-* (= *młody byk*) bull calf. *− mp* **-czk-** *pl.* **-i** *żart.* (*młody mężczyzna*) young buck.

byczki *pl. Gen.* **-ów** *kulin.* sculpins, bullheads; **puszka byczków** can of sculpins.

byczo *adv.* awesome, cool; **na wakacjach było byczo** the vacation was awesome.

byczy *a.* **1.** (*o byku*) bull; **bycza skóra** bull hide. **2.** (*jak u byka*) bull's, like a bull; **on ma taki byczy kark** he has a bull neck. **3.** *pot.* awesome, cool; **byczy facet** cool guy.

byczyć się *ipf. pot.* laze away, lay around.

być[1] *ipf.* **jestem jesteś są; będę będziesz bądź 1.** (= *znajdować się w jakimś stanie l. miejscu*) be; (= *istnieć*) exist, be there; **być na diecie** be on a diet; **być na emeryturze** be retired; **jestem po robocie** I'm finished *l.* done with work (for today); **pewnego razu był sobie król...** once upon a time there lived a king...; **w ogrodzie były róże** there were roses in the garden; **w Galaktyce są miliardy gwiazd** there are billions of stars in the Galaxy; **ile ich jest?** how many of them are there?; **być w kinie** be at the theater; **być na wycieczce** be on a trip; **być w Warszawie** be in Warsaw; **być u babci na wsi** be at grandma's house in the country; **być z kimś sam na sam** be one on one with sb; **od świtu jestem na nogach** I have been on my feet all day; **Ewa jest na ostatnich nogach** Eva is ready to drop *l.* dead on her feet; **jesteś na drodze do zawału** you are on the road to a heart attack; **wszystko jest na swoim miejscu** everything is in its place; **to było nie na miejscu** that was out of line; **być na ustach całego miasteczka** be on the lips of everyone in town; **być jedną nogą na tamtym świecie** have one foot in the grave; **co dzisiaj będzie na obiad?** what's for supper today?; **wszystko jest pod ręką** we have everything right at hand; **być u steru** *przen.* be at the wheel; **no to jestem w domu** (= *zrozumiałem*) that hits home; **być w latach** *l.* **w leciech** be up in one's years; **być w sile wieku** be in one's prime; **być w opałach** be in a bind; **teraz wszystko jest w twoich rękach** now everything is in your hands *l.* up to you; **być w siódmym niebie** be in seventh heaven; **być w swoim żywiole** be in one's element; **być na zebraniu** be at a meeting; **być na wojnie** be (fighting) in a war; **być na studiach** be at college; **być na anglistyce** be in the English Department; **nigdy nie byłem w Chicago** I've never been to Chicago; **Adam jest pod pantoflem swojej żony** Adam is henpecked; **być nie w sosie** be in a bad mood; **jest gaz i woda** we have gas and water; **jestem takiego samego zdania** I'm of the same opinion; **jestem dobrej myśli** I'm hoping for the best; **jest mi u ciebie tak dobrze** I feel so good at your place; **jest mi głupio** I feel stupid; **to jest do niczego** it's no good; **być górą**

be on top; **to nie jest czas po temu** this is not the time for that; **to nie jest mi na rękę** this is inconvenient (for me); **to nie jest po mojej myśli** that's not what I intended *l.* what I had in mind; **jestem pod wrażeniem** I'm impressed; **jestem bez pieniędzy** I'm broke; **jestem w ciąży** I'm pregnant; **Ewa jest przy nadziei** *przest.* Eva is in the family way; **jestem na służbie** I'm on duty; **byliśmy na spacerze** we were taking a walk; **dobrze wiesz, że jesteś na mojej łasce** you know fully well that you're at my mercy; **czy jesteś w stanie mnie zrozumieć?** are you able to understand me?; **jestem w dobrym humorze** I'm in a good mood; **byliśmy w kłopocie, co zrobić z...** we couldn't figure out what to do with...; **Ewa przez moment była w rozterce** for a moment Ewa was in a dilemma; **Ewa jest z Adamem w przyjaźni** Ewa is friends with Adam; **po czyjej jesteś stronie?** whose side are you on?; **Adam jest w porządku** Adam is OK *l.* alright; **to nie jest w moim guście** that's not my style; **jestem na bakier z gramatyką** I haven't a clue about grammar; **z teściową jestem na złej stopie** I'm on bad terms with my mother-in-law; **z prezesem jestem na ty** I'm on a first name basis with the president; **jestem za reformą** I'm for the reform; **oni są z sobą za pan brat** they are on familiar terms; **jestem z Ewą po słowie** *przest.* I'm engaged to Eve. **2.** (*część orzeczenia imiennego*) **jestem studentem** I am a student; **byłam piosenkarką** I was a singer; **będę generałem** I will be a general; **ta dziewczyna jest ładna** that girl is pretty; **samochód jest ojca** that's father's car; **ten długopis nie jest mój** this pen isn't mine; **bądź zdrów!** get well!; **jesteś dla mnie niczym!** you mean nothing to me; **on nie był sobą** he wasn't himself; **dwa razy dwa jest cztery** two plus two is *l.* equals four. **3.** (*w zdaniach bezosobowych*) (= *zdarzać się*) **jest piękny dzień** it's a beautiful day; **był kwiecień** it was April; **było to dość dawno** it was *l.* happened quite a long time ago; **był do ciebie telefon** you had a call; **było już późno** it was getting late; **nie ma co jeść** there's nothing to eat; **będzie z godzinę temu** it's been an hour since...; **a co będzie ze mną?** what will happen to me?; **ciekaw jestem, co z niego będzie** I'm curious (about) what will become of him; **jeżeli tak jest** if it is so; **być może** maybe, perhaps; **co będzie, to będzie** come what may; **co było, to było** let bygones be bygones; **jakoś to** (w końcu) **będzie** things will turn out fine (in the end); **co ci jest?** what's wrong *l.* the matter with you?; **z tej mąki nie będzie chleba** it's hopeless; **nie może być** that's impossible; **jest już po nim** it's too late for him; he's done for; he's a goner *l.* a has-been; **co było, a nie jest, nie pisze się w rejestr** what's done is done; **tak jest!** exactly!, precisely!, that's right; *wojsk.* yes, sir!; **to jest** (= *czyli*) that is; **było nie było** whatever happens; no matter what (happens).

być[2] *ipf. czasownik posiłkowy* **1.** *tylko* **będę będziesz** *itd.* (*w formach czasu przyszłego*) will (be); **będę pamiętał o tym** I'll remember that; **dzieci będą w ogrodzie** the kids will be in the garden; **będziemy śpiewać kolędy** we're going to sing carols. **2.** (*w formach strony biernej*) **dom był sprzedany za...** the house was sold for...; **jesteś obserwowany** you are being watched; **droga jest już naprawiona** the road has been repaired.

bydlak *mp pl.* -i *obelż.* (= *brutal, prostak, łajdak*) animal, beast, scoundrel.

bydlątko *n. emf.* (= *młode stworzenie, zwierzątko*) (little) creature, critter.

bydlę *n.* -lęci- *pl.* -lęt- *Gen.* -ąt **1.** *pot.* (= *zwierzę, zwł. rogate l. groźne*) beast, brute, animal, creature, critter; **ależ groźne bydlę!** what a fierce brute! **2.** *obelż.* animal, beast, brute; **spić się jak bydlę** get drunk as a skunk; **skończone bydlę** complete animal.

bydlęcy *a.* **1.** animal; (*o krowach*) cattle; **wagon bydlęcy** cattle truck. **2.** (= *niegodny człowieka*) beastly, inhuman; **bydlęcy upór** stubborness of a mule.

bydło *n.* **1.** *zbiorowo* (= *krowy, byki, cielęta*) cattle; **bydło mleczne** dairy cows *l.* cattle; **bydło mięsne** beef cattle; **bydło rozpłodowe** breeding stock; **bydło rasowe** pure breed cattle; **sztuka bydła** head of cattle; **stado bydła** herd of cattle; **paść bydło** feed cattle. **2.** *pot. obelż.* (*o ludziach*) animals, pigs, dogs.

byk *ma* **1.** (= *samiec bydła l. zwierzyny rogatej*) bull; **byk rozpłodowy** stud bull; **walka byków** bullfight; **jak czerwona płachta na byka** like a red flag to bull; **wziąć byka za rogi** take the bull by the horns; **z byka spadłeś?** *pot.* are you out of your mind?; **silny jak byk** strong as an ox; **przecież to stoi jak byk** but there it is, clear as day. **2.** *pot.* (*błąd*) mistake; (*ortograficzny*) spelling error; **narobić byków** make a lot of mistakes; **palnąć byka** blunder, goof. **3.** *pot.* (*uderzenie*) (head-)butt in the stomach; **zwalić kogoś bykiem** butt sb in the stomach. **4.** *astron., astrol.* **Byk** Taurus. – *mp pl.* -i *żart.* (*o mężczyźnie*) ape.

bykowiec *mi* -wc- *Gen.* -a bullwhip.

byle *conj.* **1.** (*oznaczający cel, skutek*) (in order) to; **szedłem naprzód, byle dalej** I walked ahead in order to keep moving forward; **robić byle zbyć** do sth just to get it done; **byle nie upaść** the important thing is not to fall. **2.** (*oznaczający warunek*) as long as, provided; **byle przejechać przez granicę, a będziemy bezpieczni** if we can reach the border, we'll be safe; **mów prędko, byle prawdę** make it quick, as long as you tell the truth; **byle nie** to anything but that. – *partykuła dodawana do zaimków* (just) any; **kłaść rzeczy byle gdzie** put those things down anywhere; **śmiejesz się z byle czego** laugh at anything; **nie zadaję się z byle kim** I don't associate with just anyone; **robić coś byle jak** do sth any old way; **to nie byle co** that's no small accomplishment; **to jest nie byle kto** that's not just anybody; **wszędzie byle nie tutaj** anywhere but here; **masz nie byle jaki samochód** you don't have just any (old) car; **byle jaki** crummy; **tani i byle jaki** cheapo.

byleby *conj.* as long as; **zrobię wszystko, byleby pozwolili mi wyjechać** I'd do anything as long as they let me leave.

bylejakość *f. pot.* cheapness.

byli *ipf. zob.* **być.**

bylica *f. bot.* mugwort, Artemisia.

bylina¹ *f. bot.* perennial (plant).

bylina² *f. hist.lit.* old Russian epic folk song.

był *itd. ipf. zob.* **być.**

były *ipf. zob.* **być.** – *a.* former, ex-; **były prezydent** former president, ex-president. – *mp* (= *były mąż l. partner*) ex.

bynajmniej *adv.* not at all, by no means, anything but; **bynajmniej nie gorszy, gorzej** not in the least bit worse, every bit as good; **bynajmniej nie zadowolony** far from pleased; **nie było to bynajmniej przyjemne** it was anything but pleasant.

bypass *mi med.* bypass.

bystrość *f.* **1.** (= *prędkość*) swiftness; **bystrość górskiego potoku** the swiftness of the mountain stream. **2.** (= *inteligencja*) brightness, acumen, sharpness, keenness; **bystrość umysłu** sharpness of mind; **bystrość sądu** keenness of reasoning. **3.** (*o wzroku, słuchu*) sharpness, keenness; **ten pies odznacza się szczególną bystrością słuchu** this dog is known for its particularly keen sense of hearing.

bystry *a.* **1.** (= *prędki*) swift; **bystry potok** swift-running stream; **bystry nurt** swift current; **bystra rzeka** swift river. **2.** (*o człowieku*) bright, smart, clever; **bystry chłopak** bright boy. **3.** (*o inteligencji, umyśle*) sharp, keen, quick; **bystry dowcip** clever joke; **bystry umysł** keen mind; **bystry polityk** clever politician; **bystra głowa** quick head. **4.** (*o zmyśle wzroku i słuchu*) keen, sharp; **bystry wzrok** keen sense of sight; **bystry obserwator** keen observer.

bystrzak *mp pl.* -i *pot.* smart guy.

bystrzyca *f.* rapids.

byt *mi* **1.** (= *istnienie*) existence; **byt człowieka** human existence; **zagadka bytu** riddle of existence; **walka o byt** struggle for existence; **racja bytu** raison-d'être, purpose. **2.** (= *warunki życia*) living conditions; **polepszyć sobie byt** improve one's lot (in life); **zapewnić komuś byt** provide for sb. **3.** *fil.* being; (= *obiekt istniejący*) entity.

bytność *f.* stay; **podczas mojej bytności w Krakowie** during my stay in Krakow.

bytować *ipf. lit.* dwell, live; **w tych górach bytują niedźwiedzie** bears dwell in these mountains; **bytuję na wsi** I live in the country.

bytowy *a.* living, material; **potrzeby bytowe ludzi** the material needs of humans; **sprawy bytowe** material concerns; **warunki bytowe** living conditions.

bywać¹ *ipf.* **1.** (= *być często gdzieś l. w jakimś stanie*) be (often *l.* usually *l.* sometimes), tend to be; **bywać na koncertach** often attend concerts; **bywałem smutny** I was often sad; **bywałem w złym nastroju** I tended to be in a bad mood; **bywałem bez grosza** I was often broke. **2.** (= *odwiedzać*) **bywać (na przyjęciach, imprezach)** go places; **ostatnio nie bywamy** we haven't been going out recently; **przez jakiś czas bywaliśmy u rodziców codziennie** for a while we went to our parents' house every day; **bywam między ludźmi**

I spend a lot of time with people; **bywał pan w świecie** you've been around. **3.** (= *trafiać się*) **wieczory bywają już chłodne** the evenings are geting chilling; **bywa, że nie mogę spać w nocy** there are times that I cannot sleep; **podróżowałem, bywało, po Ameryce Południowej** I travelled and spent time in South America. **4.** *przest.* **bywaj!** welcome; **bywaj zdrów!** farewell.

bywać² *ipf.* (*w formach strony biernej*) **ten film bywa pokazywany w telewizji** this movie is sometimes shown on TV.

bywalczyni *f.* patroness, frequenter, denizen.

bywalec *mp* **-lc-** *pl.* **-y** patron, frequenter, denizen.

bywały *a.* worldly, knowledgable; **bywały i wykształcony człowiek** worldly and well-educated person; **człowiek bywały w świecie** a person who has seen the world.

b.z. *abbr.* (= *bez zmian*) no change(s).

bzdet *mi Gen.* **-a** *l.* **-u** *pot.* crap.

bzdura *f.* **1.** *pot.* (= *nonsens*) bull(shit) *l.* b.s.; **opowiadać bzdury** bullshit; **wierzyć w bzdury** believe bullshit. **2.** *pot.* (= *drobiazg*) trifle; **ta plama to bzdura** that stain is no big deal.

bzdurny *a. pot.* silly, foolish, ridiculous; **bzdurne twierdzenie** silly expression; **bzdurna teoria** silly theory; **bzdurny pomysł** silly idea; **bzdurne usprawiedliwienie** ridiculous excuse.

bzdurzyć *ipf. pot.* bullshit.

bzem *itd. mi zob.* **bez¹**.

bzik *mi Gen. i Acc.* **-a** *pot.* mania, craze; **dostać bzika** go crazy; **mieć bzika** be nuts *l.* crazy, have a bee in one's bonnet (*na punkcie czegoś* about sth).

bzikować *ipf. pot.* go crazy *l.* nuts about.

bzikowaty *a. pot.* nutty, goofy; **bzikowata dziewczyna** goofy girl; **bzikowate pomysły** nutty ideas.

bzowy *a.* elder(berry); *pot.* lilac; **bzowy krzak** elderberry *l.* lilac bush; **bzowe wino** elderberry wine; **powidła bzowe** elderberry jam.

bzu *itd. mi zob.* **bez¹**.

bzyczeć *ipf.* **-ę** **-ysz** (*o owadach, maszynach*) **1.** buzz, hum. **2.** (*o pociskach*) buzz, hum.

bzyk *mi* buzz, buzzing, hum; (= *świst kuli*) whizz; **przelecieć z bzykiem** buzz past; (*o pocisku*) whizz past.

bzykać *ipf.*, **bzyknąć** *pf.* **-ij** (*o owadach*) buzz, hum; (*o pociskach*) whizz; **kule bzykały nam nad głowami** bullets were whizzing past our heads.

bździągwa *f. Gen.pl.* **-giew** *pog.* (*o kobiecie*) bitch.

bździć *ipf.* **bżdżę bździsz, bździj** *pot.* fart; *sl.* cut the cheese.

bździna *f. pot.* fart.

C

C, c *n. indecl.* (*litera*) C, c; **C jak Celina** C is for Charlie; C as in Charlie.

C¹ *n. indecl. muz.* C; **C-dur** C major; **c-moll** C minor.

C² *abbr., fiz.* (= *Celsjusza*) C, Celsius, centigrade.

ca *abbr.* (= *circa*) c., ca., circa.

cacanka *f.* **obiecanki cacanki, a głupiemu radość** promises, promises; *Br.* fine words butter no parsnips.

cackać się *ipf. pot.* **cackać się z kimś/czymś** handle *l.* treat sb/sth with kid gloves.

cacko *n. Gen.pl.* **-ek 1.** (= *bibelot*) knick-knack, trinket, bauble, piece of bric-a-brac. **2.** *przen.* gem; **jej dom to prawdziwe cacko** her house is a real gem.

cacy *a. indecl. pot., żart.* nice, lovely; *attr.* bee's knees; cat's whiskers *l.* pyjamas. – *adv. pot., żart.* nicely; **zrobić coś cacy** do a good job; **na cacy** for good.

cadyk *mp pl.* **-owie** *judaizm* zaddik (*leader of a Hasidic group*).

cajg *mi tk.* jean, drill.

cajgowy *a. tk.* jean, drill.

cal *mi Gen.* **-a 1.** inch; **deska na trzy cale** three-inch plank; **posuwać się cal po calu** inch, move inch by inch, work one's way inch by inch. **2.** *przen.* **(dżentelmen) w każdym calu** every inch (a gentleman); **on nie ustąpi ani na cal** he won't budge an inch; **być o cal od czegoś** be within an inch of sth.

cal. *abbr.* (= *kaloria*) cal., calorie.

calizna *f.* **1.** (*pokład*) bed; **calizna węgla** coal bed. **2.** (= *gleba nieorana*) unturned *l.* unploughed soil; virgin soil.

calówka *f.* **1.** (*linijka*) (folding) rule. **2.** (**deska**) **calówka** (= *na cal gruba*) one-inch plank.

calutki *a. emf. zob.* **cały; ona czyta calutki dzień** she reads morning, noon and night.

całka *f. Gen.pl.* **-ek** *mat.* integral; **całka nieoznaczona** indefinite integral; **całka elementarna** elementary integral; **całka okrężna** circulation.

całkiem *adv.* **1.** (= *całkowicie*) entirely, totally, completely. **2.** (= *dość, zupełnie*) quite, pretty; **wyglądasz całkiem nieźle** you look quite good; **wszystko zaczęło się całkiem niewinnie** everything started quite innocently; **to jest całkiem niedrogie** it's pretty cheap, it's quite inexpensive; **całkiem, całkiem** not bad, quite good; **całkiem zgłupiałeś!?** *pot.* are you out of your mind?

całkować *ipf.* **1.** *mat.* integrate. **2.** *przen.* (= *scalać*) integrate.

całkowicie *adv.* entirely, completely, totally, fully; **poświęcić się czemuś całkowicie** completely devote o.s. to sth; **całkowicie się z tobą nie zgadzam** I totally disagree with you.

całkowity *a.* entire, complete, total, full; **całkowita cisza** dead silence; **całkowite zaćmienie słońca** total eclipse of the sun; **liczba całkowita** *mat.* integer.

cało *adv.* safely; **wyjść cało z opresji** go *l.* get off scot-free; **ujść cało** escape unhurt *l.* unharmed *l.* uninjured.

całodniowy *a.* = **całodzienny**.

całodobowy *a.* twenty-four-hour, 24h; **mieć dyżur całodobowy** be on call twenty-four hours; **to sklep całodobowy** this store is open twenty-four hours.

całodzienny *a.* daylong, all-day; **całodzienne wyżywienie** full board; **całodzienny zarobek** day's pay.

całogodzinny *a.* hour-long.

całokształt *mi* the whole (of), entirety.

całomiesięczny *a.* month-long.

całonocny *a.* night-long, all-night; **całonocne czuwanie** night vigil.

całopalny *a.* **1.** (= *spalony w całości*) holocaustal; **ofiara całopalna** burnt offering; *rzad.* holocaust. **2.** (= *służący do palenia w całości*) **stos całopalny** funeral pyre.

całoroczny *a.* **1.** year-long, annual, yearly; **bilans/dochód całoroczny** *fin.* yearly *l.* annual balance sheet/income. **2.** *bot.* **roślina całoroczna** perennial (plant).

całosezonowy *a.* season-long.

całościowy *a.* comprehensive.

całość *f.* (= *wszystko razem*) whole, entirety; **całość dzieła** the work as a whole; **tworzyć zamkniętą całość** belong together; form *l.* constitute a whole; **dane układają się w logiczną całość** the data begin *l.* begins to add up; **iść na całość** go all the way, go (the) whole hog; **w całości** (= *zupełnie*) entirely, completely; (= *traktowany jako całość*) as a whole.

całotygodniowy *a.* week-long.

całować *ipf.* kiss; **całować kogoś w usta** kiss sb on the mouth; **całować babcię w rękę** kiss grandma's hand; **całować kogoś na pożegnanie** kiss sb goodbye. ~ **się** *ipf.* kiss (*z kimś* sb); **całować się namiętnie** kiss passionately.

całun *mi* shroud, pall; **całun mgły** *przen.* blanket of fog.

całus *mi Gen.* **-a** *pot.* kiss; **posłać komuś cału-**

sa blow sb a kiss; **skraść komuś całusa** kiss sb unexpectedly.

całusek *mi* **-sk-** *Gen.* **-a** *emf.* kiss.

cały *a.* **1.** (= *wszystek*) all, whole; **cały dzień** all day (long); **cały czas** all the time; **całe życie** one's whole life, all one's life; **jestem cały mokry** I'm all wet; **byłem za granicą całe sześć lat** I was abroad for six whole years; **cała prawda** the whole truth; **całymi godzinami** for hours (and hours); **cały szereg spraw do załatwienia** a number of things to do; **w tym cała rzecz** that's the problem; **z całego serca** from the bottom of one's heart; **ogród cały w kwiatach** garden full of flowers; **Ewa stała cała we łzach** Eva stood there all in tears; **na całe gardło** at the top of one's lungs; **na całej linii** all along; **w całym tego słowa znaczeniu** in the full sense of the word, literally; **z całej siły** with all one's might; as hard as one can; **cały ojciec** (*o dziecku*) like father, like son *l.* daughter; **cała matka** (*o dziecku*) like mother, like daughter *l.* son; **to cały on** *pot.* that's him all over; **na cały regulator** at full volume; **iść na całego** go all the way; go (the) whole way; go (the) whole hog; **cała nuta** *muz.* whole note, semibreve; **cała naprzód** *żegl.* full ahead. **2.** (= *jedyny*) only, all; **ten stary dom to cały mój majątek** this old house is all I have. **3.** (= *wielki*) great, whole; **całe mnóstwo zaproszeń** loads of invitations, (great) piles of invitiations; **cały stos dokumentów do podpisu** (great) piles of documents to sign; **cała masa kłopotów** lots of trouble; **całe szczęście, że...** thank goodness that..., fortunately...; **o całe niebo lepszy** far better. **4.** (= *niezniszczony*) whole, intact, unhurt; **całe buty** good shoes; **całe ubranie** good clothes; **cały i zdrów** safe and sound; **szukać dziury w całym** pick holes in sth; **i wilk syty, i owca cała** that makes everyone happy. **5.** (*wyraża lekceważenie*) **nie obchodzi mnie ten wasz cały prezes** I don't care about this President of yours.

camping *mi* campground, campsite, camping site.

campingować *pf.* camp.

canoe *n. indecl. żegl.* canoe.

Canossa *mi przen.* **iść do Canossy** go to Canossa.

canzona *f. teor.lit., muz.* canzone.

cap¹ *ma* **1.** (*o zwierzęciu*) billy goat, male goat. **2.** *pot., obelż.* (= *lubieżnik*) lecher, satyr. **3.** *myśl.* buck.

cap² *mi techn.* fishing hook, tappet hook, grab iron.

cap³ *int.* snap, smack; **a ja go cap za kołnierz** and then I grabbed him by his collar; **wtem pies mnie cap za spodnie** suddenly a dog grabbed my trouser leg; **łapu-capu** helter-skelter; **na łapu-capu** helter-skelter.

capnąć *pf.* **-ij 1.** *pot.* (= *chwycić*) grab. **2.** *pot.* (= *aresztować*) nab.

capstrzyk *mi wojsk.* (*sygnał l. parada*) tattoo.

car *mp pl. -owie hist.* czar, tsar, tzar; emperor (*in some East European countries*).

carat *mi hist.* czarism, tsarism, tzarism.

carewicz *mp pl.* **-e** *l.* **-owie** *Gen.* **-ów** *hist.* czarevitch, tsarevitch, tzarevitch.

cargo *n. indecl.* cargo.

carowa *f. hist.* czarina, tsarina, tzarina.

carówna *f. Gen.pl.* **-wien** *hist.* czarevna, tsarevna, tzarevna.

carski *a.* czarist, czaristic, tsarist(ic), tzarist(ic); **wojska carskie** czar's troops; **ukaz carski** czar's ukase; **Rosja carska** czarist Russia; **carskie wrota** *rel.* holy gate (*in Orthodox church*).

carstwo *mi hist.* czardom, tsardom, tzardom.

caryca *f. hist.* czarina, tsarina, tzarina.

casco *n. indecl. ubezp.* **1.** vehicle insurance. **2.** *żegl.* comprehensive vessel insurance.

cążki *pl. Gen.* **-ów** pliers, pincers; **cążki do manicure** clippers.

CD¹ *abbr.* (= *płyta kompaktowa*) CD (= *compact disc*).

CD² *polit.* (= *korpus dyplomatyczny*) CD (= *diplomatic corps*).

cd. *abbr.* (= *ciąg dalszy*) cont., contd., continued.

cdn. *abbr.* (= *ciąg dalszy nastąpi*) to be continued.

ceber *mi* **-br-** *Gen.* **-a** (wooden) bucket, (wooden) pail; **leje jak z cebra** the rain's coming down in buckets; *przest.* it's raining cats and dogs.

cebrzyk *mi Gen.* **-a** small bucket *l.* pail.

cebula *f.* **1.** *bot.* onion (*Allium cepa*). **2.** *bot.* **cebula morska** sea onion (*Urginea maritima*). **3.** (*warzywo*) onion; **ubierać się na cebulę** *przen.* dress in layers. **4.** *pot., przest.* (= *zegarek kieszonkowy*) pocket watch. **5.** (= *cebulka*) bulb; **cebule tulipanów** tulip bulbs.

cebulasty *a.* onion-like, onion-shaped, bulbous, bulb-shaped, oniony.

cebulica *f. bot.* squill (*Scilla*).

cebulka *f. Gen.pl.* **-ek 1.** (*warzywo*) *emf.* onion; **befsztyk z cebulką** beefsteak with onion; **sałatka z młodą cebulką** salad with green onions *l.* scallions. **2.** *bot.* (*do rozmnażania*) bulb; **cebulki tulipanów** tulip bulbs; **cebulka włosa** root.

cebulkowaty *a.* = **cebulowaty**.

cebulkowy *a. bot.* bulbous; **rośliny cebulkowe** bulbous plants.

cebulowaty *a.* = **cebulasty**.

cebulowy *a.* onion; **zupa cebulowa** onion soup; **cebulowe rośliny warzywne** *bot.* bulbous vegetables.

cech *mi* **1.** (*stowarzyszenie*) guild; **należeć do cechu** be a member of a guild. **2.** (*budynek*) guildhall.

cecha *f.* **1.** (= *właściwość*) feature, trait, attribute, character; **typowa cecha** characteristic (feature); **cecha dodatnia** positive trait, quality, virtue; **cecha ujemna** negative trait, defect; **cecha dziedziczna** hereditary trait, genetic trait; **cecha wrodzona** innate trait; **cechy płciowe** sex characters; **to jest cecha rodzinna** it runs in the family. **2.** **cecha logarytmu** *mat.* characteristic of a logarithm. **3.** (*znak*) mark, stamp; **cecha probiercza** hallmark, plate mark; **cecha legalizacyjna** *techn.* verification mark, verification stamp. **4.** *fil.* attribute. **5.** *geogr.* spot height.

cechmistrz *mp pl.* **-owie** *Gen.* **-ów** guildmaster.

cechować *ipf.* **1.** (= *charakteryzować*) characterize, be a feature of (*sb l. sth*); **Adama cechuje odwaga** courage is one of Adam's features; **wiersze te cechuje prostota** these poems are characterized by their simplicity. **2.** (= *znakować*) mark, hallmark, stamp; **cechować złoto** hallmark gold; **cechować odważniki** mark *l.* stamp weights. ~ **się** *ipf.* be characterized *l.* marked by sth; **Adam cechuje się pracowitością** Adam is a hardworking person; **ten wiersz cechuje się prostotą** this poem is characterized by its simplicity.

cechowy *a.* guild; **prawo cechowe** guild law; **chorągiew cechowa** guild flag.

cechówka *f. Gen.pl.* **-ek** *leśn.* marking hammer.

cechsztyn *mi geol.* the upper Permian.

cedent *mp prawn.* ceder.

cedować *ipf.* cede; **cedować majątek na kogoś** cede one's property to sb; cede sb one's property; **cedować weksel na kogoś** assign a bill of exchange to sb.

cedr *mi bot.* cedar (*Cedrus*); **cedr libański** cedar of Lebanon (*Cedrus libani*); **czerwony cedr** red cedar (*Juniperus Virginiana*).

cedrowy *a.* cedar; **drzewo cedrowe** cedar; **drewno cedrowe** cedar, cedarwood; **olejek cedrowy** cedarwood oil.

cedrówka *f. Gen.pl.* **-ek** *bot.* cedar waxwing (*Bombycilla cedrorum*).

ceduła *f.* **1.** *fin.* (official) (list of) quotation(s), list of prices (*spis notowań na giełdzie*). **2.** *handl.* way-bill (*spis przewożonych przedmiotów*).

cedzak *mi Gen.* **-a 1.** (*naczynie kuchenne*) colander, strainer. **2.** (*sieć rybacka*) filter *l.* trim net.

cedzić *ipf.* **1.** (= *filtrować*) strain, percolate; **odcedzić makaron** strain the water from pasta. **2.** (= *sączyć*) sip; **cedzić piwo** sip beer. **3.** (= *wymawiać powoli*) **cedzić słowa** *l.* **słowo po słowie** drawl (out) one's words; **cedzić coś przez zęby** say sth between one's teeth.

cedzidło *n. Gen.pl.* **-deł 1.** (= *filtr*) strainer, drainer, percolator. **2.** *techn.* nutsche filter.

cegielnia *f. Gen.pl.* **-i** brickyard.

cegielniany *a.* brickyard.

cegielnik *mp* **1.** (*robotnik*) brickmaker. **2.** *przest.* (= *fabrykant cegieł*) brickmaker, brickyard owner.

cegiełka *f. Gen.pl.* **-ek 1.** (*do budowy*) (small) brick; **dokładać do czegoś swoją cegiełkę** *przen.* make one's contribution to sth. **2.** *pot.* (= *datek*) contribution; share.

ceglany *a.* brick; **mur ceglany** brick wall; **ceglana posadzka** brick floor; **mączka ceglana** brick dust.

ceglarka *f. Gen.pl.* **-ek** *techn.* brick press.

ceglarski *a.* brick; **mistrz ceglarski** master brickmaker; **piec ceglarski** brick-kiln.

ceglarz *mp* brickmaker.

ceglasty *a.* brick-red; **ceglasty rumieniec** deep blush.

cegła *f. Gen.pl.* **-gieł 1.** (*do budowy*) brick; **cegła ceramiczna** *techn.* burnt brick; **cegła dziu-**

rawka *techn.* cavity brick, cellular brick; **cegła ogniotrwała** firebrick; **cegła szamotowa** *techn.* chamotte brick; **dom z cegły** brick house; **wypalać cegłę** burn bricks; **murować na dwie cegły** *bud.* lay a two brick-thick wall. **2.** *pot.* (= *gruba, poważna książka*) hefty tome.

Cejlon *mi geogr.* Ceylon (*Sri Lanka*).

Cejlonka *f. Gen.pl.* **-ek**, **Cejlończyk** *mp* Ceylonese.

cejloński *a.* Ceylonese.

cekaem *mi wojsk.* heavy machine gun, HMG; **obsługa cekaemu** heavy machine gun crew, HMG crew.

cekin *mi Gen.* **-a** *l.* **-u** (*do naszywania*) **1.** sequin. **2.** *Acc. i Gen.* **-a** *hist.* (*moneta*) sequin, zecchino, zechin.

cekinowy *a. sztuka* sequin, sequined.

cel *mi Gen.pl.* **-ów 1.** (= *punkt, do którego się zmierza*) aim, goal, purpose; **nieosiągalny cel** unattainable goal; **wspólny cel** common aim *l.* goal; **szczytne cele** laudable aims, noble aims, praiseworthy aims; **dojść do celu** reach an aim *l.* a goal; reach a destination; **cel podróży** destination; **cel życia** aim in life, aim of one's life; **błąkać się bez celu** wander, roam, ramble; **osiągnąć zamierzony cel** achieve one's aim; achieve *l.* attain *l.* realize *l.* reach a goal; accomplish *l.* achieve *l.* fulfill a purpose; **dla celów statystycznych** for statistical purposes; **na cele dobroczynne** for charity; **w celu** in order to; **w tym celu** to this end; with this end in view; **w jakim celu?** what for?; what's the purpose of this?; what's the point?; to what end?; **jakiemu celowi mogłoby to służyć?** to what purpose could we/I, etc. put it?; what purpose could it serve?; **to ma na celu...** the aim *l.* goal *l.* purpose of this is...; **bez celu** aimlessly; **celem** in order to; **chybiać celu** miss the mark; **dopiąć celu** achieve one's aim; achieve *l.* attain *l.* realize *l.* reach a goal; accomplish *l.* achieve *l.* fulfill a purpose; **to, co robisz, mija się z celem** what you do *l.* are doing is purposeless *l.* pointless *l.* useless; **przeznaczyć coś na jakiś cel** devote sth to sth; allocate sth for sth; assign sth for *l.* to sth; **stawiać sobie jakiś cel** aim to do sth; aim for sth; **zmierzać wprost do celu** take decisive steps to achieve sth; **cel uświęca środki** the end justifies the means; **okolicznik celu** *gram.* adverbial of purpose. **2.** (= *to, do czego się mierzy*) target; **cele wojskowe** military targets; **cele cywilne** civilian targets; **cel naziemny** ground target; **cel powietrzny** air(borne) target; **ruchomy cel** moving target; **atakować cel** attack a target; **trafić do celu** hit the target, hit the mark; **cel - pal!** aim - fire!; **chybić celu** miss the target; miss the mark; overshoot a target; **obrać sobie kogoś za cel** *kpin.* make sb the laughing-stock; make sb an object of ridicule; **wziąć coś za cel żartów** make sth an object of ridicule; make sth a butt of a joke; **brać kogoś/coś na cel** aim at sb *l.* sth; take aim at sb *l.* sth; aim for sth.

cela *f.* (*w więzieniu l. klasztorze*) cell.

celebra *f.* **1.** *rel.* celebration. **2.** *pot.* = **celebracja**.

celebracja *f.* celebration.

celebrans *mp rz.-kat.* celebrant, officiant.

celebrować *ipf.* **1.** *rz.-kat.* celebrate; **celebrować mszę** celebrate a mass. **2.** (= *robić coś z namaszczeniem*) make a ritual (out) of; **celebrować śniadanie wielkanocne** make a ritual out of Easter breakfast.

celiakia *f. Gen.* **-ii** *pat.* celiac disease.

celibat *mi* **1.** *rz.-kat.* celibacy; **wprowadzić celibat** introduce celibacy; **znieść celibat** abolish celibacy. **2.** (= *wstrzemięźliwość płciowa*) celibacy, continence; **żyć w celibacie** practice celibacy.

celka *f. Gen.pl.* **-ek 1.** (= *mała cela*) (small) cell. **2.** *el.* chamber. **3.** *min.* unit cell, elementary cell.

cellon *mi techn., lotn.* dope.

cellulitis *f. indecl. pat.* cellulitis.

celniczka *f. Gen.pl.* **-ek** customs officer.

celnie *adv.* **1.** (= *trafiając w cel*) accurately; **strzelać celnie** be a good marksman. **2.** (= *trafnie*) accurately, relevantly; **celnie coś sformułować** put *l.* get sth right.

celnik *mp* **1.** (*na granicy*) customs officer. **2.** *hist.* publican.

celność *f.* **1.** (*o strzale*) accuracy; **celność strzałów** *wojsk.* accuracy of fire; **celność działa** *wojsk.* hit accuracy, cannon *l.* gun accuracy. **2.** (*o rozumowaniu*) relevance, pertinence; **celność sformułowania** accuracy of a statement *l.* description; **celność argumentów** soundness of arguments. **3.** (= *doskonałość*) *rzad.* excellence; **celność wykonania koncertu** excellent performance (of a concert).

celny[1] *a.* **1.** (*o strzale*) accurate, well-aimed; **celny strzał** good shot; **celny rzut** good shot; **celne uderzenie** accurate hit; **celna broń** accurate weapon; **celny strzelec** good marksman. **2.** (= *trafny*) relevant; dead on; right on the mark *l.* money; **celna uwaga** relevant comment; **celny dowcip** good joke; **celne powiedzenie** true *l.* wise saying.

celny[2] *a. lit., rzad.* excellent, splendid; **celne wykonanie koncertu** excellent performance (of a concert); distinguished, prominent, foremost; **celna proza** excellent prose; **zbiór celniejszych utworów epoki** collection of the more prominent works of the epoch; **najcelniejsi pisarze** the most distinguished writers.

celny[3] *a.* (*o cle*) customs; **opłata celna** customs duty; **taryfa celna** tariff; **odprawa celna** customs clearance; **urząd celny** customs, customhouse, customshouse; **polityka celna** customs policy; **bariery celne** customs barriers; **unia celna** customs union; **komora celna** customs.

celofan *mi* cellophane; **kwiaty w celofanie** flowers wrapped in cellophane.

celofanowy *a.* cellophane; **torebka celofanowa** cellophane bag.

celoma *f. biol.* celom, coelom.

celować[1] *ipf.* aim, take aim; **celować w głowę** aim at the *l.* sb's head; **celować w środek tarczy** aim for the bull's eye; **celować do nieprzyjaciela** aim at the enemy; **celować wysoko** *przen.* aim high.

celować[2] *ipf. lit.* excel; **celować w sporcie** excel at sports.

celownica *f.* **1.** *astron.* (telescopic) viewfinder. **2.** *techn.* sight rail.

celowniczy *a. broń* sighting; **przyrządy celownicze** sights. – *mp wojsk.* aiming *l.* sighting man; cannon *l.* gun aimer; gun layer, trainer.

celownik *mi Gen.* **-a 1.** *gram.* dative. **2.** *broń* sight, sights; **nastawić celownik na...** set the sight at... **3.** *fot.* viewfinder. **4.** *sport* finish line. **5.** *techn.* sighthole.

celowo *adv.* deliberately, intentionally, on purpose; **robić coś celowo** do sth on purpose; **celowo nie powiedzieć czegoś** deliberately omit sth.

celowość *f.* **1.** (= *przydatność*) usefulness, purposefulness. **2.** (= *nastawienie na osiągnięcie celu*) purposefulness; **celowość czyjegoś działania** purposefulness of sb's activities. **3.** *fil.* purpose.

celowy *a.* purposeful, intentional; **celowe działanie** intentional act; **zdanie celowe** *gram.* clause of purpose.

Celsjusz *mp* Celsius.

Celt *mp pl.* **-owie** Celt, Kelt.

celtologia *f. Gen.* **-ii** Celtic studies.

celtycki *a.* Celtic; **języki celtyckie** Celtic languages.

celująco *adv.* perfectly, faultlessly; **zdać egzamin celująco** pass the exam with flying colors; **zdać na celująco** get the highest score, get an A +, get through with flying colors.

celujący *a.* excellent, exceptional, outstanding; **celujący uczeń** exceptional pupil *l.* student; **ocena celująca** A +, excellent (grade). – *mi* (*ocena*) A +, excellent; **dostać celujący** get an A +.

celuloid *mi* celluloid.

celuloza *f. biochem.* cellulose.

celulozownia *f. techn.* pulp mill.

celulozowy *a.* cellulose; **przemysł celulozowy** pulp industry; **masa celulozowa** chemical paperpulp; **papier celulozowy** cellulose paper.

ceł *mi zob.* **cło.**

cembrować *ipf.* timber, line *l.* support with stonework, bricks, concrete, etc.; **cembrowana studnia** timbered well, well lined with stonework.

cembrowanie *n.* timbering, (stonework, brick, concrete, etc.) support; **betonowe cembrowanie** concrete support.

cembrowina *f.* timber *l.* brick, stonework, concrete, etc. (support) wall.

cement *mi* cement; **cement portlandzki** waterproof Portland (cement); **brać na cement** *bud.* cement; **cement wolnowiążący** slow-setting cement; **cement szybkowiążący** fast-setting cement.

cementować *ipf.* **1.** (= *spajać*) cement. **2.** *przen.* (= *umacniać*) cement; **cementować przyjaźń między narodami** cement friendship among nations; **coś cementuje rodzinę** sth cements the family. **3.** *techn.* carbonize.

cementownia *f. Gen.pl.* **-i** cement mill, cement plant.

cementowy *a.* cement; **podłoga cementowa** cement floor; **zaprawa cementowa** cement mortar; **przemysł cementowy** cement industry; **mleko cementowe** cement grout.

cementówka *f. Gen.pl.* **-ek** *bud.* **1.** (*podkład*) cement primer. **2.** (*cegła*) cement brick.

cena *f.* price, cost, rate; **cena bieżąca/detaliczna/rynkowa** current/retail/market price; **cena hurtowa/giełdowa** wholesale/exchange price; **cena brutto/netto** gross/net price; **cena stała/nominalna** fixed/nominal price; **cena kupna/sprzedaży** purchase/sale price; **cena fabryczna** manufacturer's price; **cena zbytu** selling price; **wygórowana cena** exorbitant price, steep price; **wyśrubowana cena** inflated price, stiff price; **astronomiczna cena** *emf.* astronomical price; **słone ceny** *pot.* steep prices; **cena za kilogram** price per kilo(gram); **cena chleba** bread price; **ceny na zboże** cereal prices; **ceny konkurencyjne** competitive prices; **po cenie kosztów** at cost (price); **sprzedawać po wysokiej/niskiej cenie** sell at a high/low price; **sprzedawać po cenach obniżonych** sell at reduced prices; **kupić coś po przystępnej cenie** buy sth at an attractive price; **obliczać według aktualnych cen** calculate at current prices; **za wszelką cenę** at all *l.* any cost, at any price; **ustalać cenę na coś** set *l.* fix a price for sth; **podwyżka cen** price increase, price rise; **obniżka cen** price cut, price reduction *l.* rollback; **podwyższyć** *l.* **podnieść cenę** increase *l.* raise *l.* hike a price; **obniżyć cenę** reduce *l.* cut *l.* lower *l.* slash a price; **dyktować ceny na rynku światowym** set world prices; **ceny idą w górę** prices are rising *l.* going up *l.* skyrocketing; **ceny spadają** prices are falling *l.* going down; **nożyce cen** price bracket, price range; **ruch cen** fluctuation in prices; **zamrozić ceny** freeze prices; **zrobić coś za cenę czegoś** do sth at the expense of sth; **za pół ceny** at half price; **za żadną cenę** not for all the world; **wyznaczyć cenę za czyjąś głowę** place a price on sb's head; **honor nie ma ceny** honor is priceless; **podbijać cenę** push up a price; **być w cenie** bring *l.* command *l.* fetch *l.* get high prices; *przen.* be (highly) valued; **czyjeś akcje są w cenie** *przen.* sb is highly valued; **profesor jest u nas w cenie** we respect the professor.

cenestezja *f. psych.* cenesthesia, coenesthesia; cenesthesis, coenesthesis.

cenić *ipf.* **1.** (= *szanować, poważać*) value, esteem, respect, have a high regard for (*sb l. sth*); hold (*sb l. sth*) in high esteem; **cenić sobie kogoś/coś** think highly of sb/sth; **cenić czyjś talent** esteem sb's talent; **cenić kogoś za pracowitość** esteem sb for being hardworking; **cenić w kimś prawdomówność** esteem sb for his *l.* her truthfulness; **tej książki nie cenię sobie wysoko** I do not think much about this book; I think little of this book; **cenić kogoś jako lekarza** think highly of sb as a doctor; **ceniony fachowiec** highly valued specialist; **nisko kogoś/coś cenić** not think much of sb/sth; think little of sb/sth. **2.** (= *szacować wartość*) evaluate; estimate the value of (*sth*); **cenić czyjś majątek na pięćset tysięcy złotych** estimate the value of sb's assets at 500

thousand zloty; **cenić dom bardzo drogo** put a high price on the house. **~ się** *ipf.* **1.** (*o swojej wartości*) keep one's self-respect; **on wysoko się ceni** he thinks highly of himself; he holds himself in high esteem. **2.** (= *wyznaczać ceny*) put a price on; **w tym sklepie bardzo się cenią** this shop puts steep prices on the articles it offers.

cennik *mi Gen.* **-a** price list.

cenny *a.* valuable, precious; **cenna biżuteria** valuable jewelry; **cenny zabytek** valuable historic monument; **tracić cenny czas** lose precious time; **dawać cenne wskazówki** give valuable hints.

cenotaf *mi* cenotaph.

cenoza *f. ekol.* cenosis, coenosis.

cent *mi Acc. i Gen.* **-a 1.** (*moneta*) cent, penny; **nie mieć ani centa** be broke, be penniless; **wydać wszystko co do centa** spend all the money; **spłukać się co do centa** be flat broke. **2.** *fiz., muz.* cent.

centaur *ma mit.* **1.** centaur. **2. Centaur** *astron.* Centaurus.

center *a. sport* center, *Br.* centre

centezymalny *a.* centesimal.

centnar *mi Gen.* **-a** centner, hundredweight, cental, quintal.

centra *f. piłka nożna* cross to the center of the field.

centrala *f. Gen.pl.* **-i** *l.* **-l 1.** headquarters, head office. **2. centrala (telefoniczna)** (telephone) exchange, switchboard.

centralista *mp polit.* centralist.

centralistyczny *a. polit.* centralist.

centralizacja *f.* centralization.

centralizm *mi polit.* centralism.

centralizować *ipf.* centralize.

centralka *f. Gen.pl.* **-ek centralka telefoniczna** switchboard.

centralnie *adv.* centrally; **sklep usytuowany centralnie** centrally located shop; **budynek ogrzewany centralnie** building with central heating; **fundusze rozdzielane centralnie** centrally distributed funds.

centralność *f.* centrality.

centralny *a.* **1.** (*w centrum*) central; **centralne regiony** central regions; **położenie centralne** central location; **centralne ogrzewanie** central heating; **budowla centralna** *bud.* centrally planned building. **2.** (= *główny*) central, main, head; **władze centralne** state authorities, central authorities; **urzędy centralne** state institutions, central institutions, central authorities; **centralny układ nerwowy** *anat.* central nervous system.

centrolewica *f.* center-left party *l.* coalition, moderate left party *l.* coalition.

centrolewicowy *a.* center-left, moderate left; **rząd centrolewicowy** center-left government.

centroprawica *f.* center-right party *l.* coalition, moderate right party *l.* coalition.

centroprawicowy *a.* center-right, moderate right; **rząd centroprawicowy** center-right government.

centrosom *mi biol.* centrosome.

centrować *ipf.* **1.** *sport* cross the ball to the

center. **2.** *techn.* (= *środkować*) center. **3.** *techn.*
(= *osiować*) align, aline.
centrowiec *mp* **-wc-** *pl.* **-y** *polit.* centrist.
centrowy *a. polit.* centrist; **partia centrowa**
centrist party, moderate party; **politycy centro-wi** centrists, centrist politicians, moderates,
moderate politicians.
centrum *n. indecl. in sg. pl.* **-ra** *Gen.* **-rów 1.** (= *ośrodek*) center, *Br.* centre; **centrum miasta** city
l. town center, downtown; **centrum handlowe**
mall, shopping center; **centrum przemysłowe** industrial center; **centrum badawcze** research
center *l.* facility; **centrum komunikacyjne** communications center; **centrum kultury** cultural
center (*główny ośrodek kulturalny*), community
center (*dom kultury*); **centrum konferencyjne**
conference center; **centrum decyzyjne** *ekon.* decision-making center; **centrum obliczeniowe**
komp. computation center; **centra nerwowe**
anat. ganglions; **być** *l.* **znajdować się w centrum**
uwagi be the center of attention; be in the public
eye. **2.** *polit.* (*stronnictwo*) Center; **partie centrum** Center parties, centrist parties; **koalicja**
centrum Center coalition, centrist coalition.
centryczny *a.* centric.
centryfuga *f. przest.* centrifuge.
centrysta *mp polit.* centrist.
centrystowski *a. polit.* centrist; **polityk centrystowski** centrist politician; **centrystowskie hasła**
centrist slogans; **postawa centrystowska** centrist stance, centrist attitude; **partia centrystowska** centrist party.
centryzm *mi polit.* centrism, Centrism.
centuria[1] *f. Gen.* **-ii** *hist.* century.
centuria[2] *f. Gen.* **-ii** *bot.* centaury (*Centaurium*); **centuria pospolita** common *l.* drug centaury (*Centaurium umbellatum*); **napar z centurii** centaury infusion.
centurion *mp pl.* **-owie** *l.* **-i** *hist.* centurion;
zbroja centuriona centurion's armor.
centuś *mp żart.* miser, pennypincher, skinflint, Scrooge.
centyfolia *f. Gen.* **-ii** *bot.* cabbage rose (*Rosa centifolia*).
centygram *mi Gen.* **-a** centigram, centigramme.
centylitr *mi Gen.* **-a** centiliter, *Br.* centilitre.
centym *mi Gen.* **-a** centime.
centymetr *mi Gen.* **-a** centimeter, *Br.* centimetre; **centymetr krawiecki** tape measure.
cenzor *mp pl.* **-owie** *l.* **-rzy 1.** (*kontroler*) censor; **nadzór cenzora** censor's supervision; **uprawnienia cenzora** censor's powers. **2.** *psych.* censor. **3.** *hist.* (*w starożytnym Rzymie*) censor.
cenzorski *a.* **1.** (*o kontrolerze*) censorial, censorian; **nadzór cenzorski** censorial supervision;
skreślenia cenzorskie censorial deletions. **2.**
hist. censorial, censorian; **urząd cenzorski** censorship; **edykty cenzorskie** censorial edicts;
uprawnienia cenzorskie censorial powers.
cenzura *f.* **1.** (*kontrola*) censorship; **uprawnienia cenzury** censors' powers; **nadzór cenzury** censors' supervision; **cenzura prewencyjna** preventive censorship; **cenzura represyjna** repressive

censorship; **przejść przez cenzurę** be approved
by censors; **poddać cenzurze** censor, subject to
censorship; **cenzura obyczajowa** moral censorship; **cenzura wewnętrzna** internal censorship;
przesłać utwór do cenzury send a work for examination by censors; **cenzura kościelna** *rz.-kat.*
church censorship. **2.** *szkoln.* (*świadectwo*) report card, school report, school certificate; **dobra**
cenzura na koniec roku szkolnego good final report card. **3.** (*opinia*) opinion, reputation; **mieć**
dobrą cenzurę enjoy a fine reputation; **wystawić**
komuś złą cenzurę not think highly of sb, criticize sb. **4.** *psych.* censorship. **5.** *kość.* (= *suspensa*) suspension. **6.** *hist.* (*w starożytnym Rzymie*)
censorship.
cenzuralnie *adv.* correctly, properly; **wyrażać**
się cenzuralnie przy dzieciach use proper language in front of (the) children.
cenzuralny *a.* **1.** (*o cenzurze*) censorship; **ustawa cenzuralna** censorship act. **2.** (= *przyzwoity*)
correct, proper; **cenzuralny dowcip** clean joke;
cenzuralne zachowanie proper behavior.
cenzurka *f.* **1.** *szkoln.* (*świadectwo*) report
card, school report, school certificate; **bardzo dobra cenzurka** very good report card; **piątki na**
cenzurce A's in the report card. **2.** (*opinia*) opinion, reputation; **wystawić komuś dobrą cenzurkę**
think highly of sb.
cenzurować *ipf.* censor; **cenzurować książkę**
censor a book; **cenzurować czyjeś zachowanie**
przen. criticize *l.* censure sb's behavior; **cenzurować znajomych** *przen.* criticize one's friends,
censure one's friends.
cenzus *mi* **1.** *prawn.* qualification, requirements; **cenzus majątkowy** property requirements; **cenzus wyborczy** voter qualification;
cenzus wieku age requirements; **cenzus wykształcenia** education requirements. **2.** *hist.* (*w
starożytnym Rzymie*) census.
ceń *ipf. zob.* **cenić**.
ceownik *mi Gen.* **-a** *techn.* channel (iron *l.*
bar).
cep *mi Gen.* **-a 1.** *roln.* flail, beater; **młócić cepami** flail. **2.** *techn.* beater plate. – *mp pl.* **-y**
obelż. l. pog. blockhead, dunce, dolt.
ceper *mp* **-pr-** *pl.* **-y** *dial., pog.* plainsman (*used
by highlanders*).
cepowaty *a. obelż. l. pog.* blockheaded.
cer *mi chem.* cerium.
cera[1] *f. tylko sing.* (*twarzy*) complexion; **cera**
blada/jasna/ziemista pale/fair/sallow complexion; **cera śniada/smagła/rumiana** dark/swarthy/
ruddy complexion; **zniszczona/sucha/tłusta cera**
damaged/dry/oily complexion.
cera[2] *f. pl.* **-y** (= *ślad cerowania*) darn.
ceramiczny *a.* ceramic; **przemysł ceramiczny**
ceramic industry; **izolator ceramiczny** ceramic
insulator; **farba ceramiczna** ceramic color; **cegła**
ceramiczna ceramic brick; **pustak ceramiczny**
structural clay tile; **biżuteria ceramiczna** ceramic jewelry; **piec ceramiczny** ceramic furnace.
ceramik *mp* ceramist, ceramicist.
ceramika *f.* **1.** pottery, ware, ceramics; **ceramika wstęgowa/sznurowa/grzebykowa** *archeol.*

linear/corded/comb ware *l.* pottery. **2.** *bud., techn.* ceramics; **ceramika budowlana** structural clay products; **ceramika architektoniczna** structural clay products; **ceramika metali** powder metallurgy, metal ceramics.

cerata *f.* (*materiał*) oil-cloth; (*obrus*) plastic tablecloth.

ceratka *f. Gen.pl.* -ek piece of oil-cloth; nappy liner; **ceratka elektroizolacyjna** *el.* cambric varnished cloth.

ceratowy *a.* oil-cloth; **obrus ceratowy** plastic tablecloth; **ceratowy fartuch** oil-cloth apron; **kanapa z ceratowym obiciem** oil-cloth-upholstered couch.

Cerber *mp mit.* Cerberus, Kerberos.

cerber *mp żart.* Cerberus, formidable guard, surly keeper.

cerebracja *f. fizj.* cerebration.

cerebralny *a.* **1.** *fizj.* cerebral; **krążenie cerebralne** cerebral circulation. **2.** *jęz.* cerebral, retroflex; **spółgłoski cerebralne** cerebrals, cerebral *l.* retroflex consonants.

ceregiele *pl. Gen.* -i ceremony, formalities; **zbędne ceregiele** unnecessary formalities; **zrobić coś bez ceregieli** make no bones about sth; **robić ceregiele** make a fuss.

ceremonia *f. Gen.* -ii **1.** (*obrzęd*) ceremony; **ceremonia chrztu** baptism (ceremony); **ceremonia pierwszej komunii świętej** first (Holy) Communion (ceremony); **ceremonia bierzmowania** Confirmation (ceremony); **ceremonia koronacji** coronation (ceremony); **ceremonia ślubna** wedding ceremony; **ceremonia pogrzebowa** funeral ceremony; **ceremonia odsłonięcia pomnika** monument-unveiling ceremony; **ceremonia powitania** welcome ceremony; **ceremonia pożegnania** farewell ceremony; **ceremonia picia herbaty** tea-drinking ceremony; **dopełnić ceremonii** do sth with due ceremony; **mistrz ceremonii** master of ceremonies. **2.** (= *ostentacja*) ceremony; **ceremonia kąpieli dziecka** child-bathing ceremony; **wejść po długich ceremoniach** enter after lots of ceremony; **bez ceremonii** without ceremony, without formalities, unceremoniously; **robić ceremonie** make a fuss; **robić z kimś/czymś ceremonie** make a fuss about sb/sth.

ceremonialnie *adv.* ceremonially; **witać się z kimś ceremonialnie** greet sb ceremonially, greet sb officially *l.* formally; **kłaniać się komuś ceremonialnie** bow to sb ceremonially, bow to sb officially *l.* formally.

ceremonialność *f.* ceremoniousness, ceremony.

ceremonialny *a.* **1.** (= *konwencjonalny*) ceremonious; **ceremonialne zachowanie** ceremonious behavior; **ceremonialne stosunki** ceremonious relations; **ceremonialny ukłon** ceremonious bow, formal bow. **2.** (= *obrzędowy*) ceremonial; **strój ceremonialny** ceremonial robes *l.* clothing; **przepisy ceremonialne** ceremonial ritual.

ceremoniał *mi* ceremonial, etiquette; **dworski ceremoniał** court etiquette; **ceremoniał kościelny/dyplomatyczny** church/diplomatic ceremonial.

cerkiew *f.* -kwi- *pl.* -e **1.** *kośc.* (*świątynia*) Or-

thodox church; **nabożeństwo w cerkwi** mass in an Orthodox church. **2.** *rel.* (*wyznanie, ogół wyznawców*) the Orthodox Church; **Cerkiew prawosławna** the Eastern Orthodox Church; **Cerkiew grekokatolicka** the Greek Orthodox Church, the Church of Greece; **Cerkiew bizantyjsko-ukraińska** the Byzantine Church.

cerkiewizm *mi jęz.* Old Church Slavonic borrowing.

cerkiewka *f. Gen.pl.* -ek (*świątynia*) *emf.* small Orthodox church.

cerkiewnosłowiański *a. jęz.* Church Slavonic, Church Slavic.

cerkiewny *a. kośc.* **1.** Orthodox church; **sztuka/muzyka cerkiewna** Orthodox church art/music; **chór cerkiewny** Orthodox church choir. **2.** *jęz.* **język cerkiewny** Church Slavonic, Church Slavic.

cermetal *mi techn.* cermet.

ceroplastyczny *a. sztuka* wax, ceroplastic; **portret ceroplastyczny** wax portrait; **rzeźba ceroplastyczna** wax sculpture.

ceroplastyka *f. sztuka* ceroplastics, wax modelling.

cerowaczka *f. Gen.pl.* -ek darner.

cerować *ipf.* darn; **cerować skarpetki** darn socks.

cerowanie *n.* darning.

cerownia *f. Gen.pl.* -i **1.** darning shop. **2.** *tk.* (fabric) finishing shop *l.* department.

certacja *f. pot., przest.* pretense; **tylko bez certacji, proszę** no pretense, please.

certepartia *f. Gen.* -ii *ekon., żegl.* charter, charter party.

certolić się *ipf. pot.* = **certować się**.

certować się *ipf.* make a pretense of declining; banter.

certyfikacja *f.* certification.

certyfikat *mi* certificate; **certyfikat bezpieczeństwa** *żegl.* (ship *l.* boat) safety certificate; (cargo ship) safety construction certificate; seaworthiness certificate; **certyfikat gwarancyjny** warranty certificate; **certyfikat inwestycyjny** investment certificate; **certyfikat udziałowy** *ekon., prawn.* share *l.* stock certificate; certificate of stock; **certyfikat podatkowy** tax certificate; **certyfikat celny** customs certificate; **certyfikat walutowy** foreign exchange certificate; **certyfikat wywozowy** export certificate; **certyfikat przywozowy** import certificate, entry certificate; **certyfikat klasy statku** *żegl.* class certificate; **certyfikat rejestracyjny statku** *żegl.* certificate of registry; **międzynarodowy certyfikat jakości** international certificate of quality; **certyfikat pochodzenia towarów** *handl.* certificate of origin; **certyfikat asekuracyjny** *l.* **ubezpieczeniowy** certificate of insurance; **certyfikat depozytowy** *l.* **bankowy** *ekon.* certificate of deposit; **certyfikat okrętowy** *żegl.* certificate of registry; **certyfikat złota** gold certificate.

certyfikować *ipf.* certificate, certify.

cesarka *f. Gen.pl.* -ek *pot.* (= *cesarskie cięcie*) *chir.* Cesarean (section), C-section.

cesarski *a.* **1.** emperor's, imperial, Caesarean, Caesarian; **władza cesarska** imperial power, imperial rule; **cesarska korona** imperial *l.* emperor's crown; **pałac cesarski** imperial palace; **objąć tron cesarski** ascend to an imperial throne; **cesarscy doradcy** emperor's advisors. 2. *chir.* **cesarskie cięcie** Cesarean (section).

cesarstwo *n. gł. hist.* 1. empire; **cesarstwo rzymskie/karolińskie** the Roman/Carolingian Empire; **cesarstwo niemieckie/japońskie** the German/Japanese Empire; **Pierwsze/Drugie Cesarstwo** *hist.* the First/Second Empire (*in France*); **styl cesarstwa** the Empire style; **ubiegać się o cesarstwo** strive for the emperor's throne. 2. emperorship. 3. emperor and empress.

cesarz *mp pl.* **-e** *l.* **-owie** emperor; (*zwł. o cesarzach rzymskich*) Caesar.

cesarzowa *f. Gen.* **-ej** empress.

cesja *f.* (= *zrzeczenie się*) *t. prawn.* cession; **cesja domu** house cession; **cesja nieruchomości** real property cession; **dokonać cesji** cede; **uczynić cesję** cede.

cesjonariusz *mp prawn.* cessionary, assignee, assign.

cesze *f. zob.* **cecha**.

cetan *mi chem.* cetane.

cetanowy *a. chem.* cetane; **liczba cetanowa** cetane number.

cetnar *mi Gen.* **-a** hundredweight, cental, quintal; **cetnar angielski** cental, British hundredweight; **cetnar amerykański** American hundredweight; **lepszy funt szczęścia niż cetnar rozumu** better to be born lucky than wise; an ounce of luck is better than a pound of wisdom.

cetologia *f. Gen.* **-ii** *zool.* cetology.

cetyniak *ma ent.* pine looper moth, bordered white (*Bupalus piniarius*).

cetyniec *ma ent.* bark beetle (*Blastophagus*).

cewiarka *f. Gen.pl.* **-ek** 1. *tk.* (*robotnica*) (weft) winder operator, winder. 2. (*maszyna*) (weft) winder.

cewiarnia *f. Gen.pl.* **-i** *l.* **-ń** *tk.* winding department.

cewiarski *a. tk.* winding; **maszyna cewiarska** winder, winding machine; **robotnik cewiarski** winder.

cewić *ipf. tk.* wind, spool.

cewka *f. Gen.pl.* **-ek** 1. *anat.* tubule; **cewka moczowa** urethra; **cewka łzowa** lachrymal duct; **cewka wydalnicza** excretory tubule *l.* duct; **cewka nerwowa** nervous tubule. 2. *el.* coil; **cewka indukcyjna** induction coil, inductor; **cewka magnesująca** field coil; **cewka zapłonowa** (ignition) coil. 3. *tk.* bobbin, spool, reel; **cewka wątkowa** pirn. 4. *myśl.* (*sidła*) snare. 5. *myśl.* (= *noga sarny*) deer leg.

cewki *pl. Gen.* **-wek** *bot.* tracheids.

cewkowaty *a.* tubular.

cewkowy *a.* 1. *el.* coil; **mikrofon cewkowy** moving-coil microphone. 2. *tk.* bobbin, spool, reel; **szpula cewkowa** bobbin, spool, reel.

cewnik *mi Gen.* **-a** *chir.* catheter; **cewnik moczowy/przełykowy/żołądkowy** ureteral/esophageal/gastric catheter; **wprowadzić** *l.* **założyć cewnik** introduce *l.* insert a catheter.

cewnikować *ipf. chir.* catheterize, introduce *l.* insert a catheter into (*sth*).

cewnikowanie *n. chir.* catheterization; **cewnikowanie moczowodu** ureteral catheterization; **cewnikowanie pęcherza moczowego** catheterization of a vesica *l.* bladder.

cez *mi chem.* cesium, *Br.* caesium.

Cezar *mp hist.* Caesar; **(Gajusz) Juliusz Cezar** (Gaius) Julius Caesar.

cezar *mp pl.* **-owie** *hist. t. przen.* Caesar.

cezaropapizm *mi hist.* caesaropapism.

cezaryzm *mi polit., hist.* Caesarism; **cezaryzm demokratyczny** democratic Caesarism.

cezowy *a.* cesium, *Br.* caesium; **sole cezowe** cesium salts; **bomba cezowa** *med.* cesium therapy unit; **zegar cezowy** *fiz.* cesium clock.

cezura *f.* 1. *hist.* turning point. 2. *teor.lit., muz.* caesura.

cęgi *pl. Gen.* **-ów** *techn., zool.* pincers.

cętka *f. Gen.pl.* **-ek** spot; **futro w cętki** spotted fur, spotted fur coat; **twarz pokryta cętkami** spotted face.

cętkowany *a.* spotted; **cętkowana sierść** spotted fur *l.* coat.

chabanina *f. pot.* meat of inferior quality; bad meat.

chaber *mi* **-br-** *Gen.* **-u** *l.* **-a** *bot.* cornflower, bluebottle, bachelor's-button (*Centaurea*).

chabeta *f. pog.* jade.

chabrowy *a.* 1. (*z chabrów*) cornflower; **chabrowy wianek** cornflower garland. 2. (*kolor*) cornflower (blue).

chachar *mp pl.* **-y** *pog.* bum, hobo.

chachmęcić *ipf. pot.* (= *gmatwać*) muddle, confound.

chadecja *f. polit.* christian-democratic party *l.* movement; **rządy chadecji** christian-democratic rule.

chadecki *a. polit.* christian-democratic; **rząd chadecki** christian-democratic government.

chadek *mp polit.* christian democrat.

chadzać *ipf.* 1. (= *chodzić od czasu do czasu*) go (every now and then *l.* from time to time); **chadzać na spotkania w klubie** go to club meetings every now and then; **chadzać do kina** go to cinema from time to time. 2. **chadzać w czymś** (= *nosić*) wear sth (every now and then *l.* from time to time); **chadzać w sandałach/w słomkowym kapeluszu** wear sandals/a straw hat (every now and then).

chalaza *f. biol.* chalaza.

chalcedon *mi min.* chalcedony.

Chaldejczyk *mp*, **Chaldejka** *f. Gen.pl.* **-ek** *hist.* Chaldean.

chaldejski *a.* Chaldean; **Kościół chaldejski** *rel.* Chaldean Church.

chalkantyt *mi min.* chalcanthite, blue vitriol.

chalkograf *mp pl.* **-owie** chalcographer, chalcographist.

chalkografia *f. Gen.* **-ii** chalcography.

chalkopiryt *mi min.* chalcopyrite, copper pyrite.

chalkozyn *mi min.* chalcocite.

chała¹ *f.* = **chałka**.

chała² *f. pot.* trash, rubbish, shit; **ale chała!** what a piece of trash *l.* rubbish *l.* shit!; **ten film to skończona chała** this movie is a piece of trash; **chała nad chałami!** super trash; **nie warto oglądać tej chały** this trash isn't worth watching.

chałaciarz *mp dial., pog.* (= *człowiek źle ubrany*) ragamuffin.

chałat *mi Gen.* -a *l.* -u **1.** (*u Żydów*) gabardine. **2.** *pot.* (*fartuch*) smock, overalls.

chałka *f. Gen.pl.* -ek braided sweet white bread.

chałowaty, chałowy *a. sl.* trashy, rubbishy, shitty.

chałtura *f. pot.* **1.** slipshod *l.* slovenly work. **2.** secondary *l.* additional job; extra work; **brać chałtury** take extra work, moonlight; **łapać chałturę** chase after extra work; **uprawiać chałturę** moonlight.

chałturnictwo *n. pot.* **1.** doing slipshod work. **2.** moonlighting.

chałturniczka *f. Gen.pl.* -ek *zob.* **chałturnik**.

chałturniczy *a.* **1.** (= *wykonywany niestarannie*) slipshod, slovenly. **2.** (= *dotyczący pracy dodatkowej*) secondary, additional, extra; **zajęcie chałturnicze** extra job.

chałturnik *mi pot.* **1.** slovenly worker. **2.** moonlighter.

chałturzyć *ipf. pot.* **1.** do slipshod *l.* slovenly work. **2.** moonlight.

chałturzysta *mp*, **chałturzystka** *f. Gen.pl.* -ek *pot.* = **chałturnik**.

chałupa *f.* **1.** *pot., żart.* (*mieszkanie*) home, place. **2.** *pot.* (*budynek*) shabby building. **3.** *przest.* (*na wsi*) cottage, cabin.

chałupka *f. Gen.pl.* -ek *pot., żart.* = **chałupa** 3.

chałupnictwo *n.* cottage industry.

chałupniczka *f. Gen.pl.* -ek *zob.* **chałupnik**.

chałupniczo *adv.* **pracować chałupniczo** work at home, work in *l.* for cottage industry; **produkować coś chałupniczo** produce sth in the home.

chałupniczy *a.* cottage-industry; **produkcja chałupnicza** cottage industry.

chałupnik *mp* **1.** (*pracownik*) home worker, piece worker. **2.** *hist.* (*chłop*) serf, villein.

chałwa *f.* halvah; **chałwa waniliowa** vanilla (-flavored) halvah; **chałwa czekoladowa** chocolate (-flavored) halvah; **chałwa orzechowa** nut (-flavored) halvah.

cham *mp pl.* -y **1.** *obelż.* boor, yokel, jerk, asshole; *Br.* cad; **ty chamie!** you jerk!, you boor!; **co za cham!** what a jerk!; what an asshole!; what a boor!; **skończony cham** megajerk, megaboor; **robić coś na chama** be a dick about sth; come on (too) strong. **2.** *arch.* (*chłop*) peasant, boor.

chamedafne *f. bot.* leather leaf (*Chameadaphne*).

chamefit *ma bot.* chamaephyte.

chamicki *a.* Hamitic; **języki chamickie** *jęz.* Hamitic languages.

chamidło *n. Gen.pl.* -deł *obelż.* jerk, asshole, boor; **co za chamidło!** what a jerk *l.* boor!, what an asshole!

chamieć *ipf. pot.* become boorish *l.* rustic, coarsen, roughen.

Chamita *mp jęz.* Hamite.

chamka *f. Gen.pl.* -ek **1.** *obelż.* boorish woman. **2.** *arch.* (= *chłopka*) peasant woman.

chamowaty *a. obelż.* boorish, rude.

champion *mp pl.* -i *sport* champion, winner. − *ma pl.* -y (*pies*) champion, winner.

chamsin *mp meteor.* khamsin.

chamski *a.* **1.** *obelż.* boorish, jerky; **chamskie zagranie** jerky *l.* boorish trick; **chamski syn** boor; **chamski ryj** *sl.* jerk, asshole; **po chamsku** like a boor; in a boorish manner; unmannerly. **2.** *arch.* peasant, boorish, rustic; **chamska zagroda** peasant's farm; **chamskie nasienie** boor.

chamskość *f. obelż.* boorishness.

chamstwo *n. obelż.* **1.** (= *prostactwo*) boorishness. **2.** (= *chłopstwo*) peasantry.

chan *mp pl.* -owie *hist.* khan; **chan krymski/tatarski** Crimean/Tatar khan.

chanat *mi hist.* khanate.

chandra *f. pot.* the blues; **mieć chandrę** feel blue, have the blues; **wpaść w chandrę** get the blues.

chandrowaty *a. pot.* blue, moody, bluesy.

chandryczyć się *ipf. pot.* bicker, haggle, carp; **chandryczyć się o pieniądze** haggle over the money; **chandryczyć się z żoną** bicker with one's wife.

chanson *f. indecl. muz.* chanson.

Chanuka *f. rel. judaizm*, Hanukkah, Chanukah, the Feast of Dedication.

chaos *mi* **1.** (= *zamęt*) chaos, confusion, turmoil; **mieć chaos w głowie** be perplexed *l.* bewildered; be utterly confused; **w kraju panował totalny chaos** the country was in a state of chaos; the country was thrown into confusion; chaos reigned in the country; *mat., fiz.* chaos; **chaos molekularny** molecular chaos. **2.** *mit.* chaos (pierwotny) the abyss, the (primal) chaos; **na początku był chaos** in the beginning there was the abyss.

chaotycznie *adv.* chaotically.

chaotyczność *f.* confusion, being in a state of chaos.

chaotyczny *a.* chaotic, disorderly, disorganised; **chaotyczna rozmowa** chaotic conversation; **chaotyczne myśli** woolly thoughts; **chaotyczna polityka** inconsistent policy, wavering *l.* vacillating policy; **chaotyczny wykładowca** chaotic lecturer.

chap *int. zob.* **chaps**.

chapać *ipf.* -pię -piesz *pot.* **1.** (= *harować*) work one's hand to the bone, sweat one's guts out. **2.** *zob.* **chapnąć**.

chapnąć *pf.* -ij **1.** *pot.* (= *schwycić*) snap, snatch, grab; **pies chapnął mnie za nogawkę** the dog snapped at my trouser leg. **2.** *pot.* (= *ukraść*) grab; **złodziej chapnął torebkę i uciekł** the robber grabbed the bag and ran away.

chaps *int.* snap; **nagle pies chaps mnie za nogę** suddenly the dog snapped my leg *l.* at my leg.

charakter *mi* **1.** (= *osobowość*) (personal) character, personality; **dobry/zły charakter** good/bad character; **gwałtowny/trudny charakter** violent/difficult character; **charakter introwertyczny/**

ekstrawertyczny introvert/extrovert character; **mściwy charakter** vindictive *l.* vengeful character; **stałość charakteru** being set in one's ways, being balanced *l.* level-headed; **kształtować czyjś charakter** mould *l.* form *l.* shape sb's character; **niezgodność charakterów** irreconcilable difference of characters; **mieć charakter** be a person of (strong) character; **człowiek z charakterem** person of (strong) character; person with backbone; **człowiek bez charakteru** person of weak character; person of low moral standards; person with no backbone; **szkoła charakteru** school of hard knocks; university of life; **wyrabiać charakter** build character; shape *l.* mould character; **to nie leży w moim charakterze** it isn't in character with me; it isn't my way of doing things. **2.** (= *cecha przedmiotu l. zjawiska*) character, nature; **urzędowy charakter** official *l.* formal character; **sprawa o charakterze urzędowym** official business; **w charakterze...** in the capacity of...; in the character of...; acting as...; **pracować w charakterze wykładowcy** work as a lecturer; **spotkanie ma oficjalny/nieoficjalny charakter** it is an official/unofficial meeting; **charakter pisma** hand, handwriting, character; **coś nabiera charakteru** sth takes on character; **nadawać czemuś charakter** determine the character of sth; **mieć charakter w nogach** *żart.* be able to run fast; be the first to run away; **uchwycić charakter czegoś** capture the character *l.* nature of sth. **3.** *teor.lit.* character, hero; **komedia charakterów** commedy of characters; **charakter statyczny** static character; **charakter dynamiczny** dynamic character; **czarny charakter** *zwł. teatr l. film* villain, bad guy.

charakterek *mi* -rk- *iron.* peevish *l.* irritating person *l.* character.

charakternik *mp pot.* **1.** gutsy man. **2.** man of (strong) character.

charakterny *a. pot.* of (strong) character; **charakterna kobieta** woman of (strong) character.

charakterolog *mp pl.* -dzy *l.* -owie characterologist, person *l.* psychologist studying character (and personality).

charakterologia *f. Gen.* -ii characterology, study of character (and personality).

charakterologiczny *a.* characterological; **studium charakterologiczne** study of character and personality, character sketch; **zaburzenia charakterologiczne** *psych.* personality disorder.

charakteropata *mp psych.* characteropathic individual.

charakteropatia *f. Gen.* -ii *psych.* characteropathy.

charakterotwórczy *a.* formative, character-forming, character-moulding, character-shaping.

charakterystycznie *adv.* characteristically.

charakterystyczny *a.* **1.** characteristic (*dla kogoś / czegoś* of sb/sth); peculiar (*dla kogoś / czegoś* to sb/sth); **charakterystyczne objawy żółtaczki** symptoms characteristic of jaundice; **funkcja charakterystyczna** *mat.* characteristic function.

2. *teatr* **rola charakterystyczna** character part; **aktor charakterystyczny** character actor.

charakterystyka *f.* **1.** (*opis*) profile, description; **charakterystyka pracownika** employee profile; **ogólna/powierzchowna charakterystyka** general/superficial profile *l.* description; **szczegółowa/wnikliwa charakterystyka** detailed/in-depth profile *l.* description. **2.** *techn., mat.* characteristics, characteristic curve *l.* function; **charakterystyka silnika** engine performance; **charakterystyka spektralna** spectral(-response) characteristic; **charakterystyka światła** *żegl.* characteristics *l.* character of a light.

charakteryzacja *f.* **1.** (*zmieniony wygląd*) makeup; **charakteryzacja teatralna/filmowa** movie/theater makeup; **nominacja do Oscara za charakteryzację** Oscar nomination for best makeup; **grać w charakteryzacji** use makeup for performance. **2.** (*środki*) makeup; **nałożyć charakteryzację** apply *l.* put on makeup; **zmyć** *l.* **usunąć charakteryzację** remove makeup.

charakteryzator *mp*, **charakteryzatorka** *f. Gen.pl.* -ek makeup artist.

charakteryzatornia *f. Gen.pl.* -i makeup studio.

charakteryzatorski *a.* makeup.

charakteryzować *ipf.* **1.** (*opisywać*) characterize, profile, describe; **trafnie charakteryzować** characterize sb in well-chosen words, give an accurate description *l.* profile; **ogólnikowo charakteryzować** characterize sb in a general way, give a general description *l.* profile. **2.** (= *cechować*) characterize; **charakteryzuje go skłonność do gniewu** he is characterized by frequent outbursts of anger. **3.** *teatr* (= *zmieniać czyjś wygląd*) make (*sb*) up; **charakteryzować komuś twarz** apply makeup to one's face. ~ **się** *ipf.* **1.** (= *cechować się*) be characterized by; **klimat charakteryzuje się mroźnymi zimami** climate is characterized by frosty winters; **Adam charakteryzuje się pracowitością** Adam is a hardworking person. **2.** *teatr* (*zmieniać swój wygląd*) make (o.s.) up; **charakteryzować się na króla** make up as a king.

charci *a.* greyhound.

charcica *f.* greyhound bitch.

charczeć *ipf.* -ę -ysz **1.** (*o człowieku*) wheeze; **chory charczy** patient is wheezing. **2.** (*o przedmiocie*) sputter, knock; **silnik charczy** engine is knocking.

chargé d'affaires *mp indecl.* (*urzędnik*) chargé d'affaires.

charkać *ipf.*, **charknąć** *pf.* -ij cough up *l.* out; **charkać krwią** cough up blood; **nie charkaj!** don't cough up!

charkot *mi* wheezing voice *l.* sound, racuous voice *l.* sound.

charkotać *ipf.* -czę -czesz *l.* -cę -cesz, -cz = **charczeć** 1.

charleston *mi Acc. i Gen.* -a *taniec* Charleston.

charłacki *a.* feeble, decrepit, infirm; **charłacki wygląd** feeble appearance.

charłactwo *n. med.* cachexy, cachexia, marasmus.

charłak *mp pl.* **-i** *l.* **-cy** feeble *l.* frail *l.* decrepit *l.* infirm person.

chart *ma* greyhound; **biec** *l.* **pędzić jak chart** run very fast, run as fast as a greyhound.

charter *mi zob.* **czarter**.

charterowy *a.* zob. **czarterowy**.

charytatywnie *adv.* charitably; **działać charytatywnie** work for charity; **wspomagać charytatywnie** give to charity.

charytatywność *f.* charitableness.

charytatywny *a.* charitable; **działalność charytatywna** charity; **pomoc charytatywna** charity; **organizacja charytatywna** charity, charitable institution *l.* organization; **akcja charytatywna** charity; **koncert charytatywny** charity concert; **przeznaczyć pieniądze na cele charytatywne** give money to charity.

charyzma *f.* charisma; **ktoś obdarzony charyzmą** charismatic person; **polityk z charyzmą** charismatic politician.

charyzmat *mi* **1.** *rel.* charisma, charism; **człowiek obdarzony charyzmatem apostolstwa** person called to the charism of mission; **charyzmat ubóstwa** charism of poverty; **charyzmat prostoty** charism of simplicity; **charyzmat zakonu** religious order charism; **otrzymać charyzmat** be called to a charism. **2.** (= *charyzma*) charisma.

charyzmatyczny *a.* charismatic; **charyzmatyczny przywódca** charismatic leader; **wspólnota charyzmatyczna** *rel.* charismatic community; **charyzmatyczny uzdrowiciel** charismatic healer; **charyzmatyczny ruch odnowy** *rz.-kat.* Charismatic Movement, Roman-Catholic charismatic renewal.

charyzmatyk *mp* charismatic person.

chasyd *mp judaizm* Hasid.

chasydyzm *mi judaizm* Hasidism.

chasydzki *a. judaizm* Hasidic; **gmina chasydzka** Hasidic commune *l.* community; **zwyczaje chasydzkie** Hasidic customs.

chaszcze *pl. Gen.* **-y** *l.* **-ów** thicket.

chata *f.* **1.** (*na wsi*) cabin, hut; **urodzić się w chłopskiej chacie** be born in a peasant's cabin; **chata bobra** *l.* **bobrowa** *zool.* (beaver's) lodge; **czym chata bogata, tym rada** what's mine is yours, feel like one of the family. **2.** *pot.* (*mieszkanie*) home, place, digs.

chatka *f. Gen.pl.* **-ek** *emf.* small cabin, small hut.

chcica *f. wulg.* horniness.

chcieć *ipf.* **chcę chcesz, chciej 1.** (= *mieć chęć*) want; **chcieć coś zrobić** want to do sth; **chciałbym, żeby on przyszedł** I wish he came; **chce mi się spać** I'm (feeling) sleepy; **chce mi się jeść/pić** I'm hungry/thirsty; **chce mi się śmiać/płakać** I feel like laughing/crying; **chce mi się wyć z rozpaczy** *pot.* I feel like howling; **nie chce mi się pracować** I do not feel like working; **nic mi się nie chce** I do not feel like doing anything; **chce mi się siusiu** *pot.* I want to pee; **czego chcesz ode mnie?!** what do you want from me?!; **(czy) chcesz, czy nie chcesz** whether you like it or not; **chcę się z tobą ożenić** I want to marry you; **chciał wstać, ale mu zabrakło sił** he wanted to get

up but he lacked the strength (to do so); **jeśli chcesz, to...** if you want...; **masz, czego chciałeś** you got what you wanted, you got what you asked for; **sam tego chciał** he asked for it; **chciałbym być ptakiem** I'd like to be a bird; I wish I were a bird; **chciałbym być aktorem** I'd like to become an actor; I'd like to be an actor; I wish I were an actor; **chciałbym dożyć tego** I wish I could live long enough to see that; **chciałbym być spokojny** I'd like to be calm; **chciałbym, żeby się to nie sprawdziło** I wish it wouldn't be *l.* come true; **nie chce iść dalej** he *l.* she doesn't want to go any further; he *l.* she refuses to go any further; **sam nie wie, czego chce** even he himself doesn't know what he wants; **zrobię to, jak mi się będzie chciało** I'll do it if I feel like doing it; **ona nie chce iść za mąż** she doesn't want to get married; **chciałbym** I would like to; **chciałoby się zatańczyć** one would like to dance; **chciałoby się wyjechać na wakacje** one would like to go on holiday; **chcąc nie chcąc** willy-nilly, willingly or unwillingly; **jak sobie chcesz** as you wish; **co chcesz przez to powiedzieć?** what do you mean?; what do you mean by that?; what is that supposed to mean?; **nie chciałby, żeby mnie z nim widziano** he wouldn't want anybody to see me with him; **chciałbyś tego spróbować?** would you like to try that?; **chciałbym ci uścisnąć rękę** I'd like to shake your hand; **chciał powiedzieć coś więcej** he wanted to say more than (just) that; **chciałbym się czegoś napić** I would like something to drink; I could use a drink; **czego ona właściwie chce?** what does she really want?; **tak jest, bo tak chcę!** it is so because I want it that way!; **tak, jak chce tego zwyczaj** as custom would have it; according to custom; **chciałbym nieba ci przychylić, ale...** I would like to give you everything that you want but...; **los chciał, że...** fate decreed that...; **pech chciał, że spóźniłem się na pociąg** I had the bad luck to miss the train; unfortunately, I missed the train; **niech się dzieje, co chce** whatever is to happen, let it happen; **chcę chleba z szynką** I want bread and ham; **chciałem jak najlepiej** I tried to do my best; **niech mówi, co chce, a mnie nie przekona** whatever he *l.* she says, he *l.* she won't convice me; **niech robi, jak chce** let him do as he pleases; **chcieć to móc** where there's a will, there's way; **dla chcącego nie ma nic trudnego** where there's a will, there's way; **kto chce psa uderzyć, zawsze kij znajdzie** when you want to blame sb, you'll always find a reason. **2.** (*o rzeczach*) will *l.* would not + *verb*; **drzwi nie chcą się otworzyć** the door won't open; **ognisko nie chce się palić** the fire won't burn; **rana nie chciała się zagoić** the wound wouldn't heal; **nauka nie chce mi wchodzić do głowy** I can't remember anything I study; **nie chce mi to przejść przez gardło** I won't say that.

chciejstwo *n. lit.* wishful thinking.

chciwie *adv.* greedily; **spoglądać chciwie na coś** give sth a greedy look.

chciwiec *mp* **-wc-** *Voc.* **-wcze** *pl.* **-y** greedy person, cormorant.

chciwość *f.* greed (*na coś* for sth); **nienasycona chciwość** insatiable greed.

chciwy *a.* greedy (*na coś* for sth); **chciwy sławy** greedy *l.* craving for fame; **patrzeć chciwym okiem na coś** eye sth greedily *l.* longingly; **chłonąć coś chciwym uchem** listen to sth eagerly.

cheddar *mi Gen.* **-a** *l.* **-u** *kulin.* cheddar (cheese).

cheder *mi judaizm* heder.

cheeseburger *mi Gen.* **-a** cheeseburger.

chełbia *f. Gen.pl.* **-i** *zool.* (= *meduza*) jellyfish; **chełbia modra** common jellyfish (*Aurelia aurita*).

chełpić się *ipf.* boast, brag (*czymś* about sth); swagger, bluster; **chełpić się swoim bogactwem** boast about one's wealth; **chełpić się synem** boast about one's son; **chełpi się, że jest najpiękniejszą blondynką w klasie** she boasts that she's the most beautiful blonde in her class; **chełpić się (czymś) przed dziewczyną** boast (about sth) to a girl, boast to a girl (that...).

chełpliwie *adv.* boastfully; **opowiadać chełpliwie o swoich sukcesach** boast about one's success.

chełpliwość *f.* boastfulness, swagger, vainglory.

chełpliwy *a.* boastful; **chełpliwy facet** braggart, bragger, swaggerer; **chełpliwy uśmieszek** smirk; **chełpliwy ton głosu** boastful tone of voice.

chemia *f. Gen.* **-ii 1.** (*dziedzina wiedzy*) chemistry; **chemia analityczna/fizyczna/jądrowa/kwantowa** analytical/physical/nuclear/quantum chemistry; **chemia biologiczna** biological chemistry, biochemistry; **chemia farmaceutyczna/kliniczna** pharmaceutical/clinical chemistry; **chemia organiczna/nieorganiczna/ogólna** organic/inorganic/general chemistry; **chemia rolna** agricultural chemistry; **chemia roślin** phytochemistry, plant chemistry; **chemia spożywcza** food chemistry; **chemia stosowana/teoretyczna** applied/pure chemistry; **postępy/badania w dziedzinie chemii** advances/research in chemistry; **studiować chemię** study chemistry; **wykładać chemię** *l.* **uczyć chemii** teach chemistry; **uczyć się chemii** study chemistry; **podręcznik do chemii** chemistry textbook; **doktorat z chemii** Ph.D. in chemistry. **2.** *szkoln.* chemistry class; (= *lekcja chemii*) chemistry lesson. **3.** *pot.* (= *produkty chemiczne*) chemicals; **wszystko, co nas otacza to tylko chemia** we are surronded by nothing but chemicals. **4.** *pot., med.* chemotherapy; **leczyć chemią** treat by *l.* with chemotherapy; **być po chemii** have undergone chemotherapy. **5.** *sl.* (= *narkotyki*) chemicals, drugs.

chemiczka *f. Gen.pl.* **-ek 1.** (*specjalistka w dziedzinie chemii*) chemist. **2.** *pot.* (*nauczycielka chemii*) chemistry teacher.

chemicznie *adv.* chemically; **prać chemicznie** dry-clean; **chemicznie aktywny** chemically active; **chemicznie czysty** chemically pure.

chemiczno-fizyczny *a.* chemico-physical, chemical-physical; **badania chemicznofizyczne** chemico-physical research, chemical-physical research.

chemiczny *a.* chemical; **analiza chemiczna** chemical analysis; **budowa chemiczna cząsteczki** chemical structure of a particle; **cząsteczka chemiczna** chemical particle; **doświadczenie chemiczne** chemical experiment; **laboratorium chemiczne** chemical laboratory; **pierwiastek chemiczny** chemical element; **równanie chemiczne** chemical equation; **skład chemiczny** (chemical) composition; **symbol chemiczny** chemical symbol; **środek chemiczny** chemical agent; **wiązanie chemiczne** chemical bond; **wzór chemiczny** chemical formula; **związek chemiczny** chemical compound; **zjawisko chemiczne** chemical phenomenon; **pralnia chemiczna** dry-cleaner's; **broń chemiczna** chemical weapon; **wojna chemiczna** chemical warfare.

chemigraf *mp pl.* **-owie** zincographer.

chemigrafia *f. Gen.* **-ii 1.** (*technika*) zincography. **2.** (*klisza*) zincograph, zincotype.

chemik *mp* **1.** (*specjalista w dziedzinie chemii*) chemist. **2.** *pot.* (*nauczyciel chemii*) chemistry teacher.

chemikalia *pl. Gen.* **-ów** chemicals.

chemiluminescencja *f.* chemiluminescence.

chemioterapia *f. zob.* **chemoterapia**.

chemizacja *f.* chemicalization; **chemizacja rolnictwa** chemicalization of agriculture.

chemizm *mi* chemistry; **chemizm ścieków/roślin** sewage/plant chemistry.

chemizować *ipf.* chemicalize.

chemogeniczny *a. geol.* chemogenic; **złoża chemogeniczne** chemogenic deposits.

chemokineza *f. chem.* chemokinesis.

chemolak *mi* (*lakier*) varnish.

chemoodporny *a.* resistant to chemicals; **chemoodporna wykładzina** linoleum resistant to chemicals; **farba chemoodporna** paint resistant to chemicals.

chemoreceptor *mi Gen.* **-a** chemoreceptor.

chemosterylizacja *f.* chemosterilization.

chemosynteza *f.* chemosynthesis.

chemotaksja *f.* chemotaxis.

chemoterapeutyczny *a.* chemotherapeutic; **leki chemoterapeutyczne** chemotherapeutic medicines; **leczenie chemoterapeutyczne** chemotherapy.

chemoterapeutyk *mi* chemotherapeutic, chemotherapeutical.

chemoterapia *f. Gen.* **-ii** chemotherapy.

chemotroniczny *a.* chemotronic; **układ chemotroniczny** chemotronic system.

chemotronik *mp* chemotronist.

chemotronika *f.* chemotronics.

chemotropizm *mi* chemotropism; **dodatni/ujemny** positive/ negative chemotropism.

chemoutwardzalny *a.* chemically hardening; **lakier chemoutwardzalny** chemically hardening varnish; **tworzywo chemoutwardzalne** chemically hardening material.

cherlacki *a.* sickly; **cherlackie zdrowie** feeble health; **cherlacki chłopak** frail boy.

cherlactwo *n.* sickliness.

cherlać *ipf.* be sickly.

cherlak *mp pl.* **-i** *l.* **-cy** weakling. – *ma pl.* **-i** *myśl.* weakling.

cherlakowaty *a.* sickly.

cherlawiec *mp* **-wc-** *pl.* **-y** *pot.* weakling.

cherlawy *a.* sickly; **cherlawy chłopak** frail boy; **cherlawe zdrowie** feeble health.

cherry *f. indecl.* cherry brandy.

cherubin *mp pl.* **-y** *l.* **-i 1.** *Bibl.* cherub; **chóry cherubinów** cherubic choirs. **2.** *przen.* (*chłopiec*) cherub.

cherubinek *mp* **-nk-** *pl.* **-i** *sztuka emf.* (*chłopiec*) cherub; **piękny jak cherubinek** beautiful like a cherub.

cherubinowy *a.* cherubic; **chóry cherubinowe** cherubic choirs; **skrzydła cherubinowe** cherubic wings.

chester *mi* Cheshire *l.* Chester cheese.

chęć *f.* (= *pragnienie*) desire; (= *życzenie*) wish; **chęć posiadania** craving for money; **chęć do pracy** will to work; **chęć do życia** will to live; **chęć używania życia** lust for life; **chęć na lody** fancy for ice-cream; **chęć na tańce** fancy for dancing; **chęć poznania** curiosity to know; **chęć współpracy** cooperativeness; **nieprzeparta chęć** craving; **wielka chęć** strong desire; **okazywać chęć** express desire, show inclination; **mieć chęć porozmawiać** feel like talking; **mieć chęć na świeże truskawki** feel like eating (some) fresh strawberries; **mieć dobre chęci** have good intentions; **odebrać komuś chęć do (zrobienia) czegoś** deprive sb of the desire to do sth; **pałać chęcią zrobienia czegoś** be itching to do sth; **wzbudzić w kimś chęci** arouse sb's desire; **zrobić coś z chęci zysku** do sth for gain; **przyszła mi chęć na kino** I felt like going to the movies; **brak ci chęci** you lack will; **nigdy nie miał wielkiej chęci do tego** he's never shown much inclination for it; **zrobił to z chęci zysku** he did it for profit; **umieram z chęci zobaczenia jej** I'm dying to see her; **mimo najszczerszych chęci nie udało mi się spotkać z tobą** willing as I was I couldn't manage to meet with you; **z chęcią to zrobię** I'll be happy to do it; **liczą się dobre chęci** it's the thought that counts; **dobre chęci nie wystarczą** actions speak louder than words; fine words butter no parsnips; **w każdym razie miałem szczere chęci** anyway, I meant well; **dobrymi chęciami piekło (jest) wybrukowane** the road to hell is paved with good intentions.

chędogi *a. arch.* neat, tidy.

chętka *f. Gen.pl.* **-ek** fancy, itch; **mieć chętkę** fancy (*na coś / coś zrobić* sth/to do sth); itch (*coś zrobić* to do sth); **mieć chętkę na kogoś** (= *pożądać kogoś*) have the hots for sb; **naszła mnie chętka na kino** I felt like going to the movies; **przyszła mi chętka pograć w piłkę** I felt like playing football.

chętnie *adv.* willingly; **chętnie śpiewać/pomagać** sing/help eagerly.

chętny *a.* (= *ochoczy*) willing; **chętny uczeń** eager pupil; **chętny do pomocy** willing to help; **chętny do nauki (języka chińskiego)** eager to learn (Chinese); **słuchać chętnym uchem** lend an ear. – *mp* a person willing *l.* eager (*to do sth*);

chętnych do jej ręki nie brak she has many wooers.

chiaroscuro *n. sztuka* chiaroscuro.

chiastolit *mi min.* chiastolite, macle.

chiazm *mi ret.* chiasmus.

chiazma *f. biol.* chiasm, chiasma.

Chicago *n. indecl.* Chicago.

chicagowski *a.* Chicago.

chich *mi* śmichy-chichy giggles; **to nie żadne śmichy-chichy** it's no laughing matter.

chichocik *mi* giggle.

chichot *mi* giggle; (*zwł. stłumiony*) snigger; **głośne chichoty** loud giggles; **rozległ się chichot** somebody giggled.

chichotać *ipf.* **-czę -czesz** *l.* **-cę -cesz, -cz** giggle; (*zwł. stłumionym śmiechem*) snigger; **chichotać złośliwie** chuckle maliciously; **chichotać z byle czego** giggle at any old thing. **~ się** *ipf.* **-czę -czesz** *l.* **-cę -cesz, -cz** giggle, snigger; **bez przerwy chichoczecie się** you keep giggling all the time.

chichotka *f. Gen.pl.* **-ek** giggler.

chichotliwie *adv.* with a giggle; **opowiadać coś chichotliwie** talk about sth giggling *l.* with a giggle.

chichotliwy *a.* giggly, chuckling; **chichotliwe dziewczyny** giggling girls; **chichotliwe szepty** chuckling whispers.

chichrać się *ipf. pot.* giggle.

Chile *n. indecl.* Chile.

chili *n. indecl.* chilli.

chiliastyczny *a.* chiliastic.

chiliazm *mi rel.* chiliasm.

Chilijczyk *mp*, **Chilijka** *f. Gen.pl.* **-ek** Chilean.

chilijski *a.* Chilean; **junta chilijska** *polit.* Chilean junta; **saletra chilijska** *min.* soda niter, *Br.* soda nitre; **Chile saltpeter**, *Br.* Chile saltpetre.

Chimera *f. mit.* Chimera, chimera.

chimera *f.* **1.** *biol.*, *sztuka* chimera, chimaera; **motyw chimery** chimera theme; **chimery roślinne/zwierzęce** chimera plants/animals. **2.** *icht.* rabbitfish (*Chimaera monstrosa*). **3.** *przest.* (= *urojenie*) chimera, bogey; **gonić za chimerą** go on a wild-goose chase.

chimery *pl. Gen.* **-r** (= *dąsy*) freak, caprice; **mieć chimery** be moody; **stroić chimery** be whimsical.

chimeryczka *f. Gen.pl.* **-ek** freakish woman.

chimerycznie *adv.* freakishly, whimsically; **zachowywać się chimerycznie** behave whimsically.

chimeryczność *f.* capriciousness, moodiness.

chimeryczny *a.* **1.** (= *kapryśny*) capricious, moody; **chimeryczny mężczyzna** moody man; **chimeryczny charakter** capricious character; **usposobienie chimeryczne** capricious disposition. **2.** *przest.* (= *urojony*) fantastic, chimeric, chimerical; **chimeryczna idea/polityka** chimeric idea/policy.

chimeryk *mp* freakish man.

chinidyna *f.* quinidine.

chinina *f.* quinine.

chininowy *a.* quinine; **zastrzyk chininowy** quinine injection; **zamroczenie chininowe** quinine stupor.

Chinka f. Gen.pl. **-ek** Chinese, Chinawoman.

chinowiec mi **-wc-** Gen. **-a** bot. cinchona (Cinchona).

chinowy a. bot. cinchonic, cinchonaceous; **drzewo chinowe** cinchona (Cinchona); **kora chinowa** cinchona bark, china bark.

chintz mi tk. chintz.

Chiny pl. Gen. **-n** China; **za Chiny ludowe nie mogę tego zrobić!** pot. there is no freaking way I can do it!

Chińczyk mp Chinese, Chinaman.

chińczyk mi Acc. i Gen. **-a** Br. (gra) ludo.

chiński a. Chinese; **chińska herbata** China tea; **chińska porcelana** eggshell china; **chiński jedwab** China silk; **chińskie ceremonie** przen. oriental ceremony; **pismo chińskie** Chinese logographs; **latarnia chińska** Chinese lantern; **ogród chiński** Chinese garden; **mur chiński** the Great Wall of China; **Morze Chińskie** geogr. China Sea; **róża chińska** bot. China rose (Hibiscus rosa sinensis); **kapusta chińska** bot. Chinese cabbage, pak-choi cabbage (Brassica chinensis); **olej chiński** techn. Chinese wood oil, tung oil; **gęś chińska** zool. Chinese goose; **a ja jestem chiński cesarz** iron. and I'm a Dutchman; **nie zrobi tego za chińskiego boga** he won't do it for love or money.

chińszczyzna f. **1.** (język) Chinese; **klasyczna chińszczyzna** classical Chinese. **2.** (kultura) Chinese culture. **3.** (sztuka) Chinese art; **panuje moda na chińszczyznę** Chinese art is in fashion. **4.** (= coś niezrozumiałego) double Dutch; **to dla mnie chińszczyzna** it's all Greek to me. **5.** pot. (= dania kuchni chińskiej) Chinese food; **lubisz chińszczyznę?** do you like Chinese food?

chip mi Gen. **-a** el. (micro)chip.

chippendale mi **1.** (styl) Chippendale style; **lustro w stylu chippendale** Chippendale style mirror. **2.** (mebel) a piece of furniture in Chippendale style.

chipsy pl. Gen. **-ów** chips.

chiralność f. chem. chirality, dissymmetry.

chiralny a. chiral, dissymmetric.

chirologia f. Gen. **-ii 1.** (= język migowy) sign language. **2.** (wróżenie) palmistry.

chiromancja f. palmistry.

chiromanta mp, **chiromantka** f. Gen.pl. **-ek** palmist.

chirurg mp pl. **-dzy** l. **-owie** surgeon; **chirurg dziecięcy** pediatric surgeon; **chirurg naczyniowy** vascular surgeon; **chirurg plastyczny** plastic surgeon; **chirurg drzew** ogr. tree surgeon.

chirurgia f. Gen. **-ii 1.** (dziedzina) surgery; **chirurgia ogólna** general surgery; **chirurgia dziecięca** pediatric sugery; **chirurgia kosmetyczna** cosmetic surgery; **chirurgia plastyczna** plastic surgery; **chirurgia miękka** soft tissue surgery; **chirurgia szczękowa** dental surgery; **chirurgia twarda** l. **kostna** orthopedic surgery, bone surgery; **chirurgia urazowa** casualty surgery; **mała/wielka chirurgia** minor/major surgery; **chirurgia drzew** ogr. tree surgery. **2.** (oddział szpi-

tala) surgical ward l. department; **przyjąć pacjenta na chirurgię** admit a patient to the surgical ward; **leżeć na chirurgii** be in the surgical ward; **chirurgia urazowa** casualty ward.

chirurgicznie adv. surgically.

chirurgiczny a. surgical; **narzędzia chirurgiczne** surgery set; **klinika chirurgiczna** surgical clinic; **oddział chirurgiczny** surgical ward l. department; **zabieg chirurgiczny** surgery, surgical operation; **leczenie chirurgiczne** surgical treatment.

chiton mi hist. chiton.

chitony pl. Gen. **-ów** zool. chitons (Polyplacophora).

chityna f. chitin.

chitynowy a. chitinous; **pancerz chitynowy** chitinous shell.

chlać ipf. **-am -asz** l. **-eję -ejesz, -aj** l. **-ej, chlali** l. **chleli** wulg. booze, booze it up; **chlać na umór** drink like there's no tomorrow, drink like prohibition is coming back.

chlapa f. (= deszczowa pogoda) rainy weather; (= rozmiękły śnieg) slush; **jesienna chlapa** autumnal drizzle.

chlapać ipf. **-pię -piesz 1.** (= rozpryskiwać) splash; **chlapać pędzlem** splash paint; **chlapać farbą po podłodze** splash paint over the floor; **deszcz chlapie** the rain is splashing. **2.** pot. (= gadać bez zastanowienia) blab; **chlapać ozorem** babble. **~ się** ipf. **-pię -piesz** splash, dabble (w czymś in sth).

chlapanina f. **1.** (pogoda) drizzly weather; **przeziębić się podczas chlapaniny** catch a cold during the drizzle. **2.** (= chlapanie) splash, splashing.

chlapnąć pf. **-ij 1.** zob. **chlapać. 2.** (= rozpryskać) splash. **3.** **chlapnąć kielicha** pot. (= wypić) down one's drink; **chlapnijmy sobie jeszcze po jednym** let's have another round.

chlasnąć pf. **-ij** zob. **chlastać. ~ się** pf. **-ij** zob. **chlastać się.**

chlast int. wham!; **a ja go chlast w mordę** and wham! I punched him in the face.

chlastać ipf., **chlasnąć** pf. **-am -asz** l. **-szczę -szczesz 1.** (o cieczy) splash; **deszcz chlasta w szyby** the rain's splashing against the windows; **fala chlasnęła o burtę łodzi** a wave splashed against the boat. **2.** (= uderzać) lash, smack; **chlastać kogoś szablą** cut sb with a sabre; **gałąź chlasnęła mnie po twarzy** a twig lashed across my face; **chlasnąć konia batem** whip a horse; **chlastać językiem** l. **ozorem** pot. babble. **~ się** ipf., **chlasnąć się** pf. **-am -asz** l. **-szczę -szczesz 1.** (siebie) lash. **2.** (nawzajem) lash one another; **chlastać się nożami** slash one another with knives.

chleb mi Gen. **-a** (pieczywo) bread; **chleb biały** white bread; **chleb ciemny** l. **czarny** brown bread; **chleb pszenny** wheat bread; **chleb razowy** wholewheat bread; **chleb żytni** rye bread; **czerstwy chleb** stale bread; **świeży chleb** fresh bread; **wiejski chleb** Br. cob, cobloaf; **bochenek chleba** loaf of bread; **chleb z masłem** bread and butter; **chleb z szynką** bread and ham; **kromka chleba**

slice of bread; **skórka od chleba** crust; **suchy chleb** dry bread; **chleb powszedni** daily bread; **lekki chleb** easy living; **łaskawy chleb** charity; **rozczyniać** *l.* **miesić chleb** knead bread; **piec chleb** bake bread; **Chleb Pański** *l.* **Eucharystyczny** *rel.* the Eucharist, the Host; **chleb i wino** *rel.* bread and wine; **łamanie chleba** *rel.* fraction, breaking of the bread; **chleba naszego powszedniego daj nam dzisiaj** *Bibl.* give us our daily bread; **chleb świętojański** *bot.* (*drzewo*) carob (*Caretonia siliqua*); (*strąk*) carob; *Br. t.* Saint John's bread; **to dla mnie chleb z masłem** it's a piece of cake for me; **zwykły zjadacz chleba** an average mortal; **z niejednego pieca chleb jadał** he's seen life; **żyć o chlebie i wodzie** subsist on bread and water; **dzielić się z kimś ostatnim kawałkiem chleba** share one's last crust with sb; **pracować (ciężko) na chleb** work hard for one's bread and cheese; **robić coś dla chleba** do sth to earn a living; **odebrać komuś chleb** *l.* **pozbawić kogoś chleba** take the bread out of sb's mouth; **być bez chleba** be jobless; **wędrować za chlebem** seek livelihood; **być na cudzym chlebie** live on sb's charity; **ciężki kawałek chleba** hard bread; **zarabiać na kawałek chleba** earn one's daily bread; **chodzić po proszonym chlebie** be a beggar; **nie jem chleba za darmo** I earn my living; **nie samym chlebem człowiek żyje** man does not live on bread alone; **z tej mąki chleba nie będzie** it's no use; **przyjąć kogoś chlebem i solą** greet sb with bread and salt (*according to an old Polish tradition*); **głodnemu chleb na myśli** the tongue always *l.* ever turns to the aching tooth.

chlebaczek *mi* -czk- *Gen.* -a small haversack.

chlebak *mi Gen.* -a haversack.

chlebek *mi* -bk- *Gen.* -a *emf.* bread.

chlebodawca *mp*, **chlebodawczyni** *f.* employer; *pot.* meal ticket.

chlebowiec *mi* -wc- *Gen.* -a *bot.* breadfruit (*Artocarpus*).

chlebowy *a.* bread; **piec chlebowy** baking oven; **kwas chlebowy** kvas; **drzewo chlebowe** *bot.* = **chlebowiec.**

chlew *mi* 1. (*dla świń*) pigsty, pigpen, sty; *rzad.* piggery. 2. *pot., przen.* pigsty; **jest tu jak w chlewie** this place is a total mess!, it's a regular pigsty in here!; **ale tu chlew!** what a sty!

chlewik *mi Gen.* -a *zob.* **chlew.**

chlewnia *f. Gen.pl.* -i 1. (*budynek*) piggery. 2. (*trzoda*) swine, pigs.

chlewny *a.* **trzoda chlewna** swine, pigs.

chlipać *ipf.* -pię -piesz, **chlipnąć** *pf.* -ij 1. (= *pić*) lap up. 2. (= *płakać*) sob.

chloantyt *mi min.* chloanthite.

chlor *mi chem.* chlorine, chlorin; **związki chloru** chlorine compounds.

chloral *mi* chloral; **wodzian chloralu** chloral hydrate.

chloramina *f.* chloramine.

chloran *mi* chlorate; **chloran potasu** potassium chlorate; **chloran sodowy** sodium chlorate.

chlorargiryt *mi min.* cerargyrite.

chlorawy *a. chem.* chlorous; **kwas chlorawy** chlorous acid.

chlorek *mi* -rk- *chem., pot.* (= *wybielacz*) chloride; **chlorek amonowy** ammonium chloride; **chlorek sodu** *l.* **sodowy** sodium chloride; **chlorek potasu** potassium chloride; **chlorek etylu/metylu** ethyl/methyl chloride; **chlorek metalu** metal chloride; **chlorek niemetalu** non-metal chloride.

chlorella *f. biol.* chlorella (*Chlorella*).

chlorofil *mi biochem.* chlorophyll.

chlorofilowy *a.* chlorophyllous; **krem chlorofilowy** *kosmetyka* chlorophyll cream.

chlorofitum *mi bot.* chlorophytum (*Chlorophytum*).

chloroform *mi* chloroform.

chlorokauczuk *mi* chlorinated rubber.

chloroplast *mi bot.* chloroplast.

chlorować *ipf.* 1. (= *dodawać chlor*) chlorinate; **chlorować basen** chlorinate the water in the swimming pool; **chlorować wodę** chlorinate water; **wapno chlorowane** chlorinated lime. 2. *chem.* chlorinate.

chlorowcować *ipf. chem.* halogenate.

chlorowiec *mi* -wc- *Gen.* -a *chem.* halogen; **grupa chlorowców** halogen group.

chlorownica *f.* chlorinator.

chlorowodorek *mi* -rk- hydrochloride.

chlorowodorowy *a.* hydrochloric; **kwas chlorowodorowy** hydrochloric acid.

chlorowodór *mi* -o- hydrogen chloride.

chlorowy *a.* chloric; **pochodne chlorowe** *chem.* chlorine derivatives; **woda chlorowa** *chem.* chlorine water.

chloroza *f. bot.* chlorosis.

chloryn *mi chem.* chlorite.

chloryt *mi min.* chlorite.

chluba *f.* (= *duma*) pride; (= *chwała*) glory; (= *zaszczyt*) credit; **być chlubą narodu** be the pride of one's nation; **przynosić komuś chlubę** do sb credit.

chlubić się *ipf.* (= *być dumnym*) take pride (*kimś/czymś* in sb/sth); (= *szczycić się*) boast (*kimś/czymś* of sb/sth); **chlubić się swoimi osiągnięciami w pracy** boast of one's professional achievements; **chlubić się utalentowaną córką** boast of one's gifted daughter.

chlubnie *adv.* gloriously, illustriously; **chlubnie zdać egzamin** pass an exam with flying colors.

chlubny *a.* glorious, illustrious; **chlubny czyn** praiseworthy deed; **chlubne świadectwo** favorable testimony.

chlup *int.* 1. (*o cieczy*) splash; **a woda chlup, chlup** and the water went splish-splash. 2. (*o skoku l. upadku do wody*) plop, plunge; **wtem on do wody chlup, a ja za nim** all of a sudden he splashed into the water, and so did I; **żaba chlup do stawu** the frog jumped with a plop into the pond.

chlupać *ipf.* -pię -piesz, **chlupnąć** *pf.* -ij 1. (*o cieczy*) splash. 2. (= *uderzać w ciecz*) splash, plash; **ryba chlupnęła** a fish splashed. 3. (= *pryskać*) splash; **woda chlupnęła na podłogę** water splashed on the floor.

chlupot *mi* squelch, lap; **chlupot fal** lapping of

waves; **chlupot błota pod nogami** mud splashing under the feet.

chlupotać *ipf.* **-cze** *l.* **-ce** squelch.

chlusnąć *pf.* **-snę -śniesz, -śnij 1.** *zob.* **chlustać. 2.** *pot.* (= *skoczyć w wodę*) plunge; **chlusnąć z pomostu do jeziora** plunge from the pier into the lake. **3.** *pot.* (= *walnąć*) smack, hit; **chlusnąć kogoś w twarz** punch sb in the face. **4.** *pot.* (= *wypić alkohol*) wet the whistle; **no to chluśniem!** *pot.* bottoms up!

chlustać *ipf.* (= *rozpryskiwać się*) spurt, gush out; **krew chlustała z tętnicy** blood was gushing out from the artery.

chłam *mi pot.* crap.

chłeptać *ipf.* **-czę -czesz** *l.* **-cę -cesz, -cz** lap up; **pies chłeptał wodę** the dog was lapping up the water.

chłodek *mi emf.* chill.

chłodnawo *adv.* chilly; **wieczorami jest chłodnawo** it's chilly *l.* a bit nippy in the evenings.

chłodnawy *a.* chilly; **chłodnawe wieczory** chilly evenings.

chłodnąć *ipf.* **-ódł -odła -odli, -ij 1.** *lit.* (= *oziębiać się*) cool; **herbata chłodnie** the tea is cooling. **2.** (= *obojętnieć*) cool down; **twoja miłość chłodnie** your love is cooling down.

chłodnia *f.* *Gen.pl.* **-i** (*pomieszczenie*) cold store; (*mebel*) refrigerator; **chłodnia kominowa** cooling tower; **chłodnia składowa** cold store; **samochód chłodnia** refrigerator truck; *Br.* refrigerator lorry; **statek chłodnia** refrigerator ship; **wagon chłodnia** refrigerator car; *Br.* refrigerator truck.

chłodnica *f.* radiator; **chłodnica powietrzna** air cooler.

chłodnicowiec *mi* **-wc-** *Gen.* **-a** refrigerator ship.

chłodnictwo *n.* refrigeration engineering.

chłodniczy *a.* refrigerating, cooling; **czynnik chłodniczy** cooling agent, refrigerant; **lada chłodnicza** cool shelf; **urządzenie chłodnicze** refrigerating unit; **jajka/masło chłodnicze** refrigerator eggs/butter.

chłodnieć *ipf. zob.* **chłodnąć**.

chłodnik *mi* *Gen.* **-a 1.** (*zupa*) vegetable or fruit soup with sour milk served cold. **2.** *techn.* cooler.

chłodno *adv.* coolly; **dzisiaj jest chłodno na dworze** it's cold outside today; **chłodno tu** it's cold in here; **odezwać się do kogoś chłodno** say sth to sb with reserve; **chłodno, głodno i do domu daleko** cold, hungry and far from home.

chłodnorost *mi bot.* microtherm (*Microthermae*).

chłodny *a.* cool; **chłodny dzień** cold day; **chłodny wiatr** chilling wind; **chłodna wiosna** cold spring; **chłodna woda w basenie** cold water in the swimming pool; **mieć chłodne ręce** have cold hands; **chłodne spojrzenie** cold look; **chłodne powitanie** cold *l.* cool welcome; **chłodne słowa** cold words; **chłodne kolory** *sztuka* cold colors.

chłodzenie *n.* cooling; **chłodzenie silnika** engine cooling; **układ** *l.* **system chłodzenia** cooling system; **chłodzenie gospodarki** market cooling.

chłodziarka *f.* *Gen.pl.* **-ek** refrigerator, chiller; **chłodziarka mechaniczna** mechanical chiller; **chłodziarka sprężarkowa** compression chiller; **chłodziarka absorpcyjna** absorptive chiller.

chłodzić *ipf.* **-odź** *l.* **-ódź** cool, chill; **wiatr chłodzi** the wind is chilling; **lodówka źle chłodzi** the fridge is not working properly; *pot.* the fridge is on the fritz; **napoje chłodzące** cold drinks; **czynnik chłodzący** *techn.* refrigerant, cooling agent; **mieszanina chłodząca** *techn.* coolant. **~ się** *ipf.* **-odź** *l.* **-ódź** (*o ludziach*) refresh oneself; **chłodzić się mrożoną herbatą** refresh oneself with ice tea; (*o napojach, potrawach*) cool; **piwo chłodzi się w lodówce** the beer is cooling in the fridge.

chłodziwo *n.* refrigerant, coolant, cooling agent.

chłonąć *ipf.* **1.** (= *wchłaniać*) absorb; **chłonąć czyste powietrze** breathe in fresh air; **chłonąć woń kwiatów** inhale flowers' fragrance; **gąbka chłonie wodę** a sponge absorbs water. **2.** (= *przyswajać sobie*) absorb; **chłonąć wiedzę** absorb knowledge; **chłonąć piękne widoki** drink in beautiful sights; **rynek coś chłonie** the market absorbs sth, sth is in great demand.

chłoniak *mi* *Gen.* **-a** *pat.* lymphoma.

chłonka *f. fizj.* lymph.

chłonność *f.* absorbency; **chłonność gąbki** absorbency of a sponge; **chłonność rynku** absorptive power of the market.

chłonny *a.* **1.** (= *wchłaniający ciecz*) absorptive; **powierzchnia chłonna** absorptive area; **system chłonny** absorptive system; **jama chłonna** *zool.* mouth (*of a coelenterate*). **2.** *anat.* lymphatic; **naczynia chłonne** *anat.* lymphatic vessels; **układ chłonny** *anat.* lymphatic system; **węzły chłonne** *anat.* lymph glands *l.* nodes. **3.** (= *łatwo przyswajający*) receptive; **chłonny umysł** receptive mind; **chłonny rynek** absorptive market.

chłop *mp Dat.* **-u** (= *rolnik*) **1.** peasant; **chłop pańszczyźniany** *hist.* serf; **chłop małorolny** *hist.* smallholder; **uwłaszczenie chłopów** affranchisement of peasants; **partia chłopów** peasant party. **2.** *pl.* **-y** *pot.* (= *mężczyzna*) fellow, chap; **chłop pod wąsem** grown-up man; **swój chłop** good guy, homeboy; **równy z ciebie chłop** you're a good sort; **pięciu chłopa** five men; **chłop jak dąb** *l.* **kawał chłopa** strapping fellow, big guy; **chłop w chłopa** strapping fellows; **chłop na schwał** sturdy man, husky. **3.** *pl.* **-y** *pot.* (= *mąż, narzeczony*) man; **dbaj o swojego chłopa** take care of your man; **chce się jej chłopa** she needs a man; **tylko chłopy jej w głowie** she's only got boys on her brain.

chłopaczek *mp* **-czk-** *pl.* **-i 1.** (= *mały chłopak*) little boy. **2.** *pot., iron.* boyo.

chłopak *mp pl.* **-cy** *l.* **-i 1.** (= *dziecko płci męskiej*) (= *syn*) boy; **mam dwóch chłopaków i dziewczynkę** I've got two boys and a girl. **2.** *pot.* (= *sympatia, partner*) boyfriend; **przystojny ten chłopak Agnieszki** Agnieszka's boyfriend is really good-looking; **nie mogę przyjść, jestem umówiona ze swoim chłopakiem** I can't come, I'm seeing my boyfriend. **3.** (= *pomocnik*) boy; **chłopak stajenny** stable boy.

chłopczyca *f.* tomboy.

chłopczyk *mp pl.* **-i** *emf.* little boy; **czteroletni chłopczyk** four-year-old boy.

chłopek *mp* **-pk-** *pl.* **-owie** *l.* **-i** *uj.*, *iron.* (= *rolnik*) peasant; **chłopek roztropek** simpleton.

chłopiec *mp* **-pc-** *Dat.* **-u** *Voc.* **-cze** *pl.* **-y** **1.** (*nie dziewczynka*) boy; **urodziła zdrowego chłopca** she gave birth to a healthy boy; **mamy chłopca i dziewczynkę** we have a boy and a girl. **2.** *pot.* (= *młodzieniec*) boy, lad; **dziś nasi chłopcy świetnie sobie radzą na boisku** our boys are doing well today on the sports field; **chłopcy z lasu** guerilla. **3.** *zob.* **chłopak** 2. **4.** (= *pomocnik*) boy; **chłopiec hotelowy** hotel boy; **chłopiec okrętowy** *l.* **pokładowy** ship's boy; **służyć jako chłopiec okrętowy** (= *odbywać praktykę na statku*) sail before the mast; **chłopiec na posyłki** errand boy; **chłopiec do wszystkiego** page; **chłopiec do bicia** fall guy.

chłopieć *ipf.* become countrified.

chłopię *n.* **-pięc-** *pl.* **-piąt-** *Gen.* **-ąt** *żart.* boy.

chłopięco *adv.* boyishly; **wyglądać chłopięco** look boyish, look like a boy.

chłopięctwo *n. lit.* boyhood.

chłopięcy *a.* boyish; **chłopięcy głos** boy's voice; **chłopięcy wdzięk** boyish charm; **chór chłopięcy** boys' choir; **obuwie chłopięce** boys' footwear; **ubranie chłopięce** boy's wear; **po chłopięcemu** like a boy.

chłopisko *n. Gen.pl.* **-ów** *B.* **-ów** *l.* **-k** *emf.* chap; **poczciwe chłopisko** good old chap; **dobre z ciebie chłopisko** you're a good buddy.

chłopka *f. Gen.pl.* **-ek** **1.** (= *kobieta ze wsi*) countrywoman. **2.** (*sukienka*) dirndl.

chłopoman *mp pl.* **-i** *l.* **-y** idealizer of the peasantry.

chłopomania *f. Gen.* **-ii** idealization of the peasantry.

chłopski *a.* **1.** (*o rolniku*) peasant's; **chata chłopska** peasant cabin; **pochodzenie chłopskie** peasant origin; **partia chłopska** peasant party; **działacz chłopski** peasant activist; **bunt chłopski** peasant revolt; **powstanie chłopskie** peasant uprising; **chłopski rozum** common sense; **po chłopsku** *l.* **z chłopska** (= *w sposób podobny chłopom*) like a peasant; (= *w sposób niewyszukany*) crudely. **2.** *pot.* (*o mężczyźnie*) man's; **chłopska robota** man's job.

chłopstwo *n.* **1.** (= *chłopi*) peasantry. **2.** (= *cechy właściwe chłopom*) rusticity.

chłosnąć *pf.* **-snę** **-śniesz**, **-śnij** *zob.* **chłostać**.

chłosta *f.* whipping, lashing; **kara chłosty** the lashing; **wymierzyć chłostę** mete out the lashing; **karać chłostą** punish with lashing.

chłostać *ipf.*, **chłosnąć** *pf.* **-szczę** **-szczesz** *l.* **-am** **-asz** **1.** (= *bić batem*) whip, flog, lash. **2.** *przen.* (*o wietrze, deszczu*) lash; **wiatr chłostał twarze** the wind lashed our faces. **3.** *przen.* (= *krytykować*) lash, castigate; **chłostać ostrymi słowami** lash in sharp words; **chłostać czyjeś wady** criticise sb's vices; **chłostać kogoś publicznie** criticise sb in public, lash out at sb. **~ się** *ipf.* **-szczę** **-szczesz** *l.* **-am** **-asz** whip oneself; **średnio-**

wieczny pokutnik chłostał się aż do krwi a medieval penitent whipped himself till he bled.

chłód *mi* **-o-** **1.** (*zimno*) cold, chill; **przejmujący chłód** biting cold; **rześki chłód** brisk chill; **jesienne chłody** autumn chill; **chłód poranka** morning cold; **powiew chłodu** chilly breath; **czuć chłód** feel cold; **drżeć z chłodu** shudder with cold; **trzymać wino w chłodzie** store wine in a cool place; **od rzeki ciągnie chłód** there's a cold breeze from the river; **powiało chłodem z północy** there was a cold breeze from the north; **o głodzie i chłodzie** suffering hunger and cold. **2.** (= *brak życzliwości*) coldness; **okazywać komuś chłód** give sb a cold shoulder; **chłód w czyichś oczach** reserve in sb's eyes; **wyczuwam chłód w twoim głosie** I can hear a coldness in your voice.

chłystek *mp* **-tk-** *pl.* **-i** *pog.* whippersnapper, whipster.

chmara *f.* **1.** (= *mnóstwo*) swarms, hordes; **chmara ludzi** hordes *l.* swarm of people; **chmara owadów** swarm *l.* cloud of insects; **chmara psów** hordes of dogs; **chmara ptactwa** flock of birds. **2.** *myśl.* herd (*of deer, elks, etc.*).

chmiel *mi bot.* hop (*Humulus*); **chmiel piwowarski** (*suszone szyszki chmielu*) hops; **uprawa chmielu** hop-growing.

chmielarnia *f. Gen.pl.* **-i** *l.* **-ń** **1.** (*plantacja*) hop-field. **2.** (*przetwórnia*) oust house.

chmielarski *a.* hop-growing; **mistrz chmielarski** hop-growing expert.

chmielarz *mp* hop grower.

chmielnik *mi Gen.* **-a** (*plantacja*) hop-field.

chmielograb *mi bot.* hop hornbeam (*Ostrya*).

chmielowy *a.* hop; **szyszki chmielowe** hops; **lucerna chmielowa** *bot.* black medic, shamrock (*Medicago lupulina*); **drzewo chmielowe** *bot.* = **chmielograb**; **tyka chmielowa** *żart.* (*o kimś wysokim*) beanpole.

chmura *f.* **1.** (*na niebie*) cloud; **chmura deszczowa** rain cloud; *meteor.* nimbus (cloud); **chmura burzowa** *t. przen.* storm cloud, thundercloud; **chmura kłębiasta** *meteor.* cumulus (cloud); **chmura pierzasta** *meteor.* cirrus (cloud); **chmura kłębiasta deszczowa** *meteor.* cumulonimbus (cloud); **chmura kłębiasto-warstwowa** *meteor.* stratocumulus (cloud); **chmura pierzasto-kłębiasta** *meteor.* cirrocumulus (cloud); **chmura niska warstwowa** *meteor.* stratus (cloud); **chmura średnia warstwowa** *meteor.* altostratus (cloud); **chmury niskie** *meteor.* low clouds; **chmury wysokie** *meteor.* high clouds; **pułap chmur** *meteor.* cloud ceiling, cloud base; **pokryty** *l.* **zaciągnięty chmurami** overcast; **sięgający chmur** reaching the sky; **słońce skryło się za chmurą** the sun hid behind a cloud; **słońce wyjrzało** *l.* **zaświeciło zza chmur** the sun shone through the clouds; **urwanie** *l.* **oberwanie chmury** cloudburst. **2.** *przen.* **chodzić z głową w chmurach** have one's head in the clouds; **drapacz chmur** *bud.* skyscraper, highrise (building); **chmury gromadzą się nad kimś/czymś** *przen.* clouds are gathering over sb/sth; **przez jego twarz przebiegła chmura** a cloud came over his face; **z dużej chmury mały deszcz** the mountain has brought forth a mouse. **3.** (= *tuman*) cloud; **chmura dymu** cloud of smoke; **chmura kurzu** cloud of dust; **chmura radioaktywna** radioactive cloud *l.* plume. **4.** (= *rój*) swarm, cloud; **chmura szarańczy** swarm *l.* cloud of locust.

chmurka *f. emf.* cloudlet, little cloud.

chmurnie *adv. przen.* gloomily; **patrzeć chmurnie** frown (*na kogoś/coś* at sb/sth).

chmurnieć *ipf.* **1.** (= *stawać się chmurnym*) grow *l.* become overcast *l.* cloudy. **2.** (= *zasępiać się*) grow *l.* become gloomy; frown; **Ewa chmurniała z minuty na minutę** Ewa grew gloomier minute by minute.

chmurno *adv.* (*o pogodzie*) cloudy; **będzie zimno i chmurno** it will be cold and cloudy.

chmurny *a.* **1.** cloudy; **chmurny dzień** cloudy day; **chmurne niebo** cloudy sky; **chmurna pogoda** overcast weather. **2.** *przen.* sullen; **chmurna twarz** sullen face; **chmurne spojrzenie** sullen *l.* gloomy expression; frown; **chmurna przeszłość** clouded past.

chmurotwórczy *a. meteor.* cloud-forming.

chmurzyć *ipf. przen.* **ojciec chmurzy twarz** father's face darkens; **chmurzyć czoło** frown, knit one's brow. **~ się** *ipf.* (= *pokrywać się chmurami*) **1.** cloud over, darken, become overcast. **2.** *przen.* (*o człowieku*) grow *l.* become sullen, frown; (*o twarzy*) cloud over; **przestań się chmurzyć, wszystko się ułoży** stop looking so sullen, everything will turn out fine.

chochelka *f. Gen.pl.* **-ek** serving spoon, small ladle.

chochla *f. Gen.pl.* **-i** *l.* **-chel 1.** (= *łyżka wazowa*) ladle, dipper. **2.** (= *warząchew*) wooden spoon.

chochlik *mp pl.* **-i 1.** (= *skrzat*) elf, fairy, pixie, brownie; *Ir.* leprechaun; (= *psotnik*) puck; **złośliwy chochlik** hobgoblin. **2. chochlik drukarski** printer's devil. **3.** (= *błysk w oku*) mischievous look.

chochlikowaty *a.* elfin, elfish; (*o charakterze*) impish, puckish.

chocholi *a.* **taniec chocholi** *przen., lit.* slumber, inactivity.

chochoł *mi* **1.** *ogr.* straw covering. **2.** *roln.* capsheaf. **3.** *przest.* (= *nastroszona czupryna*) shock of hair.

chociaż *conj.* although, (even) though; while; **został dłużej w pracy, chociaż nie musiał** he stayed longer at work, although he didn't have to; **chociaż wycieczka była udana, była także bardzo męcząca** while the trip was a success, it was also very tiring. **–** *adv.* at least; just, but; **chociaż raz jesteś zadowolony** at least for once you're satisfied; **czy ty chociaż próbowałeś mówić prawdę?** did you at least try to tell the truth?; **zostań chociaż na chwilę** stay just for a moment.

chociażby *conj. i adv.* = **choćby**.

choć *conj. i part.* = **chociaż**; **ciemno choć oko wykol** it's pitch dark.

choćby *conj. i part.* even if; **pójdę na koncert, choćbym miał się zwolnić z pracy** I'm going to concert even if I have to take a day off (work); **będę u ciebie o ósmej, choćbym nawet miał iść**

pieszo I'll be at your place at eight even if I have to walk. **–** *adv.* at least, even if; as much as, just, but; **choćby na chwilę usiądźmy i porozmawiajmy** let's sit down and talk at least for a moment; **czy masz choćby jeden argument przeciwko temu?** do you have as much as one argument against it?; **powiedz choćby jedno słowo** say but one word; **choćby to było najskromniejsze** be it ever so humble; **choćby tylko (po to), żeby mu powiedzieć** even if only to tell him; **czy on choćby kiwnął palcem, żeby wam pomóc?** did he as much as lift a finger to help you?

chodaczkowy *a.* **szlachta chodaczkowa** *hist.* small freeholders (*formerly in Poland*).

chodak *mi Gen.* **-a** (= *drewniak*) clog, sabot; (= *łapeć*) moccassin; (= *kapeć*) mule.

chodliwość *f. pot.* saleability.

chodliwy *a. pot.* hot, saleable; **chodliwy towar** hot commodity.

chodniczek *mi Gen.* **-a 1.** (= *dywanik*) runner, floorcloth. **2.** (*w ogrodzie*) footpath.

chodnik *mi Gen.* **-a 1.** (*na ulicy*) sidewalk; *Br.* pavement. **2.** (*na podłodze*) (strip of) carpet, runner; **chodnik na schody** staircarpet. **3.** *górn.* (*pod ziemią*) drift, gallery; **chodnik eksploatacyjny** *l.* **wybierkowy** extraction drift; **chodnik poszukiwawczy** exploratory *l.* monkey drift; **chodnik wentylacyjny** air heading *l.* airway; **chodnik transportowy** (carrying) gangway; **ślepy chodnik** stub entry *l.* dead end. **4.** (*w drewnie*) gallery.

chodnikowy *a.* **1. płyta chodnikowa** flagstone. **2. wykładzina chodnikowa** *bud.* carpeting. **3.** *górn.* drift, gallery.

chodu *int. pot.* run!; **chłopaki, chodu!** hey guys, run!; **skończyłeś? no to chodu!** are you done? O.K., let's split!

chodziarz *mp sport* racewalker.

chodzić *ipf.* **1.** (= *stawiać kroki*) walk, go (around *l.* about); **chodzić na spacery** go for walks; **chodzić po lesie** walk *l.* take a walk in the forest; **chodzić po górach** go hiking in the mountains; **chodzić po nocy** walk at night; **chodzić ulicami** walk (along) the streets; **chodzić na palcach** walk on one's tiptoes; tiptoe; **chodzić na czworakach** crawl on all fours; **chodzić o lasce** walk with a cane; **nie chodź po trawie!** keep off the grass!; **chodź tu!** come here!; **chodź ze mną** come with me; **chodźmy!** come on!, let's go!; **chodźmy coś zjeść** let's go for a meal; **chodź, zabawimy się** let's go and have some fun; **chodzić przy nodze** (*o psie*) heel. **2.** (= *robić coś regularnie*) **chodzić na dziewczyny** *pot.* pick up girls; **chodzić po zakupy** go shopping; **chodzić na polowanie** go hunting; **chodzić na grzyby** go mushroom-picking; **chodzić po prośbie** go begging. **3.** *przen.* **chodząca encyklopedia** *żart.* walking encyclopedia; **chodzić na rzęsach** *pot.* go around raising hell; **co ci chodzi po głowie?** what's on your mind?; **pieniądze piechotą nie chodzą** money doesn't grow on trees; **wypadki chodzą po ludziach** accidents will always happen; **Adam chodzi z Ewą** Adam is going out with *l.* seeing Ewa; **nieszczęścia chodzą parami** it never rains, but it pours; **chodzić od Annasza do Kajfasza** go from one to the next; **chodzić własnymi drogami** follow one's own path; **chodzić w glorii** be bathed in glory; **ta piosenka ciągle chodzi mi po głowie** I can't get that song out of my head; **w tym wypadku talent chodzi w parze ze skromnością** in this case, talent goes hand in hand with modesty. **4.** (= *bywać gdzieś regularnie*) go to, attend; **chodzić do szkoły/pracy/kościoła** go to school/work/ church; **chodzić do teatru/kina** go to the theater/ movies; **chodzić na zebrania** attend meetings. **5.** (= *pilnować*) take care of, look after; **chodzić koło dzieci** look after the children. **6. chodzić w czymś** (= *nosić*) wear sth; **nie mam w czym chodzić** I don't have anything to wear; **chodzić w mundurze** wear a uniform. **7. o co chodzi?** what's the matter *l.* problem?, what's up?; **chodzi o to, że...** the point *l.* issue is that...; **o co ci chodzi?** what's your point *l.* problem?, what do you mean?; **chodzi o nasze życie** our lives are a stake (here); **jeśli o mnie chodzi, to...** as far as I'm concerned...; **tu nie o to chodzi, żeby...** the point *l.* issue here is not to...; **nie chodzi tu o pieniądze** money isn't the issue (here); **rozumiem, o co ci chodzi** I see what you mean; I get the picture; **jeśli chodzi o...** as regards...; **ach, o to chodzi** ah, so that's it; **(właśnie) o to chodzi** that's (just *l.* exactly) the point, that's the idea; **(właśnie) o to mi chodzi** that's (precisely) what I mean. **8.** (= *kursować*) *pot.* run; **na tej trasie pociągi chodzą bardzo rzadko** trains run along this line only every so often. **9.** (= *funkcjonować*) work, run; **mój zegarek nie chodzi** my watch stopped working *l.* running; **silnik chodzi bez zarzutu** the engine runs fine; **silnik chodzi jak w zegarku** the engine is purring like a pussycat; **klucz w zamku ciężko chodzi** the key doesn't want to turn in the lock. **10.** (= *drgać*) shake, tremble; **ściany chodzą od wybuchów** the wall are shaking from the explosions; **wino chodzi** wine ferments. **11.** (= *krążyć*) go; **chodzą słuchy, że...** word is going around that...; **dreszcze chodzą mi po plecach** I get shivers *l.* chills down my spine.

chodzik *mi Gen.* **-a 1.** (*dla dziecka*) (baby) walker. **2.** *techn.* timer.

chodzony *mi* (*taniec*) walking dance (*Polish folk dance*).

choina *f.* **1.** = **choinka** 1. **2.** (= *sośnina*) stand of young pine trees. **3.** (= *gałęzie sosnowe*) pine branches. **4.** *bot.* hemlock spruce (*Tsuga*).

choinka *f.* **1.** (= *drzewo iglaste*) evergreen tree. **2.** (*na Boże Narodzenie*) Christmas tree; **sztuczna choinka** artificial Christmas tree; **ubrać choinkę** decorate the Christmas tree; **on z choinki się urwał** *pot.*, *żart.* he's from Mars.

choinkowy *a.* Christmas-tree; **ozdoby/lampki choinkowe** Christmas-tree ornaments/lights.

chojak *mi Gen.* **-a** evergreen (tree).

chojniak *mi Gen.* **-a** young pine forest.

chojracki *a. pot.* daredevil.

chojrak *mp pl.* **-cy** *l.* **-i** *pot.* daredevil.

cholera *f.* **1.** *pat.* cholera; **cholera drobiu** *wet.* chicken *l.* fowl cholera. **2.** *pot.* (*w przekleństwach*) hell!, damn!; **do jasnej cholery!** *l.* **cholera jasna!** what the hell!; goddammit!; **po cholerę?**

what the hell for?; **o, cholera** shit; I'll be damned; **idź do cholery!** go to hell!; **boli jak cholera** it hurts like hell; **brudnych naczyń było do cholery i trochę** there were a helluva lot of dirty dishes; **zły** *l.* **wściekły jak cholera** (as) mad as hell; **cholera mnie bierze, kiedy to widzę** I get mad as hell when I see that; **cholera go wzięła** he flew off the handle.

cholernie *adv. pot.* damned; *Br.* bloody; **jestem cholernie zmęczony** I'm damned tired; **był cholernie zdolny** he was damned talented.

cholernik *mp pl.* **-cy** *l.* **-i** *pot.* **1.** = **choleryk. 2.** *pot.* (= *wyzwisko*) son-of-a-bitch.

cholerny *a. pot.* damned, hell of a *l.* helluva; *Br.* bloody; **cholerny hałas** hell of a racket; **cholerny głupiec** damned fool; **cholerny bałagan** hell of a mess; **mieć cholerne szczęście** have damned good luck.

cholerstwo *n. pot.* (= *utrapienie*) pain (in the neck), son-of-a-bitch.

choleryczka *f. Gen.pl.* **-ek** *zob.* **choleryk.**

choleryczny *a.* (= *wybuchowy*) hot-tempered, fiery, choleric; **usposobienie choleryczne** hot-tempered disposition; **temperament choleryczny** choleric temperament.

choleryk *mp* hothead; hot-tempered *l.* choleric person.

cholesterol *mi biochem.* cholesterol.

cholesterolowy *a. biochem.* cholesterol; **złogi cholesterolowe** cholesterol deposits.

cholewa *f.* top, leg; **buty z cholewami** high-top boots; **robić z gęby cholewę** *pot.* break *l.* not keep one's word.

cholewka *f. Gen.pl.* **-ek** = **cholewa; smalić do kogoś cholewki** *przest.* woo *l.* court sb.

cholewkarz *mp* boot leather stitcher.

chomąto *n. jeźdz.* (horse) collar.

chomik *ma zool.* hamster (*Cricetus*); **chomik syryjski** golden hamster (*Mesocricetus auratus*).

chomikować *ipf. pot.* squirrel away.

chora *f. Gen.* **-ej** sick woman; (*w szpitalu*) patient; *zob.* **chory.**

chorał *mi muz.* chorale; **chorał gregoriański** Gregorian chant; **chorał protestancki** *l.* **ewangelicki** *l.* **luterański** Lutheran chorale.

chorałowy *a. muz.* chorale; **śpiewy chorałowe** chorale songs; **notacja chorałowa** (system of) neumes.

chorągiew *f.* **-gwi-** *pl.* **-e 1.** (= *sztandar*) flag, banner, standard; **biało-czerwona chorągiew** white and red flag; **chorągiew kościelna** gonfalon; **wywiesić białą chorągiew** *t. przen.* raise the white flag. **2.** *harcerstwo* (*jednostka organizacyjna*) local council. **3.** *hist.* (= *oddział jazdy*) mounted company, squadron.

chorągiewka *f. Gen.pl.* **-ek 1.** (= *proporczyk*) flag, banner; **być jak chorągiewka (na wietrze** *l.* **na dachu)** *przen.* be a weathercock; **zwijać chorągiewkę** *przen.* back out. **2.** *muz.* flag. **3.** *orn.* (*część pióra*) vane.

chorągwiany *a. hist.* **szlachta chorągwiana** yeomanry (*formerly in Poland*).

chorąży *mp* **1.** *wojsk.* (*stopień wojskowy*) chief warrant officer; **młodszy chorąży** warrant officer; **starszy chorąży sztabowy** master warrant officer. **2.** *t. hist., wojsk.* (= *noszący sztandar*) standard-bearer, colors-bearer, ensign-bearer.

chordofon *mi muz.* chordophone.

choreograf *mp pl.* **-owie** choreograph.

choreografia *f. Gen.* **-ii** choreography.

choreograficznie *adv.* choreographically.

choreograficzny *a.* choreographic; **szkoła choreograficzna** school of choreography.

choroba *f. Gen.pl.* **-rób 1.** *med., pat.* disease, illness, sickness; disorder, condition; **ciężka choroba** serious illness; **choroba wrodzona/dziedziczna/nabyta** congenital/hereditary/acquired disease; **choroba ostra** *l.* **o przebiegu ostrym** acute disease; **choroba przewlekła/chroniczna** lingering/chronic illness; **nieuleczalna/śmiertelna choroba** incurable/fatal disease; **choroba zakaźna** communicable *l.* transmittable *l.* infectious *l.* contagious disease; **choroba psychiczna** *l.* **umysłowa** mental illness; **choroba nowotworowa** neoplastic disease; tumor; **choroba pasożytnicza/bakteryjna/wirusowa** parasitic/bacterial/viral disease; **choroba gardła** disease of the throat; **choroba serca** heart disease; **choroba oczu** eye disease; **choroba przewodu pokarmowego** intestinal disorder; **choroba drobiu/bydła** *wet.* poultry/cattle disease; **choroby cywilizacyjne/zawodowe** civilization/occupational diseases; **choroba odzwierzęca** zoonosis; **choroba weneryczna** venereal disease; **atak choroby** an attack of a disease; **historia** *l.* **karta choroby** case history *l.* record; **nawrót choroby** relapse of a disease; **objawy** *l.* **symptomy choroby** symptoms of a disease; **przebieg choroby** the course of a disease; **lekarz chorób wewnętrznych** internist; **lekarz chorób dziecięcych** pediatrician; **lekarz chorób kobiecych** gynecologist; **cierpieć na jakąś chorobę** suffer from a disease; **zapaść na jakąś chorobę** contract a disease; **leczyć chorobę** treat a disease; **wyleczyć kogoś z choroby** cure sb of a disease; **zapobiegać chorobom** prevent disease; **być trawionym przez chorobę** be consumed by a disease; **być ściętym** *l.* **zwalonym z nóg przez chorobę** be cut down by a disease; **być trawionym przez chorobę** be eaten away *l.* consumed by a disease; **umrzeć na jakąś chorobę** die of a disease. **2.** *pat.* (*w nazwach konkretnych schorzeń*) **choroba Addisona** Addison's disease; **choroba Alzheimera** Alzheimer's disease; **choroba Basedowa** Graves' disease; **choroba Heinego-Medina** poliomyelitis, infantile paralysis; **choroba Parkinsona** Parkinson's disease; **choroba górska** altitude sickness; **choroba kesonowa** *l.* **dekompresyjna** caisson disease *l.* decompression sickness; **choroba nurków** the bends; **choroba morska/lokomocyjna** sea/motion sickness; **choroba nadciśnieniowa** chronic hypertension; **choroba popromienna** radiation sickness; **choroba przestrzeni** agoraphobia; **choroba reumatyczna** rheumatic disease; **choroba wieńcowa** coronary disease; **choroba sieroca** orphan's syndrome. **3.** *int., pot.* hell, damn; **choroba jasna, co robisz!** what the hell are you doing!

chorobliwie *adv.* unhealthily, morbidly; insanely, obsessively; **chorobliwie zazdrosny** insanely jealous; **bać się czegoś chorobliwie** have a morbid fear of sth.

chorobliwy *a.* (= *związany z chorobą l. nienormalnie nasilony*) unhealthy, morbid, pathological; (= *o natrętnych emocjach*) insane, obsessive; **chorobliwa zazdrość** obsessive jealousy; **chorobliwe podniecenie** unhealthy excitation; **chorobliwy lęk** morbid fear, phobia.

chorobotwórczy *a.* pathogenic, pathogenetic; **czynnik chorobotwórczy** pathogen, pathogenic factor.

chorobowe *n. Gen.* **-ego** *pot.* sick leave; **iść na chorobowe** take sick leave; **być na chorobowym** be on sick leave; be off sick.

chorobowy *a.* **1.** sickness; **zasiłek chorobowy** sick *l.* sickness allowance. **2.** *med.* pathological; **zmiany chorobowe** pathological changes; **karta chorobowa pacjenta** patient's case history.

chorować *ipf.* (= *być chorym*) be sick *l.* ill (*na coś* with sth); suffer from a disease; **chorować na grypę** be sick with the flu; **chorować na wątrobę** suffer from liver problems; **chorować od wódki** be sick from drinking (too much) vodka; **chorować na nowy samochód** *przen.* be crazy about a new car.

chorowity *a.* sickly, unhealthy; **chorowite dziecko** sickly child; **chorowita bladość** unhealthy pallor.

choróbsko *n. pot.* pip.

Chorwacja *f. geogr.* Croatia.

chorwacki *a.* Croatian, Croat.

Chorwat *mp,* **Chorwatka** *f. Gen.pl.* **-ek** Croat, Croatian.

chory *a.* sick, ill; (*o części ciała*) bad; (*o bolącej części ciała*) sore, hurt; **ciężko chory** seriously ill; **chora wątroba** bad liver; **chore drzewo** sick tree; **on jest chory na serce** he has a bad heart; **jestem chory na nowy samochód** *przen.* I'm crazy about a new car. — *mp* sick person; (*w szpitalu*) patient; **izba chorych** infirmary.

chować *ipf.* **1.** (= *umieszczać, wkładać*) put (*sth*) (away), stow (*sth*) (away); **chować ręce do kieszeni** put one's hands in one's pockets; **chować ubrania w szafie** stow clothes into a wardrobe. **2.** (= *ukrywać*) hide (*sth l. sb*) away; conceal (*sth*) (*przed kimś* from sb); **chować głowę w piasek** *przen.* bury *l.* hide one's head in the sand; **chować twarz w dłoniach** bury one's face in one's hands. **3.** (= *wychowywać*) bring up, raise; *form.* rear. **4.** *roln.* (= *hodować*) breed, keep, raise; **chować świnie/owce/bydło** breed *l.* raise pigs/sheep/cattle; **chować drób** keep *l.* raise *l.* breed poultry. **5.** (= *grzebać*) bury. **6.** (= *zachowywać*) *lit.* keep, retain, cherish; **chować pamięć o kimś/czymś** cherish the memory of sb/sth; **chować coś w pamięci** keep sth in one's mind; **nie chowam do ciebie urazy** I bear you no grudge. ~ **się** *ipf.* **1.** (= *ukrywać się*) hide (away) (*przed kimś/czymś* from sb/sth). **2.** (= *wychowywać się*) be brought up; **chowałem się u dziadków** I was brought up by my grandparents. **3.** (= *miewać się*) **chować się zdrowo** keep well.

chowany *mi* (*zabawa*) hide-and-seek; **bawić się w chowanego** play hide-and-seek.

chód *mi* **-o- 1.** (= *sposób chodzenia*) gait, walk; **chwiejny chód** rolling gait, sway; **kaczy chód** waddle; **niepewny/nierówny chód** unsteady/uneven gait. **2.** *sport* (*dyscyplina*) race-walking. **3.** *jeźdz.* gait. **4.** *techn.* (= *tempo działania*) rate. **5.** (= *dobre funkcjonowanie*) **być na chodzie** *pot.* be in working order; *przen.* (*o człowieku*) be alive and kicking. **6.** *pl. pot.* (= *wpływy*) **mieć chody** have influence (*u kogoś* with sb); **uruchomić swoje chody** use one's influence. **7.** *myśl.* (= *ścieżka zwierząt*) trail. **8.** *pl. myśl.* (= *nogi psa myśliwskiego*) legs.

chór *mi* **1.** *muz.* (= *zespół śpiewaków*) choir, chorus; **chór głosów** mixed choir; **chór męski/żeński/chłopięcy/dziecięcy** men's/women's/boys'/childrens' choir; **chór mieszany** mixed choir; **chór szkolny** school chorus; **chór kościelny** church choir; **chór a capella** a capella choir; **śpiewać w chórze** sing in a choir; **chóry anielskie** *rel.* choirs of angels; **śpiewać chórem** sing in chorus. **2.** (= *kilka głosów naraz*) **chór aprobaty** chorus of approval; **przemawiać/odpowiadać chórem** speak/answer in chorus. **3.** *bud.* (*w kościele*) choir; organ loft. **4.** *lit.* (*w dramacie antycznym*) chorus.

chóralistyka *f.* choral singing.

chóralnie *adv.* in chorus; (= *razem, o głosach*) together.

chóralny *a.* choral; **zespoły chóralne** choral group; **dzieło chóralne** choral work.

chórek *mi* **-rk-** small choir, singing group; **chórek kościelny** small church choir.

chórzysta *mp* chorister, choir singer; (*chłopiec*) choirboy.

chórzystka *f. Gen.pl.* **-ek** chorister, choir singer.

chów *mi* **-o-** raising, breeding; **chów drobiu** poultry raising; **chów bydła** cattle raising; **swojskiego chowu** *przen., często pog.* homegrown, homespun.

chrabąszcz *ma zool.* cockchafer, May bug, May beetle, June bug (*Melolontha, Phyllophaga*).

chram *mi lit.* temple.

chrapa *f.* **1.** *zw. pl.* (*u zwierzęcia*) nostril. **2.** *żegl.* snorkel, breathing tube.

chrapać *ipf.* **-ię -iesz 1.** (*podczas snu*) snore; **chrapać przez sen** snore in one's sleep. **2.** (= *charczeć*) wheeze. **3.** (*o koniu*) snort.

chrapka *f. Gen.pl.* **-ek** *żart.* liking, fancy (*na coś* for sth); **nabrać chrapki na coś** take a fancy to sth; **naszła mnie chrapka, żeby się czegoś napić** I felt like (having) a drink.

chrapliwy *a.* hoarse, husky, harsh.

chrapnąć *pf.* **-ij** *zob.* chrapać.

ChRL *abbr.* (= *Chińska Republika Ludowa*) the PRC (= *People's Republic of China*).

chrestomatia *f. Gen.* **-ii** chrestomathy.

chrobot *mi* scratch, scratching, scraping, grating.

chrobotać *ipf.* **-czę -czesz** *l.* **-cę -cesz, -cz** scrape, grate, scratch.

chrobotek *mi* **-tk-** *Gen.* **-a** *bot.* (*porost*) cup moss, cup lichen (*Cladonia*); **chrobotek reniferowy** reindeer moss (*C. rangiferina*).

chrobotliwy *a.* scratching, grating.

chrobry *a. arch.* brave, gallant, valiant.

chrom *mi* **1.** *chem.* chromium. **2.** *techn.* (*lakier, powłoka*) chrome. **3.** (*skóra*) boxcalf.

chromać *ipf. lit.* limp; **chromać na prawą nogę** be lame in the right leg.

chromatofor *mi Gen.* **-a** *l.* **-u 1.** *bot.* chromoplast, chromatophore. **2.** *zool.* chromatophore.

chromatografia *f. Gen.* **-ii** *chem.* chromatography.

chromatogram *mi chem.* chromatogram.

chromatyczność *f. opt.* chromaticity.

chromatyczny *a.* chromatic; **aberracja chromatyczna** *opt.* chromatic aberration; **skala chromatyczna** *muz.* chromatic scale; **znaki chromatyczne** *muz.* chromatics; sharps and flats.

chromatyda *f. biol.* chromatid.

chromatyka *f. opt., muz.* chromatics.

chromatyna *f. biol.* chromatin.

chromian *mi chem.* chromate.

chromit *mi min.* chromite.

chromodruk *mi druk.* color printing.

chromofotografia *f. Gen.* **-ii** color photography.

chromogen *mi chem., biol.* chromogen.

chromolić *ipf. wulg.* not give a fuck about (*sb l. sth*).

chromolitografia *f. Gen.* **-ii** chromolithography.

chromoplast *mi bot.* chromoplast.

chromoproteina *f. biochem.* chromoprotein.

chromosfera *f. astron.* chromosphere.

chromosom *mi biol.* chromosome; **mapa chromosomów** chromosome map.

chromosomowy *a. biol.* chromosome, chromosomal; **aberracje chromosomowe** chromosomal aberration; **liczba chromosomowa** chromosome number.

chromować *ipf. techn.* chrome, chromium-plate.

chromowanie *n. techn.* chromium plating.

chromowce *pl. chem.* the chromium group.

chromowy *a.* **1.** *chem.* (*o związkach chromu*) chromic; **kwas chromowy** chromic acid. **2.** *chem., techn.* (= *zawierający chrom*) chrome, chromium; **stal chromowa** chrome *l.* chromium steel; **zieleń/żółcień chromowa** chrome *l.* chromium green/yellow. **3.** (*o wyrobach skórzanych*) boxcalf.

chromy *a. lit.* (*o człowieku*) lame, crippled, limping; (*o nodze*) lame, game.

chronicznie *adv.* chronically.

chroniczny *a.* chronic; *pat.* (= *nawrotowy*) recurrent, relapsing; **chroniczna bieda** chronic poverty; **chroniczny bronchit** *pat.* chronic bronchitis; **chroniczny brak czasu** chronic lack of time.

chronić *ipf.* protect, shelter (*sb l. sth*) (*przed kimś* from sb) (*przed czymś* from *l.* against sth); safeguard (*sth*) (*przed czymś* against sth); **chronić czyjeś dane osobiste** safeguard sb's personal data; **chronić zabytki** protect historical sites; **ro-**

śliny i zwierzęta chronione protected plants and animals. ~ się *ipf.* (= *szukać schronienia*) **1.** look for shelter *l.* refuge, seek shelter (*przed kimś/czymś* from sb/sth); (= *znajdować schronienie*) find protection (*przed czymś* against sth); take *l.* find shelter (*przed czymś* from sth); **chronić się przed deszczem** take shelter from the rain. **2. chronić się przed czymś** *l.* **od czegoś** (= *zapobiegać czemuś*) prevent (o.s. from) sth.

chronograf *mi Gen.* **-u** *pl.* **-y 1.** *techn.* chronograph. **2.** *hist.* (= *kronika*) chronicle, chronicle, annals. – *mp Gen.* **-a** *pl.* **-owie** *hist.* (= *kronikarz*) chronicler.

chronografia *f. Gen.* **-ii** *fiz., hist.* chronography.

chronogram *mi hist.lit.* chronogram.

chronologia *f. Gen.* **-ii 1.** (= *następstwo w czasie*) chronology, sequence, temporal order; **ustalić chronologię wypadków** establish the chronology of events. **2.** (*nauka*) chronology.

chronologicznie *adv.* chronologically, in chronological order; **uporządkować fakty chronologicznie** arrange facts chronologically.

chronologiczny *a.* chronological; **tablice chronologiczne** chronologies, chronological tables; **w porządku chronologicznym** in chronological order, chronologically.

chronologizacja *f.* chronologization.

chronologizować *ipf.* chronologize.

chronometr *mi* chronometer; **chronometr morski** *l.* **okrętowy** *żegl.* marine chronometer.

chronometraż *mi ekon.* timing, time study.

chronometria *f. Gen.* **-ii** *fiz.* chronometry.

chropawość *f.* = **chropowatość.**

chropawy *a.* = **chropowaty.**

chropowacieć *ipf.* become rough *l.* coarse.

chropowatość *f.* **1.** (*powierzchni*) roughness, coarseness, unevenness; (= *chropowate miejsce*) rough spot. **2.** (*dźwięku*) harshness, hoarseness.

chropowaty *a.* **1.** (*o powierzchni*) rough, coarse, uneven. **2.** (*o dźwięku*) harsh, hoarse.

chrumkać *ipf. pot.* (*o świni itp.*) grunt, oink.

chrupać *ipf.* **-ię -piesz 1.** (= *gryźć głośno*) munch. **2.** (= *trzeszczeć*) crunch, crack; **chrupie mi w stawach** my joints are cracking.

chrupiący *a.* (*o pieczywie itp.*) crunchy, crisp.

chrupka *f. Gen.pl.* **-ek** *zw. pl.* crisp.

chrupki *a.* crisp, crispy; (= *chrupiący*) crunchy; **pieczywo chrupkie** crisp bread.

chrupkość *f.* crispness, crunchiness.

chrupnąć *pf.* **-ij** *zob.* **chrupać.**

chrust *mi* **1.** (*gałęzie*) dry twigs *l.* sticks; **wiązka chrustu** bundle of sticks, fagot, (*Br.*) faggot. **2.** (*ciastka*) crispy fried cookies.

chruścik *mi Gen.* **-u** *l.* **-a** *ent.* (= *owad z rzędu Trichoptera*) caddis fly, trichopter.

chruśniak *mi Gen.* **-a** *l.* **-u** *lit.* (= *zarośla*) brush, thicket.

chryja *f. Gen.* **-yi** *pot.* brawl, hullabaloo (*o coś* about sth).

chrypa *f.* hoarseness; frog in the throat; **mieć chrypę** be hoarse; have a frog in one's throat; **dostać chrypy** get hoarse; get a frog in one's throat.

chrypieć *ipf.* **-ę -isz** have a husky *l.* hoarse voice.

chrypka *f. emf. zob.* **chrypa.**

chrypliwy *a.* hoarse, husky.

chrypnąć *ipf.* **-pnął -pnęła -pnęli, -ij** *l.* **-pł -pła -pli** get hoarse; **chrypnąć z krzyku** *l.* **od krzyku** get hoarse from shouting; shout o.s. hoarse.

Chryste *mp rel. zob.* **Chrystus.**

chrystiania *f. Gen.* **-ii** *narciarstwo* christiania.

chrystianizacja *f. rel.* Christianization.

chrystianizm *mi rel.* Christianity.

chrystianizować *ipf. rel.* Christianize. ~ **się** *ipf. rel.* get *l.* become *l.* be Christianized.

chrystocentryzm *mi teol.* Christocentrism.

chrystologia *f. Gen.* **-ii** *teol.* Christology.

Chrystus *mp Voc.* **Chryste** *l.* **Chrystusie** *rel.* **1.** Christ; **Jezus Chrystus** Jesus Christ. **2.** (*w wykrzyknikach*) **(Jezu) Chryste!** (Jesus) Christ!; **Chryste Panie!** Good Lord!

Chrystusowy, chrystusowy *a. rel.* Christ's *l.* of Christ; **nauka chrystusowa** teachings of Christ; **Chrystusowe cierpienia** Christ's suffering; **uczniowie Chrystusowi** Christ's disciples; **lata chrystusowe** *żart.* Christ's *l.* Jesus' age.

chryzantema *f. bot.* chrysanthemum (*Chrysanthemum*).

chryzelefantyna *f. sztuka* chryselephantine sculpture.

chryzmat *mi rel.* chrism.

chryzoberyl *mi min.* chrysoberyl.

chryzolit *mi min.* chrysolite.

chryzopraz *mi min.* chrysoprase.

chrzan *mi bot., kulin.* horseradish (*Armoracia rusticana*); **korzeń chrzanu** horseradish root; **mięso z chrzanem** meat with horseradish; **do chrzanu** *pot.* no good, lousy.

chrzanić *ipf.* **1.** *wulg.* (= *mówić od rzeczy*) bullshit; **nie chrzań** don't bullshit me. **2.** *wulg.* (= *partaczyć*) screw up.

chrzanowy *a. kulin.* horseradish.

chrząkać *ipf.,* **chrząknąć** *pf.* **-ij 1.** (*o człowieku*) clear one's throat; **chrząknąć znacząco** ahem. **2.** (*o świni*) grunt.

chrząstka *f. Gen.pl.* **-ek** (*w mięsie*) gristle; *anat.* cartilage; **chrząstki stawowe** articular cartilage; **chrząstka nosa** nasal cartilage.

chrząstkotwórczy *a. anat.* cartilagogenic; **komórki chrząstkotwórcze** cartilagogenic cells.

chrząszcz *ma Gen.pl.* **-y** *l.* **-ów** *ent.* (= *owad z rzędu Coleoptera*) beetle, coleopteran.

chrząścica *f. bot.* (*także* **chrząścica kędzierzawa**) Irish moss, carrageen, carragheen (*Chondrus crispus*).

chrzciciel *mp rel.* baptist; **Jan Chrzciciel** John the Baptist.

chrzcić *ipf.* **-czę -cisz, -ij 1.** *rel., kośc.* baptize; (*przez zanurzenie, zwł. w kościołach ewangelickich*) immerse; **ochrzczono ją imieniem Anna** she was baptized Anna. **2.** *pot., żart.* (= *rozcieńczać*) water down. **3.** *przen.* (= *nadawać nazwę*) christen, name.

chrzcielnica *f. kośc.* baptismal font.

chrzcielny *a. rel., kośc.* baptismal.

chrzciny *pl. Gen.* **-n 1.** (*ceremonia*) baptism;

(*przyjęcie z okazji chrztu*) baptism party. 2. *przen., żart.* (= *lanie, cięgi*) whipping, hiding.

chrzest *mi* **chrzt-** 1. *rel., kośc.* baptism; **trzymać kogoś do chrztu** be sb's godfather *l.* godmother; hold a child being baptized. 2. *przen.* (*oddanie do użytku*) christening. 3. *przen.* (*pierwszy udział*) baptism; **chrzest bojowy** baptism of fire.

chrzestna *f. Gen.* **-ej** *pot.* godmother.

chrzestny *a. rel., kośc.* baptismal; **imię chrzestne** baptismal name; **dziecko chrzestne** godchild; **córka chrzestna** goddaughter; **syn chrzestny** godson; **rodzice chrzestni** godparents; **matka chrzestna** godmother; **ojciec chrzestny** *t. przen.* (= *szef mafijny*) godfather. – *mp pot.* godfather.

chrześcijanin *mp pl.* **-anie** *Gen.* **-an, chrześcijanka** *f. Gen.pl.* **-ek** *rel.* Christian.

chrześcijański *a. rel.* Christian.

chrześcijaństwo *n. rel.* 1. (= *religia oparta na nauce Chrystusa*) Christianity. 2. (*ogół wyznawców*) Christiandom, Christianity; **w całym chrześcijaństwie** in all Christendom.

chrześniaczka *f. Gen.pl.* **-ek** *pot.* goddaughter.

chrześniak *mp pot.* godson.

chrzęst *mi* crunch, scrunch, grating *l.* grinding noise.

chrzęstniak *mi Gen.* **-a** *pat.* chondroma.

chrzęstny *a. anat.* cartilaginous, cartilage, chondric; **tkanka chrzęstna** cartilaginous tissue; **komórka chrzęstna** chondrocyte, cartilage cell; **ryby chrzęstne** *icht.* cartilaginous fishes (*Chondrichthyes*).

chrzęścić *ipf.* **-szczę -ścisz** crunch, scrunch, grate, grind.

chtoniczny *a. mit.* chthonic, chthonian.

chuch *mi pot.* (= *oddech*) breath; (= *chuchnięcie, dmuchnięcie*) puff.

chuchać *ipf.*, **chuchnąć** *pf.* **-ij** 1. (= *dmuchać*) blow, breathe (*na l. w coś* on sth); (= *lekko wydmuchiwać*) puff; **chuchać na zamarzniętą szybę** breathe on a window that has frozen over; **chuchnąć dymem z papierosa** puff cigarette smoke (out of one's mouth). 2. *tylko ipf.* (= *pielęgnować*) pamper, nurse (*na kogoś / coś* sb/sth).

chuchro *n. Gen.pl.* **-cher** *emf. l. pog.* wimp, milksop.

chuchrowaty *a. emf. l. pog.* frail, wimpy.

chuć *f. pl.* **-i** *l.* **-e** *lit. l. żart.* lust, desire.

chuderlak *mp pl.* **-cy** *l.* **-i** (*pog.*) weakling, wimp.

chuderlawy *a.* emaciated; *uj.* scrawny, skinny; *pred.* **(all) skin and bone** (as) thin as a toothpick; (as) lean as a rake.

chudeusz *mp Gen.pl.* **-y** *l.* **-ów** *pot. żart.* toothpick (of a man); *zob.* **chuderlak**.

chudnąć *ipf.* **-dł, -ij** lose weight, get thinner.

chudo *adv.* 1. (= *szczupło*) thinly; **wyglądać chudo** look thin. 2. *przen.* (= *mało, ubogo*) meagerly, scantily; **u niego chudo w domu** things are tight for him at home. 3. (*o jedzeniu*) (= *bez tłuszczu*) without fat.

chudoba *f. przest.* 1. (= *nędza*) indigence, misery, destitution. 2. (= *skromny dobytek*) meager possessions.

chudopachołek *mp* **-łk-** *pl.* **-i** *l.* **-owie** *arch.* 1. (= *ubogi szlachcic*) impoverished gentleman. 2. (= *człowiek niskiego stanu*) commoner.

chudy *a.* 1. (= *szczupły*) thin, lean; *uj.* skinny, scrawny; **chudy jak patyk** (as) thin as a rail *l.* a toothpick; as lean as a rake. 2. *przen.* (= *mizerny, skromny*) meager, *Br.* meagre; (= *niewystarczający*) scanty, scant; (= *nieobfity*) lean; **chude dochody** meager income; **chude lata** lean years; **chudy sezon** lean season (*na coś* for sth). 3. (= *nietłusty*) (*gł. o mięsie*) lean; (*mleko, twaróg*) low-fat. 4. (= *nieurodzajny*) barren. 5. (*ubogi w wartościowe składniki*) low-grade.

chudziak *mp pl.* **-i** *pot.* 1. = **chuderlak**. 2. *przest.* (= *biedaczysko*) poor thing *l.* soul.

chudzielec *mp* **-lc-** *Voc.* **-cze** *pl.* **-y** *l.* **-e** *pot.* thin boy *l.* man, beanpole.

chudzina *f. i mp i ma decl. like f. pot., emf.* 1. (= *wątły człowiek lub zwierzę*) frail thing. 2. (= *biedaczysko*) poor thing *l.* soul.

chudziutki *a. emf. zob.* **chudy**.

chuj *mi Acc.* **chuj** *l.* **-a** *Gen.* **-a** *Gen.pl.* **-ów** *wulg.* 1. (= *penis*) cock, dick, prick. 2. *pog.* **chuj mnie to obchodzi** the fuck I care; **chuj z nim** fuck him; **ni chuja** (= *ani trochę, nic*) not a fuck, fuck-all; **ni chuja nie zrobiłeś** you've done fuck-all; **na chuj mi to** it's no fucking use to me. – *mp Gen.pl.* **-ów** *wulg., pog.* (*o mężczyźnie*) dickhead, fuckhead; (*t. o rzeczach*) fucker, motherfucker.

chujowy *a. wulg.* shitty, fucking lousy.

chuligan *mp pl.* **-i** *l.* **-y** hoodlum, hooligan.

chuliganeria *f. Gen.* **-ii** = **chuligaństwo**.

chuliganić *ipf.* cause trouble, look for trouble.

chuligaństwo *n.* 1. (*zachowanie chuliganów*) hooliganism. 2. *zbiorowo* (gang of) hoodlums *l.* hooligans.

chusta *f.* shawl, scarf; **chusta trójkątna** *med.* triangular bandage; **blady jak chusta** (as) white as a sheet; **chusta świętej Weroniki** *sztuka, rel.* vernicle, vernacle.

chusteczka *f. Gen.pl.* **-ek** handkerchief; **chusteczka higieniczna** tissue, Kleenex®.

chustka *f. Gen.pl.* **-ek** scarf, kerchief; (*duża, kolorowa*) bandanna, bandana; (*na szyję*) neckerchief; (*na głowie*) headscarf; **chustka do nosa** handkerchief.

chutor *mi hist.* farmstead (*in Ukraine or eastern Poland*).

chwacki *a. przest.* gallant, brave.

chwalba *f. arch.* 1. (= *pochwała*) praise. 2. (= *chwalenie się, duma*) vaunt, brag.

chwalca *mp lit.* 1. (= *ten, kto chwali*) eulogist, encomiast. 2. *zw. uj.* (= *pochlebca*) flatterer, adulator.

chwalebny *a.* 1. (= *godny pochwały*) praiseworthy, commendable, laudable. 2. *lit.* (= *zaszczytny, chlubny*) glorious, meritorious.

chwalić *ipf.* 1. (= *zachwalać*) praise; **chwalić sobie coś** be satisfied with sth; **chwalić Boga** *pot.* thank God, thank goodness; **nie chwal dnia przed zachodem słońca** praise not the day before evening (*za coś* for sth). 2. (= *wielbić, czcić*) glorify, exalt; **wszelki duch Pana Boga chwali!** good God (in heaven)! ~ **się** *ipf.* brag, boast (*czymś* of sth); **nie chwaląc się**... with all due modesty...; **nie ma się czym chwalić** it's nothing to be proud of; *pot.* it's nothing to write home about.

chwalipięta *f. l. mp decl. like f. Gen.pl.* **-t** *l.* **-ów** *pot.* bigmouth, blowhard.

chwała *f.* **1.** (= *sława*) glory; **chwała Bogu!** thank God!, thank goodness!; **okryty chwałą** covered *l.* bathed in glory. **2.** (= *szacunek, cześć*) praise, credit, respect; **przynosić komuś chwałę** be to sb's credit; **do** *l.* bring sb credit. **3.** *przest.* (= *chluba, duma*) pride. **4. paść** *l.* **zginąć na polu chwały** be killed in action.

chwast[1] *mi Gen.* **-u** *bot.* weed.

chwast[2] *mi Gen.* **-u** *l.* **-a** (= *frędzel*) tassel.

chwastobójczy *a. roln.* herbicidal, weed-killing.

chwat *mp pl.* **-y** *lit.* brave boy, go-getter.

chwiać *ipf.* + *Ins.* **-eję -ejesz** shake, rock. **~ się** *ipf.* **-eję -ejesz 1.** (= *kołysać się*) shake, rock, wobble; (*o płomieniu*) flicker; **chwiać się na nogach** stagger, falter, totter; **ząb mi się chwieje** I have a loose *l.* wobbly tooth. **2.** *przen.* (= *słabnąć, upadać*) (*o państwie, gospodarce, systemie, ustroju*) totter (on the brink of collapse). **3.** *przen.* (= *wahać się*) waver, vacillate.

chwiejność *f.* **1.** (= *brak stabilności*) instability, shakiness. **2.** (= *niezdecydowanie*) (*poglądów, opinii, uczuć*) irresoluteness; **chwiejność uczuciowa** *psych.* emotional instability.

chwiejny *a.* **1.** (= *niestabilny, luźny*) shaky, rickety, wobbly, loose; **chwiejny chód, krok** unsteady *l.* staggering *l.* faltering gait. **2.** (= *niezdecydowany*) wavering, hesitant; (*pogląd, charakter*) irresolute.

chwila *f.* **1.** (= *moment*) moment, instant, while; *pot.* second, minute; **co chwila** *l.* **co chwilę** every now and then; **co chwila spoglądał na zegar** he kept looking at the clock; **krótka chwila** short moment; **lada chwila** (at) any time *l.* moment; **na chwilę** for a moment *l.* minute; **przez chwilę** for a moment *l.* minute *l.* second; **przed chwilą** *l.* **chwilę temu** a moment *l.* minute ago; **wyszła przed chwilą** she just left; she left a moment *l.* minute ago; **po chwili** a moment later; **w jednej chwili** at once; **w ostatniej chwili** at the last moment *l.* second; **w tej chwili** at the moment; (= *niezwłocznie*) right now, this instant, immediately; **w owej chwili** at that moment; **w tejże chwili** just then; **nie w tej chwili** not just now; **za chwilę** in (just) a moment *l.* second; shortly; **ani przez chwilę** not for a moment *l.* instant; **(aż) do ostatniej chwili** till the (very) last moment; **bez chwili wahania** without a moment's hesitation; **z każdą chwilą** with each moment; **zostań chwilę!** stay a moment!; **żyć chwilą** live for the moment. **2.** (= *szczególny czas*) moment, occasion, time; **chwila prawdy** moment of truth; **chwila radości** time of rejoicing; **smutna/uroczysta chwila** sad/solemn moment; **czekać na właściwą chwilę** wait for the right moment.

chwileczka, chwilka *f.* moment, (half a) second; **(czekaj) chwileczkę** wait a second *l.* minute.

chwilowo *adv.* temporarily, for the time being.

chwilowy *a.* momentary, temporary; (= *szybko mijający*) short-lived, transient.

chwost *mi* **1.** (*część ciała zwierząt*) tail. **2.** *przest.* (= *ozdoba, frędzel*) fringe.

chwościk *mi Gen.* **-a** = **chwost** 2.

chwycić *pf. zob.* **chwytać**. **~ się** *zob.* **chwytać się**.

chwyt *mi* **1.** (= *uchwycenie*) grip, hold, grasp, clutch; (= *złapanie*) catch, grab. **2.** *wspinaczka* grip. **3.** *sport* (*zapaśniczy*) grapple. **4.** (= *manewr, sposób*) trick, stratagem. **5.** *techn.* (= *uchwyt, część, za którą coś jest chwytane*) grip; **chwyt wiertła** drill shank; **chwyt pistoletu** *broń* pistol grip, gunstock. **6.** *lotn.* **chwyt powietrza** air intake.

chwytacz *mi Gen.* **-a** *techn.* catcher, arrester; (= *zabezpieczenie*) safety catch, safety stop.

chwytać *ipf.* **1.** (= *łapać*) catch, seize (*sb l. sth*) (*za coś* by sth); grab (hold of), take hold of (*sb l. sth*); (*piłkę itp.*) catch (hold of) (*sth*); **chwytać za coś** (= *sięgać po coś*) reach for sth; **chwytać za broń** take up arms; **chwytać byka za rogi** *przen.* take the bull by the horns; **chwytać kogoś za rękę** take hold of sb's hand; **chwytać kogoś za słowo** take sb at his word; **chwytać powietrze** *l.* **oddech (z trudem)** gasp for breath. **2.** (= *rozumieć, pojmować*) get, grasp; **chwytać coś w lot** grasp sth at once. **3.** *zw. pf. zob.* **chwycić**; *przen.* (= *ogarniać*) move; **chwyciło mnie to za serce** it moved me; it got to my heart; **wzruszenie chwyciło mnie za gardło** I was moved to tears. **4.** *zw. pf.* (*o rozpoczęciu się czegoś*) **mróz chwyta** its starting to freeze; **pomysł chwycił** the idea caught on; **silnik chwycił** the engine started; **to nie chwyci** it cuts no ice. **~ się** *ipf.* **1.** (= *łapać się*) seize, grasp, grab (hold of) (*za coś* sth); **tonący brzytwy się chwyta** *przen.* a drowning man will grasp at straws. **2.** (= *złapać się wzajemnie*) seize *l.* grab hold of one another; **chwycić się za ręce** take hold of each other's hand; join hands. **3.** + *Gen.* (= *uciekać się do czegoś*) resort to (*sth*). **4.** + *Gen.* (= *próbować*) **chwytać się rozmaitych zajęć** try *l.* take up odd jobs.

chwytak *mi Gen.* **-a** *techn.* grab, grapple.

chwytliwy *a.* **1.** (*o hasłach, sloganach, pomysłach*) catchy. **2.** (*o umyśle*) keen, quick, agile. **3.** *rzad.* = **chwytny**.

chwytnik *mi Gen.* **-a** *bot.* rhizoid.

chwytność *f. anat.* prehensility.

chwytny *a.* **1.** *anat.* (*o częściach ciała*) prehensile, adapted for grasping. **2.** *techn.* grabbing, grappling. **3.** *rzad.* (= *skutecznie chwytający*) **chwytny pies** seizer.

chyba *conj.* **chyba że** (= *o ile nie...*) unless; except if *l.* when; **chodzimy na spacery, chyba że pada** we go for walks except when it rains; **pójdziemy na spacer, chyba żeby padało** we'll go for a walk unless it rains. – *part.* probably; **chyba tak** I guess so; **chyba nie** I guess not; probably not; **on chyba oszalał** he must be crazy; **chyba żartujesz** you must be kidding (me) *l.* joking; you can't be serious; **chyba go znasz** you probably know him; **no chyba!** *pot.* sure!, you bet!

chybcikiem *adv.* (*także* **na chybcika**) *pot.* in a rush, in a hurry, in haste, hurriedly.

chybiać *ipf.*, **chybić** *pf.* (= *nie trafiać w cel*) **1.** miss; **chybić celu** *t. przen.* miss the mark *l.* target. **2.** (*w utartych zwrotach*) **ani chybi** surely, for sure, no doubt; **na chybił trafił** at random, randomly.

chybiony *a.* **1.** (= *nieudany*) unsuccessful, off-the-mark. **2.** (*o planie, próbie*) abortive. **3. chybiony strzał** miss.

chybki *a. lit.* (= *szybki*) swift, nimble.

chybko *adv. lit. l. arch.* swiftly.

chybnąć *pf.* -**ij** *rzad.* shake, rock. ~ **się** *pf.* -**ij** *rzad.* rock, sway.

chybotać *ipf.* -**czę** -**czesz** *l.* -**cę** -**cesz** *rzad.* -**tam** -**tasz**, -**cz** *l.* -**taj** + *Ins.* shake, rock. ~ **się** *ipf.* shake, rock, sway, wobble; (*o płomieniu*) flicker; **łódź chybotała się na falach** the boat rocked on the waves; **ten stół się chyboce** this table wobbles.

chybotliwy *a.* shaky, wobbly, unsteady; (*o płomieniu*) flickering.

chylić *ipf. lit.* bend, bow (down), incline; **chylić głowę** bow *l.* incline one's head; **chylić czoło** *l.* **czoła przed kimś** take one's hat off to sb. ~ **się** *ipf.* **1.** (= *pochylać się, zniżać się*) bend, bow down (*ku czemuś l. do czegoś* toward sth); **słońce chyli się ku zachodowi** the sun is sinking in the west. **2. chylić się ku końcowi** approach *l.* near the end; **chylić się ku upadkowi** decline; be on the decline; **chylić się ku starości** approach old age. **3. szala (zwycięstwa) chyli się na czyjąś stronę** the scale (of victory) tips *l.* turns in sb's favor.

chyłkiem *adv.* (= *niepostrzeżenie, skrycie*) stealthily, furtively.

chyłomierz *mi Gen.* -**a** *lotn., żegl., kol.* clinometer, inclinometer, level.

chytrość *f.* **1.** (= *przebiegłość*) cunning, guile, slyness. **2.** *pot.* (= *skąpstwo*) meanness.

chytrus *mp pl.* -**y** *l.* -**i** **1.** (= *osoba przebiegła*) sly dog. **2.** (= *skąpiec, sknera*) tightwad, miser.

chytrusek *mp* -**sk**- *pl.* -**i** *pot., żart.* sly dog; **lisek chytrusek** sly fox.

chytry *a.* **1.** (= *przebiegły*) cunning, crafty, sly; **chytry lis** *l.* **chytra sztuka** (= *spryciarz*) crafty *l.* sly (old) fox; **chytry jak lis** *l.* **wąż** (as) sly as a fox. **2.** *pot.* (= *skąpy*) mean, cheap, stingy. **3.** *żart.* (= *sprytnie pomyślany*) clever, ingenious; **chytra sztuczka** clever trick.

chytrze *adv.* **1.** (= *przebiegle*) slyly, craftily, cunningly. **2.** *pot.* (= *pomysłowo*) cleverly, ingeniously.

chytrzyć *ipf.* -**trz** *l.* -**yj** *pot. uj.* **1.** (= *używać podstępów*) scheme, play tricks. **2.** (= *sknerzyć*) **chytrzyć (na wydatkach)** pinch pennies; be a tightwad.

chyżo *adv.* swiftly; *żart.* (= *natychmiast*) at once, this instant.

chyżość *f. lit.* swiftness.

chyży *a. lit.* swift, fleet.

ci[1] *pron. zob.* **ten.**

ci[2] *pron. zob.* **ty.**

ciach *int.* (*ruch nożyc*) snip; (*uderzenie noża l. siekiery*) chop; (*świst kija, bata, szabli itp.*) swish; **ciach, ciach** snick-snack, snicker-snack.

ciachać *ipf.*, **ciachnąć** *pf.* -**ij** *pot.* (= *ciąć*) chop, hack; (*nożycami*) snip.

ciacho *n. pot. emf. zob.* **ciastko.**

ciałko *n. Gen.pl.* -**łek 1.** *biol., fizj.* corpuscle; **ciałko żółte** yellow body, corpus luteum; **ciałko zieleni** *bot.* chloroplast. **2.** (= *komórka krwi*) blood cell; **białe ciałka (krwi)** white blood cells, leucocytes; **czerwone ciałka (krwi)** red blood cells, erythrocytes. **3.** *emf.* body.

ciało *n. Loc.* **ciele 1.** (= *tkanki wokół szkieletu*) body, flesh; **Ciało i Krew Chrystusa** *rel.* the Body and Blood of Christ; **Boże Ciało** *rel., kośc.* Corpus Christi. **2.** (= *całość organizmu*) body; **część ciała** part of the body; body part; **język ciała** body language; **jama ciała** *anat.* body cavity; **na całym ciele** all over the body; **(na) gołe ciało** (on) one's naked body *l.* bare flesh; **na duszy i ciele** for the body and soul; **duszą i ciałem** body and soul; **a słowo stało się ciałem** and the word became flesh. **3.** *przen.* (= *grono osób, zbiorowość*) body; **ciało wykonawcze/ustawodawcze** *polit.* executive/legislative body; **ciało pedagogiczne** *szkoln.* teaching staff; **ciało polityczne** *polit.* body politic. **4.** (= *zwłoki*) (dead) body, corpse. **5.** *chem., fiz., anat.* body; **ciało ciekłe/gazowe/stałe** fluid/gaseous/solid body; **ciało obce** *med.* foreign body; **ciało szkliste** *anat.* vitreous body. **6. ciało niebieskie** *astron.* celestial *l.* heavenly body.

ciałopalny *a. gł. archeol.* crematory, cremation; **pochówek ciałopalny** cremation burial.

ciamajda *f. l. mp decl. like f. Gen.pl.* -**d** *l.* -**ów** *pot.* bungler, loser, klutz; (*o mężczyźnie*) milksop.

ciamajdowaty *a. pot.* clumsy, klutzy, gauche.

ciapa *f. l. mp decl. like f. Gen.pl.* -**p** *l.* -**ów** = **ciamajda.**

ciapać *ipf.* -**ię** -**iesz** *pot.* **1.** (= *brodzić, chlapiąc*) splash (along). **2.** (= *głośno jeść*) chomp, munch. **3.** (= *rąbać, siekać*) chop, hack.

ciapcia *f. l. mp decl. like f. Gen.pl.* -**ć** *l.* -**ów** *pot. żart.* = **ciamajda.**

ciapka *f. Gen.pl.* -**ek** *pot.* (= *plamka*) spot, speck, dot.

ciapnąć *pf.* -**ij** *zob.* **ciapać 3.**

ciapowaty *a. pot., żart.* = **ciamajdowaty.**

ciarki *pl. Gen.* -**rek** creeps, chills, shivers; **(na widok tego) ciarki mnie przechodzą** it gives me the creeps; it makes my flesh creep *l.* crawl; it sends a shiver down my spine; **strach, aż ciarki biorą** it's enough to scare you stiff.

ciasnawy *a.* cramped, confining.

ciasno *adv.* -**śniej 1.** (= *ściśle*) tight, tightly, closely, close together. **2.** *przen.* (= *w ramach ograniczeń*) narrowly; **ciasno pojmowany** narrowly conceived.

ciasnota *f.* **1.** lack of room *l.* space. **2. ciasnota umysłowa** *przen.* narrow-mindedness, parochialism.

ciasny *a.* -**śniejszy 1.** (= *ograniczony przestrzennie*) tight, cramped, confined; (*pokój*) small; (*buty, ubranie*) tight. **2.** (= *wąski*) narrow, tight; **ciasne przejście** narrow passageway.

3. *przen.* (= *ograniczony*) narrow; **ciasna defini-cja** narrow definition; **ciasny umysł** *pog.* narrow mind; **ciasne poglądy** *pog.* parochial views. **4. do jasnej ciasnej!** *pot. euf.* damn it!, dammit!
ciasteczko *n. Gen.pl.* **-ek** cookie.
ciastkarnia *f. Gen.pl.* -i *l.* **-ń** pastry shop, patisserie.
ciastkarz *mp* pastry cook.
ciastko *n. Gen.pl.* **-ek** cake, pastry, cookie.
ciasto *n. Loc.* **cieście 1.** (= *masa, z której się piecze*) dough, batter. **2.** (= *wypiek*) (*drożdżowe, kruche, biszkoptowe, owocowe*) cake; **ciasto fran-cuskie** French *l.* puff pastry. **3.** (= *masa z syp-kiego materiału z płynem*) mass; **ciasto wapien-ne** *bud.* lime putty; **ciasto skalne** *geol.* ground-mass.
ciastowaty *a.* doughy, pasty.
ciąć *ipf.* **tnę tniesz, tnij 1.** (= *kroić, t. przen.* = *skracać, cenzurować*) cut; (*mięso*) carve; (= *rą-bać*) chop. **2.** (= *ścinać*) cut down; **ciąć drzewa** cut down *l.* fell trees; **ciąć na kawałki** cut into pieces; **ciąć coś nożyczkami/nożem** cut sth with scissors/with a knife; **ciąć na plastry** slice; **ciąć w kostkę** cube, dice; **kwiaty cięte** cut flowers. **3.** (*o owadach*) bite, sting. **4. ciąć wodę/powietrze** *przen.* (*o czymś pędzącym*) cut through the wa-ter/air. – *pf.* **1.** *przen.* (= *zadać cios*) deliver *l.* strike a blow; (*nożem, szablą, mieczem*) hack, slash (*kogoś / coś* at sb/sth) (*czymś* with sth); **ciąć na oślep** slash *l.* strike out blindly; **ciąć kogoś batem** lash *l.* slash at sb with a whip; *przen.* (*o deszczu*) pelt; (*o wietrze*) bite. **2.** (= *zranić*) cut, hurt; **rana cięta** *med.* cut; **ciąć ostrym słowem** *przen.* make a cutting remark. ~ **się** *ipf.* (= *kłó-cić się*) **1.** fight (*o coś* about *l.* over sth). **2.** *pot.* (= *dokonywać samookaleczenia*) cut o.s. (up). – *pf.* (= *skaleczyć się*) cut o.s.
ciąg *mi* **1.** (= *rzeczy następujące jedna po dru-giej*) sequence, train; **ciąg myśli** train of thought; **jednym ciągiem** without a break, at a stretch, continuously. **2.** *mat.* sequence, progression; **ciąg liczbowy** sequence of numbers; **ciąg arytme-tyczny/geometryczny** arithmetic/geometric pro-gression; **ciąg rosnący/malejący** increasing/de-creasing sequence; **ciąg skończony/nieskończo-ny** finite/infinite sequence; **ciąg zbieżny** conver-gent sequence. **3.** *mat., komp.* (= *następujące po sobie znaki*) string; **ciąg znaków/liter/cyfr/symbo-li** string of characters/letters/digits/symbols. **4.** (= *rząd, szereg, pasmo*) line, row, belt; **ciąg skle-pów** row of stores; **ciąg zieleni** green belt. **5. w ciągu...** in *l.* within (the space of...); during...; **w ciągu godziny, miesiąca** in *l.* within an hour, a month; **w ciągu dnia** during the day. **6. dalszy ciąg** continuation; **dalszy ciąg powieści/filmu** se-quel to a novel/film; **ciąg dalszy nastąpi** to be continued; **robić coś w dalszym ciągu** continue *l.* keep doing sth. **7.** *techn.* **ciąg produkcyjny** pro-duction line. **8.** (= *trasa, układ dróg l. ulic*) route; **ciąg komunikacyjny** thoroughfare; **ciąg pieszy** pedestrian street. **9.** (= *ruch cieczy l. ga-zu*) flow; **ciąg powietrza** draft; **ciąg kominowy** *techn.* flue draft. **10.** *lotn.* thrust; **ciąg silnika odrzutowego** jet thrust; **ciąg śmigła** propeller

thrust; **ciąg wsteczny** reverse thrust. **11.** (= *gro-madna wędrówka zwierząt*) migration; (*łososi*) run; (*ptaków*) flight.
ciągać *ipf. pot.* **1.** (= *wlec*) haul, drag, pull. **2.** (= *prowadzić powoli*) drag; **ciągać kogoś po skle-pach** drag sb from store to store; **ciągać dzieci ze sobą** drag one's kids around with o.s.; **ciągać ko-goś po sądach** drag sb through the courts. **3. ciągać za coś** (= *szarpać*) pull (at) sth, yank (on) sth.
ciągadło *n. Gen.pl.* **-deł** *techn.* drawing die.
ciągarka *f. Gen.pl.* **-ek** *techn.* drawing ma-chine, drawbench.
ciągle *adv.* always, all the time; (= *bez prze-rwy*) continuously; (= *nieustannie*) constantly, continually, endlessly; (= *stale, wiecznie*) per-petually, permanently; **ciągle coś robić** do sth all the time; never stop doing sth.
ciągliwość *f. fiz., metal.* ductility.
ciągliwy *a. metal.* ductile.
ciągłość *f.* continuity; **ciągłość pracy** uninter-rupted period of work; **brak ciągłości** discontinu-ity, lack of continuity.
ciągły *a.* **1.** (= *stały, bezustanny*) constant, continual, endless. **2.** (= *nieprzerwany*) contin-uous, uninterrupted. **3.** *mat., fiz.* continuous; **widmo ciągłe** *fiz.* continuous spectrum; **funkcja ciągła** *mat.* continuous function. **4.** *sztuka* **układ ciągły** continuum.
ciągnąć *ipf.* **-ij 1.** (= *wlec, holować*) pull (along), drag (along), tug, tow, haul; **samochód ciągnie przyczepę** the car is pulling a trailer. **2.** *przen.* **ciągnąć kogoś za uszy** (= *zmuszać do ro-bienia postępów*) push sb (on); **ciągnąć kogoś/ coś ze sobą** (= *prowadzić*) drag sb/sth (along) with o.s.; **ciągnęła za sobą młodszą siostrę** she was pulling her younger sister behind her. **3.** (= *szarpać*) pull (*za coś* (at) sth); yank (*za coś* (on) sth); **ciągnąć kogoś za język** *przen.* cross-examine sb, question sb; **ciągnąć w swoją stronę** *przen., pot.* look after number one. **4.** (= *wydłużać, przeciągać*) stretch, extend; **ciągnąć ścianę/ulicę** extend a wall/a street; **ciągnąć linię/ przewody** *techn.* lay line/cables. **5.** (= *kontynuo-wać*) continue; go on, proceed (*coś* with sth). **6.** (= *czerpać, wyciągać, t. losować, uzyskiwać*) draw; **ciągnąć wodę ze studni** draw water from a well; **ciągnąć karty z talii** draw cards from a pack; **ciągnąć losy** draw lots; **ciągnąć nazwiska z kapelusza** draw names from a hat; **ciągnąć z cze-goś korzyść/zysk** draw *l.* derive benefit/profit from sth. **7.** *techn.* (*poddawać obróbce*) draw. **8.** (= *wciągać, wsysać*) absorb, suck (up), draw (up), draw in; **ciągnąć napój przez słomkę** suck a drink through a straw; **ciągnąć dym z fajki/pa-pierosa** draw on a pipe/cigarette; **komin dobrze/ słabo ciągnie** the flue draws well/poorly. **9.** *pot.* (= *pić, zwł. alkohol*) drink, imbibe; **ciągnąć z bu-telki** pull at a bottle. **10.** (= *pociągać, wabić, ku-sić*) attract, allure, tempt, raise (*sb's*) interest; **coś mnie ciągnie do tych ludzi** I'm attracted to those people; **nie ciągnie go do nauki** he has no inclination to study; **natura ciągnie wilka do lasu** (*przysłowie*) the leopard can't change its spots.

11. (*o powietrzu, przeciągu, zapachu*) **chłód ciągnie od rzeki** a cold draft is blowing from the river; **okropnie tu ciągnie** there's an awful draft in here; **z ogrodu ciągnęła woń bzów** the scent of lilacs drifted from the garden. **12.** (= *przemieszczać się, wędrować w określonym kierunku*) move (on *l.* along), push (on), migrate, drift, pour; **pochód ciągnął ulicą** the procession moved down the street; **pielgrzymi ciągną do Mekki** pilgrims pour into Mecca; **jesienią ptaki ciągną na południe** birds migrate south in the fall. **13.** (*o chmurach*) (= *płynąć z wiatrem*) drift. **14.** (= *podążać*) **ciągnąć za kimś/czymś** follow (in the wake of) sb/sth. **15.** *wulg.* **ciągnąć komuś druta** do a blow job on sb. **~ się** *ipf.* **1. ciągnąć się za kimś/czymś** (= *wlec się z tyłu*) trail along behind sb/sth; drag behind sb/sth; (= *pozostawać z tyłu*) trail *l.* be left behind sb/sth; **za parowozem ciągnęła się chmura dymu** a plume of smoke trailed behind the engine. **2.** (= *szarpać się wzajemnie*) **ciągnęli się za włosy** they pulled at each other's hair. **3.** (= *rozciągać się*) stretch, extend; (*o linii*) run. **4.** (= *trwać*) continue, pass, go on, proceed. **5.** (*o czasie*) (= *dłużyć się*) creep (slowly) by *l.* past; hang heavy.

ciągnienie *n.* (= *wynik losowania*) **1.** draw. **2.** *techn.* drawing; **ciągnienie na zimno/gorąco** cold/ hot drawing.

ciągnik *mi* Gen. **-a** *techn., mot.* tractor.

ciągotki *pl.* Gen. **-ek, ciągoty** *pl.* Gen. **-t** *pot.* tendency, inclination (*do czegoś* to *l.* toward sth, *do robienia czegoś* to do sth); taste, preference, fancy (*do czegoś* for sth); **perwersyjne ciągotki** perverted inclinations.

ciąża *f.* pregnancy; **być w ciąży** be pregnant; **kobieta w ciąży** pregnant woman; **zajść w ciążę** get pregnant; **przerwać ciążę** abort a pregnancy.

ciążenie *n.* *fiz.* gravitation.

ciążki *pl.* Gen. **-ów** *sport* weights.

ciążowy *a.* pregnancy; **próba ciążowa** *l.* test ciążowy pregnancy test; **suknia ciążowa** maternity dress; **zatrucie ciążowe** *pat.* gestosis.

ciążyć *ipf.* **1.** (= *wywierać ciężar, t. przen.*) weigh, lie heavy (*na czymś* on *l.* upon sth); **ciążyć komuś** (= *stanowić przykry ciężar*) weigh (heavily) on sb; **ciąży mi głowa od senności** I'm heavy with sleep; **ciążyć komuś na żołądku** (*o posiłku*) lie heavy on sb's stomach; **ciążyć na czyimś sumieniu** lie heavy on sb's conscience; **ciążą na nim poważne zarzuty** serious accusations have been laid against him; **ciąży na tobie obowiązek sprawdzenia danych** it is incumbent on *l.* upon you to verify the data; **ciąży nad nim wyrok śmierci** he's under sentence of death; **nad naszym rodem ciąży klątwa** a curse hangs over our house. **2.** (= *skłaniać się*) **ciążyć ku czemuś** gravitate toward sth; incline to *l.* toward sth.

cibora *f.* *bot.* cyperus (*Cyperus*); **cibora papirusowa** papyrus (plant) (*C. papyrus*).

cichaczem, cichcem *adv.* **1.** (= *po cichu*) stealthily, quietly, furtively. **2.** *przen.* (= *w tajemnicy*) on the sly, secretly.

cichnąć *ipf.* **-ij; cichł** *l.* **cichnął cichła cichli 1.** (*o głosach*) (= *zanikać*) die down, grow quiet. **2.**

(= *ustępować, uspokajać się*) subside, die down, calm down.

cicho *adv.* **1.** (= *bez hałasu l. ostentacji*) silently, quietly; **cicho, sza!** sh, hush!; **siedzieć cicho** sit quietly, be quiet; (= *nie rzucać się w oczy*) keep a low profile; **siedzieć cicho jak trusia** *l.* **jak mysz pod miotłą** be as quiet as a mouse; **cicho jak makiem zasiał** (it's so quiet) you could hear a pin drop; **cicho bądź!** be quiet!; quiet down! **2.** (= *dyskretnie, w sekrecie*) quietly, discreetly, secretly.

cichobieżny *a.* *techn.* silent-running, noiseless.

cichociemny *mp* *hist., wojsk.* special force paratrooper (*in wartime Poland*).

cichutki *a.* **1.** (= *ledwo słyszalny*) very low, almost inaudible. **2.** *emf. zob.* **cichy**.

cichutko *adv.* *emf. zob.* **cicho**; **po cichutku** very discreetly.

cichy *a.* **1.** (= *słabo słyszalny*) low, quiet; **po cichu** quietly; **czytać po cichu** read silently, read to o.s.; **z cicha pęk** (= *niespodziewanie*) out of the blue; *żart.* (*o człowieku*) the silent type. **2.** (= *skromny, nieśmiały*) meek, shy; **cichy adorator** silent admirer. **3.** (= *nieokazały*) quiet, modest, unassuming. **4.** (= *zakulisowy, nieoficjalny*) quiet, discreet; **cicha zgoda** silent *l.* tacit permission; **ciche porozumienie** tacit agreement *l.* understanding. **5.** (= *zaciszny, z dala od zgiełku*) tranquil, secluded. **6.** (= *spokojny*) still; **leżeć cicho** (*bez ruchu*) lie still; **cicha woda brzegi rwie** still waters run deep; **cicha woda** *żart.* the silent type. **7.** (= *beztroski, pogodny*) peaceful, serene, quiet; **ciche życie** peaceful life.

ciebie *pron. zob.* **ty**.

ciec *ipf.* **-knę -kniesz** *l.* **-kę -czesz; -kł** *l.* **-knął, -kła -kli 1.** flow; (= *sączyć się*) trickle; (*o łzach l. krwi*) (= *spływać*) run, stream; (*kroplami*) drip; **ślinka mi cieknie** my mouth is watering; **cieknie mu krew z nosa** his nose is bleeding. **2.** (= *być nieszczelnym*) leak.

ciecierzyca *f.* *bot., kulin.* chickpea, garbanzo (bean) (*Cicer arietinum*).

cieciorka[1] *f.* Gen.pl. **-ek** *myśl.* (= *samica cietrzewia*) gray hen, black grouse hen.

cieciorka[2] *bot.* crown vetch (*Coronilla varia*).

ciecz *f.* *pl.* **-e** (*stan skupienia*) liquid; (= *płyn*) fluid; **ciecz bordoska** *chem.* Bordeaux mixture; **ciecz chłodząca** *techn.* liquid coolant; **ciecz wyparta** *fiz.* displaced liquid; **ciecz zwilżająca** wetting fluid.

cieczka *f.* Gen.pl. **-ek** *zool.* heat.

cieć *mp* Gen.pl. **-ciów** *l.* **-ci** *pot.*, *często pog.* (= *dozorca*) super.

ciek *mi* watercourse.

ciekaw *a. indecl. pred. zob.* **ciekawy**.

ciekawić *ipf.* interest, arouse (*sb's*) curiosity.

ciekawie *adv.* **1.** (= *z ciekawością*) curiously, with interest. **2.** (= *interesująco, zajmująco*) interestingly, in an interesting way.

ciekawostka *f.* Gen.pl. **-ek 1.** (= *rzecz ciekawa*) curiosity. **2.** (= *nowinka*) interesting piece of news.

ciekawość *f.* curiosity, curiousness; **cieka-**

wość to pierwszy stopień do piekła curiosity killed the cat; **rozbudzić/zaspokoić czyjąś ciekawość** arouse/satisfy sb's curiosity; **umierać z ciekawości** be dying of curiosity.

ciekawski *a. pot.* prying, over-curious.

ciekawy *a.* **1.** (*także* **ciekaw**) (= *zainteresowany*) curious (*czegoś* about sth); interested (*czegoś* in sth). **2.** (= *dociekliwy*) inquisitive; (*w sposób natrętny*) prying; **ciekawe spojrzenie** inquisitive look. **3.** (= *interesujący*) interesting; **ciekawa rzecz, że...** *l.* **ciekawe, że...** interestingly enough,...

ciekły *a.* liquid.

cieknąć *ipf.* **-kł** *l.* **-knął, -kła -kli** *zob.* **ciec.**

cielak *ma* = **cielę.**

cielesność *f.* corporality, physicality.

cielesny *a.* **-śni 1.** (= *dotyczący ciała*) bodily, physical; (*o karze*) corporal. **2.** (= *seksualny*) carnal, sexual; **rozkosze cielesne** carnal pleasures; **stosunek cielesny** sexual act.

cielę *n.* **-lęci-** *pl.* **-lęt-** *Gen.* **-ąt** (*młode krowy itp., t. wieloryba*) **1.** calf; (*sarny, łani*) fawn; **głupi jak cielę** *pot.* (as) dumb as an ox; **chodzić za kimś jak cielę za krową** follow sb everywhere; **gapić się** *l.* **patrzyć jak cielę na malowane wrota** stare absently *l.* vacantly. **2.** *pot.* (= *gapa, oferma*) ninny, moron.

cielęcina *f.* **1.** (*mięso*) veal. **2.** *żart.* = **cielę** 2.

cielęcy *a.* **1.** calf's; **skóra cielęca** calfskin; **mięso cielęce** veal; **pieczeń cielęca** roast veal. **2.** *żart.* (= *nierozgarnięty, dziecinny*) silly, stupid, childish, infantile; **cielęce spojrzenie** stupid *l.* doe-eyed look; **cielęcy uśmiech** silly smile; **cielęcy zachwyt** childish delight; **cielęce lata** *żart.* young age.

cielętnik *mi Gen.* **-a** *hodowla* calf house, calf pen.

cielić się *ipf.* **1.** (*o krowie itp.*) calve; (*o sarnie, łani*) fawn. **2.** *geol.* (*o lodowcu*) calve.

cielisty *a.* (*o kolorze*) flesh(-colored).

cielna *a.* (*tylko f.*) (*o krowie itp.*) in calf; (*o sarnie, łani*) in fawn.

cielsko *n.* **1.** (= *ciało, tusza*) bulk. **2.** (= *ogromne zwierzę l. rzecz przypominająca zwierzę*) hulk.

ciem *f. zob.* **ćma.**

ciemiączko *n. Gen.pl.* **-czek** *anat.* fontanel, *Br.* fontanelle.

ciemieniowy *a. anat.* parietal; **kość ciemieniowa** parietal bone; **płat ciemieniowy** parietal lobe; **oko ciemieniowe** *l.* **narząd ciemieniowy** *zool.* (*np. u hatterii*) parietal eye.

ciemiernik *mi Gen.* **-a** *bot.* hellebore (*Helleborus*); **ciemiernik biały** black hellebore, Christmas rose, winter rose (*H. niger*).

ciemierzyca *f.* = **ciemiężyca.**

ciemię *n.* **ciemieni-** *pl.* **-on-** *anat.* crown (of the head), sinciput; **on jest nie w ciemię bity** *pot.* he's no fool.

ciemięga *f. l. mp decl. like f. Gen.pl.* **-g** *l.* **-ów** *pot.* lummox.

ciemięzca *mp,* **ciemiężczyni** *f. Gen.pl.* **-ń** *lit. zob.* **ciemiężyciel/ka.**

ciemiężyca *f. bot.* veratrum, (false) hellebore (*Veratrum*); **ciemiężyca biała** white hellebore (*V. album*).

ciemiężyciel *mp,* **ciemiężycielka** *f. Gen.pl.* **-ek** *lit.* oppressor.

ciemiężyć *ipf. lit.* oppress.

ciemku *adv.* **po ciemku** in the dark.

ciemnawy *a.* **1.** (= *pogrążony w półmroku*) dim, dusky; (= *o wodzie*) murky. **2.** (= *mroczny*) gloomy, shadowy. **3.** (= *pośredni między jasnym a ciemnym*) darkish.

ciemnia *f. Gen.pl.* **-i 1.** (*także* **ciemnia fotograficzna**) *fot.* darkroom; **ciemnia optyczna** *opt.* camera obscura. **2.** *przest.* (= *ciemność*) darkness, the dark.

ciemniactwo *n. pot., pog.* ignorance.

ciemniaczka *f. Gen.pl.* **-ek, ciemniak** *mp pl.* **-i** *l.* **-cy** *pot., pog.* dummy, dunce.

ciemnica *f.* **1.** *lit. l. hist.* (= *loch więzienny*) dungeon. **2.** *przest.* (= *ciemność*) darkness, the dark.

ciemnieć *ipf.* **1.** (= *mrocznieć*) darken, grow *l.* get dark; **ciemnieje komuś w oczach** sb's head *l.* mind is reeling. **2.** (= *czernieć*) darken, blacken; **srebro ciemnieje na powietrzu** silver darkens in the open air. **3.** (= *majaczyć jako ciemna plama*) loom dark.

ciemno *adv.* **1.** (= *mroczno*) darkly, dark; **ciemno jak w grobie** *l.* **ciemno, choć oko wykol** pitch black; **robi się ciemno** it's getting dark. **2.** (= *niezrozumiale, niejasno*) obscurely. **3. w ciemno** blind, blindly; **randka w ciemno** blind date; **strzał w ciemno** shot in the dark; **kupić coś w ciemno** buy sth sight unseen.

ciemnogród *mi* **-o-** *pog.* bigotry, obscurantism.

ciemnooki *a.* dark-eyed.

ciemnoskóry *a.* dark-skinned. – *mp* dark-skinned person.

ciemność *f.* **1.** (= *brak światła, mrok*) darkness; **w ciemności** in the dark; **egipskie ciemności** Cimmerian darkness, complete *l.* total darkness. **2.** (= *niezrozumiałość, zawiłość*) darkness, ignorance.

ciemnota *f.* **1.** (= *zacofanie, nieuctwo*) ignorance. **2.** *pot.* (= *ludzie zacofani*) ignorant *l.* uneducated people.

ciemnowłosy *a.* dark-haired.

ciemny *a.* **1.** (= *mroczny, nieoświetlony*) dark, dim; **ciemna noc** dark night; **ciemna karta** falls of fortune, bad times; **ciemny chleb** brown bread; **ciemny pokój** dim room; **łotr** *l.* **typ spod ciemnej gwiazdy** *pot.* shady character. **2.** (= *prawie czarny*) dark, dim; **ciemne okulary** dark glasses, sunglasses; *pot.* shades; **ciemna strona** dark side; **przedstawiać** *l.* **malować coś w ciemnych barwach** *l.* **kolorach** paint sth in black colors. **3.** (= *pesymistyczny*) dark; **ciemne lata wojny** dark years of the war. **4.** (= *podejrzany, nikczemny*) shady; **ciemne sprawy** shady business; **ciemny typ** shady character. **5.** (= *intensywny, nasycony*) dark. **6.** (*o skórze*) (= *śniady*) dark; **ciemna cera** dark complexion. **7.** (*o głosie*) (= *niski, gruby*) low-pitched; **samogłoski ciemne** *jęz.* dark consonants. **8.** (= *zacofany*) (*np. o okresie w historii*) dark; (*o ludziach*) unenlightened, ignorant; (= *głupi*) dumb; **ciemny jak tabaka w rogu** *pot.* nitwit, know-nothing; **ciemna masa** *pot. uj. l. żart.* dumb person, dimwit. **9.** (= *niezrozumiały, zawiły*) dark, obscure, hard to understand.

cienieć *ipf.* **1.** (= *chudnąć, kurczyć się*) thin, grow thin *l.* thinner. **2.** (*o dźwięku*) (= *podwyższać się*) *rzad.* shrill.

cieniolubny *a. bot.* shade-loving.

cieniować *ipf.* **1.** *sztuka* shade. **2.** *przen.* (= *wysubtelniać*) refine. **3.** (= *modulować*) modulate, vary the tone *l.* pitch. **4.** (= *modelować fryzurę*) layer. **5.** (*stosować makijaż*) make up, apply make-up. **6.** (*np. pokój*) shade.

cienistość *f.* shadiness.

cienisty *a.* **-szy 1.** (= *będący w cieniu*) shady, shaded, shadowy. **2.** (= *zapewniający cień*) shady; (*drzewo, altana, daszek*) shade-giving, giving shade.

cieniście *adv.* shadily.

cieniutki *a.* **1.** (= *niegruby*) thinnish. **2.** (= *wysoki*) (*o głosie, dźwięku*) high-pitched, shrill. **3.** (*o jedzeniu, piciu*) thin; **cieniutka zupa** thin soup.

cienki *a.* **-szy 1.** (= *niegruby*) thin; **mieć cienką skórę** *przen.* be thin-skinned, have a thin skin. **2.** (*o dźwięku*) (= *wysoki*) high-pitched, shrill. **3.** (*o jedzeniu, piciu*) (= *wodnisty*) thin, watery; (= *rozwodniony*) watered-down; **cienkie wino** thin wine. **4.** *pot.* (= *mierny*) run-of-the-mill; *pot.* cheesy; **cienki Bolek** *pog.* nobody.

cienko *adv.* **-niej 1.** (= *niegrubo, niepokaźnie*) thinly, thin; **cienko krajać** slice thin; **jest cienko z kimś** *pot.* he (she etc.) is not doing well; **cienko prząść** (= *żyć w biedzie*) *pot.* live from hand to mouth; (= *być bardzo chorym*) be very ill, be laid up. **2.** (*o dźwięku*) (= *wysoko*) shrill, shrilly; **cienko śpiewać** (= *żyć w biedzie*) *pot.* live from hand to mouth; (= *pokornieć*) sing small, feel small.

cienkopis *mi* fine-tip felt pen.

cienkość *f.* **1.** (= *chudość*) thinness. **2.** (*o dźwięku*) shrillness. **3.** (*o pokarmach, napojach*) thinness.

cienkusz *mi Gen.* **-a** *l.* **-u** *Gen.pl.* **-y** *l.* **-ów** *pot.* thin *l.* weak wine *l.* beer *l.* mead.

cień *mi Gen.* **-a** *Gen.pl.* **-i** *l.* **-ów 1.** (*ciemny ślad oświetlonej rzeczy*) shadow; **dawać** *l.* **rzucać cień** cast *l.* throw a shadow; **chińskie cienie** *l.* **teatr cieni** *teatr* shadow play *l.* show *l.* theater; **bać się własnego cienia** be afraid of one's own shadow; **być czyimś cieniem** be sb's shadow, be sb's inseparable companion; **chodzić za kimś jak cień** tag along behind sb; **rzucać cień na kogoś** question sb's integrity; **pozostał z niego tylko cień** he's a ghost of his former self; **gabinet cieni** *polit.* shadow cabinet. **2.** *przen.* (= *odrobina*) shadow, hint, grain; **cień prawdy** grain of truth; **cień wątpliwości** shadow of a doubt; **cień nadziei** faint hope. **3.** (*miejsce zacienione*) shade, shadow; **schować się w cień** find shelter in the shade; **być** *l.* **trzymać się** *l.* **pozostawać w cieniu** stay in the background, not stand out; **usuwać kogoś/coś w cień** overshadow sb/sth, cast *l.* put sb/sth in the shade; **być** *l.* **pozostawać w cieniu kogoś** be over-

shadowed by sb; **przekroczyć smugę cienia** cross the shadow line. **4.** *przen.* (= *ciemność*) shades, darkness. **5.** *sztuka* (= *półcień*) shadow, shade; **cienie pod oczami** dark rings under the eyes; **blaski i cienie** advantages and disadvantages. **6.** (*kosmetyk*) **cień do powiek** eye shadow. **7.** (= *kształt, sylwetka*) silhouette. **8.** (= *zjawa, duch*) shade, shadow, ghost; **cienie przodków** shades (*of ancestors*), manes; **kraina cieni** *mit.* (*świat zamieszkały przez zmarłych*) the shades, Hades; (*pośmiertna kraina błogosławionych*) Elysium, Elysian fields; **cienie elizejskie** *mit.* Elysian shades; **wyglądać jak cień** *l.* **być cieniem samego siebie** be a ghost of one's former self.

ciepać *ipf.*, **ciepnąć** *pf.* **-pię -piesz** *pot.* (= *rzucać*) fling, hurl (*czymś l. coś* sth).

ciepełko *n.* warmth.

cieplarnia *f. Gen.pl.* **-i** *l.* **-ń** *ogr.* greenhouse, hothouse.

cieplarniany *a.* **1.** (*uprawy, kwiaty, rośliny*) greenhouse; **efekt cieplarniany** greenhouse effect. **2.** *przen.* (= *wygodny, komfortowy*) comfortable, favorable; **cieplarniane warunki życia** comfortable living conditions.

cieplica *f.* hot spring.

cieplny *a. fiz., techn.* thermal, thermic; **energia cieplna** thermal energy; **izolacja cieplna** thermal insulation; **obróbka cieplna** heat treatment.

cieplutki *a.* **1.** (= *bardzo ciepły*) warm. **2.** (*mieszkanie, sweter, czapka*) warm.

ciepławy *a.* lukewarm, tepid.

ciepło[1] *n. Gen.pl.* **-peł 1.** warmth. **2.** (= *ciepła pogoda*) warm weather. **3.** *fiz.* heat; **ciepło atomowe** atomic heat; **ciepło parowania** heat of vaporization *l.* evaporation; **ciepło spalania** heat of combustion; **ciepło topnienia** heat of fusion; **ciepło właściwe** specific heat; **przewodnictwo** *l.* **przewodzenie ciepła** heat *l.* thermal conduction.

ciepło[2] *adv.* **1.** (= *między gorącem a zimnem*) warmly; **robi się ciepło** it is getting warm; **jest ciepło** it is warm; **było mi ciepło** I was warm; **ciepło, cieplej, gorąco!** (*w zabawie*) You're warm. You're getting warmer. You're hot. **2.** *przen.* (= *serdecznie*) warmly; **trzymaj się ciepło** take good care of yourself. **3.** *przen.* (*o uczuciach*) warmly; **robi mi się ciepło na duszy** *l.* **w sercu** *l.* **na sercu** it warms my soul, it warms the cockles of my heart. **4.** (*brzmieć*) nicely. **5.** *przen., pot.* (= *niebezpiecznie*) dangerously. **6.** (*o chronieniu się przed zimnem*) warmly; **ubierać się ciepło** wear warm clothes.

ciepłochłonny *a.* heat-absorbing.

ciepłokrwisty *a. zool.* warm-blooded; homoiothermic, homoiothermal.

ciepłolecznictwo *n. med.* thermotherapy.

ciepłolubny *a. biol.* thermophilic.

ciepłomierz *mi Gen.* **-a** *techn.* calorimeter.

ciepłota *f.* temperature.

ciepłownia *f. Gen.pl.* **-i** *techn.* heat-generating plant.

ciepłownictwo *n. techn.* heat engineering.

ciepły *a.* **1.** (*mający wysoką temperaturę*) warm; **ciepłe barwy** *l.* **kolory** warm colors *l.* hues; **ciepłe kraje** southern *l.* warm climes; **dać coś**

ciepłą ręką (= *dać hojnie*) be generous; **coś rozchodzi się jak ciepłe bułki** *l.* **bułeczki** *pot.* sth sells *l.* goes like hot cakes; **ciepłe kluski** *l.* **kluchy** *pot.* sluggard. **2.** *przen.* (= *serdeczny, przyjazny, życzliwy*) warm. **3.** *przen.* (*o dźwięku*) nice. **4.** *pot., przen.* (= *intratny*) profitable, rich; **ciepła posadka** cushy job. **5.** (*chroniący przed zimnem*) warm.

ciepnąć *pf.* **-ij** *zob.* **ciepać.**

ciernik *ma icht.* three-spined stickleback (*Gasterosteus aculeatus*); **trznadel ciernik** *orn.* cirl bunting (*Emberiza cirlus*).

cierniowy *a.* **1.** (= *kolczasty*) thorny; **korona cierniowa** *rel.* crown of thorns; **róża cierniowa** *bot.* dog rose (*Rosa canina*); **cierniowa korona** *zool.* crown-of-thorns starfish (*Acanthaster planci*). **2.** *przen.* (= *bolesny*) thorny.

ciernisty *a.* = **cierniowy.**

cierny *a. techn.* frictional.

cierń *mi Gen.* **-a** *Gen.pl.* **-i** *l.* **-ów** *bot., przen., pot.* thorn.

cierpiący *a.* (*dręczony chorobą*) suffering, ailing, unwell. – *mp* (*fizycznie i psychicznie*) sufferer; (*fizycznie*) ill person, patient.

cierpieć *ipf.* **-ę -isz 1.** (= *doznawać bólu*) suffer; **cierpieć z jakiegoś powodu** suffer because of sth. **2.** (= *chorować na coś*) suffer, be in pain; **cierpieć na bezsenność** suffer from insomnia; **cierpieć na brak czegoś** lack sth. **3.** (= *tolerować*) suffer, tolerate. **4.** (*zawsze z przeczeniem*) (= *nienawidzić*) hate, detest, suffer; **nie cierpię głupców** I hate fools, I do not suffer fools; **sprawa niecierpiąca zwłoki** urgent matter. **5.** (= *tracić*) suffer, lose; **cierpią na tym moje interesy** my business is suffering from it.

cierpienie *n.* (*psychiczne, fizyczne, moralne, duchowe*) suffering; **znosić cierpienia** suffer, be in pain; **przysparzać komuś cierpień** inflict suffering on sb.

cierpiętnictwo *n.* martyrdom.

cierpiętniczy *a.* martyrly.

cierpiętnik *mp* sufferer, martyr.

cierpkawy *a.* **1.** (*o smaku*) tartish. **2.** (*o zapachu*) acridish.

cierpki *a.* **1.** (*o smaku*) (= *kwaskowaty*) tart. **2.** (*o zapachu*) (= *drażniący*) acrid, rank. **3.** *przen.* (= *przykry, zgryźliwy*) tart, acrid; **cierpkie słowa** harsh words, acrid remarks.

cierpko *adv.* **1.** (= *kwaskowato*) tartly. **2.** (= *drażniąco*) acridly. **3.** *przen.* (= *ostro, zgryźliwie*) tartly, acridly.

cierpkość *f.* **1.** (= *kwaskowatość*) tartness. **2.** (*wrażenie wywołane przez zapach*) acridity. **3.** *przen.* (= *zgryźliwość*) tartness, acridity.

cierpliwie *adv.* patiently.

cierpliwość *f.* (= *opanowanie, wytrwałość*) patience; **anielska cierpliwość** the patience of an angel, endless *l.* inexhaustible *l.* infinite patience; **trzeba mieć anielską cierpliwość, żeby przez pół roku pisać doktorat po dziesięć godzin dziennie** it takes the patience of an angel to write one's Ph.D. for ten hours a day for half a year, day in and day out; **stracić do kogoś cierpliwość** lose one's patience with sb, run out of patience with sb; **jestem u kresu cierpliwości** my patience is wearing thin; **uzbroić się w cierpliwość** summon up one's patience.

cierpliwy *a.* patient.

cierpnąć *ipf.* **-ij**; **-pł** *l.* **-pnął, -pła -pli** (*o skórze*) get the creeps; (*o kończynach*) become *l.* grow numb; **skóra na kimś cierpnie** *przen.* sth makes one's flesh creep.

ciesak *mi Gen.* **-a** *techn.* adz, adze.

ciesielka *f. techn.* carpentry.

ciesielski *a.* carpenter's; **ołówek ciesielski** *techn.* carpenter's pencil.

ciesielstwo *n.* carpentry.

cieszyć *ipf.* (= *rozweselać*) make glad, gladden, delight; **bardzo mnie to cieszy** I am pleased with it, I am glad about it, I am delighted with it. **~ się** *ipf.* (= *radować się*) be pleased, be delighted (*z czegoś* with sth); be glad, be happy (*z czegoś* about sth); **cieszyć się na coś** look forward to sth; **cieszyć się jak dziecko** be as happy as a clam at hightide; *Br.* be happy as a sandboy *l.* Larry; **cieszyć się czymś** enjoy sth; **cieszyć się jak nagi w pokrzywach** *iron.* be pleased *l.* delighted *l.* happy for no apparent reason; **nic mnie nie cieszy** nothing is fun any more.

cieście *f. zob.* **ciasto.**

cieśla *mp Gen.pl.* **-i** *l.* **-ów** carpenter; **cieśla okrętowy** *żegl.* shipwright.

cieślarnia *f. Gen.pl.* **-i** *l.* **-ń** carpenter's shop.

cieśnina *f. geogr.* strait, straits, sound; **Cieśnina Kaletańska** the Straits of Dover.

cietrzew *ma* **-wi-** *orn.* black grouse; *Br. t.* black game (*Lyrurus tetrix*); **toki cietrzewi** grouses' mating rites.

cię *pron. zob.* **ty.**

cięcie *n.* **1.** (= *rozcięcie*) cut, cutting; **cesarskie cięcie** *med.* Cesarean section, Cesarean, *Br.* Caesarean section, Caesarean. **2.** (= *cios, uderzenie*) lash, slash, cut. **3.** (= *skaleczenie*) cut, gash, slash. **4.** (*kryształu, diamentu*) cut. **5.** *przen.* (= *redukcja świadczeń*) cut; **cięcia budżetowe** *l.* **w budżecie** budget cuts. **6.** *kino* (= *moment zmiany obrazu*) cut. **7.** (= *wycinanie drzew*) felling. **8.** *ogr.* pruning, trimming. **9.** *techn.* (= *dzielenie*) cutting; **cięcie mechaniczne/termiczne** mechanical/thermal cutting.

cięciwa *f.* **1.** (*w łuku*) bowstring. **2.** *mat., geom.* chord.

cięgi *pl. Gen.* **-ów 1.** *pot.* (= *kara cielesna*) (*rękami*) spanking; (*biczem, batem*) flogging; **dostać cięgi** be spanked, be flogged; **spuścić komuś cięgi** spank sb, flog sb. **2.** *przen.* (= *porażka, kłopoty*) beating.

cięgło *n. Gen.pl.* **-gieł** *techn.* link, pull rod.

cięgno *n. Gen.pl.* **-gien** *techn.* flexible connector, tension member.

cięła *itd. ipf. zob.* **ciąć.**

ciętość *f.* **1.** (= *zjadliwość, uszczypliwość*) cuttingness. **2.** (= *złość*) anger. **3.** (= *zawziętość*) doggedness, tenacity. **4.** (= *bitność*) *rzad.* bravery, valor.

cięty *a.* **1.** (= *uszczypliwy, zjadliwy*) cutting, biting. **2.** *pot.* (= *zagniewany, zły*) angry, cross.

3. *pot.* (= *zawzięty*) dogged, tenacious. 4. cut; **kwiaty cięte** cut flowers.

ciężar *mi* 1. (= *waga*) weight. 2. *fiz.* mass, weight; **ciężar atomowy** atomic weight; **ciężar cząsteczkowy** molecular weight; **ciężar pozorny** apparent weight; **ciężar właściwy** specific gravity; **ciężar gatunkowy** *przen.* importance. 3. (= *obciążenie, bagaż*) load, burden, weight; **uginać się pod ciężarem** be overburdened; **podnoszenie ciężarów** *sport* weightlifting. 4. *przen.* (= *brzemię*) burden; **być dla kogoś ciężarem** be a burden on *l.* to sb; **zdjąć** *l.* **zrzucić ciężar z serca** *l.* **z głowy** *l.* **z myśli** take a load off sb's mind, set one's heart at rest. 5. (*zwykle pl.*) (= *obowiązki*) responsibilities, duties; (= *podatki*) taxes.

ciężarek *mi* -rk- *Gen.* -a 1. (*metalowy, ołowiany*) weight; (*u wędki*) sinker; (*sondy*) plummet. 2. (= *odważnik*) weight. 3. *sport* weight, dumbbell.

ciężarna *a.* pregnant, gravid. – *f. Gen.* -ej pregnant woman, expectant mother.

ciężarowiec *mp* -wc- *Voc.* -u *l.* -cze *pl.* -y *sport* weightlifter.

ciężarowy *a.* 1. (*związany z ciężarem*) (of) weight. 2. (*do przewożenia towarów*) **pojazd** *l.* **samochód ciężarowy** truck; *Br.* **transport ciężarowy** truck transport; *Br.* lorry transport. 3. *sport* weightlifting.

ciężarówka *f. Gen.pl.* -ek *mot.* truck; *Br.* lorry.

ciężki *a.* -ższy 1. (*o dużym ciężarze*) heavy; **przemysł ciężki** heavy industry; **ciężka artyleria** *wojsk.* heavy artillery; **ciężka woda** *chem.* heavy water; **metale ciężkie** *fiz.* heavy metals; **ciężka atletyka** *sport* wrestling and weightlifting; **waga ciężka** *sport* heavyweight; **ciężkie pieniądze** *pot.* big money; **ciężki frajer** *pot.* sucker; **do ciężkiej cholery** *pot.* damn it, dammit. 2. *przen.* (= *ociężały, powolny*) heavy, slow; **ktoś ciężki do czegoś** sb clumsy at sth; **ktoś ciężki w czymś** sb slow at *l.* in sth. 3. *przen.* (*zawiły l. nieprzejrzysty styl, tekst, książka, dowcip*) heavy. 4. *przen.* (= *mocny*) heavy; **ciężki sen** heavy slumber, deep sleep; **mieć ciężką rękę** (= *bić mocno*) hit hard; **mieć ciężką rękę do czegoś** (= *źle sobie radzić*) be heavy-handed in sth, be clumsy at sth; **rządzić ciężką ręką** (= *rządzić twardo*) rule with a heavy hand, rule heavy-handedly. 5. *przen.* (= *trudny*) heavy, hard; **ciężkie życie** hard life; **ciężkie roboty** hard labor; **ciężkie więzienie** maximum security prison; **ciężki kawałek chleba** hard-earned money; **ciężka atmosfera** tense atmosphere. 6. *przen.* (= *przytłaczający*) (*o zmartwieniu, stracie, kłopocie*) serious, grave; **ciężka żałoba** deep mourning; **z ciężkim sercem** with a heavy heart, most reluctantly. 7. *med.* (*o chorobie, stanie itp.*) serious; **ciężka choroba** serious illness; **ciężka operacja** major operation; **stan ciężki** serious condition, critical condition. 8. (= *ciężkostrawny*) heavy.

ciężko *adv.* -żej 1. (*z obciążeniem*) heavily; **komuś jest ciężko** (= *ktoś niesie coś ciężkiego*) sb is carrying a heavy load; (= *ktoś ma problemy*) sb is having a hard time. 2. (= *powolnie, ociężale*) heavily, slowly. 3. *przen.* (= *niezręcznie, nie-*

udolnie) clumsily. 4. (*o ubieraniu się*) (= *grubo*) warmly; **ciężko ubrany** warmly dressed. 5. (= *z trudem*) with difficulty. 6. (= *bardzo, w najwyższym stopniu*) severely, badly; **ciężko uszkodzony** badly damaged. 7. (= *niekorzystnie, niełatwo*) hard. 8. *med.* (*niebezpiecznie dla życia i zdrowia*) seriously; **ciężko chory** seriously ill.

ciężkostrawny *a.* heavy.

ciężkość *f.* 1. *fiz.* gravity, weight; **siła ciężkości** gravity; **środek** *l.* **punkt ciężkości** center of gravity. 2. (= *opieszałość*) slowness, heaviness. 3. *przen.* (= *zawiłość, nieprzejrzystość*) obscurity, difficulty.

cinerama *f. kino* Cinerama®.

cinkciarski *a. pot.* (black market) money changer's.

cinkciarz *mp pot.* black market money changer.

ciocia *f. Voc.* -u aunt, auntie; **gdyby ciocia miała wąsy, toby był wujek** if ifs and ands were pots and pans, there'd be no work for tinkers' hands; **przyszywana ciocia** distant aunt (*a close friend of the family often referred to as 'auntie'*).

ciołek *ma* -łk- *pot.* (= *byczek*) bullock. – *mp* -łk- *pl.* -i *pot., pog.* (= *głupek*) shit-for-brains, moron, dork.

cios *mi* 1. (= *uderzenie*) blow, stroke, hit; **zadać ostateczny cios** deal a decisive blow; **jednym ciosem** at one go; **cios poniżej pasa** low blow; **zadać komuś/czemuś cios** *przen.* deal sb/sth a blow, destroy sb/sth; **iść za ciosem** follow through (on) sth, finish what one has started. 2. *techn.* ashlar, ashler. 3. *geol.* joint. 4. **ciosy** *zool.* (= *kły*) tusks. 5. *przen.* (= *nieszczęście*) blow.

ciosać *ipf.* -am -asz *l.* -szę -szesz, -aj *l.* -sz hew, carve; **ciosać komuś kołki na głowie** bug sb, nag at sb; **grubo ciosany** *t. przen.* rough-hewn, crude.

ciosak *mi Gen.* -a *techn.* pick.

ciosowy *a.* 1. (*wykonany z ciosanego kamienia lub drewna*) hewn, carved; **mur ciosowy** ashlar. 2. *geol.* joint.

ciota *f.* 1. (*o kobiecie*) witch, hag. 2. *pog., wulg.* (= *homoseksualista*) fag, faggot. 3. *pot.* (*miesiączka*) period; **mieć ciotę** be on the rag.

cioteczny *a.* 1. **cioteczny brat** *l.* **siostra** cousin, first cousin, cousin-german. 2. **cioteczny dziadek** great-uncle, granduncle; **cioteczna babka** great-aunt, grandaunt.

ciotka *f. Gen.pl.* -ek 1. (= *ciocia*) aunt. 2. *pot.* (= *miesiączka*) period.

cip, cip *int.* (*do drobiu*) cluck, cluck.

cipa *f. wulg.* 1. (*o organie*) cunt. 2. (*o kobiecie*) *pog.* bitch; **ty głupia cipo!** you stupid bitch! 3. (*o mężczyźnie*) *pog.* wanker; **ale z ciebie cipa grochowa!** gee, the sad wanker that you are!

cipka *f. Gen.pl.* -ek *wulg.* pussy.

circa *adv.* (= *około*) circa, about.

cis[1] *mi Gen.* -u *l.* -a 1. *bot.* yew (*Taxus baccata*). 2. (*drewno*) yew.

cis[2] *n. indecl. muz.* C sharp; **cis-moll** C sharp minor.

cisawy *a.* (*o maści konia*) chestnut.

ciskać *ipf.* 1. (= *rzucać*) fling, hurl, cast; **ci-**

skać groszem *l.* pieniędzmi fling money around, spend money like water; **ciskać klątwy na kogoś/coś** put a curse on sb/sth; **ciskać przekleństwa na kogoś/coś** swear at sb/sth, curse at sb/sth; **ciskać obelgi na kogoś** hurl abuse at sb, shower abuse on sb; **ciskać gromy** *l.* **pioruny na kogoś/coś** *przen.* thunder against sb/sth; **cisnąć komuś rękawicę** throw down the gauntlet to sb. 2. (= *wyrzucać*) throw away; **cisnąć w kąt** cast aside, abandon. ~ **się** *ipf.* 1. fling o.s. 2. *pot.* fume.

cisnąć¹ *ipf.* **cisnę ciśniesz, -ij** 1. (= *naciskać*) press, push. 2. (*o ubraniu*) (= *uwierać*) pinch. 3. *przen.* (= *nalegać*) insist. 4. *przen.* (= *gnębić*) pester, trouble.

cisnąć² *pf.* **cisnę ciśniesz, -ij** *zob.* **ciskać**. ~ **się** *ipf.* (*wokół czegoś*) swarm around; (*do czegoś, gdzieś*) push one's way; **cisnąć się do wyjścia** push one's way to the exit.

cisowy *a.* yew.

cisza *f.* 1. (*brak dźwięków*) silence, stillness, quiet; **cisza nocna** curfew; **cisza informacyjna** information gap, lack of information; **cisza w eterze** *pot.* (there's) no word about sb *l.* sth; **śmiertelna** *l.* **martwa** *l.* **głucha** *l.* **cmentarna** *l.* **głęboka cisza** dead *l.* stony silence; **cisza jak makiem zasiał** dead *l.* stony silence. 2. (*o atmosferze*) (= *bezruch*) calm, stillness, lull; **cisza na morzu** calm sea, lull; **cisza przed burzą** *przen.* lull before the storm. 3. *przen.* quiet, tranquility; **spokojne życie** tranquil life. 4. *przen.* (= *pokój, rozejm*) quiet, peace. 5. *przen.* (= *wewnętrzny spokój*) tranquility, peace of mind. – *int.* silence!, quiet!, hush!

ciszej *adv. zob.* **cicho**.

ciśnienie *n.* 1. *fiz.* pressure; **ciśnienie atmosferyczne** *l.* **ciśnienie powietrza** *meteor.* atmospheric pressure, barometric pressure; **wieża ciśnień** *techn.* water tower; **niskie** *l.* **wysokie ciśnienie** *pot.* high *l.* low pressure. 2. *med.* blood pressure; **ciśnienie krwi** blood pressure; **ciśnienie tętnicze** arterial blood pressure; **ciśnienie rozkurczowe** diastolic pressure; **ciśnienie skurczowe** systolic pressure; **mieć wysokie/niskie/podwyższone ciśnienie** have high/low/raised *l.* increased pressure. 3. *przen.* (= *wpływ, napór*) pressure, tension.

ciśnieniomierz *mi Gen.* **-a** *techn.* pressure gauge, manometer.

ciśnieniowy *a. fiz.*, *techn.* pressure; **aparat ciśnieniowy** autoclave.

ciuch *mi Gen.* **-a** *pot.* (= *część ubrania*) 1. garb, togs; (= *używane ubranie*) secondhand garment. 2. *zob.* **ciuchy**.

ciuchcia *f. pot.*, *żart.* steam-engine train.

ciucholand *mi pot.* secondhand clothes shop.

ciuchy *pl. Gen.* **-ów** *pot.* (*sklep*) secondhand clothes shop, (clothes) thrift shop; (*targ*) secondhand clothes market.

ciuciubabka *f.* 1. (*gra dziecięca*) blindman's buff, blindman's bluff; **grać w ciuciubabkę** play blindman's buff. 2. *pot.* (*działanie na ślepo*) acting blindfold, being in the dark; **grać z kimś w ciuciubabkę** pull the wool over sb's eyes.

ciućma *f. l. mp decl. like f. Gen.pl.* **-m** *l.* **-ów** *pot.* sluggard.

ciul *mp Gen.pl.* **-i** *l.* **-ów** *pog.* sucker, loser.

ciułacz *mp Gen.pl.* **-y** *l.* **-ów** saver, moneygrubber; **drobni ciułacze** petty savers, small-time moneygrubbers.

ciułać *ipf.* save, put aside (for the rainy day); **ciułać grosz do grosza** scrape (money) up *l.* together.

ciupa *f.* 1. *pot.* (= *klitka*) hovel. 2. *pot.* (= *więzienie*) clink, coop, pen, can; **iść do ciupy** get cooped up, get penned, get canned; **siedzieć w ciupie** do *l.* serve time.

ciupaga *f.* axe-like staff, alpenstock (*used by Polish highlanders*).

ciupasem *adv. przest.* under supervision, under guard.

ciupka *f. Gen.pl.* **-ek** (= *klitka*) hovel.

ciura *m. pl.* **-y** *Gen.* **-ów** *l.* **-r** *hist.* camp follower.

ciurczeć *ipf.* **-y** = **ciurkać**.

ciurkać *ipf.* 1. (= *ciec*) trickle, drip; **ciurkać z czegoś** trickle from sth; **ciurkać po czymś** trickle down sth. 2. (*o ptaku*) (= *ćwierkać*) chirp.

ciurkiem *adv.* (*o płynie*) *t. przen.* nonstop, continuously; **łzy płyną ciurkiem po jej policzkach** tears are trickling down her cheeks.

ciurkotać *ipf.* = **ciurkać**.

ciuszek *mi* **-szk-** *Gen.* **-a** *pot.* threads, togs.

ciut *adv.* (= *niewiele*) a (tiny little) bit (*czegoś* of sth).

cizia *f. pot.* chick; **szałowa** *l.* **fajna cizia** cool *l.* awesome chick; **poderwać cizię** pick up a chick.

ciżba *f.* crowd, throng.

ciżemka *f. Gen.pl.* **-ek** *arch.* = **ciżma**.

ciżma *f. Gen.pl.* **-żem** *l.* **-żm** *arch., hist.* shoe (*typical 12th to 15th century footwear*).

ckliwie *adv.* 1. (= *tkliwie, tęsknie*) sentimentally. 2. (= *mdło*) nauseatingly, sickeningly.

ckliwość *f.* 1. (= *sentymentalność*) sentimentality. 2. (= *uczucie mdłości*) nauseousness.

ckliwy *a.* 1. (= *sentymentalny*) sentimental. 2. (= *mdlący*) nauseating, sickening.

cle *n. zob.* **cło**.

clić *ipf.* **clij** *ekon.* clear.

clip *mi pot.* video, music video.

cło *n. Gen.pl.* **ceł** *ekon.* duty; **obłożyć coś clem** impose a duty on sth; **zwolnić coś z cła** exempt sth from duty; **cło wywozowe** *l.* **eksportowe** export duty; **cło przywozowe** *l.* **importowe** import duty; **cła preferencyjne** preference *l.* preferential duty; **cło fiskalne** financial duty.

cm *abbr.* cm (= *centimeter*).

cmentarnie *adv. przen.* gloomily, grimly.

cmentarny *a.* 1. (*kaplica, krzyż, brama*) graveyard, cemetery. 2. *przen.* (= *ponury*) gloomy, grim; **cmentarna cisza** dead silence.

cmentarz *mi Gen.* **-a** 1. (*miejsce wiecznego spoczynku*) cemetery, graveyard. 2. *hist.* (= *dziedziniec kościelny*) churchyard.

cmentarzyk *mi Gen.* **-a** (small) cemetery, (small) graveyard.

cmentarzysko *n.* 1. *hist.* (= *cmentarz pogański*) burial ground. 2. *przen.* (*zbiorowisko sta-*

rych przedmiotów) graveyard; **trafić na cmenta-rzysko historii** be tossed into the dustbin of history.

cmok *int.* smack.

cmokać *ipf.* **1.** (= *rozsmakowywać się, mla-skać*) smack; **cmokać z podziwu** *l.* **z zachwytu** smack one's lips; **cmokać fajkę** suck on a pipe. **2.** *pot.* (= *całować*) smack.

cmokier *mp pot., pog.* adulator, flatterer.

cmoknąć *pf.* **-ij** *zob.* **cmokać**.

cmoknięcie *n.* **1.** (= *mlaśnięcie*) smack. **2.** *żart.* (= *pocałunek*) peck, smack.

cmoktać *ipf.* **1.** (= *smakować, mlaskać*) smack. **2.** (= *sączyć, siorbać*) slurp, suck. **3.** (= *ssać słodycze*) suck. **4.** (= *palić fajkę, cygaro*) suck. **5.** *przn.* (= *całować*) smack.

cnota *f. Gen.pl.* **cnót** **1.** *fil.* virtue; **wzór cnoty** paragon of virtue; **iść drogą cnoty** follow a path of virtue; **sprowadzić kogoś z drogi cnoty** make sb stray from the right path; **chodząca cnota** *przen.* model of virtue, righteous person; **prawdziwa cnota krytyk się nie boi** *l.* true virtue is not afraid of *l.* touched by criticism. **2.** *lit.* (= *zaleta*) virtue; **to jest cnota nad cnotami trzymać język za zębami** a still tongue makes a wise head; keep your tongue between your teeth. **3.** *lit.* (= *dziewictwo*) virginity, virtue.

cnotka *f. Gen.pl.* **-ek** **1.** *iron.* (= *skromnisia*) modest girl *l.* woman. **2.** *pot., iron.* (= *dziewica*) virgin.

cnotliwie *adv.* **1.** (= *etycznie, pobożnie*) chastely. **2.** (= *skromnie*) modestly.

cnotliwość *f.* **1.** (= *czystość, niewinność*) chastity, virtue. **2.** *przest.* (= *szlachetność*) virtue.

cnotliwy *a.* **1.** (= *prawy, moralny*) virtuous. **2.** (= *skromny, wstydliwy*) virtuous, chaste.

c.o. *abbr. pot.* (= *centralne ogrzewanie*) central heating.

co *pron. Gen.* **czego** *Dat.* **czemu** *Ins. i Loc.* **czym** **1.** (*zastępuje rzeczowniki*) what; **rób, co chcesz** do what you want; **czego (znowu) chcesz?** what do you want (now)?; *zwł. z irytacją* what is it that you want (now)?; **co to będzie?** (= *co chcesz zrobić?*) what is it going to be?, what'll it be?; (= *co się stanie?*) what'll happen?; **po co?** what for?; **byle co** anything; **Bóg wie co** God knows what; **diabli wiedzą co** only the Devil knows; **co to, to nie** I won't have that; **jeszcze czego!** anything else?, what('s) next?; **bądź co bądź** anyway; **w czym rzecz** what's the matter; **w razie czego** (just) in case, if need(s) be; **jak przyjdzie co do czego** when the chips are down; **nie ma co!** there is no point; **co komu do tego?** it is none of anybody's business, why should it be anyone's business?, why should they care?; **co mi tam!** I don't care, I couldn't care less, who cares?; **co będzie, to będzie** happen what may; **będzie co ma być** what is to be, will be; what must be, must be; what will be, will be; **co było, a nie jest, nie pisze się w rejestr** let bygones be bygones; **co z oczu, to z serca** out of sight, out of mind; **co się stało, to się nie odstanie** what's been

done cannot be undone, let bygones be bygones; **co za dużo, to niezdrowo** too much of a good thing, too much breaks the bag; **co się odwlecze, to nie uciecze** there is luck in leisure; **co ma wisieć, nie utonie** he that is born to be hanged shall never be drowned, if you're born to be hanged then you'll never be drowned; **co nagle, to po diable** haste makes waste; **czym chata bogata, tym rada** what's mine is yours; **co ma piernik do wiatraka** what do these two things have in common?, it is quite beside the point. **2.** (*jako zaimek względny, głównie w pytaniach i zdaniach złożonych*) **co tchu** at full *l.* top speed, in all haste; **tyle, co kot napłakał** next to nothing; **co do grosza** not a penny less, not a penny more; **tyle pomoże, co umarłemu kadzidło** it won't do any good, it won't help at all. – *conj.* (*rozpoczyna zdanie podrzędne*) which. – *part.* **1.** (*wyraża powtarzalność*) every; **co krok** every step; **co godzina/co chwila/co miesiąc/co roku** every hour/every moment/every month/every year; **co prawda** admittedly; **co prawda, to prawda** you're right; **co rusz** every moment, every time; **na co dzień** every day; **co i raz** *pot.* every moment, every time; **co kraj, to obyczaj** every country has its customs; every land has its own law; so many countries, so many customs. **2.** (*wzmacnia przysłówki*) what, still; **co gorsza** what's worse, worse still; **co więcej** what's more; **co dwie głowy, to nie jedna** two heads are better than one. **3.** (*wyraża pytanie o przyczynę, cel*) why; **co się tak długo zastanawiasz?** why have you been dwelling on it so long?

coca-cola *f.* (*napój*) Coca-Cola®.

cocker-spaniel *ma kynol.* cocker spaniel.

codziennie *adv.* **1.** (= *każdego dnia*) every day, daily. **2.** (= *zwyczajnie*) *rzad.* usually, normally.

codzienność *f.* everyday life; **szara codzienność** everyday, hum-drum existence; cheerless, day to day grind.

codzienny *a.* **1.** (= *regularny*) everyday, daily; **artykuły codziennego użytku** necessities; **chleb codzienny** maintenance, livelihood. **2.** (= *powszedni, zwykły*) everyday, common; *form.* quotidian; **życie codzienne** everyday life; **codzienny strój** everyday clothes.

cofacz *mi Gen.* **-a** *komp.* backspace.

cofać *ipf.,* **cofnąć** *pf.* **-ij** **1.** (*przemieszczać ku tyłowi*) back (up), reverse, move *l.* pull *l.* draw back; **cofać zegarek** put back the clock *l.* watch. **2.** (= *wstrzymać, unieważnić*) withdraw, cancel, revoke; **cofnąć prawo jazdy** revoke a *l.* sb's driver's license; **cofnęli mi prawo jazdy** I had my driving licence revoked; **cofnąć zarządzenie** cancel *l.* revoke a regulation; **cofnąć wniosek** withdraw a motion; **cofam to** (*co powiedziałem*) I take it back. **~ się** *ipf.* **1.** (*przemieszczać się w tył*) back (up), move back; **cofać się myślą** *l.* **pamięcią do czegoś** go back to sth; **coś się komuś cofa** (*o pokarmie*) sth makes sb gag. **2.** *przen.* (= *ustępować, wycofywać się, zanikać*) recede, retire; **cofać się w rozwoju** regress. **3.** (= *uchylać się, po-*

wstrzymywać się) refrain (*przed czymś* from sth); **nie cofać się przed niczym** stop at nothing, go to any length(s).

cogodzinny *a.* hourly.

cokolwiek *pron.* **co-** *decl. like* **co, -kolwiek** *indecl.* **1.** (*zastępuje rzeczowniki*) anything; **(po prostu) zrób cokolwiek** (just) do anything. **2.** (*wprowadza zdanie podrzędne*) whatever; **cokolwiek się stanie, na pewno nie wyjadę** whatever happens I will not leave. – *adv.* a little; **przydałoby się cokolwiek więcej czasu** one could do with a little (bit) more time.

cokół *mi* **-o-** **1.** *bud.* (= *podstawa, podnóże*) base, pedestal; **cokół kontynentalny** *geol.* continental block *l.* mass. **2.** *bud.* (*postument pomnika*) pedestal. **3.** *el., techn.* socket.

cola *f. Gen.pl.* **-i** *pot.* (*napój*) Coke, cola.

comber *mi* **-br-** *Gen.* **-a** (*mięso*) saddle.

comiesięczny *a.* monthly.

conocny *a.* nightly.

consensus *mi* (= *porozumienie, zgoda powszechna*) *polit.* consensus.

copy writer *mp* copywriter.

coraz *part.* **1.** (*wyraża narastanie*) **coraz ładniejszy** prettier and prettier, nicer and nicer; **coraz szybszy** faster and faster; **coraz głośniejszy** louder and louder; **coraz bardziej** more and more; **coraz więcej** more and more; **coraz lepiej** better and better. **2.** (*wyraża powtarzalność*) repeatedly; **coraz to...** every now and again; **coraz powtarza** he keeps repeating.

corocznie *adv.* yearly, every year; annually.

coroczny *a.* yearly, annual.

correct *a. indecl.* correct, proper.

corrida *f. zob.* **korrida**.

cosinus *mi zob.* **kosinus**.

coś *pron.* **co-** *decl. zob.* **co, -ś** *indecl.* (*zastępuje rzeczownik*) (*w zdaniach twierdzących*) something; (*w zdaniach przeczących*) anything; **daj mi coś** give me something; **coś innego** something else; **coś do jedzenia** something to eat; **coś do pisania** something to write with; **coś w tym jest** there's something to it; **coś podobnego!** incredible!, is that so?; **coś ci powiem** I'll tell you what; **dojść do czegoś** (= *dotrzeć do jakiegoś miejsca*) reach sth; (= *osiągnąć pieniądze, sławę, prestiż itp.*) attain wealth, fame and prestige; **ona ma coś w sobie** there's something about her; **mieć coś do kogoś** have a problem with sb; **coś komuś leży na sercu** *l.* **wątrobie** sb has got a problem with sth; **coś tu jest nie tak** there's something wrong here, something is not quite right here; **coś ty?** you've got to be kidding. – *part.* something, somewhat, somehow; **coś mi tu nie pasuje** there's something wrong here, something is not quite right here, there seems to be something wrong here.

cotygodniowo *adv.* weekly, every week.

cotygodniowy *a.* weekly.

country *a. indecl. muz.* country, country music.

córa *f. lit.* daughter; **córa Koryntu** lady of the night.

córeczka *f. Gen.pl.* **-ek** (little) daughter.

córka *f. Gen.pl.* **-ek** daughter; **córka chrzestna** goddaughter.

cóż *pron. Gen.* **czegoż** *l.* **czegóż** *Dat.* **czemuż** *Ins. i Loc.* **czymże** **1.** (*wyraża pytanie*) what; **cóż dopiero** let alone, not to mention; **ale cóż** but. **2.** (*w funkcji względnej*) what; **cóż to za kolega** what kind of friend is he; **cóż to za pogoda** what kind of weather is that. – *part.* (*wyraża wzmocnione pytanie*) why; **cóż tak się na mnie gapisz?** why are you staring *l.* gaping at me like that?

cuchnący *a.* stinking, reeking, foul-smelling.

cuchnąć *ipf.* **-ij** stink, reek; **cuchnąć jak diabli** stink to high heaven; **cuchnie mu z ust** he has bad *l.* foul breath.

cucić *ipf.* revive; rouse (*sb*) (*z czegoś* from sth *l.* out of sth).

cud *mi pl.* **-a** (= *zjawisko nadnaturalne, t. rel.*) miracle; *przen.* (= *zdumiewające zjawisko, rzecz, osoba*) wonder, marvel, miracle, prodigy; **czynić cuda** *l.* **dokonywać cudów** *t. przen.* work *l.* perform *l.* accomplish miracles; *przen.* work marvels, do *l.* work wonders; **siedem cudów świata** the seven wonders of the world; **cud boski** God's miracle; **cud inżynierii** marvel of engineering; **cud natury** wonder of nature; **cud piękności** marvelous beauty; **cud gospodarczy** economic miracle; **to cud, że...** it's a miracle that...; **opowiadać cuda** *iron.* tell fairy stories; **dokonywać** *l.* **dokazywać cudów** do *l.* work wonders *l.* miracles (*za pomocą czegoś* with sth); **ósmy cud świata** *żart. l. iron.* cat's whiskers *l.* pyjamas; **wiara czyni cuda** faith works wonders; **wyrabiać** *l.* **wyczyniać cuda** (= *robić coś dziwnego l. nadzwyczajnego*) do magic tricks (*z czymś* with sth); (= *płatać figle*) play pranks; **nie ma cudów** (= *bądźmy realistami*) let's face it; let's be realistic; *pot.* (= *nie ma obawy*) never fear; **nie ma cudów, musi się udać** I'm sure it can't go wrong; **cuda niewidy** *iron.* the most incredible things; *int.* (and) pigs might fly.

cudacki *a.* = **cudaczny**.

cudactwo *n. uj.* bizarre thing, weirdo.

cudaczka *f. Gen.pl.* **-ek** *zob.* **cudak**.

cudaczny *a.* bizarre, weird, odd, queer.

cudaczyć *ipf.* = **cudować**.

cudak *mp pl.* **-cy** *l.* **-i** *pot.* **1.** (= *dziwak*) oddball, crank, weirdo, odd *l.* queer fish. **2.** (= *osoba o dziwnym wyglądzie*) strange-looking person.

cudem *adv.* miraculously, by (some) miracle.

cudeńko *n. Gen.pl.* **-niek** *emf.* = **cudo** 2.

cudny *a.* (= *piękny, zadziwiający*) gorgeous, marvelous, amazing; (= *przyjemny*) sweet.

cudo *n. Gen.pl.* **-ów** *pot.* **1.** (= *piękna rzecz l. osoba*) beaut, beauty, cute *l.* dandy thing. **2.** (= *osobliwość*) marvel, prodigy.

cudotwórca *mp* **1.** (= *sprawca cudów*) wonderworker; miracle man; *form.* thaumaturge; **nie jestem cudotwórcą** I can't work *l.* perform miracles. **2.** (= *iluzjonista, magik*) magician, conjuror, conjurer.

cudotwórczy *a.* wonderworking; *form.* thaumaturgic, thaumaturgical.

cudotwórczyni *f. zob.* **cudotwórca**.

cudotwórstwo *n.* wonderworking; *form.* thaumaturgy.

cudować *ipf. pot.* fuss (about *l.* around) (*z czymś* with sth).

cudownie *adv.* **1.** (= *cudem*) miraculously; (= *w niezwykły sposób*) amazingly, prodigiously; **cudownie wyzdrowieć** recover miraculously; make a miraculous recovery. **2.** (= *przepięknie, wspaniale*) gorgeously, fabulously; (= *miło, przyjemnie*) sweetly, admirably; **wyglądała cudownie** she looked gorgeous.

cudowny *a.* **1.** (= *nadprzyrodzony*) miraculous, supernatural; (= *niezwykły*) amazing, prodigious; **cudowna moc** supernatural power; **cudowny obraz/wizerunek** miraculous painting/image; **cudowne uzdrowienie** miraculous healing. **2.** (= *przepiękny, wspaniały*) gorgeous, fabulous; (= *śliczny*) cute; (= *miły, przyjemny*) sweet, admirable.

cudzołożnica *f. lit.* adulteress, adulterous woman; *zob.* **cudzołożnik**.

cudzołożnik *mp lit.* adulterer; (*w stylu biblijnym*) fornicator.

cudzołożny *a. lit.* adulterous.

cudzołożyć *ipf.* **-óż** *lit.* commit adultery (*z kimś* with sb); (*w stylu biblijnym*) fornicate.

cudzołóstwo *n. lit.* adultery; (*w stylu biblijnym*) fornicate.

cudzoziemiec *mp* **-mc-** *Voc.* **-cze** *pl.* **-y**, **cudzoziemka** *f. Gen.pl.* **-ek** foreigner, alien.

cudzoziemski *a.* foreign, alien.

cudzoziemskość *f.* foreignness.

cudzoziemszczyzna *f. uj.* foreignism, foreign fashions.

cudzożywność *f. biol.* heterotrophy.

cudzożywny *a. biol.* heterotrophic.

cudzy *a.* **1.** (= *dotyczący l. należący do kogoś innego*) someone else's, somebody else's; (= *dotyczący l. należący do innych ludzi*) other people's; others'; no one's own; **cieszyć się l. śmiać się z cudzego nieszczęścia** rejoice *l.* laugh *l.* gloat at others' misfortunes; **stroić się w cudze piórka** dress *l.* appear in borrowed plumes; **wtrącać się w cudze sprawy** meddle *l.* interfere in other people's affairs; **zabawić się cudzym kosztem** have a laugh at somebody else's expense. **2.** *przest.* (= *obcy, cudzoziemski*) foreign, alien; **cudze chwalicie, swego nie znacie** the grass is (always) greener on the other side.

cudzysłów *mi* **-o-** (*znak interpunkcyjny*) quotation mark; *Br.* inverted comma; (*para znaków*) quotes, (pair of) quotation marks *l. Br.* inverted commas; **cudzysłów otwierający/zamykający** opening/closing quotation mark; **cudzysłów pojedynczy/podwójny** single/double quotes; **otwieram cudzysłów... zamykam cudzysłów** quote... unquote; **w cudzysłowie** in quotes.

cug *mi* **1.** (= *przeciąg, przewiew*) draft, *Br.* draught. **2.** (= *okres nieprzerwanego ulegania nałogowi*) spree; **w cugu alkoholowym** (out) on a (drinking) spree. **3.** *przest., jeźdz.* set of draft horses.

cugle *pl. Gen.* **-i 1.** *jeźdz.* reins (*pl.*); rein; **ściągać cugle** draw rein; **puszczać (koniowi) cugle** give (a horse) the rein *l.* the reins; **krótkie/długie cugle** short/long rein. **2.** *przen.* (= *rygory, ryzy*) **popuścić komuś/czemuś cugli** give sb free rein; **brać kogoś/coś w cugle** *l.* **trzymać kogoś/coś w cuglach** keep a tight rein on sb/sth.

cukier *mi* **-kr- 1.** sugar; *chem., pot.* (= *sacharoza*) saccharose, sucrose; **cukier krzyształ** granulated sugar; **cukier puder** powdered sugar; **cukier w kostkach** lump sugar; **głowa cukru** *przest.* sugar loaf; **cukier w kostkach/kawałkach** cube/lump sugar; **cukier buraczany/trzcinowy/klonowy** beet/cane/maple sugar; **cukier surowy/rafinowany** raw/refined sugar; **cukier waniliowy** vanilla sugar. **2.** *chem.* sugar, saccharide; (= *węglowodan*) carbohydrate; **cukier prosty** simple sugar, monosaccharide; **cukier gronowy** (= *dekstroza*) grape sugar, dextrose; **cukier mlekowy** (= *laktoza*) milk sugar, lactose; **cukier owocowy** (= *fruktoza*) fruit sugar, fructose; **cukier słodowy** (= *maltoza*) malt sugar, maltose. **3.** *pot.* **cukier ołowiany** (= *octan ołowiowy*) sugar of lead.

cukierek *mi* **-rk-** *Gen.* **-a** candy; *Br.* sweet; **cukierek miętowy** mint.

cukierkowaty *a. uj.* = **cukierkowy**.

cukierkowość *f.* sugariness, prettiness; *pot.* cutesiness, goo.

cukierkowy *a. uj.* sugary, pretty-pretty; *pot.* cutesy, icky, gooey.

cukiernia *f. Gen.pl.* **-i** *l.* **-ń 1.** (= *kawiarnia, ciastkarnia*) café. **2.** (= *wytwórnia ciastek i słodyczy*) confectionary; (*sklep*) confectioner's store, candy store, confectionary; *Br.* sweet shop.

cukiernica *f.* sugar bowl.

cukiernictwo *n.* confectionery.

cukierniczka *f. Gen.pl.* **-ek** = **cukiernica**.

cukierniczy *a.* confectioner's, confectionary; **wyroby cukiernicze** confectionery; **zakład cukierniczy** confectionary.

cukiernik *mp* confectioner; (= *ciastkarz*) pastry cook.

cukinia *f. Gen.* **-ii** *kulin.* zucchini; *Br.* courgette.

cukromierz *mi Gen.* **-a** *techn.* saccharometer, saccharimeter.

cukrować *ipf.* (= *pokrywać cukrem*) crystallize, candy.

cukrownia *f. Gen.pl.* **-i** sugar factory.

cukrownictwo *n.* sugar industry.

cukrowy *a.* sugar; **wata cukrowa** candy-floss, cotton candy; **burak cukrowy** *roln.* sugar beet; **groszek cukrowy** *ogr.* mangetout, sugar pea; **jabłko cukrowe** *bot.* sweetsop, sugar apple, custard apple (*Annona squamosa*); **klon cukrowy** *bot.* sugar maple (*Acer saccharum*); **palma cukrowa** *bot.* black sugar palm, gomuti palm (*Arenga pinnata*); **trzcina cukrowa** *bot.* sugar cane (*Saccharum officinarum*); **rybik cukrowy** *ent.* silverfish (*Lepisma saccharina*).

cukrzyca[1] *f. pat.* diabetes; **chory na cukrzycę** *med.* diabetic (case).

cukrzyca[2] *f. cukrownictwo* massecuite.

cukrzycowy *a. med., pat.* diabetic.

cukrzyć *ipf.* (= *słodzić cukrem*) sugar, sweet-

en; (= *konserwować w cukrze*) candy. ~ **się** *ipf.*
turn into sugar; *techn.* saccharify, saccharize.

cukrzyk¹ *mp pot.* diabetic; **czekolada dla cu-**
krzyków diabetic chocolate.

cukrzyk² *ma orn.* (= *nektarnik, rodzina Necta-*
rinidae) sunbird.

cuma *f. żegl.* mooring (line), fast.

cumować *ipf. żegl.* **1.** moor, dock (*sth*) (*do cze-*
goś to sth). **2.** *lotn.* (*o statku kosmicznym*) dock
(*do czegoś* to sth).

cumowisko *n. żegl.* mooring place.

cumownica *f. żegl.* mooring post.

cumowniczy *a. żegl.* mooring; **lina cumownicza**
mooring line; **pachołek cumowniczy** mooring
post; **moduł cumowniczy** *lotn.* docking module.

cumulonimbus *mi Gen.* **-a** *l.* **-u** *meteor.* cumulonimbus (cloud).

cumulus *mi Gen.* **-a** *l.* **-u** *meteor.* cumulus
(cloud).

cumulusowy *a. meteor.* cumulous.

cupnąć *pf.* **-ij** *pot.* squat; *żart.* sit down (*na*
czymś on sth).

curry *n. indecl. kulin.* curry; (*przyprawa*) curry powder; **sos curry** curry sauce.

CV *abbr.* (= *życiorys*) CV (= *curriculum vitae*).

cwał *mi* gallop; **cwałem** *t. przen.* (= *bardzo*
szybko) at a gallop; (at) full gallop.

cwałować *ipf.* **1.** gallop (along); (*o koniu*) go at
a gallop; (*o jeźdźcu*) ride at a gallop, gallop (a
horse). **2.** *żart.* (= *biec bardzo szybko*) gallop,
speed (on *l.* along).

cwaniacki *a. pot.* smartassed.

cwaniactwo *n. pot.* smartness.

cwaniaczek *mp* **-czk-** *pl.* **-i** *pot., pog.* smarty-
pants, smarty-boots, smartass; *Br.* smartarse.

cwaniaczka *f. Gen.pl.* **-ek** *pot.* clever woman,
wiseacre.

cwaniak *mp pl.* **-cy** *l.* **-i** *pot.* wiseacre, smart
alec.

cwaniara *f. pot.* = **cwaniaczka**.

cwany *a.* **-ńszy** smart, clever.

cwel *mp sl., obelż.* fucker.

cybernetyczny *a.* cybernetic.

cybernetyk *mp* cybernetician, cyberneticist.

cybernetyka *f.* cybernetics.

cyberprzestrzeń *f. komp.* cyberspace.

cyberpunkowy *a. teor.lit.* cyberpunk.

cybeta *f. zool.* = cyweta.

cyborg *mi Gen.* **-a** cyborg.

cyborium *n. indecl. in sg. pl.* **-ria** *Gen.* **-riów**
kośc., rel., bud. ciborium.

cybuch *mi Gen.* **-a** (*część fajki*) **1.** (pipe) stem;
(= *cała fajka*) pipe. **2.** *techn.* (*do wydmuchiwa-*
nia szkła) blowpipe.

cyc¹ *mi Gen.* **-a** *wulg.* tit, boob.

cyc² *mi Gen.* **-u** *przest.* (*tkanina*) chintz.

cycata *a. pot.* busty, buxom, big-breasted.

cycek *mi* **-ck-** *Gen.* **-a 1.** *wulg.* = **cyc. 2.** *pot.* (=
sutek kobiety) nipple, breast; **dać dziecku cycka**
give suck to a baby; **dziecko przy cycku** baby at
the breast; **odstawić od cycka** *przen.* wean (*sb*).
3. *pot.* (= *sutek zwierzęcia*) teat.

cycero *mi decl. like n. druk.* (*rozmiar czcion-*
ki) pica.

cyceroński *a. hist., teor.lit.* Ciceronian.

cydr *mi* (= *jabłecznik*) cider.

cyferblat *mi* (clock) face, dial (plate).

cyfra *f.* **1.** (*znak liczby*) figure, digit, numeral;
pot. (= *liczba*) number, figure; **cyfry arabskie/**
rzymskie Arabic/Roman numerals. **2.** *przest.* (=
ozdobny monogram) cypher. **3.** *pl. przest.* (= *o-*
zdobny haft) embroidery.

cyfrować *ipf. przest.* **1.** (= *szyfrować*) encipher, encode. **2.** (= *ozdabiać haftem*) embroider.

cyfrowy *a. el., komp.* **1.** digital. **2. maszyna**
cyfrowa digital computer. **3. nagranie cyfrowe**
digital recording. **4. wskaźnik cyfrowy** digital
display.

Cygan *mp pl.* **-nie** Gypsy, Gipsy; Romany;
(*mężczyzna*) Rom.

cygan *mp pl.* **-nie 1.** *pog.* (= *włóczęga*) gypsy,
hobo, tramp, vagabond. **2.** *przest.* (= *członek cy-*
ganerii artystycznej) Bohemian. **3.** *pot.* (=
oszust, krętacz) cheat, crook, double-dealer,
swindler.

cyganeria *f. Gen.* **-ii** (= *bohema*) Bohemia.

cyganić *ipf. pot. uj.* cheat, deceive.

Cyganka *f. Gen.pl.* **-ek** Romany woman *l.* girl;
zob. **Cygan**.

cyganka *f. Gen.pl.* **-ek 1.** *żart.* (= *brunetka*)
gypsy. **2.** *uj. zob.* **cygan** 3.

cygański *a.* **1.** (= *romski, dotyczący Cyganów*)
Gypsy, Gipsy, Romany; **język cygański** Romany,
Romani. **2.** (*o stylu życia*) gypsy. **3.** (*dotyczący*
cyganerii) Bohemian.

cygaństwo *n. uj.* double-dealing, cheating.

cygaretka *f. Gen.pl.* **-ek** cigarillo.

cygarnica *f.* **1.** (= *pudełko na cygara*) cigar
box, cigar case. **2.** (= *futerał na papierosy*)
cigarette case.

cygarniczka *f. Gen.pl.* **-ek** (*ustnik*) cigar holder.

cygaro *n.* cigar; **sklep z cygarami** cigar store;
zaciągać się cygarem draw on a cigar.

cyjan *mi chem.* cyanogen; (= *dwucyjan*) di-
cyanogen.

cyjanek *mi* **-nk-** *chem.* cyanide; **cyjanek sodu/**
potasu sodium/potassium cyanide.

cyjanian *mi chem.* cyanate.

cyjanina *f. fot.* cyanin, cyanine.

cyjanit *mi min.* cyanite, disthene.

cyjanokobalamina *f. biochem.* cyanocobal-
amin.

cyjanować *ipf. techn.* cyanide.

cyjanowanie *n. techn.* cyaniding.

cyjanowodór *mi* **-o-** *chem.* hydrogen cyanide.

cyjanowy *a. chem.* cyanic.

cyjon *ma zool.* dhole, Cuon alpinus.

cykać *ipf.* **1.** (*o mechanizmie, zegarze*) tick. **2.**
(*o owadach*) chirp, chirr.

cykać się *ipf. sl.* (= *bać się*) be a chicken, be
shit-scared.

cykada *f. ent.* (= *owad z rodziny Cicadidae*) cicada.

cykas *mi Gen.* **-a** *bot.* (= *sagowiec*) cycas.

cykata *f. przest., kulin.* succade.

cykl *mi Gen.pl.* **-i** *l.* **-ów 1.** (= *okres, powtarza-*
jący się proces) cycle; **cykl księżycowy/słoneczny**

astron. the lunar/solar cycle; **cykl pór roku** the cycle of the seasons; **cykl ekonomiczny** *ekon.* business cycle; *Br.* trade cycle; **cykl produkcyjny** *ekon.* production cycle; **cykl rozwojowy** *biol.* life cycle; **cykl azotowy** *ekol.* nitrogen cycle. **2.** *teor.lit.*, *muz.* (= *seria dzieł powiązanych tematycznie*) cycle; **cykl arturiański** the Arthurian cycle. **3.** (= *seria spotkań, imprez, programów*) series.

Cyklady *pl. Gen.* **-ad** *geogr.* the Cyclades.

cyklamen *mi* **1.** *bot.* cyclamen (*Cyclamen*). **2.** (*kolor*) cyclamen.

cyklamenowy *a.* cyclamen.

cyklicznie *adv.* cyclically, in cycles.

cykliczny *a.* **1.** (= *okresowy, powtarzalny*) cyclic, cyclical, recurring (in cycles). **2.** *teor.lit.*, *muz.* (= *wieloczęściowy*) cyclic, cyclical. **3.** (= *seryjny*) serial. **4.** *chem.* cyclic; **związki cykliczne** cyclic compounds.

cyklina *f.*, **cykliniarka** *f. Gen.pl.* **-ek** *techn.* scraper.

cyklinować *ipf. techn.* scrape.

cyklista *mp*, **cyklistka** *f. Gen.pl.* **-ek** cyclist, cycler, biker.

cyklistówka *f. Gen.pl.* **-ek** cycling cap.

cyklobutan *mi chem.* cyclobutane.

cykloheksan *mi chem.* cyclohexane.

cykloida *f. mat.* cycloid.

cyklometr *mi techn.* (= *licznik obrotów koła*) cyclometer, cycle counter.

cyklon *mi meteor., chem., techn.* cyclone; **oko cyklonu** *meteor.* the eye of a cyclone; **w oku cyklonu** *przen.* in the eye of the storm.

cyklop *mp pl.* **-i** *l.* **-y** *mit.* Cyclops. – *ma pl.* **-y** *zool.* (= *oczlik*) cyclops.

cyklopentan *mi chem.* cyclopentane.

cyklopi, cyklopowy *a. mit.* Cyclopean.

cyklopropan *mi chem.* cyclopropane.

cyklorama *f. teatr* cyclorama.

cyklotron *mi fiz.* cyclotron.

cyklotymia *f. gen.* **-ii** *psych., pat.* cyclothymia.

cyklotymiczka *f. Gen.pl.* **-ek**, **cyklotymik** *mp psych.* cyclothymic, cyclothymiac.

cyklotymiczny *a. psych., pat.* cyclothymic, cyclothymiac.

cyknąć *pf.* **-ij** *zob.* **cykać**.

cykor *mi Acc. i Gen.* **-a** *no plural sl.* (= *strach*) scare; **mieć/dostać cykora** be/get shit-scared. – *mp pl.* **-y** *pot., sl.* (= *tchórz*) chicken, scaredy-cat.

cykoria *f. Gen.* **-ii** **1.** *bot., kulin.* chicory (*Cichorium*). **2.** **korzeń cykorii** chicory-root. **3.** **cykoria palona** *l.* **prażona** roasted chicory-root.

cykot *mi* (*odgłos*) ticking, tick-tock, tic-toc.

cykuta *f.* **1.** *bot.* (= *szalej jadowity*) cowbane, water hemlock (*Cicuta virosa*). **2.** (*trucizna*) hemlock.

cylinder *mi* **-dr-** *Gen.* **-a** **1.** *techn., mot.* cylinder; **blok cylindrów** cylinder block; **głowica cylindra** cylinder head. **2.** (*kapelusz*) top hat, high hat.

cylindryczny *a.* cylindrical; **pieczęć cylindryczna** *archeol.* cylindrical seal.

cyma *f. bud.* cyma.

cymbalista *mp*, **cymbalistka** *f. Gen.pl.* **-ek** *muz.* dulcimer player.

cymbał *mp pl.* **-y** *pot.* (= *głupiec*) moron, nerd, blockhead.

cymbałki *pl. Gen.* **-ów** *muz.* glockenspiel.

cymbały *pl. Gen.* **-ów** *muz.* dulcimer.

cymelium *n. indecl. in sg. pl.* **-lia** *Gen.* **-liów** *bibl.* rare book *l.* manuscript.

cymes *mi pot.* cat's whiskers *l.* pyjamas, bee's knees.

cyna *f. chem.* tin.

cynaderki *pl. Gen.* **-ek** *kulin.* kidney.

cynamon *mi kulin.* cinnamon; **kora cynamonu** cinnamon bark.

cynamonowiec *mi* **-wc-** *Gen.* **-a** *bot.* cinnamon (*Cinnamomum zeylanicum, C. cassia*).

cynamonowy *a.* (*t. o kolorze*) cinnamon; *chem.* cinnamic.

cyneraria *f. Gen.* **-ii** *bot.* cineraria (*Senecio cruentus*).

cynfolia *f. Gen.* **-ii** tinfoil.

cyngiel *mi* **-gl-** *Gen.* **-a** *pot.* (= *spust*) trigger; **pociągnąć za cyngiel** pull the trigger.

cynia *f. Gen.* **-ii** *bot.* zinnia (*Zinnia*).

cynian *mi chem.* stannate.

cyniczka *f. Gen.pl.* **-ek** *zob.* **cynik**.

cyniczny *a.* **1.** cynical; (= *szyderczy*) sarcastic, mocking. **2.** *hist., fil.* Cynic, Cynical.

cynik *mp* **1.** (= *człowiek otwarcie nieetyczny*) cynic. **2.** *hist., fil.* (= *wyznawca cynizmu*) Cynic.

cynizm *mi* **1.** (= *lekceważenie zasad*) cynicism. **2.** *hist., fil.* Cynicism.

cynk[1] *mi chem.* zinc.

cynk[2] *mi pot.* (= *ostrzeżenie, zawiadomienie*) warning, word; **dać komuś cynk** warn sb; **dostać od kogoś cynk** get a warning from sb.

cynkografia *f. Gen.* **-ii** *druk.* zincography.

cynkować *ipf. techn.* plate *l.* coat with zinc.

cynkowany *a. techn.* zinc-plated.

cynkowy *a. chem.* zinc; **maść cynkowa** *med.* zinc oxide ointment.

cynober *mi* **-br-** **1.** *min.* (*t. pigment*) cinnabar. **2.** (*barwa*) cinnabar, vermillion.

cynobrowy *a.* cinnabar, vermillion.

cynować *ipf. techn.* plate *l.* coat with tin.

cynowy *a.* tin; **kamień cynowy** *min.* (= *kasyteryt*) cassiterite.

cypel *mi* **-pl-** *Gen.* **-a** *Gen.pl.* **-i** *l.* **-ów** **1.** *geogr.* promontory, foreland, headland, point. **2.** (= *ostre, wystające zakończenie*) point, spit.

Cypr *mi geogr.* Cyprus.

Cypryjczyk *mp*, **Cypryjka** *f. Gen.pl.* **-ek** Cypriot.

cypryjski *a.* Cypriot.

cyprys *mi Gen.* **-a** *l.* **-u** *bot.* cypress (*Cupressus*).

cyprysik *mi Gen.* **-a** *l.* **-u** *bot.* cypress (*Chamaecyparis*); **cyprysik Lawsona** Lawson's cypress (*C. lawsoniana*).

cyprysowy *a.* cypress.

cypryśnik *mi Gen.* **-a** *bot.* bald *l.* swamp cypress (*Taxodium*).

cyraneczka *f. orn.* teal (*Anas crecca*).

cyranka *f. orn.* garganey (*Anas querquedula*).

cyrenajczyk *mp hist., fil.* Cyrenaic.

cyrk *mi* **1.** (*namiot, instytucja, widowisko*)

circus; *hist.* (*w starożytnym Rzymie*) circus games. **2.** *pot.* (= *heca, granda, sensacja*) circus, show; **ale cyrk!** what a lark! **3.** *geol.* **cyrk lodowcowy** cirque.

cyrkiel *mi* -kl- *Gen.* -a *Gen.pl.* -i *l.* -ów (*przyrząd kreślarski i pomiarowy*) (pair of) compasses, compass; **cyrkiel pomiarowy** *l.* **warsztatowy** (pair of) dividers.

cyrklować *ipf.* **1.** *pot.* (= *kalkulować, obliczać*) figure out. **2.** (*w krawiectwie*) hem.

cyrkon *mi* **1.** *chem.* zirconium. **2.** *min.* zircon, jargon.

cyrkonia *f. Gen.* -ii (*pot.*) = **cyrkon** 2.

cyrkowiec *mp* -wc- circus performer, circus artist.

cyrkowy *a.* circus.

cyrkówka *f. Gen.pl.* -ek *pot. zob.* **cyrkowiec.**

cyrkulacja *f.* **1.** (= *krążenie, obieg*) circulation; **cyrkulacja atmosfery** *meteor.* atmospheric circulation; **cyrkulacja pieniądza** *ekon.* money circulation, currency. **2.** *żegl.* turning motion.

cyrkulować *ipf.* circulate.

cyrkumfleks *mi jęz., druk.* circumflex (accent).

cyrograf *mi* **1.** (= *pakt z diabłem*) pact with the devil. **2.** *żart.* (= *zobowiązanie*) signed obligation.

cyrulik *mp arch.* barber.

cyrylica *f.* Cyrillic script, the Cyrillic alphabet.

cysta[1] *f. biol., pat.* cyst.

cysta[2] *f. archeol.* cist.

cysterka *f. Gen.pl.* -ek *rel.* Cistercian (nun).

cysterna *f.* (*zbiornik*) **1.** cistern, tank. **2.** (*pojazd*) tank truck, tanker.

cystersi *mp rel.* Cistercian (monk); **cystersi** the Cistercians, the White Monks.

cysterski *a. rel.* Cistercian.

cystografia *f. Gen.* -ii *med.* cystography.

cystolit *mi pat.* cystolith.

cystoskop *mi med.* cystoscope.

cystoskopia *f. Gen.* -ii *med.* cystoscopy.

cystoskopowy *a. med.* cystoscopic.

cystotomia *f. Gen.* -ii *chir.* cystotomy.

cystyna *f. biochem.* cystine.

cyt *int.* pst!, hush!

cytadela *f. Gen.pl.* -i *l.* -l *hist., bud.* citadel.

cytara *f. muz.* cittern, cither.

cytat *mi* quotation, quote, citation.

cytochemia *f. Gen.* -ii cytochemistry.

cytochrom *mi biochem.* cytochrome.

cytokinetyczny *a. biol.* cytokinetic.

cytokineza *f. biol.* cytokinesis.

cytokinina *f. biochem.* cytokinin.

cytolog *mp pl.* -dzy *l.* -owie cytologist.

cytologia *f. Gen.* -ii cytology.

cytomegalia *f. Gen.* -ii *pat.* cytomegaly.

cytomegalowirus *ma biol.* cytomegalovirus, CMV.

cytoplazma *f. biol.* cytoplasm.

cytostatyk *mi med.* cytostatic (agent).

cytować *ipf.* **1.** (= *przytaczać*) quote, cite; (= *wzmiankować*) mention. **2.** (= *wyliczać, wymieniać*) list, adduce.

cytozol *mi biol.* cytosol.

cytozyna *f. biochem.* cytosine.

cytra *f. muz.* zither.

cytral *mi chem.* citral.

cytron *mi bot.* citron (*Citrus medica*).

cytronelal *mi chem.* citronellal.

cytronelowy *a. techn.* **olejek cytronelowy** citronella oil.

cytrus *mi Gen.* -a *bot.* citrus (*Citrus*).

cytrusowy *a.* citrus; **owoce cytrusowe** citruses, citrus fruits.

cytryn *mi min.* citrine.

cytryna *f. bot.* lemon (tree) (*Citrus limon*); (*owoc*) lemon; **kwaśny jak cytryna** (as) sour as vinegar; **wycisnąć kogoś jak cytrynę** *pot., przen.* squeeze sb dry.

cytrynek *ma* -nk- (*także* **listkowiec cytrynek**) *ent.* brimstone (*Gonepteryx rhamni*).

cytrynian *mi chem.* citrate.

cytryniec *mi* -ńc- *Gen.* -a *bot.* schisandra, magnolia vine, wu-wei-zi (*Schisandra*).

cytrynowy *a.* **1.** (*smak*) lemon(-flavored), lemony; (*kolor*) lemon (yellow); **olejek cytrynowy** lemon oil. **2.** *chem.* citric; **kwas cytrynowy** (*t. kulin.*) citric acid.

cytrynówka *f. Gen.pl.* -ek (*wódka*) lemon-flavored vodka.

cytrzysta *mp*, **cytrzystka** *f. Gen.pl.* -ek *muz.* zither player.

cywet *mi techn.* civet.

cyweta *f. zool.* civet (*Viverra*); **cyweta indyjska** zibet (*V. zibetha*); **cyweta afrykańska** true civet (*V. civetta*).

cywil *mp Gen.pl.* -ów (= *osoba niesłużąca w wojsku l. policji*) **1.** civilian; (*w czasie wojny*) noncombatant. **2.** *pot.* (= *życie cywilne*) **w cywilu** in civilian life; *sl.* in civvie street; **iść do cywila** leave the service. **3.** **w cywilu** (*o policjancie = w stroju cywilnym*) in plain clothes.

cywilista *mp prawn.* civil lawyer.

cywilistyka *f. prawn.* civil law.

cywilizacja *f.* civilization; (= *świat cywilizowany*) the civilized world; **cywilizacje starożytne** ancient civilizations; **cywilizacja wschodnia/zachodnia** the Eastern/Western civilization.

cywilizator *mp*, **cywilizatorka** *f. Gen.pl.* -ek civilizer.

cywilizować *ipf.* civilize. ~ **się** *ipf.* become civilized.

cywilizowany *a.* civilized; (= *kulturalny*) cultured, polite.

cywilki *pl. Gen.pl.* -ek *pot., wojsk.* (= *ubiór cywilny*) civies, civvies.

cywilnoprawny *a. prawn.* civil legal.

cywilny *a.* **1.** (= *nienależący do wojska l. policji*) civilian; **ludność cywilna** civilian population, the civilians; **pracownicy cywilni** civilian staff; **strój cywilny** plain clothes; **po cywilnemu** in plain clothes. **2.** *prawn.* civil; **prawo cywilne** civil law; **kodeks postępowania cywilnego** civil law code; **stan cywilny** marital status; **ślub cywilny** civil marriage; **urząd stanu cywilnego** registrar's office; *Br.* register office, registry office; **urzędnik stanu cywilnego** registrar. **3.** (= *niekościel-*

ny, świecki) lay. **4.** *arch.* (= *obywatelski, osobisty*) civil; **odwaga cywilna** personal courage.

cyzelator *mp* **1.** (*rzemieślnik*) chiseler, chaser, engraver. **2.** *przen.* (= *perfekcjonista*) perfectionist.

cyzeler *mp* = **cyzelator** 1.

cyzelować *ipf.* **1.** (= *wykańczać wyroby metalowe*) chisel, chase. **2.** *przen.* (= *dopracowywać szczegóły*) perfect; finish (*sth*) to perfection; put the finishing touches to (*sth*).

cyzelunek *mi* -nk- **1.** chiseling, chiselwork. **2.** *przen.* the final touches, perfecting.

czacha *f. sl.* (= *głowa, czaszka*) nut; **prosto w czachę** right on the nut; **stuknij się w czachę** you must be off your rocker.

cza-cza *f. indecl. l. Gen.* -y *muz.* cha-cha, cha-cha-cha.

Czad *mi geogr.* Chad.

czad *mi* **1.** (= *duszący dym*) smother; *pot.* (= *tlenek węgla*) carbon monoxide. **2.** *przen., lit.* (= *coś, co osałamia l. otępia* (*czegoś* of sth). **3.** *sl.* (= *dynamika, energia*) power; **dawać czadu** (= *iść na całego*) burn some rubber; (= *grać dynamicznie*) pump up the volume; pump it up; **daliśmy czadu na imprezie** we had a blast at the party.

czadnica *f. techn.* gas generator.

czador *mi* (*islam*) chador, chuddar, veil.

czadowy *a. sl.* (= *dynamiczny, mocny*) smokin', cranking; (= *fajny, ekstra*) cool, super, jazzy.

Czadyjczyk *mp*, **Czadyjka** *f. Gen.pl.* -ek Chadian.

czadyjski *a.* (= *dotyczący Czadu l. jego mieszkańców*) **1.** Chadian. **2.** *jęz.* Chadic.

czadzić *ipf.* **1.** *pot.* (= *zadymiać pomieszczenie*) smoke out the place. **2.** *pot.* (= *głośno grać*) pump up the volume; pump it up.

czaić się *ipf.* **czaję czaisz, czaj 1.** (= *czatować*) lurk (in wait); lie in wait *l.* in ambush (*na kogoś/coś* for sb/sth); **czaić się w cieniu** *t. przen.* lurk in the shadows. **2.** (= *chować się*) hide (away) (*przed kimś/czymś* from sb/sth). **3.** *przen.* (= *majaczyć w ciemności l. we mgle, zbliżać się*) lurk, loom. **4.** *pot.* (= *wahać się*) hang back.

czajka¹ *f. orn.* lapwing, pewit, peewit (*Vanellus*).

czajka² *f. żegl., hist.* chaika (*light ship used by the Cossacks*).

czajniczek *mi* -czk- *Gen.* -a teapot.

czajnik *mi Gen.* -a kettle; **czajnik elektryczny** electric kettle, boiler jug.

czambuł *mi hist.* **1.** mounted troop (*of Tatar horsemen*). **2.** **potępić kogoś/coś w czambuł** condemn sb/sth en masse.

czapa *f.* **1.** (= *duża l. wysoka czapka*) hat; **czapa futrzana** fur hat. **2.** (= *warstwa, okrywa*) cap, layer; **czapa lodowa** icecap; **czapa polarna** polar cap; **lisia czapa** red corona *l.* halo (*around the moon*); **czapa żelazna** *geol.* gossan. **3.** *pot.* (= *głowa*) nut; **dostać** *l.* **oberwać** *l.* **zarobić w czapę** get it in the head. **4.** *pot.* (= *kara śmierci*) death sentence.

czapeczka *f. Gen.pl.* -ek (*nakrycie głowy*) small cap; (= *mycka*) skullcap; **czapeczka z papieru** paper hat.

czapka *f. Gen.pl.* -ek (*nakrycie głowy*) cap, hat; **czapka z daszkiem** peaked cap; **czapka baseballowa** baseball cap; **czapka sukienna** (*zwł. szkocka*) bonnet; **czapka błazeńska** coxcomb, fool's cap; **ośla czapka** dunce cap; **czapka niewidka** invisibility cap; **czapka frygijska** *hist.* Phrygian cap, cap of liberty; **czapki z głów** hats off (*na czyjąś cześć* to sb); **na złodzieju czapka gore** if the cap fits... (wear it).

czapkować *ipf. pog.* **czapkować komuś** *l.* **przed kimś** bow and scrape before sb.

czapla *f. Gen.pl.* -i orn. (= *ptak z rodziny Ardeidae*) heron; *arch.* hern; (*gatunek biało upierzony*) egret; **czapla siwa** grey heron (*Ardea cinerea*); **czapla biała** great egret (*Casmerodius albus*); **czapla nadobna** little egret (*Egretta garzetta*); **czapla śnieżna** snowy egret (*Leucophoyx thula*).

czapli *a.* heron; **czaple pióra** (*ozdoba*) aigrette.

czapnik *mp* capmaker.

czaprak *mi Gen.* -a *jeźdz.* horsecloth; (*t. dla innych zwierząt*) housing; (*pod siodło*) housing, pad; *hist.* (= *ozdobne okrycie konia*) caparison.

czar *mi* **1.** (= *zaklęcie*) spell; *pl.* (= *magia*) magic; **uprawiać czary** practise magic. **2.** (= *zauroczenie*) enchantment, fascination; **rzucić czar na kogoś/coś** cast a spell on *l.* over sb/sth; **zniweczyć czar** break a spell; **czar prysł** the magic was gone. **3.** *przen.* (= *wdzięk, urok*) charm, glamor, magic.

czara *f.* (*naczynie, część kielicha*) bowl, cup; **czara goryczy** cup of bitterness; **wychylić czarę goryczy** drain the bitter cup.

czarci *a.* the devil's, diabolic, satanic; **czarcie nasienie** the devil's spawn.

czarczaf *mi* purdah, purda.

czardasz *mi Gen.pl.* -y *l.* -ów *muz.* czardas.

czarka *f. Gen.pl.* -ek (*naczynko*) **1.** cup. **2.** *bot.* (*grzyb*) cup fungus (*Sarcoscypha*); **czarka szkarłatna** elf-cup (*S. coccinea*).

czarniak *ma icht.* green cod (*Pollachius virens*).

czarno *adv.* **1.** (= *bardzo ciemno, w kolorze czarnym*) black, dark; **czarno na białym** (= *wyraźnie*) in black and white; **opalić się na czarno** get a good tan; **ubierać się na czarno** dress in black; wear black. **2. na czarno** (= *nielegalnie*) off the books, illegally. **3.** (= *pesymistycznie*) black, bleak, gloomy, dismal; **czarno patrzeć na świat** look on the dark side of things; **przyszłość rysuje się czarno** the future looks gloomy.

czarno-biały *a.* black and white.

czarnobrewy *a.* black-browed.

Czarnogóra *f. geogr.* Montenegro.

czarnogórski *a.* Montenegrin.

Czarnogórzec *mp* -rc- *Voc.* -rze, **Czarnogórka** *f. Gen.pl.* -ek Montenegrin.

czarnoksięski *a.* sorcerous, necromantic; (= *magiczny*) magic, magical; **sztuka czarnoksięska** = **czarnoksięstwo**.

czarnoksięstwo *n.* sorcery, witchcraft, black

magic, black art, necromancy; (*z domniemaną pomocą diabła*) devilry.

czarnoksiężnik *mp* sorcerer, necromancer.

czarnooki *a.* black-eyed.

czarnorynkowy *a. ekon.* blackmarket.

czarnoskóry *a.* black, dark-skinned; **czarnoskóry Amerykanin** African American, Black American. – *mp* (= *Murzyn*) Black, African; Negro; *pog.* nigger.

czarnowidz *mp pl.* **-e** *l.* **-owie** (= *pesymista*) pessimist, doomsayer, prophet of doom.

czarnowłosy *a.* black-haired.

czarnowron *ma orn.* carrion crow (*Corvus corone corone*).

czarnoziem *mi geol., roln.* black earth; chernozem (*especially in eastern Europe*); **pas czarnoziemu** the black belt.

czarnuch *mp pl.* **-y** *pot., pog.* (= *Murzyn*) nigger, darky, darkie, coon.

czarnula *f.*, **czarnulka** *f. Gen.pl.* **-ek** *emf.* brunette.

czarnuszka *f. Gen.pl.* **-ek** *bot.* fennel flower (*Nigella*).

czarny *a.* **1.** (*o kolorze*) black; **czarna kawa** black coffee; **mała/duża czarna** *pot.* small/big black coffee; **czarne koszule** *hist.* (= *włoscy faszyści*) the Blackshirts; **czarna rasa** the black race, the Negroid race; **czarna ziemia** black earth; **czarny jak smoła** pitch-black, (as) black as pitch; (as) black as ink; (= *pogrążony w ciemności*) pitch-dark; **czarny jak węgiel** coal-black, (as) black as coal; **w czarną noc** in the black of the night. **2.** *her.* sable; **na czarnym polu** on sable. **3.** (= *brudny, usmolony*) dirty, sooty; **czarny jak święta ziemia** as black as a sweep. **4.** *przen.* (*często podkreśla negatywne cechy, rozpacz, pesymizm itp.*) **czarny charakter** villain; *pot.* bad guy, baddie; **czarny humor** black humor; **czarne kino** film noir; **czarna komedia** black comedy; **czarny kryminał** hardboiled detective fiction; **czarny koń** dark horse; **czarna lista** black list; **czarna magia** black magic, black art, sorcery; **czarna msza** black mass; **czarna nienawiść/rozpacz** black hatred/despair; **czarna owca** black sheep; **czarna strona czegoś** the dark side of sth; **czarny rynek** black market; **czarna śmierć** (= *zaraza, epidemia dżumy*) the Black Death; **malować kogoś/coś w czarnych barwach** paint sb/sth black; (**zachować coś**) **na czarną godzinę** (save sth) against a rainy day. **5.** (*w nazwach roślin i zwierząt*) **czarny bocian** *orn.* black stork (*Ciconia nigra*); **czarny łabędź** *orn.* black swan (*Cygnus atratus*); **czarny bez** *bot.* elder (*Sambucus nigra*); **czarna jagoda** *bot.* blueberry (*Vaccinium myrtillus*); **czarne korzonki** *bot.* (= *weżymord, skorzonera*) scorzonera, black *l.* Spanish salsify (*Scorzonera hispanica*); **czarna porzeczka** *bot.* blackcurrant (*Ribes nigrum*); **czarna wdowa** *ent.* (*pająk*) black widow (*Latrodectus mactans*); **niedźwiedź czarny** *zool.* (American) black bear (*Ursus americanus*); **olcha** *l.* **olsza czarna** *bot.* European alder (*Alnus glutinosa*); **świerk czarny** *bot.* black spruce (*Picea mariana*); **topola czarna** *bot.* black poplar (*Populus nigra*). **6.** (*w terminach*

naukowych i technicznych) **ciało czarne** *fiz.* black body; **czarna dziura** *astron.* black hole; **czarna ospa** *pat.* smallpox, variola; **czarna skrzynka** *lotn.* black box. **7.** (= *ciemnoskóry*) black, dark-skinned; (= *dotyczący Murzynów*) Black; **Czarny Ląd** *przest.* (= *Afryka*) the Dark Continent. – *mp* **1.** *pot.* (= *Murzyn*) Black. **2.** *pot., euf.* (= *diabeł*) the Black One.

czarodziej *mp Gen.pl.* **-ei** *l.* **-ów** **1.** wizard, magician; (= *czarnoksiężnik*) sorcerer, necromancer; (= *sztukmistrz*) conjuror, conjurer. **2.** *przen.* (= *cudotwórca*) miracle worker, magician.

czarodziejka *f. Gen.pl.* **-ek** sorceress, enchantress, fairy; *przen.* (*kobieta pełna uroku*) charmer, enchantress.

czarodziejski *a.* **1.** (= *magiczny, sztukmistrzowski*) magic, magical; **czarodziejska różdżka** magic wand; **czarodziejska sztuczka** magic trick; conjuring trick; **czarodziejskie zaklęcie** magic spell. **2.** (= *pełen tajemnic*) magic, enchanted.

czarodziejstwo *n.* wizardry, magic; (= *czarnoksięstwo*) witchcraft, sorcery.

czarować *ipf.* **1.** (= *uprawiać czary*) practice magic; (= *rzucać zaklęcia*) cast spells. **2.** (= *pokazywać sztuczki magiczne*) conjure, do conjuring tricks. **3.** (= *zachwycać, oczarowywać*) charm, enchant. **4.** *pot.* **czarować kogoś** (= *oszukiwać, nabierać*) take sb in, dupe sb, pull the wool over sb's eyes. **5.** *pot.* (= *kłamać*) tell fairy stories; **nie czaruj!** I want none of your fairy stories.

czarownica *f.* witch, sorceress; *przen.* (= *jędza, dokuczliwa kobieta*) witch, hag, harridan, harpy; **polowanie na czarownice** *przen.* witch hunt; **sabat czarownic** coven of witches.

czarownik *mp antrop.* medicine man, shaman.

czarowny *a.* enchanting, delightful, enthralling, entrancing.

czart *mp Dat.* **-owi** *l.* **-u** *pl.* **-y** *l.* **-ci** *przest. l. lit.* devil, fiend; **cóż to jest, do czarta?** what the deuce is that?; **a niech to czart!** to hell with it!; **(tam) do czarta!** damnation!

czarter *mi handl.* (*t.* = *kurs wynajętego samolotu l. statku*) charter; **czarter do Nowego Jorku** charter to New York.

czarterowy *a. handl.* charter, chartered; **lot czarterowy** charter flight; **samolot czarterowy** chartered airplane; **umowa czarterowa** *żegl.* charter party.

czartowski *a. lit.* deuced, devillish; **czartowskie nasienie** devil's spawn.

czartyzm *mi hist., polit.* Chartism.

czarujący *a.* charming, enchanting.

czas *mi Ins.pl.* **-ami**; *in idiomatic expressions* **-y** **1.** (*wymiar fizyczny, przemijanie*) time; **czas mija** time passes *l.* goes by; **czas płynie** time flows; **upływ czasu** the flow of time; **w czasie i przestrzeni** in time and space; **wehikuł** *l.* **maszyna czasu** time machine; **zegar pokazuje/odmierza czas** a clock shows/measures time. **2.** (= *odcinek czasu*) period, time, hours; **czas pracy** working hours; **czas wolny** leisure time; **przez cały czas** all the time; **przez ten czas** during that time *l.* period; **przez pewien czas** for a time; **po pewnym czasie** after a time; **ile mamy czasu?** how much time do we have? **3.** *przen. i w utartych zwrotach* **czas goi** *l.* **leczy rany** time heals wounds; **czas nas goni** *l.* **nagli** we're pressed for time; **czas pokaże** only time will tell; **czas pracuje dla mnie** *l.* **na moją korzyść** I have time on my side; **czas to pieniądz** time is money; **grać na czas** play for time; **ja mam czas** I can wait; **mamy dość czasu** we have enough time (on our hands); **nadrabiać stracony czas** make up for lost time; **nie ma czasu na...** there's no time for...; **nie tracić/ nie marnować czasu** lose/waste no time; **spędzać czas** spend one's time (*na czymś* on sth) (*na robieniu czegoś* doing sth); **strata czasu** waste of time; **szkoda (czyjegoś) czasu** it's a waste of (sb's) time; **szmat czasu** a long time; **tracić** *l.* **marnotrawić czas** waste one's time; **wyścig z czasem** race against time; **wytrzymać próbę czasu** stand the test of time; **zabijać czas** kill time; **zyskać na czasie** gain time. **4.** *zw. pl.* (= *epoka, okres*) times, period, days, years; **czasy starożytne/prehistoryczne** ancient/prehistoric times; **ciężkie/ trudne czasy** hard/difficult times; **dawnymi czasy** *lit.* in olden days *l.* times; in days of yore; **ostatnimi czasy** *lit.* recently; **po wszystkie czasy** *l.* **po wieczne czasy** *l.* **po wsze czasy** forever (and a day); **swego czasu** once (upon a time); **w czasach królowej Elżbiety** in Queen Elizabeth's time; in Elizabethan times; **w naszych** *l.* **obecnych czasach** in our times, nowadays; **w owym czasie** at that time; **za moich czasów** in my time; **bawić się za wszystkie czasy** have the time of one's life; **iść z duchem czasu** move *l.* keep up with the times; **jego czas się skończył** his time is over. **5. na czasie** *pot.* fashionable, trendy, in. **6.** (= *właściwa pora*) (the right) time (*na coś* for sth); **jest czas na...** there's time for...; **nie czas na żarty** it isn't the right time for joking; **najwyższy czas** high time; **od czasu do czasu** from time to time; **do czasu** only so long; **uciekaj, póki czas** run away while the going's good; **zdążyć na czas** be in time (*na coś* for sth) (*żeby coś zrobić* to do sth); **przed czasem** ahead of time; **o czasie** on time; **po czasie** behind time; **w swoim czasie** *l.* **w stosownym czasie** in due time; **czas na mnie** *l.* **komu w drogę, temu czas** I'd better go; time to go; it's (high) time I were on my way; **nadszedł czas zapłaty** the day of reckoning has come; **rychło w czas** *iron.* just in time. **7.** *fiz., astron.* (= *system rachuby czasu*) time; **czas letni/zimowy** summer/winter time; **czas lokalny** local time; **czas słoneczny** *astron.* solar time; **czas strefowy** zone time; **czas Greenwich** Greenwich mean time, GMT; **czas uniwersalny** universal time, UT; **czas uniwersalny skoordynowany** universal time coordinated, UTC; **geologiczna skala czasu** *geol.* geological time scale. **8.** *gram.* tense; **czas teraźniejszy** the present (tense); **czas przeszły** the past (tense), the preterite; **czas przyszły** the future (tense); **czas zaprzeszły** the past participle (tense).

czasami *adv.* = **czasem** 1.

czasem *adv.* **1.** (= *niekiedy*) sometimes, from

time to time, occasionally. **2.** (*w pytaniach* = *przypadkiem*) by any chance; **nie masz czasem trochę kawy?** do you by any chance have some coffee?

czasochłonny *a.* time-consuming.

czasomierz *mi Gen.* **-a 1.** *techn.* timepiece, timer. **2.** *pot.* (= *zegarek*) watch.

czasopismo *n.* periodical; journal, magazine.

czasopiśmiennictwo *n. teor.lit.* journalism.

czasoprzestrzenny *a. fiz.* spaciotemporal; **continuum czasoprzestrzenne** space-time continuum.

czasoprzestrzeń *f. fiz.* space-time.

czasownik *mi Gen.* **-a** *gram.* verb; **czasownik modalny/posiłkowy** modal/auxiliary verb; **czasownik dokonany/niedokonany** perfective/imperfective verb; **osobowa forma czasownika** finite verb.

czasownikowy *a. gram.* verb, verbal; **fraza czasownikowa** verb phrase.

czasowo *adv.* **1.** (= *pod względem czasu*) temporally. **2.** (= *przejściowo*) temporarily, for the time being.

czasowy *a.* **1.** (*dotyczący czasu*) temporal; **strefa czasowa** time zone. **2.** (= *przejściowy, okresowy*) temporary.

czasza *f.* **1.** (*naczynie, kształt półkulisty*) dish, bowl, hemisphere; **czasza anteny** antenna dish. **2.** *lotn.* **czasza spadochronu** (parachute) canopy. **3.** *mat.* **czasza kulista** spherical cap.

czaszka *f.* **1.** *anat.* skull, cranium; *pot.* brainpan; **trepanacja czaszki** *med.* skull trepanation; **trupia czaszka** (*symbol śmierci*) death's head; **(trupia) czaszka i skrzyżowane piszczele** skull and crossbones. **2.** *pot.* (= *głowa, łeb*) skull.

czaszkowiec *ma zool.* craniate.

czaszkowy *a. anat.* cranial.

czata *f. wojsk., przest.* (= *zwiad*) reconnaissance; (= *straż*) sentry.

czatować *ipf.* wait in ambush, lie *l.* lurk in wait (*na kogoś / coś* for sb/sth).

czaty *pl. Gen.* **-t** lookout; **stać na czatach** be *l.* stand on the lookout.

czawycza *f. icht.* Chinook salmon (*Oncorhynchus tschawytscha*).

cząber *mi* **-br-** *Gen.* **-a** *l.* **-u** *bot., kulin.* savory (*Satureia hortensis*).

cząsteczka *f. Gen.pl.* **-ek 1.** (= *kawałek*) fragment, particle. **2.** *chem.* molecule.

cząsteczkowy *a. chem.* molecular; **ciężar cząsteczkowy** molecular weight; **tlen/wodór cząsteczkowy** molecular oxygen/hydrogen.

cząstka *f.* **1.** (= *kawałek*) fragment, part, particle. **2.** *fiz.* molecule; **cząstka elementarna** elementary particle; **cząstka naładowana/obojętna** charged/neutral particle.

cząstkowy *a.* partial, fragmentary.

czci *itd. f. zob.* **cześć**.

czciciel *mp,* **czcicielka** *f. Gen.pl.* **-ek** worshiper, adorer.

czcić *ipf.* **czczę czcisz, -ij 1.** (= *otaczać czcią*) worship, adore. **2.** (= *świętować*) celebrate.

czcigodny *a.* honorable; venerable, reverend;

czcigodny uczony venerable scholar; **mój czcigodny kolega** (*np. w Kongresie USA*) my honorable friend; **wielce czcigodny** *Br. (tytuł używany przed nazwiskiem)* Most Honorable.

czcionka *f. druk., komp. (krój)* font; (*zestaw znaków danego kroju*) typeface; **czcionka pochyła/półgruba** italic/bold typeface.

czczo *adv.* **na czczo** with an empty stomach.

czczość *f.* **1.** (*= głód*) hunger. **2.** (*= pustka, jałowość*) emptiness, hollowness.

czczy *a.* **1.** (*o żołądku*) empty; **na czczy żołądek** with an empty stomach. **2.** *uj.* (*= jałowy, próżny*) idle, empty, futile; (*= pozbawiony sensu*) inane, meaningless; **czcza obietnica** idle promise; **czcze pogróżki** empty threats; **czcze słowa** meaningless words; **czcza rozmowa** inane conversation.

Czech *mp* Czech; *hist.* Bohemian.

czechizm *mi jęz.* Bohemism.

Czechosłowacja *f. geogr., hist.* Czechoslovakia.

Czechy *pl. Gen.* **Czech** *geogr.* the Czech Republic, Czechia; *hist.* Bohemia.

czeczota *f. stol.* burl, burr.

czeczotka[1] *f. Gen.pl.* **-ek** *orn.* redpoll (*Carduelis flammea*).

czeczotka[2] *f. Gen.pl.* **-ek** *stol.* = **czeczota**.

czego[1] *pron. zob.* **co**.

czego[2] *int. pot.* **czego?** what?, what do you want?

czegokolwiek *pron. zob.* **cokolwiek**.

czegoś *pron. zob.* **coś**.

czek *mi* check, *Br.* cheque; **płacić czekiem** pay by check; **czek bez pokrycia** dud check; *pot.* bouncer; **czek in blanco** blank check; **czek na okaziciela** check payable to bearer; **wypisać komuś czek (na jakąś sumę)** write sb a check (for a sum); **wystawić czek (na jakiś bank)** draw a check (on a bank).

czekać *ipf.* **1.** (*= oczekiwać, spodziewać się*) wait (*na kogoś/coś* for sb/sth); await (*na kogoś/coś* sb/sth); **czekać godzinami** wait for hours; **czekać, aż telefon zadzwoni** wait for the telephone to ring; **czekać z zapartym tchem** wait with bated breath; **pozostaje nam tylko czekać** we can but wait; **proszę czekać** (*w rozmowie telefonicznej*) please hang on; **tylko czekać** (*= już wkrótce*) just a moment. **2.** (*= zwlekać*) procrastinate; **czekać z założonymi rękami** play a waiting game. **3.** (*= być przeznaczonym dla kogoś*) lie ahead; await (*sb*); **ani wiedziała, co ją czeka** little did she know what awaited her; **kto wie, co nas czeka** who knows what lies ahead; **czeka go niespodzianka** he's in for a surprise. **4. czekaj (no)!** just you wait!

czekan *mi Gen.* **-a** **1.** *sport* ice ax; (*tradycyjnego typu*) alpenstock. **2.** *broń, hist.* war-hammer (*of a slender Eastern type*).

czekolada *f. kulin.* **1.** chocolate; **ciasteczko z kawałkami czekolady** chocolate chip cookie; **tabliczka czekolady** bar of chocolate. **2. gorąca czekolada** (*napój*) hot chocolate.

czekoladka *f. Gen.pl.* **-ek** chocolate; **nadziewa-**

na czekoladka chocolate cream; **pudełko czekoladek** box of chocolates.

czekoladowy *a.* (*smak, kolor*) chocolate; **o smaku czekoladowym** chocolate-flavored.

czekowy *a.* check; **książeczka czekowa** checkbook.

czeladniczy *a.* apprentice's.

czeladnik *mp* apprentice.

czeladź *f.* **1.** *hist.* the servants, the domestics. **2.** *arch.* (*= czeladnicy*) apprentices.

czele *n.* **na czele** *t. przen.* in *l.* at the forefront; in the vanguard (*czegoś* of sth); **na czele pochodu** heading the procession; **na czele grupy** (*o przywódcy*) at the head of the group; **stać na czele czegoś** be the head of sth; head sth.

czelesta *f. muz.* celesta.

czelność *f.* cheek, gall, insolence, effrontery; **masz czelność tu przychodzić?** you have the cheek *l.* gall to come here?; **co za czelność!** what cheek!

czeluść *f. pl.* **-i** *l.* **-e** (*= wielki otwór, otchłań*) depth, abyss, pit, mouth; **czeluść piekielna** the mouth of hell; (*w języku biblijnym*) the pit.

czempion *ma pl.* **-y** (*zwierzę, które zwyciężyło w konkursie l. zawodach*) champion, winner. – *mi pl.* **-i** *sport* champion, winner.

czempionat *mi* championship.

czemu[1] *pron. zob.* **co**.

czemu[2] *adv.* (*= dlaczego*) why, what for, how come; **czemu właśnie ja?** why me, of all people?; **czemu nie jesz?** why aren't you eating?; **sam nie wiem, czemu to robię** I don't know why I'm doing it.

czemukolwiek *pron. zob.* **cokolwiek**.

czemuś[1] *pron. zob.* **coś**.

czemuś[2] *adv.* for some reason, somehow; **czemuś nie mogę spać** for some reason I can't sleep.

czepek *mi* **-pk-** *Gen.* **-a** **1.** (*dziecięca czapeczka l. kobiece nakrycie głowy*) bonnet; (*staroświeckie l. zakonne nakrycie głowy*) coif. **2.** (*różne specjalne rodzaje nakrycia głowy*) cap; **czepek pływacki/kąpielowy** swimming/bathing cap; **czepek pielęgniarki** nurse's cap. **3.** *med.* (*= resztki błon płodowych na głowie noworodka*) caul; **być w czepku urodzonym** *przen.* be born with a silver spoon in one's mouth.

czepiać się *ipf.* **+** *Gen.* **1.** (*= chwytać się, trzymać się*) catch (at) (*sth*); cling to (*sth*); stick to (*sth*). **2.** (*= niesprawiedliwie krytykować*) find fault with (*sb l. sth*); pick holes in (*sth*); carp at (*sb*); pick on (*sb*); peck at (*sb*); go after (*sb*); **czego się mnie czepiasz?** why are you picking on me?; **czepiać się drobiazgów** *l.* **o drobiazgi** nitpick, pettifog; **przepraszam, że się czepiam, ale...** sorry if I'm nitpicking, but...

czepiak *ma zool.* spider monkey (*Ateles*).

czepialski *a.* nitpicking, petifogging.

czepiec *mi* **-pc-** *Gen.* **-a** **1.** (*nakrycie głowy zakonnic l. część zbroi*) coif. **2.** (*kobiece nakrycie głowy*) bonnet. **3.** *techn.* (*= osłona*) cap. **4.** *zool. anat.* (*część żołądka przeżuwaczy*) reticulum. **5.** *med.* (*porodowy*) caul.

czepigi *pl. Gen.* **-g** *roln.* plow handles, *Br.* plough handles.

czepliwy *a.* **1.** (= *mający zdolność czepiania się*) adhesive, clinging. **2.** *pot.* (*o człowieku*) grouchy, grumpy.

czepny *a. bot.* tendrilous; **organy czepne** tendrils.

czereda *f. żart.* (= *gromada*) crew, party, crowd.

czeremcha *f. bot.* bird cherry (*Prunus padus*); **czeremcha późna** black cherry (*P. serotina*); **czeremcha wirginijska** chokecherry (*P. virginiana*).

czerep *mi* **1.** *arch. l. żart.* (= *czaszka, głowa*) skull, brainpan. **2.** (= *skorupa*) potsherd, sherd, shard. **3.** *wojsk.* (= *odłamek*) shard.

czereśnia *f. Gen.pl.* -i *bot., kulin.* sweet cherry (*Prunus avium*).

czereśniowy *a.* made from sweet cherries.

Czerkies *mp*, **Czerkieska** *f. Gen.pl.* -ek Circassian.

czerkieski *a.* Circassian.

czermień *f. pl.* -nie *bot.* czermień błotna calla, wild calla lily, water arum (*Calla palustris*).

czerniak *mi Gen.* -a *pat.* melanoma.

czernica *f.* **1.** *bot.* (= *czarna jagoda*) blueberry, whortleberry, bilberry (*Vaccinium myrtillus*). **2.** *orn.* pochard (*Aithya fuligula*).

czernić *ipf.* -ń *l.* -ij make *l.* paint black. ~ **się** *ipf.* appear black.

czernidlak *mi Gen.* -a *bot.* (*grzyb*) inkcap (*Coprinus*).

czernidło *n. Gen.pl.* -deł **1.** (= *środek czerniący*) blacking, blackwash. **2.** *arch.* (= *atrament*) ink.

czernieć *ipf.* **1.** (= *stawać się czarnym*) blacken, become black. **2.** appear as black (*na tle czegoś* against sth).

czernina *f. kulin.* duck blood soup.

czerń *f. pl.* -e **1.** black; *her. l. arch.* sable; **nosić czerń** *l.* **chodzić w czerni** wear black, be dressed in black. **2.** (= *czarny barwnik*) black (dye), blacking. **3.** (= *ciemność*) darkness.

czerokeski *a.* Cherokee.

Czerokez *mp*, **Czerokezka** *f. Gen.pl.* -ek Cherokee.

czerpać *ipf.* -pię -piesz **1.** (*nabierać płyn lub coś sypkiego*) draw (*sth*), scoop (*sth*) up, scoop (*sth*) out (*skądś* from sth). **2.** *przen.* (= *uzyskiwać*) derive (*sth*) (*skądś* from sth); **czerpać zadowolenie z pracy** derive pleasure from work.

czerpadło *n. Gen.pl.* -deł *górn.* (*urządzenie wiertnicze*) bailer, bail.

czerpak *mi Gen.* -a **1.** (*łyżka do czerpania*) dipper, ladle; (*zagłębienie łyżki*) bowl. **2.** (*naczynie do wylewania wody z łodzi*) bailer. **3.** (*miarka*) scoop. **4.** *techn.* scoop, bucket.

czerpany *a. techn.* (*o papierze*) handmade.

czerstwieć *ipf.* (*o pieczywie*) go stale.

czerstwo *adv.* (= *zdrowo*) healthily.

czerstwy *a.* **1.** (*o pieczywie*) stale. **2.** (= *dziarski, rumiany*) healthy, ruddy, vigorous.

czerw *mi* -wi- *Gen.* -a *pl.* -e *przest.* (= *beznoga larwa*) grub, maggot.

czerwcowy *a.* June.

czerwiec *mi* -wc- *Gen.* -a **1.** (*miesiąc*) June. **2.**

bot. knotgrass (*Scleranthus*). – *ma* -wc- *ent.* Polish cochineal (*Porphyrophora polonica*).

czerwienić *ipf.* make *l.* color *l.* paint (*sth*) red. ~ **się** *ipf.* **1.** (= *pąsowieć, rumienić się*) blush, become red in the face; **czerwienić się ze wstydu/gniewu/zakłopotania** blush with shame/anger/embarrassment. **2.** = **czerwienieć**.

czerwienieć *ipf.* **1.** (= *stawać się czerwonym*) redden, grow *l.* become red. **2.** (= *mieć czerwony kolor*) be red.

czerwienny *a. karty* (= *kier, kierowy*) of hearts.

czerwień *f. pl.* -nie **1.** (= *kolor czerwony*) red. **2.** (= *czerwony barwnik*) red dye. **3.** **nosić czerwień** *l.* **ubierać się w czerwień** wear red. **4.** *w niektórych grach karcianych l. przest.* = *kier* hearts.

czerwonak *ma orn.* (= *ptak z rodziny Phoenicopteridae*) flamingo.

czerwonawy *a.* reddish, ruddy.

czerwonka *f. Gen.pl.* -ek *pat.* (*choroba*) dysentery; **czerwonka bakteryjna/pełzakowata** bacterial/amebic dysentery.

czerwonoskóry *a.* red-skinned. – *mp często pog.* (= *Indianin*) redskin.

czerwony *a.* **czerwieńszy 1.** (*o kolorze*) red; **czerwony jak burak** *l.* **jak rak** (as) red as a beetroot; **czerwona krew** red blood; **czerwony na twarzy** red *l.* purple in the face; **czerwona pomarańcza** blood orange; **czerwone wino** red wine; **czerwony sztandar** (*symbol komunizmu l. rewolucji*) the Red Flag; **Czerwony Krzyż** the Red Cross; **Czerwony Półksiężyc** the Red Crescent. **2.** *przen.* (*zw. wyraża ostrzeżenie*) **czerwone światło** (= *znak niebezpieczeństwa l. zakaz*) red light; **czerwony alarm** red alert. **3.** (*w nazwach roślin i zwierząt*) **czerwona porzeczka** *bot.* redcurrant (*Ribes rubrum*); **koral czerwony** *zool.* red corral (*Corrallium*). **4.** (*w terminach naukowych*) **czerwony karzeł/olbrzym** *astron.* red dwarf/giant; **krwinki czerwone** *l.* **czerwone ciałka krwi** *fizj.* red bloodcells, red corpuscles, erythrocytes. **5.** *pog.* (= *lewicowy, komunistyczny*) Red; **czerwoni** the Reds.

czerwończyk *ma ent.* (*motyl*) copper (*Lycaena, Heodes*).

czesać *ipf.* -szę -szesz **1.** (= *układać włosy*) comb, do. **2.** *tk.* comb; (*len, konopie*) hackle. ~ **się** *ipf.* comb one's hair (*czymś* with sth); (= *układać sobie fryzurę*) do one's hair; **czesać się z grzywką** wear a bang; **czesać się z przedziałkiem** make a part in one's hair.

czesak *mi Gen.* -a *tk.* comb; (*do lnu, konopi*) hackle, heckle, hatchel, flax comb.

czesalnia *f. Gen.pl.* -ni *l.* -ń *tk.* combing mill; (*lnu, konopi*) hackling house, hackling room.

czesanka *f.* (*także* **wełna czesankowa**) *tk.* combed wool.

czesarka *f. Gen.pl.* -ek *tk.* comber; (*do lnu, konopi*) hackling machine.

czeski *a.* **czeski błąd** *pot.* transposition of letters (*in typing*); **Republika Czeska** *geogr.* the Czech Republic.

czesne *n. Gen.* -ego *szkoln., uniw.* (tuition) fee.

Czeszka *f. Gen.pl.* -ek *zob.* **Czech**.

cześć¹ *f. czci- Gen. czci* **1.** (= *hołd*) honor, *Br.*

honour, homage; (= *uwielbienie*) adoration; (= *szacunek*) respect; **ku czyjejś czci** *l*. **na czyjąś cześć** in honor of sb, in sb's honor; **oddawać komuś/czemuś cześć** pay homage to sb/sth; **okazywać komuś cześć** pay homage to sb; **winniśmy im najgłębszą cześć** we owe them the deepest respect; **z wielką/niezwykłą czcią** with great/utmost respect. **2.** (= *godność*) honor, dignity, face; **stracić/ocalić swoją cześć** lose/preserve one's dignity; **odsądzać kogoś od czci i wiary** drag sb's name through the mire; **przywracać kogoś do czci** restore sb's good name.

cześć² *int.* (*powitanie*) **1.** hi; hello; **cześć, chłopaki!** hi, guys! **2.** (*pożegnanie*) see you (around); bye; bye-bye; *Br.* cheers; ta-ta; *żart.* adios (amigo); ciao; **no to cześć** see you later, then. **3. no i cześć** (= *i na tym koniec*) and that's (the end of) it; **to moja sprawa i cześć** it's my business, and that's the end of it.

cześnik *mp hist.* (*urząd tytularny*) butler.

często *adv.* often, frequently; *arch.* oft, ofttimes, oftentimes; **często gęsto** *pot.* every so often; **często cytowany** frequently cited, often cited, oft-cited; **często spotykany** frequently occurring; **często ulegający wypadkom** accident-prone; **często używany** much used; **jak często?** how often?; **niezbyt często** not too often; **o wiele za często** far too often.

częstochowski *a. geogr.* of Czestochowa, city and pilgrimage center in Poland; **rymy częstochowskie** *iron.* doggerel rhymes; **Matka Boska Częstochowska** *rel.* Our Lady of Czestochowa.

częstokół *mi* **-o-** *bud.* palisade, pale, paling.

częstokroć *adv. lit.* oftentimes, ofttimes, frequently, often; **częstokroć powtarzany** oft-repeated.

częstokrotnie *adv. przest.* frequently.

częstokrotny *a. przest.* frequent, repeated.

częstomocz *mi pat.* pollakiuria.

częstoskurcz *mi pat.* tachycardia; **częstoskurcz napadowy** paroxysmal tachycardia.

częstość *f.* **1.** (= *częste występowanie*) frequency; **częstość występowania** (*np. choroby*) incidence. **2.** *fiz.* (= *częstotliwość*) frequency; **funkcja częstości** *stat.* frequency function, probability density function; **rozkład częstości** *stat.* frequency distribution.

częstotliwość *f.* **1.** (= *częste występowanie*) frequency; **częstotliwość akcji serca** *med.* heart rate; **z coraz większą częstotliwością** with increasing frequency. **2.** *fiz.* frequency; **pasmo częstotliwości** frequency band; **zakres częstotliwości** frequency range; **wysoka/niska** *l.* **mała/średnia częstotliwość** high/low/medium frequency; **częstotliwość własna** natural frequency; **częstotliwość lustrzana** image frequency; **częstotliwość pośrednia** intermediate frequency; **częstotliwość słyszalna** audio *l.* sonic *l.* sound frequency.

częstotliwy *a.* frequent; repeated; **czasownik częstotliwy** *gram.* frequentative (verb).

częstować *ipf.* **1.** (= *proponować jedzenie, picie, papierosy itp.*) treat (*kogoś czymś* sb to sth) offer (*kogoś czymś* sth to sb). **2.** *przen.* (= *spra-*

wiać komuś przykrość) mistreat, harm; **częstować kogoś kijem/rózgą** flog sb, beat sb. **~ się** *ipf.* **1.** treat each other *l.* one another (*czymś* to sth). **2.** help o.s. (*czymś* to sth); **częstuj się!** help yourself!

częsty *a.* **-szy** frequent; common; **częsty gość** frequenter (*czegoś* of sth) frequent visitor; **częsty problem** common problem; **coraz częściej** increasingly.

częściowo *adv.* partly; **jajeczko częściowo nieświeże** curate's egg.

częściowy *a.* partial, fragmentary; **przekrój częściowy** cutaway.

część *f.* **1.** (= *fragment*) part, portion; **części ciała** *anat.* parts of anatomy, parts of the human body; **intymne części ciała** private parts; **części świata** *geogr.* continents; **części mowy** *jęz.* parts of speech; **część garderoby** article *l.* item *l.* piece of clothing; **lwia część** lion's share; **część składowa** component, constituent (part); **część frontowa** front(al) part; **część górna** upper part, upper side; **część przednia** forepart; **najważniejsza część** centerpiece, main part; **część główna** *l.* **zasadnicza czegoś** body of sth, main *l.* key *l.* vital part of sth; **część jadalna** edible *l.* eatable part; **najlepsza część** prime, choicest *l.* best part; **w części** *l.* **po części** partly; **po części spodziewał się tego** he half-expected that; **nieodłączna część czegoś** part and parcel of sth; **być nieodłączną częścią czegoś** be inherent in *l.* to sth; **być nieodłączną częścią czyjegoś życia** be a permanent fixture in sb's life; **stanowić część czegoś** form a part of sth. **2.** (= *niezbędny do funkcjonowania element maszyny*) part, unit; **rozbierać coś na części** take sth apart, dismember sth; **części zapasowe** *l.* **zamienne** *techn.* spare parts. **3.** (= *rozdział, odcinek*) (*książki*) part, chapter; (*serialu*) episode.

czkać *ipf. pot.* hiccup, hiccough.

czkawka *f. Gen.pl.* **-ek** hiccup(s), hiccough; **mieć czkawkę** hiccup, hiccough; **dostać czkawki** get the hiccups.

czknąć *pf.* **-ij** *zob.* **czkać**.

człapać *ipf.* **-pię -piesz 1.** (= *wlec się*) drag one's feet. **2.** (= *klapać, stukać*) clack.

człek *mp Dat.* **-owi** *l.* **-u** *Voc.* **-u** *l.* **-cze 1.** *pot.* (= *człowiek*) man, chap; **dobry z niego człek** he's a good chap. **2.** *pot.* (= *ja, każdy, ktokolwiek*) one, you.

człekokształtne *pl. Gen.* **-ych** *zool.* anthropoids (*Anthropoidea*).

człekokształtny *a. zool.* anthropoid; **małpa człekokształtna** pongid ape.

człon *mi Gen.* **-a** *l.* **-u 1.** (= *element, część*) part, element. **2.** *techn., mech.* (= *określona część konstrukcyjna*) module, member. **3.** *jęz.* clause.

członek *mp* **-nk-** *pl.* **-owie** (*towarzystwa, partii, rządu, rady*) member; **członek honorowy** honorary member. **–** *mi* **-nk-** *pl.* **-i** *anat.* limb; **członek męski** penis, *żart.* member.

członkini *f.* member.

członkostwo *n.* membership.

członkować *ipf.* dismember, cut up.

członkowski *a.* membership; **legitymacja/składka członkowska** membership card/fee.

człowieczek *mp* -czk- *pl.* -i *żart.* little fellow.

człowieczeństwo *n.* humanity.

człowieczy *a. lit.* human; **człowieczy los** human fate; **Syn Człowieczy** *rel.* the Son of Man.

człowiek *mp Voc.* -u *l.* -cze *pl.* **ludzie** *Gen.* **ludzi** *Ins.* **ludźmi** 1. *antrop.* human being (*Homo sapiens*); **człowiek pierwotny** primitive man; **człowiek jaskiniowy** cave man; **człowiek neandertalski** Neanderthal man; **człowiek epoki brązu** Bronze man; **biały człowiek** white man. 2. (= *osoba*) person, individual; **swój człowiek** friend, my/our man; **szary człowiek** the man in the street; **zwykły człowiek** everyman; **człowiek bez znaczenia** nobody, nonentity; **człowiek z ludu** man of the people; **dobry człowiek** good person; **święty człowiek** holy man, man of God; **człowiek gruboskórny** thick-skinned person; **człowiek interesu** businessman; **człowiek bezwartościowy** no-good; **człowiek czynu** man of action, doer; **człowiek sukcesu** achiever, hot shot; **człowiek śniegu** Abominable Snowman, Yeti; **człowiek starej daty** mossback; **człowiek-orkiestra** one-man band; **człowiek z krwi i kości** flesh and blood; **błąd człowieka** human error; **prawa człowieka** human rights; **upadek człowieka** the Fall of Man; **ani się człowiek obejrzy** before one knows; **być człowiekiem** be human; **jestem człowiekiem i nic, co ludzkie, nie jest mi obce** I am a human *l.* man and nothing that's human can be *l.* is alien to me; **człowiek strzela, Pan Bóg kule nosi** man proposes, God disposes; **człowiek uczy się przez całe życie** you never stop learning, live and learn; **góra z górą się nie zejdzie, ale człowiek z człowiekiem tak** friends may meet but mountains never greet; **niewłaściwy człowiek na niewłaściwym miejscu** a round peg in a square hole; **okazać się człowiekiem** prove human; **człowieku nie irytuj się** don't get irritated; **człowiek boże igrzysko** man, the plaything of God; **nie ma ludzi niezastąpionych** nobody is irreplaceable; **nie samym chlebem człowiek żyje** man does not live on bread alone; **człowiek człowiekowi wilkiem** man is a wolf to (his fellow-)man, one man preys on another. 3. *pot.* (= *ja, każdy, ktokolwiek*) one, you; **nie dadzą człowiekowi spokoju** they won't let a fellow be. 4. (= *dorosły*) adult, grown-up. 5. *pot.* (= *robotnik, pracownik*) worker; **nająć człowieka do kopania studni** hire a worker *l.* sb to dig a well.

czmychać *ipf.*, **czmychnąć** *pf.* -ij (= *uciekać*) flee, abscond (*przed kimś/czymś* from sb/sth).

czochra *f. tk.* ripple comb, hackle.

czochrać *ipf.* 1. (= *targać włosy*) tousle, dishevel. 2. (*o zwierzętach*) (= *ocierać*) rub. 3. *tk.* hackle, ripple. ~ **się** *ipf.* 1. (= *targać włosy*) tousle one's hair, dishevel one's hair; (= *drapać się*) scratch o.s. 2. (*o zwierzętach*) (= *ocierać się*) rub.

czołg *mi wojsk.* tank; **iść** *l.* **przeć jak czołg** *przen.* be unstoppable; **idzie mi tu czołg?** *przen.* yeah, right!, sure thing!, knock it off!

czołgać się *ipf.* 1. (= *pełzać*) crawl, creep. 2. *przen.* (*o dymie, mgle*) (= *rozprzestrzeniać się*)

sweep. 3. *pot.* (= *płaszczyć się*) grovel (*przed kimś* to *l.* before sb).

czołgista *mp wojsk.* tank crewman.

czołgowy *a. wojsk.* tank; **załoga czołgowa** tank crew.

czoło *n. Gen.pl.* **czół** 1. (= *górna część twarzy*) forehead; **z pogodnym** *l.* **rozjaśnionym czołem** with a smile; **(zdobywać coś) w pocie czoła** (achieve sth) by the sweat of one's brow; **iść z podniesionym czołem** walk with one' head high in the air; **nosić czoło wysoko** walk with one's head high in the air; **bić przed kimś czołem** kowtow to sb; **chylić przed kimś czoło** take one's hat off to sb; **marszczyć czoło** frown, furrow one's brow; **puknij się w czoło!** you must be out of your mind *l.* gourd!; **stawić komuś/czemuś czoło** meet *l.* face sb/sth, make head against sb/sth, face up to sb/sth, face sb/sth down; **mieć coś wypisane na czole** show sth. 2. (= *przednia część*) head, front; **czoło fali** *fiz.* wave front; **czoło pochodu/grupy** head of a procession/group; **na czele** at the head, at the lead; **na czele z kimś** under the leadership of sb; **postawić kogoś na czele** put sb at the head, bring sb to the fore; **stać na czele czegoś** manage sth, control *l.* head sth, lead sth; **wysunąć się na czoło** take the lead, come to the fore.

czołobitność *f.* servility, subservience, adulation, cringe.

czołobitny *a.* servile, subservient, adulatory, cringing.

czołowo *adv.* frontward, frontwards, head-on; **samochody zderzyły się czołowo** cars met *l.* crashed head-on.

czołowy *a.* 1. *anat.* frontal; **zatoki czołowe** frontal sinuses; **kości czołowe** frontal bones; **płat czołowy** frontal lobe. 2. (= *na przedzie*) front; **zderzenie czołowe** *mot.* head-on crash *l.* collision; **morena czołowa** *geol.* end *l.* terminal *l.* frontal moraine; **powierzchnia czołowa** face. 3. (*działacz, przedstawiciel, pracownik*) (= *przodujący, wybitny*) leading, main; **czołowa pozycja** leading position; **czołowe miejsce na afiszu** top billing.

czołówka *f. Gen.pl.* -ek 1. (*wyścigu, pochodu, marszu*) (= *przód*) lead, forefront; **być/znaleźć się w czołówce** be in the lead, be at the head. 2. *przen.* (= *elita, awangarda*) elite, leaders; **ścisła czołówka** leading edge. 3. *dzienn.* cover *l.* front-page story; **dać/umieścić coś na czołówce** put sth on the front page. 4. *film* (= *napisy wstępne*) titles, credits.

czop *mi Gen.* -u *l.* -a 1. (= *zatyczka*) plug, bung. 2. (= *przedmiot w kształcie stożka*) cone. 3. *pat.* (*przy anginie*) plug. 4. *techn.* (= *element łączący*) pin; journal; pivot.

czopek *mi* -pk- *Gen.* -a 1. (= *zatyczka*) plug, peg. 2. (= *przedmiot w kształcie stożka*) cone. 3. *farm.* (*doodbytniczy, dopochwowy*) suppository. 4. **czopki siatkówki** *anat.* cones. 5. *techn.* (= *element łączący*) pin; journal; pivot.

czopik *mi Gen.* -a 1. (= *przedmiot w kształcie stożka*) cone. 2. *farm., pot.* suppository.

czopować *ipf.* (= *zatykać*) plug; **czopować beczki** bung (up).

czopowy *a.* **1.** (= *dotyczący zatyczki*) plug; **piła czopowa** tennon saw. **2.** *techn.* pin; journal; pivot.

czort *mp pl.* **-y** (= *demon*) the devil, Satan; **czort go weźmie** he's going to die; he's going to get hurt; **do czorta!** what the devil *l.* hell!; **czort wie** the devil only knows; **czort z nim** *l.* **czort go bierz!** damn him!, to hell with him!; **idź do czorta!** go to hell!

czosnaczek *mi* **-czk-** *Gen.* **-a** *bot.* garlic mustard (*Alliaria officinalis*).

czosnek *mi* **-nk-** **1.** *bot.* garlic (*Allium sativum*). **2.** (= *cebulka tej rośliny*) garlic; **główka czosnku** garlic bulb; **ząbek czosnku** clove of garlic; **wyciskacz do czosnku** garlic press.

czosnkowy *a.* garlicky; alliaceous; **chlebek czosnkowy** garlic bread.

czółenko *n. Gen.pl.* **-nek 1.** (= *mała łódź*) (small) boat, (small) canoe. **2.** (= *pantofel damski*) pump, court shoe. **3.** *techn., tk.* shuttle.

czółno *n. Gen.pl.* **-łen** (= *łódź*) boat, canoe; (*drążone w pniu*) dugout.

czterdziestka *f.* **1.** (= *liczba 40*) forty; **jechać czterdziestką** *mot., pot.* drive forty kilometers per hour, be doing forty kilometers per hour. **2.** *pot.* (*o wieku*) forty; **komuś stuknęła czterdziestka** sb has turned forty; **życie zaczyna się po czterdziestce** life begins when you turn forty. **3.** *pot.* (= *tramwaj, autobus, dom, pokój nr 40*) forty; **do szpitala dojedziesz czterdziestką** the forty takes you to the hospital, streetcar/bus, etc. number forty takes you to the hospital; **mieszkamy pod czterdziestką** our house *l.* apartment number is forty. **4.** (= *rozmiar ubrania, buta*) size forty. **5.** *pot.* (= *kobieta w wieku 40 lat*) forty-year-old woman.

czterdziestodniowy *a.* **1.** (= *trwający 40 dni*) forty-day, forty days'. **2.** (= *mający 40 dni*) forty-day-old.

czterdziestogodzinny *a.* (= *trwający 40 godzin*) forty-hour, forty hours'.

czterdziestolatek *mp* **-tk-** *pl.* **-i** *l.* **-owie** *pot.* forty-year-old (man).

czterdziestolecie *n.* **1.** (= *okres 40 lat*) forty years, four decades. **2.** (= *czterdziesta rocznica*) fortieth anniversary.

czterdziestoletni *a.* **1.** (= *trwający 40 lat*) forty-year, forty years'. **2.** (= *mający 40 lat*) forty-year-old.

czterdziesty *a.* fortieth; **lata czterdzieste** the forties.

czterdzieści *num.* **-st-** *Ins.* **-oma** *l.* **-u** (= *liczba 40*) forty; **czterdziestu chłopców** forty boys.

czterdzieścioro *num. Gen.* **-rga** *Dat., Loc.* **-rgu** forty; **czterdzieścioro dzieci** forty children.

czterech *num. zob.* **cztery**.

czterechsetlecie *n.* **1.** (= *okres 400 lat*) four hundred years, four centuries. **2.** (= *czterechsetna rocznica*) four hundredth anniversary.

czterechsetny *num.* four hundredth.

czterej *num. zob.* **cztery**.

czternasta *f. Gen.* **-ej** (*godzina*) two (o'clock)

p.m.; **będę piętnaście po czternastej** I'll be there at a quarter past two; **kończę za piętnaście czternasta** I finish at a quarter to two; **mam pociąg o w pół do czternastej** my train leaves at half past one.

czternastka *f. Gen.pl.* **-ek 1.** (= *liczba 14*) fourteen. **2.** *pot.* (= *tramwaj, autobus, dom, pokój nr 14*) fourteen; **do szpitala dojedziesz czternastką** the fourteen takes you to the hospital, streetcar/bus, etc. number fourteen takes you to the hospital; **mieszkamy pod czternastką** our house *l.* apartment number is fourteen. **3.** (= *rozmiar ubrania, buta*) size fourteen. **4.** *pot.* (= *dziewczyna w wieku 14 lat*) fourteen-year-old girl. **5.** *pot.* (= *czternaste urodziny*) fourteenth birthday.

czternastodniowy *a.* **1.** (= *trwający 14 dni*) fourteen-day, fourteen days'. **2.** (= *mający 14 dni*) fourteen-day-old.

czternastogodzinny *a.* (= *trwający 14 godzin*) fourteen-hour, fourteen hours'.

czternastolatek *mp* **-tk-** *Gen.pl.* **-i** fourteen-year-old.

czternastolatka *f. Gen.pl.* **-ek 1.** (*o dziewczynce*) fourteen-year-old (girl). **2.** (*o zwierzęciu*) fourteen-year-old (animal).

czternastoletni *a.* **1.** (= *trwający 14 lat*) fourteen-year, fourteen years'. **2.** (= *mający 14 lat*) fourteen-years-old.

czternastowieczny *a.* (of) the fourteenth century; **czternastowieczny kościół** fourteenth-century church.

czternasty *a.* fourteenth. – *mi* fourteenth (*day of a month*); **umówić się z kimś na czternastego czerwca** arrange a meeting with sb on the fourteenth of June; **skończyć pracę do czternastego** finish work by the fourteenth.

czternaście *num.* **-st-** *Ins.* **-oma** *l.* **-u** (= *liczba 14*) fourteen; **czternastu studentów** fourteen students; **czternaście dziewcząt** fourteen girls; **mieć czternaście lat** be fourteen (years old); **po czternastu minutach** after fourteen minutes.

czternaścioro *num. Gen.* **-rga** *Dat., Loc.* **-rgu** fourteen; **czternaścioro dzieci** fourteen children.

czteroaktowy *a.* *teatr* four-act, in four acts; **komedia czteroaktowa** comedy in four acts, four-act comedy; **przedstawienie czteroaktowe** play in four acts, four-act play.

czteroaktówka *f. Gen.pl.* **-ek** *teatr* four-act play, play in four acts; **wystawiać czteroaktówkę** put on a four-act play.

czterochlorek *mi chem.* tetrachloride.

czterocyfrowy *a.* four-figure, four-digit.

czterocylindrowy *a.* *mot.* four-cylinder; **czterocylidrowy silnik** four.

czteroczęściowy *a.* four-part.

czterodniowy *a.* **1.** (= *trwający 4 dni*) four-day, four days'. **2.** (= *mający 4 dni*) four-day-old.

czterodrzwiowy *a.* *pot.* four-door.

czterogłosowy *a.* *muz.* four-part.

czterogodzinny *a.* (= *trwający 4 godziny*) four-hour, four hours'.

czterogwiazdkowy *a.* four-star; **czterogwiazd-**

kowy hotel four star hotel; **czterogwiazdkowy generał** *wojsk., pot.* general.

czterojajeczny *a.* four-egg; **makaron czterojajeczny** four-egg pasta.

czteroklasowy *a. szkoln.* four-grade; **szkoła czteroklasowa** four-grade school.

czterokołowy *a.* four-wheeled.

czterokondygnacyjny *a.* (*o budynku*) five-story, five-storey.

czterokonny *a.* four-horse; **zaprzęg czterokonny** four-in-hand.

czterokrotny *a.* four-times, fourfold.

czterolecie *n.* **1.** (= *okres 4 lat*) four years. **2.** (= *czwarta rocznica*) fourth anniversary.

czteroletni *a.* **1.** (= *trwający 4 lata*) four-year, four years'. **2.** (= *mający 4 lata*) four-year-old.

czterolistny *a.* four-leaved; **czterolistna koniczyna** four-leaf clover.

czteroliterowy *a.* four-letter.

czteromasztowiec *mi* -wc- *Gen.* -a *żegl.* four-masted ship, four-master.

czteromiesięczny *a.* **1.** (= *trwający 4 miesiące*) four-month, four months'. **2.** (= *mający 4 miesiące*) four-month-old.

czteroosobowy *a.* **1.** (*pokój, namiot*) (= *przeznaczony dla czterech osób*) four-person; **samochód czteroosobowy** *mot.* four-seater. **2.** (*zespół, rodzina*) (= *składający się z czterech osób*) of four persons.

czteropasmowy *a.* (*o szosie, drodze*) four-lane.

czteropiętrowy *a.* (*o budynku*) five-story, five-storey.

czteropokojowy *a.* four-room.

czteroprocentowy *a.* four-percent.

czterosilnikowy *a.* four-engine; **samolot czterosilnikowy** *lotn.* four-engine plane.

czterosuwowy *a. techn.* four-stroke; **silnik czterosuwowy** four-stroke engine.

czterosylabowy *a. jęz.* (*o wyrazie*) four-syllable.

czterościeżkowy *a. techn.* (*o magnetofonie*) four-track.

czterotaktowy *a.* **1.** *techn.* four-stroke. **2.** *muz.* four-bar, four-measure.

czterotomowy *a.* four-volume.

czterotonowy *a.* **1.** (= *ważący cztery tony*) four-ton. **2.** (= *mający udźwig czterech ton*) four-ton.

czterotygodniowy *a.* **1.** (= *trwający 4 tygodnie*) four-week, four weeks'. **2.** (= *mający 4 tygodnie*) four-week-old.

czterowartościowy *a.* *chem.* tetravalent, quadrivalent.

czterowiersz *mi Gen.* -a *teor.lit.* tetrastich.

czterowymiarowy *a.* four-dimensional.

czterozgłoskowy *a. teor.lit.* four-syllabic.

czterozmianowy *a.* four-shift.

cztery *num.* **czterej** *l.* **czterech** *Gen., Loc.* -ech *Dat.* -em *Ins.* -ema **1.** (= *liczba 4*) four; **czterej mężczyźni** four men; **dwa dodać dwa jest cztery** two and two make four; **cztery strony świata** cardinal points, four corners of the world; **cztery żywioły** the four elements; **cztery deski** coffin; **cztery ściany** room; **cztery litery** *euf.* fundament; wy-

raz na cztery litery four-letter word; **utwór na cztery ręce** *muz.* four-handed piece; **spaść na cztery łapy** land on one's feet; **zamknąć (się) na cztery spusty** lock (o.s.) up; **w cztery oczy** in private; **kuty na cztery nogi** sly old fox; **przepędzić kogoś na cztery wiatry** chase sb away (for good). **2.** *szkoln., uniw.* good, B.

czterysta *num. Ins.* -oma *l.* -u (= *liczba 400*) four hundred; **czterystu mężczyzn** four hundred men.

czterystumetrowiec *mp Gen., Acc.* -wca *sport* four-hundred-meter runner.

czub *mi Gen.* -a **1.** (= *stercząca fryzura*) mohican; **wziąć się za czuby** come to blows; **dostać po czubie** get slapped upside the head; **komuś dymi się z czuba** sb is drunk; **mieć w czubie** *pot.* be in one's cups. **2.** *zool.* crest. **3.** (= *najwyższa część*) top; **łyżka z czubem** heaping spoonful. **4.** (= *wystająca część*) point, tip. – *mp pl.* -y *pot., pog.* (= *wariat*) nut.

czubacz *ma orn.* curassow, Crax.

czubajka *f. Gen.pl.* -ek *bot.* (*grzyb*) parasol mushroom (*Lepiota*).

czubatka *f. Gen.pl.* -ek **1.** (*sikora*) **czubatka** *orn.* crested tit (*Parus cristatus*). **2.** *hodowla* (*rasa kury*) crested hen.

czubaty *a.* **1.** (*z pękiem piór, włosów*) crested. **2.** (= *ostro zakończony*) pointed, protruding. **3.** (= *pełny*) heaping, overflowing.

czubek *mi* -bk- *Gen.* -a **1.** (= *stercząca fryzura*) mohican. **2.** *zool.* crest. **3.** (= *najwyższa część*) top; **od czubka do pięt** from head to toe; **po czubek** to the top; **czubek głowy** crown of the head. **4.** (= *wystająca część*) point, tip; **łyżka z czubkiem** heaping spoonful; **czubek palca** fingertip; **sam czubek czegoś** extreme tip of sth; **na czubku nosa** on the tip of one's nose; **chodzić na czubkach palców** tiptoe, go *l.* walk on tiptoe; **postawić coś na czubku** put sth endwise. – *mp* -bk- *pl.* -i *pot., pog.* (= *wariat*) nut; **wsadzić kogoś do czubków** *l.* **zamknąć kogoś u czubków** put sb to a lunatic asylum.

czubić się *ipf.* **1.** (= *sprzeczać się*) bicker; **kto się czubi, ten się lubi** the harder they hit you, the more they like you, the more they pester *l.* nag you, the greater their affection for you. **2.** (*o ptakach*) peck each other *l.* one another.

czucie *n.* feeling, sense; **stracić czucie w rękach/nogach** lose feeling in one's hands/legs; **paść bez czucia** drop senseless.

czuciowy *a.* sensory.

czuć *ipf.* **1.** (= *odbierać bodźce*) feel, sense; **nie czuć nóg/rąk** be dead tired, be on one's last legs; **czułam na sobie czyjś wzrok** I felt *l.* sensed sb watching me. **2.** (= *wyczuwać zapach*) smell. **3.** (= *doznawać emocji*) feel; **czuć sympatię/odrazę do kogoś** have a liking/dislike for sb; **czuć do kogoś miętę** *żart.* have a crush on sb; **czuć ciężar na duszy** have one's heart in one's boots. **4.** (= *domyślać się*) get a feeling; **czuć coś przez skórę** scent sth, feel sth coming; **czuć pismo nosem** smell a rat; **czuć coś w kościach** feel sth in one's bones. **5.** realize; **czuć mores przed kimś** *l.* **wobec kogoś** awe sb; **czuć coś** (= *mieć do czegoś* *talent*) have a feel for sth. ~ **się** *ipf.* (= *być w określonym stanie*) feel; **dobrze/źle/słabo się czuć** feel well/unwell/weak; **czuć się winnym/starym/młodym** feel guilty/old/young; **czuć się na siłach** feel up to sth; **czuć się podle** feel lousy *l.* crummy; **czuć się jak w klatce** feel caged in; **czuj się jak u siebie w domu** make yourself at home; **czuć się jak u siebie w domu** feel at home; **czuć się jak ryba w wodzie** be in one's element; **czuć się zobowiązanym zrobić coś** feel obliged to do sth; **czuć się zmuszonym do zrobienia czegoś** feel compelled to do sth; **czuć się nieswojo** feel not quite o.s., feel out of it.

czuj *mi* **mieć czuja** (= *mieć wyczucie*) feel, sense, have a feeling for; (= *kierować się intuicją*) do *l.* sense by intuition, follow one's nose in doing sth; **na czuja** (= *na wyczucie*) on a hunch.

czujka *f. Gen.pl.* **-ek 1.** (= *czata*) sentry, lookout. **2.** *techn.* detector, sensor; **czujka pożarowa** fire detector.

czujnie *adv.* vigilantly, watchfully; **spać** *l.* **sypiać czujnie** sleep lightly.

czujnik *mi Gen.* **-a** *techn.* sensor.

czujność *f.* vigilance, alertness; **obudzić czyjąś czujność** put sb on guard; **uśpić/zmylić/oszukać czyjąś czujność** throw sb off guard, lull sb into a sense of security; **stracić czujność** drop *l.* lower one's guard.

czujny *a.* vigilant, alert, watchful; **pod czyimś czujnym okiem** under sb's watchful eye; **mieć czujny sen** sleep lightly, be a light sleeper.

czule *adv.* tenderly; **gruchać czule** bill and coo.

czulić się *ipf.* fondle (*do kogoś* sb).

czułek *mi* **-łk-** *Gen.* **-a 1.** *zool.* (= *wyrostek*) antenna, feeler, tentacle; (*z okiem*) ommatophore. **2.** *bot.* (= *mimoza*) mimosa (*Mimosa*).

czułostka *f. Gen.pl.* **-ek** endearment.

czułostkowość *f.* mawkishness.

czułostkowy *a.* mawkish, namby-pamby.

czułość *f.* **1.** (= *tkliwość, serdeczność*) tenderness, fondness, affection; **z czułością** tenderly. **2.** (= *objaw miłości, tkliwości itp.*) endearment; **okazywać komuś czułość** show sb affection. **3.** (= *zdolność szybkiego reagowania na bodźce*) sensitivity; (= *dokładność, precyzyjność*) precision. **4.** *techn.* sensitivity; **czułość błony fotograficznej** *l.* **filmu** *fot.* speed.

czuły *a.* **-lszy 1.** (= *serdeczny*) tender, loving, affectionate; **czułe serce** loving heart. **2.** (= *wyczulony, wrażliwy*) sensitive; **czuły punkt/miejsce** sore point/spot; **być czułym na punkcie czegoś** be sensitive *l.* defensive about sth; **trafić kogoś w czuły punkt** hit sb where it hurts. **3.** *techn.* (*waga, lampa, aparat, mikrofon*) sensitive.

czumiza *f. bot.* foxtail millet (*Setaria italica*).

czupiradło *n. Gen.pl.* **-deł** fright.

czupryna *f.* **1.** (= *bujne włosy*) mop; **bujna czupryna** bush; **ciemna czupryna** crop of dark hair; **komuś się kurzy z czupryny** sb is tipsy *l.* drunk. **2.** *pot., przen.* (= *głowa*) head; **dać po czuprynie** give sb a crack on the noggin; **oberwać po czuprynie** get beaten.

czupurnie *adv.* quarrelsomely.

czupurny *a.* quarrelsome.

czuwać *ipf.* **1.** (= *być czujnym*) be on the alert; watch over (*nad l. przy kimś/czymś* sb/sth); (*o strażnikach*) keep watch; **czuwać przy łóżku chorego** sit at sb's bedside. **2.** (= *nie spać*) keep vigil, stay awake; **czuwać całą noc** stay up all night.

czuwanie *n.* **1.** (= *pilnowanie*) watch; **całonocne czuwanie** *kośc.* vigil(s). **2.** (= *trwanie bez snu*) vigil, awakeness; **nocne czuwanie** night watch; **godziny czuwania** waking hours.

czwarta *f. Gen.* **-ej** (*godzina*) four (o'clock); **czwarta rano** four a.m.; **umówić się z kimś na czwartą** arrange to meet sb at four; **skończyć pracę do czwartej** finish work by four.

czwartek *mi* **-tk-** Thursday; **tłusty czwartek** the Thursday before Ash Wednesday; **Wielki Czwartek** *rel., kośc.* Maundy Thursday.

czwartoklasista *mp szkoln.* fourth-grader; *Br.* fourth-former.

czwartorzęd *mi geol.* Quaternary (Period).

czwartorzędny *a.* fourth-rate, inferior.

czwartorzędowy *mi geol.* Quaternary.

czwarty *a.* fourth; **czwarty wymiar** *fiz., mat.* fourth dimension; **mieć czwarty krzyżyk na karku** *pot.* be pushing forty; **czwarty bieg** *zwł. mot.* fourth gear; **jedna czwarta** one-fourth. – *mi* fourth (*day of a month*); **umówić się z kimś na czwartego czerwca** arrange to meet sb on the fourth of June. – *mp* fourth person; fourth player; **potrzebujemy czwartego do brydża** we need a fourth person to play bridge with us.

czworaczki *pl. Gen.* **-ów** quadruplets.

czworak *mi Gen.* **-a czworaki** *hist.* (*budynek*) living quarters of farm helpers; **(chodzić) na czworakach** (walk) on all fours.

czworaki *a.* fourfold; (= *w czterech rodzajach*) in four kinds *l.* types *l.* varieties.

czworo *num. decl. like n.* **-rg-** four; **czworo dzieci** four children; **dzielić włos na czworo** split hairs; **składać coś we czworo** fold in four.

czworoboczny *a.* quadrilateral.

czworobok *mi* **1.** *geom., mat.* tetragon, quadrilateral, quadrangle. **2.** (= *kształt zbliżony do czworoboku*) tetragon, square; **czworobok przegubowy** *techn.* four-bar linkage. **3.** *hist., wojsk.* square.

czworokąt *mi Gen.* **-a 1.** *geom., mat.* tetragon, quadrilateral, quadrangle. **2.** (= *kształt zbliżony do czworokąta*) tetragon, square.

czworokątny *a.* tetragonal, quadrangular.

czworomian *mi Gen.* **-u** *mat.* quadrinomial.

czworonożny *a. gł. zool.* quadruped; **czworonożny przyjaciel** four-footed friend, dog.

czworonóg *ma* **-o-** *zool.* quadruped.

czworościan *mi geom., mat., min.* tetrahedron; **czworościan foremny** regular tetrahedron.

czwórbój *mi* **-o-** *Gen.pl.* **-ów** *l.* **-oi** *sport* four-event competition.

czwórka *f. Gen.pl.* **-ek 1.** (= *cyfra 4*) four. **2.** *pot.* (= *tramwaj, autobus, dom, pokój nr 4*) four; **do szpitala dojedziesz czwórką** the four takes you to the hospital, streetcar/bus, etc. number four takes you to the hospital; **mieszkamy pod czwórką** our house *l.* apartment number is four.

3. (= *rozmiar ubrania, buta*) size four. **4.** (= *cztery osoby, przedmioty itp.*) foursome, group of four; set of four; (*np. w restauracji przy zamawianiu stolika*) party of four. **5.** *szkoln., uniw.* good, B. **6.** *wojsk.* four; **formować czwórki** form fours; **maszerować czwórkami** march in fours. **7.** *sport* (= *zespół czteroosobowy*) (crew of) four. **8.** *el.* (= *wiązka czterech przewodów*) quad. **9.** *karty* four; **czwórka pik** four of spades. **10.** (= *zaprzęg z czterech koni*) four-in-hand.

czwórnasób *adv.* fourfold, four times; **w czwórnasób** fourfold, four times.

czy[1] *part.* (*w pytaniach*) **czy pada śnieg?** is it snowing?; **czy znasz ten film?** do you know this movie?; **czy byłeś kiedyś w Anglii?** have you ever been to England?; **czy mogę już iść?** can I go now?; **czy ja wiem?** I don't know.

czy[2] *conj.* **1.** (*wprowadza zdanie podrzędne*) if, whether; **zapytaj, czy przyjdzie** ask him if he's coming. **2.** (*łączy części współrzędne*) or; **kawa czy herbata?** coffee or tea?; **prędzej czy później** sooner or later; **tak czy inaczej** *l.* **owak** *l.* **siak** one way or another, anyhow, eitherway; **świątek czy piątek** anytime.

czyhać *ipf.* **1.** (= *czaić się*) lurk waiting, wait (*na kogoś / coś* for sb/sth). **2.** *przen.* (= *zagrażać*) lurk; **tam czyha niebezpieczeństwo/śmierć** danger/death lurks there. **3.** (= *czekać w napięciu*) wait anxiously; **czyhać na okazję/sposobność** wait for an opportunity/chance.

czyj *a. Ins., Loc.* **czyim** *pl.* **czyje, czyi** *Gen., Loc.* **czyich** *Dat.* **czyim** *Ins.* **czyimi** **1.** (*wyraża pytanie: do kogo / czego coś należy?*) whose; **czyje to dziecko?** whose child is it?; **wiedziała, czyje będzie na wierzchu** she knew who'd win. **2.** (= *czyjś*) someone's, somebody's.

czyjkolwiek *a.* **czyj-** *decl. like a.,* **-kolwiek** *indecl.* anybody's, anyone's.

czyjś *a.* **czyj-** *decl. like a.,* **-kolwiek** *indecl.* somebody's, someone's.

czyli *part.* (= *to znaczy*) that is, i.e.; in other words.

czym *pron. zob.* **co.**

czymkolwiek *pron. zob.* **cokolwiek.**

czymś *pron. zob.* **coś.**

czyn *mi* deed, act; **czyn zbrojny** military action; **bohaterski czyn** heroic deed, gest; **czyn karalny** *prawn.* unlawful act; **czyn lubieżny** *prawn.* indecent liberties; **czyn hańbiący** infamy; **czyn społeczny** community work *l.* service; **człowiek czynu** man of action; **słowem i czynem** in word and deed; **wcielać** *l.* **wprowadzać w czyn** put sth into practice; **zamieniać się w czyn** come true; **przejść od słów do czynów** put one's words into action.

czynel *mi Gen.* **-a** *l.* **-u** *Gen.pl.* **-i** *l.* **-ów** *muz.* cymbal.

czynić *ipf.* **1.** (= *wykonywać coś*) do; **dobrze/źle czynić** do good/evil; **czynić cuda** work miracles; **czynić honory domu** do the honours; **czynić starania o coś** strive for sth; **czynić postępy** make progress; **czynić ustępstwa** make concessions; **czynić wysiłki** make efforts; **czynić wyznania** confide; **czynić coś w dobrej wierze** do sth in good faith; **czynić kogoś odpowiedzialnym za coś** (= *winić kogoś za coś*) hold sb accountable *l.* responsible for sth; (= *nakładać na kogoś obowiązek*) make sb responsible for sth, put sb in charge of sth. **2.** (= *zachowywać się*) behave, act; **czynić komuś dobrze** do sb good; **czynić czemuś zadość** satisfy sth; **nie czyń drugiemu, co tobie niemiło** do as you would be done by; **czyń (prędko), co masz czynić** what you are about to do, do (quickly). **3.** (= *składać się na coś*) amount.

czynienie *n.* **1.** (= *wykonywanie czegoś*) doing; **mieć z czymś/kimś do czynienia** have to do with sth/sb, deal with sth/sb. **2.** (= *zachowywanie się*) behavior.

czynnie *adv.* **1.** (= *działając osobiście*) actively; **czynnie kogoś znieważyć** hit sb on the face. **2.** (= *energicznie, z zapałem*) actively, energetically.

czynnik *mi Gen.* **-a** **1.** (= *bodziec, przyczyna, warunek*) factor; **decydujący czynnik** decisive factor; **jeden z czynników** contributory factor; **czynnik Rh** *med.* Rh factor; **najwyższe/polityczne/oficjalne czynniki** government/political/official circles; **czynnik chorobotwórczy** *pat.* pathogen; **czynnik ludzki** the human factor; **czynnik sprawczy** causative factor; **rozkładać na czynniki pierwsze** *przen.* dissect, put to pieces. **2.** *mat.* (= *wyraz iloczynu*) factor; **czynniki pierwsze** prime factors.

czynność *f.* **1.** (= *praca, obowiązki*) work, activity; **czynność prawna** *prawn.* legal act; **czynności notarialne** *prawn.* notarial acts; **zawiesić czynności** *admin.* suspend activity; **zawiesić kogoś w czynnościach** suspend sb (from their duties). **2.** (= *funkcjonowanie*) function, activity, action, operation; **czynność serca** *med.* cardiac activity, heart action. **3.** *psych.* activity; **czynność bezwiedna** automatism.

czynny *a.* **1.** (= *działający*) working, active; **pierwiastek czynny** *chem.* active element; **czynne prawo wyborcze** *prawn.* (elective) franchise; **czynna służba** *zwł. wojsk.* active duty *l.* service; **czynna zniewaga** *prawn.* (criminal) battery; **brać czynny udział w czymś** take active part in sth; **być czynnym członkiem jakiejś organizacji** be an active member of an organization; **odgrywać czynną rolę** play active part *l.* role in sth. **2.** (= *aktywny, energiczny*) active, energetic; **usunąć się z czynnego życia** retire. **3.** (= *funkcjonujący, sprawny, otwarty*) open, at work, working, operating; **czynny wulkan** *geogr.* active volcano. **4.** *jęz.* active; **imiesłów przymiotnikowy czynny** present participle; **strona czynna czasownika** active voice.

czynsz *mi Gen.pl.* **-y** *l.* **-ów** **1.** *prawn.* rent. **2.** *hist.* (= *świadczenie*) rent; **czynsz wieczysty** *l.* **wieczny** rent charge, free-farm rent.

czynszowy *a.* (= *dotyczący czynszu*) (*opłata*) rent; (*dom, kamienica*) tenemental, tenementary; **kamienica czynszowa** tenement house.

czyrak *mi Gen.* **-a** *pat.* furuncle, boil; **czyrak mnogi** carbuncle.

czysta *f. Gen.* **-ej** *pot.* (= *wódka*) vodka.

czystka *f. Gen.pl.* **-ek** (= *selekcja, odsiew*)

purge; **czystki etniczne** ethnic cleansing; **przeprowadzać czystki** purge, run a clean sweep.

czysto *adv.* **1.** (= *bez brudu*) clean; **przepisać coś na czysto** make a clean *l.* fair copy of sth. **2.** (= *przejrzyście*) clearly, clear. **3.** (= *dźwięcznie*) clearly, clear, in tune. **4.** (= *bez domieszek, wpływów*) purely; **mówić czysto po polsku** speak perfect Polish. **5.** (= *szlachetnie, fair*) fair. **6.** (= *bez obciążeń*) net; **wyjść na czysto** be square; **zarobić na czysto 100 tysięcy dolarów** make a net profit of $100 thousand. **7.** (= *prawdziwie, niewątpliwie*) clearly. **8.** (= *wyłącznie*) solely.

czystopis *mi* clean *l.* fair copy.

czystość *f.* **1.** (= *brak brudu*) cleanness, cleanliness; **coś jest nie pierwszej *l.* wątpliwej czystości** sth is far from clean, sth is soiled. **2.** (= *przezroczystość*) clarity, transparency. **3.** (= *dźwięczność*) clearness. **4.** (= *brak domieszek, wpływów*) purity; **czystość etniczna/narodowa** ethnic/national purity. **5.** (= *szlachetność*) integrity, honesty, probity; **czystość sumienia** clear conscience. **6.** (= *niewinność, celibat*) chastity; **żyć w czystości** live in celibacy. **7.** (= *regularność, wyrazistość*) precision, neatness.

czysty *a.* **-szy** *l.* **-ściejszy 1.** (= *niezabrudzony*) clean; **czysty papier** blank sheet of paper; **być czystym** *przen.* have a clear conscience. **2.** (= *przejrzysty*) clear, transparent; **czyste niebo** clear sky. **3.** (= *dźwięczny*) clear, in tune. **4.** (= *bez zniekształceń i wpływów*) pure; **czyste złoto/srebro** pure gold/silver; **czystej krwi** pure-blood, full blood; **czysta forma** *sztuka* pure form; **czyste szaleństwo/obłęd** sheer insanity/lunacy; **czysty przypadek** sheer *l.* pure coincidence; **czysty zbieg okoliczności** pure happenstance; **przez czysty przypadek** by pure coincidence; **czysty wymysł** nonsense. **5.** (= *wolny od zła, szlachetny*) upright; **czyste sumienie** clear conscience; **czysta walka** clean *l.* fair fight; **mieć czyste ręce** have clean hands; **czysty jak łza** *l.* **kryształ** as pure as the driven snow. **6.** (= *niewinny, nieskalany, cnotliwy*) clean, chaste. **7.** (= *regularny, wyrazisty*) clear, regular. **8.** (= *bez obciążeń finansowych*) in the black; **czysty zysk/dochód** net profit/income; **mieć czyste konto** have a clean sheet. **9.** *pot.* (= *niewątpliwy, oczywisty*) clear, obvious; **Adam to czysty ojciec** Adam is a spitting image of his father; **do czysta** completely.

czyszczak *mi Gen.* **-a** *Ins.* **-iem** *techn.* access eye, cleanout.

czyszczalnia *f. Gen.pl.* **-i 1.** (= *zakład oczyszczający nasiona*) chaff-removal plant. **2.** *roln.* corn cleaner.

czyszczący *a.* cleaning.

czyszczenie *n.* (= *usuwanie brudu*) cleaning; **proszek/płyn do czyszczenia** powder/liquid cleaner; **czyszczenie chemiczne** dry-cleaning; *wet.* (= *kastrowanie*) gelding.

czyścibut *mp pl.* **-y** bootblack, shoeblack.

czyściciel *mp* **1.** cleaner. **2.** *wet.* gelder.

czyścić *ipf.* **-szczę -ścisz 1.** (= *usuwać brud*) clean, cleanse; (*ryby, drób itp.*) dress; **czyścić**

chemicznie dry-clean; **czyścić szczotką** brush; **czyścić pióra** *orn.* preen, plume; **czyścić zęby szczoteczką** brush one's teeth; **czyścić zgrzebłem** curry. **2.** *med., pot.* go lax; **kogoś czyści** sb's bowels go lax. **3.** *wet.* (= *kastrować*) geld.

czyściec *mi* **-śćc-** *Gen.* **-a** *no plural* **1.** *rel.* purgatory. **2.** *przen.* (= *męka*) purgatory, ordeal, suffering. **3.** *pl.* **-e** *bot.* betony, woundwort (*Stachys*).

czyścioch *mp pl.* **-y** *pot.* stickler for cleanliness.

czyścioszek *mp* **-szk-** *pl.* **-i** *pot., żart.* stickler for cleanliness.

czyśćcowy *a. rel.* (*męki, kara, dusze*) purgatorial.

czytać *ipf.* **1.** (*książkę, gazetę, list, Sienkiewicza*) read (*o kimś/czymś* about sb/sth); **czytać po polsku/angielsku** read in Polish/English; **czytać coś w oryginale** read sth in the original; **czytać nuty** *muz.* read the score; **czytać z ruchu warg** lipread; **czytać wyrywkowo** browse, skim, scan; **czytać od deski do deski** read from cover to cover; **czytać pomiędzy wierszami** read between the lines; **czytać w czyichś myślach** read sb's mind; **czytać w kimś jak w otwartej księdze** read sb like an open book. **2.** *przen.* (= *odgadywać, wróżyć*) foretell; **czytać z ręki** read sb's palm.

czytadło *n. Gen.pl.* **-deł** *pot., pog. l. żart.* dime novel.

czytanie *n.* reading; **pierwsze/drugie/trzecie czytanie projektu ustawy** *polit.* the first/second/third reading of a bill; **czytanie z Ewangelii według św. Jana** *kośc.* reading from St. John's gospel.

czytanka *f. Gen.pl.* **-ek** *szkoln.* **1.** (= *tekst*) text. **2.** (= *książka, podręcznik*) reader.

czytelnia *f. Gen.pl.* **-i** *l.* **-ń** reading room.

czytelnictwo *n.* reading.

czytelniczka *f. Gen.pl.* **-ek** *zob.* **czytelnik**.

czytelnie *adv.* **1.** (= *wyraźnie*) legibly. **2.** *przen.* (= *zrozumiale, jasno*) legibly, clearly.

czytelnik *mp* reader.

czytelność *f.* **1.** (= *wyraźność*) legibility. **2.** (= *zrozumiałość, jasność*) legibility.

czytelny *a.* **1.** (= *wyraźny*) legible; **czytelny podpis** legible signature; **czytelny rysunek** legible drawing. **2.** (= *zrozumiały, jasny*) readable, clear; **czytelne zachowanie** legible behavior.

czytnik *mi Gen.* **-a 1.** *techn.* (*do mikrofilmów*) microreader; **optyczny czytnik znaków** optical character reader, OCR. **2.** *tel.* punched-tape reader.

czytywać *ipf.* read (*from time to time*) (*o kimś/ czymś* about sb/sth).

czyż[1] *part.* = czy.

czyż[2] *ma Gen.pl.* **-ów** *l.* **-y** *orn.* siskin (*Carduelis spinus*).

czyżby *part.* **czyżby to zgubił?** could he have lost that?; **czyżby?** really?

czyżyk *ma orn.* siskin (*Carduelis spinus*).

Ć, ć *n. indecl.* (*litera*) C with an (acute) accent.

ćma *f. Gen.pl.* **ciem 1.** *ent.* (= *nocny motyl*) moth. **2.** (= *mnóstwo*) swarm. **3.** *przest., poet.* darkness.

ćmić *ipf.* **ćmij 1.** (= *zasłaniać*) eclipse, dim; **ćmi komuś w oczach** one is blinded; **ćmić w oczy** dazzle. **2.** (= *tlić się*) glow, glimmer. **3.** (= *boleć*) ache slightly. **4.** *pot.* (= *palić*) smoke (*coś* sth) puff (*coś* on *l.* at sth). **~ się** *ipf.* **1.** (= *być mało widocznym*) be *l.* become dimmed; **ćmi się komuś w oczach** sb is blinded; **komuś ćmi się w głowie** sb is confused. **2.** (= *tlić się*) glow, glimmer.

ćmik *mi Gen.* **-a** *pot.* (= *papieros*) fag, butt.

ćpać *ipf.* **1.** *pot.* (= *obżerać się*) gobble, guzzle; (= *pałaszować*) devour, wolf, inhale. **2.** *pot.* (= *brać narkotyki*) do drugs, take drugs. **3.** *pot.* (= *rzucać*) fling, toss.

ćpun *mp pl.* **-y** *pot.* (= *narkoman*) junkie, drug addict, druggie.

ćpunka *f. Gen.pl.* **-ek** *zob.* **ćpun.**

ćwiartka *f. Gen.pl.* **-ek 1.** (= *czwarta część całości*) quarter; **złożyć coś w ćwiartkę** fold sth in four. **2.** (= *połowa części zabijanego zwierzęcia*) quarter. **3.** (= *kartka papieru*) sheet. **4.** *muz. pot.* (*o nucie*) quarter note. **5.** *pot.* (*o wódce*) 250 ml bottle of vodka; **obalić ćwiartkę** toss down a half-pint, knock back a bottle. **6.** *druk.* quarter of a sheet of composition. **7.** *druk.* (= *książka formatu ćwiartkowego*) quarto.

ćwiartkowy *a. druk.* quarto.

ćwiartować *ipf.* quarter.

ćwiczebny *a.* **1.** (*rejs, jazda, lot*) (= *szkoleniowy*) training, practice. **2.** (= *wykorzystywany przy ćwiczeniach*) training; **mundur ćwiczebny** *wojsk.* fatigues, fatigue clothes; **teren ćwiczebny** training ground; **ćwiczebna amunicja** *zwł. wojsk.* blank ammunition, blanks, dummy ammo; **broń ćwiczebna** *zwł. wojsk.* drill guns; **strzelanie ćwiczebne** *zwł. wojsk.* target practice.

ćwiczenie *n.* **1.** (= *czynność powtarzana, aby zdobyć jakąś sprawność*) exercise, practice; **ćwiczenia gimnastyczne** gymnastic exercise; **ćwiczenia wojskowe** military training, drill. **2.**

szkoln. (= *zadanie szkolne lub domowe*) exercise. **3.** *uniw.* (*rodzaj zajęć*) **ćwiczenia** classes. **4.** (= *kształcenie, szkolenie*) training. **5.** (= *powtarzanie, doskonalenie*) practice, drill. **6.** (= *gimnastykowanie się*) exercising. **7.** *muz.* study. **8.** (= *bicie*) flogging, lashing.

ćwiczeniowy *a.* (= *szkoleniowy, treningowy*) training.

ćwiczyć *ipf.* **1.** (= *kształcić, doskonalić*) train (*w czymś* sth). **2.** (= *uczyć się, powtarzać*) practice, drill. **3.** (= *gimnastykować się*) exercise; (= *uprawiać sport*) practice. **4.** (= *bić*) lash, flog. **~ się** *ipf.* practice (*w czymś* sth).

ćwiek *mi Gen.* **-a 1.** (= *gwóźdź*) tack, clout nail; **zabić komuś ćwieka w głowę** *l.* **łeb** baffle sb; **mieć ćwieka w głowie** have a bee in one's bonnet; **wybić komuś ćwieka z głowy** get sth out of sb's head, dissuade sb from doing sth. **2.** (*w szewstwie*) hobnail. **3.** *bud.* gallet.

ćwiekować *ipf.* **1.** (= *nabijać ćwiekami*) tack. **2.** *bud.* gallet. **3.** (*w szewstwie*) hobnail.

ćwierć *f.* **1.** (= *jedna czwarta*) quarter; **dzielić na ćwierci** quarter, divide into quarters; **trzy ćwierci do śmierci** *pot.* on one's last legs. **2.** (= *połowa części zabitego zwierzęcia*) quarter. **3.** *hist.* (*jednostka miary*) quarter of a bushel.

ćwierćfinalista *mp sport* quarterfinalist.

ćwierćfinał *mi sport* quarterfinal.

ćwierćinteligent *mp pog.* dolt, dummy.

ćwierćnuta *f. muz.* quarter note.

ćwierćton *mi muz.* quarter tone.

ćwierćwiecze *n. Gen.pl.* **-y** quarter of a century, twenty five years.

ćwierkać *ipf.*, **ćwierknąć** *pf.* **-ij 1.** (*o ptakach*) chirp, chirrup; **wróble na dachu o czymś ćwierkają** *pot.* a little bird told me. **2.** *przen.* (= *szczebiotać*) chirp.

ćwikła *f. kulin.* beetroot and horseradish dressing.

ćwikłowy *a. roln.* beet; **burak ćwikłowy** beet.

ćwir *int.* chirrup.

ćwok *mp pl.* **-i** *pot. pog.* dunce, blockhead.

D

D, d *n. indecl.* (*litera*) D, d; **D jak Dorota** D is for Delta; D as in Delta.

D¹ *n. indecl. muz.* (*dźwięk*) D; **d-moll** D minor; **D-dur** D major.

D² *abbr. mat.* (*rzymskie 500*) D.

d. *abbr. pot. euf.* = **de.**

dach *mi bud., mot.* roof; **dach dwuspadowy** gable *l.* saddle roof; **dach świata** *przen.* (= *Tybet, Himalaje l. Mount Everest*) roof of the world; **(mieć) dach nad głową** (have) a roof over one's head; **nie mieć dachu nad głową** have no roof over one's head, be homeless; **(dom) z czerwonym/zielonym dachem** red/green-roofed (house); **aż po dach** all the way up (to the roof); **mieszkać pod jednym dachem** live under one roof; **wróble na dachu o tym ćwierkają** *przen.* it's an open secret; a little bird told me; I heard it through the grapevine.

dacharz *mp Gen.pl.* -y *l.* -ów *bud.* roofer.

dachować *ipf. pot. mot.* roll (over), turn turtle.

dachowanie *n. pot. mot.* rollover; **mieć dachowanie** roll (over), turn turtle.

dachowy *a. bud.* roof; **więźba dachowa** roof truss; **bagażnik dachowy** *mot.* roof rack.

dachówka *f. Gen.pl.* -ek *bud.* (roofing) tile; **kryć dachówką** tile; **dach kryty dachówką** tiled roof.

dachówkarz *mp Gen.pl.* -y *l.* -ów *bud.* roofer; roof tiler.

dacie *f. zob.* **data.**

dacza *f.* dacha, cottage, summer house.

dać *pf.* **dadzą 1.** (= *przekazać*) give; **dać coś komuś** give sth to sb, give sb sth; **dać coś pod zastaw** pawn sth; **dać coś lekką ręką** give sth away freely; **dać coś na procent** (*pieniądze*) put sth in a savings account; **dać coś komuś na słowo** let sb have sth on trust, give sb sth on trust; **dać coś komuś na kredyt** *handl.* sell sb sth on credit; **kto daje i odbiera, ten się w piekle poniewiera** give a thing, and take a thing, to wear the devil's gold ring; **kto szybko daje, ten dwa razy daje** he gives twice who gives quickly; (there's) no rush to pay; **dużo bym dał za to** I'd give a lot/anything/the world/my right arm for that; **dałbym nie wiem co** I'd give anything. **2.** (= *umożliwić*) **dać zgodę na coś** agree to sth, give consent to sth; **dać komuś ślub** (*o księdzu, urzędniku*) marry sb; **dać komuś rozwód** (*o urzędniku, sądzie*) grant a divorce to sb; (*o małżonku*) agree to divorce sb; **dać do wyboru** offer a choice; **dać okazję do czegoś** create an opportunity for sth; **dać komuś wolną rękę (w czymś)** give sb a free

hand/blank check (to do sth). **3.** (= *przynosić*) **dać dochód** bring profit; **dać komuś życie** bring sb to life. **4.** (= *zapewnić*) **dać komuś wykształcenie/utrzymanie** educate/feed sb; **dać komuś pracę** employ sb. **5.** (= *pozwolić*) let; **dam sobie rękę uciąć** *przen.* I'll bet you anything; **daj, ja to zrobię** let me do it; **nie daj mu odejść/uciec** don't let him go/get away; **nie daj się prosić** don't make me/us etc. get down on my/our etc. knees; **nie dać innym dojść do głosu** hold the stage; **nie dał mi dojść do głosu** I couldn't get a word in edgeways. **6.** (= *zlecić*) **dać komputer do naprawy** get one's computer fixed/serviced; **dać ogłoszenie** place an ad. **7.** *przest. l. dial.* (= *położyć*) put; **daj to na półkę** put it on the shelf. **8.** *przest. l. dial.* (= *nastawić*) turn (over), switch; **daj telewizor na jedynkę** turn *l.* switch the TV to (channel) one; **daj to głośno** play it loud; **daj trochę głośniej/ciszej** turn *l.* crank it up/down a bit. **9.** (*w zwrotach*) **dać komuś błogosławieństwo** *zwł. kość.* give sb a blessing, bless sb; **daj Boże** let's hope (to God), would to God; **nie daj Boże/Bóg!** God forbid!; **dać komuś cynk** *pot.* tip sb off, tip sb the wink; **dać czadu** *pot.* (= *szybko jechać*) floor it, step on it, put the pedal to the metal; (= *głośno odtwarzać*) pump up the volume, play *l.* hit it up; (*o zespole* = *głośno grać*) kick out the jams, cook; **dać komuś do myślenia** make sb (stop and) think; **dać coś komuś do zrozumienia** make sth clear to sb; **dać komuś do zrozumienia, że...** make it clear to sb (that)..., give sb to understand (that)...; **dać komuś dowód miłości** prove one's love to sb; **dać komuś drapaka/chodu** *pot.* cut and run, take to one's heels; **dać dupy** *wulg. obelż. pot.* (= *uprawiać seks*) put out (*komuś* for sb); *wulg. pot. uj.* (= *spartaczyć robotę*) screw (the job) up; **daj głos!** (*do psa*) speak!; **nie dam za to głowy** I wouldn't swear to that; **dać gwarancję** guarantee, give/offer a guarantee; **dać komuś kosza** *przest. pot.* turn sb down, spurn sb, give sb the bounce; **dać komuś krzyżyk na drogę** bid sb good riddance; **dajmy na to, że...** *pot.* let's say that...; **dać na tacę** *kość.* put (some) money on the (collection) plate; **dać sobie na wstrzymanie** *pot.* let it go; **dać na zapowiedzi** *kość.* have one's/the banns published, publish the banns; **dać komuś coś odczuć** make sb feel sth; **dać ognia** fire; **dać komuś po buzi/w twarz** slap sb's face, slap sb across the face; **dać komuś po nosie** rap sb over the knuckles; **ktoś nie dał po sobie poznać czegoś** (*uczuć, strachu*) sb did not let sth show; **dać komuś popalić/wycisk/do wiwatu** *pot.* kick/whip sb's butt/ass, give sb a rough ride; **dać słowo** give one's word, make a promise; **dać słowo honoru** promise solemnly; **dać komuś święty spokój** leave sb alone; **coś komuś nie daje spokoju** sth gnaws/is gnawing at sb, sth eats away/is eating away at sb, sth haunts sb; **dać czemuś radę** manage sth; **dać komuś radę** take sb on; **dać rozkaz** give an order *l.* a command; **dać komuś w kość** *pot.* poop/wear sb out; **dać komuś w czapę** (= *zabić*) *sl.* waste sb; **dać wiarę (czemuś)** believe (sth); **dać wyraz czemuś** give expression to sth; **dać z siebie wszystko** do/give one's best; **dać za wygraną** give up; **dać komuś znać** let sb know; **dam ci znać** I'll let you know; **to nic nie da** that's no good. ~ **się** *pf.* 1. *tylko 3 os. sing. l. nieos.* (= *być realnym*) **tego nie da się zrobić** it can't be done; **ile się da** as much as possible; **na/o ile się da** as far as possible; **jak** *l.* **czym się da** by any means possible/whatsoever. 2. **dać się poznać jako ktoś** prove o.s. to be sb; **dać się ponieść (emocjom/nerwom)** get carried away; **dać się nabrać** be taken in; **dać się nabrać na coś** fall for sth; **dawać się komuś we znaki** give sb a hard time.

dadaista *mp*, **dadaistka** *f. Gen.pl.* **-ek** *sztuka* Dadaist.

dadaistyczny *a. sztuka* Dadaist.

dadaizm *mi sztuka* Dada, Dadaism.

dag *abbr.* dekagram dag (= *10 grams*).

dagerotyp *mi hist., fot.* daguerreotype.

dagerotypia *f. Gen.* **-ii** *hist., fot.* (= *technika*) daguerreotypy; (= *grafika*) daguerreotype.

daktyl *mi Gen.* **-a** *Gen.pl.* **-i** *l.* **-ów** 1. *bot.* (*owoc*) date; (*drzewo*) = **daktylowiec**. 2. *wers.* dactyl, dactylic.

daktyliczny *a. wers.* dactylic; **heksametr daktyliczny** dactylic hexameter.

daktylografia *f. Gen.* **-ii** *form.* (= *język migowy*) dactylology.

daktylogram *mi* fingerprint.

daktyloskopia *f. Gen.* **-ii** *techn.* fingerprinting, dactylography.

daktyloskopijny *a. techn.* fingerprint, dactylographic.

daktylowiec *mi* **-wc-** *Gen.* **-a** *bot.* date palm (*Phoenix dactylifera*).

daktylowy *a. bot.* **palma daktylowa** = **daktylowiec**.

dal *f. pl.* **-e** distance; **spojrzeć w dal** look into the distance, look afar; **skok w dal** *sport* long *l.* broad jump; **okulary/soczewki do dali** *opt.* distance *l.* near-sighted glasses/lenses; **w dali** in the distance; **z dala** from far away, from afar; **z dala od domu** far (away) from home, away from home; **odejść** *l.* **odjechać w siną dal** *lit.* go away for good; **trzymać się z dala od kogoś/czegoś** stay *l.* keep away from sb/sth.

dalajlama *mp pl.* **-owie** *rel., polit.* the Dalai Lama.

dalece *adv.* (= *bardzo*) very, greatly, (by) far; **dalece niewystarczający** by far insufficient; **jak dalece** to what extent; **tak dalece** to such an extent.

dalej[1] *adv.* 1. *zob.* **daleko**; (*w przestrzeni*) far-

ther, further; (*w czasie*) further; **i tak dalej** and so on; *form.* and so forth; **i co dalej?** what now?; **dalej ani rusz** we're/it's etc. stuck; **ani kroku dalej!** freeze!; don't move (a muscle)!; don't take another step!; **jak tak dalej pójdzie...** if this goes on...; **im dalej w las, tym więcej drzew** *przen.* the farther in, the deeper. 2. (*w tekście*) below; *form.* henceforth. 3. (*z czasownikiem*) on; **czytać/mówić/jechać dalej** read/talk/drive on.

dalej[2] *int.* go ahead; go on; **no dalej, rusz się!** come on, get moving!; **dalej, chodźmy już!** let's get going!; let's get a move on!; shake a leg!

dalejże *int.* 1. = **dalej**[2]. 2. (*z bezokolicznikiem l. określeniem celu*) **(oni) dalejże mnie przekonywać** they set about persuading me; **dalejże na nich!** (go) at them!; give them hell!; **dalejże na zachód!** westward ho!

daleki *a.* **-lszy** 1. (= *odległy, oddalony*) distant; *form.* remote; (*w przestrzeni*) faraway; **dalekie strony** *l.* **kraje** faraway lands; **Daleki Wschód** *geogr.* the Far East; **z daleka** from far away, from afar; **trzymać się z daleka od kogoś/czegoś** stay *l.* keep away from sb/sth. 2. (*o podróży*) long, long-distance. 3. *wojsk.* (*o pocisku, samolocie itp.*) **dalekiego zasięgu** long-range. 4. (*o związku l. pokrewieństwie*) distant; **daleki znajomy/krewny** distant acquaintance/relative. 5. (*od ideału, prawdy*) far (removed); **daleki od prawdy/od rzeczywistości** far (removed) from the truth/from reality.

daleko *adv.* **-lej** 1. (= *w oddali*) far (away); **(być/pozostawać) daleko w tyle (za kimś)** (be/stay) far *l.* way behind (sb/sth). 2. (= *na dużą odległość*) far, a long way; **ktoś wyjechał daleko** sb is far away; **daleko idący** (*o zmianach*) far-reaching; **zajść daleko** *t. przen.* go a long way; **posunąć się za daleko** go too far; **jak daleko (jest) stąd do...?** how far (is it) to...? 3. *form.* (= *znacznie*) far; **daleko bardziej/szybciej/lepiej** far more/faster/better; **daleko tańszy** far cheaper, cheaper by far.

daleko- *pref.* long-; far-.

dalekobieżny *a.* (*o pociągu, autobusie*) long-distance.

dalekodystansowy *a. sport* long-distance.

dalekomorski *a. żegl.* deep-sea; **połowy dalekomorskie** deep-sea fishing.

dalekopis *mi* 1. *techn.* (*urządzenie*) teleprinter, teletypewriter. 2. (*wiadomość*) teleprinter/teletypewriter message.

dalekosiężny *a.* (*o zmianach*) far-reaching, sweeping; (*o planach*) long-range.

dalekowidz *mp pl.* **-e** *Gen.* **-ów** *pat.* farsighted person; **być dalekowidzem** be farsighted.

dalekowschodni *a. polit.* Far-Eastern; *sztuka* oriental.

dalekowzroczność *f.* farsightedness; *pat., form.* hyperopia.

dalekowzroczny *a. t. przen.* farsighted; *pat., form.* hyperopic.

dalia *f. Gen.* **-ii** *bot., ogr.* dahlia (*Dahlia*).

Dalmacja *f. Gen.* **-ji** *geogr.* Dalmatia.

Dalmatyńczyk *mp*, **Dalmatynka** *f. Gen.pl.* **-ek** *polit., geogr.* Dalmatian.

dalmatyńczyk *ma kynol.* Dalmatian.

dalmatyński *a.* Dalmatian.

dalmierz *mi Gen.* **-a** *opt., techn.* rangefinder.

dalszy *a.* **1.** *zob.* **daleki. 2.** (= *późniejszy*) later; (= *przyszły*) future; **w swoim dalszym życiu** in my/his/her etc. later/future life; **dopełnienie dalsze** *jęz.* indirect object; **ciąg dalszy** follow-up, continuation; **ciąg dalszy nastąpi** to be continued; **ciąg dalszy na str. ...** continued on p. ...; **na dalszą metę** in the long run; **w dalszym ciągu** still; **usunąć się na dalszy plan** (*o osobie*) step back; **zejść na dalszy plan** (*o kwestii*) recede into the background, become less important.

daltonista *mp,* **daltonistka** *f. Gen.pl.* **-ek** *pat.* color-blind person; **być daltonistą** be color-blind.

daltonizm *mi pat.* color-blindness.

dama *f.* **1.** lady; **dama dworu** *arch.* lady-in-waiting; **dama do towarzystwa** (lady) companion, (lady) escort; **pierwsza dama** *polit.* First Lady; **dama serca** *przest.* ladylove. **2.** *karty* queen; **dama kier/pik** queen of hearts/spades. **3.** *warcaby* king.

damascenka *f. Gen.pl.* **-ek** *broń, hist.* (*szabla*) Damascus sword.

damasceński *a.* **1.** (= *pochodzący z Damaszku*) Damascene. **2.** **stal damasceńska** *metal.* Damascus/damask steel.

Damaszek *mi* **-szk-** *geogr.* Damascus.

damka¹ *f. Gen.pl.* **-ek** *warcaby* king.

damka² *f. Gen.pl.* **-ek** *pot.* (= *rower damski*) lady's/ladies' bike.

Damokles *mp mit.* Damocles; **miecz Damoklesa** *zwł. przen.* sword of Damocles.

damski *a.* ladies', lady's; **toaleta damska** the ladies' (room); **odzież damska** *handl.* ladies' apparel *l.* wear; **bielizna damska** lingerie; **damskie towarzystwo** female company; **jeździć (konno) po damsku** *jeźdz.* ride sidesaddle.

damsko-męski *a.* (*o salonie fryzjerskim*) unisex; **towarzystwo damsko-męskie** mixed company.

damulka *f. Gen.pl.* **-ek** *pog.* some lady, dame; *sl.* broad.

dancing *mi* = **dansing**.

dandys *mp pl.* **-i** *l.* **-y** *uj.* fop, dandy.

dandyzm *mi* foppery.

dane *pl. Gen.* **-ych** data; **dane liczbowe** numerical data, numbers; **dane osobowe** personal data; **dane personalne** personal details; **dane statystyczne** statistical data, statistics; **dane techniczne** (technical) specifications/specs, technical data; **dane demograficzne** vital statistics; **ochrona danych (osobowych)** (personal) data protection; **przetwarzanie danych** *komp.* data processing; **przybliżone dane** approximate data; **mieć wszelkie dane (po temu), by...** be fully justified in...

Dania *f. Gen.* **-ii** *geogr., polit.* Denmark.

danie¹ *n.* (= *przekazanie*) giving (*of sth*); **bez dania racji** without (proper) justification.

danie² *n. pl.* **-a** *kulin.* course; dish; **drugie danie** entrée, main course; **danie dnia** day special, dish of the day; **pierwsze danie** first course; **posiłek z trzech dań** three-course meal; **dania z drobiu/ryb/wieprzowiny** *itd.* poultry/fish/pork etc.

daniel *ma zool.* fallow deer (*Dama dama*).

danina *f. hist.* tribute, imposition; **danina (majątkowa)** (capital) levy; **obłożyć kogoś daniną** impose a levy upon sb; **pobierać od kogoś daninę** exact a tribute from sb.

danser *mp,* **danserka** *f. Gen.pl.* **-ek** *gł. przest.* dancer.

dansing, dancing *mi* **1.** (= *tańce*) dance. **2.** (= *sala taneczna*) dance hall; (= *parkiet taneczny*) dance floor.

dantejski *a.* **1.** *teor.lit.* Dantean, Dantesque. **2.** *przen.* **dantejskie sceny** shocking scenes; **dzieją się dantejskie sceny** all hell is breaking loose; **dantejskie piekło** real hell.

dany *a.* **1.** (*o faktach, dniu, osobie*) (any) given, any, a; **danego dnia** on a given day; **w danym momencie** at a given moment. **2.** (*o faktach*) relevant. **3.** (= *otrzymany*) given; **dany przez** *l.* **od Boga** *rel.* God-given.

dar *mi* (= *podarunek, talent*) gift; **dar** *l.* **dary natury** nature's bounty; **dać/dostać coś w darze** give/receive sth as a gift; **nadzwyczajny dar** unusual gift; **dar wymowy** the gift *l.* power of speech; **dar przewidywania** foresight; *zwł. polit.* vision; (= *jasnowidztwo*) second sight; **dar wyobraźni** (power of) imagination; **mieć dar wymowy/pisania** be a gifted speaker/writer, have a talent for speaking/writing; **dar niebios** *lit.* godsend.

darczyńca *mp Gen.pl.* **-ów** *prawn.* donator; (*dobroczynny*) donor, benefactor.

Dardanele *indecl.* (**cieśnina**) Dardanele *geogr.* the Dardanelles.

dardanelski *a.* **osioł dardanelski** *żart., pot.* dunderhead.

daremnie *adv. lit.* in vain, vainly, futilely.

daremność *f. lit.* futility, vanity.

daremny *a. gł. lit.* futile, vain; (= *beznadziejny*) hopeless; **daremna walka** hopeless struggle; **daremne wysiłki** futile attempts *l.* efforts.

darł *ipf. zob.* **drzeć**.

darmo *adv.* **1.** (= *bez opłat*) (**za**) **darmo** for free, free of charge, at no charge; **za pół darmo** for next to nothing; **kupić/sprzedać coś za pół darmo** buy/sell sth for a song. **2.** (= *bez skutku*) **na darmo** *lit.* in vain, to no avail; **nie na darmo ktoś coś zrobił** sb didn't do sth for nothing; **trudno i darmo** tough luck.

darmocha *f. pot.* giveaway, freebie, (free) gift; **za darmochę** (= *za darmo*) for free; (= *prawie za darmo*) for next to nothing.

darmofon *mi tel.* toll-free number, 1-800 number; *Br.* Freephone.

darmowo *adv.* for free, free of charge, at no charge.

darmowy *a.* free (of charge); **darmowy posiłek/wstęp** free meal/admission.

darmozjad *mp pl.* **-y** *zwł. pot. uj.* freeloader, sponger, scrounger.

darnina *f.* = **darń**.

darń *f. pl.* **-rnie** *Gen.pl.* **-rni** sod, turf.

darować *ipf. l. pf.* **1.** (= *dać*) give, present; (*na cele dobroczynne*) donate; **darować komuś wolność** give/grant sb freedom. **2.** (= *oszczędzić*) (*wysiłki*) spare; **darować sobie coś** spare o.s. sth; **darować komuś życie** spare sb's life; **daruj sobie!** save yourself the trouble! **3.** (= *przebaczyć*) (*karę, dług*) remit; (*winę, grzechy*) forgive; **darować komuś karę** pardon sb, let sb off; **ktoś nie może komuś czegoś darować** sb can't forgive sb; **nie mogę sobie tego darować** I could kick myself for that. **4.** (*w zwrotach*) **daruje pan/pani!** (*z oburzeniem*) excuse me!; **darowanemu koniowi nie zagląda/patrzy się w zęby** *przen.* (you) don't/ never look a gift horse in the mouth.

darowizna *f.* gift, donation, contribution; **akt darowizny** *prawn.* deed of gift.

darowywać *ipf. zob.* **darować**.

darty *ipf. pp. zob.* **drzeć**. – *a.* torn; **rana darta** *pat.* torn *l.* lacerated wound.

darwinista *mp*, **darwinistka** *f. Gen.pl.* **-ek** *biol.* Darwinian, Darwinist.

darwinizm *mi biol.* Darwinism.

darzyć *ipf.* **darzyć kogoś szacunkiem/miłością/ sympatią** have respect/love/warm feelings for sb; **darzyć kogoś zaufaniem** have trust in sb; **darzyć kogoś względami** (*lit. zwł. euf.* = *kochać się*) have a warm heart/soft spot for sb, hold sb in affection. **~ się** *ipf. arch.* **komuś się (dobrze) darzy** sb fares well.

daszek *mi* **-szk-** *Gen.* **-a** *l.* **-u 1.** *bud.* (= *mały dach*) (small) roof; (= *wysunięta osłona, zadaszenie*) canopy. **2.** (*część czapki*) peak, visor, bill; (*sama osłona bez czapki*) eye shade; **czapka z daszkiem** (*ogólnie*) peaked cap; (*sportowa płócienna*) baseball cap/hat. **3.** (= *osłona żarówki*) (lamp) shade. **4.** *druk., komp.* (= *znak ^ nad literą l.* samodzielnie*) wedge, caret, hat.

daszkowy *a.* canopy.

data *f.* date; **data urodzenia/śmierci/ukończenia** date of birth/death/completion; **data ważności** *l.* **przydatności do spożycia** *handl.* (*przed którą należy produkt zużyć*) use-by date, expiration *l. Br.* expiry date, date of expiration, best-before date; (*przed którą należy produkt sprzedać*) sell-by date, pull date; **dzisiejsza data** today's date; **pod dobrą datą** *żart.* (= *pijany*) three sheets in the wind *l.* to the wind, well-primed; **starej daty** old-fashioned, of the old school; **człowiek starej daty** old-timer, old-fashioned person.

datacja *f. form.* (*dokumentu*) date (of issue).

datek *mi* **-tk-** donation, contribution; *t. kośc.* offering; **dobrowolne datki** voluntary donations/ contributions; **prosić o datki** ask for donations/ contributions.

dativus, datiwus *mi Gen.* **-wu** *pl.* **-wy** *gram.* (= *celownik*) dative (case).

datować *ipf.* (= *oznaczać czas, stwierdzać wiek*) date; (*list*) date, date-stamp. **~ się** *ipf.* (= *rozpoczynać się*) **datować się z...** (*wieku, okresu*) date from..., date *l.* go back to...; **datować się od...** (*dnia, momentu*) date back to...

datura *f. bot.* (= *bieluń*) datura (*Datura*); *bot. l. ogr.* (= *bieluń dziędzierzawa*) *US* jimsonweed; *Br.* thorn apple (*Datura stramonium*).

Davis *mp* **Puchar Davisa** *tenis* Davis Cup.

dawać *ipf.* **daję dajesz, dawaj** *zob.* **dać**.

dawca *mp Gen.pl.* **-ów 1.** *med.* donor; **dawca**

krwi/organu blood/organ donor; **dawca uniwersalny** universal donor. **2.** (*dobroczynny*) donor, benefactor; **anonimowy dawca** anonimous donor/benefactor.

dawczyni *f.* donor, benefactor.

Dawid *mp t. Bibl.* David; **gwiazda Dawida** the star of David; **Psałterz Dawida** *l.* **Dawidów** the Davidic Psalter, the Psalter of David.

dawka *f. Gen.pl.* **-ek 1.** *med.* (*leku*) dose, dosage; **dawka dobowa** *l.* **dzienna** daily dose; **dawka zalecana** recommended dosage; **dawka leku** dose of medicine *l.* drug; **dawka przypominająca** booster dose; **dawka śmiertelna** lethal/fatal dose; **końska dawka** *t. pot.* megadose. **2.** *fiz.* (*promieniowania*) dose; **dawka pochłonięta** absorbed dose; **dawka promieniowania** radiation dose.

dawkomierz *mi Gen.* **-a** *techn., fiz.* dosimeter.

dawkować *ipf. med.* dose.

dawkowanie *n. med.* dosage.

dawniej *adv. comp. of* **dawno**; formerly, in the past, at one time; **poczuć się jak dawniej** feel like one's old self; **tak jak dawniej** like it (once) used to be.

dawniejszy *a. comp. zob.* **dawny**.

dawno *adv.* **dawno temu** a long time ago, way back; **jak dawno?** (*coś trwa*) since when?; (*coś nastąpiło*) how long ago?; **dawno, dawno temu** *lit.* once upon a time; **to było dawno i nieprawda** *żart.* but that was (so) long ago.

dawność *f.* **1.** (= *wczesność*) earliness; (= *archaiczność*) antiquity. **2.** *lit.* (= *przeszłość*) days past, days of yore, the past.

dawny *a.* **1.** (= *stary, przeszły*) old, long-ago; (= *starożytny*) ancient; (= *pierwotny*) early, primitive; (= *długo trwający*) long, longtime; (= *tradycyjny*) long-standing. **2.** (= *były*) former, past, one-time. **3. od najdawniejszych czasów** from the earliest times, since the dawn of time; **dawnymi czasy** in the old days, in years past; **dawne dzieje** old times; **od dawna** for a long time; **po dawnemu** the old-fashioned way; **z dawien dawna** *lit.* since time immemorial.

dąb *mi* **-ę- 1.** *stol.* oak. **2.** *bot.* oak (tree) (*Quercus*). **3. stanąć dęba** (*o włosach*) stand on end; (*o koniu*) prance, rear; **chłop jak dąb** *pot.* hunk, hunky guy; **zdrów jak dąb** strong as a horse *l.* as an ox, fit as a fiddle *l.* as a flea.

dąbek *mi* **-bk-** *Gen.* **-a** *leśn.* oak sapling.

dąbrowa *f. Gen.pl.* **-rów** oak forest.

dąć *ipf.* **dmę dmiesz, dmij** (= *dmuchać, wiać*) blow; **dąć w trąbkę** *muz.* blow (on) a trumpet *l.* horn.

dąsać się *ipf.* sulk, pout; **dąsać się na kogoś** be angry with sb *l.* at sb (*o coś* about sth); **dąsać się na coś** be angry at sth.

dąsy *pl. Gen.* **-ów** sulk, pout.

dążenie *n.* **dążenie do czegoś** (*do niepodległości, samodzielności*) drive for/towards sth; (*do szczęścia, sukcesu*) desire for sth, pursuing sth, striving for sth; **dążenia** aspirations.

dążność *f. form.* **dążność (do czegoś)** (= *tendencja*) tendency (towards sth); (= *aspiracja*) aspiration (for/after sth); (= *pragnienie*) desire (for sth).

dążyć *ipf.* **dążyć do czegoś** pursue sth, aim at sth, move towards sth, strive for sth.

dB *abbr. fiz., techn.* (=*decybel*) dB (= *decibel*).

db *abbr. szkoln.* (= *dobry*) B (*school grade*).

dbać *ipf.* **dbać o kogoś/coś/siebie** take care of sb/sth/o.s.; **dbać o (swoją) kondycję** keep fit, keep in shape; **dbać o linię** watch one's waistline; **dbać o (swoją) wagę** watch one's weight; **dbać o (swoje) zdrowie** be health-conscious; **nie dbać o coś** (= *traktować obojętnie*) not care about sth, not give a damn about sth.

dbałość *f.* attention, care; **dbałość o szczegóły** attention to detail.

dbały *a. lit.* (= *staranny*) diligent, conscientious, caring; (= *uważny*) careful (*o coś* of sth); (= *troskliwy*) caring, attentive.

dca, d-ca *abbr. wojsk.* = **dowódca**.

DDT *abbr. chem.* (= *dwuchlorodwufenylotrójchloroetan*) DDT, dichlorodiphenyltrichloroethane.

de, d. *abbr. euf.* (= *dupa*) ass, bottom, fanny, behind; *sl.* heinie; **coś jest (całkiem) do de** sth (really) sucks; **ktoś ma coś w de** sb doesn't give a shit about sth; **siadać na de** park one's ass *l.* fanny; **siedzieć na de** (*t.* = *nie ruszać się*) sit on one's ass.

dealer *mp* **1.** *handl.* (= *agent handlowy*) dealer, licensed distributor. **2.** (= *handlarz narkotykami*) (drug) dealer, (drug) pusher.

dealerka *f. Gen.pl.* -ek (= *handlarka narkotykami*) *zob.* **dealer** 2.

dealerski *a.* **biuro dealerskie** *handl.* dealership.

debata *f. zwł. polit.* debate (*na temat czegoś* on, over *l.* about sth); **publiczna debata** public debate.

debatować *ipf.* **debatować nad czymś** (= *dyskutować*) debate sth; (= *rozmyślać*) ponder sth.

debel *mi* -bl- *Gen. i Acc.* -a *Gen.pl.* -i *l.* -ów **1.** *sport* (= *gra podwójna*) doubles; **debel mieszany** mixed doubles; **grać debla** (*także pot.* **grać w debla**) play doubles. **2.** *sport* (*łódź*) double scull. **3.** *karty* double.

debet *mi fin.* **1.** (= *ujemny stan konta*) overdraft; **mieć debet** be overdrawn. **2.** (= *lewa strona w rachunkowości*) debit, left side.

debetowy *a. fin.* debit; **karta debetowa** debit cart; **nota debetowa** debit note.

debil *mp Gen.pl.* -i *l.* -ów, **debilka** *f. Gen.pl.* -ek *obelż. l. pat.* moron.

debilizm *mi* **1.** (= *głupota*) idiocy. **2.** *pat.* moronism.

debilka *f. Gen.pl.* -ek *zob.* **debil**.

debilnie *adv. pot., pog.* moronically.

debilny *a. pot., pog.* moronic, idiotic, stupid.

debiut *mi* **1.** (*aktorski, muzyczny, sportowy*) debut. **2.** *szachy* (= *otwarcie*) opening; (= *pierwszy ruch*) opening move.

debiutancki *a.* (*o występie, albumie*) debut, premiere, first (ever).

debiutant *mp* beginner.

debiutantka *f. Gen.pl.* -ek **1.** *zob.* **debiutant**. **2.** (= *dziewczyna wprowadzana w życie towarzyskie*) debutante.

debiutować *ipf.* make one's debut, debut.

deblista *mp*, **deblistka** *f. Gen.pl.* -ek *sport* doubles player, contestant in the doubles; (*wioślarz*) double sculler.

deblowy *a. sport* doubles.

decemwir *mp pl.* -owie *hist.* (*w starożytnym Rzymie*) decemvir.

decemwirat *mi hist.* (*w starożytnym Rzymie*) decemvirate.

decentralistyczny *a. polit.* (*o tendencjach*) decentralist, decentralization.

decentralizacja *f. polit.* decentralization.

decentralizacyjny *a. polit.* decentralist, decentralization; **zmiany decentralizacyjne** decentralization.

decentralizm *mi polit.* decentralism.

decentralizować *ipf. polit.* decentralize.

dech *mi tylko sing.* tch- **1.** (= *oddech*) breath; wind; **zapierać komuś dech w piersiach** take sb's breath away; **dech mi zaparło** it took my breath away; **zapierający dech (w piersiach)** breathtaking, stunning, breathless; **nabrać tchu** take a breath; **nie móc złapać tchu** gasp for breath, be out of breath, be short of breath; **aż ci/mu itd. tchu braknie** until you're/he's etc. blue in the face; **bez tchu** out of breath, short of breath, breathless; **być bez tchu** be out of breath, be short of breath, be breathless; **jednym tchem** in the same breath, in a single breath; at once; **nabrać tchu** draw a breath; **ostatnim tchem** with one's last *l.* dying breath; **do utraty tchu** until you're/he's etc. blue in the face; **do ostatniego tchu** to *l.* till the last (breath); **oglądać coś z zapartym tchem** watch sth keenly; **czekać z zapartym tchem** hold one's breath, wait with bated breath. **2.** *lit., rzad.* (= *powiew*) breath (of air *l.* wind).

decha *f.* **1.** *stol.* board, plank. **2.** (*w zwrotach*) **wieś zabita dechami** *pot. uj.* the sticks, the boonies, the boondocks; **gaz do dechy!** *mot., pot.* step on it!, step on the gas!, floor it!, let her rip!; **pijany w dechę** three sheets to the wind; **w dechę** *pot. przest.* (= *świetny, świetnie*) cool, swell; **płaska jak decha** *pot.* (*o kobiecie*) flat as a board.

dechrystianizacja *f. rel.* dechristianization.

deck *mi* (*część wieży hi-fi*) deck.

decybel *mi Gen.* -a *fiz.* decibel.

decybelowy *a. fiz.* decibel; **mierzony w skali decybelowej** measured on a decibel scale.

decydencki *a. polit.* (*o stanowisku*) high-ranking; of importance.

decydent *mp*, **decydentka** *f. Gen.pl.* -ek *polit.* decision-maker.

decydować *ipf.* **1.** (= *postanawiać*) **decydować** decide (*o czymś* about sth); **decydować na własną rękę** decide on one's own; **sam decyduj** it's up to you. **2.** (= *warunkować*) **decydować o czymś** determine sth, decide sth. **~ się** *ipf.* make up one's mind (*na coś l. w sprawie czegoś* about sth).

decydujący *a.* (= *rozstrzygający*) decisive, deciding; (= *najistotniejszy*) crucial, pivotal; **decydujący głos** deciding vote; *polit., parl.* casting vote; **poczynić** *l.* **zrobić decydujący krok** make a (decisive) move.

decygram *mi Gen.* **-a** *fiz.* decigram (= *0.1 grams*).

decymalny *a. mat., komp.* (= *dziesiętny*) decimal; **system decymalny** decimal system.

decymetr *mi Gen.* **-a** *fiz.* decimeter (= *10 centimeters, about 3.94 inches*); **decymetr kwadratowy/sześcienny** square/cubic decimeter.

decymetrowy *a.* decimeter; **(nadawać) na falach decymetrowych** *radio* (broadcast) at decimeter wavelengths.

decyzja *f.* decision; **decyzja administracyjna** *form.* official decision *l.* ruling; **decyzją administracyjną** *form.* through official decision *l.* ruling; **decyzja należy do kogoś** it's up to sb to decide, it's within sb's discretion; **odwlekać decyzję** delay one's decision; (= *grać na zwłokę*) keep one's options open; *form.* procrastinate; **odwoływać się od decyzji** appeal a decision; **podjąć** *l.* **powziąć decyzję** make *l.* take a decision, come to a decision, make up one's mind; **na mocy czyjejś decyzji** based on sb's decision, on the strength of sb's decision; **zostawić coś do czyjejś decyzji** leave sth for sb to decide.

decyzyjny *a.* decision; **ośrodek decyzyjny** (*organizacji*) nerve center; **proces decyzyjny** (the) decision-making (process).

dedukcja *f.* reasoning; *log.* deduction.

dedukcyjny *a. log.* (*o myśleniu, schemacie*) deductive.

dedukować *ipf. t. log.* deduce.

dedykacja *f.* (*autora*) inscription, dedication, message; **egzemplarz z dedykacją** inscribed/autographed copy.

dedykować *ipf. l. pf.* (*egzemplarz*) inscribe, autograph; (*dzieło*) dedicate; **dedykować coś komuś/czyjejś pamięci** dedicate sth to sb/sb's memory.

defekacja *f.* **1.** *fizj.* (= *wypróżnianie*) defecation. **2.** *techn.* (= *nawapnianie przy produkcji cukru*) liming.

defekator *mi Gen.* **-a** *techn.* limer, liming tank.

defekt *mi* **1.** (= *wada*) defect; *techn.* trouble, failure, malfunction. **2.** *zwł. druk.* (= *wadliwy egzemplarz*) reject.

defektoskop *mi techn.* defectoscope, flaw detector.

defektoskopia *f. Gen.* **-ii** *techn.* defectoscopy, flaw detection.

defektywny *a. techn., gram.* (= *ułomny*) defective.

defensor *mp*, **defensorka** *f. Gen.pl.* **-ek** *sport* (= *obrońca*) back, defense player; *Br.* defender.

defensywa *f.* **1.** defensive; **w defensywie** on the defensive; **zepchnąć kogoś do defensywy** put sb on the defensive. **2.** *sport* defense, *gł. Br.* defence.

defensywnie *adv.* defensively.

defensywność *f.* (= *asekuranctwo*) defensive attitude; (= *bronienie się*) the defensive.

defensywny *a.* defensive; **defensywna gra** *sport* defensive play; **linia defensywna** line of defense.

defetysta *mp*, **defetystka** *f. Gen.pl.* **-ek** *form., uj.* defeatist.

defetystyczny *a. form., uj.* defeatist; **nastroje defetystyczne** defeatist temper *l.* mood.

defetyzm *mi form.* defeatism.

defibracja *f. stol.* (= *rozwłóknienie drewna*) defibration.

defibrylacja *f. med.* (*serca*) (cardiac) defibrillation.

defibrylator *mi Gen.* **-a** *med.* defibrillator.

deficyt *mi* **1.** *zwł. ekon.* (*finansów*) deficit; (*towarów*) shortage, short supply; (*surowców*) scarcity; **deficyt budżetowy/handlowy** budget/trade deficit; **deficyt obrotów bieżących** trade gap; **deficyt rąk do pracy** labor shortage. **2.** *fiz.* shortfall, deficiency.

deficytowy *a.* **1.** *ekon.* (*o inwestycji, przedsiębiorstwie*) loss-making. **2.** *handl.* (*o towarach*) in short supply.

defiguracja *f. sztuka l. bud.* defacement, disfiguration, disfigurement.

defilada *f. zwł. wojsk.* (dress) parade, procession; march (past); **odbierać defiladę** review a parade.

defiladowy *a. zwł. wojsk.* parade; **krok defiladowy** goose step.

defilować *ipf.* **1.** (= *maszerować*) parade, march (past); **defilować przed kimś/czymś** march past sb/sth. **2.** *przen.* (= *pokazywać się ostentacyjnie*) parade, strut (*z kimś* with sb). **3.** *myśl.* cross.

definicja *f.* definition; **z definicji** *l.* **na mocy definicji** by definition.

definicyjny *a.* definitional.

definiować *ipf.* define.

definitywnie *adv.* (= *ostatecznie*) finally, conclusively; (= *zdecydowanie*) definitely.

definitywność *f.* finality.

definitywny *a.* (= *ostateczny*) final, conclusive; (= *zdecydowany*) definite.

deflacja *f.* **1.** *ekon.* deflation. **2.** *geol.* (= *erozja*) deflation, wind erosion.

deflacyjny *a.* **1.** *ekon.* (*o zjawiskach*) deflationary; (*o nastawieniu, polityce*) deflationist. **2.** *geol.* (*o erozji*) deflationary.

deflektor *mi Gen.* **-a** **1.** *mech., techn., żegl.* (= *odchylacz*) deflector, baffle. **2.** *bud.* (= *wylot kominowy*) chimney-pot.

defloracja *f. form.* defloration.

deflorować *ipf. form.* deflower.

defoliacja *f. ekol., leśn., roln.* defoliation.

defoliant *mi Gen.* **-a** *chem., roln., wojsk.* defoliant.

deformacja *f.* (= *zmiana kształtu*) deformation, distortion; (= *zniekształcenie*) deformity, disfigurement.

deformować *ipf.* deform, distort; (= *zniekształcać, szpecić*) disfigure. **~ się** *ipf.* become distorted, get out of shape; (*o konstrukcji drewnianej*) warp (out of shape).

defraudacja *f. prawn.* embezzlement, defalcation, defraudment; **dopuścić się defraudacji** commit embezzlement.

defraudant *mp*, **defraudantka** *f. Gen.pl.* **-ek**
prawn. embezzler, defrauder, peculator.
defraudować *ipf. prawn.* embezzle.
degeneracja *f.* **1.** (*moralna*) corruption, depravity, degeneracy. **2.** *biol. l. pat.* (*tkanki, gatunku, narządu*) degeneration. **3.** *fiz.* degeneration, degeneracy.
degeneracyjny *a.* (*o zmianach, procesach*) degenerative.
degenerat *mp*, **degeneratka** *f. Gen.pl.* **-ek** *pog.* degenerate.
degenerować *ipf. form.* corrupt, pervert, deteriorate. ~ **się** *ipf. form.* degenerate, deteriorate.
degradacja *f.* **1.** *geol., chem., fiz.* degradation; **degradacja gleby** *ekol. l. roln.* soil degradation/ deterioration. **2.** *gł. wojsk.* (*pozbawienie stopnia*) demotion. **3.** *socjol.* (*wartości*) degradation, corruption; (*pozycji*) degradation, comedown.
degradować *ipf.* **1.** (= *dymisjonować*) demote. **2.** (= *deprecjonować*) degrade.
degrengolada *f. form.* (= *rozprzężenie*) laxity; (= *zepsucie*) corruption, decay.
degresja *f. zwł. fin.* degression.
degustacja *f.* tasting; **degustacja win/pizzy** wine/pizza tasting.
degustator *mp*, **degustatorka** *f. Gen.pl.* **-ek** taster; **degustator win** wine taster.
degustować *ipf.* taste.
dehumanizacja *f. form.* dehumanization.
dehumanizować *ipf. form.* dehumanize.
deifikacja *f. form. l. teol.* deification.
deifikować *ipf. form. l. teol.* deify.
deista *mp*, **deistka** *f. Gen.pl.* **-ek** *fil.* deist.
deistyczny *a. fil.* deist.
deizm *mi fil.* deism.
deka[1] *indecl. pot.* (*także* **deko**) *abbr. of* **dekagram**; ten grams (= *0.358 oz*); **dziesięć deka szynki** quarter pound of ham.
deka[2] *f.* **1.** *muz.* (= *front pudła rezonansowego*) soundboard. **2.** (= *narzuta*) blanket, rug.
dekabrysta *mp*, **dekabrystka** *f. hist.* Decembrist.
dekada *f.* **1.** (= *dziesięć dni*) ten days; **w pierwszej/drugiej/trzeciej dekadzie stycznia/lutego itd.** in early/mid/late January/February etc. **2.** (= *dziesięć lat*) decade.
dekadencja *f. form.* decadence, decadency, decline.
dekadencki *a. form.* decadent.
dekadent *mp form.* decadent.
dekadentyzm *mi* decadence, decadency.
dekadowy *a.* **1.** ten-day. **2.** **opornik dekadowy** *el.* decade box.
dekagram *mi Gen.* **-a** (*jednostka masy*) decagram (= *10 grams*).
dekalitr *mi Gen.* **-a** (*jednostka objętości*) decaliter (= *10 liters*).
dekalkomania *f. Gen.* **-ii** *t. sztuka* decal, decalcomania.
dekalog *mi* **1.** *rel.* the Decalogue, the Ten Commandments. **2.** *przen.* (= *norma, reguła*) code.
dekametr *mi Gen.* **-a** (*jednostka długości*) decameter (= *10 meters*).

dekanat *mi kośc.* deanery.
dekapitacja *f. form.* (= *pozbawienie głowy*) decapitation.
dekapitalizacja *f. ekon.* decapitalization.
dekapitalizować się *ipf. ekon.* decapitalize.
dekarski *a. bud.* roof; **prace** *l.* **roboty dekarskie** roof repairs.
dekarstwo *n. bud.* roofing.
dekarz *mp Gen.pl.* **-y** roofer.
dekatyzacja *f. tk.* preshrinking.
dekatyzować *ipf. tk.* preshrink.
dekatyzowany *a. tk.* preshrunk.
dekiel *mi* **-kl-** *Gen.* **-a** *Gen.pl.* **-i** *l.* **-ów** **1.** *mot.* hubcap. **2.** (= *pokrywa*) lid, cover.
dekielek *mi* **-lk-** *Gen.* **-a** (= *pokrywka*) (small) lid.
deklamacja *f.* **1.** (= *recytacja*) recital, recitation. **2.** *przest.* (= *nieszczere przemówienie, frazes*) bombast, declamation.
deklamacyjny *a.* recitative.
deklamator *mp*, **deklamatorka** *f. Gen.pl.* **-ek** **1.** (= *recytator*) reciter. **2.** *przest.* (= *pozer*) poseur.
deklamatorski *a.* **1.** (= *recytatorski*) recitative. **2.** *przest., uj.* (= *napuszony, nieszczery*) bombastic, declamatory.
deklamować *ipf.* recite.
deklaracja *f.* **1.** (= *oświadczenie*) declaration, statement; (= *zobowiązanie*) pledge; **złożyć deklarację** issue/make a declaration/statement; **podpisać deklarację** sign a declaration; **deklaracja praw człowieka i obywatela** *polit.* Declaration of Human Rights; **deklaracja programowa** *polit.* platform. **2.** (= *formularz*) form; **wypełnić deklarację** fill out a form; **deklaracja celna** customs declaration, bill of entry; **deklaracja podatkowa** *fin.* tax form/return. **3.** **deklaracja zmiennej** *komp.* data declaration.
deklaratywizm *mi*, **deklaratywność** *f. form.* hypocrisy, insincerity.
deklaratywny *a. form., uj.* hypocritical, insincere.
deklarować *ipf.* **1.** (= *oświadczać*) declare, proclaim (*że... that...*). **2.** (= *obiecywać*) pledge, offer; **deklarować pomoc** offer help; **deklarować wsparcie dla kogoś/czegoś** pledge (one's) support for sb/sth. ~ **się** *ipf.* **1.** (= *opowiadać się*) declare (*za czymś / przeciw czemuś* for/against sth); make a commitment, commit o.s. **2.** *arch.* (= *oświadczać się*) declare o.s.
deklasacja *f. form., socjol.* degradation, declassment.
deklasować *ipf.* **1.** *sport, pot.* (*rywala*) crush, trounce. **2.** *socjol.* (= *degradować*) declass.
deklinacja *f.* **1.** *jęz.* declension. **2.** *astron.* declination.
deklinacyjny *a.* **1.** *jęz.* (*o końcówce, formie, paradygmacie*) declension, declensional. **2.** *astron.* declinational; **równoleżnik deklinacyjny** parallel of declination; **igła/busola deklinacyjna** *techn.* declinometer.
deklinować *ipf. jęz.* decline. ~ **się** *ipf. jęz.* decline.
deko *indecl.* = **deka**[1].

dekoder *mi Gen.* **-a** *techn.* decoder; (*sygnału zaszyfrowanego*) descrambler.

dekodować *ipf.* decode; (*sygnał zaszyfrowany*) descramble.

dekokt *mi arch.* (*= wywar*) decoction.

dekolonizacja *f. polit.* decolonization.

dekolonizacyjny *a. polit.* decolonize.

dekolt *mi* **1.** (*= brzeg l. kształt sukni przy szyi*) neckline, neck, décollettage; **głęboki dekolt** low neck/neckline, plunging neckline; **suknia z dekoltem** low-cut dress. **2.** (*= odsłonięte piersi*) cleavage, décolleté; **pokazywać dekolt** show cleavage.

dekompensacja *f. pat.* decompensation.

dekompletować *ipf.* (*zestaw*) break up; **dekompletować coś** (*ekipę, załogę*) thin the ranks of sth.

dekompozycja *f. form.* (*= rozkład*) decomposition, decay; (*= przebudowa*) restructuring.

dekompresja *f.* decompression; **przechodzić dekompresję** decompress.

dekompresor *mi Gen.* **-a** *techn.* decompressor.

dekompresyjny *a.* decompression, decompressive; **choroba dekompresyjna** *pat.* the bends, decompression sickness, caisson disease; **komora dekompresyjna** *żegl.* decompression chamber.

dekomunizacja *f. polit.* decommunization.

dekomunizować *ipf. polit.* decommunize.

dekoncentracja *f.* distraction, diversion, lack of concentration.

dekoncentrować *ipf.* distract.

dekoniunktura *f. ekon.* weak market, recession.

dekoniunkturalny *a. ekon.* recessive.

dekonspiracja *f.* uncovering, exposing, disclosure.

dekonspirować *ipf.* expose.

dekonstrukcja *f. teor.lit. l. fil.* deconstruction.

dekonstrukcjonista *mp*, **dekonstrukcjonistka** *f. teor.lit. l. fil.* deconstructor.

dekonstrukcjonizm *mi teor.lit. l. fil.* deconstructionism.

dekonstruktywizm *mi* = **dekonstrukcjonizm**.

dekonstruktywny *a. teor.lit. l. fil.* deconstructionist.

dekoracja *f.* **1.** (*t. = odznaczenie*) decoration; (*= ozdoba, upiększenie*) ornament; **świąteczne dekoracje** Christmas decorations; **świetlna dekoracja** decorative lights; **dekoracja wnętrz** interior decoration. **2.** *film l. teatr* scene, set, stage setting; **ustawiać dekoracje** set the stage; **zmiana dekoracji** change of scene.

dekoracyjnie *adv.* decoratively.

dekoracyjność *f.* decorativeness.

dekoracyjny *a.* decorative, ornamental.

dekorator *mp* **1.** decorator; *handl.* window dresser; **dekorator wnętrz** interior decorator. **2.** *przest., teatr l. film* (*= scenograf*) set/stage designer, decorator; (*= pomocnik scenografa*) stage hand, prop person; scene painter.

dekoratorski *a.* decorator's.

dekoratorstwo *n.* decorating, decoration.

dekorować *ipf.* (*pomieszczenie, osoby medalem*) decorate; (*odzież*) trim; (*tort*) pipe.

dekorum *n. indecl. teor.lit.* decorum; **zasada dekorum** *teor.lit.* (the principle of) decorum, the decorum principle.

dekować się *ipf. pot.* (*= ukrywać się*) hole up, lie low; (*= obijać się*) bum around, slack.

dekownik *mp pot.* slacker, dodger, shirker.

dekrement *mi mat.* decrement.

dekret *mi polit.* decree; **dekret prezydencki** executive order; **dekret z mocą ustawy** decree-law; **ogłaszać** *l.* **wydawać dekret** issue a decree.

dekretacja *f. przest.* (*= adnotacja na dokumencie*) endorsement.

dekretować *ipf.* **1.** *polit.* decree, enact. **2.** *przest.* (*= adnotować*) endorse.

dekretowy *a.* decree, decretory.

dekryptaż *mi gł. wojsk.* decryption.

dekstroza *f. biochem.* dextrose.

dekstryna *f. chem.* dextrin.

delabializacja *f. fon.* unrounding, delabialization.

delabializować *ipf. fon.* unround, delabialize.

delator *mp pl.* **-rzy** *l.* **-owie** *przest.* (*= donosiciel, oskarżyciel*) delator.

delegacja *f.* **1.** (*= reprezentacja oficjalna*) delegation. **2.** (*także* **delegacja służbowa**) (*= wyjazd służbowy*) business trip; **wyjechać w delegację** go on a business trip; **być w delegacji** *l.* **na delegacji** be away on business. **3.** (*dokument*) expense report. **4.** *form.* (*= przekazanie*) (*kompetencji, uprawnień*) delegation.

delegalizacja *f.* delegalization (*of sth*), banning (*sth*), ban (*on sth*).

delegalizować *ipf.* delegalize, ban.

delegat *mp*, **delegatka** *f. Gen.pl.* **-ek** delegate.

delegować *ipf.* **1.** (*= wysyłać*) delegate (*sb*); (*w podróż służbową*) send (*sb*) on a business trip. **2.** *form.* (*= przekazywać*) (*kompetencje*) delegate (*sth*).

delektować się *ipf.* + *Dat.* relish, savor (*sth*).

delficki *a.* Delphic; **wyrocznia delficka** *hist.* Delphic oracle.

delfin[1] *ma pl.* **-y** *Acc.* **-ów** *zool.* (*t. motyw dekoracyjny w sztuce*) dolphin; **delfin słodkowodny** (*= waleń z rodziny Platanistidae*) river dolphin; **delfin zwyczajny** common dolphin (*Delphinus delphis*). – *mi Gen. i Acc.* **-a** **1.** *sport* (*styl pływacki*) butterfly (stroke). **2. Delfin** *astron.* (*gwiazdozbiór*) Delphinus, the Dolphin.

delfin[2] *mp pl.* **-i** *hist.* (*= następca tronu*) dauphin.

delfinarium *n. sing. indecl. pl.* **-ria** *Gen.* **-riów** dolphinarium.

delfiniak *mi Gen.* **-a** *żegl.* martingale.

Delfy *pl. geogr.* Delphi.

delia *f. Gen.* **-ii** (*strój hist. = płaszcz futrzany*) pelisse.

deliberacja *f. lit.* (*= rozmyślanie*) brooding, rumination; (*= roztrząsanie*) deliberation.

deliberować *ipf. lit.* brood; deliberate (*nad czymś* over sth).

delicje *pl. Gen.* **-i** **1.** (*ciasteczka*) jaffa cakes. **2.** (*= przysmaki*) delicacies, dainties.

delikacik *mp pog., pot.* softie, wimp.

delikates *mi* (*= przysmak*) delicacy.

delikatesowy *a. kulin.* choice, dainty.

delikatesy *pl. Gen.* **-ów** (= *sklep z żywnością i garmażerką*) deli, delicatessen; (= *mały sklep samoobsługowy*) convenience store.

delikatnie *adv.* delicately, gently; (*przekonywać*) softly; (= *taktownie*) tactfully, sensitively; **delikatnie mówiąc** to put it mildly, to say the least; **delikatnie zbudowany** dainty, frail, of delicate build.

delikatnieć *ipf.* soften.

delikatność *f.* **1.** (= *łagodność*) gentleness. **2.** (= *słabość, kruchość*) delicacy, fragility, frailty. **3.** (= *takt*) tact, tactfulness. **4.** (= *drażliwość*) sensitivity. **5.** (= *wykwintność, subtelność*) finesse, subtlety.

delikatny *a.* **1.** (= *łagodny, nieagresywny*) delicate; (*o dotknięciu, powiewie, oświetleniu, traktowaniu*) gentle, soft; (*o zapachu, smaku*) mild. **2.** (= *kruchy, wrażliwy na uszkodzenia*) (*o talerzu, urządzeniu*) fragile; (*o tkaninie*) fine, delicate. **3.** (= *drażliwy, trudny*) delicate, touchy, sensitive; **delikatna sprawa/misja** sensitive matter/mission. **4.** (= *taktowny*) tactful. **5.** (= *wybredny, subtelny*) dainty, exquisite, subtle; **delikatny gust** fine *l.* exquisite taste.

delikwent *mp*, **delikwentka** *f. Gen.pl.* **-ek 1.** *pot. żart.* (= *osoba, zwł. oczekująca na coś*) soul, character, customer. **2.** *prawn.* culprit.

delimitacja *f. form.* delimitation.

delimitować *ipf. form.* delimit.

delirium *n. indecl. pat.* delirium; **delirium tremens** delirium tremens; **pogrążony w delirium** delirious.

delirka *f. pot.* (= *delirium tremens*) the D.T.'s, the jimjams, the heebiejeebies, the horrors; **mieć delirkę** have the D.T.'s, see pink elephants.

deliryczny *a.* (*o stanie umysłu*) fevered, incoherent; (*o wizji*) hallucinatory.

delta *f.* **1.** (*nazwa greckiej litery; t. geogr., mat. itp.*) delta; **delta Missisipi** *geogr.* the Mississippi Delta; **ramiona delty** *geol.* deltaic distributaries. **2.** *lotn.* (*konstrukcja skrzydła*) delta (wing); (*typ samolotu*) delta-winged aircraft.

deltoid *mi geom.* kite.

deltowaty *a.* (*o kształcie*) delta-shaped, delta, deltaic.

deltowy *a.* **1.** (= *dotyczący delty rzeki*) deltaic. **2.** *lotn.* delta(-winged).

deluwium *n. sing. indecl. pl.* **-ia** *Gen.* **-iów** *geol.* slope wash.

demagog *mp pl.* **-dzy** *l.* **-owie** *uj. l. hist.* demagogue.

demagogia *f. Gen.* **-ii** demagoguery, demagogy, demagogism.

demagogicznie *adv. uj.* demagogically.

demagogiczny *a. uj.* demagogic.

demakijaż *mi* makeup removal; **mleczko** *l.* **płyn do demakijażu** makeup remover; **płatki do demakijażu** cotton pads.

demarkacja *f. form.* demarcation.

demarkacyjny *a. form.* demarcation; **linia demarkacyjna** demarcation line, line of demarcation.

demaskacja *f.* exposing, exposal, unmasking.

demaskator *mp* exposer, unmasker.

demaskatorski *a.* exposing, unmasking.

demaskować *ipf.* expose, unmask, reveal. **~ się** *ipf.* throw off all disguise, throw off *l.* drop the mask, lift the veil.

dematerializacja *f. fiz., parapsychologia l. żart.* dematerialization.

dematerializować *ipf. fiz., parapsychologia* dematerialize. **~ się** *ipf. t. żart.* = *znikać, ulatniać się* dematerialize.

demencja *f. pat.* dementia; **demencja starcza** senile dementia.

dementi *n. indecl. polit.* denial, démenti, disavowal; *prawn.* disclaimer; **złożyć dementi** issue a denial *l.* disclaimer.

dementować *ipf. form.* deny, disavow.

demilitaryzacja *f. polit. l. wojsk.* demilitarization.

demilitaryzować *ipf. polit. l. wojsk.* demilitarize.

demineralizacja *f. chem. l. pat.* demineralizing, demineralization.

deminutiwum *n. sing. indecl. pl.* **-wa** *Gen.* **-wów** *jęz.* (= *zdrobnienie*) diminutive.

deminutywny *a. jęz.* diminutive.

demistyfikacja *f.* debunking, exposing, exposal, unmasking.

demistyfikator *mp* debunker, exposer, unmasker.

demistyfikować *ipf.* debunk, expose, unmask.

demitologizacja *f.* debunking (of myths); *form.* demythologization; (= *odzieranie z tajemnicy*) demystification.

demitologizować *ipf.* debunk; *form.* demythologize; (= *odzierać z tajemnicy*) demystify.

demiurg *mp pl.* **-owie** *fil. l. rel.* demiurge.

demo *indecl. n. i a. pot. komp. l. show-business* demo; **nagranie demo** *muz.* sample recording; **demo programu** *l.* **program w wersji demo** *komp.* demo program.

demobil *mi wojsk.* (= *zbędny sprzęt wojskowy*) army surplus; **sprzęt z demobilu** surplus army equipment; **samolot/okręt z demobilu** decommissioned aircraft/ship.

demobilizacja *f. wojsk.* demobilization; *Br. pot.* demob.

demobilizacyjny *a.* **program demobilizacyjny** *wojsk.* demobilization program.

demobilizować *ipf.* **1.** *wojsk.* demobilize, discharge from the service; *Br. pot.* demob. **2.** (= *osłabiać gotowość*) demoralize, dishearten. **~ się** *ipf.* **1.** *wojsk.* be demobilized. **2.** = *tracić gotowość* become demoralized.

demobilizująco *adv.* demoralizingly; **wpływać demobilizująco** have a demoralizing effect (*na kogoś* on sb).

demodulacja *f. el.* demodulation.

demodulować *ipf. el.* demodulate.

demograf *mp pl.* **-owie** *nauk.* demographer, demographist.

demografia *f. Gen.* **-ii** demography.

demograficzny *a.* demographic, demographical; **dane** *l.* **wskaźniki demograficzne** vital statistics; **eksplozja demograficzna** population explosion; **niż demograficzny** population slump *l.* dip; **wyż demograficzny** (*zwł. powojenny*) baby boom; *Br. pot.* (population) bulge.

demokracja *f. polit.* democracy; **demokracja ateńska** *hist.* Athenian democracy.

demokrata *mp*, **demokratka** *f. Gen.pl.* **-ek 1.** (= *zwolennik demokracji*) democrat. **2. Demokrata/ka** *polit.* (= *członek l. zwolennik amerykańskiej Partii Demokratycznej*) Democrat.

demokratycznie *adv.* democratically.

demokratyczny *a.* **1.** democratic; **Partia Demokratyczna** the Democratic Party. **2.** *polit.* (= *dotyczący Partii Demokratycznej*) Democratic.

demokratyzacja *f. polit.* democratization.

demokratyzm *mi polit.* belief in democracy.

demokratyzować *ipf.* democratize. **~ się** *ipf.* become democratized.

Demokryt *mp hist.* Democritus.

demolka *f. pot. Gen.pl.* **-ek** ruin, destruction; (= *chuligańskie niszczenie*) (act of) vandalism.

demolować *ipf.* smash up, ruin, ravage; (= *niszczyć po chuligańsku*) vandalize.

demon *mp pl.* **-y 1.** *mit., rel.* (= *zły duch*) demon. **2.** *mit.* = *duch opiekuńczy* daemon, daimon. **3.** *żart.* (= *maniak, namiętny entuzjasta*) fiend, maniac; **demon seksu** sex fiend, sex maniac; **demon szos** speed demon.

demonetyzacja *f. ekon.* demonetization.

demonetyzować *ipf. ekon.* demonetize.

demonicznie *adv.* (= *szatańsko*) demonically, diabolically; (= *niesamowicie, nieziemsko*) demoniacally.

demoniczny *a.* **1.** (= *szatański, t. przen.* = *przewrotny, tajemniczy*) demonic, diabolic; **demoniczny śmiech** demonic laughter; **moce demoniczne** demonic powers. **2.** (= *niesamowity, nadprzyrodzony*) demoniac.

demonizm *mi* **1.** *rel.* (= *wiara w demony*) demonism. **2.** (= *diaboliczność*) demonicness, diabolicalness.

demonizować *ipf.* (= *nadawać cechy diaboliczne*) demonize, villify; (*o złych cechach l. zjawiskach* = *wyolbrzymiać*) exaggerate (*sth*), blow (*sth*) out of all proportion.

demonolog *mp pl.* **-dzy** *l.* **-owie** demonologist.

demonologia *f. Gen.* **-ii 1.** (*dział etnografii i religioznawstwa*) demonology. **2.** *rel.* (*doktryna religijna*) demonism.

demonopolizacja *f. ekon.* antitrust *l.* antimonopoly regulations.

demonstracja *f.* **1.** *handl., wojsk.* (= *pokaz, manifestacja, protest uliczny*) demonstration; **demonstracja siły** display of force; **urządzić demonstrację** hold *l.* stage a demonstration. **2.** (= *ostentacja*) display, show, ostentation.

demonstracyjny *a.* ostentatious.

demonstrant *mp*, **demonstrantka** *f. Gen.pl.* **-ek** (= *uczestnik demonstracji ulicznej*) (street) demonstrator, protester.

demonstrator *mp*, **demonstratorka** *f. Gen.pl.* **-ek** (= *osoba przeprowadzająca pokaz*) demonstrator.

demonstrować *ipf.* **1.** (= *manifestować*) protest, demonstrate (*przeciw komuś/czemuś*

against sb/sth, *na rzecz czegoś* in support *l.* in favour of sth). **2.** (= *wyrażać uczucia, postawy*) manifest, display. **3.** (= *prezentować, pokazywać*) demonstrate, show, give a demonstration of (*sth*).

demontaż *mi Gen.pl.* **-y** *l.* **-ów** *techn.* disassembly, dismantling.

demontować *ipf.* (*t. przen.*) dismantle; (*urządzenie*) disassemble, take apart; (*rusztowanie itp.*) take down.

demoralizacja *f.* (moral) corruption; (*stan*) depravity; (*czynność*) depravation.

demoralizator *mp*, **demoralizatorka** *f. Gen.pl.* **-ek** corruptor, depraver.

demoralizować *ipf.* corrupt, deprave; (= *sprowadzać na złą drogę*) lead astray. **~ się** *ipf.* become corrupt *l.* depraved.

Demostenes *mp hist.* Demosthenes.

demotyczny *a. hist.* (*o systemach pisma*) demotic.

demulgować *ipf. chem.* demulsify.

den *n. zob.* **dno.**

denacjonalizacja *f. ekon.* denationalization.

denacjonalizować *ipf. ekon.* denationalize.

denar *mi Gen.* **-a** *hist.* **1.** (= *moneta rzymska l. średniowieczna*) denarius. **2.** (= *macedońska jednostka monetarna*) denar.

denat *mp*, **denatka** *f. Gen.pl.* **-ek 1.** *form.* (= *nieboszczyk*) deceased person. **2.** *pot.* (= *pijany*) drunk, dead-drunk person.

denaturacja *f. chem.* (*białka, kwasów*) denaturation.

denaturalizacja *f. prawn.* denaturalization.

denaturalizować *ipf. prawn.* denaturalize.

denaturant *mi chem.* denaturant, contaminant.

denaturat *mi chem.* denaturated alcohol, methylated spirit.

denaturować *ipf. chem.* denature, denaturize; **spirytus denaturowany** denatured (ethyl) alcohol.

denazalizacja *f. jęz.* denasalization.

denazalizować *ipf. jęz.* denasalize.

denazyfikacja *f. polit.* denazification.

denazyfikować *ipf. polit.* denazify.

dendrolog *mp pl.* **-dzy** *l.* **-owie** *bot.* dendrologist.

dendrologia *f. Gen.* **-ii** *bot.* dendrology.

dendrologiczny *a. bot.* dendrological, dendrologic; **ogród dendrologiczny** dendrological garden.

dendryt *mi* **1.** *anat.* dendrite, dendron. **2.** *min.* dendrite, arborescent/dendritic crystal. **3.** *mat.* (*wykres*) spanning tree; **dendryt decyzyjny** decision tree.

dendrytowy *a. anat., min.* dendritic.

denerwować *ipf.* **1.** (= *gniewać*) annoy, exasperate. **2.** (= *martwić*) make anxious/nervous. **~ się** *ipf.* be anxious (*czymś* about sth).

denerwująco *adv.* annoyingly; infuriatingly.

denerwujący *a.* annoying, exasperating; infuriating.

denitryfikacja *f. chem.* denitrification.

denitryfikować *ipf. chem.* denitrify.

deniwelacja *f. miern.* height difference.

denko *n. Gen.pl.* **-nek** bottom.

dennica *f.* **1.** *techn.* **dennica dyszowa** wind box; **dennica konwertora** converter bottom. **2.** (*w wozie drabiniastym*) hay-wagon floor. **3.** (= *dno ula*) hive bottom.

dennie *adv. pot.* lousily; **czuć się dennie** feel lousy.

dennik *mi Gen.* **-a** *żegl.* floor; **dennik główny/ otwarty/pełny/wysoki** main/bracket/plate/rising floor. – *ma icht.* seasnail (*Liparis liparis*).

denny *a.* **1.** (*na dnie*) ground; **fala denna** *hydrol.* ground swell; **mina denna** *wojsk.* ground mine; **morena denna** *geol.* bottom *l.* ground moraine. **2.** *żegl.* bottom; **poszycie denne** bottom plating; **wręg denny** bottom frame; **wzdłużnica denna** bottom longitudinal. **3.** *icht.* demersal. **4.** *pot.* (= *bezwartościowy*) trashy, rubbishy.

denominacja *f. rel., ekon.* denomination.

denominator *mi ekon.* denominator.

denominować *ipf. ekon.* denominate.

denotacja *f. log., fil., jęz.* denotation.

denotować *ipf. log., fil., jęz.* denote.

densometr *mi fot.* densitometer.

densytometria *f. Gen.* **-ii** *fot.* densitometry.

dentalny *a. jęz., fon.* dental.

dentysta *mp*, **dentystka** *f. Gen.pl.* **-ek** dentist; **lekarz dentysta** dental surgeon; **u dentysty** at the dentist's.

dentystyczny *a.* dental; **gabinet dentystyczny** dental surgery; *pot.* the dentist's; **technik dentystyczny** dental technician.

denuncjacja *f.* denunciation, informing.

denuncjator *mp*, **denuncjatorka** *f. Gen.pl.* **-ek** denouncer, delator; (= *donosiciel*) informer.

denuncjować *ipf.* denounce (*sb*) (*przed kimś / czymś* before sb/sth); inform (*kogoś* against *l.* on sb) (*przed kimś* to sb).

deoksyrybonukleinowy *a. biochem.* = **dezoksyrybonukleinowy.**

deontologia *f. Gen.* **-ii** *fil.* deontology.

depalatalizacja *f. jęz.* depalatalization.

depalatalizować *ipf. jęz.* depalatalize.

departament *mi* **1.** (= *dział ministerstwa*) division, office. **2.** (*w USA*) (= *ministerstwo*) ministry; **Departament Obrony** Department of Defense; **Departament Stanu** Department of State. **3.** (*jednostka administracyjna*) department.

depersonalizacja *f. lit.* (= *alienacja, uprzedmiotowienie*) *psych.* depersonalization.

depersonifikacja *f. psych.* depersonification.

depesza *f.* **1.** *tel.* (*telegraficzna*) telegram; *przest., pot.* wire; (*radiowa, telefoniczna*) cable. **2.** *dzienn.* dispatch.

depeszować *ipf.* telegraph; *US* wire (*do kogoś* sb).

depilacja *f.* depilation; (*elektrolityczna*) electrolysis.

depilacyjny *a.* (*np. o kremie, wosku*) depilatory.

depilator *mi Gen.* **-a** **1.** (*urządzenie*) depilator. **2.** (*kosmetyk*) hair remover, depilatory.

depilować *ipf.* depilate.

depolaryzacja *f. fiz.* depolarization.

depolaryzator *mi Gen.* **-a** *fiz., chem.* depolarizer.

deponent *mp prawn.* bailor.

deponować *ipf. prawn.* escrow, deposit.

deportacja *f.* **1.** *prawn.* (= *wydalenie*) deportation. **2.** *prawn.* (= *kara zesłania*) transportation.

deportować *ipf.* **1.** *prawn.* (= *wydalać za granicę*) deport. **2.** *prawn.* (= *zsyłać*) exile.

depozyt *mi* **1.** *ekon., geol.* deposit; **oddać w depozyt** deposit; *ekon.* place on deposit; **depozyt bankowy** bank *l.* banker's deposit; **depozyt sądowy** court deposit. **2.** *prawn.* escrow; **w depozycie** in escrow. **3.** (*miejsce, gdzie przechowuje się wartościowe przedmioty, pieniądze*) depository; **oddać do depozytu** deposit.

depozytariusz *mp Gen.pl.* **-y** *l.* **-ów** *prawn.* depositary.

depozytor *mp* **1.** *prawn.* bailor. **2.** *ekon.* depositor.

depozytowy *a. prawn., ekon.* deposit.

deprawacja *f.* depravity, moral corruption.

deprawator *mp* depraver.

deprawować *ipf.* deprave, corrupt. ~ **się** *ipf.* become depraved *l.* corrupt.

deprecjacja *f.* **1.** (= *pomniejszanie wartości*) deprecation, disparagement. **2.** *ekon.* depreciation.

deprecjonować *ipf.* (= *umniejszać*) belittle, deprecate, disparage. ~ **się** *ipf. ekon.* depreciate, undergo depreciation.

depresja *f.* **1.** *pot.* (= *przygnębienie*) depression, despondency, dejection. **2.** *astron., ekon., geogr., pat., psych.* depression; **depresja tektoniczna** *geol.* tectonic depression. **3.** *meteor.* depression, low.

depresyjny *a.* **1.** *pot.* (= *przygnębiający*) depressing, depressive. **2.** *psych., med.* depressive. **3.** *geogr.* depression.

deprymować *ipf.* discourage, disconcert, intimidate; *pot.* put off.

deprymujący *a.* discouraging, disconcerting; *pot.* off-putting.

deptać *ipf.* **-czę -czesz** *l.* **-cę -cesz, -cz** **1.** (*stawiać stopę*) tread (*po czymś* on sth); **nie deptać trawników!** keep off the grass!; **deptać komuś po piętach** be at sb's heels, be (hot) on sb's heels. **2.** (*niszczyć nogami*) trample (over) (*sth*). **3.** *przen.* (= *łamać, lekceważyć*) trample on (*sth*).

deptak *mi Gen.* **-u** *l.* **-a** **1.** (= *promenada*) promenade. **2.** (= *ulica tylko dla pieszych*) pedestrian precinct.

deputacja *f.* **1.** *form.* (= *poselstwo, delegacja*) deputation. **2.** *hist.* (= *komisja*) commission.

deputat[1] *mi Gen.* **-u** *pl.* **-y** *ekon.* (= *przydział*) (*węgla, opału, specjalny*) allowance.

deputat[2] *mp Gen.* **-a** *pl.* **-ci** **1.** *hist.* (= *członek trybunału*) deputy. **2.** *przest.* (= *delegat*) delegate, representative.

deputowany *mp parl.* deputy; *US* Representative; *Br.* Member of Parliament, MP.

deratyzacja *f.* (rat) disinfestation, rat destruction; **deratyzacja statku** disinfestation of a ship.

deratyzować *ipf.* disinfest.

derbista *ma*, **derbistka** *f. Gen.pl.* **-ek** *sport* (*koń*) derby winner.

derby *n. indecl. l. Gen.pl.* **-ów** *sport* (*mecz, wyścig konny*) derby.

dereń *mi Gen.* **-a** *l.* **-u** *bot.* cornel, dogwood (*Cornus*); **dereń rozłogowy** red-osier dogwood (*C. stolonifera*); **dereń właściwy** cornelian cherry (*C. mas*).

deresz *ma Gen.pl.* **-y** *l.* **-ów** *Acc.* **-ów** *zool.* roan.

dereszowaty *a.* roan; **gniado-dereszowaty** red roan; **kasztanowato-dereszowaty** strawberry roan; **karo-dereszowaty** blue roan.

derka *f. Gen.pl.* **-ek** horsecloth; blanket; **derka na nogi** *US* foot bag; *Br.* foot muff.

derkacz *ma Gen.pl.* **-y** *l.* **-ów** *orn.* corncrake, land rail (*Crex crex*).

derma *f.* American cloth, leatherette.

dermatofit *mi pat.* dermatophyte.

dermatoglifika *f. anat.* dermatoglyphics.

dermatolog *mp pl.* **-dzy** *l.* **-owie** *med.* dermatologist.

dermatologia *f. Gen.* **-ii** *med.* dermatology.

dermatologiczny *a. med.* dermatological.

dermatoza *f. pat.* dermatosis.

dermografia *f. anat.* dermography, dermatography.

dermoplastyczny *a. med.* dermatoplastic.

dermoplastyka *f. med.* dermatoplasty.

derwisz *mp Gen.pl.* **-y** *l.* **-ów** *rel.* (*członek bractwa muzułmańskiego*) dervish.

derywacja *f.* **1.** *jęz.* derivation; **derywacja wsteczna** back-formation. **2.** *lotn.* derivation. **3.** *balistyka* drift.

derywacyjny *a. jęz., mat.* derivational; **podstawa derywacyjna** base.

derywat *mi jęz.* derivative; **derywat wsteczny** back-formation.

derywować *ipf. jęz.* derive.

des *n. muz.* D-flat.

desakralizacja *f.* desecration; (= *sekularyzacja*) secularization.

desant *mi wojsk.* **1.** (= *zrzut*) airdrop; parachute operation, paratroop attack. **2.** (= *lądowanie*) landing. **3.** (= *grupa komandosów*) landing party, paratroop.

desantowiec *mp* **-wc-** *pl.* **-y** *wojsk.* (= *komandos*) paratrooper. – *mi* **-wc-** *Gen.* **-a** *pl.* **-e** *wojsk.* (*łódź, okręt*) landing craft.

desantowy *a. wojsk.* **1.** (*o barce, operacji*) landing; (*o łodzi, okręcie*) assault. **2.** (*o oddziale, wojsku*) airborne.

deseczka *f. Gen.pl.* **-ek** small board.

desegregacja *f.* desegregation.

desegregować *ipf.* desegregate.

deseniarka *f. Gen.pl* **-ek** *techn.* embossing roller.

deseń *mi Gen.* **-u** *l.* **-a** *Gen.pl.* **-i** *l.* **-ów** pattern; design; **w ten deseń** *pot.* (in) this way.

deser *mi kulin.* **1.** dessert, pudding; *Br.* sweet; *Br. pot.* afters; **na deser** for dessert. **2.** **deser lodowy** sundae; **deser bananowo-lodowy** banana split; **deser owocowy** fruit cup.

deserowy *a.* dessert; **łyżeczka deserowa** dessert spoon; **talerzyk deserowy** bread and butter plate; **widelczyk deserowy** dessert fork; **wino deserowe** dessert wine.

deska *f. Gen.pl* **-ek 1.** (*drewno*) plank; board; **deska do krojenia** cutting board, chopping block; **deska do krojenia chleba** breadboard; **deska do krojenia sera** cheeseboard; **deska do prasowania** ironing board; **deska kreślarska** drawing board; **deska podłogowa** floorboard; **deska rozdzielcza** *mot., pot.* dashboard, dash; **deska surfingowa** *sport* surfboard; **deska windsurfingowa** *sport* sailboard; **deski sceniczne** *przen.* the boards. **2.** **deska klozetowa** toilet seat; **do grobowej deski** lifelong; **leżeć na deskach** *boks* be down for the count; **ostatnia** *l.* **jedyna deska ratunku** *przen.* the last resort; **świat zabity deskami** (*także* **wieś zabita deskami**) *przen.* the back of beyond, the backwoods, the stick, the boondocks; **przeczytać coś od deski do deski** read sth from cover to cover. **3.** *pot.* (= *narta*) ski.

deskorolka *f. Gen.pl.* **-ek** *sport* skateboard.

deskować *ipf. bud.* plank, board.

deskrypcja *f. lit.* (= *opis*), *log.* description.

deskrypcyjny *a. lit.* descriptive; **gramatyka deskrypcyjna** *jęz.* descriptive grammar.

deskryptor *mi Gen.* **-a** *komp.* descriptor.

deskryptywizm *mi jęz., lit.* descriptivism.

deskryptywny *a. teor.lit., jęz.* descriptive.

desktop *mi komp.* desktop.

despekt *mi lit.* affront, offense.

desperacja *f.* desperation.

desperacki *a.* desperate; **desperacki krok** desperate measure.

desperat *mp*, **desperatka** *f. Gen.pl.* **-ek** desperate person.

despota *mp*, **despotka** *f. Gen.pl.* **-ek** *t. przen.* despot.

despotycznie *adv. t. przen.* despotically; **rządzić despotycznie** rule despotically.

despotyczny *a. t. przen.* despotic.

despotyzm *mi t. przen.* despotism.

dessous *n. indecl. żart.* = **desu**.

destabilizacja *f.* destabilization.

destabilizator *mi Gen.* **-a** *techn., lotn.* destabilizer.

destabilizować *ipf.* destabilize; unsettle.

destrukcja *f. lit.* **1.** (= *niszczenie*) destruction. **2.** (= *rozpad*) disintegration.

destrukcyjny *a.* destructive.

destylacja *f. chem.* distillation; **destylacja cząsteczkowa/ekstrakcyjna/frakcyjna/prosta/równowagowa** molecular/extractive/fractional/simple/flash distillation; **sucha destylacja drewna** destructive wood distillation; **sucha destylacja węgla** coal carbonization.

destylacyjny *a. chem.* distillatory.

destylarka *f. Gen.pl.* **-ek** *chem., techn.* still, distiller.

destylarnia *f. Gen.pl.* **-i** *l.* **-ń** *chem.* distillery, still.

destylat *mi chem.* distillate.

destylator *mi Gen.* **-a** *techn.* **1.** (*urządzenie*) distiller, still. **2.** (*człowiek*) distiller.

destylować *ipf. chem.* distill; **woda destylowana** distilled water.

desu *n. indecl.*, **desusy** *pl. Gen.pl.* **-ów** *żart.* (= *bielizna damska*) underwear, lingerie; (= *majtki*) panties.

desygnacja *f.* **1.** (= *mianowanie, powołanie*) designation. **2.** *jęz.* reference.

desygnat *mi log., jęz.* referent.

desygnować *ipf. l. pf.* appoint, designate (*na kogoś/coś* (as) sb/sth).

desygnowany *a.* (= *mianowany*) appointed, designated; (= *osoba desygnowana*) designate (*rzeczownik*); **desygnowany na stanowisko ambasadora** ambassador designate.

deszcz *mi arch. t.* **dżdż-** *Gen.pl.* **-ów 1.** rain, shower; **deszcz ze śniegiem** sleet; **kwaśny deszcz** acid rain; **przelotne deszcze** scattered showers; **rzęsisty** *l.* **ulewny deszcz** heavy rain, downpour; **pada deszcz** it's raining; **zanosi się na deszcz** it looks like rain, it looks as if it's going to rain; **schronić się przed deszczem** find shelter from the rain; **wpaść z deszczu pod rynnę** *przen.* jump/leap out of the frying pan into the fire; **rosnąć jak grzyby po deszczu** mushroom, sprout up; spread like wildfire; **z dużej** *l.* **wielkiej chmury mały deszcz** *przen.* all bark and no bite. **2.** *przen.* (= *mnóstwo, rój*) shower; **deszcz meteorów** *astron.* meteor shower.

deszczomierz *mi Gen.pl.* **-y** *meteor.* rain gauge, pluviometer.

deszczować *ipf. roln.* sprinkle.

deszczowiec *mi* **-wc-** *Gen.* **-a** (= *płaszcz przeciwdeszczowy*) raincoat; *Br.* mackintosh.

deszczownia *f. roln.* sprinkler.

deszczowy *a. form.* pluvial; (*o dniu, pogodzie*) rainy; **chmura deszczowa** rain cloud; *meteor.* nimbus; **pora deszczowa** *meteor.* rainy season; **woda deszczowa** rainwater.

deszczówka *f. Gen.pl.* **-ek** rainwater.

deszczułka *f. Gen.pl.* **-ek** (*w budownictwie*) lath; (*np. w żaluzji*) (wooden) slat.

deszczyk *mi* light rain, drizzle.

deszyfracja *f.* decoding; decipherment, decryption.

deszyfrant *mp*, **deszyfrantka** *f. Gen.pl.* **-ek** decoder; decipherer.

deszyfrator *mi Gen.* **-a** *techn.* decoder, decoding *l.* deciphering device.

deszyfrować *ipf.* decipher, decrypt; decode.

detal *mi Gen.pl.* **-i** *l.* **-ów 1.** (= *fragment*) detail (*t. bud.*). **2.** *film* big close-up. **3.** *pot.* (= *błahostka, głupstwo*) trifle. **4.** *noncount ekon., handl.* retail trade.

detalicznie *adv.* **1.** *ekon., handl.* **sprzedawać detalicznie** sell retail, retail. **2.** *pot.* (= *szczegółowo*) in detail.

detaliczny *a.* **1.** *ekon., handl.* (*o handlu, cenie, sprzedaży*) retail. **2.** *pot.* (= *szczegółowy*) detailed.

detalista *mp ekon., handl.* retailer.

detekcja *f. techn.* detection; *tel.* demodulation.

detektor *mi Gen.* **-a 1.** *techn., tel.* (= *wykrywacz*) detector. **2.** *fiz. jądrowa* detector; monitor.

detektyw *mp* detective; **prywatny detektyw** private detective *l.* investigator; *pot.* private eye.

detektywistyczny *a.* (*o filmie, powieści*) detective.

detergent *mi chem.* detergent.

determinacja *f.* **1.** (= *stanowczość*) determination, resolution. **2.** *biol., log.* determination.

determinant *mi* (= *wyznacznik*) determinant (*t. mat.*).

determinizm *mi fil.* determinism.

determinować *ipf.* determine.

detoksykacja *f. chem., med.* detoxification, detoxication.

detoksykacyjny *a. chem., med.* detoxicator, detoxicant.

detonacja *f.* **1.** (= *huk*) explosion; fulmination. **2.** *chem.* (= *eksplozja*) detonation. **3.** *muz.* discord.

detonator *mi Gen.* **-a** *techn., wojsk.* detonator, primer.

detonować *ipf.* **1.** (= *eksplodować; odpalić*) detonate; set off. **2.** (= *onieśmielać*) disconcert, unnerve, intimidate. **3.** *muz.* play *l.* sing off key.

detronizacja *f.* dethronement.

detronizacyjny *a.* **akt detronizacyjny** act of dethronement.

detronizować *ipf.* dethrone.

deuter *mi chem.* deuterium.

dewaluacja *f.* **1.** *ekon.* (= *spadek*) devaluation, depreciation. **2.** (= *spadek wartości*) (*zasad, słów, wartości*) devaluation; degradation.

dewaluować *ipf.* **1.** *ekon.* devalue, depreciate. **2.** (= *degradować, obniżać wartość*) deprecate, debase, degrade. **~ się** *ipf.* **1.** *ekon.* become devalued. **2.** (= *degradować się*) become deprecated *l.* degraded; lose value.

dewastacja *f.* vandalizing.

dewastacyjny *a.* vandalistic.

dewastator *mp* vandal.

dewastować *ipf.* vandalize.

deweloper *mp bud.* developer.

deweloping *mi bud.* developing.

dewerbalny *a. jęz.* deverbal.

dewiacja *f.* **1.** (= *odchylenie, nieprawidłowość*) deviation, anomaly; *t. fiz.* aberration. **2.** *nawigacja* deviation, error. **3.** *psych., socjol.* deviance, deviancy.

dewiacyjny *a.* **1.** *psych., socjol.* (*o zachowaniu*) deviant. **2.** *żegl.* deviation; **tabela dewiacyjna** deviation table.

dewiant *mp psych., socjol.* deviant, deviate.

dewiza *f.* (= *maksyma, motto*) motto, maxim, slogan; **życiowa dewiza** life's motto.

dewizka *f. Gen.pl.* **-ek** *arch.* (*łańcuszek*) fob, watch chain; (*przywieszka*) fob.

dewizowiec *mp* **-wc-** *pl.* **-y** *Gen.* **-ów** *pot. przest.* **1.** (= *ktoś z dewizowym kontem bankowym*) owner of a hard currency account. **2.** (= *cudzoziemiec z dewizami*) foreigner (*paying with hard currency*).

dewizowy *a. ekon.* **1.** (*o prawie, przepisach*) foreign exchange. **2.** (*o koncie*) foreign currency.

dewizy *pl. Gen.* **-z 1.** *ekon.* (foreign) exchange. **2.** *pot.* foreign currency.

dewocja *f.* **1.** (= *świętoszkowatość*) piousness;

sanctimony, sanctimoniousness. **2.** *rel.* (= *bogobojność, pobożność*) devotion, piety.

dewocjonalia *pl. Gen.* **-ów 1.** (*różańce, medaliki itp.*) devotional articles. **2.** (*sprzęt kościelny*) ecclesiastical objects.

dewocyjny *a.* **1.** (= *bigoteryjny*) sanctimonious; *pot.* churchy, holier-than-thou. **2.** *rel.* (= *pobożny*) devotional, pious.

dewon *mi geol.* the Devonian.

dewoński *a. geol.* Devonian.

dewotka *f. Gen.pl.* **-ek** *pog.* bigot, churchy woman.

dezabil *mi Gen.pl.* **-i** *l.* **-ów** *przest., żart.* dishabille; **w dezabilu** in a state of undress; half naked *l.* undressed.

dezaktualizacja *f.* superannuation.

dezaktualizować się *ipf.* become obsolete/superannuated; (*stopniowo*) become obsolescent.

dezaktywacja *f chem.* deactivation.

dezaktywować *ipf. chem.* deactivate.

dezaprobata *f.* disapproval, disapprobation, condemnation; **z dezaprobatą** disapprovingly.

dezaprobować *ipf.* disapprove (*coś* of sth) condemn (*sth* coś).

dezawuować *ipf.* disparage, deprecate.

dezercja *f. wojsk.* desertion.

dezerter *mp*, **dezerterka** *f. Gen.pl.* **-ek 1.** *wojsk.* deserter. **2.** *przen.* (*np. z partii politycznej*) defector.

dezerterować *ipf.* **1.** *wojsk.* desert, go AWOL (= *absent without leave*). **2.** *przen.* (*np. z partii politycznej*) defect, abscond.

dezinformacja *f.* misinformation; *wojsk.* disinformation; deception.

dezinformować *ipf.* misinform.

dezintegracja *f.* (= *rozpad*) disintegration (*t. fiz.*); **dezintegracja społeczna** *socjol.* social disintegration.

dezintegracyjny *a.* disintegrative.

dezintegrować *ipf.* disintegrate. ~ **się** *ipf.* disintegrate; fall apart, crumble.

dezodorant *mi* **1.** (*kosmetyk*) deodorant, antiperspirant; **dezodorant w kulce** roll-on. **2.** (= *odświeżacz powietrza*) air freshener.

dezoksyrybonukleinowy *a. biochem.* **kwas dezoksyrybonukleinowy** deoxyribonucleic acid, DNA.

dezolacja *f. przest.* **1.** (= *zniszczenie*) devastation, desolation. **2.** (= *bezsilność, rozpacz*) desolation, despair.

dezolować *ipf. przest.* **1.** (= *niszczyć*) desolate, devastate. **2.** (= *przygnębiać*) desolate.

dezorganizacja *f.* disorganization.

dezorganizacyjny *a.* (*o wpływie*) disorganizing.

dezorganizator *mp*, **dezorganizatorka** *f. Gen.pl.* **-ek** disorganizer.

dezorganizować *ipf.* disorganize.

dezorientować *ipf.* disorient; *Br.* disorientate; perplex, confuse.

dezurbanizacja *f.* deindustrialization.

dezurbanizować *ipf.* deindustrialize.

dezyderat *mi* proposition.

dezynfekcja *f.* disinfection, sanitization.

dezynfekcyjny *a.* disinfectation, disinfecting; **środek dezynfekcyjny** disinfectant.

dezynfekować *ipf.* disinfect, sanitize.

dezynfekujący *a.* disinfectant, disinfecting.

dezynsekcja *f.* (= *tępienie owadów*) disinfestation, disinsectation; (= *odwszanie*) delousing.

dezynsekować *ipf.* (= *tępić owady*) disinfest, disinsectize; (= *odwszawiać*) delouse.

dezynwoltura *f. lit.* disrespect, irreverence; **z dezynwolturą** disrespectfully, irreverently.

dęba *adv.* **stawać dęba** (*o koniu*) rear up; (*o włosach*) stand on end.

dębczak *mi Gen.* **-a 1.** (= *młody dąb*) young oak tree. **2.** (= *kij dębowy*) oak club.

dębić *ipf. pot.* (= *zdobywać*) wheedle (*coś od kogoś* sth out of sb).

dębieć *ipf.* **-eję -ejesz** (= *zdziwić się, baranieć*) be dumbfounded/flabbergasted.

dębina *f.* **1.** (*las*) oak forest/wood. **2.** (*drewno*) oakwood.

dębowy *a.* oak, oaken.

dębu *itd. mi zob.* **dąb.**

dęła *itd. ipf. zob.* **dąć.**

dętka *f. Gen.pl.* **-ek 1.** (*rowerowa, samochodowa*) (inner) tube. **2.** (*wewnątrz piłki*) bladder.

dętologia *f. Gen.* **-ii** *żart.* mumbo-jumbo, gobbledygook, gibberish.

dęty *a.* **1.** *muz.* wind; **instrumenty dęte** wind instruments; **instrumenty dęte blaszane** brass; **instrumenty dęte drewniane** woodwind; **instrumenty dęte stroikowe** reeds; **orkiestra dęta** brass band. **2.** *pot. przen.* (= *oszukańczy*) fake. **3.** *pot. przen.* (= *próżny, zarozumiały*) stuck-up, snotty, full of o.s.

diabaz *mi min.* diabase.

diabelnie *adv. pot. emf.* (= *bardzo, ogromnie*) devilish, devilishly, fiendishly; *Br.* bloody, deuced.

diabelny *a. pot. emf. l. iron.* (= *wielki, niezwykły*) whopping, whacking; **mieć diabelne szczęście** be a lucky bastard *l.* a lucky devil; **co za diabelny bałagan!** what a devil of a mess!

diabelski *a.* devilish; *pot.* (*np. o planie*) fiendish; **diabelskie nasienie** little devil, fiend; **diabelski młyn** Ferris wheel.

diabelsko *adv.* devilishly, fiendishly.

diabelstwo *n.* **1.** (= *świństwo, paskudztwo*) bastard. **2.** (= *zło, złośliwość*) wickedness, devilishness, devilry.

diabeł *mp* **-bł-** *Dat.* **-u** *Voc.* **-e** *pl.* **-y** *l.* **-i** *rel.* **1.** devil, fiend. **2. diabeł błotny** *zool.* hellbender (*Cryptobranchus alleghaniensis*); **diabeł morski** *icht.* manta ray (*Manta birostris*); **diabeł tasmański** *zool.* Tasmanian devil, ursine dasyure (*Sarcophilus harrisii*). **3.** *przen. l. w utartych zwrotach i przysłowiach* **diabeł wcielony** *l.* istny **diabeł** rascal, devil; (*o dziecku*) imp, scamp; **diabeł w niego wstąpił** (*także* **diabeł go opętał**) he's bedeviled *l.* possessed; **diabli mnie biorą** it's eating me up; it's pissing me off; **diabli nadali** shucks!; it never rains (but it pours); **diabli wzięli** (it's gone) down the drain; **diabli wiedzą** who the devil knows?; **diabła tam!** like hell he is (*l.* was, does etc.); **adwokat diabła** devil's advocate; **bać**

się czegoś jak diabeł święconej **wody** be scared out of one's wits by sth; **co/kto/dlaczego u diabła?** what/who/why the devil?; **do diabła!** dammit!; *Br.* blast!; **do diabła z czymś** to hell with sth; **idź do diabła!** go to hell!; go to the devil!; **jak (wszyscy) diabli** (*np. harować*) like the devil, like hell; **jeden diabeł** it's all the same to me; **ktoś diabła wart** a good-for-nothing; **mieć w sobie diabła** be bedeviled/possessed; **na diabła?!** (*także* **po (jakiego) diabła?!**) what the hell for?, what the devil for; **niech mnie diabli, jeżeli...** I'll be damned *l.* buggered if...; **nie taki diabeł straszny, jak go malują** it's not as bad as all that; **Panu Bogu świeczkę, a diabłu ogarek** run with the hare and hunt with the hounds; **posłać kogoś do diabła** *l.* **do wszystkich diabłów** tell sb to go to hell; **rzucić w diabły** dump, ditch; **tam, gdzie diabeł mówi dobranoc** at the back of beyond, in the backwoods *l.* the boondocks; **zaprzedać diabłu duszę** sell one's soul to the devil.

diabełek *mp* **-łk-** *Gen.* **-a** *pl.* **-i** **1.** (= *złośliwy duszek*) imp. **2.** *przen., żart.* little devil.

diabetologia *f. Gen.* **-ii** *med.* study of diabetes.

diabetyk *mp med.* diabetic.

diablę *n.* **-lęci-** *pl.* **-lęt-** *Gen.* **-ąt** = **diabełek**.

diablica *f.* **1.** *pot.* (= *jędza*) shrew, hag, witch, bitch. **2.** *pot.* (= *kociak, cizia*) vamp, foxy lady, fine bitch.

diablik *mp pl.* **-i** imp.

diablo *adv. pot. emf.* fiendishly, devilishly.

diaboliczny *a.* (*urok, spojrzenie, uśmiech*) diabolical.

diachronia *f. Gen.* **-ii** diachrony.

diachroniczny *a.* (*o analizie, językoznawstwie*) diachronic.

diadem *mi* coronet, tiara; (*królewski*) diadem.

diafragma *f.* **1.** *opt., fot.* diaphragm, lens stop. **2.** *techn.* diaphragm.

diagnosta *mp med.* diagnostician.

diagnostyk *mp Gen.* **-a** *pl.* **-cy** *med.* (*lekarz*) = **diagnosta**. – *mi Gen.* **-u** *pl.* **-i** *med., farm.* diagnostic.

diagnostyka *f.* **1.** *med.* diagnostics; diagnosis; **diagnostyka radiologiczna** radiodiagnosis; **diagnostyka rentgenologiczna** X-ray diagnosis; diagnostic roentgenology. **2.** (= *ocena, przegląd*) scrutinizing.

diagnoza *f.* **1.** *med.* diagnosis; **stawiać diagnozę** diagnose. **2.** (= *ocena, przegląd*) scrutiny.

diagnozować *ipf. med.* diagnose.

diagonal *mi tk.* diagonal, twill; **z diagonalu** twill.

diagonalnie *adv.* diagonally; across (*względem czegoś* from sth).

diagonalny *a.* **1.** *mat.* diagonal. **2.** (*w oponie*) cross-ply.

diagraf *mi techn.* diagraph.

diagram *mi* **1.** (= *wykres*) diagram; **za pomocą diagramu** diagrammatically. **2.** (= *schemat, grafik*) (*pracy, dyżurów*) schedule, timetable.

diak¹ *mp pl.* **-cy** *rel., kośc.* psalm singer (*in the Eastern Churches*); seminarian (*in the Eastern Churches*).

diak² *mi pl.* **-i** *el.* diac, trigger diode.

diakon *mp rel., kośc.* deacon.

diakonat *mi rel., kośc.* **1.** (= *urząd*) diaconate, deaconry. **2.** (= *diakoni*) deaconry.

diakonisa *f. rel., kośc.* deaconess.

diakoński *a. rel., kośc.* diaconal.

diakrytyczny *a.* diacritic; **znaki diakrytyczne** *jęz.* diacritic marks, diacritics.

dialekt *mi jęz.* dialect.

dialektalny *a. jęz.* dialectal.

dialektolog *mp pl.* **-dzy** *l.* **-owie** *jęz.* dialectologist.

dialektologia *f. Gen.* **-ii** *jęz.* dialectology.

dialektologiczny *a. jęz.* dialectological.

dialektyczny *a. fil.* dialectical.

dialektyk *mp fil.* dialectician.

dialektyka *f. fil.* **1.** (*metodologia*) dialectics. **2.** (*heglowska*) dialectic.

dialektyzacja *f. jęz., teor.lit.* use of dialectal forms.

dialektyzm *mi jęz.* dialecticism.

dialektyzować *ipf.* make dialectal, dialectize.

dializa *f. chem., med.* dialysis; **poddawać dializie** dialyze.

dializator *mi med.* dialyzer.

dializować *ipf. med., pot.* dialyze.

dialog *mi* dialog, dialogue.

dialogować *ipf.* converse; *rzad.* dialog, dialogue.

dialogowy *a.* dialog; **napisy dialogowe** *film* subtitles; **lista dialogowa** *film* script; (*czytana przez lektora*) voice-over, VO.

diamagnetyczny *a. fiz.* diamagnetic.

diamagnetyk *mi fiz.* diamagnetic material.

diamagnetyzm *mi fiz.* diamagnetism.

diament *mi* **1.** *min., druk.* diamond; **czarny diament** *przen.* (= *węgiel*) black diamond. **2.** *techn.* **diament szklarski** (= *krajak diamentowy*) diamond glass cutter; (= *krajak stalowy*) steel-wheel glass cutter.

diamentowy *a.* diamond; **diamentowe gody** diamond wedding.

diametralnie *adv.* **1.** (= *przez średnicę*) diametrally. **2.** *przen.* (= *przeciwstawnie*) diametrically; **diametralnie różny** diametrically opposed.

diametralny *a.* **1.** (*przechodzący przez średnicę*) diametral, diametric. **2.** *przen.* (= *przeciwstawny*) diametric.

diapazon *mi* **1.** *muz.* (= *skala*) diapason. **2.** *muz.* (= *kamerton*) tuning fork.

diapozytyw *mi* **1.** *fot.* slide, diapositive, transparency. **2.** *druk.* transparency.

diariusz *mi Gen.pl.* **-y** *l.* **-ów** *lit.* **1.** (= *dziennik*) diary. **2.** **diariusz parlamentarny** *parl.* parliamentary proceedings *l.* records.

diaskop *mi fot.* diascope.

diaspora *f.* **1.** (= *rozproszenie*) diaspora. **2.** *bot.* diaspore.

diastaza *f. biochem.* diastase.

diastema *f pat., dent.* diastema.

diatermia *f. Gen.* **-ii** *med.* (= *leczenie prądem*) diathermy, diathermia.

diateza *f. med., jęz.* diathesis.

diatoniczny *a. muz.* diatonic.

diatonika *f. muz.* diatonicism.

diatryba *f. lit.* diatribe (*przeciw czemuś/komuś* against sth/sb).

dicentra *f bot.* bleeding heart, dicentra (*Dicentra*).

dickensowski *a. lit.* Dickensian.

dictum *n. indecl. lit.* dictum.

didaskalia *pl. Gen.* **-ów** *teatr* stage directions.

diec. *abbr. kośc.* dioc. (= *diocese*).

diecezja *f. kośc.* diocese.

diecezjalny *a. kośc.* diocesan.

dielektryczny *a. el.* dielectric.

dieslowski *a. techn.* diesel; **silnik dieslowski** diesel engine/motor.

dieta[1] *f.* (*sposób żywienia*) diet; **dieta bezmięsna/bezsolna/bezglutenowa** vegetarian/salt-free/gluten-free diet; **dieta cud** *pot.* crash diet, wonder diet; **dieta głodowa** *uj.* starvation diet; **dieta mleczna** milk diet, lactotherapy; **dieta niskokaloryczna** calorie-controlled *l.* low-calorie diet; **dieta niskotłuszczowa** low-fat diet; **dieta odchudzająca** reducing *l.* slimming diet; **być na diecie** be on a diet, be dieting; **ścisła/zróżnicowana dieta** strict/varied diet.

dieta[2] *f.* **1.** (*pieniądze przeznaczone na utrzymanie na delegacji*) per diem, per-diem allowance. **2.** (*wynagrodzenie*) stipend; **diety poselskie** remuneration/stipend received by members of parliament.

dietetyczka *f. zob.* **dietetyk**.

dietetyczny *a.* (*o potrawie, preparacie*) dietetic; (*o błędzie, reżimie, wymaganiach*) dietary; (*o restauracji*) health-food; (= *niskokaloryczny*) calorie-controlled; (= *niskotłuszczowy*) low-fat.

dietetyk *mp* dietician; nutritionist.

dietetyka *f.* dietetics; nutrition.

dinar *mi Gen.* **-a** (*waluta, moneta, t. hist.*) dinar.

dingo *ma indecl. zool.* dingo (*Canis dingo*).

dinozaur *ma paleont.* dinosaur. – *mp pl.* **-y** *pot.* (= *twórca popularny należący do starszego pokolenia*) old-timer.

dintojra *f.* **1.** *rel.* (= *sąd rabinacki*) rabbinic court. **2.** (= *zwyczajowy sąd w świecie przestępczym*) kangaroo court.

dioda *f. el.* diode; **dioda elektroluminescencyjna** *l.* **świecąca** light-emitting diode, LED.

diodowy *a. el.* diode.

dioksyna *f. chem.* dioxin.

Dionizos *mp mit.* Dionysus.

dionizyjski *a. mit.* (*związany z Dionizosem*) Dionysian (*t. zmysłowy, bachiczny, radosny*).

diopter *mi* **-tr-** *Gen.* **-a** *techn.* sight vane.

dioptria *f. Gen.* **-ii** *opt.* diopter.

diorama *f. film, teatr, muzealnictwo* diorama.

dioryt *mi min.* diorite.

diplodok *ma paleont.* diplodocus (*Diplodocus*).

diploidalny *a. biol.* diploid.

dipol *mi Gen.* **-a 1.** *fiz.* dipole. **2.** *techn.* (= *antena*) dipole aerial, dipole.

dis *n. indecl. muz.* D sharp.

disco *n. indecl. t. muz.* (*muzyka l. klub*) disco; **muzyka disco** disco music.

display *mi Gen.pl.* **-ów** *komp.* display.

diuk *mp pl.* **-cy** *l.* **-owie** (*tytuł*) duke.

diuna *f.* (= *wydma*) dune.

diuretyczny *a. med.* diuretic.

diureza *f. med.* diuresis.

diwa *f.* **1.** (*śpiewaczka*) diva. **2.** (*aktorka*) *przest.* star.

dla *prep.* + *Gen.* **1.** for; **dla mnie/ciebie/ich** for me/you/them; **dla niej czas się nie liczy** for her, time doesn't count; **dla frajdy/przyjemności/zysku** for fun *l.* kicks/pleasure/gain; **dla twojego** *l.* **twego dobra** for your own good; **dla wspólnego dobra** for the common good; **dla zasady** on principle; **kupić/zrobić coś dla kogoś** buy/do sth for sb; **mieć coś wyłącznie dla siebie** keep sth to o.s.; **ważny dla sprawy** important for the cause. **2.** (*tłumaczone przez użycie rzeczownika jako przydawki*) **domek dla lalek** doll house; **karma dla psów** dog food. **3.** (*tłumaczone przez złożenie*) **klatka dla ptaków** birdcage; **kładka dla pieszych** footbridge; **przejście dla pieszych** crosswalk; *Br.* pedestrian crossing. **4.** to; **być grzecznym** *l.* **miłym dla kogoś** be nice to sb; **grzeczny/życzliwy dla (osób) starszych** polite/kind to the elderly; **szkodliwy dla zdrowia** harmful to your health. **5.** (*z rzeczownikiem odczasownikowym: tłumaczone bezokolicznikiem z „to"*) **dla zachowania pozorów** to keep up the pretense, *Br.* to keep up the pretence; **dla zatarcia śladów** to cover one's tracks. **6.** (*tłumaczone przez użycie końcówki dzierżawczej*) -s', -'s; **książka dla dzieci** children's book. **7.** (*w utartych zwrotach*) **dla chcącego nic trudnego** where there's a will there's a way; **dla każdego coś miłego** (there's) something for everyone; **nie dla psa kiełbasa!** *pog.* it's too good for the likes of you!

dlaczego *adv. i conj.* why; **dlaczego akurat ja?** why me, of all people?; **dlaczego nie?** why not?; **nie wiem, dlaczego** I don't know why; **powiedz, dlaczego** tell me why; **dlaczego nie lubisz jabłek?** why don't you like apples?

dlaczegoż *adv.* why (on earth), how come; **dlaczegoż mu o tym powiedziałeś?** how come you told him about it?

dlatego *adv. i conj.* (= *więc*) so, therefore, hence; **padał deszcz, dlatego wziąłem parasol** it was raining, so I took an umbrella; (= *z tego powodu*) that's why, for this reason; **dlatego też** that's why; **właśnie dlatego** that's why; **dlatego, że...** because...; **tylko dlatego, że...** just because...; **dlatego, żeby...** (in order) to...

dł. *abbr.* l. (= *length*).

dławica *f. pat.* angina; **dławica piersiowa** angina pectoris.

dławić *ipf.* **1.** (= *dusić*) choke; **coś dławi go w gardle** he has a lump in his throat; **dławiły ją łzy** she was choking with tears. **2.** (= *tłumić*) (*śmiech, strach*) stifle; **dławić coś w sobie** stifle sth. **3.** (= *uciskać*) (*naród, opozycję*) suppress. **4.** *techn.* choke, throttle. **~ się** *ipf.* (= *dusić się*) choke (*czymś* on sth); (= *zatykać się*) be choked; **dławić się ze śmiechu** choke with laughter.

dławik *mi Gen.* **-a 1.** *el.* choke (coil). **2.** *mech.* (packing) gland, gland seal. – *ma orn.* drongo (*Dicrurus*).

dłoniasty *a. gł. bot.* palmate.

dłonica *f. techn.* mitten.

dłoń *f. pl.* -e *Ins.* -niami *l.* -ńmi **1.** *t. anat.* palm; **wróżyć** *l.* **czytać z dłoni** read sb's palm. **2.** (= ręka) hand; **klaskać w dłonie** clap one's hands; **uścisnąć sobie dłonie** shake hands; **uścisnąć komuś dłonie** shake hands with sb. **3.** (*w zwrotach*) **dłoń w dłoń** hand in hand; **dłonie go świerzbią** (*bo chce uderzyć*) he is itching to hit sb, he feels like hitting somebody; (*bo jest chciwy*) he has an itching palm; **wyciągać do kogoś dłoń** (= *zaoferować pomoc*) give *l.* lend sb a (helping) hand; (= *porozumieć się z kimś*) offer peace to sb; **jak na dłoni** clear as day *l.* daylight; **ona ma czyste dłonie** her hands are clean; **mieć serce na dłoni** wear one's heart on one's sleeve; **pomocna** *l.* **bratnia dłoń** helping hand; **podać komuś pomocną dłoń** give *l.* lend sb a (helping) hand; **prędzej mi włosy na dłoni wyrosną** *l.* **kaktus na dłoni wyrośnie** I'll see you in hell first; **ująć coś w swoje dłonie** take sth in one's hands.

dłubacz *mp pot. pog.* (= *osoba powolna*) slowpoke; *Br.* slowcoach.

dłubać *ipf.* -ę -esz **1.** (= *grzebać*) pick; **dłubać w nosie/zębach/uchu** pick one's nose/teeth/ear. **2.** (= *drążyć*) pick, scoop; **dłubać w czymś** hollow sth out; **dłubać w ziemi** pick *l.* dig holes in the ground. **3.** *pot. zwł. żart.* (= *majstrować*) tinker (*przy czymś* with sth); **(on) dłubie coś przy samochodzie** he's tinkering about with his car.

dłubanina *f.* drudgery, drag; **pisanie słownika to niezła dłubanina** writing a dictionary is a hell of a drudgery.

dłubanka *f.* (*łódź*) dugout.

dług *mi fin. l. przen.* debt; **dług honorowy** debt of honor; **mieć wobec kogoś dług wdzięczności** owe a debt of gratitude to sb, be indebted to sb; **obsługa długu** *l.* **długów** debt servicing; **spłacić dług** pay back a debt, make good a debt; **siedzieć w długach po uszy** be up to one's neck *l.* ears *l.* eyeballs in debt; **wpaść** *l.* **popaść w długi** run *l.* get into debt, run up a debt; **zaciągnąć dług wobec kogoś** run up a debt with sb.

długi *a.* -ższy **1.** long; **długi na trzy metry** three meters long; **spódnica długa do kostek** ankle-length skirt; **długie spodnie** long pants; *Br.* long trousers; **długie włosy** long hair; **długie życie** long life; **długa podróż** long journey; **fale długie** *radio* long wave; **długa piłka** *sport* long ball; **długie dłuższe** *sport* long-distance running; **długie ujęcie** *film* long shot; **samogłoski długie** *fon.* long vowels. **2.** (*w zwrotach*) **jak dzień długi** all day long; **upaść jak długi** measure one's length; **mieć długi język** have a big mouth; **mieć długie uszy** have big ears; **mieć długie ręce** (= *mieć wpływy*) have long arms; (= *kraść*) have sticky fingers; **przez dłuższy czas** for a prolonged period (of time); **od dłuższego czasu** for quite a while (now), for a long while; **na dłuższą metę** in the long run.

długo *adv.* long, for a long time; **długo żyć** live long; **jak długo?** how long?; **na długo** for a long time; **tak długo, jak...** (for) as *l.* so long as...; **i żyli długo i szczęśliwie** *lit.* and they lived happily ever after.

długodystansowiec *mp* -wc- *pl.* -y *Gen.pl.* -ów *sport* long-distance runner.

długodystansowy *a. sport, tel.* long-distance; **rozmowa długodystansowa** *tel.* long-distance call, toll call; **operator długodystansowy** *tel.* long-distance operator.

długofalowo *adv.* long-term, long-range, in the long run *l.* term.

długofalowy *a.* **1.** long-term, long-range. **2.** *fiz.* long-wave.

długogrający *a. przest., muz.* long-playing; **płyta długogrająca** long-playing record, long-play(er), LP.

długoletni *a.* (*przed rzeczownikiem*) longtime, long-lived, long-standing; (*po rzeczowniku*) of many years, of long standing; **długoletnia przyjaźń** longtime friendship, friendship of many years.

długometrażowy *a. film* (*o filmie*) feature, full-feature; (*o odcinku, programie*) feature-length; **film długometrażowy** feature (film).

długonogi *a.* long-legged, leggy.

długonosy *a.* long-nosed.

długookresowy *a.* long-term, long-range.

długopis *mi* pen, ballpoint (pen); **wypełniać coś długopisem** fill sth out in pen *l.* ink.

długosz *mi Gen.pl.* -y *l.* -ów *bot.* **długosz królewski** royal fern (*Osmunda regalis*).

długoszyi *a.* long-necked.

długościomierz *mi Gen.* -a *techn.* length meter, stadiometer; (= *odległościomierz*) distance meter.

długość *f.* **1.** (*w przestrzeni*) length; **to ma 10 metrów/stóp/centymetrów długości** it is 10 meters/feet/centimeters long; **mieć tę samą długość** be of equal *l.* the same length; **miara długości** length *l.* linear *l.* long measure, measure of length; **na długość** (= *wzdłuż*) lengthwise, lengthways; **być na długość czegoś** be of the same length as sth; **na całą długość (ulicy)** throughout (the street); **na całej długości (ulicy)** all along (the street); **tej samej długości** of equal *l.* the same length, equal in length; **zwyciężyć o długość/pół długości/kilka długości** *jeźdz.* win by a length/half a length/several lengths; **długość całkowita** overall *l.* total length; **długość astronomiczna** *l.* **ekliptyczna** *astron.* celestial *l.* ecliptic longitude; **długość geograficzna** *geogr.* longitude; **długość fali** *fiz., radio* wavelength; **długość nogawki** *handl.* inside leg, leg measurement. **2.** (*w czasie*) length, duration; **długość życia** *biol.* life span, span of life; **średnia** *l.* **oczekiwana długość życia** *med., stat.* life expectancy; **długość samogłoski** *jęz.* vowel length; *fon.* vowel duration; **znak długości** *druk.* macron, long mark.

długoterminowy *a. zwł. fin.* long-term; **prognoza długoterminowa** *meteor.* long-range forecast.

długotrwały *a.* long-lasting; (*o procesie*) lengthy; (*o konflikcie*) long-lived.

długouchy *a.* long-eared.

długowieczność *f.* longevity.

długowieczny *a.* (*o osobie*) long-living; *form.* longevous; (*nie o osobie*) long-lived.

długowłosy *a.* long-haired.

dłuto *n.* **1.** *techn.* (*płaskie*) chisel; (*zaokrąglone*) gouge. **2.** *górn.* bit. **3.** *sztuka* **rzeźba (spod) dłuta Michała Anioła** sculpture by Michelangelo.

dłutować *ipf.* **1.** *techn., chir.* (*dłutem prostym*) chisel; (*dłutem okrągłym*) gouge. **2.** *roln.* ridge.

dłutownica *f. techn.* chisel.

dłużej *adv. comp. of* **długo**; longer; **dłużej nie wytrzymam** I can't stand it any longer *l.* more; **tak dłużej być nie może** it cannot go on.

dłużnik *mp*, **dłużniczka** *f. fin.* debtor; **być czyimś dłużnikiem** *dosł. i przen.* be in sb's debt, be indebted to sb.

dłużny *a.* **1.** *fin. pred.* **być komuś coś dłużnym** owe sb sth, owe sth to sb, be indebted to sb; **jesteś mi dłużna tysiąc dolarów** you owe me a thousand dollars. **2.** *fin.* **skrypt dłużny** debenture, promissory note; *pot.* IOU (*I owe you*); **rewers dłużny** bill of debt. **3. nie pozostawać komuś dłużnym** (= *zemścić się*) pay sb back (in kind).

dłuższy *a. comp. of* **długi**; longer (*od czegoś* than sth); **twój widelec jest dłuższy od mojego** your fork is longer than mine; **od dłuższego czasu** for a long time (now).

dłużyca *f.* **1.** *leśn., stol.* (= *pień*) bole, (saw) log; (= *pnie*) (long) lumber; *Br.* (long) timber. **2.** (= *długi ładunek*) long load.

dłużyć się *ipf.* (*o podróży*) drag out; (*o czasie*) drag by; **czas się komuś dłuży** time hangs *l.* lies heavy on sb's hands.

dłużyzna *f.* (*w powieści, filmie*) longueur, tedium; **pod koniec filmu są dłużyzny** the movie gets tedious towards the end.

dm *abbr.* dm (= *decimeter*).

dmę *itd. ipf. zob.* **dąć**.

dmuch *mi* **1.** blow. **2.** *metal.* blast.

dmuchacz *mp* blower; **dmuchacz szkła** glassblower.

dmuchać *ipf.* **1.** (*o osobie, wietrze*) blow; **dmuchać dymem** blow smoke; **dmuchać w trąbkę** blow (on) a trumpet. **2.** *wulg., sl.* (= *odbywać stosunek*) screw, bang. **3.** (*w zwrotach*) **dmuchać na zimne** play it safe, be extra careful; **ona nie da *l.* nie pozwoli sobie w kaszę dmuchać** she knows how to stick up for herself; **nie w kij dmuchał** *pot.* no joke, nothing to sniff at; **lepiej dmuchać niż chuchać** better safe than sorry; **kto się na gorącym sparzy, ten na zimne dmucha** once bitten, twice shy.

dmuchawa *f. techn.* blower (fan), fan.

dmuchawiec *mi* **-wc-** *Gen.* **-a** *bot.* **1.** (= *mniszek*) dandelion, blowball, puffball (*Taraxacum (officinale)*). **2.** (= *brodawnik*) hawkbit (*Leontodon*).

dmuchawka *f.* **1.** (= *rura do strzał*) blowgun; *Br.* blowpipe. **2.** *chem.* blowpipe, blow tube. **3.** *techn.* blower.

dmuchnąć *pf.* **-ij** *pf. of* **dmuchać**.

dn. *abbr. gł. form.* d. (= *dnia*); (**w**) **dn.** on; **z dn.** of; **Waszyngton, dn. 20.02.2006** Washington, Feb 20, 2006; **list wysłano dn. 5 maja** the letter was mailed on May 5; **w odpowiedzi na Pańskie/Pani/**

Państwa pismo z dn. 4 września in reply to your letter of September 4.

DNA *abbr. biochem.* DNA; **łańcuch DNA** DNA strand; **badanie DNA** (*dla celów identyfikacji*) genetic fingerprinting.

dna *f. pat.* gout.

dnia *itd. mi zob.* **dzień**.

dnieć *ipf.* **dnieje dniało** *nieos.* dawn; **dnieje/ dniało** dawn is/was breaking, day is/was dawning.

dniówka *f.* **1.** (= *dzień pracy*) workday. **2.** (*wynagrodzenie*) daily wage; **pracować za dniówkę** be paid by the day.

dno *n. Gen.pl.* **den 1.** (*naczynia, morza, doliny*) bottom; (*morza, rzeki, jaskini, doliny*) floor; (*jeziora, rzeki, morza, doliny*) bed; **na dnie morza** at the bottom of the sea; **podwójne dno** double bottom; (*ukryte dno*) false bottom; **iść na dno** *żegl.* sink (to the bottom), go down *l.* under; **wypić coś do dna** drink sth up, drink *l.* drain sth to the dregs *l.* lees. **2.** *anat.* fundus; **dno oka** (ocular) fundus, background of the eye. **3.** *pot. przen.* (= *beznadzieja*) **(kompletne *l.* totalne *l.* zupełne) dno** *pot.* the pits. **4. dno kwiatowe** *bot.* flower cup *l.* bottom. **5.** (*w zwrotach*) **bez dna** bottomless; **do dna!** bottoms up!; **stoczyć się na (samo) dno** reach rock-bottom *l.* the bottom; **na (samym) dnie** (*społeczeństwa*) down (and out); **odbić się od dna** bounce back; **worek bez dna** (*o osobie*) maw; **być na dnie rozpaczy** plumb the depths of despair.

do¹ *prep.* + *Gen.* **1.** (*dla wyrażenia kierunku ruchu*) to; **iść *l.* jechać do szkoły/pracy** go to school/work; **jechać do Warszawy/Londynu** go to Warsaw/London; **iść do dentysty/lekarza** (go) see a dentist/doctor; **chodź do mnie** come to me. **2.** (*dla wyrażenia górnej granicy*) (up) to; **od dwóch do pięciu** from two to five; **od dziewiątej do siedemnastej** (*zwł. o godzinach pracy*) (from) nine to five; **grzywna do 100 dolarów** a fine of up to 100 dollars. **3.** (*dla wyrażenia przeznaczenia*) for; **patelnia (nadająca się) do smażenia na gazie** pan (good) for gas range frying; **do czego to jest?** what is this *l.* it for?; **list/telefon do ciebie** letter/ phone for you. **4.** (*dla wyrażenia przeznaczenia; tłumaczone przez użycie rzeczownika l. imiesłowu jako przydawki*) **deska do krojenia** cutting *l.* chopping board; **deska do prasowania** ironing board; **boisko do koszykówki** basketball court; **nóż do chleba** bread knife; **pilnik do paznokci** nail file. **5.** (*dla wyrażenia przeznaczenia; tłumaczone złożeniem*) **maszyna do pisania** typewriter; **łyżeczka do herbaty** teaspoon; **opiekunka do dziecka** babysitter. **6.** (*przed rzeczownikiem odczasownikowym; tłumaczone zdaniem bezokolicznikowym*) **coś do jedzenia/picia/zrobienia** *l.* **roboty** something to eat/drink/do; **listy do wysłania** letters to be mailed; **sprawy do załatwienia** things *l.* matters to take care of, errands. **7.** (*dla wyrażenia umieszczenia czegoś w czymś*) in, into; **wrzucić list do skrzynki** put the letter in *l.* into the mailbox; **wrzucić głos do urny** put the ballot *l.* vote in *l.* into the ballot box; **wejść do rzeki** go *l.* walk into the river. **8.** (*dla wyrażenia* *limitu czasu*) until, till; by; **do tej pory** until now; **musisz to zrobić do wtorku** you must do it by Tuesday; **robić coś do upadłego** do sth until one drops; **spacerować do rana** walk until morning; **zostać do wtorku** stay until Tuesday. **9.** (*dla wyrażenia ukierunkowania uczuć*) for; **miłość do ojczyzny/matki/małżonka** love for *l.* of one's country/mother/spouse; **niechęć do zabaw** dislike for play; **tęsknić do czegoś** crave for sth; **tęsknić do kogoś** miss sb. **10.** (*dla wyrażenia przynależności*) **zaciągnąć się do wojska** join the military *l.* army, enlist, enroll; **wstąpić do związku/partii** join a union/party. **11.** (*w zwrotach*) **do jutra** see you tomorrow; **do zobaczenia** *l.* **widzenia** good bye, see you; **do diabła** *l.* **(jasnej) cholery!** *pot.* damn (it)!; **do diabła z nim/tym!** *pot.* to hell with him/that!; **co do cholery?!** *pot.* what the devil *l.* hell?!; **co do mnie** for my part, as far as I am concerned; **co tobie do tego?** that's none of your business!; **być** *l.* **nie nadawać się do niczego** be no good, be (of) no use, be useless; **raz do roku** once a year.

do² *int. i n.* indecl. *muz.* (= *dźwięk C*) doh.

doba *f. Gen.pl.* **dób** **1.** (= *24 godziny*) 24 hours, twenty-four hours; *pot.* day; **cztery razy na dobę** (*brać lekarstwo, jeść*) four times a day; **dwadzieścia cztery godziny na dobę** 24 hours a day; **dwadzieścia cztery godziny na dobę, siedem dni w tygodniu** 24 hours a day, seven days a week; 24/7; **przez trzy doby** (for) three days; **przez całą dobę** round *l.* around the clock, 24 hours a day; **otwarty całą dobę** open round the clock. **2.** (= *okres, epoka*) days, age; **w dobie Internetu/podróży kosmicznych** in the days of the Internet/space travel.

doberman *ma* *kynol.* Doberman pinscher, Doberman.

dobić *pf.* **-ję -jesz** *zob.* **dobijać.** ~ **się** *pf. zob.* **dobijać się.**

dobiec *pf.* **-gnę -gniesz -gnij -gł** *zob.* **dobiegać.**

dobieg *mi* **1.** *sport* finish. **2.** *lotn.* landing run.

dobiegać *ipf.* **1.** (= *biegnąc doganiać*) catch up (*do kogoś / czegoś* with sb/sth); reach (*do kogoś / czegoś* sb/sth). **2.** (= *prowadzić*) (*o drodze*) run, lead. **3.** (= *docierać*) (*o dźwięku*) come; **zza ściany dobiegał głośny płacz** loud crying was coming from the neighboring room. **4. dobiegać końca** come *l.* draw to an end, run its course; **dobiega pierwsza** it's almost one.

dobiegnąć *pf.* **-ij, -gł** *zob.* **dobiegać.**

dobierać *ipf.* **1.** (= *dopasować*) pick, select; match; **dobierać coś do czegoś** match sth (up) with *l.* to sth; **dobrać buty do sukienki** pick shoes to go with a dress; **dobrać coś do koloru czegoś** pick sth to match the color of sth. **2.** (= *brać jeszcze*) have *l.* take *l.* get more; **dobrać sobie zupy** have *l.* get (some) more soup. ~ **się** *ipf.* **1.** *pot.* (= *dorwać się*) get one's hands (*do czegoś / kogoś* on sth/sb); **dobrać się komuś do skóry** (= *zbić kogoś*) give sb a hiding; (= *ukarać kogoś za niecne postępki*) get one's comeuppance. **2.** *pot.* (= *przystawiać się*) hit (*do kogoś* on sb); make a pass (*do*

kogoś at sb). **3.** (= *dopasować się*) **dobierać się w pary** *l.* **parę (z kimś)** pair up (with sb); **dobrać się jak dwie krople wody** *l.* **jak w korcu maku** be two of a kind.

dobijać *ipf.* **1.** (*zabić*) finish off; **dobić kogoś** put sb out of his *l.* her *l.* their misery. **2.** *pot.* (= *doprowadzać do szału*) **dobijać kogoś** get sb's goat; **oni mnie dobijają** they really get my goat. **3.** (= *załamać*) kill, devastate. **4.** (*gwóźdź*) hit *l.* strike home. **5.** (= *docierać*) reach; **dobić do celu** reach one's destination. **6.** *sport* finish; **dobić piłkę** score a follow-up shot; (*nogą*) kick the ball home. **7.** *żegl.* reach; **przybić do portu/brzegu** reach port/the shore. **8.** *druk.* (= *dodrukować*) print (*additional copies*). **9. dobić targu (z kimś)** close *l.* strike a deal *l.* bargain (with sb). ~ **się** *ipf.* **1.** (= *stukać*) bang; **dobijać się do drzwi** bang on the door. **2.** (= *walczyć*) fight; **dobijać się o kogoś/coś** fight for sb/sth.

dobitka *f. Gen.pl.* **-ek** **1.** *sport* follow-up shot, follow-up. **2. na dobitkę** if that isn't enough, to crown it all; **stracił oko, i to na dobitkę prawe** he lost his eye, and the right eye at that.

dobitnie *adv.* (= *mocno*) forcefully, forcibly; (= *wyraźnie*) pointedly, explicitly.

dobitny *a.* (= *mocny*) forceful, forcible; (= *wyraźny*) pointed, explicit.

doborowy *a.* **1.** (= *starannie wybrany*) handpicked, specially chosen. **2.** (= *mistrzowski*) expert; **doborowe towarzystwo** select company; **doborowy strzelec** crack shot.

dobosz *mp Gen.pl.* **-ów** *l.* **-y** *muz.* drummer; **(starszy) dobosz** (*w maszerującej orkiestrze*) drum major.

dobowy *a.* (= *odbywający się co dobę*) daily; *form.* circadian, diurnal; **rytm dobowy** circadian *l.* diurnal cycle; **zalecana dawka dobowa** (*antybiotyków, witamin*) recommended daily dose.

dobór *mi* **-o-** selection; **dobór naturalny** *biol.* natural selection; **dobór kolorów** (*na obrazie, w mieszkaniu*) color scheme.

dobra¹ *a. f.* of **dobry.**

dobra² *int. pot.* OK, righty, righto; *Br.* okey-dokey.

dobra³ *n. pl.* **1.** *pl.* of **dobro. 2.** *ekon.* goods; **dobra konsumpcyjne** consumer goods. **3.** (= *majątek*) property; possessions; **dobra królewskie** *hist.* demesne; **dobra doczesne** *rel.* earthly possessions; **dobra materialne** material possessions *l.* comforts.

dobrać *pf.* **-biorę -bierzesz** *zob.* **dobierać.** ~ **się** *pf. zob.* **dobierać się.**

dobranoc *int. i n.* good night; (*int. pot.*) night-night; **pocałunek na dobranoc** goodnight kiss; **pocałować kogoś na dobranoc** kiss sb goodnight; **bajka na dobranoc** bed-time story; **gdzie diabeł mówi dobranoc** *przen.* in the middle of nowhere.

dobranocka *f. Gen.pl.* **-ek** *dziec., telew.* goodnight *l.* bedtime cartoon.

dobrany *a.* **1.** (= *dobrze wybrany*) well-chosen. **2.** (= *starannie wybrany*) hand-picked, select, choice; **dobrane towarzystwo** select company; **dobrana para** happy couple; *iron.* nice couple. **3.**

(= *dopasowany*) well matched; **dobrany kolorystycznie** color-coordinated.

dobrnąć *pf.* -**ij** **1.** (= *dotrzeć*) (finally) (manage to) reach. **2.** (= *dotrwać*) stick it out; **było ciężko, ale jakoś dobrnąłem do końca** it was hard, but somehow I managed to stick it out.

dobro *n. Loc.* -**u** *l.* -**rze 1.** (= *pożytek, szczęście*) good, welfare, well-being; **dobro i zło** good and evil *l.* bad; **dla czyjegoś (własnego) dobra** for sb's own good; **dla wspólnego dobra** for the common good; **mieć na uwadze czyjeś dobro** have sb's wellfare *l.* well-being at heart, have sb's (best) interests at heart; **dobro dziecka** child welfare; **dobro społeczne** *l.* **publiczne** public welfare. **2.** *fil., psych.* right; **odróżniać dobro od zła** know right from wrong. **3.** (= *dobroć*) goodness. **4.** *pl.* **dobra** *zob.* **dobra³.**

dobrobyt *mi* prosperity, (economic) well-being; **żyć w dobrobycie** prosper.

dobroczynność *f.* charity.

dobroczynny *a.* **1.** (= *zbawienny, pożyteczny*) beneficial. **2.** (= *leczniczy*) healing, wholesome, salubrious. **3.** (= *charytatywny*) charitable, charity; **towarzystwo dobroczynne** charity; **cele dobroczynne** charity, charities; **impreza dobroczynna** (*np. koncert, bal*) fundraiser, benefit; **marsz/bieg dobroczynny** sponsored walk/run.

dobroczyńca *mp Gen.pl.* -**ów** benefactor.

dobroć *f.* kindness, goodness; **po dobroci** *przest.* peacefully; **z dobroci serca** out of the goodness of one's heart.

dobrodusznie *adv.* kindly, good-naturedly, kind-heartedly.

dobroduszność *f.* good nature, kindness, kind-heartedness.

dobroduszny *a.* good-natured, kind-hearted, kind.

dobrodziej *mp Gen.pl.* -**ów** *l.* -**ei 1.** *gł. Voc. przest. l. żart.* (*przy zwracaniu się*) **panie dobrodzieju** my good man. **2.** *arch.* (= *dobroczyńca*) benefactor.

dobrodziejka *f.* **1.** *gł. Voc. przest. l. żart.* (*przy zwracaniu się*) **pani dobrodziejko** my dear lady; **witam panią dobrodziejkę** good morrow, my dear lady. **2.** *arch.* (= *filantropka*) benefactress, lady bountiful.

dobrodziejstwo *n.* **1.** (= *pożytek, korzyść*) benefit; **korzystać z dobrodziejstw nauki/medycyny** use the benefits of science/medicine, benefit from science/medicine. **2.** *przest.* (= *uczynność*) kindness; (= *dobry uczynek*) good deed, act of kindness. **3. dobrodziejstwo inwentarza** *prawn.* benefit of inventory; **z dobrodziejstwem inwentarza** *przest., przen.* lock, stock, and barrel.

dobrosąsiedzki *a.* neighborly, friendly; **stosunki dobrosąsiedzkie** *polit.* friendly relations.

dobrotliwie *adv. gł. przest.* kind-heartedly, good-naturedly, kindly.

dobrotliwy *a. gł. przest.* kind-hearted, good-natured, kind.

dobrowolnie *adv.* voluntarily, of one's own free will.

dobrowolność *f.* voluntary character, voluntariness; **na zasadzie** *l.* **zasadach dobrowolności**

(*o płatnościach, członkostwie*) voluntary; **zrobić coś na zasadzie dobrowolności** do sth voluntarily, volunteer to do sth.

dobrowolny *a.* (*o płatnościach, działaniach*) voluntary; (*o płatnościach*) freewill; (*o pracy*) volunteer; *zwł. prawn.* discretionary; **dobrowolny datek** voluntary donation.

dobry *a.* **lepszy 1.** (= *wysokiej jakości, prawidłowy, pozytywny, sprawny, smaczny, skuteczny, korzystny*) good; (= *uprzejmy*) good, kind (*dla kogoś* to sb). **2. dobra godzina** a good hour, the better part of an hour, at least an hour; **nie było go dobrą godzinę** he was out for at least an hour. **3.** (*w zwrotach grzecznościowych*) **bądź tak dobry i...** be so good *l.* kind and..., be a dear and...; **dzień dobry!** good morning!; **dobry wieczór!** good evening!; (*życzę ci*) **wszystkiego dobrego** *l.* **najlepszego** (I wish you) all the best. **4.** (*w innych zwrotach*) **brać** *l.* **przyjmować coś za dobrą monetę** take sth at face value; **być dobrej myśli** hope for the best; **(być) na dobrej drodze (do czegoś)** (be) on the royal road (to sth); **być pod dobrą opieką** be in good hands, be well taken care of; **być z kimś w dobrej komitywie** be well in with sb; **(być) w dobrych rękach** (be) in safe hands; **dać komuś dobrą nauczkę** teach sb a lesson; **dobra opinia** good opinion, reputability; **dobra partia** (*do małżeństwa*) good catch; **dobra robota** fine job; **dobra strona** good point, strength, advantage (*czegoś* of sth); **dobra wola** goodwill; **dobra wróżba** good *l.* happy omen, good sign; **dobra wróżka** fairy godmother; **dobre imię** good name, reputability, respectability; **dobre maniery** *l.* **obyczaje** good *l.* proper manners, social graces; **dobry humor** *l.* **nastrój** good humor, good *l.* high spirits; **dobry interes** good deal; **dobry obyczaj** good custom; **dobry omen** good *l.* happy omen; **dobry znak** good sign; **Dobry Pasterz** *rel.* the Good Shepherd; **dobrymi chęciami piekło wybrukowane** the road to hell is paved with good intentions; **dostać dobrą nauczkę** learn a lesson; **dostać się w dobre ręce** end up in good hands; **gest dobrej woli** goodwill gesture; **mieć dobrą prasę** have a good press; **mieć/utrzymywać dobrą kondycję** be/keep *l.* stay fit, be/keep *l.* stay in good shape; **mieć dobre oko (do czegoś)** have a good eye (for sth); **mieć dobre oczy** have good *l.* strong eyes; **mieć dobrego nosa (do czegoś)** have a good nose (for sth); **na dobrą sprawę** come to think of it, in fact; **na dobre** for good; **na dobre i na złe** for better or (for) worse; **na frasunek dobry trunek** *przest.* today's wine I drink today, tomorrow's sorrow I bear tomorrow; he that loves wine wants no woes; **nic dobrego (z tego nie wyjdzie** *l.* **będzie)** nothing good (will come out of this); **przedstawiać kogoś/coś w dobrym świetle** show sb/sth in a good *l.* favorable light; **stare dobre czasy** good old days; **urodzić się pod dobrą gwiazdą** be born under a lucky star; **w dobrej wierze** in good faith; **wykazać się dobrą wolą** show goodwill; **zrobić dobre wrażenie** make a good impression. – *mi szkoln.* (*ocena*) B; **dobry plus** *l.* **z plusem** B plus, B+; **bardzo dobry** A.

dobrze *int.* all right!, fine!, OK! – *adv.* **lepiej 1.**

(= *prawidłowo, dokładnie, pozytywnie, umiejętnie, ładnie, zdrowo, życzliwie*) well; **dobrze ci tak
mówić** that's easy for you to say; **dobrze coś
sprzedać** sell sth at a profit; **dobrze komuś z
oczu patrzy** sb looks honest, sb looks like a good
l. an honest person; **dobrze komuś życzyć** wish
sb well; **dobrze mu/ci tak!** (it) serves him/you
right!; **dobrze odżywiony** *t. euf.* well-fed; **dobrze
płatny** well-paid; **dobrze   poinformowany**
well-informed; **dobrze się bawić** have fun, have
a good time; **dobrze się na czymś znać** know sth
well, know sth inside out, be knowledgeable
about sth; **dobrze się uczyć** be a good student;
dobrze ubrany well-dressed; **dobrze wychowany**
well-mannered, well-behaved, well-brought-up;
dobrze wyglądać look good; **dobrze znany** well-
known; **dobrze, że...** it's a good thing (that)...,
fortunately,...; **coś komuś dobrze robi** sth does
sb good; **jak** *l.* **jeśli wszystko dobrze pójdzie** if all
l. everything goes well; **komuś dobrze poszło (w
czymś)** sb did well (at *l.* in sth); **komuś się dobrze powodzi** sb is well off, sb is doing well; **komuś w czymś dobrze** (*w stroju*) sth suits sb
(well), sth looks good on sb; **ktoś ma się dobrze**
sb is (doing) well; **wszystko dobre co się dobrze
kończy** all's well that ends well; **znać się dobrze**
know each other well. **2.** (= *znacznie*) well; **dobrze po północy** well after midnight; **dobrze
ponad normę** well above normal.
    dobrzeć *ipf.* **-ję -jesz, -yj** *przest.* recover, get
better.
    dobudowa *f. bud.* **1.** (= *dobudowywanie*) ex-
tension work (*czegoś* on sth); extending (*czegoś*
sth). **2.** *Gen.pl.* **-ów** (*budowla*) extension.
    dobudować *pf.*, **dobudowywać** *ipf.* **1.** *bud.*
(*pokój, garaż, skrzydło*) add (*coś* sth (on)) build
(*coś* sth on); annex (*coś* sth). **2.** *przen. zwł. uj.* (=
dorobić) make up; **dobudować ideologię do faktów** make up an ideology to suit the facts.
    dobudówka *f. bud.* extension; annex; *Br.* an-
nexe.
    dobudzić *pf.* wake up; **nie mogliśmy jej dobu-
dzić** we couldn't wake her up, we couldn't get
her to wake up.
    dobudzić się *pf.* wake up (*completely*).
    dobyć *pf.* **-będę -będziesz, -bądź** *zob.* **doby-
wać.**
    dobytek *mi* **-tk-** **1.** *gł. form.* (= *majątek*) be-
longings. **2.** *roln.* (= *inwentarz, bydło*) livestock,
stock.
    dobywać *ipf.* **-am -asz** **1.** (= *wyjmować*) (*np.
portfel*) produce, get out; **dobyć broni/miecza**
draw a gun/sword; **dobyć głosu** speak; **nie móc
dobyć głosu** be (left) speechless; **dobyć resztek
sił** make an all-out effort. **2.** *przest. górn.* (= *wydobywać*) mine (*coś* (for) sth).
    doc. *abbr. uniw.* asst. prof.
    docelowo *adv. form.* in prospect; as a target;
**firma ma docelowo stworzyć sto nowych miejsc
pracy** the business is expected to create a hundred new jobs.
    docelowy *a. gł. form.* **1.** (= *przewidywany,
planowany*) target; **docelowy dochód/poziom zatrudnienia** target profit/employment level. **2.** (=

będący celem) target, final; **stacja docelowa** (target *l.* final) destination.
    doceniać *ipf.*, **docenić** *pf.* appreciate, value;
nie doceniać kogoś/czegoś underestimate sb/
sth, underrate sb/sth.
    docent *mp uniw.* assistant professor; *Br.*
reader.
    dochodowość *f. ekon.* profitability.
    dochodowy *a.* **1.** *ekon.* (= *opłacalny*) prof-
itable, profit-making. **2.** *fin.* (= *dotyczący dochodów*) income; **podatek dochodowy (od osób
fizycznych/prawnych)** (personal/corporate) income tax.
    dochody *pl. Gen.* **-ów** *pl. of* **dochód**; (*osoby*) in-
come, earnings; (*państwa, spółki*) revenue.
    dochodzący *a.* **1.** visiting; **nauczyciel docho-
dzący** *szkoln.* visiting teacher. **2.** (= *niezamie-
szkały na miejscu*) nonresident; **pacjent dochodzący** *med.* nonresident patient.
    dochodzenie *n.* **1.** (= *śledztwo*) investigation,
inquiry; **wszcząć/prowadzić dochodzenie** launch/
conduct an investigation *l.* inquiry. **2.** (= *dążenie*) (*do gospodarki rynkowej, demokracji*) move
(*do czegoś* towards sth); (*do władzy, pokoju*)
drive (*do czegoś* for sth); (*do szczęścia, zamożno-
ści*) pursuit (*do czegoś* of sth); **dochodzenie do
zdrowia** recovery. **3.** (= *domaganie się*) seeking
(*czegoś* sth); search (*czegoś* for sth); pursuit (*czegoś* of sth); **dochodzenie prawdy** the search for
truth; **dochodzenie krzywd** seeking compensation. **4.** **wyścig** *l.* **wyścigi na dochodzenie** *sport
gł.* kolarstwo pursuit.
    dochodzeniowy *a.* investigative; **oficer docho-
dzeniowy** investigating officer.
    dochodzeniówka *f.* **-ek** detective bureau; in-
vestigative division (*of a police department*).
    dochodzić *ipf.* **1.** (= *docierać*) arrive; **docho-
dzić do kogoś/gdzieś** reach sb/sth; **paczka jeszcze nie doszła** the parcel hasn't arrived yet; **czy
doszedł do ciebie mój list?** did you get my letter?; **dojść do adresata** (*o przesyłce*) reach its
destination *l.* recipient; **pociąg tam nie dochodzi**
pot. trains don't go there. **2.** (= *osiągać*) reach;
dochodzić do pięćdziesiątki be approaching
fifty; **dochodzi północ/ósma** it's almost mid-
night/eight, it's getting on for midnight/eight,
it's coming up on midnight/eight. **3.** (= *uzyskiwać*) **dochodzić do zdrowia** be getting better,
turn the corner; **dojść do głosu** take one's turn
(to speak); **dochodzić do porozumienia** come to
an agreement, reach agreement; (**nie mogłem)
dojść z nim do ładu** (I couldn't) connect with him;
dochodzić do siebie (= *odzyskiwać pełnię sił,
równowagę*) pull *l.* get o.s. together, get over it;
(= *odzyskiwać przytomność*) come round *l.* to,
snap out of it; **dochodzić do siebie po czymś** get
over sth; **dojść do skutku** (= *odbyć się*) take
place, go ahead; (= *zakończyć się sukcesem*)
work out; **nie dojść do skutku** fall through. **4.**
nieos. **doszło do czegoś** (*zdarzenia*) there was
sth, sth happened; **doszło do wypadku** there was
an accident, an accident happened; **doszło do rękoczynów** it came to blows; **jak do tego doszło?**
how did this *l.* it happen? **5.** (= *przybywać do*

kompletu) be added; **pamiętaj, że dojdą jeszcze dodatkowe zajęcia** don't forget new classes will be added; **dojdzie nam dodatkowa godzina** we'll have an extra hour. **6.** (= *dociekać*) seek; pursue; search for; **dochodzić prawdy** search for the truth, seek the truth; **dochodzić krzywdy** seek compensation. **7.** (= *walczyć o*) fight for; **dochodzić swoich praw** fight for one's rights; **dojść do władzy** rise to power; **dochodzić czegoś na drodze sądowej** fight for sth in court. **8.** (= *rozumować*) **dochodzić do przekonania/wniosku** reach a conviction/conclusion; **dochodzić do sedna sprawy** get to the heart of the matter; **dojść po nitce do kłębka** *przen.* follow the thread to the end. **9.** (*o roślinach, owocach*) (= *dojrzewać*) mature, ripen. **10.** (*o potrawach*) (= *dogotowywać się*) be almost done; (= *dogotować się*) be done. **11.** *pot.* (= *przylegać*) fit tight; **okna nie dochodzą** windows won't close properly, windows are not tight. **12.** *myśl.* (*zwierzynę*) approach.

dochować *pf.*, **dochowywać** *ipf. form.* keep, be true to (*sth*); **dochować tajemnicy/przysięgi** keep a secret/an oath; **dochować wiary** be true to one's faith; **dochować zobowiązań** fulfill one's obligations. **~ się** *pf.*, **dochowywać się** *ipf. form.* (*dzieci*) be a happy father/mother of; (*pociech, plonów*) take pride in; (*plonów*) enjoy.

dochód *mi* **-o-** *ekon.* income; (*zwł. podmiotu gospodarczego*) revenue; **dochód po opodatkowaniu** disposable income; **dochód narodowy** national income; **dochód netto/brutto** net/gross income; **dochód podlegający opodatkowaniu** taxable income; **dochód wolny/zwolniony od podatku** *l.* opodatkowania tax-free/tax-exempt income; **dochód z pracy (zarobkowej)/handlu/usług** income *l.* revenue from (paid) employment/trade/services; **dochód stały** fixed income; **przynosić dochód** bring income, bring in revenue; **stały dochód** permanent *l.* steady *l.* regular income; **źródło dochodu** *l.* **dochodów** source of income; *zob. t.* **dochody.**

dochrapać się *pf.* **-pię -piesz, dochrapać się czegoś** (*np. stanowiska*) *pot.* wangle *l.* jockey *l.* maneuver one's way to sth.

dociąć *pf.* **-tnę -tniesz, -tnij** *zob.* **docinać.**

dociągać *ipf.*, **dociągnąć** *pf.* **-ij 1.** (= *zacieśnić*) (*sznurowadło, nakrętkę*) tighten. **2. dociągnąć coś do końca** (*sprawę*) carry *l.* follow *l.* see sth through. **3.** *pot.* (= *dotrwać*) hold put, last out; **dociągnąć do pierwszego** hold *l.* last out until the end of the month. **4.** (= *doholować*) (*wóz*) pull all the way (*gdzieś* to sth); **dociągnął wóz do samej stodoły** he pulled the cart all the way to the barn.

dociec *pf.* **-knę -kniesz -kł, -knij** (*prawdy, przyczyny*) find.

dociekać *ipf.* (*prawdy, przyczyny*) seek out, search for; (*przyczyn*) investigate.

dociekliwość *f.* curiosity, hunger for knowledge.

dociekliwy *a.* curious, inquiring, inquisitive.

docieplać *ipf.*, **docieplić** *pf. bud.* (*budynek, ściany, okna*) weatherize, winterize, insulate.

docieplanie, docieplenie *n. bud.* (*budynku*) weatherization, winterization, insulation.

docierać *ipf.* **1.** (= *dochodzić*) arrive; **docierać gdzieś** *l.* **do czegoś** reach sth; **dotrzeć na miejsce** arrive at *l.* reach one's destination; **dotarliśmy już na miejsce?** are we there yet? **2. docierać do kogoś** (*o osobie, wiadomości, świadomości czegoś*) get through to sb; (*o świadomości czegoś*) dawn on sb; (*o uwadze*) sink in; **uwaga do niego nie dotarła** the comment was lost on him. **3.** *mot.* (*silnik, samochód*) run in. **~ się** *ipf.* **1.** *mot.* (*o silniku, samochodzie*) be run in. **2.** *pot.* (= *dostosowywać się*) (*o ludziach w grupie*) get used to one another; (*o osobie w nowej sytuacji*) get into one's stride.

docinać *ipf.* **1.** (= *przecinać do końca*) cut all the way, cut through. **2.** (= *nacinać na zapas*) cut (some more *l.* extra) (*sth*). **3.** (= *przycinać na długość*) cut to fit. **4.** (= *dogadywać*) (*złośliwie*) gibe *l.* jibe (*komuś* at sb); (*żartobliwie*) kid (*komuś* sb); (*szyderczo, z pogardą*) taunt (*komuś* sb).

docinek *mi* **-nk-** *Gen.* **-a** gube, barb, taunt; (*niewinny*) rib.

docisk *mi* **1.** *mech.* (= *siła dociskająca*) pressure. **2.** *techn.* (= *zacisk*) clamp; (= *obciążnik*) weight.

dociskacz *mi Gen.* **-a** *techn.* (= *zacisk*) clamp; (= *obciążnik*) weight.

dociskać *ipf.*, **docisnąć** *pf.* **-ij 1.** (= *przyciskać*) press on. **2.** (*śrubę*) (= *dokręcać*) tighten. **3.** (= *zaciskać*) clamp. **4.** (= *domykać*) **docisnąć drzwi/okno/pokrywkę** close the door/window/lid firmly.

docucić *pf.* bring round.

doczekać *pf.* (= *dotrwać*) wait (*czegoś* until *l.* till sth); (= *dożyć*) (*momentu*) live (*czegoś* until *l.* till sth); (*wydarzenia*) live to see; (= *nie spać*) stay up (*czegoś* until *l.* till sth); **doczekać późnego wieku** live to an old age; **nie doczekał wiosny** he didn't live to see the spring, he died before spring came. **~ się** *pf.* wait (*czegoś* until *l.* till sth); **nie doczekać się czegoś** (*listu, wdzięczności*) never get *l.* receive sth; **doczekać się wnuków** live to have grandchildren, become a grandparent; **nie doczekała się wdzięczności/podziękowania (od kogoś)** she never received any gratitude/thanks (from sb); **nie móc się czegoś doczekać** can't wait for sth *l.* to do sth; **nie móc się kogoś doczekać** can't wait to see sb; **nie doczekał się pociechy z dzieci** his children are not much comfort to him.

doczepa *f. kol.* commuter railcar.

doczepiać *ipf.*, **doczepić** *pf.* attach (*coś do czegoś* sth to sth); (= *połączyć*) couple (*coś do czegoś* sth to *l.* with sth); (*wagony*) couple (on). **~ się** *ipf.*, **doczepić się** *pf.* **1.** *pot.* (= *przyłączać się natrętnie*) tag along (*do kogoś* with sb). **2. doczepić się do kogoś** *pot.* (= *prześladować*) get at sb, get on sb's back *l.* case, jump on *l.* over sb.

doczesność *f. form., rel.* (= *ziemskość, materialność*) worldliness, earthliness; (= *nietrwałość*) temporality.

doczesny *a. gł. form., rel.* (= *ziemski, mate-*

rialny, nie duchowy) worldly, earthly, mundane; (= *przemijający*) temporal; **dobra doczesne** earthly possessions; **życie doczesne** worldly life.

doczłapać *pf.* **-pię -piesz** waddle up (*do kogoś / czegoś* to sb/sth).

doczołgać się *pf.* crawl up (*do kogoś / czegoś* to sb/sth).

doczyścić *pf.* get cleaned, clean up; **nie mogliśmy tego doczyścić** we couldn't get it cleaned.

doczytać *pf.* (= *dokończyć czytanie*) finish reading, read sth through; (*do pewnego miejsca*) read up to (*a certain place*). ~ **się** *pf.* learn, gather (*sth from one's reading*).

dod. *abbr.* **1.** ex. (= *extra*); add. (= *additional*). **2.** add. (= *additionally*); in add. (= *in addition*).

dodać *pf. zob.* **dodawać.** − *v. indecl. mat.* (= *plus*) and, plus; **dwa dodać dwa równa się cztery** two and *l.* plus two is *l.* makes four.

dodatek *mi* **-tk- 1.** (*coś dodatkowego*) addition; supplement. **2.** (*do wynagrodzenia*) allowance, bonus, premium; **dodatek mieszkaniowy** housing allowance; **dodatek rodzinny** family allowance; **dodatek funkcyjny** executive rewards *l.* bonus; **dodatek zmianowy** shift differential. **3.** *dzienn.* supplement; **dodatek ilustrowany** *l.* **kolorowy dodatek** color supplement; **dodatek nadzwyczajny** special section. **4.** *mot. zwł. pl.* (optional) extra. **5.** *druk.* appendix. **6.** *kulin.* (*potrawa*) supplement. **7.** (*film*) extra feature. **8. w dodatku** in addition; **na dodatek** in addition, what's more; **z dodatkiem czegoś** with sth (added); **dodatek (do żywności)** (*chem.*) (food) additive; **dodatki (krawieckie)** accessories.

dodatkowo *adv.* additionally, in addition; (*płacić*) extra.

dodatkowy *a.* additional, extra; **dodatkowe połączenie** (*pociąg, autobus, samolot*) special service; **dodatkowa opinia** second opinion; **opłata dodatkowa** surcharge.

dodatni *a.* positive; **dodatni bilans** *ekon.* favorable balance, surplus; **dodatnie temperatury** *meteor.* above-freezing temperatures; **elektroda dodatnia** *el.* positive electrode; **jon dodatni** *fiz.* positive ion; **liczba dodatnia** *mat.* positive number.

dodatnio *adv.* positively; (= *korzystnie*) favorably.

dodawać *ipf.* **-ję -jesz 1.** (= *dokładać, dosypywać*) add; **dodać soli/cukru** add salt/sugar. **2.** (= *nadawać, przydawać*) add; lend; give; **dodać czemuś blasku** add luster to sth; **dodać komuś/ czemuś ducha** *l.* **życia** invigorate sb/sth; **dodać komuś wdzięku** lend grace to sb; **dodać komuś nadziei/odwagi** give sb hope/courage; **dodać komuś otuchy** lift *l.* raise sb's spirits; **dodać komuś skrzydeł** *przen.* lend wings to sb; **dodać gazu** *pot. mot.* step on the gas, step on it. **3.** (= *dopowiedzieć*) add (*że...* that...); **nic dodać, nic ująć** (= *trudno o lepszy komentarz*) what (else) can you say?, enough said; (= *dokładnie tak*) well said!; (= *to wszystko, co mam do powiedzenia*) I rest my case. **4.** *mat.* (= *sumować*) add.

dodawanie *n. mat.* addition.

dodo *ma indecl. orn.* dodo (*Raphus cucullatus*).

dodruk *mi druk.* printing of additional copies.

dodrukować *pf.* **1.** (= *powiększyć liczbę kopii*) print (*extra copies of sth*), run (*extra copies of sth*); **dodrukować dziesięć egzemplarzy** print an extra ten copies. **2.** (= *dokończyć drukowanie*) finish printing.

dodzwonić się *pf. tel.* get through (*do kogoś / czegoś* to sb/sth); **nie mogłem się do niej dodzwonić** I couldn't get through to her.

dofinansować *pf. zob.* **dofinansowywać.**

dofinansowanie *n.* **1.** *ekon.* (= *dotacja*) subsidy. **2.** *fin.* (= *wsparcie*) (financial) support.

dofinansowywać *ipf.* **1.** *ekon.* (= *dotować*) subsidize (*z czegoś* with sth). **2.** (= *wspierać*) help fund (*coś* sth); help finance (*coś* sth).

dog *ma kynol.* Great Dane.

dogadać *pf.*, **dogadywać** *ipf. pot.* **1.** (= *uzgodnić*) **dogadać coś** agree on sth; **dogadywać coś** talk sth over *l.* through. **2.** (= *dogryźć, przygadać*) (*złośliwie*) gibe *l.* jibe (*komuś* at sb); (*żartobliwie*) kid (*komuś* sb); (*szyderczo, z pogardą*) taunt (*komuś* sb); **dogadać komuś tak, że mu w pięty pójdzie** haul *l.* rake sb over the coals. ~ **się** *pf.*, **dogadywać się** *ipf.* **1.** (= *rozumieć się*) get along *l.* on (*z kimś* with sb); **dobrze się dogadywać** get along *l.* on fine; **świetnie się dogadywać** get along *l.* on famously; **nie mogę się z nim dogadać** I can't get through to him. **2.** *pot.* (= *osiągnąć porozumienie*) reach an agreement (*z kimś* with sb); **w końcu udało nam się dogadać** we finally managed to reach an agreement; (= *omówić sprawy*) talk things over (*z kimś* with sb); discuss matters (*z kimś* with sb); (= *dobić targu*) make a deal (*z kimś* with sb). **3.** (*w obcym języku*) make o.s. understood; **potrafię** *l.* **mogę się dogadać (po angielsku/polsku)** I can make myself understood (in English/Polish).

dogadzać *ipf.* (= *spełniać zachcianki*) **dogadzać komuś** *zwł. uj.* pamper sb, indulge sb (*w czymś* in sth); **dogadzać sobie** indulge o.s.; **dogodzić podniebieniu** tickle one's palate, indulge *l.* pamper one's appetite; **jeszcze się taki nie narodził, który by wszystkim dogodził** you can't please everyone.

doganiać *ipf.* catch up (*kogoś / coś* with sb/sth).

dogasać *ipf.* (*o płomieniu, uczuciu*) be dying.

dogasić *pf.* (*ogień*) put out (completely), extinguish.

doglądać *ipf.*, **doglądnąć** *pf.* **-ij** (= *pilnować*) watch (*czegoś* over sth); supervise (*czegoś* over sth); (= *opiekować się*) tend (*czegoś* sth).

dogłębnie *adv.* **1.** (= *wnikliwie, gruntownie*) in depth. **2.** (= *intensywnie*) deeply.

dogłębny *a.* **1.** (= *gruntowny, wnikliwy*) in-depth; **dogłębna krytyka** sweeping criticism. **2.** (= *intensywny*) deep.

dogmat *mi form. zwł. rel.* dogma.

dogmatycznie *adv.* dogmatically.

dogmatyczny *a.* dogmatic; *polit.* hard-line.

dogmatyk *mp* dogmatist; *polit.* hard-liner.

dogmatyka *f. teol.* (= *dogmaty*) dogma; (= *dogmatyzm*) dogmatism.

dogmatyzm *mi form., rel.* dogmatism.
dognać *pf. zwł. lit.* catch up with (*kogoś* sb).
dognić *pf.* **-ję -jesz, -ij** rot away (completely).
dogodnie *adv. form.* conveniently.
dogodność *f. form.* **1.** (= *wygoda*) convenience. **2.** (= *okazja*) opportunity.
dogodny *a. form.* **1.** (= *wygodny*) convenient. **2.** (= *korzystny*) favorable; **na dogodnych warunkach** on favorable *l.* easy terms.
dogodzić *pf.* **-gódź** *zob.* **dogadzać.**
dogonić *pf. zob.* **doganiać.**
dogorywać *ipf.* **-am -asz** *lit.* (*o ogniu, miłości, osobie*) be dying.
dogotować *pf.* **-uję -ujesz, dogotowywać** *ipf.* **1.** (= *dokończyć gotowanie*) cook fully, finish cooking. **2.** (= *ugotować więcej*) cook more; **dogotować zupy/jedzenia** cook some more soup/food.
dograć *pf.,* **dogrywać** *ipf.* **-am -asz 1.** *pot.* (= *uzgodnić*) arrange; **dograć szczegóły** arrange the details, take care of the details. **2.** (= *zagrać do końca*) play (all the way) through. **3.** (= *dodatkowo nagrać*) record (extra).
dogrywka *f.* **1.** *sport* play-off, runoff; (= *bezpośrednio po nierozstrzygniętej grze*) overtime; extra time; **rozstrzygać się w dogrywce** (*o meczu*) go into overtime; **wygrać w dogrywce** win in overtime. **2.** *fin.* extra-time trading.
dogryzać *ipf.,* **dogryźć** *pf.* **-zę -ziesz -zł -źli** (= *dokuczać*) gibe *l.* jibe, needle, pick on; **dogryzać komuś** gibe *l.* jibe at sb, needle sb, pick on sb.
dogrzać *pf.* **-eję -ejesz** *zob.* **dogrzewać.**
dogrzewać *ipf.,* **dogrzać** *pf.* **1.** (*o słońcu*) (= *przygrzewać*) beat down; **ale dogrzewa!** it's sweltering!, it's a scorcher!; **dogrzało komuś** heat is getting to sb, sb is too hot, sb is feeling hot. **2.** (*pomieszczenie*) heat.
doholować *pf.* (= *przyholować*) tow in; *pot.* (= *doprowadzić*) drag in.
doić *ipf.* **doję doisz, dój 1.** *roln.* (*krowę, kozę*) milk. **2.** *pot. przen.* (= *wykorzystywać finansowo*) milk, squeeze. **3.** *pot. przen.* (= *pić, zwł. alkohol*) knock back.
doigrać się *pf.* smart for it, bite the bullet, face the music, be rightly served, get one's comeuppance; **doigrasz się!** you're looking for trouble!; **doigrałeś się!** you've asked for it!, serves you right!
doinformować *pf.* fill in, provide additional information; **doinformować kogoś w jakiejś sprawie** fill sb in on sth. **~ się** *pf.* (= *dowiedzieć się*) find out; (= *rozpytać się*) ask around (*w jakiejś sprawie* about sth).
doinwestować *pf. ekon.* pump funds into (*coś / kogoś* sth/sb); provide additional funding *l.* finance.
dojadać *ipf.* **1.** (= *kończyć jeść*) finish one's meal, eat up. **2.** (= *najeść się*) be full; **nie dojadać** skimp on food, skip meals. **3.** (= *dokuczyć*) tease; **dojadać komuś do żywego** *przest.* cut sb to the quick.
dojarka *f. roln.* **1.** (*kobieta*) milkmaid, dairymaid. **2.** (*urządzenie*) milking machine, milker.

dojarnia *f. Gen.pl.* **-rni** *l.* **-rń** *roln.* (*duża*) milking parlor; (*mała*) milking shed.
dojazd *mi Loc.* **-eździe 1.** (= *dostęp*) access, approach (*do czegoś* to sth). **2.** (= *droga*) access *l.* approach road; (*do domu*) driveway, drive. **3.** (= *dojeżdżanie*) commute (*do czegoś* to sth); **poranny dojazd do pracy** morning commute (to work).
dojazdowy *a.* access, approach; **droga dojazdowa** access *l.* approach road; (*gospodarcza*) service road; (*do domu*) driveway, drive.
dojechać *pf.* **-jadę -jedziesz** arrive, reach; **dojechać do jakiegoś miejsca** arrive in *l.* at a place, reach a place; *zob. t.* **dojeżdżać.**
dojeść *pf.* **-jem -jesz -jedz -jadł -jedli** *zob.* **dojadać.**
dojeżdżać *ipf.,* **dojechać** *pf.* **1.** (= *jeździć regularnie*) commute; **dojeżdżać do szkoły/pracy/Warszawy** commute to school/work/Warsaw; **dojeżdżać autobusem/pociągiem/tramwajem** take the bus/train/streetcar, commute by bus/train/streetcar; **dojeżdżać samochodem (do pracy)** drive (to work); **dojeżdżać rowerem** bike in. **2.** (= *zbliżać się*) approach (*do czegoś* sth).
dojeżdżający *a.* (= *zamieszkały daleko od pracy*) commuting; (= *pracujący w kilku miejscach*) visiting, peripatetic; (= *zamieszkały poza miejscem pracy, nauki*) nonresident. – *mp* (= *osoba dojeżdżająca*) commuter.
dojmujący *a. lit.* (*o bólu, uczuciu*) sharp; (*o uczuciu*) deep, intense; **dojmujące zimno** bitter *l.* biting cold.
dojny *a. roln.* milk, milch; **dojna krowa** milk *l.* milch cow; *pot. przen.* (= *źródło łatwego dochodu*) cash cow.
dojrzale *adv.* maturely.
dojrzałość *f. biol., psych.* maturity; **dojrzałość płciowa** *biol.* puberty; **egzamin dojrzałości** *szkoln. w Polsce* secondary school final examinations; *Br.* A levels; **świadectwo dojrzałości** *szkoln. w Polsce* certificate of secondary education, secondary school graduation certificate; *US* high school diploma; *Br.* GCSE.
dojrzały *a.* **-lszy** (*o osobie, wieku, osobowości, decyzji, twórczości, serze, owocu*) mature; (*o owocu, winie*) ripe; **wiek dojrzały** maturity, adulthood.
dojrzeć[1] *pf.* **-ę -ysz, -yj 1.** (= *zobaczyć*) spot, spy; (= *rozróżnić wzrokiem*) pick out; **dojrzeć coś w oddali** spot sth in the distance. **2.** *rzad. zob.* **doglądać.**
dojrzeć[2] *pf.* **-eję -ejesz, -yj** *zob.* **dojrzewać.**
dojrzewać *ipf.* mature; (*o owocu*) ripen; (*o organizmie, pomyśle*) grow, develop; (*o winie, serze*) age.
dojrzewanie *n.* maturation; **dojrzewanie (płciowe)** *biol.* pubescence, puberty.
dojście *n.* **1.** (= *spacer*) walk (*do czegoś* to sth). **2.** (= *ścieżka*) footpath; access *l.* approach (path) (*do czegoś* to sth). **3.** *przen.* (= *zdążanie*) road, path (*do czegoś* to sth); **dojście kogoś do władzy** sb's rise to power. **4.** *zwł. pl. pot.* (= *znajomość, plecy*) connection; **mieć dojścia** be well connected, know the right people.
dojść *pf.* **dojdę dojdziesz doszedł doszła doszli**

(= *dotrzeć*) reach (*gdzieś* a place); arrive (*gdzieś* in *l.* at a place); (= *osiągnąć*) achieve sth; **nigdy do niczego nie dojdziesz** you will never get anywhere; *zob. t.* **dochodzić.**

dok *mi żegl.* dock; **dok pływający** floating dock; **suchy dok** dry *l.* graving dock; **stać w doku** be in dock; **wprowadzić statek do doku** take a ship into dock.

dokańczać *ipf.,* **dokończyć** *pf.* finish (off); **pozwól mi dokończyć (coś robić)** let me finish (doing sth); **nie dokończyć czegoś** leave sth undone.

dokapitalizować *pf. ekon.* pump *l.* channel capital into (*coś / kogoś* sth/sb); capitalize; recapitalize.

dokarmiać *ipf.,* **dokarmić** *pf.* (help) feed.

dokazywać *ipf.* (= *figlować*) frolic, romp, horse around, fool *l.* monkey around.

dokąd *adv., pron. indecl.* **1.** (= *gdzie*) where (to); **dokąd?** where (to)?; **dokąd idziesz?** where are you going (to)? **2.** (*wprowadza zdania podrzędne okolicznikowe miejsca lub celu*) (= *gdzie*) where; **nie wiem, dokąd iść** I don't know where to go; **Bóg wie dokąd** God knows where. **3.** (*wprowadza zdania podrzędne okolicznikowe miejsca lub celu*) (= *gdziekolwiek*) anywhere, wherever, any place; **pójdę, dokąd będzie trzeba** I'll go anywhere I have to; **wszędzie, dokąd pójdziesz** anywhere *l.* any place you go; **iść dokąd oczy poniosą** (go and) never look back. **4.** (= *jak długo?*) how long?, until when?; **dokąd mam czekać?** how long should I wait? **5.** (*także* **dotąd, dokąd...**) (*wprowadza zdania podrzędne określające moment, czas trwania jakiejś czynności*) (= *tak długo aż*) until; **czytała (dotąd), dokąd nie zrobiło się całkiem ciemno** she kept on reading until it was completely dark.

dokądkolwiek *adv.* (*po czasowniku*) anywhere; (*przed czasownikiem*) everywhere, no matter where; **możemy jechać dokądkolwiek** we can go anywhere; **dokądkolwiek pojedziesz/pójdziesz** everywhere you go.

dokądś *adv.* somewhere, someplace.

doker *mp* longshoreman, dockworker, stevedore.

dokerski *a.* longshoring; **prace dokerskie** cargo handling, longshoring, stevedoring.

dokleić *pf.,* **doklejać** *ipf.* stick, glue (*coś do czegoś* sth on *l.* onto sth).

dokładać *ipf.,* **dołożyć** *pf.* **1.** (= *dodawać*) add; **dołóż więcej masła** add (some) more butter; **dokładać komuś pracy** give sb (some) extra work; **dołożyć do czegoś** (= *dopłacać*) lose money on sth; **dołożyć do interesu** lose money; **dokładać do ognia** stoke (up) the fire; **dołożyć wszelkich sił** *l.* **starań by** *l.* **aby coś zrobić** do one's best to do sth, try one's hardest to do sth, make every effort to do sth. **2.** *zob. t.* **dołożyć.** ~ **się** *ipf.,* **dołożyć się** *pf. gł. pot.* chip in, pitch in.

dokładka *f. kulin.* seconds, second *l.* additional helping; **na dokładkę** *przen.* (= *dodatkowo*) on top (of that), extra, for good measure, into the bargain; (= *jakby tego było mało*) on top of everything.

dokładnie *adv.* **1.** (= *precyzyjnie*) exactly; accurately, precisely; **dokładnie coś pamiętać** remember sth well, remember sth in detail; **dokładnie ten sam** the very same. **2.** (= *starannie*) thoroughly, meticulously, well, carefully. **3.** (= *uważnie*) closely; **dokładnie kogoś/coś obserwować** watch sb/sth closely; **dokładnie kogoś/coś zbadać** examine sb/sth closely *l.* in detail. **4.** (*w określeniach czasu*) **dokładnie o piątej/siedemnastej** at five (o'clock) sharp, on the stroke of five; **dokładnie w dwie godziny** in two hours flat; **dokładnie w tej chwili** *l.* **w tym momencie** as we speak, at this very moment; **dokładnie chodzić** (*o zegarku*) run well. **5.** (*w określeniach kierunków geograficznych*) due; **dokładnie na północ/zachód** due north/west. – *int. pot.* exactly!, precisely!, dead on!, right on!, spot on!

dokładność *f.* accuracy, precision.

dokładny *a.* **1.** (= *precyzyjny*) accurate, precise, exact. **2.** (= *staranny*) meticulous, thorough. **3.** (= *szczegółowy*) detailed.

dokoła[1] *adv.* (= *naokoło*) around; **(wszędzie) dokoła** (all) around; **dokoła stały domy** there were buildings all around; **dokoła Wojtek** *pot.* again and again, on and on.

dokoła[2] *prep. + Gen.* (= *wokół*) around, round (*czegoś* sth); **siedzieć dokoła stołu** sit around *l.* round the table.

dokonać *pf. zob.* **dokonywać.** ~ **się** *pf. zob.* **dokonywać się.**

dokonanie *n. form.* **1.** (= *wyczyn*) achievement, accomplishment, feat. **2.** (= *zrobienie*) achieving, accomplishing (*czegoś* sth). **3.** *pl.* **-nia** achievements, accomplishments.

dokonany *a.* **1.** *form.* done, accomplished; **coś jest dokonane** sth is a fact; **fakt dokonany** accomplished fact, fait accompli. **2.** *gram., jęz.* perfective; **czasownik/aspekt dokonany** perfective verb/aspect; **czas dokonany** perfect tense.

dokonywać *ipf.,* **dokonać** *pf.* **-nuję -nujesz, -nuj** **1.** (= *osiągać*) achieve, accomplish (*czegoś* sth); **dokonać odkrycia** make a discovery; **dokonywać cudów** work miracles *l.* wonders. **2.** *przest.* complete, finish (off); **dokonać żywota** *lit.* breathe one's last, depart this life. ~ **się** *ipf.,* **dokonać się** *pf. gł. form.* take place; come to pass.

dokończenie *n.* conclusion.

dokończyć *pf. zob.* **dokańczać.**

dokooptować *pf.* co-opt, incorporate.

dokopać *pf.* **-ię -iesz** **1.** *pot.* boot, kick; **dokopać komuś** give sb a *l.* the boot, boot *l.* kick sb; *sl., przen.* (= *dociąć*) trash sb. **2.** (= *dokończyć kopanie*) finish digging. ~ **się** *pf.* (= *kopiąc dotrzeć*) dig all the way (*do czegoś* to sth); *przen.* (= *odszukać*) dig out; **dokopać się do prawdy** discover the truth.

dokrajać *pf. i ipf.* **-ę -esz** *zob.* **dokroić.**

dokrawać *ipf. zob.* **dokroić.**

dokrewny *a. fizj.* endocrine; **gruczoły dokrewne** *anat.* endocrine *l.* ductless glands.

dokręcać *ipf.,* **dokręcić** *pf.* tighten (up); **dokręcić wkręt/śrubę/nakrętkę** tighten (up) a screw/bolt/nut; **dokręcić kran/wodę** turn the water off all the way; **nie dokręcić kranu** leave the water running *l.* dripping; **dokręcić komuś śrubę** *pot.* *przen.* tighten *l.* turn the screws on sb. ~ **się** *ipf.,* **dokręcić się** *pf.* tighten; be turned off; **ten kran się nie dokręca** this tap *l.* faucet doesn't turn off all the way.

dokrętka *f.* **1.** *mech.* (= *kontra*) locknut. **2.** *film* retake, reshoot.

dokroić *pf.,* **dokrajać** *ipf.,* **dokrawać** *ipf.* **-ję -isz, -ój** cut (some more), slice (some more) (*czegoś* sth); **możesz (nam) dokroić chleba?** could you slice some more bread (for us)?

dokształcać się *ipf.,* **dokształcić się** *pf.* (= *douczać się*) polish up (*w czymś* on sth); (= *zdobywać nowe kwalifikacje*) acquire new skills, supplement one's education.

doktor *mp* **1.** *pl.* **-rzy** *pot.* (= *lekarz*) physician, doctor; *Voc.* **panie doktorze!** doctor! **2.** *pl.* **-rzy** *l.* **-owie** *uniw.* (= *osoba ze stopniem doktorskim*) doctor, Ph.D.; **stopień doktora** Ph.D.; **doktor nauk** Ph.D., Doctor of Philosophy; **doktor teologii/prawa/medycyny/nauk ścisłych** Doctor of Divinity/Law/Medicine/Science; **doktor habilitowany** *w Polsce* holder of a postdoctoral degree; **doktor honoris causa** doctor honoris causa.

doktorant *mp* *uniw.* Ph.D. student.

doktorantka *f.* *zob.* **doktorant.**

doktorat *mi* *uniw.* **1.** (*stopień*) Ph.D. (degree), doctorate; (**mieć**) **doktorat z fizyki/chemii** (hold *l.* have) a Ph.D. in physics/chemistry; **doktorat honorowy** honorary doctorate; **doktorat honoris causa** honorary doctorate, doctorate conferred honoris causa. **2.** (*rozprawa*) Ph.D. dissertation *l.* thesis.

doktorek -rk- *mp* *pot., t. pog.* doc.

doktorski *a.* **1.** *uniw.* (*dotyczący stopnia naukowego*) Ph.D., doctoral; **praca** *l.* **rozprawa doktorska** *l.* doctoral dissertation *l.* thesis; **otworzyć komuś przewód doktorski** admit sb into a Ph.D. program. **2.** *pot.* (*dotyczący lekarza*) doctor's.

doktoryzować się *ipf.* *l.* *pf.* get a Ph.D. (*z czegoś* in sth) (*na Harwardzie itp.* from Harvard University, etc.).

doktryna *f.* *gł. form.* doctrine.

doktrynalnie *adv.* *form.* doctrinally.

doktrynalny *a.* *form.* doctrinal, orthodox, sectarian.

doktryner *mp* doctrinaire, doctrinarian, ideologue.

doktrynerka *f.* *zob.* **doktryner.**

doktrynerski *a.* *form., uj.* doctrinaire, orthodox.

doktrynerstwo *n.* *form.* doctrinairism, orthodoxy.

dokuczać *ipf.* (= *naprzykrzać się*) bother, vex (*komuś* sb); (= *dolegać*) bother, ail, give trouble; (*zwł. o nawracającej dolegliwości*) play (sb) up; (= *mocno boleć*) be killing; (= *czynić przytyki*) tease, pick on; **komuś dokucza zimno/upał/głód** sb is suffering cold/heat/hunger; **komuś dokucza serce/kolano/krzyż** sb's heart/knee/back is playing (sb) up.

dokuczliwie *adv.* (*odczuwać*) painfully; (*przeszkadzać*) annoyingly.

dokuczliwy *a.* (*o dolegliwości*) troublesome; (*o utrudnieniach, komplikacjach*) difficult, awkward; (*o gorączce, kaszlu, katarze*) bad; (*o bólu*) nagging, acute; (*o komarze, pokrzywach*) annoying, bothersome; (*o osobie*) annoying; (*o wietrze, deszczu, bólu*) vicious.

dokuczyć *pf.* *zob.* **dokuczać.**

dokument *mi* **1.** *prawn., hist., komp.* document. **2.** *hist.* (= *zapis*) record. **3. dokumenty** (= *dowód tożsamości*) ID, identification; **dokumenty podróżne** travel documents; **lewe dokumenty** *pot.* fake ID; phony papers. **4.** *film, form.* documentary.

dokumentacja *f.* documentation.

dokumentalista *mp* *form.* **1.** *film., telew.* documentary filmmaker. **2.** *teor.lit., dzienn.* chronicler, documentary writer. **3.** (= *archiwista*) documentalist.

dokumentalistka *f.* *zob.* **dokumentalista.**

dokumentalistyka *f.* **1.** (= *archiwistyka*) documentation. **2.** *film, telew.* documentaries.

dokumentalny *a.* *telew., film, dzienn.* documentary; **film/program dokumentalny** documentary.

dokumentnie *adv.* *pot.* (= *całkowicie*) out and out, totally.

dokumentny *a.* *pot.* (= *całkowity*) out and out, total.

dokumentować *ipf.* document.

dokupić *pf.,* **dokupować, dokupywać** *ipf.* (*jedną rzecz*) get *l.* buy another; (*więcej rzeczy l. ilość*) get *l.* buy some more; **dokupić rower** get *l.* buy another bicycle; **musimy dokupić mleka** we need to get some more milk; **dokupić coś do czegoś** (*do ubrania*) get sth to go with sth; (*do urządzenia*) get sth for sth; **dokupić kartę** *karty* draw a card.

dokwaterować *pf.,* **dokwaterowywać** *ipf.* assign a new tenant *l.* occupant to a place; **dokwaterować kogoś komuś** have sb living with sb, have sb living at sb's place; **dokwaterować kogoś gdzieś** put sb (up) somewhere.

dola *f.* *lit.* **1.** (= *los*) fate, lot; **dole i niedole** ups and downs; **w doli i niedoli** through thick and thin. **2.** *pot.* (= *udział w zysku, łupie*) cut, whack, share; **dostać swoją dolę** get one's share.

dolać *pf.* **-eję -ejesz** **1.** *zob.* **dolewać. 2.** *pot.* (= *pobić, zbić kogoś*) whack (*komuś* sb).

dolar *mi* *Gen.* **-a** *fin.* dollar; **dolar amerykański/kanadyjski/australijski** US/Canadian/Australian dollar; **10 dolarów za godzinę** $10 an hour.

dolarowy *a.* *fin.* dollar.

dolatywać *ipf.* **1.** (= *lecąc docierać*) reach (*gdzieś* a place) fly (*gdzieś* as far as a place). **2.** (*o dźwiękach, zapachach*) come (in). **3.** *pot.* (= *dobiegać*) catch up.

dole *mi* *zob.* **dół.**

dolec *mi* **-lc-** *pl.* **dolce** *Gen.pl.* **-ców** *fin., pot.* *gł. pl.* buck; **kupa dolców** big bucks; **wisisz mi dwa dolce** you owe me two bucks.

dolecieć *pf.* **-ę -isz** *zob.* **dolatywać.**

dolegać *ipf.* bother, ail (*komuś* sb) give trouble; (*zwł. o nawracającej dolegliwości*) play (sb) up; (= *mocno boleć*) be killing; **co Panu/Pani do-**

lega? (*u lekarza*) what seems to be the problem *l.* trouble?; **co ci dolega?** what's wrong with you?; **nic mi/ci/mu itd. nie dolega** there's nothing wrong with me/you/him, etc.; **dolega jej noga/żołądek** her leg/stomach is bothering her, her leg/ stomach is giving her trouble.

dolegliwość *f.* **1.** *pat.* (= *choroba, ból*) complaint, ailment; *pl.* **dolegliwości** trouble; **dolegliwości żołądkowe/sercowe** stomach/heart trouble. **2.** (= *kłopot, zmartwienie*) difficulty, trouble, problem. **3.** (= *utrudnienie*) hardship.

dolegliwy *a.* **1.** *form.* (= *kłopotliwy*) burdensome, inconvenient. **2.** *przest.* (= *dokuczliwy*) acute.

dolepiać *ipf.*, **dolepić** *pf.* stick, glue (*coś do czegoś* sth on *l.* onto sth).

dolewać *ipf.* **1.** pour; **dolewać coś do czegoś** pour *l.* add sth in *l.* into *l.* on *l.* onto sth; **dolewać oliwy do ognia** *przen.* fuel the fire *l.* flames. **2.** *kulin.* (*gł. o napojach*) (= *nalewać nową porcję*) refill; **dolewać komuś** refill sb's drink/glass/cup, etc.; **dolewać komuś kawy** refill sb's coffee; **dolać?** would you like a refill? **3.** *kulin.* (*gł. o napojach*) (= *uzupełniać częściowo wypitą porcję*) top up, freshen; **dolewać komuś (do pełna)** top up sb's drink/glass/cup, etc.; **dolewać komuś kawy** top up sb's coffee; *zob. t.* **dolać**.

dolewka *f.* refill.

doleźć *pf.* **-zę -ziesz -lazł -leźli** *pot.* drag o.s. (*gdzieś* somewhere *l.* to sth).

doleżeć *pf.* **-ę -ysz 1.** (*o osobie*) (= *wytrzymać w łóżku*) stay *l.* remain in bed, lie in bed; **doleżeć do rana** stay in bed until morning. **2.** (*o zapasach, przedmiotach*) (= *przetrwać*) last; **doleżeć do wiosny** last until spring.

doliczać *ipf.*, **doliczyć** *pf.* **1.** (*koszt, kwotę*) (= *dodawać*) include, count (in), add (on *l.* in); **doliczać coś do czegoś** include sth in sth, add sth (on) to sth. **2.** (= *policzyć, wyliczyć*) count; **doliczyć do dziesięciu/stu** count (up) to ten/a hundred. **~ się** *pf.* get one's count right; **nie mogę się doliczyć dwóch talerzy** I seem to be missing two plates.

dolina *f.* **1.** *geogr.* valley; **dolina górska/lodowcowa/rzeczna** mountain/glacial/river valley. **2.** (*fali morskiej, elektromagnetycznej, akustycznej*) trough.

doliniarz *mp przest., sl.* (= *kieszonkowiec*) dip, pickpocket.

dolinka *f. Gen.pl.* **-ek** *geogr.* vale, dell.

dolmen *mi Gen.* **-a** *archeol.* (= *grobowiec*) dolmen.

dolnołużycki *a. jęz.* Lower Sorbian *l.* Wendish *l.* Lusatian. – *mi* **(język) dolnołużycki** Lower Sorbian *l.* Wendish *l.* Lusatian.

dolnoniemiecki *a. jęz.* Low German. – *mi* **(dialekt) dolnoniemiecki** Low German.

dolnopłat *mi Gen.* **-a** *lotn.* low-wing monoplane.

dolnopłuk *mi Gen.* **-a** *techn.* cistern.

dolnoprzepustowy *a. el.* low-pass; **filtr dolnoprzepustowy** low-pass filter.

dolnośląski *a. geogr.* Lower Silesian.

dolny *a.* **1.** (= *spodni, najniższy*) bottom; **dol-**

na szuflada/półka bottom drawer/shelf. **2.** (= *niższy z dwóch*) lower; **dolny pokład** *żegl.* lower deck; **dolna granica** *t. mat.* lower limit. **3.** *anat.* lower; **dolna szczęka/warga** lower jaw/lip; **dolne zęby** lower teeth; **kończyny dolne** lower extremities. **4.** *geogr., geol.* lower; **dolny bieg rzeki** lower course *l.* run of a river; **Dolna Odra** the Lower Oder; **Dolny Śląsk** Lower Silesia; **dolny trias/eocen** the Lower Triassic/Eocene.

dolomit *mi geol., min.* dolomite.

dolomitowy *a. geol., min., bud.* dolomite; dolomitic; **cegła dolomitowa** dolomite brick.

Dolomity *mi pl. geogr.* the Dolomites.

dolot *mi* **1.** *lotn.* (*połączenie*) connecting flight. **2.** *lotn.* (= *ostatni fragment lotu*) approach. **3.** *techn.* (= *doprowadzenie*) intake, inlet.

dolutować *pf.* solder (*coś do czegoś* sth on *l.* onto sth).

doładować *pf.*, **doładowywać** *ipf.* **1.** (*ciężarówkę, przyczepę*) load (a little more); **doładować czegoś** load some more sth; **doładować piasku na ciężarówkę** load some more sand on the truck. **2.** *el., mot.* (*akumulator, baterię*) recharge; *el.* (*małym prądem*) trickle-charge; **doładować akumulator** *mot.* recharge the battery; *przen.* (= *odpocząć*) recharge one's battery. **3.** *mot.* (*silnik*) supercharge, boost. **4.** *pot.* (= *dołożyć*) pile *l.* heap on. **5.** *wojsk.* (*broń*) reload.

dołączać *ipf.*, **dołączyć** *pf.* **1.** (*do przesyłki*) *załączać*) attach, enclose, append (*coś do listu / paczki / e-maila* sth to a letter/package/an e-mail). **2.** (= *przystępować*) join. **3.** (= *wyrównywać krok*) pull up (*do kogoś* to sb) fall into step (*do kogoś* with sb); **dołączać do szeregu** *zwł. wojsk.* fall in. **4.** (= *dodawać*) add; **dołączać coś (do czegoś)** add sth (to sth). **5.** (= *przyczepiać*) join, attach; **dołączać coś (do czegoś)** couple sth (to *l.* with sth). **~ się** *ipf.*, **dołączyć się** *pf.* **1.** (= *przyłączać się*) join (*do kogoś / czegoś* sb/sth). **2.** (= *dojść, pojawić się*) (*o uczuciach, objawach choroby*) set in.

dołeczek *mi* **-czk-** *Gen.* **-a 1.** *zwł. pl.* (*w policzku, brodzie*) dimple. **2.** (= *mały dołek*) pit, dimple. **3.** *anat.* foveola, pit.

dołek *mi* **-łk-** *Gen.* **-a 1.** (= *mały dół, zagłębienie*) pit, hole; **kopać pod kimś dołki** *przen.* dig a pit for sb; **kto dołki kopie, ten sam w nie wpada** *przen.* hoist *l.* thrown by *l.* with one's own petard, be shot by one's own gun, get a dose of one's own medicine. **2.** *zwł. pl.* (*w policzku, brodzie*) dimple; **kogoś ssie w dołku** (= *ktoś jest głodny*) sb has an aching void; **kogoś ściska w dołku** (= *ktoś jest wzruszony*) sb has a knot in his/her, etc. stomach, sb has a lump in his/her, etc. throat; **kogoś gniecie w dołku** sb has butterflies in his/her, etc. stomach. **3.** *pot. przen.* (= *kryzys*) hole, doldrums; (= *depresja*) doldrums; **być w dołku** be in a hole; be in the doldrums; **wyjść z dołka** bounce back. **4.** *anat.* fovea, pit; **dołek podsercowy** *l.* **sercowy** epigastric fossa; *pot.* pit of the stomach. **5.** *metal.* sprue base, well.

dołować *ipf.* **1.** *perf.* **zdołować** *pot.* (= *przygnę-**

biać) get down. **2.** *perf.* **zadołować** *t. roln.* (*warzywa, wapno*) (= *zakopywać*) pit.

dołownik *mi Gen.* **-a** *roln.* (= *sadzarka*) potato planter.

dołowy *a.* **1.** *zwł. górn.* undergound; **górnik dołowy** pitman. **2.** *roln.* (= *kopcowy*) pit, pitted.

dołożyć *pf.* **-łóż 1.** *zob.* **dokładać. 2.** *pot.* (= *uderzyć, pokonać, skrytykować*) clobber (*komuś* sb).

dołu *itd. mi zob.* **dół.**

dom *mi Loc. i Voc.* **-u 1.** (= *mieszkanie, domownicy, rodzina*) home; **w domu** at home, in the home; **być w domu** be (at) home, be in; **być poza domem** (*chwilowo*) be out; (*na dłużej*) be away (from home); **iść do domu** go home; **nikogo nie ma w domu** there's nobody home; **u kogoś w domu** at sb's house *l.* place. **2.** (= *budynek mieszkalny*) house. **3.** (= *budynek*) building. **4.** (= *gospodarstwo domowe*) household. **5.** (= *ród, dynastia*) house; kin, family; **z domu Czartoryska** (*przy podawaniu nazwiska rodowego*) née Czartoryska; **pochodzić z dobrego domu** come from a good family. **6.** (*w zwrotach*) **być panem we własnym domu** be a master of *l.* in one's own house; *pot.* rule one's roost; **ciasny, ale własny dom** a small home, but your own; **czuć się jak u siebie w domu** be *l.* feel at home; **czuj się jak u siebie w domu** make yourself at home; **czynić honory domu** do the honors; **dom i ogród** *handl.* home and garden; **dwa/trzy itd. domy dalej** two/ three, etc. doors down *l.* up *l.* over (the road); **głowa domu** head of the household; **mieć cały dom na głowie** have to run the house; **(na) po domu** (*o ubraniach*) house, indoor; **sukienka (na) po domu** house dress; **odprowadzać kogoś do domu** walk sb home; **nie ma jak w domu** *l.* wszędzie dobrze, ale w domu najlepiej east, west, home's best; home, sweet home; there's no place like home; **no to jesteśmy w domu** *pot. przen.* (= *już wszystko w porządku*) we're almost home, now we're cooking with gas, we're cool *l.* good; **pan/ pani domu** master/lady of the house, host/ hostess; **postawić cały dom na nogi** raise hell *l.* Cain; **prowadzić otwarty dom** keep open doors *l.* house; **tęsknić za domem** miss home; **szklane domy** *przen.* castles in the air, pipe dream; **wszystko dla domu** *handl.* everything for the home; **założyć dom** set up house *l.* home; **zarabiać na dom** bring home the bacon; **zaszyć się w domu** lock o.s. (away) in one's house. **7.** (*w złożeniach*) **Biały Dom** *polit.* the White House; **dom akademicki** *l.* **studencki** *uniw.* dormitory, dorm; **dom aukcyjny** auction house; **dom Boży** *l.* **modlitwy** *rel.* house of God *l.* worship; **dom dwurodzinny** duplex (house); **dom dziecka** children's home; **dom gry** gambling house; **dom kultury** community center; **dom maklerski** *fin.* brokerage (house *l.* firm), broker; **dom mody** fashion house; **dom opieki** nursing home; **dom otwarty** open house; **dom poprawczy** reformatory, reform school; **dom pogrzebowy** funeral home; **dom publiczny** house of prostitution, brothel; **dom rodzinny** family home; **dom starców** old people's home; assisted living facility *l.* home; **dom szeregowy**

bud. row house; (*w mieście*) town house; **dom towarowy** *handl.* department store; **dom wariatów** mental hospital *l.* institution; *t. przen.* madhouse; **dom wczasowy** *l.* **wypoczynkowy** resort hotel; **dom weselny** wedding house; **dom wycieczkowy** lodge; **drugi dom** home away from home, second home.

domaciczny *a. med.* intrauterine; **wkładka domaciczna** intrauterine device.

domagać się *ipf.* **1.** (= *żądać*) demand; **domagać się czegoś od kogoś** demand sth from sb, push *l.* press sb for sth; **domagać się zwrotu pieniędzy** demand a refund; **domagać się odszkodowania** claim *l.* seek compensation. **2.** (= *potrzebować*) need; **domagać się czegoś** need sth, be in need of sth; **dom domaga się remontu** house needs repair, house is in need of repair; **ziemia domaga się deszczu** soil needs rain.

domalować *pf.*, **domalowywać** *ipf.* **1.** (= *skończyć malować*) finish painting. **2.** (= *namalować dodatkowo*) add (*sth to a painting*).

domator *mp* homebody, stay-at-home.

domatorka *f. zob.* **domator.**

domatorski *a.* stay-at-home.

domawiać *ipf.* **1.** (= *uzgadniać do końca*) talk through *l.* over; **nie domówiliśmy czegoś** we didn't talk sth through *l.* over (properly). **2.** *przest.* (= *przygadywać*) chaff (*komuś* sb). **~ się** *ipf. pot.* **1.** (= *dopraszać się*) sweet-talk, cajole; **domawiać się o coś** (try to) sweet-talk sb into sth. **2.** (= *uzgadniać*) talk (things) through (*z kimś* with sb).

domek *mi* **-mk- 1.** (= *nieduży dom*) (small) house; **domek letniskowy** cabin, cottage; **domek dla lalek** doll house; **domek kempingowy** cabin, cottage; **domek dla ptaków** birdhouse; **domek z kart** *t. przen.* house of cards. **2.** (= *mieszkanko*) home; **wolnoć Tomku w swoim domku** my home is my castle.

domeldować *pf.*, **domeldowywać** *ipf.* assign a new tenant *l.* occupant to a place; **domeldować kogoś komuś** *l.* **do kogoś** have sb living with sb, have sb living at sb's place.

domena *f. komp., fiz., mat.* domain; **nazwa domeny** *komp.* domain name; **czyjaś domena** (= *dziedzina działalności*) sb's domain *l.* province *l.* preserve.

domiar *mi fin.* surtax; *gł. Br.* supertax; **na domiar** additionally, in addition, on top of; **na domiar złego** to make things *l.* matters worse.

domicyl *mi Gen.pl.* **-i** *l.* **-ów** *prawn.* domicile.

domieszać *pf.* mix in; *kulin.* stir in; **domieszać coś do czegoś** mix sth with sth; *kulin.* stir sth into sth.

domieszka *f. Gen.pl.* **-ek 1.** (= *dodatek*) admixture (*czegoś* of sth). **2.** *przen.* (= *odcień, zabarwienie, posmak*) tinge, undertone (*czegoś* of sth); **z domieszką złości** with an undertone of anger. **3.** *el., fiz.* (*w półprzewodniku*) dopant.

domieszkowanie *n. el., fiz.* (*półprzewodnika*) doping.

domięśniowo *adv. med.* intramuscularly.

domięśniowy *a. med.* intramuscular; **zastrzyk domięśniowy** intramuscular injection.

domina f. dominatrix.
dominacja f. dominance, domination.
dominanta f. **1.** (= *dominująca cecha*) dominant characteristic. **2.** *biol.*, *ekol.*, *t. muz.* dominant. **3.** *fiz.* dominant wavelength. **4.** *stat.* mode.
Dominikana f. *geogr.* Dominican Republic.
Dominikanin *mp pl.* -anie *Gen.* -anów (= *mieszkaniec Dominikany*) Dominican.
dominikanin *mp pl.* -anie *Gen.* -anów *rel.* (*zakonnik*) Dominican, Black Friar.
Dominikanka f. (= *mieszkanka Dominikany*) Dominican.
dominikanka f. *rel.* (*zakonnica*) Dominican.
dominikański a. *rel.*, *t. geogr.* Dominican.
dominium n. *sing. indecl. pl.* -nia *Gen.* -niów *polit.*, *hist.* dominion.
domino n. **1.** (*gra*) domino; **teoria domina** *polit.* domino theory. **2.** (*peleryna, t. osoba*) domino.
dominować *ipf.* **1.** (= *górować*) dominate (*nad kimś/czymś* over sb/sth). **2.** (*o poglądzie, obyczaju*) (= *cieszyć się popularnością*) prevail, predominate.
dominujący a. **1.** (= *górujący*) dominant; **cecha dominująca** dominant characteristic. **2.** (= *najpopularniejszy*) prevailing, predominant.
domknąć *pf.* -ij *zob.* **domykać**.
domniemać *pf. zob.* **domniemywać**.
domniemanie n. *form.*, *prawn.* presumption; **domniemanie niewinności** presumption of innocence.
domniemany a. alleged, presumed, suspected.
domniemywać *ipf.* -am -asz *przest.* presume, surmise (*że...* that...).
domofon *mi techn.* intercom.
domokrążca *mp przest.* door-to-door salesman; *pog.* peddler.
domorosły a. **1.** (= *niekształcony*) self-taught; **domorosły muzyk** self-taught musician; (= *samorodny*) natural; **domorosły talent** homegrown *l.* natural talent. **2.** *rzad.* homebred; homemade.
domostwo n. **1.** (= *obejście, zagroda*) homestead. **2.** *lit.* (= *dom*) residence, abode.
domownik *mp* member of a household; **domownicy** household.
domowy a. **1.** (= *dotyczący domu*) house. **2.** (= *dotyczący mieszkania*) domestic. **3.** (= *dotyczący rodziny*) family. **4.** (*w zwrotach*) **areszt domowy** house arrest; (= *kara dla dziecka*) grounding; **artykuły gospodarstwa domowego** *handl.* housewares; (*elektryczne*) household *l.* domestic appliances; **budżet domowy** family budget; **domowe ognisko** *l.* **ognisko domowe** *lit.* hearth (and home), fireside; (**wino**) **domowej roboty** homemade (wine); **piwo domowej roboty** home brew; **gospodarstwo domowe** household; **gospodyni domowa** (*mężczyzna l. kobieta*) homemaker; **obuwie** *l.* **pantofle domowe** house *l.* indoor shoes; **kura domowa** *gł. uj.* homebody; **pomoc domowa** (domestic) help; **robiony domowym sposobem** homemade; **strój domowy** house clothes; **wizyta domowa** (*lekarza*) house call; **wojna domowa** po-

lit. civil war; **zadanie domowe** *l.* **praca domowa** *szkoln.* homework; **zwierzęta domowe** pets, domestic animals.
domówić *pf. zob.* **domawiać**. ~ **się** *pf. zob.* **domawiać się**.
domyć *pf.* -ję -jesz get *l.* wash clean; **nie mogłam tego domyć** I couldn't get *l.* wash this clean.
domykać *ipf.* (*okno, drzwi*) close, shut (*sth half-open*).
domysł *mi* guess; conjecture; (**czyste**) **domysły** (pure) guesswork *l.* speculation; **snuć domysły** conjecture; **gubić się w domysłach** be guessing o.s. dizzy.
domyślać się *ipf.*, **domyślić się** *pf.* guess; **domyślać się czegoś** guess (at) sth.
domyślnie *adv.* **1.** (= *bystro*) perceptively, insightfully, perspicaciously. **2.** (= *wyjściowo*) by default.
domyślność f. sharp wits, insight, perceptiveness, perspicacity.
domyślny a. **1.** (= *bystry*) quick-witted, insightful, perspicacious. **2.** (= *wyjściowy*) default. **3.** (= *domniemany*) understood, implicit; **podmiot domyślny** *jęz.* understood subject.
donacja f. *form.* (= *darowizna, dar*) donation, contribution.
donaszać *ipf.* wear out; **donaszać rzeczy po kimś** wear sb's hand-me-downs.
donatariusz *mp Gen.pl.* -y *l.* -ów *form.* donee.
donator *mp prawn.* donor, donator.
donica f. **1.** (*na kwiaty*) planter; (*z drewna*) tub; (*ceramiczna*) (large) flower vase *l.* pot. **2.** (= *makutra*) earthenware bowl (*for mixing batter, dough etc.*). **3.** *arch.* (= *forma do ciast*) cake tin.
doniczka f. *Gen.pl.* -ek flowerpot; **sadzić w doniczce** pot.
doniczkowy a. potted; **kwiat doniczkowy** potted flower; **roślina doniczkowa** house plant, potted plant; *Br.* pot plant.
doniesienie n. **1.** (= *informacja*) report (*o czymś* of *l.* on sth); **szczegółowe doniesienia** detailed reports; **doniesienia prasowe** press reports; **najnowsze doniesienia** (**prasowe**) latest (press) reports. **2.** (= *donos*) denunciation.
donieść *pf.* -niosę -niesiesz -niósł -niosła -nieśli *zob.* **donosić**.
donikąd *adv.* nowhere; *przest.* nowhither; **donikąd się nie spieszę** I'm in no hurry (to get anywhere); **to donikąd nie prowadzi** it'll get you nowhere, it won't get you anywhere.
doniosłość f. significance, importance; *lit.* momentousness; **nie doceniać doniosłości faktu** to underestimate the significance of the fact; **wydarzenie o wielkiej doniosłości** an event of great significance; **zdawać sobie sprawę z doniosłości decyzji** to realize the momentousness *l.* significance of the decision, to realize how momentous *l.* significant the decision is *l.* was.
doniosły a. -ślejszy momentous, significant; **doniosłe wydarzenia** momentous occasions *l.* occurrences; **odgrywać w czymś doniosłą rolę** to play a significant part in sth; **doniosłe osiągnięcia naukowe** monumental scientific achievements.

donkiszot *mp pl.* **-ci** *l.* **-y** *przen.* a Don Quixote.

donkiszoteria *f. Gen.* **-ii** quixotism, quixotry; knight errantry.

donna *f. żart.* donna.

donos *mi* (*na piśmie*) incriminating letter; **złożyć na kogoś donos** inform on sb; **pisać na kogoś donos do władz** denounce sb to the authorities (*for political reasons*).

donosiciel *mp* informer, informant; *pot.* stool pigeon; *sl.* squealer, fink, stoolie; *Br. sl.* grass; *Br. szkoln., sl.* sneak; *Austr. sl.* dobber(-in).

donosicielski *a.* denunciatory.

donosicielstwo *n.* 1. informing (on people); *pot.* squealing; fingering. 2. (*polityczne*) denunciation.

donosić¹ *ipf.* **-niósł -niosła -nieśli** 1. (= *dostarczać*) replenish (*coś* with sth); supply; bring (*more*). 2. (= *informować*) report; **donosić o ostatnich wydarzeniach** report on the latest developments. 3. (= *denuncjować*) inform (*na kogoś* on sb); *pot.* tell, rat, blow the whistle (*na kogoś* on sb); *sl.* finger (*na kogoś* sb); fink (*na kogoś* on sb); *Br. sl.* grass (*na kogoś* on sb). 4. (*o pocisku, strzale*) (= *dosięgać*) reach; **nie donosić do celu** (*np. o pociskach*) fall short of the target.

donosić² *pf.* **-niósł -niosła -nieśli** *zob.* **donaszać**.

donoszony *a. med.* (*o dziecku*) full-term.

donośnie *adv.* resonantly; loudly; **mówić donośnie** speak in a resonant *l.* resounding voice; **śpiewać donośnie** sing loudly.

donośność *f.* (*głosu*) resonance; (*broni*) range.

donośny *a.* (*o głosie*) resonant, resounding; (= *grzmiący*) booming; (*o dźwięku, rozmowie*) loud.

donżon *mi bud., hist.* donjon.

donżuan *mp iron. l. żart.* Don Juan; philanderer.

doń *lit.* (= *do niego*) to him.

doodbytniczo *adv. med.* rectally, per rectum; **aplikować lek doodbytniczo** apply the medicine (intra)rectally.

doodbytniczy *a. med.* rectal, intrarectal; **czopek doodbytniczy** intrarectal suppository.

dookoła *adv.* round, around; **spojrzeć dookoła** look round *l.* around; **dookoła rozciągał się step** the steppe stretched far and wide; **dookoła Wojtek** on and on and so forth. – *prep.* + *Gen.* around, round; **kwiaty rosły dookoła domu** flowers grew around the house, there were flowers growing around the house; **sprawa kręci się dookoła zaległych wypłat** it all revolves around the overdue payments.

dookreślić *pf.* (= *podać szczegóły*) particularize; (= *wyjaśnić wątpliwości*) make unequivocal, disambiguate; **dookreślić swoje stanowisko** make one's opinion *l.* stance unequivocal.

doopłucnowo *adv. med.* intrapleurally; **podawany doopłucnowo** administered intrapleurally.

doopłucnowy *a. med.* intrapleural.

dootrzewnowo *adv. med.* intraperitoneally; **podawany dootrzewnowo** administered intraperitoneally.

dootrzewnowy *a. med.* intraperitoneal; **cewnik dootrzewnowy** intraperitoneal catheter.

dopadać *ipf.* (= *schwycić*) seize, grab ((*do*) cze-

goś sth); get hold ((*do*) czegoś of sth); (= *rzucić się*) dash ((*do*) czegoś for sth); **dopaść złodzieja** get the thief; **dopadło go nieszczęście** he was beset with misfortune.

dopalacz *mi Gen.* **-a** 1. *lotn.* afterburner; (= *zwiększacz ciągu*) thrust augmenter. 2. *techn.* afterburner; **dopalacz spalin** exhaust reheater; **dopalacz katalityczny** catalytic combustor; *mot.* catalytic converter.

dopalać *ipf.*, **dopalić** *pf.* finish burning; **dopalać papierosa** finish smoking (*a cigarette*). ~ **się** *ipf.*, **dopalić się** *pf.* (*o ogniu, płomieniu*) burn out, die down; **papieros się dopala** the cigarette has almost burned down to the end, the cigarette has almost burned itself out.

dopalanie *n. lotn.* thrust augmentation.

dopasować *pf.*, **dopasowywać** *ipf.* 1. (*w pary, kolorami, rozmiarami etc.*) match. 2. (*zmieniając*) modify, adapt. 3. (*regulując*) adjust. 4. (*brakujący kawałek*) fit in.

dopasować się *pf.*, **dopasowywać się** *ipf.* adapt (o.s.); adjust; **dopasowywać się do sytuacji** adapt *l.* adjust to the situation.

dopasowanie *n.* 1. (*w pary, kolorami, rozmiarami etc.*) matching. 2. (*ze zmianą*) modifying, modification; adapting, adaptation. 3. (*z regulacją*) adjusting, adjustment. 4. (*brakującego kawałka*) fitting in. 5. (*u krawca*) fitting.

dopasowany *a.* (*o ubraniu*) close-fitting.

dopaść *pf.* **-dnę -dniesz -dnij, -dł** *zob.* **dopadać**.

dopatrywać *ipf.*, **dopatrzyć** *pf.* (= *doglądać*) see to (*czegoś* sth); **nie dopatrzyć czegoś** neglect sth, fail to take care of sth. ~ **się** *ipf.*, **dopatrzyć się** *pf.* discern, perceive; **dopatrzeć się w czymś czegoś** (*czego nie ma*) read sth into sth.

dopchać *pf. zob.* **dopychać**. ~ **się** *pf. zob.* **dopychać się**.

dopchnąć *pf.* **-ij** *zob.* **dopychać**. ~ **się** *pf. zob.* **dopychać się**.

dopełniacz *mi Gen.* **-a** 1. *gram.* genitive. 2. *biol.* complement. 3. *fot.* replenisher solution.

dopełniaczowy *a. gram.* genitival; **przydawka dopełniaczowa** genitival modifier *l.* attribute.

dopełniać *ipf.*, **dopełnić** *pf.* **-ij** 1. (= *dodawać*) refill; *pot.* top up; **dopełnić miarki** *l.* **miary** *przen.* be the last straw; (*o czyimś działaniu*) add insult to injury. 2. (= *uzupełniać*) complement; (= *być ostatnim elementem*) complete; **modny kapelusz dopełniał jej stroju** a fashionable hat completed her outfit. 3. (= *dokonywać*) fulfil; **dopełnić obowiązku** fulfil a duty; **dopełniać formalności** attend to formalities. ~ **się** *ipf.*, **dopełnić się** *pf.* **-ij** 1. (= *uzupełniać się (nawzajem)*) complement each other *l.* one another; **barwy dopełniające się** *fiz.* complementary colors; **kąty dopełniające się** *mat.* complementary angles. 2. *lit.* (*np. o przepowiedni*) fulfill itself; **dopełnił się jego los** his fate was sealed.

dopełnienie *n.* 1. *gram.* complement; **dopełnienie bliższe** direct object; **dopełnienie dalsze** indirect object. 2. (= *dodatek*) complement. 3. *mat.* (*kąta, zbioru*) complement. 4. *astron., geogr.* colatitude. 5. (= *wypełnienie*) (*obowiązku*) fulfilment.

dopełnieniowy *a. gram.* complementary; objective; **zdanie dopełnieniowe** complementary clause, object clause.

dopędzać *ipf.*, **dopędzić** *pf.* (= *doganiać*) catch up (*coś/kogoś* with sth/sb); draw level (*coś/kogoś* with sth/sb); **biegł tak szybko, że nie mogłem go dopędzić** he was running so fast that I couldn't catch up with him.

dopiąć *pf.* **-nę -niesz, -ij** *zob.* **dopinać.** **~ się** *pf. zob.* **dopinać się.**

dopić *pf.* **-ję -jesz, -ij** *zob.* **dopijać.**

dopiec *pf.* **-kę -czesz -kł, dopiekać** *ipf.* **1.** *kulin.* (= *kończyć pieczenie*) finish baking, finish roasting. **2.** (= *dokuczać*) afflict; **bieda mu dopiekła** he was afflicted by poverty; **dopiec komuś do żywego** cut sb to the quick. **~ się** *pf.*, **dopiekać się** *ipf. kulin.* be almost done (*baking*).

dopieprzyć *pf.* **1.** (= *dodać pieprzu*) add more pepper, pepper up. **2.** *wulg.* (= *pobić*) kick *l.* beat the (living) shit (*komuś* out of sb); beat the hell (*komuś* out of sb). **~ się** *pf. wulg.* (= *zacząć krytykować*) start riding (*do kogoś* sb).

dopierdolić *pf. wulg.* (= *pobić*) give a beating, fuck up; **dalej, dopierdol mu!** come on, give it to him! **~ się** *pf. wulg.* start riding (*do kogoś* sb); **nie dopierdalaj się, co?!** fuck off, will you?!

dopiero *particle* only; not... until; **wrócę dopiero po północy** I won't be back until after midnight; **dopiero co** just now, a moment ago; *Br.* only just; **dopiero teraz/niedawno/wtedy** only now/recently/then; **dopiero wtedy zrozumiałem** only then did I understand, it was only then that I understood; **nabożeństwo dopiero się zaczęło, gdy...** the service had hardly begun when...; **najgorsze dopiero będzie** the worst is yet to come; **przeczytałem dopiero połowę książki** I've only read half of the book; **przyjadę dopiero za tydzień** I'm not coming for another week; **przyjechałem dopiero wczoraj wieczorem** I only got here last night, I got here just last night; **znaleziono ją dopiero następnego dnia** she wasn't found until the following *l.* next day; **koleje znacjonalizowano dopiero po wojnie** the railways were not nationalized until after the war; **to dopiero druga** it's only two o'clock. – *int.* **a co dopiero** let alone, not to mention; **dobrze jest mieć samochód, a co dopiero mercedesa** it's great to have a car, let alone a Mercedes, it's great to have a car, not to mention a Mercedes; **a to dopiero!** goodness me!, well I never!; *Br.* blimey!

dopieścić *pf.* **-szczę -ścisz 1.** *pot.* (= *dopracować w szczegółach*) prepare meticulously, take care of every detail. **2.** (= *okazać czułość*) show a lot of affection (*usu. to a child*), fondle.

dopijać *ipf.* drink up, finish (drinking); **dopić swoją kawę** drink up one's coffee, finish one's coffee; **nie miał czasu, by dopić drinka** he had no time to finish his drink, he had no time to drink up.

dopilnować *pf.* (= *zrobienia czegoś*) attend to, see to (*czegoś* sth); (= *zająć się, zaopiekować się*) take care (*czegoś/kogoś* of sth/sb); **dopilnować dzieci** take care of the kids; **dopilnować sprawy** see to things; **dopilnować, żeby...** see to it that...

dopinać *ipf.* **1.** (= *zapiąć całkowicie*) button up, do up; **dopiąć coś na ostatni guzik** *przen.* (*w interesach*) sew sth up; (*pracę, umowę*) wrap sth up. **2.** (= *osiągać*) **dopiąć swego** get one's (own) way; **dopiąć celu** achieve *l.* attain one's goal *l.* objective. **~ się** *ipf.* button (up); **to się nie dopina** (*o odzieży*) it won't button; (*np. o walizce*) it won't close *l.* shut.

doping *mi* **1.** (= *zachęta do walki*) encouragement; **doping publiczności** cheering. **2.** (*farmakologiczny*) doping; use of illegal stimulants *l.* steroids (*in sport*); **zawodnik przyłapany na dopingu** a competitor caught using banned *l.* prohibited substances; **zdyskwalifikować za doping** disqualify for use of banned *l.* prohibited substances (*in sport*); **stosować niedozwolony doping** use banned substances (*in sport*).

dopingować *ipf.* encourage, urge on; *pot.* push, drive (*kogoś do zrobienia czegoś* sb to do sth); **dopingować okrzykami** cheer on; **dopingować ucznia do pracy** motivate a pupil to work harder; **dobry przykład dopinguje** a good example motivates; **środek dopingujący** performance enhancer, illegal stimulant *l.* steroid. **~ się** *ipf.* push o.s.; **dopingować się do lepszej pracy** push o.s. to work better; **dopingować się niedozwolonymi środkami farmakologicznymi** use banned *l.* prohibited substances, use illegal stimulants *l.* steroids.

dopisać *pf.* **-ę -esz** *zob.* **dopisywać.** **~ się** *pf. zob.* **dopisywać się.**

dopisek *mi* **-sk-** (*na marginesie*) gloss, note; (= *adnotacja*) annotation; (= *postscriptum*) postscript; **dopiski na marginesie książki** glosses *l.* notes on the margins of the book.

dopisywać *ipf.* **1.** (= *kończyć pisanie*) finish writing; **dopisać rozdział do połowy** get half-way through (writing) the chapter. **2.** (= *uzupełniać*) annotate (*coś do czegoś* sth with sth); **dopisywać uwagi na marginesie** add notes in the margin; **dopisać kilka słów do listu** add a few words to the letter; **kąt dopisany** *geom.* escribed angle. **3.** (= *być niezawodnym*) not to fail; **nie dopisać** fail (*to do sth*); **goście dopisali** guests turned up in force *l.* in droves; **zdrowie mu dopisuje** he is in good health; **jeśli pogoda dopisze** weather permitting; **pogoda nie dopisała** the weather was bad; **publiczność wcale** *l.* **zupełnie nie dopisała** the audience stayed away; **pamięć/zdrowie mu już nie dopisuje** his memory/health is beginning to fail. **~ się** *ipf.* (*np. listy*) add one's name (*do czegoś* to sth); (*listu*) add a line or two (*do czegoś* to sth).

dopłacać *ipf.*, **dopłacić** *pf.* (= *wnieść opłatę dodatkową*) pay a surcharge (*do czegoś* on sth) (*e.g. a ticket*); (= *dołożyć*) pay extra (*do czegoś* for sth); **dopłacać do wycieczki** pay extra for the trip; **dopłacać z własnej kieszeni** pay extra out of one's own pocket; **dopłacić do interesu** sink money into a business.

dopłata *f.* surcharge (*do czegoś* on sth); extra charge (*do czegoś* for sth); **dopłata do biletów pierwszej klasy** surcharge on first-class tickets; **dopłata do wycieczki** extra charge for the excursion; **wymienić coś na nowe za dopłatą** trade sth in.

dopłynąć *pf. zob.* **dopływać.**

dopływ *mi* **1.** (*gazu, prądu, wody*) supply; (*informacji, krwi*) flow; (*kapitału, surowców*) inflow, influx; **odciąć dopływ gazu** turn the gas supply off (*at the mains*); **przerwa w dopływie prądu** power cut; **stały dopływ ciepła** constant supply of heat; **zapewnić dopływ wody** ensure a flow of water; **stały dopływ gotówki** steady inflow of cash; **zadbać o dopływ informacji** arrange a good flow of information. **2.** (*rzeki*) tributary, affluent; **prawy/lewy dopływ Warty** a tributary of the Warta on the right/left bank.

dopływać *ipf.* **-am -asz** (*np. o statku*) reach (*do czegoś* sth); **dopłynąć do portu** reach the harbor *l.* port; **gaz dopływa do wszystkich domów** gas is supplied to all the houses, gas lines run to all the houses.

dopochwowo *adv. med.* vaginally, intravaginally; **stosować dopochwowo** administer (intra)vaginally.

dopochwowy *a.* vaginal, intravaginal; **dopochwowy środek antykoncepcyjny** intravaginal contraceptive; **krążek dopochwowy** diaphragm; *pot.* (Dutch) cap; **lek dopochwowy** vaginal drug *l.* medicine; **tabletka dopochwowa** vaginal suppository, pessary; **tampony dopochwowe** vaginal tampons.

dopomagać *ipf.* **dopomagać komuś** come to sb's aid, help *l.* aid sb; **dopomagać komuś dobrą radą** aid sb with good advice *l.* counsel; **dopomagać komuś w wychowaniu dzieci** help sb rear their children; **tak mi dopomóż Bóg** so help me God.

dopominać się *ipf.*, **dopomnieć się** *pf.* **-ę -isz, -ij** insist (*o coś* on (getting) sth); demand (*o coś* sth); **dopominać się o swoje prawa** demand one's rights; **dopominać się o jedzenie** demand food; **dopominać się swojej własności** demand (the return of) one's property; **dopominać się o czyjąś krzywdę** to demand that the wrong done to sb be righted.

dopomóc *pf.* **-mogę -możesz, -móż, -mógł -mogła** *zob.* **dopomagać.**

dopompować *pf.* fill with more gas (*or liquid*); **dopompuj tę oponę** pump up that tire.

doposażyć *pf.* add more equipment (*coś* to sth).

dopowiadać *ipf.* add (*coś* sth); **dopowiedzieć coś od siebie** add sth; **nie dopowiadać wszystkiego do końca** leave the rest unsaid.

dopowiedzenie *n. gram.* apposition.

dopowiedzieć *pf.* **-em -esz** *zob.* **dopowiadać.**

dopożyczać *ipf.*, **dopożyczyć** *pf.* borrow more; **dopożyć pieniędzy od znajomych** borrow (more) money from friends.

dopóki *conj.* as *l.* so long as; **dopóki nie** until; **dopóki..., dopóty...** as *l.* so long as; **poczekamy dopóki nie wróci** we'll wait until he comes *l.* gets back; **dopóki jeszcze można** while the going is good; **dopóki śmierć nas nie rozłączy** (*powiedzenie*) 'til death do us part; **dopóki żyję, (dopóty) nie pozwolę ci na sprzedaż domu** I won't let you sell the house as *l.* so long as I live, you'll sell the house over my dead body; **czekaj dopóki nie zasną** wait until they fall asleep.

dopóty *adv.* **dopóty..., aż** until; **dopóty dzban wodę nosi, dopóki się ucho nie urwie** you can only push sb so far *l.* hard.

dopracować *pf.* **1.** (= *wykończyć*) put the finishing touch(es), put a finishing touch (*coś* on *l.* to sth); **dopracować coś w szczegółach** prepare sth in detail; **dopracować szczegóły (czegoś)** tie up the loose ends (of sth). **2.** (= *dotrwać, pracując*) work as long as it is necessary; **dopracować w szkole do emerytury** teach until retirement age. **~ się** *pf.* earn (*through hard work*); **dopracować się majątku** earn a fortune through *l.* by hard work.

dopraszać się *ipf.* plead, implore, beseech; **dopraszać się czegoś** plead one's case; **dopraszam się łaski** *arch.* begging your pardon sir/madam; **nie móc się doprosić** to plead in vain.

doprawdy *particle* really; truly, honestly; **doprawdy nie wiem, jak pani pomóc** honestly, I don't know how to help you; **doprawdy nie masz mi nic do powiedzenia?** do you really have nothing to say to me?; **To dobry chłopak. – Doprawdy?** He's a good boy. – Is he, now *l.* really?

doprawiać *ipf.*, **doprawić** *pf. kulin.* (*przyprawami*) spice, season; (*dla uzyskania konkretnego smaku*) flavor; **doprawiać sałatkę świeżą bazylią** season the salad with fresh basil; **źle doprawiony sos** poorly seasoned *l.* spiced sauce. **~ się** *ipf.*, **doprawić się** *pf.* **1.** *pot.* (= *pić zbyt wiele*) be toasted; **ale się doprawił!** he's really tanked (up)! **2.** *pot.* (= *przeziębić się*) catch a (bad) cold; **nieźle się wczoraj doprawiłeś na nartach** you caught a really bad cold while skiing yesterday.

doprecyzować *pf.* particularize; **doprecyzować swoje stanowisko** particularize one's stance *l.* stand(point).

doprosić się *pf. zob.* **dopraszać się.**

doprowadzać *ipf.* **1.** (= *przyprowadzać*) take, lead; **doprowadzać dziecko do szkoły** take a child to school; **doprowadzić konia do stajni** lead the horse to the stable; **droga doprowadzi cię do skrzyżowania z autostradą** this road will lead you to a crossroads with a highway. **2.** (*siłą*) bring forcibly (along); deliver; **doprowadzić kogoś pod eskortą (do więzienia)** escort sb (to prison). **3.** (= *powodować coś*) lead (*kogoś do czegoś* (sb) to sth); push (*kogoś do czegoś* sb to sth); (*do rozstrzygnięcia, sytuacji*) bring about (*do czegoś* sth); (*do kompromisu, przymierza*) conclude (*do czegoś* sth); make, drive (*kogoś do czegoś* sb) (+ *adj.*); (*o czymś*) result (*do czegoś* in sth); **doprowadzić do równowagi** balance; **doprowadzić do wrzenia** *kulin.* bring to a boil; **doprowadzić kogoś do ostateczności** push sb to desperate extremes; **doprowadzać kogoś do rozpaczy** drive sb to despair; **doprowadzić kogoś do ruiny** lead sb to ruin, be the ruin of sb; **doprowadzić kogoś do szaleństwa** drive sb crazy *l.* mad *l.* wild, drive sb out of their mind; **doprowadzić kogoś do wściekłości** drive sb up the wall, make sb furious; **doprowadzić kogoś do zguby** be sb's undoing; **takie zachowanie może doprowadzić do trudnej sytuacji** such behavior may bring about a difficult situation. **4.** (= *dostarczać*) connect (up) (*do czegoś coś* sth to sth); **doprowadzić gaz/ wodę do budynku** connect the building to the gas/water main; **doprowadzić prąd do domu** wire the house up to the mains. **5.** (= *osiągać cel*) bring (*coś do* sth to); **doprowadzić coś do końca** bring sth to an end, bring sth to a close *l.* conclusion; **doprowadzić dom do porządku** put the house in order. ~ **się** *ipf.* work o.s. (up) (*do czegoś* into sth); **doprowadzić się do rozpaczy** work o.s. into despair; **doprowadzić się do szału** *l.* **wściekłości** work o.s. into a rage, get all worked up; **doprowadzić się do ruiny** ruin o.s., bring about one's own downfall *l.* ruin.

doprowadzenie *n.* bringing (along); **doprowadzenie podejrzanego** bringing a suspect in.

doprowadzić *pf. zob.* **doprowadzać.** ~ **się** *pf. zob.* **doprowadzać się.**

dopust *mi* (= *plaga*) scourge, bane; **dopust boży** God's wrath; calamity, adversity; **dopust losu** blow of fate; fatality.

dopuszczać *ipf.* **1.** (= *dawać przystęp*) admit, allow, permit (*coś* sth); **nie dopuszczać do czegoś** prevent sth (from happening); **nie dopuszczać, żeby ktoś coś zrobił** keep *l.* prevent sb from doing sth, preclude sb from doing sth; **nie dopuszczać nikogo do miejsca zbrodni** admit *l.* allow nobody to the scene of the crime, bar everyone from the scene of the crime; **nie dopuszczać myśli** shut out the thought; **dopuszczamy taką hipotezę** this hypothesis is being considered; **dopuszczać możliwość** allow for the possibility, contemplate the possibility; **te fakty dopuszczają tylko jedną interpretację** these *l.* the facts admit *l.* allow *l.* permit one interpretation only; **ta reguła nie dopuszcza wyjątków** this *l.* the rule allows no exceptions; **dopuścić kogoś do tajemnicy** let sb into a secret, let sb in on a secret. **2.** (= *zezwalać*) allow, permit; **nie dopuszczać do rozmów** prevent negotiations; **nie można do tego dopuścić** this cannot be allowed *l.* tolerated; **dopuścić kogoś do egzaminu** *uniw.* permit sb to take the examination; **dopuścić do głosu** *l.* **słowa** let sb speak; (= *pozwolić na wystąpienie*) give sb the floor; **dopuścić kogoś do poufałości ze sobą** take sb into one's confidence; **dopuścić kogoś do udziału w zyskach** include sb in profit-sharing; **dopuszczony do ruchu** *mot.* roadworthy. ~ **się** *ipf.* commit, perpetrate; **dopuścić się przestępstwa** commit a criminal offence; **dopuszczać się nadużyć** (*finansowych*) commit embezzlement; **dopuścić się zbrodni** commit a crime *l.* felony; **dopuścić się zdrady małżeńskiej** commit adultery.

dopuszczalność *f.* permissibility; *prawn.* admissibility; **dyskusja nad dopuszczalnością przerywania ciąży** debate on the acceptability of abortion.

dopuszczalny *a.* permissible, allowable; *prawn.* admissible; **dopuszczalna całkowita masa pojazdu** *mot.* maximum total weight authorized; **dopuszczalna prędkość** *mot.* speed limit; **dopuszczalne obciążenie** *techn.* maximum loading capacity, safe load; **dopuszczalny poziom promieniowania** *med.* permissible level of radia-

tion; **najwyższe dopuszczalne stężenie** *chem.* maximum allowable concentration, MAC.

dopuścić *pf. zob.* **dopuszczać.** ~ **się** *pf. zob.* **dopuszczać się.**

dopychać *ipf.* push to. ~ **się** *ipf.* push one's way (*do czegoś* to sth); **dopchnąć się do lady** push one's way to the counter.

dopytać *pf.*, **dopytywać** *ipf.* make inquiries, inquire; **dopytywać o czyjeś zdrowie** inquire about *l.* after sb's health; **dopytywać kogoś o szczegóły zdarzenia** question sb closely about the details of the event. ~ **się** *pf.*, **dopytywać się** *ipf.* make inquiries, inquire; **dopytywać się o czyjeś zdrowie** inquire about *l.* after sb's health; **dopytywać się o drogę do szpitala** inquire about the way to the hospital.

dorabiać *ipf.* **1.** (= *zarabiać dodatkowe pieniądze*) earn money on the side; (*zwł. na czarno*) moonlight; **dorabiać czymś** do sth as a sideline; **dorabiać lekcjami angielskiego** give English lessons on the side. **2.** (= *uzupełniać ilość, liczbę czegoś*) replenish, restock (*coś* with sth) (*newly made*); **dorobić klucz** make a copy of a key. **3.** (= *wzbogacać coś*) add later; **dorabiać legendę do postaci prezydenta** create a legend around the president. ~ **się** *ipf.* (= *zarabiać duże pieniądze*) make it good; *pot.* grow fat (*na czymś* on sth); **dorabiać się na handlu z Rosją** grow fat on trade with Russia; **dorobić się wielkiej fortuny** make a great fortune.

dorada *f. icht.* gilthead seabrim (*Sparus aurata*).

doradca *mp* advisor, counselor; (*polityka*) aide; **doradca finansowy** financial advisor; **doradca inwestycyjny** investment analyst; **doradca prawny** legal advisor *l.* counselor; **doradca ubezpieczeniowy** insurance broker; **doradca podatkowy** tax advisor *l.* consultant; **doradca przedsiębiorstwa** management consultant; **doradca wojskowy** military advisor; **doradca zawodowy** career counselor; **sztab doradców** advisory group; **gniew jest złym doradcą** one is blinded by anger.

doradczy *a.* advisory; consultative; **ciało doradcze** advisory body; **komitet doradczy** advisory *l.* consultative board *l.* committee; **członek z głosem doradczym** non-voting member.

doradzać *ipf.*, **doradzić** *pf.* advise (*na temat* on); **mądrze komuś doradzać** advise sb wisely; **doradzać zdecydowane działanie** advise *l.* counsel taking a firm action.

doradztwo *n.* consultancy, consulting; counseling; **doradztwo ekonomiczne** economic consultancy; **doradztwo finansowe** financial consultancy; **doradztwo inwestycyjne** investment consulting; **doradztwo podatkowe** tax advice *l.* consulting *l.* counseling; **doradztwo prawne** legal counseling; **doradztwo techniczne** engineering consultancy.

dorastać *ipf.* **1.** (*o wieku*) grow up; **nasze dzieci już dorastają** our children are growing up; **mam dorastające dzieci** I have children who are almost grown. **2.** *przen.* (*np. do poziomu*) measure up (*do czegoś* to sth); **on nie dorasta mi do**

pięt *przen.* he is no match for me; **on nie dorasta do tego stanowiska** this position is beyond his capabilities.

dorastanie *n.* adolescence.

doraźnie *adv.* summarily; **pomóc doraźnie** give immediate relief; **wymierzać sprawiedliwość doraźnie** mete out summary justice.

doraźny *a.* (= *najbliższy, natychmiastowy*) immediate; (= *krótkoterminowy*) short-term; (*w sytuacji zagrożenia*) emergency; *prawn.* summary; **doraźne korzyści** immediate profits; **doraźne naprawy** emergency repairs; **doraźny cel** immediate goal; **udzielić pomocy doraźnej** give emergency first aid; **leczenie doraźne** emergency treatment; **prawo doraźne** summary justice; **sąd doraźny** summary court; (= *sąd wojenny*) court martial.

doręczać *ipf.* deliver; **doręczać list/paczkę** deliver a letter/parcel; **doręczyć komuś nakaz sądowy** *prawn.* serve sb with a writ; **doręczyć komuś pozew** *prawn.* serve a summons on sb.

doręczenie *n.* delivery; *prawn.* service.

doręczyciel *mp* mailman, postman, mail carrier.

doręczycielka *f.* mailwoman, postwoman, mail carrier.

doręczyć *pf. zob.* **doręczać.**

dorobek *mi* -bk- **1.** (= *majątek*) property (and possessions); **dorobek całego życia** life's work; **wspólny dorobek** *prawn.* gained property of spouses. **2.** *przen.* (= *osiągnięcia*) achievements, accomplishments; **dorobek naukowy** scholarly *l.* scientific achievements; **dorobek artystyczny** artistic achievements; **pokaźny dorobek twórczy** considerable artistic legacy. **3.** (= *zdobywanie majątku*) acquisition of property; **oni są na dorobku** they are still getting themselves established.

dorobić *pf.* -rób *zob.* **dorabiać.** ~ **się** *pf. zob.* **dorabiać się.**

dorobkiewicz *mp Gen.pl.* -ów upstart; *lit.* parvenu, nouveau riche.

dorocznie *adv.* annually, yearly, on a yearly basis.

doroczny *a.* annual, yearly; **doroczny konkurs** annual contest; **doroczne spotkanie** annual *l.* yearly meeting; **doroczny festiwal** annual festival.

dorodny *a.* (*o chłopaku, mężczyźnie*) strapping; robust, sturdy; (*o dziewce*) buxom; (*o owocu*) lush; (*o zwierzęciu*) robust, sturdy.

dorosła *f. Gen.* -ej adult (*woman*); grown-up (*woman*).

dorosłość *f.* adulthood; (= *dojrzałość*) maturity.

dorosły *a.* -ślejszy adult; (= *dojrzały*) mature; **dorosły chłopak** grown boy; **dorosła dziewczyna** grown girl; **mieć dorosły punkt widzenia na sprawę** have an adult point of view on the matter. – *mp* adult, grown, grown-up; **dla dorosłych** adult, grown-up; (*o filmie t.*) X-rated.

dorosnąć *pf.* -snę -śniesz *zob.* **dorastać.**

dorośle *adv.* in an adult manner *l.* way; **dorośle wyglądać** look adult *l.* grown-up; **zachowywać się dorośle** behave like an adult.

dorożka *f. Gen.pl.* -ek hackney carriage, hackney, hack; *Br.* hansom (cab).

dorożkarz *mp* hackney driver, hackie; **kląć jak dorożkarz** swear like a trooper *l.* sailor.

dorość *pf.* -rosnę -rośniesz, -rośnij -rósł -rosła -rośli *zob.* **dorastać.**

dorównać *pf.*, **dorównywać** *ipf.* equal, match (*komuś w czymś* sb in sth); be in the same class *l.* league (*komuś* as sb); be a match (*komuś* for sb); **dorównywać komuś talentem/urodą** equal sb in talent/beauty; **przekład dorównuje oryginałowi** the translation matches the original, the translation does justice to the original; **on nie dorównuje swoim kolegom** he's not a match for his friends, he cannot compete with his friends.

dorsz *ma Gen.pl.* -y *l.* -ów *icht.* cod (*Gadus morhua*); **filet z dorsza** *kulin.* cod steak.

dorszowate *a. icht.* the Gadidae family.

dorwać *pf. pot.* get one's hands (*kogoś / coś* on sb/sth); (*przestępcę*) collar, nab. ~ **się** *pf.* -ę -iesz, -ij *pot.* grab (*do czegoś* sth); get hold (*do czegoś* of sth); **dorwać się do władzy** grab power; **dorwać się do pieniędzy** get *l.* lay one's hands on some money.

dorycki *a.* **1.** *sztuka* Doric; **kolumna dorycka** Doric column; **porządek dorycki** Doric order. **2.** *jęz.* Dorian, Doric.

dorysować *pf.*, **dorysowywać** *ipf.* **1.** (= *uzupełniać rysunek*) add (*by drawing*); **dorysować wąsy** draw a moustache (*e.g. on a photo / poster*). **2.** (= *kończyć rysowanie*) finish drawing.

dorywczo *adv.* sporadically; on and off; **pracować dorywczo** do odd jobs, work off and on; **pracować dorywczo jako hydraulik/murarz** be a plumber/builder part-time.

dorywczy *a.* occasional; **praca dorywcza** off-and-on work; **dorywcza pomoc** occasional assistance.

dorzecze *n. Gen.pl.* -y *hydrol.* (river) basin; (river) catchment area; **dorzecze Odry** the Oder basin.

dorzeczny *a.* sensible; **dorzeczna dziewczynka** a sensible little girl; **powiedz wreszcie coś dorzecznego** why don't you say something sensible at last?

dorzucać *ipf.*, **dorzucić** *pf.* **1.** (= *dosięgać rzutem*) throw far enough (*to reach the target*); **dorzucić kamieniem do celu** reach one's target with a stone. **2.** (= *uzupełniać*) add; **dorzucić węgla do pieca** add some coal to the stove. **3.** *pot.* (= *dodać*) throw in; **jeśli zdecyduje się Pan na ten samochód, mogę dorzucić za darmo klimatyzację** if you decide to buy this car, I'll throw in air conditioning. **4.** (= *wtrącać*) chip in (*coś* with sth). ~ **się** *ipf.* (*do zbiórki*) chip in.

dosadnie *adv.* **1.** (= *dobitnie*) pithily, forcibly, bluntly. **2.** (= *wulgarnie*) crudely.

dosadność *f.* pithiness, bluntness.

dosadny *a.* **1.** (= *skrótowy i celny*) pithy; (= *bez ogródek*) blunt, forthright; (= *mocny*) strong, forcible. **2.** (= *wulgarny*) crude; **dosadne określenie** a rude phrase; **posługiwać się dosadnym językiem** use crude language.

dosadzać *ipf.*, **dosadzić** *pf. 3 os. pl.* -dzą **1.** add by planting; **dosadzać kwiatów w ogrodzie** plant more flowers in the garden. **2.** seat (*where there's already sb sitting*); **dosadzić kogoś do stolika** seat sb at a table (*that's already occupied*).

dosalać *ipf.* **1.** *kulin.* add (more) salt (*coś* to sth); **dosolić zupę** add (a little) more salt to the soup. **2.** *pot.* (= *dopiec*) gibe (*komuś* at sb).

dosercowy *a.* intracardiac; **iniekcja dosercowa** intracardiac injection.

dosiadać *ipf.*, **dosiąść** *pf.* -siądę -siądziesz, -siądź, -siadł **1.** (*konia, osła, wielbłąda*) mount; **dosiąść swego konika** *przen.* be on one's hobbyhorse; **dosiąść Pegaza** *przen.* mount one's Pegasus. **2.** (*do autobusu, pociągu*) get on (*a bus/train*); **na następnym przystanku dosiadło jeszcze kilka osób** a few more passengers got on at the next stop. **~ się** *ipf.*, **dosiąść się** *pf.* join (*somebody seated*); **dosiąść się do czyjegoś stolika** join a company at a table, sit down at sb's table; **na następnej stacji dosiądą się nowi podróżni** more passengers will get on at the next station.

dosiedzieć *pf.* -dzę -dzisz sit through; **dosiedzieć do końca zebrania** sit through the whole meeting.

dosięgać *ipf.*, **dosięgnąć** *pf.* -ij **1.** (= *dotknąć*) reach (up) (*coś* sth); get (*coś* at sth); **dosięgnąć do najwyższej półki** get at the top shelf, reach up to the top shelf; **dosięgnąć okiem** make out in the distance, discern in the distance; **nieszczęście dosięgło i nas** we, too, were touched by misfortune; **dosięgła go moja zemsta** he suffered my revenge; **nie dosięgnąć celu** (*o strzelającym*) undershoot; **powódź nie dosięgła wioski** the flood did not reach the hamlet; **jego przerażenie dosięgło zenitu** his terror climaxed *l.* peaked. **2.** (= *zbliżyć się*) reach; **pociski dosięgły celu** the shells reached their target; **psy dosięgły lisa** the hounds got the fox.

doskakiwać *ipf.*, **doskoczyć** *pf.* **1.** (*do jakiegoś punktu*) jump (*as far as*); **doskakiwać do 7 metrów** jump as far as 7 meters. **2.** (= *dopaść*) jump (*do kogoś/czegoś* to sb/sth); **doskoczyć do kogoś z pazurami** pounce on sb, lay into sb.

doskonale *adv.* perfectly; to perfection; (= *znakomicie*) superbly; (*rozumieć, widzieć, wiedzieć t.*) perfectly well; **doskonale!** excellent!, perfect!; **doskonale leżeć** (*o ubraniu*) be a perfect fit, fit perfectly; **doskonale cię rozumiem** I know exactly what you mean; **doskonale to rozumiem** I understand it perfectly well; **bawiliśmy się doskonale** we had a fantastic *l.* great time; **czuję się doskonale** I feel great, I'm perfectly all right; **jak zwykle jesteś doskonale poinformowany** as usual you are extremely well-informed; **jedwab doskonale miękki** perfectly soft silk.

doskonalenie *n.* **1.** (= *nadawanie ostatecznego szlifu*) (*języka, techniki, umiejętności*) perfecting, perfection; (*metody, systemu, teorii*) refinement. **2.** (= *ulepszanie*) improvement; **doskonalenie zawodowe** in-service training; **kurs doskonalenia zawodowego** refresher course, in-service course.

doskonalić *ipf.* **1.** (= *nadawać ostateczny szlif*) (*język, technikę, umiejętności*) perfect; (*metodę, procedurę, system, teorię*) refine. **2.** (= *ulepszać*) improve, better. **~ się** *ipf.* improve o.s., better o.s.; **doskonalić się w czymś** perfect one's skills at *l.* in sth; **doskonalić się zawodowo** have in-service training, take a refresher course; **doskonalić się w grze na gitarze** perfect one's guitar playing.

doskonałość *f.* **1.** (= *stan idealny*) perfection; excellence; **dążyć do doskonałości** seek perfection; **osiągnąć doskonałość** achieve *l.* attain perfection. **2.** (= *ideał*) ideal; **chodząca doskonałość** perfection itself; (*o kobiecie/mężczyźnie*) Mrs./Mr. Perfect; **zaprosić same doskonałości** invite celebrities only; **uważać się za doskonałość** regard o.s. as an ideal.

doskonały *a.* -lszy **1.** (= *idealny*) perfect, ideal; **doskonała cisza** perfect *l.* complete silence; **doskonała czystość** perfect clarity *l.* purity; **mieć doskonałą pamięć** have a memory like an elephant; **liczba doskonała** *mat.* perfect number; **małżeństwo doskonałe** a perfect marriage; **zbiór doskonały** *mat.* perfect set; **zbrodnia doskonała** the perfect crime. **2.** (= *znakomity, wspaniały*) splendid, excellent, superb; *pot.* great; **w doskonałym nastroju** in an excellent mood, in high spirits; **w doskonałym stanie** in perfect condition; **doskonały wokalista** a superb vocalist; **w doskonałej formie** *sport* in excellent *l.* top form; **cieszyć się doskonałą opinią** have an excellent reputation.

doskwierać *ipf.* annoy, plague; *pot.* get to; bother; *sl.* bug; **upał mi doskwiera** this heat is getting to me.

dosł. *abbr.* lit. (= *literal, literally*).

dosłać *pf.* -ślę -ślesz, -ślij *zob.* **dosyłać**.

dosładzać *ipf.*, **dosłodzić** *pf.* -odź *l.* -ódź sweeten more; add (more) sugar (*coś* to sth); **dosładzać kawę** add more sugar to one's coffee.

dosłownie *adv.* literally; (= *słowo w słowo*) verbatim, word for word; **cytować/pamiętać coś dosłownie** quote/remember sth verbatim; **rozumieć coś dosłownie** take/understand sth literally; **byli tam dosłownie wszyscy** literally everybody was there.

dosłowność *f.* literality.

dosłowny *a.* (*o interpretacji, przekładzie, znaczeniu*) literal; (*o cytacie*) verbatim, word for word; **dosłowna interpretacja Biblii** literal interpretation *l.* reading of the Bible; **w dosłownym znaczeniu** in the literal sense, literally.

dosłuchać *pf.* listen (*until the end*). **~ się** *pf.* hear (*while listening in*).

dosłużyć się *pf.* earn (*through long service*); **dosłużyć się stopnia generała** earn the rank of general (*through faithful service*).

dosłyszalny *a.* audible; **ledwo dosłyszalny** hardly *l.* barely audible.

dosłyszeć *pf.* -ę -ysz hear (*with difficulty*); **ledwo dosłyszeć** hear with difficulty; **przepraszam, nie dosłyszałem** sorry, I didn't catch what you said.

dosmażony *adj. kulin.* well done.

dosmażyć *pf. kulin.* fry (*more l. longer*); dosmażyć naleśników fry (some) more pancakes.

dosolić *pf. imp.* -sól *zob.* dosalać.

dospać *pf.* -śpię -śpisz, -śpij *zob.* dosypiać.

dossier *n. indecl.* file, dossier; dossier artystyczne *przen.* artistic portfolio, body of work; obszerne dossier hefty dossier.

dostać *pf.* -anę -aniesz *zob.* dostawać. ~ się *pf.* -anę -aniesz *zob.* dostawać się.

dostarczać *ipf.* supply, provide (*coś komuś* sb with sth *l.* sth to sb); *form.* furnish (*coś komuś* sb with sth); *handl.* deliver, purvey; przedstawienie dostarczyło nam wielu wzruszeń we were really moved by the show; dostarczyć dowodów/przykładów/satysfakcji provide evidence/examples/satisfaction.

dostarczyciel *mp* provider, supplier (*czegoś* of sth).

dostarczyć *pf. zob.* dostarczać.

dostatecznie *adv.* sufficiently, adequately; (*po przymiotniku lub przysłówku*) enough; dostatecznie dobrze rozumieć understand well enough; kurtka jest dostatecznie długa the coat long enough; dostać dostatecznie get a C.

dostateczny *a.* sufficient, adequate; stopień dostateczny satisfactory grade, C; zasada dostatecznej racji *log.* principle of sufficient reason; estymator/warunek dostateczny *mat.* sufficient estimator/condition. – *mi szkoln.* satisfactory, C, fair; dostateczny plus C+.

dostatek *mi* -tk- affluence, prosperity; pod dostatkiem in abundance, galore; opływać w dostatki *pot.* be flush *l.* well-heeled, be in clover; żyć w dostatku live in affluence, live in the lap of luxury; mieć czegoś pod dostatkiem have an ample supply of sth.

dostatni *a.* affluent, prosperous; wieść dostatnie życie live a life of luxury; dostatni dom affluent home; dostatnia rodzina well-to-do family.

dostatnio *adv.* affluently; żyć dostatnio live in affluence.

dostawa *f.* supply, provision; *handl.* delivery; dostawy dla wojska provisions for the army; dostawy obowiązkowe *hist., ekon.* compulsory quota; ograniczyć dostawy energii elektrycznej limit the supply of energy *l.* power supply; płatny przy dostawie *handl.* payable on delivery; z dostawą *handl.* free on board.

dostawać *ipf.* -aję -ajesz, -waj 1. (= *otrzymywać*) get; dostać buzi *pot. żart.* get a kiss, get a peck (*on the cheek*); dostać nagrodę get an award; dostać pięć lat *pot.* get five years; dostać posadę *l.* pracę get a job; dostać zielone światło get the green light; dostać awans get a promotion, be promoted; dostać brawa be applauded, meet with applause; dostać kosza *przen.* be turned down; dostać mandat be fined; dostać nauczkę learn one's lesson; niech no go dostanę w swoje ręce wait till I get may hands on him. 2. (*o dolegliwościach*) get; dostać bzika *l.* kota *l.* kręćka freak out, go loopy, lose one's grip, go ballistic; dostać gorączki get a fever; dostać grypy come down with the flu; *Br.* go down with the flu; dostać kaszlu develop a cough; dostać kataru

catch a cold; dostać mdłości feel sick; dostać na głowę *pot.* go bonkers; dostać skurczu get a cramp; dostać szału go crazy, throw a fit; dostać udaru suffer a stroke; dostać zawału have a heart attack, have a coronary; dostać zawrotu głowy reel, start to feel dizzy; dostać zawrotu głowy od czegoś *przen.* get dizzy with sth; dostał wypieków his face became flushed. 3. (*o uderzeniu*) get, receive; dostawać cięgi *l.* lanie get *l.* take a licking; dostać kamieniem w głowę be *l.* get hit on the head with a stone; dostać po łapach *przen.* get a rap on the knuckles; dostać po nosie *przen.* be brought down a peg or two; dostać w skórę get a hiding; dostać za swoje get an earful; dostać mata *mat.* be check-mated. 4. (= *sięgać*) reach; dostawać ręką do najwyższej półki reach to the top shelf. 5. nie dostawać *lit.* (= *brakować*) stand in want (*czegoś* of sth). ~ się *ipf.* 1. (*o własności*) end up (*komuś* in sb's hands); dostała się mu premia he ended up with a bonus; przestępca dostał się w ręce policji the criminal is now in the hands of the police; twój list do mnie dostał się do rąk matki your letter to me came into my mother's hands; dostać się na języki get talked about. 2. (= *dostać burę*) be in for it; dostanie ci się *l.* jeszcze dostaniesz! you're in for it, you'll catch it; dostało mi się I got a dressing-down. 3. (= *docierać gdzieś*) get (*do* to); dostać się do Warszawy pociągiem get to Warsaw by train; dostać się pod koła pociągu get under the wheels of a train; dostać się do niewoli be taken captive; dostać się na studia be admitted to a university *l.* college; dostać się na medycynę get into medical school.

dostawca *mp handl.* supplier; *handl. t.* purveyor; dostawca okrętowy shipchandler.

dostawczy *a.* delivery; samochód dostawczy panel truck, delivery van.

dostawiać *ipf.*, dostawić *pf.* 1. (= *przystawić*) (*mebel*) put (*an extra bed / chair in a room*); (*wagony*) couple (*extra railway carriages on to a train*); dostawić krzesła place extra chairs (*do czegoś* at sth). 2. (= *dostarczać*) deliver. 3. (= *doprowadzić kogoś*) hand over; dostawić skazanego do więzienia transport the convict to prison. ~ się *ipf.*, dostawić się *pf. pot.* make a pass (*do kogoś* at sb).

dostawka *f. Gen.pl.* -ek (*łóżko*) extra bed; (*siedzenie*) extra seat.

dostąpić *pf. zob.* dostępować.

dostęp *mi* access (*do czegoś* to sth); uzyskać dostęp gain *l.* get *l.* win access; z dostępem do morza with access to the sea; bez dostępu do morza landlocked; bezpośredni dostęp do pamięci *komp.* direct memory access; czas dostępu *komp.* access time; natychmiastowy dostęp *komp.* immediate *l.* rapid access.

dostępność *f.* (*miejsca*) accessibility, approachability; (*człowieka*) approachability; (*w sprzedaży / zasięgu*) availability; (= *zrozumiałość; niekosztowność*) accessibility; dostępność kultury availability *l.* accessibility of culture.

dostępny *a.* (*o miejscu*) accessible, approachable; (*o człowieku*) (= *niestwarzający dystansu*) approachable; (= *w sprzedaży/zasięgu*) available; (= *łatwo zrozumiały; niekosztowny*) accessible; **dostępny bezpośrednio** *l.* **online** *komp.* online; **dostępny dla publiczności** open to the public; **dostępny dla zwiedzających** open to visitors; **dostępny bez recepty** patent (*medicine*); **kultura powinna być dostępna dla wszystkich** culture should be available *l.* accessible to everyone; **łatwo** *l.* **powszechnie dostępny** freely accessible *l.* available; **premier jest zawsze dostępny dla dziennikarzy** journalists always have full access to the PM.

dostępować *ipf.* **1.** *lit.* (= *uzyskać*) have granted (*to one*); **dostąpić łaski** *l.* **zaszczytu** be granted the honor (*czegoś* of sth). **2.** (= *zbliżać się*) come nigh (*do czegoś* sth).

dostojeństwo *n.* respectability; dignity; **poczucie własnego dostojeństwa** feeling of self-importance; **dostojeństwo urzędu** the dignity of the office.

dostojnie *adv.* stately, grandly; **wyglądać dostojnie** look dignified, look stately.

dostojnik *mp* dignitary, high official; **dostojnik państwowy/kościelny** church/state dignitary *l.* official.

dostojność *f.* grandness, stateliness.

dostojny *a.* (= *pełen godności*) dignified, stately; (= *szacowny*) distinguished, honored; **dostojny gość** distinguished *l.* honored guest.

dostosować *pf. zob.* **dostosowywać. ~ się** *pf. zob.* **dostosowywać się.**

dostosowawczy *a.* adaptation.

dostosowywać *ipf.* (*do sytuacji*) adapt (*coś do czegoś* sth to sth); adjust (*coś do czegoś* sth to sth); (*do potrzeb indywidualnych*) customize; **dostosować ofertę do wymagań rynku** adjust the offer to market requirements; **dostosować plany do zmieniającej się sytuacji** adapt one's plans to the changing circumstances. **~ się** *ipf.* (*do sytuacji, warunków*) adapt (o.s.), adjust (o.s.) (*do czegoś* to sth); accomodate (o.s.) (*do czegoś* to sth); (*do poleceń, reguł*) conform (*do czegoś* to sth); (*do koncepcji, planu*) fall in (*czegoś* with sth).

dostrajać *ipf.,* **dostroić** *pf.* **-ój 1.** (*instrument, radioodbiornik*) tune, attune. **2.** (= *dopasować*) (*styl, samopoczucie*) adjust; *przen.* tune. **3.** *techn., el.* adjust, regulate. **~ się** *ipf.,* **dostroić się** *pf.* **1.** (= *dopasować się*) adapt, adjust; **dostroić się do otoczenia** adapt *l.* adjust to one's environment. **2.** *radio* tune in.

dostrajanie *n. techn.* tuning; **dostrajanie precyzyjne** fine-tuning.

dostrzec *pf.* **-gę -żesz -gł,** **dostrzegać** *ipf.* notice, spot (*coś* sth); perceive (*coś* sth); take note (*coś* of sth); (*np. kątem oka*) catch sight, catch a glimpse (*coś* of sth); glimpse (*coś* sth); **dostrzegam błąd w twoim rozumowaniu** I can see an error in your reasoning; **on nie dostrzega różnicy** (*np. przez nieuwagę*) he fails to see the difference; (*celowo*) he disregards the difference.

dostrzegalnie *adv.* perceptibly.

dostrzegalny *a.* (*o różnicy*) noticeable, perceptible; (*o kształcie*) discernible; **ledwie dostrzegalny błąd** mistake that's hardly noticeable.

dosunąć *pf. zob.* **dosuwać.**

dosuszyć *pf.* finish drying (*coś* sth).

dosuwać *ipf.* move closer (*coś do czegoś* sth to sth); **dosunąć krzesło do stołu** move the chair closer to the table.

dosyć *adv.* **1.** (= *w sam raz*) enough (*e.g. money, problems*); **czy już dosyć?** will it be enough?; **mieć czegoś/kogoś dosyć** have had enough of sth/sb; **mieć czegoś serdecznie dosyć** be sick and tired of sth, be fed up with sth; **ale nie dosyć na tym** not only that, it does not stop at that; **nie dosyć, że się spóźnił...** not only was he late...; **dosyć powiedzieć, że...** suffice it to say that... **2.** (= *w pewnym stopniu*) quite, fairly; **ona dosyć dobrze mówi po angielsku** she speaks English fairly *l.* quite well, she speaks fairly *l.* quite good English; **był dosyć niegrzeczny dla nas** he was quite impolite to(wards) us. – *int.* **dosyć tego!** enough is enough!, that's enough!; **dosyć, ani słowa więcej!** that's enough, not another word!

dosyłać *ipf.* (= *przysłać więcej*) send more; **doślij mu pieniędzy** send him (some) more money.

dosypać *pf.* **-ę -esz** *zob.* **dosypywać.**

dosypiać *ipf.,* **dospać** *pf.* sleep (*until*); **dospać do południa** sleep until noon; **nie dosypiać** not get enough sleep.

dosypywać *ipf.* (*trochę*) add (*by pouring more*); (*do pełna*) refill (*czegoś gdzieś* sth with sth); **dosypać cukru do cukierniczki** add sugar to the sugar bowl, pour more sugar into the sugar bowl; (= *dopełnić cukierniczkę*) refill the sugar bowl.

doszczętnie *adv.* completely, utterly; **doszczętnie rozbity** (= *np. o oddziale*) totally wiped out, totally annihilated *l.* obliterated; **doszczętnie spłonąć** burn to the ground; **powódź doszczętnie zniszczyła uprawy** the flood destroyed the crops completely.

doszedł *itd. pf. zob.* **dojść.**

doszkalać *ipf.,* **doszkolić** *pf.* **-ol** *l.* **-ól** provide supplementary training (*kogoś* to sb). **~ się** *ipf.,* **doszkolić się** *pf.* receive supplementary training.

doszlusować *pf. pot.* join up, meet up (*do kogoś* with sb).

doszorować *pf.* scrub clean.

dosztukować *pf.* add (*as a makeshift appendage*); tack on (*do czegoś* to sth).

doszukać się *pf.* **1.** detect, find; **doszukałem się w twoim wypracowaniu kilku ciekawych uwag** I detected a few interesting observations in your essay; **po ich wizycie nie mogłem się doszukać kilku wartościowych drobiazgów** I couldn't find a few valuables after their visit, a few valuables were missing after their visit; **trudno się w tym doszukać sensu** it doesn't seem to make much sense. **2.** *zob.* **doszukiwać się.**

doszukiwać się *ipf.* search out; **doszukiwać się czegoś w czymś** read sth into sth; **doszukiwać się w każdej scenie erotycznych podtekstów** read erotic undertones into every scene; **doszukiwać się ukrytych znaczeń** search for hidden meanings, try to read between the lines.

doszyć *pf.* **-ję -jesz, -yj** sew on.

doścígać *ipf.,* **doścignąć** *pf.* **-ij 1.** (= *dopędzić*) catch up (*kogoś* with sb). **2.** *przen.* (= *dorównać*) equal, rival.

dość *adv.* = **dosyć**.

dośpiewać *ipf.* finish singing; **dośpiewać sobie coś** fill in the rest of sth.

dośrodkować *pf. zob.* **dośrodkowywać**.

dośrodkowanie *n. sport* centering; **celne dośrodkowanie** well-placed centering.

dośrodkowo *adv. fiz.* centripetally.

dośrodkowy *a. fiz., med.* centripetal; **siła dośrodkowa** centripetal force; **nerwy dośrodkowe** centripetal nerves.

dośrodkowywać *ipf. sport* center, middle.

doświadczać *ipf.* **1.** (= *doznawać*) experience; (*czegoś złego*) be afflicted (*czegoś* with sth); suffer (*czegoś* sth); **doświadczać czyjejś dobroci** benefit from sb's kindness; **doświadczyć uczucia wolności** experience a feeling of freedom; **doświadczać rozkoszy czegoś** experience the ecstasy of sth; **doświadczyć wiele złego od ludzi** suffer bad treatment from people. **2.** (= *poddawać próbie*) try (*severely*); **los mnie ciężko doświadczył** fate has tried me severely, fate has played a cruel trick on me.

doświadczalnie *adv.* experimentally, through experimentation; *pot.* by experiment; **sprawdzić coś doświadczalnie** verify sth through experimentation.

doświadczalny *a.* (*np. o badaniach, fizyce, stacji*) experimental; (*o kierowcy, pilocie, zwierzęciu*) test; **królik doświadczalny** *przen.* guinea pig.

doświadczenie *n.* **1.** (*życiowe*) experience; **bez doświadczenia** (*o człowieku*) without experience, inexperienced; **brak doświadczenia** lack of experience, inexperience; **doświadczenie uczy, że...** experience shows that...; **bagaż doświadczeń** experiences; **bolesne doświadczenie** trauma, a painful experience; **brak doświadczenia** inexperience; **nabyć doświadczenia** gain *l.* get experience; **wiedzieć coś z doświadczenia** know sth by *l.* from experience; *pot.* learn sth at the university of life; **zdobyć życiowe doświadczenie** acquire life experience. **2.** (*naukowe*) experiment; **doświadczenie chemiczne/fizyczne** chemical/physical experiment; **przeprowadzać doświadczenia** carry out experiments; **robić doświadczenia** make experiments; **doświadczenia na zwierzętach** tests on animals. **3.** *fil.* experience; **doświadczenie wewnętrzne** inner experience; **doświadczenie zmysłowe** *l.* **zewnętrzne** sensory *l.* outer experience.

doświadczony *a.* (*np. o nauczycielu, pilocie, prawniku*) experienced (*w zakresie czegoś* at *l.* in sth); (*o bojowniku, podróżniku, weteranie*) seasoned, veteran; **być doświadczonym podróżnikiem** be a seasoned *l.* veteran traveler, be well-*l.* widely traveled.

doświadczyć *pf. zob.* **doświadczać**.

doświetlać *ipf.*, **doświetlić** *pf. fot.* allow better *l.* more exposure.

dot. *abbr.* (= *dotyczący*) re (= *with reference to*).

dotacja *f.* (= *pokrycie niedoboru*) subsidy (*dla kogoś / czegoś* to sb/sth); (*na konkretny cel*) grant; (= *przydzielona suma*) allocation (*na coś* for sth); **dotacja z budżetu państwa** budget grant.

dotarł *itd. pf. zob.* **dotrzeć**.

dotarty *a. mot.* run-in.

dotaszczyć *pf.* drag over, haul over (*to a place*).

dotąd *adv.* **1.** (= *potąd*) so *l.* this far *l.* high; up to here; **sięgasz mi dotąd** you reach up to here; **mieć czegoś dotąd** *przen.* be fed up with sth. **2.** (= *dotychczas*) so far, up to now; *form.* hitherto, heretofore; **jak dotąd nie miałem okazji** so far I haven't had an *l.* the opportunity; **jego spojrzenie, dotąd gniewne, złagodniało** his expression, hitherto so angry, softened. – *part.* long enough; **dotąd pisał, aż skończył rozdział** he kept on writing until he finished the chapter.

dotętniczy *a. med.* intra-arterial; **wstrzykiwanie dotętnicze** intra-arterial injection.

dotkliwie *adv.* (*pobić, ukarać*) severely; (*rozczarować*) bitterly; **dotkliwie odczuwać zimno** be *l.* feel bitterly cold.

dotkliwość *f.* (*kary*) severity; (*chłodu*) bitterness.

dotkliwy *a.* (*o karze, pobiciu*) severe; (*o bólu, braku*) grievous, acute; (*o chłodzie, ciosie, rozczarowaniu*) bitter; (*o stracie, krytyce*) heavy.

dotknąć *pf. zob.* **dotykać**. **~ się** *pf. zob.* **dotykać się**.

dotknięcie *n.* touch; **pod dotknięciem** at the touch (*czegoś* of sth); **dotknięcie ziemi** (*football amerykański, rugby*) touchdown.

dotknięty *a.* **1.** (= *urażony*) hurt; aggrieved (*czymś* at sth); *pot.* sore (*czymś* about sth). **2.** (*np. chorobą*) afflicted, stricken (*czymś* with sth); **dotknięty biedą** poverty-stricken; **dotknięty kalectwem** handicapped, suffering from a handicap; **obszar dotknięty klęską żywiołową** disaster area; **obszar dotknięty powodzią** area (hard) hit by the flood.

dotlenić się *pf.* (= *wyjść na powietrze*) get some fresh air.

dotować *ipf.* subsidize.

dotowanie *n.* subsidizing, subsidization.

dotrwać *pf.* **1.** (= *przetrwać*) survive; **ten zwyczaj dotrwał do naszych czasów** the custom has survived to the present day. **2.** (= *wytrzymać*) endure, hold out; **dotrwać do końca** stick it out.

dotrzeć *pf.* **-ę -esz, -yj -tarł** *zob.* **docierać**. **~ się** *pf. zob.* **docierać się**.

dotrzymać *pf.*, **dotrzymywać** *ipf.* (= *spełnić przyrzeczenie*) keep; abide (*czegoś* by sth); **dotrzymać obietnicy/słowa** keep one's promise/word, abide by one's promise/word; **dotrzymać przyrzeczenia/tajemnicy** keep a vow/secret; **dotrzymać warunków/terminów** keep to the conditions/deadlines; **dotrzymywać komuś kroku** keep pace with sb, keep up with sb; **dotrzymać komuś towarzystwa** keep sb company; **nie dotrzymywać** fail to keep, go back on.

doturlać się *pf.* trundle over (*to a place*).

dotychczas *adv.* (= *jak dotąd*) so far, thus far; till *l.* until now, up to this time; *form.* hitherto, heretofore; (= *do niedawna*) until recently; **dotychczas nie** as yet not; **dotychczas mieszkałem w Krakowie** until recently I lived in Cracow; **do-**

tychczas niepublikowane źródło as yet unpublished source; **dotychczas wszystko przebiega zgodnie z planem** so far everything's gone according to plan.

dotychczasowy *a.* (= *były, poprzedni*) former, previous; (*o człowieku*) former, erstwhile; **jego dotychczasowe osiągnięcia artystyczne** his artistic achievements so far; **ich dotychczasowy dom był znacznie mniejszy od tego** their previous *l.* old house was considerably smaller than this one.

dotyczyć *ipf.* concern (*czegoś/kogoś* sth/sb); (= *mieć zastosowanie, wpływać*) affect (*czegoś/kogoś* sth/sb); apply (*czegoś/kogoś* to sth/sb); **to mnie nie dotyczy** it does not concern me; **to samo dotyczy...** the same applies to...; *pot.* the same goes for...; **uwagi dotyczące...** remarks concerning...; **to nas bezpośrednio nie dotyczy** this doesn't directly concern/affect us; **nie dotyczy** (*adnotacja*) not applicable, N.A.; *Br.* n/a.

dotyk *mi* touch; **w dotyku** to the touch; **to jest gładkie w dotyku** it feels smooth, it is smooth to the touch; **zmysł dotyku** sense of touch; *med.* tactus.

dotykać *ipf.* **1.** (= *zetknąć z ręką/palcem itp.*) touch (*czegoś czymś* sth with sth); (*ręką t.*) feel (*czegoś* sth); **dotknąć drażliwego tematu** touch (up)on a sensitive subject; **ludzka noga nie dotknęła tego miejsca** no human has set foot in this place before; **nawet nie dotknąłem tych pieniędzy** I didn't even touch the money; **nie dotykać!** do not touch! **2.** (= *urazić*) hurt, upset; **dotknąć kogoś do żywego** cut sb to the quick. **3.** (= *ciężko doświadczyć*) (*o chorobie, dolegliwości*) afflict; (*o podwyżce, recesji, redukcjach*) hit. **~ się** *ipf.* be touching, touch; **czego się dotknął, robił to doskonale** he excelled at whatever he did; **niczego się nie dotknę** I won't lift *l.* raise a finger.

dotykowo *adv.* tactually.

dotykowy *a.* tactual, haptic; (*o bodźcu, narządzie, wrażeniu, wrażliwości*) tactile; **receptor dotykowy** *fizj.* tactoreceptor.

douczać *ipf.* give extra lessons (*kogoś* to sb); coach (*kogoś* sb) (*czegoś* in sth). **~ się** *ipf.* get extra training (*czegoś* in sth).

doustnie *adv.* orally; **podawać doustnie** be administered orally.

doustny *a. med.* oral; **doustny środek antykoncepcyjny** oral contraceptive, the Pill; **lek doustny** oral drug.

dowalać się *ipf. pot.* make a pass (*do kogoś* at sb).

dowalić *pf. pot.* belt, punch (*komuś* sb).

dowartościować *pf.*, **dowartościowywać** *ipf.* (*coś*) show appreciation (*coś* of sth); (*kogoś*) boost (*sb's*) self-esteem. **~ się** *pf.*, **dowartościowywać się** *ipf.* build up one's self-esteem; **dowartościowywać się w pracy charytatywnej** build up one's self-esteem by charitable work.

dowcip *mi* **1.** (= *żart*) (*opowiadany*) joke; *przest.* jest; (*robiony*) practical joke, trick; **dowcip rysunkowy** cartoon; **niesmaczny dowcip** sick joke; **niewybredny dowcip** crude joke; **nie chwycił** *l.* **zrozumiał dowcipu** the joke was lost on

him; **opowiedzieć dowcip** tell a joke; **silić się na dowcipy** try to be funny; **sypać dowcipami** reel off jokes; **zrobić komuś dowcip** play a trick on sb. **2.** (= *poczucie humoru*) wit; **cięty dowcip** keen *l.* quick *l.* sharp wit; **mieć ciężki dowcip** tell crude *l.* cack-handed jokes; **ostrzyć na kimś dowcip** make sport *l.* fun of sb; **wyostrzyć komuś dowcip** sharpen sb's wit; **cały dowcip polega na tym, że...** the whole point is that...

dowcipkować *ipf.* joke, poke fun (*z czegoś/kogoś* at sth/sb).

dowcipnie *adv.* **1.** (*z humorem*) wittily, humorously. **2.** (= *zmyślnie*) ingeniously; **dowcipnie to sobie zaplanował** he planned it with ingenuity.

dowcipniś *mp Gen.pl.* **-ów** joker, prankster.

dowcipny *a.* (*o człowieku*) witty, quick- *l.* sharp-witted, humorous; (*o opowieści*) witty.

dowiadywać się *ipf.*, **dowiedzieć się** *pf.* **1.** (= *słyszeć*) find out (*o czymś* about sth) learn (*o czymś* of *l.* about sth); **dowiedziałem się, że...** I'm told that... **2.** *tylko ipf.* (= *zasięgać informacji*) inquire (*o coś* about sth) (*o kogoś* after sb).

dowierzać *ipf.* trust (*komuś* sb); **nie dowierzać** distrust, mistrust (*czemuś/komuś* sth/sb); **nie dowierzam własnym oczym** I don't *l.* can't believe my eyes.

dowieść *pf.* **-wiodę -wiedziesz -wiódł -wiodła -wiedli** *zob.* **dowodzić**.

dowieźć *pf.* **-wiozę -wieziesz -wiózł -wiozła -wieźli** *zob.* **dowozić**.

dowlec *pf.* **-wlokę -wleczesz -włokłem -wlekli** = **dotaszczyć**. **~ się** *pf.* reach (*do czegoś* sth) (*trudging*).

dowodowy *a. prawn.* evidential; **materiał dowodowy** evidence; **moc** *l.* **wartość dowodowa** force of evidence, probative value; **postępowanie dowodowe** hearing of evidence.

dowodzenie *n.* **1.** *wojsk.* command; **przejąć dowodzenie** take command (*czymś* of sth); **przekazanie dowodzenia** passage of command; **grupa/stanowisko dowodzenia** command group/post. **2.** (*swoich racji*) *log.* argument.

dowodzić *ipf.* **-ódź** **1.** (= *przekonywać*) argue (*że...* that...). **2.** (= *dawać dowody czegoś*) prove; **to niczego nie dowodzi** this doesn't prove anything; **to zostało naukowo dowiedzione** it's been scientifically proven. **3.** *tylko ipf.* (= *przewodzić komuś*) command (*czymś* sb) be in command (*czymś* of sth); **dowodzić pułkiem** command a regiment, be in command of a regiment; **kompania dowodzona przez doświadczonego oficera** a company commanded by an experienced officer.

dowolnie *adv.* (= *bez uzasadnienia*) arbitrarily; (= *przypadkowo*) randomly, at random; **dowolnie wybrany** randomly selected, selected at random.

dowolność *f.* (= *brak uzasadnienia*) arbitrariness; (= *przypadkowość*) randomness.

dowolny *a.* (= *nieuzasadniony*) arbitrary; (= *przypadkowy*) random, randomly chosen; (= *wolny*) free; **dowolna interpretacja przepisów podatkowych** arbitrary interpretation of tax regulations; **odpowiadać na pytania w dowolnej kolej-**

ności answer the questions in a random sequence; **pisać na dowolny temat** write on a topic of one's choice; **przekład dowolny** free translation; **w stylu dowolnym** *sport* freestyle.

dowozić *ipf.*, **dowieźć** *pf.* **-żę -zisz, -oź** *l.* **-óź** transport, drive; (= *dostarczać*) deliver; **dowozić autobusami dzieci do szkoły** bus children to school; **dowieźć świeże warzywa do restauracji** deliver fresh vegetables to the restaurant.

dowód *mi* **-o-** **1.** (= *okoliczność potwierdzająca*) proof, evidence; **czy masz na to dowody?** can you prove it?; **jakie masz dowody, że...** what proof do you have that..., what evidence do you have of...; **ostateczny dowód** conclusive proof; **stanowić dowód czegoś** constitute a proof of sth. **2.** (= *przejaw*) (*miłości, uznania, wdzięczności*) token; **w dowód przyjaźni** as a mark of friendship; **w dowód wdzięczności** as a token of gratitude. **3.** (= *urzędowe zaświadczenie*) receipt; *pot.* slip; **dowód nadania** proof of posting; **dowód osobisty** *l.* **tożsamości** identification, ID; (*w formie karty*) identity card, ID; **dowód rejestracyjny** *mot.* vehicle registration card; **dowód sprzedaży** sales slip, receipt; **dowód własności** *prawn.* title deed; **dowód wpłaty** voucher, receipt; **dowód wymiany pieniędzy** currency exchange slip. **4.** *log., mat.* proof; **dowód pośredni** *l.* **nie wprost** indirect proof. **5.** *prawn.* proof, evidence; **dowód (nie)przekonywający** (in)conclusive evidence; **dowód rzeczowy** demonstrative *l.* material evidence; *pot.* exhibit; **na/w dowód czegoś** as/in proof of sth; **na dowód tego,...** to prove it,...; **z braku dowodów** for lack of evidence.

dowódca *mp wojsk.* commanding officer, commander; **naczelny dowódca** commander-in-chief.

dowództwo *n.* command; **naczelne dowództwo** high command, supreme command; **dowództwo marynarki wojennej** naval command; **Dowództwo Wojsk Lotniczych i Obrony Powietrznej** Command of the Air and Air Defense Forces; **objąć dowództwo batalionu** take *l.* assume command of a battalion; **zdać dowództwo plutonu** turn over command of the platoon; **pod czyimś dowództwem** under sb's command.

doza *f. Gen.pl.* **dóz** amount (*czegoś* of sth); measure, degree (*czegoś* of sth); **z pewną dozą niepewności/nieśmiałości** with a degree of uncertainty/shyness; **z dużą dozą prawdopodobieństwa** in all probability.

dozbrajać *ipf.*, **dozbroić** *pf.* **-ję -isz** (*armię*) supply (*with more weapons*) (*coś / kogoś* sth/sb).

dozgonnie *adv.* eternally; **będę ci dozgonnie wdzięczny** I'll be eternally grateful to you.

dozgonny *a.* (*o lojalności, miłości, poświęceniu, przyjaźni*) undying; (*o wdzięczności*) eternal; **dozgonny przyjaciel** friend for life, lifelong friend.

doznać *pf. zob.* **doznawać**.

doznanie *n.* experience; (*zmysłowe*) sensation; **doznanie estetyczne** aesthetic experience; **przykre doznania** unpleasant sensations.

doznawać *ipf.* **-aję -ajesz, -waj** sustain, suffer; experience; **doznawać cierpień** face sufferings;

doznać ciężkich strat suffer *l.* sustain heavy losses; **doznać kontuzji** receive *l.* suffer *l.* sustain a minor injury; **doznawać uczucia** experience a feeling (*czegoś* of sth); **doznać zawodu** feel disappointment.

dozorca *mp* **1.** (*w budynku, domu*) janitor, caretaker. **2.** (*więzienny*) warder, jailer.

dozorczyni *f.* **1.** cleaning woman *l.* lady, woman caretaker; (*we Francji*) concierge. **2.** (*w więzieniu*) wardress, matron.

dozorować *ipf.* oversee, supervise.

dozować *ipf.* dispense, dose.

dozowanie *n.* dosage.

dozownik *mi Gen.* **-a** **1.** dispenser; **dozownik mydła** soap dispenser. **2.** (*część maszyny*) feeder.

dozór *mi* **-o-** (= *pilnowanie*) supervision; (= *obserwacja*) surveillance; (= *sprawdzanie*) inspection; (= *ludzie dozorujący*) inspectors, inspectorate; **dozór policyjny** police supervision; **więzień pod dozorem** prisoner under surveillance; **chory bez dozoru** patient without supervision; **wyższy dozór techniczny** technical inspection; **dozór pożarowy** fire inspection; **dozór sądowy** *prawn.* probation; (= *ludzie dozorujący*) custodian service; **oddać pod dozór kuratora** put on probation; **poddać pod dozór sądowy** place under probation.

dozwalać *ipf.*, **dozwolić** *pf.* **-ól** *lit.* allow, permit.

dozwolony *a.* allowed, permitted; (*prawnie*) lawful, licit; **film dozwolony b.o.** G film (*G = general audience*); *Br.* film rated (as) U (*U = universal*); **film dozwolony dla dorosłych** X-rated film; **film dozwolony dla widzów pod opieką dorosłych** R film (*R = restricted (exhibition)*); *Br.* film rated (as) PG (*PG = parental guidance*).

dozymetr *mi fiz.* dosimeter.

dozymetria *f. Gen.* **-ii** *fiz.* dosimetry.

dozymetryczny *a. fiz.* dosimetric.

doża *mp pl.* **-owie** *hist.* doge.

dożyć *pf.* **-ję -jesz, -yj** *zob.* **dożywać**.

dożylnie *adv. med.* intravenously; **odżywiać dożylnie** drip feed; **podawany dożylnie** administered intravenously.

dożylny *a. med.* intravenous, IV; **zastrzyk dożylny** intravenous injection, IV.

dożynki *pl. Gen.* **-nek** Polish harvest festival, harvest home; (*obchodzone 1 sierpnia w Anglii*) Lammas Day.

dożynkowy *a.* harvest festival; **uroczystości dożynkowe** harvest festival celebrations; **zwyczaje dożynkowe** harvest festival customs *l.* traditions; **pieśń dożynkowa** harvest home.

dożywać *ipf.* **-am -asz** live (*czegoś* to sth); **dożyć późnej starości** live to a ripe old age; **dożywać siedemdziesiątki** live to be seventy; **ona nie dożyje jutra** she will not live *l.* last through the night; **tego już nie dożyję** I won't live to see it.

dożywiać *ipf.*, **dożywić** *pf.* give extra food (*kogoś* to sb); **dożywiać zwierzęta zimą** winterfeed wild animals.

dożywocie *n.* **1.** *prawn.* life imprisonment; **skazać kogoś na dożywocie** sentence sb to life (imprisonment). **2.** *prawn.* (*umowa*) usufruct; (*renta*) (life *l.* perpetual) annuity.

dożywotni *a.* life, lifelong; **dożywotnia renta** *prawn.* life *l.* perpetual annuity; **dożywotni urząd** office held for life; **wyrok dożywotniego więzienia** life sentence.

dożywotnio *adv.* for life, in perpetuity; **piastować godność dożywotnio** hold a post for life.

dób *f. zob.* **doba.**

dóbr *n. zob.* **dobro.**

dój *mi* -o- milking; **dój mechaniczny** mechanical milking.

dójka *f. Gen.pl.* -ek **1.** (*robotnica*) dairymaid, milker. **2.** *zool.* teat. **3.** (*krowa*) milker.

dół *mi* -o- **1.** (*zagłębienie*) hole (*in the ground*); **wykopać dół** dig a hole. **2.** *techn., bud. etc.* pit; **dół gnilny** septic tank; **dół garbarski/odlewniczy/osadowy** tanning/casting/settling pit; **dół na wapno** lime pit; **dół ustępowy** cesspit; **wilczy dół** *myśl.* pitfall. **3.** *anat.* fossa; **dół pachowy** axillary fossa, axilla, armpit; **dół biodrowy/czaszkowy/pachwinowy** iliac/cranial/inguinal fossa. **4.** (= *dolna część*) (*np. schodów, stronicy, ubioru*) bottom; (*dresu, piżamy*) bottoms; (*domu*) downstairs; **na dole** at the bottom; (*w domu*) downstairs; **na dół** down (*czegoś* sth); **u dołu** at the bottom (*czegoś* of sth); **w dół** down; (= *z górki*) downhill; **w dół rzeki** downstream, downriver; **z dołu** (*np. o patrzeniu*) from below; **od góry do dołu** (*np. pomieszczenia*) from top to bottom; (*człowieka*) from head to toe; **iść w dół** (*np. o cenach, notowaniach, temperaturze*) drop, go down; **równać w dół** (*np. w hierarchii społecznej*) let o.s. be dragged down; **w górę i w dół** up and down; **wynajmować dół** (*domu*) rent (out) the downstairs; **zaokrąglać w dół** round down. **5.** *pl* (= *biedota*) lower class(es); **pochodzić z dołów** have a lowly background, have lowly origins.

dr *abbr.* Dr., dr. (= *doctor*); **dr J. Kowalski** Dr. J. Kowalski; (*nauk humanistycznych t.*) J. Kowalski, Ph.D.; (*nauk medycznych t.*) J. Kowalski, MD.

drab *mp pl.* -y *pog.* hoodlum, thug.

drabina *f.* **1.** (*do wchodzenia*) ladder; **drabina malarska** stepladder; **drabina pożarowa** fire ladder; **drabina wysuwana** extension ladder; **schodzić z drabiny** climb down the ladder; **wchodzić po drabinie** climb the ladder; **być na samym dole drabiny społecznej** be at the bottom of the social ladder; **być na najniższym stopniu drabiny społecznej** be on the bottom rung of the social ladder. **2.** *zob.* **drabinka** 1. **3.** (*u wozu*) hayrack.

drabiniasty *a.* **wóz drabiniasty** hay cart (*with racks*).

drabinka *f. Gen.pl.* -ek **1.** (*do wchodzenia*) ladder; **drabinka sznurowa** rope ladder; **drabinka szwedzka** *l.* **drabinki** *sport* wall bars; **ćwiczyć na drabinkach** exercise on the wall bars; **drabinki** (*na placu zabaw*) climbing frame. **2.** (*w stajni*) hayrack. **3.** (*haft*) ladder stitch.

drabinkowy *a.* ladder; **haft drabinkowy** ladder stitch.

dracena *f. bot.* dracaena; **dracena smocza** *l.* **właściwa** dragon tree, dragon dracaena (*Dra-*

caena draco); **dracena wonna** fragrant dracaena (*Dracaena fragrans*).

drachma *f.* **1.** (*pieniądz*) drachma. **2.** (*aptekarska jednostka masy*) dram, drachm, drachma.

draczny *a. sl.* (= *komiczny*) droll.

draga *f. techn.* **1.** (*do pogłębiania*) dredger. **2.** (*do połowów*) drag (net), scooper.

dragon *mp hist.* dragoon.

dragować *ipf. techn.* dredge.

draka *f. pot. przest.* (= *kłótnia*) fracas, ruckus, hubbub; (= *afera*) hullabaloo; **wywołać** *l.* **zrobić drakę** kick up a fuss *l.* row; **ale draka!** that's some hullabaloo!

drakoński *a.* (= *o metodach, prawach, środkach*) draconian; **wymierzyć drakońską karę** mete out a draconian punishment.

drałować *ipf. pot.* stride.

dramat *mi* **1.** *teatr* drama; **dramat antyczny/historyczny/romantyczny/współczesny** classical/historical/Romantic/contemporary drama; **dramat muzyczny** music drama; **osoby dramatu** dramatis personae. **2.** (= *nieszczęście*) tragedy; **prawdziwy dramat** a real tragedy; **dramat rodzinny** a family tragedy, tragedy in the family; **nie rób z byle czego dramatu!** don't make a drama out of nothing!, don't make a mountain out of a molehill!

dramatis personae *pl. teatr, przen.* dramatis personae.

dramatopisarstwo *n.* playwriting, playwrighting.

dramatopisarz *mp*, **dramatopisarka** *f.* playwright, dramatist.

dramaturg *mp pl.* -dzy *l.* -owie playwright, dramatist; *form.* dramaturge, dramaturgist.

dramaturgia *f. Gen.* -ii **1.** *teor.lit.* (= *twórczość dramatyczna*) dramatic works. **2.** *teor.lit.* (= *teoria dramatu*) dramatics, dramaturgy. **3.** (= *napięcie*) dramatic tension; **dramaturgia zdarzeń** dramatic development.

dramaturgiczny *a.* dramaturgic, dramaturgical.

dramatycznie *adv.* (*np. krzyknąć, wzrastać, zmieniać się*) dramatically.

dramatyczność *f.* **1.** (*utworu*) dramatic. **2.** (*sytuacji*) dramatic character *l.* nature.

dramatyczny *a.* **1.** *teatr, muz.* dramatic. **2.** (= *wstrząsający*) startling, breathtaking; dramatic; **dramatyczna sytuacja** critical situation; **dramatyczna walka** desperate fight; **dramatyczny gest** dramatic gesture; **dramatyczny widok** breathtaking sight; **dramatyczny wpływ** startling effect.

dramatyzm *mi* (*sytuacji*) dramatic character *l.* nature.

dramatyzować *ipf.* (= *wyolbrzymiać*) overdramatize; **przestań dramatyzować** stop overdramatizing everything.

drań *mp Gen.pl.* -i *l.* -ów *pot.* scumbag, scoundrel; **zimny drań** lecherous scoundrel; **ty draniu!** you bastard!

draństwo *n. pot.* villainy; **to draństwo!** dirty trick!

drapacz *mi Gen.* -a **1.** (= *wieżowiec*) **drapacz chmur** skyscraper. **2.** *roln.* (= *brona*) harrow; (=

kultywator) grubber, cultivator. **3.** *żegl.* (*kotwicz-ka*) grapnel. **4.** *bot.* **drapacz lekarski** blessed thistle (*Cnicus benedictus*).

drapaczka *f. pot.* (*do pleców*) backscratcher.

drapać *ipf.* **-pię -piesz 1.** (*paznokciami*) scratch; (*ostrym narzędziem*) scrape. **2.** *tk.* tease, teasel. **3.** *tylko ipf.* (= *podrażniać*) irritate; sting; **dym drapie mnie w gardło** the smoke is bothering me, the smoke is bothering my throat; **ten sweter mnie drapie** the sweater is itchy. **4.** (= *swędzić*) itch. ~ **się** *ipf.* **1.** scratch (o.s.); **drapać się po plecach** scratch one's back; **drapać się po głowie** scratch one's head. **2.** *pot.* clamber; **drapać się na szczyt wzgórza** clamber up the hill.

drapak *mi Gen.* **-a** *pot.* **1. dać drapaka** cut and run. **2.** *techn.* (*strug*) toothing plane.

drapanie *n.* (*np. paznokciami*) scratching; (= *swędzenie*) itching; **drapanie w gardle** a tickle in the throat.

draperia *f. Gen.* **-ii** drapery.

drapichrust *mp pl.* **-y** *pot.* scamp.

drapieżca *mp przest.* **1.** (*zwierzę*) *zob.* **drapież-nik. 2.** (*człowiek*) plunderer.

drapieżnik *ma Acc.pl.* **-i** *zool.* predator, beast of prey.

drapieżność *f.* **1.** (*zwierząt*) predatoriness. **2.** (*u ludzi*) (= *zaborczość*) rapacity, rapaciousness.

drapieżny *a.* **1.** (*o zwierzęciu*) predatory; **ptak drapieżny** bird of prey, predatory bird; **ryba drapieżna** predatory fish. **2.** (*o człowieku*) rapacious; *przen.* predatory; **drapieżne spojrzenie** rapacious look.

drapnąć *pf.* **-ij 1.** (= *uciec*) fly the coop, *Br.* do a bunk. **2.** *zob.* **drapać.** ~ **się** *pf. zob.* **drapać się.**

drapować *ipf.* drape (*coś na czymś* sth over sth) (*coś wokół czegoś* sth around sth).

drasnąć *pf.* **-snę -śniesz, -ij** (= *skaleczyć*) graze, nick; **kula drasnęła go w ramię** a bullet grazed his shoulder. ~ **się** *pf.* nick o.s.; **drasnąłem się w kolano** I grazed my knee.

drastycznie *adv.* (*np. redukować*) drastically; **wyrażać się drastycznie** use coarse language.

drastyczny *a.* (*o kroku, ograniczeniu, środku, zmianie*) drastic; (*o scenie, widoku*) shocking.

draśnięcie *n.* graze.

dratwa *f. Gen.pl.* **-tw** *l.* **-tew** cobbler's thread.

drażetka *f. Gen.pl.* **-ek** dragée.

drażliwość *f.* **1.** (= *kontrowersyjność*) sensitivity, touchiness. **2.** (= *delikatność*) sensitivity, delicacy. **3.** (= *przeczulenie*) hypersensitivity, touchiness. **4.** (= *pobudliwość*) irritability.

drażliwy *a.* **1.** (= *kontrowersyjny*) (*np. o kwestii, pytaniu, temacie*) touchy, sensitive; **drażliwy temat** *przen.* hot potato. **2.** (= *delikatny*) (*np. o misji, problemie, sferze, sytuacji*) sensitive, delicate. **3.** (= *przeczulony*) hypersensitive, touchy; **nie bądź taki drażliwy** don't be so touchy. **4.** (= *pobudliwy*) irritable, touchy.

drażnić *ipf.* **-ij 1.** (= *podrażniać*) irritate; **dym drażnił moje oczy** the smoke irritated my eyes; **środki drażniące** *med.* irritants. **2.** (= *denerwować*) irritate, irk; get on one's nerves; **drażnił nas swoją pewnością siebie** he irritated us with his self-confidence, his self-confidence irritated us; **drażnisz mnie!** you're getting on my nerves!, you're trying my patience! ~ **się** *ipf.* tease, torment (*z kimś* sb).

drąg *mi Gen.* **-a** pole, rod; **drąg tłokowy** *techn.* piston rod.

dragal *mp pot. Gen.pl.* **-i** *l.* **-ów** a hulk of a man.

drążek *mi* **-żk-** *Gen.* **-a 1.** (*pręt*) stick, rod; **drążek flagowy** *żegl.* flagstaff; **drążek kierowniczy** *mot.* steering rod; **drążek sterowy** *lotn.* control stick *l.* column, joystick. **2.** *sport* high *l.* horizontal bar.

drążkowy *a. geom.* **cyrkiel drążkowy** beam compasses, trammel.

drążyć *ipf.* **1.** (*otwór*) drill, bore. **2.** (= *analizować, dociekać*) probe (*coś* into) sth).

dredy *pl. pot.* dreadlocks.

drelich *mi* **1.** (*materiał*) denim, drill. **2.** (*ubranie*) work clothes; (*więzienny*) prison clothes, prison uniform.

dren *mi* **1.** *roln.* drain, drain pipe *l.* tile. **2.** *med.* drain, drainage tube; **założyć dren** insert a drain.

drenaż *mi Gen.pl.* **-y** *l.* **-ów 1.** *techn., med.* (*dreny; technika*) drainage. **2.** *przen.* (*wydobywanie*) drain; **drenaż mózgów** brain drain; **drenaż rynku** *ekon.* market drain.

drenażowy *a.* drainage; **rurka drenażowa** drain, tile; **roboty drenażowe** drainage works; **drenażowe poczynania rządu** *polit., ekon.* government actions to drain the market.

drenować *ipf. techn., med., przen.* drain; **drenować kieszenie podatników** drain taxpayers' pockets.

dreptać *ipf.* **-czę** *l.* **-cę -czesz** *l.* **-cesz, -cz** (*o dziecku*) toddle; (*o dorosłym*) mince; **dreptać w miejscu** mark time, make no progress; **dreptać koło swoich spraw** *przen.* take care of one's business.

dres *mi* tracksuit *l.* track suit, sweat suit; **chodzić w dresie** *l.* **w dresach** wear a tracksuit.

dressing *mi kulin.* dressing, sauce.

dreszcz *mi* shiver, shudder; **mieć dreszcze** shiver, be shivering; **przeszedł mnie dreszcz** shiver went up *l.* down my spine, sth sent chills *l.* shivers up *l.* down my spine.

dreszczowiec *mi* **-wc-** *Gen.* **-a** *film, rzad. książka l.* sztuka thriller.

dreszczyk *mi* thrill; **ta opowieść przyprawia mnie o dreszczyk** this story gives me a thrill; **opowiadanie z dreszczykiem** thrilling story, thriller.

drewienko *n. Gen.pl.* **-nek** (little) piece of wood.

drewniak *mi Gen.* **-a 1.** (*obuwie*) clog. **2.** (*budynek*) wooden building. **3.** *ent.* garden centipede (*Lithobius forficatus*).

drewniany *a.* **1.** wooden, wood; **stół drewniany** wooden table; **instrumenty drewniane** *muz.* woodwind instruments. **2.** *przen.* wooden; **drewniany stuk** clattering sound; **drewniany głos** wooden *l.* hollow voice; **drewniana twarz** stiff face; **drewniany wiersz** wooden poem, impassive poem.

drewnieć *ipf.* **-eję -ejesz 1.** lignify, harden. **2.** *przen.* stiffen.

drewno *n. Gen.pl.* **-wien 1.** (*surowiec*) wood, timber; **drewno dębowe** oak wood, oak timber, oak; **sosnowe drewno** pine timber, pine wood, pine; **budować dom z drewna** build a house of timber; **dorzucić drewien do kominka** throw more wood on the fire; **drewno prasowane** *techn.* compressed wood; **drewno użytkowe** usable timber; **mieć nogi jak z drewna** have stiff legs; **zeschnąć się na drewno** dry up, become bone dry; (=*stwardnieć*) become as hard as wood, harden; **mięso twarde jak drewno** woody meat, tough meat. **2.** (= *polano*) piece of wood, log. **3.** *bot.* xylem, wood.

drewutnia *f. Gen.pl.* **-i** *dial.* woodshed.

drezyna *f. kol.* handcar, *Br.* trolley.

drę *ipf. zob.* **drzeć.**

dręczyciel *mp,* **dręczycielka** *f.* tormentor, tormenter.

dręczyć *ipf.* torment, plague, nag; **dręczy mnie sumienie** I have a guilty conscience, I feel pangs of conscience; **za młodu był dręczony przez nauczycieli** he was tormented by his teachers as a small boy. **~ się** *ipf.* **1.** (*siebie*) be tormented, be plagued; worry; **nie dręcz się wspomnieniami** do not let yourself be plagued by memories. **2.** (*nawzajem*) opress one another, torment one another.

drętwa *f. zool.* electric ray, crampfish (*Torpedo*).

drętwieć *ipf.* **-eję -ejesz** (*o człowieku*) stiffen; (*np. o kończynach*) go *l.* grow numb; **palce drętwiały mi z zimna** my fingers went numb with cold; **drętwieć ze strachu** be paralysed *l.* petrified with fear; **drętwieć na myśl o wizycie u dentysty** be paralysed at the thought of going to a dentist.

drętwo *adv.* dully, dryly; **mówić drętwo** speak in a dull manner.

drętwota *f.* numbness.

drętwy *a.* numb; **drętwe palce** numb fingers; **drętwa mowa** hot air, empty speech; **drętwe przemówienie** dry speech.

drgać *ipf.* **1.** (= *drżeć*) tremble; **drgająca nerwowo powieka** twitching eyelid; **ani drgnął** *l.* **nawet nie drgnął** he wouldn't turn a hair; **serce drgnęło mi ze wzruszenia** I was all choked up with emotion, I felt a sudden warmth in *l.* around my heart. **2.** (*o głosie*) tremble; **mówił głosem drgającym ze wzruszenia** his voice was trembling with emotion. **3.** (*o świetle*) flicker, twinkle; **drgający blask świecy** candle flicker *l.* twinkle.

drganie *n.* **1.** (= *drżenie*) trembling; **drganie powieki** twitch, flicker. **2.** *fiz.* vibration, oscillation; **drgania harmoniczne** harmonic vibration, sinusoidal vibration; **drgania mechaniczne** mechanic vibration; **drgania okresowe** periodic vibration; **drgania elektryczne** electric oscillation; **amplituda drgań** vibration amplitude; **okres drgań** vibration period.

drgawki *pl. Gen.* **-wek** convulsions, spasms; **dostać drgawek** go into convulsions.

drgawkowy *a.* convulsive, spasmatic.

drgnąć *pf.* **-ij** *zob.* **drgać.**

driada *f. mit.* dryad.

driakiew *f.* **-kwi-** *pl.* **-e** *bot.* scabious (*Scabiosa*).

drink *mi Gen.* **-a** drink; **pójść na drinka** go for a drink; **zaproponować komuś drinka** offer sb a drink.

drobiarski *a.* poultry; **ferma drobiarska** poultry farm; **przetwórstwo drobiarskie** poultry industry, poultry processing.

drobiarstwo *n.* poultry farming.

drobiazg *mi* **1.** (= *bibelot*) knick-knack, trinket, bauble; **wartościowe drobiazgi** valuable trinkets. **2.** (= *błahostka*) trifle. **3.** (= *małe dzieci*) the little ones, the small fry.

drobiazgowo *adv.* in detail, in a detailed manner, meticulously; **drobiazgowo rozpatrywać czyjąś prośbę** consider *l.* examine sb's application minutely; **analizować coś drobiazgowo** investigate sth meticulously; **opisać coś drobiazgowo** describe sth in great detail.

drobiazgowość *f.* detailedness, meticulousness; **opowiadać coś z drobiazgowością** give a detailed account of sth.

drobiazgowy *a.* detailed; meticulous, particular; **drobiazgowa analiza** detailed analysis; **drobiazgowe badanie** detailed examination; **on jest niezwykle drobiazgowy** he is very meticulous.

drobić *ipf.* **drób 1.** (= *kruszyć*) crumble, crush. **2.** (= *dreptać*) (*o dziecku*) toddle; (*o dorosłym*) mince.

drobina *f.* speck, particle; (*np. piasku*) grain.

drobiowy *a.* poultry; (*z kurczaka*) chicken; **wędlina drobiowa** (*z kurczaka*) cured chicken meat; (*z indyka, gęsi*) cured poultry; **szynka drobiowa** (*z indyka*) turkey ham, pressed turkey; (*z kurczaka*) pressed chicken.

drobne *pl. Gen.* **-ych** (small) change, petty cash; **rozmieniać się na drobne** *przen., pot.* focus on unimportant matters, be preoccupied with trifles.

drobnica *f.* **1.** (= *kawałeczki*) small pieces *l.* fragments, slivers. **2.** *pot.* (= *drobne pieniądze*) (small) change. **3.** *handl.* smalls; general cargo, package cargo *l.* freight; **kontenery do przewozu drobnicy** general cargo containers. **4.** (*drewno*) lumber.

drobnicowiec *mi* **-wc- Gen.** **-a** *żegl.* general cargo vessel.

drobno *adv.* finely; **drobno posiekać** chop finely, mince; **kawa drobno zmielona** finely ground coffee.

drobnomieszczanin *mp* petit bourgeois.

drobnomieszczanka *f.* petit bourgeois, petit bourgeoise.

drobnomieszczański *a.* lower middle class, petit-bourgeois; **poglądy drobnomieszczańskie** petit-bourgeois views; **gust drobnomieszczański** petit-bourgeois taste.

drobnomieszczaństwo *n.* **1.** (*warstwa społeczna*) lower middle class, petite bourgeoisie. **2.** (*poglądy*) narrow-mindedness.

drobnostka *f.* **1.** (*przedmiot*) knick-knack, trinket, gew-gaw; **gustowna drobnostka** tasteful trinket. **2.** (= *nic ważnego*) trifle, bagatelle, nothing; **to doprawdy drobnostka** it's really nothing; **nie kłóćmy się o drobnostki** let's not argue over trifles; **nie przejmuj się drobnostkami** do not worry *l.* bother about trifles.

drobnoustrój *mi* **-o-** *Gen.pl.* **-ów** *biol.* microorganism, microbe; **drobnoustrój chorobotwórczy** germ, microbe.

drobnoziarnisty *a.*   fine-grained,   finely grained; **drobnoziarnisty węgiel** fine coal, slack.

drobny *a.* **1.** (= *mały*) slight, tiny; (*o kobiecie*) petite; **drobny druk** small print; **rozbić coś na drobne kawałki** break into (little) pieces, smash into atoms; **chodzić drobnymi kroczkami** toddle, take baby steps; **drobny inwentarz** poultry and small farm animals, small livestock; **mieć drobne kłopoty** have a minor *l.* petty problem; **ogłoszenia drobne** classified ads, classifieds; **analizować najdrobniejsze szczegóły** go into detail; **drobne pieniądze** (small) change; **drobna kasza** fine groats; **pieniądze na drobne wydatki** spending money, pocket money; **rozbić wazon w drobny mak** smash a vase into smithereens *l.* a million pieces; **zalać się w drobny mak** *pot.* get blind drunk; **drobna sylwetka** fragile figure. **2.** (= *podrzędny*) small, minor; **drobny inwestor giełdowy** small trader; **drobny przedsiębiorca** small entrepreneur; **drobny producent** small manufacturer *l.* producer; **drobna szlachta** *hist.* yeomanry; **drobny przemysł** small industry; **drobny handel** retail trade.

droczyć się *ipf.* banter, chaff; **droczyć się z kimś** banter with sb.

droga¹ *f. Gen.pl.* **dróg 1.** (= *trakt*) road; **główna droga** main road; **boczna droga** side road, byroad; **droga publiczna** public road; **droga dojazdowa** access road; **skrzyżowanie dróg** intersection, junction, crossroads; **szeroka/wąska droga** broad/narrow road; **wyboista/równa droga** bumpy/smooth road; **gęsta sieć dróg** extensive road network; **zły stan dróg** bad condition of the roads; **droga bita** macadam, macadamized road; **droga gruntowa** dirt road; **swoją drogą nie masz racji** while we are at it, you're wrong; **to swoją drogą** that's a different story; **być na rozstajnych drogach** be at crossroads; **rozbój na prostej drodze** barefaced robbery; **wszystkie drogi prowadzą do Rzymu** all roads lead to Rome. **2.** (= *szlak*) route, way, track; **przewozić towary drogą morską/powietrzną/lądową** transport goods by sea/air/land; **droga żelazna** *przest.* railroad; **droga startowa** *lotn.* runway; **droga hamowania** braking distance, stopping distance; **droga strategiczna** strategic route; **drogi oddechowe** *anat.* respiratory tract; **drogi żółciowe** *anat.* bile ducts; **drogi łzowe** *anat.* lacrimal ducts, lachrymal ducts; **Droga Mleczna** *astron.* Milky Way; **przekazywać wiadomości drogą radiową** transmit messages by radio; **zgodzę się na to w drodze wyjątku** I'll agree to that by way of exception; in that case I'll make an exception; **być na drodze do sławy** be on the road to fame; **moje plany wakacyjne są na dobrej drodze** my vacation *l.* holiday plans are on the right track; **pójść niewła-**

ściwą drogą go the wrong way, take the wrong path; **kpisz, czy o drogę pytasz?** *pot.* and I'm supposed to believe you don't know a thing about it?; **nie tędy droga** that's not the way to do it. **3.** (= *trasa*) way; **zmyliłem drogę** I lost my way; **nadłożyć drogi** take a roundabout way; **czy może pani wskazać mi drogę do muzeum?** can you show me the way to the museum?, which way to the museum, please?; **dlaczego zawróciłeś z raz obranej drogi?** why have turned back from the path you took?; **tędy wiodła jedyna droga ucieczki** that was the only escape (route); **dalsza droga prowadzi przez Francję i Hiszpanię do Portugalii** then you have to travel through France and Spain to Portugal; **droga wolna** *kol.* the coast is clear; **(rób, jak chcesz -) wolna droga!** do as you please; suit yourself; it's a free country; **klasztor był o jakieś dwie godziny drogi stąd** the monastery was some two hours away; **pięć minut drogi stąd piechotą** five minutes' walk from here; **pięć minut drogi stąd samochodem** five minutes' drive from here; **to jest kawał drogi stąd** that's a long way from here; **odciąć komuś drogę odwrotu** *t. przen.* cut off sb's escape route; **torować sobie drogę do sukcesu** pave one's way to success; **stawać komuś na drodze** stand in sb's way *l.* path; **schodzić komuś z drogi** get out of sb's way; **zatrzymać się w pół drogi** stop half way there; **zamknąć komuś drogę do kariery** block *l.* stand in the way of sb's career, close the door on sb's career. **4.** (= *podróż*) journey, travel, voyage; **droga powrotna** return journey; **ruszyć w drogę** depart, set off *l.* out; *pot.* hit the road; **być gotowym do drogi** be ready to set off *l.* out; **odpoczywać po długiej drodze** rest after a long journey; **jestem w drodze od trzech dni** I have been on the road for three days; **odbyć drogę pieszo** travel on foot; **Droga Krzyżowa** *rz.-kat.* the Way of the Cross, the Stations of the Cross; **droga krzyżowa** *przen.* bearing one's cross; **dziecko jest w drodze** child is on the way; **po drodze wstąp do nich** drop in on them on your way; **w drodze do domu** on the way home; **krzyżyk na drogę** good riddance (to bad rubbish); it's your funeral; it's no skin off my nose *l.* back; **szerokiej drogi!** have a safe journey *l.* trip!; **w drogę!** let's go!, move!; **z drogi!** get out of my way!; **komu w drogę, temu czas** I, we, etc. must be off; it's high time I, we, etc. went; we should be going soon *l.* getting along now; it's about time I, we, etc. left *l.* hit the road *l.* trail. **5.** (= *metoda działania*) way; **nie sądzę, żeby to była właściwa droga do pozyskania przychylności dziekana** I don't think this is the right way to get the dean's support; **osiągnął te wyniki drogą żmudnych badań** he obtained these results after painstaking research; **przekazać coś drogą służbową** communicate sth through official channels; **rozstrzygnąć spór na drodze prawnej** settle a matter by legal action; **rozstrzygnąć spór na drodze sądowej** settle a matter in court; **dochodzić swoich praw na drodze sądowej** seek justice in court; **kroczyć swoją własną drogą** take one's own road; **chodzić własnymi drogami** follow one's own path; **ona nie mo-**

że znaleźć **drogi do swojej córki** she can't get through to her own daughter; **sprowadzać kogoś na złą drogę** lead sb astray. **6.** *fiz.* path.

droga² *f. Gen.* **-giej** dear, love, honey; **ależ moja droga, nie masz racji** but my dear, you're quite wrong *l.* mistaken; **zrobię wszystko dla mojej najdroższej** I'll do anything for my love.

drogeria *f. Gen.* **-ii** drugstore.

drogi *a.* **-ższy 1.** (= *kosztowny*) expensive; *rzad.* dear; **drogi dom** expensive house; **drogie futro** expensive fur coat; **drogie miasto** expensive city; **życie w Nowym Jorku jest bardzo drogie** it is expensive to live in New York; **drogie kamienie** precious stones; **kupić coś za drogie pieniądze** pay a lot for sth, pay for sth through the nose. **2.** (= *żądający dużej zapłaty*) expensive; **drogi adwokat/lekarz** expensive lawyer/doctor. **3.** (= *kochany*) dear; **droga Ewo!** dear Eve!; **mój drogi przyjacielu!** my dear friend!; **Ewa jest drogą memu sercu przyjaciółką** Eve is my dear friend; **moja córka jest mi droższa nad życie** my daughter is dearer to me than life itself. – *mp* dear, love, honey; **mylisz się, mój drogi** you are wrong, my dear; that's what you think, my dear; **czy mojemu najdroższemu smakował obiad?** did my honey enjoy his dinner?

drogo *adv.* **-żej 1.** *dosł.* expensively, costly; *rzad.* dearly; **to dla mnie za drogo** it is too much for me, it is too expensive for me. **2.** *przen.* dearly; **drogo za to zapłacisz!** you will pay dearly for this!; **będzie cię to drogo kosztowało** you will have to pay dearly for this; **drogo sprzedał życie** he sold his life dearly.

drogocenny *a.* precious, valuable; **drogocenna biżuteria** valuable jewelry; **drogocenny obraz** valuable picture; **dziękuję, że poświęciłeś nam trochę twojego drogocennego czasu** thank you for precious time.

drogowiec *mp* **-wc-** *pl.* **-y** road construction worker.

drogowskaz *mi t. przen.* signpost; (*podający odległość*) milestone; **wyniki tych badań służą mi za drogowskaz** the results of these tests will be a milestone for me.

drogowy *a.* road; **prace drogowe** road works; **znaki drogowe** road signs; **węzeł drogowy** interchange; **kodeks drogowy** rules of the road, highway code; **mapa drogowa** road map; **pirat drogowy** road hog; **policja drogowa** highway patrol, traffic police.

drogówka *f. Gen.pl.* **-ek** *pot.* highway patrol, traffic police.

dromader *ma zool.* dromedary (*Camelus dromedarius*).

drop *ma* **-pi-** *Gen.pl.* **-ów** *orn.* great bustard (*Otis tarda*).

dropiaty *a.* spotted; **dropiaty koń** spotted horse. – *ma* spotted horse; *rzad.* spotted dog *l.* bird.

drops *mi Gen.* **-a** drop, lozenge.

drozd *ma orn.* thrush (*Turdus*).

drozdy *pl. Gen.* **-ów** *orn.* (*rodzina ptaków*) true thrushes, turdine birds (*Turdidae*).

drożdże *pl. Gen.* **-y 1.** (*do pieczenia*) yeast;

twój syn rośnie jak na drożdżach *przen.* your son is shooting up like a weed. **2.** *bot.* yeast (*Ascomycota*).

drożdżowy *a.* (= *zawierający drożdże*) yeasty; (= *zaprawiony drożdżami*) leavened, raised; **ciasto drożdżowe** leavened dough; **babka drożdżowa** leavened pound cake.

drożdżówka *f. Gen.pl.* **-ek** sweet roll, bun.

drożdżyca *f. med.* blastomycosis, cryptococcosis.

drożeć *ipf.* **-eję -ejesz** grow (in price), go up (in price), become more expensive.

drożej *adv. zob.* **drogo.**

drożność *f. zwł. med.* patency.

drożny *a. zwł. med.* patent; **drożne przewody żółciowe** patent bile ducts.

droższy *a. zob.* **drogi.**

drożyzna *f.* inflated prices, high prices.

drób *mi tylko sing.* **-obi-** poultry; **świeży drób** (*kurczak*) fresh chicken; (*indyk, gęś itd.*) fresh poultry; **wędliny z drobiu** (*z kurczaka*) cured chicken; (*z indyka, gęsi*) cured poultry; **hodowla drobiu** poultry farming.

dróżka *f. Gen.pl.* **-ek** path, lane; **wąska dróżka** narrow path.

dróżnik *mp kol.* gateman, gatekeeper (*at a railway crossing*); **budka dróżnika** gateman's lodge.

druciany *a.* wire; **siatka druciana** wire mesh; **szkło druciane** wire glass.

drucik *mi Gen.* **-a** wire, filament.

druczek *mi* **-czk- 1.** (*litery*) (small) print. **2.** (*blankiet*) (printed) form, blank.

druga *f. Gen.* **-giej** two; **jest druga po południu** it's two o'clock p.m.; **będę piętnaście po drugiej** I'll be here/there/etc. quarter past two; **kończę za piętnaście druga** I finish quarter to two; **mam pociąg o w pół do drugiej** my train leaves half past one.

drugi *a.* **1.** (*nie pierwszy, nie trzeci*) second; **to już drugi dzień wakacji** it's already the second day of vacation *l.* holidays; **za drugim razem pójdzie ci lepiej** you'll do better the second time; **dziś mamy drugiego** *l.* **drugi maja** today is May the second, today is the second of May; **wydanie drugie poprawione** second, revised edition; **druga klasa** (*w pociągu*) second class; **druga klasa** (*w szkole*) second grade; **jabłka drugiego gatunku** second-rate apples; **drugie śniadanie** lunch; **minęła godzina druga** it is past two (o'clock); **co drugi dzień** every second *l.* other day; **na drugi dzień** on the next *l.* following day; **zająć drugie miejsce** take second place, come second; **drugi od końca** next to last, penultimate; **drugi od dołu** second from the bottom, next to the bottom; **numer drugi** number two; **program drugi** channel two; **siedem do potęgi drugiej** *mat.* seven square, seven to the power two, seven to the second power; **drugi głos** *muz.* second voice; **następnym razem zbierzemy drugie tyle pieniędzy** next time we'll collect twice as much money; **po pierwsze..., po drugie...** first(ly)..., second(ly)...; **pierwszy..., drugi...** the former..., the latter...; **coś schodzi na drugi plan** sth is of secondary importance; **grać**

w **drugiej lidze** *sport* play in the second division; **literatura drugiego obiegu** underground literature; **odpowiadali jeden po drugim** they answered one after another; **drugie danie** second *l.* main course. **2.** (= *jeden z dwóch*) other; **co drugi** every other; **statek chwiał się to w jedną, to w drugą stronę** ship was swaying *l.* rocking from side to side; **słuchaj no, jeden z drugim!** *pot.* listen, every one of you!; listen, you people!; **chłopcy zgłaszali się do odpowiedzi jeden przez drugiego** all the boys wanted to answer the teacher's question at the same time; **pasażerowie wsiadali do pociągu jeden po drugim** passengers boarded the train one after another; **na drugi raz** next time. **3.** (= *inny*) another; **staram się zrozumieć i jednych, i drugich** I am trying to understand both sides *l.* parties; **jedni chcą to, inni tamto** they want this and the others that; **wiadomości z drugiej ręki** second-hand news. **4.** (= *taki sam jak*) second, another; **pan jest dla mnie drugim ojcem** you are a second father to me. **5.** (= *przeciwny*) other; **muszę się dostać stąd na drugi koniec miasta** I have to get to the other end of the city; **na drugim brzegu rzeki** on the other bank of the river; **po drugiej stronie ulicy** on the other side of the street, across the street; **druga strona medalu** the other side of the coin; **z drugiej strony...** on the other hand...

drugoklasista *mp szkoln.* second grader.

drugoligowy *a. sport* second-division; **drużyna drugoligowa** *l.* **zespół drugoligowy** second-division team.

drugoplanowy *a. film, teatr* **1.** supporting; **aktor/-ka drugoplanow-y/a** supporting actor/actress; **rola drugoplanowa** supporting part *l.* role. **2.** minor, secondary, of secondary importance; **drugoplanowe zadania do wykonania** secondary tasks.

drugoroczny *a. szkoln.* repeating a year; **uczeń drugoroczny** pupil *l.* student repeating a year.

drugorzędny *a.* minor, secondary, second-rate; **sprawa drugorzędna** issue of secondary importance, minor issue; **drugorzędna rola** supporting part, minor part; **drugorzędny polityk** second-rate politician.

druh *mp pl.* **-owie** *l.* **-y 1.** (*harcerz*) (boy) scout; **druh drużynowy** scoutmaster, scouter. **2.** *rzad.* companion, friend.

druhna *f. Gen.pl.* **-hen 1.** (*harcerka*) (girl) scout; **druhna drużynowa** troop leader, scouter. **2.** (*na ślubie*) bridesmaid; **starsza druhna** maid of honor.

druid *mp pl.* **-dzi** *l.* **-owie** *hist., rel.* druid, Druid.

druk *mi* **1.** (= *drukowanie*) printing; **przygotować do druku** prepare for printing; **książka została oddana do druku** book is in press; **książka ukazała się drukiem** book was published *l.* printed, book appeared in print; **przemówienie wyszło drukiem** speech was published *l.* printed; **publikować drukiem** print. **2.** (= *technika drukowania*) printing technique; **druk wypukły** relief printing; **druk wklęsły** gravure printing; **druk offsetowy** offset printing; **tłusty druk** bold type *l.* typeface, boldface; **druk pochyły** italics, italic type; **druk rozstrzelony** spaced type; **druk wielobarwny** multi-color print. **3.** (*blankiet*) form, blank; (*wydawnictwa*) printed matter; **proszę wypełnić ten druk** please fill out this form, *Br.* please fill in this form; **druki akcydensowe** job printing; **druki ścisłego zarachowania** numbered (blank) forms; **druk urzędowy** official form; **druki reklamowe** advertising materials, leaflets. **4.** *techn., tk.* (= *nanoszenie deseniu*) printing; **druk ręczny** manual printing; **druk sitowy** silk-screen printing; **druk natryskowy** spray printing. **5.** *techn.* (= *deseń*) print; **druk batikowy** batik (print).

drukarka *f. Gen.pl.* **-ek 1.** *komp., techn.* printer; **drukarka igłowa** dot-matrix printer; **drukarka atramentowa** ink-jet printer; **drukarka laserowa** laser printer. **2.** *tk.* cloth printing machine.

drukarnia *f. Gen.pl.* **-i** *l.* **-ń 1.** printing house; **drukarnia dziełowa** (book) printing *l.* publishing house; **drukarnia akcydensowa** job printing house. **2.** *tk.* print works.

drukarski *a.* printing, printer's, typesetting; **błąd drukarski** typographical error, misprint; *pot.* typo; **maszyna drukarska** printing press; **arkusz drukarski** printed sheet, press sheet; **forma drukarska** printing form, printing plate; **prasa drukarska** printing press; **skład drukarski** composition; **stop drukarski** printer's alloy; **chochlik drukarski** printers's devil; **oficyna drukarska** *lit., przest.* printing shop, printing house.

drukarstwo *n.* printing.

drukarz *mp* printer; **kornik drukarz** *ent.* bark beetle, engraver beetle (*Ips typographus*).

drukować *ipf.* **1.** (= *powielać*) print; **słowo drukowane** printed word; **tkanina drukowana** printed cloth. **2.** (= *publikować*) publish; **drukować doktorat w wydawnictwie naukowym** publish a Ph.D. dissertation at an academic publishing house. **~ się** *ipf.* be in print *l.* printing, be in the press; **drugie wydanie książki już się drukuje** the second edition of the book is already in print *l.* printing, the second edition of the book is already in the press.

drukowany *a.* printed; **pisać drukowanymi literami** print; **obwód drukowany** *el.* printed circuit, printed board.

drumla *f. Gen.pl.* **-i** *muz.* Jew's harp, Jews' harp.

drut *mi* **1.** (= *cienki pręt*) wire; **drut aluminiowy/miedziany** aluminum/copper wire; **zwój drutu** coil of wire; **drut kolczasty** barbed wire, barbwire; **drut elektryczny** *pot.* electric wire; **proste jak drut** *pot.* as straight as a die, as straight as a ramrod; **pogoda jak drut** *pot.* beautiful *l.* great weather; **iść za druty** *pot.* get canned; **ciągnąć** *l.* **obciągać druta** *wulg.* give a blow job, give head, suck off. **2.** (= *przewód*) wire; **drut telefoniczny** telephone wire; **drut wysokiego napięcia** high voltage wire. **3.** (*do robótek*) knitting needle; **robić sweter na drutach** knit a sweater.

drutować *ipf.* wire.

druzgocący *a.* crushing, shattering; **druzgocą-**

ca **klęska** crushing defeat; **druzgocący cios** crushing blow.

druzgot *mi geol., górn.* breccia.

druzgotać *ipf.* **-czę -czesz** *l.* **-cę -cesz, -cz** (= *miażdżyć, kruszyć*) crush; (= *rozbić na kawałki*) shatter; (= *tłuc*) smash.

drużba *mp pl.* **-owie** best man, groomsman; **służba nie drużba** all work and no play; you're here to work not to goof off; (*zwrócenie komuś uwagi*) it's no picnic *l.* weenie roast.

drużbować *ipf.* be sb's best man.

drużyna *f.* 1. (*zespół ludzi*) team, squad; **drużyna piłkarska** football team *l.* squad; **drużyna koszykarek** (women's) basketball team; **drużyna harcerska** scouting troop; **drużyna ratownicza** search and rescue team. 2. *wojsk.* squad; **drużyna piechoty** infantry squad; **drużyna przyboczna** *hist.* household troops.

drużynowa, druhna drużynowa *f. Gen.* **-ej** troop leader, scouter.

drużynowy *a. zwł. sport* team; **klasyfikacja drużynowa** team ranking, team standings; **zwycięstwo drużynowe** team victory. – *mp* scoutmaster, scouter.

drwa *pl. Gen.* **drew** *lit.* firewood; **dorzucić drew do ognia** throw some more wood on the fire; **gdzie drwa rąbią, tam wióry lecą** you can't make an omelette without breaking eggs.

drwal *mp Gen.* **-i** *l.* **-ów** woodcutter, lumberjack, logger.

drwiąco *adv.* derisively, sneeringly, scoffingly; **uśmiechać się drwiąco** smile derisively.

drwić *ipf.* **-ij** deride, sneer, jeer, mock; **drwić z prostaka** deride a simpleton; **drwić sobie z niebezpieczeństwa** scoff at danger; **drwiąca mina** smirk; **drwiący uśmiech** derisive smile.

drwina *f.* derision, mockery, jeer; **być przedmiotem drwin** be an object of derision.

drwinka *f. Gen.pl.* **-ek** derision, mockery, jeer.

dryblas *mp pl.* **-y** *żart.* strapper, bean pole.

drybling *mi sport* dribble.

dryblować *ipf. sport* dribble.

dryf *mi* 1. *żegl.* drift, driftage; **postawić statek w dryf** lay a ship to drift; **lec w dryf** be laid to drift; **stanąć w dryf** lay to drift, heave to drift. 2. *geol.* drift; **dryf kontynentalny** continental drift.

dryfkotwa *f. Gen.pl.* **-tew** *żegl.* sea anchor, drogue.

dryfomierz *mi Gen.* **-a** *żegl.* drift meter.

dryfować *ipf. żegl.* drift; **sieć dryfująca** *ryb.* drift net.

dryg *mi* knack; **mieć dryg do gotowania** have a knack for cooking.

dryl *mi* drill, discipline, training; **wprowadzić dryl wojskowy** introduce military discipline.

drylować *ipf.* 1. *kulin.* pit, stone. 2. *roln.* drill.

drylownica *f. kulin.* pit-remover, seeder.

drynda *f. przest., dial.* (= *dorożka*) hack(ney), cab.

drzazga *f. Gen.pl.* **-zg** *l.* **-zeg** splinter, sliver, chip; **weszła mi drzazga (w palec)** I've got a splinter (in my finger); **rozbić coś w drzazgi** smash sth to a milion pieces *l.* smithereens.

drzeć *ipf.* **drę drzesz, -yj darł** 1. (*na kawałki*) tear, rend, rip; **drzeć papier** tear paper up; **drzeć mordę** *pot.* scream bloody murder; **nie drzyj tak mordy** *wulg.* shut the fuck up. 2. (= *obdzierać*) strip; **drzeć pierze** pluck down (*from a goose*); **pasy bym z niego darł!** I'd flay him alive! 3. (*tarmosić*) pull; **drzeć z kimś koty** be on the outs with sb. 4. (= *zużywać*) wear out; **drzeć buty** wear one's shoes out. ~ **się** *ipf.* 1. (= *być rozdzieranym*) tear, rip; **gęba się komuś drze** *pot.* sb is yelling. 2. (= *niszczyć się*) wear out; **buty mi się już drą** my shoes are already worn out. 3. (= *szarpać się*) pull (*each other's hair, sleeves, etc.*); **ciągle się drą jak pies z kotem** they always fight tooth and nail, they're always at each other's throat. 4. *pot.* (= *wrzeszczeć*) yell, holler, bawl; **drzeć się w niebogłosy** scream blue murder; **darł się na całe gardło** he was hollering, he was screaming to the top of his lungs; **nie drzyj się tak!** shut up, will you?

drzemać *ipf.* **-mię -miesz** 1. nap, doze, catnap. 2. *przen.* lurk, lie *l.* be dormant; **drzemią w tobie wielkie zdolności** you have great hidden talent.

drzemiący *a.* 1. (= *śpiący*) napping, dozing. 2. (= *ukryty*) dormant; **wulkan drzemiący** *geogr., geol.* dormant volcano.

drzemka *f. Gen.pl.* **-ek** nap, catnap; **uciąć sobie drzemkę** have *l.* take a nap, catch some z's.

drzewce *n.* 1. (*drążek*) (*flagi, sztandaru*) staff, pole; (*włóczni*) shaft; **drzewce sztandaru** flagstaff, flagpole. 2. *żegl.* spar.

drzewiasty *a.* (= *przypominający drzewo*) woody, ligneous; (= *mający cechy drzewa*) arborescent, arboreous; **rośliny drzewiaste** *bot.* ligneous plants.

drzewiej *adv. arch.* whilom.

drzewko *n. Gen.pl.* **-wek** 1. (= *małe drzewo*) small tree; (= *młode drzewo*) sapling; **boże drzewko** *bot.* southernwood (*Artemisia arbotanum*). 2. *dial.* (= *choinka*) Christmas tree.

drzewny *a.* 1. (= *dotyczący drzewa*) tree; **słoje drzewne** tree rings. 2. (= *dotyczący drewna*) wood; **przemysł drzewny** wood industry; **węgiel drzewny** charcoal; **wełna drzewna** wood wool; **olej drzewny** Chinese wood oil, tung oil.

drzewo *n.* 1. (*roślina*) tree; **drzewa liściaste/iglaste** deciduous/coniferous trees; **drzewa owocowe** fruit trees; **drzewo oliwkowe** common olive tree (*Olea europaea*); **drzewo figowe** fig tree, common fig (*Ficus carica l. communis*); **drzewo sandałowe** sandalwood (*Santalum album*); **drzewo sagowe** sago palm (*Metroxylon sagu*); **drzewo chlebowe** bread tree (*Artocarpus integrifolia*); **drzewo hebanowe** ebony (*Diospyros*); **drzewo kakaowe** cacao (*Theobroma cacao*); **drzewo kamforowe** camphor tree (*Cinnamomum camphora*); **korona drzewa** crown, tree top; **szum drzew** rustle of tree leaves; **aleja wysadzana drzewami** tree-lined alley *l.* lane; **jabłka prosto z drzewa** freshly picked apples; **ściąć drzewo** fell a tree, cut a tree down; **drzewo genealogiczne** family tree, genealogical tree; **drzewo wiadomości dobrego i złego** *Bibl.* tree of knowledge of good and evil; **drzewo oskrzelowe** *anat.*

bronchial tree; **im dalej w las, tym więcej drzew** the farther in, the deeper; **na pochyłe drzewo i kozy skaczą** it's no great feat to kick a fellow when he's down. **2.** (= *drewno*) wood, timber, lumber; **trumna z drzewa dębowego** oak coffin; **boazeria z drzewa sosnowego** pine panelling; **drzewo na opał** firewood; **szlachetne drzewo** hardwood.

drzeworyt *mi* (*technika l. odbitka*) wood engraving.

drzeworytnictwo *n.* wood engraving.

drzeworytnik *mp* wood engraver.

drzewostan *mi leśn.* stand, sylva *l.* silva.

drzewoznawca *mp* dendrologist.

drzewoznawczy *a.* dendrological, dendrologic.

drzewoznawstwo *n.* dendrology.

drzewożerny *a.* dendrophagous.

drzwi *pl. Gen.* -i door; **drzwi wejściowe** front door, main door; **drzwi kuchenne** back door, kitchen door; **drzwi na taras** terrace door, French windows; **drzwi otwarte na oścież** wide-open door; **pukać do drzwi** knock at the door; **dobijać się do drzwi** bang at the door, pound on the door; **zamknąć drzwi** close the door; **podsłuchiwać pod drzwiami** eavesdrop at a door; **stanąć w drzwiach** stand in the doorway *l.* on the threshold; **wyrzucić kogoś za drzwi** throw sb out; **wskazać** *l.* **pokazać komuś drzwi** show sb the door; **dom, w którym drzwi się nie zamykają** open house; **zatrzasnąć komuś drzwi przed nosem** *dosł.* slam the door in sb's face; *przen.* turn sb from one's door; **drzwi stoją przed kimś otworem** door is open to sb; **pchać się drzwiami i oknami** crowd; **wyważać otwarte drzwi** state *l.* prove the obvious; **za zamkniętymi drzwiami** behind closed doors; **rozprawa przy drzwiach zamkniętych** in camera trial; **obrady przy drzwiach otwartych** open session; **polityka otwartych drzwi** open door policy; **chodzić od drzwi do drzwi** go door-to-door, beg; **za drzwi!** out!; **nie kładź palca między drzwi** it's none of your business; don't interfere in someone else's business; **drzwi jednoskrzydłowe** single door; **drzwi dwuskrzydłowe** double doors; **drzwi obrotowe** revolving door; **drzwi rozsuwane** sliding door; **drzwi wahadłowe** swing door; **dwoje/troje drzwi** two/three doors.

drzwiczki *pl. Gen.* -czek door, small door; **trzasnąć drzwiczkami** slam the door; **drzwiczki szafy kuchennej** kitchen cupboard door.

drzwiowy *a.* door; **otwór drzwiowy** *bud.* doorway.

drżączka *f. Gen.pl.* -ek **1.** (= *dreszcze, t. med.*) shivers, tremors, trembling. **2.** *bot.* quaking grass (*Briza*).

drżeć *ipf.* -ę -ysz, -yj **1.** (= *trząść się*) tremble, shake, shiver; (*gwałtownie*) shudder; **drżeć z zimna** tremble with cold; **drżeć jak galareta** *l.* osika shake all over; **drżące ręce** trembling hands; **drżący głos** trembling voice. **2.** (= *bać się*) fear, shudder, tremble; **drżeć o zdrowie syna** fear for one's son's health; **drżeć na myśl o egzaminie** fear an exam, shudder to think *l.* at the thought of an exam.

drżenie *n.* trembling, shuddering, shaking;

(*robić coś*) **z drżeniem serca** (do sth) with a trembling heart; **opanować drżenie rąk** contain the tremble of hands.

dual *mi* **1.** (*w szachach*) double checkmate. **2.** *gram., rzad.* = **dualis**.

dualis *mi indecl. gram.* dual (number).

dualista *mp fil.* dualist.

dualistyczny *a. fil.* dualist; **światopogląd dualistyczny** dualist outlook; **ustrój dualistyczny** dualist political system.

dualizm *mi fil., rel.* dualism; **dualizm ontologiczny** ontological dualism; **dualizm teologiczny** theological dualism; **dualizm falowo-korpuskularny** *fiz.* wave-particle duality.

dualny *a. gram.* dual; **forma dualna** dual form.

dubbing *mi film* dub.

dubbingować *ipf. film* dub; **film dubbingowany** dubbed movie.

dubbingowy *a. film* dub, dubbing, dubbed; **film dubbingowy** dubbed movie.

dubeltowy *a. przest.* double; **dubeltowe piwo** (double) strong beer.

dubeltówka *f. Gen.pl.* -ek double-barreled (shot)gun; **całować się z dubeltówki** kiss with a smack on both cheeks.

dubia *pl. Gen.* -ów dubious things, materials *l.* things of dubious origin.

dubler *mp*, **dublerka** *f. teatr, film* understudy, double.

dublet *mi* **1.** (= *podwójne egzemplarze*) double, doublet; **dublet słowotwórczy** *gram.* doublet; **dublet widmowy** *fiz.* doublet. **2.** (*kamień jubilerski*) doublet. **3.** (*w bilardzie*) double. **4.** *myśl.* double.

dublon *mi hist.* (*moneta*) doubloon.

dublować *ipf.* **1.** double, duplicate. **2.** (*rolę*) understudy, double. **3.** (*w grze w karty*) double. **4.** *sport* lap.

duby *pl. Gen.* -ów **duby smalone** malarkey, nonsense; **prawić duby smalone** talk nonsense.

duch *ma* **1.** (= *wnętrze człowieka*) spirit, soul, mind; **okazać hart ducha** demonstrate *l.* display *l.* show fortitude; **spokój ducha** ease *l.* peace of mind; **w skrytości ducha** secretly, deep inside one's mind *l.* heart; **w duchu** inwardly; **w głębi ducha** secretly, inwardly; **jesteś jeszcze młody duchem** you're still young at heart, your mind is still young; **teraz mi raźniej na duchu** I am cheered *l.* heartened now; **przebywać gdzieś (daleko) duchem** be absent-minded, be engrossed in one's thoughts, seem to be far away. **2.** *fil., rel.* soul, spirit, ghost; **zły duch** (= *diabeł*) devil, Satan; (= *osoba*) jinx, evil spirit *l.* genius; **dobry duch** good spirit; **duchy opiekuńcze** attendant spirits; **oddać Bogu ducha** give up the ghost; **Bogu ducha winien** as innocent as a (new-born) babe; **wszelki duch Pana Boga chwali!** God! You scared the living daylights out of me!; (God) bless my soul!; **where the devil did you come from?!**; **nie było tam żywego ducha** there wasn't a (living) soul there; **wyzionąć ducha** give up the ghost; **upaść bez ducha** fall lifeless, drop breathless; **ledwie się duch w nim kołacze** he is on his last legs; **Duch Święty** *rel.* the Holy Spirit *l.*

Ghost. **3.** (= *zjawa*) ghost, spirit; **wywoływać duchy** conjure (up) spirits, evoke spirits; **zniknąć jak duch** disappear like a ghost. **4.** (= *usposobienie*) spirit; **człowiek wielkiego ducha** big-hearted person; **niespokojny duch** restless spirit; **buntowniczy duch** rebellious spirit. **5.** (= *nastrój*) spirit, atmosphere, climate; **spotkanie odbyło się w duchu pojednania** meeting was held in a spirit *l.* an atmosphere of reconciliation; **duch czasów** spirit of the times; **iść z duchem czasu** keep up with the times; **duch narodowy** national spirit. **6.** (= *zapał*) spirit; **brak wam ducha!** you're lacking spirit!; **dodać komuś ducha walki** hearten sb, get up sb's courage; **podnieść kogoś na duchu** cheer sb up, raise *l.* lift sb's spirits; **nabrać ducha** muster courage, be heartened; **odebrać komuś ducha** break sb's spirit, take the heart out of sb; **nowy duch wstąpił we mnie** I recovered my courage, I recovered my will to act; **nie traćcie ducha** don't lose heart; **upadać na duchu** lose heart.

duchota *f.* stuffiness, stuffy air.

duchowieństwo *n. rel.* clergy, priesthood.

duchowny *a. rel.* clerical, ecclesiastical; **seminarium duchowne** seminary; **ojciec duchowny** father confessor, confessor; **osoba duchowna** minister, clergyman. – *mp* minister, clergyman.

duchowo *adv.* spiritually; **rozwijać się duchowo** develop spiritually.

duchowość *f.* spirituality.

duchowy *a.* spiritual; **dbać o czyjś/swój rozwój duchowy** not neglect one's own/sb's spiritual *l.* personal growth; **kultura duchowa Polaków** Polish spiritual heritage; **dziedzictwo duchowe narodu** nation's spiritual heritage; **odczuwać więź duchową z kimś** commune with sb; **życie duchowe** spiritual life; **duchowy przywódca** spiritual leader; **pociecha duchowa** spiritual comfort; **pokarm duchowy** food for thought.

duda *f. pl.* dudy *Gen.pl.* dud *muz.* **1.** (*instrument ludowy*) bagpipe(s); **dudy w miech** *pot.* give up. **2.** (*organów*) pipe. – *mp pl.* **-owie** (bag)piper.

dudek *ma* **-dk-** *pl.* **-i** *orn.* hoopoe (*Upupa epops*); **wystrychnąć kogoś na dudka** *przen.* make a fool of sb.

dudka *f. Gen.pl.* **-ek** *muz.* **1.** pipe; **dąć w czyjąś dudkę** *przen.* chime in with sb. **2.** *orn.* quill, calamus.

dudlić *ipf. pot.* (= *pić łapczywie*) swill.

dudnić *ipf.* **-ij 1.** rumble (*o dźwięku*); **koła pociągu dudnią** train wheels are rumbling. **2.** *fiz.* rumble, beat.

dudu *n. indecl.* **ani dudu** (= *ani słowa*) not a word; (= *nic nie słychać*) can't hear anything.

dudziarz *mp muz.* (bag)piper.

duet *mi* **1.** *muz.* duet, duo. **2.** (= *para*) couple.

dujker *ma zool.* duiker, duyker (*Cephalophus*).

dukać *ipf. pot.* falter, stutter (*while reading*).

dukat *mi Gen.* **-a** *hist.* ducat.

dukt *mi* **1.** (*w lesie*) vista. **2.** *druk.* type duct.

dulka *f. Gen.pl.* **-ek** *żegl.* oarlock.

dulszczyzna *f.* Grundyism, priggishness.

duma¹ *f.* **1.** (= *godność osobista*) pride,

self-respect, self-esteem; **urażona duma** hurt pride; **wbijać kogoś w dumę** puff sb up, make sb proud of sth; **to zwycięstwo napawa mnie dumą** this victory makes me (really) proud; **Polacy mają poczucie dumy narodowej** Poles have a sense of national pride; **zapomnieć o swojej dumie** pocket one's pride, swallow one's pride. **2.** (= *chluba, ozdoba*) pride, boast; **czyjaś duma** sb's pride and joy; **syn jest moją dumą** my son is my pride and joy; **patrzeć na swoje dzieci z dumą** look at one's children with pride; **ten most to duma naszego miasta** this bridge is the pride of our city.

duma² *f. teor.lit.* elegy; **recytować dumę romantyczną** recite a Romantic elegy.

duma³ *f. polit.* **Duma Państwowa** State Duma (*parlament rosyjski*).

dumać *ipf.* muse (*nad czymś* about *l.* over *l.* upon sth); ponder (*nad czymś* on *l.* over *l.* upon sth); meditate (*nad czymś* on *l.* upon sth); **dumać nad przeszłością** muse about the past; **dumać nad swym losem** muse over one's own fate.

dum-dum *n. indecl.* dumdum; **pocisk dum-dum** dumdum bullet.

dumka *f. Gen.pl.* **-ek** *muz.* dumka.

dumnie *adv.* **1.** (= *z godnością*) proudly; **dumnie wypinać pierś** proudly stick out one's chest; **dumnie unieść czoło** hold one's head high. **2.** *rzad.* (= *zarozumiale*) proudly, conceitedly, vainly.

dumny *a.* **1.** (= *pełen godności*) proud; **jestem dumny z mojego syna** I am proud of my son. **2.** (= *zarozumiały*) proud, conceited, vain; **dumny jak paw** (as) proud as a peacock; **dumne spojrzenie** proud glance *l.* look.

dumping *mi ekon.* dumping; **uprawiać dumping** dump.

dumpingowy *a. ekon.* dumping-level; **cena dumpingowa** dumping-level price.

Dunaj *mi geogr.* the Danube.

dunder *mi tylko sing.* **-dr-** *Gen.* **-a** damn; **niech go dunder świśnie!** damn him!

Dunka *f. Gen. pl.* **-ek** Dane.

Dunkierka *f. geogr.* Dunkirk.

Duńczyk *mp* Dane.

duński *a.* Danish.

duo *n. indecl.* **1.** *muz.* duet. **2.** (= *para*) duo, couple.

dupa *f. wulg.* **1.** (= *pośladki*) butt, ass; **(jest) do dupy** (it's) crappy *l.* shitty; **do dupy z takim podejściem** to hell with that kind of attitude; **dać dupy** get screwed; **dać po dupie** give sb a whipping; **dostać po dupie** get (one's ass) whipped; **dać komuś w dupę** give sb an ass whipping; **możesz mnie w dupę pocałować** you can kiss my ass; **możesz sobie te pieniądze w dupę wsadzić** you can shove the money up your ass; **mam cię w dupie** I don't give a shit *l.* fuck about you; **jak cię złapię, to nogi ci z dupy powyrywam** when I catch you, I'll kick your ass inside out; **podnieś** *l.* **rusz dupę** move your ass, get your ass moving *l.* in gear; **siedź na dupie** sit on your ass; **włazić komuś w dupę** kiss sb's ass; **pocałuj mnie w dupę** kiss my ass; **bierz dupę w troki!** get lost!;

ty w dupę jebany! you fucking asshole!, you motherfucker!; **dobiorę ci się do dupy** I'll get your ass; **chodzić z gołą dupą** walk around bare-assed; (= *nie mieć pieniędzy*) not have a pot to piss in; **tam, gdzie psy dupami szczekają** where the sun never shines; **chuj ci w dupę** fuck you, up yours; **leżysz cały dzień do góry dupą** you lay (around) on your ass all day; **gadać o dupie Maryny** shoot the shit; **nie truj mi dupy** get off my ass; **nie trząś dupą** don't lose your shit, keep your shit together; **dbać tylko o swoją dupę** only worry about one's own ass; **on wyżej dupy nie podskoczy** he hasn't got it in him; **nie zawracaj mi dupy** get off my ass; **nawalony w trzy dupy** totally shitfaced; **no to dupa zimna** this is screwed; **dupa Jasiu!** bullshit! **2.** (= *żeńskie narządy płciowe*) pussy, cunt; **napalona dupa** hot bitch; **dać dupy** give it out. **3.** (= *kobieta*) piece of ass, chick; **poderwać dupę** pick up a chick; **chodzić na dupy** go looking for some ass. **4.** (= *oferma*) asshole, jerk; **dupa wołowa** asshole, chump. **5.** (= *tył*) tail; **wjechać w dupę samochodu** run into the tail of a car.

dupcia *f. Gen.pl.* **-i** *l.* **dupć 1.** *dziec.* (= *pośladki*) bottom, fanny. **2.** *pot.* (= *kobieta*) piece of ass, chick; **ale dupcia!** what a piece of ass!

dupczyć *ipf. wulg.* fuck, screw. ~ **się** *ipf. wulg.* fuck, screw; (*o prostytutkach*) turn tricks.

dupek *mp* **-pk- 1.** *pot.* (= *lizus*) kiss ass. **2.** *pot.* (= *oferma*) asshole, jerk.

duperele *pl. Gen.* **-i** *pot.* **1.** (= *brednie*) crap, bullshit *l.* b.s. **2.** (= *mało ważne szczegóły*) crap.

duplika *f. prawn.* (*oskarżonego*) rejoinder; (*druga*) rebutter; (*skarżącego*) surrejoinder; (*druga*) surrebutter.

duplikat *mi* copy, duplicate; **duplikat faktury** duplicate invoice.

dupnik *mi Gen. i Acc.* **-a** *pot.* (*zabawa*) a game involving guessing who kicked one in the rear.

dupny *a.* crappy; **dupny samochód** crappy car.

dupowaty *a.* dumb-ass(ed); **dupowaty dyrektor** dumb-ass director; **dupowaty mąż** dumb-ass husband.

dur¹ *mi pat.* typhus; **dur brzuszny** typhoid fever; **dur plamisty** typhus fever, epidemic typhus; **dur plamisty endemiczny** murine *l.* endemic typhus.

dur² *a. indecl.* major; **A-dur** A major; **tonacja C-dur** C major (key); **symfonia E-dur** symphony in E major.

duraluminium *n. indecl. techn.* duralumin.

dureń *mp* **-rni-** *Gen.pl.* **-ów** *l.* **-i 1.** *pot.* (= *głupiec*) fool, idiot; **robić z kogoś durnia** make a fool of sb; **skończony dureń** complete *l.* total fool. **2.** *karty* a card game.

durian *ma bot.* durian (*Durio zibethinus*).

durnieć *ipf. pot.* become stupid.

durnota *f.* stupidity, idiocy.

durnowaty *a.* idiotic, dumb; **durnowaty dyrektor** idiotic director; **durnowata blondynka** dumb blonde.

durny *a.* lamebrained, dumb; **durna dziewczyna** lamebrained girl; **durne sugestie** dumb suggestions.

durowy¹ *a. pat.* typhus, typhoid; **pałeczki durowe** *Salmonella bacteria*.

durowy² *a. muz.* major; **tonacja durowa** major key.

durra *f. Dat., Loc.* **-rze** *Gen.pl.* **-rr** *bot.* durra (*Sorgum durra*).

durszlak *mi Gen.* **-a** colander, strainer.

durzyć się *ipf.* have a crush (*w kimś* on sb).

dusery *pl. Gen.* **-ów** *arch.* compliments; **prawić komuś dusery** pay sb compliments.

dusiciel *mp rzad.* (= *ktoś kto dusi*) strangler. – *ma zool.* constrictor (*Boidae*).

dusić *ipf.* **-szę -sisz 1.** (*za gardło*) choke, strangle. **2.** (= *drażnić drogi oddechowe*) choke, suffocate, asphyxiate; **duszący dym** suffocating smoke; **gaz duszący** *wojsk.* asphyxiating gas. **3.** (= *cisnąć*) squeeze; (*płacz, łzy, śmiech*) suppress, hold back; **dusić podatkami** tax to death; **dusić kogoś, aby zapłacił** put pressure on sb to pay. **4.** *kulin.* (= *gotować*) stew, simmer; **dusić mięso pod przykryciem** cover and simmer meat; **mięso duszone** stewed meat. ~ **się** *ipf.* **1.** (= *oddychać z trudem*) choke, suffocate; **dusić się ze śmiechu** choke with laughter. **2.** (*za gardło*) choke *l.* strangle each other. **3.** *kulin.* stew, simmer.

dusigrosz *mp Gen.pl.* **-y** *l.* **-ów** penny pincher, scrooge.

dusza *f.* **1.** (= *wnętrze człowieka*) soul, heart; **bratnia dusza** kindred spirit; **być chorym na duszy** have an aching soul *l.* heart, be sick at heart; **jest mi ciężko/lekko na duszy** I have a heavy/light heart; **wszystko, czego dusza pragnie** everything one's heart could desire, all one's heart desires; **należę do ciebie całą duszą** *l.* **duszą i sercem** *l.* **duszą i ciałem** I belong to you heart and soul; **jestem za tym projektem duszą i ciałem** I'm for that design 110%; **Adam to dusza towarzystwa** Adam is the life of the party; **nienawidzę cię z całej duszy** I hate your guts; **włożyć w coś całą duszę** put one's heart (and soul) into sth; **ty chyba czytasz w mojej duszy** you must be reading my mind; **otworzyłem przed tobą duszę** I opened my heart to you; **w głębi duszy wierzę, że...** deep in my heart *l.* deep down I believe that...; **będę z wami duszą** I'll be with you in spirit; **dusza człowiek** good soul; **hulaj dusza** to one's heart's content; **nie ma żywej duszy** there isn't a living soul; **nie mam grosza przy duszy** I'm flat broke; **z duszą na ramieniu** with one's heart in one's mouth; **paść bez duszy** drop dead. **2.** *rel.* soul; **modlić się za dusze zmarłych** pray for the souls of the dead; **nieśmiertelna dusza** immortal soul; **wędrówka dusz** transmigration of souls. **3.** *przest.* (= *człowiek*) soul; **wieś, w której mieszka czterysta dusz** village of four-hundred souls. **4.** *arch.* (*w żelazku*) heater. **5.** *bud.* hollow newel. **6.** *muz.* sound post. **7.** *techn.* (= *rdzeń liny*) rope core.

duszek *mp* **-szk-** *pl.* **-i** fairy, elf, brownie.

duszkiem *adv.* in a (single *l.* one) gulp; **pić duszkiem** drink up (in a single *l.* one gulp), sup up.

dusznica *f. pat.* **dusznica bolesna** angina pectoris, stenocardia; **dusznica bolesna brzuszna** abdominal angina.

duszno *adv.* stifling, suffocating; **jest mi duszno** I can't breathe; **w jej mieszkaniu było duszno** her apartment was stuffy.

duszność *f.* shortness of breath, breathlessness, dyspnea; (*powietrza*) stifling heat; (*pomieszczenia*) stuffiness; **napady duszności** attacks of breathlessness.

duszny *a.* **1.** (= *utrudniający oddychanie*) stifling, suffocating; (*powietrze, pogoda*) sweltering, sultry; (*pomieszczenie*) stuffy; (*nastrój*) breathless; **duszny dzień** sweltering day. **2.** (= *odurzający*) sickly (sweet); **duszna woń jaśminu** sickly sweet fragrance of jasmine.

duszpasterski *a.* pastoral, ministerial; **opieka duszpasterska** pastoral service; **praca duszpasterska** ministry.

duszpasterstwo *n.* ministry, priesthood; **duszpasterstwo akademickie** student ministry.

duszpasterz *mp* **1.** pastor, minister. **2.** (= *ksiądz*) priest.

duszyczka *f. Gen.pl.* -ek soul.

duumwir *mp pl.* -owie *hist.* duumvir.

duumwirat *mi hist.* duumvirate.

dużo *adv.* **więcej 1.** (= *wiele*) a lot, many *l.* much; **dużo wody upłynie** not in the nearest future; **mam dużo czasu** I have a lot of time; **dużo przeszedłem w życiu** I've gone through a lot during my life; **mam dużo spraw do załatwienia** I have a lot (of things) to do *l.* take care of; **mam dużo na głowie** I have a lot on my mind; **dużo wcześniej** much earlier; **dużo palę** I smoke heavily; **powiedziałeś za dużo** you said too much; **sprzedał dużo samochodów** sell a lot of cars; **nie tak dużo** not so much *l.* many; **tak dużo, jak potrafię** as much as I can. **2.** *iron.* (= *nic*) nothing *l.* not anything; **dużo tam wiesz** you don't know anything; **dużo by to dało!** a fat lot of good that would do!

duży *a.* **-zi większy 1.** (= *wielki*) big, large; **mieć duży dom** have a big house; **zbyt duże koszty produkcji** excessive production costs; **duże piwo** large beer; **duża przerwa** *szkoln.* long break; **duży mróz** hard *l.* heavy *l.* severe frost; **duży palec** (*u ręki*) thumb; (*u nogi*) big toe; **duża litera** capital letter; **duże pieniądze** a lot of money; **duża gorączka** high fever; **duże brawa dla ciebie** *pot.* hats off to you; **duża buźka** *pot.* big kiss; **zrobić duże oczy** *pot.* make big eyes, be extremely surprised. **2.** *przen.* (= *wybitny*) great. **3.** (= *dorosły*) grown (up); **mam już dużą córkę** my daughter's already grown; **jesteś już dużym chłopcem, powinieneś to rozumieć** you're a big boy now, so you ought to understand; **małe dzieci - mały kłopot, duże dzieci - duży kłopot** small chidren - small problems, big children - big problems.

dwa *num.* **dwaj** *l.* **dwóch** *l.* **dwu** *Gen. i Loc.* **dwóch** *l.* **dwu** *Dat.* **dwom** *l.* **dwu** *l.* **dwóm** *Ins.* **dwoma** *l.* **dwu**; **dwie** *Gen. i Loc.* **dwóch** *l.* **dwu** *Dat.* **dwom** *l.* **dwu** *l.* **dwóm** *Ins.* **dwoma** *l.* **dwiema 1.** (= *liczba 2*) two; **dwa psy** two dogs; **dwa krzesła** two chairs; **dwaj bracia** *l.* **dwóch** *l.* **dwu braci** two brothers; **dwa razy** twice *l.* two times; **dwa razy dziennie** twice a day; **mój syn ma dwa lata** my son is two; **co dwa tygodnie/lata** every other week/year; **w dwóch słowach** in short *l.* brief; **dwa kroki stąd** (just) around the corner; **bez dwóch zdań** no doubt about it; **grać w dwa ognie** play dodge ball; **obiad zrobię raz, dwa** I'll have dinner ready in two shakes, I'll have dinner ready in a snap *l.* flash *l.* jiffy; **nie raz, nie dwa** more than once, many times; **wtrącić swoje dwa słowa** add *l.* put in one's two cents, add *l.* put in one's two cents' worth; **pracować za dwóch** do the work of two; **wygrać dwa do zera** win two-nil; **dwa razy daje, kto prędko daje** he gives twice who gives quickly; **kij ma dwa końce** two can play at the game; **gdzie się dwóch bije, tam trzeci korzysta** two dogs fight for a bone, and a third runs away with it; **co dwóch, to nie jeden** many hands make light work, two heads are better than one; **pokorne cielę dwie matki ssie** the still sow eats up all the draft; **trzymać dwie sroki za ogon** have too many irons in the fire; **upiec dwie pieczenie na jednym ogniu** kill two birds with one stone; **mądrej głowie dość dwie słowie** a word is enough to the wise. **2.** *szkoln., uniw.* (= *dawniej ocena niedostateczna w szkołach podstawowych i ponadpodstawowych; ocena niedostateczna na uniwersytecie*) fail, unsatisfactory, E *l.* F; (= *obecnie ocena dopuszczająca w szkołach podstawowych i ponadpodstawowych*) pass, passing, D.

dwadzieścia *num.* **dwudziest-** *Ins.* -oma *l.* -u twenty; **mam dwadzieścia lat** I'm twenty (years old); **to jakieś dwadzieścia kilometrów stąd** that's about *l.* some twenty kilometers from here.

dwadzieścioro *num. Gen.* -rga *Dat., Loc.* -rgu *Ins.* -rgiem twenty; **dwadzieścioro dzieci** twenty children.

dwaj *num. zob.* **dwa.**

dwakroć *adv. przest.* twice, two times; **dwakroć lepszy** twice as good; **dwakroć droższy** twice as expensive; **dwakroć szybszy** twice as fast, double the speed.

dwanaście *num.* **dwunast-** *Ins.* -oma *l.* -u (= *liczba 12*) twelve; **dwanaście miesięcy** twelve months; **dwunastu apostołów** *Bibl.* twelve Apostles, the Twelve; **masz dopiero dwanaście lat** you're only twelve (years old).

dwanaścioro *num. Gen.* -rga *Dat., Loc.* -rgu *Ins.* -rgiem twelve; **dwanaścioro dzieci** twelve children.

dwie *num. zob.* **dwa.**

dwieście *num.* **dwust-** *Ins.* -oma *l.* -u two hundred; **dwieście złotych** two hundred zlotys; **jechać dwieście na godzinę** drive two hundred kilometers an hour, be doing two hundred kilometers an hour; **ten kościół ma dwieście lat** that church is two hundred years old; **dom wybudowany dwieście lat temu** house built two hundred years ago.

dwoić się *ipf.* **dwoję dwoisz, dwój** double; **dwoję się i troję, ale nie nadążam** I can run around like crazy, but I still won't make it (on time); **dwoi mi się w oczach** I'm seeing double.

dwoinka *f. med.* diplococcus.

dwoistość *f.* duality *l.* dualism, doubleness; **dwoistość natury Chrystusa** *rel.* duality of

Christ's nature; **zasada dwoistości** *mat.* principle of duality.

dwoisty *a.* dual *l.* dualistic, twofold, double; **dwoista natura Chrystusa** Christ's dual nature; **dwoisty obraz** *sztuka* double image.

dwojaczki *pl. Gen.* **-ów** twins; **urodzić dwojaczki** give birth to twins.

dwojak *mi Gen.* **-a 1.** sth composed of two identical parts; (= *podwójne naczynie*) double pot. **2.** *myśl.* (= *nadlufka, dubeltówka typu bok*) over-and-under shotgun. **3.** *bud.* duplex.

dwojaki[1] *a.* double, twofold; **można to zrobić w dwojaki sposób** that can be done two ways; **powody są dwojakiej natury** reasons are twofold.

dwojaki[2] *pl. Gen.* **-ów** (= *podwójne naczynie*) double pot.

dwojako *adv.* doubly, twofold; **można to napisać dwojako** that can be written two ways.

dwojarka *f. Dat., Loc.* **-rce** *techn.* splitting machine.

dwoje *num. decl. like n.* **-jg-** two, pair; **sama wychowuję dwoje dzieci** I'm raising two children on my own; **nie ma dziś dwojga uczniów - Ani i Adama** two students are absent today - Ann and Adam; **jedno z dwojga** one or the other; **we dwoje** (just) the two of us *l.* you *l.* them; **złożyć coś we dwoje** fold sth in two; **na dwoje babka wróżyła** there's not telling how things will turn out; **zgiął się we dwoje** he doubled up; **z dwojga złego** the lesser of two evils; **pracować za dwoje** do the work of two.

dworak *mp* **1.** *arch.* courtier. **2.** (= *parobek*) farmhand.

dworcowy *a.* (train *l.* bus) station *l.* station's; **poczekalnia dworcowa** station('s) waiting lounge *l.* area; **restauracja dworcowa** station's restaurant.

dworek *mi* **-rk-** manor (house); **dworek szlachecki** noble's manor; **dworek myśliwski** hunter's lodge; **mieszkać w dworku** live in a manor.

dworka *f. Gen.pl.* **-ek 1.** *arch.* lady-in-waiting. **2.** (= *służąca*) maid.

dworować *ipf. przest.* mock, ridicule, make fun of; **dworować sobie z kolegi** ridicule one's friend.

dworski *a.* **1.** (= *dotyczący majątku ziemskiego*) estate *l.* estate's; **budynki dworskie** estate's buildings; **łąka dworska** estate's meadow. **2.** (= *dotyczący dworu królewskiego*) court *l.* courtly; **miłość dworska** courtly love; **etykieta dworska** court etiquette; **życie dworskie** court life. **3.** *przest.* (= *wytworny*) courtly, refined; **dworskie maniery** courtly manners.

dworu *itd. mi zob.* **dwór.**

dworzanin *mp pl.* **-anie** *Gen.* **-an** *hist.* courtier.

dworzec *mi* **-rc-** *Gen.* **-a** station; **dworzec kolejowy** train station; **dworzec autobusowy** bus station; **dworzec lotniczy** airport; **dworzec podmiejski** suburban station; **odjeżdżać z dworca centralnego** depart from the central station; **przyjeżdżać na dworzec główny** arrive at the central station.

dwóch *num. zob.* **dwa.**

dwóchsetlecie *n. Gen.pl.* **-i** bicentennial, bicentenary, two hundredth anniversary.

dwója *f. Gen.* **-ói** *szkoln., uniw. pot.* (= *dawniej ocena niedostateczna w szkołach podstawowych i ponadpodstawowych; ocena niedostateczna na uniwersytecie*) fail, unsatisfactory, E *l.* F; (= *obecnie ocena dopuszczająca w szkołach podstawowych i ponadpodstawowych*) pass, D; **dostać dwóję ze sprawdzianu** fail a quiz *l.* test; barely pass a quiz *l.* test; **zdać egzamin na dwóję** fail an exam; barely pass an exam.

dwójka *f.* **1.** (= *cyfra 2*) two. **2.** (= *dwie osoby, dwoje zwierząt itp.*) pair; **ustawcie się dwójkami** pair up; **zróbmy to we dwójkę** let's do it together (as a pair); **rozmawiać we dwójkę** talk one-on-one. **3.** *szkoln., uniw.* (= *dawniej ocena niedostateczna w szkołach podstawowych i ponadpodstawowych; ocena niedostateczna na uniwersytecie*) fail, unsatisfactory, E *l.* F; (= *obecnie ocena dopuszczająca w szkołach podstawowych i ponadpodstawowych*) pass, D; **dostać dwójkę ze sprawdzianu** fail a quiz *l.* test; barely pass a quiz *l.* test; **zdać egzamin na dwójkę** fail an exam; barely pass an exam. **4.** *karty* deuce; **zagrać dwójką pik** play the deuce of spades. **5.** *pot.* (= *tramwaj, autobus itp. nr 2*) two; **do dworca dojedziesz dwójką** you take *l.* ride the two to the station; (= *dom, mieszkanie, pokój nr 2*) number two; **mieszkamy pod dwójką** our house *l.* apartment is number two. **6.** *sport* (= *kajak dwuosobowy, łódź dwuosobowa*) two-person canoe *l.* kayak.

dwójkowicz *mp Gen.pl.* **-ów** *szkoln., uniw., pot.* poor *l.* failing student.

dwójkowy *a. szkoln., uniw., pot.* failing, poor; **dwójkowy uczeń** poor *l.* failing student; **system dwójkowy** *mat.* binary system.

dwójnasób *adv.* doubly; **w dwójnasób** doubly, two times as much; **powiększyć dochody w dwójnasób** double one's income.

dwójnik *mi Gen.* **-a** *el.* two-terminal network.

dwójnóg *mi Gen.* **-a** bipod.

dwóm *num. zob.* **dwa.**

dwór *mi* **-o-** **1.** (= *obszerny dom*) manor (house), mansion; **mieszkać we dworze** live in a mansion; **dwór szlachecki** estate manor. **2.** (= *majątek ziemski*) estate; **służyć we dworze** work on an estate; **powinności na rzecz dworu** obligations to the estate. **3.** (= *podwórze*) yard, courtyard; (= *miejsce pod gołym niebem*) outside, outdoors; **bawić się na dworze** play outside *l.* outdoors; **dziś jest zimno na dworze** it's cold outside today; **czy mogę wyjść na dwór?** can I go outside? **4.** (= *siedziba władcy; t. panujący z otoczeniem*) court; **dwór królewski** royal court; **dwór brytyjski** British court; **być przedstawionym na dworze** be presented at court; **podróżować z całym dworem** travel with one's entire court; **dama dworu** lady-in-waiting; **radca dworu** court advisor.

dwórka *f. Gen.pl.* **-ek** *hist.* lady-in-waiting.

dwu *num. zob.* **dwa.**

dwuaktowy *a. teatr* two-act, in two acts; **komedia dwuaktowa** comedy in two acts, two-act comedy; **przedstawienie dwuaktowe** play in two acts, two-act play.

dwuaktówka *f. Gen.pl.* **-ek** *teatr* two-act play, play in two acts; **wystawiać dwuaktówkę** put on a two-act play.

dwuaspektowy *a. gram.* biaspectual; **czasownik dwuaspektowy** biaspectual verb.

dwuatomowy *a. fiz., chem.* diatomic; **cząsteczka dwuatomowa** diatomic particle.

dwubarwny *a.* **1.** (= *w dwóch kolorach*) two-color, dichromatic; **plakat dwubarwny** two-color poster. **2.** *fiz.* dichroic, dichroitic.

dwubiegunowy *a. fiz.* bipolar.

dwuboczny *a.* bilateral; **symetria dwuboczna** *biol.* bilateral symmetry.

dwuboista *mp sport* athlete competing in a two-event competition.

dwubój *mi* **-o-** *sport* two-event competition; **dwubój zimowy** (= *biatlon*) biathlon; **dwubój klasyczny** (= *kombinacja norweska*) Nordic combined.

dwubranżowy *a.* two-division, two-branch; **sklep dwubranżowy** two-department store; **spółka dwubranżowa** company operating in two branches of industry.

dwucalowy *a.* two-inch(-long); **deska dwucalowa** two-inch board; **dwucalowa nitka** two-inch(-long) thread.

dwucukier *mi* **-kr-** *chem.* disaccharide.

dwucyfrowy *a.* two-digit; **liczba dwucyfrowa** two-digit number; **dwucyfrowy numer telefonu** two-digit (tele)phone number.

dwucylindrowy *a. mot.* two-cylinder.

dwuczęściowy *a.* two-part; (*o ubraniu*) two-piece; **film dwuczęściowy** two-part film; **dwuczęściowa sukienka** two-piece dress; **dwuczęściowy kostium kąpielowy** two-piece bathing suit.

dwuczłonowy *a.* compound, two-part; **nazwisko dwuczłonowe** double-barreled name.

dwuczub *ma Acc., Gen.* **-a** *Loc.* **-ie** *orn.* seriema, cariama (*Cariama*).

dwudaniowy *a.* two-course; **obiad dwudaniowy** two-course dinner.

dwudniowy *a.* **1.** (= *trwający dwa dni*) two-day; **dwudniowa konferencja** two-day conference. **2.** (= *w wieku dwóch dni*) **dwudniowe dziecko** two-day-old baby.

dwudrzwiowy *a.* two-door, double-doored; **samochód dwudrzwiowy** *mot.* two-door sedan.

dwudzielny *a.* two-part, bipartite; **łodyga dwudzielna** *bot.* dichotomous branch; **okno dwudzielne** *bud.* sash window; **dwudzielna zastawka serca** *anat.* mitral valve; **takt** *l.* **rytm dwudzielny** *muz.* duple meter.

dwudziesta *f. Gen.* **-ej** (*godzina*) eight p.m. *l.* in the evening; **umówić się z kimś na dwudziestą** arrange to meet sb at eight p.m.; **skończyć pracę do dwudziestej** finish work by 8 p.m.

dwudziestak *mi Gen.* **-a** *pot.* (= *banknot o nominale dwadzieścia*) twenty; **rozmienić dwudziestaka** break a twenty; **pożycz mi dwudziestaka** lend me a twenty.

dwudziestka *f. Gen.pl.* **-ek** **1.** (= *liczba 20*) twenty. **2.** (= *dwadzieścia lat*) twenty years; **je-**

stem po dwudziestce I'm in my twenties. **3.** (= *tramwaj, autobus nr 20*) twenty; **do szpitala dojedziesz dwudziestką** you take the twenty to get to the hospital. **4.** (= *dom, mieszkanie, pokój nr 20*) number twenty; **mieszkamy pod dwudziestką** we live at number twenty. **5.** (= *moneta, banknot o nominale dwadzieścia*) twenty; **rozmieni mi pani dwudziestkę?** have you got change for a twenty, ma'am? **6.** *myśl.* (= *broń kalibru 20*) twenty-millimeter shotgun. **7.** *pot.* (= *dwudziestolatka*) twenty-year-old woman.

dwudziestolatek *mp pl.* **-i** twenty-year-old man.

dwudziestolatka *f.* twenty-year-old woman.

dwudziestolecie *n. Gen.pl.* **-i** **1.** (= *20 lat*) twenty years. **2.** (= *20 rocznica*) twentieth anniversary.

dwudziestoletni *a.* twenty-year-old; **dwudziestoletni chłopak** twenty-year-old boy; **dwudziestoletnia praca na rzecz firmy** twenty years of service to the company.

dwudziestomilionowy *a.* **1.** twenty millionth. **2.** (= *liczący 20 milionów*) of twenty million; **dwudziestomilionowy naród** nation of twenty million.

dwudziestotysięczny *a.* **1.** twenty thousandth. **2.** (= *liczący 20 tysięcy*) of twenty thousand; **dwudziestotysięczne miasto** city of twenty thousand; **dwudziestotysięczny tłum** crowd of twenty thousand.

dwudziestowieczny *a.* (of the) twentieth-century; **artyści dwudziestowieczni** twentieth-century artists; **dwudziestowieczna literatura** twentieth-century literature.

dwudziestu *itd. num. zob.* **dwadzieścia**.

dwudziesty *a.* twentieth; **dwudziesty wiek** twentieth century; **dwudzieste urodziny** twentieth birthday; **lata dwudzieste dwudziestego wieku** the twenties, the 1920s; **minęła godzina dwudziesta** it just turned eight (p.m.); **urodziłem się dwudziestego maja** I was born (on) May twentieth; **jedna dwudziesta** one-twentieth. – *mi* twentieth (*day of a month*); **umówić się z kimś na dwudziestego czerwca** arrange to meet sb on the twentieth of June.

dwuelektrodowy *a. el.* two-electrode; **lampa dwuelektrodowa** diode.

dwuelementowy *a.* two-element *l.* of two elements; **zbiór dwuelementowy** *zwł. mat.* two-element set.

dwuetapowy *a.* two-stage; **konkurs dwuetapowy** two-stage competition *l.* contest; **podróż dwuetapowa** two-stage journey.

dwufazowy *a.* two-phase; **dwufazowy proces** two-phase process; **dwufazowe przygotowanie** two-phase preparation; **system dwufazowy** *el.* diphase *l.* diphasic system.

dwufenyl *mi Gen.* **-u** *chem.* biphenyl, diphenyl.

dwugarbny *a. zool.* Bactrian, two-humped; **wielbłąd dwugarbny** Bactrian camel (*Camelus bactrianus*).

dwugarmond *mi Gen.* **-u** *druk.* paragon.

dwugłos *mi* (*rozmowa*) dialog; (*śpiew*) duet.

dwugłoska *f. Gen.pl.* **-ek** *jęz.* diphthong.

dwugłosowy *a.* two-part; **utwór dwugłosowy** two-part piece, duet; **inwencja dwugłosowa** *muz.* two-part invention.

dwugłowy *a.* two-headed; **dwugłowy smok** two-headed dragon; **mięsień dwugłowy** *anat.* biceps.

dwugodzinny *a.* two-hour(-long); **dwugodzinna konferencja** two-hour-long conference; **dwugodzinna podróż** two-hour journey *l.* trip; **dwugodzinny wykład** two-hour lecture.

dwugroszówka *f.* two-grosz piece *l.* coin.

dwuizbowy *a.* 1. (= *składający się z dwóch pomieszczeń*) two-room. 2. *parl.* bicameral; **parlament dwuizbowy** bicameral parliament.

dwujajeczny *a.* two-egg; **makaron dwujajeczny** two-egg pasta.

dwujądrowy *a. biol.* binuclear.

dwujęzyczny *a.* bilingual; **kraj dwujęzyczny** bilingual country; **słownik dwujęzyczny** bilingual dictionary.

dwukadłubowiec *mi* -wc- *Gen.* -a *żegl.* catamaran, twin-hulled ship.

dwukadłubowy *a. żegl.* twin-hulled; **statek dwukadłubowy** twin-hulled ship.

dwukanałowy *a. el.* two-channel; **stereofonia dwukanałowa** two-channel stereo; **wzmacniacz dwukanałowy** two-channel amplifier.

dwukasetowy *a.* two-cassette, double-deck(ed); **magnetofon dwukasetowy** two-cassette *l.* double-deck tape recorder; **magnetowid dwukasetowy** two-cassette VCR.

dwukierunkowy *a.* 1. two-way; **ulica dwukierunkowa** two-way street; **dwukierunkowy ruch** two-way traffic. 2. *el.* bidirectional; **dwukierunkowy mikrofon** bidirectional microphone.

dwukilogramowy *a.* two-kilo(gram); **paczka dwukilogramowa** two-kilogram package; **dwukilogramowe opakowanie proszku do prania** two-kilogram package of washing powder.

dwukilometrowy *a.* two-kilometer; **dwukilometrowy pas startowy** two-kilometer runway; **dwukilometrowa trasa** two-kilometer-long route.

dwukilowy *a.* = **dwukilogramowy**.

dwuklasowy *a.* 1. *szkoln.* two-grade; **szkoła dwuklasowa** two-grade school. 2. *jęz.* two-class; **system znaków dwuklasowych** two-class system of signs.

dwukolorowy *a.* two-color; *techn.* dichromatic, dichromic; **plakat dwukolorowy** two-color poster.

dwukołowy *a.* two-wheeled, with two wheels; **pojazd dwukołowy** two-wheeled vehicle.

dwukomorowy *a.* two-chamber; **dwukomorowa torebka nasienna** *bot.* two-chamber seed pod.

dwukondygnacyjny *a.* two-story *l.* two-storey; **dwukondygnacyjny budynek** two-story building.

dwukółka *f. przest.* gig.

dwukropek *mi* -pk- *Gen.* -a colon.

dwukrotnie *adv.* twice (over), two times; **zwyciężyć dwukrotnie** win twice (over); **dwukrotnie zwiększyć dochody** double one's income.

dwukrotny *a.* two-time, twice; (*o wzroście*) twofold; **dwukrotny zwycięzca konkursu** two-time winner of a contest; **dwukrotny wzrost sprzedaży** twofold increase in sales.

dwulatek *mp* -tk- *pl.* -i (= *dwuletni chłopiec*) two-year-old (boy). — *ma* -tk- (= *dwuletnie zwierzę*) two-year-old (animal).

dwulecie *n. Gen.pl.* -i 1. (= *2 lata*) two years. 2. (= *2 rocznica*) second anniversary.

dwuletni *a.* 1. (= *trwający dwa lata*) two-year; **studia dwuletnie** two-year (course of) studies; **dwuletni okres spłat kredytu** two-year loan repayment period; **roślina dwuletnia** *bot.* biennial. 2. (= *w wieku dwóch lat*) two-year-old; **dwuletni chłopiec** two-year-old boy; **dwuletnia dziewczynka** two-year-old girl; **dwuletni pies** two-year-old dog.

dwulicowość *f.* duplicity.

dwulicowy *a.* duplicitous, two-faced; **dwulicowy człowiek** duplicitous *l.* two-faced person; **dwulicowy sposób postępowania** double-dealing ways.

dwulistnik *ma Gen.* -a *Ins.* -kiem *bot.* spider orchid (*Ophrys*).

dwuliścienny *ma bot.* **dwuliścienne** dicotyledons (*Dicotyledonae*).

dwulitrowy *a.* two-liter; **butelka dwulitrowa** two-liter bottle; **dwulitrowe opakowanie** two-liter package; **dwulitrowy silnik** two-liter engine.

dwumasztowiec *mi* -wc- *Gen.* -a *żegl.* two-masted ship.

dwumasztowy *a. żegl.* two-masted; **statek dwumasztowy** two-masted ship.

dwumecz *mi Gen.pl.* -ów *sport* doubleheader; **rozegrać dwumecz** play a doubleheader.

dwumetrowy *a.* 1. (= *mający dwa metry*) two-meter; **dwumetrowy słup** two-meter pole. 2. (= *mający dwieście kilogramów*) two hundred-kilo(gram); **dwumetrowy worek ziemniaków** two hundred-kilo bag of potatoes.

dwumian *mi mat.* binomial.

dwumiejscowy *a.* two-seat(er); **dwumiejscowy samochód sportowy** two-seater sports car.

dwumiesięcznik *mi Gen.* -a bimonthly; **prenumerować dwumiesięcznik** subscribe to a bimonthly.

dwumiesięczny *a.* 1. (= *trwający dwa miesiące*) two-month; **dwumiesięczny urlop** two-month vacation. 2. (= *w wieku dwóch miesięcy*) two-month-old; **dwumiesięczne dziecko** two-month-old child.

dwuminutowy *a.* (= *trwający dwie minuty*) two-minute; **dwuminutowa cisza** two-minute silence.

dwunasta *f. Gen.* -ej (*godzina*) twelve (o'clock); **jest dwunasta** it's twelve; **będę piętnaście po dwunastej** I'll be there a quarter after twelve; **kończę za piętnaście dwunasta** I finish at a quarter to twelve; **mam pociąg o w pół do dwunastej** my train leaves at eleven-thirty *l.* half past eleven.

dwunastka *f. Gen.pl.* -ek 1. (= *liczba 12*) twelve. 2. *pot.* (= *dwanaście lat*) twelfth birthday; **obchodzić swoją dwunastkę** celebrate one's twelfth birthday. 3. (= *tramwaj, autobus nr 12*) twelve; **do szpitala dojedziesz dwunastką** you take the twelve to the hospital. 4. (= *dom, mieszkanie, pokój nr 12*) number twelve; **mieszka-**

my pod **dwunastką** our house *l.* apartment is number twelve. **5.** (= *wielkość czcionki*) twelve-point font; **pisać dwunastką** write using a twelve-point font. **6.** *myśl.* (= *broń kalibru 12*) twelve-millimeter shotgun.

dwunastnica *f. anat.* duodenum; **wrzody** *l.* **owrzodzenie dwunastnicy** *pat.* duodenal ulcers.

dwunastogodzinny *a.*   twelve-hour(-long); **dwunastogodzinna podróż** twelve-hour journey *l.* trip; **dwunastogodzinny dzień pracy** twelve-hour work day.

dwunastoletni *a.* **1.** (= *trwający 12 lat*) twelve-year; **dwunastoletni staż pracy** twelve-year period of employment. **2.** (= *w wieku 12 lat*) twelve-year-old; **dwunastoletni chłopiec** twelve-year-old boy; **dwunastoletnia dziewczynka** twelve-year-old girl.

dwunastomiesięczny *a.* **1.** (= *trwający 12 miesięcy*) twelve-month. **2.** *rzad.* (= *w wieku 12 miesięcy*) twelve-month-old; **dwunastomiesięczny chłopiec** twelve-month-old boy.

dwunastowieczny *a.* twelfth-century; **dwunastowieczny zamek** twelfth-century castle.

dwunastozgłoskowiec *mi* -wc- *Gen.* -a *teor.lit.* poem written in dodecosyllable; **pisać dwunastozgłoskowcem** write a poem in dodecosyllable.

dwunastu *itd. num. zob.* **dwanaście**.

dwunasty *a.* twelfth; **dwunasty wiek** twelfth century; **dwunaste urodziny** twelfth birthday; **minęła godzina dwunasta** clock just struck twelve; **urodziłem się dwunastego maja** I was born (on) May twelfth, I was born (on) the twelfth of May; **jedna dwunasta** one-twelfth. − *mi* twelfth (*day of a month*); **umówić się z kimś na dwunastego czerwca** arrange to meet sb on the twelfth of June; **skończyć pracę do dwunastego** finish work by the twelfth.

dwunawowy *a. bud.* cruciform; **kościół dwunawowy** cruciform church; **bazylika dwunawowa** cruciform basilica.

dwunożny *a.* bipedal, two-legged; **zwierzę dwunożne** *zool.* biped.

dwuogniskowy *a. opt.* bifocal; **dwuogniskowe okulary** bifocals.

dwuosobowy *a.* two-person; **pokój dwuosobowy** double (room).

dwupalnikowy *a.* two-burner; **kuchenka dwupalnikowa** two-burner stove.

dwupartyjny *a. polit.* two-party; **system dwupartyjny** two-party system.

dwupasmowy *a.* two-lane; **droga dwupasmowa** two-lane road.

dwupasmówka *f. Gen.pl.* -ek *pot.* (= *droga dwupasmowa*) two-lane road.

dwupiętrowy *a.* two-story *l.* two-storey; **budynek dwupiętrowy** two-story building.

dwupłaszczyznowy *a.* on two levels; **dach dwupłaszczyznowy** *bud.* bi-level roof.

dwupłatowiec *mi* -wc- *Gen.* -a *lotn.* biplane.

dwupłatowy *a.* **1.** two-piece; **samolot dwupłatowy** *lotn.* biplane. **2.** *biol.* bilobate.

dwupłciowy *a. biol.* hermaphroditic, bisexual;

kwiat dwupłciowy *bot.* androgynous flower; **zwierzęta dwupłciowe** *zool.* hermaphroditic animals.

dwupokojowy *a.* two-room; **mieszkanie dwupokojowe** two-room apartment.

dwupolowy *a. hist., roln.* two-course rotation; **system dwupolowy** two-course rotation system.

dwupolówka *f. Gen.pl.* -ek *hist., roln.* two-course rotation system.

dwupoziomowy *a.* bi-level; **skrzyżowanie dwupoziomowe** bi-level intersection; **mieszkanie dwupoziomowe** split-level apartment.

dwuramienny *a.* two-armed; **świecznik dwuramienny** two-armed candlestick; **dźwignia dwuramienna** *fiz.* double-arm lever, double-ended lever.

dwuręczny *a.* two-handed; **miecz dwuręczny** two-handed sword; **dwuręczny bekhend** two-handed backhand; **dwuręczne pisanie na maszynie** typing with both hands.

dwurodzajowy *a.* **1.** two-type; *biol.* bigeneric. **2.** *jęz.* two-gender; **rzeczownik dwurodzajowy** two-gender noun.

dwurodzinny *a.* two-family; **dom dwurodzinny** two-family house.

dwururka *f. Gen.pl.* -ek *myśl.* double-barreled rifle *l.* shotgun.

dwurzędowy *a.* two-rowed; **marynarka dwurzędowa** double-breasted jacket; **okręt dwurzędowy** *żegl., hist.* bireme.

dwurzędówka *f. pot.* (= *marynarka dwurzędowa*) double-breasted jacket.

dwusetka *f. Gen.pl.* -ek **1.** (= *banknot o nominale dwieście*) two-hundred note; **rozmienić dwusetkę** change a two-hundred note. **2.** (= *tramwaj, autobus nr 200*) two hundred; **przy dworcu przesiądziesz się na dwusetkę** transfer to the 200 at the station. **3.** *pot.* (= *żarówka o mocy 200 wat*) 200-watt bulb.

dwusetlecie *n.* = **dwóchsetlecie**.

dwusetny *a.* two-hundredth; **dwusetna rocznica śmierci poety** two-hundredth anniversary of the poet's death; **dwusetny odcinek telenoweli** two-hundredth episode of the television serial; **rok tysiąc dwusetny** the year twelve hundred.

dwusiarczek *mi* -czk- *chem.* disulfide, bisulfide; **dwusiarczek węgla** carbon disulfide *l.* bisulfide; **dwusiarczek molibdenu** molybdenum bisulfide.

dwusieczna *f. Gen.* -ej *mat.* bisector.

dwusieczny *a.* (= *mający ostrze z obu stron*) double-edged, two-edged; **miecz dwusieczny** double-edged *l.* two-edged sword.

dwusilnikowy *a.* twin-engine, two-engine; **samolot dwusilnikowy** *lotn.* twin-engine plane.

dwuskładnikowy *a.* two-component, binary; **lakier dwuskładnikowy** two-component paint.

dwuskrzydłowy *a.*   double;   **dwuskrzydłowe drzwi** double doors.

dwuskrzydły *a. zool.* dipterous, two-winged; **dwuskrzydłe** dipterans (*Diptera*).

dwuspadowy *a.* pitched; **dach dwuspadowy** *bud.* gable *l.* pitched roof.

dwustopniowy *a.* two-tier, two-stage; **eliminacje dwustopniowe** two-stage eliminations *l.*

qualifying round; **dwustopniowa organizacja studiów** two-tier system of studies; **wybory dwustopniowe** two-tier elections.

dwustronny *a.* **1.** (= *wzajemny*) bilateral; **umowa/wymiana/korzyść dwustronna** bilateral agreement/exchange/benefit. **2.** (= *o dwu stronach*) double-sided, two-sided; **dźwignia dwustronna** *mech.* first-order lever; **materiał dwustronny** *tk.* double-faced material, reversible.

dwustu *itd. num. zob.* **dwieście.**

dwustuletni *a.* two-hundred-year old.

dwusuw *mi* **1.** *mot.* (*silnik*) two-stroke engine. **2.** *pot.* (*samochód*) two-stroker.

dwusuwowy *a.* two-stroke.

dwusylabowiec *mi* **-wc-** *Gen.* **-a** disyllable.

dwusylabowy *a.* disyllabic.

dwuszereg *mi* two rows; **ustawiać się w dwuszeregu** arrange o.s. in two rows; **zbiórka w dwuszeregu** fall-in two-deep.

dwuścian *mi geom.* dihedron.

dwuślad *mi mot.* two-track vehicle.

dwutakt *mi* **1.** *mot.* = **dwusuw. 2.** *koszykówka* two-step shot.

dwuteownik *mi Gen.* **-a** *bud., techn.* double-T bar.

dwutlenek *mi* **-nk-** *chem.* dioxide; **dwutlenek węgla** carbon di-oxide.

dwutomowy *a.* two-volume.

dwutonowy[1] *a.* (= *ważący l. mogący udźwignąć dwie tony*) two-ton.

dwutonowy[2] *a. muz.* two-tone; **akord dwutonowy** two-note chord.

dwutorowy *a. kol.* double-track.

dwutygodnik *mi Gen.* **-a** biweekly; *Br.* fortnightly.

dwutygodniowy *a.* two-week, two weeks'; *Br.* a fortnight's.

dwutysięcznik *mi Gen.* **-a** *żegl.* two-thousand-tonner.

dwutysięczny *a.* two thousandth; **w roku dwutysięcznym** in the year two thousand.

dwuwargowy *a. fon.* bilabial.

dwuwarstwowy *a.* two-ply, two-layer.

dwuwiersz *mi Gen.* **-a** couplet, distich.

dwuwierszowy *a.* two-line.

dwuwierzchołkowy *a.* twin-peaked.

dwuwiosłowy *a.* double-scull, two-oared; **łódź dwuwiosłowa** double-scull boat; two-oar.

dwuwklęsły *a.* biconcave; **soczewka dwuwklęsła** *opt.* biconcave lens.

dwuwymiarowy *a.* two-dimensional; *pot.* 2-D.

dwuwypukły *a.* biconvex; **soczewka dwuwypukła** *fiz.* a biconvex lens.

dwuwyrazowy *a.* two-word.

dwuzasadowy *a. chem.* dibasic.

dwuzłotowy *a.* two-zloty.

dwuzłotówka *f. Gen.pl.* **-ek** two-zloty piece.

dwuzmianowy *a.* two-shift.

dwuznacznie *adv.* ambiguously, equivocally; **uśmiechać sie dwuznacznie** smile quizzically; **mówić dwuznacznie** talk equivocally.

dwuznacznik *mi Gen.* **-a** double entendre.

dwuznaczność *f.* ambiguity, double meaning;

dwuznaczność sformułowania the ambiguity of the phrasing.

dwuznaczny *a.* ambiguous, equivocal; **dwuznaczna propozycja/odpowiedź** ambiguous proposal/answer; **dwuznaczny uśmiech** quizzical smile.

dwuznak *mi pismo* digraph.

dwużyłowy *a. el.* **kabel dwużyłowy** two-core cable.

dybać *ipf.* **-ię -iesz** prowl (*na coś/kogoś* after sb/sth); wait in ambush, lie in wait (*na kogoś/coś* for sb/sth).

dybel *mi* **-bl-** *Gen.* **-a** *stol., bud.* dowel.

dyblować *ipf. stol., bud.* dowel.

dyby *pl. Gen.* **-ów** *l.* **dyb** stocks; **zakuć kogoś w dyby** put sb in the stocks.

dycha *f.* **1.** *pot.* (*banknot, moneta*) tenner. **2.** *pot.* (= *dziesięć lat*) decade. **3.** *pot.* (= *tramwaj, autobus nr 10*) the number ten.

dychać *ipf. arch. l. żart.* breathe; **ledwo dycham** I can hardly breathe.

dychawica *f. pat.* asthma.

dychawiczny *a.* asthmatic; (= *łatwo tracący oddech*) short-winded; (*o koniu*) broken-winded.

dychotomia *f. Gen.* **-ii** dichotomy.

dychotomiczny *a.* dichotomous; **podział dychotomiczny** dichotomous division.

dydaktyczny *a.* didactic; **film/poemat dydaktyczny** didactic film/poem; **proces dydaktyczny** *szkoln.* didactic process; **pracownik dydaktyczny** member of the teaching staff.

dydaktyk *mp* instructor, teacher.

dydaktyka *f.* **1.** (= *nauczanie*) didactics, teaching. **2.** (= *pouczanie*) didacticism.

dydaktyzm *mi* didacticism, didacticity.

dydelf *ma zool.* (= *torbacz z rodziny Didelphidae, opos*) opossum, possum.

dyferencjacja *f. form.* (= *różnicowanie się*) differentiation; **dyferencjacja społeczna** social differentiation.

dyferencjał *mi mot.* differential (gear).

dyfrakcja *f. fiz.* diffraction.

dyfrakcyjny *a. fiz.* diffractive; **siatka dyfrakcyjna** diffraction grating; **obraz dyfrakcyjny** diffractive image.

dyfteryt *mi pat.* (laryngeal) diphtheria.

dyftong *mi fon.* diphthong.

dyftongiczny *a. fon.* diphthongal.

dyftongizacja *f. fon.* diphthongization.

dyftongizować *ipf. fon.* diphthongize. ~ **się** *ipf. fon.* diphthongize, undergo diphthongization.

dyfundować *ipf. chem.* diffuse.

dyfuzja *f. chem., fiz. l. form.* (= *przenikanie*) diffusion; **dyfuzja powierzchniowa** surface diffusion; **dyfuzja kulturowa** *socjol.* cultural diffusion.

dyfuzor *mi Gen.* **-a** *techn.* diffuser.

dyfuzyjny *a.* diffusional; **pompa dyfuzyjna** *techn.* diffusion pump.

dyg *mi* curtsy; **złożyć dyg** curtsy (*przed kimś* to sb).

dygać *ipf.* curtsy; **dygać przed królową** curtsy to the Queen.

dygestorium *n. sing. indecl. pl.* **-ria** *Gen.* **-riów** *chem.* fume cupboard.

dygnąć *pf.* **-ij** *zob.* **dygać**.

dygnitarski *a.* dignitarial, dignitary's; **po dygnitarsku** like a dignitary.

dygnitarz *mp* dignitary.

dygot *mi* tremble, quiver; **nie móc opanować dygotu rąk** inability to control trembling hands.

dygotać *ipf.* **-czę -czesz** *l.* **-cę -cesz, -cz** tremble, quiver, shiver; **dygotać z zimna** shiver with cold.

dygresja *f.* digression; **robić dygresje** digress, make digressions.

dygresyjnie *adv.* digressively, discursively.

dygresyjny *a.* digressive, discursive; **poemat dygresyjny** *teor.lit.* discursive poem.

dykcja *f.* **1.** enunciation, articulation. **2.** *teor.lit.* diction.

dykcjonarz *mi Gen.* **-a** *przest.* dictionary.

dykta *f. stol.* plywood.

dyktafon *mi el.* dictaphone.

dyktando *n.* dictation; **pisać dyktando** take dictation; **robić coś pod czyjeś dyktando** do sb's bidding.

dyktat *mi* dictate, diktat.

dyktator *mp polit., hist.* dictator; **dyktator mody** *przen.* trend-setter.

dyktatorski *a.* dictatorial; **po dyktatorsku** dictatorially.

dyktatura *f. polit.* dictatorship; **dyktatura faszystowska/Stalinowska** fascist/Stalinist dictatorship; **dyktatura proletariatu** the dictatorship of the proletariat.

dykteryjka *f. Gen.pl.* **-ek** anecdote.

dyktować *ipf.* dictate (*sth*) (*komuś* to sb); **rób, jak dyktuje serce** do what your heart dictates; **dyktować ceny** dictate prices.

dyl *mi Gen.* **-a** *Gen.pl.* **-i** *l.* **-ów 1.** (*pień, listwa*) joist. **2. dać dyla** leg it.

dylatacja *f. fiz., bud.* dilatation; **dylatacja czasu** dilatation of time.

dylatometr *mi fiz.* dilatometer.

dylatometria *f. Gen.* **-ii** *fiz.* dilatometry.

dylemat *mi* dilemma; **stanąć przed dylematem** face a dilemma; **mieć/rozwiązać dylemat** have/ solve a dilemma; **rozwiązać dylemat** solve dilemma.

dyletancki *a.* dilettantish; **po dyletancku** dilettantishly.

dyletanctwo *n.* dilettantism.

dyletant *mp*, **dyletantka** *f. Gen.pl.* **-ek** dilettante.

dyletantyzm *mi* dilettantism.

dyliżans *mi pl.* **-e** *l.* **-y** stage coach.

dylogia *f. Gen.* **-ii** *teor.lit.* dilogy.

dyluwialny *a. geol.* diluvial; **lodowiec dyluwialny** diluvial glacier; **osady dyluwialne** diluvial deposits.

dyluwium *n. indecl. przest., geol.* diluvium.

dym *mi* **1.** smoke; **gęsty/gryzący dym** thick/ acrid smoke; **kłęby/chmury dymu** puffs/clouds of smoke; **dym maskujący** *wojsk.* smoke screen; **przeszkadza mi dym z papierosa** cigarette smoke bothers me; **pójść z dymem** go up in smoke; **pu**ścić coś z dymem send sth up in smoke; **iść jak w dym** go like a shot. **2.** *arch.* homestead.

dymać *ipf.* **1.** *pot.* (= *podążać, pędzić*) run, speed, hasten. **2.** *pot.* (= *dmuchać*) blow; **dymać w miech** pump the bellows. **3.** *wulg.* (*o mężczyźnie*) (= *mieć stosunek z*) screw, fuck (*sb*). ~ **się** *ipf. wulg.* (= *kopulować*) screw, fuck (*z kimś* sb).

dymarka *f. Gen.pl.* **-ek** primitive smelting furnace.

dymić (się) *ipf.* smoke; *pot.* (= *wydzielać parę*) steam.

dymisja *f.* resignation, dismissal; **podać się do dymisji** resign, hand in one's resignation; **udzielić dymisji** dismiss; **otrzymać dymisję** be dismissed.

dymisjonować *ipf. l. pf.* dismiss.

dymka *f. Gen.pl.* **-ek** *ogr.* seed onion.

dymnica *f.* **1.** *bot.* fumitory (*Fumaria*). **2.** *techn.* smoke-box.

dymnik *mi Gen.* **-a 1.** *bud.* (*okno*) attic *l.* loft window. **2.** (*otwór wentylacyjny*) smokehole.

dymny *a.* smoke, smoked; **zasłona/świeca dymna** smoke screen/candle; **szkło dymne** smoked glass.

dymorfizm *mi biol.* dimorphism; **dymorfizm płciowy** sexual dimorphism; **dymorfizm roślin/ zwierząt** plant/animal dimorphism; **dymorfizm płciowy/sezonowy** sexual/seasonal dimorphism.

dyna *f. fiz.* (*jednostka siły*) dyne.

dynamiczny *a.* **1.** (= *żywiołowy, gwałtowny*) dynamic, lively, vigorous, rapid; **dynamiczny rozwój** dynamic *l.* lively development; **dynamiczny wzrost** dynamic *l.* rapid increase; **dynamiczna osobowość** dynamic personality. **2.** *fiz., muz.* dynamic; **ciśnienie dynamiczne** dynamic pressure; **reakcja dynamiczna** dynamic reaction; **pamięć dynamiczna** *komp.* active memory; **metamorfizm dynamiczny** *geol.* dynamic metamorphism; **oznaczenia dynamiczne** *muz.* dynamic notation; **akcent dynamiczny** *fon.* dynamic stress.

dynamika *f.* **1.** (= *żywiołowość*) dynamic, vigor. **2.** *fiz., muz.* dynamics; **zasada dynamiki** the principle of dynamics; **dynamika płynów/gazów/ plazmy** fluid/gas/plasma dynamics; **dynamika układów** system dynamics; **dynamika populacji** *biol.* population dynamics.

dynamit *mi* dynamite.

dynamizm *mi* dynamism, dynamic.

dynamizować *ipf.* dynamize; **dynamizować gospodarkę** dynamize the economy. ~ **się** *ipf.* gain momentum.

dynamo *n. el.* dynamo.

dynamometr *mi fiz.* dynamometer.

dynasta *mp form.* dynast.

dynastia *f. Gen.* **-ii** dynasty.

dynastyczny *a.* dynastic; **ród dynastyczny** ruling family; **władca dynastyczny** dynastic ruler.

dyndać *ipf.* **1.** *pot.* (= *kołysać się*) dangle, swing. **2.** (= *machać luźno*) dangle (*sth*). **3.** *pot.* (= *wisieć na szubienicy*) swing (*za coś* for sth).

dyngus *mi Gen.* **-a** *l.* **-u** water fights (*an Easter Monday tradition in Poland*).

dynia *f. bot.* pumpkin, squash (*Cucurbita*).

dyniowate *pl. bot.* the gourd family (*Cucurbitaceae*).

dyniowaty *a.* pumpkin-shaped; **dyniowata głowa** pumpkin head.

dynks *mi Gen.* -a *l.* -u *pot.* whatsit, thingummy.

dyplom *mi* diploma, certificate; **dyplom magisterski/doktorski** master's/doctoral diploma; **dyplom lekarski** medical diploma; **dyplom uznania** diploma of merit.

dyplomacja *f.* diplomacy.

dyplomata *mp t. przen.* diplomat.

dyplomatka *f. Gen.pl.* -ek **1.** (= *kobieta dyplomata*) *zob.* **dyplomata. 2.** (*teczka*) attaché case. **3.** (*płaszcz*) overcoat.

dyplomatyczny *a.* **1.** diplomatic; **kroki/rokowania/stosunki dyplomatyczne** diplomatic steps/negotiations/relations; **nota/misja/poczta dyplomatyczna** diplomatic note/mission/mail; **kurier/paszport/immunitet dyplomatyczny** diplomatic courier/passport/immunity; **służba dyplomatyczna** the diplomatic service; **język dyplomatyczny** diplomatic language; **korpus/protokół/personel dyplomatyczny** diplomatic corps/protocol/staff. **2.** *przen.* diplomatic, tactful; **dyplomatyczne milczenie** diplomatic *l.* tactful silence; **dyplomatyczna odpowiedź** diplomatic answer; **dyplomatyczne posunięcie** diplomatic move.

dyplomatyka *f. przest.* **1.** = **dyplomacja. 2.** *nauk.* (= *badanie dawnych dokumentów*) diplomatics.

dyplomowany *a.* qualified, trained, certified; **pielęgniarka dyplomowana** qualified nurse; **oficer dyplomowany** trained officer.

dyplomowy *a.* diploma; **praca dyplomowa** thesis, dissertation; **egzamin dyplomowy** final exam; **koncert dyplomowy** graduation concert.

dypodia *f. Gen.* -ii *teor.lit.* dipody.

dypsomania *f. Gen.* -ii *pat.* dipsomania.

dyptyk *mi teor.lit., sztuka* diptych.

dyr. *abbr.* (= *dyrektor*) Head.

dyrdać *ipf. pot.* scuttle (along).

dyrdymały *pl. Gen.* -ów *pot.* drivel, nonsense.

dyrekcja *f.* **1.** management; **dyrekcja przedsiębiorstwa** company management; **dyrekcja naczelna** top management; **zarządzenie dyrekcji** management ruling; **pod dyrekcją...** *muz.* conducted by... **2.** (*budynek*) head office.

dyrekcyjny *a.* of the management, manager's, managerial.

dyrektor *mp pl.* -rzy *l.* -owie **1.** (= *szef*) director, manager; **dyrektor naczelny** director general; **objąć stanowisko dyrektora** take up the position of director. **2.** *szkoln.* headperson; (*tylko o mężczyźnie*) headmaster. **3.** *hist.* director.

dyrektoriat *mi hist.* **1.** the (French) Directory. **2.** *styl* the Directoire style.

dyrektorka *f. Gen.pl.* -ek *pot.* **1.** *zob.* **dyrektor 1. 2.** *szkoln.* headmistress.

dyrektorski *a.* director's, manager's; **gabinet dyrektorski** the manager's office; **spaść z dyrektorskiego stołka** *pot.* be removed from management.

dyrektorstwo *n.* directorship.

dyrektywa *f.* directive.

dyrygencki *a.* conductorial; **pulpit dyrygencki** conductor's stand; **sztuka dyrygencka** the art of conducting.

dyrygent *mp*, **dyrygentka** *f. Gen.pl.* -ek conductor.

dyrygować *ipf.* + *Dat. muz.* conduct; *przen.* lead, supervise.

dyscyplina *f.* **1.** (= *karność*) discipline; **żelazna dyscyplina** iron *l.* harsh discipline; **utrzymywać dyscyplinę** keep *l.* maintain discipline. **2.** (= *dziedzina nauki*) discipline, field of study.

dyscyplinarka *f. Gen.pl.* -ek *pot.* disciplinary proceedings.

dyscyplinarnie *adv.* disciplinarily; **zwolniony dyscyplinarnie** disciplinarily dismissed.

dyscyplinarny *a.* disciplinary; **komisja/kara dyscyplinarna** disciplinary committee/punishment; **postępowanie dyscyplinarne** disciplinary proceedings.

dyscyplinować *ipf.* discipline.

dysertacja *f. uniw.* dissertation, thesis; **dysertacja doktorska** doctoral dissertation.

dysfunkcja *f. form.* dysfunction.

dysgrafia *f. Gen.* -ii *pat.* dysgraphy.

dysgrafik *mp* dysgraphic.

dysharmonia *f. Gen.* -ii *form.* dissonance.

dyshonor *mi* dishonor, affront; **uczynić komuś dyshonor** affront *l.* insult sb.

dysjunkcja *f. log.* disjunction; **spójnik dysjunkcji** disjunctive connective.

dysk *mi* **1.** *anat. l. kształt* disk, *Br.* disc; **wypadnięcie dysku** *pat.* slipped disk. **2.** *sport* (*konkurencja l. sprzęt*) discus. **3.** *komp.* disk; **dysk magnetyczny** magnetic disk; **twardy dysk** hard disk; **dysk elastyczny** floppy (disk), diskette; **dysk kompaktowy/optyczny** *komp.* compact/optical disc; **stacja dysków** *l.* napęd dysku disk drive.

dyskdżokej *mp Gen.pl.* -ów disc jockey, DJ.

dyskietka *f. Gen.pl.* -ek *komp.* floppy disk, floppy, diskette; **zapisać na dyskietce** save to a floppy; **drukować z dyskietki** print from a floppy.

dyskobol *mp Gen.pl.* -i *l.* -ów, **dyskobolka** *f. Gen.pl.* -ek discus thrower.

dyskografia *f. Gen.* -ii *muz.* discography.

dyskomfort *mi* discomfort, uneasiness; **odczuwać dyskomfort** feel discomfort, feel uneasy; **dyskomfort psychiczny** mental discomfort.

dyskonto *n. fin.* discount.

dyskontować *ipf.* **1.** *fin.* discount. **2.** *przen.* (= *korzystać z*) take advantage of, make the most of (*sth*).

dyskontowy *a. fin., ekon.* discount; **operacja dyskontowa** discount operation; **stopa dyskontowa** discount rate; **bank dyskontowy** discount house.

dyskopatia *f. Gen.* -ii *pat.* slipped disk.

dyskoteka *f.* disco, discotheque; **bawić się całą noc na dyskotece** disco all night; **urządzać dyskotekę** organize a disco; (*lokal*) disco.

dyskotekowy *a.* disco; **muzyka dyskotekowa** disco music; **klub dyskotekowy** disco club.

dyskrecja *f.* discretion; **liczę na twoją dyskrecję** I'm counting on your discretion; **oczekuję abso-**

lutnej dyskrecji I expect absolute discretion; **nie pytałem o nic przez dyskrecję** I didn't ask about anything out of discretion.

dyskrecjonalny *a.* **1.** *rzad.* (= *nieograniczony*) discretional, arbitrary. **2.** *przest.* (= *poufny*) confidential, private.

dyskredytacja *f. form.* discrediting.

dyskredytować *ipf. form.* discredit, compromise. **~ się** *ipf.* discredit o.s., compromise o.s.

dyskretnie *adv.* discreetly, tactfully; **rozpytywać się dyskretnie** make discreet inquiries (*o kogoś/coś* about sb/sth); **postępować dyskretnie** act discreetly.

dyskretność *f.* **1.** = **dyskrecja.** **2.** *mat.* discreteness.

dyskretny *a.* **1.** (= *dochowujący tajemnic, taktowny*) discreet. **2.** (= *skrywany, sekretny*) secret, furtive; **dyskretny kochanek** secret lover. **3.** (= *ledwo dostrzegalny*) discreet; **dyskretny aromat** discreet fragrance; **dyskretny urok** discreet charm; **dyskretne ziewnięcie** discreet yawn; **dyskretny makijaż** discreet makeup. **4.** *mat., komp.* discrete; **przestrzeń dyskretna** discrete space; **zbiór dyskretny** discrete set.

dyskryminacja *f.* discrimination, unfair treatment; **dyskryminacja rasowa** racial discrimination; **dyskryminacja kobiet** discrimination against women; **dyskryminacja wyznaniowa** religious discrimination; **dyskryminacja rolnictwa** unfair treatment of the agricultural sector; **przejawy dyskryminacji** manifestations of discrimination; **zwalczać dyskryminację** fight discrimination; **protestować przeciw dyskryminacji** protest against discrimination.

dyskryminacyjny *a.* **1.** discriminatory; **polityka dyskryminacyjna** discriminatory policy; **dyskryminacyjne ustawodawstwo** discriminatory legislation; **dyskryminacyjne cła** unfair import duties. **2.** *mat.* **analiza dyskryminacyjna** discriminant analysis.

dyskryminator *mi Gen.* **-a** *el., tel.* discriminator; **dyskryminator częstotliwości** frequency discriminator; **dyskryminator rozmów telefonicznych** phone-call discriminator.

dyskryminować *ipf.* discriminate.

dyskurs *mi ret.* discourse.

dyskursywny *a. ret.* discursive; **myślenie dyskursywne** *fil.* discursive thinking.

dyskusja *f.* discussion, debate; **burzliwa dyskusja** heated discussion; **kwestia do dyskusji** question open to discussion; **to nie podlega dyskusji** it is indisputable; **poddać coś pod dyskusję** bring sth up for discussion; **zabrać głos w dyskusji** enter a debate; **wdawać się w dyskusję** get involved in a debate.

dyskusyjny *a.* **1.** (= *dotyczący dyskusji*) discussion; **klub dyskusyjny** debating society. **2.** (= *sporny*) debatable, controversial; **kwestia dyskusyjna** disputable question; **dyskusyjne poglądy** controversial views; **dyskusyjne stanowisko** moot *l.* debatable position.

dyskutant *mp* debater.

dyskutantka *f. zob.* **dyskutant.**

dyskutować *ipf.* discuss, debate; **dyskutować**

jakiś problem discuss a problem; **dyskutować o literaturze** discuss literature; **dyskutować nad jakąś kwestią** debate a question.

dyskwalifikacja *f.* disqualification; **dożywotnia dyskwalifikacja zawodnika** *sport* life disqualification of a player, disqualification for life.

dyskwalifikować *ipf.* disqualify; **dyskwalifikować zawodnika** disqualify a player (*z zawodów* from a competition); **jego skrajne poglądy dyskwalifikują go jako obiektywnego obserwatora** his extremist views disqualify him as an objective observer.

dysleksja *f. pat., psych.* dyslexia.

dyslektyk *mp pat., psych.* dyslexic.

dyslokacja *f.* **1.** distribution; *wojsk.* deployment. **2.** *geol.* displacement.

dysocjacja *f. chem.* dissociation; **dysocjacja elektrolityczna** electrolytic dissociation; **dysocjacja termiczna** thermal dissociation; **dysocjacja jaźni** *l.* **osobowości** *psych.* dissociation.

dysocjować *ipf. chem.* dissociate.

dysolucja *f. przest., chem.* dissolution; **dysolucja soli** salt dissolution.

dysonans *mi pl.* **-e** **1.** *ret.* discordance. **2.** *muz.* discord, dissonance. **3.** *przen.* (= *niezgodność*) dissonance, discordance, discord; **dysonans między deklaracjami a czynami** discord between words and deeds; **dysonans poznawczy** *psych.* cognitive dissonance.

dysonansowy *a.* dissonant, discordant.

dyspalatalizacja *f. fon.* **1.** (= *stwardnienie*) dispalatalization. **2.** (= *przegłos*) umlaut.

dyspalatalizować *ipf. fon.* dispalatalize.

dyspensa *f. rz.-kat.* dispensation; **udzielić dyspensy** dispense (*komuś od czegoś* sb from sth); **uzyskać dyspensę** obtain dispensation.

dyspepsja *f. pat.* dyspepsia, indigestion.

dyspersja *f.* **1.** *chem.* dispersion, disperse system. **2.** *fiz.* dispersion.

dyspersyjny *a. chem., fiz.* dispersive; **układ dyspersyjny** disperse system.

dysponent *mi zwł. prawn.* holder.

dysponować *ipf.* **1.** (= *zarządzać*) administer; **dysponować czasem** have time (to spare); **dysponować gotówką** have ready cash. **2.** (= *wydawać polecenia*) give instructions. **3.** *rz.-kat.* anoint the sick, give extreme unction.

dyspozycja *f.* **1.** (= *polecenie*) order, instruction; **wydawać dyspozycje** give orders *l.* instructions; **jestem do pani dyspozycji** I'm at your disposal; **mamy do dyspozycji najnowocześniejszy sprzęt diagnostyczny** we have the most modern diagnostic equipment at our disposal. **2.** (= *konspekt*) outline; **dyspozycja wykładu** lecture outline. **3.** *med., psych.* (= *skłonność*) disposition, inclination.

dyspozycyjność *f.* time flexibility; **nieograniczona dyspozycyjność** unlimited time flexibility.

dyspozycyjny *a.* **1.** (= *zlecający*) disposing; **centrum dyspozycyjne** headquarters. **2.** (= *taki, którym można dysponować dowolnie*) discretionary, at one's disposal; **dyspozycyjny pracownik** employee prepared to work flexible hours; **fundusz dyspozycyjny** discretional fund.

dyspozytor *mp* dispatcher; **dyspozytor ruchu** traffic controller.

dyspozytorka *f. zob.* **dyspozytor**.

dysproporcja *f.* disproportion; **powiększające się dysproporcje społeczne** growing social disproportions; **dysproporcja między popytem a podażą** demand and supply disproportion.

dysproporcjonalny *a.* disproportionate; **dysproporcjonalna budowa ciała** disproportionate body.

dysproz *mi chem.* dysprosium.

dysputa *f. przest.* debate; **dysputy filozoficzne** philosophical debates; **wdawać się w dysputę** get involved in a discussion.

dystans *mi pl.* -e *l.* -y **1.** (= *odległość*) distance; **dystans między Chinami a Zachodem powoli zmniejsza się** distance between China and the West is slowly but surely decreasing; **dystans czasowy** time distance; **trzymać kogoś na dystans** keep sb at a distance; **trzymać się na dystans** keep one's distance; **zachowywać dystans** keep o.s. at a distance; **nabrać dystansu do kogoś/czegoś** distance o.s. from sb/sth; **dystans krytyczny** *biol.* critical distance; **dystans społeczny** *socjol.* social distance; **strefa dystansu** *socjol.* distance zone. **2.** *sport* distance; **krótki/średni/długi dystans** short/middle/long distance.

dystansować *ipf.* **1.** *t. przen.* (= *wyprzedzać*) distance, surpass, leave far behind. **2.** *sport* distance. ~ **się** *ipf.* distance o.s.; **dystansować się wobec bliskich** distance o.s. from one's relatives.

dystorsja *f. fiz., fot., med.* distortion.

dystrakcja *f. psych.* distraction.

dystrofia *f. Gen.* -ii *pat.* dystrophy, dystrophia; **dystrofia mięśni** muscular dystrophy.

dystrybucja *f.* **1.** (= *rozdział*) distribution; **dystrybucja towaru** goods distribution; **dystrybucja żywności** food distribution; **sieć dystrybucji** distribution network. **2.** *jęz.* distribution; **dystrybucja identyczna** identical distribution; **dystrybucja komplementarna** *l.* uzupełniająca complementary distribution; **dystrybucja krzyżująca się** cross-distribution; **dystrybucja inkluzywna** inclusive distribution. **3.** *stat.* distribution.

dystrybucjonizm *mi jęz.* distributionism.

dystrybutor *mp pl.* -rzy distributor; **dystrybutor bezpośredni** direct distributor. – *mi pl.* -ry **1.** (*na stacji benzynowej*) pump. **2.** (*do napojów*) dispenser.

dystrykt *mi* district; **Dystrykt Kolumbii** *geogr.* District of Columbia, D.C. *l.* DC.

dystych *mi teor.lit.* distich, couplet; **dystych elegijny** elegiac distich.

dystyngowany *a.* dignified, distinguished; **dystyngowane towarzystwo** distinguished society; **dystyngowane maniery** refined manners.

dystynkcje *pl. Gen.* -i insignia (of rank); **dystynkcje generalskie** general's insignia.

dysydencki *a.* dissident, dissenting; **grupa dysydencka** dissident group.

dysydent *mp* **1.** (= *opozycjonista*) dissident. **2.** *rel., hist.* (= *innowierca*) dissenter.

dysymilacja *f. biol., jęz.* dissimilation; **dysymilacja na odległość** distance dissimilation.

dysza *f. techn.* nozzle, jet; **dysza paliwowa (gaźnika)** carburetor jet.

dyszeć *ipf.* -ę -ysz pant; (*o chorym*) wheeze, gasp, rattle; **ciężko dyszeć** breathe hard; **dyszeć nienawiścią** be consumed with hatred; **ledwie** *l.* **ledwo dyszeć** be on one's last legs; have got one foot in the grave.

dyszel *mi* -szl- *Gen.* -a tongue; (*podwójny*) shaft.

dyszkant *mi Gen.* -u (*głos*) treble. – *mp Gen.* -a *pl.* -y (*śpiewak*) treble (singer).

dytyramb *mi teor.lit.* dithyramb; *przen.* (= *pochwała*) dithyramb.

dywagacja *f. lit.* divagation, digression; **snuć dywagacje** divagate, digress.

dywagować *ipf. lit.* divagate, digress.

dywan *mi* **1.** (*na podłodze*) carpet; **perski dywan** Persian rug *l.* carpet; **dywan igłowy** latch-hook carpet; **dywan** *l.* **kobierzec kwiatowy** *przen.* plant carpet *l.* layer; **latający dywan** magic carpet. **2.** *hist.* (*w Turcji osmańskiej*) divan. **3.** *teor.lit.* divan.

dywanik *mi Gen.* -a (*na podłodze*) rug, mat; **wezwać kogoś na dywanik** call sb on the carpet; **pójść na dywanik** be called on the carpet.

dywanowy *a.* **1.** carpet; **wykładzina dywanowa** fitted carpet; **nalot dywanowy** *wojsk.* carpet bombing; **kwietnik dywanowy** flowerbed; **dywanowe zbiorowiska roślinne** *biol.* carpet plant communities. **2.** *teor.lit.* divan.

dywergencja *f. lit.* divergence, divergency; **dywergencja rozwoju** *biol.* divergence; **dywergencja geomorfologiczna** *geol.* geomorphological divergence.

dywersant *mp* saboteur.

dywersja *f.* sabotage; **dywersja ideologiczna/gospodarcza** ideological/economic sabotage; **akty dywersji** acts of sabotage.

dywersyjny *a.* sabotage; **akcja dywersyjna** sabotage action; **wojna dywersyjna** guerilla war; **grupa dywersyjna** sabotage group.

dywidenda *f. ekon.* dividend; **wypłacić dywidendę** pay dividend.

dywiz *mi druk.* hyphen; **to słowo pisze się z dywizem** this word is hyphenated.

dywizja *f. wojsk.* division; **generał dywizji** major general.

dywizjon *mi wojsk.* **1.** (*w artylerii, w jednostkach zmotoryzowanych, marynarce*) command. **2.** (*w lotnictwie*) squadron.

dyzenteria *f. Gen.* -ii *pat.* dysentery.

dyżur *mi* duty hours; **całodobowy dyżur** twenty-four-hour duty; **nocny dyżur** night duty; **pełnić dyżur** be on call; **ostry dyżur** *med.* emergency service.

dyżurka *f. Gen.pl.* -ek duty-room.

dyżurny *a.* on duty; **szpital dyżurny** *med.* emergency hospital; **lekarz/oficer dyżurny** doctor/officer on duty. – *mp* person on duty; *szkoln.* monitor; **dyżurny ruchu** *kol.* traffic controller.

dyżurować *ipf.* be on duty.

dzban *mi Gen.* -a (= *naczynie*) pitcher, jug; (= *zawartość dzbana*) pitcherful, jugful; **wychylić dzban wina** *arch.* drink a pitcher *l.* jug of wine;

póty dzban wodę nosi, póki się ucho nie urwie one can only take so much.

dzbanecznik *ma Gen.* **-a** *bot.* pitcher plant (*Nepenthes*).

dzbanek *mi* **-nk-** *Gen.* **-a** pitcher, jug; **dzbanek do kawy** coffee pot; **dzbanek do herbaty** teapot; **dzbanek do mleka** milk jug *l.* pitcher.

dzbanuszek *mi* **-szk-** *Gen.* **-a** pitcher; **dzbanuszek do śmietanki** creamer, cream jug.

dziabać *ipf.* **-ię -iesz, dziabnąć** *pf.* **-ij** *pot.* jab. ~ **się** *ipf.* **-ię -iesz, dziabnąć się** *pf.* **-ij** *pot.* jab o.s.

dziać *ipf.* **-eję -ejesz** (*na drutach*) knit; (*maszynowo*) weave; **dziana spódniczka** knitted skirt.

dziać się *ipf.* **dzieje się** happen, occur, take place; **co się dzieje?** what's going on *l.* happening?; **działo się to miesiąc temu** it happened a month ago; **nic się nie dzieje** nothing's going on; **dzieje mi się krzywda** I'm being wronged; **ostatnio dobrze mi się dzieje** recently I've been doing really well; **co się z tobą dzieje?** what's the matter with you?; **dzieje się ze mną coś niezwykłego** something strange's happening to me; **niech się dzieje, co chce** come what may; **niech się dzieje wola boża** *l.* nieba God's will be done.

dziad *mp Voc.* **-dzie** *l. pot.* **-u** *pl.* **-y** 1. (= *żebrak*) beggar; **zejść na dziady** go to the dogs; **tylko dzida i baby brakuje!** everything but the kitchen sink; **przemówił dziad do obrazu, a obraz do niego ani razu** it's like talking to the wall. 2. (= *starzec*) old man. 3. *pog.* (= *mężczyzna*) guy. 4. *Voc.* **-dzie** *pl.* **-owie** (= *ojciec matki l. ojca*) grandfather; (= *przodek*) grandfather, forefather; **z dziada pradziada** for generations. 5. (= *rzep, kolczasty owoc l. koszyczek kwiatowy*) bur.

dziadek *mp* **-dk-** *pl.* **-owie** 1. grandfather, granddad, granddaddy, grandpa. 2. (= *starzec*) old man; **nie śmiej się dziadku z cudzego upadku** don't laugh at sb else's misfortune, never laugh when a hoarse goes by, you might be the next to die. 3. (= *żebrak*) beggar. 4. *karty* dummy (hand); **grać w brydża z dziadkiem** play bridge with a dummy (hand). – *mi* **-dk-** *Gen.* **-a** *pl.* **-i** (*do orzechów*) nutcracker.

dziadkowie *pl. Gen.* **-ów** grandparents.

dziadostwo *n.* 1. *pot.* (= *bieda*) slum. 2. *pog.* (= *hołota*) riffraff, the rabble. 3. *pog.* (= *tandeta*) trash, rubbish.

dziadować *ipf.* 1. *pot.* (= *żyć w nędzy*) live in poverty. 2. *rzad.* (= *żebrać*) beg.

dziadowski *a.* 1. (= *żebraczy*) beggar's; **jesteś rozpuszczony jak dziadowski bicz** you're a spoiled brat; **dziadowskie pieśni** doggerel. 2. *pot.* (= *tandetny*) trashy; (= *biedny*) poor.

dziadziuś *mp* *pl.* **-owie** *Gen.* **-ów** grandpa, granddaddy.

dział *mi* 1. (= *dziedzina działalności*) branch; **algebra jest działem matematyki** algebra is a branch of mathematics. 2. (*w czasopiśmie*) section; **dział sportowy** sports section. 3. (= *oddział jakiejś instytucji, sklepu*) department, division; **dział spożywczy** groceries; **dział kadr** human resources department; **dział wód** *l.* **wodny** *geogr.* divide. 4. (= *dzielenie czegoś*) division, dividing; *prawn.* distribution; **przeprowadzić działy mająt-**

ku distribute property. 5. *gł. prawn.* (= *przydzielona część czegoś*) share; **zrzec się swojego działu** give up one's share.

działacz *mp* activist; **działacz związkowy** trade unionist; **działacz polonijny** Polish community activist.

działaczka *f. zob.* **działacz.**

działać *ipf.* 1. (= *robić coś*) act; **działać na rzecz dzieci niepełnosprawnych** act in aid of handicapped children; **działać w imieniu bezdomnych** act on behalf of the homeless; **działać w obronie własnej** *prawn.* act in self-defense; **działać w dobrej wierze** act in good faith; **działać na szkodę przedsiębiorstwa** act to the detriment of the company, act against the interests of the company; **działać na własną rękę** *pot.* act on one's own. 2. (= *wywierać wpływ*) have an effect, influence; **muzyka działa na mnie uspokajająco** music helps me relax; **to działa na moją wyobraźnię** it inspires my imagination; **zastrzyk zaraz zacznie działać** injection will work soon; **działasz mi na nerwy** you're getting on my nerves, you're getting on my last nerve; **działać kwasem siarkowym na cynk** *chem.* treat zinc with sulfuric acid; **działać na zwłokę** play for time. 3. (*o urządzeniach*) (= *funkcjonować*) work, operate; **telefon nie działa** phone doesn't work, phone is out of order; **silnik przestał działać** engine konked out *l.* died, engine is out of order, engine won't start; **to działa na baterie** it runs on batteries. 4. (*o aktach prawnych*) (= *obowiązywać*) be in force, be effective; **to prawo nie działa wstecz** this law is not retroactive.

działalność *f.* 1. (= *działanie*) activity; **prowadzić działalność gospodarczą** run a business; **działalność artystyczna** artistic work. 2. (= *oddziaływanie*) action; **działalność wulkaniczna** volcanic activity; **erozyjna działalność wiatru** erosive action of wind.

działanie *n.* 1. (= *akcja*) action; (= *funkcjonowanie*) operation, working; (= *oddziaływanie*) effect; **mieć swobodę działania** be free to act; **liczy się skuteczność działania** what counts is effectiveness; **działania odwetowe** retaliatory action; **działania osłonowe** *ekon.* protective action; **działania interwencyjne** *ekon.* intervention; **działanie w dobrej/złej wierze** acting in good/bad faith. 2. *wojsk.* operations; **działania zaczepne** offensive actions; **działania odporne** defensive actions; **działania bojowe** warfare. 3. *mat.* operation; **działanie przemienne/łączne** commutative/associative operation; **rozdzielność działań** divisibility of operations.

działka *f. Gen.pl.* **-ek** 1. (= *parcela*) lot; **działka budowlana** building lot. 2. (= *ogródek*) fruit and vegetable garden, (garden) plot; *Br.* allotment. 3. (= *jednostka jakiejś skali*) graduation, degree; **działka elementarna** scale interval, minimum graduation. 4. *bot.* sepal. 5. *pot.* (= *udział w zysku*) cut, share. 6. *pot.* (= *przydział obowiązków*) scope of responsibility. 7. *sl.* (= *porcja narkotyku*) hit.

działko *n. Gen.pl.* **-łek** cannon, gun; **działko**

przeciwlotnicze *wojsk.* anti-aircraft cannon *l.* gun; działko *l.* armatka wodna water cannon.

działkowicz *mp Gen.pl.* -ów gardener; *Br.* allotment holder.

działkowiec *mp* -wc- *pl.* -y = działkowicz.

działkowy *a.* garden; ogródek działkowy fruit and vegetable garden, (garden) plot; *Br.* allotment.

działo *n. wojsk.* cannon, gun; działo przeciw-pancerne/przeciwlotnicze anti-tank/anti-aircraft gun; oddać salwę z dział volley; działo samobieżne self-propelled gun; działo bezodrzutowe non-recoil gun.

działon *mi Gen.* -u *wojsk.* gun section.

działowy[1] *a.* **1.** (= *częściowy*) sectional, departmental; katalog działowy *bibl.* subject catalog. **2.** (= *dzielący*) separating, dividing; ścianka działowa *bud.* partition (wall), division (wall). **3.** *prawn.* (= *związany z podziałem majątku*) distribution; intercyza działowa marital agreement.

działowy[2] *a. wojsk.* (= *armatni*) gun, cannon, artillery; salwa działowa volley, salvo. – *mp wojsk.* gunner.

dzianina *f. tk.* knitwear.

dziany *a.* **1.** knitted. **2.** *pot.* (= *zamożny*) loaded, rolling in money; dziany gość loaded guy.

dziarski *a.* spry, energetic; dziarski staruszek spry old man.

dziarsko *adv.* spryly; maszerować dziarsko march spryly.

dziatki *pl. Gen.* -tek *arch.* children.

dziatwa *f. lit.* children.

dziąsło *n. Gen.pl.* -seł gum; *anat.* gingiva; zapalenie dziąseł gingivitis.

dziąsłowy *a.* gum, gingival; *fon.* alveolar; spółgłoska dziąsłowa alveolar consonant.

dzicz *f.* **1.** (= *barbarzyńcy*) savages; (= *motłoch*) mob. **2.** *uj.* (= *odludne miejsce*) middle of nowhere.

dziczeć *ipf.* **1.** (= *wracać do stanu pierwotnego*) run wild. **2.** (*o człowieku*) (= *nabierać okrucieństwa*) grow wild.

dziczka *f. Gen.pl.* -ek (= *dziki pęd*) wilding.

dziczyzna *f. kulin.* game.

dzida *f.* spear, pike.

dzidzia *f. W.* -u *Gen.pl.* -i *l.* -dź **1.** baby. **2.** *pot.* (= *młoda kobieta*) chick, babe.

dzidziuś *mp Gen.pl.* -ów baby.

dzieci *pl. zob.* dziecko.

dzieciak *mp pl.* -i kid; *uj.* brat.

dzieciątko *n.* baby; Dzieciątko Jezus Infant Jesus.

dziecię *n.* -cięci- *pl.* -ciąt- *Gen.* -ąt *przest. l. lit.* child.

dziecięcy *a.* children's; literatura dziecięca children's books; szpital dziecięcy children's hospital; obuwie dziecięce children's footware.

dziecina *f. emf.* child.

dziecinnie *adv.* (= *w sposób właściwy dzieciom*) in a childlike manner; (= *naiwnie*) childishly; dziecinnie łatwe pytanie simple question; zachowywać się dziecinnie behave like a child.

dziecinnieć *ipf.* grow infantile.

dziecinny *a.* **1.** (= *właściwy dziecku*) childlike; pokój dziecinny nursery; wózek dziecinny baby carriage; to dziecinna igraszka it's child's play. **2.** (= *infantylny*) childish, infantile; dziecinne obawy childish fears; dziecinne wykręty childish excuses; po dziecinnemu childishly.

dzieciństwo *n.* childhood; wspomnienia z dzieciństwa childhood memories; znamy się od dzieciństwa we've known each other *l.* one another since childhood.

dzieciobójca *mp* infanticide.

dzieciobójczy *a.* infanticidal.

dzieciobójczyni *f. zob.* dzieciobójca.

dzieciobójstwo *n.* infanticide.

dzieciorób *mp* -o- *pl.* -y *pog.* baby maker.

dziecko *n. pl.* -eci *Gen.* -eci *Ins.* -ećmi child; dzieci children; dziecko szczęścia the lucky one; cudowne dziecko child prodigy; od dziecka since childhood; przecież on nie jest dzieckiem but he's not a child; zrobić komuś dziecko *pot.* knock sb up, get *l.* make sb pregnant; począć *l.* spłodzić dziecko conceive a child; dziecko niedorozwinięte retarded child; adoptować dziecko adopt a child; dziecko przyszło na świat child was born; urodzić zdrowe dziecko give birth to a healthy baby; dziecko legalne *prawn.* legitimate child, child born in wedlock; dziecko pozamałżeńskie *prawn.* illegitimate child, child born out of wedlock; dom dziecka orphanage; wyrodne dziecko wayward child; dziecko ulicy street urchin, guttersnipe, street child; jesteś jeszcze jak dziecko you're still like a child; cieszyła się jak dziecko she was as happy as a king; wylać dziecko z kąpielą throw the baby away *l.* out with the bath-water; dziecko! my dear!; dzieci i ryby głosu nie mają children should be seen, not heard; małe dzieci - mały kłopot, duże dzieci - duży kłopot small chidren - small problems, big children - big problems.

dziedzic *mp* **1.** (= *spadkobierca*) heir, inheritor; (= *następca*) heir, successor. **2.** (= *właściciel ziemski*) landlord, landowner.

dziedzictwo *n.* **1.** (= *spuścizna*) heritage, inheritance; dziedzictwo narodowe national heritage. **2.** (= *dziedziczenie*) right to inherit, right of inheritance; dziedzictwo tronu succession to the throne.

dziedziczenie *n.* **1.** *biol.* inheritance. **2.** *zwł. prawn.* right to inherit, right of inheritance; inheritance; dziedziczenie majątku property inheritance; dziedziczenie po ojcu inheriting from one's father; dziedziczenie tronu succession to the throne.

dziedziczka *f. Gen.pl.* -ek **1.** (= *spadkobierczyni*) heiress, inheritrix, inheritress; (= *następczyni*) heiress, successor. **2.** *przest.* (= *posiadaczka ziemska*) landowner.

dziedziczność *f.* **1.** *biol.* heredity, heritability. **2.** (= *przekazywalność*) succession.

dziedziczny *a.* **1.** *biol.* hereditary; choroba dziedziczna hereditary disease; cecha dziedziczna inherited *l.* hereditary trait. **2.** (= *odziedziczony*) hereditary; tron dziedziczny hereditary throne. **3.** (= *sprawujący władzę na podstawie* *sukcesji*) hereditary; **władca dziedziczny** hereditary ruler.

dziedziczyć *ipf.* **1.** *biol.* inherit. **2.** *zwł. prawn.* (= *obejmować*) inherit; **dziedziczyć po ojcu** inherit from one's father; **dziedziczyć majątek** inherit property; **dziedziczyć tron** succeed to the throne.

dziedzina *f.* (*wiedzy, nauki*) discipline, domain; (*działalności*) field, area.

dziedziniec *mi* -ńc- *Gen.* -a yard, courtyard; **dziedziniec zamkowy** bailey.

dziegieć *mi* -gci- wood tar; **łyżka dziegciu w beczce miodu** a spoon of tar in a barrel of honey.

dzieje *pl. Gen.* -ów **1.** (= *historia*) history; **dzieje Polski** Polish history; **od zarania dziejów** from the dawn of history; **Dzieje Apostolskie** Acts (of the Apostles). **2.** (= *wydarzenia, fakty*) events, vicissitudes; **to stare dzieje** this belongs to the past.

dziejowy *a.* historic; **wydarzenie dziejowe** historic event; **odpowiedzialność dziejowa** historic responsibility; **misja dziejowa** historic mission; **sprawiedliwość dziejowa** historic justice.

dziekan *mp* **1.** *uniw.* dean. **2.** (*korpusu dyplomatycznego*) doyen; (*kobieta*) doyenne. **3.** (*rady adwokackiej*) doyen; (*kobieta*) doyenne. **4.** *rz.-kat.* dean.

dziekanat *mi* **1.** *uniw.* dean's office. **2.** *rz.-kat.* deanery.

dziekanka *f. pot.* (= *urlop dziekański*) dean's leave (*a 6-month's or year's leave granted by the dean*); **wziąć dziekankę** take a dean's leave.

dziekański *a. gł. uniw.* dean's; **urlop dziekański** dean's leave.

dzielenie *n.* **1.** division, dividing. **2.** *mat.* division; **wykonać dzielenie** divide.

dzielić *ipf.* **1.** (= *dokonywać podziału*) divide; **dzielić włos na czworo** split hairs. **2.** (= *rozdzielać*) distribute, share out; **dzielić czas między pracę i dom** divide one's time between work and home; **dzielić skórę na niedźwiedziu** count one's chickens before they are hatched. **3.** *t. przen.* (= *rozgraniczać*) separate, divide; (= *różnić*) differ; **dzieli nas ocean** we're thousands of miles apart; **dzielą nas poglądy polityczne** we have different political views. **4.** (= *korzystać l. przeżywać wspólnie*) share; **dzielić z kimś mieszkanie** share an apartment with sb. **5.** *mat.* divide; **ile jest dziesięć dzielone przez dwa?** how much is ten divided by two? ~ **się** *ipf.* **1.** (= *być dzielonym*) be divided; **Włochy dzielą się na bogatą północ i biedne południe** Italy is divided into rich North and poor South. **2.** (= *dawać część czegoś*) share; **dzielić się z kimś jedzeniem** share food with sb; **dzielić się opłatkiem** share the wafer. **3.** (= *komunikować sobie coś wzajemnie*) share; **dzielić się swoimi spostrzeżeniami** share one's observations. **4.** *mat.* be divided; **czy dziesięć dzieli się przez dwa?** is ten divisible by two?

dzielna *f. Gen.* -ej *mat.* dividend.

dzielnica *f.* **1.** (= *część kraju*) province, region. **2.** (= *część miasta*) district, quarter; **dzielnica portowa** port district; **dzielnica przemysłowa** industrial zone; **dzielnica willowa** villa district, residential district. **3.** *geogr., hist.* province, region.

dzielnicowy *a.* **1.** *geogr., hist., admin.* (*w kraju*) regional; **rozbicie dzielnicowe** *hist.* regional division *l.* separation *l.* partition. **2.** *admin., policja* (*w mieście*) precinct. – *mp* constable.

dzielnie *adv.* **1.** (= *odważnie*) bravely, courageously; **dzielnie się bronić** defend o.s. bravely; **dzielnie walczyć** fight courageously. **2.** (= *zaradnie*) resourcefully; **dzielnie sobie radzić** cope resourcefully; **dzielnie się spisałaś** you did very well.

dzielnik *mi Gen.* -a *mat.* divisor.

dzielność *f.* **1.** (= *odwaga*) courage; **dzielność morska** *żegl.* sea kindliness. **2.** (= *zaradność*) resourcefulness. **3.** (= *sprawność fizyczna*) fitness.

dzielny *a.* **1.** (= *odważny*) brave, courageous; **dzielny żołnierz** brave soldier. **2.** (= *zaradny*) resourceful; **dzielna dziewczyna** resourceful girl. **3.** (= *sprawny, zręczny*) efficient; **byłaś dzielną pomocnicą** you've been very helpful.

dzieło *n.* **1.** (= *praca*) work; **dzieło zniszczenia** act of destruction; **brać się** *l.* **przystąpić do dzieła** get *l.* set to work; **koniec wieńczy dzieło** completion crowns the work. **2.** (= *efekt pracy*) result; **to dzieło przypadku** it's a (pure) coincidence. **3.** (= *utwór*) work, composition; **dzieło sztuki** work of art; **dzieło literackie** literary work; **dzieło epokowe** epoch-making work.

dziennica *f. Gen., Dat., Loc.* -y *bot.* day lily (*Hemerocallis*).

dzienniczek *mi* -czk- *Gen.* -a **1.** notebook; diary. **2.** *szkoln.* pupil *l.* student book; report card.

dziennie *adv.* daily; **cztery razy dziennie** four times a day; **pracować po dziesięć godzin dziennie** work ten hours a *l.* per day.

dziennik *mi Gen.* -a **1.** (= *gazeta*) daily. **2.** (*telewizyjny l. radiowy*) (daily) news. **3.** (*w szkole, w biurze*) register; **dziennik lekcyjny** *l.* **szkolny** *szkoln.* class *l.* school register; **dziennik okrętowy** *żegl.* logbook, log. **4.** (= *pamiętnik*) diary; **dziennik podróży** journey diary.

dziennikarka *f. Gen.pl.* -ek **1.** (= *kobieta dziennikarz*) journalist. **2.** *pot.* (= *praca dziennikarza*) journalism.

dziennikarski *a.* journalist; **kaczka dziennikarska** canard.

dziennikarstwo *n.* journalism.

dziennikarz *mp* journalist; **dziennikarz radiowy** radio reporter; **dziennikarz sportowy** sports reporter; **pracować jako dziennikarz** work as a journalist.

dzienny *a.* **1.** (= *od wschodu do zachodu słońca*) day's; **światło dzienne** daylight; **rozkaz dzienny** *wojsk.* order of the day; **zwierzęta dzienne** *zool.* diurnal animals; **ujrzeć światło dzienne** (*o ludziach*) be born, see the light of day; (*o publikacjach*) come out; **wydobyć** *l.* **wyciągać coś na światło dzienne** bring sth to light; **wyjść na światło dzienne** come to light. **2.** (= *całodobowy*) daily, day's; **utarg dzienny** daily takings; **norma dzienna** daily standard *l.* norm; **obrót dzienny**

Ziemi *astron.* Earth's diurnal motion *l.* cycle; **łuk dzienny** *astron.* diurnal arc; **porządek dzienny obrad** agenda; **być na porządku dziennym** be common; **przejść nad czymś do porządku dziennego** pass sth off lightly, pass over sth lightly.

dzień *mi* dni- *Gen.* -a *pl.* -e *l.* dni **1.** (*od wschodu do zachodu słońca*) day; **dzień dobry** (= *powitanie*) (*przed południem*) good morning; (*po południu*) good afternoon; **dzień wolny (od pracy)** day off; **dzień pracy** *l.* **roboczy** weekday; **dzień powszedni** weekday; **dzień świąteczny** holiday; **dzień polarny** *astron.* polar day; **przesilenie dnia z nocą** solstice; **do białego dnia** till dawn; **w biały** *l.* **jasny dzień** in broad daylight; **rośliny krótkiego dnia** *bot.* short-day plants; **cały boży dzień** all day long, the whole day; **dniem i nocą** day and night; **przede** *l.* **nade dniem** just before dawn; **podobny jak dzień do nocy** like night and day. **2.** (= *doba*) day and night; **dzień po dniu** day after day; **dzień w dzień** day in, day out; **dzień wczorajszy** (= *wczoraj*) yesterday; (= *przeszłość*) yesterday, past; **dzień dzisiejszy** (= *dzisiaj*) today; (= *teraźniejszość*) today, present; **dzień jutrzejszy** (= *jutro*) tomorrow; (= *przyszłość*) tomorrow, future; **szukać wczorajszego dnia** hang around; **do dnia dzisiejszego** until now; **temat dnia** headline; **bohater dnia** hero of the day; **nie znasz dnia ani godziny** you never know the day; **żyć z dnia na dzień** live from day to day, live from hand to mouth; **odkładać coś z dnia na dzień** put sth off from day to day; **co dzień** every day; **mieć dobry dzień** have one's lucky day, have a good day; **mieć zły dzień** have a lousy *l.* bad day; **dzień drogi dzieli nas od Warszawy** we are a day's journey from Warsaw; **trzy dni zwolnienia lekarskiego** three days' sick leave; **opłata za dzień** day's rate. **3.** (= *wyznaczony termin*) date; **dzień ślubu** wedding day; **dzień tygodnia** week day; **dzień imienin** nameday; **dzień urodzin** birthday; **lada dzień** any day, any time now; **po dziś dzień** till now; **do sądnego dnia** forever; **Dzień Kobiet** Women's Day; **Sądny Dzień** *rel.* Doomsday; **Dzień Zaduszny** *rz.-kat.* All Souls' Day. **4.** (= *jakiś okres*) days; **twoje dni są policzone** your days are numbered.

dziergać *ipf.* **1.** (= *obszywać*) border; **ścieg dziergany** border stitch. **2.** (= *szydełkować*) crochet. **3.** (= *haftować*) embroider.

dzierlatka *f. Gen.pl.* -ek **1.** (= *dziewczyna*) young woman. **2.** *orn.* crested lark (*Galerida cristata*).

dzierzba *f. orn.* shrike (*Lanius*).

dzierżawa *f. gł. prawn.* **1.** (= *używanie*) lease; **wziąć coś w dzierżawę** lease sth, rent sth; **oddać** *l.* **puścić** *l.* **wypuścić coś w dzierżawę** let sth, lease sth, rent sth; **wieczysta dzierżawa** ground lease, ground-rent lease, land lease. **2.** (= *opłata*) rent.

dzierżawca *mp gł. prawn.* leaseholder, lessee.

dzierżawczy *a. jęz.* possessive; **zaimek dzierżawczy** possessive pronoun; **przymiotnik dzierżawczy** possessive adjective.

dzierżawić *ipf. gł. prawn.* (= *wziąć w dzierża-*

wę) lease, take a lease, rent; (= *oddać w dzierżawę*) lease, let.

dzierżawny *a. gł. prawn.* lease; **opłata dzierżawna** rent; **kontrakt dzierżawny** lease agreement *l.* contract.

dzierżyć *ipf.* **1.** *lit. l. żart.* (= *trzymać*) hold; **dzierżyć prym** be in the lead; **dzierżyć władzę/rządy/ster władzy** wield power. **2.** *prawn.* hold.

dzierżymorda *mp pl.* -y *pot., uj.* despot.

dziesiąta *f. Gen.* -ej (*godzina*) ten o'clock; **jest dziesiąta wieczór** it's ten p.m.; **będę piętnaście po dziesiątej** I'll be there at a quarter past ten; **kończę za piętnaście dziesiąta** I finish at a quarter to ten; **mam pociąg o w pół do dziesiątej** my train leaves at half past nine.

dziesiątek *mi Ins.* -kiem *pl.* -ki decade.

dziesiątka *f. Gen.pl.* -ek **1.** (= *liczba 10*) ten; **trafić w dziesiątkę** *t. przen.* hit the *l.* score a bull's eye. **2.** (= *tramwaj, autobus, dom, pokój nr 10*) number ten; **do szpitala dojedziesz dziesiątką** the ten takes you to the hospital, streetcar/bus, etc. number ten takes you to the hospital. **3.** (= *grupa dziesięciu ludzi*) (group of) ten people; (*np. w restauracji przy zamawianiu stolika*) party of ten. **4.** (= *banknot o nominale dziesięć*) tenner, ten; (= *dziesięciocentówka*) dime. **5.** *karty* ten; **dziesiątka pik** ten of spades. **6.** **dziesiątki** (= *duża ilość, liczba*) dozens. **7.** *żegl.* (= *dezetka*) ten, ten-oared craft. **8.** (= *wielkość czcionki*) ten-point font; **pisać dziesiątką** write using a ten-point font.

dziesiątkować *ipf.* **1.** (= *zabijać co dziesiątą osobę*) decimate. **2.** *przen.* (= *niszczyć masowo*) decimate; **czarna ospa zdziesiątkowała Indian** smallpox decimated the population of American Indians.

dziesiąty *a.* tenth; **dziesiąty wiek** the tenth century; **dziesiąte urodziny** tenth birthday; **minęła już godzina dziesiąta** it's already past ten; **urodziłem się dziesiątego maja** I was born on May tenth, I was born on the tenth of May; **jedna dziesiąta** one-tenth; **dziesiąta woda po kisielu** very distant relative; **za dziesiątą górą, za dziesiątą rzeką** far, far away. – *mi* the tenth (*day of a month*); **umówić się z kimś na dziesiątego czerwca** arrange a meeting with sb for the tenth of June; **skończyć pracę do dziesiątego** finish work by the tenth.

dziesięcina *f. hist.* tithes.

dziesięcioboista *mp sport* decathlete.

dziesięciobok *mi mat.* decagon.

dziesięciobój *mi* -o- *Gen.pl.* -ów *l.* -oi *sport* decathlon.

dziesięciodniowy *a.* ten-day, ten days'; **dziesięciodniowy urlop** ten-day vacation.

dziesięciogodzinny *a.* ten-hour, ten hours'; **dziesięciogodzinna podróż** ten-hour journey.

dziesięciogroszówka *f. Gen.pl.* -ek ten-grosz coin.

dziesięciokrotnie *adv.* tenfold, ten times; **zyski wzrosły dziesięciokrotnie** profits increased tenfold.

dziesięciokrotny *a.* tenfold, ten times; **dziesięciokrotny wzrost zysków** tenfold increase in profits; **dziesięciokrotny mistrz świata** ten-time world champion.

dziesięciolatek *mp* -tk- *pl.* -i (*o chłopcu*) ten-year-old (boy). – *ma* -tk- (*o zwierzęciu*) ten-year-old (animal).

dziesięciolatka *f. Dat., Loc.* -ce **1.** (*o dziewczynce*) ten-year-old (girl). **2.** *szkoln.* ten-grade school.

dziesięciolecie *n.* **1.** (= *10 lat*) decade. **2.** (= *10 rocznica*) tenth anniversary, decennial; **dziesięciolecie małżeństwa** tenth wedding anniversary.

dziesięcioletni *a.* ten-year, ten years; **dziesięcioletni chłopiec** ten-year-old boy.

dziesięciomiesięczny *a.* ten-month, ten months; **dziesięciomiesięczne dziecko** ten-month-old baby.

dziesięciominutowy *a.* ten-minute, ten minutes; **dziesięciominutowa przerwa** ten-minute break.

dziesięcionóg *ma* **dziesięcionogi** *zool.* decapods (*Decapoda*).

dziesięciopiętrowy *a.* eleven-storey.

dziesięcioro *num. decl. like n.* -rg- ten; **dziesięcioro przykazań** the Ten Commandments.

dziesięciościan *mi Gen.* -u *mat.* decahedron.

dziesięciotysięcznik *mi Gen.* -a *żegl.* (= *statek o nośności 10 000 ton*) 10,000 DWT ship.

dziesięciozgłoskowiec *mi* -wc- *Gen.* -a *teor. lit.* decasyllable.

dziesięciozgłoskowy *a. teor.lit.* decasyllabic; **wiersz dziesięciozgłoskowy** decasyllable.

dziesięciozłotowy *a.* ten-zloty('s).

dziesięciozłotówka *f.* (*banknot*) ten-zloty note, tenner, ten; (*moneta*) ten-zloty coin.

dziesięć *num. Ins.* -oma *l.* -u ten; **dziesięciu studentów** ten students; **dziesięć dziewcząt** ten girls; **mieć dziesięć lat** be ten (years old); **mam pociąg za dziesięć minut** my train leaves in ten minutes; **po dziesięciu minutach** after ten minutes; **za dziesięć pierwsza** ten to one; **dziesięć po pierwszej** ten past one; **pracować za dziesięciu** work hard; **jeść za dziesięciu** eat like a horse.

dziesiętny *a. mat.* decimal; **ułamek dziesiętny** decimal fraction; **liczba dziesiętna** decimal number; **miary dziesiętne** metric system; **miejsce dziesiętne** decimal point; **logarytm dziesiętny** common *l.* Briggsian logarithm; **waga dziesiętna** decimal scale; **dziesiętny system miar i wag** decimal system of weights and measures, metric system.

dziewanna *f. bot.* mullein (*Verbascum*).

dziewczę *n.* -częci- *pl.* -częt- *Gen.* -ąt girl; **płoche dziewczę** shy girl; **urodziwe dziewczę** comely girl.

dziewczęcy *a.* girlish; **głos dziewczęcy** girlish voice; **dziewczęca uroda** girlish beauty.

dziewczęta *n. zob.* **dziewczę**.

dziewczyna *f.* **1.** (= *młoda kobieta*) young woman. **2.** *pot.* (= *sympatia*) girlfriend; **masz dziewczynę?** have you got a girlfriend? **3.** *przest.* (= *służąca*) maid; **dziewczyna do dziecka** baby-sitter.

dziewczynka *f. Gen.pl.* -ek **1.** (= *dziecko płci żeńskiej*) girl; **jesteś już dużą dziewczynką** you're

a big girl now. **2.** *żart.* (= *kobieta*) young woman; **ładna z ciebie dziewczynka** you're a pretty woman. **3.** *pot.* (= *kobieta lekkich obyczajów*) slut; **iść** *l.* **chodzić na dziewczynki** (= *korzystać z usług prostytutek*) whore; = *iść na podryw* go on a skirt chasing expedition, go girl-hunting.

dziewiarka *f. Gen., Loc.* -ce *tk.* **1.** (*kobieta*) knitter. **2.** (*maszyna*) knitting machine *l.* frame, knitter.

dziewiarnia *f. Gen., Dat., Loc.* -ni *tk.* knitting shop.

dziewiarski *a. tk.* knitting; **maszyna dziewiarska** knitting machine *l.* frame, knitter; **przemysł dziewiarski** knitting industry.

dziewiarstwo *n. tk.* knitting industry.

dziewiarz *mp tk. zob.* **dziewiarka** 1.

dziewiąta *f. Gen.* -ej (*godzina*) nine (o'clock); **jest dziewiąta rano** it's nine a.m.; **będę piętnaście po dziewiątej** I'll be there at a quarter past nine; **kończę za piętnaście dziewiąta** I finish at a quarter to nine; **mam pociąg o w pół do dziewiątej** my train leaves at half past eight.

dziewiątka *f. Gen.pl.* -ek **1.** (= *liczba 9*) nine. **2.** (= *tramwaj, autobus, dom, pokój nr 9*) nine; **do szpitala dojedziesz dziewiątką** the nine takes you to the hospital, streetcar/bus, etc. number nine takes you to the hospital; **mieszkamy pod dziewiątką** our house *l.* apartment number is nine. **3.** (= *wielkość obuwia*) size nine. **4.** *karty* nine; **dziewiątka pik** nine of spades. **5.** (= *grupa dziewięciu ludzi*) (group of) nine people; (*np. w restauracji przy zamawianiu stolika*) party of nine. **6.** (= *wielkość czcionki*) nine-point font; **pisać dziewiątką** write using a nine-point font.

dziewiąty *a.* ninth; **dziewiąty wiek** ninth century; **rok tysiąc dziewięćset dziewięćdziesiąty dziewiąty** the year nineteen hundred ninety nine; **dziewiąte urodziny** ninth birthday; **minęła właśnie godzina dziewiąta** clock has just struck nine; **urodziłem się dziewiątego maja** I was born on May ninth, I was born on the ninth of May; **jedna dziewiąta** one-ninth. – *mi* ninth (*day of a month*); **umówić się z kimś na dziewiątego czerwca** arrange a meeting with sb on the ninth of June; **skończyć pracę do dziewiątego** finish work by the ninth.

dziewica *f.* virgin; **Maryja Panna zawsze Dziewica** *rz.-kat.* Blessed Virgin Mary; **Święta Dziewica** *rz.-kat.* Virgin Mary, the Virgin; **Dziewica Orleańska** *hist.* the Maid of Orleans.

dziewictwo *n.* virginity; **pozbawić dziewictwa** deflower; **stracić dziewictwo** lose virginity.

dziewiczość *f.* virginity, innocence.

dziewiczy *a.* **1.** (= *dotyczący dziewicy*) virgin; **błona dziewicza** *zool., anat.* hymen; **dziewiczy rejs** maiden voyage; **wianek dziewiczy** *przest.* (= *cnota, błona dziewicza*) hymen; **dziewicza królowa** *hist.* (= *Elżbieta I*) Virgin Queen; **osobnik dziewiczy** *biol.* virgin. **2.** (= *niewinny*) chaste, intact, innocent, virgin; **dziewicza biel** virgin *l.* virginal white. **3.** (= *pierwotny*) intact, primeval.

dziewięciokrotny *a.* ninefold.

dziewięciolatek *mp* -tk- *Gen.* -i (*o chłopcu*)

nine-year-old (boy). – *ma* -**tk**- (*o zwierzęciu*) nine-year-old (animal).

dziewięciolecie *n*. nine years.

dziewięcioletni *a*. **1.** (= *trwający 9 lat*) nine-year, nine years'; **dziewięcioletnia podróż** nine-year journey. **2.** (= *w wieku 9 lat*) nine-year-old; **dziewięcioletni chłopiec** nine-year-old boy.

dziewięciomiesięczny *a*. **1.** (= *trwający 9 miesięcy*) nine-month, nine months'; **dziewięciomiesięczna podróż** nine-month journey. **2.** (= *w wieku 9 miesięcy*) nine-month-old; **dziewięciomiesięczne dziecko** nine-month-old baby.

dziewięciornik *ma Gen*. -**a** *Ins*. -**iem** *bot*. grass of Parnassus (*Parnassia*).

dziewięcioro *num. decl. like n*. -**rg**- nine; **dziewięcioro dzieci** nine children.

dziewięciozgłoskowiec *mi* -**wc**- *Gen*. -**a** *teor. lit*. nine-syllabic verse.

dziewięciozgłoskowy *a. teor.lit*. nine-syllabic; **wiersz dziewięciozgłoskowy** nine-syllabic verse.

dziewięć *num. Ins*. -**oma** *l*. -**u** (= *liczba l. cyfra 9*) nine; **dziewięciu studentów** nine students; **dziewięć dziewcząt** nine girls; **mieć dziewięć lat** be nine (years old); **mam pociąg za dziewięć minut** my train leaves in nine minutes; **po dziewięciu minutach** after nine minutes; **za dziewięć pierwsza** nine to one (o'clock); **dziewięć po pierwszej** nine past one (o'clock); **ni w pięć, ni w dziewięć** without rhyme or reason.

dziewięćdziesiąt *num*. -**ęci**- *Ins*. -**oma** *l*. -**u** (= *liczba 90*) ninety; **dziewięćdziesięciu żołnierzy** ninety soldiers; **dziewięćdziesiąt dziewczynek** ninety girls; **mam prawie dziewięćdziesiąt lat** I'm nearly ninety (years old); **do Warszawy pociąg pośpieszny jedzie dokładnie dziewięćdziesiąt minut** it takes exactly ninety minutes for a fast train to get to Warsaw; **po dziewięćdziesięciu minutach** after ninety minutes.

dziewięćdziesiątka *f. Gen.pl*. -**ek** **1.** (= *liczba 90*) ninety. **2.** (= *autobus, dom, mieszkanie nr 90*) number ninety; **do szpitala dojedziesz dziewięćdziesiątką** bus number ninety *l*. the ninety takes you to the hospital; **mieszkamy pod dziewięćdziesiątką** our house *l*. apartment number is ninety. **3.** (= *wiek 90 lat*) ninety (years of age); **babci stuknęła właśnie dziewięćdziesiątka** granny just turned ninety.

dziewięćdziesiąty *a*. ninetieth; **rok tysiąc dziewięćset dziewięćdziesiąty** the year nineteen hundred ninety; **dziewięćdziesiąte urodziny** ninetieth birthday; **dziewięćdziesiąta rocznica** ninetieth anniversary.

dziewięćdziesięcioletni *a*. **1.** (= *trwający 90 lat*) ninety-year, ninety years'. **2.** (= *w wieku 90 lat*) ninety-year-old; **dziewięćdziesięcioletni staruszek** ninety-year-old man; **dziewięćdziesięcioletni kościół** ninety-year-old church.

dziewięćset *num*. -**ciuset** (= *liczba 900*) nine hundred; **dziewięciuset mieszkańców** nine hundred inhabitants; **dziewięćset lat** nine hundred years.

dziewięćsetny *a*. nine-hundredth; **dziewięćsetna rocznica** nine-hundredth anniversary.

dziewięćsił *mi Gen*. -**a** *l*. -**u** *bot*. carline (*Carlina*).

dziewiętnasta *f. Gen*. -**ej** (*godzina*) seven (o'-clock) p.m.; **wykład kończy się o dziewiętnastej** lecture ends at seven p.m.; **jestem wolny dopiero po dziewiętnastej** I'am free only after seven p.m.; **musimy skończyć przed dziewiętnastą** we have to finish before seven p.m.

dziewiętnastka *f. Gen.pl*. -**ek** **1.** (= *liczba 19*) nineteen. **2.** (= *tramwaj, autobus, dom, mieszkanie nr 19*) number nineteen; **do szpitala dojedziesz dziewiętnastką** bus number nineteen *l*. the nineteen takes you to the hospital; **mieszkamy pod dziewiętnastką** our house *l*. apartment number is nineteen. **3.** *pot*. (= *dziewiętnaste urodziny*) nineteenth birthday. **4.** *pot*. (= *kobieta w wieku 19 lat*) nineteen-year-old woman *l*. girl.

dziewiętnastolatek *mp Gen., Acc*. -**tka** *Ins*. -**tkiem** (= *mężczyzna w wieku 19 lat*) nineteen-year-old man *l*. boy.

dziewiętnastolecie *n*. **1.** *rzad*. (= *okres 19 lat*) nineteen years. **2.** (= *dziewiętnasta rocznica*) nineteenth anniversary.

dziewiętnastoletni *a*. **1.** (= *trwający 19 lat*) nineteen-year, nineteen years'. **2.** (= *w wieku 19 lat*) nineteen-year-old; **dziewiętnastoletnia dziewczyna** nineteen-year-old girl; **dziewiętnastoletni chłopak** nineteen-year-old boy.

dziewiętnastowieczny *a*. nineteenth-century; **dziewiętnastowieczny budynek** nineteenth-century building; **dziewiętnastowieczny pisarz** nineteenth-century writer; **powieść dziewiętnastowieczna** nineteenth-century novel.

dziewiętnasty *a*. nineteenth; **dziewiętnasty wiek** nineteenth century; **rok tysiąc dziewięćset dziewiętnasty** the year nineteen hundred nineteen; **dziewiętnaste urodziny** nineteenth birthday; **minęła właśnie godzina dziewiętnasta** clock has just struck seven p.m.; **urodziłem się dziewiętnastego maja** I was born on May nineteenth, I was born on the nineteenth of May. – *mi* nineteenth (*day of a month*); **umówić się z kimś na dziewiętnastego czerwca** arrange a meeting with sb on the nineteenth of June; **skończyć pracę do dziewiętnastego** finish work by the nineteenth.

dziewiętnaście *num*. -**st**- *Ins*. -**oma** *l*. -**u** nineteen; **dziewiętnastu studentów** nineteen students; **dziewiętnaście dziewcząt** nineteen girls; **mam dziewiętnaście lat** I'am nineteen (years old).

dziewiętnaścioro *num. Gen*. -**rga** *Dat., Loc*. -**rgu** nineteen; **dziewiętnaścioro dzieci** nineteen children.

dziewka *f. Gen.pl*. -**ek** **1.** (= *dziwka*) whore. **2.** *przest*. maid.

dzieworodny *a. biol*. parthenogenetic.

dzieworództwo *n. biol*. parthenogenesis.

dziewucha *f*. gal, lass, wench.

dziewuszka *f. Gen.pl*. -**ek** *emf*. lass, gal.

dzieża *f*. kneading trough.

dzięcioł *ma orn*. woodpecker (*Picus*).

dziędzierzawa *f. bot.* **bieluń dziędzierzawa** jimsonweed (*Datura stramonium*).

dzięgiel *mi* -gl- *l.* -giel- *Gen.* -gla *l.* -u *Gen.pl.* -i *l.* -ów *bot.* angelica (*Angelica*).

dziękczynienie *n. lit.* thanksgiving; **zanosić dziękczynienie** offer thanksgiving; **Święto Dziękczynienia** *US, Can.* Thanksgiving (Day).

dziękczynność *f.* thankfulness.

dziękczynny *a.* thankful; **modlitwa dziękczynna** grace; **wotum dziękczynne** votive offering; **list dziękczynny** letter of thanks.

dzięki *pl. tylko w Nom. i Acc. lit.* thanks; **serdeczne dzięki** thanks a lot; **Bogu niech będą dzięki** thanks be to God; **dzięki Bogu** thank God. – *prep. + Dat.* thanks to; **tylko dzięki tobie zdałem ten egzamin** I passed this exam only thanks to you.

dziękować *ipf.* thank; **dziękuję ci za wszystko** thank you for everything; **z całego serca ci dziękuję** I thank you with all my heart; **dziękuję bardzo** thank you very much, much obliged; **nie ma za co dziękować** don't mention it, not at all, you're welcome; **nie, dziękuję** no, thanks; **dziękuję, chętnie** yes, please, with pleasure; **dziękuję za taką pornoc** *iron.* thank you very much indeed.

dzik *ma* 1. *zool.* wild boar, wild pig (*Sus scrofa*). 2. *ogr.* (= *pęd*) sucker. 3. *ogr.* (= *roślina*) wilding.

dziki *a.* 1. (= *pierwotny*) wild; **dzika kaczka** wild duck; **dzika róża** *bot.* dog rose (*Rosa canina*); **dzika puszcza** wilderness; **dziki koń** wild horse; **Dziki Zachód** *hist.* Wild West; **Dzikie Pola** *hist.* Wild Plains; **dzikie plemię** primitive *l.* savage tribe. 2. (= *niepohamowany*) unrestrained, wild; **dzika radość** wild joy; **dziki tłum** wild crowd; **dzikie mięso** *pat.* proud flesh; **z dziką rozkoszą** with great delight. 3. (= *przerażający, okrutny*) terrible, horrible, fierce, ferocious; **dzika walka** fierce fight; **dziki wrzask** terrible yell; **dziki wzrok** crazy look. 4. (= *nieokrzesany*) uncouth, crude; (= *nieśmiały*) shy. 5. (= *niezwykły*) strange, odd; **dzikie pomysły** crazy ideas; **dziki strój** strange clothes. 6. (= *nielegalny*) wildcat, illegal, unauthorized; **dziki strajk** wildcat strike; **dzika plaża** unguarded beach; **dziki lokator** squatter; **dzika karta** *sport* wild card. – *mp* savage, barbarian; **zwyczaje dzikich** customs *l.* traditions of savages.

dziko *adv.* wildly; **mieszkać na dziko** squat; **przyrządzać coś na dziko** *kulin.* cook *l.* prepare meat like game; **dziko wyglądająca okolica** uncivilized region, wilderness; **dziko błyszczące oczy** crazed look, wildly shining eyes; **dziko wyjące psy** dogs howling loudly; **dziko brzmiące nazwisko** strange name.

dzikość *f.* 1. (= *stan pierwotny*) wildness. 2. (= *okrucieństwo, srogość*) ferocity, fierceness.

dzikus *mp pl.* -y 1. (= *człowiek pierwotny*) savage, barbarian. 2. *pog.* (= *mruk*) uncouth person.

dzikuska *f.* 1. savage, barbarian. 2. (= *nieumiejąca się zachować dziewczyna*) shy girl.

dziobać *ipf.* -bię -biesz, -ob *l.* -ób 1. (*o ptakach*) peck, pick. 2. (= *kłuć*) prod.

dziobak *ma zool.* platypus, duckbill (*Ornithorhynchus anaticus*). – *mi Gen.* -a *żegl.* bowsprit.

dziobaty *a.* pock-marked; **dziobata twarz** pock-marked face.

dziobek *mi* -bk- *Gen.* -a 1. (*małego ptaka*) beak, bill. 2. *przen., żart.* (= *usta*) mouth. 3. (*dzbanka*) spout, lip. 4. (= *ostre zakończenie*) tip.

dziobnąć *pf.* -ij 1. *zob.* **dziobać**. 2. *pot.* (= *zjeść bardzo mało*) peck at, nibble at; **dziobnąć trochę mięsa** peck at some meat.

dziobnica *f. Gen., Dat., Loc.* -cy *żegl.* stem.

dzioborożec *ma orn.* hornbill (*Buceros*).

dziobowy *a. żegl.* bow.

dzionek *mi* -nk- *pot.* day.

dziób *mi* -o- *Gen.* -a 1. (*ptaka*) beak, bill; **ostry dziób** sharp beak; **zakrzywiony dziób** curved beak; **mieć żółto w dziobie** be a greenhorn. 2. *przen., żart.* (= *usta*) mouth; **zamknij dziób** shut your trap, shut up. 3. *Gen.* -u *l.* -a *żegl.* bow; *lotn.* nose. 4. (= *ostre zakończenie czegoś*) nose, tip; **dzioby nart** shovels. 5. (= *blizna na twarzy*) pock-mark.

dzióbek *mi* = **dziobek**.

dziryt *mi* spear; assegai.

dzisiaj *adv. zob.* **dziś**.

dzisiejszy *a.* 1. (= *dotyczący tego dnia*) today's; **spotkanie odbędzie się dzisiejszego wieczoru** meeting will take place tonight; **w dniu dzisiejszym** today; **do dnia dzisiejszego** to the present day, until now. 2. (= *współczesny*) present-day, contemporary; **dzisiejsza młodzież** the youth of today; **żyć dniem dzisiejszym** live in the present; **w dzisiejszych czasach** nowadays, these days.

dziś *adv.* 1. (= *w dniu dzisiejszym*) today; **dziś świeci słońce** the sun is shining today; **dziś jestem bardzo zajęty** I'm very busy today; **znamy się nie od dziś** we've known each other *l.* one another for years; **od dziś** from now on; **zrób dziś, co masz zrobić jutro** don't put off until tomorrow what you could do today; **na dziś** as of today. 2. (= *współcześnie, obecnie*) nowadays, presently; **dziś studiować może każdy, kto zechce** nowadays everyone who wants to study can do so; **po dziś dzień** till now, up to this day; **nie dziś, to jutro** if not today then tomorrow, in the nearest future. – *mi* 1. (= *dzień bieżący*) today. 2. (= *teraźniejszość*) today, the present.

dziupla *f. Gen.pl.* -i 1. hollow (*in a tree*). 2. *sl.* (= *miejsce ukrycia łupu przez przestępców*) stash.

dziura *f.* 1. (= *otwór*) hole; (*w zębie*) cavity; (*w materiale, ubraniu*) hole, tear; (*w statku, naczyniu*) leak; (*w płocie*) gap; (*w oponie*) puncture; **ser z dziurami** hard cheese; **wywiercić dziurę** drill a hole; **szukać dziury w całym** pick holes in sth; **on zawsze szuka dziury w całym** he's a nitpicker; **potrzebny jak dziura w moście** uncalled for, unnecessary; **wiercić komuś dziurę w brzuchu** pester sb; **schować się do mysiej dziury** run to earth; **załatać dziurę** patch a hole; **dziura ozonowa** ozone hole; **dziura w budżecie** budget hole;

dziura elektronowa *fiz.* (electron) hole; **czarna dziura** *astron.* black hole; **dziura powietrzna** *lotn.* air pocket. **2.** *pog.* (= *mała miejscowość*) shithole, jerkwater town, boondocks, Podunk. **3.** *wulg.* (= *dziewczyna*) cunt, piece of ass *l.* meat; (= *żeńskie narządy płciowe*) cunt.

dziurawić *ipf.* perforate, make holes.

dziurawiec *mi bot.* Saint-John's-wort (*Hypericum perforatum*).

dziurawka *f. Gen.pl.* -ek **1.** *bud.* cellular brick, cavity brick, hollow brick. **2.** *tel.* perforated tape, punched tape.

dziurawy *a.* (*o bucie, ubraniu*) with holes, full of holes; **był w dziurawych spodniach** his pants were torn, his pants were full of holes; (*o naczyniu, pojemniku, dachu*) leaky, leaking; (*o zębie*) decayed; **mieć dziurawe ręce** be all thumbs; **dziurawy worek** bottomless pit.

dziurka *f. Gen.pl.* -ek (little) hole; **dziurka od guzika** buttonhole; **dziurka od klucza** keyhole; **dziurki w nosie** nostrils; **mam tego po dziurki w nosie** I'm fed up with it.

dziurkacz *mi Gen.* -a punch.

dziurkować *ipf.* perforate, make holes; punch; **dziurkować bilet** cancel a ticket; **karta dziurkowana** perforated card.

dziw *mi* strange thing, wonder; **dziwy nad dziwami** the most extraordinary thing; **nie dziw, że...** no wonder; **aż dziw bierze, gdy/że...** it's a wonder.

dziwactwo *n.* **1.** (= *dziwna rzecz*) strange thing, oddity. **2.** (= *dziwne zachowanie*) eccentricity, idiosyncrasy.

dziwaczeć *ipf.* -eję -ejesz, -ej grow strange.

dziwaczek *mi bot.* **dziwaczek pospolity** four-o'clock, marvel-of-Peru, beauty-of-the-night (*Mirabilis jalapa*).

dziwaczka *f. Gen.pl.* -ek *zob.* **dziwak**.

dziwaczny *a.* bizzare, queer, strange; **dziwaczna myśl** crazy thought; **dziwaczny strój** bizzare clothes; **dziwaczny wygląd** eccentric look.

dziwak *mp* weirdo, freak.

dziwić *ipf.* surprise; **bardzo mnie to dziwi** I'm quite surprised *l.* astonished (with that). **~ się** *ipf.* be surprised; **czemu się dziwisz?** why are you surprised?; **nie ma się co dziwić** no wonder; **nie można się jej dziwić** you can't really blame her, I/you/we, etc. can't say I/you/we, etc. blame her.

dziwka *f. Gen.pl.* -ek *wulg.* whore, hooker, pro; **dziwka uliczna** streetwalker.

dziwkarz *mp wulg.* goat, whoremonger, lecher.

dziwnie *adv.* strangely; **dlaczego tak dziwnie na mnie patrzysz?** why are you looking at me in such a strange way?

dziwny *a.* strange, odd, weird, bizzare; **dziwny człowiek** strange *l.* odd man; **dziwne nazwisko** strange name; **co za dziwny zbieg okoliczności!** what a strange *l.* odd coincidence!; **dziwnym trafem** strangely enough; **nic dziwnego, że...** no wonder...; **(to) dziwne** (it's) strange *l.* weird.

dziwo *n.* **1.** strange thing, wonder; **o dziwo** would you believe it! **2.** (= *zjawa*) ghost, phantom.

dziwoląg *mp pl.* -i weirdo, freak. — *mi Gen.* -a oddity.

dziwonia *f. Gen., Dat., Loc.* -nii *pl.* -nii *orn.* common *l.* scarlet rosefinch (*Carpodacus erythrinus*).

dziwota *f.* **nie dziwota** *pot.* no wonder.

dziwować się *ipf. pot.* marvel (*komuś, czemuś* at sb/sth).

dziwowisko *n.* sight, marvel; **zrobić z siebie dziwowisko** make a sight of o.s.

dziwożona *f. mit.* goblin.

dzwon *mi* **1.** bell; **dzwon kościelny** church bell; **bicie dzwonów** toll, bell ringing; **bić w dzwon** toll *l.* ring a bell; **od wielkiego dzwonu** once in a blue moon; **serce jak dzwon** sound heart; **serce dzwonu** clapper, tongue; **dzwon alarmowy** alarm bell; **dzwon okrętowy** *żegl.* ship bell; **dzwon mgłowy** *żegl.* fog bell; **zespół dzwonów** chimes, carillon; **dzwony orkiestrowe** *l.* rurowe *muz.* tubular bells. **2.** (= *brzmienie, dźwięk dzwonu*) bell, toll; **wielkanocne dzwony** Easter bells; **dzwon pogrzebowy** death-bell; **dzwony weselne** wedding bells. **3.** *techn.* bell; **dzwon nurkowy** diving bell, bell caisson; **dzwon podwodny** *żegl.* submarine bell; **dzwon ratowniczy** *żegl.* rescue diving bell. **4. dzwony** (= *rodzaj spodni*) bell-bottoms.

dzwonek *mi* -nk- *Gen.* -a **1.** (= *sygnalizator*) bell; **dzwonek alarmowy** alarm bell; **dzwonek u drzwi** door bell; **nacisnąć dzwonek** ring a bell; **dzwonki orkiestrowe** *muz.* glockenspiel. **2.** (= *brzmienie*) ring, bell; **dzwonek na lekcję** *szkoln.* the bell; **ostatni dzwonek** the eleventh hour. **3.** (= *przedmiot o kształcie dzwonka*) bell. **4.** *bot.* bellflower (*Campanula*). **5.** *karty, pot.* (= *karo*) diamonds.

dzwonić *ipf.* **1.** (= *bić w dzwon*) ring a bell; **dzwonić na mszę** ring for church. **2.** (= *wywoływać dźwięk*) ring; (*kluczami*) jangle, clink; (*szklankami, kieliszkami*) clink; (*dzwoneczkami*) tinkle; **dzwonił zębami** his teeth were chattering. **3.** (= *rozbrzmiewać*) ring, resound; **cisza dzwoni mi w uszach** my ears are ringing with silence; **dzwoni mi w uszach** my ears are ringing. **4.** *pot.* (= *telefonować*) phone, ring up, call (*do kogoś* sb).

dzwoniec *ma* -ńc- *orn.* greenfinch (*Carduelis chloris*).

dzwonko *n. Gen.pl.* -nek *kulin.* (*kawałek ryby*) steak.

dzwonnica *f.* bell tower, belfry, campanile.

dzwonnik *mp* bell-ringer.

dzyndzel *mi* -dzl- *Gen.* -a **1.** *pot.* (= *wisiorek*) pendant. **2. dzyndzle** *pot.* (= *piersi kobiece*) jugs, melons, hooters.

dźgać *ipf.*, **dźgnąć** *pf.* -ij pierce, poke; (*łokciem*) jab. **~ się** *ipf.*, **dźgnąć się** *pf.* -ij **1.** pierce o.s., poke o.s. **2.** pierce each other *l.* one another; (*łokciem*) jab each other *l.* one another.

dźwięczeć *ipf.* -ę -ysz (= *rozbrzmiewać*) ring, sound, resound; *przen.* (= *dawać się wyczuć w* *głosie*) sound; **w głosie Adama dźwięczało powątpiewanie** Adam sounded doubtful.

dźwięcznie *adv.* sonorously.

dźwięczny *a.* sonorous, resonant; **spółgłoska dźwięczna** *jęz.* voiced consonant.

dźwięk *mi* **1.** (= *brzmienie*) sound; **dźwięk dzwonka** ring, sound of a bell; **nieartykułowane dźwięki** inarticulate sounds; **pusty dźwięk** platitude. **2.** *fiz.* sound; **zapis dźwięku** sound record; **wysokość dźwięku** sound pitch; **głośność dźwięku** sound loudness; **barwa dźwięku** timbre; **dźwięk prosty** simple tone; **dźwięk złożony** complex tone; **dźwięk rozproszony** dispersed tone; **dźwięk podsłyszalny** infrasound; **bariera dźwięku** sound barrier; **dźwięk prowadzący** *muz.* leading tone; **dźwięk nieakordowy** *muz.* inharmonic sound; **synteza dźwięku** *muz.* sound synthesis. **3.** *jęz.* (= *głoska*) sound.

dźwiękochłonny *a.* sound-absorbing.

dźwiękonaśladowczy *a.* onomatopoeic, echoic; **wyraz dźwiękonaśladowczy** onomatopoeia.

dźwiękoszczelny *a.* soundproof; **kabina dźwiękoszczelna** soundproof booth.

dźwiękowy *a.* sound, sonic; **fala dźwiękowa** sound wave; **film dźwiękowy** sound film; **kamera dźwiękowa** sound camera; **karta dźwiękowa** *komp.* sound *l.* music card; **logo dźwiękowe** sound logo; **efekty dźwiękowe** sound effects; **ścieżka dźwiękowa** soundtrack.

dźwig *mi techn.* **1.** (*maszyna*) crane; **dźwig portowy** harbor *l.* wharf crane; **dźwig bramowy** portal crane; **dźwig mostowy** bridge crane; **dźwig pływający** floating crane. **2.** (= *winda*) elevator; *Br.* lift; **dźwig towarowy** freight elevator. **3.** (= *dźwignica*) crane.

dźwigacz *mi Gen.* **-a 1.** *anat.* levator, elevator (muscle). **2.** *żegl.* cathead.

dźwigać *ipf.* **1.** (= *podnosić*) lift. **2.** *przen.* (= *wesprzeć*) uplift; **dźwigać kraj z upadku** raise one's country from decay; (= *podnosić na wyższy poziom*) improve, uplift; **dźwigać oświatę** improve the quality of education. **3.** *tylko ipf.* (= *nosić*) carry; **dźwigać walizkę** carry a suitcase; **dźwigać swój krzyż** *l.* krzyże carry one's cross; **dźwigać swoje nieszczęście** carry an albatross around one's neck. **4.** (= *odbudować*) rebuild, reconstruct; **dźwigać miasto z ruin** raise a town from ruins. **~ się** *ipf.* **1.** raise *l.* lift o.s. up. **2.** be built *l.* constructed.

dźwigar *mi Gen.* **-a** *l.* **-u** *bud., techn.* girder.

dźwigarka *f. Gen.pl.* **-ek** *techn.* winch, windlass.

dźwignąć *pf.* **-ij** *zob.* **dźwigać.** **~ się** *pf.* **-ij** *zob.* **dźwigać się.**

dźwignia *f. Gen.* **-i** *techn.* **1.** lever; **dźwignia jednoramienna** single-arm lever, single-ended lever; **dźwignia dwuramienna** double-arm lever, double-ended lever; **dźwignia zmiany biegów** *gł. mot.* gear lever. **2.** *przen.* mainspring; **reklama jest dźwignią handlu** advertising drives *l.* impels trade.

dźwignica *f. techn.* crane.

dźwignik *mi Gen.* **-a** *techn.* (lifting) jack, hoist.

dźwigowy *a.* (= *dotyczący dźwigu*) crane; (= *dotyczący windy*) elevator; *Br.* lift; **operator dźwigowy** crane operator; **szyb dźwigowy** elevator shaft. – *mp* crane operator.

Dżakarta *f. geogr.* Jakarta, Djakarta.

dżdżownica *f. zool.* earthworm (*Lumbricus*).

dżdżownik *ma orn.* plover (*Charadrius*).

dżdżu *itd. mi zob.* **deszcz.**

dżdżyć *ipf.* drizzle.

dżdżysty *a.* drizzly; **dżdżysta pogoda** drizzly weather; **dżdżysty dzień** drizzly day.

dżelada *f. zool.* gelada (*Theropithecus gelada*).

dżem *mi* jam; **dżem truskawkowy** strawberry jam; **dżem morelowy** apricot jam; **słoik dżemu** jar of jam.

dżentelmen *mp* gentleman.

dżentelmeński *a.* gentlemanly; **dżentelmeńska umowa** gentleman's *l.* gentlemen's agreement; **po dżentelmeńsku** like a gentleman, in a gentlemanly manner *l.* way.

dżersej *mi Gen.* **-u** *Gen.pl.* **-ów** *tk.* jersey. – *ma Gen.* **-a** *Gen.pl.* **-ów** *roln.* (*rasa bydła*) Jersey.

dżet *mi* **1.** (= *błyszczący paciorek*) jet. **2.** *górn.* jet.

dżez *mi muz.* jazz; **słuchać dżezu** listen to jazz; **grać dżez** play jazz; **dżez tradycyjny** classical jazz; **dżez nowoczesny** modern jazz.

dżezmen *mp muz.* jazzman.

dżezowy *a. muz.* jazz; **zespół dżezowy** *l.* dżezband jazz band; **muzyka dżezowa** jazz music.

dżihad *mi Islam* jihad, jehad.

dżin *mi* (*wódka*) gin; **dżin z tonikiem** gin and tonic.

dżingiel *mi* **-gl-** *Gen.* **-a** *Gen.pl.* **-i** jingle; **dżingiel reklamowy** advertising jingle.

dżinn *ma mit.* jinn, jinni, genie.

dżins *mi* **1.** *tk.* denim. **2.** **dżinsy** (= *spodnie dżinsowe*) (blue) jeans.

dżinsowy *a.* denim; **spodnie dżinsowe** (blue) jeans; **dżinsowa kurtka** denim jacket.

dżip *mi Gen.* **-a** *mot.* Jeep.

dżiu-dżitsu *n. indecl. sport* jujitsu, jujutsu.

dżokej *mp Gen.pl.* **-ów** *l.* **-ei** jockey.

dżokejka *f. Dat., Loc.* **-jce 1.** (= *kobieta dżokej*) (female) jockey. **2.** (= *czapka dżokejska*) jockey-cap.

dżoker *mp pl.* **-y** *karty* joker.

dżonka *f. Gen.pl.* **-ek** *żegl.* junk.

dżudo *n. indecl. sport* judo.

dżudoga *f. sport* judogi.

dżudoka *mp pl.* **-i** *l.* **-cy** *sport* judoist.

dżul *mi Gen.* **-a** *fiz.* joule.

dżuma *f. pat.* plague, bubonic fever; **dżuma dymienicza** bubonic *l.* glandular plague; **dżuma płucna** pneumonic plague, plague pneumonia; **dżuma posocznicza** septic(a)emic plague; **dżuma XX wieku** *przen.* (= *AIDS*) the plague of the twentieth century; **dżuma cynowa** *techn.* tin pest *l.* disease.

dżungla *f. Gen.pl.* **-i** jungle; **prawo dżungli** *przen.* law of the jungle.

E, e *n. indecl.* **1.** (*litera*) E, e; **E jak Ewa** E is for Echo; E as in Echo. **2.** (*samogłoska*) e.

E *n. indecl. muz.* E; **e-moll** E minor; **E-dur** E major.

e *int.* oh, well; **e! nie mam ochoty** oh, I don't feel like it; **e! ale to ładnie wygląda!** oh! that looks great!; **e tam!** oh, my foot!

ebonit *mi* ebonite, vulcanite.

ebonitowy *a.* ebonite; **pałeczka** *l.* **laska ebonitowa** ebonite rod.

ebuliometr *mi chem., fiz.* ebulliometer, ebullioscope.

ebuliometria *f. chem., fiz.* ebulliometry, ebullioscopy.

ebulioskop *f.* = ebuliometr.

ebulioskopia *f.* = ebuliometria.

ech *int.* oh, well; **ech! mam tego dość** well, I've had enough of this!; **ech! wszystko mi jedno!** oh, I don't care!

echo *n.* **1.** (= *odbicie fali dźwiękowej*) echo; **echa bitwy** echoes of battle; **budzić echo** produce *l.* cause an echo; **być czyimś echem** be sb's echo; **powtarzać jak echo** echo; **echo radarowe** radar echo; **echo radiowe** radio echo; *przen.* (= *reakcja na coś*) response; **odbijać** *l.* **odbić się (głośnym, szerokim) echem** have (far-reaching) repercussions, echo (far and wide); **przebrzmieć** *l.* **pozostać bez echa** meet with no response, make no impression. **2.** *przen.* (= *wspomnienie rzeczy dawnych*) memory, memories; **echo dni minionych** memory of days gone by. **3.** *przen.* (= *wieść, pogłoska*) word, news; **echa ostatnich wydarzeń** word on *l.* news about recent events.

echoencefalograf *mi med.* echoencephalograph.

echoencefalografia *f. Gen.* **-ii** *med.* echoencephalography.

echoencefalogram *mi med.* echoencephalogram.

echokardiograf *mi med.* echocardiograph.

echokardiografia *f. Gen.* **-ii** *med.* echocardiography, ultrasound cardiography.

echokardiogram *mi med.* echocardiogram.

echolokacja *f. biol.* echolocation; *techn.* (ultrasonic) echolocation.

echosonda *f. żegl.* echo sounder, (echo) depth finder.

ecstasy *n.* (= *metylenodioksymetamfetamina, MDMA*) ecstasy.

ecu *n. indecl. fin.* ecu (*European Currency Unit*).

edamski *a.* Edam; **ser edamski** *kulin.* Edam cheese.

eden *mi* **1.** *Bibl.* Eden, Garden of Eden. **2.** *lit.* eden, paradise.

edeński *a.* Edenic; **ogród edeński** *Bibl.* Garden of Eden.

edredon *mp Gen.* **-a** *orn.* common eider (*Somateria mollissima*). – *mi Gen.* **-u** (= *puch*) eiderdown.

edredonowy *a.* eider; **kaczka edredonowa** *orn.* common eider (*Somateria mollissima*); **puch edredonowy** eiderdown.

edukacja *f. lit.* education; **odebrać staranną edukację** receive a good education; **zakończyć edukację na poziomie szkoły średniej** have a high school education; **edukacja seksualna** sex education, sex ed; **edukacja domowa** home schooling.

edukacyjny *a.* educational; **polski system edukacyjny** Polish educational system; **program edukacyjny** educational program; **film edukacyjny** educational film.

edukować *ipf.* educate; **edukowała go ulica** he got his education on the streets. **~ się** *ipf.* be educated, receive an education.

edwardiański *a. hist.* (= *z czasów panowania Edwarda VII, tj. lat 1901–1910*) Edwardian; **epoka edwardiańska** Edwardian period.

edycja *f.* **1.** *pot.* edition; **trzecia edycja konkursu** third edition of the *l.* a contest. **2.** *druk.* publication; edition; **najnowsza edycja** latest *l.* most recent edition.

edykt *mi* edict; **ogłosić** *l.* **wydać edykt** issue an edict; **edykt mediolański** *hist.* Edict of Milan; **edykt nantejski** *hist.* Edict of Nantes.

Edynburg *mi Gen.* **-a** *geogr.* Edinburgh.

Edyp *mp mit.* Oedipus; **kompleks Edypa** *psych.* Oedipus complex.

edytor[1] *mp pl.* **-rzy 1.** (= *wydawca*) publisher. **2.** (= *osoba przygotowująca czyjeś dzieło do druku*) editor.

edytor[2] *mi pl.* **-ry** editor; **edytor tekstu** *komp.* word processor, text editor; **editor ekranowy** screen editor.

edytorski *a.* editorial; **prace edytorskie** editorial work; **szata edytorska** layout.

edytorstwo *n.* editing; **edytorstwo naukowe** academic editing.

edytować *ipf.* **1.** (= *przygotowywać do druku*) edit. **2.** *komp.* edit.

efeb *mp pl.* **-owie 1.** (= *młodzieniec*) ephebe. **2.** *hist.* ephebus.

efekciarski *a.* fancy, flashy; **efekciarski chwyt**

flashy trick; **zwrot efekciarski** fancy term; **efekciarski gest** grandiose gesture.

efekciarstwo n. showing off, grand-standing; **tanie efekciarstwo** claptrap, smoke and mirrors.

efekciarz mp show-off.

efekt mi **1.** (= wrażenie) effect, impression; **wywołać efekt** produce an effect, create l. make an impression; **efekt komiczny** comic effect; **niezamierzony efekt** unintended effect; **nie wywołać zamierzonego efektu** fall flat; **niebywały efekt** profound l. strong impression. **2.** (= chwyt) effect; **efekty dźwiękowe** sound effects; **efekty specjalne** special effects. **3.** (= wynik) effect, result; **efekt uboczny** side effect; **osiągać dobre efekty** achieve good results; **czekać na efekt czegoś** wait to see the result(s) of sth; **efekt końcowy** end result; **efekt jo-jo** yo-yo effect; **efekt cieplarniany** greenhouse effect; **efekt placeba** placebo effect.

efektownie adv. impressively, spectacularly; **wyglądać efektownie** look spectacular.

efektowny a. impressive, spectacular; **efektowny wygląd** striking good looks; **efektowna suknia** glamorous dress; **efektowne działania** spectacular job l. work.

efektywnie adv. effectively, efficiently; **pracować efektywnie** work effectively l. efficiently; **efektywnie wykonana praca** job well done.

efektywność f. effectiveness, efficiency, performance; **efektywność ekonomiczna** ekon. economic performance; **efektywność pracy** work performance; **efektywność inwestycji** efficiency of investments.

efektywny a. **1.** (= skuteczny) effective; **efektywne wyniki** positive results; **efektywni pracownicy** effective employees; **efektywny kosztowo** cost-effective. **2.** (= wydajny) efficient; **efektywna praca** efficient work. **3.** (= rzeczywisty) actual, real; **efektywna wartość** real value.

efemeryczność f. ephemerality.

efemeryczny a. ephemeral; **efemeryczne plany** short-lived plans; **efemeryczna sława** momentary fame.

efemeryda f. **1.** (= zjawisko chwilowe) ephemera, ephemeron. **2. efemerydy** bot. ephemerals. **3. efemerydy** astron. ephemerides. **4. efemerydy** ent. mayflies, ephemerids (Ephemeroptera).

efendi mp pl. **-owie** hist. effendi.

efor mp pl. **-owie** hist. ephor.

efuzja f. geol. effusion, effusive eruption; **efuzja lawy** effusion of lava; **efuzja gazu** techn. effusion.

egalitarny a. egalitarian; **ustrój egalitarny** egalitarian political system.

egalitaryzm mi egalitarianism; **egalitaryzm społeczny** social egalitarianism.

egejski a. geogr. Aegean; **kultura egejska** archeol. Aegean civilizations.

egida f. **1.** mit. aegis. **2.** (= patronat) aegis; **pod egidą** under the aegis of.

Egipcjanin mp pl. **-anie** Gen. **-an** Egyptian.

Egipcjanka f. Egyptian.

egipski a. Egyptian; **egipskie ciemności** Cimmerian darkness.

Egipt mi geogr. Egypt.

egiptolog mp pl. **-dzy** l. **-owie** uniw. Egyptologist.

egiptologia f. Gen. **-ii** uniw. Egyptology.

egiptologiczny a. uniw. Egyptological.

ego mi psych. ego.

egocentryczny a. egocentric, self-centered; **postawa egocentryczna** egocentric attitude.

egocentryk mp egocentric (person).

egocentryzm mi egocentrism.

egoista mp egoist, selfish person.

egoistka f. zob. **egoista**.

egoistycznie adv. egoistically, selfishly; **postępować egoistycznie** behave selfishly.

egoistyczny a. egoistic, egoistical, selfish; **postawa egoistyczna** selfish attitude l. behavior; **działać z pobudek egoistycznych** do sth out of selfishness.

egoizm mi egoism, selfishness.

egotyczny a. psych. egotistic, egotistical; **osobowość egotyczna** egotistical personality.

egotysta mp psych. egotist.

egotystka f. zob. **egotysta**.

egotyzm mi psych. egotism.

egzaltacja f. exaltation; **mówić z egzaltacją** speak ecstatically.

egzaltować się ipf. go into a state of ecstasy; **egzaltować się poezją** be enamoured of poetry.

egzaltowany a. **1.** (= przesadny w wyrażaniu uczuć) emotional; **egzaltowane usposobienie** emotional character l. nature. **2.** (= przewrażliwiony) highly sensitive, oversensitive; **egzaltowana dziewczyna** highly sensitive girl.

egzamin mi exam, examination; **egzamin dyplomowy** szkoln., uniw. diploma examination; **egzamin magisterski** uniw. M.A./M.Sc., etc. examination; **egzamin dojrzałości** szkoln. finals, secondary school final examinations; Br. A levels; **egzamin ustny** oral exam(ination); **egzamin pisemny** written exam(ination); **egzamin poprawkowy** retake exam(ination); **egzamin końcowy** final exam(ination); **egzaminy wstępne** entrance exams l. examinations; **egzamin do liceum** high school entrance exam(ination); **egzamin z angielskiego/matematyki** exam(ination) in English/math; **zdać egzamin** pass an exam(ination); **nie zdać egzaminu** fail an exam(ination); **oblać egzamin** pot. flunk an exam(ination); **przystąpić do egzaminu** l. **zdawać egzamin** take an exam(ination), sit an exam(ination); **dostać czwórkę z egzaminu** get a B on an exam(ination); **zaliczyć komuś egzamin** pot. pass sb; **obciąć kogoś na egzaminie** pot. fail sb, flunk sb; **zdać życiowy egzamin** przen. make the grade.

egzaminacyjny a. exam(ination); **komisja egzaminacyjna** examination committee l. board l. panel; **test egzaminacyjny** exam(ination); **pytania egzaminacyjne** exam(ination) questions; **sesja egzaminacyjna** exam(ination) session.

egzaminator mp examiner.

egzaminatorka f. zob. **egzaminator**.

egzaminować ipf. **1.** (= poddawać egzaminowi) test, give an exam(ination) (z czegoś in sth); **egzaminować z biologii** give an exam(ination) in biology. **2.** (= *badać*) examine, inspect; **egzaminować kogoś wzrokiem** look sb over, size sb up.

egzarcha *mp pl.* **-owie 1.** *hist.* exarch. **2.** *rel.* exarch.

egzarchat *mi* **1.** *hist.* exarchate. **2.** *rel.* exarchate.

egzegeta *mp* **1.** (*filolog*) exegete. **2.** (*teolog*) exegete. **3.** *hist.* exegete.

egzegetyczny *a.* exegetic, exegetical; **studia egzegetyczne** exegetical studies.

egzegetyka *f. rel.* exegesis.

egzegeza *f.* exegesis, interpretation, explanation.

egzekucja *f.* **1.** (= *wykonanie kary*) execution; **egzekucja publiczna** public execution; **masowa egzekucja** mass execution; **wykonać egzekucję** execute, carry out an execution; **zawieszenie egzekucji** stay of execution. **2.** *prawn.* (= *ściąganie należności*) enforcement, execution; **egzekucja świadczeń alimentacyjnych** enforcement *l.* execution of maintenance payments; **wszczynać egzekucję** initiate execution *l.* enforcement proceedings. **3.** *hist.* execution.

egzekucyjny *a.* **1.** *prawn.* (*o ściąganiu należności*) enforcement, executive; **postępowanie egzekucyjne** enforcement proceedings; **tytuł** *l.* **nakaz egzekucyjny** writ of execution, execution; **sprawa egzekucyjna** executory process. **2.** (*o karze śmierci*) execution; **pluton egzekucyjny** firing squad.

egzekutor *mp* **1.** *prawn.* (= *wykonawca wyroku*) executor. **2.** *prawn.* (= *komornik*) court executive *l.* enforcement officer. **3.** (= *kat*) executioner.

egzekutywa *f.* **1.** *gł. polit.* (= *władza wykonawcza*) executive. **2.** (= *wykonywanie zarządzeń*) execution, enforcement.

egzekwie *pl. Gen.* **-ii** *rz.-kat.* funeral rites.

egzekwować *ipf.* **1.** (= *wymagać wykonania*) execute, enforce, exact; (*prawo*) enforce; **egzekwować wyrok** enforce judgement; (*podatki*) collect; **egzekwować wykonanie umowy** enforce a contract; **egzekwować rzut karny** *sport* take a penalty kick. **2.** *prawn.* execute, enforce; **egzekwować należność** execute *l.* enforce a payment.

egzema *f. pat.* eczema.

egzemplarz *mi Gen.* **-a 1.** (= *jedna sztuka*) item, piece. **2.** *druk.* (*książki*) copy; **egzemplarz okazowy** presentation copy; **egzemplarz sygnalny** advance copy; **egzemplarz recenzyjny** reviewer copy; **w dwóch/trzech egzemplarzach** in duplicate/triplicate. **3.** (= *okaz*) specimen; **interesujący egzemplarz żuka** interesting specimen of beetle.

egzemplifikacja *f.* exemplification; **posługiwać się egzemplifikacją** use exemplification; **wykorzystywać egzemplifikację** make use of exemplification.

egzemplifikacyjny *a.* exemplificative; **bogaty materiał egzemplifikacyjny** rich exemplificative material.

egzemplifikować *ipf.* exemplify.

egzoderma *f. bot.* exodermis.

egzogamia *f. Gen.* **-ii** exogamy.

egzogamiczny *a.* exogamous, exogamic; **małżeństwo egzogamiczne** exogamous marriage.

egzorcysta *mp rz.-kat.* exorcist.

egzorcyzm *mi rz.-kat.* exorcism.

egzorcyzmować *ipf. rz.-kat.* exorcize.

egzorta *f. rz.-kat.* sermon, oratory; **egzorta żałobna** funeral sermon *l.* oratory; eulogy.

egzosfera *f. meteor.* exosphere.

egzotermiczny *a. chem.* exothermic; **reakcja egzotermiczna** exothermic reaction.

egzotyczny *a.* **1.** (= *daleki*) exotic; **egzotyczne wakacje** exotic vacation; **egzotyczna flora** exotic flora. **2.** (= *niecodzienny*) rare; **egzotyczna uroda** rare beauty; **egzotyczny wygląd** singular appearance.

egzotyka *f.* exoticism, exotism; *pl.* (= *rzeczy egzotyczne*) exotica.

egzotyzm *mi* **1.** (= *to, co dalekie*) exoticism, exotism. **2.** *jęz.* borrowing, loan, loanword.

egzystencja *f.* **1.** (= *istnienie*) being, living, existence; **dobre warunki egzystencji** good living conditions; **zapewnić komuś godziwą egzystencję** guarantee sb a decent standard of living; **zabiegać o minimum egzystencji** struggle to make ends meet. **2.** *fil.* existence.

egzystencjalista *mp fil.* existentialist.

egzystencjalistyczny *a. fil.* existentialist, existentialistic; **pesymizm egzystencjalistyczny** existentialist pessimism; **literatura egzystencjalistyczna** existentialist literature.

egzystencjalizm *mi fil.* existentialism.

egzystencjalny *a.* existential; **filozofia egzystencjalna** *fil.* existentialism; **zdanie egzystencjalne** *log.* existential proposition; **kwantyfikator egzystencjalny** *log.* existential quantifier *l.* operator.

egzystować *ipf.* **1.** (= *żyć w ubóstwie*) subsist; **ledwo egzystować** barely make both ends meet. **2.** *przest.* (= *istnieć*) exist.

eh *int.* oh, well; **eh! i tak tego nie zrozumiesz!** oh, you won't understand it anyway!; **eh! mam tego dosyć!** well, I've had enough of this!

einstein *mi Gen.* **-a 1.** *chem.* einsteinium. **2.** *fiz.* einstein.

ej *int.* hey; **ej! ty tam! chodź do mnie!** hey you, come here!; **ej! zaczekajcie na mnie!** hey, wait for me!; **ej! uważaj!** hey, look out!; **ej! chyba coś kręcisz** hey, you must be up to something!

ejakulacja *f. fizj.* ejaculation.

ejakulat *mi fizj.* ejaculate, ejaculation.

ejdetyczny *a.* eidetic.

ejże *int.* hey; **ejże! patrz, jak chodzisz!** hey! watch where you're going!; **ejże! mój panie! ręce przy sobie!** hey mister! keep your hands to yourself!; **ejże! dokąd to?!** hey! where do you think you're going?!; **ejże! chyba coś kręcisz!** hey, you must be up to something!

EKG *abbr. med.* ECG, EKG (*electrocardiogram*).

ekierka *f.* set square.

ekipa *f.* crew, team; **ekipa telewizyjna** television crew; **ekipa alpinistów** mountaineering expedition; **ekipa ratownicza** rescue party; **skompletować ekipę** assemble a team, form a party.

eklektyczny *a.* eclectic; **eklektyczna architektura** eclectic architecture; **eklektyczny twórca** eclectic artist.

eklektyk *mp* eclectic, eclecticist.

eklektyzm *mi* **1.** *fil.* eclecticism. **2.** *sztuka* eclecticism.

ekler *mi* **1.** *Gen.* **-a** *l.* **-u** *pot.* (= *zamek błyskawiczny*) zipper. **2.** *Gen.* **-a** *kulin.* (*ciastko*) éclair.

eklerka *f.* = **ekler** 2.

eklezjasta *mp rzad.* preacher; **Księga Eklezjasty** *Bibl.* (Book of) Ecclesiastes.

eklezjologia *f. Gen.* **-ii** *rel.* ecclesiology.

eklipsa *f. astron.* eclipse; **eklipsa Słońca** solar eclipse.

eklityczny *a. astron.* ecliptic, ecliptical; **długość/szerokość eklityczna** celestial longitude/latitude.

ekliptyka *f. Dat., Loc.* **-yce** *astron.* ecliptic.

ekloga *f. teor.lit.* eclogue.

ekoklimat *mi biol.* bioclimate.

ekokonwersja *f ekon.* ecoconversion.

ekolog *mp pl.* **-dzy** *l.* **-owie** **1.** (= *specjalista w ekologii*) ecologist. **2.** *pot.* (= *zielony*) environmentalist, green.

ekologia *f. Gen.* **-ii** ecology; **ekologia roślin** phytoecology; **ekologia zwierząt** zooecology; **ekologia ewolucyjna** evolutionary ecology; **ekologia behawioralna** behavioral ecology; **ekologia społeczna** human ecology; **ekologia systemów** systems ecology.

ekologicznie *adv.* ecologically.

ekologiczny *a.* ecological, environmental; **produkt ekologiczny** environment(ally)friendly *l.* green product; **rolnictwo ekologiczne** organic agriculture, environment(ally) friendly agriculture; **ruch ekologiczny** environmental movement; **świadomość ekologiczna** environmental awareness; **ośrodek ekologiczny** *biol.* habitat.

ekonom *mp pl.* **-owie** *l.* **-i** *hist.* steward; (*w polu*) overseer.

ekonometria *f. Gen.* **-ii** (*nauka*) econometrics.

ekonomia *f. Gen.* **-ii** **1.** (*nauka*) economics; **ekonomia normatywna** normative economics; **ekonomia dobrobytu** economics of wealth; **ekonomia polityczna** political economy. **2.** (= *oszczędność*) economy, frugality; **ekonomia języka** *jęz.* economy of language; **zasada ekonomii** *fil.* law of parsimony, Occam's *l.* Ockham's razor. **3.** *hist.* royal treasury.

ekonomicznie *f.* economically.

ekonomiczność *f.* economy, efficiency.

ekonomiczny *a.* **1.** (= *gospodarczy*) economic; **kryzys ekonomiczny** economic crisis; **rozwój ekonomiczny** economic growth; **studia ekonomiczne** economics. **2.** (= *oszczędny*) economical, efficient; **ekonomiczny samochód** economical automobile; **ekonomiczne ogrzewanie** high-efficiency heating.

ekonomika *f.* **1.** (*nauka*) economics. **2.** *pot.* (= *gospodarka*) economy.

ekonomista *mp* economist.

ekonomistka *f. zob.* **ekonomista**.

ekosfera *f. astron.* ecosphere.

ekosystem *mi biol.* ecosystem.

ekoton *mi biol.* ecotone.

ekoturystyka *f.* ecotourism.

ekotyp *mi biol.* ecotype.

ekran *mi* **1.** (= *płaszczyzna, na którą rzutuje się obraz*) screen; **ekran panoramiczny** panoramic screen; **film wszedł na ekrany** film has been released; **gwiazdy ekranu** movie stars, stars of the silver screen. **2.** (= *powierzchnia, na której wytwarza się obraz*) screen, display; **ekran telewizyjny** television screen; **ekran radarowy** radar screen *l.* display; **płaski ekran** flat-panel *l.* flatscreen display; **mały *l.* szklany ekran** *pot.* the small screen. **3.** *techn.* (= *osłona*) screen, shield; **ekran ochronny** protective screen; **ekran akustyczny** acoustic screen *l.* baffle, sound barrier; **ekran radiacyjny** radiation shield; **ekran wodny** waterwall. **4.** *el.* shield. **5.** *przest.* (*kominka*) screen.

ekranizacja *f. film* screen adaptation; **dokonać ekranizacji** adapt for the screen.

ekranizować *ipf. film* film (a screen adaptation).

ekranować *ipf. el.* shield.

ekranowy *a. film* screen; **wersja ekranowa powieści** screen adaptation of a novel; **monitor ekranowy** *komp.* visual display unit *l.* device, VDU.

ekscelencja *mp* Excellency, Excellence; **Wasza/Jego Ekscelencja** Your/His Excellency.

ekscentryczka *f.* eccentric.

ekscentrycznie *adv.* eccentrically.

ekscentryczność *f.* **1.** eccentricity, idiosyncrasy; **cechować się ekscentrycznością** be eccentric. **2.** *geom.* eccentricity.

ekscentryczny *a.* **1.** (= *ekstrawagancki*) eccentric; **ekscentryczna aktorka** eccentric actress. **2.** *geom.* eccentric; **okręgi ekscentryczne** eccentric circles.

ekscentryk *mp pl.* **-cy** eccentric. – *mi pl.* **-ki** *techn.* (= *mimośród*) eccentric.

ekscentryzm *mi rzad.* eccentricity, idiosyncrasy.

ekscerpcja *f.* excerption, extraction.

ekscerpować *ipf.* excerpt, extract.

eksces *mi Gen.* **-ów** *lit.* (= *wybryk*) excess; **ekscesy młodości** excesses of youth; (= *naruszanie porządku publicznego*) disturbance, riot; **doszło do ekscesów** sth led to disturbances.

ekscytacja *f. lit.* excitement; **nastrój pełen ekscytacji** atmosphere full of excitement; **popaść w ekscytację** become excited.

ekscytować *ipf. lit.* excite. **~ się** *ipf. lit.* be excited.

ekscytujący *a.* exciting, thrilling; **ekscytujący koncert** exciting concert.

eksfoliacja *f. Gen., Dat., Loc.* **-cji** *geol.* exfoliation.

ekshibicjonista *mp* exhibitionist, flasher.

ekshibicjonistyczny *a.* exhibitionistic; **skłonności ekshibicjonistyczne** exhibitionistic tendencies.

ekshibicjonizm *mi* exhibitionism.

ekshumacja *f.* exhumation, disinternment; **przeprowadzić ekshumację** exhume *l.* disintern.

ekshumować *ipf.* exhume, disintern.
ekskawator *mi.* **1.** *dent.* excavator. **2.** *techn.* (= *koparka*) excavator, backhoe.
ekskluzywizm *mi* exclusiveness.
ekskluzywność *f.* exclusiveness.
ekskluzywny *a.* exclusive; **ekskluzywny sklep** exclusive store.
ekskomunika *f. rel.* excommunication.
ekskomunikować *ipf. rel.* excommunicate.
ekskrementy *pl. Gen.* **-ów** excrement; feces.
ekslibris *mi* ex libris; bookplate.
eksmisja *f. prawn.* eviction; **nakaz eksmisji** eviction notice.
eksmisyjny *a. prawn.* (of) eviction; **nakaz eksmisyjny** eviction order.
eksmitować *ipf. prawn.* evict.
ekspandować *ipf. lit.* expand.
ekspansja *f.* **1.** (= *rozprzestrzenianie się*) expansion. **2.** *fiz.* expansion. **3.** *ekon.* expansion; **ekspansja gospodarcza** economic expansion.
ekspansjonistyczny *a.* expansionist; **polityka ekspansjonistyczna** expansionist policy; **hasła ekspansjonistyczne** expansionist slogans.
ekspansjonizm *mi polit.* expansionism.
ekspansywność *f.* **1.** (= *rozprzestrzenianie się*) expansiveness; **ekspansywność polityczna** political expansiveness. **2.** (= *zaborczość*) expansiveness, demonstrativeness.
ekspansywny *a.* **1.** (= *rozprzestrzeniający się*) expansive; **gospodarka ekspansywna** expansive economy. **2.** (= *zaborczy*) expansive, demonstrative; **ekspansywna osobowość** expansive personality.
ekspatriacja *f.* expatriation.
ekspatriant *mp* expatriate.
ekspatriować *ipf.* expatriate.
ekspedient *mp* sales *l.* shop assistant.
ekspedientka *f. zob.* **ekspedient.**
ekspediować *ipf.* **1.** (= *wysyłać*) ship, send; **ekspediować dzieci na kolonie** send children to a summer camp. **2.** *przest.* (= *obsługiwać klientów*) serve.
ekspedycja *f.* **1.** (= *wyprawa*) expedition; **ekspedycja naukowa** scientific expedition. **2.** (= *dział wysyłkowy*) forwarding *l.* dispatch *l.* shipping department. **3.** (= *wysyłanie*) forwarding, dispatch, shipping; **ekspedycja bagażu** baggage dispatch.
ekspedycyjny *a.* **1.** (= *o wyprawie*) expeditionary; **grupa ekspedycyjna** expeditionary group. **2.** (= *o wysłaniu*) forwarding, dispatch, shipping; **dział ekspedycyjny** forwarding *l.* dispatch *l.* shipping department.
ekspedytor *mp* **1.** (= *przedsiębiorstwo*) shipping company, freight forwarder. **2.** (= *pracownik wysyłający towar*) shipping clerk, shipping agent. **3.** (= *pracownik kontrolujący regularność kursowania pojazdów*) dispatcher.
ekspedytura *f.* forwarding *l.* dispatch *l.* shipping department.
ekspert *mp* expert, specialist; **ekspert w dziedzinie literatury polskiej** expert in Polish literature; **ekspert w zakresie logistyki** logistics expert.

ekspertyza *f.* expertise, assessment, evaluation, opinion; **ekspertyza lekarska** medical assessment; **ekspertyza prawna** legal evaluation; **zlecić ekspertyzę** commission an expert analysis; **wyniki ekspertyzy** results of expert analysis.
eksperyment *mi* **1.** (= *próba, test*) experiment; **udany eksperyment** successful experiment; **przeprowadzić eksperyment** carry out an experiment. **2.** (= *doświadczenie*) experiment, test; **eksperymenty na zwierzętach** experiments *l.* tests on animals; **eksperyment naukowy** scientific experiment.
eksperymentalista *mp* experimentalist.
eksperymentalizm *mi* **1.** *teor.lit.* experimentalism. **2.** *fil.* experimentalism.
eksperymentalny *a.* experimental; **kino eksperymentalne** experimental cinema; **fizyka eksperymentalna** experimental physics.
eksperymentator *mp* experimenter, experimentor, experimentator.
eksperymentatorski *a.* experimental, experimenter's; **czyjeś eksperymentatorskie pomysły** sb's experimental ideas.
eksperymentatorstwo *n.* experimentation.
eksperymentować *ipf.* experiment; **eksperymentować z siarką** experiment with sulphur; **eksperymentować na zwierzętach** conduct tests on animals.
ekspiacja *f.* expiation.
ekspiacyjny *a.* expiatory; **modlitwa ekspiacyjna** expiatory prayer.
eksplikacja *f. lit.* explication.
eksploatacja *f.* **1.** (= *pozyskiwanie bogactw naturalnych*) exploitation, extraction; **eksploatacja złóż węgla** coal mining, mining of coal deposits; **nadmierna eksploatacja** overexploitation; **eksploatacja odkrywkowa** *l.* **naziemna** strip *l.* open-pit mining. **2.** (= *użytkowanie*) operation, utilization; **okres eksploatacji** operating period, (useful) life; **koszty eksploatacji** operating costs; **oddać do eksploatacji** put into operation *l.* service; **wycofać z eksploatacji** withdraw from operation *l.* service, discontinue. **3.** (= *wyzysk*) exploitation; **nieludzka eksploatacja więźniów obozu** inhumane exploitation of camp prisoners; **eksploatacja sił** exploitation of labor.
eksploatacyjny *a.* **1.** of *l.* for exploitation *l.* exploiting, exploitative, exploitive. **2.** operating, operational; **materiały eksploatacyjne** supplies, consumables.
eksploatator *mp* **1.** (= *użytkownik*) operator. **2.** (= *wyzyskiwacz*) exploiter.
eksploatatorski *a.* mining, extraction; **poszukiwania eksploatatorskie** prospecting, resource exploration.
eksploatować *ipf.* **1.** (= *pozyskiwać bogactwa naturalne*) exploit, extract; (*złoże*) mine. **2.** (= *użytkować*) operate, utilize. **3.** (= *wyzyskiwać kogoś*) exploit.
eksplodować *ipf.* explode.
eksploracja *f. lit.* exploration.
eksploracyjny *a. lit.* exploratory; **prace eksploracyjne** exploratory work; **wyprawa eksploracyjna** exploratory expedition.

eksplorator *mp t. komp.* explorer.

eksploratorski *a. lit.* exploratory; **prace eksploratorskie** exploratory work.

eksplorować *ipf. lit.* explore.

eksplozja *f.* **1.** (= *wybuch*) explosion; **eksplozja gazu** gas explosion; **eksplozja bomby** bomb blast; **spowodować eksplozję** cause an explosion. **2.** *przen.* outburst; **eksplozja gniewu** outburst of anger; **eksplozja uczuć** outburst (of emotions); **eksplozja demograficzna** population explosion. **3.** *fon.* plosion.

eksplozyjny *a.* explosive; **materiał eksplozyjny** explosive; **mieszanka eksplozyjna** explosive mixture.

eksponat *mi* exhibit.

eksponent *mp* **1.** (= *wystawca*) exhibitor. **2.** *przen.* exponent, voice.

eksponować *ipf.* **1.** (= *wystawiać*) exhibit, display. **2.** (= *wystawiać na pierwszym planie*) exhibit. **3.** (= *narażać*) expose. **4.** *fot.* expose.

eksponowany *a.* **1.** prominent; **być na eksponowanym stanowisku** be in a prominent position *l.* position of prominence. **2.** (= *wystawiony*) exhibited, displayed.

eksport *mi ekon., handl.* export(s), exportation; **produkować na eksport** produce for export; **eksport węgla** coal exports; **eksport technologii** export(s) of technology; **odrzut z eksportu** *iron.* dud.

eksporter *mp* exporter.

eksportować *ipf.* export.

eksportowy *a.* export; **produkcja eksportowa** production for export; **firma eksportowa** export company.

ekspozycja *f.* **1.** (= *wystawianie*) exhibition, exhibit, exposition, expo; **ekspozycja stała** permanent exhibit(ion); **ekspozycja czasowa** temporary exhibit(ion). **2.** (= *usytuowanie w stosunku do stron świata*) exposure; **północna ekspozycja** northern exposure. **3.** *fot.* exposure. **4.** *teor.lit.* exposition. **5.** *muz.* exposition. **6.** *sport* exposure.

ekspozycyjny *a.* **1.** (= *wystawienniczy*) exhibition; **powierzchnia ekspozycyjna** exhibition space. **2.** *fot.* exposure; **czas ekspozycyjny** exposure time. **3.** *lit.* expositional; **monolog ekspozycyjny** expositional monologue. **4.** *muz.* expositional.

ekspozytura *f.* **1.** (*firmy*) branch (office), office. **2.** (*organizacji, urzędu państwowego*) local *l.* regional office.

ekspres[1] *mi* (= *list ekspresowy*) special delivery, express letter; **wysłać ekspresem** send sth special delivery.

ekspres[2] *mi* **1.** *kol.* express (train). **2.** (= *aparat do robienia kawy*) (*pod ciśnieniem*) espresso machine; (*z filtrem*) coffee maker.

ekspresja *f.* **1.** (*uczuć*) expression. **2.** *sztuka* expression.

ekspresjonista *mp sztuka* expressionist.

ekspresjonistyczny *a.* expressionist, expressionistic; **obraz ekspresjonistyczny** expressionist painting; **styl ekspresjonistyczny** expressionist style.

ekspresjonizm *mi sztuka, teor.lit.* expressionism.

ekspresowy *a.* express; **list ekspresowy** special delivery letter, express letter; **pociąg ekspresowy** *kol.* express train; **ekspresowe czyszczenie garderoby** express laundry service; **zrobić coś w ekspresowym tempie** do sth very quickly.

ekspresyjność *f.* expressiveness.

ekspresyjny *a.* expressive.

ekspresywność *f.* **1.** (= *sugestywność*) expressiveness. **2.** *biol.* expressivity.

ekspresywny *a.* expressive; **funkcja ekspresywna** *jęz.* emotive function; **znak ekspresywny** *jęz.* emotive sign.

ekspropriacja *f. lit.* expropriation.

ekspulsja *f.* expulsion.

ekstatyczność *f. rzad.* ecstatic character *l.* condition.

ekstatyczny *a.* ecstatic, rapturous; **ekstatyczny taniec** ecstatic dance; **stan ekstatyczny** *med.* ecstatic state.

ekstaza *f.* ecstasy; **ekstaza religijna** religious ecstasy; **wpaść w ekstazę** go into ecstasies; **być w stanie ekstazy** be in a state of ecstasy.

ekstensja *f.* **1.** *log.* extension. **2.** *fil.* extension.

ekstensor *mi anat.* extensor.

ekstensyfikacja *f.* extension, expansion.

ekstensywny *a.* extensive; **ekstensywna gospodarka rolna** *roln., ekon.* extensive farming system.

eksterminacja *f. zwł. hist.* extermination.

eksterminacyjny *a.* extermination.

eksterminować *ipf.* exterminate.

ekstern *mp szkoln., uniw.* extramural *l.* extension student.

eksternista *mp szkoln., uniw.* extramural *l.* extension student.

eksternistka *f. zob.* eksternista.

eksternistycznie *adv. szkoln., uniw.* as an extramural *l.* extension student; **studiować eksternistycznie** study as an extramural *l.* extension student.

eksternistyczny *a. szkoln., uniw.* extramural, extension; **studia eksternistyczne** distance learning, extramural learning.

eksterytorialność *f. prawn.* extraterritoriality.

eksterytorialny *a. prawn.* extraterritorial, extraterritorial.

ekstra *a. indecl.* **1.** (= *dodatkowy*) extra, additional; **ekstra wydatki** extra expenses. **2.** *pot.* (= *wspaniały*) great; **ekstra książka** great book. – *adv.* **1.** (= *dodatkowo*) extra; **zapłacić komuś ekstra** pay sb extra; **zrobić coś ekstra** do sth extra. **2.** (= *wspaniale*) great; **wyglądasz ekstra!** you look great!

ekstradować *pf. prawn.* extradite.

ekstradycja *f. prawn.* extradition.

ekstradycyjny *a. prawn.* extradition.

ekstrahent *mi chem.* extraction solvent, extractant.

ekstrahować *ipf. chem.* extract.

ekstrakcja f. **1.** *chem.* extraction. **2.** *med.* extraction.

ekstrakcyjny a. *chem.* extraction; **aparat ekstrakcyjny** digester; **metoda ekstrakcyjna** extraction method.

ekstraklasa f. *sport* major league, big league.

ekstrakt mi extract, essence.

ekstraktor mi **1.** *med.* extractor. **2.** *tech.* extractor.

ekstrapolacja f. (= *przewidywanie*) extrapolation; *mat.* extrapolation.

ekstrapolować ipf. **1.** (= *przewidywać*) extrapolate. **2.** *mat.* extrapolate.

ekstrawagancja f. eccentricity.

ekstrawagancki a. eccentric; **ekstrawagancki strój** outlandish outfit; **ekstrawagancka przyjaciółka** peculiar friend.

ekstrawersja f. *psych.* extroversion, extraversion.

ekstrawersyjny a. *psych.* extrovert(ed), extravert(ed); **typ ekstrawersyjny** extrovert, extravert.

ekstrawertyk mp *psych.* extrovert, extravert.

ekstremalny a. extreme; **ekstremalne warunki pogodowe** extreme weather conditions; **sytuacja ekstremalna** extreme situation; **ekstremalna opinia** extreme opinion; **sporty ekstremalne** *sport* extreme sports; **wartość ekstremalna** *mat.* extreme value.

ekstremista mp *lit.* extremist.

ekstremistyczny a. extremist; **ugrupowanie ekstremistyczne** extremist group; **poglądy ekstremistyczne** extremist views.

ekstremizm mi extremism.

ekstremum n. *indecl. in sing. pl.* **-ma** Gen. **-mów** *mat.* extremum.

ekstyrpacja f. *chir.* extirpation.

ekstyrpować ipf. *chir.* extirpate.

eksudacja f. **1.** *bot.* exudation. **2.** *geol.* exudation. **3.** *med.* exudation.

eksudat mi **1.** *bot.* exudate. **2.** *med.* exudate.

ektoderma f. **1.** *biol.* ectoderm. **2.** *zool.* ectoderm.

ektogeneza f. *Dat., Loc.* **-zie** *biol.* ectogenesis.

ektopasożyt ma Gen. **-a** *biol.* ectoparasite.

ektopia f. Gen. **-ii** *med.* ectopia.

ektoplazma f. **1.** *biol.* ectoplasm. **2.** *metafizyka* ectoplasm.

ekumena f. **1.** *geogr.* ecumene. **2.** *hist.* ecumene.

ekumeniczny a. *rel.* ecumenical; **nabożeństwo ekumeniczne** ecumenical service; **ruch ekumeniczny** ecumenism; **sobór ekumeniczny** ecumenical council.

ekumenista mp *rel.* ecumenist, ecumenicist.

ekumenizm mi *rel.* ecumenism, ecumenicism, ecumenicalism.

Ekwador mi *geogr.* Ecuador.

Ekwadorczyk mp Ecuadorian.

Ekwadorka f. Ecuadorian.

Ekwadorski a. Ecuadorian, Ecuador(e)an.

ekwilibrysta mp high-wire artist, equilibrist.

ekwilibrystyczny a. (on the) high-wire, equilibristic; **pokaz ekwilibrystyczny** high-wire act, bal-

ancing act; **ekwilibrystyczne ewolucje** high-wire acrobatics.

ekwilibrystyka f. **1.** (= *akrobatyka*) high-wire acrobatics. **2.** *przen.* (= *lawirowanie*) acrobatics; **ekwilibrystyka słowna** verbal acrobatics *l.* gymnastics.

ekwinokcjum n. *Nom.pl.* **-cja** *astron.* equinox; **ekwinokcjum jesienne** autumnal equinox; **ekwinokcjum wiosenne** vernal equinox.

ekwipaż mi **1.** *przest.* (= *wyposażenie*) equipage, outfit, paraphernalia. **2.** *arch.* (= *pojazd konny*) equipage.

ekwipolentny a. **1.** *log.* equipollent. **2.** *jęz.* equipollent; **opozycja ekwipolentna** equipollent opposition.

ekwipotencjalny a. *fiz.* equipotential; **powierzchnia ekwipotencjalna** equipotential surface.

ekwipować ipf. equip, outfit.

ekwipunek mi **-nk-** (*turystyczny, myśliwski*) equipment, gear; (*żołnierski*) equipment, accoutrement, accouterment.

ekwiwalencja f. **1.** *log.* equivalence. **2.** *jęz.* equivalence, equivalency.

ekwiwalent mi **1.** (= *odpowiednik*) equivalent; **ekwiwalent pieniężny** equivalent in money; **ekwiwalent w złocie** equivalent in gold. **2.** *ekon.* equivalent.

ekwiwalentny a. equivalent; **ekwiwalentna wartość** equivalent value.

ekwiwokacja f. Gen., Dat., Loc. **-cji** *log.* equivocation.

elaborat mi *iron.* wordy essay; comprehensive study.

Elam mi *hist.* Elam.

elamicki a. *hist.* Elamite; (*język*) Elamite, Elamitic.

elana f. *tk.* **1.** (= *włókno poliestrowe*) polyester. **2.** (= *tkanina z włókna poliestrowego*) polyester.

elanobawełna f. *tk.* polyester-cotton fabric.

elanobawełniany a. *tk.* polyester-cotton, polyester-and-cotton; **płaszcz elanobawełniany** polyester-and-cotton coat; **tkanina elanobawełniana** polyester-cotton fabric.

elanowy a. *tk.* polyester; **spódnica elanowa** polyester skirt; **tkanina elanowa** polyester (fabric).

elastomer mi *techn.* elastomer.

elastoplasty pl. *fiz.* elastoplastics.

elastoplastyczny a. *fiz.* elastoplastic; **ciało elastoplastyczne** elastoplastic body.

elastyczność f. **1.** (= *sprężystość*) elasticity, resilience, resiliency; (*mięśni*) limberness; (*tkaniny, skóry*) resiliency, resilience; **elastyczność silnika** *techn.* engine response. **2.** *przen.* flexibility, adaptability; **brak elastyczności poglądów** adamancy, unyielding views, inflexibility of one's views.

elastyczny a. **1.** (= *sprężysty*) elastic, flexible, resilient, stretch, pliable, supple; **elastyczna tkanina** *tk.* elastic *l.* stretch fabric; **bandaż elastyczny** *med.* stretch *l.* orthopedic bandage; **włókna elastyczne** *biol.* elastic tissue. **2.** *przen.* (= *zmie-*

niający się zależnie od sytuacji) flexible; **elastyczny system wynagrodzeń** flexible system of remuneration; **elastyczny system produkcyjny** *ekon.* flexible production system. **3.** *przen.* (= *łatwo przystosowujący się do nowych warunków*) versatile; **elastyczny mechanizm** versatile mechanism.

eldorado *n.* El Dorado.

eleacki *a. fil.* Eleatic; **szkoła eleacka** Eleatic school.

eleata *mp fil.* Eleatic.

eleatyzm *mi fil.* Eleaticism.

elegancja *f.* elegance; **wyszukana elegancja** sophistication; **ubierać się z elegancją** dress elegantly; (*o sposobie bycia*) refinement.

elegancki *a.* elegant; (*o ubraniu*) fine; (*o kształcie, piśmie*) graceful; (*o mieszkaniu, meblach*) posh; (*o mężczyźnie*) debonair; **elegancki świat** *żart.* the upper crust.

elegancko *adv.* elegantly; **ubierać się elegancko** dress elegantly; **zachowywać się elegancko** behave gracefully; **elegancko odnowione mieszkanie** poshly remodeled apartment.

elegant *mp* (= *mężczyzna ubierający się modnie*) man of fashion, dedicated follower of fashion; (= *mężczyzna ubierający się z przesadną elegancją*) *żart.* dandy, fop.

elegantka *f.* woman of fashion, fashion bug, sharp *l.* snappy dresser.

elegia *f. Gen.* **-ii 1.** *teor.lit.* elegy. **2.** *muz.* elegy.

elegijność *f.* elegiacness.

elegijny *a.* elegiac; **poezja elegijna** *teor.lit.* elegiac poetry; **dystych elegijny** *teor.lit.* elegiac verse.

elekcja *f. hist.* election.

elekcyjność *f. hist.* eligibility; **elekcyjność tronu** election of a king.

elekcyjny *a.* elective; **tron elekcyjny** *hist.* elective throne; **król elekcyjny** *hist.* elective king; **sejm elekcyjny** *hist.* elective Sejm *l.* parliament.

elekt *mp* the elect; **prezydent elekt** *polit.* the President elect.

elektor *mp* **1.** *polit.* (= *wyborca*) elector. **2.** *hist.* (*w Niemczech*) Elector; **książę elektor** Elector.

elektorat *mi* **1.** *polit.* (= *wyborcy*) electorate. **2.** *hist.* (*kraj*) electorate.

elektorski *a.* **1.** *polit.* (= *wyborczy*) electoral; **głosy elektorskie** electoral votes. **2.** *hist.* (*w Niemczech*) electoral.

Elektra *f. mit.* Electra; **kompleks Elektry** *psych.* Electra complex.

elektroakustyczny *a. fiz.* electroacoustic.

elektroakustyka *f. fiz.* electroacoustics.

elektroanaliza *f. techn.* electroanalysis.

elektrochemia *f. Gen.* **-ii** *chem.* electrochemistry.

elektrochirurgia *f. Gen.* **-ii** *chir.* electrosurgery.

elektrociepłownia *f.* combined heat and power plant, CHP plant.

elektrociepłowniczy *a.* heat and power; **sieć elektrociepłownicza** heat and power grid.

elektrociepłownik *mp* heat and power technician; heat and power engineer.

elektroda *f. fiz., el.* electrode; **elektroda dodatnia** positive electrode, anode; **elektroda ujemna** negative electrode, cathode.

elektrodializa *f. chem.* electrodialysis.

elektrododatni *a. fiz., el.* electropositive; **pierwiastek elektrododatni** electropositive element.

elektrodynamiczny *a. techn., el.* electrodynamic, electrodynamical; **amperomierz elektrodynamiczny** electrodynamic ammeter.

elektrodynamika *f. fiz., el.* electrodynamics; **elektrodynamika kwantowa** quantum electrodynamics.

elektroencefalograf *mi med.* electroencephalograph (*EEG*).

elektroencefalografia *f. Gen.* **-ii** *med.* electroencephalography.

elektroencefalograficzny *a. med.* electroencephalographic, electroencephalographical.

elektroencefalogram *mi Gen.* **-u** *med.* electroencephalogram (*EEG*).

elektroenergetyczny *a. techn.* electric *l.* electrical power; **linia elektroenergetyczna** (electrical) power line; **sieć elektroenergetyczna** (electrical) power grid.

elektroenergetyka *f. techn.* electric(al) power engineering.

elektrofiltr *ma Gen.* **-u** *techn.* electrostatic precipitator, electrofilter.

elektrofizjolog *ma Gen., Acc.* **-a** *med.* electrophysiologist.

elektrofizjologia *f. Gen., Dat., Loc.* **-ii** *med.* electrophysiology.

elektrofon *mi muz.* electrophone.

elektrofonia *f. Gen., Dat., Loc.* **-nii** *fiz.* electroacoustics.

elektrofor *mi Gen.* **-u** *fiz., el.* electrophorus.

elektroforeza *f. chem., fiz.* electrophoresis.

elektrografia *f. Gen., Dat., Loc.* **-fii** *fiz.* electrography.

elektroindukcja *f. fiz.* induction.

elektrokardiograf *mi med.* electrocardiograph (*ECG l. EKG*).

elektrokardiografia *f. Gen.* **-ii** *med.* electrocardiography.

elektrokardiograficzny *a. med.* electrocardiographic.

elektrokardiogram *mi med.* electrocardiogram (*ECG l. EKG*).

elektrokaustyka *f. Dat., Loc.* **-yce** *med.* electrocautery, electrocauterization.

elektrokinetyczny *a. fiz.* electrokinetic.

elektrokinetyka *f. Dat., Loc.* **-yce** *fiz.* electrokinetics.

elektrokoagulacja *f. Gen., Dat., Loc.* **-cji** *med., chir.* electrocoagulation.

elektrolit *mi chem., fiz.* electrolyte.

elektrolityczny *a. chem., fiz.* electrolytic, electrolytical; **analiza elektrolityczna** electrolytic analysis; **dysocjacja elektrolityczna** electrolytic dissociation; **miedź elektrolityczna** electrolytic copper; **wanna elektrolityczna** electrolytic tank, electrolyzer; **powłoka elektrolityczna** electrolytic coating; **kondensator elektrolityczny** electrolytic capacitor; **polaryzacja elektrolityczna** electrolytic polarization.

elektroliza *f. chem., fiz.* electrolysis; **elektroliza roztworu** electrolysis of solution.

elektrolizer *mi Gen.* **-a** *chem., fiz.* electrolytic tank, electrolyzer.

elektroluks *mi* (= *odkurzacz*) (Electrolux) vacuum cleaner.

elektroluminescencja *f. Gen., Dat., Loc.* **-cji** *fiz.* electroluminescence.

elektromagnes *mi fiz., el.* electromagnet.

elektromagnetyczny *a. fiz.* electromagnetic; **fale elektromagnetyczne** electromagnetic waves, electric waves; **indukcja elektromagnetyczna** electromagnetic induction; **pole elektromagnetyczne** electromagnetic field.

elektromagnetyzm *mi* **1.** *fiz.* (*zjawiska*) electromagnetism. **2.** *fiz.* (*dziedzina wiedzy*) electromagnetics, electromagnetism.

elektromaszynowy *a. techn.* electromechanical; **przemysł elektromaszynowy** electromechanical industry.

elektromechanik *mp* electromechanical engineer.

elektromechanika *f.* electromechanics.

elektron *mi* **1.** *fiz.* electron. **2.** *metal.* (*stop*) elektron.

elektroniczny *a. el.* electronic; **elektroniczne przetwarzanie danych** *komp.* electronic data processing, EDP; **poczta elektroniczna** *komp.* e-mail; **muzyka elektroniczna** *muz.* electronic music.

elektronik *mp el.* electronics engineer.

elektronika *f. el.* electronics; **elektronika kwantowa** quantum electronics.

elektronowy *a.* electron; **lampa elektronowa** electron tube; **wyrzutnia elektronowa** electron gun; **mózg elektronowy** *pot.* electronic brain.

elektrostatyczny *a. fiz.* electrostatic; **galwanometr elektrostatyczny** electrometer; **maszyna elektrostatyczna** electrostatic generator.

elektrostatyka *f. fiz.* electrostatics.

elektrotechniczny *a.* electrotechnical; **przemysł elektrotechniczny** electrotechnical industry.

elektrotechnik *mp* electrician.

elektrotechnika *f.* electrotechnics, electrotechnology, electrical engineering.

elektroterapia *f. Gen., Dat., Loc.* **-pii** *med.* electrotherapy.

elektrownia *f. Gen.pl.* **-i** power plant, power station; **elektrownia wodna** hydroelectric power plant; **elektrownia cieplna** thermal power plant; **elektrownia atomowa** nuclear power plant.

elektrowozownia *f. Gen.pl.* **-i** *kol.* electric locomotive *l.* engine shed.

elektrowóz *mi* **-o-** *kol.* electric locomotive *l.* engine.

elektrowstrząsy *pl. Gen.* **-ów** *med.* electroshock; **terapia elektrowstrząsowa** electroshock *l.* electroconvulsive therapy.

elektryczność *f.* **1.** (= *energia elektryczna*) electricity; **elektryczność atmosferyczna** atmospheric electricity. **2.** *pot.* (= *prąd*) power.

elektryczny *a.* electric, electrical; **opór elektryczny** electrical resistance; **obwód elektryczny** electric circuit; **pole elektryczne** electric field; **kuchenka elektryczna** electric range; **silnik elektryczny** electric motor; **pociąg elektryczny** electric train; **krzesło elektryczne** electric chair.

elektryfikacja *f.* electrification.

elektryfikować *ipf.* electrify.

elektryk *mp* **1.** (*inżynier*) electrical engineer. **2.** (*monter*) electrician.

elektryka *f.* (*dział wiedzy*) electricity.

elektryzować *ipf.* **1.** (= *wytwarzać prąd*) electrify. **2.** *przen.* (= *wstrząsać*) electrify, thrill; **elektryzować publiczność** electrify the audience. **~ się** *ipf.* become electrified.

elektryzująco *adv.* in an electrifying manner; **wiadomość o jej przyjeździe podziałała na mnie elektryzująco** news of her coming had an electrifying effect on me.

element *mi* **1.** (= *składnik*) element, component, part; **element składowy** component part; **element architektoniczny** architectural element; **elementy obce w języku** foreign elements in a language; **elementy maszyn** machine parts. **2.** (= *czynnik*) factor. **3.** *fil.* (= *żywioł*) element. **4.** *mat.* element. **5.** *pot.* (= *grupa ludzi o negatywnych cechach*) element; **przestępczy element** criminal element; **elementy radykalne** the radical element.

elementarny *a.* **1.** (= *podstawowy*) elementary, primary, basic, fundamental; **cząstka elementarna** *fiz., chem.* elementary particle; **szkoła elementarna** *hist., szkoln.* elementary *l.* primary school; **geometria elementarna** *geom.* synthetic geometry; **funkcja elementarna** *mat.* elementary function. **2.** *rzad.* (= *żywiołowy*) of the elements; **klęski elementarne** natural disasters *l.* calamities.

elementarz *mi Gen.* **-a** *szkoln.* primer.

elementy *pl. Gen.* **-ów** *szkoln., uniw.* elements, rudiments, fundamentals; **elementy fizyki** elements of physics; **elementy informatyki** introduction to computer science.

eleuzyński *a. hist.* Eleusinian; **misterium eleuzyńskie** Eleusinian mysteries.

elew *mp pl.* **-owie** **1.** *wojsk., szkoln.* cadet. **2.** *szkoln., przest.* student, disciple.

elewacja *f.* **1.** *bud.* (= *ściana zewnętrzna budynku*) facade, façade; **elewacja frontowa** facade, façade; **elewacja zachodnia** west facade *l.* façade. **2.** *bud.* (*rzut*) elevation. **3.** *astron.* elevation.

elewacyjny *a. bud.* facade, façade; **roboty elewacyjne** facade works.

elewator *mi Gen.* **-a** **1.** *roln.* (grain) elevator. **2.** *techn.* (= *przenośnik pionowy*) elevator.

elf *mp mit.* elf.

eliksir *mi przest.* elixir; **eliksir młodości** *l.* **życia** elixir of life.

eliminacja *f.* **1.** (= *selekcja*) elimination. **2.** (*w konkursie*) elimination. **3.** *sport* qualifying round, trial. **4.** *chem.* elimination. **5.** *mat.* elimination.

eliminacyjny *a.* elimination; **rozgrywki eliminacyjne** qualifying round, trials; **mecz eliminacyjny** qualifier.

eliminator *mi Gen.* **-a** *el.* suppressor, trap circuit.

eliminować *ipf.* **1.** (= *wykluczać*) eliminate. **2.** *mat.* eliminate.

elipsa *f.* **1.** *geom.* ellipse. **2.** *ret.* ellipsis.

elipsoida *f. geom.* ellipsoid; **elipsoida obrotowa** ellipsoid of revolution, spheroid; **elipsoida ziemska** reference ellipsoid.

elipsoidalny *a.* ellipsoidal, ellipsoid.

eliptyczność *f.* **1.** *geom.* ellipticity. **2.** *ret.* ellipticalness.

eliptyczny *a.* **1.** *geom.* elliptical, elliptic; **orbita eliptyczna** elliptical orbit; **tor eliptyczny** elliptical path. **2.** *ret.* elliptical, elliptic; **zdanie eliptyczne** elliptical sentence.

elita *f.* **1.** (= *wyróżniająca się grupa ludzi*) elite; **elita towarzyska** high society; **elita intelektualna** intellectual elite. **2.** *roln.* elite seed.

elitarność *f.* elitism.

elitarny *a.* **1.** (= *dostępny dla elity*) elitist; **elitarne poglądy** elitist views; **sztuka elitarna** elitist art. **2.** (= *ekskluzywny*) elite; **elitarne towarzystwo** elite company; **elitarna dzielnica** elite neighborhood.

elitaryzm *mi polit.* elitism.

elizejski *a. mit.* Elysian; **Pola Elizejskie** Elysian Fields, Elysium.

elizja *f. jęz.* elision.

elokwencja *f.* **1.** (= *krasomówstwo*) eloquence. **2.** *iron.* verbosity.

elokwentny *a.* **1.** (= *mający dar wymowy*) eloquent; **elokwentny rzecznik prasowy** eloquent spokesperson. **2.** *iron.* verbose.

eluwialny *a. geol.* eluvial; **złoża eluwialne** eluvial deposits.

eluwium *n. geol.* eluvium.

elżbietanka *f. rz.-kat.* member of the order of Franciscan Sisters of St. Elizabeth.

elżbietański *a. hist.* (= *z czasów panowania Elżbiety I*) Elizabethan; **teatr elżbietański** *teatr* Elizabethan theater; **styl elżbietański** *bud.* Elizabethan style.

emalia *f. Gen.* **-ii 1.** (= *szkliwo*) enamel; (= *ceramika*) glaze, porcelain enamel. **2.** (= *farba emaliowa*) enamel (paint). **3.** *anat., dent.* enamel.

emalier *mp* enameler, enamelist.

emaliernia *f. Gen.pl.* **-ni** *l.* **-ń** enamel shop *l.* department.

emalierski *a.* enameling; **piec emalierski** enameling furnace.

emaliować *ipf.* enamel; **emaliowany garnek** enamel pot.

emanacja *f.* **1.** (= *promieniowanie*) emanation; **teoria emanacji** *fil.* theory of emanation. **2.** *przen.* (= *oddziaływanie*) emanation. **3.** *chem., fiz.* emanation.

emancypacja *f.* emancipation, liberation; **emancypacja kobiet** emancipation of women.

emancypacyjny *a.* emancipation; **ruch emancypacyjny** emancipation movement.

emancypantka *f.* advocate of women's rights, women's lib activist *l.* advocate.

emancypować *ipf.* emancipate, liberate, free. **~ się** *ipf.* emancipate o.s., liberate o.s., free o.s.

emanować *ipf.* emanate, emit, radiate.

embargo *n.* embargo (*na coś* on sth); **nałożyć embargo** impose an embargo; **znieść embargo** lift an embargo.

emblemat *mi* emblem, logo.

embriolog *mp pl.* **-dzy** *l.* **-owie** *med.* embryologist.

embriologia *f. Gen.* **-ii** *med.* embryology.

embriologiczny *a. med.* embryological, embryologic; **badania embriologiczne** embryological examination.

embrion *mi biol.* embryo.

embrionalny *a. biol.* embryonic, embryonal, embryo; **stadium embrionalne** embryo stage; **rozwój embrionalny** embryonic development.

ementaler *mi Gen.* **-a** *kulin.* Emment(h)aler (cheese).

ementalski *a.* Emmenthaler; **ser ementalski** *kulin.* Emment(h)aler cheese.

emerycki *a.* pension, pensioner's, of retired persons; **związek emerycki** pensioners' union, union of retired persons.

emeryt *mp* (old age) pensioner, retired person, retiree.

emerytalny *a.* retirement, pension; **wiek emerytalny** retirement *l.* pensionable age; **otwarty fundusz emerytalny** public retirement *l.* pension fund.

emerytka *f. zob.* **emeryt.**

emerytowany *a.* retired; **emerytowany oficer** retired officer.

emerytura *f.* pension; **pobierać emeryturę** receive a pension; **być na emeryturze** be retired; **przejść** *l.* **odejść na emeryturę** retire; **przejść** *l.* **odejść na wcześniejszą emeryturę** take early retirement, retire early.

emfatyczny *a.* **1.** (= *wyrażany z naciskiem*) emphatic, forceful; *uj.* (= *egzaltowany*) stilted, affected, pompous. **2.** *fon.* emphatic.

emfaza *f.* emphasis; *uj.* (= *egzaltacja*) affectation.

emigracja *f.* **1.** (= *uchodźstwo*) emigration. **2.** (= *ludzie, którzy wyemigrowali*) emigrants.

emigracyjny *a.* emigration, emigrant; **rząd emigracyjny** government in exile; **urząd emigracyjny** emigration office.

emigrancki *a.* emigrant.

emigrant *mp*, **emigrantka** *f. Gen.pl.* **-ek** emigrant.

emigrować *ipf. i pf.* **1.** (= *opuszczać kraj*) emigrate. **2.** *pot.* (= *wędrować*) migrate, wander, travel.

eminencja *mp decl. like f. kośc.* (*tytuł*) eminence; **Wasza/Jego Eminencja** Your/His Eminence; **szara eminencja** *przen.* éminence grise.

emir *mp pl.* **-owie** *hist., polit.* emir.

emirat *mi* emirate; **Zjednoczone Emiraty Arabskie** *geogr.* the United Arab Emirates.

emisariusz *mp Gen.pl.* -y *l.* -ów, **emisariuszka** *f. Gen.pl.* -ek emissary.

emisja *f.* 1. *ekon.* issue; **emisja pieniędzy/akcji/ papierów wartościowych** issue of banknotes/ shares/securities. 2. *radio, tel.* broadcasting, airing; (*programów telewizyjnych*) screening. 3. *fiz.* emission. 4. *muz., fon.* **emisja głosu** voice production. 5. *ekol.* **emisja metanu/dwutlenku węgla** emission *l.* discharge of methane/carbon dioxide.

emisyjny *a.* 1. *ekon.* (of) issue; **bank/kurs emisyjny** bank/rate of issue; **prospekt emisyjny** prospectus. 2. *fiz.* emission; **widmo emisyjne** emission spectrum.

emitować *ipf.* 1. *ekon.* issue. 2. *radio, tel.* broadcast, air; *telew.* screen. 3. *fiz.* (= *wysyłać energię*) emit. 4. *ekol.* (= *wydzielać*) emit, discharge.

emocja *f.* emotion, feeling.

emocjonalizm *mi* 1. = **emocjonalność.** 2. *fil.* emotionalism.

emocjonalność *f. psych.* emotionality.

emocjonalny *a.* emotional.

emocjonować *ipf.* excite, thrill. ~ **się** *ipf.* be excited, be agog (*czymś* about sth).

emocjonujący *a.* exciting.

emotywizm *mi fil.* emotivism.

emotywny *a. psych.* emotive.

empatia *f. Gen.* -ii *psych.* empathy.

empatyczny *a. psych.* empathic, empathetic.

empire *mi Gen.* -re'u *Loc.* -rze *bud.*, **sztuka użytkowa** the Empire style.

empirowy *a.* Empire, Empire-style.

empiryczka *f. Gen.pl.* -ek *zob.* **empiryk** 1.

empiryczność *f.* empiricism.

empiryczny *a.* empirical; **dowód empiryczny** empirical proof.

empiryk *mp* 1. (= *praktyk*) empiric. 2. *fil.* empiricist.

empirysta *mp*, **empirystka** *f. Gen.pl.* -ek *fil.* empiricist.

empiryzm *mi fil.* empiricism.

emploi *n. indecl. teatr, film* acting profile.

empora *f. bud.* (internal *l.* inner) gallery.

emporowy *a. bud.* gallery.

emu *n. l. ma indecl. zool.* emu (*Dromaius novaehollandiae*).

emulacja *f. komp.* emulation.

emulator *mi Gen.* -a *komp.* emulator.

emulgator *mi Gen.* -a *chem.* emulsifier.

emulgować *ipf. chem.* emulsify.

emulgować się *ipf. chem.* emulsify.

emulsja *f.* 1. *chem.* emulsion; *pot.* (= *farba emulsyjna*) emulsion paint; **emulsja światłoczuła** *fot.* light-sensitive emulsion. 2. **emulsja do opalania** suntan lotion.

emulsyjny *a. chem.* emulsive; **farba emulsyjna** emulsion paint.

encefalograf *mi med.* encephalograph.

encefalografia *f. Gen.* -ii *med.* encephalography.

encefalograficzny *a. med.* encephalographic.

encefalogram *mi med.* encephalogram.

encefalon *mi anat.* encephalon.

encykliczny *a. kośc.* encyclical, encyclic.

encyklika *f. kośc.* encyclical.

encyklopedia *f. Gen.* -ii encyclopedia; **chodząca encyklopedia** *żart.* walking encyclopedia.

encyklopedyczność *f.* encyclopedism.

encyklopedyczny *a.* encyclopedic; **wiedza/erudycja encyklopedyczna** encyclopedic knowledge/ erudition.

encyklopedysta *mp*, **encyklopedystka** *f. Gen.pl.* -ek 1. (= *twórca encyklopedii*) encyclopedist. 2. *hist.* Encyclopedist.

encyklopedyzm *mi* 1. (= *faktografizm*) encyclopedism. 2. *hist.* (= *racjonalizm*) rationalism.

endecja *f. pot. polit.* the National Democratic Party (*in pre-war Poland*).

endecki *a. pot.* National Democratic (*in pre-war Poland*).

endek *mp pot.* National Democrat.

endemiczny *a. ekol., pat.* endemic.

endoderma *f.* 1. *bot.* endodermis. 2. *zool.* endoderm.

endodermalny *a. biol.* endodermal.

endogamia *f. Gen.* -ii endogamy.

endogamiczny *a.* endogamous.

endokrynolog *mp med.* endocrinologist.

endokrynologia *f. Gen.* -ii *med.* endocrinology.

endokrynologiczny *a. med.* endocrinological.

endometrium *a. pl.* -ia, -iów *anat.* endometrium.

endomitoza *f. biol.* endomitosis.

endomorfia *f. Gen.* -ii *biol.* endomorphy.

endomorficzny *a. biol.* endomorphic.

endonukleaza *f. biochem.* endonuclease.

endopasożyt *ma biol.* endoparasite.

endoplazma *f. biol.* endoplasm.

endoproteza *f. med.* (*proteza*) endoprosthesis.

endoskop *mi med.* endoscope.

endosmoza *f. biol.* endosmosis.

endosperm *mi bot.* endosperm.

endospora *f. bot.* endospore.

endotermiczny *a. chem.* 1. endothermal. 2. *zool.* (= *stałocieplny*) endothermal.

endywia *f. Gen.* -ii *bot.* endive (*Cichorium endyvia*).

energetyczny *a. techn., fiz.* power, energy; **przemysł energetyczny** power industry; **bilans energetyczny** energy balance; **kryzys energetyczny** energy crisis; **przerwa energetyczna** *w przewodniku itp.* energy gap.

energetyk *mp* power engineer.

energetyka *f.* (*dziedzina wiedzy*) power engineering; (*dziedzina przemysłu*) power industry; **energetyka jądrowa** nuclear power engineering.

energia *f. Gen.* -ii 1. (= *siła, witalność*) energy, strength, vigor, vitality; **tryskać energią** be bursting with energy; **pracować z energią** work with a will; **poświęcać czemuś** *l.* **na coś swoją energię** devote one's energy to sth. 2. *fiz.* energy. 3. *el.* electric energy; (= *elektryczność*) power, electricity; **dostawy energii** power supply.

energiczny *a.* energetic, vigorous.

energochłonność *f. techn.* energy consumption.

energochłonny *a.* energy-consuming.

energooszczędność *f.* energy saving.
energooszczędny *a.* energy-saving.
engagement *n. indecl.* engagement.
enharmoniczny *a. muz.* enharmonic.
enigma *f.* enigma.
enigmatyczny *a.* enigmatic.
enkaustyczny *a. mal.* encaustic.
enklawa *f.* enclave.
enklityczność *f. jęz.* encliticity.
enklityczny *a. jęz.* enclitic.
enklityka *f. jęz.* enclitic.
enkliza *f. jęz.* enclisis.
enolog *mp pl.* **-dzy** *l.* **-owie** enologist, oenologist.
enologia *f. Gen.* **-ii** enology, oenology.
enologiczny *a.* enological, enologic.
ententa *f. polit., hist.* entente (cordiale).
entomolog *mp pl.* **-dzy** *l.* **-owie** entomologist.
entomologia *f. Gen.* **-ii** entomology.
entomologiczny *a.* entomological, entomologic.
entropia *f. Gen.* **-ii** *fiz.* entropy.
entropijny, entropowy *a. fiz.* entropic.
entuzjasta *mp*, **entuzjastka** *f. Gen.pl.* **-ek** enthusiast; (= *zwolennik*) fan.
entuzjastyczny *a.* enthusiastic.
entuzjazm *mi* enthusiasm; **robić coś bez entuzjazmu** do sth half-heartedly.
entuzjazmować *ipf.* excite. ~ **się** *ipf.* be enthusiastic, be excited, be agog (*czymś* about sth).
enty *a. pot.* nth; **pytam cię po raz enty** I'm asking you for the nth time.
enumeracja *f. form.* enumeration.
enumerować *ipf. form.* enumerate, list.
enuncjacja *f. form.* enunciation, articulation.
enzym *mi biochem.* enzyme.
enzymatyczny *a.* *biochem.* enzymatic, enzymic.
enzymologia *f. Gen.* **-ii** *biochem.* enzymology.
eocen *mi geol.* the Eocene.
eoceński *a. geol.* Eocene.
eoliczny *a. geol.* aeolian.
eolit *mi archeol.* eolith.
eolityczny *a.* *archeol.* eolithic; **epoka eolityczna** the eolithic period; **wyroby eolityczne** eolithic artifacts, eoliths.
eolski[1] *a.* **1.** *mit.* Aeolian. **2.** *muz.* aeolian; **harfa eolska** aeolian harp.
eolski[2] *a.* **1.** *geogr., hist.* Aeolian; **Wyspy Eolskie** *geogr.* Aeolian Islands. **2.** *muz.* aeolian. **3.** *jęz.* Aeolic.
eon *mi* eon.
eozoiczny *a. geol.* Eozoic.
eozoik *mi geol.* the Eozoic.
eparch *mp pl.* **-owie** *hist., kośc.* eparch.
eparchia *f. Gen.* **-ii** *hist., kośc.* eparchy.
epatować *ipf.* shock, impress.
epentetyczny *a. fon.* epenthetic.
epenteza *f. fon.* epenthesis.
epicentrum *n. indecl. in sing. pl.* **-ra** *Gen.* **-rów** *geol. l. przen.* epicentre.
epicki *a. teor.lit.* epic.
epickość *f.* epic quality.
epidemia *f. Gen.* **-ii** **1.** *pat.* epidemic. **2.** *przen.*

(= *powszechne występowanie*) boom, epidemic, epidemic spread.
epidemiczny *a.* epidemic.
epidemiolog *mp pl.* **-dzy** *l.* **-owie** epidemiologist.
epidemiologia *f. Gen.* **-ii** epidemiology.
epidemiologiczny *a.* epidemiological.
epiderma *f. bot., zool.* epidermis.
epidiaskop *mi techn.* epidiascope.
epifania *f. Gen.* **-ii** epiphany.
epifora *f.* **1.** *ret.* epiphora. **2.** *med.* involuntary weeping.
epigenetyczny *a. biol., geol.* epigenetic.
epigeneza *f. biol., geol.* epigenesis.
epigon *mp form.* epigone, epigon; imitator.
epigonizm *mi* epigonism.
epigonka *f. Gen.pl.* **-ek** *zob.* **epigon**.
epigoński *a.* epigonic, epigonous; imitative, derivative.
epigramat *mi teor.lit.* epigram.
epigramatyczny *a. teor.lit.* epigrammatic, epigrammatical.
epigramatyk *mp* epigrammatist.
epik *mp* epic writer.
epika *f. teor.lit.* epic.
epikureizm *mi* **1.** *fil.* Epicureanism. **2.** *pot.* (= *hedonizm*) epicureanism.
epikurejczyk *mp* **1.** *fil.* Epicurean (philosopher). **2.** *pot.* (= *hedonista*) epicure, epicurean.
epikurejski *a.* Epicurean.
epilepsja *f. pat.* epilepsy.
epileptyczka *f. Gen.pl.* **-ek**, **epileptyk** *mp pat.* epileptic.
epileptyczny *a. med.* epileptic.
epilog *mi* **1.** *teor.lit.* epilogue. **2.** *przen.* (= *finał, koniec*) epilogue, finale.
episkopalny *a. kośc.* episcopal.
episkopat *mi kośc.* episcopate.
epistemolog *mp pl.* **-dzy** *l.* **-owie** *fil.* epistemologist.
epistemologia *f. Gen.* **-ii** *fil.* epistemology.
epistemologiczny *a. fil.* epistemological.
epistolarny *a. lit.* epistolary, epistolatory.
epistolograf *mp pl.* **-owie** *teor.lit.* epistolographer, epistolographist.
epistolografia *f. Gen.* **-ii** *teor.lit.* epistolography, letter-writing.
epistolograficzny *a. pismo* epistolographic.
epistoła *f.* **1.** *żart.* (= *list*) epistle. **2.** *rel., przest.* Epistle.
epistrofa *f. teor.lit.* epistrophe.
epitafijny *a.* epitaphial.
epitafium *n. indecl. in sing. pl.* **-ia** *Gen.* **-iów** *teor.lit., sztuka* epitaph.
epitet *mi* **1.** *teor.lit.* epithet. **2.** *pot.* insult; **obrzucić kogoś epitetami** call sb names.
epizod *mi* **1.** *teor.lit., muz., teatr, film* (*t.* = *incydent*) episode. **2.** *teatr, film* (= *drobna rola*) bit part.
epizodycznie *adv.* **1.** (= *incydentalnie*) occasionally, sporadically, at intervals. **2.** *teor.lit., teatr, film* (= *ubocznie*) episodically.
epizodyczny *a.* **1.** (= *incydentalny*) occasional,

sporadic. **2.** *teor.lit., teatr, film* (= *uboczny*) minor; (= *drugoplanowy*) small.
epizodzik *mi iron., żart.* episode.
epoka *f.* **1.** (= *okres*) epoch, period, time. **2.** *geol., archeol.* age; **epoka lodowcowa** the Ice Age; **epoka kamienia/brązu/żelaza** the Stone/Bronze/Iron Age.
epokowy *a.* epoch-making, epochal; **epokowy wynalazek** epoch-making invention.
epolet *mi zw. pl.* epaulet, epaulette, shoulder strap.
eponim *mi jęz.* eponym.
eponimiczny *a.* eponymous, eponymic.
epopeja *f. Gen.* **-ei** *teor.lit., film* epic.
epos *mi teor.lit.* epos, epic story.
era *f.* **1.** (= *okres*) era, period; **naszej ery** C.E. (= *of the common era*); A.D.; **przed naszą erą** B.C.E. (= *before the common era*); B.C. (*before Christ*). **2.** *geol.* era; **era paleozoiczna/mezozoiczna/kenozoiczna** the Palaeozoic/Mesozoic/Cainozoic era.
erb *mi chem.* erbium.
erekcja *f.* **1.** *fizj.* erection. **2.** (= *założenie, erygowanie*) erection, foundation.
erekcyjny *a.* (*dotyczący założenia, wybudowania czegoś*) (of) foundation.
erem *mi* (= *pustelnia*) hermitage.
eremita *mp* eremite, hermit; recluse.
ergonom *mp pl.* **-owie** ergonomist.
ergonomia *f. Gen.* **-ii** ergonomics.
ergonomiczność *f.* ergonomy.
ergonomiczny *a.* ergonomic.
erodować *ipf. geol.* erode.
erogenny *a. fizj.* erogenous.
erotoman *mp* erotomaniac.
erotomania *f. Gen.* **-ii** erotomania.
erotomanka *f. Gen.pl.* **-ek** *zob.* **erotoman**.
erotomański *a.* erotomanic.
erotyczny *a.* erotic, sensual; **sztuka erotyczna** erotic art.
erotyk *mi teor.lit.* erotic poem.
erotyka *f.*, **erotyzm** *mi* eroticism.
erozja *f. geol., techn.* erosion.
erozyjny *a. geol., techn.* erosive, erosional.
errata *f.* (= *arkusz poprawek*) errata.
erraty *pl. Gen.* **-ów** (= *błędy drukarskie*) errata.
ersatz *mi* substitute, imitation, ersatz.
erudycja *f.* erudition.
erudycyjny *a.* erudite.
erudyta *mp*, **erudytka** *f. Gen.pl.* **-ek** erudite.
erupcja *f.* **1.** *geol., astron.* eruption; **erupcja słoneczna/wulkaniczna** *astron.* solar/volcanic eruption. **2.** *przen.* (= *wybuch*) outburst.
erupcyjny *a. geol.* eruptive.
erygować *ipf.* (= *wznosić, fundować, zakładać*) erect, found.
erynie *pl. mit.* the Furies, the Erinyes.
erystyczny *a.* eristic.
erystyka *f.* eristic.
erytrocyt *mi biol.* erythrocyte.
es[1] *n. indecl. l. mi* (= *kształt litery s*) S.
es[2] *n. indecl. muz.* E flat.
eschatologia *f. Gen.* **-ii** *rel., fil.* eschatology.

eschatologiczny *a. rel., fil.* eschatological.
eseista *mp*, **eseistka** *f. Gen.pl.* **-ek** *teor.lit.* essayist.
eseistyczny *a. o stylu* essayistic.
eseistyka *f. teor.lit.* essay writing.
esej *mi teor.lit.* essay.
esencja *f.* **1.** *chem.* essence. **2.** (= *napar herbaciany*) strong tea brew. **3.** *fil.* (= *istota rzeczy*) essence.
esencjonalność *f.* **1.** (= *moc, stężenie*) concentration. **2.** *przen.* (= *treściwość, zwięzłość*) conciseness, brevity, succinctness.
esencjonalny *a.* **1.** (= *gęsty, stężony*) concentrated, strong. **2.** *przen.* (= *treściwy, zwięzły*) concise, succinct.
esesman *mp*, **esesmanka** *f. Gen.pl.* **-ek** *hist.* SS member (*in Nazi Germany*).
esesmański *a. hist.* SS.
eskadra *f. lotn.* **1.** flight. **2.** *wojsk.* (*w marynarce wojennej*) squadron.
eskalacja *f.* escalation.
eskalacyjny *a.* escalatory.
eskalator *mi Gen.* **-a** escalator.
eskapada *f.* escapade.
eskapista *mp*, **eskapistka** *f. Gen.pl.* **-ek** *form.* escapist.
eskapistyczny *a.* escapist.
eskapizm *mi form.* escapism.
Eskimos *mp*, **Eskimoska** *f. Gen.pl.* **-ek** Eskimo, Inuit.
eskimoski *a.* Eskimo, Inuit.
eskorta *f.* **1.** (= *konwój*) convoy. **2.** *wojsk.* escort; **pod eskortą** under escort.
eskortować *ipf.* escort.
eskortowy *a.* **1.** (= *konwojujący*) convoy. **2.** *wojsk.* escorting.
eskulap *mp pl.* **-owie** *l.* **-i** *przest., żart.* sawbones.
espadryl *mi Gen.* **-a** (*but*) espadrille.
esperanto *n. indecl. l. Gen.* **-a** Esperanto.
esperantysta *mp*, **esperantystka** *f. Gen.pl.* **-ek** Esperantist.
establishment *mi* establishment.
estakada *f.* **1.** (= *pomost komunikacyjny*) overpass. **2.** *bud.* (= *podpora*) trestle.
esteta *mp*, **estetka** *f. Gen.pl.* **-ek** esthete.
estetyczność *f.* esthetics.
estetyczny *a.* **1.** (= *piękny*) beautiful, esthetic. **2.** (= *artystyczny, dotyczący piękna*) esthetic.
estetyk *mp* esthetician.
estetyka *f.* **1.** esthetics. **2.** (= *piękno*) beauty.
estetyzm *mi* estheticism.
estetyzować *ipf.* estheticize.
Estonia *f. Gen.* **-ii** *geogr.* Estonia.
Estonka *f.*, **Estończyk** *mp* Estonian.
estoński *a.* Estonian; **język estoński** *jęz.* Estonian.
estrada *f.* stage, bandstand; **wrócić na estradę** make a comeback.
estradowiec *mp* **-wc-** *pl.* **-y** entertainter.
estradowy *a.* stage.
estragon *mi bot., kulin.* tarragon (*Artemisia dracunculus*).
estragonowy *a.* tarragon.

estriol *mi biol.* estriol.
estrogen *mi biochem.* estrogen.
estrus *mi fizj., zool.* estrus.
estryfikacja *f. chem.* esterification.
estryfikować *ipf. chem.* esterify.
estyma *f. przest., żart.* respect.
esy-floresy *pl. Gen.* **esów-floresów** *pot.* curvy lines.
eszelon *mi wojsk.* military transport.
etacik *mi żart.* job.
etamina *f. tk.* etamine.
etan *mi chem.* ethane.
etanol *mi chem.* ethanol.
etap *mi* (= *odcinek, stadium*) stage; **etap podróży/wycieczki** stage of a journey/excursion; **ostatni etap** the last stage; **etapami** by stages; **na tym etapie** at this stage.
etapowo *adv.* by stages, successively.
etapowy *a.* **1.** (= *polegający na pokonywaniu drogi odcinkami*) stage. **2.** (= *stopniowy*) successive, gradual.
etat *mi* (= *zatrudnienie*) (full-time) job; **być na etacie** be a full-time employee; **praca na pełen etat/na pół etatu** full-time/part-time job.
etatowy *a.* full-time.
etatyzacja *f.* **1.** = **etatyzm. 2.** fixing the number of full-time posts.
etatyzm *mi ekon.* State control.
eter *mi* **1.** *chem.* ether. **2.** *fil., fiz., przest.* ether; **w eterze** *l.* **na falach eteru** *radio, tel.* on the air. **3.** (= *atmosfera, powietrze*) air.
eternit *mi bud.* asbestine tile.
eternitowy *a. bud.* (of) asbestine tile.
eteryczność *f.* etherealness, airiness.
eteryczny *a.* **1.** *chem.* ethereal; **olejki eteryczne** aromatic oils. **2.** (= *zwiewny, delikatny*) ethereal, airy.
etiologia *f. Gen.* **-ii 1.** *med.* etiology. **2.** (= *wyjaśnianie, przyczyna*) etiology.
etiologiczny *a.* **1.** *med.* etiologic; **czynnik etiologiczny** aetiologic factor. **2.** (= *przyczynowy*) etiologic, causal.
Etiopczyk *mp* Ethiopian.
Etiopia *f. Gen.* **-ii** *geogr.* Ethiopia.
Etiopka *f. Gen.pl.* **-ek** *zob.* **Etiopczyk.**
etiopski *a.* Ethiopian.
etiuda *f.* **1.** *muz.* étude. **2.** (= *ćwiczenie*) study, exercise.
etniczny *a.* ethnic.
etnogeneza *f.* ethnogenesis.
etnograf *mp pl.* **-owie** ethnographer.
etnografia *f. Gen.* **-ii** ethnography.
etnograficzny *a.* ethnographic.
etnolingwistyka *f. jęz.* ethnolinguistics.
etnolog *mp pl.* **-dzy** *l.* **-owie** ethnologist.
etnologia *f. Gen.* **-ii** ethnology.
etnologiczny *a.* ethnologic.
etnonim *mi jęz.* ethnonym.
etola *f.* fur stole.
etolog *mp* ethologist.
etologia *f. Gen.* **-ii** *zool.* ethology.
etos *mi socj.* ethos.
etruski *a.* Etruscan.
Etruskowie *pl. Gen.* **-ów** *hist.* Etruscans.

etui *n. indecl.* case.
etyczny *a.* ethical.
etyk *mp* ethicist.
etyka *f.* **1.** (*nauka o moralności*) ethics. **2.** (= *moralność*) ethic; **etyka zawodowa** professional ethic; **etyka lekarska** medical ethic.
etykieta *f.* **1.** (= *savoir-vivre*) etiquette. **2.** (= *metka, nalepka, oznaczenie*) label; **przylepić komuś/czemuś etykietę** label sb/sth.
etykietka *f.* (= *nalepka, metka*) label.
etykietować *ipf.* **1.** (= *metkować, oznaczać*) label. **2.** *pot.* (= *szufladkować*) pigeonhole.
etyl *mi chem.* ethyl.
etylen *mi chem.* ethylene.
etylina *f. chem.* premium gasoline.
etylowy *a. chem.* ethyl; **alkohol etylowy** ethyl alcohol.
etymolog *mp pl.* **-dzy** *l.* **-owie** *jęz.* etymologist.
etymologia *f. Gen.* **-ii 1.** *jęz.* (= *źródłosłów*) etymology; **etymologia ludowa** folk *l.* popular etymology. **2.** *jęz.* (*nauka*) etymology.
etymologiczny *a. jęz.* etymological.
etymologizować *ipf. jęz.* etymologize.
etymon *mi jęz.* etymon.
eucharystia *f. Gen.* **-ii** *rel.* the Eucharist.
eucharystyczny *a. rel.* Eucharistic; **Kongres Eucharystyczny** Eucharistic Congress.
eufemistyczny *a. jęz.* euphemistic.
eufemizm *mi* euphemism.
eufonia *f. Gen.* **-ii** *jęz., teor.lit.* euphony.
eufoniczny *a. jęz., teor.lit.* euphonic.
euforbia *f. Gen.* **-ii** *bot.* (= *wilczomlecz*) euphorbia (*Euphorbia*).
euforia *f. Gen.* **-ii 1.** *psych.* (= *entuzjazm*) euphoria. **2.** (= *ożywienie*) excitement.
euforyczny *a. psych., med.* euphoric.
eugeniczny *a.* eugenic.
eugenika *f.* eugenics.
euglena *f. biol.* euglena (*Euglena*).
eukaliptus *mi Gen.* **-a 1.** *bot.* eucalyptus (*Eucalyptus*). **2.** *farm.* (*olejek*) eucalyptus oil.
eukaliptusowy *a. bot.* eucalyptus; **olejek eukaliptusowy** eucalyptus oil.
euklidesowy *a. mat., geom.* Euclidean; **geometria euklidesowa** Euclidean geometry.
eunuch *mp pl.* **-owie** *l.* **-y** eunuch.
Eurazja *f. geogr.* Eurasia.
eurazjatycki *a. geogr.* Eurasian.
eureka *int.* eureka.
euro *n. indecl.* Euro.
eurocentryzm *mi* Eurocentrism.
euroczek *mi ekon.* Eurocheque.
eurodolar *mi Gen.* **-a** *ekon.* Eurodollar.
eurokrata *mp polit.* Eurocrat.
europ *mi chem.* europium.
Europa *f. geogr.* (*t. jako region kulturalny*) Europe.
europeizacja *f.* Europeanization.
europeizować *ipf.* Europeanize. **~ się** *ipf.* become Europeanized.
Europejczyk *mp,* **Europejka** *f. Gen.pl.* **-ek** European.
europejski *a.* European.
europejskość *f.* Europeaness.

europocentryczny a. Eurocentric.
eurytmia f. Gen. -ii 1. teor.lit. (= eufonia) eurhythmics. 2. muz. (= harmonia) eurhythmics. 3. sztuka (= proporcjonalność) eurhythmy.
eurytmiczny a. eurhythmic, eurhythmical.
eutanazja f. euthanasia.
eutrofia f. Gen. -ii biol. eutrophy.
eutroficzny a. biol. eutrophic.
ewakuacja f. 1. (= wywożenie, przesiedlanie) evacuation. 2. med. (= usuwanie) evacuation. 3. przen., żart. (= wyjście) escape.
ewakuacyjny a. evacuative; **droga ewakuacyjna** escape route.
ewakuować ipf. evacuate. ~ **się** ipf. 1. (= opuścić zagrożony teren) be evacuated. 2. przen., żart. (= wyjść) exit, leave.
ewaluacja f. evaluation.
ewaluować ipf. evaluate.
Ewangelia f. Gen. -ii 1. rel. (= Nowy Testament) the Gospel; **Ewangelia według świętego Mateusza/Marka/Łukasza/Jana** the Gospel according to Saint Matthew/Mark/Luke/John. 2. rel. (księga zawierająca teksty czterech Ewangelii) (the book of) Gospel. 3. rel. (= Dobra Nowina) Gospel, evangel; **głosić Ewangelię** preach the Gospel; **wierzę w to jak w Ewangelię** it's gospel (truth) to me. 4. rel. (część mszy świętej) the Gospel.
ewangeliarz mi rel. lectionary.
ewangelicki a. rel. Evangelical.
ewangeliczka f. Gen.pl. -ek zob. **ewangelik**.
ewangeliczny a. rel. evangelistic, evangelical; **prawda ewangeliczna** gospel truth.
ewangelik mp rel. Evangelical.
ewangelista mp rel. evangelist.
ewangelizacja f. rel. evangelization; **nowa ewangelizacja** new evangelization.
ewangelizować ipf. rel. evangelize.
ewaporacja f. evaporation.
ewaporacyjny a. evaporative.
ewenement mi sensation.

ewentualnie[1] adv. (= ostatecznie, w razie czego) if need be.
ewentualnie[2] conj. (= albo, lub) or (alternatively).
ewentualność f. eventuality, possibility; **przygotować się na wszystkie ewentualności** get ready for every possibility.
ewentualny a. possible.
ewidencja f. admin. record, files; **ewidencja ludności** census.
ewidencjonować ipf. (= spisywać) record.
ewidencyjny a. record.
ewidentny a. evident, obvious, clear.
ewokacja f. lit. evocation.
ewokacyjny a. lit. evocative.
ewokować ipf. lit. evoke, bring (sth) to mind.
ewolucja f. 1. (= rozwój) evolution. 2. (= ruch, akrobacja) (taneczna) acrobatics; (powietrzna) aerobatics. 3. biol., socj. evolution, development; **ewolucja kulturowa** cultural evolution.
ewolucjonista mp, **ewolucjonistka** f. Gen.pl. -ek evolutionist.
ewolucjonistyczny a. evolutionistic.
ewolucjonizm mi biol., fil. evolutionism.
ewolucyjnie adv. evolutionarily.
ewolucyjność f. evolutionary character.
ewolucyjny a. evolutionary, evolutional.
ewoluować ipf. evolve.
ex aequo adv. **wygrać ex aequo** be joint winners.
exodus mi form. exodus, mass emigration.
explicite adv. explicitly, openly.
exposé n. indecl. polit. exposé; **przygotować/ wygłosić exposé** prepare/make an exposé.
ezopowy a. teor.lit. Aesopean; **bajka ezopowa** Aesopean fable; **język ezopowy** Aesopean language.
ezoteryczność f. esotericism.
ezoteryczny a. esoteric.
ezoteryzm mi esotericism.

F

F, f *n. indecl.* (*litera*) F, f; **F jak Franciszek** F is for Foxtrot; F as in Foxtrot.

F¹ *n. indecl. muz.* (*dźwięk*) F; **F-dur** F major; **f-moll** F minor.

F² *abbr. zob.* **fluor.**

F³ *abbr.* (*skala temperatury*) (= *Fahrenheit*) F, Fahrenheit scale.

F⁴ *abbr. fiz.* (*jednostka długości*) *zob.* **fermi.**

fabianin *mp hist.* Fabian, Fabianist.

fabianizm *mi hist.* Fabianism.

fabryczka *f. Gen.pl.* **-ek** (small) factory.

fabrycznie *adv.* **fabrycznie nowy** brand-new, bran-new.

fabryczny *a.* factory; **cena fabryczna** cost price; **znak fabryczny** trademark; **sklep fabryczny** factory outlet.

fabryka *f.* **1.** (= *zakład*) factory, plant; **fabryka domów** precast building units plant; **fabryka papieru** paper-mill. **2.** (= *załoga*) staff.

fabrykacja *f.* **1.** (= *wyrabianie*) manufacturing. **2.** *arch.* (= *fałszowanie*) fabrication.

fabrykancki *a. przest.* manufacturer's.

fabrykant *mp* **1.** (= *właściciel fabryki*) factory owner, manufacturer. **2.** *przest.* (= *producent*) producer, maker.

fabrykantka *f. Gen.pl.* **-ek 1.** (= *żona fabrykanta*) factory owner's wife, manufacturer's wife. **2.** (= *właścicielka fabryki, producentka*) *zob.* **fabrykant.**

fabrykat *mi* product.

fabrykować *ipf.* **1.** (= *wytwarzać*) produce, fabricate. **2.** *żart., iron.* (= *klecić, odwalać*) manufacture. **3.** (= *fałszować*) fabricate.

fabularność *f.* fictionality.

fabularny *a.* fiction; **film fabularny** *film* feature film.

fabularyzacja *f. lit.* fictionalization.

fabularyzować *ipf. lit.* fictionalize; **fabularyzowany dokument** *film* drama documentary.

fabuła *f.* **1.** *pot.* (= *treść*) plot, fable. **2.** *teor.lit., film* plot. **3.** *arch.* (= *plotka*) gossip.

facecja *f.* **1.** (= *żart*) facetiae, persiflage. **2.** *teor.lit.* facetiae.

facecjonista *mp* **1.** (= *żartowniś*) joker, wag. **2.** *teor.lit.* writer of facetiae.

facecjonistyczny *a. teor.lit.* (of) facetiae.

facet *mp* guy, dude; (*zwł. Voc.*) buddy; *Br. pot.* bloke, fellow; **czyjś facet** (= *partner*) sb's guy.

facetka *f. Gen.pl.* **-ek** *pot.* chick, girl, dame.

fach *mi* (= *zawód*) profession, calling; **kolega po fachu** professional colleague, aguy in the same line; **mieć fach w ręku** be ready for job.

fachowiec *mp* **-wc-** *pl.* **-y 1.** (= *specjalista*) specialist, expert, professional. **2.** (= *rzemieślnik*) repairman, doctor.

fachowo *adv.* **1.** (= *zawodowo*) professionally. **2.** (= *profesjonalnie*) competently, expertly.

fachowość *f.* **1.** (= *wyspecjalizowanie*) specialization. **2.** (= *profesjonalizm*) professionalism, expertise.

fachowy *a.* **1.** (= *specjalistyczny*) (*czasopismo, wiedza, wykształcenie*) specialist, professional. **2.** (= *profesjonalny*) (*pomoc, porada*) expert, professional; (*wiedza*) expertise; (*pracownik*) skilled; **fachowe oko** expert eye.

fachura *mp pot.* professional.

facio *mp pot.* guy; *Br.* bloke.

facjata *f.* **1.** (= *poddasze*) attic, garret. **2.** *pot., żart.* (= *twarz*) phiz, pan, mug. **3.** *arch.* (= *front*) facade.

faeton *mi* phaeton, chariot.

fag *ma biol.* phage, bacteriophage.

fagas *mp pl.* **-y** *l.* **-i 1.** *pot., pog.* (= *służący*) flunky. **2.** (= *pochlebca, lizus*) yes-man, hanger-on.

fagasować *ipf.* flunky.

fagasowski *a.* flunke.

fagasowstwo *n.* flunkyism.

fagocista *mp muz.* bassoonist.

fagocyt *mi biol.* phagocyte.

fagocytoza *f. biol.* phagocytosis.

fagot *mi muz.* bassoon.

fagotowy *a. muz.* bassoon.

fair *adv.* fair; **to nie fair** it's not cricket; **to nie fair w stosunku do niej** it's not fair on her.

fair play *a. i n. indecl.* fair play; **walka fair-play** clean fight.

faja *f. Gen.* **fai 1.** *iron.* (= *fajtłapa*) fumbler. **2.** *pot., szkoln.* (= *ocena niedostateczna*) failing grade; *Br.* failing mark.

fajalit *mi min.* fayalite.

fajans *mi* **1.** (*tworzywo*) faience. **2.** (*wyroby*) pottery.

fajansowy *a.* faience.

fajczarz *mp* pipe-smoker.

fajczyć *ipf. pot.* smoke a pipe. **~ się** *ipf. pot.* (= *palić się*) be on fire.

fajdać *ipf.* **1.** *wulg.* shit. **2.** *zool.* (*o ptakach*) (= *wydalać odchody*) mute.

fajerka *f. Gen.pl.* **-ek** stove lid; **zabawa na (dwadzieścia cztery) cztery fajerki** revelry, reveling.

fajerwerk *mi. Gen.* **-a** firework; *pl.* (= *pokaz sztucznych ogni, t. przen.*) fireworks.

fajka *f. Gen.pl.* **-ek 1.** (*do palenia tytoniu*)

pipe; **fajka wodna** hookah, water pipe; **kurzyć** *l.* **ćmić fajkę** smoke a pipe; **pykać z fajki** puff on a pipe; **fajka pokoju** pipe of peace, calumet. **2.** *sl.* (= *papieros*) fag, ciggy. **3.** *pot.* (*znak*) tick. **4.** (*sprzęt pływacki*) snorkel.

fajkować *ipf. pot.* (= *odznaczać*) tick off.

fajkowy *a.* pipe.

fajnie, fajno *adv. pot.* great, cool.

fajny *a. pot.* great, cool.

fajowo *adv. pot.* = **fajnie**.

fajowy *a. pot.* = **fajny**.

fajrant *mi pot.* closing time; *Br.* knock-off time.

fajtać *ipf.* + *Dat. pot.* dangle (*sth*). ~ **się** *ipf. pot.* dangle, swing.

fajtłapa *f. l. mp decl. like f. pl.* **-p** *l.* **-ów** butter-fingers, fumbler.

fajtłapowaty *a.* clumsy.

fajtnąć *pf.* **-ij 1.** *pot.* (= *machnąć*) dangle. **2.** *pot.* (= *przewrócić się*) fall over; **fajtnąć koziołka** *l.* kozła turn a somersault. **3.** *pot. emf.* (= *u-mrzeć*) kick the bucket. ~ **się** *pf. pot.* (= *przewró-cić się*) fall over.

fakir *mp pl.* **-rzy** *l.* **-owie 1.** *rel.* (*asceta w kra-jach arabskich lub w Indiach*) fakir. **2.** *pot.* (= *sztukmistrz*) conjurer, magician.

faks *mi techn.* **1.** (*urządzenie*) fax. **2.** (*wy-druk*) fax, facsimile.

faksować *ipf. techn.* fax.

faksymile *n. indecl. in sing. pl.* **-lia** *Gen.* **-liów 1.** (= *kopia*) autotype, facsimile. **2.** (= *imitacja podpisu*) stamped signature, signature facsimi-le. **3.** *tel.* (= *faks*) fax, facsimile.

faksymilowy *a.* **1.** (*będący kopią*) autotype, facsimile. **2.** *tel.* (= *faksowy*) fax.

fakt *mi* fact; **literatura faktu** *teor.lit.* non-fic-tion; **niezbity, bezsporny fakt** inescapable fact; **niepodważalne fakty** hard facts; **nagie/gołe/su-che fakty** bare/plain/dry facts; **fakt dokonany** ac-complished fact; **fakt bez znaczenia** footnote (*dla kogoś / czegoś* to sb/sth); **fakt faktem** true enough; **to fakt, że...** it's a fact that...; **przed faktem** before the event; **po fakcie** after the event; **oparty na faktach** based on facts; **trzymać się faktów** stick *l.* keep to the facts; **zgodny z faktami** factually correct; **sprzeczny z faktami** ajar with the facts; **fakty mówią same za siebie** the facts speak for themselves; **być postawionym przed faktem do-konanym** be presented with a fait accompli; **po-godzić się z faktem, że...** accept the fact that...; **liczyć się z faktami** face (the) facts; **przejść do fa-któw** get down to facts; **zwrócić uwagę na fakt, że...** draw attention to the fact that...; **nie uprze-dzajmy faktów** let's not anticipate events.

faktograf *mp pl.* **-owie** data collector.

faktografia *f. Gen.* **-ii 1.** facts. **2.** collecting facts or data.

faktograficzny *a.* fact-collecting.

faktotum *n indecl.* factotum.

faktura *f.* **1.** *ekon., handl.* invoice; **wystawiać fakturę na kwotę...** issue *l.* make out an invoice for (the amount of)... **2.** *sztuka* texture, grain, facture; **faktura materiału** material texture. **3.**

muz. fabric. **4.** *teor.lit.* (= *struktura*) structure, framework.

fakturować *ipf.* **1.** *ekon., handl.* invoice. **2.** *sztuka* grain.

fakturowany *a. sztuka* grainy.

fakturowy *a.* **1.** *ekon., handl.* invoice. **2.** *sztu-ka* grain, texture.

fakturzysta *mp*, **fakturzystka** *f. Gen.pl.* **-ek** *ekon., handl.* a person who issues invoices.

faktycznie *adv.* actually, in actual fact.

faktyczny *a.* actual, de facto, effective, practi-cal; **stan faktyczny** actuality.

faktysa *f.* factice.

fakultatywnie *adv. lit.* optionally, facultative-ly.

fakultatywność *f.* optionality.

fakultatywny *a.* optional, extracurricular, fac-ultative; **zajęcia fakultatywne** optional *l.* ex-tracurricular classes.

fakultet *mi* **1.** (= *wydział uczelni*) faculty. **2.** (= *zajęcie nieobowiązkowe*) extracurricular classes.

fala *f.* **1.** (*na wodzie*) wave; **martwa fala** *żegl.* swell; **powracająca fala** *t. przen.* returning wave. **2.** *przen.* **na fali czegoś** in the wake of sth; **płynąć z falą/przeciw fali** swim with/against the tide *l.* current *l.* stream; **być na fali** be on the crest of a wave; be on a winning streak. **3.** (*coś, co się na-sila i maleje*) wave, surge; **fala upałów** heatwave; **fala chłodów** cold wave; **fala protestów** wave of protest; **fala przestępstw** crime wave; **narastają-ca fala** (*oburzenia, protestów*) groundswell; **nowa fala** *teor.lit.*, *film* nouvelle vague, new wave; **me-ksykańska fala** *sport* Mexican wave. **4.** *przen.* (= *tłum*) influx. **5.** *fiz.* wave; **fala akustyczna** acous-tic *l.* sonic wave; **fala dźwiękowa** sonic *l.* sound wave; **fala elektromagnetyczna** electromagnetic wave; **fala uderzeniowa** shock wave; **fale radiowe** radio waves; **fale długie** long waves; **fale średnie** medium waves; **fale krótkie** short waves; **fale ultrakrótkie** ultra-high frequency waves. **6.** *pot. wojsk.* wave.

falanga *f.* **1.** (= *gromada*) phalanx, host. **2.** *hist., wojsk.* (= *zwarty szyk*) phalanx. **3.** *hist.* (*hi-szpańska organizacja faszystowska*) Falange. **4.** *hist.* (*libańska partia prawicowa*) Phalange. **5.** *hist.* (*polskie bojówki faszystowskie*) Pha-lange.

falangista *mp* **1.** *hist.* (*działacz hiszpańskiej Falangi*) Falangist. **2.** *hist.* (*działacz libańskiej partii lub polski bojówkarz*) Phalangist.

falangistowski *a.* **1.** *hist.* (*związany z hiszpań-ską Falangą*) Falange. **2.** *hist.* (*związany z li-bańską lub polską Falangą*) Phalange.

falbana *f.* falbala, flounce, furbelow; **ozdabiać falbaną** flounce.

falbaniasty *a.* flouncy, frilly.

falbanka *f. Gen.pl.* **-ek** frill, furbelow; **z falban-kami** flouncy; **falbanki** frilling.

falc *mi* **1.** *druk.* (slip-)fold. **2.** *bud.* rabbet, re-bate.

falcować *ipf.* **1.** *druk.* fold. **2.** *bud.* rabbet, re-bate.

falcówka *f. Gen.pl.* **-ek** *druk.* folding machine, folder.

faldistorium *n. indecl. kośc.* faldstool.

faleń *mi Gen.* **-a** *żegl.* guest rope.

faleza *f. geogr.* cliff.

falistość *f.* **1.** (= *pofałdowanie*) waviness. **2.** (= *pagórkowatość*) hilliness.

falisty *a.* **1.** (= *pofałdowany*) corrugated, curvy; **blacha falista** corrugated iron *l.* sheet. **2.** (= *pagórkowaty*) hilly.

Falklandy *pl. Gen.* **-ów** *geogr.* the Falkland Islands.

falliczny *a.* phallic.

fallus *mi Gen.* **-a** *anat., form.* phallus.

falochron *mi* **1.** (*budowla*) breakwater, groyne. **2.** *żegl.* (*osłona*) pier, sea wall.

falomierz *mi Gen.* **-a** *el.* ondograph, wavemeter.

falować *ipf.* **1.** (= *drgać*) wave, roll, heave. **2.** (= *fałdować*) wave. **3.** *techn.* (= *fałdować*) corrugate.

falowy *a.* wave; **teoria falowa** *jęz.* wave theory.

falsecista *mp muz.* falsetto.

falset *mi* **1.** *muz.* falsetto, head voice. **2.** *pot.* (*nienaturalnie wysoki głos męski*) falsetto.

falsetować *ipf. muz.* sing falsetto.

falsetowy *a. muz.* falsetto.

falstart *mi* **1.** *sport* false start; **zrobić falstart** jump *l.* beat the gun. **2.** *pot.* (= *nieudana próba*) failure.

falsyfikacja *f.* **1.** (= *fałszowanie*) forgery, falsification. **2.** *fil., log.* falsification.

falsyfikat *mi* forgery, fake.

falsyfikować *ipf.* **1.** (= *fałszować*) forge, falsify. **2.** *fil., log.* falsify.

falszkil *mi żegl.* false keel.

fał *mi żegl.* halyard.

fałd *mi* **1.** fold, pleat; **fałd skórny** lappet; **fałd tłuszczu** collop; **przysiąść fałdów** put one's nose to the grindstone; **trzymać się** *l.* **czepiać się czyichś fałdów** be with sb to earn a profit. **2.** *geol.* flexure, fold.

fałda *f.* crease, crimp, ply, pleat.

fałdować *ipf.* **1.** (= *marszczyć*) crease, crimp, pleat, pucker. **2.** (= *falować*) corrugate. ~ **się** *ipf.* **1.** (= *marszczyć się*) pleat, pucker. **2.** (*formować się w wypukłości lub wklęśnięcia*) corrugate.

fałdowanie *n.* **1.** (= *marszczenie*) creasing. **2.** *geol.* fold.

fałdzisty *a.* full, falling into creases.

fałsz *mi Gen.pl.* **-ów** **1.** (= *kłamstwo*) falsity, falsehood; **zadać komuś fałsz** give the lie to sb. **2.** *muz.* (= *nieczystość*) false note; **wpadać w fałsz** take a false note. **3.** *log.* falseness. **4.** *sport* pull.

fałszerstwo *n.* forgery, counterfeit, falsification.

fałszerz *mp* forger, counterfeiter, falsifier.

fałszować *ipf.* **1.** (= *podrabiać*) counterfeit, fake; **fałszować dokumenty, pieniądze** forge, falsify; (*dane*) fudge; (*facty*) misrepresent; (*rachunki, dowody*) cook, fiddle; (*wyniki, wybory*) fix. **2.** (*obniżać jakość produktów*) adulterate.

3. (*nieczysto śpiewać/grać*) sing/play out of tune.

fałszywie *adv.* **1.** (= *kłamliwie*) falsely, fraudulently; **fałszywie zeznawać** give false evidence; **fałszywie coś zrozumieć** misunderstand sth. **2.** (= *nieszczerze*) insincerely; **fałszywie się uśmiechać** smile insincerely. **3.** (*śpiewać, grać nieczysto*) out of tune.

fałszywiec *mp* **-wc-** *Voc.* **-u** *l.* **-wcze** *pl.* **-y** phony.

fałszywka *f. Gen.pl.* **-ek** *pot.* fake, phony; **fałszywki** (= *fałszywe pieniądze*) funny money.

fałszywość *f.* falsehood, falseness, falsity.

fałszywy *a.* **1.** *log., fil.* false; **fałszywe świadectwo** false testimony. **2.** (= *podrobiony, nieprawdziwy*) counterfeit, fake; (*dokumenty, pieniądze*) forged, counterfeit. **3.** (= *kłamliwy*) false; **fałszywe zeznanie** false evidence; **przedstawiać w fałszywym świetle** disguise, give false colors to sth. **4.** (= *obłudny, pozorny*) insincere; **fałszywy wstyd** false shame; **fałszywa skromność** false modesty; **fałszywy prorok** false prophet; **fałszywy świadek** false witness; **fałszywy przyjaciel** fair-weather friend. **5.** (= *błędny*) false; **fałszywe wnioski** wrong conclusion; **fałszywy ślad** wrong lead *l.* track; **fałszywy trop** wrong track; **fałszywy krok** false move; **fałszywy alarm** false alarm; **robić fałszywy alarm** cry wolf. **6.** (= *nieczysty, dysonansowy*) off-key; **grać na fałszywą nutę** take a false note, play out of tune.

fama *f.* rumor; **fama niesie** rumor *l.* gossip has it.

familia *f. Gen.* **-ii** **1.** *żart.* (= *rodzina*) family. **2.** *hist.* family.

familiarność *f.* informality.

familiarny *a.* informal.

familijny *a.* **1.** (= *rodzinny*) family. **2.** *przest.* (= *rodowy*) family.

famuła *f. żart.* (= *rodzina*) family.

fan *mp pot.* fan, adulator, devotee, follower.

fanaberie *pl. Gen.* **-ii** **1.** (= *chimery, kaprysy*) whims. **2.** (= *ekstrawagancja*) ostentation.

fanatyczka *f. Gen.pl.* **-ek** *zob.* **fanatyk**.

fanatyczny *a.* fanatical, fanatic.

fanatyk *mp* fanatic, energumen, freak; (*religijny, polityczny*) bigot.

fanatyzm *mi* fanaticism.

fanerofit *mi bot.* phanerophyte.

fanfara *f.* **1.** *muz.* (*melodia*) fanfare, flourish. **2.** *muz.* (= *trąbka*) bugle.

fanfaron *mp pl.* **-i** *l.* **-y** *przest.* braggart, coxcomb, popinjay.

fanfaronada *f.* bounce, coxcombry, fanfaronade.

fanfarowy *a. muz.* flourish; **trąbka fanfarowa** bugle.

fanfarzysta *mp muz.* bugler.

fanga *f. pot.* (*cios*) punch, stinger.

fanka *f. Gen.pl.* **-ek** *pot. zob.* **fan**.

fanklub *mi* fan club.

fant *mi Gen.* **-u** *l.* **-a** **1.** (*przedmiot do wykupu w grze*) forfeit; **dać/wykupić fant** pay/buy back a forfeit; **co z tym fantem zrobić?** *pot.* what shall I do now?; **zrobić coś z tym fantem** *pot.* do sth about it. **2.** (*wygrana na loterii*) prize.

fantasmagoria *f. Gen.* **-ii** *lit.* (= *iluzja*), *kino* phantasmagoria.

fantasmagoryczny *a.* *lit.* phantasmagoric, phantasmagorical.

fantasta *mp*, **fantastka** *f. Gen.pl.* **-ek** fantast.

fantastycznie *adv.* **1.** (= *nierealnie, baśniowo*) fantastically, fancifully. **2.** *emf.* (= *nadzwyczajnie*) fabulously, prodigiously.

fantastycznonaukowy *a.* science-fiction; **powieść fantastycznonaukowa** science-fiction novel; **film fantastycznonaukowy** science-fiction movie.

fantastyczność *f.* **1.** (= *baśniowość*) fantasticality. **2.** *emf.* (= *nadzwyczajność*) prodigiousness.

fantastyczny *a.* **1.** (= *baśniowy, nierealny*) fanciful, fantastic, fabulous; **powieść fantastyczna** *teor.lit.* fantasy novel; **film fantastyczny** *film* fantasy movie. **2.** *emf.* (= *nadzwyczajny*) prodigious, fabulous.

fantastyka *f.* **1.** (= *nierealność, baśniowość*) fantasy. **2.** *teor.lit., film* fantasy; **fantastyka naukowa** science-fiction.

fantazja *f.* **1.** (= *wyobraźnia*) fantasy, imagination; **mieć fantazję** be imaginative; **dawać się ponosić fantazji** let o.s. be carried away (by dreams); **zrobić coś z fantazją** do sth creatively; **bez fantazji** unimaginatively; **puszczać wodze fantazji** allow full play to fantasy. **2.** (= *zmyślenie*) fantasy. **3.** (= *pewność siebie*) dash; **zrobić coś z fantazją** do sth blusteringly; **robić coś dla fantazji** do sth on a whim, do sth for the fun of it; **nadrabiać fantazją** put a bold *l.* brave face on. **4.** *muz., teor.lit., film* fantasia.

fantazje *pl. Gen.* **-i** (= *kaprysy, zachcianki*) whims.

fantazjować *ipf.* **1.** (= *zmyślać*) fantasize. **2.** (= *roić, marzyć*) daydream. **3.** *muz.* (= *improwizować*) improvise.

fantazmat *mi* phantasm.

fantazyjnie *adv.* imaginatively.

fantazyjność *f.* fancifulness.

fantazyjny *a.* **1.** (= *niezwykły, wymyślny*) fanciful, imaginative; (*o stroju*) dashing. **2.** (= *baśniowy, fantastyczny*) fictitious.

fantom *mi* **1.** (= *zjawa*) phantasm, phantom. **2.** *med.* (= *model*) phantom. **3.** *med.* (*ból*) phantom (limb) pain.

fantomowy *a. med.* phantom; **bóle fantomowe** phantom limb pain.

fantowy *a.* forfeit; **loteria fantowa** lottery; *Br.* tombola.

fara *f. kośc.* parish church.

farad *mi Gen.* **-a** *fiz.* (*jednostka*) farad.

faramuszka *f. Gen.pl.* **-ek** *przest.* trifle.

faraon *mp pl.* **-owie** *l.* **-i** *hist.* (= *władca Egiptu*) pharaoh; **mrówka faraona** *zool.* pharaoh ant (*Monomorium pharaonis*). – *mi no plural Gen. i Acc.* **-a** *arch., karty* (*gra*) faro.

farba *f.* **1.** (*do malowania*) paint, color, *Br.* colour; **farba olejna** oil color *l.* paint; **farba emulsyjna** emulsion paint; **farba akwarelowa** *l.* **wodna**

watercolor; **farba podkładowa** primer; **farba drukarska** (printing) ink; **farba emaliowa** enamel paint; **farba enkaustyczna** encaustic paint; **farba klejowa** distemper; **malować ciemnymi** *l.* **czarnymi farbami** paint sth black; **farba do włosów** hair-dye. **2.** *pot.* (= *farbowanie*) dying. **3.** *pot., myśl.* (= *krew*) blood; **puścić farbę** blow the whistle.

farbiarka *f. Gen.pl.* **-ek 1.** *tk.* (*maszyna*) dyeing machine. **2.** *tk.* (*pracownica*) dyer.

farbiarnia *f. Gen.pl.* **-i** *l.* **-ń** dye house, dyeworks.

farbiarski *a. tk.* dye; **kąpiel farbiarska** dye-bath.

farbiarstwo *n. tk.* dyeing trade.

farbiarz *mp tk.* dyer.

farbka *f. Gen.pl.* **-ek** (*do prania*) blue.

farbki *pl. Gen.* **-ek** colors.

farbkować *ipf.* blue.

farbować *ipf.* **1.** (= *barwić*) dye, color, *Br.* colour; (*tkaniny*) ingrain; **farbować przez zamaczanie** dip; **farbować trwale** dye in grain; **farbować włosy** dye one's hair; **farbowany lis** turncoat. **2.** (*o tkaninie*) (= *puszczać kolor*) stain, discolor. **3.** *myśl.* bleed. **~ się** *ipf.* **1.** (*zmieniać kolor włosów*) dye one's hair. **2.** (= *barwić się*) stain.

farbownik *mi Gen.* **-a** *bot.* bugloss (*Anchusa*).

farciarz *mi Gen.* **-a** *pot.* lucky devil, lucky bastard.

farfocel *mi* **-cl-** *Gen.* **-a** (= *strzęp*) tatter; *pl.* (= *fuzle*) dregs, grounds.

farma *f.* farm.

farmaceuta *mp* pharmacist; (*pracujący w aptece*) dispenser.

farmaceutka *f. Gen.pl.* **-ek** pharmacist; (*pracująca w aptece*) dispenser.

farmaceutyczny *a.* pharmaceutical.

farmaceutyk *mi form.* pharmaceutical.

farmacja *f.* **1.** (*nauka*) pharmacy, pharmaceutics. **2.** (*wydział uczelni*) pharmacy.

farmakodynamika *f.* pharmacodynamics.

farmakognozja *f.* pharmacognosy.

farmakokinetyka *f.* pharmacokinetics.

farmakolog *mp pl.* **-dzy** *l.* **-owie** pharmacologist.

farmakologia *f. Gen.* **-ii** pharmacology.

farmakologiczny *a.* pharmacological.

farmakopea *f. Gen.* **-ei** *pl.* **-ee** *med.* pharmacopoeia.

farmakoterapia *f. Gen.* **-ii** pharmacotherapy.

farmazon *mi pl.* **-i** *l.* **-y** *pot.* (= *oszust*) cheat.

farmazony *pl. Gen.* **-ów** *pot.* (= *bzdury*) flapdoodle, balderdash; **wstawiać farmazony** talk bilge.

farmer *mp*, **farmerka** *f. Gen.pl.* **-ek** farmer.

farmerski *a.* farmer.

farmerstwo *n.* farming.

farny *a. kośc.* parish.

farsa *f.* **1.** *teor.lit.* farce; **farsa filmowa** *film* farce. **2.** *przen.* (= *głupstwo, niedorzeczność*) farce, mockery, travesty.

farsowość *f. teor.lit.* farcicality.

farsowy *a.* farcical.

farsz *mi Gen.pl.* **-y** *l.* **-ów** *kulin.* stuffing.

fart *mi pot.* luck; **mieć fart** luck out, strike (it) lucky.

fartowny *a. pot.* lucky.

fartuch *mi Gen.* **-a 1.** (*okrycie ochronne*) apron; **trzymać się czyjegoś (matczynego) fartucha** be tied to sb's apron-strings. **2.** *techn.* apron; **fartuch błotnika** *mot.* splash guard, mud flap.

fartuszek *mi* **-szk-** *Gen.* **-a** apron; (*dziecięcy*) pinafore; **trzymać się fartuszka** be tied to sb's apron-strings.

farwater *mi* **-tr-** *żegl.* fairway.

farys *mp pl.* **-owie** *l.* **-i 1.** *przest.* (= *jeździec arabski, rycerz*) Arabian horseman. **2.** *przen.* (= *śmiałek*) daredevil.

faryzeizm *mi* **1.** *hist.* Pharisaism. **2.** *przen.* (= *obłuda*) Pharisaism.

faryzejski *a.* Pharisaic.

faryzeusz *mp pl.* **-owie** *Gen.* **-y** *l.* **-ów, faryzeuszka** *f. Gen.pl.* **-ek** *hist. l. przen.* (= *obłudnik*) Pharisee.

faryzeuszostwo *n.* (= *dwulicowość*) Pharisaism.

fasa *f.* **1.** *przest.* (= *beczka*) vat. **2.** (*naczynie do garbowania skór*) tan vat.

fasada *f.* **1.** *bud.* facade, front. **2.** *przen.* (= *pozór, ułuda*) (false) front, pretense, *Br.* pretence.

fasadowość *f.* ostentation, showiness.

fasadowy *a.* **1.** *bud.* facade. **2.** *przen.* (= *efekciarski, pokazowy*) ostentatious, showy.

fascynacja *f.* fascination.

fascynować *ipf.* fascinate.

fascynująco *adv.* fascinatingly.

fascynujący *a.* fascinating.

faseta *f.,* **fasetka** *f. Gen.pl.* **-ek** facet.

fasetowy *f. jubil.* (*o szlifie*) miltifaceted.

faska *f. Gen.pl.* **-ek** firkin.

fasola *f. Gen.pl.* **-i 1.** *bot.* bean; **fasola szparagowa** string bean; **fasola wielokwiatowa** runner bean (*Phaseolus coccineus*); **fasola zwyczajna** kidney bean, green bean (*Phaseolus vulgaris*). **2.** (*strąki i nasiona*) bean.

fasolka *f. Gen.pl.* **-ek 1.** *pot.* (*roślina*) bean. **2.** (*nasiona i strąki, potrawa*) bean; **fasolka po bretońsku** baked beans in tomato sauce.

fasolowy *a.* bean.

fasolówka *f. pot.* (*zupa*) bean soup.

fason *mi* **1.** (= *krój, model*) cut, fashion. **2.** *pot.* (= *śmiałość, fantazja*) dash; **robić coś z fasonem** do sth with aplomb; **trzymać fason** keep up one's spirit; **stracić fason** lose one's spirit; **przerobić kogoś na swój fason** fashion sb after oneself.

fasonować *ipf.* shape, model, mould.

fasować[1] *ipf.* **1.** (= *porcjować*) portion. **2.** (= *przecierać*) pass through a sieve.

fasować[2] *ipf. wojsk.* draw, collect.

fastryga *f.* (*w krawiectwie*) basting.

fastrygować *ipf.* (*w krawiectwie*) baste.

fasunek *mi* **-nk-** **1.** *wojsk.* drawing, collecting. **2.** (= *przydział*) ration.

faszerować *ipf.* **1.** (= *nadziewać*) stuff. **2.** *pot., żart.* (= *karmić, wmuszać*) stuff, feed.

faszyna *f.* fascine.

faszynować *ipf.* line *l.* fill with fascine.

faszysta *mp,* **faszystka** *f. Gen.pl.* **-ek** *polit., hist.* fascist.

faszystowski *a. polit., hist.* fascist, fascistic.

faszyzacja *f. polit., hist.* introducing fascist ideology.

faszyzm *mi polit., hist.* fascism.

faszyzować *ipf.* **1.** *polit., hist.* introduce fascist ideology. **2.** lean towards fascism. **~ się** *ipf.* become *l.* grow fascist.

fatalista *mp,* **fatalistka** *f. Gen.pl.* **-ek** fatalist.

fatalistyczny *a.* fatalistic.

fatalizm *mi* **1.** *fil.* fatalism. **2.** (= *przeznaczenie*) fatality, fate.

fatalnie *adv.* **1.** (= *bardzo źle*) awfully, appallingly, disastrously; **czuć się fatalnie** feel awful; **to się fatalnie składa** this is very unfortunate. **2.** fatally, fatefully.

fatalność *f.* **1.** (= *nieszczęście*) doom. **2.** (= *los, przeznaczenie*) fate.

fatalny *a.* **1.** (= *pechowy*) unlucky, disastrous, appalling; (*o pogodzie, dniu*) foul; (*o błędzie*) capital. **2.** (= *bardzo zły, niekorzystny*) wretched. **3.** (= *nieuchronny*) fateful, unescapable.

fatałaszek *mi* **-szk-** *Gen.* **-a** *pot.* frippery.

fatamorgana *f.* **1.** *fiz.* mirage. **2.** *przen.* (= *złuda*) mirage, illusion.

fatum *n. indecl. in sing. pl.* **-ta** *Gen.* **-tów** fate, doom; **kogoś prześladuje jakieś fatum** sb is dogged by ill fortune.

fatwa *f. rel.* fatwa; **nałożyć fatwę** issue fatwa.

fatyczny *a. jęz.* phatic.

fatyga *f.* trouble; **za fatygę** for one's pains; **szkoda fatygi** it's a waste of energy.

fatygant *mp przest.* (= *adorator*) gallant.

fatygować *ipf.* bother, trouble. **~ się** *ipf.* bother, trouble (*żeby coś zrobić* to do sth).

faul *mi Gen.* **-a** *Gen.pl.* **-i** *l.* **-ów** *sport* foul.

faulować *ipf. sport* foul.

faun *mp pl.* **-owie** *l.* **-y 1.** *mit.* (= *satyr*) faun. **2. Faun** *mit.* (= *bóg pól i lasów*) Faunus.

fauna *f. zool.* fauna.

faustyczny *a.* Faustian.

fawor *mi przest., żart.* (= *życzliwość*) favor.

faworek *mi* **-rk-** *Gen.* **-a** *kulin.* dry biscuit of fried paste, light sugar fritter.

faworyt *mp* **1.** (= *ulubieniec*) favorite. **2.** *sport* front-runner, favorite. **3.** *pl.* (= *bokobrody*) whiskers.

faworyta *f.* (= *metresa*) mistress, favorite.

faworytka *f. Gen.pl.* **-ek** *zob.* **faworyt** 1, 2.

faworyzacja *f.* favor, favoritism.

faworyzować *ipf.* favor; **faworyzować kogoś** show favor to sb, discriminate in favor of sb.

fax *zob.* **faks.**

faza *f.* **1.** (= *etap*) stage, phase. **2.** *astron.* phase; **fazy Księżyca** the phases of the moon. **3.** *fiz.* phase. **4.** *chem., fiz.* phase, stage.

fazować *ipf. tech.* chamfer.

fąfel *mp* **-fl-** *Gen.pl.* **-i** *l.* **-ów** *żart.* (= *dziecko*) brat, creeper. **–** *mi* **-fl-** *Gen.* **-a,** *Gen.pl.* **-i** *l.* **-ów** (*u psa*) pendulous lips.

fe! *int.* pish, faugh; **A fe!** pah!

febra f. **1.** pot. (= gorączka) fever. **2.** pot. (= opryszczka) cold sore. **3.** med. (choroba) fever; **żółta febra** yellow fever, black vomit.

febryczny a. med. feverish.

fechtmistrz mp pl. -e l. -owie sport swordsman.

fechtować się ipf. sport fence (z kimś with sb); **fechtować się na miecze/szable/rapiery** fence with swords/sabres/rapiers; **fechtować się z kimś na słowa** przen. fence with sb.

fechtunek mi -nk- sport fencing.

federacja f. **1.** (= państwo związkowe) federation. **2.** (= związek) association.

federacyjny a. federative.

federalista mp polit. federalist.

federalistyczny a. federalist, federalistic.

federalizacja f. federalization.

federalizm mi **1.** polit. (ustrój) federalism. **2.** polit. (ruch społeczny) federalism. **3.** hist. (ruch społeczny w XIX wieku) Federalism.

Federalne Biuro Śledcze, FBI n. the Federal Bureau of Investigations.

federalny a. federal; **Republika Federalna Niemiec** the Federal Republic of Germany; **agent federalny** pot. Federal agent, Fed; **więzienie federalne** federal prison.

fedrować ipf. górn. mine.

fedrunek mi -nk- górn. output.

feeria f. Gen. -ii **feeria dźwięków/głosów** riot of sounds/voices; **feeria barw** mass of colors.

fekalia pl. Gen. -ów faeces.

felczer mp **1.** (= medyk) paramedic. **2.** arch. (= chirurg wojskowy) surgeon.

felczerka f. Gen.pl. -ek = **felczer** 1.

felczerski a. paramedic's.

feldmarszałek mp -łk- pl. -owie wojsk. field marshal.

feldmarszałkowski a. wojsk. field marshal's.

feler mi pot. flaw, snag; **mieć feler** have a flaw, be defective.

felerny a. pot. defective.

felga f. techn., pot. rim.

felieton mi dzienn. column.

felietonista mp, **felietonistka** f. Gen.pl. -ek columnist.

felietonowy a. column.

felloderma f. bot. phelloderm.

fellogen mi bot. phellogen.

felonia f. Gen. pl. -ii prawn. felony.

feluka f. żegl. felucca.

felzyt mi geol. felstone.

feminista mp feminist.

feministka f. feminist.

feministyczny a. feminist.

feminizacja f. **1.** (zdominowanie przez kobiety) feminization. **2.** med. feminization.

feminizm mi feminism.

feminizować ipf. feminize. ~ **się** ipf. feminize, become feminized.

fen mi meteor. foehn.

fenacetyna f. chem., med. phenacetin.

fenek ma -nk- zool. fennec (zerda).

fenestracja f. med. fenestration.

fenianizm mi hist. Fenianism.

Fenicja f. hist. Phoenicia.

Fenicjanin mp pl. -anie Gen. -an, **Fenicjanka** f. Gen.pl. -ek hist. Phoenician.

fenicki a. hist. Phoenician.

fenig mi Gen. -a (moneta) pfennig.

Feniks ma **1.** astron. (gwiazdozbiór) Phoenix. **2.** geogr. (grupa wysp na Pacyfiku) Phoenix Islands.

feniks mi Gen. -a **1.** mit. phenix, phoenix; **powstać** l. **odrodzić się jak feniks z popiołów** rise like the phenix from the ashes. **2.** bot. (= daktylowiec) date palm (Phoenix).

fenol mi Gen.pl. -i l. -ów chem. phenol.

fenoloftaleina f. chem. phenolophtalein.

fenolowy a. chem. phenolic.

fenomen mi Gen. -u **1.** (= osobliwość) wonder, phenomenon. **2.** fil. phenomenon. – mp Gen. -a (= geniusz, indywidualność) phenom.

fenomenalista mp fil. phenomenalist.

fenomenalistyczny a. fil. phenomenalistic.

fenomenalizm mi fil. phenomenalism.

fenomenalnie adv. (= wyjątkowo, fantastycznie) phenomenally.

fenomenalny a. **1.** (= wyjątkowy, fantastyczny) phenomenal. **2.** fil. phenomenal.

fenomenolog mp pl. -dzy l. -owie fil. phenomenologist.

fenomenologia f. Gen. -ii fil. phenomenology.

fenomenologiczny a. fil. phenomenological.

fenotyp mi biol. phenotype.

fenyl mi chem. phenyl.

fenyloalanina f. biochem. phenylalanine.

fenyloketonuria f. Gen. -ii med. phenylketonuria.

ferajna f. pot. band.

feralny a. unlucky.

feretron mi kośc. feretory.

ferie pl. Gen. -ii (szkolne, uniwersyteckie) vacation, break; **ferie zimowe** winter break.

ferma zob. **farma**.

fermata f. **1.** muz. (= pauza) pause, fermata. **2.** muz. (= przedłużenie wartości rytmicznej) fermata.

ferment mi **1.** biol., przest. (= enzym) enzyme. **2.** przen. (= wzburzenie, niepokój) unrest, ferment; **rodzić, wywołać, powodować ferment** form. foment unrest.

fermentacja f. biol., chem. fermentation.

fermentacyjny a. fermentative.

fermentować ipf. ferment.

fermi mi indecl. fiz. (jednostka) fermi.

fermion mi fiz. fermion.

fermium n. chem., fiz. fermium.

fernambuk mi (drewno) brazilwood.

fernambukowy a. (of) brazilwood.

feromon mi biol., chem. pheromone.

ferować ipf. **ferować wyrok** pass a sentence.

ferromagnetyk mi fiz. ferromagnetic metal.

ferromagnetyzm mi fiz. ferromagnetism.

ferrotyp mi fiz. ferrotype.

ferryt mi **1.** techn. (półprzewodnik) ferrite. **2.** techn. (roztwór) ferrite. **3.** geol. ferrite.

ferrytowy a. techn., geol. ferrite.

fertyczny a. lit. dapper.

ferwor *mi lit.* fervor; **w ferworze walki** in the heat of battle.

fes *n. indecl. muz.* F flat.

fest[1] *a. indecl. pot.* (= *wspaniały*) cool.

fest[2] *adv. pot.* (= *mocno*) tight, tightly; **zrobić/ przymocować coś na fest** do/fasten sth for good.

festiwal *mi Gen.pl.* **-i** *l.* **-ów** festival; **festiwal filmowy/teatralny/jazzowy** film/theater/jazz festival.

festiwalowy *a.* festival.

feston *mi* (= *girlanda*) festoon.

festyn *mi* fest.

festynowy *a.* fest.

feta[1] *f. iron.* (= *uroczystość*) extravaganza.

feta[2] *f.* (*ser*) feta.

fetor *mi* fetor, stench.

fetować *ipf.* acclaim, fete.

fetysz *mi Gen.* **-a** *Gen.pl.* **-y** *l.* **-ów** **1.** (= *amulet, talizman*) fetish, juju. **2.** (= *pamiątka*) memento.

fetyszysta *mp* **1.** (*osoba przypisująca przedmiotom magiczną moc*) fetishist. **2.** (*dewiant seksualny*) fetishist.

fetyszystyczny *a.* fetishistic.

fetyszyzacja *f.* fetishization.

fetyszyzm *mi* **1.** (*wiara w magiczną moc przedmiotów*) fetishism. **2.** (*dewiacja seksualna*) fetishism.

fetyszyzować *ipf.* have a fetish about *l.* for sth.

feudalistyczny *a.* feudalistic.

feudalizm *mi* feudalism.

feudalny *a.* feudal, feudatory.

feudał *mp pl.* **-owie** feoffor, feudalist.

fez *mi* (*nakrycie głowy*) fez.

fiakier *mp* **-kr-** *pl.* **-rzy** *przest.* (= *dorożkarz*) cabdriver. – *mi* **-kr-** *Gen.* **-a** *pl.* **-ry** *przest.* (= *dorożka*) fiacre, cab.

fiasko *n.* fiasco.

fiberoskop *mi* **1.** *med.* fiberscope.

fibra *f. Gen.pl.* **-br** *l.* **-ber** **1.** *techn.* (= *derma, skaj*) fibre. **2.** *przest.* (= *nerw*) nerve.

fibroblast *mi biol.* fibroblast.

fibroina *f. biol.* fibroin.

fibrowy *a.* fibre.

fibryna *f. biol., chem.* (= *włóknik*) fibrin.

fibrynogen *mi biol., chem.* fibrinogen.

fibrynowy *a. biol., chem.* fibrinous.

fibula *f.* **1.** *anat.* fibula. **2.** *hist.* fibula.

fideista *mp fil.* fideist.

fideistyczny *a. fil.* fideistic.

fideizm *mi fil.* fideism.

fidrygałki *pl. Gen.* **-łek** *pot.* (= *błahostki*) trivialities.

Fidżi *n. indecl.* Fiji.

Fidżyjczyk *mp*, **Fidżyjka** *f. Gen.pl.* **-ek** Fijian.

fidżyjski *a.* Fijian.

fiesta *f.* (*święto*) fiesta, festival.

fifka *f. Gen.pl.* **-ek** *pot.* cigarette holder.

figa *f.* **1.** *bot.* (*owoc*) fig. **2.** *pot.* (= *figowiec*) fig (*Ficus carica*). **3.** *żart.* (*znak odmowy*) **a figę!** forget it!; **figa z czegoś** nothing; **figa z makiem (z pasternakiem)** zilch; **dostać figę (z makiem)** get nothing.

figi *pl. Gen.* **fig** (= *majtki*) briefs, panties.

figiel *mi* **-gl-** *Gen.* **-a** *Gen.pl.* **-ów** *l.* **-i** prank; **płatać figle** play tricks *l.* pranks (*komuś* on sb); **psi figiel** childish prank; **figle-migle** pranks; **figle się kogoś trzymają** sb's fond of jokes; **o mały figiel** almost, nearly.

figlarka *f. Gen.pl.* **-ek** *zob.* **figlarz.**

figlarny *a.* impish, arch, prankish.

figlarz *mp Gen.pl.* **-y** *l.* **-ów** prankster, practical joker, trickster.

figlik *mi Gen.* **-a** **1.** (= *psota, żart*) prank, trick. **2.** *teor.lit.* short humorous poem.

figlować *ipf.* **1.** (= *swawolić*) frolic, lark about *l.* around. **2.** *żart.* (= *pieścić się, kochać się*) pet, make love.

figowiec *mi* **-wc-** *Gen.* **-a** *bot.* fig tree (*Ficus*).

figowy *a.* **1.** *bot.* fig. **2.** **liść** *l.* **listek figowy** fig leaf.

figówka *f. med.* sycosis.

figura *f.* **1.** (= *sylwetka*) figure; **mieć ładną figurę** have a fine figure; (*ubranie*) **do figury** well-cut; **chodzić do figury** go out with no overcoat on. **2.** (= *rzeźba, statua*) statue; **przydrożna figura** wayside shrine. **3.** (= *ewolucja*) figure; **taniec z figurami** figure dance. **4.** *geom.* figure. **5.** *ret.* figure of speech. **6.** *szachy* piece. **7.** *karty* court-card. **8.** *muz.* figure. **9.** *log.* figure. **10.** *pot.* (= *osobistość*) personage; **ważna** *l.* **wielka figura** VIP.

figuracja *f. muz.* figuration.

figuracyjny *a. muz.* figured.

figuralny *a.* **1.** *sztuka* (= *przedstawieniowy*) figural, figurative. **2.** *muz.* (= *wielogłosowy*) figurative.

figurant *mp*, **figurantka** *f. Gen.pl.* **-ek** **1.** *iron.* (= *marionetka, płotka*) figurehead, puppet, rubber stamp. **2.** *przest.* (= *statysta*) extra.

figuratywność *f. sztuka* figurativeness.

figuratywny *a. sztuka* figurative.

figurka *f. Gen.pl.* **-ek** **1.** (= *posążek, statuetka*) figurine. **2.** *żart.* (= *sylwetka*) figure.

figurować *ipf.* (= *znajdować się*) figure (*w czymś* in sth).

figurowy *a.* figure; **jazda figurowa na lodzie** *l.* **łyżwiarstwo figurowe** *sport* figure skating.

figurynka *f. Gen.pl.* **-ek** figurine.

fik *int.* oops!

fikać *ipf.* **1.** (= *wywijać, skakać*) frolic, gambol; **fikać kozły** turn somersaults; **fikać nogami** kick. **2.** *żart.* (= *tańczyć*) hop.

fikcja *f.* fiction; **stwarzać fikcję** invent fiction.

fikcyjnie *adv.* fictionally, fictitiously.

fikcyjność *f.* fictionality, fictitiousness.

fikcyjny *a.* fictional, fictitious.

fiknąć *pf.* **-ij** *zob.* **fikać.**

fikołek *mi* **-łk-** *Gen.* **-a** *żart.* (= *koziołek, skok*) somersault.

fiksacja *f.* **1.** *psych.* fixation. **2.** *pot.* (= *mania, bzik*) obsession, craze, bee in one's bonnet.

fiksat *mp*, **fiksatka** *f. Gen.pl.* **-ek** *przest.* maniac.

fiksatywa *f. sztuka* (= *utrwalacz*) fixative.

fiksować *ipf.* **1.** (= *ustalać, potwierdzać*) fix, determine. **2.** *pot.* (= *wariować*) be nuts (*na punkcie kogoś / czegoś* on *l.* about sb/sth).

fikus *mi Gen.* **-a** *bot.* (= *figowiec, zwł. ozdobny*) ficus, rubber plant (*Ficus*); (*drzewo*) fig-tree.

fikuśny *a. pot.* **1.** (= *dziwny, trudny w użyciu*) funny, fiddly. **2.** (= *osobliwy, wyszukany*) quaint.

Filadelfia *f. Gen.* **-ii** *geogr.* Philadelphia.

filadelfijski *a.* Philadelphia.

filakteria *f. Gen.pl.* **-ii** *rel.* phylactery, frontlet.

filantrop *mp* philantropist.

filantropia *f. Gen.* **-ii** philantropy.

filantropijność *f.* philantropism.

filantropijny *a.* philantropic.

filantropka *f. Gen.pl.* **-ek** *zob.* **filantrop.**

filar *mi Gen.* **-u** *l.* **-a 1.** *bud.* (= *słup, kolumna*) pillar. **2.** *bud.* (= *podpora*) pier; **filar mostu** bridge pier. **3.** *górn.* pillar; **filar ochronny** safety pillar. – *mp Gen.* **-a** *przen.* (*najważniejsza osoba*) pillar; **filar społeczeństwa** pillar of society *l.* the community.

filarowanie *n. bud.* pillaring.

filarowy *a.* **1.** *bud.* pillar. **2.** *górn.* pillar.

filatelista *mp*, **filatelistka** *f. Gen.pl.* **-ek** stamp collector, philatelist.

filatelistyczny *a.* stamp collecting, philatelic.

filatelistyka *f.* stamp collecting, philately.

filc *mi* **1.** *tk.* felt. **2.** *bot.* (= *meszek*) tomentum.

filcować *ipf. tk.* felt. ~ **się** *ipf.* felt.

filcowy *a. tk.* felt.

fildekos *mi Gen.* **-u** lisle.

filet *mi Gen.* **-u** *l.* **-a 1.** (*kawałek ryby lub mięsa*) fillet *l.* filet. **2.** (*potrawa*) filet. **3.** *sztuka* (*koronka*) netting, guipure *l.* filet lace. **4.** *druk.* fillet.

filetować *ipf.* fillet, bone *l.* debone.

filharmonia *f. Gen.* **-ii 1.** *muz.* (*instytucja*) philharmonic. **2.** *muz.* (*budynek*) concert hall.

filharmoniczny *a. muz.* philharmonic; **orkiestra filharmoniczna** philharmonic (orchestra).

filharmonik *mp muz.* musician in a philharmonic (orchestra).

filhellenista *mp* philhellenist, philhellene.

filhellenizm *mi* philhellenism.

filhelleński *a.* philhellenic, philhellene.

filia *f. Gen.* **-ii** branch (office).

filiacja *f.* **1.** (= *pokrewieństwo, pochodzenie*) filiation, descent. **2.** *teor.lit.* (= *związek*) relationship.

filialny *a.* branch; **kościół filialny** chapel.

filigran *mi* **1.** *sztuka* (*technika złotnicza*) filigree. **2.** *sztuka* (*wyrób*) filigree. **3.** (= *znak wodny*) watermark. **4.** *sztuka* (*koronka*) filigree, delicate openwork. **5.** *przen.* (*mały przedmiot*) small, delicate *l.* dainty object.

filigranowość *f.* delicateness.

filigranowy *a.* **1.** *sztuka* (*wykonany techniką filigranu*) filigree. **2.** *przen.* (= *mały*) dainty; **filigranowa dziewczynka** dainty young girl. **3.** *przen.* (= *drobny, misterny*) fine, delicate. **4.** (= *ażurowy, misterny*) filigree(d); **filigranowe szkło** filigree glass.

filipika *f.* **1.** *hist.* philippic. **2.** *przen.* (= *mowa oskarżycielska*) philippic, tirade.

filipin *mp rel.* philippian.

Filipinka *f. Gen.pl.* **-ek** *zob.* **Filipińczyk.**

Filipiny *pl. Gen.* **-n** *geogr.* the Philippines.

Filipińczyk *mp* Filipino.

filipiński *a.* Filipino; (*język*) Pilipino.

filister *mp* **-tr-** *pl.* **-rzy** *l.* **-owie 1.** (= *drobnomieszczanin*) Philistine. **2.** (*nie student*) non-student.

filisterski *a.* (= *drobnomieszczański*) narrow-minded.

filisterstwo *n.* (= *kołtuństwo, małostkowość*) narrow-mindedness.

filiżanka *f. Gen.pl.* **-ek 1.** (= *czarka*) cup; **filiżanka do herbaty** teacup; **filiżanka do kawy** coffee cup. **2.** (= *zawartość czarki*) cupful.

film *mi* **1.** (*utwór kinematograficzny*) movie, film, motion picture; **film fabularny** feature film; **film dźwiękowy** movie with sound; **film niemy** silent film; **film pełnometrażowy** (full-length) feature film; **film krótkometrażowy** short film; **film kostiumowy** costume drama; **film dokumentalny** documentary (film); **film reklamowy** promotional film, infomercial; **film rysunkowy** (animated) cartoon, animated film; **film panoramiczny** wide-screen film; **film animowany** animated film; **nakręcić film** make *l.* shoot a film; (= *kinematografia*) film, cinematography; *pot.* the movies; **szkoła filmu** film school. **2.** *fot.* (= *taśma, błona*) film; **film barwny/kolorowy** color film; **film czarno-biały** black and white film; **prześwietlić film** expose film; **film się komuś urwał** *pot.* sb blacked out.

filmoteka *f.* **1.** *film* (= *zbiór filmów*) film collection *l.* library. **2.** *film* (= *archiwum filmowe*) film archives.

filmować *ipf.* (*film*) film; (*scena*) shoot.

filmowiec *mp* **-wc-** *pl.* **-y** *film* filmmaker.

filmowość *f.* the qualities that make sth a good subject for a film.

filmowy *a.* **1.** *kino* movie, film, motion picture, cinematic; **aktor filmowy** movie actor; **gwiazda filmowa** movie star; **muzyka filmowa** film music; **wytwórnia filmowa** movie production company, studio; **studio filmowe** movie studio; **operator filmowy** cinematographer; **materiał filmowy** (film) footage. **2.** *fot.* film; **taśma filmowa** film; **kamera filmowa** movie camera; **klatka filmowa** frame.

filmoznawca *mp* film connoisseur *l.* connoisseur of film.

filmoznawczy *a.* film studies.

filmoznawstwo *n.* film studies.

filodendron *mi Gen.* **-u** *l.* **-a** *bot.* **1.** philodendron (*Philodendron*). **2.** *pot.* (= *monstera*) monstera (*Monstera*).

filogenetyczny *a. biol.* phylogenetic, phyletic.

filogenetyka *f. biol.* phylogeny.

filogeneza *f. biol.* phylogeny.

filogenia *f. biol.* phylogeny.

filoksera *f. ent.* grape phylloxera (*Phylloxera vitifolii*).

filolog *mp pl.* **-dzy** *l.* **-owie** philologist.

filologia *f. Gen.* **-ii 1.** (*nauka*) philology. **2.** (*wydział uczelni*) language department; **filologia angielska** English studies; **filologia francuska** French studies.

filologiczny *a.* philological.

filować *ipf.* **1.** *pot.* (= *podglądać*) watch. **2.** (*o świecy, lampie*) (= *kopcić*) smoke. **3.** *karty* lay down one's cards one by one.

filozela *f. tk.* floss silk.

filozof *mp pl.* **-owie 1.** (= *myśliciel*) philosopher; *pot.* (= *mędrzec*) thinker. **2.** *pot., iron.* (= *przemądrzalec*) Mr. Know-it-all.

filozofia *f. Gen.* **-ii 1.** (= *wiedza o mądrości*) philosophy. **2.** (*teoretyczna podstawa danej nauki*) philosophy. **3.** *pot.* (*wydział na uczelni*) philosophy. **4.** (= *umiejętność, sztuka*) art; **filozofia życiowa** philosophy of life. **5.** *pot., żart.* (= *rzecz trudna do zrozumienia*) **to żadna filozofia** there's nothing to it; it's as easy as pie.

filozoficzny *a.* philosophical; **kamień filozoficzny** philosopher's stone; **filozoficzny spokój** contemplative silence.

filozofka *f. Gen.pl.* **-ek 1.** *pot. zob.* **filozof** 1. **2.** *pot., iron.* (= *kobieta przemądrzalec*) Ms. Know-it-all.

filozofować *ipf.* **1.** *pot.* (= *rozpatrywać, zgłębiać*) philosophize. **2.** *pot., iron. l. żart.* (= *wymądrzać się*) play the philosopher.

filtr *mi Gen.* **-u** *l.* **-a 1.** *techn.* (= *sączek, cedzidło*) filter. **2.** (= *stacja filtrów*) filter station.

filtracja *f.* **1.** *techn.* filtration, filtering. **2.** *geol.* percolation.

filtracyjny *a. techn.* (*warstwa, bibuła, siatka, osad, prasa*) filter.

filtrować *ipf.* filter.

filtrowy *a. techn.* (*płótno*) filter.

filumenista *mp*, **filumenistka** *f. Gen.pl.* **-ek** matchbox label collector.

filumenistyczny *a.* matchbox label collecting.

filumenistyka *f.* matchbox label collecting.

filut *mp pl.* **-y** *pot.* **1.** (= *figlarz*) rascal. **2.** (= *frant*) joker, trickster. **3.** (= *spryciarz*) (sly) fox.

filuternie *adv.* **1.** (= *zalotnie*) playfully. **2.** (= *swawolnie*) rascally. **3.** (= *przebiegle, sprytnie*) slyly, cunningly.

filuterność *f.* **1.** (= *kokieteria, przymilność*) playfulness. **2.** (= *przebiegłość*) cunning.

filuterny *a.* **1.** (= *zalotny, żartobliwy*) playful. **2.** (= *przebiegły, sprytny*) sly, cunning.

filutka *f. Gen.pl.* **-ek** *pot.* **1.** (= *figlarka*) minx. **2.** (= *spryciarka*) sly *l.* cunning girl *l.* woman.

Fin *mp pl.* **-owie** Finn.

fin *mi Gen.* **-a** *żegl.* fin.

finalista *mp*, **finalistka** *f. Gen.pl.* **-ek** finalist.

finalizacja *f.* finalization.

finalizm *mi fil.* finalism, teleology.

finalizować *ipf.* **1.** (= *ostatecznie załatwiać*) finalize; (*interesy*) settle. **2.** (= *kończyć*) close; (*pertraktacje, rozmowy*) conclude.

finalny *a.* finished; **produkt finalny** finished product.

finał *mi* **1.** (= *koniec*) ending, close. **2.** *muz.* finale. **3.** *sport* final(s).

finałowy *a.* **1.** *muz.* finale. **2.** *sport* final.

finanse *pl. Gen.* **-ów 1.** *ekon.* finance(s); **Ministerstwo Finansów** (*w Polsce*) Ministry of Finance; (*w Stanach Zjednoczonych*) Department of the Treasury; (*w Wielkiej Brytanii*) the Trea-

sury *l.* Exchequer. **2.** *pot.* (= *oszczędności, fundusze*) finances, money.

finansista *mp*, **finansistka** *f. Gen.pl.* **-ek 1.** (= *kapitalista, milioner*) financier. **2.** *ekon.* financer.

finansjera *f.* the (high) finance.

finansować *ipf.* finance, fund.

finansowość *f. ekon.* finance.

finansowy *a.* **1.** *ekon.* financial, fiscal; **polityka finansowa** fiscal politics; **system finansowy** financial system. **2.** *pot.* (= *ekonomiczny*) financial, money; **sytuacja finansowa** financial *l.* money situation; **trudności finansowe** financial *l.* money problems *l.* trouble(s).

finezja *f.* finesse; **grać/śpiewać z finezją** play/sing with finesse.

finezyjnie *adv.* with finesse; (*wykończony, ozdobiony*) finely.

finezyjność *f.* (*dowcipu, gry*) finesse, subtlety.

finezyjny *a.* fine; (*żart, uśmiech*) subtle; (*umysł*) refined; (*rysunek, wykonanie czegoś*) fine.

fingować *ipf.* fake; (*proces, mecz*) fix.

finisz *mi Gen.pl.* **-ów** *l.* **-y 1.** *sport* finish; **lotny finisz** *sport* (*w kolarstwie*) partial spurt. **2.** *pot.* (= *koniec*) end.

finiszować *ipf.* **1.** *sport* make a dash (for the finish). **2.** *pot.* (= *kończyć*) finish.

finiszowy *a. sport* finishing, final.

Finka *f. zob.* **Fin**.

finka *f. Gen.pl.* **-ek** (*nóż*) sheath knife.

Finlandia *f. Gen.* **-ii** *geogr.* Finland.

finlandyzacja *f. hist., polit.* Finlandization.

finta *f. sport* feint, dodge.

fiński *a.* Finnish; **nóż fiński** bowie knife; **domek fiński** *bud.* framed house.

fiok *mi Gen.* **-a** *l.* **-u 1.** *iron.* (= *lok*) curls. **2.** (= *przesadna fryzura*) fancy hair-do.

fiokować się *ipf. iron.* **1.** (= *czesać się pretensjonalnie*) primp and preen. **2.** (= *ubierać się z przesadną elegancją*) bedizen oneself.

fiolet *mi* **1.** (*kolor*) purple. **2.** (*barwnik*) purple pigment *l.* dye.

fioletowieć *ipf.* **1.** (= *stawać się fioletowym*) turn *l.* become purple. **2.** (= *wyglądać fioletowo*) be *l.* look *l.* appear violet.

fioletowo *adv.* violet.

fioletowobrązowy *a.* puce.

fioletowoniebieski *a.* cadet (blue).

fioletoworóżowy *a.* heather.

fioletowy *a.* violet, purple.

fiolka *f. Gen.pl.* **-ek** vial, phial.

fioł *mi Gen.* **-a** *pot.* (= *wariactwo, obsesja*) mania; **mieć fioła na punkcie kogoś, czegoś** have a thing about sb, sth, be crazy about sb, sth. – *mp pot.* (= *oryginał, wariat*) maniac, nut.

fiołek *mi* **-łk-** *Gen.* **-a** *bot.* violet; **fiołek alpejski** *bot.* (= *cyklamen*) cyclamen.

fiołkowy *a.* **1.** (*dotyczący fiołka*) violet. **2.** (*kolor*) violet.

fiord *mi Gen.* **-u** *geogr.* fiord.

fiordowy *a. geogr.* fiord.

fiorytura *f. muz.* fioritura, roulade.

firana *f.* (= *firanka*) sheer curtain; (*z siatki*) lace *l.* net curtain.

firanka *f. Gen.pl.* **-ek** sheer curtain; (*z siatki*) lace *l.* net curtain; **zawieszać firanki** hang curtains.

fircyk *mp pl.* **-i** **1.** (= *trzpiot*) scatterbrain, birdbrain. **2.** (= *strojniś*) beau, dandy, fop.

fircykowatość *f.* dandiness, fopishness.

fircykowaty *a.* dandyish, foppish.

firet *mi druk.* em quad *l.* em space.

firletka *f. Gen.pl.* **-ek** *bot.* campion, lychnis (*Lychnis*).

firma *f.* **1.** *ekon.* (= *nazwa przedsiębiorstwa*) company; (*duża*) corporation, enterprise, concern; (*mała*) business, firm; **firma adwokacka** law firm; **firma budowlana** construction company; **firma macierzysta** parent company. **2.** *pot.* (= *przedsiębiorstwo*) company. **3.** *przen.* (= *ustalona reputacja*) name.

firmament *mi* **1.** *lit., poet.* (= *niebo*) firmament, heavens. **2.** *astron.* sky.

firmować *ipf.* **1.** (= *patronować, wspierać*) (*impreza, przedsięwzięcie*) sponsor; (*wyrób*) endorse. **2.** *przen.* (= *promować, sankcjonować*) back.

firmowy *a.* **1.** *ekon.* company; **papier firmowy** letterhead; **znak firmowy** trademark, logo. **2.** *pot.* (*dotyczący przedsiębiorstwa*) company; **danie firmowe** *kulin.* house specialty. **3.** *pot.* (= *renomowany*) brand-name.

firn *mi* firn, neve.

firnowy *a.* firn.

fis *mi indecl. muz.* F sharp; **fis-dur** F sharp major; **fis-moll** F sharp minor.

fisharmonia *f. Gen.* **-ii** *muz.* harmonium, reed organ.

fiskalizm *mi* **1.** *ekon.* fiscalism. **2.** *hist.* fiscalism.

fiskalny *a. ekon.* fiscal; **kasa fiskalna** cash register.

fiskus *mi Gen.* **-a** **1.** *ekon.* (= *skarb państwa*) treasury, fisc. **2.** *hist.* fiscus.

fistaszek *mi* **-szk-** *Gen.* **-a** *bot.* peanut.

fistuła *f.* **1.** *med.* fistula. **2.** *muz.* (= *głos*) falsetto voice.

fistułowaty *a. med.* fistulous, fistular.

fisza *f. pot.* (= *prominent*) bigwig.

fiszbin *mi* **1.** (*u wieloryba*) baleen, whalebone. **2.** (*pręt usztywniający w biustonoszach i gorsetach*) whalebone.

fiszka *f. Gen.pl.* **-ek** **1.** (= *kartka*) index card. **2.** (= *szton*) chip.

fiś *mp Gen.pl.* **-ów** *pot.* (= *świrus, szajbus*) nut. – *mi Gen.* **-a** *Gen.pl.* **-ów** *pot.* (= *obsesja*) craze, bee in one's bonnet; **dostać/mieć fisia** *żart.* go/be crazy *l.* nuts (*na punkcie kogoś / czegoś* about *l.* over sb/sth).

fitness *f. indecl.* fitness; **fitness klub** fitness club.

fitocenoza *f. biol.* phytocoenosis.

fitochemia *f. Gen.* **-ii** *chem.* phytochemistry.

fitochemiczny *a. chem.* phytochemical.

fotogeografia *f. Gen.* **-ii** *biol.* phytogeographic *l.* phytogeographical.

fitopatologia *f. Gen.* **-ii** *biol.* phytopathology.

fitoplankton *ma biol.* phytoplankton.

fitosocjologia *f. Gen.* **-ii** *biol.* phytosociology.

fitoterapia *f. Gen.* **-ii** phytotherapy.

fiu *n. indecl.* (= *ptasi gwizd*) tweet, whistling sound; **mieć fiu-fiu** *l.* **fiu-bździu w głowie** *żart.* be hair-brained. – *int.* (*wyraża podziw l. zdziwienie*) ooh!

fiut *mi Gen.* **-a** *żart.* (= *męski członek*) dick, cock.

fizjograf *mp pl.* **-owie** *biol.* physiographer.

fizjografia *f. Gen.* **-ii** *biol.* physical geography, physiography.

fizjograficzny *a. biol.* physiographic(al).

fizjokrata *mp hist., ekon.* physiocrat.

fizjokratyczny *a. hist., ekon.* physiocratic.

fizjokratyzm *mi hist., ekon.* physiocracy.

fizjolog *mp pl.* **-dzy** *l.* **-owie** physiologist.

fizjologia *f. Gen.* **-ii** **1.** (*nauka*) physiology. **2.** (*czynności życiowe organizmu*) physiology.

fizjologiczny *a.* **1.** *biol.* (= *naturalny, organiczny*) physiological; **procesy fizjologiczne** bodily functions; **płyn fizjologiczny** *med.* physiological solution. **2.** *pot.* (= *zmysłowy, erotyczny*) sensual.

fizjonomia *f. Gen.* **-ii** **1.** (= *twarz*) face, features, countenance. **2.** *przen.* (= *cecha*) character, nature.

fizjonomiczny *a.* of one's countenance.

fizjonomika *f. psych.* physiognomy.

fizjonomista *mp psych.* physiognomist.

fizjoterapeuta *mp*, **fizjoterapeutka** *f. Gen.pl.* **-ek** *med.* physical therapist.

fizjoterapeutyczny *a. med.* physiotherapeutic.

fizjoterapia *f. Gen.* **-ii** *med.* physical therapy, physiotherapy.

fizycznie *adv.* **1.** (*w sposób związany z fizyką*) physically. **2.** (= *realnie, namacalnie*) physically. **3.** (= *organicznie, cieleśnie*) physically, bodily. **4.** (*wykorzystując mięśnie*) physically; **pracować fizycznie** perform manual labor.

fizyczność *f.* corporeality.

fizyczny *a.* **1.** (= *przyrodniczy, fizykalny*) physical. **2.** (= *realny, namacalny*) physical; **coś jest fizyczną niemożliwością** sth is a physical impossibility. **3.** (= *organiczny, cielesny*) physical; **sprawność fizyczna** physical fitness; **wychowanie fizyczne** physical education; **osoba fizyczna** *prawn.* natural person. **4.** (*związany z mięśniami i ich pracą*) physical, manual; **praca fizyczna** manual labor; **pracownik fizyczny** manual laborer. **5.** (= *naturalny, geograficzny*) physical; **geografia fizyczna** physical geography; **mapa fizyczna** *geogr.* physical map.

fizyk *mp* **1.** (*specjalista*) physicist. **2.** *szkoln.* (= *nauczyciel fizyki*) physics teacher.

fizyka *f.* **1.** (*nauka*) physics. **2.** *pot.* (*przedmiot w szkole*) physics.

fizykoterapeuta *mp*, **fizykoterapeutka** *f. Gen.pl.* **-ek** *med.* physical therapist, physiotherapist.

fizykoterapeutyczny *a. med.* physiotherapeutic.

fizykoterapia *f. Gen.* **-ii** *med.* physical therapy, physiotherapy.

fizylier *mp* **1.** *wojsk.* rifleman. **2.** *hist.* fusilier.

fizylierski *a.* **1.** *wojsk.* rifleman's. **2.** *hist.* fusilier's.

flacha *f.* **1.** *pot.* (= *butelka*) bottle. **2.** *pot., żart.* (= *wódka*) bottle, booze.

flaczeć *ipf.* **1.** *pot.* (= *mięknąć, więdnąć*) get *l.* grow flabby. **2.** *pot., przen.* (= *niedołężnieć*) feel *l.* become listless *l.* lethargic.

flaczki *pl. Gen.* **-ów** *kulin.* tripe, chitterlings.

flader *mi* **-dr-** *Gen.* **-a** (*rysunek słojów w drewnie*) wood grain.

flaga *f.* flag; **biała flaga** white flag, flag of truce; **flaga państwowa** the colors; **flaga amerykańska** the Stars and Stripes, Old Glory; **flaga brytyjska** the Union Jack; **flaga piracka** the Jolly Roger; **flaga biało-czerwona** the red and white flag; **flagi sygnałowe** signal flags; **pływać pod flagą** sail under the flag; **opuścić flagę** lower the flag *l.* colors; **wywiesić flagę** fly the flag; **zatknąć flagę** hoist the flag.

flagowiec *mi* **-wc-** *Gen.* **-a** *żegl.* flagship.

flagowy *a.* flag; **statek flagowy** *żegl.* flagship; **okręt flagowy** *żegl.* flagship.

flagsztok *mi Gen.* **-a** *żegl.* flagstaff.

flak *mi Gen.* **-a 1.** (*osłonka wędliny*) casing, skin. **2.** *pot.* (*coś zwiotczałego*) rag. – *mp pl.* **-i** *pot.* (*człowiek apatyczny, zmęczony*) slug *l.* sluggard.

flaki *pl. Gen.* **-ów 1.** *pot.* (= *jelito, wnętrzności*) entrails, guts; **flaki się w kimś przewracają** be furious at sb; **wypruwać z siebie flaki** work *l.* sweat one's guts out, bust a gut; **wypruć komuś flaki** bore sb to death *l.* tears. **2.** *kulin.* tripe; **nudny jak flaki z olejem** *pot.* dull as ditchwater.

flakon *mi* **1.** (*buteleczka na perfumy*) perfume bottle. **2.** (= *wazon*) flower vase.

flakonik *mi Gen.* **-a 1.** (*buteleczka na perfumy*) small perfume bottle. **2.** (= *wazonik*) small flower vase.

flakowacieć *ipf.* **1.** *pot., przen.* (= *mięknąć, wiednąć*) get *l.* grow flabby. **2.** *pot.* (= *niedołężnieć*) feel *l.* become listless *l.* lethargic.

flakowaty *a.* *pot.* flaccid, limp.

flama *f. pot.* flame, heartthrob.

Flamand *mp Gen.* **-a** *pl.* **-owie, Flamandka** *f. Gen.pl.* **-ek** Fleming.

flamandzki *a.* Flemish.

flamaster *mi* **-tr-** *Gen.* **-a** marker (pen).

flambirowany *a. kulin.* flambé.

flamenco *n. indecl. muz.* flamenco.

flaming *ma zool.* flamingo.

flanca *f. Gen.pl.* **-c** *l.* **-y** *ogr.* seedling, set.

flancować *ipf. ogr.* plant, set.

Flandria *f. Gen.* **-ii** *geogr., hist.* Flanders.

flandryjski *a.* of Flanders.

flanela *f. Gen.pl.* **-i** *tk.* flannel.

flanelka *f. Gen.pl.* **-ek** *pot.* flannel.

flanelowy *a.* flannel, swanskin.

flanka *f. Gen.pl.* **-nk** *l.* **-nek 1.** *hist.* (*skrzydło wojska*) flank. **2.** *hist.* (= *baszta*) flanking tower. **3.** *sport* wing.

flankować *ipf.* **1.** (= *otaczać*) flank. **2.** *hist.* (=

obwarowywać) fortify. **3.** *przest.* (= *okrążać*) besiege.

flara *f. wojsk.* flare.

flaszeczka *f. Gen.pl.* **-ek** small bottle; (*na ocet, oliwę*) cruet.

flaszka *f. Gen.pl.* **-ek** *pot.* bottle; **postawić flaszkę** stand a drink; **obalić flaszkę** *sl.* knock one back.

flaszowiec *mi bot.* water apple (*Annona*); **flaszowiec łuskowaty** sweetsop (*A. squamosa*); **flaszowiec miękkociernisty** soursop (*A. muricata*); **flaszowiec siatkowy** *t. kulin.* custard apple (*A. reticulata*).

flausz *mi tk.* coating.

flauszowy *a. tk.* coating.

flauta *f. żegl.* calm.

flawina *f. biol., chem.* flavin.

flażolet *mi* **1.** *muz.* (= *flet*) flageolet, tin whistle. **2.** *muz.* (*ton*) harmonic, flageolet tone.

flądra *f.* **-dr-** *Gen.pl.* **-der 1.** *icht.* (= *jakakolwiek ryba z rodziny Pleuronectidae*) flounder, fluke (*Platichthys*); plaice (*Pleuronectes*). **2.** *pot., pog.* (= *osoba brudna, niechlujna*) slob. **3.** *pot., pog.* (= *bezwstydnica*) slut.

flądrowaty *a. pot.* slovenly.

flebologia *f. Gen.* **-ii** *med.* phlebology.

flecista *mp,* **flecistka** *f. Gen.pl.* **-ek** flutist *l.* flautist.

fleczer *mi Gen.* **-a** *l.* **-u** *dent.* filling compound.

flegma *f.* **1.** *med.* phlegm. **2.** *chem.* reflux. **3.** *psych.* (= *spokój*) sluggishness. **4.** *pot.* (= *flegmatyk*) slug.

flegmatyczka *f. Gen.pl.* **-ek** *zob.* **flegmatyk.**

flegmatyczność *f.* sluggishness, listlessness, torpidity.

flegmatyczny *a.* phlegmatic.

flegmatyk *mp psych.* phlegmatic (person).

flegmisty *a.* phlegmy; **flegmista wydzielina** phlegm; **flegmisty kaszel** productive cough.

flegmona *f. med.* phlegmon.

fleja *f. l. mp decl. like f. Gen.* **-ei** *Gen.pl.* **-j** *pot., uj.* slob.

flejtuch *mp pot., uj.* slob.

flejtuchowaty *a. pot., uj.* slobbish.

flek *mi Gen.* **-a** heelpiece, heeltap; **być na fleku** *żart.* be tipsy.

fleksja *f. jęz.* inflection; **fleksja wewnętrzna** internal flexion.

fleksografia *f. druk.* flexography.

fleksor *mi anat.* flexor muscle.

fleksura *f. geol.* flexure.

fleksyjny *a. jęz.* inflectional; **język fleksyjny** inflected language.

flesz *mi Gen.* **-a** *l.* **-u** *Gen.pl.* **-ów** *l.* **-y 1.** *fot.* flash. **2.** *sport* flèche, flash.

flet *mi* flute; **flet prosty** recorder; **flet poprzeczny** flute.

fletnia *f. Gen.pl.* **-i** **fletnia Pana** pan-pipes.

fletnista *mp,* **fletnistka** *f. Gen.pl.* **-ek** flutist.

fletowy *a.* flute; **koncert fletowy** flute concerto.

fletówka *f. Gen.pl.* **-ek** *orn.* whipbird (*Pachycephala*).

flibustier *mp hist.* filibuster.

flint *mi* flintglass.

flinta *f. przest.* shotgun.

flirciarka *f. Gen.pl.* **-ek** flirt, minx.

flirciarski *a.* flirtatious.

flirciarz *mp* flirt.

flirt *mi* (*romans*) flirtation.

flirtować *ipf.* flirt (*z kimś* with sb).

flisacki *a.* raft, rafter's; **tratwa flisacka** raft.

flisactwo *n.* rafting.

flisak *mp* rafter.

fliza *f.* **1.** (*płyta*) flagstone. **2.** *druk.* inking-table.

flizowy *a.* flagstone; **posadzka flizowa** flagstone floor.

floem[1] *mi bot.* phloem.

floem[2] *mi* (= *pływający lód*) floe.

flogiston *mi chem.* phlogiston.

flogopit *mi min.* phlogopite.

floks *mi* **-a** *l.* **-u** *bot.* phlox (*Phlox*).

flokulacja *f. chem., med.* flocculation.

flokulant *mi chem.* flocculant.

flora *f. bot.* flora; **flora bakteryjna (jelit)** *med.* intestinal flora.

florecista *mp* foilsman.

florecistka *f. Gen.pl.* **-ek** foilswoman.

floren *mi hist.* (*numizmatyka*) florin.

Florencja *f.* Florence.

florencki *a.* Florentine.

floret *mi* **1.** (*broń*) foil. **2.** *sport* (*konkurencja*) foils.

floretowy *a.* foil; **turniej floretowy** foil tournament; **drużyna floretowa** foil team.

florystyczny *a.* floristic.

florystyka *f. bot.* floristics.

flota *f.* **1.** (= *ogół statków*) the fleet. **2.** *wojsk.* fleet. **3.** *pot., przest.* (= *pieniądze*) dough, cabbage.

flotacja *f. chem.* flotation.

flotylla *f. Gen.pl.* **-lli** *l.* **-ll** (*żegl., wojsk.*) flotilla.

fluid *mi* **1.** (*parapsychologia*) aura. **2.** (= *wrażenie, nastrój*) aura. **3.** (*kosmetyka*) fluid.

fluidyzacja *f. chem.* fluidization.

fluksja *f. med.* gumboil.

fluksometr *mi fiz.* fluxmeter.

fluktuacja *f.* **1.** (= *niestałość*) fluctuation. **2.** *fiz.* fluctuation.

fluktuacyjny *a.* (of) fluctuation.

fluor *mi chem.* fluorine.

fluoran *mi chem.* fluorate.

fluorek *mi* **-rk-** *chem.* fluoride.

fluoresceina *f. chem.* fluorescein.

fluorescencja *f. fiz.* fluorescence.

fluorescencyjny *a. fiz.* fluorescent; **lampa fluorescencyjna** fluorescent lamp *l.* bulb; **analiza fluorescencyjna** fluorescence analysis; **ekran fluorescencyjny** fluorescent screen; **farba fluorescencyjna** fluorescent paint.

fluorkować *ipf. chem.* fluorinate.

fluoroskop *mi* fluoroscope.

fluoroskopia *f.* fluoroscopy.

fluorowodorowy *a. chem.* hydrofluoric; **kwas fluorowodorowy** hydrofluoric acid.

fluorowy *a. chem.* fluoric; **związek fluorowy** fluoric compound.

fluoryt *mi min.* fluorite, fluorspar.

fluoryzacja *f. dent.* fluoridation.

fluoryzować *ipf. fiz.* fluoresce.

fluwialny *a. geogr.* fluvial, fluviatile.

fluwioglacjalny *a. geol.* fluvioglacial.

fluwiometr *mi* fluviometer.

fobia *f. Gen.* **-ii** *psych.* phobia.

fochy *pl. Gen.* **-ów** sulks; **stroić fochy** sulk.

foczy *a.* seal; **siedliska focze** seal's habitat; **focza skóra** sealskin.

fok *mi Gen.* **-a** *żegl.* foresail.

foka *f. zool.* seal (*Phoca*).

foki *pl. Gen.* **fok** (*futro*) sealskin.

fokmaszt *mi żegl.* foremast.

fokreja *f. Gen.* **-ei** *żegl.* foreyard.

fokstenga *f. żegl.* fore topmast.

foksterier *ma* fox terrier.

fokstrot *mi Gen i Acc.* **-a** (*taniec*) foxtrot.

fokus *mi fiz.* focus.

folder *mi Gen.* **-u** *l.* **-a** brochure.

folgować *ipf.* **1.** (= *pozwalać sobie*) indulge (*czemuś* in sth). **2.** (= *pobłażać*) be lenient (*komuś* with sb).

folia *f. Gen.* **-ii** **1.** (*z tworzywa sztucznego*) plastic wrap. **2.** (*z metalu*) foil. **3.** (*w jubilerstwie*) foil.

foliacja *f.* **1.** *geol.* foliation. **2.** (= *numeracja kart tomu*) foliation.

foliał *mi* volume, folio.

folikulostymulina *f. biol.* follicle-stimulating hormone, FSH.

folio *n. indecl.* **1.** *druk.* folio. **2.** *handl.* folio.

foliować *ipf.* **1.** (= *pokrywać folią*) laminate. **2.** *druk., handl.* foliate.

foliowy *a.* **1.** (*z folii*) plastic; **torba foliowa** plastic bag. **2.** *druk.* folio; **wolumin foliowy** folio. **3.** *chem.* **kwas foliowy** folic acid, folacin, vitamin M.

folk *mi muz.* folk.

folklor *mi* folklore.

folklorysta *mp*, **folklorystka** *f. Gen.pl.* **-ek** folklorist.

folklorystyczny *a.* folkloric, folkloristic.

folklorystyka *f.* folklore.

folkowy *a. muz.* folk.

folować *ipf.* full.

folusz *mi* fuller.

folwarczny *a.* grange; **zabudowania folwarczne** grange, farm-buildings.

folwark *mi* grange.

fondue *n. indecl.* fondue.

fonem *mi jęz.* phoneme.

fonemowy *a. jęz.* phonemic; **grupa fonemowa** phonemic cluster.

fonetyczny *a. jęz.* phonetic; **zapis fonetyczny** phonetic transcription; **zmiany fonetyczne** phonetic changes; **wariant fonetyczny** phonetic variant.

fonetyk *mp jęz.* phonetician.

fonetyka *f. jęz.* **1.** (*dział wiedzy*) phonetics. **2.** (= *wymowa*) phonetics; **fonetyka międzywyrazowa** sandhi phonetics.

fonia *f. Gen.* **-ii** sound.

foniatra *mp med.* phoniatrist.

foniatria *f. Gen.* **-ii** *med.* phoniatrics.

foniatryczny *a. med.* phoniatric; **poradnia foniatryczna** phoniatric outpatient clinic.

foniczny *a.* phonic.

fonograf *mi* phonograph.

fonografia *f. Gen.* **-ii** phonography.

fonograficzny *a.* phonographic; **przemysł fonograficzny** music industry; **rynek fonograficzny** music market.

fonogram *mi jęz.* phonogram.

fonolog *mp pl.* **-dzy** *l.* **-owie** *jęz.* phonologist.

fonologia *f. Gen.* **-ii** *jęz.* phonology.

fonologiczny *a. jęz.* phonological, phonemic; **zapis fonologiczny** phonemic transcription; **system fonologiczny** phonological *l.* phonemic system.

fonometr *mi fiz.* phonometer.

fonon *mi fiz., chem.* phonon.

fonotaktyka *f. jęz.* phonotactics.

fonoteka *f.* record collection.

fontanna *f.* fountain; **wylewać fontanny łez** shed tears.

for *mi Gen.* **-ów** 1. *sport* handicap; **dać komuś fory** give points to sb, give sb a head start. 2. *pl.* (= *względy*) favor; **mieć u kogoś fory** enjoy sb's favor.

fora *int. pot.* get out!; **fora ze dwora!** get out of here!, get lost!

fordanser *mp* (professional) dancing partner.

fordanserka *f. Gen.pl.* **-ek** (professional) dancing partner, hostess.

foremka *f. Gen.pl.* **-ek** (*do piasku*) mold; (*do ciasta*) baking tin, cookie cutter.

foremnik *mi Gen.* **-a** *techn.* swege-block.

foremność *f.* regularity, shapeliness.

foremny *a.* regular; **foremny nos** well-shaped *l.* regular nose; **foremna bryła** regular solid; **wielokąt foremny** *geom.* regular polygon; **wielościan foremny** *geom.* regular polyhedron.

forhend *mi sport* forehand.

forma *f.* 1. (*kształt*) form, shape; **fantastyczna forma** fanciful shape; **nadać czemuś jakąś formę** shape sth, give shape to sth; **przedstawić coś w jakiejś formie** represent sth in a/the form of; **mieć/przybierać formę czegoś** take the form of sth; **transgeniczne formy roślin** *bot.* transgenic plant forms. 2. (*struktura*) form; **forma prawna** legal form; **forma własności** ownership type; **forma zastępcza** compensation; **forma biologiczna** *biol.* biological form; **forma bytu** *fil.* form of being/existence. 3. (= *konwenanse*) rules, etiquette; **zachowywać formy towarzyskie** observe the rules of social behavior; **zrobić coś pro forma** do sth as a matter of form. 4. (= *szablon*) pattern, model. 5. *fil.* form. 6. *druk.* form(e). 7. *jęz.* form; **forma gramatyczna** grammatical form; **forma hiperpoprawna** hypercorrection, hypercorrect form; **forma osobowa czasownika** personal verb form; **formy koniugacyjne** conjugational forms; **formy deklinacyjne** inflectional forms; **forma ciągła** progressive; **forma częstotliwa** frequentative; **forma (nie)dokonana** (im)perfective; **forma oboczna** alternant; **forma ściągnięta** contraction. 8. *mat.* form, quantic; **forma kwadratowa** quadratic form, quadric. 9. *sport* form, condition; **być w dobrej formie** be in good form *l.* shape; **stracić formę** lose form; **odzyskać dobrą formę** return to good form; **utrzymywać dobrą formę** keep fit; **być nie w formie** be off form; **nie w formie** out of condition *l.* form. 10. *sztuka* form. 11. *techn.* mold, matrix; **forma odlewnicza** mold; **forma piekarska** baking tin.

formacja *f.* 1. *bot.* formation. 2. *ekon.* structure. 3. *geol.* formation. 4. *jęz.* form; **formacja odrzeczownikowa** denominative forms; **formacja odczasownikowa** deverbative forms. 5. *wojsk.* formation; **formacja lotnicza** flight, flight formation. 6. *rel.* formation.

formaldehyd *mi chem.* formaldehyde.

formalina *f. chem.* formalin.

formalista *mp* 1. (= *biurokrata*) formalist, legalist. 2. (*artysta*) formalist.

formalistyczny *a.* 1. (= *biurokratyczny*) formalistic; **formalistyczne podejście** formalistic attitude. 2. *sztuka* formalistic; **malarstwo formalistyczne** formalistic painting.

formalizacja *f.* 1. (= *ujmowanie w reguły*) formalization. 2. *log., socjol.* formalization.

formalizm *mi* 1. (= *biurokracja*) formalism. 2. *sztuka* formalism.

formalizować *ipf.* formalize.

formalnie *adv.* 1. (= *pod względem formy*) structurally, formally. 2. (= *urzędowo*) formally, officially; **poinformować o czymś formalnie** inform sb about sth officially. 3. *pot.* (= *naprawdę*) literally, positively; **mam formalnie tego dosyć** I'm positively fed up with it; **formalnie padam z nóg** I'm literally dead on my feet.

formalność *f.* (= *czynność urzędowa*) formality; **to tylko formalność** it's just a formality; **formalności prawne** legal formalities.

formalny *a.* 1. (= *strukturalny*) structural; **nauki formalne** deductive sciences; **logika formalna** formal logic; **etyka formalna** formal ethics. 2. (= *urzędowy*) formal; **kwestia formalna** point of order; **formalny zapis** formal bequest; **sprzeciw formalny** formal protest; **charakter formalny** formality. 3. *pot.* literal; **formalna klęska** literal disaster.

formant *mi jęz., fiz.* formant, formative.

format *mi* format; **polityk wielkiego formatu** *przen.* politician of great caliber.

formatować *ipf. komp.* format.

formatyw *mi jęz.* formative.

formierka *f. Gen.pl.* **-ek** *techn.* moulding machine; **formierka wstrząsająca** jolter.

formiernia *f. Gen.pl.* **-i** *l.* **-ń** *techn.* foundry.

formierski *a. techn.* molding; **kaseton** *l.* **skrzynka formierska** flask.

formierstwo *n. techn.* molding.

formierz *mp techn.* former.

formista *mp sztuka* formist.

formistyczny *a. sztuka* formist.

formizm *mi sztuka* formism (*a trend in art*).

formować *ipf.* 1. (= *nadawać kształt*) shape, form, fashion; (*kapelusz*) block; (*pomysł, ideę*) gestate. 2. (= *tworzyć*) form. 3. (= *ustawiać w szyk*) form. 4. *techn.* mold. **~ się** *ipf.* form, be shaped.

formularz *mi Gen.* **-a** form, blank; **wypełnić formularz** fill *US* out/*Br.* in a form.

formuła *f.* formula; **formuła przysięgi** the words of an oath; **formuła zaklęcia** spell; **formuła chemiczna/matematyczna** chemical/mathematical formula.

formułka *f. Gen.pl.* **-ek** formula; **przywiązanie do formułek** formulism; **utarte formułki** boilerplates.

formułować *ipf.* formulate; (*pogląd*) conceptualize; (*pytanie, odpowiedź*) formulate; (*teorię*) formulate; (*zasady*) lay.

fornal *mp przest.* groom.

fornir *mi* veneer.

fornirować *ipf.* veneer; **meble fornirowane** veneered furniture.

forować *ipf.* favor.

forpik *mi żegl.* forepeak.

forpoczta *f.* outpost.

forsa *f. pot.* dough; **robić forsę** make money; **zbić forsę** make an easy buck; **mieć kupę forsy** be in fat city; **stracić kupę forsy** take a bath; **szastać forsą** be extravagant with one's money; **gruba forsa** big bucks; **nie jestem przy forsie** I am not in the chips.

forsiasty *a. pot.* well-heeled.

forsować *ipf.* **1.** (= *zdecydowanie popierać*) push, force. **2.** (= *obciążać zbyt dużym wysiłkiem*) force, extend; **forsować żaglami** *żegl.* press sails. **3.** *wojsk.* (*rzekę*) cross. **~ się** *ipf.* strain o.s., overexert o.s.

forsowny *a.* strenuous, intensive; **forsowny marsz** forced march; **forsowny dzień** heavy day.

forsycja *f. bot.* forsythia (*Forsythia*).

fort *mi* fort, stronghold.

forta *f. karty* winning card.

fortalicja *f. hist.* stronghold.

forte *n. indecl. muz.* forte. – *adv. muz.* forte; **grać forte** play loudly.

forteca *f.* fortress; **zdobyć fortecę** take a fortress; **latająca forteca** *wojsk.* flying fortress.

forteczny *a.* fortress; **mury forteczne** ramparts, battlements.

fortel *mi Gen.pl.* **-i** *l.* **-ów** stratagem, ploy, contrivance; **podejść kogoś fortelem** trick sb; **użyć fortelu** use a stratagem.

fortepian *mi* piano, grand piano; **fortepian gabinetowy** baby grand; **fortepian koncertowy** concert grand.

fortepianowy *a.* piano; **koncert fortepianowy** piano concerto; **solo fortepianowe** piano solo.

fortissimo *n. indecl. muz.* fortissimo. – *adv. muz.* fortissimo.

Fortuna *f. mit.* Fortune; **koło Fortuny** *mit.* Fortune's wheel, the wheel of Fortune; (*gra*) the wheel of Fortune.

fortuna *f.* **1.** (= *szczęście*) fortune; **ulubieniec fortuny** favorite of fortune; **fortuna kołem się toczy** fortune is fickle, every dog has its day; **kaprys fortuny** the luck of the draw. **2.** (= *majątek*) fortune; **wielomilionowa fortuna** huge fortune; **roztrwonić fortunę** squander a fortune; **wydać fortunę** spend an arm and a leg, spend a bomb; **zbić fortunę** make a fortune, make a killing.

fortunny *a. lit.* lucky, fortunate.

fortyfikacja *f. wojsk.* (*umocnienia*) fortification.

fortyfikacyjny *a. wojsk.* fortification; **system fortyfikacyjny** fortification system; **plan fortyfikacyjny** fortification plan; **prace fortyfikacyjne** defensive work.

fortyfikować *ipf. bud., wojsk.* fortify, embattle. **~się** *ipf. wojsk.* fortify, be fortified.

forum *n. pl.* **-ra** *Gen.* **-rów** **1.** (*audytorium*) audience; **na forum międzynarodowym** at an international forum; **na forum publicznym** in public. **2.** *hist.* (*w Rzymie*) forum.

fosa *f.* moat; **fosa orkiestrowa** (*w operze*) orchestra pit.

fosfat *mi chem., roln.* phosphate.

fosfatowy *a. roln.* phosphatic; **nawóz fosfatowy** phosphate.

fosfor *mi chem.* phosphorus.

fosforan *mi chem.* phosphate.

fosforawy *a. chem.* phosphorous; **kwas fosforawy** phosphorous acid.

fosforek *mi* **-rk-** *chem.* phosphide.

fosforescencja *f. fiz., biochem.* phosphorescence.

fosforowy *a. chem.* phosphoric; **kwas fosforowy** phosphoric acid; **nawozy fosforowe** phosphates.

fosforyczny *a.* phosphorescent; **światło fosforyczne** phosphorescent light.

fosforyn *mi chem.* phosphite.

fosforyt *mi górn.* phosphorite.

fosforytowy *a. chem., roln.* phosphoritic.

fosforyzować *ipf.* phosphoresce; **fosforyzujące wskazówki (zegarka)** fluorescent hands.

fosgen *mi chem.* phosgene.

fot *mi fiz.* phot.

fotel *mi Gen.* **-a** *Gen.pl.* **-i** *l.* **-ów** armchair; **fotel bujany** rocking-chair; **fotel klubowy** club chair; **fotel katapultowy** *lotn.* ejection seat; **zasiąść na fotelu ministerialnym** take ministerial office.

fotelik *mi Gen.* **-a** small armchair; **fotelik samochodowy** car seat; **fotelik dziecięcy** high chair.

fotka *f. Gen.pl.* **-ek** *żart.* photo, pic.

fotoamator *mp* amateur photographer.

fotoamatorski *a.* amateur photographic; **prace fotoamatorskie** amateur photographs.

fotochemiczny *a.* photochemical.

fotochromowy *a.* photochromic.

fotoelektryczny *a.* photoelectric; **zjawisko fotoelektryczne** photoelectric effect; **emisja fotoelektryczna** photoemission.

fotogeniczność *f.* photogenicity.

fotogeniczny *a.* photogenic; **nie jestem fotogeniczny** I am not photogenic; **fotogeniczna twarz** photogenic face.

fotograf *mp pl.* **-owie** photographer.

fotografia *f. Gen.* **-ii** **1.** (= *zdjęcie*) photograph. **2.** (*technika*) photography; **fotografia barwna** color photography, chromophotography; **fotografia czarno-biała** black and white photography; **fotografia artystyczna** art photography; **fotografia lotnicza** aerial photography; **fotografia podwod-**

na underwater photography; **fotografia korpuskularna** *fiz.* corpuscular photography; **fotografia makroskopowa** macrophotography; **fotografia mikroskopowa** microphotography; **fotografia stereoskopowa** stereoscopic photography.

fotograficzny *a.* photographic; **aparat fotograficzny** camera; **atelier fotograficzne** studio; **błona fotograficzna** film; **papier fotograficzny** photographic paper; **odbitka fotograficzna** print; **z fotograficzną dokładnością** with photographic accuracy.

fotografik *mp* photographer.

fotografika *f.* photography.

fotografować *ipf.* photograph, take a photo. ~ **się** *ipf.* be photographed, have a picture of o.s. taken; **nielubiący się fotografować** camera-shy.

fotogram *mi* (= *zdjęcie*) photograph.

fotogrametria *f. Gen.* -ii *techn.* photogrammetry.

fotograwiura *f.* 1. *druk.* (*metoda*) photogravure. 2. *druk.* (*rycina*) photogravure.

fotokineza *f. biol.* photokinesis.

fotokomórka *f. Gen.pl.* -ek *el.* photocell, photoelectric cell; **drzwi na fotokomórkę** light controlled door; **rozstrzygnięcie fotokomórką** *sport* photo finish.

fotokomórkowy *a.* (of) photocell; **system fotokomórkowy** photoelectric system.

fotokopia *f. Gen.* -ii photocopy.

fotokopiarka *f. Gen.pl.* -ek photocopier.

fotoliza *f. chem.* photolysis.

fotometr *mi fiz.* photometer.

fotometria *f. Gen.* -ii *fiz.* photometry.

fotometryczny *a.* photometric; (*badanie, pomiar*) photometric.

fotomikrografia *f. Gen.* -ii photomicrography.

fotomodelka *f. Gen.pl.* -ek model.

fotomontaż *mi* 1. (*obraz*) trick photograph, photomontage. 2. (*technika twórcza*) photomontage.

fotomontażowy *a.* photomontage.

foton *mi fiz.* photon.

fotonowy *a.* photon; (*energia*) photon; **napęd fotonowy** photon propulsion.

fotooferta *f.* ad with a photo.

fotoofset *mi druk.* photo-offset.

fotoofsetowy *a. druk.* photo-offset.

fotoplastykon *mi* peep-show.

fotoprzewodnictwo *n.* photoconductivity.

fotoprzewodnik *mi* photoconductor.

fotorealizm *mi sztuka* photorealism.

fotoreceptor *mi biol.* photoreceptor.

fotoreportaż *mi* photo essay.

fotoreporter *mp*, **fotoreporterka** *f. Gen.pl.* -ek press *l.* news photographer, photojournalist.

fotoreporterski *a.* photojournalist's.

fotos *mi* still.

fotosfera *f. astron.* photosphere.

fotoskład *mi* photosetting, filmsetting.

fotosynteza *f. bot.* photosynthesis.

fototaksja *f. biol.* phototaxis; **fototaksja ujemna/dodatnia** negative/positive phototaxis.

fototapeta *f.* photograph wallpaper.

fototerapia *f. Gen.* -ii phototherapy.

fototranzystor *mi* phototransistor.

fototropijny *a. biol.* phototropic.

fototropizm *mi biol.* phototropism, heliotropism.

fototyp *mi druk.* phototype.

fototypia *f. Gen.* -ii 1. *druk.* (*technika*) collotype. 2. (*odbitka*) heliography, phototype.

fotyczny *a. biol.* photic.

fowista *mp*, **fowistka** *f. Gen.pl.* -ek *sztuka* Fauvist.

fowizm *mi sztuka* Fauvism.

foyer *n. indecl.* foyer.

fracht *mi* 1. (*opłata*) freight. 2. (*przewóz*) freight, freightage.

frachtować *ipf.* freight.

frachtowiec *mi* -wc- *Gen.* -a *żegl.* freighter.

frachtowy *a.* freight; **statek frachtowy** *żegl.* freighter.

fragmencik *mi Gen.* -a *l.* -u small fragment *l.* excerpt.

fragment *mi* 1. (*część*) fragment; (*powieści, opery*) excerpt, fragment, extract; (*rozmowy*) fragment, scrap; **fragment konstrukcyjny** *techn.* construction fragment; **fragment rozszczepieniowy** *fiz.* fission fragment. 2. *teor.lit.* piece, excerpt.

fragmentacja *f.* fragmentation.

fragmentaryczność *f.* fragmentary character.

fragmentaryczny *a.* fragmentary.

frajda *f. pot.* fun, bang; **ale frajda!** what fun!; **sprawiać komuś frajdę** give sb a buzz; **robić coś dla frajdy** do sth for kicks; **mieć z czegoś frajdę** get a bang out of sth.

frajer *mp* 1. (*człowiek naiwny*) *pot.* sucker, gudgeon, patsy; **zrobić z kogoś frajera** take sb in. 2. *pot.* **za frajer** (= *za darmo*) as a freebie; free.

frajerka *f. Gen.pl.* -ek *zob.* **frajer** 1.

frajerski *a. pot.* sucker's.

frajerstwo *n. pot.* naiveness.

frak *mi Gen.* -a tail coat, tails.

frakcja *f.* 1. (*partii*) fraction, faction; **frakcja parlamentarna** parliamentary fraction. 2. *chem., geol., druk.* fraction.

frakcjonista *mp* member of a political fraction.

frakcyjność *f.* fractionary character.

frakcyjny *a.* 1. *polit.* factional. 2. *chem.* fractional.

frakowy *a.* dress; (*koszula, kamizelka*) dress.

fraktal *mi geom.* fractal.

fraktura *f. druk.* Fraktur.

frakturowy *a.* Fraktur, German type.

framuga *f.* frame, embrasure.

franca *f. uj.* (*choroba*) 1. bug, scrud; **złapać francę** catch a bug. 2. *uj.* (*kobieta*) bitch, slut. 3. *uj.* (*rzecz*) shit.

franciszkanin *mp pl.* -anie *Gen.* -anów Franciscan (monk), Grey Friar.

franciszkanka *f. Gen.pl.* -ek Franciscan (nun), Poor Clare.

franciszkański *a.* Franciscan.

Francja *f.* France.

francuski *a.* French; (*język, literatura, kultura*) French; **ciasto francuskie** puff pastry; **klucz francuski** monkey wrench, adjustable spanner;

miłość francuska oral sex, fellatio *l.* cunnilingus; **francuska choroba** *przest.* any venereal disease; **francuski piesek** finicky eater; **warkocz francuski** French pleat; **po francusku** (= *w języku francu-skim*) in French; (= *na francuską modłę*) after the French manner. – *mi* **1.** (*język*) French. **2.** (*lekcja*) French (lesson).

francuskojęzyczny *a.* French-speaking; (*kraj, region, literatura*) Francophone.

francuskość *f.* Frenchness.

francuszczyzna *f.* **1.** (= *język*) French. **2.** (= *obyczaje*) French manners.

Francuz *mp* Frenchman.

francuzieć *ipf.* become Frenchified.

Francuzka *f. Gen.pl.* **-ek** Frenchwoman.

Frank *mp zw. pl. hist.* (*członek ludu germań-skiego*) Frank.

frank *mi Gen.* **-a** (*waluta*) franc.

frankista *mp*, **frankistka** *f. Gen.pl.* **-ek** *hist., po-lit.* Francoist.

frankistowski *a. hist., polit.* Francoist.

franko *n. indecl. handl.* carriage-free.

frankofil *mp Gen.pl.* **-ów**, **frankofilka** *f. Gen.pl.* **-ek** Francophile.

frankofilstwo *n.* Francophilism.

frankofob *mp pl.* **-i** *l.* **-y** Francophobe.

frankofobia *n. Gen.* **-ii** Francophobia.

frankolin *ma zool.* francolin (*Francolius*).

frankoński *a.* franconian; (*o języku, kulturze*) Frankish.

frankować *ipf.* frank.

frans *mi chem.* francium.

franszyza *f. prawn.* franchise.

frant *mp pl.* **-y** **1.** (= *spryciarz*) *żart.* slyboots; **z głupia frant** *pot.* naively. **2.** (= *elegant*) dandy.

frapować *ipf.* fascinate, intrigue.

frapujący *a.* intriguing.

frasobliwy *a. przest.* sorrowful.

frasować się *ipf. przest.* worry.

frasunek *mi* worry.

fraszka *f.* **1.** (= *drobiazg*) trifle. **2.** *teor.lit.* epi-gram.

fraternizacja *f.* fraternization.

fraternizować się *ipf.* fraternize.

fraza *f.* **1.** *jęz.* phrase; **fraza intonacyjna** *fon.* intonation unit. **2.** *muz.* phrase.

frazeolog *mp pl.* **-dzy** *l.* **-owie** phraseologist.

frazeologia *f. Gen.* **-ii** **1.** *jęz.* (*dział wiedzy*) phraseology. **2.** *jęz.* (= *zwroty, wyrażenia*) id-ioms, phrases, phraseology.

frazeologiczny *a. jęz.* phraseological; **związek frazeologiczny** expression, idiom, phrase.

frazeologizacja *f. jęz.* phraseologization.

frazeologizm *mi* *jęz.* idiom, expression, phrase.

frazes *mi* platitude; **sypać frazesami** mouth/utter platitudes; **tekst pełen frazesów** boiler-plate; **puste frazesy** claptrap.

frazować *ipf. teor.lit., muz.* phrase.

frazowy *a.* phrasal.

fregata *f.* **1.** *żegl.* frigate. **2.** *zool.* frigate bird (*Fregatidae*).

frekwencja *f.* **1.** (= *liczba uczestników*) atten-dance; **niska frekwencja** low/poor attendance. **2.** *kino* frequency. **3.** *mat.* frequency.

frekwencyjny *a.* frequency; **słownik frekwen-cyjny** *jęz.* frequency dictionary.

frencz *mi Gen.* **-a** *Gen.pl.* **-y** *l.* **-ów** trench coat.

frenetyczny *a.* frenetic; (*oklaski, brawa*) wild.

frenolog *mp pl.* **-dzy** *l.* **-owie** phrenologist.

frenologia *f. Gen.* **-ii** phrenology.

frenologiczny *a.* phrenological.

freon *mi chem.* CFC, chlorofluorocarbon.

fresk *mi* **1.** (*malowidło*) fresco; **pokrywać coś freskami** fresco sth. **2.** (*technika twórcza*) fresco; **w technice freskowej** in fresco.

freskowy *a.* fresco, frescoed; (*malarstwo, tech-nika*) fresco.

fretka *f. Gen.pl.* **-ek** *zool.* ferret (*Mustela puto-rium furo*).

freudowski *a.* Freudian; **freudowskie przejęzy-czenie** Freudian slip.

freudysta *mp*, **freudystka** *f. Gen.pl.* **-ek** Freudi-an.

freudyzm *mi* Freudianism.

frez *mi techn.* cutter, fraise.

frezarka *f. Gen.pl.* **-ek** *techn.* milling machine.

frezer *mp* milling machine operator.

frezerstwo *n. techn.* milling.

frezja *f. bot.* freesia (*Freesia*).

frezować *ipf. techn.* mill.

frędzel *mi* **-dzl-** *Gen.* **-a** fringe, knotting.

friko *n. indecl. pot.* for free; **zrobić coś za friko** do sth for freebie; **towar za friko** freebie.

front *mi* **1.** (*przód*) front, face; (*kolumny sa-mochodów, kompanii*) fore part; **front atmosfe-ryczny** *meteor.* front, frontal system. **2.** (*budyn-ku*) front, facade; **mieszkać od frontu** live in the front part of the house. **3.** *wojsk.* (= *pole bitwy*) the front; **linia frontu** front line; **być na froncie** be in the front line; **na wszystkich frontach** on all fronts; **działać na kilka frontów** *przen.* play the field; **działać na dwa fronty** have a foot in both camps; **zabezpieczyć się na wszystkich frontach** cover all the bases; **zwyciężać na wszystkich frontach** *przen.* win on all fronts; **zmienić front** *przen.* change front, do about-face. **4.** *wojsk.* (= *kierunek działań strategicznych*) front; **front wschodni** Eastern front; **front narodowy** *przen.* the Popular Front; **front wyzwolenia** liberation front.

frontalnie *adv.* frontally.

frontalny *a.* **1.** (= *przedni*) frontal, front; (*atak*) frontal. **2.** *anat.* frontal; **kość frontalna** frontal bone; **arteria frontalna** frontal artery.

fronton *mi* **1.** (*budynku*) frontage, frontal. **2.** (*zwieńczenie*) pediment, frontispiece, fronton.

frontowiec *mp* **-wc-** *pl.* **-y** front-line soldier.

frontowy *a.* **1.** (= *na przedzie*) front, frontal; (*napis, elewacja*) front. **2.** *wojsk.* front; (*żoł-nierz, służba*) front-line. **3.** *meteor.* front; (*bu-rza, mgła, opady*) front. **4.** *przest.* (= *od ulicy*) front; (*mieszkanie, kamienica*) street facing.

frontyspis *mi druk.* frontispiece.

frotaż *mi sztuka* frottage.

froterka *f. Gen.pl.* **-ek** floor polisher.

froterować *ipf.* polish.

frotowy *a.* terry; (*ręcznik*) terry towel.

frotte *a. indecl.* terry; **ręcznik frotte** terry towel.

frr *int.* whirr.

fruktoza *f. chem.* fructose, laevulose, fruit sugar.

frunąć *pf. zob.* **fruwać.**

frustracja *f. psych.* frustration.

frustracyjny *a.* frustration, frustrated.

frustrat *mp,* **frustratka** *f. Gen.pl.* **-ek** frustrated *l.* disgruntled person.

frustrować *ipf.* frustrate, exasperate, infuriate. ~ **się** *ipf.* get frustrated.

frutarianin *mp* fruitarian.

fruwać *ipf.* **1.** (*o ptakach*) fly. **2.** (*o lekkich rzeczach*) flutter, fly. **3.** *przen.* (= *oddalać się*) fly away; **fruwaj stąd!** *pot.* buzz off!, beat it!

frycowe *n. Gen.* **-ego** *pot.* loss incurred because of inexperience; **zapłacić frycowe** pay for one's experience.

fryga *f.* humming-top; **zwinny jak fryga** brisk, sprightly.

Frygia *f. Gen.* **-ii** *hist.* Phrygia.

frygijski *a. hist.* Phrygian; **czapka frygijska** Phrygian *l.* liberty cap.

frykas *mi Gen.* **-a** kickshaw, delicacy.

frykatywność *f. jęz.* fricativeness.

frykatywny *a. jęz.* fricative; **spółgłoska frykatywna** fricative.

frymarczyć *ipf. pot.* (= *sprzeniewierzać*) misappropriate.

frymuśny *a.* exquisite.

frytka *Gen.pl.* **-ek** *zw. pl.* French fry; *Br.* chip.

frytkownica *f.* deep fryer; *Br.* chip pan.

frywolnie *adv.* frivolously.

frywolny *a.* frivolous.

fryz[1] *mi Gen.* **-u** **1.** *bud.* frieze. **2.** *sztuka* frieze. **3.** *techn.* parquet boards.

fryz[2] *ma Gen.* **-a** *zool.* (*krowa*) **1.** Friesian cow. **2.** *zool.* (*koń*) Friesian horse.

Fryzja *f. geogr.* Friesland.

fryzjer *mp* hairdresser; **fryzjer męski** barber; (*zakład*) barber shop; **pójść do fryzjera** go to the hairdresser *l.* barber.

fryzjerka *f. Gen.pl.* **-ek** hairdresser.

fryzjerski *a.* hairdresser's; **salon fryzjerski** hair salon.

fryzjerstwo *n.* hairdressing.

fryzura *f.* haircut, hairstyle.

Fryzyjczyk *mp,* **Fryzyjka** *f. Gen.pl.* **-ek** Frisian.

fryzyjski *a.* (*o języku itp.*) Frisian; *hodowla* (*o rasach zwierząt domowych*) Friesian.

ftalowy *a. chem., techn.* phthalic; **farba ftalowa** phthalic paint; **bezwodnik/kwas ftalowy** phthalic anhydride/acid.

fu *int.* (*wyraża naganę l. udawaną zgrozę*) fie (for shame); (*wyraża obrzydzenie*) ugh, phew; **fu, ale ohyda!** ugh, disgusting!

fucha *f.* **1.** *pot.* (*praca*) sideline, odd job. **2.** *pot.* (= *fuszerka*) bungle.

fuga[1] *f. muz.* fugue.

fuga[2] *f.* **1.** *bud.* (*wypełnienie*) jointing. **2.** *techn.* (*rowek*) rift, joint.

fugować *ipf.* joint.

fugowy *a. muz.* fugue.

fuj *int.* phew!, ugh!

fujara *f. l. mp decl. like f. Gen.pl.* **-r** *l.* **-ów** *pot.* (= *niezdara*) galoot. – *f. wulg.* (= *penis*) dick, prong, rod.

fujarka *f. Gen.pl.* **-ek** pipe.

fukać *ipf.,* **fuknąć** *pf.* **-ij** **1.** (*o zwierzętach*) snort, huff. **2.** *pot.* (= *strofować*) rate (*na kogoś* sb).

fuks *mi Gen.* **-a** *pot.* (= *szczęście*) fluke; **mieć fuksa** fluke; **fuksem** by a fluke. – *mp pl.* **-y** *pot.* (= *nowicjusz*) Johnny raw. – *ma sport* (*koń*) dark horse.

fuksja *f. bot.* fuchsia (*Fuchsia*).

fuksyna *f. chem.* fuchsine.

ful *mi Gen.* **-a** *karty* full hand, full house.

fular *mi* foulard.

fulguryt *mi min.* fulgurite.

fulmar *ma zool.* fulmar (*Fulmarus glacialis*).

fumarola *f. geol.* fumarole.

fumarowy *a. chem.* **kwas fumarowy** fumaric acid.

fumigacja *f. roln.* fumigation.

fundacja *f.* **1.** (= *fundowanie*) foundation. **2.** (*instytucja*) foundation.

fundacyjny *a.* foundation; (*statut*) charter.

fundament *mi* **1.** (*budynku*) foundation(s), groundwork. **2.** *przen.* (= *podstawa*) foundation; (*teorii*) fundament; **kłaść fundamenty pod coś** lay the foundation(s) for sth.

fundamentalista *mp* fundamentalist.

fundamentalizm *mi* fundamentalism.

fundamentalny *a.* fundamental; (*ustawa, znaczenie jakiegoś faktu*) basic, fundamental.

fundamentować *ipf. bud.* found.

fundamentowy *a. bud.* foundation; **ława fundamentowa** foundation course.

fundator *mp* **1.** (= *ofiarodawca*) founder, benefactor, endower. **2.** *żart.* (= *pokrywający koszty jakiejś rozrywki*) treater.

fundatorka *f. Gen.pl.* **-ek** **1.** (= *ofiarodawczyni*) founder, benefactor, endower. **2.** *żart.* (= *pokrywająca koszty jakiejś rozrywki*) treater.

fundnąć *pf.* **-ij,** **fundować** *ipf. pot.* (= *pokryć koszty jakiejś rozrywki*) treat (*coś komuś* sb to sth); (*stypendium*) found.

fundować *ipf.* **1.** (= *ofiarować pieniądze na cel społeczny*) endow. **2.** *pot.* (= *pokrywać koszty jakiejś rozrywki*) treat.

fundusz *mi Gen.pl.* **-y** *l.* **-ów** **1.** (= *pieniądze na cel społeczny*) fund; **fundusz dyspozycyjny** discretionary fund; **fundusz płac** wages budget; **fundusz inwestycyjny** investment fund; **fundusz socjalny** social fund; **fundusz rezerwowy** reserve fund; **otwarty fundusz emerytalny** pension/retirement fund; (*fundusze organizacji*) coffer; **fundusze publiczne** the public purse, public money; **asygnować fundusze** assign funds (*na coś* for sth); **gromadzić fundusze** raise funds/finance (*na coś* for sth); **obcinać fundusze** tighten/pull in the purse strings. **2.** *pot.* (= *zasób gotówki*) funds.

fungicyd *mi chem.* fungicide.

funkcja *f.* **1.** (= *stanowisko*) position, function;

funkcja kustosza curatorship; **funkcja redaktora** editorship; **pełnić funkcję** act as, do duty for; **pełnić kilka funkcji jednocześnie** wear several hats. **2.** (= *realizowanie czynności*) function, facility; **funkcja pamięci** (*w aparacie telefonicznym*) memory facility; **funkcja przeszukiwania** search function; **spełniać funkcję czegoś** perform a function of, serve the function of; **funkcja semantyczna** *jęz.* semantic function; **funkcja zdaniowa** *log.* propositional function; **funkcja harmoniczna** *muz.* harmonic function. **3.** *fil.* function. **4.** *mat.* function; **funkcja algebraiczna** algebraic function; **funkcja analityczna** analitic function; **funkcja ciągła** continuous function; **funkcja odwrotna** inverse function; **funkcja okresowa** periodic function; **funkcja pierwotna** primitive; **funkcja podcałkowa** integrand; **funkcja prawdopodobieństwa** probability function; **funkcja rzeczywista** real-valued function; **funkcja stała** constant function; **funkcja trygonometryczna** trigonometric function; **funkcja wielowartościowa** multivalued function; **funkcja wykładnicza** exponential function; **x jest funkcją y** x is a function of y.

funkcjonalność *f.* functionality.

funkcjonalny *a.* **1.** (= *związany z funkcjonowaniem czegoś*) functional; **semantyka funkcjonalna** *jęz.* functional semantics; **psychologia funkcjonalna** *psych.* functional psychology. **2.** (= *użyteczny*) practical, functional. **3.** *mat.* functional; **analiza funkcjonalna** functional analysis.

funkcjonariusz *mp* officer, functionary; (*państwowy*) public servant; (*policji*) policeman.

funkcjonować *ipf.* function.

funkcyjny *a.* functional, function; (*pracownik, oficer*) officer; **dodatek funkcyjny** monthly salary supplement for managerial staff; **klawisz funkcyjny** function key.

funktor *mi Gen.* **-a** *log., mat.* functor.

funt *mi Gen.* **-a** **1.** (*pieniądz*) pound; **funt szterling** (pound) sterling. **2.** (*jednostka wagi*) pound; **on nie jest wart funta kłaków** he isn't worth a crumpet *l.* a hoot.

fura *f.* **1.** *pot.* (= *wóz konny*) wagon. **2.** *sl.* (= *samochód*) wheels. **3.** *pot.* (= *mnóstwo*) heaps, lots, no end (*of sth*).

furan *mi chem.* furan.

furażerka *f. Gen.pl.* **-ek** forage cap.

furczeć *ipf.* **-ę -ysz, furknąć** *pf.* **-ij** **1.** (*o maszynie*) rumble, hum. **2.** (*o ptaku*) flutter.

furgon *mi* fourgon.

furgonetka *f. Gen.pl.* **-ek** van; **furgonetka policyjna** patrol wagon, police wagon.

furia *f. Gen.* **-ii** **1.** (= *wściekłość*) fury; **atak** *l.* **napad furii** a fit of rage; **dostać furii** go up in the air; **dzika furia** savage *l.* unbridled fury; **wpaść w furię** fly into a rage; **w (ślepej) furii** in a (blind) fury. **2.** *mit.* the Furies; **wściekły jak furia** furious.

furiacki *a.* raging.

furiat *mp uj.* madman.

furiatka *f. Gen.pl.* **-ek** *uj.* madwoman.

furknąć *pf.* **-ij** *zob.* **furczeć.**

furkot *mi* **1.** (= *odgłos skrzydeł*) flutter. **2.** (= *warkot*) whirr, buzz.

furkotać *ipf.* **-czę -czesz** *l.* **-cę -cesz, -cz** whirr, burr; (*o ptakach*) drum.

furman *mp* wagoner.

furmanka *f. Gen.pl.* **-ek** horsewagon.

furora *f.* furor; **zrobić furorę** make a hit (*wśród kogoś* with sb).

furta *f.* gate.

furtka *f. Gen.pl.* **-ek** gate; **zostawić sobie otwartą furtkę** have two strings/a second string to one's bow.

fusowaty *a.* dreggy.

fusy *pl. Gen.* **-ów** dregs; (*kawowe*) coffee grounds; (*w winie*) lees; **wróżyć z fusów** read tea leaves.

fuszer *mp pot.* botcher.

fuszerka *f. Gen.pl.* **-ek** *pot.* botch, bungle, screw-up.

fuszerować *ipf. pot.* botch, bungle, screw up.

futbol *mi sport* **1.** (= *piłka nożna*) association football, soccer. **2. futbol amerykański** American football.

futbolista *mp* football-player, footballer.

futbolowy *a.* football.

futeralik *mi Gen.* **-a** case, holder.

futerał *mi* holder, case, box.

futerko *n. Gen.pl.* **-ek** **1.** (*płaszcz*) fur coat. **2.** (*wyprawiona skóra*) fell.

futerkowy *a.* fur; (*zabawka, kołnierz*) furry; **zwierzęta futerkowe** fur-bearing animals; **tkanina futerkowa** *tk.* fur fabric.

futro *n. Gen.pl.* **-ter** **1.** *ubiór* fur; (*płaszcz*) fur coat; **futro z norek** mink coat; **futro ze srebrnych lisów** fox; **futro karakułowe** Persian lamb coat; **sztuczne futro** artificial fur. **2.** *kuśnierstwo* (= *wyprawiona skóra*) fell. **3.** *zool.* (= *sierść*) (coat of) fur, pelt, pelage, hair; **futro letnie/zimowe** summer/winter coat.

futrować *ipf. bud.* plaster, board, line.

futryna *f. bud.* door-casing, doorframe, door-trim.

futrzany *a.* (= *zrobiony z futra*) fur.

futrzarka *f. Gen.pl.* **-ek** *zob.* **futrzarz.**

futrzarski *a.* furrier's.

futrzarstwo *n.* furriery.

futrzarz *mp* furrier.

futrzasty *a.* furry.

futurolog *mp pl.* **-dzy** *l.* **-owie** futurologist.

futurologia *f. Gen.* **-ii** futurology.

futurologiczny *a.* futurological.

futurysta *mp,* **futurystka** *f. Gen.pl.* **-ek** futurist.

futurystyczny *a.* futuristic.

futuryzm *mi* futurism.

fuzja[1] *f. ekon.* merger, fusion.

fuzja[2] *f. przest.* (= *strzelba*) rifle.

fuzle *pl. Gen.* **-i** *chem.* **1.** fusel oils. **2.** *pot.* (= *męty, osad*) dregs, grounds.

fuzlowy *a. chem.* (of) fusel oil; **olej fuzlowy** fusel oil.

G

G, g *n. indecl.* (*litera*) G, g; **G jak Genowefa** G is for Golf; G as in Golf.

G *n. indecl. muz.* G; **G-dur** G major; **g-moll** G minor.

gabardyna *f.* gabardine.

gabardynowy *a.* gabardine.

gabaryt *mi* **1.** *techn.* overall dimensions. **2.** *bud.* limiting outline.

gabinet *mi* **1.** (= *pomieszczenie do pracy umysłowej*) study (room); (= *miejsce urzędowania*) office; **gabinet profesorski** professor's room. **2.** *med.* (= *pokój przyjęć*) doctor's office; *Br.* surgery; **gabinet dentystyczny** dental office, dentist's office; *Br.* dental surgery. **3.** (= *pomieszczenie mieszczące zbiór eksponatów l. miejsce rozrywki*) room, chamber; **gabinet figur woskowych** waxworks; waxwork gallery; **gabinet grozy** chamber of horror; **gabinet luster/osobliwości** mirror/curiosity room; chamber of mirrors/curiosities. **4.** *polit.* cabinet.

gabinetowy *a.* **1.** (= *służący do wyposażenia gabinetu*) study. **2.** *polit.* cabinet.

gablota *f.* **1.** showcase, display cabinet. **2.** *sl.* (= *samochód*) wheels.

gablotka *f. Gen.pl.* **-ek** = gablota 1.

Gabon *mi geogr.* Gabon.

Gabonka *f. Gen.pl.* **-ek**, **Gabończyk** *mp* Gabonese.

gaboński *a.* Gabonese; **żmija gabońska** *zool.* gaboon viper (*Bitis gabonica*).

gabro *n. indecl. geol.* gabbro.

gacek *ma* **-ck-** *zool.* long-eared bat (*Plecotus*); **gacek wielkouch** brown long-eared bat (*P. auritus*).

gach *ma* **1.** *pog.* (= *kochanek*) secret lover; *przest.* gallant. **2.** *myśl.* (= *samiec zająca*) buck hare.

gacie *pl. Gen.* **-i** *pot.* (= *majtki, szorty*) underpants, shorts; *Br.* pants; (= *długie kalesony*) drawers, long johns; *żart.* (= *spodnie*) pantaloons.

gad *ma zool.* (*t. uj. o człowieku*) reptile.

gadać *ipf. pot.* talk, speak, chat, chatter, babble; **gadać od rzeczy** talk nonsense; **gada, co mu ślina na język przyniesie** he says the first thing that comes into his head; **gadaj zdrów!** whatever you say!; **co tu dużo gadać** (there's) no need for words; **szkoda gadać** don't even ask, there's nothing to say.

gadane *n. Gen.* **-ego** *pot.* smooth talk; **mieć gadane** be a smooth talker.

gadanie *n. pot.* chat, chatter, talking; **bez gadania** without hesitation, without a word; **austriackie gadanie** *przest.* gibberish.

gadanina *f. iron.* chatter, babbling; **czcza gadanina** idle chatter, blather, (a lot of) wind.

gadatliwość *f.* talkativeness, loquacity, garrulousness.

gadatliwy *a.* talkative, loquatious, garrulous.

gadget *mi zob.* **gadżet**.

gadka *f. Gen.pl.* **-ek 1.** *pot.* chat; **gadka szmatka** empty words. **2.** *przest.* (= *opowiadanie ludowe*) folk tale.

gadolin *mi chem.* gadolinium.

gadolinit *mi min.* gadolinite.

gadożer *ma orn.* short-toed (snake) eagle (*Circaetus gallicus*).

gadu-gadu *n. indecl. pot.* chit-chat.

gadulstwo *n.* garrulousness.

gaduła *f. l. mp decl. like f. Gen.pl.* **-ł l. -ów** *pot., żart.* chatterbox, windbag, tattler.

gadzi *a. t. przen.* reptilian, reptile.

gadzina *f.* **1.** *emf.* (= *pełzające zwierzę, gad*) reptile; *zbiorowo* vermin. **2.** *pot.* (= *nikczemnik*) creep, sneak. **3.** *emf.* (= *stworzenie, zwierzę*) critter; *przest.* (= *inwentarz żywy*) livestock.

gadżet *mi* gadget.

gaelicki *a. jęz.* Gaelic.

gafa *f.* gaffe, faux pas; **strzelić gafę** make *l.* commit a gaffe; put one's foot in it *l.* in one's mouth; drop a brick.

gafel *mi* **-fl-** *Gen.* **-a** *Gen.pl.* **-ów** *żegl.* gaff.

gaflowy *a. żegl.* gaff-rigged; **żagiel gaflowy** gaffsail; **ożaglowanie gaflowe** gaff rig.

gaftopsel *mi* **-sl-** *Gen.* **-a** *żegl.* gafftopsail.

gag *mi kino* gag.

gagat *mi min.* jet.

gagatek *mp* **-tk-** *pl.* **-i** *żart.* good-for-nothing, scamp, rogue.

gailardia *f. Gen.* **-ii** *bot.* gaillardia (*Gaillardia*).

gaj *mi* grove, thicket; **święty gaj** *rel.* sacred grove.

Gaja *f. Gen.* **Gai** *mit.* Gaia.

gaja *f. Gen.* **gai** *żegl.* guy.

gajal *ma zool.* gayal (*Bos frontalis*).

gajowiec *mi* **-wc-** *Gen.* **-a** *bot.* yellow archangel (*Lamiastrum galeobdolon*).

gajowy *mp* gamekeeper.

gajówka[1] *f. Gen.pl.* **-ek** gamekeeper's lodge.

gajówka[2] *f. Gen.pl.* **-ek** *orn.* (= *pokrzewka*) warbler.

Gal *mp pl.* **-owie** Gaul.

gal[1] *mi Gen.* **-u** *tylko sing. chem.* gallium.

gal² *mi Gen.* **-a** *fiz.* (*jednostka przyśpieszenia*) gal.

gala *f.* 1. (*uroczystość*) gala. 2. (*strój*) gala dress; **w pełnej gali** in full dress, in gala. 3. **gala flagowa** *żegl.* flag display.

galabija *f. Gen.* **-bii** jellaba, jellabah.

galago *n. indecl. zool.* bush baby, galago (*Galago senegalensis*).

galaktodendron *mi bot.* cow tree (*Brosimium galactodendron*).

galaktometr *mi techn.* lactometer, lactodensimeter.

galaktoza *f. chem.* galactose.

galaktozemia *f. Gen.* **-ii** *pat.* galactosemia.

galaktyczny *a. astron.* galactic.

galaktyka *f. astron.* galaxy; **Galaktyka** the Galaxy, the Milky Way.

galalit *mi chem., techn.* galalith.

galalitowy *a.* galalith.

galant *mp przest.* dandy, gallant, man of fashion.

galanteria *f. Gen.* **-ii** 1. (= *grzeczność*) gallantry. 2. (= *wyroby ozdobne*) accessories, fancy goods; **galanteria skórzana** leather accessories.

galanteryjny *a.* accessory.

galantyna *f. kulin.* galantine.

Galapagos *pl. indecl.* (*także* **Wyspy Galapagos**) the Galàpagos Islands.

galar *mi Gen.* **-a** *żegl.* barge.

galareta *f.* (*rodzaj substancji*) jelly; *kulin.* aspic; **trząść się jak galareta** *przen.* shake like a jelly.

galaretka *f. Gen.pl.* **-ek** jelly, gelatin, gelatine; (*deser*) jello; *Br.* jelly.

galaretnica *f. bot.* (*rodzaj sinic*) nostoc (*Nostoc*).

galaretowacieć *ipf.* **-eję -ejesz** gelatinize.

galaretowaty *a.* gelatinous, jellylike; **tkanka galaretowata** *biol.* gelatinous fibre.

galaretówka *f. Gen.pl.* **-ek** *bot.* (*krasnorost*) gelidium, agarweed, agar (*Gelidium*).

galas *mi Gen.* **-a** *bot.* gall, oak-apple.

galasowy *a. bot.* gall.

galasówka *f. Gen.pl.* **-ek** *zool.* gallfly, gallwasp (*Cynips*).

galena *f.*, **galenit** *mi min.* galena.

galenowy¹ *a. chem.* galenic.

galenowy² *a. med.* Galenic.

galeon *mi żegl.* galleon.

galera *f. żegl.* 1. galley. 2. *zob.* **galery**.

galeria *f. Gen.* **-ii** 1. (= *ekspozycja, kolekcja, t. przen.*) gallery; **galeria sztuki** art gallery. 2. *bud.* gallery, ambulatory. 3. *teatr* the gallery, the gods; **na galerii** in the gallery, in the gods.

galeriowy *a. bud.* 1. gallery. 2. **las galeriowy** *ekol.* gallery forest.

galernik *mp hist.* galley slave.

galery *pl. Gen.* **-r** *hist.* (*kara*) the galleys; **skazać/zesłać kogoś na galery** condemn/send sb to the galleys.

Galia *f. Gen.* **-ii** Gaul.

Galicja *f. geogr.* Galicia (*in Spain or formerly in Poland*).

Galicjanin *mp pl.* **-anie** *Gen.* **-an**, **Galicjanka** *f. Gen.pl.* **-ek** Galician.

galicyjski *a.* Galician.

galicyzm *mi* Gallicism.

Galijka *f. Gen.pl.* **-ek** *zob.* **Gal**.

galijski *a.* Gaulish; *lit.* (= *francuski*) Gallic.

Galilea *f. Gen.* **-ei** *hist., geogr.* Galilee.

Galilejczyk *mp*, **Galilejka** *f. Gen.pl.* **-ek** Galilean.

galilejski *a.* Galilean; **Kana Galilejska** *Bibl.* Cana of Galilee.

galimatias *mi pot.* mess, muddle, pretty kettle of fish.

galion *mi żegl.* figurehead.

Galisyjczyk *mp*, **Galisyjka** *f. Gen.pl.* **-ek** Galician.

galisyjski *a. jęz.* Galician.

Gall *mp pl.* **-owie** *Gen.* **-ów** = **Gal**.

gallikanin *mp pl.* **-anie** *hist., rel.* Gallican.

gallikanizm *mi hist., rel.* Gallicanism.

gallikański *a. hist., rel.* Gallican.

galman *mi min.* zinc ore (*smithsonite or hemimorphite*).

galon¹ *mi* (*jednostka objętości*) 1. gallon. 2. (*butla*) flask.

galon² *mi* (*taśma ozdobna*) galloon (lace).

galonik *mi Gen.* **-a** = **galon²**.

galop *mi* 1. gallop; **galopem** *przen.* (= *szybko*) at a gallop; **jechać galopem** ride at a (full) gallop; gallop; **wziąć kogoś do galopu** crack the whip at sb; discipline sb. 2. *muz.* gallopade.

galopada *f.* 1. (= *jazda galopem*) gallop, galloping. 2. **galopada myśli** *przen.* brainstorm.

galopować *ipf.* (*o wierzchowcu l. jeźdźcu*) gallop (away); **galopować naprzód** *przen.* (= *robić szybkie postępy*) gallop forward; **galopujące suchoty** *pat.* galloping consumption.

galoty *pl. Gen.* **-ów** *pot.*, *żart.* (= *kalesony*) long johns; (= *spodnie*) pantaloons.

galowo *adv.* festively.

galowy *a.* gala, festal, festive; **mundur galowy** *wojsk.* gala uniform; **przedstawienie galowe** gala performance.

galtonia *f. Gen.* **-ii** *bot.* summer hyacinth, cape hyacinth (*Galtonia candicans*).

galusowy *a. chem.* gallic.

galwaniczny *a.* 1. *el., fiz.* galvanic, voltaic; **ogniwo galwaniczne** galvanic battery. 2. *techn.* electrolytic; **powłoka galwaniczna** electroplated *l.* electrolytic coating.

galwanizacja *f.* 1. *techn.* electroplating. 2. *przen. l. przest., med.* galvanization; *med.* = **galwanoterapia**.

galwanizacyjny *a. techn.* electroplating.

galwanizator *mp* electroplater, galvanizer.

galwanizernia *f. Gen.pl.* **-ni** *l.* **-ń** *techn.* galvanizing *l.* electroplating plant.

galwanizerstwo *n. techn.* electroplating, galvanizing.

galwanizować *ipf.* 1. *techn.* electroplate, galvanize. 2. *przen. l. przest., med.* galvanize.

galwanochromia *f. Gen.* **-ii** *techn.* galvanic *l.* electrolytic coloring.

galwanometr *mi fiz.* galvanometer.

galwanoplastyczny *a.* galvanoplastic.

galwanoplastyka *f. techn.* galvanoplasty, electroforming.

galwanoskop *mi fiz.* galvanoscope.

galwanotaksja *f. biol.* galvanotaxis.

galwanotechniczny *a.* electroplating.

galwanotechnik *mp techn.* electroplating specialist, galvanizer.

galwanotechnika *f. techn.* electroplating technology.

galwanoterapia *f. Gen.* **-ii** *med.* electrotherapy, galvanotherapy.

galwanotropizm *mi biol.* galvanotropism.

galwanotyp *mi druk.* electrotype.

galwanotypia *f. Gen.* **-ii** *druk.* electrotyping.

gała *f. pot. zw. pl.* (= *oko*) **1.** blinker; *pl.* (= *wyłupiaste oczy*) goggle eyes. **2.** *sl., szkoln.* (= *ocena niedostateczna*) F.

gałązka *f. Gen.pl.* **-ek** twig, branch; **gałązka oliwna** *przen.* olive branch; **gałązka wawrzynu** (*motyw zdobniczy*) sprig of laurel.

gałązkowy *a.* herring-bone; **haft gałązkowy** *tk.* herring-bone stitch.

gałąź *f.* **-ęzi-** *Nom.pl.* **-e** *Ins.pl.* **-źmi** *l.* **-ziami 1.** (*drzewa, t.* = *dziedzina*) branch; **boczna gałąź** side branch. **2.** (= *odgałęzienie*) branching. **3.** *myśl.* (= *odnoga poroża*) tine, branch.

gałęzatka *f. Gen.pl.* **-ek** *bot.* (*zielenica*) cladophora (*Cladophora*).

gałgan *mi Gen.* **-a 1.** (*szmata*) rag; *pl.* (= *zniszczone ubranie*) rags. **2.** *pot. zw. żart.* (= *łobuz*) rogue, scamp.

gałganek *mi* **-nk-** *Gen.* **-a** *pot.* piece of cloth.

gałka *f. Gen.pl.* **-ek 1.** (*uchwyt, pokrętło*) knob. **2. gałka muszkatołowa** *kulin.* nutmeg. **3. gałka oczna** *anat.* eyeball.

gałuszka *f. Gen.pl.* **-ek** *bot.* (*także* **gałuszka kulecznica**) pillwort (*Pilularia globulifera*).

gama *f.* **1.** *muz.* scale; *hist., muz.* gamut; (*gama C-dur / c-moll*) the scale of C major/C minor; **ćwiczyć gamy** practice scales. **2.** (= *zakres, skala*) gamut, range; **pełna gama wrażeń** the full gamut of impressions.

Gambia *f. Gen.* **-ii** *geogr.* The Gambia.

Gambijczyk *mp*, **Gambijka** *f. Gen.pl.* **-ek** Gambian.

gambijski *a.* Gambian.

gambit *mi szachy* gambit.

gameta *f. zool.* gamete.

gametangium *n. sing. indecl. pl.* **-ia** *Gen.* **-iów** *bot.* gametangium.

gametofit *mi bot.* gametophyte.

gamma *a. indecl.* gamma; **promieniowanie gamma** *fiz.* gamma radiation.

gamoniowaty *a. pot.* halfwitted, dull.

gamoń *mp Gen.pl.* **-i** *l.* **-ów** *pot.* halfwit, dullard.

Gandawa *f. geogr.* Gaunt.

ganek *mi* **-nk-** *bud.* **1.** (= *zadaszone wejście do domu*) porch, veranda, verandah. **2.** (= *krużganek*) gallery, arcade. **3.** *górn.* gallery. **4.** *alpinizm* ledge.

gang *mi* gang; *pot.* mob.

Ganges *mi geogr.* the Ganges.

gangesowy *a.* Gangetic.

ganglion *mi anat., pat.* ganglion.

gangrena *f. pat.* (*t. przen.*) gangrene.

gangrenowaty *a. pat.* gangrenous.

gangster *mp* gangster, mobster.

gangsterski *a.* gangster.

ganiać *ipf.* (= *biegać*) run (about *l.* around); **ganiać za kimś** (*t.* = *zalecać się do kogoś*) chase (after) sb, run after sb; **ganiać za czymś** (*t.* = *starać się o coś*) chase after sth. **~ się** *ipf. pot.* race against each other.

ganić *ipf. lit.* rebuke, reprove, reproach.

ganoid *mi icht.* ganoid (fish).

gap *mp* **-pi-** *pl.* **-e** *zw. pl. pot.* gawker, onlooker.

gapa *f. l. mp decl. like f. pot.* **1.** (= *osoba nierozgarnięta*) dunce, dope, ninny; (= *marzyciel / ka*) daydreamer. **2. podróżować na gapę** steal a ride (*czymś* on sth); dodge the fare; (*statkiem l. samolotem*) stow away. **3.** *pot.* (= *gawron*) rook.

gapić się *ipf. pot.* gawk, gape, stare (*na kogoś / coś* at sb/sth).

gapiowaty, gapowaty *a. pot.* gawkish, foolish.

gapowe *n. Gen.* **-ego** *pot.* zapłacić gapowe, pay the penalty.

gapowicz *mp Gen.pl.* **-ów**, **gapowiczka** *f. Gen.pl.* **-ek** *pot.* passenger without a ticket, faredodger; (*na statku l. w samolocie*) stowaway.

gar *mi Gen.* **-a 1.** *pot.* large pot; *pl.* (= *sprzęty kuchenne*) pots and pans; (= *naczynia do zmywania*) the dishes, the washing-up; **męczyć się przy garach** slave over a hot stove. **2.** *hutn.* hearth, crucible.

garaż *mi Gen.pl.* **-y** *l.* **-ów** garage.

garażować *ipf.* garage.

garażowy *a.* garage; **muzyka garażowa** *muz.* garage music.

garb *mi* **1.** (*na plecach człowieka l. zwierzęcia*) hump; *pat.* humpback, hunchback. **2.** (*wypukłość, wybój*) hump, bump, protuberance.

garbarnia *f. Gen.pl.* **-i** *l.* **-ń** tannery.

garbarski *a.* tanning.

garbarstwo *n.* tanning.

garbarz *mp* tanner.

garbaty *a.* **1.** (*o człowieku*) humpbacked, hunchbacked; **garbate szczęście** *żart.* rotten luck. **2.** (= *uwypuklony*) humped, arched; **garbate wzgórza** rolling hills; **garbaty nos** aquiline nose. **–** *mp* humpback, hunchback.

garbek *mi* **-bk-** *Gen.* **-a** protrusion.

garbić *ipf.* **garbić plecy/ramiona** hunch one's back/shoulders. **~ się** *ipf.* hunch (up), slouch.

garbnik *mi Gen.* **-a** *chem., techn.* tannin.

garbnikodajny *a.* tannin-rich, tanniferous.

garbnikować *ipf. techn. zwł. żegl.* bark.

garbnikowy *a. chem.* **1.** tannic; **kwas garbnikowy** tannic acid. **2.** *techn.* tanning.

garbować *ipf. techn.* tan; **garbować komuś skórę** *pot.* tan sb's hide.

garbowanie *n. techn.* tanning.

garbus *mp pl.* **-y** *l.* **-i** *pog.* hunchback, humpback. **–** *mi Gen.* **-a** *pot.* (*samochód*) Beetle.

garda *f.* **1.** *broń* (= *osłona rękojeści*) guard, hiltguard. **2.** *sport* (= *postawa obronna*) guard.

gardenia *f. Gen.* **-ii** *bot.* gardenia (*Gardenia*).

garden-party *n. indecl.* garden party.

garderoba *f. Gen.pl.* -ób 1. (= *ubrania; pomieszczenie lub szafa na odzież l. kostiumy*) wardrobe. 2. (= *szatnia*) cloakroom.

garderobiana *f. Gen.* -ej, garderobiany *mp teatr* dresser.

gardło *n. Gen.pl.* -eł 1. (*t. przednia część szyi*) throat; *anat.* gullet, pharynx; zapalenie gardła *pat.* pharyngitis; obolałe gardło sore throat; chwycić kogoś za gardło grab sb by the throat; czuć ucisk w gardle (*jako objaw wzruszenia*) have a lump in one's throat; jak psu z gardła *pot., żart.* like it's been dragged through a hedge backwards; skoczyć komuś do gardła *t. przen.* be at sb's throat; stanąć komuś (kością) w gardle stick in sb's craw *l.* throat; mieć nóż na gardle *przen.* have a knife at one's throat; poderżnąć komuś/sobie gardło cut sb's/one's throat; przepłukać gardło *pot.* (= *napić się*) wet one's throat; *Br. sl.* tickle the tonsils; śmiać się na całe gardło laugh out loud; krzyczeć/wydzierać się na całe gardło shout/yell at the top of one's voice; zdzierać (sobie) gardło *pot.* strain one's voice. 2. *przest.* (*o gwałtownej śmierci l. egzekucji*) dać (za coś) gardło *l.* zapłacić (za coś) gardłem pay (for sth) with one's head; karać kogoś gardłem *l.* na gardle put sb to the sword. 3. (= *wąskie przejście*) neck; wąskie gardło *przen.* bottleneck.

gardłować *ipf. pot.* clamor, cry out (*za czymś* for sth) (*przeciwko komuś/czemuś* against sb/sth).

gardłowy *a.* 1. *anat.* pharyngeal, guttural. 2. (*o głosie, dźwięku*) throaty, guttural. 3. *fon.* pharyngeal.

gardzić *ipf.* + *Ins.* despise, scorn, disdain; treat (*sb l. sth*) with contempt *l.* disdain.

gardziel *f. pl.* -e *anat.* 1. gullet. 2. (= *ujście, otwór*) mouth. 3. *mot.* gardziel gaźnika carburetor choke.

gargulec *mi* -lc- *Gen.* -a *bud.* gargoyle.

garkuchnia *f. Gen.pl.* -i *pot.* canteen.

garłacz *ma Gen.pl.* -y *l.* -ów hodowla (*rasa gołębi*) pouter. – *mi Gen.* -a *Gen.pl.* -y *l.* -ów *wojsk., przest.* (= *nasadka do wystrzeliwania granatów*) 1. bomb thrower. 2. *broń, hist.* blunderbuss.

garmażer *mp* delicatessen producer.

garmażeria *f. Gen.* -ii delicatessen (store), deli.

garmażerka *f. Gen.pl.* -ek 1. *zob.* garmażer. 2. (= *wyrób produktów garmażeryjnych*) delicatessen production. 3. (= *produkty garmażeryjne*) delicatessen goods, deli goods.

garmażeryjny *a.* delicatessen, deli.

garmond *mi druk.* garamond.

garmondowy *a. druk.* garamond.

garna *f. zool.* blackbuck (*Antilope cervicapra*).

garnąć się *ipf.* -ij 1. flock, stick, cling (*do kogoś l. pod czyjąś opiekę* to sb). 2. garnąć się do pracy/nauki apply o.s. to work/study.

garncarka *f. Gen.pl.* -ek 1. *zob.* garncarz. 2. *zob.* garncarstwo.

garncarski *a.* potter's; koło garncarskie potter's wheel; piec garncarski potter's kiln.

garncarstwo *n.* pottery.

garncarz *mp* (*rzemieślnik*) potter.

garnczek *mi* -czk- *Gen.* -a small pot *l.* pan, saucepan.

garnek *mi* -nk- *Gen.* -a pot, pan; gliniany garnek clay pot; nie mieć co do garnka włożyć face starvation; przyganiał kocioł garnkowi (it's a case of) the pot calling the kettle black; zaglądać w cudze garnki *pot.* poke one's nose into other people's affairs.

garnela *f. Gen.pl.* -i *l.* -l *zool.* (= *krewetka z nadrodziny Crangonoidea*) (crangonoid) shrimp.

garniec *mi* -nc- *Gen.* -a *Gen.pl.* -ów *l.* -y 1. *hist.* (*miara objętości*) gallon. 2. *arch.* = garnek.

garnieryt *mi min.* garnierite.

garnirować *ipf.* 1. *kulin.* (= *dekorować*) garnish. 2. *przest.* (= *obszywać*) trim.

garnitur *mi* 1. *ubiór* suit. 2. (*zestaw, komplet*) set.

garniturek *mi* -rk- *Gen.* -a *emf. zob.* garnitur 1.

garniturowy *a.* suit.

garnizon *mi wojsk.* garrison.

garnizonowy *a.* garrison.

garnuszek *mi* -szk- *Gen.* -a 1. = garnczek. 2. (= *kubek*) mug. 3. *przen.* (= *utrzymanie*) być u kogoś na garnuszku be maintained by sb; be dependent on sb.

garota *f. hist.* garrotte; udusić kogoś garotą garrotte sb.

garować *ipf.* 1. (*o cieście drożdżowym*) be left to rise. 2. *pot.* (= *zbyt długo spać*) stew (in bed). 3. *sl.* (= *siedzieć w więzieniu*) do time.

garsoniera *f.* bachelor apartment.

garsonka *f.* (*ubranie*) skirt suit.

garstka *f. Gen.pl.* -ek 1. (= *niewiele, mała grupa*) handful, just a few; garstka zwolenników handful of supporters. 2. *emf.* = garść 1.

garść *f. pl.* -e *l.* -i 1. (= *zawartość dłoni*) handful, fistful; (= *dłoń*) hand; pełnymi garściami *przen.* (= *obficie*) with both hands, liberally; mieć kogoś w garści *pot.* have got sb; lepszy wróbel w garści niż gołąb na dachu a bird in the hand is worth two in the bush. 2. *przen.* (= *niewielka ilość l. grupa*) handful, a few; garść szczegółów a few details.

gasić *ipf.* 1. extinguish, put out; (*płomienie, zwł. wodą*) quench; *przen.* (= *kłaść kres, tłumić*) snuff out, quench; gasić pragnienie slake *l.* quench one's thirst. 2. gasić wapno *techn.* slake lime. 3. (= *wyłączać*) turn off, switch off. 4. *el.* (= *tłumić, wygaszać*) damp. 5. *przen.* gasić spadochron *lotn.* gather up a parachute; gasić piłkę *piłka nożna* kill *l.* trap a ball.

gasidło *n. Gen.pl.* -deł *przest.* snuffer.

Gaskonia *f. Gen.* -ii *geogr.* Gascony.

Gaskonka *f. Gen.pl.* -ek, Gaskończyk *mp* Gascon.

gaskoński *a.* Gascon.

gasnąć *ipf.* -snę śniesz, -śnij gasł *l.* gasnął gasła gaśli 1. (= *przestawać się palić*) go out, be extinguished; (= *przestawać działać*) go out, go dead; silnik (mi) zgasł the engine's died (on me). 2. (= *ciemnieć, tracić blask*) fade; jego gwiazda gaśnie *przen.* his star is fading. 3. (= *marnieć, ginąć*) be dying (out); *euf.* (= *umierać*) expire;

gasnąć w oczach be wasted; **nasz ród gaśnie** our line is dying out.

gastarbeiter *mp* gastarbeiter, foreign laborer.

gastrektomia *f. Gen.* **-ii** *chir.* gastrectomy.

gastroenterolog *mp med.* gastro-enterologist.

gastroenterologia *f. med.* gastro-enterology.

gastroenterologiczny *a. med.* gastro-entero-logical.

gastrolog *mp pl.* **-dzy** *l.* **-owie** *med.* gastrolo-gist.

gastrologia *f. Gen.* **-ii** *med.* gastrology.

gastrologiczny *a. med.* gastrological.

gastronom *mp pl.* **-owie** gastronome.

gastronomia *f. Gen.* **-ii** gastronomy.

gastronomiczny *a.* gastronomic, gastronomi-cal.

gastroskop *mi med.* gastroscope.

gastroskopia *f. Gen.* **-ii** *med.* gastroscopy.

gastroskopowy *a. med.* gastroscopic.

gastrula *f. biol.* gastrula.

gastryczny *a. pat.* gastric; **dolegliwości/zabu-rzenia gastryczne** gastric problems/disorders; **gorączka gastryczna** gastric fever.

gastryk *mp med.* gastric case.

gaśnica *f.* (fire) extinguisher.

gaśniczy *a.* firefighting; **środek gaśniczy** ex-tinguishing *l.* smothering medium.

gatki *pl. Gen.* **-tek** *pot.* = **gacie.**

gatunek *mi* **-nk-** 1. (*rodzaj*) genre, type, kind; **gatunek literacki** *teor.lit.* literary genre. 2. *biol.* species. 3. (= *jakość*) quality; **kawa w najlep-szym gatunku** finest quality coffee; **pierwszy ga-tunek** top quality; **pośledni gatunek** low quality.

gatunkowy *a. biol., chem., fiz.* 1. specific. 2. (= *wyborowy*) (high-)quality.

gaucho *mp zob.* **gauczo.**

gauczo *mp pl.* **-owie** gaucho.

gaus *mi Gen.* **-a** *fiz.* gauss.

gawęda *f.* 1. (= *opowieść*) tale, yarn. 2. (= *roz-mowa, pogawędka*) conversation.

gawędziarka *f. Gen.pl.* **-ek** *zob.* **gawędziarz.**

gawędziarski *a.* (*o stylu*) conversational, story-telling.

gawędziarstwo *n.* story-telling.

gawędziarz *mp* conversationalist, story-teller.

gawędzić *ipf.* (= *rozmawiać*) 1. chat, talk, con-verse. 2. (= *snuć opowieści*) spin yarns, tell sto-ries.

gawial *ma zool.* gharial, gavial (*Gavialis gan-geticus*).

gawiedź *f.* (crowd of) onlookers.

gaworzyć *ipf.* 1. (*o niemowlęciu*) babble. 2. *lit.* (= *prowadzić pogawędkę*) chat, chatter. 3. (= *wydawać dźwięki przypominające mowę*) chat-ter, jabber.

gawot *mi muz.* gavotte.

gawron *ma orn.* rook (*Corvus frugilegus*).

gaz *mi* 1. *fiz., chem., techn.* gas; **gaz błotny** *ge-ol.* marsh gas; **gaz bojowy** *wojsk.* war gas; **gaz łzawiący** tear gas; **gaz musztardowy** *wojsk.* mus-tard gas, yperite; **gaz płynny** *l.* **skroplony** lique-fied gas; **gaz pod ciśnieniem** *l.* **sprężony** com-pressed gas; **gaz rozweselający** laughing gas; **gaz szlachetny** *chem.* noble gas, inert gas; **gaz**

świetlny *przest.* city gas, illuminating gas; **gaz węglowy** *techn.* coal gas; **gaz ziemny** *geol.* natu-ral gas; **gazy spalinowe** *mot.* exhaust fumes. 2. (*do gotowania i ogrzewania*) (fuel) gas; **gotować na gazie** cook on gas. 3. *pot.* (= *energia, rozpęd*) gas, steam; **jechać pełnym gazem** *mot.* go flat out; **gazu!** step on it! 4. *pot.* **na (lekkim) gazie** *l.* **pod gazem** (= *podpity*) tipsy, under the influ-ence. 5. *pl. fizj.* (= *gromadzenie się gazu w prze-wodzie pokarmowym*) gas, wind, flatulence; **pu-szczać gazy** discharge gas; *euf.* break wind.

gaza *f. tk., med.* gauze.

gazda *mp pl.* **-owie** hill farmer (*in the Carpa-thians*).

gazeciarka *f. Gen.pl.* **-ek** (= *roznosicielka ga-zet*) 1. papergirl. 2. *zob.* **gazeciarz** 2.

gazeciarz *mp* 1. (= *roznosiciel gazet*) paper-boy. 2. (= *kioskarz, sprzedający gazety*) news-dealer; *Br.* newsagent.

gazela *f. Gen.pl.* **-l** *l.* **-i** *zool.* gazelle.

gazeta *f.* newspaper, paper; **gazeta poranna/popołudniowa** morning/evening paper; **gazeta brukowa** tabloid.

gazetka *f. Gen.pl.* **-ek** 1. (*ścienna itp.*) news-sheet. 2. (= *ulotka*) pamphlet.

gazetowy *a.* newspaper; **papier gazetowy** newsprint, newspaper; **styl** *l.* **język gazetowy** *zw. uj.* journalese.

gazik¹ *mi Gen.* **-a** (= *tampon z gazy*) (gauze) pad, swab, sponge.

gazik² *mi Gen.* **-a** *mot.* jeep.

gazobeton *mi bud.* aerated concrete.

gazociąg *mi techn.* gas pipe; (= *instalacja za-opatrująca w gaz*) gas mains.

gazolina *f. techn.* gasoline.

gazometr *mi chem.* gasometer.

gazomierz *mi Gen.* **-a** *techn.* gas meter.

gazon *mi* lawn.

gazować *ipf.* 1. (= *nasycać dwutlenkiem wę-gla*) carbonate. 2. (= *poddawać działaniu gazu*) treat *l.* spray (*sth*) with gas. 3. (= *zabijać gazem trującym*) gas. 4. *pot.* (*biec, spieszyć się*) speed on. 5. *pot.* (= *pić alkohol*) get tanked up.

gazowany *a.* carbonated; **woda gazowana** car-bonated water.

gazowiec *mi* **-wc-** *Gen.* **-a** *żegl.* liquid gas car-rier.

gazownia *f. Gen.pl.* **-i** *techn.* gasworks.

gazowniczy *a.* gas, gaswork.

gazownik *mp* (*technik*) gasman, gasworker.

gazowy *a.* 1. *chem., fiz.* gaseous; **tlen w stanie gazowym** gaseous oxygen. 2. *techn.* gas; **butla gazowa** gas bottle; **instalacja gazowa** gas supply; **komora gazowa** gas chamber; **piecyk/palnik ga-zowy** gas oven/burner; **maska gazowa** *wojsk.* gas mask; **silnik gazowy** *techn.* gas engine. 3. *pat.* **zgorzel gazowa** gas gangrene, gaseous gan-grene.

gazpacho *n. indecl. kulin.* gazpacho.

gazyfikacja *f. techn.* gasification.

gazyfikować *ipf. techn.* gasify.

gaździna *f.* hill-farmer's wife (*in the Carpa-thians*).

gaźnik *mi Gen.* **-a** *techn.* carburetor, *Br.* carburettor.

gaźnikowy *a. techn.* carburetor.

gaża *f. Gen.pl.* gaż *l.* **-y** (= *uposażenie, zwł. artysty l. wojskowego*) salary, pay.

gąb *f. zob.* **gęba.**

gąbczasty *a.* spongy; *nauk.* spongiform; **gąbczaste zwyrodnienie mózgu** *pat.* spongiform encephalopathy.

gąbka *f. Gen.pl.* **-ek 1.** (*do mycia*) sponge; **mieć umysł chłonny jak gąbka** have a brain like a sponge; **wyciskać kogoś jak gąbkę** *przen.* squeeze sb dry. **2.** *zool.* sponge, poriferan. **3.** *przest.* (= *usta*) mouth; **pieczone gołąbki nie lecą same do gąbki** roasted chickens do not fly to one's mouth.

gądziel *f. pl.* **-e** *Gen.* **-i** *bot.* carpet bugleweed, ajuga (*Ajuga reptans*).

gągoł *ma orn.* goldeneye (*Bucephala*).

gąsienica *f. ent., mot.* caterpillar.

gąsienicowy *a.* (*o pojeździe*) caterpillar.

gąsior *ma* (*orn.*) gander. – *mi Gen.* **-a 1.** *bud.* ridge tile. **2.** (= *butla*) flagon.

gąska *f. Gen.pl.* **-ek 1.** *emf. zob.* **gęś. 2.** (= *młoda gęś*) gosling. **3.** *pog.* (= *głupia l. naiwna kobieta*) goose. **4.** *bot.* (*grzyb*) man-on-horseback (*Tricholoma*).

gąszcz *mi Gen.pl.* **-ów** *l.* **-y 1.** (*krzaków, roślinności*) thicket; *lit.* boscage. **2.** (= *plątanina*) tangle; **gąszcz słów** *przen.* verbiage.

gbur *mp pl.* **-y** *obelż.* boor, lout, oaf, yokel.

gburowaty *a. obelż.* boorish, loutish, oafish.

gdakać *ipf.* **-czę -czesz** *l.* **-kam -kasz -cz** *l.* **-kaj 1.** (*o kurze*) cluck. **2.** *przen., pog.* (*o człowieku*) (= *zbyt dużo mówić*) yack, jabber.

Gdańsk *mi Gen.* **-a** *geogr.* Gdansk.

gderać *ipf. pot.* grouch, grumble.

gdy *conj.* **1.** (*wprowadza zdanie okolicznikowe czasu*) when; (*także*) as soon as; **obudziłem się, gdy było już jasno** I awoke when it became light; **zadzwonię do ciebie, gdy tylko będę mógł** I'll call you as soon as I can; **były to czasy, gdy kobiety chodziły w długich sukniach** they were the days when women wore long dresses; **teraz gdy już wszyscy jesteśmy razem** now that we're all together. **2.** (= *jeżeli*) if; **gdy chcesz oglądać program satelitarny, musisz przełączyć kanał** if you want to watch something on satellite, you'll have to change the channel.

gdybać *ipf. pot.* speculate.

gdyby *conj.* **1.** (*wprowadza zdanie warunkowe*) if; **gdyby to planował, powiedziałby nam** if he was planning it (*l.* if he were planning it), he'd tell us; **gdybym tam był wczoraj...** if I'd been there yesterday... **2.** (*w zdaniach wyrażających życzenie*) **och, gdybyś teraz była ze mną** if only you were with me now. **3.** **jak gdyby** as if, as though.

gdybyż *conj.* if only; **gdybyż można było uratować jej życie!** if only she could have been saved.

gdyż *conj. lit.* as, because; **dyrektor nie może się z panem widzieć, gdyż jest bardzo zajęty** the director cannot see you as he's very busy.

gdzie *adv. i pron. indecl.* **1.** (*zaimek pytajny i*

względny) where; **gdzie jest twój samochód?** where's your car?; **zaparkuję tam, gdzie znajdę wolne miejsce** I'll park where I find a space; **gdzie Rzym, gdzie Krym!** (as like as) chalk and cheese. **2.** **gdzie jak gdzie** of all places, never mind other places; **gdzie jak gdzie, ale w tym pokoju musi być porządek** never mind other rooms, we have to keep this one tidy. **3.** *pot.* (= *dokąd*) where; **gdzie idziesz?** where are you going? **4.** **byle gdzie** *l.* **gdzie bądź** anywhere, any place; **połóż to byle gdzie** put it anywhere. **5.** (*także* **gdzie tylko**) (= *wszędzie, gdzie...*) wherever; **gdzie spojrzysz, wszędzie dookoła widać drzewa** wherever you look there are trees all about. **6.** *przest. l. pot. w pytaniach* = **gdzieś**; **nie widzieliście gdzie mojego pióra?** haven't you seen my pen somewhere? – *particle* (*wyraża rezygnację*) **gdzie mi (tam) myśleć o wakacjach** how can I think of the holidays; **gdzie mi się (tam) równać z tobą** how can I compete with you; **gdzie tam! ciągle nic nie wiem** sure enough, I still don't know anything.

gdziekolwiek *adv.* wherever.

gdzieniegdzie *adv.* here and there, in some places.

gdzieś *adv.* **1.** somewhere, some place; **gdzieś słyszałem już o tym** I heard about it somewhere; **kozice można jeszcze spotkać gdzieś wysoko w górach** chamois can still be found somewhere high in the mountains; **mam cię gdzieś!** *pot.* up yours!, get stuffed! **2.** (= *dokądś*) somewhere; **znów gdzieś się spieszysz** you're rushing off somewhere again. **3.** *pot.* (*także* **gdzieś tak**) (*wyraża przybliżenie*) (somewhere) about *l.* around; **w domu będę gdzieś o czwartej** I'll be home (somewhere) around four.

gdzież *adv. emf.* (*w pytaniach wyrażających zdumienie l. irytację*) where on earth, where the hell, where ever; **gdzież ja to położyłem?** where on earth did I put it? – *particle emf.* = **gdzie.**

gdzieżby *part. emf.* = **gdzie.**

gehenna *f. lit.* Gehenna, torment; **przejść gehennę** suffer agonies.

gej *mp* gay.

gejowski *a.* gay.

gejsza *f.* geisha.

gejtaw *mi*, **gejtawa** *f. żegl.* clew line.

gejzer *mi Gen.* **-a** *geol.* geyser.

gejzeryt *mi geol.* geyserite.

gekon *ma zool.* (= *jaszczurka z rodziny Gekkonidae*) gecko.

gem *mi Gen.* **-a** *sport* game.

gemma *f. jubilerstwo* gem (*in a cameo or intaglio*).

gemowy *a. sport* game; **piłka gemowa** game ball.

gen *mi biol.* gene; **gen dominujący/recesywny** dominant/recessive gene; **gen letalny** lethal gene; **geny mitochondrialne** mitochondrial genes.

gencjana *f.* **1.** *bot.* gentian (*Gentiana*). **2.** *med.* gentian violet.

genealog *mp pl.* **-dzy** *l.* **-owie** genealogist.

genealogia *f. Gen.* **-ii 1.** (= *historia rodu*) genealogy, pedigree. **2.** (= *początek, pochodzenie*) origin, genesis.

genealogiczny *a.* genealogical; **drzewo genealogiczne** family tree; **tablica genealogiczna** genealogical table.

generacja *f.* generation.

generacyjny *a.* **1.** (= *pokoleniowy*) generational. **2.** *fiz.* generating; **lampa generacyjna** *el.* generating lamp.

generalia *pl. Gen.* **-ów 1.** (*sprawy l. względy ogólne*) general aspects. **2.** *fin.* (= *wydatki związane z przedsięwzięciem*) outlays.

generalicja *f. wojsk.* the generals.

generalissimus *mp pl.* **-owie** *wojsk.* generalissimo.

generalizacja *f.* generalization.

generalizować *ipf.* generalize.

generalnie *adv.* **1.** (= *ogólnie*) generally, in general; **generalnie rzecz biorąc** generally speaking; taking everything into consideration; all in all. **2.** (= *całkowicie*) generally, entirely, wholly.

generalny *a.* **1.** (= *ogólny, całkowity*) general; **generalne wnioski/wskazówki** general conclusions/directions; **próba generalna** dress rehearsal; **remont generalny** general repair *l.* overhaul. **2.** (*zasadniczy, najważniejszy*) general, main; **dyrektor generalny** director general; **konsul generalny** consul general; **sztab generalny** general staff.

generalski *a.* general's.

generał *mp pl.* **-owie** *wojsk., kośc.* general; **generał brygady** brigadier general.

generałowa *f. Gen.* **-ej** general's wife.

generator *mi Gen.* **-a** *techn., el., komp.* generator.

generatywista *mp,* **generatywistka** *f. Gen.pl.* **-ek** *jęz.* generativist.

generatywizm *mi jęz.* generativism.

generatywno-transformacyjny *a.* *jęz.* generative-transformational.

generatywny *a. jęz.* generative; **gramatyka generatywna** generative grammar.

generować *ipf. fiz., jęz.* generate; (= *wytwarzać*) produce.

genetyczny *a. biol.* (*t. o związku, pokrewieństwie*) genetic; (*także* **przekazywany genetycznie**) (*o cechach, chorobach*) genetically transmitted; **kod/materiał genetyczny** genetic code/material; **informacja genetyczna** genetic information; **inżynieria genetyczna** genetic engineering.

genetyk *mp* geneticist.

genetyka *f.* genetics.

Genewa *f.* Geneva.

genewski *a.* **konwencja genewska** *polit.* the Geneva Convention.

geneza *f.* genesis, origin.

genialnie *adv.* brilliantly, in a masterly manner. – *int.* bravo, superb, (that's) brilliant.

genialność *f.* genius, brilliancy.

genialny *a.* brilliant; (= *mistrzowski, wybitny*) masterly, outstanding.

genitalia *pl. Gen.* **-ów** *anat.* genitals, reproductive organs.

geniusz *mp Gen.* **-a** *Gen.pl.* **-y l.** **-ów** (*człowiek nieprzeciętnie zdolny, utalentowany*) **1.** genius. **2.** *mit.* genius, guiding spirit. – *mi Gen.* **-u** (= *genialność*) genius.

genotyp *mi biol.* genotype.

genotypowy *a. biol.* genotypic, genotypical.

Genua *f. Gen.* **-ui** *geogr.* Genoa.

Genueńczyk *mp* Genoan.

genueński *a.* Genoan.

geobiont *ma biol.* soil organisms.

geocentryczny *a. astron.* geocentric; **teoria geocentryczna** geocentric theory.

geochemia *f. Gen.* **-ii** geochemistry.

geochemiczny *a.* geochemical.

geochemik *mp* geochemist.

geochronologia *f. Gen.* **-ii** *geol.* geochronology.

geochronologiczny *a.* *geol.* geochronologic, geochronological.

geociepłownia *f. Gen.pl.* **-i** *techn.* geothermal heating plant.

geoda *f. geol.* geode.

geodeta *mp miern.* geodesist, (land) surveyor.

geodezja *f. miern.* geodesy, geodetics, surveying.

geodezyjny *a. miern.* geodesic, geodetic; **pomiary geodezyjne** geodesic measurements; **linia geodezyjna** geodesic line.

geoelektrownia *f. Gen.pl.* **-i** *techn.* geothermal power plant.

geoenergetyka *f. techn.* geothermal energy engineering.

geofit *mi bot.* geophyte.

geofizyczny *a. geol.* geophysical.

geofizyk *mp geol.* geophysicist.

geofizyka *f. geol.* geophysics; **geofizyka poszukiwawcza** geophysical prospecting.

geograf *mp pl.* **-owie** (= *specjalista w zakresie geografii*) geographer; *pot.* (= *nauczyciel geografii*) geography teacher.

geografia *f. Gen.* **-ii** geography; **geografia ekonomiczna** *l.* **gospodarcza** economic geography; **geografia fizyczna** physical geography; **geografia historyczna** historical geography; **geografia lingwistyczna** *l.* **językowa** linguistic geography; **geografia regionalna** regional geography.

geograficzny *a.* geographic, geographical; **długość geograficzna** (geographic) longitude; **szerokość geograficzna** (geographic) latitude; **współrzędne geograficzne** geographic coordinates; **północ geograficzna** true north; **granica geograficzna** geographic border; **środowisko geograficzne** geographic environment; **położenie geograficzne** geographical position *l.* location.

geoida *f. geogr.* geoid.

geolog *mp pl.* **-dzy l.** **-owie** geologist.

geologia *f. Gen.* **-ii 1.** (*dział wiedzy*) geology; **geologia dynamiczna** geodynamics; **geologia stosowana** applied geology. **2.** (= *budowa geologiczna*) geology.

geologiczny *a.* geologic, geological; **epoka/era geologiczna** geological epoch/era; **okres geologiczny** geological period; **formacja geologiczna**

geological formation; **system geologiczny** geological system.

geomagnetyczny *a.* geomagnetic; **pole geomagnetyczne** geomagnetic field; **zaburzenie pola geomagnetycznego** *meteor.* magnetic disturbance.

geomagnetyzm *mi* geomagnetism, terrestrial magnetism.

geometra *mp miern.* (land) surveyor.

geometria *f. Gen.* **-ii** geometry; **geometria analityczna** analytic geometry; **geometria elementarna** elementary geometry; **geometria euklidesowa** Euclidean geometry; **geometria nieeuklidesowa** non-Euclidean geometry; **geometria wykreślna** descriptive geometry; **geometria rzutowa** projective geometry; **geometria różniczkowa** differential geometry; **geometria przestrzenna** solid geometry.

geometryczny *a.* **1.** (*o geometrii*) geometric, geometrical; **figura geometryczna** geometric figure; **postęp geometryczny** *mat.* geometric progression *l.* series; **miejsce geometryczne** *mat.* locus; **średnia geometryczna** *mat.* geometric mean. **2.** (*o ornamencie*) geometrical.

geometryzować *ipf.* geometrize.

geomorfolog *mp pl.* **-dzy** *l.* **-owie** *geogr.* geomorphologist.

geomorfologia *f. Gen.* **-ii** *geogr.* geomorphology.

geomorfologiczny *a. geogr.* geomorphological, geomorphologic.

geoplastyk *mp* relief cartographer.

geoplastyka *f.* relief cartography.

geopolityczny *a.* geopolitical.

geopolityka *f. polit.* geopolitics.

geopotencjał *mi fiz.* geopotential.

georgiański *a. hist.* Georgian.

georgika *f. teor.lit.* georgic.

georginia *f. Gen.* **-ii** *bot.* dahlia (*Dahlia*).

geosfera *f. geol.* geosphere.

geostacjonarny *a.* *astron.* geostationary, geosynchronous; **satelita geostacjonarny** geostationary satellite; **orbita geostacjonarna** geosynchronous orbit.

geosynklina *f. geol.* geosyncline.

geotektoniczny *a. geol.* tectonic, geotectonic.

geotektonika *f. geol.* tectonics.

geotermia *f. fiz.* geothermics.

geotermiczny *a. geol.* geothermal, geothermic; **energia geotermiczna** geothermal energy; **gradient geotermiczny** geothermal gradient.

geotermodynamika *f. fiz.* geothermal dynamics, geothermics.

geotropizm *mi biol.* geotropism.

geotyp *mi biol.* geotype.

gepard *ma zool.* cheetah (*Acinonyx jubatus*).

geraniol *mi chem.* geraniol.

geranium *n. indecl. bot.* geranium, crane's-bill (*Geranium*).

gerbera *f. bot.* gerbera (*Gerbera*).

gereza *f. zool.* colobus (*Colobus*).

geriatra *mp med.* geriatrician, geriatrist.

geriatria *f. Gen.* **-ii** *med.* geriatrics, geriatric medicine.

geriatryczny *a. med.* geriatric.

german *mi chem.* germanium.

germanista *mp* (= *znawca literatury, języka, historii niemieckiej*) Germanist; (= *nauczyciel języka niemieckiego*) German teacher; (= *student germanistyki*) student of German.

germanistka *f. Gen.pl.* **-ek** *zob.* **germanista**.

germanistyczny *a. uniw.* German, Germanic.

germanistyka *f. uniw.* German *l.* Germanic studies.

germanizacja *f.* Germanization.

germanizacyjny *a.* (of *l.* pertaining to) Germanization; **ruch germanizacyjny** Germanization movement; **proces germanizacyjny** Germanization.

germanizator *ma* Germanizer.

germanizm *mi jęz.* Germanism.

germanizować *ipf.* Germanize.

germanofil *mp* Germanophile.

germanofilski *a.* Germanophile.

germanofilstwo *n.* Germanism.

germanofob *mp pl.* **-i** *l.* **-y** Germanophobe.

germanofobia *f. Gen.* **-ii** Germanophobia.

germański *a.* **1.** *hist.* Germanic, Teutonic; **język germański** *jęz.* Germanic language. **2.** *przen.* (= *niemiecki*) German.

geront *mp pl.* **-ci** *l.* **-owie** *hist.* geront.

gerontofilia *f. Gen.* **-ii** *pat.* gerontophilia.

gerontokracja *f. hist.* gerontocracy.

gerontolog *mp pl.* **-dzy** *l.* **-owie** gerontologist.

gerontologia *f. Gen.* **-ii** gerontology.

gerontologiczny *a.* gerontological.

gerundium *n. sing. indecl. pl.* **-dia** *Gen.* **-diów** *jęz.* gerund.

gerundivum *n. sing. indecl. pl.* **-wa** *Gen.* **-wów** *jęz.* gerundive.

geruzja *f. hist.* gerousia.

ges *n. indecl. muz.* G flat.

gest *mi* gesture, motion; **szeroki gest** sweeping gesture; (= *hojność*) open-handedness, generosity; **mieć szeroki gest** be generous, be a big spender, be free with money; **pusty gest** empty gesture; **teatralny gest** theatrical gesture; **gest symboliczny** symbolic gesture; **gest dobrej woli** *polit.* goodwill gesture.

gestagen *mi med.* gestagen.

gestaltyzm *mi psych.* Gestalt psychology.

gestapo *n. indecl. hist.* gestapo.

gestapowiec *mp* **-wc-** *pl.* **-y** *hist.* member of the gestapo.

gestapowski *a. hist.* gestapo.

gestia *f. Gen.* **-ii** *przest.* management, administration; **leżeć w czyjejś gestii** be *l.* lie in sb's hands.

gestykulacja *f.* gesticulation, gesturing.

gestykulować *ipf.* gesticulate, make gestures.

geszefciarski *a. pog.* unscrupulous, underhanded, shady.

geszefciarstwo *n. pog.* **1.** (= *spekulacja*) wheeling and dealing. **2.** (= *szachrajstwo*) shady business (dealings).

geszefciarz *mp pog.* shady businessman.

geszeft *mi pog.* shady business.

getry *pl. Gen.* **-ów** leggings, gaiters; (*do ćwiczeń*) leg warmers; (*krótkie*) spats.

getto *n. Loc.* **-tcie 1.** *hist.* ghetto. **2.** (= *zamknięte, odizolowane środowisko*) ghetto.

Getynga *f. geogr.* Göttingen.

gęba *f. Gen.pl.* **gąb 1.** *pot.* (= *usta*) trap, yap, bazoo; (*razem ze szczęką*) kisser *l.* kisseroo, chops; **na gębę** at sb's word; **trzymaj gębę na kłódkę** keep your mouth *l.* trap shut; **iść** *l.* **lecieć z gębą** run one's mouth; **gęba się komuś nie zamyka** sb runs at the mouth, sb is a chatterbox; **być mocny w gębie** be all talk, have a big mouth, be a bigmouth *l.* loudmouth; **gębę sobie kimś wycierać** spread dirt about sb; **mieć niewyparzoną gębę** have a foul mouth; **zamknąć komuś gębę** shut sb up, keep sb quiet; **zamknij gębę!** shut your mouth *l.* trap!; **nie mam do kogo gęby otworzyć** I have no one to talk to; **nie mam co do gęby włożyć** I don't have a bite to eat; **robić z gęby cholewę** go back on one's word; **zapomnieć języka w gębie** be at a loss for words, be tongue-tied; **zapomniałeś języka w gębie?** (has the) cat got your tongue? **2.** *pot., przen.* (= *ktoś na czyimś utrzymaniu*) mouth to feed. **3.** *pot.* (= *twarz*) mug, puss, face; **straszna gęba** ugly mug; **strzelić kogoś w gębę** punch sb in the face; **skuć komuś gębę** use sb's face as a punching bag; **pan/pani całą gębą** a gentleman/lady in every sense of the word, a gentleman/lady if there ever was one *l.* if I've ever seen one; **śmiać się całą gębą** roar with laughter. **4.** (*u zwierząt*) muzzle.

gębować *ipf. pot.* shoot one's mouth off.

gębowy *a.* oral; **narządy gębowe** *zool.* mouthparts.

gęgać *ipf.* **1.** (*o gęsi*) honk, gabble. **2.** *pot.* (= *mówić niewyraźnie, bezmyślnie*) jabber.

gęgawa *f. orn.* graylag (goose); *Br.* greylag (goose) (*Anser anser*).

gęgnąć *pf.* **-ij** *zob.* **gęgać.**

gęgot *mi* honking, gabbling.

gęsi *a.* goose; **gęsia skórka** goose bumps, gooseflesh; **iść gęsiego** walk (in) Indian *l.* single file.

gęsina *f. kulin.* goose.

gęsiówka *f. Gen.pl.* **-ek** *bot.* arabis, rock cress (*Arabis*).

gęstnieć *ipf.* **1.** (= *stawać się gęstym*) thicken, get thick; (*o lesie*) get *l.* become dense; (*o śniegu, deszczu*) get heavy; (*o dymie*) get thick *l.* dense. **2.** (= *intensyfikować się*) occur *l.* appear more frequently; get *l.* become heavier.

gęsto *adv.* **gęściej 1.** (= *zwarcie*) densely, thickly; (*o śniegu*) heavily; (*o piance*) thickly; (*o dymie*) densely; **gęsto poplątany** closely intertwined; **gęsto posadzone drzewa** trees planted close together; **kartka gęsto zapisana** page heavily written on; **gęsto zaludniony** densely *l.* heavily populated. **2.** (= *tłumnie*) closely, crowded together. **3.** (= *często*) heavily, frequently; **gęsto wypijali toasty** they drank toasts one after another; **często gęsto** again and again; **tłumaczyć się gęsto** be long on excuses.

gęstościomierz *mi Gen.* **-a** *fiz.* aerometer; hydrometer.

gęstość *f.* **1.** (= *zwartość*) (*cieczy, gazu*) density; (*powietrza, zadrzewienia*) denseness; (*syropu, śmietany*) thickness; **gęstość zaludnienia** population density; **gęstość zapisu** *komp.* density. **2.** *fiz.* mass density.

gęstwa *f.* dense grouping of sth; (*zarośla*) dense vegetation, thicket; (*las*) dense forest; (*ludzie*) crowd, throng (of people); **gęstwa włosów** thick head of hair.

gęstwina *f.* thicket, dense vegetation; (*las*) dense forest.

gęsty *a.* **gęstszy** *l.* **gęściejszy 1.** (= *zwarty*) (*o lesie, mgle, tłumie*) dense; (*o włosach, zupie, sosie, dymie*) thick; (*o brodzie*) bushy; (*o trawniku, zaroślach*) lush; (*o śniegu, deszczu*) heavy; (*o siatce, sitku*) fine; (*o betonie, ziemi*) compact; (*o drzewie, krzewie*) leafy; (*o druku*) close; **gęsty grzebień** fine-toothed comb. **2.** (= *częsty*) heavy, frequent; **gęsta strzelanina** heavy firing.

gęś *f.* **1.** *orn.* goose (*Anser*); **rządzić się jak szara gęś** act like sb owns the place; **niech cię gęś kopnie!** oh brother!; **rozmawiać z kimś jak gęś z prosięciem** talk at cross-purposes. **2.** *iron.* (= *kobieta naiwna, głupia*) dumb broad. **3.** *metal.* pig sow.

gęśle *pl. Gen.* **-i** *muz.* (primitive) fiddle.

Ghana *f. geogr.* Ghana.

Ghanka *f. Gen.pl.* **-ek** *zob.* **Ghańczyk.**

Ghańczyk *mp* Ghanian.

ghański *a.* Ghanian.

giaur *mp* giaour.

giąć *ipf.* **gnę gniesz, gnij 1.** (= *pochylać*) bow; (*głowę*) lower, bow; (*kolano, rękę*) bend; **giąć kark** *l.* **grzbiet** *przen.* kowtow. **2.** (= *odkształcać*) bend, curve; **meble gięte** bentwood furniture. ~ **się** *ipf.* **1.** (= *pochylać się*) lean *l.* bend over; (*w ukłonach*) bow. **2.** (= *odkształcać się*) bend.

gibki *a.* lithe, limber; (*o ciało*) supple; (*o zwinnych ruchach*) nimble, agile.

gibon *ma zool.* gibbon (*Hylobates*).

Gibraltar *mi geogr.* Gibraltar.

gibraltarski *a.* (of *l.* pertaining to) Gibraltar; **Cieśnina Gibraltarska** *geogr.* the Strait of Gibraltar.

gicz *f. pl.* **-e** *kulin.* (veal) shank.

giczoły *pl. pot.* (= *nogi*) shanks.

giełda *f.* **1.** *ekon.* exchange, market; **giełda papierów wartościowych** stock exchange; **giełda towarowa** commodity exchange; **czarna giełda** black market. **2.** market, fair; **giełda rolno-spożywcza** farmer's market; **giełda pracy** job fair; **giełda samochodowa** car auction.

giełdowy *a. ekon.* market; **makler giełdowy** stockbroker; **kurs giełdowy** exchange quotation, market quote; **indeks giełdowy** stock exchange index.

giełdziarz *mp pot.* trader.

giemza *f.* **1.** (*skóra*) chamois. **2.** *zool.* chamois (*Rupicapra rupicapra*).

giemzowy *a.* chamois, soft leather.

gier *f. zob.* **gra.**

gierka *f. Dat.* **-rce** play, trick.

giermek *mp* **-mk-** *pl.* **-owie** *hist.* squire.

giez *ma* **gz-** *ent.* gadfly (*Hypoderma*); **giez byd-**

lęcy cattle grub, warble fly (*Hypoderma bovis l.* *Hypoderma lineatum*); **jakby go giez ugryzł** like he had a bee in his britches.

gięcie *n. techn.* bending.

giętarka *f. Gen.pl.* **-ek** *techn.* bender, bending machine.

giętki *a.* **1.** (= *elastyczny*) flexible, pliant, elastic; (*o mięśniach*) supple. **2.** *przen.* (= *łatwo dostosowujący się do sytuacji*) flexible. **3.** (= *łatwo poddający się wpływom*) malleable. **4.** *przen.* (*umysł, język*) (= *sprawny*) nimble.

giętkość *f.* **1.** (= *elastyczność*) flexibility, elasticity. **2.** (= *sprawność*) limberness; (*ciała*) suppleness.

gig *mi* **1.** (*powóz*) gig. **2.** (*łódź*) gig.

gigabajt *mi Gen.* **-a** *komp.* gigabyte.

gigaherc *mi Gen.* **-a** *el.* gigahertz.

gigant *mp pl.* **-ci** *l.* **-y** **1.** *mit.* giant, colossus. **2.** (= *rosły człowiek*) giant. – *mi Gen.* **-a** *pl.* **-y** **1.** *sport* **slalom gigant** giant slalom. **2.** (= *coś dużego*) giant. **3.** *sl.* (= *ucieczka*) runaway, getaway; **być na gigancie** be on the run.

gigantomachia *f. Gen.* **-ii** *mit.* gigantomachy, gigantomachia.

gigantyczny *a.* gigantic, giant; (*posąg, budowla, stadion*) enormous; (*wysiłek, przedsięwzięcie*) herculean.

gigantyzm *mi pat.* gigantism, giantism.

gigawat *mi fiz.* gigawatt.

gik *mi żegl.* boom.

gil *ma Gen.pl.* **-i** *l.* **-ów** *orn.* bullfinch (*Pyrrhula pyrrhula*). – *mi Gen.* **-a** *Gen.pl.* **-i** *l.* **-ów** *pot.* (*z nosa*) snot.

gildia *f. Gen.* **-ii** *hist.* guild.

gilosz *mi Gen.* **-a** *Gen.pl.* **-y** *l.* **-ów** guilloche.

gilotyna *f.* **1.** (*do egzekucji*) guillotine. **2.** *techn.* cutter, guillotine.

gilotynka *f. Gen.pl.* **-ek** **1.** (*do cygar*) cigar cutter. **2.** *druk.* guillotine, paper cutter.

gilotynować *ipf.* guillotine.

gimnastyczka *f. zob.* **gimnastyk**.

gimnastyczny *a.* gymnastic(s); (*pantofle, kostium*) gym; **ćwiczenia gimnastyczne** exercises, physical training; **sala gimnastyczna** gym, gymnasium.

gimnastyk *mp* gymnast.

gimnastyka *f.* **1.** *sport* gymnastics; (*lecznicza, zdrowotna*) calisthenics. **2.** *przen.* (= *wysiłek*) gymnastics; **gimnastyka umysłu** mental gymnastics.

gimnastykować *ipf.* **1.** *sport* exercise. **2.** *przen.* exercise. **~ się** *ipf.* **1.** *sport* exercise. **2.** *przen.* (= *głowić się*) rack one's brain; bend over backwards.

gimnazjalista *mp szkoln.* junior high school student, middle school student.

gimnazjalistka *f. zob.* **gimnazjalista**.

gimnazjalny *a. szkoln.* junior high school, middle school.

gimnazjon *mi hist.* gymnasium.

gimnazjum *n. sing. indecl. pl.* **-ja** *Gen.* **-jów** **1.** *szkoln.* junior high school, middle school. **2.** *hist.* (= *gimnazjon*) gymnasium.

gin *mi kulin.* gin; **gin z tonikiem** gin and tonic.

ginąć *ipf.* **1.** (= *przestawać istnieć*) die, perish; (*o gatunku, rodzie*) die out; **kto mieczem wojuje, ten od miecza ginie** he who lives by the sword, dies by the sword; **ginąć z głodu** die of starvation. **2.** (= *zanikać*) disappear, vanish; **samolot ginie w chmurach** plane vanishes into the clouds. **3.** (= *gubić się*) get lost; **zginęły mi rękawiczki** I lost my gloves.

gineceum *n. sing. indecl. pl.* **-ea** *Gen.* **-eów** *hist.* gynaeceum.

ginekolog *mp pl.* **-dzy** *l.* **-owie** *med.* gynecologist; *Br.* gynaecologist.

ginekologia *f. Gen.* **-ii** *med.* gynecology; *Br.* gynaecology.

ginekologiczny *a.* *med.* gynecologic, gynecological; *Br.* gynaecologic, gynaecological.

ginekomastia *f. pat.* gynecomastia, gynecomasty.

gipiura *f. tk.* guipure.

gips *mi* **1.** *min.* gypsum; (*murarski, sztukatorski*) plaster; **odlew z gipsu** plaster cast. **2.** *med.* (*opatrunek*) (plaster) cast. **3.** (= *figura z gipsu*) plaster cast figure; **ładny gips!** I'll be a monkey's uncle! **4.** *sport* (*śnieg*) soft hail, graupel.

gipsoryt *mi druk.* plaster (relief) printing.

gipsować *ipf.* plaster.

gipsowy *a.* gypsum; plaster.

gipsówka *f. Gen.pl.* **-ek** *bot.* baby's-breath (*Gypsophila*).

girlanda *f.* garland.

girobusola *f. zob.* **żyrobusola**.

girokompas *mi zob.* **żyrokompas**.

giroskop *mi zob.* **żyroskop**.

giroskopowy *a. zob.* **żyroskopowy**.

girostat *mi zob.* **żyrostat**.

girotron *mi zob.* **żyrotron**.

gis *n. indecl. muz.* G sharp.

giser *mp metal.* molder, founder.

gisernia *f. Gen.pl.* **-i** *l.* **-ń** *druk.* stereotype printing facility.

gitara *f. muz.* guitar; **gitara basowa/elektryczna** bass/electric guitar; **grać na gitarze** play the guitar; **zawracać komuś gitarę** *przen.* bug sb.

gitarowy *a. muz.* guitar.

gitarzysta *mp* guitarist, guitar player.

gitarzystka *f. Gen.pl.* **-ek** *zob.* **gitarzysta**.

giwera *f. sl.* (= *broń palna, pistolet*) piece.

glaca *f. pot.* chrome dome.

glacjalny *a. geol.* glacial; **rzeźba glacjalna** glacial relief *l.* terrain.

glacjał *mi geol.* glacial period.

glacjolog *mp pl.* **-dzy** *l.* **-owie** *geol.* glaciologist.

glacjologia *f. Gen.* **-ii** *geol.* glaciology.

glacjologiczny *a. geol.* glaciological, glaciologic.

gladiator *mp hist.* gladiator.

gladiatorski *a. hist.* gladiatorial.

gladiola *f. Gen.pl.* **-i** *zob.* **gladiolus**.

gladiolus *mi Gen.* **-a** *bot.* gladiolus, gladiola (*Gladiolus*).

glan *mi Gen.* **-a** *sl.* **1.** (*but*) shiny shoe. **2.** (*kopnięcie*) boot.

glanc *mi pot.* shine; **na glanc** *l.* **do glancu** until sth shines *l.* is brought to shine.

glancować *ipf. pot.* shine, bring to a shine.

glans *mi zob.* **glanc.**

glansować *ipf. zob.* **glancować.**

glauberski *a. chem.* Glauber; **sól glauberska** Glauber's *l.* Glauber salt.

glauberyt *mi min.* glauberite.

glaukofan *mi min.* glaucophane.

glaukonit *mi min.* glauconite.

glaukonitowy *a. min.* glauconite.

glazura *f.* **1.** (*powłoka*) glaze, glazing. **2.** (*płytka*) (glazed ceramic) tile. **3.** *kulin., rzad.* (= *lukier*) glaze, glazing.

glazurnik *mp* tile layer.

glazurować *ipf.* glaze.

gleba *f.* soil, earth, ground; **gleba ciężka** heavy soil; **gleba lekka** light soil; **gleba kwaśna** *l.* **zakwaszona** sour soil.

glebogryzarka *f. Gen.pl.* **-ek** *roln.* rototiller, rotary tiller.

glebotwórczy *a.* soil-forming.

glebowy *a.* soil, earth.

gleboznawca *mp* pedologist.

gleboznawczy *a.* pedological, pedologic.

gleboznawstwo *n.* pedology, soil science.

glej *mi* **1.** *anat.* glia, neuroglia. **2.** *roln.* gleization.

glejak *mi pat.* glioma.

glejowy *a.* **1.** *anat.* neuroglial; **tkanka glejowa** neuroglial tissue. **2.** *roln.* gleizational; (*gleba*) gleyed.

glejt *mi hist.* safe-conduct.

glejta *f. chem.* massicot.

gleda *mp l. f. pot.* bore.

głędzić *ipf.* **1.** *pot.* (= *mówić rozwlekle, nudnie*) drone (on) (*o czymś* about sth); **głędzić bez sensu** blabber (away). **2.** *myśl.* give a mating call.

gliceryd *mi chem.* glyceride.

gliceryna *f.* glycerol; glycerin, gliceryne.

glicerynowy *a.* glyceric; (*mydło, maść, krem*) glycerine.

glicyna *f. chem.* glycine.

glicynia *f. Gen.* **-ii** *bot.* wisteria, wistaria (*Wisteria*).

glif *mi bud.* (*skośny*) splay; (*prosty*) reveal; (*otwór w murze obronnym*) embrasure.

glikogen *mi chem.* glycogen.

glikol *mi chem.* glycol.

glikoproteid *mi chem.* glycoprotein, glycopeptide.

glikozyd *mi chem.* glycoside.

glin *mi chem.* aluminum, *Br.* aluminium; **tlenek glinu** aluminum oxide; (*surowiec*) corundum, alumina.

glina *f.* (*skała*) clay; **glina morenowa** *l.* **zwałowa** *geol.* boulder clay; **ulepiony z tej samej gliny** cut from the same cloth. – *mi l. f. decl. like f. pog.* (= *policjant l. policjantka*) cop.

gliniak *mi Gen.* **-a** **1.** (*piec*) earthenware stove. **2.** *pot.* (*dzbanek*) earthenware pot; (*garnek*) earthenware jug; (*duży garnek*) crock.

glinian *mi chem.* aluminate.

glinianka *f. Gen.pl.* **-ek** **1.** (*staw*) clay pit. **2.** (*chata*) mud *l.* clay hut; (*u Indian amerykańskich*) adobe hut.

gliniany *a.* clay; (*garnek, dzbanek*) earthenware; (*podłoga*) earthen; **gliniane ręce** butterfingers.

gliniarz *mp pot.* (= *policjant*) cop.

gliniasty *a.* clayey, clayish.

gliniasty *a.* **1.** (*z gliną*) clay, argillaceous. **2.** (*jak glina*) clayey; (*cera, chleb*) clay-like.

gliniec *mi* **-ńc-** *Gen.pl.* **-a** *bud.* gravelite.

glinka *f. Gen.pl.* **-ek** **1.** (*skała*) clay; (*zwł. garncarska*) argil; **glinka porcelanowa** *l.* **biała** *l.* **kaolinowa** porcelain *l.* china clay; kaolin, kaoline. **2.** (*gleba*) clay soil, loam.

glinokrzemian *mi chem.* aluminosilicate.

glinowiec *mi* **-wc-** *Gen.* **-a** *chem.* boron group element.

glinowy *a. chem.* aluminum; **tlenek glinowy** aluminium oxide.

gliptal *mi chem.* glyptal.

gliptodon *ma paleont.* glyptodont (*Glyptodon*).

gliptoteka *f.* **1.** (*zbiór kamieni*) gem collection. **2.** (*zbiór rzeźb*) sculpture collection.

gliptyka *f.* glyptics.

glissando *n. muz.* glissando.

glista *f.* **1.** *zool.* ascaris (*Ascaris*); **glista ludzka** common roundworm (*Ascaris lumbricoides*). **2.** *pot.* (= *dżdżownica*) earthworm.

glistnica *f. pat.* ascariasis.

glistnik *mi Gen.* **-a** *bot.* celandine, swallowwort (*Chelidonium maius*).

glob *mi* globe.

globalnie *adv.* (*policzyć*) in total; (*działać, traktować coś*) globally.

globalny *a.* (= *całkowity*) total, overall; (= *o całym świecie*) global; **suma globalna** sum total, aggregate.

globigeryna *f. zool.* globigerina (*Globigerina*).

globina *f. biochem.* globin.

globtroter *mp*, **globtroterka** *f. Gen.pl.* **-ek** globetrotter, world traveler.

globtroterski *a.* globetrotter's, world traveler's.

globtroterstwo *n.* globetrotting.

globula *f. astron.* globula.

globularny *a. astron.* globular.

globulina *f. chem.* globulin.

globulka *f. Gen.pl.* **-ek** globule.

globus *mi Gen.* **-a** *l.* **-u** **1.** (*model*) globe. **2.** *pot., żart.* (= *głowa*) noggin.

gloksynia *f. Gen.* **-ii** *bot.* gloxinia (*Sinningia*).

glon *mi bot.* alga (*Algae*); **glon morski** seaweed.

gloria *f. Gen.* **-ii** **1.** (= *chwała*) glory; **chodzić w glorii bohatera** have the aura of a hero. **2.** (= *aureola*) aureole, aureola; helo, gloriole. **3.** *meteor.* halo.

glorieta *f.* **1.** *bud.* (*budynku, wieży*) cupola. **2.** *bud.* (*w ogrodzie*) gazebo.

gloryfikacja *f.* glorification.

gloryfikator *mp* glorifier.

gloryfikować *ipf.* glorify.

glosa *f.* **1.** (*między wierszami*) gloss. **2.** (*komentarz*) opinion; *hist.* (*zwł. do prawa rzymskiego*) gloss.

glosarium *n. sing. indecl. pl.* **-ria** *Gen.* **-riów** *zob.* **glosariusz.**

glosariusz *mi Gen.* **-a** glossary.

glosator *mp*, **glosatorka** *f.* glosser.

glosować *ipf.* gloss.

glossematyka *f. jęz.* glossematics.

glottodydaktyka *f. jęz.* foreign language pedagogy.

glottogonia *f.* glottogony.

glukoza *f.* glucose.

glukozyd *mi chem.* glucoside.

glut *mi* snot. – *mp* snot.

glutamina *f. biochem.* glutamine.

glutaminian *mi chem.* glutamate; **glutaminian sodu** monosodium glutamate, sodium glutamate.

gluten *mi* **1.** *biol.* gluten. **2.** *techn.* gluten, glutin.

glutenowy *a. chem.* glutenous.

glutyna *f. chem.* gluten, glutin.

gładki *a.* **gładszy** **1.** (= *równy*) smooth, even; (*skóra, metal*) smooth; (*podłoga*) even; (*włosy*) straight, flat; **mięśnie gładkie** *anat.* smooth muscles, involuntary muscles. **2.** (= *bez ozdób*) plain, simple. **3.** (= *bez deseniu*) plain. **4.** *przen.* (= *udatny*) smooth; (*wiersz, tłumaczenie*) polished. **5.** *przen.* (= *uprzejmy*) smooth, suave; **gładki w mowie** silver-tongued.

gładko *adv.* **gładziej** **1.** (= *bez nierówności*) smoothly, evenly; **gładko ogolony** clean-shaven. **2.** *przen.* (= *łatwo*) smoothly, without a hitch; **wszystko poszło gładko** it all went smoothly.

gładkość *f.* smoothness.

gładkowłosy *a.* (*pies, kot*) smooth haired.

gładzak *mi techn.* hone.

gładziarka *f. Gen.pl.* **-ek** *techn.* honing machine.

gładzica *f.* **1.** *icht.* plaice (*Platessa platessa*). **2.** (*narzędzie*) scraper.

gładzić *ipf.* **1.** (= *głaskać*) stroke; (*zwierzę, zwł. psa*) pet; **gładzić kogoś po głowie** stroke sb's head. **2.** (= *wyrównywać*) smooth, even; (*beton*) level; (*metal*) file; (*drewno*) plane; (*pióra dziobem*) (*o ptaku*) preen. **3.** *lit.* (= *zabić*) kill; (= *wymazać*) efface, expunge. **~ się** *ipf.* stroke o.s.; **gładzić się po brodzie** stroke one's beard.

gładzik *mi Gen.* **-a** *techn.* calender; (*do drewna*) plane.

gładź *f. pl.* **-e** **1.** *lit.* (= *gładka powierzchnia*) smooth surface. **2.** *techn.* polished surface; **gładź szpachlowa** *l.* **tynkarska** finishing coat.

głagolica *f. jęz.* Glagolitsa, the Glagolitic alphabet.

głagolicki *a. jęz.* Glagolitic.

głaskać *ipf.* **-szczę -szczesz** *l.* **-skam -skasz**, **-szcz** *l.* **-skaj** stroke.

głasnost *f. Gen.* **-ti** *polit.* glasnost.

głaszczka *f. Gen.pl.* **-ek** *zool.* palp, palpus.

głaz *mi* boulder; **głaz narzutowy** erratic boulder, erratic; **twardy jak głaz** stone-hard; *przen.* adamant; **zimny jak głaz** stone cold; **mieć serce**

jak głaz have a heart of flint; **milczeć jak głaz** be as silent as a tomb.

głąb[1] *mi Gen.* **-a** (*np. kapusty*) heart. – *mp pl.* **-y** *Acc.* **-y** *l.* **-ów** *obelż.* (= *głupiec*) moron.

głąb[2] *f.* **-ę-** *pl.* **-ie** **1.** (= *miejsce głębokie*) depth. **2.** (= *duża odległość*) interior, heart; **w głębi kraju** in the interior.

głębia *f. Gen.pl.* **-i** **1.** (= *miejsce głębokie*) depth; (*morza, oceanu*) depths; **głębia barwy** intensity of a color. **2.** (= *duża odległość*) interior, heart; **głębia ostrości** *fot.* depth of focus; **w głębi duszy/serca** deep in one's soul/heart, deep down; **z głębi serca** from the bottom of one's heart; **wzruszyć się czymś do głębi** be taken by sth. **3.** *przen.* (= *duże zaangażowanie*) depth, keenness; (*uczuć*) intensity; (*myśli*) profoundness, profundity.

głębina *f.* depth, depths.

głębinomierz *mi Gen.* **-a** *techn.* depth gauge.

głębinowy *a.* (*w oceanie, morzu*) abyssal; **skały głębinowe** *geol.* abyssal rocks; **bomba głębinowa** *wojsk.* depth charge.

głęboki *a.* **głębszy** (= *oddalony od powierzchni*) **1.** deep; **głęboki talerz** soup plate; **głęboki oddech** deep breath; **głęboki głos** deep voice; **głęboki ukłon** low bow; **głęboki dekolt** plunging neckline. **2.** (= *rozciągły*) deep, vast; **głęboki las** deep forest. **3.** (= *daleko od brzegu*) remote, distant, far-away; **głębokie średniowiecze** distant Middle Ages; **głęboka prowincja** remote province. **4.** *przen.* (= *intensywny*) deep, intense, profound; (*ciemności, cisza, nienawiść*) utter; (*zmiany*) sweeping; (*kolor, ból*) intense; (*żal*) profound. **5.** *przen.* (= *późny*) dead; **głęboka noc/zima** dead of night/winter. **6.** *przen.* (= *przenikliwy*) profound, keen; (*spojrzenie*) penetrating.

głęboko *adv.* **głębiej** deeply, deep; (*ukłonić się*) low; (*spać*) soundly; (*świadomy*) keenly, profoundly; **głęboko podzielone** bitterly divided; **odetchnąć głęboko** take a deep breath; **głęboko osadzone oczy** deep-set eyes; **głęboko zakorzeniony** deep-rooted.

głębokość *f.* depth, deepness.

głębokościomierz *mi Gen.* **-a** *techn.* depth gauge.

głębosz *mi Gen.* **-a** *leśn.* cultivator.

głodny *a.* **1.** (= *czujący głód*) hungry; **głodny jak wilk** hungry enough to eat a horse, famished. **2.** (*wyrażający uczucie głodu*) hungry; **opowiadać głodne kawałki** *przen.* jive. – *mp* hungry person; **głodnemu chleb na myśli** the tongue always *l.* ever turns to the aching tooth; **syty głodnego nie zrozumie** it's ill speaking between a full man and a fasting.

głodomór *mp* **-o-** *pl.* **-y** **1.** (= *głodujący*) starveling. **2.** *żart.* (= *żarłok*) guzzler.

głodować *ipf.* starve; go hungry, hunger; (*celowo*) starve o.s.; (*w celach politycznych*) go on a hunger strike.

głodowy *a.* **1.** (*będący efektem głodu*) hunger, starvation; **dieta głodowa** starvation diet; **strajk głodowy** *polit.* hunger strike; **śmierć głodowa** death by starvation. **2.** (= *nędzny*) wretched, beggarly; **głodowa pensja** subsistance wages; **głodowa porcja** pitiful portion.

głodówka *f.* **1.** *polit.* hunger strike. **2.** *med.* hunger cure.

głodu *itd. mi zob.* **głód.**

głodzić *ipf.* **głodź** *l.* **głódź** starve, deprive of food. **~ się** *ipf.* **głodź** *l.* **głódź** starve o.s.

głogu *itd. mi zob.* **głóg.**

głos *mi* **1.** (*dźwięk*) voice; (= *brzmienie*) sound; (*ptaka*) call; (*trąbki, dzwonu*) sound; **na cały głos** at the top of one's voice; **płakać na cały głos** cry out loud; **stracić głos** lose one's voice; **mieć głos** (*np. do śpiewania*) have a great voice; **podnieść głos** raise one's voice; **głos wołającego na puszczy** a voice crying in the wilderness. **2.** (= *nakaz wewnętrzny*) call, voice; **głos sumienia** voice of one's consciousness; **iść za głosem serca** let one's heart rule one's head, follow the call of one's heart. **3.** *muz.* part; **utwór na cztery głosy** four-part piece. **4.** (*na zebraniu*) (= *prawo przemawiania*) permission to speak, the floor; **dojść do głosu** get a chance to speak; **mieć głos** have the floor; **prosić o głos** ask for permission to speak, ask to be recognized; **udzielić komuś głosu** give sb permission to speak, give sb the floor; **zabrać głos w sprawie...** speak out on the matter of... **5.** (= *zdanie*) voice, opinion; **głos krytyki** voice of criticism; **głos sprzeciwu** dissenting voice; **rozstrzygający głos** (*w głosowaniu, wyborach*) casting vote; (*czyjaś opinia w jakiejś sprawie*) final say; **rozstrzygający głos należy do ciebie** you have the final say; **mieć głos doradczy** act as an advisor. **6.** (= *opinia wyrażona w głosowaniu*) vote; **oddać swój głos** cast one's vote; **zwyciężyć dużą liczbą głosów** win by a large number of votes.

głosiciel *mp*, **głosicielka** *f. Gen.pl.* **-ek** *lit.* champion, torchbearer.

głosić *ipf.* **-szę -sisz** **1.** (= *upowszechniać*) promulgate, propogate; (*ewangelię, zasady*) preach; **głosić czyjąś chwałę** sound sb's praises; **fama głosi, że...** there is a rumor that..., it is rumored that... **2.** (= *wygłaszać*) deliver; **głosić kazanie** *rel.* deliver a sermon.

głosik *mi* voice.

głoska *f. Gen.pl.* **-ek** *fon.* sound, phone; **zapisać się złotymi głoskami** *przen.* record one's name in letters of gold.

głosować *ipf.* **1.** *polit.* vote, cast a vote (*na kogoś/za czymś* for sb/sth) (*przeciw komuś/czemuś* against sb/sth); **iść głosować** go to the polls. **2.** *pot.* (= *opowiadać się za czymś*) vote in favor (*za czymś* of sth); cast one's vote (*za czymś* for sth).

głosowanie *n. polit.* voting, vote; **głosowanie jawne/tajne** open/secret ballot; **poddawać coś pod głosowanie** put sth to a vote, have *l.* take a vote on sth.

głosowy *a.* **1.** (= *związany z dźwiękiem*) vocal; **fale głosowe** sound waves; **wiązadła** *l.* **struny głosowe** *anat.* vocal folds *l.* cords. **2.** *muz.* voice, vocal; **partia głosowa** vocal part. **3.** *fon.* phonetic.

głośnia *f. Gen.pl.* **-i** *anat.* glottis.

głośnik *mi Gen.* **-a** *techn.* speaker; (*uliczny*) loudspeaker; **głośnik niskotonowy** woofer; **głośnik średniotonowy** midrange speaker; **głośnik wysokotonowy** tweeter.

głośno *adv.* **1.** (= *donośnie*) loudly, loud; (*śmiać się, śpiewać*) out loud, aloud; (*protestować*) vocally; **za głośno** too loud; **głośno myśleć** think out loud. **2.** (= *z rozgłosem*) eminently; **jest o nim głośno** he is talked about a lot, he is famous; (= *otwarcie*) openly; **głośno o czymś rozmawiać** talk about sth openly.

głośność *f.* volume, loudness.

głośny *a.* **1.** (= *donośny*) loud. **2.** (= *sławny*) well-known, famous; (*np. przestępca*) notorious; **stać się głośnym** become popular.

głowa *f. Gen.pl.* **głów** **1.** (*człowieka, zwierzęcia*) head; **ból głowy** headache; **marzenie ściętej głowy** pie in the sky, wishful thinking; **trupia głowa** skull and crossbones; **od stóp do głów** from head to foot; **z odkrytą** *l.* **gołą głową** bare-headed; **bić kogoś na głowę** be more than a match for sb; **być czyimś oczkiem w głowie** be the apple of sb's eye; **chować głowę w piasek** bury *l.* hide one's head in the sand; **domagać się czyjejś głowy** call for sb's head; **drapać się w głowę** scratch one's head; **kręcić głową** shake one's head; **mieć dach nad głową** have a roof over one's head; **mieć głowę na karku** *pot.* have a good head on one's shoulders; **mieć słabą głowę** *pot.* not be able to hold one's liquor; **mieć urwanie głowy w pracy** be having a hectic time at work; **skinąć głową** nod one's head; **stawać na głowie, żeby coś robić** stand on one's head *l.* bend over backwards to do sth; **strzec kogoś/czegoś jak oka w głowie** watch sb/sth like a hawk; **zmyć komuś głowę** *pot.* rake sb over the coals; **dam sobie głowę uciąć, że...** I'd bet my life that...; **głowa mi pęka** I've got a splitting headache; **kręci mi się w głowie** my head is spinning *l.* reeling; **niech cię o to głowa nie boli** never you mind; **od przybytku głowa nie boli** there is never too much of a good thing; **ręczę za to głową** I can vouch for it; **włos z głowy mu nie spadnie** not a hair of his head shall be injured, I can vouch for his safety; **woda sodowa uderzyła mu do głowy** *pot.* sb has got a big head, sb has grown too big for his/her britches; **wszystko stoi na głowie** everything has been turned upside down *l.* topsy turvy; **głowa do góry!** cheer up! **2.** (= *rozum*) head, mind; **człowiek z głową na karku** a man with a good head on his shoulders; **łamać sobie głowę nad czymś** rack one's brains over sth; **mieć coś z głowy** have sth off one's mind; **mieć olej w głowie** have one's head screwed on right; **przychodzić do głowy** spring to mind; **przyszło mi do głowy, że... it just** came *l.* occurred to me that...; **nic mi nie przychodzi do głowy** nothing springs to mind; **robić coś z głową** use one's head to get sth done; **suszyć komuś głowę** give sb grief, bitch at sb; **tracić głowę** lose one's head; **wylecieć z głowy** slip one's mind; **zawrócić komuś w głowie** cast a spell on sb; **zawracać komuś głowę** pester *l.* bug sb about sth; **nie zawracaj sobie tym głowy** don't bother *l.* worry yourself about it; **chodzi mi po głowie pewien pomysł** I have an idea; **chyba masz coś z głową**

pot. I think you have sth wrong upstairs; **chyba masz nie po kolei w głowie** *pot.* I don't think you have all your marbles; **jego nazwisko wyleciało mi z głowy** I had his name on the tip of my tongue; **mam inne sprawy na głowie** I've got other things to worry about; **mam pustkę w głowie** my mind is a blank, I have a mental block; **moja w tym głowa, żeby...** I'll make sure that...; **nie mam głowy do interesów** I don't have a head for business; **to się nie mieści w głowie** it staggers the mind *l.* imagination; **wybij to sobie z głowy** get that idea out of your head; **spokojna głowa!** *pot.* stay cool!; **rusz głową!** use your head!; **zawracanie głowy!** nonsense!; **kto nie ma w głowie, ten ma w nogach** little wit in the head makes much work for the feet *l.* heels. **3.** (= *człowiek jako osoba myśląca*) head; **co dwie głowy, to nie jedna** two heads are better than one; **co głowa, to rozum** so many men, so many minds; **mądrej głowie dość dwie słowie** a word to the wise is sufficient. **4.** (= *człowiek jako jednostka*) head; **pół litra na głowę** a half liter per head; **płacić od głowy** pay by the head. **5.** (= *zwierzchnik*) head; **głowa państwa** head of state; **koronowana głowa** crowned head. **6.** (*np. kapusty*) head; **głowa cukru** loaf of sugar.

głowacz *ma icht.* miller's thumb (*Cottus*).

głowiasty *a.* (= *mający głowę*) headed; (= *podobny do głowy*) head-like; **sałata głowiasta** head lettuce.

głowica *f.* **1.** *techn.* (*narzędzia, sztandaru*) head; **głowica cylindra** cylinder head; **głowica nagrywająca/kasująca** recording/erase head; **głowica nożowa** cutterhead. **2.** *wojsk.* warhead. **3.** (*miecza*) hilt; (= *gałka wieńcząca rękojeść*) pommel. **4.** *bud.* (*kolumny*) capital, chapiter.

głowić się *ipf.* **głów** rack one's brains, beat one's brains out (*nad czymś* over sth).

głowienka *f.* **1.** *orn.* pochard (*Aythya ferina*). **2.** *bot.* selfheal (*Prunella vulgaris*).

głowizna *f. kulin.* headcheese; *Br.* brawn.

głownia *f. Gen.pl.* **-i** **1.** (*paląca się*) firebrand. **2.** *wojsk.* (= *klinga*) blade. **3.** *wojsk.* (= *rękojeść*) hilt. **4.** *bot.* smut (*Ustilago*).

głowniowate *pl. bot.* smuts (*Ustilaginaceae*).

głowonóg *ma* **-o-** *zool.* cephalopod (*Cephalopoda*).

głowotułów *mi* **-owi-** *Gen.* **-a** *biol.* cephalothorax.

głowowy *a.* head; (*w języku fachowym*) cephalic; **wesz głowowa** head louse.

głód *mi* **-o-** **1.** (= *łaknienie*) hunger; **morzyć kogoś głodem** starve sb; **przymierać głodem** be starving; **zaspokoić pierwszy głód** take the edge off one's appetite; **o głodzie i chłodzie** in poverty; **głód jest najlepszym kucharzem** hunger is the best sauce. **2.** (= *brak żywności*) famine, starvation; **klęska głodu** famine. **3.** *przen.* (= *pragnienie*) hunger; **głód mieszkaniowy** housing shortage; **głód wiedzy** hunger for knowledge; **głód ziemi** land hunger; **być na głodzie** *sl.* (*narkotykowym*) be strung out.

głóg *mi* **-o-** *bot.* **1.** hawthorn (*Crataegus*); **głóg**

ostrogowy cockspur (*Crataegus crus-galli*). **2.** (*owoce*) haws; *pot.* (*z dzikiej róży*) rosehip.

główka *f. Gen.pl.* **-ek** **1.** (= *mała głowa*) head; **trupia główka** skull and crossbones; **paluszek i główka to szkolna wymówka** pretended sickness is a loafer's best excuse; (*jako komentarz*) a bad workman always blames his tools; **główka pracuje!** see, I'm not that stupid! **2.** (= *część rośliny*) (*kapusty, sałaty*) head; (*czosnku*) bulb. **3.** (= *zaokrąglone zakończenie czegoś*) head; **główka zapałki** match head; **główka szpilki** pinhead. **4.** *sport* header.

główkować *ipf.* **1.** *pot.* (= *myśleć*) rake one's brains (*nad czymś* over sth). **2.** *sport* head.

główkowy *a. med.* cephalic; **poród główkowy** cephalic birth.

głównie *adv.* (= *przeważnie*) mainly, mostly, for the most part; (= *przede wszystkim*) primarily, principally, chiefly; (= *zwłaszcza*) especially.

głównodowodzący *mp* commander in chief.

główny *a.* main, primary, principal; (*rola w teatrze, filmie*) lead; (*inżynier, księgowy*) head, chief; (*specjalista*) foremost; (*schody*) grand; **główny cel** primary target; **główny akcent** primary stress; **główny podejrzany** prime suspect; **główna wygrana** first *l.* grand prize; **dworzec główny** central station; **grzech główny** *rz.-kat.* mortal sin; **konto główne** *ekon.* primary account; **kwatera główna** *wojsk.* headquarters; **liczebnik główny** numeral; **nawa główna** nave; **tętnica główna** *anat.* aorta; **zdanie główne** *gram.* main clause; **brzydki jak siedem grzechów głównych** ugly as sin.

głucha *f. Gen.* **-ej** deaf woman.

głuchnąć *ipf.* **-ij, -chł** *l.* **-chnął** be going *l.* getting deaf.

głucho *adv.* **1.** (= *bezgłośnie*) dull, with a dull sound; hollow, with a hollow sound. **2.** (= *cicho*) silently, quietly; **głucho o czymś** no word on sth; **zamknięte na głucho** locked up tight, locked up fast.

głuchoniema *f. Gen.* **-ej** deaf-mute (woman).

głuchoniemota *f.* deaf-mutism; *rzad.* surdimutism.

głuchoniemy *a.* deaf-mute, deaf and dumb; *rzad.* surdomute. – *mp* deaf-mute (man).

głuchota *f.* deafness.

głuchy *a.* **1.** (= *niesłyszący*) deaf, hearing-impaired; **głuchy jak pień** stone deaf. **2.** (= *przytłumiony*) dull, hollow, muffled; **głuchy telefon** dead call. **3.** (= *obojętny*) deaf; **głuchy na czyjeś prośby** deaf to sb's pleas. **4.** (= *cichy*) (*odgłos*) silent, quiet. **5.** *przen.* (= *daleki*) remote, distant. – *mp* deaf man.

głupek *mp* **-pk-** *pl.* **-i** **1.** *pot.* (= *głupiec*) fool, idiot. **2.** *obelż.* (= *błazen*) clown.

głupi *a.* **1.** *pog.* stupid, dumb, foolish, silly; **głupia gęś** silly cow; **głupi uśmiech** smirk; **głupi jak but** dumb as a rail; **nie bądź głupi** don't be a fool; **(spytać) z głupia frant** (ask) playing dumb. **2.** *pot.* (= *bez sensu*) stupid, dumb. **3.** *iron.* (= *naiwny*) foolish. **4.** *pot.* (= *nieważny*) trivial, piddling. **5.** *pot.* (= *kłopotliwy*) awkward. – *mp pog.* idiot, dumbass; **głupiego robota** fool's errand; **śmiać się jak głupi do sera** have a stupid mile on one's face; **nie udawaj głupiego** don't play dumb; **nie ma głupich!** nobody's that stupid!; **głupich nie sieją, sami się rodzą** fools grow *l.* folly grows without watering; **nadzieja jest matką głupich** hope often deludes the foolish man.

głupia *f. Gen.* **-ej** *pog.* idiot, fool.

głupiec *mp* **-pc-** *Voc.* **-cze** *pl.* **-y** *obelż., pog.* idiot, fool.

głupieć *ipf.* **1.** go crazy, get silly; (*od bezmyślnej pracy, bezczynności itd.*) be driven crazy; (*na starość*) get *l.* go soft in the head; **głupieję od tej roboty** this work is driving me crazy. **2.** (= *tracić głowę*) lose one's head, lose one's wits.

głupio *adv.* **1.** *pot.* (= *bezsensownie*) foolish, foolishly; stupid, stupidly; idiotic, idiotically; **głupio gadać** talk nonsense; **postąpić głupio** act like a fool. **2.** *pot.* (= *niezręcznie*) foolishly, foolish; awkwardly, awkward; **czuć się głupio** feel like a fool, feel foolish.

głupkowaty *a.* **1.** (= *nierozgarnięty*) halfwitted, retarded. **2.** (= *głupawy*) goofy, dorky.

głupol *mp pot., żart.* retard, half-wit.

głupota *f.* **1.** (= *bezmyślność*) stupidity, foolishness. **2.** *pot.* (= *bzdura*) bullshit, crap; **przestań wreszcie opowiadać głupoty, dobra?** cut that crap, will you?, will you finally cut that crap?

głupstwo *n.* **1.** (= *niedorzeczność, bzdura*) foolishness, nonsense, poppycock; **robić głupstwo** do sth foolish, do sth stupid; **palnąć głupstwo** put one's foot into it, put one's foot into one's mouth; *Br. t.* drop a brick. **2.** (= *drobnostka*) trifle, triviality; **to głupstwo!** it's no big deal.

głuptak *ma pl.* **-i** *orn.* booby (*Sula*). – *mp pl.* **-cy** *l.* **-ki** *iron.* (= *głupiec*) fool, simpleton.

głuptas *mp pl.* **-y** *żart.* (= *głupiec*) simpleton; **ty głuptasie!** you silly!

głusza *f.* **1.** (= *pustkowie*) the middle of nowhere; **leśna głusza** the backwoods. **2.** (= *cisza*) dead silence.

głuszec *ma* **-szc-** *orn.* woodgrouse; capercaillie, capercailzie (*Tetrao urogallus*).

głuszyć *ipf.* **1.** (= *tłumić*) muffle, deaden. **2.** (*o chwastach*) choke. **3.** *myśl.* knock dead.

gmach *mi* edifice, building; **gmach sądowy** courthouse.

gmatwać *ipf.* complicate, muddy. **~ się** *ipf.* **1.** (= *stać się zaplątanym*) get complicated, become complicated. **2.** (= *gubić się*) get confused, become confused.

gmatwanina *f.* tangle; (*myśli, słów, kabli, przewodów*) jumble.

gmerać *ipf.* **-ram -rasz** *l.* **-rzę -rzesz, -raj** *l.* **-rz** rummage (*w czymś* through sth). **~ się** *ipf.* stumble about, fumble about.

gmerk *mi hist.* mark.

gmin *mi przest.* the commoners.

gmina *f.* **1.** *adm.* (*w Europie*) commune; (*w Wielkiej Brytanii*) district, borough; (*w Stanach Zjednoczonych*) township; (*w Nowym Jorku*) borough. **2.** *pot.* (*urząd*) commune council. **3.** (*stowarzyszenie*) community; **gmina żydowska**

Jewish community. **4. Izba Gmin** *polit.* the House of Commons.

gminny *a.* **1.** *adm.* communal; (*droga*) local. **2.** (*dotyczący stowarzyszenia*) community. **3.** *przest.* (= *pospolity*) vulgar.

gnać *ipf.* **1.** (= *biec*) speed ahead, barrel ahead; **gnać co tchu** hotfoot it; **gnać na oślep** barrel ahead blindly; **gnać na złamanie karku** speed ahead at breakneck speed. **2.** (= *popędzać*) drive; **gnać bydło na pastwisko** drive the cattle to pasture.

gnat *mi Gen.* **-a 1.** *pot.* (= *kość*) bone; **patrzeć jak sroka w gnat** stare ahead; **połamać** *l.* **policzyć komuś gnaty** beat sb black and blue; **wyciągnąć gnaty** stretch out one's legs; **wyprostować gnaty** stretch one's legs; **sterczą mu gnaty** he's thin as a rail; **nie czuć gnatów** be dead on one's feet. **2.** *sl.* (= *pistolet*) piece.

gnejs *mi min.* gneiss.

gnejsowy *a. min.* gneissic.

gnet *mi bot.* gnetum (*Gnetaceae*).

gnębiciel *mp*, **gnębicielka** *f.* tormentor, oppressor.

gnębić *ipf.* **1.** (= *prześladować*) oppress, torment. **2.** (= *martwić*) trouble, torment.

gniadosz *ma* bay, bay horse.

gniady *a.* bay.

gniazdko *n. Gen.pl.* **-dek 1.** (= *małe gniazdo*) nest. **2.** *przen.* (= *mieszkanie*) home. **3.** *el.* socket. **4.** *górn.* pocket. **5.** (*ciastko*) donut, *Br.* doughnut.

gniazdo *n. Loc.* **-eździe 1.** (*ptaka, zwierzęcia*) nest; **gniazdo nasienne** *bot.* nidus; **bocianie gniazdo** *żegl.* crow's nest; **zły to ptak, co własne gniazdo kala** it's an ill bird that fouls its own nest. **2.** *emf.* (= *dom rodzinny, ojczyzna*) home; **gniazdo rodzinne** family nest. **3.** (= *ośrodek*) nest; **gniazdo złodziei** nest of thieves. **4.** (= *skupisko*) cluster, group; **gniazdo karabinów maszynowych** *wojsk.* machine gun nest. **5.** *bud.* nest. **6.** *el.* socket. **7.** *geol.* pocket. **8.** *techn.* socket; (*do telefonu, kabla głośnika itp.*) jack.

gniazdować *ipf. orn., zool.* nest.

gniazdowisko *n. orn., zool.* nestage.

gniazdownik *ma* **1.** *myśl.* eyas. **2.** *zool.* nidicolous bird, nest-dwelling bird.

gniazdowy *a.* nest, nesting; **instynkt gniazdowy** *psych.* nesting instinct; **ptak gniazdowy** *zool.* nesting bird; **skupisko gniazdowe** cluster of nests.

gnicie *n.* rotting, decay; (= *rozkładanie się*) decomposition.

gnić *ipf.* **-ję -jesz, -ij** rot, decay, decompose; (*o ranie*) fester; **gnić w łóżku** *pot.* languish in one's bed, be rotting in one's bed; **gnić w więzieniu** *pot.* rot in prison.

gnida *f.* **1.** (= *jajo wszy*) nit. **2.** *obelż.* louse.

gnidosz *mi Gen.* **-a** *Gen.pl.* **-y** *l.* **-ów** *bot.* lousewort (*Pedicularis*).

gnie *itd. v.* zob. **giąć**.

gnieciuch *mi* homemade plain cake.

gnieść *ipf.* **-otę -eciesz -ótł -otła -etli 1.** (= *zgniatać*) crush, squeeze; (*ciasto*) knead; (*ziemniaki*) mash. **2.** *przen.* (= *ciążyć*) (*np. o choro-*

bie, starości) weigh down. **3.** *przen.* (= *dręczyć*) oppress. **4.** (= *miąć*) crumple. **5.** (= *uwierać*) pinch. ~ **się** *ipf.* **1.** (= *tłoczyć się*) be crowded, be squeezed together; **gnieść się jak śledzie w beczce** be squeezzed together like sardines. **2.** (= *być miętym*) crease.

gniew *mi* **1.** (= *złość*) anger; **wybuch gniewu** fit of anger; **tłumić w sobie gniew** hold back one's anger; **wpaść w gniew** fall into a fit of anger; **wprawić kogoś w gniew** make sb furious; **wybuchnąć** *l.* **unieść się gniewem** explode with *l.* in anger. **2.** (= *kłótnia*) feud.

gniewać *ipf.* anger, make angry. ~ **się** *ipf.* **1.** (= *złościć się*) be angry, be mad (*na kogoś* at sb, *z powodu czegoś* about sth). **2.** (= *czuć do siebie nawzajem urazę*) be angry at one another *l.* each other, be mad at one another *l.* each other.

gniewnie *adv.* angrily.

gniewny *a.* **1.** (= *spowodowany gniewem*) angry, mad. **2.** *przen.* (= *groźny*) angry.

gniewosz *ma Gen.pl.* **-y** *l.* **-ów** *zool.* **gniewosz plamisty** smooth snake (*Coronella austriaca*).

gnieździć się *ipf.* **-żdżę -ździsz 1.** nest. **2.** *przen.* (= *skupiać się*) cluster. **3.** *przen.* (= *układać się*) nestle. **4.** *pot.* (= *mieszkać w ciasnocie*) be cooped up.

gnilec *mi* **-lc-** *Gen.* **-a 1.** *pat.* scurvy. **2.** (*u pszczół*) foulbrood.

gnilny *a.* putrefaction, rotting; **bakterie gnilne** putrefactive bacteria; **proces gnilny** putrefaction process, putrefactive process.

gniłek *mi* **-łk-** *Gen.* **-a** *bot.* Fuligo (*Fuligo*).

gniot *mi* **1.** (*wypiek*) *pot.* fallen baked good. **2.** (*książka, film*) *pot.* bore.

gniotownik *mi Gen.* **-a 1.** *roln.* (*do karmy*) mill. **2.** *techn.* crusher, grinding machine.

gnoić *ipf.* **-ję -isz, gnój 1.** *roln.* (*nawozić*) manure, fertilize with manure. **2.** *roln.* (= *pozwalać na gnicie*) rot. **3.** *pot.* (= *brudzić*) dirty, soil. **4.** *pot.* (= *upodlać kogoś*) put down, drag through the mud.

gnojak *ma ent.* dorbeetle (*Geotrupes stercorarius*).

gnojek *mp* **-jk-** *pl.* **-i** *obelż.* turd, shit.

gnojka *f. ent.* drone fly (*Eristalis tenax*).

gnojnik *mi* manure pit.

gnojowica *f.* liquid manure.

gnojowisko *n.* **1.** (*dół*) manure pit. **2.** (*kupa*) dungheap.

gnojówka *f. Gen.pl.* **-ek 1.** *roln.* (*dół*) manure pit. **2.** *roln.* (*mocz*) liquid manure.

gnom *ma mit.* (*karzeł*) gnome.

gnoma *f. teor.lit.* gnome.

gnomiczny *a. teor.lit.* gnomic.

gnomon *mi Gen.* **-a** *l.* **-u** *astron.* gnomon.

gnomoniczny *a. geom.* gnomonic; **rzut gnomoniczny** gnomonic projection.

gnomonika *f.* gnomonics.

gnoseologia *f. Gen.* **-ii** *fil.* gnoseology.

gnoseologiczny *a. fil.* gnoseological.

gnostycki *a. fil.* Gnostic.

gnostycyzm *mi fil.* Gnosticism.

gnostyczny *a. fil. zob.* **gnostycki**.

gnostyk *mp fil., rel.* Gnostic.

gnoza *f. fil., rel.* gnosis.

gnozeologia *f. Gen.* **-ii** *zob.* **gnoseologia**.

gnozeologiczny *a. zob.* **gnoseologiczny**.

gnój *mi* **-o-** *Gen.* **-u 1.** *tylko sing.* (= *odchody zwierzęce, obornik*) manure, dung, muck. **2.** *przen.* (= *bałagan, brud*) mess, muck. **3.** *przen.* (= *awantura*) quarrel, brawl; **robić gnój** pick a fight, (start a) brawl *l.* quarrel; **narobić komuś gnoju** embarass sb. – *mp* **-o-** *Gen.* **-a** *Gen.pl.* **-ów** *l.* **gnoi** *pog., wulg.* (*człowiek wzbudzający pogardę*) shithead, shit for brains.

gnu *n. l. f. indecl. zool.* (**antylopa**) gnu gnu, wildebeest (*Connochaetes*).

gnuśnie *adv.* shiftlessly, sluggishly.

gnuśnieć *ipf.* (= *stawać się gnuśnym*) laze away; (= *trwać w bezczynności*) laze around.

gnuśny *a.* shiftless, sluggish, slothful.

gnyk *mi Gen.* **-a** *anat.* hyoid.

gnykowy *a. anat.* hyoid; **kość gnykowa** hyoid bone.

go[1] *n. indecl.* (*gra*) go, I-go.

go[2] *pron. zob.* **on, ono**.

gobelin *mi sztuka* tapestry; (*zwł. oryginalny z fabryki w Paryżu*) Gobelin.

gobeliniarka *f. Gen.pl.* **-ek** *sztuka* tapestry weaver *l.* maker.

gobeliniarstwo *n. sztuka* tapestry weaving *l.* making.

gobeliniarz *mp sztuka* tapestry weaver *l.* maker.

gobelinowy *a. sztuka* tapestry, tapestried.

gocki *a. hist.* Gothic.

godecja *f. bot.* godetia, satin flower (*Godetia*).

godet *mi* (*w krawiectwie*) godet, gore.

godło *n. Gen.pl.* **-eł** (= *symbol*) emblem, badge; **godło państwowe** national emblem.

godnie *adv.* **1.** (= *właściwie, należycie*) becomingly; properly, suitably. **2.** (= *dumnie, z godnością*) stately, with dignity.

godność *f.* **1.** (= *honor, duma*) dignity, self-respect; **mieć poczucie godności** have a sense of dignity, possess dignity; **godność osobista** self-respect, dignity; **nosić się z godnością** possess self-respect; **poniżej godności** below the level of dignity. **2.** (= *stanowisko*) post, office; (= *tytuł*) title; (= *status*) status; **piastować jakąś godność** hold a post of; **nadać komuś jakąś godność** bestow *l.* confer a title on sb; **podnieść kogoś do godności** raise sb to a title, elevate sb to the rank *l.* status of; **złożyć swą godność** resign from post *l.* office, lay down sb's office. **3.** (= *nazwisko*) *przest., tylko w pytaniach* name; **(jak) Pańska godność?** what is your name, please?

godny *a.* **1.** (= *stosowny, właściwy*) adequate, suitable. **2.** (= *zasługujący na coś*) worthy; **godzien zaufania** trustworthy; **postępowanie godne nagrody** praiseworthy conduct, conduct deserving a prize; **osoba godna pożałowania** pitiful person; **(nie) być godnym takiego wyróżnienia** (not) deserve such a distinction; **godny ubolewania** regrettable, unfortunate; **godny podziwu** admirable, commendable; **godny pochwały** praiseworthy; **godny wzmianki** worth mentioning; **godny zobaczenia/obejrzenia** worth seeing/

watching; **to jest godne uwagi** it is remarkable, it is noteworthy. **3.** (= *dumny, dostojny*) proud, stately; **godne zachowanie** stately conduct; **godna postawa** stately stance.

godowy *a. biol.* mating, nuptial; **szata godowa** mating *l.* nuptial colors; (*u ptaków*) nuptial plumage; **okres godowy** mating *l.* nuptial season; **taniec godowy** mating *l.* nuptial rites *l.* dance.

gody *pl. Gen.* -ów **1.** *form.* (= *ślub, wesele*) wedding; **złote/srebrne/brylantowe gody** golden/silver/diamond (wedding) anniversary. **2.** *biol.* mating, pairing.

godzić *ipf.* **gódź 1.** (= *jednać*) reconcile. **2.** (= *łączyć*) reconcile, square (*coś z czymś* sth with sth); **godzić pracę z nauką** reconcile work and study; **godzić ogień z wodą** reconcile two opposites. **3.** (= *celować*) aim (*w kogoś / coś* at sb/sth) (*z czegoś* with sth). **4.** (= *trafiać, uderzać*) hit, strike (*w kogoś / coś* sb/sth); **godzić na czyjeś życie** threaten sb's life; **godzić w czyjś honor** be an insult *l.* affront to sb, insult *l.* affront sb. **5.** *przest.* (= *najmować*) hire, take on (*do kogoś / czegoś* to work for sb/do sth). **~ się** *ipf.* **1.** (= *jednać się*) be *l.* become reconciled (*z kimś* with sb). **2.** (= *zgadzać się*) agree (*na coś* to sth) (*z czymś* with sth); **godzić się na ciężkie warunki** accept difficult conditions; **godzić się z czymś** come to terms with sth; **godzić się z losem** be resigned to one's fate. **3.** (= *pasować, łączyć się*) agree, be compatible (*z czymś* with sth); match (*z czymś* sth). **4.** *przest.* (= *najmować się*) hire on (*do czegoś* as sb *l.* to do sth). **5.** *lit.* (= *wypada, należy, wolno, trzeba*) be suitable *l.* proper *l.* fit(ting); **to się nie godzi** it is unseemly, it it not proper.

godzien *a. indecl. zob.* **godny.**

godzina *f.* **1.** (*jednostka czasu*) hour; **pół godziny** half an hour; **dwie godziny** two hours; **parę godzin** a few hours; **dwadzieścia cztery godziny** twenty four hours; **prędkość na godzinę** miles *l.* kilometers per hour; **która godzina?** what's the time?, what time is it?; **o której godzinie?** at what time?; **jest już późna godzina** it is already late; **po godzinach** after hours, out of hours; **co godzinę** every hour; **godzina odjazdu/przyjazdu** departure/arrival time; **godziny pracy** working hours; (*np. firmy, przedsiębiorstwa*) business hours; (*np. sklepu*) opening hours; (*np. biura, urzędu*) office hours; **godziny nadliczbowe** overtime; **godziny odwiedzin** visiting hours; **godziny rektorskie** *uniw.* morning *l.* afternoon class cancellation, half-day off; **godziny szczytu** peak hour(s), rush hour(s); **godzina policyjna** curfew; **godziny urzędowe** office hours; **godziny przyjęć** opening hours, office hours; **liturgia godzin** *rel., kośc.* canonical hours; **z godziny na godzinę** hour by hour; **dobra** *l.* **bita godzina** solid *l.* full hour; **godzina z hakiem** over an hour, more than an hour; **godzina zero** H-hour, zero hour; **wybiła twoja (ostatnia) godzina** your time has come, your number is up. **2.** *lit.* (= *okres, chwila, termin*) time; **to jeszcze młoda godzina** it's still early; **szara godzina** twilight; **czarna godzina** rainy day; **chować coś na czarną godzinę** save for a

rainy day; **godzina prawdy** hour of truth; **ostatnia godzina** last hour, the last moments *l.* hours (*of sb's life*); **wymówić w dobrą/złą godzinę** say sth at the most opportune/inopportune moment; **nie być pewnym dnia ani godziny** live in uncertainty; **żyć z godziny na godzinę** live day to *l.* by day; **jej godziny są policzone** her days are numbered, her time is near. **3.** *szkoln.* (= *lekcja*) lesson, class; (= *wykład*) lecture.

godzinami *adv.* for hours; **całymi godzinami** for hours on end.

godzinka *f. Gen.pl.* -ek *emf.* hour; **z godzinkę** about an hour.

godzinki *pl. Gen.* -ek *rel.* canonical hours; **śpiewać** *l.* **odmawiać godzinki** say canonical hours.

godzinny *a.* an hour's, hourlong.

godzinowy *a.* hourly; **wskazówka godzinowa** hour hand.

godziwy *a. lit.* decent.

gofr *mi Gen.* -a *kulin.* waffle.

gofrownica *f.* waffle iron.

gogle *pl. Gen.* -i *sport* goggles.

goguś *mp pl.* -e *l.* -owie dude, fop, fancy-pants.

goić *ipf.* **goję goisz, gój 1.** *t. pat.* heal. **2.** *przen.* (= *uspokajać*) heal; **czas goi rany** time heals all wounds. **~ się** *ipf.* **goi** *t. pat.* heal.

goj *mp pog., rel.* goy, gentile.

gojka *f. pog.* goy, gentile.

gokart *mi Gen.* -a *sport* kart, go-kart.

gol *mi Gen.* -a *Gen.pl.* -i *l.* -ów **1.** *sport* goal; **gol samobójczy** own goal; **zdobyć** *l.* **strzelić gola** score a goal. **2.** *pot., szkoln.* (= *ocena niedostateczna*) fail, F.

golarka *f. Gen.pl.* -ek shaver, electric razor.

golas *mp pl.* -y **1.** *pot.* (= *nagus*) nude, naked person; **na golasa** in the nude. **2.** = **golec** 2.

golec *mp* -lc- *Voc.* -cu *l.* -cze *pl.* -y *l.* -e **1.** *pot., żart.* (= *nagus*) nude, naked person. **2.** *pot., pog.* (= *biedak*) sb without a pot to piss in; **straszny z niego golec** he doesn't even have a pot to piss in.

golem *mi Gen.* -a *rel.* golem.

golenie *n.* shaving; **maszynka do golenia** razor; **krem do golenia** shaving cream; **woda po goleniu** aftershave, after-shave.

goleniowy *a. anat.* crural, tibial; **kość goleniowa** tibia, shinbone.

goleń *f. pl.* -e *anat.* shin.

golf¹ *mi Gen.* -a *sport* **1.** golf. **2.** *zob.* **golfy.**

golf² *mi Gen.* -a *l.* -u (*sweter*) (*kołnierz*) turtleneck.

golfik *mi Gen.* -a *l.* -u *pot.* (*sweterek*) turtleneck.

golfowy¹ *a. sport* golf; **pole golfowe** golf course; **kij golfowy** golf club.

golfowy² *a.* (*dotyczący swetra*) turtleneck.

golfy *pl. Gen.* -ów (*spodnie*) golf pants.

Golgota *f. rel.* Calvary; Golgotha; **golgota** *form.* (= *cierpienie*) calvary.

goliard *mp pl.* -dzi *l.* -owie *l.* -y *hist.* goliard.

goliat *mp pl.* -ci *l.* -ty *Bibl.* **1.** Goliath. **2.** (= *olbrzym*) goliath. — *mi Gen.* -a *pl.* -y *wojsk., hist.* (*czołg*) goliath tank. — *ma pl.* -y **1.** *ent.*

(*chrząszcz*) goliath beetle (*Goliathus goliathus*). **2.** *zool.* (*żaba*) goliath frog (*Rana goliath*).

golibroda *mp pl.* **-y** *przest., pog., żart.* (= *fryzjer*) barber.

golić *ipf.* **gol** *l.* **gól** **1.** shave. **2.** *pot.* (= *pić*) booze. **3.** *pot., przen.* (= *oszukiwać*) fleece.

golizna *f.* **1.** (= *nagość*) nakedness, nudity. **2.** (*puste miejsce*) bare spot. **3.** (*skóra*) lime pelt. **4.** *przen.* (= *bieda*) poorness.

golnąć *pf.* **-ij** *pot.* (= *wypić*) have a shot; **golnąć sobie (zdrowo) wódki** have a (good) shot of vodka.

golonka *f. Gen.pl.* **-ek** *kulin.* knuckle of pork.

golutki *a.* **1.** (= *goły*) naked, nude. **2.** (= *pusty, ogołocony*) bare; (= *pozbawiony włosów*) hairless, furless. **3.** (= *bez dodatków*) basic, whole, with no extras.

gołąb *ma* **-ębi-** *orn.* pigeon (*Columba*); **gołąb pocztowy** homing pigeon; (*zwł. używany do przenoszenia wiadomości*) carrier pigeon; **gołąb pokoju** dove of peace; **siwy** *l.* **biały jak gołąb** (*o człowieku o białych włosach*) as white as snow; **lepszy wróbel w garści niż gołąb na dachu** a bird in the hand is worth two in the bush.

gołąbek *ma* **-bk-** *orn.* dove; **gołąbek pokoju** dove of peace; **siwy jak gołąbek** (*o człowieku o białych włosach*) as white as snow; **gruchają ze sobą jak dwa gołąbki** they're billing and cooing; **pieczone gołąbki nie lecą same do gąbki** he that would eat the fruit must climb the tree. – *mi Gen.* **-a** **1.** *kulin.* meat-stuffed cabbage. **2.** *bot.* (*grzyb*) russula (*Russula*). – *mp pl.* **-i** *przen.* (*bliska, kochana osoba*) darling, love, honey.

gołębi *a.* **1.** (*dotyczący ptaka*) pigeon, dove; **gołębie serce** *przen.* kind *l.* soft *l.* tender heart. **2.** (*o kolorze*) dove.

gołębiarstwo *n.* pigeon breeding.

gołębiarz *mp* (= *hodowca gołębi*) pigeon breeder. – *ma orn.* goshawk (*Accipiter gentilis*).

gołębica *f.* dove.

gołębnik *mi Gen.* **-a** (*budka dla ptaków*) dovecote, dovecot.

goło *adv.* **1.** (= *nago*) in the nude, with no clothes on; *pot.* wearing one's birthday clothes. **2.** (= *pusto*) **na polu jest goło** the field is bare. **3.** *pot.* (= *biednie*) in poverty; **goło, ale wesoło** we (I, he, they etc.) may not have a pot to piss in, but we still know how to have a good time.

gołoborze *n. Gen.pl.* **-y** **1.** *geol.* boulder *l.* block field. **2.** *leśn.* deforested area.

gołodupiec *mp* **-pc-** *Voc.* **-cu** *l.* **-cze** *pl.* **-y** *pot.* sb without a pot to piss in; **zupełny z niego gołodupiec** he's flat on his ass.

gołoledź *f. meteor.* glaze, *Br.* glaze ice, glazed frost.

gołosłowny *a.* (= *bez pokrycia, bezpodstawny*) groundless, unfounded; **gołosłowne oskarżenie** groundless accusation.

gołowąs *mp pl.* **-y** shaver, young man.

goły *a.* **1.** (= *nagi, rozebrany*) naked, nude, bare; **goły jak go Pan Bóg stworzył** in one's birthday suit; **z gołą głową** bareheaded; **robić coś gołymi rękami** do sth with bare hands; **obrać kogoś do gołej skóry** rob sb of all his/her possessions;

gołym okiem with the naked eye; **pod gołym niebem** in the open air; **gołe baby** *pot.* naked chicks. **2.** (= *pusty, ogołocony*) bare; (= *bezwłosy*) hairless; (= *pozbawiony futra*) furless; (= *pozbawiony piór*) featherless; (= *bezlistny*) leafless; **spać na gołej ziemi** sleep on the bare ground. **3.** (= *bez dodatków*) naked, bare, basic; **goła pensja** basic wage *l.* salary; **goła prawda** the naked truth; **gołe fakty** the bare facts. **4.** *pot.* (= *biedny*) poor; **goły jak święty turecki** on one's uppers, as poor as a church mouse; **goły, ale wesoły** he may not have a pot to piss in, but he still knows how to have a good time. – *mp* **1.** (= *golas*) naked person, nude; **czuć się jak goły w pokrzywach** be caught off-balance. **2.** *pot.* (= *biedak*) poor person.

gomora *f.* **sodoma i gomora** (= *zamieszanie*) utter confusion; (= *rozpusta*) debauchery.

gomółka *f. Gen.pl.* **-ek** **1.** (= *bryłka*) lump; **gomółka masła** lump of butter. **2.** *bud.* crown glass.

gonada *f. biol.* gonad; **gonada męska** male gonad, testis; **gonada żeńska** female gonad, ovary.

gonadotropina *f. biol., chem.* gonadotropin.

gondola *f. Gen.pl.* **-i** **1.** (*łódź; wagonik*) gondola. **2.** *lotn.* nacelle; (*dla pasażerów sterowca, balonu*) gondola.

gondolier *mp* gondolier.

gonfalonier *mp hist.* gonfalonier.

gong *mi* **1.** *muz.* (*instrument*) gong. **2.** (*dźwięk*) gong, chime. **3.** *sport* gong.

gongorysta *mp lit.* Gongorist.

gongoryzm *mi lit.* Gongorism.

gonić *ipf.* **1.** chase, hunt (down); (= *biec za kimś l. czymś*) run (*za kimś / czymś* after sb/sth); **jakby go kto gonił** *pot.* he is (was, etc.) in a hurry; **gonić ostatkiem pieniędzy** be almost out of money; **gonić resztkami sił** be on sb's last legs, be at the end of one's tether *l.* rope; **gonić w piętkę** *myśl.* backtrack; *przen.* lose sb's bearings; **gonić za pieniędzmi** chase after money; **gonić za sławą** chase after fame, seek fame; **gonić za sławą i pieniędzmi** seek fame and fortune; **gonić za sensacją** chase after hot stories; **gonić czas** *pot.* try to make up for lost time; **gonić za spódniczkami** *l.* **babami** *l.* **kobietami** *pot.* chase skirts. **2.** (= *spieszyć się*) hurry (*do kogoś / czegoś* to meet sb/to do sth). **3.** (= *przemieszczać się, gnać*) race; **wiatr goni chmury** wind is racing clouds; **gonić po świecie** roam around the world, wander the globe. **4.** (= *zmuszać, pędzić*) drive, urge; **gonić kogoś do nauki** urge sb to study hard, make sb study hard; **gonić kogoś do pracy** sweat sb, make sb work hard. **5.** *pot.* (*powodować rozwolnienie*) give *sb* the runs. **~ się** *ipf.* chase one another; **goń się!** *pot.* beat it!

goniec *mp* **-ńc-** *Voc.* **-cze** *pl.* **-y** **1.** (= *posłaniec*) office boy, *Br.* office junior; messenger. **2.** *wojsk.* (= *łącznik*) liaison, dispatch carrier. – *mi* **-ńc-** *Gen.* **-a** *pl.* **-e** **1.** *szachy* bishop. **2.** *techn., tk.* picker.

goniometr *mi techn., lotn., żegl.* goniometer.

goniometria *f. Gen.* **-ii** *min., mat.* goniometry.

goniometryczny a. techn., mat. goniometric, goniometrical.

gonitwa f. 1. (= bieganie, pogoń) chase, pursuit, hunt; **gonitwa myśli** pat., psych. flight of ideas. 2. sport race, run; (= wyścig konny) horse race.

gonokok mi Gen. -a biol., med. gonococcus (Neisseria gonorrhoeae).

gonokokowy a. biol., med. gonococcal, gonococcic.

gont mi Gen. -u l. -a bud. shingle.

gontowy a. bud. shingle; **dach gontowy** shingle roof.

gontyna, kontyna f. lit. pagan temple of ancient Slavs.

gończy a. **pies gończy** myśl. hound; **list gończy** zwł. prawn. arrest warrant, wanted notice. – ma myśl. hound.

GOPR abbr. **Górskie Ochotnicze Pogotowie Ratunkowe** Volunteer Mountain Rescue Service (in Poland).

goprowiec mp -wc- pl. -y member of Volunteer Mountain Rescue Service.

gorąc mi. dial., pot. (= upał) heat.

gorąco adv. -ęcej 1. (= upalnie) hot; **za gorąco** too hot; **na gorąco** immediately, directly; on the spot; (o posiłku) served hot; **wiadomości na gorąco** live news; **chwytać życie na gorąco** seize the day; (w dziennikarstwie) broadcast live, report live; **zrobiło się gorąco** it got hot; **gorąco mi** I'm hot. 2. (= serdecznie) warmly, heartily; **gorąco dziękować** thank warmly; **gorąco pragnąć** want badly; **gorąco się o coś modlić** pray fervently for sth. 3. (= niebezpiecznie) dangerously; **było gorąco** it was hot work. – n. (= upał) heat.

gorącokrwisty a. 1. (o koniu) noble. 2. przen. (= porywczy, namiętny) hot-blooded.

gorący a. -ętszy 1. (= ciepły) hot; **gorąca kąpiel** hot bath; **gorące dania** hot dishes; **gorący klimat** hot climate; **gorąca strefa** torrid area; **gorące źródło** hot spring; **gorąca linia** tel. hot line, hotline; **gorąca krew** hot blood; **gorące rytmy** Latino rhythms; **osoba w gorącej wodzie kąpana** hothead; **złapać kogoś na gorącym uczynku** catch sb red-handed l. in the act; **kuć żelazo, póki gorące** strike while the iron is hot, make hay while the sun shines. 2. (= serdeczny, namiętny) warm, hearty; **gorące brawa** warm applause, ovation; **gorąca dyskusja** heated discussion. 3. (= niebezpieczny) dangerous, risky; **gorący czas** l. **okres** hectic l. hot period l. time.

gorączka f. Gen.pl. -ek 1. pat. (= wysoka temperatura) fever; (w języku fachowym) hyperthermia, pyrexia; **mieć gorączkę** have a fever, run a temperature. 2. pat. fever; **gorączka błotna** mud fever, swamp fever; **gorączka krwotoczna** hemorrhagic fever, Br. haemorrhagic fever; **gorączka sienna** hay fever; **biała gorączka** delirium tremens; **dostać białej gorączki** pot. fly into a rage. 3. (= niepokój) excitement. 4. (= żądza) passion, want; **gorączka złota** gold rush.

gorączkować ipf. t. pat. have a fever. ~ **się** ipf. get excited, get frantic.

gorączkowy a. 1. t. pat. feverish. 2. (= nerwo-

wy) frantic, hectic; **gorączkowe przygotowania** frantic preparations.

gorbusza f. icht. pink salmon, humpback salmon (Oncorhynchus gorbuscha).

gorczyca f. bot. mustard (Brassica l. Sinapsis); **ziarnko gorczycy** mustard seed; **gorczyca biała** white mustard (Brassica alba); **gorczyca czarna** black mustard (Brassica hirta l. Sinapsis alba); **gorczyca polna** charlock, wild mustard (Brassica kaber l. Sinapsis arvensis); **gorczyca sarepska** Indian l. brown mustard (Brassica juncea).

gorczycowy a. mustard.

gorczycznik mi Gen. -a 1. bot. winter cress (Barbarea). 2. med. mustard plaster.

gording mi żegl. buntline.

gordon seter ma kynol. Gordon setter.

gordyjski a. Gordian; **węzeł gordyjski** Gordian knot; **przeciąć węzeł gordyjski** cut the Gordian knot.

gore-tex mi tk. gore-tex.

gorliwie adv. zealously, ardently, fervently.

gorliwiec mp -wc- Voc. -cze l. -cu pl. -y zealot, ardent l. devoted supporter.

gorliwość f. zeal, ardor, Br. ardour, devotion.

gorliwy a. zealous, ardent, fervent.

gors mi przest. 1. (pierś) chest, breast, bust. 2. (przednia część koszuli) plastron, shirt front. 3. (dekolt) neckline.

gorseciarka f. corsetière.

gorseciarstwo n. corset making, stays making.

gorseciarz mp corsetier.

gorsecik mi Gen. -a l. -u 1. (bielizna) corset. 2. (kaftanik) bodice.

gorset mi 1. (bielizna) corset. 2. (kaftanik) bodice. 3. med. (= pas ortopedyczny) jacket, corset, brace; **gorset gipsowy** plaster jacket.

gorsetowy a. corset.

gorszący a. (= demoralizujący) corruptive, depraving; (= oburzający) shocking, offensive; (= rażący) scandalous.

gorszy a. zob. zły.

gorszyciel mp, **gorszycielka** f. Gen.pl. -ek scandalizer; depraver.

gorszyć ipf. (= wywołać oburzenie) scandalize, shock; (= demoralizować) corrupt, deprave.

gorycz f. 1. (= gorzki smak) bitterness, bitter taste. 2. przen. (= smutek) bitterness. 3. pl. -e (= goryczka) bitter principle l. tonic; **wypić do dna kielich goryczy** drain the cup of sorrow.

goryczak mi Gen. -a **goryczak żółciowy** bot. (grzyb) bitter boletus (Tylopilus felleus).

goryczka f. tylko sing. Gen.pl. -ek (= gorzki smak) bitterness, bitter taste. – f. 1. (substancja roślinna) bitter principle l. tonic. 2. bot. gentian (Gentiana).

goryczkowate pl. bot. gentians (Gentianaceae).

goryczkowaty a. 1. bitter, bitterish. 2. bot. gentianaceous.

gorycznik mi Gen. -a = **gorczycznik** 1.

goryl ma Gen.pl. -i l. -ów zool. gorilla (Gorilla gorilla). – mp Gen.pl. -i l. -ów pot. (= ochroniarz) bodyguard.

gorylica *f. zool.* female gorilla.

gorysz *mi Gen.pl.* **-y** *l.* **-ów** *bot.* Hog's fennel (*Peucedanum officinale*).

gorzała *f. pot.* booze, the hard stuff.

gorzałka *f. Gen.pl.* **-ek** *przest.* vodka, liquor.

gorzeć *ipf.* **1.** (= *palić się*) burn, blaze; (= *stać w ogniu*) be ablaze *l.* on fire. **2.** *przen.* (= *emocjonować się*) be excited. **3.** *przen.* (= *jaśnieć, błyszczeć*) glow, shine. **4.** *przen.* (= *rumienić się*) flush, blush.

gorzej *adv. zob.* **źle.**

gorzelnia *f. Gen.pl.* **-i** *l.* **-ń** distillery.

gorzelnictwo *n.* alcohol distillation.

gorzelniczy *a.* distillatory.

gorzelnik *mp* distiller.

gorzkawy *a.* **1.** (= *gorzki*) bitterish. **2.** (= *cierpki*) (*o zapachu*) pungent, acrid.

gorzki *a.* **1.** (*o smaku gorczycy*) bitter; **gorzka herbata** unsweetened tea; **gorzka kawa** unsweetened coffee; **gorzkie zioła** bitter herbs. **2.** (= *cierpki*) (*o zapachu*) acrid, pungent. **3.** *przen.* (= *przykry, nieprzyjemny*) bitter, painful, severe; **gorzkie słowa** harsh *l.* sharp words, bitter remarks; **gorzkie żale** *rel.* Lent hymn, Lent mass; **przełknąć gorzką pigułkę** swallow a bitter pill.

gorzknia *f. Gen.pl.* **-i** *bot.* quassia wood (*Quassia amara*).

gorzknieć *ipf.* **1.** (*stawać się gorzkim*) embitter, grow bitter. **2.** *przen.* (= *markotnieć*) grow *l.* become embittered.

gorzko *adv.* **1.** (= *gorzkawo*) bitterly; **gorzko, gorzko!** kiss, kiss! (*traditional cry of guests during a wedding reception encouraging the married couple to kiss*). **2.** (= *cierpko, drażniąco*) acridly, pungently. **3.** *przen.* (= *dotkliwie, smutno*) bitterly, sadly.

gospel *mi indecl. l. Gen.* **-u** *muz.* gospel (music).

gospoda *f. Gen.pl.* **-pód** **1.** inn, public house. **2.** *arch.* (= *kwatera*) lodging(s).

gospodarczy *a.* **1.** *ekon.* economic; **mapa gospodarcza** economic map; **podmiot gospodarczy** *prawn.* economic entity. **2.** (= *przemysłowy*) industrial, manufacturing. **3.** (= *gospodarski*) farm; **samolot gospodarczy** agricultural plane; **ubój gospodarczy** home *l.* domestic slaughter(ing). **4.** (= *administracyjny*) administrative, managerial; **wykonać coś sposobem gospodarczym** do sth using one's own means.

gospodarka *f. Gen.pl.* **-ek** **1.** *ekon.* economy; **gospodarka planowa** planned economy, state-controlled economy; **gospodarka rynkowa** market economy; **gospodarka wolnorynkowa** free market economy. **2.** (= *przemysł*) industry; **gospodarka komunalna** municipal utilities management. **3.** (= *zarządzanie*) management, administration. **4.** (= *gospodarstwo rolne*) (small) farm.

gospodarnie *adv.* thriftily, frugally, economically.

gospodarność *f.* thrift, frugality.

gospodarny *a.* thrifty, frugal.

gospodarować *ipf.* **1.** (*prowadzić gospodar-*

stwo rolne) run a farm. **2.** (= *zarządzać*) manage, administer.

gospodarski *a.* **1.** (*dotyczący gospodarstwa rolnego*) farm, farming; **zwierzęta gospodarskie** livestock. **2.** (= *chłopski, wiejski*) farmer's, rural, peasant. **3.** (= *gospodarny*) thrifty, frugal, economical. **4.** (= *domowy*) house, housekeeping.

gospodarstwo *n.* **1.** (= *wiejska posiadłość*) farm; **gospodarstwo rolne** farm, farmstead; **gospodarstwo rybne** fish farm; **gospodarstwo mięsne** livestock farm; **gospodarstwo warzywne** vegetable farm; **szkoła gospodarstwa wiejskiego** university of agriculture, college of agriculture. **2.** (= *dobytek*) possessions, property; **gospodarstwo domowe** household; **prowadzenie gospodarstwa domowego** (*np. przedmiot w szkole średniej*) home economics, home ec; **artykuły** *l.* **sprzęt gospodarstwa domowego** household appliances; **zajmować się gospodarstwem domowym** keep a house. **3.** *przest.* (= *gospodarowanie*) farming.

gospodarz *mp* **1.** (= *rolnik, chłop*) farmer, peasant. **2.** (= *pan domu*) host; **gospodarz zabawy** host, party *l.* ball organizer; **gospodarz domu** (= *dozorca*) janitor; *Br.* porter; **gospodarz programu** (program) host. **3.** (= *właściciel domu*) landlord, house owner. **4.** (= *zarządca*) manager, administrator. **5.** *biol.* (= *żywiciel*) host.

gospodyni *f.* **1.** (= *pani domu*) hostess. **2.** (= *rolniczka, chłopka*) farmer, peasant; **koło gospodyń wiejskich** village women's club. **3.** (= *pomoc domowa*) housekeeper. **4.** (= *właścicielka*) landlady, owner.

gosposia *f. Voc.* **-u** *Gen.pl.* **-ś** *l.* **-i** housekeeper.

goszysta *mp polit.* gauchist, (extreme *l.* radical) leftist.

goszystowski *a. polit.* gauchist, (extreme *l.* radical) leftist.

goszyzm *mi polit.* gauchism, (extreme *l.* radical) leftism.

gościć *ipf.* **goszczę gościsz** **1.** (= *mieć gości*) entertain, have (as) guests; (*np. o hotelu*) house, accomodate. **2.** (= *być podejmowanym*) stay (*somewhere l. at sb's place*), be a guest. **~ się** *ipf.* (= *iść w gości*) be (as) a guest; (= *przyjmować gości*) have (as) a guest.

gościec *mi* **-ćc-** *Gen.* **-a** *pat.* rheumatism, rheumatoid disease.

gościna *f.* visit, stay, sojourn; **być u kogoś w gościnie** stay at sb's place; **podziękować komuś za gościnę** thank sb for his/her hospitality.

gościniec *mi* **-ńc-** *Gen.* **-a** **1.** (*droga*) track. **2.** *przest.* (= *prezent*) present, gift.

gościnnie *adv.* **1.** (= *serdecznie*) hospitably, warmly, heartily. **2.** (= *nie u siebie, przejazdem*) temporarily, as a visitor, on the way somewhere else; **wykładać gościnnie** be a visiting *l.* guest lecturer.

gościnność *f.* hospitality; **podziękować komuś za gościnność** thank sb for his *l.* her hospitality; **nadużyć czyjejś gościnności** overstay sb's welcome.

gościnny *a.* **1.** (= *otwarty, serdeczny*) hospitable, warm, friendly; **gościnne progi** open house; **gościnna ziemia** hospitable *l.* friendly land. **2.** (= *dla gości, do wynajęcia*) guest; **pokoje gościnne** guest rooms. **3.** (= *wyjazdowy, nie u siebie*) guest; **gościnne występy** guest performance *l.* appearance.

gość *mp Ins.pl.* **-mi 1.** (= *przybysz*) guest; **gość weselny** wedding guest; **częsty gość** regular guest; (*zwł. w pubie, knajpie*) regular; **nieproszony gość** unwelcome guest, uninvited guest; **niespodziewany gość** unexpected guest; **być rzadkim gościem we własnym domu** be seldom at home; **gość w dom, Bóg w dom** my home is your home; what's mine is yours; **z czym do gości** *pot.* there's nothing to brag about, it's not worth showing (off). **2.** (= *wczasowicz*) guest, visitor, holidaymaker; **hotelowi goście** hotel guests; **być stałym gościem** be a regular guest. **3.** *pot.* (= *facet*) guy, dude; **równy gość** cool guy.

gośćcowy *a. pat.* rheumatic, rheumatoid.

Got *mp pl.* **Goci** *l.* **-owie** *hist.* Goth.

Göteborg *mi Gen.* **-a** *geogr.* Gothenburg, Göteborg.

göteborski *a.* Gothenburg.

gotować *ipf.* **1.** (= *przyrządzać, kucharzyć*) cook, boil; **gotować na parze** steam. **2.** *rzad.* (= *przygotowywać*) prepare, make ready, get ready; **gotuj broń** *wojsk.* ready!; **Gotuj broń! Cel! Pal! Ready! Aim! Fire!** ~ **się** *ipf.* **1.** (= *być gotowanym*) cook, boil; **gotować się na parze** steam; **gotuje się jak w garnku** (*o pogodzie, zbiorniku wodnym*) weather/sea is stormy *l.* changing all the time; (*o zamieszkach, ruchu ulicznym*) sth is in a state of turmoil. **2.** *przen.* (= *kotłować się, miotać się*) boil, seethe; **krew się we mnie gotuje** my blood is boiling; **gotuje się w nim ze złości** he is seething with anger; **ktoś się gotuje na wspomnienie o czymś** sb gets steamed up at the memory of sth. **3.** (= *przygotowywać się*) get ready, ready o.s.; **gotować się na śmierć** prepare to die.

gotowanie *n.* **1.** (= *kucharzenie*) cooking. **2.** (= *przygotowywanie się*) getting ready, preparing o.s. (*na coś* for sth).

gotowe *n. Gen.* **-ego przyjść na gotowe** *l.* **do gotowego** get everything without lifting *l.* raising a finger.

gotowiec *mi* **-wc-** *Gen.* **-a** *szkoln.* (= *ściąga*) crib, pony.

gotowizna *f. przest.* cash.

gotowość *f.* **1.** (= *pogotowie*) readiness, preparedness; **być w gotowości** be ready, be on standby; **gotowość strajkowa** readiness to strike. **2.** (= *chęć, zamiar*) willingness; **gotowość do pomocy** willingness to help.

gotowy *a.* **1.** (= *wykończony, wykonany*) ready, finished; **wyroby gotowe** ready-made clothes, ready-to-wear clothes, off the peg clothes; **kupić coś gotowego** buy *l.* get sth ready-made. **2.** (= *chętny, skory*) willing. **3.** (= *przygotowany*) ready; **gotowe!** ready!, done!; **być gotowym na wszystko** be ready for anything. **4.** *pot., przen.* (= *(prawie) martwy*) done (in *l.* for). **5.** (*w połączeniu z bezokolicznikiem wyraża gotowość wystąpienia czynności*) ready; **jest zawsze gotów**

pomagać innym he is always ready to help other people; **dom gotowy się zawalić** house ready to collapse.

gotów *a. indecl. zob.* **gotowy**.

gotówka *f.* cash; **płacić gotówką** pay cash; **żywa gotówka** (hard) cash.

gotówkowy *a.* cash; **czek gotówkowy** *ekon.* cashier's *l.* open check.

gotycki *a.* **1.** *bud.* Gothic; **styl gotycki** Gothic style; **gotyckie budowle** Gothic buildings. **2.** *druk.* Gothic; **pismo gotyckie** Gothic, gothic type, *zwł. Br.* black letter.

gotycyzm *mi bud.* Gothicism.

gotyk *mi* **1.** *bud.* Gothic style. **2.** *druk.* Gothic, gothic type, *zwł. Br.* black letter.

gouda *f. kulin.* Gouda.

goździeniec *mi* **-ńc-** *Gen.* **-a** *bot.* clavaria (*Clavaria*); **goździeniec okółkowy** coral necklace (*Illecebrum verticillatum*).

goździk *mi Gen.* **-a 1.** *bot.* carnation, clove pink (*Dianthus caryophyllus*); **goździk chiński** China pink (*Dianthus chinensis*); **goździk brodaty** sweet william (*Dianthus barbatus*). **2.** (*przyprawa*) clove.

goździkowiec *mi* **-wc-** *Gen.* **-a** *bot.* clove (tree) (*Eugenia*).

goździkowy *a.* (*dotyczący przyprawy*) clove; **olejek goździkowy** clove *l.* caryophyllus oil.

gódź *itd. ipf. zob.* **godzić**.

gój *itd. ipf. zob.* **goić**.

gól *itd. ipf. zob.* **golić**.

góra *f.* **1.** (= *wzniesienie, szczyt*) mountain, mount; **góra lodowa** iceberg; **góry i doły** bumps; **jechać w góry** go to the mountains; **za siedmioma górami, za siedmioma lasami** *l.* **za siódmą górą, za siódmą rzeką** (*początek bajki*) once upon a time (in a distant kingdom); *przen.* (= *daleko*) far, far away; **mieć pod górę** *l.* **górkę** *pot.* have a difficult time, do sth the hard way; **góra zrodziła mysz** the mountain labors and brings forth a (ridiculous) mouse; **góra z górą się nie zejdzie, a człowiek z człowiekiem zawsze** it's a small world; friends may meet but mountains never greet; **nie chciała góra przyjść do Mahometa, przyszedł Mahomet do góry** if the mountain will not come to Mohammad, Mohammad must go to the mountain; **łatwiej z góry niż pod górę** once I (we, etc.) get over the hump, it's all downhill. **2.** (= *stos*) heap, pile; **obiecywać komuś złote góry** promise sb the moon, promise sb (all the riches of) the world. **3.** (= *górna część*) top, upper part, head; (*domu*) upstairs; **do góry** *l.* **ku górze** *l.* **w górę** up; **ręce do góry** (*np. przy zatrzymaniu przestępcy*) hands up; (*w czasie napadu*) stick'em up!; **do góry nogami** upside down; **leżeć do góry brzuchem** laze around *l.* away; **głowa do góry!** cheer up!, chin up!; **mieszkać na górze** live upstairs; **od góry do dołu** from top down, from top to bottom; **obejrzeć kogoś od góry do dołu** inspect sb from head to toe, look at sb up and down; **u góry** (*na górze czegoś*) at the top; (*w domu*) upstairs; **iść w górę** (= *wspinać się*) go uphill; (*o ludziach*) advance, make a career; (*o cenach l. wskazaniach termometru, barometru* *itp.*) go up; **w górze rzeki** upriver, upstream; **z góry** (*czegoś*) from the top; (*w domu*) from upstairs; **schodzić z góry** (*domu*) go downstairs; **płacić z góry** pay in advance; **z górą** over, more than; **było tam z górą trzydzieści osób** there were over thirty people there; **traktować kogoś z góry** patronize sb, look down one's nose at sb. **4.** *pot.* (= *kierownictwo, władza*) the authorities, the management; *pot.* the bigwigs; **wojna na górze** management infighting; **dostać kopa w górę** get bumped up a level; **polecenie z góry** order *l.* directive from the management. **5.** (= *strych*) loft, attic.

góral *mp* **1.** (= *mieszkaniec gór*) highlander. **2.** *sport* (*kolarz*) mountain biker. – *mi Gen.* **-a 1.** *pot.* (*rower*) mountain bike, MTB.

góralka *f. Gen.pl.* **-ek** highlander.

góralski *a.* highlander. – *mi* (*taniec*) fast highlanders' dance.

górą *adv.* **1.** (= *wysoko, wyżej*) high(er). **2. być górą** have the upper hand, gain advantage over sb.

górka *f. Gen.pl.* **-ek 1.** (= *pagórek*) hill, hillock; **górka rozrządowa** *kol.* hump; **iść pod górkę** go uphill; **(pobiec) z górki na pazurki** go headlong down the hill; **mieć pod górkę** *pot.* have a difficult time, do sth the hard way; **teraz mamy już z górki** *żart.* it's all downhill from here, the rest is gravy, now comes the easy part. **2.** (= *strych*) loft, attic.

górnictwo *n.* **1.** (*gałąź przemysłu*) mining; **górnictwo węglowe** coal mining; **górnictwo naftowe** oil mining; **górnictwo odkrywkowe** open-cut mining, open pit mining; **górnictwo rudowe** ore mining. **2.** (*nauka*) mining.

górniczy *a.* mining, miner's.

górnik *mp* miner.

górnolotnie *adv.* loftily, pompously.

górnolotny *a.* lofty, pompous, high-flown; *pot.* highfalutin.

górnoniemiecki *a. jęz.* High German.

górnopłat *mi lotn.* high-wing monoplane.

górnośląski *a. geogr.* Upper Silesian.

górnozaworowy *a. techn.* **silnik górnozaworowy** overhead-valve engine.

górny *a.* **1.** (= *wysoki, wierzchni*) upper, top; **kończyny górne** upper limbs; **górna granica** upper limit; **górne światło** overhead light; **górna piłka** *sport* high ball. **2.** *geogr.* (= *bliski źródła*) upstream. **3.** (= *wyżej położony, wyżynny*) upper, high(er); **Górny Egipt** Upper Egipt; **Górny Śląsk** Upper Silesia. **4.** *muz.* upper. **5.** *geol.* (= *młodszy*) upper; (*w nazwach*) Upper; **górny pliocen** Upper Pliocene.

górotwór *mi* **-o- 1.** *geol.* orogen. **2.** *górn.* rock mass, ground.

górotwórczość *f. geol.* orogeny.

górotwórczy *a. geol.* orogenic.

górować *ipf.* **1.** (= *przewyższać*) tower (*nad kimś / czymś* over sb/sth); dominate (*nad kimś / czymś* sb/sth). **2.** (*o broni palnej*) overshoot. **3.** *astron.* (= *być w zenicie*) pass the zenith. **4.** *przen.* excel, surpass (*nad kimś* sb).

górski *a.* mountain, mountainous; **górska**

miejscowość wypoczynkowa mountain resort; **pasmo górskie** mountain range.

górzysty *a.* **-szy** mountainous, hilly.

gówienko *n. Gen.pl.* **-nek** *pot.* **1.** (= *odchody*) shit, crap. **2.** *przen.* (= *drobiazg*) shitty *l.* crappy little thing, nothing.

gówniany *a. wulg.* shitty, crappy.

gówniara *f. wulg., emf.* punk, little shit.

gówniarz *mp wulg., emf.* punk, little shit, squirt.

gówno *n. Gen.pl.* **-wien 1.** *wulg.* (= *kał*) shit, crap; **wdepnąć w gówno** *przen.* be in deep shit. **2.** *wulg., przen.* (*ktoś lub coś godne pogardy*) piece of shit *l.* crap; **awanturować się o byle gówno** argue over every little piece of shit *l.* crappy thing. **3.** *wulg., przen.* (= *błahostka*) shitty *l.* crappy little thing, nothing; **gówno cię to obchodzi** it's none of your fucking business; **gówno z tego będzie** this is a fucking waste of time, this ain't gonna be worth a shit; **gówno z tego mam** I got fuck-all for my trouble, I got nothing but shit for my trouble; **dostać za coś gówno** not get jack shit for sth, get shit for sth. – *int., wulg.* (= *sprzeciw*) shit; **a gówno!** shit, no!

gra *f. Gen.pl.* **gier 1.** game, play; **gra planszowa** board game; **gra komputerowa** computer game; **gra telewizyjna** video game; **gra liczbowa** numbers game; **gra hazardowa** gamble; **gra losowa** game of chance; **dom** *l.* **salon gry** gambling house, gaming house; **gra słów** *jęz.* pun, play on words, wordplay. **2.** *sport* game; **gry zespołowe** team sports; **gra podwójna** *tenis* doubles; **gra pojedyncza** *tenis* singles; **gra mieszana** *tenis* mixed doubles; **gra o pietruszkę** *pot.* low stakes game, no stakes game. **3.** (= *drganie*) play; **gra świateł** play of lights; **gra kolorów** *l.* **barw** play of colors. – *f. tylko sing.* **1.** *sztuka* acting. **2.** (= *udawanie*) act, sham, pretense; **gra o władzę** fight for power; **określić reguły gry** specify rules of the game; **gra na giełdzie** *ekon.* speculation; **gry wojenne** *wojsk.* war games; **gra w otwarte karty** (= *uczciwe postępowanie*) square deal; (*w karty*) playing with the cards laid down faceup (*to teach sb how to play a new card game*); **ukartowana gra** sham, fixed game; **gra w kotka i myszkę** double dealing, mutual deception; **gra (nie) jest warta świeczki** the game is (not) worth the candle; **to nie wchodzi w grę** this is out of the question. **3.** *muz.* (*na fortepianie itp.*) play, performance; **gra na nerwach** getting on sb's nerves, getting on sb's last nerve.

Graal *mi Gen.* **-a święty Graal** *rel., Bibl., mit.* Holy Grail.

grab *mi* **1.** *bot.* hornbeam (*Carpinus*). **2.** (*drewno*) hornbeam (wood).

graba *f. pot., żart.* (= *ręka*) paw; **daj grabę** tip us your fin.

grabarz *mp* (*osoba*) gravedigger; **uciec grabarzowi spod łopaty** *żart.* cheat death. – *ma ent.* burying beetle, sexton (*Necrophorus*).

grabić *ipf.* **1.** (= *wyrównywać grabiami*) rake. **2.** (= *kraść*) plunder, loot, pillage.

grabie *pl. Gen.* **-i** (*narzędzie*) rake.

grabieć *ipf.* (= *kostnieć*) grow numb (*with cold*).

grabież *f. pl.* **-e** (= *kradzież*) plunder, pillage.

grabieżca *mp* plunderer, pillager.

grabki *pl. Gen.* **-bek** 1. (*narzędzie*) rake. 2. *pot. bilard* spider.

grabowy *a.* hornbeam.

graca *f.* 1. *roln., górn.* hoe. 2. *bud.* hoe, larry.

graciarnia *f. Gen.pl.* **-i** *l.* **-ń** *pot.* storage room (*in a house, usu. littered and untidy*).

gracja *f.* 1. (= *wdzięk*) grace. 2. *przen.* beautiful woman.

Gracje *pl. mit.* Graces.

gracować *ipf. roln., bud.* hoe.

gracownik *mp pl.* **-cy** *bud.* (*robotnik*) hoer. – *mi pl.* **-i** *roln.* (*narzędzie*) weeding hoe.

gracz *mp* 1. (*osoba uczestnicząca w grze*) player. 2. *przen.* (= *cwaniak, spryciarz*) sly devil, cunning person; **gracz giełdowy** speculator (*on the stock exchange*).

grać *ipf.* 1. (*uczestniczyć w grze*) play; **grać w karty** play cards; **grać w piłkę** play soccer; **grać w koszykówkę** play basketball; **grać na loterii** play the lottery; **grać na wyścigach** gamble on the horses (dogs, etc.), play the horses (dogs, etc.); **grać na giełdzie** play the stock exchange; **grać na zwłokę** play for time, stall; **grać w otwarte karty** (= *postępować uczciwie*) offer a square deal, lay one's cards on the table; (*w karty*) play with the cards laid down faceup (*to teach sb how to play a new card game*); **grać z dziadkiem** *karty* play with a dummy. 2. *muz.* play, perform; **grać na fortepianie/skrzypcach/gitarze** play the piano/violin/guitar; **grać koncert** play a concerto; **grać na cztery ręce** play a piece for four hands; **grać komuś na nosie** *przen.* thumb one's nose at sb; **grać pierwsze/drugie skrzypce** *przen.* play first/second fiddle; **w to mi graj** that's right up my alley, it's food and drink to me; **kiszki mi marsza grają** I'm starving; **szafa grająca** jukebox; **szafa gra** *pot.* everything is OK. 3. *sztuka* play, perform; **co dziś grają w kinie?** what's playing *l.* showing at the movies today? 4. (*o aktorze*) act, play; **grać główną rolę** play the main *l.* leading part; **grać komedię** *przen.* pretend, try to cover sth up. 5. (*uzewnętrzniać uczucia*) show, manifest; **w kimś gra krew** sb is excited *l.* agitated; **grać komuś na nerwach** get on sb's nerves; **grać na uczuciach** take advantage of sb's feelings *l.* emotions; **grać na słabościach** take advantage of sb's weaknesses. 6. (= *drgać, migotać*) sparkle, flicker. 7. *myśl.* (*o głuszcach, cietrzewiach*) toot; (*o ogarach*) bark ferociously (*while chasing game*).

grad *mi* 1. *meteor.* hail. 2. *przen.* (= *mnóstwo, masa*) hail, volley, shower; **grad pytań/życzeń** hail *l.* volley *l.* shower of questions/wishes; **grad pocisków** *l.* **kul** hail of bullets.

gradacja *f.* 1. (= *hierarchia, kolejność*) gradation. 2. *geol.* gradation. 3. *biol.* pest gradation.

gradient *mi fiz., mat.* gradient; **gradient ciśnienia** pressure gradient; **gradient temperatury** temperature gradient.

gradientowy *a.* gradient.

gradobicie *n. zwł. meteor.* hailstorm.

gradowy *a.* hail; **chmura gradowa** hail cloud.

gradówka *f. Gen.pl.* **-ek** *pat.* chalazion, meibomian cyst.

gradualny *a. kośc., rel.* gradual.

graduał *mi kośc., rel.* (*księga liturgiczna l. śpiew*) gradual.

graf¹ *mp Gen.* **-a** *pl.* **-owie** *hist.* count.

graf² *mi Gen.* **-u** *pl.* **-y** *mat.* graph.

grafem *mi jęz.* grapheme.

graffiti *n. indecl.* graffiti.

graficzka *f. Gen.pl.* **-ek** graphic artist.

graficznie *adv.* (= *pisemnie l. plastycznie*) graphically.

graficzny *a.* 1. (= *pisemny l. dotyczący grafiki*) graphic, graphical. 2. *mat.* graphic.

grafik¹ *mp Gen.* **-a** *pl.* **-cy** (*artysta*) graphic artist.

grafik² *mi Gen.* **-u** *pl.* **-i** (= *diagram, plan*) diagram, chart.

grafika *f.* 1. *tylko sing.* (*dziedzina*) graphic art. 2. (*dzieło sztuki*) graphic.

grafion *mi techn.* ruling pen.

grafit *mi* 1. (*część ołówka*) lead. 2. *min.* graphite.

grafitować *ipf. druk., techn.* graphitize.

grafitowy *a. techn.* graphite, graphitic; **włókna grafitowe** graphite fiber, *Br.* graphite fibre.

grafolog *mp pl.* **-dzy** *l.* **-owie** graphologist.

grafologia *f. Gen.* **-ii** graphology.

grafologiczny *a.* graphologic.

grafoman *mp*, **grafomanka** *f.* (= *kiepski pisarz*) scribbler, hack; (*osoba opanowana manią pisania*) graphomaniac.

grafomania *f. Gen.* **-ii** writing addiction, graphomania.

grafomanka *f. Gen.pl.* **-ek** *zob.* **grafoman**.

grafometria *f. Gen.* **-ii** *prawn.* graphometry.

grafometryczny *a. prawn.* graphometric.

graham *mi Gen.* **-a** *kulin.* graham bread.

grahamka *f. kulin.* graham roll.

grajdoł *mi Gen.* **-a** *l.* **-u** 1. *pot., pog.* (= *miasteczko*) hick town, shithole, noplaceville. 2. *pot., żart.* (*na plaży*) shallow hole sb digs on the beach to screen o.s. from wind and others in order to sunbathe.

grajdołek *mi* **-łk-** *Gen.* **-a** *zob.* **grajdoł**.

grajek *mp* **-jk-** *pl.* **-owie** *l.* **-i** homegrown musician.

Gral *mi zob.* **Graal**.

gram *mi Gen.* **-a** (*jednostka masy*) gram, gramme.

gramatura *f. gsm* (*gram per squared meter*).

gramatycznie *adv.* gramatically.

gramatyczny *a.* grammatical; **rodzaj gramatyczny** *jęz.* grammatical gender.

gramatyk *mp jęz.* grammarian.

gramatyka *f.* 1. (*nauka*) grammar; **gramatyka generatywna** generative grammar; **gramatyka historyczna** historical grammar; **gramatyka opisowa** descriptive grammar; **gramatyka porównawcza** contrastive grammar; **gramatyka języka polskiego/angielskiego** Polish/English grammar. 2. (*książka*) grammar book.

gramocząsteczka f. chem. mole, gram molecule.

gramofon mi record player, gramophone.

gramofonowy a. gramophone; **płyta gramofonowa** record.

gramojon mi chem. gram-ion.

gramolić się ipf. pot. clamber (na kogoś/coś up sb/sth).

gramorównoważnik mi Gen. **-a** chem. gram equivalent, equivalent weight.

gran mi Gen. **-a** miern. grain.

granat[1] mi **1.** bot. pomergranate (Punica granatum). **2.** (owoc) pomergranate.

granat[2] mi wojsk. grenade; **granat ręczny** hand grenade.

granat[3] mi sport grenade.

granat[4] mi min. garnet.

granat[5] mi (kolor) **1.** navy blue. **2.** pot. tk. navy blue cloth.

granatnik mi Gen. **-a** wojsk. grenade launcher.

granatowiec mi **-wc-** Gen. **-a** bot. pomergranate (Punica granatum).

granatowy a. navy blue.

granda f. pot., przest. (= awantura) row, brawl; (= oszustwo) deception, fraud; **robić coś na grandę** come on (too) strong, be a bit pushy.

grand prix mi indecl. sport Grand Prix.

graniastosłup mi Gen. **-a** geom. prism.

granica f. **1.** (linia wyznaczająca obszar) border, boundary, frontier; **granica państwa** state border; **wyjechać za granicę** go abroad, leave the country; **zamknąć granice** close the borders; **przejść przez zieloną granicę** cross the border illegally. **2.** (= limit) limit, bounds, confines; **być bez granic** be boundless, know no bounds; **to przekracza wszelkie granice** that's the limit; **doprowadzić kogoś do ostatecznych granic** drive sb to extremes; **trzymać się pewnych granic** stay within certain limits l. bounds; **czynić coś w granicach swoich możliwości** do sb's best, do all sb can; **wszystko ma swoje granice** there's a limit to everything. **3.** (= kres, pułap) limit, range.

graniczny a. **1.** (wyznaczający zasięg obszaru) border; **kontrola graniczna** border check; **przejście graniczne** border checkpoint, border crossing-point; **straż graniczna** border patrol; **strefa graniczna** border area l. zone. **2.** (= ostateczny, skrajny) limitary, terminal, final; **wartość graniczna** limit.

graniczyć ipf. **1.** (= sąsiadować, stykać się) border (z czymś on sth). **2.** (= zbliżać się, być podobnym) verge (do czegoś on sth).

granie n. **1.** (uczestniczenie w grach) playing, taking part in a game; **granie na zwłokę** playing for time, stalling. **2.** (wykonywanie utworów muzycznych, wydawanie dźwięków) playing, performing. **3.** (odtwarzanie roli) acting, playing.

granit mi min. granite; **serce z granitu** przen. heart of stone.

granitowy a. granite.

grant mi zwł. uniw. grant; **wnioski o granty** grant applications.

granulacja f. **1.** astron. photospheric granulation. **2.** med. granulation (tissue); **granulacja ranny** granulation. **3.** techn. (= granulowanie) granulation. **4.** techn. (skład ziarnowy substancji) graining, grain-size distribution.

granulacyjny a. techn., med. granulative.

granulat mi techn. granulated mass.

granulit mi min. granulite.

granulka f. Gen.pl. **-ek** granule, pellet.

granulocyt mi biol. granulocyte.

granulować ipf. **1.** techn. granulate; **herbata granulowana** granulated tea. **2.** med. (= ziarninować) develop granulation tissue.

grań f. pl. **-e 1.** (= kant) edge, ridge. **2.** (= krawędź górska) ridge, crest, arête.

grapefruit zob. **grejpfrut.**

grappa f. kulin. grappa.

grasica f. anat. thymus, thymus gland.

grasować ipf. **1.** (= rabować) (np. o bandzie) prowl; (np. o zbiegłym przestępcy) be at large. **2.** przen. (= szaleć) be rampant, rage.

grat mi Gen. **-a** pot. (= rupieć) (piece of) junk; mot. jalopy. – mp pl. **-y** pot., pog. (= ramol) geezer, crock.

gratis[1] adv. (= darmo) free, free of charge.

gratis[2] mi (rzecz otrzymana za darmo) complimentary.

gratisowy a. free (of charge), complimentary.

gratka f. Gen.pl. **-ek** windfall, stroke of luck, piece of good fortune.

gratulacje f. congratulations, felicitations; **złożyć komuś gratulacje z okazji czegoś** congratulate sb on sth, offer sb one's congratulations on sth.

gratulacyjny a. (list, depesza, telegram) congratulatory.

gratulować ipf. congratulate (komuś czegoś sb on sth).

gratyfikacja f. **1.** bonus, extra pay. **2.** przest. remuneration.

grawer mp engraver.

grawernia f. Gen.pl. **-i** l. **-ń** engraving shop.

grawerować ipf. engrave (coś na czymś sth on sth) (w czymś into sth).

grawerstwo n. engraving.

grawerunek mi **-nk-** engraving.

grawitacja f. fiz. gravitation; **siła grawitacji** gravitational force; **prawo grawitacji** law of universal gravitation.

grawitacyjny a. fiz. gravitational.

grawitować ipf. **1.** fiz. gravitate. **2.** przen. (= skłaniać się) gravitate (ku komuś/czemuś toward sb/sth) (do kogoś/czegoś toward sb/sth); be attracted, lean (ku komuś/czemuś to(ward) sb/sth) (do kogoś/czegoś to(ward) sb/sth).

grawiura f. druk. **1.** (technika) engraving. **2.** (rycina) engraving copy.

grażdanka f. jęz. modern Cyrillic alphabet.

grąd mi **1.** leśn. wet-ground forest. **2.** roln. (= łąka, pastwisko) valley meadow.

grążel mi Gen. **-a** Gen.pl. **-i** l. **-ów** bot. water lily (Nuphar); **grążel żółty** yellow water lily, brandy bottle (Nuphar lutea).

grdyka f. anat. Adam's apple.

Grecja f. geogr. Greece.

grecki *a.* Greek, Grecian; **ogień grecki** *hist.* Greek fire; **grecki profil** Grecian profile.

greckokatolicki *a. kośc.* Greek; **kościół greckokatolicki** Greek (Orthodox) Church.

grecysta *mp*, **grecystka** *f. uniw.* Grecian.

grecystyczny *a. uniw.* **studia grecystyczne** Greek studies.

grecystyka *f. uniw.* Greek studies.

grecyzm *mi jęz.* Grecism.

Greczynka *f. zob.* **Grek**.

gregoriański *a.* Gregorian; **chorał gregoriański** *muz.* Gregorian chant; **kalendarz gregoriański** Gregorian calendar; **kościół gregoriański** *kośc.* Armenian Gregorian church; **reforma gregoriańska** *hist., rel.* Gregorian reform.

grejpfrut *mi Gen.* -a *l.* -u **1.** *bot.* grapefruit (*Citrus paradisi*). **2.** *Gen.* -a (*owoc*) grapefruit.

grejpfrutowy *a.* grapefruit; **sok grejpfrutowy** grapefruit juice.

Grek *mp*, **Greczynka** *f.* Greek.

grek *mp pot.* **udawać greka** play dumb, play the fool.

greka *f.* (*język*) Greek, Greek language.

grekokatolik *mp rel.* Greek Catholic.

gremialnie *adv.* in a body, collectively.

gremium *n. sing. indecl. pl.* -mia *Gen.* -miów body, assembly.

Grenada *f. geogr.* Grenada.

grenadier *mp hist., wojsk.* grenadier.

grenadierski *a. hist., wojsk.* grenadier, grenadierial.

grenadyjski *a. geogr.* Grenadian.

Grenlandczyk *mp*, **Grenlandka** *f.* Greenlander.

Grenlandia *f. Gen.* -ii *geogr.* Greenland.

grenlandzki *a.* Greenlandic.

Grenoble *n. indecl. geogr.* Grenoble.

greps *mi* (= *trik, chwyt*) (*słowny*) gag; (*sytuacyjny*) practical joke.

greyhound *ma kynol.* greyhound.

grępla *f. Gen.pl.* -i *tk.* card.

gręplarka *f. tk.* carding machine.

gręplować *ipf. tk.* card; **gręplowana wełna** carded wool.

grill *mi Gen.* -a *Gen.pl.* -i *l.* -ów **1.** (= *ruszt*) barbecue, grill; **potrawy z grilla** barbecue. **2.** (*lokal*) grill (restaurant), grillroom.

grillować *ipf. pot., kulin.* barbecue, grill.

grillowy *a.* barbecue, grill; **sos grillowy** barbecue sauce.

grizli *ma indecl. zool.* grizzly bear, grizzly (*Ursus arctos horriblis*).

grizzly *ma zob.* **grizli**.

grobie *mi zob.* **grób**.

grobla *f. Gen.pl.* -i *l.* -bel (*np. rozdzielająca stawy*) causeway; (*zabezpieczająca przed wylaniem*) dike, dyke; (= *tama*) dam.

grobowiec *mi* -wc- *Gen.* -a tomb, sepulcher, *Br.* sepulchre; **rodzinny grobowiec** family vault.

grobowy *a.* grave, tomb, sepulchral; **kamień grobowy** gravestone, tombstone, headstone; **do grobowej deski** till death do us part, forever; **grobowa cisza** dead silence; **grobowa mina** gloomy face, grave expression.

groch *mi* **1.** *bot.* pea (*Pisum*); **czuć się jak groch przy drodze** feel ill at ease, be bothered all the time. **2.** (*ziarna grochu zwyczajnego*) pea(s); **rzucać grochem o ścianę** waste sb's breath; **daj spokój, to jak by rzucać grochem o ścianę** it's all falling on deaf ears; **groch z kapustą** higgledy-piggledy, hodge-podge, helter-skelter.

grochodrzew *mi bot.* locust tree, false acacia (*Robinia pseudoacacia*).

grochowy *a.* pea; **tyczka grochowa** pea stick; **zupa grochowa** pea soup.

grochówka *f.* (*zupa*) pea soup; **żołnierska** *l.* **wojskowa grochówka** *Br.* peas pottage, extra thick pea soup; **grochówka z wkładką** pea soup with sausage *l.* a piece of meat.

grochy *pl. Gen.* -ów (*wzór*) polka dots.

grodzić *ipf.* **gródź** *l.* **grodź 1.** (= *otaczać płotem*) fence, enclose with a fence. **2.** (= *dzielić*) fence off, divide, separate.

grodzki *a.* municipal, town, city; **sąd grodzki** *prawn.* magistrates' court; *hist.* borough court.

grog *mi kulin.* grog.

grom *mi lit.* thunder; **jak rażony gromem** thunderstruck; **jak grom z jasnego nieba** like a bolt from the blue; **rzucać gromy na kogoś/coś** curse sb/sth, swear at sb/sth; **jest czegoś od groma** there is plenty *l.* there are loads of sth; **jest kogoś od groma** there are loads *l.* crowds of people.

gromada *f.* **1.** (= *tłum, zgromadzenie*) group, crowd; **jest nas cała gromada** there is a whole bunch of us. **2.** *zool., bot.* (*jednostka w systematyce*) class. **3.** *astron.* cluster.

gromadka *f. Gen.pl.* -ek small group.

gromadny *a.* collective, sociable; (*o zwierzętach*) gregarious.

gromadzić *ipf.* **1.** (= *zbierać, skupiać ludzi*) gather; (= *przyciągać*) attract. **2.** (= *zbierać, kumulować*) accumulate. ~ **się** *ipf.* **1.** (= *zbierać się, skupiać się*) assemble, gather; **tłumnie się gromadzić** crowd, throng, arrive in large numbers. **2.** (*występować w większej ilości*) gather, pile up.

gromadzki *a. hist.* district.

gromić *ipf.* **1.** (= *upominać, karcić*) scold, reprimand. **2.** *lit.* (= *pokonywać, zwyciężać*) rout, defeat.

gromki *a.* booming, stentorian.

gromnica *f. zwł. rel.* (*świeca*) candle lit during storms and for dying people.

gromniczny *a.* (*dotyczący świecy*) candle; (*dotyczący święta*) Candlemas; **święto Matki Boskiej Gromnicznej** *kośc.* Candlemas (Day).

gronkowiec *ma* -wc- *biol.* staphylococcus; **mieć gronkowca** *pot.* (= *zatruć się gronkowcem*) have a staph infection.

grono *n.* **1.** (= *grupa, zespół*) team, group; **grono rodzinne** family (circle); **grono nauczycielskie** *l.* **pedagogiczne** teaching staff, teachers. **2.** *pot.* (= *kiść*) bunch, cluster; **grono winogron** bunch of grapes. **3.** *bot.* (*kwiatostan*) raceme. **4.** *fiz.* cluster.

gronorost *mi bot.* gulfweed, sargassum, sargasso (*Sargassum*).

gronostaj *ma Gen.pl.* -ai *l.* -jów *zool.* stoat, er-

mine (*Mustela erminea*). – *mi Gen.* -a *Gen.pl.* -ai
l. -jów (*skórka, futro*) ermine, ermine fur coat;
nosić gronostaje wear ermine fur coat.

gronostajowy *a.* ermine.

gronowy *a.* grape; **cukier gronowy** *chem., biol.*
grape sugar, dextrose.

gros *n. indecl.* (= *większość*) the majority.

grosik *mi Gen.* -a (*moneta*) penny, cent, farthing; *zob. t.* **grosz.**

grosular *mi min.* grossularite.

grosz *mi Gen.* -a 1. (*w Polsce*) grosz. 2. (=
drobna moneta) penny, cent, farthing; **być bez
(złamanego) grosza (przy duszy)** be penniless;
not have one penny to rub against another; not
have two pennies to rub together; **co do grosza**
not a penny less, not a penny more; to the last
penny; **nie dać złamanego grosza** give nothing;
nie wydać złamanego grosza spend nothing; **nie
być wartym złamanego grosza** not be worth a
plugged *l.* wooden nickel; **wtrącić trzy grosze** *pot.*
put in one's two cents' worth; **kupić coś za psi
grosz** buy sth dirt-cheap, buy sth for a song; pay
peanuts for sth; **nie mieć za grosz czegoś** not to
have an ounce of sth. 3. *pot.* (= *kwota*) money;
kawał grosza a good bit of money; **zarabiać grosze** earn very little; **kupić coś za ostatni grosz**
spend one's last dime on sth; **wdowi grosz** widow's mite; **liczyć się z groszem** count every penny twice; **nie liczyć się z groszem** spend money
like it's going out of style.

groszek *mi* -szk- *Gen.* -u *l.* -a 1. (*o nasionach
grochu*) pea(s); **groszek konserwowy** canned
peas. 2. *bot.* pea, vetchling (*Lathyrus*); **groszek
pachnący** sweet pea (*Lathyrus odoratus*).

groszki *pl. Gen.* -ów (*wzór*) polka dots, spots.

groszoród *mp* -o- *pl.* -y *pog.* moneygrubber.

groszowy *a.* 1. (*o wartości grosza*) grosz. 2. (=
bardzo tani, o małej wartości) dirt-cheap; **gro-
szowa powieść** dime novel; *zwł. Br.* penny-
dreadful.

groszówka *f. Gen.pl.* -ek 1. (*moneta*) one grosz
coin. 2. *dial.* large darning needle.

grot[1] *mi Gen.* -u 1. (= *ostrze*) spearhead, arrowhead. 2. *techn.* point chisel.

grot[2] *mi Gen.* -a *żegl.* mainsail; **grot sztormowy** trysail.

grota *f.* cave, grotto.

groteska *f. Gen.pl.* -ek 1. *zwł. teor.lit.* burlesque. 2. *sztuka* grotesque.

groteskowość *f.* grotesquery, grotesquerie.

groteskowy *a.* grotesque.

grotfał *mi żegl.* main halyard.

grotmars *mi żegl.* main top.

grotmarsel *mi* -sl- *Gen.* -a *żegl.* main topsail.

grotmaszt *mi żegl.* mainmast.

grotołaz *mp pl.* -i *l.* -y caver.

grotreja *f. Gen.* -ei *żegl.* main yard.

grotstenga *f. żegl.* main topmast.

grottopsel *mi* -sl- *Gen.* -a *żegl.* main topsail.

grotżagiel *mi* -gl- *Gen.* -a *żegl.* mainsail.

groza *f.* 1. (= *niebezpieczeństwo*) peril, danger. 2. (= *przerażenie, strach*) fear, awe, horror;
film grozy thriller *l.* horror (movie); **powieść grozy** thriller *l.* horror (novel).

grozić *ipf.* -żę -zisz, groź *l.* gróź 1. (= *straszyć*)
threaten, menace; **grozić komuś palcem** wag
one's finger at sb. 2. (= *zagrażać*) be imminent,
impend; **grozi nam to** it is imminent; **grozi nam,
że...** there is a danger that...

groźba *f. Gen.pl.* **groźb** 1. (= *pogróżka*) threat,
menace; **groźba użycia siły** threat to use force;
pod groźbą czegoś under threat of sth; **ani prośbą, ani groźbą** in no way. 2. (= *zagrożenie, niebezpieczeństwo*) peril, danger.

groźnie *adv.* menacingly, threateningly; **wyglądać groźnie** look menacing *l.* threatening.

groźny *a.* dangerous, formidable, menacing;
groźny człowiek dangerous person; **groźne spojrzenie** menacing look; **groźny wypadek** serious
accident; **groźna choroba** serious illness.

grób *mi* -o- grave, tomb; **grób rodzinny** family
grave; **modlić się nad grobem** prey at a grave;
składać kwiaty na grobie lay flowers at a grave;
złożyć ciało do grobu lay *l.* put sb in their grave;
Grób Nieznanego Żołnierza Tomb of the Unknown Soldier; **do (samego) grobu** till death do
us part; **zza grobu** from the other *l.* next world;
ciemno jak w grobie pitch dark; **być jedną nogą
w grobie** *l.* **stać nad grobem** be at death's door,
have (got) one foot in the grave; **kopać sobie/ko-
muś grób** be digging one's own/sb's grave; **leżeć
w grobie** rest *l.* lie in a grave; **chodzić na groby**
visit graves; **milczeć jak grób** be (as) silent as the
grave; **przewracać się w grobie** turn over in one's
grave; **wpędzać kogoś do grobu** send sb to an
early grave; **zabrać tajemnicę do grobu** carry a
secret to the grave; **on wygląda, jakby wstał z
grobu** he looks like death warmed over; he looks
like a body that's been buried and dug up again.

gród *mi* -o- 1. *hist.* stronghold, castle. 2. *lit.*
city, town; **gród Kraka** (= *Kraków*) Krak's town.

gródź *f.* -o- *pl.* -e *żegl.* bulkhead.

grubas *mp pot.* fatso, tub of lard.

grubianin *mp pl.* -anie *Gen.* -anów *przest.* boor,
rude person.

grubiański *a. przest.* boorish, rude.

grubiaństwo *n. przest.* boorishness, rudeness.

grubieć *ipf.* 1. (= *tyć*) put on weight, grow
thicker. 2. (= *twardnieć, t. przen.*) coarsen,
roughen. 3. (*o głosie*) become deeper, deepen.

grubo *adv.* 1. (= *pokaźnie, znacznie*) thickly.
2. (= *tęgo, otyło*) fattily; **wyglądać grubo** look fat.
3. (= *nisko*) in a low *l.* deep voice. 4. *przen., pot.*
much; **grubo się mylić** be gravely mistaken; **grubo więcej** much more. 5. *przen.* (= *prostacko*)
roughly, coarsely, crudely; **grubo ciosany** rough-
hewn.

grubodziób *ma* -o- *l.* -ó- *orn.* hawfinch (*Coccothraustes coccothraustes*).

grubokościsty *a.* heavy boned, big boned.

gruboskórny *a.* 1. *przen.* inconsiderate, tactless, callous. 2. *zool.* pachydermic.

grubosz *mi Gen.* -a *bot.* propeller plant (*Crassula*).

grubość *f.* 1. thickness; **mieć 30 centymetrów
grubości** be 30 centimeters thick. 2. (= *otyłość,
tęgość*) stoutness, fattiness. 3. (*o głosie*) deepness.

gruboziarnisty *a.* coarse-grained; **gruboziarnisty cukier** coarse-grained sugar; **gruboziarnista kasza/mąka** coarse-grained groats/flour; **gruboziarnista emulsja** *fot.* coarse-grained emulsion.

grubszy *a. zob.* **gruby**.

gruby *a.* 1. (= *duży, szeroki*) thick; **gruba książka** thick *l.* bulky book; **gruby zwierz** *myśl.* big game; **grube rysy** rugged features; **jelito grube** *anat.* large intestine; **szyte grubymi nićmi** self-evident, flagrant; **z grubsza** roughly. 2. (= *tęgi, otyły*) fat, obese, stout; **gruby jak beczka** as round as a barrel, as fat as a wombat. 3. (= *niski*) (*o głosie*) low, deep. 4. *przen., pot.* (= *znaczny, duży, ważny*) serious, important, big; **grube pieniądze** *l.* **gruba forsa** big money; **gruby błąd** serious *l.* grave mistake; **gruba ryba** big fish, big shot, bigwig. 5. *przen., pot.* (= *pospolity, brzydki, ordynarny*) coarse, rough, crude.

gruchać *ipf.* 1. (*o gołębiach*) coo. 2. *przen., żart.* (= *czulić się*) coo (*z kimś* to sb); **gruchać jak dwa gołąbki** bill and coo. 3. (= *gaworzyć*) coo.

gruchnąć *dk* -**ij** 1. (= *zabrzmieć, huknąć*) resound, peal. 2. *przen.* (= *rozpowszechnić się*) spread; **gruchnęła wiadomość** the news broke, the news spread like wildfire. 3. *przen.* (= *trzasnąć*) thump, pound; **gruchnąć pięścią w stół** bring *l.* slam one's fist down on the table with a thump. 4. *pot.* (= *upaść*) fall; **gruchnął jak długi** he measured his length.

gruchot *mi Gen.* -**u** (= *hałas, huk*) rattle, crash. – *mi Gen.* -**a** *pot.* (= *rupieć*) (piece of) junk; *mot.* jalopy; **stary gruchot** (piece of) junk, jalopy. – *mp Gen.* -**a** *pot., iron.* (= *starzec*) geezer, crock.

gruchotać *ipf.* -**czę** *l.* -**ocę** -**czesz** *l.* -**cesz** 1. (= *miażdżyć, łamać*) crush, break. 2. (= *turkotać, grzechotać*) rattle.

gruczolak *mi Gen.* -**a** *pat.* adenoma.

gruczoł *mi biol.* gland; **gruczoły dokrewne** endocrine glands, incretory glands, blood glands.

gruczołowy *a. biol.* glandular.

gruda *f.* 1. (= *kawał*) lump. 2. (= *zmarznięta ziemia*) frozen ground; **coś idzie jak po grudzie** it's uphill *l.* hard work, it's a thankless task. 3. *wet., pat.* sallenders.

grudka *f. Gen.pl.* -**ek** 1. (= *bryłka*) lump. 2. *pat.* (= *wyprysk*) papule.

grudkowaty *a.* 1. lumpy. 2. *pat.* papular.

grudniowy *a.* December.

grudzień *mi* -**dni**- *Gen.* -**a** December; **w grudniu po południu** *żart.* in never-never land.

grunge *mi indecl. l. Gen.* -**e'a** *muz.* grunge (music).

grunt *mi pl.* -**y** *l.* -**a** 1. (= *gleba, rola*) soil, earth; **grunty orne** *roln.* arable land. 2. (= *teren*) land, ground; **spotkać się na neutralnym gruncie** meet on neutral ground; **mieć grunt pod nogami** be on firm ground; **stracić grunt pod nogami** be out of one's depth; **trafić na podatny grunt** find favorable conditions; **przygotować grunt** create favorable conditions, ensure favorable reception; **grunt pali mu się pod nogami** the heat is on for him. 3. (= *majątek*) estate. 4. (= *dno*) bottom; **nie mieć gruntu** (= *nie sięgać dna*) be beyond *l.* out of one's depth; **do gruntu** totally, absolutely. 5. *przen.* (= *istota*) essence, point; **grunt to...** *pot.* the most important thing is..., what matters is..., what counts is...; **z gruntu** basically; **w gruncie rzeczy** in fact; **stać na gruncie czegoś** base on *l.* upon sth. 6. *zwł. sztuka* ground, base.

gruntować *ipf.* 1. (= *dotykać dna*) ground, (hit *l.* reach) bottom. 2. (= *mierzyć głębokość*) measure the depth (*of a lake, river etc. trying to stand up in water*). 3. *zwł. sztuka* cover with ground *l.* base, prime. 4. *przen., rzad.* (= *utrwalać, utwierdzać*) strenghten, consolidate.

gruntownie *adv.* thoroughly.

gruntowny *a.* thorough, in-depth.

gruntowy *a.* 1. (*związany z ziemią*) soil, land, ground; **wody gruntowe** *geol.* ground water; **uprawa gruntowa** *roln.* field culture; **warzywa gruntowe** *roln.* field vegetables; **droga gruntowa** dirt road. 2. *zwł. sztuka* ground, base; **farba gruntowa** primer.

grupa *f.* 1. (= *zespół*) group; **grupa muzyczna** band; **grupa społeczna** *socj.* social group; **grupa drzew** clump *l.* cluster of trees. 2. (= *kategoria, rodzaj*) class, category; **grupa krwi** *biol.* blood group. 3. *chem., geol.* group. 4. *wojsk.* group, squad.

grupka *f. Gen.pl.* -**ek** small group.

grupować *ipf.* 1. (= *klasyfikować*) group, classify, categorize. 2. (= *łączyć, skupiać*) group, bring together. ~ **się** *ipf.* gather (*wokół kogoś / czegoś* around sb/sth).

grupowo *adv.* collectively.

grupowy *a.* collective, joint; **zdjęcie grupowe** group photo; **zwolnienia grupowe** *ekon.* lay-offs, redundancies; **ubezpieczenia grupowe** *ekon.* group insurance; – *mp* group *l.* team leader.

grusza *f. bot.* pear tree (*Pyrus communis*).

gruszka *f. Gen.pl.* -**ek** 1. (*owoc*) pear; **nie zasypiać gruszek w popiele** use an opportunity, seize an opportunity *l.* occasion; **obiecywać komuś gruszki na wierzbie** promise sb the moon; **ni z gruszki, ni z pietruszki** all of a sudden, out of the blue. 2. *pot.* (*drzewo*) pear tree; **gruszka miłosna** *bot.* eggplant, *Br.* aubergine (*Solanum melongena*). 3. (*przedmiot w kształcie tego owocu*) pear-shaped object, bulb. 4. *techn.* converter.

gruszla *f. bot.* guava (*Psidium guajava*).

gruz *mi* rubble, debris; **gruz skalny** *geol.* debris.

Gruzin *mp*, **Gruzinka** *f. Gen.pl.* -**ek** Georgian.

gruziński *a.* Georgian.

Gruzja *f. geogr.* Georgia.

gruzobeton *mi bud.* crushed-brick concrete.

gruzowisko *n.* (= *ruiny*) ruins; (= *sterty gruzu*) rubble (heap), debris (heap).

gruzy *pl. Gen.* -**ów** (= *ruiny*) ruins, debris; **zamienić coś w kupę gruzów** turn sth into ruin, turn sth into *l.* reduce sth to a pile of rubble *l.* debris; **podnieść coś z gruzów** rebuild sth, reconstruct sth; **podnieść się z gruzów** recover; **obrócić coś w gruzy** turn sth into ruin; **lec w gruzach** crumble *l.* fall into ruin.

gruźlica *f. pat.* tuberculosis, TB, tb; **gruźlica płuc** pulmonary tuberculosis, tuberculosis of the lungs; **gruźlica kości** tuberculosis of bones; **prątki gruźlicy** Koch's bacilli, tubercle bacilli.

gruźliczy *a. pat.* tubercular, tuberculous.

gruźlik *mp med.* tuberculosis patient.

gryczany *a.* buckwheat; **kasza gryczana** buckwheat (grits).

gryf[1] *mi Gen.* **-a** *mit.* griffin, griffon, gryphon.

gryf[2] *mi Gen.* **-u** *muz.* neck.

gryfon *ma* 1. *kynol.* griffon. 2. (*mitologiczne zwierzę*) *zob.* **gryf**[1].

gryka *f. bot.* buckwheat (*Fagopyrum*); **gryka zwyczajna** buckwheat (*Fagopyrum sagittatum l. esculentum*); **gryka tatarka** (tartary) buckwheat (*Fagopyrum tataricum*).

grylaż *mi kulin.* sweet nut *l.* almond filling.

grymas *mi* (= *mina*) grimace, face; **robić grymasy** make faces.

grymasić *ipf.* **-szę -sisz** be fussy *l.* choosy, run hot and cold; (*o dziecku*) be fretful.

grymasy *pl. Gen.* **-ów** (= *kaprysy*) whims, caprices.

grymaśny *a.* fussy, finicky, choosy; (= *kapryśny*) capricious.

grypa *f. pat.* influenza; *pot.* flu.

grypowy *a. pat.* influenzal; **infekcja grypowa** flu infection.

gryps *mi pot.* secret message smuggled into *l.* out of prison.

grypsera *f. pot.* 1. (*język*) prison jargon. 2. (*więźniowie*) barons.

grypsować *ipf. pot.* (= *używać grypsery*) speak in a prison jargon; (= *należeć do grypsery*) belong to a prison gang.

grysik *mi* 1. (= *kaszka*) semolina. 2. *techn., bud.* grit.

gryzak *mi Gen.* **-a** 1. (*dla niemowląt*) teething ring, teething toy. 2. *techn.* drilling tooth.

gryzący *a.* 1. (= *piekący, ostry*) acrid, pungent; **gryzący dym** acrid smoke; **gryząca wełna** scratchy wool. 2. *przen.* (= *złośliwy*) biting, caustic. 3. *przen.* (= *dokuczliwy, przejmujący*) poignant, bitter; **gryzące wspomnienie** poignant memory.

gryzmolić *ipf.* 1. (= *bazgrać*) scrawl, scribble. 2. *przen.* (= *pisać bez talentu*) scribble.

gryzmoły *pl. Gen.* **-ów** scrawl, scribble.

gryzoń *ma zool.* rodent.

gryźć *ipf.* **-zę -ziesz -zł -źli** 1. (*przy użyciu zębów*) bite; (*np. kość*) gnaw; (= *przeżuwać*) chew, munch; **gryźć ziemię** *pot.* be pushing up the daisies, be six feet under *l.* deep. 2. (= *ranić zębami*) bite. 3. (= *żądlić*) sting. 4. (= *drażnić*) (*o dymie*) sting; (*o tkaninie*) scratch. 5. *przen.* (= *niepokoić*) torment, distress, bother; **co cię gryzie?** what's eating you?, what's wrong (with you)? ~ **się** *ipf.* (= *kąsać się*) 1. bite one another; **gryźć się w język** *przen.* hold *l.* bite one's tongue. 2. *przen.* (= *dręczyć się*) worry, fret. 3. *pot., przen.* (= *kłócić się*) fight (*o kogoś/coś* over sb/ sth). 4. *pot.* (= *nie pasować*) clash, jar (*z czymś* with sth).

grzać *ipf.* **-eję -ejesz** 1. (= *ogrzewać*) warm (up), heat; **ani mnie to ziębi, ani grzeje** *pot.* I couldn't care less, I don't give a damn. 2. (= *da-*

wać ciepło) emit heat, give off heat. 3. *pot.* (= *bić*) beat, batter. 4. *pot.* (= *strzelać*) shoot. 5. *pot.* (= *mknąć*) speed, rush. 6. *pot.* (= *pić wódkę*) booze. ~ **się** *ipf.* 1. (= *ogrzewać się*) warm o.s.; (*w słońcu*) bask (*in the sun*). 2. (= *nagrzewać się*) (*np. o wodzie, żelazku*) heat up. 3. (= *pocić się*) sweat.

grzałka *f. Gen.pl.* **-ek** travel heater, (water) heater.

grzaniec *mi* **-ńc-** *Gen.* **-a** *pot., kulin.* mulled wine.

grzanka *f. Gen.pl.* **-ek** 1. (= *tost*) toast. 2. (*napój*) mulled liquor.

grządka *f. Gen.pl.* **-ek** 1. (= *rabatka*) bed, patch. 2. (= *drążek dla ptaków*) roost.

grząski *a.* 1. (= *bagnisty*) boggy, sticky. 2. *pot.* (= *kłopotliwy, niepewny*) ticklish, awkward.

grząźć *ipf.* **-ęznę -eźniesz**, **-ij -ązł -ęzła -ęźli** *zob.* **grzęznąć**.

grzbiecista *mp*, **grzbiecistka** *f. Gen.pl.* **-ek** *sport* backstroke swimmer.

grzbiet *mi* 1. *zool.* dorsum, back, spine. 2. *pot.* (= *plecy*) back; **nie mieć co na grzbiet włożyć** not have a stitch of clothing (to cover o.s.), have nothing to wear; **dźwigać siódmy krzyżyk na grzbiecie** be (over) seventy (years old); **mieć giętki grzbiet** bow and scrape, fawn; **grzbiet dłoni** back of hand. 3. (= *krawędź*) edge, verge, ridge; **grzbiet książki** (book) back. 4. (= *szczyt*) ridge.

grzbietoród *ma* **-o-** *zool.* pipa, Surinam toad (*Pipa pipa*).

grzbietowy *a.* back; *zwł. zool., anat.* dorsal, spinal; **płetwa grzbietowa** dorsal fin; **struna grzbietowa** notochord; **styl grzbietowy** *sport* backstroke.

grzebać *ipf.* **-bię -biesz** 1. (= *rozgarniać*) rummage, search (*w czymś* through sth); **grzebać po kieszeniach** (*sobie*) rummage (through) one's pockets; (*komuś*) rummage (through) sb's pockets; (*o ptakach*) scratch (*the ground looking for worms*); (*w ogniu*) poke. 2. *pot., żart.* (= *majstrować*) fiddle, tamper (*przy czymś* with sth). 3. (= *składać do grobu*) bury. ~ **się** *ipf.* 1. (= *rozgarniać*) rummage (*w czymś* through sth). 2. (= *ociągać się, marudzić*) dawdle (away) (*z czymś* over sth).

grzebiące *pl. Gen.* **-ych** *orn.* gallinaceans (*Galliformes*).

grzebiący *pl. Gen.* **-ych** *orn.* gallinaceous; **ptaki grzebiące** gallinaceous birds.

grzebielucha *f. orn.* sand martin (*Riparia riparia*).

grzebieniowce *pl.* **-wc-** *orn.* carinates (*Carinata*).

grzebień *mi Gen.* **-a** 1. (*do czesania*) comb. 2. *anat.* (*u ptaków, gadów, płazów*) comb, crest; **grzebień fali** comb *l.* crest of a wave. 3. *anat.* (*kości, łopatki, mostka*) crest, ridge, crista. 4. *techn.* comb.

grzebiuszka *f. Gen.pl.* **-ek** *zool.* spadefoot toad (*Pelobates fuscus*).

grzech *mi* 1. *rel.* sin; **odpokutować za grzechy** atone for one's sins; **grzech pierworodny** original sin; **grzech śmiertelny** mortal sin; **grzech po-**

wszedni venial sin; **siedem grzechów głównych** (seven) deadly sins; **kobieta warta grzechu** gorgeous woman; **za jakie grzechy** what have I done?, what for? **2.** (= *wykroczenie, błąd*) sin, transgression.

grzechot *mi* rattle, clatter.

grzechotać *ipf.* **-czę** *l.* **-cę -czesz** *l.* **-cesz** rattle, clatter.

grzechotka *f. Gen.pl.* **-ek 1.** (*zabawka, kołatka*) rattle. **2.** *zool.* (*grzechotnika*) rattle.

grzechotnik *ma zool.* rattlesnake (*Crotalus l. Sistrurus*).

grzecznie *adv.* (= *uprzejmie*) politely, kindly, courteously; (= *posłusznie*) obediently; (= *spokojnie*) (*np. bawić się*) peacefully; **dzieci grzecznie bawiły się w ogrodzie** children played peacefully in the garden.

grzeczności *pl. Gen.* **-i** (= *uprzejmości*) courtesies, pleasantries; **wymieniać grzeczności** exchange courtesies.

grzecznościowy *a.* polite, courtesy; (*zwrot*) honorific; **tytuł grzecznościowy** courtesy title; **ze względów grzecznościowych** out of courtesy.

grzeczność *f.* **1.** (= *kultura osobista*) politeness, courtesy; **zrobić coś przez grzeczność** be so kind *l.* good as to do sth. **2.** (= *pomoc*) favor, *Br.* favour, kindness; **wyświadczyć komuś grzeczność** do sb a favor.

grzeczny *a.* (= *uprzejmy*) polite, kind, courteous; (= *posłuszny*) obedient; (*o dzieciach*) well-behaved.

grzejnictwo *n. techn.* heating (technology).

grzejnik *mi Gen.* **-a** *techn.* radiator, heater; **grzejnik akumulacyjny** storage heater; **grzejnik olejowy** oil heater; **grzejnik elektryczny** electric heater; **grzejnik wodny** hot-water heater.

grzejny *a. techn.* heating.

grzesznica *f.*, **grzesznik** *mp* sinner.

grzeszny *a.* sinful; **grzeszne życie** *l.* **grzeszny żywot** sinful life; **grzeszne myśli** sinful thoughts, dirty *l.* filthy thoughts.

grzeszyć *ipf.* **1.** *rel.* sin, commit a sin; **kto śpi, nie grzeszy** you're innocent when you dream; **oni nie grzeszą punktualnością** no-one would accuse them of being punctual, they're not always punctual; **ona nie grzeszy urodą** she's not exactly a stunner, no-one would accuse her of being beautiful; **on nie grzeszy mądrością** no-one would accuse him of being smart, he's a bit dumb; **lepiej grzeszyć i żałować, niż żałować, że się nie grzeszyło** it's better to have sinned and then regret it than to regret that you have not sinned. **2.** (*popełniać wykroczenia*) sin, transgress.

grzewczy *a. techn.* heating.

grzęda *f.* **1.** (= *zagon*) bed, patch. **2.** (*dla drobiu*) perch, roost; **daj kurze grzędę, ona: wyżej siędę** give sb an inch and he'll take a mile.

grzęzawisko *n.* bog, quagmire.

grzęznąć *ipf.* **-znę -źniesz, -ij -ązł -ęzła -ęźli 1.** (= *zapadać się*) get stuck, sink (*w czymś* in sth). **2.** *przen.* **grzęznąć w długach** be up to one's ears in debt.

grzmieć *ipf.* **-ę -isz, -ij 1.** thunder; **grzmi** it's

thundering. **2.** (= *głośno mówić, ryczeć*) roar, blare.

grzmocić *ipf.* (= *bić*) beat, bang, whack. **~ się** *ipf.* **1.** (*kogoś*) beat one another, fight. **2.** (*siebie*) hit o.s.

grzmot *mi* **1.** (= *wyładowanie atmosferyczne*) thunder, clap of thunder. **2.** (= *hałas*) roar, boom. **3.** *pot.* (= *wielki rupieć, grat*) (piece of) junk.

grzmotnąć *pf.* **-ij 1.** (= *uderzyć*) hit. **2.** (= *rzucić*) fling, hurl. **3.** *pot.* (= *spaść, przewrócić się*) fall; **grzmotnąć na ziemię** fall on the floor. **4.** *pot.* (= *huknąć*) thunder, boom. **~ się** *pf. pot.* (= *przewrócić się*) fall.

grzyb *mi Gen.* **-a** *bot.* fungus (*Fungi*); **grzyb skalny** *geol.* mushroom rock; **grzyb atomowy** *fiz.* mushroom (cloud); **dwa grzyby w barszcz** (= *dwa razy to samo*) the same thing twice; (= *co za dużo, to niezdrowo*) too much of a good thing; **stary jak grzyb** as old as the hills; **wyrastać jak grzyby po deszczu** spring up like weeds, mushroom; **po kiego grzyba?** *pot.* what's the point?, what for? − **mi Gen.** **-u** (= *pleśń*) mold, *Br.* mould.

grzybek *mi* **-bk- Gen.** **-a 1.** mushroom. **2.** (*przedmiot w kształcie grzyba*) mushroom; (*do cerowania*) darning egg; *techn.* valve head, jumper valve plate.

grzybiarz *mp* **1.** (*zbieracz*) mushroom picker. **2.** (*hodowca*) mushroom farmer.

grzybica *f. pat.* mycosis; **grzybica stóp** athlete's foot; (*w języku fachowym*) tinea pedis.

grzybień *mi Gen.* **-a** *bot.* water lily (*Nymphaea*).

grzybnia *f. Gen.pl.* **-i** *bot.* mycelium.

grzybobójczy *a.* fungicidal; **środek grzybobójczy** fungicide.

grzybobranie *n.* mushroom picking.

grzybowy *a.* mushroom; **zupa grzybowa** mushroom soup; **sos grzybowy** mushroom sauce.

grzyboznawca *mp biol.* mycologist.

grzyboznawczy *a. biol.* mycological, mycologic.

grzyboznawstwo *n. biol.* mycology.

grzywa *f. dosł., przen.* mane; **grzywa fali** *przen.* (wave) crest *l.* comb.

grzywacz *ma orn.* wood pigeon, ringdove (*Columba palumbus*). − **mi Gen.** **-a** (*fala*) comber, billow.

grzywka *f. Gen.pl.* **-ek** fringe, bang(s).

grzywna *f. Gen.pl.* **-wien 1.** (*kara*) fine, mulct; **wymierzyć komuś grzywnę w wysokości 100 dolarów** impose a fine of 100 dollars on sb, fine sb 100 dollars. **2.** *hist.* a monetary unit.

Guam *mi geogr.* Guam.

guamski *a.* Guamanian.

guanako *ma zool.* guanaco (*Lama guanicoe*).

guanina *f. biochem.* guanine.

guano *n.* guano.

gubernator *mp polit., hist.* governor; **gubernator generalny** governor general.

gubernatorowa *f. Gen.* **-ej** governor's wife.

gubernatorski *a.* gubernatorial, governor('s).

gubernatorstwo *n.* **1.** (*obszar*) province, state. **2.** (*urząd*) governorship.

gubernia *f. Gen.pl.* **-i** *hist.* province; (*w Rosji* *carskiej*) guberniya; **Generalna Gubernia** *l.* **Generalne Gubernatorstwo** *hist.* General-Gouvernement.

gubić *ipf.* **1.** (= *tracić*) lose; **gubić drogę** lose one's *l.* the way; **gubić oczko** drop a stitch; **gubić myśl** *l.* wątek lose the thread, lose sb's train of thought, get side-tracked; **gubić rytm** lose the rhythm *l.* beat. **2.** *biol.* (= *zrzucać*) shed. **3.** (= *narażać*) (bring to) ruin. ~ **się** *ipf.* **1.** (*np. w mieście, lesie, budynku*) lose sb's way, get lost. **2.** (*np. w sytuacji*) get confused; **gubić się w domysłach** speculate blindly; **gubić się w szczegółach** get bogged down in details. **3.** (= *tracić się z oczu*) lose sight of sb. **4.** (= *ginąć*) get lost, go missing, disappear.

gudron *mi techn.* soft asphalt, tar, pitch.

guiro *n. muz.* (*instrument*) guiro.

Gujana *f. geogr.* Guyana.

Gujanka *f.*, **Gujańczyk** *mp* Guyanese.

gujański *a.* Guyanese.

gujot *mi geogr.* guyot.

gula *f. pot.* (= *narośl, guz*) lump, bump.

gulasz *mi Gen.pl.* **-ów** *l.* **-y** *kulin.* goulash.

gulden *mi Gen.* **-a** *hist.* (*w Holandii*) guilder, gulden.

gulgot *mi* **1.** (*odgłos ptaków*) gurgle, chirp; (*indyka*) gobble. **2.** (= *bulgot*) gurgle, bubble. **3.** *pot.* (= *bełkot*) babble, mumble.

gulgotać *ipf.* **-czę** *l.* **-cę -czesz** *l.* **-cesz** **1.** (*o ptakach*) gurgle. **2.** (= *bulgotać*) gurgle, bubble. **3.** *pot.* (= *bełkotać*) babble, mumble.

gułag *mi hist.* gulag, Gulag.

guma *f.* **1.** *techn.* rubber; **guma arabska** *bot., techn.* gum arabic; **guma naturalna** *bot.* natural rubber. **2.** (*np. do majtek*) rubber band, elastic. **3.** (*podeszwa*) rubber sole. **4.** *pot.* (*do żucia*) gum; **guma do żucia** chewing gum. **5.** *pot.* (= *dętka, opona*) tire, *Br.* tyre; **złapać gumę** have a flat tire; *Br.* have a puncture. **6.** *pot.* (= *prezerwatywa*) rubber.

gumiak *mi Gen.* **-a** **1.** (= *kalosz*) galosh(e), rubber boot. **2.** *bot.* beauty leaf, Alexandrian laurel (*Calophyllum*).

gumka *f. Gen.pl.* **-ek** **1.** (*do ścierania*) eraser, rubber. **2.** (*np. do majtek*) elastic, rubber band. **3.** *pot.* (= *prezerwatywa*) rubber.

gumować *ipf. techn.* **1.** rubberize. **2.** *ogr.* gum.

gumowiec *mi* **-wc-** *Gen.* **-a** *pot.* (= *kalosz*) galosh(e), rubber boot.

gumowy *a.* **1.** (*zrobiony z gumy*) rubber; **gumowe rękawice** rubber gloves; **gumowe ucho** *pot.* eavesdropper. **2.** (*dający gumę*) gum-exuding; **drzewo gumowe** *bot.* rubber plant (*Ficus elastica*).

gumoza *f. ogr.* gummosis.

gumożywica *f. bot., techn.* gum resin.

guniak *ma ent.* **guniak czerwczyk** summer chafer (*Amphimallon solstitialis*).

gupik *ma icht.* guppy (*Lebistes reticulatus*).

gurda *f.* gourd.

gurt *mi* **1.** *bud.* buttress. **2.** (= *taśma*) petersham. **3.** (*rzemienny pas*) strap.

guru *mp indecl. rel., przen.* guru.

gusła *pl. Gen.* **-seł** sorcery, (black) magic; **wierzyć w gusła** believe in magic.

gust *mi pl.* **-y** *l.* **-a** **1.** (= *poczucie estetyczne*) taste; **o gustach się nie dyskutuje** there's no accounting for taste, to each his own; **rzecz gustu** a matter of taste; **w dobrym guście** in good taste; **w złym guście** in bad *l.* poor taste; **mieć wybredny gust** (= *być smakoszem*) have a delicate palate. **2.** (= *upodobanie*) liking, fancy; **przypaść komuś do gustu** take a fancy *l.* liking to sb; **są gusta i guściki** to each his own; **to nie jest w moim guście** it is not to my liking; **pożyczanie nie jest w moim guście** borrowing is not in my line. **3.** *pot.* (= *styl, moda*) type, sort, style; **coś w tym guście** sth of that sort.

gustować *ipf.* fancy, like (*w kimś/czymś* sb/sth) have a liking (*w kimś/czymś* for sb/sth).

gustowny *a.* tasteful.

guślarka *f. Gen.pl.* **-ek** sorceress, witch.

guślarski *a.* sorcerous, magical.

guślarstwo *n.* sorcery, (black) magic.

guślarz *mp* sorcerer.

gutaperka *f. biol.* gutta-percha.

guwernantka *f. Gen.pl.* **-ek** *przest.* governess.

guwerner *mp pl.* **-rzy** *l.* **-owie** *przest.* tutor, mentor.

guz *mi Gen.* **-a** **1.** *anat.* (= *wypukłość*) tuber, tubercle, protuberance. **2.** *t. pat.* (= *krwiak*) bump; **nabić sobie guza** bump one's head; **oberwać guza** take a beating; **szukać guza** ask *l.* look for trouble. **3.** *pat.* (= *torbiel, nowotwór*) tumor, *Br.* tumour, neoplasm. **4.** *sztuka* (*ozdoba*) boss. **5.** *przest.* (*guzik*) button. **6.** *techn.* (= *wada odlewu*) knob.

guzdrać się *ipf.* **-am** **-asz** *l.* **-rzę -rzesz** *pot.* dawdle (*z czymś* over sth); dilly-dally (*z czymś* with sth).

guzdrała *f. l. mp decl.* like *f. Gen.pl.* **-ł** *l.* **-ów** *pot.* dawdler.

guzek *mi* **-zk-** *Gen.* **-a** **1.** *anat.* (= *wypukłość*) tuber, tubercle, protuberance. **2.** *pat.* (= *nowotwór, torbiel*) tumor, neoplasm. **3.** *pat.* (= *owrzodzenie*) ulcer. **4.** *pot.* (= *wybrzuszenie*) bump.

guzik *mi Gen.* **-a** **1.** (*do zapinania*) button; **zapięty na ostatni guzik** set (to go), in trim. **2.** *techn.* (= *przycisk*) button. **3.** *pot., euf.* (= *klapa, figa*) nothing, flop, zilch; **a guzik!** no way!; **guzik z pętelką** zilch; **guzik z tego wyjdzie** nothing will come out of it, it's going to be a flop; **guzik cię to obchodzi** it's none of your business.

Gwadelupa *f. geogr.* Guadeloupe.

Gwadelupczyk *mp*, **Gwadelupka** *f. Gen.pl.* **-ek** Guadeloupian.

gwadelupski *a.* Guadeloupian.

gwajak *mi stol.* (*drewno*) **1.** guaiacum, guaiacwood, lignum vitae. **2.** *med., chem.* (*żywica*) guaiac, (gum) guaiacum.

gwajakol *mi chem.* guaiacol.

gwajakowiec *mi* **-wc-** *Gen.* **-a** *bot.* guaiacum, guaiac-tree, lignum vitae (*Guaiacum officinale, G. sanctum*).

gwajakowy *a. med., chem.* guaiacum, guaiac.

gwajawa *f. bot.* guava (*Psidium*).

gwałciciel *mp* **1.** (= *sprawca gwałtu*) rapist.

2. (= *sprawca naruszenia l. zbezczeszczenia czegoś*) violater, transgressor; desecrator, profaner.

gwałcić *ipf.* **1.** (= *popełniać gwałt*) rape. **2.** (= *naruszać*) violate, break, infringe, transgress.

gwałt *mi* **1.** (= *zgwałcenie*) rape. **2.** (= *przemoc*) violence. **3.** (= *przymus*) coercion, (brute) force; **zadawać komuś/sobie gwałt, żeby...** force sb/o.s. to... **4.** *pot.* (*gorączkowa aktywność, zamieszanie*) tumult, riot, uproar, frenzy, turmoil; **robić coś na gwałt** do sth frantically; **zrobił się/podniósł się gwałt** a tumult began/rose; **gwałtu, rety!** help!

gwałtem *adv.* **1.** (= *gwałtownie, przemocą*) forcibly, by force. **2.** (= *natychmiast, pilnie*) urgently, at once, straight away.

gwałtowny *a.* **1.** (= *wybuchowy, porywczy*) impulsive, impetuous. **2.** (= *intensywny, energiczny*) violent, intense. **3.** (= *szybki, zaskakujący*) sudden, rapid; **gwałtowna śmierć** sudden death.

gwanako *ma* = **guanako**.

gwar *mi* din, hubbub, babble (of voices); **gwar wielkomiejski** the hustle (and bustle) of the big city.

gwara *f. jęz.* local dialect, patois.

gwarancja *f.* **1.** (= *zapewnienie, pewność*) guarantee; **nie ma gwarancji, że...** there's no guarantee (that)... **2.** *prawn.* (= *rękojmia, poręczenie*) guaranty. **3.** *ekon., handl., prawn.* (= *zobowiązanie*) guarantee, guaranty, warranty; **gwarancja jakości** quality guarantee.

gwarancyjny *a.* guarantee; **naprawa gwarancyjna** repair under guarantee; **karta gwarancyjna** guarantee card.

gwarant *mp*, **gwarantka** *f. Gen.pl.* **-ek** guarantor.

gwarantować *ipf.* guarantee, guaranty, ensure.

gwardia *f. Gen.* **-ii** *gł. wojsk.* guard; **gwardia honorowa** guard of honour; **gwardia szwajcarska** the Swiss Guard (*in the Vatican*); **stara gwardia** *przen.* the old guard.

gwardian *mp pl.* **-nie** *kośc.* guardian.

gwardiański *a. kośc.* guardian.

gwardyjski *a.* (of the) guard.

gwardzista *mp*, **gwardzistka** *f. Gen.pl.* **-ek** *gł. wojsk.* guard; (*tylko o mężczyźnie*) guardsman.

gwarectwo *n. górn.* **1.** *hist.* (= *cech górników*) miner's guild, guild of miners. **2.** *przest.* (= *górnictwo*) mining.

gwarek[1] *mp* **-rk-** *pl.* **-owie** *górn., przest.* miner.

gwarek[2] *mi* **-rk-** *tylko sing. rzad.* (= *niezbyt natężony zgiełk*) hubbub, murmur.

gwarek[3] *ma* **-rk-** *zool.* hill myna *l.* mynah *l.* mina (*Gracula religiosa*).

gwarny *a.* noisy, bustling.

gwarowy *a. jęz.* dialectal.

gwarzyć *ipf. lit.* chat, converse (*z kimś* with sb, *o kimś/czymś* about sb/sth).

gwasz *mi Gen.pl.* **-ów** *l.* **-y** *sztuka* **1.** (*obraz*) gouache. **2.** *tylko sing.* (*technika, farba*) gouache, (water) body color; **malować gwaszem** paint in gouache.

Gwatemala *f. geogr.* Guatemala.

Gwatemalczyk *mp*, **Gwatemalka** *f. Gen.pl.* **-ek** Guatemalan.

gwatemalski *a.* Guatemalan.

gwelf *mp pl.* **-owie** *hist.* Guelph.

gwiazda *f. Dat. i Loc.* **gwieździe** **1.** *astron.* star; **gwiazda neutronowa** neutron star; **gwiazda zerowej/pierwszej/drugiej wielkości** zero/first/second magnitude star; **gwiazda podwójna** binary star; **gwiazda supernowa** supernova; **gwiazda zmienna** the Pole Star; **Gwiazda Polarna** the Pole Star, Polaris, the North Star. **2.** (= *nocne ciało niebieskie prócz Księżyca*) star; **Gwiazda Poranna/Wieczorna** (= *Wenus*) the Morning/Evening star; **spadająca gwiazda** shooting star; **światło gwiazd** starlight. **3.** *przen.* **czytać w gwiazdach** read the stars; **gwiazda przewodnia** guiding star; **typ spod ciemnej gwiazdy** lowlife; **urodzić się pod szczęśliwą gwiazdą** be born under a lucky star; **zobaczyć wszystkie gwiazdy** see stars before one's eyes. **4.** *przen.* (= *wybitna osoba*) star, celebrity; **gwiazda pierwszej wielkości** star of the first magnitude. **5.** (*figura, kształt, symbol, odznaczenie*) star; **gwiazda pięcioramienna** *geom.* pentagram; **Gwiazda Dawida** the Star of David. **6.** *zool.* **gwiazda morska** *przest.* (= *rozgwiazda*) starfish. **7.** *bot.* **gwiazda betlejemska** star-of-Bethlehem, starflower (*Ornithogalum umbellatum*); **gwiazda ziemna** = **gwiazdosz**.

gwiazdeczka *f. Gen.pl.* **-ek** *emf.* = **gwiazda** 2.

gwiazdka *f. Gen.pl.* **-ek** **1.** *emf.* = **gwiazda** 2; **chcieć gwiazdki z nieba** want the stars in the sky. **2.** (= *początkująca artystka*) starlet. **3.** (*figura, kształt*) star; **gwiazdka śniegowa** snowflake. **4.** *wojsk.* (*dystynkcja*) star, pip; **otrzymać kolejną gwiazdkę** be awarded another star. **5.** *druk.* asterisk, star. **6.** (*wigilia i Boże Narodzenie*) Christmastide, Christmas, Xmas; **dostać coś na gwiazdkę** get sth for Christmas.

gwiazdkowy *a.* (= *dotyczący świąt Bożego Narodzenia*) Christmas; **prezent gwiazdkowy** Christmas gift *l.* present.

gwiazdnica *f. bot.* **1.** (*roślina z rodziny goździkowatych*) stitchwort (*Stellaria*). **2.** (*glon*) zygnema (*Zygnema*).

gwiazdor *mp* **1.** (= *znakomitość*) star, celebrity. **2.** (= *święty Mikołaj*) Santa (Claus), Father Christmas.

gwiazdorski *a.* (*o przedstawieniu, popisie*) stellar; (*o zachowaniu, manierach*) star's.

gwiazdorstwo *n.* stardom, stellardom.

gwiazdosz *mi Gen.* **-a** *bot.* (*grzyb*) earthstar (*Geastrum*).

gwiazdowy *a. astron.* star, stellar; **wielkość gwiazdowa** stellar magnitude.

gwiazdozbiór *mi* **-o-** *astron.* constellation.

gwiaździsty *a.* **1.** (= *rozgwieżdżony*) starry. **2.** (= *ozdobiony gwiazdami*) star-spangled; **Gwiaździsty Sztandar** (= *flaga USA*) the Star-Spangled Banner. **3.** (= *podobny do gwiazdy*) stellar, starlike; **sklepienie gwiaździste** *bud.* lierne vault, stellar vault.

gwiezdny *a. astron.* star, stellar; **gwiezdny pył** stardust.

Gwinea *f. Gen.* **-ei** *geogr.* Guinea; **Gwinea Bis-**

sau Guinea-Bissau; **Gwinea Równikowa** Equatorial Guinea; **Nowa Gwinea** New Guinea.

gwinea *f. Gen.* **-ei** *hist.* (*moneta*) guinea.

Gwinejczyk *mp*, **Gwinejka** *f. Gen.pl.* **-ek** Guinean.

gwinejski *a.* Guinean.

gwint *mi techn.* **1.** thread; **gwint lewy/prawy** left-hand/right-hand thread. **2. z gwinta** *pot. o piciu* from the bottle. **3. jasny gwint!** *pot.* holy cow!

gwintować *ipf. techn.* thread; (*lufę broni*) rifle.

gwintownica *f. techn.* threader, (screw) die.

gwintownik *mi Gen.* **-a** *techn.* screw tap.

gwintówka *f. Gen.pl.* **-ek** *przest., broń* rifle.

gwizd *mi* whistle.

gwizdać *ipf.* **-żdżę -żdżesz 1.** whistle (*na kogoś/coś* for sb/sth); **gwizdać na psa** (= *wzywać gwizdaniem*) whistle a dog back; whistle for a dog. **2.** *przen.* **gwizdać (sobie) na kogoś/coś** (= *lekceważyć*) not give *l.* care a hoot about sb/sth.

gwizdek *mi* **-dk-** *Gen.* **-a** (*instrument l. dźwięk*) whistle; **gwizdek bosmański** *żegl.* boatswain's

whistle; **ostatni gwizdek** *sport* the final whistle; **pracować na pół gwizdka** work at half steam.

gwizdnąć *pf.* **-ij 1.** *zob.* **gwizdać. 2.** *pot.* (= *ukraść coś niewielkiej wartości*) filch (*sth*) (*komuś* from sb). **3.** *pot.* (*uderzyć znienacka*) catch, punch (*sb*) (*w coś* on sth).

gwoździk *mi Gen.* **-a** *emf.* small nail.

gwóźdź *mi* **-o-** *Gen.* **-a** *Ins.pl.* **-ami** *l.* **-mi 1.** nail; (*bez główki*) brad; **wbijać gwóźdź w coś** drive a nail into sth; **zbijać coś gwoździami** nail sth together. **2.** *przen.* **gwóźdź do trumny czyjejś/czegoś** a nail in sb's/sth's coffin; **gwóźdź programu** *pot.* the main attraction (of the evening).

gymkhana *f. sport* gymkhana.

gynerium *n. pl.* **-a** *Gen.* **-ów** *bot.* pampas grass (*Cortaderia*).

gza *itd. ma zob.* **giez.**

gzić się *ipf.* **gżę gzisz, gzij 1.** (*o zwierzętach*) mate. **2.** (*o ludziach*) *pog.* fornicate.

gzy *ma zob.* **giez.**

gzyms *mi* **1.** *bud.* cornice. **2.** (= *półka skalna*) ledge.

gżę *itd. zob.* **gzić się.**

H

H, h n. indecl. (litera) H, h; **H jak Henryk** H is for Hotel; H as in Hotel.

H n. indecl. muz. B; **H-dur** B major; **h-moll** B minor.

h abbr. = **godzina**.

ha¹ int. **1. ha! ha!** onomat. (śmiech) ha-ha, haw-haw. **2.** (wyraża zdziwienie, podziw) ha, hah. **3.** (wyraża wyzwanie) ha! **4.** (wyraża pytanie) huh?

ha² abbr. = **hektar**.

hab. abbr. uniw. = **habilitowany**.

habilitacja f. uniw. **1.** (the procedure of) granting a postdoctoral degree (in Poland). **2.** (= rozprawa habilitacyjna) postdoctoral dissertation. **3.** pot. (= stopień doktora habilitowanego) postdoctoral degree.

habilitacyjny a. uniw. postdoctoral.

habilitant mp, **habilitantka** f. Gen.pl. **-ek** uniw. postdoctoral candidate.

habilitować ipf. i pf. uniw. grant l. give a postdoctoral degree to (sb). **~ się** ipf. i pf. get a postdoctoral degree.

habilitowany a. uniw. **doktor habilitowany** postdoctoral degree (in Poland); DLitt, DSc; holder of a postdoctoral degree.

habit mi kośc. habit, frock; **przywdziać habit** przen. take the habit/frock; **zrzucić habit** przen. discard the habit/frock; **poznać mnicha po habicie** przen. a leopard can't change its spots.

hacel mi Gen. **-a** jeźdz. (= hak w podkowie konia) calk.

hacjenda f. hacienda.

haczyk mi Gen. **-a 1.** (mały hak) hook, crook. **2.** (zamknięcie drzwi) hook. **3.** pot. (= kruczek, zmyłka) catch, snag. **4.** mech. (= zaczep) crook, catch. **5.** ryb. hook, fishhook. **6.** bot. barb. **7.** (= fajka, odhaczenie) US i Can. check; Br. tick. **8.** (= pogrzebacz) poker. **9.** w zwrotach **połknąć haczyk** ryb. l. przen. swallow/take the hook, bite; **mieć na kogoś haczyk** have something on sb, have the goods on sb.

haczykowaty a. hooked; anat., bot. hamate, unciform, uncinate; **haczykowaty nos** hooknose, hooked nose.

Hades mp mit. (bóg) Hades.

hades mi mit. (= świat umarłych) Hades, the underworld; pot. (= piekło) hades, hell.

hadron mi fiz. hadron.

hafciarka f. Gen.pl. **-ek 1.** (kobieta) (woman) embroiderer; zwł. hist. embroideress. **2.** (maszyna) embroidering machine.

hafciarnia f. Gen.pl. **-i** l. **-ń** embroidery workshop.

hafciarski a. embroidery.

hafciarstwo n. embroidery.

hafciarz mp embroiderer.

hafcik mi (na ubraniu) (embroidered) edging/trim/strip.

hafn mi chem. hafnium.

haft mi **1.** embroidery, fancywork; **haft angielski** broderie anglaise, cutwork; **haft krzyżykowy** cross-stitch; **haft drabinkowy** hemstitch, drawnwork; **haft richelieu** tapestry, needlepoint. **2.** pot. (= wymioty) barf, puke; **rzucić hafta** sl. toss one's cookies, shout at the floor; zob. **haftować** 2.

haftka f. Gen.pl. **-ek** krawiectwo hook and eye.

haftować ipf. **1.** (= wyszywać) embroider. **2.** pot. (= wymiotować) barf, puke (czymś sth).

Haga f. geogr. the Hague.

hagiograf mp pl. **-owie** teor.lit. hagiographer.

hagiografia f. Gen. **-ii** teor.lit. hagiography.

hagiograficzny a. hagiographic.

haiku n. indecl. teor.lit., wers. haiku.

Haitanka f. Gen.pl. **-ek**, **Haitańczyk** mp Haitian.

haitański a. Haitian.

Haiti n. indecl. geogr. Haiti.

haj mi sl. (= euforia narkotykowa) high, buzz, trip; **na haju** high, stoned, baked.

hajcować ipf. pot. (= grzać intensywnie) keep the heat going.

hajda int. przest. come on!, forward!

hajduk mp pl. **-cy** l. **-ki** hist., wojsk. Haiduk. – mi Gen. i Acc. **-a** pl. **-i** hist. (taniec) sword dance (popular in 16c. Poland).

hajtać się ipf., **hajtnąć się** pf. **-ij** sl. (= żenić się, wychodzić za mąż) get hitched (z kimś to sb); tie the knot, jump the broom.

hak mi Gen. **-a 1.** hook; **hak holowniczy** mot. tow/towing hook; **hak rzeźnicki** (w sklepie) butcher's hook, meathook; (w zakładach mięsnych) gambrel. **2.** boks. hook. **3.** (w zwrotach) **mieć na kogoś haka** pot. have something on sb, have the goods on sb; **zagiąć/szukać na kogoś haka** pot. be gunning for sb; **... z hakiem** pot. (= ponad) ... plus.

haker mp, **hakerka** f. Gen.pl. **-ek** komp. hacker.

hakowaty a. hooked, hook-shaped.

hakownica f. broń, hist. harquebus.

hakowy a. hook.

hala f. **1.** bud. (= pomieszczenie) hall; **hala dworcowa** l. dworca station hall; **hala maszyn** (w biurze) typing pool; druk. pressroom; **hala mon-**

tażowa *mech.* assembly room; **hala przylotów/odlotów** *lotn.* arrivals/departures lounge; **hala sportowa** sports hall; **hala targowa** covered market. **2.** *geogr.* (mountain) pasture, alp. **3.** *bud., kość.* (= *kościół halowy*) hall church.

halabarda *f. broń, hist.* poleax, halberd.

halabardnik *mp gł. hist.* halberdier.

halerz *mi Gen.* **-a** (= *moneta czeska, słowacka, dawna austriacka*) haller, haler.

halibut *ma kulin.* plaice; *icht.* (*także* **halibut atlantycki**) halibut (*Hippoglossus hippoglossus*).

halka *f. Gen.pl.* **-ek** (*bielizna*) petticoat.

hall *mi* = **hol**.

halma *f.* (*gra planszowa*) halma.

halny *mi i a.* **(wiatr) halny** *meteor.* foehn (*esp. in the Tatra Mts.*).

halo *int.* **1.** *tel.* (*przy odbieraniu telefonu*) hello, yes; **halo, (słucham,) kto mówi?** yes, who is it/this? **2.** (*zawołanie*) hello. – *n. indecl. pot.* **1. wielkie (mi) halo** (= *wielka rzecz, sprawa*) big deal; *sl.* big whoop; **robić z czegoś wielkie halo** make a big deal out of sth; make a (big) fuss about sth. **2.** *meteor., fot.* halo; **efekt halo** *psych.* halo effect.

halogen *mi* **1.** *chem.* halogen. **2.** *techn.* (*żarówka*) halogen bulb. **3.** *techn., mot.* (*światło, reflektor*) halogen lamp/light.

halogenowy *a. techn., chem.* halogen; **żarówka halogenowa** halogen bulb; **reflektor halogenowy** halogen lamp.

haloid *mi chem.* haloid, halide.

haloidowy *a. chem.* haloid.

halowy *a.* **1.** *sport* (*turniej, zawody, mistrzostwa, rekord*) indoor. **2.** *bud., kość.* **kościół halowy** hall church.

hals *mi żegl.* (*kurs, lina*) tack.

halslina *f. żegl.* tack.

halsować *ipf. żegl.* tack.

halucynacja *f.* hallucination.

halucynacyjny *a.* hallucinatory.

halucynogen *mi med.* hallucinogen.

halucynogenny *a. med.* hallucinogenic.

hałas *mi* **1.** (= *wrzawa*) noise, racket; **hałas uliczny** street noise; **bez hałasu** (= *cicho*) quietly; (= *skrycie*) slyly, on the sly. **2.** (= *zamieszanie*) fuss, commotion; **narobić hałasu** make a fuss; **narobić dużo hałasu wokół czegoś** kick up a fuss about sth; **wiele hałasu o nic** much ado about nothing.

hałasować *ipf.* make (a) noise, make a racket; **przestań hałasować!** keep it down!

hałastra *f. uj., pot.* mob.

hałaśliwy *a.* noisy; (*o śmiechu, krzyku, zachowaniu*) raucous, boisterous.

hałda *f.* heap, mound, pile; *górn.* slag heap, (mine) dump.

hamak *mi Gen.* **-a** hammock.

hamburger *mi Gen.* **-a** *kulin.* burger, hamburger, patty; **hamburger drobiowy/wołowy/rybny** chicken/beef/fish burger; **hamburger wegetariański** *l.* **bezmięsny** veggieburger, soyburger.

hamować *ipf.* **1.** *zwł. mot.* (= *redukować prędkość*) brake. **2.** (= *blokować*) block. **3.** (= *spowalniać, utrudniać*) (*postęp*) slow down, restrain, impede; (*rozwój*) inhibit, stunt; (*zapał, emocje*) curb, contain; **hamować łzy** hold back one's tears. **~ się** *ipf.* (= *powstrzymywać się*) hold back; **hamuj się!** behave!, whoa!, steady!

hamownia *f. Gen.pl.* **-i** *techn.* engine test bench.

hamująco *adv.* **działać/wpływać hamująco** impede, hinder, obstruct (*na coś* sth).

hamulcowy *a. zwł. mot.* brake; **płyn hamulcowy** brake fluid; **szczęka hamulcowa** brake shoe; **układ hamulcowy** brakes. – *mp kol., sport* brakeman.

hamulec *mi* **-lc-** *Gen.* **-a** **1.** *mot.* brake; **hamulce tarczowe/bębnowe** *mot.* disk/drum brakes; **hamulec ręczny** *mot.* emergency brake, handbrake; **hamulec bezpieczeństwa** emergency brake; *kol. US* emergency cord; *kol. Br.* communication cord. **2.** *mech.* (= *blokada*) stop, pullback. **3.** *przen.* (*czynnik hamujący, utrudniający*) check, bridle, hang-up (*dla czegoś* on sth); *psych.* hang-up, inhibition, repression; **mieć hamulce** be inhibited; **on nie ma żadnych hamulców** he will stop at nothing.

han *mi chem.* hahnium (*Ha*).

handel *mi* **-dl-** *Gen.pl.* **-ów** *l.* **-i** *handl., ekon.* trade (*czymś* in sth); *zwł. form. l. na dużą skalę* commerce; (= *handlowanie*) trading; (*nielegalny*) trafficking; **handel bronią/narkotykami** drugs/arms trafficking; **handel detaliczny** *handl.* retail (trade), retailing; **handel hurtowy** *handl.* wholesale (trade), wholesaling; **handel krajowy** *l.* **wewnętrzny** *ekon.* domestic/home/internal trade; **handel morski** sea trade; **handel narkotykami** drug trafficking; **handel wymienny** barter; **handel zagraniczny** *ekon.* foreign trade; **handel żywym towarem** slave trade.

handelek *mi* **-lk-** *pot.* trade.

handicap *mi sport* handicap.

handikapować *ipf. sport* handicap.

handlara *f. pog.* (woman) huckster.

handlarka *f. Gen.pl.* **-ek** vendor; **handlarka uliczna** street vendor.

handlarski *a.* vendor's.

handlarz *mp* dealer, trader; **handlarz samochodami/antykami** *l.* **samochodów/antyków** car/antique dealer; **handlarz narkotyków** (drug) dealer; **handlarz (uliczny)** (street) vendor.

handlować *ipf.* trade, deal (*czymś* in sth); (*nielegalnie*) traffic (*czymś* in sth).

handlowiec[1] *mp* **-wc-** *pl.* **-y** *handl.* trader, dealer.

handlowiec[2] *mi* **-wc-** *pl.* **-e** *żegl.* (= *statek handlowy*) trader.

handlowy *a.* trade, commercial; **bank handlowy** merchant bank; **centrum handlowe** (shopping) mall, shopping center; **dzielnica handlowa** shopping precinct; **korzyści handlowe** trade profits; **marynarka handlowa** *żegl.* merchant marine, shipping; **nazwa handlowa** trade name; **prawo handlowe** commercial law; **port handlowy** *żegl.* commercial port; **spółka handlowa** (trading/commercial) partnership; **statek handlowy** merchant ship; **szkoła handlowa** business school/college; **tajemnica handlowa** trade secret;

znak handlowy (zastrzeżony) (registered) trademark.

handlówka f. Gen.pl. **-ek** pot. szkoln. business school.

handryczyć się ipf. gł. pot. squabble (z kimś o coś with sb about sth).

hangar mi **1.** lotn. hangar. **2.** (= magazyn portowy) shed.

haniebny a. shameful, disgraceful, dishonorable, ignoble, ignominious; przest. (= okropny) nasty, atrocious.

hantle pl. Gen. **-i** sport dumbbells, (free) weights.

hanza f. hist. Hansa, Hanse.

hanzeata mp hist. Hansa member.

hanzeatycki a. hist. Hansa, Hanseatic; **Liga Hanzeatycka** Hanseatic League; **miasto hanzeatyckie** Hansa town.

hańba f. disgrace, dishonor, shame, ignominy; **wstyd i hańba!** what a shame!; **okryć kogoś/coś hańbą** (także **przynieść komuś/czemuś hańbę**) bring disgrace/dishonor on sb/sth.

hańbiący a. disgraceful, dishonorable, shameful.

hańbić ipf. disgrace, bring disgrace on (sb); **żadna praca nie hańbi** any job's better than none. **~ się** ipf. bring disgrace upon o.s.; **mój wujek nie hańbił się pracą** iron. my uncle didn't do one tick of work.

happening mi sztuka happening.

happeningowy a. sztuka happening.

happy end mi zwł. film happy ending.

haracz mi Gen.pl. **-y** l. **-ów 1.** (= opłata za „ochronę" gangsterską) protection money; (= wymuszona opłata) squeeze; (= okup) ransom. **2.** hist. (= przymusowa danina) tribute.

harakiri n. indecl. hara-kiri.

harap mi Gen. **-u** l. **-a** jeźdz. (hunting) crop, blacksnake. – int. myśl., przest. halloo.

haratać ipf. pot. (= kaleczyć) cut (up).

harce pl. Gen. **-ów** frolic, horseplay, gambol, prancing, cavorting.

harcerka f. Gen.pl. **-ek** scout, Girl Scout; Br. Girl Guide.

harcerski a. scouting; **drużyna harcerska** scouting troop; **obóz harcerski** scouting camp; **zlot harcerski** (duży) jamboree; (mały) camporee.

harcerstwo n. scouting, the scouts; **być w harcerstwie** be a scout, be in the scouts; **Związek Harcerstwa Polskiego** Polish Scouting Association.

harcerz mp **1.** (w harcerstwie) scout, Boy Scout. **2.** iron. (= idealista) boy scout, eagle scout.

harcerzyk mp iron. = **harcerz** 2.

harcmistrz mp pl. **-owie** l. **-e** Gen. **-ów** scoutmaster.

harcować ipf. frolic, gambol, prance, cavort.

harcówka f. Gen.pl. **-ek** (zwł. zuchów) den; (zwł. starszych harcerzy) scout hut.

hardware mi Gen. **-e'u** komp. hardware.

hardwarowy a. komp. hardware.

hardy a. lit. **1.** (= dumny) haughty, proud. **2.** (= nieugięty, twardy) hardy, tough, intrepid.

hardzieć ipf. lit. grow hardy, toughen (up).

harem mi harem.

harfa f. muz. harp; **harfa eolska** aeolian harp, wind harp.

harfiany a. muz. harp.

harfiarka f. Gen.pl. **-ek**, **harfiarz** mp, **harfista** mp, **harfistka** Gen.pl. **-ek** f. harpist.

harfowy a. muz. harp.

harmider mi **-dr-** l. **-der-** pot. rumpus, racket.

harmonia f. Gen. **-ii 1.** (= zgoda, porządek) harmony, unison; **żyć w harmonii** live in harmony. **2.** muz. (= współbrzmienie) harmony, consonance. **3.** muz. (nauka) harmonics. **4.** muz. (instrument) accordion, squeeze-box; (mała) concertina.

harmoniczność f. harmony.

harmoniczny a. **1.** muz., akustyka, fiz., mat. harmonic; **drgania harmoniczne** fiz. harmonic vibrations; **średnia harmoniczna** mat. harmonic mean; **ruch harmoniczny** fiz. harmonic motion; **ton harmoniczny** muz. harmonic, overtone. **2.** (= harmonijny) harmonious.

harmonijka f. Gen.pl. **-ek 1.** muz. (także **harmonijka ustna**) (reed) harmonica, mouth organ, harp. **2.** mech. (= przegub harmonijkowy) bellows, concertina; **składać się w harmonijkę** concertina.

harmonijnie adv. harmoniously.

harmonijność f. harmoniousness, harmony.

harmonijny a. harmonious.

harmonista mp accordion/concertina player.

harmonizować ipf. **1.** (= współgrać, pasować) mesh, accord (z czymś with sth); go together. **2.** (= tworzyć całość, uzgadniać) harmonize (coś z czymś sth with sth). **3.** muz. harmonize.

harmonogram mi (zajęć) schedule, timetable, (work) plan; (osób) roster, roll; Br. rota.

harnaś mp Gen.pl. **-siów** l. **-si** przest. knight of the road (leader of highwaymen in the Tatra Mts.).

harować ipf. pot. slave (away), work hard; **harować w pocie czoła** knock o.s. out, work one's fingers to the bone, bust one's gut; sl. work one's ass off; **harować dzień i noc** work day and night; **harować jak koń** l. **wół** work like a horse/dog/mule.

harówa f. pot. = **harówka**.

harówka f. Gen.pl. **-ek** pot. grind, sweat; **codzienna harówka** daily grind.

harpagon mp pl. **-i** l. **-y** lit. (= skąpiec) Scrooge, skinflint.

harpia f. Gen. **-ii 1.** mit. Harpy. **2.** przen. (= dręczycielka) harpy. **3.** (także **harpia amerykańska**) orn. harpy eagle (Harpia harpyja).

harpun mi Gen. **-a** myśl., ryb. harpoon, lance, (barbed) spear.

harpunniczy a. harpoon.

harpunnik mp harpooner.

harpunowy a. **działko harpunowe** wielorybnictwo harpoon gun.

hart mi **1.** form. (cecha człowieka) fortitude,

moral fiber; **hart ducha/woli** stout heart. **2.** *przest. l. metal.* (= *twardość*) temper, hardness.

hartować *ipf.* **1.** *techn.* (= *utwardzać*) (*stal, szkło*) harden, temper, toughen. **2.** (= *uodparniać, wzmacniać*) (*ciało, charakter*) harden (*coś/kogoś na coś* sth/sb to/against sth); **hartować na mróz** harden to the cold. ~ **się** *ipf. t. metal.* harden.

hartowany *a.* hardened, tempered, toughened; **hartowane szkło** hardened/tempered/toughened glass.

hartowniczy *a. metal., techn.* hardening.

hartownik *mp metal.* hardener.

hartowność *f.* **1.** *metal.* (= *podatność na hartowanie*) hardening capacity, hardenability. **2.** *przest.* (= *twardość*) hardness, temper. **3.** *przest.* (= *odporność ludzi, zwierząt, roślin*) toughness.

hasać *ipf.* prance, caper, cavort.

haski *a. geogr., polit.* **konwencje haskie** the Hague Conventions; **trybunał haski** the Hague Tribunal.

hasło *n. Gen.pl.* **-seł 1.** (= *ideologia*) banner; **pod hasłem/hasłami czegoś** under the banner of sth. **2.** (*reklamowe*) catchphrase; sound bite; (= *modne słowo l. zwrot*) buzzword; (= *motto, sentencja*) watchword, slogan. **3.** (*rozpoznawcze*) *t. komp.* (= *kod dostępu*) password; **podawać hasło** give the password; **wpisać hasło** *komp.* enter the password. **4.** (= *sygnał*) code word, watchword; *wojsk.* (*w bitwie*) battle cry; (*dostępu*) countersign. **5.** (*w słowniku, encyklopedii*) entry.

hasłowy *a.* **1.** (= *dotyczący hasła*) **artykuł hasłowy** entry; **wyraz hasłowy** headword. **2.** *form.* (= *zwięzły*) concise, sententious, pithy, succinct.

hasz *mi* **1.** *sl.* (= *haszysz*) hash. **2.** *zwł. komp. l. tel.* (= *znak „#"*) pound sign, number sign, hash.

haszysz *mi* cannabis, hashish, hasheesh.

haszyszyzm *mi* cannabis addiction.

hatha-joga *f. sport* hatha yoga.

hau *int. onomat.* woof.

haubica *f. wojsk.* howitzer.

hau-hau *int. onomat.* bow-wow, woof-woof, ruff-ruff.

haust *mi* **1.** (= *łyk płynu*) gulp, swig; **wypić coś (jednym) haustem** drink sth at a gulp *l.* at one gulp. **2.** (*powietrza*) gasp.

Hawajczyk *mp* Hawaiian.

Hawaje *pl. Gen.* **-ów** *geogr., polit.* Hawaii.

Hawajka *f. Gen.pl.* **-ek** *zob.* **Hawajczyk.**

hawajski *a.* Hawaiian; **gitara hawajska** *muz.* steel guitar, Hawaiian guitar.

Hawana *f. geogr.* Havana.

hawana *f.* **1.** (*tytoń*) Havana (leaf/tobacco). **2.** (*cygaro*) Havana (cigar).

hawański *a.* Havana.

hazard *mi* **1.** (*gra*) gambling. **2.** (= *ryzyko*) gamble.

hazardowy *a.* **gry hazardowe** games of chance.

hazardzista *mp,* **hazardzistka** *f. Gen.pl.* **-ek** gambler.

he *int.* **1.** (*wyraża podziw, zdziwienie, pogar-*

dę) huh. **2.** (*śmiech*) ha-ha; **he, he, he** (*także* **he! he! he!**) ha-ha!, ha, ha!

heban *mi bot., stol.* (*drzewo, drewno, kolor*) ebony (*Diospyros ebenum*); **czarny jak heban** (as) black as coal/jet/ink/pitch/midnight, pitch-black.

hebanowy *a.* ebony.

hebel *mi* **-bl-** *Gen.* **-a** *stol.* plane.

heblarka *f. Gen.pl.* **-ek** *stol.* planer, planing machine.

heblować *ipf. stol.* plane.

hebrowiny *pl. Gen.* **-n** *stol.* shavings.

hebraista *mp,* **hebraistka** *f. Gen.pl.* **-ek** Hebrew scholar, Hebraist.

hebraistyka *f.* Hebrew, Hebraism.

hebraizm *mi jęz.* Hebraicism, Hebraism.

hebrajski *a.* Hebrew; **(język) hebrajski** *jęz.* Hebrew.

hebrajszczyzna *f.* (*język*) Hebrew; (*kultura*) Hebrew culture; (*cecha*) Hebraism.

Hebrydy *pl. Gen.* **-yd** *geogr.* the Hebrides.

heca *f.* **1.** *pot.* (= *żart, zabawa*) fun; **dla hecy** (just) for fun; for kicks; for a laugh; for the hell of it. **2.** (= *niespodzianka*) surprise; **ale heca!** *l.* **a to ci heca!** what a surprise! **3.** *przest.* (= *awantura*) uproar, brouhaha, hullabaloo.

hedonista *mp,* **hedonistka** *f. Gen.pl.* **-ek** hedonist, free-liver, libertine.

hedonistyczny *a. t. fil.* hedonist.

hedonizm *mi t. fil.* hedonism.

hegemon *mp pl.* **-i** *l.* **-owie** *form.* hegemonist, dictator, tyrant.

hegemonia *f. Gen.* **-ii** *form.* hegemony.

hegemoniczny *a. form.* hegemonic.

hej *int.* hey; **hej hop!** (*przy podnoszeniu dziecka*) up you go!; **hej ho!** (*przy podnoszeniu kotwicy*) heave-ho!; **hej ho, hej ho** (*w piosence*) hi-ho, hi-ho; **taki, że hej!** no small deal!

hejnalista *mp,* **hejnalistka** *f.* bugler.

hejnał *mi* **1.** *muz., wojsk.* (*melodia, sygnał na trąbce, pobudka*) bugle-call; **hejnał mariacki** St. Mary's Church bugle-call (*in Kraków*). **2.** *teor.lit.* aubade.

hejnałowy *a.* **1.** *teor.lit.* aubade. **2.** *muz.* **trąbka hejnałowa** bugle.

hejże *int.* **1.** (*w celu zwrócenia uwagi*) hey! **2.** (*wyraża radość l. podziw*) wow!

hekatomba *f. hist. t. przen.* (= *masakra, zagłada*) hecatomb.

heksametr *mi wers.* hexameter.

heksametryczny *a. wers.* hexametric.

hektar *mi Gen.* **-a** *zwł. roln.* hectare; **plon z hektara** *roln.* crop yield.

hektarowy *a. miern.* hectare.

hektary *pl. Gen.* **-ów** *dial. l. żart.* (= *ziemia, gospodarstwo rolne*) acres, land.

hektogram *mi* hectogram (= *100 grams or 3.53 oz.*).

hektolitr *mi Gen.* **-a** hectoliter (= *100 liters or 26.42 US gallons*).

hektometr *mi Gen.* **-a** hectometer (= *100 meters or 109.4 yards*).

hel *mi chem.* helium.

heliakalny *a. astron.* heliacal.

helikon *mi muz.* helicon.

helikopter *mi Gen.* **-a** *lotn.* helicopter; *pot.* chopper.

helikopterowy *a.* helicopter.

heliocentryczny *a. fil., astron.* heliocentric; **teoria heliocentryczna** the heliocentric system.

heliocentryzm *mi fil., astron.* heliocentrism, the heliocentric system.

heliograf *mi meteor., astron., fot., tel.* heliograph.

heliometr *mi astron., opt.* heliometer.

helioskop *mi astron., opt.* helioscope.

heliotrop *mi min., techn.* heliotrope; *bot.* (= *tomiłek*) heliotrope (*Heliotropium*).

heliotropiczny *a. bot.* heliotropic.

heliotropizm *mi bot.* heliotropism.

heliotropowy *a.* = **heliotropiczny**.

hellenista *mp*, **hellenistka** *f. Gen.pl.* **-ek** Hellenist, classical Greek scholar.

hellenistyczny *a. hist.* Hellenistic.

hellenistyka *f.* classical Greek.

hellenizacja *f.* Hellenization, Greek *l.* Hellenic influence.

hellenizm *mi* Hellenism.

hellenizować *ipf.* Hellenize.

helleński *a.* Hellenic, classical Greek; **kultura helleńska** Hellenic culture; classical Greek culture.

helota *mp hist.* helot.

helotyzm *mi* **1.** *hist.* (= *niewolnictwo*) helotism, helotage, helotry. **2.** *biol.* (= *symbioza*) helotism.

helowy *a. zwł. chem.* helium; **mowa helowa** *akust., fon.* helium speech; *pot.* munchkin voice.

Helsinki *pl. Gen.* **-ek** *geogr.* Helsinki.

helwecki *a. polit., rel.* Helvetic, Helvetian.

Helwetka *f. Gen.pl.* **-ek**, **Helweta** *mp pl.* **-ci** *l.* **-owie** *polit., rel.* Helvetic, Helvetian.

hełm *mi* **1.** (*nakrycie głowy*) helmet; **hełm tropikalny** pith helmet. **2.** *bud.* (= *kopułka*) cupola.

hełmofon *mi tel., lotn., wojsk.* headset.

hematokryt *mi med.* hematocrit (value).

hematolog *mp pl.* **-dzy** *l.* **-owie** *med.* hematologist.

hematologia *f. Gen.* **-ii** *med.* hematology.

hematologiczny *a. med.* hematological.

hematyna *f. biochem.* hematine.

hematyt *mi min.* hematite.

hemodializa *f. med.* hemodialysis.

hemofilia *f. Gen.* **-ii** *pat.* hemophilia.

hemofilik *mp pat.* hemophiliac.

hemoglobina *f. biochem.* hemoglobin.

hemoroidalny *a. pat.* hemorhoidal.

hemoroidy *pl. Gen.* **-ów** *pat.* hemorhoids, piles.

hen *adv. lit.* yonder, far away.

henna *f.* (*barwnik, farba do włosów*) *t. bot.* henna (*Lawsonia inermis*).

henr *mi Gen.* **-a** *el., fiz.* henry (*H, unit of inductance*).

Henryk *mp* Henry.

heparyna *f. biochem.* heparin.

hepatologia *f. med.* hepatology.

hepatologiczny *a. med.* hepatology; **oddział hepatologiczny** hepatology ward.

heptagon *mi geom.* heptagon.

heptatlon *mi sport* heptathlon.

heraldyczny *a.* heraldic; **barwy heraldyczne** coat of arms, blazonry.

heraldyk *mp* heraldist, armorist.

heraldyka *f.* heraldry, blazonry.

herb *mi* (*symbol*) coat of arms, blazon; (*tablica*) escutcheon.

herbaciany *a.* **1.** tea. **2. róża herbaciana** *bot.* tea rose (*Rosa odorata*).

herbaciarnia *f. Gen.pl.* **-i** *l.* **-ń** teahouse; *zwł. Br.* teashop, tearoom; (*w plenerze*) tea garden.

herbarz *mi Gen.* **-a** **1.** *her.* (*album z herbami*) armorial. **2.** *bot.* (= *zielnik*) herbarium.

herbata *f. kulin., bot.* tea; **herbata czarna/zielona** black/green tea; **herbata chińska/indyjska** China/Indian tea; **herbata ziołowa** herbal tea, herb tea; **herbata mrożona** iced tea, ice tea.

herbatka *f. Gen.pl.* **-ek** **1.** *kulin.* (*napój*) tea. **2.** (*przyjęcie*) tea party.

herbatnik *mi Gen.* **-a** butter cookie; *Br.* biscuit.

herbicyd *mi roln., chem.* herbicide.

herbicydowy *a. chem.* herbicide.

herbowy *a.* **1.** (= *heraldyczny*) armorial, emblematic; **tarcza herbowa** coat of arms, blazon, escutcheon. **2.** *hist.* (= *szlachecki*) genteel; **szlachta herbowa** gentry.

herc *mi Gen.* **-a** *fiz., el.* hertz (*Hz, unit of frequency*).

Hercegowina *f. geogr.* Hercegovina; **Bośnia i Hercegowina** *polit.* Bosnia-Hercegovina; Bosnia and Hercegovina.

heretycki *a. teol. l. przen.* heretical.

heretyczka *f. Gen.pl.* **-ek** *teol. l. przen.* heretic.

heretyk *mp teol. l. przen.* heretic.

herezja *f. teol. l. przen.* heresy.

herezjarcha *mp pl.* **-owie** *teol.* heresiarch.

Herkules *mp mit., astron.* Hercules.

herkules *mp pl.* **-i** *l.* **-y** *lit.* (= *siłacz*) Hercules. — *ma pl.* **-y** *ent.* (*chrząszcz*) hercules beetle (*Dynastes hercules*).

herkulesowy *a. mit.* Herculean; **herkulesowe prace** *t. przen.* Herculean tasks.

herma *f. sztuka* herm, herma.

hermafrodyta *mp pl.* **-ci** *pat.* (= *obojnak*) hermaphrodite. — *ma pl.* **-y** *biol.* hermaphrodite.

hermafrodytyczny *a. biol., med.* hermaphrodite, hermaphroditic.

hermafrodytyzm *mi biol., med.* hermaphroditism, hermaphrodism.

hermeneutyczny *a. teor.lit., teol.* hermeneutic, hermeneutical.

hermeneutyka *f. teor.lit., teol., fil.* hermeneutics.

Hermes *mp mit.* Hermes.

hermetycznie *adv.* hermetically; **hermetycznie zamknięty** hermetically sealed.

hermetyczność *f.* **1.** *techn.* (= *szczelność*) airtight sealing, tightness. **2.** *form.* (= *nieprzystępność*) hermetism.

hermetyczny *a.* **1.** *techn.* (= *szczelny*) airtight, hermetic. **2.** *form.* (= *nieprzystępny, tajemny*) hermetic; **dzieła hermetyczne** *hist., fil.* Hermetic Books.

hermetyzacja *f. techn.* airtight sealing.

hermetyzm *mi form., hist., fil.* hermetism.

herod-baba *f. pot., zw. obelż.* virago, dragon, snake, gorgon.

heroicznie *adv.* heroically.

heroiczny *a.* heroic; **poemat heroiczny** *teor.lit.* (*dzieło*) heroic poem; *wers.* heroic verse/meter, heroics.

heroikomiczny *a. teor.lit.* mock-heroic; **poemat heroikomiczny** mock-heroic (poem/verse).

heroikomika *f. teor.lit.* mock-heroic.

heroina *f.* **1.** (*narkotyk*) heroin. **2.** *lit.* (= *bohaterka, postać*) heroine.

heroinizm *mi pat.* heroin addiction.

heroinowy *a.* heroin.

heroizacja *f. lit.* heroization.

heroizm *mi lit.* heroism.

heroizować *ipf. lit.* heroize.

herold *mp pl.* **-owie** *l.* **-dzi 1.** *hist.* herald. **2.** *przen.* (= *prorok, zwiastun*) herald, harbinger.

heros *mp pl.* **-i** *poet.* **-owie** *l.* **-y** *mit. l. lit., przen.* hero.

herpetolog *mp pl.* **-dzy** *l.* **-owie** herpetologist.

herpetologia *f. Gen.* **-ii** *zool.* herpetology.

herszt *mp pl.* **-ci** *l.* **-owie** ringleader, gang leader.

het *adv.* (*także* **het het**) *arch.* (= *w oddali*) (over) yonder; (= *w odległej przeszłości*) long ago.

hetera *f.* **1.** *obelż. l. żart.* (= *jędza*) shrew, bitch, nag, spitfire. **2.** *hist.* (= *kurtyzana*) hetaera, hetaira.

hetero *a. pot.* (= *heteroseksualny*) hetero.

heterogenetyczny *a. biol.* heterogenetic.

heterogeneza *f. biol.* heterogenesis.

heterogeniczny *a. form.* heterogeneous, heterogenous.

heteromorficzny *a. biol.* heteromorphic.

heteromorfizm *mi biol.* heteromorphism.

heteronomia *f. Gen.* **-ii** *biol., polit.* (= *niesamodzielność*) heteronomy.

heteronomiczny *a. biol., polit.* heteronomous.

heteroseksualista *mp* heterosexual.

heteroseksualny *a.* heterosexual.

hetman *mi pl.* **-y** *szachy* queen. – *mp pl.* **-i** *l.* **-owie** *hist., wojsk.* hetman, (field) marshal.

hetmański *a.* **1.** *szachy* queen's. **2.** *hist., wojsk.* hetman's, (field) marshal's.

hetmaństwo *n. hist., wojsk.* hetmanate.

heureza *f. form.* heuristics.

heurystyczny *a. form.* heuristic.

heurystyka *f. form.* heuristics.

hę *int.* (*wyraża zdziwienie*) huh?

hi hi hi *int. onomat.* (*śmiech*) hee hee hee.

hiacynt *mi Gen.* **-a** *l.* **-u** *bot., ogr.* hyacinth (*Hyacinthus orientalis*). – *mi Gen.* **-u** *min.* hyacinth.

hialit *mi min.* hyalite.

hialuronowy *a. biol., chem.* **kwas hialuronowy** hialuronic acid.

hibernacja *f. biol.* hibernation.

hibiskus *mi Gen.* **-a** *bot., kulin.* hibiscus, roselle (*Hibiscus*).

hidżra *f. hist., rel.* the Hegira, the Hejira.

hiena *f.* **1.** *zool.* hyena; **hiena cętkowana** spotted *l.* laughing hyena (*Crocuta crocuta*); **hiena pręgowana** striped hyena (*Hyaena hyaena*). **2.** (*przen.* = *człowiek bezwzględnie żerujący na cudzym nieszczęściu*) vulture; **hiena cmentarna** grave robber.

hierarcha *mp pl.* **-owie** *kośc.* hierarch.

hierarchia *f. Gen.* **-ii** hierarchy.

hierarchiczność *f.* hierarchic structure, hierarchy.

hierarchiczny *a.* hierarchical, hierarchic.

hierarchizacja *f.* hierarchization.

hierarchizować *ipf.* hierarchize.

hieratyczny *a.* hieratic; **pismo hieratyczne** *jęz.* hieratic (writing/script).

hieroglif *mi* **1.** (*jęz.* = *pismo egipskie*) hieroglyphic, hieroglyph. **2.** (*pl. pot.* = *bazgroły*) hieroglyphics.

hieroglificzny *a. jęz., geol.* hieroglyphic; **pismo hieroglificzne** hieroglyphic script, hieroglyphics.

hieroglifika *f. jęz.* hieroglyphics.

hi-fi *abbr. techn.* hi-fi; **sprzęt hi-fi** hi-fi equipment; **wieża hi-fi** hi-fi system, stereo.

higiena *f. t. med.* (*czystość, nauka*) hygiene; **higiena jamy ustnej** dental *l.* oral hygiene; **higiena osobista** personal hygiene; **bezpieczeństwo i higiena pracy** work safety, industrial hygiene.

higienicznie *adv.* hygienically.

higieniczny *a.* hygienic; **chusteczka higieniczna** (facial) tissue.

higienista *mp med.* hygienist.

higienistka *f. Gen.pl.* **-ek 1.** *med. zob.* **higienista. 2.** *Br. szkoln.* matron.

higrometr *mi techn.* hygrometer.

higroskop *mi techn.* hygroscope.

higroskopijność *f. fiz.* moisture-absorbing capacity, hygroscopicity.

higroskopijny *a. fiz.* moisture-absorbing, moisture-absorbent, hygroscopic.

hikora *f. bot., stol.* hickory (*Carya*).

hikorowy *a. stol.* hickory.

himalaista *mp*, **himalaistka** *f. Gen.pl.* **-ek** (mountain) climber.

himalaizm *mi sport* (mountain) climbing.

Himalaje *pl. Gen.* **-ów** *geogr.* the Himalayas.

himalajski *a.* Himalayan; **niedźwiedź himalajski** *zool.* Asiatic black bear, moon/collared/Japanese black bear (*Ursus [Selenarctos] thibetanus*).

hindi *mi indecl. jęz.* Hindi.

hinduista *mp*, **hinduistka** *f. Gen.pl.* **-ek 1.** (= *indolog*) Hindu scholar. **2.** *rel.* (= *hindus*) Hindu.

hinduistyczny *a.* Hindu.

hinduistyka *f.* Hindu studies.

hinduizm *mi rel.* Hinduism.

Hindus *mp*, **Hinduska** *f. Gen.pl.* **-ek** *polit.* Indian.

hindus *mp*, **hinduska** *f. Gen.pl.* **-ek** *rel.* Hindu.

hinduski *a.* (= *indyjski*) Indian; (= *dotyczący hinduizmu*) Hindu.

Hiob *mp Bibl.* Job.

hiobowy *a.* Job's; **mieć hiobową cierpliwość**

have the patience of Job; **hiobowa wieść** grievous news.

hipcio *ma pl.* **-e, hipek** *ma* **-pk-** *pot. dziec.* (= *hipopotam*) hippo.

hiperbola *f. Gen.pl.* **-i** *l.* **-l 1.** *ret., teor.lit.* hyperbole. **2.** *geom.* hyperbola.

hiperboliczność *f.* **1.** *ret., teor.lit.* hyperbole. **2.** *geom.* hyperbolic shape.

hiperboliczny *a.* **1.** *form.* (= *przesadny*) hyperbolic, exaggerated. **2.** *geom.* hyperbolic; **funkcje hiperboliczne** *mat.* hyperbolic functions.

hiperboloida *f. geom.* hyperboloid.

hiperestezja *f. pat., psych.* hyperesthesia.

hiperinflacja *f. ekon.* hyperinflation.

hipermarket *n. handl.* superstore.

hiperon *mi fiz.* hyperon.

hiperonim *mi jęz.* hyperonym, generic term, superordinate term.

hiperpoprawność *f. jęz.* hypercorrection.

hiperprzestrzeń *f. fiz.* hyperspace.

hipertekst *mi komp., teor.lit.* hypertext.

hipertekstowy *a. komp.* hypertext.

hipertekstualność *f. teor.lit.* hypertextuality.

hipertekstualny *a. teor.lit.* hypertextual.

hipiczny *a. jeźdz.* riding, horse-riding, equestrian.

hipika *f. jeźdz.* riding, horse-riding, equestrianism.

hipis *mp,* **hipiska** *f. Gen.pl.* **-ek** hippie.

hipisowski *a.* hippie.

hipnotyczny *a.* **1.** *psych.* hypnotic; **trans hipnotyczny** hypnotic trance. **2.** (= *przykuwający uwagę*) hypnotizing.

hipnotyzer *mp,* **hipnotyzerka** *f. Gen.pl.* **-ek** hypnotist.

hipnotyzerski *a.* hypnotic.

hipnotyzować *ipf. psych. l. przen.* hypnotize.

hipnoza *f. psych.* hypnosis, hypnotism.

hipoalergiczny *a. med.* hypoallergenic.

hipocentrum *n. sejsmologia* hypocenter, ground zero.

hipochondria *f. Gen.* **-ii** *pat.* hypochondria.

hipochondryczka *f. Gen.pl.* **-ek** *zob.* **hipochondryk**.

hipochondryczny *a. pat.* hypochondriac.

hipochondryk *mp pat.* hypochondriac.

hipocykloida *f. geom.* hypocycloid.

hipoderma *f. bot., zool.* hypodermis, hypoderm.

hipodrom *mi hist., sport* hippodrome.

hipoglikemia *f. pat.* hypoglycemia.

hipokamp *mi. anat., mit.* hippocampus.

hipokorystyczny *a. jęz.* hypocoristic.

hipokorystyk *mi jęz.* hypocorism, hypocoristic.

hipokryta *mp,* **hipokrytka** *f. Gen.pl.* **-ek** hypocrite.

hipokrytyczny *a.* hypocritical.

hipokryzja *f.* hypocrisy.

hipopotam *ma zool.* hippopotamus (*Hippopotamus amphibius*); *pot.* hippo; **hipopotam karłowaty** pygmy hippopotamus (*Choeropsis liberiensis*).

hipostaza *f. fil., pat.* hypostasis.

hipostazować *ipf. fil.* hypostatize, hypostasize.

hipotaksa *f. gram.* hypotaxis.

hipotaktyczny *a. gram.* hypotactic.

hipoteczny *a. fin.* mortgage; **dług hipoteczny** mortgage; **księga hipoteczna** mortgage register.

hipoteka *f.* **1.** *fin.* mortgage. **2.** *prawn.* (= *księga wieczysta*) mortgage register; (= *wpis do księgi wieczystej*) mortgage (deed). **3.** *pot.* (= *biuro notarialne*) mortgage registry.

hipoterapia *f. Gen.* **-ii** *med.* hippotherapy, theurapeutic riding.

hipotermia *f. Gen.* **-ii** *fizj., pat.* hypothermia.

hipotetyczny *a.* hypothetical, hypothetic, conjectural; **sąd hipotetyczny** *log.* hypothetical *l.* conditional proposition.

hipoteza *f.* hypothesis, conjecture; **udowodnić/ obalić hipotezę** prove/refute a hypothesis, hypothesize; **wysuwać hipotezę** put forward a hypothesis, hypothesize.

hippika *f.* = **hipika**.

hippis, hippiska *f. Gen.pl.* **-ek** *zob.* **hipis**.

hispanista *mp,* **hispanistka** *f. Gen.pl.* **-ek** Hispanicist.

hispanistyka *f.* Spanish studies.

histereza *f. fiz.* hysteresis; **pętla histerezy** hysteresis loop.

histeria *f. Gen.* **-ii** hysteria; **zbiorowa histeria** mass hysteria; **atak/napad histerii** attack/fit of hysteria, hysterics.

histeryczka *f. zob.* **histeryk**.

histeryczny *a.* hysterical.

histeryk *mp,* **histeryczka** *f. Gen.pl.* **-ek** hysteric, hysterical person.

histeryzować *ipf.* become hysterical, behave hysterically; *pot.* have a fit; (= *wpadać w panikę*) panic.

histolog *mp pl.* **-dzy** *l.* **-owie** *med.* histologist.

histologia *f. Gen.* **-ii** *med.* histology.

histologiczny *a.* histological.

historia *f. Gen.* **-ii 1.** history; **przesiąknięty historią** steeped in history; **przejść do historii** (*także* **zapisać się w historii**) make history, go down in history (*jako ktoś / coś* as sb/sth); **historia choroby** *med.* case history; **historia naturalna** *przest.* natural history. **2.** (= *zdarzenie*) story; **historia czyjegoś życia** sb's life story; **wiecznie ta sama historia** it's the same old story; **ładna historia!** a pretty *l.* fine kettle of fish! **3.** (= *opowieść*) tale, story; **historia wyssana z palca** tall tale; **opowiadać niestworzone historie** tell tales.

historiografia *f. Gen.* **-ii** historiography.

historiograficzny *a.* (*o źródłach, dziele*) historiographic.

historiozof *mp pl.* **-owie** *fil.* philosopher of history.

historiozofia *f. Gen.* **-ii** *fil.* philosophy of history.

historiozoficzny *a.* **refleksja historiozoficzna** philosophical reflection upon history.

historyczka *f. Gen.pl.* **-ek** *zob.* **historyk**.

historycznojęzykowy *a. jęz.* (*o badaniu, opracowaniu*) historical-linguistic, diachronic.

historycznoliteracki *a. teor.lit.* (*o badaniu, opracowaniu*) in the history of literature, in literary history.

historyczność *f.* (= *autentyczność historyczna*) historicity, historicalness.

historyczny *a.* **1.** (= *dotyczący historii*) historical. **2.** (= *doniosły*) historic.

historyjka *f. Gen.pl.* **-ek** little story; *uj.* (= *wątpliwa opowieść*) cock-and-bull story; **historyjka obrazkowa** comic strip, strip; **nie opowiadaj mi historyjek** don't tell me stories.

historyk *mp* historian; *szkoln.* (= *nauczyciel historii*) history teacher.

historyzm *mi fil., sztuka* historicism.

Hiszpan *mp pl.* **-nie** Spaniard.

Hiszpania *f. Gen.* **-ii** *geogr., polit.* Spain.

hiszpanka *f. pat., przest.* (= *grypa*) influenza.

Hiszpanka *f. Gen.pl.* **-ek** *zob.* **Hiszpan**; Spanish woman.

hiszpański *a.* Spanish; **bródka hiszpańska** Vandyke beard; **hiszpańska mucha** *ent.* (*t. afrodyzjak*) Spanishfly (beetle) (*Lytta vesicatoria*). – *mi decl. like a.* (= *język hiszpański*) Spanish; **po hiszpańsku** in Spanish.

hit *mi* (= *przebój*) hit.

hitlerowiec *mp* **-wc-** *Voc.* **-cze** *l.* **-cu** *pl.* **-y** Nazi.

hitlerowski *a.* Nazi.

hitleryzm *mi* Nazism, Hitlerism.

HIV *abbr. i mi Gen.* **HIV-a** *med.* **(wirus)** HIV HIV (= *human immunodeficiency virus*); **być/nie być nosicielem (wirusa) HIV** be HIV positive/negative. – *mp pot.* (= *osoba chora na AIDS*) PWA (= *person with AIDS*).

hizop *mi* **1.** *bot.* hyssop (*Hyssopus officinalis*). **2.** (*olejek*) oil of hyssop.

hm *int.* **1.** (*zakłopotanie, niepewność*) h'm, ahem. **2.** (*powątpiewanie, niezadowolenie*) humph.

hobbista *mp*, **hobbistka** *f. Gen.pl.* **-ek** hobbyist; (= *kolekcjoner*) collector.

hobbistyczny *a.* (= *charakteryzujący hobbistę*) hobbyist's; (*o podejściu do sprawy*) casual; **zainteresowania hobbistyczne** hobbies.

hobby *n. indecl.* hobby, pastime.

hochsztapler *mp*, **hochsztaplerka** *f. Gen.pl.* **-ek** *pot. uj.* fraud, swindler; (*tylko o mężczyźnie*) confidence man, con man.

hochsztaplerski *a. pot.* crooked, fraudulent.

hochsztaplerstwo *n. pot.* fraud, confidence game.

hocki-klocki *pl. Gen.* **hocków-klocków** *pot.* fiddle-faddle; **to nie żadne hocki-klocki** it's no joke.

hodować *ipf.* **1.** raise, breed, rear; (*dla przyjemności*) keep; (*rośliny*) grow, cultivate; (*bakterie, tkanki*) culture. **2.** *przen.* (= *przechowywać*) (*nienawiść, urazę, ambicję*) cherish, nurse.

hodowca *mp* breeder; (*zboża, roślin*) grower, cultivator; **hodowca bydła/owiec/drobiu** cattle/sheep/poultry farmer; **hodowca rybek akwariowych** aquariast, aquarist.

hodowla *f.* (*bydła, pomidorów*) farming, breeding; (*nauka*) breeding; **hodowla bakteryjna/ tkanek/ostryg** bacterial/tissue/oyster culture.

hodowlany *a.* breeding, farming; **gospodarstwo hodowlane** stock *l.* animal farm; **staw hodowlany** fish pond; **odmiana hodowlana** breed; **zwierzęta hodowlane** farm animals.

ho ho *int.* (*podziw*) wow!, my!

hojnie *adv.* generously, liberally; (= *obficie*) abundantly, amply.

hojność *f.* generosity, generousness.

hojny *a.* generous, liberal; **dawać hojną ręką** give with an open hand.

hokeista *mp*, **hokeistka** *f. Gen.pl.* **-ek** *sport* hockey player.

hokej *mi* **1.** *Gen.* **-a** *sport* (*gra*) hockey; **hokej na trawie** field *l.* grass hockey. **2.** *Gen.pl.* **-ei** *sport* (*kij*) hockey stick.

hokejowy *a. sport* hockey.

hokus-pokus *n. i int. indecl.* (*zaklęcie l. sztuczki*) hocus pocus.

hol[1] *mi* (*pomieszczenie*) hall, hallway; (*w hotelu, teatrze, klubie*) lounge.

hol[2] *mi* (*do ciągnięcia*) tow; **ciągnąć na holu** tow.

hola *int. przest. l. lit.* (*sprzeciw*) whoa!, hey!

Holandia *f. Gen.* **-ii** *geogr., polit.* the Netherlands, Holland.

holding *mi ekon.* holding company.

holdingowy *a. ekon.* holding.

Holender *mp* **-dr-** Dutchman, Netherlander; **latający Holender** Flying Dutchman.

holender *mi* **-dr-** *Gen.* **-a** **1.** *techn.* hollander, beater, beating engine. **2.** (*wiatrak*) smock *l.* Dutch windmill. **3.** (*byk*) Holstein-Friesian bull. – *int. pot.* shoot!, doggone!, shucks!

Holenderka *f. Gen.pl.* **-ek** Dutchwoman, Netherlander.

holenderka *f. Gen.pl.* **-ek** *pot.* (*krowa*) Holstein, Holstein-Friesian, black-and-white cow.

holenderski *a.* Dutch. – *mi decl. like a.* (= *język holenderski*) Dutch; **mówić po holendersku** speak Dutch; **dachówka holenderska** (= *esówka*) *bud.* pantile; **sos holenderski** *kulin.* hollandaise (sauce).

holendrować *ipf.* **1.** *sport* figure skate. **2.** *lotn.* yaw. **3.** *druk.* stitch.

holistyczny *a. fil. l. med.* (*o ujęciu, teorii, założeniach*) holistic.

holizm *mi fil.* holism.

holm *mi chem.* holmium.

holocaust *mi hist., rel. l. przen.* holocaust.

holografia *f. Gen.* **-ii** *fiz.* holography.

holograficzny *a. fiz.* holographic.

holografować *ipf. fiz.* make holographic images of (*sth*).

hologram *mi fiz.* hologram.

hologramowy *a. fiz.* holographic.

holować *ipf.* tow.

holowniczy *a.* tow; **hak holowniczy** towbar; **lina holownicza** towrope; **statek holowniczy** *żegl.* towboat, tugboat, tug.

holownik *mi Gen.* **-a** **1.** *żegl.* tugboat, towboat, tug. **2.** *lotn.* glider-tug, tow-plane.

hołd *mi* **1.** (= *wyraz czci*) homage, tribute; **składać komuś hołd** pay *l.* do homage to sb. **2.** **hołd lenny** *hist.* fealty, homage.

hołdować *ipf.* + *Dat.* **1.** **hołdować czemuś** (= *wierzyć w coś*) profess sth, follow sth. **2.** *hist.* **hołdować komuś** (= *składać hołd komuś*) pay *l.*

do homage to sb, swear *l.* pledge allegiance to sb.

hołdownictwo *n. hist.* allegiance, vassalage.

hołdowniczy *a. hist.* **1.** tributary, vassal; **wierność hołdownicza** allegiance. **2.** *uj.* (= *uniżony, wiernopoddańczy*) subservient, servile.

hołdownik *mp hist.* tributary.

hołota *f.* **1.** (= *niekulturalni ludzie*) *pog.* the mob, trash, scum, rabble, riffraff. **2.** *żart.* (= *gromada dzieci*) small fry.

hołubić *ipf.* (= *rozpieszczać*) pamper, coddle.

homar *ma kulin., zool.* lobster (*Homarus vulgaris*).

homeopata *mp med.* homeopath, homeopathist; homeopathic healer; **lekarz homeopata** homeopathic physician.

homeopatia *f. Gen.* -ii *med.* homeopathy.

homeopatka *f. Gen.pl.* -ek *zob.* **homeopata**.

homeopatyczny *a. med.* (*o leku, dawce, terapii*) **1.** homeopathic. **2. magia homeopatyczna** *antrop.* homeopathic magic.

homerycki *a. teor.lit.* (*o stylu, porównaniu*) Homeric.

homeryczny *a. lit.* Homeric; **homeryczny śmiech** Homeric laughter; uproarious laughter.

homiletyczny *a. ret.* (*o tekście, poradniku*) homiletic; **sztuka homiletyczna** homiletics.

homiletyka *f. Gen.pl.* -ek *ret.* homiletics.

homilia *f. Gen.* -ii *rel.* homily, sermon.

hominid *ma zool.* hominid.

homofob *mp* homophobe.

homofobia *f. Gen.* -ii homophobia.

homofon *mi jęz.* homophone.

homofonia *f. Gen.* -ii *jęz. l. muz.* homophony.

homofoniczny *a. jęz. l. muz.* homophonic.

homogamia *f. Gen.* -ii *antrop. l. bot.* homogamy.

homogen *mi fil.* homogen.

homogenetyczny *a. form.* homogenetic.

homogenia *f. Gen.* -ii *form.* homogeny.

homogeniczność *f. form.* homogeneity.

homogeniczny *a. form.* homogeneous, homogenous; **układ homogeniczny** *fiz.* homogenous system.

homogenizacja *f.* **1.** *chem. l. socjol.* homogenization. **2.** *techn.* homogenizing treatment.

homogenizować *ipf. chem.* homogenize.

homogenizowany *a. kulin.* (*o mleku, śmietance*) homogenized; **serek homogenizowany** cream cheese.

homogram *mi jęz.* homograph.

homologacja *f.* official certification, approval, homologation.

homologacyjny *a.* certificatory, certifying; **zezwolenie homologacyjne** certificate of approval.

homologia *f. Gen.* -ii **1.** *biol. l. chem.* homology. **2.** *geom.* homology, collineation, collineatory transformation.

homologiczny *a. form.* homologous; **narządy homologiczne** *biol.* homologs, homologues; **szereg homologiczny** *chem.* homologous series.

homo-niewiadomo *n. indecl. żart.* she-male, third sexer.

homonim *mi jęz.* homonym.

homonimia *f. Gen.* -ii *jęz.* homonymy.

homonimiczny *a. jęz.* homonymous, homonymic.

homoseksualista *mp*, **homoseksualistka** *f. Gen.pl.* -ek homosexual, gay; (*tylko o kobiecie*) lesbian.

homoseksualizm *mi* homosexuality.

homoseksualny *a.* homosexual, gay.

homunkulus *ma* homunculus.

honor *mi* **1.** (= *godność osobista*) honor; self-respect, face; **na mój honor** *przest.* (= *słowo daję*) upon my honor; **punkt honoru** point of honor; **słowo honoru** one's word of honor; **to sprawa mojego honoru** my honor is at stake; **unieść się honorem** to take offense; **wyjść z honorem** save face. **2.** *karty* honor.

honorarium *n. sing. indecl. pl.* -ria *Gen.* -riów fee, honorarium; (*autorskie*) royalty.

honorować *ipf.* **1.** (= *uznawać*) honor, recognize; (*o czeku, karcie kredytowej*) accept; *form.* honor. **2.** *form.* (= *okazywać komuś szacunek*) honor, lionize.

honorowo *adv.* honorably.

honorowy *a.* (*o człowieku*) honorable; (*o długu, warunkach, tytule*) honorary; (= *bez wynagrodzenia, dobrowolny*) honorary, voluntary; **bramka honorowa** *sport* face-saver; **gość honorowy** guest of honor; **honorowy obywatel miasta** freeman of the city; **kompania honorowa** *wojsk.* guard of honor; **runda honorowa** *sport* victory lap, lap of honor; **sąd honorowy** court of honor; **sprawa honorowa** affair of honor.

honory *pl. Gen.* -ów (= *wyrazy czci*) honors; (= *pozdrowienie wojskowe, salut*) military honors, salute; **oddawać komuś honory** salute sb; **pełnić honory domu** do the honors; **przyjmować kogoś z honorami** receive sb with full honors; **przyjmować honory** (*o dostojniku*) take the salute.

hop *int.* (*zachęta do skoku l. podskoku*) jump!, hop!; **nie mów hop, póki nie przeskoczysz** don't count your chickens before they're hatched.

hop-hop *int.* (= *gdzie jesteś?*) hello!

hopla *int.* = **hopsa**.

hoplita *mp hist.wojsk.* hoplite.

hopsa *int. dziec.* upsy-daisy, oops-a-daisy.

hormon *mi biochem.* hormone; **burza hormonów** *pot.* raging hormones.

hormonalny *a. gł. med.* (*o leku, równowadze, preparacie*) hormonal, hormone; **hormonalna terapia zastępcza** hormone-replacement therapy; **układ hormonalny** *biol.* endocrine system.

hormonizacja *f. roln.* hormonization, hormone treatment.

hormonizować *ipf. roln.* hormonize.

hormonoterapia *f. Gen.* -ii *med.* hormonal *l.* hormone treatment, hormonotherapy.

hormonowy *a. med.* (*o kuracji, leku, preparacie*) hormonal, hormone.

horoskop *mi astrol.* horoscope; **stawiać komuś horoskop** cast sb's horoscope.

horoskopowy *a. astrol.* horoscopic.

horrendalny *a. form.* horrendous, horrible; (*o*

żądaniach, cenie) unreasonable; **horrendalna cena** exorbitant *l.* prohibitive price.

horrendum *n. indecl. arch.* monstrosity.

horror *mi* 1. (= *film grozy*) horror movie. 2. (= *groźna sytuacja*) nightmare.

hortensja *f. bot., ogr.* hydrangea (*Hydrangea*).

horyzont *mi* 1. horizon; **horyzont astronomiczny** celestial horizon; **horyzont fizyczny** sensible horizon, observer's horizon; **horyzont zdarzeń** *astron.* event horizon; **sztuczny horyzont** *lotn.* artificial horizon, gyro horizon; **na horyzoncie** *przen.* (= *w zasięgu wzroku*) on the horizon. 2. *hydrol.* water horizon, water level. 3. *teatr* backdrop, backcloth.

horyzontalizm *mi sztuka* horizontalism.

horyzontalność *f.* horizontality.

horyzontalny *a. form.* horizontal; **współrzędne horyzontalne** *astron.* horizontal coordinates.

horyzonty *pl. Gen.* **-ów** 1. (= *zakres wiedzy*) horizons; **poszerzać swoje/czyjeś horyzonty** broaden one's/sb's horizons *l.* mind; **wąskie/szerokie horyzonty** narrow/broad horizons. 2. (= *perspektywy*) prospects. 3. (= *środowisko*) scene.

hosanna *int. rel.* hosanna.

hospicjum *n. sing. indecl. pl.* **-ja** *Gen.* **-jów** *med.* hospice.

hospitacja *f. szkoln.* inspection.

hospitacyjny *a. szkoln.* inspection; **protokół hospitacyjny** inspection report.

hospitalizacja *f. med.* hospitalization.

hospitalizacyjny *a. med.* hospital; **leczenie hospitalizacyjne** hospital treatment.

hospitalizować *ipf. med.* hospitalize.

hospitant *mp*, **hospitantka** *f. Gen.pl.* **-ek** *szkoln.* inspector.

hospitować *ipf. szkoln.* inspect.

hossa *f.* 1. *ekon.* bull market, boom. 2. *przen.* (= *okres powodzenia*) prosperity.

hostessa *f.* hostess.

hostia *f. Gen.* **-ii** *rz.-kat.* the Host; **umoczenie hostii w winie** (*w czasie komunii*) intinction.

hot dog *mi Gen.* **-a** *kulin.* hot dog.

hotel *mi* hotel; **hotel robotniczy** workers' hostel; **hotel trzygwiazdkowy** three-star hotel; **opuścić hotel** book out.

hotelarka *f. Gen.pl.* **-ek** *zob.* **hotelarz**.

hotelarski *a.* hotel-management; **usługi hotelarskie** hotel services.

hotelarstwo *n.* hotel industry *l.* trade, hotelkeeping, hotel management.

hotelarz *mp* hotel owner, hotel-keeper, hotelier.

hotelik *mi* small hotel; (*w Europie*) pension.

hotelowy *a.* (*o pokoju, restauracji, holu*) hotel; **koniec doby hotelowej** check-out time; **goniec hotelowy** bellhop, hotel porter; **pociąg hotelowy** sleeper train; **taryfa hotelowa** hotel rate.

hoży *a. lit.* buxom, lively, bonny; **hoża dziewoja** buxom wench.

hrabia *mp Gen.* **-ego** *l.* **-i** *Dat.* **-emu** *l.* **-i** *Acc.* **-ego** *l.* **-ę** *Ins.* **-ą** *Loc.* **-i** *l.* **-im** *Voc.* **-o** *pl.* **-owie** *Gen.* **-ów** (*tytuł*) count; (*w Wielkiej Brytanii*) earl.

hrabianka *f. Gen.pl.* **-ek** count's *l.* earl's daughter.

hrabina *f.* countess.

hrabiostwo *n.* 1. (*tytuł*) countship; *w Wielkiej Brytanii* earldom. 2. (*para małżeńska*) count and countess.

hrabiowski *a.* count's; earl's.

hrabstwo *n. admin.* county; (*w Wielkiej Brytanii t.*) shire.

huba *f. bot.* bracket fungus (*Polyporus*).

hubka *f. Gen.pl.* **-ek** *przest.* amadou, tinder.

hucpa *f. pot.* chutzpah, gall.

huczeć *ipf.* **-ę -ysz** rumble; (*o grzmocie*) peal, roll; (*o grzmocie, wystrzale*) boom; (*o morzu*) roar; **huczeć od plotek** buzz with rumors; **huczy mi w głowie** my head is swimming.

hucznie *adv.* (= *głośno*) boisterously, uproariously; (= *wystawnie*) sumptuously; **hucznie się bawić** rollick.

huczny *a.* (= *bardzo głośny*) boisterous, uproarious; (*o śmiechu, oklaskach*) thunderous; (= *wystawny*) sumptuous; (*o weselu, zabawie, imieninach*) rollicking.

huf *mi arch.* (= *oddział, zastęp*) regiment, host.

hufcowa *f. Gen.* **-ej** *harcerstwo* troop leader.

hufcowy *a. harcerstwo* troop; **sztandar hufcowy** troop standard. – *mp harcerstwo* troop leader.

hufiec *mi* **-fc-** *Gen.* **-a** 1. (*harcerski*) troop. 2. *hist.* (*oddział wojsk.*) regiment.

hufnal *mi Gen.* **-a** horse-nail, horseshoe-nail.

huk *mi* 1. (*odgłos*) boom, bang; (*grzmotu*) clap, peal, roll; (*wystrzału, wybuchu*) report, crack. 2. *pot.* (= *poruszenie, zamieszanie*) fuss; **narobił wiele huku wokół tej sprawy** he's made a lot of fuss about it. 3. *pot.* (= *zatrzęsienie, bardzo dużo*) scads, lots.

hukać *ipf.* 1. (*o sowie*) hoot. 2. (= *nawoływać*) holler; (= *strofować*) bawl out, rebuke.

huknąć *pf.* **-ij** 1. (= *wydać donośny dźwięk*) boom, crump. 2. *pot.* (= *uderzyć*) whack, punch; **jak cię huknę!** wait till I smack you! 3. **huknąć na kogoś** yell at sb.

hula *mi indecl. muz.* (*taniec*) hula.

hulać *ipf.* 1. (= *zabawiać się*) revel, carouse, dissipate; **hulaj dusza!** let's party! 2. (= *wędrować*) gad about, bum around. 3. *przen.* (*o wietrze, gniewie*) rage.

hulajdusza *mp pl.* **-e** *Gen.* **-ów** *l.* **-y** *Acc.* **-ów** *l.* **-e** *przest.* fribble.

hulajnoga *f. Gen.pl.* **-nóg** scooter.

hulaka *mp pl.* **-i** *przest.* rake, spendthrift.

hulanka *f. Gen.pl.* **-ek** *lit.* revelry.

hulaszczy *a. lit.* fast, rakish; **prowadzić hulaszcze życie** lead a dissipated life.

hultaj *mp*, **hultajka** *f. Gen.pl.* **-ek** *przest. l. lit.* rogue, rascal, scoundrel; (*tylko o mężczyźnie*) knave, villain; *żart.* (= *niegrzeczne dziecko*) rogue, scamp, imp; **ty mały hultaju!** you little rogue!

hultajski *a. przest.* roguish, rascally, knavish.

hultajstwo *n. przest.* 1. (= *bycie hultajem*) roguery. 2. (= *hultaje, łajdacy*) riffraff, rabble.

humanista *mp*, **humanistka** *f. Gen.pl.* **-ek 1.** (*naukowiec*) scholar. **2.** (*renesansowy*) humanist.

humanistyczny *a.* humanistic; **nauki humanistyczne** (liberal) arts, humanities; **przedmioty humanistyczne** arts; **wydział humanistyczny** *uniw.* faculty of arts.

humanistyka *f.* **1.** (*nauka*) the humanities, the arts. **2.** *pot. uniw.* Faculty of Arts.

humanitarnie *adv.* in a humane way, with the use of humane methods.

humanitarność *f.* humanitarianism.

humanitarny *a.* humane, humanitarian; **pomoc humanitarna** humanitarian aid.

humanitarysta *mp*, **humanitarystka** *f. Gen.pl.* **-ek** humanitarian.

humanitaryzacja *f.* humanitarisation.

humanitaryzm *mi* humanitarianism.

humanizacja *f.* humanization.

humanizacyjny *a.* humanizing.

humanizm *mi* humanism.

humanizować *ipf.* humanize.

humbak *ma zool.* humpback (whale) (*Megaptera*).

hummus *mi kulin.* hummus.

humor *mi* **1.** (= *usposobienie*) humor, temper. **2.** (= *komizm*) humor; **z humorem** humorously; **bez humoru** humorlessly; **czarny humor** black humor; **poczucie humoru** sense of humor. **3.** *przest. fizj.* (= *płyn ustrojowy*) humor. **4.** (= *nastrój*) mood; (*być w dobrym / złym humorze*) be in a good/bad mood; **nie mieć humoru** be out of sorts.

humoralny *a. fizj.* humoral.

humoreska *f. Gen.pl.* **-ek 1.** *teor.lit.* humorous tale. **2.** *muz.* humoresque.

humory *pl. Gen.* **-ów** (*kaprysy*) whims; **miewać humory** be moody.

humorysta *mp*, **humorystka** *f. Gen.pl.* **-ek 1.** (*pisarz*) comic writer, humorist. **2.** (= *komik*) comedian, comic.

humorystyczny *a.* humorous; (*o scenie, opowiadaniu, monologu, postaci*) humorous, comic.

humorzasty *a. pot.* moody, temperamental.

Hun *mp pl.* **-owie** *hist.* Hun.

hungarysta *mp*, **hungarystka** *f. Gen.pl.* **-ek** Hungarologist.

hungarystyka *f.* Hungarian studies.

hungaryzm *mi jęz.* Hungarian borrowing.

hura *int.* hurray!, hooray!, hurrah!; **hip-hip, hura!** hip hip, hurray!

huragan *mi* **1.** *meteor.* (= *cyklon tropikalny*) hurricane. **2.** *pot.* (= *silny wiatr*) gale; **pędzić jak huragan** *przen.* run *l.* go like the wind. **3.** *przen.* (= *wybuch emocji*) outburst; **huragan oklasków** rapturous applause. **4.** *przen.* (*niszcząca siła*) whirlwind, cataclysm.

huraganowy *a.* **1.** hurricane; **huraganowy wiatr** hurricane wind. **2.** *przen.* (= *gwałtowny*) violent, stormy; **huraganowy ogień** *wojsk.* withering barrage.

huraoptymistyczny *a.* wildly *l.* overly optimistic; over-optimistic, over-enthusiastic.

huraoptymizm *mi* wild optimism.

hurkot *mi* din, rumble.

hurkotać *ipf.* **-czę -czesz** *l.* **-cę -cesz** rumble, rattle, make a din.

hurmem *adv.* in droves, all at once.

hurt *mi* **1.** *ekon.* wholesale (trade). **2.** *pot.* (= *duża ilość*) bulk, mass.

hurtem *adv.* in bulk, wholesale.

hurtownia *f. Gen.pl.* **-ni** wholesale store, wholesale discount; **sieć hurtowni** chain of wholesalers.

hurtownik *mp*, **hurtowniczka** *f. Gen.pl.* **-ek** wholesaler, wholesale dealer.

hurtowy *a. ekon.* wholesale.

husaria *f. Gen.* **-ii** *hist.wojsk.* husaria, husars (*a Polish type of armored cavalry*); **skrzydlata husaria** winged husars.

husarski *a. hist.wojsk.* husar; **szarża husarska** husar charge; **zbroja/kopia husarska** husar armor/lance.

husarz *mp hist.wojsk.* husar.

husky *ma indecl. kynol.* husky.

husycki *a. rel.* Hussite.

husyta *mp*, **husytka** *f. Gen.pl.* **-ek** *rel.* Hussite.

husytyzm *mi rel.* Hussitism.

huśtać *ipf.* + *Ins.* swing, rock. **~ się** *ipf.* swing, rock (o.s.).

huśtawka *f.* **1.** (*wisząca*) swing. **2.** (*pozioma*) seesaw. **3.** *przen.* (= *ciągłe zmiany*) swings; **huśtawka nastrojów** mood swings; **huśtawka cen** price swings.

huta *f.* **1.** *metal.* (*stali*) steelworks, steel mill, steel plant; **huta aluminium/cynku** aluminum/ zinc works. **2.** (*huta szkła*) glassworks.

hutnictwo *n.* metallurgical industry; (*stali*) steel industry; **hutnictwo metali nieżelaznych** nonferrous metals industry.

hutniczy *a.* metallurgical; **piec hutniczy** metallurgical furnace.

hutnik *mp* metallurgist, steelworker.

huzar *mp hist.wojsk.* hussar; **11 pułk huzarów** the 11th Hussars.

huzarski *a.* hussar, hussar's; **pieczeń huzarska** *kulin.* hussar roast.

hybryda *f. biol., jęz.* hybrid.

hybrydowy *a. biol., techn.* hybrid.

hybrydyzacja *f. biol.* hybridization.

hybrydyzować *ipf.* hybridize; *hodowla* crossbreed.

hyc, hyc-hyc *int. pot.* (*skok, podskok itp.*) **królik hyc-hyc po trawniku** the rabbit hopped about on the lawn; **kot hyc! na drzewo** the cat sprang up the tree.

hycać *ipf. pot.* hop about.

hycel *mp* **-cl-** *Gen.pl.* **-i** *l.* **-ów** *pog.* dogcatcher.

hycnąć *pf.* **-ij** leap, spring.

hydra *f. mit. l. przen.* hydra; **hydra biurokracji** hydra-headed bureaucracy.

hydrant *mi* **1.** hydrant. **2.** *pot.* (= *wąż gumowy*) water hose.

hydrat *mi chem.* hydrate.

hydrauliczny *a.* hydraulic.

hydraulik *mp* plumber.

hydraulika *f.* hydraulics.

hydrobudowa f. Gen.pl. **-ów** bud. hydroengineering.

hydrocefalia f. Gen. **-ii** pat. hydrocephaly.

hydrodynamiczny a. fiz. hydrodynamic; **siła hydrodynamiczna** hydrodynamic force.

hydrodynamika f. fiz. hydrodynamics.

hydroelektrownia f. Gen.pl. **-ni** hydroelectric power plant; **zapora hydroelektrowni** bud. hydroelectric dam.

hydroenergetyk mp waterpower engineer.

hydroenergetyka f. waterpower engineering, hydropower engineering.

hydrofil ma Gen. **-a** biol. hydrophilous species. – mi Gen. **-u** chem. hydrophile (substance).

hydrofilowy a. chem. hydrophilic, hydrophile.

hydrofob mi chem. hydrophobe.

hydrofobia f. Gen. **-ii** pat. (= wodowstręt) hydrophobia.

hydrofobowy a. chem. hydrophobic, hydrophobe.

hydrofon mi el. hydrophone.

hydrofor mi techn. water pump.

hydrofornia f. Gen.pl. **-ni** techn. water-pumping station.

hydrograf mp Gen. **-a** pl. **-owie** (specjalista) hydrographer. – mi Gen. **-u** pl. **-y** techn. (urządzenie) hydrograph.

hydrografia f. Gen. **-ii** hydrography.

hydrograficzny a. hydrographic.

hydroksylowy a. chem. hydroxyl; **grupa hydroksylowa** hydroxyl (group).

hydrolit mi chem. hydrolyte.

hydrolityczny a. chem. hydrolytic.

hydroliza f. chem. hydrolysis.

hydrolog mp pl. **-dzy** l. **-owie** hydrologist.

hydrologia f. Gen. **-ii** hydrology.

hydrologiczny a. hydrological.

hydrolokacja f. techn. (underwater) echolocation, echo-ranging, echo-sounding.

hydrolokacyjny a. echo-sounding.

hydrolokator mi Gen. **-a** hydro-sounder, hydrolocating device.

hydromechanika f. **1.** fiz. hydromechanics. **2.** techn. hydraulics.

hydromechaniczny a. hydromechanical; hydraulic.

hydrometr mi fiz. hydrometer.

hydronim mi jęz. hydronym.

hydronimia f. Gen. **-ii** jęz. hydronymy.

hydronimiczny a. jęz. hydronymic.

hydropata mp med. hydropathist.

hydropatia f. Gen. **-ii** med. hydropathy.

hydroplan mi hydroplane, seaplane.

hydroponiczny a. (o uprawie roślin) hydroponic.

hydroponika f. hydroponics.

hydrosfera f. geol. hydrosphere.

hydrostat mi techn. hydrostat.

hydrostatyczny a. fiz. hydrostatic.

hydrostatyka f. fiz. hydrostatics.

hydrotechniczny a. hydrotechnic, hydrotechnical.

hydrotechnik mp hydraulic engineer.

hydrotechnika f. hydraulic engineering.

hydroterapia f. Gen. **-ii** med. hydrotherapy.

hydrotermalny a. geol. hydrothermal.

hydrowęzeł mi **-zł-** Gen. **-a** techn. hydrotechnical system.

hymen mi anat. hymen, virginal membrane.

hymn mi hymn, anthem; **hymn państwowy** national anthem; **hymn pochwalny** lit. hymn of praise; **hymn kościelny** kośc. church hymn.

hymniczny a. teor.lit. hymnic, hymnal.

hymnografia f. Gen. **-ii** teor.lit. hymnography.

hymnolog mp pl. **-dzy** l. **-owie** hymnologist.

hymnologia f. Gen. **-ii** teor.lit. hymnology.

hyś mi Gen. **-sia**, **hyż** mi Gen. **-zia** pot. **dostać hysia** go nuts; **mieć hysia** be nuts, have a screw loose.

Hz abbr. fiz., el. Hz (= hertz); c.p.s. (= cycle per second).

I

I, i *n. indecl.* **1.** (*litera*) I, i; **I jak Irena** I is for India; I as in India; **postawić kropkę nad i** (= *zakończyć wyjaśnienia*) spell everything out; (= *dokończyć starannie*) dot the i's and cross the t's. **2.** (*głoska*) i.

i¹ *conj. i particle.* **1.** and; **mój ojciec i moja matka** my father and mother; **mąż i żona** husband and wife; **nóż i widelec** knife and fork; **widelec i łyżka** a fork and a spoon; **usiądź i słuchaj** sit down and listen. **2.** (= *plus*) and, plus; **dwa i dwa to razem cztery** two and two make four; two plus two is four. **3.** i..., i... both... and...; **lubię i psy, i koty** I like both cats and dogs. **4.** jak i... as well as...; (*zarówno*)..., jak i... both... and...; **to dotyczy zarówno ciebie, jak i mnie** it concerns both you and me; it concerns you as well as me. **5.** (= *również, nawet*) **i ja tak potrafię** I can do it too; **i specjalista może nie mieć racji** even an expert can be wrong. **6.** *emf.* (*łączy wyrazy l. zwroty powtórzone*) **jeden i ten sam** one and the same; **nic i nic** nothing whatsoever; **mówił i mówił** he talked and talked; he went on talking; **są ludzie i ludziska** there are people and people. **7.** (*wynik czynności*) **przekręciłem kluczyk i silnik ruszył** I turned the key and the engine started; **jeszcze raz mi przerwiesz i koniec** interrupt me once again and it's over. **8.** (*łączy zaimki wskazujące, powtórzone dla wyrażenia nieokreśloności*) **taki i taki** such and such; **w tym i tym miejscu** at such and such a place. **9.** *pot.* **idź i przynieś mi kawy** go and fetch me some coffee; **on znowu weźmie i zrobi coś głupiego** he'll go and do something stupid again; **weź i dokończ to** go and finish it. **10.** (*rozpoczyna zwroty wtrącone*) **mówią, i nie bez powodu, że on wygra ten wyścig** they say, and with good reason, that he'll win the race; **on gra w szachy, i to dobrze** he plays chess, and he plays well; **wyleciał z pracy, i słusznie** he was fired, and rightly so. **11.** (*w utartych zwrotach*) **(no) i już** and that's all; **nie pójdziesz i już!** you are not to go, and I mean it!; **i co teraz?** so?; well?; **no i co z tego?** so what?; **i jesteśmy kwita** and we're quits; **i tak nie zrozumiesz** you won't understand anyway.

i² *int.* (*wyraża lekceważenie*) **i! też coś!** who cares?; fiddle-de-dee!

iberoamerykański *a.* Ibero-American.

Iberyjczyk *mp*, **Iberyjka** *f. Gen.pl.* **-ek** Iberian.

iberyjski *a. geogr.* Iberian; **Półwysep Iberyjski** the Iberian Peninsula.

iberysta *mp*, **iberystka** *f. Gen.pl.* **-ek** expert in Spanish and Portuguese studies.

iberystyka *f. uniw.* Spanish and Portuguese studies.

ibis *ma orn.* (= *ptak z rodziny Threskiornithidae*) ibis; **ibis czczony** sacred ibis (*Threskiornis aethiopicus*).

ich *pron. zob.* **on**.

ichneumon *ma zool.* ichneumon, Herpestes ichneumon; *pot.* (= *mangusta*) mongoose, Herpestes.

ichnologia *f. Gen.* **-ii** *biol.* ichnology.

ichtiolog *mp pl.* **-dzy** *l.* **-owie** ichthyologist.

ichtiologia *f. Gen.* **-ii** ichthyology.

ichtiologiczny *a.* ichthyological, ichthyologic.

ichtiolowy *a.* ichthyol; **maść ichtiolowa** ichthyol ointment.

ichtioza *f. med.* ichthyosis, fishskin disease.

ichtiozaur *ma paleont.* (= *gad z rzędu Ichthyosauria*) ichthyosaur.

idea *f. Gen.* **-ei** *pl.* **-ee** *Gen.* **-ei** idea, thought; (= *koncepcja, pojęcie*) notion, concept; **idea polityczna/społeczna** political/social idea; **idea piękna/sprawiedliwości** *fil.* the idea of beauty/justice; **idea platońska** *fil.* Platonic idea; **idea postępu** the idea *l.* notion of progress; **piękna/szalona idea** beautiful/crazy idea; **kierować się ideami** to be guided by ideas.

idealista *mp*, **idealistka** *f. Gen.pl.* **-ek** **1.** (= *marzyciel*) idealist, dreamer. **2.** *fil.* idealist.

idealistyczny *a.* idealistic.

idealizacja *f.* idealization.

idealizm *mi* **1.** (= *brak realizmu*) idealism; (= *marzycielstwo*) daydreaming. **2.** *fil., sztuka, teor.lit.* idealism.

idealizować *ipf.* idealize; (= *przeceniać*) overrate, think too highly of (*sb l. sth*).

idealnie *adv.* ideally, perfectly. – *int. pot.* excellent!, super!

idealny *a.* **1.** (= *doskonały, wzorowy*) *fil.* (= *niematerialny, dotyczący idei*) ideal, perfect; **idealny ład** perfect order; **mąż idealny** perfect husband; **to idealny mąż dla niej** he's the ideal husband for her; **idealna harmonia** ideal harmony; **twór/byt idealny** *fil.* ideal construction/form; **gaz idealny** *fiz.* ideal gas; **punkt idealny** *geom.* ideal point; **próżnia idealna** *fiz.* perfect vacuum; **w idealnym świecie** in an ideal world; **w przypadku idealnym** in the ideal case; ideally. **2.** (= *wzniosły*) lofty, exalted.

ideał *mi Gen.* **-u** **1.** ideal; paragon, model; **ideał wszelkich cnót** paragon of virtue; **ideał mędrca** the ideal of a sage; **ideał pracownika** the ideal *l.* perfect employee; **uczynić kogoś swoim ideałem**

make sb one's ideal; **daleki/bliski ideału** far from/ close to the ideal; **zbliżać się do ideału** approach the ideal. **2.** (= *cel dążenia*) ideal, goal; **wzniosłe ideały** high ideals; **żyć w zgodzie ze swoimi ideałami** live up to one's ideals. **3.** *mat.* ideal.

idée fixe *f. indecl.* idée fixe, fixed idea, obsession.

identycznie *adv.* identically, in the same way; **wyglądają identycznie** they look (exactly) the same.

identyczność *f.* identity, sameness.

identyczny *a.* **1.** identical (*z kimś / czymś* with *l.* to sb/sth); **mamy identyczne upodobania** we have the same preferences. **2.** **nota identyczna** *polit.* identic note.

identyfikacja *f.* **1.** (= *rozpoznanie, ustalenie tożsamości*) identification (*kogoś / czegoś* of sb/ sth). **2.** (= *utożsamienie się*) identification (*z kimś / czymś* with sb/sth).

identyfikacyjny *a.* identity; **numer identyfikacyjny** identity number; **karta identyfikacyjna** identity card, ID (card).

identyfikator *mi Gen.* -a **1.** (= *znak l. symbol rozpoznawczy*) identifier; **identyfikator użytkownika** *komp.* user ID. **2.** (= *plakietka rozpoznawcza*) badge.

identyfikować *ipf.* identify (*kogoś / coś z kimś / czymś* sb/sth with sb/sth) (*kogoś jako... sb as...*); (= *rozpoznawać*) recognize. **~ się** *ipf.* identify (o.s.), become identified (*z kimś / czymś* with sb/ sth).

ideografia *f. Gen.* -ii *pismo* (= *system ideogramów*) ideography.

ideograficzny *a.* ideographic; **pismo ideograficzne** ideographic script.

ideogram *mi pismo* ideograph.

ideolog *mp pl.* -dzy *l.* -owie (= *propagator ideologii*) ideologue; (= *twórca l. zwolennik ideologii*) ideologist; **ideolodzy partyjni** *polit.* party ideologues.

ideologia *f. Gen.* -ii ideology.

ideologiczny *a.* ideological.

ideologizować *ipf.* ideologize, subject to ideological treatment.

ideowiec *mp* -wc- *Voc.* -cu *l.* -cze *pl.* -y idealist, enthusiast, zealot.

ideowość *f.* ideological commitment.

ideowy *a.* **1.** (= *ideologiczny*) ideological, ideologic; (= *zaangażowany ideowo*) ideologically committed. **2.** (= *oddany idei*) idealistic, devoted to an idea, enthusiastic. **3.** *techn.* **schemat ideowy** schematic diagram.

idę *itd. ipf. zob.* **iść.**

idiocieć *ipf. pog.* become demented, go mad.

idiofon *mi muz.* idiophone.

idiolatria *f. Gen.* -ii *psych.* idiolatry, self-worship.

idiolekt *mi jęz.* idiolect.

idiolektalny *a. jęz.* idiolectal.

idiom *mi jęz.* idiom; **słownik idiomów angielskich** dictionary of English idioms.

idiomatyczny *a. jęz.* idiomatic; **zwrot idiomatyczny** idiomatic expression *l.* phrase; idiom.

idiomatyka *f. jęz.* (= *nauka o idiomach*) study of idioms; (= *ogół idiomów*) idioms.

idiosynkrazja *f.* **1.** *med., przest.* (= *nadwrażliwość*) idiosyncrasy, hypersensitivity (*do czegoś* to sth). **2.** *form.* (= *niechęć, obrzydzenie*) revulsion (*do kogoś / czegoś* against *l.* from sb/sth); detestation (*do kogoś / czegoś* of sb/sth).

idiota *mp,* **idiotka** *f. Gen.pl.* -ek **1.** *pog.* (= *głupiec*) idiot, moron, imbecile, fool. **2.** *pat., przest.* idiot.

idiotyczny *a. pog.* idiotic, moronic, foolish.

idiotyzm *mi* **1.** *pog.* (= *głupota*) idiocy, foolishness. **2.** *pot.* (= *bzdura*) rubbish, nonsense. **3.** *pat., przest.* idiocy.

idol *mp Gen.pl.* -i *l.* -ów **1.** (= *bożyszcze, przedmiot kultu*) idol. **2.** *mit.* (= *bożek*) deity, pagan god.

idolatria *f. Gen.* -ii *rel.* idolatry.

idylla *f. Gen.pl.* -i *l.* -ll **1.** (= *życie beztroskie*) idyll. **2.** *teor.lit.* idyll, eclogue, bucolic.

idylliczny *a.* **1.** (= *szczęśliwy*) idyllic. **2.** *teor.lit.* idyllic, pastoral, bucolic.

idziesz *itd. ipf. zob.* **iść.**

igelit *mi chem.* (plasticized) polyvinyl chloride, PVC.

igelitowy *a.* PVC.

igielnica *f. techn., tk.* needle arm.

igielny *a.* **ucho igielne** *lit. l. przen.* the eye of a needle.

igiełka *f. Gen.pl.* -ek **1.** *techn.* (*element łożyska*) needle roller. **2.** (= *mała igła*) *zob.* **igła.**

iglak *mi Gen.* -a **1.** *pot.* (= *drzewo iglaste*) conifer. **2.** *techn.* (*pilnik*) needle file.

iglasty *a.* **1.** *bot., leśn.* coniferous; **lasy iglaste** coniferous forests. **2.** (*podobny do igły*) needle-like; *bot.* aculeate.

iglica *f.* **1.** *bud.* spire, steeple. **2.** *geol.* spire, needle. **3.** *broń* firing pin. **4.** *tk.* knitting needle. **5.** *techn.* needle, pin; **iglica zwrotnicy** *kol.* switch point. **6.** *bot.* pin clover, alfilaria (*Erodium cicutarium*).

iglicowy *a. techn.* pin, needle; **zawór iglicowy** needle valve.

iglicznia *f. Gen.pl.* -i **1.** *bot.* honey locust (*Gleditsia*). **2.** *zool.* pipefish (*Syngnathus fuscus*).

igliwie *n.* bed *l.* litter of needles.

igloo *n. indecl.* igloo.

igła *f. Gen.pl.* igieł **1.** (*t. techn., bot. i in.*) needle; **nawlekać igłę** thread a needle; **ucho igły** the eye of a needle; **igła do zastrzyków** *med.* hypodermic needle; **igła busoli** compass needle; **igła magnetyczna** magnetic needle; **igła rytownicza** *sztuka* etcher's needle, burin. **2.** (*w wyrażeniach idiomatycznych*) **jak spod igły** *l.* **prosto z igły** brand new, spick and span; **igła w stogu siana** a needle in a haystack; **robić z igły widły** make a mountain out of a molehill. **3.** (= *kolec*) spine. **4.** *bud.* (= *iglica*) spire.

igława *f. bot.* araucaria, Araucaria.

igłowy *a.* **1.** *techn.* needle; **łożysko igłowe** needle bearing. **2.** (= *zrobiony przy użyciu igły*) needle-made; **koronka igłowa** needlepoint lace.

ignam *mi bot.* yam (*Dioscorea*).

ignorancja *f.* ignorance; **dawać dowody swojej ignorancji** prove one's ignorance.

ignorancki *a.* ignorant.

ignorant *mp,* **ignorantka** *f. Gen.pl.* **-ek** ignoramus.

ignorować *ipf.* ignore; **ignorować krytykę** ignore criticism; **oni ignorują się nawzajem** they ignore each other.

igrać *ipf.* **1.** (= *traktować bez należytej powagi*) trifle (*z kimś/czymś* with sb/sth); **igrać ze śmiercią** dice with death; **igrać z ogniem** play with fire. **2.** *lit.* (= *drgać, pojawiać się i znikać*) flicker, waver; **na jej twarzy igrał uśmiech** a smile flickered on her face. **3.** *arch. l. poet.* (= *grać, bawić się, baraszkować*) play.

igraszka *f. Gen.pl.* **-ek 1.** (= *drobiazg*) trifle. **2.** (= *osoba lub rzecz na łasce jakiejś siły*) plaything; **być/stać się igraszką w czyichś rękach** be/become sb's plaything; **być igraszką żywiołów** be exposed to the fury of the elements. **3.** *lit.* (= *zabawa*) play, game; **igraszka słowna** play on words, pun; **igraszki miłosne** love play, lovemaking.

Igrek *mp pl.* **-i** *pot.* (= *osoba o nieujawnionej tożsamości*) John Doe.

igrek *mi Gen.* **-a 1.** (*litera*) Y, y. **2.** *mat.* (*jedna ze zmiennych l. niewiadomych*) y.

igrzyska *pl. Gen.* **-k** *form.* games; **(greckie) igrzyska olimpijskie** *hist.* the Olympian games; **(letnie/zimowe) igrzyska olimpijskie** *sport* the (Summer/Winter) Olympic Games; the (Summer/Winter) Olympics; **igrzyska gladiatorów** *hist.* gladiatorial games *l.* contests; **igrzyska rycerskie** *hist.* joust, tournament.

igrzysko *n. lit. l. arch.* (= *igraszka, zabawka*) plaything; **boże igrzysko** (= *zabawka w rękach bogów*) plaything of the gods.

iguana *f. zool.* (= *legwan, jaszczurka z rodziny Iguanidae*) iguana.

iguanodon *ma paleont.* iguandon (*Iguandon*).

ikebana *f.* ikebana; **naczynie** *l.* **wazon do ikebany** ikebana vase.

ikona *f. sztuka, rel.* **1.** icon. **2.** *komp.* icon; **kliknąć na ikonie** click an icon.

ikoniczny *a. nauk.* iconic.

ikonka *f. Gen.pl.* **-ek** *komp.* = **ikona** 2.

ikonografia *f. Gen.* **-ii** *sztuka* iconography.

ikonograficzny *a.* iconographic.

ikonologia *f. Gen.* **-ii** iconology.

ikonostas *mi kośc.* iconostasis (*in an Orthodox church*).

ikonowy *a. sztuka, rel.* **malarstwo ikonowe** icon painting.

ikra *f.* **1.** (*w ciele ryby*) (hard) roe; (*w wodzie*) spawn. **2.** *pot.* (= *energia, odwaga*) guts, stamina; **z ikrą** with (plenty of) guts.

ikrzak *ma icht.* spawner.

Iks *mp pl.* **-y** *pot.* (= *osoba o nieujawnionej tożsamości*) John Doe; **panowie Iks i Igrek** John Doe and Richard Roe.

iks *mi Gen.* **-a 1.** (*litera*) X, x. **2.** *mat.* (*zmienna, niewiadoma*) x; **od iks czasu** for some time; **robić coś iks razy** do sth umpteen times. **3.** (*kształt*) **nogi w iks** knock-knee, knock-knees.

Iksiński *mp,* **Iksińska** *f.,* **Iksińscy** *pl. decl. like a. pot.* = **Iks**.

iksowaty *a.* x-like; (*o nogach*) knock-kneed.

ilasty *a. geol.* loamy, clayey.

ile *pron. Nom. i Acc.* + *mp* ilu *l.* ile; *Gen.* + *count* ilu *Gen.* + *noncount* ile; *Dat. i Loc.* ilu; *Ins.* iloma *l.* ilu **1.** *zaimek pytajny l. względny* how many (*count*); how much (*noncount*); **ile mieszkań jest na tym piętrze?** how many apartments are there on this story?; **ile masz pieniędzy?** how much money do you have?; **ile masz lat?** how old are you?; **ilu ludzi widziałeś?** how many people did you see?; **pokaż, ile przeczytałeś** show me how much you have read. **2.** (*w wykrzyknikach*) **ile śniegu!** what a lot of snow! **3.** **ile tylko można** *l.* **ile się da** as much as possible; **ile wlezie** *pot.* a lot; with a vengeance. **4. po ile** (*w pytaniach o cenę*) how much; **po ile te pomarańcze?** how much are these oranges? **5. na ile** (= *do jakiego stopnia*) to what extent; **nie wiem, na ile to prawda** I don't know to what extent it's true; I don't know how much of it is true; **na ile mogę mu ufać?** how far can I trust him? **6. tyle, ile...** as much as...; as many as...; **jesz dwa razy tyle, ile ja** you eat twice as much as I do; **mam tyle lat, co ty** I'm as old as you are. **7. o tyle, o ile...** *l.* **na tyle, na ile...** in so far as...; insofar as...; inasmuch as...; to the extent that...; **powiem ci prawdę o tyle, o ile ją znam** I'll tell you the truth insofar as I know it. **8. o tyle o ile** *pot.* so-so; not very much. **9.** (*wyraża uściślenie*) **nie tyle..., ile...** not so much... as...; **jestem nie tyle śpiący, ile zmęczony** I'm not so much sleepy as tired. **10. ile razy...** every time..., whenever...; **ile razy do ciebie dzwonię, zawsze jesteś zajęty** you are always busy when I call you. **11.** (*w funkcji spójnika*) **o ile..., (to)...** provided that..., if...; **o ile chcą, (to) niech przyjdą jutro** let them come tomorrow if they want to; **o ile..., (o tyle)...** while..., whereas...; **o ile ja nie znoszę kawy, o tyle moja żona ją uwielbia** while I hate coffee, my wife loves it.

ilekolwiek *pron. decl. like* ile- + -kolwiek *indecl.* no matter how much (*noncount*); no matter how many (*count*).

ilekroć *pron.* (= *ile razy*) *form.* whenever; **ilekroć to czytam, tylekroć się śmieję** I laugh whenever I read it; I laugh every time I read it; **ilekroć się spotykamy, nigdy mnie nie poznajesz** you never recognize me when we meet.

ileś *pron. decl. like* ile- + -ś *indecl.* any number of (*count*); any amount *l.* quantity of (*noncount*); **zadali ileś (tam) pytań** they asked a number of questions.

ileż *pron. decl. like* ile- + -ż *indecl. emf.* = ile; **ileż razy mam tego wysłuchiwać?** how many times do I have to hear it?; **ileż tu kwiatów!** what a lot of flowers!

Iliada *f. hist.lit.* the Iliad.

Iliria *f. Gen.* **-ii** *hist.* Illyria.

iliryjski *a. hist.* Illyrian.

illokucja *f. jęz.* illocution.

ilmenit *n. min.* ilmenite.

iloczas *mi jęz.* quantity, duration.

iloczyn *mi mat., log.* product; **iloczyn kartezjański** Cartesian product; cross product.

iloraz *mi mat.* quotient; **iloraz różniczkowy** differential quotient; **ilorazinteligencji** *psych.* intelligence quotient, IQ.

ilościowy *a.* quantitative, numerical; **stosunek ilościowy** quantitative ratio; **analiza ilościowa** *chem.* quantitative analysis; **zmiana ilościowa** *fil.* quantitative change.

ilość *f.* amount, quantity; (= *liczba*) number; **śladowe ilości** *chem.* trace amounts.

ilu *pron. zob.* **ile**.

iluminacja *f.* **1.** (= *jasne oświetlenie*) illumination, floodlight. **2.** *sztuka* (= *barwna ilustracja*) illumination. **3.** *form.* (= *nagłe oświecenie*) enlightment, illumination, insight.

iluminacyjny *a. sztuka* illuminational.

iluminator *mp pl.* **-rzy** illuminator. – *mi Gen.* **-a** *żegl.* porthole.

iluminatorski *a. sztuka* illuminational, illuminator's.

iluminatorstwo *n. sztuka* (the art of) illumination.

iluminować *ipf.* **1.** (= *oświetlać*) illuminate, light up. **2.** *sztuka* illuminate.

ilustracja *f.* **1.** (*w książce*) illustration, picture; **ilustracja muzyczna** *l.* **dźwiękowa** incidental music; background music. **2.** (= *poglądowy przykład*) illustration, exemplification, illustrative example.

ilustracyjny *a.* illustrative; (*w książce*) pictorial; **materiał ilustracyjny** illustrations, pictorial matter; **muzyka ilustracyjna** incidental music.

ilustrator *mp*, **ilustratorka** *f. Gen.pl.* **-ek** illustrator.

ilustratorski *a.* illustrative, illustrator's.

ilustrować *ipf.* **1.** illustrate (*czymś* with sth). **2. ilustrować coś za pomocą przykładów** illustrate sth by example, exemplify sth.

ilustrowany *a.* illustrated, pictorial.

iluś *pron. zob.* **ileś**.

iluwialny *a. geol.* illuvial.

iluzja *f.* illusion; **iluzja głębi/ruchu** illusion of depth/motion; **nie mieć iluzji** have no illusions (*co do kogoś / czegoś* about sb/sth).

iluzjonista *mp*, **iluzjonistka** *f. Gen.pl.* **-ek 1.** (= *magik*) illusionist, magician, conjurer, conjuror. **2.** *sztuka* illusionist.

iluzjonistyczny *a.* **1. pokaz/popis/występ iluzjonistyczny** *cyrk* illusion *l.* magic show/act/ performance. **2.** *sztuka* illusionistic; **malarstwo iluzjonistyczne** illusionistic painting.

iluzjonizm *mi sztuka, fil.* illusionism.

iluzoryczność *a.* illusiveness, deceptiveness.

iluzoryczny *a.* illusory, illusive, deceptive.

iluż *pron. zob.* **ileż**.

ił *mi geol.* loam, clay.

iłowiec *mi* **-wc-** *Gen.* **-a** *geol.* mudstone.

iłowy *a. geol.* loam, loamy, clayey.

im¹ *conj.* **im...**, **tym...** the... the...; **im prędzej, tym lepiej** the sooner the better; **im lepiej ich znam, tym bardziej ich lubię** the better I know them the more I like them.

im² *pron. zob.* **on**.

im. *abbr.* (= *imienia*) **Towarzystwo im. Fryderyka Chopina** the Frédéric Chopin Society.

imać się *ipf.* + *Gen.* **1.** (= *wykonywać dorywczo*) take (*sth*) up; **imać się różnych zajęć** do odd jobs. **2.** (= *uciekać się do czegoś*) try, resort to (*sth*); **imać się podstępów** resort to trickery; try every trick in the book. **3.** (*o chorobach, pociskach, starości, troskach itp.*) touch, affect, afflict; **tego ostrza rdza się nie ima** this blade does not rust; **nic się go nie ima** nothing seems to affect him. **4.** *przest.* (= *chwytać*) grasp, catch hold of (*sth*).

imadło *n. Gen.pl.* **-deł** *techn.* vise, vice; **ściskać coś jak w imadle** hold sth in a vise-like grip.

image *mi Gen.* **-e'u** *polit.* (= *wizerunek publiczny*) (public) image; **poprawiać swój image** improve one's image.

imaginacja *f.* (= *wyobraźnia*) imagination; **wytwór czyjejś imaginacji** figment of sb's imagination.

imaginacyjny *a.* imaginary.

imago *n. indecl. zool., psych.* imago.

imak *mi Gen.* **-a** *techn.* gripper, clamp, jaws.

imam *mp pl.* **-owie** *rel.* imam.

imbecyl *mp pl.* **-e** *Gen.* **-i** *l.* **-ów** *pog.* imbecile, fool, idiot.

imbecylizm *mi psych., przest.* imbecility.

imbecylny *a.* imbecilic, foolish, idiotic.

imbir *mi bot., kulin.* ginger (*Zingiber officinale*).

imbirowy *a.* ginger; (*o smaku, zapachu*) gingery; **korzeń/olejek imbirowy** ginger root/oil.

imbryczek *mi* **-czk-** *Gen.* **-a**, **imbryk** *mi Gen.* **-a** tea-pot.

imelman *mi Gen.* **-a** *lotn.* Immelmann turn.

imieninowy *a.* name-day.

imieniny *pl. Gen.* **-n** (*dzień*) name day, patron saint's day; (*przyjęcie*) name-day party.

imienniczka *f. Gen.pl.* **-ek** *zob.* **imiennik**.

imiennie *adv.* (= *według imion l. nazwisk*) by name; (= *dla konkretnych osób*) individually, personally.

imiennik *mp* namesake.

imienny *a.* **1.** (= *wymieniający konkretne osoby*) personal, individual; **lista imienna** register (of names), roster; **zaproszenie imienne** personal invitation. **2.** *gram.* nominal, substantival.

imiesłowowy *a. gram.* participial.

imiesłów *mi* **-o-** *gram.* participle; **imiesłów czynny/bierny** active/passive participle; **imiesłów czasu przeszłego** past participle.

imię *n.* **imieni-** *pl.* **imiona 1.** name; (*w odróżnieniu od nazwiska*) first name, given name; **imię chrzestne** christian name; **imię zdrobniałe** pet name; **drugie imię** middle name; **nadać komuś/czemuś imię** name sb/sth; **mam na imię Robert** my name is Robert; **być z kimś po imieniu** be on first-name terms with sb; **zwracać się do kogoś po imieniu** call sb by his *l.* her first name; **znana jest pod imieniem Anna** she goes by the name Anna; **pewien człowiek imieniem William** a certain man of the name William; a certain man, William by name; **mój pies reaguje na imię Fido** my dog answers to the name Fido. **2. do-**

bre/złe imię (= *reputacja*) good/bad name *l.* reputation; **szargać czyjeś dobre imię** drag sb's name through the mud. **3.** (*w utartych zwrotach*) **w imię kogoś/czegoś** in the name of sb/sth; **w imię boże** in God's name; **w imię przyjaźni** in the name of friendship; for the sake of friendship; **w czyimś imieniu** on behalf of sb; on sb's behalf; in the name of sb; in sb's name; **nazywać rzeczy po imieniu** call a spade a spade; speak in plain words; **w imię Ojca i Syna, i Ducha Świętego** *rel.* in the name of the Father, and of the Son, and of the Holy Spirit; **wzywać czyjegoś imienia nadaremno** take sb's name in vain.

imigracja *f.* **1.** immigration; population influx. **2.** (= *ludność napływowa*) immigrants, immigrant population.

imigracyjny *a.* **wiza imigracyjna** immigration visa; **urząd imigracyjny** immigration office; **ludność imigracyjna** immigrant population.

imigrant *mp,* **imigrantka** *f. Gen.pl.* **-ek** immigrant.

imigrować *ipf.* immigrate.

imitacja *f.* imitation; (= *falsyfikat*) forgery, counterfeit, sham; **imitacja srebra** imitation silver; **nędzna/tania imitacja** poor/cheap imitation.

imitacyjny *a.* imitative.

imitator[1] *mp pl.* **-rzy** imitator.

imitator[2] *mi Gen.* **-a** *pl.* **-y** *techn.* simulator.

imitatorka *f. Gen.pl.* **-ek** *zob.* **imitator**[1].

imitatorstwo *n.* imitative art.

imitować *ipf.* **1.** (= *naśladować*) imitate. **2.** (= *wzorować się*) copy, emulate.

immanencja *f. fil.* immanence, immanency.

immanentny *a. fil.* immanent.

immaterializm *mi fil.* immaterialism.

immatrykulacja *f.* matriculation.

immatrykulacyjny *a.* matriculation.

immatrykulować *ipf.* matriculate. **~ się** *ipf.* matriculate.

immersja *f. fiz.* immersion.

immobilizer *mi Gen.* **-a** *mot.* immobilizer.

immobilizm *mi fil.* immobility.

immoralista *mp fil.* immoralist.

immoralizm *mi fil.* immoralism.

immunitet *mi prawn.* (privilege of) immunity; **immunitet dyplomatyczny** diplomatic immunity; **chroni go immunitet** he enjoys immunity; **zrezygnować z immunitetu** waive one's immunity.

immunitetowy *a.* immunity.

immunizować *ipf. biol., med.* immunize.

immunoglobulina *f. biochem.* immunoglobulin.

immunolog *mp pl.* **-dzy** *l.* **-owie** *med.* immunologist.

immunologia *f. Gen.* **-ii** *med.* immunology.

immunologiczny *a. med.* immunologic *l.* immunological; **badania immunologiczne** immunologic examination; **bariera immunologiczna** immunological barrier; **leczenie immunologiczne** immunologic treatment; **reakcja immunologiczna** immune response.

impas *mi* **1.** (= *sytuacja bez wyjścia*) deadlock, impasse; **przełamać impas** break *l.* resolve the deadlock. **2.** *karty* finesse.

impasować *ipf. karty* finesse.

impasowy *a.* finesse; (*impasowe położenie l. sytuacja*) deadlock.

impast *mi mal.* impasto.

impastować *ipf. mal.* impaste.

impeachment *mi polit.* impeachment.

impedancja *f. fiz.* impedance.

imperator *mp pl.* **-rzy** *l.* **-owie** *hist.* emperor, imperator.

imperatorowa *f. decl. like a. Voc.* **-o** *hist.* empress.

imperatorski *a.* imperatorial.

imperatyw *mi fil.* imperative; **imperatyw kategorialny** categorical imperative.

imperatywny *a. lit.* imperative.

imperialista *mp polit.* imperialist.

imperialistyczny *a. polit.* imperialist; **kraj imperialistyczny** *l.* **państwo imperialistyczne** imperialist state; **polityka/wojna imperialistyczna** imperialist policy/war.

imperializm *mi polit.* imperialism.

imperialny *a.* **1.** *polit., hist.* imperial; **polityka/wojna imperialna** imperial policy/war; **ambicje imperialne** imperial ambitions. **2.** (= *zaborczy*) aggressive.

imperium *n. sing. indecl. pl.* **-ia** *Gen.* **-iów** empire; **Imperium Brytyjskie/Osmańskie/Rzymskie** *hist.* the British/Ottoman/Roman Empire.

impertynencja *f.* impertinence *l.* impertinency, flippancy.

impertynencki *a.* impertinent, flippant, saucy; **impertynencka uwaga** impertinent remark; **impertynenckie zachowanie** saucy behavior.

impertynent *mp,* **impertynentka** *f. Gen.pl.* **-ek** impertinent.

impet *mi* **1.** impetus; (= *pęd*) momentum; (= *wstrząs, efekt uderzenia*) shock; **nabierać impetu** gain momentum; **osłabić impet** absorb *l.* reduce the shock. **2.** (= *gwałtowność*) violence; **otworzyć z impetem drzwi** fling the door open.

implant *mi med.* implant.

implantacja *f. med.* implantation.

implantacyjny *a. med.* implantation; **metoda implantacyjna** implantation method; **zabieg implantacyjny** implantation.

implantować *ipf. med.* implant.

implementacja *f. komp.* implementation.

implementować *ipf. komp.* implement.

implicite *adv. lit.* implicitly.

implikacja *f.* **1.** *form. l. log.* (= *logiczna konsekwencja, wynikanie*) implication. **2.** *form.* (= *skutek, następstwo*) consequence, ramification.

implikować *ipf.* imply, connote.

implodować *ipf. fiz.* implode.

implozja *f. fiz. l. fon.* implosion.

implozywny *a. fon.* (*o spółgłoskach*) implosive.

imponderabilia *pl. Gen.* **-liów** *fil.* imponderables.

imponować *ipf.* **1.** impress (*komuś* sb, *czymś* with sth); make an impression (*komuś* on sb). **2.** (= *popisywać się*) show off.

imponujący *a.* impressive; **imponująca przewaga** commanding lead; **imponujący widok** impressive *l.* commanding view; **imponujące zwy-**

cięstwo sweeping victory; **imponujących rozmiarów** (*o dziele, książce*) of epic *l.* impressive proportions.

import *mi* import.

importer *mp* importer.

importować *ipf.* import.

importowy *a. handl.* import; **agencja importowa** import agency; **cło importowe** *l.* **przywozowe** duty on imports; **kredyt importowy** import credit; **licencja importowa** import licence *l.* permit; **ładunek importowy** import cargo; **przepisy importowe** import regulations; **zdolność importowa** import capacity; **towary importowe** import articles *l.* imports.

impost *mi bud.* impost.

impotencja *f. pat.* impotence.

impotent *mp* impotent man.

impregnacja *f. techn.* **1.** (*powłoka ochronna*) proofing; **impregnacja przeciw wilgoci** waterproofing. **2.** (*proces*) impregnation.

impregnat *mi techn.* impregnant, repellent.

impregnować *ipf.* **1.** (*nasycać*) saturate, impregnate (*czymś* with sth); soak, steep (*w czymś* in sth). **2.** (= *zabezpieczać przed wilgocią*) waterproof. **3.** (*o substancji impregnującej*) (= *przenikać, przesycać*) permeate, imbue.

impresariat *mi* production company.

impresario *mp pl.* **-owie** impresario, production manager.

impresja *f.* impression.

impresjonista *mp*, **impresjonistka** *f. Gen.pl.* **-ek** *muz., sztuka* impressionist.

impresjonistyczny *a.* **1.** (= *oparty na subiektywnych wrażeniach*) impressionistic. **2.** *muz., sztuka, teor.lit.* (= *dotyczący impresjonizmu*) impressionist; **literatura impresjonistyczna** impressionist literature; **malarstwo impresjonistyczne** impressionist painting; **sztuka impresjonistyczna** impressionist art.

impresjonizm *mi muz., sztuka* impressionism.

impreza *f.* **1.** (*widowisko*) show; (= *wydarzenie*) event. **2.** *pot.* (= *spotkanie towarzyskie*) party; (= *spotkanie w małym l. ścisłym gronie*) get-together. **3.** *pot.* (= *plan, zamiar*) venture; **huczna impreza** brawl; **impreza charytatywna** benefit, fundraiser; **impreza składkowa** bottle party, bring-your-own-bottle *l.* bring-your-own-booze party, BYOB (party); **impreza sportowa** sporting event; **impreza zamknięta** invitational.

imprezować *ipf. pot.* (= *brać udział w spotkaniach towarzyskich*) party.

imprezowy *a.* **1.** (*dotyczący widowiska*) show; (*sala*) auditorium. **2.** *pot.* (*dotyczący spotkania towarzyskiego*) party; **imprezowy chłopak** party animal; **imprezowa dziewczyna** party girl.

imprimatur *n. indecl. kośc.* imprimatur.

impromptu *n. sing. indecl. muz.* impromptu.

improwizacja *f.* **1.** (*muzyczna, literacka, aktorska*) improvisation; *pot.* improv. **2.** *przen.* (= *działanie bez przygotowania*) extemporisation. **3.** *muz.* (*w jazzie*) jam.

improwizacyjny *a.* improvisational; **talent improwizacyjny** improvisational talent.

improwizator *mp*, **improwizatorka** *f. Gen.pl.* **-ek** improviser.

improwizować *ipf.* **1.** (= *tworzyć utwór muzyczny, literacki bez przygotowania*) improvise. **2.** (= *działać bez przygotowania*) extemporise. **3.** *muz.* (*w jazzie*) jam.

impuls *mi* **1.** (= *bodziec*) stimulus. **2.** *fiz. l. fizj.* impulse; **impuls nerwowy** nerve impulse; **działać pod wpływem impulsu** *l.* **kierować się impulsem** act on (an) impulse; act on the spur of the moment.

impulsowy *a. fiz., techn.* pulse; **laser impulsowy** pulse laser; **reaktor impulsowy** pulsed reactor; **technika impulsowa** *el.* impulse technique, pulse electronics.

impulsywność *f.* impulsiveness.

impulsywny *a.* **1.** (= *pobudliwy*) excitable, impulsive. **2.** (= *odruchowy*) instinctive. **3.** (= *spontaniczny*) spontaneous, impulsive; **impulsywna osoba** impulsive person; **impulsywna reakcja** impulsive *l.* instinctive reaction.

imputować *ipf.* impute.

inaczej *adv.* **1.** (= *odmiennie*) differently, in a different way; **tak czy inaczej** anyhow. **2.** (= *w przeciwnym razie*) otherwise. **3.** (= *czyli*) or; **bo inaczej...** (*pogróżka*) or else...; **inaczej zaśpiewać** (= *zmienić zdanie pod naciskiem*) change one's tune; **jakżeby inaczej!** how else!; **nie inaczej!** how else!, no other way!

inauguracja *f.* inauguration.

inauguracyjny *a.* inaugural; **mowa inauguracyjna** inaugural speech; **wykład inauguracyjny** opening lecture.

inaugurować *ipf.* inaugurate; (= *zapoczątkować*) initiate.

in blanco *adv.* in blank; **czek in blanco** blank check.

incest *mi* **1.** *prawn.* incest. **2.** *biol.* (= *kojarzenie krewniacze*) inbreeding.

inchoatywny *a. jęz.* inchoative.

incipit *mi* incipit.

incognito *adv.* incognito, anonymously. – *n. indecl.* incognito.

incydencja *f. geom.* incidence.

incydent *mi* incident.

incydentalny *a. form.* (= *przypadkowy*) incidental, fortuitous; **sprawa incydentalna** incidental issue; **wydatki incydentalne** incidental expenses; *prawn.* incidental; (*skarga*) incidental.

ind *mi chem.* indium.

indagacja *f.* questioning, interrogation.

indagować *ipf.* question, interrogate (*kogoś o coś* sb about sth).

indeks *mi* **1.** (= *skorowidz*) index. **2.** (*studenta*) credit book. **3.** *stat. l. mat.* index; **indeks cen** price index; **indeks dolny/górny** *druk.* lower/upper index; **indeks nazw geograficznych** gazetteer; **indeks ksiąg zakazanych** index of forbidden books; *kośc.* Index Librorum Prohibitorum.

indeksacja *f. ekon.* indexation, index-linking.

indeksacyjny *a. ekon.* indexation; **system indeksacji** indexation system; **zasady indeksacji** indexation basis.

indeksować *ipf. ekon.* index, index-link.

indeksowanie *n. komp.* indexing.

indeksowy *a. komp.* index; **błąd indeksowy** index error, indexing error; error in indexing; **pamięć indeksowa** index storage; **plik indeksowy** index file; **pole indeksowe** index field; **pozycja indeksowa** index entry; **słownik indeksowy** indexing vocabulary.

indemnizacja *f. prawn.* indemnity.

indemnizować *ipf. prawn.* indemnify.

Indianin *mp pl.* -anie *Gen.* -an Native American, Amerindian, (American) Indian; **bawić się w Indian** play Indians.

indianista *mp* Amerindianist, Native American studies expert.

indianistyka *f.* Native American studies, Amerindian studies.

indianizm *mi jęz.* Indianism.

Indianka *f. Gen.pl.* -ek *zob.* **Indianin**.

indiański *a.* Native American, Amerindian, (American) Indian; **kultura indiańska** Native American *l.* Indian culture; **plemię indiańskie** Native American *l.* Indian tribe; **wódz indiański** Native American *l.* Indian chief.

Indie *pl. Gen.* -ii *geogr.* India; **Indie Zachodnie** the West Indies.

indoaryjski *a. jęz.* Indo-Aryan.

Indochiny *pl. Gen.* -n *geogr.* Indochina.

indochiński *a.* Indochinese; **Półwysep Indochiński** *geogr.* Indochina.

indoeuropeista *mp*, **indoeuropeistka** *f. Gen.pl.* -ek Indo-Europeanist, Indo-European linguist.

indoeuropeistyka *f.* Indo-European studies, Indo-European linguistics.

indoeuropejski *a. jęz.* Indo-European; **języki/ludy/studia indoeuropejskie** Indo-European languages/peoples/studies.

indogermański *a. jęz., przest.* (= *indoeuropejski*) Indo-Germanic.

indoirański *a.* Indo-Iranian.

indoktrynacja *f. form. l. polit.* indoctrination.

indoktrynować *ipf.* indoctrinate.

indolencja *f. uj.* (= *niedołęstwo*) indolence; (= *bierność*) sloth.

Indonezja *f. geogr.* Indonesia.

Indonezyjczyk *mp*, **Indonezyjka** *f. Gen.pl.* -ek Indonesian.

indonezyjski *a.* Indonesian; **język indonezyjski** *jęz.* Indonesian, the Indonesian language, Bahasa Indonesia.

indor *mp* turkey cock.

indos *mi prawn., fin.* endorsement.

indosant *mp prawn., fin.* endorser.

indosatariusz *mp prawn., fin.* endorsee.

indosować *ipf. prawn., fin.* endorse.

indukcja *f.* 1. *log.* induction; **zasada indukcji** induction; **indukcja matematyczna** mathematical induction. 2. *fiz., el.* induction; **indukcja elektromagnetyczna/elektrostatyczna** electromagnetic/electrostatic induction; **indukcja elektryczna/magnetyczna** electric/magnetic induction; **współczynnik indukcji** inductance.

indukcyjny *a.* 1. *log.* inductive; **wnioskowanie indukcyjne** inductive reasoning. 2. *fiz., el.* in-

duction; **cewka indukcyjna** induction coil; **piec indukcyjny** induction furnace.

indukować *ipf.* 1. *log.* induce. 2. *fiz.* induce, induct.

induktor *mi Gen.* -a 1. *chem.* inductor. 2. *el.* (*prądnica*) magneto. 3. *el.* (*cewka*) coil.

induktywny *a. mat.* inductive.

indult *mi rz.-kat.* indult.

industrializacja *f.* industrialization.

industrializm *mi* industrialism.

industrializować *ipf.* industrialize.

industrialny *a.* industrial; **społeczeństwo industrialne** industrial society; **sektor industrialny** industrial sector.

indyczka *f. Gen.pl.* -ek turkey hen.

indyczy *a.* turkey; **choroba indycza** *pat.* blackhead; **mięso indycze** turkey (meat).

indyczyć się *ipf.* get one's feathers ruffled.

indygenat *mi hist.* right of citizenship; Polish peerage (*granted to a foreign nobleman*).

indygo *n.* 1. (*barwnik*) indigo. 2. *bot.* indigo (*Indigofera tinctoria*); **dzikie indygo** wild indigo (*Baptisia tinctoria*).

indygowiec *mi* -wc- *Gen.* -a *bot.* anil (*Indigofera suffruticosa*).

indygowy *a.* indigo; (*błękit*) indigo; **biel indygowa** *chem.* indigo white.

indyjski *a.* Indic, Indian, Hindustani; **języki indyjskie** *jęz.* Indic *l.* Indo-Aryan languages; **Półwysep Indyjski** the Indian Subcontinent.

indyk *ma* turkey; **indyk dziki** *orn.* wild turkey (*Meleagris gallopavo*).

indykator *mi Gen.* -a *chem. l. techn.* indicator.

indywiduacja *f. psych.* individuation.

indywidualista *mp*, **indywidualistka** *f. Gen.pl.* -ek individualist.

indywidualizm *mi* individualism.

indywidualizować *ipf. form.* individualize. ~ **się** *ipf.* become individualized.

indywidualnie *adv.* individually, on an individual basis, one by one.

indywidualność *f.* 1. (= *oryginalność*) individuality. 2. (= *człowiek wybitny*) (prominent) personality.

indywidualny *a.* 1. (= *oryginalny, osobisty*) individual; **odpowiedzialność indywidualna** individual responsibility. 2. (= *pojedynczy*) single, individual; **budownictwo indywidualne** independent building; **gospodarstwo indywidualne** family farm.

indywiduum *n. sing. indecl. pl.* -ua *Gen.* -uów 1. (= *osoba, osobnik*) individual. 2. *pog.* (= *podejrzany osobnik*) shady character.

indziej *adv.* else; **kiedy indziej** some other time; *pot.* (= *w bliżej nieokreślonej przyszłości*) mañana; **gdzie indziej** somewhere else; **nigdzie indziej** nowhere else; **być myślami gdzie indziej** be miles away.

inercja *f.* (= *bezwład*) inertia; **siła inercji** force of inertia.

inercyjny *a.* inertial.

inertny *a. chem.* inert.

infamia *f. Gen.* -ii *hist.* infamy.

infant *mp hist.* infante.

infantka *f. Gen.pl.* **-ek** *hist.* infanta.

infantylizm *mi* **1.** (= *zdziecinnienie*) childishness, puerility. **2.** *med.* infantilism.

infantylizować *ipf.* make childish *l.* infantile.

infantylność *f.* childishness.

infantylny *a.* childish, infantile, babyish, puerile; **infantylna odpowiedź** childish response *l.* answer; **infantylna osoba/reakcja** childish person/reaction; **infantylne zachowanie** childish behavior.

infekcja *f. pat.* infection; **w ranę wdała się infekcja** the wound has gone septic.

infekcyjny *a. pat.* infectious; **choroba infekcyjna** infectious *l.* contagious disease; **droga infekcyjna** means of transmission.

infibulacja *f. chir.* infibulation.

infiks *mi jęz.* infix.

infiltracja *f. polit., wojsk.* infiltration.

infiltrować *ipf. polit., wojsk.* infiltrate (*coś* into sth).

inflacja *f. ekon.* inflation; **inflacja jednocyfrowa** single-digit inflation; **inflacja wynosi 10%** inflation stands at 10%; **galopująca/pełzająca inflacja** runaway/creeping inflation; **stopa inflacji** inflation rate; **ukryta inflacja** hidden inflation.

inflacyjny *a. ekon.* inflationary; **inflacyjny wzrost cen** inflationary price upsurge; **luka inflacyjna** inflationary gap; **mechanizm inflacyjny** inflation mechanism.

inflancki *a.* Livonian; **szlachta inflancka** Livonian nobility; **wojna inflancka** *hist.* the Livonian War (*of 1558-1582*); **zakon inflancki** *hist.* (= *zakon kawalerów mieczowych*) the Livonian Knights, the Livonian Brothers of the Sword.

Inflantczyk *mp*, **Inflantka** *f. Gen.pl.* **-ek** Livonian.

Inflanty *pl. Gen.* **-ów** *hist.* Livonia.

influencja *f. astrol.* influence; *fiz., przest.* induction.

influent *mi ekol.* influent.

infolinia *f. Gen.* **-ii** helpline.

informacja *f.* **1.** (= *wiadomość*) information, piece of news, datum; **biuro informacji** information service; **system informacji** information system; **źródło informacji** source of information, information source; **informacja genetyczna** genetic information; **informacja naukowa** scientific information; **teoria informacji** information theory. **2.** (= *punkt informacyjny*) information desk, help desk; **informacja kolejowa** information; **informacja turystyczna** visitor center, visitor's *l.* visitors' center. **3.** *komp.* information; **przetwarzać informacje** process information; **udzielić informacji** provide information; **zbierać informacje** collect information; **informacja z pierwszej ręki** inside story; **poufna informacja** confidence, confidential information; **strzępy informacji** scraps of information.

informacyjny *a.* informational; **agencja informacyjna** news agency; **biuletyn informacyjny** news bulletin; **biuro informacyjne** (*znanej osoby*) public relations; **broszura informacyjna** factsheet; **embargo informacyjne** D-notice; **prospekt informacyjny** prospectus; **punkt informacyjny** information service; **redakcja informacyjna** news desk, newsdealer; **serwis informacyjny** news bulletin.

informator[1] *mi Gen.* **-a** *pl.* **-ry** (= *przewodnik*) guide; (*wyższej uczelni*) prospectus.

informator[2] *mp pl.* **-rzy** **1.** (= *źródło informacji*) informant. **2.** (*policyjny, więzienny*) informer.

informatorka *f. Gen.pl.* **-ek** *zob.* **informator**[2].

informatyczka *f. Gen.pl.* **-ek** *zob.* **informatyk**.

informatyczny *a.* IT (information technology); **instytut informatyczny** IT institute; **firma informatyczna** computer company, IT company, software company; **studia informatyczne** IT studies; **usługi informatyczne** IT *l.* computer services; *zob.* **informatyka**.

informatyk *mp* computer scientist, information technologist.

informatyka *f.* (= *technologia komputerowa*) computer technology; (= *dyscyplina naukowa zajmująca się budową komputera oraz programami i systemami komputerowymi*) computer science, information science, informatics; (= *technika informacyjna*) information technology.

informatyzować *ipf. komp.* introduce information technology (*np. w przemyśle, handlu*).

informować *ipf.* inform; (= *pouczyć*) instruct; (= *wyjaśnić*) illuminate; (= *zawiadomić*) notify. **~ się** *ipf.* inquire.

infostrada *f. komp.* information superhighway.

infradźwięk *mi akustyka* infrasound.

infrastruktura *f.* infrastructure; **infrastruktura ekonomiczna** economic infrastructure; **infrastruktura społeczna** social infrastructure.

infratest *mi socjol.* viewer *l.* listener survey, (program) ratings.

infuła *f.* **1.** (*nakrycie głowy*) miter. **2.** *przen.* (*stanowisko*) episcopal office. **3.** *hist.* infula (*w starożytnym Rzymie*).

infułat *mp rz.-kat.* mitered prelate.

infuzja *f. med.* infusion.

infuzorie *pl. Gen.* **-riów** *biol., przest.* infusoria.

infuzyjny *a. med.* infusive; **igła infuzyjna** infusion needle; **płyn infuzyjny** infusion.

ingerencja *f.* (= *interwencja*) **1.** interference, intervention. **2.** (= *mieszanie się*) encroachment.

ingerować *ipf.* (= *interweniować*) **1.** interfere, intervene (*w coś* in sth); step in. **2.** (= *mieszać się*) encroach (*w coś* on *l.* upon sth).

ingres *mi kośc.* inauguration.

ingresja *f. geol.* ingression.

ingresywny *a. fon.* ingressive.

Ingusz *mp*, **Inguszka** *f. Gen.pl.* **-ek** Ingush.

Inguszetia *f. geogr.* Ingushetia.

inhalacja *f. med.* inhalation.

inhalator *mi Gen.* **-a** *med.* inhaler, inhalator; *pot.* spray, puffer.

inhalować *ipf. med.* inhale.

inhibicja *f. chem., fizj.* inhibition.

inhibitor *mi Gen.* **-a** *chem.* inhibitor, anticatalyst, negative catalyst; **inhibitor korozji** corrosion *l.* rust inhibitor.

inhumacja *f.* inhumation.

inicjacja *f.* **1.** (= *wtajemniczenie*) initiation; (= *wkroczenie w dorosłe życie*) rite of passage. **2.** *techn.* (= *zapoczątkowanie*) initiation.

inicjacyjny *a.* **1.** initiatory; **ceremonia inicjacyjna** initiation ceremony; **obrzęd inicjacyjny** *antrop.* initiation rite. **2. substancja inicjacyjna** *techn.* initiator.

inicjalny *a.* initial; **litera inicjalna** initial; **komórka inicjalna** *bot.* initial, meristematic cell; **akcent inicjalny** *fon.* initial accent; **rym inicjalny** *teor.lit.* initial rhyme.

inicjał *mi* **1.** (= *monogram*) initial. **2.** (*w rękopisie średniowiecznym*) initial, swash letter.

inicjator[1] *mp pl.* **-rzy** initiator; **inicjator ustawy** *parl.* sponsor.

inicjał[2] *mi Gen.* **-a** *pl.* **-ry** *chem.* initiator; **inicjator polimeryzacji** initiator of polymerization.

inicjatorka *f. Gen.pl.* **-ek** *zob.* **inicjator**[1].

inicjatywa *f.* **1.** (= *propozycja*) initiative, move; **wystąpić z inicjatywą** put forward an initiative; **inicjatywa ustawodawcza** legislative initiative; **podjąć inicjatywę** take the initiative; **robić coś z własnej inicjatywy** do sth on one's own initiative. **2.** (= *przedsiębiorczość*) enterprise; **wykazywać inicjatywę** show initiative; **mieć inicjatywę** have initiative. **3.** (= *działalność*) enterprise, drive. **4.** (= *prymat*) initiative, lead; **przejąć inicjatywę** take the initiative, take the lead; **inicjatywa pokojowa** peace initiative; **prywatna inicjatywa** private initiative; **wolna inicjatywa** free initiative; **osoba z inicjatywą** self-starter; **pełen inicjatywy** proactive.

inicjować *ipf.* initiate, start, launch.

iniekcja *f. med.* injection.

Inka *mp pl.* **-owie** Inca; **imperium Inków** *hist.* the Inca Empire.

inkantacja *f.* incantation.

inkarnacja *f. rel.* incarnation.

Inkas *mp,* **Inkaska** *f. Gen.pl.* **-ek** *rzad.* = **Inka**.

inkasent *mp* collector (of payments).

Inkaska *f. Gen.pl.* **-ek** *zob.* **Inka**.

inkaski *a.* Inca, Incan, Incaic; **cywilizacja inkaska** the Inca civilisation; **kultura inkaska** Inca *l.* Incan culture.

inkaso *n. ekon.* collection (of payments); **inkaso dokumentowe** documentary collection; **inkaso finansowe** collection of financial items; **waluta inkasa** collection currency; **zlecenie inkasa** collection order.

inkasować *ipf.* **1.** (*należności*) collect. **2. inkasować ciosy** *boks* take blows.

inkasowy *a. ekon.* **rozliczenie inkasowe** cashless settlement.

inkaust *mi arch.* ink.

inklinacje *pl. Gen.* **-i** inclinations, predilections.

inkorporacja *f. form., prawn., med.* incorporation.

inkorporować *ipf.* incorporate (*coś do czegoś* sth into sth).

inkrustacja *f.* **1.** *sztuka* encrustation, incrustation, inlay, buhl. **2.** *biol.* incrustation.

inkrustować *ipf. sztuka* encrust, incrust, inlay.

inkubacja *f.* **1.** *roln.* incubation; **inkubacja jaj** incubation of eggs. **2.** *med.* incubation; **okres inkubacji** *pat.* latent period.

inkubator *mi Gen.* **-a 1.** *roln.* (= *wylęgarka*) incubator. **2.** *med.* incubator, couveuse. **3.** *ekon.* incubator.

inkunabuł *mi hist.* incunabulum.

inkwizycja *f. hist.kośc.* the Inquisition.

inkwizycyjny *a. kośc.* **1.** inquisitional. **2.** *prawn.* inquisitorial.

inkwizytor *mp hist.kośc.* inquisitor.

inność *f.* (= *odmienność*) otherness, distinctness, individuality.

innowacja *f.* **1.** (= *nowatorstwo, ulepszenie*) innovation. **2.** (= *nowość*) novelty.

innowacyjny *a.* innovative.

innowator *mp* innovator.

innowierca *mp rel.* infidel, heretic, dissenter.

innowierczy *a. rel.* heretical, heretic.

inny *a.* another, other, different; **innym razem** some other time, another time; **ktoś inny** someone *l.* somebody else; **nikt inny** no one *l.* nobody else; **coś innego** something else; **nic innego** nothing else; **wszystko inne** everything else; **a, to co innego** ah, that makes a difference; **inny od kogoś/czegoś** different from sb/sth; **między innymi** among others, among other things, inter alia; **być innego zdania** take a different view, be of a different opinion, have a different opinion; **nie było innej rady** *l.* **innego wyjścia** there was no other way; **każdy z innej parafii** *pot.* poles apart, apples and oranges; **zacząć z (całkiem) innej beczki** change tack; change the subject; switch to something (completely) different; **inna para kaloszy** *pot.* another pair of shoes, a horse of another colour *l.* of a different colour; **to zupełnie inna historia** that's a different story; that's another story; **innymi słowy** in other words, to put it another way; **w taki czy inny sposób** one way or another, one way or the other.

inochód *mi* **-o-** *jeźdz., zool.* amble.

inscenizacja *f. teatr* **1.** (= *przedstawienie*) performance, mis-en-scene, staging. **2.** (= *reżyseria, adaptacja*) production.

inscenizator *mp,* **inscenizatorka** *f. Gen.pl.* **-ek** stage-manager, producer.

inscenizować *ipf.* **1.** (*dokonywać inscenizacji*) stage, perform. **2.** (= *odgrywać, pozorować*) act out, put on.

insekt *ma* insect.

inseminacja *f. zool.* **1.** insemination. **2.** *med.* semination, insemination.

inseminator *mp zool.* inseminator.

inseminować *ipf. zool.* (= *unasienniać*) inseminate.

inskrypcja *f.* (*napis*) inscription, engraving.

insolacja *f. fiz., meteor.* insulation.

inspekcja *f.* **1.** (= *kontrola*) inspection, visitation, audit (*budynku, toku produkcji*). **2.** (= *organ kontroli*) inspectorate body.

inspekcjonować *ipf.* (= *kontrolować*) inspect, visit.

inspekt *mi ogr.* hotbed, frame.

inspektor *mp pl.* -**rzy** *l.* -**owie 1.** (= *kontroler*) inspector, superintendent, supervisor. **2.** (*stopień w policji*) police inspector; *Br.* superintendent; **główny inspektor** inspector general.

inspektorka *f. Gen.pl.* -**ek** (= *kontrolerka*) *zob.* **inspektor 1.**

inspektorat *mi* inspectorate.

inspektowy *a. ogr.* (of a) hotbed, (of a) frame.

inspicjent *mp,* **inspicjentka** *f. Gen.pl.* -**ek** *teatr* stage manager, stage-hand, call boy.

inspiracja *f.* **1.** (= *natchnienie*) inspiration, stimulation. **2.** (= *impuls, podnieta*) incentive, stimulus, spur. **3.** *lit.* afflatus. **4.** *fizj.* (= *wdech*) inspiration.

inspiracyjny *a.* **1.** (= *sugestywny*) inspiring, inspirative. **2.** *jęz.* inspiratory.

inspirator *mp,* **inspiratorka** *f. Gen.pl.* -**ek** inspirer.

inspirować *ipf.* (= *pobudzać*) inspire, stimulate, animate (*kogoś do czegoś* sb to sth, *do zrobienia czegoś* to do sth). ~ **się** *ipf.* (= *pobudzać się*) be inspired (*czymś* by sth); draw inspiration (*czymś* from sth).

inspirujący *a.* inspiring, stimulating.

instalacja *f.* **1.** *techn.* (= *zespół urządzeń*) installation, system; **instalacja elektryczna** *el.* wiring; electric installation; **instalacja grzewcza** heating installation. **2. instalacja sanitarna** sanitary system. **3.** *techn.* (= *montaż*) installation. **4.** *sztuka* installation.

instalacyjny *a. techn.* installation; **puszka instalacyjna** installation box; **dysk/pakiet/program instalacyjny** *komp.* installation disk/package/program.

instalator *mp,* **instalatorka** *f. Gen.pl.* -**ek** installer, fitter.

instalować *ipf.* **1.** *techn.* (= *montować*) install, fix. **2.** (= *urządzać, lokować*) put in, place.

instancja *f.* instance; **wyższa/niższa instancja** higher/lower instance; **sąd pierwszej instancji** court of first instance.

instant *a. indecl. kulin.* instant; **kawa/herbata instant** instant coffee/tea.

instrukcja *f.* **1.** (= *pouczenie*) instruction, order, command. **2.** (*zasady działania, użytkowania*) directions for use, instructions; **instrukcja obsługi** user's guide, instruction leaflet, operation manual. **3.** (= *przepis*) instruction, prescription, guidance.

instruktaż *mi* briefing, instruction, training.

instruktor *mp,* **instruktorka** *f. Gen.pl.* -**ek 1.** instructor. **2.** *sport* trainer, coach.

instrument *mi* **1.** *muz.* instrument; **instrumenty klawiszowe/perkusyjne/strunowe** keyboard/percussion/stringed instruments. **2.** (= *narzędzie, przyrząd*) tool, device, instrument, appliance. **3.** (= *środek, metoda działania*) means; **instrumenty ekonomiczne** *ekon.* economic instruments.

instrumentacja *f.* **1.** *muz.* (= *aranżacja*) instrumentation, orchestration. **2.** *teor.lit.* instrumentation.

instrumentalista *mp muz., fil.* instrumentalist.

instrumentalistka *f. Gen.pl.* -**ek** *muz. zob.* **instrumentalista.**

instrumentalny *a.* **1.** *muz.* instrumental; **muzyka instrumentalna** instrumental music; **zespół instrumentalny** instrumental ensamble. **2.** (= *narzędziowy*) instrumental; **analiza instrumentalna** *chem.* instrumental analysis. **3.** (= *pomocniczy*) instrumental, helpful; **instrumentalne traktowanie** *uj.* exploitation.

instrumentariuszka *f. Gen.pl.* -**ek** *med.* instrumenter, operating-theater attendant.

instruować *ipf.* (= *pouczać*) instruct, teach.

instynkt *mi* **1.** (= *motyw, odruch*) instinct; **instynkt macierzyński** maternal instinct; **instynkt samozachowawczy** self-preservation instinct; **instynkt przetrwania** survival instinct; **instynkt seksualny** sexual drive. **2.** (= *zdolność, nakaz wewnętrzny*) aptitude, gift, intuition.

instynktownie *adv.* instinctively, intuitively, on the spur of the moment.

instynktowny *a.* instinctive, intuitive, spur-of-the-moment; **instynktowna reakcja** instinctive reaction; gut reaction.

instytucja *f.* **1.** (= *organizacja, zakład, biuro*) institution, society, organization, establishment. **2.** (= *funkcja, urząd*) institution.

instytut *mi* **1.** institute. **2.** *uniw.* institute, school, department.

instytutowy *a.* **1.** institute. **2.** *uniw.* departmental.

insulina *f. biochem., med.* insulin.

insulinowy *a. biochem.* insulin.

insygnia *pl. Gen.* -**iów** insignia; **insygnia królewskie** royal insignia, regalia; **insygnia papieskie** papal insignia.

insynuacja *f.* insinuation, innuendo.

insynuować *ipf.* insinuate (*że ktoś coś zrobił* that sb did sth); impute (*coś komuś* sth to sb).

intarsja *f.* **1.** *sztuka* (*technika zdobienia*) intarsia, tarsia. **2.** *sztuka* (= *inkrustacja*) intarsia, tarsia, inlay.

intarsjować *ipf. sztuka* intarsiate.

integracja *f.* (= *tworzenie całości*) integration.

integracyjny *a.* integrative.

integralizm *mi form., polit.* integralism.

integralność *f.* integrality.

integralny *a.* integral.

integrator *mi Gen.* -**a** *el.* integrator.

integrować *ipf.* integrate, consolidate, unite.

integrysta *mp,* **integrystka** *f. Gen.pl.* -**ek** *rel.* integrist.

integryzm *mi rel.* integrism.

intelekt *mi* intellect, intelligence.

intelektualista *mp,* **intelektualistka** *f. Gen.pl.* -**ek 1.** (= *inteligent, uczony*) intellectual, academic. **2.** *fil.* intellectualist.

intelektualizm *mi fil.* intellectualism.

intelektualny *a.* (= *umysłowy, myślowy*) intellectual.

inteligencik *mp pl.* -**i** *iron., pog.* (*o osobie wykształconej*) **1.** egghead, geek, nerd. **2.** *pog.* (=

zarozumialec, ćwierćinteligent) Mr. Know-it-all, smart Aleck, smarty pants.

inteligencki *a.* intellectual.

inteligencja *f.* **1.** intelligence, brightness, cleverness. **2.** *biol., psych.* (= *zdolność rozumienia, umysł*) intelligence, intellect; **sztuczna inteligencja** *komp.* artificial intelligence, AI; **iloraz inteligencji** intelligence quotient, IQ; **test na inteligencję** IQ test *l.* intelligence test. **3.** *socjol.* (= *pracownicy umysłowi*) intelligentsia.

inteligent *mp* intellectual, educated person.

inteligentka *f. Gen.pl.* -ek *zob.* **inteligent**.

inteligentnie *adv.* intelligently, shrewdly, cleverly.

inteligentny *a.* **1.** (= *mądry*) intelligent, shrewd, bright, clever; **broń inteligentna** *wojsk.* smart weapon, intelligent weapon. **2.** (= *świadczący o inteligencji*) (*wzrok, twarz, spojrzenie, zachowanie*) intelligent.

intencja *f.* **1.** (= *cel, zamiar*) intention, intent, aim, objective; **mieć dobre/złe intencje** have good/bad intentions; **robić coś w najlepszej intencji** mean well; **zrobienie czegoś jest czyjąś intencją** it is sb's intention to do sth. **2.** *rel.* intention; **modlitwa w czyjejś intencji** prayer on behalf of sb; **intencje mszalne** intentions.

intencjonalny *a.* **1.** (= *celowy, zamierzony*) intentional, deliberate, purposeful. **2.** *fil.* intentional.

intendent *mp*, **intendentka** *f. Gen.pl.* -ek **1.** (= *pracownik administracyjny zajmujący się działem gospodarczym*) steward, housekeeper. **2.** (= *dyrektor l. kierownik administracyjny*) intendant.

intendentura *f.* **1.** (= *dział gospodarczy*) intendancy, ordnance. **2.** *wojsk.* (= *kwatermistrzostwo*) commissariat.

intensyfikacja *f.* intensification.

intensyfikować *ipf.* intensify, strengthen, enhance. ~ **się** *ipf.* become intense, get intensified.

intensywnie *adv.* intensely, strongly.

intensywność *f.* intensity, intensiveness.

intensywny *a.* (= *nasilony, wyraźny, mocny*) **1.** intense, strong, sharp. **2.** (*o kursie, uprawie*) intensive; (*o kolorze*) deep; (*o opadach*) heavy; **intensywna terapia** *l.* **opieka medyczna** *med.* intensive care.

interchampion *ma kynol.* interchampion.

InterCity *mi indecl.* InterCity train.

intercom *mi zob.* **interkom**.

intercyza *f. prawn.* marriage settlement, marriage articles.

interdykt *mi* **1.** *hist.* (= *nakaz, zakaz*) interdict, interdiction, prohibition, ban. **2.** *rel., kośc.* (*kara*) interdict.

interdyscyplinarny *a.* (= *wielokierunkowy*) interdisciplinary.

interes *mi* **1.** (= *sprawa, prośba*) business, matter, affair; **mieć do kogoś interes** *pot.* have sth to talk to sb about; have a matter to take up with sb; have a little business (to discuss) with sb; **mieszać się do czyichś interesów** *pot.* meddle with sb's affairs; poke *l.* pry into sb's affairs; **(to) nie twój interes** *pot.* (it's) not your business; (it's)

no business of yours; (it's) none of your business. **2.** (= *zysk, korzyść*) bargain; **interes polityczny** *polit.* political matter; **chodzić koło swoich interesów** go about one's business; serve one's own interests; **coś leży w czyimś interesie** sth is to sb's (best) interest(s); sth is in sb's interest; **mieć w czymś (swój) interes** have an axe to grind in sth; have a vested interest in sth; **sprzeczność interesów** clash of interests, conflict of interest(s). **3.** (= *działalność gospodarcza*) business activity; **człowiek interesu** businessman; (*kobieta*) businesswoman; **nieczysty interes** shady deal; **uczciwy interes** square deal; **ruch w interesie** business is booming, flourishing *l.* brisk; **robić na czymś interes** do a roaring trade in sth; profit from sth; **wziąć się do interesu** get down to business. **4.** *pot.* (= *prywatne przedsiębiorstwo, sklep, zakład*) business; **otworzyć własny interes** open up a business, start a business; **rozkręcić interes** set up in business. **5.** *sl.* (= *penis*) one's thing.

interesant *mp*, **interesantka** *f. Gen.pl.* -ek (= *petent*) inquirer; (= *klient*) customer, client.

interesik *mi* **1.** (*mała sprawa, prośba*) small matter, a little request, question. **2.** (*nieduże przedsięwzięcie l. przedsiębiorstwo*) small business.

interesować *ipf.* interest; **to mnie nie interesuje** I am not interested in it; I don't take interest in it. ~ **się** *ipf.* **1.** (= *być zainteresowanym*) be interested, take an interest (*czymś* in sth). **2.** (= *okazywać zainteresowanie*) be concerned (*kimś / czymś* about sb/sth).

interesowny *a.* (= *wyrachowany*) self-seeking, calculating, interested.

interesujący *a.* interesting, absorbing, fascinating, attractive.

interesy *pl. Gen.* -ów (= *przedsięwzięcia finansowe*) business affairs *l.* matters, dealings, ventures; **prowadzić interesy** do business, engage in business; **w interesach, służbowo** on business.

interfejs *mi komp.* interface.

interferencja *f. fiz.* interference.

interferencyjny *a. fiz.* interferential; **obraz interferencyjny** interference pattern.

interferometr *mi fiz.* interferometer.

interferon *mi biochem.* interferon.

interferować *ipf. fiz.* interfere.

interfiks *mi jęz.* infix.

interfiksalny *a. jęz.* infixal.

interglacjalny *a. geol.* interglacial.

interglacjał *mi geol.* interglacial period.

interior *mi geogr.* interior.

interkom *mi techn.* intercom, interphone, intercommunication system.

interkomunikacja *f. techn.* intercommunication.

interkontynentalny *a.* intercontinental.

interliga *f. sport* interleague.

interlinearny *a.* (= *międzywierszowy*) interlinear.

interlinia *f. Gen.* -ii *druk.* space, lead, leading.

interliniować *ipf. druk.* lead.

interludium *n. sing. indecl. pl.* **-ia** *Gen.* **-iów** *muz., teor.lit., teatr* interlude.

intermedium *n. sing. indecl. pl.* **-ia** *Gen.* **-iów** **1.** *teor.lit., teatr* interlude. **2.** *muz.* (= *wstawka muzyczna*) interlude, intermezzo.

intermezzo *n. muz., teatr* intermezzo.

interna *f.* **1.** *med., pot.* (*dział medycyny*) internal medicine. **2.** *med., pot.* (*oddział szpitalny*) department of internal diseases.

internacjonalista *mp*, **internacjonalistka** *f.* *Gen.pl.* **-ek** internationalist.

internacjonalistyczny *a.* (= *kosmopolityczny*) international, cosmopolitan.

internacjonalizm *mi* internationalism.

internacjonalny *a.* international.

internat *mi* dormitory, dorm; **szkoła z internatem** boarding school.

internauta *mp komp.* surfer, Internet user, internaut.

Internet *mi komp.* the Internet; **surfować po Internecie** *l.* **buszować w Internecie** surf the Internet.

internetowy *a. komp.* Internet.

internista *mp*, **internistka** *f. Gen.pl.* **-ek** *med.* internist.

internistyczny *a. med.* (of) internal medicine, internistic.

internować *ipf.* intern.

internowana *f. Gen.* **-ej**, **internowany** *mp* internee; **obóz dla internowanych** detention camp, internment camp.

interpelacja *f. polit.* interpellation, question; **czas na interpelacje poselskie** question time (*in parliament*).

interpelacyjny *a.* interpellative.

interpelator *mp form.* interpellator.

interpelować *ipf.* (*pytać*) interpellate.

interpersonalny *a. psych.* (= *międzyludzki*) interpersonal.

Interpol *mi* the Interpol.

interpretacja *f.* **1.** (= *wytłumaczenie, komentarz*) interpretation, explanation, exegesis. **2.** (= *odegranie, kreacja*) interpretation, rendition, rendering. **3.** *komp.* interpretation.

interpretacyjny *a.* **1.** (= *komentatorski, wyjaśniający*) interpretative. **2.** (= *wykonawczy*) interpretational.

interpretator *mp*, **interpretatorka** *f. Gen.pl.* **-ek** interpreter.

interpretować *ipf.* **1.** (= *wyjaśniać, komentować*) interpret. **2.** (= *wykonywać, odtwarzać, grać*) render, interpret.

interpunkcja *f.* punctuation.

interpunkcyjny *a.* punctuation; **błąd/znak interpunkcyjny** punctuation error/mark.

interregnum *n. sing. indecl. pl.* **-a** *Gen.* **-ów** *polit., hist.* interregnum.

interreks *mp pl.* **-owie** *hist.* interrex.

interview *n. l. mi indecl. l. Gen.* **-u** (= *wywiad*) interview.

interwał *mi nauk., muz.* interval; **interwał czasoprzestrzenny** *fiz.* space-time interval.

interwencja *f.* **1.** (= *ingerencja*) intervention, interference. **2.** *polit.* intervention; **interwencja**

zbrojna/dyplomatyczna armed/diplomatic intervention.

interwencyjny *a.* interventional; **ceny/zakupy interwencyjne** *ekon.* intervention prices/buying.

interweniować *ipf.* **1.** (= *wstawiać się*) intervene, intercede (*u kogoś* by sb). **2.** (= *mieszać się*) interfere (*w coś* in sth); meddle (*w coś* with sth).

intestat *mp prawn.* intestate.

intonacja *f.* **1.** *fon.* intonation, pitch modulation. **2.** *muz.* intonation.

intonować *ipf.* **1.** (= *rozpoczynać śpiew*) intone, chant, cantillate. **2.** (= *wymawiać, akcentować*) stress, intonate.

intrata *f. przest.* profit.

intratny *a.* (= *dochodowy*) lucrative, profitable, paying.

introdukcja *f. muz., biol., roln.* introduction.

introligator *mp*, **introligatorka** *f. Gen.pl.* **-ek** *druk.* bookbinder.

introligatornia *f. Gen.pl.* **-ni** *l.* **-ń** bookbindery.

introligatorski *a. druk.* bookbinding, bookbinder's; **prasa introligatorska** binding press.

introligatorstwo *n. druk.* bookbinding.

intronizacja *f.* **1.** (= *koronacja*) enthronement. **2.** *kośc.* (= *ingres*) inauguration.

intronizować *ipf.* enthrone.

introspekcja *f.* **1.** *psych.* (= *samoobserwacja*) introspection, insight. **2.** *teor.lit., film* introspection.

introspekcyjny *a.* introspective.

introwersja *f. psych.* introversion.

introwersyjny *a. psych.* introvert; **typ introwersyjny** introversive *l.* introvertive type.

introwertyczka *f. Gen.pl.* **-ek**, **introwertyk** *mp* *psych.* introvert.

intruz *mp pl.* **-i** *l.* **-y** (= *nieproszony gość*) **1.** intruder; (= *osoba wkraczająca bezprawnie na czyjś teren*) tresspasser. **2.** *prawn.* (= *osoba naruszająca czyjeś prawo*) interloper, encroacher.

intryga *f.* **1.** (= *podstęp, manipulacja*) plot, scheme, intrigue, machination. **2.** *teor.lit., film* plot.

intrygancki *a.* plotting, scheming, mischief-making.

intrygant *mp*, **intrygantka** *f. Gen.pl.* **-ek** schemer, intriguer, machinator, mischief-maker.

intrygować *ipf.* **1.** (= *zaciekawiać*) puzzle, intrigue, interest. **2.** (= *knuć, spiskować*) plot, scheme, machinate (*przeciw komuś/czemuś* against sb/sth).

intrygujący *a.* (= *interesujący*) intriguing, piquant.

intubacja *f. med.* intubation.

intuicja *f.* **1.** (= *przeczucie, przewidywanie*) intuition, foreboding, hint, feeling. **2.** *psych., fil.* intuition.

intuicjonista *mp fil.* intuitionist.

intuicjonizm *mi fil., log., mat.* intuitionism.

intuicyjny *a.* (= *podświadomy, irracjonalny*) intuitive; (*o przeczuciu, obawie*) visceral.

intymnie *adv.* intimately.

intymność *f.* (= *prywatność, poufałość*) intimacy, privacy.

intymny *a.* intimate; (= *prywatny, osobisty*) private.

inwalida *mp*, **inwalidka** *f. Gen.pl.* -ek invalid, disabled person.

inwalidzki *a.* invalid's; **renta inwalidzka** disability pension; **wózek inwalidzki** wheelchair, invalid chair.

inwalidztwo *n.* disability.

inwazja *f.* 1. (= *najazd, agresja*) invasion, aggression. 2. (= *masowe występowanie szkodników*) invasion, plague.

inwazyjny *a.* 1. (= *napastniczy*) aggressive; **siły inwazyjne** *wojsk.* invasion forces. 2. *med.* invasive.

inwencja *f.* 1. (= *pomysłowość*) inventiveness, creativity. 2. (= *wynalazek*) invention. 3. *muz.* invention.

inwentaryzacja *f.* stock-taking, taking inventory.

inwentaryzator *mp*, **inwentaryzatorka** *f. Gen.pl.* -ek stock taker.

inwentaryzować *ipf.* make an inventory, take stock *l.* inventory of (*sth*).

inwentarz *mi Gen.* -a *Gen.pl.* -y *l.* -ów 1. (= *mienie*) stock. 2. (= *wykaz mienia*) inventory. 3. *hodowla* stock, livestock; **inwentarz hodowlany** breeding stock.

inwentura *f.* (= *remanent*) stock-taking.

inwersja *f. jęz., chem., mat., muz.* inversion.

inwertor *mi Gen.* -a *el.* inverter.

inwestor *mp*, **inwestorka** *f. Gen.pl.* -ek investor.

inwestować *ipf.* invest (*w coś* in sth).

inwestycja *f.* investment; **dobra/rozsądna inwestycja** good/sound investment.

inwestycyjny *a. fin.* capital, investment; **fundusz inwestycyjny** investment fund; **wydatki inwestycyjne** capital expenditure.

inwigilacja *f.* surveillance.

inwigilować *ipf.* keep under surveillance.

inwit *mi brydż* invitation bid.

inwokacja *f. teor.lit.* invocation.

inwolucja *f. biol.* (= *zanik*) involution.

inwoluta *f. geom.* involute.

inżynier *mp pl.* -owie *l.* -rzy engineer; **inżynier budownictwa lądowego** civil engineer; **inżynier elektronik/górnik** electronics/mining engineer.

inżynieria *f. Gen.* -ii engineering; **inżynieria budowlana** *przen.* construction engineering; **inżynieria społeczna** *przen.* social engineering; **inżynieria genetyczna** *biol.* genetic engineering.

inżynieryjny *a.* engineering.

ipekakuana *f. med.* ipecac.

iperyt *mi wojsk., chem.* mustard gas.

ippon *mi sport* ipoon.

iracki *a.* Iraqi.

Irak *mi geogr.* Iraq.

Irakijczyk *mp*, **Irakijka** *f. Gen.pl.* -ek Iraqi.

Iran *mi geogr.* Iran.

Iranka *f. Gen.pl.* -ek, **Irańczyk** *mp* Iranian.

irański *a.* Iranian; **języki irańskie** *jęz.* Iranian languages.

ircha *f.* chamois (leather), chammy *l.* shammy (leather).

irchowy *a.* chamois, chammy, shammy.

irga *f. bot.* cotoneaster (*Cotoneaster*).

Irlandczyk *mp* Irishman.

Irlandia *f. Gen.* -ii *geogr.* Ireland; **Irlandia Północna** Northern Ireland.

Irlandka *f. Gen.pl.* -ek Irishwoman.

irlandzki *a.* Irish; **język irlandzki** Irish Gaelic; **Irlandzka Armia Republikańska** *polit.* Irish Republican Army, IRA.

irokeski *a.* Iroquois, Iroquoian.

Irokez *mp* Iroquois, Iroquoian.

irokez *mi Gen. i Acc.* -a *pot.* (*fryzura*) punk hairstyle.

irokezka *f. Gen.pl.* -ek *zob.* **Irokez**.

ironia *f. Gen.* -ii 1. (= *drwina*) irony, sarcasm; **jak na ironię** ironically; **ironia losu** ironic twist (of fate). 2. *teor.lit.* irony.

ironiczny *a.* ironic, ironical.

ironista *mp*, **ironistka** *f. Gen.pl.* -ek ironist.

ironizować *ipf.* to be ironic.

irracjonalizm *mi*, **irracjonalność** *f.* irrationality, irrationalism.

irracjonalny *a.* irrational.

irradiacja *f. fiz.* irradiation.

iryd *mi chem.* iridium.

irygacja *f. roln., med.* irrigation.

irygacyjny *a.* irrigational; **kanał/rów irygacyjny** irrigation canal/ditch.

irygator *mi Gen.* -a *med.* irrigator.

irys *mi Gen. i Acc.* -a 1. *bot.* iris (*Iris*). 2. (*cukierek*) toffee.

irytacja *f.* (= *gniew, zdenerwowanie*) irritation.

irytować *ipf.* irritate, annoy, upset. ~ **się** *ipf.* get irritated; get annoyed *l.* upset.

irytujący *a.* irritating, provoking, annoying.

iryzacja *f.* (= *połysk tęczowy*) iridescence; *techn.* iridization.

iryzować *ipf.* 1. (= *mienić się*) iridesce. 2. *techn.* iridize.

ischias *mi pat.* sciatica.

iskać *ipf.* groom. ~ **się** *ipf.* groom o.s.

iskierka *f. Gen.pl.* -ek spark, scintilla; (= *rozbłysk*) flicker, sparkle; **ani iskierki prawdy** not a scintilla of truth; **iskierka nadziei/zainteresowania** flicker of hope/interest.

iskiernik *mi el.* spark gap.

iskra *f. Gen.pl.* **iskier** spark; (= *rozbłysk*) flicker, sparkle; **krzesać iskry** strike sparks; **iskra elektryczna** *fiz.* electric spark; **iskra zapłonowa** *techn.* ignition spark; **iskra boża** divine sparkle; **iskra entuzjazmu** spark of enthusiasm; **iskra nadziei** flicker of hope.

iskrochron *mi techn.* spark arrester.

iskrownik *mi Gen.* -a *techn.* magneto.

iskrowy *a.* spark, sparkling.

iskrzyć, ~ **się** *ipf.* 1. (= *sypać iskrami*) sparkle, spark, give out sparks. 2. **iskrzy się między nimi** *przen.* sparks are flying between them.

islam *mi rel.* Islam.

islamista *mp*, **islamistka** *f. Gen.pl.* -ek *rel.* Muslim.

islamistyczny *a. rel.* Islamic, Muslim.

islamizacja f. Islamization.
islamizować v. Islamize.
islamski a. Islamic, Muslim.
Islandczyk mp Icelander.
Islandia f. Gen. -ii geogr. Iceland.
Islandka Gen.pl. -ek zob. **Islandczyk**.
islandzki a. Icelandic.
Istambuł mi geogr. Istanbul.
istnieć ipf. be, exist.
istniejący a. existent, existing, extant.
istnienie n. (= byt) existence, being; (= życie ludzkie) life, existence; **istnienie wieczne** eternal life.
istny a. real, veritable.
istota f. **1.** (= treść, sens) essence, core, gist; **w istocie (rzeczy)** as a matter of fact; **pojąć istotę sprawy** get the point; **zbadać istotę rzeczy** explore the heart of the matter. **2.** (= stworzenie) creature, being; **istota nadprzyrodzona/ludzka** supernatural/human being; **istota pozaziemska** extraterrestrial (being), ET; alien (from outer space); **Istota Najwyższa** fil., rel. the Supreme Being. **3.** (= natura, osobowość) nature. **4. istota biała/szara** anat. white/gray matter.
istotka f. Gen.pl. -ek (= stworzonko) little creature, little thing, critter.
istotnie adv. **1.** (= całkowicie, zasadniczo) crucially, vitally, essentially. **2.** (= naprawdę, rzeczywiście) indeed, really, in fact, actually, truly. **3.** (= znacząco) significantly, considerably.
istotny a. **1.** (= ważny) crucial, vital, fundamental. **2.** (= rzeczywisty, prawdziwy) real, actual. **3.** (= duży, znaczny) significant, considerable.
iście adv. lit. (= rzeczywiście) truly, veritably.
iść ipf. idę idziesz, idź szedł szła szli **1.** (= kroczyć pieszo) go, walk, stride; **iść pieszo** l. **piechotą** go on foot, walk (it), foot it; **iść drogą** walk l. go down the road, follow the road; **iść pod górę** walk uphill l. up the hill; **iść przez park** walk across the park; **iść raźnym/niepewnym krokiem** walk briskly/unsteadily; **iść parami/dwójkami** go in pairs/in twos; **iść przy (czyjejś) nodze** (o psie) heel (sb). **2.** (= poruszać się, posuwać się) go (on), go ahead l. along, move (on), run; **iść prosto przed siebie** go straight ahead; **iść w górę/w dół** go up/down; rise/fall; **idziemy?** shall we go?; **patrz, jak idziesz!** look where you go!; **idź dalej** go on, move on, keep walking; **iść na czele czegoś** head sth, lead sth; **iść przodem** lead the way; **iść na oślep** grope one's way; **iść pod żaglami** żegl. sail on, sail along; **iść z wiatrem** żegl. run free; sail before the wind. **3.** (= podążać) **iść za kimś/czymś** follow sb/sth; **iść za tropem** myśl. l. przen. follow the scent; **iść za czyjąś radą** follow sb's advice; **iść za czyimś przykładem** follow sb's example l. lead; follow in sb's footsteps; **iść za najnowszą modą** follow the latest fashion; **iść za głosem serca** listen to one's heart; **iść za głosem sumienia/rozsądku** listen to the voice of conscience/reason. **4.** (= udawać się w jakieś miejsce) go; **iść do domu** go home; **iść na miasto** go into town; **iść do szkoły/pracy/kościoła** go to school/work/church; **iść do kina** go to the movies; **iść na przy-**

jęcie go to a party; **iść do łóżka** go to bed; **iść z kimś do łóżka** euf. go to bed with sb. **5.** (= udawać się gdzieś przymusowo) go, be taken to (a place); **iść do szpitala** go l. be taken to hospital; **iść do więzienia** go to prison, go to jail; be imprisoned; **iść do nieba/piekła** go to heaven/hell; **iść na dno** founder, sink, go to the bottom; **iść na zasiłek** go on the dole; **iść na zieloną trawkę** pot. be given the sack; be sacked l. fired. **6.** (= wychodzić z zamiarem zrobienia czegoś) go (out); **iść na lunch** go (out) for lunch; **iść na przechadzkę** l. **na spacer** go for a walk; **iść na zakupy** go shopping; **iść na ryby/na polowanie** go fishing/hunting; **iść na narty/na łyżwy** go skiing/skating; **iść popływać** go for a swim; go swimming; **iść spać** go to sleep. **7.** (= odchodzić) go (away); **idź sobie!, idź precz!** l. **idź stąd!** go away!; pot. get lost!; **idź do diabła!** emf. go to hell!, go to the devil!; **idź się utop!** pot. go jump in the lake! **8.** (= przemijać) **iść w niepamięć** be forgotten; **iść w zapomnienie** fall l. sink into oblivion. **9.** (= wstępować do jakiejś instytucji) **iść do college'u** go to college; **iść na studia wyższe** go to university; **iść na medycynę** take up medicine; **iść do wojska** join the army; enlist, sign on l. up. **10.** (= rozpoczynać coś) **iść na urlop/przepustkę** go on leave/furlough; **iść na emeryturę** retire. **11.** (= atakować) **iść do szturmu** wojsk. charge (na coś at sth); be on the attack; **idź na niego!** go at him! **12.** (= ciągnąć się, prowadzić) lead, run, stretch, extend; **ścieżka idzie pod górę** the path runs uphill; **droga szła milami przez pustynię** the road stretched for miles across the desert. **13.** (o filmie, sztuce, programie) (= być pokazywanym) be on, be played; (= być nadawanym) be on the air; **co idzie dziś wieczorem?** what's on tonight?; **sztuka idzie bez przerwy od dwóch lat** the play has been produced continuously for two years. **14.** (= zbliżać się) come, approach; **idzie burza** a storm is coming; **idzie deszcz** it's going to rain; **idzie lato** the summer is approaching; **idą trudne czasy** hard times are coming. **15.** (= wykazywać tendencję) **iść w górę** rise, soar, increase, go up, be on the rise; **iść w dół** drop, fall, dip, decrease, go down; **idzie ku lepszemu** things are looking up. **16.** (= działać, pracować) run, work; **iść w ruch** be set in motion; start up, start working; **silnik szedł na pełnych obrotach** the engine was running at full speed. **17.** (o sprawach) (= toczyć się, posuwać się) go, proceed, be doing; **nie idzie mi** I'm stuck (z czymś with sth); **interesy idą dobrze** the business is doing well; **jak (ci) idzie?** (= jak się masz?) how are you doing?; **idzie jak po maśle/jak po grudzie** it's going swimmingly/hard; **wszystko idzie jak z płatka** everything's (coming up) roses; **idzie nam opornie** it's slow l. tough going; **iść pełną parą** be in full swing; go full steam l. speed ahead; **sprawiać, że coś idzie dobrze** make sth tick; **nie idzie tego zrobić** sl. it can't be done. **18.** (= sprzedawać się) sell, go; **iść jak ciepłe bułeczki** l. **jak woda** go like hot cakes; **iść pod młotek** come l. go under the hammer. **19.** (= brzmieć) **jak ta piosenka idzie?** how does the song go? **20.** (= chodzić o coś) **idzie o to, że...**

what I mean is that...; the problem is that...; **tu idzie o życie** it's a matter of life and death; **tu idzie o twój honor** your honor is at stake. **21.** (*w różnych wyrażeniach idiomatycznych*) **iść na całego** go the whole hog; **iść na coś** (= *zadowalać się czymś*) settle for sth; **iść na kompromis** make a compromise (*z kimś* with sb); compromise; **iść na układy** pact (*z kimś* with sb); **iść (z kimś) o zakład** bet (sb) (*że...* that...); **iść na noże** *l.* na udry be at daggers drawn (*z kimś* with sb) (*z kimś* with sb); **iść na łatwiznę** take the easy way out; cut corners.

Itaka *f. geogr.* Ithaca.

Italia *f. Gen.* **-ii** *geogr.* Italy.

italianista *mp*, **italianistka** *f. Gen.pl.* **-ek** Italianist.

italianistyka *f.* Italian studies.

italianizm *mi jęz.* Italianism; *sztuka* Italianate *l.* Italianesque trait.

italika *f.*, **italiki** *pl. Gen.* **-ów** *druk.* italics.

italski *a.* Italic.

itd. *abbr.* (= *i tak dalej*) etc., et cetera (= *and so on*); **itd., itp.** *pot.* and so on, and so forth.

iteracja *f. mat., komp.* iteration; **dokonywać iteracji** iterate.

iteracyjny *a. mat., komp.* iterative; **krok iteracyjny** iterative step, iteration.

iteratywny *a. jęz.* iterative.

iterb *mi chem.* ytterbium.

iterować *ipf. mat., komp.* itaerate.

itp. *abbr.* (= *i tym podobne*) etc. (= *and so on; and so forth*); and the like; or similar.

itr *mi chem.* yttrium.

iwa *f. bot.* goat willow (*Salix caprea*).

Izaak *mp Bibl.* Isaac.

izabelowaty *a. jeźdz.* palomino; **koń izabelowaty** palomino (horse).

Izajasz *mp Bibl.* Isaiah.

izba *f.* **1.** (= *pokój, pomieszczenie*) room, chamber; **izba chorych** infirmary; **izba dziecka** children shelter; **izba porodowa** delivery room; **izba przyjęć** admission room, reception room; **izba wytrzeźwień** detoxification center; *pot.* drunk tank; **izba pamięci** memorial room; **izba żołnierska** barrack room. **2.** (*jednostka organizacyjna, instytucja*) chamber; **izba handlowa** chamber of commerce; **izba lekarska** physicians' chamber; **izba adwokacka** lawyers' chamber; **izba morska** marine chamber; **izba rozrachunkowa** clearinghouse. **3.** *polit.* (*organ państwowy*) house, chamber; **Izba Reprezentantów** *parl.* the House of Representatives; **Izba Lordów/Gmin** *parl.* the House of Lords/Commons; **izba niższa/wyższa parlamentu** *parl.* the lower/upper house of parliament; **Izba Gwiaździsta** *hist.* the Star Chamber; **Izba Skarbowa** the Internal Revenue Service; **Najwyższa Izba Kontroli** the Supreme Control Chamber.

izbica *f.* **1.** *arch.* (= *pokój*) chamber. **2.** *techn.* ice-apron, icebreaker. **3.** *bud.* the upper floor (*of a tower*).

izobara *f. meteor.* isobar, pressure contour.

izobaryczny *a. meteor.* isobaric.

izobata *f. geogr.* isobath, depth curve.

izobutan *mi chem.* isobutane.

izochroniczny *a. fiz.* isochronous.

izochronizm *mi fiz.* isochronism, isochrony.

izodynamiczny *a. fiz.* isodynamic.

izoglosa *f. jęz.* isogloss.

izoklina *f. geogr.* isoclinic line.

izolacja *f.* **1.** (= *oddzielenie*) isolation, separation (*od czegoś* from sth). **2.** (= *odizolowanie się*) seclusion; **w izolacji** in seclusion; incommunicado. **3.** *fiz., techn.* (= *osłona*) insulation; **izolacja cieplna/elektryczna** thermal/electric insulation; **izolacja akustyczna** sound insulation.

izolacjonista *mp*, **izolacjonistka** *f. Gen.pl.* **-ek** *polit.* isolationist.

izolacjonizm *mi polit.* isolationism.

izolacyjny *a.* **1.** (= *dotyczący separacji politycznej*) isolationist. **2.** (= *dotyczący izolacji, osłony*) insulating; **materiały izolacyjne** insulating materials; **taśma izolacyjna** insulating band.

izolat *mi chem.* isolate.

izolatka *f. Gen.pl.* **-ek 1.** (*w szpitalu*) isolation ward. **2.** (*w więzieniu*) seclusion cell, solitary confinement.

izolator *mi Gen.* **-a** *el.* insulator, non-conductor; *techn.* insulation, insulating material.

izolować *ipf.* **1.** (= *oddzielać, odłączać*) isolate, separate (*od kogoś/czegoś* from sb/sth). **2.** (= *zaopatrywać w izolację*) *techn.* insulate. **~ się** *ipf.* seclude o.s.

izomer *mi chem.* isomer.

izomeria *mi chem.* isomerism.

izomeryczny *a. chem.* isomeric.

izometria *f. Gen.* **-ii** *mat., muz., techn.* isometry.

izometryczny *a. mat., techn.* isometric.

izooktan *mi chem.* isooctane.

izopentan *mi chem.* isopentane.

izoterma *f.* **1.** *fiz.* isotherm. **2.** *meteor.* isothermal line.

izotermia *f. Gen.* **-ii** *meteor.* isothermy.

izotermiczny *a. fiz.* isothermal.

izotop *mi chem., fiz.* isotope; **izotop promieniotwórczy** radioactive isotope, unstable isotope; **izotop trwały** stable isotope; **masa atomowa izotopu** isotopic mass *l.* weight.

izotopowy *a. chem., fiz.* isotopic.

izotropia *f. Gen.* **-ii** *fiz.* isotropy.

izotropowy *a. fiz.* isotropic.

Izrael *mi Gen.* **-a** *geogr.* Israel.

Izraelczyk *mp* Israeli.

Izraelita *mp*, **Izraelitka** *f. Gen.pl.* **-ek** *hist.* Israelite.

Izraelka *f. Gen.pl.* **-ek** *zob.* **Izraelczyk**.

izraelski *a.* Israeli.

Izyda *f. mit.* Isis.

iż *conj. lit.* = *że*; **przypuszczam, iż to prawda** I suppose that it is true; **sądzę, że to prawda, iż on żyje** I believe that it is true that he is alive.

iżby *conj.* = *żeby*.

J

J, j *n. indecl.* (*litera*) J, j; **J jak Jadwiga** J is for Jig; J as in Jig.

J *abbr. fiz.* = dżul.

j. *abbr.* **1.** *geogr.* = jezioro. **2.** *jęz.* = język.

ja *pron. i n. Gen. i Loc.* **mnie** *Dat.* **mnie** *l.* **mi** *Acc.* **mnie** *Ins.* **mną** (= *własna osoba*) I, me; **ja też** same here; **ja nie mogę!** (*okrzyk rezygnacji l. niedowierzania*) give me strength!; **ja cię kręcę!** *pot.* holy cow!; **a ja?/a co ze mną?** what about me?; **jak ja** like me; **to (tylko) ja** it's (just/only) me; **ja sam** *l.* **ja osobiście** I myself; **drugie ja** one's other *l.* second self; **moje własne ja** my own self.

jabłecznik *mi Gen.* **-a** *kulin.* **1.** (*ciasto*) apple pie. **2.** (*napój*) cider.

jabłeczny *a. kulin.* apple.

jabłko *n. Gen.pl.* **-ek 1.** *kulin.* (*owoc*) apple. **2.** (*także* **jabłko królewskie**) *hist.* (*insygnia władzy*) orb. **3.** (*w zwrotach*) **jabłko Adama** *anat.* Adam's apple; **jabłko niezgody** bone of contention; **złote jabłko** (= *kokosowy interes*) golden apple, gold mine; **zbić kogoś na kwaśne jabłko** beat sb to a jelly; **niedaleko pada jabłko od jabłoni** like father like son; the apple doesn't fall far from the tree.

jabłkowity *a.* (*o koniu*) dapple-grey.

jabłkowy *a.* **1.** *kulin.* apple; **mus jabłkowy** apple sauce. **2. kwas jabłkowy** *chem.* malic acid.

jabłoniowy *a.* apple-tree.

jabłonka *f. Gen.pl.* **-ek** apple tree.

jabłoń *f. pl.* **-nie** apple tree; *bot.* apple (*Malus*); **dzika/rajska jabłoń** crab apple; **niedaleko pada jabłko od jabłoni** like father like son; the apple doesn't fall far from the tree.

jabłuszko *n. Gen.pl.* **-ek** *pot.* apple; **zielone jabłuszko** (*odmiana jabłka*) Granny Smith apple; (*zapach*) green apple; **rajskie jabłuszko** crab apple.

jabol *mi Gen. i Acc.* **-a** *sl.* apple wine; vino; *Br.* plonk.

jacht *mi żegl.* yacht, sailboat; *Br.* sailing-boat.

jachting *mi żegl.* yachting, sailing.

jachtklub *mi żegl.* yacht club, sailing *l.* yachting club.

jachtowy *a. żegl.* sailing, yachting; **przystań jachtowa** marina.

jad *mi* (*t. przen.*) venom, poison; *pat.* toxin; **jad kiełbasiany** *chem.* botulin; **jad trupi** cadaveric poison; **ziać jadem** (*także* **sączyć jad**) *przen.* spout *l.* spew venom.

jadaczka *f. Gen.pl.* **-ek** *pog., sl.* (= *usta*) trap, yap; **drzeć jadaczkę** yell, bawl out; **otworzyć/ zamknąć jadaczkę** open/shut one's trap; **trzymać jadaczkę na kłódkę** put a sock in it, keep one's cakehole shut.

jadać *ipf.* (= *jeść*) eat (from time to time); **jadać na mieście** dine out; **jadać w drogich restauracjach** go to expensive restaurants; **on z niejednego pieca chleb jadał** *przen.* he has seen a great deal (in his life).

jadalnia *f. Gen.pl.* **-ni** *l.* **-ń 1.** (= *pokój stołowy*) dining room. **2.** (*meble*) dining/dinner set, dining table and chairs.

jadalny *a.* **1.** (*który można jeść bezpiecznie*) edible; **grzyby jadalne** edible mushrooms. **2.** *pot.* (= *smaczny*) eatable. **3.** (*w którym się je*) dining; **pokój jadalny** (*także* **jadalny**) (= *jadalnia*) dining room; **sala jadalna** dining hall.

jadę *itd. ipf. zob.* **jechać**.

jadł *itd. ipf. zob.* **jeść**.

jadło *n.* (= *jedzenie*) *form.* food, edibles, nourishment, victual.

jadłodajnia *f. Gen.pl.* **-i** *l.* **-ń** (= *stołówka*) cafeteria, commissary; (= *bar*) eatery.

jadłospis *mi kulin.* menu.

jadłowstręt *mi pat.* anorexia (nervosa), sitophobia.

jadowitość *f.* (*zwierzęcia l. przen.*) venomousness, poisonousness; (*toksyny*) virulence.

jadowity *a.* (*t. przen.*) venomous, poisonous; (*o toksynie*) virulent; **szalej jadowity** *bot.* water hemlock, cowbane (*Cicuta virosa*).

jadowy *a. anat., zool.* (*wydzielający jad*) venomous, poisonous; **gruczoł jadowy** venom gland, venomous gland; **kolec jadowy** poisonous spine; (*u dzioba*) poison spur; **ząb jadowy** (venom) fang, venomous fang.

jagielloński *a. gł. hist.* Jagiellonian; **Uniwersytet Jagielloński** *uniw.* the Jagiellonian University (*in Kraków*).

jaglany *a.* millet; **kasza jaglana** *kulin.* millet (seed).

jagnić się *ipf. wet.* (*o owcy*) lamb (down).

jagnię *n.* **-nięci-** *pl.* **-niąt-** *Gen.* **-ąt** lamb; **potulny jak jagnię** (as) meek as a lamb.

jagnięcy *a. zool., kulin.* lamb; **kotlet jagnięcy** lamb chop; **skóra jagnięca** lambskin; **wilk w jagnięcej skórze** *przen.* wolf in sheep's clothing.

jagoda *f. Gen.pl.* **-ód 1.** *bot.* (*typ owocu*) berry. **2.** (*także* **czarna jagoda**) *bot., kulin.* (*niektóre gatunki borówek*) blueberry, huckleberry (*Vaccinium*); whortleberry (*Vaccinium myrtillus*); **placek z jagodami** blueberry pie. **3.** (*pokrzyk*) **wilcza jagoda** deadly nightshade, belladonna (*Atropa belladonna*).

jagodowy *a.* blueberry; **dżem jagodowy** blueberry jam.

jagodówka *f. Gen.pl.* **-ek 1.** *anat.* (= *błona naczyniowa oka*) uvea. **2.** *przest., kulin.* (= *nalewka jagodowa*) blueberry vodka.

jagodzianka *f. Gen.pl.* **-ek** *gł. kulin.* **1.** (*ciastko*) blueberry muffin. **2.** (*zupa*) blueberry soup. **3. jagodzianka na kościach** *pot. żart.* rotgut (= *methylated spirit*).

jagódka *f. Gen.pl.* **-ek 1.** (= *czarna jagoda*) blueberry. **2.** (*owoc*) berry.

jaguar *ma zool.* jaguar (*Panthera onca*). – *mi Gen. i Acc.* **-a** *mot.* (*samochód*) Jaguar.

jaja *pl. Gen.pl.* **jaj 1.** *pl. of* **jajo. 2.** *pot. wulg.* (=*jądra*) balls, nuts; **kopnąć kogoś w jaja** kick sb in the balls *l.* nuts. **3.** *pot. obsc.* (= *odwaga*) balls, spunk; **z jajami** ballsy, spunky; **bez jaj** weedy; **facet** *l.* **gość bez jaj** chickenshit; **mieć jaja** have balls; **nie mieć jaj** have no balls. **4.** *pot. czas. obsc.* (= *żarty*) **robić coś dla jaj** do sth for kicks; **bez jaj!** no shit!; **robić sobie z kogoś/czegoś jaja** take the piss out of sb/sth; **jaja sobie ze mnie robisz?** are you shitting me? **5.** *pot.* (= *przeboje, perypetie*) pisser; **ale/niezłe jaja!** what a pisser!

jajcarski *a. sl.* (= *śmieszny, zwariowany*) wacky.

jajcarz *mp*, **jajcara** *f. sl.* (= *zabawna osoba*) artist, joker.

jajczarka *f. Gen.pl.* **-ek**, **jajczarz** *mp roln.* egg farmer, egg producer.

jajczarski *a. roln.* egg; **przemysł jajczarski** the egg industry; **ferma jajczarska** egg farm.

jajczarstwo *n. roln.* egg farming, egg production.

jajeczko *n. Gen.pl.* **-czek 1.** *biol.* (= *żeńska komórka rozrodcza*) ovum. **2.** *dimin.* (= *jajko*) egg. **3.** (= *przedmiot w kształcie jajka*) egg. **4. jajeczko częściowo nieświeże** *żart.* curate's egg.

jajeczkować *ipf. fizj.* ovulate.

jajeczkowanie *n. fizj.* ovulation.

jajecznica *f. kulin.* scrambled eggs; **jajecznica na boczku** bacon and eggs.

jajeczny *a. kulin.* egg; **proszek jajeczny** egg powder.

jajko *n. Gen.pl.* **-ek 1.** *kulin.* egg; **jajko na miękko/twardo** soft-boiled/hard-boiled egg; **jajka sadzone** eggs sunny-side up, fried eggs; **jajka na boczku** bacon and eggs; **jajko wielkanocne** Easter egg. **2.** *orn., zool.* = **jajo** 2. **3.** *biol.* (= *żeńska komórka rozrodcza*) = **jajo** 3. **4.** (= *przedmiot l. figura w kształcie jajka*) egg, oval. **5.** (*w zwrotach*) **jajko Kolumba** the obvious solution; **kura znosząca złote jajka** the goose that lays the golden egg; **obchodzić się z kimś/czymś jak z jajkiem** handle *l.* treat sb/sth with kid gloves.

jajnik *mi Gen.* **-a** *anat.* ovary.

jajnikowy *a. anat.* ovarian.

jajo *n.* **1.** = **jajko** 1, 4, 5. **2.** *orn., zool.* egg; **jajo ptasie/ptaka** bird/bird's egg; **jajo gada** reptile egg; **jajo węża** snake's egg; **wysiadywać jaja** (*także* **siedzieć na jajach**) *orn.* brood; **znosić jaja** lay eggs. **3.** *biol.* (= *żeńska komórka rozrodcza*) ovum. **4.** *pot. obsc. zob.* **jaja.**

jajogłowy *mp pog.* (= *intelektualista*) egghead. – *a.* (*o głowie w kształcie jajka*) eggheaded.

jajorodność *f. biol., zool.* oviparity.

jajorodny *a. biol., zool.* oviparous.

jajowaty *a.* (*o kształcie jaja*) egg-shaped.

jajownik *mi Gen.* **-a** *bud., sztuka* egg-and-dart.

jajowód *mi* **-o-** *anat.* Fallopian tube.

jajowy *a. biol.* ovarian.

jajożyworodność *f. zool.* ovoviviparity.

jajożyworodny *a. zool.* ovoviviparous.

jak¹ *adv. i conj.* **1.** (*w pytaniach*) how; **jak dawno?** how long ago?; **jak daleko?** how far?; **jak długo?** how long?; **jak mu tam?** what was his name?, what's his name?; **jak ona wygląda?** what does she look like?; **jak się czujesz?** how are you feeling; **jak to?** how so?, how do you mean? **2.** (*w pytaniach o instrukcje*) how do I..., how does one...; **jak dojść do dworca?** how do I get to the station?; **jak po niemiecku powiedzieć „dziękuję”?** how do you say "thank you" in German?; **jak się robi bigos?** how do you make bigos?; **jak to włączyć?** how do you turn this thing on?; **jak jej o czymś takim powiedzieć?** how does/ should one tell her about something like this? **3.** (*w zdaniach podrzędnych*) how, as; **wiem, jak to działa** I know how this works; **jest (akurat) takie, jak lubisz** it's just the way you like it; **nie wiem, jak wam podziękować** I don't know how I can (ever) thank you. **4.** (*w wykrzyknieniach*) how; **jak tu cicho!** how quiet (this place is)!; **jak pięknie śpiewasz!** how beautifully you sing!, what a great singer you are! **5.** (= *kiedy, w chwili gdy*) when; **dam ci znać, jak przyjdzie/zadzwoni** I'll let you know when she comes/calls; **jak tylko...** as soon as..., directly... **6.** (= *jeśli*) if; **jak nie** if not, unless; **jak nie przestaniesz, (to)...** if you don't stop..., unless you stop...; **kto, jak nie ja/ty/my/on/ona** who, if not me/you/us/him/her; **jak nie teraz, to kiedy?** if not now, when? **7.** (= *dopóki*) as long as; **jak świat światem** as long as the world keeps turning; **jak żyję, nie widziałem czegoś takiego** I've never seen **brzydki jak noc** (as) ugly as sin, butt ugly; **(niezłe) jak na niego** (not bad) for him; **zimny jak lód** (as) cold as ice; **serce jak kamień** heart of stone. **9.** (= *dokąd*) as far as; **jak okiem sięgnąć** as far as the eye can see. **10.** (*z przymiotnikiem l. przysłówkiem w stopniu najwyższym*) as... as possible; **jak najprędzej/najszybciej/najlepiej** as soon/fast/well as possible; **jak najwięcej** (*z rzeczownikiem w liczbie pojedynczej*) as much as possible; (*z rzeczownikiem w liczbie mnogiej*) as many as possible. **11. jak gdyby** as if, as though, like; **patrzył tylko, jak gdyby nie rozumiał** he just stared as if he didn't understand. **12. jak i** (*także* **jak również**) as well as; and also. **13. byle jak** (= *niestarannie*) crudely, anything like it. **8.** (*przy porównaniach*) as, for; any old way, any which way; (= *słabo, źle*) badly, poorly. **14.** (*w innych zwrotach*) **czuć się jak u siebie w domu** feel at home; **jak amen w pacierzu** sure as death; **jak Boga kocham!** I swear to God!, honest to God!; **jak cię widzą, tak cię piszą** fine feathers make fine birds; **jak jeden mąż** as one (man); with one accord; **(wszystko) idzie jak z**

płatka everything is coming up roses; **jak po maśle** smoothly; **nie ma jak w domu** (there's) no place like home; home sweet home; **tak jak zawsze** same as usual.

jak² *ma zool.* yak (*Bos grunniens*).

jakby *conj. i adv.* **1.** (*także* **tak jakby**) (= *niby*) as if, as though, like; **jakby nigdy nic** as if nothing happened; **skakał, jakby zwariował** he was jumping like (he was) crazy. **2.** (= *w rodzaju*) sort of, kind of; **czuła się jakby dziwnie** she felt sort *l.* kind of funny; **coś jakby** something like, sort of (like); **to było coś jakby rurka** it was sort of (like) a pipe. **3.** (= *jeżeliby*) if; **jakby ktoś przyszedł/dzwonił** if anybody comes/calls.

jaki *a. i conj.* **1.** (*tożsamość, t. w zdaniach podrzędnych*) what, which; **jaka książka?** what book?; **jakim prawem?** by what right?; **wiesz, na jakiej półkuli leży Australia?** do you know which hemisphere Australia is in? **2.** (*cechy, t. w zdaniach podrzędnych*) what... like; **jaki on jest?** what is *l.* what's he like?; **jaka tam jest pogoda?** what is *l.* what's the weather like over there?; **nie wiem, jaki jest ten film** I don't know what this movie is like. **3.** (*zdziwienie z zaprzeczeniem*) **jakie pieniądze?** what money, who said anything about money? **4.** (*w wykrzyknieniach*) (*z rzeczownikiem policzalnym w liczbie pojedynczej*) what a; (*z rzeczownikiem niepoliczalnym l. policzalnym w liczbie mnogiej*) what; (*z przymiotnikiem*) how; **jaki miły piesek!** what a nice doggie!; **jaka ładna pogoda!** what nice weather!; **jaka ona jest miła!** how nice she is! **5.** (*wyraża lekceważenie*) **jaki tam z niego specjalista** some expert!, he's not much of an expert. **6. byle jaki** (= *kiepski*) crummy, tacky, poor; (= *dowolny*) any; **nie byle jaki...** not just your ordinary..., some...; **coś jest nie byle jakie** sth is really something. **7.** (*w innych zwrotach*) **jaki taki** so-so; **jaki pan, taki kram** like master, like man; **po jakiemu on mówi?** what language is he speaking?; **po jaką cholerę...?** (*także* **po jakie licho...?**) why the hell...?

jakieś *a. indecl.* (= *około*) some, around; **to będzie kosztowało jakieś pięćset dolarów** that'll cost some *l.* around 500 dollars.

jakikolwiek *a. i pron.* **jaki-** *decl. like a.* **-kolwiek** *indecl.* any, a; **potrzebny mi jest jakikolwiek samochód** I need any car *l.* a car; **może być jakikolwiek** any (one) will do.

jaki- *decl. like a.,* **-ś** *indecl.* (= *dowolny, nieważne jaki*) (*w zdaniach twierdzących*) some, a; (*w zdaniach pytających*) any; **tam jest jakaś tabliczka** there's some sign *l.* a sign over there; **masz jakiś pomysł?** do you have any ideas?; **jakiś tam** some.

jaki- *decl. like a.,* **-ż** *indecl.* what; **jakaż przyszłość nas czeka?** what does the future hold in store for us?

jakkolwiek *adv.* (= *obojętnie jak*) no matter how, however; **jakkolwiek to zrobisz, będzie zadowolona** no matter how you do it, she'll be happy; **jakkolwiek głupie to się może wydawać** however stupid that may seem, stupid as it may seem. – *conj.* (= *chociaż, mimo że*) although; **jak-**kolwiek **zrobiliśmy wszystko, co mogliśmy, (to)...** although we did everything in our power,...

jako *conj.* **1.** (= *jak*) as; **jako dziecko** (= *w dzieciństwie*) as a child; **mówię do ciebie jako twój ojciec** I am speaking to you as your father. **2. jako że** (= *ponieważ*) since, as; **jako tako** (= *przeciętnie*) so-so; **jako żywo** *lit.* (= *naprawdę*) upon my life.

jakobin *mp hist., polit.* Jacobin.

jakobinizm *mi hist.* Jacobinism.

jakobinka *f. bot., ogr.* (= *cynia*) zinnia (*Zinnia*).

jakobiński *a. hist.* Jacobin.

jakoby *conj.* **1.** (= *że ponoć*) **mówiono, jakoby zamierzał wyjechać** they said he was about to leave; **zaprzecza, jakoby go widziała** she denies ever having seen him. **2.** (= *rzekomo, podobno*) supposedly, professedly; **rzeczy, które jakoby miały się zdarzyć** things that supposedly happened. **3.** *przest.* (= *tak jakby*) as though, as if.

jakoś *adv.* (= *w jakiś sposób*) somehow (or other); **jakoś to będzie** (*także* **jakoś sobie poradzimy**) we'll manage (it somehow); **jakoś nie umiałam się z nim dogadać** somehow we didn't get along; **jakoś się trzymam** still surviving; **jakoś tak** something like this; **... czy jakoś tak ...** or something.

jakościowo *adv.* **1.** (= *jeśli chodzi o jakość*) quantity-wise; **dobry jakościowo** good/high-quality, quality; **zły jakościowo** poor-quality. **2.** *form.* (= *nie ilościowo*) qualitatively.

jakościowy *a.* **1. różnica jakościowa** a difference in kind. **2.** *form.* (= *nie ilościowy*) qualitative; **analiza jakościowa** *chem.* qualitative analysis.

jakość *f.* **1.** *t. handl.* quality; **gwarancja jakości** *handl.* quality assurance, guaranty; **jakość życia** *med., socjol.* quality of life; **wysokiej/niskiej jakości** high/low-quality; **towary dobrej jakości** *handl.* high-quality goods, quality goods; **produkt wysokiej jakości** *handl.* quality product; **złej jakości** poor-quality. **2.** *handl.* (= *sort*) grade.

jakoż *conj. przest.* and indeed.

jaksztag *mi żegl.* jackstay.

jakubka *f. Gen.pl.* **-ek** *żegl.* Jacob's ladder.

jakże *adv. i int. emf. zwł. lit.* how, however; **jakże to?** how so?; **jakże tak można?** how could you (do that)?; **jakże się cieszę, że cię widzę!** how happy I am to see you!; **a jakże!** of course!, certainly!, by all means!

jakżeby *adv.* (*wyraża oczekiwanie*) *emf., zwł. lit.* how; **jakżeby inaczej?** how else?

jakżeż *adv. i int.* **1.** *emf., zwł. lit.* however, how. **2.** (*także* **jakżeż to?**) how so?

jałmużna *f. gł. uj.* (= *pomoc biednym*) alms, charity; (= *datek*) handout; **wyciągać rękę po jałmużnę** (= *prosić się, żebrać*) hold out one's hand.

jałmużnik *mp przest.* **1.** (= *dający jałmużnę*) almoner. **2.** (= *żebrak*) almsman.

jałowcowy *a. bot.* juniper; **kiełbasa jałowcowa** *kulin.* juniper-smoked sausage; **olejek jałowcowy** juniper oil; **wódka jałowcowa** gin.

jałowcówka *f.* (= *wódka*) gin.

jałowiec *mi* **-wc-** *Gen.* **-a** *bot.* juniper (*Juniperus*).

jałowieć *ipf. roln., ekol.* (*o glebie*) become impoverished.

jałowizna *f. roln.* **1.** (= *młode bydło*) calves, young cattle. **2.** (= *nieużytek*) idle land, barren field, wasteland.

jałowość *f. t. roln., pat.* sterility.

jałowy *a.* (*o glebie, osobniku, dyskusji, narzędziach*) sterile; (*o dyskusji, silniku*) idle; (*o posiłku*) bland; **bieg jałowy** *mot.* neutral.

jałówka *f. Gen.pl.* **-ek** *roln.* (= *młoda krowa*) heifer.

jama *f.* **1.** (= *dół, dziura*) pit, hole. **2.** (= *nora*) burrow, hole. **3.** (= *pieczara*) cave, cavern; **Smocza Jama** *geogr.* Dragon's Cave (*in Kraków*). **4.** *anat.* cavity; **jama ustna/nosowa/brzuszna** oral/ nasal/abdominal cavity; **jama gardłowa** pharynx. **5.** *metal.* (*w odlewie*) pipe. **6.** *pot.* (= *kryjówka*) den.

Jamajczyk *mp*, **Jamajka** *f. Gen.pl.* **-ek** Jamaican.

Jamajka *f. geogr., polit.* Jamaica.

jamajka *f.* (*rum*) Jamaica rum.

jamajski *a. geogr., polit.* Jamaican; **dolar jamajski** *fin.* Jamaica dollar.

jamb *mi wers.* iamb.

jambiczny *a. wers.* iambic.

jamboree *n. indecl.* (*zlot, koncert*) (*zlot harcerski*) jamboree.

jamisty *a. anat.* cavernous; **ciało jamiste** (*w penisie, łechtaczce*) corpus cavernosum, cavernous body.

jamkowaty *a. anat.* lacunar.

jamnik *ma kynol.* dachshund. – *mi Gen. i Acc.* **-a** *pot.* **1.** (*radio, magnetofon*) boombox. **2.** (*torba sportowa*) gym bag.

jamochłon *ma zool.* coelenterate.

jams *mi bot.* yam (*Dioscorea*).

jam session *f. indecl. muz.* jam session.

janczar *mp pl.* **-owie** *l.* **-rzy** *hist.* janissary, janizary.

janczary *pl. Gen.* **-ów** *dial. l. hist.* (= *dzwonki*) bells.

Jankes *mp hist.* Yankee.

jankes *mp zw. pog.* (= *Amerykanin*) Yankee.

jankeski *a. hist.* Yankee.

janowiec *mi* **-wc-** *Gen.* **-a** **1.** *bot.* broom, genista (*Genista*); **janowiec barwierski** dyer's greenweed, woodwaxen (*Genista tinctoria*). **2.** *przest., tk.* greenweed.

jansenista *mp*, **jansenistka** *f. Gen.pl.* **-ek** *rel.* Jansenist.

jansenistyczny *a. rel.* Jansenistic.

jansenizm *mi rel.* Jansenism.

jantar *mi lit., min.* (= *bursztyn*) amber.

jantarowy *a. lit.* (= *bursztynowy*) amber; **szlak jantarowy** *hist.* the Amber Route.

japa *f. sl., zwł. pog.* (= *usta*) yap, kisser, trap.

Japonia *f. Gen.* **-ii** *geogr., polit.* Japan.

Japoniec *mp* **-ńc-** *Voc.* **-cze** *l.* **-cu** *pl.* **-y** *l.* **-e** *obelż.* (= *Japończyk*) Jap, Nip.

japonista *mp*, **japonistka** *f. Gen.pl.* **-ek** scholar in Japanese studies, expert on Japanese.

japonistyka *f. uniw.* (= *filologia japońska*) Japanese studies.

japonizm *mi jęz.* Japanese borrowing *l.* loan.

Japonka *f. Gen.pl.* **-ek** *zob.* **Japończyk**.

japonki *pl. Gen.* **-ek** *pot.* (= *klapki*) thongs, flipflops.

japonolog *mp pl.* **-owie** *l.* **-dzy** = **japonista**.

japonologia *f. Gen.* **-ii** = **japonistyka**.

Japończyk *mp* Japanese.

japoński *a.* Japanese; **język japoński** *jęz.* Japanese; **ogród japoński** *ogr.* Japanese garden; **pismo japońskie** *jęz.* the Japanese writing system.

japońskość *f.* the Japanese character, being Japanese.

japońszczyzna *f.* Japanese art *l.* objects.

jar *mi geogr.* (= *wąwóz*) ravine, gulch, gorge.

jarać *ipf. sl.* (= *palić*) drag, smoke. ~ **się** *ipf. sl.* burn.

jard *mi Gen.* **-a** *l.* **-u** (*jednostka długości*) yard.

jareccy *pl. Gen.* **-ckich** *sl., żart.* (= *rodzice*) the (old) folks.

jarecka *f. decl. like a. sl., żart.* (= *mama*) the old lady.

jarecki *mp decl. like a. pot. żart.* (= *tata*) the old man, pops.

jarmarczność *f. uj.* (= *kiczowatość*) trashiness.

jarmarczny *a.* **1.** *uj.* (= *kiczowaty*) trashy; **literatura jarmarczna** trash. **2.** (= *targowy*) fair, market.

jarmark *mi* fair.

jarmułka *f.* (= *mycka*) yarmulke, yarmulka.

jarmuż *mi bot., kulin.* collard, kale (*Brassica oleracea acephala*).

jarosz *mp*, **jaroszka** *f. Gen.pl.* **-ów** *l.* **-y** (= *wegetarianin*) vegetarian; (= *półwegetarianin*) demi-vegetarian, demi-veg.

jarski *a. kulin.* (= *bezmięsny*) vegetarian.

jary *a.* **1.** *roln.* spring; **zboże jare** spring crop. **2.** *przest.* (= *krzepki*) sprightly; **stary, ale jary** there's life in the old dog yet.

jarząb *mi Gen.* **-ębu** *l.* **-ąba** *Loc.* **-ąbie** *l.* **-ębiu** *pl.* **-ąby** *l.* **-ębie** *bot.* (= *jarzębina*) mountain ash, rowan (tree) (*Sorbus*).

jarząbek *ma* **-bk-** *orn.* hazel grouse, hazelhen (*Tetrastes bonasia*); (*samiec*) hazelcock.

jarzeniowy *a. fiz., el.* glow; *pot.* fluorescent; **lampa jarzeniowa** *el.* glow lamp.

jarzeniówka *f. Gen.pl.* **-ek** *el.* glow lamp; *pot.* (= *świetlówka*) fluorescent tube.

jarzębiak *mi* (*wódka*) rowan(berry) vodka.

jarzębina *f. bot.* **1.** (*owoc*) rowan, rowanberry. **2.** (*drzewo*) (European) mountain ash, rowan (tree) (*Sorbus aucuparia*).

jarzębinowy *a.* rowan, rowanberry.

jarzmo *n. Gen.pl.* **-rzm** *l.* **-rzem** *t. roln., mech., techn.* yoke; **jarzmo małżeńskie** *lit.* the yoke of marriage; **zrzucić jarzmo (niewolnictwa)** *lit.* cast/ throw off the yoke (of slavery).

jarzmowy *a.* **1.** *mech.* (= *spajający*) yoke, linking. **2.** *anat.* malar, jugular; **kość jarzmowa** malar *l.* jugular bone. **3.** **łuk jarzmowy** *bud.* transverse arch.

jarzyć się *ipf.* glow.

jarzyna *f. kulin.* vegetable.

jarzynka *f. kulin.* veg, veggie.

jarzynowy *a. zwł. kulin.* vegetable; **sałatka/zupa jarzynowa** *kulin.* vegetable salad/soup.

jasełka *pl. Gen.* -łek *rz.-kat.* (*przedstawienie*) nativity play; (= *szopka*) nativity scene.

jasiek¹ *mi* -śk- *Gen.* -a (= *poduszeczka*) throw pillow; *Br.* scatter cushion.

jasiek² *mi* -śk- *Gen.* -a *kulin.* (= *duża fasola*) butter bean.

jasieniec *mi* -ńc- *Gen.* -a *bot.* sheep's bit (*Jasione*).

jaskier *mi* -kr- *Gen.* -u *l.* -a *bot.* buttercup, crowfoot (*Ranunculus*).

jaskinia *f.* **1.** *t. geol.* (= *grota*) cave; *geol., sport* pothole. **2.** (= *kryjówka*) den. **3. jaskinia lwa** *zwł. przen.* lion's den; **jaskinia zła/rozpusty** *przen.* seat of evil/vice.

jaskiniowiec *mp* -wc- *Voc.* -cze *l.* -cu *pl.* -y (*t. pot.* = *brutal, prymityw*) caveman; *paleont.* cave dweller, troglodyte.

jaskiniowy *a.* cave; **człowiek jaskiniowy** *paleont.* cave dweller, troglodyte; **malarstwo** *l.* malowidło jaskiniowe *sztuka* cave painting.

jaskółczy *a.* **1.** *orn.* swallow's, swallow; **jaskółcze gniazdo** swallow's nest. **2. jaskółcze ziele** *bot.* swallowwort, celandine (*Chelidonium maius*).

jaskółka *f. Gen.pl.* -ek **1.** *orn.* swallow; **jaskółka brzegówka** bank swallow, sand martin (*Riparia riparia*); **jaskółka dymówka** barn/chimney swallow (*Hirundo rustica*); **jaskółka oknówka** house martin (*Delichon urbica*); **pierwsza jaskółka** *przen.* (= *zwiastun*) harbinger; **jedna jaskółka wiosny nie czyni** (*przysłowie*) one swallow does not make a summer. **2.** *teatr, przest. l. żart.* (= *balkon*) the gods, family circle. **3.** *pot.* (= *frak*) tails. **4.** *sport* (*skok do wody*) swan dive; *Br.* swallow dive. **5.** *sport* (*figura w gimnastyce, łyżwiarstwie*) arabesque.

jaskra *f. med.* glaucoma.

jaskrawić się *ipf. lit.* glitter, shimmer.

jaskrawo *adv.* (= *jasno, rażąco*) glaringly; (= *pstrokato*) garishly.

jaskrawość *f.* (= *oczywistość*) flagrancy; (= *jasność*) glare; (= *pstrokatość*) garishness.

jaskrawy *a.* **1.** *gł. uj.* (= *jasny*) glaring, bright; (= *pstry*) garish. **2.** *uj.* (= *rażący*) glaring, flagrant.

jasne *n. decl. like a. pot.* (= *piwo jasne*) lager; (= *kufel piwa*) pint; **jedno jasne!** I'll have a lager!; one pint, please. – *int. pot.* sure (thing)! – *a. zob.* jasny.

jasno *adv.* jaśniej **1.** (= *widno*) brightly; **jasno świecić** shine brightly. **2.** (= *zrozumiale, wyraźnie*) clearly; **jasno jak na dłoni** crystal-clear; **jasno się wyrażać** make o.s. clear.

jasnobeżowy *a.* light beige, putty, stone, buff.

jasnobrązowy *a.* light brown, walnut, biscuit.

jasnoczerwony *a.* light red, vermillion, scarlet.

jasnofioletowy *a.* pale purple, lavender, lilac, mauve.

jasnogórski *a. rz.-kat,* Jasna Góra (*referring to a celebrated monastery in Częstochowa, Poland*); **jasnogórskie sanktuarium** the shrine of

Jasna Góra; **Jasnogórska Pani** (= *Matka Boska*) (our) Lady of Jasna Góra; (*obraz*) the Black Madonna (of Jasna Góra).

jasnoniebieski *a.* light blue, baby blue.

jasność *f.* **1.** (*światła, koloru, pomieszczenia, głosu*) brightness; (*światła*) brilliance. **2.** (= *zrozumiałość*) clarity, clearness; **jasność umysłu** clarity of mind. **3.** *astron., fiz.* luminosity. **4.** jasność obiektywu *fot.* lens speed.

jasnota *f. bot.* dead nettle (*Lamium*).

jasnowidz *mp,* jasnowidzka *f. Gen.pl.* -ek psychic, clairvoyant, seer.

jasnowidzący *a.* psychic, clairvoyant.

jasnowidzenie *n.* psychic powers, clairvoyance.

jasnowłosy *a.* fair-haired; (*o mężczyźnie*) blond; (*o kobiecie*) blonde.

jasnozielony *a.* light green, jade (green), lime (green), apple green, moss green.

jasnożółty *a.* light yellow, wheat.

jasny *a.* jaśniejszy **1.** (= *świecący, mocno oświetlony*) bright; (= *jaskrawy*) brilliant; **jasne światło** bright/brilliant light; **jasny dzień** bright day; (= *pełne światło dzienne*) full daylight; **jasna noc** bright night. **2.** (*o kolorze, odcieniu*) light; (*o włosach*) fair. **3.** (= *zrozumiały, wyraźny, prosty*) clear; **jasny dowód** clear evidence; **jasny cel** clear goal; **jasne jak słońce** clear as daylight; **rzecz jasna,...** of course,... **4.** *przen.* (= *szczęśliwy*) bright; **jasna przyszłość** bright future. **5.** (*o głosie*) bright. **6.** (*w zwrotach*) **jak grom z jasnego nieba** like a bolt from/out of the blue; **jasna cholera!** *pot.* holy shit!; **Jasna Góra** *geogr., rz.-kat.* Jasna Góra (*RC monastery in Częstochowa, Poland*); **jasna sprawa!** sure (thing)!; **do jasnej (ciasnej)!** (*także* **jasny gwint!**) *pot. euf.* holy cow!; **jasne piwo** light beer, lager.

jaspis *mi min.* jasper.

jaspisowy *a.* jasper.

jastrząb *ma* -ębi- *orn. t. przen.* hawk (*Accipiter*).

jastrzębi *a.* hawkish; **jastrzębi nos** hawk nose, hooknose; **jastrzębi wzrok** hawkeye.

jastrzębiec *mi* -bc- *Gen.* -a *bot.* hawkweed (*Hieracium*).

jasyr *mi hist.* (= *niewola*) (Turkish) captivity; **brać w jasyr** capture.

jaszczur *ma Gen.* -a *paleont.* saurian; *pot.* (= *dinozaur*) dinosaur; *zool., mit., her.* (= *salamandra*) salamander. – *mi Gen.* -u *bibl.* (= *skóra do oprawy*) roan.

jaszczurczy *a.* **1.** *paleont.* saurian. **2.** *przen.* (= *podstępny*) reptilian.

jaszczurka *f. Gen.pl.* -ek *zool.* lizard.

jaśmin *mi bot.* jasmine (*Jasminum*); *pot.* = jaśminowiec.

jaśminowiec *mi* -wc- *Gen.* -a *bot.* mock orange, syringa (*Philadelphus*).

jaśminowy *a.* jasmine; **herbata jaśminowa** jasmine tea.

jaśnie *int. i adv. przest.* **jaśnie Pani** her Ladyship; **jaśnie (wielmożny) Pan** his Lordship; *Voc.* **jaśnie Panie/Pani** my Lord/Lady.

jaśnieć *ipf.* **1.** (= *świecić, promienieć*) shine,

brighten; **jaśnieć radością** (*o twarzy*) light up with joy. **2.** (= *rozjaśniać się*) lighten. **3.** (= *blaknąć*) pale.

jaśniej *adv. zob.* **jasno.**

jaśniejszy *a. zob.* **jasny.**

jatka *f. Gen.pl.* **-ek 1.** (= *bijatyka*) free-for-all. **2.** (= *krwawy dramat*) carnage, butchery. **3.** *arch.* (= *sklep mięsny*) butcher's, butcher shop; (= *kram z mięsem, rzeźnia*) shambles.

jaw *mi* **wyjść na jaw** (*o faktach*) come to light, surface; **wyciągnąć coś na jaw** bring sth to light, expose sth.

Jawa *f. geogr.* Java.

jawa[1] *f. lit.* (= *rzeczywistość*) reality; **na jawie** for real; **sen na jawie** waking dream; **śnić na jawie** daydream; **czy to jawa, czy sen?** is this for real?

jawa[2] *f. mot.* Jawa (bike) (*motorcycle brand*).

Jawajczyk *mp*, **Jawajka** *f. Gen.pl.* **-ek** Javanese.

jawajka *f. Gen.pl.* **-ek** *teatr* (*lalka*) puppet.

jawajski *a. t. jęz.* Javanese.

jawić się *ipf. lit.* (= *ukazywać się, wydawać się*) appear.

jawnie *adv.* publicly, openly, in the open.

jawnogrzesznica *f. przest. l. rel., lit.* notorious sinner; (= *rozpustnica*) jezebel, harlot; (= *cudzołożnica*) adulteress.

jawnogrzesznik *mp przest. l. rel., lit.* notorious sinner; (= *rozpustnik, cudzołożnik*) adulterer.

jawność *f.* (= *otwartość*) openness; (= *szczerość*) frankness.

jawny *a.* **1.** (= *nieutajniony*) open; **jawne głosowanie** *parl., polit.* open vote. **2.** (= *wyraźny*) explicit; (= *szczery*) frank, undisguised. **3.** (= *bezczelny*) (*o kłamstwie*) barefaced, brazen.

jawor *mi bot., leśn., stol.* sycamore (*Acer pseudoplatanus*).

jaworowy *a. leśn., stol.* sycamore.

jaz *mi hydrol.* weir.

jazda[1] *f. Dat. i Loc.* **jeździe 1.** (*samochodem jako pasażer, autobusem, rowerem, pociągiem*) ride; (*samochodem jako kierowca*) drive; **jazda próbna** *mot.* test drive, road test. **2.** (= *droga, podróż*) trip, journey. **3.** *mot.* (= *lekcja prowadzenia samochodu*) driving lesson; (= *egzamin na prawo jazdy*) road test. **4.** *hist., wojsk.* cavalry, horse; **lekka/ciężka jazda** light/heavy cavalry. **5.** *sl.* (= *halucynacja narkotykowa*) trip. **6.** **jazda figurowa/szybka (na lodzie)** *sport* figure/speed skating; **jazda na łyżwach** *sport* ice-skating; **jazda na nartach** *sport* skiing; **jazda na rolkach** *sport* rollerblading; **jazda na wrotkach** *sport* skating; **jazda konna** *jeździ.* horse(back) riding; **prawo jazdy** *mot.* driver's license; **rozkład jazdy** timetable, schedule.

jazda[2] *int. pot. zwł. pog.* get out!, get lost!; **jazda (mi) stąd!** get the hell out of here!

jazgarz *ma Gen.pl.* **-y** *l.* **-ów** *icht., ryb.* pope, ruffe (*Acerina cernua*).

jazgot *mi* (= *hałas*) clamor; (= *gadanie*) cackle.

jazgotać *ipf.* **-czę** *l.* **-cę -czesz** *l.* **-cesz** (= *hałasować*) rattle; (= *gadać*) cackle.

jazgotliwy *a. uj.* **1.** (= *kłótliwy, krzykliwy*)

rumbustious. **2.** (*o głosie, dźwięku*) (= *ostry, przenikliwy*) shrill, grating.

jazz *mi muz.* (*także* **dżez**) jazz; **słuchać jazzu** listen to jazz; **grać jazz** play jazz; **jazz nowoczesny/tradycyjny** modern/classical jazz.

jazzman *mp muz.* jazzman.

jazzować *ipf. muz.* play jazz.

jazzowy *a.* jazz; **muzyka jazzowa** jazz (music); **zespół jazzowy** jazz band.

jaź *ma Gen.pl.* **-i** *l.* **-ów** *icht., ryb.* ide, orfe (*Leuciscus idus*).

jaźń *f. Gen.pl.* **-i** *psych.* ego; *fil.* self.

ją *pron.* (*o kobiecie, samicy*) her; (*o rzeczy, pojęciu*) it; *zob.* **ona.**

jąć *pf.* **jął jęła jęli** *arch. lit.* **1.** (= *zacząć*) **jąć robić coś** enter/embark upon sth. **2.** (= *chwycić*) seize, grasp. **~ się** *pf. gł. lit.* **jąć się czegoś** (= *zabrać się do czegoś*) engage in sth.

jąderko *n. Gen.pl.* **-rek 1.** *biol.* nucleolus. **2.** (= *ziarnko, pestka*) kernel.

jądro *n. Gen.pl.* **-der 1.** *anat.* testicle. **2.** (= *ziarno, pestka*) kernel. **3.** *przen.* (= *środek, istota, sedno*) core, heart. **4.** *astron.* (*komety, galaktyki*) nucleus; (*planety*) core; **jądro Ziemi** *l.* **ziemskie** Earth's core; *geol.* centrosphere, barosphere. **5.** *biol., fiz.* nucleus; **jądro atomowe** atomic nucleus; **jądro komórkowe** (cell) nucleus. **6.** *komp.* (*Linuksa*) kernel.

jądrowy *a. fiz., wojsk., biol.* nuclear; **bomba jądrowa** nuclear bomb; **broń jądrowa** nuclear arms/weapons; **energia jądrowa** nuclear energy; **fizyka jądrowa** nuclear physics; **elektrownia jądrowa** nuclear power plant.

jąkać się *ipf.* **1.** *pat.* (= *zacinać się*) stutter, stammer. **2.** (= *nie móc się wypowiedzieć*) falter.

jąkała *f. l. mp decl. like f. Gen.pl.* **-ł** *l.* **-ów** *pot.* stutterer, stammerer.

jątrzyć *ipf.* **1.** (= *drażnić, denerwować*) fester, rankle. **2.** *pat.* (= *utrudniać gojenie*) fester. **~ się** *ipf. t. pat.* (= *zaogniać się, ropieć*) fester.

je[1] *pron. zob.* **ona, ono.**

je[2] *ipf. zob.* **jeść.**

jebać *ipf.* **jebię jebiesz** *wulg. pot.* (= *mieć stosunek z*) fuck; **jebać to!** (= *do licha z tym!*) the fuck with that! **~ się** *ipf. wulg. pot.* **1.** (= *mieć stosunek*) fuck (*z kimś sb*). **2.** (= *certolić się*) fuck around (*z czymś* with sth). **3.** **jeb się!** *obelż.* (= *spadaj, odczep się*) go fuck yourself!

jebaka *mp pl.* **-i** *Gen.* **-ów** *wulg. sl.* (= *mężczyzna bardzo aktywny seksualnie*) ass-man, cunt-chaser; (= *mężczyzna jako obiekt seksualny*) stud, fuck.

jebanie *n. wulg. pot.* (= *stosunek*) fuck.

jebany *a. wulg. pot.* fucking; **kurwa jebana!** fucking shit!; **(o ty) w dupę jebany!** (you) fucking asshole!

jebnąć *pf.* **-ij** *wulg. pot.* **1.** (= *uderzyć*) whack, slam, bash. **2.** (= *rzucić*) chuck. **3.** (= *ukraść*) nip, lift, snatch. **4.** (= *rozbić się*) go bust, smash up. **5.** (= *rozlecieć się*) (*o gospodarce, kraju*) go tits/belly up, go bust. **~ się** *pf. wulg.* **1.** *pot.* (= *uderzyć się*) bang/smash o.s.; **jebnąć się w głowę/kolano (o coś)** bang/slam one's head/knee (against sth). **2.** *sl.* (= *pomylić się*) fuck up, goof up, slip up.

jebnięty *a. pot. wulg., obelż.* (= *głupi, pomylony*) fucked, screwed.

jechać *ipf.* **jadę jedziesz 1.** (= *udawać się*) go; (*samochodem jako kierowca*) drive; (*rowerem, konno*) ride; **jechać samochodem** (*jako kierowca*) drive; (*jako pasażer*) ride; **jechać rowerem** cycle, bike; **jechać pociągiem/autobusem** take the train/bus, go by train/bus; **jechać na koniu/konno** go on horseback, ride (*do... to...*). **2.** (= *przemieszczać się*) (*o osobie, pojeździe*) go, travel; (*o pojeździe*) move; **jechać na rowerze** ride a bicycle; **jechać autobusem** ride in a bus; **jechać pociągiem** ride on a train; **jechać na nartach** ski; **jechać na koniu/konno** ride a horse; **jechać na gapę** *pot.* beat one's way; (*w ukryciu w dużym pojeździe*) stow away. **3.** *pot.* (= *śmierdzieć*) stink; **czymś jedzie od kogoś** sb stinks of sth; **ale (tu) jedzie!** what a stink! **4. jechać (z kimś) na jednym wózku** *przen.* be in the same boat (as sb); **jechać do Rygi** *przest., przen., pot., euf.* (= *wymiotować*) lose one's lunch.

jeden *num. decl. like a. tylko sing.* **-dn- 1.** (= *1*) one, a, single; **jedna osoba** one person; **(bilet) w jedną stronę** one-way (ticket). **2.** (*w zwrotach*) **jeden na jeden** *l.* **na jednego** one on one; **jednym słowem** in a word, in sum; **jednym tchem** in the same breath; **słuchać jednym uchem** listen with half an ear; **skoczyć (dokądś) na jednej nodze** run (somewhere); **być jedną nogą w grobie** *l.* **na tamtym świecie** have one foot in the grave; **co dwie głowy, to nie jedna** two heads are better than one; **postawić wszystko na jedną kartę** put all one's eggs in one basket; **za jednym zamachem** at a/one blow, at one go, all in one go; **z jednej strony..., (ale) z drugiej strony...** on (the) one hand..., (but) on the other (hand)... – *a.* **-dn- 1.** (= *jakiś, pewien*) a, some, one; **(taki) jeden gość** some guy. **2.** (= *wspólny, łączny*) one, shared, common; **jedna łazienka** shared/common bathroom. **3.** (= *taki sam*) same; *zob.* **jedno** 1. – *mp decl. like a.* **-dn-** (= *ktoś*) one, someone; **co jeden, to lepszy** *iron.* any one (of them) is as bad as the other, they're all alike/the same; **jeden do drugiego** to each other, to one another, one to another; **jeden z drugim** *zwł. pog.* both of you/them; **jeden z wielu** one of many; **jeden za wszystkich, wszyscy za jednego** all for one and one for all; **siła złego na jednego** tough luck, it's rough luck on him. – *mi decl. like a.* **-dn-** *pot.* (= *kieliszek alkoholu*) shot; **wstąpić na jednego** stop in for a drink; **wypić jednego** have a shot, throw one down; **wypić po jednym** have a shot (each).

jedenasta *f. decl. like a.* (*godzina*) eleven; **jest za pięć jedenasta** it's five to eleven; **jest kwadrans po jedenastej** it's a quarter past/after eleven.

jedenastka *f. Gen.pl.* **-ek 1.** (*liczba l. coś o numerze 11*) eleven. **2.** *sport* (= *zespół*) eleven, team (of eleven). **3.** *piłka nożna* (= *rzut karny*) penalty (kick).

jedenastobok *mi geom.* hendecagon.
jedenastokąt *mi Gen.* **-a** *geom.* hendecagon.

jedenastolatek *mp* **-tk-** *pl.* **-i, jedenastolatka** *f. Gen.pl.* **-ek** eleven-year-old.

jedenastoletni *a.* (*o dziecku, samochodzie*) eleven-year-old; (*o okresie*) eleven-year, of eleven years.

jedenastozgłoskowiec *mi* **-wc-** *Gen.* **-a** *wers.* hendecasyllable.

jedenasty *a.* eleventh.

jedenaście *num.* **-st-** *Ins.* **-oma** *l.* **-u** (*liczba*) eleven.

jedenaścioro *num. decl. like n.* **-rg-** *Loc.* **-u** eleven.

jedli *itd. ipf. zob.* **jeść**.

jedlina *f. gł. arch. l. dial.* (= *jodła*) fir (tree); (*gałązki jodły*) fir branches; (= *zagajnik jodłowy*) fir grove.

jedna *num. i a.* **1.** *zob.* **jeden. 2.** *mat.* (*w ułamkach zwykłych*) one, a; **jedna dziesiąta/setna** (one) tenth/hundredth; **jedna druga/czwarta** (one) half/quarter.

jednać *ipf. lit.* **1.** (= *godzić*) reconcile. **2.** (= *zjednywać*) **jednać sobie kogoś** win sb for o.s. ~ **się** *ipf. lit.* **jednać się z kimś** (= *godzić się*) make (one's) peace with sb, become reconciled with sb; (*łączyć się*) unite; **jednać się z Bogiem** *rel.* make peace with God.

jednak *conj.* **1.** (= *mimo to*) however, still, nevertheless; **nie był jednak zupełnie pewien** he wasn't, however, quite sure; **a jednak** anyway, still, all/just the same, (and) yet; **a jednak to zrobił** he did it anyway *l.* all the same; still, he did it; **a jednak się kręci!** (*powiedzenie przypisywane Galileuszowi*) and yet it does move! (*eppur si muove!*). **2.** (*także* **ale jednak**) but (still), though, yet; **był kolorowy, jednak nie do przesady** it was colorful, but not too colorful. **3.** (= *okazuje się, że*) it turns out (that); **jednak jest za duży** it turns out that it's too big, it turns out to be too big. **4. a jednak!** (= *a widzisz?*) see?, didn't I tell you?

jednaki *a. przest., lit.* = **jednakowy**.

jednako *adv. przest., lit.* = **jednakowo**.

jednakowo *adv.* **1.** (= *tak samo*) alike; **myśleć/wyglądać jednakowo** think/look alike. **2.** (= *(po) równo*) equally.

jednakowość *f.* **1.** (= *identyczność*) sameness. **2.** (= *podobieństwo*) uniformity.

jednakowy *a.* equal, identical, the same.

jednakże *conj. zwł. form.* **1.** (= *mimo to*) nevertheless, however, still, notwithstanding. **2.** (= *wszak*) yet, but.

jednia *f. Gen.pl.* **-ni** *lit.* (= *jedność, całość*) oneness, unity.

jedno *n. Gen.* **-ego 1.** (= *to samo*) same; **jedno i to samo** one and the same (thing); **na jedno wychodzi** it amounts to the same, no difference; **wszystko (mi) jedno** it's all the same (to me); who cares?; it's six of one and half a dozen of the other; **wszystko jedno kto/co/jak** *itd.* no matter who/what/how etc.; **jedno jest pewne** one thing is for sure; this much is certain. **2.** (= *coś*) one; **jedno z dwojga** one or the other. **3.** *form.* (= *jedność, całość*) oneness, unity; **łączyć w jedno** unite.

jednoaktowy *a. teatr* one-act.
jednoaktówka *f. Gen.pl.* **-ek** *teatr* one-act play.

jednobarwny a. monochrome; *opt., fiz.* monochromatic; **światło jednobarwne** *opt., fiz.* monochromatic light.

jednobiegunowy a. *el., fiz.* unipolar.

jednobrzmiący a. (*o wyroku, decyzji*) unanimous.

jednocyfrowy a. *mat.* single-digit; **numer jednocyfrowy** single-digit number; **jednocyfrowa inflacja** *ekon.* single-digit inflation.

jednocylindrowy a. *mot.* single-cylinder; **silnik jednocylindrowy** single-cylinder engine.

jednoczesność f. simultaneity, concurrence.

jednoczesny a. simultaneous, concurrent.

jednocześnie adv. **1.** (= *równocześnie*) simultaneously, concurrently. **2.** (= *także, również*) at the same time, simultaneously.

jednoczęściowy a. one-piece; **strój jednoczęściowy** swimsuit, one-piece suit.

jednoczyć *ipf.* (= *łączyć*) unite (*kogoś/coś z kimś/czymś* sb/sth with sb/sth, *wokół kogoś/czegoś* for sth). **~ się** *ipf.* (= *łączyć się*) unite.

jednodaniowy a. *kulin.* one-course, single-course; **jednodaniowy posiłek** one-course meal.

jednodniowy a. **1.** (= *trwający jeden dzień*) one-day; (= *mający jeden dzień*) one-day-old. **2.** *przen.* (= *krótkotrwały*) five-minute.

jednodniówka f. *Gen.pl.* **-ek 1.** *dzienn.* special issue. **2.** (*także* **jętka jednodniówka**) *ent.* dayfly, mayfly (*Ephemerida*).

jednofazowy a. *el.* single-phase; **prąd jednofazowy** single-phase current.

jednogarbny a. *zool.* (*o wielbłądzie*) one-humped; **wielbłąd jednogarbny** Arabian camel, dromedary (camel) (*Camelus dromedarius*).

jednogłosowość f. *muz.* monophony.

jednogłosowy a. *muz.* monophonic.

jednogłośnie adv. *zwł. polit.* unanimously.

jednogłośny a. *zwł. polit.* unanimous.

jednogodzinny a. one-hour, one-hour-long.

jednoimienny a. **1.** (*o jednym imieniu*) single-name. **2. ładunki jednoimienne** *el.* same-sign charges.

jednoizbowy a. *parl.* unicameral, single-house; **parlament jednoizbowy** unicameral parliament.

jednojajowy a. *biol.* **bliźnięta** *l.* **bliźniaki jednojajowe** identical twins.

jednojęzyczny a. monolingual.

jednokierunkowość f. **1.** *mot.* (*ulicy*) one-way traffic. **2.** *techn.* unidirectionality.

jednokierunkowy a. **1.** *mot.* one-way; **ulica jednokierunkowa** one-way street. **2.** *techn.* unidirectional.

jednokładność f. *geom.* homothety.

jednokładny a. *geom.* homothetic.

jednokolorowy a. same-color, monochrome, uniform (in color); *techn.* monochromatic.

jednokomórkowy a. *biol.* single-celled, one-celled, single-cell, one-cell, unicellular.

jednokonny a. (*o powozie, zaprzęgu*) one-horse.

jednokopytne pl. *Gen.* **-ych** *zool.* perissodactyls.

jednokopytny a. *zool.* single-hoofed.

jednokrotny a. **1.** (= *zdarzający się raz*) one-time, single, single-time. **2.** (= *mający jedną warstwę*) single.

jednokształtny a. *form.* uniform.

jednolatek *mp* **-tk-** *pl.* **-owie 1.** (*dziecko*) one-year-old. **2.** (= *rówieśnik*) contemporary, coeval, peer. – *ma* **-tk-** *pl.* **-i** *zool., myśl.* (= *zwierzę jednoroczne*) one-year-old.

jednoletni a. **1.** (= *mający jeden rok*) one-year-old. **2.** (= *trwający jeden rok*) one-year, one-year-long.

jednolistny a. *bot.* single-leaf, unifoliate, monophyllous.

jednoliścienne pl. *Gen.* **-ych** *bot.* monocotyledons.

jednolitość f. uniformity.

jednolity a. uniform.

jednomian *mi* *mat.* monomial.

jednomianowy a. *mat.* monomial.

jednomiesięczny a. **1.** (= *trwający jeden miesiąc*) one-month, one-month-long. **2.** (= *mający jeden miesiąc*) one-month-old.

jednominutowy a. one-minute, one-minute-long.

jednomyślnie adv. unanimously.

jednomyślność f. unanimity.

jednomyślny a. unanimous.

jednonasienny a. *bot.* monospermous.

jednonogi a. one-legged.

jednoobiektywowy a. *fot.* single-lens; **lustrzanka jednoobiektywowa** single-lens reflex (camera).

jednoocze n., **jednooczność** f. *pat., opt.* monocular vision.

jednooczny a. *opt.* monocular.

jednooki a. one-eyed.

jednoosobowy a. **1.** (*o kierownictwie, odpowiedzialności*) single-person, one-person, unipersonal. **2.** (*o pokoju, bilecie, kajaku*) single. **3.** *prawn.* **spółka jednoosobowa** sole proprietorship.

jednopalcowy a. **1.** *zool.* monodactylous. **2. rękawiczki jednopalcowe** mittens, mitts.

jednopartyjny a. *polit.* single-party; **system jednopartyjny** single-party system.

jednopiętrowy a. *bud.* (= *dwukondygnacyjny*) two-storied.

jednopłaszczyznowy a. *geom.* single-plane.

jednopłat *mi* *Gen.* **-a** *lotn.* monoplane.

jednopłatowiec *mi* **-wc-** *Gen.* **-a** *lotn.* monoplane.

jednopłciowy a. *biol.* unisexual.

jednopokojowy a. one-room, single-room; **mieszkanie jednopokojowe** one-room apartment, efficiency (apartment), studio (apartment).

jednopokoleniowy a. **rodzina jednopokoleniowa** *socjol.* nuclear family.

jednopręcikowy a. *bot.* monandrous.

jednorazowo adv. once.

jednorazowy a. **1.** (*także* **jednorazowego użytku**) disposable. **2.** (= *jednokrotny*) single, one-time, one-off.

jednorazówka f. *Gen.pl.* **-ek** *pot.* (= *chusteczka,* *kubek, strzykawka itp. jednorazowego użytku)* disposable.

jednoręki *a.* one-handed; **jednoręki bandyta** *(automat do gry)* one-armed bandit, fruit machine.

jednoroczny *a. ogr., bot.* annual; **roślina jednoroczna** annual.

jednorodność *f.* homogeneity, uniformity.

jednorodny *a.* homogeneous, uniform.

jednorodzinny *a.* single-family; **domek jednorodzinny** *bud.* detached house.

jednorożec *ma -żc- mit.* unicorn.

jednorurka *f. Gen.pl.* **-ek** *myśl.* (= *śrutówka)* shotgun; (= *broń palna jednolufowa)* single-barreled gun.

jednorzędowy *a.* **1.** single-row. **2.** *krawiectwo* single-breasted; **garnitur jednorzędowy** single-breasted suit; **marynarka jednorzędowa** single-breasted jacket.

jednorzędówka *f. Gen.pl.* **-ek** *pot. (marynarka)* single-breasted jacket; *(płaszcz)* single-breasted coat.

jednosilnikowy *a. lotn., techn.* single-engine.

jednosłupkowy *a. bot.* monogynous.

jednostajnie *adv.* **1.** *gł. uj.* (= *monotonnie)* monotonously. **2.** (= *równomiernie)* uniformly; **ruch jednostajnie przyspieszony/opóźniony** *mech.* uniformly accelerated/retarded motion.

jednostajność *f.* **1.** (= *monotonność)* monotony. **2.** (= *równomierność)* uniformity.

jednostajny *a.* **1.** *gł. uj.* (= *monotonny)* monotonous. **2.** (= *równomierny)* uniform; **ruch jednostajny** *mech.* uniform motion.

jednostka *f. Gen.pl.* **-ek** **1.** (= *moduł, sztuka, egzemplarz, oddział)* unit. **2.** (= *osoba)* individual; **kult jednostki** *polit., socjol.* personality cult. **3.** *(w pomiarach)* unit; **jednostka miary/masy/natężenia** unit of measure/mass/intensity; **jednostka pochodna** derived unit. **4.** *(także* **jednostka pływająca)** *żegl.* vessel. **5.** *fil.* entity. **6.** **jednostka badawcza** research unit; **jednostka monetarna** *fin.* currency unit, unit of currency; **jednostka wojskowa** military unit.

jednostkowość *f. form.* (= *niepowtarzalność)* individuality.

jednostkowy *a.* **1.** (= *liczony na jednostkę)* unit; **cena jednostkowa** *handl.* unit price; **koszt jednostkowy** *ekon.* unit cost. **2.** (= *sporadyczny)* isolated. **3.** (= *indywidualny, pojedynczy)* individual.

jednostopniowy *a. (o procesie)* one-stage, single-stage.

jednostronność *f.* **1.** (= *stronniczość)* one-sidedness. **2.** *(uznanie przez jedną ze stron)* unilaterality. **3.** *techn.* (= *jednokierunkowość)* unidirectionality.

jednostronny *a.* **1.** (= *dotyczący jednej strony)* *polit., anat., techn.* unilateral; **jednostronna deklaracja** unilateral declaration; **jednostronne zobowiązanie** *prawn.* unilateral deed, deed poll. **2.** *uj.* (= *stronniczy)* one-sided. **3.** **dźwignia jednostronna** *mech.* second-order *l.* second-kind lever. **4.** (= *dotyczący jednej powierzchni)* sin-

gle-sided; **kopia jednostronna** single-sided copy. **5.** (= *jednokierunkowy)* unidirectional.

jednosylabowy *a. jęz.* monosyllabic; **wyraz jednosylabowy** monosyllable.

jednoszynowy *a. kol.* single-rail, monorail; **kolej jednoszynowa** monorail.

jedność *f.* **1.** (= *spójność, zgoda)* unity; **w jedności siła** united we stand, divided we fall. **2.** (= *całość)* *fil.* oneness, wholeness; **stawać się jednością** become one. **3.** *teatr., teor.lit.* unity; **zasada trzech jedności** the three unities; **jedność akcji/czasu/miejsca** unity of action/time/place. **4.** *mat.* (= *1)* unity, unit.

jednoślad *mi* **1.** *mot.* one-track/single-track vehicle. **2.** *lit. l. żart.* (= *rower)* bicycle.

jednośladowiec *mi* **-wc-** *Gen.* **-a** *mot.* single-track vehicle.

jednośladowy *a. mot.* single-track; **pojazd jednośladowy** single-track vehicle.

jednotomowy *a. bibl.* single-volume.

jednotonowy *a.* **1.** *muz.* monotone. **2.** (= *ważący jedną tonę, przystosowany do ciężaru jednej tony)* one-ton.

jednotorowość *f.* (= *jednostronność)* narrowness, lack of breadth.

jednotorowy *a.* **1.** (= *jednostronny)* one-track. **2.** *kol.* one-track; **kolejka jednotorowa** one-track rail.

jednotygodniowy *a.* **1.** (= *trwający jeden tydzień)* one-week, one-week-long. **2.** (= *mający jeden tydzień)* one-week-old.

jednowarstwowy *a. techn.* single-layer.

jednowartościowy *a.* **1.** *chem. (o pierwiastku)* monovalent, univalent. **2.** *mat.* single-valued; **funkcja jednowartościowa** single-valued function.

jednowątkowy *a. komp., teor.lit., film* single-thread.

jednowymiarowy *a.* one-dimensional.

jednowyrazowy *a.* one-word.

jednozasadowy *a. chem.* monobasic.

jednozgłoskowy *a. jęz.* = **jednosylabowy**.

jednozłotowy *a. fin. (o monecie, opłacie)* one-zloty.

jednozmianowy *a.* single-shift; **praca jednozmianowa** single-shift system.

jednoznacznie *adv.* (= *wyraźnie)* explicitly, unambiguously.

jednoznaczność *f.* **1.** (= *wyrazistość)* explicitness, unambiguity, unequivocalness. **2.** *log.* equivalence of meaning, meaning equivalence, synonymy.

jednoznaczny *a.* **1.** (= *wyraźny, określony)* *(o sformułowaniu, prawie)* explicit, unambiguous; *(o rozróżnieniu, różnicy)* clear-cut. **2.** *log.* equivalent in meaning, synonymous.

jednożeństwo *n. form.* monogamy.

jednożyłowy *a. el.* single-core; **kabel jednożyłowy** single-core/single cable.

jedwab *mi* **-bi-** *Gen.pl.* **-i** *l.* **-ów** **1.** *tk.* silk; **jedwab naturalny** natural silk; **sztuczny jedwab** rayon, artificial silk. **2.** *przen.* (= *gładkość, połysk)* silkiness.

jedwabisty *a.* silky, silken.

jedwabnictwo *n. tk.* sericulture.

jedwabnik *ma ent., tk.* silkworm (*Bombyx mori*); (*także* **jedwabnik dębowy** *l.* **chiński**) tussah, tussore (*Antheraea paphia*).

jedwabny *a.* **1.** (*zrobiony z jedwabiu*) silk, silken. **2.** *tk.* (*związany z produkcją jedwabiu i handlem jedwabiem*) silk, sericultural; **szlak jedwabny** *hist.* the Silk Road *l.* Route. **3.** *przen.* (= *gładki, delikatny*) silken, silky; **jedwabne życie** life of luxury, dolce vita.

jedyna *f. decl. like a.* (= *ukochana*) sweetheart, love. – *a. zob.* **jedyny**.

jedynaczka *f. Gen.pl.* **-ek**, **jedynak** *mp* only child.

jedynie *adv.* **1.** (= *wyłącznie*) only; **mogę jedynie próbować** I can only try; **jedynie ty możesz mnie uratować** only you can save me, you alone can save me. **2.** (= *zaledwie*) merely; **był jedynie umiarkowanie szczęśliwy** he was merely moderately happy.

jedynka *f. Gen.pl.* **-ek 1.** (= *1, coś o numerze jeden*) (number) one. **2.** *szkoln.* F (*failing grade*); **dostać jedynkę** get an F. **3.** *dent.* front tooth. **4.** *mot., gł. pot.* (= *pierwszy bieg*) first (gear); **jechać na jedynce** drive in first; **wrzucić jedynkę** put it in first. **5.** *gł. pot.* (= *pokój jednoosobowy*) (*pomieszczenie dla jednej osoby*) single room. **6.** *gł. pot. sport* (*kajak, sanie, zaprzęg itp. dla jednego zawodnika*) single.

jedynowładca *mp polit., form.* monocrat.

jedynowładczy *a. polit., form.* monocratic.

jedynowładztwo *n. polit., form.* monocracy.

jedyny *a.* **1.** (= *jednostkowy*) only, one; **jeden jedyny** *emf.* one and only; **jedyny w swoim rodzaju** one of a kind, unique. **2.** (= *wyjątkowy*) special. – *mp decl. like a.* (= *ukochany*) sweetheart.

jedz *itd. ipf. zob.* **jeść**.

jedzenie *n.* **1.** (= *pokarm*) food; **jedzenie i picie** food and drink. **2.** (= *konsumpcja*) eating; **coś do jedzenia** something to eat; **apetyt rośnie w miarę jedzenia** the more you get the more you want.

jedzie *itd. ipf. zob.* **jechać**.

jeep *mi Acc. i Gen.* **jeepa** (*także* **dżip**) jeep; *pot.* (= *jakikolwiek samochód terenowy*) all-purpose automobile.

jego *pron. zob.* **on, ono**.

jegomość *mp Gen.* **-ci** *l.* **-cia** *pl.* **-cie** *l.* **-ciowie** *Gen.* **-ci** *l.* **-ciów 1.** *przest.* (= *pan, nieznajomy osobnik, szlachcic*) gentleman; *arch.* (= *pan domu*) host, master; **król Jegomość** His Majesty. **2.** *arch.* (= *ksiądz*) reverend.

Jehowa *mp rel.* Jehovah; **świadek Jehowy** = jehowita.

jehowita *mp*, **jehowitka** *f. Gen.pl.* **-ek** *rel.* Jehovah's Witness.

jej¹ *int.* **o jej!** gee!

jej² *pron. zob.* **ona**.

jejku *int.* **o jejku!** geeze!, gee whiz!

jejmość *f. pl.* **-e** *przest.* (= *pani, kobieta, szlachcianka*) lady; *arch.* (= *gospodyni*) goodwife, mistress (of the household); **królowa Jejmość** Her Majesty.

jelec¹ *mi* **-lc-** *Gen.* **-a** (= *garda*) guard, cross.

jelec² *ma* **-lc-** *icht.* dace (*Leuciscus leuciscus*).

jeleni *a.* cervine; (*o porożu*) deer; (*o mięsie*) venison; **jelenia szyja** (*u konia*) ewe-neck; **jelenie rogi** antlers, attire; *myśl.* head; *her.* attire.

jelenina *f.* venison.

jeleniowaty *a. zool.* cervid.

jeleń *ma* **1.** *zool.* deer (*Cervus*); (*samiec*) stag, hart; **jeleń bagienny** (*południowoamerykański*) marsh deer, swamp deer (*Blastocerus dichotomus*); **jeleń brazylijski** brocket (deer), forest deer (*Mazama*); **jeleń olbrzymi** *paleont.* Irish elk (*Megaloceros giganteus*); **jeleń szlachetny** red deer (*Cervus elaphus*); **jeleń wirginijski** white-tailed deer (*Odocoileus virginianus*). **2.** *pot.* (= *obiekt oszustwa*) (easy) mark, soft touch; (= *człowiek nabrany*) dupe; (= *frajer, naiwniak*) sap, fall guy; sucker; **zrobić z kogoś jelenia** put one over on sb; pull a fast one on sb.

jelito *n. anat.* intestine, bowel; *pot.* gut; **jelito cienkie** small intestine; **jelito grube** colon, large intestine/bowel; **jelito ślepe** caecum, typhlon; blind gut; **nieżyt jelit** *pat.* enteritis; **skręt jelit** *med.* intestinal torsion/volvulus.

jelitodyszec *ma zool.* acorn worm (*Balanoglossus*).

jelitowy *a. anat.* intestinal, enteric.

jelonek *ma* **-nk- 1.** (= *młody jeleń*) buck. **2.** (= *skóra z jelonka*) deerskin. **3.** *ent.* stag beetle (*Lucanus* (*cervus*)).

jełczeć *ipf.* (*o maśle, słoninie, tłuszczu*) go rancid.

jełop *mp pl.* **-y** *pog.* twerp; fathead, bonehead, blockhead.

jem *itd. ipf. zob.* **jeść**.

jemioła *f. bot.* (European) mistletoe (*Viscum album*).

jemiołuszka *f. Gen.pl.* **-ek** *orn.* waxwing (*Bombycilla garrulus*).

jemu *pron. zob.* **on**.

jen *mi Gen.* **-a** (= *japońska jednostka monetarna*) yen.

jeniec *mp* **-ńc-** *pl.* **-y** captive; prisoner; **jeniec wojenny** prisoner of war, POW.

jeniecki *a.* prisoner-of-war, POW; **obóz jeniecki** POW camp.

jenot *ma zool.* raccoon dog (*Nyctereutes procyonoides*).

jer¹ *ma orn.* brambling (*Fringilla montifringilla*).

jer² *mi gram.* jer, yer (*in Slavic*); **jer miękki/twardy** front/back jer.

jeremiada *f. lit.* jeremiad, bitter lament.

Jeremiasz *mp Bibl.* Jeremiah.

Jerozolima *f. geogr.* Jerusalem.

jerozolimski *a.* Jerusalem; **krzyż jerozolimski** Jerusalem cross.

jersey *tk.* jersey. – *ma hodowla* (*rasa bydła*) Jersey.

jerseyowy *a.* jersey; **jerseyowa garsonka** jersey suit.

Jeruzalem *n. Bibl.* Jerusalem.

Jerycho *n. Bibl., geogr.* Jericho.

jerychoński *a.* Jericho; **trąba jerychońska** *pot.* (*o człowieku*) nincompoop; **trąby jerychońskie**

Bibl. the trumpets of Jericho; **róża jerychońska** *bot.* rose of Jericho, resurrection plant (*Anastatica hierochuntica*).

jerzyk *ma orn.* (common) swift (*Apus apus*); **jerzyk alpejski** alpine swift (*A. melba*); **jerzyk blady** pallid swift (*A. pallidus*).

jesienny *a.* autumnal; fall, autumn; **jesienne zrównanie dnia z nocą** autumnal equinox, autumnal point.

jesień *f. pl.* -e fall; autumn; **złota jesień** indian summer; **jesienią** (*także* **na jesieni**) in the fall, in (the) autumn; **jesień życia** the autumn of one's life; **pod jesień** towards the beginning of fall.

jesion *mi* **1.** *bot.* ash (*Fraxinus*); **jesion amerykański** white ash (*F. americana*); **jesion mannowy** flowering ash, manna ash (*F. ornus*); **jesion pensylwański** red ash (*F. pennsylvanica*); **jesion wyniosły** European ash (*F. excelsior*). **2.** (*drewno*) ash.

jesionka *f. Gen.pl.* -ek overcoat (*as worn in the autumn*).

jesionowy *a.* ashen; ash.

jesiotr *ma icht.* sturgeon; **jesiotr amerykański** white sturgeon, Pacific sturgeon (*Acipenser transmontanus*); **jesiotr sachaliński** green sturgeon (*A. medirostris*); **jesiotr zachodni** common sturgeon, Baltic sturgeon (*A. sturio*).

jest *itd. ipf. zob.* **być.**

jestestwo *n. fil.* existence; *pot.* being; **całym (swoim) jestestwem** with every fiber of one's being.

jeszcze *particle* **1.** (= *wciąż*) still; **był już niemłody, ale jeszcze w pełni sił** he wasn't young, but still going strong. **2.** (= *ponownie*) more, again; **jeszcze jeden** one more; another one; **jeszcze raz** one more time, once again; **jeszcze się zobaczymy** we'll meet again; **jeszcze trochę herbaty?** (would you like some) more tea?; **muszę poczekać jeszcze kilka dni** I have to wait a few more days. **3.** (= *nawet*) even; **jest jeszcze lepsze niż wczoraj** it's even better than yesterday; **jeszcze teraz wzdrygam się, jak o tym pomyślę** even now I shudder when I think of it; **poznaliśmy się jeszcze przed studiami** we met even before college. **4.** (= *poza tym*) else; **kto jeszcze?** who else?; **Bóg wie, co jeszcze** God only knows what else. **5.** yet; **jeszcze cię dopadnę** I'll get you yet; **jeszcze jeden** yet another; **jeszcze nie** not yet; **jeszcze nie skończyłem książki** I haven't finished the book yet; **jeszcze nigdy** never yet, never before; **nie odchodź jeszcze** don't go yet; **jeszcze nie teraz** not now; **jeszcze zaczekaj** hold on, wait a minute. **6.** (*w utartych zwrotach*) **jeszcze czego!** *pot.* like hell I will *l.* would; **jeszcze tego brakowało!** I should think not!; that would be the limit!; **jeszcze jak!** and how!; I'd love to!; I sure do *l.* will (*etc.*); **jeszcze śmiesz pytać!** how dare you ask!; **jeszcze do niedawna** until recently.

jeść *ipf.* **jem jesz jedzą, jedz, jadł jedli 1.** (= *spożywać*) eat; **daj mi jeść!** *pot.* give me something to eat!; **jeść z apetytem** eat heartily; **jeść na mieście** eat out; **jeść kolację** *przest.* sup; **jeść obiad** dine; **jeść za dwóch** eat like a horse. **2.** *przen.* **jeść komuś z ręki** eat out of sb's hand; **on jej je z**

ręki she has him eating out of her hand; **z niejednego pieca chleb jadł** he's been around; **jedz, pij i popuszczaj pasa** eat, drink and be merry, for tomorrow we die.

jeśli *conj.* if; **jeśli nie** unless; **jeśli chcesz, pójdziemy do kina** we can go to the movies if you like; **jeśli mnie pamięć nie myli** if my memory serves me; **jeśli można** if I may; if that's OK (with you); **jeśli nie będzie padać** unless it rains; **jeśli pani pozwoli** if you don't mind; **jeśli wcześniej skończę pracę, zadzwonię do ciebie** if I finish work earlier, I'll call you; **któż, jeśli nie on?** if not him, who?

jeśliby *conj.* if (+ *would*/*should*); **jeślibym wcześniej skończył pracę, zadzwonię do ciebie** if I should finish work earlier, I'll call you; **jeśliby pan poczekał, zobaczę co się da zrobić** if you (will *l.* would) wait, I'll see what I can do.

jezdnia *f. Gen.pl.* -i roadway; street, road; **przejść przez jezdnię** cross the street *l.* road.

jezdny *a.* **koło jezdne** *techn.* vehicle wheel; **lina jezdna** *techn.* track cable; **sieć jezdna** *el., kol.* overhead wires; **tabor jezdny** *kol.* rolling stock; **układ jezdny** *techn., mot.* wheels and suspension.

jeziorko *n. Gen.pl.* -ek tarn; small lake, lakelet.

jeziorny *a. biol.* lacustrine.

jezioro *n.* lake; *arch., poet.* mere; *Scot.* loch; *Ir.* lough; **Jezioro Bodeńskie** Lake Constance; **Wielkie Jeziora** *US geogr.* the Great Lakes; **Kraina Jezior** *Br. geogr.* Lake District, the Lakes.

Jezu *int.* **Jezu Chryste!** (*także* **o Jezu!** *l.* **Jezu miłosierny!**) Jesus Christ!; *pot.* Jesus H. Christ!, gee!, geeze!

jezuicki *a. rz.-kat.* (*o zakonie, kolegium, klasztorze, kościele*) Jesuit; (= *charakterystyczny dla jezuitów*) Jesuitic, Jesuitical; **jezuickie wykręty** Jesuitry, Jesuitism; **po jezuicku** Jesuitically.

jezuicko *adv.* Jesuitically.

jezuita *mp rz.-kat.* Jesuit priest; Jesuit.

jezuityzm *mi rz.-kat.* Jesuitism, Jesuitry.

Jezus *mp Voc.* **Jezu** *l.* **Jezusie** *rel.* Jesus; **Jezus Chrystus** Jesus Christ; **Jezus Nazareński** Jesus of Nazareth; **Dzieciątko Jezus** Christ child. – *int.* **Jezus Maria!** Jesus Christ!; Jesus, Mary and Joseph!

Jezusowy *a.* Jesu; **Towarzystwo Jezusowe** *rz.-kat.* the Society of Jesus; **mieć Jezusowe lata** be thirty-three years old.

jeździć *ipf.* **jeżdżę jeździsz 1.** (= *podróżować*) travel; (*autobusem, w samochodzie l. pociągu t.*) ride; **jeździć za granicę** travel abroad. **2.** (= *kierować np. pojazdem*) ride; **jeździć konno** ride (a horse); **jeździć na motocyklu** ride a motorbike *l.* motorcycle; **jeździć na rowerze** ride a bicycle/bike, cycle; **jeździć na wrotkach** roller-skate; **jeździć samochodem** drive (a car); **łaska pańska na pstrym koniu jeździ** you can't count on the higher-ups' favours to last. **3.** (= *kursować*) run; **o tej porze tramwaje już nie jeżdżą** streetcars don't run at this time of night. **4.** *pot.* (= *ślizgać się, posuwać się*) slide, run. **5.** *przen.* (= *wodzić*) run (*po czymś* along, down *l.* through sth); **jeździć wzrokiem po czymś** run one's eyes over sth; **przejechał ręką po jej plecach** he ran his hand down her back.

jeździec *mp* -dźc- *Voc.* -cze *l.* -cu *pl.* -y rider; horseman; *rzad.* equestrian.

jeździecki *a.* riding; *form.* equestrian; **instruktor/klub/sport/sprzęt jeździecki** riding instructor/club/sport/gear; **strój jeździecki** riding dress *l.* kit; (*damski*) riding habit.

jeździectwo *n.* horseback riding; horsemanship; *form.* equitation, equestrianism; *sport* riding sport.

jeż *ma* **1.** *zool.* hedgehog (*Erinaceus*). **2.** (*fryzura*) crew cut; flat top; **mieć włosy** *l.* **strzyc się na jeża** wear a crew cut.

jeżeli *conj.* = **jeśli.**

jeżogłówka *f. Gen.pl.* -ek *bot.* burr reed (*Sparganium*).

jeżokrab *ma zool.* king crab (*Lithodes*).

jeżowaty *a. biol.* erinaceous.

jeżowiec *ma* -wc- **1.** *zool.* sea urchin, echinus (*Echinus*). **2.** *bot.* hedgehog cactus (*Echinocactus*).

jeżozwierz *ma zool.* porcupine (*Hystrix*).

jeżówka *f. Gen.pl.* -ek *icht.* puffer, globefish, porcupine fish (*Diodon hystrix*).

jeżyć *ipf.* bristle; **jeżyć komuś włosy** make sb's hair stand on end; make sb's hair curl. ~ **się** *ipf.* **1.** (= *sterczeć*) bristle (up); (*o włosach*) prickle. **2.** *przen.* (= *być nieufnym*) sulk. **3.** *przen.* (= *być usianym*) be beset (*czymś l. od czegoś* with sth).

jeżyk *ma* (= *mały jeż*) **1.** young hedgehog. **2.** *pot.* = **jeż 2.**

jeżyna *f. bot.* (*krzew*) blackberry, dewberry (bush), bramble (*Rubus*); (*owoc*) blackberry, dewberry.

jeżynowy *a.* (*o nalewce, soku*) blackberry, dewberry; **zarośla jeżynowe** bramble thicket.

jęczeć *ipf.* -ę -ysz moan, groan; **jęczeć z bólu** groan in pain, moan with pain; **jęczał, że...** he moaned that...; **jęczeć pod ciężarem czegoś** groan under (the weight of) sth; **jęczeć w niewoli** *przen.* groan under the weight of oppression.

jęczmienny *a.* barley.

jęczmień *mi Gen.* -a **1.** *bot., roln.* barley (*Hordeum*). **2.** *pat.* sty, stye.

jędrność *f.* firmness.

jędrny *a.* (*o ciele, piersiach*) firm; (*o języku, stylu*) powerful, robust; lively; (*o owocu*) full.

jędza *f.* **1.** (= *złośnica*) bitch, shrew, vixen, scold; nag, harridan; *przest.* beldam. **2.** (*w bajce*) old witch.

jędzowaty *a.* bitchy, shrewish, vixenish, vixenly; nagging, scolding.

jęk *mi* moan, groan; **jęk bólu** groan *l.* moan of pain; **jęk rozpaczy/zawodu** groan of despair/disappointment; **wydać jęk** let out a groan *l.* moan; give a moan.

jękliwy *a.* moanful; moaning, groaning.

jęknąć *pf.* -ij *zob.* **jęczeć.**

jętka *f.* **1.** *ent.* ephemerid; dayfly, mayfly (*Hexagenia limbata*). **2.** *bud.* collar beam.

jęzor *mi Gen.* -a **1.** *pot. uj.* tongue, clapper; **le-**

cieć z wywieszonym jęzorem run hotfoot; **mleć jęzorem** *l.* **strzępić jęzor** jaw; blabber (on), prattle (on); **jęzor ją świerzbi** *pot.* she's bursting to say it. **2.** *geol.* scree, talus; **jęzor lodowca** névé.

języczek *mi* -czk- *Gen.* -a **1.** (= *mały język*) (little) tongue. **2.** *anat.* (*u człowieka*) uvula. **3.** *bot.* lingula. **4.** *muz.* tongue. **5.** **języczek u wagi** pointer.

języczkowaty *a.* lingulate, linguiform.

języcznik *ma bot.* **języcznik zwyczajny** hart's-tongue (*Phyllitis scolopendrium*).

język *mi Gen.* -a **1.** (*w jamie ustnej*) tongue; **wino rozwiązało mu język** wine (has) loosened his tongue; **dostać się na języki** become the talk of the town/village; **język ją świerzbi** she's bursting to say it; **łamać sobie język na czymś** twist one's tongue around sth; **mieć coś na końcu języka** have sth on the tip of one's tongue; **mieć długi język** not be able to keep a secret; **mieć ostry język** have a sharp tongue; **mówić, co ślina na język przyniesie** blabber; **pociągnąć kogoś za język** tap sb for information; **pokazać komuś język** stick *l.* put one's tongue out at sb; **trzymaj język za zębami!** hold your tongue!; **ugryźć się w język** *dosł. l. przen.* bite one's tongue; **zapomnieć języka w gębie** lose one's tongue; **co, zapomniałeś języka w gębie?** lost your tongue, eh?; cat got your tongue?; **złe języki** (= *plotkarze, potwarcy*) evil tongues. **2.** language; *lit.* tongue; (= *mowa*) speech; **język ojczysty** native language *l.* tongue; mother tongue; **język obcy** foreign language *l.* tongue; **język angielski** English, the English language; **język mówiony** spoken language, speech; **język pisany** written language; **język literacki/potoczny** literary/colloquial language; **języki indoeuropejskie** the Indoeuropean languages; **język programowania** *komp.* programming language; **kaleczyć język francuski** speak broken French; **nauczanie języków obcych** *edukacja* foreign language teaching, FLT; **władać dobrze językiem niemieckim** have a good command of the German language; **znajdować z kimś wspólny język** find a common interest with sb. **3.** (= *sposób mówienia*) language; *rzad.* parlance; (= *słownictwo*) vocabulary. **4.** (= *coś w kształcie języka*) (*w bucie*) tongue; **język spustowy** *wojsk.* trigger; **język rumowiskowy** *geol.* scree, talus; **języki płomieni** tongues of fire. **5.** *arch.* (= *jeniec informator*) prisoner (*who can be interrogated*); **zasięgnąć języka** ask around.

językowo-zębowy *a. fon.* dentilingual, linguodental.

językowy *a.* (*o barierze, laboratorium, sprawnościach*) language; (*o poprawności, pożyczkach, rozwoju*) linguistic; (*o dźwiękach, mięśniach*) *anat., fon.* lingual; **zdolności językowe** flair, gift, talent *l.* knack for languages.

językoznawca *mp* linguist.

językoznawczy *a.* linguistic.

językoznawstwo *n.* linguistics; **językoznawstwo ogólne/porównawcze/stosowane/strukturalne** general/contrastive/applied/structural linguistics.

jidysz *mi indecl. l. Gen.* -u *jęz.* Yiddish.

JKM *abbr.* **Jego/Jej Królewska Mość** HM (*His / Her Majesty*).

joannita *mp hist.* knight of St. John.

jod *mi chem.* iodine.

jodan *mi chem.* iodate.

jodek *mi* **-dk-** *chem.* iodide.

jodełka *f. Gen.pl.* **-ek** 1. (= *mała jodła*) little fir-tree. 2. (*wzór tkaniny, układ cegieł*) herringbone (pattern).

jodła *f. Gen.pl.* **-deł** *bot.* fir (*Abies*); **jodła balsamiczna** balsam fir (*A. balsamea*); **jodła jednobarwna** *l.* **kalifornijska** Colorado (white) fir (*A. concolor*); **jodła pospolita** (European) silver fir (*A. alba*); **jodła wspaniała** red fir (*A. magnifica*); (*drzewo*) fir-tree.

jodłować *ipf. muz.* warble, yodel.

jodłowy *a.* fir; firry; (= *z drewna jodłowego*) deal.

jodoform *mi chem.* iodoform.

jodować *ipf. chem.* iodize, iodate.

jodowy *a. chem.* iodic; iodine; **kolba jodowa** iodine flask; **kwas jodowy** iodic acid; **liczba jodowa** iodine number *l.* value.

jodyna *f. med.* (tincture of) iodine.

jodynować *ipf. med.* paint with iodine.

jog *mp pl.* **-owie** *Ind.* = **jogin**.

joga *f. Ind.* (*system filozoficzny l. zespół ćwiczeń*) yoga.

jogging *mi* jogging.

jogin *mp Ind.* yogi.

joginka *f. Gen.pl.* **-ek** *Ind.* yogini.

jogiński *a.* yogic.

jogurt *mi* yogurt, yoghurt.

joker *ma* = **dżoker**.

jolka *f. Gen.pl.* **-ek** *żegl.* 1. (*jacht*) yawl. 2. (*łódź*) jolly boat.

jon *mi chem., fiz.* 1. ion. 2. **jon dodatni/ujemny** positively/negatively charged ion; cation/ anion.

Jonatan *mp Bibl., ogr.* Jonathan.

Jonia *f. hist.* Ionia.

joniczny *a. wers.* Ionic.

jonizacja *f. chem., fiz.* ionization; **akt jonizacji** ionizing event.

jonizacyjny *a.* (*o czujniku, komorze, liczniku, potencjale*) ionization.

jonizator *mi Gen.* **-a** *chem., fiz.* 1. (*czynnik*) ionizing agent. 2. (*aparat*) ionizer.

jonizować *ipf. chem., fiz.* ionize; **promieniowanie jonizujące** ionizing radiation.

Jonka *f. Gen.pl.* **-ek** *hist. zob.* **Jończyk**.

jonoforeza *f. med.* iontophoresis.

jonosfera *f. fiz.* ionosphere.

jonosferyczny *a. fiz.* ionospheric.

jonowy *a.* ionic; ion; **silnik jonowy** ion engine; **pułapka jonowa** ion trap; **sieć jonowa** ionic lattice; **wiązanie jonowe** ionic bond; **wymiana jonowa** ion exchange.

Jończyk *mp hist.* Ionian.

joński *a.* 1. *bud.* Ionic; **kolumna jońska** Ionic column; **porządek joński** Ionic order. 2. *muz.* **skala jońska** Ionian mode. 3. *jęz., geogr.* Ionian, Ionic; **dialekt joński** the Ionic (Greek) dialect; **Morze/Wyspy Jońskie** Ionian Sea/Islands.

Jordania *f. Gen.* **-ii** *geogr.* Jordan.

jordanowski *a.* **ogródek jordanowski** children's playground.

Jordańczyk *mp*, **Jordanka** *f. Gen.pl.* **-ek** Jordanian.

jordański *a.* Jordanian.

jota *f.* (*litera*) iota; (= *szczegół, odrobina t.*) jot; **co do joty** to the letter; **ani na jotę** not one iota; **jota w jotę** precisely.

jotacja *f. jęz.* iotacism.

jowialność *f.* joviality, conviviality.

jowialny *a.* jovial, convivial.

Jowisz *mp* 1. *mit.* Jupiter, Jove; **na Jowisza!** *przest.* by Jove! 2. *astron.* Jupiter; **księżyc Jowisza** Jupiter's moon; Jovian moon; moon of Jupiter.

jowiszowy *a. mit., astron.* Jovian.

joystick *mi komp.* joystick.

Józef *mp t. Bibl.* Joseph.

juan *mi Gen.* **-a** (= *chińska jednostka monetarna*) yuan.

jubel *mi* **-bl-** *Gen.* **-a** *pot.* 1. (= *pijatyka*) wild party; bout of fun; drinking bout, spree, binge. 2. (= *wielka radość*) bout of joy.

jubilat *mp*, **jubilatka** *f. Gen.pl.* **-ek** one celebrating his/her birthday etc.; *żart.* birthday boy/girl; **para jubilatów** the anniversary couple.

jubiler *mp* jeweler; *form.* lapidary; **u jubilera** at the jeweler's (store).

jubilerski *a. form.* (*dot. kamieni*) lapidary; (*sklep, wyrób, rzemiosło*) jeweller's.

jubilerstwo *n.* jeweller's craft *l.* trade.

jubileusz *mi Gen.pl.* **-y** *l.* **-ów** jubilee; **srebrny/ złoty/brylantowy jubileusz** silver/golden/diamond jubilee; **obchodzić jubileusz** celebrate a jubilee, jubilate; **urządzić komuś jubileusz** arrange a jubilee celebration for sb.

jubileuszowy *a.* (*przemówienie, obchody*) jubilee; **wydanie jubileuszowe** anniversary edition.

jucha *f. pot.* (= *krew*) blood. – *f. l. mp decl. like f. Gen.pl.* **-ch** *l.* **-ów** *obelż.* (= *drań*) son of a gun.

jucht *mi* Russian leather.

juchtowy *a.* Russian leather.

juczny *a.* **koń juczny** packhorse; **zwierzę juczne** pack animal; beast of burden; *przest.* sumpter.

juczyć *ipf.* load up (*czymś* with sth).

Juda *mp Bibl.* Jude.

judaika *pl. Gen.* **-ów** Judaica.

judaista *mp*, **judaistka** *f. Gen.pl.* **-ek** *rel.* follower of Judaism.

judaistyczny *a. rel.* Judaistic; Judaic.

judaizm *mi rel.* Judaism.

Judasz *mp Bibl.* Judas (Iscariot).

judasz *mp Gen.pl.* **-y** *l.* **-ów** *pog.* (= *zdrajca*) Judas. – *mi Gen.* **-a** *Gen.pl.* **-y** *l.* **-ów** (*w drzwiach*) peephole, spyhole, eyehole; (*w więzieniu t.*) judas (window *l.* hole).

judaszowiec *mi* **-wc-** *Gen.* **-a** *bot.* Judas tree (*Cercis*).

judaszowy *a.* Judas', Judas's; **judaszowe srebrniki** blood money; thirty pieces of silver.

Judea *f.* 1. *geogr., hist.* Judea, Judaea. 2. *przen.* (=) Jewry.

Judejczyk *mp*, **Judejka** *f. Gen.pl.* -ek *hist.* Judean, Judaean.

judejski *a. hist.* Judean, Judaean.

judo *n. indecl.* judo.

judoka *mp* judoka.

judykatura *f. prawn.* judicatory.

judzić *ipf.* incite; goad, egg on; **judzić do niezgody** foment discord.

jufers *mi żegl.* deadeye.

Jugol *mp*, **Jugolka** *f. Gen.pl.* -ek *sl., pog.* (= *Jugosłowian-in/ka*) Yugo.

Jugosławia *f. Gen.* -ii *geogr.* Yugoslavia.

Jugosłowianin *mp pl.* -anie *Gen.* -an, **Jugosłowianka** *f. Gen.pl.* -ek Yugoslav, Yugoslavian.

jugosłowiański *a.* Yugoslav, Yugoslavian.

juhas *mp* shepherd (*in the Tatra Mountains*).

juhaski *a.* shepherd's.

juhasować *ipf.* tend sheep (*in the Tatra Mountains*).

jujuba *f. bot.* jujube (*Ziziphus*).

juk *mi przest.* (*na zwierzęciu jucznym*) pannier, pack; (*u siodła*) saddlebag.

juka *f. bot.* yucca (*Yucca*); **juka krótkolistna** Joshua tree (*Yucca brevifolia*); *tk.* (= *włókno jukowe*) yucca fiber.

jukka *f. bot.* = **juka** 1.

jukowy *a. tk.* yucca.

juliański *a. kośc.* Julian; **kalendarz juliański** Julian calendar.

jumpsztag *mi żegl.* jackstay.

junacki *a.* **1.** (= *młodzieńczy*) youthful; (= *dzielny*) gallant. **2.** (= *dotyczący hufców pracy*) work-brigade.

junaczka *f. Gen.pl.* -ek *zob.* **junak** 2.

junak *mp* **1.** *arch.* (= *zuch, młodzieniec*) gallant stripling *l.* youth. **2.** (*w hufcu pracy*) (male) work-brigade volunteer (*esp. in Stalinist Poland*).

junior *mp*, **juniorka** *f. Gen.pl.* -ek **1.** (*w rodzinie*) Junior. **2.** *sport* junior.

junkier *mp* -kr- **1.** *hist.* (*zwł. w Prusach*) Junker. **2.** *hist.* (*w armii carskiej*) cadet; nobleman serving as noncomissioned officer.

junkierski *a.* **1.** *hist.* (*zwł. w Prusach*) Junker. **2.** *hist.* (*w armii carskiej*) cadet.

junkierstwo *n. hist.* (= *obszarnicy pruscy*) Junkerdom.

Junona *f. mit.* Juno.

junta *f. polit.* (military) junta.

jupiter *mi Gen.* -a *film* sun lamp.

Jura *f. geogr.* the Jura (Mountains).

jura *f. geol.* the Jurassic (period).

jurajski *a. geol.* Jurassic.

jurność *f.* sexual vigor, libido; (*męska*) virility, machismo.

jurny *a.* sexually vigorous, lustful; (*o mężczyźnie*) virile, macho.

juror *mp*, **jurorka** *f. Gen.pl.* -ek juror, member of the jury.

jurta *f.* yurt.

jury *n. indecl.* jury.

jurysdykcja *f. prawn.* jurisdiction.

jurysdykcyjny *a. prawn.* jurisdictional, jurisdiction.

jurysprudencja *f. prawn.* jurisprudence.

jurysta *mp przest.* jurist, jurisprudent.

justować *ipf.* **1.** *druk.* justify. **2.** *opt.* align; collimate.

justowanie *n.* **1.** *druk.* justification. **2.** *opt.* alignment; collimation.

justunek *mi* -nk- *druk.* blank material, spacing material.

jusznica *f. ent.* horsefly, cleg (*Chrysops, Tabanus*).

juści *particle przest.* = **jużci**.

juta *f.* **1.** *bot.* jute (*Corchorus capsularis, C. olitorius*). **2.** (*tkanina*) hessian; gunny, burlap.

Jutlandczyk *mp*, **Jutlandka** *f. Gen.pl.* -ek Jutlander.

Jutlandia *f. Gen.* -ii *geogr.* Jutland.

jutlandzki *a.* Jutlandish.

jutowy *a.* gunny, burlap.

jutro *n. t. przen.* tomorrow; **od jutra** as of tomorrow; (starting) from tomorrow; **marzyć o lepszym jutrze** dream of a better tomorrow. – *adv.* tomorrow; **do zobaczenia jutro** (I'll) see you tomorrow; **jeśli nie dziś, to jutro** (either) today or tomorrow.

jutrzejszy *a.* tomorrow's.

jutrzenka *f. Gen.pl.* -ek *poet.* (= *świt*) **1.** aurora, dawn. **2. Jutrzenka** (= *gwiazda zaranna*) the Morning Star.

jutrznia *f. Gen.pl.* -i *kośc.* matins.

juwenalia *pl. Gen.* -ów (*studenckie*) student festival.

juwenilia *pl. Gen.* -ów *form.* (= *dzieła l. utwory młodzieńcze*) juvenilia.

już *adv. i particle* **1.** already; **jak już mówiłem** as I have already said; **już idziesz?** are you leaving already?; **już jestem spóźniony** I'm late already. **2.** yet (*w pytaniach ogólnych*); **czy już jadłeś?** have you eaten yet?; **czy Tom już przyjechał?** has Tom arrived yet? **3. już nie** not any more. **4. to już koniec** it's all over; **już po mnie** I've had it; I'm done; **nie i już!** the answer is no!; no means no!; **już ja cię nauczę!** I'll teach you a lesson!; **tego już za wiele!** that's the last straw!; **już cię nie ma!** out you go!; **już idę!** I'm just coming!; **już miałem powiedzieć...** I was just about to say...

jużci *particle przest.* **a jużci** forsooth, iwis.

jw. *abbr.* **jak wyżej** do. (*ditto*); see above.

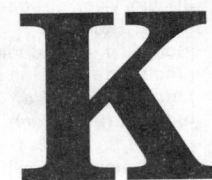

K, k n. *indecl.* (*litera*) K, k; **K jak Kazimierz** K is for Kilo; K as in Kilo.

K *abbr. komp.* K (= *kilobyte*).

kabaczek *mi* **-czk-** *Gen.* **-a** *bot.* marrow squash, vegetable marrow (*Cucurbita pepo*).

kabalarka *f. Gen.pl.* **-ek** cab(b)alist, kab(b)alist.

kabalista *mp* cab(b)alist, kab(b)alist.

kabalistyczny *a.* cab(b)alistic, kab(b)alistic.

kabalistyka *f.* cab(b)alism, kab(b)alism.

kabała *f.* **1.** (*wróżenie*) *rel.* cab(b)ala, kab(b)ala. **2.** (= *tarapaty*) predicament; **wpakować** *l.* **wplątać się w (niezłą) kabałę** get into a pretty *l.* fine mess.

kaban *ma dial.* fatso.

kabanos *mi Gen.* **-a** *kulin.* thin dried smoked pork sausage.

kabareciarz *mp pot.* entertainer.

kabarecik *mi* short floor show.

kabaret *mi* cabaret; **kabaret literacki** literary cabaret.

kabaretki *pl. pot.* (*o pończochach*) fishnet stockings; (*o rajstopach*) fishnet tights.

kabareton *mi* cabaret contest.

kabaretowy *a.* (*o piosence, programie, scenie*) cabaret; **aktor kabaretowy** (stand-up) comedian; **artysta kabaretowy** entertainer.

kabel *mi* **-bl-** *Gen.* **-a 1.** (= *grubszy przewód*) cable; *pot.* (= *sznur sieciowy*) lead, cord; *Br.* flex; **kabel jednożyłowy/koncentryczny/wielożyłowy** single-core/coaxial/multicore cable; **kabel podmorski** submarine cable. **2.** *żegl.* (*jednostka odległości*) cable, cable('s) length.

kabelek *mi* **-lk-** *Gen.* **-a** (thin) lead, cord; *Br.* flex.

kabelgat *mi żegl.* cable tier.

kabeltaw *mi żegl.* hawser.

kabestan *mi żegl.* capstan; **kabestan szotowy** winch.

kabina *f.* (*np. projekcyjna, telefoniczna, do głosowania*) booth; (*kolejki linowej, pasażerska na pokładzie samolotu l. statku*) cabin; (*ciężarówki, lokomotywy*) cab; (*np. dźwigu, suwnicy*) cage, cabin; **kabina kierowcy** driver's cab; **kabina prysznicowa** shower cubicle; **kabina pilota** cockpit; **kabina radiooperatora/radiotelegrafisty** radio room; **kabina telefoniczna** telephone booth *l.* kiosk, call box.

kabinet *mi* cabinet; writing desk (*esp. 17th century*); *Br. t.* bureau.

kabinowy *a.* **tłumacz kabinowy** simultaneous interpreter.

kablogram *mi* cablegram, cable.

kablować *ipf.* **1.** *tel.* cable. **2.** *pot.* (= *donosić*) fink, squeal (*na kogoś* on sb); *Br.* grass (*na kogoś* on sb).

kablowiec *mi* **-wc-** *Gen.* **-a** *żegl.* cable-layer.

kablowy *a.* cable; **telewizja kablowa** cable television; **lokalna telewizja kablowa** community antenna television, CATV.

kablówka *f. Gen.pl.* **-ek** *pot.* cable TV, CATV.

kabłąk *mi Gen.* **-a** *techn.* arch; (*wiadra, opuszczanej budy*) bail; **kabłąk ochronny** *techn.* finger guard; **kabłąk spustu** trigger guard.

kabłąkowaty *a.* arched; (*o nogach*) bandy; **o kabłąkowatych nogach** bandy-legged, bowlegged.

kaboszon *mi sztuka* (*kamień*) (*motyw*) cabochon.

kabotaż *mi żegl.* (= *żegluga morska*) cabotage; (= *żegluga przybrzeżna*) coasting.

kabotażowiec *mi* **-wc-** *Gen.* **-a** *żegl.* coaster.

kabotażowy *a.* coasting.

kabotyn *mp* (= *kiepski aktor*) play-actor; (= *pozer*) poseur.

kabotynizm *mi* (= *kiepskie aktorstwo*) play-acting; *rzad.* cabotinage.

kabotynka *f. Gen.pl.* **-ek** (= *kiepska aktorka*) play-actress; (= *pozerka*) poseuse.

kabotyński *a.* play-acting.

kabotyństwo *n. zob.* **kabotynizm**.

kabriolet *mi* **1.** *mot.* (*nadwozie*) convertible; *Br. t.* drophead coupé. **2.** *hist.* (*powóz*) cabriolet.

kabura *f.* holster; **kabura pod pachą** shoulder holster.

kabza *f. przest.* pouch, purse; **nabić sobie kabzę** line one's (own) pockets, feather one's (own) nest.

kac *mi Gen.* **-a** *pot.* hangover, the morning after; **mieć kaca** have a hangover, be hung over; **na kacu** hung over.

kacap *mp pl.* **-y, kacapka** *f. Gen.pl.* **-ek** *pog.* Russky.

kacenjamer *mi przest. zob.* **kac**.

kacerz[1] *mp Gen.pl.* **-y** *l.* **-ów** *rel.* heretic.

kacerz[2] *mi Gen.* **-a** *Gen.pl.* **-y** (*sieć*) crab pot.

kacheksja *f. pat.* cachexy, cachexia.

kacyk *mp pl.* **-owie 1.** (*wódz*) cacique. **2.** *pot.* (= *prominent*) cacique, jack-in-office.

kacykostwo *n. pot.* caciquism; absolute rule by a local official.

kaczan *mi Gen.* **-a** (*kukurydzy*) corncob, cob; (*kapusty*) (cabbage) stump.

kaczątko n. Gen.pl. -tek duckling; **brzydkie kaczątko** przen. ugly duckling.

kaczenica f. zool. goose barnacle (Lepas).

kaczeniec mi -ńc- Gen. -a bot. marsh marigold, cowslip; Br. t. kingcup (Caltha palustris).

kaczę n. -częci- pl. -częt- Gen. -ąt zob. **kaczątko.**

kaczka f. Gen.pl. -ek 1. orn. duck (Anatidae); **puszczać kaczki** play ducks and drakes; **kaczka dziennikarska** przen. canard, journalistic hoax. 2. (do oddawania moczu) bed urinal. 3. lotn. canard, tail-first aircraft.

kaczkowaty a. ducklike; **kaczkowaty chód** waddle, ducklike walk.

kaczor ma (= samiec kaczki) drake; **kaczor Donald** Donald Duck.

kaczuszka f. Gen.pl. -ek little duck, duckling; **kaczuszka gumowa** (do zabawy w kąpieli) rubber duck.

kaczy a. duck's; **kaczy chód** waddle, ducklike walk; **kaczy dziób** duck bill; **kaczy kuper** (fryzura) duck's ass; Br. duck's arse, DA.

kadecki a. cadet.

kadencja f. 1. (okres) term, tenure; (parlamentu, sądu) term; (rządu) life; (sędziego) prawn. judicature. 2. (= czas sprawowania urzędu) term of office, tenure; **połowa kadencji** midterm; **odbyć kadencję** serve the term. 3. muz. (zakończenie) cadence. 4. muz. (improwizacja) cadenza. 5. jęz. cadence.

kadencyjny a. tenurial.

kadet mp 1. wojsk. cadet; **kadet marynarki** midshipman; **korpus kadetów** cadet corps; **szkoła kadetów** cadet school. 2. polit., hist. (w Rosji) Kadet, Constitutional Democrat.

kadi mp pl. -owie prawn. cadi, kadi.

kadisz mi judaizm Kaddish; **odmawiać kadisz** say Kaddish.

kadłub mi Gen. -a 1. anat. trunk. 2. (statku) hull; (samolotu) fuselage; techn. body. 3. (= obudowa) casing. 4. (= skorupa) shell.

kadłubowy a. 1. (= poobcinany) truncated; **parlament kadłubowy** polit., hist. Rump Parliament, the Rump (1648–1653). 2. (= odnoszący się do kadłuba) żegl. hull; lotn. fuselage.

kadm mi chem. cadmium.

kadmować ipf. chem. cadmium plate.

kadmowy a. chem. cadmium; **brąz kadmowy** cadmium copper; **czerwień/żółcień kadmowa** cadmium red/yellow; **siarczan/siarczek kadmowy** cadmium sulfate/sulfide.

kadr mi fot., film frame; **poza kadrem** off screen, out of shot.

kadra f. 1. (= zespół pracowników) personnel, staff; **dział kadr** human resources department, personnel department. 2. (w wojsku) cadre. 3. sport **kadra narodowa** national team.

kadrowa f. Gen. -ej pot. human resources officer, personnel officer.

kadrować ipf. kino frame.

kadrowicz mp Gen.pl. -ów sport member of the (men's) national team.

kadrowiczka f. Gen.pl. -ek sport member of the (women's) national team.

kadrowiec mp -wc- pl. -y pot. human resources officer, personnel officer.

kadrowy a. human resources, personnel; **rezerwy kadrowe** staff reserves; **polityka kadrowa** employment policy. – mp Gen. -ego pot. zob. **kadrowiec.**

kadry pl. Gen. -r (biuro) human resources department, personnel department.

kadryl mi Gen. i Acc. -a Gen.pl. -i l. -ów 1. muz. quadrille. 2. (taniec) quadrille; (taniec ludowy) square dance. 3. jeźdz. French equestrian display, quadrille.

kaduceusz mi Gen. -a Gen.pl. -y l. -ów 1. mit. caduceus. 2. (u błazna) bauble.

kaduk mi Gen. -a prawn., hist. escheat; **prawem kaduka** unlawfully, illegitimately.

kadysz mi zob. **kadisz.**

kadzić ipf. 1. (wonnym dymem) burn incense. 2. (= przesadnie pochlebiać) lay it on (a bit thick); **kadzić komuś** pot. massage sb's ego.

kadzidełko n. Gen.pl. -ek joss stick, incense stick.

kadzidlany a. incense.

kadzidło n. Gen.pl. -eł incense; **pomoże to, jak umarłemu kadzidło** it's about as much help as a kick in the teeth.

kadzielnica f. kośc. censer, thurible.

kadź f. pl. -e 1. (naczynie) chem. vat; met. ladle; papiernictwo chest; (filtracyjna, hartownicza) tank; (zlewna) tub. 2. (ciecz) chem. vat.

kaem mi pot. (karabin) MG (= machine gun).

kaemista mp pot. machine gunner.

kafar mi Gen. -a techn. piledriver.

kafejka f. Gen.pl. -ek pot. café.

kafel mi -fl- Gen. -a (stove) tile.

kafelek mi -lk- Gen. -a (ścienny) (wall) tile; (podłogowy) (floor) tile.

kafelkarz mp tiler.

kafelkować ipf. tile.

kafelkowy a. (np. o podłodze) tiled.

kaflarz mp tilemaker.

kaflowy a. tiled; **piec kaflowy** tiled stove.

kaftan mi Gen. -a 1. (roboczy) smock; hist. pourpoint; (obcisły) doublet; (krótki) jerkin; **kaftan bezpieczeństwa** straitjacket. 2. (typu bliskowschodniego) caftan.

kaftanik mi Gen. -a 1. (dziecięcy) matinée coat. 2. (kobiecy) type of nightgown.

kaganek mi -nk- Gen. -a oil-lamp; **nieść kaganek oświaty** przen. spread enlightenment.

kaganiec mi -ńc- Gen. -a 1. (np. dla psa) muzzle. 2. (lampa) zob. **kaganek.**

kahał mi judaizm kahal.

kaik mi Gen. -a caique.

kainit mi min. kainite.

Kair mi geogr. Cairo.

kairczyk mp Cairene.

kairski a. Cairene.

kajać się ipf. (żałować czegoś) repent; (wyznać coś) confess with contrition; **kajać się za grzechy** repent of one's sins.

kajak mi Gen. -a canoe; zwł. sport kayak; **pływać kajakiem** kayak; canoe.

kajakarka f. Gen.pl. -ek sport woman canoeist.

kajakarstwo n. sport canoeing; **kajakarstwo sportowe** sport canoeing.

kajakarz mp sport canoeist.

kajakowy a. (o mistrzostwach, przystani, spływie, wyprawie) canoe; (o zawodach) canoeing.

kajdaniarz mp prisoner in chains.

kajdanki pl. Gen. -ów handcuffs; **założyć komuś kajdanki** l. **skuć kogoś kajdankami** handcuff sb.

kajdany pl. Gen. -n **1.** (do skuwania rąk i nóg) shackles, manacles; hist. irons; **zakuć kogoś w kajdany** clap sb in irons. **2.** lit. (= niewola) chains; **zrzucić kajdany** przen. cast off one's chains.

kajet mi przest. exercise-book, notebook.

Kajfasz mp Bibl. Caiaphas.

kajmak mi kulin. butterscotch.

kajman ma zool. cayman, caiman (Caiman).

kajtek mp -tk- pl. -i żart. kid, lad.

kajuta f. cabin.

kajutowy a. cabin.

kajzer mp iron. kaiser.

kajzerka f. Gen.pl. -ek kulin. kaiser roll.

kakadu f. indecl. orn. cockatoo (Kakatoe).

kakao n. indecl. kulin. cocoa.

kakaowiec mi -wc- Gen. -a bot. cacao (Theobroma cacao).

kakaowy a. cocoa; **ziarno kakaowe** cocoa beans; **drzewo kakaowe** zob. **kakaowiec**.

kakofonia f. Gen. -ii muz., przen. cacophony.

kakofoniczny a. muz. cacophonous, cacophonic.

kaktus mi Gen. -a bot. cactus (Cactaceae).

kaktusowate pl. Gen. -ych bot. cactaceans, cactaceae.

kaktusowy a. cactus.

kalabasa f. (owoc) (naczynie) calabash.

kalać ipf. lit. befoul, soil, tarnish; **kalać honor** l. **dobre imię rodziny** soil l. tarnish the family reputation; **zły to ptak, co swoje gniazdo kala** it's an ill bird that fouls its own nest. **~ się** ipf. przen. (= brudzić się) soil; **nie skalać się czymś** not to soil one's hands with sth.

kalafa f. dial., pot. kisser, mug; **zarobić w kalafę** get one in the kisser.

kalafior mi bot. cauliflower (Brassica oleracea botrytis).

kalafiorowy a. cauliflower; **sałatka/zupa kalafiorowa** kulin. cauliflower salad/soup.

kalafonia f. Gen. -ii rosin, colophony; **smarować kalafonią** rosin.

kalambur mi equivoque, equivoke; (zwł. utworzony dla uzyskania efektu komicznego) pun.

kalamburzysta mp punster.

kalamin mi min. calamine.

kalamit mi paleont. calamite, Calamites.

kalander mi -dr- Gen. -a techn. calender.

kalandrować ipf. techn. calender.

kalarepa f. bot. kohlrabi (Brassica oleacera gongolydes).

kalcyferol mi Gen.pl. -i l. -ów med. calciferol.

kalcynacja f. metal., techn. calcination.

kalcynator mi metal. calciner.

kalcynować ipf. metal. calcine.

kalcynowany a. metal. **soda kalcynowana** calcined soda, soda ash.

kalcyt mi min. calcite.

kaldera f. geol. caldera.

kalebasa f. bot. bottle gourd, calabash (Lagenaria siceraria).

kalectwo n. physical disability, handicap; **spowodować u kogoś kalectwo** cripple l. incapacitate sb; **zrobienie tego grozi kalectwem** doing that poses a threat of serious injury; **kalectwo życiowe** shiftlessness, languor.

kaleczyć ipf. (np. nożem) cut; (= ranić) wound; (dotkliwie) lacerate; **kaleczyć język francuski/niemiecki** murder the French/German language, speak broken French/German. **~ się** ipf. cut o.s., hurt o.s.

Kaledonia f. Gen. -ii hist. **1.** Caledonia. **2.** geogr. **Nowa Kaledonia** New Caledonia.

kaledonidy pl. Gen. -ów geogr. Caledonian mountains.

kaledoński a. Caledonian; **orogeneza kaledońska** geol. Caledonian orogeny l. orogenesis; **Kanał Kaledoński** geogr. Caledonian Canal.

kalejdoskop mi kaleidoscope; **zmieniać się jak w kalejdoskopie** be changeable.

kalejdoskopowy a. kaleidoscopic.

kaleka f. l. mp decl. like f. pl. -i l. -cy Gen. -k l. -ów cripple, invalid; **kaleka emocjonalna** pot. emotional cripple; **kaleka życiowa** l. życiowy pot. born loser, ne'er-do-well.

kaleki a. **1.** (= niedołężny) crippled, disabled. **2.** przen. (= niedoskonały) (found) wanting, flawed. **3.** przen. lame.

kalendarium n. sing. indecl. pl. -ria Gen. -riów **1.** (spotkań, imprez) calendar. **2.** (= zestawienie wydarzeń) (w historii kraju, życiu pisarza) chronology.

kalendarz mi Gen. -a **1.** (rachuba czasu) (t. drukowany) calendar; **kalendarz gregoriański/juliański/republikański** Gregorian/Julian/Revolutionary calendar; **kalendarz ścienny** wall calendar; **kalendarz reklamowy** advertising l. publicity calendar. **2.** (= terminarz, plan) calendar; **kalendarz biurowy** desk calendar; Br. (desk) diary; **kalendarz wyborczy** voting calendar.

kalendarzowy a. calendar; **miesiąc kalendarzowy** calendar month; **rok kalendarzowy** calendar l. civil year; **kalendarzowa wiosna/zima** astronomical spring/winter.

kalendarzyk mi Gen. -a **1.** (= terminarz) calendar; Br. diary. **2.** pot. (metoda antykoncepcyjna) rhythm method.

kalendy pl. Gen. -d hist. calends, kalends.

kalenica f. (roof) ridge.

kalesony pl. Gen. -ów (długie) long underwear; pot. long johns; (krótkie) briefs; Br. trunks.

kaletka f. anat. bursa.

kaletnictwo n. purse- and bagmaking.

kaletniczy a. (warsztat, mistrz) purse- and bagmaking; **galanteria kaletnicza** bags and purses.

kaletnik mp purse- and bagmaker.

kalia *f. Gen.* -**ii** *bot.* calla, calla lily (*Zantedeschia aethiopica*).

kaliber *mi* -**br**- 1. (*wielkość*) caliber; **człowiek wielkiego kalibru** a high caliber man, man of a high caliber; **humor ciężkiego kalibru** *przen.* heavy humor. 2. (= *rozmiar lufy*) caliber; (*zwł. w dubeltówkach*) gauge, bore; **dużego/małego kalibru** large/small caliber, large/small bore; **dubeltówka kalibru 12** 12-gauge shotgun; **pocisk kalibru 7,63** 7.63-caliber bullet; **rewolwer kalibru 45** a forty-five.

kalibrator *mi Gen.* -**a** *techn.* calibrator; **kalibrator kwarcowy** *el.* quartz frequency standard.

kalibromierz *mi Gen.* -**a** calibrator.

kalibrować *ipf. techn.* 1. (*rozmiar*) size. 2. (*podziałkę*) calibrate.

kalibrowanie *a. techn.* 1. (*rozmiaru*) sizing. 2. (*podziałki*) calibration.

kalif *mp pl.* -**owie** caliph, calif.

kalifat *mi* caliphate, califate.

kaliforn *mi chem.* californium.

Kalifornia *f. Gen.* -**ii** *geogr.* California.

Kalifornijczyk *mp*, **Kalifornijka** *f. Gen.pl.* -**ek** Californian.

kalifornijski *a.* Californian.

kaligraf *mp pl.* -**owie** calligrapher, calligraphist; penman.

kaligrafia *f. Gen.* -**ii** calligraphy, penmanship.

kaligraficzny *a.* calligraphic.

kaligrafować *ipf.* (= *pisać starannie*) write in one's best handwriting; (= *pisać zgodnie z zasadami kaligrafii*) write calligraphically.

kaliko *n. indecl.* 1. *tk.* calico. 2. *papiernictwo* chintz, calico paper.

kalikować *ipf.* blow (*a pipe organ*).

kalimagnezja *f. chem., roln.* sulfate of potash magnesia.

kalina *f. bot.* cranberry bush *l.* tree (*Viburnum*); **kalina hordowina** wayfaring tree (*Viburnum lantana*); **kalina koralowa** cramp bark, European cranberry bush (*Viburnum opulus*).

Kalipso *f. mit.* Calypso.

kalipso *n. muz.* calypso.

kalka *f. Gen.pl.* **kalk** *l.* **kalek** 1. (*do pisania na maszynie*) carbon paper; *Br. t.* carbon; **pisać coś przez kalkę** make a carbon copy of sth. 2. (*przezroczysta*) tracing paper; **rysunek przez kalkę** traced design. 3. *jęz.* calque.

kalkomania *f. Gen.* -**ii** decalcomania, decal; (*proces t.*) transfer printing.

kalkować *ipf.* trace; (= *odciskać kolor*) calk.

kalkulacja *f.* (*rachunek*) (*planowanie*) calculation; **kalkulacja kosztów** costing, cost accounting, cost calculation.

kalkulacyjny *a.* calculation, calculating; **arkusz kalkulacyjny** spreadsheet; **maszyna kalkulacyjna** calculating machine.

kalkulator *mi* calculator; **kalkulator kieszonkowy** pocket calculator.

kalkulować *ipf.* 1. (*obliczać*) calculate. 2. (*rozważać*) reckon. ~ **się** *ipf. pot.* (= *opłacać się*) pay; **to mi się nie kalkuluje** it's not worth my trouble.

kalla *f.* 1. *bot.* water arum (*Calla palustris*). 2. *zob.* **kalia**.

kalmar *ma zool.* squid, calamary (*Loligo*).

kalomel *mi chem.* calomel, mercurous chloride.

kaloria *f. Gen.* -**ii** calorie, calory, cal.

kaloryczność *f.* calorific value, caloricity.

kaloryczny *a.* caloric, calorific.

kaloryfer *mi Gen.* -**a** radiator, heater.

kalorymetr *mi fiz.* calorimeter.

kalorymetria *f. Gen.* -**ii** calorimetry.

kalorymetryczny *a.* calorimetric; **bomba kalorymetryczna** *fiz.* oxygen-bomb calorimeter, bomb calorimeter.

kalosze *Gen.pl.* -**y** wellingtons, rubber boots; (*nakładane na buty*) galoshes; **to inna para kaloszy** *pot.* that's a different cup of tea, that's a different story; **sędzia kalosz!** *pog.* we got screwed!, are you blind?

kalota *f.* 1. *anat.* calvaria. 2. *bud.* calotte.

kalotka *f. kośc.* calotte.

kalumet *mi* calumet.

kalumnia *f. Gen.* -**ii** calumny, aspersion; **rzucać na kogoś kalumnie** cast aspersions on sb.

kalwaria *f. Gen.* -**ii** 1. *rz.-kat.* Calvary, the Way of the Cross; **Góra Kalwaria** Calvary. 2. *przen.* (= *cierpienie*) calvary.

kalwaryjski *a.* Calvary; **stacja kalwaryjska** station of the Cross; **dziad kalwaryjski** beggar.

kalwin *mp* Calvinist.

kalwinista *mp* Calvinist.

kalwinizm *mi* Calvinism.

kalwinka *f. Gen.pl.* -**ek** *zob.* **kalwin**.

kalwiński *a.* Calvinistic, Calvinistical.

kał *mi* (= *odchody*) excrement; *med.* feces, *Br.* faeces; **oddawać kał** defecate.

kałamarnica *f. zool.* squid, calamary (*Loligo*).

kałamarz *mi Gen.* -**a** (*buteleczka*) inkpot, inkbottle; (*w pulpicie*) inkwell.

kałasznikow *mi Gen.* -**a** *broń* Kalashnikov, AK-47.

kałdun *mi Gen.* -**a** *pot.* belly, paunch.

kałmucki *a.* Kalmuck, Kalmyk.

Kałmuk *mp* Kalmuck, Kalmyk.

kałmuk *ma zool.* Kalmyk horse.

kałowy *a.* faecal, excremental.

kałożerny *a.* coprophagous, scatophagous.

kałożerstwo *n.* coprophagy.

kaługa *f. icht.* kaluga (*Huso dauricus*).

kałuża *f.* puddle, pool.

kałużnica *f. ent.* great silver beetle (*Hydrous piceus*).

kama *f. zool.* red hartebeest (*Alcelaphus buselaphus caama*).

kamamber *mi kulin.* Camembert.

kamaryla *f.* camarilla, cabal.

kamasze *Gen.pl.* -**y** gaiters.

kambialny *a. bot.* cambial.

kambium *n. indecl. bot.* cambium.

Kambodża *f.* Cambodia.

kambodżański *a.* Cambodian.

kambr *mi geol.* the Cambrian period, the Cambrian.

kambryjski *a. geol.* Cambrian.

kambuz *mi Gen.* -**a** *żegl.* caboose.

kamea *f. Gen.* -**ei** *jubilerstwo* cameo.

kamedulski a. Camaldolese.

kameduła mp Camaldolese; **zakon kamedułów** Congregation of Monk Hermits of Camaldoli.

kameleon ma zool. chameleon (*Chamaeleontidae*). – mp pl. -y przen. chameleon.

kameleonowy a. chameleonic.

kamelia f. Gen. -ii bot. camellia (*Camellia*).

kameliowy a. camellia; **dama kameliowa** przest. courtesan, courtezan.

kamena f. mit. Camena.

kamera f. 1. camera; **kamera filmowa** movie camera, Br. cine camera; **kamera lotnicza** aerial camera; **kamera telewizyjna** TV camera; **kamera wideo** camcorder, video camera; **kamera obskura** camera obscura; **ukryta kamera** candid camera. 2. hist. HM Treasury. 3. przest. (*pomieszczenie*) chamber.

kameralista mp, **kameralistka** f. Gen.pl. -ek chamber musician.

kameralistyka f. chamber music.

kameralnie adv. (= w sposób niedostępny dla ogółu) privately; (= przytulnie) intimately.

kameralność f. privacy.

kameralny a. 1. (*nastrój*) cozy, Br. cosy, intimate; teatr small audience; **kameralne spotkanie** (= zamknięte spotkanie) in camera meeting. 2. muz. chamber; **koncert kameralny** concert of chamber music; **orkiestra kameralna** chamber orchestra.

kamerdyner mp 1. (= starszy lokaj) butler. 2. hist. (= pokojowiec osobisty) valet.

kamerdynerski a. butler's; valet's.

kamerher mp hist. chamberlain.

kamerling mp pl. -owie rz.-kat. camerlengo.

kamerowy a. ujęcie kamerowe take, shot.

kamerton mi 1. muz. (*przyrząd*) tuning-fork; **kamerton dęty** pitch-pipe. 2. muz. (*dźwięk*) standard pitch.

kamertonowy a. tuning-fork; **dźwięk kamertonowy** standard pitch.

Kamerun mi Cameroon.

Kamerunka f. Gen.pl. -ek **Kameruńczyk** mp Cameroonian.

kameruński a. Cameroonian.

kamerzysta mp cameraman.

kamerzystka f. Gen.pl. -ek camerawoman.

kamfora f. chem. camphor; **zniknąć jak kamfora** vanish into thin air.

kamforowiec mi -wc- Gen. -a bot. camphor tree (*Cinnamomum camphora*).

kamforowy a. camphor; (o olejku t.) camphorated; (o kwasie) camphoric.

kamgarn mi 1. tk. (*przędza*) worsted yarn. 2. tk. (*tkanina*) worsted fabric.

kamica f. med. lithiasis; **kamica nerkowa** nephrolithiasis; **kamica żołądkowa** gastrolithiasis.

kamieniarka f. 1. bud. (*budulec*) stonework. 2. bud. (*rzemiosło*) stonework, stone-masonry, stone-cutting.

kamieniarski a. stonemason's, stonecutter's; **roboty kamieniarskie** stonework.

kamieniarstwo n. zob. **kamieniarka**.

kamieniarz mp stone-mason, stonecutter.

kamienica f. tenement, tenement house.

kamieniczka f. Gen.pl. -ek small tenement house.

kamienicznik mp tenement house owner.

kamieniec mi -ńc- Gen. -a geol. gravel-bank.

kamienieć ipf. 1. (*twardnieć*) geol. petrify. 2. przen. (np. ze strachu) be petrified; przen. (= stawać się nieczułym) be petrified, petrify.

kamieniołom mi quarry, stone pit.

kamienioryt mi stone engraving.

kamienistość f. stoniness.

kamienisty a. stony, rocky; **kamienista plaża** shingle beach.

kamiennictwo n. quarrying.

kamienny a. 1. (z kamienia) of stone, stony; **węgiel kamienny** hard coal, bituminous coal. 2. (= twardy) stony, stone hard. 3. przen. (= nieczuły) stony, stony-hearted; **kamienna twarz** impassive face; **kamienne serce** heart of stone. 4. przen. (= głęboki, niczym niezmącony) dead; (o śnie) deep.

kamienować ipf. stone.

kamienowanie n. stoning.

kamień mi -ni-; Gen. -a 1. (kawałek skały) stone, rock; **kamień brukowy** paving stone, cobble-stone; **kamień budowlany** building stone; **kamień ciosowy** bud. cut stone, ashlar; **kamień drogowy** road stone; **kamień do zapalniczek** flint; **kamień nagrobny** gravestone, tombstone, headstone; **kamień milowy** dosł. i przen. milestone; **kamień młyński** millstone; **kamień pamiątkowy** memorial stone; **kamień węgielny** cornerstone; **siny kamień** min. blue vitriol, blue-stone; **kamień litograficzny** druk. lithographic stone; **okres** l. **epoka kamienia łupanego** geol. Stone Age, the palaeolithic period; **okres** l. **epoka kamienia gładzonego** geol. the neolithic period; **kamień probierczy** touchstone; **kamień filozoficzny** philospher's stone; **siedzieć gdzieś kamieniem** not move l. stir from the spot; **zmarznąć na kamień** freeze stiff; **spać jak kamień** sleep like a log; **przepaść jak kamień w wodę** disappear into thin air; **spadł mi kamień z serca** that's a load l. weight off my mind; **być komuś kamieniem u szyi** be a burden to sb; **kamień na kamieniu nie został** (o miastach, budowlach) not a stone was left standing; **kląć się w żywy kamień** to swear up and down; **mieć serce z kamienia** have a heart of stone; **trafiła kosa na kamień** diamond cut diamond. 2. (w jubilerstwie) gemstone, stone. 3. (w czajniku) scale. 4. med. calculus, stone; **kamień nerkowy** renal calculus; **kamień żółciowy** gallstone, bilestone; **kamień nazębny** tartar. 5. (= pionek) (playing-) piece.

kamikadze mp indecl. kamikaze.

kamionka f. Gen.pl. -ek 1. (*naczynie*) stoneware. 2. (*substancja*) stoneware clay. 3. roln. (= stos kamieni) stone pile. 4. bot. stone bramble (*Rubus saxatilis*). 5. zool. stone marten (*Martes foina*).

kamionkowy a. stoneware.

kamizelka f. Gen.pl. -ek 1. vest; Br. waistcoat. **kamizelka ratunkowa** life-jacket; **kamizelka kuloodporna** bulletproof jacket; **płakać komuś w ka-**

mizelkę confide one's troubles to sb. **2.** *hist.* (= *przodzik*) camisole.

kamlot¹ *mi* (*tkanina*) camlot.

kamlot² *mi Gen.* **-a** *dial. pot.* (= *kamień*) rock, stone.

kamlotowy *a.* camlet.

kamora, kamorra *f. hist.* (= *mafia*) Camorra.

kampania *f. Gen.* **-ii** **1.** (= *ukierunkowane działanie*) campaign; **kampania cukrownicza** sugar (beet) harvest; **kampania reklamowa** advertising campaign; **kampania wyborcza** electoral campaign; (*zwł. na skalę lokalną*) canvassing; **prowadzić kampanię na rzecz kogoś/czegoś/przeciwko komuś/czemuś** campaign for/against sb/sth. **2.** *wojsk.* military campaign; **Kampania Wrześniowa** *hist.* September campaign (*of 1939*).

kampanijny *a.* campaign.

kampanila *f. Gen.pl.* **-i** *bud.* campanile.

kampanula *f. bot.* campanula, bell flower (*Campanula*).

kampesz *mi bot., techn.* logwood (*Haematoxylon campechianum*).

kampus *mi uniw.* campus; **poza kampusem** off-campus.

kamrat *mp* (= *towarzysz*) companion; (= *kolega*) mate, buddy.

kamuflaż *mi* camouflage.

kamuflet *mi wojsk.* (*mina*) (*wybuch*) camouflet.

kamuflować *ipf.* camouflage.

kamuszek *mi zob.* **kamyczek.**

kamusznik *ma orn.* ruddy turnstone (*Arenaria interpres*).

kamyczek *mi* **-czk-** *Gen.* **-a** pebble, shingle.

kamyk *mi Gen.* **-a** **1.** (*odłamek skały*) pebble, shingle; **wrzucić kamyk do czyjegoś ogródka** *przen.* drop a broad hint. **2.** (*w jubilerstwie*) gemstone, stone. **3.** (*pionek*) (playing-)piece.

Kanaan *f. hist., geogr.* Canaan.

Kanada *f. geogr.* Canada.

kanada *f. pot., żart.* land of milk and honey; **ale kanada!** this is gorgeous!

Kanadyjczyk *mp* Canadian.

Kanadyjka *f. Gen.pl.* **-ek** *zob.* **Kanadyjczyk.**

kanadyjka *f. Gen.pl.* **-ek** *sport* canoe, Canadian canoe.

kanadyjkarski *a.* canoe.

kanadyjkarstwo *n.* canoeing.

kanadyjkarz *mp* canoeist.

kanadyjski *a.* Canadian.

kanalarz *mp* **1.** *pot.* (*robotnik*) sewerman. **2.** *pog.* (= *bezdomny*) bum, hobo.

kanalia *f. Gen.* **-ii** (= *łotr*) scoundrel, rascal.

kanalik *mi Gen.* **-a** **1.** (*rów*) channel. **2.** (*otwór*) duct, conduit. **3.** (*w organizmie*) canal, tubule.

kanalikowy *a.* canal; **promienie kanalikowe** *fiz.* canal rays.

kanalizacja *f.* **1.** (*sanitarna*) sewerage, sewage system. **2.** (*odwadniająca*) drainage; **kanalizacja rzeki** river canalization.

kanalizacyjny *a.* sewerage.

kanalizator *mp* sewer builder.

kanalizować *ipf.* (*miasto*) provide with a sewer system; (*rzekę*) canalize.

kanał *mi* **1.** (*rów*) canal, ditch. **2.** (*ściek*) drain, sewer; **kanał burzowy** storm-water drain, storm sewer. **3.** (*do żeglugi*) canal, waterway; **kanał portowy** harbor channel; **kanał morski** (*łączący dwa morza*) channel. **4.** (*cieśnina*) channel; **kanał La Manche** the English Channel. **5.** *techn.* (*przewód*) duct, conduit. **6.** (*w organizmie*) canal, duct. **7.** *komp.* channel. **8.** *el.* conduit; **kanał radiofoniczny** broadcasting channel; **kanał telewizyjny** television channel. **9.** *mot.* (*do napraw podwozia*) pit. **10.** *teatr* (*dla orkiestry*) pit. **11.** *jęz., pot.* (= *droga przekazywania informacji*) channel. **12.** *pot.* (= *impas*) dead end; **wpuścić kogoś w kanał** *pot.* pull a fast one on sb; **no to kanał!** that's done it!

kanałowy *a.* canal; **leczenie kanałowe** root canal therapy, root canal.

kanapa *f.* sofa, couch.

kanapka *f.* **1.** (*do siedzenia*) small sofa, settee. **2.** (*do jedzenia*) sandwich.

kanapowy *a.* sofa, couch; **partia kanapowa** fringe political party.

kanar¹ *mi* **1.** *bot.* canary grass (*Phalaris canariensis*). **2.** (*ziarno*) canary seed.

kanar² *mp Gen.* **-a** *pog.* (= *kontroler*) ticket inspector, ticket cop.

kanarek *ma* **-rk-** **1.** *orn.* canary (*Serinus canaria*). **2.** (= *łobuz*) rogue, scamp.

kanarkowy *a.* (*dotyczący kanarka*) canary's; (*o kolorze*) canary-colored, bright yellow.

kanaryjski *a.* **mozga kanaryjska** *bot. zob.* **kanar¹**; **Wyspy Kanaryjskie** the Canary Islands.

kanasta *f. karty* canasta.

kancelaria *f. Gen.* **-ii** **1.** (*pomieszczenie*) office; (*ambasady l. konsulatu*) chancellery; (*prawna*) law firm; **kancelaria adwokacka** *Br.* chambers; **kancelaria notarialna** notary's office. **2.** (*zbiór akt*) registry.

kancelaryjny *a.* (*o pracy, urzędniku*) office; (*o stylu pisania*) legalese; **papier kancelaryjny** foolscap.

kancelaryzm *mi jęz.* legalese.

kancelista *mp*, **kancelistka** *f.* clerk.

kancera *f.* damaged stamp.

kancerofobia *f. Gen.* **-ii** *med.* cancerophobia.

kancerogenny *a.* carcinogenic.

kancerować *ipf. pot.* damage, mangle.

kanciarstwo *n. pot.* swindling, dirty pool.

kanciarz *mp pot.* conman, con artist, crook.

kanciastość *f.* angularity.

kanciasty *a.* (*o wyglądzie*) angular, boxy; (*o ruchach*) awkward, angular; (*o zachowaniu*) rough, coarse.

kancik *mi Gen.* **-a** **1.** (*krawędź*) edge. **2.** *pot.* (= *oszustwo*) swindle, cheat.

kancjonał *mi rel.* psalm book, hymn book.

kanclerski *a.* chancellor's; **urząd kanclerski** chancellorship.

kanclerstwo *n.* chancellorship.

kanclerz *mp* **1.** *hist., polit.* chancellor; **Lord Kanclerz** (= *sędzia najwyższy i Przewodniczący Izby Lordów*) Lord Chancellor. **2.** (= *kurator uczelni*) chancellor.

kancona *f. muz., lit.* canzone.

kanconeta f. 1. muz. canzonetta, canzonet. 2. lit. = **kancona**.

kand mi (= pokarm dla pszczół) candy.

kandela f. Gen.pl. -i fiz. candela, candle.

kandelabr mi Gen. -u l. -a candelabrum, candelabra.

kandydat mp **kandydatka** f. Gen.pl. -ek (na urząd, stanowisko polityczne) candidate; (osoba ubiegająca się o przyjęcie do pracy, na studia) applicant; **kandydat na wiceprezydenta** (w wyborach prezydenckich w USA) running mate; **kandydat nauk** uniw. canidate of science (holder of a university degree equivalent to Ph.D.).

kandydatura f. 1. (= kandydowanie) candidacy, candidature; **wysuwać czyjąś kandydaturę** nominate sb, put sb up as a candidate. 2. (stopień naukowy) candidate of science degree (equivalent to Ph.D.).

kandydować ipf. be a candidate, run for; **kandydować na prezydenta** run for president; **mogący kandydować** eligible.

kandyzować ipf. candy.

kandyzowany a. candied.

kanele pl. bud. flute.

kanelować ipf. bud. flute.

kanelowanie n. bud. fluting.

kanelura f. bud. flute.

kangur ma zool. kangaroo; pot. Austr. roo (Macropus). – mi Gen. -a lotn. bounce.

kangurzyca f. female kangaroo.

kania f. 1. orn. kite (Milvus). 2. bot. parasol mushroom (Lepiota procera).

kanianka f. bot. dodder (Cuscuta).

kanibal mp 1. (= ludożerca) cannibal, man-eater. 2. (= okrutnik) shark.

kanibalizm mi cannibalism.

kanibalski a. cannibal.

kanikuła f. 1. (= okres upałów) dog days; (= upały) summer heat. 2. (u Rzymian) dog days.

kanion mi geogr., geol. canyon; **Wielki Kanion** geogr. Grand Canyon.

kanister mi -tr- Gen. -a jerrycan.

kaniuk ma **kaniuk amerykański** swallow-tailed kite (Elaonides fortificatus).

kaniula f. med. cannula, canula.

kanka f. 1. (rurka) canulla, canula; nozzle. 2. (naczynie) can.

kankan mi Gen. -a cancan.

kanoe n. indecl. 1. sport canoe. 2. (łódź eskimoska) kayak.

kanon mi 1. (norma, zasada) canon. 2. druk., muz., rel. canon. 3. (= podstawowy zasób, indeks) canon; **nieobjęty kanonem** (o pismach) extracanonical.

kanonada f. cannonade.

kanonia f. Gen. -ii (= urząd kanonika) canonry.

kanoniczka f. Gen.pl. -ek kośc. canoness.

kanoniczny a. 1. (= wzorcowy) canonical. 2. mat., prawn., rel. canonical; **prawo kanoniczne** canon law; **godziny kanoniczne** canonical hours.

kanonier mp wojsk. gunner.

kanonierka f. gunboat; **dyplomacja kanonierek** polit. gunboat diplomacy.

kanonik mp kośc. canon; **kanonik regularny** canon regular.

kanonikat mi kośc. = **kanonia**.

kanonista mp prawn. canonist.

kanonistyczny a. prawn. canonistic.

kanonistyka f. the science of canon law; **studiować kanonistykę** study canon law.

kanonizacja f. rel., kośc. canonization.

kanonizacyjny a. rel., kośc. canonization.

kanonizować ipf. rel., kośc. canonize (kogoś sb); confer sainthood (kogoś on sb).

kanonowy a. 1. (= zgodny z regułami) canonical. 2. muz., rel. canonical. 3. druk. (o czcionce) canon.

kanopa f. hist. (= urna grobowa) Canopic jar l. vase.

kant mi 1. (= krawędź, załamanie) edge; (spodni) crease; **puścić kogoś/coś kantem** chuck sb/sth up; **postawić się komuś kantem** stand up to sb. 2. pot. (= oszustwo) swindle, cheat; **robić kanty** swindle, cheat.

kantak mi (narzędzie) cant hook, cant dog.

kantal mi metal. kanthal.

kantalup mi Gen. -a bot. cantaloupe, cantaloup (Cucumis melo cantalupensis).

kantar mi Gen. -a 1. (= uździenica) halter; (= uzda, wędzidło) headstall, head collar. 2. orn. (przy dziobie) lore.

kantaryda f. 1. ent. Spanish fly (Lytta vesicatoria). 2. med. = **kantarydyna**.

kantarydyna f. med. cantharides, Spanish fly.

kantata f. muz., teor.lit. cantata.

kantatowy a. cantata.

Kanton mi geogr. Canton.

kanton mi (w Szwajcarii i Francji) canton; **dzielić na kantony** canton; **Jezioro Czterech Kantonów** geogr. Lucerne Lake, Lake of the Four Cantons.

kantonalny a. cantonal.

kantonka f., **kantończyk** ma Cantonese.

kantoński a. Cantonese; **język kantoński** Cantonese.

kantor[1] mp pl. -owie l. -rzy rel. (w synagodze) cantor; hazan, chazan, hazzan; (w kościele katolickim) precentor, cantor; (w kościele anglikańskim) vicar choral.

kantor[2] mi pl. -y 1. (biuro, kancelaria) office; **kantor wymiany walut** exchange office, currency exchange; **pracowni-k/ca kantoru** money changer. 2. (przedstawicielstwo handlowe, agencja) bureau, agency.

kantorek mi -rk- Gen. -a 1. (biuro) office. 2. (mebel) writing desk; Br. t. bureau.

kantoria f. Gen. -ii kośc. cantorate.

kantować ipf. 1. pot. (= oszukiwać) swindle, cheat; sl. do, rip off. 2. techn. (= obracać) tilt, turn. 3. techn. (= nadawać kant) edge.

kantowski a. fil. Kantian.

kantówka f. Gen.pl. -ek 1. (linijka) square ruler. 2. bud. squared timber.

kantyczka f. Gen.pl. -ek 1. rel. (pieśń) canticle. 2. rel. (książka) hymn book.

kantyk mi rel. canticle, chant.

kantylena f. muz. cantilena.

kantyna *f.* (*bufet*) canteen, cafeteria; **kantyna oficerska** officers' mess; (*sklepik*) canteen, commissary.

kantysta *mp* Kantian.

kantyzm *mi* Kantianism, Kantism.

kanu *n. zob.* **kanoe.**

kanwa *f.* **1.** (*do wyszywania*) canvas. **2.** (= *tło*) groundwork; **osnuty na kanwie czegoś** *przen.* based on sth.

kańczug *mi Gen.* **-a** (*bicz*) whip; (*uderzenie*) lash.

kaodaizm *mi rel.* Caodaism.

kaolin *mi min., med.* kaolin, china clay.

kaolinit *mi min.* kaolinite.

kaowiec *mp* -wc- *pl.* -y *pot.* (= *instruktor kulturalno-oświatowy*) party coordinator *l.* organizer (*at community centers, companies etc.*).

kap *int.* **kap, kap** drip, drip.

kapa *f.* **1.** (= *narzuta*) bedspread, counterpane, coverlet. **2.** (*na konia*) horse-cloth. **3.** (*w walce byków*) capa, cape. **4.** (= *okap*) cowl, bonnet, hood. **5.** *żegl.* companionway. **6.** (*szata liturgiczna*) cope.

kapać *ipf.* -ę -esz **1.** drip (*z czegoś* from sth); (= *ściekać kroplami*) (*o wodzie, deszczu, pocie*) trickle; (*o świecy*) gutter; **kapie z kurka** the tap drips; **kapie mu z nosa** his nose is running, he has a runny nose; **kapać od złota** *przen.* be all ablaze with gold; **kapiący od złota** gorgeous in gold. **2.** (*płacić małymi sumami*) pay by driblets.

kapar *mi Gen.* -a *bot., kulin.* caper (*Capparis*); **kapar ciernisty** spineless caper (*Capparis spinosa*).

kapcan *mp pl.* -y *pot.* gawk, crock.

kapcanieć *ipf. pot.* go downhill, flag.

kapciuch *mi Gen.* -a *przest.* (*na tytoń*) tobacco pouch.

kapeador *mp pl.* -rzy *l.* -owie capeador.

kapeć *mi* -pci- *Gen.* -a **1.** (*pantofel*) slipper; (*muzealny*) overshoe. **2.** *pot.* (*but*) old worn-out shoe.

kapela *f. Gen.pl.* -i *l.* -l **1.** (= *zespół ludowy*) folk group. **2.** *pot.* (= *zespół młodzieżowy*) band; **kapela jazzowa** jazz band, combo.

kapelan[1] *mp pl.* -i (*duchowny*) chaplain; **kapelan wojskowy** military chaplain; *pot.* padre; **kapelan więzienny** prison chaplain.

kapelan[2] *ma pl.* -y *icht.* capelin, caplin (*Mallotus villosus*).

kapelański *a.* chaplain's.

kapelaństwo *n.* chaplaincy.

kapelmistrz *mp pl.* -e *l.* -owie *Gen.* -ów (= *kierujący orkiestrą, chórem etc.*) conductor; *US t.* director; (= *kierujący orkiestrą*) bandmaster; (= *kierujący chórem*) choirmaster.

kapelmistrzostwo *n.* conductorship.

kapelmistrzować *ipf.* conduct (*an orchestra, choir etc.*).

kapelmistrzowski *a.* conductor's.

kapelusik *mi Gen.* -a *zob.* **kapelusz.**

kapelusz *mi Gen.* -a **1.** (*na głowie*) hat; **kapelusz filcowy** felt hat, *zwł. Br.* trilby; **kapelusz kardynalski** *dosł. i przen.* cardinal's hat; **kapelusz**

dwurożny bicorn; **kapelusz trójrożny** *l.* trójgraniasty tricorn, tricorne; **kapelusz słomkowy** straw hat; **kapelusz panamski** *l.* **panama** Panama hat, Panama, panama; **kapelusz tyrolski** Tyrolean hat; **kapelusz rybacki** *żegl.* sou'wester, nor'wester; **kapelusz pszczelarski** bee hat; **kapelusz od słońca** sun hat; **kapelusz tesalski** *hist.* petasus, petasos; **kapelusz kowbojski** cowboy hat; **przekrzywić kapelusz** (*na bok l. na bakier*) cock one's hat; **bez kapelusza** hatless; **szpilka do kapelusza** hatpin; **uchylić kapelusza** raise one's hat; *pot.* dip one's lid; **(jak) z kapelusza** (= *jak w czarnej magii; przypadkowo*) out of a hat; (= *zmyślony*) off the top of one's head; **pudło na kapelusze** hatbox, bandbox; **wieszak na kapelusze** hat-stand; **mieć na głowie kapelusz** have one's hat on. **2.** (*grzyba*) (mushroom) cap, pileus; (*niedojrzałego grzyba*) button.

kapelusznictwo *n.* hat making.

kapelusznik *mp* hatter.

kapeluszowy *a.* (*dotyczący nakrycia głowy*) hat; (*o grzybach*) capped, pileate.

kaper *mp* -pr- *pl.* -rzy *l.* -owie *hist.* privateer; *pot.* pirate.

kaperka *f. hist.* = **kaperstwo.**

kaperować *ipf.* **1.** *hist.* privateer. **2.** (= *przekupywać*) win over (*esp. players of a rival sports club by bribe*).

kaperski *a. hist.* privateer; **list kaperski** *hist.* letter(s) of marque, letter of marque and reprisal; **sąd kaperski** prize court; **statek kaperski** privateer.

kaperstwo *n. hist.* privateering.

kapibara *f. zool.* capybara (*Hydrochoerus hydrochaeris*).

kapilara *f. anat., fiz., geol.* capillary; **kapilara termometru** thermometer capillary.

kapilarność *f. fiz., geol.* capillarity.

kapilarny *a.* capillary; **ściana kapilarna** *anat.* capillary wall; **rurka kapilarna** *fiz.* capillary tube; **wody kapilarne** *geol.* capillary water.

kapiszon *mi Gen.* -u *l.* -a **1.** (*spłonka*) percussion cap. **2.** *hist.* (*kaptur*) hood.

kapiszonowy *a., attr.* percussion-cap.

kapiszonówka *f. Gen.pl.* -ek *hist.* percussion-cap gun.

kapitalik *mi* **1.** *zob.* **kapitał. 2.** *druk.* small capital.

kapitalista *mp*, **kapitalistka** *f. Gen.pl.* -ek capitalist.

kapitalistyczny *a.* capitalist.

kapitalizacja *f.* capitalization; **stopa kapitalizacji** rate of capitalization; **kapitalizacja siły nabywczej** capitalization of earning power; **kapitalizacja odsetek** capitalization of interest.

kapitalizm *mi* capitalism; **kapitalizm państwowy** state capitalism; **kapitalizm monopolistyczny** monopoly capitalism; **kapitalizm korporacyjny** collective capitalism; **kapitalizm menedżerski** managerial capitalism.

kapitalizować *ipf.* capitalize.

kapitalny *a.* **1.** (= *istotny*) cardinal, fundamental, capital; **o kapitalnym znaczeniu** of paramount importance; **kapitalny remont** (*samo-*

chodu, maszyny) major overhaul; (*domu*) extensive redecoration; **ściana kapitalna** *bud.* main wall. **2.** (= *znakomity*) brilliant, splendid; *pot.* smashing, stunning. **3.** (= *śmieszny*) priceless.

kapitał *mi ekon.* (= *środki finansowe*) **1.** capital; (*przy naliczaniu odsetek*) principal; **kapitał akcyjny** share capital; **kapitał obcy** debt capital; **kapitał obrotowy** working capital; **kapitał podwyższonego ryzyka** venture capital; **kapitał rezerwowy** reserve (capital); **kapitał statutowy** authorized capital; **kapitał własny** equity, shareholders' funds, shareholders' equity; **kapitał wniesiony** paid-up share capital, paid-in capital; **kapitał wyemitowany** issued capital; **kapitał wykorzystywany** capital employed; **kapitał zakładowy** initial capital; **kapitał ludzki** human capital; **lokata kapitału** capital investment; **przekształcać w kapitał** capitalize; **zbić na czymś kapitał** *przen.* make capital (out) of sth. **2.** (= *kapitaliści*) capital.

kapitała *f.* capitals.

kapitałka *f. Gen.pl.* **-ek** *introl.* headband.

kapitałochłonność *f. ekon.* capital intensity.

kapitałochłonny *a. ekon.* capital-intensive.

kapitałowy *a.* capital; **środki kapitałowe** capital resources; **zyski kapitałowe** capital gains.

kapitan *mp pl.* **-owie** *lotn., wojsk., sport* captain; **kapitan żeglugi wielkiej** deep-sea captain; **kapitan marynarki** lieutenant commander; **kapitan marynarki handlowej** merchant navy captain; **kapitan portu** harbor master.

kapitanat *mi* (*portu*) port authority.

kapitanostwo *n.* the captain and his wife.

kapitanować *ipf.* serve as a captain.

kapitański *a.* captain's; **mostek kapitański** the bridge.

kapitaństwo *n.* (*stopień wojskowy*) captaincy, captainship.

kapitel *mi Gen.* **-a** *l.* **-u** *Gen.pl.* **-i** *l.* **-ów** *bud.* capital, chapiter, cap.

Kapitol *mi* (*siedziba Kongresu USA*) the Capitol.

kapitulacja *f. dosł. i przen.* capitulation, surrender (*przed kimś/czymś l. wobec kogoś/czegoś* to sb/sth); **bezwarunkowa kapitulacja** unconditional surrender; **ostateczna kapitulacja** ultimate *l.* final capitulation; **akt kapitulacji** capitulation, capitulation act.

kapitulacyjny *a.* capitulation; **akt kapitulacyjny** capitulation, capitulation act.

kapitulancki *a.* defeatist.

kapitulanctwo *n.* defeatism.

kapitulant *mp* **1.** (= *poddający się*) capitulator. **2.** (= *defetysta*) defeatist.

kapitularz *mi Gen.* **-a** **1.** *rel.* (*sala*) chapterhouse. **2.** *rel.* (= *wyciąg z przepisów kościelnych*), *hist.* (= *ustawa królewska we Francji za Karolingów*) capitulary.

kapitulny *a.* capitular.

kapitulować *ipf.* **1.** (= *kończyć wojnę*) capitulate, surrender (*przed kimś* to sb). **2.** (= *poddawać się, wycofywać się*) surrender, give up; **no dobra, kapituluję** *żart.* (= *nie mam nic więcej do powiedzenia*) OK, I rest my case.

kapituła *f.* (= *kolegium honorowe*) (= *zgromadzenie duchownych*) chapter; **członek kapituły** capitulary; **zgromadzenie kapituły** (*kolegiaty, katedry, zakonu*) chapter.

kapka *f. Gen.pl.* **-ek** **1.** (= *kropla*) driblet, drop. **2.** (= *odrobina*) wee bit, tad; **on jest kapkę za niski** he's a tad short; **kapka czegoś** (*np. rozsądku, trudności*) a mite of sth.

kaplica *f.* chapel; (*wzniesiona na cześć męczennika*) martyry; (*z relikwiarzami*) feretory; **kaplica boczna** side chapel; **prywatna kaplica** private chapel, oratory; **Kaplica Sykstyńska** the Sistine Chapel.

kaplicowy *a.* chapel.

kapliczka *f. Gen.pl.* **-ek** (= *mała kaplica*) chapel; **kapliczka przydrożna** wayside shrine.

kapłan *mp rel.* priest; **najwyższy kapłan** *hist., kośc.* (*w starożytnym Rzymie*) pontiff; **kapłan Bachusa** *hist.* (*t. przen.*) bacchant; **rządy kapłanów** hierocracy, hagiarchy; **kapłan sztuki** *przen.* priest of art.

kapłanka *f. Gen.pl.* **-ek** *rel.* priestess.

kapłański *a.* priestly, hieratic, hieratical; **święcenia kapłańskie** holy orders; **nadanie święceń kapłańskich** ordination; **nadać komuś święcenia kapłańskie** confer holy orders upon sb, ordain sb; **przyjmować święcenia kapłańskie** take holy orders, be ordained.

kapłaństwo *n.* priesthood; **sakrament kapłaństwa** sacrament of priesthood; **pozbawić kogoś kapłaństwa** (*zwł. za karę*) unfrock sb, defrock sb.

kapłon *ma* capon.

kapłonić *ipf.* caponize.

kapnąć *pf.* **-ij** *zob.* **kapać**. **~ się** *pf. pot.* (= *zrozumieć, zorientować się*) figure out (*że...* that...).

kapo *f. l. mp indecl.* prisoner foreman (*in Nazi camps*).

kapodaster *mi muz.* capo, capo tasto.

kapok *mi Gen.* **-a** **1.** *żegl.* life jacket. **2.** (= *włókno puchowca*) ceiba; (= *włókno nasienne*) kapok.

kaponiera *f. wojsk.* caponier.

kapota *f. pot.* (*okrycie wierzchnie*) coat.

kapotaż *mi lotn.* rollover, overturn.

kapotować *ipf.* roll over, overturn.

kapować *ipf.* **1.** *pot.* (= *rozumieć*) twig (*że...* that...) catch on; **on chyba jeszcze nie kapuje** it looks like he hasn't twigged yet; **kapujesz?** are you with me?, do you follow? **2.** *pot.* (= *donosić*) squeal (*komuś na kogoś* on sb to sb).

kapral *mp* corporal.

kapralski *a.* corporal's.

kaprawy *a.* (*o oczach*) bleary.

kapryfolium *n. sing. indecl. pl.* **-lia** *Gen.* **-liów** *bot.* honeysuckle (*Lonicera caprifolium*).

kaprys *mi* **1.** (= *zachcianka*) caprice, whim, fancy; **pod wpływem kaprysu** on a whim; **zrobić coś pod wpływem kaprysu** have a whim to do sth; **zależnie od czyjegoś kaprysu** at sb's will and pleasure; **miewać kaprysy** be wayward. **2.** *przen.* (= *odmiana, zmiana*) quirk, twist; **kaprysy pogody** vagaries of weather, weather vagaries; **kaprys losu/historii** quirk *l.* twist of fate/

history; **kaprys natury** freak. **3.** *muz.* capriccio, caprice.

kaprysić *ipf.* **-szę -sisz** (= *miewać kaprysy*) be capricious, be fickle; (= *grymasić*) fuss; (= *być wybrednym*) pick and choose.

kapryśność *f.* (= *zmienność usposobienia*) whimsicality, capriciousness, fickleness; (= *grymaśność*) fussiness.

kapryśny *a.* (= *o zmiennym usposobieniu*) capricious, whimsical; (= *grymaśny*) fussy; (*o dziecku, zachowaniu*) petulant; (*zwł. o kobiecie*) flighty; (*o pogodzie*) freakish, unpredictable.

kapsel *mi* **-sl-** *Gen.* **-a 1.** (*od butelki*) crown cap. **2.** (= *spłonka*) percussion cap.

kapslować *ipf.* (*butelki*) cap (*bottles*).

kapslownica *f. techn.* capping machine.

kapsuła *f. astron.* (space) capsule; **kapsuła ratownicza** emergency capsule.

kapsułka *f. Gen.pl.* **-ek 1.** (*z lekiem*) capsule. **2.** *fiz.* tube.

kapsułkować *ipf.* capsule, encapsulate.

Kapsztad *mi* Cape Town.

kapsztadzki *a.* Cape Town.

kaptować *ipf.* win *l.* bring over, win round; **kaptować klientów** tout for customers.

kaptur[1] *mi Gen.* **-a 1.** (*na głowie*) hood; **kurtka/ płaszcz z kapturem** hooded jacket/coat. **2.** (*osłona*) cap, cover; (*nad kominem*) cowl. **3.** *myśl.* hood.

kaptur[2] *mi Gen.* **-a 1.** *hist.* (*konfederacja*) interregnum vigilance committee. **2.** *hist.* (*sąd*) = **sąd kapturowy**.

kapturek *mi* **-rk-** *Gen.* **-a** bonnet, hood; **Czerwony Kapturek** Little Red Riding Hood; **kapturek dopochwowy** *med.* diaphragm, Dutch cap.

kapturnica *f. bot.* pitcher plant, huntsman's-cup (*Sarracenia*).

kapturowy *a.* (= *podobny do kaptura*) hood-shaped; **konfederacja kapturowa** interregnum vigilance committee; **sąd kapturowy** *hist.* (*zwł. w Niemczech*) vehmgricht, fehmic court; *przen.* (= *niesprawiedliwy trybunał*) star chamber.

kapturzyć *ipf. myśl.* hood (*a hawk or falcon*).

kapucyn[1] *mp pl.* **-i** (*zakonnik*) Capuchin.

kapucyn[2] *ma pl.* **-y** (*gołąb*) capuchin.

kapucynka *f.* **1.** (*zakonnica*) Capuchin nun. **2.** *zool.* capuchin, sapajou (*Cebus*).

kapucyński *a.* Capuchin's, Capuchin.

kapusta *f. bot.* cabbage (*Brassica oleracea*); **kapusta brukselska** Brussels sprouts (*Brassica oleracea gemmifera*); **kapusta włoska** savoy (*Brassica oleracea sabuda l. capitata*); **kapusta pekińska** Chinese cabbage, pe-tsai cabbage (*Brassica pekinensis*); **kapusta chińska** Chinese cabbage, pak-choi cabbage (*Brassica chinensis*); **kapusta morska** sea kale (*Crambe maritima*); **kapusta czerwona** *l.* **modra** red cabbage; **kapusta kiszona** *l.* **kwaszona** sauerkraut; **główka kapusty** cabbage head; **kiła kapusty** *pat.* clubroot; **groch z kapustą** *przen.* higgledy-piggledy, pell-mell.

kapustnica *f. ent.* cabbage moth (*Mamestra brassicae*).

kapustnik *mi Gen.* **-a** *roln.* (*pole*) cabbage field.

– **ma** *ent.* (*motyl*) **bielinek kapustnik** cabbage white (*Pieris brassicae*).

kapuś *mp Gen.pl.* **-ów** *pog.* snitch, rat; (*zwł. pracujący dla policji*) stool pigeon, fink.

kapuściany *a.* cabbage; **kapuściana głowa** *pot.* blockhead, cabbage head, numskull.

kapuścisko *n.* **1.** *zob.* **kapusta. 2.** *roln.* cabbage field.

kapuśniaczek *mi* **-czk- 1.** (*zupa*) = **kapuśniak 1. 2.** (*deszcz*) sprinkle, drizzle. **3.** (*pasztecik*) cabbage pasty.

kapuśniak *mi Gen.* **-a 1.** (*zupa*) cabbage soup. **2.** (*deszcz*) drizzle, sprinkle.

kaput *int. pot.* kaput.

kar *mi geol.* glacial cirque.

kara *f.* punishment (*za coś* for (doing) sth); *prawn., sport* penalty (*za coś* for (doing) sth); **kara chłosty** flogging, whipping; **kara cielesna** corporal punishment; **kara grzywny** fine, pecuniary penalty; **kara pieniężna** fine, mulct; **kara nagany** reprimand; **kara dyscyplinarna** disciplinary punishment; **kara ograniczenia wolności** penalty of restricted liberty; **kara pozbawienia wolności** custodial sentence; **kara aresztu** penalty of arrest; **kara więzienia** imprisonment; **kara dożywocia** life sentence; **kara dożywotniego więzienia** life imprisonment; **kara śmierci** capital punishment, death penalty; **najwyższy wymiar kary** capital punishment; **podlegający karze** subject *l.* liable to penalty, under penalty; **kara zaostrzona** increased penalty; **darowanie kary** remission of penalty, pardon; **okoliczność wpływająca na złagodzenie kary** circumstance affecting the mitigation of punishment; **surowa kara** heavy *l.* harsh sentence; **zasłużona kara** deserts, comeuppance; **wymierzyć komuś karę** inflict a punishment on sb; **mieć karę za coś** be punished for sth; **potulnie przyjąć karę** submit meekly to one's punishment, kiss the rod; **odbyć karę** (*więzienia*) serve one's sentence; **kara boska** *pot.* divine retribution; **kara boska z tym chłopakiem/samochodem!** this boy/car is a nuisance!

karabela *f. Gen.pl.* **-i** *l.* **-l** *hist.* carabella (*type of curved sword*).

karabin *mi Gen.* **-u** *l.* **-a** rifle; **karabin automatyczny** automatic rifle; **karabin samopowtarzalny** semi-automatic rifle; **karabin myśliwski** hunting gun; **karabin maszynowy** machine-gun; **ciężki/ lekki karabin maszynowy** heavy/light machine-gun; **karabin wielostrzałowy** magazine gun *l.* rifle.

karabinek *mi* **-nk-** *Gen.* **-a 1.** (*broń*) carbine; (*kawaleryjski t.*) carabin, carabine; **karabinek pneumatyczny** air rifle; **karabinek sportowy** sporting rifle. **2.** (*klamra*) karibiner, snaplink.

karabinier *mp* **1.** (*policjant*) carabiniere. **2.** *hist.* (*żołnierz*) carbineer, carabinier, carabineer.

karabinowy *a.* rifle; **ogień karabinowy** rifle fire; **granat karabinowy** rifle grenade; **zamek karabinowy** gunlock.

karabińczyk *mi* = **karabinek 2.**

karacena *f. hist.* scale armor.

karaczany *pl. Gen.* **-ów** *ent.* cockroaches (*Blat-*

todea); **karaczan wschodni** oriental cockroach, black beetle (*Blatta orientalis*).

karać *ipf.* **-rzę -rzesz** punish (*kogoś za coś* sb for (doing) sth); *prawn., sport* penalize; **karać fizycznie** chastise; **karać grzywną** *l.* **mandatem** fine, mulct; **karać kogoś śmiercią** sentence sb to death; **karać suspensą** (*duchownego*) defrock, unfrock.

karafka *f. Gen.pl.* **-ek** decanter.

karagana *f. bot.* caragana, pea tree (*Caragana*); **karagana syberyjska** Siberian pea tree (*Caragana arborescens*).

karaibski *a.* Caribbean; **Morze Karaibskie** Caribbean Sea, the Caraibbean; Spanish Main.

Karaiby *a. pl. pot. geogr.* the Caribbean.

Karaim *mp pl.* **-owie, Karaimka** *f. Gen.pl.* **-ek** *rel.* Karaite.

karaimski *a. rel.* Karaite.

karakal *ma zool.* caracal, desert lynx (*Felis l. Lynx caracal*).

karakol *mi hist.* (*manewr bitewny*) caracole.

karakon *ma pot.* = **karaluch**.

karakuł *ma Gen.* **-a** (*owca*) (*futro*) karakul, caracul; Persian lamb.

karakułowy *a.* karakul, caracul.

karalność *f.* punishability; *zwł. prawn.* penality.

karalny *a.* punishable, penal; **karalny grzywną** punishable with a fine.

karaluch *ma ent.* oriental cockroach, black-beetle (*Blatta orientalis*).

karambol *mi* **1.** (= *kraksa*) multiple crash, pileup. **2.** *bilard* (*gra*) carom biliards; (*uderzenie*) carom; *zwł. Br.* cannon; (*bila*) red ball.

karambolować *ipf. bilard* carom; *Br.* cannon.

karany *mp* person with a criminal record, convict. – *a.* punishable (*czymś* by sth); **przestępstwo karane więzieniem** *l.* **pozbawieniem wolności** penitentiary offence; **przestępstwo karane śmiercią** capital offence; **przestępstwo karane śmiercią przez powieszenie** hanging offence; **być poprzednio karanym** have a criminal record; **to przestępstwo jest karane więzieniem/śmiercią** this offence is punishable by a prison sentence/death.

kararyjski *a.* **marmur kararyjski** Carrara marble.

karaś *ma icht.* crucian carp, crucian (*Carassius carassius*).

karat *mi Gen.* **-a 1.** (*jednostka masy kamieni szlachetnych*) carat. **2.** (*miara zawartości złota w stopie*) karat, *Br.* carat.

karate *n. indecl. sport* karate.

karateka *mp sport* karate fighter.

karatowy *a.* (*w odniesieniu do kamieni szlachetnych*) carat; (*w odniesieniu do złota*) karat, *Br.* carat; **24-karatowe złoto** 24-karat gold.

karawaka *f. hist., rel.* Caravaca cross.

karawan *mi* hearse.

karawana *f. dosł. i przen.* caravan; (*pionierów amerykańskich*) wagon train; **psy szczekają, karawana idzie dalej** the dogs bark but the caravans move on.

karawaniarski *a.* (= *ponury, pogrzebowy*) dismal, funereal; (*firma, koń*) undertaker's.

karawaniarz *mp* undertaker's man.

karawaning *mi* **1.** (*podróżowanie*) caravanning. **2.** (*pojazd*) camper.

karawaningowy *a.* caravanning.

karawanowy *a.* caravan.

karawanseraj *mi Gen.pl.* **-ów** caravanserai, caravansary; (*zwł. w Turcji i krajach arabskich*) khan.

karawela *f. żegl.* caravel, carvel.

karawelowy *a. żegl.* caravel.

karb *mi* (= *nacięcie*) notch, nick; (*na brzegu liścia*) crenation; **kłaść** *l.* **złożyć coś na karb czegoś** put sth down to (sb's) sth, attribute sth to (sb's) sth; **składam to na karb jej niedoświadczenia** I put it down to her inexperience, I attribute it to her inexperience; **wziąć kogoś/coś w karby** bring *l.* whip sb/sth into line, bring sb/sth under control; **trzymać kogoś w karbach** keep sb in line.

karbamid *mi chem.* carbamide.

karbazol *mi chem.* carbazole.

karbid *mi chem.* carbide, calcium carbide.

karbidownia *f. Gen.pl.* **-i** carbide factory.

karbidowy *a.* carbide; **lampa karbidowa = karbidówka**.

karbidówka *f. Gen.pl.* **-ek** carbide lamp, acetylene lamp.

karbieniec *mi bot.* bugleweed, horehund (*Lycopus*); **karbieniec pospolity** gipsywort (*Lycopus europaeus*).

karbocykliczny *a. chem.* carbocyclic; **związki karbocykliczne** carbocyclic compounds.

karboksyl *mi chem.* carboxyl.

karboksylowy *a. chem.* carboxyl, carboxylic; **grupa karboksylowa** carboxyl group, carboxylic group.

karbol *mi chem.* phenol, carbolic acid.

karbolineum *n. indecl. bud., chem.* Carbolineum.

karbolować *ipf.* phenolate, carbolize.

karbolowy *a. chem.* carbolic; **kwas karbolowy** phenol, carbolic acid.

karbon *mi geol.* the Carboniferous, Carboniferous period.

karbonado *mi min.* carbonado, black diamond.

karbonariusz *mp hist.* Carbonaro.

karbonarski *a. hist.* Carbonarist.

karbonaryzm *mi hist.* Carbonarism.

karbonatyzacja *f. geol.* carbonatization.

karbonit *mi górn.* carbonite.

karbonizacja *f. chem., druk., tk.* carbonization.

karbonizować *ipf. chem., druk., tk.* carbonize.

karbonowy *a. chem.* carbonic; **kwas karbonowy** carbonic acid.

karbonylowy *a.* carbonyl, carbonylic; **grupa karbonylowa** carbonyl group.

karboński *a. geol.* Carboniferous; **okres karboński** Carboniferous period, the Carboniferous.

karborund *mi* **1.** *chem.* silicon carbid. **2.** *techn.* (*materiał ścierny*) Carborundum.

karborundowy *a. techn.* Carborundum.

karbować *ipf.* **1.** (= *nacinać*) notch, nick; **karbować sobie w pamięci** remember. **2.** (= *fałdować*) corrugate, wrinkle, crease.

karbunkuł *mi* **1.** *pat.* carbuncle. **2.** *przest.* (= *czerwony kamień szlachetny*) carbuncle.

karbunkułowy *a. pl. pat.* carbuncular; **objawy karbunkułowe** carbuncular symptoms.

karburacja *f. mot.* carburetion, carburation.

karburator *mi Gen.* **-a** *mot.* carburetor, carbureter.

karburyzacja *f. techn.* (*metalu, paliwa*) carburization.

karburyzator *mi Gen.* **-a** *chem., techn.* carburetant.

karburyzować *ipf. techn.* carburize, carburet, carburate.

karcący *a.* reproachful; **karcąca mina** reproachful expression; **karcąca ręka sprawiedliwości** the long arm of the law *l.* justice; **karcące spojrzenie** reproachful look.

karcer *mi* solitary confinement cell; *pot.* the hole.

karciany *a.* card; **dług karciany** gaming debt; **stolik karciany** card-table; **sztuczka karciana** card trick.

karciarski *a.* gambling; **pasja karciarska** passion for cards, passion for gambling.

karciarstwo *n.* compulsive card-playing.

karciarz *mp* compulsive card-player.

karcić *ipf.* **1.** (= *skrzyczeć*) rebuke, scold. **2.** (= *uderzyć*) smack.

karcinogenny *a. pat.* carcinogenic.

karcz *mi Gen.* **-a** *Gen.pl.* **-ów** (= *pniak z korzeniami*) stump, stub.

karczek *mi* **-czk-** *Gen.* **-a** **1.** (= *mały kark*) little neck. **2.** *tk.* neck.

karczemny *a.* bar, inn; **karczemna awantura** brawl, free-for-all.

karczma *f. Gen.pl.* **-czm** *l.* **-czem** inn, tavern.

karczmarka *f. zob.* **karczmarz**.

karczmarz *mp* innkeeper.

karczoch *mi Gen.* **-a** **1.** *bot.* artichoke, globe artichoke (*Cynara scolymus*). **2.** *bud.* type of ornament resembling artichoke.

karczować *ipf.* grub (out), stump, stub.

karczowisko *n. leśn.* clear-cut, clear cutting.

karczownik *mp pl.* **-cy** (= *robotnik zajmujący się karczowaniem*) grubber. – *mi Gen.* **-a** *pl.* **-i** (= *narzędzie do karczowania*) grubber, grub hoe. – *ma pl.* **-i** *zool.* water vole (*Arvicola terrestris*).

karczunek *mi* **-nk-** grubbing (out).

kard *mi Gen.* **-a** *bot.* cardoon, cardon (*Cynara cardunculus*).

kardamon *mi* **1.** *bot.* cardamom (*Elettaria cardamon*). **2.** (= *nasiona kardamonu*) cardamom.

kardamonowy *a.* cardamom; **nasiona kardamonowe** cardamom seeds; **owoc kardamonowy** cardamom fruit.

kardan *mi Gen.* **-a** *techn.* cardan shaft.

kardanowy *a. techn.* cardan; **przegub kardanowy** cardan joint.

kardiochirurg *mp pl.* **-dzy** *l.* **-owie** *med.* cardiac surgeon.

kardiochirurgia *f. Gen.* **-ii** *med.* cardiac surgery.

kardiochirurgiczny *a. med.* cardiac; **klinika kardiochirurgiczna** cardiac clinic; **leczenie kardiochirurgiczne** cardiac treatment; **oddział kardiochirurgiczny** cardiac ward *l.* unit; **operacja kardiochirurgiczna** open-heart surgery.

kardiograf *mi* **1.** *med.* electrocardiograph, cardiograph. **2.** *techn.* cardioidograph.

kardiografia *f. Gen.* **-ii** *med.* electrocardiography, cardiography.

kardiogram *mi med.* electrocardiogram, cardiogram.

kardiolog *mp pl.* **-dzy** *l.* **-owie** *med.* cardiologist.

kardiologia *f. Gen.* **-ii** *med.* cardiology.

kardiologiczny *a. med.* cardiologic, cardiological; **klinika kardiologiczna** cardiological clinic; **leczenie kardiologiczne** cardiological treatment; **oddział kardiologiczny** cardiological ward *l.* unit; **operacja kardiologiczna** cardiological surgery.

kardiostymulator *mi Gen.* **-a** *med.* pacemaker.

kardiotachometr *mi med.* cardiotachometer.

kardiowersja *f. med.* cardioversion.

kardynalny *a.* cardinal; **kardynalny błąd** cardinal error; **cnoty kardynalne** cardinal virtues; **liczby kardynalne** *mat.* cardinal numbers; **kardynalne punkty horyzontu** *astron.* cardinal points; **kardynalne punkty układu optycznego** *fiz.* cardinal points.

kardynalski *a. rz.-kat.* cardinal's; **czerwień kadynalska** cardinal red; **godność kardynalska** cardinalate, cardinalship; **kapelusz kardynalski** cardinal's hat; **kolegium kardynalskie** College of Cardinals; **urząd kardynalski** cardinalate, cardinalship.

kardynalstwo *n. rz.-kat.* cardinalate.

kardynał *mp pl.* **-owie** *rz.-kat.* cardinal. – *ma pl.* **-y** *orn.* cardinal (*Cardinalis cardinalis*).

Karel *mp pl.* **-owie** Karelian.

Karelia *f. geogr.* Karelia.

Karelka *f. zob.* **Karel**.

karelski *a.* Karelian.

karenaż *mi żegl.* careen.

karencja *f.* **1.** (= *okres wyczekiwania*) waiting period. **2.** *ubezp.* waiting period. **3.** *fin.* (*dotycząca kredytu*) grace period. **4.** *roln.* preharvest interval. **5.** *sport* waiting period.

karesy *pl. Gen.* **-ów** *przest.* coaxing.

kareta *f.* **1.** carriage; **to pasuje jak wół do karety** it's like a square peg in a round hole. **2.** *karty* four of a kind.

karetka *f.* (= *mała kareta*) small carriage; **karetka pocztowa** mail truck; **karetka pogotowia** ambulance; **karetka więzienna** prison van; *pot.* paddy *l.* patrol wagon, Black Maria.

karetta *f. Dat., Loc.* **-tcie** *zool.* loggerhead turtle (*Caretta caretta*).

kariatyda *f. bud.* caryatid.

karibu *n. l. ma indecl. zool.* caribou (*Rangifer tarandus caribou*).

kariera *f.* **1.** (*zawodowa*) career; **robić karierę**

work one's way up; **światowa kariera** international career; **zrobić karierę** make a career. **2.** (= *powodzenie życiowe*) success.

karierowicz *mp Gen.pl.* **-ów** careerist.

karierowiczka *f. zob.* **karierowicz**.

karierowiczostwo *n.* careerism, pushing one's way up.

karierowiczowski *a.* careerist; **karierowiczowskie ambicje** careerist ambitions.

karimata *f.* foam pad; *Br.* carrimat.

kariogamia *f. Gen.* **-ii** *biol.* karyogamy.

kariokinetyczny *a. biol.* karyokinetic; **wrzeciono kariokinetyczne** spindle.

kariokineza *f. biol.* karyokinesis.

kariolimfa *f. biol.* karyolymph.

kariolka *f. hist.* (= *odkryty pojazd konny*) cariole, carriole.

kariologia *f. Gen.* **-ii** *med.* karyology.

kariomitoza *f. biol.* karyomitosis.

karioplazma *f. biol.* karyoplasm.

kariotyp *mi biol.* karyotype.

kark *mi* **1.** nape (of the neck); **pędzić na złamanie karku** run *l.* rush headlong; **mieć głowę na karku** have one's head screwed on; **mieć sztywny kark** be stiff-necked; **mieć kogoś/coś na karku** be bothered *l.* pestered by sb/sth; **nadstawiać za kogoś/coś karku** risk one's neck for sb/sth; **ukręcić czemuś kark** put an end to sth; **skręcić kark** break one's neck; **ugiąć przed kimś karku** bend low before sb; **na karku** *pot.* (*o czymś, co nadchodzi, zbliża się*) approaching, imminent. **2.** *zool., anat.* nucha.

karkołomność *f.* recklessness.

karkołomny *a.* breakneck, reckless; **karkołomna jazda** reckless driving; **karkołomna prędkość** breakneck speed.

karkówka *a. kulin.* (*wieprzowa*) shoulder; (*wołowa*) chuck.

karleć *ipf.* dwarf.

karli *a.* dwarfish; **karli wzrost** dwarfish height.

karlica *f. zob.* **karzeł**.

karła *itd. mp zob.* **karzeł**.

karłowacieć *ipf.* dwarf.

karłowatość *f.* dwarfism.

karłowaty *a.* dwarfish, dwarf; **jabłoń karłowata** dwarf apple; **sosna karłowata** *bot.* dwarf pine, mugho pine (*Pinus mugo mugo*); **wierzba karłowata** dwarf willow; **gospodarstwo karłowate** *ekon., roln.* farm of no more than two hectares; **ludy karłowate** *antrop.* dwarf peoples, small-statured peoples.

karma¹ *f.* (= *pasza*) fodder, feed, forage, provender; **karma dla kotów/psów** cat/dog food.

karma² *f. rel., fil.* karma.

karman *mi* = **karma**².

karmaniola *f. hist.* **1.** (= *pieśń rewolucyjna z 1792 r., taniec*) carmagnole. **2.** (= *strój piemoncki*) carmagnole.

karmazyn *mi Gen.* **-u** *pl.* **-y** (= *kolor czerwony*) crimson. – *mp Gen.* **-a** *pl.* **-i** *hist.* (= *szlachcic ze starożytnego rodu*) Polish nobleman of an ancient house. – *ma Gen.* **-a** *pl.* **-y** **1.** *icht.* redfish, rosefish, ocean perch, Norway haddock (*Seba-*

stes marinus). **2.** *zool.* (*rasa kur*) Rhode Island Red.

karmazynowy *a.* **1.** crimson; **karmazynowy kolor** crimson. **2. karmazynowy szlachcic** *zob.* **karmazyn**.

karmel *mi kulin.* caramel.

karmelarski *a.* candymaker's; **mistrz karmelarski** master candymaker; **pracownia karmelarska** candymaker's workshop.

karmelarstwo *n.* candymaking.

karmelarz *mp* candymaker.

karmelek *mi* **-lk-** *Gen.* **-a** *kulin.* caramel.

karmelicki *a. rz.-kat.* Carmelite; **klasztor karmelicki** Carmelite monastery; **kościół karmelicki** Carmelite church; **reguła karmelicka** Carmelite rule; **zakon karmelicki** Carmelite order.

karmelita *mp rz.-kat.* Carmelite, White Friar; **zakon karmelitów** Carmelite Order.

karmelitanka *f. rz.-kat.* Carmelite.

karmelitański *a. zob.* **karmelicki**.

karmelizacja *f. chem.* caramelization.

karmelizować *ipf. kulin.* caramelize.

karmelowy *a. kulin.* caramel; **cukierek karmelowy** caramel; **lody karmelowe** caramel ice-cream; **polewa karmelowa** caramel icing.

karmiący *a.* feeding; **matka karmiąca** nursing mother.

karmiciel *mp przest.* feeder, breadwinner.

karmicielka *f. zob.* **karmiciel**.

karmić *ipf.* **1.** (*butelką*) bottle-feed. **2.** (*łyżką l. łyżeczką*) spoon-feed. **3.** (*piersią*) breast-feed, nurse, suckle. **4.** (= *żywić*) feed. **5.** *przen.* (= *dostarczać czegoś niematerialnego*) feed, nurture; **karmić kogoś obietnicami** beguile sb with promises. **~ się** *ipf.* **1.** (= *żywić się*) feed on. **2.** (= *dostarczać sobie czegoś niematerialnego*) feed on; **karmić się wspomnieniami** cherish one's memories.

karmidło *n. Gen.pl.* **-deł** *roln.* animal feeder.

karmin *mi* (= *czerwony barwnik l. kolor*) carmine.

karminowy *a.* carmine; **karminowy kolor** carmine; **karminowe policzki** carmine cheeks; **karminowe usta** carmine lips.

karmnik *mi Gen.* **-a** (*dla ptaków*) bird table. – *ma roln.* (= *tucznik*) porker.

karnacja *f.* **1.** (= *cera*) complexion; **jasna karnacja** pale complexion; **śniada karnacja** swarthy *l.* dark complexion. **2.** *sztuka* rendition of the color of human flesh on a painting, carnation.

karnalit *mi min.* carnallite.

karnawał *mi* carnival.

karneol *mi min.* carnelian.

karnet *mi* **1.** (= *abonament*) subscription card; (= *bloczek biletów*) book of tickets; (= *bloczek z kuponami*) coupon *l.* voucher book. **2.** *przest.* dance card.

karniak *mi Gen.* **-a** *pot.* shot of vodka (*to be had by a latecomer to a party to catch up*); **musisz wypić** *l.* **walnąć karniaka** you must have a penalty shot to catch up.

karnie *adv.* **1.** (= *za karę*) by way of punishment; **zwolnić kogoś karnie ze służby** *wojsk.* discharge dishonorably. **2.** (= *w sposób zdyscypli-*

nowany) in an orderly manner; **zachowywać się karnie** behave o.s.

karnik *mp pot.* (= *specjalista w zakresie prawa karnego*) criminal lawyer, criminalist.

karnisz *mi Gen.* -a *l.* -u *Gen.pl.* -y *l.* -ów curtain rail, cornice.

karność *f.* discipline, obedience; **wychowywać kogoś w karności** bring sb up in a disciplined way.

karny *a.* **1.** *gł. prawn.* (= *dotyczący kary*) criminal, penal; **kodeks karny** criminal code, penal code; **kolonia karna** penal colony; **mandat karny** fine; **podlegać odpowiedzialności karnej** be liable to prosecution; **prawo karne** criminal law, penal law; **sprawa karna** *l.* **proces karny** criminal trial; **wyprawa karna** punitive expedition; **zakład karny** *l.* **penitencjarny** penitentiary; **pole karne** *piłka nożna* penalty area; **punkt karny** *sport* penalty point; **rzut karny** *piłka nożna* penalty kick; **rzuty karne** *piłka nożna* (*w celu rozstrzygnięcia meczu*) penalties; **oddział karny** *wojsk.* penal unit. **2.** (= *zdyscyplinowany*) disciplined; **karne dziecko** well-behaved child; **karny pies** obedient dog; **karny żołnierz** disciplined soldier.

karo *n. indecl. karty* (= *kolor oznaczony czerwonym rombem*) diamonds; **as karo** ace of diamonds. – *n. karty* (= *karta koloru karo*) diamond; **mieć cztery kara** have four diamonds. – *n. indecl.* (= *dekolt w kształcie kwadratu*) diamond-shaped neckline.

karoca *f. przest.* carriage, coach.

Karoling *mp pl.* -owie *hist.* Carolingian.

karoliński *a. hist.* Carolingian, Carlovingian; **dynastia karolińska** Carolingian Dynasty; **renesans karoliński** Carolingian Renaissance.

karoseria *f. Gen.* -ii *mot.* body (*of a car*).

karoseryjny *a. mot.* car body; **blacha karoseryjna** car body sheet; **element karoseryjny** car body part; **prasa karoseryjna** car body press.

karoten *mi biol., chem.* carotene, carotin.

karotenoid *mi biol., chem.* carotenoid, carotinoid.

karowy *a. karty* diamonds; **as karowy** *l.* **karo** ace of diamonds.

karp *ma* -pi- *icht.* carp (*Cyprinus carpio*); **karp w galarecie** *kulin.* carp in jelly, jellied carp; **karp po żydowsku** *kulin.* sweet-boiled carp.

karpacki *a. geogr.* Carpathian.

Karpaty *pl. Gen.* -ów *geogr.* the Carpathian Mountains, the Carpathians.

karpi *a.* carp's; **krycie dachu w karpią łuskę** *bud.* plain *l.* plane tile roofing.

karpiówka *f. bud.* plain *l.* plane tile.

karpologia *f. Gen.* -ii *bot.* carpology.

kart *mi Gen.* -u *l.* -a *mot.* kart, go-kart.

karta *f.* **1.** (= *arkusz papieru*) sheet (of paper); **karta do głosowania** ballot paper; **karta gwarancyjna** warranty (card); **karta katalogowa** *bibl.* index card; **karta biblioteczna** *bibl.* library card; **karta mobilizacyjna** *wojsk.* draft card; **karta powołania** *l.* **wcielenia** *wojsk.* draft card; **karta pracy** work card; **karta pocztowa** postcard; **karta rejestracyjna** registration card; **karta wstępu** *l.* **wejścia** pass, admission ticket. **2.** (*w książce*) page,

leaf; **karta tytułowa** title page. **3.** (= *menu*) menu; **danie z karty** à la carte dish; **karta win** wine list. **4.** *karty* (playing) card; **domek z kart** *przen.* house of cards; **grać w otwarte karty** put one's cards on the table; **odkrywać karty** *przen.* show one's cards; **postawić wszystko na jedną kartę** stake everything on one roll of the dice; **stawiać karty** tell sb's fortune, read the cards; **talia kart** deck (of cards); **znać czyjeś karty** know sb's intentions; **karta mi dziś nie idzie** I'm out of luck today; **mieć ukrytą kartę w rękawie** have a card up one's sleeve; **kto gra w karty, ten ma łeb obdarty** a fool and his money are soon parted; **kto nie ma szczęścia w kartach, ten ma szczęście w miłości** unlucky at cards, lucky in love. **5.** *przen.* (= *pewien okres dziejów*) chapter; **nowa karta w historii narodu** new chapter in a nation's history; **mroczna karta czyjejś biografii** dark chapter of one's life. **6.** *komp.* card; **karta dźwiękowa** sound card; **karta graficzna** graphic card; **karta wideo** video card. **7.** *fin.* card; **karta debetowa** debit card; **karta kredytowa** credit card. **8.** *polit.* charter, card; **Karta Atlantycka** *hist.* the Atlantic Charter; **Wielka Karta Swobód** *hist.* the Great Charter; **Karta Narodów Zjednoczonych** the United Nations Charter; **Karta 77** Charter 77; **zielona karta** *US* (= *zezwolenie na pracę*) green card; *ubezp., mot.* (= *międzynarodowe ubezpieczenie komunikacyjne*) green card.

kartacz *mi Gen.* -a *Gen.pl* -y *l.* -ów *hist.*, *wojsk.* grapeshot.

Kartagina *f. hist. geogr.* Carthage.

kartagiński *a. hist.* Carthaginian, Punic.

kartel *mi* **1.** *ekon.* cartel; **kartel narkotykowy** drug cartel. **2.** *prawn.* cartel.

karteluszek *mi* -szk- *Gen.* -a *pot.* scrap of paper.

karter *mi mot.* crankcase.

kartezjanin *mp pl.* -anie *Gen.* -an *fil.* Cartesian.

kartezjanizm *mi fil.* Cartesianism.

kartezjański *a. fil.* Cartesian; **iloczyn kartezjański** *mat.* Cartesian product; **myśl kartezjańska** Cartesian thought; **kartezjański układ współrzędnych** *mat.* Cartesian coordinates; **przestrzeń kartezjańska** *geom.* Cartesian space.

karting *mi sport, mot.* (go-)kart racing.

kartingowy *a. sport, mot.* (go-)kart; **sport kartingowy** (go-)kart racing; **tor kartingowy** (go-)kart racetrack; **zawody kartingowe** (go-)kart race.

kartka *f.* **1.** (= *arkusz papieru*) sheet (of paper), piece of paper; **kartka pocztowa** postcard. **2.** (= *pocztówka*) postcard; **kartka świąteczna** (*bożonarodzeniowa*) Christmas card; (*wielkanocna*) Easter card; **kartka z życzeniami** *l.* **pozdrowieniami** greetings card; **żółta/czerwona kartka** *sport* yellow/red card; **dostać żółtą kartkę** be booked; **dostać czerwoną kartkę** *sport* be sent off. **3.** (*w książce*) page, leaf.

kartkować *ipf.* **1.** (= *przeglądać pobieżnie*) leaf through, flick through. **2.** (= *przeglądać w poszukiwaniu informacji*) thumb through.

kartkowy *a.* of or referring to sheets of paper; **system kartkowy** rationing system.

kartkówka *f. szkoln., pot.* pop quiz.

kartofel *mi* -fl- *Gen.* -a *bot.* potato (*Solanum tuberosum*); **kartofle w mundurkach** *kulin.* jacket potatoes.

kartoflanka *f. kulin.* 1. (= *zupa z kartofli*) potato soup. 2. (= *mąka ziemniaczana*) potato flour.

kartoflany *a.* potato; **mąka kartoflana** potato flour; **pole kartoflane** potato field; **zupa kartoflana** potato soup; **kartoflany nos** bulbous nose.

kartoflisko *n.* potato field.

kartograf *mp pl.* -owie cartographer.

kartografia *f. Gen.* -ii cartography.

kartograficzny *a.* cartographic, cartographical; **rzut kartograficzny** projection; **siatka kartograficzna** graticule.

kartogram *mi geogr.* cartogram.

karton *mi* 1. (= *pudło z tektury*) carton, cardboard box. 2. (= *tektura*) cardboard. 3. *sztuka* cartoon.

kartoniarka *f. techn.* board machine.

kartonik *mi Gen.* -a 1. (= *pudełko z tektury*) small carton, small cardboard box. 2. (= *kawałek kartonu*) piece *l.* scrap of cardboard.

kartonowy *a.* cardboard; **opakowanie kartonowe** cardboard box *l.* packaging; **pudełko kartonowe** cardboard box; **teczka kartonowa** file, folder; **maszyna kartonowa** *techn.* board machine.

kartoteka *f.* 1. (= *zbiór fiszek*) card index; (= *zbiór danych*) files. 2. (= *zbiór informacji na czyjś l. jakiś temat*) dossier; **kartoteka policyjna** police record(s), rap sheet. 3. *komp.* file directory.

kartuski *a. rz.-kat.* Carthusian; **klasztor kartuski** Carthusian monastery.

kartusz *mi Gen.* -a *Gen.pl.* -y *l.* -ów 1. *sztuka* cartouche, cartouch. 2. *hist., wojsk.* (= *ładownica*) pouch. 3. *wojsk.* (= *pojemnik z ładunkiem prochowym*) cartouche, cartouch, cartridge.

kartuz *mp rz.-kat.* Carthusian.

kartuzja *f. bud.* Carthusian monastery.

kartuzjański *a. rz.-kat.* Carthusian; **habit kartuzjański** Carthusian habit; **klasztor kartuzjański** Carthusian monastery; **reguła kartuzjańska** Carthusian rule; **zakon kartuzjański** Carthusian order.

karuk *mi* isinglass.

karuzel *mi hist.* carrousel.

karuzela *f.* 1. (*w wesołym miasteczku*) carousel, merry-go-round; *Br.* roundabout. 2. *komp.* round robin. 3. *techn.* whirling arm.

kary *a.* black; **kary koń** black horse.

karygodność *f.* scandalousness, reprehensibility.

karygodny *a.* scandalous, reprehensible; **karygodny błąd** gross error; **karygodna ignorancja** crass ignorance; **karygodny nietakt** deplorable gaffe; **karygodne zaniedbanie** unpardonable *l.* criminal negligence.

karykatura *f.* 1. (= *ośmieszający rysunek*) caricature. 2. *przen.* (= *coś zdeformowanego, przejaskrawionego*) caricature, travesty, parody; **karykatura człowieka** travesty of a human being; **karykatura męża stanu** caricature of a statesman.

karykaturalnie *adv.* caricaturely, caricaturally.

karykaturalność *f.* quality of being caricatural.

karykaturalny *a.* caricatural; **karykaturalna postać** caricatural figure; **karykaturalny wygląd** caricatural appearance.

karykaturować *ipf.* caricature.

karykaturzysta *mp* caricaturist.

karzeł *mp* -rł- *pl.* -y 1. (= *człowiek bardzo niskiego wzrostu o nienaturalnie dużej głowie i krótkich kończynach*) dwarf. 2. (= *karzeł o proporcjonalnej budowie ciała*) midget. 3. (*w bajkach*) (= *skrzat*) dwarf, brownie. – *mi* -rł- *Gen.* -a *ogr.* dwarf.

karzełek *mp* -łk- *pl.* -i 1. (= *liliput*) dwarf. 2. (*w bajkach*) (= *skrzat*) dwarf, brownie.

kasa *f.* 1. (= *skrzynka l. szafa do przechowywania pieniędzy*) strongbox; **kasa pancerna** strongbox, safe; **kasa ogniotrwała** fireproof strongbox; **kasa fiskalna** cash register. 2. (= *czyjś fundusz*) treasury; **prowadzić kasę** keep accounts; **zamknąć kasę** close accounts; **kasa się nie zgadza** accounts do not tally; **zrobić kasę** *pot.* (*o filmie*) be a box-office success *l.* hit, be a blockbuster; **zrobić** *l.* **zbić kasę na czymś** *pot.* (*o człowieku*) make a fortune from sth. 3. (= *pomieszczenie, miejsce gdzie wypłaca/wpłaca się pieniądze*) (*w sklepie*) cash desk; (*w supermarkecie*) check-out, checkout counter; **kasa biletowa** (*na dworcu*) ticket office; (*w kinie, teatrze, na stadionie*) box office. 4. *fin.* (= *instytucja finansowa*) bank, fund, society; **kasa chorych** healthcare fund; **kasa mieszkaniowa** building society; **kasa oszczędności** savings bank; **kasa zapomogowo-pożyczkowa** provident society. 5. *pot.* (= *pieniądze, gotówka*) cash, a few bucks; **masz kasę na browar?** got any beer money?

kasacja *f.* 1. (= *rozwiązanie*) dissolution, disbandment; (*zakonu*) suppression. 2. (= *unicestwienie*) scrapping; (*o samochodzie, samolocie*) scrapping; **samochód nadaje się tylko do kasacji** car is only fit for writing off. 3. *prawn.* final appeal, last resort appeal; **kasacja orzeczenia** annulment of a decision.

kasacyjny *a.* 1. dissolutive; suppresive; **bulla kasacyjna** brief of suppression. 2. scrapping, write-off. 3. *prawn.* final, last resort; annulment; **sąd kasacyjny** Supreme Court (of Appeal); **wniosek kasacyjny** *prawn.* final appeal petition.

Kasandra *f. mit. t. przen.* Cassandra.

kaseciak *mi Gen.* -a *pot.* (= *magnetofon kasetowy*) tape recorder.

kaseta *f.* 1. (*do słuchania, oglądania*) cassette, tape. 2. (= *pojemnik*) case, box. 3. *fot.* cartridge.

kasetka *f.* 1. (= *pojemnik*) case, box. 2. *fot.* cartridge.

kaseton *mi bud.* coffer, caisson, lacunar.

kasetonować *ipf. bud.* coffer.

kasetonowy *a. bud.* coffer; **strop** *l.* **sufit kasetonowy** lacunar.

kasetowy a. tape, casette; **magnetofon kasetowy** tape recorder.

kasiarz mp pot. safecracker, yegg.

kasja f. bot. cassia (Cassia).

kasjer mp **1.** (w banku) teller, cashier. **2.** (na
dworcu) booking clerk. **3.** (w sklepie) cashier.
4. (w supermarkecie) checker.

kasjerka f. zob. **kasjer.**

kasjop mp chem. lutetium.

kask mi **1.** (ochronny) helmet; hard hat; (rowerowy, motocyklowy) crash helmet; **kask tropikalny** pith helmet, topee, topi. **2.** hist. (= hełm
stalowy z grzebieniem) casque.

kaskada f. **1.** (= wodospad) cascade; **kaskada
śmiechu** przen. ripple of laughter. **2.** hydrotechnika cascade. **3.** el., komp. cascade.

kaskader mp **1.** film stuntman. **2.** cyrk acrobat.

kaskadowy a. cascade; **układ kaskadowy** cascade system; **wzmacniacz kaskadowy** cascade
amplifier.

kasłać ipf. cough.

kasować ipf. **1.** (= unieważniać) annul, cancel. **2.** (bilet w autobusie, tramwaju) punch,
cancel. **3.** (znaczek) cancel. **4.** (nagranie) erase;
komp. (plik, dane itp.) delete. **5.** prawn. annul,
quash, make null and void; **kasować wyrok** annul a sentence. **6.** pot. (w sklepie) total, add up
(the price for all products purchased).

kasownik mi Gen. **-a 1.** (do biletów) ticket
puncher. **2.** muz. natural. **3.** techn. reset.

kasowy a. **1.** (= związany z kasą, obrotem pieniędzmi) cash; **księga kasowa** cashbook; **raport
kasowy** cash report; **wpływy kasowe** cash receipts. **2.** (= związany z pomieszczeniem kasy)
till; cash desk; box office; **okienko kasowe** cash
desk. **3.** (= dochodowy) profitable; **kasowy film**
box-office success l. hit; **kasowe przedstawienie**
box-office success l. hit.

kaspijski a. geogr. Caspian; **Morze Kaspijskie**
the Caspian Sea.

kassata f. kulin. cassata.

kasta f. **1.** Ind. caste. **2.** (= grupa społeczna)
caste. **3.** biol. caste.

kastaniety pl. Gen. **-ów** bones, castanets.

kastet mi (broń) brass knuckles, knuckle-
duster.

kastowość f. caste system.

kastowy a. caste.

kastracja f. castration, emasculation, gelding.

kastracyjny a. castratory, gelding.

kastrat mp pl. **-ci 1.** (= eunuch) castrate, eunuch. **2.** (= kastrowany śpiewak) castrato. – ma
pl. **-y** (samiec zwierzęcia) gelding.

kastrować ipf. (człowieka) castrate, emasculate; (zwierzę) castrate, cut, geld; (zwł. psa l. kota) alter, fix.

kasyno n. **1.** (= dom gry) casino. **2.** (oficerskie, wojskowe) (= klub) mess (hall).

kasyteryt mi min. cassiterite, tinstone.

kasza f. (produkt) groats, kasha; (potrawa)
kasha, porridge; **kasza jaglana** millet; **kasza
jęczmienna** pearl barley; **kasza gryczana** buckwheat; **kasza manna** semolina; **nie dać sobie w**
kaszę dmuchać not let o.s. be led by the nose,
know how to stick up for o.s.

kaszak mi Gen. **-a** pat. atheroma, sebaceous
cyst.

kaszalot ma zool. sperm whale, cachalot (Phy-
seter catodon).

kaszanka f. Gen.pl. **-ek** kulin. blood sausage,
blood l. black pudding.

kaszarnia f. Gen.pl. **-i** l. **-ń** oat mill.

kaszel mi **-szl-** Gen.pl. **-i** l. **-ów** cough; pat. tus-
sis; **suchy kaszel** dry cough; **kaszel z odkrztusza-
niem** productive cough.

kaszka f. Gen.pl. **-ek** kulin. porridge; Br. stir-
about; **kaszka manna** semolina; **kaszka z mlekiem** przen. (= łatwa, nieskomplikowana sprawa) piece of cake; **rozbić coś w drobną kaszkę**
smash sth to atoms l. smithereens.

kaszleć ipf. **-ę -esz, -l** l. **-aj, kaszlnąć** pf. **-ij**
cough.

kaszmir mi **1.** tk. cashmere, kashmir. **2.** geogr. Kashmir, Cashmere.

kaszmirowy a. tk. cashmere.

kaszmirski a. geogr. Kashmiri.

kaszta f. druk. type case.

kasztan mi Gen. **-a 1.** bot. (drzewo) chestnut
(Castanea sativa). **2.** (owoc tego drzewa) chestnut. **3.** pot. = **kasztanowiec. 4.** Gen. **-u** (kolor)
chestnut. – ma (koń) chestnut.

kasztanowaty a. (kolor) chestnutty, brown,
maroon.

kasztanowcowate pl. Gen. **-ych** bot. horse
chestnut family (Hippocastanaceae).

kasztanowiec mi **-wc-** Gen. **-a** bot. horse chestnut (Aesculus).

kasztanowy a. **1.** (= odnoszący się do kasztana
l. kasztanowca) chestnut. **2.** (kolor) chestnut,
maroon, sorrel.

kasztany pl. Gen. **-ów** zool. (= narośle na kończynie koniowatych) chestnuts.

kasztel mi Gen.pl. **-i** l. **-ów** hist. castle.

kasztelan mp pl. **-owie** l. **-i** hist. castellan,
chatelain.

kasztelania f. Gen. **-ii** hist. (urząd l. obszar)
castellany.

kasztelanka f. Gen.pl. **-ek** hist. castellan's
daughter.

Kaszub mp pl. **-i** l. **-owie** Kashubian.

Kaszuba mp pl. **-i** l. **-owie** zob. **Kaszub.**

kaszubić ipf. jęz. speak in the Kashubian dialect.

Kaszubka f. Gen.pl. **-ek** zob. **Kaszub.**

kaszubski a. Kashubian.

kat mp Dat. **-u** l. **-owi** pl. **kaci** l. **-y** (= osoba wykonująca wyroki śmierci) executioner, hang-
man, headsman, decapitator; hist. (= wykonawca tortur, kar) torturer; **stać jak kat nad dobrą
duszą** keep pestering sb.

kataboliczny a. biol. catabolic.

katabolizm mi biol. catabolism.

katachreza f. teor.lit. catachresis.

katafalk mi catafalque.

kataklizm mi **1.** (= klęska żywiołowa) disaster,
calamity, cataclysm, catastrophe. **2.** przen. cataclysm, upheaval.

katakumby *pl. Gen.* **-b** catacombs.

kataleksja *f. wers.* catalectic.

katalektyczny *a. wers.* catalectic; **stopa katalektyczna** *zob.* **kataleksja.**

katalepsja *f. med.* catalepsy.

kataleptyczny *a. med.* cataleptic.

kataleptyk *mp med.* cataleptic.

katalityczny *a. chem.* catalytic.

kataliza *f. chem.* catalysis; **kataliza dodatnia** positive catalysis; **kataliza ujemna** negative catalysis.

katalizator *mi Gen.* **-a** **1.** *chem.* catalyst, catalytic agent; **katalizator dodatni** accelerator, positive catalyst; **katalizator ujemny** negative catalyst, inhibitor. **2.** *mot.* catalytic converter.

katalog *mi* catalog; *bibl.* catalog; *komp.* directory; **katalog centralny** *bibl.* union catalog; **katalog działowy** *bibl.* classified catalog; **katalog fiszkowy** *gł. bibl.* card catalog; **katalog sprzedaży wysyłkowej** mail catalog; **katalog gwiazd** *astron.* catalog of stars.

katalogować *ipf.* catalog.

katalogowy *a.* catalog; **cena katalogowa** sticker price, list price.

Katalonia *f. Gen.* **-ii** *geogr.* Catalonia.

Katalonka *f. Gen.pl.* **-ek** *zob.* **Katalończyk.**

Katalończyk *mp* Catalan.

kataloński *a.* Catalan.

katamaran *mi żegl.* catamaran.

katana *f. pot.* jacket, coat.

katapulta *f.* **1.** *hist.* catapult, onager, trebuchet. **2.** *lotn.* (*startowa*) catapult. **3.** *lotn.* ejector, ejection seat.

katapultować *ipf.* **1.** *lotn.* (*by ratować*) eject. **2.** *lotn.* (*przy starcie*) catapult. **~ się** *ipf. lotn.* (*by się ratować*) eject.

katapultowy *a. lotn.* ejection; **fotel katapultowy** ejection seat.

Katar *mi geogr.* Quatar.

katar[1] *mi Gen.* **-u** *pl.* **-y** *pat.* catarrh, coryza, rhinitis; *pot.* runny nose; **katar chroniczny** chronic runny nose; **katar sienny** hay fever; **mam katar** my nose is running.

katar[2] *mp Gen.* **-a** *pl.* **-owie** *l.* **-rzy** *rel.* Cathar, Catharist.

katarakta *f.* **1.** *pat.* cataract. **2.** *geol.* cataract.

kataryniarz *mp* organ grinder.

katarynka *f. Gen.pl.* **-ek** barrel organ, hand organ, hurdy-gurdy; **mówić jak katarynka** talk a blue streak, patter, chatter.

kataster *mi* **-tr-** *admin.* cadastre, cadaster.

katastralny *a. admin.* (*o podatku, księdze*) cadastral; **mapa katastralna** cadastral map.

katastrofa *f.* **1.** (= *wypadek, klęska*) catastrophe, calamity, disaster; **katastrofa lotnicza** (plane) crash; **katastrofa kolejowa** railway accident. **2.** *teor.lit.* (*w tragedii antycznej*) catastrophe.

katastrofalny *a.* catastrophic, catastrophical, disastrous.

katastroficzny *a.* catastrophic, disastrous, calamitous; **katastroficzny ton** ominous tone.

katastrofista *mp* catastrophist.

katastrofistka *f. Gen.pl.* **-ek** *zob.* **katastrofista.**

katastrofizm *mi fil., biol., geol.* catastrophism.

katatonia *f. Gen.* **-ii** *pat.* catatonia.

katatoniczny *a. pat.* catatonic.

katatonik *mp Gen., Acc.* **-a** *pat.* catatonic.

katecheta *mp rz.-kat.* catechist.

katechetka *f. Gen.pl.* **-ek** *zob.* **katecheta.**

katechetyczny *a. rz.-kat.* catechistic, catechistical; **katechetyczna metoda nauczania** *hist., szkoln.* catechetic(al) instruction, catechism.

katechetyka *f. rz.-kat.* catechesis.

katecheza *f. rz.-kat.* catechesis, religious instruction.

katechizacja *f. rz.-kat.* catechization.

katechizm *mi* **1.** *rz.-kat.* catechism. **2.** *przen.* (= *podstawy czegoś*) ABCs, ABC's, ABC, fundamentals, rudiments; (*polityczny, etyczny*) tenets, catechism.

katechizmowy *a.* catechismal.

katechizować *ipf. rz.-kat.* catechize.

katechumen *mp rz.-kat.* catechumen, neophyte.

katechumenat *mi rz.-kat.* catechumenate.

katechumenka *f. Gen.pl.* **-ek** *zob.* **katechumen.**

katedra *f.* **1.** (= *pulpit wykładowcy*) desk; lectern. **2.** *uniw.* (= *jednostka organizacyjna*) department; (= *stanowisko*) chair. **3.** *rel.* (= *główny kościół diecezji*) cathedral.

katedralny *a. rel.* cathedral.

kategoria *f. Gen.* **-ii** **1.** (= *typ*) category, class, type, group; *ekon.* (*wiekowa, zarobkowa*) bracket; **kategoria gramatyczna** *jęz.* form class; **kategoria E** (= *niezdolny do służby wojskowej*) 4-F; **kategoria pojęciowa** *log.* intention; **restauracja pierwszej kategorii** first-class restaurant. **2.** *fil.* category.

kategorycznie *adv.* categorically, emphatically; (*zaprzeczyć*) flatly, vehemently.

kategoryczność *f.* categorical character.

kategoryczny *a.* (*o zakazie, żądaniu, tonie*) emphatic; (*o odmowie*) downright, flat; (*o zaprzeczeniu*) categorical, flat, stiff, square; **imperatyw kategoryczny** *fil.* categorical imperative.

kategoryzować *ipf.* categorize, compartmentalize, classify.

kateter *mi med.* catheter.

katetometr *mi techn.* cathetometer.

katgut *mi chir.* catgut.

katgutowy *a. chir.* catgut; **szew katgutowy** catgut suture.

katharsis *n. indecl.* **1.** *teor.lit.* catharsis. **2.** *psych.* catharsis.

kation *mi fiz.* cation, positive ion.

kationowy *a. fiz.* cationic; **barwnik kationowy** cationic dye.

katiusza *f. hist., wojsk.* Stalin Organ (*a Soviet mobile rocket launcher used during WW II*).

katoda *f. fiz.* cathode; **katoda wtórna** dynode; **katoda żarzona** thermionic cathode.

katodowy *a. fiz.* cathodic; **promienie** *l.* **promieniowanie katodowe** cathode rays.

katolicki *a. rz.-kat.* Catholic; **Kościół Katolicki** the Roman Catholic Church.

katolickość *f. rz.-kat.* Catholicity.

katolicyzm *mi rz.-kat.* Catholicism.

katoliczka f. Gen.pl. **-ek** zob. **katolik.**

katolik mp Catholic.

katolikos mp rel. Catholicos, Catholicus, Katholikos.

katorga f. **1.** toil, ordeal, murder. **2.** hist. penal servitude.

katorżniczy a. murderous; (praca) backbreaking.

katorżnik mp hist. convict sentenced to hard labor.

katować ipf. torture, torment.

katownia f. Gen.pl. **-i** (= miejsce tortur) place of torture.

katowski a. executioner's.

katusze pl. Gen. **-y** agony, grueling; **cierpieć katusze** suffer agony.

kaucja f. deposit; security; surety; bond; prawn. bail; **zwolnić kogoś za kaucją** release sb on bail.

kauczuk mi caoutchouc, (natural) rubber; **kauczuk naturalny** India l. natural rubber; **kauczuk syntetyczny** synthetic rubber.

kauczukodajny a. (o roślinie) rubber-yielding.

kauczukonośny a. zob. **kauczukodajny.**

kauczukowiec mi **-wc-** Gen. **-a** bot. rubber tree (Hevea).

kauczukowy a. rubber, caoutchouc.

kaukaski a. Caucasian, Caucasic.

Kaukaz mi geogr. (góry) the Caucasus, the Caucasus Mountains; (region) the Caucasus, the Caucasia.

kaulifloria f. Gen. **-ii** bot., pot. cauliflory.

kaustyczny a. caustic; **soda kaustyczna** chem. caustic soda, sodium hydroxide; **powierzchnia kaustyczna** opt. caustic surface.

kaustyka f. opt. caustic surface.

kauter mi med. cautery.

kauteryzacja f. med. cauterization.

kauteryzować ipf. med. cauterize.

kauzalista mp fil. causationist.

kauzalistyczny a. fil. causationist.

kauzalizm mi fil. causationism.

kauzatywny a. jęz. causative.

kauzyperda mp pl. **-dzi** l. **-y** pog. lame-duck lawyer.

kawa f. **1.** bot. (roślina) coffee (Coffea). **2.** (nasiona tej rośliny) coffee (beans); **kawa mielona** ground coffee. **3.** (napój) coffee; (porcja napoju) (cup of) coffee; **biała kawa** white coffee, café au lait; **czarna kawa** black coffee, café noir; **kawa po turecku** coffee Turkish style; **kawa rozpuszczalna** instant coffee; **kawa z ekspresu** filter coffee; **kawa ze śmietanką** coffee with cream; **kawa zbożowa** ersatz coffee; **ekspres do kawy** coffee maker, espresso machine; **wykładać kawę na ławę** przen. not mince words, say openly.

kawalarka f. Gen.pl. **-ek** zob. **kawalarz.**

kawalarstwo n. jesting, joking, prankishness, waggishness.

kawalarz mp joker, practical joker, prankster, clown, cutup.

kawalątek mi **-tk-** Gen. **-a** little bit, small piece.

kawaler mp pl. **-owie** l. **-rzy** **1.** (= nieżonaty mężczyzna) bachelor; **kawaler do wzięcia** elligi-

ble bachelor; **stary kawaler** confirmed bachelor. **2.** (= młodzieniec) young man. **3.** przest. (= adorator) cavalier. **4.** (orderu) knight; **odznaczać tytułem kawalera (orderu)** knight. **5.** hist. (= rycerz zakonnik) knight.

kawaleria f. Gen. **-ii** wojsk. cavalry; **lekka kawaleria** hist. light cavalry; **ciężka kawaleria** hist. heavy cavalry.

kawalerka f. Gen.pl. **-ek** **1.** (mieszkanie) studio (apartment), efficiency apartment. **2.** pot. (= młodzieńcy) young men. **3.** pot. (= okres przedmałżeński) bachelorhood.

kawalerski a. (o stanie) unmarried, single; (o gospodarstwie) bachelor's; **wieczór kawalerski** stag party l. night.

kawalerstwo n. bachelorhood.

kawaleryjski a. wojsk. cavalry; **koń kawaleryjski** trooper; **koszary kawaleryjskie** horse-barracks.

kawalerzysta mp cavalryman, trooper, cavalier.

kawalkada f. cavalcade; **kawalkada samochodów** autocade, motorcade.

kawał mi **1.** Gen. **-a** (= część) piece; (= duży kawałek) hunch; (chleba, sera) chunk, hunk; **kawał czasu** ages; **kawał drogi** long way, miles; **kawał chłopa** big l. strapping guy, husky; **kawał drania** rake, rascal; **kawał grosza** a pretty penny, a tidy sum; **kawał życia** better part of one's life. **2.** Gen. **-u** (= dowcip) joke; **kawał z brodą** wheeze; **opowiedzieć kawał** tell a joke; **sypać kawałami** crack jokes. **3.** Gen. **-u** (= figiel) practical joke, prank, trick; **zrobić coś dla kawału** do sth for a joke l. a laugh l. fun; **zrobić komuś kawał** play a joke l. trick on sb.

kawałeczek mi **-czk-** Gen. **-a** (= część) little bit l. piece, tiny bit l. piece; **kawałeczek drogi stąd** not far away, very near.

kawałek mi **-łk-** Gen. **-a** **1.** (= część) bit, fragment, patch, piece; (kredy) stick; (listwy, rury) length; (= odłamek) sliver, shiver, splinter; (zwł. mięsa) slice, collop; **ładny kawałek drogi** long way, miles; **zobaczył kawałek świata** he's been around, he's seen a lot; **dzielić się z kimś ostatnim kawałkiem chleba** share one's last crust with sb; **opowiadać głodne kawałki** pot. jive; **pracować ciężko na kawałek chleba** work hard to earn one's living; **po kawałku** bit by bit; **rozlecieć się na kawałki** fall to pieces. **2.** pot. (= utwór muzyczny) piece, number.

kawałkować ipf. cut up; divide.

kawarniany a. café.

kawerna f. **1.** pat. cavity. **2.** geol. cavern, cave, cavity.

kawiarenka f. Gen.pl. **-ek** small café; **kawiarenka internetowa** Internet café.

kawiarnia f. Gen.pl. **-i** l. **-ń** café, coffee shop, coffeehouse.

kawior mi kulin. caviar, caviare.

kawka[1] f. Gen.pl. **-ek** **1.** coffee. **2.** pot. (= spotkanie towarzyskie) coffee klatsch.

kawka[2] f. Gen.pl. **-ek** orn. jackdaw (Corvus monedula).

kawon mi Gen. **-u** l. **-a** **1.** bot. watermelon (Ci-

trullus lanatus l. vulgaris). **2.** (*owoc tej rośliny*) watermelon.

kawowiec *mi* **-wc-** *Gen.* **-a** *bot.* coffee (*Coffea*).

kawowy *a.* coffee.

kazać *ipf.* **każę każesz** (= *wydawać polecenie*) command, direct (*komuś zrobić coś* sb to do sth); have (*coś zrobić* sth done); order; make (*komuś coś zrobić* sb do sth); **kazać komuś coś zrobić** tell sb to do sth; **kazać komuś czekać** keep sb waiting; **rób co ci każę!** do as you're told!; **kazać się komuś kłaniać** ask sb to give sb else one's regards.

kazalnica *f.* **1.** *kośc.* pulpit. **2.** *alpinistyka* pulpit.

kazamata *f. hist.* (*w twierdzy, na okręcie*) casemate.

kazanie *n.* **1.** *rel.* sermon, homily, preachment; **wygłaszać kazanie** sermonize, preach; **siedział jak na tureckim kazaniu** it was all Greek to him. **2.** *przen.* (= *pouczenie umoralniające*) lecture, talking-to; **lubiący prawić kazania** preachy; **prawić komuś kazanie** lecture sb, preach at sb.

kazeina *f. biochem.* casein.

kazeinowy *a. biochem.* casein; **farba kazeinowa** casein.

kazić *ipf.* **każę kazisz** *przest.* **1.** (= *psuć, szpecić*) mar. **2.** (= *demoralizować*) corrupt, debauch.

kazirodca *mp* incestuous person.

kazirodczy *a.* incestuous.

kazirodztwo *n.* incest.

kaznodzieja *f. Gen.* **-ei** *Gen.pl.* **-ów 1.** *rel.* preacher. **2.** *przen.* (= *moralista*) preacher.

kaznodziejski *a.* predicatory, preacher's; **po kaznodziejsku** in a sermonizing manner.

kaznodziejstwo *n. rel.* **1.** (= *wygłaszanie kazań*) preaching. **2.** (= *twórczość kaznodziejska*) homilies.

kazualizm *mi fil.* casualism.

kazualny *a. jęz.* case.

kazuar *ma orn.* cassowary (*Casuarius*).

kazuista *mp* casuist.

kazuistyczny *a.* casuistic, casuistical.

kazuistyka *f.* casuistry.

kaźń *f. lit., przest.* **1.** (= *męka*) torture, torment. **2.** (= *kara śmierci*) execution.

każdorazowo *adv.* each time, every time.

każdorazowy *a.* each, every.

każdy *a.* every; (= *poszczególny, z osobna*) each; **być na każde skinienie** *l.* **wezwanie** be at sb's beck and call; **o każdej porze** anytime; **pod każdym względem** in every respect; **każdego dnia** every day; **każdego wieczoru** nightly; **każdego roku** every year, yearly, annually; **w każdej chwili** at any time; **z każdą minutą** every minute; **na każdym kroku** every step of the way, at every turn, wall-to-wall; **w każdym razie** at any rate, anyhow, at all events, in any case. – *mp* (= *każdy człowiek*) everybody; **każdy z nas** each of us; **wystarczy dla każdego** there's enough to go round; **każdy ma swoje pięć minut** every dog has its day; **każdy sobie rzepkę skrobie** it's every man for himself; **każdy z każdym** *sport* (*rozgrywki*) round robin; **płacić każdy za siebie** go Dutch.

kącik *mi Gen.* **-a 1.** (= *róg pokoju*) corner, nook; **kącik ust** corner of the mouth; **zewnętrzny kącik oka** tail of the eye. **2.** (= *lokum*) place of one's own; **mieć własny kącik** have a place of one's own; **przytulny kącik** snuggery. **3.** (= *rubryka w czasopiśmie*) column, section; **kącik złamanych serc** agony column; **kącik sportowy** sports column.

kądziel *f. pl.* **-e 1.** *tk.* distaff. **2.** *przest.* (= *linia żeńska*) distaff (side); **po kądzieli** on the distaff side; **krewny po kądzieli** enate.

kąkol *mi bot.* corn cockle (*Agrostemma githago*).

kąpać *ipf.* **-ię -iesz 1.** (= *myć*) bathe, wash, lave, tub; **w gorącej wodzie** *l.* **ukropie kąpany** hot-blooded, hotheaded. **2.** *chem., techn.* bathe. **~ się** *ipf.* **1.** (= *myć się*) bathe; **kąpać się w słońcu** bathe *l.* bask in the sun. **2.** (= *pływać*) swim.

kąpiel *f. pl.* **-e 1.** bath; **kąpiel lecznicza** healing bath; **kąpiel słoneczna** sun bath; **wylać dziecko z kąpielą** throw the baby away *l.* out with the bath-water; **wziąć kąpiel** take a bath. **2.** (= *pływanie*) swim, bath. **3.** *chem., techn.* bath; **kąpiel barwiąca** dye-bath; **kąpiel bieląca** bleaching bath; **kąpiel przędzalnicza** spinning bath.

kąpielisko *n.* **1.** (*zespół urządzeń*) watering place; (*plaża*) bathing beach; (*basen*) swimming pool. **2.** (*miejscowość*) seaside resort, watering place.

kąpielowy *a.* bathing; swimming; **ręcznik kąpielowy** bath towel; **basen kąpielowy** swimming pool; **kostium kąpielowy** bathing suit; **czepek kąpielowy** bathing cap; **miejscowość kąpielowa** *zob.* **kąpielisko** 2.

kąpielówki *pl. Gen.* **-wek** (swimming) trunks.

kąsać *ipf.* **1.** (= *gryźć*) bite. **2.** *przen.* (= *dokuczać*) nettle, gall; (*o mrozie*) bite, nip.

kąsek *mi* **-sk-** *Gen.* **-a** bite, morsel; **łakomy** *l.* **smaczny kąsek** *przen.* tidbit; (= *przystojny mężczyzna*) stud muffin; (= *przystojna kobieta*) cookie; **tłusty kąsek** *przen.* plum.

kąśliwie *adv.* cuttingly, sharply; **wyrażać się o kimś/czymś kąśliwie** make biting *l.* cutting remarks about sb/sth, speak about sb/sth with malice.

kąśliwość *f.* acerbity, malice.

kąśliwy *a.* (*uwaga, stwierdzenie, żart*) biting, cutting.

kąt *mi Gen.* **-a 1.** (= *zetknięcie się dwu płaszczyzn, np. ścian*) corner. **2.** *geom.* angle; **kąt ostry** acute angle; **kąt prosty** right angle; **kąt rozwarty** obtuse angle; **kąt graniczny** *fiz.* critical angle; **kąt odbicia** *fiz.* reflection angle; **kąt padania promieni** *fiz.* incidence angle. **3.** (= *lokum*) *pot.* place; **mieć własny kąt** have a place of one's own; **mieszkać kątem u kogoś** put up at sb's place; **odwiedzić stare kąty** visit old haunts. **4.** (*w zwrotach*) **cisnąć w kąt** *pot.* (= *rzucić byle gdzie, odrzucić*) throw in the corner; (= *zaniechać, zaprzestać*) give up, throw up, abandon; **patrzeć kątem oka** watch out of the corner of one's eye; **płakać po kątach** sniffle; **postawić kogoś do kąta** stand sb in the corner, send sb to the corner; **rozstawiać kogoś po kątach** *pot.* order sb around;

rozważyć coś pod jakimś kątem examine sth from a certain angle *l.* perspective; **snuć się z kąta w kąt** *pot.* moon.

kątnica *f. anat.* cecum, caecum, blind gut.

kątomierz *mi Gen.* **-a 1.** *geom., szkoln.* protractor. **2.** *wojsk.* panoramic sight.

kątownica *f.* **kątownica nastawna** *bud.* sine bar.

kątownik *mi Gen.* **-a 1.** *bud.* (= *element konstrukcyjny*) angle iron *l.* steel; (*do mierzenia*) bevel (square). **2.** *druk.* composing stick.

kątowy *a.* angular; **minuta kątowa** *astron.* minute; **prędkość kątowa** *fiz.* angular velocity; **stopień kątowy** *geom.* degree.

kciuk *mi Gen.* **-a** *anat.* thumb.

kebab *mi kulin.* kebab, kabob, kebob.

kecz *mi Gen.* **-a** *żegl.* ketch.

keczup *mi kulin.* ketchup, catchup, catsup.

kedyw *mp pl.* **-owie** *hist.* (= *tytuł tureckich władców Egiptu 1867–1914*) khedive.

kefir *mi kulin.* kefir.

kefirowy *a. kulin.* kefir; **grzybek kefirowy** kefir grains.

kegel *mi* **-gl-** *Gen.* **-a** *druk.* type *l.* point size.

keja *f. Gen.* **kei** *żegl.* quay.

keks *mi Gen.* **-u** *l.* **-a** *kulin.* fruit cake.

kelner *mp* waiter.

kelnerka *f.* waitress.

kelnerować *ipf. pot.* wait.

kelnerski *a.* waiting, waiter's; **obsługa kelnerska w pokojach** room service.

kelnerstwo *n.* waitering.

kelwin *mi fiz.* kelvin.

kem *mi geol.* kame.

kemping *mi* campsite, camp-site; (*dla karawaningów*) RV park.

kempingowy *a.* camping; **domek kempingowy** cabin, cottage; **przyczepa kempingowa** trailer, mobile home; **samochód kempingowy** recreational vehicle, RV, camper.

kendo *n. indecl. sport* kendo.

kenel *mi górn.* cannel (coal).

kenelski *a. górn.* cannel; **węgiel kenelski** cannel (coal).

Kenia *f. Gen.* **-ii** *geogr.* Kenya.

Kenijczyk *mp* Kenyan.

Kenijka *f.* Kenyan.

kenijski *a.* Kenyan.

kenozoiczny *a. geol.* Cenozoic, Cainozoic; **era kenozoiczna** the Cenozoic (Era), the Cainozoic (Era).

kenozoik *mi geol.* the Cenozoic (Era), the Cainozoic (Era).

kent *ma roln.* (= *rasa kent l. owca rasy kent*) Romney (Marsh).

kentumowy *a. jęz.* centum; **języki kentumowe** *l.* **kentum** centum languages.

kepi *n. indecl.* kepi.

keramzyt *mi bud.* gravelite.

keramzytowy *a. bud.* gravelite; **kruszywo keramzytowe** gravelite.

keratyna *f. biol.* keratin.

kermes *mi chem.* kermes.

keson *mi* **1.** *bud.* caisson. **2.** *lotn.* torque *l.* torsion box.

kesonowy *a.* caisson, decompression; **choroba kesonowa** *pat.* (= *choroba dekompresyjna*) caisson disease, decompression sickness; *pot.* the bends; **komora kesonowa** decompression chamber.

ket *mi żegl.* **1.** (*statek*) catboat. **2.** (*ożaglowanie*) cat rig.

ketmia *f. Gen.* **-ii 1.** *bot.* hibiscus (*Hibiscus*); **ketmia jadalna** okra (*Hibiscus esculentus*); **ketmia konopiowata** kenaf (*Hibiscus cannabinus*). **2.** *tk.* kenaf.

keton *mi chem.* ketone.

ketonowy *a. chem.* ketonic; **ciałka ketonowe** *biochem.* ketone bodies, acetone bodies.

kędzierzawić *ipf.* **1.** (= *układać loki*) crimple, curl. **2.** *tk.* (= *kosmacić*) frieze. **3.** *tk.* (= *teksturować*) texture.

kędzierzawka *f.* (= *choroba roślin powodująca zwijanie się liści*) curl.

kędzierzawy *a.* curly; *bot.* (*o liściach*) crispate.

kędzior *mi Gen.* **-a** curl, ringlet.

kędziorek *mi* **-rk-** *Gen.* **-a** lock of hair.

kępa *f.* **1.** (*drzew, krzaków*) clump, cluster. **2.** (= *wzniesienie na podmokłym terenie*) holm.

kępka *f.* **1.** (*traw, kwiatów*) tuft, tussock. **2.** (*włosów*) tuft.

kęs *mi Gen.* **-a 1.** (= *kawałek czegoś do jedzenia*) bite, morsel. **2.** *rzad.* (= *kawałek, część*) bit, part. **3.** *hutn.* billet. **4.** *myśl.* laniary.

kęsisko *n. hutn.* **kęsisko kwadratowe** bloom; **kęsisko płaskie** slab.

kęsy *mi pl. górn.* rounds.

khaki *a. indecl.* khaki.

ki *a.* **ki diabeł** what the heck.

kibel *mi* **-bl-** *Gen.* **-a 1.** *pot.* (= *toaleta*) john. **2.** *pot.* (= *kubeł na śmieci*) trash can. **3.** *sl.* (= *więzienie*) can, cooler.

kibic *mp* **1.** *sport* supporter, fan. **2.** *przen.* (= *obserwator*) onlooker.

kibicować *ipf.* **1.** *sport* support (*komuś/czemuś* sb/sth). **2.** *przen.* (= *wspierać*) back, support.

kibić *f. pl.* **-e** *lit.* waist.

kiblować *ipf.* **1.** *sl.* (= *odbywać karę więzienia*) serve *l.* do time. **2.** *sl.* (= *powtarzać klasę w szkole*) repeat. **3.** *wulg.* (= *oddawać stolec*) shit, crap.

kibuc *mi Gen.* **-u** *l.* **-a** kibbutz.

kicać *ipf.* hop, jump.

kicha *f.* **1.** *pot.* (= *jelito*) gut. **2.** *pot.* (= *kaszanka*) blood sausage. **3.** *pot.* (= *dętka*) tube; **złapać kichę** get a puncture, get a flat (tire). **4.** *sl.* (= *beznadziejna sytuacja*) screwup.

kichać *ipf.* sneeze; **kichać na coś** *pot.* not to give a hoot about sth.

kichawa *f. pot., żart.* (= *nos*) schnoz(zle).

kichnąć *pf.* **-ij** *zob.* **kichać.**

kichnięcie *n.* sneeze.

kicia *f. dziec.* (= *kotek*) pussy.

kiciuś *mi Gen.pl.* **-ów 1.** *dziec.* (= *kotek*) pussy. **2.** *przen.* (= *osoba kochana*) sweetie.

kicz *mi Gen.pl.* **-ów** kitsch.

kiczowato *adv.* in a kitschy manner *l.* way; **wyglądać kiczowato** look cheap *l.* tawdry.

kiczowaty *a.* kitschy, schlocky.

kić *mi Gen.* -a *Gen.pl.* -ów *sl.* (= *więzienie*) can, cooler; **siedzieć w kiciu** be in the cooler, serve *l.* do time.

kićkać się *ipf. pot.* (= *mylić się*) get confused, get all mixed up.

kidnaper *mp* kidnapper.

kidnaperstwo *n.* kidnapping.

kidnaping *mi* kidnapping, abduction.

kiecka *f. pot.* dress.

kiedy *adv.* when; **kiedy się zobaczymy?** when do we meet next?; **kiedy bądź** whenever, any time; **kiedy indziej** some other time; **kiedy tylko** as soon as; **rzadko kiedy** hardly ever; **od kiedy?** since when?; **do kiedy?** till when?; **na kiedy?** by when? – *conj.* 1. (= *gdy*) when; **kiedy już byłem gotowy** when I was (finally) ready, once ready; **spałem już, kiedy zadzwonił telefon** I was sleeping, when the phone rang. 2. (= *skoro*) as, since; **kiedy już zdecydowałeś się na ten wyjazd, nie zapomnij o ubezpieczeniu** as you decided to take this trip, don't forget about the insurance. 3. (= *podczas gdy*) while.

kiedykolwiek *adv.* 1. whenever, (at) any time; **kiedykolwiek ją widzę...** every time I see her...; **lepszy niż kiedykolwiek** better than ever (before); **najmądrzejsza osoba, jaką kiedykolwiek spotkałam** the wisest person I've ever met. 2. (*w pytaniach*) ever; **czy kiedykolwiek z nim rozmawiałaś?** have you ever talked to him?

kiedyś *adv.* (*w przeszłości*) once, sometime; (*w przyszłości*) one *l.* some day, sometime.

kielich *mi Gen.* -a 1. (*naczynie*) goblet; (*mszalny*) chalice; **pójść na kielicha** *pot.* go and have a drink; **wypić kielich goryczy** drink the cup of sorrow; **wznieść kielich za coś** raise one's glass to sth. 2. *bot.* (*kwiatu*) calyx. 3. *techn.* (*rury*) pipe bell *l.* socket.

kielichowaty *a.* 1. *bot.* calycate. 2. (*kształt*) cup-shaped.

kielichowiec *mi* -wc- *Gen.* -a *bot.* sweet shrub (*Calycanthus*); **kielichowiec wonny** Carolina allspice (*Calycanthus floridus*).

kielichowy *a.* cup-shaped; **rura kielichowa** *techn.* flared *l.* socket tube.

kieliszek *mi* -szk- *Gen.* -a 1. (*naczynie*) glass; **kieliszek do brandy** *l.* **koniaku** snifter; **kieliszek do wina** wineglass; **kieliszek do jajek** eggcup; **kieliszek przed snem** nightcap; **zaglądać do kieliszka** be fond of the bottle, be fond of a drop, hit the bottle; **opróżnić kieliszek** drain a glass; **skoczyć na kieliszek** *pot.* go and have a drink; **szukać zapomnienia w kieliszku** drown one's sorrows; **trącić się kieliszkami** clink glasses. 2. (= *porcja mocnego alkoholu*) *pot.* shot.

kielnia *f. Gen.pl.* -i 1. *bud.* trowel; **nakładać/wyrównywać kielnią** trowel. 2. *myśl.* beaver's tail.

kieł *mi* kł- *Gen.* kła 1. *anat., dent.* (*u człowieka*) canine (tooth), eye tooth, dog tooth; (*u zwierzęcia*) fang; (*u dzika, morsa, słonia*) tusk;

szczerzyć kły grin from ear to ear. 2. *techn.* center.

kiełb *ma* -bi- *icht.* gudgeon (*Gobio*); **mieć kiełbie we łbie** *pot.* be scatterbrained.

kiełbasa *f. kulin.* sausage; **nie dla psa kiełbasa** it's too good for the likes of you.

kiełbasiany *a.* sausage; (= *podobny do kiełbasy*) sausage-like; **choroba kiełbasiana** *pat.* botulism; **jad kiełbasiany** *biochem.* botulin.

kiełbasić się *ipf. pot.* (= *gmatwać się*) get complicated; get confused.

kiełbaska *f.* hotdog, frankfurter.

kiełbaśnica *f.* 1. *kulin.* (= *osłonka*) sausage casing. 2. *techn.* sausage filler *l.* machine.

kiełek *mi* -łk- *Gen.* -a *bot.* germ, sprout; **kiełki pszenicy** wheat germ.

kiełkować *ipf.* 1. *bot.* (*o nasionach*) germinate, sprout. 2. (*o pomysłach, ideach*) germinate.

kiełznać *ipf.* (*konia*) bit; *przen.* (*uczucia, pożądanie*) curb, quell.

kiełzno *n.* bit.

kiep *mp* kp- *pl.* kpy *pog., przest.* dumbbell, dunce.

kiepski *a.* lousy.

kiepsko *adv.* lousily, poorly; **czuć się kiepsko** feel lousy, feel under the weather.

kier *a. indecl. karty* (*o asie, damie, piątce*) of hearts; **as kier** ace of hearts. – *mi Gen.* -a (= *karta kier*) heart(s).

kierat *mi hist. t. przen.* treadmill; **chodzić jak w kieracie** keep *l.* have one's nose to the grindstone.

kierdel *mi* -dl- *Gen.* -a *dial.* (= *stado owiec*) fold.

kiermasz *mi Gen.pl.* -ów fair, bazaar.

kiermaszowy *a.* fair; **stoisko kiermaszowe** stall.

kiernoz *ma roln.* boar.

kierować *ipf.* 1. (= *zwracać, wysyłać kogoś, coś dokądś, w jakimś kierunku*) direct; (*do lekarza, do rozpatrzenia, do pracy, do szkoły, na przesłuchanie*) send, refer; (*broń, wysiłki*) aim; (*skargę*) file; **kieruje nim ambicja** he's driven by ambition; **kierować rozmowę na coś** lead a conversation in a particular direction, steer a conversation towards sth/a certain topic; **kierować uwagę na coś** focus on sth. 2. (= *prowadzić pojazd*) (*samochodem*) drive; (*samolotem*) fly; (*statkiem, samolotem*) steer, navigate. 3. (= *zarządzać pracami grupy ludzi*) manage; (*pracami, badaniami*) supervise. ~ **się** *ipf.* 1. (= *iść w określonym kierunku*) go towards, make for, head towards *l.* for. 2. (*rozumem, rozsądkiem, uczuciem*) (= *postępować według czegoś*) follow; **kierować się rozsądkiem** be guided by (common) sense; **kierować się uczuciem** follow one's heart, do as one's heart tells one.

kierowca *mp* driver; (*osobisty*) chauffeur.

kierownica *f.* 1. *mot.* (steering) wheel; **za kierownicą** *t. przen.* at the wheel; **zmieniać kogoś za kierownicą** take over at the wheel from sb. 2. (*roweru, motoru*) handlebars. 3. *żegl.* lead-in pier. 4. *geom.* directrix.

kierownictwo *n.* **1.** (= *zarządzanie l. zarząd*) management; **kierownictwo produkcji** line management; **kierownictwo średniego szczebla** middle management; **pracować pod czyimś kierownictwem** work under sb's supervision. **2.** (= *przywództwo*) leadership.

kierowniczka *f.* manageress, manager.

kierowniczy *a.* (*o stanowisku*) managerial, executive; **mechanizm kierowniczy** *mot.* steering mechanism *l.* gear; **układ kierowniczy** *mot.* steering system; **układ kierowniczy ze wspomaganiem** power steering (system).

kierownik *mp* manager, supervisor.

kierowy *a. karty* of hearts.

kierpec *mi* -pc- *Gen.* -a moccasin (*of Tatra highlanders*).

kierunek *mi* -nk- **1.** (*drogi, marszu*) direction; (*wiatru, prądu*) set; (*dochodzenia, badań, rozumowania*) line; **iść w jakimś kierunku** go *l.* make towards sth, make for sth, head towards *l.* for sth; **kierunek działania** course of action; **kierunek studiów** *uniw.* major; **mieć zdolności w jakimś kierunku** have a gift for sth; **nadawać ton** *l.* **kierunek** set the trend; **w kierunku Warszawy** towards Warsaw; **w przeciwnym kierunku** in the other *l.* opposite direction. **2.** *sztuka* trend. **3.** (= *zarządzanie*) management, leadership; **pracować pod czyimś kierunkiem** work under sb's guidance *l.* instruction. **4.** *wojsk.* front.

kierunkowskaz *mi* **1.** (= *znak drogowy, drogowskaz*) signpost. **2.** *mot.* turn signal, directional; *Br.* indicator, blinker.

kierunkowy *a.* directional, of or pertaining to direction; *uniw.* (*o przedmiocie studiów*) major; (*o antenie, mikrofonie*) directional; **numer kierunkowy** *tel.* area code; **ruch kierunkowy** *biol.* tropism; **ster kierunkowy** *lotn.* rudder.

kierz *mi* krz- *Gen.* **krza** *arch.* (= *krzak*) bush, shrub.

kierznia *f. Gen.pl.* -i *kulin., dial.* churn.

kiesa *f.* **1.** *przest.* (= *sakiewka*) purse. **2.** *przen.* (= *kapitał, majątek*) purse; **kiesa publiczna** the public purse; **wydatki z kiesy państwowej** public spending; **mieć pełną kiesę** have a heavy purse; **potrząsnąć kiesą** dig into one's purse.

kieszeń *f. pl.* -e **1.** (*np. w ubraniu*) pocket; **kieszeń magnetofonu** cassette compartment; **schować coś do kieszeni** pocket sth, put sth into a pocket; **trzymać ręce w kieszeni** have one's hands in one's pockets; **znać coś jak własną kieszeń** know sth like the back of one's hand, know sth inside out. **2.** (= *własne zasoby pieniężne*) finance, money, funds; **bić kogoś po kieszeni** set sb back (a bit); **mieć węża w kieszeni** be tight-fisted; **mieć kogoś w kieszeni** have sb in one's pocket; **napchać sobie kieszenie** line one's (own) pockets; **płacić z własnej kieszeni** pay out of one's own pocket; **siedzieć u kogoś w kieszeni** be in sb's pocket; **to nie na moją kieszeń** it's more than my pocket can stand, it's beyond my means, I can't afford it. **3.** *teatr* scene dock *l.* bay.

kieszonka *f.* small pocket; **kieszonka na zegarek** fob.

kieszonkowe *n. Gen.* -ego pocket money, allowance.

kieszonkowiec *mp* -wc- *pl.* -y pickpocket.

kieszonkowy *a.* pocket.

kij *mi Gen.* -a *Gen.pl.* -ów **1.** stick; **kij baseballowy** *sport* (baseball) bat; **kij bilardowy** *sport* cue; **kij hokejowy** *sport* hockey stick; **kij golfowy** *sport* (golf) club; **kij narciarski** *sport* ski stick *l.* pole; **jakby kij połknął** as stiff as a poker *l.* ramrod; **nie kijem go, to pałką** it is six of one and half a dozen of the other; **nie w kij dmuchał** no small beer; **wetknąć kij w mrowisko** stir up a hornet's nest; **każdy kij ma dwa końce** every coin has two sides, there are two sides to everything, there are two sides to every question. **2.** beating, flogging, whipping; **kij będzie w robocie** sb's gonna get a good whipping.

kijanka *f. zool.* tadpole, polliwog.

kijek *mi* -jk- *Gen.* -a stick; **kijek narciarski** *sport* ski stick *l.* pole.

kiks *mi Gen.* -a **1.** *sport* miss, muff. **2.** *muz.* false note.

kiksować *ipf.* **1.** *sport* miss, muff. **2.** *muz.* be/play/sing off key, be/play/sing out of tune.

kikut *mi Gen.* -a (*kończyny, zęba*) stump; (*ogona*) stub.

kil *mi Gen.* -u *l.* -a *Gen.pl.* -ów *żegl.* keel.

kilak *mi Gen.* -a *pat.* gumma.

kilblok *mi żegl.* keel block.

kilim *mi tk.* kilim, rug.

kilimiarka *f. tk.* kilim *l.* rug weaver.

kilimiarstwo *n. tk.* kilim *l.* rug weaving.

kilka *num. Ins.* -oma *l.* -u a few, some, several; **kilka dni temu** the other day; **kilka razy** a few times; **pięćdziesiąt kilka dolarów/mil** fifty odd dollars/miles, fifty dollars/miles or so.

kilkadziesiąt *num.* **kilkudziesięci-** *Ins.* -oma *l.* -u a few dozen.

kilkakroć *adv. lit.* divers times.

kilkakrotnie *adv.* several times, on several occasions.

kilkakrotny *a.* multiple; repeated.

kilkanaście *num.* **kilkunast-** *Ins.* -oma *l.* -u a dozen or so.

kilkanaścioro *num. decl. like n.* -rg- *zob.* **kilkanaście.**

kilkaset *num.* **kilkuset** a few hundred.

kilkoro *num. decl. like n.* -rg- *zob.* **kilka.**

kilkudniowy *a.* **1.** (= *trwający kilka dni*) a few days', of several days; **kilkudniowy pobyt** a few days' stay. **2.** (= *w wieku kilku dni*) a few days old; **kilkudniowy zarost** stubble.

kilkudziesięciu *num. zob.* **kilkadziesiąt.**

kilkugodzinny *a.* a few hours', of several hours; **kilkugodzinna jazda (samochodem)** a few hours' drive.

kilkuletni *a.* **1.** (= *trwający kilka lat*) a few years', of several years. **2.** (= *w wieku kilku lat*) a few years old; **kilkuletni chłopiec** a few years old (boy), small boy.

kilkumetrowy *a.* (= *wysoki / długi / szeroki na kilka metrów*) a few meters high/long/wide; (*odległość*) of a few meters.

kilkumiesięczny *a.* **1.** (= *trwający kilka mie-*

sięcy) of several months, a few months long, a few months'. **2.** (= *w wieku kilku miesięcy*) a few months old; **kilkumiesięczne niemowlę** a few months old baby.

kilkuminutowy *a.* a few minutes long, of several minutes.

kilkunastodniowy *a.* **1.** (= *trwający kilkanaście dni*) of a dozen days or so. **2.** (= *w wieku kilkunastu dni*) a dozen days old.

kilkunastogodzinny *a.* of a dozen hours or so.

kilkunastolatek *mp* -tk- *pl.* -i teenager, teenage boy, teen.

kilkunastolatka *f.* teenager, teenage girl, teen.

kilkunastoletni *a.* **1.** (= *trwający kilkanaście lat*) of a dozen years or so. **2.** (= *w wieku kilkunastu lat*) a dozen years or so old; (*samochód, dom, drzewo*) of a dozen years or so, a dozen years or so old; (*chłopiec, dziewczynka*) teenage.

kilkunastu *num. zob.* **kilkanaście.**

kilkuosobowy *a.* of *l.* for several persons.

kilkupiętrowy *a.* several-story, of several stories.

kilkuset *num. zob.* **kilkaset.**

kilkusetletni *a.* a few hundred years old.

kilkusetmetrowy *a.* (= *wysoki / długi / szeroki na kilkaset metrów*) a few hundred meters high/long/wide; (*odległość*) of a few hundred meters.

kilkutygodniowy *a.* **1.** (= *trwający kilka tygodni*) a few weeks long, of a few weeks, a few weeks'. **2.** (= *w wieku kilku tygodni*) a few weeks old; **kilkutygodniowe niemowlę** a few weeks old baby.

kilkutysięczny *a.* of a few thousand.

kilkuwiekowy *a.* a few centuries old.

kilo *n. indecl. pot.* kilo.

kilobajt *mi Gen.* -a *komp.* kilobyte (*KB*).

kilof *mi Gen.* -a pickax, pick.

kilogram *mi Gen.* -a kilogram (*kg*); **trzy złote za kilogram** three zloty a *l.* per kilogram.

kilogramowy *a.* one-kilo.

kiloherc *mi Gen.* -a *fiz.* kilohertz (*kHz*).

kilokaloria *f. Gen.* -ii *fiz.* kilocalorie (*kcal*).

kilometr *mi Gen.* -a kilometer (*km*); **trzydzieści kilometrów na godzinę** thirty kilometers an *l.* per hour; **w odległości dziesięciu kilometrów** ten kilometers away.

kilometraż *mi* mileage.

kilometrowy *a.* **1.** (= *długości jednego kilometra*) one-kilometer(-long). **2.** (= *związany z kilometrem*) kilometric, kilometrical. **3.** *pot.* (= *niekończący się*) never-ending, lengthy.

Kilonia *f. Gen.* -ii *geogr.* Kiel.

kilowat *mi Gen.* -a *fiz.* kilowatt (*kW l. kw*).

kilowatogodzina *f. el.* kilowatt-hour (*kWh l. kwh*).

kilowolt *mi Gen.* -a *fiz.* kilovolt (*kV l. kv*).

kilowy *a.* **1.** (= *ważący kilogram*) one-kilo. **2.** *żegl.* keel; **jacht kilowy** keel boat, keeler.

kilson *mi żegl.* keelson, kelson.

kilt *mi Scot.* kilt.

kilwater *mi żegl.* wake.

kiła *f. pat.* **1.** (= *syfilis*) syphilis, lues; **kiła wrodzona** congenital syphilis. **2. kiła kapusty** *bot.* clubroot.

kiłowy *a. pat.* syphilitic, luetic.

kim *pron. zob.* **kto.**

kimać *ipf. pot.* snooze; *sl.* catch a few Zs; *Br.* kip.

kimberlit *mi geol.* kimberlite.

kimkolwiek *pron. zob.* **ktokolwiek.**

kimnąć *pf.* -ij *zob.* **kimać.**

kimograf *mi med.* kymograph.

kimografia *f. Gen.* -ii *med.* kymography.

kimono[1] *n.* **1.** (*strój*) kimono. **2.** (*krój rękawów*) kimono (sleeve).

kimono[2] *n. pot.* (= *sen*) snooze; **uderzać w kimono** hit the sack, hit the hay.

kimonowy *a.* kimono.

kimś *pron. zob.* **ktoś.**

kimże *pron. zob.* **któż.**

kinderbal *mi Gen.pl.* -ów *l.* -i *pot.* children's ball.

kindżał *mi broń* kinjal, Caucasian dagger.

kinematograf *mi przest.* **1.** (= *kino*) cinema, movie theater; *Br.* the pictures. **2.** (= *projektor*) cinematograph.

kinematografia *f. Gen.* -ii (= *produkcja*) **1.** filmmaking, moviemaking. **2.** (= *technika*) cinematography.

kinematograficzny *a.* filmmaking, moviemaking.

kinematyczny *a. fiz.* kinematic, kinematical.

kinematyka *f. fiz.* kinematics.

kineskop *mi techn.* picture tube, kinescope; **kineskop o obniżonej radiacji** low radiation kinescope.

kineskopowy *a.* kinescope; **lampa kineskopowa** picture tube.

kinestetyczny *a. fizj.* kinesthetic; **zmysł kinestetyczny = kinestezja.**

kinestezja *f. fizj.* kinesthesia, kinesthesis.

kinetoterapia *f. Gen.* -ii *med.* kinetotheraphy.

kinetoza *f. pat., wet.* kinetosis.

kinetyczny *a. fiz.* kinetic; **energia kinetyczna** kinetic energy; **tarcie kinetyczne** kinetic friction.

kinetyka *f. fiz.* kinetics; **kinetyka chemiczna** chemical *l.* reaction kinetics.

kineza *f. biol.* kinesis.

kinkiet *mi* wall light *l.* lamp.

kino *n.* **1.** (*budynek*) (movie) theater, motion-picture theater, cinema; the movies; **kino dla zmotoryzowanych** drive-in (movie) theater; **kino objazdowe** mobile (movie) theater, mobile cinema; **co grają w kinie?** what's on *l.* what's playing at the movies?; **iść do kina** go to the movies. **2.** (= *sztuka filmowa*) cinema, the movies; **kino artystyczne** art cinema; **kino autorskie** art film; **kino awangardowe/eksperymentalne** avant-garde/experimental cinema; **kino dokumentalne** documentary cinema; **kino moralnego niepokoju** cinema of moral concern; **kino dźwiękowe/nieme** sound/silent cinema; **kino zaangażowane** socially conscious *l.* aware cinema. **3.** (= *seans*) movie (show); **dam ci parę złotych na kino** I'll give you some money for the movies. **4.** *pot.* (= *niesamowita, zabawna sytuacja*) fun, blast; **ale kino!** what a blast!, what a good time!; **niezłe kino!** that's fun!

kinol *mi Gen.* **-a** *pot.* (= *nos*) snout, nozzle.

kinoman *mp*, **kinomanka** *f. Gen.pl.* **-ek** movie-goer.

kinooperator *mp* motion-picture projector operator, projectionist.

kinowy *a.* movie, cinema, film; **kasa kinowa** box office; **sala kinowa** theater, screen.

kiosk *mi* 1. (*z prasą*) kiosk, stand, stall, booth. 2. *bud.* kiosk. 3. *żegl.* conning tower.

kioskarka *f. Gen.pl.* **-ek**, **kioskarz** *mp* newsdealer, newsagent.

kipa *f.* 1. *techn.* (*kadź*) dyeing vat. 2. *żegl.* padeye, fairlead, fairleader.

kiper[1] *mp pl.* **-rzy** *kulin.* (*testujący*) taster.

kiper[2] *mi pl.* **-y** *kulin.* (*zwł. śledź*) kipper.

kiperski *a. kulin.* taster, taster's.

kiperstwo *n. kulin.* tasting.

kipieć *ipf.* **-ię** **-isz** 1. (= *bulgotać*) seethe, surge, churn. 2. (= *przelewać się*) boil (over). 3. (= *złościć się*) seethe, boil; **kipieć ze złości** boil with anger. 4. (= *tętnić życiem*) bustle, be full of life, be active. 5. *myśl.* scurry, scamper.

kipiel *f. Gen.pl.* **-i** welter, surf, surge.

kipnąć *pf.* **-ij** *pot., żart.* (= *umrzeć*) kick the bucket, buy the farm, cash in one's chips.

kir *mi* pall; **okryć się kirem** *lit.* go into mourning.

kirasjer *mp hist., wojsk.* cuirassier.

kirasjerski *a. hist., wojsk.* cuirassier.

kirgiski *a.* Kirgiz, Kirghiz.

Kirgiz *mp*, **Kirgizka** *f. Gen.pl.* **-ek** Kirgiz, Kirghiz.

Kirgizja *f. geogr.* Kirghizia.

Kirke *f. indecl. mit.* Circe, Kirke.

kirkut *mi rel.* Jewish cemetery.

kirys *mi hist., wojsk.* cuirass.

kisić *ipf.* **-szę** **-sisz** 1. (= *kwasić*) pickle. 2. *pot.* (= *przetrzymywać*) hang on to (*sth*). ~ **się** *ipf.* (= *kwasić się*) 1. pickle. 2. *pot.* (= *przebywać w domu*) rot away at home, not go out at all.

kisiel *mi Gen.pl.* **-i** *l.* **-ów** fruit-flavored starch jelly; **dziesiąta woda po kisielu** very distant relative; very distant affinity *l.* relation.

kisnąć *ipf.* **-snę** **-śniesz**, **-ij**; **-sł** **-sła** **-śli** *l.* **-snął** **-snęła** **-snęli** 1. (= *kwaśnieć*) turn sour. 2. *pot.* (= *przebywać w domu*) rot away at home, not go out at all.

kiszka *f. Gen.pl.* **-ek** 1. *anat.* intestine, bowels; **ślepa kiszka** appendix; **skręt kiszek** intestinal torsion *l.* volvulus; **katar kiszek** enteritis; **kiszki komuś marsza grają** sb is starving. 2. *kulin.* blood sausage, black pudding; kishke. 3. *pot.* (tire) tube. 4. *przen.* (= *coś wąskiego, długiego*) long and narrow object *l.* room.

kiszkowaty *a.* long and narrow; **kiszkowaty pokój** long and narrow room.

kiszonka *f. Gen.pl.* **-ek** 1. *roln.* silage, ensilage. 2. (*z warzyw*) pickled vegetables.

kiszony *a.* pickled; **kiszona kapusta** sauerkraut; **kiszony ogórek** (dill) pickle.

kiść *f. pl.* **-e** (*gałązka*) 1. spray; (*grono*) bunch; *bot.* (*kwiatostan*) raceme. 2. (= *frędzel, pióropusz*) crest; brush; **kiść ręki** *lit.* hand and wrist.

kit *mi* putty; glazier's putty; **kit szpachlowy** hard putty; **kit pszczeli** propolis; **do kitu!** *pot.* this sucks!; **wciskać komuś kit** bullshit sb.

kita *f.* 1. (*ogon*) brush, tail; **odwalić kitę** *wulg.* kick the bucket, cash in one's chips. 2. (*pęk*) bunch, bundle. 3. (*kwiatostan*) spray; raceme.

Kitajec *mp* **-jc-** *pl.* **-e** *pog.* (= *Chińczyk*) Chink.

kitara *f. muz.* kithara, cithara.

kitarzysta *mp*, **kitarzystka** *f. Gen.pl.* **-ek** kithara player.

kitel *mi* **-tl-** *Gen.* **-a** *Gen.pl.* **-i** *l.* **-ów** smock.

kitka *f.* 1. (*ogon*) brush; tuft; ponytail (*fryzura*). 2. (*pęk*) bunch. 3. (*kwiatostan, wiecha*) spray; raceme.

kitować *ipf.* 1. (*uszczelniać*) putty. 2. *pot.* (= *kłamać*) bullshit.

kiur *mi Gen.* **-u** *chem.* curium. – *mi Gen.* **-a** *fiz.* curie.

kiurowce *pl. Gen.* **-ów** *chem.* transamericium elements.

kiwać *ipf.* (= *poruszać czymś w tę i z powrotem*) 1. wag, swing; **kiwać głową** nod; **kiwać na kogoś** beckon sb; **kiwać nogami** swing *l.* dangle sb's legs; **ptak kiwał ogonkiem** the bird wagged its tail; **nie kiwnąć palcem** not lift *l.* raise a finger. 2. *pot.* (= *oszukiwać*) double-cross. ~ **się** *ipf.* 1. (= *kołysać się*) (*człowiek, głowa*) swing; (*mebel*) be rickety. 2. (= *bujać się*) swing, rock.

kiwi *n. indecl.* 1. (*owoc*) kiwi (fruit). 2. *orn.* kiwi (*Apteryx*).

kiwnąć *pf.* **-ij** *zob.* **kiwać**. ~ **się** *pf. zob.* **kiwać się**.

klacz *f.* mare.

klaczka *f. Gen.pl.* **-ek** (= *młoda klacz*) filly.

klad *mi biol.* clade.

kladogram *mi biol.* cladogram.

kladystyczny *a. biol.* cladistic.

kladystyka *f. biol.* cladistics.

klajster *mi* **-tr-** *pot.* glue, paste, stickum.

klajstrować *ipf. pot.* mend *l.* smear (*sth*) with glue.

klajstrowaty *a. pot.* gluey, jelly-like, pasty.

klaka *f. pot.* claque.

klakier *mp* claquer, claqueur.

klakson *mi mot.* horn.

klamerka *f. Gen.pl.* **-ek** 1. (= *sprzączka*) clasp. 2. clothespin (*do wieszania ubrań*). 3. *med.* clip, clasp.

klamka *f. Gen.pl.* **-ek** doorknob; (*podłużna*) handle; (*okrągła*) knob; **klamka zapadła** it's too late now; you can't turn back time.

klamoty *pl. Gen.* **-ów** *pot.* stuff, rummage, odds and ends.

klamp *mi med.* clamp, (artery) clip.

klamra *f. Gen.pl.* **-mer** 1. (= *sprzączka*) buckle, clasp. 2. (*nawias*) curly bracket, bracket; square bracket; **ująć coś w klamry** put sth in brackets. 3. *sport* (*przy wspinaczce*) staple. 4. *sport* (= *klincz*) clinch.

klamrować *ipf.* 1. (= *zakładać klamry*) clamp, clasp. 2. *sport* (*w boksie*) clinch.

klamrowy *a.* 1. fastened with a buckle *l.* clamp. 2. **nawias klamrowy** curly *l.* square bracket.

klan *mi* **1.** *Scot., Ir.* clan, family. **2.** (= *grupa ludzi o wspólnych interesach*) clan, clique.

klang *mi żegl.* clang.

klangor *mi* (= *głos żurawi*) clangor.

klanowy *a.* clan; clannish; **system klanowy** clan system; **społeczeństwo klanowe** clan society.

klap *int.* clap, slap.

klapa *f.* **1.** (= *pokrywa*) cover, hatch, trapdoor, flap; tailgate (*ciężarówki, półciężarówki*). **2.** (*płaszcza, marynarki*) lapel; **chwycić kogoś za klapy** grab sb by the lapels. **3.** *techn.* valve; **klapa bezpieczeństwa** safety *l.* escape valve. **4.** *muz.* stop, piston. **5.** *pot.* (= *fiasko*) flop, washout; **zrobić klapę** flop.

klapać *ipf.* -pię -piesz **1.** (= *uderzać czymś płaskim*) clap, slap. **2.** (*dziobem, zębami*) snap. **3.** *myśl.* toot.

klapka *f. Gen.pl.* -ek **1.** *strój* small lapel. **2.** (*element urządzenia*) valve; **klapka telefoniczna** *techn.* drop indicator.

klapki *pl. Gen.* -ek (*obuwie*) flip-flops.

klapnąć *pf.* -ij **1.** *zob.* **klapać. 2.** *pot.* (= *usiąść*) flop (down). **3.** *pot.* (= *uderzyć miękko*) flop.

klapować *ipf. pot.* be all right, be cool; **coś tu nie klapuje** there's something wrong with it.

klaps[1] *mi Gen.* -a (*uderzenie*) smack, slap; **dać komuś klapsa** smack *l.* slap sb.

klaps[2] *mi Gen.* -a *kino* clapper boards, clap sticks.

klapsa *f.* (*gruszka*) Clapp pear, Clapp's favorite.

klapser *mp kino* clapper boy.

klapserka *f. Gen.pl.* -ek *kino* clapper girl.

klark[1] *mp pl.* -owie *żegl.* clerk.

klark[2] *mi Gen.* -a *chem.* **klark pierwiastków** the Clarke concentration number.

klarnecista *mp*, **klarnecistka** *f. Gen.pl.* -ek *muz.* clarinettist, clarinetist.

klarnet *mi muz.* clarinet.

klarnetowy *a. muz.* clarinet.

klarować *ipf.* **1.** (*oczyszczać*) clarify, clear, refine. **2.** *pot.* (= *wyjaśniać*) clear up, clarify. **3.** *żegl.* (*przy wyjściu w morze*) clear. **4.** *żegl.* (*po zawinięciu do portu*) stow. ~ **się** *ipf.* **1.** (*oczyszczać się*) clarify, clear, refine. **2.** *pot.* (= *stawać się jasnym*) clear up, clarify.

klarowność *f.* clarity.

klarowny *a.* clear, lucid, limpid; **mówić w klarowny sposób** speak in a clear way.

klaryska *f. rz.-kat.* nun of the order of St. Clare.

klasa *f.* **1.** (*kategoria*) class; **pierwsza/druga klasa** first/second class; **klasa turystyczna** tourist class; **wagon pierwszej klasy** first-class car; **podróżować pierwszą klasą** travel first class. **2.** (= *jakość, poziom*) class, quality; **sportowiec najwyższej klasy** top-class athlete; **posiłek pierwszej klasy** *l.* **pierwsza klasa** (= *pierwszorzędny*) first-rate *l.* first-class meal; **odznaczać się wysoką klasą** be of high quality; **ona ma klasę** she has class; **stanowić klasę dla samego siebie** be in a class by o.s.; be in a class of one' own. **3.** (= *grupa uczniów w szkole*) class; (= *rocznik*) grade; **zdolna/miła klasa** talented/nice students; **przejść do następnej klasy** be promoted to the next grade. **4.** (= *sala szkolna*) classroom; **w klasie** in the classroom. **5.** (= *przedmiot w szkole artystycznej*) class; **klasa fortepianu/śpiewu/dyrygentury** piano/singing/conducting class. **6.** *socjol.* class; **klasa rządząca/uprzywilejowana** the ruling/privileged class; **klasa wyższa/niższa** the upper/lower class; **klasa średnia/robotnicza** the middle/working class. **7.** *techn.* class, grade. **8.** *bot.* class. **9.** *mat.* class, set. **10.** *sport* division, league.

klaser *mi Gen.* -a stamp album.

klaskać *ipf.* -szczę -szczesz *l.* -am -asz, -szcz *l.* -aj, **klasnąć** *pf.* -snę -śniesz, -ij **1.** clap, applaud; **klaskać w ręce** *l.* **dłonie** clap one's hands. **2.** + *Ins.* (= *kłapać*) smack, snap (*sth*). **3.** *myśl.* (= *wydawać trele*) trill.

klasowość *f.* belonging to a class; class divisions.

klasowy *a.* **1.** class, category. **2.** class; **społeczeństwo klasowe** class society; **świadomość klasowa** class consciousness; **walka klasowa** class struggle. **3.** class; **dziennik klasowy** class *l.* attendance register; **praca klasowa** test; **wycieczka klasowa** class trip.

klasówka *f. Gen.pl.* -ek *szkoln.* test, quiz.

klaster *mi Gen.* -a *muz.* **1.** tone cluster. **2.** *chem.* cluster.

klastyczny *a. geol.* clastic; **skała klastyczna** clastic rock.

klasy *pl.* (*gra dziecięca*) hopscotch.

klasycysta *mp*, **klasycystka** *f. Gen.pl.* -ek classicist.

klasycystyczny *a.* classicistic; **sztuka klasycystyczna** classicistic art; **klasycystyczna budowla** classicistic building.

klasycyzm *mi* classicism.

klasycyzować *ipf.* classicize.

klasyczność *f.* classic(al) character.

klasyczny *a.* **1.** (*antyczny*) classical; **filologia klasyczna** Classics; **języki klasyczne** classical languages. **2.** (= *klasycystyczny*) classical, classicistic; **tragedia klasyczna** classical tragedy; **literatura klasyczna** classical literature; **balet klasyczny** classical ballet. **3.** (= *typowy*) classic; **klasyczny przykład** classic example, typical example. **4.** (= *tradycyjny*) classical; **fizyka klasyczna** classical physics; **metoda klasyczna** classical method; **kombinacja klasyczna** *narciarstwo* Nordic combined; **styl klasyczny** *pływanie* breaststroke.

klasyfikacja *f.* **1.** (*podział*) classification, categorization, division. **2.** *szkoln.* awarding (final) marks *l.* grades. **3.** *sport* presenting *l.* compiling standings *l.* ranking. **4.** *log.* classification.

klasyfikacyjny *a.* classificatory, classification.

klasyfikator *mp pl.* -rzy classifier. – *mi pl.* -y *techn.* classifier.

klasyfikować *ipf.* **1.** (= *dokonywać podziału*) classify, categorize. **2.** (= *dokonywać oceny*) grade, mark. **3.** *sport* rank, compile standings.

klasyk *mp* **1.** (*artysta wzorcowy*) classic; **kla-**

syk jazzu jazz classic. **2.** (= *pisarz okresu klasy-cyzmu*) classicistic writer.

klasyka *f.* classics.

klasztor *mi* **1.** (*budynek*) cloister, priory; (*męski*) monastery; (*żeński*) convent, nunnery. **2.** (*zgromadzenie*) religious order; (*męski*) monastery; (*żeński*) convent, nunnery.

klasztorny *a.* monastic, cloistral; **szkoła klasztorna** convent *l.* religious school; **sklepienie klasztorne** *bud.* cloister vault.

klata *f. pot. emf.* (= *klatka piersiowa*) chest.

klatka *f. Gen.pl.* **-ek 1.** (*dla zwierząt*) cage; **klatka piersiowa** rib cage, chest; **klatka schodowa** staircase. **2.** *pot.* (*filmu*) frame. **3.** *el.* cage. **4.** *górn.* cage.

klatrat *mi chem.* clathrate.

klaun *mp pl.* **-i** *l.* **-y** clown.

klaunowski *a.* clownish; **klaunowskie wygłupy** clowning.

klaustrofobia *f. Gen.* **-ii** *pat.* claustrophobia.

klaustrofobiczny *a.* claustrophobic.

klauzula *f. prawn.* clause, provision, proviso; **klauzula egzekucyjna** *l.* **wykonalności** enforcement clause; **klauzula największego uprzywilejowania** most favored nation clause.

klauzulowy *a.* clausal.

klauzura *f. rz.-kat.* **1.** (*przepisy*) rules of enclosure. **2.** (*część klasztoru*) enclosure, inclosure.

klauzurowy *a. rz.-kat.* enclosed; **zakon klauzurowy** enclosed order.

klawesyn *mi muz.* harpsichord.

klawesynista *mp*, **klawesynistka** *f. Gen.pl.* **-ek** harpsichordist.

klawesynowy *a. muz.* harpsichord.

klawiatura *f.* keyboard; **klawiatura fortepianu/ komputera** computer/piano keyboard.

klawikord *mi muz.* clavichord.

klawikordzista *mp*, **klawikordzistka** *f. Gen.pl.* **-ek** clavichordist.

klawisz *mi Gen.* **-a** *Gen.pl.* **-y** *l.* **-ów 1.** (*w klawiaturze*) key. **2.** *sl.* (= *dozorca więzienny*) screw.

klawiszowy *a.* key; **instrument klawiszowy** *muz.* keyboard.

klawo *adv. pot., przest.* (= *świetnie, w porządku*) groovy, swell.

klawy *a. pot., przest.* (= *świetny*) swell, groovy, spiffy, far-out; **klawy film** groovy movie.

kląć *ipf.* **klnę klniesz, klnij; klą klęła** swear, curse; **kląć na czym świat stoi** swear like a trooper. **~ się** *ipf.* swear (*na coś* by sth); **kląć się na wszystkie świętości** swear to God.

kląskać *ipf.* **1.** (*o słowiku*) trill. **2.** (= *kłapać*) slog, tramp. **3.** smack one's lips.

kląskawka *f. Gen.pl.* **-ek** *orn.* stonechat (*Saxicola torquata*).

klątwa *f.* **1.** (= *ekskomunika*) excommunication, curse, anathema; **klątwa kościelna/papieska** ecclesiastical/papal excommunication. **2.** curse; **rzucić na kogoś klątwę** put a curse on sb.

kle *mi zob.* **kieł.**

klecha *mp pl.* **-y** *Gen.* **-ów** *l.* **-ch** *pog.* (= *ksiądz*) padre, sky pilot, Holy Joe.

klechda *f. lit.* folk story; fairy tale.

klechdowy *a.* folk-story.

klecić *ipf.* **1.** piece together, cobble (together). **2.** *przen.* throw together, improvise; **klecić rymy** *l.* **wiersze** *żart.* cobble rimes.

kleić *ipf.* **-ję -isz** (*łączyć*) glue (together). **~ się** *ipf.* **1.** (= *lepić się*) stick; **kleją mi się powieki** my eyelids are drooping; **wszystko mu się klei do rąk** *przen.* he has sticky fingers; **rozmowa się nie klei** the conversation is heavy-going. **2.** *pot.* (= *łączyć się w logiczną całość*) make sense; **twoje opowiadanie zupełnie się nie klei** your story doesn't make any sense at all.

kleik *mi kulin.* gruel, loblolly.

kleistość *f.* glueyness, stickiness, viscosity.

kleisty *a.* gluey, sticky, glutinous; **kleista maź** gunk.

klej *mi Gen.pl.* **-ów** glue, cement, adhesive; **klej biurowy** library paste; **klej stolarski** carpenter's *l.* joiner's glue; **klej roślinny** vegetable glue, mucilage; **klej zwierzęcy** animal glue.

klejarka *f. Gen.pl.* **-ek** *druk.* **1.** gluing machine. **2.** *stol.* glue spreader. **3.** *tk.* dressing machine.

klejarnia *f. Gen.pl.* **-i** *l.* **-ń** *techn.* gluing shop; glue shop.

klejarski *a.* glue.

klejarz *mp* gluer.

klejnocik *mi Gen.* **-u** *l.* **-a** gem, bijou.

klejnot *mi* **1.** (*wyrób jubilerski*) gem, jewel; **klejnot herbowy** family crest. **2.** (= *cenna rzecz*) gem, jewel.

klejodajny *a. biol.* mucilaginous.

klejonka *f. Gen.pl.* **-ek 1.** (*płótno*) buckram. **2.** (*deska*) plywood. **3.** *sztuka* collage. **4.** *tk.* dressing.

klejowaty *a.* = **kleisty.**

klejowy *a.* glue; **farba klejowa** glue *l.* sized color, distemper.

klejstogamia *f. Gen.* **-ii** *bot.* cleistogamy.

klejstogamiczny *a. bot.* cleistogamous, cleistogamic.

klekot *mi Gen.* **-u 1.** (*bociana*) clatter. **2.** (= *terkot*) clatter, rattle. – *mi Gen.* **-u** *l.* **-a** *pot.* (= *gruchot*) piece of junk.

klekotać *ipf.* **-czę -czesz** *l.* **cę -cesz, -cz 1.** (*o bocianie*) clatter. **2.** (= *terkotać*) clatter, rattle. **3.** *pot.* (= *trajkotać*) chatter.

klekotka *f. Gen.pl.* **-ek** *przen., pot.* (= *gadatliwa kobieta*) chatterbox.

klekotliwy *a.* clattering, rattling; **klekotliwy dźwięk** rattling sound.

kleks *mi Gen.* **-a 1.** (*z atramentu*) blot. **2.** *rzad.* (= *barwna plama na obrazie*) splash.

klematis *mi Gen.* **-u** *l.* **-a** *bot.* clematis (*Clematis*).

kleń *ma pl.* **-e** *icht.* chub (*Leuciscus cephalus*).

klepać *ipf.* **-ię -iesz 1.** (*uderzać*) pat, tap; **klepać kogoś po ramieniu** pat sb on the shoulder. **2.** (= *rozpłaszczać*) hammer, chase; **klepać kosę** *roln.* sharpen a scythe by hammering; **klepać len** *roln.* scutch; **klepać biedę** *przen.* be hard up. **3.** chatter, prattle. **~ się** *ipf.* (= *uderzać siebie*) **1.** pat o.s.; **klepać się po brzuchu** pat sb's belly. **2.** (= *klepać się nawzajem*) pat each other.

klepadło n. Gen.pl. -**deł** techn. stake, sett.
klepak mi Gen. -**a 1.** (młot) chasing hammer.
2. tk. willow, willower, willey.
kleparka f. Gen.pl. -**ek** tk. willow, willower, willey.
klepisko n. **1.** roln. threshing floor, barn floor.
2. techn. (część młocarni) concave.
klepka f. Gen.pl. -**ek** (beczki) stave; (podłogowa) floorboard; **brak mu piątej klepki** he has a screw loose.
klepnąć pf. -**ij** zob. **klepać**. ~ **się** pf. zob. **klepać się**.
klepsydra f. **1.** (do mierzenia czasu) hourglass. **2.** (= zawiadomienie o pogrzebie) obituary notice.
kleptoman mp, **kleptomanka** f. Gen.pl. -**ek** kleptomaniac, cleptomaniac.
kleptomania f. Gen. -**ii** kleptomania.
kler mi clergy, priesthood.
klerk mp pl. -**owie** hist. l. arch. clerk, scholar.
klerycki a. kośc. clerical; **strój klerycki** clerical garments, (suit of) clericals.
kleryk mp rz.-kat. seminarist.
klerykalizacja f. clericalization.
klerykalizm mi clericalism.
klerykalizować ipf. clericalize. ~ **się** ipf. become clericalized.
klerykalny a. clerical.
klerykał mp pl. -**owie** clerical.
kleszcz ma ent. (= pajęczak zwł. z rodziny Ixodidae) tick.
kleszcze pl. Gen. -**y 1.** (= szczypce, cęgi) pincers, tongs, pliers; **kleszcze dentystyczne** med. extractor, extracting forceps; **kleszcze porodowe** med. forceps. **2.** bud. roof tie. **3.** zool., anat. claws, pincers, forceps.
kleszczowy a. **poród kleszczowy** med. forceps delivery, instrumental delivery.
kleszczyki pl. Gen. -**ów** small tongs l. forceps, tweezers.
kleszy a. pog., przest. priestish.
klezmer mp muz. (członek kapeli żydowskiej) klezmer; pot. musician for hire.
klęczeć ipf. -**ę -ysz** kneel, be on one's knees.
klęczki pl. Gen.pl. -**ek na klęczkach** on one's knees, on bended knees; **paść na klęczki** drop l. sink to one's knees; **powstać z klęczek** rise from one's knees.
klęcznik mi Gen. -**a** (rodzaj krzesła) kneeling chair; kośc. kneeler, prie-dieu.
klęczny a. sport kneeling; **siad klęczny** kneeling squat.
klękać ipf. kneel down.
klęknąć pf. -**ij** kneel down.
klępa f. **1.** (= samica łosia) (moose) cow. **2.** pog. (o kobiecie) hag, (old) cow.
klęska f. Gen.pl. -**sk 1.** (= porażka) defeat; **ponieść klęskę** suffer defeat. **2.** (= nieudane przedsięwzięcie) fiasco, failure, disaster; **przyjęcie okazało się kompletną klęską** the party was a total fiasco. **3.** (= katastrofa) disaster, calamity, plague; **klęska głodu/suszy** disastrous famine/drought.

klęsnąć ipf. -**snę -śniesz, klęsł klęsła** l. -**snął -snęła** rzad. cave in, collapse.
klient mp **1.** (= interesant) client, customer; **stały klient** (restauracji, sklepu) regular customer, patron. **2.** sl. (= osoba) guy.
klientela f. customers, custom; clientele.
klientka f. Gen.pl. -**ek** zob. **klient**.
klif mi geol. cliff; **klif nadmorski** sea-cliff.
klifowy a. cliffy; **wybrzeże klifowe** cliff shoreline.
klika f. pog. clique, coterie.
klimaks mi pot. zob. **klimakterium**.
klimakterium n. sing. indecl. med. climacteric, menopause.
klimakteryczny a. med. climacteric, climacterical; **zaburzenia/objawy klimakteryczne** climacteric disorder/symptoms.
klimat mi **1.** meteor., geogr. climate; **klimat łagodny/ciepły** mild/warm climate; **klimat ostry/surowy** harsh/severe climate; **klimat kontynentalny/oceaniczny** continental/oceanic climate; **klimat monsunowy/pustynny/śródziemnomorski** monsoon/desert/Mediterranean climate; **klimat równikowy/zwrotnikowy/podzwrotnikowy** equatorial/tropical/subtropical climate; **klimat umiarkowany/subpolarny/polarny** moderate/subpolar/polar climate. **2.** przen. (= nastrój) atmosphere; **klimat miejscowy** local atmosphere; **przyjazny/nieprzyjemny klimat** friendly/unpleasant atmosphere; **klimat intelektualny/moralny** intellectual/moral atmosphere; **zmienia się klimat wokół czegoś** the atmosphere is changing around sth.
klimatolog mp pl. -**dzy** l. -**owie** climatologist.
klimatologia f. Gen. -**ii** climatology.
klimatologiczny a. climatologic, climatological; **dane/prognozy klimatologiczne** climatological data/forecasts.
klimatoterapia f. Gen. -**ii** climatotherapy.
klimatyczny a. climatical, climatic; **strefa klimatyczna** geogr. climatic zone l. belt; **leczenie klimatyczne** med. climatic treatment, climatotherapy.
klimatyzacja f. techn. **1.** (= regulacja temperatury) air-conditioning. **2.** (urządzenie) air-conditioner.
klimatyzacyjny a. air-conditioning.
klimatyzator mi Gen. -**a** techn. air-conditioner.
klimatyzować ipf. air-condition.
klimatyzowany a. air-conditioned.
klin mi Gen. -**a** (przedmiot l. kształt) **1.** wedge. **2.** (podkładany pod koło l. beczkę) chock; **wbijać się klinem** wedge in (między l. pomiędzy... between...). **3. zabić komuś klina** przen. put sb on the spot; **wbić klin między...** (= poróżnić, podzielić) drive a wedge between...; **wybijać klin klinem** fight fire with fire; (= wypijać klina) drink the hair of the dog; start the day with a drink. **4.** druk. quoin. **5.** meteor. wedge; **klin wysokiego ciśnienia** high-pressure wedge. **6.** lotn. vee formation. **7.** wojsk. wedge. **8.** (= trójkąt tkaniny l. skóry) wedge, gore; **spódnica w kliny** gored skirt. **9.** Gen. i Acc. -**a** pot. (= kieliszek wódki jako sposób na kaca) hair of the dog (that bit you). **10.** (wstawka wzmacniająca szwy) gusset.

klincz *mi boks* clinch.

klinczować *ipf. boks* get into a clinch.

klinga *f. broń* sword *l.* saber blade.

klingeryt *mi techn.* klingerite.

klinicysta *mp,* **klinicystka** *f. Gen.pl.* -ek clinician.

kliniczny *a. med.* 1. clinical; **objawy kliniczne** clinical symptoms; **obraz kliniczny schorzenia** the clinical picture of a disorder; **śmierć kliniczna** *pat.* clinical death. 2. *przen.* (= *odbiegający od normy, chorobliwy*) pathological, extreme, abnormal; **kliniczny przykład głupoty** example of pathological stupidity.

kliniec *mi* -ńc- *Gen.* -a *bud.* 1. voussoir, archstone. 2. *górn.* (*kruszywo*) key aggregate.

klinika *f. med.* clinic; **klinika dentystyczna/dziecięca** dental/pediatric clinic; **klinika kardiologiczna/onkologiczna** heart/cancer clinic.

klinkier *mi techn.* clinker; (*cegła*) clinker brick.

klinkiernia *f. Gen.pl.* -i clinker works.

klinkierowy *a.* 1. clinker; **nawierzchnia klinkierowa** *bud.* clinker surface. 2. *żegl.* **poszycie klinkierowe** clinker plating.

klinometr *mi geol., miern.* clinometer.

klinować *ipf.* wedge *sth* (up) (*czymś* with sth); chock, quoin; (= *zabezpieczać kołkiem*) nog; **klinować działo** *wojsk.* wedge a gun.

klinowy *a.* 1. wedge-shaped, wedge-like; arrow-headed, V-shaped, vee-shaped; (*o znakach pisma*) cuneiform; *anat.* sphenoid, sphenoidal; **pismo/napisy klinowe** *hist., jęz.* cuneiform script/inscriptions; **szyk klinowy** *wojsk.* vee formation. 2. *techn.* **połączenie klinowe** cleft joint; **pas klinowy** V-belt, vee belt; **próba klinowa** *metal.* wedge test.

klip *mi film* video clip.

klipa *f.* 1. *numizmatyka* polygonal coin. 2. (*gra*) tipcat.

kliper *mi* -pr- *Gen.* -a *żegl.* clipper.

kliprowy *a. żegl.* clipper; **dziób kliprowy** clipper bow.

klips *mi Gen.* -a 1. (*ozdoba ucha*) ear clip. 2. (*zacisk, uchwyt*) clip.

kliring *mi ekon.* clearing.

kliringowy *a. ekon.* clearing; **rozliczenie kliringowe** clearing of accounts; **umowa kliringowa** clearing agreement.

klisza *f.* 1. *fot.* film. 2. *druk.* (printing) plate. 3. = *stereotyp, frazes* cliché.

klitka *f. Gen.pl.* -ek *pot.* (= *ciasny pokoik*) den.

klituś-bajduś *mi indecl. pot.* (= *trele-morele*) fiddle-faddle, fiddlededee; (*o człowieku*) fiddle-faddler; **co ty mi opowiadasz? klituś-bajduś!** what are you telling me? it's all fiddlededee.

kliważ *mi geol.* cleavage.

kliwer *mi* -wr- *Gen.* -a *żegl.* jib, jibsail; headsail.

kliwerbom *mi żegl.* jib boom.

kliwerfał *mi żegl.* jib halyard.

kliwerszot *mi żegl.* jib sheet.

kliwia *f. Gen.* -ii *bot.* clivia, Kaffir lily (*Clivia*).

kloaczny *a.* 1. cesspool; **dół kloaczny** cesspit, latrine; **odór kloaczny** cesspool stench. 2. *zool., anat.* (= *stekowy*) cloacal.

kloaka *f.* 1. (= *zbiornik na nieczystości*) cesspool, sump; (= *odpływ ścieków*) sewer. 2. *przen.* (= *bagno moralne*) cesspool. 3. *zool., anat.* (= *stek*) cloaca.

kloc *mi Gen.* -a 1. (= *ociosany pień*) block, chump; *przen.* (= *bryła, ciężar*) block, lump, dead weight; **gruby/ciężki jak kloc** hefty. 2. *żart.* (= *osiłek*) bruiser, muscleman. 3. *wulg.* (= *stolec*) turd.

klocek *mi* -ck- *Gen.* -a 1. (= *kawałek twardego materiału*) block, chunk. 2. (*do zabawy*) (building-)block, brick; **zbudować zamek z klocków** build a castle with blocks. 3. *pl. pot.* (= *czynność, umiejętność*) **nie bawię się w te klocki** I'm not playing this game; **jestem dobry w te klocki** I'm good at it. 4. *druk.* **klocek drzeworytniczy** printing block. 5. *techn.* **klocek hamulcowy** brake shoe *l.* block. 6. *tk.* (*do haftów*) bobbin.

klockowy *a.* **hamulec klockowy** *techn.* shoe brake; **koronka klockowa** *tk.* bobbin lace, pillow lace.

klocowaty *a.* (= *ciężki, barczysty*) bulky, heavyset.

klomb *mi* flower bed.

klon[1] *mi* 1. *bot.* maple (*Acer*); **klon cukrowy** sugar maple (*A. saccharum*). 2. *stol.* maple wood.

klon[2] *mi Gen.* -u *pl.* -y 1. *biol.* clone. 2. *przen.* (= *wierne naśladownictwo, imitacja*) clone; **klon Elvisa Presleya** *żart.* Elvis Presley clone; **klon komputera osobistego IBM** *komp.* IBM clone PC.

kloniczny *a. pat.* clonic; **skurcz kloniczny** clonic spasm.

klonować *ipf. biol.* clone.

klonowanie *n. biol.* cloning.

klonowy *a.* maple; (= *obsadzony szpalerem klonów*) maple-lined, maple-bordered; **syrop klonowy** maple syrup; **aleja klonowa** maple-bordered lane.

klop *mi Gen.* -a *pot.* (= *ubikacja*) john.

klops *mi Gen.* -a *l.* -u 1. *kulin.* (= *klopsik*) meat ball; (= *pieczeń rzymska*) meat loaf. 2. *pot.* (= *klapa, koniec*) dead end; **no to klops z nami** so we're done.

klopsik *mi Gen.* -a *kulin.* meat ball.

klosz *mi Gen.* -a *Gen.pl.* -y *l.* -ów (*lampy*) 1. lamp shade. 2. (*patera*) epergne. – *mi Gen.* -u *Gen.pl.* -y *l.* -ów (*krój sukni*) flare.

kloszard *mp* hobo, tramp, vagrant.

kloszowy *a.* bell-shaped; **spódnica kloszowa** flared skirt; **spodnie** bell-bottoms.

klotoida *f. fiz., mat.* clothoid, Cornu spiral.

klown *mp zob.* **klaun.**

klozet *mi pot.* lavatory, toilet.

klozetowy *a.* toilet; **muszla klozetowa** toilet bowl; **babcia klozetowa** *pot.* restroom attendant.

klub *mi* 1. (= *stowarzyszenie*) club, association; **klub żeglarski/piłkarski/golfowy/młodzieżowy** sailing/soccer/golf/youth club; **klub książki** book club; **klub poselski** *l.* **parlamentarny** *polit.* parliamentary club (*in Poland*); **Klub Rzymski/Londyński/Paryski** *ekon.* the Rome/London/

Paris Club; **wstąpić** *l.* **zapisać się do klubu** join a club. **2.** (*budynek*) clubhouse. **3.** (*lokal*) club; **klub nocny** night-club.

kluba *f. hist.* **1.** thumbscrew; **brać kogoś w kluby** *przen.* discipline sb. **2.** *przest., techn.* (= *imadło*) vise; (= *blok*) block (and tackle).

klubowiec *mp* **-wc-** *pl.* **-cy** club-member.

klubowy *a.* club; **fotel klubowy** easy chair.

klucha *f.* **1.** *pot.* (= *kluska*) dumpling; **ciepłe kluchy** *przen., pog.* milksop. **2.** *pot.* (= *niewypieczony chleb, ciasto*) half-baked bread/cake, gooey bread/cake. **3.** *pog.* (= *ktoś otyły*) obese, plump as a dumpling.

kluchowaty *a.* gooey; (*o mężczyźnie*) unmanly, effete.

klucz *mi Gen.* **-a 1.** (*do zamykania, otwierania, uruchamiania*) key; **klucz do drzwi frontowych** the key to the front door; **klucze do samochodu** car keys; **klucz uniwersalny** master key; **zamknąć coś na klucz** lock sth; **podglądać przez dziurkę od klucza** peep through the peephole; **pod kluczem** (= *w zamknięciu*) under lock and key; **budynek oddany pod klucz** (= *gotowy do użytku*) turn-key building. **2.** *przen.* (= *środek do osiągnięcia czegoś*) key, passport; **klucz do sukcesu** the key to success. **3.** (= *zasada rozwiązania szyfru; zbiór rozwiązań l. odpowiedzi*) key; **klucz do szyfru** key to a code; **podręcznik z kluczem** textbook with a key; **powieść z kluczem** *teor.lit.* roman à clef. **4.** *biol.* (= *tekst służący do identyfikacji roślin l. zwierząt*) key. **5.** (= *schemat postępowania*) rule, system; **klucz rozdzielania stanowisk** nomination rules; **kandydat z klucza partyjnego** *polit.* party nominee. **6.** (*ptaków*) wedge, skein. **7.** *bud.* keystone. **8.** *lotn.* vee formation. **9.** *muz.* clef; **klucz wiolinowy/basowy** treble/bass clef. **10.** *techn.* (*do uchwytu wiertarki itp.*) chuck key. **11.** *techn.* (*do śrub, nakrętek*) wrench; *Br.* spanner; **klucz nasadowy/oczkowy/ampulowy** socket/ring/pin wrench; **klucz nastawny** adjustable wrench; **klucz francuski** monkey wrench; **klucz dynamometryczny** torque wrench. **12.** *tel.* (= *przycisk zamykający obwód*) key. **13.** *hist.* (= *majątek, zespół folwarków*) demesne.

kluczka *f. Gen.pl.* **-ek 1.** (*węzeł*) noose, loop, hitch. **2.** *myśl.* dodging.

klucznica *f. arch.* housekeeper.

klucznik *mp hist.* house-steward, butler.

kluczowy *a.* key, pivotal, crucial; **kluczowe zagadnienie** key issue; **kluczowy problem** crucial problem.

kluczyć *ipf.* **1.** (= *zmieniać kierunek*) zigzag; weave *l.* wind (one's way) (*wśród czegoś l. przez coś*) through sth). **2.** (= *unikać mówienia wprost*) hedge.

kluczyk *mi Gen.* **-a 1.** (= *mały klucz*) key; (= *do śrub, nakrętek*) wrench, spanner; **kluczyk zapłonu** *mot.* ignition key; **kluczyk do nakręcania** (*mechanizmu*) winding key. **2.** *bot.* (= *pierwiosnek lekarski*) cowslip (primrose) (*Primula veris*).

kluć się *ipf.* **1.** (*o pisklęciu*) hatch. **2.** *przen.* (= *kształtować się*) take shape; **coś się kluje** there's something in the air; something' brewing.

klusek *mi Gen.* **-a, kluska** *f. Gen.pl.* **-ek** *kulin.*

(*o okrągłym kształcie*) dumpling; *pl.* (*lane, krajane, kładzione*) noodles; **ciepłe kluski** *pog.* (*o mężczyźnie*) milksop.

kluza *f. żegl.* hawse-hole.

kła *itd. mi zob.* **kieł.**

kłaczasty *a.* shaggy.

kłaczek *mi* **-czk-** *Gen.* **-a 1.** flake; tuft. **2.** *chem.* floccule.

kłaczkowaty *a.* **1.** flaky, fluffy; tufty. **2.** *chem.* flocculent.

kłaczyć się *ipf.* mat.

kład *mi geom.* rabattement.

kładka *f. Gen.pl.* **-ek** footbridge; (*nad sceną teatru, wzdłuż mostu*) catwalk; *żegl.* plank.

kłak *mi Gen.* **-a 1.** wisp of hair; (= *pęczek włosów*) tuft. **2.** *pl. żart. l. uj.* (= *włosy*) straggly hair.

kłam *mi lit.* falsehood; **zadać kłam czemuś** give the lie to sth.

kłamać *ipf.* **-ię -iesz** lie, tell lies; **kłamać gładko** *l.* **jak z nut** lie glibly; **kłamać jak najęty** lie like a conjurer; **kłamać w żywe oczy** lie in one's teeth *l.* throat.

kłamca *mp* liar.

kłamczuch *mp pl.* **-y, kłamczucha** *f. pot.* liar, fibber.

kłamliwie *adv.* falsely, untruthfully.

kłamliwość *f.* falseness, untruthfulness, mendacity.

kłamliwy *a.* **1.** (= *skłonny do kłamstwa*) deceitful, mendacious. **2.** (= *fałszywy*) false, untrue.

kłamstewko *n. Gen.pl.* **-wek** fib; white lie.

kłamstwo *n.* lie, falsehood; **złapać kogoś na kłamstwie** catch sb lying.

kłaniać się *ipf.* **1.** bow (down) (*komuś / czemuś* to sb/sth, *przed kimś / czymś* before sb/sth); **kłaniać się w pas** *l.* **do ziemi** make a low *l.* reverent bow; *pog.* (= *okazywać uległość*) bow and scrape; **kłaniam się (uniżenie)** *przest.* your (humble *l.* obedient) servant. **2.** (= *pozdrawiać listownie*) send one's regards (*komuś* to sb).

kłap *int.* snap!

kłapaczka *f. pot.* (= *usta*) yap, trap.

kłapać *ipf.* **-pię -piesz, kłapnąć** *pf.* **-ij 1.** (*szczękami*) snap (*na coś / kogoś* at sb/sth). **2.** (= *stukać, szczękać*) rattle, clatter, chatter.

kłapouch *ma żart.* (= *osioł l. królik*) lop-ear.

kłapouchy *a.* lop-eared.

kłaść *ipf.* **kładę kładziesz kładł 1.** (= *umieszczać w pozycji leżącej*) lay, place; (= *odkładać*) put down; **kłaść karty na stół** show one's cards; **kłaść kogoś spać** *l.* **do łóżka** put sb to bed. **2.** (= *wkładać, wtykać*) put, stuff (*do czegoś* in sth). **3.** *przen.* **kłaść coś na karb czegoś** attribute sth to sth; put sth down to sth; **kłaść krzyżyk na kimś czymś** *l.* (*pot.*) **lachę na kogoś/coś** give up on sb/sth, write sb/sth off; **kłaść coś komuś łopatą do głowy** *pot.* cram sth into sb's head. **4.** (= *zakładać na siebie*) put (*sth*) on; don. **5.** *bud.* (= *układać*) lay; **kłaść kafelki/zaprawę/cegły** lay tiles/mortar/bricks; **kłaść tynk na ścianę** plaster a wall. **6.** (= *przechylać, przyginać*) bend down; (= *przewracać*) knock down; **kłaść kogoś/coś pokotem** mow sb/sth down. **7.** *pot.* (= *zaprzepaszczać,* niweczyć) ruin. ~ **się** *ipf.* **1.** (= *przyjmować po-zycję leżącą*) lie down (*na czymś* on sth); **kłaść się krzyżem** lie prostrate. **2. kłaść się (do łóżka)** (= *iść spać*) go to bed; **kłaść się wcześnie/późno** go to bed early/late; **kłaść się z kurami** keep early hours. **3.** (= *rozpościerać się*) spread, lie, hang (*na czymś l. nad czymś* over sth); **kłaść się cieniem na czymś** cast a shadow on *l.* over sth. **4.** (= *ciążyć*) weigh (*na kimś / czymś* on *l.* upon sb/ sth); **kłaść się ciężarem na czyimś sercu** weigh upon sb's heart; weigh down sb's heart. **5.** (= *przewracać się*) fall down.

kłąb *mi* **-ę- 1.** (= *plątanina*) tangle. **2.** (= *kłębek*) ball. **3.** (= *obłok*) cloud. **4.** *zool., anat.* withers; **wysokość w kłębie** height at the withers.

kłącze *n. bot.* rhizome, rootstock, rootstalk.

kłębek *mi* **-bk-** *Gen.* **-a 1.** ball; **kłębek wełny/ sznurka/przędzy** ball of wool/string/yarn; **kłębek nerwów** bundle of nerves; **trafić po nitce do kłębka** learn the truth little by little; **zwinąć się w kłębek** curl up. **2.** (= *obłoczek*) wisp, swirl, twist, cloudlet; **kłębek dymu/mgły** wisp of smoke/mist.

kłębiasty *a.* swirling; *meteor.* cumulous; **chmura kłębiasta** cumulus (cloud).

kłębić się *ipf.* (= *tworzyć kłębowisko*) whirl, swirl; (= *wzbierać*) surge, swell; (*o kurzu*) fluff; (*o chmurach*) cumulate.

kłębowisko *n.* **1.** (= *zamęt, wir*) whirl, swirl, vortex. **2.** (= *plątanina*) tangle; (= *zbity rój*) swarm.

kłębu *itd. mi zob.* **kłąb.**

kłębuszek *mi* **-szk-** *Gen.* **-a** *emf. zob.* **kłębek.**

kłęk *mi bot., stol.* Kentucky coffeetree (*Gymnocladus dioicus*).

kłoda *f. Gen.pl.* **kłód 1.** log, block; **zwalać się/ leżeć/spać jak kłoda** *przen.* fall/lie/sleep like a log; **rzucać komuś kłody pod nogi** *przen.* put a spoke in sb's wheel. **2.** (*do pętania zwierząt*) clog. **3.** *hist.* (*narzędzie tortur*) stocks.

kłonica *f.* stanchion, stake.

kłonić *ipf. lit.* bend; **kłonić głowę** bow one's head. ~ **się** *ipf. lit.* bend down, incline.

kłopot *mi* problem, trouble; embarrassment; **mieć kłopot** have a problem; **być w kłopotach** *l.* **mieć kłopoty** be in trouble; **być w kłopocie** (= *nie wiedzieć, co robić*) be at a loss; be embarrassed; **wprawić kogoś w kłopoty** get sb in trouble.

kłopotać *ipf.* **-czę -czesz** *l.* **-cę -cesz -cz** *lit.* trouble, bother (*sb*). ~ **się** *ipf.* worry, bother (*o kogoś / coś* about sb/sth).

kłopotliwy *a.* (= *sprawiający kłopot*) troublesome, inconvenient; (= *wprawiający w zakłopotanie, niezręczny*) awkward, embarrassing, uneasy, uncomfortable; **kłopotliwy gość** troublesome visitor; **kłopotliwe milczenie** awkward silence; **kłopotliwe pytanie** embarrassing question.

kłos *mi Gen.* **-a** ear; *bot.* spike, spica.

kłosić się *ipf.* ear.

kłosować *ipf. roln.* (= *młócić*) thresh.

kłosowy *a.* **opatrunek kłosowy** *med.* spica.

kłócić się *ipf.* **1.** (= *spierać się*) quarrel, argue, fight. **2.** (= *nie pasować*) clash, jar, disagree (*z czymś* with sth).

kłód *f. zob.* **kłoda.**

kłódka *f.* padlock; **buzia** *l.* **gęba na kłódkę!** *pot.* keep your mouth shut, not a word!

kłótliwy *a.* quarrelsome, belligerent; (*żona*) quarrelsome wife; (*ton*) belligerent tone.

kłótnia *f. Gen.pl.* **-i** quarrel, argument, row.

kłótnica *f.* shrew; *zob.* **kłótnik.**

kłótnik *mp* squabbler.

kłucie *n.* **1.** *zob.* **kłuć. 2.** stabbing pain.

kłuć *ipf.* **kłuję kłujesz** *l.* **kolę kolesz, kłuj** *l.* **kol 1.** (= *nakłuwać*) pierce, stab; **rana kłuta** *pat.* punctured wound. **2.** (= *boleć jak ukłucie*) stab. **3.** (*o owadach*) bite; (= *żądlić*) sting. **4.** *przen.* **kłuć w oczy** be an eyesore; **prawda w oczy kole** nothing hurts more than truth.

kłujący *a.* **1.** (= *kolczasty, ciernisty*) prickly, thorny. **2.** (*ból*) stabbing. **3.** (*owad*) biting, stinging.

kłujka *f. Gen.pl.* **-ek** *ent.* proboscis.

kłus *mi Gen.* **-a** trot; **jechać kłusem** *jeźdz.* trot, ride at a trot; **biec** *l.* **pędzić kłusem** trot (along).

kłusak *ma jeźdz.* trotter.

kłusować[1] *ipf. jeźdz.* (= *biec kłusem*) trot (along).

kłusować[2] *ipf.* (= *polować nielegalnie*) poach.

kłusownictwo *n.* poaching.

kłusownik *mp* poacher.

kłykcina *f. anat.* condyle.

kłykieć *mi* **-kci-** *Gen.* **-a** *Gen.pl.* **-i** *l.* **-ów** *anat.* condyle.

KM *abbr. mech., mot.* hp, HP (= *horsepower*).

km *abbr.* **1.** km (= *kilometer*). **2.** *wojsk.* MG (= *machine gun*).

km/h *abbr.* kph, km/h (= *kilometers per hour*).

kmieć *mp* **1.** *pog.* hick, bumpkin, yokel. **2.** *hist.* peasant.

kmin *mi bot., kulin.* cumin (*Cuminum cyminum*).

kminek *mi* **-nk-** *kulin.* caraway (seed); *bot.* caraway (*Carum carvi*); **chleb z kminkiem** caraway-seed bread.

kminkowy *a. kulin.* caraway-seed.

kminkówka *f. Gen.pl.* **-ek** *kulin.* kümmel.

kmiot, kmiotek *mp pl.* **-i** *pog.* hick, bumpkin, yokel.

knaga *f. żegl.* (*do lin*) cleat; (*do dulek*) rigger.

knajpa *f. pot.* joint.

knajpka *f. Gen.pl.* **-ek** *pot.* joint, hole-in-the-wall.

knebel *mi* **-bl-** *Gen.* **-a** gag.

kneblować *ipf.* gag.

knecht *mp* **1.** *żegl.* (= *słupek*) bollard. **2.** *hist.* landsknecht (= *German foot soldier*).

knedel *mi* **-dl-** *Gen.* **-a** *kulin.* dumpling.

kniaź *mp pl.* **-owie** *l.* **-e** *Gen.* **-ów** *hist.* knez, duke (*in Russia*).

knieć *f. pl.* **-e** *bot.* (*także* **knieć błotna**) marsh marigold, cowslip (*Caltha palustris*).

knieja *f. Gen.* **-ei** *Gen.pl.* **-j** *l.* **-ei** *zwł. lit.* forest.

knocić *ipf. pot.* botch. ~ **się** *ipf. pot.* go to pieces, get screwed up.

knot *mi Gen.* **-a 1.** (*świecy, lampy*) wick. **2.** *pot.* (= *fuszerka*) bungle, botch.

knować *ipf.* = **knuć.**

knuć *ipf.* plot, connive.

knur *ma zool., roln.* boar.

knut *mi Gen.* -a *arch.* (= *bicz*) knout.

knykieć *mi* -kci- *Gen.* -a *Gen.pl.* -i *l.* -ów *anat. l. arch.* knuckle.

knyp *mi Gen.* -a *dial. l. sl.* (= *nóż*) chiv, shiv.

knypek *mp pot., gł. pog.* (= *niski osobnik*) squirt, shortie, shrimp.

knypel *mi* -pl- *Gen.* -a 1. *lotn.* (= *dźwignia*) joystick. 2. (= *młotek rzeźbiarza*) mallet.

koadiutor *mp kośc.* (= *biskup pomocniczy*) coadjutor.

koadiutoria *f. Gen.* -ii *kośc.* coadjutorship.

koadiutorka *f. Gen.pl.* -ek *kośc.* coadjutor, coadjutrix.

koagulacja *f. chem.* coagulation.

koagulant *mi chem.* coagulant.

koagulat *mi chem.* coagulate, coagulum.

koagulator *mi Gen.* -a 1. *chem.* coagulator. 2. *techn.* coagulator; **koagulator laserowy** laser coagulator.

koagulować *ipf. chem.* coagulate.

koala *f. Gen.pl.* -i **(niedźwiadek) koala** *zool.* koala (bear) (*Phascolarctos cinereus*).

koalicja *f. polit.* coalition; **koalicja rządowa** government coalition.

koalicyjny *a. polit.* (*o rządzie, gabinecie*) coalition.

koartykulacja *f. fon.* coarticulation.

koartykulacyjny *a. fon.* coarticulatory.

kobalt *mi chem.* cobalt.

kobaltawy *a. chem.* cobaltous; **chlorek kobaltawy** cobalt chloride.

kobaltować *ipf. metal.* cobalt-plate.

kobaltowy *a.* cobalt; *chem. t.* cobaltic; **bomba kobaltowa** *med.* cobalt bomb; **błękit kobaltowy** *sztuka* cobalt blue.

kobiałka *f. Gen.pl.* -ek basket; (*na owoce*) punnet.

kobieciarz *mp pot.* womanizer.

kobiecina *f. emf.* (poor old) woman.

kobieco *adv.* in a feminine way, like a woman.

kobiecość *f.* femininity.

kobiecy *a.* (*o wyglądzie, cechach charakteru, chodzie*) feminine; (*o elektoracie, narządach*) female; (*o literaturze, chorobach, modzie*) women's; **po kobiecemu** like a woman.

kobierzec *mi* -rc- *Gen.* -a *przest.* carpet; **stanąć na ślubnym kobiercu** *przen.* (= *zawrzeć związek małżeński*) tie the knot.

kobieta *f.* woman; *zwł. form.* female; *pot.* (= *dziewczyna, żona*) lady; **kobieta lekkich obyczajów** woman of easy virtue; **kobieta pracująca** working woman; **kobieta z przeszłością** woman with a past; **moja kobieta** my lady; **samotna kobieta** single woman.

kobietka *f. Gen.pl.* -ek *emf.* woman.

kobita *f. dial. l. pot.* woman.

kobitka *f. Gen.pl.* -ek *dial. l. żart.* woman; **lubić kobitki** like the ladies.

kobra *f. zool.* cobra (*Naja*).

kobuz *ma orn.* hobby (*Falco subbuteo*).

kobyła *f.* 1. (= *klacz*) mare. 2. *pot.* (= *coś dużego*) whopper. 3. *w zwrotach* **jeździć na kimś jak**

na łysej kobyle *pot.* trample upon sb; **znać kogoś jak łysą kobyłę** *pot.* know sb like the back of one's hand, know sb inside out.

kobyłka *f. Gen.pl.* -ek 1. (= *klacz*) (small) mare. 2. *zwł. stol.* (*podpora*) trestle.

kobza *f. muz.* bagpipes, pipes.

kobziarz *mp* piper.

koc *mi Gen.pl.* -ów blanket.

kocanka *f. Gen.pl.* -ek *bot.* helichrysum (*Helichrysum*).

kochać *ipf.* love; **kocham Cię** I love you; **jak Boga kocham!** so help me God!

kochać się *ipf.* 1. (= *darzyć się wzajemną miłością*) love each other, love one another. 2. (= *darzyć miłością*) **kochać się w kimś** be in love with sb. 3. (= *uprawiać seks*) make love (*z kimś* to *l.* with sb). 4. **kochają się jak pies z kotem** *iron.* there's no love lost between them.

kochana *f. Gen.* -ej love.

kochaneczek *mp* -czk- *pl.* -owie *żart.* sweetie pie.

kochaneczka *f. Gen.pl.* -ek *żart.* sweetie pie.

kochanek *mp* -nk- *pl.* -owie lover.

kochanica *f. arch.* mistress.

kochanie *n.* 1. (= *miłość*) love. 2. (= *osoba kochana*) love, sweetheart. 3. *Voc.* (= *moja droga, mój drogi*) (my) dear, (my) darling. 4. **kochanie się** lovemaking.

kochaniutka *f. Gen.* -ej *gł. Voc.* my dear.

kochaniutki *mp gł. Voc.* my dear.

kochanka *f. Gen.pl.* -ek lover.

kochany *a.* dear; **kochana mamo** dear mom; **moja kochana** my dear; **kochana pani!** my dear lady! – *mp* love.

kochaś *mp Gen.pl.* -ów *gł. Voc.* (= *mój drogi*) sweetheart.

kocher *mi Gen.* -a (= *kuchenka turystyczna*) portable cooking stove, primus stove.

kochliwy *a.* amorous.

koci *a.* (= *kota*) feline, cat's; (= *przypominający kota*) catty, feline; **kocie łby** (= *kostka brukowa*) cobblestones; (= *dziury w drodze*) potholes; **kocie oczy** (*na szosie*) cat's-eyes; **kocia muzyka** cacophony; **żyć z kimś na kocią łapę** *zwł. uj.* shack up with sb.

kociak *ma* 1. (= *kotek*) kitty, puss, pussy. 2. *pot.* (*dziewczyna*) chick; (*na plakacie*) pinup girl. 3. *myśl.* (= *młode zająca*) young hare.

kociątko *n. Gen.pl.* -tek (= *kotek*) kitty, puss, pussy.

kocica *f.* 1. (= *kotka*) (she) cat, tabby; (*podstarzała, dostojna*) grimalkin. 2. *myśl.* (= *zajęczyca*) doe (*of a hare*).

kocić się *ipf.* have kittens, kitten.

kocimiętka *f. Gen.pl.* -ek *bot.* catmint, catnip (*Nepeta*).

kocioł *mi* -tł- *Gen.* -a 1. *techn.* boiler; **kocioł parowy** steam boiler. 2. *gł. przest.* (= *duży garnek*) (big) kettle, (big) pot; (= *bardzo duży garnek*) cauldron; (= *zawartość garnka*) kettleful, potful. 3. *muz.* kettledrum. 4. *pot.* (= *zamieszanie*) hurly-burly; **w szkole huczało jak w kotle** the school was bursting with noise. 5. *geol.* cirque. 6. *rugby* scrum. 7. *wojsk.* encirclement. 8. (=

pułapka policyjna) trap. **9. przyganiał kocioł garnkowi** (it's) the pot calling the kettle black, you're a fine one to talk.

kociołek *mi* -**łk**- *Gen.* -**a** pot, kettle.

kocisko *n. emf.* tomcat.

kocmołuch *mp pl.* -**y** *pog.* slob.

kocować *ipf. przest. med.* pack.

kocówa *f. sl.* the blanket treatment (*hazing practise*).

kocur *ma* **1.** (= *kot samiec, duży kot*) tomcat. **2.** *myśl.* tom.

kocyk *mi* rug, (small) blanket.

koczkodan *ma zool.* guenon (*Cercopithecus*).

koczować *ipf.* **1.** *antrop.* (*o ludach pierwotnych*) lead a nomadic life; **plemię koczujące** nomadic tribe. **2.** *pot.* (= *mieszkać w prymitywnych warunkach*) camp; (= *oczekiwać*) be stuck; **koczować na lotnisku** be stuck at an airport.

koczowisko *n.* camp.

koczownictwo *n. antrop.* nomadism.

koczowniczy *a. antrop.* nomadic.

koczownik *mp antrop.* nomad.

kod *mi* code; **kod (pocztowy)** postal code; *US* zip code; *Br.* postcode; **kod genetyczny** *biol.* genetic code; **kod alfanumeryczny** *komp.* alphanumeric code; **kod binarny** *komp.* binary code; **kod źródłowy** *komp.* source code; **kod paskowy** *l.* **kreskowy** *handl.* bar code; **złamać kod** crack a code.

koda *f. muz.* coda.

kodeina *f. chem.* codeine.

kodeks *mi* **1.** (= *zbiór norm*) *t. prawn.* code; **kodeks cywilny/karny/handlowy** civil/penal/commercial code; **kodeks drogowy** rules of the road; *Br.* highway code; **kodeks etyczny/moralny** ethics/moral code. **2.** *bibl.* codex.

koder *mi Gen.* -**a** *tel., komp.* encoder, coder.

kodować *ipf.* code, encode.

kodowany *a.* coded.

kodycyl *mi Gen.pl.* -**i** *l.* -**ów** *prawn.* codicil.

kodyfikacja *f. prawn. l. form.* codification.

kodyfikator *mp*, **kodyfikatorka** *f. Gen.pl.* -**ek** *prawn.* codifier.

kodyfikować *ipf. prawn. l. form.* codify.

koedukacja *f. szkoln.* coeducation.

koedukacyjny *a.* coeducational, coed.

koegzystencja *f. gł. form.* coexistence.

koegzystować *ipf. gł. form.* coexist.

koenzym *mi biochem.* coenzyme.

koercja *f. fiz.* coercive force.

kofeina *f. chem.* caffeine; **kawa bez kofeiny** decaffeinated (coffee); *pot.* decaf.

kofeinizm *mi pat.* caffeine addiction.

koga *f. żegl., hist.* cog.

kogel-mogel, kogiel-mogiel *mi* -**gl**- -**gl**- *Gen.* -**a** -**a** *kulin.* yolk stirred with sugar.

kognitywizm *mi jęz.* cognitivism.

kognitywny *a. jęz.* cognitive.

kogo *pron. Gen. i Acc. of* **kto**; who; *form.* whom; **dla kogo to jest?** who is this for?; **kogo widziałaś/spotkałaś itd.?** who did you see/meet etc.?; **kogo masz na myśli?** who do you have in mind?; **kogo (to) widzimy!** look who's here!; **na kogo się patrzysz?** who are you looking at?; **na kogo wypada?** whose turn is it?; **ktoś, kogo spot-**

kałam (*w zdaniu podrzędnym przydawkowym*) somebody (that *l.* who *l.* whom) I've met.

kogokolwiek *pron. Gen. i Acc. of* **ktokolwiek**; whoever; *form.* whomever; **wybierz kogokolwiek chcesz** pick whoever you want.

kogoś *pron. Gen. i Acc. of* **ktoś**; somebody, someone; (*w pytaniach*) anybody, anyone; **spotkałem kogoś** I met somebody; **widziałaś kogoś?** did you see anybody?

kogoż, kogóż *pron. Gen. i Acc. of* **któż**; *emf.* whoever, who, whomever; **kogóż to interesuje?** whoever needs to know this?

koguci *a.* cock's, rooster's; **waga kogucia** *boks, zapasy* bantam weight.

kogucik *ma orn.* (= *młody kogut*) cockerel; (= *mały kogut*) small rooster, small cock.

kogut *ma* **1.** *orn.* (*samiec kury*) rooster, cock. **2.** *pot.* (= *kobieciarz*) stud. **3.** *pot. uj.* (= *zawadiaka*) fighting cock, turkey cock. **4.** *pot.* (= *sterczące włosy*) cowlick. **5.** *pot.* (flashing) roof-top sign (*on a police car, etc.*).

kogutek *ma* -**tk**- **1.** *orn.* = **kogucik**. **2.** (*na dachu*) weathercock. **3.** *pot.* (= *sterczące włosy*) cowlick.

koherencja *f. form. zwł. fiz., log.* coherence.

koherentność *f. form. zwł. fiz., log.* coherence.

koherentny *a. form. zwł. fiz., log.* coherent.

kohezja *f. fiz.* cohesion.

kohorta *f. gł. hist.* cohort.

koić *ipf.* **kój** *gł. lit.* (*ból, cierpienie*) soothe, relieve; (*nerwy*) calm.

koincydencja *f. form.* coincidence.

koincydencyjny *a. form.* coincident.

koine *f. indecl. jęz.* (= *ponadregionalna odmiana języka*) koine.

koja *f. Gen.* **koi** *żegl.* berth.

kojarzyć *ipf.* **1.** (= *widzieć powiązanie*) associate (*coś z czymś* sth with sth); (*fakty*) piece together; **(nie) kojarzysz?** *pot.* (don't you) get it? **2.** (= *swatać*) match, pair (*kogoś z kimś* sb with sb). **~ się** *ipf.* **1. to mi się kojarzy z czymś** it brings to mind sth, it makes me think of sth; **to mi się z niczym nie kojarzy** (*także* **nic mi się z tym nie kojarzy**) it doesn't ring the bell. **2.** (= *łączyć się w parę*) pair up.

kojąco *adv.* (*działać*) soothingly.

kojący *a.* soothing.

kojec *mi* -**jc**- *Gen.* -**a** (*dla dziecka*) playpen; *dla drobiu* coop; (*dla owiec, świń*) pen.

kojfnąć *pf. sl.* (= *umrzeć*) croak.

kojot *ma zool.* coyote, prairie wolf (*Canis latrans*).

kojpu *ma indecl. zool.* nutria (*Myocastor coypus*).

kok[1] *mi Gen.* -**a** (*fryzura*) bun.

kok[2] *mp żegl.* (= *kucharz okrętowy*) cook.

koka *f.* **1.** *sl.* (= *kokaina*) coke, snow. **2.** *bot.* coca (*Erythroxylum coca*). **3.** *pot.* (= *Coca-Cola*) coke.

kokaina *f. chem.* cocaine.

kokainizm *mi pat.* cocaine addiction, cocainism.

kokainowy *a.* **1.** (= *dotyczący kokainy*) cocaine. **2. krzew kokainowy** *bot.* coca (shrub *l.* plant) (*Erythroxylum coca*).

kokarda *f.* bowknot, knot, bow.

kokardka *f. Gen.pl.* **-ek** (small) bowknot, (small) knot, (small) bow; **zawiązać coś na kokardkę** (*buty, sznurowadła*) tie sth in a bow.

kokieteria *f. Gen.* **-ii** coquetry.

kokieteryjnie *adv.* coquettishly, flirtatiously.

kokieteryjny *a.* coquettish, flirtatious.

kokietka *f. Gen.pl.* **-ek** coquette.

kokietować *ipf.* **1.** (= *uwodzić*) flirt (*kogoś* with sb). **2.** (*wyborców, widownię*) woo.

kokila *f. Gen.pl.* **-i** *l.* **-l** *metal.* chill, permanent mold; *Br.* chill, permanent mould.

koklusz *mi pat.* whooping cough, pertussis.

kokon *mi zwł. ent.* cocoon.

kokonizacja *f. techn.* cocooning, spray webbing.

kokoryczka *f. Gen.pl.* **-ek** *bot.* Solomon's seal (*Polygonatum*).

kokos *mi Gen.* **-u** *l.* **-a** **1.** *bot., kulin.* (= *orzech kokosowy*) coconut. **2.** *bot.* (= *palma kokosowa*) = **kokosowiec. 3. zbijać** *l.* **robić** *l.* **zarabiać kokosy** *pot.* (= *zarabiać duże pieniądze*) make a bundle (*na czymś* on sth).

kokosić się *ipf. pot.* fidget.

kokosowiec *mi* **-wc-** *Gen.* **-a** *bot.* (= *palma kokosowa*) coconut palm (*Cocos nucifera*).

kokosowy *a.* **1.** *kulin., bot.* coconut; **masło kokosowe** coconut butter; **mleko kokosowe** coconut milk; **olej kokosowy** coconut oil; **palma kokosowa** = **kokosowiec**; **wiórki kokosowe** desiccated coconut; **włókno kokosowe** *tk.* coir, coconut fibre. **2. kokosowy interes** *pot.* (= *świetny interes*) gold mine.

kokoszka *f. Gen.pl.* **-ek** (broody) hen.

kokpit *mi lotn., żegl.* cockpit.

koks *mi* **1.** (*na opał*) coke. **2.** *pot.* (= *narkotyk, środek dopingujący*) dope.

koksiak *mi* (*piecyk*) salamander.

koksować *ipf. techn.* coke.

koksownia *f. Gen.pl.* **-i** *techn.* coking plant.

koksownictwo *n. techn.* cokemaking, coke engineering.

koksowniczy *a. techn.* **bateria koksownicza** *techn.* coke oven battery; **piec koksowniczy** *techn.* coke oven *l.* kiln, coking oven *l.* kiln; **przemysł koksowniczy** cokemaking, coke engineering.

koksownik *mp pl.* **-cy** (*robotnik*) coke plant worker. – *mi pl.* **-i** (*piec*) salamander.

koksowy *a.* **piec koksowy** coke oven *l.* kiln, coking oven *l.* kiln.

koksujący *a. techn.* **węgiel koksujący** coking coal.

koktajl *mi* **1.** *kulin.* (*napój*) cocktail; (*mleczny*) (milk) shake. **2.** (*przyjęcie*) cocktail party. **3. koktajl Mołotowa** Molotov cocktail.

koktajlbar *mi* (= *bar alkoholowy w hotelu*) cocktail lounge; (= *bar z koktailami mlecznymi*) ice-cream parlor.

koktajlowy *a.* (*o sukni, przyjęciu, barze*) cocktail.

kol. *abbr.* **1.** *zwł. form.* = **kole-ga/żanka**. **2.** RR (= *railroad*).

kola *f. Gen.pl.* **-i** **1.** *pot.* (*napój*) coke. **2.** *bot.* cola (*Cola*); **orzeszki kola** cola nuts.

kolaboracja *f. polit.* collaboration (*with an enemy*).

kolaboracyjny *a. polit.* (*o rządzie*) collaborationist.

kolaborancki *a. polit.* (*o postawie*) collaborationist.

kolaborant *mp*, **kolaborantka** *f. Gen.pl.* **-ek** *polit.* collaborator.

kolaborować *ipf. polit.* collaborate (*with an enemy*).

kolacja *f.* **1.** *kulin.* (= *posiłek późnym wieczorem*) supper; (= *posiłek wczesnym wieczorem z wielu dań; przyjęcie*) dinner; **kolacja przy świecach** candlelit dinner; **zaprosić kogoś na kolację** ask sb to dinner; (*do swojego domu*) have sb over to dinner. **2.** *form.* (= *porównanie, zestawienie*) (*zwł. tekstów*) collation.

kolacyjka *f. Gen.pl.* **-ek** *zwł. żart., kulin.* (= *posiłek późnym wieczorem*) (little) supper; (= *posiłek wczesnym wieczorem z wielu dań; przyjęcie*) (little) dinner.

kolagen *mi biochem.* collagen.

kolagenowy *a. biochem.* collagen; **choroba kolagenowa** *pat.* collagen disease; **implant kolagenowy** *med.* collagen implant; **płat kolagenowy** (*zabieg kosmetyczny*) collagen patch.

kolanko *n. Gen.pl.* **-ek** **1.** (small) knee. **2.** *kulin.* (*makaron*) elbow macaroni. **3.** *techn.* (*złączka rurowa o kącie prostym*) elbow, ell; (*w odpływie pod zlewem, wanną*) U-bend. **4.** *bot.* knot, node.

kolankowy *a.* **1.** (= *zakrzywiony*) elbow-shaped. **2.** *bot.* knotty, nodular.

kolano *n.* **1.** (*nogi*) knee; **do kolan** (*także* **po kolana**) (*na wysokość*) knee-high; (*na głębokość*) knee-deep; **w śniegu po kolana** up to one's knees in snow; **na kolanach** *t. przen.* on bended knee; **u kogoś na kolanach** in *l.* on sb's lap, on sb's knee; **klękać na jedno kolano** drop down on one knee; **kolana się pod kimś ugięły** *przen.* sb went weak in the knees; **napisać** *l.* **zrobić coś na kolanie** *pot. przen.* dash sth off; **paść na kolana (przed kimś)** drop *l.* go *l.* fall down on one's knees (to sb); **prosić kogoś na kolanach** be on one's knees; **rzucić kogoś na kolana** *przen.* bring *l.* force sb to sb's knees; **łysy jak kolano** bald as an egg; **przełożyć kogoś przez kolano** put sb over one's knee. **2.** (= *zakole*) elbow. **3.** *techn.* = **kolanko** 3. **4.** *mech.* (*przegub*) knee joint.

kolanowy *a.* knee; **staw kolanowy** *anat.* knee joint; **odruch kolanowy** *fizj.* knee jerk; **prasa kolanowa** *mech.* knuckle joint press, toggle press.

kolanówka *f. Gen.pl.* **-ek** **1.** *gł. pl.* (= *skarpeta do kolan*) knee sock, knee-high. **2.** (= *podszewka w nogawkach*) trouser-lining.

kolarski *a.* cycling; **tor kolarski** velodrome.

kolarstwo *n. sport* cycling; **kolarstwo szosowe** road racing.

kolarz *mp sport* cyclist.

kolaudacja *f.* **1.** *bud.* terminal inspection. **2.** *film* producers' screening of a new film.

kolaż *mi sztuka* collage.

kolba *f.* **1.** *bot.* spadix; *kulin.* (*kukurydzy*) cob; **kukurydza w kolbach** corn on the cob. **2.** *wojsk.* (*karabinu*) butt; (*pistoletu*) grip. **3.** *techn.* (= *lutownica*) soldering iron. **4.** *chem.* flask.

kolcolist *mi* **kolcolist (zachodni)** *bot.* gorse, furze, whin (*Ulex (Europaeus)*).

kolczasty *a. bot.* thorny, spiny, prickly; **drut kolczasty** barbed wire; **brona kolczasta** *roln.* = **kolczatka** 3.

kolczatka *f. Gen.pl.* -ek **1.** *zool.* echidna, spiny anteater (*Tachyglossus*). **2.** (*obroża*) choke chain. **3.** (*także* **brona kolczatka**) *roln.* rotary harrow.

kolczuga *f. hist.* chain armor, chain mail, (coat of) mail.

kolczyk *mi Gen.* -a **1.** (*biżuteria*) earring. **2.** *wet., roln.* earmark.

kolczykować *ipf. wet., roln.* (*inwentarz*) earmark.

kole[1] *mi zob.* **koło.**

kole[2] *ipf. zob.* **kłuć.**

kolebać *ipf.* -ę -esz *arch.* rock. ~ **się** *ipf. arch.* rock.

kolebka *f. Gen.pl.* -ek *t. przen.* cradle; **kolebka cywilizacji** cradle of civilization; **od kolebki** from the cradle.

kolebkowaty *a. bud.* (*o belkowaniu*) arched.

kolebkowy *a.* **sklepienie kolebkowe** *bud.* barrel *l.* wagon vault.

kolec *mi* -lc- *Gen.* -a **1.** *bot.* thorn, spike; *zool.* spine. **2.** *sport* (*w bucie lekkoatlety*) spike; (*w bucie piłkarza*) stud; **kolce** (*buty sportowe*) spikes. **3.** (*w oponie*) stud.

kolega *mp* friend, buddy; (*gdy płeć jest ważna*) boy *l.* male friend; **kolega z klasy** *l.* **ze szkolnej ławy** classmate; **kolega szkolny** *l.* **ze szkoły** schoolmate; **kolega z pokoju** roommate; **kolega z pracy** fellow worker, colleague; **kolega po fachu** fellow (in the trade); **panie kolego** Mr...

kolegiacki *a. kośc.* collegiate; **kościół kolegiacki** collegiate church.

kolegialnie *adv. form.* (*decydować*) jointly, collegially.

kolegialność *f. form.* collegiality.

kolegialny *a. form.* (*o decyzji, ciele, władzy*) joint, collegial.

kolegiata *f. kośc.* collegiate church.

kolegium *n. sing. indecl. pl.* -gia *Gen.* -giów **1.** *uniw., polit.* college; **kolegium nauczycielskie** *uniw.* teachers' college, teacher (training) college; **kolegium elektorów** *l.* **elektorskie** *polit.* electoral college; **Kolegium Kardynalskie** *rz.-kat.* College of Cardinals. **2.** (*sąd*) court (*for minor civil offenses*); **kolegium sędziowskie** jury. **3.** (= *rada*) board, committee; **kolegium redakcyjne** editorial board. **4.** *hist.* (*szkoła średnia*) college; **kolegium jezuickie** Jesuit college.

kolegować się *ipf.* be friends (*z kimś* with sb).

koleina *f. mot.* rut.

kolej *f. Gen.* -ei **1.** (*system transportu*) rail, railroad; *Br.* railway; (*pociąg*) train; **jechać ko-**

leją take the train, go *l.* travel by rail; **kolej jednoszynowa** monorail; **kolej linowa** cable railway; (*naziemna*) funicular (railway); (*podwieszana*) suspension railway; **kolej parowa** steam rail; **kolej podmiejska** commuter train; **kolej podziemna** subway, metro; *gł. Br.* underground; **kolej wąskotorowa** narrow-gauge railroad; **kolej zębata** rack *l.* cog railroad; **szybka kolej** high-speed train, rapid rail. **2.** (*instytucja*) rail. **3.** (= *kolejność*) turn; **z kolei** (= *następnie*) next; in turn; (= *z rzędu*) in a row; **po kolei** in order, in turn, by turns; **nie po kolei** in the wrong order; **czyjaś kolej** sb's turn; **czyja kolej?** whose turn is it?, who's next?; **ktoś ma nie po kolei w głowie** *pot.* sb's got a screw loose somewhere. **4.** (= *bieg zdarzeń*) **koleje losu** vicissitudes, ups and downs; **kolej rzeczy** course of nature; **zwykłą koleją rzeczy** as a matter of course.

kolejarz *mp* railroader; *Br.* railwayman.

kolejka *f. Gen.pl.* -ek **1.** (*pociąg*) train; (*system transportu*) rail; **jechać kolejką** take the train; **kolejka dojazdowa** *l.* **podmiejska** commuter train; **kolejka górska** (*w wesołym miasteczku*) roller coaster, big dipper; **kolejka linowa** cable railway; (*wagonik*) cable car; (*naziemna*) funicular (railway); (*podwieszana*) suspension railway; **kolejka wąskotorowa** narrow-gauge railroad; **kolejka zębata** rack *l.* cog railroad. **2.** (*zabawka*) model railroad; *Br.* model railway. **3.** (*oczekujących*) line; *Br.* queue (*po coś* for sth); **stać w kolejce** stand in line; *Br.* queue (up); **bez kolejki** *l.* **poza kolejką** without waiting (for one's turn), without any waiting; **wpychać się bez kolejki** jump the line. **4.** *pot.* (= *drink*) round (of drinks); **stawiać komuś kolejkę** buy *l.* stand sb a round (of drinks).

kolejnictwo *n.* railroad, rail; *Br.* railway; *techn.* railroad engineering.

kolejno *adv.* (= *w kolejności*) in turn, by turns; (= *pojedynczo*) individually, one by one.

kolejność *f.* order, sequence; **poza kolejnością** without waiting (for one's turn), without any waiting; **w kolejności alfabetycznej/rosnącej/malejącej** in alphabetical/ascending/descending order.

kolejny *a.* (= *następny*) next; (= *następujący*) consecutive, successive; (= *jeszcze jeden*) another; **kolejny raz** yet again.

kolejowy *a.* (*o linii*) railroad; *Br.* railway; (*o bilecie, połączeniu*) train; (*o transporcie*) rail; **dworzec kolejowy** *l.* **stacja kolejowa** train station; *Br.* railway station; **przejazd kolejowy** grade crossing, level crossing.

kolekcja *f.* collection; **kolekcja mody** fashion collection *l.* line; **kolekcja wiosenna/zimowa** spring/winter collection *l.* line.

kolekcjoner *mp*, **kolekcjonerka** *f. Gen.pl.* -ek collector; **kolekcjoner pocztówek** postcard collector.

kolekcjonerski *a.* collector's.

kolekcjonerstwo *n.* collecting.

kolekcjonować *ipf.* collect.

kolekta *f.* **1.** *kośc.* (*modlitwa*) collect. **2.** *kośc.* (= *zbiórka pieniędzy*) collection.

kolektiwum *n. sing. indecl. pl.* **-wa** *Gen.* **-wów** *jęz.* collective (noun *l.* pronoun).

kolektor *mi Gen.* **-a** *pl.* **-ry** **1.** *mot.* manifold; **kolektor wydechowy/wylotowy** *mot.* exhaust manifold; **kolektor ssący** *mot.* suction manifold. **2.** *techn., el., chem.* collector; (*sanitarny, kanalizacyjny, ściekowy*) collector, collecting pipe. – *mp pl.* **-rzy** (*w kolekturze*) lottery agent *l.* broker.

kolektura *f.* lottery office.

kolektyw *mi form.* (= *zespół ludzki*) body, team, group.

kolektywizacja *f. ekon.* collectivization; **kolektywizacja rolnictwa** collectivization of agriculture.

kolektywizm *mi* collectivism.

kolektywizować *ipf. ekon.* collectivize.

kolektywnie *adv. form.* (*decydować, odpowiadać*) collectively.

kolektywność *f. form.* collectivity.

kolektywny *a. form.* collective.

kolendra *f.* coriander (*Coriandrum sativum*).

koleś *mp Gen.pl.* **-ów** *pot., zwł. pog.* (= *kolega*) buddy; (= *facet*) guy, dude; *zwł. polit.* crony; *Voc.* buddy, bud, pal; **słuchaj, koleś** listen, buddy.

koleżanka *f. Gen.pl.* **-ek** friend; girl *l.* female friend; **koleżanka z klasy** *l.* **ze szkolnej ławy** classmate; **koleżanka szkolna** *l.* **ze szkoły** schoolmate; **koleżanka z pokoju** roommate; **koleżanka z pracy** colleague, fellow worker.

koleżeński *a.* friendly; **spotkanie koleżeńskie** meeting of friends; **(postępować) po koleżeńsku** (act) like a friend; **sąd koleżeński** peer court.

koleżeńskość *f.* friendliness.

koleżeństwo *n.* **1.** (*przyjaźń*) friendship. **2.** (= *koleżanki i koledzy*) friends.

koleżka *mp pl.* **-owie** *zwł. żart. l. pog.* buddy.

kolęda *f. gł. rz.-kat.* **1.** (*pieśń*) (Christmas) carol. **2.** (*chodzenie po domach*) wassail. **3.** (*wizyta księdza*) Christmas call (*by a priest*). **4. chodzić po kolędzie** (*o kolędnikach*) wassail; (*o księdzu*) pay Christmas calls.

kolędnik *mp rz.-kat.* caroler, wassailer; **kolędnicy** waits.

kolędować *ipf. rz.-kat.* **1.** (*śpiewać*) sing carols. **2.** (*chodzić po domach*) wassail.

kolia *f. Gen.* **-ii** necklace.

koliber *ma* **-br-** *orn.* hummingbird (*Trochilus*).

kolidować *ipf.* **kolidować z czymś** clash with sth; **kolidować z prawem** be against the law.

koligacja *f. lit.* (= *pokrewieństwo, związek*) relationship.

kolimacja *f. opt.* (= *nadanie zbieżności*) collimation; (= *błąd*) collimation error.

kolimacyjny *a. opt.* collimation; **błąd kolimacyjny** collimation error.

kolimator *mi Gen.* **-a** *opt.* collimator.

kolisty *a.* (*o kształcie*) round, circular; (*o ruchu*) circular.

kolizja *f. form.* **1.** (= *zderzenie pojazdów*) collision. **2.** (= *sprzeczność*) conflict; **pozostawać w kolizji z czymś** be in conflict with sth; **kolizja przepisów** *prawn.* conflict of laws.

kolizyjny *a. form.* **1.** (*o skrzyżowaniu*) accident-prone. **2.** (*o prawach*) conflicting.

kolka *f. Gen.pl.* **-ek** *pat.* (= *chwilowe kłucie w boku*) stitch; (*poważniejsza dolegliwość*) colic; **kolka jelitowa/wątrobowa/nerkowa** intestinal/hepatic/nephritic colic.

kolkowy *a.* colicky.

kolnąć *pf.* **-ij** stab.

kolodium *n. indecl. chem.* collodion.

kolofon *mi bibl.* colophon.

koloid *mi chem.* colloid.

koloidalny, koloidowy *a. chem.* colloidal, colloid; **roztwór koloidowy** colloidal solution.

kolokwializm *mi jęz.* colloquialism.

kolokwialność *f. form.* colloquialism, colloquialness.

kolokwialny *a. form.* colloquial.

kolokwium *n. sing. indecl. pl.* **-wia** *Gen.* **-wiów** *uniw.* **1.** (= *sprawdzian*) test. **2. kolokwium habilitacyjne** postdoctoral examination. **3.** (*sympozjum*) colloquium.

kolon¹ *mi Gen.* **-u** *pl.* **-y** *wers.* colon.

kolon² *mp Gen.* **-a** *pl.* **-owie** *hist.* serf.

kolonat *mi hist.* colonate.

kolonel *mi druk.* minion.

Kolonia *f. Gen.* **-ii** *geogr.* Cologne.

kolonia *f. Gen.* **-ii** **1.** (*posiadłość, grupa ludzi*) *t. biol.* colony; (*osiedle*) settlement. **2.** (*także pl.* **kolonie**) (*wczasy dla dzieci*) camp; **kolonie letnie** summer camp.

kolonialista *mp polit.* colonialist.

kolonializm *mi polit.* colonialism.

kolonialny *a.* colonial; (*o celach, polityce*) colonialist; **posiadłość kolonialna** colony; **styl kolonialny** *bud., sztuka* Colonial style.

kolonista *mp,* **kolonistka** *f. Gen.pl.* **-ek** **1.** (*osadnik*) colonist, settler. **2.** (*dziecko na wakacjach*) camper.

kolonizacja *f.* colonization, settlement.

kolonizacyjny *a.* colonization.

kolonizator *mp polit.* colonizer.

kolonizatorski *a.* colonialist.

kolonizować *ipf.* colonize, settle.

koloński *a. geogr.* Cologne; **woda kolońska** (eau de) cologne.

kolor *mi* **1.** color; **jakiego koloru jest...?/jaki kolor ma...?** what color is...?; **do koloru** (*także pod kolor*) in matching color; **dobór kolorów** color scheme; **gama kolorów** variety of colors; **kolory podstawowe/pochodne** fundamental *l.* primary/secondary colors; **w jaskrawych/żywych/spokojnych/stonowanych kolorach** in garish/vivid/soft/subdued colors; **ciepły/zimny kolor** warm/cold color; **przedstawiać coś w jasnych/ciemnych kolorach** *przen.* paint sth in bright/dark colors. **2. kolory** (= *pranie kolorowe*) coloreds. **3.** *karty* suit. **4. kolory** (*na policzkach*) color; **odzyskać kolory** regain color; **stracić kolory** lose color.

koloratka *f. Gen.pl.* **-ek** *kośc.* clerical collar.

koloratura *f. muz.* coloratura.

koloraturowy *a. muz.* coloratura; **sopran koloraturowy** coloratura (soprano).

kolorować *ipf.* **1.** (= *barwić*) color; (*książeczkę, rysunek*) color in. **2.** *film* colorize.

kolorowo *adv.* colorfully.

kolorowy *a.* **1.** (= *nie czarno-biały*) color; **foto-**

grafia kolorowa color photography; **kolorowy monitor** *komp., telew.* color monitor. **2.** (= *wielobarwny*) colorful. **3.** (*o mężczyznach, kobietach, imigrantach*) *cz. obelż.* colored; **ludność kolorowa** people of color. **4. kolorowy ołówek** crayon; **metale kolorowe** *metal.* non-ferrous metals. – *mp* (= *człowiek rasy innej niż biała*) person of color; *cz. obelż.* colored.

kolorymetr *mi chem.* colorimeter.

kolorymetria *f. Gen.* **-ii** *chem.* colorimetry.

kolorymetryczny *a. chem.* colorimetric.

kolorysta *mi,* **kolorystka** *f. Gen.pl.* **-ek 1.** *sztuka* colorist. **2.** (= *blagier*) embroiderer.

kolorystycznie *adv.* (*interesujący*) in terms of color, color-wise; **dobrany kolorystycznie** color-coordinated.

kolorystyczny *a.* (*o zestawieniu*) color; (*o zdolnościach, uroku*) coloristic.

kolorystyka *f.* color.

koloryt *mi* **1.** (*kolory*) color, colors; **ciepły/zimny koloryt** *sztuka* warm/cold colors. **2.** (*charakter*) color; **koloryt lokalny** local color.

koloryzować *ipf.* **1.** (= *przesadzać*) exaggerate; (*fakty, opowieść*) embellish, embroider. **2. szampon koloryzujący** shampooing colorant.

kolos *mi Gen.* **-a** (*posąg*) colossus; *przen.* giant, colossus; **kolos na glinianych nogach** weak-kneed giant.

kolosalnie *adv.* colossally, hugely, enormously.

kolosalność *f.* hugeness, enormousness.

kolosalny *a.* colossal, huge, enormous.

koloseum *n. indecl. bud.* coliseum, colosseum.

kolportaż *mi* circulation, distribution.

kolportażowy *a.* circulation, distribution.

kolporter *mp,* **kolporterka** *f. Gen.pl.* **-ek** distributor (*of newspapers, magazines*).

kolporterski *a.* distributor.

kolportować *ipf.* distribute (*newspapers, magazines*).

Kolumbia *f. Gen.* **-ii** *geogr., polit.* Colombia.

Kolumbijczyk *mp,* **Kolumbijka** *f. Gen.pl.* **-ek** Colombian.

kolumbijski *a.* Colombian.

kolumienka *f. Gen.pl.* **-ek** *bud.* (small) column.

kolumna *f.* **1.** column; **kolumna destylacyjna/kapilarna** *chem.* distillation/capillary column; **kolumna kierownicy** *mot.* steering column; **kolumna marszowa** *wojsk.* column of route; **kolumna masztu** *żegl.* lower mast; **kolumna parnikowa** *roln.* steamer column. **2.** (*zespół*) unit; **kolumna sanitarna** hospital unit. **3.** (*także* **kolumna głośnikowa**) speaker; **kolumna 2-** *l.* **3-drożna** 2 *l.* 3-way speaker.

kolumnada *f. bud.* collonade.

kolumnowy *a.* columnar.

kołacz *mp Gen.* **-a 1.** *przest., kulin.* round wheat cake; **bez pracy nie ma kołaczy** no pain, no gain. **2.** *roln.* oilcake.

kołatać *-czę* *l.* **-cę -czesz** *l.* **-cesz, -cz 1.** (= *stukać*) knock (*do drzwi* at the door). **2.** (*o sercu*) throb, pound. **3. kołatać do kogoś o coś** (= *prosić*) appeal to sb for sth. **~ się** *ipf.* **1.** (= *telepać się*) joggle along. **2.** (= *błąkać się*) knock about.

3. (= *nie opuszczać*) linger; **myśl kołacze się w głowie** the thought still lingers.

kołatanie *n.* **kołatanie serca** *przest., pat.* palpitation.

kołatek *ma* **-tk-** *ent.* deathwatch (*Anobium pertinax*).

kołatka *f. Gen.pl.* **-ek 1.** (*u drzwi*) (door) knocker. **2.** (*do hałasowania*) clapper.

kołchoz *mi hist., ekon.* kolkhoz, collective farm.

kołchozowy *a. hist., ekon.* kolkhoz, collective.

kołchoźnica *f. hist.* kolkhoznik.

kołchoźniczy *a. hist., ekon.* kolkhoz, collective.

kołchoźnik *mp hist.* kolkhoznik.

kołczan *mi* quiver, arrow case.

kołdra *f. Gen.pl.* **-der** (continental) quilt, duvet; **kołdra puchowa** eiderdown.

kołduny *pl. Gen.* **-ów** *kulin.* meat dumplings.

kołek *mi* **-łk-** *Gen.* **-a 1.** (*do wbijania, t. do ubrań, namiotu, u szewca*) peg; (= *bolec*) pin; (*gwintowany*) stud; **kołek strojeniowy** tuning peg. **2.** (*w zwrotach*) **ciosać komuś kołki na głowie** (= *dręczyć*) tyrannize sb; ; **nie siedź jak kołek!** don't sit there like a bump on a log!; **samotny jak kołek** all alone; **stać jak kołek** stand like a post.

kołem *adv.* in a circle.

kołkować *ipf.* peg; pin; stud.

kołkowaty *a. uj.* (*o figurze, części ciała*) stocky; (= *sztywny*) stiff; (= *niezgrabny*) awkward.

kołkownica *f. żegl.* pin rail.

kołkowy *a.* (*o butach*) pegged.

kołnierz *mi Gen.* **-a 1.** (*część ubrania*) collar; **kołnierz marynarski** sailor collar; **kołnierz ortopedyczny** *med.* orthopedic collar; **ktoś nie wylewa za kołnierz** *żart.* sb enjoys a drink. **2.** (= *krój przy szyi*) neck. **3.** *zool., orn.* collar. **4.** *mech.* collar; **kołnierz masztu** *żegl.* mast coat.

kołnierzowy *a.* **1.** (= *przy kołnierzu*) collar; (= *przy szyi*) neck. **2.** *mech.* flange, collar.

kołnierzyk *mi Gen.* **-a** (small) collar.

koło¹ *n. Gen.pl.* **kół 1.** (*krąg*) circle; ring. **2.** *geom., geogr.* circle; **koło wielkie/małe** great/small circle; **koło podbiegunowe** *l.* **polarne** *geogr.* polar circle; **koło podbiegunowe północne/południowe** *geogr.* Arctic/Antarctic circle. **3.** (*pojazdu, maszyny*) wheel; **koło garncarskie** *przest.* potter's wheel, kick wheel; **koło łopatkowe** *żegl.* paddle wheel; **koło młyńskie** millwheel; **koło napędowe** drive-wheel, driving wheel; **koło pasowe** pulley; **koło ogonowe** *lotn.* tailwheel; **koło sterowe** *żegl.* steering wheel; **koło zamachowe** flywheel; **koło zapasowe** spare wheel; **koło zębate** cog (wheel); **napęd na przednie/tylne/cztery koła** *mot.* front-/rear-/four-wheel drive; **wolne koło** freewheel. **4.** (*narzędzie tortur*) rack. **5.** (*środowisko*) circle; **koła polityczne** political circles. **6.** (*zainteresowań*) circle, club. **7.** *pot.* (= *tysiąc złotych*) grand; **dwa koła** two grand. **8.** *pot.* (= *zero*) zilch, zip, nil; **dwa do koła** two-nil. **9.** (*w zwrotach*) **błędne koło** *log.* vicious circle; **piąte koło u wozu** fifth wheel; **koło fortuny** wheel of fortune; **koło ratunkowe** life buoy; *przen.* lifeline; **w koło** (= *ciągle*) all the time; (= *dokoła*) round (in circles); **zataczać koła** *l.* **koło nad czymś** circle over sth.

koło² *prep.* + *Gen.* **1.** (= *obok, w pobliżu*) **koło czegoś** by sth, near sth; **dom koło poczty** the house near *l.* by the post office. **2.** (= *około, w przybliżeniu*) around, about; **koło 40** around 40, about 40; **coś koło tego** something like that.

kołodziej *mp Gen.pl.* **-ów** *przest.* cartwright.

kołomyja *f. Gen.* **-yi** (= *zamieszanie*) hurlyburly.

kołowacieć *ipf.* **1.** *pot.* (= *głupieć*) be stumped. **2.** *arch.* (= *sztywnieć*) stiffen. **3.** *wet.* get *l.* catch the gid.

kołowacizna *f.* **1.** *wet.* staggers; (*u owiec*) gid. **2.** *pot.* (= *zamieszanie*) hurly-burly. **3.** *pot.* (= *zamęt w głowie*) confusion; **można dostać kołowacizny z tymi świętami** all those holidays can drive you nuts.

kołować *ipf.* **1.** *lotn.* (*w powietrzu*) circle; (*na ziemi*) taxi. **2.** (= *zataczać koła*) circle.

kołowanie *n. lotn.* (*w powietrzu*) circling; (*na ziemi*) taxiing.

kołowaty *a.* **1.** *wet.* staggery; (*o owcach*) affected with the gid. **2.** *pot.* (= *ogłupiały, skołowany*) dazed.

kołowiec *mi* **-wc-** *Gen.* **-a 1.** *żegl.* paddleboat, paddle wheeler. **2. dwunastokołowiec/osiemnastokołowiec itd.** *mot.* 12-/18-wheeler etc.

kołowrotek *mi* **-tk-** *Gen.* **-a 1.** *tk.* spinning wheel. **2.** *ryb.* reel. **3.** (= *bramka*) turnstile. **4.** *mech.* windlass, winch. **5.** (= *powtarzalność wydarzeń*) routine.

kołowrotowy *a. mech.* windlass, winch.

kołowrót *mi* **-o-** *Gen.* **-u** *l.* **-a 1.** *mech.* windlass, winch, wheel and axle. **2.** (*bramka*) turnstile. **3.** *sport* turn. **4.** (*narzędzie tortur*) rack. **5.** (= *powtarzalność wydarzeń*) routine.

kołowy *a.* **1.** (*o kształcie koła*) circular; **orbita kołowa** *astron.* circular orbit; **ruch kołowy** *mech.* rotary *l.* circular motion; **stożek kołowy** *geom.* circular cone; **wykres kołowy** piechart. **2.** (*na kołach*) wheeled; **pojazd kołowy** wheeled vehicle; **ruch kołowy** road *l.* vehicular traffic.

kołpak *mi Gen.* **-a 1.** *mot.* hubcap. **2.** (*czapka*) calpac. **3.** *techn.* cap.

kołtun *mi Gen.* **-a** (*splątane włosy*) shag, matted hair, elflocks; *pat.* plica; **kołtuny** *żart.* (= *włosy*) wig. – *mp pl.* **-y** *uj. przest.* obscurantist.

kołtuneria *f. Gen.* **-ii** *uj. przest.* **1.** (= *ciemnota*) obscurantism, ignorance. **2.** (= *obskuranci*) obscurantists.

kołtunowaty *a.* (*o włosach*) matted.

kołtuński *a. uj. przest.* obscurant(ist).

kołtuństwo *n. uj. przest.* obscurantism, ignorance.

kołysać *ipf.* **-ę -esz 1.** (*drzewami*) sway, swing; (*łodzią*) rock (*czymś* sth). **2.** (*dziecko, wózek*) rock; **kołysać dziecko do snu** rock *l.* lull a baby to sleep. **3.** (*o statku*) roll. **~ się** *ipf.* **-ę -esz** (*o drzewie*) sway; *żegl., lotn.* (= *na boki*) roll; (*w fotelu*) rock.

kołysanka *f. Gen.pl.* **-ek** lullaby.

kołyska *f. Gen.pl.* **-ek** (*niemowlęca*) t. *żegl., wojsk.* cradle.

koma *f.* **1.** *opt.* coma. **2.** *przest. mat.* point (*in decimal fractions*); **dwa koma pięć** two point five.

komando *n. hist.* Kommando (*member of the labor gang at German concentration camps during WW II*).

komandor *mp wojsk.* commodore; **komandor orderu** (Knight) Commander.

komandoria *f. Gen.* **-ii 1.** (= *krzyż komandorski*) Commander's Cross. **2.** *hist.* command(e)ry.

komandorski *a.* **1.** *wojsk.* commodore's. **2. krzyż komandorski (z gwiazdą)** Commander's Cross (with star).

komandos *mp* commando.

komar *ma ent.* mosquito (*Culex*); **płyn** *l.* **emulsja** *l.* **spray na komary** *l.* **przeciw komarom** mosquito repellent.

komarzyca *f. ent.* female mosquito.

komasacja *f. form.* aggregation.

komasacyjny *a. form.* aggregate, aggregative.

komasować *ipf. form.* aggregate.

komatyczny *a. pat.* comatose.

kombajn *mi* **1.** *roln.* (combine) harvester, combine; **kombajn zbożowy/buraczany/ziemniaczany** grain/beet/potato harvester. **2. kombajn górniczy** *górn.* LHD unit *l.* machine, loading-hauling-dumping machine. **3. kombajn kuchenny** *kulin.* food processor.

kombajnista *mp*, **kombajnistka** *f. Gen.pl.* **-ek** harvester *l.* combine operator.

kombatancki *a.* (war) veteran, vet.

kombatant *mp*, **kombatantka** *f. Gen.pl.* **-ek** (war) veteran, vet.

kombi *n. indecl. mot.* station (wagon); *Br.* estate car.

kombinacja *f.* **1.** (= *połączenie*) combination. **2.** *pot.* (= *oszustwo*) scam, fraud, trickery. **3.** *sport* **kombinacja alpejska** Alpine combined; **kombinacja norweska** *l.* **klasyczna** Nordic combined.

kombinacyjny *a. form.* combinatorial, combinatory, combinative.

kombinat *mi* **1.** (= *duży zakład*) industrial complex, plant. **2.** *przen.* (= *kolos, moloch*) giant.

kombinator *mp*, **kombinatorka** *f. Gen.pl.* **-ek** *pot., czas. obelż.* (= *spryciarz*) (smooth) operator, schemer; (= *oszust*) scammer.

kombinatorski *a. pot. zwł. uj.* shifty, double-dealing, scheming.

kombinatorstwo *n. pot.* trickery, double-dealing.

kombinatoryczny *a. form., mat.* combinatorial; **wariant kombinatoryczny** *jęz.* combinatorial variant.

kombinatoryka *f. mat.* combinatorics, combinatorial analysis.

kombinatowy *a.* industrial complex.

kombinerki *pl. Gen.* **-rek** *techn.* lineman's pliers; *Br.* combination pliers.

kombinezon *mi* (*także* **kombinezon roboczy**) overalls, coveralls, boiler suit; (*ubranie damskie*) jump suit; (= *ogrodniczki*) dungarees;

(*dziecięcy*) rompers; (*dziecięcy zimowy*) snow-suit; **kombinezon kosmiczny** space suit; **kombinezon lotniczy** *lotn.* flying suit; **kombinezon narciarski** ski suit; **kombinezon przeciwprzeciążeniowy** *lotn.* G-suit.

kombinować *ipf.* **1.** (= *łączyć*) combine, compose, mix. **2.** *pot.* (= *kręcić*) wheel and deal, be up to something; **kombinować z kimś** have something going with sb; **on/ona coś kombinuje** he/she is up to something. **3.** *pot.* (= *oszukiwać*) cheat. **4.** (*także* **kombinować sobie**) *pot.* (= *główkować*) be figuring. **5.** *pot.* (= *majstrować*) tinker, meddle (*przy l. w czymś* with sth).

komedia *f. Gen.* -ii **1.** *film, teatr* comedy; **komedia muzyczna/romantyczna** musical/romantic comedy; **komedia dell'arte** commedia dell'arte; **grać/wystawiać komedię** play/stage a comedy. **2.** (= *udawanie*) game, act; **po co ta komedia?** who are you kidding?; **robić** *l.* **stroić** *l.* **wyprawiać komedie** put on an act. **3.** (= *śmieszna l. absurdalna sytuacja*) farce.

komediancki *a. uj.* grotesque, farcical.

komedianctwo *n.* farce.

komediant *mp* **1.** (= *udawacz*) fraud. **2.** (= *aktor komediowy*) comedy actor; (= *komik*) comedian.

komediantka *f. Gen.pl.* -ek **1.** (= *udawaczka*) fraud. **2.** (= *aktorka komediowa*) comedy actress; (= *komiczka*) comedienne.

komediofarsa *f. teatr* low comedy, slapstick.

komediopisarstwo *n. teor.lit.* comedy (writing).

komediopisarz *mp teor.lit.* comedy writer.

komediowość *f. form.* comedy.

komediowy *a.* comic.

komedyjka *f. Gen.pl.* -ek *teatr, film* (short) comedy.

komenda *f.* **1.** (= *rozkaz*) *t. wojsk., komp.* command; **(jak) na komendę** (right) on cue. **2.** (= *siedziba dowodzenia*) headquarters; **komenda policji** police department. **3.** (= *dowództwo*) command; **pod czyjąś komendą** under sb's command; **objąć/sprawować komendę nad kimś/czymś** take/have command over sb/sth.

komendant *mp,* **komendantka** *f. Gen.pl.* -ek (= *dowódca*) *wojsk.* commanding officer; (*w harcerstwie*) scoutmaster; **komendant straży pożarnej** fire chief.

komendantura *f.* headquarters.

komenderować *ipf.* **1.** (= *dowodzić*) command. **2.** *pot.* **komenderować kimś** (= *rozkazywać komuś*) push sb about.

komensal *ma biol.* commensal.

komensaliczny *a. biol.* commensal.

komensalizm *mi biol.* commensalism, commensality.

komentarz *mi Gen.* -a **1.** (= *objaśnienie, interpretacja*) commentary; (= *tekst publicystyczny, narracja*) commentary; **komentarz polityczny** political commentary. **2.** (= *uwaga, ocena*) comment; **bez komentarza** no comment; **coś nie wymaga komentarza** sth requires no comment; **odmówić komentarza** *dzienn.* decline *l.* refuse to

comment; **wywoływać komentarze** provoke comments. **3.** *komp.* comment.

komentator *mp,* **komentatorka** *f. Gen.pl.* -ek *zwł. dzienn.* commentator.

komentatorski *a.* commentarial.

komentować *ipf.* **1.** (= *objaśniać, interpretować*) commentate (*coś* on sth). **2.** (= *omawiać, robić krytyczne uwagi*) comment (*coś* on sth).

komercja *f.* commercialism.

komercjalizacja *f. t. ekon.* commercialization.

komercjalizm *mi* commercialism.

komercjalizować *ipf. t. ekon.* commercialize. -- **się** *ipf. t. ekon.* commercialize.

komercyjny *a. zwł. ekon.* commercial.

kometa *f. astron.* comet.

kometka *f. Gen.pl.* -ek *sport* badminton.

komfort *mi* comfort; **komfort fizyczny/materialny/psychiczny** physical/financial/psychological comfort.

komfortowo *adv.* comfortably.

komfortowy *a.* (= *wygodny*) comfortable; (= *luksusowy*) luxury.

komicznie *adv.* comically.

komiczność *f.* comedy.

komiczny *a.* **1.** (= *wesoły, zabawny*) comical. **2.** (= *komediowy*) comic; **aktor komiczny** comic actor; **opera komiczna** comic opera.

komik *mp* (= *aktor komediowy*) comic *l.* comedy actor, comedian; (= *satyryk, wesoły człowiek*) comedian.

komiks *mi* (= *historyjki obrazkowe*) (comic) strip; (*książeczka*) comic book.

komiksowy *a.* (*o bohaterze, formie*) comic-strip.

komin *mi Gen.* -a **1.** (*w budynku*) chimney; (*na statku, lokomotywie*) chimney, funnel; (*wolno stojący, fabryczny*) smokestack, stack; **komin dachowy** chimney top; **dym z komina** chimney smoke. **2.** *meteor., lotn.* ascending (air) current. **3.** *geol.* chimney; **komin wulkaniczny** volcanic pipe. **4.** (*w zwrotach*) **kominy płacowe** *fin.* runaway salaries; **kurzyć jak komin** smoke like a chimney.

kominek *mi* -nk- *Gen.* -a **1.** (= *ognisko w domu*) fireplace, fire; **przy kominku** at *l.* by the fireside; **napalić w kominku** light the fire. **2.** (*spotkanie*) evening get-together. **3.** *lotn.* (parachute) vent. **4.** (= *mały komin*) (small) chimney.

kominiarka *f. Gen.pl.* -ek (*czapka*) balaclava.

kominiarski *a.* chimney.

kominiarz *mp* chimney sweep.

kominkowy *a.* **1.** (*związany z kominkiem*) fireplace; **sala kominkowa** room *l.* hall with a fireplace. **2.** (*o spotkaniu, imprezie*) fireside.

kominowy *a.* chimney; **przewód** *l.* **kanał kominowy** flue.

komis *mi* **1.** *handl.* (*sklep*) consignment store; (*system handlu*) consignment; **brać coś w komis** take sth on consignment; **oddawać towary w komis** consign goods. **2.** *uniw., pot.* (= *egzamin komisyjny*) final resit *l.* retake.

komisant *mp form.* (= *prowadzący komis*) commission merchant, consignee.

komisariat *mi* **1.** (= *posterunek, komenda*) station; **komisariat policji** police station. **2.** (= *komitet*) (*wystawy, festiwalu*) committee. **3.** *hist.* (*w Związku Radzieckim*) commissariat.

komisaryczny *a.* **zarząd komisaryczny** *prawn.* receivership.

komisarz *mp* **1.** (*w policji*) chief of police, police commissioner; *Br.* police superintendent. **2.** *polit.* commissioner; **wysoki komisarz** high commissioner. **3.** *hist.* (*w Związku Radzieckim*) commissar.

komisja *f. admin.* committee, board, commission; **członek komisji** committee member; **komisja budżetowa** budget committee; **Komisja Edukacji Narodowej** National Board of Education; **Komisja Europejska** *polit.* European Commission; **komisja egzaminacyjna** *szkoln.* examination board; **komisja kwalifikacyjna** selection committee; **komisja odwoławcza** review committee; **komisja parlamentarna** parliamentary committee; **Komisja Praw Człowieka Organizacji Narodów Zjednoczonych** United Nations Human Rights Commission; **komisja wyborcza** electoral board *l.* committee; **stała komisja** standing committee; **zasiadać w komisji** serve on a committee.

komisowe *n. Gen.* **-ego** *handl.* (*opłata*) commission.

komisowy *a. handl.* consignment.

komisyjnie *adv.* (= *w komisji, przez komisję*) by a committee; (= *w obecności komisji*) in the presence of a committee.

komisyjny *a.* (= *dokonany w komisji l. przez komisję*) (done) by a committee *l.* board; (= *dokonany w obecności komisji*) done in the presence of a committee; (*o spotkaniu*) committee; **egzamin komisyjny** *szkoln.* examination conducted before an examination board.

komitent *mp handl.* consignor, consigner.

komitet *mi admin., polit.* committee, board; **komitet blokowy** *l.* **osiedlowy** citizens' board *l.* association; **komitet naukowy** scientific committee; **komitet organizacyjny** planning committee; **komitet redakcyjny** *dzienn.* editorial board; **komitet rodzicielski** *szkoln.* PTA, Parent Teacher Association; **komitet strajkowy** strike committee; **komitet wyborczy** electoral committee.

komitetowy *a.* committee.

komitywa *f.* good *l.* friendly terms; **być z kimś w dobrej komitywie** be on friendly terms with sb.

komiwojażer *mp pl.* **-owie** *l.* **-rzy** *handl.* (= *domokrążca*) traveling salesman.

komiwojażerka *f. handl.* **1.** (= *akwizytorka*) *Gen.pl.* **-ek** traveling saleswoman. **2.** (*zajęcie*) traveling sales.

komiwojażerstwo *n. handl.* (*zajęcie*) traveling sales.

komizm *mi* comedy.

komnata *f.* (= *sala*) chamber.

komoda *f.* chest of drawers, bureau; (*stylowa*) commode; (*wysoka*) highboy; (*z lustrem*) dresser.

komodor *mp pl.* **-rzy** *l.* **-owie** *wojsk.* (= *dowódca eskadry okrętów*) commodore.

komonica *f. bot.* lotus (*Lotus*); **komonica zwyczajna** bird's-foot trefoil (*Lotus corniculatus*).

komora *f. Gen.pl.* **-mór 1.** *zwł. techn.* (= *pomieszczenie, wnęka*) chamber; **komora chłodnicza** cold room; **komora dekompresyjna** decompression chamber; **komora gazowa** gas chamber; **komora iskrowa** spark chamber; **komora jonizacyjna** ionization chamber; **komora niskich ciśnień** low-pressure (test) chamber; **komora spalania** combustion chamber; **komora sprężania** compression chamber. **2.** *anat.* ventricle; **komora serca** ventricle; **migotanie komór** *pat.* ventricular fibrillation. **3. komora celna** customs house.

komorne *n. Gen.* **-ego** (= *czynsz*) rent.

komornik *mp* (*debt*) collector.

komorowy *a.* **1.** *anat., fizj., pat.* ventricular; **częstoskurcz komorowy** *pat.* ventricular tachycardia. **2.** *techn.* chamber; **piec komorowy** chamber furnace.

komosa *f. bot.* goosefoot (*Chenopodium*).

komosowate *pl. Gen.pl.* **-ych** *bot.* chenopods (*Chenopodiaceae*).

komódka *f. Gen.pl.* **-ek** (*mebel*) (small) chest of drawers; lowboy.

komórczak *mi Gen.* **-a** *biol.* syncytium.

komórka *f. Gen.pl.* **-ek 1.** *biol.* cell; **komórka mięśniowa/nerwowa/tłuszczowa/rozrodcza** muscle/nerve/fat/generative cell; **komórka roślinna/zwierzęca** plant/animal cell; **szare komórki** *t. przen.* gray matter. **2.** *techn.* cell; **komórka fotoelektryczna** *el.* photoelectric cell, photocell; **komórka pamięci** *komp.* memory cell. **3.** *tel.*, *gł. pot.* cell phone, mobile phone. **4.** (= *schowek*) closet; (= *marny pokoik*) den. **5.** (= *jednostka organizacyjna*) unit.

komórkowy *a.* cellular; **beton komórkowy** *bud.* cellular concrete; **błona/ściana komórkowa** *biol.* cell membrane/wall; **telefon komórkowy** *tel.* cellular phone, cell phone, mobile phone.

kompakt *mi pot.* **1.** (= *płyta*) CD. **2.** (= *odtwarzacz*) CD player. **3.** (= *muszla ze spłuczką*) toilet.

kompaktowy *a.* compact; **nagranie kompaktowe** CD recording; **odtwarzacz kompaktowy** CD player, compact disc player; **płyta kompaktowa** compact disc, CD.

kompan *mp pot.* (= *kolega*) buddy.

kompania *f. Gen.* **-ii 1.** *wojsk.* company; **kompania honorowa** (*towarzysząca*) honor guard, guard of honor; (*oddająca salwę*) firing party *l.* squad. **2.** *gł. arch.* (= *towarzystwo*) company; **dotrzymać komuś kompanii** keep sb company. **3.** *arch.* (= *spółka*) company.

kompanijny *a. wojsk.* company.

komparator *mi el.* comparator.

komparatysta *mp*, **komparatystka** *f.* (= *wyznawca metody porównawczej*) comparatist.

komparatystyczny *a.* comparative.

komparatystyka *f.* (*nauka*) comparative studies.

komparatywizm *mi* (*podejście*) comparative approach.

komparatywny *a. form.* comparative.

kompas *mi techn.* compass.

kompasowy *a.* compass; **róża kompasowa** (*tarcza*) compass card; (*na mapie*) compass rose.

kompatybilny *a. komp. l. form.* compatible.

kompendium *n. sing. indecl. pl.* **-dia** *Gen.* **-diów** *form.* (= *podsumowanie wiedzy*) compendium, compend.

kompensacja *f. form. t. fiz., techn., psych.* compensation.

kompensacyjny *a.* (= *wyrównawczy*) *form.* compensatory.

kompensata *f. form.* (= *wyrównanie*) compensation.

kompensator *mi Gen.* **-a** *techn.* compensator.

kompensować *ipf. form. t. fiz., techn., psych.* (= *wyrównywać*) compensate (*coś* for sth). ~ **się** *ipf.* (= *równoważyć się*) balance out.

kompetencja *f.* **1.** (= *fachowość, wiedza*) competence; **brak kompetencji** lack of competence, incompetence; **kompetencja językowa** *jęz.* linguistic competence. **2.** *pl.* **kompetencje** (= *władza*) authority, power; (= *zakres uprawnień*) jurisdiction, purview, province; (*sądu*) cognizance; **coś leży/nie leży w czyichś kompetencjach** sth comes *l.* falls within/outside sb's jurisdiction *l.* authority; **coś należy do czyichś kompetencji** sth falls within sb's jurisdiction *l.* authority; **przekroczyć swoje kompetencje** overstep one's authority, exceed one's power. **3.** *biol.* competence.

kompetencyjny *a.* (*dotyczący zakresu uprawnień*) power, jurisdiction; **spór kompetencyjny** jurisdiction dispute.

kompetentnie *adv.* (= *fachowo*) competently.

kompetentny *a.* **1.** (= *właściwy, uprawniony*) pertinent. **2.** (= *profesjonalny, fachowy*) competent. **3.** *biol.* competent.

kompilacja *f. t. komp.* compilation.

kompilacyjny *a.* (= *nieoryginalny*) compilatory.

kompilator *mi Gen.* **-a** *pl.* **-ry** *komp.* compiler. – *mp pl.* **-rzy** (= *autor niesamodzielnego dzieła*) compiler.

kompilatorka *f. Gen.pl.* **-ek** (= *autorka niesamodzielnego dzieła*) compiler.

kompilatorski *a.* (= *nieoryginalny*) compilatory.

kompilować *ipf. t. komp.* compile.

kompleks *mi* **1.** *form.* (= *zespół*) complex; **kompleks budynków/szkół/sklepów** building/school/shopping complex; **kompleks przemysłowy** industrial complex; **kompleks sportowy/rekreacyjny** sports/leisure complex; **kompleks leśny** forest complex. **2.** *pl.* **kompleksy** (= *poczucie niższości*) feeling of inferiority, inferiority complex; **mieć kompleksy (w stosunku do kogoś)** feel inferior (to sb); **pozbawić kogoś kompleksów** restore sb's self-confidence; **pozbyć się kompleksów** regain one's self-confidence; **wpędzić kogoś w kompleksy** give sb a complex, undermine sb's self-confidence. **3.** *psych.* complex; **kompleks Edypa** Oedipus complex; **kompleks niższości/wyższości** inferiority/superiority complex; **mieć kompleks na punkcie czegoś** have a complex about sth. **4.** *chem.* complex.

kompleksowo *adv.* (= *całościowo*) comprehensively, globally.

kompleksowość *f.* (= *całościowość*) comprehensiveness.

kompleksowy *a.* (= *całościowy*) (*o rozwiązaniu*) global, comprehensive; **kompleksowe usługi** full service.

komplement *mi* (= *grzeczność, pochlebstwo*) compliment; **powiedzieć komuś komplement** pay sb a compliment, pay a compliment to sb, compliment sb (*na temat czegoś* about sth); **obsypywać kogoś komplementami** shower compliments on sb.

komplementarność *f. form.* complementarity; **zasada komplementarności** *fiz.* (principle of) complementarity, complementarity principle.

komplementarny *a. form.* (= *uzupełniający*) complementary.

komplementować *ipf.* (= *chwalić*) **komplementować kogoś** compliment sb, shower compliments on sb. ~ **się** *ipf.* (= *wzajemnie się chwalić*) exchange compliments.

komplet *mi* **1.** (= *zestaw*) set; (*ubrania*) suit; **komplet sztućców** cutlery set; **stawiać się w komplecie** turn out *l.* come in full force; **szukam czegoś do kompletu z...** I'm looking for something to go with... **2.** (= *brak wolnych miejsc*) *kino, teatr* (*także* **komplet widzów**) full house; *lotn.* (*także* **komplet pasażerów**) full flight; **mieć komplet** be booked up, be fully booked.

kompletnie *adv.* completely, totally.

kompletność *f.* completeness.

kompletny *a.* (= *pełny, zupełny*) complete, total; **kompletna bzdura** complete nonsense; **kompletna porażka** utter failure; **kompletne zero** *l.* **dno** *pot.* the pits; **kompletny idiota** complete *l.* perfect idiot.

kompletować *ipf.* (= *zbierać, gromadzić*) collect; (*zespół, załogę*) assemble; (*wykaz*) compile.

komplety *pl. Gen.* **-ów** (*także* **tajne komplety**) *hist.* secret classes.

komplikacja *f.* complication.

komplikować *ipf.* complicate; **komplikować sobie/komuś życie** make life difficult for o.s./sb. ~ **się** *ipf.* (= *gmatwać się*) get complicated.

komponent *mi* component, element.

komponować *ipf.* (*muzykę, wiersz*) compose, write.

kompost *mi ogr., roln.* compost.

kompot *mi* **1.** *kulin.* (*deser*) stewed fruit, compote; **kompot z jabłek** stewed apples; **wpaść jak śliwka w kompot** *przen.* be cooked, get into a jam. **2.** *pot.* (*narkotyk*) black tar (*Polish home-made drug*).

kompotierka *f. Gen.pl.* **-ek** (dessert) bowl.

kompozycja *f.* composition.

kompozycyjny *a. form.* (= *strukturalny*) compositional.

kompozytor *mp*, **kompozytorka** *f. Gen.pl.* **-ek** *muz.* composer.

kompozytorski *a.* composer's.

kompozytowy *a. zwł. techn.* composite.

kompres *mi med.* (= *okład*) compress.

kompresja *f. techn., komp.* compression.

kompresor *mi Gen.* **-a** *techn.* compressor.

kompromis *mi* (= *zgoda, ustępstwo*) compromise; **iść na kompromis** compromise, agree to a compromise; **osiągać kompromis** reach compromise.

kompromisowo *adv.* (*negocjować*) flexibly; (*postanowić*) by way of compromise.

kompromisowy *a.* (*o stanowisku, stronie*) flexible; (*o porozumieniu*) compromise.

kompromitacja *f.* embarrassment, discredit.

kompromitować *ipf.* (= *zawstydzić*) embarrass; (= *dyskredytować*) discredit. **~ się** *ipf.* **1.** (= *błaźnić się*) disgrace o.s. **2.** (= *wzajemnie się ośmieszać, ubliżać sobie*) discredit one another.

kompromitujący *a.* (*o materiałach, faktach*) compromising; (*o postępku*) discreditable.

komputer *mi Gen.* **-a** *techn.* computer; **komputer klasy IBM** IBM compatible; **komputer osobisty/stacjonarny** personal/desktop computer; **pisać/przepisywać na komputerze** type/type up on a computer; **umieć obsługiwać komputer** be computer-literate; **wpisywać** *l.* **wprowadzać do komputera** key in.

komputerowiec *mp* **-wc-** *pl.* **-y** *pot.* computer guy; (= *informatyk*) computer expert; (= *maniak komputerowy*) computer nerd.

komputerowo *adv. komp.* with a computer; **sterowany komputerowo** computer-controlled; **wspomagany komputerowo** computer-aided; **projektowanie wspomagane komputerowo** computer-aided design.

komputerowy *a. komp.* computer; **skład komputerowy** *druk.* computer typesetting; **tomograf komputerowy** *med.* CAT scanner; **tomografia komputerowa** *med.* (*badanie*) CAT scan; (*metoda*) CAT scanning.

komputeryzacja *f. komp.* computerization.

komputeryzować *ipf. komp.* computerize.

komu *pron. Dat. of* **kto**; (to) who; *form.* whom; **komu to dałaś?** who did you give it to?; **komu na tym zależy?** who wants that?

komuch *mp pl.* **-y** *pot. pog.* (= *komunista*) commie.

komukolwiek *pron. Dat. of* **ktokolwiek**; (to) anybody, (to) whoever; *form.* whomever; **daj to komukolwiek** give it to anybody; **daj to komukolwiek chcesz** give it to anybody *l.* whoever *l.* whomever you want.

komuna[1] *f. tylko sing. pot. polit.* **1.** (= *komunizm*) communism. **2.** (= *komuniści*) commies.

komuna[2] *f.* (= *wspólnota*) commune; **Komuna Paryska** *hist.* the (Paris) Commune.

komunalny *a.* (= *miejski*) municipal; **budownictwo** *l.* **mieszkania** *l.* **mieszkanie komunalne** public housing; **public services usługi komunalne**.

komunał *mi* (= *banał*) cliché, platitude, banality.

komunard *mp hist.* Communard.

komunia *f. Gen.* **-ii** *rel.* communion; **Pierwsza Komunia (Święta)** first (Holy) Communion; **iść** *l.* **przystępować do komunii** (*także* **przyjmować komunię**) take communion.

komunikacja *f.* **1.** (= *transport*) transportation, transit; *Br.* transport; **komunikacja miejska** city transit (system); **komunikacja publiczna** public trasportation; *Br.* public transport; **środki komunikacji** means of transportation *l.* transit; *Br.* means of transport; **komunikacja autobusowa/kolejowa** (= *połączenie*) bus/train service. **2.** (= *łączność, porozumienie*) communication.

komunikacyjny *a.* **1.** (= *transportowy*) transport, transportation, transit; **węzeł komunikacyjny** hub. **2.** (= *związany z porozumiewaniem się*) communication; **protokół komunikacyjny** *tel.* communication protocol; **umiejętności komunikacyjne** communication skills.

komunikant *mi Gen.* **-a** *pl.* **-y** *rel.* (= *hostia*) Host. – *mp pl.* **-ci** *rel.* (*osoba przystępująca do komunii*) communicant.

komunikat *mi zwł. dzienn.* announcement; *polit. t.* communiqué; **komunikat meteorologiczny** weather forecast; **komunikat prasowy** press release; **komunikat radiowy** radio announcement.

komunikatywność *f. form.* (= *czytelność*) clarity, perspicuity.

komunikatywny *a. gł. form.* **1.** (= *jasno mówiący*) articulate. **2.** (= *dotyczący komunikacji*) communicative; **funkcja komunikatywna** *jęz.* communicative function. **3.** (= *czytelny, zrozumiały*) clear, perspicuous.

komunikować *ipf. gł. form.* communicate (*coś komuś* sth to sb). **~ się** *ipf.* (= *porozumiewać się*) communicate; (= *być w kontakcie*) stay *l.* be in touch (*z kimś* with sb).

komunista *mp*, **komunistka** *f. Gen.pl.* **-ek** *polit.* communist.

komunistyczny *a. polit.* communist.

komunizm *mi polit.* communism.

komunizować *ipf. polit.* communize. **~ się** *ipf. polit.* communize, become communist.

komuś *pron. Dat. of* **ktoś**; (to) somebody, (to) someone; (= *komukolwiek*) (to) anybody; **dać coś komuś** give sth to somebody, give somebody sth.

komutacja *f. el., tel., jęz.* commutation.

komutator *mi Gen.* **-a** *techn.* commutator.

komutatywny *a. mat.* commutative.

komutować *ipf. el., tel.* commutate.

komuż *pron. Dat. of* **któż**.

komża *f. Gen.pl.* **-y** *l.* **-ż** *kośc.* surplice.

konać *ipf. lit.* (= *umierać*) be dying; **konać z tęsknoty za kimś/czymś** yearn for sb/sth; **konać ze śmiechu** be dying of laughter.

konar *mi Gen.* **-a** *l.* **-u 1.** (= *gałąź*) bough, limb. **2.** *myśl.* antler.

koncelebra *f. kośc.* concelebration.

koncelebrować *ipf. kośc.* concelebrate.

koncentracja *f.* (= *centralizacja, skupienie, stężenie*) concentration; **koncentracja władzy** *polit.* concentration of power; **koncentracja wojsk** *wojsk.* troop concentration.

koncentracyjny *a.* concentration; **obóz koncentracyjny** concentration camp.

koncentrat *mi* concentrate; **koncentrat pomidorowy** *kulin.* tomato paste *l.* purée, tomato concentrate.

koncentrować *ipf.* concentrate. **~ się** *ipf.* concentrate; **koncentrować się na czymś** concentrate on sth.

koncentryczny *a.* **1.** *el.* coaxial; **przewód** *l.* **ka-**

bel **koncentryczny** coaxial cable. **2.** *geom.* concentric; **koła koncentryczne** concentric circles.

koncentryk *mi pot. el.* (= *kabel koncentryczny*) coaxial cable.

koncepcja *f.* **1.** (= *pomysł*) idea; **mam pewną koncepcję** I have an idea. **2.** (= *pojęcie*) conception, concept.

koncepcyjny *a.* **1.** (= *twórczy*) creative; **praca koncepcyjna** creative work. **2.** (= *dotyczący koncepcji*) conceptual.

koncept *mi zwł. lit. l. żart.* (= *pomysł*) idea; (= *pomysłowość*) ideas; **komuś brak konceptu** sb lacks ideas; **ruszyć konceptem** use one's head.

konceptualista *mp* **1.** *fil.* conceptualist. **2.** *sztuka* conceptual artist, conceptualist.

konceptualistyczny *a. fil., sztuka* conceptualist.

konceptualizm *mi* **1.** *fil.* conceptualism. **2.** *sztuka* conceptual art.

konceptualny *a. form., fil., sztuka* conceptual.

koncern *mi ekon.* concern; **koncern międzynarodowy** multinational concern, multinational.

koncert *mi* **1.** *muz.* (*występ*) concert; **koncert popowy/rockowy** pop/rock concert; **koncert kameralny/symfoniczny** chamber/symphony concert; **uroczysty koncert** special *l.* gala concert; **koncert życzeń** *radio* listeners' choice, request program. **2.** *muz.* (*utwór*) concerto. **3.** (*ptaków, słowików, żab*) singing. **4.** (= *popis*) feat; **koncert organizacji/aktorstwa** feat of organization/acting.

koncertant *mp*, **koncertantka** *f.* concert performer.

koncertmistrz *mp Gen.pl.* **-ów** *muz.* concertmaster; *Br. t.* leader.

koncertować *ipf.* perform, give concerts.

koncertowo *adv. pot.* (= *znakomicie*) smashingly, beautifully.

koncertowy *a.* **1.** (*dotyczący koncertu*) concert; **sala koncertowa** concert hall; **trasa koncertowa** concert tour. **2.** *pot.* (= *znakomity*) smashing, beautiful; **koncertowy występ** smashing performance.

koncertyna *f. hist., muz.* concertina.

koncesja *f. prawn.* (*np. na sprzedaż alkoholu*) license; *handl.* (*np. na rozprowadzanie i sprzedaż produktów firmowych*) franchise.

koncesjonariusz *mp Gen.pl.* **-y** *l.* **-ów** *prawn.* licensee, license holder; *handl.* franchise holder, franchisee.

koncesjonować *ipf. prawn.* license; *handl.* franchise.

koncesjonowany *a. prawn.* (= *autoryzowany*) licensed.

koncesyjny *a. prawn.* (= *licencyjny*) licensing, license; **przepisy koncesyjne** licensing regulations; **umowa koncesyjna** *handl.* franchise.

koncha *f.* **1.** (= *muszla, naczynie, trąbka*) conch. **2.** *anat., bud.* concha, conch; **koncha uszna** *anat.* auricle, pinna.

konchiolina *f. biol.* conchiolin.

konchiologia *f.* conchology.

konchoida *f. mat.* conchoid.

konchowy *a.* conchiform.

koncyliacja *f. prawn.* conciliation.

koncyliarysta *mp hist., rel.* conciliarist.

koncyliaryzm *mi hist., rel.* conciliarism.

koncypować *ipf. arch. l. żart.* (= *myśleć*) cogitate, ponder.

kondemnacja *f. żegl.* condemnation.

kondensacja *f. chem., fiz.* (= *zagęszczenie*) condensation.

kondensacyjny *a.* condensation; **smuga kondensacyjna** *lotn.* vapor *l.* condensation trail, contrail.

kondensat *mi chem., fiz.* condensate.

kondensator *mi Gen.* **-a** **1.** *el.* capacitor. **2.** *techn.* (= *skraplacz*) condenser.

kondensor *mi opt.* condenser.

kondensować *ipf. techn.* condense. **~ się** *ipf. techn.* condense.

kondolencje *pl. Gen.* **-i** (= *wyrazy współczucia*) condolences; sympathy, sympathies; **składać (komuś) kondolencje** offer *l.* extend one's condolences *l.* sympathy *l.* sympathies (to sb).

kondolencyjny *a.* condolatory; **list kondolencyjny** letter of condolence, letter of sympathy.

kondom *mi* (= *prezerwatywa*) condom.

kondominium *n. sing. indecl. pl.* **-nia** *Gen.* **-niów** *polit.* condominium.

kondor *ma orn.* condor; **kondor kalifornijski** California condor (*Gymnogyps californianus*); **kondor królewski** king condor *l.* vulture (*Sarcorhamphus papa*); **kondor olbrzymi** Andean condor (*Vultur gryphus*).

kondotier *mp hist.* condotierre.

konduita *f. przest. l. żart.* (= *prowadzenie się*) conduct.

kondukt *mi* procession; **kondukt żałobny** *l.* **pogrzebowy** cortege, cortège; funeral procession.

konduktor *mp* (= *kontroler*) conductor, ticket inspector.

konduktorka *f. Gen.pl.* **-ek** **1.** (= *kontrolerka*) conductress, ticket inspector. **2.** (*torebka*) shoulder bag.

konduktorski *a.* conductor's.

kondycja *f.* **1.** (= *sprawność, forma, sytuacja*) shape, condition; (= *dobra sprawność*) fitness; **kondycja psychiczna/fizyczna** mental/physical condition; **w dobrej/złej kondycji** in good/bad shape, in/out of condition; **kondycja finansowa** financial standing. **2.** *przest.* (= *status społeczny*) condition.

kondycyjnie *adv.* in terms of fitness; **wytrzymać kondycyjnie** keep it up; **nie wytrzymać kondycyjnie** tire out, run out of breath.

kondycyjny *a.* (= *wytrzymałościowy*) fitness; **trening kondycyjny** fitness training; **obóz kondycyjny** fitness camp.

kondygnacja *f. bud.* (= *piętro*) story, *Br.* storey, floor.

koneksje *pl. Gen.* **-i** (= *znajomości*) connections.

koneser *mp*, **koneserka** *f. Gen.pl.* **-ek** (= *znawca*) connoisseur.

koneserski *a.* connoisseur.

koneserstwo *n.* (= *znawstwo*) connoisseur-ship.

konewka *f. Gen.pl.* **-ek** *ogr.* watering can *l.* pot.

konfabulacja *f. psych.* confabulation.

konfabulować *ipf. psych.* confabulate.

konfederacja *f.* (= *związek, przymierze*) confederacy; *polit.* confederation; **konfederacja targowicka/barska** *hist.* Confederation of Targowica/Bar.

konfederacki *a. hist.* confederate.

konfederacyjny *a.* confederate.

konfederat *mp hist.* confederate.

konfederatka *f.* (*czapka*) four-cornered cap, square cap.

konfederować *ipf. polit.* confederate. ~ **się** *ipf. polit.* confederate.

konfekcja *f. handl.* (= *ubrania*) off-the-rack *l.* ready-made *l.* ready-to-wear clothes *l.* clothing; *Br. t.* off-the-peg clothes; **konfekcja damska/męska** womenswear/menswear; **konfekcja damska** *Br. t.* ladies' wear.

konfekcjonować *ipf.* **1.** (= *pakować gotowe produkty*) package. **2.** (= *produkować*) produce (*ready-to-wear clothes, ready-to-use furniture*).

konfekcyjny *a.* (= *odzieżowy*) clothing.

konferansjer *mp* (= *prezenter*) master of ceremonies; *pot.* MC, emcee.

konferansjerka *f.* (= *zapowiadanie*) acting as a master of ceremonies; *pot.* emceeing.

konferansjerski *a.* (= *prezenterski*) master of ceremonies; *pot.* MC, emcee.

konferansjerstwo *n.* acting as a master of ceremonies; *pot.* emceeing.

konferencja *f.* conference; **konferencja na szczycie** *polit.* summit conference; **konferencja rozbrojeniowa** *polit.* conference on disarmament; **konferencja naukowa** scientific conference; **konferencja prasowa** press conference.

konferencyjny *a.* conference; **sala konferencyjna** conference room, conference hall; **stół konferencyjny** conference table; **tłumacz konferencyjny** conference interpreter.

konferować *ipf. form.* (= *debatować*) confer (*z kimś* with sb, *o czymś* about sth).

konfesja *f. rel., sztuka* confession.

konfesjonał *mi rz-kat.* confessional.

konfetti *n. indecl.* confetti.

konfidencjonalność *f.* **1.** (= *zażyłość, poufałość*) familiarity, intimacy. **2.** (= *tajność*) confidentiality.

konfidencjonalny *a.* **1.** (= *zażyły, poufały*) familiar, intimate. **2.** (= *tajny, dyskretny*) confidential.

konfident *mp*, **konfidentka** *f. Gen.pl.* **-ek** *gł. pog.* (= *donosiciel/ka*) informer.

konfiguracja *f. chem., astron., komp.* configuration; *komp. t.* setup; **konfiguracja polityczna** political configuration.

konfigurować *ipf. komp.* configure, set up.

konfirmacja *f. rel., log.* confirmation.

konfirmacyjny *a. form.* confirmatory.

konfirmant *mp*, **konfirmantka** *f. Gen.pl.* **-ek** *rel.* confirmand.

konfirmować *ipf. rel.* confirm.

konfiskata *f. prawn.* confiscation, forfeit.

konfiskować *ipf. prawn.* confiscate, forfeit.

konfitura *f. kulin.* preserve; **konfitura wiśniowa** cherry preserve.

konflikt *mi* conflict; **konflikt interesów** conflict *l.* clash of interest *l.* interests; **konflikt międzynarodowy** international conflict; **konflikt pokoleń** generation gap; **konflikt serologiczny** *pat.* blood group incompatibility; **konflikt zbrojny** armed conflict; **wejść w konflikt z prawem** infringe the law.

konfliktowość *f.* (= *kłótliwość*) irascibility, disagreeableness.

konfliktowy *a.* **1.** (= *kłótliwy*) disagreeable, confrontational. **2.** (*dotyczący konfliktu*) conflict; **sytuacja konfliktowa** conflict situation.

konfluencja *f. geogr.* confluence, conflux.

konfokalny *a. mat.* confocal.

konforemny *a. geom.* conformal.

konformista *mp rel., socjol.* conformist.

konformistyczny *a.* conformist.

konformizm *mi rel., socjol.* conformism.

konfrontacja *f.* **1.** (= *porównanie*) confrontation, comparison (*z kimś/czymś* with sb/sth). **2.** (= *konflikt*) confrontation, face-off; **konfrontacja zbrojna** armed confrontation. **3. konfrontacja świadków** *prawn.* (witness) confrontation (*for the purposes of cross-examination*); **konfrontacja (świadków) z podejrzanym** *prawn.* (*dla identyfikacji podejrzanego*) line-up; *Br.* identification *l.* identity parade.

konfrontować *ipf.* **1.** (= *porównywać, zestawiać*) compare (*kogoś/coś z kimś/czymś* sb/sth with sb/sth). **2.** *prawn.* (*zeznania, świadków*) confront; (*podejrzanego*) parade.

konfucjanista *mp*, **konfucjanistka** *f. fil.* (= *wyznawca konfucjanizmu*) Confucian, Confucianist.

konfucjanizm *mi fil.* Confucianism.

konfucjański *a. fil.* Confucian.

kongenialny *a.* (*o umysłach, duszach*) congenial; **kongenialny przekład** (= *doskonały przekład*) masterly translation.

konglomeracja *f.* **1.** *form., socjol., geol.* conglomeration. **2.** *geol.* (= *konglomerat*) conglomerate.

konglomerat *mi form., geol., ekon.* conglomerate.

kongregacja *f. rel.* congregation.

kongregacyjny *a. rel.* congregational.

kongres *mi* (= *narada, konferencja, organizacja, ciało ustawodawcze*) congress; **Kongres Polonii Amerykańskiej** Polish American Congress; **Kongres Polonii Kanadyjskiej** Canadian Polish Congress; **Kongres Stanów Zjednoczonych** United States Congress; **kongres wiedeński** *hist.* Congress of Vienna.

kongresman, **kongresmen** *mp* (= *członek Kongresu, parlamentarzysta*) congressman.

kongresowy *a.* congress; **centrum kongresowe** congress center; **języki kongresowe** congress languages; **Królestwo Kongresowe** *hist.* Congress Kingdom of Poland.

Kongresówka *f. hist.* Congress Poland.

kongruencja *f. form.* congruity; *mat., jęz.* congruence.

kongruentny *a. form., mat., jęz.* congruent; **figury kongruentne** *geom.* congruent figures.

koniak *mi* brandy; *(francuski)* cognac.

koniakówka *f. Gen.pl.* **-ek** *(kieliszek)* (brandy) snifter.

koniara *f.*, **koniarz** *mp pot.* (= *miłośniczka l. miłośnik koni*) horse lover.

koniczyna *f.* **1.** *bot.* clover *(Trifolium)*; **czterolistna koniczyna** four-leaf clover. **2.** *mot.* *(skrzyżowanie)* cloverleaf. **3.** (= *symbol Irlandii*) shamrock.

konidiofor *mi bot.* conidiophore.

konidium *n. bot.* conidium.

koniec *mi* **-ńc-** *Gen.* **-a 1.** (= *kres*) end. **2.** (= *czubek*) tip. **3.** *(w zwrotach)* **bez końca** without end, endlessly; **do końca świata** till the end of time; **do (samego) końca** until the (very) end; **iść na koniec świata** go to the ends of the earth; **gadać bez końca** talk for hours on end; **to jest na końcu świata** it is at the back of beyond; **każdy kij ma dwa końce** two can play at that game; **koniec końców** when all is said and done; **koniec wieku** fin de siècle, end of century; **koniec wieńczy dzieło** the end crowns all *l.* the work; **ktoś ma coś na końcu języka** sth is on the tip of sb's tongue; **mieć się ku końcowi** come *l.* draw to a close; **na końcu świata** at the end of the world; **na szarym końcu** at the very end; **na tym koniec** that's it; that's the end of it; **nie koniec na tym** that's not all, wait till you hear the rest (of it); **od końca** from the end; **to już koniec** it's all over now; (= *w odwrotnej kolejności*) in reverse order; **od końca do końca** from end to end, from one end to the other; **od początku do końca** from beginning to end, from start to finish; **początek końca** beginning of the end; **pod koniec tygodnia/miesiąca** at the end of the week/month; **w końcu** finally, at last; **koniec świata** (= *zamieszanie*) chaos, (utter) confusion; *(okrzyk)* my word!; **wiązać koniec z końcem** make (both) ends meet; **położyć czemuś koniec** put a stop to sth; **(no to) koniec pieśni!** this is it!

koniecznie *adv.* necessarily, absolutely; **koniecznie musisz przyjść!** you simply must come!

konieczność *f.* necessity; **konieczność dziejowa** historical necessity; **smutna konieczność** sad necessity; **stan wyższej konieczności** absolute necessity; **z konieczności** (out) of necessity, by necessity; **jeśli zajdzie konieczność** *l.* **w razie konieczności** if necessary; **znaleźć się w obliczu konieczności zrobienia czegoś** be faced with the necessity to do sth.

konieczny *a.* necessary; **warunek konieczny** *log., mat.* necessary condition; **obrona konieczna** *prawn.* *(siebie)* necessary self-defense; *(osoby trzeciej)* necessary defense; **(działać) w warunkach obrony koniecznej** (act) in necessary self-defense/defense.

konik *ma* (= *mały koń*) **1.** little horse; *dziec.* horsie, gee-gee. **2.** *(zabawka)* hobbyhorse. **3.** *szachy* knight, horse. **4.** (= *hobby*) hobby; **dosiąść** *l.* **wsiąść na swego konika** ride one's hob-

byhorse. **5.** *mech.* tailstock. **6. konik morski** *icht.* sea horse *(Hippocampus)*; **konik polny** *ent.* grasshopper *(Locusta)*. – *mp pl.* **-i** *pot.* (= *spekulant*) ticket tout, scalper.

konina *f.* *(mięso)* horseflesh, horse meat.

koniokrad *mp pl.* **-y** (horse) rustler, horse thief.

koniokradztwo *n.* (horse) rustling, horse stealing *l.* theft.

konisko *n.* (= *stary koń*) hack, jade, nag; **stare konisko** *żart.* (= *dorosły mężczyzna*) big boy.

konitrut *mi bot.* hedge hyssop *(Gratiola officinalis)*.

koniuch *mp pl.* **-y** *l.* **-owie** *przest.* hostler.

koniugacja *f.* **1.** *jęz.* conjugation; **koniugacja czasowników** conjugation of verbs, verb conjugation. **2.** *biol.* conjugation; **koniugacja mejotyczna chromosomów** synapse.

koniugacyjny *a.* *jęz.* conjugational, conjugation.

koniugować *ipf.* **1.** *jęz.* conjugate *(przez coś* for sth). **2.** *biol.* conjugate *(z czymś* with sth).

koniunkcja *f. log., jęz., astron.* conjunction.

koniunktiwus *mi Gen.* **-wu** *gram.* subjunctive (mood), conjunctive (mood).

koniunktor *mi Gen.* **-a** *komp., log.* AND operator.

koniunktura *f.* **1.** *ekon.* (= *sytuacja ekonomiczna*) economic situation *l.* conditions; (= *dobra sytuacja ekonomiczna*) (economic) boom, (economic) prosperity; **nakręcać koniunkturę** power the economy; **poprawa koniunktury** upturn in the economy. **2.** (= *pomyślność*) prosperity. **3.** (= *położenie*) situation, conditions; **koniunktura polityczna** political situation *l.* conditions.

koniunkturalista *mp*, **koniunkturalistka** *f. Gen.pl.* **-ek** *uj.* timeserver, opportunist.

koniunkturalizm *mi* timeserving, opportunism.

koniunkturalnie *adv.* **1.** (= *zależnie od całokształtu*) according to situation. **2.** (= *oportunistycznie*) opportunistically.

koniunkturalność *f.* **1.** (= *zależność od całokształtu*) condition-dependence. **2.** (= *okresowość*) ups and downs, cyclicity. **3.** (= *oportunizm*) timeserving, opportunism.

koniunkturalny *a.* **1.** (= *zależny od koniunktury*) condition-dependent. **2.** (= *wahliwy*) up-and-down. **3.** (= *wyrachowany*) timeserving, opportunistic.

koniunktyw *mi gram.* = **koniunktiwus**.

koniuszek *mi* **-szk-** *Gen.* **-a** tip.

koniuszy *mp pl.* **-owie** *hist.* equerry.

konklawe *n. indecl.* *rz.-kat.* conclave.

konkludować *ipf. form.* conclude.

konkluzja *f. form.* conclusion; **w konkluzji** in conclusion.

konkordancja *f. t. jęz.* (= *indeks, zestawienie*) concordance.

konkordat *mi polit.* concordat.

konkrecja *f. geol.* concretion.

konkrecyjny *a. geol.* concretionary.

konkret *mi* **1.** (= *fakt*) fact; **porozmawiajmy o**

konkretach let's talk facts; **przejść do konkretów** get down to business. **2.** *fil.* the concrete.

konkretnie *adv.* (= *jasno*) specifically, clearly; (= *rzeczowo*) concretely; **mało konkretnie** vaguely.

konkretność *f.* (= *jasność*) clarity; (= *rzeczowość*) substance, concreteness; **twojej propozycji brak konkretności** your proposal lacks substance.

konkretny *a.* **1.** (= *jasny*) clear, concrete. **2.** (= *określony*) specific. **3.** (*o osobie*) businesslike. **4.** (= *porządny*) substantial; **zjeść coś konkretnego** have a substantial meal, have something substantial. **5.** (= *nieabstrakcyjny*) concrete; **muzyka konkretna** *muz.* concrete music; **sztuka konkretna** *sztuka* concrete art.

konkretyzacja *f.* **1.** (= *uściślenie*) detailed specification; **potrzebna jest konkretyzacja** details need to be worked out. **2.** (= *wprowadzenie w życie*) implementation. **3.** *fil.* concretization.

konkretyzm *mi fil.* (= *radykalny realizm*) concretism.

konkretyzować *ipf.* **1.** (= *precyzować*) work out the details (*coś* of sth). **2.** (= *wprowadzać w życie*) implement. **3.** *fil.* concretize. **~ się** *ipf.* (= *nabierać wyrazistości, realności*) take shape, jell; (= *pojawiać się*) emerge.

konkubent *mp pl.* **-nci** **1.** *prawn., socjol.* spousal equivalent. **2.** = **konkubin**.

konkubin *mp pl.* **-owie** (= *partner ogniska domowego*) (male) partner, live-in partner; (= *kochanek*) (male) lover.

konkubina *f.* **1.** *prawn., socjol.,* spousal equivalent. **2.** (= *partnerka ogniska domowego*) (female) partner, live-in partner, concubine; (= *kochanka*) (female) lover.

konkubinat *mi* living together; *prawn.* concubinage; **żyć (z kimś) w konkubinacie** co-habit with sb.

konkurencja *f.* **1.** (= *współzawodnictwo*) *ekol.* competition; **konkurencja rynkowa** *ekon.* (= *rywalizacja*) market competition; (= *wolny rynek*) free market. **2.** *sport* (= *dyscyplina*) event.

konkurencyjność *f.* competitiveness.

konkurencyjny *a.* **1.** (= *atrakcyjny*) competitive; **konkurencyjna cena/oferta** *ekon.* competitive price/offer. **2.** (= *rywalizujący*) rival, competing.

konkurent *mp*, **konkurentka** *f.* **1.** (= *rywal, przeciwnik*) competitor, rival. **2.** *przest.* (= *zalotnik*) suitor.

konkurować *ipf.* **1.** (= *rywalizować*) compete (*z kimś / czymś* with *l.* against sb/sth) (*o kogoś / coś* for sb/sth). **2.** *przest.* (= *zalecać się*) court (*o kogoś* sb).

konkurs *mi* **1.** (= *rozgrywka, turniej*) competition, contest; **konkurs audiotele** viewer competition; (*w którym odpowiedzi udziela się przez telefon*) phone-in competition; **konkurs hipiczny** *jeźdz.* show jumping; **konkurs otwarty/zamknięty** open/closed competition; **konkurs piękności** beauty contest; **stawać do konkursu** enter a contest *l.* competition; **uczestni-k/czka konkursu** contestant. **2.** *prawn.* (= *przetarg*) invitation for

tenders *l.* offers; **ogłaszać konkurs na coś/na zrobienie czegoś** invite tenders *l.* offers for sth/to do sth.

konkursowy *a.* competitive, competition; contest; **egzamin konkursowy** competitive examination; **jury konkursowe** *l.* **komisja konkursowa** jury, jury panel.

konkury *pl. Gen.* **-ów** *przest.* (= *zaloty*) courtship; **uderzać w konkury do kogoś** court sb.

konkwista *f. hist.* conquest (*of Latin America*).

konkwistador *mp hist.* conquistador.

konnica *f. hist., wojsk.* (= *kawaleria*) cavalry, horse.

konno *adv.* (= *na koniu*) on horseback; **jeździć konno** ride (on horseback).

konny *a.* **1.** (= *na koniach*) horse, horseback; **jazda konna** horse *l.* horseback riding; **piechota/policja konna** mounted infantry/police; **wyścigi konne** horse racing. **2.** (*o powozie, zaprzęgu*) horse-drawn.

konoida *f. geom.* conoid.

konopie *pl. Gen.* **-i** *bot., tk.* hemp, cannabis (*Cannabis*); **konopie indyjskie** Indian hemp, cannabis (*Cannabis indica*); **wyskoczyć** *l.* **wyrwać się jak Filip z konopi** *przen.* put one's foot in it; *Br. t.* drop a brick.

konopny *a.* **1.** (*z konopi*) hemp, hempen; **nić konopna** hempyarn; **olej konopny** hemp *l.* hempseed oil; **sznur konopny** hempstring. **2.** (= *płowy, jasny*) (*o włosach*) flaxen.

konosament *mi handl.* bill of lading.

konotacja *f. form., log., jęz.* connotation.

konotować *ipf. form., log., jęz.* connote.

konował *mp pl.* **-y** *pot., pog.* (= *lekarzyna*) quack doctor.

konsekracja *f. rel.* consecration.

konsekrować *ipf. rel.* consecrate.

konsekwencja *f.* **1.** (= *systematyczność*) consistency; **konsekwencja w działaniu** consistent action. **2.** (= *następstwo*) consequence (*czegoś* of sth); *zob. t.* **konsekwencje**. **3.** *log.* (= *konkluzja*) consequence.

konsekwencje *f. pl.* consequences; **wyciągać konsekwencje z czegoś** (= *zareagować stosownie*) not let sth pass; (= *ukarać winnych*) find those responsible for sth; **ponieść konsekwencje (czegoś)** take *l.* suffer the consequences (of sth); **liczyć się z konsekwencjami** face the consequences.

konsekwentnie *adv.* (= *systematycznie*) consistently.

konsekwentny *a.* (= *systematyczny*) consistent.

konsensus *mi* (= *zgoda, kompromis*) consensus; **brak (jest) konsensusu (wśród kogoś co do czegoś)** there is no consensus (among sb on sth); **osiągać konsensus** reach a consensus.

konserwa¹ *mi* (= *produkt spożywczy*) canned food *l.* goods (*usually meat, fish or vegetables*).

konserwa² *mp tylko sing. pot.* (= *konserwatysta*) stick-in-the-mud, old fog(e)y.

konserwacja *f.* (*maszyn i urządzeń, dróg*) maintenance; (*zabytków*) conservation; (*żywności*) preservation.

konserwacyjny *a.* (*o maszynach i urządzeniach, drogach*) maintenance; **prace konserwacyjne** maintenance works; (*o zabytkach*) conservational; (*o żywności*) preservation.

konserwant *mi* (= *środek konserwujący*) preservative.

konserwator *mp* **1.** (= *restaurator, renowator*) restorer, conservator. **2.** (= *mechanik*) maintenance technician.

konserwatorium *n. sing. indecl. pl.* **-ria** *Gen.* **-riów** (= *szkoła muzyczna*) conservatory, conservatoire.

konserwatorski *a.* (= *dotyczący konserwatora zabytków*) restorer's; **prace konserwatorskie** restoration (works).

konserwatorstwo *n.* (= *renowacja*) renovation, restoring; (= *opieka nad zabytkami*) preservation of historical buildings and objects.

konserwatysta *mp* **1.** (= *tradycjonalista*) conservative. **2.** *polit.* (= *członek partii konserwatywnej*) Conservative.

konserwatystka *f. Gen.pl.* **-ek** *zob.* **konserwatysta**.

konserwatywnie *adv.* (= *tradycjonalistycznie*) conservatively.

konserwatywność *f.* (= *tradycjonalizm*) conservativeness; (= *konserwatyzm*) conservativeness.

konserwatywny *a.* **1.** (= *tradycjonalistyczny*) conservative. **2.** *polit.* (= *prawicowy*) conservative; **Partia Konserwatywna** *Br.* Conservative Party, Tory Party.

konserwatyzm *mi* **1.** (= *tradycjonalizm, zachowawczość*) conservatism. **2.** (= *prawicowość*) conservatism.

konserwować *ipf.* **1.** (= *odnawiać*) restore. **2.** (= *remontować*) maintain. **3.** (= *wekować*) preserve; can. ~ **się** *ipf.* **1.** (= *nie psuć się*) preserve; **ogórki dobrze się konserwują** cucumbers preserve well. **2.** (= *trzymać się*) age gracefully *l.* with dignity; **on dobrze się konserwuje** *l.* trzyma he ages gracefully *l.* with dignity.

konserwowy *a.* (= *konserwowany*) (*o mięsie, rybach*) canned; (*o ogórkach*) pickled.

konsjerżka *f. rzad.* concierge.

konsola *f. Gen.pl.* **-i** **1.** (= *ozdobny stolik*) console table. **2.** *bud.* console. **3.** *techn.* console. **4.** *komp.* console.

konsolacja *f.* **1.** *lit.* (= *pocieszenie, współczucie*) consolation. **2.** *przest.* (= *stypa*) funeral banquet.

konsolacyjny *a. lit.* (= *pocieszający*) consolatory.

konsoleta *f.* **1.** (= *stół mikserski*) console. **2.** *komp.* console.

konsolidacja *f.* **1.** (= *zespolenie*) consolidation. **2.** *ekon., prawn.* consolidation.

konsolidacyjny *a.* **1.** (= *łączący*) consolidative. **2.** *ekon., prawn.* consolidative.

konsolidować *ipf.* **1.** (= *jednoczyć*) consolidate. **2.** *ekon., prawn.* consolidate. ~ **się** *ipf.* (= *łączyć się*) consolidate (*w coś* into sth).

konsonans *mi pl.* **-e** **1.** *teor.lit.* (*rym*) consonance. **2.** *muz.* consonance.

konsonant *mi jęz.* (= *spółgłoska*) consonant.

konsonantyczny *a. jęz.* consonantal.

konsonantyzm *mi jęz.* consonantism.

konsonantyzować się *ipf. jęz.* consonantize.

konsorcjum *n. sing. indecl. pl.* **-ja** *Gen.* **-jów** *ekon.* consortium.

konspekt *mi* (= *szkic, plan, zarys*) outline.

konspiracja *f.* **1.** (= *spiskowanie*) conspiracy. **2.** (= *tajna organizacja*) undergound, Underground.

konspiracyjność *f.* **1.** (= *tajność*) secrecy. **2.** (= *dyskrecja*) confidentiality.

konspiracyjny *a.* **1.** (= *tajny*) secret, conspirational. **2.** (= *dyskretny*) confidential.

konspirator *mp* (= *spiskowiec*) conspirer.

konspiratorka *f. Gen.pl.* **-ek** *zob.* **konspirator**.

konspiratorski *a.* conspiratorial, conspiratory.

konspiratorstwo *n.* (= *spiskowanie*) conspiracy, conspiring.

konspirować *ipf.* **1.** (= *spiskować*) conspire, plot (*przeciw komuś* against sb). **2.** (= *kamuflować*) keep secret (*przed kimś* from sb). ~ **się** *ipf.* (= *ukrywać się, maskować się*) hide (*przed kimś* from sb).

konstabl *mp pl.* **-e** *l.* **-owie** *Gen.* **-i** *l.* **-ów** (= *policjant*) police officer; *Br.* constable.

Konstancja *f. geogr.* Constance; **Sobór w Konstancji** *hist.* Council of Constance (*1414-1418*).

konstanta *f.* (= *element trwały*) constant.

konstantan *mi techn.* constantan.

konstatować *ipf. lit.* (= *stwierdzać*) establish; **konstatować nieścisłości** establish inconsistencies.

konstelacja *f.* **1.** *astron.* (= *gwiazdozbiór*) constellation. **2.** *przen.* (= *układ*) state of affairs; **konstelacja sił politycznych w parlamencie** political make-up of the parliament.

konsternacja *f.* (= *zdziwienie*) consternation, confusion, dismay.

konsternować *ipf.* (= *deprymować*) consternate, confuse, dismay.

konstrukcja *f.* **1.** (= *struktura*) construction, structure; **konstrukcja nośna** *techn.* supporting structure, load-bearing structure; **konstrukcja psychiczna** mental make-up. **2.** (= *budowanie*) construction. **3.** *mat.* construction. **4.** *jęz.* construction.

konstrukcyjny *a.* constructional, structural; **stal konstrukcyjna** *techn.* structural steel; **zadanie konstrukcyjne** *mat.* ruler-and-compass problem.

konstrukt *mi* construct.

konstruktor *mp* (= *budowniczy, architekt*) designer; (= *wykonawca*) constructor.

konstruktorka *f. Gen.pl.* **-ek** *zob.* **konstruktor**.

konstruktorski *a.* designer.

konstruktywista *mp sztuka* constructivist.

konstruktywistyczny *a. sztuka* constructivist.

konstruktywizm *mi sztuka* constructivism.

konstruktywnie *adv.* (= *twórczo*) constructively.

konstruktywny *a.* (= *twórczy*) constructive; **konstruktywna krytyka** constructive criticism.

konstruować *ipf.* (= *budować*) construct, build (*z czegoś* of sth).

konstruowanie *n.* (= *zespalanie*) construction.

konstytuanta *f. polit.* constituent assembly.

konstytucja *f.* 1. *prawn.* (= *ustawa zasadnicza*) constitution; niezgodny z konstytucją unconstitutional; poprawka do konstytucji constitutional amendment; zawrzeć w konstytucji constitutionalize; zgodność z konstytucją constitutionality. 2. *biol.* (= *struktura, anatomia*) constitution; konstytucja psychiczna mental constitution *l.* make-up.

konstytucjonalista *mp* 1. *polit.* constitutionalist. 2. *psych.* constitutional psychologist.

konstytucjonalizm *mi* 1. *polit.* constitutionalism. 2. *psych.* constitutional psychology.

konstytucjonalny *a. med., psych.* constitutional.

konstytucyjnie *adv. prawn.* (= *zgodnie z konstytucją*) constitutionally.

konstytucyjność *f. prawn.* (= *praworządność*) constitutionality.

konstytucyjny *a.* 1. *prawn.* (= *dotyczący konstytucji*) constitutional; Trybunał Konstytucyjny Constitutional Tribunal; monarchia konstytucyjna constitutional monarchy. 2. (= *dotyczący budowy ciała*) constitutional; woda konstytucyjna *chem.* chemically combined water.

konstytuować *ipf.* (= *ustanawiać*) constitute, establish. ~ się *ipf.* (= *tworzyć się*) be set up, be established; ukonstytuowała się komisja rządowa government committee has been set up.

konstytutywny *a.* 1. (= *zasadniczy, podstawowy*) constituent, constitutive. 2. (= *stanowiący o czymś*) constitutive. 3. *fiz., chem.* constitutive.

konsubstancjacja *f.* *rz.-kat.* consubstantiation.

konsul *mp pl.* -owie *Gen.* -ów 1. (*dyplomata*) consul; konsul generalny consul general; konsul honorowy honorary consul. 2. *hist.* consul (*in the ancient Roman republic*). 3. *hist.* consul (*in the French First Republic*).

konsularny *a.* 1. consular; biuro konsularne consular agency; patent konsularny commission of appointment. 2. *hist.* consular.

konsulat *mi* 1. (= *placówka konsularna*) consulate; konsulat generalny consulate general. 2. *hist.* consulate.

konsultacja *f.* 1. (= *porada*) consultation; konsultacje indywidualne *uniw.* tutorial. 2. (= *narada rzeczoznawców*) consultation. 3. (= *badanie lekarskie*) (medical) examination.

konsultacyjny *a.* (= *doradczy*) consultative, consultatory, consultive.

konsultant *mp* (= *ekspert*) consultant.

konsultantka *f. Gen.pl.* -ek *zob.* konsultant.

konsulting *mi ekon.* consulting.

konsultingowy *a. ekon.* consulting; firma konsultingowa consultancy; usługi konsultingowe consulting services.

konsultować *ipf.* (= *radzić, opiniować*) consult (*z kimś* with sb). ~ się *ipf.* (= *zasięgać opinii, rady*) 1. consult (*z kimś l. u kogoś* with sb). 2. (= *naradzać się*) advise (*z kimś* with sb).

konsumacja *f.* consummation.

konsumenci *pl. Gen.* -ów *biol.* consumers; konsumenci pierwotni *l.* pierwszego rzędu primary consumers.

konsumencki *a.* consumer.

konsument *mp* (= *nabywca*) consumer; ochrona praw konsumenta consumer protection; rzecznik praw konsumenta consumer advocate.

konsumentka *f. Gen.pl.* -ek *zob.* konsument.

konsumeryzm *mi ekon.* consumerism.

konsumować *ipf.* 1. (= *jeść, pić*) consume. 2. (= *korzystać, używać*) use.

konsumpcja *f.* 1. (= *spożywanie*) consumption. 2. (= *używanie*) use.

konsumpcjonizm *mi* (= *komercjalizm*) consumerism.

konsumpcyjny *a.* 1. (= *spożywczy*) consumable. 2. (= *użytkowy*) consumer; dobra konsumpcyjne *ekon.* consumer goods; kredyt konsumpcyjny *ekon.* consumer credit. 3. (= *dążący do zdobywania dóbr materialnych*) consumerist; społeczeństwo konsumpcyjne consumerist society.

konsygnacja *f.* 1. *handl.* (= *specyfikacja towarów*) shipping specification. 2. *handl.* (= *sprzedaż komisowa*) consignment.

konsygnacyjny *a. handl.* consignment.

konsygnant *mp handl.* consignor.

konsygnatariusz *mp Gen.pl.* -y *l.* -ów *handl.* consignee.

konsygnować *ipf. handl.* (= *przesłać, przekazać*) consign.

konsylium *n. sing. indecl. pl.* -lia *Gen.* -liów consultation; konsylium lekarskie medical consultation.

konsystencja *f.* (= *stopień spoistości*) consistency.

konsystorski *a. rel., rz.-kat.* consistorial, consistorian; sąd konsystorski consistory.

konsystorz *mp rel., rz.-kat.* consistory.

konszachty *pl. Gen.* -ów (= *machinacje*) shady dealings, collusions.

kontakt *mi* 1. (= *łączność, styczność*) contact; kontakty (= *znajomości*) connections; żeby się dostać na prawo, musisz mieć kontakty you have to know the right people to get into *l.* admitted to a law school; kontakt listowny correspondence; kontakt wzrokowy eye contact; kontakty gospodarcze business contacts; kontakty kulturalne cultural relations; być w kontakcie keep in touch (*z kimś/czymś* with sb/sth); stracić kontakt lose contact (*z kimś/czymś* with sb/sth); tracić kontakt z rzeczywistością lose one's grasp on reality; utrzymywać kontakty towarzyskie socialize (*z kimś* with sb); lekarz pierwszego kontaktu primary care physician. 2. *el.* (= *gniazdko wtykowe*) socket; włączać do kontaktu plug in. 3. *el., pot.* (= *włącznik*) switch. 4. *chem.* (= *katalizator kontaktowy*) contact, contact agent, solid catalyst.

kontaktować *ipf.* 1. (= *uzyskiwać łączność*) put in touch (*z kimś/czymś* with sb/sth). 2. (= *stykać*) contact, touch; żarówka nie kontaktuje bulb has a loose connection. 3. *pot.* (= *rozumieć*) get, dig. ~ **się** *ipf.* (= *spotykać się*) be in touch (*z kimś / czymś* with sb/sth).

kontaktowy *a.* **1.** (= *umożliwiający zetknięcie*) contactual, contact; **skrzynka kontaktowa** dead letter box *l.* drop; **lokal kontaktowy** safe house; **sport kontaktowy** contact sport; **szkła kontaktowe** *opt.* contact lenses. **2.** *el.* socket. **3.** *chem.* contact; **katalizator kontaktowy** contact (agent), solid catalyst; **metoda kontaktowa** contact process. **4.** *pot.* (= *towarzyski*) sociable.

kontaminacja *f.* **1.** (= *połączenie*) blending, mixture. **2.** *jęz.* contamination.

kontaminować *ipf.* **1.** (= *łączyć*) blend. **2.** *jęz.* blend.

kontekst *mi* **1.** *jęz.* context. **2.** (*społeczny, kulturowy*) matrix, framework; **w kontekście czegoś** in the context of sth; **wyrwany z kontekstu** taken out of context.

kontekstowy *a.* contextual.

kontekstualizm *mi sztuka, teor.lit.* contextualism.

kontemplacja *f.* **1.** (= *zaduma*) contemplation. **2.** *fil., rel.* contemplation.

kontemplacyjność *f.* **1.** (= *refleksyjność*) contemplativeness. **2.** *fil., rel.* contemplativeness.

kontemplacyjny *a.* **1.** (= *refleksyjny*) contemplative. **2.** *fil., rel.* contemplative; **zakon kontemplacyjny** contemplative order.

kontemplować *ipf.* **1.** (= *medytować*) contemplate. **2.** *fil.* contemplate.

kontener *mi Gen.* **-a** (*opakowanie*) container.

kontenerowiec *mi* **-wc-** *Gen.* **-a** *żegl.* containership.

kontenerowy *a.* container; **terminal kontenerowy** containership terminal.

konteneryzacja *f.* containerization.

kontent *a. tylko w Nom.* (= *zadowolony*) content, satisfied.

konterfekt *mi przest.* (= *portret, obraz*) counterfeit, portrait.

kontestacja *f.* (= *opór, dezaprobata*) contestation, defiance, calling into question, opposition.

kontestacyjny *a.* (= *przeciwny*) contesting, defiant, opposing, disapproving.

kontestator *mp* (= *antagonista*) contester, contender, adversary.

kontestować *ipf.* (= *oponować, sprzeciwiać się*) contest, defy, call into question, oppose.

kontinuum *n. sing. indecl. pl.* **-nua** *Gen.* **-nuów** **1.** *fil., mat.* continuum. **2.** *przen.* (= *ciąg*) continuum.

konto *n.* **1.** *fin.* account; **konto bankowe** bank account; **konto bieżące** checking account; **konto debetowe** drawing account; **konto gotówkowe** cash account; **konto kredytowe** credit account, charge account; **konto zbiorcze** control account; **mieć konto w banku** have an account at *l.* with a bank; **otwierać** *l.* **zakładać konto** open an account; **sprawdzać stan konta** check one's account balance; **wpłacić pieniądze na konto** pay *l.* put money into an account; **zamknąć** *l.* **zlikwidować konto** close an account; **zapisać na czyjeś konto** chalk up to sb. **2.** *komp.* account; **konto e-mailowe** e-mail account. **3.** *przen.* record; **mieć czyste**

konto have a clean sheet *l.* record; **zapisać na czyjeś konto** chalk up to sb.

kontorsja *f. rzad.* contortion.

kontorsjonista *mp* contortionist.

kontorsjonistka *f. Gen.pl.* **-ek** *zob.* **kontorsjonista.**

kontować *ipf. ekon.* (= *księgować*) enter.

kontra[1] *prep.* + *Nom.* (= *przeciw*) versus; **Gołota kontra Tyson** Gołota vs. Tyson.

kontra[2] *f.* **1.** (= *sprzeciw*) retort. **2.** *karty* double. **3.** *boks* (= *cios*) counterpunch, counterblow. **4.** *sport* (= *kontratak*) counterattack.

kontrabanda *f.* (= *przemyt*) contraband; **kontrabanda wojenna** contraband of war.

kontrabandzista *mp* (= *przemytnik*) contrabandist, smuggler.

kontrabas *mi muz.* double bass, contrabass, bass viol.

kontrabasista *mp muz.* double bass player, contrabassist.

kontrabasowy *a. muz.* double bass, contrabass.

kontradmirał *mp pl.* **-owie** *wojsk.* commodore admiral.

kontrafagot *mi muz.* contrabassoon, double bassoon.

kontrafał *mi żegl.* downhaul.

kontrafałda *f.* box pleat.

kontrahent *mp prawn.* (= *strona umowy*) contracting party, party to a contract.

kontrahentka *f. Gen.pl.* **-ek** *zob.* **kontrahent.**

kontrahować *ipf.* (= *współpracować*) enter into a contract (*z kimś* with sb).

kontrakcja[1] *f.* **1.** *fiz.* (= *kurczenie się*) contraction. **2.** *geol.* contraction. **3.** *jęz.* (= *ściągnięcie*) contraction.

kontrakcja[2] *f.* (= *reakcja*) counteraction.

kontrakt *mi prawn.* (= *umowa*) contract; **podpisać kontrakt** sign a contract (*z kimś* with sb); **zawrzeć kontrakt** enter into a contract (*z kimś* with sb).

kontraktacja *f. roln.* (= *forma skupu*) type of contract for the supply of agricultural products.

kontraktować *ipf.* (= *zawierać transakcję*) enter into a contract (*for supply of sth*) (*z kimś* with sb).

kontraktowy *a.* (= *ustalony, umowny*) contractual; **profesor kontraktowy** *uniw.* adjunct professor; **pracownik/robotnik kontraktowy** casual.

kontralt *mi Gen.* **-u** *muz.* (*głos*) contralto. – *mp Gen.* **-a** *pl.* **-y** *muz.* (*śpiewaczka*) contralto.

kontraltowy *a. muz.* contralto.

kontramarka *f. numizmatyka* countermark, counterstamp.

kontraoktawa *f. muz.* contraoctave.

kontrapost *mi sztuka* contrapposto.

kontrapozycja *f. log.* contraposition.

kontrapunkcista *mp muz.* contrapuntist.

kontrapunkt *mi muz.* counterpoint.

kontrapunktować *ipf. muz.* counterpoint.

kontrapunktowy *a. muz.* contrapuntal.

kontrargument *mi* (= *argument przeciwny*) counterargument.

kontrargumentować *ipf.* (= *oponować*) counter, oppose.

kontrast *mi* **1.** (= *przeciwieństwo*) contrast; **uderzający kontrast** striking contrast. **2.** *fiz., opt.* contrast; **kontrast oświetlenia** *fot.* lighting contrast; **bez kontrastu** (*o fotografii*) flat. **3.** *psych.* contrast. **4.** *med.* (*przy zdjęciach rentgenowskich*) contrast medium.

kontrastować *ipf.* (= *odróżniać się*) contrast, stand in contrast (*z czymś* with *l.* to sth).

kontrastowość *f.* **1.** (= *odróżnianie się*) contrast. **2.** *fot.* (= *wyrazistość*) contrast.

kontrastowy *a.* contrastive, contrasting; **wywoływacz kontrastowy** *fot.* contrast developer; **środek kontrastowy** *med.* contrast medium.

kontrastujący *a.* contrasting.

kontrasygnata *f.* (= *współpodpisanie*) countersign, countersignature.

kontrasygnować *ipf.* countersign.

kontraszot *mi Gen.* **-a** *żegl.* preventer.

kontratak *mi wojsk., sport* counterattack.

kontratakować *ipf.* counterattack.

kontredans *mi pl.* **-e** *l.* **-y** (*taniec lub muzyka do niego*) contredanse, contradance.

kontrgambit *mi szachy* countergambit.

kontrkandydat *mp* (= *rywal*) rival.

kontrkultura *f.* (= *kontestatorski ruch społeczny*) counterculture.

kontrmanewr *mi wojsk.* countermaneuver.

kontrmina *f. wojsk.* countermine.

kontrnatarcie *n. wojsk.* (= *kontrofensywa*) counteroffensive.

kontrnegatyw *mi fot.* copy negative.

kontrofensywa *f. wojsk.* (= *przeciwnatarcie*) counteroffensive.

kontroferta *f. ekon.* (= *kontrpropozycja*) counteroffer.

kontroktawa *f. muz.* contraoctave.

kontrola *f. Gen.pl.* **-i 1.** (= *przegląd, inspekcja*) control, check, checkup, inspection, examination; **kontrola bandery** verification of flag; **kontrola celna** (= *punkt kontrolny l. czynność*) customs; (= *czynność*) customs examination; **kontrola cen** price control; **kontrola dentystyczna** dental checkup *l.* examination; **kontrola kasowa** cash audit; **kontrola graniczna** immigration control; **kontrola jakości** quality control; **kontrola** *l.* **rewizja ksiąg rachunkowych** audit; **kontrola lotów** flight control, air-traffic control; **kontrola osobista** strip search; **kontrola paszportowa** passport control; **kontrola ruchu powietrznego** air-traffic control; **kontrola urodzeń** birth control; **kontrola techniczna** product-quality control; **kontrola zbrojeń** arms control; **kontrola wyrywkowa** spot check; **podlegać kontroli** be subject to control. **2.** (= *władza*) control; **rozciągać** *l.* **mieć nad czymś kontrolę** have control over sth; **wymykać się spod kontroli** get out of control. **3.** *pot.* (= *kontroler*) inspector.

kontroler[1] *mp pl.* **-rzy** (= *inspektor*) inspector; **kontroler biletów** ticket inspector; (= *nadzorca*) supervisor.

kontroler[2] *mi Gen.* **-a** *pl.* **-ry** *techn.* (= *urządzenie kontrolne*) controller, governor.

kontrolerka *f. zob.* **kontroler[1]**.

kontrolerski *a.* inspector's.

kontrolka *f.* **1.** (= *notes*) checklist. **2.** *pot.* (= *lampka sygnalizacyjna*) indicator, pilot lamp; *el.* pilot lamp *l.* light.

kontrolny *a.* of or related to control *l.* inspection; **eksperyment kontrolny** control experiment; **lampka kontrolna** pilot lamp; *el.* pilot light; **jazda kontrolna** *mot.* test drive; **obraz kontrolny** *telew.* test pattern; **odcinek kontrolny** (*czeku, biletu*) counterfoil, stub; **organ kontrolny** supervisory body; **pakiet kontrolny akcji** *ekon.* controlling interest *l.* stake; **posterunek kontrolny** checkpoint; **próba kontrolna** *med.* sample check; **wieża kontrolna** *lotn.* control tower; **badania kontrolne** *med.* medical checkup.

kontrolować *ipf.* **1.** (= *sprawdzać*) control, check, check up, inspect; (*rachunki, księgi*) audit; **kontrolować bilety** inspect tickets. **2.** (= *nadzorować*) supervise, superintend. **3.** (= *decydować, panować*) command; (*np. większość w parlamencie*) hold sway (*coś* over sth). ~ **się** *ipf.* (= *pilnować się*) control o.s.; (*nawzajem*) control each other *l.* one another.

kontroskarżenie *n. prawn.* countercharge.

kontrować *ipf.* **1.** (= *oponować*) counter, oppose. **2.** *karty* double. **3.** *boks* counter.

kontrowersja *f.* (= *polemika, sprzeczność*) controversy.

kontrowersyjnie *adv.* (= *dyskusyjnie*) controversially.

kontrowersyjność *f.* (= *problematyczność*) controversialism, state of being controversial.

kontrowersyjny *a.* (= *problematyczny, niejednoznaczny*) controversial; **kwestia kontrowersyjna** controversial issue, debatable issue.

kontrpropozycja *f.* (= *przeciwny wniosek*) counterproposal.

kontrreformacja *f. rz.-kat.* Counter Reformation.

kontrreformacyjny *a. rz.-kat.* Counter-Reformation.

kontrrewolucja *f.* counterrevolution.

kontrrewolucjonista *mp* counterrevolutionary.

kontrrewolucyjny *a.* counterrevolutionary.

kontrtorpedowiec *mi* **-wc-** *Gen.* **-a** *wojsk.* torpedo boat destroyer.

kontrtytuł *mi druk.* collective *l.* general title.

kontruderzenie *n. wojsk.* (= *przeciwnatarcie*) counteroffensive.

kontrwalacja *f. hist.* contravallation.

kontrwywiad *mi* counterintelligence, counterespionage; **kontrwywiad wojskowy** military counterintelligence.

kontrwywiadowca *mp* (= *agent*) counterspy.

kontrybucja *f.* **1.** *polit.* (= *trybut*) tribute. **2.** *polit.* (= *danina nakładana przez okupanta*) contribution. **3.** *hist.* (*w społeczeństwie feudalnym*) tribute.

kontrybucyjny *a.* **1.** *polit.* tribute. **2.** *polit.* (= *reparacyjny*) contribution. **3.** *hist.* tribute.

kontuar *mi* (= *lada*) counter.

kontur *mi* **1.** (= *kształt*) contour. **2.** *sztuka* (=

obrys) contour. **3.** *fon.* contour; **kontur intonacyjny** intonation contour.

konturować *ipf.* (= *obrysowywać*) contour, trace.

konturowy *a.* contour; **mapa konturowa** *geogr.* contour map; **pióro konturowe** *orn.* contour feather.

konturówka *f. Gen.pl.* **-ek 1.** (= *kredka do ust*) lip liner. **2.** *geogr.* (= *mapa konturowa*) contour map.

kontusz *mi Gen.* **-a** *Gen.pl.* **-y** *l.* **-ów** *hist.* (*ubranie*) type of old Polish robe worn by noblemen.

kontuzja *f.* (= *uraz*) injury; **ulec kontuzji** suffer an injury; **doznać kontuzji nogi** injure one's leg.

kontuzjować *ipf.* (= *spowodować kontuzję*) injure.

kontuzjowany *a.* (= *ranny*) injured.

kontynent *mi* **1.** *zwł. geogr.* (= *część świata*) continent; **czarny kontynent** the Dark Continent, Africa. **2.** (= *Europa*) (*dla Brytyjczyków*) the Continent. **3.** *przest.* (= *ląd*) mainland, continent; **kontynent europejski** mainland Europe; **dryf** *l.* **przesuwanie się kontynentów** *geogr.* continental drift.

kontynentalny *a.* **1.** (= *dotyczący lądu*) continental; **blokada kontynentalna** *hist.* the Continental System; **klimat kontynentalny** *meteor.* continental climate; **Kongres Kontynentalny** *hist.* Continental Congress; **skorupa kontynentalna** *geogr.* continental crust; **Wododział Kontynentalny** *geogr.* Continental Divide; **wzniesienie kontynentalne** *geogr.* (*dna morskiego*) continental rise. **2.** (= *dotyczący Europy*) Continental; **finał kontynentalny** continental final *l.* championships; **śniadanie kontynentalne** continental breakfast.

kontyngent *mi* **1.** *rzad.* (= *przydział*) contingent, ration. **2.** *ekon.* (= *limit*) quota; **kontyngent bezcłowy** duty free quota. **3.** *polit., wojsk.* levy. **4.** *polit.* (= *dostawy obowiązkowe*) levy; **nałożyć na kogoś kontyngent** levy sb, impose a levy on sb.

kontyngentowy *a.* **1.** (= *przydziałowy*) rationed. **2.** *ekon.* quota. **3.** *polit., wojsk.* levied, imposed.

kontynuacja *f.* (= *przedłużanie, ciąg dalszy*) continuation.

kontynuant *mi jęz.* continuant.

kontynuanta *f. fon.* continuant.

kontynuator *mp* continuator.

kontynuatorka *f. Gen.pl.* **-ek** *zob.* **kontynuator**.

kontynuować *ipf.* (= *nie przerywać*) continue, keep, go on; **kontynuować pracę** continue working, keep working, go on with one's work.

kontysta *mp ekon.* (= *księgowy*) bookkeeper.

kontystka *f. Gen.pl.* **-ek** *zob.* **kontysta**.

konurbacja *f.* (= *zespół miejski*) conurbation.

konus *mp pl.* **-y** *pog., iron.* (= *kurdupel*) peanut.

konwalescencja *f. prawn.* coming into effect.

konwalia *f. Gen.* **-ii konwalia majowa** *bot.* lily of the valley (*Convallaria maialis l. majalis*).

konwalidacja *f. prawn.* (= *legalizacja*) validation.

konwaliowy *a.* lily, of or related to lily of the valley.

konwejer *mi Gen.* **-a 1.** *techn.* (= *taśmociąg*) conveyor, conveyer, conveyor belt. **2.** (*sposób przesłuchania*) extended interrogation with sleep deprivation.

konwekcja *f. fiz.* convection.

konwekcyjny *a. fiz.* convectional, convective; **grzejnik konwekcyjny** *techn.* convector.

konwektor *mi Gen.* **-a** *techn.* (= *grzejnik konwekcyjny*) convector.

konwenans *mi pl.* **-e** (= *zwyczaj*) convention; (*in plural*) convenances, etiquette; **odrzucać konwenanse** defy *l.* flout convention.

konwencja[1] *f.* **1.** (= *zwyczaj*) convention. **2.** *polit.* (= *umowa międzynarodowa*) convention; **Konwencja Genewska** Geneva Convention. **3.** *sztuka* (*literacka, filmowa, artystyczna*) (= *styl*) convention; **łamać obowiązujące konwencje** break with conventions.

konwencja[2] *f. polit.* (= *zjazd przedwyborczy*) convention.

konwencjonalizacja *f.* conventionalization.

konwencjonalizm *mi* **1.** (= *konwencjonalność*) conventionalism. **2.** *fil.* conventionalism.

konwencjonalizować *ipf.* (= *czynić konwencjonalnym*) conventionalize.

konwencjonalnie *adv.* (= *kurtuazyjnie*) conventionally.

konwencjonalność *f.* **1.** (= *umowność; kurtuazyjność*) conventionality. **2.** (= *tradycyjność*) conventionalism.

konwencjonalny *a.* **1.** (= *umowny, tradycyjny*) conventional; **broń konwencjonalna** *wojsk.* conventional weapons; **konwencjonalne metody leczenia** *med.* conventional treatment methods. **2.** (= *kurtuazyjny*) conventional.

konwencyjny *a. polit.* conventional.

konwent *mi* **1.** *rel., kośc.* (= *zakon, zgromadzenie*) convent. **2.** *rel., kośc.* (= *kolegium*) chapter, assembly. **3.** *polit.* (= *zebranie*) convention; **konwent seniorów** (*w Sejmie*) Sejm Council of Seniors; (*w Senacie*) Senate Council of Seniors.

konwentowy *a.* **1.** *rel., kośc.* (= *dotyczący zakonu*) conventual. **2.** *rel., kośc.* (= *kolegialny*) conventual. **3.** *polit.* convention.

konwentykiel *mi przest.* conventicle.

konwergencja *f.* **1.** (= *zbieżność*) convergence. **2.** *biol.* convergence. **3.** *med.* (= *ruch zbieżny oka*) convergence.

konwers *mp pl.* **-i** *rel.* person living permanently in a monastery without taking religious vows and usu. performing menial tasks. – *mi pl.* **-y** *log.* converse.

konwersacja *f.* **1.** (= *rozmowa, dialog*) conversation; *rzad.* converse. **2.** *szkoln.* (= *lekcja j. obcego polegająca na rozmowie*) speaking class.

konwersacyjnie *adv.* conversationally.

konwersacyjny *a.* conversational.

konwersatorium *n. sing. indecl. pl.* **-ria** *Gen.* **-riów 1.** *uniw.* seminar. **2.** *kośc.* (= *rozmównica*) parlor, locutorium, locutory.

konwersatoryjny *a.* **1.** *uniw.* seminarial. **2.** *kośc.* of or related to parlor.

konwersja *f. form.* conversion; **dokonać konwersji** convert.

konwersować *ipf. przest.* (= *rozmawiać*) converse (*z kimś* with sb) (*o kimś/czymś* about sb/sth).

konwerter *mi Gen.* **-a 1.** *komp.* converter. **2.** *el.* converter.

konwertor *mi Gen.* **-a 1.** *el.* converter. **2.** *chem.* converter. **3.** *metal.* converter; **konwertor Bessemera** *l.* **bessemerowski** Bessemer converter.

konwertorownia *f. Gen.pl.* **-i** *metal.* converter house *l.* bay.

konwertować *ipf.* **1.** *ekon.* convert. **2.** *komp.* convert.

konwertyta *mp rel.* (= *neofita*) convert, neophyte.

konwikt *mi hist.* (= *szkoła z internatem*) convent school.

konwisarstwo *n.* (= *ludwisarstwo*) foundry.

konwisarz *mp Gen.pl.* **-y** *l.* **-ów** (= *ludwisarz*) founder.

konwojent *mp* (= *członek eskorty*) escort.

konwojować *ipf.* (= *eskortować*) escort.

konwój *mi* **-o-** *Gen.pl.* **-ów 1.** (= *eskorta*) escort. **2.** (= *kolumna pojazdów*) convoy.

konwulsje *pl. Gen.* **-i** (= *drgawki*) convulsions; **doprowadzać kogoś do konwulsji** make sb curl up; **dostać konwulsji** *l.* **drgawek** go into convulsions.

konwulsyjnie *adv.* (= *spazmatycznie*) convulsively.

konwulsyjny *a.* **1.** (= *spazmatyczny*) convulsive. **2.** (= *przypominający konwulsje*) convulsionary.

koń *ma Ins.pl.* **-mi** *zool.* horse (*Equus caballus*); **dosiadać konia** mount a horse; **jeździć na koniu** ride a horse; **koń arabski** Arab horse; **koń angielski** English Thoroughbred; **koń Przewalskiego** *zool.* Przewalski's horse (*Equus caballus przewalskii*); **koń morski** *zool.* walrus, morse (*Odobenus rosmarus*); **koń mechaniczny** *fiz.* horsepower; **żołnierz/policjant na koniu** mounted soldier/policeman; **na koń!** to horse!, mount up!; **konia z rzędem temu, kto zna odpowiedź** I'll give half my kingdom to the one who knows the answer; **jechać co koń wyskoczy** ride like the wind; **koń by się uśmiał** it's so funny I forgot to laugh; **można z nim konie kraść** he'd lay down in traffic for you, he'd walk a mile in the rain to help you out; **zjadłbym konia z kopytami** I could eat a horse; **pracować jak koń** work like a dog *l.* horse; **napracowałem** *l.* **naharowałem się jak koń** I feel like I've been ridden hard and put away wet; **znamy się jak łyse konie** I know him/her like I know myself, I know him/her better than I know myself; **robić kogoś w konia** pull a fast one on sb; **być czarnym koniem** be a dark horse; **koń trojański** Trojan horse; **zdrowy jak koń** as fit as a fiddle; **uradowany, jakby go kto na sto koni wsadził** happy as a clam at high tide; **baba z wozu, koniom lżej** one down and easier to go, every little bit helps; **królestwo za konia** my kingdom for a horse; **darowanemu koniowi nie zagląda się w zę-** by you don't look a gift horse in the mouth; **jeśli spaść, to z dobrego konia** it's better to fail aiming high than to succeed aiming low; **koń ma cztery nogi, a potknie się** it's a good horse that never stumbles; **łaska pańska na pstrym koniu jeździ** being in your master's good graces doesn't last forever, your good fortune can be changed by a twist of fate; **pańskie oko konia tuczy** looking after your possessions brings good results, the eye of a master does more work than both his hands; **koń jaki jest każdy widzi** it's as plain as the nose on your face. – *mi Gen.* **-a** *Ins.pl.* **-mi 1.** (*zabawka*) toy horse; **koń na biegunach** rocking horse. **2.** *sport* (= *kozioł*) (vaulting *l.* long) horse. **3.** *szachy* (= *skoczek*) knight, horse. **4.** *wulg.* (= *penis*) prick, dick; **walić konia** jerk off; *Br.* toss off.

końca *itd.* *mi zob.* **koniec.**

końcowy *a.* (= *ostatni*) final, closing, latter; **końcowy gwizdek** final whistle; **końcowy rozdział książki** closing chapter of a book; **końcowa część filmu** closing scenes; **efekt końcowy** end result; **egzaminy końcowe** *uniw., szkoln.* finals; **przystanek końcowy** terminus; **rym końcowy** tail-rhyme.

końcówka *f. Gen.pl.* **-ek 1.** (= *resztka*) remnant, end; (*np. cygara, ołówka*) stub. **2.** *el.* (= *element na końcu przewodu*) terminal. **3.** *jęz.* ending, termination; **końcówka fleksyjna** desinence. **4.** *sport* finish; **wyrównana końcówka** close finish. **5.** *szachy* end game. **6.** *techn.* tip; end; terminal.

kończyć *ipf.* **1.** (= *finalizować*) finish, end, conclude; **kończyć obiad** finish one's dinner; **kończyć książkę** finish one's book; **kończyć na czymś** stop at sth; **skończyć pracę** finish work, knock off, call it a day; **skończyć szkołę średnią** graduate (from secondary school); **kończyć studia** graduate (from university *l.* college); **jutro kończę 25 lat** I will be *l.* turn 25 tomorrow; **skończyła naukę w wieku 15 lat** she left school at 15; **skończył medycynę/geografię** he has a degree in medicine/geography. **2.** (= *zrywać z czymś*) be through (*z kimś/czymś* with sb/sth). **3.** *rzad.* (= *umierać*) die. **~ się** *ipf.* **1.** (= *dobiegać końca*) end, come to an end; **skończyć się fiaskiem/sukcesem** result in *l.* lead to failure/success; **skończyć się rozwodem** end in divorce; **świat się na tym nie kończy** it's not the end of the world; **wszystko dobre, co się dobrze kończy** all's well that ends well; **niekończący się** neverending. **2.** (= *wyczerpywać się*) run out; **kończą nam się pieniądze** we're running out of money, the money's running out; **moja cierpliwość się kończy** my patience is wearing thin. **3.** *pot.* (= *tracić energię*) become dead beat, become dog-tired, be done in.

kończyna *f.* (= *ręka, noga, łapa*) limb, extremity; **kończyna dolna** lower extremity; **kończyna górna** upper extremity, forelimb; **kończyna przednia** foreleg; **kończyna tylna** hind leg; **kończyna fantomowa** *med.* (*po amputacji*) phantom limb.

koński *a.* **1.** (= *dotyczący konia*) equine, horsy; horse; **włosie końskie** horsehair. **2.** (= *podobny do konia*) horse-like; **koński ogon** (*fryzura*) ponytail; **końska dawka** mammoth dose, heroic dose; **końskie zdrowie** robust health; **mieć końskie zdrowie** be (as) fit as a fiddle; **koński śmiech** horselaugh; **końskie okulary** blinkers; (*przen.*) narrow-mindedness; **końska twarz** horsy face.

kooperacja *f.* (= *współpraca*) cooperation.

kooperacyjny *a.* cooperative.

kooperant *mp* (= *podwykonawca*) subcontractor.

kooperować *ipf.* (= *współpracować*) cooperate (*z kimś* with sb).

kooptacja *f.* (= *dołączenie*) co-option, co-optation.

kooptować *ipf.* (= *dołączać*) coopt, co-opt.

koordynacja *f.* (= *zharmonizowanie, współdziałanie*) coordination; **koordynacja ruchowa** *l.* **motoryczna** *fizj.* motor coordination; **brak koordynacji ruchów** *pat.* incoordination.

koordynacyjny *a.* coordinative.

koordynata *f. mat.* coordinate.

koordynator *mp pl.* **-rzy** (= *organizator*) coordinator. – *mi Gen.* **-a** *pl.* **-ry** (= *instytucja, rzecz itp. koordynująca*) coordinator; (= *czynnik koordynujący*) coordinating factor.

koordynować *ipf.* (= *harmonizować*) coordinate.

kop *mi* (*pot.*) **1.** (= *kopnięcie, kopniak*) kick; **dać komuś kopa** kick sb, give sb a kick. **2.** (= *bodziec, zachęta do działania*) kick, spur; **potrzeba mu dobrego** *l.* **porządnego kopa** he needs a good kick in the pants. **3.** (= *efekt działania alkoholu, narkotyków*) kick, rush; **dawać niezłego kopa** give a good kick.

kopa *f. Gen.pl.* **kop** *l.* **kóp 1.** *przest.* (= *sześćdziesiąt sztuk*) threescore. **2.** (= *mnóstwo*) dozens; **kopę lat!** (*przy spotkaniu dawno niewidzianej osoby*) long time no see!; **kopę lat go nie widziałem** I haven't seen him for donkey's years, I haven't seen him for ages; **czegoś jest na kopy** there are dozens *l.* loads of sth. **3.** *roln.* (= *stóg*) stack; **kopa siana** haystack. **4.** (= *góra*) dome.

kopacz *mp Gen.pl.* **-y** *l.* **-ów 1.** (= *osoba kopiąca*) digger. **2.** *górn.* (= *rębacz*) hewer. **3.** *pot.* (= *marny piłkarz*) third-rate *l.* lousy soccer player.

kopaczka[1] *f. Gen.pl.* **-ek** *roln.* (*maszyna rolnicza*) digger, crop-lifter; (= *motyka*) hoe.

kopaczka[2] *f. Gen.pl.* **-ek** *roln.* (= *kobieta kopiąca ziemniaki*) potato digger.

kopać *ipf.* **-ię -iesz 1.** (= *uderzać nogą*) kick; **kopać leżącego** kick sb when they are down; **niech cię gęś kopnie!** damn you! **2.** (= *ryć*) dig, excavate; **kopać łopatą** dig with a spade, spade; **samemu sobie grób kopać** dig one's own grave; **kto pod kim dołki kopie, sam w nie wpada** hoist with one's own petard. **3.** (= *wykopywać*) dig, excavate; **kopać kartofle** lift *l.* dig up potatoes. **4.** *pot.* (*o broni*) (= *odrzucać*) kick, recoil, jerk back. **5.** *pot.* (*o płodzie*) kick. **6.** *pot.* (= *porażać*) zap, bite.

kopaiwa *f.* **1.** *bot.* copaiba, copaiva (*Copaifera*). **2.** (= *balsam z kopaiwy*) copaiba, copaiva.

kopaiwowy *a.* copaiba, copaiva; **balsam kopaiwowy** copaiba balm *l.* resin.

kopal *mi* (*żywica*) copal.

kopalina *f. górn.* mineral (*obtained by mining*).

kopalnia *f. Gen.pl.* **-i** *l.* **-ń 1.** *górn.* mine, pit; **kopalnia odkrywkowa** strip *l.* open-pit mine; **kopalnia złota/soli/węgla** gold/salt/coal mine; **kopalnia złota** *przen.* (= *źródło wielkich dochodów*) gold mine. **2.** *przen.* (= *źródło wiedzy*) mine, store; **kopalnia wiedzy** mine of information.

kopalniak *mi Gen.* **-a** *górn.* pitwood, pitprop, pit timber.

kopalniany *a. górn.* mining, of or related to a mine *l.* pit; **gaz kopalniany** firedamp; **szyb kopalniany** pit shaft, pit; **wózek kopalniany** tram, tub.

kopalnictwo *n. górn.* (= *górnictwo*) mining.

kopalny *a.* **1.** (= *górniczy, wydobywczy*) mined; min(e)able; **paliwo kopalne** fossil fuel. **2.** (= *prehistoryczny*) fossil; **człowiek kopalny** fossil man (*any of the extinct primitive species of man*).

kopanina *f.* **1.** (= *kopanie w ziemi*) aimless and/or chaotic digging. **2.** *iron.* (= *marna gra w piłkę nożną*) shitty play, crappy performance.

kopara *f. pot. pog. l. żart.* **1.** (= *koparka*) excavator, steam shovel. **2.** (= *szczęka*) jaw; **kopara** *l.* **szczęka mu opadła** (*ze zdziwienia*) his jaw dropped.

koparka *f. Gen.pl.* **-ek** (*maszyna*) excavator, steam shovel.

kopcić *ipf.* **1.** (= *dymić*) smoke. **2.** *pot.* (= *palić papierosy*) smoke, puff (on); **kopcić fajkę** puff on a pipe. **~ się** *ipf.* (= *tlić się*) smoke, smolder.

kopciuszek *mp* **-szk- 1.** (*postać*) Cinderella. **2.** (= *popychadło*) Cinderella. – *ma* **-szk-** *orn.* redstart (*Phoenicurus*).

kopcować *ipf.* (= *dołować*) pit; *Br.* clamp; **kopcować warzywa** pit vegetables.

kopczyk *mi Gen.* **-a** (= *mała górka*) mound, hillock.

kopczykować *ipf. ogr., roln.* (= *okopywać*) earth up.

kopeć *mi* **-pci-** *Gen.* **-a** *l.* **-u 1.** (= *sadza*) soot. **2.** (= *dym z sadzą*) soot-filled smoke.

Kopenhaga *f. geogr.* Copenhagen.

kopenhaski *a.* Copenhagen.

kopenhażanin *mp* Copenhagener.

kopenhażanka *f. zob.* **kopenhażanin.**

koper *mi* **-pr-** *bot.* dill (*Anethum graveolens*); **koper morski** *bot.* samphire (*Crithmum maritimum*); **koper włoski** *bot.* fennel (*Foeniculum vulgare*).

koperek *mi* **-rk-** *kulin.* dill; **pęczek koperku** bunch of dill leaves.

koperkowy *a. kulin.* dill; **zupa koperkowa** dill soup; **sos koperkowy** dill sauce.

Kopernik *mp* Copernicus; **Mikołaj Kopernik** Nicolaus Copernicus.

kopernikański *a. zob.* **kopernikowski.**

kopernikowski *a. astron.* Copernican; **system kopernikowski** Copernican System.

koperta *f.* **1.** (*na list*) envelope. **2.** (= *powłoka*) quilt cover. **3.** (= *płaska torebka*) clutch (bag *l.* purse. **4.** (*zegarka*) watchcase; **zegarek z kopertą** hunter *l.* hunting watch. **5.** *pot.* (= *łapówka*) bribe (*esp. a sum of money given in an envelope*).

kopertować *ipf.* (= *wkładać do kopert*) put into envelopes and seal.

kopertówka *f. Gen.pl.* **-ek 1.** (= *płaska torebka*) clutch (bag *l.* purse). **2.** bribe (*esp. a sum of money given in an envelope*).

kopia[1] *f. Gen.* **-ii** (= *duplikat*) copy; (*dzieła sztuki, obrazu*) reproduction; (*rzeźby*) replica; (*dokumentu*) counterpart, copy; (= *odbitka*) print; **wierna kopia** faithful copy; (*o osobie*) clone; *komp.* backup (copy).

kopia[2] *f. Gen.* **-ii 1.** *hist.* (= *lanca*) (tilting) lance; **kruszyć kopie** lock horns, go to battle (*o kogoś/coś* over sb/sth). **2.** *hist.* (= *drużyna*) knight's entourage.

kopiał *mi* **1.** (= *bloczek pozwalający zachować kopię*) copybook. **2.** *techn.* (= *wzornik*) template, templet.

kopiarka *f. Gen.pl.* **-ek 1.** *techn.* (= *kopiorama*) printing frame. **2.** *film* printer, printing machine. **3.** *techn.* (= *obrabiarka*) tracing machine, tracer *l.* copying lathe. **4.** *pot.* (= *kserokopiarka*) copier, copy(ing) machine.

kopiasto *adv.* (= *czubato*) in a heap.

kopiasty *a.* (= *czubaty*) heaping; *Br.* heaped; **kopiasta łyżka** heaping spoonful.

kopiec *mi* **-pc-** *Gen.* **-a 1.** (= *pryzma*) mound, heap. **2.** (= *sztuczne wzniesienie*) mound, hill; **usypać kopiec** mound, heap, hill; **Kopiec Wandy** a large mound created in honor of Wanda, a legendary Polish heroine; **Kopiec Kościuszki** a large mound created in honor of Tadeusz Kosciuszko; **Kopiec Piłsudskiego** a large mound created in honor of Jozef Pilsudski. **3.** *archeol.* barrow, tumulus. **4.** *roln.* mound; *Br.* clamp.

kopiejka *f. Gen.pl.* **-ek** (*moneta*) kopeck, kopek, copeck.

kopieniactwo *n. hist., archeol.* manually tilling fields with a hoe.

kopijnik *mp hist.* (= *rycerz uzbrojony w kopię*) lance-armed knight.

kopiorama *f. druk.* printing-down frame.

kopiować *ipf.* **1.** (= *powielać*) copy, duplicate, reproduce. **2.** *przen.* (= *naśladować*) copy, imitate. **3.** *komp.* copy.

kopiowy *a.* copying; **ołówek kopiowy** indelible pencil; **rama kopiowa** *druk.* zob. **kopiorama**.

kopista *mp* (= *osoba sporządzająca kopie; skryba*) copyist, copier.

kopnąć *pf.* **-ij** zob. **kopać**; **kopnąć w kalendarz** *pot.* kick the bucket, croak. **~ się** *pf.* **1.** (= *uderzyć siebie nogą*) kick o.s. **2.** (= *pobiec*) trot off; **kopnąć się po kogoś/coś** trot off to fetch sb/sth.

kopniak *mi Gen.* **-a** kick; **dostać kopniaka** (= *zostać uderzonym nogą*) get a kick; (= *zostać wyrzuconym z pracy*) get the sack, be *l.* get fired.

kopnięcie *n.* **1.** (= *kopniak*) kick. **2.** *pot.* (= *odrzut*) kick, recoil. **3.** *pot.* (= *ruch płodu*) kick.

kopnięty *a.* **1.** (= *uderzony*) kicked. **2.** *pot.* (= *szalony*) nuts.

kopny *a.* (*śnieg, piasek*) obstructive, blocking, hindering.

kopolimer *mi chem.* copolymer.

kopolimeryzacja *f. chem.* copolymerization.

kopra *f.* (= *wysuszony miąższ kokosów*) copra.

koprocesor *mi Gen.* **-a** *komp.* coprocessor.

koproducent *mp* (= *kooperant*) coproducer.

koprodukcja *f.* (= *współpraca*) coproduction.

koprodukcyjny *a.* coproduction.

koprofag *ma biol.* coprophagist.

koprofagia *f. Gen.* **-ii** *biol., pat.* coprophagia, coprophagy.

koprolalia *f. psych.* coprolalia.

koprolit *mi* **1.** *roln.* (= *nawóz naturalny*) coprolith. **2.** *paleont.* (= *ekskrementy zwierząt kopalnych*) coprolite.

kopsnąć *pf.* **-ij 1.** *pot.* (= *dać*) give; **kopsnij no szluga** gimme a fag, will you? **2.** *pot.* (= *kopać*) kick.

Kopt *mp pl.* **-owie** Copt.

Koptyjka *f. Gen.pl.* **-ek** zob. **Kopt**.

koptyjski *a.* Coptic; **kościół koptyjski** *rel.* Coptic Church.

kopula *f. Gen.pl.* **-i 1.** *jęz.* (= *łącznik*) copula. **2.** *muz.* coupler.

kopulacja *f. fizj.* (= *stosunek płciowy*) copulation, coitus.

kopulacyjny *a. fizj.* copulatory; **narządy kopulacyjne** copulatory organs.

kopulasty *a.* (= *wypukły*) cupola-shaped, cupolaed, dome-shaped.

kopulować *ipf. fizj.* copulate (*z kimś/czymś* with sb/sth).

kopuła *f.* **1.** *bud.* (= *sklepienie*) dome, cupola. **2.** *geol.* dome.

kopułka *f. Gen.pl.* **-ek** *bud.* (= *mała kopuła*) cupola.

kopułowy *a. bud.* domical, domic, cupola-shaped.

kopystka *f. Gen.pl.* **-ek** (= *łyżka, łopatka*) paddle.

kopytka *pl. Gen.* **-tek** *kulin.* (= *kluski z kartofli*) potato dumplings.

kopytne *pl. Gen.* **-ych** *zool.* ungulates (*Ungulata*).

kopyto *n.* **1.** (= *racica*) hoof; **zaryć kopytami** (*o koniu*) balk (*przed czymś* at sth); **ruszyć z kopyta** light out, tear off; **zjadłbym konia z kopytami** I could eat a horse; **wyciągnąć kopyta** *pot.* kick the bucket; **skarżypyta bez kopyta** *pog.* tattletale, snitch. **2.** *techn.* (*przyrząd szewski*) last; **robić wszystko na jedno kopyto** do everything after one fashion; **przerobić kogoś na swoje kopyto** fashion sb after one's own mold.

kopytowy *a.* ungual, ungular.

kora[1] *f.* **1.** *bot.* bark; **kora chinowa** *med.* cinchona (bark). **2.** *anat.* cortex; **kora mózgowa** cerebral cortex; **kora nadnercza** renal cortex. **3.** *tk.* seersucker.

kora[2] *f. sztuka* (= *posąg dziewczyny*) kore.

korab *mi* **-bi-** *Gen.* **-a** *Gen.pl.* **-ów** *l.* **-i** *poet.* (= *łódź, okręt*) vessel.

koral *ma Gen.* **-a** *Gen.pl.* **-i** *l.* **-ów** *zool.* (= *koralowiec*) coral (*Anthozoa*); **koral szlachetny** *l.* **czerwony** precious coral, red *l.* rose coral (*Corallium rubrum*). **– mi Gen.** **-a** *Gen.pl.* **-i** *l.* **-ów 1.** (*zwykle pl.*) (= *naszyjnik*) (necklace of) beads. **2.** *orn.* (*zwykle pl.*) (= *narośl u ptaków*) wattle. **– mi Gen.** **-u** *tylko sing.* (*kolor*) coral.

koralik *mi Gen.* **-a** (= *paciorek*) bead.
koralka *f. bot.* coral weed (*Corallina*).
koralowce *pl. Gen.* **-ów** *zool.* anthozoans (*Anthozoa*).
koralowina *f.* (= *szkielet korala czerwonego*) coral.
koralowy *a.* 1. *zool.* (= *związany z koralowcami*) coral, coralline; **rafa koralowa** coral reef; **Wielka Rafa Koralowa** *geogr.* the Great Barrier Reef; **wyspa koralowa** coral island. 2. (= *dotyczący koralowiny*) coral, coralline. 3. (*kolor*) coral-red; **drzewo koralowe** *bot.* coral tree, coral bean tree (*Erythrina collarodendron*); **bez koralowy** *bot.* European red elder (*Sambucus racemosa*); **kalina koralowa** *bot.* guelder rose (*Viburnum opulus*).
Koran *mi rel.* Koran, Quran; **wyznawcy Koranu** followers of the Koran.
koraniczny *a. rel.* Koranic.
korba *f. techn.* crank, winch; **kręcić korbą** crank; **odbiła mu korba** *pot.* he went nuts.
korbka *f. Gen.pl.* **-ek** (= *mała korba*) crank, winch.
korbowód *mi* **-o-** *techn.* connecting rod, link rod.
korbowy *a. techn.* (= *związany z korbą*) crank; (= *napędzany korbą*) cranked; **czop korbowy** crankpin; **wał korbowy** crankshaft.
korcić *ipf.* (= *kusić, intrygować*) tempt; **korci mnie, żeby to zrobić** I am itching to do it.
kord[1] *mi Gen.* **-u** *tk.* cord.
kord[2] *mi Gen.* **-a** *hist.* (= *miecz*) sword.
kordegarda *f. hist.* (= *odwach*) guardhouse.
kordelas *mi Gen.* **-a** (= *nóż myśliwski*) hunting knife (*usu. ornamented*); bowie knife.
Kordelierzy *pl. Gen.* **-ów** *hist.* Cordeliers (*political club in Paris*).
kordialność *f. lit.* (= *serdeczność*) cordiality.
kordialny *a. lit.* (= *serdeczny*) cordial.
kordiał *mi* 1. *przest. l. lit.* (= *nalewka*) cordial. 2. *przest.* (= *stymulujący lek*) cordial.
kordieryt *mi min.* cordierite.
kordon *mi* 1. (= *obstawa, szpaler*) cordon; **otoczyć kordonem** cordon off. 2. (= *posterunki straży granicznej*) border guards. 3. *przen.* (= *bariera*) border.
kordonek *mi* **-nk-** *Gen.* **-u** *l.* **-a** *tk.* (*nić*) chenille.
Kordyliery *pl. Gen.* **-ów** *geogr.* the Cordilleras.
kordylina *f. bot.* dracaena, dracena (*Cordyline*).
kordyt *mi* (= *proch*) cordite.
kordzik *mi Gen.* **-a** (= *sztylet*) dagger, poniard (*worn e.g. by Polish air force officers*).
Korea *f. Gen.* **-ei** *geogr.* Korea; **Korea Południowa** South Korea; **Korea Północna** North Korea.
Koreanka *f. Gen.pl.* **-ek** *zob.* **Koreańczyk**.
Koreańczyk *mp* Korean.
koreański *a.* Korean.
koreczek *mi kulin.* canapé.
koreferat *mi* (= *polemika*) polemic report.
korek *mi* **-rk-** *Gen.* **-a** 1. *bot.* cork. 2. (= *surowiec z kory*) cork. 3. (= *zamknięcie butelki*) cork. 4. *pot.* (= *zator*) jam; **korek uliczny** traffic jam. 5.

pot. (= *bezpiecznik*) fuse. 6. *pot.* (= *zatyczka*) plug.
korekcja *f. rzad.* (= *korekta, naprawa*) correction.
korekcyjny *a.* corrective; **papier korekcyjny** correction paper; **gimnastyka korekcyjna** remedial *l.* corrective exercises.
korekta *f.* 1. (= *poprawianie*) correction. 2. *druk.* (= *adiustacja*) proofreading. 3. *med.* (= *operacja plastyczna*) plastic surgery. 4. *pot.* (= *odbitka korektorska*) proof.
korektor[1] *mp pl.* **-rzy** (= *adiustator*) proofreader.
korektor[2] *mi Gen.* **-a** *pl.* **-ry** 1. (= *pisak do korekty*) whiteout marker; (= *płyn do korekty*) whiteout. 2. *el., tel.* equalizer; **korektor graficzny** graphic equalizer. 3. (*w kosmetyce*) cover stick.
korektorka *f. Gen.pl.* **-ek** *zob.* **korektor[1]**.
korektorski *a.* proofreader's; **znaki korektorskie** proofreader's marks.
korektura *f.* (= *korekta*) (*w kodeksie, ustawie*) amendment; (= *adiustacja*) proofreading.
korektywa *f. lit.* (= *poprawka*) correction.
korelacja *f. form.* (= *współzależność*) correlation.
korelacyjny *a.* (= *współzależny*) correlate, correlational.
korelat *mi* (= *odpowiednik*) correlate.
korelatywny *a.* (= *współzależny*) correlative.
korelować *ipf.* (= *łączyć, łączyć się*) correlate.
korepetycje *pl. Gen.* **-i** 1. (= *prywatne lekcje*) private lessons, tutoring, coaching; **udzielać korepetycji** give private lessons, coach. 2. (= *przygotowanie śpiewaków, chóru, baletu do występu*) coaching.
korepetytor *mp* 1. (= *nauczyciel*) coach, private instructor, tutor. 2. (*chóru, baletu*) coach.
korepetytorka *f. Gen.pl.* **-ek** *zob.* **korepetytor**.
korespondencja *f.* 1. (= *pisanie listów*) correspondence; **prowadzić** *l.* **utrzymywać z kimś korespondencję** carry on *l.* keep up a correspondence with sb. 2. (= *zbiór listów*) mail, letters, correspondence. 3. (= *rodzaj reportażu*) correspondence, report.
korespondencyjnie *adv.* (= *listownie*) by mail.
korespondencyjny *a.* (= *listowy; reporterski*) correspondence; **kurs korespondencyjny** correspondence course.
korespondent *mp* 1. (= *osoba pisząca listy*) correspondent. 2. (= *reporter*) correspondent; **korespondent wojenny** war correspondent; **korespondent zagraniczny** foreign correspondent; **członek-korespondent** corresponding member.
korespondentka *f. Gen.pl.* **-ek** *zob.* **korespondent**.
korespondować *ipf.* 1. (= *pisać listy*) correspond, exchange letters (*z kimś* with sb). 2. *przest.* (= *odpowiadać czemuś*) correspond (*z czymś* with *l.* to sth).
korgi *ma indecl. kynol.* (Welsh) corgi.
korki[1] *pl. Gen.* **-ów** *piłka nożna* (= *buty piłkarskie*) cleats.

korki² *pl. Gen.* **-ów** *pot.* (= *korepetycje*) private lessons.

korkociąg *mi* **1.** (*do butelek*) corkscrew. **2.** *lotn.* (*figura akrobacji*) spin, tailspin.

korkodąb *mi bot.* (= *dąb korkowy*) cork oak (*Quercus suber*).

korkowacieć *ipf. bot.* suberize.

korkować *ipf.* **1.** (= *zamykać butelkę*) cork (up). **2.** (= *blokować*) jam. **3.** *pot.* (= *umierać*) kick the bucket.

korkowiec *mi* **1.** (*zabawka*) popgun. **2.** *zool.* soft coral, red finger coral, red duster coral (*Alcyonium palmatum*). **3.** *bot.* **korkowiec amurski** Amur corktree (*Phallodendron amurense*).

korkowina *f. bot.* cork, phellem.

korkownica *f.* bottle corker.

korkowy *a.* (= *zrobiony z korka*) cork; (= *podobny do korka*) cork-like; **drewno korkowe** cork wood; **dąb korkowy** *bot.* cork oak, cork tree (*Quercus suber*); **kwas korkowy** *chem.* suberic acid.

kormofit *mi. bot.* cormophyte.

kormoran *ma orn.* cormorant (*Phalacrocorax*); **kormoran czubaty** green cormorant, shag (*Ph. aristotelis*); **kormoran czarny** great cormorant (*Ph. carbo*); **kormoran peruwiański** Guanay cormorant (*Ph. bougainvillii*).

kornak *mp* (= *dozorca słoni*) mahout.

kornecista *mp* (*muzyk*) cornetist, cornettist.

kornel *mi* (*drewno*) dogwood.

korner *mi Gen.* **-a 1.** *sport* (= *rzut rożny*) corner kick, corner. **2.** *ekon.* corner.

kornet¹ *mi Gen.* **-u** (= *czepiec*) (*t. zakonnicy*) cornet.

kornet² *mi Gen.* **-a** *hist., wojsk.* (*oficer*) (*jednostka*) cornet.

kornet³ *mi Gen.* **-u** *muz.* (*instrument*) cornet, cornet à pistons.

kornie *adv.* (= *pokornie*) humbly.

kornik *ma ent.* bark beetle (*Scolytidae*).

korniszon *mi Gen.* **-a** (= *ogórek marynowany*) gherkin, cornichon.

Kornwalia *f. Gen.* **-ii** *geogr.* Cornwall.

Kornwalijczyk *mp* Cornishman.

Kornwalijka *f. Gen.pl.* **-ek** Cornishwoman.

kornwalijski *a.* Cornish.

korny *a. żart., lit.* (= *pokorny*) humble.

korodować *ipf.* corrode.

korona *f.* **1.** (*symbol władzy*) crown; **korona królewska** king's crown, royal crown; **korona cesarska** emperor's crown, imperial crown; **strącić komuś koronę z głowy** dethrone sb, overthrow sb's rule; **korona ci z głowy nie spadnie** *iron.* it won't tarnish your reputation, it won't bring any dishonor to you. **2.** (= *władza*) crown, Crown; **zdobyć koronę** establish one's rule, seize power; **sięgać po koronę** win the crown, take the crown; **pretendent do korony** pretender to the throne. **3.** (= *przybranie głowy*) crown, wreath; **korona z liści laurowych** laurel wreath; **korona Słońca** *l.* **słoneczna** *astron.* corona; **korona** *l.* **szachownica cesarska** *bot.* crown imperial (*Fritillaria imperialis*); **korona cierniowa** crown of thorns; **korona męczeństwa** crown of martyr-

dom. **4.** (= *konary i gałęzie*) crown, tree top. **5.** *bot.* (*część okwiatu*) corolla. **6.** (*waluta*) crown; (*w Danii i Norwegii*) krone; (*w Szwecji*) krona; (*w Islandii*) króna; (*w Czechach i na Słowacji*) koruna; *hist.* (*w Austrii*) krone. **7.** *przen.* (= *uwieńczenie*) crown, culmination; **zdobyć koronę Himalajów** climb all the 8000 m peaks of the Himalayas. **8.** *anat.* (*część zęba*) crown. **9.** *dent.* (= *koronka*) crown, artificial crown. **10.** *bud.* coping, crown; **korona drogi** crown. **11.** (= *monarchia*) crown. **12.** *muz.* (= *fermata*) fermata, hold, pause. **13.** *karty* (= *pięć honorów*) five honors; (= *cztery asy*) four aces.

koronacja *f.* coronation, crowning.

koronacyjny *a.* coronation.

koronarografia *f. Gen.* **-ii** *med.* coronarography.

koronarograficzny *a. med.* coronarographic.

koroner *mp prawn.* (= *sędzia śledczy*) coroner.

koroniec *ma* crowned pigeon (*Goura*).

koronium *n. chem.* coronium.

koronka *f.* **1.** (*tkanina*) lace; **koronka igłowa** point lace, needlepoint lace, needlepoint; **koronka klockowa** bobbin lace. **2.** *rel.* (*modlitwa*) chaplet; **odmawiać koronkę** say chaplets. **3.** *dent.* (= *proteza*) crown. **4.** *górn.* core bit.

koronkarka *f. Gen.pl.* **-ek 1.** (*kobieta wyrabiająca koronki*) lace maker. **2.** *tk.* (*maszyna produkująca koronki*) lace machine.

koronkarski *a.* lace-making.

koronkarstwo *n. tk.* lace making.

koronkarz *mp* lace maker.

koronkowy *a.* **1.** (= *ażurowy*) lacy, openwork. **2.** (= *kunsztowny*) fine, delicate; **koronkowa robota** meticulous work.

koronny *a.* **1.** *hist.* (*dotyczący monarchy*) royal, crown; **dobra koronne** royal lands, royal property, crown land; **insygnia koronne** royal insignia. **2.** *hist.* (*dotyczący Korony*) Crown. **3.** (= *najważniejszy*) key, major; **koronny argument** conclusive argument; **świadek koronny** key witness.

koronograf *mi astron.* coronagraph, coronograph.

koronować *ipf.* **1.** (*przekazywać władzę monarsze*) crown. **2.** *przen.* (= *finalizować*) crown. **~ się** *ipf.* (= *stawać się królem*) be crowned; **koronować się na króla** be crowned king.

koronowany *a.* crowned; **koronowana głowa** (= *monarcha*) crowned head.

koronowy *a.* (*dotyczący korony*) crown; *bot.* corollaceous; **nakrętka koronowa** *techn.* castellated nut.

korować *ipf. techn.* (*usuwać korę*) bark, decorticate. **~ się** *ipf.* (*o pniu, drewnie*) bark, peel.

korowarka *f. Gen.pl.* **-ek** *techn.* (*maszyna*) barker, barking machine.

korowiec *mi ent.* flatbug (*Aradus*); **korowiec sosnowy** pine bark bug (*A. cinnamomeus*).

korowina *f. bot.* outer bark.

korowodowy *a.* (= *orszakowy*) pageant, processional.

korowody *pl. Gen.* **-ów** *pot.* (= *ceregiele*) rigmarole, rigamarole.

korowód *mi* -o- (= *orszak*) pageant, parade.
korowódka *f. Gen.pl.* -ek *ent.* (*ćma*) European caterpillar moth (*Thaumetopoea pityocampa*).
korowy *a.* 1. *bot.* bark. 2. *anat.* cortical.
korozja *f.* 1. *techn.* (= *rdzewienie*) corrosion. 2. *geol.* (= *erozja*) corrasion.
korozyjny *a.* 1. *techn.* corrosive. 2. *geol.* corrasive.
korówka *f. Gen.pl.* -ek **bawełnica korówka** *ent.* wooly apple aphid (*Eriosoma lanigerum*).
korówkowy *a.* **osiec korówkowy** *ent.* woolly apple aphid parasitoid (*Aphelinus mali*).
korporacja *f.* 1. *ekon.* corporation, company. 2. (= *stowarzyszenie*) corporation, society; **korporacja studencka** (*męska*) fraternity; (*żeńska*) sorority.
korporacyjny *a.* corporate, corporative.
korporał *mi rel., kość.* corporal, corporale.
korporant *mp,* **korporantka** *f. Gen.pl.* -ek student fraternity member.
korpulentny *a.* (= *gruby*) stout, corpulent.
korpus *mi* 1. *anat.* (= *tułów*) trunk, torso. 2. *bud., techn.* (= *trzon*) body. 3. *wojsk.* corps; **korpus oficerski** officers' corps. 4. (= *zespół*) corps; **korpus dyplomatyczny** *polit.* diplomatic corps; **korpus konsularny** *polit.* consular corps. 5. *druk.* long primer. 6. *jęz.* corpus; **korpus tekstów** text corpus.
korpuskularny *a. fiz.* (= *cząsteczkowy*) corpuscular; **promieniowanie korpuskularne** corpuscular radiation.
korral *mi* (*zagroda*) corral.
korrida *f.* (*walka z bykiem*) bullfight, corrida.
korsak *ma zool.* corsac fox (*Vulpes corsac*).
korsarski *a.* (= *piracki*) piratical, piratic; corsair.
korsarstwo *n.* (= *piractwo*) piracy.
korsarz *mp* (= *pirat*) pirate, corsair. – *mi Gen.* -a (*statek*) privateer, pirate, corsair.
korso *n. indecl. l. Gen.* -a 1. (= *aleja*) alley (*of an Italian city*). 2. (= *pochód*) parade (*in an Italian city*).
Korsyka *f. geogr.* Corsica.
Korsykanin *mp,* **Korsykanka** *f. Gen.pl.* -ek Corsican.
korsykański *a.* Corsican.
kort[1] *mi tenis* (tennis) court; **kort trawiasty** grass court; **kort twardy** hard court; **kort ziemny** clay court.
kort[2] *mi tk.* (*tkanina*) cord.
kortezy *pl. Gen.* -ów *hist., polit.* Cortes.
kortyzol *mi fizj., med.* (*hormon*) hydrocortisone, cortisol.
kortyzon *mi fizj., med.* (*hormon*) cortisone.
korumpować *ipf.* (= *przekupywać*) corrupt.
korund *mi min.* corundum.
korupcja *f.* (= *łapownictwo*) corruption.
korupcyjny *a.* (= *łapówkarski*) corrupt; **afera korupcyjna** corruption scandal.
korweta *f.* 1. *żegl.* (*okręt eskortujący*) corvette. 2. *żegl., hist.* (*statek*) corvette.
korybant *mp mit.* Corybant.
koryfeusz *mp Gen.pl.* -y *l.* -ów 1. (= *znakomitość*) outstanding personality. 2. (= *czołowy*

**przedstawiciel*) (*np. dziedziny w nauce, kierunku w sztuce*) caryphaeus. 3. (*tancerz*) ballet soloist. 4. *hist.* (= *przewodnik chóru*) coryphaeus.
korygować *ipf.* 1. (= *poprawiać*) correct, rectify; (*zwł. zapisy księgowe*) adjust. 2. (= *adiustować*) proofread. 3. *muz.* (= *naprawiać*) repair; (= *stroić*) tune (up).
koryncki *a.* Corinthian; **porządek koryncki** *bud.* Corinthian order; **kapitel koryncki** *bud.* Corinthian capital.
Korynt *mi geogr., hist.* Corinth.
Koryntczyk *mp,* **Koryntyjka** *f. Gen.pl.* -ek Corinthian.
Koryntianin *mp pl.* -anie *Gen.* -an, **Koryntianka** *f. Gen.pl.* -ek *Bibl.* Corinthian; **listy do Koryntian** *Bibl.* Corinthians.
koryntka *f. Gen.pl.* -ek (= *rodzynka*) currant.
korytarz *mi Gen.* -a 1. (*pomieszczenie*) corridor, hall; **korytarz powietrzny** *lotn.* air corridor; **korytarz eksterytorialny** extraterritorial corridor. 2. (= *przejście podziemne*) tunnel.
korytko *n.* 1. (*małe koryto*) trough. 2. (= *rynienka*) channel. 3. (= *skrzynka na kwiaty*) flower box. 4. (= *przybornik*) pen tray.
koryto *n.* 1. (= *poidło, żłób*) trough; **dorwać się do koryta** put on the feeding bag, line up at the trough; **leźć** *l.* **pchać się jak świnia do koryta** push one's way, barge; **być przy korycie** have the feeding bag on, be in the mainstream. 2. *techn.* (= *pojemnik*) trough. 3. *techn.* (*wlewowe, spustowe*) spout. 4. *geol.* bed; **koryto rzeki** river bed; **koryto wielkiej wody** (*budowane przy regulacji rzeki*) flood bed, inundation area.
korzec *mi* -rc- *Gen.* -a 1. *arch.* (*miara objętości*) 120 liters; **dobrać się w korcu maku** be cast in the same mold. 2. *arch.* (*naczynie*) vessel for storing grain; **chować coś pod korcem** keep sth under one's hat.
korzenić się *ipf. bot.* (= *ukorzeniać się*) *przen.* (= *krzewić się*) root, take root.
korzenionóżki *pl. Gen.pl.* -ek *zool.* rhizopods (*Rhizopoda*).
korzeniowy *a. bot., dent.* root; **przewód korzeniowy** root canal.
korzeniówka *f. Gen.pl.* -ek 1. spice-flavored vodka. 2. *bot.* **korzeniówka pospolita** pinesap, false beechdrops; *Br.* yellow bird's nest (*Monotropa hypopitys*).
korzenny *a.* (*związany z przyprawami*) spicy; **przyprawy korzenne** spice; **kupiec korzenny** spice merchant.
korzeń *mi Gen.* -a 1. *bot., dent., przen.* (= *podstawa, źródło*) root; **korzeń główny** primary root; **korzeń boczny** secondary root; **korzeń przybyszowy** adventitious root; **korzeń spichrzowy** tuber, tuberous root; **czarny korzeń** *bot.* scorzonera, black salsify (*Scorzonera hispanica*); **zapuścić korzenie** take root; **wyrwać coś z korzeniami** uproot sth; **średniowieczna filozofia sięga korzeniami starożytności** the medieval philosphy has its roots in antiquity. 2. *pl. kulin.* (= *przyprawy, korzonki*) spice. 3. *pl. przen.* (= *źródło, początek*) roots; **tkwić w czymś korzeniami** be rooted in sth.

korzonek *mi* -nk- *Gen.* -a 1. (*mały korzeń*) rootlet. 2. *anat.* (*część organu, narządu*) root, radix, radicle; **korzonki nerwowe** nerve radicles; **ból korzonków** radicular pain; *pot.* pain in the lower back; **bolą mnie korzonki** I have this pain in the lower back.

korzonkowy *a.* 1. (= *korzeniowy*) root. 2. (*dotyczący korzonków nerwowych*) radicular.

korzyć się *ipf.* (= *okazywać uległość*) humble o.s. (*przed kimś/czymś* before sb/sth); (= *kłaniać się*) prostrate o.s. (*przed kimś/czymś* before sb/sth).

korzystać *ipf.* (= *używać*) use (*z czegoś* sth); make use (*z czegoś* of sth); avail o.s. (*z czegoś* of sth); (*z sytuacji*) take advantage (*z czegoś* of sth); **korzystać ze swoich praw** exercise one's rights; **gdzie dwóch się bije, tam trzeci korzysta** two dogs fight *l.* strive for a bone, and a third runs away with it.

korzystanie *n.* (= *używanie*) use; (*z prawa/przywileju*) enjoyment (*of a right/privilege*).

korzystnie *adv.* (= *pożytecznie*) 1. beneficially. 2. (= *przychylnie, pozytywnie*) favorably.

korzystny *a.* 1. (= *opłacalny*) profitable, lucrative; **korzystna umowa** profitable *l.* lucrative contract. 2. (= *pożyteczny, sprzyjający*) beneficial, favorable, advantageous; **korzystne warunki** favorable conditions. 3. (= *pozytywny, pochlebny*) favorable; **korzystny wygląd** good looks; **przedstawiać coś w korzystnym świetle** present sth in a favorable light, put a favorable spin on sth.

korzyść *f.* (= *pożytek*) advantage, benefit; (= *zysk*) profit; **korzyści materialne** financial profits; **czerpać** *l.* **ciągnąć** *l.* **odnosić korzyści z czegoś** reap profit from sth, benefit from sth; **przynosić korzyści** be beneficial; (*materialne*) bring profit; **na czyjąś korzyść** to sb's advantage, in sb's favor; **zmienić się na korzyść** change for the better; **korzyści z używania dobrej encyklopedii są bardzo liczne** the benefits *l.* advantages of using a good encyclopedia are numerous.

kos *ma orn.* blackbird (*Turdus merula*).

kosa *f.* 1. (*narzędzie rolnicze*) scythe; **trafiła kosa na kamień** diamond cut diamond. 2. *pot.* (= *nóż*) shiv. 3. *geogr.* (= *mierzeja*) spit.

kosaciec *mi* -ćc- *Gen.* -a *bot.* iris (*Iris*).

kosaćcowate *pl.* *Gen.* -ych *bot.* iridaceous plants.

kosarz *ma zool.* (*pajęczak*) daddy longlegs; *Br.* harvestman (*Opilio*).

kosatka *f. Gen.pl.* -ek *bot.* false asphodel (*Tofieldia*).

kosekans *mi mat.* cosecant.

kosiarka *f. Gen.pl.* -ek *techn.* (*maszyna rolnicza*) mower; **kosiarka do trawy** lawn mower.

kosiarz *mp* (= *żniwiarz*) haymaker.

kosić *ipf.* **koszę kosisz** 1. (= *ścinać*) mow; **kosić trawę** mow grass; **kosić pszenicę** mow *l.* cut *l.* harvest *l.* reap wheat; **kosić trawnik** mow lawn; **lot koszący** *lotn.* hedgehopping; **lecieć lotem koszącym** hedgehop. 2. *przen.* (= *zabijać*) mow down. 3. *przen., pot.* (= *oblewać*) fail (*plenty of students during an exam*). 4. *sport, pot.* (=

faulować) foul. 5. *pot.* (= *zdobywać*) gain, earn; **kosić forsę** be raking it in.

kosinus *mi Gen.* -a *mat.* cosine.

kosinusoida *f. mat.* cosine curve.

kosisko *n.* 1. *żart.* (= *kosa*) scythe. 2. (= *trzonek kosy*) snath, snathe.

kosmaczek *mi bot.* **jastrzębiec kosmaczek** mouse-ear hawkweed (*Hieracium pirosella*).

kosmatka *f. Gen.pl.* -ek *bot.* woodrush (*Luzula*).

kosmaty *a.* (= *włochaty*) hairy, shaggy, hirsute; **kosmate myśli** *przen.* dirty thoughts.

kosmek *mi anat. zob.* **kosmki**.

kosmetologia *f. med.* cosmetology.

kosmetyczka *f.* 1. (*kobieta*) beautician. 2. (*torebka*) vanity case *l.* bag *l.* box.

kosmetyczny *a.* 1. (= *pielęgnacyjny, upiększający*) cosmetic; **chusteczki kosmetyczne** (soft) tissues; **gabinet kosmetyczny** beauty parlor; **chirurgia kosmetyczna** *med.* cosmetic surgery. 2. *przen.* (= *drobny, nieznaczny*) cosmetic; **zmiany kosmetyczne** cosmetic changes.

kosmetyk *mi* cosmetic.

kosmetyka *f.* 1. (*sztuka pielęgnacji ciała*) cosmetology. 2. *przen.* (= *upiększanie, poprawianie*) beautifying.

kosmiczny *a.* 1. (*dotyczący kosmosu*) cosmic; **lot kosmiczny** space flight; **prom kosmiczny** space shuttle; **pył kosmiczny** *astron.* cosmic dust; **przestrzeń kosmiczna** (outer) space; **medycyna kosmiczna** space medicine; **pierwsza prędkość kosmiczna** orbital velocity; **druga prędkość kosmiczna** escape velocity; **promieniowanie kosmiczne** *fiz.* cosmic ray; **sonda kosmiczna** space probe; **stacja kosmiczna** space station; **statek** *l.* **pojazd kosmiczny** spacecraft. 2. *przen.* (= *ogromny*) cosmic, vast; **kosmiczny problem** major *l.* serious problem.

kosmita *mp,* **kosmitka** *f. Gen.pl.* -ek alien, extraterrestrial.

kosmki *pl. Gen.* -ów *biol.* (= *wypustki*) villi; **kosmki jelitowe** *anat.* intestinal villi.

kosmobiologia *f.* space biology, cosmobiology.

kosmochemia *f.* cosmochemistry, space chemistry.

kosmodrom *mi astron.* (= *wyrzutnia rakietowa*) launching pad, launch pad; (= *port kosmiczny*) space center; (*w byłym ZSRR*) cosmodrome; **Kosmodrom Bajkonur** the Baikonur Cosmodrome.

kosmofizyka *f.* space physics, cosmophysics.

kosmogonia *f. Gen.* -ii *astron., rel.* cosmogony.

kosmogoniczny *a.* cosmogonic; **mit kosmogoniczny** cosmogonic myth.

kosmograf *mp pl.* -owie *astron.* cosmographer, cosmographist.

kosmografia *f. Gen.* -ii *astron.* (= *astronomia*) cosmography.

kosmograficzny *a.* (= *astronomiczny*) cosmographic, cosmographical.

kosmolog *mp pl.* -dzy *l.* -owie *astron.* (= *astronom*) cosmologist.

kosmologia *f. Gen.* -ii *astron., rel.* cosmology.

kosmologiczny *a. astron., rel.* cosmological, cosmologic.

kosmonauta *mp*, **kosmonautka** *f.* astronaut; (*w byłym ZSRR*) cosmonaut.

kosmonautyka *f.* astronautics, cosmonautics.

kosmopolita *mp* **1.** (= *internacjonalista*) cosmopolitan, cosmopolite. **2.** *biol.* cosmopolite.

kosmopolityczny *a.* cosmopolitan; **organizm kosmopolityczny** *biol.* cosmopolitan.

kosmopolityzm *mi* (= *internacjonalizm*) cosmopolitanism.

kosmos *mi* **1.** (= *wszechświat*) universe, cosmos. **2.** *fil.* cosmos. **3.** *pot.* (= *przestrzeń pozaziemska*) outer space.

kosmotron *mi* *fiz.* Cosmotrone.

kosmówka *f. Gen.pl.* **-ek** *anat.* (*błona płodowa*) chorion.

kosmyk *mi Gen.* **-a 1.** (= *lok*) wisp, strand; **kosmyk włosów** wisp of hair. **2.** *myśl.* hare's tail.

koso *adv. przest.* (= *krzywo*) slantingly, slantly; obliquely; **patrzeć na kogoś koso** frown on sb.

kosodrzewina *f. bot.* dwarf mountain pine, Swiss mountain pine (*Pinus montana l. mugus*).

kosówka *f. Gen.pl.* **-ek** = **kosodrzewina**.

Kostaryka *f. geogr.* Costa Rica.

Kostarykanin *mp*, **Kostarykanka** *f. Gen.pl.* **-ek** Costa Rican.

kostarykański *a.* Costa Rican.

kosterowate *pl. icht.* trunkfish, boxfish (*Ostracion*).

kostium *mi* **1.** (= *garsonka*) (woman's) suit, two-piece, two-piecer. **2.** (= *przebranie, strój*) costume, outfit; **strój kąpielowy** bathing suit, swimsuit.

kostiumer *mp teatr* costumer, costumier.

kostiumolog *mp pl.* **-dzy** *l.* **-owie** costume studies expert.

kostiumologia *f. Gen.* **-ii** costume studies.

kostiumowy *a.* **1.** (= *garniturowy*) suit. **2.** (*związany z kostiumem - specjalnym strojem*) costume; **film kostiumowy** *kino* historical movie; **próba kostiumowa** *teatr* dress rehearsal; **bal kostiumowy** costume ball *l.* party.

kostka *f. Gen.pl.* **-ek 1.** (= *kość*) bone; **kostki słuchowe** *anat.* auditory ossicles, ear ossicles *l.* bones. **2.** (*część nogi*) ankle; **woda po kostki** ankle-deep water. **3.** (*część ręki*) knuckle. **4.** (*o kształcie sześcianu*) cube; **cukier w kostkach** lump sugar; **kostka brukowa** sett; **krajać w kostkę** dice; **składać coś w kostkę** fold sth neatly; **kostka do gry** dice; **kostka toaletowa** toilet freshener. **5.** (= *płytka do gitary*) pick, plectrum.

kostkować *ipf.* **1.** (= *brukować*) pave (*with setts*). **2.** (*obrabiać metal*) spot.

kostkowy *a.* (*o kształcie sześcianu*) cubic, cubical.

kostnica *f.* morgue; *Br. t.* mortuary.

kostnieć *ipf.* **1.** (= *zmieniać się w tkankę kostną*) ossify; (= *twardnieć*) harden. **2.** *przen.* (= *utrwalać się*) fossilize; (*zwł. o przyzwyczajeniach*) ossify. **3.** *przen.* (= *marznąć*) freeze, grow numb with cold.

kostnina *f. biol.* callus.

kostniwo *n. anat.* cementum, cement.

kostnoszkieletowe *pl. Gen.* **-ych** *icht.* teleosts, teleosteans (*Teleostei*).

kostny *a.* bone, bony; **tkanka kostna** *anat.* bone tissue, osseous tissue; **komórki kostne** *anat.* osteocytes, osseous *l.* bone cells; **mączka kostna** bone meal; **popiół kostny** bone ash; **układ kostny** *anat.* osseous *l.* skeletal system; **ryby kostne** *icht.* bony fishes (*Osteichthyes*).

kostołuskie *pl. Gen.* **-ich** *icht.* holostean fishes, holosteans (*Holostei*).

kostotom *mi chir.* (*narzędzie*) costotome.

kostotomia *f. Gen.* **-ii** *chir.* costotomy.

kostropaty *a.* (= *szorstki*) rough, coarse, harsh.

kostrzewa *f. bot.* fescue, fescue grass (*Festuca*).

kostucha *f. pot.* (= *śmierć*) the Grim Reaper, Death; **uciec kostusze spod kosy** have a close brush with death, cheat death.

kostur *mi Gen.* **-a 1.** (= *laska*) (walking) stick. **2.** (= *pogrzebacz*) poker.

kostycznie *adv.* (= *zgryźliwie*) caustically, scathingly.

kostyczność *f.* (= *zgryźliwość*) causticity.

kostyczny *a.* (= *zgryźliwy, złośliwy*) caustic, scathing.

kosy *a.* (= *krzywy*) slanting, oblique; **kose spojrzenie** frown, frowning look; **patrzeć na kogoś kosym okiem** frown on sb.

kosynier *mp hist.* scythe bearer.

kosz *mi Gen.* **-a** *Gen.pl.* **-y** *l.* **-ów 1.** (= *koszyk*) basket; **kosz na śmieci** garbage can; *Br.* dustbin; **worek do kosza na śmieci** bin liner; **kosz do bielizny** clothes hamper; *Br.* laundry basket; **kosz na papiery** wastepaper basket; **kosz piknikowy** picnic basket, picnic hamper; **zostać** *l.* **siąść na koszu** (= *doznać zawodu*) be thwarted in sb's expectations; (= *nie ożenić się* *l. nie wyjść za mąż*) remain single; **dostać kosza** be rejected, be given a rebuff; **coś nadaje się do kosza** sth is useless, sth is no good. **2.** (= *ażurowa osłona*) basket; **kosz kwiatowy** *ogr.* flower basket; **kosz dziobowy** *żegl.* bow pulpit; **kosz masztowy** *żegl.* top; **kosz rufowy** *żegl.* stern pulpit. **3.** (*gondola balonu*) basket. **4.** (*na plaży*) roofed wicker beach chair. **5.** (*motocykla*) sidecar. **6.** (= *koksownik*) brazier, salamander. **7.** *myśl.* (*zasłona*) hunting screen. **8.** *sport* basket; **rzucać do kosza** shoot at the basket. **9.** *sport* (*celny strzał w koszykówce*) basket, field goal. **10.** *pot. sport* (= *koszykówka*) basketball; **grać w kosza** play basketball.

koszałki-opałki *pl. Gen.* **-ek -ek** *l.* **-ów -ów** *pot.* (= *bzdury*) fiddle-faddle.

koszara *f. dial.* sheep pen.

koszarować *ipf. wojsk.* accommodate in barracks.

koszarowy *a.* barracks.

koszary *pl. Gen.* **-r** *wojsk.* barracks.

koszatka *f. Gen.pl.* **-ek** *zool.* forest dormouse (*Dryomys nitedula*).

koszenila *f.* **1.** *ent.* cochineal, cochineal insect (*Dactylopius coccus*). **2.** *techn.* (*barwnik*) cochineal.

koszenilina *f.* = koszenila 2.

koszer *mi rel.* (*w judaizmie*) (= *czystość*) kosher condition; (*przepisy*) kosher rules.

koszerny *a. rel.* (*w judaizmie*) kosher.

koszerować *ipf.* **1.** *rel.* kosher, kasher. **2.** *żart.* (= *myć*) wash (*thoroughly*); scrub.

koszka *f. Gen.pl.* -ek (*rodzaj ula*) skep.

koszmar *mi* **1.** (*sen*) nightmare. **2.** (= *coś strasznego*) nightmare, drag; **ta podróż była koszmarem** this journey was a nightmare.

koszmarek *mi* -rk- *Gen.* -a *pot.* (= *tandeta, brzydactwo*) eyesore.

koszmarnie *adv.* (= *strasznie*) horribly, terribly, ghastly.

koszmarny *a.* **1.** (*budzący grozę*) scary, nightmarish; **mieć koszmarne sny** have nightmares; **koszmarne warunki** terrible conditions. **2.** (= *brzydki*) hideous, horrid; **koszmarny wygląd** hideous appearance.

koszówka *f. Gen.pl.* -ek **1.** *ent.* bagworm moth (*Psychidae*). **2.** *bud.* (= *karpiówka*) plane *l.* plain tile.

koszt *mi pl.* -y *l.* -a (= *wydatek, cena*) cost, price, expense; **koszty eksploatacji** operating costs; **koszty podróży** travelling expenses; **koszty utrzymania** cost of living; **koszty własne** prime costs; **kosztem kogoś lub czegoś** at the cost *l.* expense of sb *l.* sth; **bawić się czyimś** *l.* **cudzym kosztem** have a laugh at sb's expense *l.* cost; **bez względu na koszty** at all costs, at any price; **małym** *l.* **tanim kosztem** cheaply; **na koszt firmy** on the house; **narazić kogoś na koszty** put sb to expense; **na własny koszt** at sb's own expense; **zawyżać koszty** inflate costs.

kosztorys *mi* (= *kalkulacja*) cost estimate.

kosztorysant *mp*, **kosztorysantka** *f.* cost estimator.

kosztorysować *ipf.* (= *szacować*) (make a) cost estimate.

kosztorysowy *a.* (= *kalkulacyjny*) estimative.

kosztować *ipf.* **1.** (= *stanowić koszt*) cost; **coś dużo kosztuje** sth costs a lot, sth is expensive; **coś mało kosztuje** sth is cheap; **ile to kosztuje?** how much is it?, how much does it cost? **2.** (= *być przyczyną*) cost; **drogo go to kosztowało** *dosł.* it cost him a lot; *przen.* it cost him a lot, he paid for it through the nose; **kosztować wiele czasu** cost a lot of time; **kosztować wiele trudu** *l.* **zachodu** cost a great deal of trouble. **3.** (= *degustować*) try, taste. **4.** *przen.* (= *doświadczać*) experience; **kosztować wolności** enjoy freedom.

kosztownie *adv.* expensively.

kosztowności *pl. Gen.* -i (= *klejnoty*) valuables.

kosztowny *a.* (= *drogi, cenny*) expensive, costly.

koszula *f.* (*odzież*) shirt; **koszula damska** women's shirt; **koszula męska** (men's) shirt; **koszula nocna** nightgown, nightdress; **brunatne koszule** *hist.* Brownshirts, *Br.* Brown Shirts; **czarne koszule** *hist.* Black Shirts, *Br.* Blackshirts; **wziąć żonę w jednej koszuli** marry a dowerless woman; **zgrać się do ostatniej koszuli** gamble all the money away; **zostać w jednej koszuli** lose sb's shirt; **nosić koszulę w zębach** *żart.* be a small kid; **bliższa ciału koszula niż sukmana** near is my shirt but nearer is my skin.

koszulka *f. Gen.pl.* -ek **1.** (= *mała koszula*) shirt. **2.** (= *podkoszulek*) T-shirt; **żółta koszulka** *kolarstwo* yellow jersey. **3.** (= *pokrowiec, osłona*) cover, jacket; **jajko w koszulce** *kulin.* poached egg. **4.** *techn.* (*w reaktorze jądrowym*) can, clad; **koszulka wodna** (*w silniku*) water jacket.

koszulowy *a.* shirt.

koszyczek *mi* -czk- *Gen.* -a **1.** (= *mały koszyk*) basket, punnet. **2.** *bot.* (*rodzaj kwiatostanu*) capitulum, head. **3.** *ent.* (*na nodze pszczoły*) pollen basket, corbicula.

koszyk *mi Gen.* -a basket, hamper.

koszykarka *f. Gen.pl.* -ek **1.** *sport* (*zawodniczka*) basketball player. **2.** (*kobieta wyplatająca koszyki*) basket maker *l.* weaver. **3.** (*wiklina*) basket wicker.

koszykarski *a.* **1.** (*dotyczący koszykarstwa*) basket-making, basketry; **narzędzia koszykarskie** basketry tools. **2.** *sport* (*związany z koszykówką*) basketball.

koszykarstwo *n.* (*rzemiosło*) basketry.

koszykarz *mp* **1.** *sport* (*zawodnik*) basketball player. **2.** (*mężczyzna wyplatający koszyki*) basket maker *l.* weaver.

koszykowy *a.* basket; **piłka koszykowa** *sport* basketball; **haft koszykowy** basket weave.

koszykówka *f. sport* basketball.

kośba *f. lit.* (= *koszenie*) mowing.

kości *pl.* **1.** (*gra*) dice. **2.** (*zwłoki*) dead body.

kościany *a.* (*z kości*) bone.

kościec *mi* -śćc- *Gen.* -a **1.** (= *szkielet*) skeleton. **2.** *przen.* (= *istota*) essence, basis; (= *trzon*) framework; **brak mu kośćca** he has no backbone.

kościelny *a.* **1.** (*dotyczący budynku*) church; **pieśni kościelne** church songs *l.* hymns; **wieża kościelna** church tower; **biedny jak mysz kościelna** as poor as a church mouse. **2.** (*dotyczący instytucji*) ecclesiastical, church; **święto kościelne** church holiday, holy day; **Państwo Kościelne** the Holy See, Vatican; **ślub kościelny** church *l.* white wedding. – *mp* (= *zakrystian*) sexton, sacristan.

kościogubny *a. biol.* osteoclastic; **komórka kościogubna** osteoclast.

kościotrup *mi Gen.* -a *dosł., przen.* skeleton.

kościotwórczy *a. biol.* osteoblastic; **komórka kościotwórcza** osteoblast.

kościół *mi* -o- *Gen.* -a *Loc.* -ele **1.** (= *świątynia*) church; **kościół parafialny** parish church; **kościół garnizonowy** garrison church; **iść pod kościół** *przen.* start begging; **chodzić do kościoła** go to church; **słyszał, że dzwonią, ale nie wie, w którym kościele** in the right church but in the wrong pew; wrongly heard, wrongly answered. **2.** (= *wierni*) Church, Christendom. **3.** (= *wyznanie chrześcijańskie*) Church; **Kościół anglikański** the Anglican Church, the Church of England; **Kościół grekokatolicki** the Greek Orthodox Church; **Kościół katolicki** the Catholic Church; **Kościół prawosławny** the (Eastern) Orthodox Church; **Kościół rzymskokatolicki** the Roman-

Catholic Church; **Kościół unicki** the Uniate Church; **Ojciec/Doktor Kościoła** *rel.* Father/Doctor of the Church.

kościsty *a.* (= *chudy*) bony, skinny.

kość *f. Ins.pl.* **-mi 1.** (*część szkieletu*) bone; **kość słoniowa** ivory; **kość niezgody** bone of contetion; **skóra i kości** bag of bones; **do szpiku kości** *l.* **do kości** to the marrow *l.* bone; **z krwi i kości** trueborn; **on jest poczciwy z kościami** he's a good *l.* honest person; **rozejść się po kościach** come to nothing, be (just) a flash in the pan; **stanąć komuś kością w gardle** be bothered by sth, be annoyed by sth, be fed up with sth; **zmarznąć na kość** be chilled to the bone, freeze stiff; **porachować komuś kości** beat sb black and blue, trounce sb; **nie czuć kości** be done in; **czuć coś w kościach** feel sth in sb's bones; **wygrzewać kości na słońcu** bask in the sun; **dać komuś w kość** give sb a hard time; **dostać w kość** be put through it, be given a hard time; **być przy kości** be plump; **psiakość** *pot.* shoot. **2.** (= *kostka do gry*) die; **kości zostały rzucone** the die is cast; *zob. t.* **kości.**

koślawić *ipf.* **1.** (= *krzywić*) crook, distort. **2.** (= *przekręcać, przeinaczać*) distort, misrepresent. **~ się** *ipf.* (= *wykrzywiać się*) crook, bend.

koślawo *adv.* (= *krzywo, kulawo*) crookedly, awry.

koślawość *f.* **1.** (= *krzywość, kulawość*) crookedness. **2.** *pat.* valgity.

koślawy *a.* **1.** (= *krzywy, niezgrabny*) crooked, bent; **mający koślawe nogi** knock-kneed, bowlegged; **koślawe krzesło** rickety chair. **2.** (= *niepoprawny*) sloppy. **3.** *pat.* valgus.

kośnik *ma orn.* hoatzin, stinkbird (*Opisthocomus hoazin*).

kośny *a.* (*przeznaczony do koszenia*) harvestable.

kot *ma Dat.* **-u 1.** *zool.* cat (*Felis domestica*); **kupować kota w worku** buy a pig in a poke; **drzeć z kimś koty** fight like cat and dog, be at loggerheads with sb; **żyć jak pies z kotem** lead a cat-and-dog life, be at loggerheads with sb; **tyle co kot napłakał** next to nothing; **bawić się z kimś jak kot z myszką** play a cat-and-mouse game with sb; **odwracać kota ogonem** *pot.* (= *przeinaczać swoje słowa*) shift one's ground; (= *przeinaczać czyjeś słowa*) distort the facts; **latać jak kot z pęcherzem** be running back and forth like a cat on hot bricks; **pogonić komuś kota** throw sb out; **mieć kota na jakimś punkcie** be crazy about sth; **kot zawsze spada na cztery łapy** a cat has nine lives; a cat falls *l.* lands on its feet *l.* legs; **myszy tańcują, kiedy kota nie czują** while the cat's away, the mice will play; **pierwsze koty za płoty** the first try is just for practice; I was just warming up; **w nocy wszystkie koty szare** all cats are grey in the dark. **2.** *myśl.* hare. – *mi Gen.* **-a** *Dat.* **-u** *żegl.* (= *kotwica czterołapowa*) grapnel. – *mp Dat.* **-u** *pl.* **-y** *pot.* **1.** (= *nowicjusz*) newbie, cherry. **2.** (= *młody żołnierz*) plebe. **3.** (= *uczeń pierwszej klasy, student pierwszego roku*) freshman.

kota *f. wojsk., miern.* spot height.

kotangens *mi Gen.* **-a** *mat.* cotangent.

kotangensoida *f. mat.* cotangent curve.

kotara *f.* (= *zasłona*) curtain.

kotbelka *f. żegl.* cathead.

koteczek *ma* **-czk-** (= *kotek*) kitten, pussy(cat). – *mp* **-czk-** *pl.* **-i** (*pieszczotliwie o kochanej osobie*) honey, sweetie.

kotek *ma* **-tk-** (*mały kot*) kitten, pussy(cat). – *mp* **-tk-** *pl.* **-i** (*pieszczotliwie o kochanej osobie*) honey, sweetie. – *mi* **-tk-** *Gen.* **-a** *żegl.* grommet, grummet.

koteria *f. Gen.* **-ii** (= *klan, klika*) coterie, clique.

koteryjność *f.* cliquishness.

koteryjny *a.* cliquish.

kotew *f.* **-twi-** *pl.* **-e 1.** *bud.* (= *klamra*) anchor, tie. **2.** *techn.* (*śruba*) tie. **3.** *żegl.* (= *kotwica*) anchor.

kotik *ma* Northern fur seal (*Callorhinus ursinus*).

kotka *f. Gen.pl.* **-ek 1.** *zool.* (= *samica kota*) she-cat. **2.** *bot.* (= *bazia*) catkin, ament.

kotlarnia *f. Gen.pl.* **-i** *l.* **-ń** *techn.* boiler forge.

kotlarstwo *n.* (*rzemiosło*) coppersmithing.

kotlarz *mp Gen.pl.* **-y** *l.* **-ów** (*produkujący kotły*) boiler maker, boiler smith; (*produkujący rondle itp.*) coppersmith.

kotle *mi zob.* **kocioł.**

kotlecik *mi Gen.* **-a** *kulin.* chop.

kotlet *mi Gen.* **-a** *kulin.* (*z kością*) chop; (*bez kości*) fillet; (*zwł. z mięsa najwyższej jakości*) cutlet; **kotlet mielony** *l.* **siekany** hamburger; **kotlet schabowy** pork chop; **kotlet drobiowy** poultry fillet *l.* cutlet; **grać do kotleta** (*o zespole muzycznym l. piosenka-rzu / -rce*) play dinner music, go commercial.

kotlina *f.* **1.** *geogr.* (= *dolina, niecka*) valley. **2.** (= *zagłębienie*) hollow, hole. **3.** *metal.* hearth.

kotlinny *a. geogr.* valley.

kotlinowaty *a.* valley-like.

kotlista *mp,* **kotlistka** *f.* kettledrummer.

kotła *itd. mi zob.* **kocioł.**

kotłować *ipf. pot.* (= *mieszać*) roil. **~ się** *ipf. pot. przen.* (= *kłębić się*) mill about *l.* around; (*o cieczy*) roil; **w kraju się kotłuje** the country is in a state of flux.

kotłowanina *f. pot.* (= *kłębienie się, chaos*) turmoil; **kotłowanina ludzi** huddle.

kotłownia *f. Gen.pl.* **-i** boiler room *l.* house; *żegl.* stokehold, stokehole; fire-room.

kotłowy *a.* (*dotyczący kotła*) boiler; (*dotyczący kotłowni*) boiler-room, boiler-house; **kamień kotłowy** boiler scale; *Br. t.* fur. – *mp* (= *palacz*) stoker, fireman.

kotna *a.* (= *ciężarna*) (big *l.* heavy) with young, pregnant; (*o kotce*) in *l.* with kitten; (*o owcy*) in lamb.

kotonizacja *f. tk.* cottonization.

kotonizować *ipf. tk.* cottonize.

kotować *ipf. wojsk., miern.* (spot-)height.

kotowate *pl. Gen.* **-ych** *zool.* felines, felids (*Felidae*).

koturn *mi Gen.* **-u** *l.* **-a 1.** (*podeszwa*) wedge (heel). **2.** (*obuwie*) wedge (heel), wedgie. **3.** *hist.* (*obuwie w antycznym teatrze*) cothurnus, buskin. **4.** *przen., przest.* (= *patos*) cothurnus, (the) buskin.

koturnowość f. (= górnolotność, patetyczność) grandiloquence, stiltedness.

koturnowy a. 1. (dotyczący obuwia) wedge. 2. przen. (= napuszony, górnolotny) grandiloquent, stilted.

kotuś mp Gen.pl. -ów (pieszczotliwie o kochanej osobie) honey(baby), sugar.

kotwa f. = **kotew**.

kotwica f. żegl. (w zegarku) anchor; **kotwica admiralicji** stocked anchor; **kotwica martwa** sinker, mooring; **kotwica patentowa** stockless l. patent anchor; **stać na kotwicy** lie l. ride at anchor; **rzucić kotwicę** drop l. cast anchor; **podnieść kotwicę** raise l. weigh anchor.

kotwicowisko n. żegl. (= reda) anchorage, anchor ground.

kotwiczka f. Gen.pl. -ek 1. żegl. grapnel, small anchor. 2. techn. (w zegarku) anchor. 3. (w wędkarstwie) fisherman's anchor. 4. (= haczyk) fish-hook.

kotwiczny a. żegl. anchor; **kluza kotwiczna** hawsehole, hawse; **światło kotwiczne** anchor lights; **talia kotwiczna** cat(head), anchor tackle; **winda kotwiczna** windlass.

kotwiczyć ipf. żegl. (= stawać na kotwicy) anchor, cast anchor.

kotwić ipf. bud. (= łączyć) anchor, brace.

kotylion mi Gen. -a 1. muz. (taniec) cotillion. 2. (ozdoba) favor.

kotylionowy a. 1. (o tańcu) cotillion. 2. (o ozdobie) favor.

kowadełko n. Gen.pl. -ek 1. (narzędzie) anvil. 2. anat. anvil, incus. 3. wojsk. detonator cap.

kowadło n. Gen.pl. -eł (narzędzie) anvil; **być/ znaleźć się między młotem a kowadłem** be/find o.s. between a rock and a hard place, be/find o.s. between the devil and the deep (blue) sea; rzad. be/find o.s. between the hammer and the anvil.

kowal mp (rzemieślnik) smith, blacksmith; **każdy jest kowalem swojego losu** everyone is the architect of his own fortune. – ma 1. ent. fire bug (Pyrrhocoris apterus). 2. orn. olivaceous woodcreeper (Sittasomus griseicapillus).

kowalik ma orn. nuthatch (Sitta europaea).

kowalność f. techn. malleability, forgeability.

kowalny a. techn. malleable, forgeable.

kowalski a. smith's; **miech kowalski** forge bellows; **młot kowalski** sledgehammer, sledge.

kowalstwo n. (rzemiosło) smithery; **kowalstwo artystyczne** metal craftwork.

kowar mi techn. kovar.

kowarka f. Gen.pl. -ek techn. (= młotkownica) swaging machine, swager.

kowboj mp Gen.pl. -ów cowboy.

kowbojski a. cowboy; **kowbojskie buty** cowboy boots; **kowbojski film** cowboy movie, western; **kowbojski kapelusz** cowboy hat.

koza f. Gen.pl. kóz 1. zool. goat (Capra); **koza domowa** domestic goat (Capra hircus); pot. (= samica kozy) nanny goat, she-goat; **na pochyłe drzewo każda koza skacze** poverty begets poverty, it's no great feat to kick a fellow when he's down; **przyjdzie koza do woza** I shall catch you some day carrying corn to our mill, you're going to need my help someday; **przyszła koza do woza!** so you've come (to beg) for my help, haven't you?; **raz kozie śmierć** a man can die but once; come what may! 2. pot. (= nastolatka) filly. 3. pot. (= więzienie) jug, can; **siedzieć w kozie** be in the can. 4. pot., szkoln. detention. 5. pot. (= piecyk) iron stove. 6. pot. (do noszenia cegieł) hod. 7. muz. (instrument) bagpipes. 8. icht. (= kózka) spined loach (Cobitis taenia).

kozacki a. (hist.) Cossack.

kozactwo n. 1. hist., wojsk. the Cossacks. 2. przen. (= brawura) bravado.

kozaczki pl. Gen. -ów (obuwie) winter boots.

Kozak mp Voc. -u l. -cze Cossack; **złapał Kozak Tatarzyna, a Tatarzyn za łeb trzyma** the biter bit.

kozak mp Voc. -u l. -cze pl. -cy 1. hist., wojsk. Cossack. 2. przen. (= zawadiaka) swaggerer; **ale z ciebie kozak** don't be such a swaggerer. – mi Gen. -a pl. -i 1. muz. (taniec) Cossack dance. 2. (obuwie) winter boot. 3. bot. (grzyb) birch bolete, shaggy boletus (Leccinum scabrum).

kozera f. **nie bez kozery** with a good reason.

kozetka f. Gen.pl. -ek (mebel) couch.

kozi a. goat; **kozia bródka** goatee; **kozie mleko** goat's milk; **ser kozi** goat cheese; **zapędzić kogoś w kozi róg** drive l. force sb into a (tight) corner; **taka z niej aktorka jak z koziej dupy trąba** as an actress she ain't worth a shit l. wiping your ass on.

koziarz mp (hodowca) 1. goatherd. 2. muz. (muzyk) piper.

kozibród mi -o- bot. goatsbeard (Tragopogon); **kozibród łąkowy** Jack-go-to-bed-at-noon (Tragopogon pratensis).

kozica f. zool. chamois (Rupicapra rupicapra).

kozieradka f. Gen.pl. -ek bot. fenugreek (Trigonella foenum-graecum).

kozik mi Gen. -a (= scyzoryk) pocketknife (with a wooden handle).

kozina f. (= kozie mięso) goat meat.

kozioł ma -zł- 1. zool. (= samiec kozy) billy goat; **kozioł ofiarny** scapegoat; **uparty jak kozioł** stubborn as a mule; **kozioł śnieżny** Rocky Mountain goat, mountain goat (Oreamnos americanus). 2. myśl. (= samiec sarny) roebuck. – mi -zł- Gen. -a 1. (siedzenie dla woźnicy) box. 2. sport (= skrzynia) horse, buck; **skakać przez kozła** vault the horse. 3. sport (odbicie piłki) rebound, bounce. 4. pot. (= fikołek) somersault. 5. (= krzyżak, stojak) trestle. 6. (do przenoszenia cegieł) hod. – mp -zł- pl. -y pot. (= uparciuch) mule.

koziołek ma -łk- zool., myśl. kid. – mi -łk- -a 1. (dla woźnicy) box. 2. pot. (= fikołek) somersault; **fikać koziołki** somersault; przen. (= dokazywać) caper. 3. (= krzyżak, stojak) trestle.

koziołkować ipf. (= przewracać się) tumble.

koziorożec ma -żc- zool. ibex (Capra ibex). – mi -żc- Gen. -a 1. astrol. (znak zodiaku) Capricorn; Goat, Capricornus, Capricorn; **osoba spod znaku Koziorożca** a Capricorn; **zwrotnik Koziorożca** geogr. tropic of Capricorn. 2. astron. (konstelacja) Capricornus, Capricorn.

kozioróg ma ent. lognicorn, long-horned beetle (*Cerambyx*); **kozioróg dębosz** cerambyx longicorn (*Cerambyx cerdo*).

kozłek *mi* -złk- *Gen.* -a *bot.* valerian; *Br. t.* allheal (*Valeriana*); **kozłek lekarski** garden heliotrope, common valerian (*Valeriana officinalis*).

kozłkowate *pl. bot.* valerianas (*Valerianaceae*).

kozłować *ipf.* **1.** *sport* (= *odbijać piłkę*) dribble. **2.** *lotn.* (= *podskakiwać przy lądowaniu*) bounce.

kozodój *ma* -o- *Gen.pl.* -ów *orn.* nightjar, goatsucker (*Caprimulgidae*); **lelek kozodój** *orn.* goatsucker, European nightjar (*Caprimulgus europaeus*).

koźlak *mi Gen.* -a *bot.* birch bolete, shaggy boletus (*Leccinum scabrum*).

koźlarz *mi Gen.* -a *zob.* **koźlak**.

koźlę *n.* -ęci- *pl.* -ęt- *Gen.* -ąt kid.

koźli *a.* goatish; **koźla skórka** kidskin, kid; **koźli upór** *przen.* mulishness.

koźlina *f.* (= *kozina*) goat meat.

kożuch *mi Gen.* -a **1.** (*ubranie*) sheepskin coat; **kwiatek do kożucha** *przen.* a square peg in a round hole. **2.** (*na mleku, farbie; na stawie*) skin.

kożuchować *ipf.* **1.** *ogr.* (*szczepić*) scion graft. **2.** *bud.* (*szalować*) board.

kożusznik *mp* (*rzemieślnik*) furrier.

kół *mi* -o- *Gen.* -u *l.* -a (= *pal, żerdź*) stake.

kółeczko *n. Gen.pl.* -ek *zob.* **kółko**.

kółko *n. Gen.pl.* -ek **1.** (= *małe koło l. okrąg*) circlet, ringlet; (*mebla, fotela itd.*) caster *l.* castor, truckle. **2.** (*figura w tańcu*) circle; **kółko i krzyżyk** tick-tack-toe, tic-tac-toe; *Br.* noughts and crosses; **kółko się zamyka** we come full circle; **kręcić się w kółko** go *l.* run around in circles; **powtarzać w kółko to samo** harp on the same string. **3.** (*element w kształcie koła*) ring, wheel; **dom na kółkach** mobile home, trailer; **cztery kółka** *pot.* wheels; **kółko na klucze** key *l.* split ring; **kółko na serwetkę** napkin ring; **kółko nosowe** (*np. u byka*) nose ring; **meble na kółkach** rollaway furniture. **4.** *techn.* (= *wałek, trybik*) wheel; **kółko zębate** pinion, gear wheel. **5.** (= *grupa*) circle; **kółko zainteresowań** interest group. **6.** *pot.* (= *kierownica*) wheel; **siedzieć za kółkiem** be at the wheel; **w kółko** (*chodzić, biegać*) round and round, in circles; (= *wciąż*) over and over (again), again and again, time and again.

kółkować *ipf.* (*np. byka*) ring.

kóz *f. zob.* **koza**.

kózka *f. Gen.pl.* -ek **1.** *zool.* kid; **żeby kózka nie skakała, to by nóżki nie złamała** better safe than sorry. **2.** *pot.* (= *nastolatka*) filly. **3.** *icht.* (= *koza*) spined loach (*Cobitis taenia*). **4.** *ent.* lingicorn (beetle), long-horned beetle (*Cerambycidae*).

kózkowate *pl. ent.* longicorns (*Cerambycidae*).

kpiarski *a.* derisive, mocking.

kpiarstwo *n.* derision, mockery.

kpiarz *mp* (= *szyderca*) scoffer, tease; (= *żartowniś*) joker.

kpiąco *adv.* (= *drwiąco*) derisively, mockingly.

kpiący *a.* (= *drwiący*) derisive, mocking.

kpić *ipf.* -ij (= *drwić*) mock (*z kogoś / czegoś* sb/sth) jeer (*z kogoś / czegoś* at sb/sth); **kpisz, czy o drogę pytasz** you must be joking!, you're putting me on!

kpina *f.* (= *drwina*) derision, mockery; **przedmiot kpin** object of ridicule; **to są kpiny!** this is ridiculous!

kra[1] *f. Gen.pl.* **kier** (*tafla lodu*) ice floe, floe.

kra[2] *int.* (*dźwięk wydawany przez wrony*) caw!

krab *ma zool.* (*skorupiak*) crab (*Cancer*). – *mi Gen.* -a *kulin.* crab, crabmeat.

krach *mi* **1.** (= *kryzys gospodarczy*) slump, crash; (= *bankructwo firmy*) crash, bankruptcy; **krach na giełdzie** stock-market crash. **2.** (= *klęska*) failure; **krach marzeń/planów** failure of dreams/plans.

kraciasty *a.* (= *w kratę*) checked, checkered.

kradnę *itd. ipf. zob.* **kraść**.

kradzież *f. pl.* -e theft; *prawn.* larceny; **drobna kradzież** petty theft; **kradzież w sklepie** shoplifting; **kradzież z włamaniem** burglary; **popełnić kradzież** commit a theft.

kradziony *a. zob.* **kraść**.

kraik *mi* small country.

kraina *f.* **1.** (= *kraj*) country, land. **2.** (= *region l. ekosystem*) region; **kraina mlekiem i miodem płynąca** land of milk and honey, land of plenty. **3.** (= *teren*) land; **kraina baśni** fairyland; **kraina marzeń** dreamland, never-never land.

kraj *mi Gen.pl.* -ów **1.** (= *państwo*) country; **kraj członkowski** member country; **kraj pochodzenia** country of origin; **kraj rozwijający się** developing country; **kraj rozwinięty** developed country; **kraje trzeciego świata** Third World countries. **2.** (= *ojczyzna*) homeland, native country. **3.** (= *teren*) land; **co kraj, to obyczaj** so many countries, so many customs; every country has its customs; **egzotyczne/ciepłe kraje** exotic/hot countries; **kraj lat dziecinnych** land of childhood memories. **4.** (= *krawędź, brzeg*) edge, verge; **iść na kraj świata** go to the ends of the earth.

krajać *ipf.* -ę -esz **1.** (= *ciąć*) cut; (*mięso w plastry*) carve; (*na plastry l. kromki*) slice; (*w kostkę*) cube, dice; **krawiec tak kraje, jak mu materii staje** one must cut one's coat according to one's cloth. **2.** *pot.* (= *operować*) cut up. ~ **się** *ipf.* (= *być dzielonym*) cut; **serce mi się kraje** my heart bleeds *l.* breaks.

krajalnia *f. Gen.pl.* -i *l.* -ń cutting-room.

krajalnica *f.* slicer, cutter.

krajalność *f.* (*właściwość szkła l. minerału*) sectility.

krajan *mp* (= *rodak*) compatriot, coutryman.

krajanka *f. Gen.pl.* -ek (= *rodaczka*) compatriot, countrywoman.

krajarka *f. Gen.pl.* -ek **1.** (= *krajalnica*) cutter, slicer. **2.** *druk.* (= *gilotyna*) paper cutter. **3.** *techn.* (*do blachy, papieru*) guillotine; (*do tkanin*) cutter.

krajka *f. Gen.pl.* -ek **1.** (= *wstążka*) ribbon (*usu. patterned*). **2.** (= *lamówka*) selvage, list.

krajobraz *mi* **1.** (= *widok*) landscape, scenery; **krajobraz miejski** cityscape, townscape; **krajobraz morski** seascape; **krajobraz księżycowy** *dosł. i przen.* moonscape; **krajobraz wiejski** rural landscape, countryside; **piękno krajobrazu** scenic beauty. **2.** *sztuka* (= *pejzaż*) landscape.

krajobrazowy *a.* landscape, scenic; **atrakcja krajobrazowa** beauty spot; **malarstwo krajobrazowe** landscape painting; **malar-z/ka krajobrazow-y/a** landscape painter; **park krajobrazowy** scenic park; **trasa krajobrazowa** scenic route.

krajowiec *mp* **-wc-** *pl.* **-y** (= *tubylec*) native; indigene, indigen.

krajowy *a.* domestic, home, national; **gazeta krajowa** domestic newspaper; **produkt krajowy brutto** *ekon.* gross domestic product; **produkt krajowy netto** *ekon.* net domestic product; **przemysł/rynek krajowy** domestic industry/market; **sprzedaż krajowa** home sales; **średnia krajowa** *mat.* national average; **Armia Krajowa** *hist.* Home Army.

krajoznawca *mp* hiker, sightseer.

krajoznawczy *a.* hiking, sightseeing; **czasopisma krajoznawcze** travel magazines; **film krajoznawczy** *kino* travelog, *Br.* travelogue; **szlak krajoznawczy** interpretive walk; **wycieczka krajoznawcza** sightseeing tour.

krajoznawstwo *n.* (= *turystyka*) tourism, sightseeing.

krakać *ipf.* **-czę -czesz 1.** (*o ptakach*) caw, croak; **kiedy wejdziesz między wrony, musisz krakać jak i one** when in Rome do as the Romans do, when in Rome do as Rome does. **2.** *przen., pot.* (= *przepowiadać klęskę*) croak.

krakers *mi Gen.* **-a** (*ciastko*) cracker, water biscuit.

kraking *mi chem.* cracking.

krakowiak *mp pl.* **-cy** (= *krakowianin*) Cracovian, inhabitant of Cracow. – *mi Gen. i Acc.* **-a** *pl.* **-i** *muz.* (*taniec*) cracovienne, krakowiak.

krakowianin *mp pl.* **-anie** *Gen.* **-an** Cracovian.

krakowianka *f. Gen.pl.* **-ek** Cracovian, inhabitant of Cracow.

krakowski *a.* Cracovian, of Cracow; **kasza krakowska** buckwheat grits; **kiełbasa krakowska** Cracow pork sausage; **pogodzić się krakowskim targiem** split the difference.

Kraków *mi* **-o-** *Gen.* **-a** Cracow; **nie od razu Kraków zbudowano** Rome was not built in a day.

kraksa *f.* (= *wypadek*) crash.

krakus *mp pl.* **-i** *l.* **-y 1.** *żart.* (= *krakowianin*) Cracovian, inhabitant of Cracow. **2.** *hist.* (= *kawalerzysta*) light cavalryman.

krakuska *f. Gen.pl.* **-ek** (*czapka*) fur-lined four-cornered cap.

krakwa *f. orn.* gadwall (*Anas strepera*).

kram *mi* **1.** (= *stragan*) stall, stand; (= *budka*) booth; **jaki pan, taki kram** like author like book. **2.** *pot.* (= *bałagan*) clutter; **cały ten kram** the whole kit and caboodle. **3.** (= *zamęt, chaos*) trouble.

kramarka *f. Gen.pl.* **-ek** (= *straganiarka*) huckstress, stall-keeper.

kramarski *a.* (= *straganiarski*) huckster's, huckstering.

kramarstwo *n.* (= *handel*) huckstering.

kramarz *mp* (= *straganiarz*) huckster, stall-keeper.

kran[1] *mi* (= *kurek*) faucet; *Br.* tap.

kran[2] *mi* (= *dźwig*) crane.

kraniec *mi* **-ńc-** *Gen.* **-a** (= *kres, koniec*) end, limit, extreme; **kraniec miasta** city limits, outskirts; **kraniec świata** world's end, ends of the earth; **stać na dwóch krańcach** to be at opposite poles.

kraniolog *mp pl.* **-dzy** *l.* **-owie** craniologist.

kraniologia *f. Gen.* **-ii** craniology.

kraniologiczny *a.* craniological.

kraniometr *mi* craniometer.

kraniometria *f. Gen.* **-ii** craniometry.

kraniometryczny *a.* craniometric, craniometrical.

kranioskopia *f.* cranioscopy.

kraniotabes *mi pat.* craniotabes.

kraniotomia *f. Gen.* **-ii** *med.* (= *trepanacja*) craniotomy.

kranówa *f. Gen.pl.* **-ek** *pot.* (= *woda z kranu*) tap water.

krańcowo *adv.* (= *skrajnie, ekstremalnie*) radically, extremely.

krańcowość *f.* (= *skrajność, ekstremalność*) extremity.

krańcowy *a.* **1.** (= *końcowy*) final; **krańcowy przystanek** terminal stop. **2.** (= *skrajny, ekstremalny*) extreme, ultimate.

kras *mi geol.* karst.

krasa *f.* (= *piękno*) *lit.* beauty; (*zwł. piękno fizyczne*) pulchritude; **w całej swojej krasie** in all its beauty.

krasić *ipf.* (*tłuszczem*) add fat (*to a dish*); (*sosem*) add gravy (*to a dish*).

kraska *f. Gen.pl.* **-ek** *orn.* European roller (*Corracias garrulus*).

kraski *pl. orn.* rollers (*Coraciidae*).

krasnal *mp Gen.pl.* **-i** *l.* **-ów** = krasnoludek.

krasnodrzew *mi bot.* coca (*Erythroxylon coca*).

krasnolicy *a. poet.* (= *piękny*) beauteous.

krasnoludek *mp* **-dk-** *pl.* **-i 1.** (*postać bajkowa*) dwarf; (*zwł. pomagający ludziom w pracy*) brownie; (*zwł. mieszkający pod ziemią*) gnome; **Królewna Śnieżka i siedmiu krasnoludków** Snow White and the Seven Dwarfs. **2.** (= *drobny, niski człowiek*) sprite; *obelż.* gnome.

krasnopiórka *f. icht.* rudd (*Scardinius erythrophthalmus*).

krasnorost *mi bot.* red algae, red seaweed (*Rhodophyceae*).

krasomówca *mp* (= *orator*) elocutionist.

krasomówczy *a.* (= *oratorski*) elocutionary.

krasomówstwo *n.* (= *oratorstwo*) elocution.

krasowy *a. geol.* karstic; **jaskinia krasowa** dripstone cave; **zapadlisko krasowe** doline, dolina.

krasula *f. pot.* (= *krowa*) cow.

kraszanka *f. Gen.pl.* **-ek** (= *pisanka*) Easter egg.

kraść *ipf.* **-dnę -dniesz, -ij, -dł** (= *przywłaszczać*) steal; **kraść coś komuś** steal sth from sb;

kradzione nie tuczy ill-gotten gains never prosper.

krata *f.* **1.** (*przegroda*) (*ozdoba*) grill; (*w ścianie, ogrodzeniu*) grating; (*w oknie, w więzieniu*) bars; **trafić za kraty** *pot.* end up behind bars; **za kratami** *pot.* behind bars. **2.** (*wzór*) check, checker; **szkocka krata** tartan.

krater *mi* crater.

kratka *f. Gen.pl.* **-ek 1.** (= *mała krata*) grate; **kratka wentylacyjna** *bud.* air grating; **siedzieć za kratkami** *pot.* be behind bars. **2.** (*wzór*) check, checker. **3.** (= *czworokąt*) square; (= *w formularzu*) box; **papier w kratkę** squared paper; **w kratkę** (*np. pracować, chodzić do szkoły*) irregularly, on and off.

kratkować *ipf.* checker, square.

kratownica *f.* **1.** (= *przegroda*) grate, grating, lattice. **2.** *techn., bud.* (= *układ konstrukcyjny*) framework.

kraul *mi Gen.* **-a** *sport* crawl; **pływać kraulem do** *l.* swim the crawl, crawl.

krawaciarka *f.* tie-maker.

krawaciarstwo *n.* tie-making.

krawaciarz *ma* tie-making.

krawat *mi Gen.* **-a** *l.* **-u 1.** (*element ubrania*) tie; **chodzić w krawacie** wear a tie; **spinka do krawata** tiepin, tie tack, tie clasp. **2.** *sport* (*w zapasach*) stranglehold, Japanese stranglehold. **3.** *żegl.* lazy jack, tier.

krawcowa *f. Gen.* **-ej** (= *szwaczka*) seamstress, dressmaker.

krawędziarka *f. Gen.pl.* **-ek 1.** *techn.* (= *prasa*) bending brake, folding brake. **2.** *techn.* (= *heblarka*) edger.

krawędź *f. pl.* **-e 1.** (= *kant, brzeg*) edge, verge; (*naczynia*) brink, rim. **2. na krawędzi przepaści/ bankructwa** on the brink of a precipice/ bankruptcy; **krawędź skrawająca** *l.* **tnąca** *techn.* cutting edge.

krawężnica *f. bud.* hip rafter, angle rafter.

krawężnik *mi Gen.* **-a 1.** (*przy jezdni i chodniku*) curb; *Br.* kerb. **2.** *techn.* (= *strug*) rebate plane, sash plane. – *mp pl.* **-i** *pot., żart.* (= *policjant*) flatfoot, cop.

krawiec *mp* **-wc-** *pl.* **-y** (*rzemieślnik*) (*męski*) tailor; (*damski*) dressmaker; **krawiec tak kraje, jak mu materii staje** one must cut one's coat according to one's cloth.

krawiecki *a.* tailor's; *form.* sartorial; **dodatki krawieckie** passementerie, trimmings; **kreda krawiecka** French chalk, tailor's chalk; **mięsień krawiecki** *anat.* sartorius; **żelazko krawieckie** goose.

krawiectwo *n.* (*zwł. męskie*) tailoring; (*zwł. damskie*) dressmaking.

krąg *mi* **-ę- 1.** (= *okrąg*) circle; **kamienny krąg** *archeol.* cromlech, stone circle; **kręgi pod oczami** rings *l.* circles under the *l.* one's eyes; **świetlisty krąg** ring of light; **w krąg** around, in a circle; **zaklęty** *l.* **zaczarowany krąg** charmed circle; **otoczyć kręgiem** encircle; **zataczać szerokie kręgi** spread far and wide. **2.** (= *koło, krążek*) ring; **krąg światła** ring *l.* pool of light. **3.** (= *grupa ludzi, znajomych*) circle; **w rodzinnym kręgu** in family circle. **4.** (= *zwój*) (*np. kabla*) coil. **5.** (= *zakres, sfera*) domain; **krąg kulturowy** culture.

krągłość *f.* **1.** (= *kulistość*) roundness, rotundity. **2.** (= *wypukłość*) swell; **ponętne krągłości kształtów** curvaceousness.

krągłouste *pl. zool.* cyclostomes (*Cyclostomata*).

krągły *a.* **1.** (= *okrągły*) round. **2.** (*o formie pisania i mówienia*) (= *gładki, piękny*) round, flowing. **3.** (= *pełny, dorodny*) (*o osobie*) rotund.

krąp *ma* **-pi-** *zool.* (*ryba*) silver bream, white bream (*Blicca bjoerkna*).

krążek *mi* **-żk-** *Gen.* **-a 1.** (= *kółko, plasterek*) disk; **krążek cebuli** onion ring; **krążek kiełbasy** slice of sausage; **krążek wewnątrzmaciczny** *med.* intrautrine device, IUD; **krążek pochwowy** *med.* pessary; **krążek międzykręgowy** *anat.* intervertebral disc. **2.** *sport* (*w hokeju*) puck. **3.** *techn.* (= *walec*) roller. **4.** *pot.* (= *płyta*) (*analogowa*) record; (*CD*) disc.

krążenie *n.* **1.** (= *kołowanie*) (*przed pozwoleniem na lądowanie*) holding pattern. **2.** (= *błądzenie*) cruising. **3.** (*o płynach ustrojowych, pokarmach itp.*) circulation; **krążenie krwi** *fizj.* blood circulation; **niewydolność krążenia** *pat.* circulatory failure; **układ krążenia** *fizj.* circulatory system.

krążeniowy *a.* circulatory.

krążkopławy *pl. zool.* scyphozoan (*Scyphozoa*).

krążkować *ipf. techn.* roller finish, roller burnish.

krążnik *mi Gen.* **-a** *techn.* runner, muller, roller.

krążownik *mi Gen.* **-a 1.** *wojsk.* (*okręt wojenny*) cruiser. **2.** *pot.* (*zwł.*) **krążownik szos** (= *samochód*) cruiser.

krążyć *ipf.* **1.** (= *kołować*) (*o samolocie, ptakach*) circle, make circles; (*wokół własnej osi*) rotate; (*po orbicie*) orbit. **2.** (= *kluczyć*) wander, cruise (about); **krążyć bez celu** wander aimlessly. **3.** (*o płynach ustrojowych, pokarmach*) *fizj.* circulate. **4.** (= *rozchodzić się*) circulate, be passed around; **krążyć z rąk do rąk** pass from hand to hand.

krążyna *f. bud.* (= *podpora*) centering.

kreacja *f.* **1.** (= *rola*) creation. **2.** (= *strój*) outfit, creation; **modna kreacja** stylish gown; **kreacja wieczorowa** party dress. **3.** (= *tworzenie*) creation.

kreacjonista *mp fil., lit., rel.* creationist.

kreacjonistyczny *a. fil., lit., rel.* creationist, creationistic.

kreacjonizm *mi fil., lit., rel.* creationism.

kreacyjny *a.* (= *twórczy*) creative.

kreator *mp pl.* **-rzy** *l.* **-owie 1.** *fil.* (= *stwórca*) Creator. **2.** (= *twórca*) creator; **kreator mody** couturier, fashion designer.

kreatura *f.* **1.** *pot., obelż.* (= *nikczemnik*) scoundrel, toad. **2.** *przest.* (= *osobnik*) individual.

kreatyna *f. chem.* creatine, creatin.

kreatynina *f. chem.* creatinine.

kreatywny *a.* (= *twórczy, dynamiczny*) creative.

krecha f. (= *gruba kreska*) thick line; **mieć u kogoś krechę** pot. be in sb's bad l. black books, be on sb's black list; **na krechę** pot. on credit.

kreci a. 1. (= *dotyczący kreta*) mole. 2. *przen.* (= *podstępny, fałszywy*) underhand; **krecia robota** scheming.

kreda f. 1. geol. (*skała*) chalk. 2. (*do pisania, w przemyśle*) chalk; **biały jak kreda** as white as a sheet l. ghost; **kolorowa kreda** colored chalk; **kreda do tablicy** chalk; **pisać kredą** write in chalk. 3. geol. (*okres ery mezozoicznej*) the Cretaceous, Cretaceous period.

kredens mi 1. (*mebel*) cupboard. 2. hist. (*izba*) butler's pantry.

kredka f. Gen.pl. **-ek** 1. (= *ołówek*) colored pencil, crayon. 2. (*kosmetyk*) pencil; **kredka do brwi** eyebrow pencil; **kredka do oczu** eyeliner, liner; **kredka do ust** lip pencil, lip liner; **kredka świecowa** wax crayon.

kredo n. indecl. l. Gen. **-a** (= *przekonanie*) rel. (= *wyznanie wiary*) credo, creed.

kredować ipf. techn. (*papier*) apply white pigment coating.

kredowy a. 1. (= *zawierający kredę*) chalky; techn. cretaceous; **farba kredowa** distemper. 2. geol. cretaceous; **okres kredowy** Cretaceous period, the Cretaceous. 3. pot. (*o papierze*) coated, glossy.

kredyt mi 1. (= *pożyczka*) credit, loan; **kredyt bankowy** bank loan, bank credit; **kredyt handlowy** trade credit; **kredyt hipoteczny** mortgage; **kredyt inwestycyjny** investment credit; **kredyt konsumpcyjny** consumer credit; **kredyt mieszkaniowy** home loan; **kredyt zaufania** confidence, trust; **obdarzyć kogoś kredytem zaufania** take sb into one's confidence; **okres spłaty kredytu** credit period; **ubiegać się o kredyt** apply for a loan; **umowa kredytowa** l. **o kredyt** credit agreement; **zaciągnąć/dostać/spłacić kredyt** take up/get/repay (one's) credit. 2. handl. (= *rubryka należności*) credit. 3. pot. (*obrót handlowy bez pieniędzy*) credit; **na kredyt** on credit.

kredytobiorca mp borrower, debtor.

kredytodawca mp creditor, lender.

kredytować ipf. (= *pożyczać*) credit, give credit.

kredytowy a. credit; **karta kredytowa** credit card; **list kredytowy** ekon. letter of credit; **rachunek kredytowy** ekon. loan account; **towarzystwo kredytowe** ekon. credit society; **zdolność kredytowa** ekon. creditworthiness.

krem mi 1. (*deser*) cream; **ciastko z kremem** cream slice, éclair; **krem budyniowy** custard; **krem czekoladowy** chocolate cream. 2. (*w kosmetyce*) cream; **krem do golenia** shaving cream; **krem do rąk/twarzy** hand/face cream; **krem na noc/dzień** night/day cream; **krem nawilżający** moisturizing cream; **krem ochronny** barrier cream; **krem do opalania** suntan lotion; Br. suncream; **krem do opalania z filtrem ochronnym** sunscreen, sunblock. 3. (= *zupa*) cream; **krem ze szparagów** cream of asparagus. 4. (*kolor*) cream.

kremacja f. cremation; **poddać kremacji** cremate.

kremacyjny a. crematory; **piec kremacyjny** crematory, crematorium; **zakład kremacyjny** crematory.

krematorium n. sing. indecl. pl. **-ria** Gen. **-riów** crematorium, crematory.

krematoryjny a. crematory; **piec krematoryjny** crematorium, crematory.

Kreml mi Gen. **-a** polit. the Kremlin.

kreml mi Gen. **-a** hist. kremlin.

kremować[1] ipf. (*smarować kremem*) cream.

kremować[2] ipf. (*dokonywać kremacji*) cremate.

kremowy a. 1. (= *zrobiony z kremu, zawierający krem*) cream, creamy; **śmietana** l. **śmietanka kremowa** heavy l. whipping cream. 2. (*kolor*) creamy, cream.

kremówka f. Gen.pl. **-ek** 1. (*rodzaj śmietany*) heavy l. whipping cream. 2. (*ciastko*) cream cake.

krenelaż mi hist., bud. crenels, crenelles.

kreodonty pl. paleont. creodonts (*Creodonta*).

Kreol mp Gen.pl. **-ów**, **Kreolka** f. Gen.pl. **-ek** Creole.

kreolski a. Creole.

kreować ipf. 1. (= *tworzyć*) create. 2. (= *odgrywać rolę*) (*o aktorze*) create, perform the role of.

kreozot mi chem. creosote.

krepa f. 1. tk. crepe; (*żałobna*) crape; **krepa chińska** crepe de Chine. 2. (= *guma krepowa*) techn. crepe rubber, crepe.

krepdeszyn mi tk. crepe de Chine.

krepina f. (= *bibułka ozdobna*) crepe paper, crepe.

krepitacja f. pat. crepitus.

krepon mi tk. crepon.

krepować ipf. techn. (*tkaninę, papier*) crepe.

krepowy a. tk. crepe; (= *marszczony*) techn. crepe; **bibułka krepowa** crepe paper, crepe.

kres mi 1. (= *granica, kraniec*) limit, end; **kres dolny zbioru** mat. greatest lower bound, infimum; **kres górny zbioru** mat. least upper bound, supremum; **kres zbioru liczb** mat. bound; **kres funkcji** mat. limit. 2. (*o czasie*) end; **być u kresu sił** be completely exhausted; **dobiegać kresu** be coming l. drawing to a close; **kres cierpienia** limits of suffering; **kres wytrzymałości** limit of endurance; **mieć swój kres** come to an end; **położyć czemuś kres** put an end to sth; **położyć kres czyimś nadziejom** extinguish sb's hopes.

kreska f. Gen.pl. **-ek** 1. (= *linia*) line; (= *łącznik między wyrazami*) hyphen; (= *myślnik*) dash; kartogr. hachure; **cienka kreska** thin l. fine line; **gruba kreska** thick l. heavy line; **mieć u kogoś kreskę** pot. be in sb's black l. bad books. 2. (*znak graficzny*) stroke; **o z kreską** o acute. 3. techn. (*oznaczenie na skali*) mark; **kreska taktowa** muz. bar; **kreska ułamkowa** mat. line of a fraction; **być pod kreską** pot. be in the red; **przyjdzie na kogoś kreska** sb's turn will come. 4. (*znak w alfabecie Morse'a*) dash.

kreskować *ipf.* (= *rysować kreski*) line, hatch; *kartogr.* hachure.

kreskowy *a.* line; **linia kreskowa** dashed line; **kod kreskowy** bar code.

kreskówka *f. Gen.pl.* **-ek** *film, pot.* (= *film rysunkowy*) (animated) cartoon.

kresomózgowie *n. Gen.pl.* **-i** *anat.* telencephalon, endbrain.

kresowiak *mp* = **kresowianin.**

kresowianin *mp pl.* **-anie** *Gen.* **-an** frontiersman (*esp. of the Polish eastern frontier*).

kresowianka *f. Gen.pl.* **-ek** frontierswoman (*esp. of the Polish eastern frontier*).

kresowy *a.* (= *dotyczący kresów*) borderland, frontier.

kresy *pl. Gen.* **-ów** (= *pogranicze*) frontier, borderland; **Kresy Wschodnie** *hist.* Polish eastern frontier.

kresz *mi tk.* crash.

kreślarka *f.* draftswoman, *Br.* draughtswoman.

kreślarnia *f. Gen.pl.* **-i** *l.* **-ń** drawing office, drafting room.

kreślarski *a.* draftsman's; **deska kreślarska** drawing board; **papier kreślarski** drawing *l.* drafting paper; **tusz kreślarski** drawing ink.

kreślarstwo *n.* technical drawing.

kreślarz *mp Gen.pl.* **-y** *l.* **-ów** draftsman, *Br.* draughtsman.

kreślić *ipf.* **1.** (= *wykreślać, projektować*) draft. **2.** (= *rysować, bazgrać*) draw. **3.** (= *przekreślać, usuwać*) cross out. **4.** (= *pisać ręcznie*) write, handwrite. **5.** *lit.* (= *opisywać, przedstawiać*) depict. **~ się** *ipf.* **1.** (= *odcinać się od tła*) stand out. **2.** *przest.* (= *podpisywać się*) sign.

kret *ma zool.* **1.** mole (*Talpa europaea*); **ślepy jak kret** blind as a mole *l. bat.* **2.** *przen.* (*podstępny człowiek*) schemer, plotter; **ryć pod kimś jak kret** scheme against sb. **3.** *techn.* mole plow *l.* drainer, mole.

Kreta *f. geogr.* Crete.

Kretenka *f. Gen.pl.* **-ek, Kreteńczyk** *mp* Cretan.

kreteński *a.* Cretan; **byk kreteński** *mit.* Cretan bull; **kultura kreteńska** *hist.* Minoan culture; **pismo kreteńskie** *jęz.* Cretan script.

kretesem *adv.* **z kretesem** completely, utterly.

kreton *mi tk.* cretonne.

kretować *ipf. roln.* (*napowietrzać glebę*) aerate; mole drain, mole.

kretowisko *n.* molehill.

krety *pl. Gen.* **-ów** (*futro*) moleskin fur.

kretyn *mp pl.* **-i** *l.* **-y** **1.** *pot.* (= *dureń, głupek*) moron, blockhead; *rzad.* cretin. **2.** *med.* cretin.

kretynizm *mi* **1.** *pot.* (= *głupota*) stupidity. **2.** *med.* cretinism, infantile hypothyroidism.

kretynka *f. pot.* = **kretyn.**

kretyński *a. pot.* moronic, stupid.

krew *f.* **krwi-** **1.** *fizj.* blood; **krew tętnicza/żylna** arterial/venous blood; **analiza krwi** blood test; **białe/czerwone ciałka krwi** white/red blood cells; **grupa krwi** blood group *l.* type; **płytka krwi** blood platelet; **przepływ krwi** blood flow; **pobrać krew** draw blood; **skrzep krwi** blood clot; **puszczać komuś krew** bleed sb; (*za pomocą pijawek*) leech

sb; **zatamować krew** arrest bleeding, staunch the flow of blood; **biorca/dawca krwi** blood recipient/donor; **bez kropli krwi** (= *bardzo blady*) as white as a sheet; **bez rozlewu krwi** without bloodshed; **do krwi** till first blood; **do ostatniej kropli krwi** to the *l.* one's last *l.* dying breath; **krew z mlekiem** *przen.* (*o cerze*) peaches and cream; **za cenę krwi** for the price of blood; **z krwi i kości** (= *prawdziwy*) true, to the core; **tonąć we krwi** be bathed in blood; **napsuć komuś krwi** *przen.* try sb's patience; **coś idzie jak krew z nosa** *przen.* sth is a drag; **przelewać niewinną krew** shed innocent blood; **wysysać krew** suck blood; **przypieczętować coś krwią** seal sth with blood; **splamić ręce krwią** *l.* **mieć krew na rękach** *l.* **mieć krew na sumieniu** have blood on one's hands; **mrozić komuś krew w żyłach** make sb's blood curdle, make sb's blood run cold; **mrożący krew w żyłach** blood-curdling; **krew uderzyła komuś do głowy** *przen.* sb saw red; **kogoś krew zalewa** *pot.* sb sees red; **krew się w kimś burzy** *przen.* sb's blood boils; **żądza krwi** blood lust. **2.** (= *temperament, osobowość*) temperament, nature; **zew krwi** call of blood; **gorąca krew** hot blood; **coś weszło komuś w krew** sth has become second nature with sb; **mieć coś we krwi** have sth in one's blood; **krew nie woda** (= *związki rodzinne są silne*) blood is thicker than water; (*o czymś gorącym temperamencie*) he (she etc.) is so hot-blooded *l.* hot-tempered; **krew się w kimś odzywa** sb's blood tells; **zachować/stracić zimną krew** keep/lose one's cool; **z zimną krwią** in cold blood. **3.** (= *pochodzenie, pokrewieństwo*) blood, kinship; **błękitna krew** blue blood; **braterstwo krwi** *przen.* blood brotherhood; **czystej** *l.* **pełnej krwi** thoroughbred, full blood; **krew z krwi, kość z kości** flesh and blood; **więzy krwi** blood ties; **książę krwi** a prince of the blood; **w czyichś żyłach płynie Polska/obca krew** there is Polish/foreign blood in sb's veins.

krewa *f. pot.* (= *niepowodzenie*) flop.

krewetka *f. Gen.pl.* **-ek** *zool., kulin.* shrimp (*Crangon*); prawn (*Palaemon*).

krewetkowy *a.* shrimp; prawn.

krewki *a.* (= *porywczy*) hot-blooded.

krewkość *f.* (= *temperament*) hot temper *l.* blood.

krewna *f. Gen.* **-ej** kinswoman; relation, relative.

krewniaczka *f. Gen.pl.* **-ek** *pot.* = **krewna.**

krewniak *mp pl.* **-cy** *l.* **-i** *pot.* = **krewny.**

krewny *mp* kinsman; relation, relative; **bliski/daleki krewny** close/distant relation; **najbliższy krewny** next of kin; **traktować kogoś jak ubogiego krewnego** treat sb as a leper, treat sb like dirt.

kreza *f.* **1.** *orn.* (= *pióra wokół szyi ptaka*) ruff, ruffle. **2.** *techn.* orifice, diaphragm. **3.** *hist.* (*kołnierz*) ruff.

krezka *f. Gen.pl.* **-ek** **1.** *anat.* mesentery; **krezka jajnika** mesovarium; **krezka jądra** mesorchium; **zapalenie krezki** mesenteritis. **2.** *arch.* (= *falbanka, kołnierz*) ruff, flounce.

krezol *mi chem.* cresol.

krezolowy *a. chem.* cresol.

Krezus *mp mit.* Croesus.

krezus *mp pl.* -i *l.* -y (= *bogacz*) Croesus.

kręcić *ipf.* **1.** (= *obracać*) turn, spin; **kręcić piruety** pirouette; **kręcony fotel** swivel chair; **kręcone schody** spiral staircase; **coś kręci w nosie** sth makes one feel like sneezing; **kręcić bicz na własny grzbiet** *l.* **kręcić na siebie bat** *przen.* make a rod for one's own back; **ja cię kręcę!** *pot.* jeez!, gee!; **kręcić głową** shake one's head; **kręcić młynka palcami** twiddle one's thumbs, twirl one's fingers; **kręcić komuś głowę** *l.* **gitarę** bother sb; **kręcić na coś nosem** turn up one's nose at sth. **2.** (= *skręcać*) (*włosy*) curl, frizz; (*papierosa*) roll up; **kręcić wąsa** twist one's mustache. **3.** (= *ucierać*) *kulin.* mix; **kręcić ciasto** mix dough; **kręcić mak** grind poppy seed. **4.** *pot.* (= *kłamać*) pussyfoot, blur the facts. **5.** *pot.* (= *rządzić*) manipulate, boss. **6.** *pot.* (*w kolarstwie*) (= *jechać na rowerze, pedałować*) pedal. **7.** *pot.* (= *filmować*) shoot, film. **8.** *pot.* (= *flirtować*) hang out; **kręcimy ze sobą od paru tygodni** we've been hanging out for a few weeks; (= *spotykać się*) date (*z kimś* sb); **kręcę z nią od pół roku** I've been dating her for half a year. **9.** *pot.* (= *podniecać*) turn on; **to mnie kręci** it turns me on. **~ się** *ipf.* **1.** (= *obracać się dookoła*) twirl, spin, whirl; **kręcić się w tańcu** twirl; **kręcić się jak chorągiewka na dachu** be a weathercock; **kręcić się jak piskorz** squirm; **kręcić się w kółko** turn round and round; **komuś kręci się w głowie** sb is dizzy *l.* giddy; **łza się komuś w oku kręci** tears well up in sb's eyes. **2.** *przen.* go *l.* run (around) in circles; **coś się kręci wokół czegoś** sth centers on sth, sth hinges on sth. **3.** (= *wałęsać się*) wander, roam; **kręcić się jak w ukropie** make frantic haste, bustle around. **4.** *pot.* (= *wiercić się*) fidget; **kręcić się jak kot z pęcherzem** be in a twitter. **5.** *pot.* (= *interesować się, zajmować się*) busy oneself (*wokół kogoś / czegoś* with sb/sth). **6.** *pot.* (= *prosperować*) run *l.* go smoothly. **7.** (= *skręcać się*) (*o włosach*) curl, be curly; **włosy jej się kręcą** she's got curly hair; (*o dymie*) wreathe.

kręciek *mi* -ćk- *Gen. i Acc.* -a (*choroba*) (*zwł. u owiec i kóz*) gid; **mieć/dostać kręćka** *pot.* be/go nuts.

kręcz *mi pat.* **kręcz karku** torticollis; *pot.* wryneck.

kręg *mi anat.* vertebra; **kręg obrotowy** axis; **kręg szczytowy** atlas.

kręgarstwo *n.* chiropractic.

kręgarz *mp* (= *terapeuta*) chiropractor.

kręgiel *mi* -gl- *Gen.* -a (bowling) pin; (*w grze z dziewięcioma kręglami*) ninepin; *Br. t.* skittle; (*w grze z dziesięcioma kręglami*) tenpin.

kręgielnia *f. Gen.pl.* -i *l.* -ń bowling alley.

kręglarski *a.* bowling.

kręgle *pl. Gen.* -i (*gra*) bowling; (*gra z dziewięcioma kręglami*) ninepins; *Br. t.* skittles; (*gra dziesięcioma kręglami*) tenpins; **grać w kręgle** bowl.

kręgosłup *mi Gen.* -a **1.** *anat.* backbone, spine; (*w języku fachowym*) spinal *l.* vertebral column; **skrzywienie kręgosłupa** *pat.* curvature of the spine; **uraz/złamanie kręgosłupa** *pat.*

spinal injury/fracture. **2.** *przen.* (= *moralność*) backbone, spine; **być pozbawionym kręgosłupa moralnego** have no backbone, be invertebrate.

kręgowiec *ma* -wc- *zool.* vertebrate (*Vertebrata*).

kręgowy *a. anat.* spinal, vertebral; **kanał kręgowy** spinal *l.* vertebral canal; **rdzeń kręgowy** spinal cord.

kręgu *itd. mi zob.* **krąg** *l.* **kręg**.

krępacja *f. pot.* self-consciousness.

krępować *ipf.* **1.** (= *wiązać*) bind, tie up. **2.** (= *uwierać*) (*o ubraniu*) constrain. **3.** (= *ograniczać, utrudniać*) constrain, hamper. **4.** (= *onieśmielać, peszyć*) embarrass. **~ się** *ipf.* (= *wstydzić się*) be embarrassed, be bashful; **nie krępuj się!** (*w odpowiedzi na pytanie*) go (right) ahead!; **nie krępuj się i napisz/powiedz/przyjedź** don't hesitate to write/say/come; **proszę się nie krępować** make yourself at home.

krępujący *a.* (= *zawstydzający*) embarassing, awkward; (= *wprowadzający w zakłopotanie*) awkward, uneasy; **krępująca cisza** uneasy silence; **krępujący klient/gość** awkward customer/guest.

krępulec[1] *mi* -lc- *Gen.* -a *med.* (= *opaska uciskowa*) tourniquet.

krępulec[2] *mi* -lc- *Gen.* -a (*w rzemiośle*) tongue.

krępy *a.* stocky, chunky, thickset.

kręt *mp pot., dial.* = **krętacz**.

krętacki *a. pot.* crooked, shady.

krętactwo *n. pot.* crookedness, shadiness.

krętacz *mp*, **krętaczka** *f. Gen.pl.* -ek *pot.* cheater, crook; *zwł. Br.* twister.

krętaki *pl. ent.* whirligig beetles (*Gyrinidae*).

krętarz *mi anat.* trochanter.

krętek *ma* -tk- *biol.* spirochete (*Spirochaetales*); **krętek blady** treponema (*Treponema pallidum*).

krętogłów *ma* -o- *orn.* wryneck (*Jynx torquilla*).

kręty *a.* (*o drodze, rzece, schodach*) winding, meandering; (*o włosach*) curly.

kriochirurgia *f. Gen.* -ii *med.* cryosurgery.

kriofit *mi bot.* cryophyte.

kriolit *mi min.* cryolite, ice stone.

kriologia *f. Gen.* -ii *geol.* cryology.

kriometr *mi chem., fiz.* cryometer.

kriometria *f. Gen.* -ii *chem., fiz.* cryometry.

kriometryczny *a. chem., fiz.* cryometric.

krioplankton *ma biol.* cryoplankton.

kriosfera *f. geol.* cryosphere.

kriostat *mi techn.* cryostat.

krioterapia *f. Gen.* -ii *med.* cryotherapy.

kris *mi* (*sztylet*) kris; *rzad.* crease, creese.

krnąbrność *f.* defiance, fractiousness.

krnąbrny *a.* defiant, fractious.

krochmal *mi* **1.** *pot.* (= *mączka ziemniaczana*) starch. **2.** *biol., chem.* starch, amylum.

krochmalić *ipf.* **1.** starch. **2.** (= *mieć gdzieś*) *przen.* not give a toss (*kogoś / coś* about sb/sth).

krocie *pl. Gen.* -i *lit.* myriad (*czegoś* of sth); **zarobić krocie** (**na czymś**) to make a fortune (out of sth).

krocień *mi bot.* croton (*Croton*).

krocionogi *pl. zool.* millipedes, millepedes (*Diplopoda*).

krociowy *a. przest.* exorbitant.

krocze *n. anat.* crotch, perineum.

kroczny *a.* gressorial, walking; **odnóża kroczne** walking legs.

kroczyć *ipf.* **1.** (*dumnie*) strut; (*regularnymi krokami*) pace; **kroczył w stronę stacji** he headed toward the station. **2.** *przen.* (= *dążyć*) head (*do czegoś* for sth); **kroczyć utartą drogą** *przen.* keep to the beaten track.

kroćset *num. indecl. pot.* many hundred thousands; **do kroćset piorunów/diabłów/katów!** dammit!, the hell with it!

krogulec *ma* -**lc**- *orn.* sparrow hawk (*Accipiter nisus*).

kroić *ipf.* **krój 1.** (= *ciąć*) cut; (*w plastry, na kromki*) slice; **kroić coś na kawałki** cut sth to pieces; **kroić w kostkę** cube, dice. **2.** (= *wykrawać*) (*np. sukienkę*) cut out, tailor. ~ **się** *ipf.* **1.** *przen.* (= *zapowiadać się*) be in the air; **kroi ci się lanie** you're after a good whipping. **2.** (= *ciąć się*) (*o mięsie, drewnie*) cut.

krojczy *mp* cutter (*of clothes*).

krok *mi* **1.** (= *stąpnięcie*) step; (*ciężki*) plod, tramp; (= *sposób chodzenia*) gait, walk; **krok defiladowy** parade step; **niepewny krok** unsteady gait; **równać krok** fall into step; **dotrzymywać komuś kroku** *t. przen.* keep pace with sb; **chodzić za kimś krok w krok** follow sb around, dog sb's footsteps; **posuwać się krok za krokiem** go step by step; **przyspieszać/zwalniać kroku** speed up/slow down; **skierować dokądś swoje kroki** turn one's steps somewhere; **wlec się żółwim krokiem** lag on *l.* move at a snail's pace; **od miłości do nienawiści tylko jeden krok** there's a thin line between love and hate; **ani kroku dalej!** freeze!, hold it right there!; **nie idę ani kroku dalej!** I'm not going *l.* moving a step further! **2.** (= *odcinek drogi*) step; **być o krok od** be one step away from; **co krok** at every step, every step of the way; **dwa kroki stąd** within a stone's throw of here; **nie ruszyć się ani na krok** not to move a step; **spotykać coś na każdym kroku** *l.* **co krok** encounter sth at every step *l.* every step of the way; **wielki/milowy krok naprzód/wstecz** a great/enormous step forward/back. **3.** (= *działanie*) step; **desperacki/fałszywy krok** desperate/false step; **krok po kroku** step by step; **podjąć konieczne/pilne kroki** take necessary/urgent steps; **podjąć odpowiednie kroki** (*prawn.*) take due steps; **zrobić pierwszy krok** take the first steps. **4.** *pot.* (*część ubrania*) crotch.

krokiet[1] *mi Gen.* -**a** *kulin.* croquette.

krokiet[2] *mi Gen.* -**a** *sport* croquet.

krokietowy[1] *a. kulin.* croquette.

krokietowy[2] *a. sport* croquet.

krokiew *f.* -**kwi**- *pl.* -**e** *bud.* rafter.

krokodyl *ma Gen.pl.* -**i** *l.* -**ów** *zool.* crocodile (*Crocodylus*); *pot.* croc; **krokodyl nilowy** Nile crocodile (*Crocodylus niloticus*); **krokodyl różańcowy** salt-water crocodile (*Crocodylus porosus*). – *mi Gen.* -**a** *Gen.pl.* -**i** *l.* -**ów** *lotn.* split flap.

krokodylek *ma* -**lk**- *zool.* little crocodile. – *mi* -**lk**- *Gen.* -**a** *med., el.* (= *zacisk, żabka*) alligator clip; *Br.* crocodile clip.

krokodyli *a.* **1.** *zool.* crocodile, crocodile's; (= *należący do rzędu krokodyli*) crocodilian. **2.** *przen.* (= *fałszywy, dwulicowy*) (*w zwrocie*) **krokodyle łzy** crocodile tears.

krokodylowy *a. zool.* crocodile, crocodile's; (*należący do rzędu krokodyli*) crocodilian; **buty/torebka z krokodylowej skórki** crocodile shoes/purse.

krokoit *mi min.* crocoite; *Br. t.* red-lead ore.

krokosz *mi Gen.* -**a** *l.* -**u** *Gen.pl.* -**y** *l.* -**ów** *bot.* safflower (*Carthamus tinctorius*).

krokoszowy *a. bot.* safflower; **olej krokoszowy** safflower oil.

krokowy *a.* **1.** *anat.* **gruczoł krokowy** prostate gland. **2.** *techn., el.* **silnik krokowy** stepper *l.* stepping motor.

kroksztyn *mi bud.* corbel, console, bracket.

krokus *mi Gen.* -**a** **1.** *bot.* crocus (*Crocus*). **2.** (*do polerowania stali*) jeweller's rouge, crocus.

krokwiowy *a. bud.* raftered.

krokydolit *mi min.* crocidolite.

kromka *f. Gen.pl.* -**ek** (*chleba*) slice (*of bread*).

kromlech *mi Gen.* -**a** *l.* -**u** *bud.* cromlech.

kronika *f.* **1.** (= *annały*) chronicle, annals. **2.** *teor.lit.* (*gatunek literacki*) chronicle. **3.** (= *przegląd wydarzeń*) chronicle; **kronika towarzyska** society column, gossip column; **kronika tygodniowa** weekly news. **4.** *film* newsreel.

kronikarski *a.* **1.** (*dotyczący kroniki*) chronicle. **2.** (*dotyczący kronikarza*) chronicler's. **3.** *przen.* (= *krótki, zwięzły*) succinct.

kronikarstwo *n.* (*zwł. dawniej*) chronicle writing; (= *zapisywanie wydarzeń*) recording of events.

kronikarz *mp* chronicler.

Kronos *mp mit.* Cronus, Cronos, Kronos.

kropeczka *f. Gen.pl.* -**ek** dot, spot.

kropelka *f. Gen.pl.* -**ek 1.** (= *mała kropla*) droplet. **2.** (= *mała ilość*) drop; **ani kropelki** not a drop; **może jeszcze kropelkę wina?** a little more wine?

kropelki *pl. Gen.* -**ek kropelki do oczu** eye drops.

kropelkowy *a.* droplet; **zakażenie kropelkowe** *l.* **drogą kropelkową** *med.* droplet infection.

kropić *ipf.* **1.** (= *zwilżać*) sprinkle. **2.** *pot.* (= *bić*) beat, whip. **3.** *pot.* (= *strzelać*) shoot. **4.** (*o deszczu*) spit, rain lightly. ~ **się** *ipf.* **1.** (= *pryskać się*) (*siebie*) sprinkle o.s. (*czymś* with sth); (*kogoś*) sprinkle one another (*czymś* with sth). **2.** *pot.* (= *bić się*) fight.

kropidlak *mi Gen.* -**a** *bot.* aspergillus (*Aspergillaceae*).

kropidło *n. Gen.pl.* -**eł 1.** (*narzędzie*) aspersorium; aspergillum, aspergill. **2.** *bot.* water dropwort (*Oenanthe*).

kropielnica *f.* (*naczynie*) stoup.

kropka *f. Gen.pl.* -**ek 1.** (*znak interpunkcyjny*) period; *Br.* full stop *l.* point; **trzy kropki** ellipsis. **2.** (*znak diakrytyczny*) dot; **postawić kropkę nad i** *przen.* spell it out. **3.** (*znak mnożenia*) multiplication sign. **4.** (*znak w alfabecie Morse'a*) dot.

5. *muz.* dot; **półnuta z kropką** dotted half note. **6.** (= *okrągła plamka*) dot, spot; **spódnica w kropki** dotted skirt. **7.** *pot., przen.* (= *koniec*) period; **koniec i kropka** that's that, this is it. **8.** (= *trudna sytuacja*) spot; **znaleźć się w kropce** be put on the spot.

kropkować *ipf.* dot, spot; **kropkować wypowiedź** *przen.* bleep a comment.

kropkowany *a.* specled, dotted; **linia kropkowana** dotted line.

kropla *f. Gen.pl.* **-i** *l.* **-pel 1.** (*cieczy*) drop; **kropla deszczu** raindrop; **kropla goryczy** drop of bitternes; **kropla w morzu** *przen.* a drop in the bucket *l.* ocean; **krople łez** tear drops; **krople potu** beads of sweat *l.* perspiration; **podobni jak dwie krople wody** as *l.* like peas in a pod; **walczyć do ostatniej kropli krwi** fight to the *l.* one's last *l.* dying breath, fight to the bitter end; **wypić do ostatniej kropli** drain to the dregs, drink up; **kropla drąży skałę** drops of water wear away a stone. **2.** *bud.* (*ornament stylu doryckiego*) gutta. **3.** *techn.* (*w szklarstwie*) gather.

krople *pl. Gen.* **-i** *l.* **-pel** (*mieszanka leków*) drops; **krople do nosa** nose drops; **krople walerianowe** tincture of valerian, valerian tincture.

kroplik *mi Gen.* **-a** *bot.* monkey-flower, musk (*Mimulus*).

kroplisty *a.* (falling, flowing etc.) in heavy drops; **kroplisty pot** beads of sweat; **kroplista rosa** dew drops.

kroplomierz *mi Gen.* **-a** *techn.* dropper, dropping tube.

kroplówka *f. Gen.pl.* **-ek 1.** *med.* (*zabieg l. płyn do zabiegu*) drip feed; *Br.* drip; **kroplówka dożylna** intravenous drip, (an) IV; **stosować kroplówkę** administer drip feed, drip-feed. **2.** *pot.* (*zestaw do zabiegu*) drip feed; **podłączyć kogoś pod kroplówkę** put sb on a drip feed *l.* IV.

kropnąć *ipf.* **-ij 1.** *pot.* (= *zabić*) hit; **kropnąć sobie w łeb** blow out one's brains. **2.** *pot.* (= *wypić*) wet one's whistle; **kropnąć po jednym** have a shot. **3.** *pot.* (= *szybko coś napisać*) dash off. ~ **się** *ipf.* **1.** *pot.* (= *pomylić się*) blunder, goof. **2.** *pot.* (= *iść*) dash; **kropnąć się spać** *l.* **do łóżka** tumble into bed.

kros *mi sport* (*wyścig motocyklowy*) **1.** motocross. **2.** *sport* (*bieg przełajowy*) cross-country race. **3.** *sport* (*w tenisie*) cross-shot.

krosno *n. Gen.pl.* **-sien** *techn., tk.* loom.

krosowiec *mp* **-wc-** *pl.* **-y** *sport* (*w wyścigu motocyklowym*) **1.** motocross rider. **2.** *sport* (*w biegu przełajowym*) cross-country runner.

krosowy *a.* **1.** *sport* (*o wyścigach motorowych*) motocross. **2.** *sport* (*o biegach przełajowych*) cross-country.

krosta *f. pat.* pustule, pimple.

krostka *f. Gen.pl.* **-ek** *pat.* pimple, pustule.

krostowaty *a.* pimply, pimpled.

krośniarka *f.,* **krośniarz** *mp* loom weaver.

krotność *f. mat.* factor.

krotochwila *f. teor.lit.* burlesque, farce.

krotochwilny *a. przest. l. żart.* facetious, hilarious.

kroton *mi bot.* croton (*Croton*).

krowa *f. Gen.pl.* **krów 1.** (*samica*) cow; **krowa mleczna** milk *l.* milch cow; **cielna krowa** springer, springing cow; **dojna krowa** *dosł. i przen.* milk *l.* milch cow; *przen.* cash cow; **choroba szalonych krów** mad cow disease; **krowa morska** *zool.* (Steller's) sea cow (*Hydrodamalis gigas*); **krowa, która dużo ryczy, mało mleka daje** (*jako powiedzenie*) big talkers are little doers; (*jako komentarz o kimś*) he (she etc.) is all bark and no bite; **święta krowa** *rel., przen.* sacred cow. **2.** *pot.* (*o niezgrabnej kobiecie*) cow.

krowi *a.* cow, cow's; (= *podobny do krowy*) cowlike; (*w języku fachowym*) bovine; **krowie mleko** cow milk; **krowi placek** cow pie, meadow muffin.

krowianka *f.* **1.** *wet., pat.* cowpox, vaccinia. **2.** *wet.* (*szczepionka*) cow-pox inoculation.

krowiarka *f. Gen.pl.* **-ek, krowiarz** *mp* cattle farmer, stock breeder.

krowiasty *a.* cowlike.

krowieniec *mi* **-ńc-** *Gen.* **-a** (= *nawóz krowi*) cow dung (*usu. in a liquid form*).

krowieńczak *ma ent.* horned dung beetle (*Copris lunaris*).

króbka *f. Gen.pl.* **-ek** *druk.* letter-case.

krócej *adv. zob.* **krótko**.

króciak *mi Gen.* **-a** *techn., bud.* short board, short.

króciec *mi* **-ćc-** *Gen.* **-a** *techn.* **króciec kielichowy** socket ferrule; **króciec rurowy** stub *l.* connector pipe.

króciuchno *adv.* **1.** (= *bardzo krótko*) briefly. **2.** (= *przez bardzo krótki czas*) for a very short time. **3.** (= *w niewielu słowach*) very briefly.

króciuchny *a.* **1.** (*o małej długości*) very short. **2.** (*o krótkim czasie*) very short, very brief. **3.** (= *niewielki*) tiny, wee, itsy-bitsy.

króciutki *a.* = **króciuchny**.

króciutko *adv.* = **króciuchno**.

krój *mi* **-o-** *Gen.pl.* **-ów 1.** (= *wzór*) cut, fashion, style. **2.** (= *krojenie ubrań*) cutting; **kurs kroju i szycia** sewing course. **3.** *druk.* typeface; **krój liter** lettering.

król[1] *mp pl.* **-owie** *Gen.* **-ów 1.** (= *władca*) king; **król elekcyjny** elected king; **umarł król, niech żyje król** *l.* **król umarł; niech żyje król!** the king is dead; long live the king!; **król zwierząt** king of beasts *l.* the jungle; **poszedł tam, gdzie król chodzi piechotą** *żart.* he had a little business to attend to; **muszę iść tam, gdzie król piechotą chodzi** I have some business to attend to, I'll be in my office if you need me; **Trzej Królowie** the Magi, Three Wise Men; **Święto Trzech Króli** Epiphany; **za króla Ćwieczka** *żart.* when the world was young. **2.** (= *ktoś najlepszy w danej dziedzinie*) master; **król bawełny** cotton lord; **król strzelców** *sport* top scorer. – *mi Gen.* **-a** *pl.* **-e** *Gen.* **-i** *karty, szachy* king; **król pik/karo** king of spades/diamonds.

król[2] *ma pl.* **-e** *Gen.* **-i** (= *królik*) rabbit.

królestwo *n. Loc.* **-e 1.** (= *monarchia*) kingdom; **królestwo niebieskie** *l.* **boże** *rel.* kingdom of heaven *l.* God, heavenly kingdom; **królestwo za konia!** my kingdom for a horse! **2.** (= *dziedzina, domena*) realm. **3.** *biol.* kingdom; **królestwo ro-**

ślin/zwierząt plant/animal kingdom. **4.** *Loc.* **-u** (= *para królewska*) the Royal Couple.

królewicz *mp Gen.pl.* **-ów 1.** (= *syn króla*) prince. **2.** (= *laluś*) dandy.

królewna *f. Gen.pl.* **-wien 1.** (= *córka króla*) princess; **królewna Śnieżka** Snow White; **śpiąca królewna** Sleeping Beauty. **2.** *pot. żart. l. pieszczotliwie* princess.

królewski *a.* **1.** (*dotyczący króla l. królowej*) royal, regal; (*dotyczący króla*) kingly; (*dotyczący królowej*) queenly; **błękit królewski** *chem.* cobalt blue; **insygnia władzy królewskiej** regalia; **królewskie obowiązki** kingly *l.* queenly duties; **pałac królewski** Royal Palace; **woda królewska** *chem.* aqua regia, nitrohydrochloric acid; **Wasza Królewska Mość** Your Royal Highness, Your Majesty. **2.** (= *wspaniały*) royal; **królewskie powitanie** royal welcome; **po królewsku** royally.

króliczek *ma* **-czk-** (= *mały królik*) bunny, small rabbit. – *mp* **-czk-** *pl.* **-i** *pot.* (*kobieta pozująca do śmiałych zdjęć*) Playboy bunny.

królik *ma zool.* **1.** rabbit (*Oryctolagus cuniculus*); **królik amerykański** cottontail (*Sylvilagus*); **klatka na króliki** hutch; **królik doświadczalny** guinea pig; **oczy jak u królika** red eyes; **mnożyć/ pieprzyć się jak króliki** multiply/fuck like rabbits. **2.** *zob.* **króliki**.

królikarnia *f. Gen.pl.* **-i** *l.* **-ń 1.** (*ferma*) rabbit breeding farm. **2.** (*pomieszczenie*) rabbitry.

króliki *mi Gen.* **-ów** (*futro*) rabbit *l.* cony fur.

królobójca *mp* regicide, king killer.

królobójczy *a.* regicidal.

królobójstwo *n.* regicide.

królowa *f. Gen.* **-ej 1.** (= *monarchini*) queen; **królowa matka** queen mother; **królowa serc** *przen.* queen of hearts; **Królowa Śniegu** Ice Queen; **królowa nocy** *bot.* night-blooming cereus (*Cereus grandiflorus*); **paź królowej** *ent.* swallowtail (*Papilio machaon*). **2.** (= *kobieta wyróżniająca się*) queen. **3.** *szachy* queen. **4.** *ent.* (*u pszczół, mrówek, termitów*) queen.

królować *ipf.* **1.** (= *panować*) reign, rule. **2.** (= *dominować*) *przen.* prevail; **uprzedzenia rasowe nadal tu królują** racial prejudice still prevails here. **3.** (= *górować, wznosić się*) overlook (*nad czymś* sth).

królówka *f. szachy* queen.

krótki *a.* **-tszy 1.** (= *niedługi*) short; **biegi krótkie** *sport* short-distance running; **broń krótka** *wojsk.* small arm; **fale krótkie** *fiz., radio* shortwave; **krótkie włosy** short hair; **krótki wzrok** *med.* short-sightedness, near-sightedness; myopia; **krótkie spięcie** *el.* short (circuit), shorting; *przen.* (*kłótnia*) miff; **mieć krótki rozum** be thickheaded; **kłamstwo ma krótkie nogi** lies have short wings *l.* legs. **2.** (= *krótkotrwały*) brief, short; **krótki oddech** short breath *l.* wind; **samogłoska krótka** *fon.* short vowel; **mieć krótką pamięć** have a short memory; **krótki termin** (*data oddania jakiejś pracy itd.*) tight deadline; **na krótką metę** *przen.* in the short term *l.* run; **w krótkim czasie** in a short time. **3.** (= *zwięzły*) short, brief, concise; **w krótkich słowach** briefly.

krótko *adv.* **-cej 1.** (= *o małej długości*) short;

krótko ostrzyżony close-cropped; **ostrzyc się krótko** crop one's hair short; **krótko kogoś trzymać** *przen.* to keep a tight rein on sb. **2.** (= *przez krótki czas*) shortly; **na krótko** for a short time, for a little while; **krótko potem** shortly after; **krótko trwać** last for a short time; **deszcz padał krótko** it didn't rain for long. **3.** (= *w niewielu słowach*) briefly, shortly; **krótko mówiąc** briefly put; **mówiąc krótko i węzłowato...** to give you the long and short of it... **4.** (= *blisko*) at a short distance.

krótkodystansowiec *mp* **-wc-** *pl.* **-y** *sport* short-distance runner.

krótkodystansowy *a. sport* short-distance; **bieg krótkodystansowy** short-distance run.

krótkofalowiec *mp* **-wc-** *pl.* **-y** short-wave radio user.

krótkofalowy *a.* **1.** (= *krótkotrwały*) short-term. **2.** *fiz.* short-wave.

krótkofalówka *f.* **1.** *pot.* (*radiostacja*) short-wave radio *l.* transmitter. **2.** *med., pot.* short-wave diathermy.

krótkometrażowy *a. film* short; **film krótkometrażowy** short subject, short.

krótkonogi *a.* short-legged.

krótkoogniskowy *a. fot.* short-focus.

krótkookresowy *a.* short-term.

krótkość *f.* shortness.

krótkoterminowy *a.* short-term; **kredyt krótkoterminowy** short-term credit.

krótkotrwałość *f.* (= *ulotność*) transience.

krótkotrwały *a.* short-lived; **krótkotrwały sukces** short-lived success, flash in the pan.

krótkowąsy *a.* **kiełb krótkowąsy** *icht.* gudgeon (*Gobio gobio*).

krótkowidz *mp* (= *niedowidzący*) short-sighted *l.* near-sighted person; **być krótkowidzem** be short-sighted *l.* near-sighted; *przen.* (*nie umieć przewidywać*) be short-sighted.

krótkowidztwo *n. zob.* **któtkowzroczność**.

krótkowłosy *a.* (*np. o rasie psa, kota, królika*) short-haired; (*mający krótko obcięte włosy*) short-haired, close-cropped.

krótkowzroczność *f.* **1.** *med.* short-sightedness, near-sightedness; myopia. **2.** *przen.* (= *niezdolność przewidywania*) short-sightedness; myopia.

krótkowzroczny *a.* **1.** *pat. l. przen.* shortsighted, myopic. **2.** *przen.* (*nieprzewidujący*) short-sighted.

krówka *f. Gen.pl.* **-ek 1.** *emf.* (= *krowa*) cow. **2.** (*cukierek*) fudge. **3.** **boża krówka** (= *biedronka*) ladybug; *Br.* ladybird.

krówsko *n. pog.* (*o kobiecie*) cow.

krtaniowy *a. anat., fon.* laryngeal.

krtań *f. pl.* **-e** *anat.* larynx; **zapalenie krtani** *pat.* laryngitis.

krucho *adv.* **1.** fragilely. **2.** *pot.* (= *marnie*) **krucho ze mną** I'm in the soup; I'm done for; **krucho u nas z forsą** we're hard up (for money).

kruchość *f.* **1.** (= *łamliwość*) fragility, britleness. **2.** *przen.* (= *słabość*) frailty.

kruchta *f. bud., kośc.* **1.** porch, galilee. **2.** *uj.*

(= *przesadne przywiązanie do Kościoła*) church-iness, orthodoxy.

kruchy *a*. **1.** (= *łamliwy*) brittle, fragile; (= *chrupiący*) crispy, crunchy; **kruche ciasto** short-cake; **kruche mięso** tender meat. **2.** *przen*. (= *słaby, wątły*) frail, fragile, flimsy; (= *niepewny*) precarious, uncertain; **kruche zdrowie** frail health.

krucjata *f. hist. l. przen.* crusade.

krucyfiks *mi* crucifix.

kruczek *mi* -czk- *Gen.* -a (= *sztuczka prawna*) **1.** loophole; (= *wybieg, zwód*) trick, ruse. **2.** *przest.* (= *haczyk*) hook, crook; (= *pogrzebacz*) poker.

kruczoczarny *a*. raven black.

kruczowłosy *a*. raven-haired.

kruczy *a*. **1.** (= *dotyczący kruka*) raven's, corvine. **2. wyrostek kruczy** *anat.* coracoid process; **kość krucza** *zool.* coracoid (bone). **3.** (*kolor*) raven black. **4.** *poet.* (= *złowróżbny*) grim, ominous.

kruk *ma orn.* raven (*Corvus corax*); **kruk kru-kowi oka nie wykole** *przen.* crows don't pick crows' eyes; dog does not eat dog; **biały kruk** *przen.* rarity, rara avis. − *mp pl.* -cy *l.* -owie *przen. uj.* (= *czarnowidz*) prophet of doom.

krukowate *pl. decl. like a. orn.* (= *rodzina Cor-vidae*) corvids, the crow family.

krup *mi Gen.* -a *pat.* (= *błonica*) croup.

krupa *f.* **1.** *pl.* (*kasza*) barley groats. **2.** *pot.* (= *okruch*) crumb; (= *grudka*) lump; **liczyć krupy** *przen.* pinch and scrape. **3.** *meteor.* snow pellet.

krupczatka *f.* (*mąka*) coarse-ground whole-wheat flour.

krupić się *ipf.* lump, become lumpy.

krupier *mp* croupier.

krupierski *a*. croupier's.

krupnik *mi* **1.** *kulin.* (*zupa*) barley gruel. **2.** (*napój alkoholowy*) honey-flavoured spiced vod-ka.

krupniok *mi kulin.* (= *kaszanka*) blood sausage, black pudding (*in Silesia*).

krupon *mi* (*skóra*) sole-leather.

krupowy *a. pat.* (= *błoniczny*) croupous.

kruszarka *f. Gen.pl.* -ek *techn.* crusher.

kruszcowy *a*. ore.

kruszczyca *f. ent.* (*różne chrząszcze z rodziny Scarabaeidae*) goldsmith beetle; **kruszczyca zło-tawka** rose chafer (*Cetonia aurea*).

kruszczyk *mi Gen.* -a *bot.* helleborine (*Epipac-tis*).

kruszec *mi* -szc- **1.** *min.* (= *cenna ruda*) valu-able metal ore. **2.** *przest.* (= *metal szlachetny*) precious metal.

kruszeć *ipf.* **1.** (= *stawać się kruchym*) crum-ble (away), grow brittle *l.* friable; *kulin.* become tender *l.* tenderized. **2.** (*o człowieku*) (= *pokor-nieć, mięknąć*) soften, relent.

kruszon *mi* (*napój alkoholowy*) cup.

kruszonka *f. Gen.pl.* -ek *kulin.* crumble top-ping.

kruszyć *ipf.* (*rozdrabniać*) **1.** crumble, pulver-ize, break up. **2.** *przen.* **kruszyć kopię** (= *toczyć bój l. spór*) break a lance (*z kimś* with sb); **kru-**

szyć czyjeś serce soften sb's heart; **kruszyć czyjś opór** break down sb's resistance. ~ **się** *ipf.* crumble, fall apart, fall to pieces.

kruszyna *f.* **1.** (= *okruch*) crumb; (= *ziarno, drobina*) grain. **2.** *emf.* (*o dziecku*) mite. **3.** *bot.* buckthorn (*Rhamnus*).

kruszynek *ma* -nk- *ent.* trichogramma wasp (*Trichogramma*).

kruszywo *n. bud.* aggregate.

kruża *f. arch.* (*naczynie*) cruse, bowl.

krużganek *mi* -nk- *Gen.* -a *l.* -u *bud.* gallery, cloister.

krużgankowy *a. bud.* (surrounded by a) gallery.

krwawiączka *f. przest., pat.* hemophilia.

krwawica *f.* **1.** *emf.* (= *harówka, wysiłek*) hard work. **2. to wszystko moja krwawica** I sweated blood for all this.

krwawić *ipf.* **1.** (= *wydzielać krew*) bleed. **2.** (= *ranić do krwi*) make (*sb l. sth*) bleed, wound. **3.** *poet.* (= *zabarwiać czerwono*) redden, taint (*sth*) blood-red.

krwawienie *n.* bleeding; *pat.* (= *krwotok*) hem-orrhage; **krwawienie miesięczne** *fizj.* menstrua-tion.

krwawnica *f.* **1.** *bot.* loosestrife (*Lythrum*). **2.** *pat.* (= *hemoroidy*) piles, hemorrhoids.

krwawnik *mi Gen.* -a **1.** *bot.* yarrow (*Achillea*). **2.** *min.* bloodstone, heliotrope; decorative hematite.

krwawo *adv.* **1.** (= *z rozlewem krwi*) bloodily; **stłumić coś krwawo** drown sth in blood. **2.** (= *w kolorze krwi*) blood-red.

krwawy *a*. **1.** (= *z krwią*) blood, bloody; (= *krwawiący*) bleeding; **krwawa kiszka** *kulin.* blood sausage, black pudding; **krwawa biegunka** *med.* dysentery. **2.** (= *okrutny*) bloody, blood-thirsty. **3.** *przen.* **krwawy chrzest** baptism of fire; **krwawy pot** bloody sweat; **krwawa łaźnia** (= *masakra*) blood bath. **4.** (= *czerwony jak krew*) blood-red.

krwi *itd. f. zob.* krew.

krwiak *mi Gen.* -a *pat.* hematoma, blood tu-mor.

krwinka *f. Gen.pl.* -ek *fizj.* blood cell; **biała krwinka** white blood cell, leukocyte; **czerwona krwinka** red blood cell, erythrocyte.

krwiobieg *mi biol.* blood circulation.

krwiodawca *mp*, **krwiodawczyni** *f. med.* blood donor.

krwiodawstwo *n. med.* blood donation.

krwiomocz *mi pat.* hematuria.

krwionośny *a. anat.* circulatory; **naczynia krwionośne** blood vessels; **układ krwionośny** cir-culatory system.

krwiopijca *mp*, **krwiopijczyni** *f. pot.* (= *wyzyski-wacz/ka*) bloodsucker.

krwiotwórczy *a. fizj.* hemopoietic.

krwiożerczość *f.* **1.** (= *drapieżność*) fierceness, ferocity. **2.** (= *okrucieństwo*) bloodthirstiness.

krwiożerczy *a*. **1.** (= *drapieżny, dziki*) fierce, ferocious, savage. **2.** (= *okrutny*) bloodthirsty.

krwistoczerwony *a*. (*kolor*) blood-red.

krwisty *a*. **1.** (= *krwawy*) bloody. **2.** (*rumiany,* *zdrowy*) ruddy. **3.** (= *energiczny, pełen życia*) full-blooded. **4.** (*czerwony*) blood-red.

krwiściąg *mi bot.* burnet (*Sanguisorba*).

krwotoczny *a. pat.* hemorrhagic; **gorączka krwotoczna** hemorrhagic fever.

krwotok *mi pat.* hemorrhage; **krwotok wewnętrzny/zewnętrzny** internal/external hemorrhage.

kryć *ipf.* **-ję -jesz 1.** (= *chować*) hide. **2.** (= *skrywać, zasłaniać*) cover (up), conceal; (= *przesłaniać, osłaniać*) cover, screen; **kryć coś pod maską** *l.* **płaszczykiem (czegoś)** hide sth behind *l.* under a mask (of sth); **kryć twarz w dłoniach** bury one's face in one's hands. **3.** (= *osłaniać przed odpowiedzialnością*) cover up for (*sb*). **4.** (= *powlekać*) coat (*sth*) (over) (*czymś* with sth). **5.** *sport* (= *pilnować*) mark, cover. **6.** (= *zawierać w sobie*) contain, hold. **7.** (*pokrywać, zabezpieczać*) cover, protect, shield. **8.** *hodowla* (= *kopulować z samicą*) cover; (*o baranie*) tup. **~ się** *ipf.* **1.** (= *chować się, pozostawać w ukryciu*) hide (*przed kimś / czymś* from sb/sth); **kryć się z czymś** conceal sth. **2.** (= *ukrywać się za pozorami*) be behind (*sth*); **co się kryje za tym przyjaznym uśmiechem?** what's behind this friendly smile? **3.** (= *czaić się, majaczyć*) lurk. **4.** (= *znajdować się w niewidocznym miejscu*) be *l.* lie (hidden) (*w czymś* in sth, *za czymś* behind sth).

krygować się *ipf. uj.* put on airs.

kryjówka *f. Gen.pl.* **-ek** hideaway, hideout, hiding-place; (= *skrytka*) cache.

krykiet *mi Gen.* **-a** *sport* cricket.

krykietowy *a. sport* cricket.

kryl *ma zw. sing. zool.* (= *skorupiak z rzędu Euphausiacea*) krill.

Krym *mi geogr.* the Crimea.

kryminalista *mp*, **kryminalistka** *f. Gen.pl.* **-ek 1.** (*przestępca*) criminal. **2.** (*prawnik*) criminal lawyer.

kryminalistyczny *a.* criminal.

kryminalistyka *f. prawn.* criminology.

kryminalny *a.* criminal; **policja kryminalna** criminal police; **powieść kryminalna** crime story, detective story; **film kryminalny** crime movie.

kryminał *mi pot.* **1.** (= *więzienie*) prison. **2.** (= *przestępstwo kryminalne*) crime. **3.** (= *utwór kryminalny*) whodunit.

kryminogenność *f. socjol.* criminogenicity.

kryminogenny *a. socjol.* criminogenic, crimogenic.

kryminolog *mp pl.* **-dzy** *l.* **-owie** criminologist.

kryminologia *f. Gen.* **-ii** criminology.

kryminologiczny *a.* criminological.

krymka *f. Gen.pl.* **-ek** (*czapka*) skull-cap.

krymski *a.* Crimean.

krynica *f. poet.* (= *zdrój, źródło*) spring, fountain, fount.

kryniczny *a.* **woda kryniczna** spring water.

krynolina *f. strój* crinoline.

krypa *f. żegl.* **1.** (= *płaskodenna łódź*) scow, punt. **2.** (= *dłubanka*) dugout. **3.** *żart.* (= *łajba*) tub.

krypta *f.* crypt.

kryptofit *mi bot.* cryptophyte.

kryptograf *mp pl.* **-owie** cryptographer, cryptographist.

kryptografia *f. Gen.* **-ii** cryptography.

kryptograficzny *a.* cryptographic.

kryptogram *mi* cryptogram.

kryptolog *mp pl.* **-dzy** *l.* **-owie** cryptologist.

kryptologia *f. Gen.* **-ii** cryptology.

krypton *mi chem.* krypton.

kryptonim *mi* (= *tajny pseudonim*) codename; *wojsk.* (= *tajne oznaczenie l. hasło*) codeword.

krystaliczność *f.* **1.** *fiz., chem.* crystallinity. **2.** *przen.* (= *czystość, przejrzystość*) (crystal) clarity.

krystaliczny *a.* **1.** *fiz., chem.* crystalline; **ciało krystaliczne** crystalline body. **2.** *przen.* (*kryształowy, czysty*) crystal clear.

krystalizacja *f.* **1.** *fiz., chem.* crystallization. **2.** *przen.* (= *formowanie się*) crystallization, formation.

krystalizacyjny *a. fiz., chem.* crystallization.

krystalizator *mi Gen.* **-a 1.** *chem.* crystallizer. **2.** *techn.* (*forma odlewnicza*) continuous casting mold.

krystalizować *ipf. fiz., chem.* crystallize. **~ się** *ipf. przen.* (= *klarować się, nabierać kształtu*) crystallize, take form.

krystalografia *f. Gen.* **-ii** *fiz., chem.* crystallography.

krystalograficzny *a. fiz., chem.* crystallographical.

krystaloid *mi bot.* crystalloid.

kryształ *mi* **1.** crystal; **kryształ górski** *min.* rock crystal; **czysty jak kryształ** (as) clear as crystal; crystal clear. **2.** (*szkło*) crystal (glass). **3.** (*cukier*) granulated sugar.

kryształowy *a.* **1.** (*krystaliczny, zrobiony z kryształu*) crystal. **2.** (= *czysty, przejrzysty*) crystal clear. **3.** (= *uczciwy, szlachetny*) spotless.

kryterium *n. sing. indecl. pl.* **-ria** *Gen.* **-riów 1.** (= *miernik*) criterion. **2.** *kolarstwo* criterium.

kryty *a.* covered; (= *zadaszony*) roofed; **być krytym** *pot.* be covered.

krytycyzm *mi* criticism.

krytycznie *adv.* critically; (= *sceptycznie*) sceptically.

krytycznoliteracki *a.* literary critical.

krytyczny *a.* **1.** critical; **wydanie krytyczne** critical edition; **krytyczny umysł** critical mind; **sytuacja krytyczna** critical situation, crisis. **2.** (= *rozstrzygający*) crucial, decisive. **3.** *nauk.* (= *graniczny, ekstremalny*) critical; **masa/temperatura krytyczna** *fiz.* critical mass/temperature; **punkt krytyczny** critical point; **osiągnąć stan krytyczny** (*o reaktorze jądrowym*) go critical.

krytyk *mp* critic.

krytyka *f.* **1.** criticism; **krytyka tekstu** textual criticism; **nie wytrzymywać krytyki** not stand up to criticism; **poniżej wszelkiej krytyki** beneath (all) criticism. **2.** (= *ogół krytyków*) the critics; **zdaniem krytyki...** the critics say that... **3.** (= *tekst krytyczny*) critique, review.

krytykancki *a. uj.* nit-picking.

krytykanctwo *n. uj.* nit-picking.

krytykant *mp*, **krytykantka** *f. Gen.pl.* **-ek** *uj.* nitpicker.

krytykować *ipf.* criticize.

kryza *f.* **1.** (*kołnierz*) ruff. **2.** *techn.* flange, rim.

kryzys *mi* **1.** crisis; **kryzys energetyczny** energy crisis; **kryzys polityczny/gabinetowy** *polit.* political/cabinet crisis; **kryzys gospodarczy** *ekon.* economic crisis. **2.** **kryzys wieku średniego** *psych.* midlife crisis.

kryzysowy *a. zwł. polit.* crisis; **rozmowy kryzysowe** crisis talks.

krza *itd. mi zob.* **kierz.**

krzaczasty *a.* (*o brwiach*) bushy; (*o roślinności*) shrubby, bushy.

krzaczek *mi* **-czk-** *Gen.* **-a** (small) bush, shrub.

krzak *mi Gen.* **-a** *l.* **-u** (= *krzew*) **1.** bush, shrub; **krzak róży** rosebush; **krzak gorejący** *Bibl.* burning bush. **2.** *pl.* (= *zarośla*) thicket, bushes, shrubbery.

krzątać się *ipf.* busy o.s., bustle.

krzątanina *f.* bustler*ze f. zob.* **kra.**

krzeczot *ma orn.* (= *białozór*) gyrfalcon (*Falco rusticolus*).

krzem *mi chem.* silicon; **dwutlenek krzemu** silicon dioxide; silica.

krzemek *mi* **-mk-** *chem.* silicide.

krzemian *mi chem.* silicate.

krzemica *f. pat.* silicosis.

krzemienny *a.* flint.

krzemień *mi Gen.* **-nia** *min.* flint, flintstone, chert.

krzemionka *f. chem., min.* silica.

krzemionkowy *a. geol.* siliceous.

krzemowodór *mi* **-wodor-** *chem.* silane, silicon hydride.

krzemowy *a.* silicon; *chem.* silicic; **kwas krzemowy** silicic acid; **stal krzemowa** *metal.* silicon steel; **pylica krzemowa** *med.* silicosis; **Dolina Krzemowa** Silicon Valley (*in California*).

krzepa *f.* vigor; (= *tężyzna fizyczna*) brawn; *pot.* kick.

krzepiący *a.* (= *pocieszający, optymistyczny*) optimistic, comforting.

krzepić *ipf.* (= *wzmacniać*) **1.** strengthen, invigorate, fortify. **2.** (= *dodawać otuchy*) comfort, reassure. **~ się** *ipf.* (= *posilać się*) refresh o.s. (*czymś* with sth).

krzepki *a.* vigorous, robust, stout.

krzepliwość *f. fizj.* coagulation.

krzepliwy *a.* coagulable.

krzepnąć *ipf.* **-ij, -pł** *l.* **-pnął -pła -pli** (= *twardnieć, tężeć*) **1.** harden, set, fix; *form.* solidify. **2.** *chem., fizj.* coagulate. **3.** *lit.* (= *nabierać siły*) gather strength; (= *stabilizować się*) become established.

krzesać *ipf.* **-szę -szesz krzesać iskry/ogień** strike sparks/fire.

krzesełko *n. Gen.pl.* **-ek** *emf.* (small) chair.

krzesełkowy *a. techn.* chair; **wyciąg krzesełkowy** chair lift.

krzesiwo *n.* (fire) striker, steel (*for a tinderbox*).

krzesło *n. Gen.pl.* **-eł** **1.** (*mebel*) chair; **krzesło**

obrotowe swivel chair; **krzesło elektryczne** electric chair. **2.** *przest., teatr* seat in the stalls. **3.** *przest.* (= *godność, urząd*) office.

krzew *mi bot.* shrub, bush.

krzewiasty *a.* shrub-like, shrubby; *bot.* frutescent.

krzewiciel *mp*, **krzewicielka** *f. Gen.pl.* **-ek** *lit.* propagator.

krzewić *ipf.* (= *rozpowszechniać*) propagate, spread. **~ się** *ipf.* **1.** (*o roślinach*) (= *rozrastać się*) spread, grow, ramble. **2.** (= *rozpowszechniać się*) propagate, spread.

krzewinka *f. Gen.pl.* **-ek** *bot.* low shrub.

krzta *f.* ani krzty not a whit.

krztusić się *ipf.* choke (*czymś* on sth, *od czegoś* from sth); (= *kaszleć*) cough.

krztusiec *mi* **-ść-** *Gen.* **-a** *pat.* whooping cough.

krztyna *f.* tiny bit, grain, a little (*czegoś* of sth); **krztynę** a little bit.

krzyczący *a.* (= *prowokacyjny, jaskrawy*) loud; **krzycząca niesprawiedliwość** howling injustice.

krzyczeć *ipf.* **-ę -ysz** **1.** shout (*na kogoś* at sb, *do kogoś* to sb); **krzyczeć na cały głos** shout at the top of one's voice; **krzyczeć na całe gardło** shout o.s. hoarse. **2.** (*o dziecku*) (= *głośno płakać*) wail. **3.** *myśl.* (*o ptakach*) shriek.

krzyk *mi* **1.** shout. **2.** (= *awantura, zamieszanie*) fuss, ado; **narobić krzyku** make *l.* kick up a fuss (*o coś* about *l.* over sth). **3.** *pot.* (= *głośny płacz dziecka*) wail. **4.** *myśl.* (*głos ptaka*) shriek.

krzykacz *mp*, **krzykaczka** *f. Gen.pl.* **-ek** *pot.* bigmouth, loudmouth.

krzykliwy *a.* (*hałaśliwy*) **1.** loud, loudmouthed. **2.** (= *jaskrawy, rażący*) loud, garish, gaudy.

krzyknąć *pf.* **-ij** *zob.* **krzyczeć.**

krzyna *f.* = **krztyna.**

krzywa *f. decl. like a. mat.* curve; **krzywa dzwonowa** bell curve, normal curve; **krzywa płaska** plane curve; **krzywa wzrostu** (*wykres*) growth curve.

krzywda *f.* harm, wrong, injustice; **wyrządzić komuś krzywdę** do sb wrong; **doznać krzywdy** be wronged; suffer harm; **nie stanie ci się żadna krzywda** you'll suffer no wrong; **upomnieć się o swoją krzywdę** to forgive and forget; **wynagrodzić krzywdę** redress an injustice; make up for the wrong done; **z czyjąś krzywdą** to sb's detriment.

krzywdzić *ipf.* wrong, misuse, do (*sb*) wrong.

krzywica *f. pat.* rickets.

krzywiczny *a. pat.* rickety.

krzywić *ipf.* bend, curve; (*twarz, usta*) twist, contort. **~ się** *ipf.* **1.** (= *zakrzywiać się, zginać się*) bend, curve. **2.** (= *robić miny*) make *l.* pull faces, grimace (*do kogoś* at sb); (= *wyrażać niezadowolenie*) frown (*na kogoś / coś* at sb/sth).

krzywik *mi Gen.* **-a** (= *wzornik*) French curve.

krzywizna *f.* **1.** *mat.* curvature. **2.** *pot.* (= *koślawość*) crookedness.

krzywka *f. Gen.pl.* **-ek** *mech.* cam.

krzywo *adv.* **1.** *zob.* **krzywy. 2.** (= *z niechęcią*) **patrzeć krzywo na kogoś/coś** look askance at sb/sth; frown at sb/sth.

krzywoprzysięgać *ipf.* perjure o.s., commit perjury.

krzywoprzysięstwo *n.* perjury.

krzywoprzysięzca *mp*, **krzywoprzysiężczyni** *f.* perjurer.

krzywy *a.* **1.** (= *koślawy, wygięty*) crooked, curved, bent, oblique; (= *powykrzywiany*) contorted, twisted; (= *zniekształcony*) distorted; **krzywe zwierciadło** *t. przen.* fairground mirror. **2.** (= *niechętny, niezadowolony*) disapproving, wry; **krzywe spojrzenie** disapproving look; **krzywa mina** frown; **krzywy uśmiech** wry smile.

krzyż *mi Gen.* -a **1.** cross; (= *symbol chrześcijaństwa*) the Cross; **Czerwony Krzyż** the Red Cross; **Krzyż Chrystusa** *rel.* Christ's Cross; **jak z krzyża zdjęty** like death warmed up; **leżeć krzyżem** prostrate o.s. **2. na krzyż** criss-cross, crosswise; **przekroić coś na krzyż** cut sth crosswise *l.* on the cross. **3.** *rel.* (= *krucyfiks*) crucifix, cross. **4.** *rel.* (= *gest wyrażający znak krzyża*) (the sign of) cross; **uczynić znak krzyża** make a cross; **krzyż na drogę** *pot.* good riddance. **5.** *przen.* (= *cierpienie*) cross; **ona ma z nim krzyż pański** he is the cross she has to bear; **dźwigać swój krzyż** bear one's cross. **6.** (*odznaka, order*) cross; **krzyż harcerski** scouting cross; **Krzyż Walecznych** the Cross of Valor; **Krzyż Zasługi** the Cross of Merit. **7.** small of the back; lower back; *anat.* sacrum; **ból krzyża** *l.* **w krzyżu** lower back pain, lumbago.

krzyżacki *a.* Teutonic; **zakon krzyżacki** *hist.* the Teutonic Order.

Krzyżak *mp hist.* Teutonic knight.

krzyżak *mi Gen.* -a **1.** *techn.* (*element konstrukcyjny w kształcie krzyża*) cross, crosspiece. **2.** *techn.* (*uchwyt kluczy nasadowych*) X-shaped base. **3.** (*świecznik*) cross candlestick. – *ma zool.* (*pająk*) garden spider, cross spider (*Araneus diadematus*).

krzyżmo *n. rel.* **1.** *rz.-kat. i prawosławie* (= *olej święty*) chrism. **2.** (= *szata chrzcielna*) chrisom.

krzyżodziób *ma* -dziob- *orn.* crossbill (*Loxia*).

krzyżować *ipf.* **1.** (*układać na krzyż*) cross; **krzyżować ramiona** cross one's arms; **krzyżować szpady** *t. przen.* cross swords (*z kimś* with sb). **2.** (= *przybijać do krzyża*) crucify. **3.** *biol.* cross, crossbreed, hybridize. **4.** *przen.* (= *niweczyć*) cross, thwart, obstruct; **krzyżować czyjeś plany** thwart sb's plans. **~ się** *ipf.* **1.** (= *przecinać się*) cross, intersect. **2.** *biol.* (= *dawać mieszane potomstwo*) interbreed, crossbreed.

krzyżowiec *mp* -wc- *pl.* -y *hist.* crusader.

krzyżownica *f.* **1.** *bot.* milkwort (*Polygala*). **2.** *techn.* intersection.

krzyżowy *a.* **1.** (= *o kształcie krzyża*) cross(-shaped), X-shaped; **sklepienie krzyżowe** *bud.* cross vault. **2.** (= *naprzemienny*) **krzyżowy ogień** *wojsk.* crossfire; **krzyżowy ogień pytań** *prawn.* cross-examination, cross-questioning; **zapylenie krzyżowe** *bot.* cross-pollination. **3.** *rel.* of the Cross; **Droga Krzyżowa** the Stations of the Cross. **4.** *anat.* sacral; **kość krzyżowa** sacrum. **5.** *hist.* **wyprawa krzyżowa** crusade.

krzyżówka *f. Gen.pl.* -ek **1.** (*rozrywka umysłowa*) crossword (puzzle); **rozwiązywać krzyżówki** do *l.* solve crosswords. **2.** *orn.* mallard (*Anas platyrhynchos*). **3.** *biol.* hybrid, cross. **4.** *pot.* (= *skrzyżowanie*) crossroads.

krzyżulec *mi* -lc- *Gen.* -a **1.** *techn.* crosshead, cross-brace. **2.** *żegl.* mooring swivel.

krzyżyk *mi Gen.* -a **1.** (= *mały krzyż*) (small) cross; **haftować krzyżykami** cross-stitch; **stawiać krzyżyk** (*zamiast podpisu*) make one's cross. **2.** *rel.* (= *znak krzyża*) cross; **dać komuś krzyżyk na drogę** *przen.* send sb away empty-handed; **krzyżyk na drogę** *pot.* good riddance. **3.** *muz.* sharp. **4.** *druk.* dagger, obelisk. **5.** *pot.* (= *dziesięć lat życia*) decade; **mieć ósmy krzyżyk na karku** be in one's seventies.

krzyżykowy *a.* crossed; **haft krzyżykowy** cross-stitch.

ksanten *mi chem.* xanthene.

ksantofil *mi Gen.pl.* -i *l.* -ów *biochem.* xanthophyl.

ksantogenian *mi chem.* xanthogenate.

ksantogenowy *mi chem.* **kwas ksantogenowy** xanthogenic acid.

ksantorea *f. Gen.* -ei *bot.* grass tree (*xanthorrhoea*).

ksantyna *f. chem.* xanthine.

ksantypa *f. żart.* (= *sekutnica*) shrew, nagging wife, Xanthippe.

ksenofil *mp Gen.pl.* -i *l.* -ów xenophile.

ksenofilia *f. Gen.* -ii (*internacjonalizm*) xenophilia.

ksenofob *mp pl.* -i *l.* -owie xenophobe.

ksenofobia *f. Gen.* -ii xenophobia.

ksenon *mi chem.* (*pierwiastek*) xenon.

ksero *n. indecl.* **1.** (= *kserokopiarka*) photocopier, xerox. **2.** (= *kserokopia*) photocopy, xeroxed copy.

kserofit *mi bot.* xerophyte.

kserograf *mi* photocopier, xerox.

kserografia *f. Gen.* -ii xerography.

kserograficzny *a.* xerographic, photocopying; **papier kserograficzny** photocopier paper; **odbitka kserograficzna** photocopy.

kserokopia *f. Gen.* -ii (*odbitka kserograficzna*) photocopy.

kserokopiarka *f.* (*kserograf*) photocopier, xerox.

kserować *ipf.* photocopy, xerox.

ksiądz *mp* -ę- *Dat.* -u *Voc.* -że *pl.* -ża *Gen.* -ży *Ins.* -żmi *kośc.* priest; **ksiądz katolicki/prawosławny** Catholic/Orthodox priest.

książeczka *f. Gen.pl.* -ek **1.** booklet; **książeczki dla dzieci** children's books; **książeczka do nabożeństwa** prayerbook. **2.** (= *dokument z luźnych lub zszytych kartek*) book, booklet; **książeczka oszczędnościowa** savings book; **książeczka czekowa** checkbook; **książeczka wojskowa** military ID.

książę *mp decl. like n.* **księci-** *pl.* **książęt-** *Gen.* **-ąt** (*zwł. członek rodziny królewskiej*) prince; duke; **książę małżonek** prince consort; **wielki książę** *hist.* grand duke; **udzielny książę** *hist.* sovereign prince; **książę ciemności** (= *Szatan*) the Prince of Darkness.

książęcy *a.* prince's, princely; duke's, ducal.

książka *f. Gen.pl.* **-ek 1.** book; **książka dla dzieci** children's book; **książka dla młodzieży** book for young people; **książka z obrazkami** picture book; **książka adresowa** address book; **książka kucharska** recipe book, cookbook; **półka na książki** bookshelf; **czytać w kimś jak w otwartej książce** read sb like an open book; **mówić jak z książki** talk like a book; **siedzieć** *l.* **ślęczeć nad książką** pore over a book. **2.** (*dokumentacja, rejestr*) book, register; **książka skarg i zażaleń** complaints book; **książka telefoniczna** phone directory.

książkowy *a.* **1.** (*wydawniczy*) book; **debiut książkowy** literary debut; **publikacja książkowa** book publication. **2.** (= *literacki*) bookish; **styl książkowy** bookish style. **3. mól książkowy** (= *nałogowy czytelnik l. chrząszcz z rodziny Bostrychidae*) bookworm.

ksieni *f. przest., kośc.* abbess.

księga *f. Gen.pl.* **-ąg 1.** *emf. l. form.* (= *duża książka*) book, volume, tome; **ciężka księga** hefty volume; **księga gości** guestbook; **czytać w kimś jak w otwartej księdze** read sb like an open book. **2.** (= *część utworu literackiego*) book. **3.** (= *zbiór dokumentów, rejestr*) book, register; **księga główna** *fin.* ledger; **księga inwentarzowa** inventory book; **fałszować księgi** cook the book; **księgi wieczyste** real-estate register; **biała/czarna księga** *polit.* white/black book; **czerwona księga** (= *lista zagrożonych gatunków itp.*) red book.

księgarnia *f. Gen.pl.* **-ni** *l.* **-ń** bookstore; *Br.* bookshop; **księgarnia antykwaryczna** second-hand bookstore; **księgarnia wirtualna** *l.* **internetowa** *komp.* on-line bookstore.

księgarski *a.* bookseller's; **składnica księgarska** (*handl.*) bookseller's warehouse.

księgarstwo *n.* **1.** (*handl.*) bookselling, the book trade. **2.** (= *zawód księgarza*) bookselling.

księgarz *mp* bookseller.

księgi *pl. Gen.* **ksiąg** *zool., anat.* psalterium, omasum.

księgosusz *mi zool., pat.* rinderpest.

księgowa *f. decl. like a. zob.* **księgowy²**.

księgować *ipf. fin.* keep the books, do the accounts.

księgowanie *n. fin.* accounting, bookkeeping.

księgowość *f.* **1.** *fin.* = **księgowanie**. **2.** (*dział przedsiębiorstwa*) bookkeeping *l.* accounting department.

księgowy¹ *a. fin.* accounting, bookkeeping; **wartość księgowa** book value.

księgowy² *mp* accountant, bookkeeper.

księgozbiór *mi* **-zbior-** book collection, library; **księgozbiór podręczny** *bibl.* reference library.

księgoznawczy *a.* bibliological, bibliographic.

księgoznawstwo *n.* book-lore, bibliology, bibliography.

księstwo *n.* **1.** (*jednostka polityczna*) principality; duchy. **2.** (*tytuł l. urząd*) princedom; dukedom. **3.** (*książę z żoną*) princely couple.

księżna *f. Gen.* **-y** *l.* **-ej** *Acc.* **-ę** *l.* **-ą** *Dat. i Loc.* **-ie** *l.* **-ej** *Voc.* **-o** *pl. decl. like a.* duchess; *rzad.* princess; **księżna regentka** princess regent.

księżniczka *f. Gen.pl.* **-ek** (= *królewna, t. przen.*) princess.

księżowski *a.* priest's, priestly, clerical.

księżulek *mp* **-lk-** *pl.* **-owie**, **księżulo** *mp pl.* **-owie** *pot. emf.* padre.

księży *a.* priestly, clerical.

księżyc *mi Gen.* **-a 1.** (*także* **Księżyc**) (= *satelita Ziemi*) the Moon; (*jako zjawisko na niebie l. źródło światła*) moon; **blask** *l.* **światło księżyca** moonlight, moonshine; **złoty księżyc** golden moon; **wyprawa na Księżyc** lunar mission; **księżyc w pełni/nowiu** full/new moon; **księżyc w pierwszej/ostatniej kwadrze** the moon in its first/last quarter; **przy księżycu** *l.* **w świetle księżyca** by the light of the moon; **jakby spadł z księżyca** *przen.* as if he were from the moon; **wyglądać jak księżyc w pełni** be moon-faced. **2.** *astron.* (= *naturalny satelita planety*) moon, (natural) satellite.

księżycowy *a.* lunar; **krajobraz księżycowy** lunar landscape, moonscape; **miesiąc księżycowy** lunar month; **kamień księżycowy** (*pochodzący z Księżyca*) moonrock; *min.* moonstone.

księżycówka *f. Gen.pl.* **-ek** (= *bimber*) moonshine.

księżyna *mp Gen.pl.* **-n** *l.* **-ów** = **księżulek**.

ksylem *mi bot.* xyleme.

ksylen *mi chem.* xylene.

ksylit *mi geol.* lignite.

ksylofag *ma biol.* xylophage.

ksylofon *mi muz.* xylophone.

ksylograf *mi druk.* xylograph.

ksylografia *f. Gen.* **-ii** *druk., sztuka* xylography.

ksylograficzny *a.* xylographic.

ksylol *mi chem.* xylol, xylene.

ksyloza *f. chem.* xylose.

ksywa *f. pot.* nickname.

ksywka *f. Gen.pl.* **-ek** *pot.* (*pseudonim*) nickname.

kształcenie *n.* **1.** (= *nauka, edukacja*) education, training; **kształcenie nauczycieli** teacher training. **2.** (= *doskonalenie*) development, improvement.

kształcić *ipf.* **1.** (= *uczyć*) teach, train (*na kogoś* as sb). **2.** (= *rozwijać, doskonalić*) develop, improve. **~ się** *ipf.* **1.** (= *uczyć się*) train, study, learn (*w czymś* sth). **2.** (= *doskonalić się*) improve one's skills.

kształt *mi* **1.** shape, form; (= *zarys*) outline, contour; **nadać kształt czemuś** give shape to sth; **przybierać realne kształty** take shape. **2.** (= *sylwetka, budowa ciała*) figure, shape, build.

kształtka *f. Gen.pl.* **-ek** *techn.* profile; (*element hydrauliczny*) fitting; (*kształtka kamienna*) *bud.* shaped stone.

kształtny *a.* well-proportioned; (*zwł. o ciele kobiety*) shapely, good-figured.

kształtować *ipf.* shape, mold, model. **~ się** *ipf.* **1.** (= *formować się*) take shape, develop. **2.** *form.* (= *osiągać daną wartość*) run (*na poziomie... at a level of...*); **inflacja kształtuje się na poziomie 10%** inflation is running at (a level of) 10%.

kształtownik *mi Gen.* **-a** *techn.* section.

kszyk *ma orn.* common snipe (*Gallinago gallinago*).

kto *pron. Gen. i Acc.* **kogo** *Dat.* **komu** *Ins. i Loc.* **kim** **1.** who; (*po przyimkach i czasem w przypadkach zależnych*) whom; **kto tam?** who's there?; **kto to powiedział?** who said that?; **jeśli nie ty, to kto?** if not you, then who?; **nie wiadomo kto** *l.* **bóg wie kto** God knows who; **stój, kto idzie?** stop, who goes there?; **kto wie...** who knows...; **kto by pomyślał** who would have thought; **do kogo piszesz?** who are you writing (to)?; *form.* to whom are you writing?; **kogo masz na myśli?** who do you mean?; *form.* whom do you mean?; **dla kogo to?** who is it for?; **z kim mam przyjemność?** *form.* with whom do I have the pleasure?; **kto jest kim?** *l.* **kto jest kto?** who's who?; **kto pierwszy, ten lepszy** the winner takes all; **komu w drogę, temu czas** I must be on my way; **kto śpi, nie grzeszy** he who sleeps, sins not. **2.** (= *ktoś, ktokolwiek*) **kto inny** somebody else; **kto jak kto, byle nie ty** anyone but you; **jest tam kto?** is anybody there?

ktokolwiek *pron.* **kto-** *decl. zob.* **kto,** **-kolwiek** *indecl.* (*zaimek względny*) **1.** whoever; (*czasem w przypadkach zależnych*) whomever; no matter who *l.* whom; **ktokolwiek to powiedział, kłamał** whoever said it was lying. **2.** (= *wszystko jedno kto*) anybody, anyone.

ktoś *pron.* **kto-** *decl. zob.* **kto,** **-ś** *indecl.* **1.** somebody, someone; (*w pytaniach*) anybody, anyone; **ktoś wypił moją kawę** someone drank my coffee; **czy jest ktoś w domu?** is there anybody *l.* anyone home? **2.** (= *ważna osoba*) somebody; **on myśli, że jest kimś** he thinks he's somebody. – *mp Gen.pl.* **-ów** *żart.* (= *osoba nienazwana po imieniu*) somebody; **chciałbym poznać tego ktosia** I'd like to meet that somebody.

którędy *adv.* which way.

którędykolwiek *adv.* (*wprowadza zdanie podrzędne*) whichever way, no matter which way; (= *wszystko jedno którędy*) any which way; (= *którąkolwiek z dwu dróg*) either way.

który *pron.* **1.** (*wyraża pytanie*) which; **o której godzinie?** at what time?; **który to?** which one is it?; **którego dzisiaj mamy?** what's the date today? **2.** (*rozpoczyna zdanie podrzędne*) (*odnosząc się do osoby*) who; (*czasem w przypadkach zależnych*) whom; (*odnosząc się do rzeczy*) which; (*w zdaniu przydawkowym definiującym*) that; **dziewczyna, którą spotkałem** the girl who I met, the girl I met, the girl that I met, the girl whom I met; **książka, którą czytam** the book I'm reading, the book that I'm reading, the book which I'm reading; **John, który widział mnie wcześniej, od razu mnie poznał** John, who had seen me before, recognized me at once.

którykolwiek *pron.* **który-** *decl. like a.,* **-kolwiek** *indecl.* (*zaimek względny*) **1.** whichever, no matter which. **2.** (= *obojętnie który*) any; (*z dwóch*) either; **weź którykolwiek z tych dwóch** take either of these two.

któryś *a.* **który-** *decl. like a.,* **-ś** *indecl.* one; **któregoś dnia** one day; **któryś z nich** *l.* **spośród nich** one of them.

któryż *pron.* **który-** *decl. like a.,* **-ż** *indecl. emf.* (*w pytaniach*) *zob.* **który.**

któż *pron. Gen.* **kogóż** *Dat.* **komuż** *Ins. i Loc.* **kimże** *emf.* (*w pytaniach*) *zob.* **kto**; who ever, who on earth; **któż to jest, u diabła?** who the hell is that?

ku *prep. + Dat.* (= *do, w stronę*) **1.** toward; **mieć się ku sobie** be attracted toward each other. **2.** *lit.* (= *gwoli, dla*) **ku pamięci...** to commemorate...; **ku przestrodze** as a cautionary example; **ku uciesze widowni** to the amusement of the audience; **ku mojemu wielkiemu zaskoczeniu** to my great surprise.

Kuba *f. geogr.* Cuba.

Kubanka *f. Gen.pl.* **-ek, Kubańczyk** *mp* Cuban.

kubański *a.* Cuban.

kubas *mi Gen.* **-a** *pot. emf.* mug.

kubatura *f.* (= *objętość*) cubature, cubage.

kubeba *f. bot.* cubeb (*Piper cubeba*).

kubek *mi* **-bk-** *Gen.* **-a** (*naczynie*) **1.** mug; **gorący kubek** *kulin.* instant soup; **podobni kubek w kubek** *pot.* as like as two peas in a pod. **2.** (*pojemność*) mugful. **3.** *anat.* **kubki smakowe** tastebuds.

kubeł *mi* **-bł-** *Gen.* **-a** **1.** (= *wiadro*) bucket, pail; **wylać na kogoś kubeł zimnej wody** *przen.* throw a bucket of cold water on sb; **wylać na kogoś kubeł pomyj** *przen.* sling mud at sb; **morda w kubeł!** *sl.* shut your gob! **2.** *techn.* (*pojemnik, czerpak*) bucket.

kubiczny *a.* (= *sześcienny*) cubic; (*o kształcie*) cubical, cubiform.

kubik *mi Gen.* **-a** (= *metr sześcienny*) cubic meter.

kubista *mp,* **kubistka** *f. Gen.pl.* **-ek** cubist.

kubistyczny *a.* cubist.

kubizm *mi sztuka* cubism.

kubrak *mi Gen.* **-a** (*strój*) doublet.

kubryk *mi żegl.* forecastle.

kuc *ma zool.* pony; **kuc szetlandzki** Shetland pony.

kucać *ipf.* squat (down), crouch.

kucharka *f. Gen.pl.* **-ek** cook; **gdzie kucharek sześć, tam nie ma co jeść** too many cooks spoil the broth.

kucharski *a.* culinary, cook's; **sztuka kucharska** culinary art; **książka kucharska** cookbook, recipe book.

kucharz *mp* cook; (= *kuchmistrz, szef kuchni*) chef; **głód to najlepszy kucharz** hunger is the best sauce.

kucharzyć *ipf. żart.* play the cook; mess around in the kitchen.

kuchcik *mp pl.* **-i** kitchen boy; *arch.* scullion.

kuchenka *f. Gen.pl.* **-ek** **1.** (= *piecyk do gotowania*) cooker; **kuchenka elektryczna/gazowa** electric/gas cooker; **kuchenka mikrofalowa** microwave oven. **2.** (= *mała kuchnia*) kitchenette.

kuchenny *a.* **1.** (= *związany z kuchnią*) kitchen, cooking; **sprzęty kuchenne** kitchenware; **zlew/stół kuchenny** kitchen sink/table; **nóż kuchenny** cook's knife; **kuchenne wejście/schody** kitchen entrance/stairs; **dziewczyna** *l.* **dziewka kuchenna** *przest.* kitchen maid; **łacina kuchenna**

przest. kitchen Latin, dog Latin; **sól kuchenna** cooking salt. **2.** *techn.* (= *dotyczący piecyka*) baking.

kuchmistrz *mp Gen.pl.* **-ów** chef.

kuchmistrzowski *a.* chef's.

kuchnia *f. Gen.pl.* **-i** *l.* **-chen 1.** (= *miejsce, gdzie przygotowuje się posiłki*) kitchen; **szef kuchni** head cook, chef; **ślepa kuchnia** windowless kitchen; **kuchnia okrętowa** cookroom; **kuchnia polowa** mobile kitchen; (*serwująca posiłki dla bezdomnych l. ubogich*) soup kitchen. **2.** (= *piec do gotowania*) stove, cooker; **kuchnia węglowa** coal stove. **3.** (*sztuka kulinarna*) cuisine; **kuchnia jarska** vegetarian cuisine; **znać się na kuchni** be a good cook.

kuchta *f. pog.* kitchen servant, drudge; *Br.* skivvy.

kucie *n. metal. zob.* **kuć**.

kucki *pl. Gen.* **kucek** squatting position, squat; **siedzieć w kucki** squat.

kucmerka *f. Gen.pl.* **-ek** *bot.* skirret, Sium sisarum.

kucnąć *pf.* **-ij** *zob.* **kucać**.

kucyk *ma* = **kuc**. – *mi Gen.* **-a** (= *kitka*) pony tail.

Kuczki *pl. Gen.* **Kuczek** *judaizm* the Feast of Tabernacles; Sukkot, Succoth.

kuczny *a. sport* **siad kuczny** squat.

kuć *ipf.* **1.** (*obrabiać metal*) forge, hammer; **kucie na gorąco/na zimno** hot/cold forging; **kuć żelazo, póki gorące** *przen.* strike while the iron's hot. **2.** (*podkuwać*) shoe; **kuty (na cztery nogi)** *pot.* (= *zaradny, sprytny*) resourceful; (= *przebiegły*) cunning, as wily as a fox. **3.** (*np. o dzięciole*) (= *stukać*) tap (*w coś* sth). **4.** *pot. szkoln.* (= *uczyć się intensywnie*) cram, plod, grind (away); *Br.* swot (up).

kudłacz *mp pot.* (*o człowieku*) mophead; (*o zwierzęciu*) shaggy thing.

kudłaty *a.* hairy, shaggy; **kudłate myśli** *żart.* dirty thoughts.

kudły *pl. Gen.* **-ów** *l.* **-deł** *pot.* mat (of hair), shaggy hair.

kufa *f.* **1.** (*beczka*) (storage) cask. **2.** *myśl.* (= *pysk psa*) muzzle.

kufajka *f. Gen.pl.* **-ek** *pot.* (= *waciak*) quilted work jacket.

kufel *mi* **-fl-** *Gen.* **-a** tankard, stein; beer jug, beer mug; = *szklanka do piwa* beer glass; (*porcja piwa*) pint; **rozmawiać przy kuflu** talk over a pint.

kufelek *mi* **-lk-** *Gen.* **-a** *emf. zob.* **kufel**; **chodźmy na kufelek** let's go for a pint.

kufer *mi* **-fr-** *Gen.* **-a 1.** (*skrzynia, sakwojaż*) chest, trunk. **2.** *pot.* (= *bagażnik samochodowy*) trunk; *Br.* boot.

kuferek *mi* **-rk-** *Gen.* **-a 1.** (= *walizka, sakwojaż*) trunk. **2.** (= *damska torebka*) handbag.

kuglarka *f. Gen.pl.* **-ek** *zob.* **kuglarz**.

kuglarski *a.* **1.** conjuring, conjurer's; **kuglarskie sztuczki** conjuring tricks. **2.** *przen.* (= *oszukańczy*) tricky.

kuglarstwo *n. t. przen.* conjuring (tricks), sleight of hand.

kuglarz *mp* **1.** (*magik*) conjurer. **2.** *przen.* (= *oszust*) trickster, con-man.

kuguar *ma zool.* (= *puma*) cougar, puma, mountain lion (*Puma concolor*).

kujawiak *mi Gen. i Acc.* **-a** (*taniec*) kujawiak (*a Polish folk dance*).

kujawski *a.* Kujavian (*from the Kujavia region in Poland*).

kujność *f. techn.* forgeability.

kujon *mp pl.* **-y** *pot.* grind; *Br.* swot.

kukać *ipf.* (*o kukułce*) **1.** cuckoo. **2.** *sl.* (= *zerkać*) peep (*na kogoś/coś* at sb/sth).

kukiełka *f. Gen.pl.* **-ek** puppet.

kukiełkowy *a.* puppet; **teatrzyk kukiełkowy** puppet theater.

kuklik *mi Gen.* **-a** *bot.* avens (*Geum*).

kukła *f. Gen.pl.* **kukieł 1.** (= *lalka, manekin*) effigy, figure, doll. **2.** *pog.* (*o kimś bezwolnym*) puppet.

kuknąć *pf.* **-ij** *zob.* **kukać**.

kuks *mi Gen.* **-a** = **kuksaniec**.

kuksać *ipf.* **-ij** (= *szturchać*) nudge, elbow.

kuksaniec *mi Gen.* **-a** nudge, elbow.

kuksnąć *pf.* **-ij** *zob.* **kuksać**.

kuku *int.* cuckoo; **a kuku** *dziec.* boo, peekaboo. – *n. indecl.* **zrobić sobie kuku** *dziec.* hurt o.s.; **mieć kuku (na muniu)** *pot.* be off one's nut; have bats in the belfry.

kukułka *f. Gen.pl.* **-ek** *orn.* cuckoo (*Cuculus, Coccyzus*); **zegar z kukułką** cuckoo clock.

kukurydza *f. bot.* corn; *Br.* maize (*Zea mays*).

kukurydziany *a.* corn, maize; **mąka kukurydziana** corn flour; **kukurydziane kolby** corn cobs.

kukuryku *int.* cock-a-doodle-doo.

kula¹ *f.* **1.** (*bryła*) ball, sphere; **kula śniegowa** snowball; **kula ziemska** globe; **kryształowa kula** (*do wróżenia*) crystal ball; **kula u nogi** ball and chain. **2.** *lekkoatletyka* shot; **pchnięcie kulą** shot put. **3.** *broń* (= *pocisk*) bullet; **kula armatnia** cannonball; **wpakować sobie kulę w łeb** *pot.* blow one's brains out; **trafić jak kulą w płot** *przen.* be wide of the mark; **a niech mnie kule biją!** blow me!; **człowiek strzela, Pan Bóg kule nosi** man proposes, God disposes. **4.** *jeźdz.* (*u siodła*) pommel.

kula² *f.* (*szczudło, podpora*) crutch; **kule** a pair of crutches; **chodzić o kulach** go (about) on crutches.

kulać *ipf. pot.* (= *turlać*) roll. **~ się** *ipf.* (= *toczyć się*) roll.

kulas *mi Gen.* **-a** *żart.* (= *noga*) leg. – *mp pl.* **-y** *obelż.* = **kulawiec**.

kulawiec *mp* **-wc-** *Voc.* **-cu** *l.* **-cze** *obelż.* cripple, hobbler.

kulawy *a.* **1.** (= *ułomny, kulejący*) lame; (*o nodze*) game; **pies z kulawą nogą** *pot.* not a living soul. **2.** (= *koślawy, chybotliwy*) wonky. **3.** *przen.* (= *niedoskonały, nieregularny*) ragged, halting. **4.** *przen.* (= *kiepski, marny*) lame, poor; **kulawa wymówka** lame excuse.

kulbaczyć *ipf.* (= *siodłać*) saddle.

kulbak *ma icht.* Greenland halibut (*Reinhardtius hipoglossoides*).

kulbaka *f.* (= *siodło*) saddle.

kulczyba *f. bot.* strychnos (*Strychnos*); kulczyba wronie oko nux vomica (*S. nux-vomica*).
kulczyk *ma orn.* serin (*Serinus serinus*).
kuleczka *f. Gen.pl.* -ek *emf. zob.* kulka.
kuleć *ipf.* 1. (= *utykać*) hobble (along), limp. 2. *przen.* (= *szwankować*) be deficient.
kulfon *mi Gen.* -a 1. *pl. pot.* (= *bazgroły*) scrawl. 2. *pot.* (= *nochal*) beak.
kulić się *ipf.* huddle o.s. up, curl o.s. up; (*ze strachu*) cower, cringe.
kulig *mi* sleigh ride.
kulik *ma zool.* (*ptak*) curlew (*Numenius*); kulik mniejszy whimbrel (*N. phaeopus*).
kulinarny *a.* culinary; sztuka kulinarna culinary art; high cuisine; przepis kulinarny recipe.
kulis *mp pog. przest.* coolie.
kulisa *f. rzad., teatr zob.* kulisy.
kulistość *f.* roundness, sphericity, sphericalness.
kulisty *a.* spherical, round.
kulisy *pl. Gen.* -s 1. *teatr* wings; wejść za kulisy go behind the scenes; grać od kulis *uj.* overact. 2. *pot.* (= *szczegóły, nieujawnione okoliczności*) the inside story; za kulisami (= *niejawnie*) behind the scenes, behind the closed doors.
kulka *f. Gen.pl.* -ek 1. (= *mała kula*) ball, pellet; kulka z chleba bread pellet. 2. (*do gry l. zabawy*) marble. 3. lecieć sobie z kimś w kulki *pot.* pull sb's leg. 4. *pot.* (= *pocisk, kula*) bullet; wpakować komuś kulkę w łeb put a bullet in sb's head; zarobić kulkę be shot. 5. *techn.* (*element łożyska*) ball.
kulkowy *a.* ball; pióro kulkowe ballpoint pen, ballpen; łożysko kulkowe *techn.* ball bearing.
kulminacja *f.* 1. (= *maksimum*) culmination, climax. 2. *astron.* culmination. 3. *geogr.* highest point, peak.
kulminacyjny *a.* 1. culminating; kulminacyjna fala powodzi the high point of a flood; punkt kulminacyjny culminating point, climax. 2. *geogr.* highest.
kulminować *ipf.* culminate, come to a head.
kulnąć (się) *pf.* -ij *zob.* kulać (się).
kulnik *mi Gen.* -a *bot.* globe daisy, Globularia.
kulomb *mi Gen.* -a *fiz.* coulomb.
kulombometr, kulometr *mi fiz.* voltameter, coulometer.
kulomiot *mp sport* (*zawodnik*) shotputter. – *mi przest., wojsk.* machine gun.
kulomiotka *f. Gen.pl.* -ek *sport zob.* kulomiot *mp.*
kulon *ma orn.* stone curlew (*Burhinus oedicnemus*).
kuloodporny *a.* bulletproof; kuloodporna kamizelka bulletproof vest *l.* jacket; kuloodporne szkło bulletproof glass.
kulowy *a. techn.* ball; zawór kulowy ball valve.
kulsza *f. Gen.pl.* -sz *l.* -y *anat., przest.* hipbone.
kulszowy *a. anat.* sciatic; kość kulszowa hipbone; nerw kulszowy sciatic nerve; rwa kulszowa *pat.* sciatica.
kult *mi* 1. (*otaczanie czcią*) cult, worship; kult zmarłych cult *l.* worship of the dead; kult ognia cult of fire, fire-worship; kult szatana satanic

cult; kult muzyki popularnej pop-music cult; kult jednostki *polit.* personality cult. 2. *rel.* (*liturgia*) cult.
kultowy *a.* 1. (*obrzędowy, religijny*) cult, cultic; obrzędy kultowe cult rituals. 2. *pot.* cult; kultowy film cult film; kultowa postać cult personality.
kultura *f.* 1. (*cywilizacja, tradycja*) culture; kultura europejska/amerykańska/afrykańska European/American/African culture; kultura grecka/rzymska/starożytna Greek/Roman/ancient culture; kultura ludowa folk culture; dom kultury community center, arts center. 2. (*wysoki poziom sprawności, wykształcenia*) culture, cultivation, refinement; kultura fizyczna physical culture; kultura umysłowa culture of the mind; kultura osobista sophistication. 3. (= *maniery*) manners, politeness; kultura towarzyska social manners; brak kultury bad manners. 4. *biol., roln.* (= *hodowla*) culture; kultura bakterii/wirusów *biol.* bacterial/viral culture.
kulturalny *a.* 1. (= *dotyczący kultury*) cultural; życie kulturalne cultural life; prąd kulturalny cultural tendencies. 2. (= *taktowny, wyrobiony*) polite; kulturalne towarzystwo/zachowanie polite company; kulturalne zachowanie polite behaviour. 3. (= *wyrafinowany, wykształcony*) cultured, refined, sophisticated.
kulturolog *mp pl.* -dzy *l.* -owie culture expert.
kulturologia *f. Gen.* -ii cultural studies.
kulturotwórczy *a.* culture-producing, culturally active.
kulturowy *a. socjol.* cultural; wartości/procesy kulturowe cultural values/processes; antropologia kulturowa cultural anthropology.
kulturoznawca *mp* culture expert.
kulturoznawczy *a.* related to cultural studies.
kulturoznawstwo *n.* cultural studies.
kulturysta *mp*, kulturystka *f. Gen.pl.* -ek bodybuilder.
kulturystyczny *a.* bodybuilding.
kulturystyka *f.* bodybuilding.
kultywacja *f. roln.* cultivation.
kultywacyjny *a. roln.* cultivational.
kultywator *mi Gen.* -a *roln., ogr.* cultivator.
kultywować *ipf.* 1. (*pielęgnować, hołubić*) cultivate, cherish; kultywować tradycje cultivate traditions. 2. *roln.* (= *uprawiać*) cultivate.
kuluarowy *a.* unofficial, behind-the-scenes.
kuluary *pl. Gen.* -ów 1. (= *westybul*) lobby. 2. *przen.* rozmowy w kuluarach talks behind the scenes.
kułacki *a. hist.* kulak.
kułactwo *n. hist.* the kulaks.
kułaczka *f. Gen.pl.* -ek *zob.* kułak².
kułak¹ *mi Gen.* -a *pl.* -i 1. (= *pięść*) fist; rzucić się na kogoś z kułakami raise one's fists at sb; śmiać się w kułak laugh up one's sleeves. 2. (= *uderzenie pięścią*) blow, punch.
kułak² *mp pl.* -cy *hist.* kulak.
kum¹ *mp pl.* -owie *l.* -y 1. *żart.* (= *ojciec chrzestny*) godfather. 2. *pot.* (= *przyjaciel*) friend, chum, buddy, pal, crony.
kum² *int.* croak.

kuma *f. zob.* **kum¹**.
kumać *ipf. pot.* (= *rozumieć*) dig; **nie kumam tego** I don't dig it, I don't follow.
kumać się *ipf. pot.* (= *spoufalać się*) hobnob (*z kimś* with sb).
kumak *ma zool.* fire-bellied toad (*Bombina*).
kumaryna *f. chem.* coumarin.
kumberland *mi kulin.* Cumberland sauce.
kumkać *ipf.* (*o żabie*) (= *rechotać*) croak.
kumkwat *ma bot.* kumquat (*Fortunella*).
kumoszka *f. Gen.pl.* **-ek 1.** *pot. arch.* (= *plotkarka, trajkotka*) gossip, tattler; **chodzić po kumoszkach** chatter, tattle. **2.** *pot. żart.* (= *przyjaciółka*) mate, pal, gossip.
kumoter *mp* **-tr-** *pl.* **-rzy** *l.* **-owie** *l.* **-ry 1.** *pot.* (= *sojusznik, przyjaciel*) crony, companion; *polit.* logroller. **2.** *dial.* friend.
kumoterski *a.* logrolling.
kumoterstwo *n. pot.* cronyism, logrolling, favoritism, nepotism.
kumpel *mp* **-pl-** *Gen.pl.* **-i** *l.* **-ów** *pot.* (= *kolega*) buddy, mate, pal.
kumpela *f. Gen.pl.* **-i** *zob.* **kumpel**.
kumpelka *f. Gen.pl.* **-ek** *zob.* **kumpel**.
kumplować się *ipf. pot.* (= *kolegować się*) be buddies (*z kimś* with sb).
kumplowski *a. pot.* buddy-buddy, chummy, friendly.
kumulacja *f.* (= *gromadzenie; gromadzenie się*) accumulation, cumulation.
kumulacyjny *a.* accumulative, cumulative.
kumulować *ipf.* (= *zbierać, gromadzić*) accumulate, cumulate.
kumys *mi kulin.* kumiss, koumis(s).
kuna *f. zool.* marten (*Martes*); **kuna leśna** pine marten (*Martes martes*); **kuna domowa** stone marten, beech marten (*Martes foina*).
kundel *ma* **-dl-** *Gen.pl.* **-i** *l.* **-ów** (= *pies mieszaniec*) mongrel, cur, mutt.
kundlowaty *a.* mongrel.
kung-fu *n. indecl. sport* kung fu.
kuni *a.* marten.
kunktator *mp lit.* (= *asekurant*) cunctator, dilator, procrastinator.
kunktatorski *a. lit.* (= *asekurancki*) cunctatious, cunctatory, dilatory.
kunktatorstwo *n. lit.* (= *asekuranctwo*) cunctation, dilatoriness, procrastination.
kunszt *mi* **1.** (= *artyzm*) artistry, art. **2.** (= *rzemiosło, zawód*) craft.
kunsztownie *adv.* (= *artystycznie*) artistically.
kunsztowność *f.* (= *artyzm*) artistry.
kunsztowny *a.* (= *artystyczny*) artistic.
kupa *f.* **1.** *pot.* (= *duża liczba, ilość*) loads of sth, pile, buttload of sth, mound, heap; **leżeć na kupie** be piled up; **zebrać na kupę** pile up; **trzymać się kupy** *l.* **w kupie** stick together; **do kupy** together. **2.** *pot.* (= *odchody*) turd; **zrobić kupę** poop, crap, shit. – *adv.* (= *dużo*) a lot, lots.
kupalnik *mi Gen.* **-a** *bot.* arnica (*Arnica*).
kupała *f. hist.* (= *sobótka*) Midsummer Eve *l.* Night, St. John's Eve *l.* Night.
kupczyć *ipf. lit.* trade, traffic.
kupela *f. metal.* cupel furnace.

kupelacja *f. metal.* cupellation.
kupelacyjny *a. metal.* cupeling.
kupelka *f. metal.* cupel.
kupelować *ipf. metal.* cupel.
kuper *mi* **-pr-** *Gen.* **-a 1.** (*u ptaków*) rump; *orn.* uropygium; **bić** *l.* **strzelać jak w kaczy kuper** fire point-blank. **2.** *pot.* (= *pośladki*) buttocks.
kupić *pf. zob.* **kupować**.
Kupidyn *mp mit.* Cupid.
kupidyn *mp sztuka* (= *amorek*) cupid.
kupiec *mp* **-pc-** *Voc.* **-u** *l.* **-cze** *pl.* **-y 1.** (= *nabywca*) buyer, purchaser. **2.** (= *handlowiec, przedsiębiorca*) merchant, trader.
kupiecki *a.* merchant, merchant-like; **talent kupiecki** salesmanship.
kupiectwo *n.* (= *handel*) trade, business, commerce.
kupka *f. Gen.pl.* **-ek** *por.* **kupa**.
kupkówka *f.* **kupkówka pospolita** *bot.* orchard grass, cocksfoot grass (*Dactylis glomerata*).
kuplecista *mp przest.* cabaret singer.
kuplecistka *f. Gen.pl.* **-ek** *zob.* **kuplecista**.
kupler *mp rzad.* (= *stręczyciel*) procurer, pimp.
kuplerstwo *n. rzad.* (= *stręczycielstwo*) procuration.
kuplet *mi* **1.** verse (*of a satirical l. cabaret song*). **2.** *muz.* couplet.
kupno *n.* purchase; **akt kupna** purchase agreement, sales contract; **cena kupna** purchase *l.* buying price.
kupny *a. pot.* (= *kupiony*) bought, purchased.
kupon *mi* **1.** (= *blankiet w grze*) coupon; **zbierać kupony** collect coupons. **2.** (= *odcinek kontrolny biletu*) counterfoil. **3.** (= *kawałek tkaniny*) length of cloth. **4.** (= *talon, asygnata*) voucher.
kupować *ipf.* **1.** (= *nabywać*) buy, purchase (*u kogoś* at sb's) (*od kogoś* from sb) (*za coś* for sth); **kupować kota w worku** buy a pig in a poke; **kupować na wyprzedaży** buy in a sale; **kupować przez pośrednika** buy through an agent. **2.** *pot.* (= *zjednać sobie*) win (over); **każdego można kupić** everyone may be bought. **3.** *karty* (= *dobrać kartę*) draw.
kuprowy *a. orn.* uropygial; **gruczoł kuprowy** uropygial gland, oil gland.
kuprówka *f. Gen.pl.* **-ek** *ent.* brown-tail moth (*Euproctis chrysorrhoea*).
kupryt *mi min.* cuprite, red copper ore, ruby copper.
kuprytowy *a. min.* cuprite.
kupujący *mp* (= *nabywca*) buyer, purchaser; (= *klient*) customer, client, shopper, buyer.
kur¹ *ma Gen.* **-a 1.** *dial.* (= *kogut*) cock, rooster; **czerwony kur** fire, conflagration. **2.** *icht.* sculpin (*Myoxocephalus*). – *mi Gen.* **-a** (= *ptak z blachy w formie chorągiewki*) weathercock.
kur² *mi Gen.* **-u** *pat.* = *różyczka*.
kura *f.* **1.** *orn.* chicken (*Gallus domesticus*). **2.** (= *samica koguta*) hen; **kura domowa** *pot., przen.* housewife, homebody, stay-at-home; **kura znosząca złote jajka** goose that lays the golden eggs; **obnosić się z czymś jak kura z jajem** ponder a problem, be undecided; **pisać jak kura pazurem**

write illegibly, (scribble) chicken scratch; **cho-dzić spać z kurami** go to bed with the chickens; **wyglądać jak zmokła kura** look like a drowned rat; **co było na początku: jajo czy kura?** which came first: the chicken or the egg?; **daj kurze grzędę, ona: wyżej siędę** give him an inch and he'll take a mile; **trafiło się jak ślepej kurze ziarno** he/she/etc. got sth by a fluke. **3.** *orn.* (= *samica kurowatych*) hen.

kuracja *f.* (= *terapia*) treatment, therapy; **kuracja odchudzająca** diet.

kuracjusz *mp Gen.pl.* **-y** *l.* **-ów** health resort visitor; patient.

kuracjuszka *f. Gen.pl.* **-ek** *zob.* **kuracjusz.**

kuracyjny *a.* curative, therapeutical; **miejscowość kuracyjna** health resort.

kurak *ma* **1.** (= *kurczak*) chicken. **2.** *orn.* gallinaceous bird (*Galliformes*).

kurant *mi Gen.* **-a 1.** *muz.* (= *melodia*) chimes; **wygrywać kuranty** chime, ring the chimes. **2.** (= *mechanizm wygrywający melodię*) chimes, glockenspiel; **zegar z kurantem** chiming clock.

kurara *f.* (*trucizna*) curare, curari.

kuratela *f.* **1.** *prawn.* (= *nadzór*) guardianship; **oddać kogoś/coś pod kuratelę** appoint a guardian for sb/sth. **2.** *przen.* (= *opieka*) tutelage; **wziąć w kuratelę** take sb under one's wing.

kurator *mp pl.* **-rzy** *l.* **-owie 1.** *szkoln.* superintendent of schools. **2.** *prawn.* (*prawo cywilne*) guardian, custodian; (*prawo karne*) probation officer. **3.** *prawn.* (= *osoba zarządzająca interesami instytucji, grupy ludzi*) trustee.

kuratorium *n. sing. indecl. pl.* **-ria** *Gen.* **-riów** *szkoln.* (= *jednostka administracji szkołami*) board of education.

kuratorka *f. Gen.pl.* **-ek** *zob.* **kurator.**

kuratorski *a.* *prawn.* (*prawo cywilne*) guardian's, custodian's; (*prawo karne*) probation officer's.

kuratoryjny *a. szkoln.* pertaining to a board of education.

kuraż *mi arch.* courage; **dla kurażu** to summon up courage.

kurbel *mi Gen.* **-a** *techn.* crank, winch.

kurbet *mi jeźdz.* curvet.

kurcz *mi Gen.pl.* **-ów** *l.* **-y** (= *skurcz, spazm*) cramp, spasm.

kurczak *ma* chicken; **kurczak z rożna** *kulin.* spitroasted chicken.

kurczatow *mi Gen.* **-a** *chem.* kurchatovium; *US* unnilquadium, rutherfordium.

kurczę *n.* **-ęci-** *pl.* **-ęt-** *Gen.* **-ąt 1.** (= *kurczak*) chicken. **2.** *przen.* (*o dziecku*) chick. – *int. pot., euf.* damn, shit; **o kurczę!** oh shit!

kurczliwość *f. zwł. techn.* contractibility, retractability.

kurczliwy *a. zwł. techn.* contractible, contractile, retractable, shrinkable.

kurczowo *adv.* tightly; **kurczowo ściskać** hold tight.

kurczowy *a.* convulsive, spasmodic; **kurczowy uścisk** tight grip.

kurczyć *ipf.* (= *maleć*) contract, shrink. **~ się** *ipf.* **1.** (= *zmniejszać się*) shrink; **kurczyć się ze**

strachu cringe from fear. **2.** (= *ściągać się*) shrink; (*o metalu, mięśniu*) contract; **kurczyć się po praniu** shrink after washing. **3.** (= *zawężać się*) narrow down.

Kurd *mp pl.* **-owie** Kurd.

kurde *int. pot., euf.* shit; **o kurde!** oh shit!

kurdebelans *int.* shit.

kurdesz *mi Gen.* **-a** *Gen.pl.* **-ów** *arch.* lively folksong *l.* dance (*popular in Poland in the 18th century*).

kurdupel *mp* **-pl-** *Gen.pl.* **-i** *l.* **-ów** *pot.* runt.

kurduplowaty *a. pot.* runtish.

kurdyban *mi sztuka* cordovan.

kurdybanek *mi* **-nk-** *Gen.* **-a bluszczyk kurdybanek** *bot.* ground ivy (*Glechoma hederacea*).

kurdybanowy *a. sztuka* cordovan.

Kurdyjka *f. zob.* **Kurd.**

kurdyjski *a.* Kurdish.

kurek *mi* **-rk-** *Gen.* **-a 1.** (= *kurczak*) chicken. **2.** (= *figurka wyobrażająca koguta*) wooden/tin/metal cock; **kurek na kościele** *przen.* weathercock. **3.** *techn.* (= *kran*) faucet, tap, (stop)cock; **zakręcić kurek** turn the faucet off. **4.** *wojsk.* cock. **5.** *icht.* gurnard (*Trigla*).

kurenda *f. przest.* (= *zawiadomienie*) circular.

kurewka *f. Gen.pl.* **-ek** *wulg.* tart.

kurewski *a. wulg.* (= *dotyczący kurwy*) whorish; (= *niewygodny, niekorzystny*) fucked up; **to wszystko przez to jego kurewskie podejście** it's all due to this fucked up attitude of his.

kurewsko *adv. wulg.* whorishly; fucking.

kurewstwo *n. wulg.* **1.** (= *nierząd*) whoredom. **2.** (= *rozwiązłość*) fucking around, sleeping around. **3.** (= *świństwo, draństwo*) a fucking dirty trick; **to co mi zrobił, to było kurewstwo** it was a fucking dirty trick that he played on me.

kurhan *mi* **1.** *archeol.* (= *mogiła*) tumulus, barrow, burial mound. **2.** (= *kopiec*) mound.

kuria *f. Gen.* **-ii 1.** *kośc.* curia; **Kuria Rzymska** *rz.-kat.* Curia Romana. **2.** *hist.* curia. **3.** *admin., polit.* (= *okręg wyborczy; kategoria wyborców*) constituency.

kurialny *a.* curial.

kurier *mp pl.* **-rzy** (= *posłaniec*) courier, messenger. – *mi Gen.* **-a** *pl.* **-ry 1.** *przest.* (= *gazeta codzienna*) daily. **2.** *przest.* (= *pociąg pośpieszny*) fast train.

kurierski *a.* courier; **przesyłki kurierskie** delivery mail; **usługi kurierskie** (express) delivery service.

kuriozalnie *adv.* (= *dziwacznie*) oddly, weirdly, curiously.

kuriozalny *a.* (= *dziwaczny*) odd, strange, weird, curious.

kuriozum *n. sing. indecl. pl.* **-za** *Gen.* **-zów** (= *osobliwość*) oddity, curiosity; (*o człowieku*) weirdo.

kurka *f. Gen.pl.* **-ek 1.** *zob.* **kura; kurka wodna** *orn.* moorhen, water hen (*Gallinula chloropus*). **2.** *bot.* chanterelle (*Cantharellus cibarius*).

kurkowy *a.* **1.** (= *związany z figurką wyobrażającą koguta*) cock; **zawody kurkowe** shooting contest (*where the target resembles a rooster*); **bractwo kurkowe** rifle club; **król kurkowy** champion shot. **2.** *techn.* faucet; **zawór kurkowy** plug valve, cock.

kurkuma *f. bot.* curcuma, turmeric (*Curcuma*).

kurkumina *f. chem.* curcumin.

Kurlandia *f. geogr., hist.* Courland, Kurland.

kurlandzki *a.* Courlandic.

kurnik *mi Gen.* **-a 1.** (= *pomieszczenie dla drobiu*) chicken coop, henhouse. **2.** *przen.* (= *buda, barak*) hovel; **mieszkać w kurniku** live in a hovel.

kurny *a.* smoky; **kurna chata** chimneyless cabin *l.* hut.

kuropatwa *f. orn.* partridge (*Perdrix perdrix*).

kuropatwi *a.* partridge's, of a partridge.

kurort *mi* (= *uzdrowisko*) health resort, spa.

kurować *ipf.* (= *leczyć*) cure, treat, heal. **~ się** *ipf.* (= *leczyć się*) undergo treatment.

Kurp *mp* **-pi-** *Gen.pl.* **-ów** Kurp.

Kurpianka *f. Gen.pl.* **-ek** *zob.* **Kurp.**

Kurpie *pl. Gen.* **-ów** *l.* **-i** *geogr.* Kurpie.

kurpiowski *a.* of the Kurpie region *l.* the Kurpie.

kurs *mi* **1.** (= *droga, trasa*) route, road; (*przejazd*) ride; **zapłacić za kurs** pay for the (cab) ride. **2.** (= *trasa samolotu l. statku*) course; **trzymać się kursu** stay on course; **zmienić kurs** change (the) course; **zboczyć z kursu** go off (the) course; **wziąć kurs na południe** head southwards. **3.** *polit., przen.* (= *kierunek działania*) course, direction, policy. **4.** (= *obieg*) circulation; **wyjść z kursu** be no longer in use, be no longer popular. **5.** (= *cena*) rate; **kurs bankowy** bank rate; **kurs dolara** dollar exchange rate; **kurs złota** price of gold; **kurs walutowy** foreign exchange rate; **kurs giełdowy** market rate; **kurs dnia** day's rate. **6.** (= *kształcenie*) course; **kurs języka angielskiego** English course; **kurs komputerowy** computer course *l.* classes. **7.** *uniw.* (= *cykl ćwiczeń i wykładów*) course; **kurs gramatyki** grammar course.

kursant *mp* student.

kursantka *f. Gen.pl.* **-ek** *zob.* **kursant.**

kursor *mi Gen.* **-a** *komp.* cursor.

kursować *ipf.* **1.** (*o pojazdach*) (= *jeździć*) run; (*o środkach transportu wodnego*) ply. **2.** *żart.* (= *przemieszczać się*) cruise; circulate. **3.** (*o pieniądzach*) (= *być w obiegu*) be in circulation. **4.** (*o wiadomościach*) (= *krążyć*) be passed around, pass from mouth to mouth.

kursowy *a.* **1.** (= *dotyczący jazdy*) ride, drive. **2.** (= *dotyczący ceny*) of an exchange rate. **3.** *uniw.* course.

kursywa *f. druk.* (= *pismo pochyłe*) italics.

kurtaczek *ma orn.* pitta (*Pitta*).

kurtka *f. Gen.pl.* **-ek** jacket; **kurtka zimowa** winter jacket; **kurtka na wacie** wadded jacket.

kurtuazja *f.* (= *grzeczność*) courtesy.

kurtuazyjny *a.* courteous, courtesy; **złożyć kurtuazyjną wizytę** pay a courtesy visit.

kurtyna *f.* **1.** *teatr* curtain; **podnosić/opuścić kurtynę** raise/lower *l.* drop the curtain; **żelazna kurtyna** *hist., polit.* the Iron Curtain; **opuścić na coś kurtynę** draw a curtain over sth. **2.** (= *zasłona*) curtain, drape.

kurtyzana *f.* (= *kochanka, prostytutka*) courtesan, courtezan.

kurulny *a. hist.* curule; **krzesło kurulne** curule chair.

kurwa *f. Gen.pl.* **kurw** *l.* **kurew** *wulg.* **1.** (= *prostytutka*) whore. **2.** (*przekleństwo*) fuck; **kurwa mać!** fuck!, fuck it!

kurwiarz *mp Gen.pl.* **-y** *l.* **-ów** *wulg.* (= *dziwkarz*) whoremonger, rake, roué.

kurwica *f. wulg.* state of being totally pissed off; **dostać kurwicy** get totally pissed off.

kurwić się *ipf. wulg.* (= *puszczać się*) fuck around (*z kimś* with sb).

kurwiszcze *n. wulg.* (= *prostytutka*) slut, bitch, whore.

kurwiszon *mp* = **kurwiszcze.**

kurz *mi Gen.pl.* **-ów** dust; **zmiatać przed kimś kurz** be sb's devoted servant.

kurzajka *f. Gen.pl.* **-ek** *med.* (= *brodawka*) wart.

kurzawa *f.* whirling cloud, swirl; **kurzawa śniegu** blizzard, snowstorm.

kurzawka *f. Gen.pl.* **-ek 1.** = **kurzawa. 2.** *geol.* quicksand.

kurzy *a.* hen's; **kurze jaja** hen's eggs; **kurza ferma** chicken farm; **kurze ziele** *bot.* tormentil (*Potentilla erecta l. tormentilla*); **kurza ślepota** *pat.* twilight blindness, aknephascopia; **kurze łapki** crow's feet; **domek na kurzej nóżce** chicken leg hut; **kurzy móżdżek** *l.* rozum birdbrain.

kurzyć *ipf.* **1.** (= *pylić*) raise dust. **2.** *pot.* (= *palić papierosa*) smoke, puff. **~ się** *ipf.* **1.** (*o kurzu*) be raised; **kurzyło się za samochodem** car raised a cloud of dust; **kłamać aż się kurzy** lie like a gas-meter, tell blatant lies; **uciekać** *l.* wiać aż **się kurzy** run as fast as legs can carry. **2.** (= *dymić się*) smoke. **3.** (= *wydzielać kłęby pary*) steam; **komuś się kurzy z czupryny** *l.* ze łba sb is tipsy *l.* drunk.

kurzyślad *mi bot.* pimpernel (*Anagallis*).

kusiciel *mp* **1.** (= *podjudzacz*) tempter, inciter. **2.** *przen.* (= *diabeł*) the Tempter.

kusicielka *f. Gen.pl.* **-ek** (= *uwodzicielka*) temptress, seducer, siren.

kusicielski *a.* tempting, luring, seducing.

kusicielsko *adv.* seductively.

kusić *ipf.* **kuszę kusisz** (= *zachęcać, wabić*) tempt, allure; **kusi mnie, żeby to zrobić** I am tempted to do it; **kusić los** take unnecessary risk(s), tempt providence *l.* fate.

kuskus[1] *mi Gen.* **-u** *kulin.* (*potrawa, kasza*) couscous.

kuskus[2] *ma Gen.* **-a** *zool.* spotted cuscus (*Phalanger maculatus*).

kuso *adv.* shortly.

kustodia *f. Gen.* **-ii 1.** *rel.* (= *zespół klasztorów*) group of monasteries supervised by one custos. **2.** *kość.* (*naczynie*) custodial.

kustosz *mp Gen.pl.* **-y** *l.* **-ów 1.** (*pracownik muzeum lub biblioteki*) curator. **2.** *kość.* custos, custodian.

kusy *a.* (= *przykrótki*) short. **–** *mp* (= *diabeł*) devil.

kusza *f.* **1.** *hist.* (*broń*) crossbow, arbalest; **ku-**

sza młot *icht.* smooth hammerhead (*Sphyrna zygaena*). **2.** *hist.* (= *machina oblężnicza*) ballista.

kuszący *a. zob.* **kusicielski.**

kuszetka *f. Gen.pl.* **-ek** *kol.* (= *wagon z miejscami do spania*) sleeping car; (= *miejsce do spania w takim wagonie*) couchette, sleeping berth.

kuszetkowy *a. kol.* sleeping, couchette; **wagon kuszetkowy** sleeping car.

kuśka *f. Gen.pl.* **-ek** *pot., żart.* penis.

kuśnierski *a.* furriery.

kuśnierstwo *n.* furriery.

kuśnierz *mp* (= *futrzarz*) furrier, fur dresser.

kuśtykać, kusztykać *ipf. pot.* (= *utykać*) limp, hobble.

kutafon *mp pl.* **-y** *wulg.* (= *wredna osoba*) prick.

kutas *mp pl.* **-y** *wulg.* (= *kutafon*) prick. – *mi Gen.* **-a 1.** *wulg.* (= *penis*) dick, prick, cock. **2.** *przest.* (= *ozdoba z nici, sznurka itp. w kształcie pędzla*) tassel.

kuter *mi* **-tr- 1.** (= *statek rybacki*) fishing boat. **2.** *żegl.* (*jacht*) cutter. **3.** *wojsk.* (= *okręt wojenny*) cutter; **kuter torpedowy** torpedo boat.

kuternoga *f. l. mp decl. like f. Gen.pl.* **-nóg** *l.* **-ów** *pot.* (= *człowiek kulejący*) lame person.

kutia *f. Gen.* **-ii** *kulin.* traditional festive Slavonic dish (*made of honey, poppy seeds and wheat*).

kutner *mi Gen.* **-a** *l.* **-u 1.** *bot.* (= *meszek*) tomentum. **2.** *tk.* nap, fluff.

kutnerować *ipf. tk.* nap.

kutwa *f. l. mp Gen.pl.* **kutw** *l.* **-ów** *pog., żart.* (= *skąpiec*) niggard, stingy old miser.

kuty *a.* **1.** (*z metalu*) forged; **kute żelazo** wrought iron. **2.** (*o zwierzętach*) (= *podkuty*) shod; **on jest kuty na cztery nogi** he's a sly old fox.

kutykula *f.* **1.** *bot.* cuticle. **2.** *zool.* (= *oskórek*) cuticle.

kutyna *f. bot.* cutin.

kuwejcki *a.* Kuwaiti.

Kuwejt *mi geogr.* Kuwait.

Kuwejtczyk *mp* Kuwaiti.

Kuwejtka *f. Gen.pl.* **-ek** *zob.* **Kuwejtczyk.**

kuwertura *f. kulin.* (= *polewa czekoladowa*) chocolate coating *l.* icing.

kuweta *f.* **1.** *fot.* developing dish *l.* tray. **2.** (*dla kota*) sandbox.

kuzyn *mp pl.* **-owie** *l.* **-i** cousin.

kuzynka *f. Gen.pl.* **-ek** *zob.* **kuzyn.**

kuzynostwo *n. Loc.* **-wie** (= *pokrewieństwo*) kinship. – *n. Loc.* **-wu** (= *kuzyn z żoną*) cousin and his wife.

kuzynowski *a.* cousin's.

kuźnia *f. Gen.pl.* **-i** (= *warsztat kowala*) forge, smithy, blacksmith's shop.

kwadra *f. astron.* quarter; **kwadra księżyca** quarter.

kwadrans *mi pl.* **-e** (= *piętnaście minut*) quarter, fifteen minutes; **za kwadrans czwarta** quarter to four; **kwadrans po siódmej** quarter past seven; **kwadrans akademicki** *uniw.* fifteen minutes' grace.

kwadrant *mi Gen.* **-u** *l.* **-a 1.** *astron., żegl., techn.*

(*przyrząd pomiarowy*) quadrant. **2.** *mat.* (= *ćwiartka płaszczyzny*) quarter, quadrant. **3.** *sport* (= *palant*) baseball.

kwadrat *mi* **1.** *geom.* square; **kwadrat logiczny** *log.* square of opposition; **kwadrat magiczny** *stat.* magic square. **2.** *mat.* (= *druga potęga*) square, the second power; **podnieść do kwadratu** square, raise to the second power; **osioł do kwadratu** *pot.* jackass, pudding head.

kwadratowy *a.* **1.** *geom.* square; **metr kwadratowy** square meter. **2.** *mat.* square; **pierwiastek kwadratowy** square root. **3.** (= *w kształcie kwadratu*) square(-shaped); **nawias kwadratowy** square brackets.

kwadratura *f.* **1.** *astron.* quadrature. **2.** *geom.* quadrature; **kwadratura koła** squaring the circle.

kwadryga *f. hist.* (*wóz konny*) quadriga.

kwadrylion *mi Gen.* **-a** (= *tysiąc trylionów*) septillion.

kwakać *ipf.* **-cze** (*o kaczce*) quack.

kwakier *mp* **-kr-** *pl.* **-rzy** *l.* **-owie** *rel.* Quaker.

kwakierka *f. Gen.pl.* **-ek 1.** *rel.* Quakeress; *zob.* **kwakier. 2.** (*kapelusz*) broadbrim.

kwakierski *a. rel.* Quaker, Quakerish, Quakerly.

kwakierstwo *n. rel.* Quakerism.

kwaknąć *pf. zob.* **kwakać.**

kwa-kwa *int.* quack-quack.

kwalifikacja *f.* (= *zaliczenie*) qualification; **kwalifikacja prawna** *prawn.* legal qualification.

kwalifikacje *pl. Gen.* **-i** (= *wykształcenie*) **1.** qualifications, training. **2. kwalifikacje do ubiegania się o coś** eligibility for sth; **zdobyć kwalifikacje** acquire *l.* gain qualifications; **nie mieć żadnych kwalifikacji** have no qualifications, be unqualified.

kwalifikacyjny *a.* qualifying, qualificatory, qualification; **wymagania kwalifikacyjne** qualification requirements; **turniej kwalifikacyjny** tryout, trial, qualification contest; **komisja kwalifikacyjna** selection committee; **rozmowa kwalifikacyjna** interview.

kwalifikator *mp pl.* **-rzy** (= *klasyfikator*) classifier. – *mi Gen.* **-a** *pl.* **-ry** *jez.* qualifier, modifier.

kwalifikować *ipf.* **1.** (= *klasyfikować*) classify (*do czegoś* for/as sth) categorize, systematize. **2.** (= *uznawać*) qualify, certify, authorize. **~ się** *ipf.* (= *nadawać się*) qualify (*na kogoś* to be sb *l.* as sb); meet the requirements, be eligible *l.* fit (*do czegoś* for sth); (*o rzeczy*) lend itself (*do czegoś* to sth).

kwalifikowany *a.* **1.** (= *wyszkolony*) qualified, competent; **kwalifikowany pracownik** qualified worker, skilled worker. **2.** (= *doborowy*) high-quality, accomplished, proficient, select; **kwalifikowana większość** qualified majority.

kwant *mi fiz.* quantum; **kwant energii** energy quantum; **teoria kwantów** quantum theory.

kwantowy *a. fiz.* quantum; **fizyka/mechanika kwantowa** quantum physics/mechanics.

kwantum *n. sing. indecl. pl.* **-ta** *Gen.* **-tów** *lit.* quantum, amount; **kwantum wiedzy** amount of knowledge.

kwantyfikacja *f. nauk., log.* quantification.

kwantyfikator *mi Gen.* **-a** *log., gram.* quantifier.

kwantytatywny *a. form.* (= *ilościowy*) quantitative.

kwantyzacja *f. fiz.* quantization.

kwapić się *ipf.* be eager *l.* willing *l.* anxious (*do czegoś* to do sth); be quick (*z czymś* with sth); **nie kwapić się do (zrobienia) czegoś** be in no hurry to do sth; linger to do sth; be slow *l.* reluctant to do sth; **nie kwapić się z pomocą komuś** be slow to help sb.

kwarantanna *f. Gen.pl.* **-nn** quarantine; **poddać kwarantannie** put *l.* hold in quarantine; subject to quarantine.

kwarc *mi min.* quartz.

kwarcowy *a.* quartz, quartzitic; **szkło kwarcowe** quartz glass; **zegar kwarcowy** *el.* quartz clock; **lampa kwarcowa** *techn.* sunlamp.

kwarcówka *f. Gen.pl.* **-ek** **1.** *pot.* (*lampa*) sunlamp. **2.** *pot.* (*zabieg*) sunlamp treatment.

kwarcyt *mi min.* quartzite.

kwarcytowy *a.* quartzite; **łupki kwarcytowe** quartz schist.

kwark *mi Gen.* **-a** *fiz.* quark.

kwarkowy *a. fiz.* quark.

kwarta *f.* **1.** *muz.* fourth. **2.** *sport* quarter. **3.** *szerm.* carte. **4.** *przest.* (*miara objętości*) quart.

kwartalnie *adv.* (= *co trzy miesiące*) quarterly, every three months, trimonthly.

kwartalnik *mi Gen.* **-a** quarterly (magazine *l.* journal).

kwartalny *a.* (= *trzymiesięczny*) quarterly, trimonthly; **premia kwartalna** quarterly bonus; **opłata kwartalna** *fin.* quarterage, quarterly payment.

kwartał *mi* **1.** (= *trzy miesiące*) quarter, three months. **2.** (= *dzielnica*) district, quarter, square. **3.** *przest.* (*część roku szkolnego*) term.

kwartet *mi* **1.** *muz.* (*utwór*) quartet, quartette; **kwartet fortepianowy/skrzypcowy** piano/violin quartet. **2.** *muz.* (*zespół*) quartet; **kwartet wokalny/smyczkowy** vocal/string quartet.

kwartetowy *a. muz.* (of a) quartet.

kwas *mi* **1.** *chem.* acid; **kwas siarkowy/azotowy** sulfuric/nitric acid; **kwas askorbinowy** ascorbic acid; **kwas solny** hydrochloric acid, muriatic acid; **kwas pruski** prussic acid, hydrocyanic acid, hydrogen cyanide. **2.** (= *zaczyn, zakwas*) leaven. **3.** (*coś kwaśnego*) sourness; **kwas chlebowy** kvas, kvass. **4.** *zw. pl.* (= *niesnaski*) bitterness, sourness, bad blood, bickering, clashing.

kwasek *mi* **-sk-** *pot.* acid; **kwasek cytrynowy** *kulin.* citric acid.

kwasica *f. pat.* acidosis.

kwasić *ipf.* **1.** (= *kisić*) pickle, leaven, subject to fermentation. **2.** *pot.* (= *psuć*) sour, embitter, disenchant. **~ się** *ipf.* **1.** (= *kisić się*) ferment, turn sour, pickle. **2.** *przen.* (= *nudzić się*) idle, loiter, laze about.

kwasja *f. Gen.pl.* **-i** **1.** *bot.* quassia (*Quassia amara*). **2.** *chem.* quassia.

kwaskowaty *a.* sourish, vinegary; *form.* acidulous.

kwasochłonny *a. biol.* acidophilic, acidophilous.

kwasomierz *mi Gen.* **-a** *techn.* acidometer.

kwasoodporność *f. chem.* acid resistance.

kwasoodporny *a. chem.* acid-proof; (= *odporny na odbarwienie kwasem*) acid-fast.

kwasoryt *mi* etching.

kwasorytnictwo *n. sztuka* etching.

kwasotwórczy *a.* acid-forming.

kwasowość *f. chem.* acidity.

kwasowy *a. chem.* acidic.

kwaszony *a.* pickled, sour; **kwaszone ogórki** pickled cucumbers; **kapusta kwaszona** sauerkraut.

kwaśnieć *ipf.* **1.** (= *kwasić się*) acidify, turn sour. **2.** *przen.* (= *wpadać w zły humor*) become embittered *l.* resentful; sulk.

kwaśność *f.* **1.** (= *kwaskowatość*) sourness, sour taste, acidity. **2.** *chem., med., roln.* (= *kwasowość*) acidity.

kwaśny *a.* **1.** (*o cierpkim smaku*) sour, acid, sourish; **kwaśne mleko** sour milk; **kwaśne winogrona** sour grapes; **amator kwaśnych jabłek** *przen.* odd bird *l.* fish; person marching to the beat of a different drummer; maverick; **kwaśny jak cytryna** *l.* jak ocet (as) sour as a lemon; **sprać kogoś na kwaśne jabłko** give sb a good hiding, beat sb to jelly *l.* to a pulp, beat sb black and blue. **2.** (= *o cechach kwasu*) acidic, acid; **kwaśne deszcze** acid rains; **kwaśna gleba** *roln.* sour soil, acidic soil. **3.** *przen.* (= *ponury, niezadowolony*) sour-tempered, peevish; **kwaśna mina** wry mouth, long face, long nose, vinegar countenance.

kwatera *f.* **1.** (= *lokal*) lodgings, accommodation, quarters; **mieszkać na kwaterze** take up lodgings *l.* quarters, quarter; **wolne kwatery** rooms for rent; **kwatera prywatna** private apartments; **kwatera główna** headquarters; **stać na kwaterze** *wojsk.* be billeted *l.* quartered. **2.** (= *działka, pole*) plot; **kwatera na cmentarzu** cemetery section *l.* plot. **3.** (*w ogrodzie*) garden bed *l.* plot.

kwatermistrz *mp pl.* **-owie** *l.* **-e** *Gen.* **-ów** **1.** (= *zaopatrzeniowiec*) supply manager. **2.** *wojsk.* quartermaster.

kwatermistrzostwo *n. wojsk.* **1.** (*służba*) quartermaster department, commissariat. **2.** (*specjalność*) logistics.

kwatermistrzowski *a. wojsk.* logistic, quartermaster's.

kwaternion *mi mat.* quaternion.

kwaterować *ipf.* **1.** (= *mieszkać na kwaterze*) quarter, dwell. **2.** *wojsk.* be quartered, be billeted. **3.** *przest.* (= *wynajmować lokal*) lodge, rent accommodations.

kwaterunek *mi* **-nk-** housing; *wojsk.* billeting, quartering.

kwaterunkowy *a.* housing; **urząd kwaterunkowy** housing office; **mieszkanie kwaterunkowe** *l.* **lokal kwaterunkowy** public housing; *Br.* council flat.

kwazar *mi astron.* quasar.

kwazarowy *a. astron.* quasar.

kwef *mi* (*zasłona na twarz*) **1.** yshmak, veil. **2.** (*nakrycie głowy*) wimple.

kwerenda *f.* **1.** *lit.* (= *zbieranie informacji*) search query. **2.** *komp.* query.

kwesta *f.* (= *zbiórka*) collection (of money for charity), quest, fundraising; **chodzić po kweście** collect funds *l.* contributions.

kwestarka *f. Gen.pl.* **-ek, kwestarz** *mp* collector of funds.

kwestia *f. Gen.* **-ii 1.** (= *problem*) issue, matter, affair, problem, question. **2. omówić delikatną kwestię** touch upon *l.* discuss a delicate matter, touch a sensitive nerve; **to kwestia gustu** it's a matter of taste; **to tylko kwestia czasu** it's only a matter *l.* a question of time; **nie ulega kwestii, że...** there's no doubt about it that..., there's no question that; **w tej kwestii** in this regard; **otwarta kwestia** open question; **kwestia sporna** bone of contention; **kontrowersyjna kwestia** burning question, controversial question, moot point; **drażliwa kwestia** sensitive question; **kwestia życia i śmierci** a matter of life and death; **poruszyć kwestię** raise *l.* bring up a question. **3.** *teatr, film* line; **powiedzieć swoje kwestie** deliver one's lines.

kwestionariusz *mi Gen.* **-a** (= *ankieta*) questionnaire, questionary.

kwestionować *ipf.* call into question, doubt, challenge.

kwestor *mp* **1.** (= *główny księgowy*) bursar. **2.** *hist.* quaestor, questor.

kwestorski *a.* bursarial; *hist.* quaestorial.

kwestować *ipf.* (= *zbierać datki*) collect funds *l.* money.

kwestura *f.* **1.** (= *dział finansowo-księgowy*) bursar's office, bursarship. **2.** *hist.* quaestorship.

kwękać *ipf. pot.* (= *narzekać*) grumble, be ailing, bellyache, grouch, moan.

kwiaciarka *f. Gen.pl.* **-ek 1.** (= *sprzedawczyni kwiatów*) flower girl, flower vendor. **2.** (*kobieta wyrabiająca sztuczne kwiaty*) artificial flower maker.

kwiaciarnia *f. Gen.pl.* **-i l.** **-ń** florist's.

kwiaciarski *a.* florist's (shop).

kwiaciarstwo *n.* **1.** (*dział ogrodnictwa*) floriculture. **2.** (= *wyrób sztucznych kwiatów*) artificial flower manufacture.

kwiat *mi Loc. i Voc.* **kwiecie 1.** (= *roślina ozdobna*) flower, plant; **kwiaty cięte** cut flowers; **kwiaty doniczkowe** pot flowers; **bukiet kwiatów** bunch of flowers; **sztuczne kwiaty** artificial flowers; **kwiat papuzi** *bot.* parrot flower (*Heliconia psittacorum*); **dzieci-kwiaty** flower people. **2.** (*część rośliny*) flower, blossom; (= *część kwiatu złożonego*) floret; **kwiat złożony** composite flower. **3.** (*motyw*) flower (pattern); **kwiaty (mrozu) na szybach** frostwork. **4.** *przen.* (= *elita, najlepsza część*) the cream *l.* flower *l.* pick of (*sb l. sth*); **kwiat młodzieży** the flower of youth; **w kwiecie wieku** in the prime of life; in the pink of life. **5.** *chem.* flower (of sulphur).

kwiatek *mi* **-tk-** *Gen.* **-a 1.** (= *roślina ozdobna*) flower; **pasować jak kwiatek do kożucha** be out of place *l.* out of keeping; fit like a square pig into a round hole. **2.** *przen.* **ładne kwiatki** *iron.* a fine

thing, indeed!; **wąchać kwiatki od spodu** *pot., żart.* push up the daisies. **3.** *bot.* (= *część kwiatu złożonego*) floret. **4.** (*motyw*) fleuret, fleurette. **5.** *pot.* (= *błąd*) blunder, bloomer, botch, flub; **sadzić kwiatki** make blunders, blunder, slip up.

kwiaton *mi Gen.* **-u l.** **-a** *bud.* fleuron, finial.

kwiatostan *mi bot.* inflorescence.

kwiatostanowy *a. bot.* floral.

kwiatowy *a.* (of a) flower, flowery; (*o organie rozmnażania się roślin, o motywie dekoracyjnym*) floral; **ogród kwiatowy** flower garden; **korona kwiatowa** corolla; **roślina kwiatowa** flowering plant; **woda kwiatowa** flower scent; **motyw kwiatowy** flowery motif, millefleurs.

kwiatuszek *mi* **-szk-** *Gen.* **-a 1.** *emf.* (*roślina*) little flower; *lit.* floweret. **2.** (*o kochanej osobie*) sweetie, honey, sugar.

kwiczeć *ipf.* **-y 1.** (*o zwierzętach*) squeak, squeal. **2.** *pot.* (= *śmiać się*) roar *l.* shriek with laughter; **kwiczeć jak zarzynane prosię** cry blue murder; **leżeć i kwiczeć** *pot.* be in dire straits, be in a fix, be in hot water.

kwiczoł *ma zool.* (*ptak*) fieldfare (*Turdus pilaris*).

kwieciak *ma ent.* **kwieciak jabłkowiec** appleblossom weevil (*Anthonomous pomorum*).

kwiecić *ipf. lit.* adorn with flowers. **~ się** *ipf. lit.* (= *zakwitać*) blossom.

kwiecie *n. lit.* flowers, blossom.

kwiecień *mi* **-tni-** *Gen.* **-a** *Gen.pl.* **-i** (*miesiąc*) April; **kwiecień plecień, bo przeplata trochę zimy, trochę lata** April weather, rain and sunshine both together.

kwiecistość *f. przen.* (= *ozdobność*) floridity, florid style, luxuriance, ornateness.

kwiecisty *a.* **1.** (= *ukwiecony*) flowered. **2.** (*w kwiaty*) flowery, flowered. **3.** *przen.* (= *ozdobny*) colorful, flowery; **kwieciste zwroty** flowers of speech, flowery phrases; **kwiecisty styl/język** flowery style/language.

kwietnik *mi Gen.* **-a 1.** (= *klomb*) flower bed, parterre. **2.** (*półka na doniczki z kwiatami*) flower shelf; flower-pot stand.

kwietnikowy *a. ogr.* bedding; **kwietnikowe rośliny** bedding plants.

kwietniowy *a.* April.

kwietysta *mp*, **kwietystka** *f. Gen.pl.* **-ek** quietist.

kwietystyczny *a.* quietistic.

kwietyzm *mi* **1.** (= *apatia, obojętność*) indifference. **2.** *fil.* quietism.

kwik *mi* squeak, squeal; **wydać (z siebie) kwik** utter *l.* let out a squeal.

kwiknąć *pf. zob.* **kwiczeć.**

kwilić *ipf.* **1.** (= *płakać*) whimper, whine, wail, mewl. **2.** (*o ptakach*) (= *ćwierkać*) twitter, chirp, chirrup, warble.

kwinta *f. muz.* fifth; **kwinta zmniejszona** diminished fifth; **spuścić nos na kwintę** make *l.* pull a long face.

kwintal *mi Gen.* **-a** (*jednostka masy*) (= *100 kg*) quintal, hundredweight.

kwintesencja *f.* (= *sedno sprawy, meritum*) essence, gist, crux, quintessence.

kwintet *mi* **1.** *muz.* (*utwór*) quintet; **kwintet fortepianowy/skrzypcowy** piano/violin quintet. **2.** *muz.* (*zespół*) quintet; **kwintet smyczkowy/wokalny** string/vocal quintet.

kwintylion *mi Gen.* **-a** *l.* **-u** *mat.* nonillion; *Br.* quintillion.

kwit *mi* (= *pokwitowanie*) receipt, voucher, check; (= *paragon*) chit, slip; **kwit bagażowy** baggage check *l.* ticket; **kwit celny** docket, customs receipt; **kwit pocztowy** postal receipt.

kwita *adv.* quits, square, even; **no to jesteśmy kwita** so we're quits; **no i kwita** and that's the end of it; **kwita z nami** we are through; this is where it ends.

kwitariusz *mi Gen.* **-a** receipt book.

kwitek *mi* **-tk-** *Gen.* **-a** (= *dowód, odcinek*) receipt, chit; **odprawić** *l.* **odesłać kogoś z kwitkiem** send sb away empty-handed, rebuff sb; **odejść z kwitkiem** go empty-handed.

kwitnący *a.* (= *zdrowy, urodziwy*) thriving, flourishing, blooming, exuberant.

kwitnąć *ipf.* **-tnął** *l.* **-tł -tła 1.** (*o roślinach*) (= *zakwitać*) blossom, bloom, flourish, be in flower. **2.** (*o ludziach*) (= *pięknieć*) be flourishing *l.* exuberant, thrive. **3.** (= *rozwijać się*) flourish, thrive, prosper; **interes kwitnie** business is flourishing *l.* booming *l.* brisk.

kwitować *ipf.* **1.** (= *poświadczać*) confirm, acknowledge; **kwitować odbiór czegoś** acknowledge receipt of sth. **2.** (*przen.* = *lekceważyć*) **kwitować coś wzruszeniem ramion** shrug sth off; **kwitować coś śmiechem** laugh sth off.

kwiz *mi* (= *konkurs*) quiz.

kwoka *f.* **1.** (= *kokoszka*) clucking hen, mother hen; **kwoka z pisklętami** brood hen, broody hen; **sztuczna kwoka** incubator. **2.** (*z lekceważeniem o kobiecie*) hen, grouser, grumbler.

kworum *n. indecl.* (= *wymagana liczba*) quorum.

kwota *f.* (= *suma pieniędzy*) amount, sum; **łączna kwota** total amount; **należna kwota** amount due; **kwota pieniężna** sum of money.

kwotowy *a.* (= *pieniężny*) money.

kynolog *mp pl.* **-dzy** *l.* **-owie** cynologist.

kynologia *f. Gen.* **-ii** cynology.

kynologiczny *a.* kennel; **związek kynologiczny** kennel club.

kysz *int.* **a kysz!** shoo!, away!, begone!

L

L, l *n. indecl.* (*litera*) L, l; **L jak Leon** L is for Lima; L as in Lima.

l *abbr.* (= *litr*) l, l. (*liter*).

la, LA *abbr.* (= *lekkoatletyka*) track and field.

la *n. indecl.* **1.** *muz.* (= *dźwięk a*) la. **2.** (*zastępuje słowa w piosence*) la; **tra, la, la** tra, la, la.

laba *f. pot.* time off, R and R; (*w szkole*) break; **mieć labę** have some time off; **chodzić na labę** skip school, cut classes.

labarum *n. hist.* labarum.

labializacja *f. jęz.* labialization.

labializować *ipf. jęz.* labialize.

labialny *a. jęz.* labial.

labilność *f.* lability.

labilny *a.* labile.

labiodentalny *a. jęz.* labiodental.

labiowelarny *a. jęz.* labiovelar.

labirynt *mi* **1.** *bud.* labyrinth, maze. **2.** *przen.* (= *plątanina dróg, ulic itp.*) maze. **3.** *przen.* (= *powikłana sytuacja*) morass. **4.** *ogr.* labyrinth, maze. **5.** *anat.* (= *błędnik*) labyrinth.

labiryntowy *a.* labyrinthine, labyrinthian, labyrinthic.

laboga *int. dial.* oh, Jesus; oh, my God.

laborant *mp* **1.** (= *pracownik laboratorium*) lab(oratory) assistant *l.* technician. **2.** *przest.* (= *pomocnik w aptece*) pharmacist's assistant.

laborantka *f. Gen.pl.* **-ek** *zob.* **laborant**.

laboratorium *n. sing. indecl. pl.* **-ria** *Gen.* **-riów** laboratory; *pot.* lab; **laboratorium językowe** language laboratory.

laboratoryjny *a.* lab, laboratory; **szkło laboratoryjne** laboratory glassware.

labrador *mi Gen.* **-u** *Loc.* **-orze** *miner.* labradorite. – *ma Gen.* **-a** *Loc.* **-orze** *kynol.* Labrador, Labrador retriever.

laburzysta *mp Br.* (= *zwolennik Partii Pracy*) Labourite, Labour (Party) supporter; (= *członek Partii Pracy*) Labourite, Labour (Party) member.

laburzystowski *a. Br.* Labour (Party).

Lach *mp pl.* **-owie** *l.* **-y** *arch.* (= *Polak*) Pole; **strachy na Lachy** nothing to be afraid of *l.* get alarmed about, empty threats, just talk.

lacha *f. pot.* **1.** walking stick, walking cane; (*zwł. z giętą rączką*) heavy cane; (*długi*) staff; **kłaść lachę na kogoś/coś** (*rezygnować*) give up on sb/sth, write sb/sth off. **2.** *wulg.* (= *członek męski*) rod, dick. **3.** *pot.* (= *dziewczyna*) chick, babe.

laczki *pl. Gen.* **-ów** *pot.* (*domowe*) slippers; (*plażowe*) thongs, flip-flops.

lać *ipf.* **leję lejesz** **1.** (= *nalewać*) pour; **lać krew** spill blood; **lać łzy** shed tears; **lać wodę** *przen.* (= *pisać l. mówić mało treściwie*) lay it on thick; **lać w siebie alkohol** drink one's fill, get tanked up; **lać w kogoś alkohol** get sb tanked up. **2.** (*dzwony, świece*) cast. **3.** *pot.* (= *bić*) pound, hammer. **4.** (*o deszczu*) pour (down); **leje jak z cebra** it's raining cats and dogs, it's coming down in buckets *l.* sheets, it's *l.* the rain's pouring down. **5.** *wulg.* (= *oddawać mocz*) piss. ~ **się** *ipf.* **1.** (= *spływać*) gush, pour; **żar się leje z nieba** it's sweltering hot. **2.** *pot.* (= *bić się*) hammer each other *l.* one another, pound each other *l.* one another. **3.** be cast.

lada[1] *f.* (= *kontuar*) counter; **lada chłodnicza** refrigerated display case, refrigerated counter; **spod lady** under the counter.

lada[2] *particle* **1.** (= *byle*) any (old), least (little); **nie będzie mnie lada kto obrażał** I'm not going to have some nobody offending me; **lada trudność go zniechęca** he gets discouraged by the least little difficulty. **2.** (*z jednostkami czasu*) any; **lada moment** any moment *l.* second *l.* time; **lada dzień** any day; **nie lada** no small; **nie lada wyczyn** no mean feat; **nie lada okazja** a real opportunity.

ladaco *mp l. n. indecl. żart.* bum, good-for-nothing.

ladacznica *f. przest.* (= *nierządnica*) harlot, strumpet.

lady *f. indecl.* lady.

lafirynda *f. pog.* hussy, floozy.

laga *f. pot.* staff.

lagier *mi* **-gr-** *hist., pot.* Nazi concentration camp.

laguna *f. t. geogr.* lagoon.

laicki *a.* **1.** (= *świecki*) secular, lay. **2.** (= *dyletancki*) layman's.

laickość *f.* secularity, secular nature.

laicyzacja *f.* secularization.

laicyzm *mi* secularity.

laik *mp* layman.

laikat *mi* laity.

lajkonik *ma* hero on a hobbyhorse (*associated with mumming plays held after Corpus Christi in Kraków*).

lak *mi* **1.** (*do pieczętowania listów*) sealing wax. **2.** *bot.* gillyflower, gilliflower (*Cheiranthus*); **lak pospolity** wallflower (*Cheiranthus cheiri*).

laka *f.* **1.** (*żywica*) lacquer. **2.** (*przedmiot*) lacquer, lacquerware.

lakier *mi* varnish, lacquer; (*do samochodu*) paint; **lakier błyszczący/półmatowy** gloss/semi-gloss varnish; **lakier do podłóg** floor varnish; **lakier do paznokci** (finger)nail polish; **lakier do włosów** hair spray; **lakier pustyniowy** *l.* **pustynny** *geol.* desert varnish, desert polish.

lakierki *pl. Gen.* **-ów** patent leather shoes.

lakiernia *f. Gen.pl.* **-i** paint shop.

lakiernictwo *n.* **1.** (= *produkowanie lakierów*) varnish *l.* paint production. **2.** (= *zajęcie lakiernika*) varnishing, painting.

lakierniczy *a.* varnish, paint; (*o lakiernictwie*) varnishing, painting; (*o lakierniku*) varnisher's, painter's.

lakiernik *mp* varnisher, painter.

lakierować *ipf.* **1.** (= *powlekać lakierem*) varnish, lacquer; (*paznokcie, samochód*) paint; (*meble, podłogę*) varnish. **2.** *pot.* (= *przedstawiać w sposób nieprawdziwy*) dress up the truth, varnish the truth; (*zwł. ukrywając prawdę*) whitewash, gloss over.

lakmus *mi zwł. chem.* litmus.

lakmusowy *a.* litmus; **papierek lakmusowy** *chem.* litmus *l.* test paper.

lakoniczność *f.* laconism, laconicism.

lakoniczny *a.* laconic; **lakoniczna odpowiedź** laconic reply.

lakować *ipf.* seal.

lakowy *a.* **1.** (*pieczęć*) sealing wax. **2.** (*stolik*) lacquer, lacquered, lacquerware.

lakrymator *mi wojsk.* tear gas.

laktacja *f. biol.* lactation.

laktaza *f. biol.* lactase.

laktoalbumina *f. biol.* lactalbumin.

laktoza *f. chem.* lactose.

lala *f.* (= *duża lalka*) **1.** doll. **2.** *przen.* (*o kobiecie*) (baby) doll; **stać/siedzieć jak malowana lala** stand/sit there looking pretty; stand/sit like a bump on a log; **jak ta lala** top-notch.

lalczyny *a.* doll's.

laleczka *f. Gen.pl.* **-ek** (= *mała lalka*) dolly; *pot.* (*o dziewczynie*) (baby) doll.

lalka *f. Gen.pl.* **-ek** **1.** (*zabawka*) doll, dolly. **2.** *przen.* (*o kobiecie*) (baby) doll. **3.** (= *kukiełka*) puppet; **teatr lalek** puppet show.

lalkarka *f. Gen.pl.* **-ek** *zob.* **lalkarz.**

lalkarski *a.* **1.** doll-maker's. **2.** puppeteer's.

lalkarstwo *n.* **1.** (= *wyrób lalek*) doll making. **2.** *teatr* puppetry.

lalkarz *mp* **1.** (= *osoba wyrabiająca lalki*) doll maker. **2.** *teatr* puppeteer.

lalkowy *a.* puppet; **teatr lalkowy** puppet show.

lalunia *f.* doll, baby, babe.

lalusiowaty *a.* duded up.

laluś *mp Gen.pl.* **-ów** *iron.* dude.

lama[1] *mp pl.* **-owie** *rel.* lama.

lama[2] *f. pl.* **-y** *zool.* llama (*Lama glama*).

lama[3] *f. tylko sing. tk.* lamé.

lamaistyczny *a. rel.* Lamaistic.

lamaita *mp rel.* Lamaist.

lamaizm *mi rel.* Lamaism.

lamarkizm *mi Gen.* **-u** *biol.* Lamarckism.

lambrekin *mi Gen.* **-u** *l.* **-a** lambrequin.

lament *mi* **1.** (= *zawodzenie*) lament, lamentation; (*głośny*) wail. **2.** *teor.lit.* elegy, lament.

lamentacja *f. muz.* dirge; (*krótka*) elegy.

lamentacyjny *a.* lamentatory, mourning, wailing.

lamentować *ipf.* lament, mourn; (*głośno*) wail (*nad kimś/czymś* sb/sth).

lameta *f.* tinsel garland.

laminaria *f. bot.* laminaria (*Laminaria*).

laminat *mi* **1.** *techn.* (*tworzywo*) laminate, lamination; (*materiał*) Formica. **2.** *tk.* laminate.

laminatowy *a.* **1.** *techn.* (*płyta*) Formica, laminate(d). **2.** *tk.* (*płaszcz*) laminate.

laminować *ipf.* laminate.

laminowany *a.* laminated, plastic-coated.

lamować *ipf.* (= *obszywać brzeg materiału*) border, edge (*with piping l. trim*).

lamówka *f. Gen.pl.* **-ek** trim, piping.

lampa *f.* lamp; *el.* (*w radiu, telewizorze*) tube; **lampa błyskowa** *fot.* flash (lamp); **lampa elektronowa** electron *l.* vacuum tube, valve; **lampa elektronopromieniowa** cathode-ray tube; **lampa kineskopowa** picture tube; **lampa kwarcowa** quartz lamp, sunlamp; **lampa fluorescencyjna** fluorescent lamp *l.* tube; **lampa jarzeniowa** neon lamp; (*w reklamach*) neon light; **lampa łukowa** arc lamp *l.* light; **lampa naftowa** kerosene *l.* oil lamp; **lampa stojąca** floor lamp; **lampa żarowa** incandescent light bulb; **lampa Aladyna** *mit.* Aladdin's lamp; **gadać do lampy** *pot.* waste one's breath, talk to the walls.

lampart *ma zool.* leopard (*Panthera pardus*).

lampas *mi Gen.* **-a** **1.** (*na spodniach*) stripe. **2.** (*na ścianie*) frieze.

lamperia *f. Gen.* **-ii** dado; (*z drewna*) wainscot(ting).

lampiarnia *f. Gen.pl.* **-i** *l.* **-ń** *górn.* lamp room.

lampion *mi* (Chinese) lantern.

lampka *f. Gen.pl.* **-ek** **1.** (= *mała lampa*) lamp, light; **choinka z czerwonymi lampkami** Christmas tree with red lights; **lampka kontrolna** indicator light, pilot light; **lampka nagrobkowa** eternal *l.* memorial lights; **lampka nocna** bedside lamp; **lampka wieczysta** *l.* **wieczna** *rel.* sanctuary lamp, eternal light *l.* flame. **2.** (= *kieliszek*) glass; (*do wina*) wineglass. **3.** (= *zawartość kieliszka*) glassful; **lampka wina** glass of wine.

lampownia *f. Gen.pl.* **-i** *zob.* **lampiarnia.**

lampowy *a.* lamp; (*o lampie elektronowej*) tube; **radio lampowe** tube radio.

lamus *mi Gen.* **-a** *przest.* (= *rupieciarnia*) storeroom; **odłożyć coś do lamusa** junk sth, discard sth; **wyciągać z lamusa** dig sth out (of the attic).

lanca *f.* **1.** (*broń*) lance. **2.** *ogr.* lance.

lancet *mi chir.* lancet.

lancetnik *ma zool.* lancelet, amphioxus (*Amphioxus*).

lancetowaty *a.* lanceolate; **łuk lancetowaty** *bud.* lancet arch.

landara *f. Dat., Loc.* **-arze** **1.** (= *coś dużego i niezgrabnego*) jumbo. **2.** *przest.* carriage.

lando *n.* (*powóz*) landau.

landrynka f. Gen.pl. **-ek** fruit drop.

landrynkowaty a. zob. **landrynkowy**.

landrynkowy a. **1.** (= przypominający landrynkę) fruit flavored. **2.** przen. (= sentymentalny) syrupy, mawkish.

landszaft mi (= bohomaz) tacky l. cheesy landscape.

landtag mi polit. Landtag.

langusta f. zool. spiny lobster, langouste (Palinurus vulgaris).

lanie n. **1.** (= wylewanie) pouring; **lanie wody** przen. laying it on thick. **2.** (= bicie) beating, licking, thrashing; (jako kara dla dziecka) spanking; **dostać lanie** get a spanking; **spuścić komuś lanie** give sb a licking. **3.** (= zwycięstwo) sport beating, pounding; **dostawać lanie** take a pounding; **spuścić komuś lanie** clobber sb.

lanolina f. chem., med. lanolin, lanoline, wool fat.

lanolinowy a. lanolin.

lansada f. (= łukowaty skok konia) gambado, gambade.

lansjer mp pl. **-rzy** hist. (= ułan) lancer, lance. – mi Gen. **-a** pl. **-ry** hist. (taniec) lancers.

lansjerski a. lancer's.

lansować ipf. promote, publicize; (kandydata na stanowisko) back, support.

lantan mi chem. lanthanum.

lantana f. Dat., Loc. **-nie** bot. lantana (Lantana).

lantanowce pl. Gen. **-ów** chem. lanthanides, lanthanide series l. elements.

lanugo n. (= meszek płodowy) lanugo.

lany a. (= półpłynny) cast; (o wyrobach metalowych) molten; **żelazo lane** cast iron; **beton lany** poured concrete; **lane ciasto** batter; **lane kluski** spaetzle(s), batter dumplings; **lany poniedziałek** Easter Monday.

Laos mi geogr. Laos.

laparoskop mi med. laparoscope.

laparoskopia f. Gen. **-ii** med. laparoscopy.

laparotomia f. Gen. **-ii** chir. laparotomy.

lapidarium n. sing. indecl. pl. **-ria** Gen. **-riów** lapidarium, stone collection.

lapidarnie adv. concisely, tersely, curtly, pithily.

lapidarność f. conciseness, terseness, pithiness.

lapidarny a. concise, terse, curt, pithy.

Laponia f. Gen. **-ii** geogr. Lapland.

Laponka f. Gen.pl. **-ek** zob. **Lapończyk**.

Lapończyk mp Laplander, Lapp.

lapoński a. Lapp, Lappish.

lapsus mi lit. slip; **popełnić lapsus** make a slip; **lapsus linguae** slip of the tongue.

laptop mi komp. laptop (computer).

lar mi zool. lar (Hylobates lar).

larum n. indecl. **1.** przest. (= wrzawa) uproar, turmoil; **podnieść larum** create an uproar. **2.** hist. (= sygnał bojowy) alarum, larum, alarm.

larwa f. zool. larva.

larwalny a. zool. larval.

larwicyd mi chem. larvicide.

lary pl. Gen. **-ów** mit. Lares; **lary i penaty** Lares and Penates.

laryngalny a. anat. laryngeal; **spółgłoski laryngalne** jęz. laryngeal l. glottal consonants.

laryngofon mi techn. laryngophone.

laryngolog mp med. laryngologist.

laryngologia f. Gen. **-ii** med. laryngology.

laryngologiczny a. med. laryngological, laryngologic.

laryngoskop mi med. laryngoscope.

laryngoskopia f. Gen. **-ii** med. laryngoscopy.

las mi Loc. **lesie** forest, wood(s); **las iglasty** coniferous forest; **las liściasty** deciduous forest; **las pierwotny** primeval l. virgin forest; **las tropikalny** tropical rainforest; **las rąk/sztandarów** przen. sea of hands/flags; **za górami, za lasami** (w bajkach) in a land far, far away; **nauka nie poszła w las** it was a lesson well learned; **być z czymś w lesie** be a mile behind with sth.

laseczka f. Gen.pl. **-ek** **1.** (= mała laska) walking stick, cane; **laseczka szklana** glass rod. **2.** (= pałeczka czegoś) stick. **3.** biol. bacillus. **4.** pot. (o dziewczynie) chick, babe.

lasek mi **-sk-** grove (of trees).

laser mi techn. laser.

laserować ipf. sztuka (= powlekać obraz) glaze.

laserowy a. laser.

laserunek mi **-nk-** sztuka glaze.

laska f. **1.** (= kij do podpierania) walking stick; (ciężka, spacerowa) cane; (długa) staff; **laska pasterza** shepherd's crook; **laska marszałkowska** parl. speaker's staff; **złożyć projekt do laski marszałkowskiej** parl. present a bill to the speaker; **chodzić o lasce** walk with (the help of) a cane. **2.** (= pałeczka czegoś) stick; **laska dynamitu** stick of dynamite; **laska cynamonu** cinnamon stick. **3.** bud. mullion. **4.** pot. (o dziewczynie) chick, babe. **5.** wulg. (= członek męski) rod, dick; **zrobić komuś laskę** wulg. give sb head l. a blow job, suck sb off.

laskarz mp sport field hockey player.

laskowy a. **1.** (= w postaci pałeczki) stick. **2.** (= leszczynowy) hazel, filbert; **orzech laskowy** hazelnut, filbert.

lasostep mi geogr. wooded steppe.

lasotundra f. geogr. wooded tundra.

lasować ipf. slake. **~ się** ipf. slake.

lasso n. lasso, lariat.

lastrykarski a. terrazzo laying.

lastrykarstwo n. terrazzo laying.

lastrykarz mp terrazzo layer.

lastryko n. indecl. l. Gen. **-a** terrazzo.

lastrykować ipf. lay terrazzo.

lastrykowy a. terrazzo.

laszować ipf. lotn. release.

l.at. abbr. (= liczba atomowa) atomic number.

lata pl. Gen. **lat** **1.** (= liczba mnoga rzeczownika rok) years; **lata dziewięćdziesiąte** the nineties, the 90s; **lata chude** lean years; **lata tłuste** good years; **kopę lat!** long time no see!; **sto lat!** many happy returns!; **od wielu lat** for (many) years; **od niepamiętnych lat** as far back as anyone can remember; **po latach** years later; **z bie-**

giem lat as the years went by, with the passage of time. **2.** (= *czas przeżyty przez kogoś*) years; **lata** *l.* **latka lecą** we're getting older; **ile masz lat?** how old are you?; **mieć** *l.* **liczyć sobie dwadzieścia lat** be twenty years old; **mieć najlepsze lata za sobą** be over the hill; **mieć swoje lata** be long in the tooth; **(nie) wyglądać na swoje lata** (not) look one's age; *zob. t.* **rok.**

latacz *mi Gen.* **-a** *Gen.pl.* **-y** *l.* **-ów** *żegl.* flying jib.

latać *ipf.* **1.** (= *fruwać*) fly. **2.** (= *odbywać podróż statkiem powietrznym*) fly. **3.** (= *trząść się*) shake; (*o rękach*) tremble. **4.** *pot.* (= *udawać się gdzieś pospiesznie*) run; **latać jak kot z pęcherzem** run around like a chicken with its head cut off; **latać za babami** *l.* **spódniczkami** go chasing after women *l.* anything in a skirt.

latający *a.* flying; **latający Holender** Flying Dutchman; **latająca forteca** *lotn.* flying fortress; **latające ryby** *icht.* flying fish; **latający spodek** *l.* **talerz** flying saucer.

latanina *f. pot.* running around; (*kilkakrotnie w to samo miejsce*) running back and forth.

latarka *f. Gen.pl.* **-ek** flashlight; *Br.* torch.

latarnia *f. Gen.pl.* **-i** *l.* **-ń 1.** (*urządzenie świetlne*) lantern, lamp; (*słup*) lamppost; **latarnia uliczna** street lamp; **latarnia morska** lighthouse; **latarnia lotnicza** landing beacon; **latarnia chińska** Chinese lantern. **2.** *bud.* lantern.

latarnik *mp* **1.** (= *pracownik latarni morskiej*) lighthouse keeper. **2.** *przest.* (= *człowiek obsługujący latarnie uliczne*) lamplighter.

latawica *f. pot.* social butterfly, gadabout; bimbo.

latawiec *mi* **-wc-** *Gen.* **-a** *pl.* **-e** (*zabawka*) kite. — *mp* **-wc-** *Voc.* **-cze** *pl.* **-y** *pot.* (= *człowiek lubiący się włóczyć*) social butterfly, gadabout.

lateks *mi chem.* latex.

lateksowy *a. chem.* latex.

lateralny *a. anat.* lateral.

lato *n. Loc.* **lecie** summer; **babie lato** Indian summer; **lato stulecia** summer of the century; **latem** *l.* **w lecie** in the summer; **a ja na to jak na lato** well, I'd love to.

latorośl *f. pl.* **-e 1.** (= *młody pęd*) shoot, sprig. **2.** *żart.* (*o potomku*) scion, offspring.

latryna *f.* latrine.

latyfundium *n. sing. indecl. pl.* **-dia** *Gen.* **-diów** *hist.* latifundium.

latynista *mp szkoln., uniw.* Latinist.

latynizacja *f.* Latinization.

latynizm *mi jęz.* Latinism.

latynizować *ipf.* Latinize.

latynoamerykański *a.* Latin-American.

Latynos *mp* Latino; *US* Hispanic, Hispanic American.

latynoski *a.* Latin-American.

latyński *a.* Latin.

laufer *mi* **-fr-** *Gen.* **-a** *szachy przest.* (= *goniec*) bishop.

laur *mi* **1.** *bot.* laurel, (sweet) bay (*Laurus nobilis*). **2.** (= *liść laurowy*) bay leaf; (= *wieniec laurowy*) laurel; **laur olimpijski** Olympic laurels;

spocząć na laurach rest on one's laurels; **zdobywać laury** win *l.* reap laurels.

laureat *mp* laureate, prizewinner, winner.

laureatka *f. Gen.pl.* **-ek** *zob.* **laureat.**

laurka *f. Gen.pl.* **-ek** (*powinszowanie*) paper with child's hand-decorated name day or birthday greetings, hand-made greetings card; *przen.* (*przesadnie pochlebna opinia*) flattery; **wystawić komuś laurkę** overpraise sb, flatter sb.

laurowy *a.* (*liść*) bay; (*wieniec*) laurel.

lawa *f. geol.* lava.

lawenda *f. bot.* lavender (*Lavandula*).

lawendowy *a.* lavender.

laweta *f.* **1.** (= *podstawa armaty*) (gun) carriage. **2.** (= *platforma do przewożenia samochodów*) car carrier.

lawina *f.* **1.** avalanche; **lawina śnieżna** avalanche; **lawina błotna** mudslide; **lawina skalna** rockslide; **lawina lodowa** ice fall. **2.** *przen.* (= *mnóstwo*) avalanche, cornucopia; **lawina listów** avalanche of letters; **lawina oklasków** storm of applause; **lawina gości** flood of guests; **lawina obelg** shower of abuse.

lawinisko *n. geol.* (deposit of) avalanche *l.* landslide debris.

lawinowy *a.* **1.** (= *dotyczący lawiny*) avalanche; **zagrożenie lawinowe** avalanche threat. **2.** (= *gwałtownie narastający*) snowball, snowballing, avalanche; **efekt lawinowy** snowball effect; **reakcja lawinowa** snowball reaction; **lawinowy wzrost** snowballing increase; **przepływ lawinowy** avalanche flow; **przebicie lawinowe** *el.* avalanche breakdown; **dioda lawinowa** *el.* avalanche diode; **jonizacja lawinowa** *fiz.* cumulative ionization.

lawirant *mp*, **lawirantka** *f. Gen.pl.* **-ek** *pot. uj.* maneuvrer, trimmer, fox.

lawirować *ipf.* **1.** *żegl.* tack (about); **lawirować pod wiatr** tack against the wind. **2.** (= *zręcznie omijać przeszkody*) zigzag, slalom (*między czymś* between sth); *przen.* (= *używać wykrętów, unikać narażania się*) maneuver, tack (about *l.* around), dodge.

lawowy *a. geol.* lava, laval; **pokrywa lawowa** lava crust.

lawsonia *f. Gen.* **-ii** *bot.* henna (*Lawsonia inermis*).

lazaret *mi przest., wojsk.* field hospital, ambulance.

lazł *itd. ipf. zob.* **leźć.**

lazulit *mi min.* lazulite.

lazur *mi* azure; *poet.* (= *firmament, błękitne morze*) the azure, the blue.

lazura *f. szklarstwo* staining.

lazurować *ipf. szklarstwo* stain.

lazurowy *a.* azure; **Lazurowe Wybrzeże** *geogr.* Côte d'Azur.

lazuryt *mi min.* lazurite; (*kamień ozdobny*) lapis lazuli.

ląc się *ipf.* = **lęgnąć się.**

ląd *mi* land; **Czarny Ląd** (= *Afryka*) the Dark Continent; **stały ląd** continent, mainland; **na ląd** ashore, to the shore, onto the shore; **na lądzie**

ashore, on shore; **lądem** by land, overland; **zejść na ląd** disembark, get ashore, land.

lądolód *mi* -lod- *geol.* continental ice sheet, continental glacier.

lądotwórczość *f. geol.* epeirogeny, epeirogenesis.

lądotwórczy *a. geol.* epeirogenic.

lądować *ipf.* **1.** land; *lotn. t.* touch down; *żegl. t.* take land. **2.** *przen. pot.* (= *wydobywać się z trudnej sytuacji*) fall *l.* land on one's feet; **on miewa kłopoty, ale zawsze jakoś ląduje** he sometimes gets into trouble but always manages to land on his feet; **jak lądujesz finansowo?** how are you doing financially? **3.** *pot.* (= *dostawać się gdzieś*) land, end up; **lądować w areszcie** end up in detention.

lądowanie *n.* landing; *lotn. t.* touchdown; **lądowanie awaryjne** *l.* przymusowe emergency landing; crash landing; **miękkie lądowanie** soft landing; **podchodzenie do lądowania** *lotn.* landing approach; **przelot bez lądowania** no-landing flight.

lądowisko *n.* landing strip, landing field; (*dla helikoptera*) landing pad.

lądownik *mi Gen.* -a (*astronautyka*) lander, landing module.

lądowy *a.* land, ground; *biol.* (= *żyjący na lądzie*) land, terrestrial; **droga lądowa** land route; **przewozić coś drogą lądową** transport sth by land; **atak lądowy** *wojsk.* ground attack; **siły lądowe** *wojsk.* ground forces, land forces; **ssak lądowy** *zool.* land mammal, terrestrial mammal; **inżynieria lądowa** *techn.* civil engineering; **szczur lądowy** *żegl., żart.* landlubber; **pomost lądowy** *geogr.* landbridge.

ląg *mi* -ę- **1.** (= *wykluwanie się*) hatching; **pora lęgu** *orn.* hatching time. **2.** *orn.* (= *jaja wysiadywane jednocześnie*) brood.

lągł *itd. ipf. zob.* **lęgnąć się.**

leader *mp* = **lider.**

leasing *mi* leasing; **wziąć coś w leasing** lease sth (*od kogoś* from sb).

leasingowy *a.* leasing.

lebiega *f. l. mp decl. like f. Gen.pl.* -g *l.* -ów *pot. pog.* sluggard.

lebioda *f. bot.* (= *komosa biała*) lamb's-quarters, pigweed, goosefoot (*Chenopodium album*).

lebiodka *f. Gen.pl.* -ek *bot.* oregano, wild marjoram (*Origanum vulgare*).

lec *pf.* **legnę** -niesz, -nij, **legł** *lit.* **1.** (= *położyć się*) lie down; **lec w grobie** lie down in one's grave. **2.** (= *paść*) **lec u czyichś stóp** fall at sb's feet; **lec w gruzach** lie *l.* fall in ruins. **3.** (= *zginąć*) fall, perish, die; **lec w boju** *l.* **walce** fall in battle; **lec w obronie ojczyzny** lay down one's life in defense of one's country.

lechicki *a. jęz.* Lekhitic.

lecie *n. zob.* **lato.**

lecieć *ipf.* -cę -cisz **1.** (= *przemieszczać się w przestrzeni*) fly (along); (*na skrzydłach*) wing one's way; (*o dźwięku itp.*) travel; **iskry lecą** sparks are flying. **2.** (= *podróżować samolotem*) fly. **3.** (= *wznosić się; przen.* = *rosnąć*) rise, soar;

ceny lecą w górę prices are soaring. **4.** (= *poruszać się szybko, pędzić*) run, go, speed (on *l.* along); **lecę po niego** I'll fetch him; **leć, bo się spóźnisz na autobus** get a move on or you'll miss your bus; **lecieć na kogoś/coś** *pot.* go chasing after sb/sth. **5.** (= *płynąć, spływać*) run, flow; **leci mu krew z nosa** his nose is bleeding; **woda leci z kranu** water is running from the faucet; **łzy leciały mi z oczu** tears ran from my eyes. **6.** (= *upływać*) fly by, fly past; **lata lecą** years fly by. **7.** (= *powodzić się*) **jak (ci) leci?** how's it going?, how are things? **8.** *pot.* **(wszystko) jak leci** the whole lot *l.* caboodle; **bierz jak leci** take all the lot. **9.** (= *spadać, upadać*) fall, drop; **wszystko leci mi z rąk** I'm dropping things; **lecieć komuś przez ręce** collapse in sb's arms; **lecieć z nóg** collapse, sink to the ground; *pot.* (= *padać ze zmęczenia*) feel ready to drop; **lecieć z konia/z siodła** fall from the horse/from one's saddle. **10.** *przen.* (= *tracić wartość*) fall, drop; **lecą ceny akcji** share prices are falling. **11.** (*o filmie, programie itp.*) be on; **co leci w kinie dziś wieczorem?** what's on at the movies tonight?; **leci moja ulubiona piosenka** they're playing my favorite song.

leciutki *a. emf. zob.* **lekki.**

leciutko *adv. emf. zob.* **lekko.**

leciwy *a. przest. l. żart.* aged, elderly.

lecytyna *f. biochem.* lecithin.

lecytynaza *f. biochem.* lecithinase.

lecz *conj. form.* but.

leczenie *n. med.* treatment (*kogoś* of sb, *czegoś* for sth); therapy, care; **leczenie chirurgiczne/farmakologiczne** surgical/drug treatment; **leczenie objawowe/zachowawcze** symptomatic/conservative treatment; **leczenie długotrwałe** long-term care *l.* treatment; **leczenie pooperacyjne** aftercare; **leczenie snem** hypnotherapy; **wydatki na leczenie** medical expenses.

lecznica *f.* infirmary, hospital; (= *klinika*) clinic; **lecznica dla zwierząt** veterinary clinic, animal hospital *l.* clinic, pet clinic.

lecznictwo *n. med.* medical care; (= *medycyna*) medicine; **lecznictwo otwarte/zamknięte** outpatient/inpatient care.

leczniczy *a.* medicinal; therapeutic, curative, medical; (*o kosmetykach*) medicated; **zabieg leczniczy** medical *l.* curative treatment; **roślina lecznicza** medicinal plant; **właściwości lecznicze** medicinal properties; **w celach leczniczych** for medicinal purposes.

leczo *n. indecl. kulin.* lecso (*Hungarian spicy stew*).

leczyć *ipf.* (*pacjenta l. chorobę*) **1.** treat; (= *uzdrawiać, t. przen.* = *naprawiać*) cure, heal; **leczyć kogoś na zapalenie płuc** *l.* **z zapalenia płuc** treat sb for pneumonia; **hipnoza nie leczy raka** hypnosis doesn't cure cancer; **leczyć złamane serca** *przen.* heal broken hearts. **2.** *przen.* (= *odzwyczajać*) cure (sb) (*z czegoś* of sth). **3.** (*o lekarzu*) (= *uprawiać medycynę*) practice. **~ się** *ipf.* **1.** (= *poddawać się kuracji*) be treated, undergo treatment (*na coś l. z czegoś* for sth); **leczyć się na serce** undergo treatment for a heart condition; **leczyć się u kogoś** be sb's patient. **2.** (=

wracać do sił l. zdrowia) recover, convalesce; **le-
czę się z ran** I'm recovering from wounds. **3.** (=
leczyć samego siebie, t. z nawyków, wad itp.)
cure oneself (*z czegoś* of sth).

ledwie, ledwo *conj.* as soon as, the moment
(that), the minute (that); **ledwie przyłożył głowę
do poduszki, już spał** he fell asleep as soon as his
head touched the pillow; **uciekł, ledwieśmy go
zobaczyli** he ran away the moment we saw him;
**ledwo odłożyłem słuchawkę, telefon znów za-
dzwonił** no sooner had I hung up than the phone
rang again; I had no sooner hung up than the
phone rang again. – *adv.* (= *zaledwie, prawie
nie*) barely, scarcely, (only) just; **ledwo, ledwo**
just barely; **ledwie żywy** barely alive; **dom jest
ledwie widoczny** the house is barely visible; **ledwo zdążył na pociąg** he nearly missed his train.

legalista *mp*, **legalistka** *f. Gen.pl.* **-ek** legalist.

legalistyczny *a.* legalistic.

legalizacja *f. prawn.* legalization.

legalizacyjny *a.* (of) legalization; **dokument
legalizacyjny** certificate of legalization.

legalizm *mi* legalism.

legalizować *ipf.* legalize.

legalnie *adv.* legally; lawfully; **legalnie wybra-
ni reprezentanci** legally elected representatives;
na pół legalnie half-legally.

legalność *f.* legality, lawfulness.

legalny *a.* legal; (= *prawnie dopuszczalny*)
lawful, licit; (= *prawnie uznany*) rightful; **legal-
na władza** legal authority; **legalne przedsięwzięcie** lawful enterprise; **legalny właściciel** rightful
owner.

legar *mi bud.* joist; groundbeam, sleeper; **legar podłogowy** floor joist.

legat *mp hist., polit.* (= *poseł*) legate, envoy,
ambassador; **legat papieski** *rz.-kat.* papal legate.
– *mi prawn.* (= *zapis w testamencie*) bequest,
legacy.

legato *adv. i n. indecl. muz.* legato.

legator *mi pl.* **-rzy** *l.* **-owie**, **legatorka** *f. Gen.pl.*
-ek *prawn.* legator.

legawiec *ma* **-wc-** *myśl.* pointer.

legenda *f.* **1.** (= *opowieść fantastyczna; przen.*
= *fama, pogłoska*) legend (*o kimś/czymś* of sb/
sth); **według legendy...** legend has it that...; **krą-
żą o nim legendy** stories are going around about
him; **rozprawić się z legendą** debunk a legend. **2.**
pot. (= *osoba sławna*) legend (*czegoś* of sth); **żywa legenda** living legend. **3.** (= *objaśnienie
oznaczeń na mapie, wykresie itp.*) legend, key; (=
objaśnienie rysunku) caption; (= *napis na monecie*) legend.

legendarny *a. t. pot.* (= *słynny*) legendary.

legginsy *pl. Gen.* **-ów** *strój* leggings.

leghorn *ma hodowla* Leghorn.

legia *f. Gen.* **-ii** legion; **Legia Cudzoziemska** the
(French) Foreign Legion; **Legia Honorowa** the
Legion of Honor.

legion *mi wojsk. zwł. hist.* **1.** legion. **2.** *przen.*
(= *rzesza*) legions, host; **legion zwolenników/wiel-
bicieli** legions of supporters/admirers.

legionista *mp* legionary.

legionowy *a.* legionary.

legislacja *f. prawn.* legislation.

legislacyjny *a. prawn.* legislative.

legislatura, legislatywa *f. polit.* (= *władza ustawodawcza*) legislature; **legislatura stanowa**
state legislature.

legitymacja *f.* **1.** (*organizacji, klubu*) membership card; (= *dowód tożsamości*) identification,
ID, identity card. **2.** (= *uprawnienie*) authorization, legitimation (*do czegoś* for sth, *do robienia
czegoś* to do sth); **legitymacja społeczna** social legitimation *l.* legitimatization *l.* legitimization.

legitymacyjny *a.* **zdjęcie legitymacyjne** ID photograph.

legitymista *mp*, **legitymistka** *f. Gen.pl.* **-ek** legitimist.

legitymistyczny *a.* legitimist.

legitymizm *mi* legitimism.

legitymować *ipf.* **1.** (= *sprawdzać dokumenty*)
check sb's documents *l.* identification *l.* papers.
2. (= *uprawniać*) legitimate, legitimatize, legit-
imize; authorize (*sb*) (*do czegoś* for sth, *do robienia czegoś* to do sth). **3.** (= *motywować, uzasadniać*) justify. **~ się** *ipf.* **1.** (= *okazywać dokumenty*) show one's documents *l.* identification; prove
one's identity. **2.** + *Ins. form.* (= *posiadać*) hold;
legitymować się paszportem niemieckim hold a
German passport; **rząd legitymuje się poparciem
społecznym** the government enjoys popular
support.

legnąć *pf.* **-ij**, **legł** = **lec**.

lego *n. indecl.* Lego; **klocki lego** Lego bricks.

legowisko *n.* sleeping-place, (makeshift) bed,
pallet; **legowisko z liści** bed of leaves; (= *miejsce
snu zwierząt, barłóg*) den, lair.

legumina *f. przest.* dessert.

legwan *ma zool.* iguana (*Iguana*).

leiszmania *f. Gen.* **-ii** *biol.* leishmania (*Leishmania*).

leiszmanioza *f. pat.* leishmaniasis.

leizna *f. techn.* **leizna kamienna** *l.* **skalna** cast
rock.

lej[1] *mi Gen.* **-a** *Gen.pl.* **-ów** **1.** *techn.* funnel;
(*załadowczy, dozujący*) hopper. **2.** (= *zagłębie-
nie*) crater; **lej po pocisku** shell crater, shell hole.

lej[2] *mi Gen.* **-a** *Gen.pl.* **lei** (= *rumuńska
jednostka monetarna*) leu.

lejce *pl. Gen.* **-ów** reins.

lejdejski *a. fiz.* **butelka lejdejska** Leyden jar.

lejek *mi* **-jk-** *Gen.* **-a** funnel.

leję *itd. ipf. zob.* **lać**.

lejkowaty *a.* funnel-shaped; (= *klinowaty*)
wedge-shaped, V-shaped; *anat.* infundibular;
bot. infundibuliform; **lejkowate ujście rzeki** *hydrol.* coastal-plain estuary.

lejtmotyw *mi* leitmotif, leitmotiv.

lejtnant *mp wojsk., przest.* (= *porucznik*) lieutenant.

lek[1] *mi med.* (= *lekarstwo*) medicine, medication, drug (*na coś l. przeciwko czemuś* against
sth); *t. przen.* remedy (*na coś* for sth); **podawać
leki** administer drugs *l.* medicines; **lek przeciwko
zapaleniu płuc** drug against pneumonia, pneumonia drug; **leki ziołowe** herbal remedies; **lek
uspokajający** tranquilizer; **lek przeciwbólowy**

pain-killing drug; *form.* analgesic; **oporność na leki** drug resistance.

lek² *mi Gen.* **-a** (= *albańska jednostka monetarna*) lek.

lek. *abbr.* (= *lekarz*) **lek. med.** (= *lekarz medycyny*) M.D. (= *medicinae doctor*); **lek. wet.** (= *lekarz weterynarii*) M.V.D. (= *medicinae veterinariae doctor*).

lekarka *f. Gen.pl.* **-ek** *zob.* **lekarz.**

lekarski *a.* doctor's; medical; **gabinet lekarski** doctor's office; *Br.* (doctor's) surgery; **badanie lekarskie** medical check *l.* examination; **zalecenia lekarskie** doctor's orders; **zaświadczenie lekarskie** medical certificate.

lekarstwo *n.* **1.** drug, medicine, medication; **lekarstwo od kaszlu** *l.* **na kaszel** cough medicine; **lekarstwo na serce** heart medication. **2.** *przen.* cure, remedy (*na coś* for sth); **lekarstwo na samotność** cure for loneliness. **3.** *pot.* **ani na lekarstwo** not a trace; **jak na lekarstwo** a tiny bit, (just) a tad; **w tym roku śniegu ani na lekarstwo** there's not a trace of snow this year.

lekarz *mp* physician; doctor; *pot.* medic; (*w marynarce wojennej*) surgeon; **lekarz ogólny** general practitioner, G.P.; **lekarz rodzinny** family doctor; **lekarz weterynarii** veterinarian; *pot.* vet; *Br.* veterinary surgeon; **lekarz okrętowy** ship's surgeon *l.* doctor; **iść do lekarza** go to a doctor, visit a doctor; **wzywać lekarza** call *l.* summon a doctor.

lekce *adv. przest.* lightly, lightheartedly; **ważyć coś sobie lekce** make light of sth.

lekceważący *a.* disrespectful, dismissive, disparaging, scornful, flippant; **lekceważąca uwaga** scornful *l.* disparaging remark; **lekceważący ton głosu** dismissive tone of voice; **lekceważący stosunek do czegoś** flippant attitude toward sth.

lekceważenie *n.* disrespect, disparagement, disregard.

lekceważyć *ipf.* scorn, disparage, ignore, disregard; pay no attention to, take no notice of (*sb l. sth*); **lekceważyć swoje obowiązki** neglect one's duties; **lekceważyć prawo** flout the law; **lekceważyć niebezpieczeństwo** ignore danger; **lekceważyć czyjeś uczucia** ignore *l.* disregard sb's feelings.

lekcja *f.* **1.** lesson; *szkoln.* (*z grupą uczniów*) class; **lekcja angielskiego/matematyki** English/math class; **dawać lekcje gry na fortepianie** give piano lessons; **udzielać komuś lekcji** tutor sb. **2.** *przen.* (= *nauczka*) **niech to będzie dla ciebie lekcją** let this be a lesson to you; **zapamiętać sobie lekcję** learn one's lesson; **lekcja pokory** lesson in humility. **3.** *pl.* (= *praca domowa*) homework; **odrabiać lekcje** do one's homework. **4.** *rel.* (= *czytanie*) lesson, lection. **5.** *teor.lit.* (= *odczytanie tekstu*) lection (*reading*).

lekcyjny *a. szkoln.* class, teaching; **sala lekcyjna** classroom; **godzina lekcyjna** teaching period.

lekki *a.* **lżejszy 1.** (= *niecięźki, niegruby*) light; **lekki jak piórko** (as) light as a feather; **lekki jak puch** *l.* **powietrze** (as) light as air; **lekki ubiór** light clothes; **podróżować z lekkim bagażem** travel light; **z lekkim sercem** *przen.* with a light heart; **waga lekka** *sport* lightweight; **przemysł lekki** light industry; **broń lekka** *wojsk.* small arms; **lekka kawaleria** *wojsk.* light cavalry. **2.** (= *nieduży*) light; **lekki posiłek** light meal. **3.** (= *nieociężały, zwinny*) light, nimble; **lekkie kroki** light footfalls. **4.** (= *delikatny*) light, slight, slender, frail, fine; **lekkie rusztowanie** light *l.* slight scaffolding; **lekki jak pajęczyna** (as) fine as cobweb. **5.** (= *nieznaczny, nienasilony*) faint, light, slight; **lekki uśmiech** faint smile; **lekki zapach** faint smell; **lekki sen** light sleep; **lekki ból głowy** slight headache; **lekki wietrzyk** gentle *l.* light breeze; **lekkie zdziwienie** slight surprise. **6.** (= *łatwy, znośny*) easy, light; **lekka praca** easy work; **lekka kara** light punishment; **lekkie ćwiczenia fizyczne** light physical exercise; **lekki kawałek chleba** *przen.* easy money; **lekka śmierć** easy death. **7.** (= *niezbyt mocny*) light; **lekkie wino** light wine. **8.** (= *niepoważny, niefrasobliwy, frywolny*) light, lighthearted; (*o obyczajach*) (= *rozwiązły*) loose; **lekka komedia** light comedy; **rozdawać coś lekką ręką** be liberal with sth; **lekkie prowadzenie się** loose conduct.

lekko *adv.* **lżej 1.** (= *nieciężko, niegrubo*) lightly, light; **lekko mu na duszy** he's in high spirits; **ubierać się lekko** dress lightly. **2.** (= *zwinnie, nieociężale*) lightly, nimbly. **3.** (= *delikatnie, nieznacznie, trochę*) lightly, slightly, gently; **lekko ranny/uszkodzony** slightly injured/damaged; **lekko pukać do drzwi** knock (at the door) gently; **lekko licząc** at the very least; **z lekka** slightly. **4.** (= *łatwo*) easily; **lekko poszło** *pot.* it was an easy job. **5.** (= *niepoważnie, lekkomyślnie*) lightly, flippantly, lightheartedly; **lekko coś traktować** treat sth with levity. **6.** (= *niemoralnie*) loosely; **prowadzić się lekko** conduct o.s. loosely.

lekkoatleta *mp*, **lekkoatletka** *f. Gen.pl.* **-ek** (track and field) athlete.

lekkoatletyczny *a.* athletic.

lekkoatletyka *f.* track and field (sports), athletics.

lekkoduch *mp pl.* **-y** playboy; *przest.* rake.

lekkomyślnie *adv.* (= *beztrosko*) lightheartedly, frivolously; (= *pochopnie*) rashly, recklessly.

lekkomyślność *f.* (= *beztroska*) lightheartedness, frivolity; (= *pochopność*) rashness, recklessness.

lekkomyślny *a.* (= *beztroski, niepoważny*) **1.** lighthearted, frivolous, carefree. **2.** (= *działający pochopnie*) rash, reckless; (= *czyniony pochopnie*) rash, reckless, precipitous, hasty.

lekkopółśredni *a. sport* welterweight.

lekkostrawny *a.* light, easy to digest.

lekkość *f.* **1.** (= *mały ciężar*) lightness. **2.** (= *delikatność, subtelność, zręczność*) lightness, nimbleness. **3.** (= *łatwość*) ease. **4.** (= *brak powagi l. rozsądku*) levity, frivolity, flippancy.

lekkośredni *a. sport* light middleweight.

lekkozbrojny *a. hist., wojsk.* lightly armed.

lekoman *mp* drug addict.

lekomania *f. Gen.* **-ii** drug dependency *l.* addiction.

lekomanka *f. Gen.pl.* **-ek** *zob.* **lekoman.**

lekospis *mi* pharmacopeia.

leksem *mi jęz.* lexeme.
leksyka *f. jęz.* lexicon.
leksykalizacja *f. jęz.* lexicalization.
leksykalizować się *ipf. jęz.* become lexicalized, undergo lexicalization.
leksykalny *a. jęz.* lexical.
leksykograf *mp pl.* **-owie** lexicographer.
leksykografia *f. Gen.* **-ii** lexicography.
leksykograficzny *a.* lexicographic.
leksykolog *mp pl.* **-dzy** *l.* **-owie** lexicologist.
leksykologia *f. Gen.* **-ii** *jęz.* lexicology.
leksykologiczny *a.* lexicological.
leksykon *mi* dictionary, lexicon.
lektor *mp* **1.** (= *prelegent*) lecturer. **2.** *film* voice-over. **3.** *uniw.* instructor, teacher; **lektor języka obcego** foreign language instructor. **4.** *rel.* lector.
lektorat *mi* **1.** *uniw.* (= *kurs języka obcego*) foreign language course. **2.** *rel.* lectorship.
lektorka *f. Gen.pl.* **-ek** *zob.* **lektor** 1, 2, 3.
lektura *f.* **1.** (= *czytanie, coś do czytania*) reading; **nie mogę oderwać się od lektury** I can't put this book down. **2.** *szkoln.* (book for) required reading; **ta książka to lektura obowiązkowa** this book is required reading; **lista lektur** reading list.
lektyka *f.* sedan (chair), litter; (*typu orientalnego*) palanquin.
lelek *ma* **-lk-** *orn.* (= *ptak z rodziny Caprimulgidae*) goatsucker, nightjar; **lelek kozodój** (European) nightjar (*Caprimulgus europaeus*); **lelek krzykliwy** whippoorwill (*Caprimulgus vociferus*); **lelek karoliński** chuck-will's-widow (*Caprimulgus carolinensis*).
lemat *mi mat.* lemma.
lemiesz *mi Gen.* **-a** **1.** *roln.* plowshare, *Br.* ploughshare; *techn.* share. **2.** *anat.* vomer.
lemieszowy *a. anat.* vomerine.
leming *ma zool.* lemming (*Lemmus*).
lemoniada *f.* lemonade.
lemur *ma zool.* (*małpiatka, zwł. z rodziny Lemuridae*) lemur.
len *mi* **ln-** **1.** *bot.* (*t. włókno*) flax (*Linum usitatissimum*). **2.** (= *płótno lniane*) linen.
lenicja *f. jęz.* lenition.
lenić się[1] *ipf.* shirk.
lenić się[2] *ipf.* = **lenieć**.
leniec *mi* **-ńc-** *Gen.* **-a** *bot.* bastard-toadflax (*Thesium*).
lenieć *ipf.* molt.
leninizm *mi polit., hist.* Leninism.
leninowiec *mp* **-wc-** *pl.* **-y** *polit., hist.* Leninist.
leninowski *a. polit., hist.* Lenin's; (= *dotyczący leninizmu*) Leninist.
leninówka *f. Gen.pl.* **-ek** (*czapka*) Lenin cap.
lenistwo *n.* (*cecha charakteru*) laziness, indolence; *form.* sloth; (= *próżnowanie, bezczynność*) idleness; **słodkie lenistwo** sweet idleness; **oddawać się lenistwu** laze around, laze one's time away.
leniuch *mp pl.* **-y** *pot.* lazybones, sluggard.
leniuchować *ipf.* laze (about *l.* around), loaf (around).
leniuszek *mp* **-szk-** *emf. zob.* **leniuch**.

leniwie *adv.* lazily, idly; (= *powoli*) unhurriedly, slowly.
leniwiec *mp* **-wc-** *Voc.* **-cu** *l.* **-cze** *pl.* **-y** *l.* **-e** *pot.* = **leniuch**. – *ma* **-wc-** *pl.* **-e** *zool.* (*szczerbak*) sloth; **leniwiec olbrzymi** *paleont.* giant ground sloth.
leniwieć *ipf.* grow lazy.
leniwy *a.* **1.** (= *gnuśny*) lazy, indolent; *form.* slothful; (*atmosfera, nastrój*) idle, relaxed. **2.** (= *powolny*) slow, sluggish, unhurried. **3. leniwe pierogi** *kulin.* cottage-cheese dumplings (*a Polish dish*).
lennictwo *n. hist.* vassalage.
lenniczka *f. Gen.pl.* **-ek** *hist.* = **lennik**.
lenniczy *a. hist.* vassal, feudatory.
lennik *mp hist.* vassal, liege, feudatory.
lenno *n. hist.* fee, fief.
lenny *a. hist.* feudal; **hołd lenny** homage liege *l.* feudal.
leń *mp Gen.pl.* **-ni** *l.* **-niów** idler, sluggard, lazybones.
lep *mi* (*na muchy*) flypaper; (*na ptaki*) birdlime; *przen.* (= *przynęta*) bait; (*chwytać coś na lep*) lime sth; **brać l. chwytać kogoś na lep** (*czegoś*) lure sb (with sth); **iść l. łapać się na lep** rise to the bait.
lepianka *f. Gen.pl.* **-ek** mud hut.
lepić *ipf.* **1.** (= *łączyć klejem*) glue, paste (up); (*o kleju*) (= *trzymać*) stick. **2.** (= *formować*) make, form, shape; **lepić bałwana** make a snowman; **lepić kulki z plasteliny** shape plasticine into balls. **~ się** *ipf.* **1.** (= *być lepkim*) be sticky (*od czegoś* with sth). **2.** (= *sklejać się*) bind (up *l.* together). **3.** (= *przyklejać się*) stick, adhere (*do czegoś* to sth); *pot.* (= *lgnąć, przywierać*) cling (*do kogoś / czegoś* to sb/sth); **wszystko lepi się mu do rąk** *przen.* he has sticky fingers; **lepić się do kogoś** cling *l.* stick to sb (like a leach).
lepidolit *mi min.* lepidolite.
lepidozaury *pl. Gen.* **-ów** *zool.* (*nadrząd gadów*) lepidosaurs (*Lepidosauria*).
lepiej *adv.* **1.** better; **coraz lepiej** better and better; **jeszcze lepiej** even better; better still; **tym lepiej, że on mnie nie zna** it's just as well that he doesn't know me; **im prędzej, tym lepiej** the sooner the better; **lepiej późno niż wcale** better late than never; **tak (już) lepiej** (*pochwała*) that's better; *por.* **dobrze. 2.** (*wyraża radę l. postanowienie podyktowane rozsądkiem*) had better; **lepiej nic nie ruszaj** you'd better not touch anything; **lepiej sobie pójdę** I'd better go.
lepiężnik *mi Gen.* **-a** *bot.* butterbur (*Petasites*).
lepik *mi bud.* adhesive, cement; **lepik dachowy** (coal-tar) roofing pitch.
lepiszcze *n. Gen.* **-y** *techn.* binder, binding agent.
lepki *a.* **1.** sticky, tacky, gummy; **lepkie ręce** *przen.* (= *skłonność do kradzieży*) sticky fingers. **2.** *fiz.* viscous.
lepkość *f.* **1.** stickiness, tackiness. **2.** *fiz.* viscosity.
lepnica *f. bot.* catchfly (*Silene*).
lepra *f. pat.* (= *trąd*) leprosy.
leprozorium *n. sing. indecl. pl.* **-ia** *med.* leprosarium; *hist.* leper-house, lazar-house.

lepsze *n. decl. like a.* the better; **na lepsze** *l.* **ku lepszemu** for the better; **zmiana na lepsze** change for the better; **iść z kimś o lepsze** compete with sb.

lepszość *f.* superiority.

lepszy *a.* better, superior; preferable; **o niebo lepszy** *pot.* miles better; **kto pierwszy, ten lepszy** first come, first served; *por.* **dobry.**

lesbijka *f. Gen.pl.* **-ek** lesbian.

lesbijski *a.* lesbian.

leser *mp sl.* slacker, shirker, gold brick.

leserować *ipf. pot.* goof off, shirk.

lesie *mi zob.* **las.**

lesistość *f.* woodiness.

lesisty *a.* woody, forested.

less *mi geol.* loess.

lessowy *a. geol.* loess.

leszcz *ma Gen.pl.* **-y** *l.* **-ów** *icht.* bream (*Abramis brama*).

leszczyna *f.* 1. *bot.* hazel (*Corylus*); **leszczyna południowa** *l.* **lambertowska** filbert (*C. maxima*); **krzak leszczyny** hazelbush. 2. (= *gaik leszczynowy*) hazelwood, hazel copse.

leszczynowy *a.* hazel.

leśnictwo *n.* 1. (*gałąź gospodarki, nauka*) forestry. 2. (*obszar leśny*) forest district.

leśniczówka *f. Gen.pl.* **-ek** ranger's station, forester's lodge.

leśniczy *mp* forest ranger, forester.

leśnik *mp* 1. forest officer. 2. *pot.* = **leśniczy.**

leśny *a.* forest, woodland; (= *mieszkający w lesie*) forest-dwelling; *form.* sylvan; **ścieżka leśna** forest path; **robotnik leśny** forest worker; **sceneria leśna** woodland scenery.

letarg *mi pat.* lethargy; *przen.* apathy, listlessness, torpor, stupor; **otrząsać się z letargu** shake off (one's) lethargy; **wyrywać kogoś z letargu** rouse sb from lethargy; **zapadać w letarg** fall into a lethargy.

letargiczny *a.* lethargic; (= *bezwolny, apatyczny*) apathetic, listless, torpid.

letejski *a.* **woda letejska** *mit.* the water of Lethe.

letni *a.* 1. (właściwy latu) summer; **czas letni** daylight savings time, daylight saving time, daylight time; **przesilenie letnie** the summer solstice, Midsummer Day. 2. (= *ciepławy*) lukewarm, tepid. 3. *przen.* (= *słabo zaangażowany*) half-hearted.

letniczka *f. Gen.pl.* **-ek** *zob.* **letnik.**

letniak *mi Gen.* **-a** *pot.* (= *domek letni*) summer house.

letnik *mp* vacationer.

letnio *adv.* 1. tepidly, lukewarmly. 2. (*bez zaangażowania*) half-heartedly.

letnisko *n.* summer resort.

letniskowy *a.* summer-resort.

leukemia *f. Gen.* **-ii** *pat.* leukemia.

leukocyt *mi biol.* leucocyte.

leukocytoza *f. fizj.* leucocytosis.

leukoplast *mi bot.* leucoplast.

lew¹ *ma* **lw-** *Dat.* **lwu** *zool.* 1. lion (*Panthera leo*). 2. *przen.* **lew salonowy** ladies' man; **dzielny jak lew** (as) brave as a lion; **włazić lwu w paszczę**

put one's head into the lion's mouth; **jaskinia lwa** (= *niebezpieczne miejsce*) lion's den. 3. *zool.* **lew morski** (*nazwa niektórych uchatek*) sea lion. 4. **Lew** *astron., astrol.* Leo.

lew² *mi Gen.* **-a** (*jednostka monetarna Bułgarii*) lev.

lewa¹ *f. Gen.* **-y** *karty* trick; **brać lewy** take a trick, win a trick.

lewa² *f. Gen.* **-ej** 1. (= *lewa strona*) left side, left-hand side; **z lewej** from the left. 2. *wojsk.* (*w komendzie marszowej - lewa noga*) left; **lewą naprzód marsz!** left march!

lewacki *a. polit., uj.* extreme leftist.

lewactwo *n. polit., uj.* extreme leftist attitude.

lewak *mp polit., uj.* extreme leftist.

lewar *mi Gen.* **-a** 1. (*podnośnik*) jack. 2. (*rurka do przelewania cieczy*) syphon.

lewarek *mi* **-rk-** *Gen.* **-a** 1. (= *mały podnośnik*) jack; **lewarek samochodowy** car jack; **podnieść coś lewarkiem** jack sth up. 2. (*rurka do przelewania cieczy*) syphon. 3. *dent.* pelican.

lewatywa *f. med.* enema; **zrobić lewatywę** give an enema.

lewiatan *ma Bibl. l. przen.* leviathan.

lewica *f.* 1. *polit.* the left, left wing. 2. *przest.* (= *lewa ręka*) left hand.

lewicować *ipf.* have leftist tendencies.

lewicowiec *mp* **-wc-** *pl.* **-y** left-winger.

lewicowy *a.* left-wing, leftist.

lewitacja *f.* levitation.

lewitować *ipf.* levitate.

lewizna *f. pot.* illegal work.

lewkonia *f. Gen.* **-ii** *bot.* stock, gillyflower (*Matthiola*).

lewo *adv.* **na** *l.* **w lewo** (= *w lewą stronę*) left; (= *po lewej stronie*) on the left; **na prawo i lewo** right and left, all over the place; **na lewo** *pot.* (= *nielegalnie*) under the table, on the q.t.

lewobrzeżny *a.* left-bank.

leworęczność *f.* left-handedness.

leworęczny *a.* left-handed. – *mp* left-hander, lefty.

lewoskrętny *a. chem.* levorotatory, levogyrous; *bot.* sinistrorse.

lewoskrzydłowy *a.* left-wing. – *mp sport* left wing.

lewostronny *a.* left-hand; **ruch lewostronny** left-hand traffic, left-hand driving.

lewy *a.* 1. (*o stronie ciała*) left, left-hand; **lewy pas** *mot.* fast lane; **lewy gwint** *techn.* left-hand thread; **po lewej stronie** on the left, on the left-hand side; **z lewej strony** *l.* **od lewej strony** from the left; **mieć dwie lewe ręce** *żart.* be clumsy, be ambilevous; **wstać lewą nogą** *pot.* get out of bed on the wrong side. 2. (= *wewnętrzny*) inside; **wywrócić coś na lewą stronę** turn sth inside out. 3. *pot.* (= *fałszywy*) phony, phoney, fake; **lewe dokumenty** fake ID.

leźć *ipf.* **lezę leziesz lazł leźli** 1. *pot.* (= *wlec się*) trudge, plod along, trail, traipse. 2. *pot.* (= *wspinać się*) climb. 3. *pot.* (= *pchać się*) jostle one's way; **patrz, gdzie leziesz!** look where you're going!; **leźć komuś w łapy** get into sb's hands.

leżak *mi Gen.* **-a** beach chair.

leżakować *ipf.* **1.** (= *odpoczywać na leżaku*) lie in a beach chair. **2.** (*o trunkach*) mature, mellow.

leżakownia *f. Gen.pl.* -i storage cellar.

leżanka *f. Gen.pl.* -ek (= *tapczan*) couch.

leżąco *adv.* na leżąco lying down.

leże *n. Gen.pl.* -y **1.** (= *legowisko*) place to lie down. **2.** (*miejsce snu zwierząt*) lair, den.

leżeć *ipf.* -ę -ysz **1.** (*być w pozycji leżącej*) lie; leżeć plackiem lie flat; leżeć w szpitalu stay in the hospital; leżeć w grobie lie burried; leżeć na pieniądzach be rolling in money. **2.** (= *znajdować się*) lie; Warszawa leży nad Wisłą Warsaw lies on the Vistula; to nie leży w moim interesie it is not in my interest; pieniądze leżą na ulicy the streets are paved with gold. **3.** (= *rozpościerać się, pokrywać*) spread; leży jak ulał fits like a glove; ich dobro leży mi na sercu I have their welfare at heart; leży mi to na sumieniu it lies heavy on my conscience. **4.** (= *być niewykorzystanym*) lie idle; leżeć odłogiem (*o ziemi*) lie fallow; *przen.* (= *leniuchować*) idle around; robota leży the work remains undone. **5.** *pot.* (= *znajdować się w trudnej sytuacji*) have trouble; gospodarka leży the economy is down; jeśli mi nie pomożesz, leżę! if you don't help me I'm cooked!; leżeć bez jednej/dwóch *karty* be one/two down.

leżnik *mi Gen.* -a *bud.* transom pole.

lędźwie *pl. Gen.* -i **1.** (*część pleców pomiędzy żebrami a miednicą*) loins. **2.** *pot.* (= *uda*) loins.

lędźwiowy *a.* loin.

lęg *mi* = ląg.

lęgnąć się *ipf.* -ij, lągł lęgła lęgli, ląc się *ipf.* lęgnę lęgniesz, -ij, ląkł lęgła lęgli (= *wykluwać się*) hatch; (= *rodzić się*) breed; *przen.* (= *powstawać po kryjomu*) arise secretly, spring up.

lęgowisko *n.* hatchery.

lęgowy *a.* breeding; sezon lęgowy breeding season.

lęk *mi* fear, anxiety, apprehension; lęk wysokości fear of heights, acrophobia; odczuwać lęk (przed kimś, przed czymś) fear sb, sth, be afraid of sb, sth.

lękać się *ipf.* be afraid.

lękliwość *f.* timidity, apprehensiveness.

lękliwy *a.* apprehensive, faint-hearted.

lękowy *a. med.* stany lękowe anxiety neurosis.

lgnąć *ipf.* -ij **1.** (= *przylepiać się*) cling. **2.** (= *garnąć się*) be attracted (*do kogoś, do czegoś* to sb, sth); lgnąć jak mucha do miodu be attracted like a bee to a flower.

li *particle przest.* li tylko only, exclusively.

liana *f.* liana.

lias *mi geol.* lias.

liasowy *a. geol.* liassic.

libacja *f.* booze-up, drinking spree; urządzać libacje throw a booze-up.

Liban *mi geogr.* Lebanon.

Libanka *f. Gen.pl.* -ek, Libańczyk *mp* Lebanese.

libański *a.* Lebanese.

liberalizacja *f.* liberalization.

liberalizm *mi* **1.** *polit., ekon.* liberalism. **2.** (= *wyrozumiałość*) liberality.

liberalizować *ipf.* liberalize.

liberalnie *adv.* liberally.

liberalność *f.* liberality, liberalness.

liberalny *a.* **1.** (*zgodny z doktryną liberalizmu*) liberal. **2.** (= *wyrozumiały*) liberal.

liberał *mp pl.* -owie **1.** (= *zwolennik liberalizmu*) liberal. **2.** (= *członek partii liberalnej*) Liberal.

liberia *f. Gen.* -ii livery.

libertyn *mp* **1.** (= *zwolennik libertynizmu*) libertine, free thinker. **2.** (= *osoba nieprzestrzegająca norm obyczajowych, religijnych*) libertine.

libertynizm *mi* libertinism.

libertyński *a.* libertarian.

Libia *f. Gen.* -ii *geogr.* Libya.

libido *n. indecl. psych.* libido.

Libijczyk *mp*, Libijka *f. Gen.pl.* -ek Libyan.

libijski *a.* Libyan.

libra *f.* **1.** (*miara papieru*) quire. **2.** (*typ wagi*) scales.

librecista *mp* librettist.

libretto *n. Loc.* -tcie libretto.

licealista *mp*, licealistka *f. Gen.pl.* -ek high school student.

licealny *a.* high school.

licencja *f.* **1.** (= *zezwolenie na wykonywanie czynności*) license; mieć licencję pilota to have pilot's license. **2.** (= *zezwolenie na korzystanie z praw*) license; mieć licencję na produkcję czegoś have a license to produce sth; telewizor na licencji Sony TV set under license from Sony. **3.** licencja poetycka poetic license.

licencjat *mi Gen.* -u *pl.* -y **1.** (*typ studiów*) BA course. **2.** (*tytuł niższy od magistra*) bachelor's degree, bachelor's. – *mp Gen.* -a, -ci (*osoba mająca licencjat*) BA (Bachelor of Arts), BSC (Bachelor of Science).

licencjonowany *a.* licensed.

licencyjny *a.* license.

liceum *n. sing. indecl. pl.* -ea *Gen.* -eów high school.

lichenolog *mp pl.* -dzy *l.* -owie lichenologist.

lichenologia *f. Gen.* -ii *bot.* lichenology.

licho[1] *n. pot.* (*coś złego*) deuce, dickens; licha wart trashy; pal to licho! to hell with it!; do licha (ciężkiego)! hang it!; do licha i trochę (= *w nadmiarze*) no end of (*sth*); po kiego licha... why on earth..., why the heck...; licho wie goodness knows; licho nie śpi better be safe, accidents will happen; niech cię licho porwie hell with you!

licho[2] *adv.* (= *marnie*) poorly.

lichota *f.* **1.** (= *tandeta*) trash, junk. **2.** (= *marna jakość*) trash.

lichtarz *mi Gen.* -a candlestick.

lichtarzyk *mi Gen.* -a sconce.

lichtuga *f. żegl.* lighter, coasting barge.

lichwa *f.* usury.

lichwiarka *f. Gen.pl.* -ek *zob.* lichwiarz.

lichwiarski *a.* usurious.

lichwiarstwo *n.* usuriousness.

lichwiarz *mp* usurer.

lichy *a.* **1.** (= *zaniedbany*) miserable; (*o glebie*) poor; (*o pożywieniu*) poor. **2.** (= *niewielki*) poor.

3. (= *kiepski, niewiele wart*) shoddy, poor; (*o filmie, obrazie*) trashy; (*ubranie*) flimsy.

lico *n.* **1.** *lit.* (= *twarz*) face. **2.** *bud.* face. **3.** *przest.* (*zewnętrzna powierzchnia czegoś*) face, front; **lico skóry** grain.

licować *ipf.* **1.** *form.* be compatible (*z czymś* with sth); **to nie licuje z kodeksem honorowym** it's incompatible with the code of honor. **2.** *bud.* face, veneer.

licowy *a.* **1.** (= *zewnętrzny*) right. **2.** *bud.* (*używany do licowania*) facing. **3.** *bud.* (= *frontowy*) front.

licówka *f. Gen.pl.* -**ek** *bud.* facing brick, facing tile.

licytacja *f.* **1.** (= *przetarg*) tender, auction; **wystawiać coś na licytację** put sth up for auction. **2.** *karty* bidding.

licytacyjny *a.* bidding.

licytant *mp* bidder, offerer.

licytator *mp* auctioneer.

licytować *ipf.* **1.** (= *dokonywać licytacji*) auction, bid. **2.** (= *zgłaszać na licytacji jakąś sumę*) bid a given sum, offer a given sum. **3.** *karty* bid. ~ **się** *ipf.* (= *prześcigać się*) try to outdo one another (*w czymś* at sth).

liczący *a.* **maszyna licząca** calculator; **liczący się naukowiec** eminent scholar.

liczba *f.* **1.** *mat.* number; **liczba całkowita** integer; **liczba naturalna/kardynalna** natural/cardinal number; **liczba wymierna/niewymierna** rational/surd number; **liczba rzeczywista/urojona/zespolona** real/imaginary/complex number; **liczba dziesiętna/dwójkowa** decimal/binary number; **liczba atomowa** *chem.* atomic number; **liczba porządkowa** ordinal number, ordinal; **liczba parzysta/nieparzysta** even/odd number. **2.** *jęz.* number; **liczba pojedyncza/podwójna/mnoga** singular/dual/plural (number). **3.** (= *suma takich samych jednostek*) number. **4.** **znaleźć się w liczbie (zwycięzców)** be counted among (the winners), class among (the winners).

liczbowo *adv.* **1.** (*za pomocą liczb*) in numbers; **jak to wygląda liczbowo?** what are the figures? **2.** (= *arytmetycznie, rachunkowo*) numerically, arithmetically.

liczbowy *a.* numerical; **oś liczbowa** *mat.* coordinate axis.

liczebnie *adv.* in number.

liczebnik *mi Gen.* -**a** numeral; **liczebnik główny** cardinal number; **liczebnik porządkowy** ordinal number.

liczebnikowy *a.* numeral.

liczebność *f.* number.

liczebny *a.* numerical; **mieć przewagę liczebną nad kimś** outnumber sb; **stan liczebny** number.

liczman *mp żegl.* tallyman.

licznie *adv.* in large numbers.

licznik *mi Gen.* -**a 1.** (*urządzenie*) meter; (*w taksówce*) taxi meter. **2.** *mat.* numerator.

liczny *a.* **1.** (*składający się z wielu jednostek*) numerous. **2.** (= *częsty*) abundant, plentiful.

liczyć *ipf.* (= *sumować*) **1.** count, total. **2.** (= *rachować*) calculate; **liczyć do dwudziestu** count (up) to twenty; **lekko licząc** at the lowest esti-

mate. **3.** (= *wliczać*) count, include; **na pokładzie jest 10 osób, nie licząc załogi** there are 10 people on the board beside the crew. **4.** (= *wynosić*) amount to, total; **zespół liczy 4 muzyków** the band numbers 4 musicians. **5.** (= *spodziewać się*) count on; **liczył na (to, że dostanie) podwyżkę** he counted on getting a rise; **liczyć na kogoś, na coś** (= *polegać*) count on sth, sb. **6.** (= *wyznaczać cenę*) charge; **ile pan liczy za poradę?** what do you charge for a consultation? ~ **się** *ipf.* **1.** (= *liczyć siebie wzajemnie*) count each other. **2.** (= *być liczonym*) be counted; **liczyć się na setki** run into hundreds. **3.** (= *mieć znaczenie*) count, matter; **to się nie liczy** it doesn't count, it counts for nothing. **4.** (= *brać pod uwagę*) take into account, count on; **liczyć się z kimś** hold sb in high esteem; **nie liczyć się z czymś** ignore sth, disregard sth; **liczyć się ze słowami** watch one's tongue, mind one's tongue; **liczyć się z (każdym) groszem** be careful of every penny one spends.

liczydło *n. Gen.pl.* -**eł 1.** (*przyrząd do obliczeń*) abacus. **2.** *techn.* (*mechanizm wskazujący licznika*) counter.

liczykrupa *f. l. mp decl. like f. Gen.pl.* -**p** *l.* -**ów** *pog.* scrooge, tightwad.

lider *mp* **1.** (= *przywódca*) leader. **2.** *sport* leader.

Liechtenstein *mi geogr.* Liechtenstein.

liga *f.* **1.** (*organizacja*) league; **Liga Narodów** *hist.* the League of Nations. **2.** *sport* league.

ligatura *f. druk., med., muz.* ligature.

lignina *f.* **1.** (= *wata celulozowa*) cellucotton. **2.** (= *drzewnik*) lignin.

ligninowy *a.* **1.** (*dotyczący waty celulozowej*) cellucotton. **2.** (*dotyczący drzewnika*) lignin.

ligowiec *mp* -**wc-** *pl.* -**y** *sport* league player.

ligowy *a.* league.

ligustr *mi bot.* privet (*Ligustrum*).

ligustrowy *a. ogr.* privet.

lik[1] *mi żegl.* edge of sail.

lik[2] *mi* **bez liku** countless, innumerable.

likaon *ma zool.* African hunting dog (*Lycaon pictus*).

likier *mi* liqueur.

likierowy *a.* liqueur.

likwidacja *f.* **1.** (= *zniesienie*) abolition, abrogation. **2.** *prawn.* liquidation. **3.** **likwidacja szkód** liquidation of damages. **4.** *pot.* (= *uśmiercenie*) liquidation, elimination.

likwidacyjny *a. prawn.* **1.** clearing. **2.** **postępowanie likwidacyjne** liquidation proceedings.

likwidator *mp prawn.* liquidator.

likwidatura *f. fin.* (= *wydział instytucji finansowej*) payments department.

likwidować *ipf.* **1.** (= *usuwać*) liquidate, wind up. **2.** *prawn.* liquidate, do away with. **3.** *pot.* (= *uśmiercać*) eliminate, liquidate.

likwor *mi przest. l. żart.* (= *napój, zwł. alkoholowy*) liquor, beverage.

likworowy *a.* (*o słodyczach*) liqueur.

lila *a. indecl.* (*kolor*) lilac.

lilak *mi Gen.* -**a** *bot.* lilac (*Syringa*).

lilia *f. Gen.* -**ii 1.** *bot.* lily (*Lilium*); **biały jak lilia** lily-white. **2.** *her.* fleur-de-lys.

lilijka *f.* **1.** (= *mała lilia*) little lily. **2.** (*znak harcerski*) scout badge.

liliowiec *mi* **-wc-** *Gen.* **-a** *bot.* day lily (*Hemerocallis*). – *ma* **-wc-** *zool.* (= *szkarłupień z gromady Crinoidea*) sea lily.

liliowoniebieski *a.* lilac-blue.

liliowy *a.* **1.** (*mający związek z liliami*) lily. **2.** (= *lila*) lilac.

lilipuci *a.* Lilliputian, tiny, midgety.

liliput *mp pl.* **-y** *l.* **-ci** **1.** (= *karzełek*) Lilliputian, dwarf. **2.** (*przedmiot o niewielkich rozmiarach*) midget; **domek liliput** tiny house.

liliputka *f. Gen.pl.* **-ek** (*rasa kur*) bantam hen.

liman *mi geogr.* coastal salt lake.

limba *f. bot.* Swiss pine (*Pinus cembra*).

limeryk *mi lit.* limerick.

limes *indecl. mat.* limes.

limfa *f. fizj.* lymph.

limfatyczny *a. fizj., anat.* lymphatic; **układ limfatyczny** lymphatic system; **węzły limfatyczne** lymph nodes, lymph glands.

limfocyt *mi fizj.* lymphocyte.

limfocytoza *f. med.* lymphocytosis.

limit *mi* limit; **limit czasu** time limit.

limitacja *f.* limitation.

limitować *ipf.* limit, restrict.

limitowy *a.* limit.

limuzyna *f.* limousine.

lin *ma icht.* tench (*Tinca tinca*).

lina *f.* rope; **lina holownicza** tow-rope; **chodzić po linie** walk a tightrope; **przeciągać linę** play tug-of-war; **przeciąganie liny** tug-of-war.

lincz *mi Gen.pl.* **-ów** lynch.

linczować *ipf.* lynch.

linearność *f.* linearity.

linearny *a.* linear; **pismo linearne** linear script.

lingwista *mp*, **lingwistka** *f. Gen.pl.* **-ek** linguist.

lingwistyczny *a.* **1.** (= *językoznawczy*) linguistic. **2.** (= *językowy*) linguistic.

lingwistyka *f.* **1.** linguistics. **2.** **lingwistyka stosowana** applied linguistics.

linia *f. Gen.* **-ii** **1.** *geom.* line; **linia prosta** (straight) line; **linia krzywa** curve; **linia kropkowana** dotted line; **linia przerywana** dashed line, broken line; **w jednej linii** in a line; **w linii prostej** in a straight line, as the crow flies; **linia demarkacyjna** line of demarcation; **linie papilarne** *anat.* papillary lines; **linia brzegowa** *geogr.* coastline; **linia autowa** *sport* touch line; **linia bramkowa** *sport* goal line; **papier w linie** lined paper. **2.** (= *szereg, rząd*) row, rank. **3.** *wojsk.* line; (= *front*) the front (line); **walczyć w pierwszej linii** be in the forefront of the fighting line; **zwycięstwo/klęska na całej linii** *t. przen.* sweeping victory/defeat. **4.** (= *trasa*) route; **linie lotnicze** airlines; **linia produkcyjna** assembly line, production line. **5.** (= *kontur*) contour; **dbać o linię** watch one's weight. **6.** (= *kierunek działania*) line; **iść po linii najmniejszego oporu** take the line of least resistance. **7.** (= *ród*) lineage; **przodek/potomek w linii prostej** ancestor/descendant in a direct line, lineal ancestor/descendant. **8.** (= *liniał*) ruler. **9.** *miern.* straight-edge. **10.** (= *wiersz w tekście*) line.

linieć *ipf.* molt.

linijka *f. Gen.pl.* **-ek** **1.** (= *liniał*) ruler. **2.** (= *wiersz w tekście*) line.

liniować *ipf.* line.

liniowiec *mi* **-wc-** *Gen.* **-a** *pl.* **-e** **1.** (*statek pasażerski lub towarowy*) liner. **2.** *wojsk.* (*okręt bojowy*) ship of the line. – *mp* **-wc-** *Voc.* **-u** *l.* **-cze** *pl.* **-y** (= *frontowiec*) front-line soldier.

liniowy *a.* **1.** (*związany z linią*) linear; **podziałka liniowa** *geogr.* linear scale; **równanie liniowe** *mat.* linear equation; **sędzia liniowy** *sport* linesman; **żegluga liniowa** line traffic. **2.** *wojsk.* (= *frontowy*) front-line; **wojska liniowe** troops of the line; **służba liniowa** front-line service.

linka *f. Gen.pl.* **-ek** cord.

linkowy *a.* (= *dotyczący linki*) cord, rope, line.

linoleum *n. sing. indecl. pl.* **-ea** *Gen.* **-eów** linoleum.

linoryt *mi* **1.** (*technika graficzna*) linoleum block printing. **2.** (*odbitka*) linoleum print.

linorytowy *a.* linoleum-block.

linoskoczek *mp* **-czk-** *pl.* **-i** *l.* **-owie** tightrope walker, acrobat, equilibrist.

linotyp *mi druk.* linotype.

linotypista *mp druk.* linotyper, linotypist.

linotypowy *a. druk.* linotype.

linownica *f. techn.* cableway.

linowy *a.* rope, cable, line; **kolejka linowa** cable railway.

liofilizacja *f. techn.* lyophilization, freeze-drying.

liofilizator *mi Gen.* **-a** *techn.* lyophilizing chamber.

liofilizować *ipf. techn.* lyophilize, freeze-dry.

liofilizowany *a. techn.* lyophilized.

lipa *f.* **1.** *bot.* linden (*Tilia*). **2.** *pot.* (= *oszustwo, kłamstwo*) eyewash, bunk. **3.** *pot.* (= *tandeta*) trash, junk.

lipaza *f. biol.* lipase.

lipcowy *a.* July.

lipid *mi biol., chem.* lipid, lipide.

lipidowy *a. biol., chem.* lipid, lipide.

lipiec *mi* **-pc-** *Gen.* **-a** July.

lipień *ma icht.* grayling (*Thymallus thymallus*).

lipina *f.* (= *drewno lipy*) linden (wood).

lipny *a.* **1.** *pot.* (= *nieprawdziwy*) fake(d), phony; **lipne papiery** *l.* **dokumenty** phony papers. **2.** *pot.* (= *tandetny*) trashy, cheap, junky.

lipoma *f. pat.* lipoma.

liposom *mi biochem.* liposome.

lipowy *a.* linden, lime.

lir *mi Gen.* **-a** (*jednostka monetarna Włoch*) lira.

lira *f. muz.* lyre; **lira korbowa** hurdy-gurdy.

lirnik *mp t. przen.* lyrist.

lirogon *ma orn.* lyrebird (*Menura*).

liryczka *f. Gen.pl.* **-ek** *zob.* **liryk**.

liryczny *a.* **1.** (= *odnoszący się do liryki*) lyric, lyrical; **głos liryczny** *muz.* lyric voice. **2.** (= *uczuciowy*) lyric, emotional, sentimental.

liryk *mp Gen.* **-a** *pl.* **-cy** (= *poeta*) lyrist, lyric poet. – *mi Gen.* **-u** *pl.* **-i** (= *utwór liryczny*) lyric.

liryka *f. teor.lit.* lyric poetry.

liryzm *mi* lyricism.

lis *ma* **1.** *zool.* fox (*Vulpes*); **lis srebrny** silver fox; **sprytny jak lis** (as) cunning *l.* sly as a fox. **2.** (= *futro z lisa*) fox fur. – *mp pl.* **-y** (= *człowiek przebiegły*) **1.** cunning person, crafty person; **farbowany lis** turncoat, wolf in sheep's clothing; **stary lis** old busy-body, old fog(e)y. **2.** *zob.* **lisy.**

lisi *a.* **1.** (= *odnoszący się do lisa*) fox; **lisia czapa** *l.* **czapka** (= *otoczka wokół Księżyca*) halo round the moon. **2.** (= *zrobiony z futra z lisa*) fox-fur. **3.** *przen.* (= *właściwy komuś przebiegłemu*) foxy, sly.

lisica *f.* **1.** *zool.* vixen. **2.** = **kurka** 2. **3.** *icht.* European hook-nose (*Agonus cataphractus*).

list *mi* letter; **list gończy** arrest warrant, warrant of arrest; **list otwarty** open letter; **list polecający** letter of recommendation; **list zwykły** surface-mail letter; **list polecony** certified letter *l.* mail; *Br.* registered letter; **list lotniczy** airmail letter; **list pasterski** *rel.* pastoral; **listy uwierzytelniające** credentials; **list żelazny** safe-conduct; **list miłosny** love letter.

lista *f.* list; **lista obecności** attendence list, roll; **lista płac** payroll; **lista przebojów** (= *spis utworów*) the charts; (= *program radiowy, telewizyjny*) hit parade; **lista wyborcza** register of voters; **znajdować się na czarnej liście** be blacklisted, be on the black list.

listek *mi* **-tk-** *Gen.* **-a 1.** (= *mały liść*) (little) leaf; **listek figowy** fig leaf. **2.** (= *część liścia złożonego*) leaflet; *pot.* (= *płatek kwiatu*) petal. **3.** *rzad.* (= *cienki arkusik czegoś*) sheet; **listki złota** gold leaves.

listera *f. bot.* twayblade (*Listera*).

listewka *f. Gen.pl.* **-ek 1.** (= *wąska deseczka*) strip of wood. **2.** (= *paseczek tkaniny*) list, border, selvage.

listonosz *mp Gen.pl.* **-y** *l.* **-ów** letter carrier, mailman.

listonoszka *f. Gen.pl.* **-ek** letter carrier.

listopad *mi Gen.* **-a** November.

listopadowy *a.* November; **listopadowy deszcz** November rain.

listowie *n.* foliage, leafage.

listownica *f. bot.* laminaria (*Laminaria*).

listownie *adv.* by mail, by letter.

listowny *a.* written.

listowy *a.* letter; **papier listowy** writing paper, stationery; **skrzynka listowa** mailbox.

listwa *f. Gen.pl.* **-ew 1.** (= *wąska deseczka*) strip of wood, slat, batten; **listwa przypodłogowa** baseboard; *Br.* skirting (board). **2.** (= *pasek tkaniny*) list, border, salvage. **3.** (= *występ muru lub skały*) ledge.

lisy *pl. Gen.* **-ów** (= *futro z lisa*) fox fur.

liszaj *mi Gen.* **-a** *Gen.pl.* **-ów** *l.* **-ai** *pat.* lichen.

liszajec *mi* **-jc-** *Gen.* **-a** *pat.* impetigo.

liszajowaty *a. pat.* lichenous.

liszka[1] *f. Gen.pl.* **-ek** *pot.* (= *gąsienica*) caterpillar.

liszka[2] *f. Gen.pl.* **-ek** *myśl.* (= *samica lisa*) vixen.

liściak *ma Gen.* **-a** *Ins.* **-iem** *bot.* **1.** phyllode. **2.** phillophora (*Phillophora*).

liściasty *a.* **1.** (= *pokryty liśćmi*) leafed, leafy; **drzewo liściaste** deciduous tree; **las liściasty** deciduous forest. **2.** (= *mający kształt liścia*) leaflike, foliaceous.

liście[1] *mi zob.* **list.**

liście[2] *f. zob.* **lista.**

liścień *mi Gen.* **-a** *bot.* cotyledon.

liścik *mi Gen.* **-a** *l.* **-u** note.

liściowy *a.* leaf, foliaceous.

liść *mi Gen.* **-a** *Ins.pl.* **-mi** leaf; **liść bobkowy** *l.* **laurowy** bay leaf; **drżeć** *l.* **trząść się jak liść osiki** *l.* **osiny** tremble like a leaf; **puszczać liście** leaf, put forth leaves; **tracić liście** shed leaves.

lit *mi chem.* lithium.

litania *f. Gen.* **-ii 1.** *rz.-kat.* litany. **2.** *pot.* (= *długi spis*) litany, endless list; **litania skarg** litany of complaints.

litanijny *a.* litany.

litera *f.* letter; **duża litera** capital letter, uppercase letter; **mała litera** small letter, lowercase letter; **litery drukowane** printed letters; **litera prawa** *prawn.* letter of the law, litera legis; **cztery litery** *euf.* rump; *Br.* bum; **łykać litery** slur.

literacki *a.* literary; **język literacki** literary language; **kierownik literacki** art editor; **salon literacki** reading hall.

literackość *f.* literary character.

literalny *a.* (= *dosłowny*) literal.

literat *mp* writer, man of letters.

literatka *f. Gen.pl.* **-ek 1.** *zob.* **literat. 2.** *pot.* (= *szklaneczka*) chaser glass.

literatura *f.* **1.** (= *twórczość piśmiennicza*) literature, writings; **literatura faktu** factual literature; **literatura ludowa** folk literature; **literatura piękna** belles-lettres. **2.** (= *ogół prac pisemnych z jednej dziedziny*) literature.

literaturoznawca *mp* literature specialist.

literaturoznawczy *a.* literature-specialist.

literaturoznawstwo *n.* literary studies.

literka *f. Gen.pl.* **-ek** (= *mała litera*) (small) letter.

liternictwo *n.* lettering.

liternik *mp* letterer.

literować *ipf.* spell; **czy mógłby pan przeliterować swoje nazwisko?** could you spell your name, please?

literowiec *mi* **-wc-** *Gen.* **-a** *jęz.* acronym.

literowy *a.* literal.

literówka *f. Gen.pl.* **-ek** typo.

litewski *a.* Lithuanian.

litofilny *a. chem.* lithophile; **pierwiastek litofilny** lithophile (element).

litogeneza *f. geol.* lithogenesis.

litograf *mp pl.* **-owie** lithographer.

litografia *f. Gen.* **-ii 1.** *druk.* (*technika druku*) lithography. **2.** *druk.* (*odbitka*) litograph.

litograficzny *a. druk.* lithographic, lithographical.

litografować *ipf. druk.* litograph.

litologia *f. Gen.* **-ii** *min.* lithology.

litologiczny *a. min.* lithologic, lithological.

litopon *f. chem.* lithopone.

litoral *mi geogr.* littoral (region).

litoralny *f. geogr.* littoral; **strefa litoralna** littoral (region).

litosfera *f. geol.* lithosphere.

litościwie *a.* mercifully, compassionately.

litościwość *f.* mercifulness, compassionateness.

litościwy *a.* merciful, compassionate.

litość *f.* (= *łaska*) mercy; (= *współczucie*) compassion; **litości!** (have) mercy!; **bez litości** without mercy, merciless; **na litość boską!** for goodness' sake!, for heaven's sake!; **(robić coś) z litości** (do sth) out of pity; **mieć litość nad kimś** take pity on sb; **wzbudzać litość** arouse pity.

litota *f. teor.lit.* litotes, meiosis.

litotomia *f. Gen.* **-ii** *chir.* lithotomy.

litotrypsja *f. Gen.* **-ji** *med.* lithotripsy.

litotryptor *mi med.* lithotripter.

litować się *ipf.* have mercy (*nad kimś/czymś* on sb/sth).

litr *mi Gen.* **-a** liter; **postawić (pół) litra** *pot.* stand *l.* buy (half) a liter of vodka.

litraż *mi* liter capacity; **litraż silnika** *mot.* (engine) cubic capacity.

litrowy *a.* one-liter.

lituanista *mp* Lithuanian studies expert.

lituanistyka *f.* Lithuanian studies.

lituanizacja *f.* acquiring Lithuanian features.

lituanizm *mi jęz.* word/phrase/form/etc. of Lithuanian origin.

liturgia *f. Gen.* **-ii** *rel.* liturgy.

liturgiczny *a. rel.* liturgical, liturgic.

liturgika *f. rel., uniw.* liturgics.

Litwa *f. geogr.* Lithuania.

Litwin *mp,* **Litwinka** *f. Gen.pl.* **-ek** Lithuanian.

litwor, arcydzięgiel litwor *mi bot.* angelica (*Angelica archangelica*).

litworowy *a.* angelica; **olejek litworowy** angelica oil.

lity *a.* **1.** (= *masywny*) solid; **lita skała** solid rock; **lite złoto** pure gold. **2.** *lit.* (= *lany*) cast. **3.** *lit.* (= *dziergany złotem*) gold-laced. **4.** (= *jednogatunkowy*) pure, homogeneous.

liwistonia *f. Gen.* **-ii** *bot.* fan palm (*Livistona*).

lizać *ipf.* **1.** (= *przesuwać po czymś językiem*) lick; **palce lizać!** yummy!, finger-licking good!; **lizać rany** lick one's wounds; **lizać czyjeś buty** *l.* **stopy** *pot.* (= *zabiegać o czyjeś względy*) bow and scrape, lick one's shoes *l.* boots *l.* heel, brownnose, kiss ass, be an apple-polisher; **pies ci mordę lizał!** *pot.* get stuffed!, I don't give a damn about you! **2.** (= *muskać*) brush against, graze; **kula liznęła mu rękę** bullet grazed his hand; **ogień lizał dach** fire swept across the roof. **~ się** *ipf.* **1.** (= *lizać siebie*) lick o.s. **2.** *przen.* (= *leczyć się z czegoś*) recover, get better; **lizać się z ran** recover from one's wounds. **3.** (= *lizać siebie nawzajem*) lick each other *l.* one another. **4.** *pot.* (= *całować się, zwłaszcza publicznie*) make out, neck, suck face.

lizak *mi Gen.* **-a 1.** (= *cukierek na patyku*) lollipop, lollypop. **2.** *pot.* (= *tarcza sygnalizacyjna*) signal board.

lizawka *f. Gen.pl.* **-ek 1.** (*koryto dla zwierzyny*) salt lick. **2.** (*dodatek do paszy*) salt lick.

lizawość *f. wet.* licking.

lizawy *a. wet.* licking.

Lizbona *f. geogr.* Lisbon.

liznąć *pf.* **-znę -źniesz,-źnij 1.** *zob.* **lizać. 2.** *pot.* (= *skosztować*) taste, take a bite. **3.** *pot.* (= *poznać coś powierzchownie*) get a smattering of sth, dabble in. **~ się** *pf. zob.* **lizać się**.

lizol *mi* Lysol.

lizus *mp pl.* **-y lizuska** *f. Gen.pl.* **-ek** *pot.* toady, brown-noser, bootlicker, apple-polisher, asskisser.

lizusostwo *n. pot.* toadyism, boot-licking, asskissing.

lizusować *ipf. pot.* act toady, butter up.

lizusowski *a. pot.* toadyish.

lizymetr *mi geol.* lysimeter.

lizyna *f. biochem.* **1.** (*aminokwas*) lysine. **2.** (*przeciwciało*) lysin.

lm. *abbr. jęz.* (= *liczba mnoga*) pl. (*plural*).

lnianowłosy *a.* flaxen-haired.

lniany *a.* **1.** (= *zrobiony z lnu*) linen; **lniana marynarka** linen jacket; **olej lniany** flaxseed *l.* linseed oil. **2.** (= *w kolorze lnu*) flaxen.

lniarski *a.* flax, flax-processing.

lniarstwo *n.* flax (processing) industry.

lnica *f. Gen., Dat., Loc.* **-cy** *bot.* toadflax, spurred snapdragon (*Linaria*).

lnicznik *ma Gen.* **-a Ins.** **-iem** *bot.* **lnicznik siewny** gold-of-pleasure, false flax (*Camelina sativa*).

lnisko *n.* flax stubbles.

lnu *itd. mi zob.* **len**.

LO *abbr.* (= *liceum ogólnokształcące*) H.S. (*high school*).

lob *mi sport* lob.

lobby *n. indecl. zwł. polit.* lobby.

lobektomia *f. Gen.* **-ii** *chir.* lobectomy.

lobelia *f. Gen.* **-ii** *bot.* lobelia (*Lobelia*).

lobować *ipf. sport* lob.

loch *mi* dungeon.

locha *f. myśl., roln.* (= *maciora*) sow.

locja *f. żegl.* **1.** (*dział wiedzy*) pilotage. **2.** (= *podręcznik nawigacji*) Sailing Directions; *US* Coast Pilot; *Br.* Pilot, Admirality Pilot.

loco *n. indecl. handl.* ex; **loco magazyn** ex warehouse; **cena loco (fabryka/magazyn)** ex (works/warehouse) price.

loczek *mi* **-czk-** *Gen.* **-a** curl, lock.

lodołam *mi techn.* ice-apron.

lodołamacz *mi Gen.* **-a** *żegl.* icebreaker.

lodospad *mi Gen.* **-u** *Loc.* **-zie** *geogr.* icefall.

lodoszreń *f.* ice-sheet snow.

lodowacieć *ipf.* **1.** (= *zamarzać*) freeze. **2.** (= *marznąć*) freeze. **3.** *pot.* (= *drętwieć*) freeze, stiffen. **4.** *pot.* (= *obojętnieć*) become frigid *l.* indifferent.

lodowaty *a.* **1.** (= *zimny*) ice-cold, icy. **2.** *pot.* (= *oziębły*) icy, frigid; **lodowaty ton** harsh tone; **lodowate milczenie** eerie silence; **lodowate przyjęcie** chilly *l.* reserved welcome.

lodowcowy *a. geol., geogr.* glacial; **dolina lodowcowa** glacial valley; **epoka lodowcowa** *l.* **okres lodowcowy** ice age, glacial epoch *l.* period.

lodowica *f. Gen., Dat., Loc.* **-cy** black ice.

lodowiec *mi* **-wc-** *Gen.* **-a** *geogr.* glacier.

lodowisko *n.* (ice *l.* skating) rink.

lodownia *f. Gen.pl.* **-i 1.** (= *chłodnia*) icehouse, cold storage. **2.** *pot.* (= *niedogrzane pomieszczenie*) underheated place *l.* room *l.* apartment.

lodownik *mi Gen.* **-a** *techn.* ice generator *l.* maker.

lodowy *a.* **1.** (= *utworzony z lodu*) ice; **góra lodowa** iceberg. **2.** (= *związany z lodem*) ice; **żeglarstwo lodowe** iceboating. **3.** *przest.* (= *lodowaty*) ice-cold.

lodówka *f. Gen.pl.* **-ek 1.** refrigerator, fridge. **2.** *orn.* old squaw (*Clangula hyemalis*).

lodu *itp. mi* zob. **lód**.

lody *pl. Gen.* **-ów** ice cream; **lody na patyku** ice cream on a stick; *por.* **lód**.

lodziarka *f. Gen.pl.* **-ek** *zob.* **lodziarz**.

lodziarnia *f. Gen.pl.* **-i** *l.* **-ń** ice cream parlor.

lodziarski *a.* ice-cream.

lodziarstwo *n.* ice-cream production *l.* making.

lodziarz *mp* ice cream seller *l.* vendor.

lodżia *f. Gen.* **-ii 1.** (*balkon*) balcony. **2.** (*budynek; część budynku*) loggia.

loftka *f. myśl.* shot.

loftkowy *a. myśl.* shot.

log *mi żegl.* log.

logarytm *mi mat.* logarithm; **logarytm dziesiętny** common logarithm, Briggsian logarithm; **logarytm naturalny** natural logarithm, Naperian logarithm.

logarytmiczny *a. mat.* logarithmic; **równanie logarytmiczne** logarithmic equation; **suwak logarytmiczny** slide rule; **tablice logarytmiczne** logarithmic tables.

logarytmować *ipf. mat.* find the logarithm.

logicznie *a.* logically.

logiczność *f.* soundness, logicalness.

logiczny *a.* **1.** (= *dotyczący logiki*) logical; **kwadrat logiczny** square of opposition. **2.** (= *sensowny*) sound, sensible, reasonable; **układać się w logiczną całość** make sense, fit together.

logik *mp log.* logician.

logika *f.* **1.** (*nauka*) logic; **logika dwuwartościowa** two term logic; **logika formalna** formal logic; **logika symboliczna** symbolic logic, mathematical logic; **logika trójwartościowa** three term logic; **logika zdaniowa** propositional logic. **2.** (= *zdrowy rozsądek*) common sense; **postępować zgodnie z logiką** act reasonably. **3.** (= *sensowność*) reason; **żelazna logika** irrefutable logic.

logistyczny *a. zwł. wojsk.* logistic, logistical.

logistyka *f. zwł. wojsk. t. ekon.* logistics.

logizować *ipf.* logicize.

logo *n. indecl.* logo, logotype.

logometr *mi el.* quotient meter, ratio meter.

logopatia *f. Gen.* **-ii** speech impediment.

logopatolog *mp pl.* **-dzy** *l.* **-owie** speech pathologist.

logopatologia *f. Gen.* **-ii** speech pathology.

logopeda *mp* speech therapist.

logopedia *f. Gen.* **-ii** logopedics, logopedia, speech therapy.

logopedyczny *a.* logopedic.

logos *mi fil., rel.* logos.

logotyp *mi druk.* logotype, logo.

logować się *ipf. komp.* log in.

lojalista *mp* loyalist.

lojalizm *mi* loyalism.

lojalka *f. Gen.pl.* **-ek** *pot.* loyalty oath.

lojalnie *adv.* **1.** (= *praworządnie*) legally. **2.** (= *uczciwie*) honestly.

lojalność *f.* **1.** (= *praworządność*) loyalty. **2.** (= *uczciwość wobec kogoś*) loyalty, integrity.

lojalny *a.* **1.** (= *praworządny*) loyal, law-abiding. **2.** (= *uczciwy wobec kogoś*) loyal, honest.

LOK *abbr.* (= *Liga Obrony Kraju*) National Defense League (*in Poland*).

lok *mi Gen.* **-a** lock, curl.

lokacja *f.* **1.** *hist.* foundation of a town. **2.** *techn.* ranging, location.

lokacyjny *a.* **1.** *hist.* foundation; **przywilej lokacyjny** foundation privilege; (*dokument*) foundation charter. **2.** *techn.* ranging, locational.

lokaj *mp Gen.pl.* **-ów** *l.* **-ai** lackey, footman, flunk(e)y.

lokajski *a.* **1.** (= *właściwy lokajowi*) lackey's. **2.** *pot.* (= *służalczy*) servile.

lokajstwo *n.* **1.** (= *zawód lokaja*) post of a lackey. **2.** *pot.* (= *służalczość*) flunkyism, servility.

lokal *mi Gen.pl.* **-i** *l.* **-ów 1.** (= *pomieszczenie*) premises, place; **lokal biurowy** office; **lokal mieszkalny** apartment; **lokal użytkowy** business premises; **lokal wyborczy** polls; *Br.* polling station. **2.** (= *restauracja*) restaurant; **lokal nocny** night club; **iść do lokalu** go out.

lokalizacja *f.* **1.** (= *umiejscowienie*) location. **2.** (= *ograniczenie skutków*) containment. **3.** (= *dokonywanie tłumaczenia wraz z przystosowaniem do warunków lokalnych*) localization.

lokalizacyjny *a.* **1.** locational, location. **2.** (= *dotyczący dokonywania tłumaczenia wraz z przystosowaniem do warunków lokalnych*) localization.

lokalizator *mi Gen.* **-a 1.** finder, locator. **2.** (= *specjalista w zakresie lokalizacji*) localization specialist *l.* expert; localization engineer.

lokalizm *mi Gen.* **-u** (= *wyrażenie, zwrot właściwy danemu regionowi, miejscowości itp.*) localism.

lokalizować *ipf.* **1.** (= *umiejscawiać*) locate. **2.** (= *ustalać położenie*) locate. **3.** (= *ograniczać zasięg zjawisk*) contain; **lokalizować ogień** contain a fire. **4.** (= *dokonywać tłumaczenia wraz z przystosowaniem do warunków lokalnych*) localize.

lokalnie *adv.* locally, regionally.

lokalny *a.* local, regional; **lokalne opady/lokalny wiatr** local rainfall/wind; **koloryt lokalny** local color; **patriotyzm lokalny** localism; **wizja lokalna** *prawn.* inspection at the scene of the crime.

lokalowy *a.* **1.** (= *dotyczący pomieszczeń*) housing, dwelling; **prawo lokalowe** housing (management) regulations. **2.** (= *dotyczący restauracji*) restaurant.

lokata *f.* **1.** *ekon.* investment; **lokata bankowa** deposit; **lokata kapitału** capital investment. **2.** (= *miejsce w klasyfikacji*) position, place, rank; **zdobyć pierwszą lokatę** finish in the first place; *pot.* come first.

lokator *mp* **1.** occupant, resident; **dziki lokator** squatter. **2.** = **lokalizator** 1.

lokatorka *f. Gen.pl.* -ek *zob.* **lokator** 1.

lokatorski *a.* occupant's, resident's.

lokaut *mi ekon.* lockout.

lokomocja *f.* locomotion; **środek lokomocji** means of transportation; *Br.* means of transport.

lokomocyjny *a.* locomotive, transportive; **choroba lokomocyjna** *pat.* motion sickness.

lokomotywa *f. kol.* locomotive, engine.

lokomotywownia *f. Gen.pl.* -i *kol.* engine *l.* locomotive depot.

lokomotywowy *a.* engine, locomotive.

lokować *ipf.* **1.** (= *umieszczać*) place, put; (= *kwaterować*) house, accomodate. **2.** *ekon.* invest; **lokować pieniądze w czymś** invest money in sth. **3.** *hist.* locate. ~ **się** *ipf.* **1.** (= *sadowić się*) sit. **2.** (= *zajmować jakieś miejsce w klasyfikacji*) come, rank (*first, second, last, etc.*).

lokówka *f. Gen.pl.* -ek curler.

lokum *n. indecl.* quarters, lodgings.

lollard *mp hist.* Lollard.

lombard *mi* pawnshop.

lombardowy *a.* pawn.

Londyn *mi geogr.* London.

londynka *f.*, **londyńczyk** *mp* Londoner.

londyński *a.* London.

longan *mi bot.* longan, lungan (*Euphoria longana*).

longplay *mi Gen.* -a *Gen.pl.* -ów long-playing record, LP.

lont *mi* fuse; (*zwł. dawniej*) match.

lonża *f. jeździ.* longe, lunge.

looping *mi lotn.* loop.

LOP *abbr.* (= *Liga Ochrony Przyrody*) the League for the Conservation of Nature.

lora *f.* (*wagon*) gondola car, gondola; *zwł. Br.* lorry.

loran *mi lotn.* loran (*Long Range Navigation*).

lord *mp pl.* -owie lord; **Izba Lordów** *parl.* House of Lords.

lordowski *a.* lordly.

lordoza *f. pat.* lordosis, anterior spinal curvature.

lorenc *mi Gen.* -a *fiz.* c.

lorens *mi chem.* lawrencium.

lorneta *f.* binoculars, field glasses.

lornetka *f. Gen.pl.* -ek binoculars, field glasses; **lornetka polowa** field binoculars; **lornetka teatralna** opera glasses.

lornion *n. przest.* lorgnette, lorgnon.

los *mi* **1.** (= *dola*) lot, fortune; **koleje losu** vicissitudes, ups and downs; **zły los** bad fortune; **ważą się losy kraju** the future of the country is at stake, the fate of the country hangs in the balance. **2.** (= *przeznaczenie*) fate, destiny; **na los szczęścia** (= *licząc na szczęście*) hoping for the best; (= *na chybił trafił*) at random; **uśmiech** *l.* zrządzenie losu stroke of luck; **ironia losu** irony of fate; **ofiara losu** loser, sad sack; **wybraniec losu** (sb) born under a lucky star; **być zdanym na łaskę losu** be at the mercy of fate; **kusić los** push *l.* crowd sb's luck; **masz ci los!** too bad!; **los spra-**

wił, że... it so happened that...; **los tak chciał** it was written in the stars. **3.** (= *bilet loteryjny*) (lottery) ticket; **ciągnąć losy** draw lots; **wygrać los na loterii** *przen.* be blessed by luck.

losować *ipf.* (*zwycięzcę, liczbę*) **1.** draw. **2.** (= *ciągnąć losy*) draw lots.

losowanie *n.* drawing.

losowo *adv.* at random, randomly.

losowy *a.* **1.** (*związany z wydarzeniami życia*) of fate *l.* lot; **wypadek losowy** act of God. **2.** (*związany z przypadkowością*) random, chance; **gra losowa** game of chance.

lot *mi* (= *lecenie*) flight; **lot czarterowy** charter flight; **lot rejsowy** scheduled flight; **lot kosmiczny** space flight; **lot koszący** hedgehopping; **lot nurkowy** dive; **lotem błyskawicy** in a flash; **w lot** instantly; **widok z lotu ptaka** bird's eye view; **niskiego lotu** *przen.* mediocre, of low quality; **obniżyć loty** be off sb's peak, go *l.* run to seed.

lotek *mi* -tk- *Gen.* -a *pot.* lotto, (national) lottery; **grać w lotka** enter a lotto *l.* lottery.

loteria *f. Gen.* -ii **1.** (*gra losowa*) lottery; **loteria fantowa** raffle; **wygrać na loterii** win a lottery. **2.** *pot.* (= *sytuacja niepewna*) lottery; **życie to loteria** life is a lottery.

loteryjka *f. Gen.pl.* -ek (*gra towarzyska*) lotto, lottery.

loteryjny *a.* lottery.

lotka *f. Gen.pl.* -ek **1.** *orn.* flight feather. **2.** *lotn.* aileron. **3.** *sport* shuttlecock, shuttle.

lotnia *f. Gen.pl.* -i hang glider.

lotniarstwo *n.* hang gliding.

lotniarz *mp* hang glider.

lotnictwo *n.* **1.** (*dziedzina techniki*) aviation; **lotnictwo cywilne** civil aviation; **lotnictwo wojskowe** air force. **2.** (= *samoloty*) (air)plane fleet.

lotniczy *a.* air, aerial; **linie lotnicze** airline, air carrier; **port lotniczy** airport; **pokaz lotniczy** airshow; **zdjęcie lotnicze** aerial photograph; (**wysłać coś) pocztą lotniczą** (send sth) by airmail.

lotnik *mp* pilot, aviator; (*zwł. wojskowy*) airman.

lotnisko *n.* (= *port lotniczy*) airport; (= *lądowisko*) airfield.

lotniskowiec *mi* -wc- *Gen.* -a *wojsk., żegl.* aircraft carrier.

lotniskowy *a.* airport.

lotność *f.* **1.** *chem., fiz.* volatility. **2.** (= *zwiewność*) lightness. **3.** (= *szybkość*) swiftness. **4.** (= *polot*) sharpness, cleverness.

lotny *a.* **1.** *chem., fiz.* volatile, gaseous. **2.** (= *zwiewny*) light, airy. **3.** (= *ruchliwy*) mobile; **lotny piasek** quicksand; **lotny oddział policji** flying police squad; **lotny finisz** *sport* flying finish. **4.** (*umożliwiający latanie*) flight, flying, volant; **błona lotna** *anat., zool.* patagium. **5.** (= *inteligentny*) clever, sharp.

lotos *mi bot.* lotus (*Nelumbo*).

lotosowy *a. bot.* lotus.

lotto *n. indecl.* lotto; **grać w lotto** enter a lotto.

lottomat *mi* lotto machine.

lowelas *mp pl.* -i *l.* -y *pog.* ladies' man; flirter, flirt.

loża *f. Gen.pl.* lóż **1.** (*wyodrębnione miejsce*)

box, gallery; **loża honorowa** VIP box; **loża praso-wa** press gallery; **loża rządowa** government bench. **2.** (*jednostka organizacyjna masonerii*) lodge; **loża masońska** Masonic lodge; **należeć do loży** belong to a lodge.

lód *mi* -o- **1.** (= *zamarznięta woda*) ice; **sztucz-ny lód** artificial ice; **suchy lód** *chem.* dry ice; **ho-kej na lodzie** *sport* ice hockey; **jazda szybka na lodzie** *sport* speed skating; **jazda figurowa na lo-dzie** *sport* figure skating; **zimny jak lód** as cold as ice, ice-cold; **budować l. stawiać zamki na lodzie** build castles in the air; **mieć forsy jak lodu** have money to burn; **przełamać pierwsze lody** break the ice; **zostać na lodzie** be left out in the cold; **zostawić kogoś na lodzie** leave sb out in the cold. **2.** (= *porcja lodów*) ice cream; *por.* **lody**.

lp. *abbr. jęz.* (= *liczba pojedyncza*) sing. (*sin-gular*); (= *liczba porządkowa*) (item) no. (*(item) number*).

LSD *n. t. chem* LSD; *pot.* acid.

lśniący *a.* glittering, shining; (*włosy, sierść*) sleek, glossy; (*źrenice*) glistening; **lśniący czy-stością** spick-and-span.

lśnić *ipf.* -ij glitter, shine; (*o wodzie, brylancie, oczach*) glisten; **lśnić czystością** be spick-and-span, be spotlessly clean. ~ **się** *ipf.* glitter, shine; (*o wodzie, brylancie, oczach*) glisten.

lu *int. pot.* **1.** (*odgłos wylewanej wody*) whoosh, splash. **2.** (*odgłos uderzenia*) slap. **3.** (*zachęta do czegoś*) c'mon, let's do it; **no to lu!** bottoms up!, drink up!

lub *conj.* or; **lub też** or else.

luba *f. Gen.* -ej *żart.* (= *ukochana*) love, dear, darling, sweetheart.

lubczyk *mi bot.* lovage (*Levisticum officinale*).

lubczykowy *a. bot.* lovage.

lubiany *a.* (= *popularny*) popular; **być lubia-nym** enjoy popularity, be popular.

lubić *ipf.* **1.** (= *czuć sympatię do kogoś*) like (*kogoś* sb); (= *mieć w czymś upodobanie*) like, en-joy (*coś* sth); be fond (*coś* of sth); be keen (*coś* on sth); **(nie) lubić czegoś robić** (not) like *l.* enjoy doing *l.* to do sth, (not) be fond of doing sth; **co kto lubi** everybody to their taste. **2.** *pot.* (= *mieć zwyczaj coś robić*) be liable *l.* apt to; **historia lubi się powtarzać** history repeats itself. ~ **się** *ipf.* (*siebie*) like o.s.; (*nawzajem*) like one another.

lubieżnik *mp* lecher, wanton.

lubieżność *f.* lasciviousness, lewdness.

lubieżny *a.* lascivious, lewd, wanton; **czyn lu-bieżny** *zwł. prawn.* lewd *l.* indecent conduct.

lubo *conj. arch.* (= *chociaż*) albeit.

lubość *f.* **z lubością** *przest.* with pleasure *l.* de-light; **robić coś z lubością** take delight in (doing) sth.

lubować się *ipf.* take delight, delight (*w czymś* in sth).

luby *a. przest.* (= *przyjemny*) pleasant, likable. – *mp żart.* (= *ukochany*) love, dear, darling, sweetheart.

lucerna *f. bot.* alfalfa, lucerne (*Medicago*).

lucyfer *mp pl.* -y **1.** *rel.* Lucifer. **2.** *uj.* (= *zły człowiek*) devil, mischief-maker.

lud *mi* **1.** (*grupa społeczna*) commonalty, peo-ple; **pochodzić z ludu** be of common origin, have sb's roots in the peasantry *l.* working class. **2.** (= *plemię, wspólnota*) people; **wędrówka ludów** *hist.* wanderings *l.* migration of peoples; *przen.* droves of people (*traveling l. moving*); **lud Boży** *rel.* the People of God. **3.** *pot.* (= *tłum*) crowd.

ludek *mi Gen.* -u **1.** *iron.* (= *lud*) commonalty. **2.** (= *tłumek*) small crowd. – *mp Gen.* -a *pl.* -i (= *ludzik, figurka*) little man; (*człowiek*) little guy *l.* man.

ludno *adv.* crowdedly.

ludnościowy *a.* populational.

ludność *f.* population.

ludny *a.* crowded.

ludobójca *mp* genocide, person commiting genocide.

ludobójczy *a.* genocidal.

ludobójstwo *n.* genocide.

ludojad *ma* (*zwierzę*) man-eater; **żarłacz ludo-jad** *icht.* great white shark, man-eating shark (*Carcharodon carcharias*). – *mp* (*człowiek*) can-nibal, man-eater.

ludowiec *mp* -wc- *pl.* -y *polit.* member of a peasant party.

ludowładztwo *n.* democracy.

ludowodemokratyczny *a.* people's democratic.

ludowość *f.* folk *l.* rural *l.* country character.

ludowy *a.* **1.** (*dotyczący ludu*) people; **demo-kracja ludowa** *polit.* people's democracy; **partia ludowa** *polit.* peasant party. **2.** (= *wiejski*) folk, country; **literatura ludowa** folk literature; **muzy-ka ludowa** folk music.

ludoznawca *mp* ethnologist.

ludoznawczy *a.* ethnologic, ethnological.

ludoznawstwo *n.* ethnology.

ludożerca *mp* cannibal, man-eater.

ludożerczy *a.* cannibalistic.

ludożerstwo *n.* cannibalism.

ludwisarnia *f. Gen.pl.* -i bell foundry.

ludwisarski *a.* bell-foundry.

ludwisarstwo *n.* bell founding.

ludwisarz *mp* bell founder.

ludyczność *f. lit.* ludic character, playfulness.

ludyczny *a. lit.* ludic, playful.

ludyzm *mi lit.* ludic character; *rzad.* ludicism; playfulness.

ludzie *pl. Gen.* -i *Ins.* -mi people, persons; **lu-dzie pracy** working people; **młodzi ludzie** young people; **przy ludziach** in public; **nieszczęścia cho-dzą po ludziach** accidents happen; *pot.* shit hap-pens; **będą z ciebie ludzie** you will grow into a good person, you will make a good... (*person, teacher, student, etc.*); **wyjść na ludzi** be a decent *l.* good person; **wykierować kogoś na ludzi** help sb to be a success; *por.* **człowiek**.

ludzik *mp pl.* -i (*figurka*) little man; (*człowiek*) little guy *l.* man.

ludziska *pl. Gen.* -k *żart.* folks, people.

ludzki *a.* **1.** (*mający związek z człowiekiem*) human; **istota ludzka** human being; **rodzaj ludzki** humankind, the human race; **to przechodzi ludzkie pojęcie** this is unbelievable, it's beyond belief. **2.** (= *humanitarny*) humane; **być ludzkim dla kogoś** treat sb in a humane way; **(traktować**

kogoś) po ludzku (treat sb) in a humane way, (treat sb) kindly. **3.** (*odpowiedni dla ludzi*) appropriate, suitable; **(mieszkać itp.) po ludzku** (live, etc.) in suitable conditions.

ludzkość *f.* **1.** (= *ród ludzki*) humankind, mankind. **2.** (= *natura ludzka*) humanity, kindness.

lufa *f.* **1.** (*część broni palnej*) barrel. **2.** *pot.* (*najniższa ocena w szkole*) flunk.

lufcik *mi Gen.* **-a** window vent.

lufka *f. Gen.pl.* **-ek** *pot.* (= *prosta cygarniczka*) cigarette holder.

luft *mi* **do luftu** *pot.* good for nothing, no good.

lugier *mi* **-gr-** *Gen.* **-a** **1.** *żegl.* (*żaglowiec*) lugger. **2.** *żegl.* (*statek rybacki*) drifter.

lugrotrawler *mi Gen.* **-a** *żegl.* trawler drifter, combination lugger.

lugrowy *a. żegl.* lugger; drifter.

Luizjana *f. geogr.* Louisiana.

luk *mi* **1.** *żegl.* (*pomieszczenie na statku*) hatch. **2.** *żegl.* (*otwór w pokładzie*) hatchway, hatch.

luka *f.* **1.** (*miejsce niezapełnione*) gap, break; *form.* (= *brakujący fragment tekstu*) hiatus, lacuna; **luka prawna** *l.* **w prawie** legal loophole; **zapełnić lukę** *t. przen.* fill in a gap. **2.** (= *niedobór*) deficiency, shortcoming; **luka w pamięci** blackout.

lukier *mi* **-kr-** *kulin.* icing, frosting, glazing.

lukowy *a. żegl.* hatch.

lukratywność *f.* lucrativeness.

lukratywny *a.* lucrative, profitable.

lukrecja *f. bot.* licorice, *Br.* liquorice (*Glycyrrhiza*).

lukrecjowy *a.* licorice.

lukrować *ipf.* **1.** *kulin.* ice, frost, glaze. **2.** *przen.* (= *chwalić nadmiernie*) varnish.

lukrowy *a.* icing, frosting, glazing.

luks *mi Gen.* **-a** *fiz.* lux, meter-candle.

Luksemburczyk *mp*, **Luksemburka** *f.* Luxembourger.

Luksemburg *mi Gen.* **-a** *geogr.* Luxembourg.

Luksemburka *f. zob.* **Luksemburczyk.**

luksemburski *a.* Luxembourgian.

luksfer *mi Gen.* **-a** *bud.* glass tile, Luxfer tile.

luksomierz *mi Gen.* **-a** *fiz.* lux meter.

luksosekunda *f. fiz.* lux-second.

luksus *mi* luxury; **pozwolić sobie na luksus czegoś** afford the luxury of sth; **żyć w luksusie** *l.* **opływać w luksusy** live in the lap of luxury.

luksusowy *a.* luxury, luxurious.

lulać *ipf. pot.* (= *usypiać dziecko*) **1.** lull. **2.** *żart.* (= *spać*) (*zwł. w zwrotach do dzieci*) sleep.

lulek *mi* **-lk-** *Gen.* **-a lulek czarny** *bot.* henbane (*Hyoscyamus niger*).

luli (**laj**) *int.* bye-bye, hushaby.

lulu *int. żart.* (= *spać*) (*t. w zwrotach do dzieci*) bye-bye.

lumbago *n. indecl. pat.* lumbago, lumbar back pain.

lumen *mi Gen.* **-a** *fiz.* lumen.

lumenomierz *mi Gen.* **-a** *fiz.* lumen meter.

lumenosekunda *f. fiz.* lumen-second.

luminarz *mp emf.* luminary, personage.

luminescencja *f. fiz.* luminescence.

luminescencyjny *a. fiz.* luminescent.

luminizm *mi sztuka* luminism.

luminofor *mi fiz., chem.* luminophore, luminophor.

lump *mp pl.* **-y** *pot.* (= *człowiek z marginesu społecznego*) down-and-out, down-and-outer.

lumpenproletariacki *a. polit., socjol.* lumpenproletarian, lumpen.

lumpenproletariat *mi polit., socjol.* lumpenproletariat.

lumpenproletariusz *mp polit., socjol.* lumpenproletarian, lumpenprole.

lumpowski *a.* down-and-out.

lunacja *f. astron.* lunation, lunar month.

lunapark *mi* amusement park.

lunatyczka *f. Gen.pl.* **-ek** *zob.* **lunatyk.**

lunatyczny *a.* sleepwalking, somnambulistic.

lunatyk *mp*, **lunatyczka** *f.* sleepwalker, somnambulist.

lunatyzm *mi* sleepwalking, somnambulism.

lunąć *pf.* **1.** (*o deszczu*) pour, lash down; **lunęło** rain started lashing down, it started pouring. **2.** *pot.* (= *chlusnąć*) spurt; **lunąć wodą** spurt water. **3.** *pot.* (= *uderzyć mocno*) whack, thwack.

lunch *mi Gen.pl.* **-ów** lunch, luncheon.

luneta *f.* **1.** (*przyrząd optyczny*) telescope. **2.** *bud.* lunette.

lunit *mi astron.* lunar soil, lunar rock.

lupa *f.* magnifying glass; **brać kogoś/coś pod lupę** examine *l.* investigate sth/sb closely; **brać coś pod lupę** probe sth.

lura *f. pot.* wish-wash.

lurowaty *a. pot.* wishy-washy.

lusterko *n. Gen.pl.* **-rek** mirror; **lusterko boczne** *mot.* outside mirror; **lusterko wsteczne** *mot.* rearview mirror.

lustracja *f.* **1.** (= *kontrola*) inspection. **2.** *polit.* vetting.

lustracyjny *a.* **1.** (= *kontrolny*) inspectional. **2.** *polit.* vetting; **ustawa lustracyjna** vetting act.

lustrator *mp*, **lustratorka** *f. Gen.pl.* **-ek** **1.** (= *kontroler*) inspector. **2.** (= *zwolennik lustracji politycznej*) supporter of political vetting.

lustro *n. Gen.pl.* **-er** mirror, looking glass; **lustro weneckie** two-way mirror; **lustro wody** water level; **pić do lustra** drink alone.

lustrować *ipf.* **1.** (= *kontrolować*) inspect. **2.** *polit.* vet. **~ się** *ipf.* (= *przyglądać się bacznie jeden drugiemu*) survey each other.

lustrzanka *f. Gen.pl.* **-ek** *fot.* reflex camera.

lustrzany *a.* **1.** (= *mający związek z lustrem*) mirror; **lustrzane odbicie** mirror image. **2.** (= *błyszczący*) shining, glossy.

lut *mi techn.* solder.

luteranin *mp pl.* **-anie** *Gen.* **-anów**, **luteranka** *f. rel.* Lutheran.

luteranizm *mi rel.* Lutheranism, Lutherism.

luterański *a. rel.* Lutheran.

lutet *mi chem.* lutetium.

lutnia *f. Gen.pl.* **-i** *muz.* lute.

lutnictwo *n.* violin making.

lutniczy *a.* violin-making.

lutnik *mp* violin maker, luthier.

lutniowy *a. muz.* lute.

lutnista *mp*, **lutnistka** *f. Gen.pl.* **-ek** *muz.* lutenist; *rzad.* lutist.

lutowacz *mp techn.* solderer.

lutować *ipf. techn.* solder.

lutowina *f. techn.* soldered joint.

lutownica *f. techn.* soldering iron.

lutowniczy *a. techn.* solder, soldering; **kolba lutownicza** soldering tool; **lampa lutownicza** blowtorch.

lutowy *a.* February.

luty *mi* February.

luwers *mi żegl.* cringle.

luz *mi* **1.** (= *wolne miejsce*) (free) room, (free) space; *pot.* (= *wolny czas*) (free) time; **mam trochę luzu między zajęciami** I've got some free time between classes. **2.** *techn.* (*wolna przestrzeń między częściami urządzenia*) play, clearance. **3.** *techn.* (*odcinek ruchu jałowego*) play; **na luzie** *mot.* in neutral gear; **wrzucić luz** *mot.* shift to neutral (gear). **4.** *pot.* (= *swoboda zachowania*) ease; **luz psychiczny** freedom from anxiety; **(być) na luzie** (be) laid back, (be) free and easy.

luzak *mp pl.* **-cy** **1.** *hist.* (= *ordynans konny*) groom. **2.** *pot.* (*osoba zachowująca się swobodnie*) cool dude. – *ma pl.* **-i** (= *nieosiodłany koń*) led horse.

luzem *adv.* **1.** (= *bez obciążenia*) without any load; **prowadzić konia luzem** lead a horse. **2.** (= *bez opakowania*) loose; **kupować coś luzem** buy sth loose. **3.** (= *swobodnie*) loosely, loose; **puścić dziecko luzem** let the child loose.

luzować *ipf.* **1.** (= *zastępować*) relieve, replace (*kogoś* sb); take over (*kogoś* from sb). **2.** (= *zmniejszać naprężenie*) slacken, loosen; **luzować linę/nakrętkę** slacken a rope/nut.

luźno *adv.* loosely; **luźno zawiązany** loosely tied; **luźno wypowiedziany** said casually *l.* detachedly; **w autobusie było luźno** *pot.* the bus was not packed.

luźność *f.* looseness.

luźny *a.* **1.** (= *nieobcisły*) loose, loose-fitting. **2.** (= *niezwarty*) loose; **luźne kartki** loose pages *l.* sheets of paper; **luźna zabudowa** scattered buildings. **3.** (*o linie*) slack. **4.** (= *swobodny*) casual; **luźna uwaga** casual remark; **luźne notatki** casual notes; **luźny kontakt** occasional contacts; **luźna fabuła** loosely-constructed plot. **5.** *pot.* (*o człowieku*) (= *pozbawiony zahamowań*) cool, laid back.

lwa *itd. ma zob.* **lew.**

lwi *a.* lion('s); *form.* leonine; **lwia część** lion's share; **lwia czupryna** mane; **mieć lwie serce** be lionhearted; **mieć lwi pazur (do czegoś)** have a great talent (for sth); **lwia paszcza** *bot.* snapdragon (*Antirrhinum maius*).

lwiątko *n. Gen.pl.* **-ek** lion cub, lionet.

lwica *f.* lioness.

lwowiak *mp pot.* = **lwowianin.**

lwowianin *mp*, **lwowianka** *f.* inhabitant of Lvov.

lwowski *a.* (of) Lvov, (of) Lviv.

Lwów *mi* **-o-** *Gen.* **-a** *geogr.* Lvov, Lviv.

LWP *abbr. hist.* (= *Ludowe Wojsko Polskie*) Polish People's Army.

lycra *f.* lycra.

lżej *adv. zob.* **lekko.**

lżejszy *a. zob.* **lekki.**

lżyć *ipf.* **-yj** swear (*kogoś* at ab); revile (*kogoś* sb). **~ się** *ipf.* **-yj** swear at one another, revile one another.

J K L

Ł, ł *n. indecl.* (*litera*) L with a bar, L-bar.

Łaba *f. geogr.* the Elbe.

łabędzi *a.* (*o piórach, jeziorze*) swan; **łabędzi puch** swan's-down; **łabędzia szyja** swan-neck, swanlike neck; **łabędzi śpiew** *przen.* swansong.

łabędziarnia *f. Gen.pl.* -i *l.* -ń swannery.

łabędziątko *n. orn.* cygnet.

łabędzica *f. orn.* pen, female swan.

łabędź *ma orn.* **1.** swan (*Cygnus*); **łabędź niemy** mute swan (*C. olor*); **łabędź krzykliwy** whooper (swan) (*C. cygnus*); **łabędź mały** *l.* **czarnodzioby** tundra swan, whistling swan (*C. columbianus*); **łabędź trębacz** trumpeter swan (*C. buccinator*); (= *samiec łabędzia*) cob, male swan. **2.** *astron.* **Łabędź** Cygnus.

łac. *abbr.* (= *łaciński*) Lat. (*Latin*).

łach *mi Gen.* -a *pot.* (= *zniszczone ubranie, szmata*) rag; (= *zniszczony kawałek tkaniny*) tatter.

łacha *f.* **1.** (= *odnoga rzeki*) backwater, bayou. **2.** (= *ławica*) shoal, sandbank.

łachman *mi Gen.* -a *pot.* (= *zniszczone ubranie, szmata*) rag; (= *zniszczony kawałek tkaniny*) tatter.

łachmaniarz *mp przest.* **1.** (= *obszarpaniec*) *lit.* ragamuffin. **2.** (= *zbieracz szmat*) ragpicker.

łachmyta *f. l. mp decl. like f. Gen.pl.* -t *l.* -ów *pog.* **1.** (= *obszarpaniec*) *lit.* ragamuffin. **2.** (= *człowiek bezwartościowy*) scoundrel, scamp.

łachudra *f. l. mp decl. like f. Gen.pl.* -der *l.* -ów *pot. pog.* scoundrel, rascal, scamp.

łaciaty *a.* piebald; (*o koniu*) pinto.

łacina *f.* **1.** (= *język łaciński*) Latin. **2.** *szkoln., pot.* (= *lekcja łaciny*) Latin class *l.* lesson. **3.** *pot.* (= *przekleństwa*) swear words, cursing, foul language.

łacinka *f.* **1.** (= *pismo łacińskie*) Roman *l.* Latin alphabet. **2.** *hist.* (= *kursywa*) italics.

łacinnik *mp* **1.** (= *znawca łaciny*) Latinist, Latin scholar. **2.** (= *nauczyciel łaciny*) Latin teacher.

łaciński *a.* Latin; **alfabet łaciński** Roman *l.* Latin alphabet; **krzyż łaciński** *rel.* Latin cross; **obrządek łaciński** *rel.* Latin rite; **Ameryka Łacińska** *geogr.* Latin America.

łacińskość *n.* Latinity.

ład *mi* order; **bez ładu i składu** (= *nieporządnie*) higgledy-piggledy, pell-mell; (= *bez związku*) without rhyme or reason; **dojść z kimś do ładu** come to terms with sb; **dojść z czymś do ładu** get sth straight, straighten *l.* sort sth out; **zaprowadzić ład w czymś** order sth, put sth in order.

ładnie *adv.* **1.** (= *estetycznie*) nicely, lovely, prettily; **ładnie ci w tym swetrze** this sweater suits you well, you look nice *l.* pretty *l.* lovely in this sweater. **2.** (*o pogodzie*) nice, fine, lovely; **jest ładnie** it's nice *l.* lovely outside, (it's) beautiful *l.* nice weather. **3.** *pot.* (= *dużo*) pretty, a great deal, fairly. **4.** *iron.* (= *kiepsko*) fine, pretty; **ładnie się spisałeś!** you can be proud of yourself!, are you proud of yourself?!

ładnieć *ipf.* -eję -ejesz grow pretty.

ładniutki *a.* pretty-pretty.

ładny *a.* **1.** (= *odznaczający się urodą*) pretty, attractive, good-looking, cute, beautiful; (*o pogodzie, dniu*) nice, fine, lovely. **2.** *pot.* (= *znaczny*) pretty, fair, good, handsome; **ładny grosz** pretty penny, a nice round sum; **ładny wiek** pretty age; **ładnych parę lat** a good many years. **3.** *iron.* (= *kiepski*) fine, pretty; **ładny gips** *l.* **numer!** a pretty *l.* fine kettle of fish!, a fine trick!

ładowacz *mp* (*robotnik*) loader. – *mi Gen.* -a (*urządzenie*) loader.

ładować *ipf.* (= *obciążać ładunkiem*) load; **ładować w coś pieniądze** pump *l.* sink money into sth; (*broń*) load; (*akumulator*) charge. ~ **się** *ipf. pot.* (= *wpychać się*) force one's way, work one's way, barge (*gdzieś* into *l.* in sth); (*o akumulatorze*) be charging.

ładowarka *f. Gen.pl.* -ek **1.** (*do towarów*) loader, loading machine. **2.** (*do baterii*) (battery) charger.

ładownia *f. Gen.pl.* -i **1.** *żegl.* (cargo) hold. **2.** *kol.* loading station.

ładownica *f.* **1.** *wojsk.* (ammunition) pouch, (cartridge) pouch. **2.** *el.* (battery) charger.

ładowniczy *a.* (*o dźwigu*) loading. – *mp wojsk.* loader.

ładownik *mi Gen.* -a **1.** *wojsk.* (= *przyrząd do ładowania*) cartridge clip. **2.** *wojsk.* (*zasobnik*) cartridge holder, cartridge clip, charger clip.

ładowność *f.* load capacity, carrying capacity, cargo capacity.

ładowny *a.* capacious.

ładunek *mi* -nk- **1.** (*towary*) load, cargo, freight, shipload. **2.** (= *materiał wybuchowy*), charge; (= *bomba*) bomb, stick; *pot.* (= *nabój*) shell, cartridge. **3.** *el.* electric charge.

ładunkowy *a.* **1.** (*o urządzeniu*) loading. **2.** (*o dokumentach*) shipping.

łagier *mi* -gr- *hist.* labor camp (*in the USSR*).

łagiewka *f. Gen.pl.* -ek *anat., bot.* utricle; **łagiewka pyłkowa** *bot.* pollen tube.

łagodnie *adv.* **1.** (= *dobrotliwie*) softly, mildly, kindly, leniently. **2.** (= *delikatnie*) softly, gently, tenderly.

łagodnieć *ipf.* **1.** soften, grow milder *l.* gentler. **2.** (*o uczuciu, wietrze*) ease off, subside, relent.

łagodność *f.* **1.** (= *dobrotliwość*) gentleness, tenderness, kindness. **2.** (*klimatu*) mildness, moderateness.

łagodny *a.* **1.** (= *dobrotliwy*) gentle, mild, good-natured, suave. **2.** (*o karze*) mild, lenient. **3.** (*o dźwięku, świetle, wzgórzu*) gentle, soft, gradual; **nowotwór łagodny** *pat.* benign tumor. **4.** (= *nie żrący*) non-corrosive.

łagodzący *a.* **1.** mitigating, mitigatory, soothing, assuasive; **okoliczności łagodzące** extenuating *l.* mitigating circumstances. **2.** (= *kojący*) palliative, alleviative, lenitive.

łagodzić *ipf.* **-odź** *l.* **-ódź** **1.** (= *zażegnywać*) soothe, appease, ease. **2.** (*karę*) mitigate, moderate. **3.** (*ból, cierpienie*) alleviate, soften, relieve, assuage, palliate.

łajać *ipf.* **-ę -esz** scold, rebuke, reprimand, dress down. **~ się** *ipf.* pounce on each other *l.* one another, squabble, jump down each other's throats.

łajba *f. żegl., żart.* hooker, bucket, tub.

łajdacki *a.* scoundrelly, villainous, blackguardly.

łajdactwo *n.* scoundrelism, roguery, villainy.

łajdaczka *f. Gen.pl.* **-ek** **1.** *przest.* slut, whore, woman of easy virtue. **2.** *rzad. zob.* **łajdak.**

łajdaczyć się *ipf.* bedkop, swing, sleep around, lead a dissolute life.

łajdak *mp pl.* **-i** *l.* **-cy** scoundrel, villain, scumbag, rogue.

łajno *n. Gen.pl.* **-en** dung, manure.

łajza *f. l. mp decl. like f. Gen.pl.* **-z** *l.* **-ów** *pot.* (= *niedołęga*) oaf, gawk, galoot.

łaknąć *ipf.* **-ij** (= *pragnąć*) starve, crave, yearn (*czegoś* for sth); hunger (*czegoś* for *l.* after sth).

łaknienie *n.* **1.** (= *pragnienie*) hunger, thirst, desire, yearning. **2.** *med.* appetite, hunger.

łakocie *pl. Gen.* **-i** sweets, candies, sweetmeats, confectionery.

łakomczuch *mp pl.* **-y** gourmand, greedy-guts.

łakomić się *ipf.* feel greed (*na coś* for sth) be greedy, be avid (*na coś* of sth) covet (*na coś* sth) be tempted (*na coś* by sth).

łakomstwo *n.* gourmandism, greediness, greed.

łakomy *a.* **1.** (= *lubiący jeść*) gourmand, lickerish. **2.** (= *zachłanny*) greedy (*na coś* for sth) avaricious, avid, covetous (*na coś* of sth); **łakomy kąsek** *przen.* tasty bit, morsel, dainty.

łam *mi* column; **na łamach gazet** *l.* **pism** in the papers.

łamacz *mi Gen.* **-a** *Gen.pl.* **-y** (*maszyna*) breaker, crusher. – *mp pl.* **-y** *l.* **-ów** *druk.* maker-up, make-up hand.

łamać *ipf.* **-ę -esz** **1.** (= *kruszyć*) break, smash, crack; **łamać sobie język na czymś** twist one's tongue trying to pronounce sth; **łamać sobie głowę nad czymś** puzzle one's head over sth, rack one's brains, beat out *l.* cudgel one's brains; **ła-**

mie mnie w krzyżu *pot.* my back is killing me, I have shooting pains in my back; **łamać (pierwsze) lody** break the ice. **2.** (*opór, przeszkody*) (= *przezwyciężać*) break (down), overcome. **3.** (= *naruszać*) break, violate, transgress, infringe; (*umowę*) breach; (*zasady*) flout; (*obietnicę*) break, go back on; **łamać prawo** break the law, infringe upon the law; **łamać tradycję** fly in the face *l.* teeth of tradition. **4.** (= *zaprzepaszczać*) ruin, spoil; **łamać sobie karierę** ruin *l.* spoil one's career, bring one's career to an end. **5.** *druk.* make up. **~ się** *ipf.* **1.** (= *dzielić się*) share; **łamać się opłatkiem** share the wafer. **2.** (= *być łamanym*) break; **głos się komuś łamie** sb's voice falters. **3.** *przen.* (*o fali, świetle*) refract, be refracted. **4.** *przen.* (= *załamywać się*) break down, get depressed, go to pieces. **5.** (*o falach*) (= *rozpryskiwać się*) break. **6.** (= *wahać się*) waver, be in two minds. **7.** *pot.* (= *zamartwiać się*) eat one's heart out, fret; **nie łam się, wszystko będzie dobrze** don't worry, it's going to be fine *l.* all right.

łamaga *f. l. mp decl. like f. Gen.pl.* **-g** *l.* **-ów** *pot.* all fingers and thumbs, ham-handed person, goon.

łamany *a.* broken; **łamana angielszczyzna** broken English; **linia łamana** broken line; **akord łamany** *muz.* broken chord, arpeggio, arpeggiated chord; **7 łamane przez 26** seven stroke twenty six.

łamańce *pl. Gen.* **-ów** **1.** (= *skręty ciała*) twists, figures; **łamańce językowe** *przen.* tongue twisters. **2.** (= *zakrętasy*) flourishes, zigzag lines.

łamigłówka *f. Gen.pl.* **-ek** (*zadanie*) puzzle, brain-twister, brain-teaser, poser; *przen.* (= *skomplikowany problem*) puzzle, enigma, problem.

łamistrajk *mp pl.* **-i** strikebreaker, blackleg, fink, scab.

łamistrajkowy *a.* strikebreaker, blackleg.

łamliwość *f.* fragility, brittleness.

łamliwy *a.* breakable, brittle, fragile, frail.

łan *mi* **1.** (= *ziemia obsiana zbożem*) field. **2.** *hist.* fee, feud, fief.

łania *f. Gen.pl.* **łań** *l.* **-i** (= *samica jelenia l. daniela*) doe; hind; **dziewczyna jak łania** comely girl.

łanowy *a.* field.

łańcuch *mi Gen.* **-a** **1.** (= *szereg ogniw*) chain; **łańcuchy** (= *okowy, kajdany*) chains, shackles; **trzymać psa na łańcuchu** chain the dog up, keep the dog chained up; **zakuć w łańcuchy** clap in irons *l.* chains *l.* fetters. **2.** (*ozdoba choinkowa*) Christmas tree chain. **3.** (= *ciąg*) chain, sequence, series, succession; **łańcuch gór** *l.* **górski** mountain range *l.* chain; **łańcuch zdarzeń** sequence *l.* series *l.* chain of events; **utworzyć łańcuch** (= *ustawić się w szereg*) line up. **4.** *chem.* chain.

łańcuchowy *a.* **1.** chain; **pies łańcuchowy** watchdog, bandog; **przekładnia łańcuchowa** *techn.* chain transmission; **(linia) łańcuchowa** *geom.* catenary. **2.** *chem.* chain; **reakcja łańcuchowa** chain reaction.

łańcuszek *mi* -szk- *Gen.* -a **1.** (= *mały łańcuch*) chain; **łańcuszek szczęścia** chain letter. **2.** (*ścieg*) chain stitch.

łańcuszkowy *a.* chain; **ścieg** *l.* **haft łańcuszkowy** chain stitch, chain work.

łapa *f.* **1.** (= *noga zwierzęcia*) paw, forefoot; **daj łapę!** (*komenda do psa*) give me the paw!, shake! **2.** *pot. żart.* (= *ręka ludzka*) paw; **dawać komuś w łapę** grease *l.* oil sb's palm *l.* hand; **dostać kogoś w łapy** get sb in one's clutches; **położyć łapę na czymś** lay one's hands on sth, clap one's hand on sth; **spadać (jak kot) na cztery łapy** fall *l.* land on one's (four) feet; **żyć z kimś na kocią łapę** *pot.* shack up (with sb), play house; **precz z łapami!** hands off! **3.** *techn.* lug; arm; **łapa kotwicy** *żegl.* fluke.

łapacz *mp Gen.pl.* -y *l.* -ów **1.** *pot.* catcher. **2.** *baseball* catcher. – *mi Gen.* -a *Gen.pl.* -y **1.** *techn.* catcher; arrester; separator; collector; trap. **2.** *chem.* drip tube.

łapać *ipf.* -ę -esz **1.** (= *chwytać*) catch, seize, grasp, snatch; **łapać kogoś za słowa** *l.* **słówka** use *l.* turn sb's words against them; **łapać oddech** catch one's breath, gasp for breath; **łapać stację** *pot.* pick up a (radio) station. **2.** *pot.* (= *zatrzymywać*) catch, apprehend; **łapać złodzieja!** thief! thief!, stop the thief!; **łapać kogoś na gorącym uczynku** catch sb red-handed, catch sb in the act; **łapać kogoś na czymś** catch sb doing sth. **3.** (*o uczuciach, bólu*) catch, seize, captivate; **kurcz mnie złapał** I was seized with a cramp; **łapać grypę** catch a cold, come down with a cold. **4.** *pot.* (= *rozumieć*) catch on, follow, grasp, get the drift of; **on nic nie łapie** he doesn't follow at all, he doesn't get it. ~ **się** *ipf.* **1.** (= *chwytać się*) grasp, clutch, catch hold of; **łapać się na coś** be deceived by sth, be led down the garden path; **łapać się na czymś** catch o.s. doing sth; **łapać się za jakieś zajęcie** take up an occupation; **łapać się za głowę** clutch one's head. **2.** (*o zwierzętach*) (= *dawać się schwytać*) fall into traps/snares/nets, get caught.

łapanka *f. Gen.pl.* -ek *zwł. hist.* roundup, raid.

łapcie *pl. Gen.* -i slippers.

łapczywie *adv.* greedily, avidly, ravenously, voraciously.

łapczywość *f.* greed, greediness, avidity.

łapczywy *a.* greedy (*na coś* for sth) avid, desirous (*na coś* of sth).

łapiduch *mp pl.* -y *przest., żart.* pill-pusher, doc.

łapka *f. Gen.pl.* -ek **1.** (= *mała łapa*) paw; **kurze łapki** (= *zmarszczki wokół oczu*) crow's feet; **służyć** *l.* **skakać przed kimś na dwóch łapkach** *przen.* wait upon sb's hand and foot, dance attendance on sb, cringe to *l.* before sb. **2.** (= *packa*) (fly) swatter. **3.** (= *pułapka na zwierzęta*) trap, snare; **łapka na myszy** mousetrap.

łapownictwo *n.* bribery, corruption.

łapowniczy *a.* bribery.

łapownik *mp* briber.

łapówa *f. pot.* bribe, soap; *Br.* bung.

łapówka *f. Gen.pl.* -ek *pot.* bribe, payola, hush money; **brać łapówkę** take *l.* accept a bribe; **da-**

wać łapówkę bribe sb, grease *l.* oil sb's palm, grease the wheels.

łapówkarstwo *n.* bribery, corruption.

łapówkarz *mp* briber, grafter, itching palm.

łapówkowy *a.* (of a) bribe.

łapserdak *mp pl.* -i *pog.* **1.** *przest.* ragamuffin. **2.** (= *łobuz, łotr*) scoundrel, rogue.

łapsko *n.* paw, mutton-fist, mitt.

łapu-capu *adv.* helter-skelter; **na łapu-capu** helter-skelter, slap-dash, hurry-scurry.

łasica *f.* **1.** *zool.* weasel (*Mustela*). **2.** **łasice** (= *futro z łasic*) weasel fur coat.

łasić się *ipf.* **łaszę łasisz** (*o zwierzętach*) fawn; *przen.* (*o ludziach*) fawn (*do kogoś* over sb) cringe, toady (*do kogoś* to sb).

łaska *f.* **1.** (= *przychylność*) favor, grace, goodwill; **zaskarbić sobie czyjąś łaskę** win sb's favor; **bez łaski** *l.* **łaski bez!** *pot.* I can do without it!, big deal!; **co łaska** any amount is appreciated, I leave it to your generosity; **z łaski swojej** *l.* **jeśli łaska** if you please; **artysta z bożej łaski** (= *utalentowany artysta*) born artist; (= *amator*) amateur (artist); **a pomóc mi nie łaska?** *pot.* you're not gonna help me?; **być u kogoś w łaskach** be in favor with sb, be in sb's good graces; **być zdanym na łaskę losu** be at the mercy of fortune *l.* fate; **być na łasce kogoś/czegoś** be at the mercy of sb/sth; **robić coś z łaski** *pot.* do sth grudgingly *l.* reluctantly; **wkraść się** *l.* **wkupić się w czyjeś łaski** worm o.s. into sb's favor, ingratiate o.s. with sb. **2.** (= *ułaskawienie*) pardon, amnesty; **prawo łaski** *prawn.* power of pardon; **w drodze łaski** (= *przez złagodzenie kary*) by act of pardon; (= *wyjątkowo*) as an exception, exceptionally; **w niełasce** in sb's black books, in sb's bad graces. **3.** *rel.* grace, divine *l.* God's grace; **stan łaski** state of grace.

łaskawca *mp iron.* philanthropist.

łaskawie *adv.* **1.** (= *życzliwie*) kindly, favorably, amicably. **2.** (*w zwrotach grzecznościowych*) if you please, will you please; **czy mógłbyś mi łaskawie pomóc?** would you be so kind as to help me?, would you kindly help me?

łaskawość *f.* graciousness, kindness, benevolence, benignity.

łaskawy *a.* (*np. o uśmiechu*) favorable, benignant, encouraging; (*o losie*) favorable, propitious; (*o klimacie*) mild; **bądź łaskaw mi pomóc** be so kind and help me.

łaskotać *ipf.* -czę *l.* -cę -czesz *l.* -cesz, -cz tickle, titillate.

łaskotki *pl. Gen.* -ek tickles; **mieć łaskotki** be ticklish.

łaskotliwy *a.* ticklish.

łasować *ipf.* eat/drink on the sly.

łasuch *mp pl.* -y gourmand, sweet-toothed person.

łasy *a.* greedy (*na coś* for sth) fond, avid (*na coś* of sth).

łasza *f. Gen., Dat., Loc.* -szy *zool.* (= *jakikolwiek drapieżnik z rodziny Viverridae*) viverrine civet (cat).

łaszczyć się *ipf.* covet (*na coś* sth) hunger (*na coś* after sth).

łaszek *mi* **-szk-** *Gen.* **-a** *pot.* garment, tog.

łata[1] *f.* **1.** (= *naszyty kawałek czegoś*) patch, scrap, mend; **przypiąć komuś łatę** *l.* **łatkę**, put a black mark on sb. **2.** (*u zwierząt*) spot, speckle, stain; **brązowy pies w białe łaty** white-spotted brown dog, brown dog with white spots.

łata[2] *f.* **1.** *bud.* lath, batten, scantling. **2.** *miern.* (measuring) staff, (measuring) rod.

łatać *ipf.* **1.** (= *przyszywać łaty*) patch; (*buty*) cobble. **2.** (= *naprawiać*) patch (up), repair, mend. **3.** *przen.* patch up; **łatać budżet** patch up a *l.* the budget.

łatanina *f.* **1.** (= *rzecz połatana*) patchwork, patching up. **2.** *przen.* (= *partactwo*) bungle, botch, botched *l.* bungled job.

łatka *f. Gen.pl.* **-ek** *zob.* **łata**[1].

łatwiutki *a.* easy-peasy, awfully *l.* dead easy.

łatwizna *f.* **1.** cutting corners; **iść na łatwiznę** cut corners, follow *l.* choose the line of least resistance. **2.** (= *łatwa rzecz*) piece of cake, cinch, pushover.

łatwo *adv.* **1.** (= *bez trudu*) easily, effortlessly, without difficulty; **nie jest jej łatwo** she's having a hard time. **2.** (= *szybko*) readily, soon; **łatwo się męczyć** tire quickly.

łatwopalność *f.* inflammability, flammability.

łatwopalny *a.* inflammable, flammable, combustible.

łatwość *f.* **1.** (= *brak trudności*) ease, facility; **z łatwością** easily, with ease, with one's eyes closed. **2.** (= *zrozumiałość*) clarity.

łatwowierność *f.* gullibility, credulity.

łatwowierny *a.* gullible, credulous, overtrusting.

łatwy *a.* **1.** (= *niewymagający trudu*) easy, simple; **łatwy chleb** easy money; **łatwa kobieta** easy woman; **łatwy w obsłudze** (*maszyna*) easy to use; *komp.* user friendly. **2.** (= *bezkonfliktowy*) agreeable, relaxed, easy; **człowiek łatwy w pożyciu** easygoing person. **3.** (= *osiągnięty bez rzetelnej pracy*) effortless.

ława *f.* **1.** (*siedzenie*) bench; **ława przysięgłych** *prawn.* jury, petit *l.* petty *l.* common *l.* traverse *l.* trial jury; **ława oskarżonych** *prawn.* dock; **na ławie oskarżonych** in the dock; **ława szkolna** school desk; **ława poselska** parliamentary bench; **wyłożyć kawę na ławę** *l.* kawa na ławę lay it on the line, talk turkey. **2.** (*stolik*) coffee table. **3.** (= *zwarty szereg*) compact mass, close array.

ławą *adv.* in a mass, in streams, in their dozens.

ławeczka *f. Gen.pl.* **-ek** **1.** (= *mała ława*) (small) bench, (long) seat. **2.** *sport* bench.

ławica *f.* **1.** (= *mielizna*) sandbank, shoal, shallow. **2.** (= *grupa zwierząt morskich*) shoal, school; *przen.* (*chmur itp.*) bank. **3.** *geol.* stratum, bed.

ławicowy *a.* (= *dotyczący ławicy ryb*) shoal, school.

ławka *f. Gen.pl.* **-ek** (*w parku*) bench; (*w szkole*) desk; (*w kościele*) pew; **ośla ławka** *przest.* dunce's bench; **ławka bosmańska** *żegl.* boatswain's chair, bo'sun's chair; **ławka kar** *ho-*

kej penalty box; **ławka rezerwowych** *sport* (substitute) bench.

ławkowiec *mi* **-wc-** *Gen.* **-a** paintbrush.

ławniczy *a. prawn.* juror's.

ławnik *mp prawn.* juror.

łazanka *f. Gen.pl.* **-ek** *kulin.* fettuccine.

łazarz *mp Gen.pl.* **-y** *l.* **-ów** down-and-out(er), beggar, pauper.

łazęga *f. l. mp decl. like f. Gen.pl.* **-g** *l.* **-ów** *pot.* (= *osoba lubiąca się włóczyć*) vagrant, vagabond, tramp. – *f. Gen.pl.* **-g** (= *włóczenie się*) wandering.

łazęgować *ipf.* wander, rove.

łazić *ipf.* **1.** *pot.* (= *chodzić*) walk; *pot.* (= *wlec się*) drag on. **2.** (= *wspinać się*) climb (*po czymś* sth).

łazienka *f. Gen.pl.* **-ek** bathroom.

łazienkowy *a.* bathroom.

łazik *mp pl.* **-i** (= *włóczęga*) vagrant, tramp, rover, loiterer. – *mi Gen.* **-a** (*samochód*) Jeep, all-terrain vehicle.

łazikować *ipf.* rove, loiter, ramble.

łaźnia *f. Gen.pl.* **-i** **1.** (= *zakład kąpielowy*) baths, bathhouse; **łaźnia rzymska** Turkish bath; **sprawić komuś łaźnię** give sb a (sound) thrashing. **2.** *chem.* bath.

łączący *a.* **1.** conjunctive, connective. **2.** *gram.* conjunctive; **tryb łączący** *gram.* subjunctive.

łącze *n. Gen.pl.* **-y** *techn.* link, connection.

łączeń *ma Gen.* **-cznia** *bot.* flowering rush (*Butomus umbellatus*).

łączka *f. Gen.pl.* **-ek** *zob.* **łąka**; **ośla łączka** *narty* bunny hill, nursery slope.

łączliwość *f.* connectivity.

łączliwy *a.* connective, conjunct.

łączniarka *f. Gen.pl.* **-ek** *tk.* doubler.

łącznica *f. tel.* switchboard; **łącznica kolejowa** *kol.* (railway) siding.

łączniczka *f. Gen.pl.* **-ek** *zob.* **łącznik**[1].

łącznie *adv.* all in, including, inclusively, cumulatively; **pisać coś łącznie** spell *l.* write sth as one word; **łącznie ze mną** me included, including me.

łącznik[1] *mp pl.* **-cy** *wojsk.* messenger; (*zmotoryzowany*) dispatch rider.

łącznik[2] *mi Gen.* **-a** *pl.* **-i** **1.** (= *to, co łączy*) link, copula, tie, connective. **2.** (*znak graficzny*) hyphen. **3.** *bud.* connecting passage(way) (*between two buildings*). **4.** *jęz.* copula, linking verb. **5.** *muz.* tie.

łącznikowy *a.* linking, connective; *jęz.* copulative; **oficer łącznikowy** *wojsk.* liasion officer.

łącznościowiec *mp* **-wc-** *Voc.* **-cu** *l.* **-y** **1.** *pot.* (= *pracownik telekomunikacji*) telecommunications worker. **2.** *wojsk.* communications specialist.

łącznościowy *a.* (of) (tele)communications; **satelita łącznościowy** (tele)communications satellite.

łączność *f.* **1.** (= *kontakt*) contact; (= *wspólnota*) unity; **nawiązać łączność z kimś/czymś** make *l.* establish contact with sb/sth; **stracić łączność z kimś/czymś** lose contact with sb/sth; **utrzymy-**

wać (stałą) łączność z kimś/czymś keep in touch with sb/sth, be in contact with sb/sth. **2.** (*dział komunikacji*) communications, telecommunications; **łączność satelitarna** satellite communications. **3.** *wojsk.* communications units.

łącznotkankowy *a.* *biol.* (of) connective tissue.

łączny *a.* **1.** (= *wspólny*) total; **pisownia łączna** unhyphenated spelling; **w łącznej punktacji prowadzi Polak** Pole is in the lead in the overall standings. **2.** (= *taki, który łączy*) connective, conjunctional, conjunctive; **tkanka łączna** *biol.* connective tissue.

łączyć *ipf.* **1.** (= *spajać*) join, unite, couple; (*drogę, linię*) connect, join; **nic nas z sobą nie łączy** we're perfect strangers, there's nothing between us; **łączyć w sobie** combine various characteristics *l.* traits. **2.** (= *umożliwiać rozmowę telefoniczną*) connect, put through; **łączę z dyrektorem!** I'm putting you through to the director! **3.** (= *dopuszczać zwierzęta do spółkowania*) mate. **4.** (= *mieszać*) mix, blend; **łączę pozdrowienia** (*w liście*) (with) kind *l.* best regards; **łączyć przyjemne z pożytecznym** combine business with pleasure. **~ się** *ipf.* **1.** (= *stanowić całość*) be joined; (*o dłoniach, gałęziach*) meet, join; (*o drogach, rzekach*) merge. **2.** (= *uzyskiwać połączenie*) get a connection. **3.** (*o zwierzętach*) (= *łączyć się w pary*) mate. **4.** (= *kojarzyć się*) be associated *l.* connected, associate (*z czymś* with sth). **5.** (= *jednoczyć się*) unite; **proletariusze wszystkich krajów, łączcie się!** proletarians of all countries, unite! **6.** *chem.* combine.

łąka *f.* meadow, grassland, lea.

łąkarski *a.* (of) meadow cultivation.

łąkarstwo *n.* meadow cultivation.

łąkarz *mp* meadow cultivation specialist.

łąkowy *a.* meadow.

łątka *f. Gen.pl.* **-ek** *ent.* demoiselle, damselfly (*Agrion*).

łeb *mi* **łb-** *Gen.* **-a** *Dat.* **-u** **1.** (= *głowa zwierzęcia*) head, frontlet; **kocie łby** cobblestones. **2.** *pot.* (= *głowa ludzka*) pate; **łeb w łeb** neck and neck, nip and tuck; **na łeb, na szyję** headlong, headfirst, hurry-scurry; **coś wzięło w łeb** sth has fizzled out, sth has ended in smoke; **brać się za łby** come to grips, come to loggerheads; **palnąć sobie w łeb** blow one's brains out; *pot.* (= *rozum*) brains, head; **ten to ma łeb** he has the brains, he's a man of brains; **kłaść coś komuś do łba** drive sth home. **3.** (*zakończenie śruby itp.*) head.

łebek *mi* **-bk-** *Gen.* **-a** **1.** *zob.* **łeb** 1, 2; **od łebka** per head *l.* person, each; **wziąć kogoś na łebka** give sb a lift; **robić coś po łebkach** scratch the surface of sth, scamp, do sth superficially *l.* cursorily *l.* perfunctorily. **2.** *iron.* (= *chłopak*) lad, youth. **3.** (*zakończenie szpilki itp.*) head.

łebski *a. pot.* brainy, clever.

łechtaczka *f. Gen.pl.* **-ek** *anat.* clitoris.

łechtać *ipf.* **-czę** *l.* **-cę** *l.* **-am** **-czesz** *l.* **-cesz** *l.* **-asz, -cz** *l.* **-aj** **1.** (= *łaskotać*) tickle, titillate. **2.** (= *pochlebiać*) flatter, coax (*sb*); **łechtać czyjąś próżność** tickle *l.* flatter sb's vanity.

łepek *mi* **-pk-** *Gen.* **-a** = **łebek**.

łepetyna *f. żart.* bean.

łez *f. zob.* **łza**.

łezka *f. Gen.pl.* **-ek** *zob.* **łza**; **z łezką w oku** with a tear in one's eye, sentimentally; **historia z łezką** tearjerking story, tearjerker.

łęg *mi* marshy meadow, fen; *Br.* carr.

łęgowy *a.* marshy, swampy; **las łęgowy** riparian *l.* riverine forest.

łęk *mi* **1.** (*część siodła*) pommel; (*przedni*) saddlebow; (*tylny*) cantle. **2.** *bud.* arch. **3.** *geol.* syncline. **4.** *sport* pommel; **koń z łękami** pommel horse.

łękotka, łąkotka *f. Gen.pl.* **-ek** *anat.* meniscus.

łęty, łęciny *pl. roln., ogr.* tops, haulm.

łgać *ipf.* **łżę łżesz, łżyj** *pot.* lie, tell lies.

łgarski *a.* lying, mendacious.

łgarstwo *n. pot.* lie, mendacity; (= *kłamanie, skłonność do kłamania*) mendacity.

łgarz *mp pot.* liar.

łkać *ipf.* sob, weep, whimper, snivel.

łkanie *n.* sobbing, whimper.

łoboda *f. Dat., Loc.* **-odzie** *bot.* saltbush, orach (*Atriplex*).

łobuz *mp pl.* **-y** **-i** **1.** (= *urwis*) urchin. **2.** (= *łajdak*) scoundrel, scalawag, scamp.

łobuzeria, łobuzerka *f. Gen.* **-ii** gang *l.* band of rascals; rascals, scoundrels (*collectively*).

łobuzerski *a.* **1.** (= *filuterny*) playful, impish, mischievous. **2.** (= *chuligański*) roguish, raffish.

łobuzerstwo *n.* roguery, rascality, devilment.

łobuziak *mp pl.* **-i** *pot.* scamp.

łobuzować *ipf.* be up to mischief, play pranks.

łobuzowaty *a.* scampish, mischievous.

łochynia *f. Gen.* **-ni** *bot.* bog billberry (*Vaccinium uliginosum*).

łodyga *f.* stalk, stem.

łodygowy *a.* of or pertaining to stem *l.* stalk; *bot.* cauline.

łodyżka *f. Gen.pl.* **-ek** (little) stem, (little) stalk.

łodzi *itd. f. zob.* **łódź**.

łodzik *ma zool.* nautilus (*Nautilus*).

łodziowy *a.* boat; **wodnosamolot łodziowy** *lotn.* flying boat.

łoić *ipf.* **łój** **1.** *pot.* wallop; **łoić komuś skórę** *przen.* tan sb's hide. **2.** *pot.* (= *pić alkohol*) booze.

łojotok *mi pat.* seborrhea.

łojowaty *a.* tallowy.

łojowy *a.* tallowy; *fizj.* sebaceous; **gruczoły łojowe** *anat.* sebaceous glands.

łoju *itd. mi zob.* **łój**.

łokciowy *a. anat.* elbow, ulnar, cubital; **nerw łokciowy** ulnar nerve; **staw łokciowy** elbow joint.

łokieć *mi* **-kci-** *Gen.* **-a** **1.** (*część ręki*) elbow; **rozpychać się łokciami** (**w tłumie**) elbow one's way (through the crowd); **urabiać sobie ręce po łokcie** work one's fingers to the bone. **2.** *arch.* (*miara długości*) (= *17-22 cali*) cubit; (= *ok. 45 cali*) ell.

łom *mi* **1.** (= *drąg stalowy*) crowbar; (*krótki, zwł. złodziejski*) jimmy; **podważać coś łomem**

crowbar sth; jimmy sth. **2.** (= *cios skalny*) ashlar. **3.** (= *złom, zwł. metalowy*) scrap.

łomot *mi* (= *głuchy odgłos*) thud, thump; (= *dudnienie*) rumble; (= *huk*) bang; (= *hałas*) din; **łomot serca** heart throb.

łomotać *ipf.* **-czę** *l.* **-cę -czesz** *l.* **-cesz, -cz** (= *hałasować*) knock; (*o sercu*) throb; **łomotać do drzwi/w ścianę** bang *l.* hammer on the door/wall.

łono *n. poet.* (= *pierś*) bosom; (= *podołek*) lap; *anat.* womb; **na łonie natury** in the open; **na łonie rodziny** in the bosom of one's family, en famille; **przenieść się na łono Abrahama** *żart.* meet one's Maker.

łonowy *a. zwł. anat.* pubic; **kość łonowa** pubic bone; **wesz łonowa** *ent.* crab louse, pubic louse (*Phthirius pubis*); **włosy łonowe** pubic hair, pubes; **wzgórek łonowy** mons pubis; (*u kobiet*) mons veneris.

łopata *f.* **1.** (*do przerzucania*) shovel; (*do kopania*) spade; **kłaść łopatą do głowy** explain in the simplest terms. **2.** (= *ilość mieszcząca się na łopacie*) shovelful; spadeful. **3.** *górn.* (*ładowarki*) loading head. **4.** (*wirnika, śmigła*) blade.

łopatka *f. Gen.pl.* **-ek 1.** (= *mała łopata*) scoop; (*w kuchni*) spatula; (*ogrodnicza*) trowel. **2.** *anat., zool.* shoulder blade, scapula; **położyć kogoś na (obie) łopatki** pin sb's shoulders to the ground; *przen.* floor sb. **3.** *zwł. kulin.* (= *przednia ćwiartka zwierzęcia*) shoulder. **4.** (*wirnika*) blade; *żegl.* (*koła łopatkowego*) paddle.

łopatkowy *a.* **1.** *anat., zool.* scapular. **2.** (= *o kształcie łopatki*) spatular; **koło łopatkowe** *żegl.* paddle wheel.

łopatologia *f. Gen.* **-ii** *żart.* explanations for dummies.

łopatologicznie *a. żart.* in the simplest possible terms; **tłumaczyć coś łopatologicznie** explain sth in the simplest terms.

łopian *mi bot.* burdock (*Arctium*).

łopot *mi* flap, flutter.

łopotać *ipf.* **-cze** *l.* **-ce** flap, flutter.

łopuch *mi Gen.* **-a** *l.* **-u** *zob.* łopian.

łopucha *f. bot.* wild radish, jointed charlock (*Raphanus raphanistrum*).

łosi, łosiowy *a.* (= *dotyczący łosia*) moose; *Br.* elk; **łosiowa skóra** moose skin; **łosie rogi** moose antlers; *bot.* (*paproć*) stag-horn fern, elk-horn fern (*Platycerium*).

łoskot *mi* bang, boom, crash, dump; (*burzy, wybuchów*) roll, peal; (*pociągu*) clatter, rumble.

łoskotać *ipf.* **-czę** *l.* **-cę -czesz** *l.* **-cesz, -cz** rumble, bang, clatter.

łososiowy *a.* **1.** (= *dotyczący łososia*) salmon. **2.** (= *koloru mięsa łososia*) salmon (pink).

łosoś *ma* **1.** *icht.* salmon (*Salmo*); **łosoś pacyficzny** Pacific salmon (*Oncorhynchus*). **2.** *kulin.* **łosoś wędzony** lox.

łosza *f. myśl.* moose cow; *Br.* elk cow.

łoszak *ma* moose calf; *Br.* elk calf.

łoś *ma zool.* moose; *Br.* elk (*Alces alces*).

łotewski *a.* Latvian; (*o języku*) Latvian, Lettish.

łotr *mp pl.* **-ry** *l.* **-rzy** scoundrel; **łotr spod ciemnej gwiazdy** blackhearted villain.

łotrostwo *n.* knavery.

łotrowski *a.* knavish, scoundrelly.

Łotwa *f. geogr.* Latvia.

Łotysz *mp Gen.pl.* **-y** *l.* **-ów, Łotyszka** *f. Gen.pl.* **-ek** Latvian, *przest.* Lett.

łowca *mp* hunter; **łowca głów** headhunter; **łowca posagów** fortune hunter.

łowczy *a.* hunting; **ptak łowczy** hawking bird. — *mp* **1.** (= *urzędnik związku łowieckiego*) gamekeeper. **2.** *hist.* Master of the Royal Hunt.

łowczyni *f. Gen.pl.* **-ń** *zob.* łowca.

łowicki *a.* of or pertaining to Łowicz.

łowić *ipf.* **łów 1.** (= *łapać zwierzęta*) hunt, catch, chase; **łowić ryby** fish, hook; **łowić ryby w mętnej wodzie** *przen.* fish in troubled waters. **2.** (= *natężać uwagę*) heed, be heedful; **łowić dźwięki** strain one's ears to catch sounds; **łowić coś wzrokiem** watch for sth.

łowiecki *a.* hunting; **sezon łowiecki** open season; **teren łowiecki** game preserve.

łowiectwo *n.* hunting, game shooting.

łowisko *n. ryb.* fishery, fishing ground.

łowność *f.* hunting ability.

łowny *a.* game; **zwierzyna łowna** *myśl.* game; **łowny kot** good mouser; **ptak łowny** *myśl.* game bird.

łowy *pl. Gen.* **-ów** *por.* łów; *lit.* chase, hunt; **bezkrwawe łowy** wildlife photography; **wyruszyć na łowy** go hunting.

łoza *f. Gen.pl.* **łóz 1.** *bot.* grey willow (*Salix cinerea*). **2.** (= *zarośla wierzbowe*) osier clump. **3.** (= *witka wierzbowa*) osier, withe.

łoże *n. Gen.pl.* **łóż 1.** (= *duże łóżko*) bed; **łoże z baldachimem** four-poster bed; **z nieprawego łoża** adulterine, bastard, illegitimate, born out of wedlock; **na łożu śmierci** on one's deathbed. **2.** *techn.* bed; cradle; (*działa, silnika*) mounting; **łoże karabinu** *wojsk.* (gun)stock.

łożnica *f. przest.* chamber.

łożyć *ipf.* **łóż** lay out (*na coś* on sth) provide (*na coś* for sth).

łożysko *n.* **1.** (= *koryto rzeki*) riverbed. **2.** *anat.* placenta. **3.** *techn.* bearing.

łożyskowy *a.* **1.** (*o ssaku*) placental, placentary. **2.** (*o pierścieniu, stopie*) bearing.

łódka *f. Gen.pl.* **-ek** boat.

łódź *f.* **-o-** *pl.* **-e** boat; **łódź latająca** *lotn.* flying boat; **łódź motorowa** motorboat; **łódź podwodna** submarine; **łódź ratunkowa** lifeboat; **łódź wycieczkowa** pleasure boat; **łódź żaglowa** sailboat; *Br.* sailing boat.

łój *mi* **-o-** **1.** (= *tłuszcz*) (*przemysłowy*) tallow; (*jadalny*) suet. **2.** *fizj.* (*wydzielina*) sebum.

łów *mi* **-o-** chase, hunt, hunting.

łóżeczko *n. Gen.pl.* **-ek 1.** (small) bed. **2.** (= *łóżko dla niemowlaka l. małego dziecka*) crib; *Br.* cot.

łóżko *n. Gen.pl.* **-ek** bed; **łóżko polowe** cot, camp bed; **łóżko piętrowe** bunk bed; **w nogach łóżka** at the foot of the bed; **być przykutym do łóżka** be bedridden; **iść z kimś do łóżka** *pot.* go to bed with sb, sleep with sb.

łóżkowy *a. pot.* (= *dotyczący seksu*) bedroom.

łubianka *f. Gen.pl.* **-ek** chip basket; *Br.* trug.

łubin *mi bot.* lupine; *Br.* lupin (*Lupinus*).

łubinowy *a.* lupine.

łubki *pl. Gen.* **-ów** *med.* splints.

łubu-du *int. pot.* thumpety thump.

łuczek *mi* **-czk-** *Gen.* **-u** *l.* **-a** *zob.* **łuk** 1, 2.

łucznictwo *n. sport* archery.

łuczniczka *f. Gen.pl.* **-ek** *zob.* **łucznik** 1.

łuczniczy *a.* archery; archer's, toxophilitic.

łucznik *mp* 1. *hist., wojsk., sport* archer, bow-man. 2. *hist.* (*rzemieślnik*) bowyer.

łuczywo *n.* resinous chip.

łudząco *adv.* deceptively, delusively; **być łudząco podobnym do kogoś** be a spitting image of sb.

łudzić *ipf.* beguile; **łudzić (kogoś) obietnicami** shower (sb) with promises. **~ się** *ipf.* deceive o.s., delude o.s.; **łudzić się, że...** labor under the illusion *l.* delusion that...

ług *mi* 1. *techn., chem.* lye. 2. (*do prania*) lye; *Br.* buck.

ługoodporny *a. techn.* lyeproof, alkali-resisting.

ługować *ipf.* 1. *chem.* leach, lixiviate. 2. *tk.* boil in lye.

ługownik *mi techn.* lye vat, extraction apparatus.

łuk *mi* 1. (= *krzywizna*) curve, arc, arch; **łuk brwiowy** eyebrow ridge; **łuk elektryczny** *el.* electric arc; **zatoczyć łuk** curve; **obejść łukiem** circumvent, bypass, go around; **wygiąć się w łuk** arch, bow. 2. (*broń*) bow; **strzelać z łuku** shoot with a bow. 3. *bud.* arch; **łuk przyporowy** flying buttress; **łuk triumfalny** triumphal arch. 4. *mat.* arc. 5. *muz.* tie, ligature. 6. *narty* turn.

łukować *ipf. żegl.* swing.

łukowato *adv.* curvedly, arcuately.

łukowaty *a.* arcuate, curved.

łukowy *a.* 1. (*o kształcie*) arched, curved. 2. *bud.* (*sklepienie*) arch. 3. *el.* arc; **lampa łukowa** arc lamp; **piec łukowy** arc furnace. 4. *geom.* arc.

łuna *f.* glow, afterglow.

łunochod *mi* lunar vehicle.

łup[1] *mi* (= *zdobycz wojenna*) booty, loot, pillage, plunder; **paść łupem kogoś/czegoś** fall prey to sb/sth.

łup[2] *int.* bang! whang!

łupać *ipf.* **-ę -esz** 1. *pot.* (*o bólu*) kill; **łupie mnie w krzyżu** I have shooting pains in my back, my back is killing me. 2. (= *rozszczepiać*) split, chip, crack, cleave; **łupać orzechy** crack nuts; **epoka** *l.* **okres kamienia łupanego** *archeol.* Paleolithic (period). **~ się** *ipf.* split, chip, crack, fissure.

łuparka *f. Gen.pl.* **-ek** *techn.* splitting machine.

łupek *mi* **-pk-** *geol.* schist, slate.

łupiarka *f. Gen.pl.* **-ek** *techn.* splitting machine.

łupić *ipf.* 1. (= *grabić*) pillage, plunder, loot. 2. (= *wykorzystywać materialnie*) rip off, flay; **łupić kogoś ze skóry** bleed sb white *l.* dry, rip sb off. 3. *przen.* (= *zadawać klęskę*) beat; **łupić w karty** *pot.* play cards.

łupieski *a. przest.* pillaging, predatory.

łupiestwo *n.* pillage.

łupież *mi* 1. *pat.* dandruff. 2. (= *płatki łuszczącego się naskórka*) scurf.

łupieżca *mp przest.* looter, pillager, plunderer, despoiler.

łupieżczy *a. przest.* predatory.

łupina *f.* 1. (= *skórka owocu*) peel, skin, hull; (*np. kukurydzy*) husk; (*np. arbuza, melona, cytryny*) rind; (*twarda*) shell; **łupina orzecha** nutshell; *przen.* (= *mała łódka*) cockleshell, tiny boat. 2. *bud.* shell construction.

łupinka *f. Gen.pl.* **-ek** (= *cienka, mała łupina*) thin peel *l.* skin; *przen.* (= *łódeczka*) cockleshell.

łupinowy *a. bud.* shell; **konstrukcja łupinowa** shell construction.

łupkowatość *f. geol.* schistosity.

łupkowaty *a. geol.* schistose, schistous.

łupkowy *a. geol.* schistose, schistous.

łupliwość *f. min.* cleavage, fissility.

łupliwy *a.* cleavable, fissile.

łupnąć *pf.* **-ij** 1. *zob.* **łupać.** 2. *pot.* (= *walnąć*) bang; **łupnąć komuś karę** inflict a fine on sb. 3. *pot.* (= *wystrzelić z hukiem*) shoot. **~ się** *pf. pot.* (= *uderzyć się*) knock o.s., bash o.s.

łupnia, łupień *mi pot.* (*tylko w wyrażeniach*) **dać komuś łupnia** crump sb, give sb a pasting; **dostać (od kogoś) łupnia** get a pasting (from sb), get a licking (from sb).

łupu-cupu *int.* whip-whop.

łuska *f. Gen.pl.* **-ek** 1. *zool.* scale. 2. *bot.* (= *okrywa*) hull, shell, husk, scutellum; **łuska spadła mi z oczu** scales fell from my eyes. 3. *bot.* (*liść*) scale, bud scale. 4. *geol.* flake, broken fold. 5. *med.* squama, scale; **rybia łuska** *pat.* ichthyosis, fish skin disease. 6. *wojsk.* (*część naboju*) shell, cartridge. 7. *hist., wojsk.* (*w zbroi*) scale.

łuskać *ipf.* husk; shell; hull; peel; shuck.

łuskiewnik *mi Gen.* **-a** *bot.* toothwort (*Lathraea*).

łuskoskóre *pl. decl. like a. zool.* (*rząd gadów*) lizards and snakes (*Squamata*).

łuskowaty *a.* husky; scaly; *zool.* sclerous.

łuskowiec *ma* **-wc-** 1. *orn.* pine grosbeak (*Pinicola enucleator*). 2. *zool.* (= *ssak z rzędu Pholidota*) pangolin, scaly anteater.

łuszczaki *pl. orn.* (*rodzina ptaków*) finches (*Fringillidae*).

łuszczarka *f. Gen.pl.* **-ek** 1. *techn.* (= *tokarka do prętów*) bar turning machine, bar turner. 2. *techn.* (= *maszyna do otrzymywania łuszczki*) veneer slicer. 3. *techn.* (= *maszyna do obłuskiwania ziarna*) hulling machine.

łuszczarnia *f. Gen.pl.* **-i** *techn.* pearling mill.

łuszczka *f. Gen.pl.* **-ek** *techn.* veneer.

łuszczyca *f. pat.* psoriasis.

łuszczycowy *a. pat.* psoriatic.

łuszczyć *ipf.* 1. = **łuskać.** 2. *techn.* (= *odzierać z kory*) decorticate, debark. **~ się** *ipf.* flake, scale; (*o naskórku, skórze*) desquamate; (*o farbie, korze*) peel off.

łuszczyna *f. bot.* silique.

łut *mi hist., miern.* half an ounce; **łut szczęścia** a bit *l.* stroke of luck.

łuza *f. bilard* pocket; **wbijać do łuzy** pocket.

łuzowy *a. bilard* pocket; **bilard łuzowy** pocket billiards.

Łużyce *pl. geogr.* Lusatia.

łużycki *f.* Lusatian; (*język*) Sorbian, Wendish; **kultura łużycka** *archeol.* Lusatian Culture, Lausitz Culture.

łycha *f.* large spoon; ladle.

łyczek *mi* -czk- *Gen.* -a swallow, gulp; **pić łyczkami** sip, sup.

łydka *f. Gen.pl.* -ek *anat.* calf.

łyk *mi* gulp, swallow; (*powietrza, napoju*) draft; **pić dużymi łykami** swig, quaff; **pić małymi łykami** sip, sup; **łyk świeżego powietrza** breath of fresh air.

łykać *ipf.*, **łyknąć** *pf.* swallow; **łykać ślinkę** lick one's chops; **łykać łzy** gulp back one's tears; **łykać końcówki** swallow one's endings.

łyko *n. bot.* phloem.

łykowaty *a.* 1. (*zawierający łyko*) stringy, fibrous. 2. (*o mięsie*) leathery.

łypać *ipf.* -ę -esz, **łypnąć** *pf.* -ij leer (*na kogoś / coś* at sb/sth).

łysawy *a.* 1. (= *łysiejący*) baldish. 2. (= *rzadko porośnięty*) bare, barren.

łysek *ma* -sk- *pog.* baldhead, baldy, baldie.

łysieć *ipf.* 1. (= *tracić włosy*) go bald, grow bald, be getting thin on top. 2. *przen.* (*o polach, pagórkach*) become barren.

łysiejący *a.* balding.

łysina *f.* 1. (= *miejsce pozbawione włosów*) bald patch, bald spot; (*wyłysiała głowa*) bald head. 2. (= *plamka na czole krowy lub klaczy*) blaze, star.

łysinka *f. Gen.pl.* -ek bald spot.

łyso *adv.* baldly; **czuć się łyso** *pot.* feel like a heel.

łysol *mp pot.* baldhead.

łysy *a.* 1. (*o człowieku*) bald; **łysy jak kolano** as bald as a coot; (*łysa opona*) *pot.* worn tire. 2. (*o zwierzęciu mającym strzałkę*) bald-faced animal; **jeździć na kimś jak na łysej kobyle** ill-treat sb, trample on sb; **znać się jak łyse konie** be as thick as thieves. 3. *pot.* (= *pozbawiony roślinności*) bare, barren. – *mp* (*człowiek*) baldy, baldie, baldhead.

łyszczec *ma Gen.* -czca *bot.* baby's breath (*Gypsophila*).

łyżeczka *f. Gen.pl.* -ek 1. teaspoon; **łyżeczka chirurgiczna** *chir.* curette. 2. (= *zawartość łyżeczki*) teaspoonful; **dwie łyżeczki cukru** two teaspoonfuls of sugar.

łyżeczkować *ipf. med.* curette.

łyżka *f. Gen.pl.* -ek 1. spoon; **łyżka do zupy** soup spoon; **łyżka wazowa** ladle; **łyżka do butów** shoehorn; **łyżka do (nakładania) lodów** scoop; **utopiłby go w łyżce wody** he would kill him with his bare hands. 2. (= *zawartość łyżki*) spoonful. 3. *techn.* (*część koparki*) scoop, bucket. 4. *górn.* bailer.

łyżkować *ipf. górn.* bail.

łyżkowy *a.* 1. *techn.* scoop, bucket. 2. *górn.* bail.

łyżwa *f. Gen.pl.* -ew *sport* 1. (*but z płozą*) ice skate; **łyżwa figurowa** rocker; **jeździć na łyżwach** ice-skate. 2. *narty* V-skate stride; **biegać łyżwą** use V-skate.

łyżwiarka *f. Gen.pl.* -ek *zob.* **łyżwiarz**.

łyżwiarski *a.* skating; **tor łyżwiarski** (*do jazdy szybkiej*) skating course.

łyżwiarstwo *n. sport* ice-skating; **łyżwiarstwo figurowe** figure skating; **łyżwiarstwo szybkie** speed skating.

łyżwiarz *mp* ice skater.

łyżworolka *f. Gen.pl.* -ek roller blade.

łyżwowy *a.* skate; **krok łyżwowy** V-skate stride.

łza *f. Gen.pl.* **łez** tear, teardrop; **krokodyle łzy** crocodile tears; **być czystym jak łza** be as clear as crystal; **na otarcie łez** as a consolation; **szkoda łez** it's no use crying; **doprowadzać kogoś do łez** bring sb to tears, bring tears to sb's eyes; **nie uronić ani jednej łzy** not shed a single tear; **połykać łzy** gulp back one's tears; **ronić łzy** shed tears; **śmiać się do łez** laugh till one cries, laugh one's head off; **zalewać się łzami** weep buckets; **ze łzami w oczach** with tears in one's eyes.

łzawiący *a.* lachrymatory, lacrimatory; **gaz łzawiący** tear gas, lachrymator, lacrimator.

łzawić *ipf.* tear, stream, water; **oczy mi łzawią** my eyes are running.

łzawnica *f. Gen., Dat., Loc.* -cy *hist.* lachrymatory, lachrymal.

łzawość *f.* corniness, mushiness; (*np. filmu*) weepiness.

łzawy *a.* 1. (= *pełen łez*) tearful. 2. (= *skłaniający do łez*) mushy; **łzawy film** tearjerker, tearjerking movie.

łzowy *a. anat.* lacrimal, lachrymal; **gruczoły łzowe** lacrimal glands.

łżę *itd. ipf. zob.* **łgać**.

M, m *n. indecl.* (*litera*) M, m; **M jak Maria** M is for Mike; M as in Mike.

M *abbr.* (*cyfra rzymska*) M (= *thousand*).

M. *abbr.* n. (= *nominative*).

m *abbr.* m (= *meter*).

m.[1] *abbr. zob.* **miasto.**

m.[2] *abbr. zob.* **mieszkanie.**

m.[3] *abbr. zob.* **morze.**

m.[4] *abbr.* (= *rodzaj męski*) m. (= *masculine*).

Ma *abbr.* Mach (= *Mach number*).

ma[1] *a.* (= *moja*) *zob.* **mój.**

ma[2] *ipf. zob.* **mieć.**

maca *f.* (*spożywana przez Żydów w święto Paschy*) matzo, mathoh; matza, matzah.

macać *ipf.* **1.** (= *badać*) feel, finger. **2.** *pot.* (= *obmacywać*) paw, grope. ~ **się** *ipf. pot.* (= *obmacywać się*) paw, grope; *Br. t.* snog.

maccartyzm *mi polit.* McCarthyism.

Macedonia *f. Gen.* **-ii** Macedonia.

Macedonka *f. Gen.pl.* **-ek, Macedończyk** *mp* Macedonian.

macedoński *a.* Macedonian.

macek *mi zob.* **macka.**

maceracja *f. kulin., techn.* maceration.

macerować *ipf.* macerate, steep (*w czymś* in sth).

mach *mi Gen.* **-a 1.** *fiz.* Mach, Mach number. **2.** (= *zaciągnięcie się*) *pot.* drag, puff; **pociągnąć macha** drag a puff.

machabejski *a. hist.* Maccabean.

Machabeusze *mp Gen.pl.* **-ów** *hist.* Maccabees.

machać *ipf.* **1.** (= *kiwać*) (*ręką, chusteczką*) wave; (*szablą, mieczem*) brandish; (*nogami*) swing, sweep; (*skrzydłami*) flap; (*ogonem*) wag; **machać do kogoś** wave to sb. **2.** *pot.* (= *robić szybko*) dispatch.

macher *mp* **1.** *pot.* (= *fachowiec*) master hand. **2.** *pot.* (= *fuszer, oszust*) trickster, bluffer.

machina *f.* **1.** (= *maszyna*) engine, machine. **2.** (= *system, organizacja*) the system; **machina oblężnicza** *hist.* siege engine; **machiny wojenne** *hist.* enginery; **dostać się w tryby machiny** get caught *l.* crushed in the cog-wheels of the machine.

machinacja *f.* machination.

machinalnie *adv.* mechanically.

machinalność *f.* automaticity.

machinalny *a.* mechanical, automatic.

machlojka *f. Gen.pl.* **-ek** *pot.* dirty trick.

machnąć *pf.* **-ij 1.** (= *kiwnąć*) wave; **machnąć koziołka** *l.* **kozła** turn a somersault; **machnąć na coś ręką** give sth up; **przez jakiś czas próbowa-**

łem go przekonać, ale w końcu machnąłem na to ręką I've been trying to convince him to do it for some time, but I finally decided to give it up. **2.** *pot.* (= *zrobić szybko*) dispatch; **machnąć list** whip off a letter. **3.** *pot.* (= *uderzyć*) hit. ~ **się** *pf.* **-ij 1.** (= *pójść, pojechać*) run, hop over; **machnąć się na piechotę** go on foot. **2.** *pot.* (= *spudłować*) miss one's mark. **3.** *pot.* (= *pomylić się*) blow it, botch it, fumble; **machnąć się w rachunkach** screw up one's calculations.

machometr *mi lotn., techn.* Machmeter, Mach indicator.

machorka *f.* (*tytoń*) shag.

macica *f. anat.* uterus, matrix; **w macicy** in utero; **macica perłowa** *biol.* mother-of-pearl, nacre.

maciczny *a. anat., biol., med.* uterine.

macie[1] *ipf. zob.* **mieć.**

macie[2] *f. zob.* **mata.**

maciejka *f. Gen.pl.* **-ek** *bot.* night-scented stock, evening-scented stock (*Matthiola bicornis*).

macierz *f. pl.* **-e 1.** *lit.* (= *ojczyzna*) motherland. **2.** *mat.* array, matrix. **3.** *el.* matrix. **4.** *arch.* (= *matka*) mother.

macierzanka *f. Gen.pl.* **-ek** *bot.* thyme (*Thymus*).

macierzowy *a. mat.* matrix; **rachunek macierzowy** matrix calculus.

macierzyński *a.* maternity, maternal, motherly; **instynkt macierzyński** maternal instinct; **miłość macierzyńska** maternal love; **urlop macierzyński** maternity leave.

macierzyństwo *n.* maternity, motherhood; **świadome macierzyństwo** birth control; **radość macierzyństwa** joy of motherhood.

macierzysty *a.* **1.** (= *pierwotny*) mother, parent; **spółka macierzysta** parent company; **skała macierzysta** *geol.* matrix, bedrock; **ług macierzysty** *chem.* leach. **2.** (= *rodzimy, rodzinny*) mother, vernacular.

maciora *f.* (= *samica świni*) sow.

maciupeńki *a. emf.* teenie-weenie, teenie-tiny, itty-bitty, itsy-bitsy; *Br. t.* tiddly, titchy.

maciupki *a. emf. zob.* **maciupeńki.**

macka *f. Gen.pl.* **-ek** (= *czułek*) palpus; (*ośmiornicy*) tentacle.

macki *pl. Gen.* **macek 1.** *dosł., przen.* (= *presja, zakusy*) tentacles, feelers. **2.** *techn.* callipers.

mackowaty *a.* tentacled.

macocha *f.* stepmother.

macoszy *a.* novercal, stepmotherly; **traktować po macoszemu** treat harshly *l.* unfairly, neglect.

maczać *ipf.* dip, toss, dunk (*w czymś* in sth); **maczać mięso w panierce** sop *l.* dip meat in batter; **maczać w czymś palce** meddle with sth, have a hand in sth.

maczek *mi* -czk- **1.** *bot.* small poppy. **2.** *pot.* (*drobny deszcz*) drizzle.

maczeta *f.* (*nóż*) machete.

maczkiem *adv.* **pisać (drobnym) maczkiem** write in a tiny hand.

maczuga *f.* **1.** *hist.* (*broń*) bludgeon, club. **2.** *sport* Indian club. **3.** *wulg.* (= *penis*) dick.

maczugowiec *ma* -wc- *biol.* (*bakteria*) corynebacterium.

mać *f. pl.* -e *arch.* (= *matka*) mother; **psia mać!** *wulg.* dammit!; **kurwa mać** *wulg.* fuck!, fuck it!

mada *f. roln.* alluvial soil, valley alluvium.

Madagaskar *mi geogr.* Madagascar.

Madagaskarczyk *mp*, **Madagaskarka** *f. Gen.pl.* -ek Madagascan.

madagaskarski *a.* Madagascan.

madapolam *mi tk.* madapollam.

madejowy *a.* **madejowe łoże** *przen.* the rack; (*w bajkach*) bed of nails.

madera *f.* **1.** (*wino*) Madeira. **2.** (*sos*) Madeira sauce. **3.** *tk.* (*tkanina*) Madeira fabric.

maderyzacja *f.* maderization.

maderyzowany *a.* **wino maderyzowane** maderized wine.

Madonna *f. sztuka* the Madonna.

madowy *a. roln.* alluvial.

madras *mi* **1.** *tk.* (*tkanina*) madras. **2.** (*herbata*) Madras tea.

madrasa *f. zob.* **medresa**.

madrycki *a.* (of) Madrid.

madrygalista *mp muz.* madrigalist.

madrygał *mi muz., teor.lit.* madrigal.

madrygałowy *a. muz., teor.lit.* madrigalian.

Madryt *mi geogr.* Madrid.

madrytczyk *mp*, **madrytka** *f. Gen.pl.* -ek inhabitant of Madrid.

Madziar *mp pl.* -rzy *l.* -owie, **Madziarka** *f. Gen.pl.* -ek (= *Węgier*) Magyar.

madziarski *a.* (= *węgierski*) Magyar.

maestria *f. Gen.* -ii *lit.* masterly skill, mastership.

maestro *mp pl.* -owie (= *mistrz*) maestro.

mafia *f. Gen.* -ii **1.** (*sycylijska*) the Mafia. **2.** (= *organizacja przestępcza*) Mafia, mob. **3.** *przen.* (= *klika, koteria*) Mafia, clique.

mafijny *a.* mafia; **boss mafijny** mafia boss.

mafioso *mp* mafioso.

mag *mp pl.* -owie **1.** (= *magik*) mage, sorcerer. **2.** *rel.* (= *kapłan, wróżbita*) Magus.

magazyn *mi* **1.** (*budynek*) warehouse, storehouse. **2.** (*pomieszczenie*) stockroom, storeroom. **3.** (*czasopismo, audycja, program*) magazine; **magazyn informacyjny** news bulletin. **4.** (*sklep*) store. **5.** *wojsk., myśl.* (= *magazynek*) cartridge clip, magazine.

magazynek *mi* -nk- *Gen.* -a *l.* -u **1.** *wojsk., myśl.* cartridge clip, magazine. **2.** (= *składzik*)

storeroom; **magazynek pomocy dydaktycznych** resource room.

magazynier *mp* storeman, storehousekeeper.

magazynierka *f. Gen.pl.* -ek storehousekeeper.

magazynować *ipf.* **1.** (= *przechowywać*) store; (*w składzie celnym*) warehouse. **2.** (= *zbierać*) store up, stockpile.

magazynowy *a.* storage; **gospodarka magazynowa** stock management.

magdeburczyk *mp*, **magdeburka** *f. Gen.pl.* -ek inhabitant of Magdeburg.

Magdeburg *mi* Magdeburg.

magdeburka *f. Gen.pl.* -ek *zob.* **magdeburczyk**.

magdeburski *a.* Magdeburg.

Maghreb *mi* Maghreb, Maghrib.

magia *f. Gen.* -ii **1.** (= *czary*) magic, sorcery; **biała/czarna magia** white/black magic; **to dla mnie czarna magia** this is all double Dutch *l.* Greek to me. **2.** (= *moc, urok*) magic; **magia słów/wiosny** the magic of words/springtime.

magicznie *adv.* magically.

magiczny *a.* **1.** (= *czarodziejski*) magic, magical; **magiczna różdżka** magic wand; **magiczne sztuczki** magic tricks; **magiczne zaklęcie** incantation, magic charm *l.* spell; **kwadrat magiczny** *mat.* magic square. **2.** (= *cudowny, tajemniczy*) magic, magical; **magiczne piękno** magic beauty; **mieć na kogoś magiczny wpływ** have sb under one's spell *l.* thumb.

magiel *mi* -gl- *Gen.* -a **1.** (= *maglownica, prasowarka*) mangle. **2.** *pot.* (= *tłok*) crush.

magik *mp* **1.** (= *sztukmistrz*) conjurer, magician. **2.** (= *spryciarz*) dodger.

magister *mp* -tr- *pl.* -owie master; (*nauk ekonomicznych*) Master of Business and Administration, MBA; (*nauk humanistycznych*) Master of Arts, MA; (*nauk ścisłych i przyrodniczych*) Master of Science, MSc.

magisterium *n. indecl. in sing. pl.* -ria *Gen.* -riów **1.** (*stopień*) master's degree. **2.** (= *nauczanie Kościoła*) magisterium.

magisterski *a.* master's; **egzamin magisterski** Master's exam; **praca magisterska** Master's thesis; **seminarium magisterskie** Master's seminar.

magistracki *a.* municipal; (*dotyczący budynku*) townhall.

magistrala *f. Gen.pl.* -i *l.* -l **1.** (*droga*) major highway; **magistrala kolejowa** main line. **2.** (= *główna sieć*) main; **magistrala gazowa** gas main; **magistrala wodociągowa** water main. **3.** *komp.* bus.

magistrancki *a.* postgraduate.

magistrant *mp*, **magistrantka** *f. Gen.pl.* -ek postgraduate, graduate student.

magistrat *mi* (= *ratusz*) town hall; (= *władze miasta*) municipality, municipal council.

magistratura *f. hist.* municipality.

magla *itd. zob.* **magiel**.

maglować *ipf.* **1.** (= *prasować*) mangle. **2.** *pot.* (= *wypytywać*) grill. **3.** *pot.* (= *powtarzać się*) harp on; **maglować coś w kółko** *l.* **bez przerwy** keep harping on the same string.

maglownica *f.* **1.** (= *magiel*) hand mangle. **2.** *techn.* mangle.

maglownik *mi Gen.* **-a 1.** (*materiał*) mangling cloth. **2.** (= *wałek*) mangling roller.

magma *f. geol.* magma.

magmatyzm *mi geol.* magmatism.

magmowy *a. geol.* igneous, magmatic; **skała magmowa** igneous rock, whinstone.

magnacki *a.* lordly.

magnal *mi techn.* magnal.

magnat *mp* **1.** (= *arystokrata*) magnate, lord. **2.** (= *bogacz*) mogul, magnate; **magnat prasowy** press baron, press tycoon.

magnateria *f. Gen.* **-ii** *hist.* nobility, magnates.

magnatka *f. Gen.pl.* **-ek** (= *arystokratka*) great lady.

magnes *mi fiz., przen.* magnet.

magnesować *ipf. fiz.* magnetize.

magnesowanie *n. fiz.* magnetization.

magnesowy *a. fiz.* magnetic.

magneśnica *f. el., fiz.* field magnet.

magnet *mi pot.* (= *magnetofon*) tape recorder.

magnetochemia *f. Gen.* **-ii** magnetochemistry.

magnetofon *mi* tape recorder, cassette recorder; (*bez wzmacniacza*) tape deck.

magnetofonowy *a.* **taśma magnetofonowa** audiotape; **nagranie magnetofonowe** tape recording.

magnetograf *mi fiz.* magnetograph.

magnetogram *mi fiz.* magnetogram.

magnetokaloryczny *a. fiz.* magnetocalorific.

magnetometr *mi fiz.* magnetometer.

magnetometria *f. Gen.* **-ii** *fiz.* magnetometry.

magneton *mi fiz.* magneton.

magnetorezystor *mi Gen.* **-a** *fiz.* magnetoresistor.

magnetosfera *f. astron.* magnetosphere.

magnetoskop *mi fiz.* magnetoscope.

magnetostrykcja *f. fiz.* magnetostriction.

magnetoterapia *f. Gen.* **-ii** *med.* magnetotherapy.

magnetowid *mi* video cassette recorder, video recorder, VCR.

magnetron *mi fiz.* magnetron.

magnetronowy *a. fiz.* magnetronic.

magnetyczny *a.* **1.** *fiz.* magnetic; **pole magnetyczne** magnetic field; **igła magnetyczna** magnetic needle; **karta magnetyczna** magnetic card, swipe card; **taśma magnetyczna** magnetic tape. **2.** (= *hipnotyczny*) mesmerizing; **mieć magnetyczny wpływ na kogoś/coś** mesmerize sb/sth, cast a spell on sb/sth.

magnetyka *f. fiz., geol.* magnetics.

magnetyt *mi min.* magnetite.

magnetyzm *mi* **1.** *fiz.* magnetism. **2.** (= *mesmeryzm*) mesmerism.

magnez *mi chem.* (*pierwiastek*) magnesium.

magnezja *f.* **magnezja palona** *chem.* magnesia.

magnezowy *a. chem.* magnesian; **tlenek magnezowy** magnesium oxide.

magnezyt *mi min.* magnesite.

magnezytowy *a. min.* magnesitic.

magnificat *n. indecl.* Magnificat.

magnificencja *mp* (= *rektor*) **Jego Magnificencja** Rector Magnificus.

magnolia *f. Gen.* **-ii** *bot.* magnolia (*Magnolia*).

magot *ma zool.* Barbary ape, magot (*Macaca sylvana*).

maharadża *mp pl.* **-owie** maharaja, maharajah.

maharani *f.* maharani, maharanee.

mahatma *mp pl.* **-owie** mahatma.

mahdi *mp rel.* Mahdi.

Mahomet *mp* (*prorok*) Mohammed, Muhammad.

mahometanin *mp pl.* **-anie** *Gen.* **-an, mahometanka** *f. Gen.pl.* **-ek** *rel.* (= *muzułmanin*) Mohammedan, Mahometan.

mahometanizm *mi rel.* (= *islam*) Mohammedanism, Mahometanism.

mahometański *a. rel.* Mohammedan, Mahometan.

mahonia *f. Gen.* **-ii** *bot.* mahonia (*Mahonia*).

mahoniowiec *mi* **-wc-** *Gen.* **-a** *bot.* (= *mahoń*) mahogany (*Swietenia mahagoni*).

mahoniowy *a.* mahogany; **drzewo mahoniowe** *bot. zob.* **mahoniowiec.**

mahoń *mi Gen.pl.* **-i** *l.* **-ów 1.** *bot. zob.* **mahoniowiec. 2.** (*drewno*) (*kolor*) mahogany.

maić *ipf.* **maję maisz, maj** adorn with verdure.

maik *mi* (*obyczaj*) **1.** spring festival. **2.** *zool.* oil beetle (*Meloe*).

maj *mi Gen.* **-a** *Gen.pl.* **-ów** (*miesiąc*) May.

Maja *mp Gen.* **Mai** *pl.* **-owie** Maya.

majaczenie *n.* **1.** *med.* delirium; **majaczenie alkoholowe** delirium tremens. **2.** (= *urojenie, przywidzenie*) hallucinations. **3.** (= *brednie*) ravings.

majaczyć *ipf.* **1.** (= *prześwitywać*) loom; **coś majaczy we mgle** sth looms in the fog. **2.** (*np. w gorączce*) be delirious.

majak *mi Gen.* **-a** (= *urojenie*) hallucination.

mają *ipf. zob.* **mieć.**

majątek *mi* **-tk- 1.** (= *posiadłość*) property. **2.** (= *dorobek, bogactwo*) fortune, wealth; *prawn.* estate; **majątek obrotowy** *fin.* current assets, working capital; **majątek ruchomy** *prawn.* movable property, personal estate; **majątek trwały** fixed assets; **majątek narodowy** national wealth; **majątek własny** *fin.* equity, own capital; **zarobić (na czymś) majątek** make a fortune (on sth); **roztrwonić cały majątek** squander a fortune.

majątkowy *a. prawn.* material; **podatek majątkowy** property tax; **poręczenie majątkowe** (*pieniężne*) bail; (*papierami wartościowymi*) appearance bond; **szkoda majątkowa** pecuniary prejudice; **wspólnota majątkowa** communalism.

majcher *mi* **-chr-** *Gen.* **-a** (= *nóż*) sticker.

majdan *mi Gen.* **-a** *l.* **-u** (= *graty*) caboodle.

majeranek *mi* **-nk-** *bot.* marjoram (*Majorana hortensis*).

majerankowy *a.* marjoram.

majestat *mi* **1.** (= *powaga*) majesty; **w majestacie prawa** in the name of the law. **2.** (= *okazałość*) grandeur. **3.** *arch.* (= *władza, władca*) majesty; **obraza majestatu** lese-majesty.

majestatycznie *adv.* majestically.

majestatyczność *f.* majesty, stateliness.

majestatyczny *a.* majestic, august, stately.

majętność *f. przest.* **1.** (= *posiadłość*) estate.

2. (= *majątek*) property. **3.** *przest.* (= *bogactwo*) wealth.

majętny *a.* wealthy, affluent.

majolika *f. sztuka* (= *fajans*) majolica, maiolica.

majonez *mi kulin.* mayonnaise.

majonezowy *a. kulin.* mayonnaise.

major[1] *mp pl.* **-owie** *l.* **-rzy** *wojsk.* major.

major[2] *a. indecl. muz.* major.

majorat *mi hist., prawn.* primogeniture.

majordom *mp pl.* **-owie** *hist.* constable.

majordomus *mp pl.* **-owie** *hist.* major-domo.

Majorka *f. geogr.* Majorca.

majorowa *f. Gen.* **-ej** major's wife.

majorowy *a. muz.* major.

majoryzować *ipf.* (= *przegłosowywać*) outvote; (= *zdobyć przewagę głosową*) outnumber.

Majowie *pl. zob.* **Maja**.

majowy *a.* May; **konwalia majowa** lily of the valley (*Convallaria majalis*); **nabożeństwo majowe** *kośc.* daily May service in the Catholic Church.

majówka *f. Gen.pl.* **-ek** (*wycieczka*) picnic.

majster *mp* **-tr-** *pl.* **-owie** *l.* **-rzy 1.** (= *rzemieślnik*) master; **majster ciesielski** master carpenter. **2.** (= *brygadzista*) foreman. **3.** *pot.* (= *specjalista*) master; **majster do wszystkiego** jack-of-all-trades; **majster-klepka** (*w sensie negatywnym*) tinker; (*w sensie pozytywnym*) handyman.

majster-klepka *mp zob.* **majster**.

majsterkować *ipf.* do (some) DIY.

majsterkowanie *n.* DIY, do-it-yourself.

majsterkowicz *mp Gen.pl.* **-ów** do-it-yourselfer, DIY-man.

majstersztyk *mi* **1.** (= *arcydzieło*) masterpiece. **2.** *pot.* (*o sprytnym posunięciu*) smart move.

majstrować *ipf.* **1.** *pot.* (= *naprawiać, manipulować*) tinker, tamper, fiddle (*przy czymś* with sth). **2.** *iron.* (= *kombinować*) scheme.

majtać *ipf. pot.* (= *wymachiwać*) swing; **majtać nogami** swing one's legs; **pies majtał ogonem** the dog was wagging its tail. **~ się** *ipf.* dangle, swing.

majtasy *pl. Gen.* **-ów** *pot., żart.* (= *majtki*) undies, panties.

majtek *mp* **-tk-** *pl.* **-owie** (= *marynarz*) deck hand.

majtki *pl. Gen.* **-ek** (*długie*) underpants, drawers; (*krótkie*) briefs; (*damskie, dziecięce*) panties; *Br.* (*damskie*) knickers; **robić w majtki (ze strachu)** be scared shitless, be scared out of one's wits, wet *l.* piss (in) one's pants.

majtnąć *pf.* **-ij 1.** *pot.* (= *machnąć*) wave; swing; (*ogonem*) wag. **2.** *pot.* (= *rzucić*) fling. **~ się** *pf.* **-ij** swing.

majuskuła *f.* **1.** *druk.* uppercase letter, capital letter. **2.** *hist.* majuscule.

majuskułowy *a.* **1.** *druk.* uppercase, capital. **2.** *hist.* majuscular.

mak *mi* **1.** *bot.* poppy (*Papaver*); **mak kalifornijski** California poppy (*Eschscholzia californica*); **mak lekarski** opium poppy (*Papaver somni-*

ferum); **mak polny** corn poppy, field poppy (*Papaver rhoeas*); **mak wschodni** Oriental poppy (*Papaver orientale*). **2.** (= *nasiona maku*) poppy seed; **cicho jak makiem zasiał** deathly still; **było cicho jak makiem zasiał** you could hear a pin drop; **cisza jak makiem zasiał** deathly hush; **dobrać się w korcu maku** take to each other right off the bat; **rozbić coś w drobny mak** smash sth to smithereens; **figę z makiem!** nothing doing! **3.** *Gen.* **-a** (= *kwiat maku*) poppy (flower).

makabra *f. pot.* nightmare, horror.

makabreska *f. Gen.pl.* **-ek** *teor.lit.* tale of the macabre.

makabrycznie *adv.* gruesomely.

makabryczność *f.* gruesomeness, goriness.

makabryczny *a.* (*o widoku, zdarzeniu*) macabre, grisly, gruesome; (*o temacie, szczegółach*) morbid; (*o dowcipie*) sick.

makadam *mi Gen.* **-u** *Loc.* **-ie** *techn.* macadam.

makak *ma zool.* macaque (*Macacus*).

makaron *mi kulin.* pasta; (*nitki*) vermicelli, spaghetti; (*rurki*) macaroni; (*paski*) noodles, fettucine *l.* fettucini; (*muszelki*) shells; (*kolanka*) rigatoni, elbows; **zupa z makaronem** noodle soup; **makaron zapiekany z serem** macaroni and cheese.

makaroniarz *mp pog.* (= *Włoch*) wop, dago.

makaroniczny *a. teor.lit., jęz.* macaronic; **wiersz makaroniczny** macaronics, macaronic verse.

makaronik *mi kulin.* (= *ciastko migdałowe*) macaroon.

makaronista *mp teor.lit.* writer *l.* user of macaronics.

makaronizm *mi jęz.* macaronicism.

makaronizować *ipf. jęz.* use macaronicisms.

makaronowy *a. kulin.* pasta.

makata *f.* tapestry, wall hanging.

makatka *f. Gen.pl.* **-ek** (small) tapestry, (small) wall hanging.

Makau *n. geogr.* Macao, Macau.

makia *f. Gen.* **-ii** *bot.* maquis.

makiaweliczny *a. polit.* Machiavellian.

makiawelizm *mi polit.* Machiavellianism, Machiavellism.

makieta *f.* **1.** (= *model*) model; (*rzeźby*) maquette; (*maszyny*) mock-up; *wojsk.* deception device, decoy; **makieta czołgu** dummy tank; **makieta działa** Quaker gun. **2.** *film, teatr* (= *dekoracja*) mock-up. **3.** *druk.* dummy.

makijaż *mi Gen.pl.* **-y** *l.* **-ów** makeup; maquillage; **robić (sobie) makijaż** make up.

makkartyzm *mi polit. zob.* **maccartyzm**.

makler *mp ekon.* broker; **makler giełdowy** stockbroker, exchange broker; **makler morski** *l.* **okrętowy** ship-broker, shipping agent.

maklerski *a. ekon.* broker's; **dom maklerski** brokerage house *l.* firm; **biuro maklerskie** broker's office.

maklerstwo *n. ekon.* brokerage, brokering.

makolągwa *f. orn.* linnet (*Carduelis l. Acanthis cannabina*); **makolągwa żółtodzioba** twite (*Carduelis l. Acanthis flavirostris*).

makowaty *a. bot.* papaveraceous.

makowiec *mi* **-wc-** *Gen.* **-a** *kulin.* poppyseed cake.

makowy *a.* poppy; poppyseed; **główki makowe** poppyheads; **ciasto makowe** poppyseed cake.

makówka *f. Gen.pl.* **-ek 1.** (= *owoc maku*) poppyhead. **2.** *pot.* (= *głowa*) bean, noodle.

makrama *f. tk.* macramé.

makrela *f. Gen.pl.* **-i** *l.* **-i** *icht.* mackerel (*Scomber scombrus*).

makro *a.* (= *wielki*) macro.

makroanaliza *f. chem.* macroanalysis.

makrobiotyczny *a.* macrobiotic.

makrobiotyka *f.* macrobiotics.

makrocefalia *f. Gen.* **-ii** *pat.* macrocephaly, macrocephalia.

makrocząsteczka *f. Gen.pl.* **-ek** *chem.* macromolecule.

makrodefinicja *f. komp.* macrodefinition.

makroekonomia *f. Gen.* **-ii** *ekon.* macroeconomics.

makroekonomiczny *a. ekon.* macroeconomic.

makroelement *mi biol., chem.* macronutrient.

makroewolucja *f. biol.* macroevolution.

makrofag *mi Gen.* **-a** *biol.* macrophage.

makrofizyka *f. fiz.* macrophysics.

makrofotografia *f. Gen.* **-ii** *fot.* macrophotography.

makrogameta *f. biol.* macrogamete.

makrografia *f.* macrography.

makroinstrukcja *f.* = **makropolecenie**.

makroklimat *mi meteor.* macroclimate.

makroklimatologia *f. Gen.* **-ii** *meteor.* macroclimatology.

makrokomórka *f. Gen.pl.* **-ek** *komp.* macrocell.

makrokosmiczny *a. fil.* macrocosmic.

makrokosmos *mi fil.* macrocosm.

makromolekularny *a. chem.* macromolecular.

makromolekuła *f.* = **makrocząsteczka**.

makron *mi chem., fiz.* molecule larger than 0.1mm in diameter.

makroorganizm *mi biol.* macroorganism.

makroplankton *mi biol.* macroplankton.

makropolecenie *n. komp.* macro(instruction).

makropsja *f. pat.* macropsia, macropsy.

makroregion *mi admin.* macroregion.

makroregionalny *a. admin.* macroregional.

makroskala *f.* macroscale; **w makroskali** on a macroscale.

makroskopia *f. Gen.* **-ii** *metal.* macroscopy.

makroskopowy *a.* macroscopic, macroscopical, megascopic; **fotografia makroskopowa** *fot.* macroscopic photography.

makrospora *f. bot.* macrospore, megaspore.

makrostruktura *f.* macrostructure.

maks *mi pot.* **na maksa** (at) full blast, to the max.

maksi *a. indecl.* maxi; **spódnica maksi** maxiskirt.

maksimum *n. indecl. in sing. pl.* **-ma** *Gen.* **-mów** maximum; **do maksimum** to the maximum, to the full(est); **maksimum dobrej woli** abundant goodwill.

maksyma *f.* (= *aforyzm*) maxim, saying, dictum.

maksymalista *mp* maximalist.

maksymalistyczny *a.* favoring direct action to achieve all the goals and rejecting compromise.

maksymalizacja *f.* maximization, maximation.

maksymalizm *mi* rejection of compromise.

maksymalizować *ipf.* maximize.

maksymalnie *adv.* **1.** (= *najpełniej*) to the maximum, to the full(est), to the utmost; (= *krańcowo*) most possible; **maksymalnie dużo** most possible. **2.** (= *nie więcej niż*) maximum.

maksymalny *a.* maximum; *t. techn.* maximal; **maksymalna ilość punktów** full marks; **prędkość maksymalna** maximum speed; **z maksymalną prędkością** at full speed.

makuch *mi Gen.* **-a** *l.* **-u** *roln.* oil(seed) cake; **makuch sprasowany** presscake.

makulatura *f.* **1.** (= *surowiec wtórny*) scrap *l.* waste paper; **punkt skupu makulatury** paper recycling center, paper drop. **2.** *przen., pog.* (= *podrzędna literatura*) pulp fiction.

makulaturowy *a.* of or pertaining to scrap *l.* waste paper; **papier makulaturowy** recycled paper.

makutra *f.* (= *donica*) earthenware mixing bowl.

malachit *mi min.* malachite.

malachitowy *a.* malachite; **zieleń malachitowa** *techn.* malachite green.

malaga *f. kulin.* (= *słodkie wino hiszpańskie*) Malaga.

Malaj *mp pl.* **-e** *l.* **-owie** Malay.

Malajczyk *mp* Malay, Malayan.

Malaje *pl. geogr.* Malaya.

Malajka *f. Gen.pl.* **-ek** *zob.* Malajczyk.

malajski *a.* Malay(an); **Półwysep Malajski** *geogr.* Malay Peninsula.

malakologia *f. Gen.* **-ii** *zool.* malacology.

malakser *mi Gen.* **-a** food processor.

malamut *ma kynol.* (Alaskan) malamute, malemute.

malaria *f. Gen.* **-ii** *pat.* malaria.

malarka *f. Gen.pl.* **-ek** (woman) painter.

malarnia *f. Gen.pl.* **-i** *techn.* paint shop; *teatr* set design shop.

malarski *a.* (*o przyborach, technice*) painting; (*o wizji, wyobraźni*) painterly; **pracownia malarska** (painter's) studio.

malarskość *f.* painterly quality.

malarstwo *n. sztuka* painting; **malarstwo jaskiniowe/olejne/rodzajowe/sztalugowe** cave/oil/genre/easel painting.

malaryczny *a.* malarial, malarian, malarious; *pat.* paludal; **gorączka malaryczna** *pat.* ague.

malarz *mp* (= *artysta zajmujący się malarstwem; rzemieślnik trudniący się malowaniem*) painter; **malarz pokojowy** house painter, decorator.

malarzyna *mp iron.* dauber.

malatura *f. sztuka* painting.

malec *mp* **-lc-** little boy, kid; (*uczący się chodzić*) toddler.

maleć *ipf.* (*o natężeniu, rozmiarze, ważności*) diminish; (*o ilości, rozmiarze, sile*) decrease, be on the decrease; dwindle (away), ebb (away); **funkcja malejąca** *mat.* decreasing function.

Malediwy *pl. Gen.* **-ów** *geogr.* the Maldives, Maldive Islands.

maleinowy *a. chem.* maleic; **kwas maleinowy** maleic acid; **żywice maleinowe** maleates.

maleńka *f. Gen.* **-iej** *emf.* babe.

maleńki *a.* (*o dziecku, rozmiarze*) tiny; *pot.* little tiny; (*o ilości, rozmiarze*) minute; (*o człowieku, rozmiarze*) diminutive; (*o kobiecie*) petite. – *mp emf.* baby.

maleńkość *f.* (*dziecka, rozmiaru*) tininess; (*ilości, rozmiaru*) minuteness; **od maleńkości** from the cradle, since childhood.

maleństwo *n. emf.* little one; baby.

Malezja *f. geogr.* Malaysia.

Malezyjczyk *mp*, **Malezyjka** *f. Gen.pl.* **-ek** Malaysian.

malezyjski *a.* Malaysian.

malgaski *a. t. jęz.* Malagasy.

Malgasz *mp pl.* **-e** *l.* **-owie** *Gen.* **-ów**, **Malgaszka** *f. Gen.pl.* **-ek** Malagasy.

maligna *f.* delirium; **w malignie** delirious; **bredzić jak w malignie** rave, ramble.

malina *f. bot.* **1.** raspberry (*Rubus*); **malina kamionka** stone bramble (*Rubus saxatilis*); **malina moroszka** cloudberry, salmonberry, yellowberry (*Rubus chamaemorus*); **malina właściwa** (red) raspberry (*Rubus idaeus*); **wpuścić kogoś w maliny** lead sb up *l.* down the graden path. **2.** (= *owoc tej rośliny*) raspberry; **sok z malin** raspberry juice; **dziewczyna jak malina** peach of a girl, comely girl.

maliniak *mi Gen.* **-a** (= *zarośla malin*) raspberry bush.

malinka *f. Gen.pl.* **-ek** **1.** (*owoc*) raspberry (fruit). **2.** (*cukierek*) raspberry candy. **3.** *pot.* (= *ślad po pocałunku*) hickey.

malinnik *mi Gen.* **-a** raspberry garden.

malinowy *a.* **1.** (*związany z maliną*) raspberry. **2.** (*kolor*) raspberry-red.

malinówka *f.* (*alkohol*) raspberry liqueur.

malizna *f. pot.* (= *coś małego*) sth small; (= *mało czegoś*) scarcity, shortage.

malkontencki *a.* malcontent.

malkontenctwo *n.* (permanent) discontentment, (permanent) discontentedness.

malkontent *mp* malcontent, discontent; *pot.* (= *osoba psująca innym nastrój*) wet blanket, party-pooper, stick-in-the-mud.

malkontentka *f. Gen.pl.* **-ek** *zob.* **malkontent**.

malm *mi geol.* Late Jurassic Epoch, Malm, White Jurassic (sequence).

malonowy *a. chem.* malonic; **kwas malonowy** malonic acid.

malować *ipf.* **1.** (= *powlekać farbą*) paint; (= *remontować*) decorate; **malować mieszkanie** (*samemu*) decorate *l.* paint one's apartment; (*wynająwszy kogoś*) have one's apartment decorated *l.* painted; **malować paznokcie** paint *l.* varnish one's nails; **malowana lala** *przen.* bimbo; **świeżo malowane** (*ostrzeżenie*) wet paint; **malowany król** *przen.* puppet king; **patrzeć jak cielę na malowane wrota** *przen.* gawk, goggle, gape. **2.**

sztuka (= *tworzyć obraz*) paint; **malować obrazy** paint pictures. **3.** (= *robić makijaż*) make up; **malować usta** put on lipstick; **malować oczy** put on eye make-up. **4.** (= *obrazowo relacjonować*) paint, portray; **nie taki diabeł straszny jak go malują** devils are not so black as they are painted. **~ się** *ipf.* **1.** (= *robić sobie makijaż*) make up. **2.** (= *odzwierciedlać się*) be manifest *l.* visible, appear, show.

malowanie *n.* **1.** (*czynność*) painting; (= *remont*) decoration. **2.** *przest.* picture; **ładny** *l.* **śliczny jak malowanie** pretty as a picture.

malowanka *f. Gen.pl.* **-ek** **1.** (= *ozdoba, rysunek*) color picture. **2.** (= *kolorowanka*) coloring book.

malowidło *n. Gen.pl.* **-eł** *sztuka* (= *obraz*) painting; **malowidło skalne** cave *l.* rock painting; **malowidło ścienne** wall painting, mural.

malowniczo *adv.* **1.** (= *atrakcyjnie*) picturesquely. **2.** (= *obrazowo*) graphically.

malowniczy *a.* **1.** (= *atrakcyjny*) picturesque; (*o krajobrazie*) scenic. **2.** (= *obrazowy*) graphic; (*o stylu*) pictorial.

malstrom *mi geogr.* Maelstrom.

Malta *f. geogr.* Malta.

Maltanka *f. Gen.pl.* **-ek** Maltese (woman).

Maltańczyk *mp* **1.** (= *mieszkaniec Malty*) Maltese. **2.** *kynol.* Maltese (dog).

maltański *a.* Maltese; **kawaler maltański** *rel.* Knight of Malta; **krzyż maltański** Maltese cross; **zakon maltański** *rel.* Order of Malta.

maltaza *f. biol., chem.* maltase.

maltoza *f. chem.* maltose, malt sugar.

maltretować *ipf.* maltreat, ill-treat; abuse (physically); *pot.* knock about; *pot.* (*zwł. dziecko, żonę*) batter.

maltretowanie *n.* maltreatment, ill-treatment; (physical) abuse; *pot.* (*dzieci, żony*) battering.

maltuzjanizm *mi ekon.* Malthusianism.

maltuzjańczyk *mp ekon.* Malthusian.

maltuzjański *a. ekon.* Malthusian.

maluch *mp* (= *małe dziecko*) little one, kiddie *l.* kiddy; (*uczący się chodzić*) toddler. – *mi Gen.* **-a** *mot., pot.* Fiat 126p (*a Polish-manufactured compact car*).

maluchny *a. emf.* wee.

maluczki *a.* lesser. – *mp* lesser mortal.

malunek *mi* **-nk-** *pot.* painting.

malusieńki *a. emf.* teeny, itty-bitty, itsy-bitsy, teenie-weenie.

maluśki *a. emf.* teeny, itty-bitty, itsy-bitsy, teenie-weenie.

malutki *a. emf.* (*o dziecku, rozmiarze*) tiny; *pot.* little tiny; (*o ilości, rozmiarze*) minute; (*o człowieku, rozmiarze*) diminutive; (*o rozmiarze*) minuscule.

malwa *f. bot.* **1.** mallow (*Malva*). **2.** alth(a)ea (*Althaea*).

malwersacja *f. zwł. fin.* embezzlement, peculation.

malwersant *mp zwł. fin.* embezzler, peculator.

malwersantka *f. Gen.pl.* **-ek** *zob.* **malwersant**.

malwersować *ipf. zwł. fin.* embezzle, peculate.

mała *f. Gen.* **-ej** (*o dziewczynce, kobiecie*) little girl; (*przy zwracaniu się*) baby, babe, dear; **mała czarna (kawa)** demitasse.

małe *n. Gen.* **-ego** young (one).

małmazja *f. kulin., przest.* malmsey, malvasia.

mało *adv.* **mniej** 1. (= *niewiele*) not much, little (*niepoliczalne*); not many, few (*policzalne*); **o mało co** pretty *l.* very nearly, narrowly; **o mało co nie upadłem** I nearly fell; **mało brakowało** it was a close call; **mało tego, że...** not only...; **mało tego** that's not all; **jeszcze ci mało?** had enough yet?; **ni mniej ni więcej tylko...** nothing less than...; **co najmniej** at least; **za mało** too few (*policzalne*); too little (*niepoliczalne*). 2. (= *rzadko*) hardly; **mało kiedy** hardly ever; **mało kto** hardly anybody *l.* anyone; **mało kto wie, że...** hardly anybody *l.* anyone knows that..., (very) few people know that...

małodusznie *adv.* pusillanimously.

małoduszność *f.* pusillanimity.

małoduszny *a.* pusillanimous.

małogłowie *n pat.* microcephaly, microcephalia.

małogłowy *a. biol.* microcephalous.

małokalibrowy *a.* (*o broni palnej*) small-caliber.

małolat *mp pl.* **-y** *pog.* squirt.

małolata *f. zob.* **małolat.**

małoletni *a. prawn.* underage, minor. – *mp prawn.* minor.

małoletniość *f. prawn.* minority, nonage.

małolitrażowy *a. mot.* subcompact, compact; **samochód małolitrażowy** compact car.

małomiasteczkowość *f. rzad.* small-town ways.

małomiasteczkowy *a.* small-town.

małomówność *f.* taciturnity, reticence.

małomówny *a.* taciturn, reticent.

małomózgowie *n pat.* microencephaly, microencephalia.

małoobrazkowy *a. fot.* 35mm; **aparat małoobrazkowy** 35mm camera.

Małopolanin *mp pl.* **-anie** *Gen.* **-an** inhabitant of Małopolska (*Little Poland*).

Małopolanka *f. Gen.pl.* **-ek** *zob.* **Małopolanin.**

Małopolska *f. geogr., hist.* Małopolska, Little Poland (*a region and province in southern Poland*).

małopolski *a.* of Little Poland.

małorolny *a. roln.* small-farm; **chłop małorolny** smallholder; **małorolne gospodarstwo** smallholding.

małoseryjny *a.* low-volume; **produkcja małoseryjna** low-volume production *l.* manufacture.

małosolny *a.* low-salt; **małosolna dieta** low-salt diet; **ogórek małosolny** *kulin.* low-salt pickle.

małostkowość *f.* pettiness, small-mindedness.

małostkowy *a.* petty, pettish, mean, small-minded.

małość *f.* 1. (= *mały rozmiar*) small size, smallness. 2. (= *przeciętność, niepozorność*) meanness.

małotonażowy *a. żegl.* small-tonnage.

małowartościowy *a.* of little value.

małpa *f.* 1. *zool.* monkey, simian; *t. pot.* ape; **małpy człekokształtne** anthropoid *l.* great apes, pongids (*Pongidae*); **małpy nadrzewne** arboreal monkeys; **małpy szerokonose** New World monkeys, platyrrhines (*Platyrrhini*); **małpy wąskonose** Old World monkeys, catarrhines (*Catarrhini*). 2. *przen.* (*obelżywie o człowieku*) monkey, ape. 3. *przen.* (= *naśladowca*) copycat, ape.

małpi *a.* apish; simian; **małpia zręczność** cat-like agility; **małpie figle** monkeyshines; **dostać małpiego rozumu** go ape.

małpiarnia *f. Gen.pl.* **-i** *l.* **-ń** monkey house.

małpiatka *f. zool.* prosimian (*Prosimii*).

małpiszon *ma żart.* (= *małpa*) monkey. – *mp pl.* **-y** *przen., obelż.* (= *kreatura, brzydal*) ape.

małpka *f. Gen.pl.* **-ek** 1. little monkey. 2. *pot.* (= *mała butelka alkoholu*) small flask (*of usu. vodka*).

małpolud *mp pl.* **-y** 1. (= *australopitek*) apeman. 2. *przen., obelż.* (= *kreatura, brzydal*) ape, apeman.

małpować *ipf.* copycat, ape.

małpowanie *n.* apery, mimicry.

małpożer *ma orn.* monkey-eating eagle (*Pitecophaga jefferyi*).

mały *a.* **mniejszy** 1. (= *nieduży*) small; little; **mały palec** *anat.* little finger; **mała litera** small letter; (*w maszynie do pisania*) lowercase letter; **małymi literami** in lowercase; **Mały Wóz** *astron.* Little Dipper; **małe piwo** *przen.* piece of cake, no big deal; **mała czarna** demitasse; **na małym ekranie** on TV; **o mały włos** just barely; **o mały włos nie zrobić czegoś** be within a hair's breadth of doing sth; **o mały włos bym zginął** I missed being killed by a hair; **mieć coś w małym palcu** have sth at one's fingertips; **małe jest piękne** small is beautiful. 2. (= *młody*) little; **mała dziewczynka** little girl; **małe dzieci - mały kłopot, duże dzieci - duży kłopot** small children cause small problems, big children cause big problems. – *mp* (*o chłopcu*) little boy; **od małego** since childhood.

małż *ma Gen.pl.* **-y** *l.* **-ów** mussel, clam.

małże *pl. zool.* bivalves (*Lamellibranchia*).

małżeński *a.* matrimonial, marital, married; **para małżeńska** married couple; **pożycie małżeńskie** married life; **problemy małżeńskie** matrimonial troubles; **przysięga małżeńska** marital vows; **scena** *l.* **sprzeczka małżeńska** argument between a husband and wife; **trójkąt małżeński** ménage à trois; **związek małżeński** marriage.

małżeństwo *n.* 1. (= *stan*) matrimony, wedlock; **małżeństwo mieszane** intermarriage; **małżeństwo z rozsądku** marriage of convenience; **kojarzyć małżeństwo** match a marriage; **unieważnić małżeństwo** annul a marriage; **zawrzeć małżeństwo** marry, get married. 2. *Loc.* **-u** (= *małżonkowie*) married couple, husband and wife; **oni są udanym małżeństwem** they are a good couple.

małżonek *mp* **-nk-** *pl.* **-owie** (= *mąż*) husband, spouse; **książę małżonek** (= *mąż królowej*) prince consort.

małżonka *f. Gen.pl.* **-ek** (= *żona*) wife, spouse.

małżonkowie *pl. Gen.* **-ów** (= *małżeństwo*) married couple, husband and wife.

małżoraczek *ma* **-czk-** *zool.* ostracod (*Ostracoda*).

małżowina *f.* 1. (= *muszla*) (mollusk's) shell. 2. *anat.* **małżowina uszna** auricle, pinna; **małżowina nosowa** turbinate, turbinate bone; nasal concha.

mam[1] *ipf. zob.* **mieć**.

mam[2] *f. zob.* **mama**.

mama *f.* mam, mom; **nie ma jak u mamy** home sweet home, east west home is best; **jak mamę kocham!** *pot.* on my mother's grave!

mamałyga *f.* 1. *kulin.* (= *ugotowana kaszka kukurydziana*) hominy, grits. 2. *uj.* (= *nieapetyczna papka*) slop.

mamba *f. zool.* mamba (*Dendroaspis*).

mambo *n.* (*taniec*) mambo.

mamcia *f. Voc.* **-u** *pot.* mommy, mamma, mam.

mameluk *mp pl.* **-cy** *l.* **-owie** *hist.* Mameluke, Mamaluke.

mamer *mi* **-mr-** *Gen.* **-a** *pot.* (= *więzienie*) cooler.

mamić *ipf.* 1. (= *zwodzić, łudzić*) beguile, delude. 2. (= *wabić, kusić*) lure, entice; **mamić kogoś obietnicami** lure sb with promises.

mamilaria *f. bot.* mammillaria (*Mammillaria*).

maminsynek *mp* **-nk-** *pl.* **-owie** *l.* **-i** mama's boy.

maminy *a.* mam's; **mamina córeczka** mama's girl; **maminy synek** mama's boy.

mamka *f. Gen.pl.* **-ek** (= *karmiąca*) wet nurse.

mamlać *ipf.* **-ę -esz** 1. (= *mamrotać*) mumble, mutter. 2. (= *jeść powoli*) mumble.

mammograf *mi med.* mammograph.

mammografia *f. Gen.* **-ii** *med.* mammography.

mammologia *f. Gen.* **-ii** mammalogy.

mammologiczny *a.* mammalogical.

mamona *f. żart.* (= *pieniądze*) mammon; *pot.* dough, mazuma.

mamra *itd. mi zob.* **mamer**.

mamraj *mi Gen.pl.* **-ów** *techn.* mud.

mamro *mi zob.* **mamer**.

mamrot *mi* (= *mruczenie*) mutter.

mamrotać *ipf.* **-czę** *l.* **-cę -czesz** *l.* **-cesz, -cz** (= *mruczeć*) mutter, murmur.

mamuci *a.* mammoth; **mamucia skocznia** *sport* mammoth ski jump; **mamucie drzewo = mamutowiec**.

mamunia *f. Voc.* **-u** mammy, mamma.

mamusia *f. Voc.* **-u** mammy, mam.

mamut *ma zool.* mammoth (*Mammuthus*); **mamut wielki** wooly mammoth (*Mammuthus primigenius*). – *mi Gen.* **-a** *bot.* (*fasola*) large-sized beans. – *mp pl.* **-y** *przen.* (= *ciemniak, tradycjonalista*) old fogy, old fogey.

mamutowiec *mi* **-wc-** *Gen.* **-a** *bot.* giant sequoia, big tree (*Sequoiadendron giganteum*).

mamy[1] *ipf. zob.* **mieć**.

mamy[2] *f. zob.* **mama**.

mana *f. antrop.* mana.

mañana *f.* mañana.

manat *zool.* manatee (*Trichechus*).

manatki *pl. Gen.* **-ów** *pot.* stuff; *Br. t.* clobber; **pakować/zabrać swoje manatki** pack/take one's stuff.

manczester *mi* **-tr-** *l.* **-ter-** (*tkanina*) corduroy.

manczesterowy *a.* corduroy.

mandala *f. rel., sztuka* mandala.

mandaryn *mp* mandarin.

mandarynka *f. Gen.pl.* **-ek** 1. *bot.* tangerine (*Citrus reticulata*); mandarin (*Citrus nobilis*). 2. (*owoc*) tangerine, mandarin. 3. *orn.* mandarin duck (*Aix galericulata*).

mandarynkowy *a.* tangerine, mandarin.

mandat *mi* 1. *polit.* (= *pełnomocnictwo*) mandate. 2. (*w parlamencie*) seat; **sprawować mandat** carry out a mandate; **stracić mandat (w parlamencie)** lose one's seat (in Parliament). 3. *prawn.* (*wezwanie do zapłacenia kary*) (*kara*) fine; **dać komuś mandat** give sb a ticket; **ukarać kogoś mandatem** fine sb (*usu. for a traffic offense*); **słony mandat** heavy fine, hefty fine.

mandatariusz *mp Gen.pl.* **-y** *l.* **-ów**, **mandatariuszka** *f. Gen.pl.* **-ek** *polit.* mandatary, mandatory.

mandatowy *a.* 1. *polit.* mandate; **komisja mandatowa** mandates committee; **terytorium mandatowe** mandated territory, mandate. 2. *prawn.* **postępowanie mandatowe** proceedings by police penal orders.

mandola *f. muz.* mandola.

mandolina *f. muz.* mandolin, mandoline.

mandolinista *mp*, **mandolinistka** *f. Gen.pl.* **-ek** mandolinist.

mandolinowy *a. muz.* mandolin.

mandorla *f. Gen.pl.* **-i** *sztuka* (= *aureola*) mandorla, vesica.

mandragora *f. bot.* mandrake, mandragora (*Mandragora officinarum*).

mandryl *ma zool.* mandrill (*Mandrillus sphinx*).

Mandżuria *f. Gen.* **-ii** *geogr.* Manchuria.

mandżurski *a.* Manchurian.

manekin *mi Gen.* **-a** (*krawiecki*) (tailor's) dummy; (*sklepowy*) mannequin.

manele *pl. Gen.* **-i** *pot.* stuff; *Br. t.* clobber.

manetka *f. Gen.pl.* **-ek** *techn.* throttle.

manewr *mi* 1. (= *zwrot*) maneuver; *Br.* manoeuvre; move. 2. (= *fortel*) maneuver; *Br.* manoeuvre; stratagem; **manewr polityczny** political maneuver. 3. *wojsk. zob.* **manewry**.

manewrować *ipf.* 1. (= *poruszać, lawirować*) maneuver; *Br.* manoeuvre; steer. 2. *pot.* (= *kombinować*) maneuver; *Br.* manoeuvre.

manewrowy *a. t. wojsk.* maneuver; *Br.* manoeuvre; **plac manewrowy** driver training ground; **lokomotywa manewrowa** *kol.* shunting locomotive, switching locomotive.

manewry *pl. Gen.* **-ów** *wojsk.* maneuvers; *Br.* manoeuvres.

maneż *mi Gen.* **-u** *l.* **-a** (= *ujeżdżalnia*) manège, manege; riding school.

mangan *mi chem.* manganese.

manganawy *a. chem.* manganous.

manganian *mi chem.* manganate.

manganin *mi techn.* Manganin®.

manganit *mi min.* manganite.

manganowiec *mi* **-wc-** *Gen.* **-a** *chem.* manganese group element.

manganowy a. chem. manganic; **kwas manganowy** manganic acid.

mango n. indecl. bot. (drzewo) (owoc) mango (Mangifera indica).

mangowy a. mango; **drzewo mangowe** zob. mango.

mangrowiec mi -wc- Gen. -a bot. mangrove (Rhizopoda).

mangrowy a. bot. mangrove.

mangusta f. zool. mongoose (Herpestes).

mania f. Gen. -ii **1.** (= namiętność) mania (czegoś for sth). **2.** pat. mania; **mania prześladowcza** persecution complex, persecution mania; **mania wielkości** pat. megalomania; przen. delusions of grandeur.

maniacki a. maniacal, maniac.

maniactwo n. mania, fad.

maniaczka f. Gen.pl. -ek, **maniak** mp maniac.

maniakalny a. pat. manic; **psychoza maniakalno-depresyjna** manic-depressive psychosis, bipolar disorder.

manicheizm mi fil. Manichaeism, Manicheism.

manichejczyk mp Manichaean, Manichean.

manichejski a. Manichaean, Manichean.

manicure mi zob. **manikiur**.

manicurzystka f. Gen.pl. -ek zob. **manikiurzystka**.

maniera f. **1.** (= styl) manner, style. **2.** (= pretensjonalność) mannerism.

manierka f. Gen.pl. -ek canteen, flask.

manierować ipf. make sb l. sth manneristic. ~ **się** ipf. get manneristic, become affected.

maniery pl. Gen. -r manners; **mieć dobre/złe maniery** good-/bad-mannered; **bez manier** without manners.

manieryczność f. mannerism.

manieryczny a. mannered, manneristic.

manierysta mp sztuka mannerist.

manierystyczny a. sztuka manneristic.

manieryzm mi **1.** (= manieryczność) mannerism. **2.** sztuka mannerism.

manifest mi **1.** (= odezwa) (= program) manifesto. **2.** żegl. manifest.

manifestacja f. **1.** (= demonstracja, wiec) demonstration. **2.** (= uzewnętrznienie) manifestation; **manifestacja uczuć** manifestation, expression.

manifestacyjnie adv. ostentatiously.

manifestacyjny a. ostentatious.

manifestant mp, **manifestantka** f. Gen.pl. -ek demonstrator.

manifestować ipf. **1.** (= demonstrować) demonstrate, stage a demonstration; **manifestować przeciw wojnie** demonstrate against the war, stage an anti-war demonstration. **2.** (= uzewnętrzniać) manifest.

manikiur mi manicure.

manikiurzystka f. Gen.pl. -ek manicurist.

manila f. tk. (włókno) Manila hemp, abaca.

maniok mi bot. cassava, manioc (Manihot).

manipulacja f. **1.** (czynność wykonywana ręcznie) manipulation, handling. **2.** (= propaganda) manipulation.

manipulacje pl. Gen. -i (= procedura) procedure.

manipulacyjny a. **1.** (dotyczący ręcznego działania) manipulative. **2.** (= perswazyjny) manipulative. **3.** (dotyczący procedury) procedural; **opłata manipulacyjna** handling charges.

manipulant mp manipulator.

manipularz mi Gen. -a kość. maniple.

manipulator mp pl. -rzy manipulator. – mi pl. -y komp., techn. manipulator.

manipulować ipf. **1.** (= wykonywać czynność) manipulate, handle. **2.** (= sterować ludźmi) manipulate. **3.** (= fałszować) manipulate.

manipuł mi wojsk., hist. maniple.

manitu mp indecl. manitou, manitu.

mankament mi shortcoming, drawback.

mankiet mi **1.** (u rękawa) cuff; (u spodni) (trouser) cuff; Br. turn-up; **spinki do mankietów** cuff links. **2.** żegl. button (of an oar). **3.** med. (= urządzenie do pomiaru ciśnienia krwi) blood pressure cuff.

manko n. ekon. cash shortage, deficit.

manna f. **1.** (kasza) cream of wheat. **2.** bot. (trawa) manna grass (Glyceria). **3.** bot. (porost) manna lichen (Lecanora esculenta); **manna z nieba** manna from heaven.

mannica f. bot. **mannica nadmorska** Nuttall's alkaligrass (Puccinellia nuttalliana).

mannoza f. biochem. (cukier) mannose.

manometr mi techn. manometer, pressure gauge.

manometria f. Gen. -ii techn. manometry.

manometryczny a. techn. manometric.

manowce pl. Gen. -ów (= bezdroża) back country, backwoods; **zejść na manowce** go astray; **sprowadzić kogoś na manowce** lead sb astray.

mansarda f. **1.** (= poddasze) attic, garret. **2.** (= dach) mansard, mansard roof.

mansardowy a. **1.** (= strychowy) attic. **2.** mansard; **dach mansardowy** mansard roof.

manta f. icht. (= diabeł morski) manta, devilfish (Manta birostris).

manto n. hiding; **dostać manto** take a hiding; **spuścić komuś manto** give sb a good hiding.

mantolet mi kość. mantelletta.

mantra f. rel. mantra.

mantyka[1] mp l. f. decl. like f. Gen.pl. -k l. -ów pot. (= zrzęda) moan, grumbler; **jezu, ale z ciebie mantyka!** jeez, don't be such a moan!

mantyka[2] f. tylko sing. (= wróżbiarstwo) divination.

mantyla f. **1.** (= chusta) mantilla. **2.** arch. (= pelerynka) mantelet.

mantysa f. mat. mantissa.

manualny a. lit. (= ręczny) manual.

manuał mi muz. (= klawiatura) manual.

manufaktura f. (zakład) workshop.

manuskrypt mi (= rękopis) druk. manuscript.

mańka f. Gen.pl. -niek przest. (= lewa ręka) left hand; **zażyć** l. **zajść kogoś z mańki** dupe sb, hoodwink in.

mańkuctwo n. left-handedness.

mańkut mp pl. -ci l. -y pot. lefty, south paw.

maoista *mp*, **maoistka** *f. Gen.pl.* **-ek** *polit.* Maoist.

maoistowski *a. polit.* Maoist.

maoizm *mi polit.* Maoism.

Maorys *mp*, **Maoryska** *f. Gen.pl.* **-ek** Maori.

maoryski *a.* Maori.

mapa *f.* map, chart; **mapa administracyjna** administrative map; **mapa fizyczna** physical map; **mapa geologiczna** geologic map; **mapa historyczna** historical map; **mapa konturowa** relief map; **mapa polityczna** political map; **mapa topograficzna** topographic map; **mapa samochodowa** road map; **mapa sztabowa** ordnance map; **mapa pogody** weather chart; **legenda mapy** map legend.

mapka *f. Gen.pl.* **-ek** map, plan.

mapnik *mi Gen.* **-a** map-case.

mara *f.* 1. (= *widzenie senne*) dream. 2. (= *duch*) apparition.

marabut *mp pl.* **-ci** *rel.* marabout. − *ma pl.* **-y** *orn.* marabou (*Leptoptilos crumeniferus*).

marakas *mi muz.* (*instrument*) maraca.

marakuja *f. Gen.* **-ui** *bot.* maracuja (*Passiflora edulis*).

maranta *f. bot.* maranta (*Maranta*).

maraskino *mi* (*likier*) maraschino.

maraton *mi* 1. *sport* marathon. 2. (*długa impreza*) marathon; **maraton filmowy/kabaretowy** movie/cabaret marathon.

maratonka *f. Gen.pl.* **-ek**, **maratończyk** *mp* *sport* marathon runner.

maratoński *a. sport* marathon; **bieg maratoński** marathon race.

marazm *mi* 1. (= *apatia*) torpor, apathy. 2. *pat.* marasm.

marcato *adv. muz.* marcato.

marcepan *mi Gen.* **-a** (*masa*) (*wyrób*) marzipan.

marcepanowy *a.* marzipan.

marchew *f.* **-chwi-** *pl.* **-e** *bot.* carrot (*Daucus carota*).

marchewka *f. Gen.pl.* **-ek** 1. (*korzeń*) carrot. 2. **zasada/polityka kija i marchewki** the carrot and stick method/policy. 3. *kulin.* (*potrawa*) carrots; **marchewka z groszkiem** peas and carrots.

marchia *f. Gen.* **-ii** *hist.* March.

marchwianka *f. Gen.pl.* **-ek** (*zupa*) carrot soup.

marcować *ipf. pot.* (*o kotach*) be in the heat.

marcowy *a.* March; **marcowa pogoda** changeable weather.

marek *mi* **-rk-** *Gen.* **-a** *bot.* water parsnip (*Sium*). − *mp* **-rk-** **nocny marek** nighthawk; **tłuc się jak marek po piekle** make a hell of a noise; **tłukłeś się wczoraj jak marek po piekle** I thought you were going to wake the dead last night.

marengo¹ *n. indecl. l. Gen.* **-a** *tk.* pepper-and-salt woollen cloth.

marengo² *a. indecl.* (*kolor*) pepper-and-salt.

mareograf *mi techn.* mareograph, tide gauge.

margaryna *f. kulin.* margarine.

margerytka *f. Gen.pl.* **-ek** *bot.* daisy, oxeye daisy; marguerite (*Chrysanthemum leucanthemum*).

margiel *mi* **-gl-** *geol.* marl.

marginalia *pl. Gen.* **-ów** 1. *lit.* (= *drobiazgi*) trifles, trivia, matters of lesser importance. 2. *druk.* marginal notes.

marginalny *a.* 1. (= *nieistotny*) marginal, peripheral. 2. (= *marginesowy*) marginal.

margines *mi* 1. (= *brzeg*) margin, edge. 2. (*to, co nie jest istotne*) margin; **margines błędu** margin of error; **na marginesie czegoś** on the margin of sth; **uwaga na marginesie** side note; **zrobić uwagę na marginesie** mention sth in passing; **być na marginesie** play a secondary role; **tak na marginesie,...** by the way,... 3. (= *półświatek*) underworld; **margines społeczny** the dregs of society.

marglisty *a. geol.* marl.

marglować *ipf. roln.* marl.

marglowy *a. geol.* marl.

margrabia *mp Gen.* **-ego** *l.* **-i** *Dat.* **-emu** *l.* **-i** *Acc.* **-ego** *l.* **-ę** *Ins.* **-ą** *Loc.* **-i** *l.* **-im** *Voc.* **-o** *pl.* **-owie** *Gen.* **-ów** *hist.* margrave.

margrabina *f.* margravine.

margrabiowski *a.* margrave's, margravial.

mariacki *a.* Virgin Mary, Our Lady; **hejnał mariacki** bugle-call from the Our Lady Church Tower in Cracow; **Kościół Mariacki** Our Lady Church.

marianin *mp pl.* **-anie** *Gen.* **-an** *rel.* Marist.

mariański¹ *a. rel.* Marist.

mariański² *a. geogr.* Mariana; **Rów Mariański** Mariana Trench.

mariasz *mi Gen. i Acc.* **-a** *karty* marriage.

mariaż *mi Gen.pl.* **-y** *l.* **-ów** (= *małżeństwo*) (= *scalenie*) marriage.

marihuana *f.* (*narkotyk*) marijuana, marihuana.

marimba *f. muz.* (*instrument*) marimba.

marina *f. żegl.* marina.

marines *mp indecl.* (= *amerykańska piechota morska*) Marines.

marionetka *f. Gen.pl.* **-ek** 1. (= *lalka*) marionette, puppet. 2. (= *figurant*) figurehead, puppet.

marionetkowy *a.* 1. (= *lalkowy*) puppet; **teatrzyk marionetkowy** puppet theater. 2. (= *podporządkowany*) puppet; **marionetkowy rząd** puppet government; **marionetkowy sąd** cangaroo court.

marka¹ *f. Gen.pl.* **-ek** 1. (= *znak firmowy*) trade mark. 2. (= *wartość, gatunek*) brand, quality. 3. (= *uznanie*) name. 4. (*samochodu*) make. 5. *przest.* (= *znaczek*) stamp.

marka² *f. Gen.pl.* **-ek** (*waluta*) mark, (*niemiecka*) Deutschmark; (*fińska*) markka.

markazyt *mi min.* marcasite.

marker *mi Gen.* **-a** 1. (= *pisak*) marker pen, highlighter. 2. *med.* (= *wskaźnik*) index, indicator.

market *mi* (*sklep*) market.

marketing *mi ekon.* marketing.

marketingowy *a. ekon.* marketing.

markierant *mp* shirker, slacker.

markietan *mp*, **markietanka** *f. Gen.pl.* **-ek** *hist.* sutler.

markieteria *f. D* **-ii** (= *inkrustacja*) marquetry.

markiz *mp pl.* **-owie** marquis.
markiza *f.* **1.** (*tytuł*) marchioness, marquise.
2. (*daszek*) (*nad wejściem do domu*) awning, canopy; (*nad wejściem do teatru, hotelu*) marquee, marquise. **3.** (*namiot*) marquee. **4.** (*ciastko*) cream-filled cookie.
markotnie *adv.* sadly.
markotnieć *ipf.* get blue, grow melancholy.
markotny *a.* blue, down, sad.
markować *ipf.* **1.** (= *udawać*) feign. **2.** *sport* feint.
markowy *a.* trade-mark, brand-name, quality.
marksista *mp* Marxist.
marksistowski *a.* Marxist.
marksistowsko-leninowski *a.* Marxist-Leninist.
marksizm *mi fil., polit.* Marxism.
marksizm-leninizm *mi fil., polit.* Marxism-Leninism.
markur *ma zool.* markhor (*Capra falconeri*).
marla *f. Gen.pl.* **-i** *tk.* gauze, leno.
marlin *ma icht.* marlin, spearfish (*Makaira l. Tetrapterus*); **marlin biały** white marlin (*Tetraptus albidus l. Makaira albida*).
marlinka *f. Gen.pl.* **-ek** *żegl.* marline, marlin.
marlować *ipf. żegl.* marl.
Marmara *indecl. geogr.* **Morze Marmara** the Sea of Marmara *l.* Marmora.
marmolada *f.* **1.** (= *dżem*) jam; (*z owoców cytrusowych*) marmalade. **2.** *przen., pot.* (= *zmasakrowane ciało*) massacred body.
marmoladka *f. Gen.pl.* **-ek 1.** (*cukierek*) jelly candy. **2.** (= *dżem, galaretka*) jam, jelly.
marmoryzacja *f.* **1.** *sztuka* (= *stiuk*) marbling. **2.** *sztuka, bud.* (*czynność*) marble, marbleizing.
marmoryzować *ipf. sztuka, bud.* marble, marbleize.
marmozeta *f. zool.* marmoset (*Callithrix*); **marmozeta biała** silvery marmoset (*C. argentata*).
marmur *mi geol.* marble; **marmur onyksowy** onyx marble; **marmur zielony** verd(e) antique.
marmurek *mi* **-rk-** *Gen.* **-a 1.** (*kamień dekoracyjny*) marble. **2.** (= *osełka*) whetstone. **3.** *pot.* (*odzież*) stonewashed denim garment.
marmurkować *ipf.* **1.** (= *wykładać marmurem*) line with marble. **2.** (= *malować w deseń naśladujący marmur*) marble.
marmurkowy *a.* marble, marbled, marboreal; **papier marmurkowy** marbled *l.* marble paper; **dżins marmurkowy** stonewashed denim *l.* jean; **szkło marmurkowe** marbled *l.* marble glass; **kot marmurkowy** *zool.* marbled (tiger) cat (*Felis marmorata*).
marmurołom *mi* marble quarry.
marmurowy *a.* **1.** (= *zrobiony z marmuru*) marble, marmoreal, marmorean. **2.** *przen.* (= *twardy, blady*) marmoreal, marmorean, marble.
marne *adv. zob.* **marnie**.
marnie *adv.* (= *źle, kiepsko*) poorly; **czuć się marnie** feel crummy; **marnie skończyć** come to a sticky end.
marnieć *ipf.* (= *stawać się marnym*) deteriorate, decay; (= *marnować się*) run to waste; (*o*

roślinach) wilt, wither; (= *mizernieć*) waste away; **marnieć w oczach** go downhill.
marność *f.* **1.** (= *bezwartościowość*) paltriness, meagerness, flimsiness. **2.** (= *vanitas*) vanity; **marność nad marnościami i wszystko marność** vanity of vanities, all is vanity.
marnotrawca *mp* squanderer, prodigal, wastrel.
marnotrawić *ipf.* waste, squander, dissipate; **marnotrawić czas** waste time.
marnotrawnie *adv.* wastefully, prodigally.
marnotrawny *a.* prodigal; **syn marnotrawny** prodigal son.
marnotrawstwo *n.* prodigality, waste.
marnować *ipf.* waste, fritter away; **marnować siły** waste one's energy; **marnować czas** waste time, fritter away time, trifle, burn the daylight; (*o czasie, pieniądzach*) squander, dissipate, misspend; **marnować czyjś czas** waste sb's time, give sb the runaround; *pot.* jack *l.* jerk sb around; **marnować sobie życie** waste one's life. **~ się** *ipf.* **1.** (= *zaniedbywać się*) languish, waste away; **marnujesz się w tej pracy** you're above this sort of work, this sort of work is beneath you. **2.** (= *psuć się*) deteriorate, go to waste.
marny *a.* **1.** (= *kiepski, małowartościowy*) lousy, flimsy; **marny dochód** miserable income; **marny film** lousy movie; **marna wymówka** flimsy excuse; **marny twój los** *l.* **widok** *pot.* you'll live to regret this, you'll rue the day; **czeka kogoś marny koniec** sb's going to meet a sticky end, sb's in for a sticky end; **nie powiedzieć o kimś marnego słowa** never speak ill of sb. **2.** *lit.* (*dziś tylko we frazach*) (= *bezcelowy*) vain, futile; **marne nadzieje** vain expectations; **pójść na marne** go down the drain; **wyrzucać pieniądze na marne** squander money. **3.** (= *słaby, chorowity*) sickly, weak, ailing.
Marokanka *f. Gen.pl.* **-ek**, **Marokańczyk** *mp* Moroccan.
marokański *a.* Moroccan; **skóra marokańska** *l.* **marokin** morocco.
Maroko *n. geogr.* Morocco.
maron[1] *mi Gen.* **-a** *pl.* **-y** (= *kasztan jadalny*) marron.
maron[2] *mp pl.* **-i** *l.* **-owie** (= *zbiegły niewolnik*) Maroon.
maronicki *a. rel.* Maronite; **kościół maronicki** Maronite Church.
maronita *mp rel.* **maronitka** *f. Gen.pl.* **-ek** Maronite.
Marrakesz *mi geogr.* Marrakech, Marrakesh.
Mars *mi Gen.* **-a** *astron.* Mars. – *mp mit.* Mars.
mars[1] *mi Gen.* **-a** (*mina*) frown.
mars[2] *mi Gen.* **-u** *żegl.* top.
marsel *mi* **-sl-** *Gen.* **-a** *żegl.* topsail.
Marsjanin *mp pl.* **-anie** *Gen.* **-an Marsjanka** *f. Gen.pl.* **-ek** Martian.
marsjański *a. astron.* Martian.
Marsjasz *mp mit.* Marsyas.
marski *a. pat.* cirrhotic.
marskość *f. pat.* cirrhosis; **marskość wątroby** cirrhosis of the liver.

marsowy *a.* stern; **marsowa mina** stern face; **marsowe spojrzenie** stern look.

marspikiel *mi* -kl- *Gen.* -a *żegl.* marlinespike, marline spike.

marsylczyk, marsylianin *mp* Marseillais.

Marsylia *f. Gen.* -ii *geogr.* Marseilles.

Marsylianka *f.* (= *hymn Francji*) the Marseillaise.

marsylka, marsylianka *f. zob.* **marsylczyk.**

marsz[1] *mi Gen.pl.* -ów **1.** (*chód*) march; **biegiem marsz!** double!; **naprzód marsz!** quick march!; **marsz do domu/do szkoły** off you go home/to school! **2.** (= *demonstracja*) march; **czarny marsz** anti-violence march *l.* demonstration; **Marsz Żywych** (= *marsz ofiar holocaustu*) March of the Living. **3.** *Gen.* -a *muz.* march; **marsz weselny** wedding march; **marsz żałobny** funeral march; **kiszki mi marsza grają** *pot., żart.* I'm starving.

marsz[2] *mi Gen.* -a *Gen.pl.* -y *l.* -ów *geol.* marsh soil.

marszałek *mp* -łk- *pl.* -owie **1.** *wojsk.* marshal; **marszałek polny** field marshal. **2.** *parl.* speaker, president; **marszałek sejmu** Speaker of the Sejm; **marszałek senatu** Speaker of the Senate; *US* President of the Senate. **3.** *hist.* marshal; **marszałek dworu** knight marshal.

marszałkostwo *n.* **1.** (*urząd*) marshalcy, marshalship. **2.** *Loc.* -u (= *marszałek z żoną*) marshal and his wife.

marszałkowski *a.* marshal; **buława marszałkowska** marshal's baton; *przen.* marshalcy, marshalship; **laska marszałkowska** *parl.* Speaker's Staff; **straż marszałkowska** *parl.* Speaker's Guard; **złożyć projekt (ustawy) do laski marszałkowskiej** *parl.* present a bill to the Speaker of the Sejm.

marszand *mp* art merchant.

marszczyć *ipf.* **1.** (= *fałdować*) (*o materiale*) gather; (*o wodzie*) ruffle, ripple. **2.** (= *robić zmarszczki*) crease, wrinkle; **marszczyć brwi** knit one's brow; **marszczyć czoło** frown. ~ **się** *ipf.* (= *fałdować się*) crease, wrinkle; (*o brwiach*) contract; (*o tafli wody*) ripple, ruffle; (*o tkaninie*) ruck up; (*o tkaninie, papierze*) cockle.

marszobieg *mi* interval training, fartlek.

marszowy *a.* **1.** (= *rytmiczny*) march; **marszowy krok** *wojsk.* military pace. **2.** (*o zorganizowanym ruchu*) march; **kolumna marszowa** column of route; **szyk marszowy** marching order. **3.** *muz.* march.

marszruta *f.* (= *trasa*) route, itinerary.

marszrutowy *a.* of or related to route *l.* itinerary.

marsżagiel *mi żegl.* topsail.

marten *mi Gen.* -a *metal.* (= *piec martenowski*) open-hearth furnace.

martenowski *a. metal.* open-hearth; **piec martenowski** open-hearth furnace; **stal martenowska** open-hearth steel.

martensy *pl. Gen.* -ów (*buty*) Doc Martens.

martenzyt *mi metal.* martensite.

martini *n. indecl. kulin.* martini; **wytrawne martini** martini dry.

martleta *f. her.* martlet.

martwak *mi pat.* sequestrum.

martwica *f.* **1.** *pat.* necrosis. **2.** *leśn.* (= *korowina*) outer bark. **3.** *geol.* sinter; **martwica krzemionkowa** siliceous sinter; **martwica wapienna** calcareous sinter.

martwiczy *a. pat.* necrotic; **tkanka martwicza** necrotic tissue.

martwić *ipf.* (= *smucić*) sadden; (= *przysparzać trosk*) worry; (= *niepokoić*) upset, trouble; (= *nękać, gnębić*) vex, trouble. ~ **się** *ipf.* worry (*o kogoś/coś* about sb/sth); **nie martw się** don't worry; **nie ma się czym martwić** there's nothing to worry about; **później będziemy się o to martwić** we'll cross that bridge when we come to it.

martwieć *ipf.* **1.** (= *tracić czucie*) become numb. **2.** *pat.* (= *obumierać*) undergo necrobiosis.

martwienie *mi* **1.** (= *utrata czucia*) numbing. **2.** *pat.* necrobiosis.

martwo *adv.* (= *bez życia*) lifelessly; **martwo urodzony** *pat.* stillborn.

martwota *f.* (= *brak objawów życia*) deadness; (= *bezwład*) inertia; (= *odrętwienie*) numbness; (= *otępienie*) torpor.

martwy *a.* **1.** (= *bez życia*) dead; **martwy kapitał** *ekon.* dead *l.* barren capital; **martwy inwentarz** *roln.* dead stock, farm equipment; **martwa natura** *sztuka* still life; **martwe pole** *wojsk.* dead ground; **martwa ręka** *prawn.* mortmain, dead hand; **martwy punkt** standstill; *techn.* dead center, dead point; **martwa litera (prawa)** dead letter; **martwe dusze** (*people whose names are fictitiously entered on lists, registers etc., usu. to obtain illegal financial gains*) dummy IDs; (*osoby korzystające bezprawnie np. z opieki zdrowotnej*) phantom applicants; **coś utknęło w martwym punkcie** sth has come to a standstill; **martwy jak kłoda** as dead as a doornail. **2.** (= *bez wyrazu*) dead; **martwy wzrok** dead look. **3.** (= *nieożywiony*) dead; **martwa cisza** dead calm; **martwa woda** *geogr.* dead water; **martwa fala** *żegl.* swell; **martwa piłka** *sport* dead ball; **martwy poród** *l.* poród martwego płodu *pat.* stillbirth; **Morze Martwe** *geogr.* the Dead Sea; **zwoje znad Morza Martwego** the Dead Sea Scrolls; **martwy sezon** dog days, low season, off-season. **4.** (= *skostniały*) dead; **martwy język** *jęz.* dead language. **5.** (= *zmarły*) the dead; **powstać z martwych** rise from the dead.

martyrolog *mp pl.* -owie *l.* -dzy *kośc.* martyrologist.

martyrologia *f. Gen.* -ii **1.** (= *cierpienie*) martyrdom. **2.** *kośc.* (*księga*) martyrology.

martyrologiczny *a.* martyrological, martyrologic; **muzeum martyrologiczne** museum of martyrdom.

martyrologium *mi. kośc.* martyrology.

maruda *f. l. mp decl. like f. Gen.pl.* -d *l.* -dów **1.** *pot.* (= *męczydusza*) grouch, whiner. **2.** *pot.* (= *ślamazara*) dawdler, slug.

maruder *mp* **1.** *wojsk.* (= *dezerter*) marauder. **2.** (= *ślamazara*) dawdler, laggard.

maruderski *a.* of or related to marauding; **grupy maruderskie** bands of marauders.

maruderstwo *n.* (= *dezercja*) marauding; (= *ociąganie się*) dawdling.

marudny *a.* **1.** *pot.* (= *zrzędliwy*) grouchy, whining. **2.** (*o dziecku*) fretful. **3.** *pot.* (= *ślamazarny*) dawdling, sluggish.

marudzić *ipf.* **1.** *pot.* (= *zrzędzić*) grouch, whine; **nie marudź!** stop whining!, don't you start! **2.** *pot.* (= *guzdrać się*) dawdle, lag behind.

maruna *f. bot.* złocień **maruna** feverfew (*Chrysanthemum parthenium*).

Mary *kulin.* **Krwawa Mary** Bloody Mary.

mary *pl. Gen.* **mar** *lit.* (= *nosze, trumna*) **1.** bier; **leżeć na marach** be dead. **2. czary mary** (= *magia*) wizardry; (*zaklęcie*) hocus-pocus.

marycha *f. pot.* (= *marihuana*) Mary Jane, ganja.

maryjny *a. rz.-kat.* Marian.

marynarka *f. Gen.pl.* **-ek 1.** (= *górna część garnituru*) jacket; **marynarka jednorzędowa** single-breasted jacket; **marynarka dwurzędowa** double-breasted jacket. **2.** (= *flota*) marine, navy; **marynarka handlowa** merchant marine; **marynarka wojenna** navy; **baza marynarki wojennej** naval base; **szkoła marynarki wojennej** Naval Academy.

marynarkowy *a.* of or related to jacket.

marynarski *a.* naval, sailor, sailor's; **marynarski chód** sailor's gait; **marynarska czapka** sailor hat; **marynarski kołnierz** sailor collar; **marynarskie ubranie** sailor suit; **marynarski węzeł** reef knot, square knot.

marynarz *mp* seaman, sailor; **zostać marynarzem** go to sea. – *mi Gen. i Acc.* **-a** (*gra*) rock-paper-scissors; **zagrać w marynarza** draw lots *l.* straws.

marynata *f.* **1.** *kulin.* (*potrawa*) marinade. **2.** (= *zalewa*) marinade; (*np. do ogórków*) pickle.

marynista *mp* *sztuka* (= *malarz*) seascapist, marine painter; (= *pisarz*) marine writer.

marynistyczny *a. sztuka* marine; **obraz marynistyczny** seascape.

marynistyka *f. sztuka* (*o malarstwie*) seascape painting; (*o pisarstwie*) marine fiction.

marynować *ipf.* **1.** *kulin.* (*o mięsie, rybie*) marinate, marinade; (*o warzywach*) pickle; **grzyby marynowane** pickled mushrooms. **2.** *przen., pot.* (= *przechowywać*) keep, store.

marzanka *f. Gen.pl.* **-ek** *bot.* woodruff (*Asperula*); **marzanka wonna** sweet woodruff (*Asperula odorata*).

marzanna[1] *f. bot.* madder (*Rubia*).

marzanna[2] *f.* (*kukła*) straw dummy representing winter; **topienie marzanny** traditional drowning of a straw dummy symbolizing winter.

marzanowate *pl. Gen.* **-ych** *bot.* Rubiaceae family (*Rubiaceae*).

marzec *mi* **-rc-** *Gen.* **-a** March; **w marcu jak w garncu** March enters as a lamb and leaves like a lion.

marzenie *n.* **1.** (= *fantazjowanie*) dream. **2.** (= *uługa*) dream, fantasy; **marzenie ściętej głowy** pie in the sky; **szczyt marzeń** climax of one's dreams; **być u szczytu marzeń** achieve the ultimate success; **marzenie senne** dream; **marzenie** *l.* **sen na jawie** daydreaming; **pożegnać się z marzeniami** kiss one's dreams goodbye. **3.** (= *mrzonka*) daydream. **4.** *pot.* (= *doskonałość*) knockout.

marzłoć *f. geol.* permafrost.

marznąć *ipf.* **-nij, -zł** *l.* **-znął -zła -zli 1.** (= *zamarzać*) freeze. **2.** (= *ziębnąć*) freeze.

marzyciel *mp*, **marzycielka** *f. Gen.pl.* **-ek** daydreamer, stargazer.

marzycielski *a.* dreamy.

marzycielstwo *n.* daydreaming.

marzyć *ipf.* **1.** (= *roić*) dream (*o kimś/czymś* about sth/sb); **nie ma co o tym marzyć** dream on!, in your dreams!, it is out of the question; **marzę o wakacjach** I'm dying for a vacation; **marzyć o zrobieniu czegoś** ache to do sth; **głupi marzy o bogactwie, a mądry o szczęściu** a fool dreams of wealth, a sage of happiness. **2.** (= *fantazjować*) daydream, fantasize; **marzyć o niebieskich migdałach** daydream, build castles in the air. **~ się** *ipf.* **1.** (= *nęcić wyobraźnię*) occupy one's thoughts; **marzy mi się nowy samochód** I can't stop dreaming about a new car, I'm dying for a car. **2.** (= *śnić się*) dream.

marzymięta *f. bot.* elshotzia (*Elsholtzia*).

marża *f. ekon.* margin, mark-up; **marża hurtowa** wholesale margin; **marża detaliczna** retail margin.

masa *f.* **1.** (= *substancja*) mass; **masa bituminczna** *bud.* bituminous mix; **masa ceramiczna** body; **masa perłowa** mother-of-pearl; **masa plastyczna** plastic; **zbijać (się) w gęstą masę** mat. **2.** (= *mnóstwo*) masses; **cała masa czegoś** masses of sth, bags of sth; *Br.* loads of sth; **masa pieniędzy** a mint; **kosztować masę pieniędzy** cost a bundle. **3.** *chem., fiz.* mass; **masa atomowa** atomic mass; **masa cząsteczkowa** molecular mass; **masa krytyczna** critical mass; **masa molowa** molar mass; **masa spoczynkowa** rest mass; **masa właściwa** mass density. **4.** (= *ogół ludzi*) masses; **masy robotnicze** the working classes; **ciemna masa** *pot.* meatball, fathead. **5.** *el.* ground; *Br.* earth. **6.** *prawn.* estate; **masa spadkowa** inheritance, estate; **masa upadłościowa** estate (*of a bankrupt*); **zarządca masy upadłościowej** receiver in bankruptcy.

Masaj *mp pl.* **-owie, Masajka** *f. Gen.pl.* **-ek** Masai, Maasai.

masakra *f.* massacre; (*np. w bitwie*) carnage; (*np. bezbronnego tłumu*) battue.

masakrować *ipf.* **1.** (= *mordować*) massacre. **2.** (= *ranić*) beat up, batter, maul.

masarnia *f. Gen.pl.* **-i** *l.* **-ń** butcher's shop.

masarski *a.* of or related to butcher *l.* butcher's shop.

masarz *mp* butcher.

masaż *mi Gen.pl.* **-y** *l.* **-ów** massage; **masaż erotyczny** erotic massage; **masaż stóp** foot massage; **masaż serca** *med.* heart massage; **zrobić komuś masaż** give sb a massage.

masażysta *mp* masseur.

masażystka *f. Gen.pl.* **-ek** masseuse.

mascara *f.* (= *tusz do rzęs*) mascara.

maseczka *f. Gen.pl.* **-ek** **1.** (= *maska*) mask; **maseczka chirurgiczna** surgical mask. **2.** (*kosmetyczna*) face pack, mask, facial; **maseczka błotna** mud pack.

maselnica *f.* **1.** (= *urządzenie do wyrobu masła*) churn. **2.** (= *naczynie na masło*) butter dish.

maselniczka *f. Gen.pl.* **-ek** butter dish.

maselko *n. Gen.pl.* **-łek** butter.

maser *mi Gen.* **-a** *techn., fiz.* maser.

maserowy *a. techn., fiz.* maser.

maska[1] *f. Gen.pl.* **-ek** **1.** (= *ozdobna osłona twarzy*) mask. **2.** *przen.* (= *poza, kostium*) mask, guise; **maska obojętności** mask of indifference; **pod maską przyjaźni** under the guise of friendship; **przywdziewać maskę** masquerade; **zrzucić maskę** take off one's mask, drop one's mask, show one's true colors; **zdzierać z kogoś maskę** unmask sb, expose sb. **3.** (= *odlew twarzy*) mask; **maska pośmiertna** death mask. **4.** (= *ochrona twarzy*) mask; **maska chirurgiczna** *med.* surgical mask; **maska przeciwgazowa** gas mask; **maska do nurkowania** diving mask, scuba mask. **5.** *mot.* (= *pokrywa silnika*) hood; *Br.* bonnet. **6.** *med.* (*część aparatu tlenowego*) oxygen mask. **7.** *fot.* mask.

maska[2] *f. Gen.pl.* **-ek** (= *śpiewogra*) masque, mask.

maskarada *f.* (*zabawa*) masquerade.

maskonur *ma orn.* puffin (*Fratercula arctica*).

maskotka *f. Gen.pl.* **-ek** **1.** (= *talizman*) mascot. **2.** (= *zabawka*) stuffed animal, soft toy.

maskować *ipf.* **1.** (= *zakrywać*) (*o uczuciach*) mask, hide, suppress; (*o zapachu*) mask; *wojsk.* camouflage. **2.** (= *udawać*) assume a disguise, dissemble. **3.** *chem.* mask. ~ **się** *ipf.* **1.** (= *konspirować się*) camouflage. **2.** (= *ukrywać się*) masquerade, dissemble.

maskownica *f. fot.* easel.

maskowniczy *a.* masking, camouflaging; **siatka maskownicza** *l.* **maskująca** camouflage netting.

maskowy *a.* mask; **bal maskowy** masked ball, masque.

maskujący *a.* masking; **siatka maskująca** *wojsk.* camouflage netting; **taśma maskująca** masking tape.

maskulinizacja *f.* **1.** (*np. w miejscu pracy*) (= *antyfeminizacja*) male domination. **2.** *biol., med., jęz.* masculinization.

maskulinizm *mi* **1.** (= *naśladowanie mężczyzn*) masculinity. **2.** *med.* masculinity.

maskulinizować *ipf.* **1.** (*np. o miejscu pracy*) (= *zdominować*) dominate by males. **2.** *biol., med., jęz.* masculinize. ~ **się** *ipf.* (*np. o niektórych zawodach*) become male-dominated, give way to male domination.

masło *n. Gen.pl.* **maseł** **1.** *kulin.* (*tłuszcz*) butter; **masło kakaowe** cocoa butter; **masło kokosowe** coconut butter; **masło orzechowe** peanut butter; **masło roślinne** vegetable butter; **to bułka z masłem** it's a piece of cake; **coś idzie jak po maśle** it's a plain sailing; **wyglądać jak pączek w maśle** be a picture of health; **masło maślane** *przen.* tautology. **2.** (*kostka*) slab of butter; **smarować masłem** spread with butter, butter.

masłosz *mi bot.* shea (*Butytrospermum parkii*).

masłowy *a.* butter; *chem.* butyric; **fermentacja masłowa** butyric fermentation; **kwas masłowy** butyric acid.

masochista *mp* masochist.

masochistka *f. Gen.pl.* **-ek** *zob.* **masochista**.

masochistyczny *a.* masochist, masochistic.

masochizm *mi pat. t. przen.* masochism.

mason *mp* (= *wolnomularz*) Freemason, Mason.

masoneria *f. Gen.* **-ii** Freemasonry, Masonry.

masonka *f. Gen.pl.* **-ek** *zob.* **mason**.

masoński *a.* Masonic, Freemasonic; **loża masońska** Masonic lodge.

masować *ipf.* massage. ~ **się** *ipf.* **1.** massage. **2.** get a massage.

masowiec *mi* **-wc-** *Gen.* **-a** *żegl.* bulk carrier, bulker.

masowo *adv.* in large quantities *l.* numbers; **produkować masowo** mass produce.

masowość *f.* (*demonstracji, produkcji*) large scale *l.* character.

masowy *a.* **1.** (= *liczny*) mass; **broń masowej zagłady** *l.* **masowego rażenia** *wojsk.* weapons of mass destruction; **środki masowego przekazu** mass media; **masowe deportacje** mass deportation; **masowy wykup czegoś** run on sth. **2.** (*dla ogółu*) popular; **kultura masowa** popular *l.* pop culture; **masowy odbiorca** (*zwłaszcza podatny na manipulację*) admass. **3.** *chem., fiz.* mass; **liczba masowa** mass number.

masówka *f. Gen.pl.* **-ek** **1.** *pot.* (= *wiec*) rally, mass meeting. **2.** *pot.* (= *produkcja masowa*) mass production.

massasauga *f. zool.* massasauga (*Sistrurus catenatus*).

mass media *pl. Gen.* **-ów** mass media.

mastaba *f.* (= *grobowiec*) mastaba, mastabah.

mastektomia *f. chir.* mastectomy.

mastiff *ma zob.* **mastyf**.

mastodont *ma paleont.* mastodon (*Mastodon l. Mammut*).

masturbacja *f.* masturbation; **uprawiać masturbację** masturbate.

masturbacyjny *a.* masturbation.

masturbować się *ipf.* masturbate.

mastyf *ma kynol.* mastiff.

mastyka *f. zob.* **mastyks**.

mastyks *mi* (= *żywica*) mastic, mastic gum; **mastyks asfaltowy** asphalt mastic.

mastyksowy *a.* mastic; **drzewo mastyksowe** *bot.* mastic tree *l.* shrub, mastic (*Pistacia lentiscus*).

maswerk *mi bud., sztuka* tracery.

masyw *mi* **1.** (= *duży obiekt*) pile; large object occupying a substantial area (*e.g. a large building*); **masyw katedry/budynku** large *l.* massive cathedral/edifice. **2.** *geol.* massif; **masyw centralny** massif; **Masyw Centralny** Massif Central (*in France*). **3.** *techn.* solid tire.

masywnie *adv.* **1.** (= *mocno, trwale*) massively, solidly. **2.** (= *muskularnie*) heftily.

masywny *a.* **1.** (= *mocny, wielki*) massive, solid, bulky. **2.** (= *muskularny*) hefty.

masz *ipf. zob.* **mieć.**

maszerować *ipf.* march; **maszerować w miejscu** *muz., wojsk.* mark time; **maszerować w takt czegoś** march in step with sth.

maszkara *f.* **1.** (= *pokraka*) eyesore, monster. **2.** *zob.* **maszkaron.**

maszkaron *mi Gen.* **-a** *bud.* mask, mascaron.

maszt *mi* **1.** (= *słup*) pole; **maszt antenowy** aerial mast; **maszt cumowniczy** *lotn.* (*np. dla sterowców*) mooring mast; **maszt flagowy** flagpole, flagstaff; **opuścić flagę do połowy masztu** (*na znak żałoby*) half-mast a flag; **wciągnąć flagę na maszt** hoist a flag, run up a flag. **2.** *żegl.* mast; **maszt przedni** foremast; **maszt tylni** aftermast.

masztalerz *mp pl. Gen. i Acc.* **-y** *l.* **-ów** *przest.* stableman, groom; hostler, ostler; *rzad.* currier.

masztowiec *mi* **-wc-** *Gen.* **-a** *żegl.* sailing ship.

masztowy *a. żegl.* of or related to a mast, -masted; **trójmasztowy** three-masted.

maszyna *f.* **1.** *techn.* machine; **maszyna parowa** steam engine; **maszyna do szycia** sewing machine; **maszyna do pisania** typewriter; **pisać na maszynie** typewrite; **maszyna analogowa** *komp.* analog computer; **maszyna cyfrowa** *komp.* digital computer; **maszyna prosta** (simple) machine; **budowa maszyn** mechanical engineering; **trybik w maszynie** (*o człowieku*) a cog in the wheel. **2.** *przen.* (*o człowieku*) (= *automat*) machine. **3.** *pot.* (*o samochodzie, samolocie*) machine.

maszyneria *f. Gen.* **-ii 1.** *techn.* machinery. **2.** *przen.* (= *system, machina*) machinery. **3.** *teatr* set changer.

maszynista *mp* **1.** *kol.* (engine) driver; (*elektrowozu*) motorman. **2.** (= *operator maszyny*) machine operator. **3.** *teatr* scene shifter.

maszynistka *f.* **1.** (= *kobieta zawodowo pisząca na maszynie*) typist. **2.** *zob.* **maszynista** 1.

maszynka *f. Gen.pl.* **-ek 1.** *techn.* (= *maszyna*) machine; **maszynka do golenia** (*elektryczna*) electric razor *l.* shaver; (*zwykła*) safety razor; **maszynka do mięsa** mincer; **maszynka do strzyżenia** hair trimmer *l.* clipper; **maszynka do robienia pieniędzy** (*np. korupcjogenna ustawa*) a license to print money; **przepuścić kogoś przez maszynkę** (= *poddać kogoś ciężkiej próbie*) put sb through the mill. **2.** (= *kuchenka, piecyk*) cooker; **maszynka spirytusowa** propane *l.* Coleman stove.

maszynopis *mi* typescript; **w maszynopisie** typewritten.

maszynopisanie *mi* typewriting, typing.

maszynownia *f. Gen.pl.* **-i** engine room.

maszynowo *adv.* (= *automatycznie*) by means of a machine, mechanically; **obrabiać maszynowo** machine; **wykonany maszynowo** machine-made.

maszynowy *a.* **1.** (= *dotyczący maszyny*) machine; **karabin maszynowy** *wojsk.* machine gun; **gniazdo karabinów maszynowych** *wojsk.* ma-

chine gun nest; **papier maszynowy** typing *l.* typewriter paper; **pistolet maszynowy** *wojsk.* machine gun; **park maszynowy** plant and machinery. **2.** (= *mechaniczny*) machine; **błąd maszynowy** *l.* drukarski typo, typing error; **język maszynowy** *komp.* machine language; **tłumaczenie maszynowe** *komp.* machine translation.

maść¹ *f. med.* (= *krem, smarowidło*) ointment, unguent; **maść gojąca** salve.

maść² *f.* **1.** (= *barwa sierści*) color. **2.** *przen.* (= *typ, gatunek*) description; **wszelkiej maści** of every description.

maślacz *mi Gen.* **-a** *l.* **-u** *kulin.* (*wino*) type of sweet or semi-dry Tokay wine.

maślak *mi Gen.* **-a** *bot.* boletus (*Boletus*).

maślan *mi chem.* butyrate.

maślanka *f. Gen.pl.* **-ek 1.** *kulin.* (*napój*) buttermilk. **2.** *bot.* **maślanka wiązkowa** (*grzyb*) Naematoloma fasciculare (*Naematoloma fasciculare*).

maślany *a.* (= *z masła, zawierający masło*) buttery; **herbatnik maślany** butter cookie, shortbread; **maślane oczy** *przen.* cloudy *l.* hazy *l.* filmy eyes; **mieć maślane ręce** *przen.* be a butterfingers.

maślnica *f.* butter dish.

mat¹ *mi Gen.* **-u** *tylko sing.* (= *brak połysku*) matte, matt, mat; **na mat** matte-finished.

mat² *mi Gen.* **-a** *tylko sing. szachy* checkmate; *rzad.* mate; **dostać mata** be checkmated; **dać komuś mata** checkmate sb; **szach i mat** checkmate.

mat³ *mp Gen.* **-a** *pl.* **maci** *wojsk.* petty officer third class; *Br.* leading seaman.

mata *f.* **1.** (= *materac, słomianka*) mat. **2.** *sport* mat; **rzucić kogoś na matę** throw sb on the mat.

matactwo *n.* jiggery-pokery, hocus-pocus, trickery.

matacz *mp pot.* (= *oszust*) swindler, con man.

mataczyć *ipf. pot.* (= *oszukiwać*) trick, dupe.

matador *mp* **1.** (= *toreador*) matador. **2.** *przen., iron.* (= *znakomitość*) bigwig, heavyweight.

matczyny *a. lit.* motherly; **matczyna miłość** motherly love; **trzymać się matczynej spódnicy** be tied to one's mother's apron strings.

matczysko *n. emf.* old woman, mam(m)a.

mate *n. indecl.* **1.** *bot.* maté, mate (*Ilex paraguariensis*). **2.** *kulin.* (*napój*) maté, mate, yerba maté.

mateczka *f. Gen.pl.* **-ek 1.** *emf.* (= *matka*) mommy, mommie. **2.** *pot.* (*o kobiecie*) ma'am, m'am.

matecznik *mi Gen.* **-a 1.** (= *gęstwina*) virgin forest. **2.** *przen.* (= *kryjówka*) lair, den.

mateczny *a. bot., zool.* parent, parental; **komórka mateczna** *pszczelarstwo* queen cell; **roślina mateczna** *ogr., leśn.* parent plant.

matematyczka *f. Gen.pl.* **-ek** *zob.* **matematyk.**

matematycznie *adv.* **1.** (= *rachunkowo*) mathematically. **2.** (= *dokładnie*) mathematically, precisely.

matematyczny *a.* (= *dotyczący matematyki*) **1.** mathematical, mathematic; **analiza matematy-**

czna analysis, calculus; **formuła matematyczna** mathematic fomula; **tablica matematyczna** calculator. **2.** (= *dokładny*) mathematical, mathematically precise; **mieć umysł matematyczny** be mathematically minded.

matematyk *mp* **1.** (*naukowiec*) mathematician. **2.** *pot.* (*nauczyciel*) mathematics *l.* math teacher.

matematyka *f.* **1.** mathematics; **matematyka wyższa** higher mathematics; **mieć głowę do matematyki** have a good head for figures. **2.** *uniw.*, *pot.* (= *wydział matematyki*) faculty of mathematics. **3.** *szkoln.*, *pot.* (= *lekcja matematyki*) math class.

matematyzacja *f. lit.* mathematicization.

materac *mi* Gen. -a Gen.pl. -y *l.* -ów **1.** (*do leżenia, do ćwiczeń, do pływania*) mattress; **dmuchany materac** air mattress, inflatable mattress; **materac przeciwodleżynowy** mattress for prevention of bedsores. **2.** *wojsk.* (= *osłona*) mat.

materacyk *mi* Gen. -a small mattress.

materia *f.* Gen. -ii **1.** (*ogół przedmiotów*) matter; **materia międzygwiezdna/międzyplanetarna** interstellar/interplanetary matter; **przemiana materii** *biol.* metabolism. **2.** *fil.* matter, the material. **3.** (= *problematyka*) matter; **w tej materii** on this point. **4.** *arch.* (= *materiał*) material, fabric. **5.** *arch.* (= *ropa*) matter.

materialista *mp*, **materialistka** *f.* Gen.pl. -ek *fil.*, *pot.* materialist.

materialistyczny *a. fil.*, *pot.* materialistic; **filozofia materialistyczna** *fil.* materialism.

materializm *mi fil.*, *pot.* (= *komercjalizm*) materialism.

materializować się *ipf.* (= *urzeczywistniać się*) materialise.

materialnie *adv.* materially.

materialność *f.* materiality.

materialny *a.* **1.** (= *fizyczny, konkretny*) material; **kultura materialna** material culture. **2.** (= *finansowy*) material; **pomoc materialna** material help; **korzyści materialne** material gains; **od strony materialnej** on the financial side. **3.** *prawn.* substantive; **prawo materialne** substantive law.

materiał *mi* **1.** (= *surowiec*) material; **materiały biurowe** office supplies; **materiały budowlane** building materials; **materiał wybuchowy** explosive; **zmęczenie materiału** fatigue (*e.g. metal fatigue*); **dobry materiał na żonę/męża** good wife/husband material. **2.** (= *wiadomości, dokumentacja*) material; **materiał dowodowy** body of evidence; **materiał obciążający** incriminating evidence; **materiał archiwalny** archive material. **3.** (= *tkanina*) material, fabric.

materiałochłonność *f.* material intensity.

materiałochłonny *a.* material intensive.

materiałooszczędny *a.* material-saving.

materiałowy *a.* (of) materials; **gospodarka materiałowa** materials management.

materiałoznawca *mp* materials expert.

materiałoznawstwo *n.* materials science.

matka *f.* Gen.pl. -ek **1.** (= *rodzicielka*) mother;

rodzona **matka** natural mother; **matka chrzestna** godmother; **Matka Boska** *l.* **Boża** Heavenly Mother, Mother of Jesus; **dzień matki** mother's day; **jak go matka zrodziła** in his birthday suit; **matka jest tylko jedna** you only have one mother; **mieć coś po matce** take after one's mother; **powtarzać jak za panią matką** (= *powtarzać bezmyślnie*) repeat sth parrot-fashion; (= *naśladować zachowanie*) take a leaf from sb's book; **wyssać coś z mlekiem matki** take sth in with your mother's milk; **jak matkę kocham** on my mother's grave; **zbić kogoś tak, że go rodzona matka nie pozna** beat sb so badly that their own mother wouldn't recognise them; **potrzeba jest matką wynalazków** necessity is the mother of invention; **drugiej matki nie znajdziesz** you only have one mother; **nadzieja jest matką głupich** hope is the mother of all fools; **czcij ojca swego i matkę swoją** honor thy mother and thy father. **2.** (= *samica*) mother. **3.** (= *przeorysza*) mother; **matka przełożona** mother superior. **4.** (*określenie głównego obiektu*) mother. **5.** *ent.* (*u pszczół, mrówek*) queen. **6.** *sport* (= *kapitan*) team leader. **7.** *pot.*, *żart.* (= *żona*) the missis, the missus.

matkobójca *mp*, **matkobójczyni** *f.* matricide.

matkobójczy *a.* matricidal.

matkobójczyni *f.* zob. **matkobójca.**

matkobójstwo *n.* matricide.

matkować *ipf.* mother (*komuś* sb).

matma *f. pot.* (= *matematyka*) math, *Br.* maths.

matnia *f.* Gen.pl. -i **1.** (= *sidła*) snare. **2.** (*część sieci*) cod end. **3.** (= *sytuacja bez wyjścia*) cul de sac; **wpędzić kogoś w matnię** draw sb into a trap; **wyjść z matni** escape from a trap.

matoł *mp pl.* -y **1.** *pat.* moron. **2.** *pog.*, *pot.* (= *głupek*) moron, halfwit.

matołectwo *n. pat.* moronism.

matołek *mp* -łk- *pl.* -i *l.* -owie zob. **matoł.**

matować[1] *ipf. techn.* mat, matt.

matować[2] *ipf. szachy* mate.

matowieć *ipf.* become matt.

matowy[1] *a.* **1.** (= *bez połysku*) matt; **matowa cera** dull complexion. **2.** (= *przytłumiony*) (*o głosie*) dull. **3.** (= *nieprzezroczysty*) (*o szkle*) frosted.

matowy[2] *a. szachy* mate.

matówka *f.* Gen.pl. -ek *fot.* viewfinder, focusing screen.

matriarchalny *a.* matriarchal.

matriarchat *mi* matriarchy.

matrioszka *f.* matrioshka.

matrona *f.* **1.** *hist.* matron. **2.** *lit.* matriarch; *żart.* matron.

matronimik *mi jęz.* metronymic.

matryca *f. druk., komp., techn.* matrix.

matrykuła *f. hist.* register of students.

matrymonialny *a.* matrimonial; **biuro matrymonialne** marriage bureau; **ogłoszenie matrymonialne** singles ad; **oszust matrymonialny** matrimonial fraud.

matuchna *f.* Gen.pl. -chen mater.

matula *f.* mater.

matura *f.* **1.** (*egzamin*) high school finals (*in*

Poland). **2.** (= *świadectwo dojrzałości*) high school diploma (*in Poland*).

maturalny *a.* graduation; **bal maturalny** graduation ball; **świadectwo maturalne** high school diploma (*in Poland*); **egzamin maturalny** high school finals (*in Poland*).

maturzysta *mp*, **maturzystka** *f. Gen.pl.* **-ek** high school graduate (*in Poland*).

matuś *f. pl.* **-e** *emf.* mom.

matuzalem *mp pl.* **-owie** Methuselah.

Maur *mp pl.* **-owie** Moor.

Mauretania *f.* Mauritania.

Mauretanka *f. Gen.pl.* **-ek, Mauretańczyk** *mp* Mauritanian.

mauretański *a.* Mauritanian.

Mauritius *mi* Mauritius.

mauzer *mi Gen.* **-a** *broń* Mauser.

mauzoleum *n. sing. indecl. pl.* **-ea** *Gen.* **-eów** mausoleum.

mawiać *ipf.* always say; **jak mawiał mój ojciec** as my father used to say.

mazać *ipf.* **mażę mażesz 1.** (= *smarować*) smear. **2.** (= *gryzmolić*) scrawl. **3.** (= *ścierać*) wipe. **~ się** *ipf.* **1.** (= *smarować się*) smear o.s. **2.** (= *rozcierać się*) become smudged. **3.** *pot.* (= *płakać*) blubber.

mazagran *mi* (*napój*) iced coffee with rum.

mazak *mi Gen.* **-a 1.** (= *pisak*) felt tip pen. **2.** (= *pędzel*) large paintbrush.

mazanina *f.* (= *bazgranina*) scrawl.

mazdaizm *mi rel.* Zoroastrianism, Zoroastrism; Mazdaism.

mazdajski *a. rel.* Zoroastrian; Mazdean.

mazer *mi* **1.** (*wzór*) grain. **2.** (*technika*) graining.

mazgaić się *ipf.* **-ję -isz** (= *płakać*) sob.

mazgaj *mp Gen.pl.* **-ów** *l.* **-ai** crybaby.

maziczka *f. bot.* madia (*Madia*).

mazidło *n. Gen.pl.* **-deł 1.** (= *maść*) liniment. **2.** *pot.* (= *smarowidło*) ointment.

maziowy *a.* gungy; **błona maziowa** *anat.* synovial membrane; **kaletka maziowa** *anat.* synovial bursa.

mazistość *f.* gunginess.

mazisty *a.* gungy.

maznąć *pf.* **maznę maźniesz, -ij** *zob.* **mazać.**

mazowiecki *a.* Mazovian; **dialekt mazowiecki** *jęz.* Mazovian dialect.

Mazowszanin *mp pl.* **-anie** *Gen.* **-an, Mazowszanka** *f. Gen.pl.* **-ek** Mazovian.

Mazowsze *n. geogr.* Mazovia.

mazu *ma icht.* cherry salmon (*Oncorhynchus masu*).

Mazur *mp*, **Mazurka** *f. Gen.pl.* **-ek 1.** (= *mieszkaniec Mazur*) Masurian. **2.** (= *mieszkaniec Mazowsza*) Mazovian.

mazur *mi Gen. i Acc.* **-a** *muz.* (*taniec*) (*melodia*) mazurka; **biały mazur** the last mazurka (*danced at dawn*).

mazurek *mi* **-rk-** *Gen.* **-a 1.** *muz.* mazurka; **Mazurek Dąbrowskiego** Dabrowski's Mazurka. **2.** (*ciasto*) traditional Polish Easter cake. – *ma* **-rk-** *orn.* tree sparrow (*Passer montanus*).

Mazurka *f. Gen.pl.* **-ek** *zob.* **Mazur.**

mazurski *a.* Masurian; **Pojezierze Mazurskie** *geogr.* Masurian Lakeland.

Mazury *pl. Gen.* **-r** *geogr.* Masuria.

mazurzenie *n. jęz.* the Mazovian pronunciation (*of Polish sibilants*), the mazurzenie pronunciation.

mazut *mi chem.* mazout, mazut; heavy fuel oil.

maź *f. pl.* **-e 1.** (*substancja*) gunge; **maź płodowa** *fizj.* vernix caseosa; **maź stawowa** *anat.* synovial fluid. **2.** *pot.* (= *smar*) axlegrease.

maźnica *f.* **1.** (*naczynie*) greasepot. **2.** *techn.* journal box.

mąciciel *mp*, **mącicielka** *f. Gen.pl.* **-ek** troublemaker, disturber of the peace.

mącić *ipf.* **1.** (= *mieszać*) stir up. **2.** *przen.* (= *niepokoić, zakłócać*) disturb; **mącić komuś spokój** upset sb, worry sb; **mącić komuś w głowie** put ideas into sb's head. **~ się** *ipf.* **1.** (= *kotłować się*) be stirred up; **komuś mąci się w oczach** sb's eyes are blearing; **wzrok się komuś mąci** sb's sight is failing. **2.** *przen.* (= *gmatwać się*) muddy; **mąci mi się w głowie** I feel giddy.

mąciwoda *f. l. mp decl. like f. Gen.pl.* **-ód** *l.* **-ów** troublemaker.

mączka *f. Gen.pl.* **-ek** *techn.* flour, meal; **mączka ziemniaczana** potato flour; **mączka rybna** fish meal; **mączka kostna** bone meal.

mączniak *mi Gen.* **-a 1.** *bot.* powdery mildew (*Erysiphaceae*). **2.** (*choroba*) powdery mildew.

mącznica *f.* **1.** (*skrzynia*) meal chest. **2.** (*otwór*) flour hopper. **3.** *bot.* **mącznica lekarska** bearberry (*Arctostaphylos uvaursi*).

mącznik *ma ent.* mealworm (*Tenebrio*); **mącznik młynarek** common mealworm, yellow mealworm (*Tenebrio molitor*).

mączny *a.* flour, floury; **produkty mączne** flour products; **jarząb mączny** *bot.* whitebeam (*Sorbus aria*).

mądrala *f. l. mp decl. like f. Gen.pl.* **-i** *l.* **-ów** *pot., iron.* smart aleck.

mądralińska *f. Gen.* **-ej, mądraliński** *mp pot., iron.* smart aleck.

mądrość *f.* **1.** (= *rozsądek*) wisdom; **mądrość książkowa** book learning; **mądrość życiowa** the wisdom of experience; **zęby mądrości** *anat.* wisdom teeth; **Księga Mądrości** *Bibl.* Wisdom of Solomon. **2.** (= *przemyślność*) wisdom. **3.** *zw. pl.* (= *mądre poglądy, powiedzenia*) wise saying; **ludowe mądrości** folk wisdom.

mądry *a.* **1.** (= *rozumny*) wise; **mądra głowa** a wise head; **nie bądź taki mądry!** *pot.* don't try to be so smart!, don't be such a smart aleck!; **bądź tu mądry i pisz wiersze** how am I going to get out of this one?; **mądrej głowie dość dwie słowie** a word to the wise is enough; **mądry Polak po szkodzie** wise after the event. **2.** (= *rozważny*) smart; **mądry wykład** smart lecture; **mądra książka** smart book. **3.** (= *sprytny*) smart; **mądry pies** smart dog. **4.** (= *trudny*) tough; **to dla mnie za mądre** it's too tough for me. – *mp* a wise man; **co u mądrych w myśli, to u głupich w ustach** a fool says what a wise man thinks; **głupi marzy o bo-**

gactwie, mądry o szczęściu a fool dreams of riches, a wise man of happiness.

mądrze *adv.* wisely; **mądrze coś robić** do sth wisely.

mądrzeć *ipf.* become wiser.

mądrzyć się *ipf.* play the wise guy; **nie mądrzyj się, co?** don't be such a smart aleck!

mąk[1] *f. zob.* **męka.**

mąk[2] *f. zob.* **mąka.**

mąka *f.* 1. *(ze zboża)* flour; **mąka pszenna/żytnia/ryżowa** wheat/rye/rice flour; **mąka kukurydziana** cornflour; **mąka tortowa** cake flour; **z tej mąki chleba nie będzie** nothing will come of this, this will come to nothing. 2. *(proszek)* flour; **mąka kartoflana** *l.* **ziemniaczana** potato flour.

mąkinia *f. Gen.pl.* **-i** *bot.* whitebeam *(Sorbus aria).*

mątew *f.* **-twi-** *pl.* **-e, mątewka** *f. Gen.pl.* **-ek** whisk.

mątwa *f. zool.* cuttlefish *(Sepia).*

mąż *mp* **-ę-** *pl.* **-owie** 1. *(= małżonek)* husband; **wyjść za mąż** get married; **złapać męża** *pot.* make a catch; **nazywać się po mężu** take one's husband's name; **trzymać męża pod pantoflem** keep one's husband under one's thumb; **mąż głową domu, a żona szyją** the woman is the power behind the throne. 2. *lit.* *(= mężczyzna)* man; **mąż zaufania** intermediary; **mąż stanu** statesman; **mąż opatrznościowy** savior, man of the moment; **jak jeden mąż** as one man, with one accord.

mchu *itd.* *mi zob.* **mech.**

mdleć *ipf.* 1. *(= tracić przytomność)* faint; **mdleć ze strachu** faint from fear; **mdleć z zachwytu** go into ruptures. 2. *(= słabnąć)* flag, droop. 3. *(= drętwieć)* go numb.

mdlić *ipf.* nauseate, make sick; **mdli mnie** I feel sick.

mdławy *a.* 1. *(= mdlący)* nauseating, sickly. 2. *(= blady)* *(o świetle)* faint. 3. *(= mglisty)* *(o kolorach)* muddy.

mdłości *pl. Gen.* **-i** *(= nudności)* nausea; **dostawać mdłości** feel nauseous, feel sick; **przyprawiać kogoś o mdłości** *l.* **wywoływać u kogoś mdłości** make sb feel nauseous, make sb feel sick.

mdły *a.* 1. *(= wywołujący nudności)* nauseating. 2. *(= słaby, niewyrazisty)* *(o świetle)* faint. 3. *(= nijaki, bez wyrazu)* *(o książce, filmie, utworze muzycznym)* bland. 4. *(= bez smaku)* *(o jedzeniu)* bland, insipid. 5. *(= nudny)* *(o osobie, rozmowie)* vapid.

me *a.* *(= moje)* *zob.* **mój.**

meander *mi* **-dr-** *Gen.* **-a** *bud., geogr.* meander.

meandry *pl. Gen.* **-ów** *przen.* *(= komplikacje)* twists and turns.

mebel *mi* **-bl-** *Gen.* **-a** a piece of furniture; **meble** *(pl.)* furniture.

meblarski *a.* furniture making, furniture maker's.

meblarstwo *n.* furniture making.

meblarz *mp* furniture maker.

meblościanka *f. Gen.pl.* **-ek** *(mebel)* wall unit, shelf unit.

meblować *ipf.* furnish.

meblowóz *mi* **-o-** furniture van.

meblowy *a.* furniture.

mecenas *mp pl.* **-i** *l.* **-owie** 1. *(= opiekun)* patron; **mecenas sztuki** a patron of the arts. 2. *(= adwokat)* polite form of address for a lawyer.

mecenasowski *a.* benevolent.

mecenat *mi* patronage.

mech *mi* **mch-** 1. *bot.* moss *(Muscus).* 2. *(= meszek, puszek)* fluff, down. 3. *przen.* *(= kurz)* fluff. 4. *myśl.* *(= scypuł)* velvet.

mechacenie (się) *n.* pilling.

mechacić się *ipf.* pill.

mechanicyzm *mi fil.* mechanism.

mechanicznie *adv.* *(= maszynowo)* *(= odruchowo)* mechanically.

mechaniczny *a.* 1. *fiz., techn.* mechanical; **energia mechaniczna** mechanical energy; **koń mechaniczny** horsepower. 2. *(= maszynowy)* mechanical; **instrumenty mechaniczne** *muz.* mechanical instruments; **mechaniczna muzyka** mechanical music. 3. *(= automatyczny, odruchowy)* mechanical.

mechanik *mp* 1. *(robotnik)* mechanic; **mechanik samochodowy** car mechanic; **mechanik pokładowy** *lotn.* flight engineer; **mechanik samolotowy** *lotn.* aircraft engineer. 2. *(= inżynier)* mechanic, engineer; **inżynier mechanik** mechanical engineer.

mechanika *f. fiz., techn.* mechanics; **mechanika kwantowa** quantum mechanics; **mechanika precyzyjna** precision engineering.

mechanizacja *f. techn.* mechanization.

mechanizator *mp* mechanizer.

mechanizm *mi* 1. *techn.* mechanism. 2. *(= ciąg procesów)* mechanism; **mechanizm rynkowy** market mechanism; **mechanizmy obronne** *med., psych.* defense mechanisms.

mechanizować *ipf. techn.* mechanize.

mechanochemia *f. Gen.* **-ii** *chem.* mechanochemistry, mechanical chemistry.

mechanoreceptor *mi Gen.* **-a** *anat.* mechanoreceptor.

mechanoskopia *f. Gen.* **-ii** toolmark examination science.

mechanoskopijny *a.* badanie **mechanoskopijne** toolmark examination.

mechanoterapia *f. Gen.* **-ii** *med.* mechanotherapy.

mechatronika *f. techn.* mechatronics.

mechaty *a.* shaggy.

meches *mp pl.* **-owie** *l.* **-i** *(= przechrzta)* Jew who has converted to Christianity.

mecz *mi Gen.pl.* **-ów** *sport* match, game; **mecz piłkarski** football match; **mecz finałowy** final; **mecz półfinałowy** semifinal; **mecz międzypaństwowy** international; **mecz towarzyski** friendly, friendly match.

meczbol *mi Gen.* **-a** *sport* match point.

meczet *mi bud., rel.* mosque.

medal *mi* medal; **złoty/srebrny/brązowy medal** gold/silver/bronze medal; **otrzymać medal za coś** be awarded a medal for sth; **odwrotna strona medalu** *(przeciwna cecha)* the other side of the coin;

(*ujemna cecha*) the downside of sth; **każdy medal ma dwie strony** there are two sides to every coin, there's a downside to everything; **być na medal** be top notch; **zrobiłeś to na medal** this was a fantastic job on your part; **moja była dziewczyna jest kierowcą na medal** my ex-girlfriend is a top notch driver.

medalier *mp* medalist, *Br.* medallist.

medalierski *a.* medalist's, *Br.* medallist's.

medalierstwo *n.* medal making.

medalik *mi Gen.* **-a** holy medal.

medalion *mi* (= *ozdoba, wisior*) *bud., sztuka, kulin.* medallion.

medalionik *mi Gen.* **-a** **1.** (= *ozdoba, wisior*) *bud., sztuka, kulin.* medallion. **2.** (= *medalik*) holy medal.

medalista *mp,* **medalistka** *f. Gen.pl.* **-ek** *sport* medalist, medal winner; **złoty/srebrny/brązowy medalista** gold/silver/bronze medalist; **medalista olimpijski** Olympic medalist.

medalowy *a. sport* medal; **klasyfikacja medalowa** medal ranking; **konkurencja medalowa** medal-ranking event.

media *pl. Gen.* **-ów** mass media.

mediacja *f.* mediation.

mediacyjny *a.* mediatory.

medialny[1] *a.* **1.** (= *hipnotyczny*) psychic. **2.** *jęz.* reflexive.

medialny[2] *a.* (*dotyczący mediów*) media.

mediana *f. mat., geom.* median.

medianta *f. muz.* mediant.

mediator[1] *mp pl.* **-rzy** *l.* **-owie** mediator.

mediator[2] *mi Gen.* **-a** *pl.* **-ry** *biol.* mediator.

mediatorski *a.* mediatory.

mediewista *mp,* **mediewistka** *f. Gen.pl.* **-ek** medievalist.

mediewistyczny *a.* (= *średniowieczny*) medieval.

mediewistyka *f.* medieval studies.

Mediolan *mi geogr.* Milan.

mediolańczyk *mp,* **mediolanka** *f.* Milanese.

mediolański *a.* Milanese.

mediować *ipf.* mediate.

medium *n. sing. indecl. pl.* **-dia** *Gen.* **-diów** **1.** (*w parapsychologii, w spirytyzmie*) medium. **2.** *jęz.* the reflexive voice, the reflexive. **3.** *fiz.* (= *środowisko*) medium. **4.** *muz.* middle register.

mediumistyczny *a.* psychic.

mediumizm *mi* psychism.

medresa *f.* madrasa, madrasah.

Meduza *f. mit.* Medusa.

meduza *f. zool.* jelly fish, medusa (*Scyphozoa*).

medycejski *a.* Medicean.

medycyna *f.* **1.** (*nauka*) medicine; **medycyna kosmiczna** space medicine; **medycyna lotnicza** aviation medicine; **medycyna morska** maritime medicine; **medycyna pracy** industrial medicine; **medycyna sądowa** forensic medicine; **medycyna sportowa** sports medicine; **medycyna szkolna** school medicine; **medycyna tropikalna** tropical medicine; **medycyna wypadkowa** accident and emergency medicine; **medycyna ludowa** folk medicine. **2.** (= *akademia medyczna, wydział*

lekarski) medicine; **studiować medycynę** study medicine, be a medical student.

medyczny *a.* medical; **akademia medyczna** medical academy.

medyk[1] *mp pl.* **-cy** **1.** *żart.* (= *lekarz*) medic. **2.** *pot.* (= *student medycyny*) medic.

medyk[2] *mi Gen.* **-a** *pl.* **-i** *pot.* (*szkoła*) nurse training school.

medykament *mi lit.* medicament, medication.

medytacja *f.* (= *rozmyślanie*) *rel.* meditation.

medytacyjny *a.* meditational.

medytować *ipf.* (= *rozważać*) meditate (*o kimś/czymś* on sb/sth).

Mefistofeles *mp* Mephistopheles.

mefistofelesowski *a.* Mephistophelean, Mephistophelian.

megabajt *mi Gen.* **-a** *komp.* megabyte.

megafon *mi techn.* (*pojedynczy głośnik*) megaphone; (*zespół głośników*) public address system, PA system; **mówić przez megafon** speak over a megaphone *l.* PA system.

megaherc *mi Gen.* **-a** *el.* (*jednostka częstotliwości*) megahertz.

megakaloria *f. Gen.* **-ii** *fiz.* (*jednostka*) megacalorie.

megalit *mi archeol., geol.* megalith.

megalityczny *a.* megalithic.

megaloman *mp,* **megalomanka** *f.* megalomaniac.

megalomania *f. Gen.* **-ii** (= *mania wielkości*) *pat.* megalomania.

megalomanka *f. Gen.pl.* **-ek** *zob.* **megaloman.**

megalomański *a.* megalomaniacal, megalomaniac.

megalomaństwo *n.* megalomania.

megantrop *mi Gen.* **-a** *antrop.* Java Man (*Meganthropus palaeojavanicus*).

megaplankton *mi biol.* megaplankton.

megaron *mi bud.* megaron.

megasam *mi* superstore, supermarket.

megawat *mi Gen.* **-a** *fiz.* (*jednostka*) megawatt.

megiera *f.* (= *złośnica*) shrew.

mejoza *f. biol.* meiosis.

Mekka *f. Dat. i Loc.* **Mekce** *geogr.* Mecca.

mekka *f. Dat. i Loc.* **mekce** mecca.

Meksyk *mi geogr.* Mexico.

meksyk *mi pot.* (= *bałagan*) mess; **ale meksyk!** what a mess!

Meksykanin *mp pl.* **-anie** *Gen.* **-an, Meksykanka** *f. Gen.pl.* **-ek** Mexican.

meksykański *a.* Mexican.

melamina *f. chem., techn.* melamine.

melaminowy *a. chem., techn.* melamine.

melancholia *f. Gen.* **-ii** **1.** (= *smutek*) (= *zaduma*) melancholy; **czarna melancholia** black bile. **2.** *pat.* depression, melancholia.

melancholiczka *f. Gen.pl.* **-ek** *zob.* **melancholik.**

melancholijny *a.* melancholy.

melancholik *mp,* **melancholiczka** *f. Gen.pl.* **-ek** melancholic.

Melanezja *f. geogr.* Melanesia.

Melanezyjczyk *mp,* **Melanezyjka** *f. Gen.pl.* **-ek** Melanesian.

melanezyjski *a.* Melanesian.

melaniczny *a. zool.* = **melanotyczny**.
melanina *f. biol.* melanine.
melanit *mi min.* melanite.
melanizm *mi biol.* melanism.
melanocyt *mi* melanocyte.
melanofor *mi biol.* melanophore.
melanoma *f. pat.* melanoma.
melanotropina *f. biochem.* melanotropin.
melanotyczny *a. zool.* melanotic, melanic.
melanteryt *mi min.* melanterite.
melanż *mi Gen.pl.* **-ów 1.** (= *mieszanina*)
melange, medley, mixture. **2.** *tk.* melange, fabric with mingled colours.
melasa *f.* molasses.
melasowy *a.* molasses; (= *przypominający me-
lasę*) molassy.
melatonina *f. biol., med.* melatonin.
melba *f.* (*lody*) fruit sundae.
meldować *ipf.* **1.** (= *zgłaszać*) report (*sth*) (*komuś* to sb). **2.** (= *rejestrować*) register. **3.** *karty*
declare. **~ się** *ipf.* **1.** (= *zgłaszać się*) report (*u
kogoś* to sb). **2.** (*rejestrować się*) register. **3.** *pot.*
(= *zjawiać się*) show one's face.
meldunek *mi* **-nk- 1.** (= *zgłoszenie, raport*) report, dispatch; **złożyć meldunek** submit a report;
report back (*komuś* to sb); **przesyłać meldunek**
send a dispatch. **2.** (= *zameldowanie*) registration. **3.** *karty* declaration.
meldunkowy *a.* **1.** (= *ewidencyjny*) registration. **2. księga meldunkowa** registration book.
meliczny *a. teor.lit.* melic.
melika *f. teor.lit.* melic.
melina *f. pot.* **1.** (= *kryjówka, podejrzany lokal*) den, hole. **2.** (= *miejsce nielegalnej sprzedaży alkoholu*) speakeasy.
meliniara *f. pot. zob.* **meliniarz**.
meliniarski *a. pot.* bootlegger's.
meliniarz *mp pot.* bootlegger.
melinit *mi chem.* melinite.
melinować się *ipf. pot.* conceal o.s.
melioracja *f. roln.* land improvement; land
melioration; **melioracja wodna** drainage.
melioracyjny *a. roln.* soil-improving; **rów melioracyjny** drainage ditch.
meliorant *mp*, **meliorantka** *f. Gen.pl.* **-ek** land
improvement expert.
meliorować *ipf. roln.* improve, meliorate.
melisa *f. bot.* lemon balm (*Melissa officinalis*).
melizmat *mi muz.* melisma.
melizmatyczny *a. muz.* melismatic.
melizmatyka *f. muz.* melismatics.
melodia *f. Gen.* **-ii** *muz.* **1.** tune, melody;
przest. air. **2.** (*głosu*) tune, intonation. **3.** *przen.*
melodia *l.* **pieśń przyszłości** thing of the future.
melodramat *mi teor.lit., film t. przen.* melodra-
ma; **robić z czegoś melodramat** make a drama
out of sth.
melodramatyczny *a.* melodramatic.
melodyczny *a. muz.* melodic.
melodyjka *f. Gen.pl.* **-ek** (light) tune.
melodyjny *a.* melodious, melodical.
melodyka *f. muz.* melodics.
meloman *mp*, **melomanka** *f. Gen.pl.* **-ek** music
lover, melomaniac.

melomania *f. Gen.* **-ii** craze for music.
melon *mi Gen.* **-a** (*owoc*) melon; *bot.* musk melon (*Cucumis melo*).
melonik *mi Gen.* **-a** bowler (hat).
melonowiec *mi* **-wc-** *Gen.* **-a** *bot.* pawpaw, pa-
paw, papaya, melon tree (*Carica papaya*).
melonowy *a.* melon; **drzewo melonowe** *bot.* =
melonowiec.
Melpomena *f. mit.* Melpomene.
melton *mi tk.* melton (cloth).
mełł *itd. ipf. zob.* **mleć**.
membrana *f.* **1.** *techn.* diaphragm, membrane. **2.** *anat.* (= *błona bębenkowa*) tympanic
membrane.
membranofon *mi muz.* (*instrument*) membra-
nophone.
membranowy *a.* membranous; **pompa mem-
branowa** *techn.* diaphragm pump.
memento *n. indecl. Lat.* reminder, warning;
memento mori memento mori.
memłać *ipf. pot.* chew slowly, cud.
memorabilia *pl. Gen.* **-ów** *lit.* memorable
events, memorabilia.
memorandum *n. sing. indecl. pl.* **-a** *Gen.* **-ów**
polit. memorandum, aide-mémoire.
memoriał *mi* **1.** (= *pismo skierowane do
władz*) memorial, petition. **2.** *sport* memorial
sporting event. **3.** *handl.* ledger.
memoriałowy *a.* memorial.
memuar *mi przest.* memoir, diary.
menada *f. mit. l. przen.* menad, maenad.
menarche *n. indecl. fizj.* menarche.
menaż *mi Gen.pl.* **-y** *l.* **-ów**, **menaża** *f. przest.*,
wojsk. mess.
menażeria *f. Gen.* **-ii** menagerie.
menażka *f. Gen.pl.* **-ek** mess kit; *Br.* mess tin.
menda *f.* **1.** *pot.* = **mendoweszka**. **2.** *przen.*,
obelż. louse.
mendel *mi* **-dl-** *Gen.* **-a** (= *piętnaście sztuk*) fifteen.
mendelew *mi chem.* mendelevium.
mendoweszka *f. Gen.pl.* **-ek** *ent.* crab louse,
pubic louse (*Phthirus pubis*).
menedżer *mp pl.* **-owie** (= *szef, impresario,
opiekun*) manager.
menedżerski *a.* managerial.
menedżerstwo *n.* management.
menedżeryzm *mi ekon.* managerialism.
menel *mp Gen.pl.* **-i** *l.* **-ów** *pot.* bum.
menelstwo *n. pot.* company of bums.
menhir *mi archeol.* menhir.
meningokok *ma biol., pat.* meningococcus
(*Neisseria meningitidis*).
menisk *mi* **1.** *fiz.* meniscus; **menisk wklęsły/
wypukły** concave/convex meniscus. **2.** *opt.*
meniscus lens. **3.** *anat.* (= *łękotka*) meniscus; (=
dysk) disk.
mennica *f.* mint.
menniczy *a.* minting.
menonicki *a. rel.* Mennonite.
menonita *mp*, **menonitka** *f. Gen.pl.* **-ek** *rel.*
Mennonite.
menopauza *f. fizj.* menopause.
menopauzalny *a. fizj.* menopausal.

menora *f.* menorah.

mensa *f. kość.* mensa, altar top.

menstruacja *f. fizj.* menstruation.

menstruacyjny *a. fizj.* menstrual.

mentalność *f.* mentality.

mentalny *a.* mental.

mentol *mi chem.* menthol.

mentolowy *a.* mentholated; (*o smaku*) menthol.

mentor *mp pl.* -rzy 1. *przest.* (= *wychowawca, doradca*) mentor. 2. *iron.* (= *moralista*) moralizer. – *mi Gen.* -a *pl.* -ry *ogr.* grafting a young plant on to an older one so that it copies its charcteristics.

mentorka *f.* 1. *arch.* (*nauczycielka*) mentor. 2. *iron.* (*moralistka*) moralizer.

mentorować *ipf.* 1. *ogr.* (*szczepić*) graft a young plant on to an old one. 2. *przest.* (*wychowywać, nauczać*) mentor.

mentorski *a.* moralizing; mentorski ton moralizing tone.

mentorstwo *n.* mentoring.

mentos *mi Gen.* -a *pot.* (*cukierek*) mint.

menu *n. indecl. t. komp.* menu.

menuet *mi Gen. i Acc.* -a *muz.* minuet.

menzura *f.* 1. *muz.* measure. 2. *szermierka* (fencing) measure, distance.

menzuralny *a. muz.* mensural.

menzurka *f. chem.* measuring flask, graduated cylinder *l.* flask.

mer¹ *mp pl.* -owie mayor.

mer² *mi Gen.* -a *pl.* -y *chem.* mer unit.

merc *mi Gen.* -a *pot.* (= *mercedes*) Merc.

merceryzacja *f. tk.* mercerization.

merceryzarka *f. Gen.pl.* -ek *tk.* (*maszyna*) mercerizer.

merceryzować *ipf. tk.* mercerize.

merdać *ipf.* (*o psie*) wag; merdać ogonem wag one's tail.

merenga *f.* (*ciastko*) meringue.

mereżka *f. Gen.pl.* -ek drawnwork, hemstitch.

mereżkować *ipf.* drawnwork, hemstitch.

meritum *n. sing. indecl. pl.* -ta *Gen.* -tów (= *istota*) crux, the heart of the matter.

merkantylista *mp*, merkantylistka *f. Gen.pl.* -ek mercantilist.

merkantylizacja *f.* mercantilization.

merkantylizm *mi ekon.* mercantilism.

merkantylność *f.* mercantility.

merkantylny *a.* mercantile.

merkaptan *mi chem.* mercaptan.

Merkury¹ *mp mit.* Mercury.

Merkury² *mi astron.* (*planeta*) Mercury.

merkuryjski *a. mit., astrol.* 1. Mercurial. 2. *astron.* Mercurian.

merla *f. Gen.* -i *tk.* gauze.

merlan *ma icht.* whiting (*Gadus merlangus*).

merostwo *n.* 1. (*urząd*) mayoralty. 2. (= *magistrat*) the Mayor's office. 3. *Loc.* -u (= *mer z żoną*) the Mayor and his wife.

Merowingowie *pl. Gen.* -ów *hist.* the Merovingians.

merowiński *a. hist.* Merovingian.

merynos *ma Gen.* -a *zool.* (*owca*) merino. – *mi Gen.* -u (*przędza*) merino (wool).

merystem *mi bot.* meristem.

merytoryczny *a.* pertaining to the content *l.* to the subject matter; uwaga merytoryczna remark about the content.

mesa *f. żegl.* mess, mess-cabin; mesa oficerska officer's mess, wardroom.

mesjanista *mp*, mesjanistka *f. Gen.pl.* -ek Messianist.

mesjanistyczny *a.* Messianic.

mesjanizm *mi rel., fil.* Messianism; mesjanizm żydowski Jewish Messianism.

mesjański *a.* = mesjanistyczny.

Mesjasz *mp rel.* the Messiah.

mesjasz *mp Gen.pl.* -y *l.* -ów (= *zbawca*) messiah.

meskalina *f. chem., med.* mescaline.

mesmeryczny *a.* mesmeric.

mesmerysta *mp*, mesmerystka *f. Gen.pl.* -ek *hist., psych.* mesmerist.

mesmeryzm *mi hist., psych.* mesmerism.

mesz *mi hodowla* (*pasza*) mash.

meszek *mi* -szk- down, fluff.

meszka *Gen.pl.* -ek *f. ent.* (= *muchówka z rodziny Simuliidae*) sandfly.

meta *f.* 1. *zwł. sport* (= *koniec*) finish (line *l.* post); być pierwszym/drugim/ostatnim na mecie come in first/second/last; dobiec do mety finish (the race). 2. *przen.* na krótką metę in the short term; na dalszą metę in the long run. 3. *pot.* (= *kryjówka*) bolt-hole, hideout.

metabaza *f. teor.lit.* apostrophe.

metabola *f. teor.lit.* rephrasing, repetition with variation; (= *zmiana rytmu*) metrical variation.

metaboliczny¹ *a. biol.* metabolic.

metaboliczny² *a. teor.lit.* strofa metaboliczna metrically varied stanza.

metabolit *mi Gen.* -u *biol.* metabolite. – *ma Gen.* -a *ent.* metabolous insect.

metabolizm *mi biol.* metabolism.

metafaza *f. biol.* metaphase.

metafilozofia *f. Gen.* -ii *fil.* metaphilosophy, theory of philosophy.

metafizyczny *a.* 1. *fil.* metaphysical. 2. (= *pozazmysłowy, duchowy*) metaphysical, supernatural, spiritual. 3. *pot., iron.* (= *zawiły*) abstract, arcane.

metafizyk *mp* metaphysician.

metafizyka *f.* 1. *fil.* metaphysics. 2. *pot., iron.* arcane stuff.

metafora *f. teor.lit.* metaphor.

metaforycznie *adv.* metaphorically.

metaforyczność *f.* metaphoric quality.

metaforyczny *a.* metaphoric, metaphorical.

metaforyka *f.* metaphor.

metagalaktyka *f. astron.* metagalaxy.

metageneza *f. biol.* metagenesis.

metajęzyk *mi Gen.* -a *jęz., log.* metalanguage.

metajęzykowy *a.* metalinguistic.

metakrylan *mi chem.* methacrylate.

metal¹ *mi* metal; płynny metal liquid metal; metal rodzimy *min.* native metal; metale koloro-

we *chem.* non-ferrous metals; **metale ciężkie/lekkie** heavy/light metals; **metale nieszlachetne** base *l.* common metals; **metale szlachetne** noble *l.* precious metals; **rudy metali** *min.* metal ores.
metal² *mi muz.* (heavy) metal.
metaldehyd *mi chem.* metaldehyde.
metaliczny *a.* metallic.
metalik¹ *a. indecl.* (*barwa lakieru*) metallic.
metalik² *mi mot., pot.* metallic (blue) car.
metalimnion *mi hydrol.* metalimnion.
metalingwistyczny *a. jęz., log.* metalinguistic.
metalingwistyka *f. jęz.* metalinguistics.
metalizacja *f. techn.* metalization.
metalizować *ipf. techn.* metalize.
metalofon *mi muz.* metallophone.
metalografia *f. Gen.* **-ii** *techn., druk.* metallography.
metaloid *mi chem.* metalloid.
metaloplastyczny *a. sztuka* metalwork.
metaloplastyka *f. sztuka* metalwork.
metalowiec¹ *mp* **-wc-** *pl.* **-y** (= *mechanik*) metalworker.
metalowiec² *mp* **-wc-** *pl.* **-y** *pot.* (*muzyk*) heavy-metal musician, heavy-metallist.
metalowy¹ *a.* (= *z metalu*) metal.
metalowy² *a. pot. muz.* (heavy-)metal.
metaloznawca *mp* physical metallurgist.
metaloznawstwo *n.* metal science, physical metallurgy.
metalurg *mp pl.* **-dzy** *l.* **-owie** metallurgist.
metalurgia *f. Gen.* **-ii** metallurgy.
metalurgiczny *a.* metallurgic, metallurgical.
metamatematyczny *a. mat., log.* metamathematical.
metamatematyka *f. mat., log.* metamathematics.
metamer *mi zool.* (= *segment*) metamere.
metameria *f. Gen.* **-ii** **1.** *chem.* metamerism. **2.** *zool.* (= *segmentacja*) metamerism.
metamorficzny *a. geol.* metamorphic.
metamorfizm *mi geol.* metamorphism.
metamorfoza *f. t. biol., geol.* (= *przemiana*) metamorphosis.
metan *mi chem.* methane.
metanauka *f. fil.* metascience.
metanaukowy *a.* metascientific.
metanol *mi chem.* methanol.
metanomierz *mi Gen.* **-a** *górn.* methanometer.
metanowy *a.* methane; **bakterie metanowe** *biol.* methane bacteria, Methanobacteria.
metapleks *mi chem., techn.* plexiglas.
metapleksowy *a.* plexiglas.
metapsychiczny *a.* metapsychic, metapsychical.
metapsychika *f.* metapsychics.
metapsychologia *f. Gen.* **-ii** **1.** (= *teoria psychologii*) metapsychology. **2.** (= *parapsychologia*) parapsychology.
metasekwoja *f. Gen.* **-oi** *bot.* metasequoia, dawn redwood (*Metasequoia glyptostroboides*).
metasomatoza *f. geol.* metasomatism, metasomatosis.
metastaza *f. pat.* metastasis.
metatekst *mi teor.lit.* metatext.

metateza *f.* **1.** *jęz.* (= *przestawka*) metathesis. **2.** *gram., teor.lit.* (= *inwersja*) inversion, transposition.
metatonia *f. Gen.* **-ii** *jęz.* metatony.
metempsychoza *f. rel., fil.* metempsychosis.
meteo *a. indecl. żegl., lotn.* = **meteorologiczny**; **służby meteo** meteorological services.
meteonawigacja *f. żegl.* meteorological navigation.
meteor *mi* meteor, shooting star; (= *bolid*) fireball, bolide; **deszcz meteorów** meteor *l.* meteoric shower; *pot.* = **meteoryt**.
meteorograf *mi meteor.* meteorograph.
meteorografia *f. meteor.* meteorography.
meteorogram *mi meteor.* meteorogram.
meteoroid *mi astron.* meteoroid, meteoritic body.
meteorolit *mi geol.* meteorolite.
meteorolog *mp pl.* **-dzy** *l.* **-owie** meteorologist.
meteorologia *f. Gen.* **-ii** meteorology.
meteorologiczny *a.* meteorological; **prognoza meteorologiczna** meteorological forecast, weather forecast; **stacja meteorologiczna** meteorological station; **satelita meteorologiczny** meteorological satellite.
meteoropata *mp* weather-sensitive person.
meteoropatia *f. Gen.* **-ii** *pat.* weather sensitivity.
meteoropatologia *f. Gen.* **-ii** *med.* weather-sensitivity studies.
meteorowy *a.* meteoric.
meteoryt *mi geol.* meteorite.
meteorytowy *a.* meteoritic; **żelazo pochodzenia meteorytowego** meteoritic iron.
meteorytyka *f.* meteoritics.
meteosatelita *mi* weather satellite.
methemoglobina *f. biochem.* methemoglobin.
metka¹ *f. Gen.pl.* **-ek** (= *etykietka*) label, tag.
metka² *f. Gen.pl.* **-ek** (*wędlina*) raw-meat sausage.
metkować *ipf.* label.
metkownica *f.* labeler, labeling device.
metoda *f.* (= *sposób, procedura*) method (*czegoś* of sth); **metoda kolejnych przybliżeń** *mat.* the method of successive approximations; **metoda porównawcza** comparative method; **metodą prób i błędów** by trial and error.
metodolog *mp pl.* **-dzy** *l.* **-owie** methodologist.
metodologia *f. Gen.* **-ii** methodology.
metodologiczny *a.* methodological.
metodyczka *f. Gen.pl.* **-ek** *zob.* **metodyk**.
metodycznie *adv.* methodically, systematically.
metodyczność *f.* methodicalness, systematicality.
metodyczny *a.* **1.** (*dotyczący metodyki*) methodic, methodical. **2.** (= *systematyczny*) methodical, systematic.
metodyk *mp* methodologist.
metodyka *f.* **1.** (= *ogół reguł*) method, methodology. **2.** (= *dydaktyka*) methodology, teaching methods.
metodysta *mp*, **metodystka** *f. Gen.pl.* **-ek** *rel.* Methodist.

metodystyczny *a. rel.* Methodist.
metodyzm[1] *mi* = **metodyczność**.
metodyzm[2] *mi rel.* Methodism.
metonimia *f. Gen.* -ii *ret.* metonymy.
metonimiczny *a. ret.* metonymic, metonymical.

metr *mi Gen.* -a **1.** *miern., fiz.* (*jednostka długości*) meter, *Br.*, metre; **metr bieżący** running meter; **metr kwadratowy/sześcienny** square/cubic meter; **metr na sekundę** meter per second. **2.** (= *miarka o długości metra*) meter stick; **metr krawiecki** tapeline, tape measure; **metr stolarski** carpenter's rule; **sprzedawać coś z metra** sell sth by the meter; **mieć czegoś od metra** *pot.* have no end of sth. **3.** *pot.* (= *100 kg*) one hundred kilos.

metraż *mi Gen.pl.* -y *l.* -ów (*powierzchnia*) **1.** metric area; (*długość*) length in meters. **2.** *film* length; **krótki metraż** short movies, short films; **długi** *l.* **pełny metraż** full-length movies *l.* films.

metresa *f. przest.* mistress, favourite.

metro *n.* subway; *Br.* underground; **jeździć metrem** travel *l.* go by subway.

metrologia *f. Gen.* -ii metrology.

metronom *mi muz.* metronome.

metropolia *f. Gen.* -ii *polit., kośc., hist.* metropolis.

metropolita *mp kośc.* metropolitan.

metropolitalny *a. kośc.* metropolitan.

metrówka *f. Gen.pl.* -ek *pot.* (= *miarka metrowa*) meter stick.

metrum *n. indecl. muz., teor.lit.* meter; *Br.* metre.

metryczny *a. miern.* **1.** metric. **2.** *teor.lit.* metrical.

metryka *f.* **1.** (= *świadectwo*) certificate; **metryka urodzenia/chrztu/ślubu/śmierci** certificate of birth/baptism/marriage/death. **2.** (= *informacja o pochodzeniu*) certificate of origin. **3.** (*dane dotyczące eksponatu, pojazdu itp.*) specification. **4.** (= *rejestr, archiwum*) register (book), archives; (= *akta stanu cywilnego*) public records; *hist.* (= *archiwum koronne*) royal archives. **5.** *mat.* metric. **6.** *teor.lit.* metrics.

metrykalny *a.* registral.

metyl *mi chem.* methyl.

metylen *mi chem.* methylene.

metylowy *a. chem.* methyl, methylic; **alkohol/oranż metylowy** methyl alcohol/orange.

Metys *mp*, **Metyska** *f. Gen.pl.* -ek Métis, half-breed; (*kobieta*) Métisse.

mewa *f. orn.* gull, sea-gull (*Larus*); **mewa śmieszka** black-headed gull (*L. rigibundus*).

mezalians *mi pl.* -e *l.* -y misalliance, mésalliance, mismarriage.

mezoblast *mi biol.* mesoblast.

mezoderma *f. biol.* mesoderm.

mezofit *mi bot.* mesophyte.

mezolit *mi archeol.* the Mesolithic (period).

mezolityczny *a. archeol.* Mesolithic.

mezon *mi fiz.* meson.

mezoplankton *mi biol.* mesoplankton.

Mezopotamia *f. Gen.* -ii *geogr., hist.* Mesopotamia.

mezopotamski *a.* Mesopotamian.

mezosfera *f. meteor.* mesosphere.

mezozaur *ma paleont.* (= *gad z rzędu Mesosauria*) mesosaur.

mezozoiczny *a. geol., paleont.* Mesozoic; **era mezozoiczna** the Mesozoic (era).

mezozoik *mi geol.* the Mesozoic.

mezzosopran *mi muz.* (*głos l. śpiewaczka*) mezzo-soprano, mezzo.

mezzosopranistka *f. Gen.pl.* -ek *muz. zob.* **mezzosopran**.

mezzosopranowy *a. muz.* mezzo-soprano, mezzo.

męczarnia *f. Gen.pl.* -i torture, torment.

męczący *a.* wearisome, tedious, tiresome, fatiguing.

męczennica *f.* **1.** (*kobieta*) *zob.* **męczennik**, **2.** *bot.* passionflower (*Passiflora*).

męczennik *mp* **1.** *rel., polit.* martyr (*za coś* for sth); **robić z siebie męczennika** *iron.* make a martyr of o.s. **2.** *emf.* (= *człowiek cierpiący*) sufferer, martyr.

męczeński *a.* martyr's; **zginąć śmiercią męczeńską** die a martyr.

męczeństwo *n.* martyrdom.

męczyć *ipf.* **1.** (= *poddawać torturom*) torture. **2.** (= *gnębić, dręczyć*) nag, torment. **3.** (= *pozbawiać sił*) tire (out), exhaust, fatigue. **4.** (= *denerwować, nużyć*) weary, annoy. **5.** (= *naprzykrzać się*) pester, badger (*sb*) (*czymś* with sth, *o coś* for sth). ~ **się** *ipf.* **1.** (*cierpieć*) suffer. **2.** (= *tracić siły*) lose one's strength, become exhausted, tire. **3.** (= *trudzić się*) drudge, work hard (*nad czymś* at sth).

męczydusza *f. l. mp decl. like f. Gen.pl.* -sz *l.* -y *l.* -ów *żart.* pest, bore.

mędrek *mp* -rk- *pl.* -owie *pot.* smart aleck, smart-ass, know-all.

mędrkować *ipf. pot.* play the philosopher, smart-ass.

mędrzec *mp* -drc- *pl.* -y sage, thinker.

męka *f. Gen.pl.* mąk **1.** (= *cierpienie*) suffering, torment. **2.** (= *tortury*) torture. **3.** (= *utrapienie*) nuisance.

męski *a.* **1.** (= *będący mężczyzną*) male, masculine; (= *cechujący mężczyznę*) manly, manlike, virile; (= *przeznaczony dla mężczyzn*) man's, men's, for men; **dziecko płci męskiej** male child; **uroda męska** male beauty; **wiek męski** *l.* **lata męskie** manhood, virility; **fryzjer męski** men's hairdresser; **kosmetyki męskie** cosmetics for men; **odzież męska** men's wear, menswear; **po męsku** like a man; **porozmawiajmy po męsku** let's talk man to man. **2.** *gram.* masculine; **rodzaj męski** masculine gender. **3.** *teor.lit.* **rym męski** masculine rhyme. **4.** *biol., fizj.* male; **męskie narządy płciowe** *anat.* male sexual organs; **gameta męska** male gamete; **kwiat męski** *bot.* male flower.

męskoosobowy *a. gram.* masculine-personal, virile.

męskość *f.* manhood, virility; maleness, masculinity; *euf.* (= *męskie narządy płciowe*) male parts.

męstwo *n.* manliness, courage.

męt *mi Gen.* -u *zw. pl.* (= *zanieczyszczenie*)

scum, dregs. – *mp Gen.* **-a** *pl.* **-y** *pog.* (= *człowiek z marginesu społecznego*) bum; **męty społeczne** scum; riff-raff; dregs of society.

mętlik *mi pot.* mess, confusion, topsy-turvy.

mętnieć *ipf.* **1.** (= *stawać się mętnym*) become turbid. **2.** (= *zacierać się*) become blurred.

mętny *a.* **1.** (= *nieprzejrzysty*) turbid, cloudy. **2.** (= *zatarty*) blurred, vague, hazy, unclear. **3.** (= *niejasny, wątpliwy*) dubious, ambiguous, obscure, vague; (= *niespójny*) incoherent.

męża *itd. mp zob.* **mąż**.

mężatka *f. Gen.pl.* **-ek** married woman.

mężczyzna *mp Gen.pl.* **-n** man; *form.* male; **rozmawiać jak mężczyzna z mężczyzną** talk man to man; **bądź mężczyzną!** be a man!

mężnie *adv.* courageously, bravely; **stawać mężnie** *lit.* make a brave stand (*przeciwko komuś / czemuś* against sb/sth).

mężnieć *ipf.* **1.** (= *dorastać jako mężczyzna*) grow into a man. **2.** (= *stawać się silnym*) grow into power.

mężny *a.* brave, courageous, manly.

mężobójca *mp arch.* homicide, murderer.

mężobójczyni *f.* husband-killer.

mężobójstwo *n.* **1.** killing one's husband. **2.** *arch.* homicide, murder.

mężowski *a.* husband's.

mężulek *mp* **-lk-** *pl.* **-owie**, **mężuś** *mp pot., żart. l. iron.* hubby.

mgiełka *f. Gen.pl.* **-ek** haze, mist; *przen. zob.* **mgła**.

mglejarka *f. Gen.pl.* **-ek** *bot.* (*grzyb*) amanitopsis (*Amanitopsis*).

mglistość *f.* **1.** (= *zamglenie*) haziness, mistiness. **2.** (= *zatarcie konturów*) blur. **3.** (= *niezrozumiałość*) obscurity, vagueness.

mglisty *a.* **1.** (= *przesycony mgłą*) foggy, hazy, misty. **2.** (= *niewyraźny*) blurred, dim. **3.** (= *niejasny*) obscure, vague.

mgła *f. Gen.pl.* **mgieł 1.** fog, haze, mist; **widzieć jak przez mgłę** see dimly; **zachodzić mgłą** cloud over, become misted over. **2.** (*coś zwiewnego l. niewyraźnego*) mist. **3.** (= *opar*) vapor.

mgławica *f. astron.* nebula; **Mgławica Andromedy** the Andromeda Nebula *l.* Galaxy.

mgławicowy *a. astron.* (*materia, widmo*) **1.** nebular. **2.** *lit.* (= *mglisty, niejasny*) nebulous.

mgławy *a. lit.* = **mglisty**.

mgłowy *a. żegl.* fog; **sygnał mgłowy** fog signal; **syrena mgłowa** foghorn.

mgnienie *n.* **1.** (= *mrugnięcie*) blink, wink; **w mgnieniu oka** in the twinkling of an eye. **2.** (= *chwila*) instant, moment.

miał¹ *mi* dust; **miał węgla** coaldust.

miał² *itd. ipf. zob.* **mieć**.

miałki *a.* **1.** fine, powdered. **2.** *przen.* (= *pozbawiony wyrazu, nijaki*) shallow, worthless.

miałkość *f.* **1.** fineness. **2.** (= *brak wyrazu*) shallowness, worthlessness.

miano *n.* **1.** *lit.* (= *imię, godność, tytuł*) name, denomination, designation, title; **nosić miano** bear a name; **pretendować do miana czegoś** have pretensions to being sth. **2.** *chem.* titer. **3.** *mat., fiz.* denomination.

mianować *ipf. l. pf.* **1.** nominate, designate (*sb*) (*czymś* as sth). **2.** *chem.* titrate. ~ **się** *ipf. l. pf.* + *Ins.* (= *uzurpować sobie miano*) call oneself, pretend to be (*sth*).

mianowanie *n.* nomination.

mianowany *a.* **1.** *mat.* (*o liczbie*) denominated. **2.** *chem.* (*o roztworze*) titrated.

mianowicie *adv.* namely, to wit, to be precise, that is (to say); **miał dobry zawód, był mianowicie lekarzem** he had a good job: namely, he was a physician; **odwiedziłem obie stolice, (a) mianowicie Paryż i Londyn** I have visited both capitals, that is to say Paris and London.

mianownik *mi Gen.* **-a 1.** *gram.* nominative. **2.** *mat.* denominator; **sprowadzić ułamki do wspólnego mianownika** reduce *l.* bring fractions to a common denominator.

miara *f. Dat. i Loc.* **mierze 1.** *miern.* (*jednostka porównawcza*) (unit of) measure; **system miar i wag** system of weights and measures; **wzorzec miary** measurement standard; **miary metryczne** metric measures. **2.** (*przyrząd do mierzenia*) measure, gauge. **3.** (= *rozmiar*) size. **4.** (= *pomiar krawiecki*) measure; **brać miarę** take measure; **ubranie na miarę** clothes made to measure. **5.** (*ilość, liczba*) quantity, amount, number. **6.** (= *umiar*) moderation; **ponad miarę** to excess; **nie znać miary w jedzeniu/piciu** eat/drink beyond limits. **7.** (= *jakość, wartość*) value, quality; **talent dużej miary** talent of high caliber. **8.** (*w utartych wyrażeniach*) **w miarę jak... as...**; **apetyt rośnie w miarę jedzenia** *przen.* the more you get, the more you want; **nad wszelką miarę** beyond measure; **w miarę** moderately; **byli w miarę grzeczni** they were rather polite; **ze wszech miar** *lit.* by all means, on all accounts; **żadną miarą** by no means.

miareczkować *ipf. chem.* titrate.

miareczkowanie *n. chem.* titration, titrimetry.

miareczkowy *a. chem.* titrimetric.

miarka *f. Gen.pl.* **-ek 1.** yardstick, standard; **mierzyć kogoś swoją miarką** evaluate sb according to one's standards. **3.** (= *odmierzona ilość*) measure, amount. **3.** *przen.* **miarka za miarkę** measure for measure; **ziarnko do ziarnka, zbierze się miarka** take care of the pennies and the dollars will take care of themselves.

miarkować *ipf.* **1.** (= *hamować, uspokajać*) restrain, moderate. **2.** *przest.* (= *rozumieć, domyślać się*) understand. **3.** *rzad.* (= *odmierzać*) measure out, deal out.

miarodajność *f.* reliability, credibility.

miarodajny *a.* reliable, credible.

miarowość *f.* regularity, steadiness.

miarowy *a.* **1.** (= *równomierny, rytmiczny*) regular, steady; measured, rhythmical. **2.** (= *służący do odmierzania*) mensural. **3.** *teor.lit.* cadenced.

miast *prep.* + *Gen. lit.* instead of.

miasteczko *n. Gen.pl.* **-ek** (little) town; **wesołe miasteczko** amusement park, funfair.

miastenia *f. Gen.* **-ii** *pat.* myasthenia.

miasteniczny *a. pat.* myasthenic.

miasto *n. Loc.* **mieście 1.** town, city; **miasto**

stołeczne capital city; **miasto-państwo** *polit.,* *hist.* city-state; **ojcowie miasta** the city fathers. **2.** (= *teren l. centrum danego miasta*) town; **stare miasto** the old town; **wyjść na miasto** go out; go into town; **być na mieście** be in town; **być poza miastem** be out of town; **pojechać do miasta** go downtown. **3.** (= *ludność miasta*) the town, townspeople, townsfolk; **całe miasto o tym wie** the whole town knows about it.

miastowy *mp pot., zw. uj.* towny, townee.

miau *int.* miaow, meow, miaou.

miauczeć *ipf.* **-ę -ysz** miaow, meow, miaou, miaul.

miauk *mi* = **miauknięcie**.

miauknąć *pf.* **-ij** *zob.* **miauczeć**.

miauknięcie *n.* miaow, meow, miaou.

miazga *f.* pulp; **rozgnieść** *l.* zetrzeć coś na miazgę reduce sth to a pulp; **zetrzeć kogoś na miazgę** *przen.* beat sb to a mummy; **miazga zębowa** *anat.* dental pulp; **miazga korkotwórcza** *bot.* cambium.

miazmat *mi form.* miasma.

miażdżarka *f. Gen.pl.* **-ek** *techn.* crusher.

miażdżący *a.* (= *druzgocący, przygniatający*) crushing, devastating, sweeping.

miażdżyca *f. pat.* sclerosis.

miażdżycowy *a. pat.* sclerotic.

miażdżyć *ipf.* **1.** crush. **2.** *przen.* (= *unicestwiać, zgniatać*) crush, suppress, annihilate; **miażdżyć kogoś spojrzeniem** crush sb with a look; **miażdżyć powstanie** suppress *l.* crush an uprising.

miażdżysty *a. anat.* **jądro miażdżyste** pultaceous nucleus.

miąć *ipf.* **mnę mniesz, mnij** crumple, crease. ~ **się** *ipf.* become crumpled *l.* creased.

miąższ *mi* **1.** flesh, pulp, squash. **2.** *anat., zool., bot.* parenchyma.

miąższość *f. geol.* thickness.

micela *f. biochem., fiz.* micelle.

micha *f. emf. zob.* **misa**.

michałki *pl. Gen.* **-ów** *pot. żart.* trifles, trivialities.

midi *a. indecl.* medium; medium-length. – *n. indecl.* medium-length; **nosić midi** wear medium-length.

miech *mi Gen.* **-a 1.** bellows. **2.** *przest.* (= *wór*) sack.

miechunka *f. Gen.pl.* **-ek** *bot.* **miechunka rozdęta** winter cherry, chinese lantern, alkekengi (*Physalis alkekengi*); **miechunka peruwiańska** Cape gooseberry, goldenberry (*P. peruviana*); **miechunka pomidorowa** tomatillo (*P. ixocarpa*).

miecz *mi Gen.* **-a** *Gen.pl.* **-y** *l.* **-ów 1.** *broń* sword; **miecz dwuręczny/obosieczny** two-handed/double-edged sword; **dobyć miecza** draw the sword. **2.** *przen.* **krewny po mieczu** spear-side relative; **prawo miecza** law of the sword. **3.** *bud.* angle brace, diagonal brace, counter clamp. **4.** *żegl.* centerboard, dropkeel, sliding keel.

miecznik *mp pl.* **-cy 1.** *hist.* (*urząd*) swordbearer. **2.** *hist.* (*rzemieślnik*) sword-maker, sword-cutler, swordsmith. – *ma pl.* **-i 1.** *icht.*

swordfish (*Xiphias gladius*). **2.** *zool.* (= *orka*) killer whale, orca (*Orcinus orca*).

mieczować *ipf. bud.* brace.

mieczowy *a.* **kawalerowie mieczowi** *hist.* the Knights of the Sword; **wiązanie mieczowe** *bud.* bracing; **jacht mieczowy** *żegl.* centerboard yacht.

mieczyk *mi Gen.* **-a 1.** (*broń*) short sword. **2.** *bot.* gladiolus, sword lilly (*Gladiolus*). – *ma icht.* swordtail (*Xiphophorus*).

mieć *ipf.* **mam masz, miej 1.** (*oznacza posiadanie, cechę, związek z czymś l. kimś, władzę nad czymś*) have, have got; **mieć coś na sobie** have sth on; **masz dużo pieniędzy/czasu** you have *l.* you've got a lot of money/time; **mieć niebieskie oczy** have blue eyes; **czy masz samochód?** do you have a car?; have you got a car?; **nie mam przy sobie pieniędzy** I have *l.* I've got no money on me; **masz przy sobie paszport?** do you have your passport with you?; **mam pomysł** I have an idea; **nie mam pojęcia, o czym mówisz** I have no idea what you're talking about; **mam brata i siostrę** I have a brother and a sister; **co masz w ręce?** what are you holding in your hand?; **mieć dużo do zrobienia** have a lot to do; **mieć coś do powiedzenia** have sth to say; **mieć coś do dyspozycji** have sth at one's disposal; **mam sprawę do załatwienia** I have some business to do; **nie mam na nowy samochód** *pot.* I cannot afford a new car; **masz jeszcze pięć minut** you still have five minutes; **mam teraz wykład** I'm lecturing right now; **mam gości** I am having guests; **ona ma kochanka** she has a lover. **2.** (*w różnych utartych zwrotach*) **mam już dość** I've had enough; **mieć kogoś/czegoś po dziurki w nosie** be fed up with sb/sth; **mieć kogoś po swojej stronie** have sb on one's side; **mieć coś za sobą** have sth over; **mieć coś z głowy** *pot.* be rid of sth; **czy masz coś przeciwko mnie?** do you have something against me?; **mieć coś komuś za złe** hold sth against sb; **mieć z kimś/czymś do czynienia** deal with sb/sth; **mam z kimś na pieńku** *pot.* have a bone to pick with sb; **mieć w czubie** *pot.* be tipsy; **mieć fioła** *l.* **bzika** *żart.* be crazy, have a bee in one's bonnet; **mieć coś w nosie** *pot.* not give a hoot about sth; **mieć coś w dupie** *wulg.* not give a shit about sth; **ona ma to do siebie, że...** it is characteristic of her that...; **mieć z kimś dziecko** have a child with sb; **mam cię w garści** I have you on toast; **mieć kogoś w kieszeni** have sb in one's pocket; **mieć głos** have the floor; **mieć znajomości** have connections; **mieć kogoś/coś na oku** keep an eye on sb/sth; **mieć coś na sumieniu** have sth on one's conscience; **mieć coś na uwadze** *l.* **w pamięci** bear sth in mind; **mieć coś na myśli** have sth in mind; **co masz na myśli?** what do you mean?; **mieć czelność coś zrobić** have the cheek to do sth; **mieć czyste ręce** have clean hands; **mieć czyste/nieczyste sumienie** have a clear/guilty conscience; **mieć coś pod ręką** have sth at hand; **mieć coś w zanadrzu** have sth up one's sleeve; **mieć szczęście/pecha** be lucky/unlucky; **nie mieć grosza przy duszy** be penniless, be broke. **3.** (*choroby, dolegliwości*) **mieć odrę** have measles; **mieć kaszel** have a cough; **mieć zakatarzony nos** have a running nose. **4.** *pot.* (= *uwieść, odbyć stosunek seksualny z*) have (*sb*); **czy już ją miałeś?** have you had her yet? **5.** (*w wykrzyknikach*) **masz!** (= *proszę!*) here you are!; **a masz!** take this!; **masz za swoje** get your desert!; **mam cię!** I got you!; gotcha!; **masz ci los!** too bad! **6.** (*dane osobiste, wymiary itp.*) **mam na imię Tomasz** my name is Thomas; **ile masz lat?** how old are you?; **ona ma siedemnaście lat** she's seventeen years old; **ta łódź ma pięć metrów długości** this boat is five meters long; **mam metr osiemdziesiąt wzrostu** I am one hundred and eighty centimeters tall; **godzina ma sześćdziesiąt minut** there are sixty minutes in an hour; **pociąg ma dziesięć minut spóźnienia** the train is ten minutes late. **7.** mieć miejsce happen, occur, take place. **8.** (*z przeczeniem i zaimkiem*) **nie mieć co jeść** have nothing to eat; **nie mam co ze sobą zrobić** I don't know what to do with myself; **nie mieć gdzie się podziać** have no place to go; **nie mieć nic do powiedzenia** have nothing to say; **nie mieć nic do stracenia** have nothing to lose. **9.** (*z przeczeniem w trzeciej osobie czasu teraźniejszego: oznacza brak l. nieistnienie*) **jej tu nie ma** she isn't here; **nie ma tu nikogo** there's nobody here; **nie ma co płakać** there's no need to cry; it's no use crying; **nie ma to jak w domu!** (there's) no place like home!; **nie ma sprawiedliwości na tym świecie** there is no justice in this world; **nie ma mnie dla nikogo** tell everyone I am out; **nie ma deszczu** there's no rain; it isn't raining; **nie ma jej w domu** she's not at home; she's out; **nie ma sprawy** no problem. **10.** (*wyraża powinność*) be to, be supposed to; **co mam teraz zrobić?** what am I supposed to do now?; **mam wyjechać o czwartej** I am to leave at four; **to mam być ja?** is this supposed to be me?; **mam przyjechać czy nie?** should I come or not?; **czas mało pokazać, że...** time was to show that...; **co ma wisieć, nie utonie** if you're born to be hanged you shall never be drowned. **11.** (*wyraża niespełnione oczekiwania*) **miałem zostać inżynierem** I was to have been an engineer. **12.** (*wyraża spełnienie, ukończenie*) mieć coś zrobione have sth done; **mam zebrane materiały** I have some materials collected. **13.** (*wyraża przypuszczenie*) **miałbym żałować tego?** should I regret it?; **gdybym miał wybierać...** if I were to chose... ~ się *ipf.* **1.** (= *czuć się*) be; **jak się masz?** how are you?; **on ostatnio ma się nie najlepiej** he hasn't been well lately; **masz się teraz z pyszna** you have to pay the devil now. **2.** (*wyraża stan rzeczy*) **ma się na deszcz** it's going to rain; **sprawy tak się mają** the things are going like this; this is how the matter stands; **dzień ma się ku końcowi** the day is drawing to an end. **3.** (= *uważać się*) **za kogo ty się masz?** who do you think you are? **4.** (*w utartych wyrażeniach*) **mieć się na baczności przed kimś/czymś** beware sb/sth; **mieć się ku sobie** be attracted to each other; **ma się rozumieć** sure, certainly, of course.

miednica *f.* **1.** (*naczynie*) basin, bowl. **2.** *anat.* pelvis.

miednicowy *a. anat.* pelvic; **pas miednicowy** pelvic girdle.

miedniczka *f. Gen.pl.* -**ek** *anat.* **miedniczka nerkowa** renal pelvis.

miedza *f.* boundary strip.

miedziak *mi Gen.* -**a** copper (coin).

miedzianka *f. Gen.pl.* -**ek** *zool.* (= *gniewosz*) smooth snake (*Coronella austriaca*).

miedzianobrody *a.* red-bearded.

miedzianowłosy *a.* red-haired.

miedziany *a.* copper; (= *koloru miedzi*) copper-colored.

miedziawy *a. chem.* (*chlorek, siarczek, tlenek*) cuprous.

miedzionośny *a. geol.* copper-bearing, cupriferous.

miedzioryt *mi sztuka* copperplate.

miedziorytnictwo *n. sztuka* copperplate engraving, chalcography.

miedziorytniczy *a.* copperplate, chalcographic.

miedziorytnik *mp* copper engraver.

miedziować *ipf. techn.* copper, coat with copper.

miedziowanie *n. techn.* coppering.

miedziowce *pl. Gen.* -**ów** *chem.* the copper group.

miedziowiec *mp* -**wc**- *pl.* -**y** (*górnik*) copper miner.

miedziowy *a. chem.* cupric.

miedź *f.* **1.** *chem.* copper. **2.** *pl.* -**dzie** (*wyrób z miedzi*) copper.

miejscami *adv.* **1.** (= *gdzieniegdzie*) here and there. **2.** (= *częściowo*) partially, partly.

miejsce *n.* **1.** (= *punkt, lokalizacja*) place, point, spot; **miejsce pracy/zamieszkania** place of work/residence; **miejsce spotkań** meeting place; **miejsce zdarzenia** the spot; **miejsce do zabawy** playground; **miejsce przeznaczenia** destination; **miejsce widokowe** beauty spot; **miejsce wiecznego spoczynku** *lit.* last resting-place; **miejsce chorobowo zmienione** *pat.* pathologically changed spot; **miejsce przecięcia** intersection; **miejsce publiczne** public place; **to nie czas ani miejsce, by...** it's not the right time nor place to...; **chodzić z miejsca na miejsce** walk from place to place; **miejsce artykulacji** *fon.* place l. point of articulation. **2.** (= *sytuacja*) **gdybym był na twoim miejscu...** if I were in your place...; if I were in your shoes...; **na twoim miejscu poczekałbym** if I were you, I'd wait. **3.** miejsce geometryczne *mat.* locus. **4.** (= *właściwy stan l. położenie*) **na swoim** *l.* **właściwym miejscu** in the right place; **właściwy człowiek na właściwym miejscu** the right man in the right place; **nie mogę sobie znaleźć miejsca** I can't find a place for myself; **znaleźć swoje miejsce na ziemi** find one's place on earth; **znać swoje miejsce** know one' place; **odłóż to na miejsce** put it back; **na miejsca!** *sport* ready! **5.** na miejscu (= *nie ruszając się*) in the same place; **zostań na miejscu** stay where you are. **6.** na miejscu (= *natychmiast*) on the spot; **paść trupem na miejscu** die on the spot; **zabić kogoś na miejscu** kill sb on the spot. **7.** *przen.* (*o aktywności*) **dreptać w miejscu** make no progress; **nie móc usiedzieć na miejscu** *l.* **w miejscu** be forever on the move; **ruszyć z miejsca** (=

podjąć działanie) stir up, break a deadlock, move ahead; **ruszyć coś z miejsca** proceed with sth. **8. z miejsca** *pot.* straight away, at once. **9. w miejsce czegoś** (= *zamiast*) in place of sth; **zachowanie nie na miejscu** improper behavior. **10.** (= *fragment przestrzeni*) space, room; **there's enough room for both of us** jest dość miejsca dla nas obu. **11.** (= *siedzenie, krzesło*) place, seat; **miejsce zarezerwowane** reserved seat; **rezerwacja miejsc** seat reservation; **wszystkie miejsca są zajęte** all the seats are occupied; **ustąpić komuś miejsca** yield a place to sb; **miejsce w parlamencie** *polit.* (parliamentary) seat; **honorowe miejsce** seat of honor. **12.** (= *lokata, kolejność*) place, position; **miejsce w kolejce** position in a line; **zająć pierwsze/drugie/ostatnie miejsce** *sport* come first/second/last. **13.** (*fragment utworu*) passage. **14.** (= *posada, etat*) vacancy, job; **starać się o miejsce** look for a job; **nie mamy miejsc** we have no vacancies; **wymówić komuś miejsce** give sb notice.

miejscownik *mi Gen.* **-a** *gram.* locative.

miejscowo *adv.* locally.

miejscowość *f.* locality, place; **miejscowość wypoczynkowa** holiday resort.

miejscowy *a.* (*lokalny*) local; **czas miejscowy** local time; **ludność miejscowa** local people, the locals; **znieczulenie miejscowe** *med.* local anesthesia.

miejscówka *f. Gen.pl.* **-ek** (*bilet*) reserved seat ticket.

miejski *a.* town, city, municipal, urban; **komunikacja miejska** city transport, municipal transport; **rada miejska** city council; **folklor miejski** urban folklore.

miel *itd. ipf. zob.* **mleć**.

mielec *mi* **-lc-** *Gen.* **-a** *orn., anat.* gizzard, gigerium.

mielić *ipf.* **-ę -esz** = **mleć**.

mielizna *f.* **1.** shoal, shallow; **osiąść na mieliźnie** *żegl. l. przen.* run aground. **2.** *przen.* (= *słabe l. banalne miejsce w książce, utworze itp.*) shallow fragment.

mielone *n. Gen.* **-ego** *kulin.* meat loaf.

mielonka *f. Gen.pl.* **-ek** *kulin.* luncheon meat.

mielony *mi* (*kotlet*) meat loaf, meatball.

mienić *ipf. lit.* call. **~ się** *ipf.* + *Ins. lit.* call o.s., purport *l.* claim to be (*sth*); **i on się mieni moim przyjacielem!** and he purports to be a friend of mine!

mienić się *ipf. lit.* sparkle, iridesce, be iridescent; **mienić się w blasku słońca** sparkle in sunlight; **mienił się na twarzy** his colors came and went.

mienie *n. prawn.* property, possessions, estate; **mienie ruchome/nieruchome** movable/immovable property; **przepadek mienia** confiscation of property.

mieńszewik *mp hist., polit.* Menshevik.

miernictwo *n.* (= *teoria pomiarów*) metrology; *geodezja* land measuring, land surveying.

mierniczy *a.* measuring. – *mp* land surveyor.

miernie *adv. uj.* poorly.

miernik *mi Gen.* **-a** **1.** (= *miara*) measure, gauge (*czegoś* of sth). **2.** (= *kryterium*) standard, criterion (*czegoś* of sth). **3.** *techn.* meter, gage, gauge, measuring instrument; **miernik uniwersalny** *el.* multimeter.

miernikowiec *ma* **-wc-** *ent.* (= *motyl z rodziny Geometridae*) geometrid, geometer (moth); **gąsienica miernikowca** inchworm, loopworm, measuring worm.

mierność *f.* mediocrity, average range.

miernota *f. pog.* person of mediocre ability, dullard.

mierny *a.* (= *przeciętny*) mean, average; (= *niewybitny*) mediocre, indifferent; (= *słaby, byle jaki*) poor. – *mi szkoln.* admissible.

mierzalny *a.* measurable.

mierzarka *f. Gen.pl.* **-ek** *techn.* measuring machine.

mierzchnąć *ipf.* **-ch-** *lit., rzad.* grow dusky; *t. przen.* dwindle, wane.

mierze *f. zob.* **miara**.

mierzeja *f. Gen.* **-ei** spit, sand bar.

mierzić *ipf.* **-rżę -rzisz** *lit.* disgust, sicken, nauseate, fill (*sb*) with disgust.

mierznąć *ipf.* **-znę -zniesz** *l.* **-źniesz, -znij** *l.* **-źnij, -zł -zli** *l.* **-źli** *lit.* pall (*komuś* on sb).

mierzwa *f.* **1.** *roln.* (*nawóz*) muck, farm manure. **2.** *roln.* (*ściółka*) matted straw. **3.** **mierzwa ludzka** *pog.* the common crowd.

mierzwić *ipf.* **-w** *l.* **-ij** ruffle, shag. **~ się** *ipf.* get ruffled, shag.

mierzyć *ipf.* **1.** (= *odmierzać*) measure (out). **2.** (= *liczyć sobie*) measure; **korytarz mierzy dwa metry szerokości** the corridor measures two meters across. **3.** *przen.* **mierzyć kogoś wzrokiem** eye sb; **mierzyć kogoś własną miarą** measure sb by one's own yardstick. **4.** (= *przymierzać*) try (*sth*) on. **5.** (= *celować*) aim, take aim (*do kogoś l. czegoś l. w kogoś/coś* at sb/sth); **mierzyć do kogoś z pistoletu** aim *l.* point a gun at sb; **wysoko mierzyć** *przen.* aim high. **~ się** *ipf.* **1.** (= *sprawdzać swój wzrost*) check one's height. **2.** **mierzyć się wzrokiem** eye each other. **3.** *lit.* **mierzyć się z kimś** measure one's strength with *l.* against sb; (= *walczyć*) measure swords with sb. **4.** *lit.* **mierzyć się z czymś** cope with sth.

mierzyn *ma*, **mierzynek** *ma* **-nk-** *przest.* draft horse.

mies. *abbr.* = **miesiąc**.

miesiąc *mi Gen.* **-a** *Gen.pl.* **-ęcy** **1.** (= *dwunasta część roku*) month; **miesiąc kalendarzowy/księżycowy** calendar/lunar month; **miesiące zimowe/letnie** winter/summer months; **w tym miesiącu** this month; **w ubiegłym** *l.* **zeszłym miesiącu** last month; **w przyszłym miesiącu** next month; **co miesiąc** every month; **po miesiącu** after a month; a month later; **za miesiąc** in a month; in a month's time; **czekać miesiącami** *l.* **przez długie miesiące** wait for months; **czekam od miesiąca** I've been waiting for a month; **z miesiąca na miesiąc** month by month; **miesiąc za miesiącem** month after month; **jestem w czwartym miesiącu (ciąży)** I am four months pregnant; **miodowy miesiąc** honeymoon; **popamiętasz ruski**

miesiąc *pot.* you won't forget it for a long time. **2.** *poet.* (*księżyc*) moon.

miesiączka *f. Gen.pl.* **-ek** *fizj.* menstruation, period.

miesiączkować *ipf. fizj.* menstruate.

miesiączkowy *a. fizj.* menstrual.

miesiącznica *f. bot.* honesty, satin-flower (*Lunaria*).

miesięcznie *adv.* monthly; **tysiąc dolarów miesięcznie** one thousand dollars a month.

miesięcznik *mi Gen.* **-a 1.** (= *pismo ukazujące się raz na miesiąc*) monthly; **miesięcznik ilustrowany** illustrated monthly. **2.** *bot.* moonseed (*Menispermum*).

miesięczny *a.* monthly; **urlop/pobyt miesięczny** one month's vacation/stay; **pensja miesięczna** salary; **abonament miesięczny** monthly subscription *l.* service fee; **miesięczne dziecko** month-old baby.

mieszacz *mp* (*robotnik*) mixer. – *mi Gen.* **-a** *techn., telew., radio* mixer.

mieszać *ipf.* **1.** stir; (= *łączyć ze sobą*) mix, blend; (= *potrząsać*) shake; **mieszać kogoś z błotem** hurl abuse at sb, cast a slur on sb. **2.** (= *dodawać coś*) add; **mieszać niemieckie słowa do swojej wypowiedzi** incorporate German words into one's utterance. **3.** (= *wciągać*) involve (*kogoś w coś* sb in sth); **nie mieszaj mnie w swoje interesy** leave me out of your business. **4.** (= *nie rozróżniać*) mix up, confuse; **mieszać pojęcia/fakty/nazwiska/wyrazy** confuse issues/facts/names/words. **5.** (= *peszyć*) confuse, disconcert, abash. **6.** *przest.* interfere; **mieszać komuś szyki** thwart *l.* cross sb's plans. **~ się** *ipf.* **1.** (= *łączyć się w całość*) mix, blend. **2.** (= *wtrącać się do czegoś*) meddle, interfere, butt in; **nie mieszaj się w nie swoje sprawy** don't poke your nose into somebody else's business; **nie chcę się w to mieszać** I don't want to be a part of it. **3.** (= *być mylonym*) be mixed up with, be taken for somebody else; **mieszają mi się daty/nazwiska/fakty** I confuse dates/names/facts. **4.** (= *peszyć się*) be confused, be abashed.

mieszadło *n. Gen.pl.* **-eł** *techn.* stirrer, mixer, agitator.

mieszak *mi Gen.* **-a** *techn.* agitator.

mieszalnia *f. Gen.pl.* **-i** mixing plant; **mieszalnia pasz** feed *l.* fodder mixing plant.

mieszalnik *mi Gen.* **-a 1.** *techn.* (*zbiornik*) mixer, agitator. **2.** *metal.* mixer.

mieszaniec *ma* **-ńc-** *pl.* **-e** *biol.* hybrid, crossbred. – *mp* **-ńc-** *pl.* **-y** *zw. pog.* half-breed.

mieszanina *f.* mix, mixture; **mieszanina gazów** gas mixture; **mieszanina stylów/myśli/uczuć** mixture of styles/thoughts/feelings; **mieszanina narodów/ras** medley of nationalities/races; **mieszanina chłodząca** *l.* **oziębiająca** *fiz.* freezing mixture; **mieszanina piorunująca** *fiz.* detonating gas.

mieszanka *f. Gen.pl.* **-ek** mix, mixture; **mieszanka owocowa/ziołowa/warzywna** fruit/herb/vegetable mix; **mieszanka czekoladowa** assorted chocolates; **mieszanka pastewna** *roln.* fodder crop mixture; **mieszanka paszowa** *roln.* fodder

mixture; **mieszanka palna** *l.* **paliwowo-powietrzna** *techn., mot.* air-fuel mixture; **mieszanka bogata** *techn., mot.* rich mixture; **mieszanka uboga** *techn., mot.* weak mixture, lean mixture, poor mixture.

mieszany *a.* mixed; **las mieszany** mixed forest; **chór mieszany** mixed choir; **małżeństwo mieszane** mixed marriage, intermarriage; **ludność mieszana** mixed population; **deklinacja mieszana** *gram.* mixed declension; **gra mieszana** *sport* mixed doubles.

mieszarka *f. Gen.pl.* **-ek** *techn.* mixer; **mieszarka bębnowa/łopatkowa/spiralna** drum/paddle/ribbon mixer.

mieszczanin *mp pl.* **-anie** *Gen.* **-an** burgher, townsman; *pot., pog.* bourgeois.

mieszczanka *f. Gen.pl.* **-ek** *zob.* **mieszczanin**.

mieszczański *a.* **1.** burgher, middle-class. **2.** (*moralność, gust, przyzwyczajenia*) (= *drobnomieszczański*) bourgeois, narrow-minded.

mieszczaństwo *n.* bourgeoisie, middle class.

mieszczka *f. Gen.pl.* **-ek 1.** *przest.* townswoman, burgher. **2.** *pog.* bourgeois.

mieszczuch *mp pl.* **-y** *pog.* big-city man, city man.

mieszek *mi* **-szk-** *Gen.* **-a 1.** (= *mały miech*) bellows. **2.** *fot.* bellows. **3.** *bot.* follicle. **4.** *przest.* (= *sakiewka*) pouch, moneybag.

mieszkać *ipf.* live; **mieszkać w willi/pod mostem** live in a villa/under the bridge; **mieszkać w hotelu** stay at a hotel; **mieszkać na wsi/w mieście** live in the country/in the town; **mieszkać w Londynie/w Polsce/za granicą** live in London/in Poland/abroad; **mieszkać przy** *l.* **na ulicy Traugutta** live at *l.* in Traugutta street; **mieszkać na parterze/drugim piętrze** live on the ground *l.* first floor/third floor; *Br.* live on the ground floor/second floor; **mieszkać z kimś pod jednym dachem** live with sb under the same roof, share an apartment with sb; **mieszkać kątem u kogoś** put up at sb's place; **mieszkać o miedzę z kimś** live next door to sb, live cheek by jowl with sb; **mieszkać na kupie** coop up; **radość i pokój mieszkają we mnie** *przen.* joy and peace are with me.

mieszkalnictwo *n.* housing policy.

mieszkalny *a.* (*dom, budynek*) residential; (*dzielnica*) residential, living.

mieszkanie *n.* apartment; *Br.* flat; **ciepłe/zimne mieszkanie** warm/cold apartment; **suche/wilgotne mieszkanie** dry/damp apartment; **słoneczne mieszkanie** sunny apartment; **widne/ciemne mieszkanie** bright/dark apartment; **przestronne/ciasne mieszkanie** roomy *l.* spacious/small *l.* cramped apartment; **mieszkanie samodzielne/prywatne/służbowe** self-contained/private/company apartment; **mieszkanie spółdzielcze** cooperative apartment; **mieszkanie własnościowe** condominium; **mieszkanie kwaterunkowe** public housing apartment; *Br.* community housing flat; **wynająć komuś/wynająć od kogoś mieszkanie** let/rent an apartment; **urządzić mieszkanie** decorate one's apartment; **odnowić mieszkanie** redecorate one's apartment; **sprzątnąć mieszkanie** clean up one's apartment; **przydział**

mieszkania apartment allocation; **mieszkanie z przydziału** assigned apartment.

mieszkaniec *mp* -ńc- *pl.* -y (*domu*) occupant, resident; (*miasta, wsi, osiedla*) inhabitant, resident; (*kraju*) resident.

mieszkaniowy *a.* housing; **spółdzielnia mieszkaniowa** housing cooperative.

mieszkaniówka *f. Gen.pl.* -ek *pot.* housing policy.

mieszkanka *f. Gen.pl.* -ek *zob.* **mieszkaniec**.

mieszkanko *n. Gen.pl.* -ek apartment.

mieścić *ipf.* -szczę -ścisz (*o naczyniu, pojemniku*) hold; (*o budynku*) house; (*o sali, samochodzie*) seat. ~ **się** *ipf.* (= *znajdować się*) be situated, be located; (= *znajdować dość miejsca*) fit; **to się w głowie nie mieści!** the mind boggles!

mieście *n. zob.* **miasto**.

mieścina *f. pog.* Podunk, jerkwater town, hicksville.

mieść *ipf.* **miecie miótł miotła miotły** *lit.* sweep.

mietelnik *f. bot.* kochia (*Kochia*).

mietlica *f. bot.* bent grass (*Agrostis*).

miewać *ipf.* have (*every now and then*); **miewać bóle głowy** have headaches; **miewać ochotę na coś** feel like doing sth. ~ **się** *ipf. lit.* be feeling, be doing; **jak się pan miewa?** how are you feeling?

mięcho *n. pot.* meat; **rzucać mięchem** cuss, curse, swear, use four-letter words.

mięczak *ma zool.* mollusk, mollusc (*Mollusca*). – *mp pl.* -**i** *pog.* wimp.

międlarka *f. Gen.pl.* -ek **1.** *tk.* breaker, breaking machine. **2.** (*maszyna garbarska*) staking machine.

międlica *f.* swingle.

międlić *ipf.* -l *l.* -lij **1.** (*len*) swingle, scutch. **2.** *pot.* (= *gnieść*) crumple, crush. **3.** (= *mamrotać*) mutter. **4.** *pot.* (= *rozwodzić się nad czymś*) drag out. **5.** (*skóry*) stake.

między *prep.* + *Ins.* **1.** (*przy lokalizacji kogoś / czegoś*) between; **między domami** between the houses; **między lasem a szosą** between the forest and the road; **między młotem a kowadłem** *przen.* between the devil and the deep blue sea, between a rock and a hard place; **czytać coś między wierszami** *przen.* read between the lines. **2.** (*kiedy ktoś / coś jest otoczone ze wszystkich stron*) in the middle of, among; **między drzewami znajdowało się małe jeziorko** there was a little lake surrounded by trees. **3.** (*dla wyróżnienia jednego z wielu*) (= *wśród*) among; **najzdolniejszy między studentami pierwszego roku** the most talented among the first year students; **między innymi** among other things. **4.** (*dla oznaczenia relacji, w jakiej pozostają jakieś osoby, przedmioty*) between; **między nami mówiąc** between you and me; **między sobą** between ourselves/yourselves/ themselves; **kłótnie między małżonkami** nuptial rows, arguments between the spouses. **5.** (*dla oznaczenia czasu*) between; **będę między pierwszą a drugą po południu** I'll be there between 1 and 2 p.m. **6.** + *Acc.* (*dla oznaczenia kierunku*) (= *pomiędzy*) between, among; **odłożyć coś między książki** put sth among the books; **włożyć coś**

między bajki *przen.* dismiss sth. **7.** + *Acc.* (*przy podziale*) between, among; **rozdzielić majątek między syna i córkę** divide one's property between one's son and one's daughter. **8.** + *Ins.* (*przy wyborze*) between; **wybierać między dobrem a złem** choose between the good and the bad.

międzyczas *mi sport* (*mierzony po każdym okrążeniu*) lap time; (*mierzony w różnych punktach trasy*) split time; **w międzyczasie** in the meantime.

międzycząsteczkowy *a. fiz., chem.* intermolecular; **oddziaływania międzycząsteczkowe** intermolecular forces.

międzygatunkowy *a. biol.* interspecific; **krzyżówka międzygatunkowa** interspecific crossing.

międzygórze *n. Gen.pl.* -y *geol.* basin.

międzygwiazdowy, międzygwiezdny *a. astron.* interstellar; **pył międzygwiazdowy** interstellar dust.

międzykomorowy *a. anat.* interventricular; **przegroda międzykomorowa** (inter)ventricular septum.

międzykomórkowy *a. biol.* intercellular.

międzykontynentalny *a.* intercontinental.

międzykostny *a. anat.* interosseous.

międzykręgowy *a. anat.* intervertebral.

międzylądowanie *n.* stopover; **rejs z dwoma międzylądowaniami** flight with two stopovers.

międzylekcyjny *a.* inter-lesson.

międzylodowcowy *a. geol.* interglacial; **okres międzylodowcowy** interglacial (period).

międzyludzki *a.* interpersonal, human.

międzymiastowa *f. Gen.* -ej *tel.* long-distance call.

międzymiastowy *a. tel.* long-distance; **centrala/ rozmowa międzymiastowa** long-distance operator/call.

międzymorze *n. Gen.pl.* -y *geogr.* isthmus.

międzymózgowie *n. Gen.pl.* -i *anat.* diencephalon, interbrain.

międzynarodowy *a.* international; **prawo międzynarodowe** *prawn.* international law.

międzynarodówka *f. Gen.pl.* -ek **1.** *polit., hist.* International; **I Międzynarodówka** the First International, the International Working Men's Association; **II Międzynarodówka** the Second International, the Socialist International; **III Międzynarodówka** the Third International, the Comintern, the Communist International; **IV Międzynarodówka** the Fourth International. **2.** (*pieśń*) the Internationale.

międzypalcowy *a. zool.* interdigital; **błona międzypalcowa** interdigital membrane.

międzypaństwowy *a.* international; **mecz międzypaństwowy** *sport* international.

międzypartyjny *a.* inter-party.

międzypiętro *n. Gen.pl.* -er intermediate landing.

międzyplanetarny *a. astron.* interplanetary; **materia międzyplanetarna** interplanetary matter; **przestrzeń międzyplanetarna** outer space; **lot międzyplanetarny** space flight; **statek między-**

planetarny spaceship; **sonda międzyplanetarna** space probe.

międzyplemienny *a.* intertribal.

międzyplon *mi roln.* intercrop, catch crop.

międzypłciowość *f. biol.* intersexuality.

międzypokład *mi żegl.* **1.** (*pokład*) tweendeck. **2.** (*przestrzeń*) tween deck.

międzypokoleniowy *a.* intergenerational; **konflikt międzypokoleniowy** generation gap.

międzyreligijny *a.* interdenominational; **dialog międzyreligijny** interdenominational dialogue *l.* dialog.

międzyresortowy *a.* interdepartmental; **umowa/współpraca międzyresortowa** interdepartmental agreement/cooperation.

międzyrządowy *a.* intergovernmental; **Konferencja Międzyrządowa** (*Unia Europejska*) Intergovernmental Conference, IGC.

międzyrzecze *n. Gen.pl.* **-y** *geogr.* interfluve, interamnian region.

międzysemestralny *a. uniw., szkoln.* intersession; **przerwa międzysemestralna** term break, semester break.

międzystanowy *a.* interstate; **droga międzystanowa** *US* Interstate (Highway).

międzyszczękowy *a. anat.* intermaxillary; **kość międzyszczękowa** intermaxillary bone.

międzyszkolny *a. szkoln., uniw.* interschool; **zawody międzyszkolne** interschool competition.

międzytkankowy *a. biol.* intertissue.

międzytorze *n. Gen.pl.* **-y** *kol.* intertrack space.

międzyuczelniany *a. uniw.* interuniversity, intercollegiate.

międzywęźle *n. bot.* internode.

międzywierszowy *a.* interlinear; *przen.* (to be) read between the lines.

międzywojenny *a.* interwar; **dwudziestolecie międzywojenne** Poland's twenty years of independence after World War I.

międzywojewódzki *a.* interprovincial.

międzywojnie *n. Gen.pl.* **-i** *lit.* interwar period.

międzywyrazowy *a. fon.* word sandhi; **upodobnienie międzywyrazowe** assimilation across word boundaries.

międzywyznaniowy *a.* interfaith, interdenominational; **dialog międzywyznaniowy** interfaith dialogue *l.* dialog.

międzyzakładowy *a.* interfactory; **międzyzakładowy komitet strajkowy** interfactory strike committee.

międzyzwiązkowy *a.* interunion.

międzyzwrotnikowy *a. geogr.* intertropical, tropical.

międzyżebrowy *a. anat.* intercostal; **mięsień międzyżebrowy** intercostal (muscle).

miękczyć *ipf.* **1.** *t. przen.* (= *sprawiać, że coś jest miękkie*) soften. **2.** *fon.* palatalize. ~ **się** *ipf. fon.* be *l.* become palatalized.

miękisz *mi* **1.** (= *miękka część czegoś*) pulp. **2.** *bot.* parenchyma; **miękisz asymilacyjny** *l.* **zieleniowy** chlorenchyma; **miękisz gąbczasty** spongy mesophyll; **miękisz palisadowy** palisade parenchyma.

miękiszowy *a. bot.* parenchymal, parenchymatous; **tkanka miękiszowa** parenchyma.

miękki *a.* **-kcy, -kszy 1.** (= *nietwardy*) soft; (*mięso*) tender; **miękki dywan** thick carpet; **miękkie meble** upholstered furniture; **miękka woda** soft water; **podniebienie miękkie** *anat.* soft palate; **chirurgia miękka** *chir.* soft tissue surgery; **miękkie lądowanie** *astron.* soft landing; **spółgłoska miękka** *fon.* palatal (consonant); **metale miękkie** *techn.* soft metals; **mieć miękkie serce** be soft-hearted, be tender-hearted, have a soft heart; **jestem dla ciebie za miękki** I am too soft *l.* lenient *l.* easy on you. **2.** *przen.* (= *mało stanowczy*) soft, weak. **3.** *przen.* (= *harmonijny*) soft, gentle, mellow.

miękko *adv.* **-kcej** softly; gently; **jajko na miękko** *kulin.* soft-boiled egg.

miękkopłetwe *pl. Gen.* **-ych** *icht.* malacopterygians, soft-finned fishes (*Malacopterygii*).

miękkość *f. Gen.* **-i** softness; (*dywanu*) thickness; *fon.* (*spółgłoski*) palatality.

miękkotematowy *a. jęz.* soft-stemmed.

miękławka *f. Dat.* **-wce** *icht.* bowfin (*Amia calva*).

mięknąć *ipf.* **-ij, -kł** *l.* **-knął -kła -kli** (= *stawać się miękkim*) *t. przen.* soften.

mięsak *mi Gen.* **-a** *pat.* sarcoma.

mięsień *mi* **-śni-** *Gen.* **-a** *t. anat.* muscle; **mięsień gładki** smooth muscle; **mięsień czworoboczny** trapezius muscle; **mięsień prosty** straight muscle; **mięsień sercowy** myocardium, cardiac *l.* heart muscle; **skurcz mięśnia** muscular contraction; **zanik mięśnia** muscular atrophy; **niedowład mięśnia** muscular paresis.

mięsisty *a.* **1.** fleshy; **mięsista twarz** plump face. **2.** *bot.* succulent; **mięsiste liście** succulent leaves. **3.** (*o tkaninach, skórach*) thick; **mięsisty dywan** thick carpet.

mięsiwo *n.* meat dish.

mięsny *a.* meat; **sklep mięsny** butcher's, meat shop; **danie mięsne** meat dish; **konserwa mięsna** canned meat, spam; **gospodarstwo mięsne** *roln.* stock farm; **bydło mięsne** *roln.* beef cattle.

mięso *n.* **1.** (*zwierząt*) meat; **mięso wieprzowe** pork; **mięso cielęce** veal; **mięso wołowe** beef; **mięso baranie** mutton; **mięso jagnięce** lamb; **miękkie/twarde mięso** tender/tough meat; **soczyste mięso** juicy meat; **przypieczone mięso** well-done meat; **smażone mięso** fried meat; **gotowane mięso** boiled meat; **duszone mięso** stewed meat; **pieczone mięso** roasted meat; **wędzone mięso** smoked meat; **mięso świeże/mrożone** fresh/frozen meat; **białe mięso** white meat; **sztuka mięsa** lump of meat, piece of meat; **pierogi z mięsem** meat-stuffed piroshki *l.* dumplings. **2.** *pot.* (*człowieka*) flesh; **mięso armatnie** *przen.* cannon fodder; **dzikie mięso** *pat.* granulation, proud flesh; **rzucać mięsem** cuss, curse, use four-letter words.

mięsopust *mi* carnival.

mięsopustny *a.* carnival.

mięsożerca *mp* **1.** *zool.* carnivore. **2.** *żart.* (*o człowieku*) meat-eater.

mięsożerny *a. zool.* carnivorous.

mięśniak *mi Gen.* **-a** *pat.* myoma. – *mp pl.* **-i** *pog.* iron pumper, beefcake.

mięśniolot *mi lotn.* man-powered aircraft.

mięśniowy *a.* muscular; **żołądek mięśniowy** *zool.* gizzard, ventriculus.

mięta *f.* **1.** *bot.* mint (*Mentha*); **mięta pieprzowa** peppermint (*Mentha piperita*); **mięta karbowana** *l.* **kędzierzawa** *l.* **zielona** spearmint (*Mentha spicata*); **czuć do kogoś miętę** have a crush on sb. **2.** *kulin.* mint tea.

miętosić *ipf.* crumple.

miętowy *a.* mint; **likier miętowy** crème de menthe.

miętówka *f. Gen.pl.* **-ek 1.** (*cukierek*) mint, mint candy. **2.** (*wódka*) mint-flavored vodka.

miętus *ma icht.* burbot (*Lota lota*). – *mi Gen.* **-a** *pot.* (*cukierek*) mint, mint candy.

mig *mi* sign; **rozmawiać na migi** sign, speak by signs; **zrobić coś w mig** *pot.* do sth in a jiffy, do sth in no time.

migacz *mi Gen.* **-a** *zwł. mot.* turn signal, directional, blinker; *Br.* indicator.

migać *ipf.* **1.** (= *błyskać*) flash. **2.** (= *poruszać szybko czymś*) breeze. **3.** (*o głuchoniemych*) (= *porozumiewać się*) sign. ~ **się** *ipf. pot.* shirk; **migać się od pracy/obowiązków** swing the lead, shirk work/duty.

miganie *n.* (*język*) sign language.

migawka *f. Gen.pl.* **-ek 1.** *fot.* shutter. **2.** short report, flash.

migawkowy *a.* **1.** *fot.* shutter; **zdjęcie migawkowe** snapshot. **2.** (= *krótki*) brief, short; **migawkowe spojrzenie** cursory look. **3.** *żegl.* quicklight, flashing-light; **sygnalizacja migawkowa** quick (flashing) light signals, flashing light signals.

migdalić się *ipf. pot.* neck, make out.

migdał *mi* **1.** *bot.* (*roślina*) almond (tree) (*Amygdalus communis l. Prunus amygdalus*); **migdał ziemny** yellow nutsedge (*Cyperus esculentus*). **2.** (*nasiono*) almond; **gorzki/słodki migdał** bitter/sweet almond; **marzyć o niebieskich migdałach** daydream.

migdałek *mi* **-łk-** *Gen.* **-a 1.** almond. **2.** *anat.* tonsil; **migdałek gardłowy** pharyngeal tonsil, third tonsil; **zapalenie migdałków** *pat.* tonsilitis.

migdałowiec *mi* **-wc-** *Gen.* **-a 1.** *bot.* almond (tree) (*Amygdalus communis l. Prunus amygdalus*). **2.** *min.* amygdaloid.

migdałowy *a.* almond, almondy.

migiem *adv.* in a jiffy.

miglanc *mp pot.* slacker, shirker.

migmatyt *mi geol.* migmatite.

mignąć *pf.* **-ij** *zob.* **migać**.

mignon *mi Gen.* **-u** *druk.* minion.

migot *mi* gleam, glimmer, flicker.

migotać *ipf.* **-czę -czesz** *l.* **-cę -cesz, -cz 1.** (= *błyskać*) shimmer, glisten. **2.** (*o przedmiocie, zwłaszcza metalicznym*) (= *szybko się poruszać*) flicker.

migotanie *n.* flicker; (= *lśnienie*) shimmer, glisten; **migotanie komór (serca)** *pat.* ventricular fibrillation; **migotanie przedsionków (serca)** *pat.*

auricular fibrillation, atrial fibrillation; **migotanie gwiazd** *astron.* scintillation, twinkling.

migotliwy *a.* flickering, glimmering, twinkling; **migotliwy blask** flickering shimmer; **migotliwy płomyk** glimmering flame; **migotliwe światło** flashing light.

migowy *a.* **1.** (= *odnoszący się do znaków*) sign; **język migowy** sign language. **2.** (*w sygnalizacji świetlnej*) flashing; **kierunkowskaz migowy** flashing indicator; **lampka migowa** flashing light.

migracja *f.* **1.** (= *wędrówka*) migration. **2.** *bot.* migration. **3.** *zool.* migration.

migracyjny *a.* migration, migrational, migratory.

migrena *f. pat.* migraine.

migrować *ipf.* **1.** (*o ludziach*) migrate. **2.** *biol.* migrate.

mijać *ipf.* **1.** (= *przemieszczać się obok czegoś*) pass, go past; **minęła mnie okazja do spotkania się z twoimi rodzicami** I missed the chance to meet your parents; **kara cię nie minie** you won't escape the punishment, you won't get away with this. **2.** (= *upływać*) pass, elapse, lapse; **minęła godzina trzecia** it is past three; **przeziębienie minęło** cold is gone; **występ minął bez echa** the performance did not evoke a response, the performance was a flop. ~ **się** *ipf.* **minąć się 1.** (= *przemieszczać się obok siebie*) pass (each other *l.* one another). **2.** (= *nie spotykać się*) miss each other; **to mija się z celem** there is no point in it, it's pointless; **minąłeś się z powołaniem** you have missed your vocation; **mijać się z prawdą** (*o człowieku*) depart from the truth; (*o informacji*) be untrue.

mijanie *n.* passage, lapse; **światła mijania** *mot.* low beams, dimmed headlights; *Br.* dipped headlights.

mijanka *Gen.pl.* **-ek** *f.* turnout.

mika *f. min.* mica.

mikado *mp pl.* **-owie** mikado, Mikado.

mikanit *mi techn.* micanite.

mikocki *a. archeol.* Micoquian; **kultura mikocka** Micoquian Culture.

mikolog *mp pl.* **-dzy** *l.* **-owie** *bot.* mycologist.

mikologia *f. Gen.* **-ii** *bot.* mycology.

mikologiczny *a. bot.* mycological, mycologic.

Mikołaj *mp Gen.pl.* **-ów** Nicholas; **Święty Mikołaj** Santa Claus, Santa; *Br.* Father Christmas; **dostać prezent na Mikołaja** get a present from Santa Claus.

mikołajki *pl. Gen.* **-ów** December 6 gift-shower.

mikoryza *f. Dat.* **-zie** *bot.* mycorrhiza.

mikotoksyna *f. bot.* micotoxin.

mikowy *a. min.* mica, micaceous.

mikoza *f. pat.* mycosis.

mikroamper *mi Gen.* **-a** *fiz.* microampere.

mikroanaliza *f. chem.* microanalysis.

mikrob *ma* **1.** *przest.* microbe. **2.** *przen.* bug.

mikrobiolog *mp pl.* **-dzy** *l.* **-owie** microbiologist.

mikrobiologia *f. Gen.* **-ii** microbiology.

mikrobiologiczny *a.* microbiological, microbiologic.

mikrobus *mi mot.* minibus, van.

mikrocefalia *f. Gen.* **-ii** *pat.* microcephaly, microcephalia.

mikrochemia *f. Gen.* -ii *chem.* microchemistry.

mikrochirurgia *f. Gen.* -ii 1. *biol.* micrurgy. 2. *chir.* microsurgery.

mikrochirurgiczny *a.* 1. *biol.* micrurgical. 2. *chir.* microsurgical.

mikrocysta *f.* 1. *med.* microcyst. 2. *bot.* microcistis (*Microcistis*).

mikrocyt *mi pat.* microcyte.

mikrocząstka *f. fiz.* micromolecule.

mikrodruk *mi druk.* microprint.

mikroekonomia *f. Gen.* -ii *ekon.* microeconomics.

mikroelektronika *f. el.* microelectronics.

mikroelement *mi biol., chem.* micronutrient.

mikroewolucja *f. biol.* microevolution.

mikrofag *ma biol.* microphage.

mikrofala *f.* 1. *fiz.* microwave. 2. *pot.* (= *kuchenka mikrofalowa*) microwave (oven).

mikrofalowy *a. fiz.* microwave; **kuchenka mikrofalowa** microwave oven.

mikrofalówka *f. Gen.pl.* -ek 1. *tel.* (*nadajnik*) microwave transmitter. 2. *pot.* (*kuchenka*) microwave (oven).

mikrofauna *f. zool.* microfauna.

mikrofilm *mi fot.* microfilm.

mikrofilmować *ipf. fot.* microfilm.

mikrofilmowy *a. fot.* microfilm.

mikrofizyka *f. fiz.* microphysics.

mikroflora *f. bot.* microflora.

mikrofon *mi techn.* microphone; **mikrofon cieplny** hot-wire *l.* thermal microphone; **mikrofon ciśnieniowy** pressure microphone; **mikrofon dynamiczny** dynamic *l.* moving-coil microphone; **mikrofon elektroakustyczny** electrostatic *l.* condenser microphone; **mikrofon kierunkowy** directional microphone.

mikrofonowy *a.* microphonic.

mikrofotografia *f. Gen.* -ii *fot.* 1. (*technika*) microphotography. 2. (*zdjęcie*) microphotograph.

mikrofotograficzny *f. Gen.* -ii *fot.* microphotographic.

mikrofotogram *mi fot.* microphotograph.

mikrofotometr *mi fiz., fot.* microphotometer.

mikrogameta *f. biol.* microgamete.

mikrografia *f. Gen.* -ii 1. *fot.* micrograph. 2. (= *opis drobnych przedmiotów*) micrography. 3. *sztuka* micrography.

mikroklimat *mi meteor.* microclimate.

mikroklimatyczny *a. meteor.* microclimatic.

mikroklin *mi min.* microcline.

mikrokomputer *mi Gen.* -a *komp.* microcomputer.

mikrokomputerowy *a. komp.* microcomputer.

mikrokosmos *mi fil., biol., fiz.* microcosm, microcosmos.

mikrokrystaliczny *mi krystal.* microcrystalline.

mikrolit *mi Gen.* -u 1. *archeol.* microlith. 2. *krystal.* microlite.

mikrolityczny *a. archeol.* microlithic.

mikromanipulacja *mi Gen.* -cji *techn.* micromanipulation.

mikromer *mi biol.* micromere.

mikrometr *mi* 1. *techn.* micrometer, micrometer caliper, mike. 2. *astron.* micrometer. 3. *miern.* micrometer, micron.

mikrometryczny *a.* micrometrical, micrometric.

mikrominiaturowy *a.* microminiature.

mikrominiaturyzacja *f. Gen.* -cji microminiaturization.

mikromoduł *mi techn.* micromodule.

mikron *mi miern.* micron, micrometer.

Mikronezja *f. geogr.* 1. (*część Oceanii*) Micronesia. 2. (*państwo*) **Federacja Mikronezji** Federated States of Micronesia.

Mikronezyjczyk *mp* Micronesian.

Mikronezyjka *f. zob.* **Mikronezyjczyk.**

mikronezyjski *a.* Micronesian.

mikroorganizm *mi biol.* microorganism.

mikropaleontolog *mp Gen.* -a *paleont.* micropaleontologist.

mikropaleontologia *f. Gen.* -gii *paleont.* micropaleontology.

mikropaleontologiczny *mp Gen.* -a *paleont.* micropaleontological, micropaleontologic.

mikropipeta *a. chem.* micropipette, micropipet.

mikroplankton *mi biol.* microplankton.

mikroprocesor *mi Gen.* -a *komp.* microprocessor.

mikroprogram *mi komp.* microprogram.

mikropyle *n.* 1. *bot.* micropyle. 2. *zool.* micropyle.

mikroreprodukcja *f.* microreproduction.

mikrosejsmiczny *a. geol.* microseismic; **wstrząs mikrosejsmiczny** microseismic tremor.

mikrosejsmy *pl. geol.* microseisms.

mikrosekunda *f. Dat.* **-ndzie** microsecond.

mikroskala *f.* microscale.

mikroskop *mi opt.* microscope; **mikroskop elektronowy** electron microscope; **mikroskop jonowy** ion microscope.

mikroskopia *f. Gen.* -ii microscopy.

mikroskopijny *a.* 1. (= *dający się widzieć tylko przez mikroskop*) microscopic, microscopical. 2. (= *bardzo mały*) *przen.* microscopic, tiny.

mikroskopowy *a.* microscopic, microscope.

mikrosocjologia *f. Gen.* -ii *socjol.* microsociology.

mikrosom *mi biol.* microsome.

mikrosonda *f. techn.* microprobe.

mikrospora *f. bot.* microspore.

mikrostruktura *f.* microstructure.

mikroślad *mi kryminalistyka* microtrace.

mikrotelefon *mi techn.* handset.

mikrotom *mi techn.* microtome.

mikroukład *mi el., komp.* integrated circuit, microcircuit.

mikrowaga *f.* microbalance.

mikrowzór *mi komp.* dither.

mikrus *mp pl.* -y *żart.* shrimp; *Br. pot.* midget.

mikry *a.* small, minute.

mikrynit *mi min.* micrinite.

mikryt *mi min.* micrite.

mikser *mi Gen.* **-a** *pl.* **-ry 1.** (*kuchenny*) blender, mixer; *Br.* liquidizer. **2.** *radio, telew., film* (*urządzenie*) mixer. **3.** *druk.* mixer. – *mp pl.* **-rzy 1.** (*w barze*) barkeeper. **2.** *radio, telew., film* (*pracownik*) mixer.

mikserski *a.* mixing; **stół mikserski** mixing console *l.* desk; **studio mikserskie** mixing room.

miksomatoza *f. wet.* myxomatosis.

miksować *ipf.* **1.** (= *mieszać, ubijać*) blend; (*owoce, warzywa*) liquidize; (*napój*) mix. **2.** *radio, telew., film* mix.

mikst *mi sport* mixed doubles.

mikstura *f.* **1.** (= *napój*) potion, concoction. **2.** *muz.* (*w organach*) mixture.

mila *f.* mile; **mila angielska** *l.* **lądowa** (statute) mile (*1609 m*); **mila chińska** li (*500 m*); **mila morska** nautical mile (*1852 m*); **mila norweska** *l.* **szwedzka** Norwegian *l.* Swedish mile (*10 000 m*).

milczący *a.* **1.** (= *małomówny*) silent, tacit, tight-lipped. **2.** (= *odbywający się bez słów*) tacit; **milcząca większość** *polit.* silent majority; **milcząca zgoda** tacit consent; **milczące przyznanie się do winy** tacit admission of guilt.

milczeć *ipf.* **-ę -ysz** be silent, remain silent; **milczeć jak grób** *l.* **kamień** *l.* **zaklęty** be silent as the grave; **milcz!** be quiet!

milczek *mp* **-czk-** *pl.* **-i** *pot.* clam; *lit.* man of few words.

milczenie *n.* silence; **mowa jest srebrem, a milczenie złotem** speech is silver(n) but silence is golden; **pominąć coś milczeniem** pass over sth (in silence); **przerwać milczenie** break the silence; **spuścić zasłonę milczenia** draw a veil (*na coś* over sth); **zmusić kogoś do milczenia** silence sb.

milczkiem *adv.* quietly, tacitly.

mile *adv.* **1.** (= *życzliwie*) nicely, warmly; **coś byłoby mile widziane** sth would not come *l.* go amiss; **jesteś tu zawsze mile widziany** you are always welcome here, you have a standing invitation to visit us; **mile wspominać coś/kogoś** remember sth/sb fondly, recall sth/sb with fondness. **2.** (= *przyjemnie*) pleasantly; **być mile zaskoczonym czymś** be pleasantly surprised by sth.

milenijny *a.* (*o obchodach, uroczystościach*) millennial; **pluskwa milenijna** *komp.* millennium bug; **rok milenijny** millennial anniversary.

milenium *n. sing. indecl. pl.* **-nia** *Gen.* **-niów** millennium.

mileryt *mi min.* millerite, capillary pyrite.

miliamper *mi Gen.* **-a** *Loc.* **-rze** *fiz.* miliampere.

miliard *mi Gen.* **-a 1.** (= *1 000 000 000*) billion; *Br. t.* milliard. **2.** **miliardy** *przen.* (= *całe mnóstwo*) zillions.

miliarder *mp,* **miliarderka** *f. Gen.pl.* **-ek** billionaire.

miliardowy *a.* billionth; (*o inwestycji, majątku, wydatkach*) in the order of a billion; in the order of a few billions.

milibar *mi fiz., meteor.* millibar.

milicja *f.* **1.** (= *wojskowy oddział rezerwy, np. w Szwajcarii*) militia. **2.** *hist.* (= *policja*) police.

milicjant *mp* **1.** *hist.* (= *policjant*) policeman. **2.** (= *żołnierz milicji*) militiaman.

milicjantka *f. Gen.pl.* **-ek** *hist.* (= *policjantka*) policewoman.

milicyjny *a. hist.* (*o patrolu, radiowozie, szkole*) police.

miligram *mi Gen.* **-a** milligram; *Br.* milligramme.

mililitr *mi Gen.* **-a** milliliter.

milimetr *mi Gen.* **-a** millimeter; **milimetr słupa rtęci** millimeter of mercury (*millihg*); **co do milimetra** to a hair.

milimetrowy *a.* millimeter; **papier milimetrowy** graph *l.* plotting paper.

milin *mi bot.* trumpet creeper (*Campsis*).

milion *mi Gen.* **-a 1.** (= *1 000 000*) million; **jeden na milion** one in a million. **2.** **miliony** *przen.* (= *całe mnóstwo*) zillions.

milioner *mp,* **milionerka** *f. Gen.pl.* **-ek** millionaire.

milionowy *a.* (*np. o inwestycji, stratach*) in the order of a million, in the order of a few millions; (*z kolei*) (*np. o pasażerze*) millionth.

milisekunda *f.* millisecond.

militaria *pl. Gen.* **-ów** militaria.

militarny *a. wojsk.* military.

militarysta *mp* militarist.

militarystyczny *a.* militaristic.

militaryzacja *f.* militarization.

militaryzm *mi* militarism.

militaryzować *ipf.* militarize. **~ się** *ipf.* become militarized.

miliwat *mi fiz.* milliwatt.

miliwolt *mi fiz.* millivolt.

milknąć *ipf.* **-ij, -kł** *l.* **-knął -kła -kli 1.** (= *przestać mówić*) become silent. **2.** (= *ucichnąć*) (*nagle*) stop; (*o tłumie*) fall silent; (*stopniowo*) become *l.* grow quiet; (*np. o muzyce, śmiechu*) fade (away); (*o hałasie*) die down.

milord *mp pl.* **-owie** milord; **milordzie** my lord.

milowy *a.* mile; **kamień milowy** *t. przen.* milestone; **zrobić milowy krok** *przen.* make a great stride *l.* leap (*ku czemuś* toward sth).

milu *ma zool.* Père David's deer (*Elaphurus davidianus*).

milusińscy *pl. Gen.* **-ich** *żart.* the little ones; brood (of children).

miluśki *a.* = **milutki**.

milutki *a.* (*np. o dziewczynce, pokoju*) cute(sy); (*o dziecku, zwierzątku*) cuddly.

miła *f. Gen.* **-ej** sweetheart, (true)love, beloved; **miła ma** my truelove, my beloved.

miłek *mi Gen.* **-a** *bot.* **miłek jesienny** pheasant's eye, red morocco (*Adonis autumnalis*); **miłek wiosenny** sweet vernal, yellow adonis (*A. vernalis*).

miło *adv.* **1.** (= *życzliwie*) pleasantly, warmly, nicely; **miło było Pana poznać** it's been nice meeting you; **miło mi Pana poznać** nice to meet you; **miło cię widzieć** (it's) good to see you; **miło, że przyszedłeś** it was nice of you to come; **to bardzo miło z twojej strony** it's very kind *l.* nice of

you, you're very kind. **2.** (= *z przyjemnością*)
with pleasure; **miło będzie odpocząć po pracy**
it'll be nice to have some rest after work; **że aż
miło** with great pleasure; **zajadać aż miło** eat
heartily.

miłorząb *mi -ę- bot.* **miłorząb japoński** ginkgo,
maidenhair tree (*Ginkgo biloba*).

miłosierdzie *n.* (=*litość*) mercy; charity; (*w stosunku do winnego*) clemency; **akt miłosierdzia**
act of mercy, lenity; **bez miłosierdzia** mercilessly; **siostra miłosierdzia** *rz.-kat.* Sister of Charity.

miłosiernie *adv.* mercifully; charitably; (*w stosunku do winnego*) clemently.

miłosierny *a.* (= *litościwy*) merciful; **Boże miłosierny!** Good God!, Good(ness) gracious!; (= *tolerancyjny*) lenient; (*w stosunku do winnego*)
clement.

miłosny *a.* (*o liście, napoju, pieśni*) love; (*o
przygodzie*) romantic; (*o podboju, zapędach*)
amorous; (*o spojrzeniu*) loving.

miłostka *f. Gen.pl.* **-ek** affair; *Fr.* affaire
d'amour, affaire de coeur; *pot.* fling.

miłościwie *adv. arch.* graciously; **miłościwie
panujący** His/Her Majesty.

miłościwy *a. arch.* (= *łaskawy*) gracious; (= *litościwy*) merciful.

miłość *f.* **1.** (*uczucie*) love (*do czegoś / kogoś* for
sth/sb); **miłość braterska/małżeńska/ojcowska**
brotherly/marital/paternal love; **gorąca/nie-
szczęśliwa/pierwsza/platoniczna/ślepa miłość**
deep/unrequited/first/platonic/blind love; **miłość od pierwszego wejrzenia** love at first sight;
miłość własna amour-propre, self-love; **szczenięca miłość** puppy love, calf love; **wolna miłość** free
love; **na miłość boską!** good(ness) gracious!, for
God's sake!; **uprawiać miłość** *pot.* make love; **Wasza Miłość!** *arch.* Your Grace!; **z miłością** loving-
ly, adoringly. **2.** (= *ukochana osoba*) (true)love.

miłośniczka *f. Gen.pl.* **-ek** *zob.* **miłośnik.**

miłośnik *mp* lover; *pot.* buff; **miłośnik filmu**
film lover, movie buff; **miłośnik opery/przyrody/
psów/sztuki** opera/nature/dog/art lover.

miłować *ipf. lit.* love, cherish. **~ się** *ipf. lit.*
love each other.

miły *a.* **1.** (= *przyjemny*) nice; (*np. o chłodzie,
człowieku, niespodziance*) pleasant; (*o wspomnieniach*) fond; (*o tonie głosu*) kindly; (*o od-
mianie*) refreshing; **miły dla oka** pleasing to the
eye; **miły w obejściu** personable; **być miłym dla
kogoś** be pleasant to sb; **do miłego zobaczenia!**
till we meet again!; **bądź tak miły i...** would you
be so kind and *l.* as to... **2.** (= *kochany*) dear,
beloved; **jak mi Bóg miły** honest to God; **na miły
Bóg!** for God's sake!; **miły sercu** dear. – *mp* dear,
darling, sweetheart, (true)love, beloved; **miły
mój** my truelove, my beloved.

mim *mp pl.* **-owie** mime, mime artist, mummer. – *mi pl.* **-y** *teor.lit.* mime.

mimesis *f.* mimesis, mimicry.

mimetyczny *a. biol., krystal., sztuka* mimetic.

mimetyzm *mi* **1.** *biol.* mimesis, mimicry. **2.**
sztuka mimesis.

mimezja *f. krystal.* pseudosymmetry.

mimiczny *a.* mimic.

mimik *mp Gen., Acc.* **-a** *Ins.* **-iem** mimic.

mimika *f.* facial movements *l.* expressions.

mimikra *f. biol.* mimicry, mimesis.

mimo *prep.* + *Gen.* in spite (*czegoś* of sth) despite (*czegoś* sth); **mimo wszystko** in spite of all;
mimo woli unwittingly, inadvertently, unawares; **mimo to** still, even so, despite (all) that.
– *conj.* although, though; **mimo że** (even)
though; **postanowiliśmy zostać, mimo że było już
bardzo późno** we decided to stay, even though it
was very late. – *adv. przest.* past; **Adam przeszedł mimo niezauważony** Adam walked past
unnoticed.

mimochodem *adv.* by the way, in passing, en
passant; **powiedzieć coś mimochodem** mention
sth in passing, mention sth en passant, say sth
parenthetically.

mimośrodowość *f. mech.* eccentricity.

mimośrodowy *a. mech.* eccentric.

mimośród *mi -o-* **1.** *techn.* eccentric. **2.** *mech.*
circular cam.

mimowolnie *adv.* unwittingly, inadvertently,
unintentionally, involuntarily.

mimowolny *a.* unwitting, unintentional, involuntary.

mimoza *f.* **1.** *bot.* mimosa (*Mimosa*); **mimoza
wstydliwa** sensitive plant, humble plant (*Mimosa pudica*). **2.** *przen.* (*o człowieku*) sensitive
plant.

min. *abbr.* **1.** (= *minimum, minimalny*) min.
(*minimum*). **2.** (= *minuta*) min. (*minute*).

mina[1] *f.* (= *wyraz twarzy*) (facial) expression;
przen. face; **grobowa mina** long face; **z kwaśną** *l.*
ze skwaszoną miną sour-faced; **mina mu zrzedła**
his face fell; **mieć rzadką minę** be down in the
mouth; **z miną niewiniątka** with a look of pure innocence; **nadrabiać miną** put on a brave face; **robić miny** make *l.* pull faces; **robić dobrą minę do
złej gry** make the best of a bad job.

mina[2] *f. wojsk.* mine; **mina lądowa/morska/
przeciwpiechotna/przeciwczołgowa** land/float-
ing/antipersonnel/antitank mine; **mina-pułapka**
booby trap; **rozbroić minę** render a mine safe;
stawiacz min (*okręt*) minelayer; **wykrywacz min**
mine detector.

minaret *mi bud.* minaret.

minąć *pf. zob.* **mijać.**

mincerz *mp hist.* coiner, minter.

miner *mp* **1.** *wojsk.* (= *saper*) sapper. **2.**
przest. (= *górnik*) miner.

mineralizacja *f. chem., geol., biol.* mineraliza-
tion.

mineralizować *ipf. chem., geol., biol.* mineral-
ize. **~ się** *ipf. chem., geol., biol.* become mineral-
ized.

mineralny *a.* mineral; **olej mineralny** *mot.* mineral oil; **wełna mineralna** *techn., bud.* rock wool,
mineral wool; **woda mineralna** *kulin.* mineral
water; **zasoby mineralne** mineral resources.

mineralog *mp pl.* **-dzy** *l.* **-owie** mineralogist.

mineralogia *f. Gen.* **-ii** mineralogy.

mineralogiczny *a.* mineralogical, mineralogic.

minerał *mi geol., chem.* mineral; **minerał ciężki/
ilasty/kruszconośny/towarzyszący** heavy/clay/

ore/accessory mineral; **mineral księżycowy** KREEP (*Kalium, Rare Earth Elements, Phosphorus*).

mineta *f. wulg.* (= *pieszczota oralno-genitalna*) (*na kobiecie*) cunnilingus, cunnilinctus; (*na mężczyźnie*) blow job, fellatio.

mini *a. indecl.* (*o sukience, spódnicy*) mini. – *n. indecl.* mini(skirt); **nosić mini** wear a mini.

minia *f. Gen.* **-ii** *chem.* (*ołowiana*) red lead, minium; (*żelazowa*) iron oxide red.

miniatura *f.* **1.** (= *model*) miniature; **w miniaturze** in miniature. **2.** *sztuka* (= *mały obraz*) miniature. **3.** *hist.* (= *iluminacja*) miniature, illumination.

miniaturowy *a.* **1.** (= *maleńki*) miniature; (*np. o samochodzie, aparacie fotograficznym*) baby. **2.** *sztuka* miniature; **malarstwo miniaturowe** miniature painting.

miniaturyzacja *f.* miniaturization.

miniaturyzować *ipf.* miniaturize.

miniaturzysta *mp sztuka* miniaturist.

minibus *mi mot.* minibus, van.

minigolf *mi sport* pitch-and-putt.

minimalista *mp* minimalist.

minimalistyczny *a.* minimalist.

minimalizacja *f.* minimization; **minimalizacja ryzyka** risk management.

minimalizm *mi* minimalist policy; minimalism.

minimalizować *ipf.* minimize.

minimalnie *adv.* marginally, minimally; (*np. przegrać*) by a hair's breadth, narrowly.

minimalny *a.* (= *najmniejszy z dopuszczalnych/możliwych/wymaganych*) minimum, least possible; (= *bardzo niewielki*) negligible, minimal; (*o zmianie*) fractional, minute; (*o różnicy*) hairbreadth; **płaca minimalna** *ekon.* minimum wage.

minimum *n. sing. indecl. Gen.* **-ma** *Gen.* **-mów** minimum; **minimum socjalne** subsistence level; **absolutne minimum** absolute *l.* bare minimum; **ograniczać do minimum** keep to a minimum, reduce to a minimum; **słownik minimum** mini-dictionary; **zmniejszać do minimum** minimize. – *adv.* minimum, at least; **minimum 4 godziny** four hours (at the) minimum.

miniony *a.* (*era, stulecia*) bygone, past; (*rok, miesiąc, tydzień*) past, last; **w minionym tygodniu** last week.

miniówa *f. pot.* mini(skirt).

miniserial *mi telew.* miniseries.

minispódniczka *f. Gen.pl.* **-ek** miniskirt.

minister *mp* **-tr-** *pl.* **-owie** *polit.* minister; *US* Secretary; *Br.* Secretary of State; **minister bez teki** minister without portfolio; **minister finansów** minister of finance; **minister skarbu** minister of the treasury; *US* Secretary of the Treasury; *Br.* Chancellor of the Exchequer; **minister obrony narodowej** defense minister; *US* Defense Secretary; *Br.* Defence Secretary; **minister pełnomocny** minister plenipotentiary; **minister spraw wewnętrznych** minister of the interior, minister of internal affairs; *Br.* Home Secretary; **minister spraw zagranicznych** minister of

foreign affairs, foreign minister; *US* Secretary of State; *Br.* Foreign Secretary; **minister sprawiedliwości** minister of justice; *US* Attorney General; *Br.* Lord Chancellor; **Rada Ministrów** Council of Ministers; *US* the Administration; *Br.* the Cabinet.

ministerialny *a. polit.* ministerial; departmental.

ministerstwo *n.* ministry; *US* department; *Br.* department, office; **ministerstwo finansów** ministry of finance; **ministerstwo skarbu** ministry of the treasury; *US* Department of the Treasury; *Br.* the Treasury; **ministerstwo obrony narodowej** ministry of defense; *US* Department of Defense; *Br.* Ministry of Defence; **ministerstwo spraw wewnętrznych** ministry of the interior, ministry of internal affairs; *Br.* Home Office; **ministerstwo spraw zagranicznych** ministry of foreign affairs; *US* State Department; *Br.* Foreign and Commonwealth Office; **ministerstwo sprawiedliwości** ministry of justice; *US* Department of Justice; *Br.* Lord Chancellor's office.

ministrant *mp rz.-kat.* acolyte, altar boy, server.

ministrantura *f. rz.-kat.* serving.

minojski *a. archeol.* Minoan; **cywilizacja minojska** Minoan civilization.

minorat *mi hist., prawn.* ultimogeniture.

minorowy *a.* **1.** *muz.* minor; **skala minorowa** minor scale; **tonacja minorowa** minor key. **2.** *przen.* (= *smutny*) sullen, gloomy; **nastrój minorowy** sullen mood.

minoryta *mp rz.-kat.* Minorite, Franciscan.

minować *ipf. wojsk.* mine.

minowiec *mi* **-wc-** *Gen.* **-a** *wojsk., żegl.* minelayer.

minowy *a. wojsk.* mine; **pole minowe** mine field.

minóg *ma* **-o-** *icht.* lamprey, lamper eel (*Petromyzon*); **minóg morski** sea lamprey (*Petromyzon marinus*); **minóg rzeczny** river lamprey (*Lampetra fluviatilis*); **minóg strumieniowy** brook lamprey (*Lampetra planeri*); **minóg ukraiński** Ukrainian lamprey (*Eudontomyzon mariae*).

minstrel *mp hist.* minstrel.

mintaj *ma icht.* wall-eye pollock (*Theragra chalcogramma*).

minus *mi Gen.* **-a** *mat.* minus; **minus dwa stopnie Celsjusza** minus 2 degrees centigrade; **minus podatek** less tax; **być Rh-minus** be Rhesus negative; **cztery** *l.* **czwórka minus** *szkoln.* B–; **plus minus 300** three hundred, give or take a few; **plus minus** more or less; **znak minus** minus sign. – *mi Gen.* **-u** (= *wada*) drawback, disadvantage; **mieć same minusy** have only minuses; **samochód ma swoje plusy i minusy** car has its pluses and minuses.

minuskuła *f. druk.* minuscule.

minuskułowy *a. druk.* minuscule, minuscular.

minusowy *a.* negative; (*o temperaturze*) sub-zero, below-zero; (*o saldzie, bilansie*) debit.

minuta *f.* **1.** (*jednostka czasu*) minute; **minuta ciszy** minute of silent tribute; **co do minuty** to the minute, dead on time, on the dot; **co minutę**

once a *l.* every minute; **po kilku minutach** within minutes, after a few minutes; **z minuty na minutę** minute by minute, by the minute; **za parę minut** in a few minutes. **2.** *geom.* (*jednostka kąta*) minute (*of arc*).

minutnik *mi Gen.* **-a** (*w kuchni*) timer.

minutowy *a.* minute; one-minute; **wskazówka minutowa** minute hand.

miocen *mi geol.* the Miocene (Epoch).

mioceński *a. geol.* Miocene.

miodarka *f.* (*urządzenie*) honey extractor.

miodla *f. bot.* **miodla pospolita** chinaberry, China tree (*Melia azedarach*).

miodnik *mi Gen.* **-a** *bot.* nectary.

miodobranie *n.* honey harvest.

miododajny *a.* melliferous.

miodojad *ma orn.* honeyeater (*Meliphaga*).

miodokwiat *mi bot.* musk orchid (*Herminium*).

miodowód *ma orn.* black-throated honey guide (*Indicator indicator*).

miodowy *a.* honey; **miodowy miesiąc** honeymoon.

miodówka *f. Gen.pl.* **-ek** *ent.* jumping plant louse (*Psylla*); **miodówka jabłoniowa** apple sucker (*Psylla mali*).

miodunka[1] *f. bot.* lungwort (*Pulmonaria*).

miodunka[2] *f. ent.* flower piercer (*Diglossa*).

mioglobina *f. biol.* myoglobin.

miograf *mi med.* myograph.

miografia *f. med.* myography.

miogram *f. med.* myogram.

miolog *mp med.* myologist.

miologia *f. Gen.* **-ii** *med.* myology.

miologiczny *a. med.* myologic, myological.

mion *mi Gen.* **-u** *Loc.* **-ie** *fiz.* muon.

miot *mi zool.* litter.

miotacz *mi Gen.* **-a** *wojsk.* thrower, mortar; **miotacz ognia** flamethrower. – *mp sport* thrower; *baseball* pitcher; (*kuli*) shot putter.

miotać *ipf.* **1.** (= *ciskać*) hurl, fling, sling; **miotać przekleństwa** hurl abuse *l.* insults (*na kogoś* at sb). **2.** (= *chwiać, kołysać*) (*np. łodzią*) rock, toss; (*np. gałęziami*) lash; **gniew miota kimś** *przen.* sb is raging with anger. **~ się** *ipf.* (*np. we śnie*) toss and turn; (*np. z bólu*) writhe; (*np. po pokoju*) jiggle about; (*w złości*) flail about.

miotełka *f.* whisk broom.

miotła *f. Gen.pl.* **-eł** broom; **nowa miotła** *przen.* a new broom (sweeps clean); **siedzieć cicho jak mysz pod miotłą** be as quiet as a mouse.

miotonia *f. pat.* myotonia.

miozyna *f. biol.* myosin.

miód *mi* **-o-** **1.** (= *produkt pszczół*) honey; **miód akacjowy/lipowy/pszczeli/wielokwiatowy** acacia/linden/bee *l.* natural/wildflower honey; **plaster miodu** honeycomb; **sztuczny miód** honey ersatz; **kraina mlekiem i miodem płynąca** *Bibl.* land of milk and honey; **lgnąć do kogoś/czegoś jak mucha do miodu** be drawn to sb/sth like a bee to honey; **cud, miód (ultramaryna)** a real beauty. **2.** *kulin.* mead.

mira *f. zob.* **mirra.**

mirabel(k)a *f. bot.* yellow *l.* mirabelle plum (*Prunus domestica insititia*).

mirabilit *mi min.* mirabilite.

miraż *mi Gen.pl.* **-y** *l.* **-ów** *opt. t. przen.* mirage.

miriady *pl. Gen.* **-d** myriads.

mirkina *f. zool.* douroucouli, douricouli, durukuli, owl monkey, night monkey (*Aotus trivirgatus*).

mirra *f. Dat. i Loc.* **mirrze** myrrh; **mirra, kadzidło i złoto** *Bibl.* gifts of gold and of incense and of myrrh.

mirt *mi bot.* myrtle (*Myrtus*).

mirtowy *a.* myrtle.

mirza *mp pl.* **-owie** mirza.

misa *f.* **1.** (= *duża miska*) (large) bowl. **2.** *techn.* pan, tray, bowl. **3.** *geogr.* basin.

miseczka *f. Gen.pl.* **-ek** **1.** (= *mała miska*) (small) bowl; (*t. w biustonoszu*) cup. **2.** *biol.* cupule, cup.

misecznik *ma Gen., Acc.* **-a** *ent.* oyster scale (*Lecanium*).

misiek *ma* **-śk-** *emf.* (= *niedźwiedź*) bear; (*zabawka*) teddy bear.

misio *ma Gen.pl.* **-ów** *emf.* (= *niedźwiedź*) bear; (*zabawka*) teddy bear.

misiu *ma l. mp zob.* **misio.**

misja *f.* **1.** (= *zadanie*) mission. **2.** *dyplomacja* mission, legation; **misja pokojowa** peace(-keeping) mission. **3.** *rel.* mission.

misjonarski *a. rel.* missionary.

misjonarz *mp rel.* missionary, missioner.

miska *f. Gen.pl.* **-ek** bowl; (*do mycia*) washbasin, washbowl; **miska klozetowa** toilet bowl; **miska olejowa** *mot.* oil sump; *mech.* drip pan; **miska soczewicy** *Bibl., przen.* mess of pottage.

miss *f. indecl.* (= *najpiękniejsza kobieta*) Miss; **Miss Polonia** Miss Poland.

misterium *n. sing. indecl. pl.* **-ria** *Gen.* **-riów** **1.** *teatr, rel.* mystery play; **misterium wielkanocne** Passion play. **2.** *hist., rel. t. przen.* mysteries.

misternie *adv.* meticulously; elaborately, intricately; subtly, delicately, finely.

misterność *f.* meticulousness; elaborateness, intricateness; subtleness, delicateness, fineness.

misterny *a.* (*robota*) meticulous; (*fryzura, plan*) elaborate, intricate; (*haft, rzeźba*) subtle, delicate, fine.

mistral *mi Gen.* **-u** *l.* **-a** *meteor.* mistral.

mistrz *mp pl.* **-owie** *Gen.* **-ów** **1.** (= *znawca w swojej dziedzinie*) master; adept; **mistrz ceremonii** master of ceremonies, MC; **mistrz fortepianu** master of the piano; **mistrz noweli** master of the short story; **mistrz nad mistrze** past master; **być mistrzem w czymś** be adept at sth. **2.** (= *rzemieślnik samodzielnie wykonujący swój zawód*) master; **mistrz cechowy/ciesielski/kamieniarski/piekarski** master craftsman/carpenter/stonemason/baker; **wyzwolić się na mistrza** earn one's master craftsman's certificate. **3.** (*zwierzchnik w fabryce*) foreman; **mistrz zmianowy** shift foreman. **4.** *rel.* master; **wielki mistrz** Grand Master. **5.** *sport* champion; **mistrz świata/Europy** world/European champion; **aktualny mistrz** reigning champion.

mistrzostwo *n.* **1.** (= *doskonałość*) mastery. **2.** *sport* championship; **mistrzostwa świata w lekkiej atletyce** world track-and-field championship(s).

mistrzowski *a.* **1.** (= *znakomicie wykonany*) masterly; **mistrzowskie posunięcie** master stroke; **mistrzowskie wykonanie** masterly performance; **po mistrzowsku** excellently, superbly. **2.** *rzemiosło* master's; **dyplom mistrzowski** master craftsman's certificate; **dyplom mistrzowski elektryka/hydraulika** master electrician's/ plumber's certificate; **egzamin mistrzowski** master craftsman's examination. **3.** *sport* champion, winning; **tytuł mistrzowski** championship.

mistrzowsko *adv.* in a masterly way; excellently, superbly.

mistrzyni *f. zob.* **mistrz** 1, 2, 3, 5.

mistycyzm *mi rel., fil.* mysticism.

mistyczka *f. Gen.pl.* **-ek** *zob.* **mistyk**.

mistyczny *a.* mystical, mystic; **mistyczna otoczka** mystique.

mistyfikacja *f.* hoax, mystification.

mistyfikator *mp,* **mistyfikatorka** *Gen.pl.* **-ek** hoaxer, mystifier.

mistyfikatorka *f.*

mistyfikować *ipf.* hoax, mystify.

mistyk *mp rel., fil.* mystic.

mistyka *f.* **1.** mysticalness. **2.** = **mistycyzm**.

misyjny *a. rel.* mission; missionary; **działalność misyjna** missionary work; **placówka misyjna** mission.

miszmasz *mi pot.* hodgepodge, jumble.

miś *ma Gen.pl.* **-ów** *emf.* (= *niedźwiedź*) bear; (*zabawka*) teddy bear. – *mi Gen.* **-a** *Gen.pl.* **-ów** *tk.* artificial fur.

Miśnia *f* **1.** *geogr.* Meissen. **2.** (*porcelana*) Dresden china, Meissen porcelain.

miśnieński *a.* Meissen; **miśnieńska porcelana** Dresden china, Meissen porcelain.

mit *mi rel. t. przen.* myth, mythos; **mity greckie** Greek mythology; **mit o Dedalu i Ikarze** the myth of Daedalus and Icarus; **rozwiać mit** explode *l.* dispel a myth.

mitel *mi druk.* English.

mitenka *f. Gen.pl.* **-ek** mitt.

mitochondria *pl. Gen.* **-ów** *biol.* mitochondria.

mitolog *mp pl.* **-dzy** *l.* **-owie** mythologist.

mitologia *f. Gen.* **-ii** mythology, mythos; **mitologia rzymska** Roman mythology.

mitologiczny *a.* mythological, mythologic.

mitologizacja *f.* mythicization, mythologization.

mitologizować *ipf.* mythicize, mythologize.

mitoman *mp psych.* mythomaniac.

mitomania *f. Gen.* **-ii** *psych.* mythomania.

mitomanka *f. Gen.pl.* **-ek** *zob.* **mitoman**.

mitomański *a. psych.* mythomaniac.

mitotwórczy *a.* mythopoeic.

mitotwórstwo *n. teor.lit.* mythopoeia; *przen.* mythmaking.

mitoza *f. biol.* mitosis.

mitra *f. rz.-kat.* miter; **otrzymać mitrę** *przen.* be mitered; **mitra książęca** *her.* ducal *l.* duke's coronet.

mitralieza *f. wojsk.* mitrailleuse.

mitręga *f. pot.* drudgery; *lit.* travail.

mitrężyć *ipf. pot.* idle away, waste.

mitu *ma orn.* **mitu zwyczajny** razor-billed currassow (*Crax mitu*).

mityczny *a. t. przen.* mythical.

mitygować *ipf. lit.* mitigate, moderate, restrain. ~ **się** *ipf. lit.* restrain o.s.

mityng *mi* **1.** (= *wiec*) meeting, rally. **2.** *sport* meeting, meet.

mizantrop *mp* misanthrope, misanthropist.

mizantropia *f. Gen.* **-ii** misanthropy.

mizantropijny *a.* misanthropic, misanthropical.

mizantropka *f. Gen.pl.* **-ek** *zob.* **mizantrop**.

mizdra *f. Dat.* **-drze** *garbarstwo* flesh side.

mizdrować *ipf. garbarstwo* flesh, scour.

mizdrownica *f. Gen.* **-cy** *garbarstwo* fleshing machine.

mizdrzyć się *ipf.* cajole, wheedle (*do kogoś* sb); (*np. przed lustrem*) preen.

mizerak *mp pl.* **-i** *pot.* starveling, weakling.

mizeria *f. Gen.* **-ii** *kulin.* cucumber salad.

mizernie *adv.* **1.** (*wyglądać*) wanly, haggardly, scrawny, sickly. **2.** (= *marnie*) poorly, wretchedly, badly, miserably.

mizernieć *ipf.* grow wan *l.* haggard *l.* feeble, lose flesh, waste away.

mizerny *a.* **1.** (*o twarzy, dziecku*) wan, pallid, sickly. **2.** (= *nędzny*) poor, wretched, mean.

mizerota *f. l. mp decl. like f. Gen.pl.* **-t** *l.* **-ów** *pot.* starveling, weakling.

mizerykordia *f. Gen.* **-ii** *hist.* misericord, misericorde.

mizoandria *f. Gen.* **-ii** **mizoandryzm** *mi psych.* misandry.

mizogamia *f. Gen.* **-ii** *psych.* misogamy.

mizogin *mp psych.* misogynist.

mizoginia *f. Gen.* **-ii** *psych.* misogyny.

mizoginiczny *a. psych.* mysogynic, misogynous, misogynistic.

mizoginizm *mi zob.* **mizoginia**

mjr *abbr.* (= *major*) Maj. (*Major*).

mklik *ma Gen.* **-a** *ent.* **mklik mączny** Mediterranean flour moth (*Ephestia kuehinella*).

mknąć *ipf.* **-ij** speed, scurry, scud.

mlask *mi* smack.

mlaskać *ipf.* **-am** *l.* **-szczę** **-asz** *l.* **-szczesz, -aj** *l.* **-szcz** **1.** (*przy jedzeniu*) smack, smack one's lips, champ. **2.** (*o błocie itp.*) plash, splash.

mlasnąć *pf.* **-snę** **-śniesz, -ij** *zob.* **mlaskać**.

mlaśnięcie *n.* smack.

mlecz *mi Gen.* **-u** *l.* **-a** *Gen.pl.* **-y** *l.* **-ów** **1.** *bot.* sow thistle (*Sonchus*). **2.** *fizj.* (*w jelitach*) chyle. **3.** *fizj.* (*w żołądku*) chyme. **4.** *icht.* milt, roe.

mleczaj *mi Gen.pl.* **-ów** *bot.* (*grzyb*) milky cap (*Lactarius*).

mleczak *ma* **1.** *icht.* milter. **2.** *zool.* suckling. – *mi Gen.* **-a** *anat.* deciduous tooth, milk tooth, baby tooth.

mleczan *mi chem.* lactate.

mleczarka f. Gen.pl. -ek 1. zob. **mleczarz** 1. 2. arch. (= dojarka, dójka) milkmaid, dairymaid.

mleczarnia f. Gen.pl. -i l. -ń 1. (przetwórnia) dairy, creamery. 2. (w gospodarstwie wiejskim) dairy.

mleczarski a. (o zakładzie, przemyśle, spółdzielni) dairy.

mleczarstwo n. dairy industry, dairying.

mleczarz mp 1. (= roznosiciel mleka) milkman. 2. (= osoba zajmująca się mleczarstwem) dairyman.

mleczko n. Gen.pl. -ek 1. milk. 2. (= ciecz podobna do mleka) milk; **mleczko kosmetyczne** lotion, cleansing milk. 3. bot. milk; **mleczko kauczukowe** latex. 4. zool. (= płyn, pokarm dla młodych) milk; **pszczele mleczko** royal jelly; **mleczko maciczne** uterine milk. 5. icht. milt, roe. 6. kulin. pudding; **ptasie mleczko** chocolate-covered marshmallows.

mlecznobiały a. milky white.

mleczność f. Gen. -ści 1. ability to lactate. 2. roln. milking capacity, lactation yield. 3. whiteness.

mleczny a. 1. (= dotyczący mleka) milk; **bar mleczny** milk bar; **bydło mleczne** dairy cattle; **gruczoły mleczne** anat. mammary glands; **zęby mleczne** anat. deciduous teeth, milk teeth, baby teeth; **Droga Mleczna** astron. Milky Way. 2. (podobny do mleka) milky; (o szkle, żarówce) frosted. 3. bot. lactescent.

mleć ipf. **mielę mielisz mełł mełli** mill; (kawę, orzechy) grind; (mięso) mince; **mleć językiem** l. **ozorem** pot. prattle, talk one's head off, talk nineteen to the dozen; **kawa mielona** ground coffee.

mleko n. 1. (u ssaków) milk; **mleko chude** skim l. skimmed milk; **mleko pełne** l. **tłuste** whole milk; **mleko półtłuste** semi-skimmed milk; **kwaśne mleko** sour milk; **zsiadłe mleko** curdled milk, clabber; **mleko skondensowane** condensed milk; **mleko pasteryzowane** pasteurized milk; **mleko homogenizowane** homogenized milk; **mleko humanizowane** humanized milk; **mleko w proszku** dry l. dried milk, powdered milk, instant milk; **mleko waniliowe** vanilla milk; **wyssać coś z mlekiem matki** imbibe l. drink in l. suck sth with one's mother's milk; **kraina mlekiem i miodem płynąca** land of plenty, land of milk and honey; **masz jeszcze mleko pod nosem** you are still wet behind the ears; **krowa, która dużo ryczy, mało mleka daje** great talkers are little doers. 2. (= ciecz podobna do mleka) milk; **mleko wapienne** chem. milk of lime, whitewash; **mleko cementowe** bud. cement grout. 3. bot. milk; latex; **mleko palmowe** palm milk; **mleko kokosowe** coconut milk.

mlekodajny a. lactescent.

mlekowiec mi -wc- Gen. -a bot. cow tree (Brosimum galactodendron).

mlekowy a. lactic, milk; **fermentacja mlekowa** chem. lactic fermentation; **kwas mlekowy** chem. lactic acid; **cukier mlekowy** chem. lactose, milk sugar.

mlewnik mi Gen. -a roln. roller mill.

młaka f. dial. marsh, swamp, bog.

młocarnia, młocarka f. Gen.pl. -i l. -ń roln. threshing machine, thresher, grain separator.

młocarz, młocek f. roln. thrasher.

młociarz mp sport hammer thrower.

młocka f. tylko sing. threshing.

młockarnia f. Gen.pl. -i l. -ń zob. **młocarnia**.

młode n. Gen. -ego young, offspring; (psa, foki, myszy, szczura) pup; (niedźwiedzia, wilka, lwa, wieloryba) cub; (lisa, bobra) kit.

młodnieć ipf. get younger.

młodnik, młodniak mi Gen. -a l. -u zwł. leśn. young stand, young growth.

młodo adv. young, youthfully; **umrzeć młodo** die young; **wyglądać młodo** look young.

młodociany a. 1. (o człowieku) youthful, adolescent, juvenile; **młodociany przestępca** prawn. juvenile delinquent. 2. (o zwierzętach i roślinach) young; (o trawie, liściach) early. – mp zwł. prawn. (prawo cywilne, rodzinne) minor, infant; (prawo karne) juvenile.

młodopolski a. teor.lit. of or related to Young Poland, neoromantic.

młodość f. 1. youth, adolescence, early life; **błędy młodości** misspent youth. 2. (= początki) beginning(s), early years.

młodszy mp younger; **mój młodszy brat** my younger brother; **młodszy rangą/stopniem** junior; **Jan Kowalski młodszy** Jan Kowalski junior.

młody a. 1. (= niestary) young, youthful; **młoda para** young marrieds, newly married couple, newlyweds; **panna młoda** bride; **pan młody** bridegroom, groom; **państwo młodzi** bride and groom; **młody talent** budding talent; **młody geniusz** whiz kid; **być wiecznie młodym** be ageless; **za młodu** in one's young years. 2. (= młodzieńczy) adolescent, boyish, youthful; **młode lata** youth, adolescence, teens, the springtime of life. 3. (= świeży) new, fresh; **młode ziemniaki** new potatoes; **młode wino** young wine. 4. (= dopiero co powstały) new, recent, young. 5. (= niedoświadczony) inexperienced, wet behind the ears. – mp 1. young man; **młoda** young woman; **młodzi** youth. 2. bridegroom, groom; **młoda** bride; **młodzi** (przed ślubem) bride and groom; (po ślubie) newlyweds.

młodziak mp pl. -i 1. pot. youngster, shaver. 2. (= młode zwierzę) youngster, young.

młodzian mp pl. -y l. -ie lit. youth, sapling.

młodzieniaszek mp -szk- pl. -owie l. -i przest. sapling, stripling, sprig.

młodzieniec mp -ńc- pl. -y lit. youth, lad, sapling.

młodzieńczy a. youthful, adolescent, juvenile; **wiek młodzieńczy** adolescence.

młodzież f. 1. (o ludziach) young people, the young, youth, teenagers; **młodzież szkolna** schoolchildren; **trudna młodzież** troubled youth; **złota młodzież** przest. gilded youth. 2. (o zwierzętach) young, youngsters. 3. (o drzewach) young growth.

młodzieżowiec mp -wc- pl. -y 1. (działacz)

youth activist. **2.** *sport* young athlete (*aged between 21–23*).

młodzieżowy *a.* (*o muzyce, organizacji*) youth; (*o literaturze*) juvenile.

młodzieżówka *f. Gen.pl.* **-ek** *zwł. sport* junior team.

młodzik *mp pl.* **-i 1.** (*chłopak*) shaveling, shaver, youngster. **2.** (*zwierzę*) youngling, youngster. **3.** *sport* young athlete (*aged between 13–17*).

młokos *mp pl.* **-y** *pot.* cub, hobbledehoy.

młot *mi Gen.* **-a 1.** (*narzędzie*) hammer; **znaleźć się między młotem a kowadłem** be between the devil and the deep (blue) sea, be a piggy in the middle, be caught between a rock and a hard place, be between Scylla and Charybdis; **serce waliło mi młotem** I had my heart in my mouth, my heart leapt *l.* pounded. **2.** *sport* hammer; **rzut młotem** hammer throw. **3.** *techn.* hammer, stamp; **młot kafarowy** drop weight; **młot pneumatyczny** pneumatic hammer. – *ma icht.* hammerhead shark (*Sphyrna zygaena*).

młoteczek *mi* **-czk-** *Gen.* **-a 1.** (*narzędzie*) (little) hammer. **2.** *anat.* malleus, hammer. **3.** *el.* tap. **4.** *muz.* hammer.

młotek *mi* **-tk-** *Gen.* **-a 1.** (*narzędzie*) hammer; (*drewniany*) mallet; **młotek licytacyjny** gavel; **pójść pod młotek** come *l.* go under the hammer. **2.** *krokiet* mallet. **3.** *techn.* hammer. **4.** *muz.* hammer. **5.** *pot.* moron, idiot.

młotownia *f. Gen.pl.* **-i** *techn.* hammer forge, hammer forging department.

młócić *ipf.* **1.** *roln.* thresh; **młócić cepem** flail. **2.** *pot.* (= *bić*) larrup, pound. **3.** *pot.* (= *powtarzać coś*) harp on *l.* upon. **4.** *pot.* (= *jeść*) tuck into, put away, scoff.

młódka *f. Gen.pl.* **-ek 1.** (= *dziewczyna*) lass, young woman, miss. **2.** *myśl.* fledgling.

młódź *f.* **-o-** *arch.* **1.** (*o ludziach*) youth, young people, the young. **2.** (*o zwierzętach*) young, youngsters. **3.** (*o drzewach*) young growth.

młyn *mi Gen.* **-a 1.** (*zakład*) mill; **młyn wodny** water mill; **diabelski młyn** Ferris wheel. **2.** (*maszyna*) mill; grinder. **3.** *przen.* (= *wir spraw*) stir, bustle; **woda na czyjś młyn** grist to sb's mill. **4.** *rugby* scrum, scrummage.

młynarczyk *mp* miller's apprentice.

młynarka *f. Gen.pl.* **-ek** *zob.* **młynarz.**

młynarstwo *n.* **1.** milling. **2.** milling industry.

młynarz *mp* miller.

młynek *mi* **-nk-** *Gen.* **-a 1.** mill, grinder; **młynek do kawy** coffee mill *l.* grinder; **młynek do pieprzu** pepper mill; **młynek modlitewny** *rel.* prayer wheel. **2.** *roln.* winnower, winnow mill. **3.** (*gra planszowa*) pachisi. **4.** *arch.* spin, reel, whirl; **wywijać** *l.* **kręcić** *l.* **robić młynka** spin, reel, whirl.

młyński *a.* mill; **kamień młyński** *t. przen.* millstone; **koło młyńskie** (*w młynie wodnym*) waterwheel; (*w młynie żarnowym*) millstone.

mną *pron. zob.* **ja.**

mnemotechniczny *a.* mnemonic.

mnemotechnika, mnemonika *f.* mnemonics.

mnę *itd. ipf. zob.* **miąć.**

mniam-mniam *int.* yummy.

mnich *mp pl.* **-si** (= *zakonnik*) monk. – *mi Gen.* **-a** *pl.* **-y 1.** *techn.* outlet box, monk. **2.** *bud.* barrel tile.

mnie *pron. zob.* **ja.**

mniej *adv.* (*wody, pieniędzy*) less; (*ludzi, krzeseł*) fewer; **coraz mniej** less and less; fewer and fewer; **mniej więcej** more or less; **nie mniej** no less than; no fewer than; **ni mniej, ni więcej, tylko...** not less and not more than...; *zob.* **mało.**

mniejszościowy *a.* minority; **rząd mniejszościowy** *polit.* minority government.

mniejszość *f.* **1.** minority; **znak mniejszości** *mat.* less-than sign; **być w mniejszości** be in the minority; **stanowić mniejszość czegoś** constitute the minority of sth. **2.** (= *grupa ludzi różniąca się od większości obywateli danego państwa*) minority; **mniejszość religijna** religious minority; **mniejszość wyznaniowa** denominational minority; **mniejszość etniczna** ethnic minority; **mniejszość narodowa** national minority.

mniejszy *a.* less, lesser; **mniejsza o to** *l.* **mniejsza z tym** never mind; **iść po linii najmniejszego oporu** cut corners, follow the line of least resistance; **Azja Mniejsza** *geogr.* Asia Minor; *zob.* **mały.**

mniemać *ipf. lit.* presume, assume, suppose.

mniemanie *n.* judgement, opinion; **mieć dobre mniemanie o sobie** think highly of o.s., have a high opinion of o.s.; **mieć wysokie mniemanie o kimś** hold sb in high esteem, think highly of sb; **w jego mniemaniu** in his opinion *l.* judgment *l.* view, according to him; **w mniemaniu, że...** thinking *l.* believing that...

mnisi *a.* monkish, monastic.

mniszek *mi* **-szk-** *Gen.* **-a** *bot.* dandelion (*Taraxacum*).

mniszka *f. Gen.pl.* **-ek 1.** (= *zakonnica*) nun. **2.** *bud.* barrel tile. **3.** *ent.* nun moth (*Lymantria monacha*).

mnogi *a. lit.* numerous, multiple; **liczba mnoga** *gram.* plural; **ciąża mnoga** *med.* multiple *l.* plural pregnancy.

mnogość *f.* **1.** (= *mnóstwo*) multitude, multiplicity, plurality. **2.** *mat.* set; **teoria mnogości** set theory.

mnożenie *n. mat.* multiplication; **tabliczka mnożenia** multiplication table.

mnożna *f. Gen.* **-ej** *mat.* multiplicand.

mnożnik *mi Gen.* **-a** *mat.* multiplier.

mnożyć *ipf.* **mnóż 1.** (= *powiększać*) multiply, increase, augment, intensify. **2.** (= *rozmnażać*) multiply, reproduce, breed, proliferate. **3.** (= *rozplenić*) reproduce, propagate, spread. **4.** *mat.* multiply. ~ **się** *ipf.* **mnóż 1.** (= *powiększać się*) multiply, increase, augment, intensify. **2.** (= *wydawać potomstwo*) multiply, proliferate, breed, procreate.

mnóstwo *n.* a lot of, a great many, multitude, plenty, a whale of; **on mnóstwo zarabia** he earns a (whole) lot; **mamy mnóstwo czasu** we have plenty of time.

moa *ma orn.* moa (*Dinornithiformes*).

mobilizacja *f.* **1.** *wojsk.* (= *powołanie rezerwistów*) call-up, mobilization. **2.** *wojsk.* (= *przej-*

ście *w stan wojny*) mobilization; **ogłosić stan mobilizacji** order (a) mobilization. **3.** (= *uaktywnienie*) activation, activization. **4.** (= *gotowość*) readiness.

mobilizować *ipf.* **1.** *wojsk.* mobilize, call up. **2.** (= *pobudzać do działania*) muster up; stimulate. ~ **się** *ipf.* **1.** *wojsk.* mobilize. **2.** (= *zbierać w sobie*) pull o.s. together; (= *organizować się*) get o.s. organized.

mobilność *f.* mobility.

mobilny *a.* mobile.

moc *f. pl.* **-e 1.** (= *siła*) power, strength, force; **złe** *l.* **piekielne** *l.* **nieczyste moce** the powers of darkness; **to nie jest w mojej mocy** it's beyond my powers, it's not within my powers; **zrobiłem wszystko, co było w mojej mocy** I did my utmost *l.* (very) best. **2.** (= *zdolność*) might, power, strength; **z całej mocy** with all one's might; **uzdrawiająca moc ziół** revitalizing power of herbs; **stracić moc oddziaływania** lose power, lose influence; **moc produkcyjna** capacity; **moc przerobowa** processing capacity. **3.** *zwł. prawn.* (= *ważność*) effective force, effectuality, vigor; **na mocy prawa** by the law, ipso iure; **nabrać mocy (prawnej)** become legally binding; **pozostawać w mocy** be *l.* remain in effect *l.* force, be effective *l.* legally binding; **moc prawna** force and effect, legal efficacy, vigor. **4.** (= *wytrzymałość*) strength, durability. **5.** *zwł. chem.* (= *stężenie*) strength, concentration; (*alkoholu*) proof, strength. **6.** (= *mnóstwo*) plenty, lots of, a lot of, a whale of; **moc ludu** crowds *l.* throngs *l.* masses of people; **moc kwiatów** masses *l.* multitude of flowers. **7.** *fiz.* power; **moc elektryczna** electric power.

mocarny *a. lit.* (*o dłoniach*) strong; (*o państwie, władcy*) strong, powerful, mighty.

mocarstwo *n.* power; **wielkie mocarstwo** world power, superpower; **mocarstwo morskie** sea power.

mocarstwowy *a.* imperialistic; **dążenia mocarstwowe** imperialistic policy.

mocarz *mp* **1.** *lit.* (= *władca*) ruler. **2.** *lit.* (= *siłacz*) strongman.

mocno *adv.* **1.** (= *silnie*) (*trzymać, przyklejać, wtykać*) fast, firmly; (*uderzać, kopnąć, naciskać*) hard; (*zakręcać, nakładać, uścisnąć*) tightly, tight; **stanąć mocno na nogach** have *l.* keep one's *l.* both feet on the ground; **trzymać kogoś mocno w garści** have sb under one's thumb, have sb on toast. **2.** (= *intensywnie*) strongly, intensely; (*zdziwiony, spóźniony, zaniedbany*) very; (*pachnieć, świecić*) intensely, strongly; (*kochać, tęsknić*) very much, a lot, strongly; (*spać*) sound, fast; **mocno spał** he was sound *l.* fast asleep; **mocno czerwony** intensely red, deeply red; **najmocniej przepraszam** I am awfully *l.* terribly sorry; **najmocniej dziękuję** thank you so much, thank you very much; **mocno przekonany** strongly convinced; **mocno padało** it rained hard *l.* heavily. **3.** (= *solidnie*) firmly, well, strongly; **mocno zbudowany** strongly built, well-knit, sturdy. **4.** (= *dobitnie*) clearly, forcibly; **mocno powiedziane** bluntly said.

mocny *a.* **1.** (= *silny*) (*ramię, cios, światło, argument*) strong, powerful; (*człowiek, zwierzę*) strong, muscular, sturdy; (*uścisk*) firm, tight; (*silnik*) powerful; **spółgłoska mocna** *fon.* strong *l.* fortis consonant; **sylaba mocna** *fon.* strong syllable; **mocny kolor** *karty* strong hand in trumps; **mocna karta** *karty* trump; **mocne uderzenie** *muz.* big beat; **mieć mocną rękę** have a firm *l.* a heavy *l.* an iron hand; **stanąć na mocnych nogach** stand on one's own legs *l.* two feet. **2.** (= *intensywny, skondensowany*) (*o winie, wódce, zapachu*) strong, heavy; (*o papierosie, truciźnie*) strong; (*o kawie, herbacie*) strong, strongly-flavored; (*o kolorze*) deep, intense, vivid; (*o śnie*) sound, deep; **kieliszeczek czegoś mocniejszego** short drink, short one. **3.** (= *odporny*) strong, durable; (*o butach, ubraniu roboczym*) hard-wearing, heavy-duty; (*o konstrukcji*) solid, strong; (*o kościach*) strong, thick; **to moja mocna strona** it's my forte, it's my strong point *l.* suit; **mieć mocną głowę** have a strong head, be able to hold one's drink *l.* liquor. **4.** (= *niezachwiany*) (*o postanowieniu*) firm; (*o argumencie*) cogent, sound; (*o dowodzie*) strong; (*o wrażeniu*) strong, powerful. **5.** (= *dobitny*) strong, expressive, forceful; (*o sformułowaniu, zwrocie*) straightforward, bold, explicit; **używać mocnych słów** use bold *l.* strong words. **6.** (= *biegły*) good at, competent; **mocny w geografii** good at geography; **on jest tylko mocny w gębie** *l.* **języku** he is all mouth (and no action).

mocodawca *mp prawn.* principal; *pot.* boss, employer.

mocować *ipf.* fasten, fix, mount, clamp. ~ **się** *ipf.* **1.** (= *walczyć*) wrestle, grapple (*z kimś* with sb). **2.** (= *zmagać się*) struggle, fight. **3.** (= *trudzić się*) exert o.s., make every effort, fall all over o.s., fall *l.* bend over backwards.

mocz *mi* urine; **oddawać mocz** urinate, pass water.

moczan *mi chem., med.* urate.

moczarka *f. Gen.pl.* **-ek** *bot.* pondweed, waterweed, elodea (*Elodea*).

moczarowaty *a.* marshy, boggy, quaggy, swampy.

moczary *pl. Gen.* **-ów** swamp, marsh, fen.

moczenie *n.* steeping, soak(ing); **moczenie nocne** *pat.* nocturia, bed wetting.

mocznica *f. pat.* ur(a)emia.

mocznik *mi Gen.* **-a** *chem.* urea.

mocznikowy *a. chem.* ureal, ureic.

moczopędny *a.* diuretic; **lek moczopędny** diuretic.

moczopłciowy, moczowo-płciowy *a. anat.* genitourinary, urogenital.

moczowód *mi* **-o-** *anat.* ureter.

moczowy *a.* urinary, uric; **pęcherz moczowy** *anat.* urinary bladder; **cewka moczowa** *anat.* urethra; **kwas moczowy** *anat.* uric acid; **kamienie moczowe** *pat.* urinary calculuses, uroliths.

moczówka *f. Gen.pl.* **-ek** *med.* diabetes insipidus.

moczyć *ipf.* **1.** (= *czynić mokrym*) wet. **2.** (= *trzymać w płynie*) soak, drench, steep. ~ **się** *ipf.* **1.** (= *być moczonym*) soak, steep. **2.** *żart.* (= *ką-*

pać się) bathe. **3.** (= *oddawać bezwiednie mocz*) wet one's bed, wet o.s.

moczygęba *f. l. mp decl. like f. Gen.pl.* **-ów** *l.* **-ąb** *pot.* soak, tosspot, lush, sot.

moczymorda *f. l. mp decl. like f. Gen.pl.* **-ów** *l.* **-d** *pot.* boozer, soak, lush.

moda *f. Gen.pl.* **mód 1.** (= *nowy trend*) fashion, trend, vogue. **2.** (= *styl ubierania się*) fashion, look; **coś jest w modzie** sth is in vogue *l.* fashion; **coś wyszło z mody** sth has gone out of fashion; **ostatni krzyk mody** the latest craze *l.* fashion, all the go *l.* vogue, dernier cri.

modalność *f. fil., jęz.* modality.

modalny *a. fil., jęz., muz.* modal.

model *mi Gen.* **-u** *Gen.pl.* **-i 1.** (= *prototyp, wzór*) model; (*ekonomiczny, matematyczny*) model. **2.** (= *typ*) make, brand. **3.** (= *sposób*) mode. **4.** *metal.* pattern, mold. – *mp Gen.* **-a** *Gen.pl.* **-i** *l.* **-ów 1.** *sztuka* (= *osoba pozująca artyście*) model. **2.** (= *osoba uczestnicząca w pokazach mody*) (fashion) model.

modelarnia *f. Gen.pl.* **-i** *l.* **-ń 1.** (*pracownia*) modeler's room. **2.** *metal.* pattern shop.

modelarski *a.* model-making; (*o klubie, pracowni*) modeler's; (*o pokazach*) model, modeling.

modelarstwo *n.* **1.** (*hobby*) model making. **2.** *metal.* pattern making.

modelarz *mp* **1.** (*hobbysta*) modeler, model maker. **2.** *metal.* pattern maker.

modelator *mp teatr* modeler.

modelina *f.* modeling clay.

modelka *f. Gen.pl.* **-ek 1.** (*pozująca artyście*) model. **2.** (*na pokazie mody*) (fashion) model.

modelować *ipf.* mould, pattern, model; (*włosy*) do, set.

modelowy *a.* **1.** (= *wzorcowy*) model, standard, exemplary. **2.** (= *wykonywany z użyciem modelu*) model; (*o ćwiczeniach*) sample, specimen, model. **3.** *metal.* pattern.

modelunek *mi* **-nk-** modeling.

modem *mi komp.* modem; **modem kablowy** cable modem.

moderna *f. sztuka, teor.lit.* **1.** modernism. **2.** (= *grupa artystów*) modernist group, group of modernists.

modernista *mp sztuka, teor.lit.* modernist.

modernistyczny *a. sztuka, teor.lit.* modernistic, modernist.

modernizacja *f.* modernization, upgrading.

modernizm *mi sztuka, teor.lit.* modernism.

modernizować *ipf.* modernize, upgrade. ~ **się** *ipf.* modernize.

modlić się *ipf.* **módl** say one's prayers, pray (*o coś* for sth) (*za kogoś* for sb).

modliszka *f. Gen.pl.* **-ek 1.** *ent.* European *l.* praying mantis (*Mantis religiosa*). **2.** *przen.* (*o kobiecie*) man-eater, ball buster *l.* breaker.

modlitewnik *mi Gen.* **-a** *rel.* prayer book.

modlitewny *a. rel.* prayer.

modlitwa *f. rel.* prayer, orison; (*zwł. przed posiłkiem*) blessing; **Modlitwa Pańska** the Lord's Prayer.

modła *f. Gen.pl.* **modeł** *przest.* (= *wzór*) fash-

ion, model; **na jakąś modłę** after the fashion of sth.

modły *pl. Gen.* **modłów** *przest.* prayers, devotions.

modnie *adv.* fashionably, stylishly.

modnisia *f. żart. l. iron.* fashion bug *l.* queen, walking fashion show, clothes horse.

modniś *mp Gen.pl.* **-ów** *żart. l. iron.* fop, dandy, coxcomb.

modny *a.* (*o płaszczu, butach, tańcu*) fashionable, in fashion *l.* vogue, trendy, stylish; (*o przeboju*) top; (*o artyście*) popular.

modrak *mi Gen.* **-a** *bot.* **1.** *dial.* (= *chaber*) cornflower, bluebottle, bachelor's-button (*Centaurea cyanus*). **2.** sea kale (*Crambe maritima*).

modraszek *ma Gen.* **-szka** *ent.* copper (*Lycaena*).

modry *a.* cornflower blue, deep blue.

modrzew *mi* **-wi-** *Gen.* **-a 1.** *bot.* (*drzewo*) larch (*Larix*). **2.** (*drewno*) larch (wood).

modrzewiowy *a.* (*o lesie, podłodze*) larch.

modrzewnica *f. Gen.* **-cy** *bot.* bog rosemary (*Andromeda*).

modulacja *f.* **1.** modulation. **2.** (*głosu*) inflection. **3.** *muz.* modulation, transition. **4.** *fiz.* modulation.

modulacyjny *a.* **1.** (*o głosie*) inflectional. **2.** *muz.* modulatory. **3.** *fiz.* modulative, modulatory.

modularny *a.* modular.

modulator *mi Gen.* **-a** *techn.* modulator.

modulować *ipf.* **1.** (*głos*) inflect. **2.** *muz., fiz.* modulate.

moduł *mi* **1.** (= *jednostka, element*) module, unit. **2.** *mat.* absolute value, modulus. **3.** *komp.* module, unit; **moduł pamięci** memory *l.* storage module *l.* unit. **4.** *fiz.* modulus.

modyfikacja *f.* **1.** (= *poprawka*) modification, qualification, change; **wprowadzać modyfikacje** modify, qualify. **2.** *biol.* modification.

modyfikator *mi Gen.* **-a 1.** modifier. **2.** *metal.* inoculator.

modyfikować *ipf.* **1.** (= *wprowadzać zmiany*) modify, change, qualify. **2.** *metal.* inoculate. ~ **się** *ipf.* modify, change.

modylion *mi bud.* modillion.

modystka *f. Gen.pl.* **-ek** milliner, hatter.

modzel *mi Gen.* **-u** *pat.* callus, callosity.

mogę *itd. ipf. zob.* **móc.**

mogiła *f. lit.* (= *grób*) grave, tomb.

mogoł *mp pl.* **-owie** *hist.* Mogul, Moghul.

Moguncja *f. geogr.* Mainz.

mohar *ma bot.* foxtail millet (*Setaria italica*).

moher *mi* **1.** (*włóczka*) mohair. **2.** (*wyrób*) mohair.

Mohikanin *mp pl.* **-anie** *Gen.* **-anów** Mohican.

moi *itd. a. zob.* **mój.**

Mojra *f. mit.* Moira.

Mojżesz *mp Bibl.* Moses.

mojżeszowy *a. Bibl.* Mosaic, Mosaical, of Moses; **Księgi Mojżeszowe** Pentateuch.

mokasyn *mi Gen.* **-u** *l.* **-a 1.** (*indiański*) moccasin. **2.** (*damski l. męski*) loafer, moccasin.

mokiet *mi Dat.* **-u** *tk.* moquette.

mokka f. Dat. i Loc. **mokce** mocha (coffee).

moknąć ipf. **-ij, moknął** l. **mókł mokła mokli** get wet, soak.

mokradła pl. Gen.pl. **-eł** wetlands, swamp, morass.

mokro adv. wetly, humidly; **jest mokro** it is wet; **zetrzeć coś na mokro** wipe sth (up) with a wet cloth; **dziecko ma mokro** pot. the baby is wet.

mokry a. wet, humid; (o ziemi, trawie, śniegu, jezdni, ciele, włosach) wet; (o lecie) wet, rainy, damp; **cały byłem mokry ze strachu** I was all soaked with fear; **mokra robota** pot. rubout.

mokrzyca f. Gen. **-cy** bot. sandwort (Minuartia).

mokrzycznik ma Gen. **-a** bot. jagged chickweed (Holosteum umbellatum).

mol mi Gen. **-a** chem., fiz. **1.** mole, mol. **2.** (= gramocząsteczka) gram-molecule.

mola itd. ma zob. **mól**.

molalny a. chem., fiz. molal.

molekularny a. (o fizyce, biologii) molecular.

molekuła f. fiz. molecule.

moleskin mi Gen. **-u** tk. moleskin.

molestować ipf. **1.** (= prześladować) molest, harass, abuse. **2.** (= naprzykrzać się) pester, molest.

molestowanie n. harassment, abuse; **molestowanie dzieci** child abuse; **molestowanie seksualne** sexual harassment.

molibden mi chem. molybdenum.

molibdenian mi chem. molybdate.

molibdenit mi min. molybdenite.

molik ma ent. **1.** (clothes) moth, tineid (Tineola). **2.** Mediterranean flour moth (Ephestia kuehinella).

molinezja f. icht. molly (Mollienisia).

moll a. indecl. muz. minor; **tonacja a-moll** A-minor (key).

molo n. **1.** żegl. pier, jetty; (nabrzeże) wharf, quay. **2.** (pomost spacerowy) pier.

moloch mp **1.** Bibl. Moloch, Molech. **2.** przen. juggernaut, behemoth.

molowy[1] a. chem. molal, molar; **roztwór molowy** molar solution.

molowy[2] a. muz. minor; **tonacja molowa** minor key; **skala molowa** minor scale.

Mołdawia f. Gen. **-ii** geogr. Moldova.

Mołdawianin mp pl. **-anie** Gen. **-an** Moldovan.

Mołdawianka f. Gen.pl. **-ek** zob. **Mołdawianin**.

mołdawski a. Moldovan.

momencik mi moment, second, minute; **za momencik** pot. in a jiffy, in a second; **momencik!** just a moment l. second l. minute!

moment mi **1.** (= chwila) moment, instant, second; **moment!** just a moment l. second l. minute!; **chwila, moment!** wait a minute l. second l. moment!; **czekać na odpowiedni moment (żeby coś zrobić)** wait for the most opportune moment (to do sth); **czekać na właściwy moment** bide one's time; **decydujący moment** decisive moment; **moment kulminacyjny** climax, culmination; **moment przełomowy** turning point; **dobry** l. **świetny moment sobie wybrałeś żeby...** iron. it's not exactly the best moment to...; **do-**

brze wybrać moment choose the right time l. moment, choose the most opportune moment; **lada moment** l. **chwila** (at) any moment; **moment krytyczny** crunch, critical moment; **na** l. **przez moment** for a while l. moment; **pokonać krytyczny moment** l. **punkt** turn the corner; **trudno o gorszy moment na robienie komentarzy** there could scarcely be a worse moment to make a comment; **wybrać zły moment na coś** choose a bad l. the wrong l. the most inopportune moment for sth; **mieć dobre momenty** have one's moments; **to nie jest odpowiedni moment (na robienie czegoś)** this is hardly the time (to do sth); **dokładnie w tym momencie** (at) this very moment, as we speak; **nie zareagować w odpowiednim momencie** miss one's cue; **przeszkodzić komuś w najbardziej nieodpowiednim momencie** interrupt sb at the most inopportune moment; **w danym momencie** at a given moment; **w każdym** l. **dowolnym momencie** at any time; **w krytycznym momencie** when the crunch comes; **w momencie gdy** (= w czasie gdy) while; (= skoro tylko) the (very) moment; **w ostatnim momencie** at the last moment, in the nick of time; **w tym momencie** (= teraz) at the moment; (= wtedy) at that moment; (= w tej sytuacji) at this point l. juncture; **w tym samym momencie** at the same time; **w złym** l. **nieodpowiednim momencie** untimely, at the most inopportune moment; **zaskoczyć kogoś w najmniej odpowiednim momencie** catch sb with their pants down; **zrobić coś w odpowiednim momencie** time sth well; **doprowadzić coś do momentu rozstrzygającego** bring sth to a head; **od tego momentu** from this moment on. **2.** fiz., mech., mat. moment; **moment magnetyczny** fiz. magnetic moment; **moment bezwładności** fiz. moment of inertia; **moment siły** fiz. moment of force; **moment bezwzględny** mat. absolute moment; **moment spinowy** fiz. spin; **moment odśrodkowy (układu materialnego)** mech. product of inertia, moment of deviation; **moment obrotowy** mech. torque; **moment pędu** mech. angular momentum, moment of momentum.

momentalnie adv. instantly, in an instant, instantaneously.

momentalny a. split-second, immediate; (o odpowiedzi, odruchu, reakcji) instantaneous; (o reakcji) instant; **czasownik momentalny** jęz. momentary verb; **momentalna** l. **natychmiastowa decyzja** split-second decision.

Monachium n. indecl. geogr. Munich.

monada f. fil. monad.

monadyczny a. fil. monadic, monadical, monadal.

Monako n. geogr. Monaco; **mieszkaniec** l. **mieszkanka Monako** Monegasque, Monégasque.

monarcha mp pl. **-owie** monarch, sovereign; **monarcha absolutny** absolute monarch.

monarchia f. Gen. **-ii** monarchy; **monarchia absolutna** absolute monarchy; **monarchia konstytucyjna** constitutional l. limited monarchy; **ustanowić monarchię** establish l. set up a monarchy; **obalić monarchię** overthrow a monarchy.

monarchiczny a. monarchical, monarchic.

monarchini *f. pl.* -inie *Gen.pl.* -iń *l.* -yń *zob.* **monarcha**.

monarchista *mp* monarchist.

monarchistyczny *a.* monarchistic.

monarchizm *mi* monarchism.

monarszy *a.* monarchal, monarchial, regnal, regal, royal; **insygnia monarsze** royal insignia.

monaster, monastyr *mi rel.* Orthodox monastery.

moneta *f.* coin, specie; **brać** *l.* **przyjmować** *l.* **wziąć coś za dobrą monetę** *przen.* take sth at face value; **brzęcząca moneta** cash; **moneta zdawkowa** *ekon.* token (coin); **bicie monet** coinage, mintage; **podrobiona moneta** counterfeit coin, slug; *pot.* wooden nickel; **rzucać monetą (o coś)** toss (for sth); **rzucać** *l.* **rzucić monetę** *l.* **monetą** flip a coin; **rzut monetą** flip of a coin; (*przy losowaniu*) toss-up; **automat na monety** coin machine; **płacić** *l.* **odpłacać się równą** *l.* **podobną** *l.* **tą samą monetą** *przen.* pay back in kind.

monetarny *a. ekon.* monetary; **jednostka monetarna** monetary unit; **polityka monetarna** monetary policy.

monetka *f. Gen.pl.* -ek 1. *rzad.* (small) coin. 2. *zool.* money cowrie (*Cypraea moneta*).

Mongolia *f. Gen.* -ii *geogr.* Mongolia.

mongolizm *mi pat.* Down *l.* Down's syndrome; **dotknięty mongolizmem** affected with Down syndrome.

mongoloid *mp Gen., Acc.* -a 1. *antrop.* Mongoloid. 2. *pot.* (= *człowiek dotknięty mongolizmem*) person affected with Down syndrome.

mongoloidalny *a. antrop.* Mongoloid; **osoba typu mongoloidalnego** Mongoloid.

mongolski *a.* Mongolian, Mongol; **język mongolski** Mongolian, Mongol; **fałda mongolska** *antrop.* epicanthus, epicanthic (eye)fold.

Mongoł *mp pl.* -owie, **Mongołka** *f. Gen.pl.* -ek Mongolian, Mongol.

moniaki *pl. Gen.* -ów *dial.* change; money.

monista *mp fil.* monist.

monistka *f. Gen.pl.* -ek *zob.* **monista**.

monistyczny *a. fil.* monistic, monistical.

monit *mi* 1. (= *wezwanie do zapłaty*) reminder, dun. 2. *komp.* (= *znak zgłoszenia*) prompt, message; **monit o błędzie** error message.

monitor *mi Gen.* -a 1. (= *czasopismo urzędowe*) official journal. 2. *telew.* monitor, display screen; **monitor kontrolny** control monitor. 3. *komp.* (= *ekran komputera*) video monitor, visual display unit, VDU, display, screen; **monitor kineskopowy** cathode ray tube *l.* CRT display; **monitor ciekłokrystaliczny** liquid crystal display, LCD; **monitor alfanumeryczny** alphanumeric display; **monitor graficzny** graphic-display unit; **monitor monochromatyczny/czarno-biały** monochromatic/black-and-white monitor; **monitor kolorowy** color monitor *l.* display; **monitor niskoemisyjny** low emissions monitor; **monitor z klawiaturą** visual display terminal, VDT; **podstawka monitora** monitor stand. 4. *komp.* (= *program zarządzający*) monitor; **monitor systemu baz danych** database system monitor; **monitor zdarzeń**

event monitor. 5. *techn.* hydraulic monitor *l.* giant. 6. *hist., żegl.* (*mały okręt pancerny*) monitor.

monitoring *mi* monitoring; **monitoring wód podziemnych** *hydrol.* groundwater monitoring; **monitoring częstości serca** *med.* heart-rate monitoring.

monitorować *ipf.* monitor.

monitorowanie *n. techn., komp.* monitoring; **automatyczne monitorowanie bezpieczeństwa** automated security monitoring; **monitorowanie ruchu** traffic monitoring; **monitorowanie napięcia** voltage monitoring; **monitorowanie sprzętu** hardware monitoring; **monitorowanie sieci** network monitoring; **monitorowanie zdalne** telemonitoring.

monitować *ipf.* dun; **monitować kogoś** send sb a reminder, dun sb.

monizm *mi fil.* monism.

mono *a. indecl.* mono, monophonic. – *adv.* in mono. – *n.* mono, monophony, monophonic sound.

monochord *mi muz.* monochord.

monochrom *mi sztuka* monochrome.

monochromatyczność *f.* monochromaticity.

monochromatyczny *a.* monochromatic, monochrome.

monochromatyzm *mi sztuka* monochromaticity, painting in monochrome.

monocyt *pl. Gen.* -ów *biol.* monocyte.

monodia *f. Gen.* -ii *muz.* monody.

monodram *mi teatr* monodrama.

monofag *ma biol., zool.* monophagous animal.

monofagizm *mi biol.* monophagy.

monofiletyzm *mi biol.* monophyletism.

monofonia *f.* monophony.

monofoniczny *a.* (*telewizor, radio, sprzęt*) mono, monophonic, monaural; *el.* monaural; *muz.* monophonic.

monoftong *mi fon.* monophthong.

monoftongizacja *f. fon.* monophthongization.

monogamia *f. Gen.* -ii *t. zool.* monogamy.

monogamiczny *a.* (*o ludziach, o zwierzętach*) monogamous, monogamistic.

monogamista *mp* monogamist.

monografia *f. Gen.* -ii monograph; **pisać monografię na temat (kogoś** *l.* **czegoś)** write a monograph (about sb *l.* sth), monograph (sb *l.* sth).

monograficzny *a.* monographic.

monografista *mp pl.* -ści *rzad.* monographer.

monogram *mi* monogram, cipher; **podpisać się monogramem na czymś** initial sth; **ozdabiać coś monogramem** monogram sth; **oznaczać coś monogramem** personalize sth; **z monogramem** (*o ręczniku, piórze, papeterii*) personalized.

monokl *mi Gen.* -a 1. *opt.* monocle, simple lens. 2. *przest.* (*okulary*) monocle, eyeglass; **z monoklem w oku** monocled.

monokultura *f. roln.* monoculture.

monokulturowy *a. roln.* monocultural.

monolit *mi* 1. (= *jednolity blok kamienny, t. rzeźba z takiego bloku*) monolith. 2. *przen.* (= *zwarta całość*) monolith.

monolityczny *a. t. przen.* monolithic.

monolog *mi* monologue, monolog; **monolog dramatyczny** dramatic monologue; **monolog satyryczny** standup comedy; **monolog sceniczny** soliloquy; **monolog wewnętrzny** interior monologue.

monologować *ipf.* soliloquize.

monologowy *a.* monologic, monological.

monoman *mp* monomaniac.

monomania *f. Gen.* -ii monomania.

monomanka *f. Gen.pl.* -ek *zob.* **monoman**.

monomer *mi chem.* monomer.

monometalizm *mi ekon.* monometallism.

mononukleoza *f. pat.* mononucleosis; (= *mononukleoza zakaźna*) infectious mononucleosis, glandular fever.

monopol *mi* **1.** *ekon.* (= *wyłączne prawo*) monopoly (*na coś* on *l.* of *l.* over sth); **przełamać monopol** break (up) a monopoly; **mieć monopol na coś** have *l.* hold monopoly on *l.* of *l.* over sth; **monopol skarbowy** state monopoly; **monopol rządowy** government monopoly. **2.** (= *zrzeszenie przedsiębiorstw*) monopoly. **3.** *pot.* (= *wódka*) vodka, alcohol.

monopolista *mp* monopolist.

monopolistka *f. Gen.pl.* -ek *zob.* **monopolista**.

monopolistyczny *a.* monopolistic.

monopolizować *ipf.* monopolize; **monopolizować rynek** monopolize a market.

monopolowy *a.* monopoly; **sklep monopolowy** package store, liquor store; *Br.* off-licence.

monopolówka *f. Gen.pl.* -ek *pot.* (= *wódka*) vodka.

monosacharyd *pl. Gen.* -ów *chem.* monosaccharide.

monospermia *f. Gen.* -ii *biol.* monospermy.

monostych *mi Gen.* -u *teor.lit.* monostich.

monosylaba *f. Dat., Loc.* -bie monosyllable; **mówić/odpowiadać monosylabami** speak/ answer monosyllabically *l.* reluctantly.

monosylabiczny *a.* monosyllabic.

monoteista *mp rel.* monotheist.

monoteistka *f. Gen.pl.* -ek *zob.* **monoteista**.

monoteistyczny *a. rel.* monotheistic, monotheistical, monotheist.

monoteizm *mi rel.* monotheism.

monotematyczny *a.* monothematic.

monotonia *f. Gen.* -ii (*życia, stylu, rutynowej czynności*) monotony; (*w głosie, stylu pisania*) flatness, sameness, drabness; **przerwać monotonię** break the monotony.

monotoniczny *a.* monotonic; *muz.* monotone; **funkcja monotoniczna** *mat.* monotonic function.

monotonny *a.* (*zadanie, praca, osoba*) monotonous, humdrum; (*czynność*) drab; **monotonna egzystencja** humdrum existence; **monotonna mowa** drone; **monotonna intonacja** chant; **zespół** *l.* **syndrom monotonnych ruchów** *pat.* repetitive strain injury.

monotyp *mi* **1.** *biol.* monotype. **2.** *druk.* monotype. **3.** *żegl.* one-design (class) (boat), monotype (class).

monstrancja *f. rz.-kat.* monstrance.

monstrualność *f.* monstrousness, monstrosity.

monstrualny *a.* monstrous.

monstrum *n. sing. indecl. pl.* -ra *Gen.* -rów monster, monstrosity.

monsun *mi meteor.* monsoon.

monsunowy *a.* monsoonal; **las monsunowy** monsoon forest.

montaż *mi Gen.pl.* -y *l.* -ów **1.** *techn.* (= *składanie*) assembly, assemblage; (= *zakładanie instalacji*) installation, fitting, instal(l)ment; **montaż bezpłatny** *l.* **gratis** *handl.* free installation; **montaż instalacji (wodno-kanalizacyjno-gazowych)** pipe fitting. **2.** *film, radio* editing; **okres montażu i udźwiękowienia** postproduction; **montaż roboczy** *l.* **wstępny** rough cut. **3.** *film, radio* (*rodzaj programu*) montage.

montażownia *f. Gen.pl.* -i **1.** (= *montownia*) assembly shop, assembly plant. **2.** *film, radio* cutting *l.* editing room.

montażowy *a. techn.* **1.** assembly; **hala montażowa** assembly shop; **linia** *l.* **taśma montażowa** assembly line; **pracować przy linii** *l.* **taśmie montażowej** work on an assembly line, be an assembly line worker; **brygada montażowa** assembly crew; **taśma montażowa** assembly belt. **2.** *film, radio* editing; **stół montażowy** editing table.

montażysta *mp* **1.** *film, radio* editor. **2.** *bud.* construction worker, erector. **3.** *techn.* (= *osoba składająca coś z elementów*) assembler; (= *wykonawca instalacji*) fitter.

montażystka *f. Gen.pl.* -ek *zob.* **montażysta** 1.

monter *mp techn.* (= *osoba składająca coś z elementów*) assembler; (= *wykonawca instalacji*) fitter.

monterski *a.* fitter's; assembler's; **leżanka monterska** *mot.* creeper, cradle.

montować *ipf.* **1.** *techn.* (= *składać*) assemble; (= *instalować*) install, fit; (= *konstruować*) construct, erect; **montować maszyny** assemble machinery. **2.** *film, radio* edit. **3.** *pot.* (= *organizować, zbierać*) muster, get together.

montownia *f. Gen.pl.* -i *techn.* assembly shop, assembly plant.

monument *mi* **1.** *lit.* (= *pomnik*) monument (*poświęcony komuś / czemuś* to sb/sth). **2.** *przen.* (= *przedmiot o wartości zabytkowej*) (historical) monument; (= *świadectwo czegoś*) monument.

monumentalizm *mi* monumentalism.

monumentalność *f.* monumentality.

monumentalny *a.* monumental.

mop *mi* (*do podłogi*) mop.

mops *ma kynol.* pug; **nudzić się jak mops** *pot.* be bored stiff, be bored to death.

mora[1] *f. tk.* moire, tabby.

mora[2] *f. teor.lit.* mora.

mora[3] *f.* **1.** *druk.* moiré. **2.** *telew.* moiré effect, interference pattern.

morale *n. indecl.* morale; **podnosić morale** boost *l.* raise *l.* lift morale; **żołnierskie morale** morale of the troops.

moralista *mi* moralist.

moralistka *f. Gen.pl.* -ek *zob.* **moralista**.

moralistyka *f.* moralizing, moralism.

moralitet *mi teor.lit.* morality (play).

moralizator *mp* moralizer.

moralizatorka *f. Gen.pl.* **-ek** *zob.* **moralizator**.

moralizatorski *a.* moralistic, didactic.

moralizm *mi* moralism.

moralizować *ipf.* moralize (*na temat czegoś* on *l.* about *l.* over *l.* upon sth); (*obłudnie*) cant.

moralnie *adv.* morally; **czuć się moralnie zobowiązanym (zrobić coś)** be *l.* feel honor bound (to do sth); **moralnie zepsuty** morally tainted, scrofulous, rotten; **podbudowywać kogoś moralnie** uplift sb's spirits.

moralność *f.* morals, morality; **obraza moralności** indecency, indecent act; **poczucie moralności** moral sense; **obrońca moralności publicznej** custodian of public morals; **stróż moralności** guardian of morality; **moralność publiczna** public morals.

moralny *a.* **1.** (= *etyczny*) moral, ethical; **podwójny kodeks moralny** double moral standards; **normy moralne** moral standards; **nauka moralna** moral; **moralne zwycięstwo** moral victory; **pozbawiony kręgosłupa moralnego** lacking moral backbone *l.* fiber, spineless; **rozprzężenie moralne** lax morals; **upadek moralny** moral decay; **ze względów moralnych** on ethical *l.* moral grounds. **2.** (= *duchowy*) moral, spiritual; **kredyt moralny** trust; **krzywda moralna** moral damages; **odpowiedzialność moralna** moral responsibility; **poparcie** *l.* **wsparcie moralne** moral support.

morał *mi* (= *nauka umoralniająca*) moral; (= *końcowy wniosek*) tag line; **prawić komuś morały** preach at sb; **płynie z tego morał, że...** and the moral of/to the story is...; **wysnuć morał z czegoś** draw a moral from sth.

moratorium *n. sing. indecl. pl.* **-ria** *Gen.* **-riów** *prawn.* moratorium (*na coś* on sth); **moratorium płatnicze** grace period.

moratoryjny *a. prawn.* moratory; **ustawa moratoryjna** moratory law.

Morawianin *mp pl.* **-anie** *Gen.* **-an** Moravian.

Morawianka *f. Gen.pl.* **-ek** *zob.* **Morawianin**.

morawski *a.* Moravian; **dialekt morawski** *jęz.* Moravian; **kościół morawski** *rel.* Moravian Church; **członek/członkini kościoła morawskiego** *rel.* Moravian.

Morawy *pl. Gen.* **-w** *geogr.* Moravia.

mord *mi* murder, killing; (*zwł. na tle politycznym*) assassination; **mord rytualny** sacrifice, ritual killing; **mord masowy** mass murder.

morda *f.* **1.** (*zwierzęcia*) muzzle, snout. **2.** *wulg. t. pot.* (*człowieka*) mug; **zamknij** *l.* **stul mordę!** shut your face *l.* trap!, keep your trap shut!; **morda w kubeł!** shut your face *l.* trap!, keep your trap shut!; **wyskoczyć na kogoś z mordą** bawl sb out, lash out at sb; **dostać w mordę** *l.* **oberwać po mordzie** get beaten up; **dać komuś w mordę** punch sb in the face; **pies ci mordę lizał** I couldn't care less about you; **trzymać kogoś za mordę** boss sb, order sb about; **padać na mordę** be dogtired, be done in, be bushed *l.* pooped; **wyrzucić** *l.* **wywalić kogoś na zbitą mordę** bounce sb, throw sb out.

morderca *mp* murderer, killer; (*zwł. na tle politycznym*) assassin; **zawodowy morderca** contract killer; **najemny morderca** hired killer, bra-

vo; **płatny morderca** gun, hit man; **seryjny morderca** serial killer; **wielokrotny morderca** multiple killer *l.* murderer; **wynająć płatnego mordercę do zabicia kogoś** put a contract on sb.

morderczy *a.* (= *właściwy mordercy*) murderous; (*o broni*) murderous; (*o ataku*) vicious; (*o instynkcie, spojrzeniu, wyrazie twarzy*) murderous, killer; (*o ciosie*) crippling, devastating; (*o pośpiechu*) deadly; (*o rywalizacji, metodach walki z konkurencją*) cutthroat, ruthless; (= *wyczerpujący*) killing, exhausting; **to był morderczy wyścig** this race was a killer.

morderczyni *f. Gen.pl.* **-ń** murderess; *zob. t.* **morderca**.

morderstwo *n. por.* **zabójstwo**; (= *intencjonalne pozbawienie kogoś życia*) murder, killing; (*zw. na tle politycznym*) assassination; (*zwł. na zlecenie*) hit; **popełnić morderstwo** commit murder; **potrójne morderstwo** triple murder *l.* killing; **pod zarzutem morderstwa** on suspicion of murder; **postawić kogoś w stan oskarżenia pod zarzutem morderstwa** indict sb on murder; **przyznać się do morderstwa** confess to murder; **seryjne morderstwa** serial killings; **trzy zarzuty morderstwa** three counts of murder.

mordęga *f. pot.* drag; drudgery; **zajmowanie się nim to mordęga** it's a bitch having to take care of him.

mordobicie *n. pot.* (fist-)fight, brawl.

mordoklejka *f. pot.* (*cukierek*) (candy) kiss.

mordować *ipf.* **1.** (= *zabijać*) murder, kill, slay; (*z powodów politycznych*) assassinate; **mordować masowo** slaughter. **2.** *pot.* (= *męczyć*) pester, bother, bug. **~ się** *ipf.* **1.** (= *zabijać się wzajemnie*) kill each other *l.* one another. **2.** (= *męczyć się*) struggle (*z czymś* with sth); *pot.* kill o.s. (*robiąc coś l. żeby coś zrobić* doing sth *l.* to do sth).

mordownia *f. Gen.pl.* **-i** *pot.* (= *speluna*) dive, hole in the wall.

morela *f. Gen.pl.* **-i** *l.* **-l** **1.** *bot.* (*roślina*) apricot (tree) (*Prunus armeniaca*). **2.** (*owoc tej rośliny*) apricot.

morelowy *a.* **1.** (*o dżemie, drzewie*) apricot. **2.** (*o kolorze*) apricot.

morena *f. geol.* moraine, till; **morena denna** ground *l.* basal moraine; **morena boczna** lateral *l.* bank moraine; **morena czołowa** end *l.* terminal *l.* frontal moraine.

morenowy *a. geol.* morainal, morainic.

mores *mi* *przest.* obedience, disciplined behaviour; **nauczyć kogoś moresu** teach sb good manners.

morf *mi* *jęz.* morph.

morfem *mi* *jęz.* morpheme; **morfem słowotwórczy** *l.* **derywacyjny** derivational morpheme; **morfem fleksyjny** inflectional morpheme; **morfem zerowy** zero morpheme; **morfem wolny** free morpheme; **morfem (z)wiązany** bound morpheme.

morfemowy *a. jęz.* morphemic.

Morfeusz *mp mit.* Morpheus; **być w objęciach Morfeusza** be in the arms of Morpheus, be in the land of Nod.

morfina *f.* morphine, morphia.

morfinizm *mi* addiction to morphine.

morfogeneza *f. biol.* morphogenesis.

morfografia *f. Gen.* **-ii** *geogr.* orography, orology.

morfologia *f. Gen.* **-ii** **1.** *biol., jęz.* morphology. **2.** *geol.* morphology, geomorphology. **3.** *med., pot.* (= *skład krwi*) blood count.

morfologiczny *a. biol., geol., jęz., med.* morphologic, morphological.

morfonologia *f. Gen.* **-ii** *jęz.* morpho(pho)nology, morpho(pho)nemics.

morfotaktyka *f. Gen.* **-i** *jęz.* morphotactics.

morga *f. Gen.pl.* **mórg** *hist.* unit of land measure (*approx. 5600 sq.m*).

morganatyczny *a.*   *hist.*   morganatic, left-handed; **małżeństwo morganatyczne** morganatic *l.* left-handed marriage.

morion¹ *mi min.* (= *czarna odmiana kwarcu*) morion.

morion² *mi hist.* (= *hełm bez przyłbicy*) morion.

morka *f. Gen.pl.* **-ek** *meteor.* seawind.

mormon *mp rel.* (= *wyznawca mormonizmu*) Mormon.

mormonizm *mi rel.* Mormonism.

mormonka *f. Gen.pl.* **-ek** *zob.* **mormon.**

mormoński *a. rel.* Mormon.

mornel *ma orn.* Eurasian dotterel (*Eudromias morinellus*).

moro *n. indecl. pot.* (= *mundur polowy*) fatigues, fatigue clothes.

moroszka *f. Gen.pl.* **-ek** *bot.* cloudberry (*Rubus chamaemorus*).

morowanie *ipf. tk.* watering, waving, tabbying.

morowy¹ *a. tk.* tabby, moiré; **wzór morowy** moiré.

morowy² *a.* **1.** *pot.* (= *przyzwoity*) fine, plucky; **morowy chłop** good *l.* great guy; (= *przyjemny*) nice; **morowa robota** nice work. **2.** *przest.* (= *niosący mór*) pestilential; **morowe powietrze** plague.

morowy³ *a.* (= *iloczasowy*) mora.

mors¹ *ma zool.* walrus (*Odobenus rosmarus*).

mors² *mi Gen.* **-a** *pot.* (= *alfabet Morse'a*) *tel.* Morse, Morse code, Morse alphabet; **nadawać morsem** send (messages) in Morse code.

morski *a.* sea; (*np. o nawigacji*) nautical; (*np. o bitwie, szkole, siłach*) naval; (*np. o potędze, handlu, klimacie, muzeum*) maritime; (*np. o roślinach, ssakach, ubezpieczeniu*) marine; (*o podróży, transporcie*) sea, seafaring; **choroba morska** *pat.* seasickness; **brzeg morski** seashore; **wybrzeże morskie** seacoast, seaside; **klimat morski** maritime climate; **latarnia morska** lighthouse; **mila morska** *żegl.* (international) nautical mile (*1,852 m*); **prąd morski** (sea *l.* ocean) current; **kolor morski** sea green; **gwiazda morska** starfish; sea star; **cebula morska** *bot.* squill (*Urginea maritima*); **dno morskie** seafloor, seabed; **drogą morską** by sea; **trawa morska** *bot.* grass weed, grass wrack (*Zostera marina*); **konik morski** *icht.* sea horse (*Hippocampus*); **koń morski** = **mors¹**; **krowa morska** *zool.* sea cow, Steller's sea

cow (*Hydrodamalis gigas*); **lew morski** *zool.* California sea lion (*Zalophus californianus*); **pejzaż morski** *t. sztuka* seascape; **piechota morska** *wojsk.* marines; *US* Marine Corps; **podróż morska** sea voyage; **port morski** seaport; **potęga morska** (*o państwie*) sea power; **prawo morskie** *prawn.* maritime law, admiralty (law); (*międzynarodowe*) law of the sea; **słoń morski** *zool.* elephant seal (*Mirounga leonina*); **szlak morski** seaway; **sól morska** sea salt; **świnka morska** *zool.* guinea pig (*Cavia porcellus*); **wilk morski** *żegl.* sea dog, salt; **woda morska** brine, salt water, seawater.

morszczuk *ma icht.* hake (*Merluccius merluccius*); **morszczuk srebrzysty** silver hake (*Merluccius bilinearis*).

morszczyn *mi bot.* fucus (*Fucus*).

morświn *ma zool.* porpoise (*Phocoena phocoena*).

mortadela *f. kulin.* mortadella.

morusać się *ipf. zob.* **umorusać się.**

morwa *f.* **1.** *bot.* (*roślina*) mulberry (*Morus*). **2.** (*owoc tej rośliny*) mulberry.

morwowy *a.* mulberry; **jedwabnik morwowy** *ent.* silkworm moth (*Bombyx mori*).

moryna *f. chem.* morin.

morze *n. Gen.pl.* **mórz** **1.** *t. geogr.* sea; **morzem** by sea; **na morzu** (*pływać, znajdować się*) on the sea; (*służyć, pracować*) at sea; **nad morzem** (= *blisko morza*) by the sea; (*o wakacjach*) at *l.* by the seaside; **brzeg morza** seashore; **dno morza** seafloor, seabed; **otwarte** *l.* **pełne morze** high seas, open sea; **morze przybrzeżne** littoral *l.* marginal sea; **morze śródziemne** inland sea, land-locked sea; **morze terytorialne** territorial waters; **poziom morza** sea level; **na poziomie morza** at sea level; **nad poziomem morza** above sea level; **cisza na morzu** calm; **kropla w morzu** a drop in the ocean; **za siódmym morzem** *l.* **za siedmioma morzami** far, far away; **jechać nad morze** go to the seaside; **owoce morza** *kulin.* seafood; **ta rzeka wpada do morza** this river flows to the sea; **zew morza** call of the sea; **wzburzone morze** rough *l.* choppy sea; **spokojne morze** calm sea; **gładkie morze** smooth sea; **pływać w morzu** swim in the sea; **wychodzić w morze** *żegl.* put out to sea; **Morze Adriatyckie** the Adriatic Sea; **Morze Arktyczne** the Arctic Ocean; **Morze Azowskie** the Sea of Azov; **Morze Bałtyckie** the Baltic Sea; **Morze Barentsa** the Barents Sea; **Morze Chińskie** the China Sea; **Morze Czerwone** the Red Sea; **Morze Egejskie** the Aegean Sea; **Morze Irlandzkie** the Irish Sea; **Morze Japońskie** the Sea of Japan; **Morze Karaibskie** the Caribbean Sea, Spanish Main; **Morze Kaspijskie** the Caspian Sea; **Morze Liguryjskie** the Ligurian Sea; **Morze Marmara** the Sea of Marmara; **Morze Martwe** the Dead Sea; **Morze Południowochińskie** the South China Sea; **Morze Północne** the North Sea; **Morze Śródziemne** the Mediterranean Sea; **Morze Tyrreńskie** the Tyrrhenian Sea; **Morze Wschodniochińskie** the East China Sea. **2.** *przen.* (= *mnóstwo*) sea, myriads, zillions, loads; **morze głów** sea of heads; **morze łez** oceans of tears; **morze krwi** river(s) of blood. **3.** *astron.* mare.

morzyć *ipf. przest.* torment, torture (*to death*); **morzyć kogoś głodem** starve sb, hunger sb; **sen mnie morzył** I was overcome with sleep. ~ **się** *ipf.* **morzyć się głodem** starve o.s., go on a crash diet.

mosiądz *mi Gen.pl.* **-ów** *metal.* brass.

mosiek *mp* **-śk-** *pog.* (= Żyd) kike.

mosiężnictwo *n.* brasswork.

mosiężnik *mp* brazier.

mosiężny *a.* **1.** (= *zrobiony z mosiądzu*) brass, brassy, brazen. **2.** (= *mający barwę mosiądzu*) brassy, brazen; *rzad.* (= *brzmiący jak mosiądz*) brazen.

Moskal *mp Nom.pl.* **-le, Moskalka** *f. Gen.pl.* **-ek** *zwł. hist., pog.* Muscovite, Russ.

moskit *ma ent.* mosquito.

moskitiera *f.* mosquito net.

Moskwa *f. geogr.* Moscow.

Moskwianin *mp pl.* **-anie** *Gen.* **-an, Moskwianka** *f. Gen.pl.* **-ek** (= *mieszkaniec Moskwy*) Muscovite.

most *mi* **1.** *bud.* bridge; **most powietrzny** airlift; **most pontonowy** *gł. wojsk.* pontoon bridge; **most dla pieszych** footbridge; **most kratowy** truss bridge; **most łukowy** arch bridge; **most obrotowy** swing *l.* turn bridge; **most wiszący** suspension bridge; **most wspornikowy** cantilever bridge; **most zwodzony** drawbridge; **powiedzieć coś prosto z mostu** tell sth straight out, not beat around *l.* about the bush; **prosto z mostu** bluntly, curtly, straight from the shoulder; **walić prosto z mostu** mouth off, be a square shooter; **spalić za sobą mosty** burn one's bridges *l.* boats (behind one); **o jeden most za daleko** a bridge too far; **coś jest komuś potrzebne jak dziura w moście** sb needs sth like a hole in the head. **2.** *dent.* bridgework, (dental) bridge.

mostek *mi* **-tk-** **1.** (= *mały most*) (small) bridge, footbridge. **2.** *kulin.* brisket. **3.** *anat.* sternum, breastbone. **4.** *żegl.* bridge. **5.** *żegl.* (= *trap*) gangplank, gangway. **6.** *muz.* bridge. **7.** *sport* (*ćwiczenie gimnastyczne*) bridge. **8.** *dent.* (dental) bridge, bridgework.

mostowe *n. decl. like a. przest.* (= *opłata za przejazd*) (bridge) toll.

mostownica *f.* **1.** *bud., kol.* bridge sleeper *l.* tie. **2.** *techn.* travelling transporter.

mostowy *a.* (*o filarze, przęśle*) bridge; **przyczółek mostowy** *wojsk.* bridgehead.

moszcz *mi kulin.* must; **moszcz winny** stum.

moszna *f. Gen.pl.* **-en** *anat.* scrotum.

mosznowy *a. anat.* scrotal; **worek mosznowy** scrotum; **przepuklina mosznowa** *pat.* scrotal hernia.

mościć *ipf.* moszczę mościsz pad; **mościć poduszkami** cushion. ~ **się** *ipf.* settle o.s. comfortably.

mość *f. pl.* **-e** *przest.* (*w zwrotach*) **Jego/Jej Królewska Mość** His/Her Majesty; **Jego/Wasza Lordowska Mość** His/Your Lordship; **Jej/Jego/Wasza Królewska Mość** Your Majesty.

motać *ipf.* **1.** (*nici*) reel, wind, spool. **2.** (= *plą-*

tać) tangle, snarl. **3.** *pot.* (= *robić intrygi*) intrigue, scheme. ~ **się** *ipf.* (= *plątać się*) **1.** entangle, become entangled. **2.** *pot.* (= *być zdezorientowanym*) become snarled up.

motek *mi* **-tk-** *Gen.* **-a** *tk.* **1.** (*np. wełny, nici*) skein, hank. **2.** (= *szpulka*) spool, reel.

motel *mi* motel.

motelowy *a.* motel.

motet *mi muz.* motet.

motłoch *mi uj.* riffraff, rabble; **rządy motłochu** mob rule, mobocracy; ochlocracy.

motocross *mi zob.* **motokros**.

motocykl *mi Gen.* **-a** *Gen.pl.* **-i** *l.* **-ów** motorcycle; (*duży z wysoką kierownicą*) chopper; **motocykl terenowy** dirt bike; **motocykl szosowy** speed bike.

motocyklista *mp*, **motocyklistka** *Gen.pl.* **-ek** *f.* motorcyclist, motorcycle rider.

motocyklowy *a.* motocycle.

motodrom *mi* motordrome.

motokros *mi* motocross.

motolotnia *f. Gen.pl.* **-i** *lotn.* powered hang glider.

motopompa *f. techn.* motor pump.

motor *mi* **1.** (= *silnik*) motor, engine; **motor elektryczny/parowy/spalinowy** electric/steam/internal combustion engine; **motor zmian** *przen.* (*o osobie, idei*) prime mover; **być motorem czegoś** *przen.* be the driving force behind sth. **2.** *pot.* (= *motocykl*) motorbike, bike.

motorniczy *mp* motorman; *Br.* tram driver.

motorower *mi* moped.

motorowiec *mi* **-wc-** *Gen.* **-a** (*statek*) motor ship. – *mp* **-wc-** *pl.* **-y** (*sportowiec*) motorcycle racer; (= *żużlowiec*) speedway rider.

motorowodniak *mp sport* motorboater.

motorowodny *a.* motorboat; **sport motorowodny** motorboating.

motorowy *a.* motor; **łódź motorowa** motorboat.

motorówka *f. Gen.pl.* **-ek** motorboat, powerboat.

motoryczny *a. anat.* motor; **nerw/mięsień motoryczny** motor nerve/muscle.

motoryka *f. fizj.* motor activity.

motorynka *f.* motor scooter, scooter.

motoryzacja *f. mot.* motorization.

motoryzacyjny *a.* automotive, motor; **przemysł motoryzacyjny** automotive industry; **sklep motoryzacyjny** automobile accessory shop.

motoryzować *ipf. mot.* motorize.

motoszybowcowy *a.* motor-glider.

motoszybowiec *mi* **-wc-** *Gen.* **-a** *lotn.* motor glider, powered glider.

motowidło *n. Gen.pl.* **-eł** *tk.* (*do nici*) **1.** reeling-machine, spool. **2.** *roln.* pick-up reel.

motto *n. Dat. i Loc.* **motcie** motto; **motto życiowe** life's philosophy.

motyka *f.* hoe; **porywać się z motyką na słońce** try to square the circle, bite off more than one can chew.

motyl *ma ent.* butterfly (*Lepidoptera*). – *mi Gen.* **-a** **1.** *żegl.* spinnaker. **2.** *pl. metal.* (*wada stali*) butterflies.

motylek *ma* **-lk-** *Gen.* **-a** (= *mały motyl*) butterfly. – *mi* -lk- *Gen.* -a *sport, pot.* (*styl pływania*) butterfly.

motylica *f.* **1.** *zool.* (= *motylica wątrobowa*) liver fluke (*Fasciola hepatica*). **2.** *wet.*, *pat.* fascioliasis.

motylkowate *pl. bot.* the papilionaceous family (*Papilionaceae*).

motylkowaty *a.* (= *przypominający motyla*) (*t. o roślinie*) papilionaceous.

motylkowy *a.* **1.** butterfly, butterfly's; **styl motylkowy** *sport* butterfly stroke; **nakrętka motylkowa** *mech.* wing nut, butterfly nut. **2.** *zob.* **motylkowaty**.

motyw *mi* **1.** (= *pobudka*) motive; **motyw działania** driving force; **motywy popełnienia przestępstwa** motives of a crime; **główny motyw** leading motive; **ukryte motywy** ulterior motives *l.* ends. **2.** (*muzyczny, literacki*) motif, theme; (*zdobniczy*) motif, motive; **motyw przewodni** *lit.*, *muz.* leitmotiv, leitmotif.

motywacja *f.* **1.** motivation; **mieć (silną) motywację** be (highly) motivated; **dostarczać motywacji (komuś)** motivate (sb). **2.** (= *uzasadnienie*) justification.

motywować *ipf.* **1.** (= *pobudzać*) motivate (*kogoś do czegoś* sb to do sth); **motywować (kogoś) do działania** motivate (sb) to act, motivate (sb) to action. **2.** (= *ukazywać motywy*) give reasons *l.* grounds (*coś* for sth). **3.** (= *uzasadniać*) justify; **motywować coś czymś** put sth down to sth.

mowa *f.* **1.** (= *język*) language, tongue; (*zwł. obca*) *pot.* lingo; (*język określonego środowiska*) parlance, idiom; (*język określonego regionu*) dialect; **mowa ojczysta** mother tongue; **mowa potoczna** colloquial speech; **w mowie prawniczej** legal parlance. **2.** (= *to, co się mówi*) talk, speech; **skoro o tym mowa** in connection with this; **skoro mowa o wakacjach...** speaking of holidays...; **artykuł, o którym mowa...** the article in question...; **nie było mowy o czymś** there was no mention of sth; **nie ma mowy o tym, żeby się mylił** there is no possibility of his being wrong; **mowa była o przyszłej współpracy** the subject (of the discussion) was future cooperation; **o wilku mowa** speak of the devil; **mowy nie ma!** *l.* **nie ma mowy!** *pot.* that's out of the question!, no way!, forget it!, no dice! **3.** (= *zdolność mówienia*) speech; **narządy mowy** *l.* **aparat mowy** speech organs, organs of speech; **zaburzenie mowy** speech disorder; **rozpoznawanie mowy** speech recognition; **synteza mowy** speech synthesis; **system rozpoznawania mowy** voice recognition system; **mowa ciała** (*psych.*) body language; **odbierać komuś mowę** dumbfound sb; **odebrało mu mowę** he was left speechless; **odzyskać mowę** find one's tongue; **mowa jest srebrem, milczenie złotem** speech is silver, silence is gold. **4.** *gram.* speech; **część mowy** part of speech; **mowa zależna** indirect *l.* reported speech; **mowa niezależna** direct speech. **5.** (= *wymowa*) pronunciation. **6.** *Gen.pl.* **mów** (= *przemówienie*) speech, address; **mowa inauguracyjna** inaugural speech; **mowa pochwalna** eulogy; **mowa pogrzebowa** funeral oration; **mowa pożegnalna** valediction; **mowa**

obrończa defence; **wygłosić mowę** (*zwł. polityczną*) make *l.* give *l.* deliver a speech.

mozaika *f.* **1.** (*ozdoba*) (*z kostek kamienia, szkła*) mosaic; (*z kostek drewna, kości słoniowej*) inlay; **mozaika liściowa** *bot.* leaf mosaic. **2.** *bot.*, *pat.* mosaic, mosaic disease.

mozaikowy *a.* mosaic; **posadzka mozaikowa** *bud.* inlaid floor; **choroba mozaikowa** *bot.*, *pat.* mosaic disease.

mozaistyczny *a. rel.* Mosaic; **prawo mozaistyczne** Mosaic law.

mozaizm *mi rel.* Mosaism.

mozazaur *ma paleont.* mosasaur, mosasaurus (*Mosasaurus*).

mozga *f. bot.* **mozga (kanaryjska)** canary grass (*Phalaris canariensis*); **mozga trzcinowata** reed canary grass (*Phalaris arundinacea*).

mozolić się *ipf.* -ól (*fizycznie*) slog (*nad czymś* at sth); toil (*nad czymś* at *l.* over sth); (*umysłowo*) rack one's brains (*nad czymś* over sth); **mozolić się nad odpowiedzią** rack one's brains for an answer.

mozolnie *adv.* arduously, laboriously, with great effort; **pracować mozolnie i bez efektu** plow the sands *l.* the air.

mozolny *a.* (*o pracy, zadaniu*) laborious, strenuous; (*o podróży*) arduous; **mozolna praca** toil, hard labor.

mozół *mi* -o- *lit.* toil, travail; **z mozołem** arduously.

moździerz *mi Gen.* -a (*działo*) (*naczynie*) mortar.

może *part.* **1.** *3 os. sing. zob.* **móc**. **2.** (*wyraża ewentualność*) maybe, possibly; **być może** perhaps, possibly, maybe; **być może, że...** it's possible that...; **(być) może przyjdę** I may come; **może się mylę, ale...** correct me if I'm wrong but...; **może tak, (a) może nie** perhaps I do, perhaps I don't; **może i jest inteligentna, ale...** she might be smart, but...; **może go porwano** he could have been kidnapped; **może wyjdę na głupka, ale...** at the risk of sounding stupid,...; **nie może być!** that's impossible! **3.** (*wyraża zachętę, prośbę*) how *l.* what about...?, suppose..., what would you say if...?, would you like...?, would you mind...?; **(a) może byśmy (tak) poszli do kina?** why don't we go to the movies?; **(a) może napilibyśmy się kawy?** how about some coffee?; **może byś zjadł kawałek ciasta?** what would you say to a piece of cake?; **może pójdziemy do mnie?** why don't we go to my place?; **(a) może byśmy wzięli taksówkę?** let's take a taxi, shall we?; **może trochę więcej szczegółów?** could you be a bit more specific?; **może cię zainteresuje, że...** it may interest you to know that..., you may find it interesting that...; **(a) może by (tak) trochę ciszej?** keep *l.* pipe it down, please!; **może dolać?** (*drinka, kawę, piwo*) would you like a refill?; **może komuś drinka?** who wants a drink?; **może piwko?** want a beer?

możesz *itd. ipf. zob.* **móc**.

możliwe *adv.* **to możliwe** that's possible; **bardzo możliwe, że...** it's possible that..., it may well be that...; **całkiem możliwe, że będzie padać** it can always rain; **możliwe, że to zrobiła** she may have done it, it's possible that she has done it.

możliwie *adv.* **1.** (= *w miarę możliwości*) possibly, if possible; **możliwie najlepszy** the best possible; **możliwie najszybciej** as soon as possible, ASAP, asap; **zrób to możliwie dobrze** do it as well as you possibly can, give it your best; **zrób to możliwie szybko** do it as soon as you possibly can. **2.** *pot.* (= *znośnie*) not too badly, tolerably; **wyglądali całkiem możliwie** they didn't look too bad; **zachowuj się możliwie!** behave yourself!

możliwość *f.* **1.** (= *prawdopodobieństwo*) possibility, chance; **możliwość wygranej** chance of winning; **możliwość nauki** chance to learn; **możliwość wybuchu gazu** possibility of gas explosion; **do granic możliwości** to the limit; **w miarę możliwości** if (at all) possible; **znikoma możliwość** slight possibility; **istnieje znikoma możliwość, że** it is just possible that...; **istnieje możliwość, że...** there is a possibility that... **2.** (= *zdolność, potencjał*) ability, capability, potential; **możliwości finansowe** financial means; **w zasięgu czyichś możliwości finansowych** within sb's means; **osiągnąć pełnię swoich możliwości** achieve one's full potential; **osiągnąć szczyt swoich możliwości** (*w karierze*) be at the top of the tree, be at the height of one's power; **przerastać czyjeś możliwości** be beyond sb's capabilities; **w granicach czyichś możliwości** within sb's power; **stwarzać możliwości czegoś** open the door to sth; **wyczerpać możliwości** exhaust one's resources, shoot one's bolt; **znać swoje możliwości** know one's limits. **3.** (= *sposobność*) chance, opportunity; **miałem możliwość rozmawiać z nim** I had a chance *l.* an opportunity to talk to him; **czy będę miał możliwość wykorzystania moich umiejętności?** will there be any opportunity for me to use my skills? **4.** (= *ewentualność*) contingency, eventuality; **być przygotowanym na wszelkie możliwości** be prepared for all contingencies. **5.** (= *perspektywy*) chances, prospects; **możliwość powodzenia** chances of success.

możliwy *a.* **1.** (= *dający się urzeczywistnić*) possible, likely; **możliwy do wyobrażenia** conceivable; **możliwy do przyjęcia** acceptable; **o ile to (w ogóle) możliwe** if (at all) possible; **na tyle, na ile (to) możliwe** as far as possible; **to może nie być możliwe** it may not be possible; **czy to możliwe?** is that possible?, could that be true?; **jak to możliwe?** is that possible?, how come?; **wszelkimi możliwymi sposobami** by any means possible, by any means available. **2.** (= *ewentualny*) possible, potential; **uniknąć możliwego niebezpieczeństwa** avoid a possible *l.* potential danger; **możliwe, że zadzwonią jutro** they may give us a ring tomorrow; **możliwe, że spóźnili się na pociąg** they may have missed the train; **szukałem w każdym możliwym miejscu** I searched in every likely place. **3.** *pot.* (= *znośny*) passable, so-so.

można *v.* **1.** (*wyraża możliwość urzeczywistnienia czegoś*) it is possible to..., one (you etc.) can *l.* may...; **rzec by można, że...** one (you etc.) could *l.* can say that...; **można się cieszyć, że...** it is fortunate that...; **można już iść** you (we etc.)

may *l.* can go now; **można śmiało powiedzieć, że...** it is safe to say that...; **można wykazać, że...** it is arguable that...; **można jej wybaczyć, że...** she could be forgiven for...; **czego (innego) można się (było) spodziewać?** what (else) can *l.* do you expect?; **można było tego uniknąć** it was avoidable; **nie można się jej oprzeć** she is irresistible; **można mieć wątpliwości** there is room for doubt; **gdyby tylko było można** if it was only possible, given half a chance; **można tam dojść piechotą** it is within walking distance; **można się było tego spodziewać** small *l.* little wonder; **wszystko co można sobie wyobrazić** everything under the sun, everything but the kitchen sink; **można wytrzymać** *pot.* it's O.K. *l.* okay, it's alright *l.* all right; **jak można...?** (*coś zrobić*) how to...?, how can one...?; (*wyraz oburzenia*) how can *l.* dare you...? **2.** (*dla wyrażenia przyzwolenia*) one (you etc.) may..., one (you etc.) is (are etc.) allowed *l.* free to...; **czy można?** may I?, do you mind?; **czy tu można palić?** may *l.* can I smoke here?; **czy można zapalić?** do you mind if I smoke?; **tak nie można!** that's wrong!; **jeśli można** if that's OK; **czy można zamknąć okno?** do you mind if I close the window?; **nie można tak myśleć** you mustn't think that; **można by pójść do kina** how *l.* what about going to the cinema?, why don't we go to the cinema?

możni *mp pl.* magnates, aristocracy.

możność *f.* (= *możliwość, zdolność*) **1.** possibility; **w miarę możności** as far as possible. **2.** (= *sposobność*) opportunity, chance; **mieć możność coś zrobić** have the opportunity to do sth; **miałem możność z nim to omówić** I had the chance *l.* opportunity to discuss it with him.

możnowładca *mp* magnate; (*zwł. monarcha*) potentate.

możnowładczy *a.* magnate's, potentate's.

możnowładztwo *n.* **1.** (= *magnateria, arystokracja*) magnates, aristocracy. **2.** (= *oligarchia*) oligarchy.

możny *a.* powerful and wealthy, mighty.

możylinek *mi bot.* sandwort (*Moehringia*).

móc *ipf.* **mogę możesz mógł mogła mogli 1.** (= *być w stanie*) can (*coś zrobić* do sth); be able (*coś zrobić* to do sth); be capable (*coś zrobić* of doing sth); **nie móc czegoś zrobić** be unable to do sth; **nie móc przestać o czymś myśleć** can't get sth out of one's head; **nie móc się komuś/czemuś oprzeć** find sb/sth irresistible; **jeśli tylko możesz** if you possibly can; **gdybym tylko mógł** if only I could; **będzie mógł wam pomóc** he will be able to help you; **nie możemy sobie na to pozwolić** we cannot afford it; **szkoda, że nie możesz przyjść** it is a pity that you can't come; **kto mógł coś takiego zrobić?** who could have done a thing like that?; **staram się jak mogę** I'm doing my best, I'm doing the best I can; **nie mogę zaprzeczyć, że...** I don't *l.* can't deny (that)...; **nie mogę się z tym nie zgodzić** I can't quarrel with that; **dziękuję, (ale) już nie mogę** (*odmowa poczęstunku*) I couldn't; no, thanks, I'm full; **mógłby być twoim ojcem** he is old enough to be your father; **może być albo**

jeden, albo drugi either will do; tak nie może być! that will never do!; może być? is it OK?; chcieć to móc where there's a will there's a way. 2. (= być uprawnionym, mieć pozwolenie) be permitted *l.* allowed (coś zrobić to do sth); can (coś zrobić do sth); czy mogę wyjść wcześniej? may *l.* can I leave early?; możesz robić, co chcesz you can do whatever you like *l.* want; możesz iść do domu you can go home, it's OK for you to go home; kiedy będziemy mogli ją zobaczyć? when do we get to see her? 3. (nadaje odcień prawdopodobieństwa, możliwości) can, may; czego ona może chcieć? what can she want?; mógł zostać porwany he could have been kidnapped; to nie może być ona it couldn't be her; to mógł być ktoś inny it could have been someone else. 4. (w prośbach, ofertach pomocy, wykrzyknieniach) can, may; jeśli mogę if I may; czy mógłbym... is it *l.* would it be all right if I...; czy mogę z tobą porozmawiać? can I talk to you?; w czym mogę pomóc? (how) can I help you?; mogę prosić o otwarcie okna? would you mind opening the window?; czy mógłbyś to powtórzyć? could you say it again?; czy mogę prosić o sól? could you pass the salt?; czy mogę prosić o uwagę? can *l.* could I have your attention?; ja nie mogę! *pot.* (reakcja na coś irytującego) gimme a break!, give me strength! 5. (wyraz pretensji) can, may; mógłby przynajmniej przeprosić he might at least apologize; mogła przynajmniej zadzwonić she could *l.* might at least have called; jak mogłeś (mi to zrobić)? how could you (do this to me)?

mód *f. zob.* moda.

módl się *itd. ipf. zob.* modlić się.

mój *a.* moj- *l.* m- *Ins. i Loc.* moim *l.* mym *pl.* moi *Gen., Acc. i Loc.* moich *l.* mych *Dat.* moim *l.* mym *Ins.* moimi *l.* mymi (z rzeczownikiem, który precyzuje) my; mój pies my dog; moja dziewczyna my girlfriend; to są moje książki these are my books; ten idiota mój szef my idiot *l.* fool of a boss; (z rzeczownikiem, który nie precyzuje) of mine; pewien mój znajomy a friend of mine; chyba masz kilka moich książek, prawda? you have several of mine books, don't you?; (bez rzeczownika) mine; te książki są moje these books are mine; to (nie) moje! it's (not) mine!, this is (not) mine! mój *mp,* moja *f. pot.* (= mąż/żona) my husband/wife; (= narzeczony/narzeczona) my fiancé/fiancée; (= chłopak/dziewczyna) my boyfriend/girlfriend. moje *n.* (moja własność) what belongs to me, my property; po mojemu if you ask me, for my money; wyszło na moje *l.* moje na wierzchu told you so!, what'd I tell you?

mókł *itd. ipf. zob.* moknąć.

mól *ma* -o- *ent.* 1. tineid (Tineidae); *pot.* moth; mól odzieżowy clothes moth (Tineola bisselliella); mól książkowy bookworm. 2. (= zmartwienie) worry; każdu ma swojego mola, co go gryzie we all have our worries.

mór *mi* -o-, morze *przest.* (= dżuma) 1. plague. 2. (= zaraza bydlęca) murrain.

mórg *f. zob.* morga.

mórz *n. zob.* morze.

mówca *mp,* mówczyni *f. Gen.pl.* -ń speaker; mówca uliczny soap-box orator, soap-boxer.

mówiący *mp* (= mówca) speaker.

mówić *ipf.* 1. (= wypowiadać słowa) say (coś komuś sth to sb) (że... that...); (= opowiadać, informować) tell (komuś sb sth *l.* sth to sb) (komuś o kimś/czymś sb about sb/sth *l.* of sb/sth) (komuś, że... sb that...); (= odzywać się, rozmawiać, przemawiać) speak, talk (z kimś with *l.* to sb, o kimś/czymś about *l.* of sb/sth) (do kogoś to sb); (= wspominać) refer (o kimś/czymś to sb/sth); mention (komuś o kimś/czymś sb/sth to sb); mów dalej! keep talking!; mów za siebie! speak for yourself!; mówcie (trochę) ciszej! keep it down!; to put it mildly; mówi się, że... they say that...; the story goes that...; it is reported *l.* rumored that...; mówić dobrze/źle o kimś/czymś speak well/ill of sb/sth; mówić komuś dzień dobry say hello to sb; mówić do siebie talk to o.s.; mówić otwarcie speak one's mind; mówić po próżnicy waste one's breath; mówić w czyimś imieniu speak for sb; mówić z przekonaniem speak with authority; mówisz poważnie? are you serious?; a nie mówiłem? did't I tell you?; co mówiłeś? what did you say?; dobrze mówi! hear, hear!; do mnie mówisz? are you talking to me?; fakty mówią same za siebie *przen.* the facts speak for themselves; i kto to mówi? look who's talking!; lepiej nie mówić the less said, the better; nie ma o czym mówić (w odpowiedzi na podziękowanie) don't mention it; forget it; nie mów nic don't say anything; nie mów z pełnymi ustami don't talk with your mouth full; nie musisz mówić nic więcej (= wszystko rozumiem) enough said. 2. (= wyrażać słowami) tell; mówić (całą) prawdę tell the (whole) truth; mówić kłamstwa tell lies. 3. (= wyrażać się w dany sposób) talk, speak; mówić bzdury *l.* nonsensy *l.* od rzeczy talk nonsense; mówić do rzeczy talk sense; mówić na temat speak to the point; nareszcie mówisz do rzeczy now you're talking sense. 4. (= nakazywać) tell (komuś, żeby coś zrobił sb to do sth); mówiłem mu, żeby przyszedł I told him to come; nienawidzę, jak mi się mówi, co mam robić I hate people telling me what to do; rób, co ci mówię! do what I tell you! 5. (= posługiwać się językiem) speak; mówić dobrze/biegle po japońsku speak good/fluent Japanese; mówić po angielsku kiepsko/z obcym akcentem speak English badly/with a foreign accent; nie mówię *l.* nie umiem mówić po węgiersku I can't speak Hungarian; osoba mówiąca po angielsku/polsku English/Polish speaker; mówić tym samym językiem (= dobrze się rozumieć) speak the same language. 6. (= sugerować, wywoływać wspomnienie) mean, ring a bell; czy to ci coś mówi? does this mean anything to you?; does it ring a bell?; jego nazwisko nic mi nie mówi his name doesn't ring a bell. 7. (przedstawiając się przez radio *l.* telefon) cześć, mówi Marta hi, it's Martha (speaking); tu mówi Londyn *radio* this is London calling. 8. (= zwracać się do kogoś) mów mi Ed call me Ed; możesz mi mówić po imieniu you can call me by my first name. **9.** (*w komentarzach na temat wypowiedzi*) **mówiąc delikatnie** to say the least; **mówiąc poważnie** joking aside; **mówiąc szczerze** frankly (speaking); to be frank; **mówiąc w przenośni** metaphorically speaking; **inaczej mówiąc** to put it differently; **jak (już) mówiłem** like I said; **kiedy już o tym mówimy** while we are at it; **krótko mówiąc** to make *l.* cut a long story short; in brief; **między nami mówiąc** between ourselves; between you and me (and the gatepost); **nawiasem mówiąc** by the way; by the bye; incidentally; **nie mówiąc (już) o kimś/czymś** not to mention sb/sth; to say nothing of sb/sth; let alone sb/sth; **prawdę mówiąc** to tell the truth; as a matter of fact; **przykro mi to mówić** I hate to say it; **skoro już o tym mówimy** while we're at it; **ściśle mówiąc** strictly speaking.

mówiony *a.* (*o języku*) (= *nie pisany*) spoken, oral.

mówka *f. Gen.pl.* **-ek** *iron.* speech, talk; **gładka mówka** glib speech; **palnąć mówkę** come out with a speech.

mównica *f.* rostrum, lectern.

mózg *mi* **1.** *anat.* brain, cerebrum, encephalon; **lewa/prawa półkula mózgu** the left/ right hemisphere; **płaty mózgu** cerebral lobes. **2.** *pat.* **gąbczaste zwyrodnienie mózgu** spongiform encephalopathy; **guz mózgu** encephaloma, brain tumour; **obrzęk mózgu** cerebral edema; **udar mózgu** apoplexy; **ustanie czynności mózgu** brain death; **uszkodzenie mózgu** brain damage; **wstrząs** *l.* **wstrząśnienie mózgu** concussion (of the brain); **wylew krwi do mózgu** cerebral hemorrhage; *pot.* stroke; **zapalenie mózgu** brain fever, encephalitis; **zapalenie mózgu i rdzenia** encephalomyelitis. **3.** *przen.* **burza mózgów** brainstorming; **drenaż mózgów** brain drain; **poddać praniu mózgu** brainwash; **pranie mózgu** brainwashing; **trust mózgów** brain trust; think tank. **4.** *pot. przen.* (= *autor planu*) mastermind, the brains; **mózg spisku/operacji** the brains behind the plot/operation. **5. mózg elektronowy** *przest.* (= *komputer*) electronic brain.

mózgoczaszka *f. Gen.pl.* **-ek** *anat.* brain box, cranium.

mózgowie *n. Gen.pl.* **-wi** *anat.* brain, encephalon; **pień mózgowia** brain stem.

mózgowiec *mp* **-wc-** *pl.* **-y** *iron.* egghead, highbrow.

mózgownica *f.* (= *czaszka*) **1.** brainpan. **2.** *żart.* (= *intelekt*) brains; **wytężać mózgownicę** beat out *l.* cudgel one's brains.

mózgowo-rdzeniowy *a. anat.* cerebrospinal; **płyn mózgowo-rdzeniowy** cerebrospinal fluid.

mózgowy *a. anat.* **1.** cerebral, encephalous, encephalic; **kora mózgowa** cortex; **opona mózgowa** meninx; **półkula mózgowa** cerebral hemisphere; **przysadka mózgowa** hypophysis, pituitary gland *l.* body; **puszka mózgowa** cranium. **2.** *pat.* **krwotok mózgowy** cerebral hemorrhage; **porażenie mózgowe** cerebral palsy; **zapalenie opon mózgowych** meningitis, brain fever.

móżdżek *mi* **-dżk-** **1.** *anat.* cerebellum. **2.** *ku-*

lin. brains; **móżdżek cielęcy** calves' brains. **3.** *iron.* **ptasi móżdżek** (*o osobie*) nitwit, birdbrain.

mroczek *mi* **-czk-** *Gen.* **-a** *zw. pl. pat.* scotoma. – *ma* **-czk-** *zool.* bat, serotine (*Eptesicus serotinus*).

mroczkowate *pl. Gen.* **-ych** *zool.* vespertilionids (*Vespertilionidae*).

mrocznieć *ipf.* **-eję -ejesz** darken, dusk; grow dark *l.* dusky.

mroczny *a.* **1.** (= *ciemny*) dark, darkling, dusky, dim, murky, somber. **2.** (= *ponury*) gloomy, glum, dismal, somber.

mroczyć się *ipf. poet.* = **mrocznieć**.

mrok *mi* (= *ciemność*) darkness, the dark; (= *zmierzch*) dusk, twilight; (= *ponurość*) gloom, murk, murkiness; **w mroku nocy** in the dead of night; **mroki średniowiecza** *przen.* the Dark Ages.

mrowić *ipf.* (*o częściach ciała*) tingle. **~ się** *ipf.* (= *roić się*) swarm, teem (*od kogoś / czegoś* with sb/sth).

mrowie *n.* **1.** (= *mnóstwo*) multitude, plenty, plethora, myriad; (*ludzi*) swarm, crowd. **2.** = **mrowienie**.

mrowienie *n.* (= *ciarki*) chill, tingling, tingle; (*w zdrętwiałych kończynach*) *pot.* pins and needles.

mrowisko *n.* anthill, ant colony; *form.* (*t.* = *hodowla mrówek*) formicary, formicarium; **ludzkie mrowisko** *przen.* warren; **wetknąć kij w mrowisko** *przen. pot.* set the cat among the pigeons; stir up a hornets' nest.

mrozić *ipf.* **-żę -zisz** **1.** (= *ziębić*) chill, freeze; (*o lodówce*) freeze; *zob.* **mrożony**; **mrozić komuś krew w żyłach** *przen.* curdle one's blood. **2.** (= *paraliżować*) freeze, transfix, paralyse. **~ się** *ipf.* (= *chłodzić się*) chill.

mrozoodporny *a. techn.* **1.** frost-proof, frost-resistant. **2.** (*o roślinie*) hardy.

mroźny *a.* frosty; nippy, chilly.

mrożący *a.* **mrożący krew w żyłach** blood-curdling.

mrożonka *f. Gen.pl.* **-ek** frozen food, chilled food.

mrożony *a.* frozen, chilled; (= *przechowywany w zamrażarce*) deep-frozen; (*o herbacie, kawie*) iced; (*o napojach*) cooled, frappé.

mrówczan *mi chem.* formate.

mrówczy *a.* **1.** ant's, ants'. **2.** *przen.* **mrówcza praca** *l.* **mrówczy trud** painstaking work *l.* labor.

mrówka *f. Gen.pl.* **-ek** **1.** *ent.* ant; *arch.* emmet; **mrówka faraona** pharaoh('s) ant (*Monomorium pharaonis*); **mrówka rudnica** wood ant (*Formica rufa*); **mrówka królowa/żołnierz/robotnica/niewolnica** queen/soldier/worker/slave ant; **latająca mrówka** antfly; **pracowity jak mrówka** (as) busy as a bee. **2. mrówki** (= *mrowienie*) tingling, tingle; (*w kończynach*) pins and needles; **na ten widok mrówki przeszły mi po plecach** the view sent a tingle down my spine.

mrówkojad *ma zool.* anteater; **mrówkojad wielki** great *l.* giant anteater; ant bear (*Myrmecophaga tridactyla*).

mrówkojadek *ma* -dk- *zool.* pygmy *l.* silky *l.* two-toed anteater (*Cyclopes didactylus*).

mrówkolew *ma* -lw- *ent.* antlion (*Myrmeleon*); **larwa mrówkolwa** doodlebug.

mrówkowy *a. chem.* formic.

mrównik *ma zool.* aardvark (*Orycteropus afer*).

mróz *mi* -o- **1.** (= *zimno, ziąb*) frost, freeze, frostiness; (*personifikacja*) Jack Frost; **dziś w nocy będzie mróz** it'll freeze tonight; **siarczysty** *l.* **trzaskający mróz** hard *l.* heavy frost; **20 stopni mrozu** 20 degrees of frost; **w największy mróz** in the depth of winter. **2.** (= *szron*) hoarfrost, white frost; **mróz na szybie** frostwork.

mruczando *n. żart.* mormorando, humming.

mruczeć *ipf.* -ę -ysz **1.** hum, lip, murmur; (*o kocie, t. zadowolonej l. rozmarzonej osobie*) purr. **2.** **mruczeć (pod nosem)** (= *mówić cicho i niewyraźnie*) mutter. **3.** *pot.* (= *narzekać*) grumble, murmur (*na kogoś/coś* against sb/sth).

mrugać *ipf.*, **mrugnąć** *pf.* -ij **1.** (*o oku*) blink, nictate, nictitate; **mrugać (okiem)** wink (*do kogoś* at sb); **nawet nie mrugnąć (okiem)** not bat an eye *l.* eyelid, not flicker an eyelid; (= *nie okazać zdziwienia*) not turn a hair. **2.** (*o gwiazdach, świetle*) twinkle, wink. **3.** + *Ins.* (= *włączać i wyłączać*) flash; **mrugać światłami** *mot.* flash one's headlights *l.* brights.

mrugnięcie *n.* blink, wink.

mruk *mp pl.* -i **1.** (= *odludek, milczek*) loner, clam, misanthrope; (= *osoba opryskliwa*) curmudgeon. **2.** *icht.* (= *ryba z rodziny Mormyridae*) elephant-nose fish.

mrukliwość *f.* (= *małomówność*) **1.** taciturnity. **2.** (= *opryskliwość*) gruffness, surliness.

mrukliwy *a.* (= *małomówny*) **1.** taciturn. **2.** (= *opryskliwy*) gruff, surly.

mruknąć *pf.* -ij *zob.* **mruczeć**.

mru-mru *int. pot.* **ani mru-mru** mum's the word; hush.

mrużyć *ipf.* **mrużyć oczy** blink, squint (one's eyes); narrow one's eyes; screw up one's eyes. ~ **się** *ipf.* (*o oczach*) blink, narrow.

mrzeć *ipf.* **mrę mrzesz**, -yj, **marł** *lit.* die, perish.

mrzonka *f. Gen.pl.* -ek chimera, daydream, pipe dream, flight of fancy, castle in the air; **gonić za mrzonkami** build castles in the air; catch at shadows; chase the sun *l.* wind.

mrzyk *ma ent.* carpet beetle (*Anthrenus*).

msza *f.* **1.** *rel.* (church) service; *gł. rz.-kat.* mass, Mass; **msza zwykła/uroczysta** Low/High Mass; **chodzić na mszę** go to Mass; **dawać na mszę** offer a Mass (intention) (*za kogoś/coś* for sb/sth); **odprawiać mszę** celebrate *l.* say Mass; **spóźnić się na mszę** be late for church; **wysłuchać mszy** hear Mass; **po mszy** after church; **czarna msza** black mass. **2.** *muz.* mass.

mszak *mi Gen.* -a *bot.* bryophyte.

mszalny *a. kośc.* of the mass; **kielich mszalny** chalice; **wino mszalne** sacramental wine; **sprzęty mszalne** implements of the mass, mass-requisites.

mszał *mi kośc.* missal.

mszczę *itd. ipf. zob.* **mścić**.

mszyca *f. ent.* aphis, aphid, ant cow, plant louse; **środek przeciwko mszycom** *l.* **na mszyce** aphicide.

mszywioł *ma zool.* bryozoan.

mściciel *mp*, **mścicielka** *f. Gen.pl.* -ek avenger; *lit.* nemesis.

mścić *ipf.* **mszczę mścisz**, -ij (= *wywierać zemstę*) revenge (*kogoś/coś* sb/sth); **mścić krzywdę/zbrodnię** avenge a wrong/a crime. ~ **się** *ipf.* **1.** avenge o.s. (*na kimś* on sb) avenge (*za coś* sth); revenge o.s. (*na kimś* on sb, *za coś* for sth); get *l.* take (one's) revenge; take vengeance (*na kimś* on sb, *za coś* for sth). **2.** (*o okolicznościach, czynach*) rebound (*na kimś* on *l.* upon sb); (*o wypowiedzianych słowach*) come home to roost.

mściwy *a.* revengeful, vindictive, vengeful, unforgiving.

mu *pron. zob.* **on**.

mucha *f.* **1.** *ent.* fly; **mucha domowa** housefly (*Musca domestica*); **mucha końska** horsefly, cleg, gadfly; **mucha tse-tse** tsetse fly (*Glossina*); **lep na muchy** flypaper; **packa na muchy** flyswatter, swatter; **pełen jajeczek** *l.* **larw much** fly-blown; **upstrzony przez muchy** flyspecked; **Władca Much** (= *Belzebub*) Lord of the Flies. **2.** **hiszpańska mucha** (*afrodyzjak*) Spanish fly. **3.** (*w wyrażeniach idiomatycznych*) **zachowuje się, jakby go mucha ugryzła** he's like a bear with a sore head; **mucha nie siada** everything's in apple-pie order; **on (nawet) muchy by nie skrzywdził** he wouldn't harm *l.* hurt a fly; **padać jak muchy** drop (off) like flies; **ruszać się jak mucha w smole** *pot.* move at a snail's pace. **4.** *wędkarstwo* **łowienie ryb na muchę** flyfishing; **sztuczna mucha** *ryb.* fly lure, doctor; (*z piór*) hackle; (*imitacja larwy muchy*) dunfly. **5.** (*krawat*) bow tie; **pod muchą** wearing a bow tie.

muchołapka *f. Gen.pl.* -ek flytrap.

muchołówka *f. Gen.pl.* -ek **1.** *bot.* flytrap, Venus'(s) fly-trap (*Dionaea muscipula*). **2.** *orn.* flycatcher (*Muscicapa*).

muchomor, muchomór *mi* -mor- *Gen.* -a *bot.* amanita (*Amanita*); *pot.* toadstool; **muchomor czerwony** fly agaric, red amanita (*A. muscaria*); **muchomor sromotnikowy** death cap (*A. phalloides*); **muchomor jadowity** destroying angel (*A. virosa*).

muchotrzew *mi bot.* spurry (*Spergularia*).

muchówka *f. Gen.pl.* -ek *ent.* (= *owad z rzędu Diptera*) dipteran, dipterous insect.

mucyna *f. biochem.* mucin.

muczeć *ipf.* -y moo, low.

mudżahedin *mp islam* mujaheddin, mujahedeen, mujahideen.

muezin, muezzin *mp islam* muezzin, crier.

mufa *f. techn.* pipe coupling, muff, coupler, sleeve; **mufa nuplowa redukcyjna** reducing coupling; **mufa kablowa** cable box, joint box; **mufa rozdzielcza** bifurcating box, branching box.

mufka *f. Gen.pl.* -ek **1.** *strój* muff. **2.** *techn.* coupling.

mufla *f. Gen.pl.* -i *techn.* (*pieca*) muffle.

muflon *ma zool.* mouflon (*Ovis musimon*).

muflowy *a. techn.*, *hutn.* muffle; **piec muflowy** muffle furnace.

mufti, mufty *mp islam* Mufti.

Mulat *mp*, **Mulatka** *f. Gen.pl.* **-ek** mulatto.

mulda *f. sport* **1.** mogul. **2.** *hutn.* charging pan, charging box.

mulica *f. zool.* she-mule; *zob.* **muł**.

mulina *f. tk.* embroidery floss.

mulisty *a.* muddy, sludgy, slimy, oozy.

multanka *f. Gen.pl.* **-ek** *gł. pl. muz.* Moldavian bagpipe.

multikino *n.* cineplex, multiplex.

multilateralny *a.* multilateral.

multimedialny *a.* multimedia; **komputer multimedialny** multimedia computer; **multimedialne pomoce naukowe** multimedia teaching aids.

multimilioner *mp*, **multimilionerka** *f. Gen.pl.* **-ek** multimillionaire.

multipleks *mi el.* multiplex.

multiplekser *mi el.* multiplexer, multiplexor; **multiplekser przekaźnikowy** relay multiplexer.

multiplikator *mi Gen.* **-a** *techn.* multiplier; **multiplikator ciśnienia hydraulicznego** hydraulic intensifier.

multiplikatywny *a. mat.* multiplicative.

multiwitamina *f. med.* multivitamin.

multum *n. indecl.* plenty, galore.

muł¹ *mi Gen.* **-u** (*szlam*) mud, ooze, sludge, slime, sullage; (*rzeczny*) sullage; **muł pokarbidowy** carbide residue; **muł rudny** ore pulp; **muł wapienny gęsty** lime paste.

muł² *ma Gen.* **-a** (= *krzyżówka klaczy z osłem*) mule; (= *potomek konia i oślicy*) hinny; **poganiacz mułów** muleteer; **uparty jak muł** (as) obstinate *l.* stubborn as a mule, mulish. – *mp Gen.* **-a** *pl.* **-y** *obelż.* idiot, ass; **ty mule!** you fool!; you silly ass!

mułła *mp Dat. i Loc.* **mulle** *pl.* **-owie** *islam* mullah, mulla.

mumia *f. Gen.* **-ii** mummy.

mumifikacja *f.* mummification.

mumifikować *ipf. t. przen.* mummify. **~ się** *ipf.* mummify, undergo mumification.

mundial *mi Gen.pl.* **-i** *l.* **-ów** *piłka nożna* (FIFA) World Cup.

mundur *mi* **1.** uniform; **mundur wojskowy/marynarski/policyjny** military/naval/police uniform; **mundur galowy** dress uniform; **mundur polowy** battledress, service uniform; **mundur pułkowy** *l.* pułku regiments; **mundur roboczy** fatigue dress. **2.** fatigues; **mundur z khaki** khakis, olive drab; **przywdziać mundur** (= *wstąpić do wojska*) join the army; **zrzucić mundur** (= *wyjść z wojska*) quit the service.

mundurek *mi* **-rk-** *Gen.* **-a** **1.** uniform; **mundurek szkolny** *szkoln.* school uniform; *zob.* **mundur. 2. ziemniaki w mundurkach** *kulin.* jacket potatoes.

mundurowy¹ *a.* uniform; **bluza mundurowa** tunic; **płaszcz mundurowy** greatcoat.

mundurowy² *mp* (*osoba*) uniformed person.

municypalny *a.* municipal; **policja municypalna** municipal police.

munsztuk *mi Gen.* **-a** *jeźdz.* curb, curb bit, curb chain.

mur *mi* **1.** *bud.* (*ściana*) wall; (*konstrukcja*) masonry; (*z cegieł*) brickwork; **mur ceglany/kamienny** brick/stone wall; **mur z kamienia ciosanego/łamanego** ashlar/rubble masonry; **mur suchy** dry wall, dry masonry; **mur obronny** defensive wall; **mur pruski** half-timbered wall; **mur szczelinowy** *l.* **podwójny** cavity wall; **mur chiński** the Great Wall of China; **odgradzać** *l.* **odseparowywać murem** wall (*sth*) off. **2.** *przen.* **budować mur wokół siebie** *l.* **otaczać się murem** *przen.* build a wall around o.s.; **na mur-beton** with one hundred per cent certainty; **przyparty do muru** with one's back against the wall; hard-pressed; **przypierać kogoś do muru** pin sb down, drive *l.* push sb to the wall, corner sb, force *l.* paint sb into a corner; **walić głową w mur** bang one's head against a brick wall; **stać za kimś murem** give unanimous support to sb. **3.** *pl.* (*przen.*) (= *miasto, domy*) the (town *l.* city) walls; **w murach (miasta)** in the (town) walls. **4.** *piłka nożna* wall.

murarka *f. pot.* **1.** bricklaying, masonry. **2.** *Gen.pl.* **-ek** *zob.* **murarz**.

murarski *a.* bricklayer's, mason's; **zaprawa murarska** mortar; **packa murarska** hawk, mortarboard; **plansza murarska** (*do rozrabiania zaprawy itp.*) banker; **mistrz murarski** master builder; **pomocnik murarski** hod-carrier, laborer.

murarstwo *n.* bricklaying, masonry.

murarz *mp* **1.** bricklayer, mason. **2.** *górn.* **murarz dołowy** waller.

murawa *f.* grass, the green, turf.

murek *mi* **-rk-** *Gen.* **-u** *l.* **-a** parapet, low wall.

murena *f. icht.* moray (*Muraena helena*).

murgrabia *mp Gen.* **-ego** *l.* **-i** *Dat.* **-emu** *l.* **-i** *Acc.* **-ego** *l.* **-ę** *Ins.* **-ą** *Loc.* **-i** *l.* **-im** *Voc.* **-o** *pl.* **-owie** *Gen.* **-ów** burgrave, burggrave.

murować *ipf.* **1.** build (in bricks/stone); mason (*sth*); lay bricks. **2.** *przen., krykiet, piłka nożna* stonewall.

murowany *a.* **1.** *bud.* brick, stone, made of brick/stone. **2.** *pot.* (= *pewny*) absolutely sure.

murszeć *ipf.* **-eję -ejesz** rot, decay.

murzyn *mp* **1. Murzyn** Black (person *l.* man); (= *Afrykanin*) African; Negro; **Murzyn amerykański** African American, Afro-American. **2.** *przen.* dark-skinned person; **opalić się na murzyna** get a deep tan. **3.** (= *nielegalny robotnik*) illegal worker; (= *wynajęty autor*) ghostwriter.

Murzynek *mp* **-nk-** *pl.* **-i** Black boy.

murzynek *mi* **-nk-** *Gen.* **-a** *kulin.* **1.** chocolate cake. **2.** *pot.* (*kawa*) black coffee with whipped cream.

Murzynka *f. Gen.pl.* **-ek** *zob.* **Murzyn**; Black woman, African woman; *przest. l. pog.* Negress.

murzyński *a.* Black, Negro; **murzyńskie pieśni religijne** *muz.* Negro spirituals.

mus¹ *mi* (= *przymus, konieczność*) necessity, must; **jak mus, to mus** needs must when the devil drives; **robić coś z musu** do sth out of necessity *l.* under constraint; **małżeństwo z musu** shotgun marriage.

mus² *mi* (*deser*) spumoni, mousse; (*owocowy ze śmietaną*) fool; **mus jabłkowy** applesauce; **mus czekoladowy/truskawkowy** chocolate/strawberry mousse.

musical *mi Gen.pl.* -i *l.* -ów musical (comedy).

musicalowy *a.* musical.

music-hall *mi Gen.pl.* -i *l.* -ów **1.** (*widowisko*) vaudeville; music hall. **2.** (*budynek*) music hall.

musieć *ipf.* **muszę musisz 1.** (*wyraża konieczność lub chęć*) have (got) to, must, need; **muszę iść do dentysty** (*wewnętrzny przymus, chęć*) I must go to the dentist; (*zewnętrzny przymus, np. ponieważ jestem umówiony*) I have to go to the dentist; **nie muszę iść do dentysty** I don't have to go to the dentist; I don't need to go to the dentist; I needn't go to the dentist; **będę musiał iść do dentysty** I'll have to go to the dentist; **musiałem tam iść** (*wewnętrzny lub zewnętrzny przymus*) I had to go there; (*zewnętrzny przymus*) I was forced *l.* compelled *l.* obliged to go there; **nie musiałem tam iść** I didn't have to go there; **muszę powiedzieć/przyznać/wyznać, że...** I must *l.* have to say/admit/confess (that)...; **nie musisz mi tego ciągle wypominać** *l.* **powtarzać** no need to rub it in; **on musi odejść** (*np. ze stanowiska*) he has to go; **czy muszę to zrobić?** must I do it?; do I have to do it?; (= *czy to konieczne*) need I do it?; **czy naprawdę musisz być taki okrutny?** do you have to be so cruel?; **czy muszę mówić więcej?** need I say more?; **to się musiało stać** it was bound to happen. **2.** (*coś jest nieuniknione*) **ona zawsze musi się martwić** she must always worry; **faceci muszą się wyszumieć** boys will be boys; **morderstwo musi wyjść na jaw** murder will out. **3.** (*wyraża prawdopodobieństwo*) **on musi być starszy od ciebie** he must be older than you; **musiała zajść jakaś pomyłka** there must be some mistake; **musiałem się pomylić** I must have made a mistake; **musiało mi się to przyśnić** *l.* **przywidzieć** I must have dreamt it. **4.** (= *nie móc się powstrzymać*) **musiałem spróbować** I couldn't help trying; I (just) had to try.

muskać *ipf.* **1.** (= *delikatnie dotykać*) skim, brush, graze. **2.** (= *głaskać*) stroke; (*pióra*) preen. **~ się** *ipf.* (= *dotykać się przelotnie*) **1.** brush, graze; **zderzaki naszych samochodów musnęły się** our car bumpers grazed. **2.** (*o ptaku*) preen (one's feathers).

muskularny *a.* athletic, muscular, brawny; **muskularne ramiona** beefy shoulders, brawny shoulders, hard-muscled shoulders.

muskulatura *f.* musculature.

muskuł *mi* muscle.

musli *n. indecl. kulin.* muesli.

musnąć *pf.* **musnę muśniesz, -ij** *zob.* **muskać.**

musować *ipf.* sparkle, fizz, effervesce.

mustang *ma* (*koń*) mustang.

mustrować *ipf. żegl.* take on, hire (*as a ship's crew member*).

mustyk *ma* **mustyki** *ent.* black flies (*Simuliidae*).

musujący *a.* sparkling, fizzy, effervescent; **wino musujące** sparkling wine; **tabletka musująca** effervescent tablet; **napój musujący** fizzy drink; *pot.* (soda) pop.

musze *f. zob.* **mucha.**

muszelka *f. Gen.pl.* -ek shell.

muszę *itd. ipf. zob.* **musieć.**

muszka *f. Gen.pl.* -ek **1.** (= *mała mucha*) (small) fly; **muszka owocowa** *ent.* fruit fly, drosophila, vinegar fly, pomace fly (*Drosophila*). **2.** (*krawat*) bow tie. **3.** (*celownicza*) sight; **trzymać kogoś na muszce** hold sb at gunpoint. **4.** (= *sztuczny pieprzyk na twarzy kobiety*) beauty spot, patch.

muszkatel *mi* **1.** (*wino*) muscatel. **2.** *bot.* (= *pelargonia*) pelargonium, geranium, stork's-bill (*Pelargonium*).

muszkatołowiec *ma bot.* nutmeg (*Myristica*).

muszkatołowy *a.* muscat, muscatel; **gałka muszkatołowa** nutmeg; **wino muszkatołowe** muscatel.

muszkiet *mi Gen.* -u *Loc.* -ecie *hist.* musket.

muszkieter *mp pl.* -rzy *l.* -owie *hist.* (= *żołnierz uzbrojony w muszkiet; żołnierz francuskiej gwardii królewskiej*) musketeer.

muszla *f. Gen.pl.* -i **1.** *zool.* shell. **2.** (*kształt*) shell; **muszla koncertowa** (concert) bowl; **muszla uszna** *anat.* auricular concha. **3.** bowl; **muszla klozetowa** toilet bowl; **muszla umywalki** (wash)bowl, (wash)basin.

muszlowaty *a.* shell-like.

muszlowy *a.* shell; shell-shaped.

musztarda *f. kulin.* mustard; **teraz to już musztarda po obiedzie** you're a day late and a dollar short.

musztardowy *a. kulin.* mustard; **sos musztardowy** mustard sauce; **gaz musztardowy** *chem., wojsk.* mustard gas.

musztardówka *f. Gen.pl.* -ek *pot.* glass (*mustard jar used chiefly as a vodka glass*).

musztra *f. wojsk.* drill.

musztrować *ipf. wojsk. t. przen.* drill.

muszy *a.* fly, of or pertaining to flies; **waga musza** *sport* flyweight.

muślin *mi tk.* muslin.

muślinowy *a. tk.* muslin; **muślinowy szal** muslin shawl.

mutacja *f.* **1.** (*głosu*) cracking of sb's voice, breaking of sb's voice; **przeszedł mutację w zeszłym roku** his voice cracked *l.* broke last year. **2.** (= *zmiana*) mutation, change, alteration. **3.** *biol.* mutation.

mutacyjny *a.* mutative, mutational.

mutagen *mi biol.* mutagen.

mutant *ma biol.* mutant.

mutować *ipf.* **1.** (*o głosie chłopięcym*) crack, break. **2.** *biol.* mutate.

mutualizm *mi biol.* mutualism.

muza *f.* **1.** *mit.* Muse. **2.** *lit.* (= *natchnienie*) muse, inspiration; **dziesiąta muza** cinema. **3.** *pot.* (= *muzyka*) music; **zapuść jakąś muzę** put on *l.* play some music.

muzealia *n. tylko pl. Gen.* -liów museum collections.

muzealnictwo *n.* museology.

muzealnik *mp* (= *specjalista w zakresie muze-*

alnictwa) museologist; (= *pracownik muzeum*) museum employee.

muzealny *a.* museum; **zbiory muzealne** museum collections; **eksponat muzealny** museum exhibit, museum piece; **wartość muzealna** historical value *l.* importance; **okaz muzealny** *iron.* museum piece, old fogey.

muzeum *n. sing. indecl. pl.* **-ea** *Gen.* **-eów** museum; **muzeum sztuki nowoczesnej** museum of modern art; **muzeum morskie** maritime museum; **muzeum historii naturalnej** natural history museum; **muzeum archeologiczne** archeological museum.

muzułmanin *mp pl.* **-anie** *Gen.* **-anów** *rel.* Muslim.

muzułmanka *f. Gen.pl.* **-ek** *zob.* **muzułmanin.**

muzułmański *a. rel.* Muslim.

muzycznie *adv.* musically; **muzycznie uzdolniona osoba** person gifted for music, musically gifted person.

muzyczny *a.* musical, music; **utwór muzyczny** piece of music, musical composition; **teatr muzyczny** music theatre; **ilustracja muzyczna** (= *muzyka do filmu, sztuki, słuchowiska, programu itp.*) score; **instrument muzyczny** musical instrument; **notacja muzyczna** musical notation; **szkoła muzyczna** school of music, music school; **słuch muzyczny** ear for music; **talent muzyczny** gift for music; **pamięć muzyczna** good memory for music.

muzyk *mp* (= *odtwórca utworów muzycznych*) musician; (= *kompozytor*) composer.

muzyka *f.* 1. *sztuka* music; **muzyka poważna** classical music; **muzyka rozrywkowa** pop music; **muzyka taneczna** dance music; **muzyka ludowa** folk music; **muzyka filmowa** movie music; (= *ścieżka dźwiękowa*) soundtrack, score; **muzyka kameralna** chamber music; **muzyka instrumentalna** instrumental music; **muzyka sfer** *fil.* music of the spheres; **kocia muzyka** *pot.* caterwauling. 2. *pot.* orchestra, band.

muzykalność *f.* 1. (= *uzdolnienie*) musicality, musicalness. 2. (= *melodyjność, śpiewność*) (*np. wiersza*) melodiousness.

muzykalny *a.* musical; **muzykalna rodzina** musical family.

muzykant *mp pot.* musician.

muzykolog *mp pl.* **-dzy** *l.* **-owie** musicologist.

muzykologia *f. Gen.* **-ii** musicology.

muzykologiczny *a.* musicological; **zbiory muzykologiczne** musicological collections; **badania muzykologiczne** musicological research.

muzykoterapia *f. Gen.* **-ii** musicotherapy.

muzykować *ipf.* perform music (*as an amateur l. amateurs*).

my *pron. Gen., Acc. i Loc.* **nas** *Dat.* **nam** *Ins.* **nami** we; **to my** it's us; **było nas pięcioro** there was five of us, we were five; **wpadnijcie do nas jutro** pop in tomorrow, drop by tomorrow, call on us tomorrow; **u nas w domu** in/at our house/ home/place; **My, Król...** We, the King...

mycie *n.* washing; **mycie naczyń** washing up; **maszyna do mycia naczyń** dishwasher.

mycka *f. Gen.pl.* **-ek** skullcap.

myć *ipf.* **-ję -jesz** (*ręce, twarz, talerz*) wash; (*okna, podłogę*) clean; (*zęby*) brush, clean; **ręka rękę myje** one hand washes the other, you scratch my back and I'll scratch yours. ~ **się** *ipf.* wash, wash up, have a wash.

mydelniczka *f. Gen.pl.* **-ek** soap dish.

mydlany *a.* soap, soapy; **płatki mydlane** soap flakes; **bańka mydlana** *t. przen.* soap bubble; **woda mydlana** soapy water; **opera mydlana** *telew., radio* soap opera.

mydlarnia *f. Gen.pl.* **-i** *l.* **-ń** *pot.* toiletry store.

mydlarski *a.* soap; **przemysł mydlarski** soap industry.

mydlarstwo *n.* soapworking, soap boiling.

mydlić *ipf.* soap; **mydlić komuś oczy** pull the wool over sb's eyes. ~ **się** *ipf.* 1. (*o człowieku*) soap o.s. 2. (*o mydle*) lather.

mydliny *pl. Gen.* **-n** suds.

mydlnica *f. Gen., Dat., Loc.* **-cy** *bot.* soapwort, bouncing Bet *l.* Bess (*Saponaria officinalis*).

mydłek *mp* **-łk-** *pl.* **-i** *pot., przest.* whippersnapper.

mydło *n. Gen.pl.* **-eł** 1. soap; **mydło toaletowe** toilet soap; **mydło w płynie** liquid soap; **kostka mydła** bar of soap; **włazić komuś w dupę bez mydła** *wulg.* kiss one's ass, suck up to sb, suck sb's hind tit; **wyjść na czymś jak Zabłocki na mydle** make a bad business of sth. 2. (= *kredka krawiecka*) French chalk. 3. *domino* blank.

mydłodrzew *ma Gen.* **-u** *bot.* soapbark (*Quillaja*).

myjka *f. Gen.pl.* **-ek** washcloth.

myjnia *f. Gen.pl.* **-i** (*samochodowa*) car wash; (*wagonów, maszyn itp.*) washing stand; **samochodowa myjnia automatyczna** automatic car wash.

mykeński *a. hist.* Mycen(a)ean; **kultura mykeńska** *archeol.* Mycenaean civilization.

mylić *ipf.* 1. (= *mieszać, plątać*) confuse, mix up. 2. (= *wprowadzać w błąd*) mislead; **pozory mylą** appearances are misleading, looks can be deceiving; **jeśli mnie oczy nie mylą** if my eyes do not deceive me; **jeśli pamięć mnie nie myli** if I remember it right *l.* correctly. ~ **się** *ipf.* 1. (= *popełniać błędy*) make mistakes, make errors. 2. (= *być w błędzie*) be wrong; **ciągle mylą mi się te nazwiska** I always mix up these names, I always confuse these names; **jeśli się nie mylę** if I am not wrong, unless I am mistaken; **grubo się mylisz** you are entirely wrong.

mylnie *adv.* mistakenly, wrongly, erroneously; **mylnie poinformować** misinform; **mylnie tłumaczyć** misinterpret; **mylnie zrozumieć** misunderstand.

mylny *a.* mistaken, erroneous; **mylny pogląd** misconception.

mysi *a.* mouse; **mysia nora** mouse hole; **mysi kolor** mouse-gray; **schowałbym się w mysią dziurę** I'd like to curl up and die; **mysi ogonek** *żart.* pigtail.

mysikrólik *ma orn.* goldcrest (*Regulus regulus*).

mysz *f.* 1. *zool.* mouse (*Mus musculus*); **biedny jak mysz kościelna** as poor as a church mouse;

siedzieć cicho jak mysz pod miotłą be as still as a mouse, lie low; **spocić się jak (ruda) mysz** be bathing in sweat; **myszy tańcują gdy kota nie czują** when the cat's away the mice will play. **2.** *komp.* mouse.

myszaty *a.* (*kolor*) mouse-gray.

myszka *f. Gen.pl.* **-ek 1.** (= *mała mysz*) (small) mouse; **bawić się z kimś w kotka i myszkę** play cat and mouse with sb; **chyba widzi białe myszki** he must be seeing things. **2.** (= *ciemne znamię*) mole, nevus. **3.** *przest.* (= *zapach starego wina*) aroma, bouquet; **trącić myszką** be out of date, be going gray.

myszkować *ipf.* ferret, poke about *l.* around.

myszołów *ma* **-o-** *orn.* buzzard (*Buteo*).

myśl *f.* **1.** thought, idea. **2.** (= *myślenie*) thinking; **to mi nawet przez myśl nie przeszło** it never occurred to me; **coś/ktoś komuś przywodzi na myśl kogoś/coś** sth/sb reminds sb of *l.* about sb/sth; **bądź dobrej myśli** hope for the best, think positive; **kogo/co masz na myśli?** who(m)/what do you mean?; **na myśl o tym robi mi się niedobrze** the very thought *l.* idea of it makes me sick; **często wracam myślą do tamtych dni** I often recall those days; **błądzić gdzieś myślami** be far away, fantasize about sth; **być pochłoniętym (jakąś) myślą** *l.* (jakimiś) myślami be absorbed in thought. **3.** (= *umysł*) mind; **przyszło mi na myśl, że...** it came to me that..., it came to my mind that..., it occurred to me that..., it crossed my mind that...; **nie mogę się pogodzić z myślą, że...** I cannot reconcile myself with the thought of... **4.** (= *pojęcie, sąd*) opinion, view; **czarne myśli** gloomy thoughts; **wymiana myśli** exchange of ideas *l.* views; **czytać komuś w myślach** read sb's mind; **muszę zebrać myśli** I need to concentrate; **złota myśl** aphorism; **w myśl tej zasady** according to this principle. **5.** (= *idea*) idea, concept; **błysnęła mi myśl, że...** it crossed my mind that...; **podzieliła się z nami swoimi myślami na temat...** she shared with us her ideas *l.* thoughts concerning *l.* on...; **myśl przewodnia** main *l.* central idea; **iść za czyjąś myślą** share sb's opinion; **genialna myśl** brilliant idea; **bić się z myślami** be of *l.* in two minds about sth; **wszystko idzie po mojej myśli** everything is going just as I planned; **nosić się z myślą kupna domu** consider *l.* contemplate buying a house; **podsunął mi świetną myśl** he gave me a great idea; **robimy wszystko z myślą o**

ludziach potrzebujących pomocy we do everything to help the needy.

myślący *a.* thinking, intelligent.

myśleć *ipf.* **-ę -isz 1.** (= *rozumować*) think, reason; **o czym myślisz?** what are you thinking about?; **co o tym myślisz** *l.* **sądzisz?** what do you think about it?; **myśleć rozsądnie** be sensible; **myśleć logicznie** think logically; **zawsze mówi to, co myśli** he always speaks his mind; **myśleć głośno** think aloud, think out loud; **niewiele myśląc** without much thought, not thinking much, on the spur of the moment; **i kto by pomyślał, że...** and who would have thought that...; **myśleć o niebieskich migdałach** *żart., iron.* daydream, indulge in daydreams. **2.** (= *troszczyć się o kogoś / coś*) think of, care for; **on myśli tylko o sobie** he thinks of nobody but himself; **muszę myśleć o przyszłości mojej rodziny** I must have the future of my family in mind, I have got to think of my family's future. **3.** (= *mieć zamiar coś zrobić*) intend, be going to, think of; **myślę o wycieczce do Hiszpanii w lipcu** I am thinking of going on a trip to Spain in *l.* this July; **ani myślę o wyjeździe do Warszawy** I have no intention to go to Warsaw, I am not going to go to Warsaw; **czy ty myślisz o niej poważnie?** are you serious about her?; **co ty sobie myślisz?!** what do you think you are doing?!; **myślę, że tak** I think so; **myślę, że nie** I don't think so.

myślenie *n.* thinking, reasoning; **logiczne myślenie** logical thinking; **myślenie abstrakcyjne** abstract thinking; **to daje dużo do myślenia** it makes one think, it gives one food for thought.

myśliciel *mp* thinker.

myślistwo *n.* hunting.

myśliwiec *mi* **-wc-** *Gen.* **-a** *lotn., wojsk.* fighter (plane). – *mp* **-wc-** *pl.* **-y** *lotn., wojsk.* (= *pilot myśliwca*) fighter pilot.

myśliwski *a.* hunting; **pies myśliwski** hunting dog; **tereny myśliwskie** hunting grounds; **karta myśliwska** hunting license; **samolot myśliwski** *lotn., wojsk.* fighter (plane).

myśliwy *mp* hunter.

myślnik *mi Gen.* **-a** hyphen, dash.

myślowy *a.* intellectual; thinking.

myto *n. hist.* toll.

mżawka *f. Gen.pl.* **-ek** drizzle.

mżyć *ipf.* drizzle; **mży** it's drizzling.

mżysty *a.* drizzly.

N, n *n. indecl.* (*litera*) N, n; **N jak Natalia** N is for November; N as in November.

N *abbr.* (*w kalendarzu*) = **niedziela**.

N. *abbr.* (*w skrótach nazw geograficznych*) = **Nowy**.

n. *abbr.* (*z nazwą rzeki*) = **nad**.

na *prep.* + *Loc.* **1.** (*miejsce*) on, at, in (*często nie tłumaczony jako przyimek*); **na stole** on the table; **na ścianie** on the wall; **na górze/na dole** up/down; at the top/bottom (*czegoś* of sth); (= *na piętrze/na parterze*) upstairs/downstairs; **na ulicy** on the street; *Br.* in the street; **na Siódmej Ulicy** on Seventh Street; *Br.* in Seventh Street; **na Pennsylvania Avenue pod numerem 10** *Br.* at 10 Pennsylvania Avenue; **na Alasce/Litwie** in Alaska/Lithuania; **na deszczu** (out) in the rain; **na dworze** (= *na zewnątrz*) outside, outdoors; **na koniu** on a horse, on horseback; **na korytarzu** in the corridor; **na palcu/głowie** on one's finger/head; **mieć mnóstwo spraw na głowie** *przen.* have a lot on one's mind *l.* shoulders; **na początku/końcu czegoś** at the beginning/end of sth; **na polu** in the field; **na uniwersytecie/poczcie** at the university/post office; **na zachodzie** in the west. **2.** (*sytuacja*) **gdybym był na twoim miejscu** if I were you, if I were in your shoes. **3.** (= *podczas*) at, during, on; **na zebraniu/koncercie** at a meeting/concert; **na wakacjach** on vacation; *Br.* on holiday; **na wycieczce** on a trip *l.* excursion; **spędzać czas na czytaniu** spend one's time reading. **4.** (*środek lokomocji*) **jechać na koniu** ride (on) a horse; **jeździć na nartach** ski, go skiing; **jeździć na rowerze** ride (on) a bicycle, ride a bike. **5.** (*ruch lub pozycja ciała*) on; **chodzić na rękach** walk on one's hands; **leżeć na boku** lie on one's side; **na nogach** (*t. przen.* = *w dobrej kondycji*) on one's feet. **6.** (*instrument*) on; **grać na skrzypcach/fortepianie** play the violin/piano; **grać melodię na fortepianie** play a tune on the piano. **7.** (*narzędzie*) **pisać na maszynie** type, typewrite; **robić na drutach** knit. **8.** (*precyzowanie znaczenia rzeczownika*) **buty na wysokich obcasach** high-heeled shoes; **ciasto na drożdżach** yeast dough; **nalewka na wiśniach** cherry liqueur; **koń na biegunach** rocking horse. **9.** (*po czasownikach l. przymiotnikach*) **oszczędzać na czymś** economize on sth; **wprawiać się na czymś** cut one's teeth on sth; **wychowany na czymś** brought up *l.* raised on sth. – *prep.* + *Acc.* **1.** (*kierunek l. cel*) to, toward(s), on, upon (*często nie tłumaczony jako przyimek*); **na Alaskę/Litwę** to Alaska/Lithuania; **na stolicę** (*o celu marszu, operacji wojskowej*) toward *l.* on the capital; **na górę/na dół** up/down; (*po schodach*) upstairs/downstairs; **na pocztę/dworzec kolejowy** to the post office/railroad station; **na ulicę** (out) into the street; **na zachód** west, westward(s); **wyjść na ulicę** (*euf.* = *zacząć uprawiać prostytucję*) go on the streets. **2.** (*po czasownikach l. przymiotnikach*) **chory na głowę** (*pot.* = *szalony*) sick in the head, brainsick; **chorować l. cierpieć na coś** suffer from sth; **cieszyć się na coś** look forward to sth; **krzyczeć na kogoś** shout at sb; **patrzeć na kogoś/coś** look at sb/sth; **zanosi się na deszcz** it's going to rain; **zły na kogoś/coś** angry at/with sb/sth. **3.** (*stan*) **postawić kogoś na nogi** *przen.* put sb on their feet (again). **4.** (*okres*) for; **na chwilę** for a moment, for a while; **na miesiąc** for a month. **5.** (*termin, wyznaczony czas*) (**dokładnie**) **na czas** (right) on time; **obiad będzie na piątą** dinner will be (ready) at five; **umówić się na środę** agree to meet on Wednesday, schedule an appointment for Wednesday; **wracam na Wielkanoc** I'll be back *l.* returning for Easter; **zrobię to na jutro** I'll do it for tomorrow. **6.** (*napęd, zasilanie*) **silnik na benzynę** gasoline engine; **zegar na baterię** battery-powered clock. **7.** (*przeznaczenie*) **kosz na śmieci** waste-paper basket; **materiał na sukienkę** dress material; **koncert na fortepian** *muz.* piano concerto; **skrzynka na listy** mailbox; *Br.* letter-box. **8.** (*sposób*) with, by; **walczyć na miecze** fight with swords; **kupować na raty** buy on installments; **kupować/sprzedawać na sztuki** buy/sell by the piece. **9.** (*miara*) **100 kilometrów na godzinę** a hundred kilometers an hour/per hour; **szeroki na dwa metry** two meters wide; **raz na rok** once a year. **10.** (*przyczyna, bodziec*) on, upon, at, to; **co ty na to?** what do you say?, what would you say to that?; **na żądanie** on demand; **na czyjąś prośbę/czyjś rozkaz** on *l.* at sb's request/order; **na widok kogoś/czegoś** at the sight of sb/sth; **na wieść o wypadku** upon the news of the accident; **odpowiedzieć na pytanie** answer a question. **11.** (*podział*) into, in; **drzeć coś na kawałki** tear sth into *l.* to pieces; **dzielenie włosa na czworo** *przen.* hair-splitting; **dzielić/łamać/składać coś na pół** divide/break/fold sth in half. **12.** (*dzielenie liczb*) **sto na dziesięć** one hundred (divided) by ten. **13.** (*wymiary*) **pięć na dziesięć cali** five by ten inches. **14.** (*cel*) to, for, into; **być przyjętym na (Uniwersytet) Yale** be accepted at *l.* by Yale (University); **dostać się na wydział chemii** get into the chemistry department; **iść na przyjęcie/zebranie** go to a party/

meeting; **iść na ryby** go fishing; **iść na spacer** go for a walk; **jechać na wycieczkę** go on an excursion; **wyskoczyć na miasto** go out, go into town. **15.** (*w utartych zwrotach*) **na dobitkę** to crown it all, to top it (all) off, on top of all that; **na domiar złego** to make matters worse; **na przykład** for example, for instance; **jak na złość** ironically; **na zakończenie** finally; **na złamanie karku** at breakneck speed *l.* pace, helter-skelter. **16.** (*w równoważnikach zdań*) **na pomoc!** help!; **na koń!** mount up!; **na zdrowie!** (*toast*) cheers!; (*odpowiedź na kichnięcie*) bless you! – *prep. z przysłówkami, przymiotnikami i wyrazami nieodmiennymi* **1.** (*z nazwami kolorów*) **pomalować coś na biało** paint sth white. **2.** (*okres*) for; **na długo/krótko** for a long/short time; **na zawsze** forever. **3.** (*sposób*) **na czczo** on an empty stomach; **na leżąco** lying (down), reclining, prone; **jajko na twardo** hard-boiled egg; **na wznak** on the back. **4.** (*relacje przestrzenne*) **na zewnątrz** (*czegoś*) outside (sth); **na wprost** (straight) on *l.* ahead; (= *naprzeciw*) opposite; **na zachód/lewo** (*o położeniu*) to the west/left (*od czegoś* of sth). **5.** (*w utartych zwrotach*) **wszystko na nic/na próżno** (it's) all for nothing/in vain.

nabab *mp pl.* **-owie** *hist. l. żart.* (= *bogacz*) nabob.

nabajać *pf. zob.* **bajać**.

nabajdurzyć *pf. zob.* **bajdurzyć**.

na bakier *adv.* **1.** (*o nakryciu głowy*) askew. **2.** *pot.* (= *w złych stosunkach*) on bad terms, at odds (*z kimś* with sb); **jestem na bakier z chemią** chemistry is not my game *l.* not exactly up my alley; **być na bakier z prawem** be in trouble with the law.

nabałaganić *pf.* make a mess.

nabarłożyć *pf. pot.* = **nabałaganić**.

nabawiać się *ipf.*, **nabawić się** *pf.* + *Gen.* (*choroby*) contract, catch, get; **nabawić się kłopotów** get into trouble.

nabazgrać *pf. zob.* **bazgrać**.

nabiał *mi tylko sing.* dairy produce and eggs.

nabiałowy *a.* **sklep nabiałowy** dairy store.

nabić *pf.* **-biję -bijesz 1.** *zob.* **nabijać**. **2.** *rzad.* (= *zbić*) beat up, thrash; **nabić sobie/komuś guza** get/give sb a bump (on the head).

nabiec *pf.* **-gnę -gniesz, -gnij, -gł** *zob.* **nabiegać**.

nabiedzić się *pf. pot.* take (great) pains (*nad czymś* over sth, *z kimś / czymś* with sb/sth); have a devil of a time *l.* job (*robiąc coś* with sth).

nabiegać *ipf.* **1.** (= *nabrzmiewać*) swell (*czymś* with sth); **nabiegać krwią** *pat.* engorge with blood. **2.** **nabiegać komuś do oczu** (*o łzach*) well up in sb's eyes. **3.** *lit.* **nabiegać przerażeniem/gniewem** (*o oczach*) flash terror/anger; **nabiegać rumieńcem ze wstydu/zażenowania** (*o twarzy, policzkach*) flush with shame/embarrassment. **~ się** *pf.* **1.** (= *biegać do woli*) have a (good) run. **2.** *pot.* = **nachodzić się**.

nabiegły *a.* (= *nabrzmiały*) swollen (*czymś* with sth); **nabiegły krwią** (*o oczach*) bloodshot (*wskutek czegoś* from sth).

nabieracz *mp pot.* (= *naciągacz, oszust*) trickster, con man, con artist.

nabierać *ipf.* **1.** (*t.* = *wdychać*) take in; (= *zagarniać, czerpać*) pick up, scoop up; (*łyżką*) spoon up; (= *wchłaniać*) absorb, take up; (= *wciągać*) draw in; **nabierać na widelec** *l.* widły fork; **nabierać oczka** (*robótki*) pick up stitches; **nabierać tchu** breathe in, inhale; **nabierać wody** *żegl.* (*o statku*) take in water; **nabierać wody w usta** *przen.* keep mum, hold one's tongue; *pot.* clam up. **2.** (= *zdobywać więcej, uzyskiwać*) gain, gather; **nabierać ciała** gain weight; **nabierać kształtu** take shape; **nabierać przekonania/pewności** grow convinced/certain; **nabierać rozgłosu** gain fame; **nabierać rumieńców** (*o człowieku*) get more color; *przen.* (*o dyskusji itp.*) warm up; **nabierać sił/rozumu/doświadczenia** gain strength/wisdom/experience; **nabierać szybkości/rozpędu** *t. przen.* gather *l.* gain speed/momentum; **nabierać wysokości** *lotn.* gain altitude *l.* height, climb; **nabierać znaczenia/wartości** grow in importance/value. **3.** *pot.* (= *oszukiwać*) take (sb) in, dupe, fool, trick. **~ się** *ipf.* (= *dawać się wprowadzić w błąd*) be duped *l.* fooled, be had; **nabierać się na coś** fall for sth.

nabieżnik *mi Gen.* **-a** *żegl.* leading marks.

nabijać *ipf.* **1.** (= *napychać*) pack, cram, stuff; (= *napełniać*) fill (*czymś* with sth); (*broń*) load; **nabijać fajkę** fill one's pipe; **nabijać sobie/komuś kabzę** line one's/sb's pocket; **nabijać sobie/komuś głowę czymś** put sth into one's/sb's head; **nabijać kogoś w butelkę** *pot.* (= *oszukiwać*) make a fool of sb, play sb for a fool, put sb on. **2.** (= *ozdabiać, wysadzać*) stud (*czymś* with sth). **3.** (= *nadziewać*) skewer, transfix (*na coś* with *l.* on sth); (*t. jako sposób egzekucji*) impale (*na coś* on *l.* upon sth). **4.** (= *mocować, nasadzać*) fasten, mount, fix (*na coś* on *l.* upon sth). **~ się** *ipf.* **1.** (= *nadziewać się*) become *l.* get impaled (*na coś* on *l.* upon sth). **2.** **nabijać się z kogoś/czegoś** *pot., uj.* jeer *l.* mock (at) sb/sth.

nabiodrek *mi* **-drk-** *Gen.* **-a** *broń, hist.* cuisse.

nabity *a.* **1.** *pot.* (= *przepełniony*) packed, crammed, stuffed (*kimś / czymś* with sb/sth); (= *zatłoczony*) overcrowded. **2.** (*o broni*) loaded (*czymś* with sth). **3.** (*o mięśniach itp.*) lumpy; (*o policzkach itp.*) fleshy; (= *krępy*) heavy-set, stout.

nabla *f. mat.* del, nabla.

nabluzgać *pf.* + *Dat.* curse loudly at (sb), heap obscenities on (sb).

nabłocić *pf.* track mud.

nabłonek *mi* **-nk-** *Gen.* **-a 1.** *anat.* epithelium; **nabłonek cylindryczny/płaski** columnar/squamous epithelium. **2.** (*bot.* = *kutykula*) cuticle.

nabłoniak *mi Gen.* **-a** *pat.* epithelioma.

nabłonkowy *a.* **1.** *anat.* epithelial. **2.** *bot.* cuticular.

nabłyszczać *ipf.* gloss, polish, buff; *tk.* (*t. skórę*) glaze.

nabłyszczarka *f. Gen.pl.* **-ek** *techn.* glazing machine.

nabłyszczyć *pf. zob.* **nabłyszczać**.

naboczny *a.* **linia naboczna** (*t.* **linia boczna**) *icht., anat.* lateral line.

nabojowy *a. broń* **komora nabojowa** cartridge chamber, gun chamber.

na bok *adv.* aside; (= *z drogi*) out of the way, away; **odłożyć na bok** *t. przen.* put (*sth*) to one side *l.* aside, set (*sth*) aside; **żarty na bok** (= *mówiąc serio*) (all) joking *l.* kidding aside; *Br.* joking apart.

na bosaka *adv.* (*pot.* = *boso*) barefoot, barefooted.

nabożeństwo *n.* **1.** *kośc.* liturgy, office, (church) service; **książeczka do nabożeństwa** prayer book, church-book; **odprawiać nabożeństwo** conduct a service, celebrate a liturgy, say office; **nabożeństwo za zmarłych** service for the dead. **2.** (= *cześć, uwielbienie*) reverence, veneration; (= *powaga*) solemnity; **odnosić się z nabożeństwem do kogoś/czegoś** treat sb/sth with reverence, revere sb/sth.

nabożnisia *f.*, **nabożniś** *mp pog.* bigot, pietist.

nabożny *a.* (= *pobożny*) pious; (= *poważny*) devout, sincere; **nabożny lęk** *l.* **nabożna cześć** awe; **pełen nabożnego lęku** awed; **słuchać w nabożnym skupieniu** *przen.* listen with devout attention.

nabój *mi* **-o-** *Gen.pl.* **-oi** *l.* **-ojów** **1.** (= *jednostka amunicji*) round (of ammunition), cartridge; **pas z nabojami** cartridge belt; (*noszony przez ramię*) bandoleer; **ostry nabój** live round; **ślepy nabój** blank (cartridge), dummy round. **2.** (= *ładunek; hutn.* = *wsad*) charge.

nabór *mi* **-o-** recruitment.

nabrać (się) *pf.* **-biorę -bierzesz** *zob.* **nabierać (się)**.

nabroić *pf.* **-ój** *pot.* get into mischief.

nabrudzić *pf.* make a mess, scatter dirt all over the place.

nabrzeże *n. Gen.pl.* **-y** **1.** *żegl.* wharf, berth, jetty, quay; **cumować coś do nabrzeża** dock sth; **nabrzeże przeładunkowe/rozładunkowe** loading/discharging berth. **2.** *rzad.* = **nadbrzeże** 1.

nabrzeżny *a.* **1.** *żegl.* dockside, quayside. **2.** = **nadbrzeżny**.

nabrzmiałość *f.* swelling; *form.* distention, tumescence; *pat.* intumescence.

nabrzmiały *a.* **1.** (= *spuchnięty, powiększony*) swollen; *form.* distended, tumescent. **2.** *przen.* (= *ciężki, brzemienny*) pregnant (*czymś* with sth); (*o problemie, konflikcie*) acute, severe.

nabrzmieć *pf.* **-eję -ejesz**, **nabrzmiewać** *ipf.* swell (*czymś* with sth); *form.* distend; *pat.* intumesce.

nabujać *pf.* **1.** + *Acc.* (*pot.* = *okłamać, oszukać*) dupe. **2.** + *Dat.* (= *naopowiadać kłamstw*) tell lies to (*sb*); **nabujać komuś ile wlezie** take sb for a ride; *sl.* bullshit sb.

naburmuszać się *ipf.* pout, sulk, bristle, get moody.

naburmuszony *a. pot.* sulky, moody.

naburmuszyć się *pf. zob.* **naburmuszać się**.

nabuzować się *pf. sl.* = **nachlać się**.

nabuzowany *a. sl.* **1.** (= *wzburzony, odurzony narkotykiem*) lit, stoned, high, doped up. **2.** (= *pijany*) blind drunk, tanked, wasted; *Br.* sloshed, pissed.

nabycie *n.* acquisition; *form.* (= *kupno*) purchase; **do nabycia** obtainable.

nabyć *pf.* **-będę -będziesz, -bądź** *zob.* **nabywać**.

nabytek *mi* **-tk-** (= *osoba l. rzecz pozyskana*) acquisition; *form.* accession; (= *zakup*) purchase.

nabyty *a.* **1.** acquired; **cecha nabyta** *biol.* acquired trait; **nabyty zespół zaniku odporności** *pat.* (= *AIDS*) acquired immune deficiency syndrome; **odporność nabyta** *fizj.* acquired immunity. **2.** *form.* (= *kupiony*) purchased, obtained.

nabywać *ipf.* **-am -asz** **1.** *form.* (= *kupować*) purchase, obtain. **2.** (= *uzyskiwać*) acquire; **nabywać wiedzy/biegłości** acquire knowledge/proficiency; **nabywać prawa** *l.* **prawo do czegoś** acquire a right to sth.

nabywca *mp form.* purchaser, buyer; *prawn.* vendee.

nabywczy *a.* **siła nabywcza** *ekon.* purchasing power.

nabywczyni *f. form. zob.* **nabywca**.

nabzdyczać się *ipf.*, **nabzdyczyć się** *pf. sl.* = **naburmuszać się**.

nacechowany *a.* **1.** characterized (*czymś* by sth). **2.** *jęz.* marked. **3.** *rzad.* (= *oznakowany*) stamped (*czymś* with sth).

nachalny *a. emf.* pesky, pushy, pestering.

nachapać się *pf.* **-ię -iesz** *pot., zw. uj.* **1.** (= *wzbogacić się*) hit the jackpot, make a pile. **2.** + *Gen.* (= *nagromadzić do woli*) heap up.

nachlać się *pf.* **-eję -ejesz** *pot.* **1.** (= *spić się*) get wasted *l.* tanked, booze it up, hit the bottle. **2.** (= *wypić za dużo*) drink too much (*czegoś* of sth).

nachlapać *pf.* **-ię -iesz** splash water about; + *Dat.* slop (*sth*) all over the place.

nachmurzyć *pf.* **nachmurzyć twarz** *l.* **czoło** = **nachmurzyć się** 1. **~ się** *pf.* **1.** (*o człowieku*) frown, scowl; *lit.* lour, lower. **2.** (*o twarzy*) cloud over.

nachodzić *ipf.* **1.** (= *odwiedzać bez zaproszenia*) intrude on *l.* upon (*sb*); *form.* make incursions into *l.* upon sb's leisure time; *przen.* (*o uczuciach, nastrojach* = *opanowywać*) come over (*sb*); *przen.* (= *przychodzić do głowy*) occur to (*sb*). **2.** *lit.* (= *atakować, napadać*) overcome, raid, make incursions *l.* inroads into (*sth*). **~ się** *pf.* walk one's legs off, run o.s. ragged, run all over town (*za czymś* looking for sth).

nachorować się *pf.* suffer from (chronic *l.* lasting) illness.

nachwalić się *pf.* **nie móc się nachwalić kogoś/czegoś** extoll sb/sth, praise sb/sth to the skies; **nie mogę się (dość) nachwalić ich gościnności** I just can't praise their hospitality enough.

na chybcika *adv. pot.* in a rush, hastily; **robota na chybcika** rush job.

nachylać *ipf.* bend (down), incline; (*głowę*) bow (down). **~ się** *ipf.* lean (over), bend down; (*t. o linii, powierzchni*) incline, tilt, slant.

nachylenie *n.* inclination, tilt, slant; (= *przechył*) list; (*terenu, drogi*) gradient; (*dachu*) pitch; (*ściany*) *bud.* batter; (*greenu*) *golf* borrow; **pod nachyleniem** at *l.* on a tilt, at a pitch *l.* slant.

nachylić (się) *pf. zob.* **nachylać (się)**.

nachylony *a.* bent, inclined, sloping.

naciąć *pf.* **-tnę -tniesz, -tnij** **1.** *zob.* **nacinać. 2.** (= *ściąć dużo*) cut down. **3.** *pot.* (= *okpić, oszukać*) **naciąć kogoś na duże pieniądze** trick sb out of a lot of money. **~ się** *pf.* **1.** (= *oszukać się*) trick o.s. (*na czymś* at sth). **2.** (= *natknąć się*) stumble (*na kogoś/coś* on *l.* upon sb/sth); (*o przeciwniku*) find *l.* meet one's match (*na kogoś* in sb).

naciąg *mi* **1.** (= *naprężenie*) tension, pull. **2.** *sport, muz.* (*rakiety tenisowej, instrumentu*) stringing. **3.** *techn.* (*w zegarku*) winding mechanism, remontoir.

naciągacz *mp*, **naciągaczka** *f. Gen.pl.* **-ek** *pot.* swindler, cheat, con artist, hustler.

naciągać *ipf.* **1.** (= *naprężać, napinać*) stretch, tighten (up), draw tight, tauten; (= *rozciągać niebezpiecznie*) strain, stretch to the limit, extend; (*cięciwę*) pull back, draw; **naciągać mięsień** *pat.* strain *l.* pull a muscle; **naciągać fakty/przepisy** *przen.* stretch the truth/the regulations. **2.** (= *zakładać, nasuwać*) pull on. **3.** (*pokrowiec, koc*) pull up, draw up (*na coś* over sth). **4.** *pot.* **naciągać kogoś na coś** (= *wyłudzać coś od kogoś*) wheedle *l.* coax sth out of sb; (= *namówić kogoś na zrobienie czegoś*) cajole *l.* badger sb into doing sth. **5.** (*o herbacie, ziołach*) brew, infuse, draw. **~ się** *ipf.* tighten (up), stretch.

naciągany *a. pot.* (= *nierzetelny, sztuczny*) farfetched, strained.

naciągnąć *pf.* **-ij** **1.** *zob.* **naciągać. 2.** (= *naczerpać, ciągnąć*) draw. **~ się** *pf. zob.* **naciągać się.**

naciec *v.* **-knę -kniesz, -knij** *zob.* **naciekać.**

naciek *mi* **1.** accumulation; *geol.* deposit, encrustation; (= *stalaktyt l. stalagmit*) dripstone. **2.** *pat.* infiltration.

naciekać *ipf.* **1.** (= *gromadzić się wskutek ściekania*) collect (*do czegoś* in sth). **2.** *med.* infiltrate.

naciekły *a.* (= *nabrzmiały*) swollen (*czymś* with sth).

nacieknąć *pf.* = **naciec.**

naciekowy *a.* **1.** *med.* infiltrative. **2.** *geol.* encrustant.

nacierać[1] *ipf.* (= *trzeć*) rub; (= *masować*) massage; *med.* embrocate (*czymś* with sth).

nacierać[2] *ipf.* (= *ruszać do ataku*) charge (*na kogoś/coś* at sb/sth); (*kopią; t. przen. piórem l. słownie*) tilt (*na kogoś* at sb). **~ się** *ipf.* rub (o.s.) down (*czymś* with sth).

nacierpieć się *pf.* **-ię -isz** suffer (much).

nacieszyć się *pf.* (*kimś*) have (*sb*) for o.s.; (*czymś*) enjoy (*sth*) to the full *l.* to one's heart's content.

nacięcie *n.* **1.** (= *rowek, wgłębienie*) notch, nick, score; (*piłą*) kerf; *zwł. chir.* (*t.* = *czynność cięcia*) incision. **2.** **nacięcie pilnika** *techn.* file cut.

nacinać *ipf.* **1.** (*ciało, gwint, zęby pilnika*) cut; (= *karbować*) notch, nick; *chir.* incise; (*mięso, rybę*) *kulin.* crimp. **2.** *pot.* (= *oszukiwać*) *zob.* **naciąć.**

nacios *n.* *leśn.* blaze.

naciowy *a.* *ogr., kulin.* **pietruszka naciowa** green parsley; **seler naciowy** (stalk) celery.

nacisk *mi* **1.** (= *napór, ciśnienie, presja*) pressure; *techn.* thrust; **nacisk boczny/wzdłużny** side/axial thrust; **grupa nacisku** pressure group; **reagować na naciski** respond to pressure; **pod naciskiem** under pressure (*kogoś/czegoś* from sb/sth); **ulegać naciskowi** yield to pressure; **wywierać na kogoś nacisk** bring pressure to bear on sb, put sb under pressure, put pressure on sb (*żeby coś zrobił* to do sth). **2.** (= *akcent*) stress, emphasis; **kłaść nacisk na coś** emphasize *l.* stress sth, lay stress on sth, put/lay/place emphasis on sth; **nacisk położony jest na coś** the emphasis is on sth; **z naciskiem** emphatically.

naciskać *ipf.*, **nacisnąć** *pf.* **-śnij** (= *atakować, nalegać, wywierać presję, t. przen.*) press (*na kogoś* sb, *w sprawie czegoś* for sth); (*pedał, przycisk, spust itp.*) push, press (down *l.* in), squeeze; **naciskać czapkę/kapelusz na uszy** *pot.* ram one's cap/hat on one's head.

naciułać *pf.* (*czegoś*) *pot.* save (*sth*) up.

nacja *f. Gen.pl.* **-ji** *rzad.* **-yj** nation.

nacjonalista *mp*, **nacjonalistka** *f. Gen.pl.* **-ek** nationalist.

nacjonalistyczny *a.* nationalist, nationalistic.

nacjonalizacja *f.* nationalization.

nacjonalizacyjny *a.* concerned with nationalization.

nacjonalizm *mi* nationalism.

nacjonalizować *ipf.* nationalize.

naczekać się *pf.* spend a long time waiting (*na kogoś/coś* for sb/sth).

na czele *adv. i prep.* + *Gen.* at the head (of); **stać** *l.* **iść na czele czegoś** head sth.

naczelna *f. zob.* **naczelny.**

naczelne *pl. zool.* (*rząd ssaków*) primates (*Primates*).

naczelniczka *f. Gen.pl* **-ek** *pot. zob.* **naczelnik; naczelniczka poczty** postmistress.

naczelnik *mp* **1.** (= *zarządca, kierownik; form. t. o kobiecie*) head, manager; **naczelnik policji** chief of police; **naczelnik poczty** postmaster; **naczelnik stacji** *kol.* stationmaster, station manager; **naczelnik więzienia** prison governor. **2.** *hist.* (= *dowódca powstania*) (insurrection) leader.

naczelny *a.* **1.** (= *kierujący, główny*) chief, head; **dyrektor naczelny** chief executive; **redaktor naczelny** *dzienn.* chief editor, editor in chief; **wódz naczelny** *wojsk.* commander in chief. **2.** (= *najważniejszy*) (*hasło, zadanie*) main, chief, principal; **na naczelnym miejscu** first and foremost. **3.** **ssak naczelny** *zool.* primate. – *mp* **-ego** *pot.* (= *dyrektor naczelny, szef*) boss.

naczepa *f. mot.* semitrailer.

naczerpać *pf.* **-ię -iesz, naczerpywać** *ipf.* (*czegoś*) scoop (*sth*) up.

naczółek *mi* **-łk-** *Gen.* **-a** (*dachu*) *bud.* jerkin head.

na czworakach *adv.* on all fours.

naczyniak *mi Gen.* **-a** *pat.* angioma, hemangioma; **naczyniak limfatyczny** lymphangioma.

naczynie *n.* **1.** (= *talerz, miska itp.*) dish; *form.* vessel; **naczynia (kuchenne)** the dishes; **naczynie liturgiczne** *rel.* liturgical vessel; **zmywać naczynia** wash up, wash the dishes. **2.** *anat.* (*t. bot.*)

vessel; **naczynie krwionośne/limfatyczne** blood/lymphatic vessel; **naczynie wieńcowe** coronary artery. **3.** *bot.* trachea.

naczyniowy *a. anat., bot.* vascular; **rośliny naczyniowe** *bot.* vascular plants; **tkanka naczyniowa** *bot.* vascular tissue; **układ naczyniowy** *anat.* vascular system; **naczyniowa choroba wiązów** *bot., pat.* Dutch elm disease; **zapaść naczyniowa** *pat.* circulatory collapse.

naczyniówka *f. Gen.pl.* **-ek** *anat.* choroid.

naczytać się *pf.* **1.** + *Gen.* read a lot of (*sth*). **2.** (= *znużyć się czytaniem*) be tired of reading.

nać *f.* tops, leaves.

naćpać się *pf. pot.* stuff *l.* gorge o.s., feed one's face (*czymś l. czegoś* with sth); *pog.* pig out.

naćpany *a. pot.* (stuffed) full (*czymś* of sth); *sl.* (= *odurzony narkotykiem*) high (*czymś* on sth).

nad *prep.* + *Ins.* **1.** (= *powyżej, ponad*) above, over; **nad głową** (= *w górze*) overhead. **2.** (= *na brzegu l. krawędzi, blisko*) **nad (samą) granicą** at the (very) border, near the border; **nad grobem** at the graveside; *przen.* (= *blisko śmierci*) at death's door, with one foot in the grave; **nad morzem** at the seaside, on the sea; **nad rzeką/jeziorem** on the river/lake; **Waszyngton leży nad Potomakiem** Washington lies *l.* is located on the Potomac River; **nad przepaścią** *t. przen.* on the edge of a precipice; **nad ranem** in the early morning. **3.** (*przedmiot uwagi l. kontroli*) **litować się nad kimś** feel pity for sb; (= *okazywać komuś miłosierdzie*) have *l.* take pity on sb; **mieć przewagę nad kimś** have the advantage on *l.* over sb, have the upper hand over sb; **opieka nad dziećmi** child care; **pastwić się nad kimś** torment sb; **płakać nad czymś** cry over sth; **rozpaczać nad kimś/czymś** lament for sb/sth; **sprawować władzę nad kimś/czymś** rule sb/sth; *form.* have/hold dominion over sb/sth; **stracić panowanie nad sobą** lose one's temper; *pot.* blow one's top, blow a gasket, hit the ceiling. **4.** (*temat rozważań l. dyskusji*) **debata nad ustawą/wnioskiem** debate on a bill/motion; **zastanawiać się nad czymś** consider sth, pause over sth. **5.** (*cel badań l. wysiłków*) **pracować nad czymś** work on sth. **6.** *lit.* (*podkreślenie wyjątkowości; często z archaiczną formą narzędnika*) **mistrz nad mistrzami** *l.* **nad mistrze** master of *l.* over masters; **Pieśń nad Pieśniami** *Bibl.* the Song of Songs. – *prep.* + *Acc.* **1.** (*cel w przestrzeni*) over, above; **nad głowę** above one's head; (= *w górę*) up; **nad miasto** over the town *l.* city. **2.** (= *na brzeg*) **nad jezioro/morze/rzekę** to the lake/sea/river. **3.** *lit.* (*porównanie lub wybór*) than, above; **cenić coś nad życie** value sth above life; **cóż jest (lepszego) nad wino?** what (is) better than wine?; **nade wszystko** above all.

nadać (się) *pf.* **1.** *zob.* **nadawać (się)**. **2.** *pot.* **diabli nadali!** damn!, the hell with it!; **diabli nadali taką robotę** to hell with such a job; **kogo tam diabli nadali?** who the hell is that?

nadajnik *mi* **-a** *tel.* transmitter; **nadajnik radiowy/telewizyjny** radio/television transmitter; **nadajnik-odbiornik** transceiver.

nadal *adv.* still; **grać/mówić/żyć nadal** play/talk/live on.

nadanie *n.* (*czynność*) conferral, conferment, bestowal; (= *akt obdarowania*) grant, investiture; **nadanie praw/przywilejów** (*dokument*) charter of rights/privileges; **nadanie praw miejskich** incorporation; **nadanie ziemi** grant of land.

nadaremnie, nadaremno *adv.* in vain, vainly, futilely.

nadaremny *a.* futile, vain.

na darmo *adv.* = **nadaremnie**.

nadarzać *ipf.*, **nadarzyć** *pf. lit.* (*o losie, Bogu* = *zesłać*) send (*coś komuś* sth to sb *l.* sb sth). ~ **się** *ipf.* (*o sposobności, gratce*) turn up, present itself, occur (*komuś* to sb).

nadawa *f.* **nadawa (surowca)** *techn.* amount (of raw material) to be processed.

nadawać *ipf.* **-daję -dajesz, -dawaj 1.** (= *wysyłać*) send; (*list, przesyłkę*) post. **2.** (= *przyznawać, dawać*) grant (*coś komuś* sth to sb *l.* sb sth); (*wyróżnienie, przywilej, prawo*) confer (*coś komuś* sth on *l.* upon sb); (*imię, nazwę, formę, znaczenie*) give; **nadawać komuś szlachectwo** confer knighthood on *l.* upon sb, knight, ennoble sb. **3.** (*cechę*) **nadawać bieg** initiate, launch (*sth*), set (*sth*) going; **nadawać czemuś inny/nowy tok** set sth on a different/new course; **nadawać ton** set the tone (*czemuś* for *l.* of sth). **4.** *tel.* transmit; (*audycję*) broadcast; (*o stacji radiowej l. telewizyjnej*) be on the air. **5.** *pot.* (= *nastręczać, załatwiać*) fix (*sth*) up (*komuś* for sb). **6.** *tylko ipf. pot.* (= *mówić szybko*) chatter (on *l.* away), tattle (*o czymś* about sth); *pot.* (= *donosić, skarżyć*) tell (*na kogoś* on sb). ~ **się** *ipf.* be suitable, be fit, be apt (*do czegoś* for sth); **ona nadaje się na żonę** she'll make a good wife; **to się nada** this will do.

nadawca *mp* (*listu, przesyłki*) sender; (*przekazu pieniężnego*) remitter; *handl.* consigner; **w razie niedoręczenia zwrócić nadawcy** *poczta* if undeliverable, return to sender.

nadawczy *a.* (*o sprzęcie, aparacie*) *tel.* transmitting, broadcasting.

nadawczyni *f. zob.* **nadawca**.

nadąć (się) *pf. zob.* **nadymać (się)**.

nadąsać się *pf.* (= *obrazić się*) take offense (*o coś* at sth); (= *naburmuszyć się*) sulk; *pot.* throw a tantrum.

nadąsany *a.* (looking) hurt *l.* offended, sulky.

nadążać *ipf.*, **nadążyć** *pf.* **1.** (= *dotrzymywać kroku*) keep up, keep pace (*za kimś / czymś* with sb/sth); **nie nadążać (za kimś/czymś)** fall *l.* lag behind (sb/sth); **nie nadążać (za czymś)** (= *nie rozumieć, tracić wątek*) not follow (sth). **2.** (= *być gotowym na czas*) meet the deadline (*z czymś* for sth); **nadążać z robotą** keep up *l.* cope with the work.

nadbagaż *mi lotn.* excess baggage.

nadbałtycki *a.* located on the Baltic coast.

nadbić *pf.* **-biję -bijesz** *zob.* **nadbijać**.

nadbiec *pf.* **-gnę -gniesz, -gnij** *zob.* **nadbiegać**.

nadbieg *mi mot.* overdrive; **uruchamiać** *l.* **wrzucać nadbieg** go into overdrive.

nadbiegać *ipf.* **1.** (= *przybywać biegiem*) come running. **2.** (= *zbliżać się szybko*) approach (fast); (*o falach*) roll in, surge. **3.** (*o dźwięku* = *docierać z odległości*) come, be heard.

nadbiegnąć *pf.* **-gnij** *rzad.* = **nadbiec**; *zob.* **nadbiegać**.

nadbijać *ipf.* **1.** (= *nadtłukiwać*) chip. **2.** *rzad.* (= *przybijać dodatkowo*) nail *l.* tack (*sth*) on. **3.** *druk.* offprint, reprint separately.

nadbitka *f. Gen.pl.* **-ek** *druk.* offprint.

nadboran *mi chem.* perborate.

nadbrzeże *n. Gen.pl.* **-y 1.** (= *obszar nad brzegiem wód*) waterfront; (*rzeki*) bank; (*umocnione*) embankment; (*jeziora*) lakefront; (*morskie*) seafront; (= *wybrzeże*) coast. **2.** *rzad.* = **nabrzeże 1.**

nadbrzeżny *a.* **1.** waterfront; (= *nadrzeczny*) riverside; (= *nadmorski*) coastal, seaside. **2.** *ekol., hydrol.* littoral.

nadbrzusze *n. Gen.pl.* **-y** *anat.* epigastrium.

nadbrzuszny *a. anat.* epigastric.

nadbudowa *f. Gen.pl.* **-ów** *t. przen.* superstructure.

nadbudować *pf.*, **nadbudowywać** *ipf.* build (*sth*) (*nad czymś* over, on *l.* upon sth).

nadbudówka *f. Gen.pl.* **-ek** *t. żegl.* superstructure.

nadburcie *n. żegl.* bulwark.

nadchloran *mi chem.* perchlorate.

nadchodzący *a.* **1.** (= *zbliżający się*) approaching, upcoming, oncoming; (*o burzy*) gathering. **2.** (*form.* = *mający nastąpić*) imminent, impending, forthcoming. **3.** (*o miesiącu, roku itp.* = *przyszły*) coming, next; **w nadchodzących latach** in the years to come.

nadchodzić *ipf.* **1.** (= *zbliżać się, t. przen.*) come (on), approach; *form.* be at hand. **2.** (*o burzy, chmurach, zmroku* = *nadciągać*) gather. **3.** (*o wiadomości, liście* = *docierać do adresata*) arrive. **4.** (= *następować*) follow; (*o porze roku, okresie*) come around *l.* on, near, draw near; (*o nocy, zimie, mrozie*) draw on; (*o śnie, śmierci*) come.

nadciągać *ipf.*, **nadciągnąć** *pf.* **-ij 1.** (= *zbliżać się, t. przen.*) approach, draw near; (*o wojsku*) march in. **2.** (*o burzy, chmurach, zmroku*) gather. **3.** (*o tłumie* = *gromadzić się*) collect; (*o czymś groźnym l. nieprzyjemnym*) draw on; *arch.* be *l.* draw nigh; (*o nocy*) fall.

nadciekłość *f. fiz.* superfluidity.

nadciekły *a. fiz.* superfluid.

nadciśnienie *n.* **1.** *pat.* hypertension, high blood pressure; **nadciśnienie tętnicze napadowe/utrwalone** labile/essential hypertension. **2.** *fiz.* excess pressure; (*fali uderzeniowej*) overpressure; *techn., zwł. lotn.* superpressure.

nadciśnieniowiec *mp* **-wc-** *Voc.* **-wce** *pot.* hypertensive (case).

nadciśnieniowy *a.* **1.** *pat.* hypertensive. **2.** *techn.* superpressure.

nadczłowiek *mp pl.* **nadludzie** superman, superhuman being.

nadczułość *f.* hypersensitivity.

nadczuły *a.* hypersensitive.

nadczynność *f. pat.* excess activity, hyperactivity; **nadczynność śledziony** hypersplenism; **nadczynność tarczycy** hyperthyroidism.

nadczynny *a. pat.* hyperactive.

naddać *ipf. zob.* **naddawać**.

naddatek *mi* **-tk-** **1.** (= *nadwyżka*) surplus, excess; **z naddatkiem** *przen.* with a vengeance, with interest. **2.** *techn.* allowance, excess material.

naddawać *ipf.* **-daję** **-dajesz, -dawaj** *techn.* (*materiał*) supply (*sth*) with an allowance.

naddunajski *a. t. archeol.* Danubian.

naddzierać *ipf.* make a tear in (*sth*).

naddźwiękowiec *mi* **-wc-** *Gen.* **-a** *lotn., pot.* supersonic jet.

naddźwiękowy *a.* supersonic.

nade *prep.* (*w utartych zwrotach*) = **nad**; + *Ins.* **nade dniem** *lit.* before dawn, at daybreak; **nade mną** (*miejsce*) over *l.* above me; + *Acc.* **nade mnie** (*kierunek*) above me; *lit.* (more) than I; **nade wszystko** above all.

nadecznik *ma zool.* freshwater sponge (*Spongilla lacustris*).

nadedrzeć *pf.* **-drę** **-drzesz, -drzyj, naddarł** *zob.* **naddzierać**.

nadejście *n.* coming, approach, arrival, advent, onset.

nadejść *pf.* **-jdę** **-jdziesz, nadszedł** *zob.* **nadchodzić**.

nadenerwować się *pf.* fret (o.s.), get upset (*z powodu czegoś* over *l.* about sth).

nadeń *adv.* (*w pozycji nieakcentowanej*) *lit.* = **nad niego**.

nadepnąć *pf.* tread, step (*na coś* on *l.* upon sth); **nadepnąć komuś na odcisk** *przen.* tread on sb's corns *l.* toes; **słoń mu na ucho nadepnął** *pot.* he has no ear for music.

nadeptać *pf.* **-pczę** **-pczesz** *l.* **-pcę** **-pcesz, -pcz 1.** (= *nabłocić*) track mud. **2.** *rzad.* = **nadepnąć**. **~ się** *pf. pot.* = **nachodzić się**.

nadeptywać *ipf. zob.* **nadepnąć**.

nader *adv. lit.* (*z przymiotnikami*) very, most, exceedingly; (*z czasownikami i imiesłowami*) greatly, highly, very much.

naderwać *pf.* **-rwę** **-rwiesz, -rwij** *zob.* **nadrywać**. **~ się** *pf.* **1.** *zob.* **nadrywać się**. **2.** (= *nadwerężyć sobie plecy*) strain *l.* pull one's back.

naderwany *a.* half-torn, damaged; (*o uchwycie, guziku itp.*) (hanging) loose, coming off; (*o ścięgnie, mięśniu*) strained, torn.

naderżnąć *pf.* **-nę** **-niesz, -nij** *zob.* **nadrzynać**.

nadesłać *pf.* **-ślę** **-ślesz, -ślij** *zob.* **nadsyłać**.

nadeżreć *pf.* **-żrę** **-żresz, -żryj, nadżarł** *zob.* **nadżerać**.

nadęcie *n.* **1.** (= *zarozumiałość*) pomposity, conceit. **2.** (= *sztuczność*) affectation, stiltedness, airs and graces.

nadętość *f.* = **nadęcie**.

nadęty *a.* (= *nadąsany*) sulky; (= *zarozumiały*) pompous, conceited; (= *sztuczny, przesadny*) affected, stilted.

nadfiolet *mi fiz.* ultraviolet (light); **fotografia w nadfiolecie** ultraviolet photography.

nadfioletowy *a.* *fiz.* ultraviolet; **mikroskop nadfioletowy** ultraviolet microscope; **promieniowanie nadfioletowe** ultraviolet radiation.

nadfiołkowy *a. przest.* = **nadfioletowy**.

nadfruwać *ipf.*, **nadfrunąć** *pf.* (*o ptakach, motylach*) come flying *l.* fluttering.

nadganiać *ipf.* (= *nadrabiać opóźnienie l. zaległości*) catch up (*z czymś* on sth); *pf.* **nadgonić.**

nadgarstek *mi* -**tk**- *Gen.* -**a** wrist; *anat.* carpus; **kości nadgarstka** carpal bones.

nadgarstkowy *a. anat.* carpal.

nadgarstnik *mi Gen.* -**a** *sport* wrist guard.

nadgnić *pf.* -**gniję** -**gnijesz**, -**gnij** begin to rot *l.* decay, decay partially.

nadgniły *a.* partially rotten *l.* decayed.

nadgodzina *f. zw. pl.* overtime; **płatne nadgodziny** paid overtime; **pracować w nadgodzinach** work overtime, be on overtime; **wynagrodzenie za nadgodziny** overtime (payment).

nadgonić *pf. zob.* **nadganiać.**

nadgorliwiec *mp* -**wc**- *Voc.* -**wcze** *l.* -**wcu** *uj.* eager beaver.

nadgorliwość *f. uj.* overeagerness.

nadgorliwy *a. uj.* overeager.

nadgórnik *mp górn.* overman.

nadgraniczny *a.* border, frontier; **strefa/wioska nadgraniczna** frontier zone/village.

nadgryzać *ipf.*, **nadgryźć** *pf.* **1.** (= *napoczynać, gryząc*) take a bite out of; (= *skubać zębami*) nibble at. **2.** (*o rdzy, substancji żrącej*) eat into, corrode (*sth*).

nadinspektor *mp pl.* -**rzy** *l.* -**owie** *policja* (*stopień l. funkcja*) superintendent.

nadinterpretacja *f.* overinterpretation.

nadir *mi astron.* nadir.

nadjechać *v.* -**jadę** -**jedziesz** *zob.* **nadjeżdżać.**

nadjeziorny *a. rzad.* lakeside, lakefront; *ekol.* lacustrine.

nadjeżdżać *ipf.* (*konno*) come riding; (*o pojeździe l. ludziach w pojeździe*) approach, come, draw near; *pot.* roll up; (*o pociągu = wjeżdżać na stację*) draw in.

nadjodan *n. chem.* periodate.

nadkład *mi górn.* overburden.

nadkładać *ipf.* **nadkładać drogi** take a roundabout way; **nadkładać parę mil** go several miles out of one's way; *pf.* **nadłożyć.**

nadkole *n. mot.* body-fixing frame.

nadkomisarz *mp policja* chief superintendent, assistant commissioner.

nadkomplet *mi* excess, overplus, oversupply.

nadkwas *mi chem.* peracid.

nadkwasota *f.* hyperacidity; **mieć nadkwasotę** suffer from hyperacidity.

nadkwasowość *f.* *chem.* superacidity, overacidity.

nadkwaśność *f. zob.* **nadkwasota.**

nadkwaśny *a.* hyperacidic.

nadlatywać *ipf.*, **nadlecieć** *pf.* **1.** (= *przybywać, lecąc w powietrzu*) (*o ptaku*) come flying; (*o samolocie*) arrive. **2.** *pot.* (= *przybywać ze znaczną prędkością*) rush (at), fly.

nadległy *a. bot.* overlaying.

nadleśnictwo *n.* forest inspectorate, forestry management.

nadleśniczówka *f. Gen.pl.* -**ek** forest inspector's office.

nadleśniczy *mp decl. like a. Nom.pl.* -**owie** forest inspector, forest manager.

nadliczbowy *a.* **1.** additional; **godziny nadliczbowe** overtime. **2.** *mat.* supernumerary.

nadludzie *pl. zob.* **nadczłowiek.**

nadludzki *a.* **1.** (= *przekraczający ludzkie możliwości*) superhuman. **2.** (= *nadprzyrodzony*) superhuman, divine.

nadłamać *pf.*, **nadłamywać** *ipf.* **1.** (= *złamać częściowo*) break sth, crack sth. **2.** (= *ułamać*) break sth off.

nadłożyć *pf. zob.* **nadkładać.**

nadłubać się *pf. pot.* hammer (away), peg away (*przy czymś* at sth).

nadłupać *pf.*, **nadłupywać** *ipf.* **1.** (= *odłupać*) chip a bit off. **2.** (= *nieznacznie rozłupać*) crack, split.

nadłupany *a.* chipped, cracked.

nadmanganian *mi chem.* permanganate.

nadmanganowy *a.* **kwas nadmanganowy** *chem.* permanganic acid.

nadmarznięty *a.* frost-bitten.

nadmetraż *mi* excess of living area, extra space.

nadmiar *mi* excess, surplus; **nadmiar szczęścia** too much of a good thing, excessive happiness; **mieć czegoś w nadmiarze** have sth enough and to spare.

nadmiarowość *f. med.* presbyopia.

nadmiarowy *a. med.* presbyopic.

nadmieniać *ipf.*, **nadmienić** *pf.* mention.

nadmiernie *adv.* excessively.

nadmierny *a.* (*wysiłek, praca*) **1.** undue; (*cena, żądanie*) exorbitant, inordinate; (*wzruszenie, szczęście*) excessive; (*wzrost*) immoderate, excessive. **2.** **nadmierna ekspozycja** *fot.* over-exposure.

nadmorski *a.* seaside, maritime.

nadmuch *mi mot.* demister, defogger.

nadmuchać *pf.*, **nadmuchiwać** *ipf.* inflate, blow out, fill (*czymś* with sth).

nadmuchiwany *a.* inflatable.

nadmurszeć *pf.* -**eję** -**ejesz** rot, moulder.

nadnapięcie *n. el.* overvoltage, overpotential.

nadnaturalność *f.* supernatural.

nadnaturalny *a.* supernatural.

nadnerczak *mi med.* renal adenocarcinoma, clear cell renal carcinoma.

nadnercze *n. med.* adrenal gland, suprarenal gland, surrenal gland.

nadnerczowy *a. zob.* **nadnerkowy.**

nadnerkowy *a.* adrenal, suprarenal.

nadobny *a. arch. l. żart.* comely, fair; **nadobne dziewczę** fair maiden; **płacić** *l.* **odpłacać komuś pięknym za nadobne** pay sb back in the same coin; play tit for tat with sb.

nadobowiązkowo *adv.* optionally.

nadobowiązkowy *a.* optional.

nadoczodołowy *a. anat.* supraorbital.

nadokiennik *mi Gen.* -**a** *bud.* dripstone, dripmoulding, label.

nadoknie *n. Gen.pl.* -**ni** *bud.* window head.

nadokuczać *pf.* annoy, tease.

nadopiekuńczy *a.* overprotective.

nadpalać *ipf.* burn (*sth*) partly *l.* in part, scorch. ~ **się** *pf.* burn partly.

nadpalić (się) *pf. zob.* **nadpalać (się).**

nadpalony *a.* partly burnt, scorched.

nadpiłować *pf.*, **nadpiłowywać** *ipf.* saw into sth.

nadplastyczność *f. fiz.* superplasticity.

nadpleśniały *a.* mildewy.

nadpleśnieć *pf.* mildew.

nadpłacać *ipf.*, **nadpłacić** *pf.* (= *płacić ponad należność*) make an excess payment; (= *przepłacać, płacić ponad wartość*) overpay.

nadpłata *f.* (= *zapłata ponad należność*) excess payment; (= *zapłata ponad wartość*) overpayment.

nadpłynąć *pf. zob.* **nadpływać.**

nadpłynność *f. fiz.* superfluidity.

nadpłynny *a. fiz.* superfluid.

nadpływać *ipf.* (*o statku*) arrive; (*o człowieku*) swim up; (*o chmurach*) float up.

nadpobudliwość *f.* hyperactivity.

nadpobudliwy *a.* hyperactive.

nadpodaż *f.* excessive supply.

nadpotencjał *mi el.* overpotential.

nadprodukcja *f.* overproduction.

nadprogram *mi* supplement.

nadprogramowo *adv.* additionally.

nadprogramowy *a.* additional, supplementary.

nadproże *n. Gen.pl.* **-y** *bud.* lintel.

nadpróchniały *a.* partly decayed *l.* moldered, carious.

nadpróchnieć *pf.* **-eję -ejesz** begin to decay *l.* molder.

nadprzewodnictwo *n. fiz.* superconductivity.

nadprzewodnik *mi Gen.* **-a** *fiz.* superconductor.

nadprzewodnikowy *a. fiz.* superconducting, superconductive.

nadprzyrodzoność *f.* supernaturalness, the supernatural.

nadprzyrodzony *a.* supernatural.

nadpsuć się *pf.* **-uję -ujesz** taint.

nadrabiać *ipf.* (*czas*) make up for; **nadrabiać zaległości** reduce a backlog; **nadrabiać miną** put on a brave face, put a happy/glad face on sth.

nadrdzewiały *a.* rusty.

nadrdzewieć *pf.* **-eję -ejesz** rust, get rusty.

nadrealista *mp* surrealist.

nadrealistyczny *a.* surrealistic.

nadrealizm *mi sztuka* surrealism.

nadrobić¹ *pf. zob.* **nadrabiać.**

nadrobić² *pf.* (= *pokruszyć*) crumble.

nadruk *mi* **1.** (= *drukowany napis*) printed inscription. **2.** (*barwny wzór*) printed design. **3.** **nadruk ochronny** *tk.* overprinted resist.

nadrukować *pf.*, **nadrukowywać** *ipf.* **1.** (= *pokrywać wzorem*) print. **2.** (= *drukować jedno na drugim*) overprint. **3.** (= *drukować dużą liczbę czegoś*) print.

nadrywać (się) *ipf. zob.* **naderwać (się).**

nadrząd *mi* **-ę** *zool.* superorder.

nadrzecze *n. Gen.pl.* **-y** riverside.

nadrzeczny *a.* riverside; *form.* riparian.

nadrzeć *pf.* **-drę -drzesz, -drzyj, -darł 1.** (*wy-*

szarpać pewną ilość czegoś) tear out. **2.** (*drąc, zniszczyć dużo czegoś*) tear up.

nadrzewny *a.* arboreal.

nadrzędnie *adv.* superiorly.

nadrzędność *f.* superiority.

nadrzędny *a.* (*instytucja, stanowisko*) superior; (*wartość, racja*) imperative, overriding; **zdanie nadrzędne** *gram.* main clause.

nadrzynać *ipf.* incise, make a cut in sth.

nadskakiwać *ipf.* dance attendance, fawn (*komuś* on sb).

nadsłuchiwać *ipf.* listen out (*czegoś* for sth).

nadspodziewanie *adv.* **1.** (= *niespodziewanie*) unexpectedly. **2.** (= *lepiej niż oczekiwano*) beyond expectation.

nadspodziewany *a.* **1.** (*wynik*) (= *lepszy niż oczekiwano*) unhoped for. **2.** (*gość, wyjazd*) (= *niespodziany*) unexpected.

nadstawiać *ipf.* **1.** present; **nadstawiać drugi policzek** *przen.* turn the second cheek; **nadstawiać policzek do pocałunku** *przen.* present a cheek (to kiss *l.* to be kissed); **nadstawiać głowy** *l.* **karku (za coś, za kogoś)** risk one's neck. **2.** **nadstawiać ucha** *l.* **uszu** (= *nasłuchiwać*) prick up one's ears; (= *słuchać z chęcią*) be all ears, lend one's ears. ~ **się** *ipf.* **1.** **nadstawiać się do czegoś** present o.s. for sth. **2.** (= *ryzykować*) run a risk.

nadstawka *f. Gen.pl.* **-ek** (*część mebla*) top.

nadsterowność *f. techn.* oversteer.

nadsterowny *a. techn.* oversteering.

nadstępka *f. żegl.* keelson.

nadstruktura *f. krystal.* superlattice, superstructure.

nadsyłać *ipf.* send in.

nadszarpnąć *pf.*, **nadszarpywać** *ipf.* **1.** (= *uszkodzić, nadwerężyć, pogorszyć*) damage, impair; (*zdrowie*) undermine; (*nerwy*) stretch; (*reputację*) tarnish. **2.** (= *uszczuplić*) reduce, make a dent in (*sth*).

nadsztukować *pf.*, **nadsztukowywać** *ipf.* (= *wydłużać*) lengthen; (= *łatać, uzupełniać*) patch.

nadsztygar *mp górn.* chief foreman.

nadszybie *n. Gen.pl.* **-i** *górn.* shaft top, pit bank, pit brow, pit-head.

nadtapiać *ipf.* make (*sth*) begin to melting. ~ **się** *ipf.* begin to melt, start melting.

nadtlenek *mi chem.* peroxide.

nadtlenowy *a. chem.* peroxide.

nadtłuc *pf.* **-kę -czesz, nadtłukiwać** *ipf.* chip, crack.

nadto *conj. lit.* (= *poza tym*) moreover, besides. – *adv. przest.* (= *zbyt*) too, overly; **aż nadto** more than enough, amply; **tego już nadto** that's enough.

nadtopić (się) *pf. zob.* **nadtapiać (się).**

nadtytuł *mi* **1.** (*na karcie tytułowej*) head. **2.** (*w tekście prasowym*) headline.

nadużycie *n.* **1.** (= *nieumiarkowane użycie*) overuse; **nadużycie prawa** abuse of the law. **2.** (= *malwersacja*) embezzlement, misuse of funds.

nadużyć *pf.*, **nadużywać** *ipf.* **1.** (= *używać nieumiarkowanie*) overuse. **2.** (= *wykorzystywać niewłaściwie*) abuse, misuse.

nadwaga *f.* **1.** (= *nadwyżka ciężaru*) overweight; **nadwaga bagażu** excess luggage; **mieć nadwagę** be overweight. **2.** (= *towar dodany ponad wagę*) extra weight.

nadważkość *f. lotn.* increased gravity.

nadwątlać *ipf.* weaken.

nadwątleć *pf.* **-eję -ejesz** weaken.

nadwątlić *pf. zob.* **nadwątlać.**

nadwerężać *ipf.*, **nadwerężyć** *pf. lit.* (= *osłabiać*) weaken, impair, injure; (*wzrok*) weaken; (*zdrowie*) undermine; (*siły, fundusze*) tax, strain.

nadwerężać się *ipf.* strain oneself, overtax oneself.

nadwęglan *mi chem.* percarbonate.

nadwodny *a.* **1.** (= *nadbrzeżny*) aquatic, riverside, lakeside. **2.** (= *unoszący się nad wodą*) above water.

nadwodzie *n. Gen.pl.* **-i 1.** *żegl.* deadworks, abovewater body. **2.** (= *teren nadmorski niezalewany falami*) backshore.

nadworny *a.* court; **nadworny dostawca** purveyor in ordinary.

nadwozie *n. Gen.pl.* **-i** bodywork.

nadwoziowy *a.* bodywork.

nadwrażliwość *f.* **1.** (= *przewrażliwienie*) over-sensitivity. **2.** *med.* hypersensitivity.

nadwrażliwy *a.* **1.** (= *przewrażliwiony*) over-sensitive. **2.** *med.* hypersensitive.

nadwymiar *mi* oversize.

nadwymiarowy *a.* oversize.

nadwytrzymałość *f.* superstrength.

nadwyżka *f. Gen.pl.* **-ek** surplus; **wykonać z nadwyżką** do *l.* make more than needed, exceed the target figures.

nadwzroczność *f. med.* hypermetropia, hyperopia.

nadwzroczny *a. med.* hypermetropic, hyperopic.

nadymać *ipf.* puff out. **~ się** *ipf.* **1.** (= *wciągać powietrze*) draw in a lungful of air. **2.** (= *przybierać wypukły kształt*) bulge, swell, plump out *l.* up. **3.** *pot.* (= *dąsać się*) sulk. **4.** *pot.* (= *puszyć się*) puff up; put on airs; **nadymać się jak paw** strut like a peacock.

nadymić *pf.* make a lot of smoke; (*dymem z papierosa*) smoke up; **nadymić w pokoju** smoke the room.

nadymka *f. Gen.pl.* **-ek** *icht.* smooth puffer (*Lagocephalus laevigatus*).

nadzbieżność *f. mat.* overconvergence.

nadziać (się) *pf. zob.* **nadziewać (się).**

nadziany *a. pot.* filthy rich, well-heeled.

nadziąślak *mi Gen.* **-a** *pat.* epulis.

nadzieja *f. Gen. i Gen.pl.* **-ei** hope; **mieć nadzieję** hope (*na coś* for sth); **mam nadzieję, że...** I hope that...; **dawać** *l.* **robić komuś nadzieje** raise sb's hopes, build up sb's hopes; **iskierka nadziei** flicker of hope; **karmić się** *l.* **żyć nadzieją** live in hope(s) (*czegoś* of sth); **mieć nadzieję wbrew nadziei** hope against hope; **pokładać w kimś/czymś nadzieję** pin one's hopes on sb/sth; put (one's) faith in sb/sth; **porzucić** *l.* **stracić (wszelką) nadzieję** give up (all) hope; lose heart; **rokować**

nadzieje show promise; **rozwiać czyjeś nadzieje** dispel sb's hopes; **w nadziei, że...** hoping that..., in the hope that...; **w tobie cała moja nadzieja** you are my only hope; **wiązać nadzieje z czymś, z kimś** place one's hopes on sth/sb, put one's hopes on sth/sb; **zawieść czyjeś nadzieje** dash sb's hopes; **żywić nadzieję** *lit.* cherish the hope.

nadziemny *a.* overhead, above ground, overground.

nadziemski *a.* heavenly.

nadzienie *n.* stuffing, filling, forcemeat.

nadziewać *ipf.* **1.** (= *wypełniać nadzieniem*) stuff, skewer. **2.** (= *nasadzać na coś ostrego*) stick, fix. **~ się** *ipf.* **1.** (= *nabijać się na coś ostrego*) stick o.s., get impaled (*na coś* on sth). **2.** *pot.* (= *spotykać niespodzianie*) run, bump (*na kogoś/coś* into sb/sth).

nadziewarka *f. Gen.pl.* **-ek** *techn.* stuffer.

nadziwić się *pf.* **nie móc się nadziwić** be unable to stop wondering, be amazed (*komuś/czemuś* at sb/sth).

nadzmysłowy *a.* extrasensory.

nadzorca *mp* overseer, supervisor.

nadzorczy *a.* supervisory; **rada nadzorcza** board of supervisors.

nadzorować *ipf.* oversee, supervise.

nadzór *mi* **-o- 1.** (= *sprawowanie kontroli*) supervision, inspection; **nadzór policyjny** (police) surveillance; **nadzór techniczny** engineering supervision; **być pod nadzorem** be under surveillance; **sprawować nadzór nad kimś/czymś** supervise *l.* oversee sb/sth. **2.** (= *urząd sprawujący kontrolę*) supervisory board *l.* office.

nadzwyczaj *adv.* = **nadzwyczajnie** 1.

nadzwyczajnie *adv.* **1.** (= *nader, niesłychanie*) exceptionally, extremely, extraordinarily, remarkably. **2.** (= *dobrze, świetnie*) excellently; *pred.* fine, wonderful, excellent, cool, great; **poszło ci nadzwyczajnie** you did excellently; **czuję się nadzwyczajnie** I'm feeling wonderful.

nadzwyczajny *a.* **1.** (= *nieprzeciętny*) extraordinary, exceptional, unusual, remarkable. **2.** (= *nadprogramowy, specjalny*) special, extra; **nadzwyczajne środki ostrożności** extra precautions; **dodatek nadzwyczajny** special supplement; **wydanie nadzwyczajne** special issue. **3.** *uniw.* **profesor nadzwyczajny** associate professor. **4.** *prawn.* **rewizja nadzwyczajna** extraordinary appeal.

nadźwigać się *pf.* + *Gen.* get tired carrying (*sth*).

nadżerać *ipf.* **1.** (= *zniszczyć częściowo*) corrode sth. **2.** (= *napoczynać, jedząc*) bite into sth.

nadżerka *f. Gen.pl.* **-ek 1.** *pat.* erosion, ulcer, sore. **2.** *metal.* speck, pit.

nadżerkowy *a. pat.* erosional.

naelektryzować *pf.* electrify. **~ się** *pf.* get *l.* become electrified.

nafajdać *pf. wulg.* crap, shit.

nafaszerować *pf. kulin.* stuff, fill (*sth*) (*czymś* with sth); *pot.* (= *napchać, napełnić*) fill (*sth*) up (*czymś* with sth); **nafaszerować kogoś kulami** *pot.* shoot sb full of holes.

nafciarski *a.* petroleum.

nafciarstwo *n. pot.* = **naftownictwo**.

nafciarz *mp pot.* oilman.

nafta *f.* **1.** *techn. US* kerosene *l.* kerosine; *Br.* paraffin. **2.** *pot.* (= *ropa naftowa*) (crude) oil, petroleum.

naftalen *mi chem.* naphthalene.

naftalina *f.* mothballs.

naftociąg *mi* oil pipeline.

naftodajny *a.* oil-rich.

naftonośny *a.* oil-producing.

naftopochodny *a. chem.* petroleum-derived.

naftowiec *mp* -wc- oil worker.

naftownictwo *n. górn.* oil *l.* petroleum industry.

naftowy *a.* **1.** (*dotyczący nafty*) oil, petroleum; **pole naftowe** oilfield; **przemysł naftowy** oil *l.* petroleum industry; **ropa naftowa** (crude) oil, petroleum; **szyb naftowy** oil well. **2.** (*wykorzystujący naftę jako paliwo*) *US* kerosene, kerosine; *Br.* paraffin; **lampa/latarnia naftowa** kerosene lamp/lantern.

nagabnąć *pf.*, **nagabywać** *ipf.* **1.** *uj.* (= *zaczepiać*) pester; *pot.* hound, dog; accost. **2.** (= *zwracać się z prośbami, żądaniami*) approach, solicit (*sb*) (*o coś* for sth).

nagadać *pf. pot.* **1.** *często uj.* talk, chatter, babble, prattle; (= *naopowiadać*) tell (*sb*) a lot (*o czymś* about sth); **nagadać głupstw** talk nonsense; **nagadać na kogoś (niestworzonych rzeczy)** tell tales about sb. **2.** + *Dat.* (= *nakrzyczeć na kogoś*) tell (*sb*) off, chew (*sb*) out, come down on (*sb*). ~ **się** *pf.* say a lot (at one sitting), talk to one's heart's content.

nagana *f.* reprimand, rebuke; **dostać naganę** receive a reprimand; **powiedzieć coś tonem nagany** say sth reproachfully; **udzielić komuś nagany** reprimand sb, give sb a reprimand.

naganiacz *mp* **1.** *myśl.* beater. **2.** *uj.* (= *osoba nastręczająca klientów*) solicitor; (= *stręczyciel*) pimp.

naganiać *ipf.* (= *zapędzać*) drive; **naganiać kogoś do roboty** *pot.* force sb to work. ~ **się** *pf. pot.* = **nachodzić się**.

naganka *f. Gen.pl.* -ek *myśl. zob.* **nagonka**.

naganność *f.* culpability, blameworthiness.

naganny *a.* **1.** (= *zasługujący na naganę*) reprehensible, culpable, blameworthy. **2.** (= *wyrażający naganę*) reproachful.

nagapić się *pf. pot.* get an eyefull (*na coś* of sth); gape at will (*na coś* at sth).

nagar *mi techn.* carbon deposit.

nagardłować się *pf. pot.* shout to one' heart's content.

nagarnąć *pf.*, **nagarniać** *ipf.* pile (up), heap (up), rake (up).

nagazować się *pf. pot.* (= *spić się*) get plastered *l.* smashed.

nagderać *pf. pot.* bellyache, moan and groan. ~ **się** *pf. pot.* (= *zaspokoić chęć gderania*) be through *l.* finished bellyaching.

nagi *a.* **1.** (= *nieubrany*) nude, naked; *pot.* in the buff, in the raw; **rozebrać się do naga** strip (down) naked. **2.** (= *pozbawiony pokrycia, ozdób*) bare; (*góra*) bald; (*miecz*) unsheathed; *pot.*

(= *pozbawiony upiększeń*) plain, undisguised; **naga prawda** the naked truth; **nagie fakty** hard facts.

nagiąć (się) *pf.* -gnę -gniesz, -gnij, -giął -gięła -gięli *zob.* **naginać (się)**.

nagietek *mi* -tk- *Gen.* -a *bot.* marigold (*Tagetes*).

nagimnastykować się *pf.* **1.** (= *zmęczyć się gimnastyką*) have enough exercise. **2.** *pot.* (= *zrobić coś z trudem*) go through a lot of trouble.

naginać *ipf.* **1.** (= *zginać*) bend (down). **2.** (= *dowolnie interpretować*) bend, stretch; **naginać fakty** stretch the facts; **naginać przepisy** bend the rule. **3.** (= *dopasowywać na siłę*) make (*sth*) fit; **naginać fakty do teorii** make the facts fit the theory; **naginać sens do rymu** sacrifice meaning for the sake of rhyme. ~ **się** *ipf.* **1.** (= *zginać się*) bend. **2.** (= *dostosowywać się*) adapt, adjust (*do czegoś, kogoś* to sth, sb).

naglący *a.* urgent, pressing.

nagle *adv.* **1.** (= *nieoczekiwanie*) suddenly, abruptly, all of a sudden; **umrzeć nagle** die unexpectedly. **2.** (= *szybko*) quickly; **co nagle, to po diable** haste makes waste.

naglić *ipf.* press (*kogoś do czegoś* sb to do sth, *o coś* for sth); **naglić, że...** insist that...; **czas nagli** time is pressing.

nagłaśniać *ipf.* **1.** (= *wyposażać w sprzęt elektroakustyczny*) amplify. **2.** (= *nadawać rozgłos*) publicize.

nagłos *mi jęz.* initial sound.

nagłosowy *a. jęz.* initial.

nagłość *f.* suddenness, abruptness.

nagłośnia *f. anat.* epiglottis.

nagłośnić *pf. zob.* **nagłaśniać**.

nagłośnieniowy *a.* amplifying, amplification.

nagłowić się *pf.* -łów nagłowić się nad czymś spend much time puzzling over sth; *zob.* **głowić się**.

nagłówek *mi* -wk- **1.** (= *tytuł*) heading; (*w gazecie*) headline. **2.** *jeźdz.* (*część uzdy*) crownpiece.

nagły *a.* **1.** (= *nieoczekiwany*) sudden, abrupt; **nagły wydatek** unexpected expense; **z nagła** all of a sudden; **nagła krew go zalała** he blew his top, he went wild; **do nagłej cholery!** damn it all! **2.** (= *naglący*) urgent; **w nagłym przypadku** in case of emergency.

nagminnie *adv.* commonly.

nagminny *a.* **1.** (= *częsty*) common. **2.** *med.* pandemic.

nagnać *pf. zob.* **naganiać**.

nagniatać *ipf.*, **nagnieść** *pf.* (= *lekko nacisnąć*) press.

nagnieść *pf.* (= *zgnieść dużo czegoś*) crush a lot of.

nagniotek *mi* -tk- *Gen.* -a *pat.* corn.

nago *adv.* **1.** (= *bez ubrania*) naked, nude. **2.** (= *bez pokrycia, ozdób*) bare.

nagolennik *mi Gen.* -a **1.** (= *ochraniacz na goleń*) shin guard. **2.** *hist.* (*część zbroi*) greave.

nagonasienne *pl. bot.* the gymnosperms.

nagonić *pf. zob.* **naganiać**.

nagonka *f. Gen.pl.* -ek *myśl.* battue; (*kampa-*

nia przeciwko komuś) campaign; **prowadzić nagonkę na kogoś** *l.* **przeciwko komuś** carry on a campaign against sb.

nagość *f.* **1.** (= *bycie nagim*) nudity, nakedness. **2.** (= *brak pokrycia, ozdób*) nakedness, bareness. **3.** (= *występowanie bez osłonek*) openness.

nagotować *pf.* + *Gen.* cook a lot of (*sth*).

nagozalążkowe *pl. bot.* gymnospermae.

nagrabić *pf.* **1.** (= *nazbierać grabiami*) rake up. **2.** (= *narabować*) plunder.

nagrać (się) *pf. zob.* **nagrywać (się).** ~ **się** *pf.* (= *zmęczyć się graniem*) play enough.

nagradzać *ipf.* **1.** (= *przyznawać nagrodę*) award. **2.** (= *rekompensować*) reward.

nagranie *n.* **1.** (= *to, co zostało nagrane*) recording. **2.** *sport* set up.

nagraniowy *a.* (*sesja, studio*) recording.

nagrobek *mi* -**bk**- *Gen.* -**a 1.** (= *pomnik nagrobny*) gravestone, tombstone. **2.** *lit.* (= *epitafium*) epitaph.

nagrobkarstwo *n.* monumental *l.* memorial stonemasonry.

nagrobkowy, nagrobny *a.* sepulchral.

nagroda *f.* **1.** (= *wyróżnienie*) prize, award; **Nagroda Nobla** the Nobel Prize; **nagroda pocieszenia** consolation prize; **w nagrodę (za coś)** in reward (for sth), as a reward (for sth); **wręczanie nagród** award presentation *l.* ceremony. **2.** (= *zapłata za zasługi*) reward.

nagrodzić *pf. zob.* **nagradzać.**

nagromadzenie *n.* gathering, collection, accumulation.

nagromadzić *pf.* collect, accumulate, amass; (*o zapasach*) stock-pile. ~ **się** *pf.* **1.** (= *zostać nagromadzonym*) accumulate, pile up. **2.** *pot.* (= *zebrać się w gromadę*) gather.

nagrymasić *pf.* -**szę** -**sisz** *pot.* make a lot of fuss.

nagrywać *ipf.* **1.** (= *rejestrować*) record; (*na taśmę wideo, na magnetofon*) tape. **2.** *sport* (= *podawać piłkę*) set up. **3.** *pot.* (= *załatwiać*) set up, fix up (*komuś coś* sb with sth). ~ **się** *ipf.* be recorded.

nagrywarka *f. komp.* CD-writer.

nagryzmolić *pf.* scribble, scrawl.

nagrzać (się) *pf.* -**eję** -**ejesz** *zob.* **nagrzewać (się).**

nagrzany *a.* **1.** *pot.* (= *pijany*) *US* sloshed; *Br.* pissed. **2.** *pot.* (= *podniecony*) turned on.

nagrzeszyć *pf.* commit many sins.

nagrzewać *ipf.* **1.** (= *ogrzewać*) heat, warm. **2.** (= *przygotowywać pewną ilość czegoś grzanego*) heat (up), warm (up). ~ **się** *ipf.* heat up, warm up.

nagrzewarka *f. Gen.pl.* -**ek** *techn.* heating unit.

nagrzewnica *f.* **1.** *mot.* heater. **2.** *hutn.* hot-blast stove, blast-furnace stove.

nagus *mp pl.* -**y** naked person.

nagusieńki *a. dimin.* bare-naked, stark-naked.

nagwintować *pf. techn.* thread; (*wnętrze rury*) tap.

nahaj *mi* -**a**, **nahajka** *f. Gen.pl.* -**ek** *przest.* whip.

nahałasować *pf.* make a ruckus, make a lot of noise.

naharować się *pf.* work one's hands *l.* tail off.

nahulać się *pf.* carouse about the town, paint the town red.

naigrawać się *pf.* **naigrawać się z kogoś/czegoś** make fun of sb/sth, ridicule *l.* deride *l.* taunt sb/sth.

naiwniactwo *n. pot.* simple-mindedness.

naiwniak *mp pot.* sucker, dupe.

naiwnie *adv.* naively.

naiwność *f.* **1.** (= *łatwowierność*) gullibility. **2.** (= *prostota, ograniczenie*) naivety, naiveté (*myśli, stylu*) artlessness. **3.** *zw. pl.* (= *naiwne poglądy*) unsophisticated views.

naiwny *a.* **1.** (= *łatwowierny*) gullible. **2.** (*odznaczający się naiwnością*) naive; (*wypowiedź, tekst*) artless; **naiwna sztuka** naive art.

naj-naj *a. tylko pred. pot.* top quality, superb.

najada *f. mit.* naiad, river nymph.

najazd *mi Loc.* **najeździe 1.** (= *zbrojna napaść*) (*na dużą skalę*) invasion, incursion; (*na małą skalę*) raid, foray. **2.** *pot.* (= *tłumne przybycie*) invasion. **3.** *narciarstwo* (= *górna część skoczni*) inrun. **4.** *narciarstwo* (*nabieranie szybkości przed skokiem*) approach to take-off. **5.** (*ujęcie filmowe*) close up, zoom in.

najazdowy *a.* **hamulec najazdowy** *mot.* overrunning brake.

najać (się) *pf. zob.* **najmować (się).**

najądrze *n. Gen.pl.* -**y** *anat.* epididymis.

najbardziej *adv. sup.* most (of all), best; **jak najbardziej!** *pot.* sure!, you bet!; *zob.* **bardzo.**

najbliższy *a. sup.* **1.** (= *sąsiedni*) (the) next. **2.** (= *niedaleki w czasie*) next; **przy najbliższej okazji** (at) the first chance possible; **w najbliższych dniach** within the next few *l.* couple of days; **w najbliższym czasie** in the (very) near future. **3.** (= *zażyły*) closest; **najbliższa rodzina** immediate family; **najbliższy krewny** next of kin; *zob.* **bliski.**

najdalej *adv.* **1.** *sup.* (= *w największej odległości*) farthest, furthest; **najdalej na północ położona część kraju** the northernmost part of the country; *zob.* **daleko. 2.** (= *nie dalej niż*) at the furthest, at the farthest. **3.** (= *nie później niż*) (*o trwaniu czasu*) at the longest; (*o terminie ostatecznym*) at the latest.

najebać *pf.* -**ię** -**iesz najebać komuś** kick *l.* beat sb's ass, beat the shit out of sb.

najebany *a. wulg.* (= *pijany*) fucked up, shit-faced.

najechać *pf.* -**jadę** -**jedziesz** *zob.* **najeżdżać.**

najedzony *a.* full, stuffed.

najem *mi* -**jm**- (*o robotnikach*) hire; (*o nieruchomości*) lease, rent; *Br.* let; **oddać w najem** lease (out), rent (out); *Br.* let (out); **wziąć w najem** rent, hire.

najemca *mp* lessee, tenant.

najemniczy *a.* (*o pracownikach*) hired; (*o płatnych żołnierzach*) mercenary.

najemnik *mp* **1.** (= *żołnierz*) mercenary, soldier of fortune. **2.** (= *robotnik*) hired hand. **3.** *pog.* (= *sprzedawczyk*) sell-out, turncoat, benedict arnold.

najemny *a.* **1.** (= *płatny*) hired; **najemny robotnik** hired hand; **najemny morderca** hired killer, hit man. **2.** (= *opłacany*) paid. **3.** (= *przekupiony przez kogoś*) be in sb's pocket.

najeść się *pf.* **1.** (= *zaspokoić głód*) eat one's fill, have enough to eat. **2.** (= *doświadczyć czegoś nieprzyjemnego*) experience, endure; **najeść się strachu, wstydu** suffer from fear, shame, experience fear, shame.

najeździć się *pf.* **1.** (= *dużo podróżować*) travel a lot, do a lot of travelling. **2. najeździć się samochodem, na motorze, na nartach** do a lot of driving, riding, skiing, drive, ride, ski a lot. **3.** (= *zmęczyć się jeżdżeniem*) be (sick and) tired of travelling, driving etc., have enough of travelling, driving etc.

najeźdźca *mp* invader.

najeżać *ipf. zob.* **najeżyć.**

najeżać się *ipf. zob.* **najeżyć się.**

najeżdżać *ipf.* **1.** (= *wpadać pojazdem*) hit, run into (*na coś, na kogoś* sth, sb). **2.** (= *dokonywać napaści*) attack, invade. **3.** *pot.* (= *przybywać tłumnie*) invade. **4.** *pot.* (= *krytykować*) attack (*na kogoś* sb).

najeżka *f. Gen.pl.* **-ek** *icht.* porcupine puffer, spiny puffer (*Diodon hystrix*).

najeżony *a.* **1.** (= *nastroszony*) bristling. **2.** *pot.* (= *nadąsany*) sulky, sullen. **3. najeżony trudnościami** beset with obstacles.

najeżyć *pf.* (= *stroszyć*) bristle; (*o piórach*) ruffle; **strach najeżył mu włosy** fear set his hair on end.

najeżyć się *pf.* **1.** (= *stroszyć się*) (*o ptakach*) ruffle its feathers; (*o zwierzętach*) bristle its hair. **2.** (= *dąsać się*) bristle (up). **3.** (= *stanąć dęba*) (*o włosach, sierści*) bristle; (*o piórach*) ruffle.

najęty *a.* **gadać, kłamać itp. jak najęty** talk, lie, etc. one's head off.

najgorsze *n.* **-ego** the worst, worst of all; **być przygotowanym na najgorsze** be prepared for the worst; **najgorsze jest to, że...** the worst (thing) is that...; **najgorsze mamy ze sobą** the worst is over.

najgorszy *a. sup.* the worst; **w najgorszym razie** at (the) worst; **w najgorszym wypadku** if worst comes to worst, in the worst case; **wymyślać komuś od najgorszych** think the worst of sb; **to nie najgorszy pomysł** that is not a bad idea (at all); *zob.* **zły.**

najgorzej *adv. sup.* (the) worst (of all); **nie najgorzej** not (too) bad *l.* badly; *zob.* **źle.**

najlepiej *adv. sup.* (the) best (of all); **nie najlepiej** not (too) good *l.* well; **najlepiej jak tylko mogłem** as well as *l.* best I could; **najlepiej będzie, jeżeli ja pójdę, zrobię to** I had better go, do it, it would be better if I went, did it; *zob.* **dobrze.**

najlepsze *n.* **-ego** (the) best; **najlepsze, co możemy zrobić, to...** the best (that) we can do is...; **wszystkiego najlepszego!** best wishes; **coś ty najlepszego zrobił?** what have you ever done?; **spałem w najlepsze** I could not have slept better; **bawiłem się w najlepsze** I could not have had a better time.

najlepszy *a. sup.* best, greatest; **najlepszy aktor pod słońcem** the greatest living actor; **mimo jego najlepszych chęci** in spite of his best intentions; **w najlepszym razie** at (the) best; *zob.* **dobry.**

najmniej *adv. sup.* (the) least, the fewest; **jak najmniej** as little as possible, as few as possible; *zob.* **mało.** – *adv.* (= *przynajmniej*) (the) least; **co najmniej** at (the very) least, to say the least.

najmniejszy *a. sup.* (the) smallest, (the) least; **iść po linii najmniejszego oporu** take the path of least resistance; **nie mamy najmniejszych szans** we haven't got the slightest *l.* a ghost of a chance; **nie mam najmniejszego pojęcia** I don't have *l.* haven't got the slightest idea; **w najmniejszym stopniu** least of all; *zob.* **mały.**

najmocniej *adv. sup.* strongest; **najmocniej dziękuję, przepraszam** I (most) sincerely thank you, apologize; *zob.* **mocno.**

najmować *ipf.* (*lokal*) rent, lease; *Br.* let; (*ludzi*) hire (*do czegoś* to do sth). **~ się** *ipf.* be hired (*do czegoś* to do sth); **najmować się do pracy** take work *l.* a job.

najnowszy *a. sup.* (the) latest, (the) most recent, (the) newest; **najnowsza moda** the latest fashion, the new look; **najnowszy wynalazek** the latest thing.

najogólniej *adv. sup.* **najogólniej mówiąc** (speaking) in the most *l.* very general terms; *zob.* **ogólnie.**

najpierw *adv.* first (of all), in the first place, to begin with, first and foremost.

najpóźniej *adv. sup.* (the) latest, at the (very) latest; **najpóźniej za tydzień** in a week at the (very) latest.

najprawdopodobniej *adv.* most probably, in all likelihood; *zob.* **prawdopodobnie.**

najprzód *n. przest.* = **najpierw.**

najstarszy *a. sup.* oldest; (*o synu, siostrze*) eldest; *zob.* **stary.**

najście *n.* **1.** (= *niespodziewana wizyta*) intrusion; **przepraszam za najście** pardon the intrusion, sorry for the intrusion. **2.** (= *napaść zbrojna*) incursion.

najść *pf.* **-jdę -jdziesz, -szedł -szła -szli** *zob.* **nachodzić.**

najwidoczniej *adv.* (very) clearly, (quite) evidently.

najwięcej *adv. sup.* (the) most, most of all; *zob.* **dużo, wiele.**

najwyraźniej *adv.* **1.** *sup. zob.* **wyraźnie. 2.** (very) clearly; (= *bezsprzecznie*) (quite) evidently.

najwyżej *adv.* **1.** *sup. zob.* **wysoko. 2.** (the) highest. **3.** (= *nie więcej niż*) at (the very) most; **nie będzie mnie (co) najwyżej godzinę** I will be gone for an hour at the most. **4.** (= *najpóźniej*) at the latest, at the outside. **5.** *pot.* (= *w najgorszym razie*) at worst; **poproszę ją, najwyżej mi odmówi** I'll ask her, the worst she can do is say "no".

najwyższy *a. sup.* **1.** (= *największy wzrostem*) (the) highest; (*człowiek*) (the) tallest; (*budynek*) (the) highest, (the) tallest. **2.** (= *położony najwyżej*) (the) top, (the) highest, (the) uppermost.

3. (= *najważniejszy*) chief, paramount, supreme; **Sąd Najwyższy** *prawn.* the Supreme Court; **stopień najwyższy** *jęz.* superlative; **najwyższy czas (coś zrobić)** high time (to do sth); **sprawa najwyższej wagi** a matter of the utmost importance. **4.** (= *naintensywniejszy*) extreme, maximum; **w najwyższym stopniu** extremely.

nakadzić *pf.* **-dzę -dzisz 1.** (= *napełnić wonią kadzidła*) fill the air with (the smell of) incense. **2.** *pot.* (= *nadymić*) smoke up a room, fill a room with smoke.

nakapać *pf.* **-ię -iesz 1.** drip. **2. nakapał barwnika do farby** he poured drops of dye into the paint.

nakarmić *pf.* **-ię -isz** feed.

nakaz *mi* **1.** (= *zarządzenie*) order, command; (= *rozporządzanie*) decree, warrant; **nakaz aresztowania** arrest warrant; **nakaz rewizji** search warrant; **nakaz sądowy** injunction, writ, warrant; **nakaz mody** *przen.* dictate of fashion; **znak nakazu** *mot.* regulatory sign. **2.** (= *bodziec*) dictate; **nakaz moralny** moral dictate.

nakazać *pf. zob.* **nakazywać**.

nakazowy *a.* **postępowanie nakazowe** by (means of an) order of the court.

nakazywać *ipf.* **1.** (= *wydawać nakaz*) order, command; **nakazywać komuś coś robić** order sb to so sth. **2.** (*o sytuacji itp., wymagać*) require, demand; **nakazywać szacunek** command respect; **sytuacja nakazuje ostrożność** the sitution requires caution; **grzeczność nakazuje nam tak postąpić** politeness demands that we do so.

nakierować *pf.*, **nakierowywać** *ipf.* **1.** (= *nastawiać na cel*) (*o ogniu, dziale*) direct; (*o broni*) aim; (*teleskopie, lornetce*) point (*na coś* at sth). **2.** (= *nadawać kierunek rozmowie itp.*) direct, lead (*na coś* to sth).

naklać *pf.* **-klnę -klniesz, -klnij, -klął -klęła -klęli** curse, swear (*na kogoś / coś* at sb/sth).

nakleić *pf.*, **naklejać** *ipf.* stick (up), paste (up) (*na czymś* on sth); **nakleić znaczek na kopercie** stamp an envelope.

naklejka *f. Gen.pl.* **-ek** (= *etykieta*) label; (= *nalepka*) sticker.

nakład *mi* **1.** *zw. pl.* (*wkład pieniądzy*) expenditure, outlay; (*wkład pracy, energii*) expenditure; **robić coś wielkim nakładem sił** expend a great deal of energy doing sth. **2.** (= *liczba egzemplarzy*) (*o książce*) edition; (*o gazecie, czasopiśmie*) circulation; **książka ukazała się w wielotysięcznym nakładzie** the book was released in an edition of several thousand copies. **3.** (= *ogłoszenie drukiem*) release, edition; **książka ukaże się nakładem wydawnictwa** the book will appear as a release of the publishing house; **nakładem własnym** published by the author.

nakładać *ipf.* **1.** (= *kłaść*) put, place, set, lay (*sth*) (*na coś* on sth); (*jedzenie*) serve; **nakładać sobie czegoś** help o.s. to sth. **2. nakładać deski na siebie** overlap boards; **nakładać psu kaganiec** muzzle a dog; (= *ubierać*) put on. **3.** (= *rozsmarowywać*) apply, spread, smear. **4.** (= *obarczać*) impose; (*podatki, cło*) impose, put; (*obowiązek*)

impose; (*karę*) inflict. **~ się** *ipf.* (= *pokrywać się w przestrzeni l. czasie*) overlap.

nakładca *mp* publisher.

nakładka *f. Gen.pl.* **-ek 1.** (= *nasadka*) cap, covering. **2.** *bud.* lap. **3.** *komp.* overlay. **4.** *piłka nożna* (*rodzaj faulu*) high kick; *Br.* high foot.

nakłamać *pf.* **-ię -iesz** tell a lot of lies (*komuś* to sb).

nakłaniać *ipf.* induce, incline (*kogoś do czegoś* sb to do sth); prevail (*kogoś do czegoś* upon sb to do sth); **nakłaniać kogoś do zrobienia złego** tempt sb to do evil.

nakłaść *pf.* **-kładę -kładziesz** (= *umieszczać dużo czegoś*) pile (up), put a lot of (*sth*); (= *napchać*) load, fill, cram (*do czegoś* into sth); **nakłaść coś komuś do głowy** beat sth into sb's head. **– *pf. pot.*** (= *zbić*) beat up; **nakłaść komuś po pysku** give it to sb (right) in the mouth.

nakłonić *pf. zob.* **nakłaniać**.

nakłucie *n.* **1.** (= *ukłucie*) puncture, prick; (= *ślad po ukłuciu*) puncture. **2.** *med.* puncture.

nakłuć *pf.*, **nakłuwać** *ipf.* **1.** (= *przekłuwać*) prick (holes), perforate, pierce. **2.** (= *nabijać*) stick (*na coś* on sth).

nakolannik *mi Gen.* **-a** knee-pad.

nakopać *pf.* **1.** + *Gen.* (= *wydobyć, kopiąc*) dig up, excavate. **2.** + *Dat. pot.* (= *zbić, kopiąc*) kick, boot. **3.** + *Dat. pot. piłka nożna* (= *zwyciężyć z dużą przewagą punktów*) whip.

nakopcić *pf. pot.* (= *nadymić*) smoke the room, smoke up.

nakostniak *mi Gen.* **-a** *wet.* (*na kończynach*) ringbone; (*na górnych częściach nóg*) splint.

nakostnik *mi Gen.* **-a** *sport* ankle pad, ankle guard.

nakrajać *pf.* **-aję -ajesz** = **nakroić**.

nakrapiać[1] *ipf.* moisten, sprinkle.

nakrapiać[2] *ipf.* speckle, mark with spots.

nakrapiany *a.* (= *cętkowany*) speckled, spotted.

nakraść *pf.* **-kradnę -kradniesz, -kradnij** + *Gen.* thieve, steal a lot of (*sth*). **~ się** *pf. pot.* make a fortune by thieving.

nakres *mi żegl.* plot.

nakreślać *ipf.* **1.** (= *szkicować*) sketch. **2.** (= *wytyczać*) outline, lay out.

nakreślić *pf.* **1.** *zob.* **nakreślać**. **2.** (= *napisać coś szybko*) scrawl, scribble. **3.** (= *narysować, naszkicować, t. przen.*) sketch, draw, outline.

nakręcać *ipf.*, **nakręcić** *pf.* **1.** (= *wprawiać w ruch, kręcąc*) wind (up); **nakręcać numer** dial *l.* pick a number; **nakręcać film** shoot a movie; **robić/powtarzać coś jak nakręcony** do/repeat sth mechanically. **2.** (= *nawijać*) wind, reel (*sth*) (*na coś* on sth). **3.** *tylko pf. pot.* (= *nakłamać*) cheat, twist. **4.** *tylko pf. pot.* (= *podburzyć*) talk into.

nakrętka *f. Gen.pl.* **-ek 1.** (= *mutra*) nut; **nakrętka motylkowa** wing nut. **2.** (*pokrywka z gwintem*) (screw-on) cap, (screw) top.

nakroić *pf.* **-kroję -kroisz, -krój** + *Gen.* slice, cut (a lot of) (*sth*).

nakropić *pf. zob.* **nakrapiać**[2].

nakruszyć *pf.* **1.** (= *naśmiecić okruchami*) leave crumbs (behind). **2.** (= *rozdrobnić, krusząc*) crumble (*sth*), break (*sth*) up into crumbs.

nakrycie *n.* **1.** (= *komplet zastawy stołowej*) (place *l.* table) setting; **podać dwa dodatkowe nakrycia** set two more places. **2.** (= *okrycie, pokrycie*) cover, covering; **nakrycie głowy** headgear; **nakrycie łóżka** bedspread; **nakrycie budynku** *bud.* roofing.

nakryć *pf.* **-yję -yjesz, -yj 1.** (= *przykrywać*) cover; **diabeł ogonem nakrył** (*przen. o rzeczy, której nie można znaleźć*) where is it hiding?; **nakrywać (stół) do obiadu** set *l.* lay the table for dinner. **2.** *pot.* (= *przyłapać*) nail, nab (*sb*) (*na czymś* doing sth). ~ **się** *pf.* cover oneself; **nakryć się nogami** *przen.* take a tumble, fall headlong; **stoliczku, nakryj się** (*zaklęcie z baśni*) table, spread yourself.

nakrywać (się) *ipf.* **-am -asz** *zob.* **nakryć (się)**.

nakrzyczeć *pf.* **-ę -ysz nakrzyczeć na kogoś** scold *l.* berate sb, give sb a scolding. ~ **się** *pf.* get tired of shouting, yell one's lungs out; **nakrzyczeć się do woli** yell and shout to one's heart's content.

nakupić *pf.* + *Gen.* buy a bunch *l.* a load of (*sth*).

nakurzyć *pf.* **1.** raise (a lot of *l.* a cloud of) dust. **2.** (= *zadymić*) fill (*sth*) with smoke; *pot.* (= *nadymić, paląc papierosy*) smoke the room, smoke up.

nalać *pf.* **-leję -lejesz 1.** *zob.* **nalewać; nalej sobie drinka** pour yourself a drink; **nalałem im dwie filiżanki** I filled *l.* poured two cups for them; **z pustego i Salomon nie naleje** *przen.* nothing comes from nothing. **2.** (= *rozlać niechcący*) spill (*sth*) (*na coś* on *l.* all over sth). **3.** *pot.* (= *nasikać*) pee, piss (*na coś* on *l.* all over sth, *do czegoś* into sth). **4.** *pot.* (= *zbić, sprać*) beat (*sb*) up.

nalany *a.* (= *nabrzmiały*) obese, fat, bloated.

nalatać się *pf.* **1.** (= *zmęczyć się lataniem*) get tired of flying; (= *odbyć wiele lotów*) fly many times. **2.** *pot. zob.* **nachodzić się**.

nalatywać *ipf.* **1.** (= *zbliżać się, lecąc*) come flying; (= *gromadzić się, lecąc*) swarm; (*o ptakach*) flock. **2.** *pot.* **nalatywać na kogoś** (= *napastować słownie*) get on sb's back.

naleciałość *f.* (= *obcy wpływ, zwł. językowy*) (foreign) influence, loan.

nalecieć *pf.* **-cę -cisz 1.** *zob.* **nalatywać. 2.** *rzad.* (= *biegnąc szybko, wpaść*) slam, crash (*na kogoś/coś* into sb/sth).

nalegać *ipf.* insist (*na coś* on *l.* upon sth); **nalegać, żeby ktoś coś zrobił** insist on sb's doing sth, urge sb to do sth.

naleganie *n.* insistence, urgency; **z naleganiem w głosie** insistently, with a note of urgency in one's voice.

nalepiać *ipf.*, **nalepić** *pf.* **1.** (= *przyklejać*) stick, paste, glue, affix (*na coś/do czegoś* on/onto sth). **2.** *tylko pf.* (= *lepiąc, zrobić wiele*) make a lot *l.* plenty of (*sth*).

nalepka *f. Gen.pl.* **-ek** label, sticker.

naleśnik *mi Gen.* **-a** *kulin.* US crêpe; *gł. Br.* pancake.

naleśnikowy *a. kulin.* **ciasto naleśnikowe** (crêpe *l.* pancake) batter.

nalewać *ipf.* **1.** (= *wlewać*) pour (*do czegoś* into sth). **2.** *pot.* (= *napełniać, lejąc*) fill, replenish.

nalewka *f. Gen.pl.* **-ek 1.** (*alkohol*) liqueur. **2.** *med., przest.* tincture.

należeć *ipf.* **-ę -ysz 1.** (= *być własnością l. częścią*) belong (*do kogoś/czegoś* to sb/sth); **należeć do najlepszych/najgorszych** rank among *l.* be one of the best/worst; **należeć do spisku** be involved in *l.* take part in a plot; **należeć do przeszłości** belong to the past, lie in the past; **oni do siebie należą** *przen.* they belong together. **2.** (= *stanowić obowiązek, być czyjąś sprawą*) **to do ciebie należy** that's none of your business; **to nie należy do moich obowiązków** that's not my job *l.* my responsibility; **zrobię, co do mnie należy** I'll do my part *l.* my duty. **3.** *tylko bezosobowo* (= *trzeba, powinno się*) **jak (się) należy** well, properly; **należy szanować starszych** one's elders should be respected, you ought to *l.* should respect your elders; **nie należy wpadać w panikę** there's no need to panic; **należałoby podkreślić, że...** it should be emphasized that... ~ **się** *ipf. nieos.* (= *przysługiwać*) be owed *l.* due (*komuś* to sb); **ile się panu należy (ode mnie)?** how much do I owe you?; **należy mu się awans** he's due for promotion; **należy mu się nagroda/kara** he deserves a prize/to be punished; **to mi się nie należy** I don't deserve that; **oddać, co się komuś należy** give sb what they deserve; *przen.* (= *oddać sprawiedliwość*) give sb their due (reward).

należność *f.* amount *l.* balance due, charge; **uregulować należności za coś** pay the amount *l.* balance due for sth.

należny *a.* (= *należyty, t. przen.*) due; (= *do zapłaty*) owed.

należycie *adv.* (= *właściwie*) properly, appropriately, suitably; (= *starannie*) accurately, carefully.

należyty *a.* due, proper, appropriate.

naliczać *ipf.*, **naliczyć** *pf.* **1.** (= *obliczać*) calculate, reckon; (*odsetki*) *fin.* charge; **naliczać punkty karne** *sport* subtract penalty points (*for sth* za coś). **2.** *tylko pf.* (= *określić liczbę*) count (up) (*x sztuk czegoś* x of sth).

nalot *mi* **1.** (= *powłoka*) coating; (*kurzu, rdzy, pleśni*) layer; (*na języku*) fur. **2.** *wojsk.* (= *atak lotniczy*) air raid, bombing raid; **dokonać nalotu** make *l.* launch a bombing raid; **nalot dywanowy** carpet bombing raid. **3.** *pot.* (= *wtargnięcie*) raid (*na kogoś, coś* on sb, sth).

naładować *pf.* **1.** *zob.* **ładować. 2.** *pot.* **naładować kieszeń** (= *wzbogacić się, obłowić się*) fill *l.* line one's pockets. ~ **się** *pf.* **1.** *el.* be charged (up). **2.** *pot. żart.* (= *najeść się*) be full, be stuffed.

naładowany *a.* **1.** (= *pełen*) jam-packed, crammed full; (*o pojeździe*) loaded (up), laden (*czymś* with sth *l.* full of sth). **2.** *fiz., el.* charged; **cząstka naładowana ujemnie/dodatnio** negatively/positively charged particle. **3.** *broń* loaded.

nałamać *pf.* **-ię -iesz** + *Gen.* break a large number of (*sth*).

nałapać *pf.* **-ię -iesz** + *Gen.* catch a lot *l.* a large number of (*sth*).

nałazić się *pf.* -żę -zisz *pot.* 1. spend a long time wandering *l.* roving (*po czymś* about *l.* around sth). 2. = **nachodzić się**.

nałogowiec *mp* -wc- *Voc.* -wcze *l.* -wcu addict.

nałogowy *a.* habitual, compulsive; **wywołujący nałogowe uzależnienie** addictive.

nałokietnik *mi Gen.* -a *sport* elbow pad.

nałowić *pf.* -ów + *Gen.* catch a lot of *l.* plenty of (*sth*).

nałożnica *f. przest. l. lit.* concubine.

nałożyć (się) *pf. zob.* **nakładać (się)**.

nałóg *mi* -o- *t. przen.* addiction (*używania czegoś* to sth); (= *niepożądany nawyk*) bad habit; (= *przyzwyczajenie*) habit; **nałóg alkoholowy** alcohol addiction, addiction to alcohol; **paść ofiarą nałogu** succumb *l.* fall victim to one's addiction; **stać się nałogiem** become a habit; **wejść komuś w nałóg** become sb's habit; **wpaść w nałóg** become addicted, develop an addiction; **zwalczyć nałóg** overcome one's addiction.

nałykać się *pf.* + *Gen.* gulp down; (= *objeść l. opić się*) be full of (*sth*); **nałykać się wstydu** *przen.* be full of embarassment *l.* shame.

nam *pron. zob.* **my**.

namacać *pf.* feel; **namacać drogę (w ciemności)** *t. przen.* feel one's way (in the dark).

namacalny *a.* 1. (= *dotykalny, t. przen.* = *konkretny*) tangible, concrete. 2. *przen.* (= *wyraźny, jasny*) clear; (*o świadectwie, fakcie*) palpable.

namaczać *pf.* soak (*sth*) (*w czymś* in sth).

namagnesować (się) *pf.*, **namagnesowywać (się)** *ipf. zob.* **magnesować (się)**.

namagnesowany *a.* magnetized, magnetic.

namakać *ipf.* get soaked *l.* drenched.

namalować *pf. zob.* **malować**.

namarszczyć *pf.* (*tkaninę*) pleat.

namarzać *ipf. rzad.* (= *pokrywać się szronem*) frost over.

namarznąć *pf.* -ij 1. *zob.* **namarzać**. 2. (*o wielu ludziach l. zwierzętach*) freeze *l.* be frozen to death; (*o roślinach uprawnych*) be destroyed by frost. ~ **się** *ipf.* freeze through and through.

namaszczać *ipf.* (= *smarować*) smear, rub, grease (*czymś* with sth); *zwł. rel.* anoint (*czymś* with sth); **namaścić kogoś na króla** anoint sb king. ~ **się** *ipf.* (*czymś*) smear *l.* rub (*sth*) over oneself, anoint o.s. with (*sth*).

namaszczenie *n.* 1. anointment; **ostatnie namaszczenie** *l.* **namaszczenie chorych** *rel.* last rites, anointment of the sick. 2. *lit.* (= *powaga*) solemnity; **z namaszczeniem** solemnly.

namaszczony *a.* -eni 1. (= *naznaczony przez namaszczenie*) anointed. 2. (= *podniosły*) solemn.

namaścić (się) *pf.* -szczę -ścisz *zob.* **namaszczać (się)**.

namawiać *ipf.* persuade; **namawiać kogoś do zrobienia czegoś** talk sb into doing sth, convince *l.* persuade sb to do sth; **namawiać kogoś do buntu** incite sb to riot; **namawiać kogoś do grzechu** tempt sb to do evil *l.* to commit a sin. ~ **się** *ipf.* 1. (= *zachęcać się wzajemnie*) encourage one another, egg each other on. 2. *pot.* (= *uzgadniać plany*) make a deal, decide beforehand; (= *spi-*

skować) conspire (together), collude (*z kimś* with sb, *przeciw komuś/czemuś* against sb/sth).

namaz *mi islam* salat.

namącić *pf. pot.* (= *wprowadzać zamieszanie*) mix things up, confuse the issue; **namącić komuś w głowie** get sb (all) confused *l.* mixed up.

nameczyć się *pf.* have a hard time (*z czymś* with sth); go through o lot.

nami *pron. zob.* **my**.

namiar *mi zw. pl.* bearings, position, coordinates; **brać namiar** *żegl.* take a bearing; *pl.* **daj mi swoje namiary** *sl.* tell me how I can get in touch with you.

namiastka *f.* substitute, surrogate; **namiastka wolności** *przen.* a poor substitute for freedom.

namiernik *mi Gen.* -a *żegl., lotn.* bearing-finder, direction-finder, D/F.

namierzać *ipf.*, **namierzyć** *pf.* 1. *wojsk., lotn., żegl.* (= *ustalać położenie obiektu*) locate, determine the location of (*sth*); *pot.* (= *ustalać miejsce pobytu*) find, track down. 2. (= *odmierzać pewną ilość*) measure (*sth*) out.

namiestnik *mp gł. hist.* 1. (= *pełnomocnik*) representative, plenipotentiary. 2. *wojsk.* (= *dowódca chorągwi*) lieutenant.

namieszać *pf.* 1. (= *przygotować, mieszając*) mix; (= *zmieszać, używając wielu składników*) mix (up), blend (together). 2. *pot.* = **namącić**.

namiętnie *adv.* 1. (= *z namiętnością*) passionately, intensely, ardently; **lubić namiętnie** have a passion for (*sth*), be passionately fond of (*sth*). 2. (= *gwałtownie*) vehemently.

namiętność *f.* passion (*ku czemuś l. do czegoś* for sth); **wzniecić w kimś namiętność** kindle a passion in sb.

namiętny *a.* 1. (= *zmysłowy, uczuciowy*) passionate; (= *zapalony, zamiłowany*) ardent; **namiętny kochanek/pocałunek** passionate lover/kiss. 2. (= *gwałtowny*) vehement; **namiętny sprzeciw** vehement protest.

namiot *mi* tent; **namiot cyrkowy** circus tent; **namiot tlenowy** *med.* oxygen tent; **rozbić namiot** put up a tent; **spać pod namiotem** sleep in a tent.

namiotnik *ma ent.* ermine moth (*Yponomeuta*).

namiotnikowiec *ma* -wc- *zw. pl. ent.* (= *motyl z rodziny Yponomeutidae*) ermine moth.

namiotowy *a.* **płótno namiotowe** tent cloth; **pole namiotowe** campsite, camping site; *US* campground.

namnażać *ipf.* 1. + *Acc.* (= *rozmnażać*) multiply, breed. 2. + *Gen.* (= *wytwarzać dużo*) create a lot of (*sth*). ~ **się** *ipf.* (= *rozmnażać się*) multiply, breed (in great numbers); (= *pojawiać się masowo*) proliferate.

namnożyć (się) *pf.* -óż *zob.* **namnażać (się)**.

namoczyć *pf. zob.* **namaczać**.

namoknąć *pf.* -ij *zob.* **namakać**.

namolność *f.* pushiness.

namolny *a. pot.* pushy, annoying.

namordować *pf.* + *Gen.* slaughter, mow down. ~ **się** *pf. pot.* (= *napracować się*) kill oneself (*czymś* with sth).

namorzyn *mi bot.* mangrove.

namorzynowy *a.* **bagno namorzynowe** *ekol.* mangrove swamp.

namotać *pf.* **1.** (= *nawinąć*) wind (*na coś* onto sth). **2.** (*pot.* = *uknuć*) plot, scheme. **3.** *pot.* = **namącić.**

namowa *f. Gen.pl.* **-ów** persuasion, insistence; **za czyjąś namową** at sb's insistence; **opierać się czyimś namowom** resist sb's efforts to persuade; **ulegać czyimś namowom** give in *l.* yield to sb's persuasion.

namówić (się) *pf. zob.* **namawiać (się).**

namulisko *n. geol.* alluvium, alluvial deposit.

namuliskowy *a. geol.* alluvial.

namulnik *mi Gen.* **-a** *bot.* mudwort (*Limosella*).

namuł *mi geol.* silt, mud.

namydlać *ipf.* soap (up), lather (up). ~ **się** *ipf.* soap o.s. up, lather o.s. up.

namydlić (się) *pf. zob.* **namydlać (się).**

namysł *mi* thought, reflection, consideration; **bez (chwili) namysłu** without a (moment's) thought, without (a moment's) reflection; **czas do namysłu** time to think about sth *l.* to think sth over; **po namyśle** on reflection, on second thought *l.* (*Br.*) thoughts; **po dojrzałym namyśle** after mature consideration; **z namysłem** deliberately.

namyślać się *ipf.*, **namyślić się** *pf.* reflect (*nad czymś* on *l.* upon sth); think deeply (*nad czymś* about sth).

nandu *ma indecl. orn.* rhea (*Rhea americana, Pterocnemia pennata*); *pl.* (*rząd ptaków*) rheas (*Rheiformes*).

nanercz *mi Gen.* **-a** *bot., kulin.* cashew (*Anacardium occidentale*); **orzech/owoc nanercza** cashew nut/apple.

nanerczowate *pl. bot.* the cashew *l.* sumac family (*Anacardiaceae*).

nanieść *pf.* **-niosę -niesiesz -niósł -niosła -nieśli 1.** *zob.* **nanosić. 2.** (*o kurze itp.*) **nanieść (dużo) jaj** lay (a lot of) eggs.

nanizać *pf.* **-żę -żesz** *zob.* **nizać.**

nankin *mi tk.* nankin.

nanogram *mi Gen.* **-a** nanogram.

nanometr *mi Gen.* **-a** nanometer.

nanoplankton *mi biol.* nanoplankton.

nanosekunda *f.* nanosecond.

nanosić -szę -sisz *ipf.* **1.** (*warstwę, np. farby*) spread (*na coś* on *l.* over sth). **2.** (*geol. o wodzie, wietrze* = *osadzać*) deposit. **3.** (= *umieszczać, wpisywać*) mark, plot (*coś na coś l. na czymś* sth on sth); **nanosić poprawki/uwagi** make corrections/annotations (*na czymś* on sth). – *pf.* **1.** (*pot.* = *nanieść na butach*) track; **nanosić błota do kuchni** track mud into the kitchen. **2.** (= *zgromadzić dużo*) bring *l.* carry a lot of (*sth*); (*węgla, drewna*) haul.

nań *adv. lit.* (*w pozycji nieakcentowanej*) = **na niego.**

naobiecywać *pf.* **naobiecywać komuś wiele** *l.* **różnych rzeczy** make all sorts of promises to sb, promise sb the earth.

naobierać *pf.* + *Gen.* (*owoców, ziemniaków*) peel a lot of (*sth*).

naocznie *adv.* **1.** (= *na własne oczy*) with one's own eyes, personally. **2.** (= *dobitnie*) clearly, distinctly, palpably.

naoczny *a.* **1. naoczne świadectwo** first-hand testimony; **naoczny świadek** eye witness. **2.** (= *jasno widoczny*) evident, clear, palpable. **3.** (= *dokonywany za pomocą wzroku*) visual.

na odchodnym *adv.* on parting, taking one's leave.

na odczepnego *adv.* paying *l.* humoring lipservice; **obiecać komuś coś na odczepnego** promise sth in order to get rid of sb.

na odjezdnym *adv.* making *l.* saying one's farewells.

naokoło *prep.* + *Gen.* (all) around; *Br.* round. – *adv.* **1.** (= *dookoła*) all around, on all sides; *Brit.* all round; **naokoło ciągnął się las** woods extended all around *l.* on all sides. **2.** (= *okrężną drogą*) **iść** *l.* **jechać naokoło** take a roundabout route. **3.** (*emf.* = *ciągle, w kółko*) again and again.

naoliwiać *ipf.*, **naoliwić** *pf.* oil, grease, lubricate.

na opak *adv.* the wrong way, contrariwise; **wszystko poszło na opak** all went awry; **zrozumiałeś wszystko na opak** you've got the wrong end of the stick.

naopowiadać *pf.* **naopowiadać (komuś) bzdur** *l.* **niestworzonych rzeczy** *pot.* tell (sb) cock-and-bull stories *l.* tall tales (*o kimś/czymś* about sb/sth); run off at the mouth.

na osobności *adv.* in private.

naostrzyć *pf.* sharpen.

na oścież *adv.* wide.

na oślep *adv.* **1.** (= *po omacku*) blindly. **2.** (= *bez opamiętania*) full tilt, headlong.

naówczas *adv. przest. l. lit.* (= *w owej chwili*) then, thereupon; (= *w owym czasie*) at that time, in those days.

napa *f.* (*pot.* = *zatrzask krawiecki*) snap.

napaćkać *v.* **1.** (*pot.* = *nabazgrać, nachlapać*) daub, smear (*czymś* sth *l.* with sth, *na czymś* on sth). **2.** (= *nabrudzić, nabłocić*) make a mess *l.* (*zwł. Br.*) a muck.

napad *mi* **1.** (= *napaść*) attack, assault; **napad rabunkowy** robbery, mugging; **napad zbrojny** armed assault *l.* robbery; **dokonać napadu na kogoś/coś** make an assault on sb/sth; (*w celach rabunkowych*) rob sb/sth. **2.** (= *atak choroby, gwałtowna reakcja*) fit, seizure, attack, paroxysm; **napad kaszlu** fit of coughing; **napad padaczki** *pat.* epileptic seizure, attack of epilepsy; **dostać napadu śmiechu** go into a fit of laughter *l.* of (the) giggles; **w napadzie wściekłości/szału** in a fit of rage/fury. **3.** *sport* forward offense *l.* line.

napadać *ipf.* **1.** (*t. przen.* = *atakować*) attack, assault; (*w celach rabunkowych*) rob, mug (*kogoś/coś l. na kogoś/coś* sb/sth). **2.** (*o stanach psychicznych* = *opanowywać*) overcome, come over (*sb*); **co cię napadło?** what's gotten into you?, what has come over you? – *pf. nieos.* (*o opadach*) fall heavily; **napadało (dużo) deszczu/śniegu** there has been a heavy rainfall/snowfall.

napadowy *a. pat.* (= *nagły, gwałtowny*) paroxysmal, occurring in fits; (= *niestały, nawracający*) labile, unstable.

napakować *pf.* cram *l.* stuff full, pack full (*czymś* of sth). **~ się** *pf.* (*o ludziach*) crowd, throng (*do czegoś* into sth, *do środka* in *l.* inside).

napakowany *a.* (*o walizce, worku*) crammed *l.* packed full (*czymś* of sth); (*pot. = muskularny*) built, buff, brawny, burly.

napalać się *ipf. pot.* (= *nabierać ochoty*) be hot *l.* (*Br.*) keen (*na coś/na zrobienie czegoś* on (the idea of) sth/doing sth); *zob.* **napalony**.

napalić *pf.* (*w piecu, na kominku*) light *l.* make a fire; **aleście tu napalili** (*pot. = nakopcili dymem tytoniowym*) you've smoked up the place. **~ się** *pf.* 1. *zob.* **napalać się**. 2. (= *nasycić się paleniem*) have enough cigarettes.

napalm *mi wojsk.* napalm.

napalmowy *a.* **bomba napalmowa** *wojsk.* napalm bomb.

napalony *a.* 1. (*pot. = ogarnięty chęcią*) hot (to trot), fired, keyed up, gung-ho; *US sl.* psyched; *Br.* keen (*na coś/na zrobienie czegoś* on (the idea of) sth/doing sth). 2. (*sl. = podniecony seksualnie*) horny, turned on, frisky, in heat.

napar *mi* infusion, brew.

naparsteczek *mi* -czk- *Gen.* -a (*żart. = odrobina, kieliszeczek*) thimbleful, dram.

naparstek *mi* -tk- *Gen.* -a 1. thimble. 2. *żart.* = **naparsteczek**.

naparstnica *f. bot., med.* digitalis (*Digitalis*); **naparstnica purpurowa** (common) foxglove (*D. purpurea*).

naparstnik *mi Gen.* -a *sport* tab.

naparzać *ipf.* 1. (*zioła itp.*) brew, infuse. 2. *tk.* steam. 3. (*pot. = bić*) whip, thrash. **~ się** *ipf.* 1. (= *o ziołach itp.*) brew, infuse, steep. 2. (*pot. = bić się*) go at it, fight, scrap.

naparzyć *pf. zob.* **naparzać** 1, 2. **~ się** *pf. zob.* **naparzać się** 1.

napaskudzić *pf.* (*pot. = nabrudzić, zwł. odchodami*) make a mess *l.* (*zwł. Br.*) a muck; **kto napaskudził na dywan?** who has messed up the carpet?

napastliwość *f.* (= *zaczepność*) agressiveness, belligerence; (= *złośliwość*) bitterness, malice.

napastliwy *a.* (= *zaczepny*) aggressive, belligerent, fierce; (*o słowach, tonie wypowiedzi* = *ostry, złośliwy*) bitter, cutting, malicious.

napastnik *mp* 1. (= *agresor*) agressor, assailant; (= *najeźdźca*) invader. 2. *sport* forward, attack player.

napastować[1] *ipf.* 1. (= *napadać*) attack, assault. 2. (= *naprzykrzać się*) harass, pester, badger, plague (*sb*). 3. (= *molestować seksualnie*) molest, assault (*sb*) sexually.

napastować[2] *pf.* (= *natrzeć pastą*) polish, shine, wax, buff.

napaść[1] *f.* = **napad** 1; **być obiektem napaści** be assaulted, come under attack.

napaść[2] *pf.* -padnę -padniesz, -padnij, -padł *zob.* **napadać**.

napaść[3] *pf.* -pasę -pasiesz -pasł -paśli (*hodowla = nakarmić paszą*) feed, give fodder to; (*na pastwisku*) put out to grass; *żart.* (= *nakarmić do syta*) feed (*sb*) up. **~ się** *pf.* (*o zwierzęciu l. żart. o człowieku = najeść się*) eat one's fill; (= *objeść się do rozpuku*) stuff o.s., feed one's face (*czymś* with sth); pig out, gorge o.s. (*czymś* on sth).

napatoczyć się *pf. pot.* (*o ludziach*) pop up; (*o sprawach, kłopotach*) crop up.

napatrzeć się, napatrzyć się *pf.* -ył -yli *rzad.* -ał -ali have *l.* take a good look (*na kogoś/coś* at sb/ sth); **nie mogę się na nią napatrzyć** I can't take my eyes off her.

napawać *ipf.* 1. (*lit. = przejmować, napełniać*) fill, inspire, imbue (*kogoś czymś* sb with sth). 2. *form.* **napawać oczy widokiem czegoś** feast one's eyes on (the sight of) sth. 3. *tk.* (= *nasycać*) impregnate, pad (*with sth* czymś). **~ się** *ipf. form.* gloat (*czymś* about *l.* over sth).

napchać (się) *pf. zob.* **napychać (się)**.

napełniać *ipf.* (*t. przen. o uczuciach itp.*) fill (up) (*czymś* with sth); (*naczynie*) refill, replenish; (= *nadmuchiwać*) inflate; **napełnia nas duma/radość** we are filled with pride/happiness. **~ się** *ipf.* fill up, be filled (*czymś* with sth).

napełnić (się) *pf.* -ij *zob.* **napełniać (się)**.

naperfumować (się) *pf. zob.* **perfumować (się)**.

napęcznieć *pf. zob.* **pęcznieć**.

napęd *mi* 1. (*techn. = urządzenie napędzające*) drive; **napęd bezpośredni** direct drive; **napęd dyskietki/dysku twardego** *komp.* diskette/harddisk drive; **napęd na przednie/tylne koła** mot. front-wheel/rear-wheel drive; **napęd na cztery koła** *mot.* four-wheel drive. 2. (= *siła napędzająca*) driving force; (*rakietowy, odrzutowy*) *lotn.* propulsion; **o napędzie odrzutowym** *lotn.* jet-propelled; **o napędzie ręcznym** hand-driven; **okręt podwodny o napędzie jądrowym** *wojsk.* nuclear-powered submarine.

napędowy *a.* (*techn. = napędzający*) driving, propulsive; **olej napędowy** diesel fuel; **siła napędowa** driving force; **wał napędowy** drive shaft.

napędzać *ipf.,* **napędzić** *pf.* 1. (= *zaganiać*) round up; **napędzać (kogoś/coś) z powrotem** drive (sb/sth) back (*do czegoś* into sth). 2. *zw. pf. przen.* **napędzić komuś stracha** *l.* **strachu** give sb a scare; **napędzić komuś rozumu do głowy** teach sb a lesson. 3. (*pot. = nakłaniać, zapędzać*) **napędzać kogoś** incite sb, goad sb on (*do zrobienia czegoś* to do sth). 4. (*techn. l. przen. = wprawiać w ruch*) propel, drive, impel; **samochód napędzany elektrycznie** electric car. 5. (= *powodować zwiększenie intensywności*) push, increase; **napędzać inflację** create inflationary pressures.

napiąć (się) *pf.* -pnę -pniesz, -pnij, -piął -pięła -pięli *zob.* **napinać (się)**.

napić się *pf.* -piję -pijesz, -pij (= *wypić nieco napoju*) have a drink; (= *ugasić pragnienie*) have enough to drink, quench one's thirst; **napije się pani kawy?** would you like some coffee, ma'am?

napiec *pf.* -kę -czesz, -kł + *Gen.* (*chleba, ciastek*) bake a lot of (*sth*); (*mięsa, ziemniaków*) roast a lot of (*sth*).

napierać *ipf.* **1.** (= *przeć, atakować*) press (*na kogoś* sb, *na coś* against sth). **2.** (= *nalegać*) insist (*na kogoś, aby zrobił coś* on sb('s) doing sth). ~ **się** *ipf.* + *Gen. pot.* (= *domagać się*) clamor for (*sth*), demand.

napierśnik *mi Gen.* **-a 1.** (*część fartucha*) bib. **2.** (*część uprzęży*) breast collar. **3.** *hist.* (*część zbroi*) breast plate.

napięcie *n.* **1.** (= *naprężenie, sytuacja konfliktowa, zdenerwowanie*) tension; **napięcie mięśniowe** *fizj.* muscle tone; **napięcie nerwowe** nervous tension, stress; **napięcie powierzchniowe** *fiz.* surface tension; **napięcie tektoniczne** *geol.* tectonic tensional forces; (= *denerwująca niepewność*) suspense, anxiousness; **oczekiwać w napięciu** wait anxiously; **trzymać w napięciu** keep in suspense. **2.** *el.* voltage, current; **wysokie napięcie** high voltage; **pod napięciem** live current.

napiętek *mi* **-tk-** *Gen.* **-a 1.** (*obcas*) heel. **2.** *anat.* (= *kość skokowa*) talus, ankle bone.

napiętnik *mi Gen.* **-a** *rzad. zob.* **napiętek** 1.

napiętnować *pf. zob.* **piętnować**.

napięty *a.* **1.** (= *naprężony*) tense; (*mięśnie*) tense; (*lina*) taut. **2.** (= *natężony*) intense; (*uwaga*) rapt. **3.** (= *wymagający wysiłku*) demanding; (*termin*) tight. **4.** (= *pełny niepokoju*) distraught; (*atmosfera*) tense.

napinać *ipf.* tighten, tauten; (*tkaninę*) stretch; (*linę*) take up the slack in (*sth*), haul in; **napinać łuk** string a bow; **napinać mięśnie** flex *l.* tense one's muscle. ~ **się** *ipf.* **1.** (= *naprężać się*) tighten (up). **2.** (= *naprężać mięśnie*) flex one's muscle.

napis *mi* inscription; **napisy** *film* subtitles.

napisać *pf.* **-szę -szesz** *zob.* **pisać**.

napitek *mi* **-tk-** *zw. pl.* (*pot.* = *alkohol*) booze; (*przest.* = *napój*) beverage.

napity *a. pot.* = **pijany**.

napiwek *mi* **-wk-** tip; **dać komuś napiwek** leave sb a tip, tip sb.

napleść *pf.* **-plotę -pleciesz -plótł -plotła -pletli 1.** (= *upleść wiele*) plait a lot. **2.** *pot.* (= *nagadać głupstw*) talk a lot of gibberish, talk a load of nonsense.

napletek *mi* **-tk-** *Gen.* **-a** *anat.* prepuce, foreskin.

naplotkować *pf.* spread a lot of gossip. ~ **się** *pf.* spend much time gossiping.

napluć *pf.* **-pluję -plujesz** = **plunąć**; *zob.* **pluć**; **napluć komuś w twarz** spit in sb's face.

napłakać *pf.* **-czę -czesz tyle, co kot napłakał** *pot.* very little; **płacą mi, co kot napłakał** they pay me next to nothing; **zrobiłeś tyle, co kot napłakał** you've done hardly any work at all. ~ **się** *pf.* cry one's eyes *l.* heart out.

na płask *adv.* flat; **leżeć/padać na płask** lie/fall flat *l.* prone.

napłodzić *pf.* + *Gen.* **1.** (= *spłodzić dużą liczbę*) beget, procreate. **2.** *pot.* (= *stworzyć, napisać*) produce, put out, release, come out with.

napłynąć *pf. zob.* **napływać**.

napływ *mi* **1.** (= *napłynięcie, gromadzenie się*) inflow, influx; **napływ krwi** *pat.* blood congestion.

2. *przen.* (= *gromadne przybywanie*) immigration, arrival, influx. **3.** (*uczuć, doznań*) surge.

napływać *ipf.* **1.** (*o cieczach, gazach, t. przen.* = *docierać licznie*) flow in, pour in; (*o krwi*) rush; (*o łzach*) well up (*do oczu* in one's eyes). **2.** + *Dat.* (= *napełniać się*) fill (*with sth* czymś); **jego twarz napłynęła krwią** he flushed *l.* blushed, his face reddened. **3.** *przen.* (= *gromadzić się tłumnie*) flock in, gather, come together *l.* in droves.

napływowy *a.* **1.** (*o ludności l. społeczności*) immigrant, non-native, foreign. **2.** *geol.* alluvial, drifted; **gleba napływowa** alluvial soil.

napocić się *pf. pot.* work night and day, slave away (*nad czymś* at sth); sweat blood, exert o.s., knock o.s. out, work one's fingers to the bone (*robiąc coś* doing sth).

napocząć *pf.* **-cznę -czniesz** begin, start (on); (*jedzenie*) cut *l.* bite into; (*butelkę, puszkę*) open.

na poczekaniu *adv.* immediately, promptly, as soon as possible; (*o usłudze*) while you *l.* U wait.

napoczynać *ipf. zob.* **napocząć**.

na podorędziu *adv.* at hand, within (one's *l.* arm's) reach, at one's fingertips.

na pohybel *adv.* + *Dat. zw. żart.* death to (*sb*), down with (*sb*).

napoić (się) *pf.* **-poję -poisz, -pój** *zob.* **poić (się)**.

napoleonka *f. Gen.pl.* **-ek** *kulin.* napoleon; *Br.* millefeuille.

napoleoński *a. hist.* Napoleonic.

na poły *adv. lit.* half, partly, in part.

napominać *ipf.* admonish, rebuke, reprove.

napomknąć *pf.* **-ij** *zob.* **napomykać**.

napomknienie *n.* (= *krótka wzmianka*) (brief) mention; (= *aluzja*) hint, allusion, intimation.

napomnieć *pf.* **-ę -isz, -ij** *zob.* **napominać**.

napompować *pf. zob.* **pompować**.

napomykać *ipf.* (= *wspominać mimochodem*) mention (*o kimś/czymś* sb/sth); allude (*o kimś/czymś* to sb/sth); hint (*o czymś* at sth, *komuś o czymś* sth to sb, *że...* that...); intimate (*że...* that...).

napotkać *pf. zob.* **napotykać**.

napotny *a. med.* diaphoretic, sudorific, sudatory.

napotykać *ipf.* encounter; (*ludzi*) meet, run into; *pot.* bump into; (*opór*) meet with; (*trudności, przeszkody*) come across, face.

napowietrzać *ipf. techn.* aerate; **beton napowietrzony** *bud.* air-entrained concrete.

napowietrzanie *n. techn.* aeration; (*betonu*) air entrainment.

napowietrzny *a.* (= *odbywający się nad ziemią*) aerial; *techn.* (*zwł. o linii energetycznej*) overhead; **napowietrzna kolej linowa** aerial cableway.

napowietrzyć *pf. zob.* **napowietrzać**.

napożyczać *pf.* + *Gen.* **1.** (= *spłodzić dużą liczbę*) lend a large number or amount of (*sth*) (*komuś* to sb). **2.** borrow a large number or amount of (*sth*) (*od kogoś* from sb).

napój *mi* **-o-** *Gen.pl.* **-jów** *l.* **-i** drink; *form.* beverage; **napój bezalkoholowy** soft drink; **napój chłodzący** cool drink; **napój wyskokowy** *l.* **alko-**

holowy hard drink, liquor; *form.* alcoholic beverage; *żart.* libation.

napór *mi* **-o- 1.** (= *nacisk, presja, ciśnienie*) pressure; (*fal, wiatru*) impact; **pod naporem czegoś** under the impact *l.* pressure of sth. **2.** *przen.* (*bólu, emocji*) spasm, twinge.

napracować się *pf.* do a lot of (hard) work, work hard (*przy czymś l. nad czymś* at sth *l.* on sth).

napraszać się *ipf.* + *Dat.* importune (*sb*) (*o coś* for sth); pester, badger (*sb*) (*z czymś* with sth) (*o coś* for sth).

naprawa *f.* **1.** (= *reperacja*) repair, mending; **naprawa gwarancyjna** warranty service; **oddać coś do naprawy** get *l.* have sth fixed *l.* repaired; **być w naprawie** be under repair; **nie do naprawy** (damaged) beyond repair. **2.** (= *ulepszanie*) improvement, reform.

naprawczy *a.* **punkt** *l.* **warsztat naprawczy** repair shop; **stacja naprawcza** *mot.* garage, service station.

naprawdę *adv.* **1.** (= *rzeczywiście, bardzo, zgodnie z prawdą*) really, truly, genuinely; **naprawdę piękny dzień** a really fine day; **co o tym naprawdę myślisz?** what do you really think about it?; **czyś ty naprawdę oszalał?** have you really gone crazy?; **ją ją naprawdę lubię** I really like her; **on jest naprawdę chory** he is really sick. **2.** (= *prawdę mówiąc, w rzeczywistości*) in (actual) fact, as a matter of fact, actually, to tell the truth; **tak naprawdę nie nazywam się Brown** in actual fact, my name isn't Brown; **tak naprawdę to po prostu nie chce mi się tego robić** to tell the truth, I simply don't feel like doing it. **3.** (= *w samej rzeczy*) indeed; **naprawdę?** (*niedowierzanie*) oh, really?, indeed?; **byłem naprawdę zadowolony** I was very happy indeed; **on naprawdę dobrze gotuje** he cooks very well indeed; **to naprawdę dziwne** that is indeed strange.

naprawiacz *mp*, **naprawiaczka** *f. Gen.pl.* **-ek** *zw. iron.* reformer.

naprawiać *ipf.*, **naprawić** *pf.* **1.** (= *reperować*) repair, mend, fix, refit. **2.** (= *poprawiać, udoskonalać*) improve, amend; (= *reformować*) reform. **3.** (= *usuwać skutki*) **naprawiać błędy/pomyłki** correct one's errors/mistakes; **naprawiać szkody/wyrządzone (komuś) zło** make amends, make restitution *l.* make up for damage/for the wrong done (to sb).

naprędce *adv.* hastily, slapdash, impromptu; **naprędce sklecony** improvised, rough and ready, makeshift, thrown together; **naprędce sklecony posiłek** hastily concocted meal.

naprężać *ipf.* tighten, strain, tauten, tense; (= *rozciągać*) stretch; **naprężać mięśnie** tense one's muscles; (= *demonstrować siłę*) flex one's muscles. **~ się** *ipf.* tense, tauten; (= *wysilać się*) strain; (= *nie szczędzić starań*) put one's shoulder to the wheel.

naprężenie *n.* tension, strain; *fiz., techn.* stress; **naprężenie krytyczne** buckling *l.* critical stress; **naprężenie ścinające/ściskające/rozciągające** shearing/compressive/tensile stress.

naprężyć (się) *pf. zob.* **naprężać (się).**

napromieniać *ipf. rzad.* = **napromieniowywać.**

napromieniować *pf. zob.* **napromieniowywać.**

napromieniowanie *n. fiz.* irradiation, exposure (to radiation).

napromieniowywać *ipf. fiz.* irradiate, expose *l.* subject to radiation.

naprosić *pf.* + *Gen.* (= *sprosić*) invite a great number of (*sb*).

naprosić się *pf.* + *Gen.* **naprosić się (kogoś) o coś** beg (sb) for sth, beg sth (of sb).

naprostować *pf.*, **naprostowywać** *ipf.* straighten out, put/set (*sth*) straight; *przen.* (= *skorygować*) correct.

naprowadzać *ipf.*, **naprowadzić** *pf.* **1.** (= *nakierowywać*) direct, lead; (*lunetę, lufę broni*) aim (*na coś* at sth). **2.** *wojsk., nawigacja* home, guide; **naprowadzać działo (na cel)** lay the gun; **naprowadzać samolot/statek** guide an airplane/ship; **naprowadzanie radiolokacyjne** radar homing; **urządzenia naprowadzające** homing devices. **3.** *przen.* **naprowadzić kogoś na ślad** *l.* **trop kogoś/czegoś** set sb on sb's trail/on the trail of sth; **naprowadzać dyskusję na temat czegoś** steer the discussion towards (the subject of) sth.

naprzeciw *adv.* **1.** (= *ku komuś, czemuś*) **wyjść (komuś) naprzeciw** = **wyjść naprzeciw komuś. 2.** (= *po przeciwnej stronie*) opposite, on the opposite side; (= *po drugiej stronie ulicy*) across the street; **mieszkać naprzeciw** live across the street *l.* opposite. – *prep.* **1.** + *Dat.* (= *ku komuś, czemuś*) **wyjść naprzeciw komuś** go out to meet sb (halfway); **wyjść naprzeciw czyimś potrzebom/życzeniom** *przen.* meet sb's needs/wishes. **2.** + *Gen.* (= *po przeciwnej stronie*) opposite; **mieszkać naprzeciw szkoły** live opposite *l.* (*US*) across from the school.

naprzeciwko *adv. i prep.* = **naprzeciw; z naprzeciwka** (= *z sąsiedztwa*) from across (the street); **nadchodzić z naprzeciwka** approach from the opposite direction.

naprzeciwległy *a.* opposite, diametrically opposed; **ulistnienie naprzeciwległe** *bot.* opposite leaves.

naprzeć *pf.* **-prę -przesz, -przyj, -parł** *zob.* **napierać.**

na przedzie *adv.* at the head, in the lead, in *l.* at the front.

na przekór *adv.* contrarily, obstinately, wilfully.

na przełaj *adv.* across, cross-country; **bieg na przełaj** *sport* cross-country run; **iść na przełaj** take a short cut.

na przemian *adv.* by turns, in (successive) turns, alternately.

naprzemianległy *a.* alternate; **ulistnienie naprzemianległe** *bot.* alternate leaves.

naprzemienny *a.* alternating, alternate, happening by turns.

naprzód *adv.* **1.** (= *do przodu*) forward, onward, on, ahead; **naprzód!** (*komenda*) forward!; **cała naprzód** *żegl.* full (steam) ahead; **iść naprzód** go on, advance; *przen.* (= *czynić postępy*) make progress; **technika posuwa się naprzód** technology advances *l.* goes ahead; **wielki krok/**

skok naprzód a giant step/leap forward; **to odkrycie oznacza krok naprzód** this discovery marks a quantum leap forward; **wybiegać myślą naprzód** (= *w przyszłość*) look *l.* plan ahead. **2.** (= *zawczasu, z wyprzedzeniem*) in advance; **kupić sobie bilety pięć dni naprzód** get one's tickets five days in advance.

na przychodne *adv.* **mamy kucharkę/sprzątaczkę na przychodne** we have a woman who comes to cook/clean; **pielęgniarka na przychodne** visiting nurse.

naprzyjmować *pf.* + *Gen.* accept a lot of (*sth*); **naprzyjmować ludzi do pracy** *pot.* employ (too) many people.

naprzykrzać się *ipf.* + *Dat.* pester, badger, bug (*sb*) (*o coś* for sth, *z czymś* with sth); bother (*sb*) (*czymś* with sth, *w sprawie czegoś* about sth).

naprzykrzony *a.* **-eni** annoying, pesky.

naprzykrzyć się *pf.* *zob.* **naprzykrzać się.**

naprzynosić *pf.* bring *l.* haul in a lot of (*sth*).

naprzywozić *pf.* **-woź** *l.* **wóź** + *Gen.* cart in a lot of (*sth*), bring boatloads of (*sth l. sb*).

napsioczyć *pf.* *pot.* grumble, beef, bitch, bellyache (*na kogoś/coś* about sb/sth).

napsocić *pf.* get into mischief; **coście tu napsocili?** what have you been up to?

napstrzyć *pf.* **-yj 1.** (*o muchach*) leave specks. **2.** *pot.* overdecorate (*sth*) (*czymś* with sth).

napsuć *pf.* **1.** + *Gen.* (= *zepsuć wiele*) ruin, damage a lot of (*sth*). **2. napsuć komuś krwi** *pot.* be a nuisance to sb.

napuchnąć *pf.* **-ij** swell (up) (*od czegoś* with *l.* from sth).

napuchnięty *a.* swollen, bloated.

napuszać *ipf.* puff up, puff out. **~ się** *ipf.* **1.** (= *stawać się puszystym*) become puffy *l.* puffed out; **ptak napuszył się** the bird ruffled up its feathers. **2.** *przen.* (= *stawać się wyniosłym*) puff up (with pride).

napuszczać *ipf.* **1.** + *Gen.* (= *nalewać z kranu*) pour (*sth*) (*do czegoś* into sth); **napuszczać wody do wanny** fill the tub with water, run a bath. **2.** + *Acc.* *pot.* (= *podburzać*) set (*sb*) (*na kogoś* on sb).

napuszenie *f.*, **napuszoność** *f.* pomposity, haughtiness, vainglory; (= *nienaturalność*) mannerism, pretension; (*stylu, języka*) stiltedness, turgidity.

napuszony *a.* **-eni** pompous, haughty, puffed up; (= *pretensjonalny*) pretentious; (*styl, mowa*) stilted, turgid, bombastic.

napuszyć (się) *pf.* *zob.* **napuszać (się).**

napuścić *pf.* *zob.* **napuszczać.**

napychać *ipf.* **1.** (= *wypełniać szczelnie*) stuff, cram, pack; **napychać kieszenie** (= *wzbogacać się*) line one's pockets, make one's pile. **2.** *pot.* (= *przekarmiać*) stuff. **~ się** *ipf.* *pot.* (= *objadać się*) gorge (o.s.) (*czymś* on sth) stuff o.s. (*czymś* with sth).

napylać *ipf.*, **napylić** *pf.* **1.** *techn.* deposit (*sth*) by spraying *l.* dusting; **napylać farbę na powierzchnię** spray a surface with paint, spray paint on a surface. **2.** *el.* (= *nanosić*) sputter

(*sth*) (*na coś* on sth); (= *pokrywać*) sputter(-coat) (*sth*) (*czymś* with sth).

napyskować *pf.* + *Dat.* *pot.* (= *odpowiedzieć niegrzecznie*) sass, smart-mouth, talk back to (*sb*); (= *skląć, skrzyczeć*) berate, bark at (*sb*).

napytać *pf.* **napytać sobie biedy** *pot.* get into hot water.

narada *f.* council, meeting, consultation; **narada wojenna** *t. przen.* council of war; **toczyć** *l.* **wieść z kimś narady** consult with sb, confer with sb, hold counsel with sb.

naradzać się *ipf.*, **naradzić się** *pf.* (= *odbywać naradę*) hold a meeting *l.* a council; **naradzać się z kimś nad czymś** *l.* **w sprawie czegoś** consult sb about sth, confer with sb about *l.* on sth, seek sb's advice on sth.

naraić *pf.*, **narajać** *ipf.* *pot.* **narajać komuś coś** get *l.* find sth for sb; **narajać komuś kogoś** (= *swatać*) match sb with sb, get sb and sb together.

naramiennik *mi* *Gen.* **-a 1.** (= *epolet*) shoulderstrap. **2.** *broń, hist.* pauldron. **3.** *sport* shoulder-pad.

naramienny *a.* shoulder; **mięsień naramienny** *anat.* deltoid muscle.

narastać *ipf.* (= *potęgować się*) grow, increase; (= *nawarstwiać się*) accumulate, gather, pile up.

naraz *adv.* **1.** (= *niespodziewanie*) suddenly, all of a sudden, unexpectedly. **2.** (= *jednocześnie*) at the same time, at one time, all at once, simultaneously; **po dwa naraz** two at a time.

narazić (się) *ipf.* *zob.* **narażać (się).**

narażać *pf.* endanger, jeopardize, put (*sb l. sth*) at a risk; **narażać kogoś/się na ryzyko/ośmieszenie** expose sb/o.s. to a risk/to ridicule; **narażać życie** risk one's life (*dla kogoś/czegoś* for sb/sth). **~ się** *pf.* **1.** (= *wystawiać się na niebezpieczeństwo*) run risks; expose o.s. (*na coś* to sth). **2. narażać się komuś/czemuś** fall foul of sb/sth.

narąbać *pf.* **-ię -iesz** + *Gen.* chop (a lot of) (*sth*). **~ się** *pf.* *pot.* (= *spić się*) get screwed, sozzled, ripped, waxed *l.* knackered, tie one on.

narąbany *a.* *pot.* (= *pijany*) screwed, sozzled.

narciarka *f.* *Gen.pl.* **-ek 1.** *zob.* **narciarz. 2.** (= *czapka narciarska*) ski hat. **3.** *zw. pl. pot.* (= *but narciarski*) ski boot. **4.** (*spodnie*) ski pants.

narciarski *a.* ski, skiing; **bieg narciarski** ski race; **instruktor narciarski** ski instructor; **kijek/ kombinezon narciarski** ski pole/suit; **skocznia narciarska** jumping hill; **warunki narciarskie** skiing conditions.

narciarstwo *n.* skiing; **narciarstwo akrobatyczne** acroski; **narciarstwo alpejskie/zjazdowe** Alpine/downhill skiing; **narciarstwo klasyczne** Nordic *l.* cross-country skiing; **narciarstwo wodne** water skiing; **uprawiać narciarstwo** ski.

narciarz *mp* skier.

narcystyczny *a.* narcissistic.

narcyz *mi* *Gen.* **-a** *bot.* daffodil, narcissus (*Narcissus*). – *mp* (= *człowiek zakochany w sobie*) narcissist.

narcyzm *mi* narcissism.

nard *mi bot.* spikenard, nard (*Nardostachys jatamansi*).

narecznica *f. bot.* male fern (*Dryopteris filix-mas*).

nareperować *pf. pot.* fix, repair.

nareszcie *adv.* at last, finally; *int.* **nareszcie (jesteś)!** there you are!

naręcze *n. Gen.pl.* **-y** armful (*czegoś* of sth).

nargile *pl. Gen.* **-i** *l.* **-ów** hookah, narghile, hubble-bubble.

narkolepsja *f. pat.* narcolepsy.

narkoleptyczny *a. pat.* narcoleptic.

narkoman *mp* drug addict.

narkomania *f. Gen.* **-ii** *pat.* drug addiction, drug abuse.

narkomanka *f. Gen.pl.* **-ek** *zob.* **narkoman**.

narkotyczny *a.* narcotic; **głód narkotyczny** *pat.* drug withdrawal; **sen narkotyczny** narcosis, drug-induced sleep.

narkotyk *mi* drug; *med.* narcotic; **handel/handlarz narkotykami** drug trade/dealer; **przemyt narkotyków** drug smuggling.

narkotykowy *a.* **kartel narkotykowy** drug cartel.

narkotyzować *ipf. form.* narcotize.

narkotyzować się *ipf.* take drugs.

narkoza *f. chir.* (*zabieg*) general anesthesia; (*sen*) narcosis; **operacja pod narkozą** surgery under a general anesthetic.

narobić *pf.* **-rób 1.** + *Gen.* (= *zrobić dużo czegoś*) make *l.* produce a lot of (*sth*). **2.** + *Gen.* (= *spowodować, wywołać*) make, cause, produce, bring about; **coś ty narobił (najlepszego)!** look what you've done!; **narobić długów** incur debts, go into debt; **narobić hałasu/krzyku** *t. przen.* make a lot of noise, make *l.* kick up a fuss (*o coś* about *l.* over sth); **narobić komuś smaku na coś** *przen.* whet sb's appetite for sth; **narobić komuś wstydu** bring shame on sb, embarrass sb; **narobić (niezłego) bigosu** *l.* kłopotu make a (fine) mess. **3.** *euf.* **narobić na coś** *l.* **do czegoś** (= *zabrudzić kałem lub moczem*) soil sth. **~ się** *pf.* **1.** *pot.* (= *napracować się*) slave away, work hard (*nad czymś* at *l.* over sth). **2. ale się narobiło!** (*pot. o nieprzyjemnej sytuacji*) what a pretty kettle of fish!

narodowiec *mp* **-wc-** *Voc.* **-wcze** *pl.* **-y** *polit., często uj.* nationalist.

narodowościowy *a.* ethnic.

narodowość *f.* **1.** (= *przynależność etniczna*) ethnicity, nationality; **być narodowości polskiej** be of Polish nationality, be an ethnic Pole, be Polish. **2.** *lit.* (= *naród*) nation.

narodowowyzwoleńczy *a. polit.* **front/ruch narodowowyzwoleńczy** national liberation front/movement; **walka narodowowyzwoleńcza** struggle for national independence.

narodowy *a.* **dzień żałoby narodowej** day of national mourning; **gwardia narodowa** *US* the National Guard; **hymn narodowy** national anthem; **park narodowy** national park.

narodzenie *n. arch.* birth; **Boże Narodzenie** Christmas, Xmas.

narodzić się *pf.* (= *przyjść na świat*) be born; *lit.* (= *powstać*) arise, emerge, originate.

narodziny *pl. Gen.* **-n** birth; *form.* (= *pojawienie się czegoś*) origin, emergence; **narodziny nowej epoki** the beginning of a new epoch; **w chwili narodzin** at the moment of birth.

narodzony *a.* **-eni** born; **nowo narodzone dziecko** newborn baby; **jak nowo narodzony** (*o samopoczuciu*) restored to life, like a new-born babe, as fresh as a daisy; **naiwny/niewinny jak nowo narodzone dziecię** as naive/innocent as a babe in arms.

narosnąć *pf.* **-snę -śniesz**, **-śnij**, **-rósł -rosła -rośli** *zob.* **narastać**.

narośl *f. pl.* **-e** *gł. pat.* excrescence, growth.

narowić *ipf.* **-ów** *jeźdz.* make restive. **~ się** *ipf.* (*o koniu*) become restive.

narowisty *a.* (*o koniu*) restive, vicious; (*o usposobieniu*) contrary, uncontrollable.

narozlewać *pf.* + *Gen.* spill a lot of (*sth*).

narozrabiać *pf.* **1.** + *Gen.* (= *rozrobić dużo czegoś*) mix (up) a lot of (*sth*). **2.** *pot.* (= *spsocić, wywołać zamieszanie*) *zob.* **rozrabiać**.

naroże *n. Gen.pl.* **-y** *bud.* corner, quoin; (*dachu*) hip.

narożnik *mi Gen.* **-a 1.** (= *styk ścian l. powierzchni, kąt*) angle, quoin; (*t. = róg pomieszczenia, ringu, ulicy itp.*) corner. **2.** *bud.* (= *wzmocnienie styku*) gusset. **3.** (= *kanapa narożna*) corner sofa, L-shaped sofa.

narożny *a.* **1. sklep narożny** (= *umiejscowiony na rogu ulicy*) corner store. **2. stolik narożny** (= *przeznaczony do umieszczenia w rogu*) corner table.

naród *mi* **-o-** nation; *przest.* (= *mrowie ludzi*) many people, multitude; **Liga Narodów** *hist.* the League of Nations; **Narody Zjednoczone** the United Nations, UN.

narów *mi* **-o-** vice, fault, bad habit; **tępić** *l.* **wykorzeniać narowy** eradicate vices.

narracja *f. teor.lit.* (= *przebieg akcji*) narration; *form.* (= *opowieść*) narrative; **narracja w pierwszej osobie** first-person narration.

narracyjny *a.* narrative.

narrator *mp*, **narratorka** *f. Gen.pl.* **-ek** narrator.

narratorski *a.* **1.** (= *pochodzący od narratora*) **komentarz narratorski** narrator's comments. **2.** (= *dotyczący narracji*) **talent narratorski** narrative gift.

narta *f. często pl. sport* ski; **narty biegowe/turystyczne/zjadowe** cross-country/tourist/Alpine skis; **narty wodne** water skis; **jeździć na nartach** ski.

nartnik *ma ent.* (= *owad z rodziny Gerridae*) water strider.

nartorolki *pl. Gen.* **-ek** roller skis.

nartostrada *f.* ski slope.

naruszać *ipf.*, **naruszyć** *pf.* **1.** (= *przekraczać, łamać, zaburzać*) (*dyscyplinę, reguły, postanowienia*) violate; (*granicę, terytorium*) encroach on (*sth*); (*plan, harmonogram*) interfere with (*sth*); (*równowagę*) disturb; **naruszać prawo** break *l.* infringe the law; **naruszać zasady** break *l.* violate the rules. **2.** (*napoczynać*) break into (*sth*). **3.** (= *nadłamywać*) break; (= *lekko uszkadzać*) chip, damage; (= *lekko ranić*) injure. **4.** (= *ujawniać*) reveal, betray.

narwać *pf.* -rwę -rwiesz, -rwij pick *l.* pluck a lot of (*sth*).

narwal *ma zool.* narwhal (*Monodon monoceros*).

narwaniec *mp* -ńc- *Voc.* -ńcze *l.* -ńcu *pl.* -y *pot.* hothead.

narwany *a. pot.* reckless, crazy, madcap, hotheaded; *przest.* harum-scarum; *pred.* nuts.

narybek *mi* -bk- **1.** (= *młode ryby*) fry. **2.** *pot.* (= *młodzi pracownicy, nowicjusze*) rookies, novices.

narysować *pf. zob.* **rysować** 1.

narząd *mi anat.* organ; **narząd ruchu/słuchu/ wzroku** organ of locomotion/hearing/vision; **narządy mowy/zmysłów** speech/sense organs; **narządy płciowe** reproductive organs.

narzecze *n. Gen.pl.* -y (regional) dialect.

narzeczeński *a.* **okres narzeczeński** (the period of) engagement.

narzeczeństwo *n.* engagement; *form.* betrothal.

narzeczona *f. Gen.* -ej fiancée.

narzeczony *mp pl.* -eni fiancé; *pl.* the betrothed (couple).

narzekać *ipf.* complain, grumble (*na kogoś/ coś* about sb/sth); **nie narzekam** *l.* **nie mogę narzekać** (= *jestem zadowolony*) I can't complain; **nie można narzekać na brak czegoś** there's no shortage of sth; **jeśli on na coś narzeka, to nie na brak pieniędzy** if there's anything he lacks it isn't money.

narzędnik *mi Gen.* -a *gram.* instrumental.

narzędzie *n. Gen.pl.* -i tool, implement, utensil; (= *przyrząd*) instrument, device; (= *środek służący do osiągnięcia celu*) means; **narzędzie ręczne** hand tool; **być (ślepym) narzędziem w czyichś rękach** *przen.* be a tool in sb's hands.

narzędziowiec *mp* -wc- *pl.* -y *techn.* toolmaker.

narzędziownia *f. Gen.pl.* -i *techn.* toolroom, toolmaker's shop.

narzędziowy *a. techn.* **stal narzędziowa** tool steel; **stop narzędziowy** tool alloy.

narznąć *pf.* -ij *rzad.* = **narżnąć**.

narzucać *ipf.*, **narzucić** *pf.* **1.** (= *rzucać na wierzch*) throw, fling, pile (*sth*) (*na coś* on, onto, on top of *l.* over sth); **narzucać tynk na ścianę** *bud.* roughcast a wall. **2. narzucać coś na siebie** (= *okrywać się pospiesznie*) fling, throw *l.* slip sth on. **3.** (= *wymuszać*) impose, force (*sth*) (*komuś on l.* upon sb); **narzucać ograniczenia** impose limitations *l.* constraints (*na coś on l.* upon sth); **narzucać (ostre) tempo** force the pace; **narzucać swoją wolę** get *l.* have one's way (*komuś* with sb); **narzucać warunki** dictate conditions *l.* terms (*komuś* to sb). **~ się** *ipf.*, **narzucić się** *pf.* (= *napraszać się*) impose o.s., inflict o.s. *l.* one's company (*komuś* on *l.* upon sb); **mam nadzieję, że się państwu nie narzucam** *form.* I hope I'm not imposing on you.

narzut *mi* **1.** *handl.* extra charge. **2.** *bud.* (= *warstwa tynku*) floating.

narzuta *f.* bedspread, coverlet.

narzutka *f. Gen.pl.* -ek (= *lekkie okrycie*) cape, cloak.

narzutowiec *mi* -wc- *Gen.* -a *geol.* erratic.

narzutowy *a.* **głaz narzutowy** = **narzutowiec**.

narzygać *pf. pot.* (= *zwymiotować*) vomit, puke; *sl.* barf, ralph, loose ones lunch; + *Ins.* puke (*sth*) (up), throw (*sth*) up (*na coś* over *l.* all over sth).

narzynać *ipf.* notch, cut (*sth*) (*w czymś* in sth) (*na czymś* on sth).

narzynka *f. Gen.pl.* -ek *techn.* (threading) die.

narżnąć *pf.* -ij **1.** *zob.* **narzynać**. **2.** + *Gen.* (= *pociąć*) cut (up); (= *pozabijać nożem*) butcher, slaughter. **3.** *wulg.* (= *nasrać*) crap.

nas *pron. zob.* **my**.

nasada *f.* **1.** base, root; **nasada języka** *anat.* the root of the tongue; **nasada liścia/łodygi** *bot.* leaf/stem base; **nasada nosa/ogona** the base of the nose/tail; **u nasady (czegoś)** at the base (of sth). **2.** = **nasadka** 2.

nasadka *f. Gen.pl.* -ek **1.** (= *skuwka*) ferrule, cap. **2.** *techn.* (= *przystawka, głowica*) attachment, head, nozzle.

nasadowy *a.* **klucz nasadowy** *techn.* socket wrench.

nasadzać *ipf.*, **nasadzić** *pf.* **1.** (= *osadzać, nakładać*) fix, set, mount (*sth*) (*na coś* on *l.* upon sth); **nasadzać kapelusz na głowę** put on *l.* don a hat. **2.** *pf.* + *Gen.* (= *posadzić wiele roślin*) plant. **3.** *pf.* **nasadzić błędów** *pot.* make (many) mistakes.

nasączać *ipf.* soak (*sth*) (*czymś* in sth); saturate (*sth*) (*czymś* with *l.* in sth). **~ się** *ipf.* soak (*czymś* in sth).

nasączyć (się) *pf. zob.* **nasączać (się)**.

na schwał *adj. przest.* manly; **chłop na schwał** *pot.* big guy, macho.

nasenny *a. med.* soporific, somniferous; **proszki** *l.* **pigułki nasenne** sleeping-pills, tranquilizers, sleep-producing sedatives.

nasercowy *a.* **leki nasercowe** *med.* heart drugs.

nasi *a. zob.* **nasz.** – *mp pl.* -szy- *Gen.* -ch *pot.* our boys, our folks; **górą nasi!** hurray for our boys!

nasiać *pf.* -sieję -siejesz -siali *l.* -eli + *Gen.* sow a lot of (*sth*).

nasiadówka *f. Gen.pl.* -ek **1.** *med.* sitz bath. **2.** *pot.* (= *nudne zebranie*) boring meeting.

nasiąkać *ipf.* **1.** (= *wchłaniać wilgoć*) soak (up), absorb, imbibe. **2.** (= *przechodzić czymś*) become permeated, become saturated; **słowa nasiąknięte goryczą** words full of bitterness.

nasiąkający *a.* saturable, spongy.

nasiąkanie *n.* imbibition, impregnation, soaking.

nasiąkliwość *f.* absorbability, impregnability.

nasiąkliwy *a.* absorbent.

nasiąknąć *pf.* -ij -kł *l.* -knął *zob.* **nasiąkać**.

nasiąknięty *a.* soaked, saturated; **nasiąknięty wodą** waterlogged.

nasiec *pf.* -kę -czesz -kł **1.** (= *ściąć dużo czegoś*) cut; (*trawy*) mow. **2.** *przest.* (= *namordować, siekąc*) cut down, saber, slaughter.

nasiedzieć się *pf.* -dzę -dzisz -dzą **1.** (= *przez długi czas siedzieć*) sit long enough. **2.** (= *przez długi czas przebywać*) stay long enough.

nasiekać *pf. zob.* **nasiec** 1.

nasieniak *mi Gen.* -a *pat.* seminoma, dysgerminoma.

nasienie *n. pl.* -on- **1.** (= *zarodek rośliny*) seed. **2.** (= *sperma*) sperm, semen. **3.** *arch.* offspring, issue; **diabelskie nasienie** spawn of the devil.

nasieniotok *mi pat.* spermatorrh(o)ea.

nasieniowodowy *a. anat.* deferent.

nasieniowód *mi* -o- *anat.* vas deferens, deferent *l.* spermatic duct.

nasiennictwo *n. roln.* seed production.

nasienniczy *a. roln.* seed-producing, (of *l.* pertaining to) seed production.

nasiennik *mi Gen.* -a **1.** *ogr., roln.* seedling. **2.** *leśn.* seed-tree.

nasienny *a.* **1.** (= *dotyczący nasion*) seed, seminiferous; **rośliny nasienne** *bot.* seed plants, spermatophytes. **2.** (= *dotyczący spermy*) seminal, spermatic.

nasierdzie *n. Gen.pl.* -i *anat.* epicardium.

nasiębierny *a.* **koło nasiębierne** *techn.* overshot water wheel.

nasięźrzał *mi bot.* adder's-tongue (*Ophioglossum*).

nasikać *pf. pot.* piss.

nasilać się *ipf.* intensify, escalate.

nasilenie *n.* intensification, escalation.

nasilić się *pf. zob.* **nasilać się.**

nasionko *n. Gen.pl.* -ek seedlet.

nasionoznawstwo *n.* seed science.

nasiusiać *pf. pot.* pee.

naskakiwać *ipf.* **1.** (= *skacząc, nacierać*) thrust (*na kogoś* at sb). **2.** *pot.* (= *atakować słownie*) assault (*na kogoś* sb).

naskalny *a.* rock; **malowidła naskalne** rock paintings.

naskarżyć *pf. zob.* **skarżyć.**

naskładać *pf.* **1.** (= *zgromadzić*) collect. **2.** (= *ułożyć w stertę*) pile up, heap up. **3.** (= *zaoszczędzić pieniędzy*) save.

naskoczyć *pf.* **1.** *zob.* **naskakiwać. 2.** (*o kości*) go back in place.

naskorupienie *n. geol.* efflorescence.

naskórek *mi* -rk- *Gen.* -a **1.** *anat.* epidermis; **obetrzeć sobie naskórek** rub *l.* scrape one's skin. **2.** *bot.* cuticle, epidermis. **3.** *techn.* skin.

naskórkowanie *n. med.* epidermisation.

naskórkowaty *a. anat.* epidermoid.

naskórkowość *f. el.* (Kelvin *l.* conductor) skin effect.

naskórkowy *a.* **1.** *anat.* epidermal, epidermic. **2.** *bot.* cuticular.

naskórny *a.* (= *występujący na skórze*) situated on the skin; (= *działający na skórę*) skin.

naskórzak *mi pat.* epidermoma, epidermoid tumour.

naskrobać *pf.* -bię -biesz **1.** (= *obrać, skrobiąc*) (*warzyw*) scrape, peel; (*ryb*) scale. **2.** *pot.* (= *napisać niedbale*) scribble, scrawl.

naskubać *pf.* -bię -biesz **1.** (*o ptactwie*) (= *oczyścić, skubiąc*) pluck. **2.** (*wełnę, włosie*) (= *rozerwać*) tease. **3.** (= *nagryźć*) nibble.

nasłać *pf.* -ślę -ślesz *zob.* **nasyłać.**

nasłoneczniać *ipf.*, **nasłonecznić** *pf.* -ij insolate, expose to the sun's rays. ~ **się** *ipf.* be insolated; (*o ludziach*) sunbathe, bask in the sun.

nasłonecznienie *n. t. meteor.* insolation.

nasłoneczniony *a.* insolated, sunlit, sunny.

nasłuch *mi* intercept, interception, listening (in); **nasłuch radiowy** radio intercept *l.* watch, listening watch; **prowadzić nasłuch** monitor, listen (in).

nasłuchać się *pf.* listen to, hear; (*opowieści*) hear enough of; (*wymówek, komplementów*) get an earful of.

nasłuchiwać *ipf.* listen (out) for (*kogoś / czegoś* sb/sth).

nasłuchowy *a.* interceptive.

nasłupny *a.* pillared.

nasłużyć się *pf.* serve long enough.

nasmarować *pf. zob.* **smarować.**

nasmażyć *pf. kulin.* (*w tłuszczu*) fry; (*w cukrze*) make jam.

nasmołować *pf. zob.* **smołować.**

nasmrodzić *pf. pot.* **1.** (= *zepsuć powietrze nieprzyjemnym zapachem*) stink (up); (= *puszczać wiatry*) fart. **2.** *pot.* (= *zaszkodzić komuś obmową*) slander, backbite.

nasobaczyć *pf. pot.* abuse, revile (*komuś* sb).

nasolenie *n.* saltness, saltiness.

nasolić *pf.* -ól salt, preserve with salt.

naspędzać *pf.* bring together, gather; (*bydło*) round up.

naspraszać *pf.* invite.

nasprowadzać *pf.* (*ludzi*) bring; (*towarów*) buy, order; (*z zagranicy*) import.

nasrać *pf. wulg.* shit, poop.

nasrożyć *pf.* **1.** (= *nadać srogi wygląd*) assume a stern look *l.* expression. **2.** (= *nastroszyć*) (*o zwierzęciu*) bristle; (*o ptaku*) ruffle. ~ **się** *pf.* scowl.

nassać się *pf.* suck one's fill.

nastać *pf.* -anę -aniesz, -ań *zob.* **nastawać.**

nastanie *n.* advent, coming, onset; **z nastaniem nocy** at nightfall; **z nastaniem dnia** at daybreak, at dawn.

nastarczać *ipf.*, **nastarczyć** *pf.* make *l.* provide enough of; **nie (móc) nastarczyć z czymś** fail to provide enough of sth, be unable to meet the demand for sth.

nastawa *f.* **1.** *bud.* retable. **2.** *techn.* setting.

nastawać *ipf.* -aję -ajesz, -awaj **1.** (= *następować*) come, follow; (*o pogodzie, porze roku, dnia*) set in, come; **nastało milczenie** silence fell *l.* followed. **2.** *pot.* (= *obejmować funkcję*) take over. **3.** (= *nalegać*) insist (*na coś* on sth); press (*na kogoś, żeby coś zrobił* sb to do *l.* into doing sth). **4.** *przest.* (= *dybać*) have designs (*na kogoś / coś* on sb/sth); **nastawać na czyjeś życie** threaten sb's life.

nastawczy *a. techn.* adjusting, setting.

nastawiać *ipf.*, **nastawić** *pf.* **1.** (= *wysuwać w jakimś kierunku*) point, direct, turn; **nastawić**

kołnierz raise *l.* put up one's collar; **nastawiać ucha** prick up one's ears. **2.** (= *stawiać na płycie kuchenki*) place, put; **nastawiać wodę na herbatę** put the kettle on. **3.** (= *regulować*) fix, set, adjust; **nastawiać budzik na szóstą** set the alarm-clock for six o'clock; **nastawiać ostrość** bring into focus, adjust the focus; **nastawiać płytę** play *l.* put on a record; **nastawić radio** turn the radio on; **nastawiać radio na jakąś stację** tune in to a station; **nastawiać zwrotnicę** *kol.* switch. **4.** (= *usposabiać*) dispose (*do kogoś/czegoś* to *l.* towards sb/sth); **nastawiać kogoś życzliwie do kogoś** dispose sb well to *l.* towards sb; **nastawiać kogoś wrogo do kogoś** dispose sb ill to *l.* towards sb. **5.** *med.* (*złamaną kość*) set; (*zwichnięty staw*) reduce. **6.** (= *umieścić wiele czegoś*) put, place (*a lot of sth*); **nastawiać domów** build a lot of houses. **~ się** *ipf.*, **nastawić się** *pf.* **1.** (= *poddawać się działaniu czegoś*) dispose o.s. (*do czegoś* to sth). **2.** (= *przygotowywać się*) expect (*na coś* sth); prepare (*do czegoś* for sth); **nastawiać się na poważną rozmowę** prepare for a serious conversation.

nastawienie *n.* **1.** attitude (*do l. wobec kogoś/ czegoś* to *l.* towards sb/sth). **2.** *med.* reduction, reposition.

nastawiony *a.* **-eni 1.** (= *mający jakieś nastawienie*) disposed (*do kogoś/czegoś* towards sb/ sth); **nastawiony na karierę** career-minded; **życzliwie nastawiony do ludzi** well-disposed towards people; **wrogo nastawiony do kogoś** ill-disposed towards sb. **2.** (= *nakierowany*) set, fixed, pointed. **3.** (= *przystosowany*) oriented; **zakład nastawiony na produkcję eksportową** export-oriented *l.* -orientated company.

nastawnia *f. Gen.pl.* **-i** *techn.* control station, control room; *kol.* switch tower.

nastawnica *f. kol.* interlocking frame.

nastawniczy *mp kol.* (= *pracownik nastawiający zwrotnice*) signalman, signaler.

nastawnik *mi Gen.* **-a** *techn.* controller; (*w zegarku*) pusher, push-piece.

nastawność *f. med.* **nastawność oka** accommodation.

nastawny *a. techn.* adjustable.

nastąpić *pf. zob.* **następować**.

następ *mi techn.* pedal.

następca *mp* successor; (= *dziedzic*) heir; **następca tronu** heir to the throne, Crown Prince.

następczyni *f.* heiress; **następczyni tronu** heiress to the throne, Crown Princess.

następnie *adv.* then, next, subsequently.

następnik *mi Gen.* **-a 1.** *fil., mat., muz.* consequent. **2.** *jęz.* apodosis, consequent clause.

następny *a.* next, following; **następny proszę!** next please!; **następnego dnia** the next *l.* following day; **w następnym tygodniu** next week; **następnym razem** next time; **następny co do ważności** next in rank *l.* importance.

następować *ipf.* **1.** (= *nadeptywać*) step, tread (*na coś* on sth); **następować komuś na pięty** tread on sb's heels; **nastąpić komuś na odcisk** step *l.* tread on sb's corns. **2.** (= *pojawiać się w kolejności*) follow, succeed (*po czymś* sth); **powiedział,**

co następuje... he said as follows...; **ciąg dalszy nastąpi** to be continued. **3.** (= *obejmować władzę, tron*) succeed, take over. **4.** (= *zdarzać się*) follow, ensue, happen, take place; (*o mrozach*) come; **następować szybko po sobie** follow *l.* happen in quick succession.

następstwo *n.* **1.** (= *konsekwencja*) result, consequence, outcome, after-effect; **w następstwie czegoś** in the aftermath of sth, as a result of sth, as a *l.* in consequence of sth; **być następstwem czegoś** be due to sth, result from sth. **2.** (= *kolejność*) sequence, succession, order; **następstwo czasów** *jęz.* sequence of tenses. **3.** (= *sukcesja*) succession; **następstwo tronu** succession to the throne.

następująco *adv.* as follows, in the following way; **list brzmi następująco...** the letter reads as follows...

następujący *a.* following; **następujący po sobie** successive; **dostała list następującej treści...** she received a letter to the effect that...

nastia *f. Gen.* **-ii** *biol.* nastic movement.

nastolatek *mp* **-tk-** *pl.* **-i** teenager, adolescent.

nastolatka *f. zob.* **nastolatek**.

nastoletni *a.* teenage, adolescent.

nastój *mi* **-o-** *Gen.pl.* **-ów** *przest.* (= *napar*) infusion.

nastrajać *ipf.* **1.** (= *stroić instrument*) tune (up); (*o strunach*) key. **2.** (= *usposabiać*) dispose, incline (*do kogoś/czegoś* to *l.* towards sb/ sth). **~ się** *ipf.* dispose o.s. (*do kogoś/czegoś* to sb/sth); **nastrajać się przychylnie do kogoś** dispose o.s. well to *l.* towards sb.

nastraszyć *pf.* frighten, scare. **~ się** *pf.* be *l.* get frightened *l.* scared.

nastręczać *ipf.*, **nastręczyć** *pf.* **1.** (= *dostarczać*) present, offer; (*kłopotów, trudności*) cause. **2.** *pot.* (= *rekomendować*) recommend; (*posadę*) find.

nastroić *pf.* **-ję -isz, -ój** *zob.* **nastrajać**. **~ się** *pf.* **-ję -isz, -ój** *zob.* **nastrajać się**.

nastrojowo *adv.* romantically.

nastrojowość *f.* romantic atmosphere.

nastrojowy *a.* romantic.

nastrosz *ma bot.* epacris (*Epacris*).

nastroszyć *pf.* (*o zwierzęciu, włosy*) bristle; (*o ptaku, pióra*) ruffle; (*uszy*) prick up. **~ się** *pf.* **1.** (= *najeżyć się*) bristle. **2.** (= *przyjąć postawę obronną*) bristle.

nastrój *mi* **-o- 1.** (= *stan psychiczny*) mood, humour, frame of mind; **huśtawka nastrojów** swinging moods; **nagła zmiana nastroju** mood swing; **być w dobrym/złym nastroju** be in a good/ bad mood; **(nie) być w nastroju do czegoś** (not) be in the mood for sth; **wprawiać kogoś w zły nastrój** put sb in a bad mood. **2.** (= *atmosfera*) atmosphere, ambiance.

nastrzępić *pf.* fray.

nastrzyc *pf. zob.* **strzyc**.

nasturcja *f. bot.* nasturtium (*Tropaeolum*).

nasturcjowate *pl. Gen.* **-ych** *bot.* the nasturtium family (*Tropaeolaceae*).

nastyczny *a. bot.* nastic; **ruch nastyczny** nastic movement.

nasunąć *pf.*, **nasuwać** *ipf.* **1.** (= *naciągnąć*) draw, pull; (= *założyć*) put on; **nasunąć czapkę na oczy** pull one's cap *l.* hat over one's eyes. **2.** (= *podsunąć*) suggest; **nasunąć coś komuś na myśl** suggest sth to sb; **to nasuwa mi na myśl** this brings to my mind; **nasuwać wątpliwości** raise doubts. **~ się** *pf.*, **nasuwać się** *ipf.* **1.** (= *przykryć, posuwając się*) overlap, slide onto. **2.** (= *powstać*) arise, emerge; (*o myśli, propozycji, refleksji*) come to mind.

nasuszyć *pf.* (*grzybów*) dry.

naswawolić *pf.* gambol, frolic.

nasycać *ipf.* **1.** (= *zaspokajać głód*) appease, satisfy, gratify. **2.** (= *zadowalać*) satisfy, gratify, sate; **nasycić ciekawość** satisfy one's curiosity; **nasycić czymś oczy** feast one's eyes on sth. **3.** (*o wilgoci itp., przepajać*) permeate, pervade. **4.** (= *wprowadzać substancję do czegoś*) saturate; impregnate; imbue; soak. **5.** *lit.* (= *wprowadzać dużo elementów*) fill; **nasycić film scenami przemocy** fill a film with violence. **~ się** *ipf.* **1.** (= *najadać się*) eat one's fill, appease one's hunger. **2.** (= *zadowalać się*) have one's fill, enjoy sth to the full, gratify o.s. to the full, gratify one's desire. **3.** (= *być nasycanym*) be permeated; be saturated.

nasycalnia *f. techn.* **nasycalnia drewna** wood treating plant, timber preserving plant.

nasycalnik *mi Gen.* -a *chem.* saturator.

nasycanie *n. chem.* saturation, impregnation; **nasycanie drewna** wood treatment, pickling of timber; **nasycanie dwutlenkiem węgla** carbonation.

nasycenie *n.* saturation, satiation; **nasycenie barwy** chromaticity, colour saturation; **nasycenie rynku** *ekon.* market saturation.

nasycić *pf. zob.* **nasycać**. **~ się** *pf. zob.* **nasycać się**.

nasycony *a.* **1.** (*o kolorze, parze, roztworze*) (= *intensywny*) saturated; **para nasycona** *chem.* saturated vapor; **roztwór nasycony** *chem.* saturated solution; **związki nasycone** *chem.* saturated compounds. **2.** (= *syty*) full, satiated, replete. **3.** (= *wypełniony*) full, replete.

nasyp *mi* embankment, bank; **nasyp kolejowy** railway embankment.

nasypać *pf.* -ię -iesz, **nasypywać** *ipf.* **1.** (= *nagromadzić, sypiąc*) pour. **2.** (= *rozsypać na powierzchni*) strew.

nasz *a.* (*z rzeczownikiem*) our; (*samodzielnie*) ours; **nasz wspólny przyjaciel** our mutual friend; **wasze przygody są ciekawsze od naszych** your adventures are more interesting than ours; **pewien nasz przyjaciel** a friend of ours; **po naszemu** *pot.* (= *zgodnie ze zwyczajem*) after our fashion, as we do it; (= *tak, jak nam odpowiada*) our way; (= *na polską modłę*) Polish fashion; (= *po polsku*) in Polish, in our tongue; **nie nasz** foreign; **przed naszą erą** before Christ, BC; **dobra nasza!** hurray!; **nasz człowiek** our man.

naszarpać *pf.* -ię -iesz *pot.* pull; pluck. **~ się** *pf.* -ię -iesz *pot.* (= *czynić ogromne wysiłki*) exert o.s.

naszatkować *pf.* shred, slice.

naszczać *pf. wulg.* piss.

naszczekiwać *ipf.* bark.

naszczekiwanie *n.* barking.

naszczuć *pf.* **1.** (*psa*) set (*na kogoś* at sb). **2.** *przen.* (= *nastawić przeciwko komuś*) set (*kogoś przeciw komuś* sb against sb).

naszczytnik *mi Gen.* -a *bud.* acroterium.

naszedł, naszła *itd. pf. zob.* **najść**.

naszelnik *mi Gen.* -a (*część uprzęży*) trace.

naszkicować *pf. zob.* **szkicować**.

naszkliwny *a. techn.* enamel.

naszkodzić *pf.* **1.** (= *spowodować szkody*) cause damage. **2.** (= *zepsuć swoim postępowaniem*) harm, hurt; **naszkodzić sobie** *l.* **komuś** damage one's *l.* sb's reputation.

naszperać się *pf.* rummage.

naszpikować *pf.* **1.** *kulin.* lard. **2.** *pot.* (= *przesycić*) lard; **naszpikować przemówienie cytatami** lard *l.* embellish a speech with quotations; (*lekami*) stuff. **~ się** *pf. pot.* (*lekami, wiadomościami*) stuff o.s.

naszukać się *pf.* + *Gen.* look for a long time; **naszukać się kogoś/czegoś** look for sb/sth for a long time; be weary of looking for sb/sth.

naszyć *pf.* -ję -jesz, -yj **1.** *zob.* **naszywać**. **2.** (= *uszyć dużo*) sew a lot (*czegoś* of sth).

naszyjnik *mi Gen.* -a **1.** (*ozdoba*) necklace. **2.** (= *pas, łańcuch nakładany na szyję zwierzęcia*) collar.

naszykować *pf. pot.* prepare.

naszywać *ipf.* **1.** (= *przyszywać na wierzch*) sew (*na coś* on *l.* onto sth). **2.** (= *ozdabiać*) trim (*czymś* with sth).

naszywka *f.* badge; **naszywki sierżanta** sergeant's stripes; **naszywki generała** general's stars.

naście *num.* -st- *mp* -u *Ins.* -u *l.* -oma *pot.* umpteen.

naścienny *a.* wall.

naścinać *pf.* cut.

naśladować *ipf.* **1.** (= *wzorować się*) copy, emulate; **naśladować kogoś** follow *l.* tread in sb's footsteps. **2.** (= *imitować*) imitate, emulate. **3.** (= *udawać kogoś*) imitate, mimic.

naśladowca *mp* imitator.

naśladowczy *a.* **1.** (= *odnoszący się do naśladowania*) imitative. **2.** (= *nieoryginalny*) unoriginal, imitative.

naśladownictwo *n.* **1.** (= *naśladowanie*) imitation. **2.** (= *wytwór naśladowania*) imitation, copy. **3.** *biol.* (= *mimetyzm*) mimicry, mimesis.

naśladownik *mi Gen.* -a *techn.* simulator; **naśladownik lotu** flight simulator.

naślęczeć się *pf.* peg away (*nad czymś* at sth).

naślinić *pf.* lick, moisten with saliva.

naśmiać się *pf.* -eję -ejesz (= *śmiać się do woli*) have a good laugh.

naśmiecić *pf.* litter.

naśmiewać się *ipf.* poke fun, laugh, scoff (*z kogoś / czegoś* at sb/sth).

naśnieżny *a.* nival, hiemal; **organizmy naśnieżne** *biol.* nival organisms.

naśnieżyć *pf.* **1.** (= *oprószyć śniegiem*) snow over. **2.** (= *nanieść śniegu, np. na podłogę*) soil with snow.

naświetlacz *mi Gen.* **-a** floodlight.

naświetlać *ipf.* **1.** *med., techn.* insolate; expose to light. **2.** (= *tłumaczyć*) elucidate, explain; (*temat, sprawę, fakty*) throw light on. **3.** *fot.* expose. ~ **się** *ipf.* get insolated; be exposed to light.

naświetlanie *n.* **1.** *med., techn.* insolation; exposure to light. **2.** (= *objaśnianie*) elucidation, explanation, clarification. **3.** *fot.* exposure.

naświetlenie *n. techn.* exposure, quantity of illumination.

naświetlić *pf. zob.* **naświetlać.** ~ **się** *pf. zob.* **naświetlać się.**

naświnić *pf. pot.* **1.** (= *nabrudzić*) make a mess. **2.** (= *zaszkodzić komuś*) traduce, slander (*komuś* sb).

natapirować *pf.* (*włosy*) backcomb, tease.

natarcie *n.* **1.** (= *tarcie*) rubbing. **2.** (= *atak*) attack; *wojsk.* offensive, attack.

natarczywie *adv.* importunately, obtrusively, insistently.

natarczywość *f.* importunity, obtrusiveness, insistence.

natarczywy *a.* **1.** (= *nachalny*) importunate, obtrusive; (*klient*) importunate, pressing, persistent; (*prośba*) persistent, urgent, pressing. **2.** (= *dokuczliwy*) troublesome, annoying; (*dźwięk, dzwonek*) insistent, obtrusive; (*ból*) persistent.

nataskać *pf. pot.* lug.

nataszczyć *pf. pot.* lug.

natchnąć *pf.* **1.** (= *zainspirować*) inspire, prompt (*kogoś do czegoś* sb to do sth). **2.** (= *wzbudzić*) inspire, infuse (*kogoś czymś* sb with sth).

natchnienie *n.* **1.** (= *poryw twórczy*) inspiration; **w natchnieniu** *l.* **pod wpływem natchnienia** inspirationally; **w chwili natchnienia** in an inspired moment. **2.** (= *impuls twórczy*) inspiration; **czerpać natchnienie z czegoś** draw inspiration from sth; **budzący natchnienie** inspiring.

natchniony *a.* **-eni** (*utwór, artysta*) inspired; (*twarz*) rapt.

natenczas *adv. przest.* (= *wtedy*) then.

natężać *ipf.* **1.** (= *wysilać*) (*siły, słuch, wzrok*) strain; (*uwagę, pamięć*) exert. **2.** (= *potęgować*) intensify, enhance, magnify. ~ **się** *ipf.* **1.** (= *wysilać się*) strain o.s., exert o.s. **2.** (= *wzmagać się*) intensify, heighten; (*o hałasie, ulewie*) intensify, increase; (*o konfliktach*) escalate.

natężenie *n.* **1.** (= *intensywność*) intensity; **natężenie dźwięku** volume; **natężenie hałasu** noise level; **natężenie barwy** colour intensity; **natężenie prądu** *el.* current intensity *l.* strength; **natężenie pola** *fiz.* field intensity *l.* strength; **natężenie pola elektrycznego** *fiz.* electric field intensity *l.* strength; **natężenie pola magnetycznego** *fiz.* magnetic field strength, magnetic intensity; **natężenie obciążenia** load intensity; **natężenie oświetlenia** *opt.* illumination; **natężenie ruchu** traffic congestion *l.* volume *l.* density. **2.** (= *napięcie nerwów*) tension, strain. **3.** (= *koncentracja uwagi*) focus, concentration; **słuchać z natężeniem** listen attentively.

natężyć *pf. zob.* **natężać.** ~ **się** *pf. zob.* **natężać się.**

natka *f.* top leaves, tops; **natka pietruszki** parsley.

natkać *pf.* **1.** (= *utkać dużo czegoś*) weave. **2.** *pot.* (= *napchać*) cram, stuff.

natknąć się *pf. zob.* **natykać się.**

natleniać *ipf.* oxygenate, oxygenize.

natlenienie *n.* oxygenation.

natłoczyć *pf.* **1.** (= *naupychać*) cram. **2.** (= *napompować*) pump; (*piwo, wino z beczki*) draft.

natłok *mi* **1.** (= *tłum*) crowd, throng. **2.** (= *mnóstwo czegoś*) congestion, loads of; (*myśli, spraw*) rush; **natłok myśli** teeming thoughts; (*wrażeń, informacji*) avalanche, flood.

natłuc *pf.* **-kę -czesz 1.** (= *rozdrobnić, tłukąc*) pound. **2.** (= *rozbić dużo czegoś*) break. **3.** *pot.* (= *zabić wiele zwierząt, wielu ludzi*) slaughter. **4.** *pot.* (= *zbić*) thump, thwack (*komuś* sb). **5.** *pot.* (= *dużo zarobić*) make; **natłuc kasy** make shitloads of money. ~ **się** *pf.* **-kę -czesz 1.** (= *ulec stłuczeniu*) break. **2.** *pot.* (= *zmęczyć się długą drogą*) have a long and tiring journey.

natłuszczać *ipf.*, **natłuścić** *pf.* **-szczę -ścisz** oil, grease.

natłuszczony *a.* greasy, oily.

NATO *abbr.* (= *Organizacja Paktu Północnoatlantyckiego*) NATO (*North Atlantic Treaty Organization*).

natomiast *conj.* whereas, while.

natopić *pf.* **1.** (= *rozpuścić*) melt. **2.** (= *utopić*) drown.

natowski *a.* (of *l.* pertaining to) NATO.

natracić *pf.* (*pieniędzy, czasu*) waste; (*ludzi*) lose.

natrafiać *ipf.*, **natrafić** *pf.* come across, happen on *l.* upon; encounter (*na kogoś/coś* sb/sth); (*przeszkodę*) come across, meet, encounter; (*trop, ślady*) find, come across; (*na ropę*) strike.

natręctwo *n.* **1.** (= *natarczywość*) obtrusiveness, importunity. **2.** *pat.* (= *obsesja*) obsessive compulsive disorder; **natręctwo lękowe** phobia, morbid fear; **natręctwo myślowe** compulsive thinking.

natręt *mp* pushy person.

natrętnie *adv.* obtrusively, importunately, persistently.

natrętny *a.* **1.** obtrusive, intrusive; (*interesant*) importunate; (*myśl*) obsessive; (*prośba*) persistent; (*mucha*) troublesome. **2.** *pat.* obsessive-compulsive, obsessional, obsessive; **natrętna czynność** compulsive activity.

natrolit *mi min.* natrolite.

natron *mi* **1.** *min.* natron. **2.** *druk.* sulfate paper.

natrudzić *pf.* trouble, bother (*kogoś czymś* sb with sth). ~ **się** *pf.* go to the trouble, take (the) trouble, exert o.s.

natrysk *mi* **1.** (*urządzenie*) shower. **2.** (*kąpiel*) shower (bath). **3.** *techn.* (*powlekanie*) spraying. **4.** *techn.* (*warstwa*) coat.

natryskiwacz *mi Gen.* **-a** *techn.* spray gun.

natryskiwać *ipf.* **1.** (= *polewać*) shower. **2.** *techn.* spray; **natryskiwać beton** *bud.* gunite.

natryskowy *a.* **1.** (= *służący do kąpieli*) shower, showery. **2.** (= *służący do powlekania*) spray, spraying.

natrząsać się *ipf.* **1.** (= *wyśmiewać się*) sneer, scoff (*z kogoś/czegoś* at sb/sth). **2.** (= *dokuczać*) poke fun (*z kogoś/czegoś* at sb/sth).

natrząść *pf.* shake; **natrząść jabłek** shake apples from the tree.

natrzeć *pf.* -**trę** -**tarł**, -**trzyj** *zob.* **nacierać**. ~ **się** *pf.* -**trę** -**tarł**, -**trzyj** *zob.* **nacierać się**.

natura *f.* **1.** (= *przyroda*) nature; **martwa natura** *mal.* still life; **wybryk natury** a freak of nature; **na łonie natury** in the open; **rysować z natury** draw from nature; **wbrew naturze** against nature, contrary to nature; **prawa natury** natural laws, the laws of nature. **2.** (= *stan nietknięty cywilizacją*) nature; **w stanie naturalnym** in the natural state; **powrót do natury** return to nature. **3.** (= *organizm*) body, organism; **silna natura** strong organism. **4.** (= *usposobienie*) nature, temper; **natura ludzka** human nature; **być bojaźliwym z natury** be a coward by nature; **to nie leży w mojej naturze** it's not in my nature; **przyzwyczajenie jest drugą naturą człowieka** habit is *l.* becomes second nature. **5.** (= *istota, rodzaj*) nature, character; **problem natury technicznej** a problem of a technical nature; **z natury rzeczy** in the nature of things. **6. w naturze** (= *w towarach*) in kind.

naturale *adv. muz.* naturale.

naturalista *mp teor.lit., fil., sztuka* naturalist.

naturalistka *f. zob.* **naturalista**.

naturalistycznie *adv.* naturalistically.

naturalistyczny *a. teor.lit., fil., sztuka* naturalistic.

naturalizacja *f. admin.* naturalization.

naturalizm *mi teor.lit., fil., sztuka* naturalism.

naturalizować *ipf. admin.* naturalize. ~ **się** *ipf. admin.* naturalize, become naturalized.

naturalnie *adv.* **1.** (= *jak w naturze*) naturally. **2.** (= *normalnie*) naturally. **3.** (= *swobodnie*) naturally, unaffectedly. **4.** (= *oczywiście*) of course; **mogę się przysiąść? - naturalnie!** may I join you? - but of course!

naturalność *f.* **1.** (= *brak sztuczności*) naturalness, unaffectedness. **2.** (= *pierwotność*) naturalness, natural state.

naturalny *a.* **1.** (= *niesztuczny*) natural; **bogactwa naturalne** natural resources; **dobór naturalny** natural selection, survival of the fittest; **jedwab naturalny** silk; **przyrost naturalny** population growth rate; **umrzeć śmiercią naturalną** die of natural causes; **śmierć naturalna** natural death; **potrzeba naturalna** (= *oddanie moczu l. kału*) call of nature. **2.** (= *przyrodzony*) natural, inborn; **naturalnej wielkości** life-size(d), full-size(d). **3.** (= *normalny*) regular, ordinary, natural; **liczby naturalne** *mat.* natural numbers; **skala minorowa naturalna** *muz.* natural minor scale; **jest rzeczą naturalną, że...** it's (only) natural to *l.* that... **4.** (= *swobodny, niewymuszony*) natural, unaffected. **5.** *przest.* barter, in-kind; **gospodarka naturalna** *ekon.* barter economy.

naturszczyk *mp film* untrained actor.

naturysta *mp* nudist, naturist.

naturystka *f. zob.* **naturysta**.

naturystyczny *a.* nudist, naturist.

naturyzm *mi* nudism, naturism.

natworzyć *pf.* -**órz** produce, create, invent.

natychmiast *adv.* immediately, instantly, at once, straight away, right away.

natychmiastowy *a.* immediate, instant.

natykać się *ipf.* encounter, come up against (*na kogoś/coś* sb/sth).

natyrać się *pf. pot.* fag (out).

natywista *mp fil., psych.* nativist.

natywistyczny *a. fil., psych.* nativist, nativistic.

natywizm *mi fil., psych.* nativism.

nauce *f. zob.* **nauka**.

nauczać *ipf. lit.* teach, preach.

nauczanie *n. szkoln.* instruction, teaching; **nauczanie początkowe** primary education.

nauczka *f.* lesson; **dać komuś nauczkę** teach sb a lesson; **dostać nauczkę** learn a lesson; **masz nauczkę!** let it be a lesson!, it serves you right!

nauczyciel *mp* teacher; **nauczyciel chemii** chemistry teacher; **doświadczenie jest najlepszym nauczycielem** *przen.* experience is the best teacher.

nauczycielka *f. zob.* **nauczyciel**.

nauczycielski *a.* teacher's, teachers', teacherly; **kolegium nauczycielskie** teachers college, teacher training college; **pokój nauczycielski** teachers' room; **ciało** *l.* **grono nauczycielskie** teachers, teaching staff, faculty.

nauczycielstwo *n.* **1.** (= *nauczyciele*) teachers, teaching staff, faculty. **2.** (= *zawód nauczyciela*) teaching.

nauczyć *pf.* teach, train; **nauczony doświadczeniem** taught by experience; **nauczyć kogoś moresu** show sb their place; **nauczyć kogoś rozumu** teach sb a lesson; **ja cię/was nauczę!** I'll show you!, now, get *l.* eat this!; *por.* **nauczać**, **uczyć**. ~ **się** *pf.* learn.

nauganiać się *pf.* run about; **nauganiać się za kimś/czymś** chase (after) sb/sth.

naujadać się *pf.* yap.

nauka *f.* **1.** (= *ogół wiedzy*) science; **nauki humanistyczne** the humanities; **nauki przyrodnicze** natural science; **nauki społeczne** social studies; **nauki stosowane** applied sciences; **nauki ścisłe** exact science; **nauki wyzwolone** *hist.* liberal arts. **2.** (= *doktryna*) teachings, theory. **3.** (= *uczenie się*) study, education, learning; **nauka jazdy** (*kurs*) driving school; (*napis na samochodzie*) L; **pobierać nauki** *lit.* learn, study. **4.** (= *przestroga*) lesson; **wyciągnąć z czegoś naukę** learn a lesson from sth; **nauka nie poszła w las** the lesson has not been forgotten. **5.** *rel.* (= *kazanie kościelne*) sermon. **6.** *pot. rel.* (= *kurs przedmałżeński*) premarital instruction; **chodzić na nauki** attend a premarital instruction course.

naukładać *pf.* **1.** (= *ułożyć jedno na drugim*) heap up. **2.** (= *ułożyć na jakimś miejscu*) place. **3.** (*o wierszach, muzyce*) (= *napisać dużo*) compose.

naukowiec *mp* -wc- *pl.* -y scientist, scholar, researcher.

naukowo *adv.* 1. (= *w sposób naukowy*) scientifically; naukowo udowodniony scientifically proven. 2. (= *w dziedzinie nauki*) in the field of research, scientifically; pracować naukowo do research.

naukowy *a.* 1. (= *badawczy*) scientific, scholarly; badania naukowe research; pracownik naukowy research worker; ośrodek naukowy research centre; stopień naukowy university degree. 2. (= *dydaktyczny*) educational; pomoce naukowe teaching aids.

naukoznawstwo *n.* science of science.

naumieć się *pf. pot.* (= *nauczyć się*) learn, familiarize o.s.

naumyślnie *adv.* deliberately, intentionally, on purpose.

naumyślny *a.* deliberate, intentional, purposeful.

nauplius *ma zool.* nauplius.

naurański *a. geogr.* Nauruan.

naurągać *pf. pot.* hurl abuse (*komuś* at sb); insult, abuse (*komuś* sb).

Nauru *n. indecl. geogr.* Nauru.

nauru *mi indecl. jęz.* Nauruan.

nauszniki *pl.* 1. (*część czapki*) earmuffs, earflaps; czapka z nausznikami cap with earflaps. 2. *hist.* (*część hełmu*) earpieces.

nautilus *mi Gen.* -a (*puchar*) nautilus cup. – *ma zool.* (pearly *l.* chambered) nautilus (*Nautilus*).

nautofon *mi żegl.* nautophone.

nautyka *f. żegl.* nautics.

nauwijać się *pf.* bustle about.

naużerać się *pf. pot.* wrangle, bicker (*z kimś* with sb).

naużywać się *pf.* make the most of, live it up, enjoy o.s.

nawa *f.* 1. *bud.* aisle; nawa boczna aisle; nawa główna nave; nawa poprzeczna transept. 2. *arch.* ship, vessel; nawa państwowa ship of state.

nawab *mp pl.* -owie *zob.* nabab.

nawadniać *ipf.* irrigate, water.

nawadnianie *n.* irrigation, watering.

nawaga *f. icht.* navaga (*Eleginus navaga*).

nawalacz *mp pot.* flake.

nawalać *ipf.* 1. *pot.* (= *psuć się*) conk (out). 2. *pot.* (= *nie wywiązywać się z czegoś*) blow it.

nawalanka *f. pot.* 1. (= *partactwo*) botchery, bungle. 2. (= *bezładna walka*) scuffle.

nawalić *pf.* 1. *zob.* nawalać. 2. (= *zgromadzić wiele czegoś*) heap up, amass. 3. *pot.* (= *oddać kał*) shit. ~ się *pf.* 1. *pot.* (= *zebrać się w wielkiej liczbie*) throng. 2. *pot.* (= *upić się*) get loaded.

nawalny *a.* (= *gwałtowny*) violent, heavy; nawalny deszcz heavy rain.

nawalony *a.* -eni *pot.* (= *pijany*) loaded.

nawał *mi* (= *ogrom*) multitude; (*pracy, zajęć*) mountains, spate; (*klientów*) crowd, host; (*myśli*) rush; w nawale zajęć zapomniał o wszystkim in a spate of work he forgot about everything; nawał pracy mountains *l.* a mountain of work.

nawała *f. lit.* (= *najeżdżające wojsko*) invading army; (= *najazd*) invasion; nawała ogniowa *wojsk.* shelling.

nawałnica *f.* (= *burza*) storm; (= *śnieżyca*) snowstorm, blizzard; (= *gwałtowna ulewa*) rainstorm; nawałnica wojenna *przen.* ravages of war.

nawałnik *ma orn.* nawałnik burzowy stormy petrel (*Hydrobates pelagicus*).

nawaniać *ipf. chem.* odorize.

nawanianie *n. chem.* odorizing.

nawapniać *ipf. techn.* lime.

nawapnianie *n. techn.* liming.

nawar *mi* (= *kamienny osad na ściankach naczyń*) scale; nawar krzemionkowy *geol.* geyserite.

nawarstwiać się *ipf.*, nawarstwić się *pf.* 1. (= *układać się warstwami*) stratify. 2. (= *kumulować się*) accumulate; (*o problemach, sprawach*) accumulate, pile up.

nawarstwienie *n.* stratification.

nawarstwiony *a.* 1. (= *ułożony warstwowo*) overlaid, stratified. 2. (= *nagromadzony*) accumulated, piled up.

nawarzyć *pf.* 1. *przest.* (= *ugotować*) concoct. 2. (= *pędzić piwo*) brew; nawarzyć (komuś) piwa *przen.* get (sb) into trouble.

naważka *f. Gen.pl.* -ek *chem.* weighed amount.

naważyć *pf.* weigh (out).

nawąchać się *pf.* snuff up.

nawbijać *pf.* 1. (*gwoździ*) drive in, hammer. 2. (= *wmówić, przekonać, poinformować*) hammer in; nawbijać sobie/komuś czegoś do głowy *przen.* get sth into one's/sb's head.

nawdychać się *pf.* inhale, snuff up.

nawet *adv.* even; nawet, nawet not bad at all; nawet o tym nie wspominaj! don't (you) even mention it!

nawęd *ma icht.* angler (fish), white monkfish (*Lophius piscatorius*).

nawęglać *ipf. techn.* carburize, case-harden.

nawęglanie *n. techn.* carburizing, case-hardening.

nawiać *pf.* -wieję -wiejesz *zob.* nawiewać.

nawiany *a. pot.* (= *pijany*) fuddled, three sheets in the wind.

nawias *mi* 1. (*znak graficzny*) parenthesis; *Br.* bracket; w nawiasie in parenthesis; otworzyć/zamknąć nawias open/close the parenthesis; umieścić słowo w nawiasie put a word into parentheses; wziąć w nawias parenthesize; nawiasem mówiąc by the way, incidentally; być *l.* znaleźć się poza nawiasem społeczeństwa be on the margin(s) of society. 2. *mat.* bracket; nawias klamrowy brace, curly bracket; nawias kwadratowy square bracket; nawias okrągły parenthesis, round bracket.

nawiązać *pf.* -żę -żesz *zob.* nawiązywać. ~ się *pf.* -żę -żesz *zob.* nawiązywać się.

nawiązanie *n.* w nawiązaniu do czegoś with reference to sth.

nawiązka *f. prawn.* discretionary damages; z nawiązką (= *z nadwyżką*) with interest; (= *więcej niż oczekiwano*) with a vengeance.

nawiązywać *ipf.* 1. (= *przyczepiać, wiążąc*) tie, bind, fasten, attach. 2. (= *rozpoczynać*) (*kon-*

takt, łączność, stosunki) establish; (*korespondencję, rozmowy*) enter into. **3.** (= *odnosić się*) refer (*do czegoś* to sth); **nawiązując do pańskiego listu** with reference to your letter.

nawicert *mi żegl.* navicert.

nawiedzać *ipf.*, **nawiedzić** *pf.* **1.** (*o kataklizmach itp.*) hit, descend upon, strike. **2.** *lit.* (= *odwiedzać*) visit. **3.** (*o myślach itp.*) appear. **4.** (*o duchach*) haunt.

nawiedzenie *n.* (*przez ducha, zjawę*) visitation; **Nawiedzenie Najświętszej Maryi Panny** *rz.-kat.* the Visitation.

nawiedzony *a.* **-eni 1.** *pot.* (= *fanatyczny*) obsessed, fanatical. **2.** (= *dotknięty nieszczęściem, klęską*) stricken; **nawiedzone miejsce** (= *miejsce nawiedzane przez duchy*) haunted place. – *mp pl.* **-eni** (= *fanatyk*) crank.

nawiercać *ipf.*, **nawiercić** *pf.* **1.** (= *nawiercić*) bore, drill. **2.** (= *rozszerzyć nawiercony otwór u wlotu*) countersink.

nawiercanie *n. techn.* spot drilling, spotting.

nawiertak *mi Gen.* **-a** *techn.* spotting drill, spotter.

nawierzchnia *f. Gen.pl.* **-i** pavement; **nawierzchnia asfaltowa** asphalt pavement; **nawierzchnia betonowa** concrete pavement; **nawierzchnia brukowa** cobble pavement; **nawierzchnia tłuczniowa** crushed-stone *l.* macadam pavement; **Uwaga! Śliska nawierzchnia!** Caution! Slippery road!

nawierzchniowy *a.* pavement; **roboty nawierzchniowe** road works.

nawietrzak *mi Gen.* **-a** *bud.* register.

nawietrzna *f. Gen.* **-ej** *żegl.* windward.

nawietrzność *f. żegl.* weather helm.

nawietrzny *a. żegl.* windward.

nawiew *mi* **1.** (*urządzenie*) ventilator, fan. **2.** (= *nawiewanie*) ventilation.

nawiewać *ipf.* **1.** (= *nanosić*) blow in. **2.** (= *zalatywać, ciągnąć od*) blow, come. **3.** *pot.* (= *uciekać*) scoot, dart away.

nawiewnik *mi Gen.* **-a** *żegl.* ventilator.

nawiewny *a. techn.* ventilating, ventilative, ventilatory.

nawieźć *pf.* **-wiozę -wieziesz -wiózł -wieźli** *zob.* **nawozić.**

nawigacja *f.* **1.** *żegl., lotn.* navigation; **nawigacja astronomiczna** celestial navigation; **nawigacja radiowa** radio navigation; **nawigacja satelitarna** satellite navigation. **2.** (= *żeglowanie*) sailing, navigation.

nawigacyjny *a.* navigational.

nawigator *mp* navigator.

nawigować *ipf.* navigate.

nawijać *ipf.* **1.** (= *zwijać*) wind, reel, coil. **2.** *pot.* (= *mówić dużo*) twaddle, prate. **~ się** *ipf.* **1.** (= *zwijać się*) reel, coil, wind. **2.** *pot.* (= *pojawiać się niespodzianie*) turn up, show up; **nawijać się (komuś) pod rękę** come to hand, come sb's way; **co tylko mi się nawinie** whatever I lay my hands on.

nawijarka *f. techn.* winder, reeler, wind-up reel.

nawijka *f.* (= *gadka, paplanina*) twaddle, blather.

nawilgacać *ipf.*, **nawilgocić** *pf.* humidify.

nawilgać *ipf.*, **nawilgnąć** *pf.* moisten, absorb moisture.

nawilgocenie *n.* humidification.

nawilżacz *mi Gen.* **-a 1.** (*pojemnik na kaloryfer*) (eco-)humidifier. **2.** (*aparat do rozpylania wody*) humidifier. **3.** (*w żelazku*) steamer.

nawilżać *ipf.*, **nawilżyć** *pf.* (*skórę*) moisturize, moisten; (*powierzchnię czegoś, chusteczkę*) moisten, damp, dampen; (*powietrze*) humidify.

nawinąć *pf. zob.* **nawijać.** **~ się** *pf. zob.* **nawijać się.**

nawis *mi* **1.** (= *zwieszająca się masa*) overhang; **nawis inflacyjny** *ekon.* inflation bias. **2.** *żegl.* overhang.

nawlatywać *pf.* fly in.

nawlec *pf.* **-wlekę -wleczesz -wlókł** *l.* **-wlekł -wlekli, nawlekać** *ipf.* **1.** (= *nizać*) (*igłę*) thread; (*korale*) string. **2.** (= *nakładać*) slip (*coś na coś* sth on sth). **3.** (= *przyciągnąć, wlokąc*) drag.

nawłazić *pf.* get inside; (*o kolcach*) stick in.

nawłoć *f. pl.* **-e** *bot.* goldenrod (*Solidago*); **nawłoć kanadyjska** tall goldenrod (*Solidago canadensis*); **nawłoć późna** late goldenrod (*Solidago gigantea*).

nawodnić *ipf. zob.* **nawadniać.**

nawodny *a.* **1.** (*położony na wodzie l. nad wodą*) water; **nawodna część statku** *żegl.* upper works. **2.** (*żyjący nad wodą l. na wodzie*) aquatic; **ptactwo nawodne** waterfowl.

nawodorowanie *n. metal.* hydriding.

nawoływać *ipf.* **1.** (= *wołać*) call. **2.** (= *zachęcać*) exhort, incite, urge (*kogoś do (zrobienia) czegoś* sb to (do) sth).

nawoływanie *n.* **1.** (= *wołanie*) call, calling. **2.** (= *zachęcanie*) exhortation, incitement.

nawoskować *pf. zob.* **woskować.**

nawoskowany *a.* waxen.

nawozić *ipf.* **-żę -zisz, -woź** *l.* **-wóź 1.** (= *użyźniać*) fertilize. **2.** (= *gromadzić, wożąc*) bring, cart (in), truck (in).

nawozowy *a.* fertilizing.

nawożenie *n.* fertilization.

nawój *mi* **-o-** *techn.* yarn packing, beam.

nawóz *mi* **-o-** fertilizer; **nawóz naturalny** manure, dressing; **nawóz organiczny** organic fertilizer; **nawóz zielony** green manure; **nawóz sztuczny** chemical fertilizer.

nawpieprzać się *pf. pot.* (= *najeść się*) eat a bloody lot *l.* hell of a lot.

nawpierdalać się *pf. wulg.* (= *najeść się*) eat a fucking lot.

nawpychać się *pf. pot.* (= *najeść się*) stuff o.s., cram.

nawracać *ipf.* **1.** (= *zawracać*) return, turn back. **2.** (= *nakłaniać do zmiany wyznania*) convert (*kogoś na coś* sb to sth). **3.** (= *wracać*) return; **nawracać do tematu** *przen.* keep returning to the same subject. **4.** *tech.* reverse. **~ się** *ipf.* **1.** (= *zmienić religię, wyznanie*) convert, be converted; **nawracać się na chrześcijaństwo** convert to Christianity. **2.** (= *porzucić błędy*) reform, be reformed, mend one's ways. **3.** (= *wrócić do* *dawnych przekonań*) return, convert (*na coś to sth*).

nawrot *mi bot.* gromwell (*Lithospermum*).

nawrotnik *mi Gen.* **-a** *el.* reversing switch, reverser.

nawrotny *a.* recurrent.

nawrotowy *a. med.* recurrent, relapsing.

nawrócenie *n.* **1.** (*z innego wyznania*) conversion. **2.** (*grzesznika*) reformation.

nawrócić *pf. zob.* **nawracać.** ~ **się** *pf. zob.* **nawracać się.**

nawrócony *a.* **-eni 1.** (*z innego wyznania*) converted. **2.** (*grzesznik*) reformed.

nawrót *mi* **-o- 1.** (= *ponowne wystąpienie*) recurrence, relapse, regression; **zrobić coś za drugim nawrotem** do sth at the second attempt. **2.** *techn.* reverse, reversal.

nawrzeszczeć *pf.* **-ę -ysz** *pot.* scream, yell (*na kogoś* at sb).

nawrzucać *pf.* **1.** (= *wrzucić dużo czegoś*) throw. **2.** *pot.* (= *zwymyślać*) rate, scold (*komuś* sb).

nawtranżalać się *pf. pot.* (= *najeść się*) tuck away.

nawtykać *pf.* **1.** *pot.* (= *wetknąć dużo czegoś*) insert, stuff; (*o igłach, patykach*) stick. **2.** *pot.* (= *zwymyślać*) chide, rag (*komuś* sb).

nawychwalać *pf.* praise, extol. ~ **się** *pf.* praise, extol; **nawychwalać się kogoś pod niebiosa** praise sb to the skies; **nie móc się nawychwalać kogoś/czegoś** not have words enough to praise sb/sth.

nawyczyniać *pf. pot.* do; **coś ty nawyczyniała?** what on earth have you done?

nawydziwiać *pf.* (= *kaprysić*) be whimsical, be capricious, make a fuss; **nawydziwiać na coś** make a fuss about sth.

nawygadywać *pf.* **1.** *pot.* (= *opowiadać nieprawdę*) talk rubbish; **nawygadywać głupot** talk nonsense; **coś ty jej nawygadywał?** what sort of trash have you told her? **2.** *pot.* (= *powiedzieć wiele przykrych rzeczy*) lash (out), sneer.

nawygrażać *pf.* threaten.

nawygrzebywać *pf.* **1.** (= *wygrzebać dużą ilość czegoś*) dig out. **2.** (= *wyciągnąć skądś*) pull out. **3.** (= *wyszukać*) ferret out.

nawyk *mi* habit; (= *nałóg*) vice; **z nawyku** out of habit; **siłą nawyku** by force of habit; **mieć nawyk spania po obiedzie** have a habit of sleeping after dinner; **wejść komuś w nawyk** become sb's habit; **wyrobić sobie nawyk** get into a habit, acquire *l.* develop a habit; **zerwać z nawykiem** kick a habit; **zły nawyk** bad habit; **irytujący nawyk** annoying habit; **obrzydliwy nawyk** repulsive habit.

nawykać *ipf. lit.* become accustomed, get used (*do czegoś* to sth).

nawykły *a.* accustomed, used (*do czegoś* to sth).

nawyknąć *pf.* **-ij, -kł** *l.* **-knął** *zob.* **nawykać.**

nawykowy *a.* habitual.

nawymyślać *pf.* (= *skrzyczeć*) insult, abuse, revile; **nawymyślać komuś od ostatnich** shower abuse on sb, call sb names; **nawymyślać komuś**

od złodziei call sb a thief; (= *wymyślić wiele czegoś*) invent.

nawyrabiać *pf.* **1.** (= *wyprodukować dużo czegoś*) produce. **2.** (*ciasta*) knead. **3.** (= *nawyczyniać*) *pot.* do; **coś ty nawyrabiał?** what have you done? ~ **się** *pf. pot.* happen, fall out, come about; **ale się nawyrabiało!** what a mess!

nawyszukiwać *pf.* find, search out.

nawzajem[1] *adv.* (= *obopólnie*) each other, one another, reciprocally.

nawzajem[2] *int.* the same to you; **dziękuję, nawzajem** thank you, same to you.

nazabijać *pf.* (*ludzi*) kill; (*zwierząt*) kill, slaughter.

nazad *adv. pot.* back, backwards; **tam i nazad** to and fro; **iść nazad** go back.

nazadawać *pf.* **1.** (= *wyznaczyć zadanie*) assign. **2.** (*pytań*) ask. **3.** (*bólu*) inflict.

nazajutrz *adv. lit.* the next *l.* following day.

nazalizacja *f. fon.* nasalization.

nazalizować *ipf. fon.* nasalize.

Nazarejczyk *ma rel.* (= *Jezus*) the Nazarene.

nazareńczyk *mp mal.* (*członek grupy malarskiej*) Nazarene.

Nazaret *mi geogr.* Nazareth.

nazaretanka *f.* **1.** *zob.* **nazaretańczyk. 2.** *zob.* **nazaretanki.**

nazaretanki *pl. Gen.* **-ek** *rz.-kat.* Sisters of the Holy Family of Nazareth.

nazaretańczyk *ma* (= *mieszkaniec Nazaretu*) Nazarene.

nazbierać *pf.* (= *zgromadzić*) gather; (*o znaczkach, monetach*) collect; (*o pieniądzach*) raise, collect; (*o doświadczeniu*) gain; (*o materiałach, wiadomościach, plotkach*) compile, collect, glean; (*o kwiatach, owocach*) pick. ~ **się** *pf.* **1.** (= *zejść się*) gather, assemble. **2.** (= *nagromadzić się*) (*o pracy, żalu, powodach*) accumulate, heap up.

nazbijać *pf.* (= *połączyć gwoździami*) nail together; **nazbijać bąków** (= *lenić się*) *przen.* idle away.

nazbyt *adv.* too, excessively; **aż nazbyt** too much; **nie nazbyt** not so much *l.* very.

nazewnictwo *n.* **1.** *jęz.* onomastics. **2.** (= *słownictwo fachowe*) terminology, nomenclature.

nazewniczy *a.* **1.** *jęz.* onomastic. **2.** (= *związany z fachową terminologią*) terminological, nomenclatural.

nazębny *a.* located *l.* situated on the teeth, teeth; **kamień nazębny** calculus, tartar.

naziemny *a.* **1.** (= *znajdujący się na ziemi*) ground; **obsługa naziemna** *lotn.* ground crew *l.* staff. **2.** *bot.* overground. **3.** *zool.* terrestrial.

naziom *mi bud.* surcharge, overburden.

nazista *mp*, **nazistka** *f. Gen. pl.* **-ek** Nazi.

nazistowski *a.* Nazi.

nazizm *mi* Nazi(i)sm.

nazjeżdżać (się) *pf.* arrive.

nazlatywać się *pf.* **1.** (= *zlecieć się*) fly in, come flying. **2.** *pot.* (= *zejść się*) flock (together).

nazłazić się *pf.* **-żę -zisz 1.** (= *zgromadzić się*) *pot.* crowd in. **2.** (= *naschodzić się w dół*) (*z drze-*

wa, po drabinie) climb down; (*ze schodów*) go *l.* come down.

nazłorzeczyć *pf.* curse (*komuś* sb).

nazmyślać *pf.* invent, make up.

naznaczać *ipf.*, **naznaczyć** *pf.* **1.** (= *oznaczać*) mark, indicate. **2.** (= *zostawiać ślad*) mark, scar; **twarz naznaczona bliznami** scarred face. **3.** (= *ustalać, wyznaczać*) set, fix, appoint; **naznaczać kogoś na swego następcę** appoint sb one's successor; **naznaczać cenę na czyjąś głowę** set *l.* put a price on sb's head.

naznosić *pf.* **-szę -sisz 1.** (= *nagromadzić*) gather, bring. **2.** (= *przynosić z góry na dół*) carry down. **3.** (= *znieść dużo jajek*) lay.

nazrywać *pf.* pick.

nazwa *f.* name; designation, appelation; **o nazwie...** of *l.* by the name of...; **istnieć tylko z nazwy** exist in name only; **występować pod nazwą** appear as; **być znanym pod nazwą...** be known as...; **nazwa firmowa** brand name; **nazwa handlowa** trade name; **nazwa ogólna** generic name; **nazwa potoczna** customary name; **nazwa zastrzeżona** registered trade name; **nazwa zwyczajowa** common name; **błędna nazwa** misnomer; **nosić nazwę X** be named X; **nadawać czemuś nazwę** name sth, give sth a name.

nazwać *pf.* **-ę -iesz** *zob.* **nazywać.** ~ **się** *pf.* **-ę -iesz** *zob.* **nazywać się.**

nazwisko *n.* surname, (last *l.* family) name; **nazwisko panieńskie** maiden name; **nazwisko rodowe** family name; **pod cudzym nazwiskiem** under somebody else's name; **paszport na czyjeś nazwisko** a passport in sb's name; **ktoś nazwiskiem** *l.* **o nazwisku...** sb by the name of...; **tylko bez nazwisk, proszę** no names, please; **nie wymieniać z nazwiska** not name names; **wyrobić sobie nazwisko** (= *zostać sławnym, uznanym*) make a name for o.s.; **znać kogoś tylko z nazwiska** know sb by name.

nazwozić *pf.* **-żę -zisz 1.** (= *przywieźć dokądś*) bring. **2.** (*z góry na dół*) take down.

nazyrejczyk *mp hist., judaizm* Nazarite, Nazirite.

nazywać *ipf.* **1.** (= *określać nazwą*) call, name, term; **nazywać kogoś po imieniu** call sb by their first *l.* Christian name; **nazywać rzeczy po imieniu** call a spade a spade. **2.** (= *nadawać imię*) name, christen. ~ **się** *ipf.* **1.** (= *nosić imię, nazwisko*) be called; **jak się pani nazywa?** what is your name, please? **2.** (= *być określanym jakąś nazwą*) be called; **jak się to nazywa?** what is it called?, what do you call it?; **to się nazywa pech!** that's what you call bad luck!, tough luck! **3.** (= *nadawać sobie miano*) call o.s. **4.** (= *nadawać sobie nawzajem miano*) call one another *l.* each other.

nażarty *a. pot.* full.

nażąć *pf.* **-żnę -żniesz, -żnij, -ął -ęli** reap *l.* cut a lot of.

nażłopać się *pf.* **-ię -iesz** *pot.* swill, drink one's fill.

nażreć się *pf.* **-żrę -żresz, -żryj, -żarł** *pot.* (*o zwierzętach*) eat one's fill; *wulg.* (*o ludziach*) gobble, gulp.

nb. *abbr.* (= *notabene*) by the way, incidentally.

NBP *abbr.* (= *Narodowy Bank Polski*) the National Bank of Poland.

ndst. *abbr. szkoln.* (= *niedostateczny*) F (*failure l. fail*).

n.e. *abbr.* (= *naszej ery*) C.E. (*common era*); A.D. *l.* AD (*anno Domini*).

neandertalczyk *mp antrop.* Neandertal, Neanderthal (man).

neandertalski *a. antrop.* Neandertal, Neanderthal; **człowiek neandertalski** Neandertal man.

Neapol *mi geogr.* Naples.

Neapolitanka *f. zob.* **Neapolitańczyk.**

Neapolitańczyk *mp* Neapolitan.

neapolitański *a.* Neapolitan.

nearktyczny *a. zool.* Nearctic; **kraina nearktyczna** Nearctic region.

nebularny *a. astron.* nebular, nebulous.

nebulizacja *f. med.* nebulization, spraying.

nefelin *mi min.* nepheline.

nefelinit *mi min.* nephelinite.

nefelometr *mi chem.* nephelometer.

nefelometria *f. Gen.* **-ii** *chem.* nephelometry.

Nefertiti, Nefretete *f. indecl.* Nefertiti, Nofretete.

nefoskop *mi meteor.* nephoscope.

nefrektomia *f. Gen.* **-ii** *chir.* nephrectomy.

nefroblastoma *f. med.* nephroblastoma, Wilms' tumor.

nefrolepis *f. indecl. bot.* nephrolepis, ladder fern, Boston fern (*Nephrolepis*).

nefrolog *mp med.* nephrologist.

nefrologia *f. Gen.* **-ii** *med.* nephrology.

nefrologiczny *a. med.* nephrological.

nefron *mi anat.* nephron.

nefropatia *f. Gen.* **-ii** *pat.* nephropathy.

nefrotoksyczność *f. med.* nephrotoxicity.

nefrotomia *f. Gen.* **-ii** *chir.* nephrotomy.

nefroza *f. pat.* nephrosis.

nefrydia *pl. Gen.* **-ów** *zool.* nephridia.

nefryt *mi min.* nephrite.

negacja *f.* **1.** *lit.* (= *przeczenie*) negation. **2.** *log.* negation.

negaton *mi chem., fiz.* negatron, negative electron.

negatyw *mi* **1.** *fot.* negative. **2.** *techn.* negative mold. **3.** *paleont.* mold.

negatywistyczny *a.* negativistic.

negatywizm *mi* negativism.

negatywnie *adv.* **1.** (= *z dezaprobatą*) negatively, disapprovingly; **być nastawionym negatywnie do kogoś/czegoś** disapprove of sb/sth. **2.** (= *odmownie*) in the negative; **odpowiedzieć negatywnie** answer in the negative.

negatywny *a.* **1.** (= *przeczący*) negative; (*sąd, postawa*) negative. **2.** (= *niekorzystny, ujemny*) negative. **3.** (= *odmowny*) negative.

negatywowy *a. fot.* negative.

negliż *mi* **1.** (= *swobodny strój*) negligée, undress. **2.** (= *całkowite lub częściowe obnażenie*) undress; **w negliżu** in a state of undress.

negocjacje *pl. Gen.* **-i** negotiations; **prowadzić**

negocjacje conduct negotiations; **rozpocząć negocjacje** start negotiations; **zerwać negocjacje** break off negotiations; **negocjacje pokojowe** peace talks *l.* negotiations.

negocjacyjny *a.* negotiation.

negocjator *mp* negotiator.

negocjować *ipf.* negotiate.

negować *ipf.* (= *zaprzeczać*) deny; (= *nie uznawać*) negate.

negowanie *n.* (= *zaprzeczanie*) denial; (= *nieuznawanie*) negation.

Negr *mp przest.* Negro; *wulg.* nigger.

negroid *mp antrop. zw. pl.* Negroid.

negroidalny *a. antrop.* Negroid.

nekrobioza *f. biol.* necrobiosis.

nekrofag *ma zool.* necrophage.

nekrofil *mp pat.* necrophile, necrophiliac.

nekrofilia *f. Gen.* -ii *pat.* necrophilia.

nekrofilski *a. pat.* necrophilic, necrophiliac.

nekrofobia *f. Gen.* -ii necrophobia.

nekrolatria *f. Gen.* -ii *rel.* (= *oddawanie zmarłym czci religijnej*) ancestor worship; (= *kult zmarłych*) cult of the dead.

nekrolog *mi* obituary.

nekromancja *f.* necromancy.

nekromanta *mp* necromancer.

nekropolia *f. Gen.* -ii *hist.* necropolis.

nekroskopia *f. Gen.* -ii necroscopy.

nekrotyczny *a. pat., biol.* necrotic.

nekroza *f. pat., biol.* necrosis.

nektar *mi mit., bot., kulin.* nectar.

nektaria *pl. Gen.* -ów *bot.* nectaries.

nektarniki *pl. Gen.* -ów *orn.* sunbirds (*Nectariniidae*).

nektarowy *a.* nectarous.

nektarynka, nektaryna *f. ogr.* nectarine.

nekton *mi ekol.* nekton.

nelma *f icht.* inconnu, Alaska sheefish (*Stenodus leucichthys nelma*).

nelson *mi Gen.* -a *sport* half nelson; **podwójny nelson** full nelson.

nematologia *f.* nematology.

nemezis *f. indecl.* **1.** *mit.* Nemezis. **2.** nemesis.

nemrod *mp żart.* nimrod.

nenia *f. Gen.* -ii *teor.lit.* dirge.

nenufar *mi Gen.* -a *bot.* spatterdock, water lily (*Nuphar*).

neo- *pref.* neo-.

neoanarchizm *mi fil.* neo-anarchism.

neobarok *mi sztuka* neo-Baroque.

neobehawioryzm *mi psych.* neobehaviorism.

neodarwinista *mp* Neo-Darwinist.

neodarwinistyczny *a.* Neo-Darwinist.

neodarwinizm *mi biol., fil.* Neo-Darwinism.

neodym *mi chem.* neodymium.

neofaszysta *mp polit.* neofascist.

neofaszystowski *a. polit.* neofascist.

neofaszyzm *mi polit.* neofascism.

neoficki *a.* neophytic.

neofilologia *f. Gen.* -ii modern languages studies.

neofilologiczny *a.* (of *l.* pertaining to) modern languages *l.* modern languages studies.

neofita *mp* neophyte.

neofitka *f. zob.* **neofita**.

neofityzm *mi* neophytism.

neofobia *f.* neophobia.

neogea *f. geogr., biol.* Neogea, Neogaea.

neogen *mi geol.* the Neogene (Period).

neogeniczny *a. geol.* Neogene.

neogotycki *a. sztuka, bud.* neo-Gothic.

neogotyk *mi sztuka, bud.* neo-Gothic.

neografia *f.* neography.

neoheglizm *mi fil.* Neo-Hegelism.

neoheglowski *a. fil.* Neo-Hegelian.

neohellenista *mp sztuka* neo-Hellenist.

neohellenizm *mi sztuka* Neo-Hellenism.

neohumanizm *mi fil.* neo-humanism.

neoimpresjonizm *mi sztuka* neo-impressionism, Neo-Impressionism.

neokantyzm *mi fil.* neo-Kantianism.

neoklasycyzm *mi sztuka* neoclassicism, Neo-classicism.

neoklasyczny *a. sztuka* neoclassical, Neoclassical, neoclassic, Neoclassic.

neoklasyk *mp* neoclassicist.

neokolonialista *mp polit., ekon.* neocolonialist.

neokolonializm *mi polit., ekon.* neocolonialism.

neokolonialny *a. polit., ekon.* neocolonial.

neokonserwatyzm *mi polit.* neoconservatism.

neolamarkizm *mi biol.* neo-Lamarckism.

neoliberalizm *mi ekon.* neoliberalism.

neolit *mi geol.* the Neolithic.

neolityczny *a. geol.* Neolithic.

neologizm *mi jęz.* neologism.

neomaltuzjanizm *mi ekon.* neo-Malthusianism.

neomerkantylizm *mi ekon.* neo-mercantilism.

neomycyna *f. med.* neomycin.

neon *mi* **1.** *chem.* neon. **2.** *pot.* (*lampa*) neon light; (= *napis świetlny*) neon (sign).

neonazista *mp polit.* neo-Nazi.

neonazistowski *a. polit.* neo-Nazi.

neonazizm *mi polit.* neo-Nazism.

neonek -nk- *Gen.* -ów *icht.* tetra (*Paracheirodon*); **neonek Innesa** neon tetra (*P. innesi*).

neonowy *a.* neon.

neonówka *f. pot.* neon light.

neontologia *f. Gen.* -ii *zool.* neontology.

neoplastycyzm *mi sztuka* neoplasticism.

neoplatonik *mp fil.* Neoplatonist.

neoplatonizm *mi fil.* Neoplatonism.

neoplatoński *a. fil.* Neoplatonic.

neopozytywista *mp fil.* neopositivist.

neopozytywistyczny *a. fil.* neopositivist.

neopozytywizm *mi fil.* neopositivism.

neopren *mi techn.* neoprene.

neorealista *mp fil., sztuka* neorealist.

neorealistyczny *a. fil., sztuka* neorealist.

neorealizm *mi fil., sztuka* neorealism.

neorenesans *mi sztuka* neo-Renaissance.

neoromantyczny *a. sztuka* neoromantic.

neoromantyk *mp sztuka* neoromantic.

neoromantyzm *mi sztuka* neoromanticism.

neoscholastyczny *a. fil.* neo-Scholastic.

neoscholastyk *mp fil.* neo-Scholastic.

neoscholastyka *f. fil.* neo-Scholasticism.

neosemantyzm *mi jęz.* semantic neologism.
neoslawizm *mi hist.* neo-Slavism.
neotektonika *f. geol.* neotectonics.
neotenia *f. Gen.* -ii *biol.* neoteny.
neotomista *mp fil.* neo-Thomist.
neotomistyczny *a. fil.* neo-Thomist, neo-Thomistic.
neotomizm *mi fil.* neo-Thomism.
neotrockizm *mi polit.* neo-Trotskyism.
neotropikalny *a. geogr., zool.* Neotropical.
nep *abbr. hist.* (= *nowa polityka ekonomiczna*) NEP (*New Economic Policy, in Soviet Russia*).
Nepal *mi geogr.* Nepal.
Nepalczyk *mp*, **Nepalka** *f. Gen.pl.* -ek Nepali.
nepalski *a.* (*o ludziach*) Nepalese; (*o języku*) Nepali.
nepotysta *mp* nepotist.
nepotyzm *mi* nepotism.
neptek *mp* -tk- *pl.* -i *pot.* (= *ciapa*) loser, wimp.
Neptun *mp mit.* Neptune. − *mi astron.* Neptune.
neptun *mi chem.* neptunium.
nerczyca *f. pat.* nephrosis.
nerczycowy *a. pat.* nephrotic.
nerecznica *f. bot.* shield fern, wood fern, buckler fern (*Dryopteris*).
nereida *f.* 1. *mit.* Nereid. 2. *zool.* clamworm (*Nereis*).
nerka *f.* 1. *anat.* kidney; **sztuczna nerka** artificial kidney (device). 2. (*naczynie szpitalne*) kidney-shaped basin.
nerki *pl. Gen.* -rek *kulin.* kidneys.
nerkowaty *a.* kidney-shaped.
nerkowiec *mi* -wc- *Gen.* -a 1. *bot.* cashew (*Anacardium*). 2. *zool.* giant kidney worm (*Dioctophyma renale*).
nerkowy *a.* kidney; *med.* renal; **kamienie nerkowe** kidney stones; **miedniczka nerkowa** *anat.* renal pelvis.
nerkówka *f. kulin.* loin of veal.
Neron *mp hist.* Nero.
nerpa *f. zool.* ringed seal (*Pusa hispida*).
nerw *mi* 1. *anat.* nerve; **nerw błędny** vagus nerve; **nerw kulszowy** ischiadic *l.* sciatic nerve; **nerw obwodowy** peripheral nerve; **nerw ruchowy** motor nerve; **nerw trójdzielny** trigeminal nerve. 2. *bot.* vein; **nerw główny** midrib. 3. *pot.* (= *predyspozycja*) knack, talent, skill; **mieć nerw pisarski** have a talent *l.* skill for writing; **robić coś z nerwem** put verve into sth one does. 4. *zob.* **nerwy**.
nerwacja *f. Gen.* -cji *bot.* venation.
nerwiak *mi Gen.* -a *pat.* neuroma.
nerwica *f. pat.* neurosis; **nerwica żołądka** nervous stomach.
nerwicowiec *mp* -wc- *pl.* -y *pot.* excitable *l.* edgy person; *pat.* neurotic.
nerwicowy *a. pat.* neurotic.
nerwoból *mi Gen.pl.* -ów *l.* -i *pat.* neuralgia.
nerwowo *adv.* 1. nervously, fretfully; (*w odniesieniu do stanu nerwów*) neurotically; **nerwowo chory** neurotic. 2. (= *niespokojnie*) nervously, restlessly.
nerwowość *f.* 1. nervousness. 2. (= *drażli-*

wość) irritability. 3. (= *gorączkowość*) feverishness.
nerwowy *a.* 1. *anat.* (= *dotyczący nerwu*) nervous; **komórka nerwowa** neuron, nerve cell; **tkanka nerwowa** nervous *l.* nerve tissue; **układ** *l.* **system nerwowy** nervous system; **zakończenia nerwowe** nerve endings. 2. (*rozstrój, tik*) nervous. 3. (= *niespokojny*) (*człowiek*) nervous, anxious; (*sen, ruchy*) restless. 4. (= *łatwo ulegający rozdrażnieniu*) irritable, edgy, jumpy.
nerwówa, nerwówka *f. Gen.pl.* -ek *pot.* tense situation.
nerwus *mp pl.* -y *pot.* edgy person.
nerwy *pl.* (= *system nerwowy*) nerves; **stalowe** *l.* **żelazne nerwy** nerves of steel; **nerwy jak postronki** strong nerves; **kłębek nerwów** (*o człowieku*) a bundle of nerves; **wojna nerwów** war of nerves; **szkoda nerwów** it's not worth the worry *l.* stress; **działać komuś na nerwy** get on sb's nerves; **grać komuś na nerwach** play on sb's nerves; **mieć silne/słabe nerwy** have strong/weak nerves; **szarpać sobie nerwy** rack one's nerves; **tracić nerwy** lose one's nerve; **panować nad nerwami** keep (one's) cool.
nerytyczny *a. geogr.* neritic; **strefa nerytyczna** neritic zone.
neseser *mi* 1. (= *teczka, aktówka*) briefcase. 2. (= *torba podręczna*) overnight bag. 3. (= *kosmetyczka*) toiletries bag.
neseserek *mi* -rk- *Gen.* -a 1. (= *torba podręczna*) (small) overnight bag. 2. (= *kosmetyczka*) toiletries bag.
neska *f. pot.* (= *kawa rozpuszczalna*) instant (coffee).
nestor *mp pl.* -rzy *lit.* nestor. − *ma pl.* -ry *orn.* kea (*Nestor notabilis*).
nestorianizm *mi rel.* Nestorianism.
net *mi sport* net.
netto *a. indecl.* net; **dochód/zysk netto** net income/profit; **waga/cena netto** net weight/price; **płaca** *l.* **wynagrodzenie netto** net pay.
neuma *f. muz.* neume.
neuralgia *f. Gen.* -ii *pat.* neuralgia.
neurastenia *f. Gen.* -ii *pat.* neurasthenia.
neurasteniczny *a. pat.* neurasthenic.
neurastenik *mp pat.* neurasthenic.
neuroblast *mi biol.* neuroblast.
neurochemia *f. chem., med.* neurochemistry.
neurochirurg *mp chir.* neurosurgeon.
neurochirurgia *f. Gen.* -ii *chir.* neurosurgery.
neurochirurgiczny *a. chir.* neurosurgical.
neurofibryl *mi biol.* neurofibril.
neurofizjolog *mp med.* neurophysiologist.
neurofizjologia *f. Gen.* -ii *med.* neurophysiology.
neurofizjologiczny *a. med.* neurophysiological, neurophysiologic.
neurogeniczny *a.* neurogenic, neurogenous.
neurohormony *pl. Gen.* -ów *biol.* neurohormones.
neuroleptyki *pl. Gen.* -ów *med.* antipsychotics, neuroleptics.
neurolog *mp med.* neurologist.
neurologia *f. Gen.* -ii *med.* neurology.

neurologiczny *a. med.* neurological.

neuroma *f. pat.* neuroma.

neuron *mi anat.* neuron, nerve cell; *Br.* neurone.

neuropata *mp pat.* neuropath.

neuropatia *f. Gen.* -ii *pat.* neuropathy.

neuropatolog *mp med.* neuropathologist.

neuropatologia *f. Gen.* -ii *med.* neuropathology.

neuropatyczny *a. pat.* neuropathic.

neuropsychiatria *f. med., psych.* neuropsychiatry.

neuropsychiatryczny *a. med., psych.* neuropsychiatric.

neuropsychologia *f. med., psych.* neuropsychology.

neurotyczny *a.* 1. *pat.* neurotic. 2. *przen.* nervous.

neurotyk *mp pat.* neurotic.

neuroza *f. pat.* neurosis, psychoneurosis.

neurula *f. zool.* neurula.

neuryt *mi anat.* axon.

neuston *ma biol.* neuston.

neutralizacja *f. chem., polit., fon.* neutralization.

neutralizator *mi Gen.* -a *techn.* neutralizer.

neutralizm *mi polit.* neutralism, nonalignment.

neutralizować *ipf.* 1. (= *ustanawiać neutralność*) neutralize. 2. *chem.* neutralize. 3. (= *czynić nieszkodliwym*) neutralize. ~ **się** *ipf.* neutralize.

neutralnie *adv.* neutrally; **zachować się neutralnie** remain neutral.

neutralność *f.* 1. *polit.* neutrality, nonalignment. 2. (= *bezstronność*) impartiality.

neutralny *a.* 1. *polit.* neutral, nonaligned; **spotkać się na neutralnym gruncie** meet on neutral ground; **pas neutralny** no-man's-land; **strefa neutralna** neutral zone. 2. (= *bezstronny*) impartial, unbiased. 3. *chem.* (= *obojętny*) neutral. 4. (*kolor, odpowiedź*) (= *stonowany*) subdued.

neutrino *n. fiz.* neutrino.

neutrofil *mi biol.* neutrophil, neutrophile.

neutron *mi fiz.* neutron.

neutronowy *a. fiz.* neutron; **gwiazda neutronowa** *astron.* neutron star.

neutrum *n. jęz.* neuter.

newralgia *f. Gen.* -ii *pat.* neuralgia.

newralgiczny *a.* 1. *pat.* (= *związany z newralgią*) neuralgic. 2. *przen.* dangeorus, troublesome; **punkt/rejon newralgiczny** trouble spot/area.

nęcący *a.* tempting, inviting, seductive.

nęcić *ipf.* 1. (= *kusić*) allure, entice, tempt. 2. *ryb.* (= *zanęcać*) bait.

nędza *f.* 1. (= *niedostatek*) extreme poverty, indigence; **nędza moralna** degradation, abasement; **w skrajnej nędzy** in utmost poverty; **obraz nędzy i rozpaczy** a pitiful *l.* sorry sight; **cierpieć nędzę** be poverty-stricken, live in poverty. 2. (= *tandeta*) trash, garbage.

nędzarka *f. zob.* **nędzarz**.

nędzarz *mp* pauper, beggar.

nędznie *adv.* 1. (= *ubogo*) in (utmost *l.* utter) poverty; (*żyć, wyglądać*) miserably, wretchedly. 2. (= *skąpo*) scantily, skimpily; (*płacić*) stingily. 3. (= *nieudolnie*) carelessly, negligently.

nędznieć *ipf.* waste away.

nędznik *mp* rascal, scoundrel.

nędzny *a.* 1. (= *znamionujący nędzę*) miserable, wretched; (*ubiór, wygląd*) shabby. 2. (= *zabiedzony*) frail, gaunt; (*dziecko, szkapa*) emaciated. 3. (= *lichy*) sorry, wretched; (*hotel, posiłek*) mean. 4. (= *niewystarczający*) paltry; (*zarobek, zbiory*) measly. 5. (= *bezwartościowy*) trashy. 6. (= *podły*) mean, base; (*tchórz, postępek*) worthless.

nękać *ipf.* plague, haunt. ~ **się** *ipf.* torment o.s.

NFI *abbr.* (= *Narodowy Fundusz Inwestycyjny*) National Investment Fund.

ni *conj.* nor; **ni... ni...** neither... nor...; **ni stąd, ni zowąd** out of the blue, for no reason (whatsoever); **ni z tego, ni z owego** out of the blue; **ni mniej, ni więcej** no less than; **ni pies, ni wydra** neither fish nor flesh; **ni w pięć, ni w dziewięć** without any sense whatsoever; **ni cholery!** *pot.* for the life of me!; *por.* **ani**.

niacyna *f. chem.* nicotinic acid, niacin.

Niagara *f. geogr.* Niagara (Falls).

niania *f.* nanny.

niańczyć *ipf.* nurse.

niańka *f.* nursemaid, nursery maid.

nią *pron. zob.* **ona**.

niby *adv.* supposedly, allegedly; as if, as though; like; **niby przypadkiem** as if by chance; **poszedł niby do pracy** he supposedly went to work; **on jest niby bystry** he is supposed to be clever; **on jest niby geniuszem** he's (supposed to be) some kind *l.* sort of genius.

nibygwiazda *f. Gen.* -wieździe *astron.* quasar, quasi-stellar object.

nibynóżki *pl. Gen.* -żek *biol.* pseudopodia.

nic *pron. Gen.* **niczego** *Dat.* **niczemu** *Loc. i Ins.* **niczym** 1. (= *żadna rzecz*) nothing; (*z innym wyrazem przeczącym*) anything; **nic dobrego** (*o człowieku*) no good, good for nothing; **nic dziwnego** no wonder; **nic podobnego!** nothing of the sort *l.* kind!, no way!; **nic takiego** nothing really; **niczego sobie** *pot.* (= *całkiem niezły*) not bad (at all); **nic z tego** it's no use, nothing doing; **to nic nie pomoże** it's not going to help; **nic ci do tego!** it's none of your business!, mind your own business!; **nic tu po nas** we won't help here, we won't be of any use here; **to nic, że przegraliśmy** never mind that we lost; **być do niczego** be useless, be no good, be good for nothing; **nic nie szkodzi** never mind, it's nothing; **być niczym** be worthless; **nic mi nie jest** I'm alright, I'm O.K.; **nic mu nie będzie** he'll be fine *l.* alright *l.* O.K.; **nic a nic** not a thing; **mieć kogoś/coś za nic** not think much of sb/sth; **nie mieć nic do powiedzenia** have nothing to say; **nie mieć nic do stracenia** have nothing to lose; **nie mieć nic przeciw komuś/czemuś** have nothing against sb/sth; **zrobić coś z niczego** make sth out of nothing. 2. (= *wcale, w najmniejszym stopniu*) nothing at all, not at all; **jak nic** (= *na pewno*) for sure; (= *bez trudu*) without any effort, like nothing; **wszystko na nic** (all) for nothing; **za nic (w świecie)** not for anything (in the world); **to nie ma nic do rzeczy** that is immaterial *l.* irrelevant; **na nic się (nie) zdać** be useless; **jakby** *l.* **jak gdyby (nigdy) nic** as if nothing happened; **nie miałem nic w ustach od tygodnia** I haven't eaten for a week. – *n. indecl.* nothing; **wielkie nic** big (fat) zero; **zupa nic** *kulin.* milk soup with egg yolk, sugar and vanilla.

Nicea *f. Gen.* -ei *geogr.* Nice.

nichrom *mi metal.* Nichrome.

niciany *a.* made of thread.

niciarka *f.* **1.** *tk.* (= *maszyna do wyrobu nici*) twisting machine, ply-twist. **2.** *druk.* (= *maszyna do zszywania książek*) thread sewing *l.* stitching machine. **3.** *techn.* (= *maszyna do nitowania*) riveting machine *l.* press, riveter.

niciarnia *f. Gen.pl.* -i *l.* -ń *tk.* twisting shop.

nicie *mi zob.* **nit**.

nicielnica *f. Gen.pl.* -i *l.* -ń *tk.* harness.

nicienie *pl. zool.* nematodes (*Nematoda*).

nicień *ma zool.* nematode, roundworm (*Nematoda*).

nicość *f.* **1.** (= *niebyt*) nothingness. **2.** (= *bycie bezwartościowym*) worthlessness.

nicować *ipf.* **1.** (= *przerabiać ubranie*) turn. **2.** (= *krytykować*) pick to pieces.

nicpoń *mp Gen.pl.* -i *l.* -ów (a) good-for-nothing.

niczego *itd. pron. zob.* **nic**.

niczyj *a. Loc. i Ins.* -yim *pl.* -yje, -yi *Gen. i Loc.* -yich *Dat.* -yim *Acc.* -yje, -yich *Ins.* -yimi nobody's, no-one's; **ziemia niczyja** no-man's-land.

niczym¹ *conj.* (= *jak*) as if.

niczym² *pron. zob.* **nic**.

nić *f. Ins.pl.* -mi **1.** (= *włókno do szycia*) thread; **(coś jest) szyte grubymi nićmi** (sth is) perfectly obvious, (sth is) thinly disguised; **trzymać nici czegoś** pull the strings of sth; **nici z czegoś** *pot.* nothing will come of it, it will all go up in smoke; **nić opowieści** thread of the story. **2.** (*wydzielina pająków*) thread, cobweb.

Niderlandy *pl.* -ów *hist.* the Netherlands.

niderlandzki *a.* Netherlandic, Netherlandian.

nie *particle* **1.** (*z czasownikami*) not; **nie martw się!** don't worry!; **nie poszlibyśmy do kina?** why don't we go to the movies?, wouldn't you like to go to the movies?; **nie uda ci się!** you won't make it!; **nie ma co dłużej czekać** there's no point in waiting any longer, it's no good *l.* use waiting any longer; **być albo nie być** to be or not to be; **nie ma go tutaj** he is not here; **nie ma jej** she is not in. **2.** (*z rzeczownikami*) not, no; **nie koniec na tym** but that's not all; **nie do śmiechu nam** we don't feel like laughing; **diabeł nie człowiek** (he's) a devil of a man; **nie w porę** at an inopportune moment; **nie w porządku** (= *niesprawiedliwie*) unfair, not right; (= *zepsuty*) out of order; **nie na rękę (komuś)** not convenient (for sb); **nie do wiary** past belief; **nie do wytrzymania** past endurance; **nie do złamania** unbreakable; **nie do pojęcia** incomprehensible. **3.** (*z przymiotnikami, przysłówkami*) not; **nie teraz** not now; **je-**

szcze nie not yet; **nie dość** not enough; **nie całkiem** not quite; **nie warto** it's not worth it; **nie wiadomo** nobody knows; **wyszedł, nie płacąc** he left without paying. **4.** (*zaprzeczenie*) no; **Idziesz? - Nie.** Are you coming? - No, I'm not; **nie i nie** no way; **co to, to nie** it is out of the question, no way; **nie, bo nie** no and that's it; **czemu nie** why not. **5.** *pot.* (*prośba o potwierdzenie*) not; **znasz go, nie?** you know him, don't you?

nie- *pref.* (*z przymiotnikami, przysłówkami, rzeczownikami*) un-, in-, im-, ir-, il-; (*z rzeczownikami*) non-.

nieadekwatnie *adv.* inadequately.

nieadekwatność *f.* inadequacy.

nieadekwatny *a.* inadequate, inappropriate.

nieagresja *f.* non-aggression; **pakt o nieagresji** *polit.* non-aggression pact.

nieagresywny *a.* unaggressive.

nieakademicki *a.* unacademic.

nieaktualny *a.* (*bilet*) invalid; (*informacja*) out-of-date; (*paszport, prawo jazdy*) expired; (*oferta*) unavailable.

nieaktywny *a.* inactive.

nieakuratny *a.* **1.** *pot.* (= *niedokładny*) inaccurate. **2.** (= *nieuważny*) careless. **3.** (= *niepunktualny*) unpunctual.

niealfabetycznie *adv.* unalphabetically, not alphabetically.

nieambitny *a.* unambitious.

nieantagonistyczny *a.* unantagonistic.

nieapetycznie *adv.* **1.** (= *nie wzbudzając apetytu*) unappetizingly. **2.** (= *niepowabnie*) uninvitingly.

nieapetyczny *a.* **1.** (= *niewzbudzający apetytu*) unappetizing. **2.** (= *niepowabny*) uninviting.

nieartykułowany *a.* inarticulate.

nieatrakcyjnie *adv.* **1.** (= *nieinteresująco*) uninterestingly. **2.** (= *niepowabnie*) unattractively.

nieatrakcyjność *f.* **1.** (= *nieinteresujący charakter*) uninterestingness. **2.** (= *niepowabność*) unattractiveness.

nieatrakcyjny *a.* **1.** (= *nieinteresujący*) uninteresting. **2.** (= *niepowabny*) unattractive.

nieautentycznie *adv.* inauthentically, unauthentically, spuriously.

nieautentyczność *f.* inauthenticity, unauthenticity, spuriousness.

nieautentyczny *a.* inauthentic, unauthentic, spurious.

nieautoryzowany *a.* unauthorized.

niebacznie *adv.* **1.** (= *bez zastanowienia*) rashly, incautiously, imprudently, inconsiderately; **niebacznie coś powiedzieć** say sth imprudently. **2.** (= *nieuważnie*) inconsiderately, inadvertently.

niebaczny *a.* **1.** (= *nieroztropny*) rash, incautious, imprudent, inconsiderate; (*słowa*) unguarded, inadvertent; **być niebacznym na coś** be heedless of sth. **2.** (= *nieuważny*) inconsiderate, inadvertent.

niebagatelny *a.* considerable, substantial.

niebanalnie *adv.* originally.

niebanalny *a.* original.

niebarwny *a.* colourless.

niebawem *adv. lit.* anon, soon, shortly.

niebezpieczeństwo *n.* **1.** (= *zagrożenie*) danger, peril, jeopardy, menace; **być** *l.* **znaleźć się w niebezpieczeństwie** be in danger; **narazić kogoś/coś na niebezpieczeństwo** endanger sb/sth, imperil sb/sth, bring *l.* put sb/sth into danger; **narazić się na niebezpieczeństwo** expose o.s. to danger; **niebezpieczeństwo dla kogoś/czegoś** danger to sb/sth; **stanowić niebezpieczeństwo dla kogoś/czegoś** constitute *l.* be a danger to sb/sth; **istnieje niebezpieczeństwo, że...** there is a danger that...; **śmiertelne niebezpieczeństwo** mortal *l.* deadly danger. **2.** (= *ryzyko*) risk, hazard; **niebezpieczeństwo pożaru** fire hazard; **niebezpieczeństwo wybuchu** explosion hazard; **niebezpieczeństwo utraty życia** life hazard. **3.** (= *sytuacja awaryjna*) emergency.

niebezpiecznie *adv.* dangerously, perilously.

niebezpieczny *a.* **1.** (= *stwarzający zagrożenie*) (*sytuacja, bandyta*) dangerous; (*ładunek, substancja*) hazardous; **niebezpieczny dla otoczenia** posing a threat to society. **2.** (= *ryzykowny*) risky. **3.** (= *drażliwy*) ticklish, thorny, spiny.

niebezpośredni *a.* indirect.

niebianin *mp pl.* **-anie** *Gen.* **-an** *poet.* heavenly being.

niebianka *f. zob.* **niebianin**.

niebiański *a.* **1.** *lit.* (= *właściwy niebu*) heavenly, celestial. **2.** *lit.* (= *zachwycający*) heavenly, divine.

niebiańsko *adv. lit.* divinely, delightfully.

niebiańskość *f. lit.* heavenliness.

niebiedny *a.* well-to-do.

niebiegunowy *a.* non-polar.

niebielistka *f. Gen.pl.* **-ek** *bot.* **niebielistka trwała** swertia (*Swertia perennis*).

niebieskawy *a.* bluish.

niebieski *a.* **1.** (*kolor*) blue; **lis niebieski** *zool.* blue fox (*Alopex lagopus*); **śnić o niebieskich migdałach** daydream. **2.** (= *związany z niebem jako sklepieniem nad Ziemią*) heavenly, celestial; **ciała niebieskie** *astron.* heavenly bodies; **niebieski ptak** *l.* **ptaszek** *przen.* sponger. **3.** (= *związany z niebem jako miejscem pobytu bóstw*) heavenly, divine; **królestwo niebieskie** the Kingdom of Heaven; **zastępy niebieskie** heavenly host, hosts of heaven.

niebiesko *adv.* in blue; **pomalować coś na niebiesko** paint sth blue.

niebieskolila *a. indecl.* lilac-blue.

niebieskooki *a.* blue-eyed.

niebieskoszary *a.* blue-gray.

niebieskozielony *a.* blue-green.

niebieszczeć *ipf.*, **niebieścieć** *ipf.* **1.** (= *stawać się niebieskim*) become *l.* turn blue. **2.** *zob.* **niebieszczyć się**.

niebieszczenie *n. tk.* blueing.

niebieszczyć *ipf.*, **niebieścić** *ipf.* (= *nasycać niebieską barwą*) blue, tint blue. **~ się** *ipf.*, **niebieścić się** *ipf.* (= *być widocznym dzięki niebieskiej barwie*) show blue.

niebieściuchny *a.*, **niebieściutki** *a. emf.* blue.

niebiosa *pl. Gen.* **-os** *Loc.* **-osach** *l.* **-esiech** *poet.* heaven(s); **wychwalać kogoś/coś pod niebiosa** praise *l.* laud sb/sth to the skies; **o niebiosa!** by heaven(s)!, in heaven's name!

niebłahy *a.* important, serious.

niebo *n.* **1.** (= *firmament*) sky; **jak grom z jasnego nieba** like a bolt out of *l.* from the blue; **na niebie** in the sky; **między niebem a ziemią** in midair; **o (całe) niebo lepszy** far better; **pod gołym niebem** in the open air; **spać pod gołym niebem** sleep rough; **różnić się o całe niebo** *l.* jak **niebo i ziemia** be as different as chalk from cheese; **manna z nieba** manna from heaven; **z nieba mi spadłeś!** you're a godsend!; **nic z nieba nie spada** nothing is for free. **2.** *rel.* heaven; **w niebie** in heaven; **wielkie nieba!** good heavens!; **być w siódmym niebie** be in heaven; **(chcieć) przychylić komuś nieba** (want to) do anything to make sb happy; **poruszyć niebo i ziemię** move heaven and earth; **to woła o pomstę do nieba** it cries to heaven; **niebo w gębie!** *pot.* delicious!, finger-licking good!

nieboga *f. Gen.pl.* **-óg** *lit.* poor dear.

niebogaty *a.* **1.** (= *niezamożny*) unwealthy. **2.** (= *mało zróżnicowany*) unvaried, dull.

niebojaźliwy *a.* fearless.

niebojowy *a.* unaggressive.

niebolesny *a.* painless.

nieboraczek *mp* **-czk-** *emf.* = **nieborak**.

nieboraczka *f. zob.* **nieboraczek**.

nieborak *mp pl.* **-cy** *l.* **-ki** poor thing.

niebosiężny *a. lit.* sky-high.

nieboski *a.* **jak nieboskie stworzenie** dreadfully, terribly.

nieboskłon *mi lit.* horizon.

nieboszczka *f. zob.* **nieboszczyk**.

nieboszczyk *mp pl.* **-cy** *l.* **-ki** dead person, the deceased.

niebotyczność *f. lit.* loftiness.

niebotyczny *a.* **1.** *lit.* (= *bardzo wysoki*) sky-high, lofty. **2.** *lit.* (= *niezwykły*) great, eminent.

niebożątko *n.*, **niebożę** *n.* poor thing.

niebrzydki *a.* **1.** (= *dość ładny*) rather pretty. **2.** (= *niezły*) not bad, passable.

niebrzydko *a.* **1.** (= *dość ładnie*) in a not unsightly way. **2.** (= *nieźle*) passably.

niebyły *a.* non-existent; unreal; **uważać** *l.* **uznać coś za niebyłe** consider sth null and void; **uważaj moją uwagę za niebyłą** forget my remark.

niebyt *mi* non-existence.

niebywale *adv.* unusually.

niebywały *a.* (most) unusual.

niecałkowicie *adv.* incompletely, not completely, not quite, not altogether.

niecałkowity *a.* incomplete, fragmentary; **liczby niecałkowite** *mat.* fractions.

niecały *a.* **1.** (= *niecałkowity*) incomplete, fragmentary. **2.** (= *niepełny*) less than; **niecały rok** less than a year; **mieć niecałe 18 lat** be just under 18.

niecelnie *adv.* wide.

niecelny *a.* **1.** (= *chybiony*) wide. **2.** (= *nietrafiający w sedno*) pointless, irrelevant.

niecelowość *f.* futility, inexpediency.

niecelowy *a.* futile, inexpedient, aimless.

niecenzuralnie *adv.* obscenely, indecently.

niecenzuralny *a.* 1. (= *nieprzyzwoity*) obscene, indecent. 2. (= *niezgodny z cenzurą*) unprintable.

niech *adv.* 1. **niech wejdą** let them come in; **niech żyje (król)**! long live (the King)!; **niech się dzieje, co chce** come what may; **niech cię ręka boska broni, jeśli...** God help you if...; **niech będzie pochwalony (Jezus Chrystus)** praised be Jesus Christ; **niech będzie** let it be, so be it; **niech ci będzie** all right; **a niech go!** (*z podziwem*) some lucky devil!; **niech to szlag!** damnation!; **niech mi wolno będzie (powitać/zaprosić)** let me (welcome/invite); **niech stracę** my loss!; **niech pomyślę** let me think *l.* see; **niech żyje...!** three cheers for...!; **a niech to!** what a nuisance!; **niech cię o to głowa nie boli** don't worry, I'll take care of everything. 2. *pot.* (= *przypuśćmy, że*) **a niech ktoś się o tym dowie** suppose *l.* what if sb learns about it; **a niech ci się nie uda** suppose *l.* what if you fail.

niechaj *adv. lit. zob.* **niech**.

niechajże *adv. lit. zob.* **niech**.

niechby *adv. zob.* **niech**.

niechcący *a.* unintentionally, accidentally, by accident.

niechcenie *n.* **od niechcenia** (= *przypadkiem*) by accident, accidentally; (= *niedbale*) casually, negligently; (= *z łatwością*) easily, without effort.

niechciany *a.* unwanted.

niechęć *f.* 1. (= *brak ochoty*) reluctance, unwillingness (*do zrobienia czegoś* to do sth); **z niechęcią** reluctantly; **czuć niechęć do nauki** have an aversion to learning. 2. (= *antypatia*) dislike (*do kogoś/czegoś* of *l.* for sb/sth); aversion (*do kogoś/czegoś* to sb/sth); **okazywać komuś niechęć** show a dislike for sb, manifest one's aversion to sb; **żywić niechęć do kogoś/czegoś** dislike sb/sth; **poczuć niechęć do czegoś** take a dislike to sth.

niechętnie *adv.* 1. (= *opieszale*) reluctantly. 2. (= *nieprzyjaźnie*) with animosity, unfavourably.

niechętny *a.* 1. (= *opieszały*) reluctant (*do zrobienia czegoś* to do sth). 2. (= *nieprzyjazny*) unfriendly, unfavourable (*komuś/czemuś* to sb/sth).

niechlorowany *a.* unchlorinated, not chlorinated.

niechlubnie *adv. lit.* shamefully, disgracefully, ingloriously.

niechlubny *a. lit.* shameful, disgraceful, inglorious.

niechluj *mp pot.* slob, sloven.

niechlujnie *adv.* sloppily, slovenly, in a slovenly manner.

niechlujność *f.* sloppiness, slovenliness.

niechlujny *a.* sloppy, slovenly.

niechlujstwo *n.* sloppiness, slovenliness.

niechodliwy *a. pot.* unsalable; *Br.* unsaleable.

niechorobotwórczy *a. med.* non-pathogenic.

niechrześcijański *a.* 1. (= *inny niż chrześci-jański*) non-Christian, unchristian. 2. (= *niezgodny z zasadami chrześcijaństwa*) unchristian.

niechrześcijańsko *adv.* unchristianly.

niechybnie *adv.* for sure, for certain, without fail.

niechybny *a.* certain, inescapable, inevitable.

niechże *part. zob.* **niech**.

nieciągłość *f.* discontinuity; **nieciągłość Mohorovicicia** *geol.* Mohorovicic discontinuity, Moho.

nieciągły *a.* discontinuous, discrete; **funkcja nieciągła** *mat.* discontinuous function; **linia nieciągła** broken line.

niecić *ipf.* 1. *lit.* (= *rozpalać*) light, kindle. 2. *lit.* (= *wzbudzać*) stir up; (*bunt*) incite; (*radość*) arouse, excite.

nieciekawie *adv.* 1. (= *nie wzbudzając zainteresowania*) in an uninteresting way, uninterestingly. 2. *pot.* (= *niedobrze*) bad; **twoja sprawa wygląda nieciekawie** your case *l.* business looks bad.

nieciekawy *a.* 1. (= *niezainteresowany*) uninterested. 2. (= *niebudzący zainteresowania*) uninteresting. 3. *pot.* (= *nieprzyjemny*) shady, bad, suspect; **obracać się w nieciekawym towarzystwie** have shady friends.

niecielesny *a.* incorporeal.

niecierpek *mi* -pk- *Gen.* -a *bot.* impatiens, jewelweed, touch-me-not (*Impatiens*); **niecierpek ogrodowy** balsam (*Impatiens balsamina*).

niecierpliwić *ipf.* make impatient. ~ **się** *ipf.* grow *l.* get impatient.

niecierpliwie *adv.* impatiently.

niecierpliwość *f.* impatience; **z niecierpliwością** impatiently.

niecierpliwy *a.* 1. (= *niewytrwały*) impatient. 2. (= *będący oznaką zniecierpliwienia*) impatient.

niecka *f.* 1. (*naczynie*) trough, pan. 2. *geol.* basin, trough, syncline; **niecka węglowa** coal basin.

nieckowaty *a.* channelled.

niecnota *f. l. mp decl. like f. Gen.pl.* -t *l.* -ów *przest.* 1. (= *łotr*) scoundrel, rogue. 2. (= *nicpoń*) good-for-nothing.

niecny *a. lit.* ignoble, ignominious.

nieco *adv.* somewhat; **nieco silniejszy** somewhat stronger; **co nieco** a little; **małe co nieco** a little something; **mieć nieco czasu** have some time.

niecodziennie *adv.* 1. (= *wyjątkowo*) uncommonly, unusually. 2. (= *oryginalnie*) uncommonly, unusually; (*ubierać się*) originally.

niecodzienność *f.* uncommonness, unusualness, originality.

niecodzienny *a.* 1. (= *wyjątkowy*) uncommon, unusual. 2. (= *oryginalny*) extraordinary, original.

niecoś *adv.* **coś niecoś** something, a thing or two.

niecukry *pl. Gen.* -ów *chem.* non-sugars.

niecykliczny *a.* 1. (= *nieregularny*) irregular. 2. *chem.* non-cyclic.

niecywilizowany *a.* uncivilized.

nieczęsto *adv.* infrequently.

nieczęsty *a.* infrequent.

nieczułość *f.* **1.** (= *brak czułości, obojętność*) heartlessness, insensitivity, insensibility. **2.** (= *brak czucia*) numbness, insensitivity, insensibility.

nieczuły *a.* **1.** (= *niewrażliwy*) insensitive, insensible (*na coś* to sth); heartless, callous. **2.** (= *odporny*) impervious (*na coś* to sth).

nieczynny *a.* **1.** (= *niedziałający*) inactive, inoperative; (*telefon, winda*) out of order; (*kino, biuro*) closed; (= *wygasły*) extinct. **2.** *chem., fiz.* inert, inactive.

nieczysto *adv.* **1.** (= *fałszywie*) out of tune. **2.** (= *niezgodnie z przepisami*) foully; (*grać, uderzać*) unfairly.

nieczystości *pl. Gen.* **-i 1.** (= *śmieci*) garbage; *Br.* rubbish; (= *odpady*) waste. **2.** (= *odchody*) waste, f(a)eces.

nieczystość *f.* **1.** (= *brak czystości*) uncleanliness. **2.** (= *nieuczciwość*) dishonesty. **3.** (= *nieprzyzwoitość*) impurity, inchastity; **grzech nieczystości** *rz.-kat.* the sin of impurity. **4.** (= *w sporcie, naruszenie zasad*) foul play. **5.** (= *skażenie*) impurity, contamination; (*rasy, zboża*) impurity. **6.** (*dźwięku*) (= *fałszywość*) being out of tune.

nieczysty *a.* **1.** (= *brudny*) dirty, unclean. **2.** (= *nieuczciwy*) dishonest. **3.** (= *nieprzyzwoity*) impure, unclean; (**mieć**) **nieczyste myśli** (have) warped *l.* impure thoughts; (**mieć**) **nieczyste sumienie** (have) guilty conscience; **moc** *l.* **siła nieczysta** (= *diabeł*) unclean spirit. **4.** *sport* foul. **5.** (= *skażony*) impure, contaminated; (*rasa, zboże*) impure. **6.** (*dźwięk, śpiew*) (= *fałszywy*) out of tune.

nieczytelnie *adv.* **1.** (= *nie do odczytania*) illegibly. **2.** (= *niezrozumiale*) unclearly.

nieczytelność *f.* **1.** (*podpisu*) illegibility. **2.** (*przesłania, poezji*) unclearness.

nieczytelny *a.* **1.** (= *niedający się odczytać*) illegible. **2.** (= *niezrozumiały*) unclear.

niedaleki *a.* **1.** (= *położony w pobliżu*) nearby; **z niedaleka** from not far away; **być niedalekim od prawdy** be near the truth. **2.** (= *krótko trwający*) short; **niedaleka podróż** short journey. **3.** (= *mający wkrótce nastąpić*) near, prospective, coming; **w niedalekiej przyszłości** in the near *l.* foreseeable future.

niedaleko *adv.* **1.** (= *w pobliżu*) near; **to niedaleko (stąd)** it's not far (from here). **2.** (= *w pobliże*) not far; **niedaleko pada jabłko od jabłoni** the apple never falls far from the tree. **3.** (= *niezadługo*) soon, not far off; **już niedaleko do świąt** Christmas is (quite) near (now).

niedawno *adv.* recently, not (so) long ago.

niedawny *a.* **1.** (= *nieodległy w przeszłości*) recent; **do niedawna** until recently. **2.** (= *trwający od krótkiego czasu*) recent; **od niedawna** since recently. **3.** (= *były*) former.

niedbale *adv.* **1.** (= *byle jak*) slapdash, sloppily; (*pracować, sprzątać*) neglectfully, sloppily. **2.** (= *nonszalancko*) carelessly, nonchalantly.

niedbalstwo *n.* negligence, neglect.

niedbaluch *mp pl.* **-y** *pot.* slob, sloven.

niedbałość *f.* **1.** (= *niestaranność*) negligence, sloppiness. **2.** (= *nonszalancja*) nonchalance, carelessness.

niedbały *a.* **1.** (= *nierzetelny*) negligent; (*pracownik*) negligent, inattentive. **2.** (= *niechlujny*) slapdash, sloppy. **3.** (= *nonszalancki*) casual; (*strój*) untidy, sloppy; (*poza, gest*) offhand.

niedefiniowalny *a.* undefinable.

niedelikatnie *adv.* tactlessly, indelicately, rudely.

niedelikatność *f.* tactlessness, indelicacy, rudeness.

niedelikatny *a.* (= *nietaktowny*) (*człowiek*) tactless, rude; (*uwaga, postępowanie*) indelicate, tactless, rude.

niedemokratyczny *a.* undemocratic.

niedługi *a.* **1.** (= *niezbyt długi*) short. **2.** (= *krótkotrwały*) short, brief; **w niedługim czasie** in a short time, shortly.

niedługo *adv.* **1.** (= *przez krótki czas*) a little while; **to potrwa niedługo** it won't take long; **niedługo pociągnie** *pot.* he won't last long. **2.** (= *wkrótce*) soon, before long.

niedobarwliwość *f.* *pat.* hypochromia, hypochromatism.

niedobiałczenie *n.* *pat.* hypoproteinia.

niedobitek *mp* **-tk-** *pl.* **-i** survivor.

niedobór *mi* **-o- 1.** (= *niedostatek*) (*witamin*) deficiency; (*żywności*) shortage, scarcity; (*pieniędzy, siły roboczej*) shortage; **niedobór witamin** vitamin deficiency; **niedobór elektronowy** *fiz.* electron deficiency; **niedobór masy** *fiz.* mass defect; **niedobór tlenowy** oxygen want; **niedobór siły roboczej** shortage of labor. **2.** (= *deficyt*) deficit.

niedobrany *a.* **1.** (= *nieodpowiedni*) (*kapelusz, meble*) ill-matched; (*małżeństwo*) mismatched, ill-suited. **2.** (= *niestosowny*) inappropriate.

niedobry *a.* **1.** (= *pozbawiony dobroci*) bad, not good, evil. **2.** (= *nieszlachetny*) bad, wicked; (*intencje, zwyczaj*) bad. **3.** (= *niepomyślny*) bad. **4.** (= *niesumienny*) bad. **5.** (= *nieodpowiedni*) improper; (*materiał, surowiec*) improper, substandard; (*rozmiar, ubranie*) unsuitable, ill-fitting. **6.** (= *niesmaczny*) bad. **7.** (= *niewesoły*) bad; (*nastrój, myśli*) gloomy.

niedobrze *adv.* **1.** (= *nie tak, jak trzeba*) wrong, wrongly, badly; **mieć niedobrze w głowie** have a screw loose. **2.** (= *niezdrowo*) unwell, sickly; **niedobrze mi** I feel sick; **czuć się niedobrze** feel unwell *l.* sick. **3.** (= *nieprzychylnie*) unkindly; **niedobrze mu z oczu patrzy** he doesn't look like a good person. **4.** (= *niepomyślnie*) badly; **niedobrze z nim** he is in trouble; **to się niedobrze skończy** it's going to end badly; **niedobrze to wygląda** it looks pretty bad. **5.** (= *nieprzyjemnie*) not well, badly; **coś niedobrze pachnie** *przen.* sth stinks, sth is not right.

niedoceniany *a.* underestimated.

niedochodowy *a.* **1.** (= *nieprzynoszący dochodów*) unprofitable. **2.** (= *nienastawiony na dochód*) non-profit.

niedociągnięcie *f.* shortcoming, defect.

niedocieczony *a. lit.* unfathomable, incomprehensible.

niedociśnienie *n. pat.* hypotension; **niedociśnienie tętnicze** arterial hypotension.

niedocukrzenie *n. pat.* **niedocukrzenie krwi** hypoglyc(a)emia.

niedoczas *mi szachy* time trouble.

niedoczekanie *n.* **niedoczekanie twoje!** that will be the day!

niedoczulica *f. pat.* hyp(a)esthesia.

niedoczynność *f. pat.* hypofunction, hypoactivity, deficient function; **niedoczynność tarczycy** hypothyroidism, hypothyreosis.

niedodma *f. pat.* atelectasis, airlessness of the lungs.

niedogodnie *adv.* inconveniently.

niedogodność *f.* inconvenience.

niedogodny *a.* inconvenient.

niedogon *mi chem.* tails.

niedogotowany *a. kulin.* underdone, half-cooked, half-baked.

niedoinformowany *a.* underreported, uninformed.

niedoinwestowanie *n.* undercapitalization, underfunding.

niedoinwestowany *a.* undercapitalized, underfunded.

niedojda *f. l. mp decl. like f. Gen.pl.* **-d** *l.* **-ów** *pog.* twerp, goof.

niedojdowaty *a.* goofy.

niedojrzałość *f.* **1.** (= *stadium poprzedzające dojrzałość*) (*człowieka*) immaturity; (*sera, owocu*) unripeness. **2.** (= *brak dojrzałości psychicznej*) immaturity.

niedojrzały *a.* **1.** (= *niebędący w pełni rozwoju*) immature; (*owoc, zboże*) unripe, green; (*ser*) unripe, immature; (*wino*) immature, green. **2.** (= *nieukształtowany psychicznie*) immature. **3.** (= *niedoświadczony*) green, raw; (*artysta, polityk*) unfledged. **4.** (= *będący w trakcie fermentacji*) immature, aging.

niedokarmiony *a.* underfed, undernourished.

niedokładnie *adv.* **1.** (= *niestarannie*) sloppily, negligently, carelessly. **2.** (= *ogólnikowo*) inaccurately.

niedokładność *f.* **1.** (= *niestaranność*) negligence, carelessness, sloppiness. **2.** (= *ogólnikowość*) inaccuracy.

niedokładny *a.* **1.** (= *niestaranny*) sloppy; (*człowiek*) careless, negligent; (*tłumaczenie, pomiar*) inaccurate, incorrect. **2.** (= *ogólnikowy*) inaccurate.

niedokonany *a. jęz.* imperfective, imperfect.

niedokończony *a.* unfinished, incomplete.

niedokrwienie *n. pat.* isch(a)emia; **niedokrwienie mózgu** cerebral isch(a)emia.

niedokrwiony *a. pat.* isch(a)emic.

niedokrwistość *f. pat.* an(a)emia.

niedokrwisty *a. pat.* an(a)emic.

niedokształcony *a.* undereducated.

niedokwasota, niedokwaśność *f. pat.* achlorhydria.

niedola *f. lit.* misery; **w doli i niedoli** through thick and thin.

niedolew *mi metal.* misrun (casting), short run casting.

niedolot *mi lotn.* undershoot, short landing.

niedoludnienie *n.* underpopulation.

niedoładowanie *n.* **1.** (= *niepełne obciążenie*) underloading. **2.** (= *niepełne naładowanie ładunkiem elektrycznym*) undercharge, undercharging.

niedołęga *f. l. mp decl. like f. Gen.pl.* **-g** *l.* **-ów** *pot.* twerp, goof.

niedołęstwo *n.* **1.** (= *niesprawność fizyczna*) disability, infirmity. **2.** (= *nieudolność*) incompetence. **3.** (= *niezdarność*) awkwardness.

niedołężnie *adv.* **1.** (= *niesprawnie ruchowo*) infirmly. **2.** (= *nieudolnie*) incompetently. **3.** (= *niezdarnie*) awkwardly.

niedołężnieć *ipf.* (= *tracić sprawność ruchową*) grow *l.* become infirm.

niedołężny *a.* **1.** (= *niesprawny ruchowo*) infirm. **2.** (= *nieudolny*) incompetent. **3.** (= *niezdarny*) awkward.

niedomagać *ipf.* **1.** (= *podupadać na zdrowiu*) languish. **2.** (= *być chorym*) be ailing; **on niedomaga na serce** he has a heart condition. **3.** (= *szwankować*) malfunction.

niedomaganie *n.* **1.** (= *dolegliwość*) indisposition, ailment. **2.** (= *usterka*) defect, shortcoming.

niedomiar *mi* insufficiency, defficiency; **niedomiar tlenu** *biol.* oxygen depletion.

niedomoga *f. Gen.pl.* **-óg 1.** *pat.* insufficient function, weakness. **2.** (= *niedociągnięcie*) defect, shortcoming.

niedomówienie *n.* **1.** (= *aluzja*) hint, undertone; **bez niedomówień** in plain terms, straightforwardly. **2.** (= *nieporozumienie*) misunderstanding. **3.** *ret.* pause.

niedomykalność *f. pat.* incompetence, insufficiency, defective closure; **niedomykalność zastawek serca** valvular incompetence *l.* insufficiency.

niedomyślny *a.* slow on the uptake.

niedomyty *a. pot.* slovenly.

niedonoszony *a.* (= *urodzony przed terminem*) preterm, premature, born before term.

niedookreślony *a.* underspecified.

niedopałek *mi* **-łk-** *Gen.* **-a** (cigarette) butt, (cigarette) stub.

niedopałka *f. bud.* underburnt brick.

niedopatrzenie *n.* oversight; **przez niedopatrzenie** through an oversight; **z powodu niedopatrzenia** due to an oversight.

niedopieczony *a. kulin.* underdone, rare.

niedopieszczony *a.* **1.** *pot.* (= *niedoceniony*) underappreciated. **2.** (= *odczuwający brak czułości*) not caressed enough. **3.** *pot.* (= *niedopracowany*) half-baked, patchy, scrappy.

niedopity *a.* **1.** *pot.* (= *taki, który nie zdążył się upić*) not having had enough, not quite canned, not quite fuddled; **jestem niedopity** I need another drink. **2.** (= *niewypity do końca*) left unfinished *l.* undrunk; **został tylko niedopity sok** there is only some juice left.

niedopłata *f.* short payment; **ma Pan/Pani jesz-**

cze 100 zł **niedopłaty** you still have to pay 100 PLN of the amout due, there's still 100 PLN of the amout due to be paid.

niedopompowanie *n. mot.* underinflation.

niedopowiedzenie *n.* **1.** (= *niedokończenie wypowiedzi*) understatement, allusion. **2.** *ret.* pause.

niedopracowany *a.* half-baked.

niedoprasowanie *n. techn.* short moulding.

niedoprzęd *mi tk.* roving.

niedoprzędzarka *f. tk.* roving frame.

niedopuszczalnie *adv.* inadmissibly, unacceptably.

niedopuszczalność *f.* inadmissibility.

niedopuszczalny *a.* unacceptable, inadmissible; **to niedopuszczalne!** that's unacceptable!

niedorajda *f. l. mp decl. like f. Gen.pl.* **-d** *l.* **-ów** *pog.* goof, wimp.

niedoręczenie *n.* non-delivery; **w przypadku niedoręczenia** if undelivered.

niedorobiony *a.* **1.** (= *nieskończony, niegotowy*) unfinished, incomplete. **2.** (= *głupawy*) *pot.* deficient.

niedorosły *a.* minor, under age.

niedorozwinięty *a.* **1.** (= *upośledzony psychicznie*) retarded, mentally handicapped *l.* deficient. **2.** (= *niecałkowicie rozwinięty*) underdeveloped. **3.** (= *głupkowaty*) *pot.* moronic.

niedorozwój *mi* **-o- 1.** (= *upośledzenie psychiczne*) mental deficiency. **2.** (= *nieprawidłowość budowy organu*) underdevelopment.

niedoróbka *f. pot.* (= *coś niezrobione do końca*) bungle, botchery; (= *usterka*) fault.

niedorzecznie *adv.* preposterously, absurdly.

niedorzeczność *f.* nonsense, preposterousness, absurdity.

niedorzeczny *a.* nonsensical, preposterous, absurd.

niedosięgły, niedosiężny *a.* **1.** (= *taki, którego nie można dotknąć*) inaccessible. **2.** (= *taki, którego nie można osiągnąć*) unattainable. **3.** (= *taki, któremu nie można dorównać*) unrivalled, matchless.

niedoskonałość *f.* imperfection, flaw; **niedoskonałość punktowa** *krystal.* point defect; **niedoskonałość sieciowa** *krystal.* lattice defect.

niedoskonały *a.* imperfect; flawed, faulty.

niedosłyszalnie *adv.* inaudibly.

niedosłyszalny *a.* inaudible.

niedosłyszący *a.* hard-of-hearing. – *mp* hard of hearing.

niedosłyszeć *ipf.* **-ę -ysz** be hard of hearing.

niedosłyszenie *n.* partial deafness.

niedospany *a.* sleepy, drowsy; **jest niedospany** he needs more sleep.

niedostatecznie *adv.* **1.** (= *niewystarczająco*) insufficiently, scantily. **2.** (= *niezadowalająco*) inadequately, unsatisfactorily.

niedostateczność *f.* insufficiency, scantiness.

niedostateczny *a.* **1.** (= *niewystarczający*) insufficient, scanty. **2.** (= *niezadowalający*) inadequate, unsatisfactory; **ocena niedostateczna** *szkoln.* fail, failure, unsatisfactory *l.* failing

grade. – *mi szkoln.* fail, failure, unsatisfactory *l.* failing grade.

niedostatek *mi* **-tk- 1.** (= *nędza*) want, poverty; **cierpieć niedostatek** live in want *l.* poverty. **2.** (= *mankament*) shortcoming, deficiency. **3.** *przest.* (= *brak*) shortage, scarcity.

niedostępność *f.* **1.** (*szczytu, osoby*) inaccessibility. **2.** (*twierdzy, zamku*) impenetrability.

niedostępny *a.* **1.** (= *taki, do którego dostęp jest utrudniony*) inaccessible; (*gęstwina lasu, twierdza*) impenetrable, impervious. **2.** (= *taki, do którego dostęp jest zabroniony*) prohibited. **3.** (= *taki, do którego wstęp jest niemożliwy*) inaccessible. **4.** (= *nieprzystępny*) (*o ludziach*) unapproachable, aloof. **5.** (= *nieosiągalny*) unobtainable, unattainable; beyond *l.* out of reach; **nieprzystępna cena** prohibitive price.

niedostosowanie *n.* (*czyjeś*) unadjustedness.

niedostosowany *a.* (*o człowieku*) unadjusted.

niedostrzegalnie *adv.* imperceptibly.

niedostrzegalność *f.* imperceptibility.

niedostrzegalny *a.* imperceptible, unnoticeable.

niedosyt *mi* (= *stan nienasycenia*) insufficiency, deficiency; (= *odczuwanie braku*) want; **mieć niedosyt czegoś** be wanting in sth; **odczuwać niedosyt miłości/spokoju** thirst *l.* hunger for love/peace.

niedoszły *a.* **1.** (= *niezrealizowany*) unrealized, unattained; **niedoszłe małżeństwo** a marriage that might have been. **2.** (= *taki, który nie urzeczywistnił zamierzeń*) would-be; **niedoszły artysta** would-be artist, artist manqué.

niedościgły, niedościgniony *a.* **1.** (= *nieosiągalny*) unattainable. **2.** (= *niezrównany*) unparalleled, unequaled; peerless. **3.** *przest.* (= *niedający się doścignąć*) swift.

niedoświadczenie *n.* inexperience.

niedoświadczony *a.* **-eni** inexperienced, unexperienced.

niedoświetlenie *n. fot.* underexposure.

niedoświetlony *a. fot.* underexposed.

niedotlenienie *n. pat.* oxygen deficiency; (*tkanek*) hypoxia; (*tkanek i organów*) anoxia.

niedotlenowanie *n. pat.* (*krwi*) hypoxemia; (*krwi tętniczej*) anoxemia.

niedotrenowanie *n. sport* inadequate training.

niedouczony *a.* undereducated.

niedouk *mp pl.* **-i** *pog.* undereducated person.

niedowaga *f.* underweight.

niedowarzony *a.* (= *nie w pełni dojrzały*) immature.

niedoważkość *f. fiz.* reduced gravity.

niedowcipny *a.* **1.** (= *nieśmieszny*) unamusing. **2.** (= *pozbawiony poczucia humoru*) having no sense of humor.

niedowiarek *mp* **-rk-** *pl.* **-i 1.** (= *osoba mająca wątpliwości w wierze*) doubter, skeptic. **2.** *żart.* (= *sceptyk*) doubting Thomas.

niedowidzenie *n. pat.* amblyopia.

niedowidzieć *ipf.* **-dzę -isz** be short-sighted, have poor vision; **on niedowidzi** his sight is failing.

niedowierzająco *adv.* **1.** (= *z niedowierza-*

niem) incredulously. **2.** (= *podejrzliwie*) distrustfully, mistrustfully.

niedowierzanie *n.* **1.** (= *powątpiewanie*) incredulity, disbelief; **z niedowierzaniem** in disbelief. **2.** (= *nieufność*) distrust, mistrust.

niedowład *mi* **1.** *pat.* paresis. **2.** (= *indolencja*) inertia, sluggishness.

niedozwolony *a.* **1.** (= *wzbroniony*) prohibited, forbidden. **2.** *praw.* illicit, unlawful.

niedożywienie *n.* malnutrition.

niedożywiony *a.* **-eni** malnourished, undernourished.

niedrapieżny *a.* non-predatory.

niedrogi *a.* (= *tani*) inexpensive, cheap.

niedrogo *adv.* inexpensively, cheaply; **kupić coś niedrogo** get sth at a reasonable price.

niedrożność *f.* **1.** *pat.* occlusion; **niedrożność jelit** intestinal occlusion. **2.** *techn.* obstruction.

niedrożny *a.* **1.** *pat.* occluded. **2.** *techn.* obstructed.

niedużo *adv.* not much, not many.

nieduży *a.* **-zi** **1.** (= *mały*) rather small, not large. **2.** (= *niewysoki*) rather short.

niedwuznacznie *adv.* unambiguously.

niedwuznaczność *f.* unambiguousness.

niedwuznaczny *a.* unambiguous.

niedyplomatycznie *adv.* undiplomatically.

niedyplomatyczny *a.* undiplomatic.

niedyskrecja *f.* indiscretion; **popełnić niedyskrecję** be indiscreet.

niedyskretnie *adv.* indiscreetly.

niedyskretny *a.* **1.** (= *nieumiejący dochować tajemnicy*) indiscreet. **2.** (= *niedelikatny, nietaktowny*) indelicate, tactless.

niedysponowany *a.* indisposed, unwell.

niedyspozycja *f.* indisposition, ill health.

niedziedziczny *a.* non-hereditary.

niedziela *f.* Sunday; **Wielka Niedziela** *rel.* Easter Sunday; **Niedziela Palmowa** *rel.* Palm Sunday; **urodzony w niedzielę** (= *leniwy*) lazybones; (= *szczęściarz*) lucky devil.

niedzielny *a.* Sunday; **niedzielny kierowca** Sunday driver.

niedzisiejszy *a.* **1.** (= *nieodnoszący się do dnia dzisiejszego*) not today's. **2.** (= *przestarzały*) old-fashioned.

niedźwiadek *ma* **-dk-** **1.** (= *mały niedźwiedź*) little bear; (= *młode niedźwiedzia*) bear cub. **2.** (*zabawka*) Teddy bear.

niedźwiadki *pl.* *ent.* scorpions (*Scorpionida*).

niedźwiedziątko *n.* bear cub.

niedźwiedzi *a.* **1.** (*trop, sadło*) bear's; **niedźwiedzia skóra** bearskin; **niedźwiedzia przysługa** disservice. **2.** (*siła, ruchy*) bearish; *form.* ursine.

niedźwiedzica *f.* she-bear; **Wielka Niedźwiedzica** *astron.* Ursa Major, Great Bear; **Mała Niedźwiedzica** *astron.* Ursa Minor, Little *l.* Lesser Bear.

niedźwiedziowaty *a.* bearish.

niedźwiedziówka *f.* *ent.* garden tiger (*Arctia caja*).

niedźwiedź *ma* *zool.* bear; **niedźwiedź biały** *l.* **polarny** polar bear (*Thalarctos maritimus*); **nie-**

dźwiedź brunatny brown bear (*Ursus arctos*); **niedźwiedź malajski** sun bear, honey bear (*Helarctos malayanus*); **niedźwiedź morski** Northern fur seal (*Callorhinus ursinus*); **niedźwiedź szary** grizzly bear (*Ursus arctos horribilis*); **niedźwiedź jaskiniowy** *paleont.* cave bear (*Ursus spelaeus*); **nie dziel skóry na niedźwiedziu** don't count your chickens before they are hatched; catch the bear before you sell his skin. – *mp* **1.** *żart.* (= *człowiek niezgrabny*) oaf. **2.** *ekon.* (*gracz giełdowy*) bear.

nieefektownie *adv.* **1.** (= *nie wywołując efektu*) unattractively. **2.** (= *niepozornie*) modestly.

nieefektowny *a.* **1.** (= *niewywołujący efektu*) unattractive. **2.** (= *niepozorny*) modest.

nieefektywny *a.* inefficient, ineffectual.

nieekonomiczny *a.* uneconomical.

nieelastyczny *a.* **1.** (= *niesprężysty*) inelastic. **2.** (= *z trudem się przystosowujący*) inflexible. **3.** (= *nieidący na ustępstwa*) steadfast.

nieelegancki *a.* **1.** (= *niegustowny*) inelegant, lacking style. **2.** (= *niekulturalny*) impolite.

nieelegancko *adv.* **1.** (= *niegustownie*) inelegantly. **2.** (= *niekulturalnie*) impolitely.

nieestetycznie *adv.* unaesthetically.

nieestetyczny *a.* unaesthetic, unsightly.

nieetatowy *a.* (= *półetatowy*) part-time; (= *pomocniczy, dodatkowy*) supernumerary.

nieetycznie *adv.* unethically.

nieetyczny *a.* unethical.

nieeuklidesowy *a.* *geom.* **geometria nieeuklidesowa** non-Euclidean geometry.

nieeuropejski *a.* non-European.

niefachowo *adv.* **1.** (= *bez znajomości fachu*) unprofessionally, amateurishly. **2.** (= *nieumiejętnie*) incompetently.

niefachowość *f.* lack of professionalism, lack of competence.

niefachowy *a.* **1.** (= *niezawodowy*) unprofessional, amateur. **2.** (= *niewykwalifikowany*) unqualified, untrained. **3.** (= *nieumiejętny*) incompetent, amateurish.

niefart *mi* *pot.* tough luck; **mieć niefart** have tough luck, have bad luck.

niefartowny *a.* *pot.* **1.** (*np. osoba*) unlucky. **2.** (*np. dzień*) tough, bad.

niefiguratywny *a.* *sztuka* non-figurative.

nieforemnie *adv.* irregularly, misshapenly.

nieforemność *f.* **1.** (= *brak prawidłowego kształtu*) irregularity, malformation. **2.** (= *brak określonej formy*) shapelessness.

nieforemny *a.* **1.** (= *niemający prawidłowego kształtu*) irregular, malformed; **nieforemny trójkąt** irregular triangle. **2.** (= *niemający określonej formy*) shapeless.

nieformalnie *adv.* **1.** (= *nieoficjalnie*) informally. **2.** (= *niezgodnie z przepisami, nieprawnie*) illicitly, illegally.

nieformalność *f.* **1.** (= *nieoficjalność*) (*np. spotkania*) informality. **2.** (= *niezgodność z przepisami*) illicitness, illegality.

nieformalny *a.* **1.** (= *nieoficjalny*) informal; **załatwić coś drogą nieformalną** take care of sth going through the back door. **2.** (= *nielegalny*) illicit, illegal.

niefortunnie *adv.* **1.** (= *pechowo*) unfortunately, unluckily. **2.** (= *niepomyślnie*) unhappily.

niefortunny *a.* **1.** (= *pechowy*) unfortunate, unlucky. **2.** (= *nieudany*) unfortunate, unsuccessful.

niefrasobliwie *adv.* light-heartedly, unconcernedly.

niefrasobliwość *f.* light-heartedness, unconcern.

niefrasobliwy *a.* **1.** (= *świadczący o braku zmartwienia*) light-hearted, unconcerned. **2.** (= *nieskłonny do martwienia się*) care-free, easy-going.

niefunkcjonalny *a.* **1.** (= *niespełniający swojej roli*) non-functional. **2.** (= *nieużyteczny*) impractical.

niegaszony *a.* **niegaszone wapno** quicklime.

niegazowany *a.* still, noncarbonated.

niegdysiejszy *a.* *przest.* bygone.

niegdyś *adv.* *lit.* once, in bygone days, in days *l.* years gone by; **był sobie niegdyś...** once upon a time there was *l.* lived...

niegładki *a.* **1.** (= *nierówny, chropowaty*) uneven, rough. **2.** (= *nieuprzejmy*) unrefined, crude.

niegłęboki *a.* **1.** (= *płytki*) rather shallow, not deep. **2.** (= *nieznaczny*) shallow, not intense. **3.** (= *mało wnikliwy*) shallow, superficial.

niegłośno *adv.* quietly, not loudly; **mówić niegłośno** speak in a low voice.

niegłośny *a.* (*muzyka, dźwięk*) soft, gentle; (*rozmowa, dzwonek do drzwi, instrument*) quiet, barely audible.

niegłupi *a.* **1.** (= *bystry*) quite clever. **2.** (= *rozsądny*) sensible. **3.** *pot.* (= *niezły*) pretty good, not bad; **to niegłupi pomysł** that's not a bad idea.

niegłupio *adv.* **1.** (= *sensownie*) sensibly, quite cleverly. **2.** *pot.* (= *nieźle*) not bad.

niegodny *a.* **1.** (= *niewart czegoś*) unworthy, undeserving; **być niegodnym czegoś** be unworthy of sth; **zachowanie niegodne dżentelmena** behavior unbecoming of a gentleman. **2.** *lit.* (= *nikczemny*) vile, base.

niegodziwie *adv. lit.* vilely, ignobly.

niegodziwiec *mp* **-wc-** *Voc.* **-wcze** *pl.* **-y** *lit.* scoundrel, rogue.

niegodziwość *f. lit.* vileness, ignobility.

niegodziwy *a. lit.* vile, ignoble.

niegospodarnie *adv.* uneconomically, wastefully.

niegospodarność *f.* uneconomical management.

niegospodarny *a.* uneconomical, wasteful.

niegościnnie *adv.* inhospitably.

niegościnność *f.* inhospitality.

niegościnny *a.* **1.** (*o osobie, okolicy*) inhospitable. **2.** (*o terenie*) forbidding, bleak.

niegotowy *a.* **1.** (= *jeszcze niewykonany*) not ready, not finished. **2.** (= *nieprzygotowany*) unprepared.

niegramatycznie *adv.* ungrammatically.

niegramatyczność *f.* ungramaticality.

niegramatyczny *a.* ungrammatical.

niegroźnie *adv.* **1.** (= *nie budząc grozy*) not dangerously. **2.** (= *nie zagrażając*) not seriously.

niegroźny *a.* **1.** (= *niebudzący grozy*) (*np. pies*) not dangerous. **2.** (= *niezagrażający*) (*np. choroba*) not serious.

niegrzecznie *adv.* **1.** (= *nieuprzejmie*) unkindly, discourteously. **2.** (= *szorstko*) rudely, impolitely. **3.** (*o dziecku*) naughtily.

niegrzeczność *f.* **1.** (= *nieuprzejmość*) incivility, discourtesy. **2.** (= *brak grzeczności*) impoliteness, rudeness. **3.** (*np. dziecka*) naughtiness.

niegrzeczny *a.* **1.** (= *nieuprzejmy*) unkind, discourteous. **2.** (= *szorstki*) impolite, rude. **3.** (*o dziecku*) naughty.

niegustownie *adv.* tastelessly.

niegustowny *a.* tasteless, in bad taste.

nieharmoniczny *a. muz.* inharmonic.

nieharmonijnie *adv.* inharmoniously.

nieharmonijny *a.* inharmonious, disharmonious; discordant.

niehigienicznie *adv.* unhygienically.

niehigieniczny *a.* unsanitary, unhygienic.

niehomogeniczny *a.* unhomogeneous.

niehonorowo *adv.* dishonorably, *Br.* dishonourably.

niehonorowy *a.* dishonorable, *Br.* dishonourable; foul; *sport* unsportsmanlike.

niehumanitarny *a.* inhumane.

nieingerencja *f. polit.* non-interference.

nieinteligentnie *adv.* unintelligently.

nieinteligentny *a.* unintelligent.

nieinteresująco *adv.* uninterestingly, uninspiringly.

nieinteresujący *a.* uninteresting.

nieinterwencja *f. polit.* non-intervention.

nieistotny *a.* **1.** (= *nieważny*) unimportant. **2.** (= *niepowiązany*) irrelevant, immaterial.

niej *pron. zob.* **ona.**

niejadalny *a.* **1.** (= *nienadający się do jedzenia*) inedible. **2.** (= *niesmaczny*) uneatable.

niejadek *mp* **-dk-** *pl.* **-i** *pot.* fussy eater.

niejadowity *a.* nonvenomous.

niejaki *a.* **1.** *lit.* (= *nieznaczny*) (a) certain, some; **od niejakiego czasu** for some time; **z niejaką trudnością** with some difficulty. **2.** *lit.* (= *bliżej nieznany*) a certain; **niejaki Nowak** a (certain) Mr. Nowak.

niejako *adv.* (= *poniekąd*) to some extent, to some degree; somehow.

niejasno *adv.* **1.** (= *niewyraźnie*) vaguely, ambiguously. **2.** (= *niezrozumiale*) obscurely, unclearly.

niejasność *f.* (= *coś niejasnego*) ambiguity, vagueness.

niejasny *a.* **1.** (= *ledwie widoczny*) dim, dark. **2.** (= *nieprecyzyjny*) unclear, vague; (*przeczucie*) indefinite.

niejawnie *adv.* secretly.

niejawny *a.* secret; **posiedzenie niejawne** *prawn.* closed session.

niejeden *a.* **-dn-** many a, quite a number; **niejeden raz** many a time. – *mp* **-dn-** *Gen.* **-ego**

many a man; **niejeden się w niej kochał** no few had loved her; **niejeden by sobie nie poradził** many a man wouldn't manage.

niejednakowo *adv.* differently, variously.

niejednakowy *a.* different, various.

niejedno *adv.* (= *wiele*) many, a number of, a lot of; **niejedno widziałem** I have seen a lot; **mieć niejedno na sumieniu** have a lot on one's conscience; **niejedno mógłbym opowiedzieć** I could tell you a thing or two.

niejednoczesność *f.* non-concurrence.

niejednoczesny *a.* nonconcurrent, not simultaneous.

niejednokrotnie *adv.* more than once, many a time; repeatedly.

niejednokrotny *a.* repeated, recurrent.

niejednolicie *adv.* non-uniformly, not uniformly.

niejednolitość *f.* non-uniformity, nonuniformity; lack of uniformity.

niejednolity *a.* non-uniform, nonuniform.

niejednomyślny *a.* not unanimous.

niejednorodnie *adv.* heterogeneously.

niejednorodność *f.* heterogeneity.

niejednorodny *a.* heterogeneous.

niejednostajność *f.* unevenness, lack of regularity.

niejednostajny *a.* uneven, irregular; **ruch niejednostajny** *fiz.* non-uniform motion.

niejednoznacznie *adv.* ambiguously, equivocally; **mówić o czymś niejednoznacznie** be ambiguous on sth.

niejednoznaczny *a.* ambiguous, equivocal.

niekaralność *f.* unpunishability.

niekaralny *a.* unpunishable.

niekarany *a.* *prawn.* without a criminal record.

niekarność *f.* lack of discipline, disobedience.

niekarny *a.* undisciplined, disobedience.

niekatolicki *a.* non-Catholic.

niekiedy *adv.* at times, now and them.

nieklarowny *a.* **1.** (= *nieprzejrzysty*) unclarified. **2.** (= *niejasny*) unclear.

niekłamany *a.* *lit.* unfeigned, genuine; **z niekłamanym podziwem** with genuine admiration.

niekłopotliwy *a.* **1.** (= *dogodny*) convenient. **2.** (= *nieprzysparzający kłopotu*) not troublesome. **3.** (*o człowieku*) easy to get along with.

niekobiecy *a.* unwomanly.

niekoleżeński *a.* **1.** (= *nieprzyjazny*) unfriendly. **2.** (= *niechętnie zawierający znajomości*) unsociable.

niekoleżeńskość *f.* unfriendliness.

niekompatybilność *f.* *komp.* incompatibility.

niekompatybilny *a.* *komp.* incompatible.

niekompetencja *f.* incompetence.

niekompetentnie *adv.* incompetently.

niekompetentny *a.* incompetent.

niekompletność *f.* incompleteness.

niekompletny *a.* incomplete.

niekomunikatywny *a.* uncommunicative.

niekoniecznie *adv.* **1.** (*bez konieczności*) unnecessarily. **2.** *pot.* (= *nie całkiem*) not necessarily.

niekonieczny *a.* unnecessary.

niekonsekwencja *f.* inconsistency.

niekonsekwentnie *adv.* inconsistently.

niekonsekwentny *a.* inconsistent.

niekontrastowy *a.* (*o zdjęciu*) blurred.

niekontrolowany *a.* uncontrolled.

niekonwencjonalny *a.* unconventional; **medycyna niekonwencjonalna** alternative medicine.

niekorzystnie *adv.* **1.** (= *niepomyślnie*) unfavorably, *Br.* unfavourably; **wpływać na coś niekorzystnie** have an adverse influence on sth. **2.** (= *brzydko*) badly; **w tej sukience wyglądała niekorzystnie** the dress she was wearing didn't do her justice.

niekorzystny *a.* **1.** (= *nieprzynoszący korzyści*) unprofitable. **2.** (= *niepomyślny*) unfavorable, *Br.* unfavourable; **niekorzystne warunki** adverse conditions; **być w niekorzystnej sytuacji** be at a disadvantage; **zrobić na kimś niekorzystne wrażenie** fail to impress sb. **3.** (= *niepochlebny*) disadvantageous (*dla kogoś* for sb).

niekorzyść *f.* disadvantage; **na czyjąś niekorzyść** to sb's disadvantage; **rozstrzygnąć sprawę na czyjąś niekorzyść** (*w sądzie*) decide a case against sb.

niekowalny *a.* *techn.* unmalleable.

niekrępujący *a.* **1.** (= *taki, który nie krępuje*) unembarrassing. **2.** (*o wejściu, pokoju*) private.

niekrystaliczny *a.* non-crystalline.

niekrzepliwość *f.* incoagulability.

niekrzepliwy *a.* incoagulable.

niekształtnie *adv.* misshapenly.

niekształtny *a.* misshapen; (*o ciele*) unshapely.

niektórzy *pl. Gen.* **-rych** some, some people.

niekulturalnie *adv.* uncivilly, unmannerly.

niekulturalny *a.* uncivil, unmannered.

niekurczliwy *a.* (*tkanina, materiał*) nonshrink.

niekwestionowany *a.* indisputable, unquestionble.

nieledwie *adv.* *przest.* little short of being; almost.

nielegalnie *adv.* illegally.

nielegalność *f.* illegality.

nielegalny *a.* illegal.

nielekki *a.* **-kcy** **1.** (= *ciężki*) rather heavy, not light. **2.** (= *niełatwy*) rather hard, not easy.

nielekko *adv.* not lightly; **nielekko mi z tym żyć** it's something it's not easy to live with.

nieletni *a.* juvenile; *prawn.* minor. – *mp* juvenile; *prawn.* minor; **przestępczość nieletnich** juvenile delinquency *l.* crime; **sąd dla nieletnich** juvenile court.

nieletniość *f.* minority.

nielękliwy *a.* fearless.

nielicho *adv.* **1.** *pot.* (= *nieźle*) not bad, quite well. **2.** *pot.* (= *sporo*) quite a lot.

nielichy *a.* *pot.* (= *niezły*) not bad.

nielicznie *adv.* sparsely.

nieliczny *a.* sparse, scanty.

nieliniowy *a.* **1.** (= *nietworzący linii*) non-linear; **równanie nieliniowe** *mat.* non-linear equation. **2.** *wojsk.* non-combatant.

nieliteracki *a.* non-literary.

nieliterowy *a.* letterless.
nielitościwy *a.* merciless, unmerciful.
niello *n. indecl. sztuka* niello.
nielogicznie *adv.* illogically.
nielogiczność *f.* illogicality.
nielogiczny *a.* illogical.
nielojalnie *adv.* disloyally.
nielojalność *f.* disloyalty.
nielojalny *a.* disloyal.
nielot *ma orn.* flightless bird, ratite (*Apterygiformes*).
nielotny *a.* **1.** (= *nieulatniający się*) non-volatile. **2.** (*o ptakach*) flightless, ratite. **3.** (*np. o pogodzie*) (= *niesprzyjający lotom*) unflyable. **4.** (= *nierozgarnięty*) dull-witted.
nieludzki *a.* **1.** (= *okrutny*) inhuman, inhumane. **2.** (= *nadludzki*) superhuman; **z nieludzką siłą** with superhuman strength.
nieludzko *adv.* **1.** (= *okrutnie*) cruelly, inhumanly. **2.** (= *ponad ludzką wytrzymałość*) awfully; **nieludzko zmęczony** dead tired.
nieludzkość *f.* inhumanity.
nieład *mi* disarray; **nieład artystyczny** creative chaos; **ubranie/włosy w nieładzie** clothes/hair in disarray.
nieładnie *adv.* **1.** (= *brzydko*) unpleasingly; (*np. ubierać się*) unbecomingly; **on nieładnie pisze** his handwriting is ugly; **ona nieładnie się porusza** her movements are clumsy. **2.** (*postępować, zachowywać się*) unfairly.
nieładny *a.* **1.** (= *brzydki*) ungly, unsightly; **nieładna pogoda** bad *l.* ugly weather. **2.** (*np. postępek*) unfair.
niełamliwość *f.* unbreakability.
niełamliwy *a.* unbreakable.
niełaska *f.* disgrace; disfavor, *Br.* disfavour; **być w niełasce** be in disgrace, be out of favor; **popaść w niełaskę** fall into disgrace; **zdać się na czyjąś łaskę i niełaskę** throw o.s. upon sb's mercy.
niełaskawy *a.* **1.** (= *nieżyczliwie usposobiony*) unkind (*dla kogoś* to sb). **2.** (= *nieprzychylny*) adverse, hostile; (*pogoda*) inclement; (*wyrok*) unfavorable, *Br.*unfavourable.
niełatwo *adv.* not easily; **niełatwo jest...** it is not easy to...
niełatwy *a.* **1.** (= *trudny*) not easy, quite difficult. **2.** (*w obejściu, współżyciu*) not easy to get along with. **3.** (= *nieskory*) slow (*do czegoś* to do sth); **niełatwy do śmiechu/płaczu** slow to laugh/cry.
niełaz *ma zool.* (= *torbacz z rodziny Dasyuridae*) dasyure.
niełowny *a.* non-game.
niełupka *f. bot.* achene, akene.
niemagnetyczność *f. techn.* non-magnetism.
niemagnetyczny *a. techn.* non-magnetic.
niemajętny *a.* unwealthy.
niemal *adv.* almost, nearly.
niemalejący *a.* **ciąg niemalejący** *mat.* non-decreasing sequence; **funkcja niemalejąca** *mat.* non-decreasing function.
niemalże *particle emf. zob.* **niemal**.

niemało *adv.* quite a lot (*kogoś/czegoś* of sb/sth).
niemały *a.* substantial, pretty big.
niemarksistowski *a.* non-marxist.
niematerialistyczny *a.* non-materialistic.
niematerialny *a.* **1.** (= *bezcielesny*) immaterial, incorporeal. **2.** (= *niepieniężny*) non-materialistic.
niemądry *a.* unwise.
niemądrze *adv.* unwisely.
Niemcy *pl. Gen.* **-miec** *Ms.* **-czech** *geogr.* Germany; **Republika Federalna Niemiec** Federal Republic of Germany.
niemczeć *ipf.* become Germanized, Germanize.
niemczyć *ipf.* Germanize. ~ **się** *ipf.* become Germanized, Germanize.
niemczyzna *f.* **1.** (= *język niemiecki*) German language. **2.** (= *kultura niemiecka*) German culture.
niemelodyjny *a.* tuneless.
niemetal *mi chem., fiz.* nonmetal.
niemetaliczny *a.* non-metallic.
niemetalowy *a.* non-metal.
niemetodyczny *a.* unmethodical.
niemetryczny *a.* non-metric, non-metrical.
niemęski *a.* unmanly.
niemęskoosobowy *a. jęz.* **rodzaj niemęskoosobowy** non-virile gender, non-masculine-human gender.
niemęskość *f.* unmanliness.
niemianowany *a.* **liczba niemianowana** *mat.* abstract number.
niemiara *f.* **co niemiara** (= *wiele*) no end of; (= *bez ograniczeń*) without limit; **kłopotów co niemiara** a world of trouble.
niemiarodajny *a.* unreliable.
niemiarowość *f.* **1.** (= *nierytmiczność*) irregularity. **2.** *pat.* arrhythmia.
niemiarowy *a.* **1.** (= *nierytmiczny*) irregular. **2.** *pat.* arrhythmic.
Niemiec *mp* **-mc-** *pl.* **-y** German.
niemiec *mi pot. szkoln.* German class.
niemiecki *a.* German; **owczarek niemiecki** *kynol.* German shepherd, Alsatian; **prawo niemieckie** *hist.* German law; **Niemiecka Republika Demokratyczna** *hist.* German Democratic Republic.
niemieckość *f.* German character.
niemieć *ipf.* become dumb.
niemierzalny *a.* unmeasurable.
niemieszkalny *a.* non-residential.
niemile, niemiło *adv.* unpleasantly; **niemile widziany** unwelcome; **być czymś niemile zaskoczonym** be unpleasantly surprised by sth.
niemiłosiernie *adv.* **1.** (= *bezlitośnie*) mercilessly, unmercifully. **2.** (= *okropnie*) (*np. prażyć, dłużyć się*) terribly, awfully.
niemiłosierny *a.* **1.** (= *bezlitosny*) merciless, unmerciful. **2.** (= *uciążliwy*) (*np. upał*) terrible, awful.
niemiły *a.* **1.** (= *przykry*) unpleasant, disagreeable; **życie mu niemiłe** life has lost its value

for him. **2.** (= *niesympatyczny*) unkind (*dla kogoś* to sb).

Niemka *f. Gen.pl.* **-ek** German (woman); *zob.* **Niemiec.**

niemłody *a.* oldish.

niemnący *a.* crease-resistant.

niemniej *conj.* still, however; **niemniej jednak** nevertheless, even so.

niemo *adv.* dumbly, speechlessly.

niemoc *f.* **1.** (= *osłabienie fizyczne*) infirmity, feebleness; **niemoc płciowa** *pat.* impotence. **2.** (= *bezsilność*) incapacity, powerlessness; **niemoc twórcza** creativity crisis.

niemodnie *adv.* unfashionably.

niemodny *a.* (= *niezgodny z modą*) unfashionable; (= *przestarzały*) out-of-date.

niemoralnie *adv.* immorally.

niemoralność *f.* immorality.

niemoralny *a.* immoral.

niemota *f.* (= *brak zdolności mówienia*) muteness. – *f. l.* mp *decl. like f. Gen.pl.* **-t** *l.* **-ów** *pot.* (= *osoba nierozgarnięta*) dumbo, dumbhead.

niemowa *f. l.* mp *decl. like f. Gen.pl.* **-mów** *l.* **-mowów 1.** (= *osoba pozbawiona umiejętności mówienia*) mute. **2.** *żart.* (= *osoba małomówna*) clam.

niemowlak *mp pl.* **-i** *pot.* = **niemowlę.**

niemowlę *n.* **niemowlęci-** *pl.* **-ęt-** *Gen.* **-ąt** baby; **od niemowlęcia** from the cradle; **odstawić niemowlę od piersi** wean an infant.

niemowlęctwo *n.* babyhood.

niemowlęcy *a.* baby; **wiek niemowlęcy** babyhood.

niemożebny *a. pot.* unbearable; **niemożebne kłopoty** a world of trouble.

niemożliwie *adv.* (= *nieznośnie*) intolerably, unbearably; (*gorąco*) awfully, terribly; (*zachowywać się*) outrageously, intolerably.

niemożliwość *f.* impossibility; **do niemożliwości** to the extreme.

niemożliwy *a.* **1.** (= *niedający się zrealizować*) impossible; **to niemożliwe!** that's impossible!; **to niemożliwe, żeby...** it is impossible that... **2.** *pot.* (= *okropny*) awful, outrageous; (= *nieznośny*) intolerable, unbearable; **jesteś niemożliwy!** you're impossible!

niemożność *f.* impossibility.

niemrawo *adv.* sluggishly.

niemrawość *f.* sluggishness.

niemrawy *a.* sluggish.

niemuzykalność *f.* unmusicality, unmusicalness.

niemuzykalny *a.* unmusical.

niemy *a.* **1.** (= *pozbawiony zdolności mówienia*) mute, dumb. **2.** (= *oniemiały*) speechless; **niemy z rozpaczy** speechless with despair; **niemy świadek (czegoś)** silent witness (of sth). **3.** (= *niemogący wydawać głosu*) silent; **film niemy** silent film. **4.** (= *niewyrażony słowami*) tacit, silent; **niema zgoda** tacit agreement, tacit consent. – *mp* mute.

nienacechowaność *a. jęz.* unmarkedness.

nienacechowany *a. jęz.* unmarked.

nienadaremnie *adv.* not in vain.

nienadzwyczajnie *adv.* ordinarily.

nienadzwyczajny *a.* ordinary.

nienagannie *adv.* impeccably; **nienagannie ubrany** impeccably dressed.

nienaganność *f.* impeccability, faultlessness.

nienaganny *a.* (*strój, zachowanie*) impeccable.

nienależycie *adv. przest.* inadequately.

nienależyty *a. przest.* inadequate.

nienarodzony *a.* **-eni** unborn.

nienaruszalność *f.* (*np. korespondencji*) inviolability; (*np. granic*) integrity; (*np. małżeństwa*) sanctity.

nienaruszalny *a.* (*granice*) unalterable; (*prawa*) inalienable.

nienaruszony *a.* intact.

nienasycenie *adv.* insatiably. – *n.* insatiability.

nienasycony *a.* **1.** **-eni** (= *stale głodny*) unsated, voracious; (*o pragnieniu*) unquenchable. **2.** (*ciekawość, kolekcjoner*) insatiable. **3.** *chem., fiz.* unsaturated; **roztwór nienasycony** unsaturated solution; **para nienasycona** unsaturated steam.

nienaśladowczy *a.* non-imitative.

nienaturalnie *adv.* unnaturally, artificially.

nienaturalność *f.* unnaturalness, artificiality.

nienaturalny *a.* **1.** (= *nienormalny*) unnatural; **nienaturalna śmierć** violent death. **2.** (= *udawany*) unnatural, artificial; (*gest, śmiech*) unnatural, affected.

nienaukowo *adv.* unscientifically.

nienaukowy *a.* unscientific.

nienaumyślnie *adv.* unintentionally.

nienawidzić *ipf.* hate, detest. **~ się** *ipf.* **1.** (= *nienawidzić jeden drugiego*) hate one another. **2.** (= *mieć żal do siebie*) hate o.s.

nienawistnie *adv.* hatefully.

nienawistny *a.* **1.** (= *wzbudzający nienawiść*) (*np. wróg*) odious. **2.** (= *pełen nienawiści*) (*np. spojrzenie*) hateful.

nienawiść *f.* hatred, hate (*do kogoś / czegoś* for *l.* towards sb/sth); **budzić w kimś nienawiść** instill hatred in sb; **być chorym z nienawiści** be consumed with hatred; **czuć** *l.* **żywić nienawiść do kogoś/czegoś** feel hatred to sb/sth; **wzniecić nienawiść** arouse hatred.

nienawykły *a.* unaccustomed (*do czegoś* to sth).

nienazwany *a.* (= *niewyrażalny*) inexpressible.

nienażarty *a. pot.* (= *nienasycony*) insatiable, gluttonous.

nieniszczący *a. techn.* non-destructive.

nienormalnie *adv.* abnormally.

nienormalność *f.* abnormality.

nienormalny *a.* **1.** (= *niezgodny z normą*) abnormal. **2.** (= *niezgodny z oczekiwanym rezultatem*) anomalous. **3.** (= *chory psychicznie*) insane.

nienowoczesność *f.* antiquatedness.

nienowoczesny *a.* antiquated, old-fashioned.

nienowy *a.* **1.** (= *dość stary*) oldish. **2.** (= *znany od dawna*) not new.

nieobcy *a.* familiar.

nieobecność *f.* **1.** (= *brak kogoś gdzieś*) absence; **pod czyjąś nieobecność** in sb's absence. **2.** *szkoln.* (= *opuszczona lekcja*) absence.

nieobecny *a.* absent; **nieobecny duchem** absent in soul. – *mp* absentee.

nieobelżywy *a.* unabusive.

nieobeznanie *n.* ignorance (*z czymś* of sth); unacquaintance (*z czymś* with sth).

nieobeznany *a.* ignorant (*z czymś* of sth); unacquainted (*z czymś* with sth).

nieobfity *a.* unabundant.

nieobiektywny *a.* unobjective, non-objective.

nieobliczalnie *adv.* **1.** (= *nieprzewidywalnie*) unpredictibly. **2.** (= *nieprzeliczenie*) incalculably.

nieobliczalność *f.* **1.** (= *nieprzewidywalność*) unpredictibility. **2.** (= *ilość nie do policzenia*) incalculability.

nieobliczalny *a.* **1.** (= *nieprzewidywalny*) (*skutek, człowiek*) unpredictable. **2.** (= *niedający się policzyć*) incalculable.

nieobłaskawiony *a.* untamed.

nieobojętny *a.* **1.** (= *podatny*) not indifferent (*na coś* to sth). **2.** (= *istotny*) important.

nieobopólny *a.* unreciprocal.

nieobowiązkowość *f.* negligence.

nieobowiązkowy *a.* **1.** (= *dobrowolny*) optional, voluntary. **2.** (= *niesumienny*) negligent.

nieobronny *a.* unfortified.

nieobrotny *a.* unresourceful, unenterprising.

nieobuty *a.* unshod.

nieobycie *n.* **1.** (= *brak ogłady*) roughness, crudeness. **2.** (= *nieoswojenie*) unacquaintance (*z czymś* with sth).

nieobyczajnie *adv.* indecently.

nieobyczajność *f.* indecency.

nieobyczajny *a.* indecent.

nieobyty *a.* **1.** (= *nieumiejący się zachować*) uncultured, unsophisticated. **2.** (= *niezaznajomiony*) unacquainted (*z czymś* with sth).

nieobywatelski *a.* uncivil.

nieoceniony *a.* invaluable.

nieoczekiwanie *adv.* unexpectedly.

nieoczekiwany *a.* unexpected.

nieoczytany *a.* unread.

nieodczuwalny *a.* imperceptible.

nieoddanie *n.* **pożyczyć coś na wieczne nieoddanie** *pot.* (*komuś*) lend sth for keeps; (*od kogoś*) borrow sth for keeps.

nieodgadniony *a.* *lit.* inscrutable.

nieodłącznie *adv.* inseparably.

nieodłączny *a.* (*przyjaciel*) inseparable; (*cecha*) inherent; **stanowić nieodłączną część czegoś** be an inseparable part of sth; *przen. t.* be part and parcel of sth.

nieodmiennie *adv.* invariably.

nieodmienność *f.* **1.** (= *stałość*) invariance, invariability. **2.** *jęz.* inflectionlessness.

nieodmienny *a.* **1.** (= *stały*) invariable, invariant. **2.** *jęz.* uninflected.

nieodparcie *adv.* irresistibly.

nieodparty *a.* (*chęć, urok*) irresistible; (*argument*) irrefutable, compelling.

nieodpłatnie *adv.* free of charge.

nieodpłatny *a.* free.

nieodporny *a.* **1.** (*na choroby*) not immune (*na coś* to sth). **2.** (= *niewytrzymały*) non-resistant (*na coś* to sth); (*o roślinie*) intolerant (*na coś* of sth).

nieodpowiedni *a.* inappropriate, unsuitable.

nieodpowiednio *adv.* inappropriately, unsuitably.

nieodpowiedzialnie *adv.* irresponsibly.

nieodpowiedzialność *f.* irresponsibility.

nieodpowiedzialny *a.* irresponsible.

nieodrodny *a.* true; **być nieodrodnym dzieckiem epoki** be a true child of one's time.

nieodstępny *a.* inseparable.

nieodwołalnie *adv.* irrevocably, beyond recall.

nieodwołalność *f.* irrevocability.

nieodwołalny *a.* irrevocable.

nieodwracalnie *adv.* irreversibly.

nieodwracalny *a.* (*decyzja, zmiany*) irreversible; (*szkody*) irreparable.

nieodzownie *adv.* indispensably.

nieodzowność *f.* indispensability.

nieodzowny *a.* indispensable.

nieodżałowany *a.* (*strata*) much regretted; (*o zmarłym*) late lamented.

nieoficjalnie *adv.* unofficially.

nieoficjalny *a.* unofficial.

nieogarniony *a.* **1.** (= *niezmierzony*) limitless. **2.** (= *niepojęty*) inconceivable.

nieoględnie *adv.* inconsiderately, rashly.

nieoględny *a.* inconsiderate, rash.

nieograniczenie *adv.* **1.** (= *bez ograniczeń*) unrestrictedly, unlimitedly. **2.** (= *bezgranicznie*) absolutely.

nieograniczoność *f.* limitlessness.

nieograniczony *a.* **1.** (*władza, wolność*) unrestricted, absolute. **2.** (*wydatki, czas*) unlimited. **3.** (= *ogromny*) infinite.

nieokazały *a.* inconspicuous.

nieokiełznany *a.* *lit.* unbridled, reinless.

nieokresowo *adv.* non-periodically.

nieokresowy *a.* non-periodical; **ułamek nieokresowy** *mat.* non-periodic fraction.

nieokreśloność *f.* **1.** (= *niejasność*) indeterminacy, vagueness. **2.** (= *brak określonych granic*) indefiniteness.

nieokreślony *a.* **1.** (= *niejasny*) (*lęk, uczucie*) vague; (*kolor, wiek*) indeterminate. **2.** (= *nieograniczony*) indefinite; **przedimek nieokreślony** *jęz.* indefinite article; **zaimek nieokreślony** *jęz.* indefinite pronoun; **umowa o pracę na czas nieokreślony** permanent employment contract.

nieokrzesanie *n.* crudeness, loutishness.

nieokrzesaniec *mp* **-ńc-** lout.

nieokrzesany *a.* coarse, crude.

nieomal *adv.* = **niemal**.

nieomylnie *adv.* infallibly.

nieomylność *f.* infallibility; **nieomylność papieża** *rel.* papal infallibility.

nieomylny *a.* infallible.

nieopanowanie *n.* (= *gwałtowność*) lack of self-restraint, vehemence.

nieopanowany *a.* **1.** (= *wybuchowy*) (*człowiek*) quick-tempered; (*reakcja*) vehement. **2.** (= *niekontrolowany*) uncontrollable, unrestrained

nieopatrznie *adv.* recklessly.

nieopatrzność *f.* recklessness.

nieopatrzny *a.* reckless.

nieopierzony *a.* **1.** (= *bez piór*) unfledged. **2.** (= *niedoświadczony*) unfledged, callow.

nieopisanie *adv.* indescribably, inexpressibly.

nieopisany *a.* indescribable, inexpressible.

nieopłacalność *f.* unprofitability.

nieopłacalny *a.* **1.** (= *nierentowny*) unprofitable. **2.** (= *niewspółmierny do korzyści*) unremunerative; (*wysiłek*) unrewarding.

nieopodal *adv.* (= *w pobliżu*) nearby. – *prep.* + *Gen.* near, close to.

nieopodatkowany *a.* untaxed.

nieoprawny *a.* (*książka*) unbound; (*obraz*) unframed; (*klejnot*) unset.

nieoprocentowany *a.* without interest.

nieorganiczny *a.* inorganic; **chemia nieorganiczna** inorganic chemistry.

nieortodoksyjny *a.* unorthodox.

nieortograficznie *adv.* in bad spelling; **pisać nieortograficznie** be a bad speller.

nieortograficzny *a.* misspelled.

nieoryginalny *a.* **1.** (= *fałszywy*) unauthentic. **2.** (= *wtórny*) unoriginal.

nieosiągalność *f.* unattainability.

nieosiągalny *a.* **1.** (= *niedościgniony*) (*cel, ideał*) unattainable; (*szczyt*) unreachable. **2.** (= *nie do kupienia, dostania*) (*wydanie, płyta*) unobtainable.

nieosłonięty *a.* (*miejsce*) unsheltered.

nieosobiście *adv.* not personally.

nieosobowo *adv.* impersonally.

nieosobowy *a. jęz.* impersonal.

nieostrość *f.* **1.** (= *brak ostrości*) (*narzędzia*) bluntness. **2.** (= *łagodność*) (*klimatu*) mildness. **3.** *fot.* blurring, unsharpness. **4.** (= *brak precyzji*) (*o kryteriach*) vagueness, indistinctness.

nieostrożnie *adv.* carelessly.

nieostrożność *f.* **1.** (= *brak rozwagi*) carelessness; **przez nieostrożność** through carelessness. **2.** (= *postępek*) negligence; **popełnić nieostrożność** take an unguarded step.

nieostrożny *a.* careless.

nieostry *a.* **1.** (= *tępy*) (*np. nóż*) blunt. **2.** (= *łagodny*) (*klimat*) mild. **3.** (= *rozmazany*) (*zdjęcie*) out of focus, unsharp; (*obraz*) blurred. **4.** (= *nieprecyzyjny*) (*kryteria*) vague, indistinct.

nieoswojony *a.* **1.** (*o zwierzęciu*) untamed. **2.** (*o człowieku*) (= *niezaznajomiony*) unaccustomed (*z czymś* to sth); unacquainted (*z czymś* with sth).

nieoszacowany *a.* inestimable, priceless.

nieoszczędny *a.* thriftless.

nieoświecony *a.* **-eni** unenlightened.

nieowłosiony *a.* hairless.

nieoznaczony *a.* indeterminate; **nieoznaczony układ równań** *mat.* indeterminate system of equations.

nieoznakowany *a.* unmarked.

nieożywiony *a.* **1.** (= *martwy*) *t. jęz.* inanimate; **przyroda nieożywiona** inanimate nature. **2.** (= *nudny, powolny*) lifeless, spiritless; (*dyskusja*) unanimated.

niepakowny *a.* not capacious, incapacious.

niepalatalny *a. jęz.* non-palatal.

niepalący *a.* non-smoking. – *mp* non-smoker; **przedział dla niepalących** non-smoking compartment.

niepalny *a.* non-flammable, incombustible.

niepamięć *f.* **1.** (= *zapomnienie*) oblivion; **do niepamięci** *lit.* (= *szalenie*) passionately; **pójść w niepamięć** sink *l.* fall into oblivion; **puścić coś w niepamięć** forgive and forget sth. **2.** *pat.* amnesia.

niepamiętliwy *a.* forgiving.

niepamiętny *a.* (= *niebywały*) most exceptional; **od niepamiętnych czasów** from time immemorial.

nieparka *f. ent.* **brudnica nieparka** gypsy moth (*Lymantria dispar*).

nieparlamentarnie *adv.* in unparliamentary language.

nieparlamentarny *a.* unparliamentary; **nieparlamentarny język** unparliamentary language.

nieparzystokopytne *pl. Gen.* **-ych** *zool.* perissodactyls (*Perissodactyla*).

nieparzystość *f.* oddness.

nieparzysty *a.* **1.** (= *niepodzielny przez dwa*) odd. **2.** (= *nie do pary*) unpaired.

niepedagogiczny *a.* uneducational.

niepełnoletni *a.* minor.

niepełnoletni *a.* under-age.

niepełnoletniość, niepełnoletność *f.* minority.

niepełnoprawny *a.* not fully legitimate.

niepełnosprawność *f.* disability, handicap.

niepełnosprawny *a.* **1.** (= *nie w pełni sprawny*) (*fizycznie lub psychicznie*) disabled, handicapped. **2.** (= *funkcjonujący wadliwie*) malfunctioning. – *mp* a handicapped *l.* disabled person.

niepełnowartościowy *a.* deficient; (*produkt*) defective; (*pracownik*) incompetent.

niepełny *a.* **1.** (= *nienapełniony*) not full. **2.** (= *niecałkowity*) incomplete.

nieperiodyczny *a.* non-periodical.

niepewnie *adv.* uncertainly.

niepewność *f.* uncertainty; **niepewność jutra** uncertain future; **trzymać kogoś w niepewności** keep sb in suspense; **żyć w niepewności** live a life of uncertainty.

niepewny *a.* **1.** (= *nie całkiem bezpieczny*) insecure, unsafe; (*pogoda*) treacherous; **niepewne jutro** uncertain future; **chodzić po niepewnym gruncie** skate on thin ice. **2.** (= *niebudzący zaufania*) unreliable, doubtful; (*wiadomość*) undependable; (*pamięć*) treacherous. **3.** (= *niemający pewności*) uncertain; **być niepewnym jutra** be uncertain of one's future. **4.** (= *niezdecydowany*) hesitant; (*krok*) unsteady; (*głos*) faltering.

niepijący *a.* teetotal. – *mp* teetotaler, *Br.* teetotaller.

niepisany *a.* (*prawo, kodeks, umowa*) unwritten.

niepiśmienny *a.* illiterate.

nieplanowo *adv.* in an unplanned way.

nieplanowy *a.* unplanned.

nieplatoniczny *a.* non-platonic.

niepłatny *a.* unpaid.

niepłochliwy *a.* not timid.
niepłodność *f.* **1.** (= *bezpłodność*) infertility, sterility. **2.** (= *jałowość*) (*o glebie*) barrenness.
niepłodny *a.* **1.** (= *bezpłodny*) infertile, sterile. **2.** (= *jałowy*) (*o glebie*) barren.
niepłynny *a.* **1.** (= *niebędący płynnym*) nonliquid. **2.** *ekon.* (= *zamrożony*) unavailable.
niepobłażliwy *a.* unindulgent.
niepochlebnie *adv.* unfavorably, *Br.* unfavourably; critically.
niepochlebny *a.* unfavorable, *Br.* unfavourable; critical.
niepociągający *a.* unattracive.
niepocieszający *a.* not comforting.
niepocieszony *a.* disconsolate, inconsolable.
niepoczytalność *f.* insanity.
niepoczytalny *a.* insane.
niepoczytny *a.* not widely read.
niepodatny *a.* impervious (*na coś* to sth).
niepodejrzliwy *a.* unsuspecting.
niepodległościowy *a.* (of) independence; **ruch niepodległościowy** independence movement.
niepodległość *f.* independence.
niepodległy *a.* independent.
niepodobieństwo *n.* impossibility; **opór był niepodobieństwem** resistance was impossible.
niepodobna *adv.* **niepodobna pracować w taki skwar** it is impossible to work in such heat; **niepodobna, żeby...** it is unlikely that...
niepodobny *a.* unlike (*do kogoś*/*czegoś* sb/sth); dissimilar (*do kogoś*/*czegoś* to sb/sth).
niepodważalność *f.* (*twierdzenia, tezy*) irrefutability; (*wyroku, dowodu*) unquestionability.
niepodważalny *a.* (= *niemożliwy do obalenia*) irrefutable; (= *niekwestionowany*) unquestionable.
niepodzielnie *adv.* (*rządzić, władać*) absolutely.
niepodzielność *f.* **1.** (= *niemożliwość podziału*) indivisibility. **2.** (= *absolutyzm*) absolutism.
niepodzielny *a.* **1.** (*wyraz, własność*) indivisible; **niepodzielny przez dwa/siedem** indivisible by two/seven. **2.** (*władza*) absolute.
niepoetycki *a.* non-poetic.
niepoetyczny *a.* unpoetic.
niepogoda *f.* bad weather.
niepogodny *a.* **1.** (= *deszczowy*) rainy. **2.** (= *smutny*) sad.
niepohamowany *a.* uncontrollable.
niepojemny *a.* not capacious, incapacious.
niepojęcie *adv.* inconceivably.
niepojętny *a.* slow-witted, dull.
niepojęty *a.* inconceivable.
niepokalanie *adv.* immaculately.
niepokalany *a. lit.* (= *nieskazitelny*) (= *bez grzechu*) immaculate; **niepokalane poczęcie** *rel.* Immaculate Conception.
niepokaźnie *adv.* insignificantly.
niepokaźny *a.* insignificant.
niepokoić *ipf.* **-ję -isz, -ój 1.** (= *wzbudzać obawę*) worry. **2.** (= *nękać*) bother. **~ się** *ipf.* worry (*o kogoś*/*coś* about sb/sth) (*czymś* about sth).
niepokojąco *adv.* alarmingly, disturbingly.

niepokojący *a.* alarming, disturbing.
niepokoje *pl. Gen.* **-ów** *l.* **-oi** (= *zamieszki*) unrest.
niepokonany *a.* invincible.
niepokorny *a.* rebellious, disobedient.
niepokój *mi* **-o-** *Gen.pl.* **-ów** *l.* **-oi 1.** (= *obawa*) anxiety (*o kogoś*/*coś* about *l.* for sb/sth); **wzbudzać w kimś niepokój** set sb worrying; **żyć w ciągłym niepokoju** live in constant anxiety; **nie ma powodów do niepokoju** there is no reason for concern. **2.** (= *brak spokoju*) unrest, turmoil; **w kraju panuje niepokój** the country is in turmoil, the country is troubled.
niepoliczalny *a.* (= *niezliczony*) countless; *jęz.* uncountable.
niepolitycznie *adv.* **1.** (= *w sposób niezwiązany z polityką*) non-politically. **2.** (= *niestosownie*) improperly, indecorously.
niepolityczny *a.* **1.** (= *niezwiązany z polityką*) non-political. **2.** (= *niestosowny*) improper, indecorous.
niepomierny *a.* extreme, excessive.
niepomny *a. lit.* unmindful (*na coś l.* *czegoś* of sth).
niepomyślnie *adv.* unsuccessfully.
niepomyślność *f.* adversity, unsuccess.
niepomyślny *a.* (*wiadomość*) bad; (*wiatr, pogoda, sytuacja*) adverse; (*próba, wyniki*) unsuccessful; (*warunki*) unfavorable, *Br.* unfavourable.
nieponętny *a.* unattractive.
niepopłatny *a.* unprofitable.
niepoprawnie *adv.* **1.** (= *błędnie*) incorrectly, wrongly. **2.** (= *zatwardziale*) incorrigibly.
niepoprawność *f.* **1.** (= *błąd*) incorrectness. **2.** (= *zatwardziałość*) incorrigibility.
niepoprawny *a.* **1.** (= *błędny*) incorrect, wrong. **2.** (= *zatwardziały*) incorrigible.
niepopularność *f.* unpopularity.
niepopularny *a.* unpopular.
nieporadnie *adv.* incapably, incompetently.
nieporadność *f.* **1.** (= *bezbronność*) helplessness. **2.** (= *niezręczność*) awkwardness. **3.** (= *niedołęstwo, niezaradność*) incapability, incompetence.
nieporadny *a.* **1.** (= *bezbronny*) helpless. **2.** (= *niezręczny*) awkward. **3.** (= *niedołężny, niezaradny*) incapable, incompetent.
nieporęcznie *adv.* inconveniently; **nieporęcznie mi zwracać się z taką prośbą** I find it awkward to have such a favor to ask.
nieporęczny *a.* unwieldy.
nieporowaty *a.* non-porous.
nieporozumienie *n.* **1.** (= *pomyłka*) misunderstanding; **zaszło nieporozumienie** there was a misunderstanding. **2.** (= *kłótnia*) disagreement, misunderstanding; **położyć kres nieporozumieniom** put an end to disagreement. **3.** (= *coś nieudanego*) flop; **ten film to kompletne nieporozumienie** this movie is a complete flop.
nieporównany *a.* incomparable, matchless.
nieporównywalnie *adv.* incomparably.
nieporównywalność *f.* incomparability.
nieporównywalny *a.* incomparable.

nieporuszony *a.* **1.** (= *nieruchomy*) motionless. **2.** *lit.* (= *niewzruszony*) unaffected, untouched (*wobec czegoś* by sth).

nieporządek *mi* **-dk-** disorder, mess.

nieporządnie *adv.* untidily, messily; (*wyglądać*) slovenly.

nieporządny *a.* **1.** (= *nieutrzymujący porządku*) untidy, slovenly. **2.** (= *nieuporządkowany*) disorderly, messy.

nieposkromiony *a.* **-eni 1.** (*apetyt, temperament*) uncontrollable; (*ciekawość, ambicja*) unrestrained. **2.** (*zwierzę*) untamed.

nieposłuszeństwo *n.* disobedience; **nieposłuszeństwo obywatelskie** civil disobedience.

nieposłuszny *a.* disobedient.

niepospolicie *adv.* **1.** (= *wyjątkowo*) exceptionally. **2.** (= *w sposób niepospolity*) uncommonly.

niepospolity *a.* **1.** (= *wyjątkowy*) exceptional. **2.** (= *ponad zwykły poziom*) uncommon.

niepostępowy *a.* unprogressive.

niepostrzegalny *a.* imperceptible.

niepostrzeżenie *adv.* imperceptibly; **wyjść niepostrzeżenie** leave unnoticed.

nieposzanowanie *n.* disrespect (*kogoś/czegoś* for sb/sth); disregard (*kogoś/czegoś* of sb/sth).

nieposzlakowanie *adv.* spotlessly.

nieposzlakowany *a.* spotless.

niepośledni *a.* not unworthy of notice.

niepoświęcony *a.* unconsecrated.

niepotrzebnie *adv.* unnecessarily.

niepotrzebny *a.* **1.** (= *niekonieczny*) unnecessary. **2.** (= *niechciany*) unwanted.

niepotwierdzony *a.* unconfirmed.

niepowabny *a.* unattractive.

niepoważnie *adv.* (*podchodzić do czegoś*) unseriously; (*zachowywać się*) silily.

niepoważny *a.* (*podejście*) unserious; (*człowiek*) silly.

niepowetowany *a.* irreparable; **niepowetowana strata** irreparable loss.

niepowodzenie *n.* failure; **skazany na niepowodzenie** destined *l.* doomed to fail; **doznać niepowodzenia** fail; **(nie) zrażać się niepowodzeniami** (not) lose heart.

niepowołany *a.* **1.** (= *niekompetentny*) unfit (*do czegoś* for sth); incompetent (*do robienia czegoś* to do sth). **2.** (= *niepożądany*) undesirable, improper; **dostać się w niepowołane ręce** fall into the wrong hands.

niepowstrzymany *a.* uncontrollable, unrestrained.

niepowszechny *a.* uncommon, infrequent.

niepowszedni *a.* uncommon, unusual.

niepowściągliwość *f.* immoderation, intemperance.

niepowściągliwy *a.* immoderate, intemperate.

niepowtarzalność *f.* uniqueness.

niepowtarzalny *a.* unique.

niepozbywalny *a.* inalienable, unalienable.

niepoznaka *f.* **dla niepoznaki** to distract (sb's) attention.

niepoznanie *n.* **do niepoznania** beyond *l.* past all recognition.

niepoznawalność *f.* inscrutability.

niepoznawalny *a.* inscrutable.

niepozornie *adv.* inconspicuously; **wyglądać niepozornie** look inconspicuous.

niepozorny *a.* inconspicuous.

niepożądany *a.* undesirable, unwelcome.

niepożyteczny *a.* useless, unprofitable.

niepożywny *a.* innutritious.

niepracowity *a.* indolent.

niepracujący *a.* unemployed.

niepraktycznie *adv.* impractically, unpractically.

niepraktyczność *f.* impracticality, unpracticality.

niepraktyczny *a.* impractical, unpractical.

nieprawda *f.* untruth; **to nieprawda!** that's not true!; **nieprawda!** (= *niemożliwe*) don't tell me!; **mówić nieprawdę** tell lies. – *particle* **to jest ślicz-ne, nieprawda?** it's lovely, isn't it it?; **widziałeś się z nim wczoraj, nieprawda?** you met him yesterday, didn't you?

nieprawdaż *particle zob.* **nieprawda**.

nieprawdopodobieństwo *n.* **1.** (= *niewiarygodność*) incredibility, improbability. **2.** (= *nieprawdopodobne zdarzenie*) improbability.

nieprawdopodobny *a.* incredible, improbable.

nieprawdziwie *adv.* **1.** (= *niezgodnie z prawdą*) untruthfully, falsely. **2.** (= *sztucznie*) falsely, artificially.

nieprawdziwość *f.* **1.** (= *niezgodność z prawdą*) untruthfulness, untruth; fallacy. **2.** (= *nierzeczywistość*) unreality. **3.** (= *sztuczność*) falseness, artificiality.

nieprawdziwy *a.* **1.** (= *niezgodny z prawdą*) untrue. **2.** (= *nierzeczywisty*) unreal. **3.** (= *sztuczny*) (*np. biżuteria, futro*) false, artificial.

nieprawidłowo *adv.* **1.** (= *niepoprawnie*) incorrectly. **2.** (= *niezgodnie z normą*) irregularly. **3.** (= *niezgodnie z przepisami*) against the rules.

nieprawidłowość *f.* **1.** (= *brak prawidłowości*) incorrectness. **2.** (= *odstępstwo od normy*) irregularity.

nieprawidłowy *a.* **1.** (= *niepoprawny*) incorrect. **2.** (= *niezgodny z normą*) irregular. **3.** (= *niezgodny z przepisami*) against the rules.

nieprawnie *adv.* unlawfully, illegally.

nieprawny *a.* unlawful, illegal.

nieprawomocny *a. prawn.* (*o wyroku*) not (yet) legally binding, non-final; (*od którego toczy się postępowanie odwoławcze*) pending appeal.

nieprawomyślność *f.* disloyalty.

nieprawomyślny *a.* disloyal.

niepraworządny *a.* (*własność*) not rightful; (*władza*) illegitimate; (*obywatel*) law breaking.

nieprawość *f.* **1.** *lit.* (= *występek*) wrongdoing, misdeed. **2.** *lit.* (= *nielegalność*) illegality.

nieprawowierność *f.* unorthodoxy.

nieprawowierny *a.* unorthodox.

nieprawowity *a.* illegitimate.

nieprawy *a.* **1.** *lit.* (= *nieślubny*) illegitimate; **z nieprawego łoża** born out of wedlock, illegitimate. **2.** *lit.* (= *nieprawny*) illegal.

nieprecyzyjnie *adv.* imprecisely, inaccurately.

nieprecyzyjny *a.* imprecise, inaccurate.

nieprędki *a.* not quick, sluggish.

nieprędko *adv.* not soon.

nieprodukcyjny *a.* (= *niezwiązany z produkcją*) not connected with production, unproductive.

nieproduktywny *a.* **1.** (= *niewydajny*) unproductive. **2.** (= *nieprzynoszący korzyści*) unprofitable; (*np. gadanina*) empty. **3.** *jęz.* unproductive.

nieprofesjonalista *mp*, **nieprofesjonalistka** *f.* non-professional.

nieprofesjonalny *a.* unprofessional, non-professional.

nieproletariacki *a.* non-proletarian.

nieproliferacja *f. polit.* non-proliferation.

nieproporcjonalnie *adv.* disproportionally, disproportionately.

nieproporcjonalność *f.* disproportion, disproportionateness.

nieproporcjonalny *a.* **1.** (= *nieforemny*) disproportionate. **2.** (= *niewspółmierny*) disproportionate (*do czegoś* to sth).

nieproszony *a.* **-eni** unwelcome; **nieproszony gość** uninvited guest; unwelcome guest, unwelcome visitor; *pot.* gatecrasher.

nieprzebaczalny *a.* unpardonable.

nieprzebity *a.* impenetrable.

nieprzebłagany *a.* unpropitiated.

nieprzebrany *a.* countless, innumerable.

nieprzebyty *a.* impassable, impenetrable; (*o rzece*) unfordable.

nieprzechodni *a.* **1.** (*o pomieszczeniu*) not connecting. **2.** *jęz.* intransitive.

nieprzeciętnie *adv.* outstandingly.

nieprzeciętny *a.* outstanding.

nieprzegadany *a.* not wordy.

nieprzejednanie *n.* implacability. – *adv.* implacably, uncompromisingly.

nieprzejednany *a.* implacable, uncompromising.

nieprzejezdny *a.* (*np. o drodze z powodu robót*) closed; (*np. o drodze z powodu złych warunków*) impassable.

nieprzejrzany *a.* **1.** (= *rozległy*) immeasurable. **2.** (= *nieprzenikniony*) impenetrable.

nieprzejrzysty *a.* **1.** (= *nieprzezroczysty*) opaque. **2.** (= *niezrozumiały*) obscure.

nieprzekładalność *f.* untranslatability.

nieprzekładalny *a.* untranslatable.

nieprzekonująco *adv.* unconvincingly.

nieprzekonujący *a.* unconvincing.

nieprzekraczalny *a.* impassable; **nieprzekraczalny termin** deadline.

nieprzekupny *a.* incorruptible.

nieprzeliczony *a.* innumerable, countless.

nieprzemakalny *a.* (*o odzieży*) rainproof; (*o opakowaniu*) waterproof; **płaszcz nieprzemakalny** raincoat.

nieprzemijający *a.* everlasting, imperishable.

nieprzemijalność *f.* imperishability, everlastingness.

nieprzemysłowy *a.* non-industrial.

nieprzenikliwość *f.* **1.** (= *niedomyślność*) lack of discernment, obtuseness. **2.** (= *nieprzepuszczalność*) imperviousness.

nieprzenikliwy *a.* **1.** (= *niedomyślny*) undiscerning, obtuse. **2.** (= *nieprzepuszczalny*) impervious.

nieprzenikniony *a.* **-eni** **1.** (= *nieprzejrzysty*) impenetrable. **2.** (= *nieodgadniony*) unfathomable, inscrutable.

nieprzenośny *a.* **1.** (= *dosłowny*) literal. **2.** (= *niedający się przenosić*) immobile, non-portable.

nieprzeparty *a.* irresistible.

nieprzepisowy *a.* (*zagranie*) foul; (*zachowanie*) non-conforming.

nieprzepuszczalność *f.* impenetrability, imperviousness; (*dla światła*) opacity; (*dla powietrza*) air-tightness.

nieprzepuszczalny *a.* (*dla wody*) waterproof; (*dla światła*) opaque; (*dla powietrza*) air-tight.

nieprzerwanie *adv.* **1.** (= *ciągle*) incessantly, continuously. **2.** (= *bez odstępów*) uninterruptedly.

nieprzerwany *a.* **1.** (= *trwający bez przerwy*) incessant, continuous. **2.** (= *niemający przerw, jednolity*) uninterrupted.

nieprzestępny *a.* (*o roku*) non-leap, ordinary.

nieprześcigniony *a.* **-eni** unsurpassed, unexcelled.

nieprzetłumaczalność *f.* untranslatability.

nieprzetłumaczalny *a.* untranslatable.

nieprzewidywalny *a.* unpredictable, unforeseeable.

nieprzewidzianie *adv.* unexpectedly.

nieprzewidziany *a.* unforeseen, unexpected.

nieprzewodnik *mi fiz.* non-conductor.

nieprzezornie *adv.* improvidently.

nieprzezorność *f.* improvidence.

nieprzezorny *a.* improvident.

nieprzezroczystość *f.* opacity.

nieprzezroczysty *a.* opaque.

nieprzezwyciężony *a.* **1.** (= *nie do przezwyciężenia*) (*np. przeszkoda*) insurmountable. **2.** (= *nieprzeparty*) (*pokusa*) irresistible; (*wstręt, senność*) overwhelming.

nieprzychylnie *adv.* unfavorably, *Br.* unfavourably; disapprovingly; **być nastawionym nieprzychylnie do kogoś/czegoś** be prejudiced *l.* biased against sb/sth.

nieprzychylność *f.* disfavor, *Br.* disfavour.

nieprzychylny *a.* **1.** (= *nastawiony nieżyczliwie*) unfriendly, hostile. **2.** (= *negatywny*) (*opinia, decyzja*) unfavorable, *Br.* unfavourable; (*o wietrze, pogodzie*) foul, adverse.

nieprzyczepny *a.* non-cohesive.

nieprzydatność *f.* uselessness.

nieprzydatny *a.* useless.

nieprzyjaciel *mp pl.* Gen. i Acc. **-ół** Dat. **-ołom** Ins. **-ółmi** Loc. **-ołach** **1.** (= *wróg*) enemy, foe. **2.** (= *wroga armia*) the enemy.

nieprzyjacielski *a.* enemy; **oddziały nieprzyjacielskie** enemy troops.

nieprzyjaciółka *f.* enemy, foe.

nieprzyjazny *a.* **1.** (= *wrogi*) hostile, unfriendly. **2.** (= *niesprzyjający, niedostępny*) inhospitable; (*wiatr, pogoda*) foul, adverse. **3.** (*klimat, brzeg, okolica*) inhospitable.

nieprzyjaźnie *adv.* in an unfriendly way; **odnosić się nieprzyjaźnie do kogoś** be hostile to sb.

nieprzyjemnie *adv.* **1.** (= *niemile*) unpleasantly; **nieprzyjemnie zdziwiony** unpleasantly surprised; **było mi nieprzyjemnie** I felt bad. **2.** (= *niesympatycznie*) unpleasantly.

nieprzyjemność *f.* trouble; **mieć nieprzyjemności** be in trouble; **narazić kogoś na nieprzyjemności** put sb in trouble.

nieprzyjemny *a.* **1.** (= *niemiły*) (*atmosfera, wrażenie*) unpleasant; (*smak, zapach*) unpleasant, disagreeable. **2.** (= *niesympatyczny*) unpleasant.

nieprzylepny *a.* non-adhesive.

nieprzymiotnikowy *a. jęz.* non-adjectival.

nieprzymusowy *a.* voluntary, optional.

nieprzymuszony *a.* **-eni** voluntary, spontaneous; **z własnej i nieprzymuszonej woli** of one's own free will.

nieprzypadkowo *adv.* not accidentally.

nieprzypadkowy *a.* not accidental.

nieprzystawalność *f.* incompatibility.

nieprzystawalny *a.* incompatible; *geom.* non-congruent.

nieprzystępnie *a.* **1.** (*o zachowaniu*) (= *z dystansem*) unapproachably, standoffishly. **2.** (*o wyjaśnieniach itp.*) (= *zawile*) inaccessibly.

nieprzystępność *f.* **1.** (= *wyniosłość*) unapproachability, standoffishness. **2.** (= *niedostępność*) inaccessibility.

nieprzystępny *a.* **1.** (= *wyniosły*) unapproachable, standoffish. **2.** (= *niedostępny*) (*tekst, szczyt*) inaccessible; (*cena*) prohibitive, outrageous.

nieprzystojny *a.* (= *niewłaściwy*) indecorous, improper; (= *nieprzyzwoity*) indecent.

nieprzystosowanie *n.* non-adjustment.

nieprzystosowany *a.* unadjusted.

nieprzytomnie *adv.* **1.** (= *bez udziału świadomości*) unconsciously; **nieprzytomnie pijany** blind drunk, dead drunk; **patrzeć nieprzytomnie** stare vacantly. **2.** (= *gorączkowo*) feverishly. **3.** *pot.* (= *z wielką intensywnością, gwałtownością*) franticly; **nieprzytomnie zakochany** madly in love.

nieprzytomność *f.* unconsciousness; **być zmęczonym do nieprzytomności** be dead tired; **pobić kogoś do nieprzytomności** beat sb unconscious *l.* senseless; **upić się do nieprzytomności** get blind *l.* dead drunk.

nieprzytomny *a.* **1.** (= *bez świadomości*) unconscious; **nieprzytomny wzrok** vacant stare. **2.** (= *oszołomiony*) frantic, wild (*z czegoś* about sth); **nieprzytomny ze strachu** scared stiff, scared out of one's wits. **3.** (= *intensywny*) wild, mad.

nieprzytulnie *adv.* not cozily, *Br.* not cosily.

nieprzytulny *a.* not cozy, *Br.* not cosy.

nieprzywykły *a.* unaccustomed, not accustomed (*do czegoś* to sth).

nieprzyzwoicie *adv.* **1.** (= *niezgodnie z panującymi obyczajami*) indecently, obscenely. **2.** (= *niezgodnie z panującymi zasadami*) improperly,

in an unseemly fashion. **3.** *pot.* (= *bardzo*) obscenely.

nieprzyzwoitość *f.* **1.** (= *bezwstydność*) immodesty, indecency. **2.** (= *coś nieprzyzwoitego*) impropriety.

nieprzyzwoity *a.* **1.** (= *niezgodny z panującymi obyczajami*) indecent, obscene; (*język*) filthy, profane; (*dowcip*) dirty. **2.** (= *niezgodny z panującymi zasadami*) improper, unseeming.

niepunktualność *f.* unpunctuality.

niepunktualny *a.* unpunctual.

niepylak, niepylak apollo *ma ent.* apollo, apollo butterfly (*Parnassius apollo*).

niepyszny *a.* **jak niepyszny** crestfallen; **wyszedł jak niepyszny** he left with his tail between his legs.

nieracjonalnie *adv.* irrationally, unreasonably.

nieracjonalność *f.* (= *nierozumność*) irrationality; (*gospodarki, zarządzania*) inefficiency.

nieracjonalny *a.* **1.** (= *nieoparty na rozumie*) irrational; (*argument*) unreasonable. **2.** (= *przynoszący straty*) irrational; (*gospodarka*) inefficient.

nierad *a. tylko pred. przest.* (= *niezadowolony*) discontented; **nierad komuś** annoyed to see sb. – *adv. przest.* (= *niechętnie*) reluctantly, unwillingly; **rad nierad** willy-nilly, like it or not.

nierasowy *a.* (*pies, kot*) non-pedigree; (*koń*) non-thoroughbred, not thoroughbred.

nieraz *adv.* **1.** (= *wielokrotnie*) many times, repeatedly. **2.** (= *czasami*) sometimes.

nierdzewny *a.* rustproof; **stal nierdzewna** stainless steel.

nierealistyczny *a.* **1.** (= *nieoparty na trzeźwym sądzie*) unrealistic. **2.** *sztuka* nonrealistic.

nierealny *a.* **1.** (= *fikcyjny*) unreal. **2.** (= *nieoparty na realnych podstawach*) unrealistic. **3.** (= *niemożliwy do zrealizowania*) unfeasible.

niereformowalny *a. pot.* set in one's ways, hard-headed.

nieregularnie *adv.* irregularly; (*np. kursować, spotykać się*) on an irregular basis.

nieregularność *f.* irregularity.

nieregularny *a.* (*t. puls, odmiana*) irregular; **oddziały nieregularne** irregular troops; **wiersz nieregularny** irregular verse.

niereligijny *a.* unreligious.

nierentowność *f.* unprofitability.

nierentowny *a.* unprofitable.

nierogacizna *f.* swine.

nierolniczy *a.* non-agricultural.

nieromantyczny *a.* **1.** (*człowiek, sceneria*) unromantic. **2.** (*twórczość, poeta*) non-romantic.

nierozciągliwy *a.* inextensible; (*o materiale*) non-stretch.

nierozdzielnie *adv.* inseparably.

nierozdzielność *f.* inseparability.

nierozdzielny *a.* inseparable.

nierozerwalnie *adv.* inseparably, inextricably.

nierozerwalność *f.* (= *nierozłączność*) inseparability; (*związku, więzi*) indissolubility.

nierozerwalny a. (= *nierozłączny*) inseparable; (*związek, więź*) indissoluble.

nierozgarnięty a. slow-witted, dense.

nierozłączka f. *orn.* budgerigar, budgie (*Melopsittacus undulatus*); **papużki nierozłączki** *przen.* Siamese twins.

nierozłącznie adv. inseparably.

nierozłączny a. inseparable.

nierozmowny a. incommunicative, taciturn.

nierozmyślnie adv. unintentionally.

nierozmyślny a. unintentional.

nierozpoznawalny a. (= *niemożliwy do odróżnienia*) undistinguishable; (= *niemożliwy do rozpoznania*) unrecognizable.

nierozpuszczalny a. insoluble.

nierozsądnie adv. 1. (= *nie mając rozsądku*) unwisely, foolishly. 2. (= *niezgodnie z rozsądkiem*) unreasonably, imprudently.

nierozsądny a. 1. (= *pozbawiony rozsądku*) unwise, foolish. 2. (= *niezgodny z rozsądkiem*) unreasonable, imprudent.

nierozstrzygalny a. unsolvable.

nieroztropnie adv. imprudently.

nieroztropność f. imprudence.

nieroztropny a. imprudent.

nierozumny a. 1. (= *niemądry*) unreasonable. 2. (= *nieprzemyślany*) foolish. 3. (= *bezrozumny*) irrational; **nierozumne zwierzę** irrational animal.

nierozwaga f. rashness, imprudence.

nierozważnie adv. rashly, recklessly.

nierozważny a. 1. (= *lekkomyślny*) thoughtless, inconsiderate. 2. (= *nieprzemyślany*) rash, reckless.

nierozwiązalny a. (*o problemie*) intractable; (*o zagadce*) insoluble.

nierozwikłany a. insoluble.

nierozwinięty a. 1. (= *opóźniony w rozwoju*) backward; (*umysłowo*) retarded. 2. *jęz.* simple.

nierób *mp* **-o-** *pl.* **-y** *pot.* loafer, do-nothing.

nieróbstwo n. idleness, loafing.

nierówno adv. 1. (= *krzywo*) crookedly, unevenly. 2. (= *niejednakowo*) unevenly; (= *nierytmicznie*) irregularly.

nierównoboczny a. *geom.* inequilateral.

nierównoległy a. non-parallel.

nierównomiernie adv. (*np. podzielić*) unequally; (*np. bić*) (*o sercu*) irregularly.

nierównomierność f. (*podziału*) inequality; (*pulsu*) irregularity.

nierównomierny a. (*podział*) unequal; (*puls*) uneven, irregular.

nierówność f. 1. (= *niegładkość powierzchni*) unevenness, irregularity. 2. (= *dysproporcja*) inequality, disparity; **nierówność społeczna** social inequality. 3. (*jezdni, chodnika*) roughness, bumpiness. 4. *mat.* inequality.

nierównouprawnienie n. inequality.

nierównowaga f. imbalance.

nierówny a. 1. (= *niegładki*) uneven; (*teren*) broken, hilly; (*droga*) rough, bumpy. 2. (= *krzywy*) crooked. 3. (= *zróżnicowany*) varied; (*poziom, jakość*) inconsistent; **toczyć nierówną walkę** fight a one-sided battle. 4. (= *niemiarowy*)

uneven, erratic; (*oddech*) irregular. 5. (= *nierównoważony*) unbalanced; (*charakter, usposobienie*) inconsistent.

nieruchawy a. 1. (= *powolny, ociężały*) sluggish, torpid. 2. (= *mało lotny*) slow, slow-witted.

nieruchliwy a. sluggish, torpid.

nieruchomieć *ipf.* become motionless, freeze.

nieruchomo adv. motionlessly.

nieruchomość f. 1. (= *bezruch*) stillness. 2. (= *bycie nieruchomym*) motionlessness. 3. (*akcentu*) fixedness. 4. (= *dobra nieruchome*) real estate; *Br.* real property; **biuro obrotu nieruchomościami** real estate agency; **podatek od nieruchomości** property tax.

nieruchomy a. 1. (= *nieporuszający się*) motionless, still; **majątek nieruchomy** real estate; *Br.* real property. 2. (= *związany z określoną pozycją*) immovable, stationary. 3. (*akcent*) fixed.

nierytmicznie adv. unrhythmically.

nierytmiczność f. lack of rhythm.

nierytmiczny a. unrhythmic.

nierzadki a. not infrequent, not uncommon.

nierzadko adv. not infrequently, not uncommonly.

nierząd *mi* prostitution; **uprawiać nierząd** be a prostitute.

nierządnica f. *przest.* harlot, prostitute.

nierządny a. **czyn nierządny** *prawn.* indecent act.

nierzeczowy a. pointless, futile.

nierzeczywisty a. unreal.

nierzetelnie adv. 1. (= *niesumiennie*) unconscientiously. 2. (= *nieuczciwie*) dishonestly.

nierzetelność f. 1. (= *niesumienność*) unconscientiousness. 2. (= *nieuczciwość*) dishonesty.

nierzetelny a. 1. (= *niesumienny*) unconscientious. 2. (= *niestaranny*) unreliable. 3. (= *nieuczciwy*) dishonest.

niesamodzielnie adv. not independently, with assistance.

niesamodzielność f. dependence.

niesamodzielny a. 1. (= *stale potrzebujący pomocy*) dependent. 2. (= *niewykonany samodzielnie*) not done independently. 3. *jęz.* dependent.

niesamowicie adv. 1. (= *niepokojąco*) eerily, uncannily. 2. *pot.* (= *bardzo*) incredibly, amazingly; **niesamowicie pięknie oczy** incredibly pretty eyes.

niesamowitość f. 1. (= *niezwykłość*) strangeness. 2. (= *niepokojący charakter czegoś*) eeriness, uncanniness.

niesamowity a. 1. (= *budzący lęk*) uncanny. 2. (= *nadzwyczajny*) amazing, incredible.

niesamożywny a. *biol.* heterotrophic.

niesceniczny a. not suitable for theatrical adaptation.

niesforność f. unruliness.

niesforny a. unruly, boisterous.

nieskalany a. 1. *lit.* (= *idealnie czysty*) immaculate, pristine. 2. *lit.* (= *nieposzlakowany*) unsullied, unblemished.

nieskazitelnie adv. 1. *lit.* (= *idealnie*) impeccably; (*czysty, biały*) immaculately. **2.** *lit.* (= *szlachetnie*) irreproachably.

nieskazitelność *f.* **1.** *lit.* (= *idealna czystość*) immaculacy. **2.** *lit.* (= *prawość, nienaganność*) spotlessness, impeccability.

nieskazitelny *a.* **1.** *lit.* (= *idealny*) immaculate; (*wymowa, elegancja*) flawless. **2.** (= *nieposzlakowany*) impeccable, spotless.

nieskładnie *adv.* awkwardly, clumsily.

nieskładność *f.* awkwardness, clumsiness.

nieskładny *a.* **1.** (= *nieukładający się harmonijnie*) discordant, inharmonious; (= *nierówny, nierytmiczny*) uneven. **2.** (= *niezgrabny*) clumsy, awkward.

niesklonny *a.* disinclined, reluctant (*do czegoś* to do sth).

nieskomplikowany *a.* uncomplicated.

nieskończenie *adv.* **1.** (= *ciągle*) infinitely, endlessly. **2.** (= *wiecznie*) eternally, everlastingly. **3.** *pot.* (= *ogromnie*) extremely, incredibly.

nieskończoność *f.* **1.** (= *bezmiar*) infinity; (*kosmos*) boundlessness; **w nieskończoność** endlessly, ad infinitum. **2.** *mat.* infinity.

nieskończony *a.* **1.** (= *bezkresny*) infinite, endless; (*przestrzeń*) boundless. **2.** (= *niekończący się*) endless, never-ending. **3.** *mat.* infinite.

nieskory *a.* not eager, not inclined (*do czegoś* to do sth).

nieskracalny *a.* **ułamek nieskracalny** *mat.* irreducible fraction.

nieskromnie *adv.* **1.** (= *bezwstydnie*) indecently. **2.** (= *chełpliwie*) immodestly.

nieskromność *f.* **1.** (= *bezwstydność*) indecency. **2.** (= *chełpliwość*) immodesty.

nieskromny *a.* **1.** (= *bezwstydny*) indecent. **2.** (= *zarozumiały*) immodest.

nieskutecznie *a.* to no avail.

nieskuteczność *f.* ineffectiveness, inefficacy.

nieskuteczny *a.* **1.** (= *bezskuteczny*) ineffective, ineffectual. **2.** (= *daremny*) futile.

niesława *f.* infamy, disrepute; **okryć kogoś/coś niesławą** bring sb/sth into disrepute.

niesławny *a.* infamous, disgraceful.

niesłodki *a.* not sweet.

niesłony *a.* not salty.

niesłowiański *a.* non-Slavic; *Br.* non-Slavonic.

niesłowność *f.* unreliability.

niesłowny *a.* unreliable, undependable.

niesłusznie *adv.* unfairly, wrongly; **niesłusznie oskarżony** falsely accused.

niesłuszność *f.* **1.** (= *bezpodstawność*) groundlessness. **2.** (= *niesprawiedliwość*) injustice, unfairness.

niesłuszny *a.* **1.** (= *bezpodstawny*) groundless. **2.** (= *niesprawiedliwy*) unjust, unfair.

niesłychanie *adv.* outrageously, extremely.

niesłychany *a.* (= *zdumiewający*) unheard of, outrageous; (= *nadzwyczajny*) unprecedented, unparalleled; **to niesłychane!** that's incredible!, that's unbelievable!

niesłyszalnie *adv.* inaudibly.

niesłyszalny *a.* inaudible; **prawie niesłyszalny** barely audible.

niesłyszący *a.* hearing impaired, deaf.

niesmacznie *adv.* **1.** (= *nieapetycznie*) unpalatably. **2.** (= *wzbudzając niesmak*) tastelessly.

niesmaczny *a.* **1.** (= *nieapetyczny*) unpalatable, tasteless. **2.** (= *wzbudzający niesmak*) tasteless, in bad taste; (*żart*) sick.

niesmak *mi* **1.** (= *przykry smak w ustach*) bad *l.* unpleasant taste (*in the mouth*); **mieć niesmak po czymś** be left with a bad taste in one's mouth. **2.** (= *obrzydzenie*) disgust, repugnance; **czuć niesmak** be disgusted; **wzbudzać niesmak** be disgusting.

niesnaski *pl. Gen.* **-ek** *lit.* disagreements; **niesnaski rodzinne** family feuds.

niesolidarny *a.* disloyal, not in solidarity.

niesolidnie *adv.* unreliably.

niesolidność *f.* **1.** (= *nierzetelność*) unreliability. **2.** (= *nietrwałość*) flimsiness.

niesolidny *a.* **1.** (= *nierzetelny*) unreliable, unconscientious. **2.** (= *nietrwały*) flimsy.

niespecjalnie *adv. pot.* (= *nieszczególnie*) not really.

niespecjalny *a. pot.* (= *nieszczególny*) so-so.

niespełna *particle* (= *prawie*) (somewhat) less than; **niespełna rozumu** out of one's mind; **za niespełna tydzień** in less than a week; **mieć niespełna czterdzieści lat** be just forty years old.

niespieralny *a.* irremovable.

niespiesznie *adv.* in a leisurely manner; **niespiesznie mi** I'm in no hurry.

niespieszny *a.* leisurely.

niesplik *mi bot.* medlar (*Mespilus germanica*).

niespłacalny *a.* unpayable.

niespodzianka *f.* surprise; **miła/przykra niespodzianka** pleasant/unpleasant surprise; **zrobić komuś niespodziankę** (*np. wizytą*) surprise sb; (= *kupić mały prezent*) give sb a surprise present; **mam dla ciebie niespodziankę** I have a surprise for you.

niespodziewanie *adv.* unexpectedly.

niespodziewany *a.* unexpected.

niespokojnie *adv.* **1.** (= *nerwowo*) nervously; (*np. spać*) uneasily. **2.** (= *z niepokojem*) (*spoglądać, rozglądać się*) anxiously; (*np. siedzieć*) fretfully.

niespokojny *a.* **1.** (= *ruchliwy, zmienny*) uneasy; (*człowiek*) restless; (*morze, dzielnica*) rough; (*koń*) skittish; (*sen*) uneasy, restless; **niespokojne czasy** turbulent times; **niespokojne sumienie** guilty conscience. **2.** (= *zdenerwowany*) anxious, uneasy; **być niespokojnym o kogoś/coś** be anxious about sb/sth. **3.** (= *wyrażający niepokój*) anxious.

niespołeczny *a.* anti-social, asocial.

niesporczak *ma zool.* tardigrade; *pot.* water bear (*Tardigrada*).

niesporny *a.* **1.** (= *bezsprzeczny*) indisputable, incontestable. **2.** *prawn.* not under dispute.

niesportowy *a.* unsportsmanlike.

niespotykany *a.* (*okaz*) rare; (*uprzejmość*) unprecedented.

niespożyty *a.* indefatigable; **niespożyta energia** indefatigable energy.

niespójność *f.* **1.** (= *brak spójności*) incohesion. **2.** (= *brak związku logicznego*) incoherence.

niespójny *a.* **1.** (= *niespoisty*) incohesive. **2.** (= *nietworzący logicznej całości*) incoherent.

niesprawdzalność *f.* indeterminability.

niesprawdzalny *a.* indeterminable.

niesprawiedliwie *adv.* unjustly, unfairly; (*podzielić*) inequitably.

niesprawiedliwość *f.* **1.** (= *brak sprawiedliwości*) injustice, iniquity. **2.** (= *niesprawiedliwy postępek*) (an) injustice; **krzycząca niesprawiedliwość** flagrant injustice; **doznać niesprawiedliwości** experience injustice; **wyrządzić komuś niesprawiedliwość** do sb an injustice.

niesprawiedliwy *a.* **1.** (= *postępujący wbrew sprawiedliwości*) unfair, unjust; (*podział*) inequitable; **być niesprawiedliwym wobec** *l.* **dla kogoś/czegoś** treat sb/sth unfairly *l.* unjustly. **2.** (= *krzywdzący*) (*np. wyrok*) wrongful.

niesprawność *f.* **1.** (= *brak sprawności*) disability; **niesprawność ręki/nogi** hand/leg disability. **2.** (= *złe funkcjonowanie*) (*urządzenia*) malfunction, malfunctioning.

niesprawny *a.* **1.** (= *niewyćwiczony*) unfit, out of shape; (*np. o kończynie*) disabled. **2.** (= *źle funkcjonujący*) malfunctioning; (= *zepsuty*) out of order.

niesprzeczny *a.* consistent.

niesprzyjający *a.* unfavorable, *Br.* unfavourable; (*okoliczność*) adverse; (*wiatr, pogoda*) foul, adverse.

niestabilność *f.* instability.

niestabilny *a.* unstable, insecure.

niestałość *f.* **1.** (= *brak stałości*) impermanence, instability; (*uczuć*) fickleness. **2.** (= *nieregularność*) inconsistency, irregularity; (*opadów*) intermittence.

niestały *a.* **1.** (= *zmienny, kapryśny*) changeable, inconsistent; (*charakter*) fickle. **2.** (= *nieregularny*) unsteady; (*pogoda*) unstable.

niestarannie *adv.* carelessly.

niestaranność *f.* carelessness.

niestaranny *a.* careless.

niestary *a.* quite young.

niestateczny *a.* **1.** *techn.* unstable. **2.** *przest.* (= *niezrównoważony*) unstaid.

niestawiennictwo *n.* failure to appear.

niestety *adv.* unfortunately; **niestety, nie mogę ci pomóc** I'm afraid I can't help you, unfortunately I can't help you.

niestosownie *adv.* inappropriately, unsuitably; (= *nietaktownie*) tactlessly; **niestosownie do okoliczności** (*np. ubrać się*) inappropriately for the occasion; **zachować się niestosownie** forget one's manners.

niestosowność *f.* inappropriateness, unsuitability.

niestosowny *a.* inappropriate, unsuitable; (= *nietaktowny*) tactless.

niestrawność *f.* indigestion, dyspepsia; **dostać niestrawności** get indigestion.

niestrawny *a.* (= *niedający się trawić*) (= *trudny w odbiorze*) indigestible.

niestrudzenie *adv.* indefatigably, untiringly.

niestrudzony *a.* **-eni** indefatigable, tireless.

niestrzęp, niestrzęp głogowiec *ma ent.* black-veined white (*Aporia crataegi*).

niestworzony *a.* incredible; **niestworzone historie** *pot.* tall tales.

niesubiektywny *a.* non-subjective.

niesubordynacja *f.* insubordination.

niesumienność *f.* unconscientiousness.

niesumienny *a.* unconscientious.

nieswojo *adv.* **czuć się nieswojo** feel uncomfortable *l.* uneasy, not feel o.s.

nieswój *a.* **-o-** *Ins. i Loc.* **-oim** *pl.* **-oje -oi** *Gen. i Loc.* **-oich** *Dat.* **-oim** *Acc.* **-oje -oich** *Ins.* **-oimi** uneasy, ill at ease.

niesylabiczny *a.* *fon.* non-syllabic.

niesymetrycznie *adv.* asymmetrically.

niesymetryczność *f.* asymmetry.

niesymetryczny *a.* asymmetrical.

niesympatycznie *adv.* unpleasantly, uncongenially; **zachować się niesympatycznie wobec kogoś** be unfriendly to sb.

niesympatyczny *a.* unpleasant, unlikable.

niesystematycznie *adv.* unsystematically, unmethodically.

niesystematyczność *f.* haphazardness.

niesystematyczny *a.* **1.** (= *nieodznaczający się systematycznością*) unsystematic, unmethodical. **2.** (= *nieregularny*) irregular; (*tryb życia*) disorganized, chaotic.

niesyty *a.* (*wrażeń, doznań*) insatiate.

nieszablonowo *adv.* originally.

nieszablonowy *a.* unorthodox, original.

nieszczególnie *adv.* not particularly well, so-so; **wyglądała dziś nieszczególnie** she didn't look very well today.

nieszczególny *a.* not particularly good, so-so.

nieszczelnie *adv.* (*zamknięty*) not shut tight.

nieszczelność *f.* **1.** (= *brak szczelności*) leakiness. **2.** (= *przeciek, wyciek*) leak.

nieszczelny *a.* leaky; (*drzwi, okna*) drafty, *Br.* draughty; **dach jest nieszczelny** the roof is leaking.

nieszczerość *f.* (*słów, wypowiedzi*) insincerity; (*zachowania, uczuć*) inauthenticity.

nieszczery *a.* insincere; (*uśmiech*) false.

nieszczerze *adv.* insincerely.

nieszczęsny *a.* **1.** *lit.* (= *doświadczony przez los*) ill-fated. **2.** (= *niepomyślny, niefortunny*) misfortunate; (*pomysł*) hapless. **3.** *pot.* (= *pechowy, godny politowania*) unfortunate.

nieszczęście *n.* (= *zły los, niepowodzenie*) bad luck, misfortune; (= *tragedia*) disaster; (= *wypadek*) accident; **na nieszczęście** unfortunately; **pasmo nieszczęść** (*niepowodzeń*) stroke of bad luck; **seria nieszczęść** (*wypadków*) chapter of accidents; **sprowadzić na kogoś/coś nieszczęście** bring misfortune on *l.* upon sb/sth; **wyglądać jak siedem nieszczęść** look like something the cat dragged in; **nieszczęścia chodzą parami** it never rains but it pours; when it rains, it pours; **nie ma nieszczęścia** it's no (big) loss, it's no (great) tragedy.

nieszczęśliwie *adv.* **1.** (= *żałośnie*) unhappily,

miserably. **2.** (= *fatalnie*) hopelessly. **3.** (= *niepomyślnie*) unsuccessfully.

nieszczęśliwy *a.* **1.** (= *taki, którego spotkało nieszczęście*) unfortunate, luckless; *(kaleka, mina)* miserable. **2.** (= *świadczący o nieszczęściu*) miserable. **3.** *(pomysł, zbieg okoliczności)* unfortunate; *(miłość, małżeństwo, człowiek)* unhappy; **nieszczęśliwy wypadek** unfortunate accident, mishap.

nieszczęśnik *mp* poor wretch, poor soul.

nieszkodliwie *adv.* harmlessly; (= *niegroźnie*) not seriously.

nieszkodliwość *f.* harmlessness.

nieszkodliwy *a.* harmless; *(o substancji)* innoxuous; **nieszkodliwy wariat** harmless lunatic; **nieszkodliwy dla środowiska** environmentally friendly, environment-friendly.

nieszlachetnie *adv.* basely; dishonorably; *Br.* dishonourably.

nieszlachetność *f.* baseness.

nieszlachetny *a.* base; dishonorable; *Br.* dishonourable; **metal nieszlachetny** base metal.

nieszpory *pl. Gen.* **-ów** *rz.-kat.* vespers.

nieszpułka *f. bot.* medlar *(Mespilus germanica)*.

niesztowica *f. pat.* ecthyma.

nieściągalny *a.* uncollectible; **nieściągalne długi** bad debts.

nieścieralny *a.* indelible.

nieścisłość *f.* **1.** (= *brak ścisłości*) *(informacji, danych)* imprecision, inexactness. **2.** (= *niedokładność*) *(rachunków, sprawozdania)* inaccuracy. **3.** (= *brak spoistości*) *(tkaniny, gleby)* incoherence.

nieścisły *a.* **1.** (= *nieprecyzyjny*) inexact, imprecise. **2.** (= *niespoisty*) *(gleba)* incoherent; *(tkanina)* loose.

nieściśle *adv.* (= *niedokładnie*) inaccurately, imprecisely.

nieściśliwość *f. fiz.* incompressibility.

nieściśliwy *a. fiz.* incompressible.

nieść *ipf.* **niosę niesiesz niósł niosła nieśli 1.** (= *iść, trzymając coś*) carry, take; **nieść torbę w ręku** carry a bag in one's hand; **nieść bieliznę do pralni** take one's underwear to the laundry; **nieść głowę wysoko** carry one's head high. **2.** (= *przynosić*) bring; *(o wodzie)* carry; **nieść komuś radość/pociechę/pomoc** bring sb joy/consolation/help; **iść, gdzie oczy** *l.* **nogi niosą** follow one's nose; **gdzie cię znowu niesie?!** where are you going now?! **3.** (= *być przyczyną czegoś*) bring; **wojna niesie śmierć** war brings death. **4.** *(o impulsie, emocji)* lead. **5.** *(jaja)* lay. **6.** *(o pocisku, głosie)* carry; **nieść na 1000 metrów** *(o broni)* carry a 1000 meters. **7.** *(o plotce, wieści)* spread; **wieść niesie, że...** it is rumored that... ~ **się** *ipf.* **1.** (= *rozprzestrzeniać się*) *(o zapachu, dźwiękach, mgle itp.)* spread, waft. **2.** (= *o środkach lokomocji*) move along; *(o łodzi)* be borne; *(o pociągu)* roll; *(o rzece)* flow. **3.** (= *składać jaja*) lay eggs.

nieślubny *a.* illegitimate, born out of wedlock.

nieśmiało *adv.* (= *niepewnie*) shyly, coyly; (= *wstydliwie*) timidly, sheepishly.

nieśmiałość *f.* shyness, timidity.

nieśmiały *a.* **1.** (= *wstydliwy*) timid, sheepish. **2.** (= *będący wyrazem nieśmiałości*) shy, coy.

nieśmiertelnie *adv.* immortally.

nieśmiertelnik *mi Gen.* **-a** *bot.* strawflower *(Helichrysum bracteatum)*.

nieśmiertelność *f.* **1.** (= *wieczne życie*) immortality, life everlasting. **2.** (= *wiekopomność*) immortality.

nieśmiertelny *a.* **1.** (= *żyjący wiecznie*) immortal, everlasting. **2.** (= *wiekopomny*) immortal.

nieśna *a.* *(o kurze)* laying.

nieśność *f.* egg laying.

nieświadomie *adv.* **1.** (= *bezwiednie*) unawares; (= *bez udziału świadomości*) unconsciously. **2.** (= *nie znając czegoś*) unknowingly.

nieświadomość *f.* **1.** (= *niewiedza*) ignorance; **być w nieświadomości czegoś** be ignorant of sth, be unaware of sth; **trzymać kogoś w nieświadomości** keep sb in ignorance *l.* in the dark; **żyć w nieświadomości (czegoś)** live in ignorance (of sth). **2.** (= *brak świadomości*) unconsciousness.

nieświadomy *a.* **1.** (= *nieuświadamiający sobie*) unaware, ignorant *(czegoś* of sth). **2.** (= *mimowolny*) *(ruch, gest)* involuntary. **3.** (= *bez udziału świadomości*) unconscious.

nieświąteczny *a.* *(dzień)* working.

nieświeży *a.* **1.** *(o żywności)* (= *zepsuty*) bad; *(o chlebie)* stale; *(o maśle)* rancid. **2.** *(o odzieży)* (= *długo używany*) soiled, dirty. **3.** *(o człowieku, twarzy)* (= *zmęczony*) faded. **4.** *(o zapachu)* (= *nieprzyjemny*) bad. **5.** (= *nienowy*) outdated; *(o wiadomości)* stale, old.

nieświszczuk *ma zool.* black-tailed prairie dog *(Cynomys ludovicianus)*.

nietakt *mi* faux pas, gaffe; **popełnić nietakt** commit *l.* make a faux pas, make a blunder.

nietaktownie *adv.* tactlessly.

nietaktowny *a.* tactless.

nietechniczny *a.* non-technical.

nietegoroczny *a.* not this year's.

nietematyczny *a.* non-thematic.

nieterminowo *adv.* past the deadline, unpunctually.

nieterminowość *f.* unpunctuality.

nieterminowy *a.* past the deadline, unpunctual.

nietęgi *a.* **1.** *pot.* (= *lichy*) mediocre, poor; **nietęga mina** long face. **2.** (= *szczupły*) quite slim.

nietęgo *a.* poorly.

nietknięty *a.* **1.** (= *nienaruszony*) intact; *(o człowieku)* (= *nieraniony*) unharmed, sound. **2.** (= *nierozpoczęty*) *(śniadanie, praca)* untouched. **3.** (= *niezbadany*) intact, untouched; **nietknięty ludzką stopą** untrodden.

nietłukący *a.* unbreakable, non-breakable.

nietłusty *a.* *(np. ser)* low-fat.

nietłuszczowy *a.* fat-free.

nietoksyczny *a.* non-toxic, nontoxic.

nietolerancja *f.* **1.** (= *brak tolerancji*) intolerance *(dla l. wobec kogoś / czegoś* of sb/sth); **nietolerancja religijna/rasowa** religious/racial intolerance. **2.** *med.* intolerance *(na coś* to *l.* for sth).

nietolerancyjnie *adv.* intolerantly (*dla l. wobec kogoś / czegoś* of sb/sth).
nietolerancyjny *a.* intolerant (*dla l. wobec kogoś / czegoś* of sb/sth).
nietoperz *ma zool.* bat (*Chiroptera*).
nietopliwość *f.* infusibility.
nietopliwy *a.* infusible.
nietowarzyski *a.* **1.** (*o ludziach*) unsociable. **2.** (*o zwierzętach*) non-gregarious, solitary.
nietradycyjny *a.* untraditional.
nietrafiony *a.* missed, wrong.
nietrafnie *adv.* irrelevantly, inappropriately.
nietrafny *a.* **1.** (= *nieprzekonujący*) irrelevant, pointless. **2.** (= *chybiony*) missed.
nietreściwy *a.* **1.** (*o wykładzie, książce*) lacking substance. **2.** (*o pożywieniu*) lacking nourishing substance.
nietrudno *adv.* without difficulty, easily; **nietrudno zgadnąć** it is an easy guess, it is easy to guess.
nietrudny *a.* **1.** (= *łatwy*) not difficult, rather easy. **2.** (*o człowieku*) (= *nieuciążliwy*) easy; **nietrudny w pożyciu** easy to live with.
nietrwale *adv.* impermanently.
nietrwałość *f.* impermanence; (*uczuć*) fickleness; (*żywności*) perishability.
nietrwały *a.* impermanent; (*o uczuciach*) fleeting; (*o żywności*) perishable; (*o kolorze*) fast-fading.
nietrzeźwość *f.* insobriety, intoxication; **w stanie nietrzeźwości** in a state of intoxication, in a state of drunkenness.
nietrzeźwy *a.* **1.** (= *pijany*) intoxicated, drunk; (*oddech*) drunken; **być w stanie nietrzeźwym** be in a state of intoxication, be in a state of drunkenness; **prowadzenie pojazdu w stanie nietrzeźwym** driving under the influence; *Br.* drink driving. **2.** (= *pozbawiony zdrowego sądu*) unsound. – *mp* drunk.
nietutejszy *a.* foreign; (*produkt*) non-domestic; **jestem nietutejszy** I am a stranger here.
nietuzinkowy *a.* extraordinary.
nietykalność *f.* inviolability, immunity; **nietykalność cielesna** bodily inviolability; **nietykalność osobista** personal immunity; **nietykalność poselska** *US* congressional immunity; *Br.* parliamentary immunity; **naruszenie nietykalności cielesnej** battery, assault and battery.
nietykalny *a.* inviolable; (*o osobie*) untouchable.
nietypowo *adv.* atypically; (*np. rozpocząć rozmowę*) unusually.
nietypowy *a.* (= *niezgodny z normą*) atypical; (*np. rozmiar*) non-standard.
nietzscheanizm *mi* Nietzscheism.
nieubezpieczony *a.* uninsured.
nieubłaganie *adv.* **1.** (= *bezlitośnie*) unrelentingly. **2.** (= *nieuchronnie*) inevitably.
nieubłagany *a.* **1.** (= *bezlitosny*) implacable, relentless. **2.** (= *nieuchronny*) inevitable.
nieuchronnie *adv.* inevitably, inescapably.
nieuchronność *f.* inevitability, inescapability.
nieuchronny *a.* inevitable, inescapable.
nieuchwytność *f.* elusiveness.

nieuchwytny *a.* **1.** (= *niedający się chwycić*) elusive; **być nieuchwytnym dla kogoś** be unattainable for sb. **2.** (= *niedający się określić*) indefinable, elusive.
nieuciążliwy *a.* (= *niekłopotliwy*) not troublesome.
nieuctwo *n.* ignorance.
nieuczciwie *adv.* dishonestly.
nieuczciwość *f.* dishonesty.
nieuczciwy *a.* dishonest.
nieuczesany *a.* uncombed.
nieuczony *a.* **-eni** *pot.* unschooled, uneducated.
nieuczuciowy *a.* unemotional.
nieuczynny *a.* disobliging.
nieudacznik *mp pot.* loser.
nieudany *a.* unsuccessful.
nieudolnie *adv.* awkwardly, clumsily.
nieudolność *f.* **1.** (= *nieporadność*) awkwardness. **2.** (*stylu, formy*) inefficiency, incompetence.
nieudolny *a.* clumsy, awkward.
nieufnie *adv.* distrustfully, mistrustfully.
nieufność *f.* distrust, mistrust (*do l. wobec l. w stosunku do kogoś / czegoś* of sb/sth); **wotum nieufności** vote of no confidence; **podchodzić do kogoś/czegoś z nieufnością** approach sb/sth with reserve; **wzbudzać nieufność w kimś do kogoś/czegoś** arouse sb's mistrust towards sb/sth.
nieufny *a.* **1.** (= *sceptyczny*) distrustful (*do l. wobec l. w stosunku do kogoś / czegoś* of sb/sth). **2.** (= *świadczący o nieufności*) distrustful; (*spojrzenie*) suspicious.
nieugaszony *a.* unquenchable, inextinguishable.
nieugięcie *adv.* relentlessly.
nieugiętość *f.* relentlessness.
nieugięty *a.* relentless.
nieugodowy *a.* unconciliatory.
nieujarzmiony *a.* unsubjugated, unsubdued.
nieuk *mp pl.* **-i** *pog.* ignoramus.
nieukojony *a.* **-eni** inconsolable.
nieukontentowany *a. lit.* discontented.
nieukrócony *a.* uncurbed.
nieuleczalnie *adv.* (*chory, głupi*) incurably.
nieuleczalny *a.* **1.** (= *niedający się wyleczyć*) incurable. **2.** (= *niepoprawny*) (*optymista, lenistwo*) incorrigible.
nieuległy *a.* unsubmissive.
nieulękle *adv.* fearlessly.
nieulękły *a. lit.* fearless.
nieumiarkowanie *adv.* immoderately, excessively. – *n.* immoderation (*w czymś* in sth); (*zwł. w piciu*) intemperance.
nieumiarkowany *a.* (*żądanie*) immoderate; (*apetyt, optymizm*) intemperate.
nieumiejętnie *adv.* incompetently, unskilfully.
nieumiejętność *f.* inability, unskilfulness.
nieumiejętny *a.* incompetent, unskilful.
nieumyślnie *adv.* unintentionally, inadvertently.
nieumyślny *a.* unintentional, inadvertent; **nieumyślne spowodowanie śmierci** *prawn.* manslaughter.

nieunikniony *a.* unavoidable, inescapable.
nieuporządkowany *a.* disorderly.
nieupoważniony *a.* **-eni** unauthorized (*do czegoś* to do sth); **(osobom) nieupoważnionym wstęp wzbroniony** no entry.
nieuprawniony *a.* unauthorized (*do czegoś* to do sth).
nieuprawny *a.* unarable, waste.
nieuprzedzony *a.* **1.** (= *bez uprzedzeń*) unbiased. **2.** (= *którego nie uprzedzono*) uninformed.
nieuprzejmie *adv.* **1.** (= *niegrzecznie*) impolitely. **2.** (= *nieżyczliwie*) unkindly.
nieuprzejmość *f.* **1.** (= *niegrzeczność*) impoliteness. **2.** (= *nieżyczliwość*) unkindness.
nieuprzejmy *a.* **1.** (= *niegrzeczny*) impolite. **2.** (= *nieżyczliwy*) unkind.
nieuregulowany *a.* unregulated.
nieurodzaj *mi* **1.** (= *złe zbiory*) crop failure; **był nieurodzaj na gruszki** the pear crop failed. **2.** *przen.* scarcity (*czegoś l. na coś* of sth).
nieurodzajny *a.* infertile; **nieurodzajny rok** lean year.
nieurodziwy *a.* uncomely.
nieurzędowy *a.* unofficial, informal.
nieusłuchany *a. pot.* disobedient.
nieuspołeczniony *a.* **1.** (= *prywatny*) private. **2.** (*o człowieku*) devoid of civic spirit.
nieusposobiony *a.* (= *źle usposobiony*) ill-disposed.
nieusprawiedliwiony *a.* unjustified, unexcused.
nieustający *a.* incessant, continuous.
nieustannie *adv.* unceasingly, continuously.
nieustanny *a.* incessant, unceasing; continuous.
nieustawny *a.* (*o pomieszczeniu*) incommodious.
nieustępliwie *adv.* persistently, tenaciously.
nieustępliwość *f.* persistence, persistency; tenacity.
nieustępliwy *a.* persistent, tenacious.
nieustraszony *a.* **-eni** fearless, intrepid.
nieusuwalny *a.* irremovable.
nieuszanowanie *a.* disrespect (*kogoś / czegoś* for sb/sth).
nieuszkodzony *a.* undamaged.
nieuśmierzony *a.* **1.** (*o bólu*) not soothed. **2.** (*o rozruchach*) not quelled.
nieutrudzony *a.* indefatigable.
nieutulony *a.* **-eni** inconsolable, disconsolate; **pozostali w nieutulonym żalu...** (*w nekrologu*) the bereaved...
nieutwardzony *a.* unhardened.
nieuwaga *f.* inattention; **przez nieuwagę** through inattention; **chwila nieuwagi** an unguarded moment.
nieuważnie *adv.* **1.** (= *z roztargnieniem*) inattentively, absent-mindedly. **2.** (= *niedbale*) carelessly, neglectfully.
nieuważny *a.* **1.** (= *roztargniony*) inattentive, absent-minded. **2.** (= *spowodowany brakiem uwagi*) careless, neglectful.
nieuwzględniony *a.* not taken into consideration.

nieuzasadniony *a.* groundless, unfounded.
nieuzbrojony *a.* **-eni** **1.** (= *niemający broni*) unarmed. **2.** *bud.* undeveloped.
nieuzdolniony *a.* untalented.
nieużyteczny *a.* useless.
nieużytki *pl. Gen.* **-ów** wastelands.
nieużytkowy *a.* non-utilitarian.
nieużyty *a.* disobliging.
niewart *a. tylko pred.* **1.** (= *bezwartościowy*) worthless. **2.** (= *niegodny*) unworthy (*kogoś / czegoś* of sb/sth); **gra niewarta świeczki** the game is not worth the candle, it's not worth it; **on jest niewart złamanego grosza** *l.* **funta kłaków** he is not worth a hoot.
nieważkość *f.* **1.** *lit.* (= *błahość*) insignificance, triviality. **2.** *fiz.* weightlessness, zero gravity.
nieważność *f.* **1.** (= *błahość*) insignificance, triviality. **2.** (= *nieprawomocność*) invalidity.
nieważny *a.* **1.** (= *błahy*) unimportant, insignificant. **2.** (*o ludziach*) (= *niewpływowy*) insignificant. **3.** (= *nieprawomocny*) invalid, null and void.
niewąski *a. pot.* (= *nie byle jaki*) not bad.
niewąsko *adv. pot.* (= *nie byle jak*) not badly.
niewątpliwie *adv.* undoubtedly.
niewątpliwy *a.* undoubted, unquestionable.
niewczas *mi* **po niewczasie** too late.
niewczesny *a.* untimely, inopportune.
niewdzięcznica *f.* ungrateful girl *l.* woman.
niewdzięcznik *mp* ungrateful boy *l.* man.
niewdzięczność *f.* ingratitude.
niewdzięczny *a.* **1.** (= *niepoczuwający się do wdzięczności*) ungrateful, thankless. **2.** (= *niedający satysfakcji*) thankless, unrewarding.
niewerbalny *a.* non-verbal.
nieweryfikowalny *a.* unverifiable.
niewesoło *adv.* sadly; **sytuacja wygląda niewesoło** the situation is quite bad, things are looking pretty bad.
niewesoły *a.* joyless, sad; **niewesoła mina** long face; **niewesołe myśli** gloomy thoughts; **niewesoła przyszłość** bleak future.
niewiadoma *f. mat.* unknown; **równanie z jedną niewiadomą/dwoma niewiadomymi** equation in one unknown/two unknowns; **coś jest wielką niewiadomą** *przen.* sth is a great unknown.
niewiadomy *a.* unknown.
niewiara *f. Dat. i Loc.* **-erze** disbelief (*w kogoś / coś* in sb/sth).
niewiarygodnie *adv.* **1.** (= *niesamowicie*) unbelievably, incredibly. **2.** (= *w sposób niezasługujący na zaufanie*) unreliably.
niewiarygodność *f.* **1.** (*np. świadka, zeznań*) unreliability. **2.** (= *niesamowitość*) incredibility.
niewiarygodny *a.* **1.** (*świadek, relacja*) unreliable. **2.** (= *niesamowity*) unbelievable, incredible.
niewiasta *f. Dat. i Loc.* **-eście** *lit.* woman.
niewiązany *a.* **mowa niewiązana** prose.
niewiążący *a.* unbinding.
niewidka *f.* **czapka niewidka** cap of invisibility.
niewidocznie *adv.* invisibly.

niewidoczny *a.* invisible.

niewidomy *a.* blind. – *mp* a blind person.

niewidy *pl.* **cuda niewidy** *pot.* wonders.

niewidzący *a.* **1.** (= *niewidomy*) blind. **2.** (*o wzroku*) (= *który nie widzi*) unseeing; **niewidzące oczy** unseeing eyes.

niewidzenie *n.* (= *rozłąka*) separation; **spotkać się po długim niewidzeniu** meet after a long time.

niewidzialnie *adv.* without being seen.

niewidzialny *a.* invisible.

niewiedza *f.* ignorance.

niewiele *num. Ins.* **-oma** *l.* **-u** (*przy rzeczowniku policzalnym*) few, not many; (*przy rzeczowniku niepoliczalnym, czasowniku, przymiotniku*) little, not much. – *adv.* (= *mało*) little, not much; **niewiele sobie robić z kogoś/czegoś** not to care much about sb/sth; **niewiele myśląc** not thinking much; **niewiele mówiący tytuł** a title that doesn't say much; **niewiele brakowało, żeby zginął** he nearly got killed.

niewielki *a.* **1.** (= *nieokazały*) not big, not large. **2.** (= *niemający dużego znaczenia*) (*zysk, majątek*) insignificant; (*kłopot, nadzieja*) little.

niewielu *num. zob.* **niewiele**.

niewierność *f.* **1.** (= *wiarołomstwo*) infidelity, unfaithfulness. **2.** (= *nielojalność*) disloyalty. **3.** (= *nieścisłość*) (*np. przekładu*) inaccuracy.

niewierny *a.* **1.** (= *wiarołomny*) unfaithful. **2.** (= *nielojalny*) disloyal. **3.** *lit.* (= *sceptyczny*) doubting; **niewierny Tomasz** doubting Thomas. **4.** (= *nieścisły*) (*kopia, przekład*) inaccurate. – *mp* (= *ktoś, kto nie jest wyznawcą jakiejś religii*) infidel.

niewierzący *a.* unbelieving, non-believing. – *mp* unbeliever, non-believer.

niewieści *a. lit.* womanly.

niewieścieć *ipf.* become effeminate.

niewiniątko *n. Gen.pl.* **-tek** *żart.* innocent; **rzeź niewiniątek** *rel.* Massacre of the Innocents; *przen.* slaughter of the innocents, massacre of the innocents; *żart.* (*o egzaminie itp.*) massacre; **na egzaminie była prawdziwa rzeź niewiniątek** the exam was a freaking massacre; **udawać niewiniątko** play innocent.

niewinnie *adv.* **1.** (= *niesłusznie*) innocently; **niewinnie ukarany** unjustly punished. **2.** (= *z prostotą*) ingenuously; (*uśmiechać się*) innocently. **3.** (= *niegroźnie*) harmlessly; (*żartować*) inoffensively.

niewinność *f.* **1.** (= *brak winy*) innocence. **2.** (= *skromność*) innocence, purity. **3.** (= *naiwność*) ingenuousness.

niewinny *a.* **1.** (= *taki, który nie zawinił*) innocent; *prawn.* not guilty; **uznany za niewinnego** presumed innocent. **2.** (= *czysty, nieskalany*) innocent. **3.** (= *błahy*) trifling. **4.** (= *naiwny*) ingenuous.

niewładny *a.* **1.** (= *bezwładny*) numb, inert. **2.** *lit.* (= *niemający władzy*) not having the authority; **być niewładnym zrobić coś** have no authority *l.* power to do sth.

niewłaściwie *adv.* **1.** (= *błędnie*) wrongly. **2.** (= *niestosownie*) inappropriately.

niewłaściwość *f.* **1.** (= *bycie niewłaściwym*) inappropriateness. **2.** (= *gafa*) impropriety.

niewłaściwy *a.* **1.** (= *nieprawidłowy*) wrong, inappropriate; **ułamek niewłaściwy** *mat.* improper fraction. **2.** (= *niestosowny*) improper, inappropriate; **w niewłaściwym czasie** untimely; **dostać się w niewłaściwe ręce** fall into the wrong hands; **to było niewłaściwe** that was out of place.

niewłóknisty *a.* non-fibrous.

niewnikliwy *a.* careless.

niewodny *a.* (*np. roztwór*) non-aqueous.

niewojowniczy *a.* unwarlike.

niewola *f.* **1.** (= *brak wolności*) captivity; **dostać się do niewoli** (*np. o żołnierzu*) be taken captive, be taken prisoner; **popaść w niewolę** be taken captive; **wziąć kogoś do niewoli** take sb captive; **żyć w niewoli** (*np. o zwierzętach*) live in captivity. **2.** (= *uzależnienie*) addiction; **być w niewoli nałogu** be in chains of addiction.

niewolić *ipf.* **-ól** *lit.* constrain.

niewolnica *f.* slave; **niewolnica mody** *przen.* fashion slave, slave of fashion.

niewolnictwo *n.* slavery.

niewolniczo *adv.* **1.** (= *służalczo*) slavishly, servilely. **2.** (= *z przesadną wiernością*) (*np. naśladować*) slavishly.

niewolniczy *a.* **1.** (= *właściwy niewolnikowi*) slavish; **niewolnicza praca** slave labor, *Br.* slave labour. **2.** (= *uległy*) servile. **3.** (= *przesadnie wierny*) slavish.

niewolnik *mp* slave; **handel niewolnikami** slave-trade; **niewolnik nałogu** *przen.* slave to an addiction; **być niewolnikiem czegoś** be a slave to sth; **uczynić kogoś swoim niewolnikiem** enslave sb.

niewonny *a.* odorless, *Br.* odourless.

niewód *mi* **-o-** *ryb.* dragnet.

niewprawnie *adv.* unskilfully, ineptly.

niewprawny *a.* unskilful, inept.

niewrażliwie *adv.* insensibly.

niewrażliwość *f.* **1.** (= *brak reakcji*) insensitivity. **2.** (= *nieczułość, obojętność*) insensibility (*na coś* to sth).

niewrażliwy *a.* **1.** (= *niereagujący*) insensitive. **2.** (= *nieczuły, obojętny*) insensible (*na coś* to sth).

niewskazany *a.* inadvisable.

niewspółczesny *a.* uncontemporary.

niewspółmiernie *adv.* incommensurately (*do czegoś* with sth).

niewspółmierność *f.* incommensurability (*do czegoś* with sth).

niewspółmierny *a.* incommensurate (*do czegoś* with sth).

niewspółrzędny *a.* non-co-ordinate.

niewstrzemięźliwy *a.* immoderate, intemperate.

niewulkaniczny *a.* non-volcanic.

niewybaczalny *a.* unpardonable, unforgivable.

niewybredny *a.* **1.** (= *niekapryśny*) (*np. klient*) not fastidious. **2.** (= *niewymagający*) (*np. widownia*) undemanding. **3.** (= *prymitywny*) (*żart, gust*) unrefined.

niewybuch *mi wojsk.* unexploded shell, dud.

niewychowany *a.* ill-mannered.

niewyczerpany *a.* inexhaustible.

niewyczuwalny *a.* impalpable; *(napięcie, zagrożenie)* imperceptible; *(puls)* weak.

niewydajnie *adv.* inefficiently.

niewydajny *a.* inefficient.

niewydarzony *a.* **-eni** *pot.* mediocre.

niewydolność *f.* **1.** *pat.* failure, failure of function; **niewydolność krążenia/nerek** circulatory/renal failure. **2.** (= *złe funkcjonowanie*) malfunction.

niewydolny *a.* **1.** *pat.* failing, inefficient. **2.** (= *źle funkcjonujący*) malfunctioning.

niewygadany *a.* inarticulate, close-mouthed.

niewygasły *a.* unextinguished; *(pamięć)* immortal.

niewygoda *f. Gen.pl.* **-ód 1.** (= *brak wygody*) discomfort. **2.** (= *niedogodność*) inconvenience, trouble; **znosić niewygody** suffer hardships.

niewygodnie *adv.* uncomfortably.

niewygodny *a.* **1.** (= *niezapewniający wygody*) uncomfortable; *(dojazd)* inconvenient. **2.** (= *niepożądany*) *(np. świadek)* inconvenient; **być niewygodnym dla kogoś** be inconvenient to sb.

niewygórowany *a.* not excessive.

niewykluczony *a.* conceivable; **niewykluczone, że będę mieć trochę wolnego czasu** it is not out of the question that I'll have some spare time.

niewykonalny *a.* unworkable, unfeasible.

niewykrywalny *a.* undetectable.

niewykształcony *a.* **-eni** uneducated.

niewykwalifikowany *a.* unskilled, unqualified.

niewykwintny *a.* inelegant.

niewyłączny *a.* non-exclusive.

niewymagający *a.* undemanding.

niewymawialny *a.* **1.** (= *niedający się wymówić*) unpronounceable. **2.** (= *którego nie wolno wymawiać*) unmentionable.

niewymiarowy *a.* non-standard size.

niewymienny *a.* *(pieniądz)* inconvertible; *(część, element)* non-interchangeable.

niewymierny *a.* immeasurable; **liczba niewymierna** *mat.* irrational number.

niewymowny *a. lit.* unspeakable.

niewymuszony *a.* casual, unconstrained.

niewymyślny *a.* plain.

niewyobrażalny *a.* unimaginable.

niewypał *mi* **1.** *wojsk.* (= *pocisk, który nie został odpalony*) dud, misfire. **2.** *pot.* (= *niewybuch*) unexploded shell. **3.** (*coś nieudanego*) flop, wash-out, fiasco; **spektakl okazał się niewypałem** the performance turned out to be a complete wash-out.

niewyparzony *a.* **mieć niewyparzoną gębę** *l.* **niewyparzony język** *pot.* be foul-mouthed.

niewypłacalność *f.* insolvency.

niewypłacalny *a.* insolvent.

niewypoczęty *a.* unrested.

niewypowiedziany *a. lit.* inexpressible, unspeakable.

niewyrazisty *a.* unclear, vague.

niewyraźnie *adv.* **1.** (= *niewyraziście, niejasno*) indistinctly, faintly; *(pisać, pamiętać)* indis-

tinctly. **2.** *pot.* (= *nieswojo*) unwell, seedily; *(uśmiechać się)* faintly; **czuć się niewyraźnie** (= *czuć się źle*) feel out of sorts; (= *odczuwać strach*) feel insecure. **3.** *pot.* (= *podejrzanie*) suspiciously; *(usprawiedliwiać się)* vaguely.

niewyraźny *a.* **1.** (= *słaby, niewyrazisty*) indistinct; *(cień, głos, dźwięk)* faint; *(zarys, wypowiedź)* vague. **2.** *pot.* (= *nieswój*) unwell, seedy. **3.** *pot.* (= *niepewny*) vague, uncertain; *(wzrok)* insecure. **4.** *pot.* (= *podejrzany*) suspicious; *(towarzystwo, przeszłość)* shabby.

niewyrażalny *a.* inexpressible.

niewyrobiony *a.* **1.** **-eni** (= *niemający ogłady*) unrefined, unsophisticated. **2.** (= *niewypracowany*) untrained; *(gust)* unrefined.

niewyrośnięty *a.* **1.** (*o człowieku*) small, short. **2.** (*o cieście*) unrisen. **3.** (*o roślinach*) dwarf.

niewyrozumiały *a.* strict.

niewysłowiony *a. lit.* inexpressible, unutterable.

niewysoki *a.* **1.** (= *niski*) not (very) tall. **2.** (= *znajdujący się nisko, na niską wysokość*) not (very) high; *(sufit, skok)* (quite) low. **3.** (= *niewielki*) small, little; *(zarobek, cena)* not (very) high; *(jakość, poziom)* (quite) low.

niewysoko *adv.* **1.** (= *nisko*) low. **2.** (= *słabo*) low; **niewysoko sobie cenić kogoś/coś** not think much of sb/sth; **nisko opłacany** low paid.

niewyspany *a.* sleepy.

niewystarczająco *adv.* insufficiently.

niewystarczający *a.* insufficient.

niewystarczalność *f.* insufficiency.

niewystawny *a.* modest.

niewyszkolony *a.* untrained.

niewyszukany *a.* simple.

niewytłumaczalny *a.* inexplicable.

niewytrawny *a.* inexperienced.

niewytrwały *a.* unpersevering.

niewytrzymały *a.* **1.** (= *nieodznaczający się wytrzymałością*) *(człowiek)* not persevering; *(organizm)* unenduring; *(materiał)* not resistant. **2.** (= *nieodporny*) sensitive *(na coś* to sth).

niewytworny *a.* inelegant.

niewywrotny *a.* stable; *(o łodzi)* uncapsizable.

niewyznaczalny *a.* undeterminable.

niewyżyty *a.* unappeased, unsatisfied.

niewzruszoność *f.* inflexibility.

niewzruszony *a.* **-eni** inflexible, rigid; *(spokój)* imperturbable; *(poglądy, zasady)* firm; **być niewzruszonym na coś** be insensitive to sth.

niezaangażowanie *n.* lack of commitment, non-commitment; **polityka niezaangażowania** *polit.* non-alignment policy.

niezaangażowany *a.* uncommitted *(w coś* to sth); unengaged *(w coś* in sth); **państwo niezaangażowane** *polit.* non-aligned country *l.* state.

niezabawny *a.* unamusing.

niezachwiany *a.* undeterred, unwavering.

niezadługo *adv.* before long, soon.

niezadowolenie *n.* discontent, dissatisfaction *(z kogoś/czegoś* with sb/sth); **okazywać komuś swoje niezadowolenie** show sb one's dissatisfaction.

niezadowolony *a.* **-eni 1.** (= *nierad*) discontented, dissatisfied, unhappy (*z kogoś/czegoś* with sb/sth). **2.** (= *świadczący o niezadowoleniu*) unhappy, dissatisfied.

niezakłócony *a.* undisturbed.

niezakrzepły *a.* uncoagulated.

niezależnie *adv.* **1.** (= *samodzielnie*) independently. **2.** (= *bez względu na coś*) irrespective, regardless (*od kogoś/czegoś* of sb/sth).

niezależność *f.* independence (*od kogoś/czegoś* of *l.* from sb/sth); **niezależność materialna** self-sufficiency; **cieszyć się niezależnością** be independent.

niezależny *a.* **1.** (= *niezawisły*) (*państwo, związek, sąd, sędzia*) independent; (*opinia, osąd*) detached; **niezależny materialnie** financially independent; **niezależny w sądach** unbiased, impartial. **2.** (= *samodzielny*) independent (*od kogoś/czegoś* of sb/sth); self-sufficient; **z powodów ode mnie niezależnych** for reasons beyond my control; **to (jest) ode mnie niezależne** it's beyond my control; **mowa niezależna** *jęz.* direct speech.

niezamężna *a.* unmarried, single. – *f. Gen.* **-ej** single *l.* unmarried woman.

niezamienny *a.* unexchangeable, non-exchangeable.

niezamierzony *a.* unintentional.

niezamieszkany *a.* uninhabited.

niezamożność *f.* indigence.

niezamożny *a.* indigent.

niezaplanowany *a.* unplanned.

niezapobiegliwość *f.* improvidence.

niezapobiegliwy *a.* improvident.

niezapominajka *f. bot.* forget-me-not (*Myosotis*).

niezapomniany *a.* unforgettable, memorable.

niezaprzeczalnie *adv.* undeniably.

niezaprzeczalny *a.* undeniable, undisputed.

niezaradność *f.* helplessness, resourcelessness.

niezaradny *a.* helpless, resourceless.

niezasadny *a.* unjustified, unfounded, groundless.

niezasłużenie *adv.* undeservedly.

niezasłużony *a.* undeserved.

niezasobny *a.* **1.** (= *ubogi*) poor. **2.** (= *niemający zasobów*) of limited means, scantily provided (*w coś* with sth).

niezaspokojony *a.* unsatisfied; (*o pragnieniu*) unquenched.

niezastąpiony *a.* **-eni** irreplaceable; **nie ma ludzi niezastąpionych** nobody is irreplaceable.

niezatapialny *a.* unsinkable.

niezatarty *a.* indelible, memorable.

niezauważalnie *adv.* imperceptibly.

niezauważalny *a.* (= *niedostrzegalny*) imperceptible; (= *niezwracający uwagi*) inconspicuous.

niezauważony *a.* unnoticed.

niezawiły *a.* uncomplicated.

niezawiniony *a.* non-culpable, faultless.

niezawisłość *f.* independence; **niezawisłość sędziowska** *prawn.* independence of the judiciary.

niezawisły *a.* (*państwo, sąd*) independent.

niezawodnie *adv.* **1.** (= *z pewnością*) unfailingly, without fail. **2.** (= *sprawnie, bez usterek*) efficiently.

niezawodność *f.* reliability.

niezawodny *a.* **1.** (= *pewny*) (*przyjaciel*) reliable, dependable; (*urządzenie, kuracja, lek*) reliable, trustworthy; (*środek*) unfailing. **2.** (= *sprawny*) efficient, reliable.

niezawodowiec *mp* non-professional.

niezbadany *a.* (*tajemnica, przyszłość*) unfathomable, fathomless; (*terytorium*) unexplored; **niezbadane są wyroki losu** you never know what befalls you.

niezbędnie *adv.* indispensably; **niezbędnie potrzebny** indispensable.

niezbędnik *mi Gen.* **-a 1.** (*łyżka i widelec*) combination spoon and fork. **2.** (*komplet przyborów*) kit.

niezbędny *a.* indispensable, essential.

niezbicie *adv.* irrefutably.

niezbity *a.* irrefutable, incontrovertible.

niezborność *f.* **1.** (= *niespójność*) incoherence, incongruence. **2.** *pat.* astigmatism, astigmia.

niezborny *a.* **1.** incoherent, incongruent. **2.** *pat.* astigmatic.

niezbyt *adv.* not very, not too.

niezbywalny *a. prawn.* inalienable.

niezdara *f. l. mp decl. like f. Gen.pl.* **-r** *l.* **-ów** *pot.* duffer; **to skończony niezdara** he's all thumbs.

niezdarnie *adv.* clumsily.

niezdarność *f.* clumsiness.

niezdarny *a.* **1.** (= *niezręczny*) clumsy; (*pracownik*) inept, ineffectual; (*ruchy*) awkward. **2.** (= *wykonany nieumiejętnie*) botched, bungled.

niezdatność *f.* inaptitude, unfitness (*do czegoś* for sth).

niezdatny *a.* unfit (*do czegoś* for sth); **woda niezdatna do picia** water unfit for drinking; **niezdatny do pracy/służby wojskowej** unfit for work/military service.

niezdecydowanie¹ *n.* **1.** (*stan*) indecision. **2.** (*cecha*) indecisiveness.

niezdecydowanie² *adv.* irresolutely.

niezdecydowany *a.* **1.** (= *niemogący się zdecydować*) hesitant, undecided, irresolute. **2.** (= *świadczący o niezdecydowaniu*) hesitant, irresolute. **3.** (*kolor*) indefinite.

niezdolność *f.* **1.** (= *brak zdolności*) inability, incapability; **niezdolność do kłamstwa** incapability of lying. **2.** (= *niezdatność*) unfitness (*do czegoś* for sth); **niezdatność do pracy/służby wojskowej** unfitness for work/military service.

niezdolny *a.* **1.** (= *nieinteligentny*) unintelligent. **2.** (= *niebędący w stanie czegoś zrobić*) incapable. **3.** (= *niezdatny*) unfit (*do czegoś* for sth); **niezdolny do pracy/służby wojskowej** unfit for work/military service.

niezdrowo *adv.* **1.** (= *w sposób świadczący o chorobie*) unhealthily; **wyglądać niezdrowo** look sick *l.* ill. **2.** (= *niekorzystnie dla zdrowia*) unhealthily.

niezdrowy *a.* **1.** (= *trochę chory*) unwell, unhealthy. **2.** (= *chorobliwy*) sickly, unhealthy;

(*cera*) sallow. **3.** (= *szkodliwy dla zdrowia*) unhealthy, unwholesome; (*klimat, miejsce*) insalubrious. **4.** (= *niewłaściwy*) morbid, unwholesome; **niezdrowa wyobraźnia** morbid imagination; **niezdrowy pogląd** morbid opinion.

niezdyscyplinowany *a.* undisciplined, recalcitrant.

niezgłębiony *a.* **1.** (= *bezdenny*) unfathomable, fathomless. **2.** (= *nieprzenikniony*) inscrutable, impenetrable; (*ciemność, lasy*) impenetrable. **3.** (= *niepojęty*) inscrutable, unfathomable.

niezgłoskotwórczy *a. jęz.* non-syllabic.

niezgoda *f.* disagreement, discord; **kość niezgody** bone of contention; **jabłko niezgody** apple of discord; **być w niezgodzie z czymś** be in conflict *l.* at variance with sth; **być** *l.* **żyć z kimś w niezgodzie** be at loggerheads with sb; **siać niezgodę** sow dissension *l.* division, spread discord.

niezgodnie *adv.* **1.** (= *kłótliwie*) quarrelsomely. **2.** (= *wbrew*) inconsistently (*z czymś* with); **postępować niezgodnie z prawem** violate the law. **3.** (= *rozbieżnie*) inconsistently, incompatibly.

niezgodność *f.* **1.** (= *kłótliwość*) quarrelsomeness. **2.** (= *sprzeczność*) inconsistency; **niezgodność czegoś z czymś** discrepancy *l.* disagreement between sth and sth. **3.** (= *rozbieżność*) inconsistency; (*charakterów, opinii*) incompatibility.

niezgodny *a.* **1.** (*małżeństwo, charakter*) quarrelsome. **2.** (= *sprzeczny*) inconsistent, not in agreement *l.* in keeping (*z czymś* with sth); **niezgodny z prawdą** contrary to the truth. **3.** (= *rozbieżny*) incompatible; (*poglądy, zeznania*) inconsistent.

niezgorszy *a. pot.* passable.

niezgrabnie *adv.* **1.** (= *nieforemnie*) shapelessly. **2.** (= *niezręcznie, nieporadnie*) clumsily, awkwardly.

niezgrabny *a.* **1.** (= *nieforemny*) unshapely, shapless. **2.** (= *niezręczny*) clumsy, awkward. **3.** (= *będący objawem nieudolności*) clumsy, awkward; (*ruch, ukłon*) ungainly. **4.** (= *pozbawiony elegancji*) ungainly, uncouth; (*styl*) awkward.

niezguła *f. l. mp decl. like f. Gen.pl.* -l *l.* -**ów** *pot.* oaf.

niezidentyfikowany *a.* unidentified; **niezidentyfikowany obiekt latający** unidentified flying object.

nieziemski *a.* **1.** (= *zachwycający*) unearthly, ethereal, heavenly. **2.** *pot.* (= *niezwykły*) unearthly; (*awantura, smród*) horrid.

nieziemsko *adv.* **1.** (= *zachwycająco*) ethereally, enchantingly. **2.** *pot.* (= *bardzo*) uncommonly, awfully.

nieziszczalny *a. lit.* unrealizable.

niezjadliwy *a.* **1.** (= *pozbawiony zjadliwości*) not virulent, unscathing. **2.** *pot.* (= *niesmaczny*) inedible.

niezliczony *a.* -**eni** innumerable, countless.

niezłomnie *adv.* steadfastly, unwaveringly.

niezłomność *f.* steadfastness, firmness.

niezłomny *a.* steadfast, unwavering, unshaken.

niezłośliwy *a.* **1.** (= *niedokuczliwy*) not malicious. **2.** *med.* benign.

niezłożony *a.* uncomplicated.

niezły *a.* **1.** (= *dość sumienny, dość dobry*) pretty good, not bad. **2.** (= *poczciwy, zacny*) quite nice; **niezły z niego numer!** *iron.* he's a fine bit of a knave. **3.** (= *dość dobrej jakości*) pretty good, not bad. **4.** (= *pozytywny*) pretty good; (*wiadomość, opinia, wrażenie*) positive. **5.** (*interes*) quite profitable. **6.** (*zarobek, kawałek, porcja*) considerable, quite large *l.* big.

niezmącony *a.* unbroken, undisturbed.

niezmiennie *adv. lit.* invariably.

niezmiennik *mi mat.* invariant.

niezmienność *f. lit.* invariability, permanence.

niezmiennotematowy *a. jęz.* of unchanging stem.

niezmienny *a.* invariable, permanent.

niezmiernie *adv. lit.* extremely, immensely.

niezmierny *a. lit.* extreme, immense, immeasurable.

niezmierzony *a.* immeasurable; (*bogactwa, tłum, obszar*) immense, vast.

niezmordowany *a.* unfatigued, persistent.

niezmysłowy *a.* unsensual.

niezmywalny *a.* indelible, ineffaceable.

nieznacznie *adv.* insignificantly.

nieznaczny *a.* insignificant.

nieznajomość *f.* ignorance (*czegoś* of sth).

nieznajomy *a.* unknown, unfamiliar. – *mp* stranger.

nieznane *n. Gen.* -**ego** the unknown; **jechać w nieznane** go into the unknown.

nieznany *a.* unknown; **Grób Nieznanego Żołnierza** Tomb of the Unknown Soldier.

niezniszczalność *f.* indestructibility.

niezniszczalny *a.* indestructible.

nieznośnie *adv.* **1.** (*hałaśliwy*) unbearably. **2.** (= *niegrzecznie*) annoyingly, unbearably, intolerably.

nieznośny *a.* **1.** (= *dokuczliwy*) unbearable, unendurable, trying, nagging. **2.** (*dziecko, uczeń*) unbearable.

niezobowiązujący *a.* (*strój*) casual, informal.

niezorganizowany *a.* disorganized, unorganized.

niezorientowany *a.* uninformed, not informed, ignorant.

niezrażony *a.* undeterred.

niezręcznie *adv.* **1.** (= *niezgrabnie*) clumsily, awkwardly, unskilfully. **2.** (= *niezbyt sprytnie, w sposób nieprzemyślany*) impoliticly. **3.** (= *żenująco*) embarrassingly.

niezręczność *f.* **1.** (= *niezdarność*) clumsiness, awkwardness. **2.** (= *niezręczny postępek, słowa*) blunder; **popełnić niezręczność** blunder. **3.** (= *brak sprytu, przemyślności*) impoliticness.

niezręczny *a.* **1.** (= *niezgrabny, niezdarny*) clumsy, awkward. **2.** (*dowcip, pytanie, sytuacja*) embarrassing. **3.** (= *pozbawiony sprytu,* *przemyślności*) unwise; (*polityk, wypowiedź*) impolitic, inexpedient.

niezrozumiale *adv.* **1.** (= *w sposób niezrozumiały*) incomprehensibly, unintelligibly. **2.** (= *w sposób nieuzasadniony*) unaccountably.

niezrozumiały *a.* **1.** (= *niejasny, zawiły*) incomprehensible, obscure. **2.** (= *nieuzasadniony*) unaccountable, inexplicable.

niezrozumienie *n.* lack of understanding, incomprehension; **spotkać się z niezrozumieniem** meet with incomprehension.

niezrównanie *adv.* exceedingly.

niezrównany *a.* unmatched, unequalled.

niezrównoważony *a.* **-eni 1.** (= *nieobliczalny*) unbalanced, ustable; (*człowiek, charakter, zachowanie*) unpredictable. **2.** (= *któremu brakuje równowagi*) unbalanced.

niezupełnie *adv.* not quite.

niezupełny *a.* incomplete; **przeobrażenie niezupełne** *ent.* incomplete metamorphosis.

niezwłocznie *adv.* promptly, immediately.

niezwłoczny *a.* prompt, immediate.

niezwrotny *a.* **1.** (= *z trudem się obracający*) unwieldy. **2.** (= *bezzwrotny*) non-returnable.

niezwyciężony *a.* **-eni 1.** (= *niepokonany*) invincible. **2.** *lit.* (*kłopoty, senność*) insurmountable.

niezwyczajny *a.* unusual.

niezwykle *adv.* **1.** (= *niecodziennie*) unusually. **2.** (= *bardzo*) extremely.

niezwykłość *f.* **1.** (= *bycie niezwykłym*) unusualness, uncommonness, extraordinariness. **2.** (= *niezwykły fakt*) oddity.

niezwykły *a.* unusual.

niezyskowny *a.* unprofitable.

nieźle *adv.* pretty *l.* fairly well.

nieżartobliwy *a.* unhumorous.

nieżeglowny *a. żegl.* unnavigable.

nieżelazny *a.* non-ferrous; **metale nieżelazne** *l.* **kolorowe** non-ferrous metals.

nieżonaty *a.* single, unmarried. – *mp* single *l.* unmarried man, bachelor.

nieżyciowy *a.* **1.** (= *niezaradny*) unrealistic. **2.** (= *niepraktyczny*) impracticable, unworkable.

nieżyczliwie *adv.* unkindly, unfriendly.

nieżyczliwość *f.* unkindness, unfriendliness.

nieżyczliwy *a.* **1.** (= *nieprzychylnie usposobiony*) unfriendly, unkind. **2.** (= *świadczący o braku przychylności*) unfavorable, unfriendly.

nieżyt *mi pat.* catarrh, inflammation of the mucuous membrane; **nieżyt nosa** rhinitis; **nieżyt żołądka** gastritis.

nieżywotny *a.* inanimate; **rzeczownik nieżywotny** *jęz.* inanimate noun.

nieżywy *a.* dead; **padł jak nieżywy** he dropped like dead (weight).

nigdy *adv.* never; (*w przeczeniach*) ever; **jak gdyby nigdy nic** as if nothing had happened; **jak nigdy** like never before; **nigdy w życiu** never in my life; **na święty nigdy** in the Never-Never Land, in your dreams; **z nim nigdy nic nie wiadomo** you never know with him; **(już) nigdy więcej** never again.

nigdzie *adv.* nowhere; (*w przeczeniach i pytaniach*) anywhere; **nigdzie indziej** nowhere else.

Niger *mi* **-gr-** *geogr.* Niger.

Nigeria *f. Gen.* **-ii** *geogr.* Nigeria.

Nigeryjczyk *mp* Nigerian.

Nigeryjka *f. zob.* **Nigeryjczyk**.

nigeryjski *a.* Nigerian.

nihilista *mp fil., polit.* nihilist.

nihilistyczny *a. fil., polit.* nihilist, nihilistic.

nihilizm *mi fil., polit.* nihilism.

nijak *adv. pot.* in no way; **nijak nie mogę cię zrozumieć** there is no way I can understand you.

nijaki *a.* (= *przeciętny*) nondescript, mediocre; **rodzaj nijaki** *jęz.* neuter.

nijako *adv.* **1.** (= *w sposób nijaki*) nondescriptly. **2.** *pot.* (= *niezbyt dobrze*) unwell. **3.** *pot.* (= *nietaktownie, niezręcznie*) improperly; **nijako iść z wizytą w takim stroju** it's improper to pay a visit in the clothes like these.

NIK *abbr.* (= *Najwyższa Izba Kontroli*) Supreme Board of State Audit; (*oficjalnie zalecana nazwa*) Supreme Chamber of Control.

Nikaragua *f. Gen.* **-ui** *geogr.* Nicaragua.

nikaraguański *a.* Nicaraguan.

nikczemnie *adv.* meanly.

nikczemnik *mp* scoundrel, villain.

nikczemność *f.* **1.** (= *bycie nikczemnym*) meanness. **2.** (= *nikczemny postępek*) meanness, villainy.

nikczemny *a.* **1.** (*człowiek*) mean, villainous. **2.** (= *będący oznaką podłości*) mean, villainous.

Nike *f. indecl. mit.* Nike.

nikiel *mi* **-kl-** *chem.* nickel.

nikielin *mi min.* niccolite.

nikielina *f. metal.* nickeline.

nikim *pron. zob.* **nikt**.

niklować *ipf.* nickel(-plate).

niklowanie *n.* nickel-plating.

niklowany *a.* nickel-plated.

niklowce *pl. Gen.* **-ów** *chem.* nickel group.

niklowy *a.* **1.** (= *zrobiony z niklu*) nickelic. **2.** *pot.* (= *niklowany*) nickel-plated.

nikły *a.* (= *słaby*) (*blask, woń, zarys, światło*) faint; (*szansa, nadzieja*) slender.

niknąć *ipf.* **-ij, -nął** *l.* **-kł 1.** (= *znikać*) vanish. **2.** (= *przestawać istnieć*) fade away, perish. **3.** *lit.* (*o chorym, słabnąć*) sink; **niknąć w oczach** sink fast.

nikogo *pron. zob.* **nikt**.

nikomu *pron. zob.* **nikt**.

nikotyna *f. chem.* nicotine.

nikotynizm *mi pat.* nicotinism.

nikotynowy *a.* nicotine; **kwas nikotynowy** *chem.* nicotinic acid.

Nikozja *f. geogr.* Nicosia.

nikt *pron. Gen. i Acc.* **nikogo** *Dat.* **nikomu** *Ins. i Loc.* **nikim** nobody, no one; (*w przeczeniach i pytaniach*) anybody, anyone; **nikt a nikt** not a soul; **nikt inny** nobody else; **nikt z nas** none of us; **być nikim** be nobody; **umie tańczyć jak nikt** he is an unmatched dancer, no one can dance as good as him.

Nil *mi geogr.* the Nile.

nim¹ *pron.* (*on*) him; (*ono*) it; *por.* **on, ono.**

nim² *conj.* before; *por.* **zanim.**

nimb *mi* **1.** *lit.* (= *aureola*) halo, aureole, nimbus. **2.** *lit.* (= *świetność*) glory; **otoczony nimbem sławy** in a blaze of glory.

nimbostratus *mi Gen.* **-a** *meteor.* nimbostratus.

nimbus *a. meteor.* nimbus, rain cloud.

nimfa *f.* **1.** *mit.* nymph; **nimfa morska** nereid, sea nymph; **nimfa leśna** wood nymph. **2.** *zool., ent.* nymph.

nimfetka *f.* nymphet.

nimfomania *f. Gen.* **-ii** *pat.* nymphomania.

nimfomanka *f.* nymphomaniac.

nimi *pron.* them; *por.* **one, oni.**

niniejszy *a. lit.* present; **niniejszym oświadczam, że...** I hereby declare that...; **niniejszym zaświadcza się, że...** this is to certify that...

Niniwa *f. hist.* Nineveh.

ninja *mp* ninja.

niob *mi chem.* niobium.

Niobe *f. indecl. mit.* Niobe.

niobit *mi min.* columbite, niobite.

niosę *itd. ipf. zob.* **nieść.**

nioska *f.* laying hen.

niósł *itd. ipf. zob.* **nieść.**

NIP *abbr.* (= *numer identyfikacji podatkowej*) Tax *l.* Taxpayer Identification Number.

nipa *f. bot.* nipa (*Nypa fruticans*).

nirwana *f.* nirvana.

niski *a.* **1.** (= *mający niewielką wysokość, wzrost*) (*dom, drzewo*) low; (*człowiek*) short. **2.** (= *znajdujący się niewysoko*) low; **niski ukłon** deep bow. **3.** (= *pośledni*) low, humble; **ktoś/coś niskiego lotu** sb/sth mediocre. **4.** (*cena, temperatura, ciśnienie*) low. **5.** (= *nikczemny*) mean, base. **6.** (*o głosie*) low, deep.

nisko *adv.* **1.** (= *niewysoko*) low. **2.** (= *niewysoko w hierarchii*) low; **nisko kogoś cenić** not think much of sb; **upaść nisko** be debased. **3.** (= *o cenach itp.*) low; **on jest nisko notowany** he is rated low. **4.** (*o głosie*) low, deeply.

niskoalkoholowy *a.* low-proof, low-alcohol.

niskobiałkowy *a.* low-protein.

niskociśnieniowy *a. techn.* low-pressure.

niskogatunkowy *a.* low-grade, poor quality.

niskokaloryczny *a.* low-calorie.

niskonapięciowy *a. el.* low-voltage.

niskopienny *a.* (*o roślinach*) dwarf.

niskopodwoziowy *a. gł. mot.* low-clearance.

niskoprężny *a. techn.* low-compression; **silnik niskoprężny** low-compression engine.

niskoprocentowy *a.* **1.** (= *zawierający niewielki procent*) low-grade; (*alkohol, roztwór*) weak. **2.** (*kredyt, pożyczka*) low-interest.

niskostopowy *a. metal.* low-alloyed.

niskotłuszczowy *a.* low-fat.

niskotopliwy *a. techn.* fusible, low-melting.

niskowęglowy *a. metal.* low-carbon.

niskowrzący *a. techn.* low-boiling.

nisza *f.* niche; **nisza ekologiczna** *biol.* ecological niche.

niszczarka *f.* (*dokumentów*) shredder.

niszcząco *adv.* destructively.

niszczeć *ipf.* **-eje** become spoiled *l.* ruined, deteriorate.

niszczuka *f. icht.* longnose gar (*Lepisosteus osseus*).

niszczyciel *mp* destroyer, demolisher. – *mi Gen.* **-a** *wojsk., żegl.* destroyer.

niszczycielski *a.* destructive, devastating.

niszczyć *ipf.* **1.** (= *burzyć, psuć*) destroy, devastate. **2.** (= *zużywać*) wear (out). **3.** (= *unicestwiać*) exterminate, anihilate; (*akta, dokumenty, chwasty*) destroy; **niszczyć czyjś spokój** *przen.* ruin sb's peace. **4.** (= *osłabiać*) shatter; (*organizm, włosy*) ruin. **5.** *pot.* (= *zwalczać*) fight. **~ się** *ipf.* **1.** (= *ulegać uszkodzeniu*) deteriorate, get spoiled. **2.** (= *tracić zdrowie, osłabiać się*) ruin one's health. **3.** (= *niszczyć siebie wzajemnie*) destroy each other *l.* one another.

nit *mi techn.* rivet.

nitka *f.* **1.** (= *nić*) thread; **nitka dentystyczna** dental floss; **dojść** *l.* **trafić po nitce do kłębka** unravel sth; **nie zostawić na kimś suchej nitki** pick sb to pieces; **zgrać się do nitki** lose one's shirt; **przemoknięty do suchej nitki** dripping *l.* soaking wet. **2.** (= *coś, co przypomina nić*) thread; **nitka rurociągu** pipe, pipeline; **nitka pajęczyny** thread, cobweb; **makaron nitki** *kulin.* vermicelli. **3.** *bot.* (*pręcika*) filament.

nitkowaty *a.* thread-like; **tętno nitkowate** *med.* filiform *l.* thready pulse.

nitnikowce *pl. Gen.* **-ów** *zool.* hairworms (*Gordiacea*).

nitować *ipf.* rivet.

nitowanie *n.* riveting.

nitownica *f.* riveting machine, riveter.

nitownik *mi Gen.* **-a** squeeze riveter.

nitratyn *mi min.* Chile nitre.

nitroanilina *f. chem.* nitroaniline.

nitrobakterie *pl. biol.* nitrobacteria.

nitrobenzen *mi chem.* nitrobenzene.

nitroceluloza *f. chem.* nitrocellulose.

nitrocelulozowy *a. chem.* nitrocellulosic, nitrocellulous.

nitrofenol *mi chem.* nitrophenol.

nitrofil *ma bot.* nitrophilous plant.

nitrogliceryna *f. chem.* nitroglycerin, nitroglycerine.

nitrować *ipf. chem.* nitrate.

nitrowanie *n. chem.* nitration.

nitrowy *a. chem.* nitric; **grupa nitrowa** nitro group.

nitrozwiązek *mi Gen. pl.* **-ów** *chem.* nitro compound.

nitryfikacja *f. chem.* nitrification.

nitryfikacyjny *a. biol.* nitrification, nitrifying; **bakteria nitryfikacyjna** nitrifying bacteria.

nitryfikator *ma biol.* nitrifier.

nitryfikować *ipf. chem.* nitrify.

nitryt *mi min.* niter, *Br.* nitre; potassium nitrate.

niuans *mi pl.* **-e** nuance.

niuch *mi Gen.* **-a 1.** *przest.* (= *szczypta tabaki*) pinch (*of snuff*). **2.** *żart.* (= *nos*) nose; **mieć niucha (do czegoś)** *pot.* (= *mieć wyczucie*) have a nose (for sth).

niuchać *ipf.* **1.** *pot.* (= *wąchać*) sniff. **2.** *pot.* (= *szukać*) nose around (*za czymś* for sth).

niuton *mi Gen.* **-a** *fiz.* newton.

niwa *f.* **1.** *poet.* (= *pole*) field. **2.** *lit.* (= *dziedzina*) arena; **działać/pracować na niwie (społecznej)** *przen.* be active/work in the (public) arena.

niwacja *f. geol.* nivation.

niwalny *a. geol.* nival.

niweczyć *ipf.* (*plany*) thwart; (*nadzieje*) dash; (*spokój*) shatter.

niwelacja *f.* (= *wyrównywanie terenu*) *miern.* (= *pomiary*) levelling.

niwelacyjny *a.* levelling.

niwelator *mi Gen.* **-a** *miern.* surveyor's level.

niwelować *ipf.* (*teren, różnicę*) *miern.* (= *dokonywać pomiarów*) level.

nizać *ipf.* **niżę niżesz** (*na sznurek*) string; (*na nitkę*) thread.

nizaryta *mp rel., hist.* Assassin, Nizari Isma'ilite.

nizina *f.* lowland.

nizinny *a.* lowland; (*region*) low-lying; **bydło nizinne** Holsteins; *Br.* Friesians.

niziuteńki *a. zob.* **niziutki.**

niziutki *a.* (*o człowieku*) knee-high, tiny; (*o murze, stole*) very low; (*o ukłonie*) down to the ground; (*o poziomie*) pitifully low.

niż[1] *conj.* than; **(nie) więcej niż** (no) more than; **jest wyższy niż jego brat** he is taller than his brother; **jest więcej niż ładna** she is more than just pretty.

niż[2] *mi Gen.pl.* **-ów 1.** (= *nizina*) lowland. **2.** (= *niski poziom*) low; **niż demograficzny** drop in the birth rate. **3.** (= *obszar niskiego ciśnienia*) depression, low; **niż baryczny** barometric low.

niżby *conj.* than.

niżej *adv. comp.* lower, below; **niżej podpisany** the undersigned; **niżej wymieniony** mentioned below; **piętro niżej** downstairs; *por.* **nisko.**

niżeli *conj przest.* = **niż**[1].

niżeliby *conj., przest.* = **niżby.**

niżowy *a.* **1.** (*dotyczący niziny*) lowland. **2.** (*dotyczący atmosferycznego*) low.

niższość *f.* inferiority; **kompleks niższości** inferiority complex; **mieć poczucie niższości** have a sense *l.* feeling of inferiority.

niższy *a. comp.* **1.** (= *mniej wysoki*) (*przedmiot*) lower; (*człowiek*) shorter. **2.** (= *gorszy, pośledniejszy*) (*jakość*) inferior; (*kategoria*) subordinate; (*ranga*) junior, lower; **izba niższa** *parl.* lower house; *por.* **niski.**

NMP *abbr.* BVM (= *Beata Virgo Maria*) (= *Blessed Virgin Mary*).

no *particle* **1.** *pot.* (*w trybie rozkazującym*) o.k., alright; **no już!** come on!; **no dalej!** go on! **2.** *pot.* (= *tak*) o.k., yeah, sure; **Chcesz jeść? - No.** Do you want something to eat? - Sure. **3.** *pot.* (*zastępuje pytanie*) what; **Wiesz co się stało? - No?** You know what happened? - What? **4.** *pot.* (*wtrącenie wewnątrz wypowiedzi*) well; **no nie?** right?, o.k.?, yeah?; **no to co?** so what?; **no to do jutra** o.k., see you tomorrow; **no dobrze, pojedziemy** o.k. *l.* alright, we'll go; **no wiesz, jak mogłeś?** jeez, how could you? – *int.* **1.** (*wyraża pogróżkę*)

now; **no, no, tylko nie tak ostro** now, now, not so hard. **2.** (*wyraża podziw, zdumienie*) well; **no, no, niezły z niego numer!** well, well, isn't he something; **no proszę!** there you go!; **no pewnie!** you bet!

Nobel *mi* **-bl-** *Gen.* **-a** *pot.* (= *Nagroda Nobla*) Nobel prize.

nobel *mi* **-bl-** *Gen.* **-a** *chem.* nobelium.

nobil *mp pl.* **-owie** *hist.* noble.

nobilitacja *f.* **1.** (= *nadanie szlachectwa*) ennoblement. **2.** (= *podniesienie prestiżu, rangi*) distinguishment.

nobilitować *ipf.* **1.** (= *nadawać szlachectwo*) ennoble, knight. **2.** (= *podnosić rangę*) distinguish, dignify.

noblista *mp* Nobel prize winner.

nobliwy *a.* distinguished.

noc *f. pl.* **-e** night; **noc polarna** arctic night; **noc świętojańska** midsummer night; **noc zimowa/letnia** winter/summer night; **białe noce** white nights; **gwiaździsta noc** starry night; **nocą** *l.* **w nocy** at night; **Paryż nocą** Paris by night; **(w) dzień i noc** day and night; **co noc** every night, nightly; **noc w noc** night after night; **od świtu do nocy** from morning till night; **pracować od świtu do nocy** burn the candle at both ends; **po nocy** at night; **brzydki jak noc** ugly as the devil; **w nocy z czwartku na piątek** the night from Thursday to Friday; **uczyć się po nocach** study at night, burn the midnight oil studying; **zostać na noc** stay for the night; **życzyć komuś dobrej nocy** say goodnight to sb.

nocek *ma* **-ck-** *zool.* a bat of the genus Myotis.

nochal *mi Gen.* **-a** beak, hooter.

nocka *f. pot.* (= *nocna zmiana*) night shift; *pot.* graveyard shift.

nocleg *mi* a place to spend the night, lodgings; **dawać komuś nocleg** put sb up for the night; **zatrzymać się (gdzieś) na nocleg** stop (somewhere) for the night.

noclegownia *f. Gen.pl.* **-i** lodgings.

noclegowy *a.* **dom noclegowy** lodging house.

nocnicówki *pl. ent.* noctuids (*Noctuidae*).

nocnik *mi Gen.* **-a** chamber pot; (*dla dzieci*) potty.

nocny *a.* night; (*zwierzę*) nocturnal; **nocny autobus** night bus; **nocny marek** night owl, nighthawk; **koszula nocna** nightshirt.

nocoświetlik *ma zool.* Noctiluca miliaris (*Noctiluca miliaris*).

nocować *ipf.* **1.** (= *spędzać gdzieś noc*) spend the night, stay for the night. **2.** (= *dawać komuś nocleg*) put up (for the night).

Noe *mp Gen.* **Noego** *Bibl.* Noah; **arka Noego** Noah's Ark.

noga *f. Gen.pl.* **nóg 1.** (= *kończyna dolna*) leg; **do nogi!** here!, come!; **w nogi!** run!; **do nogi broń!** ground arms!; **kula u nogi** ball and chain, albatross; **do góry nogami** upside down; **na jednej nodze** (= *szybko*) on the double; **co sił w nogach** as fast as one's legs can carry one; **ktoś kuty na cztery nogi** a sly old fox; **brać nogi za pas** take to one's heels; **bronić się przed czymś rękami i nogami** fight sth tooth and nail; **być (od rana) na**

nogach to be one one's feet (all day); **być jedną nogą na tamtym świecie** have one foot in the grave; **dać nogę** *pot.* make tracks; **iść noga za nogą** walk at a snail's pace; **lecieć** *l.* **padać z nóg** be on one's last legs; **mieć iksowate nogi** be bow-legged; **nakryć się nogami** *pot.* (= *przewrócić się*) take a tumble, fall head over heels; **poczuć grunt pod nogami** feel on solid ground; **tracić grunt pod nogami** be out of one's depth; **podstawić komuś nogę** trip sb up; **postawić kogoś na nogi** get *l.* put sb on his *l.* her feet; **powłóczyć nogami** shuffle one's feet; **przewrócić coś do góry nogami** (= *rozrzucić bezładnie*) turn sth upside down; **rzucać komuś kłody pod nogi** put a spoke in sb's wheel; **stanąć na nogi** *l.* **nogach** (= *dorobić się*) stand on one's feet (again); (= *wyzdrowieć*) get back on one's feet; **ściąć kogoś z nóg** knock sb off his *l.* her feet; **traktować kogoś per noga** *żart.* not give sb an ounce of respect; **wstać lewą nogą** get up on the wrong side of the bed; **wyciągać nogi** pick up one's pace; **wyciągnąć nogi** (= *umrzeć*) kick the bucket; **wybić co do nogi** kill every last one; **choroba ścięła go z nóg** he was off his feet with an illness; **moja noga tu więcej nie postanie** I'll never set foot here again; **noga mu się powinęła** (= *przewrócił się*) he tripped over himself; (= *popełnił błąd*) he slipped up; **nie czuję nóg** my legs are failing me. **2.** (= *stopa*) foot. **3.** (*część sprzętu*) foot; **w nogach łóżka** at the foot of the bed. **4.** *pot.* (= *niedołęga*) twerp, goof; **noga z chemii** sb hopeless at chemistry.

nogawka *f.* (pant) leg; *Br.* (trouser) leg.

nokaut *mi sport* knockout; **nokaut techniczny** technical knockout; **przegrać przez nokaut** lose by knockout.

nokautować *ipf.* knock out.

nokdaun *mi sport* knockdown.

noks *mi Gen.* **-a** *fiz.* nox.

noktowizja *f.* noctovision, night vision.

noktowizor *mi Gen.* **-a** night vision device.

noktowizyjny *a.* noctovision, night vision.

nokturn *mi mal., muz., teor.lit.* nocturne.

NOL *abbr.* (= *niezidentyfikowany obiekt latający*) UFO (= *unidentified flying object*).

nomada *mp pl.* **-owie** *l.* **-dzi** nomad.

nomadyczny *a.* nomadic.

nomadyzm *mi* nomadism.

nomenklatura *f.* **1.** (= *nazewnictwo*) nomenclature. **2.** (*zwł. postkomunistyczna*) nomenklatura.

nomen omen *indecl.* nomen omen, the name is the sign of the thing.

nominacja *f.* **1.** (*na stanowisko*) appointment; **dostać nominację na ministra** be appointed minister. **2.** (*w wyborach, do nagrody*) nomination (*do czegoś* for sth).

nominacyjny *a.* (*na stanowisko*) appointment; (*w wyborach, do nagrody*) nomination; **pismo nominacyjne** letter of appointment.

nominalista *mp fil.* nominalist.

nominalistyczny *a. fil.* nominalist.

nominalizm *mi fil.* nominalism.

nominalnie *adv.* nominally.

nominalny *a.* **1.** (= *formalny*) nominal; **płaca**

nominalna nominal wages; **wartość nominalna** face value. **2.** *techn.* (= *znamionowy*) duty.

nominał *mi* **1.** *ekon.* denomination; **banknot o nominale 100 złotych** a 100 zloty bill. **2.** (*cena książki*) list price.

nominatywny *a. gram.* nominative.

nominować *ipf.* (*w wyborach, do nagrody*) nominate; (*na stanowisko, stopień*) appoint.

nominowany *a.* (*w wyborach, do nagrody*) nominated; (*na stanowisko, stopień*) appointed (*do czegoś* to (do) sth).

nomogeneza *f. biol.* nomogenesis.

nomografia *f. Gen.* **-ii** *mat.* nomography.

nomogram *mi mat.* nomogram, nomograph.

nomokanon *mi hist.* nomocanon.

nomokracja *f. polit.* nomocracy.

nomologia *f.* nomology.

nomologiczny *a.* nomological.

nomos *mi muz.* nomos.

nomotetyczny *a.* nomothetic, nomothetical.

nona *f. muz.* ninth.

nonajron *a. indecl.* noniron. – *mi* noniron fabric.

nonet *mi muz.* (*utwór*) (*zespół*) nonet.

noniusz *mi Gen.* **-a** *Gen.pl.* **-y** *l.* **-ów** vernier.

nonkonformista *mp* **1.** (= *człowiek niestosujący się do norm*) nonconformist. **2.** *rel.* Nonconformist.

nonkonformistyczny *a.* **1.** (= *niestosujący się do norm*) nonconformist. **2.** *rel.* Nonconformist.

nonkonformizm *mi* **1.** (= *niestosowanie się do norm*) nonconformism. **2.** *rel.* Nonconformity, Nonconformism.

nonowy *a. muz.* **akord nonowy** ninth chord, ninth.

nonparel *mi druk.* nonpareil.

nonsens *mi* **1.** (= *brak sensu*) nonsense, absurdity. **2.** (= *niedorzeczne słowa, postępek*) nonsense.

nonsensowność *f.* nonsensicalness, nonsensicality; absurdity.

nonsensowny *a.* nonsensical.

non stop *adv.* (*grać, jechać*) nonstop; (*być otwartym*) (*o sklepie, barze*) round-the-clock, around-the-clock. – *a. indecl.* nonstop.

nonszalancja *f.* nonchalance.

nonszalancki *a.* nonchalant.

nonszalancko *adv.* nonchalantly.

nora *f.* **1.** (*królika, lisa*) burrow; (*wilka*) den; (*myszy*) hole. **2.** *pot.* (= *obskurne pomieszczenie*) hole.

noradrenalina *f. biochem.* noradrenaline, noradrenalin.

nordycki *a.* Nordic.

nordyk *mp antrop.* Nordic.

noria *f.* (*narzędzie*) noria.

norka *f.* **1.** (= *mała nora*) burrow. **2.** *zool.* mink (*Mustela*); **norka amerykańska** American mink (*Mustela vison*); **norka europejska** European mink (*Mustela lutreola*).

norki *pl. Gen.* **-ek** (= *futro z norek*) mink.

norma *f.* **1.** (= *reguła*) norm, standard; **norma językowa** linguistic norm; **norma moralna** moral standard; **norma techniczna** technical norm;

zgodny z normą in accordance with a standard. **2.** (= *ustalona ilość, granica*) quota; (= *ilość pracy*) norm; **norma czasu** time quota; **wykonać normę** meet *l.* fulfill a quota; **wracać do normy** be back to normal. **3.** *druk.* signature.

normalizacja *f.* **1.** (= *standaryzacja*) standardization. **2.** (= *uporządkowanie*) normalization.

normalizacyjny *a.* standardization.

normalizować *ipf.* **1.** (= *standaryzować*) standardize. **2.** (= *porządkować, normować*) normalize. **~ się** *ipf.* normalize.

normalka *f. pot.* sth normal; **nie przejmuj się, to normalka** don't worry, that's normal.

normalna *f. Gen.* **-ej** *geom.* normal.

normalnie *adv.* normally.

normalnieć *ipf.* (= *stawać się normalnym*) normalize; (= *powracać do normy*) return to normal.

normalność *f.* **1.** (= *zgodność z normą*) normality, normalcy. **2.** (= *pełnia władz umysłowych*) normality, sanity.

normalnotorowy *a. kol.* standard-gauge.

normalny *a.* **1.** (= *zgodny z normą*) normal. **2.** (= *zwykły*) normal, usual; (*godziny pracy, odjazdu*) regular; (*bilet*) full fare. **3.** (= *zdrowy psychicznie*) normal, sane.

Normandia *f. Gen.* **-ii** *geogr.* Normandy.

normandzki *a.* Norman.

Normanowie *pl. Gen.* **-nów** the Normans.

normatyw *mi* standard, norm.

normatywista *mp prawn.* normativist.

normatywistyczny *a. prawn.* normativist.

normatywizm *mi prawn.* normativism.

normatywność *f.* normativeness.

normatywny *a.* **1.** (= *ustalający normy*) normative; **nauki normatywne** normative sciences. **2.** (= *zgodny z normą*) standard.

normować *ipf.* standardize. **~ się** *ipf.* return to normal, normalize.

nornica ruda *f. zool.* bank vole (*Clethrionomys glareolus*).

nornik *ma* **1.** *zool.* vole (*Microtus*). **2.** *myśl.* dog for pursuing fox or badger below ground (*such as dachshund or terrier*).

Norweg *mp pl.* **-owie** *l.* **-dzy** Norwegian.

Norwegia *f. Gen.* **-ii** *geogr.* Norway.

norweski *a.* Norwegian; **kombinacja norweska** *sport* Nordic combination.

Norweżka *f.* Norwegian (woman).

Norymberga *f. geogr.* Nuremberg.

norymberski *a.* Nuremberg; **procesy norymberskie** *hist.* Nuremberg trials.

nos *mi Gen.* **-a 1.** (= *narząd powonienia*) nose; **orli nos** Roman nose, hook nose; **zadarty nos** pug nose; **pod nosem** (= *blisko*) (right) under one's nose; (= *niewyraźnie*) (*powiedzieć coś*) under one's breath; (= *w czyjejś bliskości*) in one's face; **dać komuś po nosie** cut sb down to size, take sb down a peg (or two); **kręcić nosem (na coś)** tun one's nose up (at sth); **mieć mleko pod nosem** be wet behind the ears; **mieć muchy w nosie (z powodu czegoś)** be ticked off (about sth); **mieć (dobrego) nosa (do czegoś)** have a (good) nose (for sth); **mieć kogoś/czegoś po dziurki w nosie** be

sick and tired of sb/sth; **mieć kogoś/coś w nosie** not care less about sb/sth, not give a darn *l.* hoot about sb/sth; **mówić przez nos** talk through one's nose; **nie widzieć dalej niż czubek własnego nosa** not see past the end of one's nose; **pilnować własnego nosa** mind one's own business; **podtykać coś komuś pod nos** put sth in sb's face; **przytrzeć** *l.* **utrzeć komuś nosa** rake sb over the coals; **sprzątnąć coś komuś sprzed nosa** grab sth (out) from under sb's nose; **wodzić kogoś za nos** lead sb (around) by the nose, play with sb; **wtykać** *l.* **wściubiać nos w coś** (= *wtrącać się*) stick *l.* poke one's nose into sth; **zadzierać nosa** go around with one's nose (up) in the air; **zatrzasnąć komuś drzwi przed nosem** slam the door in sb's face; **zaryć nosem** fall on one's face; **zwąchać pismo nosem** smell a rat; **zwiesić nos na kwintę** hang one's head down; **idzie jak krew z nosa** it is a real drag. **2.** (= *spiczasty koniec*) nose; (*buta*) toe; (*nart*) tip.

nosacizna *f. pat., wet.* glanders.

nosacz *ma zool.* proboscis monkey (*Nasalis larvatus*).

nosek *mi* **-sk-** *Gen.* **-a 1.** (= *mały nos*) little nose. **2.** (= *czubek*) (*buta, narty*) tip. **3.** *sport* (= *uchwyt na pedał roweru*) toe cap.

nosiciel *mp,* **nosicielka** *f.* **1.** (*ten, kto nosi*) carrier; (*noszący ubranie*) wearer. **2.** (= *reprezentant idei itp.*) apostle, advocate. **3.** *med.* carrier.

nosicielstwo *n. pat.* carrier state.

nosić *ipf.* **-szę -sisz 1.** (= *dźwigać*) carry; **nosić kogoś na barana** give sb a piggyback ride; **nosić kogoś na rękach** (= *dogadzać komuś*) dote on sb; **nosić kogoś/coś w pamięci** *przen.* cherish the memory of sb/sth; **nosić żal** *l.* **urazę** *przen.* bear a grudge; **gdzie cię znowu (licho) niesie?** *pot.* where (the heck) are you off to this time? **2.** (= *mieć przy sobie*) carry. **3.** (= *ubierać się w coś*) wear; **nosić żałobę** wear black; **tego się już nie nosi** that's out of style; **jaki numer butów pani nosi?** what size shoe do you wear, madam? **4.** (= *mieć coś jako cechę*) bear, have; **nosić brodę/wąsy/długie włosy** have *l.* wear a beard/mustache/long hair; **nosić głowę wysoko** hold one's head high; **nosić nazwisko/tytuł** bear a name/title; **nosić ślady (dawnej świetności)** bears signs (of former glory). **~ się** *ipf.* **1.** (= *zachowywać się w określony sposób*) carry o.s.; **nosić się z czymś jak kura z jajkiem** (= *afiszować się*) go around bragging about sth; (= *rozważać*) sit on the fence; **nosić się z zamiarem (zrobienia czegoś)** (= *zamierzać*) intend (to do sth); (= *rozważać*) contemplate (doing sth). **2.** (= *ubierać się w określony sposób*) dress; **nosić się elegancko** dress elegantly.

nosidełko *n. Gen.pl.* **-ek** baby carrier.

nosidło *n. Gen.pl.* **-deł** yoke.

nosorożec *ma* **-żc-** *zool.* rhinoceros (*Rhinocerotidae*).

nosowo *adv.* nasally.

nosowość *f. jęz.* nasality.

nosowy *a.* nasal; **głos nosowy** nasal voice; **głoska nosowa** *jęz.* nasal.

nosówka f. 1. jęz. nasal. 2. pat., wet. distemper.

nostalgia f. Gen. -ii nostalgia.

nostalgiczny a. nostalgic.

nostryfikacja f. recognition (of a foreign academic degree or diploma).

nostryfikacyjny a. recognition.

nostryfikować ipf. recognize (a degree or diploma).

nostrzyk mi Gen. -a bot. melilot, sweet clover (Melilot).

nosze pl. Gen. -y stretcher.

noszenie n. lotn. lift.

nośnik mi Gen. -a 1. (czynnik, urządzenie przenoszące coś) carrier; **nośnik ciepła** heat carrier, heating medium; **nośnik danych** komp. data carrier; **nośnik transportowy** transportation carrier. 2. chem. carrier.

nośność f. 1. (= dopuszczalne obciążenie) carrying capacity; (statku) deadweight; (mostu) load capacity. 2. (= zdolność przenoszenia) (rzeki, wiatru) force, strength. 3. (= donośność) (broni, głosu) range. 4. (o kurze) egg production.

nośny a. 1. (= znoszący duże obciążenie) bearing, carrying. 2. (= przenoszący) carrying; **płat nośny** lotn. wing; **rakieta nośna** booster rocket; **siła nośna** carrying capacity. 3. (= donośny) (broń) wide-range; (głos) loud. 4. (= nieśny) egg laying. 5. (= wyrazisty) expressive.

NOT abbr. (= Naczelna Organizacja Techniczna) Polish Federation of Engineering Associations.

nota f. 1. polit. (pismo) note; **nota dyplomatyczna** diplomatic note; **nota protestacyjna** note of protest. 2. (= ocena) grade; **nota redakcyjna** editor's note. 3. ekon. note.

notabene adv. indecl. by the way, incidentally.

notable pl. Gen. -i l. -ów lit. (the) notables.

notacja f. notation.

notarialnie adv. before a notary; **uwierzytelnić notarialnie** notarize.

notarialny a. notarial; **akt notarialny** notarial deed; **biuro notarialne** notary public's office.

notariat mi notary public's office.

notariusz mp pl. -e l. -owie Gen. -y l. -ów notary public.

notatka f. note; **robić notatki** take notes.

notatnik mi Gen. -a 1. (zeszyt) notebook. 2. (np. z podróży) notes.

notebook mi Gen. -a komp. laptop, notebook computer.

notes mi notebook, diary; (z adresami) address book.

notka f. 1. (= przypis) footnote; **notka edytorska** editor's note. 2. (= notatka prasowa) note.

notorycznie adv. notoriously.

notoryczny a. 1. (= niepoprawny) notorious. 2. (= powtarzający się) habitual, chronic.

notować ipf. 1. (= robić notatki) write down, take notes (coś of sth). 2. (= rejestrować) record (coś sth); keep a record (coś of sth); (na giełdzie)

quote; **notować coś w pamięci** make a mental note of sth.

notowanie n. 1. (np. wykładu) taking notes. 2. (= rejestrowanie) recording. 3. ekon. quotation.

notowany a. (= rejestrowany) recorded; (kurs, cena) quoted; **być notowanym** (w kartotekach policji) have a record; **być wysoko/nisko notowanym** be highly/poorly regarded.

notyfikacja f. prawn. notification.

notyfikować ipf. prawn. notify.

noumenon mi fil. noumenon.

novum n. indecl. novelty.

nowa f. astron. nova.

Nowa Anglia f. Gen. -ii geogr. New England.

Nowa Fundlandia f. Gen. -ii geogr. Newfoundland.

Nowa Gwinea f. Gen. -ii geogr. New Guinea.

nowalijka f. early vegetable.

Nowa Szkocja f. geogr. Nova Scotia.

nowator mp innovator.

nowatorka f. innovator.

nowatorski a. innovative.

nowatorstwo n. innovation.

Nowa Zelandia f. Gen. -ii geogr. New Zealand.

nowe n. Gen. -ego wind of change; **idzie nowe** the wind of change is blowing.

nowe n. decl. like a. (= to co nowe) the new; **walka starego z nowym** the battle between the old and the new.

nowela[1] f. teor.lit. short story, novella.

nowela[2] f. prawn. amendment.

nowelista mp, **nowelistka** f. short-story writer.

nowelistyka f. short-story writing.

nowelizacja f. prawn. amendment.

nowelizować ipf. prawn. ammend.

nowenna f. rz.-kat. novena.

nowicjat mi novitiate, noviciate.

nowicjusz mp Gen.pl. -y l. -ów, **nowicjuszka** f. t. rel. novice; **być nowicjuszem w czymś** be a novice at sth.

nowik mi bot. closterium (Closterium).

nowina f. 1. (= wieść) (piece of) news; **dobra nowina** (= ewangelia) the Good News; **to mi** l. **dla mnie nie nowina** that's nothing new to me. 2. (= teren świeżo wzięty pod uprawę) virgin land.

nowinka f. 1. (= błaha nowina) (bit of) news. 2. (= nowość) novelty.

nowinkarstwo n. (= wprowadzanie nowości, nowinek) innovating, innovation.

nowinkarz mp 1. (= człowiek lubiący nowości) innovator. 2. (= ten, kto powtarza plotki, nowinki) gossip monger.

nowiu itd. mi zob. **nów**.

nowiutki a. brand-new.

nowo adv. newly; **nowo mianowany** newly appointed; **na nowo** (= od początku) anew, from the beginning; **czuć się jak nowo narodzony** feel like a newborn; **być jak nowo narodzone dziecko** be like a newborn.

nowobogacki a. nouveau riche. – mp nouveau riche.

nowoczesność f. modernity, modernness; **no-**

woczesność koncepcji innovativeness of an idea.

nowoczesny *a.* modern; (= *współczesny, teraźniejszy*) current, contemporary, present-day; (= *postępowy*) novel, innovative, pioneering, new; (= *uwzględniający najnowsze osiągnięcia*) advanced; **nowoczesne poglądy** progressive views, new thinking; **nowoczesne rozwiązania** innovative *l.* fresh solutions; **nowoczesna technologia** advanced technology; **najnowocześniejsze metody** the latest methods.

nowocześnie *adv.* modernly, in a modern way; innovatively.

nowocześnieć *ipf.* modernize.

nowofalowy *a. film* new wave.

nowofundlandczyk *mp* (= *mieszkaniec Nowej Fundlandii*) Newfoundlander. – *ma kynol.* Newfoundland.

nowogrecki *a.* modern Greek.

nowojorczyk *mp* New Yorker.

nowojorski *a.* New York.

nowołaciński *a.* New Latin.

nowomodny *a.* (= *dostosowany do nowej mody*) trendy, in vogue; (= *dotąd niestosowany*) *iron.* newfangled.

nowomowa *f. iron.* newspeak; **urzędnicza nowomowa** gobbledygook.

noworoczny *a.* New Year's.

noworodek *mp* -dk- newborn, neonate.

nowość *f.* **1.** (= *bycie nowym*) newness. **2.** (= *to, co jest nowe*) novelty; **nowość z firmy X** new product by company X; **nowości wydawnicze** new releases *l.* publications.

nowotworowy *a. pat.* cancerous, neoplastic.

nowotwór *mi* -o- *pat.* tumor, neoplasm; **nowotwór niezłośliwy** *l.* **łagodny** benign tumor; **nowotwór złośliwy** malicious tumor.

nowożeńcy *pl. Gen.* -ów newlyweds.

nowożytny *a.* modern.

nowy *a.* **1.** (= *dopiero co zrobiony*) new; **zupełnie nowy** brand-new; **jak nowy** as good as new. **2.** (= *inny niż przedtem, nastający*) new; **Nowy Rok** New Year; **Nowy Testament** *Bibl.* New Testament; **nowy księżyc** *pot.* new moon; **co nowego?** what's new?; **od nowa** *l.* **na nowo** from the beginning, over again, anew. **3.** (= *świeżo przybyły, dopiero co poznany*) new; **nowa twarz** new *l.* fresh face. **4.** (= *nowoczesny, odkryty*) new, recent; **nowa fala** *film* New Wave; **Nowy Świat** *geogr.* New World, Western Hemisphere; **po nowemu** innovatively. **5.** (= *kolejny*) new, next. – *mp* newcomer, sb new.

Nowy Jork *mi geogr.* (*miasto*) New York (City); (*stan*) New York (State).

Nowy Meksyk *mi geogr.* New Mexico.

Nowy Orlean *mi geogr.* New Orleans.

nozdrze *n. Gen.pl.* -y nostril; (*wieloryba, delfina*) blowhole.

noża *itd. mi* zob. **nóż**.

nożny *a.* foot, pedal; **piłka nożna** *sport* soccer; *Br.* football; **hamulec nożny** *mot.* footbrake; **rozrusznik nożny** *mot.* (*w motocyklu*) kick-starter.

nożownik *mp* **1.** (= *bandyta używający noża*)

knife-wielding assailant. **2.** (= *rzemieślnik wyrabiający noże*) cutler.

nożyce *pl. Gen.* -c **1.** (*narzędzie do cięcia*) shears; **nożyce ogrodnicze** pruning shears; **nożyce blacharskie** (tin) snips; **nożyce do cięcia drutu** wire cutters; **nożyce cen** *ekon.* price scissors; **uderz w stół, a nożyce się odezwą** if the cap fits, wear it. **2.** *techn.* cutter. **3.** *sport* scissors *l.* flutter kick.

nożyczki *pl. Gen.* -czek scissors; **nożyczki do (obcinania) paznokci** nail scissors.

nożyk *mi Gen.* -a **1.** (= *mały nóż*) (small) knife. **2.** (= *ostrze w maszynce do golenia*) blade.

nóg *f.* zob. **noga**.

nów *mi* -o- new moon.

nówka *f. pot.* sth (brand-spanking) new.

nóż *mi* -o- *Gen.* -a **1.** (*narzędzie do cięcia*) knife; **nóż kuchenny** kitchen knife; **nóż chirurgiczny** *chir.* scalpel, lancet; **nóż sprężynowy** switchblade; *Br.* flick knife; **nóż do papieru** paper cutter; **jak nożem uciął** all of a sudden; **iść na noże** be at loggerheads; **iść pod nóż** go under the knife; **mieć nóż na gardle** be in a tight spot *l.* corner; **postawić coś na ostrzu noża** give an ultimatum; **przykładać komuś nóż do gardła** put a knife to sb's throat; **wbić komuś nóż w plecy** *przen.* stab sb in the back, backstab sb. **2.** *techn.* (= *sprzęt do cięcia*) cutter; (= *ostrze maszyny*) blade.

nóżka *f.* **1.** (= *mała noga*) leg; **nóżki cielęce** *kulin.* calve's foot; **nóżka kurczaka** *kulin.* drumstick. **2.** (= *mała podpora, trzonek*) (*kieliszka, grzyba*) stem; (*stolika, cyrkla*) foot.

np. *abbr.* (= *na przykład*) e.g. (*for example*).

n.p.m. *abbr.* (= *nad poziomem morza*) above sea level.

nr *abbr.* (= *numer*) no. (*number*).

NRD *abbr. hist.* (= *Niemiecka Republika Demokratyczna*) GDR (*German Democratic Republic*).

NRF *abbr. hist.* (= *Niemiecka Republika Federalna*) FRG (*Federal Republic of Germany*).

NSA *abbr.* (= *Naczelny Sąd Administracyjny*) Supreme Administrative Court (*in Poland*).

NSZ *abbr. hist.* (= *Narodowe Siły Zbrojne*) National Armed Forces (*in Poland*).

NSZZ *abbr.* (= *Niezależny Samorządny Związek Zawodowy*) Independent Self-Governing Trade Union (*Solidarity*).

n-ty *a.* umpteenth; **po raz n-ty** for the umpteenth time.

nucić *ipf.* **1.** (= *śpiewać tylko melodię*) hum; (= *śpiewać półgłosem*) sing under one's breath; (*dziecku*) croon. **2.** (*o ptakach*) warble.

nucie *f.* zob. **nuta**.

nuda *f.* **1.** (= *stan znudzenia*) boredom; **nudy na pudy** *żart.* snore; **umierać z nudów** be bored stiff *l.* to death; **robić coś z nudy** *l.* **nudów** do sth just to pass *l.* kill the time, do sth out of boredom. **2.** (*coś nieciekawego*) sth boring *l.* tedious, bore.

nudności *pl. Gen.* -i nausea, queasiness.

nudny *a.* boring, dull; **nudny jak flaki z olejem** (as) dull as ditchwater.

Ł M N

nudysta *mp* nudist.

nudystka *f. zob.* **nudysta.**

nudyzm *mi* nudism.

nudziara *f. zob.* **nudziarz.**

nudziarstwo *n.* **1.** (= *nudzenie*) boredom. **2.** (*coś nudnego*) bore.

nudziarz *mp pot.* bore.

nudzić *ipf.* **1.** (= *wzbudzać nudę*) bore; **to mnie nudzi** I'm bored with that, that bores me. **2.** *pot.* (= *nagabywać*) bore (*kogoś o coś* sb with sth). ~ **się** *ipf.* **1.** (= *odczuwać nudę*) be bored; **nudzi mi się** I'm bored. **2.** (= *przykrzyć się*) be tired; **nudzi mi się ta gra** I'm tired of this game.

nugat *mi kulin.* nougat.

nuklearny *a.* nuclear, atomic; **broń nuklearna** *wojsk.* nuclear weapons.

nukleaza *f. biochem.* nuclease.

nukleinowy *a. biochem.* **kwas nukleinowy** nucleic acid.

nukleoid *mi biochem.* nucleoid, prokaryotic nucleus.

nukleon *mi fiz.* nucleon.

nukleonika *f. fiz.* nucleonics.

nukleoproteiny *pl. Gen.* **-n** *biol.* nucleoproteins.

nukleotydy *pl. Gen.* **-ów** *biol.* nucleotides.

nukleozyd *mi Gen.pl.* **-ów** *biol.* nucleoside.

nuklid *mi fiz.* nuclide.

numer *mi* **1.** (= *liczba*) number; **numer kierunkowy** *tel.* area code; **numer rejestracyjny** *mot.* (*w dowodzie*) registration number; (*na tablicach*) license plate number. **2.** (= *rozmiar*) size. **3.** (= *przedmiot oznaczony liczbą*) number. **4.** (= *egzemplarz czasopisma*) issue, number. **5.** (= *element programu*) act; **numer popisowy** main act. **6.** *pot.* (= *nieoczekiwane zachowanie*) trick; **ale numer!** some trick!; **wykręcić jakiś numer** play a trick; **ten numer nie przejdzie!** nothing doing!, no way! **7.** *pot.* (*o człowieku, gagatek*) character, number; **ale z niego numer!** he's quite a character! **8.** *pot.* (= *stosunek płciowy*) number. **9.** *przest.* (= *pokój hotelowy*) (hotel) room.

numeracja *f.* numeration, numbering.

numerant *mp pot.* operator.

numerantka *f. zob.* **numerant.**

numerek *mi* -rk- *Gen.* -a **1.** (= *liczba*) number. **2.** (= *przedmiot oznaczony liczbą*) number. **3.** (*w szatni, u lekarza*) ticket, number. **4.** *pot.* (= *stosunek płciowy*) number.

numerować *ipf.* number.

numerowy *a.* number.

numeryczny *a. lit.* numerical, numeric.

numizmat *mi* old *l.* antique coin.

numizmatyczny *a.* numismatic, numismatical.

numizmatyk *mp* numismatist.

numizmatyka *f.* numismatics.

nunatak *mi geol.* nunatak.

nuncjatura *f. rz.-kat.* **1.** (= *przedstawicielstwo* *dyplomatyczne Watykanu*) nunciature. **2.** (= *urząd nuncjusza*) nunciature.

nuncjusz *mp Gen.pl.* -y *l.* -ów *rz.-kat.* nuncio.

nur *mi Gen. i Acc.* -a dive; **dać nura** (= *zanurkować*) dive. – *ma orn.* loon (*Gavia*).

nurek *mp* -rk- *pl.* -owie diver, frogman. – *mi* -rk- *pl.* -i dive; **dać nurka** (= *zanurkować*) dive.

nurki *pl. Gen.* -ów mink coat.

nurkować *ipf.* **1.** (= *skakać do wody*) dive. **2.** (= *pływać pod wodą*) dive. **3.** (= *kryć się*) duck. **4.** *lotn.* (nose)dive.

nurkowanie *n.* **1.** (= *skakanie do wody*) diving. **2.** (= *pływanie pod wodą*) diving. **3.** *lotn.* (nose)diving.

nurnik *mi techn.* plunger. – *ma orn.* **nurnik białoskrzydły** guillemot (*Cepphus grylle*).

nurogęś *f. orn.* common merganser (*Mergus merganser*).

nurt *mi* **1.** (= *prąd rzeki*) current; **nurt wydarzeń** *przen.* series of events. **2.** (= *tendencja rozwojowa*) trend. **3.** (= *odmęty*) waters.

nurtować *ipf.* bother; **nurtuje mnie wątpliwość** I have a nagging doubt.

nurzać *ipf.* dip; immerse, submerse. ~ **się** *ipf.* wallow (*w czymś* in sth); **nurzać się w rozpuście** *przen.* wallow in debauchery.

nurzyk *ma orn.* **nurzyk podbielały** common murre (*Uria aalge*).

nuta *f.* **1.** *muz.* (*znak graficzny*) note; *por.* **nuty.** **2.** (= *ton*) key. **3.** *pot.* (= *melodia*) tune. **4.** (= *zabarwienie*) tone, note; **nuta triumfu** note of triumph.

nutacja *f. astron., fiz., bot.* nutation.

nutka *f. Gen.pl.* -ek **1.** note; (= *ton*) key. **2.** (= *zabarwienie*) tone, note.

nutowy *a. muz.* note; **papier nutowy** music paper; **zapis nutowy** score.

nutria *f. Gen.* -ii *zool.* nutria, coypu (*Myocastor coypus*); **futro z nutrii** nutria *l.* coypu coat.

nuty *pl. Gen.* nut score; **grać/śpiewać z nut** play/sing from the score; **kłamać jak z nut** lie through one's teeth.

nuworysz *mp Gen.pl.* -ów nouveau riche.

nuż *particle* and if, what if; **a nuż przyjdzie?** and what if he/she comes?

nużący *a.* tiring, tiresome.

nużyca *f. wet., pat.* demodecosis.

nużyć *ipf.* tire, weary, fatigue. ~ **się** *ipf.* tire, grow weary.

nygus *mp pl.* -y *pot.* (= *wałkoń*) layabout, loafer, lazybones.

nyktalopia *f. pat.* nyctalopia, night blindness.

nykturia *f. pat.* nocturia.

nylon *mi tk.* nylon.

nylonowy *a.* nylon.

nylony *pl.* (*pończochy*) nylons, nylon stockings.

NZS *abbr.* (= *Niezależne Zrzeszenie Studentów*) Independent Student Association (*in Poland*).

O, o *n. indecl.* (*litera*) O, o; **O jak Olga** O for Olive, O as in Olive.

O *abbr. chem. zob.* **tlen.**

o¹ *int.* **1.** (*wyraża zdziwienie*) oh; **o rety!** oh boy!, oh my!; **o Boże!** oh my God!, **o nie!** oh no! **2.** (*wyraża gest wskazywania*) look!; **o tam!** over there!

o² *prep.* **1.** *+ Acc. l. Loc.* (*cel myślenia, mówienia, pytania*) about; **mówić o kimś/czymś** talk about sb/sth; **myśleć o kimś/czymś** think about sb/sth; **pytać o kogoś/coś** ask about sb/sth; **prosić o coś** ask for sth; **gniewać się o coś** be angry about sth, be angry over sth; **kłócić się o coś** quarrel about sth; **przyprawiać kogoś o mdłości** make sb sick; **być zazdrosnym o kogoś/coś** be jealous of sb/sth; **oskarżać kogoś o coś** accuse sb of sth, charge sb with sth; **mieć o czymś pojęcie** have an idea of sth; **nie mieć zielonego pojęcia o czymś** not to have the foggiest *l.* faintest idea of sth. **2.** *+ Acc.* (*obiekt, na który skierowana jest czynność*) against, on; **opierać się o kogoś/coś** lean against sb/sth; **uderzać o coś** hit against sth, hit sth; **potykać się o coś** trip over sth, trip on sth, stumble on sth. **3.** *+ Acc.* (*różnica wielkości*) by; **większy o metr** one meter longer, longer by one meter; **starszy/młodszy o rok** one year older/younger. **4.** *+ Loc.* (*termin*) at; **o godzinie szóstej** at six (o'clock); **o północy** at midnight; **o świcie** at dawn. **5.** *+ Loc.* (*określone cechy*) with, of; **człowiek o silnych nerwach** man with strong nerves; **roślina o pięknych kwiatach** plant with beautiful flowers; **dziewczyna o ujmującym uśmiechu** girl with a charming smile; **człowiek o dużych wymaganiach** demanding person, person of high expectations; **chodzić o kulach** walk on crutches; **chodzić o lasce** walk with a stick; **chodzić o własnych siłach** walk on one's own; **żyć o chlebie i wodzie** live on bread and water.

oaza *f.* **1.** (*na pustyni*) oasis. **2.** *przen.* (*miejsce spokoju*) oasis, haven; **oaza ciszy** *l.* **spokoju** oasis of calm.

oba *num. Ins.* **-oma** *l.* **-u** both.

obaj *num. Ins.* **oboma** *l.* **obu** both.

obalać *ipf.*, **obalić** *pf.* **1.** (= *przewracać*) knock down, knock over, bring down. **2.** (= *odsuwać od władzy*) overthrow, depose; **obalić rząd** overthrow the government. **3.** (= *oddalać, odpierać*) refute, disprove; **obalić zarzut** rebut a charge; **obalić wyrok** reverse a sentence. **4.** (= *delegalizować*) abolish.

obandażować *pf.* bandage, dress.

obarczać *ipf.*, **obarczyć** *pf.* **1.** (= *obciążać*) burden, encumber. **2.** (= *nakładać obowiązki*) burden sb with a duty. **3.** hold sb responsible for sth; **obarczyć winą** put the blame on sb.

obawa *f.* (= *niepokój, strach*) anxiety; concern (*o kogoś/coś* for sb/sth); fear (*przed kimś/czymś* of sb/sth); **żywić** *l.* **mieć obawę** fear; **żyć w obawie** live in fear of; **robić coś w obawie przed czymś** do sth for fear of sth; **w obawie o własne życie** in fear of one's life; **zachodzi obawa, że** there are grounds to fear that; **I am afraid that; bez obawy** no fear!, don't worry, never fear.

obawiać się *ipf.* fear, dread (*kogoś/czegoś* sb/sth); be concerned (*o kogoś/coś* about sb/sth); fear (*o kogoś/coś* for sb/sth); **obawiać się, że** be afraid that; **tego się właśnie obawiam** this is what I fear; **tego się właśnie obawiałem** it is just as I feared; **obawiam się, że tak** I'm afraid so; **obawiam się, że nie** I'm afraid not.

obcas *mi Gen.* **-a** heel; **buty na wysokich obcasach** high-heeled shoes, (high) heels.

obcążki *pl. Gen.* **-ów** (pair of) pliers.

obcesowo *adv.* bluntly, brusquely, offhandedly.

obcesowość *f.* bluntness, offhandedness.

obcesowy *a.* blunt, brusque, offhand.

obcęgi *pl. Gen.* **-ów** (pair of) pincers.

obchody *pl. Gen.* **-ów** (= *uroczystość*) celebrations.

obchodzić *ipf.* **1.** (= *chodzić wokół*) walk round; **obchodzić przepisy/prawo** circumvent the regulations/law; **obchodzić zakaz** evade a ban; **obchodzić przeszkodę** get round an obstacle. **2.** (= *kontrolować, sprawdzać*) make a round. **3.** (= *interesować*) interest, concern, be of interest; **to mnie nie obchodzi** I don't care, I don't give a damn; **mało mnie to obchodzi** I couldn't care less; **co cię to obchodzi!** it's none of your business! **4.** (= *świętować*) celebrate. **~ się** *ipf.* **1.** (= *traktować kogoś/coś*) treat sb/sth; handle (*z czymś* sth); do (*bez kogoś/czegoś* without sb/sth); **obejdzie się!** thanks a lot. **2.** (= *używać, obsługiwać*) use, handle (*z czymś* sth). **3.** (= *zadowalać się*) make do (*czymś* with sth).

obchód *mi* **-o-** (= *kontrola*) round.

obciach *mi pot.* shame, come-down, dump; **narobić komuś obciachu** come down on sb.

obciąć *pf.* **obetnę obetniesz**, **-ij** *zob.* **obcinać. ~ się** *pf. zob.* **obcinać się.**

obciągać *ipf.*, **obciągnąć** *pf.* **-ij 1.** (= *powlekać, obijać*) upholster. **2.** (*o odzieży*) (= *naciągać*) straighten one's clothes, smooth one's clothes.

3. *wulg.* (= *odbywać stosunek oralny*) give sb a blow job, suck sb off, suck the sugar stick.

obciążać *ipf.* **1.** (= *objuczać, obładowywać*) burden, load down, weigh down. **2.** (= *zaopatrzyć w balast*) weigh, load; **obciążać sobie pamięć** burden one's memory. **3.** (*wymuszać działanie ponad normę*) overburden; **obciążona sieć/linia** overloaded network/line *l.* connection. **4.** (= *nakładać obowiązki*) burden sb with duties. **5.** (= *obwiniać*) blame, put the blame on; **obciążyć kogoś odpowiedzialnością** hold sb responsible; **obciążyć kogoś zarzutami** lay charges on sb; **obciążyć kogoś kosztami** charge expenses to sb; **obciążyć czyjeś konto** charge sb's account, debit sb's account; **obciążyć hipoteką** mortgage sth. ~ **się** *ipf.* **1.** (= *objuczyć się*) burden o.s. **2.** (= *podejmować się obowiązków*) saddle o.s. with duties, take up duties, assume responsibilities. **3.** (= *obwiniać się*) blame o.s. **4.** (= *wzajemnie się oskarżać*) blame each other.

obciążalność *f.* *techn.* load capacity, load-carrying ability.

obciążenie *n.* **1.** (= *objuczenie*) burden, load. **2.** (= *praca do wykonania*) workload; **nadmierne obciążenie** overburden, overload. **3.** *techn.* load. **4.** *el.* inductive load. **5.** (= *powierzenie obowiązków*) burdening sb with duties. **6.** (= *obciążenie finansowe*) strain on sb's finances.

obciążyć *pf. zob.* **obciążać.** ~ **się** *pf. zob.* **obciążać się.**

obciec *pf.* -knę -kniesz, -knij, **obciekać** *ipf.*, **obcieknąć** *pf.* -ij drip dry, trickle.

obcierać *ipf.* **1.** (= *wycierać*) wipe. **2.** (= *skaleczyć*) graze, scrape. **3.** (*o butach*) pinch.

obcinać *ipf.* **1.** cut off; prune, trim, clip. **2.** *pot.* (= *zmniejszać*) trim, prune; **obcinać wypłatę** deduct from the salary. ~ **się** *ipf. pot.* (= *ostrzyc się*) have one's hair cut.

obcinak *mi Gen.* -a *techn.* cutter; cut-off tool, parting tool.

obciosać *pf.* -ciosam *l.* -ciosę -ciosasz *l.* -ciosa -ciosają *l.* -cioszą *l.* -cieszą, -ciosaj *l.* -ciosz *l.* -ciesz, **obciosywać** *ipf.* trim.

obciskać *ipf.* **1.** (= *owijać*) wrap tightly. **2.** (= *przylegać, opinać*) fit tight, cling.

obcisły *a.* tight-fitting, close-fitting.

obcisnąć *pf.* -ij *zob.* **obciskać.**

obco *adv.* (= *nieswojo*) strangely, strange; **czuć się obco** not to feel at home, feel like a stranger.

obcojęzyczny *a.* foreign language.

obcokrajowiec *mp* -wc- *Voc.* -cze *l.* -u *pl.* -y foreigner.

obcopylność *f. bot.* allogamy.

obcopylny *a. bot.* allogamous.

obcość *f.* strangeness.

obcować *ipf.* **1.** (= *przebywać*) mix, associate, rub shoulders (*z kimś / czymś* with sb/sth); **obcować z przyrodą** *l.* **naturą** commune with nature. **2.** *rzad.* (= *współżyć, odbywać stosunek płciowy*) have an intercourse, have sex (*z kimś* with sb).

obcy *a.* **1.** strange, foreign, alien; **zupełnie obcy człowiek** perfect stranger. **2.** (= *cudzy*) other people's, sb else's. **3.** (= *zagraniczny*) foreign;

obce wpływy oudside influence; **ciało obce** *med.* foreign body; **czuć się obcym** feel like a stranger; **uprzejmość jest mu obca** kindness is foreign *l.* alien to him. – *mp* stranger; foreigner, alien.

obcyndalać się *ipf.* *pot.* loaf about, loaf around.

obczyzna *f.* foreign lands; (= *wygnanie*) exile; **na obczyźnie** in exile.

obdarować *pf.*, **obdarowywać** *ipf.* present sb with sth. ~ **się** *pf.*, **obdarowywać się** *ipf.* give each other *l.* one another presents.

obdartus *mp pl.* -y ragamuffin, scruff.

obdarty *a.* ragged, tattered.

obdarzać *ipf.* endow; give; bestow; **obdarzać kogoś uczuciem** give one's affection to sb, bestow one's affection on sb; **obdarzyć kogoś zaufaniem** place one's trust in sb, trust sb; **obdarzyć kogoś uśmiechem** smile at sb, give sb a smile; **obdarzyć kogoś spojrzeniem** give sb a glance.

obdarzony *a.* -eni endowed; **obdarzona inteligencją i urodą** endowed with beauty and brains; **ktoś hojnie obdarzony przez naturę** *pot.* sb well-endowed, sb well-equipped by nature.

obdarzyć *pf. zob.* **obdarzać.**

obdrapać *pf.* -ę -esz, **obdrapywać** *ipf.* scratch.

obdukcja *f. Gen.pl.* -ji *med., prawn.* **1.** (= *badanie poszkodowanego*) forensic examination. **2.** (= *sekcja zwłok*) postmortem (examination), autopsy.

obdzielać *ipf.*, **obdzielić** *pf.* hand out sth to sb, deal sth out to people.

obdzierać *ipf.* **1.** (= *zrywać*) strip (*z czegoś* of sth). **2.** (= *ogałacać*) strip; **obdzierać kogoś ze skóry** rip sb off; **obdzierać zwierzę ze skóry** skin an animal; **obdzierać kogoś ze złudzeń** deprive sb of delusions, strip sb of their illusions.

obecnie *adv.* **1.** now, at present, currently. **2.** (= *w dzisiejszych czasach*) nowadays, these days.

obecność *f.* **1.** presence; attendance; **obecność na zajęciach** attendance; **lista obecności** roll, roster; **sprawdzać obecność** call the roll; **sprawdzanie obecności** roll call, calling the roll; **w czyjejś obecności** in sb's presence, in sb's hearing. **2.** (= *istnienie*) existence.

obecny *a.* **1.** (*będący gdzieś*) present; **obecny!** present!, here!; **być obecnym na zajęciach** attend classes. **2.** (= *teraźniejszy*) current, present; **w obecnej chwili** at present, at the moment.

obedrzeć *pf.* -drę -drzesz, -drzyj, **obdarł** *zob.* **obdzierać.**

obejma *f. techn.* clamping ring, clasp, grip.

obejmę *itd. pf. zob.* **objąć.**

obejmować *ipf.* -ę -esz, -ij **1.** (= *otaczać ramionami*) embrace, hug; **obejmować kogoś/coś wzrokiem** *l.* **spojrzeniem** take sb/sth in. **2.** (= *przejmować*) take over; **obejmować władzę** take power, come to power. **3.** (= *rozprzestrzeniać się*) spread. **4.** (= *rozumieć*) comprehend, grasp. **5.** (= *zawierać*) include, encompass; **cena obejmuje wszystkie koszty** all costs included, price is all-inclusive.

obejrzeć *pf.* **-ę -ysz, -yj** *zob.* **oglądać. ~ się** *pf. zob.* **oglądać się.**

obejście *n.* **1.** (= *obchód*) round. **2.** (= *gospodarstwo*) farmyard. **3.** (= *sposób bycia*) manner; **miły w obejściu** well-mannered; **łatwy w obejściu** easy to deal with. **4.** (= *droga, która coś omija*) bypass.

obejść *pf.* **-dę -dziesz obszedł obeszła obeszli** *zob.* **obchodzić. ~ się** *pf. zob.* **obchodzić się.**

obelga *f.* insult, invective, offence, abuse.

obelisk *mi bud.* obelisk.

obeliskowy *a. bud.* obelisk.

obelżywie *adv.* insultingly, offensively.

obelżywy *a.* insulting, offensive, abusive.

oberek *mi* **-rk-** *Gen. i Acc.* **-a** *muz.* (*taniec*) lively Polish folk dance.

obertas *mi Gen. i Acc.* **-a** *żart. zob.* **oberek.**

oberwać *pf.* **-ę -esz, -ij** *zob.* **obrywać. ~ się** *pf. zob.* **obrywać się.**

oberwanie *n.* (= *odłączenie*) tear-off; **oberwanie chmury** cloudburst.

oberwaniec *mp* **-ńc-** *Voc.* **-cze** *l.* **-u** *pl.* **-y** *l.* **-e** *pot.* ragamuffin, scruff.

oberwany *a.* torn off.

oberża *f. Gen.pl.* **-y** *l.* **-ż** *przest.* inn, tavern.

oberżnąć *pf.* **-ij** *zob.* **obrzynać.**

oberżyna *f.* **1.** *bot.* (*roślina*) eggplant (*Solanum melongena esculentum*); *Br.* aubergine. **2.** (*owoc*) eggplant; *Br.* aubergine. **3.** *pot.* (*kolor*) aubergine.

oberżysta *mp przest.* innkeeper.

obeschnąć *pf.* **-nij, -nął** *l.* **obsechł obeschła obeschli** *zob.* **obsychać.**

obeszła *itd. pf. zob.* **obejść.**

obetnę *itd. pf. zob.* **obciąć.**

obetonować *pf.* concrete; strengthen with concrete.

obetrzeć *pf.* **-rę -rzesz, -rzyj, obtarł** *zob.* **obcierać. ~ się** *pf. zob.* **obcierać się.**

obeznać się *pf. przest.* familiarize o.s., acquaint o.s. (*z czymś* with sth).

obeznany z czymś *a.* familiar with sth, acquainted with sth.

obezwładniać *ipf.* overpower, overwhelm.

obezwładniający *a.* overwhelming, incapacitating; **obezwładniający strach** paralysing fear.

obezwładnić *pf.* **-ij** *zob.* **obezwładniać.**

obeżreć *pf.* **-ę -esz, -yj, obżarł** *zob.* **obżerać. ~ się** *pf. zob.* **obżerać się.**

obędę *itd. pf. zob.* **obyć.**

obficie *adv.* profusely, abundantly, copiously; **padać obficie** rain heavily, pour.

obfitość *f.* abundance, profusion, copiousness; **rosnąć w obfitości** grow in profusion.

obfitować *ipf.* abound (*w coś* in *l.* with sth).

obfitujący *a.* abounding (*w coś* in sth).

obfity *a.* abundant, plentiful, copious, profuse, heavy; **obfite kształty** curvaceous body, curves.

obfotografować *pf.*, **obfotografowywać** *ipf.* take numerous photographs *l.* photos of, shoot from every possible angle.

obgadać *pf.*, **obgadywać** *ipf.* **1.** *pot.* (= *obmawiać*) backbite. **2.** *pot.* (= *rozpatrzeć*) talk over.

obgotować *pf.*, **obgotowywać** *ipf.* parboil.

obgryzać *ipf.*, **obgryźć** *pf.* **-zę -ziesz -zł -źli** bite; (*o człowieku*) pick; (*o psie*) gnaw at; **pies obgryza kość** dog gnaws at a bone; **obgryzać paznokcie** bite one's nails; **obgryźć liście** eat (up) leaves.

obiad *mi Loc.* **-edzie** **1.** (*posiłek*) dinner; lunch; **proszony obiad** dinner; **musztarda po obiedzie** a day after the fair; **jeść obiad** have dinner, have lunch; **wydać obiad** give dinner. **2.** (= *pora obiadowa*) lunchtime; **przed obiadem** before dinner, before lunch; **po obiedzie** after dinner, after lunch; **co jest na obiad?** what's for dinner?, what are we having for dinner?, what's for lunch?

obiadowy *a.* lunch, dinner; **pora obiadowa** lunchtime, dinner time; **przerwa obiadowa** lunch break.

obibok *mp pl.* **-i** *pot. żart.* (= *leń*) lazybones.

obicie *n.* **1.** (= *obtłuczenie*) chip, crack. **2.** (*na owocu*) bruise. **3.** (= *pokrycie mebla*) upholstery, coating; **pokrycie drzwi** padding. **4.** (= *pobicie*) beating, hiding, thrashing. **5.** (= *materiał, tapicerka*) upholstery.

obiciowy *a.* upholstery; **tkanina obiciowa** upholstery.

obić *pf.* **obiję obijesz, obij** *zob.* **obijać. ~ się** *pf. zob.* **obijać się.**

obie *num. Ins.* **-ema** *l.* **-u** *l.* **-oma** both.

obiec *pf.* **obiegnę obiegniesz, obiegnij, obiegł** *zob.* **obiegać.**

obiecać *pf. zob.* **obiecywać.**

obiecanka *f. Gen.pl.* **-ek** empty promise; **obiecanki cacanki, a głupiemu radość** promises, promises!

obiecująco *adv.* promisingly; **przedstawiać się obiecująco** look promising.

obiecujący *a.* promising.

obiecywać *ipf.* **1.** (= *przyrzekać*) promise (*coś komuś* sth to sb *l.* sb sth); **ziemia obiecana** promised land; **obiecywać złote góry** promise the moon, promise the earth; **obiecywać gruszki na wierzbie** promise wonders; **obiecujesz?** promise?; **obiecywać coś sobie** promise o.s. **2.** (= *zapowiadać*) promise.

obieg *mi* **1.** (= *ruch dokoła czegoś*) rotation, revolution around sth. **2.** (= *krążenie cieczy*) circulation; **obieg krwi** *med.* blood circulation. **3.** (= *wymiana, obrót*) turnover, circulation; **obieg pieniądza** currency circulation; **wycofać z obiegu** withdraw from circulation; **puścić plotkę w obieg** spread a rumor; **być w obiegu** circulate, be in circulation; **wyjść z obiegu** get out of circulation; **wprowadzić w obieg** put into circulation.

obiegać *ipf.*, **obiegnąć** *pf.* **obiegnę obiegniesz, obiegnij, obiegł** **1.** (= *okrążać*) circle, run around. **2.** *astron.* (= *obiegać po orbicie*) orbit, circle. **3.** (*o plotkach*) (= *rozchodzić się*) spread.

obiegowy *a.* **1.** (*dotyczący ruchu*) rotary, rotative, circular. **2.** (= *powszechny, używany*) common, general; **obiegowa opinia** commonplace opinion, hackneyed opinion; **waluta obiegowa** legal tender.

obiegówka *f. Gen.pl.* **-ek** *pot.* clearance slip.

obiekcja *f. Gen.pl.* **-ji** objection.

obiekt *mi* **1.** (= *przedmiot*) object; **obiekt zain-**

teresowania object of interest, target; **niezidentyfikowany obiekt latający** unidentified flying object, UFO. **2.** (= *budynek*) building, structure; **obiekty sportowe** sports facilities; **obiekty wojskowe** military installations; **obiekt przemysłowy** industrial works, industrial plant; **obiekt historyczny** historic building; **obiekty użyteczności publicznej** public buildings.

obiektyw *mi opt.* lens.

obiektywizm *mi* **1.** (= *obiektywność*) objectivity. **2.** (= *bezstronność*) impartiality, objectivity.

obiektywnie *adv.* **1.** (= *bezstronnie*) impartially, objectively. **2.** (= *prawdziwie*) objectively.

obiektywność *f.* **1.** (= *obiektywizm*) objectivity. **2.** (= *realność*) objectiveness.

obiektywny *a.* **1.** (= *bezstronny*) impartial, objective; **obiektywny sąd** objective judgement; **obiektywny sprawozdawca** impartial commentator. **2.** (= *realny*) objective.

obielmo *n. bot.* perisperm.

obiema *num. zob.* **obie**.

obierać *ipf.* **1.** (*zdejmować zewnętrzną warstwę*) peel; **obierać owoce/warzywa/ziemniaki** peel fruits/vegetables/potatoes. **2.** (= *wybierać*) choose, elect. **3.** (= *pozbawiać*) strip (*czegoś* of sth).

obieralność *f.* (= *wybieralność*) eligibility.

obieralny *a.* elective; **przedmiot obieralny** elective *l.* facultative *l.* optional course; **urząd obieralny** elective office.

obierki *pl. Gen.* **-rek** peelings.

obierze *pf. zob.* **obrać**.

obierzyna *f. zob.* **obierki**.

obietnica *f.* promise; **złożyć obietnicę** make a promise; **złamać obietnicę** break a promise; **dotrzymać obietnicy** keep a promise.

obieżyświat *mp pl.* **-y** *pot.* globetrotter.

obijać *ipf.* **1.** (*o kubku, garnku*) (= *obtłukiwać*) chip, crack; (*o owocach*) (= *obtłukiwać*) bruise. **2.** (*o meblach*) (= *pokrywać, obciągać*) upholster. **3.** (= *bić*) thrash, batter, flog. **~ się** *ipf.* **1.** (*uderzając, uszkodzić się*) chip, crack. **2.** (*o owocach*) get bruised; **obiło mi się** *o uszy* I heard that..., it came to my ears that...; **obijać się jak groch o ścianę** make no impression whatsoever on sb. **3.** *tylko ipf.* (= *próżnować*) loaf about.

obiorę *itd. pf. zob.* **obrać**.

objadać *ipf.* sponge (*kogoś* on sb); eat sb out of house and home. **~ się** *ipf.* gorge, stuff o.s.

objaśniać *ipf.*, **objaśnić** *pf.* explain, interpret.

objaśnienie *n.* **1.** (= *wyjaśnienie*) explanation. **2.** (= *komentarz*) commentary, interpretation.

objaw *mi* symptom.

objawiać *ipf.*, **objawić** *pf.* **1.** (= *wyrazić, uzewnętrznić*) display. **2.** (= *ujawniać*) reveal, display, manifest. **~ się** *ipf.*, **objawić się** *pf.* manifest itself.

objawienie *n.* **1.** (= *uzewnętrznienie*) display, manifestation. **2.** (= *zjawisko, olśnienie*) revelation. **3.** *rel.* (= *ukazanie się*) revelation.

objawowo *adv.* symptomatically.

objawowy *a.* symptomatic; **leczenie objawowe** *med.* symptomatic treatment.

objazd *mi Loc.* **-eździe** **1.** (= *droga okrężna*) di-

version. **2.** (*tymczasowa droga*) detour; *Br.* diversion. **3.** (= *objeżdżanie*) tour.

objazdowy *a.* detour; **droga objazdowa** *l.* **okrężna** detour; **trasa objazdowa** (*np. zespołu muzycznego, teatru*) tour; **objazdowy teatr** roadshow, road show.

objąć *pf.* **obejmę obejmiesz, obejmij** *zob.* **obejmować**. **~ się** *pf. zob.* **obejmować się**.

objechać *pf.* **-jadę -jedziesz** *zob.* **objeżdżać**.

objeść *pf.* **-jem -jesz, -jedz, -jadł -jedli** *zob.* **objadać**. **~ się** *pf. zob.* **objadać się**.

objeździć *pf. zob.* **objeżdżać**.

objeżdżać *ipf.*, **objeździć** *pf.* **-jeżdżę -jeździsz, -jeźdź 1.** (= *okrążać*) circle, go around; **objeżdżać miasto** bypass the city. **2.** (= *odwiedzać*) tour, visit; **objechać cały kraj** tour the whole country, travel around the whole country; **objechać całą rodzinę** visit the whole family (*esp. in one tour around the country / an area, etc.*). **3.** *pot.* (= *opieprzać*) dress down. **4.** *tylko ipf.* (= *testować samochód*) test-drive.

objęcie *n.* **1.** (*gest*) embrace. **2.** (*stanowiska, władzy*) assumption; (*urzędu*) taking (over), assumption. **3.** (= *uścisk*) embrace; **padli sobie w objęcia** they started embracing; **rzucić się w czyjeś objęcia** fall into sb's arms, throw o.s. in sb's arms; **popaść w objęcia kogoś/czegoś** fall into sb's/sth's arms, fall for sb/sth hook, line and sinker; **trzymać kogoś w objęciach** *l.* **ramionach** hold sb in an embrace; **wyrwać się z objęć czegoś** extricate o.s. from sth; **wyrwać się z objęć kogoś** get out from under sb's influence; **wziąć kogoś w objęcia** *l.* **ramiona** clasp sb in one's arms; **być w objęciach Morfeusza** be in the arms of Morpheus, be in the land of Nod; **wyrwać kogoś z objęć śmierci** snatch sb back from the jaws of death.

objętościowo *adv.* cubically.

objętościowy *a.* cubical; **analiza objętościowa** *chem.* volumetric analysis.

objętość *f.* **1.** (= *pojemność, kubatura*) volume. **2.** (= *rozmiar*) volume; **objętość wydawnictwa** *druk.* publication *l.* edition size. **3.** *chem., fiz.* volume; **objętość atomowa** atomic volume; **objętość molowa** molar volume; **objętość oddechowa** *fizj.* tidal volume; **objętość skokowa** *techn.* volumetric displacement, swept volume. **4.** *mat.* volume; **wzór na objętość** volume formula.

objuczać *ipf.*, **objuczyć** *pf.* burden, load.

objuczać się *ipf.*, **objuczyć się** *pf.* burden o.s.

obkleić *pf.* **-ej**, **obklejać** *ipf.* paste, stick; **obkleić coś papierem** plaster sth with paper, stick paper over sth; **obkleić pokój plakatami** paste posters all over the room.

obkładać *ipf.* **1.** (= *owijać*) cover with; **obkładać książki** put covers on one's books. **2.** *myśl.* (*o człowieku – otoczyć zwierzynę*) bay, surround; **obłożyć pole** (*o psie*) search the hunting area. **~ się** *ipf.* bury o.s.; **obkładać się książkami/notatkami** bury o.s. in one's books/notes (*in order to study*).

obkopać *pf.*, **obkopywać** *ipf.* earth up.

obkuć *pf.* -**ję** -**jesz** *zob.* **obkuwać**. ~ **się** *pf.*, **obkuwać się** *ipf.* cram (*esp. for an examination*).

obkupić się *pf.* buy a lot of things (*usu. for a certain purpose*); **obkupił się już na wakacje** he has already bought all he needs for his vacation.

obkupiony *a.* -**eni** stocked up (*w coś* on sth); **jestem już obkupiony na wakacje** I've already bought all I need for my vacation.

obkuwać *ipf.* 1. (= *obciosać*) hew, trim. 2. *pot.* (= *nauczyć się*) cram. ~ **się** *ipf. pot.* cram.

oblać *pf.* -**eję** -**ejesz** -**ali** *l.* -**eli** *zob.* **oblewać**. ~ **się** *pf. zob.* **oblewać się**.

obladzać *ipf.* cover with ice, ice. ~ **się** *ipf.* become covered with ice, ice over.

oblamować *pf. zob.* **oblamowywać**.

oblamowanie *n.* hem.

oblamowywać *ipf.* hem.

oblanie *n. pot.* (= *niezaliczenie komuś*) failing sb, flunking sb.

oblat *mp rel.* oblate.

oblatać *pf. zob.* **oblatywać**.

oblatany *a.* 1. (= *doświadczony*) at home with *l.* on *l.* in, well-versed in; **oblatany z niego człowiek** he knows all this backwards and forwards, he's been around. 2. *lotn.* (= *przetestowany*) test-flown.

oblatka *f. Gen.pl.* -**ek** *zob.* **oblat**.

oblatywacz *mp* test pilot.

oblatywać *ipf.* 1. (= *okrążać*) fly around; **oblecieć coś spojrzeniem** glance at sth, cast one's eye over sth; **wieść obleciała miasto** it's going round town that..., the word on the street is that...; **strach** *l.* **tchórz go obleciał** he got cold feet; **obleciał mnie dreszcz** an attack of shivers came over me, I had an attack of shivers; **ponure myśli mnie obleciały** I succumbed to gloomy thoughts. 2. (= *obchodzić*) go *l.* run round. 3. *pot.* (= *odwiedzać*) visit; **oblecieć sklepy** shop around; **oblecę jeszcze paru znajomych** I'll just pop into a couple of places. 4. *pot.* (= *odpadać*) chip off, flake. 5. *pot.* (= *być zaakceptowanym*) be sufficient, do; **dobra, jakoś to obleci** all right, it will do. 6. *lotn.* (*testować samolot*) test-fly.

oblec[1] *pf.* -**okę** *l.* -**ekę** -**eczesz** -**ókł** *l.* -**ekł** -**ekła** -**ekli** *zob.* **oblekać**.

oblec[2] *pf.* -**gnę** -**gniesz**, -**gnij**, -**gł** *l.* -**gnął** -**gła** -**gli** *zob. pf. zob.* **oblekać się**.

oblecieć *pf.* -**cę** -**cisz** *zob.* **oblatywać**.

oblegać *ipf.*, **oblegnąć** *pf.* -**nij**, -**ł** *l.* -**nął** -**ła** -**li** 1. (= *otaczać wojskiem*) besiege, lay siege to, beleaguer. 2. (= *obstąpić*) mob, crowd around. 3. *pot.* (= *nagabywać*) beleaguer.

oblekać *ipf.* clothe, attire (*w coś* in sth); **oblec ciało** don one's clothes; **oblec jakąś postać/kształt** assume the shape; **oblec coś w ciało** lend substance to sth; **oblec wilka w owczą skórę** put a good face on sb, be a wolf in sheep's clothing (*give a vile character good appearance*). ~ **się** *ipf.* (= *ubrać się*) don (*w coś* sth); **oblec się w jakąś postać** *l.* **formę** assume the shape *l.* form of; **oblec się w ciało** come into being; **oblec się w owczą skórę** pretend innocence, play the innocent, be a wolf in sheep's clothing.

oblence *pl. Gen.* -**ów** *zool.* nemathelminths (*Nemathelminthes*).

oblepiać *ipf.*, **oblepić** *pf.* 1. (= *obklejać*) plaster (*np. papierem*). 2. (= *smarować*) plaster, coat (*np. gliną*). 3. (= *pokrywać*) cake (*np. zaschniętym błotem*). 4. (*o owadach*) swarm. 5. (= *obciskać, przylegać*) cling. ~ **się** *ipf.*, **oblepić się** *pf.* 1. (= *polepić się*) become sticky, become covered with a sticky substance. 2. (= *przylegać*) cling.

obleśnie *adv.* (= *lubieżnie*) lecherously, lustfully; (= *obrzydliwie*) disgustingly.

obleśność *f.* (= *lubieżność*) lecherousness, lustfulness; (= *obrzydliwość*) disgustedness.

obleśny *a.* (= *lubieżny*) lecherous, lustful; (= *obrzydliwy*) disgusting.

oblewać *ipf.* 1. (= *polewać*) pour, splash; **oblewać kogoś łzami** mourn sb; **oblać kogoś zimną wodą** pour *l.* throw cold water on sb; **zimny pot mnie oblewał** I was bathed in cold sweat. 2. (= *pokrywać*) coat; **oblany czekoladą** chocolate-coated. 3. (= *wystąpić*) suffuse; **twarz oblał jej rumieniec** her cheeks reddened. 4. (*o wodzie*) (= *otaczać*) surround, wash (*a land*). 5. *pot.* (= *uczcić, opić*) celebrate (*usu. by heavy drinking*); **trzeba to oblać** we have to drink to it. 6. *pot.* (= *nie zdać*) fail, flunk. 7. *pot.* (*nie zaliczyć komuś*) fail sb, flunk sb. ~ **się** *ipf.* 1. (= *polać się*) spill over o.s., pour on o.s.; **oblewać się potem** be bathed in sweat, sweat all over; **oblać się rumieńcem** blush, flush. 2. *pot.* (= *nie zdać*) fail, flunk.

oblewanie *n.* 1. (= *polewanie*) pouring, splashing. 2. (= *pokrywanie*) coating. 3. *pot.* (= *niezaliczanie*) failing; **oblewanie studentów to jego hobby** failing *l.* flunking students is his hobby. 4. *pot.* (= *uczczenie czegoś*) bash, blast, spree, booze-fest (*celebrating sth, e.g. passing an important exam, by means of organising a lavish party*); **oblewanie mieszkania** house-warming.

obleźć *pf.* -**ezę** -**eziesz** -**azł** -**eźli** *zob.* **obłazić**.

oblężenie *n.* 1. (= *otoczenie, okrążenie*) siege; **stan oblężenia** state of siege. 2. (= *obstąpienie*) siege, crowding round; **autobus był zupełnie oblężony** there were swarms of people hoping to get on the bus.

oblężniczy *a.* or of related to a siege; **drabina oblężnicza** scaling ladder; **wieża oblężnicza** siege tower.

oblężony *a.* -**eni** the besieged.

obliczać *ipf.* 1. (= *rachować*) calculate, compute; **obliczać głosy** poll; **obliczać** *l.* **ustalać koszty** cost. 2. (= *planować, uwzględniać*) estimate; **straty obliczono na 1 milion złotych** losses have been estimated at 1 million zlotys. ~ **się** *ipf.* 1. (= *rozliczać się*) settle; **muszę się obliczyć z gospodynią** I have to settle with the landlady. 2. (= *uwzględniać, planować*) estimate the cost, cost.

obliczalny *a.* calculable, computable.

oblicze *n. Gen.pl.* -**y** 1. *lit.* (= *twarz*) countenance, visage; **znaleźć się w obliczu klęski** face *l.* meet with defeat; **(równy) w obliczu prawa**

(equal) before the law; **w obliczu śmierci** in the article of death, at death's door; **stanąć przed czymś obliczem** be admitted into sb's presence; **stanął w obliczu ruiny** ruin stared him in the face; **zniknąć z oblicza ziemi** disappear from the face of the earth; **wszyscy są równi w obliczu śmierci** death is a great leveller. **2.** (= *charakter, kształt, wygląd*) nature; face; shape; **nadać czemuś nowe oblicze** put a new face to sth; **ujawnić swoje prawdziwe oblicze** show one's true colors.

obliczenie *n.* **1.** (= *naliczenie, policzenie*) calculation, computation. **2.** (= *wynik, dane*) calculation; **obliczenie szacunkowe** estimate.

obliczeniowy *a.* calculative, computational; **centralna jednostka obliczeniowa** *komp.* central processing unit, CPU.

obliczony *a.* calculated, computed; **obliczony na osiągnięcie czegoś** calculated to do sth; **obliczony na pokaz** played to the gallery; **obliczony na zwłokę** dilatory; **nieobliczony na zysk** non-profit.

obliczyć *pf. zob.* **obliczać**. ~ **się** *pf. zob.* **obliczać się**.

obligacja *f. ekon.* bond, debenture; **obligacja imienna** non-negotiable bond; **obligacja na okaziciela** bearer bond; **obligacja skarbowa** *l.* **skarbu państwa** treasury bond; **obligacja oszczędnościowa** savings bond.

obligatoryjnie *adv.* obligatorily.

obligatoryjny *a.* obligatory.

obligować *ipf. przest.* oblige (*do czegoś* to do sth).

obliteracja *f. t. pat.* obliteration.

oblizać *pf.* -**żę** -**żesz** -**zał**, **oblizywać** *ipf.* lick. ~ **się** *pf.*, **oblizywać się** *ipf.* (*o człowieku*) lick one's lips; (*o zwierzęciu*) lick its mouth; **oblizywać się na myśl o czymś** lick one's lips *l.* chops thinking of sth.

oblodzenie *n.* icing.

oblodzić *pf. zob.* **obladzać**. ~ **się** *pf. zob.* **obladzać się**.

oblodzony *a.* icy; **oblodzona jezdnia** icy road.

oblot *mi* **1.** (= *oblecenie*) flight around, flyby, flyover. **2.** *lotn.* (= *próbny lot*) test flight. **3.** *ent.* (*lot owadów*) reconnaissance, reconnoiter (*of insects, before e.g. laying eggs*). **4.** *myśl.* teaching a falcon or other bird used for hunting game to fly according to the hunter's orders.

oblubienica *f. lit., żart.* betrothed.

oblubieniec *mp* -ńc- *pl.* -**y** *lit., żart.* betrothed.

oblubieńcy *pl. Gen.* -**ów** *lit.* (= *narzeczeni*) the betrothed.

obluzgać *ipf. pot.* bawl out, give sb a dressing-down.

obluzować *pf. zob.* **obluzowywać**. ~ **się** *pf. zob.* **obluzowywać się**.

obluzowany *a.* loosened, slackened.

obluzowywać *ipf.* loosen (up), slacken. ~ **się** *ipf.* come loose.

obładować *pf.*, **obładowywać** *ipf.* burden, load, pack. ~ **się** *pf.*, **obładowywać się** *ipf.* load *l.* burden o.s.; **obładować się książkami** load o.s. down with books.

obładowany *a.* laden; **ciężko obładowany czymś** heavy-laden with sth.

obłamać *pf.* -**ę** -**esz**, **obłamywać** *ipf.* **1.** (= *odrywać*) break off. **2.** *druk.* wrap (*text around an image*); **tekst obłamany** wrapped text. ~ **się** *pf.*, **obłamywać się** *ipf.* break off.

obłapiać *ipf.*, **obłapić** *pf.* (= *obmacywać*) paw, maul. ~ **się** *ipf.*, **obłapywać się** *pf.* suck face; *Br.* snog.

obłaskawiać *ipf.*, **obłaskawić** *pf.* **1.** (= *oswajać zwierzę*) tame, domesticate. **2.** (*uczynić kogoś przyjaznym*) tame, domesticate. ~ **się** *ipf.*, **obłaskawić się** *pf.* (= *oswajać się*) become tamed *l.* domesticated.

obława *f.* **1.** *myśl.* (= *polowanie z nagonką*) hunt, surround. **2.** *myśl.* (= *nagonka*) hunt. **3.** (*akcja policyjna l. wojskowa*) manhunt; **obława policyjna** raid; **obława na przestępcę** hunt for a criminal.

obłazić -**żę** -**zisz** *ipf.* **1.** (*o owadach*) (= *obsiąść*) swarm over. **2.** *pot.* (= *odpadać*) peel, come off, flake.

obłączek *mi anat.* lunula, lunule, half-moon.

obłąk *mi Gen.* -**a** *l.* -**u** **1.** (= *pałąk*) bail *l.* bale. **2.** *bud.* straining *l.* strainer arch. **3.** *techn.* straining strap.

obłąkaniec *mp* -ńc- *pl.* -**y** **1.** (= *umysłowo chory*) lunatic, madman. **2.** *przen.* (= *pomyleniec*) loony.

obłąkany *a.* **1.** (= *wariacki, szaleńczy*) mad, insane. **2.** *przen.* (= *pomylony*) crazy. – *mp* (= *obłąkaniec*) loony.

obłąkańczy *a.* lunatic, insane; **obłąkańczy strach** mad fear.

obłęd *mi* **1.** *pat.* paranoia. **2.** (= *obłąkanie*) madness; **czysty** *l.* **istny obłęd** sheer lunacy; **napad obłędu** fit of madness; **dostać obłędu** go mad; **miał obłęd w oczach** his eyes were wild; **doprowadzić kogoś do obłędu** drive sb mad; **przyprawiać kogoś o obłęd** craze sb.

obłędnie *adv.* **1.** (= *szaleńczo*) madly, insanely; **kochać kogoś obłędnie** *l.* **do szaleństwa** love sb madly, be madly in love with sb. **2.** *pot.* (= *wyjątkowo, wspaniale*) fantastically, excellently.

obłędny *a.* **1.** (= *wariacki*) mad, insane. **2.** *pot.* (= *nadzwyczajny*) fantastic, super, excellent.

obło *n. żegl.* bilge.

obłocić *pf.* muddy; **obłocić sobie buty** get one's shoes muddy. ~ **się** *pf.* get muddy.

obłoczek *mi* -czk- *Gen.* -**a** *l.* -**u** **1.** (= *chmura*) cloudlet. **2.** *przen.* (*coś w powietrzu*) whiff, puff, waft. **3.** *pat.* nebula.

obłoczniaki *pl. Gen.* -**ów** *bot.* hymenomycetes (*Hymenomycetes*).

obłok *mi* **1.** *meteor.* (= *chmura*) cloud; **pod obłoki** sky-high; **chwalić kogoś pod obłoki** sing the praises of sb, praise sb to the skies; **zstąpić z obłoków** wake up to life *l.* reality, wake up and smell the coffee, get one's feet back on the ground; **bujać w obłokach** have one's head in the clouds. **2.** *przen.* (*coś w powietrzu*) cloud; **obłok** *l.* **tuman kurzu** cloud of dust.

obłowić się *pf.* -ów *pot.* (= *zarobić*) make a killing; **obłowić się na czymś** cash in on sth.

obłożnie *adv.* bedridden; **człowiek obłożnie chory** bedridden person.

obłożny *a.* bedridden; **choroba obłożna** severe illness (*during which one is bedridden*).

obłożony *a. pat.* coated; **obłożony język** coated *l.* furry *l.* furred tongue; **mieć obłożony język** have fur on one's tongue.

obłożyć *pf.* -óż 1. (= *pokryć*) cover. 2. (= *ostrzelać*) shell. 3. (= *obciążyć*) burden, load; **jestem obłożony pracą** I've got loads of work to do; **obłożyć akcyzą** excise, impose an excise on; **obłożyć kogoś grzywną** impose *l.* lay a fine on sb, fine sb; **obłożyć kogoś karą** inflict punishment on sb; **obłożyć kogoś klątwą** lay a curse on sb, anathematize sb. ~ **się** *pf.* put sth around o.s.; **obłożyć się książkami** bury in one's books (*in order to study*).

obłuda *f.* cant, unctuousness, hypocrisy.

obłudnica *f.* canter.

obłudnie *adv.* unctuously, cantingly.

obłudnik *mp* canter.

obłudny *a.* unctuous, canting.

obłupać *pf.* -ę -esz *zob.* **obłupywać.** ~ **się** *pf.* *zob.* **obłupywać się.**

obłupić *pf.* 1. *zob.* **obłupać; obłupić** *l.* obedrzeć **kogoś ze skóry** flay sb, skin sb. 2. (= *obrabować*) rob; **obłupić kogoś ze skóry** (= *wyzyskać*) flay sb, fleece sb, rip sb off.

obłupywać *ipf.* (*o jajkach*) shell; (*o korze, drzewach*) bark. ~ **się** *ipf.* chip, break off.

obłuskać *pf.*, **obłuskiwać** *ipf.* (*o jajkach, grochu*) shell; (*o kukurydzy*) husk.

obły *a.* 1. (= *walcowaty*) cylindrical. 2. (= *jajowaty*) oval, ovoid.

obmacać *pf.*, **obmacywać** *ipf.* 1. (= *dotykać*) feel, grope. 2. (= *dotykać lubieżnie*) fondle, grope. ~ **się** *pf.* (= *przeszukać*) feel, search; **obmacać się po kieszeniach** rummage through one's pockets.

obmacywać się *ipf.* (= *obłapiać się*) suck face, make out; *Br.* snog.

obmalować *pf.*, **obmalowywać** *ipf.* 1. (= *pomalować*) paint sth all over. 2. *pot.* (= *obsmarowywać*) backbite, defame.

obmawiać *ipf.* backbite. ~ **się** *ipf.* backbite each other *l.* one another.

obmiatać *ipf.* sweep.

obmierzać *ipf.*, **obmierzyć** *pf.* measure up (*e.g. the whole room, building, etc.*).

obmierzać *ipf.*, **obmierzić** *pf.* -rżę -rzisz -rził make hateful; **obmierzić komuś życie** make sb's life hateful; **obmierzić komuś mięso** put sb off meat.

obmierzłość *f.* 1. (= *brzydota, ohyda*) repulsiveness, abhorrence. 2. (= *wstręt*) repulsion, disgust, hatred.

obmierzły *a.* -rźli horrid, detestable; **obmierzły pokój** horrid room; **obmierzły nudziarz** awful bore.

obmierzyć *pf.* *zob.* **obmierzać.**

obmierźle *adv.* horridly, detestably.

obmieść *pf.* -otę -eciesz -ótł -otła -etli *zob.* **obmiatać.**

obmowa *f. Gen.pl.* -ów obloquy, backbiting.

obmówić *pf.* *zob.* **obmawiać.** ~ **się** *pf.* *zob.* **obmawiać się.**

obmurować *pf.*, **obmurowywać** *ipf.* 1. (= *obłożyć cegłą*) line (*with brick*). 2. *przest.* (= *otoczyć murem*) wall in *l.* up.

obmyć *pf.* -ję -jesz, -yj *zob.* **obmywać.** ~ **się** *pf.* *zob.* **obmywać się.**

obmyślać *ipf.*, **obmyślić** *pf.* devise, contrive, conceive.

obmywać *ipf.* 1. (= *umyć*) dabble, splash; **obmywać stopy** wash sb's feet. 2. (*o wodzie*) (= *zalewać, moczyć*) wash. ~ **się** *ipf.* have a wash (*w czymś* in sth); **obmywać się z czegoś** wash sth off.

obnażać *ipf.*, **obnażyć** *pf.* 1. (= *rozebrać*) strip (*sb of their clothes*), unclothe. 2. (= *odsłaniać*) expose, bare; **obnażać miecz** unsheathe one's sword. 3. *geol.* denude. 4. (*o ubraniu*) (= *nie zakrywać*) expose. 5. *przen.* (= *demaskować*) unmask, divulge; **obnażyć czyjąś głupotę** expose *l.* lay bare sb's stupidity, shine a spotlight on sb's stupidity. ~ **się** *ipf.*, **obnażyć się** *pf.* expose o.s., strip (*przed kimś* in front of sb).

obnażanie *n.* exposure; denudation; **obnażanie się w miejscu publicznym** *prawn.* indecent exposure.

obnieść *pf.* -osę -esiesz -ósł -osła -eśli *zob.* **obnosić.**

obniżać *ipf.* 1. (= *zniżać*) lower; **obniżać głos** lower one's voice; **obniżać lot** descend; **obniżyć o pół tonu** *muz.* flat, flatten; **obniżyć poprzeczkę** *przen.* lower the requirements; **obniżyć loty** *przen.* lower one's sights. 2. (= *zmniejszać*) reduce, diminish; **obniżać ceny** reduce prices, mark down; **obniżyć cenę czegoś o 10%** take 10% off sth; **obniżyć cenę o 10 złotych** lop 10 zlotys off the price; **obniżyć ocenę** *szkoln.* mark sb down (*za coś* for sth); **obniżyć temperaturę** (*np. w piekarniku, kaloryferów*) turn down the heat. ~ **się** *ipf.* 1. (= *zniżać się*) drop, sink, lower. 2. (= *zmniejszać się*) decrease, decline, diminish; **obniżyć się o 20%** come down by 20%; **temperatura obniżyła się o 3 stopnie** the temperature has fallen by 3 degrees.

obniżka *f. Gen.pl.* -ek reduction, cut; **obniżka cen** price cut; **obniżka kosztów** cost reduction.

obniżyć *pf.* *zob.* **obniżać.** ~ **się** *pf.* *zob.* **obniżać się.**

obnosić *ipf.* -szę -sisz 1. (= *pokazywać, przenosząc*) take sth round; **obnosić kogoś na językach** *pot.* backbite. 2. *tylko ipf. pot.* (= *demonstracyjnie okazywać*) sport, flaunt; **obnosić swoje szczęście** make a parade of one's happiness. ~ **się** *ipf.* sport, flaunt, flash (*z czymś* sth); **obnosić się z pieniędzmi** flash money around, flaunt one's wealth.

obnośny *a.* peddling; **handel obnośny** *l.* sprzedaż obnośna peddlery.

obnóże *n. Gen.pl.* -y **obnóże pyłkowe** *biol., ent.* load of pollen (*on the hind leg of a bee*).

obocznik *mi Gen.* -a *jęz.* alternant, allomorph.

oboczność *f. jęz.* alternation.

oboczny *a. jęz.* alternant; **temat oboczny** stem alternant.

oboista *mp muz.* oboist.

obojczyk *mi Gen.* **-a 1.** *anat.* clavicle, collarbone. **2.** (= *koloratka*) amice. **3.** (= *zbroja*) gorget.

obojczykowy *a. anat.* clavicular, claviculate.

oboje *num. decl. like n.* **-jg-** both (*he and she*); **my oboje** both of us.

obojętnie *adv.* **1.** (= *biernie*) indifferently, detachedly; **pachnieć obojętnie** smell inoffensive. **2.** (= *bez znaczenia*) no matter, doesn't matter; **obojętnie gdzie** no matter where; **obojętnie kiedy** no matter when; **obojętnie kto** no matter who. **3.** *chem.* inertly, inactively. **4.** *fiz.* neutrally.

obojętnieć *ipf.* (*stawać się obojętnym*) inure o.s. (*na coś* to sth); (= *powszednieć*) grow indifferent.

obojętność *f.* **1.** (= *niewrażliwość, bierność*) indifference; **udawać obojętność** affect indifference; **z udawaną obojętnością** with feigned indifference. **2.** *chem.* inertness, inactiveness. **3.** *fiz.* neutrality.

obojętny *a.* **1.** (= *niewrażliwy*) indifferent; **obojętny na coś** indifferent to sth, dead to sth; **obojętny widz** indifferent spectator; **obojętny stosunek** detached attitude; **obojętne spojrzenie** vacant stare; **obojętny na cierpienie** untouched by suffering; **to mi jest obojętne** it's all just the same to me, I don't care. **2.** (= *nieistotny*) indifferent, immaterial. **3.** (= *nijaki*) indifferent, neutral. **4.** *chem.* inert, inactive; **sól obojętna** normal salt; **odczyn obojętny** neutral reaction; **roztwór obojętny** neutral solution. **5.** *fiz.* (= *nienaelektryzowany*) neutral; **cząstka obojętna** neutral particle.

obojnacki, obojnaczy *a. biol.* hermaphrodite.

obojnactwo *n.*   *biol.*   (=   *dwupłciowość*) hermaphroditism.

obojnaczy *a. zob.* **obojnacki**.

obojnak *mp pl.* **-i** *biol.* hermaphrodite, bisexual.

obok[1] *prep.* + *Gen.* (= *blisko*) by, near, close to; (= *oprócz*) beside.

obok[2] *adv.* close by, near by, beside, alongside; **tuż obok** close by, next door, (close) at hand; **ktoś/coś jest obok** sb/sth is close by; **istnieć** *l.* **występować obok czegoś** coexist with sth; **przebiec/przelecieć/przejść obok czegoś** run/fly/go by *l.* past sth.

obol *mi Gen.* **-a** *Gen.pl.* **-i** *l.* **-ów 1.** *hist.* (*moneta*) obol, obolus. **2.** *hist.* (*jednostka masy*) obol, obolus.

obolały *a.* **1.** (= *zbolały*) sore, aching, achy. **2.** (= *cierpiący*) grievous, racked, sad; **powiedzieć coś obolałym głosem** say sth in a voice racked with pain.

oboma *num. zob.* **oba** *l.* **obaj**.

obopólnie *adv.* mutual.

obopólny *a.* mutual; **obopólny zysk** mutual gain; **obopólna korzyść** mutual benefit; **dla obopólnej korzyści** to the mutual advantage; **za obopólną zgodą** by mutual agreement *l.* consent.

obora *f. Gen.pl.* **obór** *roln.* (cow) shed, (cow) barn; **ostatnie cielę z obory** (*ostatnie pieniądze*) one's bottom dollar; (*ostatnia karta*) one's last ace in the hole; **patrzeć na księżą oborę** *przest.* have one foot in the grave, be about to kick the bucket *l.* buy the farm; **wpuścić wilka do obory** get a drunk to tend the bar.

oborać *pf.* **-rzę -rzesz -rał** *zob.* **oborywać**.

obornik *mi Gen.* **-a** (*nawóz*) manure, dung.

oborowy[1] *a. roln.* of a (cow) shed *l.* barn; (cow-)shed, (cow-)barn.

oborowy[2] *mp* cowherd, cattleman.

oborywać *ipf. roln.* plow round (*e.g. a tree*).

obosieczny *a.* **1.** (*mający ostrze z obu stron*) double-edged, two-edged; **miecz obosieczny** double-edged *l.* two-edged sword. **2.** (*niebezpieczny dla obu stron*) double-edged, two-edged.

obostrzać *ipf.* (= *zaostrzać*) tighten, bolster, strengthen; **więzienie o obostrzonym rygorze** high security prison.

obostrzenie *n.* (= *zaostrzenie*) tightening, bolstering, strengthening; **wprowadzić obostrzenia w przepisach drogowych** tighten traffic laws.

obostrzyć *pf. zob.* **obostrzać**.

obowiązany *a.* obliged.

obowiązek *mi* **-zk-** (= *powinność*) obligation, duty; **obowiązek moralny** moral duty *l.* obligation; **obowiązek obywatelski** civic duty; **psi obowiązek** bounden duty (*a usu. upleasant but unquestionable duty*); **święty obowiązek** bounden *l.* sworn duty; **codzienne obowiązki** *l.* **harówka** the daily round *l.* grind; **najpierw obowiązek, potem przyjemność** duty before pleasure; **lekceważyć obowiązki** make light of one's duties; **mieć obowiązek coś robić** have an obligation *l.* a responsibility to do sth; **mieć poczucie obowiązku** have a sense of duty; **poczuwam się do obowiązku, by...** I feel it is my duty to...; **spełnić swój obowiązek** do one's duty; **wywiązać się z obowiązków** do one's duty; **wypełniać obowiązki** fulfill one's duties; **zaniedbywać obowiązki** neglect one's duties, be remiss in one's duties; **zrobiłem to z (poczucia) obowiązku** I did it out of duty, I felt it was my duty to do it; **z obowiązku** (*z przymusu*) dutifully; **spoczywa na nim obowiązek zrobienia tego** he was burdened *l.* saddled with the responsibility to do it; **zostać zwolnionym z obowiązków** be relieved of one's responsibilities; **spełniać obowiązki gospodarza** officiate as host, host; **obowiązek płatności** *prawn.* obligation to pay; **obowiązek udzielenia pomocy** *prawn.* obligation to give assistance.

obowiązki *pl. Gen.* **-ów** (= *powinności, zobowiązania*) responsibilities, duties, obligations; **obowiązki rodzinne** obligations *l.* duties to one's family; **obowiązki ministra** ministerial duties; **obowiązki premiera** mantle of the prime minister; **pełniący obowiązki prezesa** acting chairman *l.* president; **przejąć czyjeś obowiązki** take over from sb; **zaniedbywać się w obowiązkach** be remiss in one's duties; **pełnić obowiązki prezydenta** act as president; **zawiesić kogoś w obowiązkach** suspend sb; **zakres obowiązków** scope of responsibility, one's responsibilities; (*w formie listy -*

opisu stanowiska pracy) job description; **wchodzić w czyjś zakres obowiązków** come *l.* be within the scope of one's responsibility.

obowiązkowo *adv.* **1.** (= *przymusowo*) obligatorily, compulsorily. **2.** *pot.* (= *koniecznie*) absolutely, it goes without saying.

obowiązkowość *f.* **1.** (= *sumienność*) conscientiousness. **2.** (= *rygor, przymus*) compulsoriness.

obowiązkowy *a.* **1.** (= *obowiązujący*) obligatory, compulsory; **obowiązkowe szkolenie** obligatory training; **obowiązkowa służba wojskowa** compulsory military service. **2.** *szkoln.* curricular, compulsory, obligatory. **3.** (= *sumienny*) conscientious, dutiful; **obowiązkowy pracownik** conscientious worker *l.* employee. **4.** (= *nie do przegapienia*) unmissable.

obowiązujący *a.* (*o prawie, umowie, przepisie*) effective; (= *wiążący*) binding; (*o prawie*) in force, in vigor; (*o rozporządzeniu*) operative; (*o umowie*) valid; **prawnie obowiązujący** legally binding *l.* valid; **mieć moc obowiązującą** be (legally) binding; **moc obowiązująca umowy** *prawn.* obligation of a contract.

obowiązywać *ipf.* (= *być obowiązkiem, być zasadą*) be compulsory; **obowiązuje strój wieczorowy** evening dress is de rigueur; (= *mieć ważność*) hold good, apply to; **ta zasada obowiązuje wszystkich** this rule applies to everyone, this rule holds good for everyone; (= *mieć moc prawną*) be effective, be in force, be valid.

obozować *ipf.* camp out; encamp.

obozowicz *mp Gen.pl.* **-ów** camper.

obozowisko *n.* campsite.

obozowy *a.* **1.** (= *kempingowy*) camping; **sprzęt obozowy** camping equipment. **2.** (= *wypoczynkowy*) camp, leisure. **3.** (= *koalicyjny*) of or related to a (political) camp or bloc, bloc, coalition. **4.** (= *więzienny*) of or related to a concentration or labor camp; **obozowe baraki** camp barracks; **literatura obozowa** *teor.lit.* literature describing the life in concentration, labor and POW camps.

oboźny *mp* **1.** (= *kierownik obozu harcerskiego*) camp leader, camp counselor. **2.** *hist.* high-ranking army official responsible for munitions, equipment, etc., quartermaster.

obój *mi* **-o-** *Gen.pl.* **oboi** *l.* **-ów** *muz.* oboe.

obóz *mi* **-o-** **1.** camp. **2.** (= *miejsce wypoczynku lub szkolenia*) camp; **obóz harcerski** scout camp; **obóz językowy** language camp; **obóz letni** summer camp; **obóz wędrowny** camping trip; **obóz wojskowy** army *l.* military camp. **3.** (= *koalicja, ugrupowanie*) camp; **obóz lewicowy** the leftist camp. **4.** (= *miejsce izolacji, więzienie*) camp; **obóz dla internowanych** detention *l.* internment camp; **obóz dla uchodźców** refugee camp; **obóz jeniecki** prisoner-of-war *l.* P.O.W. camp; **obóz koncentracyjny** concentration camp; **obóz pracy** labor camp; **obóz przejściowy** temporary refugee camp; **obóz śmierci** death camp.

obrabiać *ipf.* **1.** (= *kształtować*) work; (*ręcznie za pomocą narzędzi*) tool; (= *poddać obróbce*) process; (*maszynowo*) machine. **2.** (= *uprawiać*

ziemię) till, cultivate. **3.** (= *obdziergać, podszywać*) hem. **4.** *pot.* (= *plotkować*) gossip; **obrabiać komuś dupę** *l.* **tyłek** bitch about sb, bad-mouth sb. **5.** *pot.* (= *okradać*) knock off, do; **obrobić** *l.* **zrobić bank** *pot.* stick up *l.* do a bank; **obrobić** *l.* **zrobić komuś chatę** *pot.* hit sb's apartment *l.* house.

obrabialny *a.* *techn.* workable, machin(e)able.

obrabiarka *f. Gen.pl.* **-ek** *techn.* machine tool; **obrabiarka do drewna** woodworking machine; **obrabiarka do metalu** metalworking machine.

obrabować *pf.,* **obrabowywać** *ipf.* (= *okradać*) rob, strip (*z czegoś* of sth); (*świątynię, grobowiec*) despoil.

obracać *ipf.* **1.** (= *kręcić, przewracać*) turn; **obrócić klucz w zamku** turn the key in the lock; **obracać oczami** roll one's eyes; **obracać w tańcu** whirl *l.* spin sb (*dancing*); **obracać coś w palcach** twiddle with sth, finger sth; **obracać pieniędzmi** conduct financial *l.* business transactions; **obracać językiem** *pot.* blabber, jabber; **to się obróci przeciwko tobie** it will turn against you. **2.** (= *kierować, zwracać ku czemuś*) turn; **obrócić** *l.* **skierować na kogoś wzrok** turn one's eyes to sb; **obrócić na bok** turn to the side; **obracać kota ogonem** blow smoke over sth (*usu. twist the meaning of one's own words, statements, promises, etc.*). **3.** (= *przeznaczać, inwestować*) make use (*coś na jakiś cel* of sth for a certain purpose); **obrócić coś na swój pożytek** turn sth to one's profit. **4.** (= *przemieniać*) turn into; **obracać coś w gruzy** *l.* **perzynę** bring sth to ruin, lay waste to sth; **obrócić coś wniwecz** shatter, crush sth to smithereens; **obrócić wniwecz czyjeś nadzieje** shatter one's hopes; **obracać coś w żart** turn sth into a joke. **5.** *pot.* (= *chodzić tam i z powrotem*) go there and back. **6.** *wulg.* (*mieć stosunek z kobietą*) bang, grind; *Br.* shag. **~ się** *ipf.* **1.** (= *kręcić się*) turn, revolve, rotate; **obracać się w koło** spin; **obracać się wokół osi** pivot; **obrócić się na pięcie** turn *l.* spin on one's heel; **Ziemia obraca się wokół własnej osi** *astron.* the earth rotates on its axis; **a jednak się obraca** and yet it does move (*words of Galileo*). **2.** (= *odwracać się*) turn; **obracać się na drugi bok** roll over; **obrócić się tyłem** *l.* **plecami do kogoś** turn one's back on sb; **obracać się przeciwko komuś** turn against sb; **obracać się jak chorągiewka** change one's views or loyalties (*political, etc.*). **3.** (= *zmieniać się*) turn into; **obrócić się w gruzy** *l.* **perzynę** be shattered, be crushed into smithereens. **4.** (= *przebywać, znajdować się*) mingle, mix; **obracać się wśród kogoś** mingle *l.* socialize with sb, rub elbows *l.* shoulders with sb; **obracać się w różnych kręgach** move in different circles. **5.** (= *dotyczyć*) revolve; **jego zainteresowania obracają się wokół leksykografii** his interests revolve around lexicography.

obrachować *pf.,* **obrachowywać** *ipf.* calculate, compute. **~ się** *pf.,* **obrachowywać się** *ipf.* **1.** (= *obliczyć się*) estimate (*e.g. one's financial situation*). **2.** (= *rozliczać się*) settle *l.* square accounts (*z kimś* with sb); **obliczyć się z właścicielem** settle with the landlord.

obrachunek *mi* -nk- calculation, computation; **zrobić obrachunek z przeszłością** *przen.* square accounts with one's past.

obrachunkowy *a.* financial; **okres obrachunkowy** *fin.* accounting period; **rok obrachunkowy** *fin.* fiscal *l.* financial year, FY.

obrać *pf.* **obiorę obierzesz** *zob.* **obierać**.

obradować *ipf.* debate (*nad czymś* sth); **parlament właśnie obraduje** parliament is just in session.

obrady *pl. Gen.* -d proceedings, session; **porządek obrad** *l.* **dnia** *t. parl.* agenda, order of the day; **sala obrad** *l.* posiedzeń sessions-chamber; **przerwa w obradach** recess; **otworzyć obrady** open the proceedings *l.* session; **przerwać** *l.* **zawiesić obrady** adjourn the proceedings; **przewodniczyć obradom** be in the chair, chair a session; **zakończyć obrady** close *l.* adjourn the proceedings *l.* session.

obramienie *n.* **1.** (= *wykonanie ramy*) framing. **2.** (= *rama*) frame.

obramować *pf. zob.* **obramowywać**.

obramowanie *n.* (= *otoczenie*) border, framing; *bud.* (= *wykończenie*) fringe.

obramowywać *ipf.* **1.** (= *otaczać, okalać*) encircle, surround. **2.** (= *utworzyć ramę*) fringe, border.

obrastać *ipf.* **1.** (= *zarastać*) overgrow, grow over. **2.** (= *pokrywać się*) grow *l.* become covered (*by plants*); **obrastać w fortunę** make a pile *l.* bundle; **obrastać w piórka** feather one's nest; **obrastać w tłuszcz** run to fat; make a pile *l.* bundle; **obrosnąć brudem** get dirt caked on, get caked in dirt.

obraz *mi* **1.** (= *malowidło*) picture, painting; **namalować obraz** do a painting; **galeria obrazów** picture gallery; **wpatrywać się w kogoś jak w obraz** (= *patrzeć z zachwytem*) never to take one's eyes off sb; (= *uwielbiać*) look up to sb, set sb on a pedestal; **przemawiał dziad do obrazu, a obraz do niego ani razu** I may as well talk to the wall. **2.** (= *wizerunek*) image; **obrazy z przeszłości** images of the past; **obrazy z młodości** images of one's youth; **(człowiek został stworzony) na obraz i podobieństwo Boga** (man was created) in God's own image; **obraz nędzy i rozpaczy** sorry *l.* pitiful sight; **żywy obraz kogoś** living *l.* spitting image of sb. **3.** (= *całość spraw*) picture; **mieć jasny obraz sytuacji** have a clear picture of the situation; **ogólny obraz sytuacji** the big picture; **przedstawiać pesymistyczny obraz czegoś** paint a gloomy picture of sth; **fałszować obraz** misrepresent (*kogoś / czegoś* sb/sth); **obraz kliniczny** *med.* clinical *l.* nosological picture. **4.** *teatr* (= *akt*) act; **żywy obraz** tableau vivant. **5.** *techn.* (*na ekranie*) picture; **obraz telewizyjny** television picture; **obraz kontrolny** test pattern; **częstotliwość odświeżania obrazu** *komp.* refresh rate. **6.** *film* (= *film*) motion picture, movie, picture. **7.** *fiz., fot., opt.* (= *zdjęcie*) picture, image; **obraz optyczny** *fiz.* optical image; **obraz pozorny** *opt.* virtual image.

obraza *f.* **1.** (= *zniewaga*) insult, offense. **2.** (= *obrażenie się*) resentment, grudge; **kamień obra-** zy rock of offense. **3.** (*wykroczenie przeciw czemuś*) offense, outrage; **obraza munduru** disgrace to the uniform; **obraza moralności** indecency; **obraza majestatu** lese majesty *l.* lèse majesté; **obraza sądu** *prawn.* contempt of court; **uznać kogoś winnym obrazy sądu** *prawn.* hold sb in contempt of court; **bez obrazy** no offense; **(toż) to obraza boska!** *pot.* it's outrageous!

obrazek *mi* -zk- *Gen.* -a **1.** (= *mały obraz*) small picture; **święte obrazki** pictures *l.* portraits of the saints; **książeczka z obrazkami** picture book; **piękny jak z obrazka** *l.* **jak malowanie** pretty as a picture. **2.** (= *scenka*) picture; **sielankowy obrazek** idyllic picture *l.* scene. **3.** *teor.lit.* (= *opowiadanie*) sketch.

obrazić *pf.* -żę -zisz *zob.* **obrażać**. ~ **się** *pf. zob.* **obrażać się**.

obrazki *pl. Gen.* -ów *bot.* arums (*Arum*); **obrazki plamiste** cuckoopint, lords-and-ladies (*Arum maculatum*).

obrazkowate *pl. Gen.* -ych *bot.* the family Araceae (*Araceae*).

obrazkowy *a.* pictorial; **historyjka obrazkowa** (*np. w gazecie*) comic strip; **pismo obrazkowe** picture writing; **słownik obrazkowy** pictorial dictionary.

obrazoburca *mp rel., t. przen.* iconoclast.

obrazoburczy *a. rel., t. przen.* iconoclastic.

obrazoburczyni *f. zob.* **obrazoburca**.

obrazoburstwo *n. rel., t. przen.* iconoclasm.

obrazować *ipf.* picture, depict, portray.

obrazowanie *n.* **1.** depiction, representation. **2.** *lit., sztuka* imagery; **obrazowanie oniryczne** *teor.lit.* oneiric imagery. **3.** *med.* imaging; **obrazowanie mózgu** brain scan.

obrazowo *adv.* vividly, picturesquely, pictorially.

obrazowość *f.* vividness, picturesqueness.

obrazowy *a.* **1.** (= *malowniczy*) vivid, picturesque, pictorial, graphic; **obrazowy opis** vivid *l.* graphic account. **2.** *fiz., fot.* picture; **lampa obrazowa** *techn.* television *l.* picture tube.

obraźliwie *adv.* offensively, insultingly.

obraźliwość *f.* **1.** (= *obelżywość*) offensiveness. **2.** (= *drażliwość*) touchiness.

obraźliwy *a.* **1.** (= *obrażający*) offensive, insulting. **2.** (= *drażliwy, obrażalski*) touchy.

obrażać *ipf.* **1.** (= *ubliżać*) offend, insult; (*słownie*) abuse; **obrazić kogoś śmiertelnie** offend sb gravely; **obrazić kogoś do żywego** cut sb to the quick. **2.** (= *naruszyć coś*) offend; **obrażać czyjeś uczucia** hurt sb's feelings. ~ **się** *ipf.* (= *żywić urazę*) take offence, be in a huff, be miffed (*na kogoś / coś* at sb/sth) (*za coś* for sth) (*o coś* at sth); **obrazić się na cały świat** turn one's back on the world *l.* one's fellow man, become bitter and twisted.

obrażalski *a. pot.* huffy, huffish.

obrażenie *n.* **1.** (= *znieważenie*) insult, offense. **2.** (= *rana*) injury; **odnieść obrażenia** suffer injuries; **poważne obrażenia wewnętrzne** serious internal injuries.

obrażony *a.* -eni **1.** (= *urażony*) offended, insulted, resentful (*na kogoś / coś* at sb/sth). **2.** (=

niechętny) sullen, huffy; **zrobić obrażoną minę** give a sullen look, make an offended face, look offended; **obrażony na cały świat** bitter and twisted.

obrąbać *pf.* **-ę -esz, obrąbywać** *ipf.* chop off.

obrączka *f. Gen.pl.* **-ek 1.** (*biżuteria*) ring; **obrączka ślubna** wedding ring *l.* band. **2.** (*u zwierząt*) ring. **3.** (= *obwódka*) band.

obrączkować *ipf.* **1.** (*o zwierzętach*) ring. **2.** *ogr.* ring *l.* ringbark, girdle.

obrączkowanie *n.* **1.** (*u zwierząt*) ringing. **2.** *ogr.* ringing *l.* ringbarking, girdling.

obrączkowy *a.* **1.** (*o wyrobie obrączek*) ring, band; **złoto obrączkowe** wedding ring *l.* band gold. **2.** (*o kształcie*) ring-shaped, annular; *anat.* circinate; **zaćmienie obrączkowe** *astron.* annular eclipse.

obręb *mi* **1.** (= *teren*) premises, area; **w obrębie zakładu/szkoły** on the company/school premises. **2.** (= *granica*) limit; **w obrębie czegoś** within the limits *l.* compass of sth; **w obrębie miasta** within the city limits. **3.** (= *zakres, zasięg*) extent, reach, compass; **wyrzucić kogoś poza obręb** *l.* **nawias społeczeństwa** ostracize sb, exclude sb. **4.** (= *lamówka, obszycie*) hem. **5.** *przen.* (= *dziedzina, sfera*) sphere, area; **to jest w obrębie moich zainteresowań** it is an area of interest to me. **6.** *leśn.* compartment; **obręb leśny** forest district.

obrębiać *ipf.*, **obrębić** *pf.* hem.

obręcz *f. pl.* **-e 1.** (= *obejma*) (*np. beczki*) hoop; **obręcz barkowa** *anat.* shoulder girdle; **obręcz biodrowa** *anat.* pelvic girdle. **2.** *mot.* (= *felga*) rim. **3.** (*ozdoba*) circlet. **4.** *gimnastyka* (gymnastic) hoop. **5.** *koszykówka* hoop.

obrobić *pf.* **-ób** *zob.* **obrabiać.** ~ **się** *pf.* (= *uwinąć się*) get everything done (*usu. get one's household duties done quickly*).

obrodzić *pf.* **1.** (= *zaowocować*) yield a rich crop; **sady w tym roku obrodziły** orchards are abounding *l.* abundant in fruit this year. **2.** *przen.* (= *dopisać*) be in plenty; **talenty w tym roku nie obrodziły** there were few talented ones this year (*e.g. of candidates to an arts or film college*).

obrok *mi* **1.** (= *pasza*) feed, fodder, provender. **2.** *przest.* (= *jedzenie*) provender.

obrona *f.* **1.** (= *bronienie się, ochrona*) defense; *Br.* defence; **obrona konieczna** *prawn.* necessary defense; **obrona własna** *prawn.* self-defense. **2.** (= *obrońca*) defender. **3.** (*wstawianie się za kimś, odpieranie oskarżeń*) defense, advocacy; **wziąć kogoś w obronę** come *l.* spring to sb's defense; **stanąć w obronie kogoś/czegoś** rise to sb's defense/in the defense of sth, stand up for sb/sth; **nie mieć nic na swoją obronę** have nothing in one's defense; **obrona pracy magisterskiej/doktorskiej** defense of one's master's/doctoral thesis. **4.** (= *osłona*) protection. **5.** *prawn.* the defense, defense counsel(s), counsel(s) for the defense; **obrona z urzędu** (*czynność*) public defense; (*osoba*) assigned counsel, court-appointed attorney, public defender. **6.** *wojsk.* defense; **obrona przeciwlotnicza** air defense; **ob-**

rona cywilna civil defense; **najlepszą obroną jest atak** attack is the best defense, the best defense is a good offense. **7.** *sport* (= *defensywa*) the defense. **8.** *szachy* defense; **obrona sycylijska** Sicilian Defense.

obronić *pf.* **1.** (= *odeprzeć atak*) defend (*przed kimś/czymś* against sb/sth). **2.** (= *wziąć w obronę*) defend, stand up for. **3.** (= *zdać egzamin*) defend (*usu. one's master's or doctoral thesis*); pass. **4.** *sport* (*strzał na bramkę*) save. **5.** (= *osłonić*) protect, deliver from. ~ **się** *pf.* **1.** (= *odeprzeć atak*) defend o.s. (*przed kimś/czymś* against sb/sth). **2.** (= *obronić rozprawę*) defend (*one's doctoral dissertation*); pass; **kiedy się bronisz?** when are you having your PhD defense?; **już się obroniłeś?** have you defended your dissertation yet?; *pot.* have you been PhDed yet? **3.** (= *ochronić się*) protect o.s., deliver o.s. from.

obronność *f.* **1.** (*o bezpieczeństwie państwa*) defense; **wydatki na obronność** defense spending. **2.** *biol.* (= *odporność*) resistance.

obronny *a.* defensive; **pies obronny** guard dog; **mechanizm obronny** defense mechanism; **wał obronny** bulwark; **mury obronne** ramparts; **wyjść z czegoś obronną ręką** get off the tiger *l.* the tiger's back.

obrońca *mp* **1.** (= *występujący w obronie*) defender, champion; **obrońca uciśnionych** champion of the oppressed. **2.** (= *orędownik*) defender, advocate. **3.** *prawn.* (= *adwokat*) defense counsel, counsel for the defense, defender, defense attorney, defense lawyer; **obrońca z urzędu** assigned counsel, court-appointed attorney, public defender. **4.** *sport* defender.

obrończy *a.* advocatory; **mowa obrończa** *prawn.* closing argument *l.* statement, final argument, jury summation, summing up.

obrończyni *f. zob.* **obrońca.**

obrosnąć *pf.* **-rosnę -rośniesz, -rośnij, -rósł -rosła -rośli** *zob.* **obrastać.**

obrostnica *f. bot.* (= *wiązowiec*) hackberry (*Celtis*).

obrośnięty *a.* overgrown, covered (*with grass, dust, etc.*).

obrotność *f.* go-aheadness, enterprise, resourcefulness.

obrotny *a.* **1.** (= *przedsiębiorczy*) enterprising; *pot.* street-smart. **2.** *przest.* (= *szybki*) nimble, agile; **mieć obrotny język** have a glib tongue.

obrotomierz *mi Gen.* **-a** *techn.* tachometer, rev counter.

obrotowy *a.* **1.** (= *wirowy*) rotary, revolving, rotatory, rotative; *astron.* revolutionary; *anat.* trochoid; **bryła obrotowa** *geom.* solid of revolution; **kręg obrotowy** *anat.* axis; **moment obrotowy** *mech.* torque; **ruch obrotowy** *mech.* circumvolution; **staw obrotowy** *med.* trochoid joint; **talerz obrotowy** (*w gramofonie*) turntable. **2.** (= *obracający się*) revolving; **drzwi obrotowe** revolving door; **krzesło obrotowe** swivel chair; **scena obrotowa** revolving *l.* rotating stage. **3.** *ekon.* sales, turnover; **fundusz** *l.* **kapitał obrotowy** working capital; **podatek obrotowy** sales *l.* turnover tax; **środki obrotowe** circulating *l.* current *l.* floating *l.* short term assets, circulating capital.

obroża *f. Gen.pl.* **-y 1.** (*dla psa*) collar *l.* dog collar. **2.** *zool.* (= *kołnierz*) collar, torque.

obróbka *f. Gen.pl.* **-ek 1.** *techn.* (= *przetwarzanie*) processing; (= *nadawanie kształtu*) working, tooling, machining; (*poddawanie działaniu temperatury, kwasów itp.*) treatment; **obróbka chemiczna** chemical treatment; **obróbka cieplna** heat treatment; **obróbka danych** *komp.* data processing; **obróbka drewna** woodworking; **obróbka metali** metalworking; **obróbka plastyczna** plastic working; **obróbka skrawaniem** machining; **obróbka ścieków** sewage treatment; **obróbka termiczna** heat treatment. **2.** *roln.* (= *uprawa*) cultivation.

obrócić *pf. zob.* **obracać.** ~ **się** *pf. zob.* **obracać się.**

obróść *pf.* **-osnę -ośniesz, -ośnij, -ósł -osła -ośli** *zob.* **obrastać.**

obrót *mi* **-o- 1.** (= *ruch wokół własnej osi*) turn, spin; *mat., mech.* rotation; *astron., mech.* revolution; *mech.* rev; *astron.* revolution, roll; **na najwyższych obrotach** in high *l.* top gear; **na pełnych obrotach** at full speed; **pracować na pełnych obrotach** (*np. o firmie, fabryce*) work at full capacity, be in full swing; **pracować na najwyższych obrotach** (*np. o czyjejś wyobraźni*) go into overdrive; **życie na pełnych obrotach** life in the fast lane; **brać kogoś w obroty** work sb; **w przyszłym roku biorę moich studentów w obroty** I'm going to work my students next year. **2.** (= *kierunek, zwrot*) turn; **obrót spraw** the state of affairs; **przybrać zły obrót** (*np. o planach*) go adrift; **sprawy przybrały nowy obrót** things have taken a new turn; **sprawy między nimi przybrały fatalny obrót** things between them have come to a dreadful pass. **3.** *ekon.* sales, turnover; **obrót detaliczny** retail sales; **obrót towarowy** sales of goods; **wzrost obrotów** increase in sales; **zwiększać obroty handlowe** drum up business.

obrugać *pf. pot.* (= *skarcić*) scold.

obrumieniać *ipf.*, **obrumienić** *pf.* brown (*na patelni* in a frying-pan) (*w maśle* in butter).

obrus *mi Gen.* **-u** *l.* **-a** tablecloth, spread.

obruszać *ipf.*, **obruszyć** *pf.* **1.** (= *poruszać*) stir, shake. **2.** (= *rozchwiać*) work loose, loosen. ~ **się** *ipf.*, **obruszyć się** *pf.* **1.** (= *denerwować się*) bridle (*na kogoś / coś* at sb/sth). **2.** (= *poluzować się*) loosen, slacken.

obryć *pf.* **-ję -jesz, -yj 1.** (*o kretach, dzikach*) burrow. **2.** *pot.* (= *nauczyć się*) cram; **być obrytym** be well-crammed (*for a test*). ~ **się** *pf.* **-ję -jesz, -yj** = **obryć** 2.

obrys *mi* (= *kontur*) outline, contour.

obrysować *pf.*, **obrysowywać** *ipf.* (= *obliniować, szkicować*) outline, contour.

obryty *a.* **1.** (= *zryty*) burrowed, hollowed out. **2.** (= *obkuty, nauczony*) well-crammed (*for a test*).

obryw *mi* **1.** (= *oberwanie się*) landslide *l.* landslip; **obryw skalny** rockfall. **2.** (= *urwisko*) precipice. **3.** *pot.* (= *wysoki dochód*) good money;

ma w tej pracy niezłe obrywy he's raking it in in this job.

obrywać *ipf.* **1.** (= *urywać*) tear off; (*owoce*) pick; (*np. liście z gałęzi*) pluck. **2.** *ogr.* (*pączki lub pędy*) pinch. **3.** *pot.* (= *dostawać*) get; **oberwać dwóję** get *l.* earn a D; **oberwać nauczkę** catch it, catch hell. **4.** *pot.* (= *dostawać lanie*) get it in the neck; **oberwać po głowie** get a knock on the head. ~ **się** *ipf.* (= *urywać się, odpadać*) tear off, fall off.

obryzgać *pf.*, **obryzgiwać** *ipf.* **1.** (= *chlapać*) splash, splotch. **2.** (= *wyzywać*) chide, lash (out) (*kogoś* at sb). ~ **się** *pf.*, **obryzgiwać się** *ipf.* (= *opryskiwać się*) splash o.s., splotch o.s.

obrządek *mi* **-dk- 1.** (= *rytuał*) ritual. **2.** *rel.* (= *ryt liturgiczny*) rite; **obrządek łaciński** the Latin rite; **obrządek wschodni** the Greek rite. **3.** (= *wyznanie religijne*) denomination. **4.** *pot.* (= *oporządzanie*) farm chores.

obrządzać *ipf.*, **obrządzić** *pf.* tend (*farm animals*).

obrzezać *pf. zob.* **obrzezywać.**

obrzezanie *n.* circumcision; **święto Obrzezania Pańskiego** *rel.* Circumcision.

obrzezaniec *mp* **-ńc-** *pl.* **-y** circumcised person.

obrzezywać *ipf.* circumcise.

obrzeże *n. Gen.pl.* **-y** outer edge(s), fringe; **obrzeża miasta** outskirts.

obrzeżki *pl. Gen.* **-ów** *zool.* (*kleszcze*) soft ticks (*Argasidae*).

obrzęd *mi* (= *ceremoniał, rytuał*) ceremony.

obrzędowość *f.* rituals, rites (*esp. folk or ethnic traditional ceremonies*).

obrzędowy *a.* ritual.

obrzęk *mi* **1.** *pat.* edema; **obrzęk mózgu/płuc** *pat.* cerebral/pulmonary edema; **obrzęk złośliwy** *wet.* blackleg. **2.** *pot.* (= *miejsce spuchnięte*) swelling, puff.

obrzękać *ipf.* swell, tumefy.

obrzęki *pl. Gen.* **-ów** *zool.* (*pająki*) gall mites (*Eriophyidae*).

obrzękły *a.* swollen, tumid.

obrzęknąć *pf.* **-ij** *zob.* **obrzękać.**

obrzmiałość *f.* swelling.

obrzmiały *a.* swollen.

obrzmieć *pf. zob.* **obrzmiewać.**

obrzmienie *n.* swelling.

obrzmiewać *ipf.* swell.

obrzucać *ipf.*, **obrzucić** *pf.* **1.** (= *obsypywać*) hurl, pelt, throw; **obrzucać kogoś granatami** pelt grenades at sb; **obrzucić kogoś kwiatami** throw *l.* hurl flowers at sb; **obrzucić kogoś pytaniami** flood *l.* inundate sb with questions. **2.** (= *obłożyć, otulić*) cover (*e.g. with earth or clay, in order to protect from the cold, etc.*). **3.** (= *wyzywać*) hurl; **obrzucić kogoś błotem** throw *l.* sling *l.* fling *l.* hurl mud at sb, drag sb's name through *l.* in the muck *l.* mud; **obrzucać kogoś przekleństwami** shower sb with abuse, hurl abuse at sb; **obrzucić kogoś wyzwiskami** swear at sb, call sb names; **obrzucić kogoś stekiem wyzwisk** hurl a volley of abuse at sb. **4.** (= *obszywać*) overcast. ~ **się** *ipf.*, **obrzucić się** *pf.* **1.** (= *zarzucać się*) hurl at each other *l.* one another, throw at each other *l.* one another. **2.** (= *wyzywać się*) hurl; **obrzucać się wyzwiskami** hurl insults at each other *l.* one another.

obrzutka *f. bud.* render.

obrzydlistwo *n.* sth nauseating or hideous; **ten placek to obrzydlistwo** this pie is damn yucky; **to, co zrobił, to obrzydlistwo** what he did was hideous.

obrzydliwie *adv.* hideously, sickeningly.

obrzydliwiec *mp* -wc- *Voc.* -cze *l.* -u *pl.* -y crud.

obrzydliwość *f.* **1.** (= *ohyda, szkaradność*) *zob.* **obrzydlistwo. 2.** (= *obrzydzenie*) disgust, revulsion.

obrzydliwy *a.* (= *ohydny*) disgusting, revolting, sickening.

obrzydły *a.* disgusting, revolting, sickening.

obrzydnąć *pf.* -ij, -dł *l.* -dnął -dła -dli become loathsome *l.* abhorrent; **życie mi obrzydło** I'm plain sick and tired of my life.

obrzydzać *ipf.* make repugnant, gross out, repulse; **obrzydzić sobie kogoś** *l.* **coś** become disgusted with sb *l.* sth.

obrzydzenie *n.* disgust, revulsion; **napełniać** *l.* **napawać obrzydzeniem** fill with disgust, gross out, repulse.

obrzydzić *pf. zob.* **obrzydzać.**

obrzygać *pf. pot.* puke (*kogoś/coś* all over sb/sth *l.* on sb/sth).

obrzyn *mi Gen.* -a **1.** *pot.* (*broń*) sawed-off gun. **2.** (= *skrawek*) paring; (*metalu*) scissel, clippings.

obrzynać *ipf.* **1.** (= *okroić*) trim. **2.** (= *obcinać*) cut off, saw off.

obrzynek *mi* -nk- *Gen.* -a **1.** (= *ścinek*) paring; (*metalu*) scissel, clippings; (*np. jedzenia*) dribs and drabs. **2.** *pot.* (*broń*) sawed-off gun.

obsada *f.* **1.** (= *obsadzenie*) appointment, assignment. **2.** (= *załoga*) crew. **3.** (= *personel*) staff. **4.** (*w filmie, teatrze*) cast. **5.** *myśl., zootechnika* (*ilość zwierzyny na łowisku, stan inwentarza*) stock. **6.** *techn.* (= *oprawa*) holder; mounting; housing.

obsadka *f. Gen.pl.* -ek *przest.* (*do pisania*) penholder.

obsadzać *ipf.,* **obsadzić** *pf.* **1.** (= *sadzić rośliny*) plant out (*a piece of land with flowers, bushes, etc.*); **obsadzić drogę drzewami** line a road with trees. **2.** (= *przytwierdzać*) fix, fit. **3.** (= *angażować*) appoint, assign; **obsadzić stanowisko** appoint sb to a post, man a post; **obsadzić aktora w roli** cast an actor in a part, cast an actor as; **obsadzić załogą** (*fort, statek*) man; **obsadzić garnizonem** *wojsk.* garrison; **obsadzać sztukę** cast a play. **4.** *rzad.* (= *obsiadać*) take one's seat, sit down (*e.g. around sb/sth*). **5.** (= *zajmować pozycje*) take up positions.

obscena *pl. Gen.* -ów obscenities.

obsceniczność *f.* obscenity.

obsceniczny *a.* obscene.

obserwacja *f.* **1.** (= *przyglądanie się*) observation, scrutiny; (*np. policyjna*) surveillance; **być pod ścisłą obserwacją** (*np. w miejscu pracy*) be under close scrutiny. **2.** (= *opinia*) observation,

remark. **3.** *med.* observation; **pacjent poddany obserwacji** a patient under observation.

obserwacyjny *a.* (*służący do obserwacji, empiryczny*) observational; **punkt obserwacyjny** vantage point; **samolot obserwacyjny** *wojsk.* reconnaissance plane.

obserwator *mp pl.* -rzy *l.* -owie **1.** (= *widz*) observer; spectator; **przenikliwy obserwator życia politycznego** an acute observer of the political life. **2.** (= *wysłannik, delegat*) observer; (*np. przy wyborach*) watcher, scrutineer. **3.** *wojsk.* (= *zwiadowca*) spotter.

obserwatorium *n. sing. indecl. pl.* -ria *Gen.* -riów observatory; **obserwatorium astronomiczne** astronomical observatory.

obserwatorka *f. Gen.pl.* -ek *zob.* **obserwator.**

obserwatorski *a.* observatory.

obserwować *ipf.* **1.** (= *dokonywać obserwacji*) observe. **2.** (= *śledzić coś*) watch; keep track of. **3.** (= *przyglądać się, nadzorować*) monitor, scrutinize; **bacznie kogoś obserwować** keep a close eye *l.* watch on sb; **obserwować ptaki** (*jako hobby*) birdwatch. **~ się** *ipf.* **1.** (= *patrzeć na siebie*) observe *l.* watch each other *l.* one another. **2.** (= *oglądać się samemu*) observe *l.* watch o.s.

obsesja *f.* obsession (*na punkcie kogoś/czegoś* with *l.* about sb/sth); **mieć obsesję na punkcie kogoś/czegoś** be obsessed *l.* obsessive about sb/sth, obsess over *l.* about sb/sth, fixate on sb/sth.

obsesyjnie *adv.* obsessively.

obsesyjność *f.* obsessiveness.

obsesyjny *a.* obsessive.

obsiać *pf.* -eję -ejesz *zob.* **obsiewać. ~ się** *pf.* **1.** (= *zakończyć siew*) have completed one's sowing. **2.** (*o chwastach*) get self-sown.

obsiadać *ipf.,* **obsiąść** *pf.* -siądę -siądziesz -siadł -siedli gather around, cluster around, sit around (*e.g. a table, etc.*).

obsiany *a.* sown over (*with seeds of a plant*); **obsiany pszenicą** under wheat.

obsiew *mi* **1.** (= *obsianie*) sowing. **2.** (= *wysiane ziarno*) seeds sown (*over an area*).

obsiewać *ipf.* sow over (*a piece of land*); **obsiać kukurydzą** corn over; **obsiać trawą** grass over.

obsikać *pf.,* **obsikiwać** *ipf.* **1.** (*o moczu*) wet (*coś* sth); pass water (*coś* on sth). **2.** *pot.* (= *pryskać*) spray, squirt.

obsiusiać *pf.* pass water (*coś* on sth).

obskakiwać *ipf.,* **obskoczyć** *pf.* **1.** (= *otaczać*) beset (*kogoś/coś* sb/sth); close in (*kogoś/coś* on sb/sth). **2.** *pot.* (= *iść w kilka miejsc*) hit, cruise. **3.** (= *skakać*) jump around. **4.** *pot.* (= *usługiwać*) wait hand and foot (*komuś* on sb); treat with kid gloves.

obskrobać *pf.* -ę -esz, **obskrobywać** *ipf.* scrape off, peel off (*z czegoś* sth).

obskubać *pf.* -ę -esz, **obskubywać** *ipf.* **1.** (= *obrywać*) pluck (*z czegoś* sth off). **2.** *pot.* (= *wyłudzać, grabić*) fleece.

obskurancki *a.* obscurant, obscurantist.

obskurant *mp,* **obskurantka** *f. Gen.pl.* -ek obscurant, obscurantist.

obskurantyzm *mi* obscurantism.

obskurnie *adv.* sordidly, shabbily.

obskurny *a.* sordid, shabby.

obsługa *f.* 1. (= *obsługiwanie*) service, attendance; obsługa klientów customer service; obsługa długu *fin.* debt servicing; obsługa techniczna maintenance. 2. (= *załoga, personel*) service, staff; obsługa naziemna ground crew *l.* staff; obsługa techniczna maintenance staff.

obsługiwać *ipf.* 1. (= *pomagać, spełniać polecenia*) serve. 2. (*np. klienta w sklepie*) attend to, help. 3. (*np. gościa w restauracji*) wait on *l.* upon. 4. (*np. maszynę*) operate. 5. (*dług*) service. 6. (= *działać, mieć zasięg*) serve, service; tę linię obsługują dwa autobusy this line is served *l.* serviced by two buses. ~ się *ipf.* help o.s.; w tym barze obsługujemy się sami this is a self-service bar.

obsługowy *a.* servicing.

obsłużyć *pf. zob.* obsługiwać. ~ się *pf. zob.* obsługiwać się.

obsmarować *pf.*, obsmarowywać *ipf.* 1. (= *brudzić*) smear, bedaub. 2. *pot.* (= *obmawiać*) blacken, vilify, drag sb's same through the mud; (*w prasie*) libel. ~ się *pf.*, obsmarowywać się *ipf.* 1. (= *ubrudzić się*) smear o.s., bedaub o.s. 2. (= *oczerniać się*) blacken one another, vilify one another.

obsmażać *ipf.*, obsmażyć *pf.* lightly brown sth. ~ się *ipf.*, obsmażyć się *pf.* 1. (= *przyrumieniać się*) get lightly browned. 2. *pot.* (= *opalać się na słońcu*) bake (*in the sun*).

obstalować *pf.*, obstalowywać *ipf. przest.* (= *zamawiać*) order.

obstalunek *mi* -nk- *przest.* (= *zamówienie*) order; zrobiony na obstalunek made to order.

obstawa *f.* (= *ochrona*) guards, bodyguards.

obstawać *ipf.* -aję -ajesz, -waj 1. (= *upierać się*) persist (*przy czymś* in sth) stick (*przy czymś* to sth). 2. *przest.* (= *ujmować się*) support, stand by, back (*za kimś l. czymś* sb *l.* sth).

obstawiać *ipf.*, obstawić *pf.* 1. (= *otaczać*) surround. 2. *sport* (= *kryć*) guard. 3. (*w hazardzie, wyścigach*) bet on, back. 4. *pot.* (= *ochraniać*) guard; bodyguard. ~ się *ipf.*, obstawić się *pf.* (= *otaczać się*) surround o.s.

obstąpić *pf.*, obstępować *ipf.* (= *otaczać*) surround, form *l.* gather in a circle around.

obstrukcja *f.* 1. (= *utrudnianie*) obstruction; obstrukcja parlamentarna *polit.* filibuster, parliamentary obstruction. 2. *med.* (= *zatwardzenie*) constipation; (*zwł. ostra*) obstipation.

obstrukcyjny *a.* 1. (= *dotyczący utrudniania*) obstructive. 2. *med.* constipation, obstipation.

obstrzał *mi* 1. *wojsk.* fire; być pod obstrzałem be under fire. 2. *górn.* firing. 3. *przen.* (= *nagonka, atak*) fire; być pod obstrzałem prasy *l.* mediów be *l.* come under fire from the press *l.* mass media.

obstrzępić *pf.* (= *obszarpać*) fray, tatter.

obstrzyc *pf.* -gę -żesz -gł -gła -gli, obstrzygać *ipf.* cut (sb's) hair, shear.

obstukać *pf.*, obstukiwać *ipf.* 1. (= *opukać*) tap. 2. *przen., pot., szkoln.* (= *wyuczyć się*) cram, learn.

obsunąć *pf. zob.* obsuwać. ~ się *pf. zob.* obsuwać się.

obsuszać *ipf.*, obsuszyć *pf.* dry. ~ się *ipf.*, obsuszyć się *pf.* 1. (= *wysuszać się*) dry. 2. (= *obsychać z wierzchu*) dry on the surface.

obsuwać *ipf.* slide, sink. ~ się *ipf.* 1. (= *zsuwać się*) slide; sink. 2. (= *przewracać się*) fall, drop (*na coś* onto sth); obsuwać się na kolana *l.* ziemię drop *l.* sink to one's knees *l.* the ground. 3. *przen.* (= *nie udać się*) fail.

obsuwisko *n. geol.* landslide.

obsychać *ipf.* dry, get dry.

obsydian *mi min.* obsidian.

obsypać *pf.* -ę -esz, obsypywać *ipf.* 1. (= *oprószyć*) sprinkle; obsypywać pocałunkami shower with kisses; obsypywać komplementami shower with compliments; obsypywać obelgami shower *l.* pelt with insults. 2. (= *usiać*) cover. 3. (= *obdarowywać*) shower; obsypywać kogoś prezentami shower sb with gifts *l.* presents. 4. *roln.* (= *obkopywać*) ridge, hill, earth up. ~ się *pf.*, obsypywać się *ipf.* 1. (= *oprószyć się*) become covered. 2. (= *pokrywać się*) sprinkle o.s., cover o.s. 3. (= *obrzucać się*) (*np. piaskiem*) throw at each other; (*np. obelgami*) shower each other, pelt each other. 4. (= *odrywać się*) drop, fall (*z czegoś* from sth).

obszar *mi* 1. (= *teren*) area; territory. 2. *mat.* closed and connected set. 3. *przen.* (= *dziedzina*) area, field.

obszarnictwo *n.* 1. (= *feudalizm*) feudalism, landowning. 2. (= *obszarnicy*) landowners, landed gentry *l.* aristocracy.

obszarniczy *a.* landowning.

obszarnik *mp* landowner.

obszarpać *pf.* -ę -esz *zob.* obszarpywać. ~ się *pf. zob.* obszarpywać się.

obszarpaniec *mp* -ńc- *pl.* -y *pog.* ragamuffin.

obszarpany *a.* ragged, tattered.

obszarpywać *ipf.* fray, tatter. ~ się *ipf.* become frayed, become tattered.

obszczekać *pf.*, obszczekiwać *ipf.* 1. (*o psie*) bark at. 2. *pot.* (= *obgadywać*) run down, crab about.

obszedł *pf. zob.* obejść.

obszernie *adv.* (= *długo*) at length; (= *dokładnie, drobiazgowo*) comprehensively, in great detail.

obszerność *f.* 1. (= *przestronność*) spaciousness, ampleness. 2. (= *szczegółowość*) comprehensiveness, detailedness.

obszerny *a.* 1. (= *przestronny*) large, broad, spacious. 2. (= *szczegółowy*) comprehensive, detailed.

obsztorcować *pf.*, obsztorcowywać *ipf. pot.* tell off, dress down.

obszukać *pf.*, obszukiwać *ipf.* 1. (= *przejrzeć, przeszukać*) search, go through. 2. (= *zrewidować*) frisk.

obszycie *n.* 1. (= *przyszycie*) hemming. 2. (= *lamówka*) hem. 3. *techn.* (= *osłona*) sheathing.

obszyć *pf.* -ję -jesz, obszywać *ipf.* -am -asz 1. (= *przyszywać*) hem. 2. (= *obrębiać*) edge, fringe. 3. (= *zaszyć*) sew up. 4. *żegl.* plank.

obszywka *f. Gen.pl.* **-ek** hem, border, fringe.

obściskać *pf.*, **obściskiwać** *ipf.* hug, squeeze. **~ się** *pf.*, **obściskiwać się** *ipf.* hug each other, squeeze each other.

obśliniać *ipf.*, **obślinić** *pf.* cover with saliva. **~ się** *ipf.*, **obślinić się** *pf.* cover o.s. with saliva.

obśmiać *pf.* **-eję -ejesz**, **obśmiewać** *ipf. pot.* laugh, scoff, jeer (*kogoś/coś* at sb/sth). **~ się** *pf.*, **obśmiewać się** *ipf. pot.* have a good laugh.

obtaczać *ipf.* **1.** (= *obklejać*) coat; **obtoczyć w mące** coat with flour; **obtoczyć w bułce** bread. **2.** (*np. kamień*) (= *wygładzać*) wear. **3.** *techn.* turn. **4.** *rzad.* (= *okrążać*) roll around, go around.

obtańcować *pf.*, **obtańcowywać** *ipf.* **1.** *przest.* (= *tańczyć*) (*wiele tańców z jedną osobą*) dance again and again with sb; (*kolejno z wieloma osobami*) dance with all the women present. **2.** *pot.* (= *rugać, karcić*) scold, dress down.

obtarcie *n.* **1.** (= *wytarcie*) wipe, rub. **2.** (= *zdarcie, uszkodzenie*) scratch, scrape; **otarcie lakieru** scratched paint. **3.** (= *rana*) sore; **otarcie naskórka** graze.

obtarł *itd. pf. zob.* **obetrzeć**.

obtłuc *pf.* **-kę -czesz -kł -kli**, **obtłukiwać** *ipf.* **1.** (= *wyszczerbić*) chip. **2.** (= *kaleczyć, uszkodzić*) bruise, beat. **~ się** *pf.*, **obtłukiwać się** *ipf.* **1.** (= *wyszczerbić się*) become chipped. **2.** (= *kaleczyć się*) bruise.

obtoczyć *pf. zob.* **obtaczać**.

obu *num. zob.* **oba, obaj, obie**.

obuch *mi Gen.* **-a 1.** (*część narzędzia*) head; **obuch siekiery** head of an ax(e). **2.** *hist.* (*broń*) battle-ax(e); **dostać obuchem w głowę** *przen.* be stunned *l.* staggered.

obuć *pf. zob.* **obuwać**.

obudowa *f. Gen.pl.* **-ów 1.** (= *osłona*) housing, casing. **2.** (= *zabudowa*) surrounding buildings. **3.** (= *obudowanie*) housing *l.* casing construction. **4.** *górn.* lining.

obudować *pf.*, **obudowywać** *ipf.* **1.** (= *zabudowywać*) build round, surround with buildings. **2.** (= *osłaniać*) encase. **3.** (*o kuchni, przedpokoju*) have fitted.

obudzić *pf.* **1.** (= *zbudzić*) wake (up), waken (up), awake, awaken. **2.** (= *wywołać, wzbudzić*) rouse. **~ się** *pf.* **1.** (= *zbudzić się*) wake (up), waken (up), awake, awaken; **obudzić się z ręką w nocniku** *pot.* have *l.* get *l.* receive *l.* experience a rude awakening. **2.** (= *pojawić się*) (*o emocjach*) arise, come to life.

obumarły *a.* **1.** (= *martwy*) dead. **2.** (= *wygasły*) extinct.

obumierać *ipf.*, **obumrzeć** *pf.* **-mrę -mrzesz, -mrzyj, -marł 1.** (= *zamierać*) atrophy, necrose. **2.** (= *zanikać, wygasać*) die, die out, wither.

obunogi *pl. Gen.* **-ów** *zool.* amphipods (*Amphipoda*).

obunożny *a.* of both feet *l.* legs.

obunóż *adv. sport* on both feet *l.* legs.

obupłciowość *f. biol.* hermaphrodism, hermaphroditism; bisexuality, bisexualism.

obupłciowy *a. biol.* hemaphroditic, bisexual.

oburącz *adv.* with both hands; **trzymać się czegoś oburącz** hold onto sth with both hands.

oburzać *ipf.* (= *gniewać*) shock, apall, outrage. **~ się** *ipf.* be *l.* feel indignant (*na kogoś l. coś* with sb *l.* at sth).

oburzająco *adv.* outrageously.

oburzający *a.* outrageous.

oburzenie *n.* indignation, outrage; **święte oburzenie** righteous indignation.

oburzony *a.* **-eni** indignant, outraged.

oburzyć *pf. zob.* **oburzać**. **~ się** *pf. zob.* **oburzać się**.

obustronny *a.* **1.** (*na dwóch stronach*) bilateral, two-sided, double-sided. **2.** (= *wzajemny*) mutual, reciprocal.

obuwać *ipf.* shoe.

obuwie *n.* footwear.

obuwik *mi Gen.* **-a** *bot.* lady's-slipper, ladyslipper (*Cypripedium*).

obuwnictwo *n.* shoe industry.

obuwniczy *a.* shoe; **przemysł obuwniczy** shoe industry.

obuwnik *mp* (= *szewc*) shoemaker.

obwałować *pf. zob.* **obwałowywać**.

obwałowanie *n.* **1.** (= *wzniesienie wału*) embanking. **2.** (= *wały przeciwpowodziowe*) levee.

obwałowywać *ipf.* embank.

obwarować *pf. zob.* **obwarowywać**. **~ się** *pf. zob.* **obwarowywać się**.

obwarowanie *n.* **1.** (= *otoczenie wałem*) embankment. **2.** fortification, entrenchment. **3.** (= *zagwarantowanie*) guarantee, security.

obwarowywać *ipf.* **1.** (= *umacniać*) fortify, entrench. **2.** (= *zagwarantować*) guarantee, secure.

obwarzanek *mi* **-nk-** *Gen.* **-a 1.** (*ciastko*) pretzel. **2.** (= *kółko*) pretzel-shaped object.

obwąchać *pf.*, **obwąchiwać** *ipf.* (= *powąchać*) sniff (*kogoś/coś* at sb/sth); snuff (*kogoś/coś* at sb/sth).

obwiązać *pf.* **-żę -żesz**, **obwiązywać** *ipf.* (= *owijać*) tie; wrap around. **~ się** *pf.*, **obwiązywać się** *ipf.* (= *zawijać się*) wrap (*sth around sb's head, shoulders, etc.*).

obwiesić *pf.*, **obwieszać** *ipf.* (= *zawieszać*) hang; (= *udekorować*) decorate; (= *upstrzyć*) festoon. **~ się** *pf.*, **obwieszać się** *ipf.* deck o.s. out.

obwieszczać *ipf.* (= *ogłaszać*) announce, proclaim.

obwieszczenie *n.* (= *informowanie l. komunikat*) announcement, proclamation.

obwieś *mp Gen.pl.* **-i** *l.* **-ów** *pot.* (= *nicpoń, gagatek*) good-for-nothing.

obwieścić *pf. zob.* **obwieszczać**.

obwieść *pf.* **-wiodę -wiedziesz -wiódł -wiodła -wiedli** *zob.* **obwodzić**.

obwieźć *pf.* **-wiozę -wieziesz -wiózł -wiozła -wieźli** *zob.* **obwozić**.

obwiniać *ipf.*, **obwinić** *pf.* (= *zarzucić*) blame (*kogoś o coś* sb for sth); (= *oskarżyć*) accuse (*kogoś o coś* sb of sth).

obwiniony *a.* **-eni** accused. **– mp** *prawn.* the accused, defendant.

obwisać *ipf.* droop, hang down, flag.

obwisłość *f.* droopiness.

obwisły *a.* drooping.

obwisnąć *pf.* **-sł** *l.* **-snął -sła** *zob.* **obwisać**.

obwodnica *f.* (*trasa*) beltway, bypass; *Br.* ring road.

obwodowy *a.* **1.** (*dotyczący zamkniętej linii*) circumferential, circular; **trasa obwodowa** beltway, bypass; *Br.* ring road; **obwodowy układ nerwowy** *anat.* peripheral nervous system. **2.** district; **obwodowa komisja wyborcza** (district) polling station.

obwodzić *ipf.* **-ódź 1.** (= *otaczać*) encircle, surround. **2.** (= *oprowadzać*) show around (*po czymś* sth).

obwoluta *f.* jacket, dust cover.

obwołać *pf.*, **obwoływać** *ipf.* **1.** (= *ogłaszać, proklamować*) announce, proclaim. **2.** *przest.* (= *uznawać, nazywać*) proclaim.

obwozić *ipf.* drive around, show around.

obwoźny *a.* mobile; **handel obwoźny** door-to-door *l.* house-to-house sales.

obwód *mi* **-o- 1.** (*zamknięta linia*) circumference, periphery; **obwód trójkąta** periphery of a triangle; **obwód okręgu** circumference of a circle; **obwód elektryczny** electric circuit. **2.** (= *teren*) district; **obwód wyborczy** polling district; **obwód łowiecki** hunting ground.

obwódka *f. Gen.pl.* **-ek** border.

oby *particle* (= *aby*) may you, he, etc.; I wish *l.* hope you, he, etc.; **oby tak było** I wish it were so; **obyś był szczęśliwy** may you be happy.

obycie *n.* **1.** (= *przyzwyczajenie się*) familiarity (*z czymś* with sth). **2.** (= *ogłada*) manners, cultivation, refinement; **obycie towarzyskie** cultivation.

obyczaj *mi Gen.pl.* **-ów 1.** (= *zwyczaj*) custom; **ludowe obyczaje** folk customs; **obyczaje bożonarodzeniowe** Christmas customs; **co kraj, to obyczaj** so many countries, so many customs; every country has its customs; **inne czasy, inne obyczaje** other times, other manners *l.* customs. **2.** (= *nawyk*) habit.

obyczaje *pl. Gen.* **-ów** (= *obyczajowość*) morals; **kobieta lekkich obyczajów** woman of easy virtue; **upadek obyczajów** decline of moral standards; **muzyka łagodzi obyczaje** music soothes *l.* calms the savage beast.

obyczajowość *f.* **1.** (*ogół obyczajów*) customs, tradition. **2.** (= *prowadzenie się*) morals. **3.** (= *maniery*) manners.

obyczajowy *a.* **1.** (*dotyczący obyczaju*) customary; **film obyczajowy** *film* film drama; **powieść obyczajowa** *teor.lit.* novel of manners. **2.** (*dotyczący prowadzenia się*) moral; **policja obyczajowa** vice squad.

obyczajówka *f. Gen.pl.* **-ek** *pot.* vice squad; *sl.* pussy posse.

obyć się *pf.* **obędę obędziesz obędą, obądź**, **obył** *zob.* **obywać się**.

obydwa *num. Gen. i Loc.* **-óch** *l.* **-u** *Dat.* **-om** *l.* **-u** *l.* **-óm** *Ins.* **-oma** *l.* **-u** both.

obydwaj *num. Gen. i Loc.* **-óch** *l.* **-u** *Dat.* **-om** *l.* **-u** *l.* **-óm** *Ins.* **-oma** *l.* **-u** both.

obydwie *num. Gen. i Loc.* **-óch** *l.* **-u** *Dat.* **-om** *l.* **-u** *l.* **-óm** *Ins.* **-ema** *l.* **-oma** both.

obydwoje *num. decl. like n.* **-jg-** both.

obyty *a.* **1.** well-mannered, cultured, cultivated; **człowiek obyty w świecie** person who has been around. **2.** (= *przyzwyczajony*) familiar (*z czymś* with sth).

obywać się *ipf.* **1.** (= *radzić sobie*) go, do, manage (*bez kogoś l. czegoś* without sb *l.* sth); dispense (*bez czegoś* with sth). **2.** (= *zadowalać się*) make do (*czymś* with sth).

obywatel *mp*, **obywatelka** *f. Gen.pl.* **-ek 1.** (*państwa*) citizen; **obywatel świata** citizen of the world, cosmopolite; **szary obywatel** the man in the street. **2.** (= *mieszkaniec*) inhabitant, citizen; **honorowy obywatel** honorary citizen.

obywatelski *a.* citizenly; civic, civil; **prawa obywatelskie** civil rights; **obowiązki obywatelskie** civic duties.

obywatelstwo *n.* citizenship; **obywatelstwo polskie** Polish citizenship; **podwójne obywatelstwo** dual citizenship; **obywatelstwo honorowe** honorary citizenship; **nadać obywatelstwo** grant citizenship; **pozbawić obywatelstwa** revoke citizenship; **uzyskać obywatelstwo** receive *l.* acquire citizenship; **zrzec się obywatelstwa** give up *l.* renounce citizenship.

obznajamiać *ipf.*, **obznajomić** *pf.* inform (*z czymś* of *l.* about sth); acquaint (*z czymś* with sth). **~ się** *ipf.*, **obznajomić się** *pf.* acquaint o.s., become acquainted, familiarize o.s. (*z czymś* with sth).

obżarstwo *n.* gluttony.

obżartuch *mp* **-y** glutton, gourmand.

obżerać *ipf.* **1.** (*o zwierzętach*) (= *objadać*) gnaw (*coś* at *l.* upon sth). **2.** *pot.* (= *objadać*) **obżerać kogoś** eat sb else's food, sponge food off sb. **~ się** *ipf. pot.* binge, gorge.

ocalać *ipf.* save, rescue, salvage (*przed kimś l. czymś* from sb *l.* sth); deliver (*od czegoś* from sth); **ocalić od zapomnienia** save from oblivion. **~ się** *ipf.* survive (*z czegoś* sth).

ocaleć *pf.* survive (*z czegoś* sth).

ocalenie *n.* **1.** (= *uratowanie*) salvation. **2.** (= *ratunek*) rescue.

ocalić *pf. zob.* **ocalać**. **~ się** *pf. zob.* **ocalać się**.

ocean *mi* **1.** *geogr.* ocean; **Ocean Atlantycki** the Atlantic (Ocean); **Ocean Indyjski** the Indian Ocean; **Ocean Spokojny** the Pacific (Ocean). **2.** *przen.* (= *bezmiar, ogrom*) ocean.

oceanarium *n. sing. indecl. pl.* **-ria** *Gen.* **-riów** oceanarium.

Oceania *f. Gen.* **-ii** *geogr.* Oceania, Oceanica.

oceaniczny *a.* oceanic.

oceanografia *f. Gen.* **-ii** oceanography.

oceanograficzny *a.* oceanographic, oceanographical.

oceanolog *mp Gen.pl.* **-dzy -***l.* **-owie** oceanologist.

oceanologia *f. Gen.* **-ii** oceanology.

oceanotechnika *f.* ocean engineering, oceaneering.

ocechować *pf.* brand, mark.

ocelot *ma zool.* ocelot (*Felis pardalis*).

oceloty *pl. Gen.* **-ów** (*skóry, futro*) ocelot fur.

ocembrować *pf.* reinforce (*a well, river bank, etc. with bricks, concrete, etc.*).

ocena *f.* **1.** (= *opinia, sąd*) opinion, assessment, judgment; **poddać coś ocenie** evaluate sth, assess sth; **przychylna ocena** favorable opinion. **2.** (= *stopień, nota*) grade, mark; **ocena niedostateczna** fail; **ocena pozytywna** pass. **3.** (= *wycena*) valuation, appraisal; (*wstępna, pobieżna*) estimate.

oceniać *ipf.*, **ocenić** *pf.* **1.** (= *opiniować, krytykować*) judge, assess. **2.** (= *wyceniać, szacować*) estimate, appraise, value; (*szkoln., uniw.* (*klasówkę, pracę semestralną*) grade, mark; **oceniać straty na 10 mln zł** estimate the losses at 10 million PLN.

ocenzurować *pf.* **1.** (= *skontrolować*) censor; **ocenzurować powieść/artykuł/film** censor a novel/article/movie. **2.** (= *ocenić*) evaluate.

ocet *mi* oct- *kulin.* vinegar; **kwaśny jak ocet siedmiu złodziei** as sour as vinegar *l.* a crab.

och[1] *int.* ooh.

och[2] *n. sing. indecl.* ooh; **achy i ochy** expressions of admiration, amazement, excitement, etc.

ochlać się *pf. pot.* booze it up, drown one's whistle.

ochlaj *mi Gen.* **-u** *Gen.pl.* **-ów** *pot.* (= *popijawa, libacja*) carusal, brash, bender. – *mp Gen.* **-a** *Gen.pl.* **-ów** *pot.* (= *pijak*) boozer.

ochlapać *pf.* **-ę -esz** *zob.* **ochlapywać**. ~ **się** *pf.* *zob.* **ochlapywać się**.

ochlapus *mp pl.* **-y** *pot.* (= *pijak*) boozer, drunkard.

ochlapywać *ipf.* **1.** (= *pryskać*) splash, spatter, dabble. **2.** *pot.* (= *malować niestarannie*) paint in a slovenly way. ~ **się** *ipf.* **1.** (= *opryskiwać się*) spatter o.s.; get spattered. **2.** *pot.* (= *niedokładnie się myć*) splash (a little) water on o.s.

ochlokracja *f. polit.* ochlocracy.

ochlokratyczny *a. polit.* ochlocratic.

ochładzać *ipf.* **1.** cool; chill. **2.** refresh, cool. **3.** (= *obojętnieć, rozluźniać stosunki*) cool, chill. ~ **się** *ipf.* **1.** cool; cool down; **ochładza się** it's getting colder. **2.** cool off; refresh o.s. **3.** (= *rozluźniać się*) (*o kontaktach*) cool.

ochłap *mi Gen.* **-a** *l.* **-u** **1.** *pot.* (*mięso*) scrap of meat. **2.** *pot.* (= *resztka, byle co*) scrap.

ochłoda *f.* cool(ness); refreshment; **lody dla ochłody** ice cream for refreshment.

ochłodnąć *pf.* **-ij** **1.** (= *ostudzić się*) cool (down *l.* off). **2.** (= *zobojętnieć*) cool. **3.** (= *uspokoić się*) cool *l.* calm down.

ochłodzenie *n.* **1.** cooling. **2.** *meteor.* cold(er) weather; **w przyszłym tygodniu nadejdzie ochłodzenie** it will be colder next week. **3.** (*zanik serdeczności, zażyłości*) cooling.

ochłodzić *pf.* **-ódź** *zob.* **ochładzać**. ~ **się** *pf. zob.* **ochładzać**.

ochłonąć *pf.* **1.** (= *uspokoić się*) cool down, recover (*z czegoś* from sth). **2.** (= *ostygnąć*) cool off.

ochmistrz *mp pl.* **-e** *l.* **-owie** *Gen.* **-ów** **1.** *żegl.*

purser, (chief) steward. **2.** *hist.* steward, chamberlain.

ochmistrzyni *f. hist.* high maid-in-waiting.

ochoczo *adv.* **1.** (= *chętnie*) willingly. **2.** (= *radośnie*) cheerfully.

ochoczy *a.* **1.** (= *chętny*) willing. **2.** (= *radosny*) cheerful.

ochojnik *ma ent.* gall aphid (*Chermes*).

ochota *f.* (= *gotowość*) willingness, readiness; (= *pragnienie*) desire; (= *pożądanie*) desire, lust; (= *zapał, gorliwość*) zest, eagerness; **mieć ochotę na coś** feel like sth; **mieć na kogoś ochotę** (= *pożądać kogoś*) have hots for sb; **nabierać ochoty do czegoś** begin to like sth; **nie mieć na nic ochoty** do not feel like doing anything; **czy masz** *l.* **miałbyś ochotę na coś?** would you like sth?; **pracować z ochotą** work eagerly.

ochotniczka *f. Gen.pl.* **-ek** *zob.* **ochotnik**.

ochotniczo *adv.* voluntarily.

ochotniczy *a.* voluntary, volunteer; **Ochotnicza Straż Pożarna** Voluntary Fire Brigade.

ochotnik *mp* volunteer; **kto na ochotnika?** any volunteers?; **zgłosić się** *l.* **pójść na ochotnika** volunteer.

ochra *f. min., barwnik* ocher; *Br.* ochre.

ochraniacz *mi Gen.* **-a** *Gen.pl.* **-y** *l.* **-ów** guard; **ochraniacz na kolana** knee pad.

ochraniać *ipf.* protect, guard (sb *l.* sth) (*przed kimś/czymś l. od kogoś/czegoś* against sb/sth).

ochrona *f.* **1.** (= *ochranianie*) protection, preservation, conservation; **ochrona zwierząt** animal protection; **ochrona przyrody** nature preservation *l.* conservation; **ochrona danych osobowych** personal data protection; **ochrona przeciwpożarowa** fire protection; **ochrona przeciwpowodziowa** flood control; **gatunek pod ochroną** protected species. **2.** (= *osłona*) protection, guard, shield. **3.** (= *straż*) guard, security; **ochrona osobista** bodyguard.

ochroniarski *a.* security; (body)guard; **agencja ochroniarska** security agency.

ochroniarz *mp* **1.** *pot.* (= *strażnik, goryl*) bodyguard. **2.** *pot.* (= *ekolog*) (= *działacz ochrony przyrody*) conservationist; (= *działacz ochrony środowiska*) environmentalist.

ochronić *pf. zob.* **ochraniać**. ~ **się** *pf. zob.* **ochraniać się**.

ochronnik *mi Gen.* **-a** **1.** *techn.* (= *bezpiecznik*) protector. **2.** (*do ochrony uszu przed hałasem*) hearing protector.

ochronny *a.* protective; **kask ochronny** hard hat, crash helmet; **odzież ochronna** *l.* **ubranie ochronne** protective clothing; **krem ochronny do rąk** protective hand cream; **filtr ochronny** (*przeciwsłoneczny*) sunblock, sunscreen; **okres ochronny** *myśl.* close season; **znak ochronny** *handl.* trademark; **barwy ochronne** *wojsk.* khaki; *zool.* protective coloration, protective coloring; **szczepienia ochronne** *med.* prophylactic *l.* preventive vaccination; **parasol ochronny** *przen.* umbrella.

ochryple *adv.* (*o głosie*) hoarsely.

ochrypły *a.* (*o głosie*) hoarse.

ochrypnąć *pf.* **-nij**, **-nął** *l.* **-ł -ła** **-nęli** *l.* **-li** get *l.*

grow hoarse, hoarsen; **ochrypnąć od krzyku/mówienia** shout/talk o.s. hoarse.

ochrypnięty *a.* (*o głosie*) hoarse.

ochrzan *mi pot.* (= *upomnienie*) dressing-down; **dać/dostać ochrzan** give/be given a dressing-down.

ochrzaniać *ipf.*, **ochrzanić** *pf. pot.* (= *karcić*) give a dressing-down, roast. ~ **się** *ipf.* **1.** *pot.* (= *oskarżać się*) give a dressing-down to each other. **2.** *pot.* (= *leserować*) do nothing, loaf around.

ochrzcić *pf.* -ij **1.** *rel.* bapitze. **2.** *pot., żart.* (= *rozcieńczyć*) thin (out). **3.** *przen.* (= *nazwać*) name, give a name to. ~ **się** *pf. rel.* be baptized.

ochrzęstna *f. Gen.* -ej *anat.* perichondrium.

ochwacić *pf.* founder. ~ **się** *pf.* (*o koniu*) founder.

ochwat *mi wet.* founder, laminitis.

ociągać *ipf.*, **ociągnąć** *pf.* -ij *myśl.* (= *oskórowywać*) skin.

ociągać się *ipf.* (= *zwlekać*) delay, procrastinate (*z czymś* doing sth).

ociekać *ipf.*, **ociec, ocieknąć** *pf.* -knę *l.* -kę -kniesz *l.* -czesz, -knij *l.* -ciecz, -kł *l.* -knął -kła -kli **1.** (= *spływać*) drip; **ociekać krwią** drip *l.* soak with blood; **ociekać potem** drip *l.* soak with sweat; **ociekać złotem** drip with gold. **2.** (= *schnąć*) drain.

ocielić się *pf.* (*o krowie, lodowcu*) calve.

ociemniały *a.* (= *niewidomy*) blind. – *mp* (= *niewidomy*) blind person; **ociemniali** the blind.

ociemnieć *pf.* (= *oślepnąć*) go blind.

ocieniać *ipf.*, **ocienić** *pf.* shade.

ocieplacz *mi Gen.* -a **1.** (= *podpinka*) lining. **2.** (*strój*) jumpsuit. **3.** *techn.* (= *termoizolator*) thermal insulator.

ocieplać *ipf.* **1.** (= *docieplać*) insulate; weatherize. **2.** (= *ogrzewać, grzać*) warm; **ocieplić stosunki** warm up relations. ~ **się** *ipf.* **1.** (= *ogrzewać się*) grow warm(er). **2.** (*o pogodzie*) get warm(er); **jutro się ocieplił** it will be warmer tomorrow. **3.** *przen.* (*ulegać złagodzeniu*) warm up.

ocieplenie *n.* **1.** (= *zaizolowanie, docieplenie*) insulation; weatherization. **2.** (= *izolacja, termoizolacja*) (thermal) insulation. **3.** (= *ogrzanie*) warming up. **4.** (*o pogodzie*) warmer weather; **po południu nastąpi ocieplenie** it will be warmer in the afternoon; **globalne ocieplenie** *ekol.* global warming.

ocieplić *pf. zob.* **ocieplać**. ~ **się** *pf. zob.* **ocieplać się**.

ocierać *ipf.* **1.** (= *wycierać*) wipe, rub. **2.** (= *kaleczyć*) graze. ~ **się** *ipf.* **1.** (= *wycierać się*) wipe o.s., dry o.s. **2.** (= *dotykać się*) brush *l.* rub against. **3.** *przen.* (= *być bliskim*) rub; **ocierać się o kogoś** rub shoulders with sb; **ocierać się o prawdę** come close to the truth. **4.** become cultivated *l.* cultured.

ociężale *adv.* heavily, languidly.

ociężałość *f.* heaviness, languidness; **ociężałość umysłowa** retardation.

ociężały *a.* heavy, languid.

ociosać *pf.* -sam -sasz *l.* -szę -szesz, -saj *l.* -sz, **ociosywać** *ipf.* (= *obrabiać, wygładzać*) hew.

ocipieć *pf. pot.* (= *zwariować*) be out of sb's mind; **ocipiałeś?** are you out of your fucking mind?

ociupina *f. pot.* a tiny bit, dash, smidgen.

ociupinka *f. Gen.pl.* -ek *pot.* a tiny little bit, dash.

ocknąć *pf.* -ij **1.** (= *obudzić*) wake (up), awake. **2.** (= *wyrwać z zadumy*) rouse. ~ **się** *pf.* **1.** (= *obudzić się*) wake (up), awake, be roused (*z czegoś* from sth). **2.** (= *oprzytomnieć*) rouse o.s. (*z czegoś* from sth).

oclić *pf.* -ij *ekon.* levy, impose duty (*coś* on sth); **czy ma Pan/-i coś do oclenia?** do you have anything to declare?

octan *mi chem.* acetate.

octowiec *mi* -wc- *Gen.* -a *bot.* **sumak octowiec** staghorn sumac (*Rhus typhina*).

octowy *a.* vinegar, acetic; **zalewa octowa** vinegar pickle *l.* marinade; **marynata octowa** vinegar marinade; **kwas octowy** *chem.* acetic acid.

octówka *f. Gen.pl.* -ek *ent.* vinegar fly (*Drosophila funebris*).

ocucać *ipf.*, **ocucić** *pf.* revive, bring around *l.* round. ~ **się** *pf. rzad.* come around *l.* round.

ocukrować *pf. rzad. zob.* **ocukrzyć**.

ocukrzyć *pf.* (= *posypać cukrem*) sprinkle with sugar; (= *posłodzić*) sugar, sweeten.

ocyganić *pf. pot.* (= *oszukać*) bamboozle, hoodwink.

ocynkować *pf. techn.* galvanize.

ocynować *pf. techn.* tin.

oczadzieć *pf.* **1.** (= *zaczadzieć*) asphyxiate. **2.** (*ulec oszołomieniu*) be stunned.

oczar *mi bot.* witch hazel (*Hamamelis*).

oczarować *pf. zob.* **oczarowywać**.

oczarowanie *n.* **1.** (= *zachwycenie*) charm, enchantment. **2.** (= *zachwyt*) fascination.

oczarowate *pl. Gen.* -ych *bot.* the family Hamamelidaceae (*Hamamelidaceae*).

oczarowywać *ipf.* charm, enchant; put *l.* cast a spell on.

oczekiwać *ipf.* **1.** (= *czekać*) await (*na kogoś/coś* sb/sth); wait (*na kogoś l. coś* for sb *l.* sth). **2.** (= *spodziewać się*) expect (*czegoś od kogoś* sth from sb).

oczekiwanie *n.* **1.** (= *czekanie*) awaiting, waiting. **2.** (= *spodziewanie się*) expecting. **3.** (= *nadzieja, pragnienie*) expectation; **spełniać czyjeś oczekiwania** meet sb's expectations; **coś przechodzi najśmielsze oczekiwania** sth exceeds *l.* surpasses all expectations.

ocznice *pl. ent.* the family Satyridae (*Satyridae*).

oczepiny *pl. Gen.* -n (*obrzęd weselny*) ceremonial putting on of a cap by the bride at wedding.

oczeret *mi* **1.** *bot.* Schoenoplectus (*Schoenoplectus*). **2.** **oczerety** *pot.* (= *szuwary*) rushes.

oczerniać *ipf.*, **oczernić** *pf.* -ń *l.* -nij (= *szkalować*) defame, traduce, run down. ~ **się** *ipf.*, **oczernić się** *pf.* **1.** (= *szkalować się samemu*) defame o.s., run o.s. down. **2.** (= *szkalować się wzajemnie*) defame each other, run each other down.

oczko *n. Gen.pl.* **oczek** **1.** (*małe oko*) eye; **pa-**

wie oczko ocellus, eyelike spot; **pawie oczko** *icht.* guppy (*Lebistes reticulatus*); **świńskie oczka** small eyes, piggy eyes; **być oczkiem w głowie** be the apple of sb's eye; **oczka się komuś kleją** sb's eyelids are drooping, sb is falling asleep; **puścić do kogoś oczko** wink at sb. **2.** (*kamień szlachetny*) stone. **3.** (*w zupie, rosole*) ring, patch. **4.** *tk.* stitch; **oczko w rajtuzach** run; *Br.* ladder; **zgubić oczko** drop a stitch; **komuś poleciało oczko** (*na pończosze*) sb's stocking ran; (*na rajstopie*) sb's tights ran; **podnosić oczka** mend runs. **5.** (= *dziurka*) small hole; mesh. **6.** *pot.* (= *punkt*) spot, point. **7.** (= *stawek*) small pond, pool; **oczko wodne** water hole. **8.** *ogr.* eye. **9.** *tylko sing.* *karty* blackjack, twenty-one. **10.** *druk.* face of type, typeface.

   oczkować *ipf. ogr.* bud.

   oczlik *ma zool.* **oczliki** cyclops (*Cyclopoidea*).

   oczny *a.* eye, optic; **gałka oczna** *anat.* eyeball; **plamka oczna** *biol.* eyespot.

   oczodołowy *a. anat.* orbital.

   oczodół *mi* **-o-** *anat.* orbit, orbital cavity, eye socket.

   oczopląs *mi pat.* nystagmus.

   oczyszczać *ipf.* **1.** (*usuwać brud*) clean, cleanse, clear (*coś z kogoś/czegoś* sth off sb/sth) purify; **oczyszczać ranę** *med.* clean *l.* cleanse a wound; **oczyścić teren** clear the area; **soda oczyszczona** baking soda; **krem oczyszczający** cleansing cream. **2.** (= *uniewinniać*) clear (*z czegoś* of sth); exonerate (*z czegoś* from sth). **3.** (= *usuwać*) remove. **~ się** *ipf.* **1.** (= *usuwać brud z siebie*) get cleaned (*z czegoś* of sth). **2.** (= *być oczyszczanym*) be *l.* get cleaned. **3.** (= *zrehabilitować się*) be cleared (*of guilt l. charges*).

   oczyszczalnia *f. Gen.pl.* **-i** *techn.* refinery; purification plant; **oczyszczalnia ścieków** sewage treatment plant.

   oczyszczarka *f. Gen.pl.* **-ek** *techn.* fettling machine.

   oczyścić *pf. zob.* **oczyszczać**. **~ się** *pf. zob.* **oczyszczać się**.

   oczytanie *n.* (= *erudycja*) literariness, erudition.

   oczytany *a.* literate, literary, well-read.

   oczywistość *f.* obviousness, patency.

   oczywisty *a.* obvious, patent, evident; **oczywista prawda** plain truth.

   oczywiście *adv.* (= *niewątpliwie*) obviously, evidently. *– particle* (= *no pewnie*) certainly, of course, by all means.

   od *prep. + Gen.* **1.** (*przy określaniu kierunku*) from; **od drzwi** from the door; **od wschodu** from the east; **okno od ulicy** front window. **2.** (*przy określaniu trwania*) for; **od pięciu lat** for five years; **od dawna** for a long time. **3.** (*przy określaniu punktu początkowego*) from, since; **od świtu do nocy** from dawn till dusk; **od a do zet** from A to Z; **od rana do wieczora** all day long; **od stóp do głów** from head *l.* crown *l.* top to toe *l.* foot; **od początku do końca** from the start till the end; **od dziecka** since childhood; **od wtorku** since Tuesday; **od poniedziałku do piątku** Monday through Friday. **4.** (*przy wyrażaniu strony*)

from; **od lewej do prawej** from the left to the right. **5.** (*przy określaniu punktu wyjściowego*) (away) from; **500 kilometrów od Nowego Jorku** 500 kilometers away from New York. **6.** (*przy określaniu dolnej granicy*) from; **od czterech do pięciu minut** from four to five minutes; **od 100 do 150 dolarów** from 100 to 150 dollars. **7.** (*przy określaniu przyczyny*) with, from; **czoło mokre od potu** forehead damp with sweat. **8.** (*przy określaniu pochodzenia*) from; **list od mojej dziewczyny** letter from my girlfriend; **wiedzieć coś od kogoś** know sth from sb. **9.** (*przy określaniu przeznaczenia*) for; **dziurka od klucza** keyhole; **tabletka od bólu głowy** headache pill, painkiller. **10.** (*przy określaniu specjalizacji*) **nauczyciel od angielskiego** English teacher, teacher of English; **fachowiec od komputerów** computer technician. **11.** (*przy porównaniach*) than; **lepszy od kogoś** better than sb. **12.** (*przy wyrażaniu odejścia od czegoś*) from, to; **zwolnienie od opłat** exemption from charges; **odstępstwo od reguły** exception to the rule. **13.** (*przy wyrażaniu czynnika*) by; **stawka od godziny** hourly rate; **cena od sztuki** item *l.* unit price; **praca płatna od godziny** work paid by the hour; **czegoś jest od metra** *pot.* there's loads *l.* plenty of sth, there's shitloads of sth. **14.** (*przy wyrażaniu powtarzalności*) from; **od domu do domu** from house to house.

   oda *f. Gen.pl.* **ód** *muz., teor.lit.* ode.

   odaliska *f. Gen.pl.* **-ek** *hist.* (= *niewolnica*) odalisque, odalisk.

   odautorski *a.* (= *autorski*) author's; **komentarz odautorski** author's commentary; (= *pierwszoosobowy*) first-person.

   odbarwiać *ipf.*, **odbarwić** *pf.* discolor, decolor, bleach. **~ się** *ipf.*, **odbarwić się** *pf.* discolor, become decolored.

   odbąkiwać *ipf.*, **odbąknąć** *pf.* **-ij** *pot.* mumble *l.* mutter in response.

   odbezpieczać *ipf.*, **odbezpieczyć** *pf.* (= *uruchamiać, t. o broni palnej*) unlock.

   odbębniać *ipf.*, **odbębnić** *pf.* **-ij** **1.** (*grać na bębnie*) drum. **2.** (*nieudolnie grać na fortepianie*) thump out. **3.** *pot.* (= *odwalać*) dash off, rattle off.

   odbędzie *itd. pf. zob.* **odbyć**.

   odbicie *n.* **1.** (*zmiana kierunku*) deflection, reflection; **odbicie światła** *fiz.* reflection of light. **2.** (= *odzwierciedlenie*) reflection, reflex. **3.** (= *otwarcie*) hitting sth open, opening. **4.** (= *odłamanie*) breaking off. **5.** (= *stłuczenie*) chipping. **6.** (= *powielenie*) copying. **7.** (*o statku*) departure, setting sail. **8.** (= *skręcenie*) turning. **9.** *tenis* return. **10.** *koszykówka* bounce. **11.** *pot.* (= *uwiedzenie*) stealing. **12.** *przen.* (= *przedstawienie*) representation. **13.** (= *refleks*) reflection, reflex. **14.** (= *beknięcie*) belch. **15.** (= *obraz*) picture, image; **być czyimś odbiciem** be sb's image. **16.** (= *kopia*) copy. **17.** (*ciosu*) parry. **18.** (*więźniów, zakładników*) rescue, freeing.

   odbić *pf.* **-biję -bijesz, -bij** *zob.* **odbijać**. **~ się** *pf. zob.* **odbijać się**.

   odbiegać *ipf.*, **odbiec, odbiegnąć** *pf.* **-gnę**

-gniesz, -gnij, -gł -gli 1. (= *odchodzić biegiem*) run off *l.* away. 2. (*od tematu*) depart, stray (away); **odbiegać od tematu** stray (away) *l.* depart from the subject, stray off the subject. 3. (= *różnić się*) differ; **odbiegać od czegoś** differ from sth.

odbierać *ipf.* 1. (= *zabrać*) take away, deprive of; **kto daje i odbiera, ten się w piekle poniewiera** give a thing, and take a thing, to wear the devil's gold ring; give a thing and take again, and you shall ride in hell's wain; (= *zabierać przemocą*) seize; (= *konfiskować*) confiscate. 2. (= *odzyskiwać*) get back, reclaim. 3. (= *zabierać z powrotem*) collect, pick up (*od kogoś* from sb); **odebrać pranie z pralni** pick one's wash(ing) up from the laundry *l.* cleaners; **odbierać dzieci z przedszkola** pick the children up from the kindergarten; **odebrać buty od szewca** pick sb's shoes up from a shoe repair shop. 4. (= *otrzymać*) receive, get, pick up; **odbierać listy** pick up sb's letters; **odebrać nagrodę** receive a prize *l.* an award; **odbierać życzenia** receive wishes *l.* greetings; **odebrać staranne wychowanie** receive a thorough education; **odbierać gości z dworca** pick up one's guests from the station, meet one's guests at the station. 5. (= *uzyskiwać, przyjmować*) receive; obtain; take; **odebrać dziecko** *l.* **poród** deliver a baby; **odbierać telefon** answer the phone *l.* a call, pick up the phone; **odebrać od kogoś przysięgę** *l.* **ślubowanie** swear sb in, administer an oath to sb. 6. (= *zabierać*) take away, steal; **odebrać komuś żonę** steal sb's wife; **odbierać komuś złudzenia** disillusion sb; **odebrać komuś wiarę** shake sb's faith; **odbierać komuś głos** cut sb off from speaking; **wzruszenie odebrało mu głos** he was speechless with emotion; **odebrać komuś życie** take sb's life; **odebrać sobie życie** take one's own life; **odbierać komuś sen** keep sb up; **odebrać komuś spokój** drive sb to distraction, tip sb off their balance; **kogo Bóg chce ukarać, temu rozum odbiera** whom God will destroy, He first makes mad; whom God would ruin, He first deprives of reason. 7. (= *pozbawiać uprawnień*) revoke; **odbierać prawo jazdy** revoke a driver's license; **odbierać uprawnienia adwokackie** disbar. 8. (= *przyjmować, zrozumieć*) get, understand; **odebrać wiadomość** get a message; **odbierać coś jako wyraz sympatii** take sth as a manifestation of support. 9. (*o sprzęcie radiowo-telewizyjnym*) receive; **odbierać na tej samej fali** *pot.* be on the same wavelength.

odbierak *mi Gen.* -a *techn., el.* collector.

odbijacz *mi Gen.* -a *żegl.* fender; **odbijacz dziobowy** bow fender.

odbijać *ipf.* 1. (*o zmianie kierunku*) reflect, deflect; **odbić piłkę** return a ball; **odbijać piłkę** bounce a ball; **odbijać głos** reflect the voice, echo, resound, reverberate; **odbijać światło** reflect light. 2. (= *odzwierciedlać*) reflect. 3. (= *otwierać*) hit open, open; **odbić butelkę** *pot.* hit a bottle open. 4. (= *odrywać*) break *l.* force open; break off, detach; **odbijać tynk** hammer down. 5. (= *uszkodzić, ranić*) beat (up), rough up; **odbić komuś nerki** kidney punch sb. 6. (= *powielać*)

copy; print; **odbijać ślady** leave traces; **odbijać pieczątkę** put a stamp, stamp. 7. (= *odpierać*) ward off, repulse, repel; **odbijać cios** parry a blow. 8. (*o statku*) (= *odpływać*) set sail, depart. 9. (= *skręcać*) turn; **odbijać w prawo** turn right. 10. (= *uwalniać*) free, rescue; **odbić więźniów/jeńców** free *l.* rescue prisoners/prisoners of war. 11. (= *odzyskać własność*) recapture, retake, win back. 12. (*w tańcu*) cut in on. 13. *pot.* (= *uwodzić cudzą żonę, dziewczynę*) steal. 14. (= *powetować*) recoup, make up for, compensate. 15. **odbić na kimś swój gniew** vent one's anger on sb. 16. (= *kontrastować*) contrast, differ (*od czegoś* from sth). 17. (*o broni palnej*) recoil, kick back. 18. *pot.* (= *wariować*) go crazy; **szajba komuś odbiła** sb went crazy *l.* berserk; **palma komuś odbiła** sb went crazy *l.* berserk. ~ **się** *ipf.* 1. (*zmieniać kierunek*) be reflected *l.* deflected; **odbijać się jak groch od ściany** fall on deaf ears; **odbijać się głośnym echem** reverberate. 2. (= *skakać*) take off; **odbić się od dna** rebound, bounce back. 3. (*wytworzyć obraz w wodzie, szybie*) be reflected. 4. (= *przejawiać się*) manifest o.s. 5. (= *odciskać się*) leave a trace, be impressed *l.* imprinted. 6. *przen.* leave a mark, influence, have an impact on. 7. (= *odłączać się*) break away, leave. 8. *pot.* (= *powetować sobie*) recoup o.s., make o.s. up for. 9. (= *bekać*) belch, burp.

odbijak *mi Gen.* -a *techn.* (= *młot*) scaling hammer, scaler.

odbijany *a.* reflected *l.* deflected; **odbijany taniec** switch-partners dance. – *mi* (*taniec*) switch-partners dance.

odbiorca *mi* (*informacji, przesyłki*) recipient, receiver, addressee; (*produktu*) consumer, user, end user; (*sztuki, literatury, programu itp.*) audience; (*zamówionego towaru*) consignee; (*przekazu pieniężnego, czeku itp.*) payee.

odbiorczy *a.* (*dotyczący odbierania*) receiving; **antena odbiorcza** receiving antenna.

odbiorczyni *f. zob.* **odbiorca**.

odbiorę *itd. pf. zob.* **odebrać**.

odbiornik *mi Gen.pl.* -a *techn., fiz.* receiver; **odbiornik radiowy** radio, radio receiver; **odbiornik telewizyjny** TV set, television receiver.

odbiór *mi* -o- 1. (= *odebranie*) receipt, collection; **pokwitować odbiór czegoś** sign for sth, acknowledge the receipt of sth. 2. *fiz., radio* reception. 3. (= *reagowanie, percepcja*) reception; **książka została odebrana życzliwie** book met with a favorable reception. 4. (*sygnał*) reception; **bez odbioru** over and out. 5. (= *kontrola*) acceptance; **odbiór techniczny** technical acceptance.

odbitka *f. Gen.pl.* -ek 1. (= *kopia*) print; copy; **odbitka kserograficzna** photocopy; **odbitka fotograficzna** print. 2. *jęz.* calque, loan translation. 3. *teor.lit.* (= *przedtakt*) anacrusis. 4. *muz.* upbeat. 5. *druk.* (= *nadbitka*) offprint.

odblask *mi t. fot.* (= *odbicie*) reflex, reflection.

odblaskowy *a.* 1. (= *świecący*) reflective; **światełka odblaskowe** *mot.* reflectors. 2. *pot.* (*jaskrawy kolor*) fluorescent, garish.

odblokować *pf.*, **odblokowywać** *ipf.* 1. (=

udrażniać) clear, free, unblock. **2.** *wojsk.* (= *usunąć wojska nieprzyjaciela*) repel; (= *przerwać oblężenie*) break; (= *oczyścić z min*) clear.

odbłysk *mi rzad.* reflex, reflection.

odbłyskiwać *ipf.* **1.** (*o świetle*) be reflected. **2.** (= *zamrugać, sygnalizować*) flash, blink.

odbłyskowy *a. rzad.* reflective, reflecting.

odbłysnąć *pf.* -snę -śniesz, -śnij, -sł -sła *l.* -snął -snęła -snęli *zob.* **odbłyskiwać**.

odbłyśnik *mi Gen.* -a *techn.* reflector.

odbojnica *f.* **1.** *żegl.* rubrail, sheerguard. **2.** *kol.* check *l.* guard rail. **3.** *pot.* (= *listwa ochronna*) guard timber.

odbojowy *a.* fender, guard; **listwa odbojowa** *żegl.* rubrail, sheerguard.

odbój *mi* -o- *techn., bud.* fender, bumping block; **odbój drzwiowy** door stop; **odbój okienny** window stop.

odbrązawiać *ipf.*, **odbrązowić** *pf.* -ów (= *zdjąć z piedestału*) demythologize, debunk.

odbudowa *f. tylko sing.* **1.** *bud.* rebuilding, reconstruction. **2.** *przen.* (= *przywrócenie*) restoration; **odbudowa zaufania** restoration of trust.

odbudować *pf.*, **odbudowywać** *ipf.* **1.** *bud.* reconstruct, rebuild. **2.** *przen.* (= *przywracać*) restore. ~ **się** *pf.*, **odbudowywać się** *ipf. bud.* be reconstructed, be rebuilt.

odburkiwać *ipf.*, **odburknąć** *pf.* -ij answer *l.* talk back.

odbyć *pf.* -będę -będziesz, -bądź *zob.* **odbywać**. ~ **się** *pf. zob.* **odbywać się**.

odbyt *mi anat.* anus, anal orifice; **sztuczny odbyt** *med.* artificial *l.* preternatural anus.

odbytnica *f. anat.* rectum.

odbytniczy *a. anat.* rectal.

odbytowy *a. anat.* anal.

odbywać *ipf.* do; serve; hold; have; make; **odbywać kurs** do a course; **odbywać karę** serve a sentence; **służbę wojskową** serve in the army; **odbyć rozmowę** have a conversation, talk; **odbyć stosunek** have an intercourse; **odbyć naradę** hold a conference; **odbyć podróż** make a journey. ~ **się** *ipf.* take place, be held.

odcedzać *ipf.*, **odcedzić** *pf.* strain, drain; **odcedzać coś przez sitko** strain with a sieve.

odchodne *n. Gen.* -ego **na odchodnym** upon leaving.

odchody *pl. Gen.* -ów excrement, feces; *Br.* faeces.

odchodzić *ipf.* **1.** (= *oddalać się*) go away, walk away, leave; **odchodzić bez słowa** leave without a word; **odejść z pracy na własną prośbę** resign from sb's job, give up *l.* leave *l.* quit sb's job; **odchodzić w siną dal** vanish without a trace, leave no forwarding address; **odchodzić z kwitkiem** go away empty-handed, be turned down; **odejść w przeszłość** belong to the past; **odchodzić od rozumu** be out of sb's mind *l.* senses (*with worry, apprehension, etc.*). **2.** (= *porzucać*) depart, stray (away); **odchodzić od tematu** depart *l.* stray (away) from the subject, stray off the subject. **3.** *tylko ipf. przen.* (= *rozwidlać się*) diverge, branch off. **4.** (= *odjechać*) leave, depart;

pociąg odchodzi z toru przy peronie pierwszym the train departs from platform one. **5.** (= *zostawiać*) leave; **odejść od żony** leave sb's wife. **6.** (= *zwolnić się*) leave; **odchodzić z pracy** leave from work; **odejść na emeryturę** retire (from work). **7.** (= *umierać*) pass away; **odejść z tego świata** depart from this world. **8.** (= *skończyć się, mijać*) wear off, disappear, go away; **ból odchodzi** the pain is going away. **9.** (= *odpadać*) come off, flake off, peel (off). **10.** (= *oddzielać się*) come apart. **11.** *pot.* (= *przeznaczać*) be spent on. **12.** *tylko ipf. pot.* (= *odbywać się*) be going on.

odchorować *pf.*, **odchorowywać** *ipf.* be sick (at heart), have a nervous breakdown, be down in the mouth.

odchować *pf.*, **odchowywać** *ipf.* raise, rear.

odchów *mi* -o- *roln.* battening, fattening.

odchrzanić się *pf. pot.* (= *odczepić się*) give a break; **odchrzanić się od kogoś** give sb a break; **odchrzań się!** get off my back!, give me a break!

odchrząkiwać *ipf.*, **odchrząknąć** *pf.* clear sb's throat, hawk (up).

odchudzać *ipf.* **1.** put on a diet. **2.** (= *ograniczać, oszczędzać*) limit, reduce. ~ **się** *ipf.* diet, be on a diet.

odchudzanie *n.* dieting, slimming.

odchudzić *pf. zob.* **odchudzać**. ~ **się** *pf. zob.* **odchudzać się**.

odchwaszczać *ipf.*, **odchwaścić** *pf.* **1.** (= *usuwać chwasty*) weed. **2.** (= *oczyszczać*) weed out.

odchylać *ipf.* **1.** (= *rozsuwać*) pull *l.* draw back *l.* apart. **2.** (= *odginać, przechylać*) bend; tilt. ~ **się** *ipf.* bend *l.* swing aside.

odchylenie *n.* **1.** (= *rozsunięcie*) pulling *l.* drawing apart. **2.** (= *przechylenie, odgięcie*) bending; tilting. **3.** (= *nieprawidłowość*) deviation, aberration.

odchylić *pf. zob.* **odchylać**. ~ **się** *pf. zob.* **odchylać się**.

odchyłka *f. Gen.pl.* -ek **1.** *miern.* deviation. **2.** *pot.* (= *dziwactwo, anomalia*) oddity, peculiarity.

odciąć *pf.* **odetnę odetniesz, odetnij, odciął** *zob.* **odcinać**. ~ **się** *pf. zob.* **odcinać się**.

odciąg *mi* **1.** *bud.* ventilating hood. **2.** *techn.* guy, stay.

odciągacz *mi Gen.* -a **1.** (= *ściągaczka*) liquid pump, sucker; **odciągacz pokarmu** breast pump. **2.** *techn.* guy, stay.

odciągać *ipf.*, **odciągnąć** *pf.* -ij **1.** (= *odsuwać*) pull away (*od czegoś* from sth); **odciągać czyjąś uwagę** divert sb's attention. **2.** (= *zniechęcać*) discourage, put off. **3.** (= *napinać*) tighten. **4.** (= *odsysać*) suck. **5.** (= *odwlekać*) put off, delay.

odciążać *ipf.*, **odciążyć** *pf.* **1.** (= *zmniejszać ciężar*) lighten, reduce load. **2.** (= *wyręczać, ulżyć*) relieve (*od czegoś* of sth).

odciekać *ipf.*, **odciec, odcieknąć** *pf.* -cze *l.* -knie -kł **1.** (= *spływać*) flow away. **2.** (= *osuszać się*) drain.

odcień *mi Gen.* -a **1.** (= *zabarwienie*) hue, shade, shading, cast; **bielszy odcień bluesa** *muz. przen.* whiter shade of blues. **2.** (= *subtelna róż-*

nica) shade, tinge; **odcienie miłości** shades of love.

odcierpieć *pf.* **-ę -isz** expiate, atone; **odcierpieć swoje** *pot.* endure one's suffering; **odcierpieć za swoje** *pot.* get what one deserves.

odcięta *f. Gen.* **-ej** *mat., geom.* abscissa.

odcięty *a.* **1.** (= *odkrojony*) cut off. **2.** (= *odizolowany*) detached, cut off, isolated; **odcięty od świata** cut off from the world.

odcinać *ipf.* **1.** (= *odkrawać, odrąbywać*) cut, cut off; **dać sobie odciąć rękę za to, że** count *l.* bank *l.* bet on sth. **2.** (= *odizolować*) dissociate; **odciąć od świata** cut off from the world; **odcinać kupony od czegoś** *przen.* reap the benefits of one's earlier efforts. **~ się** *ipf.* **1.** (= *zdystansować się*) dissociate o.s. (*od kogoś / czegoś* from sb/ sth). **2.** (= *odgryzać się*) retort, talk back. **3.** *tylko ipf.* (= *wyróżniać się*) stand out; **odcinać się od tła** stand out against the background.

odcinek *mi* **-nk-** *Gen.* **-a 1.** (= *ogniwo, człon*) segment, section, portion. **2.** (= *kwit*) stub; (= *odcinek czeku, przekazu*) counterfoil. **3.** (*drogi, rzeki, wybrzeża*) (= *fragment*) stretch; **powieść w odcinkach** serial; **odcinek pilotażowy serialu/programu/audycji cyklicznej** pilot; **odcinek serialu** episode. **4.** *mat., geom.* segment. **5.** *wojsk.* sector.

odcinkowy *a.* **1.** (= *częściowy*) sectorial, segmental. **2.** (= *w odcinkach*) serial.

odcisk *mi* **1.** (= *ślad*) print, imprint, trace; **odciski palców** fingerprints. **2.** (= *nagniotek*) corn, callus; **nadepnąć komuś na odcisk** tread on sb's corns *l.* toes.

odciskać *ipf.*, **odcisnąć** *pf.* **-snę -śniesz, -śnij 1.** (= *zostawiać ślad*) impress (*w czymś* in sth) (*na czymś* on sth); **odcisnąć piętno** set a mark, imprint. **2.** (= *wyciskać*) squeeze out (*z czegoś* from sth); **odciskać sok** squeeze out juice. **~ się** *ipf.*, **odcisnąć się** *pf.* **1.** (= *odbijać się*) leave a trace (*na czymś* on sth). **2.** (= *upamiętniać się*) be impressed on sb's mind.

odcumować *pf.*, **odcumowywać** *ipf. żegl.* unmoor, cast loose, loose (*od czegoś* from sth).

odcyfrować *pf.*, **odcyfrowywać** *ipf.* decipher, make out.

odczarować *pf.*, **odczarowywać** *ipf.* disenchant.

odczasownikowy *a. jęz.* deverbative, verbal.

odczekać *pf.*, **odczekiwać** *ipf.* (= *poczekać*) wait sth out.

odczepiać *ipf.*, **odczepić** *pf.* detach (*od czegoś* from sth); unpin; (*przyczepę*) unhitch. **~ się** *ipf.* (= *odłączać się*) disengage. **~ się** *pf.* **1.** *zob.* **odczepiać się. 2.** *pot.* (= *uwolnić się*) get off sb's back, get rid (*od kogoś / czegoś* of sb/sth). **3.** *pot.* (= *dać spokój*) leave alone.

odczepka *f. Gen.pl.* **-ek na odczepkę** to get rid of sb; **coś na odczepkę** sop.

odczepne *n. Gen.* **-ego na odczepne** offhandedly; **zrobić coś na odczepnego** give sth a lick and a promise.

odczucie *n.* **1.** (= *doświadczenie*) feeling, sensation, sense. **2.** (= *przeżycie*) experience; **w mo-**

im odczuciu... my own feeling is..., in my estimation... **3.** (= *wrażenie, doznanie*) impression.

odczuć *pf. zob.* **odczuwać.**

odczulać *ipf. med., fot.* desensitize.

odczulanie *n. med.* desensitization.

odczulić *pf. zob.* **odczulać.**

odczuwać *ipf.* (= *doświadczać*) experience, feel; **odczuwać niepokój** be *l.* feel anxious (*w związku z czymś* about sth); **odczuwać pieczenie** prickle; **odczuwać potrzebę zrobienia czegoś** feel like doing sth, feel the need to do sth; **odczuwać przygnębienie** feel low; **odczuwać swędzenie** itch; **odczuwać wyrzuty sumienia** feel guilty; **dać komuś coś odczuć** make sb feel sth, bring sth home to sb; **dać się odczuć** communicate itself.

odczuwalny *a.* sensible.

odczyn *mi chem., med.* reaction; **odczyn alergiczny** allergic reaction.

odczyniać *ipf.*, **odczynić** *pf.* break (*a spell*).

odczynnik *mi Gen.* **-a** *chem.* reagent.

odczynnikowy *a. chem.* reactive, reagent.

odczynowość *f. med.* reactivity.

odczyt *mi* **1.** (= *wykład*) talk, lecture, prelection, presentation. **2.** (= *odczytanie wyniku, zapisu*) reading.

odczytać *pf. zob.* **odczytywać.**

odczytowy *a.* **1.** (= *wykładowy*) lecture. **2.** (= *wskaźnikowy*) reading.

odczytywać *ipf.* **1.** (= *przeczytać*) read out; **odczytywać listę obecności** call the roll. **2.** (= *sprawdzić stan, zapis*) take the readings. **3.** (= *odgadywać*) interpret.

oddać *pf.* **-dzą** *zob.* **oddawać. ~ się** *pf. zob.* **oddawać się.**

oddalać *ipf.* **1.** (= *odsuwać*) avert; carry away; remove (*od kogoś / czegoś* from sb/sth); **oddalać niebezpieczeństwo** avert *l.* stave off a danger; **oddalać zmartwienie** cast a worry from one's mind. **2.** (= *opóźniać*) put off. **3.** (= *zwalniać z pracy*) dismiss, send away. **4.** (= *rozluźniać kontakty*) drift apart, grow apart. **5.** *prawn.* (= *odrzucać*) dismiss; **oddalać powództwo** nonsuit, dismiss a petition *l.* suit. **~ się** *ipf.* **1.** (= *odsuwać się*) grow away (*od kogoś / czegoś* from sb/ sth). **2.** go *l.* walk away, leave; **oddalać się samowolnie** go AWOL; **oddalać się szybko** (*o człowieku*) hasten away; (*o pojeździe*) dash away.

oddalenie *n.* **1.** remoteness. **2. samowolne oddalenie się** *wojsk.* absence without leave, AWOL. **3.** (= *zwolnienie z pracy*) dismissal. **4.** *prawn.* (= *odrzucenie*) dismissal; **oddalenie powództwa** nonsuit. **5.** (= *odległość*) distance; **być w oddaleniu** be at a distance.

oddalić *pf. zob.* **oddalać. ~ się** *pf. zob.* **oddalać się.**

oddalony *a.* **-eni** (= *odległy*) remote, distant.

oddany *a.* **1.** (= *przywiązany, ofiarny*) committed, devoted, stalwart, true-hearted; (*o przyjacielu*) affectionate, true-blue; (*o zwolenniku idei*) staunch, ardent. **2.** (= *całkowicie oddany*) wedded (*czemuś* to sth). **3.** (= *zaangażowany*) committed, dedicated (*czemuś* to sth). **4.** (*o głosie*) cast.

oddawać *ipf.* **-aję -ajesz 1.** (= *zwracać*) give

back, return; **oddawać długi** pay back debts, repay. **2.** (= *przekazywać, powierzać*) check; **oddawać na przechowanie** deposit; **oddać walizkę do przechowalni** check one's luggage at the checkroom; **oddawać komuś głos** give sb the floor. **3.** (*władzę, uprawnienia*) hand over, cede; (*twierdzę, miasto*) surrender, give up, render (up); **oddać krew** give *l.* donate blood; **oddawać ostatnią koszulę** give away the shirt off one's back; **oddać życie za kogoś** lay down one's life for sb. **4.** (= *doręczać*) deliver. **5.** (= *odwzajemniać*) return, requite; **oddać, co się komu należy** do sb justice; **oddawać honory wojskowe** salute; **oddawać hołd** pay tribute, salute; **oddać głos** cast a vote; **oddać komuś pierwszeństwo** yield precedence to sb; **oddać komuś niedźwiedzią przysługę** do sb an ill turn; **oddać komuś ostatnią przysługę** pay one's last respects to sb; **oddać komuś sprawiedliwość** do justice to sb; **oddawać komuś serce** give one's heart to sb; **oddawać strzały** fire shots, volley. **6.** (= *wyprawiać*) send; **oddać chorego do szpitala** send an ill person to hospital; **oddać dziecko do szkoły z internatem** send a child to boarding school; **oddawać coś w czyjeś ręce** surrender sth to sb; **oddawać w dzierżawę** put out to lease; **oddawać w zastaw** hock, give *l.* put in pledge; **oddawać w ajencję** *handl.* franchise; **oddać kogoś pod sąd** bring sb to justice; **oddać pod sąd wojenny** court-martial. **7.** (= *wyrażać*) render; **oddać coś w jakiś sposób** render sth as. **8.** (= *wydalić*) excrete; **oddać kał** defecate; **oddać mocz** urinate, micturate. **~ się** *ipf.* **1.** (= *podporządkowywać się*) surrender; **oddawać się do czyjejś dyspozycji** put o.s. at sb's disposal; **oddawać się w ręce policji** turn o.s. in. **2.** (= *zaangażować się, poświęcać się*) indulge, devote o.s. (*czemuś* to sth). **3.** (*o kobiecie*) give o.s. away, surrender; **oddać się za pieniądze** sell o.s.

oddech *mi* **1.** (= *oddychanie*) breath, breathing; **brak oddechu** breathlessness; **złapać drugi oddech** *zwł. sport* shift into second gear, catch the draft; **wstrzymać oddech** hold one's breath; **z zapartym oddechem** with bated breath. **2.** (= *wydech*) exhalation; **nieświeży oddech** bad breath, halitosis; **czuć czyjś oddech na plecach** feel sb breathing down one's neck. **3.** (= *odpoczynek*) rest; **chwila oddechu** break, pause.

oddechowy *a.* respiratory; **układ oddechowy** *anat.* respiratory system; **drogi oddechowe** *anat.* respiratory tract.

oddelegować *pf.*, **oddelegowywać** *ipf.* delegate, designate.

oddepeszować *pf.* wire back.

oddolny *a.* bottom-up; (*o inicjatywie*) grass roots.

oddychać *ipf.* breathe, respire; **oddychać pełną piersią** breathe deeply; **ciężko oddychać** gasp; **odetchnąć z ulgą** sigh with relief; **odetchnąć innym powietrzem** *przen.* have a change of air, change one's surroundings.

oddychanie *n.* breathing, respiration; **sztuczne oddychanie** *med.* artificial respiration, resuscitation; **oddychanie usta-usta** *med.* mouth-to-mouth resuscitation; **sztuczne oddychanie z masażem serca** *med.* cardiopulmonary resuscitation, CPR.

oddział *mi* **1.** (= *grupa*) unit, group; *wojsk.* unit, detachment; (*policyjny*) squad; **oddziały pokojowe** peacekeeping force; **oddziały szturmowe** *wojsk.* assault troops, shock troops; *handl.* branch office. **2.** (= *filia, wydział*) branch, agency; division, department. **3.** *med.* ward, unit; **oddział intensywnej opieki** intensive care unit; **oddział odwykowy** detoxification center; **leżeć na oddziale wewnętrznym** be treated in the department of internal diseases.

oddziałać *pf. zob.* **oddziaływać.**

oddziałowy *a.* departmental, divisional; **siostra oddziałowa** *med.* ward nurse.

oddziaływać -łuję *l.* **-ływam -łujesz** *l.* **-ływasz, -łuj** *l.* **-ływaj** *ipf.* act, impinge, operate (*na kogoś / coś* on sb/sth); **wzajemnie na siebie oddziaływać** interact, interplay.

oddziaływanie *n.* impingement; *chem.* interaction.

oddzielacz *mi Gen.* **-a** *techn., chem.* separator.

oddzielać *ipf.*, **oddzielić** *pf.* **1.** (= *odgradzać*) separate (*od kogoś / czegoś* from sb/sth). **2.** (= *odrywać, odłączać*) cut off, detach, disjoin (*od czegoś* from sth). **3.** (= *rozłączać*) divide, interspace, set apart; **oddzielić ziarno od plew** separate the wheat from the chaff. **~ się** *ipf.*, **oddzielić się** *pf.* **1.** (= *odłączać się*) dissociate o.s., separate o.s., disconnect o.s. (*od czegoś* from sth). **2.** (= *odizolowywać się, rozłączać się*) isolate o.s., cut o.s. off (*od kogoś / czegoś* from sb/sth).

oddzielnie *adv.* apart, separately, severally.

oddzielny *a.* separate, discrete.

oddzierać *ipf.* rip away (*od czegoś* from sth).

oddzwaniać *ipf.*, **oddzwonić** *pf.* return a call, call back.

oddźwięk *mi* response, echo.

ode *prep. zob.* **od.**

odebrać *pf.* **odbiorę, odbierzesz** *zob.* **odbierać.**

odechcieć się *pf.* **-chce -chciało, odechciewać się** *ipf.* lose all liking for sth, no longer feel like doing sth.

odedrzeć *pf.* **odedrę odedrzesz, odedrzyj, oddarł** *zob.* **oddzierać.**

odegnać *pf. zob.* **odganiać.**

odegrać *pf. zob.* **odgrywać. ~ się** *pf. zob.* **odgrywać się.**

odejmować *ipf.* **1.** (= *pomniejszać, odliczać*) deduct, subtract, diminish; **odejmować sobie od ust** scrimp and save; **odjąć sobie lat** subtract *l.* shave off a few years, lie about one's age. **2.** *mat.* deduct, subtract. **3.** (= *oddzielać*) separate; disconnect; remove; **jak ręką odjął** as if by magic. **4.** (= *odbierać, zabierać*) take away, deprive (*sb of sth*).

odejmowanie *n.* subtraction, deduction.

odejście *n.* **1.** (= *oddalenie się*) departure, leaving. **2.** *przen.* (= *porzucenie*) breakaway; (*od tematu*) digression. **3.** (= *rozłączenie się*) departure; **odejście na emeryturę** retirement. **4.** (= *zwolnienie się z pracy*) quitting one's job. **5.** (= *śmierć*) passing, demise. **6.** (= *odchylenie*) deviation, divergence.

odejść *pf.* **odejdę odejdziesz odszedł odeszła odeszli** *zob.* **odchodzić.**

odeń *pron.* (= *od niego*) from him.

odeon *mi* (= *amfiteatr*) odeum, odeon.

odepchnąć *pf.* **-ij** *zob.* **odpychać.** **~ się** *pf. zob.* **odpychać się.**

odeprzeć *pf.* **odeprę odeprzesz, odeprzyj, odparł** *zob.* **odpierać.**

oderwać *pf.* **-ę -esz, -ij** *zob.* **odrywać.** **~ się** *pf. zob.* **odrywać się.**

oderwany *a.* **1.** (= *oddzielny*) separate, stray; **oderwany od rzeczywistości** unreal, bookish; **oderwany od świata** unwordly; **oderwany od tematu** off (the) topic. **2.** (= *nierealny, abstrakcyjny*) abstract.

oderżnąć *pf.* **-ij** *zob.* **odrzynać.**

odeskortować *pf.* escort, convoy.

odeskować *pf. zob.* **odeskowywać.**

odeskowanie *n. bud.* timbering, boarding, planking.

odeskowywać *ipf. bud.* timber, plank, board.

odesłać *pf.* **-ę -esz, -ij** *zob.* **odsyłać.**

odespać *pf.* **-śpię -śpisz, -śpij** *zob.* **odsypiać.**

odetchnąć *pf.* **-ij 1.** *zob.* **oddychać. 2.** (= *odreagować, uspokoić się*) have a break, take a break.

odetkać *pf. zob.* **odtykać.** **~ się** *pf. zob.* **odtykać się.**

odezwa *f.* proclamation.

odezwać się *pf.* **-ę -esz, -ij** *zob.* **odzywać się.**

odfajkować *pf.,* **odfajkowywać** *ipf.* **1.** *pot.* (= *zaznaczać*) tick, check, mark off. **2.** *pot.* (= *odwalać*) cross sth off one's list, wrap sth up.

odfiltrować *pf.,* **odfiltrowywać** *ipf.* filter out, filter off. **~ się** *pf.,* **odfiltrowywać się** *ipf.* be filtered.

odfrunąć *pf.,* **odfruwać** *ipf.* fly away, take flight.

odgadnąć *pf.* **-ij, -dł** *l.* **-dnął -dła -dli, odgadywać** *ipf.* **1.** (= *rozwiązywać, zgadywać*) make out, puzzle out. **2.** (= *przewidywać*) foretell, predict; **odgadnąć czyjeś zamiary** read sb's mind, second-guess sb.

odgałęziać się *ipf.,* **odgałęzić się** *pf.* branch off.

odgałęzienie *n.* branch, embranchement, offshoot.

odganiać *ipf.* drive away (*od kogoś / czegoś* from sb/sth); **odganiać od siebie złe myśli** chase away bad *l.* negative thoughts, chase the clouds away.

odgarnąć *pf.* **-ij, odgarniać** *ipf.* sweep aside *l.* away; **odgarniać włosy z czoła** sweep *l.* comb back sb's hair; **odgarniać śnieg** clear the snow, shove the snow away.

odgazować *pf.,* **odgazowywać** *ipf. techn.* degas, outgas.

odgazowywanie *n. techn.* degasification.

odgiąć *pf.* **odegnę odegniesz, odegnij, odgiął, odginać** *ipf.* straighten. **~ się** *pf.,* **odginać się** *ipf.* bend.

odgławiać *ipf. techn.* behead.

odgłos *mi* **1.** (= *dźwięk*) noise, sound; **odgłos kroków** footstep, footfall; **odgłos ciszy** sound of silence; **odgłos walki** sound of fighting; **odgłosy**

niezadowolenia rumblings. **2.** (= *echo, odzew*) echo.

odgłowić *pf.* **-ów** *zob.* **ogławiać.**

odgniatać *ipf.* crease, wrinkle; (*o owocu*) bruise.

odgniecenie *n.* dent; (*na owocu*) bruised spot.

odgnieść *pf.* **-gniotę -gnieciesz, -gnieć, -gniótł -gniotła -gnietli** *zob.* **odgniatać.**

odgonić *pf. zob.* **odganiać.**

odgotować *pf.,* **odgotowywać** *ipf.* (= *usunąć przez gotowanie*) boil off.

odgórnie *adv.* top-down.

odgórny *a.* top-down; **odgórna decyzja** directive (from above).

odgradzać *ipf.* fence off, mark off, separate (*od kogoś / czegoś* from sb/sth). **~ się** *ipf.* (= *odgraniczać się*) separate o.s., shut o.s. off (*od kogoś / czegoś* from sb/sth).

odgraniczać *ipf.,* **odgraniczyć** *pf.* **1.** (= *być granicą*) separate, demarcate, delimit. **2.** (= *rozgraniczać*) differentiate. **~ się** *ipf.,* **odgraniczyć się** *pf.* (= *odgradzać się*) separate o.s., shut o.s. off.

odgrażać się *ipf.* make threats, bluster.

odgrodzić *pf.* **-ódź** *l.* **-odź** *zob.* **odgradzać.** **~ się** *pf. zob.* **odgradzać się.**

odgromnik *mi Gen.* **-a** *techn.* (= *piorunochron*) lightning arrester.

odgruzować *pf.,* **odgruzowywać** *ipf.* clear of rubble *l.* debris.

odgrywać *ipf.* **-am -asz 1.** (= *grać*) play. **2.** (*w przedstawieniu*) (= *występować*) act, perform, personate; **odgrywać rolę** act a role, enact; **odgrywać pantomimę** mime; **odgrywać głupiego** play dumb *l.* stupid; **odegrać ważną rolę** play a vital part. **3.** *karty* (= *wygrywać, odzyskać*) take it out of sb, win back. **~ się** *ipf.* **1.** (= *wygrywać, odzyskać*) strike back. **2.** (= *rewanżować się*) have one's revenge (*na kimś* on sb) (*za coś* for sth).

odgryzać *ipf.,* **odgryźć** *pf.* **-zę -ziesz -zł -źli** bite off. **~ się** *ipf.,* **odgryźć się** *pf.* **1.** (*o zwierzętach*) bite *l.* snap back. **2.** *pot.* (= *kontratakować*) snap back, strike back; (*w rozmowie*) retort. **3.** *pot.* (= *powetować sobie*) come back into one's own. **4.** *pot.* (= *wyzdrowieć*) get well.

odgrzać *pf.* **-eję -ejesz** *zob.* **odgrzewać.**

odgrzebać *pf.* **-ię -iesz, odgrzebywać** *ipf.* **1.** (= *odkopywać*) dig out, unearth. **2.** *przen.* (= *odnajdywać*) fish up, rake up; (*dawne urazy*) dredge; (*stare pomysły*) reincarnate, exhume; **odgrzebać w pamięci** search *l.* jog one's memory, dig sth out from one's memory.

odgrzewać *ipf.* **1.** (= *podgrzewać*) warm over, reheat. **2.** (= *odświeżyć*) rehash; **odgrzewany dowcip** stale joke; **odgrzewane kotlety** (*rzecz znana od dawna*) mutton dressed as a lamb.

odgrzybiać *ipf.,* **odgrzybić** *pf.* eliminate dry-rot.

odgwizdać *pf.* **-żdżę -żdżesz, -żdż, odgwizdywać** *ipf.* **1.** (= *odpowiadać gwizdaniem*) whistle back. **2.** (= *sygnalizować*) whistle, pipe. **3.** (*o melodii*) whistle.

odhaczać *ipf.,* **odhaczyć** *pf.* **1.** (= *odczepiać*) unhook. **2.** (= *zaznaczać, odfajkowywać*) tick off, check off.

odholować *pf.* **1.** (= *odprowadzić na holu*) tow away, haul away; **odholować na parking** tow away to a parking lot. **2.** *żart.* (*odprowadzić kogoś, zwykle nietrzeźwego*) have to take sb home in a wheel-barrow, escort a drunk home.

odhumanizować *pf.* dehumanize.

odimienny *a.* **1.** *jęz.* (*od rzeczownika, przymiotnika, zaimka*) substantival. **2.** *jęz.* (*od nazwy własnej*) eponymous.

odimiesłowowy *a. jęz.* participial.

odiskiernik *mi Gen.* -a *techn.* spark arrester.

odium *n. indecl. lit.* odium; **wziąć na siebie całe odium** accept *l.* bear the odium.

odizolować *pf.*, **odizolowywać** *ipf.* **1.** (= *oddzielać*) isolate, separate. **2.** (= *zaizolować*) insulate. ~ **się** *pf.*, **odizolowywać się** *ipf.* isolate o.s. (*od kogoś/czegoś* from sb/sth).

odjazd *mi Loc.* -eździe **1.** (= *wyjazd*) departure; **czekać na odjazd pociągu** wait for the train's departure; **autobus gotowy do odjazdu** the bus is ready to depart. **2.** *pot.* (= *czad, odlot*) trip; **totalny odjazd!** that's a killer, that's wicked *l.* hellacious *l.* phat.

odjazdowy *a.* **1.** (*związany z odjazdem*) departure; **przystanek odjazdowy** departure stop. **2.** *pot.* (= *wspaniały, odlotowy*) cool, awesome; **odjazdowe ciuchy** cool clothes.

odjąć *pf.* **odejmę odejmiesz, -ij** *zob.* **odejmować**.

odjechać *pf.* -jadę -jedziesz, -jedź *zob.* **odjeżdżać**.

odjemna *f. Gen.* -ej *mat.* minuend, negative.

odjemnik *mi Gen.* -a *mat.* subtrahend.

odjezdne *n. Gen.* -ego **na odjezdnym** when leaving, at parting.

odjeżdżać *ipf.* **1.** (= *oddalać się, wyruszać*) depart, leave; (*o pojeździe*) pull out. **2.** *pot.* (= *naćpać się*) trip (out).

odkarmiać *ipf.*, **odkarmić** *pf.* feed well; **odkarmione dziecko** well-fed child.

odkazić *pf.*, **odkażać** *ipf.* disinfect; **środki odkażające** disinfectants.

odkażalnik *mi Gen.* -a *chem.* disinfectant.

odkażanie *n.* disinfection.

odkąd *adv.* **1.** (= *od kiedy*) since. **2.** (= *od jakiego miejsca*) where... from. **3.** (= *od kiedy*) since when.

odkleić *pf.*, **odklejać** *ipf.* unstick. ~ **się** *pf.*, **odklejać się** *ipf.* come unstuck (*od kogoś/czegoś* off sb/sth).

odklepać *pf.* -ę -esz, **odklepywać** *ipf.* **1.** *pot.* (= *wyrecytować mechanicznie*) rattle off; **odklepać pacierz/wiersz** rattle off a prayer/poem. **2.** *pot.* (= *załatwić*) do a quickie, throw sth together at the last minute; **odklepać lekcje** scribble homework; **odklepać pracę/obowiązki** do a rush job.

odkład *mi* **1.** *bud.* spoil. **2.** *ogr.* layer.

odkładać *ipf.* **1.** (= *przesuwać, przemieszczać*) move, shift; **odkładać na bok** put away, put aside; **odłożyć coś na półkę** put sth back on the shelf; **odłożyć słuchawkę** hang up (the phone). **2.** (= *odwlekać*) delay, put off, postpone; **odkła-**

dać decyzję put off a decision; **odkładać wyjazd** put off a journey, postpone a trip; reschedule an exam; **odkładać na później/na jutro** put sth off till later/tomorrow; **nie odkładaj na jutro tego, co masz zrobić dziś** don't put off till tomorrow what you can do now. **3.** (= *oszczędzać, gromadzić*) save, put aside *l.* by; **odkładać na samochód** put aside *l.* save for a car; **odkładać pieniądze** save (money), put (money) aside; **odkładać na czarną godzinę** keep sth against a rainy day. **4.** *fizj.* (*o organizmie*) (= *gromadzić*) accumulate; **odkładać tłuszcze** accumulate fat. **5.** *ogr.* layer. ~ **się** *ipf.* (= *gromadzić się*) accumulate.

odkłaniać się *ipf.*, **odkłonić się** *pf.* return sb's greeting, acknowledge sb's greeting.

odkochać się *pf.*, **odkochiwać się** *ipf.* fall out of love (*w kimś* with sb).

odkomenderować *pf.*, **odkomenderowywać** *ipf. zwł. wojsk.* detach, detail.

odkopać *pf.* -ę -esz *zob.* **odkopywać**.

odkopnąć *pf.* -ij *zob.* **odkopywać**.

odkopywać¹ *ipf.* (= *wykopać*) dig up, unearth.

odkopywać² *ipf.* **1.** (= *usunąć, oddalić nogą*) kick away, kick aside, kick off. **2.** *sport* (= *oddać piłkę kopnięciem*) kick back, return.

odkorkować *pf.*, **odkorkowywać** *ipf.* (= *otworzyć*) open; uncork; unplug; **odkorkować butelkę** uncork a bottle.

odkotwiczać *ipf.*, **odkotwiczyć** *pf. żegl.* weigh anchor, lift anchor.

odkrajać *pf.* -ę -esz, **odkrawać** *ipf.* cut off; carve.

odkręcać *ipf.*, **odkręcić** *pf.* **1.** (= *otwierać, odłączać*) open; (*śrubę, zakrętkę, pokrywkę*) unscrew; (*słoik*) twist off; (*kran, kurek, wodę, gaz*) turn on; **odkręcić butelkę** open a bottle. **2.** *pot.* (= *odwikłać*) undo. ~ **się** *ipf.*, **odkręcić się** *pf.* **1.** (= *odłączać się*) come off. **2.** (= *otwierać się*) open. **3.** (= *obrócić się*) turn around.

odkroić *pf.* -ój *zob.* **odkrawać**.

odkrycie *n.* **1.** (= *wynalazek*) invention; (= *odnalezienie*) discovery; **odkrycia geograficzne** geographical discoveries; **odkrycie Ameryki** discovery of America; **odkrycie nowego pierwiastka** discovery of a new element. **2.** (= *odsłonięcie, obnażenie*) exposure. **3.** (= *zauważenie, poznanie, ujawnienie*) disclosure.

odkryć *pf.* -ję -jesz *zob.* **odkrywać**. ~ **się** *pf. zob.* **odkrywać się**.

odkryty *a.* **1.** invented; discovered. **2.** open; uncovered; **odkryty samochód** convertible; **odkryty wóz** open carriage; **odkryty teren** open area, open ground.

odkrywać *ipf.* **1.** (= *odsłaniać, obnażać, zdejmować*) uncover; **odkryć głowę** uncover one's head; **odkrywać karty** put *l.* lay one's cards on the table. **2.** (= *wynaleźć, poznawać*) discover; invent; **odkryć Amerykę** discover America; **odkrywać nowe metody badań** invent *l.* develop new research methods. **3.** (= *zauważyć, uświadomić, ujawnić*) realize, notice; **odkryć sekret** uncover a secret, ferret out a secret; **odkrywać Amerykę** *pot.* reinvent the wheel. ~ **się** *ipf.* **1.** (=

odsłaniać się, obnażać się) uncover. **2.** (= *objawiać się, ujawniać się*) appear.

odkrywca *mp* discoverer, explorer; inventor.

odkrywczość *f.* innovativeness, innovative character.

odkrywczy *a.* **1.** (= *badawczy*) exploratory. **2.** (= *twórczy, nowatorski*) innovative; revealing, insightful.

odkrywczyni *f. zob.* **odkrywca.**

odkrywka *f. Gen.pl.* **-ek** *górn.* open pit, exposure; *geol.* outcrop, exposure.

odkrywkowy *a. górn.* open-pit, strip; **górnictwo odkrywkowe** open-pit mining, strip mining; **kopalnia odkrywkowa** open-pit mine, strip mine.

odkrztusić *pf.*, **odkrztuszać** *ipf.* cough up.

odkształcać *ipf.* deform, misshape. **~ się** *ipf.* deform, misshape (*od czegoś* by *l.* due to *l.* as a result of sth).

odkształcalność *f. techn.* deformability.

odkształcalny *a. techn.* deformable.

odkształcenie *n.* **1.** (= *zmienienie kształtu*) deformation, misshapenness. **2.** *techn.* strain; deformation; **odkształcenie sprężyste** elastic sprain.

odkształcić *pf. zob.* **odkształcać.** **~ się** *pf. zob.* **odkształcać się.**

odkuć *pf. zob.* **odkuwać.** **~ się** *pf. zob.* **odkuwać się.**

odkup *mi* repurchase; buyback; **prawo odkupu** *prawn.* option of *l.* to repurchase, right of repurchase.

Odkupiciel *mp rel.* the Redeemer.

odkupić *pf. zob.* **odkupywać.**

odkupienie *n.* **1.** *rel.* (= *zbawienie*) redemption. **2.** (= *wykupienie*) buyout. **3.** (= *zakupienie*) buyback, repurchase (*od kogoś* from sb). **4.** (= *zadośćuczynienie*) satisfaction, compensation. **5.** (*win, grzechów*) atonement.

odkupywać *ipf.* **1.** *tylko pf. rel.* (= *zbawić*) redeem. **2.** (= *wykupić, odkupić*) buy back, repurchase. **3.** (= *zadośćuczynić*) satisfy, compensate; **odkupię ci tę książkę** I'll replace that book. **4.** (= *okupić*) expiate, atone for (*coś* sth).

odkurzacz *mi Gen.* **-a** vacuum cleaner, vacuum sweeper; *Br.* hoover.

odkurzać *ipf.*, **odkurzyć** *pf.* (= *wycierać z kurzu*) dust; (= *czyścić odkurzaczem*) vacuum; *Br.* hoover.

odkuwać *ipf.* **1.** (= *wykuwać*) forge, hammer; **odkuwać mosiądz** hammer brass. **2.** (= *odkruszać, odrąbywać*) break off (*od czegoś* of sth); **odkuwać zamek** break a lock off. **~ się** *ipf.* **1.** *pot.* (= *wzbogacać się*) make up for a loss, recover from a loss. **2.** *pot.* (= *mścić się*) take revenge (*na kimś* on sb) (*za coś* for sth).

odkuwka *f. Gen.pl.* **-ek** *metal.* forging.

odkwasić *pf.*, **odkwaszać** *ipf.* deacidify.

odlać *pf.* **-eję -ejesz** *zob.* **odlewać.** **~ się** *pf. zob.* **odlewać się.**

odlatywać *ipf.*, **odlecieć** *pf.* **-ę -isz** **1.** (= *oddalić się*) (*o ptaku*) fly away *l.* off; (*o samolocie*) take off, depart; **odlecieć do ciepłych krajów** fly south for the winter; **odlatywać do Warszawy** take a

plane to Warsaw. **2.** (= *odpadać*) fall off (*od czegoś* sth). **3.** *pot.* (= *być odurzonym*) trip.

odlegle *adv.* (= *daleko*) distantly, remotely.

odległościomierz *mi Gen.* **-a** *Gen.pl.* **-y** *l.* **-ów** *opt.* rangefinder.

odległość *f.* **1.** (*w przestrzeni*) distance; **na odległość ramienia** at arm's length; **trzymać się od kogoś/czegoś w pewnej odległości** keep one's distance from sb/sth; **robić coś na odległość** do sth from a (long) distance. **2.** (*w czasie*) remoteness.

odległy *a.* **1.** (*w przestrzeni*) (= *daleki*) distant, remote. **2.** (*w czasie*) remote, distant in time; **odległa przeszłość/przyszłość** distant past/future.

odlepiać *ipf.*, **odlepić** *pf.* unstick. **~ się** *ipf.*, **odlepić się** *pf.* come unstuck.

odlew[1] *mi* **1.** *techn.* cast, casting. **2.** (= *odlewanie*) casting, molding.

odlew[2] **na odlew** hard; **uderzyć kogoś na odlew** hit sb a hard blow.

odlewać *ipf.* **1.** (= *odcedzać*) drain, strain. **2.** (= *przelewać*) pour; (= *wylewać*) pour out. **3.** (= *formować*) cast, mold; **odlewać pomnik** cast a monument; **odlać dzwon** cast a bell; **odlewać monety** cast coins. **~ się** *ipf.* **1.** (= *kształtować się*) mold, shape. **2.** *pot., wulg.* (= *oddać mocz*) take a leak, piss.

odlewnia *f. Gen.pl.* **-i** *metal.* foundry.

odlewnictwo *n. metal.* founding, foundry.

odlewniczy *a. metal.* casting.

odlewnik *mp metal.* caster, founder.

odleźć *pf.* **-lezę -leziesz -lazł -lazła -leźli** *zob.* **odłazić.**

odleżały *a. pat.* covered in bedsores.

odleżeć *pf.* **-ę -ysz** **1.** (= *wykurować się, leżąc*) nurse; **odleżeć grypę** nurse the flu. **2.** (= *odparzyć*) develop bedsores. **~ się** *pf.* **1.** (= *poleżeć*) lie in bed. **2.** *roln.* (*o ziemi*) rest, lie fallow *l.* unworked. **3.** (*o żywności*) (= *dojrzeć, leżakować*) mature. **4.** *pot.* (= *ulec zwłoce*) be shelved, lie gathering dust.

odleżyna *f. pat.* bedsore, decubitus ulcer; **zapobiegać odleżynom** prevent bedsores.

odliczać *ipf.*, **odliczyć** *pf.* **1.** (= *odmierzać*) measure; count. **2.** (= *odejmować, umniejszać*) deduct. **3.** (= *liczyć po kolei*) count; **kolejno odlicz!** count off!; **odliczyć do dziesięciu** count to ten.

odlot *mi* **1.** (= *wylot*) departure; **hala odlotów** departure hall; **odlot ptaków** *orn.* migration of birds. **2.** *pot.* (= *odurzenie*) trip. **3.** *pot.* (= *coś wspaniałego*) sth awesome.

odlotowy *a. pot.* (= *wspaniały*) awesome, cool.

odludek *mp* **-dk-** *pl.* **-i** recluse.

odludnie *adv.* solitarily, in isolation.

odludny *a.* lonely, desolate; secluded; **odludny teren** secluded area.

odludzie *n. Gen.pl.* **-i** secluded spot; middle of nowhere; **mieszkać na odludziu** live miles from nowhere, live off the beaten track.

odłam *mi* **1.** (= *kawał, część*) block, mass. **2.** *zwł. polit.* (= *frakcja, ugrupowanie*) faction; splinter group; *sztuka* trend, current.

odłamać *pf.* -ę -esz *zob.* **odłamywać. ~ się** *pf. zob.* **odłamywać się.**

odłamek *mi* -mk- *Gen.* -a **1.** (= *kawałek*) sliver, splinter. **2.** *wojsk.* shrapnel; **raniony odłamkami** injured by shrapnel.

odłamkowy *a.* sliverlike; **pocisk odłamkowy** *wojsk.* shrapnel.

odłamywać *ipf.* break off. **~ się** *ipf.* break off.

odławiać *ipf.* catch (*fish, game*).

odłazić *ipf.* fall off; flake, peel off.

odłączać *ipf.*, **odłączyć** *pf.* **1.** (= *oddzielać, oddalać*) disconnect, separate (*od kogoś/czegoś* from sb/sth); **odłączyć dziecko (od piersi)** wean. **2.** (= *odseparowywać*) separate (*od kogoś/czegoś* from sb/sth). **~ się** *ipf.*, **odłączyć się** *pf.* break away, straggle (*od kogoś/czegoś* from sb/sth).

odłogowy *a. roln.* fallow.

odłowić *pf.* -ów *zob.* **odławiać.**

odłożyć *pf.* -óż *zob.* **odkładać. ~ się** *pf. zob.* **odkładać się.**

odłóg *mi* -o- *roln.* uncultivated *l.* unworked land, fallow land; **leżeć odłogiem** lie fallow.

odłów *mi* -o- *zwł. ryb., t. myśl.* catch; **odłowy hodowlane** *ryb.* fish crop.

odłupać (się) *pf.* -pię -piesz *zob.* **odłupywać (się).**

odłupek *mi* -pk- *Gen.* -a (= *w drewnie, metalu*) splinter, chip; (= *w kamieniu, porcelanie*) chip, sliver; (= *na powierzchni lakierowanej*) flake.

odłupywać *ipf.* split off, chip off, break off (*od czegoś* from sth) (*z czegoś* sth). **~ się** *ipf.* split off, chip off, break off.

odma *f. pat.* emphysema; **odma czaszkowa** pneumatocele, pneumocephalus; **odma opłucnowa** pneumothorax, aerothorax; **odma osierdzia** pneumopericardium; **odma podskórna** subcutaneous emphysema; **odma zaotrzewnowa** retropneumoperitoneum.

odmachiwać *ipf.*, **odmachać, odmachnąć** *pf.* **-ij 1.** (= *odkiwnąć ręką*) wave back. **2.** *pot.* (= *odfajkować, szybko zrobić*) get done with quickly, do quickly, do a rush job.

odmagnesować *pf.*, **odmagnesowywać** *ipf.* demagnetize; degauss. **~ się** *pf.*, **odmagnesowywać się** *ipf.* be demagnetized; become demagnetized.

odmalować *pf.*, **odmalowywać** *ipf.* **1.** (= *pomalować na nowo*) repaint; **odmalować mieszkanie** redecorate an appartment. **2.** *przest.* (= *namalować*) paint, picture; portray. **3.** (= *opisać*) depict, portray. **~ się** *pf.*, **odmalowywać się** *ipf.* show; **na jej twarzy odmalowała się radość** she beamed with joy.

odmarzać *ipf.*, **odmarznąć** *pf.* **-ij** -zł *l.* -znął -zła (= *rozmrażać się, topnieć*) defrost, thaw.

odmaszerować *pf.*, **odmaszerowywać** *ipf.* march off.

odmawiać *ipf.* **1.** (= *sprzeciwiać się*) refuse, decline; **odmówić pomocy** refuse help; **odmawiać sobie czegoś** deny o.s. sth; **odmówić posłuszeństwa** refuse to obey, defy; **wszystkiego sobie odmawiać** deny o.s. everything. **2.** (= *wyperswadować, zniechęcać*) dissuade (*od czegoś* from doing sth). **3.** (= *wyrecytować, zmówić*) say; recite;

odmawiać pacierz/modlitwę/różaniec say one's prayer/rosary. **4.** *pot.* (= *odwoływać, wycofywać się*) cancel.

odmeldować się *pf.*, **odmeldowywać się** *ipf.* report one's departure (*u kogoś* with sb).

odmęt *mi* **1.** (= *głębia, toń*) depths (of the sea). **2.** (= *wzburzenie, zamieszanie, chaos*) turmoil, confusion, chaos.

odmiana *f.* **1.** (= *zmiana*) change, modification, alteration; **odmiana losu** change of fate; **dla odmiany** *l.* **na odmianę** for a change. **2.** (= *wariant*) variety. **3.** *biol.* variety. **4.** *jęz.* (= *fleksja*) inflection.

odmieniać *ipf.*, **odmienić** *pf.* **1.** (= *zmieniać*) change, alter, modify. **2.** *jęz.* inflect (*przez coś* sth); **odmieniać przez przypadki/rodzaje/liczby/osoby** decline; **odmieniać przez czasy/tryby** conjugate. **~ się** *ipf.*, **odmienić się** *pf.* **1.** (= *zmieniać się*) change. **2.** *jęz.* inflect.

odmieniec *mp* -ńc- *Voc.* -cze *l.* -u *pl.* -y (= *cudak, dziwak*) eccentric, freak, weirdo. — *ma* -ńc- *pl.* -e **odmieniec jaskiniowy** *zool.* olm (*Proteus anguinus*).

odmiennie *adv.* differently.

odmienność *f.* **1.** (= *różność, odrębność*) distinctness. **2.** (= *zmienność*) changeability. **3.** *jęz.* inflectedness.

odmienny *a.* **1.** (= *inny, różny*) different, dissimilar; **być w odmiennym stanie** *przest.* be expecting, be pregnant. **2.** (= *zmienny*) changeable. **3.** *jęz.* inflected; **odmienne części mowy** inflected parts of speech.

odmierzać *ipf.*, **odmierzyć** *pf.* measure, determine by measuring; (= *wydzielać*) measure out; **odmierzać takt** *muz.* beat time; **odmierzać słowa** weigh one's words; **jaką miarką mierzysz, taką ci odmierzą** do to others as you would be done by.

odmiękać *ipf.*, **odmięknąć** *pf.* -ij, -kł *l.* -knął -kła soften (*usu. in liquid*).

odmitologizować *pf.* demythologize, dispel the myth of.

odmładzać *ipf.* **1.** (= *nadawać młodszy wygląd*) make look younger. **2.** (= *odnawiać*) bring new blood into; **odmładzać załogę** bring new life into the staff. **3.** (= *czynić młodszym*) rejuvenate. **~ się** *ipf.* rejuvenate.

odmładzający *a.* rejuvenating; **zabiegi odmładzające** rejuvenating treatment.

odmłodnieć *ipf.* rejuvenate, feel younger; look younger.

odmłodzić *pf.* -ódź *zob.* **odmładzać. ~ się** *pf. zob.* **odmładzać się.**

odmowa *f. Gen.pl.* -ów refusal; **kategoryczna/stanowcza odmowa** flat/outright refusal; **odmowa (składania) zeznań** refusal to testify; **spotkać się z odmową** meet with a refusal.

odmownie *adv.* negatively.

odmowny *a.* negative; **odmowna odpowiedź** negative answer, refusal of request, rejection of request.

odmówić *pf. zob.* **odmawiać.**

odmrażacz *mi Gen.* -a defroster.

odmrażać *ipf.*, **odmrozić** *pf.* -óż *l.* -oź **1.** (= *uszkodzić ciało na mrozie*) freeze, get frostbitten;

odmroziłem sobie ręce/uszy my hands/ears are frostbitten. **2.** (= *usuwać skutki mrozu*) defrost; de-ice. **3.** *przen.* (= *liberalizować*) thaw, liberalize; **stosunki uległy odmrożeniu** relations thawed.

odmrożenie *n.* **1.** (= *uszkodzenie ciała przez mróz*) frostbite; **odmrożenie rąk/nóg** chilblain; **odmrożenia pierwszego/drugiego/trzeciego/czwartego stopnia** first/second/third/fourth degree frostbite. **2.** (= *roztopienie*) defrosting; de-icing; melt. **3.** *przen.* (*kapitału, środków*) release, unfreezing.

odmulać *ipf.*, **odmulić** *pf.* elutriate, remove silt.

odnająć *pf.* -mę -miesz, -mij *zob.* **odnajmować**.

odnajdować *ipf.* find; **odnajdować zgubę** find sth lost; **odnaleźć spokój** find (inner) peace; **odnaleźć kogoś/coś wzrokiem** catch sight of sb/sth. ~ **się** *ipf.* **1.** (= *wrócić, pojawiać się*) come back, turn up, show up. **2.** (= *odszukać się*) find each other *l.* one another. **3.** (= *odzyskać spokój*) find peace, regain inner peace. **4.** (= *znaleźć się*) be found; **książka się odnalazła** book was found.

odnajdywać *ipf. zob.* **odnajdować**. ~ **się** *ipf. zob.* **odnajdować się**.

odnajmować *ipf.* **1.** (= *wynajmować od kogoś*) rent (*od l. u kogoś* from sb); **odnajmować mieszkanie/pokój** rent an apartment/a room. **2.** (= *wydzierżawiać komuś*) let; **odnajmować komuś sklep/pokój** let a store/room to sb.

odnaleźć *pf.* -jdę -jdziesz -azł -eźli *zob.* **odnajdować**. ~ **się** *pf. zob.* **odnajdować się**.

odnawiać *ipf.* **1.** (= *odświeżać, remontować*) renovate, refurbish. **2.** (= *ulepszać*) improve. **3.** (= *podejmować na nowo, przywracać*) renew, revive. **4.** (= *uzupełniać*) replenish; **odnawiać zapasy** replenish supplies. ~ **się** *ipf.* **1.** (= *polepszać się, poprawiać się*) improve, get better. **2.** (= *reaktywować się, odtwarzać się*) revive, regenerate. **3.** (= *odradzać się*) revive.

odnawialny *a.* renewable; **odnawialne źródła energii** renewable sources of energy.

odniesienie *n.* **1.** (= *zaniesienie*) taking back, carrying back. **2.** (= *dostąpienie*) achievement, attainment; **odniesienie sukcesu** achievement of success. **3.** (*o ranach, obrażeniach*) suffering. **4.** (= *relacja, zależność*) reference; **w odniesieniu do czegoś** with reference to; **punkt odniesienia** point of reference; **układ odniesienia** frame of reference.

odnieść *pf.* -osę -esiesz -ósł -osła -eśli *zob.* **odnosić**. ~ **się** *pf. zob.* **odnosić się**.

odnoga *f. Gen.pl.* -óg (*pnia, drogi*) branch; (*rzeki*) arm; (*łańcucha górskiego*) spur; *bot.* offshoot.

odnosawiać *ipf. jęz.* denasalize.

odnosić *ipf.* **1.** (= *zanosić*) take back, bring back, carry back; **odnosić książki do biblioteki** take books back to the library. **2.** (= *osiągać*) achieve; **odnosić sukcesy** achieve success, succeed, be a success; **coś odnosi skutek** sth produces an effect, sth gives a result. **3.** (*o ranach, obrażeniach*) suffer, sustain; **odnieść obrażenia** sustain injuries. **4.** (= *porównywać*) compare

(*do kogoś/czegoś* with *l.* to sb/sth). ~ **się** *ipf.* **1.** (= *traktować*) treat (*do kogoś/czegoś* sb/sth). **2.** (= *mieć związek*) relate (*do czegoś* to sth).

odnosowić *pf.* -ów *zob.* **odnosawiać**.

odnośnie *adv.* in relation (*do kogoś/czegoś* to sb/sth).

odnośnik *mi Gen.* -a **1.** (= *odsyłacz*) reference; (= *przypis*) footnote. **2.** *chem.* reference material.

odnośny *a. lit.* (= *właściwy, odpowiedni*) pertinent, relevant, appropriate.

odnotować *pf.*, **odnotowywać** *ipf.* **1.** (= *zapisywać*) write down, take down. **2.** (= *zarejestrować, zapamiętywać*) notice, take heed of; **odnotować w pamięci** remember.

odnowa *f. tylko sing.* **1.** (= *regeneracja*) revival, regeneration; **odnowa biologiczna** biological regeneration. **2.** (= *naprawa, remont*) renovation; **odnowa zabytków** restoration. **3.** (= *poprawa, ulepszenie*) improvement.

odnowić *pf.* -ów *zob.* **odnawiać**. ~ **się** *pf. zob.* **odnawiać się**.

odnowienie *n.* **1.** (= *odświeżenie, wyremontowanie*) redecoration, refurbishment; renovation. **2.** (= *ulepszenie*) improvement, upgrade; modernization. **3.** (= *wznowienie działalności*) resumption. **4.** (= *uzupełnienie*) replenishment.

odnóże *n. Gen.pl.* -y *l.* -ż **1.** *zool.* (jointed) limb. **2. odnóża** *żart.* (= *nogi*) stumps, underpinnings.

odnóżka *f. Gen.pl.* -ek (= *sadzonka*) sprout.

odojcowski *a. jęz.* (= *patronimiczny*) patronymic.

odontolog *mp pl.* -dzy *l.* -owie *dent.* odontologist.

odontologia *f. Gen.* -ii *dent.* odontology.

odontologiczny *a. dent.* odontological.

odosobniać *ipf.*, **odosobnić** *pf.* -ij isolate. ~ **się** *ipf.*, **odosobnić się** *pf.* isolate o.s., seclude o.s.

odosobnienie *n.* **1.** (= *odizolowanie*) isolation; **odosobnienie chorego** isolation of a sick person. **2.** isolation, seclusion; (*miejsce*) solitude, lonely place; **miejsce odosobnienia** *prawn.* penal institution, penitentiary.

odosobniony *a.* **1.** (= *na uboczu, samotny; t. żyjący w odosobnieniu*) secluded, lonely. **2.** (= *rzadki, wyjątkowy*) exceptional, unusual; isolated.

odór *mi* -o- (= *smród*) stench, stink, reek.

odpad *mi* waste (material); scrap; **odpady promieniotwórcze** radioactive waste.

odpadać *ipf.* **1.** (= *odrywać się*) come off, fall off; **odpaść od ściany** come off (the wall), peel off (the wall); **ręce mi odpadają** I'm dead tired, I'm done in. **2.** (*o terytoriach*) be separated, be severed (*od czegoś* from sth); **odpadło mi trochę obowiązków** *przen.* I was relieved of some duties *l.* responsibilities; I finished some of my numerous assignments; I don't have that much to do anymore. **3.** (= *rezygnować, być wyeliminowanym*) drop out; **odpaść z rozgrywek** be eliminated; **odpaść w eliminacjach** be eliminated in the qualifying round; **odpaść z konkursu** be eliminated from a contest; **ktoś/coś odpada** sb/sth is out (of the question).

odpadki *pl. Gen.* **-ów** (*przemysłowe*) waste; (*domowe, kuchenne*) garbage, refuse; trash.

odpadkowy *a.* waste, scrap.

odpadowy *a.* waste.

odpakować *pf.*, **odpakowywać** *pf.* open, unwrap.

odpalać *ipf.*, **odpalić** *pf.* **1.** (= *zapalać papierosa, fajkę, zapałkę*) light. **2.** (= *strzelić*) fire. **3.** (= *wystrzelić*) launch. **4.** (= *spowodować zapłon rakiety*) ignite, blast off. **5.** *pot.* (= *uruchamiać, włączać silnik w samochodzie*) start. **6.** *pot.* (= *odcinać się*) riposte. **7.** *pot.* (= *dzielić się, dawać*) fork over *l.* out *l.* up, give o.s. one's cut.

odparować¹ *pf.*, **odparowywać** *ipf.* **1.** (= *spowodować utratę wody*) evaporate, vaporize; **odparować roztwór** evaporate a solution. **2.** (= *zmienić się w parę*) evaporate, vaporize. **3.** (= *wyparować*) evaporate; **woda odparowała** water evaporated.

odparować² **1.** (= *odbić cios*) parry, ward off; **odparować atak** repel an attack. **2.** *pot.* (= *odciąć się, zripostować*) retort, riposte; **odparować komuś** chat back to sb; **odparować zarzuty** refute charges.

odparzać *ipf.* chafe. **~ się** *ipf.* be chafed, become chafed.

odparzelina *f.* chafe.

odparzenie *n.* **1.** (= *wywołanie zaczerwienienia i bólu*) chafing. **2.** (= *miejsce*) intertrigo, chafe, chafed spot *l.* area.

odparzyć *pf. zob.* **odparzać. ~ się** *pf. zob.* **odparzać się.**

odpasać¹ *ipf.*, **odpaść** *pf.* **-sę -siesz -sł -śli 1.** *roln.* fatten. **2.** *pot.* (= *odżywić*) feed well.

odpasać² *pf.*, **odpasywać** *ipf.* (= *odpiąć, zdjąć pas*) unbelt, ungird; take off.

odpaść¹ *pf.* **-dnę -dniesz, -dnij, -dł** *zob.* **odpadać.**

odpaść² *pf. zob.* **odpasać¹.**

odpędzać *ipf.*, **odpędzić** *pf.* **1.** (= *odganiać*) chase away, repel; (= *zmuszać do cofnięcia się*) drive *l.* force back; **odpędzić głód** suppress hunger; **odpędzić (od siebie) złe myśli** chase away bad thoughts. **2.** *chem., techn.* expel; repel.

odpiąć *pf.* **odepnę odepniesz, odepnij** *zob.* **odpinać. ~ się** *pf.* **odepnij** *zob.* **odpinać się.**

odpicować się *pf. pot.* spruce up, deck o.s. out.

odpicowany *a. pot.* spruced up, decked out, swanky.

odpieczętować *pf.*, **odpieczętowywać** *ipf.* unseal, break *l.* remove seal, open.

odpieprzać się *ipf.*, **odpieprzyć się** *pf. wulg.* (= *odwalić się*) fuck off.

odpierać *ipf.* **1.** (*atak, natarcie*) fight off, ward off; (*nieprzyjaciela*) fight back, repulse; (*ciosy*) fight off; (*argumenty, zarzuty*) refute, rebut. **2.** *tylko pf. lit.* (= *odpowiedzieć*) answer, say.

odpierdolić *pf. wulg.* (= *zrobić niestarannie*) fuck up. **~ się** *pf. wulg.* (= *odczepić się*) fuck off.

odpierdolony *a.* **-eni** *wulg.* (= *spartaczony, zrobiony niedbale*) fucked up.

odpierniczony *a. pot.* (= *ubrany elegancko*) spruced up, slicked up.

odpierniczyć się *pf. pot.* **1.** (= *ubrać się elegancko*) slick up. **2.** (= *odczepić się*) buzz off, bug off.

odpiłować *pf.*, **odpiłowywać** *ipf.* (*piłą*) saw off; (*pilnikiem*) file off.

odpinać *ipf.* **1.** (*guziki, spodnie, koszulę*) undo, unbutton; (*zamek*) unzip, unfasten, undo; (*pas, szelki*) unbuckle, take off; (*broszkę, spinkę*) unclasp. **2.** (= *odczepiać, usuwać*) take off. **~ się** *ipf.* get undone.

odpis *mi* **1.** (= *kopia*) copy, transcript; **odpis uwierzytelniony** *zwł. prawn.* certified (true) copy. **2.** *ekon., handl.* write-off, charge-off; **odpis podatkowy** tax deduction.

odpisać *pf.* **-szę -szesz, odpisywać** *ipf.* **1.** (= *pisemnie odpowiedzieć*) answer, write back. **2.** (= *przepisać*) copy, make a copy of; **odpisywać** (= *ściągać; t. przepisywać zadanie domowe*) copy. **3.** *zwł. prawn.* (= *zapisać coś komuś*) transfer, grant, cede; **odpisać wnukom dom** give one's house to one's grandchildren. **4.** *ekon., handl.* (= *odliczyć, odjąć*) write off, charge off.

odplamiacz *mi Gen.* **-a** stain remover.

odplątać *pf.*, **odplątywać** *ipf.* disentangle, unravel. **~ się** *pf.*, **odplątywać się** *ipf.* get disentangled, get unravelled; set o.s. free.

odplunąć *pf.*, **odpluwać** *ipf.* spit (out).

odpłacać *ipf.*, **odpłacić** *pf.* repay, pay back, return (*za coś* for sth); **odpłacać dobrem za zło** return good for evil; **odpłacić pięknym za nadobne** get even, pay back in kind; **odpłacić tą samą** *l.* **podobną** *l.* **równą monetą** give tit for tat. **~ się** *ipf.*, **odpłacić się** *pf.* repay, pay back (*za coś* for sth).

odpłatnie *adv.* for a payment, for a fee, against payment.

odpłatność *f.* fee, charge; payment; price.

odpłatny *a.* paid.

odpłynąć *pf. zob.* **odpływać.**

odpływ *mi* **1.** (*o cieczy*) (= *odpływanie*) outflow, drainage. **2.** (= *ubytek, odchodzenie*) loss; **odpływ fachowców** brain drain; **odpływ gotówki** cash drain, drain on sb's income; **odpływ ludzi** emigration. **3.** (= *ścieki*) effluence. **4.** (= *otwór*) outlet. **5.** *geogr.* ebb (tide), low tide; **strefa przypływów i odpływów** high and low tide area. **6.** *geogr.* (= *ilość odpływającej wody*) runoff. **7.** *geogr.* (= *ujście rzeki*) mouth, outlet; (= *odnoga rzeki*) (river) arm; (= *ujście jeziora*) outlet.

odpływać *ipf.* **-am -asz 1.** (= *płynąc, oddalać się*) swim away; sail away *l.* out (*od kogoś/czegoś* from sb/sth); (*o przedmiotach*) float away. **2.** (*o cieczach*) (= *wyciekać*) drain; flow away; **krew odpłynęła komuś z twarzy** sb turned pale.

odpływowy *a.* **1.** outflow, drain; **przewód odpływowy** drainpipe; **otwór odpływowy** drainhole. **2.** *geogr.* ebb, tidal; **prąd odpływowy** tidal current.

odpocząć *pf.* **-nę -niesz, -nij** *zob.* **odpoczywać.**

odpoczynek *mi* **-nk-** rest, relaxation; **zimowy/letni odpoczynek** winter/summer vacation; **odpoczynek po pracy** rest after work; **zasłużony**

odpoczynek well-earned rest; **nie dawać chwili odpoczynku** keep pestering sb; **wieczny odpoczynek** eternal rest.

odpoczynkowy *a.* rest, resting.

odpoczywać *ipf.* rest, have *l.* take a rest.

odpodobnienie *n. jęz.* dissimilation.

odpokutować *pf.*, **odpokutowywać** *ipf.* atone (*za coś* for sth); suffer the consequences (*za coś* of sth).

odpolityczniać *ipf.*, **odpolitycznić** *pf.* -ij depoliticize.

odpompować *pf.*, **odpompowywać** *ipf.* pump (out).

odpornościowy *a. zwł. med.* immunologic, immunological; immune; **ciała odpornościowe** antibodies; **mechanizm odpornościowy** immune mechanism; **reakcja odpornościowa organizmu** immune reaction; **surowica odpornościowa** immune *l.* specific serum.

odporność *f.* resistance; *med.* resistance, immunity; **wysoka/niska odporność** high/low resistance; **wrodzona/nabyta odporność** inborn/acquired resistance; **odporność na choroby** resistance to diseases.

odporny *a.* unaffected (*na coś* by sth); resistant (*na coś* to sth); *med.* immune; *bot.* tolerant; **odporny na ból** resistant to pain; **odporny na działanie kwasów** acid-resistant.

odpowiadać *ipf.* **1.** (= *dawać odpowiedź*) answer, reply; **odpowiadać listownie/ustnie/pisemnie** answer in a letter/orally/in writing; **odpowiedzieć wymijająco** answer evasively; **odpowiadać grzecznie/bezczelnie/niechętnie** answer politely/insolently/reluctantly. **2.** (= *reagować na uwagi*) respond; **odpowiadać na apel/wezwanie** respond to an appeal/a call; **odpowiedzieć na krytykę** respond to criticism; **odpowiadać na zarzuty** respond to accusations. **3.** *szkoln.* say one's lesson, give a report, be quizzed; **odpowiadać z matematyki** be quizzed on maths, give maths; **odpowiadać ustnie/pisemnie** answer orally/in writing; **odpowiedzieć na dobrą ocenę** get a good grade *l.* mark. **4.** (= *odpłacać*) return, reciprocate; **odpowiedzieć grzecznością na grzeczność** reciprocate favors. **5.** (= *ponosić odpowiedzialność*) be responsible (*za coś* for sth); (= *ponosić karę*) be held responsible, answer (*za coś* for sth); **odpowiadać za morderstwo** be held responsible for murder; **odpowiadać przed sądem** be brought to trial, be tried; **odpowiadać za uczniów** be responsible for one's pupils *l.* students; **odpowiadać głową/majątkiem/życiem za kogoś/coś** vouch for sb/sth (with one's head/money/life); **odpowiadać z wolnej stopy** *prawn.* be released pending trial. **6.** (= *pasować, być odpowiednim*) suit; match; fulfill; **to mi odpowiada** it suits me (fine). **7.** (= *być zgodnym z czymś*) correspond; **odpowiadać rzeczywistości/prawdzie** correspond with the facts/truth.

odpowiedni *a.* appropriate, suitable, adequate, right; **odpowiednia chwila** *l.* pora opportune moment; **odpowiedni człowiek** the right man *l.* person; **odpowiednie kwalifikacje** the necessary qualifications; **odpowiednie leczenie** adequate *l.* appropriate treatment; **odpowiednie słowa** right *l.* adequate words; **dostać się w odpowiednie ręce** get in the right hands.

odpowiednik *mi Gen.* -a equivalent; counterpart.

odpowiednio *adv.* suitably, adequately.

odpowiedniość *f.* conformity, correspondence.

odpowiedzialnie *adv.* responsibly; **zachowywać się odpowiedzialnie** behave responsibly, act responsibly.

odpowiedzialność *f.* responsibility; liability; **odpowiedzialność cywilna** *prawn.* civil liability; **odpowiedzialność karna** *prawn.* criminal responsibility; **odpowiedzialność konstytucyjna** *prawn.* constitutional accountability; **odpowiedzialność osobista/zbiorowa** personal *l.* individual/collective responsibility; **odpowiedzialność za słowa** responsibility for one's words; **brak odpowiedzialności** irresponsibility; **pociągnąć kogoś do odpowiedzialności za coś** bring *l.* call sb to account for sth; **poczucie odpowiedzialności** sense of responsibility; **poczuwać się do odpowiedzialności** feel responsible; **spółka z ograniczoną odpowiedzialnością** *prawn., handl.* limited liability company; **uchylać się od odpowiedzialności** shirk responsibility; **za coś grozi odpowiedzialność sądowa** *l.* karna *prawn.* sth is liable to prosecution.

odpowiedzialny *a.* **1.** (= *solidny, rzetelny*) reliable, trustworthy, responsible; **odpowiedzialny pracownik** reliable employee. **2.** (= *ważny, niełatwy, znaczący*) responsible; challenging, difficult; **odpowiedzialne stanowisko** responsible position; **odpowiedzialne zadanie** difficult task.

odpowiedzieć *pf.* -wiem -wiesz -wiedzą, -wiedz *zob.* odpowiadać.

odpowiedź *f.* **1.** (*na pytanie*) answer, reply; **krótka odpowiedź** brief answer; **pisemna/ustna odpowiedź** written/oral answer; **odpowiedź na pytanie/list** answer to a question/letter; **negatywna/pozytywna odpowiedź** negative/positive answer; **udzielić komuś odpowiedzi** answer sb, provide sb with an answer; **dać komuś odpowiedź** give sb an answer; **zostawić coś bez odpowiedzi** leave sth unanswered; **mieć na wszystko gotową odpowiedź** have a reply to everything; **w odpowiedzi na Pański list** in reply to your letter. **2.** (*na lekcjach*) (= *odpowiadanie*) report, lesson; **wziąć kogoś do odpowiedzi** quiz sb. **3.** (= *reakcja*) response; **w odpowiedzi na strajki** in response to strikes; **odpowiedź immunologiczna** *med.* immune response. **4.** *szachy* response.

odpowietrzać *ipf. techn.* deaerate.

odpowietrznik *mi Gen.* -a *techn.* deaerator; vent; air-escape; breather.

odpowietrzyć *pf. zob.* odpowietrzać.

odpór *mi* -o- resistance, opposition; **dać odpór** resist, oppose; **słowny odpór** verbal resistance.

odpracować *pf.*, **odpracowywać** *ipf.* work off *l.* out; make up for.

odprasować *pf.*, **odprasowywać** *ipf.* iron.

odprawa *f.* **1.** (= *narada*) briefing, meeting. **2.** (= *riposta*) riposte. **3.** (= *wynagrodzenie*) severance pay; **odprawa emerytalna** retirement bonus; **odprawa pośmiertna** bereavement (pay). **4.** (*przy wyjazdach za granicę*) clearance; **odprawa celna** customs clearance.

odprawiać *ipf.*, **odprawić** *pf.* **1.** (= *usuwać, oddalać*) send away, dismiss, send packing; **odprawić kogoś z kwitkiem** send sb away *l.* back empty-handed. **2.** (= *wysyłać, wyprawiać*) dispatch, send; (= *clić*) clear. **3.** (= *odbywać, wykonywać*) carry out; **odprawiać mszę** say *l.* celebrate a mass; **odprawić ślub** officiate at a wedding; **odprawić pogrzeb** conduct a funeral; **odprawić modły** say prayers.

odprężać *ipf.* **1.** (= *rozluźniać*) relax. **2.** (= *uspokajać*) relax, unwind. **3.** *techn.* decompress. **4.** *techn.* anneal. ~ **się** *ipf.* relax, unwind.

odprężenie *n.* relaxation; **odprężenie psychiczne/fizyczne** mental/physical relaxation; *polit.* détente, detente; **odprężenie w stosunkach międzynarodowych** détente, detente.

odprężyć *pf. zob.* **odprężać**. ~ **się** *pf. zob.* **odprężać się**.

odprowadzać *ipf.*, **odprowadzić** *pf.* **1.** (= *towarzyszyć*) see off, escort, accompany; **odprowadzać dziewczynę do domu** see one's girlfriend home, walk one's girlfriend home; **odprowadzić na dworzec** see sb to the station; **odprowadzić na cmentarz** attend sb's funeral; **odprowadzić kogoś na bok** take sb aside; **odprowadzać wzrokiem** *l.* **spojrzeniem** follow sb with one's eyes. **2.** (= *eskortować*) escort, take; **odprowadzać więźnia/oskarżonego** escort a prisoner/the accused; **odprowadzić kogoś do więzienia/na komisariat** take sb to prison/a police station. **3.** (= *usuwać, wypompowywać*) pipe; pump; **odprowadzać ścieki** discharge sewage. **4.** *zwł. ekon.* (= *przekazywać, oddawać*) transfer; **odprowadzać pieniądze do banku** transfer money to a bank. ~ **się** *ipf.*, **odprowadzić się** *pf.* accompany each other *l.* one another.

odpruć *pf.*, **odpruwać** *ipf.* unsew, unseam, undo, rip apart. ~ **się** *pf.*, **odpruwać się** *ipf.* come unsewn, come undone, rip apart.

odprysk *mi* (= *kawałek*) piece; (*szkła, kamienia, tynku, węgla*) splinter, chip; (*farby*) flake.

odpryskiwać *ipf.*, **odprysnąć** *pf.* -snę -śniesz, -śnij, -snął *l.* -sł -snęła *l.* -sła -snęli chip off; (*o farbie*) flake.

odprzymiotnikowy *a. jęz.* adjectival.

odpukać *pf.*, **odpukiwać** *ipf.* **1.** (= *odstukać*) knock back. **2.** **odpukać w niemalowane drewno** touch wood.

odpust *mi* **1.** *kośc.* (= *uroczystość, święto*) church fete, church fair. **2.** *rel.* indulgence, pardon; **udzielić odpustu** grant indulgence; **uzyskać odpust** receive indulgence; **odpust zupełny** plenary indulgence; **odpust częściowy** indulgence.

odpustowy *a.* **1.** (= *dotyczący odpustu*) church-fair, church-fete; **odpustowe uroczystości** church-fair celebrations; **odpustowe nabożeństwo** church-fair service; **zabawa odpustowa** church-fair (dancing) party; **odpustowy jarmark** church-fair market. **2.** *przen.* (= *jarmarczny, kiczowaty*) kitschy.

odpuszczać *ipf.* **1.** *przest.* (= *przebaczać, roz-*

grzeszać) forgive; **odpuszczać komuś grzechy** absolve sb from sins. **2.** *techn.* soften. **3.** *pot.* (= *rezygnować*) give up, let go; **odpuścić sobie** let go.

odpuszczenie *n.* remission, pardon, forgiveness.

odpuścić *pf. zob.* **odpuszczać**.

odpychać *ipf.* **1.** (= *odsuwać*) push back *l.* away. **2.** (= *powodować niechęć*) repel, disgust, repulse (*od kogoś / czegoś* from sb/sth); **odpychać swoim zachowaniem/wyglądem** repel with one's behavior/appearance. **3.** (= *odtrącać*) reject. ~ **się** *ipf.* **1.** (= *odsuwać się*) push back; shove off; (= *przepychać się*) push each other. **2.** *fiz.* repel each other.

odpychająco *adv.* repulsively, disgustingly.

odpychający *a.* repulsive, repellent, disgusting.

odpylacz *mi Gen.* **-a** *techn.* dust collector, dust extractor, deduster.

odpylać *ipf.*, **odpylić** *pf. t. techn.* dedust, extract *l.* remove dust.

Odra *f. geogr.* the Oder (River).

odra *f. pat.* measles.

odrabiać *ipf.* **1.** (= *wykonywać*) do, perform, get one's work done; **odrabiać lekcje** do homework; **odrobić zaległości w pracy** catch up on one's work. **2.** (= *naprawiać, zrekompensować*) make up for, correct; undo; **odrobić szkody** undo the damage. **3.** *pot.* (= *odpracować*) work off *l.* out; **odrabiać nieobecności** make up for one's absences. **4.** *pot.* (= *wycyzelować*) give a fine finish.

odraczać *ipf.* postpone, put off, defer, adjourn; **odraczać termin płatności** defer payment; **odroczyć na miesiąc** postpone for a month, put off for a month; **odroczyć rozprawę** adjourn a trial; **odraczać służbę wojskową** defer.

odradzać[1] *ipf.*, **odradzić** *pf.* dissuade; **odradzać komuś coś** advise sb against sth.

odradzać[2] *ipf.*, **odrodzić** *pf.* -odź *l.* -ódź (= *odnawiać, regenerować*) revitalize, bring back to life; revive. ~ **się** *ipf.*, **odrodzić się** *pf.* **1.** (= *ożywać, odmieniać się*) revive, be reborn, be restored to life, come back to life. **2.** *biol.* regenerate. **3.** (= *wyrodzić się*) be unlike, be different than (*one's mother l. father*).

odradzić *pf. zob.* **odradzać**[1].

odrastać *ipf.* **1.** (= *wyrastać*) grow back *l.* again; **włosy odrosły** hair has grown back *l.* again. **2.** grow; **jeszcze nie odrósł od ziemi** he's still wet behind the ears, he's just out of the cradle.

odratować *pf.*, **odratowywać** *ipf.* save, rescue.

odraza *f.* disgust, repugnance; **budzić** *l.* **wzbudzać w kimś odrazę** fill sb with disgust, make sb sick; **czuć do kogoś/czegoś odrazę** feel disgust at *l.* with sb/sth.

odrażająco *adv.* repulsively, disgustingly.

odrażający *a.* disgusting, repulsive, repugnant.

odrąbać *pf.* -ę -esz, **odrąbywać** *ipf.* chop off, cut off.

odrdzewiacz *mi Gen.* **-a** *techn.* rust remover.

odrdzewiać *ipf.*, **odrdzewić** *pf. techn.* derust, remove rust.

odreagować *pf.*, **odreagowywać** *ipf.* get over, recover from stress. ~ **się** *pf.*, **odreagowywać się** *ipf.* recover from stress.

odrealniać *ipf.*, **odrealnić** *pf.* -ij make unreal, render unreal.

odredakcyjny *a.* editorial; **komentarz odredakcyjny** editorial; editor's note.

odremontować *pf.* redecorate, refurbish; renovate.

odrestaurować *pf.* restore, renovate; **odrestaurowane zabytki** renovated historic monuments.

odrębnie *adv.* 1. (= *inaczej, samoistnie*) differently, separately. 2. (= *szczególnie, oddzielnie*) individually, distinctly.

odrębność *f.* autonomy; distinction.

odrębny *a.* 1. (= *osobny, oddzielny*) separate. 2. (= *suwerenny*) autonomous. 3. (= *odmienny, inny*) different.

odręcznie *adv.* 1. (= *manualnie*) manually, by hand. 2. (= *natychmiast, od razu*) immediately, instantly.

odręczny *a.* 1. (= *wykonany własnoręcznie*) freehand, by hand; **odręczny list** handwritten letter. 2. (= *natychmiastowy, doraźny*) instant; while-you-wait.

odrętwiały *a.* 1. (= *zdrętwiały*) numb. 2. *przen.* (= *sparaliżowany, zobojętniały*) torpid, apathetic; indifferent.

odrętwieć *pf.* 1. (= *ścierpnąć, zesztywnieć*) become *l.* grow numb. 2. *przen.* (= *zobojętnieć*) become torpid *l.* indifferent, grow indifferent.

odrętwienie *n.* 1. (= *bezwład, sztywność*) numbness. 2. *przen.* (= *apatia, zobojętnienie*) stupor, apathy; indifference.

odrobaczać *ipf.*, **odrobaczyć** *pf. med., wet.* worm, deworm.

odrobić *pf.* -ób *zob.* **odrabiać**.

odrobina *f.* 1. (= *kawałeczek*) bit; particle. 2. (= *garstka*) handful. 3. *przen.* (*o uczuciach, cechach*) (= *krzta*) ounce, bit, iota; **odrobina szczęścia** a bit of luck; **odrobinę** a little (bit); **w tej historii nie ma ani odrobiny prawdy** there's not an iota of truth to this story.

odrobinka *f. Gen.pl.* -ek 1. (= *kawałeczek, garsteczka*) very little, tiny bit. 2. *przen.* (*o uczuciach, cechach*) (= *krzyna*) bit.

odroczenie *n.* (*posiedzenia, sprawy*) adjournment; (*wykonania wyroku*) reprieve, respite, stay; (*służby wojskowej*) deferment.

odroczyć *pf. zob.* **odraczać**.

odrodzenie *n.* 1. (= *odnowienie, ożywienie*) rebirth, revival; **odrodzenie moralne** moral revival. 2. *hist.* (= *renesans*) the Renaissance.

odrodzeniowy *a.* 1. *hist.* (= *renesansowy*) Renaissance. 2. (= *odrodzeńczy, ozdrowieńczy*) revival; reviving.

odrodzić *pf.* -odź *l.* -ódź *zob.* **odradzać**. ~ **się** *pf. zob.* **odradzać się**.

odrosnąć *pf.* -snę -śniesz, -śnij, -ósł -osła -ośli *zob.* **odrastać**.

odrost *mi* 1. *ogr.* sucker, shoot. 2. *roln.* regrowth.

odrosty *pl. Gen.* -ów *pot.* (*o włosach*) roots.

odróżniać *ipf.*, **odróżnić** *pf.* -ij 1. (= *rozróżniać*) distinguish, differentiate; **nie odróżniać kolorów** be color-blind; **odróżniać złe od dobrego** distinguish the bad from the good. 2. (= *rozpoznawać*) recognize, discriminate. 3. (= *odróżniać się*) differentiate (*od kogoś / czegoś* from sb/sth). ~ **się** *ipf.*, **odróżnić się** *pf.* be different, be distinct (*od kogoś / czegoś* from sb/sth).

odróżnienie *n.* distinction; **w odróżnieniu od kogoś/czegoś** as opposed to sb/sth, distinct from sb/sth.

odruch *mi* 1. *psych.* reflex; **odruch bezwarunkowy** unconditioned *l.* inborn reflex; **odruch kolanowy** knee reflex; **odruch warunkowy** conditioned *l.* trained reflex. 2. (= *reakcja*) impulse; reaction; **ludzkie odruchy** normal reactions.

odruchowo *adv.* 1. (= *mimowolnie*) involuntarily, spontaneously. 2. (= *instynktownie*) instinctively.

odruchowy *a.* 1. (= *machinalny, bezwiedny, instynktowny*) reflex, reflexive. 2. (= *nieumyślny, mimowolny*) involuntary, instinctive, spontaneous.

odrutować *pf.* 1. wire, bind with wire, fasten with wire. 2. fence; surround with (barbed) wire.

odrwić *pf.* -ij deceive, cheat, take in.

odrysować *pf.*, **odrysowywać** *ipf.* copy; draw, sketch.

odrywać *ipf.* 1. (= *oddzierać*) tear off, rip off; **oderwać guziki** tear *l.* rip off buttons; **nie odrywać** *l.* **nie móc oderwać od kogoś/czegoś oczu** *l.* **wzroku** have one's eyes riveted on sb/sth; be fascinated with sb/sth. 2. (= *oddzielić*) detach, separate. 3. (= *przeszkadzać*) distract, draw away; **odrywać od pracy/nauki** distract *l.* draw away from work/studying. ~ **się** *ipf.* 1. (= *odpaść*) come off. 2. (= *odłączać się*) break away, draw away (*od czegoś* from sth); **oderwać się od rzeczywistości** *l.* **życia** *l.* **ziemi** lose touch with reality; **samolot oderwał się od ziemi** plane took off. 3. (= *przerywać*) interrupt, stop, take a break; **nie móc oderwać się od czegoś** can't tear away from sth.

odrzec *pf.* -knę -kniesz, -knij, -kła *lit.* (= *odpowiedzieć*) reply, answer.

odrzeczownikowy *a. jęz.* substantive, substantival.

odrzeć *pf.* odrę odrzesz, odrzyj, odarł 1. (= *zerwać, obedrzeć*) tear away *l.* off, strip (off); *przen.* (= *pozbawić*) deprive, strip; **odrzeć ze złudzeń** disillusion. 2. *przen.* (= *obłupić*) steal, rob; **odrzeć kogoś ze skóry** *l.* **do ostatniej skóry** fleece sb, flay sb.

odrzekać *ipf. zob.* **odrzec**.

odrzucać *ipf.*, **odrzucić** *pf.* 1. (= *odsuwać, wyrzucać*) throw aside, cast away; **coś odrzuca kogoś od kogoś/czegoś** sth puts sb off sb/sth. 2. (= *rzucać z powrotem*) throw back, return. 3. (= *usuwać*) get rid of, throw away; **odrzucić troski na bok** *przest.* stop worrying, stop thinking about sth. 4. (= *odtrącać, kwestionować*) reject, decline, turn down; **odrzucać ofertę/propozycję/**

podanie reject *l.* turn down an offer/proposal/application; **odrzucać wniosek** defeat a motion. **5.** (*o wojsku*) repel, drive back.

odrzut *mi* **1.** (*np. broni palnej*) (= *siła*) recoil, kick, reaction. **2.** (= *rzut z powrotem*) throw back. **3.** (= *wadliwa, wyeliminowana rzecz*) reject.

odrzutowiec *mi* **-wc-** *Gen.* **-a** *lotn.* jet (air)plane, jet.

odrzutowy *a.* jet; **silnik odrzutowy** jet engine; **samolot odrzutowy** jet plane.

odrzwia *pl. Gen.* **-i** *bud.* doorframe.

odrzynać *ipf.* cut off; saw off. ~ **się** *ipf.* (= *odróżniać się*) be distinct.

odsadzać *ipf.*, **odsadzić** *pf.* (= *odsuwać, odstawiać*) separate; drive away (*od kogoś / czegoś* from sb/sth); **odsadzać cielęta/prosięta/szczenięta** wean lambs/piglets/pups. ~ **się** *ipf.*, **odsadzić się** *pf.* (= *oddalać się, odrywać się*) draw away.

odsalać *ipf. techn.* desalt, desalinize, desalinate.

odsalutować *pf. zwł. wojsk.* return a salute.

odsapnąć *pf.* **-ij** breathe (*po czymś* after sth).

odsączać *ipf.*, **odsączyć** *pf.* drain (off); (*przez sito*) strain; **odsączać ryż/makaron/warzywa** drain *l.* strain rice/noodles/vegetables; **odsączać ser/twaróg** strain milk. ~ **się** *ipf.*, **odsączyć się** *pf.* drain off (*z czegoś* from sth).

odsączanie *n.* draining, straining; *górn.* (*wody*) bleeding.

odsądzać *ipf.*, **odsądzić** *pf.* deny (*kogoś od czegoś* sb sth); **odsądzić kogoś od czci i wiary** drag sb's name through muck and mire; **odsądzać kogoś od talentu/rozumu** deny sb (any) talent/reason.

odseparować *pf.*, **odseparowywać** *ipf.* separate; isolate (*od kogoś / czegoś* from sb/sth). ~ **się** *pf.*, **odseparowywać** *ipf.* separate, keep separate (*od kogoś / czegoś* from sb/sth).

odsetek *mi* **-tk-** *Gen.* **-a 1.** *t. ekon.* (= *procent*) percentage; proportion; **znaczny odsetek pracowników** significant percentage *l.* proportion of workers. **2.** (= *procent, zysk; kara pieniężna*) interest; **narosłe odsetki** accrued interest; **odsetki bankowe/roczne** bank/annual interest; **odsetki ustawowe** statutory interest; **odsetki za zwłokę** interest for default; **zaległe odsetki** outstanding interest.

odsiać *pf.* **-eję -ejesz 1.** (= *przesiać*) sieve, sift. **2.** (*osobę z grupy*) (= *wyizolować*) comb out. **3.** *pot.* (*kandydatów*) (= *oblać, wyeliminować*) screen (out); (*na egzaminie*) flunk, fail.

odsiadka *f. Gen.pl.* **-ek** *pot.* time; **mieć odsiadkę** serve *l.* do time.

odsiadywać *ipf.* **1.** (= *gdzieś długo przebywać, czekając*) sit out. **2.** (= *odbywać karę więzienia*) serve *l.* do time (*za coś* for sth).

odsiarczać *ipf.*, **odsiarczyć** *pf.* **1.** *chem.* desulphurize. **2.** *techn.* (*paliwo*) sweeten.

odsiecz *f. pl.* **-e** relief; **odsiecz wiedeńska** *hist.* the Succor of Vienna; **iść na odsiecz** bring relief; **przyjść z odsieczą** to relieve; **ruszyć z odsieczą** hasten to the relief.

odsiedzieć *pf.* **-ę -isz** *zob.* **odsiadywać**.

odsiew *mi* **1.** (*zboża, mąki*) (= *przesiewanie*) sifting. **2.** *roln.* (= *pozostałość po oczyszczeniu*) shorts. **3.** *pot.* (*kandydatów*) (= *eliminowanie*) screening, selection. **4.** (*osoby nieprzyjęte*) throw-outs, rejects.

odsiewacz *mi Gen.* **-a** *techn.* sifter.

odsiewać *ipf. zob.* **odsiać**.

odsikać się *pf. pot.* take a piss *l.* leak.

odskakiwać *ipf.* **1.** (= *odsuwać się*) spring (*od kogoś / czegoś* away from sb/sth). **2.** (*o piłce*) (= *odbić się*) bounce, rebound. **3.** (*o zamknięciu*) (= *otwierać się*) spring back. **4.** (*o broni palnej, sprężynie*) recoil. **5.** (= *oddalać się*) break away; **odskoczyć od peletonu** break away from the main group. **6.** (*o kuli*) (= *rykoszetować*) ricochet, rebound.

odskocznia *f. Gen.pl.* **-i 1.** *t. przen.* springboard. **2.** (= *miejsce do wypoczynku*) retreat, refuge. **3.** (= *relaks*) relaxation; **odskocznia od obowiązków/pracy/problemów** refuge from duties/work/problems.

odskoczyć *pf. zob.* **odskakiwać**.

odskok *mi* **1.** (= *odskoczenie*) leap, jump. **2.** (*broni palnej, sprężyny*) recoil. **3.** (*piłki*) bounce, rebound. **4.** (= *rykoszet*) ricochet, rebound.

odsłaniać *ipf.* **1.** (*piersi, ramiona*) (= *odkrywać*) expose, bare; (*pomnik, tablicę pamiątkową*) unveil; **odsłonić duszę przed kimś** *przen.* bare one's soul to sb; **odsłonić karty** *przen.* show one's cards *l.* hand; **odsłonić przyłbicę** *przen.* drop *l.* throw off the mask. **2.** (= *ujawniać*) reveal, disclose. **3.** (*zasłonę, kotarę*) (= *odsuwać*) draw; (*w teatrze*) raise. ~ **się** *ipf.* **1.** (= *ukazywać się, pokazywać się*) come into view, appear; **odsłonił się widok** view appeared. **2.** (= *zdemaskować się*) drop *l.* throw off the mask; show true colors. **3.** (= *odsuwać się*) rise; **kurtyna się odsłania** curtain is rising.

odsłona *f.* **1.** (*w teatrze*) (= *akt, scena*) scene; **ostatnia odsłona** the final curtain. **2.** *sport* (*w szachach l. szermierce*) opening; **szach z odsłony** discovered check.

odsłonić *pf. zob.* **odsłaniać**. ~ **się** *pf. zob.* **odsłaniać się**.

odsłonięcie *n.* **1.** (= *ukazanie, ujawnienie*) disclosure, revelation (*czegoś* of sth); **odsłonięcie pomnika/tablicy** unveiling of a monument/plaque; **zmusić kogoś do odsłonięcia kart** force sb's hand. **2.** (= *odsunięcie*) drawing; **odsłonięcie kurtyny** curtain rise.

odsłuchać *pf.*, **odsłuchiwać** *ipf.* **1.** (*śpiewaczkę, aktora itp.*) (= *przesłuchać przed występem*) audition. **2.** (= *posłuchać*) listen (*coś* to sth); **odsłuchać taśmę** play a tape.

odsługiwać *ipf.*, **odsłużyć** *pf.* (= *odbywać służbę w wojsku; t. odpracowywać, odrabiać*) serve (out); **odsłużyć wojsko** serve in the army. ~ **się** *ipf.*, **odsłużyć się** *pf.* (= *rewanżować się, odwdzięczać się*) repay; **odsłużyć się komuś przysługą za przysługę** return sb's favor.

odsmażać *ipf.*, **odsmażyć** *pf.* refry; **odsmażyć dowcip** *przen.* warm over *l.* rehash a joke.

odsolić *pf.* **-ól** *zob.* **odsalać**.

odsprzedać *pf.*, **odsprzedawać** *ipf.* -aję -ajesz resell.

odsprzedaż *f. pl.* -e resale.

odstać się *pf.* -ę -esz **1.** (*o cieczy*) (= *wyklarować się*) settle, clarify; (*o winie*) mature. **2.** *przen.* (= *odmienić się*) change; **co się stało, to się nie odstanie** things done cannot be undone, it's no use crying over spilt milk.

odstający *a.* protruding; **odstające uszy** protruding ears.

odstawać *ipf.* -aję -ajesz, -waj **1.** (= *oddzielać się*, *sterczeć*) protrude, jut out, stick out. **2.** (= *nie pasować*, *różnić się*) stand out; **odstawać od otoczenia** stick out like a sore thumb.

odstawiać *ipf.*, **odstawić** *pf.* **1.** (*meble, szafę*) (= *przesuwać, przenosić*) move (*od czegoś* away from sth). **2.** (= *odłożyć*) set aside, put away. **3.** (*zastrzyki, leki*) (= *skończyć brać, robić coś*) discontinue; **odstawić dziecko od piersi** wean a baby; **odstawić narkotyki/wódkę** come off drugs/vodka; **odstawić numer** *pot.* pull a fast one. **4.** *pot.* (= *zwolnić, odsunąć*) **odstawić na boczny tor** put on the shelf. **5.** (= *dostarczać*) deliver. **6.** (= *zaprowadzić, odprowadzić*) take; **odstawić dzieci do szkoły** take the kids to school; **odstawić samochód do warsztatu** take one's car to a garage; **odstawić samochód do wypożyczalni** return a (rented) car. **7.** *pot.* (= *udawać*) play, act. **8.** *pot.* (= *robić, pracować*) do, carry out; **odstawiać fuchę** botch a job.

odstawka *f. Gen.pl.* -ek fire, sack, dismissal; **pójść w odstawkę** *pot.* be put on the shelf, be thrown on the scrap-heap.

odstąpić *pf. zob.* **odstępować**.

odstęp *mi* **1.** (*w przestrzeni l. czasie*) interval, space. **2.** *druk.* (*między literami, słowami, liniami*) space, spacing; **pojedynczy/podwójny odstęp** single/double spacing.

odstępca *mp* traitor, renegade.

odstępne *n. Gen.* -ego **1.** (= *zapłata*) compensation, restitution. **2.** *prawn.* (= *odszkodowanie*) compensation for loss of contract.

odstępować *ipf.* **1.** (= *odsuwać się*) move away; **nie odstępować kogoś ani na krok/ani na chwilę** dog sb's footsteps. **2.** (*od zamiaru*) (= *zrezygnować*) abandon, give up; (*od umowy*) withdraw, retract (*od czegoś* from sth). **3.** (= *ustępować, zrzekać się*) give up; **odstępować komuś swoje miejsce** give up one's seat to sb. **4.** (= *odsprzedawać*) sell (*coś komuś* sth to sb *l.* sb sth). **5.** *przest.* (= *opuszczać, pozostawiać*) abandon.

odstępstwo *n.* **1.** (*od zwyczaju, zasady, reguły*) (= *odrzucenie wartości*) departure (*od czegoś* from sth); (*od wiary, opcji politycznej*) apostasy; (*w religii, polityce*) (= *nonkonformizm*) dissent. **2.** (= *zmiana*) deviation; **odstępstwo od normy** aberration; **odstępstwo od reguł** violation of the rules.

odstojnik *mi Gen.* -a *techn.* sedimentation tank; clarifier.

odstraszać *ipf.* **1.** scare off *l.* away. **2.** (*komary, drapieżniki*) repel, keep away.

odstraszający *a.* deterrent; **czynniki odstra-**

szające deterrents; **środek odstraszający owady** insect repellent.

odstraszyć *pf. zob.* **odstraszać**.

odstręczać *ipf.*, **odstręczyć** *pf.* **1.** (= *działać odstraszająco*) deter, dissuade (*kogoś od zrobienia czegoś* sb from doing sth). **2.** (= *nie dopuszczać*) keep off *l.* away (*od kogoś / czegoś* from sb/sth).

odstręczający *a.* (= *odpychający*) repulsive.

odstrzał *mi* **1.** *myśl.* shooting off, cull. **2.** *górn.* blasting. **3.** *pot.* (= *degradacja, dymisja*) elimination; **iść na odstrzał** be doomed; **przeznaczyć kogoś na odstrzał** earmark sb for elimination.

odstrzelić *pf.*, **odstrzeliwać** *ipf.* **1.** (= *odrywać strzałem*) shoot off. **2.** *myśl.* cull, shoot off. **3.** *górn.* blast, shoot. ~ **się** *pf.*, **odstrzeliwać się** *ipf.* shoot back.

odstrzelony *a.* shot off.

odstukać *pf.*, **odstukiwać** *ipf.* **1.** (= *odpowiadać na stukanie*) knock back. **2.** **odstukać w niemalowane** touch wood. **3.** (= *wystukać rytm*) tap (*a rhythm*).

odsunąć *pf.* **1.** (= *przesunąć, oddalić*) move away *l.* back (*od kogoś / czegoś* from sb/sth). **2.** oust; dismiss; **odsunąć od władzy** oust *l.* remove from power; **odsuwać od siebie przykre wspomnienia** brush aside sad memories. **3.** (= *otworzyć, odsłonić*) open; uncover; **odsuwać zasłonę** draw a curtain; **odsunąć zamek błyskawiczny** unzip. ~ **się** *pf.* **1.** (*o zamku błyskawicznym*) (= *otworzyć się*) unzip. **2.** (= *oddalić się*) move *l.* stand back (*od kogoś / czegoś* from sb/sth); move *l.* step aside; **proszę się odsunąć!** stand back, please! **3.** (= *odseparować się*) seclude o.s.; **odsunąć się od swoich przyjaciół** distance o.s. from one's friends.

odsupłać *pf.*, **odsupływać** *ipf.* unknot, untie; *przen.* disentangle.

odsuwać *ipf. zob.* **odsunąć**. ~ **się** *ipf. zob.* **odsunąć się**.

odsyłacz *mi Gen.* -a **1.** (= *znak graficzny*) reference (mark). **2.** (= *przypis, objaśnienie*) reference, note. **3.** (= *tekst odsyłający lub hasło odsyłające do innego*) cross-reference.

odsyłać *ipf.* **1.** (= *wysyłać z powrotem*) send back. **2.** (= *kierować dokądś*) refer (*do kogoś / czegoś* to sb/sth); **odsyłać do specjalisty** refer to a specialist; **odsyłać od Annasza do Kajfasza** drive from pillar to post; **odsyłać z kwitkiem** send back empty-handed. **3.** (= *wskazywać miejsce w tekście dla uzyskania informacji*) cross-refer, cross-reference.

odsypać *pf.* -ę -esz *zob.* **odsypywać**.

odsypiać *ipf.* (*nieprzespaną noc*) make up for.

odsypywać *ipf.* pour off.

odszczekać, odszczeknąć *pf.* -ij, **odszczekiwać** *ipf.* **1.** (*o psie*) bark. **2.** *pot.* (= *pyskować, odciąć się*) talk back. **3.** *pot.* (= *odwołać*) take back, eat crow, eat one's words. ~ **się, odszczeknąć się** *pf.*, **odszczekiwać się** *ipf.* **1.** (*o psie*) bark. **2.** *pot.* (= *odciąć się, opryskliwie odpowiedzieć*) talk back (*komuś* to sb).

odszczepieniec *mp* -ńc- *pl.* -y *rel., polit.* apostate, dissident.

odszczepieństwo *n. rel., polit.* apostasy, dissidence.

odszczurzać *ipf.* exterminate rats.

odszczurzanie *n.* rat-extermination.

odszczurzyć *pf. zob.* **odszczurzać**.

odszedł *itd. pf. zob.* **odejść**.

odszkodowanie *n.* 1. (= *ubezpieczenie*) compensation, indemnity; **złożyć wniosek o odszkodowanie (tytułem ubezpieczenia)** put in *l.* make a claim on the insurance. 2. (= *kara*) damages, compensation; **przyznać komuś odszkodowanie** award *l.* grant sb damages; **ubiegać się o odszkodowanie** claim *l.* seek compensation; **wypłacić komuś odszkodowanie** pay sb compensation; **zaskarżyć kogoś o odszkodowanie** *prawn.* sue sb for damages. 3. (= *zadośćuczynienie*) settlement; redress, remedy.

odsznurować *pf.*, **odsznurowywać** *ipf.* undo, untie; **odsznurowywać buty** unlace shoes.

odszraniać *ipf.*, **odszronić** *pf.* defrost; **płyn odszraniający** defroster.

odszukać *pf.*, **odszukiwać** *ipf.* find; hunt out; **odszukać słowo w słowniku** look up a word in a dictionary.

odszyfrować *pf.*, **odszyfrowywać** *ipf.* 1. (= *odczytać szyfr*) decode, decrypt. 2. (= *odgadnąć*) decipher; **odszyfrować czyjeś gryzmoły** decipher sb's scribble.

odśnieżać *ipf.* clear of snow, remove snow; (*pługiem*) plow snow; (*szuflą*) shovel snow.

odśnieżarka *f. Gen.pl.* -ek *techn.* snow plow; snow blower; snow-clearing machine.

odśnieżny *a.* snow-clearing.

odśnieżyć *pf. zob.* **odśnieżać**.

odśpiewać *pf.*, **odśpiewywać** *pf.* sing.

odśrodkowy *a.* 1. (= *od środka*) centrifugal; **ruch odśrodkowy** centrifugal movement; **siła odśrodkowa** *fiz.* centrifugal force. 2. (= *decentralizacyjny*) decentralizing, devolutionary; **tendencje odśrodkowe** devolutionary tendencies.

odśrubować *pf.*, **odśrubowywać** *ipf.* unscrew, screw off.

odświeżacz *mi Gen.* -a freshener; **odświeżacz do ust** breath freshener; **odświeżacz powietrza** air freshener.

odświeżać *ipf.*, **odświeżyć** *pf.* 1. (*mieszkanie, łazienkę*) (= *odnawiać*) freshen up; redecorate. 2. (= *przywracać świeżość*) refresh; **odświeżająca kąpiel/prysznic** refreshing bath/shower. 3. (= *uaktualniać, odmładzać*) infuse new blood; **odświeżyć drużynę** infuse new blood into a team. 4. (= *ożywiać, przywracać*) refresh; **odświeżać komuś pamięć/wspomnienia** refresh sb's memory/recollections; **odświeżyć dawną przyjaźń** revive *l.* renew old friendship. 5. (*stronę, grafikę, pamięć, obraz na ekranie*) refresh. ~ **się** *ipf.*, **odświeżyć się** *pf.* (= *doprowadzać się do właściwego stanu, regenerować siły*) freshen up, refresh (o.s.); **odświeżyć się po podróży** freshen up after a journey.

odświętnie *adv.* festively; **odświętnie ubrany** wearing one's Sunday best.

odświętność *f.* festive character.

odświętny *a.* 1. (= *związany ze świętem*) festive, holiday; **odświętny posiłek** special meal; **odświętny strój** one's (Sunday) best. 2. (= *uroczysty, podniosły*) celebratory; **odświętny nastrój** holiday *l.* festive mood, holiday spirit.

odtajać *pf.* 1. (= *odmarznąć*) thaw. 2. (*o człowieku*) (= *ogrzać się*) thaw (out), get warm.

odtańczyć *pf.* dance; **odtańczyć taniec radości** do a dance of joy.

odtąd *adv.* 1. (= *od tego miejsca*) (starting) from here, (starting) from this point. 2. (= *od tamtego czasu*) since then; **odtąd żyli długo i szczęśliwie** and they lived happily ever after. 3. (= *od obecnej chwili*) from now on. 4. **odtąd** *l.* **odkąd** from that time on.

odtelefonować *pf.* (= *oddzwonić*) call back.

odtelegrafować *pf.* (= *oddepeszować*) wire back.

odtłuc *pf.* -tłukę -tłuczesz, -tłucz, -tłukł, **odtłukiwać** *ipf.* knock off; chip. ~ **się** *pf.*, **odtłukiwać się** *ipf.* get knocked off; chip.

odtłuszczać *pf.* 1. (*mleko*) skim. 2. (*powierzchnię, wełnę, skórę*) degrease. 3. defat.

odtłuszczony *a.* 1. (*o mleku*) skim(med). 2. (*o powierzchni, wełnie, skórze*) degreased. 3. defatted.

odtransportować *pf.*, **odtransportowywać** *ipf.* 1. (*towar*) deliver. 2. (*człowieka*) take, escort.

odtrąbić *pf.* 1. (= *odegrać na trąbie, trąbce*) trumpet; **odtrąbić capstrzyk/hejnał** sound the tattoo/bugle-call; **odtrąbiono!** *wojsk.* route march!; **zrobić coś na odtrąbiono** *pot.* scamp sth. 2. (= *odpowiedzieć trąbieniem*) trumpet (back).

odtrącać *ipf.*, **odtrącić** *pf.* 1. (= *odsuwać, odpychać*) shove away. 2. (= *utrącić, obtłuc*) knock off, break off. 3. (= *potrącać, odliczać*) deduct. 4. (= *odrzucać, nie przyjmować*) reject; **odtrącać czyjąś pomoc/przyjaźń** reject sb's help/ friendship.

odtrutka *f. Gen.pl.* -ek 1. (= *antidotum*) antidote, counterpoison. 2. (= *środek zaradczy*) antidote (*na coś* to sth).

odtruwać *pf. med.* (*od alkoholu, narkotyków*) detoxify.

odtwarzacz *mi Gen.* -a player; **odtwarzacz przenośny** personal stereo; **odtwarzacz samochodowy/kasetowy** radio/cassette player; **odtwarzacz wideo/kompaktowy/DVD** video/CD/DVD player.

odtwarzać *ipf.*, **odtworzyć** *pf.* -órz 1. (*skórę, nabłonek*) (= *regenerować, odradzać*) regenerate. 2. (= *rekonstruować, odbudowywać*) reconstruct; reproduce; (*domy, obrazy*) restore; **odtworzyć przebieg wypadków** reconstruct the train of events; **odtwarzać zalesienie** *leśn.* reforest. 3. (= *odzwierciedlać w sztuce*) capture; **odtwarzać rolę** perform a role. 4. (*o taśmie magnetofonowej, wideo, płycie*) play, play back; **odtwarzać nagrany mecz** play a recorded match. ~ **się** *ipf.*, **odtworzyć się** *pf.* (*o tkankach*) (= *odradzać się*) regenerate.

odtwarzanie *n.* (*budynku, obrazu*) reconstruction, recreation; (*tkanek*) regeneration; (*dźwię-*

ku, obrazu) playing, playback; **jakość odtwarzania** picture *l.* sound quality; **wysoka wierność odtwarzania dźwięku** *techn.* high fidelity, hi-fi.

odtwórca *mp* **1.** (= *wykonawca*) performer; **odtwórca głównej roli** lead actor; **odtwórca muzyki Chopina** performer of Chopin's music. **2.** (= *imitator*) reproducer.

odtwórczość *f.* reproductiveness, imitativeness.

odtwórczy *a.* **1.** (= *dotyczący odtwarzania*) reproductive; **odtwórcze zdolności** imitative skills. **2.** (= *naśladujący, wtórny*) imitative.

odtwórczyni *f.* **1.** (= *wykonawczyni*) performer; **odtwórczyni głównej roli** lead actress; **odtwórczyni muzyki Chopina** performer of Chopin's music. **2.** (= *imitatorka*) reproducer.

odtykać *ipf.* **1.** unstop. **2.** (= *wyjmować korek*) uncork. **3.** (*coś zatkanego, zablokowanego*) unclog. **~ się** *ipf.* **1.** (*o zatyczce*) (= *otwierać się*) fall out. **2.** (= *przestać być zapchanym*) unclog.

odtylcowy *a.* breech-loading; **broń odtylcowa** breechloader.

oduczać *ipf.*, **oduczyć** *pf.* unteach, teach not to; **oduczać kogoś robienia czegoś** teach sb not to do sth. **~ się** *ipf.*, **oduczyć się** *pf.* unlearn; **oduczać się robienia czegoś** unlearn sth, teach o.s. not to do sth.

odurzać *ipf.* **1.** (*narkotykami*) drug; (*alkoholem, narkotykami*) intoxicate. **2.** (= *oszałamiać, otumaniać*) stupefy, overpower; **odurzający zapach** overpowering smell. **~ się** *ipf.* take; **odurzać się chemikaliami** abuse solvents; **odurzać się narkotykami** take *l.* abuse drugs.

odurzająco *adv.* intoxicatingly, overpoweringly, headily.

odurzający *a.* intoxicating, overpowering, heady; **środki odurzające** *med.* intoxicants; drugs; stupefacients.

odurzenie *n.* (*alkoholem*) intoxication; (*alkoholem, narkotykiem*) stupor.

odurzyć *pf. zob.* **odurzać**. **~ się** *pf. zob.* **odurzać się**.

odwach *mi arch.* guardhouse.

odwadniać *ipf.* **1.** (= *usuwać wodę, osuszać*) drain; **odwadniać łąki/bagna** drain meadows/ swamps; **odwadniać ścieki/ropę naftową** dewater sewage/crude oil; **kanał** *l.* **rów odwadniający** ditch, trench. **2.** *chem., pat.* dehydrate. **~ się** *ipf. chem., pat.* dehydrate.

odwaga *f.* (= *męstwo*) courage, bravery; **nie grzeszyć odwagą** be soft-hearted; **mieć odwagę coś zrobić** have courage to do sth; **odwaga cywilna** moral courage; **stracić odwagę** lose heart *l.* one's nerve; **to wymaga odwagi** it takes courage; **zebrać się na odwagę** muster (up) *l.* summon up the courage.

odwalać *ipf.*, **odwalić** *pf.* **1.** (= *odsuwać*) move *l.* heave aside; **odwalić kitę** *pot.* croak. **2.** *pot.* (= *wykonywać*) do; **odwalić kawał roboty** do a whole lot of work; **odwalić za kogoś brudną robotę** do sb's dirty work. **3.** *pot.* (= *pracować bez zaangażowania*) botch (up); **odwalać robotę** *l.* **fuszerkę** botch a job. **4.** *pot.* (= *eliminować, odrzucać*) eliminate; reject; **odwalić kogoś na egzaminie**

flunk sb; **odwalić prośbę/podanie** turn down a request/application. **5.** *pot.* (= *ściągać*) crib (*od kogoś/z czegoś* from sb/sth); **odwalać na sprawdzianie** crib during a test. **6.** *pot.* (= *udawać, naśladować*) pretend, sham.

odwalić *pf.* **1.** *zob.* **odwalać**. **2.** *pot.* (= *odciąć, odrąbać*) chop *l.* lop off. **~ się** *pf. pot.* (= *odczepić się*) shove off; get off (*od kogoś* sb's back); **odwal się!** get off my back!, buzz off!, bug off!

odwapniać *ipf.*, **odwapnić** *pf.* **-ij** (= *usuwać wapń z kości, zębów, skór*) decalcify.

odwapnienie *n.* **1.** (= *usunięcie wapnia z kości, zębów*) decalcification, loss of calcium. **2.** *techn.* (*w garbarstwie*) decalcification, deliming.

odwar *mi chem.* decoction.

odwarstwiać *ipf.*, **odwarstwić** *pf. med.* exfoliate; detach. **~ się** *ipf.*, **odwarstwić się** *pf. pat.* exfoliate; detach.

odwarstwienie *n.* *pat.* exfoliation; detachment; **odwarstwienie siatkówki** retinal detachment.

odważać *ipf.* weigh out; **odważyć kilogram jabłek** weigh out a kilo of apples. **~ się** *ipf.* find courage, venture (*na zrobienie czegoś* to do sth); **odważyć się zaprzeczyć** dare to deny.

odważniak *mp pl.* **-cy** *l.* **-i** *pot.* redhot.

odważnie *adv.* bravely, courageously.

odważnik *mi Gen.* **-a** (= *ciężarek*) weight; **odważnik kilogramowy** kilo weight.

odważny *a.* **1.** courageous, brave; (*o krytyce*) unflinching; **odważny strażak** brave fire-fighter. **2.** (*o scenach erotycznych, filmie*) explicit.

odważyć *pf. zob.* **odważać**. **~ się** *pf. zob.* **odważać się**.

odwdzięczać się *ipf.*, **odwdzięczyć się** *pf.* return a favor; repay (*komuś za coś* sb for sth); **odwdzięczać się za czyjąś pomoc/hojność** repay sb's kindness/generosity; **odwdzięczyć się pięknym za nadobne** pay back in kind; **odwdzięczyć się z nawiązką** repay with interest.

odwet *mi* (= *zemsta, rewanż*) retaliation, revenge; **w odwecie** in reprisal *l.* retaliation (*za coś* for sth); **wziąć na kimś odwet** take revenge on sb.

odwetowiec *mp* **-wc-** *pl.* **-y** retaliationist.

odwetowy *a.* retaliatory.

odwiązać *pf.* **-żę -żesz**, **odwiązywać** *ipf.* untie, undo; **odwiązać buty** unlace shoes; **odwiązać paczkę** undo a parcel. **~ się** *pf.*, **odwiązywać się** *ipf.* come untied, come undone.

odwidzieć się *pf.* **-i** *pot.* **odwidziało mi się** I've changed my mind.

odwieczny *a.* (= *od wieków, prastary*) (*zamek*) ancient; (*prawda*) eternal; (*problem*) perennial; (*puszcza*) primeval; (*zwyczaje*) immemorial.

odwiedzać *ipf.*, **odwiedzić** *pf.* **1.** (*z wizytą*) visit; call on; **odwiedzać znajomych/rodzinę** visit friends/family. **2.** (= *bywać, przebywać w celu zobaczenia, zwiedzania*) go to; (*często*) frequent; **odwiedzać muzea/teatry/wystawy** go to *l.* frequent museums/theaters/exhibitions; **odwiedź mnie jutro** come and see me tomorrow; **regularnie odwiedzać nocne kluby** go clubbing. **~ się**

ipf., **odwiedzić się** *pf.* visit each other *l.* one another.

odwiedziny *pl. Gen.* **-n** (= *wizyta*) visit, call; **być w odwiedzinach u kogoś** be on a visit to sb; **przyjść w odwiedziny do kogoś** pay *l.* make a call on sb, pay sb a visit; come to visit sb.

odwiercać *ipf.*, **odwiercić** *pf. górn.* drill, bore.

odwiert *mi* 1. *górn.* (= *odwiercenie*) drilling, boring. 2. *górn.* (*otwór*) borehole, well; **odwiert naftowy** oil well.

odwiesić *pf.*, **odwieszać** *ipf.* (*o słuchawce, płaszczu*) hang up.

odwieść *pf.* **-wiodę -wiedziesz, -wiódł -wiodła -wiedli** *zob.* **odwodzić**.

odwieźć *pf.* **-wiozę -wieziesz, -wiózł -wiozła -wieźli** *zob.* **odwozić**.

odwijać *ipf.* 1. (*coś zapakowanego w papier*) unwrap. 2. (= *rozwijać*) (*o sznurku, niciach*) unreel, unwind. 3. (= *zawijać w drugą stronę*) fold back; *med.* (*o powiece*) evert; (*o rękawach*) unroll. ~ **się** *ipf.* unreel, unwind.

odwilż *f. pl.* **-e** thaw.

odwilżacz *mi Gen.* **-a** *techn.* dehumidifier.

odwinąć *pf. zob.* **odwijać**. ~ **się** *pf.* 1. *pot.* (= *zamachnąć się*) swing one's arm (*to deal a blow*). 2. (= *uderzyć*) deal a blow.

odwirować *pf.*, **odwirowywać** *ipf.* (*o praniu*) spin, spindry; **odwirować coś** give sth a spin.

odwlec *pf.* **-wlokę** *l.* **-wlekę -wleczesz -wlókł** *l.* **-wlekł -wlokła** *l.* **-wlekła -wlekli, odwlekać** *ipf.* 1. (= *odsuwać, przemieszczać*) drag away. 2. (= *opóźniać*) delay (*zrobienie czegoś* doing sth); **nie odkładaj do jutra, co możesz zrobić dziś** never put off till tomorrow what you can do today. ~ **się** *pf.*, **odwlekać się** *ipf.* be put off; **co się odwlecze, to nie uciecze** there is luck in leisure.

odwłok *mi Gen.* **-u** *l.* **-a** *ent.* abdomen.

odwodnić *pf.* **-ij** *zob.* **odwadniać**. ~ **się** *pf. zob.* **odwadniać się**.

odwodnienie *n.* (*pola*) 1. drainage. 2. *med.* dehydration.

odwodowy *a. wojsk.* reserve, backup.

odwodzić *ipf.* **-ódź** 1. (= *odciągać*) take; (*spust pistoletu*) cock; *fizj.* (*o mięśniu*) abduct; **odwodzić kogoś na stronę** take sb aside. 2. (= *powstrzymywać kogoś przed czymś*) discourage *l.* dissuade (*kogoś od zrobienia czegoś* sb from doing sth).

odwołać *pf. zob.* **odwoływać**. ~ **się** *pf. zob.* **odwoływać się**.

odwołanie *n.* (*zarządzenia*) 1. cancellation, repeal. 2. (= *dymisja*) (*urzędnika*) dismissal; (*ambasadora*) recall. 3. *prawn.* (*od wyroku*) appeal; **aż do odwołania** until further notice.

odwoławczy *a.* 1. *prawn.* appellate; **postępowanie odwoławcze** appeal proceedings; **procedura odwoławcza** appellate procedure; **sąd odwoławczy** court of appeal. 2. (= *unieważniający*) cancelling.

odwoływać *ipf.* (= *przywoływać do siebie*) 1. call; **odwołać kogoś na stronę** call sb aside. 2. (= *dymisjonować*) dismiss; (*ambasadora*) recall. 3. (*wykład, lot*) cancel; (*słowo, obietnicę*) withdraw, retract. ~ **się** *ipf. prawn.* 1. appeal; **od-**

wołać się do sądu appeal to the court; **odwołać się od decyzji** appeal from *l.* against a decision, lodge an appeal against a decision. 2. (= *przywoływać jakiś autorytet*) refer (*do kogoś / czegoś* to sb/sth); (*do uczuć, do rozumu, do doświadczenia*) appeal (*do czegoś* to sth).

odwozić *ipf.* (= *zawozić*) 1. take, drive; **odwozić dzieci do szkoły** take *l.* drive children to school. 2. (= *odwozić z powrotem*) take back, drive back; **odwieźć kogoś do domu** take *l.* drive sb back home.

odwód *mi* **-o-** *wojsk.* 1. reserve. 2. *przen.* **mieć coś w odwodzie** hold *l.* keep sth in reserve.

odwracać *ipf.* 1. (*o głowie*) turn (away); (*o kartkach*) turn; (*o ubraniach, pościeli*) turn over, reverse; **odwrócić wzrok** avert one's eyes *l.* gaze; **stać odwrócony plecami do kogoś** stand with one's back turned to sb. 2. (*zmieniać stan czegoś*) (*o biegu rzeki*) reverse; (*o ubraniu*) turn inside out; **odwracać czyjąś uwagę od czegoś** divert sb's attention from sth; **odwrócić nieszczęście** avert a disaster; **odwracać kota ogonem** *pot.* (= *przeinaczać swoje słowa*) shift one's ground; (= *przeinaczać czyjeś słowa*) distort the facts. ~ **się** *ipf.* 1. (= *obracać się*) turn round; (*tyłem*) turn away; (*na bok*) turn to one's side; **karta się odwróciła** *przen.* my luck has run out *l.* turned; **odwrócić się na pięcie** turn on one's heel. 2. (= *zerwać z kimś, z czymś*) turn one's back (*od kogoś* on sb) turn away (*od kogoś* from sb); **szczęście się ode mnie odwróciło** luck has deserted me.

odwracalność *f.* reversibility.

odwracalny *a.* reversible; **film odwracalny** *fot.* reversal film; **reakcja odwracalna** *chem.* reversible *l.* balanced reaction.

odwrotnie *adv.* (= *przeciwnie*) on the contrary, contrarily, in contrast; **odwrotnie proporcjonalny** *mat.* inversely proportional; **włożyłaś bluzkę odwrotnie** (= *na lewą stronę*) you've put the blouse on inside out; (= *tyłem do przodu*) you've put the blouse on backwards *l.* back to front.

odwrotność *f.* (= *przeciwieństwo*) the opposite, the reverse; (*liczby, ułamka*) *mat.* inverse.

odwrotny *a.* 1. (= *przeciwny*) opposite, reverse; **odnieść odwrotny skutek** (*np. o planach*) backfire; **odwrotna strona medalu** *przen.* the other side of the coin; **przesłać odwrotną pocztą** send by return mail. 2. (= *w przeciwnym kierunku*) in the opposite direction; **w odwrotnej kolejności** in reverse order.

odwrócenie *n.* reversion, inversion; (*polityki, decyzji*) reversal.

odwrócić *pf. zob.* **odwracać**. ~ **się** *pf. zob.* **odwracać się**.

odwrót *mi* **-o-** 1. *wojsk.* retreat, withdrawal; **być w odwrocie** be in retreat; **odciąć komuś odwrót** intercept sb's retreat. 2. *przen.* (= *zmiana stanowiska, poglądów*) turn (*od czegoś* (away) from sth); move (*od czegoś* (away) from sth). 3. (= *przeciwna strona czegoś*) reverse; **na odwrocie** on the reverse; **na odwrocie strony** on the reverse side, overleaf; **na odwrót** on the contrary, the other way round; **włożyłeś koszulę na odwrót**

(= *na lewą stronę*) you're wearing the shirt inside out; (= *tyłem do przodu*) you're wearing the shirt backwards *l*. back to front.

odwszawiać *ipf.*, **odwszawić** *pf.* delouse.

odwyk *mi pot.* (*zwł. od alkoholu*) drying-out; (*od alkoholu, narkotyków*) detox; **być na odwyku** *pot.* (= *odstawić alkohol l. narkotyki*) be drying out, be in detox; (= *przebywać w klinice odwykowej*) be in rehab, be in detox.

odwykać *ipf.*, **odwyknąć** *pf.* **-ij** lose the habit (*od robienia czegoś* of doing sth); get out of the habit (*od robienia czegoś* of doing sth); **przez ten rok zupełnie odwykłem od pracy** during the year I grew completely disaccustomed to work.

odwykowy *a.* drying-out, detox, rehab; **leczenie odwykowe** rehab; **oddział odwykowy** detoxification center.

odwykówka *f. Gen.pl.* **-ek** *pot.* drying-out ward *l*. clinic, detox center.

odwzajemniać *ipf.*, **odwzajemnić** *pf.* **-ij** (*o uczuciach, sympatii, miłości*) reciprocate, requite; (*o uśmiechu*) return; (*o przysłudze*) return, repay. **~ się** *ipf.*, **odwzajemnić się** *pf.* reciprocate, return; repay (*komuś za coś* sb for sth).

odwzorować *pf. zob.* **odwzorowywać**.

odwzorowanie *n.* mapping; (*o rysunku*) transfer; (*na kalce*) tracing.

odwzorowywać *ipf.* **1.** (= *tworzyć coś na wzór czegoś*) imitate, copy. **2.** *mat.* map. **3.** *opt.* image.

odymiać *pf.*, **odymić** *ipf.* **1.** (= *odkazić dymem*) fumigate. **2.** (*o pszczołach*) smoke.

odyniec *ma* **-ńc-** *zool.* boar.

odyseja *f.* odyssey.

Odyseusz *mp mit.* Odysseus, Ulisses.

odzew *mi* **1.** (*na hasło*) countersign. **2.** (= *odpowiedź, reakcja*) response; **apel o pomoc pozostał bez odzewu** there was no response to the appeal for help.

odziać *pf.* **-eję -ejesz** *zob.* **odziewać**. **~ się** *pf. zob.* **odziewać się**.

odziedziczyć *pf.* (*w spadku, po przodkach*) inherit (*coś po kimś* sth from sb).

odzienie *n. przest.* attire.

odzierać *ipf.* **1.** (= *zdzierać coś z czegoś*) strip (*z czegoś* of sth); **odzierać ze skóry** skin, flay; **odarty ze złudzeń** *przen.* disillusioned; **wrzeszczał, jakby go odzierali ze skóry** he was screaming bloody murder. **2.** (= *doprowadzać do ubóstwa*) skin, rip off; **odarli mnie ze skóry** they ripped me off.

odziewać *ipf. przest.* attire; **nędznie odziany** meanly attired; **odziewać w habit** frock. **~ się** *ipf. przest.* attire oneself.

odzież *f.* clothes, clothing; **odzież codzienna** *l*. **swobodna** casual wear *l*. clothes; **gotowa odzież** off-the-rack clothes; *Br.* off the peg clothes; **odzież damska/męska/zimowa** ladies'/men's/winter wear; **odzież ochronna** protective clothing.

odzieżowiec *mp* **-wc-** *pl.* **-y** clothing industry expert.

odzieżowy *a.* clothes; **przemysł odzieżowy** clothing industry; **sklep odzieżowy** clothes de-

partment store; *Br.* clothes shop; **wesz odzieżowa** body *l*. clothes louse (*Pediculus corporis*).

odzieżówka *f. Gen.pl.* **-ek** *pot.* (*szkoła*) **1.** dressmaking school. **2.** *pot.* (= *przemysł odzieżowy*) clothing industry. **3.** (= *fabryka odzieżowa*) clothing factory.

odznaczać *ipf.* award; (*medalem, orderem*) decorate (*kogoś za coś* sb for sth). **~ się** *ipf.* **1.** (= *charakteryzować się*) be characterized (*czymś* by sth); **odznacza się inteligencją** she's remarkably intelligent. **2.** (= *wyróżniać się*) distinguish oneself; (= *uwidaczniać się*) stand out; **obraz odznaczał się na tle białej ściany** the picture stood out on a white wall.

odznaczenie *n.* decoration, distinction; **nadać komuś odznaczenie** decorate sb.

odznaczyć *pf. zob.* **odznaczać**. **~ się** *pf. zob.* **odznaczać się**.

odznaka *f.* **1.** (= *wyróżnienie*) distinction, decoration. **2.** (= *znak przynależności*) badge.

odzwierciedlać *ipf.* reflect, mirror; **wiernie odzwierciedlać rzeczywistość** be true to life. **~ się** *ipf.* (= *wyrażać*) be reflected.

odzwierciedlenie *n.* reflection.

odzwierciedlić *pf. zob.* **odzwierciedlać**. **~ się** *pf. zob.* **odzwierciedlać się**.

odzwierzęcy *a.* (*o chorobie*) animal-borne, animal-transmitted.

odzwyczaić *pf.*, **odzwyczajać** *ipf.* break *l*. lose a habit; disaccustom (*kogoś od czegoś* sb to sth). **~ się** *pf.*, **odzwyczajać się** *ipf.* break *l*. lose a habit; disaccustom oneself (*od czegoś* to sth).

odzysk *mi* **1.** (= *coś odzyskanego*) recovered material; **cegły z odzysku** reused bricks. **2.** (= *odzyskiwanie czegoś*) recovery, reuse; **odzysk metali** metal recovery *l*. winning; **odzysk surowców wtórnych** by-product recovery.

odzyskać *pf.*, **odzyskiwać** *ipf.* recover, win *l*. get back, regain; **odzyskać linię** get one's figure back; **odzyskać mowę** find one's tongue; **odzyskać panowanie nad sobą** regain *l*. recover one's composure; **odzyskać przytomność** regain consciousness, come round *l*. to; **odzyskać władzę** regain power; **odzyskać zdrowie** recover from an illness, regain one's health.

odzywać się *ipf.* **-am -asz** **1.** (= *mówić coś*) speak; (*o uczuciach*) awake; **odezwij się do mnie!** speak to me! **2.** (= *rozlegać się*) sound; **uderz w stół, a nożyce się odezwą** the hit dog howls; methinks thou dost protest too much. **3.** *karty* (*w licytacji*) call; bid.

odzywka *f. Gen.pl.* **-ek** **1.** *pot.* (= *niegrzeczna reakcja słowna*) mouth, back talk. **2.** *karty* (*w licytacji*) call, bid.

odźwiernik *mi Gen.* **-a** *anat.* pylorus.

odźwierny *mp* doorkeeper; *Br.* porter.

odżałować *pf.* **1.** (= *przeboleć*) (*o stracie*) get over. **2.** (= *zdecydować się na znaczny wydatek*) (*o pieniądzach*) part with.

odżegnać się *pf.*, **odżegnywać się** *ipf.* distance oneself (*od czegoś* from sth).

odżyć *pf.* **-ję -jesz**, **odżywać** *ipf.* **-am -asz** **1.** (= *odzyskiwać siły*) come back to life; *przen.* get a new lease on life. **2.** (= *odnawiać się*) regenerate; (*o przyjaźni, nadziei*) be revived.

odżywczy *a.* nourishing, nutritional, nutritious; **krem odżywczy** nourishing cream; **wartość odżywcza** nutritional value.

odżywiać *ipf.* nourish, feed. ~ **się** *ipf.* (*o człowieku*) eat; feed oneself; (*o zwierzęciu*) feed; **odżywiać się prawidłowo** eat right.

odżywianie *n.* nutrition, nourishment, diet; *gł. med.* alimentation; **odżywianie piersią** breast feeding; **sztuczne odżywianie** *med.* artificial feeding; **zdrowe/urozmaicone odżywianie** healthy/varied diet.

odżywić *pf. zob.* **odżywiać.** ~ **się** *pf. zob.* **odżywiać się.**

odżywiony *a.* **-eni** fed, nourished; **dobrze odżywiony** well-fed, well-nourished; **źle odżywiony** poorly-fed, ill-nourished.

odżywka *f. Gen.pl.* **-ek** (*dla dzieci*) formula; (*dla sportowców*) supplement; **odżywka do włosów** hair-conditioner; **szampon z odżywką** shampoo and conditioner.

oenzetowski *a.* UN, United Nations; **oenzetowska misja pokojowa** UN peace-keeping mission.

ofensywa *f.* **1.** *wojsk.* offensive, offense; **przejść do ofensywy** take the offensive; **przypuścić ofensywę** launch an offensive. **2.** *sport* offense; **grać w ofensywie** play on offense.

ofensywnie *adv.* offensively, aggressively.

ofensywność *f.* aggressiveness.

ofensywny *a.* offensive, agressive; **gra ofensywna** offensive play.

oferent *mp* bidder, tenderer.

oferma *f. l. mp decl. like f. pl.* **-m** *l.* **-ów** *pog.* loser, klutz, schlep; **oferma życiowa** born loser.

ofermowaty *a. pog.* klutzy.

oferować *ipf.* offer; (*o cenie*) bid; (*o pomocy, radzie*) offer, volunteer.

oferta *f.* offer; proposal; **oferta specjalna** special offer.

offset *mi* **1.** *druk.* (*technika*) offset. **2.** *druk.* (*maszyna*) offset press.

offsetowy *a. druk.* offset.

ofiara *f. Dat. i Loc.* **-erze 1.** (= *datek*) contribution, donation. **2.** (= *poświęcenie czegoś*) sacrifice; **najwyższa ofiara** the final *l.* supreme sacrifice. **3.** (= *osoba poszkodowana*) casualty, victim; **ofiara śmiertelna** fatality; **padać ofiarą czegoś** fall victim to sth. **4.** *pog.* (= *niezdara*) loser, klutz, schlep; **ofiara losu** born loser. **5.** *rel.* sacrifice, offering; **składać coś w ofierze** make an offering of sth.

ofiarnie *adv.* (*pracować*) with dedication, unsparingly.

ofiarność *f.* (= *szczodrość*) **1.** generosity. **2.** (= *oddanie, skłonność do poświęceń*) (*np. w pracy*) dedication, devotion.

ofiarny *a.* **1.** (= *pełen poświęcenia*) dedicated, devoted, selfless. **2.** *rel.* (*o zwierzęciu, stosie, ogniu, ołtarzu*) sacrificial; **kozioł ofiarny** scapegoat.

ofiarodawca *mp*, **ofiarodawczyni** *f.* donor.

ofiarować *pf. l. ipf. zob.* **ofiarowywać.** ~ **się** *pf. l. ipf. zob.* **ofiarowywać się.**

ofiarowanie *n.* (*o upominkach, nagrodach*) **1.** presentation; (*o pieniądzach, darach*) donation. **2.** *rel.* offertory, oblation.

ofiarowywać *ipf.* **1.** (= *podarować coś*) present (*komuś coś* sb with sth); give, offer; (*o datkach*) donate. **2.** *rel.* (= *złożyć w ofierze*) offer up. ~ **się** *ipf.* (= *deklarować swoje uczucia, chęci*) offer, volunteer; **ofiarowywać się z pomocą** offer one's help.

oficer *mp pl.* **-owie** (commissioned) officer; **oficer dowodzący** commanding officer; **oficer liniowy** line officer; **oficer łącznikowy** liaison officer; **oficer rezerwy** reserve officer; **oficer sztabowy** staff officer; **młodszy oficer** subaltern; **starszy oficer** general officer; **ranga** *l.* **stopień oficera** comission.

oficerki *pl. Gen.* **-rek** *pot.* jackboots.

oficerski *a.* officer's; officers'; **nominacja oficerska** commission; **kasyno oficerskie** officers' mess; **szkoła oficerska** military academy.

oficjalista *mp* clerk.

oficjalnie *adv.* officially, formally.

oficjalność *f.* official character, formality.

oficjalny *a.* **1.** (= *urzędowy, formalny*) official, formal; **oficjalny przedstawiciel** accredited representative; **wizyta oficjalna** *l.* **państwowa** state visit; **wersja oficjalna** (*dokumentu, wydarzeń*) official version. **2.** (= *niedopuszczający poufałości*) reserved.

oficjał *mp rz.-kat.* official.

oficjel *mp* official; *pot.* bigwig.

oficyna *f.* **1.** (*dobudówka*) annex; *Br.* annexe. **2.** (= *drukarnia, wydawnictwo*) publishing house.

ofierze *f. zob.* **ofiara.**

oflag *mi hist.* oflag.

oflagować *pf.* put up flags on (*sth*).

oflagowy *a. hist.* oflag.

ofsajd *mi sport* offside.

ofsajdowy *a. sport* offside.

oftalmologia *f. Gen.* **-ii** *med.* ophthalmology.

oftalmologiczny *a. med.* ophthalmological.

oftalmoskopia *f. Gen.* **-ii** *med.* ophthalmoscopy.

ofukiwać *ipf.* rate, scold.

ofuknąć *pf.* **-ij** *zob.* **ofukiwać.**

ogałacać *ipf.* bare, strip (*z czegoś* of sth); *form.* denude; deprive of; (*z pieniędzy*) *pot.* clean out; **drzewa ogołocone z liści** trees denuded of their leaves.

oganiać *ipf.* brush away. ~ **się** *ipf.* brush (*od kogoś/czegoś* sb/sth away *l.* off).

ogar *ma myśl.* hound.

ogarek *mi* **-rk-** *Gen.* **-a** stump, end; **ogarek świecy** candle-end; **Panu Bogu świeczkę i diabłu ogarek** (try to) serve two masters; have one face to God and another to the devil; run with the hare and hunt with the hounds.

ogarnąć *pf.* **-ij**, **ogarniać** *ipf.* **1.** (= *obejmować ramionami*) embrace. **2.** (= *widzieć, rozumieć całość*) comprehend; **ogarniać kogoś/coś spojrzeniem** take sb/sth in; **staram się ogarnąć złożo-**

ność sytuacji I'm trying to fathom the complexity of the situation; **trudno to ogarnąć umysłem** it's difficult to grasp, it's mind-boggling. **3.** (= *przenikać kogoś*) grip, overcome, sweep; **ogarnęła mnie panika** I was panic stricken, panic gripped me. **4.** (= *otaczać kogoś, coś*) surround, encompass; **ogarnęły nas kompletne ciemności** we were left in total darkness. **5.** (= *rozprzestrzeniać się*) (*epidemia, pożar*) spread *l.* sweep across. **6.** *pot.* (= *porządkować, sprzątać*) (*mieszkanie, obejście*) *pot.* tidy (up), spruce up. ~ **się** *pf.* -**ij**, **ogarniać się** *ipf.* spruce up, freshen up; **muszę się trochę ogarnąć przed obiadem** I have to spruce up a bit before dinner.

ogień *mi* **ogni-** *Gen.* **-a 1.** (= *palenie się*) fire; **dolać oliwy do ognia** add fuel to the flames; **języki ognia** tongues of fire; **na wolnym ogniu** *kulin.* on a low heat; **nie igraj z ogniem!** don't play with fire!; **nie ma dymu bez ognia** *przen.* there's no smoke without fire; **ogień i woda** *przen.* fire and water; **słomiany ogień** *l.* zapał short-lived enthusiasm; **ściana ognia** wall of fire; **upiec dwie pieczenie na jednym ogniu** *przen.* kill two birds with one stone; **wpaść jak po ogień** make a whirlwind visit. **2.** (= *pożar*) fire; **coś stoi w ogniu** sth is in flames; **łuna ognia** glow; **skoczyć dla kogoś w ogień** go through fire and water for sb; **ugasić ogień** put out a fire; **zaprószyć gdzieś ogień** set sth on fire. **3.** (= *ognisko, stos*) fire; (*ofiarny*) pyre. **4.** (= *płomień*) fire, flame; (*zapalniczki, zapałki*) light; **masz ogień?** *pot.* do you have a light?, got a light?; **sztuczne ognie** fireworks; **zimne ognie** sparklers. **5.** (= *strzały z broni*) fire; **być na linii ognia** be in the line of fire; **krzyżowy ogień pytań** *przen.* cross-examination; **ognia!** *wojsk.* fire!; **ogień artyleryjski** shellfire; **ogień armatni** gunfire; **ogień krzyżowy** *wojsk.* crossfire; **otworzyć ogień** *wojsk.* open fire; **przerwać ogień!** *wojsk.* cease fire! **6.** *przen.* (= *namiętność, pasja*) (*gniewu, nienawiści, żądzy*) fire, fervor. **7.** *przen.* (= *żar*) heat. **8.** *przen.* (= *rumieniec*) blush. **9.** *przen.* (= *łuna*) glow.

ogier *ma* (*koń*) stallion; (= *ogier rozpłodowy*) stud. – *mp pl.* -**y** *wulg.* (*kochanek*) stud, stallion.

oglądać *ipf.* **1.** (= *przyglądać się*) (*o filmie, telewizji*) watch; (*o obrazie, książce*) look at, examine; (*o zabytkach, mieście*) see; (*o towarze w sklepie*) look through, browse; **oglądać wystawy** window-shop. **2.** (= *widzieć kogoś, coś*) see; **chciałbym cię oglądać w dobrym zdrowiu** I'd like to see you in good health. ~ **się** *ipf.* **1.** (= *przyglądać się sobie*) look at oneself. **2.** (= *zwracać oczy w jakimś kierunku*) (*do tyłu*) look back; (*na boki*) look around; **oglądać się za kimś** (*kobietami, mężczyznami*) have a roving *l.* wondering eye. **3.** (= *liczyć na kogoś, coś*) *przen.* count on; **nie oglądaj się na rodziców, oni ci nie mogą pomóc** don't count on your parents, they can't help you. **4.** (= *zwracać uwagę na*) have regard for; **nie oglądał się na jej uczucia** he had no regard for her feelings. **5.** (= *szukać*) look for; **oglądam się za mieszkaniem** I'm looking for an apartment.

oglądalność *f.* ratings, viewing figures; **okresowe badania oglądalności** sweeps.

oględnie *adv.* **1.** (= *ostrożnie*) guardedly, delicately. **2.** (= *umiarkowanie*) moderately.

oględność *f.* **1.** (= *umiar*) moderation. **2.** (= *ostrożność*) caution; (*w mowie*) guardedness.

oględny *a.* (*o mowie, stwierdzeniach*) guarded; (*o krytyce, ocenie*) understated; **w oględny sposób** in a guarded manner; **w oględnych słowach** in guarded language.

oględziny *pl. Gen.* -**n 1.** (= *badanie*) examination; **oględziny lekarskie** medical examination; **oględziny zwłok** postmortem (examination), autopsy. **2.** (= *inspekcja*) inspection, survey.

ogłada *f.* good manners, refinement; **bez ogłady** coarse, unrefined; **ogłada towarzyska** polish; **pełen ogłady** urbane.

ogłaszać *ipf.* **1.** (= *podać do wiadomości*) announce; (*dekret, manifest, odezwę*) publish, issue; (*niepodległość, stan wyjątkowy*) declare; **ogłaszać wyrok** pronounce sentence; **ogłosić zawieszenie broni** call a truce. **2.** (= *opublikować*) publish. ~ **się** *ipf.* **1.** (= *przekazywać o sobie jakąś wiadomość*) advertise. **2.** *przest.* (= *uzurpować sobie tytuł*) declare oneself.

ogławiacz *mi Gen.* -**a** *roln.* root topper.

ogławiać *ipf.* **1.** *roln.* (*np. buraki*) top. **2.** *leśn.* head, poll.

ogłosić *pf. zob.* **ogłaszać**. ~ **się** *pf. zob.* **ogłaszać się**.

ogłoszenie *n.* announcement; (*niepodległości, zawieszenia broni*) declaration; (*pisemne*) notice; (*matrymonialne, reklamowe*) advertisement, ad; **ogłoszenia drobne** the classifieds; **ogłoszenie towarzyskie** personal columns *l.* ads, the personals.

ogłoszeniodawca *mp* advertiser.

ogłoszeniowy *a.* advertisement; **słup ogłoszeniowy** kiosk; **strona ogłoszeniowa** advertisement page; **tablica ogłoszeniowa** bulletin board.

ogłowić *pf.* -**ów** *zob.* **ogławiać**.

ogłuchnąć *pf.* -**ij** go *l.* grow deaf; **ogłuchnąć na jedno ucho** go *l.* grow deaf in one ear.

ogłupiać *ipf.* stupefy; (*za pomocą propagandy*) stupefy.

ogłupiająco *adv.* (*działać na kogoś*) stupefyingly.

ogłupiający *a.* stupefying; (*o pracy, zadaniu*) mind-numbing; **ogłupiająca propaganda** stupefying propaganda.

ogłupiały *a.* (*ze zmęczenia, z nudów*) stupefied; (*po narkotykach, środkach odurzających*) dopey; (*o narodzie*) confused.

ogłupić *pf. zob.* **ogłupiać**.

ogłupieć *pf.* go mad, be stunned; **ogłupieć ze szczęścia** go mad for joy.

ogłupienie *n.* stupefaction; **stan ogłupienia** stupor.

ogłuszać *ipf.* **1.** (= *uniemożliwiać słyszenie*) deafen. **2.** (= *pozbawiać przytomności*) stun, knock out.

ogłuszający *a.* (*hałas, muzyka, salwa*) deafening, earsplitting.

ogłuszyć *pf. zob.* **ogłuszać**.

ogniący się *a.* (*rana, skaleczenie*) inflamed.

ognicha *f. bot.* charlock, wild mustard (*Sinapis arvensis*).

ognik *mi Gen.* -a 1. (= *płomień*) flame; **błędny ognik** will-o'-the-wisp. 2. (= *odblask*) sparkle, glow; **ogniki w oczach** sparkle in the eyes.

ogniomistrz *mp Gen.pl.* -ów sergeant of artillery.

ognioodporność *f.* fire-resistance.

ognioodporny *a.* fireproof, fire-resistant.

ognioszczelność *f.* fire-tightness.

ognioszczelny *a.* fire tight, flame-proof; (*o drzwiach, pokrywie, śluzie, przegrodzie*) flameproof, FLP.

ogniotrwałość *f.* refractoriness.

ogniotrwały *a.* (*o ceramice, naczyniu, kasie*) fireproof, fire-resistant; *tech.* refractory; **materiał ogniotrwały** refractory.

ogniowy *a.* 1. (*o paleniu się*) fire, fiery, igneous; (*o blasku*) fiery. 2. (*o straży, bezpieczeństwie*) fire. 3. *wojsk.* (*o ostrzale, gnieździe*) fire; **zapora ogniowa** fire curtain; **próba ogniowa** crucible, trial by fire; **oficer ogniowy** GPO, Gun Position Officer; **chrzest ogniowy** ordeal, acid test; (*stanowisko*) gun site.

ognisko *n.* 1. (*ogień*) fire; (*duże pod gołym niebem*) bonfire; **ognisko domowe** *poet.* hearth and home, home; **ognisko kowalskie** *techn.* smith's hearth, (smithy) forge. 2. (*impreza*) campfire; **ognisko sygnalizacyjne** *l.* **obrzędowe** **rozpalić ognisko** make *l.* light a fire. 3. (= *centrum*) center, seat; (*muzyczne, artystyczne, plastyczne*) group, circle. 4. *fot.* focus. 5. *pat.* focus, focal spot; **ognisko gruźlicze** tuberculous focus; **ognisko zapalne** inflammatory focus; **ognisko zakażenia** *l.* **infekcyjne** focus of infection; **ropne** purulent focus, suppurative focus. 6. **ognisko zapalne** *polit.* trouble spot; **ognisko niepokoju** hot spot; **ognisko trzęsienia ziemi** earthquake focus, seismic focus.

ogniskowa *f. Gen.* -ej *fot.* focal length, focal distance; *opt.* focal distance; **stała ogniskowa** fixed focus.

ogniskować *ipf.* (= *skupiać*) concentrate, focus. ~ **się** *ipf.* (= *skupiać się*) concentrate, be focused, be concentrated.

ogniskowy *a. fot., pat.* focal.

ognistoczerwony *a.* (*o ustach, róży*) flaming red, scarlet.

ognistość *f.* (*o barwie*) fieriness; (*o spojrzeniu*) passionateness, intensity.

ognistowłosy *a.* ginger-haired.

ognisty *a.* 1. (= *rozżarzony*) fiery, flaming, blazing; (*o błyskawicy, łunie, lawie*) fiery, burning; **woda ognista** *żart.* firewater. 2. (*o kolorze*) flaming red, scarlet; (*o włosach*) flaming red, ginger; (*o maku, róży*) carmine, claret. 3. (= *z temperamentem*) passionate, intense, hot-tempered; (*o kochanku*) passionate, ardent; (*o ogierze*) wild, impetuous; (*o tańcu*) fervent, passionate; (*o spojrzeniu*) passionate, eager.

ogniście *adv.* (*o kolorze*) 1. fiery; (*lśnić*) flamingly, blazingly. 2. (*o temperamencie*) ardently, passionately; (*kochać*) passionately, ardently; (*grać, tańczyć*) passionately.

ogniwo *n.* 1. (*łańcucha*) link. 2. (*organizacji społecznej, politycznej*) cell. 3. (*bateria*) battery, cell; **ogniwo słoneczne** solar battery *l.* cell; **ogniwo łączące** nexus, sequential link; **brakujące ogniwo** *biol.* missing link; **stanowić ogniwo pośrednie** mediate, moderate (*pomiędzy czymś a czymś* between sth and sth).

ogolić *pf.* -ol *l.* -ól shave, give sb a shave. ~ **się** *pf.* shave, have a shave.

ogolony *a.* -eni shaved; (*o twarzy, nodze*) shaved, shaven; **starannie ogolony** cleanshaven; **nieogolony** unshaven, unshaved.

ogołacać *ipf. zob.* **ogałacać**.

ogołocić *pf. zob.* **ogałacać**.

ogon *mi Gen.* -a 1. (*u zwierząt*) tail; (*w języku fachowym*) cauda; (*lisi*) brush; (*zająca*) bun; **odwracać kota ogonem** *pot.* (= *przeinaczać swoje słowa*) shift one's ground; (= *przeinaczać czyjeś słowa*) distort the facts; **przyczepić się jak rzep do psiego ogona** stick *l.* cling to sb like a leech, cling to sb like a barnacle; **koński ogon** (*fryzura*) ponytail; **jaskółczy ogon** *bud.* dovetail; **chwytać dwie sroki za ogon** have *l.* keep several *l.* many irons in the fire. 2. (= *tył czegoś*) tail; (*samolotu*) tail; (*fraka*) trail; (*sukienki*) train, trail; **bez ogona** tailless; **zostawać w ogonie** lag behind. 3. *teatr* (= *epizodyczna rola*) bit part; **grać ogony** play bit parts.

ogonek *mi* -nk- *Gen.* -a 1. (= *mały ogon*) tail; **mysi ogonek** (*fryzura*) pigtail, queue; **każda sroczka swój ogonek chwali** everybody blows his own horn. 2. (*liścia*) *bot.* peduncle, petiole, footstalk; (*owocu, kwiatu*) stem; (*kwiatu, grzyba, liścia*) stalk; (= *szypułka*) hull; **bez ogonka** (*o owocu, kwiecie*) stemmed. 3. (*u dołu liter ą, ę*) hook. 4. *pot.* (= *kolejka*) line; *Br.* queue.

ogoniasty *a.* taillike, tailed; (*o płazach, małpach*) caudate; (*o komecie*) tailed.

ogonice *pl. Gen.* -c *bot.* appendicularians (*Appendicularia*).

ogonowy *a.* caudal, tail; (*o płetwie*) tail fin; **kość ogonowa** (*anat.*) tailbone, coccyx; **zupa ogonowa** *kulin.* oxtail soup.

ogończe *pl. Gen.* -y *icht.* marbled stingray (*Dasyatis chrysonota marmorata*).

ogorzałka *f. Gen.pl.* -ek *orn.* scaup *l.* scaup duck (*Aythya marila*).

ogorzały *a.* weather-beaten, sunburnt.

ogorzeć *pf.* get tanned.

ogólniak *mi Gen.* -a *pot.* high, hi; (*prywatny*) prep; *Br.* comprehensive school.

ogólnie *adv.* 1. (= *powszechnie*) generally, universally, widely. 2. (= *nie wdając się w szczegóły*) generally, in general, by and large; **ogólnie mówiąc** broadly *l.* generally speaking; **ogólnie biorąc** on the whole, altogether, all in all; **ogólnie przyjęty** widely-accepted.

ogólnik *mi Gen.* -a generality, truism; (*o frazesie*) cliché; **mówić ogólnikami** talk in abstractions, generalize; **zbyć kogoś ogólnikami** put sb off with sweeping statements, cut sb short, stall sb off.

ogólnikowo *adv.* (*np. omawiać coś*) broadly, in

broad *l.* general terms; (*wypowiadać się*) vaguely.

ogólnikowość *f.* generality, general character; (*rozważań, odpowiedzi*) vagueness.

ogólnikowy *a.* general, broad, circumlocutory; (*o stwierdzeniu, odpowiedzi, wypowiedzi*) vague; (*o ocenie*) sweeping.

ogólnodostępny *a.* open-access, public access; **ogólnodostępne środki komunikacji** public transport.

ogólnojęzykoznawczy *a.* linguistic, (of) general linguistics; (*o studium, badaniach, rozważaniach*) linguistic.

ogólnokrajowy *a.* countrywide, nationwide; (*o zjeździe, porozumieniu, akcji*) nationwide, countrywide; (*o zasięgu ogólnokrajowym*) national.

ogólnokształcący *a.* general education; **liceum ogólnokształcące** high school; *Br.* grammar school.

ogólnoludzki *a.* (*o problemie, katastrofie, potrzebach*) universal.

ogólnonarodowy *a.* national, nationwide; (*o akcji, zrywie*) nationwide; (*o dobrach kultury*) national.

ogólnopaństwowy *a.* national, nationwide, state; (*o planie, problemach*) state, nationwide.

ogólnopolski *a.* all-Polish; (*o zjeździe, konferencji, konkursie, festiwalu*) all-Polish, Polish; **język ogólnopolski** general Polish.

ogólność *f.* generality, general character; **w ogólności** broadly *l.* generally speaking.

ogólnoświatowy *a.* worldwide, global, universal; (*o kryzysie, problemie*) global; (*o kongresie*) worldwide; **nadawać ogólnoświatowy zasięg** globalize.

ogólny *a.* **1.** (= *powszechny*) general, universal, usual; (*o dobrach*) common; (*o użytku*) general. **2.** (= *nieszczegółowy*) general; (*o wykształceniu, wnioskach, osłabieniu, przemęczeniu*) general; (*o pojęciu*) general, broad; (*o widoku*) general, sweeping; (*o wrażeniu*) overall, general; **lekarz ogólny** general practitioner, GP; **szpital ogólny** general hospital; **ogólny dostęp** open access, public access; **wiedza ogólna** general knowledge; **tendencja ogólna** prevailing trend, prevalent trend; **ogólny zarys** general outline; **nazwa ogólna** *log.* general term; **pojęcie ogólne** umbrella term; **zasada ogólna** general rule *l.* principle; **Zgromadzenie Ogólne** *parl.* General Assembly. **3.** (= *końcowy, łączny*) total, global; (*o kosztach budowy, liczbie mieszkańców*) total; **ogólna suma** *mat.* sum total.

ogół *mi* **1.** (= *całość*) totality, generality; (*o normach, zjawiskach*) total, sum. **2.** (*społeczeństwo*) the general public; **ogół ludności** people at large, the community; **leżeć w interesie ogółu** be in the general interest; **dobro ogółu** the common good; **na ogół** on the whole, in general; **w ogóle** (= *w sumie*) in sum, in total; **co to w ogóle znaczy?** what's that supposed to mean?; **w ogóle** (= *wcale*) (not) at all, whatsoever; **nie mam w ogóle żadnych planów** I have no plans at all *l.* whatsoever; **w ogóle nie mam o tym pojęcia!** I don't know anything about it at all!

ogółem *adv.* all in all, altogether, on the whole; **ogółem jesteś mi winien pięć dolarów** altogether you owe me five dollars.

ogórecznik *mi Gen.* -a *bot.* **ogórecznik lekarski** borage (*Borago officinalis*).

ogórek *mi* -rk- *Gen.* -a **1.** (*roślina*) cucumber (*Cucumis sativus*). **2.** (*owoc*) cucumber; (*kiszony*) dill pickle; (*konserwowy*) pickle.

ogórkowy *a.* cucumber; **zupa ogórkowa** *kulin.* cucumber soup; **sezon ogórkowy** *przen.* silly season, dog days.

ograbiać *ipf.*, **ograbić** *pf.* **1.** (*kraść*) rob (*kogoś z czegoś* sb of sth); (= *splądrować*) loot; (*miejsce, krajobraz*) despoil. **2.** (*grabiami*) rake up.

ograć *pf. zob.* **ogrywać**.

ogradzać *ipf.* **1.** (*działkę, pastwisko*) enclose; (*płotem*) fence in; (*murem*) wall in; (*żywopłotem*) hedge; (*sztachetami*) rail in. **2.** (= *być ogrodzeniem*) surround, enclose.

ograniczać *ipf.* **1.** (= *ujmować w granice, zakreślać granice*) delimit, border; (*swobodę, zakres*) restrict, confine. **2.** (= *uszczuplać, redukować*) limit, reduce; (*o piciu, paleniu, wydatkach*) cut down (*coś* on sth) reduce; (*o wydatkach, inflacji*) reduce, keep a tight rein (*coś* on sth); **ograniczać do minimum** keep *l.* reduce sth to the minimum, cut sth to the bone. **3.** (= *być granicą czegoś*) restrict, border. **~ się** *ipf.* **1.** (*zakres działań, możliwości*) confine oneself (*do czegoś* to sth); restrict oneself (*do czegoś* to sth). **2.** (= *poprzestać na czymś*) content oneself (*do czegoś* with sth). **3.** (*o czyichś obowiązkach*) confine, be confined (*do czegoś* to sth). **4.** (*oszczędzać*) economize, cut down on spending; **kończą nam się pieniądze; musimy się ograniczać** we're running out of money; we have to economize *l.* cut down on spending.

ograniczenie *n.* **1.** (= *limit*) limitation, restriction; **ograniczenie prędkości** speed limit; **ograniczenie swobód obywatelskich** limitation on civil liberties; **korzystać z czegoś bez ograniczeń** make free use of sth; **nakładać ograniczenia na coś** impose *l.* place restrictions *l.* constraints *l.* limits on sth; **ograniczenie czasowe** time limit; **bez ograniczeń** without restraint *l.* limits, freely. **2.** (= *tępota*) dullness, narrow-mindedness; **ograniczenie umysłowe** *pat.* mental retardedness, mental deficiency. **3.** *jęz.* constraint.

ograniczoność *f.* **1.** (= *niedobór*) scantiness, paucity; (*rezerw, funduszy, zasobów*) shortage, scarcity. **2.** (= *tępota*) narrow-mindedness.

ograniczony *a.* -eni **1.** (= *niewielki, niewystarczający*) limited, restricted; **ograniczony miejscowo** *med.* local; **ograniczona odpowiedzialność** limited liability. **2.** (= *o wąskich horyzontach myślowych*) narrow-minded; (*o poglądach, horyzontach*) narrow.

ograniczyć *pf. zob.* **ograniczać**. **~ się** *pf. zob.* **ograniczać się**.

ograny *a.* **1.** (*o instrumencie*) worn out; (*o utworze muzycznym*) played-out. **2.** *pot.* (= *nieoryginalny*) hackneyed, run-of-the-mill; (*o dowcipie*) corny.

ogrodnictwo *n.* **1.** (*gałąź gospodarki*) horticulture. **2.** (*uprawa*) gardening.

ogrodniczka *f. Gen.pl.* **-ek** *zob.* **ogrodnik**.

ogrodniczki *pl. Gen.* **-ów** dungarees.

ogrodniczy *a.* horticultural, gardening; (*o sklepie, narzędziach*) garden, gardening; (*o szkole*) gardening; **centrum ogrodnicze** garden center.

ogrodnik *mp* gardener, horticulturist.

ogrodowy *a.* (*o róży, altanie, ławce, sztuce, malinie*) garden; **meble ogrodowe** garden furniture; **krasnal ogrodowy** garden gnome.

ogrodzenie *n.* enclosure, fence; (*murowane*) wall; (*ze sztachet*) railing; (*z drutu kolczastego*) barbed wired fence; (*pod napięciem*) electrified fence.

ogrodzeniowy *a.* (*o siatce, słupku, kracie*) fence; **materiał ogrodzeniowy** fencing.

ogrodzić *pf.* **-odź** *l.* **-ódź** *zob.* **ogradzać**.

ogrom *mi* (*rozmiar*) enormity, vastness; (*miasta, budowli*) hugeness, enormity; (= *wielka ilość*) multitude; (*problemów, pracy*) bulk, load; (*klęsk, nieszczęść*) enormity, vastness.

ogromnie *adv.* enormously, tremendously, immensely.

ogromnieć *ipf. lit.* assume enormous proportions.

ogromny *a.* **1.** (= *wielki*) (*o domu, majątku, długu, drzewie*) huge, enormous; (*o jeziorze, wiedzy, liczbach*) huge, vast. **2.** (= *silny, intensywny*) (*o bólu, radości*) intense, extreme; (*o smutku*) deep, extreme; (*o powodzeniu, sukcesie, trudnościach*) huge, great; **to ma ogromne znaczenie** it's of (the) utmost importance; **ogromna ilość czegoś** large *l.* huge amount of sth.

ogród *mi* **-o-** garden; (*na tyłach domu*) backyard; *Br.* back garden; **ogród miejski** town garden; **ogród warzywny** vegetable *l.* kitchen garden; **ogród botaniczny** botanic gardens, botanical garden; **ogród zoologiczny** zoological garden; **ogród skalny** rock garden, rockery; **rajski ogród** *Bibl.* the Garden of Eden; **uprawiać ogród** garden.

ogródek *mi* **-dk-** *Gen.* **-a 1.** (= *mały ogród*) garden, garden plot; (*działkowy*) allotment; (*jordanowski*) (children's) playground; **wrzucić kamyk do czyjegoś ogródka** have a broad hint *l.* dig at sb. **2.** (*latem przed restauracją, kawiarnią*) open-air café; **ogródek piwny** beer garden.

ogródek, bez *adv.* bluntly, explicitly; **mówić bez ogródek** speak straight from the shoulder, speak bluntly *l.* outright.

ogrywać *ipf.* **-am -asz 1.** (= *wygrać pieniądze od kogoś*) win money from sb. **2.** *sport* (= *pokonać*) beat. **3.** (= *zbanalizować*) hackney.

ogryzać *ipf. zob.* **obgryzać**.

ogryzek *mi* **-zk-** *Gen.* **-a 1.** (*jabłka*) core. **2.** *przen.* (*ołówka*) stub.

ogryźć *pf.* **-zę -ziesz -zł -źli** *zob.* **obgryzać**.

ograć *pf.* **-eję -ejesz** *zob.* **ogrzewać**. ~ **się** *pf. zob.* **ogrzewać się**.

ogrzewacz *mi Gen.* **-a** *techn.* heater.

ogrzewać *ipf.* heat, warm (up). ~ **się** *ipf.* **1.** (= zacząć czuć ciepło) warm oneself. **2.** (= *stawać się ciepłym*) heat up, get warm.

ogrzewanie *n.* heating; **centralne ogrzewanie** central heating; **ogrzewanie podłogowe** floor *l.* underfloor heating.

ogrzewczy *a.* (*o urządzeniu, sezonie*) heating.

ogrzewnictwo *n.* heating technology.

ogumienie *n.* tires; *Br.* tyres.

ohajtnąć się *pf.*, **ohajtać się** *ipf.* **-ij** *pot.* (= *ożenić się*) get hitched, tie the knot.

ohar *ma orn.* common shelduck (*Tadorna tadorna*).

oheblować *pf.* plane.

oho *int.* **1.** (*wyraża podziw, zdziwienie*) oho!, well, well!; **pogoda, że oho!** ahh, what beautiful weather!, ahh, the weather is nice! **2.** (*podkreśla dezaprobatę*) uh-oh; **oho, będzie padać** uh-oh it's going to rain.

ohyda *f.* **1.** (*obrzydliwość*) monstrosity, atrocity; (*o widoku*) eyesore; **ale ohyda, aż zbiera mi się na wymioty** ugghh, how disgusting. **2.** (*zbrodni, czynu, postępowania*) atrocity, baseness.

ohydnie *adv.* atrociously, hideously, disgustingly; (*kląć*) badly, terribly; **wyglądać ohydnie** look hideous, look atrocious.

ohydny *a.* hideous, atrocious; (*o postaci*) horrid, loathsome, hideous; (*o postępowaniu, zachowaniu się*) vile, atrocious; (*o pogodzie*) wretched, filthy; (*o kolorze, zapachu*) horrible, abominable, offensive.

oj *int.* **1.** (*wyraża emocjonalne zaangażowanie*) oops!, oh!; **oj, ale wstrętne** ugh, how disgusting!; **oj, jaki długi** wow, how long!; **oj, ale pachnie** ah, how nice it smells; **oj tak, zgadzam się z tobą** oh yes *l.* yeah, I agree. **2.** (*wyraża pogróżkę, dezaprobatę, naganę*) oh; **oj, bo będziesz żałował!** oh, you'll regret it!; **oj, nieładnie!** oh, that's not very nice!; **oj, wy lenie!** oh, you lazy people! **3.** (*w piosenkach ludowych*) blah-de-blah; **oj dana, dana** blah-de-blah.

ojciec *mp* ojc- *Dat.* **-u** *Voc.* **ojcze** *pl.* **-owie 1.** (*wobec swoich dzieci*) father; (*przodek*) ancestor, forefather; **ojciec chrzestny** godfather; **przybrany ojciec** foster father, nursing father; **ojcowie miasta** city fathers; **Bóg Ojciec** *rel.* God the Father; **Ojciec Święty** Holy Father; **ojciec kościoła** Church Father; **Ojcze Nasz** Our Father, paternoster; **wykapany ojciec** he's the spitting image of his father; **tradycje ojców** ancestral traditions. **2.** (*samiec zwierząt*) sire. **3.** (= *inicjator, założyciel*) founding father, originator; (*teatru, literatury, dramatu*) father; **jaki ojciec, taki syn** like father, like son. **4.** *pot.* (= *mąż*) hubby, my man, mister. **5.** *pot.* (= *mężczyzna, zwłaszcza starszy*) old man. **6.** *rel.* (*zakonnik, duchowny*) father.

ojcobójca *mp* patricide.

ojcobójstwo *n.* patricide.

ojcostwo *n.* paternity, fatherhood; **ustalić ojcostwo** *prawn.* establish fatherhood.

ojcować *ipf.* father.

ojcowizna *f.* patrimony.

ojcowski *a.* fatherly, paternal; (*o uczuciach*) fatherly; (*o domu, majątku*) father's.

ojczulek *mp* -lk- *pl.* -owie *emf.* daddy; (*o zakon-niku*) dear Father, soul saver, sin-hound.

ojczym *mp pl.* -owie stepfather.

ojczysty *a.* native, mother; (*o dziejach, kultu-rze*) native; **język ojczysty** native language, mother tongue; **kraj ojczysty** homeland, father-land, motherland; **ziemia ojczysta** native soil, homeland.

ojczyzna *f.* 1. (= *kraj rodzinny*) homeland, fa-therland, motherland. 2. *przen.* (= *miejsce po-chodzenia*) home; **ojczyzną impresjonizmu jest Francja** France is the cradle of impressionism. 3. *zool., bot.* (*siedlisko*) habitat.

ojej *int.* (oh) dear!, gosh!, oops!; **ojej, to boli** ouch, it hurts!; **ojej, ale piękne** oh *l.* ah, how beautiful!; **ojej, boję się!** eek, I'm scared!; **ojej, co ci się stało?** oh dear, what happened to you?

ojoj *int.* oh; **ojoj, ale tu duszno** oh, how stuffy.

okablować *pf.*, **okablowywać** *ipf. techn.* wire.

okadzać *ipf.*, **okadzić** *pf.* 1. (*wonnościami*) in-cense, cense. 2. *ogr.* fumigate. 3. *przen.* (= *schlebiać*) flatter, butter up.

okalać *ipf.* 1. (= *okrążać*) surround, encircle. 2. (= *oblamować*) edge, hem. 3. (= *obramować*) border.

okaleczać *ipf. zob.* **okaleczyć**.

okaleczenie *n.* 1. (*kalectwo*) lameness, crip-pledom. 2. (*zranienie*) injury, wound, mutila-tion. 3. *prawn.* mayhem.

okaleczyć *pf.* 1. (= *uczynić kaleką*) cripple, lame; (= *pozbawić kończyny lub kończyn*) muti-late, maim; (*zranić*) injure. 2. *przen.* (= *uszko-dzić*) damage. ~ **się** *pf.* injure oneself.

okamgnienie *n.* twinkling (of an eye), twink, split second; **w okamgnieniu** in a flash, in the twinkling of an eye.

okantować *pf.* 1. *pot.* (= *oszukać*) con, chisel, bunco. 2. *sport* (*narty*) edge.

okap *mi* 1. (*na zewnątrz budynku*) eaves. 2. (*w kuchni*) ventilation hood. 3. *górn.* overhang. 4. *leśn.* canopy.

okapi *f. l. ma indecl. zool.* okapi (*Okapia john-stoni*).

okapnik *mi Gen.* -a *bud.* drip; (*murowany*) wa-ter table; (*pod drzwiami*) weatherboard.

okaryna *f.* ocarina.

okaz *mi* 1. (= *egzemplarz*) specimen, piece; (= *wzór*) exemplar, paragon; (*na wystawie*) exhibit, showpiece; **piękny okaz** showpiece; **rzadki okaz** collector's item. 2. (= *ideał*) picture; **okaz zdro-wia** a picture of health; **autentyczny okaz** the genuine article; **okaz głupoty** a perfect fool.

okazać *pf.* -żę -żesz *zob.* **okazywać**. ~ **się** *pf. zob.* **okazywać się**.

okazale *adv.* (= *wspaniale*) imposingly, mag-nificently, splendidly; (= *wystawnie, bogato*) sumptuously, grandly; **wyglądać okazale** look splendid, look magnificent.

okazałość *f.* glory, grandiosity, splendor; (*wy-stawność*) sumptuousness, grandeur; **w całej okazałości** in all its glory.

okazały *a.* (*o domu, ogrodzie*) grand, magnifi-cent, imposing; (*o wzroście*) grand, portly; (*o przyjęciu*) grand, splendid; (*o człowieku*) big, portly.

okaziciel *mp* holder, bearer; **czek na okaziciela** check to the bearer; *Br.* cheque to the bearer, bearer check; **bilet okresowy na okaziciela** (hold-er) season ticket.

okazja *f.* 1. (= *sposobność*) opportunity, chance; **znakomita okazja** golden opportunity; **dobra okazja** bargain, plum; **zmarnowana okazja** missed *l.* lost opportunity, fumble; **korzystać z okazji** take an opportunity *l.* the chance; **skwa-pliwie korzystać z okazji** grab a chance, seize an opportunity, leap at the chance *l.* opportunity; **przegapić okazję** miss one's *l.* a chance, miss the boat *l.* bus; **zaprzepaścić okazję** let sth *l.* it slip through one's fingers; **a przy okazji...** and by the way,...; **odwiedzę go przy okazji** (*po drodze*) I'll go to see him on my way; **okazja czyni złodzieja** opportunity makes a thief. 2. (= *uroczystość, sy-tuacja niezwyczajna*) occasion; **nie byle jaka oka-zja** quite an occasion; **sukienka na specjalną oka-zję** dress for a special occasion; **serdeczne życze-nia z okazji urodzin** many happy returns of the day. 3. (= *przypadkowy środek lokomocji*) *pot.* free ride; **łapać okazję** hitch *l.* thumb a lift *l.* ride; **przyjechałem tu okazją** I hitched a ride *l.* lift here.

okazjonalizm *mi fil.* occasionalism.

okazjonalnie *adv. lit.* occasionally.

okazjonalny *a.* 1. (= *okolicznościowy*) on occa-sion; (*o koncercie, wierszu*) occasional, on occa-sion. 2. (= *przypadkowy*) accidental, casual.

okazowy *a.* typical, classic; **okazowy przykład bezmyślności** classic example of thoughtless-ness; **egzemplarz okazowy** (*podpisany przez au-tora*) presentation copy; (*do recenzji*) review copy.

okazyjnie *adv.* **kupić/sprzedać coś okazyjnie** buy/sell at a good *l.* bargain price, make a good bargain *l.* deal on sth.

okazyjny *a.* (*o ocenach, kupnie, sprzedaży*) bargain.

okazywać *ipf.* 1. (= *pokazywać*) (*bilet, legity-mację*) show, produce, present. 2. (= *uzewnętrz-niać*) (*zdumienie, zdenerwowanie, szacunek, ra-dość, gniew*) show, demonstrate, evince; **okazać komuś współczucie** have *l.* take pity on sb; **oka-zać komuś czułość** show sb one's affection; **oka-zywać szacunek** pay respect; **okazywać pomoc** provide help *l.* assistance, lend *l.* give a (help-ing) hand. ~ **się** *ipf.* turn out, prove; **powieść okazała się arcydziełem** the novel turned out to be a masterpiece; **okazało się, że można na nim polegać** he proved to be reliable; **okazało się, że świeci słońce** it turned out that the sun was shining; **jak się okazało** as it turned out; **jak się okazuje** apparently; **to się jeszcze okaże** it re-mains to be seen, that is yet to be seen; **okazuje się że...** it appears that...

okcydentalista *mp* occidentalist.

Okeanos *mp mit.* Okeanos.

okej *particle. pot.* OK, okay.

okiełznać *pf.* **1.** (*konia*) break in, tame. **2.** *przen.* (= *powściągnąć*) curb, bridle, restrain.

okienko *n. Gen.pl.* **-ek 1.** (= *małe okno*) window. **2.** (*na poczcie, w banku*) counter; **przy okienku** (*np. płacić*) at the counter. **3.** (*otwór*) window; (*w dachu*) skylight; (*nad drzwiami*) transom; *Br.* fanlight; **koperta z okienkiem** window envelope; **okienko formularza** blank. **4.** *szkoln.* gap. **5.** *druk.* inset. **6.** *komp.* window.

okiennica *f.* shutter; **otworzyć okiennicę** unshutter the window.

okienny *a.* window; **parapet okienny** windowsill; **rama okienna** window frame; **szyba okienna** window pane.

okiść *f. pl.* **-e** *l.* **-i** *lit.* snow formations, tuft of snow.

oklapnąć *pf.* **-ij, -nął** *l.* **-ł -nęła** *l.* **-ła -nęli** *l.* **-li 1.** *pot.* (= *zwiesić się, zwisnąć*) droop, hang down; (*o kwiatach*) wilt. **2.** *pot.* (= *stracić energię*) wilt, sink.

oklaski *pl. Gen.* **-ów** applause, clapping; **burza oklasków** burst *l.* round of applause; **wywołać burzę oklasków** *teatr* bring the house down; **zbierać oklaski** meet with applause; **nagrodzić kogoś/coś oklaskami** give sb/sth an ovation *l.* a hand.

oklaskiwać *ipf.* applaud (*kogoś / coś* sb/sth); **oklaskiwać kogoś/coś** give sb/sth a hand.

okleić *pf. zob.* **oklejać**.

okleina *f. stol.* veneer.

okleinowy *a.* veneer.

oklejać *ipf.* stick, paste; *stol.* veneer; **okleić pokój plakatami** paste posters onto the wall.

oklep *mi indecl.* bareback; **jechać na oklep** ride bareback.

oklepany *a. pot.* commonplace, well-worn; (*o kawale*) twice-told, corny; (*o melodii, temacie*) well-worn, worn out; (= *banalny*) trite; **oklepany frazes** cliché, bromide.

okludować *ipf. chem., meteor.* occlude.

okluzja *f. chem., meteor.* occlusion.

okład *mi med.* compress, pack; **gorący okład** stupe; **zimny okład** cold pack; **okład z lodu** ice pack; **z okładem** over, or more, odd; **tysiąc z okładem** a good thousand, over a thousand, a thousand or more.

okładać *ipf.* **1.** (= *przykrywać*) cover (up), wrap; **okładać chleb serem** make a cheese sandwich. **2.** *pot.* (= *bić*) batter, belabor, thrash; (*pałką*) club, truncheon; **okładać kogoś pięściami** rain *l.* deliver blows on sb, pummel sb. **~ się** *ipf.* **1.** (= *przykrywać się*) surround o.s.; **okładać się książkami/notatkami** bury oneself in one's books/notes (*in order to study*). **2.** (= *bić się nawzajem*) rain blows on each other, pummel one another.

okładka *f. Gen.pl.* **-ek** cover; (*płyty gramofonowej*) jacket; **książka w papierowej** *l.* **miękkiej okładce** paperback; **książka w twardej okładce** hardback.

okładkowy *a.* cover.

okładzina *f.* **1.** (*materiał*) facing, lining; **okładzina dębowa/kamienna/marmurowa** oak/stone/ marble lining; **okładzina cierna** *techn.* friction lining. **2.** *górn.* shaft lining.

okładzinowy *a.* facing, lining; **kamień okładzinowy** facing stone.

okłamać *pf.* **-ę -esz, okłamywać** *ipf.* lie, tell a lie (*kogoś* to sb); deceive (*kogoś* sb); **okłamywać siebie samego** deceive o.s., delude o.s. **~ się** *pf.*, **okłamywać się** *ipf.* **1.** (*siebie wzajemnie*) tell lies to each other, lie to each other, deceive each other. **2.** (*samego siebie*) deceive o.s., delude o.s.

okno *n. Gen.pl.* **okien 1.** (*w ścianie*) window; **okno wystawowe** shop window, display window; **okno weneckie** Venetian window; **ślepe okno** blind window; **okno opuszczane** drop window; **okno rozetowe** rose window; **okno tektoniczne** *geol.* tectonic window; **okno widokowe** picture window; **okno witrażowe** leaded window; **okno na świat** window on the world; **włazić drzwiami i oknami** *pot.* come in streams, pour in. **2.** (*inspektu*) cold frame, garden frame. **3.** *górn.* (*regulacyjne*) regulator. **4.** *komp.* window.

oknówka *f. Gen.pl.* **-ek** *orn.* jaskółka oknówka house martin (*Delichon urbica*).

oko *n. pl.* **ocz-** *Nom.* **-y** *Gen.* **-u** *Ins.* **-ami** *l.* **-yma 1.** (*narząd wzroku*) eye, optic (*arch.*); **piwne/brązowe/niebieskie oczy** hazel/brown/blue eyes; **podbite oko** black eye, shiner, mouse; **bystre oko** sharp *l.* keen eye; **mieć bystre oko** be sharp *l.* keen eyed *l.* eyesighted; **zaczerwienione oko** reddish eye; **kocie oczy** (*na drodze*) cat's eyes; **kocie oko** *min.* cat's eye; **tygrysie oko** *min.* tiger's eye; **dno oka** *anat.* eyegrounds, fundus of the eye; **oko cyklonu** *meteor.* bull's eye, the eye of the storm; **sokole oko** eagle eye; **maślane oczy** filmy eyes; **wprawne oko** practiced eye; **w mgnieniu oka** in a blink of an eye, in a twinkling, in a flash *l.* crack; **na pierwszy rzut oka** at first glance; **coś widać na pierwszy rzut oka** sth can be seen at first glance; **bez zmrużenia oka** without batting an eye; **na moich oczach** before *l.* under my eyes, in front of my very eyes; **słabnąć** *l.* **niknąć w oczach** (*o człowieku*) be fading away, be wasting away; **ale masz oko!** good eye!; **cieszący oko** easy on the eye; **cieszyć oko** please the eye; **klapki na oczach** blinders, tunnel vision; **klapki na oczy** (*konia*) blinders; *Br.* blinkers; **w moich oczach to jest nic niewarte** it's not worth a penny in my eyes *l.* to my mind; **z zamkniętymi oczami** with one's eyes closed; **pożerać kogoś oczami** devour sb with one's eyes; **patrzeć na coś krzywym okiem** frown upon sth, look askance at sth; **być komuś solą w oku** be a thorn in sb's side *l.* flesh, be the stone in sb's shoe; (**szkolić się**) **pod okiem instruktora** (train) under the supervision of the instructor; **ciemno, choć oko wykol** the night is inky black; **rzucać się w oczy** stick out a mile, stick out like a sore thumb; **spędza mi to sen z oczu** I can't get it out of my mind; **czytam w twoich oczach, że...** I can see *l.* read it in your eyes that...; **dobrze ci z oczu patrzy** you have a kind look in your eyes; **iść, gdzie oczy poniosą** go and never look back, walk and don't look back; **jak okiem sięgnąć** as far as the eye can see; **mieć oczy wokół głowy** have eyes at the back of one's head; **zrobiło mi się ciemno przed oczami** I was seeing spots before my eyes; **mam to na oku** I'm keeping a (sharp) eye on it; **mieć coś na oku** (*np. o pracy*) set sights on sth; **mam babcię ciągle przed oczyma** I can still see grandma before my eyes; **miej oczy i uszy otwarte!** keep your eyes and ears open!; **powiedzieć** *l.* **wygarnąć komuś prawdę w oczy** tell sb the truth to his/her face, speak the truth to sb's face; **wspominać kogoś/coś z łezką w oku** think softly *l.* affectionately *l.* nostalgically about sb/sth, think about sb/sth with affection; **mydlić komuś oczy** pull the wool over sb's eyes, throw dust in sb's eyes; **nawet nie mrugnął okiem** he didn't flicker an eyelid; **nie mogłem od niej oderwać oczu** I couldn't take my eyes off her; **nie mogę spojrzeć jej w oczy** I can't look her in the eye/face; **mieć oko na coś** keep one's eyes open *l.* peeled *l.* skinned for sth; **nie spuszczaj z oka dzieci** keep your eye on the children, keep a close eye *l.* watch on the children; **podbić komuś oko** give sb a black eye *l.* a shiner; **własnym oczom nie wierzę!** I can't believe my eyes!; **nie zmrużyłem oka** I didn't sleep a wink; **otworzył szeroko oczy** open one's eyes wide; **widzieć kątem oka** see sth out of the corner of one's eye; **strzec kogoś/czegoś jak oka w głowie** keep a close eye on sb/sth; **rzut oka na coś** glimpse at sth; **kiedy ty wreszcie przejrzysz na oczy?** when will you finally take the blinds off?; **przewracać oczami** turn up *l.* roll one's eyes; **robić do kogoś perskie oko** give sb the eye, give sb a glad eye, make eyes at sb; **kłamać w żywe oczy** lie through one's teeth, lie in one's throat; **na piękne oczy** on trust; **w cztery oczy** in private; **rozmawiać z kimś w cztery oczy** talk heart to heart to sb, talk eye to eye; **rzuć na to okiem** have *l.* take a look *l.* glance at it, cast an eye over it, please; **gołym okiem** with the naked eye; **stanąć z kimś oko w oko** stand face to face with sb, confront sb eyeball to eyeball; **stracić kogoś z oczu** lose sight of sb; **spuścić oczy** lower one's eyes, cast one's eyes down; **spojrzeć prawdzie w oczy** face the truth; wake up and smell the coffee; see things for what they really are; **świecić oczami za kogoś** blush for sb, take the rap; **widzieć coś gołym okiem** see sth with the naked eye; **widzieć coś na własne oczy** see sth with one's own eyes; **widzieć coś oczami duszy** see sth in one's mind's eyes; **wpaść komuś w oko** catch sb's fancy *l.* eye, take *l.* tickle *l.* catch sb's fancy; **zamknąć oczy** close one's eyes, breathe one's last; **przymykać na coś oczy** turn a blind eye to sth; **zejdź mi z oczu!** get out of my sight!; **oczy mi się kleją** I have heavy eyes *l.* eyelids; **pi razy oko** sth in the neighborhood of, more or less; **pasuje to jak pięść do oka** it's like a square peg in a round hole; **oczy wychodzą mu na wierzch** (*ze zdziwienia*) his eyes popped out; **oko ci zbieleje** it'll leave you open-mouthed; **kruk krukowi oka nie wykole** crows don't pick crows' eyes; dog does not eat dog; **oko za oko, ząb za ząb** an eye for an eye and a tooth for a tooth; **pańskie oko konia tuczy** the eye of the master does more work than both his hands; **prawda w oczy kole** the greater the truth, the greater the libel; **strach ma wielkie oczy** fear has big eyes; **czego oko nie widzi, tego sercu nie żal** what the eye doesn't see, the heart doesn't grieve over; what the eye sees not, the heart craves not. **2.** *pl.* **oka** *Gen.* **ok** (= *coś jak oko*) eye; (*w rosole*) keep your eyes; **pawie oko** peacock's eye, ocellus, eyespot. **3.** (*w sieci rybackiej*) mesh. **4.** *żegl.* (*wachta*) watch, lookout. **5.** *żegl.* (*pętla na linie*) eye-splice, loop.

okocić się *pf.* (*o kotce*) kitten, have kittens; (*o owcy*) lamb (down).

okolica *f.* **1.** (= *otoczenie*) surroundings, neighborhood, vicinity; **okolice Gdyni** the area around Gdynia. **2.** (= *obszar*) region, area; **lesista okolica** forest area; **górzysta okolica** mountainous *l.* hilly region; **ładne okolice** pleasant surroundings; **w okolicy czegoś** in the vicinity of sth, in the neighborhood of sth; **najbliższa okolica** immediate surroundings. **3.** (= *najbliżsi sąsiedzi*) neighborhood; **jutro będzie o tym mówić cała okolica** tomorrow the whole neighborhood will be talking about it. **4.** (= *miejsce w organizmie*) region, area; **w okolicy krzyża** in the lower back region.

okolicznik *mi Gen.* **-a** *gram.* adverbial.

okolicznikowy *a. gram.* adverbial; **zdanie okolicznikowe** adverbial clause.

okolicznościowy *a.* occasional, on occasion; (*o literaturze, poezji, utworze, przemówieniu*) occasional; **urlop okolicznościowy** (*w wypadku śmierci, choroby itp.*) compassionate leave.

okoliczność *f.* circumstance, occasion; **smutna/radosna okoliczność** sad/happy occasion; **okoliczności wypadku** the circumstances of the accident; **okoliczności wymagają natychmiastowego działania** the circumstances call for *l.* require immediate reaction *l.* attention; **okoliczności łagodzące** *prawn.* mitigating *l.* extenuating circumstances; **okoliczności obciążające** aggravating circumstances; **zbieg okoliczności** coincidence; **niesprzyjające okoliczności** adverse circumstances *l.* conditions; **w tych okolicznościach** under those circumstances; **z kim mam okoliczność?** *żart.* with whom do I have the pleasure?

okoliczny *a.* (= *otaczający*) surrounding; **okoliczne łąki** surrounding meadows; (= *przyległy*) neighboring; **okoliczne domy** neighboring houses; (= *miejscowy*) local; **okoliczna ludność** local people, locals.

okolić *pf. zob.* **okalać**.

okolnica *f. bot.* pericycle.

około *prep.* + *Gen.* about, around, roughly, approximately; **około dwóch godzin** about two hours; **około połowy maja** somewhere round mid-May; **około dwóch kilogramów** around *l.* about two kilos; **około dwóch mil** around *l.* about two miles, two miles or thereabout; **gdzieś około południa** somewhere around noon, noonish; **około dwustu ludzi** roughly two hundred people; **on ma około 45 lat** he's in his mid-forties.

okołobiegunowy *a.* circumpolar; (*o morzu, krajobrazie*) polar.

okołorównikowy a. circumequatorial, equatorial; (*o strefie, klimacie, pustyni*) equatorial.

okołosłoneczny a. circumsolar, heliocentric; (*o przestrzeni, ruchu*) circumsolar; **orbita okołosłoneczna** heliocentric orbit.

okołoziemski a. circumterrestrial; **orbita okołoziemska** circumterrestrial orbit.

okoniokształtne *pl. Gen.* **-ych** *icht.* perch-likes (*Perciformes*).

okoniowate *pl. Gen.* **-ych** *icht.* percids (*Percidae*).

okoń *ma icht.* perch (*Perca fluviatilis*); **stawać okoniem** *pot.* stand pat, stand one's ground.

okop *mi wojsk.* trench, entrenchment.

okopać *pf.* **-ę -esz** *zob.* **okopywać.** **~ się** *pf. zob.* **okopywać się.**

okopcić *pf.* blacken with smoke, smoke. **~ się** *pf.* get black with smoke.

okopcować *pf. ogr.* earth up.

okopowe *pl. Gen.* **-ych** *roln.* root crops.

okopowy a. root; **rośliny okopowe** root crops.

okopywać *ipf.* **1.** *wojsk.* entrench. **2.** *roln.* earth up. **~ się** *ipf. wojsk.* entrench o.s., dig in.

okostna *f. Gen.* **-ej** *anat.* periosteum; **zapalenie okostnej** *pat.* periostitis.

okowita *f. pot.* (= *wódka*) fire water.

okowy *pl. Gen.* **-ów** **1.** *lit.* (= *kajdany*) fetters, shackles. **2.** *przen.* fetters; **w okowach lodu** icebound.

okólnik *mi Gen.* **-a** **1.** (*pismo*) circular letter, circular; memo. **2.** (*ogrodzenie*) cattle-yard.

okólny a. (*o piśmie*) circular; **okólna droga** detour.

okpić *pf.* **-ij** befool, cozen. **~ się** *pf.* deceive o.s.

okradać *ipf.* rob (*kogoś z czegoś* sb of sth).

okrajać *pf.* **-ę -esz** *zob.* **okrawać.**

okrakiem *adv.* astraddle, astride; **siedzieć okrakiem na krześle** be sitting astride a chair.

okrasa *f. kulin.* (= *tłuszcz*) fat; (= *sos*) gravy.

okrasić *pf. zob.* **okraszać.**

okraszać *ipf. kulin.* (*tłuszczem*) add fat (*to a dish*); (*sosem*) add gravy (*to a dish*).

okraść *pf.* **-dnę -dniesz, -dnij, -dła** *zob.* **okradać.**

okratować *pf.* grate.

okratowanie *n.* grille *l.* grill, grillwork.

okrawać *ipf.* **1.** (*np. chleb ze skórki*) cut, edge. **2.** *przen.* (= *uszczuplić, zmniejszyć*) clip, pare; (*tekst*) abridge, expurgate.

okrawek *mi* **-wk-** *Gen.* **-a** cutting, clipping, trimming; **okrawek sera** cheeseparing.

okrąg *mi* **-ę-** **1.** *geom.* (= *koło*) circle; **okrąg opisany** circumcircle. **2.** (= *obwód*) circumference.

okrąglak *mi Gen.* **-a** **1.** (*pień*) log. **2.** (*budowla*) rotunda.

okrągło *adv.* roundly, spherically; **na okrągło** round the clock, twenty-four/seven, 24-7.

okrągłości *pl. Gen.* **-i** *pot.* rotundity, full shape.

okrągłość *f.* roundness, circularity.

okrągły a. **1.** (*w kształcie koła, kuli*) circular, ringed. **2.** (= *pulchny, gruby*) chubby, plumpy; (*o biodrach, kształtach*) full-figured, rotund.

okrążać *ipf.* **1.** (= *obchodzić, objeżdżać*) circle,

encircle, orbit. **2.** (= *ogradzać*) ring round, surround. **3.** *wojsk.* envelop, bottle up.

okrążenie *n.* **1.** circuit, encirclement; *sport* lap. **2.** *wojsk.* envelopment.

okrążyć *pf. zob.* **okrążać.**

okres *mi* **1.** (= *określony czas trwania*) period, season; **okres godowy** *biol.* mating season; **okres istnienia** *l.* **życia** lifetime; **okres najwyższej oglądalności** *telew.* prime time; **okres prolongaty** grace period; **okres przechowywania** (*produktu*) shelf life; **okres urzędowania** incumbency; **okres ochronny** *myśl.* fence season, closed season. **2.** (= *epoka*) period; **epoka baroku** Baroque period. **3.** *szkol.* (= *semestr*) semester, term. **4.** *fizj.* (= *menstruacja*) period. **5.** *astron.* cycle. **6.** *geol.* period; **okres lodowcowy** glacial period; **okres kambryjski** the Cambrian period, the Cambrian. **7.** *ret.* period, sentence. **8.** *muz.* passage, phase.

okresowo *adv.* periodically, intermittently.

okresowość *f.* periodicity, intermittence.

okresowy a. **1.** (= *powtarzający się*) periodic, periodical, recurring. **2.** (= *tymczasowy, chwilowy*) temporary. **3.** *chem.* periodic; **układ okresowy pierwiastków** periodic table *l.* system. **4.** **ułamek okresowy** *mat.* circulating *l.* repeating *l.* recurring decimal.

określać *ipf.* define, determine; (*wartość*) assess; (*na oko*) guesstimate.

określenie *n.* **1.** (= *epitet*) definition, designation; **określenie pieszczotliwe** term of endearment. **2.** (*sąd*) appellation, designation. **3.** *jęz.* attribute.

określić *pf. zob.* **określać.**

określnik *mi Gen.* **-a** *jęz.* determiner, modifier.

określony a. definite, specific; (*o przyczynach*) specifiable; **przedimek określony** *gram.* definite article.

okręcać *ipf.* (= *owijać*) twist, loop, wrap (*sth around sb/sth*). **~ się** *ipf.* **1.** (= *obracać się dookoła*) swivel, swirl. **2.** (= *owijać się*) twist, wrap.

okręcić *pf. zob.* **okręcać.** **~ się** *pf. zob.* **okręcać się.**

okręg *mi* **1.** (*obszar*) region, area, district; (*rolniczy, górniczy, wydobywczy, przemysłowy*) region, belt. **2.** (*administracyjny*) district; **okręg policyjny** (*w mieście*) precinct; **okręg sądowy** judicial district; **okręg wyborczy** constituency.

okręgowy a. district, regional; (*o sądzie*) circuit, district; **okręgowa komisja wyborcza** district electoral committee.

okręt *mi* sail, ship; *wojsk.* vessel; **okręt desantowy** assault ship; **okręt flagowy** flagship; **okręt liniowy** battleship; **okręt podwodny** submarine; **okręt Marynarki Wojennej USA** USS, United States Ship; **być sobie sterem, żeglarzem, okrętem** *przen.* paddle one's own canoe, be the captain of one's soul.

okrętka *f. Gen.pl.* **-ek** buttonhole stitch; **szyć na okrętkę** sew overhand.

okrętować *ipf.* (*angażować; przebywać*) ship.

okrętowiec *mp* **-wc-** *pl.* **-y** (*specjalista*) shipbuilder, shipwright. – *ma* **-wc-** *zool.* **świdrak okrętowiec** shipworm (*Teredo navalis*).

okrętownictwo n. shipbuilding.

okrętowy a. marine, naval, shipborne; **dziennik okrętowy** journal; **ładunek okrętowy** shipload; **chłopiec okrętowy** ship's boy; **służyć jako chłopiec okrętowy** (= *odbywać praktykę na statku*) sail before the mast.

okrężnica f. 1. *anat.* colon; **zapalenie okrężnicy** colitis; **okrężnica zstępująca** descending colon. 2. (*sieć rybacka*) purse seine. 3. *techn.* blast pipe. 4. *bot.* water-violet, feather foil (*Hottonia palustris*).

okrężnie *adv.* circuitously.

okrężny a. circuitous, circular; (*o drodze*) roundabout, indirect; **mięsień okrężny** *anat.* orbicular muscle.

okroić *pf.* **-ój** *zob.* **okrawać**.

okropieństwo n. hideousness, atrocity.

okropnie *adv.* 1. (= *przerażająco*) horribly, dreadfully, horridly. 2. *pot.* (= *bardzo, w dużym stopniu, ogromnie*) terribly, awfully; **okropnie się cieszę** I'm terribly *l.* awfully happy.

okropność f. abhorrence, hideousness, atrocity.

okropny a. 1. (= *straszny, przerażający*) horrible, terrible, awful; (*o warunkach*) miserable; (*o zachowaniu, charakterze, pogodzie*) awful, vile; (*o zapachu, przyzwyczajeniu*) obnoxious, nasty. 2. (= *bardzo intensywny*) immense, extreme, intense. 3. (= *zły, brzydki*) atrocious, horrid, wretched.

okruchy *pl. Gen.* **-ów** 1. (= *kawałeczki*) crumbs, scrubs, pieces. 2. (*nadziei*) *przen.* crumbs.

okrucieństwo n. 1. (= *sadyzm*) cruelty, atrocity, ruthlessness. 2. (= *okrutne czyny*) atrocities, excesses.

okruszek mi **-szk-** *Gen.* **-a** crumb; **okruszek chleba** breadcrumb.

okruszyna f. (*pieczywa*) crumb; (= *drobina*) particle.

okrutnica f. bully, brute, tormentor.

okrutnie *adv.* 1. (= *bezlitośnie*) atrociously, cruelly, ruthlessly. 2. *pot.* (= *bardzo, ogromnie*) awfully, terribly.

okrutnik mp bully, brute, tormentor.

okrutność f. (= *sadyzm*) cruelty, ruthlessness.

okrutny a. 1. (= *nieubłagany*) cruel, ruthless. 2. (= *przerażający*) diabolical, savage. 3. *pot.* (= *ogromny*) excessive, extreme.

okrwawić *pf.* stain with blood, spill blood; **okrwawiona koszula** blood-stained shirt.

okrycie n. 1. (*ubranie*) coat. 2. (= *przykrycie*) cover, covering; **spać bez okrycia** sleep uncovered.

okryć *pf.* **-ję -jesz** *zob.* **okrywać**. **~ się** *pf. zob.* **okrywać się**.

okrytonasienne *pl. Gen.* **-ych** *zob.* **okrytozalążkowe**.

okrytozalążkowe *pl. Gen.* **-ych** *bot.* angiosperms (*Angiospermae*).

okrywa f. coat, encasement; (*nasienna*) involucre, operculum; **okrywa kwiatostanu** husk.

okrywać *ipf.* 1. (= *otulać*) cover, envelop, wrap; **okrywać całunem** shroud; **śmierć prezy-**

denta okryła naród żałobą the whole nation mourned over the president's death; **okryć kogoś hańbą** cover sb with shame, bring disgrace *l.* dishonor on sb; **okryć kogoś niesławą** bring sb into disrepute. 2. *przen.* (= *pokrywać*) cover; (*płatkami, np. śniegu*) flake; (*ziemią*) earth up. **~ się** *ipf.* 1. (= *otulać się*) cover o.s. up; (*kocem*) wrap o.s. up with a blanket; **okryć się żałobą** mourn, grieve; **okryć się hańbą** cover o.s. with shame. 2. *przen.* (= *pokrywać się*) cover o.s.

okrzemki *pl. Gen.* **-ów** *bot.* diatoms (*Diatomae*).

okrzemkowy a. (*o skale, ziemi*) diatomaceous.

okrzepnąć *pf.* **-ij, -nął** *l.* **-ł -ła -li** congeal, stiffen.

okrzesanie n. polish, polished manners; **brak mu okrzesania** he's coarse *l.* ill-mannered.

okrzyczany a. acclaimed, renowned.

okrzyczeć *pf.* **-ę -ysz** *zob.* **okrzyknąć**.

okrzyk mi cry, exclamation, shout, interjection; (*dopingujący*) cheer; **okrzyk bojowy** battle cry; **okrzyk zachwytu/radości/bólu** cry of delight/joy/pain.

okrzyknąć *pf.* **-ij** hail (*kogoś / coś czymś* sb/sth as sth); acclaim (*kogoś / coś czymś* sb/sth as sth).

Oksford mi Oxford.

oksybiont ma *biol.* aerobe, oxybiont.

oksybioza f. *biol., chem.* aerobic process.

oksydacja f. *chem.* oxidation.

oksydacyjny a. *chem.* oxidizing.

oksydaza f. *biol.* oxidase.

oksydoreduktazy *pl. Gen.* **-z** *biol.* oxireductase enzymes.

oksydować *ipf. chem.* oxidize. **~ się** *ipf. chem.* oxidize.

oksydowanie n. *chem.* oxidizing, blueing.

oksydowany a. *chem.* (*o srebrze, zegarku*) oxidized.

oksyhemoglobina f. *biol.* oxyhemoglobin, *Br.* oxyhaemoglobin.

oksymoron mi *teor.lit.* antilogy, oxymoron.

oksytocyna f. *biol.* oxytocin.

oksyton mi *jęz.* oxytone.

oksytoneza f. *jęz.* oxytonesis.

oksytoniczny a. *jęz.* oxytonical.

oktan mi *chem.* octane.

oktanowy a. *chem.* octane; **liczba oktanowa** octane number, antiknock rating.

oktawa f. 1. *muz.* eighth, octave. 2. *rz.-kat.* octave. 3. *wers.* octonary, octet.

oktet mi muz. (*zespół, utwór*) octet.

oktrojować *pf. polit.* decree.

oktylion mi mat. octillion.

okucie n. ferrule, fitting.

okuć *pf. zob.* **okuwać**.

okulant mi *ogr.* shoot of budded plant.

okular mi *opt.* eyepiece, ocular, eyeglass.

okularnik ma *pl.* **-i** *zool.* (*kobra*) Indian cobra (*Naja naja*). — *mp pl.* **-cy** *żart.* four-eyes.

okulary *pl. Gen.* **-ów** 1. (*do korekcji wzroku*) eyeglasses, glasses; spectacles, specs; (*przeciwsłoneczne*) sunglasses, shades; **okulary w rogowej oprawie** horn-rimmed glasses; **okulary dwuogniskowe** bifocals; **patrzeć na coś/świat przez różowe okulary** look at sth/the world through rose-tinted *l.* colored glasses *l.* spectacles. **2.** (*dla konia*) blinders; *Br.* blinkers.

okulawić *pf.* cripple, lame.

okulbaczyć *pf.* saddle.

okuleć *pf.* go lame.

okulista *mp*, **okulistka** *f. Gen.pl.* **-ek** oculist, ophthalmologist.

okulistyczny *a.* ophthalmological.

okulistyka *f.* ophthalmology.

okulizacja *f. ogr.* bud grafting, budding.

okulizak *mi Gen.* **-a** *ogr.* budding knife.

okulizator *mi Gen.* **-a** *ogr. zob.* **okulizak.**

okulizować *ipf. ogr.* graft, bud.

okultysta *mp* occultist.

okultystyczny *a.* cabbalistic, occult; **wiara okultystyczna** cabbala.

okultyzm *mi* cabbalism, the occult, occultism.

okup *mi* ransom; **porwać kogoś dla okupu** kidnap sb for ransom.

okupacja *f.* **1.** *polit.* (*państwa, terenów*) occupation; **być pod okupacją** be under occupation. **2.** *prawn.* occupancy.

okupacyjny *a.* occupation, occupying; **strajk okupacyjny** stay-in *l.* sit-down strike.

okupant *mp* occupier.

okupić *pf. zob.* **okupywać.** ~ **się** *pf. zob.* **okupywać się.**

okupować *ipf.* **1.** *polit., prawn.* occupy. **2.** (*np. łazienkę*) *żart.* hog.

okupywać *ipf.* **1.** (= *opłacać coś kosztem czegoś*) obtain (*coś czymś* sth at the price of sth); **drogo coś okupić** pay a high price for sth, pay dearly for sth. **2.** (= *wynagradzać*) compensate (*coś* for sth). ~ **się** *ipf.* compensate (*za coś* for sth) pay (*a high price for sth*).

okutać *pf. pot.* wrap up, muffle up. ~ **się** *pf. pot.* wrap o.s. up, muffle o.s. up.

okuwać *ipf.* ferrule; **okuwać konia** shoe *l.* calk a horse.

okwiat *mi bot.* perianth.

okwitać *ipf.*, **okwitnąć** *pf. bot.* (*o kwitnących kwiatach, drzewach*) cease blooming; (*o kwiatach*) shed petals.

olać *pf.* **-eję -ejesz** *zob.* **olewać.**

olbrzym[1] *mp pl.* **-i** *l.* **-y** giant.

olbrzym[2] *mi Gen.* **-a** *pl.* **-y** jumbo; (*o budynku*) colossus; **gwiazda olbrzym** *astron.* giant star.

olbrzymi *a.* **1.** (= *bardzo duży*) colossal, enormous, giant; (*o wiedzy, kosztach*) vast; (*o sukcesie*) rip-roaring, huge; (*o wzroście*) spectacular. **2.** (= *intensywny*) tremendous, excessive.

olbrzymieć *ipf.* **1.** (= *stawać się wielkim, bardzo dużym*) grow to gigantic proportions. **2.** *lit.* (= *stawać się coraz bardziej intensywnym*) increase, swell.

olbrzymka *f.* **1.** giantess. **2.** *ogr.* (*drzewo*) tree that bears large fruits.

olcha *f. bot.* alder (*Alnus*).

olchowy *a.* (*o drewnie, meblach*) alder, aldern.

oldboj *mp Gen.pl.* **-ów** *pot. żart.* seasoned professional.

oldenburgi *pl. Gen.* **-ów** *zool.* Oldenburg horses.

oleander *mi* **-dr-** *Gen.* **-a** *bot.* oleander, rosebay (*Nerium oleander*).

oleandrowy *a.* oleander.

olefiny *pl. Gen.* **-n** *chem.* olefins.

oleica *f. zool.* oil beetle (*Meloe proscarabeus*).

oleić *ipf. techn.* oil, lubricate.

oleina *f. chem.* olein.

oleinowy *a. chem.* oleic.

oleistość *f.* oiliness.

oleisty *a.* **1.** (= *podobny do oleju*) oily. **2.** (= *bogaty w olej*) (*o nasionach*) oleaginous; **roślina oleista** oil plant.

olej *mi Gen.pl.* **-ei** *l.* **-ów** **1.** (*pochodzenia roślinnego*) oil; **olej lniany** linseed oil; **olej rycynowy** castor oil; **olej maszynowy** lube; **olej żywiczny** resin oil, resinol; **oleje święte** *rz.-kat.* holy oil; **mieć olej w głowie** *żart.* have quick wits; **mieć na tyle oleju w głowie, żeby coś zrobić** have the gumption *l.* wit to do sth; **nudny jak flaki z olejem** dry as dust, dull as ditchwater. **2.** (*pochodzący z ropy naftowej, węgla, smoły*) oil; **olej napędowy** fuel oil, diesel oil; **olej smarowy** lubricant. **3.** *mal.* (*farba*) oil-paint. **4.** *mal.* (*obraz*) oil painting.

olejarka *f. Gen.pl.* **-ek** *techn.* oiler.

olejarnia *f. Gen.pl.* **-i** *l.* **-ń** *techn.* oil mill.

olejarski *a.* oil; (*o zakładzie, przemyśle*) oil producing.

olejarstwo *n. techn.* oil manufacture, oil milling.

olejek *mi* **-jk-** essence, oil; **olejek eteryczny** essential oil, ethereal oil; **olejek różany** attar of roses; **olejek piżmowy** musk oil; **olejek miętowy** peppermint; **olejek do opalania** suntan oil.

olejkodajny *a.* (*o roślinie*) oliferous.

olejniczka *f. Gen.pl.* **-ek** *techn.* oiler.

olejny *a.* oil; **farba olejna** oil paint; **obraz olejny** *mal.* oil painting; **technika olejna** *mal.* oil painting.

olejowiec *mi* **-wc-** *Gen.* **-a** *bot.* oil palm (*Elaeis guineensis*).

olejowy *a.* oil; **ogrzewanie olejowe** oil heating; **pompa olejowa** oil pump.

oleodruk *mi* oleograph.

oleografia *f. Gen.* **-ii** oleography.

oleomargaryna *f.* oleomargarine.

oleożywice *pl. Gen.* **-c** *chem.* oleoresins.

olewać *ipf. pot.* (= *lekceważyć*) blow off; **olewam to** I don't give a damn about it.

olicować *pf. bud.* face.

oligarcha *mp pl.* **-owie** oligarch.

oligarchia *f. Gen.* **-ii** *polit.* oligarchy.

oligarchiczny *a. polit.* oligarchic.

oligocen *mi geol.* the Oligocene, the Oligocene epoch.

oligofagi *pl. Gen.* **-ów** *zool.* oligophagous animals.

oligofrenia *f. Gen.* **-ii** *psych.* oligophrenia.

oligofreniczny *a. psych.* (*dziecko, uszkodzenie*) oligophrenic.

oligofrenik *mp psych.* oligophrenic.

oligofrenopedagogika *f.* oligophrenic pedagogy.

oligomer *mi chem.* oligomer.

oligosacharyd *mi chem.* oligosaccharide.

oligotrof *mi bot.* oligotrophic plant.

oligotroficzny *a.* (*o roślinie, jeziorze*) oligotrophic.

oligotrofizm *mi biol.* (*w zbiornikach wodnych*) oligotrophy.

oliguria *f. Gen.* -ii *med.* oliguria, oliguresis.

Olimp *mi* Olympus; (*świata mody, muzyki*) *przen.* stratosphere.

Olimpia *f. Gen.* -ii Olympia.

olimpiada *f.* **1.** *sport* Olympiad, Olympic Games, Olympics; **olimpiada zimowa** Winter Olympics; **olimpiada letnia** Summer (Olympic) Games. **2.** *szkoln.* contest.

olimpijczyk *mp* **1.** *sport* Olympian. **2.** *szkoln.* contestant.

olimpijka *f. Gen.pl.* -ek **1.** *sport* (*zawodniczka*) *zob.* **olimpijczyk. 2.** *szkoln.* contestant. **3.** (*kurtka*) sports jacket.

olimpijski *a.* **1.** *sport* Olympic. **2.** *mit.* Olympian; **olimpijski spokój** *przen.* Olympian composure.

olinowanie *n. żegl.* cordage; *lotn.* wiring; (*spadochronu*) shroud lines.

oliwa *f.* **1.** (*tłuszcz roślinny*) oil; **oliwa z oliwek** olive oil; **dolać oliwy do ognia** add fuel to the flames; rub salt into the wound; **oliwa sprawiedliwa, zawsze na wierzch wypływa** the truth will out. **2.** (*olej mineralny*) mineral oil.

oliwiarka *f. Gen.pl.* -ek *techn.* lubricator, oil cup, oiler.

oliwić *ipf.* lubricate, oil.

oliwin *mi min.* olivine.

oliwka *f. Gen.pl.* -ek **1.** *bot.* (*drzewo*) olive tree (*Olea europanea*). **2.** (*owoc*) olive.

oliwkowate *pl. Gen.* -ych *bot.* the olive family (*Oleaceae*).

oliwkowy *a.* olive; **kolor oliwkowy** olive, green; **drzewo oliwkowe** olive tree; **cera oliwkowa** olive complexion; **olej oliwkowy** olive oil.

oliwnik *mi Gen.* -a **1.** (*gaj*) olive grove. **2.** *bot.* oleaster (*Elaeaganus*).

oliwny *a.* olive; **lampka oliwna** olive oil lamp; **gałązka oliwna** olive branch; **Góra Oliwna** Mount of Olives; **palma oliwna** *bot.* oil palm (*Elaeis*).

ols *mi* (*las*) alder swamp.

olstro *n. Gen.pl.* -ter (*kabura*) holster.

olsza *f. Gen.pl.* -y *l.* **olsz** *bot.* alder (*Alnus*).

olszówka *f.* (*grzyb*) poison paxillus, naked brimcap (*Paxillus involutus*).

olszyna *f.* **1.** (*las*) alder forest. **2.** (*drewno*) alder wood.

olszynka *f. Gen.pl.* -ek (*las*) alder grove *l.* forest.

olszynowy *a.* alder; **las olszynowy** alder forest.

olśnić *pf.* -ij *zob.* **olśniewać.**

olśnienie *n.* **1.** dazzle. **2.** flash of insight, revelation; **i wtedy doznałem olśnienia** and then it dawned on me.

olśniewać *ipf.* **1.** (= *razić światłem*) dazzle, daze, blind. **2.** (= *wzbudzić zachwyt*) dazzle, overwhelm.

olśniewająco *adv.* dazzlingly.

olśniewający *a.* dazzling; **olśniewający występ** breathtaking performance; **olśniewająca uroda** dazzling beauty; **olśniewająca inteligencja** outstanding intelligence; **olśniewający widok** magnificent view.

ołowianoszary *a.* lead-grey, leaden.

ołowiany *a.* **1.** (*z ołowiem*) lead, leaden; **ołowiany żołnierzyk** tin soldier; **blacha ołowiana** lead sheet; **biel ołowiana** *chem.* white lead; **minia ołowiana** *chem.* minium, red lead. **2.** (*kolor*) leaden; **ołowiane niebo** leaden skies. **3.** *przen.* (= *ciężki*) leaden; **ołowiane nogi** *l.* **stopy** leaden feet.

ołowiawy *a. chem.* plumbous; **siarczek ołowiawy** plumbous sulfide.

ołowica *f. med.* lead poisoning, saturnism; (*przewlekła*) plumbism.

ołowiować *ipf. techn.* lead.

ołowiowanie *n. techn.* leading.

ołowiowy *a.* lead, plumbic; **szkło ołowiowe** lead glass; **związki ołowiowe** plumbic compounds.

ołów *mi* -owi- **1.** *chem.* lead. **2.** (*pocisk, kula, śrut*) lead.

ołówek *mi* -wk- *Gen.* -a **1.** (*do pisania*) pencil; **ołówek kreślarski** drafting pencil; **ołówek kopiowy** indelible pencil; **ołówek kolorowy** colored pencil; **ołówek automatyczny** propelling *l.* automatic pencil; **ołówek miękki** soft pencil; **ołówek twardy** hard pencil; **ołówek do brwi** eyebrow pencil; **obliczać coś** *l.* **żyć z ołówkiem w ręku** calculate one's expenses accurately, be very economical. **2.** (*rysunek*) pencil drawing; **portret w ołówku** pencil portrait.

ołówkowy *a.* pencil; **szkic ołówkowy** pencil sketch.

ołtarz *mi Gen.* -a *rel.* altar; **ołtarz główny** high altar, (apse) altar; **ołtarz boczny** side altar; **ołtarz gotycki** Gothic altar; **ołtarz szafkowy** *l.* **szafiasty** winged altarpiece; **iść z kimś do ołtarza** lead sb to the altar, marry sb; **złożyć życie na ołtarzu ojczyzny** offer one's life for one's homeland, die for one's homeland.

ołtarzowy *a.* altar; **rzeźba ołtarzowa** altar sculpture, altarpiece.

ołtarzyk *mi Gen.* -a **1.** *rel.* (= *mały, prowizoryczny ołtarz*) altar. **2.** *rel.* (= *figura noszona w procesji*) feretory.

om *mi Gen.* -a *fiz.* ohm.

omacku *adv.* **po omacku** blindfold; **szukać czegoś po omacku** grope for sth.

omacywanie *n. med.* palpation.

omal *adv.* almost, nearly; **omal nie zemdlała** she almost fainted; **to jest omalże niemożliwe** it's almost impossible.

omamiać *ipf.*, **omamić** *pf.* beguile. ~ **się** *ipf.*, **omamić się** *pf.* beguile o.s.

omamy *pl. Gen.* -ów hallucinations; **omamy wzrokowe** visual hallucinations; **omamy słuchowe** auditory hallucinations.

Oman *mi geogr.* Oman.

oman *mi bot.* elecampane, scabwort (*Inula*).

omasta *f. dial., kulin.* (= *tłuszcz*) fat; (= *sos*) gravy.

omaszczać *ipf. kulin.* (*tłuszczem*) add fat (*to a dish*); (*sosem*) add gravy (*to a dish*).

omasztować *pf. zob.* omasztowywać.

omasztowanie *n. żegl.* spars.

omasztowywać *ipf. żegl.* spar.

omaścić *pf. zob.* omaszczać.

omawiać *ipf.* discuss, talk over; omawiać kwestię discuss a question *l.* matter.

ombrofil *mi Gen.pl.* -i *l.* -ów *bot.* ombrophile.

ombrofilny *a. bot.* ombrophilous; tropikalny las ombrofilny ombrophilous rain forest.

ombrofob *mi Gen.* -a *bot.* ombrophobe.

ombrometr *mi meteor.* pluviometer, rain gauge, ombrometer.

omdlały *a.* faint, languid; omdlały głos faint voice.

omdleć *pf. zob.* omdlewać.

omdlenie *n.* 1. (= *utrata przytomności*) fainting, faint; (*w języku fachowym*) syncope; ocknąć się z omdlenia come around *l.* round. 2. (= *słabość, niemoc*) faintness, languor, weakness; ręce komuś omdlewają sb's hands feel faint *l.* weak.

omdlewać *ipf.* 1. (= *tracić przytomność*) faint, swoon. 2. (= *tracić siły*) feel faint, languish, weaken; ręce omdlewają mi ze zmęczenia my hands feel faint *l.* feeble from exertion.

omdlewający *a.* faint, languid; omdlewające spojrzenie withering look.

omega *f.* 1. (*litera*) omega; alfa i omega (the) alpha and omega. 2. *żegl.* type of centerboard Bermudan *l.* Marconi sloop. 3. (*zegarek*) Omega watch.

omen *mi* omen, portent, augury; dobry *l.* szczęśliwy omen good omen; zły omen bad *l.* ill omen; nomen omen aptly named.

omiatać *ipf.* sweep; omiatać coś wzrokiem scan sth.

omieszkać *pf.* 1. nie omieszkam powiadomić pani o decyzji I'll remember to inform you about my decision. 2. *prawn.* omit, neglect, fail.

omieść *pf.* -otę -eciesz -ótł -otła -etli *zob.* omiatać.

omijać *ipf.,* ominąć *pf.* 1. (= *mijać kogoś l. coś*) go around *l.* round; pass; walk *l.* go *l.* drive past; omijać trudności avoid difficulties; omijać przepisy go around regulations, evade regulations. 2. (= *nie stawać się czyimś udziałem*) pass over; ominął mnie awans I was passed over for promotion. 3. (= *nie brać kogoś l. czegoś pod uwagę*) overlook, pass over, avoid; omijać temat sprzedaży w rozmowie avoid mentioning the sale; omijać kogoś przy awansie pass sb over for promotion. 4. *tylko ipf.* (= *unikać kogoś l. czegoś*) avoid; omijać kogoś szerokim łukiem *pot.* steer clear of sb, avoid sb studiously. ~ się *ipf.* (= *unikać się*) avoid each other.

omlet *mi kulin.* omelet; *Br.* omelette.

omłot *mi roln.* 1. (= *młocka*) threshing. 2. (*ziarno*) grain yield.

omłócić *pf. roln.* thresh.

omnibus *mi Gen.* -u *pl.* -y *hist.* (*pojazd*) omnibus, bus. – *mp Gen.* -a *pl.* -i *żart.* brain; ale z niego omnibus! he's got brains!

omocznia *f. Gen.pl.* -i *anat.* allantois.

omometr *mi fiz.* meter ohm.

omomierz *mi Gen.* -a *fiz.* ohmmeter.

omotać *pf.* 1. (= *owinąć*) wrap, wind, lap. 2. (= *otulić*) wrap up, tuck. 3. (= *usidlić, opętać*) entrap, entangle. ~ się *pf.* 1. (= *owinąć się*) wrap o.s. up. 2. (= *wplątać się*) get entangled.

omówić *pf. zob.* omawiać.

omówienie *n.* 1. (*artykuł w prasie*) review, report. 2. (= *szczegółowa prezentacja czegoś*) presentation, description. 3. *teor.lit.* (= *peryfraza*) periphrasis.

omsknąć się *pf.* -ij *pot.* (= *obsunąć się*) slip.

omszały *a.* mossy; musty, moldy; *Br.* mouldy; omszałe drzewo mossy tree; omszała butelka wina moldy bottle of wine.

omszeć *pf.* cover with moss; cover with mold, *Br.* cover with mould.

omszony *a. zob.* omszały.

omułek *ma* -łk- *zool.* omułek jadalny blue mussel (*Mytilus edulis*).

omurować *pf.,* omurowywać *ipf.* line with bricks; wall.

omyć *pf.* -ję -jesz *zob.* omywać.

omylić *pf.* deceive, mislead. ~ się *pf. przest.* make a mistake *l.* an error, be mistaken.

omylność *f.* fallibility; erroneousness.

omylny *a.* fallible; człowiek jest omylny we all make mistakes, nobody is perfect.

omyłka *f. Gen.pl.* -ek error, mistake; przez omyłkę by mistake.

omyłkowo *adv.* by mistake, mistakenly.

omyłkowy *a.* mistaken, erroneous, wrong.

omywać *ipf.* -am -asz wash.

on[1] *pron. Gen. i Acc.* jego *l.* go *l.* niego *Dat.* jemu *l.* mu *l.* niemu *Ins. i Loc.* nim *pl.* oni, one *Gen.* ich *l.* nich *Dat.* im *l.* nim *Acc.* ich *l.* nich, je *Ins.* nimi *Loc.* nich he; him; it; on jeden mógł to zrobić he's the only one who could have done it; jak to on what do you mean it's him?; a niech go! damn him!; patrzcie go! look at him!; Jego Magnificencja Rector Magnificus; Jego Ekscelencja His Excellency; Jego Wysokość His Highness; Jego Królewska Mość His Majesty the King, His Royal Highness; Jego Świątobliwość His Holiness.

on[2] *a. arch.* (= *tamten*) this, that; onego czasu long time ago.

ona[1] *pron. Gen. i Dat.* jej *l.* niej *Acc.* ją *Ins.* nią *Loc.* niej *pl.* one *Gen.* ich *l.* nich *Dat.* im *l.* nim *Acc.* je *l.* nie *Ins.* nimi *Loc.* nich she; her; it; ona jedna mogła to zrobić she's the only one who could have done it; jak to ona what do you mean it's her?; a niech ją! damn her!; patrzcie ją! look at her!; Jej Magnificencja Rector Magnificus; Jej Ekscelencja Her Excellency; Jej Wysokość Her Highness; Jej Królewska Mość Her Majesty the Queen, Her Royal Highness.

ona[2] *a.* (= *tamta*) *arch.* this, that; onej godziny long time ago.

onager *ma* 1. *zool.* onager (*Equus hemionus onager*). 2. *hist.* onager.

onanizm *mi* masturbation, onanism.

onanizować się *ipf.* masturbate.

ondulacja *f. przest.* coiffure; **trwała ondulacja** permanent wave.

ondulować *ipf. przest.* coiffure; perm.

one *pron. zob.* **on** *l.* **ona** *l.* **ono.**

onegdaj *adv. przest.* the other day, the day before yesterday.

ongi *adv. przest.* erst(while), aforetime.

ongiś *adv. przest.* erst(while), aforetime.

oni *pron. zob.* **on.**

oniemiały *a.* speechless, dumbfounded; **oniemiały z zachwytu** speechless with delight.

oniemieć *pf.* be (left) speechless.

onieśmielać *ipf.* embarass, abash.

onieśmielenie *n.* embarrassment; **wywołać czyjeś onieśmielenie** embarass sb.

onieśmielić *pf. zob.* **onieśmielać.**

onieśmielony *a.* **-eni** embarassed, abashed.

onkogen *mi pat.* oncogene.

onkolog *mp pl.* **-dzy** *l.* **-owie** *med.* oncologist.

onkologia *f. Gen.* **-ii** *med.* oncology.

onkologiczny *a.* oncologic, oncological.

ono *prep. Gen.* **jego** *l.* **go** *l.* **niego** *Dat.* **jemu** *l.* **mu** *l.* **niemu** *Acc.* **je** *l.* **nie** *Ins. i Loc.* **nim** *pl.* **one** *Gen.* **ich** *l.* **nich** *Dat.* **im** *l.* **nim** *Acc.* **je** *l.* **nie** *Ins.* **nimi** *Loc.* **nich** it.

onomasta *mp jęz.* onomastician.

onomastyczny *a. jęz.* onomastic.

onomastyka *f. jęz.* onomastics, onomatology.

onomastykon *mi jęz.* onomasticon.

onomatopeiczny *a. teor.lit.* onomatopoeic.

onomatopeja *f. Gen.* **-ei** *teor.lit.* onomatopoeia.

onomazjologia *f. Gen.* **-ii** *jęz.* onomasiology.

onomazjologiczny *a. jęz.* onomasiologic, onomasiological.

ontogenetyczny *a. biol.* ontogenetic; **antropologia ontogenetyczna** ontogenetic anthropology.

ontogeneza *f. biol.* ontogeny, ontogenesis.

ontologia *f. Gen.* **-ii** *fil.* ontology.

ontologiczny *a. fil.* ontologic, ontological; **dowód ontologiczny** ontological argument *l.* proof.

ontyczny *a. fil.* ontic, noumenal.

onuca *f. przest., zwł. wojsk.* a piece of cloth wrapped round the foot as a sock.

onyks *mi min.* onyx.

onyksowy *a.* onyx; **waza onyksowa** onyx vase.

oń *pron. lit.* (= *o niego*) about him.

oogamia *f. Gen.* **-ii** *biol.* oogamy.

oogeneza *f. biol.* oogenesis.

oolit *mi min.* oolite, egg stone.

oolitowy *a. min.* oolitic; **wapień oolitowy** oolite.

oologia *f. Gen.* **-ii** *orn.* oology.

ooplazma *f. biol.* ooplasm.

opactwo *n. rel.* abbey.

opacznie *adv.* wrongly, mistakenly; **opacznie coś zrozumieć** get sth wrong.

opaczny *a.* wrong, erroneous, mistaken; **robić coś w sposób opaczny** do sth the wrong way.

opad *mi* **1.** *meteor.* precipitation; **opady atmosferyczne** precipitation; **opady deszczu** rainfall; **opady przelotne** occasional precipitation; **opad promieniotwórczy** *l.* **radioaktywny** fallout. **2.** *med.* sedimentation rate, hypostasis; **opad krwi** erythrocyte sedimentation rate. **3.** *sport* (*ćwi-*

czenie) bend. **4.** (= *upadanie, spadek*) fall, drop; **opad liści** leaf-fall; **opad wód** water subsidence.

opadać *ipf.* **1.** (= *osuwać się, obniżać się*) fall, drop; (*o głowie*) droop; (*o wodzie w rzece, emocjach*) subside; (*o cieście*) collapse; (*o zawiesinie, roztworze*) settle; **ręce opadają** it's hopeless; **opadać z sił** lose one's strength; **zmęczenie ze mnie opadło** fatigue is gone. **2.** (= *spadać*) (*o liściach, owocach*) fall; (*o kwiatach*) die. **3.** (= *napadać na kogoś*) assail, beset; **opadły ją wątpliwości** she was beset with doubts. **4.** *tylko ipf.* (= *okrywać*) hang loose; **zasłony opadają do podłogi** curtains hang loose to the floor.

opadanie *n.* fall, drop; subsidence; **opadanie krwinek** *med.* erythrocyte sedimentation, erythrocyte hypostasis.

opadowy *a.* precipitation, rain, snow, hail; **chmura opadowa** rain *l.* snow *l.* hail cloud.

opak *adv.* wrongly, mistakenly; **na opak** wrong, the wrong way, the other way round; **zrozumieć na opak** get hold of the wrong end of the stick.

opakować *pf. zob.* **opakowywać.**

opakowanie *n.* packaging; **opakowanie jednorazowe** disposable packaging; **opakowanie jednostkowe** unit packaging.

opakowywać *ipf.* package, wrap (*czymś l. w co* sth up (in sth)).

opal *mi min.* opal.

opalacz *mi Gen.* **-a** beach suit, beachwear.

opalać *ipf.* **1.** (= *ogrzewać*) heat (*czymś* with sth). **2.** (= *nadpalać ogniem*) char, singe; (*drób*) singe. **3.** (*ciało*) sunbathe. **4.** *pot.* (= *palić cudze papierosy*) bum cigarettes off sb; **nie chcę cię opalać** I don't want to bum cigarettes off you. **~ się** *ipf.* (sun)tan; get a (sun)tan.

opalenizna *f.* (sun)tan.

opalescencja *f. opt.* opalescence.

opalić *pf. zob.* **opalać.** **~ się** *pf. zob.* **opalać się.**

opalizacja *f.* opalescence.

opalizować *ipf.* opalesce.

opalony *a.* **-eni** (sun)tanned.

opalowy *a.* opal; **opalowy połysk** opalescence.

opał *mi* (*paliwo*) fuel.

opałowy *a.* fuel; **skład opałowy** fuel yard; **materiał opałowy** fuel; **wartość opałowa** calorific value.

opały *pl. Gen.* **-ów** trouble; **wpaść w opały** get in trouble; **być w opałach** be in trouble, be in distress; **wyjść z opałów** overcome trouble.

opamiętać się *pf.* come to sb's senses, bring o.s. to reason; pull o.s. together.

opamiętanie *n.* reflection, reason; **bez opamiętania** with abandon.

opancerzać *ipf.* armor, plate, cuirass.

opancerzony *a. zwł. wojsk.* armored; **samochód opancerzony** armored car *l.* vehicle; **transporter opancerzony** armored personnel carrier, APC.

opancerzyć *pf. zob.* **opancerzać.**

opanować *pf. zob.* **opanowywać.** **~ się** *pf. zob.* **opanowywać się.**

opanowanie *n.* **1.** (= *zawładnięcie*) capture, seizure; (= *podporządkowanie sobie*) containment; (= *nauczenie się*) mastery. **2.** (= *spokój*) self-control, composure.

opanowany *a.* **1.** (*o mieście, twierdzy*) captured; (*o pożarze*) contained; (*o strachu*) overcome; **teren opanowany przez Niemców** German-controlled area; **pożar został opanowany** fire was contained. **2.** (= *spokojny*) composed, cool.

opanowywać *ipf.* **1.** (= *zdobywać nad czymś władzę*) capture, seize. **2.** (= *przejmować kontrolę nad czymś*) contain, bring under control. **3.** (= *poddawać się wpływowi uczuć*) be overcome; **opanowała mnie radość** I was overcome with joy. **4.** (= *zdobywać jakąś umiejętność, wiedzę*) master, learn. **5.** *sport* (*piłkę*) control. **~ się** *ipf.* control o.s., contain o.s., calm down.

opar *mi* **1.** (= *mgła*) mist. **2.** (= *wyziew*) vapor, fume.

oparcie *n.* **1.** (*podpora*) support, footing; **szukać w kimś oparcia** ask for sb's support; **oparcie dla nogi** foothold. **2.** (*krzesła, kanapy itp.*) back(rest); (*na głowę*) headrest; (*na rękę, ramię*) armrest. **3.** (= *podstawa*) basis, base; **w oparciu o** on the basis of.

oparł *itd. pf. zob.* **oprzeć.**

op-art *mi sztuka* op art, Op Art.

opartowski *a. sztuka* op-art.

oparzelina *f.* **1.** *pat.* scald(ing). **2.** *leśn.* sunscald.

oparzelisko *n.* morass, bog, marsh.

oparzenie *n. pat.* burn, scald(ing); **oparzenie pierwszego/drugiego/trzeciego stopnia** first-/second-/third-degree burn; **oparzenie słoneczne** sunburn.

oparzeniowy *a.* burn, scald; **oddział oparzeniowy** burn ward.

oparzyć *pf.* **1.** (*skórę*) burn, scald, scorch; (*pokrzywą*) sting; **zerwać się jak oparzony** jump to sb's feet. **2.** *zwł. kulin.* scald. **~ się** *pf.* get burned; **oparzyć się w rękę** burn sb's hand.

opas *mi Gen.* **-u** *roln.* (*karmienie*) fattening. – *ma Gen.* **-a** *roln.* (= *tucznik*) fattener; porker.

opasać[1] *pf.* **-szę -szesz** *zob.* **opasywać.**

opasać[2] *pf. roln.* (= *tuczyć*) fatten. **~ się** *pf. zob.* **opasywać się.**

opaska *f. Gen.pl.* **-ek** band; (*na głowę*) headband; (*na oko*) patch; (*na rękę*) armband; (*na czoło*) sweatband; **opaska do włosów** hairband; **opaska biodrowa** loincloth; **opaska uciskowa** *med.* torniquet, pressure band; **opaska żałobna** weed, mourning band.

opasły *a.* **-śli** obese, fat; **opasły chłopak** obese boy; **opasła twarz** round face.

opasowy *a. roln.* fattening, fattenable; **wieprz opasowy** porker.

opasywać *ipf.* **1.** (= *obwiązywać*) tie, bind; belt, gird. **2.** (= *otaczać*) gird, surround, enclose, encircle; **otoczyć miasto fosą** dig a moat around a town. **~ się** *ipf.* (= *obwiązywać się*) **1.** belt o.s., gird o.s. **2.** be surrounded *l.* girded.

opaść[1] *pf.* **-dnę -dniesz, -dnij, -dł** *zob.* **opadać.**

opaść[2] *pf.* **-sę -siesz -sł -śli** *zob.* **opasać**[2].

opat *mp rel.* abbot.

opatentować *pf.* patent.

opatrunek *mi* **-nk-** *med.* **1.** dressing; **opatrunek**

jałowy aseptic dressing; **opatrunek uciskowy** pressure dressing; **opatrunek gipsowy** cast; **zmiana opatrunku** change of dressing. **2.** (= *opatrywanie*) dressing (of a wound); **chodzić na opatrunki** go to have sb's dressings changed.

opatrunkowy *a. med.* dressing; **materiały opatrunkowe** dressings; **gaza opatrunkowa** gauze; **wata opatrunkowa** dressing cotton.

opatrywać *ipf.* **1.** (= *sprawdzać stan czegoś*) fix, put in a working order; **opatrywać okna** seal windows. **2.** (*ranę*) dress (a wound), bandage. **3.** (= *wyposażać w coś*) provide with, supply with, equip with; **opatrzyć dokument pieczęcią** affix a stamp *l.* seal to a document; **opatrzyć dokument podpisem** affix a signature to a document; **książka opatrzona przedmową** book with a foreword; **opatrywać chorego sakramentami** *rz.- kat.* administer sacraments to an ill person.

opatrznościowy *a.* providential; **mąż opatrznościowy** white knight, savior; *Br.* saviour.

opatrzność *f. rel.* Providence; **oko opatrzności** the eye of Providence.

opatrzony *a.* **1.** fixed. **2.** dressed, bandaged. **3.** provided *l.* supplied *l.* equipped with; **list opatrzony podpisem dyrektora** letter with director's signature affixed thereto; **chory opatrzony sakramentami** ill person to whom sacraments have been administered.

opatrzyć *pf. zob.* **opatrywać.**

opatrzyć się *pf.* (*pot.* = *znudzić się*) be seen too often; **coś się komuś opatrzyło** sb has seen too much of sth.

opatulać *ipf.,* **opatulić** *pf. pot.* tuck (*sb*) in, wrap (*sb*) (up) snugly. **~ się** *ipf.,* **opatulić się** *pf. pot.* wrap o.s. up.

opchać się *pf. zob.* **opychać się.**

opchnąć *pf.* **-ij** **1.** *sl.* (= *sprzedać*) flog. **2.** *pot.* (= *zjeść*) stuff.

opcja *f.* **1.** option; *polit.* clean start. **2.** *komp.* option. **3.** (*prawn.* = *wybór obywatelstwa*) option (of nationality). **4.** *prawn.* (*w prawie autorskim*) copyright. **5.** (*prawn.* = *uprawnienie do kupna lub sprzedaży*) option. **6.** *żegl.* ship's option.

opera *f.* **1.** *muz.* opera; **opera komiczna/tragiczna** comic/grand opera; **opera buffa/seria** opera buffa/seria. **2.** (*teatr, gmach*) opera (house). **3.** (*przedstawienie*) opera; **pójść na operę** go to an opera. **4.** (*żart.* = *śmieszna sytuacja*) funny *l.* comic situation; **opera mydlana** *film* soap opera.

operacja *f.* **1.** *med.* operation, surgery; **operacja plastyczna** plastic surgery; **poddać kogoś operacji** operate on sb. **2.** (*ekon.* = *czynność, szereg czynności*) operation, transaction; **operacje finansowe** financial operations; **operacje handlowe** business transactions. **3.** *mat.* operation. **4.** *techn.* operation, action, process. **5.** *wojsk.* operation; **plan operacji** operation plan.

operacjonizm *mi fil.* operationalism.

operacyjnie *adv. med.* surgically, operationally; **leczyć kogoś operacyjnie** operate on sb, perform a surgery on sb.

operacyjny *a.* **1.** *med.* operative, operation, operating; surgical; **zabieg operacyjny** surgery;

sala operacyjna operating room *l.* theater; **stół operacyjny** operating table; **blok operacyjny** operating room; **leczenie operacyjne** surgical treatment. **2.** *ekon.* operational, transactional; **rachunek operacyjny** current account. **3.** *wojsk.* operational, combat. **4.** *komp.* operating; **system operacyjny** operating system.

operator *mp pl.* **-rzy 1.** *med.* (*chirurg*) operating surgeon, operator. **2.** *film* (*kamerzysta*) cameraman. **3.** *techn.* (*wykwalifikowany robotnik*) operator; **operator dźwigu** crane operator. **4.** (= *zarządzający*) operator; **operator telefonii komórkowej** mobile phone company. – *mi pl.* **-ry** *log., mat.* operator.

operatorka *f. Gen.pl.* **-ek** *techn.* (*wykwalifikowana robotnica*) operator.

operatywnie *adv.* efficient; **działać** *l.* **pracować operatywnie** work efficiently.

operatywny *a.* efficient; **operatywny pracownik** efficient employee *l.* worker; **operatywne działanie** efficient operations.

operetka *f. Gen.pl.* **-ek 1.** (*utwór sceniczny*) operetta. **2.** (*teatr, gmach*) operetta house. **3.** (*przedstawienie*) operetta.

operetkowy *a.* **1.** (*związany z utworem muzycznym*) operetta; **śpiewak operetkowy** operettist; **aktor operetkowy** operettist. **2.** (*przen.* = *groteskowy, niepoważny*) farcical.

operon *mi biol.*, *genetyka* operon.

operować *ipf.* **1.** *med.* operate; **operować chorego** operate on a patient. **2.** (= *działać*) operate, work; act; (*o słońcu*) beat down. **3.** + *Ins.* (= *posługiwać się*) use, manipulate. **4.** + *Ins. ekon.* circulate, trade in. **5.** *wojsk.* operate, carry out military operations; **operować w rejonie umocnień nieprzyjaciela** operate near enemy positions.

operowy *a.* opera; operatic; **głos operowy** firm voice.

opędzać *ipf.*, **opędzić** *pf.* **1.** (= *odganiać*) drive away. **2.** (*pot.* = *z trudem zaspokajać* *l.* *oddalać od siebie*) appease, relieve; **opędzić głód** appease hunger. ~ **się** *ipf.*, **opędzić się** *pf.* **opędzić się od kogoś/czegoś** (= *bronić się, odganiać*) drive *l.* chase sb/sth away; (= *uwolnić się od niepożądanych osób* *l.* *rzeczy*) get rid of sb/sth; **nie mogę opędzić się od wielbicieli** I can't get rid of my fans.

opędzlować *pf.* **1.** (*pot.* = *dużo zjeść*) eat up, finish off. **2.** (*sl.* = *sprzedać*) unload.

opętać *pf. zob.* **opętywać**.

opętana *f. Gen.* **-ej** *rzad.* **1.** lunatic, crazy woman. **2.** (*przez diabła*) possessed woman.

opętaniec *mp* **-ńc-** *Voc.* **-ńcze** *pl.* **-y** maniac, fan.

opętany *a.* wild, crazy, frantic. – *mp rzad.* **1.** lunatic, madman; **latać jak opętany** *pot.* run around like crazy *l.* like a chicken with its head cut off. **2.** (*przez diabła*) possessed man.

opętańczy *a.* wild, crazy, frenzied.

opętywać *ipf.*, **opętać** *pf.* (= *owładnąć*) obsess, captivate, come over (*sb*); (*o diable, demonie*) possess.

opiat *mi* opiate.

opiąć *pf.* **opnę opniesz, opnij, opiął opięła opięli** *zob.* **opinać**. ~ **się** *pf. zob.* **opinać się**.

opić *pf.* **-ję -jesz** *zob.* **opijać**. ~ **się** *pf. zob.* **opijać się**.

opiec *pf.* **opiekę opieczesz, opiecz, opiekł** *zob.* **opiekać**. ~ **się** *pf. zob.* **opiekać się**.

opieczętować *pf.* seal, stamp.

opieka *f.* **1.** (= *troska, troskliwa dbałość*) care, protection; **opieka lekarska** medical care *l.* assistance; **opieka rodzicielska** parental care; **powierzam go twojej opiece** I entrust him to your care; **powierzam ci pod opiekę mojego kota** I put my cat in your care; **jest pod opieką babci** he is in his grandmother's care; **opieka społeczna** social welfare; **opieka zdrowotna** health care. **2.** (*dozór*) care, charge. **3.** *prawn.* (*nadzór*) custody, guardianship; **opieka prawna** legal custody; **opieka rodzicielska** parental custody.

opiekacz *mi Gen.* **-a** toaster.

opiekać *ipf.* (*w piekarniku*) roast; (*na wolnym ogniu*) broil, grill; (*na grillu*) barbecue; (*na patelni*) fry. ~ **się** *ipf.* roast; broil; be barbecued *l.* barbecuing.

opiekany *a.* (*w piekarniku*) roasted; (*na wolnym ogniu*) broiled, grilled; (*na grillu*) barbecued; (*na patelni*) fried.

opiekować się *ipf.* take care (*czymś l. kimś* of sth *l.* sb); look after (*czymś l. kimś* sth *l.* sb).

opiekun *mp pl.* **-owie**, **opiekunka** *f. Gen.pl.* **-ek** carer; **opiekun prawny** guardian; **opiekun społeczny** social worker; **opiekunka do dzieci** babysitter.

opiekuńczy *a.* caring, protective; **władza opiekuńcza** *prawn.* guardianship authority; **państwo opiekuńcze** welfare state.

opielać *ipf. ogr.* weed.

opieńka *f. Gen.pl.* **-ek** *biol.* **opieńka miodowa** honey mushroom (*Armillaria mellea*).

opieprzać *ipf.* **1.** (= *posypywać pieprzem*) pepper. **2.** (*pot.* = *wymyślać komuś*) jump on (*sb*). ~ **się** *ipf. pot.* (= *lenić się*) fart around.

opieprzyć *pf. zob.* **opieprzać**.

opierać¹ *ipf.* **1.** (= *wspierać coś na czymś*) prop, lean (*o coś* against sth); rest, put (*na czymś* on sth). **2.** (= *brać za podstawę*) base; **oprzeć wnioski na wynikach badań** base one's conclusions on research results; **film oparty na powieści** movie based on a novel.

opierać² *ipf.* **opierać kogoś** (= *prać czyjąś odzież*) wash sb's clothes. ~ **się** *ipf.* **1.** (= *wspierać się*) prop, lean (*o coś* against sth). **2.** (= *brać za podstawę*) base (*na czymś* on *l.* upon sth); **opierać się na wynikach badań** base on research results; **sprawa oparta się o prokuratora** case was referred to a prosecutor. **3.** (= *liczyć na pomoc, polegać*) rely (*na kimś/czymś* on sb/sth); **wiem, że mogę się na nim oprzeć** I know that I can rely on him. **4.** (= *stawiać opór*) resist; **opierać się pokusom** resist temptations; **nie mogę oprzeć się wrażeniu, że już panią widziałem** I can't resist the impression that I've seen you before *l.* that we've already met. **5.** *tylko ipf.* (= *spoczywać na podporach*) be supported, rest; **most opiera się na filarach** bridge is supported by pillars.

opierdalać *ipf. wulg.* (= *wymyślać komuś*) chew out (*sb's*) ass. ~ **się** *ipf. wulg.* (= *lenić się, zwlekać*) fuck around, screw off.

opierdol *mi wulg.* a fucking chewing out, the fucking third degree.

opierdolić *pf. zob.* **opierdalać**.

opierdzielać *ipf.*, **opierdzielić** *pf. pot.* (= *wymyślać komuś*) chew out, harsh out on, give hell.

opierniczać *ipf.*, **opierniczyć** *pf. pot.* (= *wymyślać komuś*) chew out.

opierunek *mi* -nk- *żart.* washing, wash; **wikt i opierunek** *żart.* full board and washing.

opierzać się *ipf.*, **opierzyć się** *pf. orn.* fledge, grow feathers.

opierzony *a.* -eni fledged.

opierzyć się *pf. zob.* **opierzać się**.

opieszale *adv.* tardily, sluggishly.

opieszałość *f.* tardiness, sluggishness.

opieszały *a.* tardy, sluggish.

opiewać *ipf.* **1.** (*lit.* = *sławić*) exalt, extol. **2.** (*o rachunku*) (= *wynosić, równać się*) amount to; **rachunek opiewa na 250 złotych** the bill amounts to 250 zlotys.

opięty *a.* tight, skintight.

opijać *ipf.* (= *pić alkohol, by uczcić coś*) drink to, celebrate (with drink); **dziś opijamy mój nowy dom** today we're drinking to my new house. ~ **się** *ipf.* (= *pić do woli l. zbyt wiele*) drink to excess; (= *upijać się*) get drunk.

opilczy *a.* **obłęd opilczy** *pat.* delirium tremens.

opilstwo *n.* alcohol addiction; drunkenness, intoxication; **opilstwo okresowe** *pat.* dipsomania.

opiłek *mi* -łk- *Gen.* -a shaving; **opiłki metalu** metal filings.

opinać *ipf.* cling *l.* cleave to (*sth*). ~ **się** *ipf.* be (skin-)tight.

opinia *f. Gen.* -ii **1.** (= *pogląd, sąd*) opinion, view; **przychylna opinia** positive opinion; **sprzeczne opinie** dissenting *l.* conflicting opinions *l.* views; **podzielam twoją opinię** I agree with you, I share your views; **polegam na twojej opinii** I trust your judgement; **zyskałeś w mojej opinii** now I have a high opinion of you; **według opinii specjalistów nie możemy zaciągnąć kolejnego kredytu** according to experts we cannot take out another loan; **opinia publiczna** public opinion. **2.** (= *reputacja*) reputation, opinion; **tą historią z kradzionym samochodem zepsuł sobie opinię** this story about the stolen car earned him a bad name *l.* ruined his reputation; **doktor Kowalski cieszy się opinią doskonałego chirurga** doctor Kowalski enjoys a fine reputation as a surgeon; **ktoś stara się zszargać mi opinię** sb is trying to tarnish my reputation. **3.** (= *ocena przełożonego*) opinion, assessment, reference; **wydać komuś opinię** provide sb with a (letter of) reference; **załączyć opinię z poprzedniego miejsca pracy** enclose references from the previous employer; **opinia biegłego rewidenta** *handl., prawn.* auditor's report.

opiniodawca *mp* expert, adviser *l.* advisor; (= *wystawiający opinię o pracowniku*) referee, reference.

opiniodawczy *a.* consultative; **komisja opiniodawcza** consultative committee.

opiniotwórczy *a.* opinion-forming.

opiniować *ipf.* express an opinion (*coś* on sth); pass a judgement (*coś* on sth).

opis *mi* description; (= *opowieść, relacja*) account; **opis techniczny** specification; **opis bibliograficzny** bibliographic description; **opis patentowy** (patent) specification; **opis techniczny projektu** design specifications.

opisać *ipf.* -szę -szesz *zob.* **opisywać**.

opisanie *n.* description; **nie do opisania** beyond words; **zamieszanie nie do opisania** indescribable confusion.

opisowo *adv.* descriptively.

opisowy *a.* descriptive; **ocena opisowa** *szkoln.* descriptive grade; **gramatyka opisowa** *jęz.* descriptive grammar; **stopniowanie opisowe** *gram.* periphrastic comparison; **anatomia opisowa** *med.* descriptive anatomy.

opisywać *ipf.* **1.** (= *dokładnie przedstawiać słowami*) describe, delineate; characterize; **wielokąt opisany** *geom.* circumscribed polygon; **koło opisane** *geom.* circumscribed circle; **tej tragedii nie da się opisać słowami** this tragedy is indescribable *l.* defies description; **tego nie da się opisać** it defies description. **2.** *prawn.* inventory.

opity *mp pot.* (= *pijany*) drunk.

opium *n. indecl.* opium.

opiumowany *a.* opiate.

opiumowy *a.* opium.

oplatać *ipf.* **1.** (= *obwiązywać*) tie, bind. **2.** (= *obejmować*) hug, embrace. **3.** (= *okręcać się wokół czegoś*) twist around, wind *l.* coil around (*sth*). ~ **się** *ipf.* twist around o.s.; (*o roślinach*) entwine; **oplatać się ramionami** wrap sb's arms around each other.

oplątać *pf.* **oplączę oplączesz** *ipf.* **1.** (= *owijać*) entwine. **2.** (*przen.* = *osaczać*) ensnare, entrap; **oplątany siecią intryg** ensnared by intrigues.

opleć *pf.* **opielę opielesz opełł opełli** *zob.* **opielać**.

opleść *pf.* -otę -eciesz -ótł -otła -etli *zob.* **oplatać**. ~ **się** *pf. zob.* **oplatać się**.

oplombować *pf.* seal.

oplot *mi techn.* (*kabla*) braid, plait.

opluć *pf. zob.* **opluwać**. ~ **się** *pf. zob.* **opluwać się**.

opluskać *pf.* -skam *l.* -szczę -skasz *l.* -szczesz, **opluskiwać** *ipf.* splash; **opluskać sobie twarz** splash some water on one's face. ~ **się** *pf.*, **opluskiwać się** *ipf.* splash o.s. (*czymś* with sth).

opluwać *ipf.* **1.** (*śliną*) spit on *l.* at (*sb/sth*). **2.** (*przen.* = *oczerniać*) sling *l.* throw mud at (*sb/sth*). ~ **się** *ipf.* **1.** slaver *l.* slobber o.s. **2.** *przen.* sling *l.* throw mud at each other.

opłacać *ipf.* (= *uiszczać należność*) *przen.* (= *ponosić konsekwencje*) pay (*za coś czymś* for sth with sth); **opłacić chwilę zapomnienia śmiertelną chorobą** pay for a moment of indulgence with a fatal disease. ~ **się** *ipf.* **1.** (= *przynosić zysk*) pay; **nie opłaca się tego robić** it's not worth doing; **to się nie opłaca** it's not worth the trouble;

opłaciło się! it was worth my while! **2.** (= *prze-kupywać kogoś*) pay off; **opłacać się mafii** pay the mafia off.

opłacalność *f.* profitability.

opłacalny *a.* profitable.

opłacić *pf. zob.* **opłacać.** ~ **się** *pf. zob.* **opłacać się.**

opłakany *a.* lamentable, pitiful, deplorable; **opłakany stan** pitiful state.

opłakiwać *ipf.* lament, bemoan, mourn.

opłata *f.* **1.** (*kwota*) payment, charge, fee; (*za naukę*) tuition; (*za przejazd*) fare; **opłata celna** customs duty; **opłata drogowa** toll; **opłata pocztowa** postage; **opłata sądowa** court fee; **opłata skarbowa** stamp duty; **za niewielką opłatą** for a small fee. **2.** (= *uiszczanie należności*) payment; **zalegać z opłatą** be in arrears.

opłatek *mi* -tk- *Gen.* -a wafer; **dzielić się opłatkiem** share the wafer; **blady jak opłatek** as pale as death.

opłotki *pl. Gen.* -ów **1.** hurdles, fencing. **2.** *przest.* village lane (*usu. between fences*).

opłucna *f. Gen.* -ej *anat.* pleura.

opłucnowy *a. pat.* pleural; **odma opłucnowa** pneumothorax.

opłukać *pf.* -czę -czesz -kał, **opłukiwać** *ipf.* rinse, wash. ~ **się** *pf.*, **opłukiwać się** *ipf.* wash o.s.

opłynąć *pf. zob.* **opływać.**

opływ *mi fiz., lotn.* flow round *l.* past.

opływać *ipf.* -am -asz **1.** (= *okrążać, płynąc*) sail around, circumnavigate; swim around. **2.** *tylko ipf.* (= *obfitować*) flow with; **opływać w dostatki** live off the fat of the land, live in clover, live in the lap of luxury.

opływowy *a.* streamlined.

opodal *adv.* nearby; **opodal przepływała rzeka** river flew nearby. – *prep.* + *Gen.* near; **nie opodal = nieopodal.**

opodatkować *pf. zob.* **opodatkowywać.** ~ **się** *pf. zob.* **opodatkowywać się.**

opodatkowany *a.* taxed, taxable; **opodatkowane przychody** taxable income.

opodatkowywać *ipf.* tax, impose *l.* levy a tax (*coś* on sth). ~ **się** *ipf.* subscribe (*na rzecz czegoś* to sth).

opoka *f.* **1.** *min.* (bed)rock. **2.** (*przen.* = *podwalina, podstawa*) foundation, bedrock.

opole *n. Gen.pl.* -i *hist.* union of settlements.

opona *f.* (*np. samochodowa*) tire; *Br.* tyre; **opona bezdętkowa** tubeless tire; **opona zimowa** snow tire; **opony mózgowo-rdzeniowe** *anat.* cerebro-spinal meninges; **zapalenie opon mózgowych** *pat.* meningitis.

oponent *mp*, **oponentka** *f. Gen.pl.* -ek opponent, adversary.

oponować *ipf.* oppose; object.

oponowy *a.* **1.** tire; *Br.* tyre; **przemysł oponowy** tire-making industry. **2.** *pat.* **objawy oponowe** meningeal symptoms.

opończa *f. Gen.pl.* -y *hist.* cloak.

opornie *adv.* with difficulty, slowly; **nauka mu idzie opornie** he's making slow progress in his studies.

opornik *mi Gen.* -a **1.** *el.* resistor. **2.** *wojsk.* buffer, recoil brake.

oporność *f.* **1.** (= *nieustępliwość*) restiveness, balkiness, stubbornness. **2.** (= *niewrażliwość*) (*t. med. o drobnoustrojach*) resistance (*na coś* to sth); **oporność na wysoką temperaturę** resistance to high temperature; **oporność na mróz** resistance to frost. **3.** *el.* (electric) resistance.

oporny *a.* **1.** (= *nieustępliwy*) restive, balky, stubborn. **2.** (= *niepoddający się działaniu siły*) resisting, unyielding. **3.** **oporny na krytykę/argumenty** (= *niewrażliwy*) impervious to criticism/arguments. – *mp* (= *oporny człowiek*) **oporni** the disobedient.

oporować *ipf. narciarstwo* snowplow; *Br.* snowplough, use a braking wedge.

oporowy *a. techn.* resisting, resistance; **mur oporowy** revetment; **łuk oporowy** flying buttress; **stop oporowy** resistor alloy; **termometr oporowy** resistance thermometer; **technika oporowa** *narciarstwo* braking wedge.

oportunista *mp* opportunist.

oportunistyczny *a.* opportunistic.

oportunizm *mi* opportunism.

oporządzać *ipf.* **1.** *roln.* groom, tend. **2.** *kulin.* (*zwierzynę*) dress; (*rybę*) clean.

oporządzenie *n. wojsk.* equipment, gear.

oporządzić *pf. zob.* **oporządzać.**

opos *ma zool.* opossum (*Didelphys*).

oposowy *a.* opossum; **futro oposowe** opossum fur coat.

oposy *pl. Gen.* -ów (*futro*) opossum fur coat.

opowiadać *ipf.* tell, relate, describe; **długo by opowiadać** it's a long story; **opowiadać bzdury** talk nonsense *l.* rubbish; **opowiadać dziecku bajkę** tell a child a story; **opowiadać bajki** *przen.* fable; **opowiadać dowcipy** tell jokes. ~ **się** *ipf.* **1.** (= *popierać*) support (*za l. przy kimś / czymś* sb/sth); opt (*za l. przy kimś / czymś* for sb/sth); subscribe (*za l. przy kimś / czymś* to sb/sth). **2.** (*informować*) inform, tell; **dlaczego nie opowiedziałeś się, dokąd wychodzisz?** why didn't you tell us where you were going?

opowiadanie *n.* story, tale, narrative; *teor.lit.* short story.

opowiastka *f. Gen.pl.* -ek tale, story.

opowiedzieć *pf.* -wiem -wiesz -wiedzą, -wiedz *zob.* **opowiadać.** ~ **się** *pf. zob.* **opowiadać się.**

opowieść *f.* tale, story.

opozycja *f.* **1.** (= *przeciwstawianie się*) opposition, resistance; **czy jesteś w opozycji do socjaldemokratów?** do you oppose the Social Democrats? **2.** *polit.* (*partia, partie*) opposition; **opozycja parlamentarna** parliamentary opposition, the opposition. **3.** *astron.* opposition. **4.** *jęz.* opposition.

opozycjonista *mp polit.* oppositionist; member of the opposition.

opozycyjnie *adv. rzad.* in opposition, oppositely.

opozycyjny *a.* **1.** opposing, resisting. **2.** opposition; **partia** *l.* **ugrupowanie** *l.* **stronnictwo opozycyjna/-e** opposition party. **3.** **formy opozycyj-**

ne *jęz.* alternative units, opposing forms; *fon.* minimal pairs.

opój *mp* **-o-** *Gen.pl.* **-ów** *pog.* soak, lush, sot.

opór *mi* **-o-** **1.** (= *przeciwstawianie się*) resistance, opposition; (*czynny, zacięty*) defiance; **stawiać komuś/czemuś opór** resist *l.* oppose sb/sth, offer resistance to sb/sth; **bierny opór** passive resistance; **ruch oporu** resistance movement; (*w czasie drugiej wojny światowej we Francji*) the Resistance. **2.** (*wahanie, niechęć*) reservation; **mam opory w stosunku do tego projektu** I have my reservations about this project; **mieć opory przed zrobieniem czegoś** be reluctant to do sth; **iść po linii najmniejszego oporu** take *l.* follow the line *l.* path of least resistance, take the easy way out. **3.** *fiz.* resistance; **opór ośrodka** resistance of the medium; **opór aerodynamiczny** drag; **opór elektryczny** electric resistance. **4.** *narciarstwo* braking wedge.

opóźniacz *mi Gen.* **-a** *wojsk.* delayer, delay pellet.

opóźniać *ipf.*, **opóźnić** *pf.* **-ij** delay, postpone, put off; (*postęp, rozwój*) retard. **~ się** *ipf.*, **opóźnić się** *pf.* **-ij** be late, be delayed; be behind time, lag behind; **zegarek mi się opóźnia** my watch is slow.

opóźnienie *n.* delay; **nasz pociąg ma opóźnienie** our train is delayed.

opóźniony *a.* **-eni** (*pociąg*) delayed; late; **opóźniony w rozwoju** retarded; *euf.* slow.

opracować *pf. zob.* **opracowywać**.

opracowanie *n.* **1.** (= *przygotowanie*) preparation. **2.** (= *rozprawa*) (*naukowe*) study; (= *zarys*) survey; (= *analiza*) analysis.

opracowywać *ipf.* (= *przygotowywać*) prepare; (*plan*) work out; (*książkę, podręcznik*) compile; (*pozew, list*) draw up.

oprać *pf.* **opiorę opierzesz oprał** *zob.* **opierać**.

oprawa *f.* **1.** (*książki*) binding. **2.** (= *obramowanie*) frame; **metalowa oprawa** metal frame; **oprawa muzyczna** musical setting; **oprawa oczu** eyebrows and (eye)lashes. **3.** (= *oprawianie książki*) (book)binding; (= *oprawianie w ramę*) framing. **4.** (*upolowanego zwierzęcia*) dressing; (= *zdjęcie skóry*) skinning.

oprawca *mp* (= *ten, kto torturuje*) torturer; (= *morderca*) murderer.

oprawiać *ipf.*, **oprawić** *pf.* **1.** (*książkę*) bind. **2.** (*w obramowanie*) frame. **3.** (*upolowane zwierzę*) dress; (= *zdjąć skórę*) skin.

oprawka *f. Gen.pl.* **-ek** frame, rim; (*okularów*) frames; (*żarówki*) socket.

oprawny *a.* (*o książkach*) bound; (= *osadzony w ramy*) framed, set; **oprawny w złoto** set with *l.* in gold.

opresja *f.* trouble, plight; **znaleźć się w opresji** be in trouble, be left in a sorry plight; **wyjść cało *l.* obronną ręką z opresji** get through sth in one piece, make it through.

oprocentować *pf. zob.* **oprocentowywać**.

oprocentowanie *n. zwł. ekon.* interest, interest rate; **niskie oprocentowanie** low rate of interest; **oprocentowanie w skali roku *l.* w stosunku rocznym** annual interest rate, annual *l.* annual-

ized percentage rate, APR; **stopa oprocentowania wynosi 7%** the interest rate is 7%.

oprocentowywać *ipf. zwł. ekon.* calculate percentage; calculate interest.

oprofilować *pf. zob.* **oprofilowywać**.

oprofilowanie *n.* **1.** molding, forming. **2.** *bud.* mold(ing).

oprofilowywać *ipf.* **1.** *bud.* mold. **2.** *techn.* mold, form.

oprogramowanie *n. komp.* software.

opromieniony *a.* radiant; **opromieniony szczęściem** radiant *l.* bright with joy.

oprowadzać *ipf.*, **oprowadzić** *pf.* show (*sb*) around, give (*sb*) a tour.

oprócz *prep.* + *Gen.* **1.** (= *obok, poza*) aside from, besides, apart from; **oprócz palm rosły tam także cyprysy** aside from palm trees, cypresses grew there as well; **oprócz tego** (= *dodatkowo, ponadto*) aside from that. **2.** (= *z wyjątkiem*) except; (*po przeczeniach*) besides, but; **oprócz matki nie miał żadnej rodziny** he didn't have any relatives besides *l.* aside from his mother; **oprócz niego nikogo więcej tam nie było** there was nobody else there except *l.* besides him; **nic jeszcze nie piłem oprócz porannej kawy** I haven't had anything but my morning coffee so far; **pokazano im wszystkie pokoje oprócz sypialni** they were shown all the rooms except *l.* save the bedroom; **wszyscy się śmiali oprócz Ewy** everybody laughed, except *l.* save Eve.

oprószać *ipf.*, **oprószyć** *pf.* dust, sprinkle.

opróżniać *ipf.*, **opróżnić** *pf.* **-ij** (*butelkę, kieszenie, szufladę*) empty; (*wagon, ciężarówkę itp.*) unload; (*mieszkanie*) vacate. **~ się** *ipf.*, **opróżnić się** *pf.* **-ij** empty, become empty.

oprych *mp pl.* **-y** *pog.* thug, ruffian.

opryskać *pf. zob.* **opryskiwać**. **~ się** *pf. zob.* **opryskiwać się**.

opryskiwacz *mi Gen.* **-a** *ogr.* sprinkler; *roln.* sprayer.

opryskiwać *ipf.* **1.** (= *skrapiać*) sprinkle, splash, spatter. **2.** *ogr., leśn.* spray. **~ się** *ipf.* **1.** (= *skrapiać siebie*) sprinkle o.s. **2.** (= *skrapiać jeden drugiego*) sprinkle each other.

opryskliwie *adv.* surlily, grumpily.

opryskliwość *f.* surliness, grumpiness.

opryskliwy *a.* surly, grumpy, crabby; **opryskliwy człowiek** (a) grump, (a) crab, (a) grumpuss; **opryskliwa odpowiedź** curt reply.

opryszczka *f. Gen.pl.* **-ek** *pat.* herpes.

opryszek *mp* **-szk-** *pl.* **-i *l.* -owie** thug, ruffian.

oprzeć *pf.* **oprę oprzesz, oprzyj, oparł oparli** *zob.* **opierać**. **~ się** *pf. zob.* **opierać się**.

oprzęd *mi ent.* cocoon.

oprzyrządowanie *n. techn.* instruments, tools.

oprzytomnieć *pf.* regain consciousness, come round *l.* to; *t. przen.* wake.

opsoniny *pl. Gen.* **-n** *med.* opsonines.

opsyny *pl. Gen.* **-n** *med.* opsines.

optant *mp prawn.* person opting.

optatiwus *mi Gen.* **-wu** *jęz.* optative.

optimum *n. sing. indecl. pl.* **-ima** *Gen.* **-imów** optimum.

optoelektronika *f. techn.* optoelectronics.

optować *ipf.* opt (*za czymś* for sth).

optyczny *a.* optical; **dysk optyczny** optical disk; **przyrządy optyczne** optical instruments; **złudzenie optyczne** optical illusion.

optyk *mp* **1.** (*fizyk*) opticist. **2.** (*rzemieślnik*) optician.

optyka *f.* **1.** *fiz.* optics; **optyka elektronowa** electron optics; **optyka fizyczna** physical optics; **optyka geometryczna** geometrical optics; **optyka kryształów** crystal optics. **2.** *pot.* (= *punkt widzenia*) perspective, view.

optymalizacja *f.* optimization; **optymalizacja wydatków** expenditure optimization.

optymalizator *mi Gen.* -a *techn., komp.* optimizer.

optymalizować *ipf.* optimize.

optymalnie *adv.* optimally.

optymalny *a.* optimal, optimum.

optymista *mp*, **optymistka** *f. Gen.pl.* -ek optimist.

optymistycznie *adv.* optimistically.

optymistyczny *a.* optimistic, hopeful.

optymizm *mi* **1.** (*postawa życiowa*) optimism; **być pełnym optymizmu** be full of optimism. **2.** *fil.* optimism.

opublikować *pf.* (= *wydać*) publish; (= *podać do wiadomości*) announce.

opuchlizna *f.* swelling, turgidity.

opuchły *a.* swollen, turgid.

opuchnąć *pf.* -ij, -ł *l.* -nął -ła -li swell.

opuchnięty *a.* swollen.

opukać *pf.*, **opukiwać** *ipf.* percuss, sound, tap.

opukiwanie *n. med.* percussion.

opukowo *adv. med.* by percussion; **badać opukowo** examine by percussion.

opukowy *a. med.* percussion, percussive; **opukowe badanie** percussion *l.* percussive examination; **opukowy odgłos** percussion sound.

opuncja *f. bot.* prickly pear, cholla (*Opuntia*).

opus *n. decl. like mi muz.* opus.

opust *mi handl.* discount, price reduction, rebate.

opustoszały *a.* (= *opuszczony*) deserted, desolate; (= *pusty*) empty.

opustoszeć *pf.* become deserted; empty.

opuszczać *ipf.* **1.** (= *spuszczać, zniżać coś*) lower; **opuszczać głowę** lower sb's head; **opuszczać oczy** *l.* lower sb's eyes; **opuszczać szybę w samochodzie** roll *l.* wind a window down; **opuścić ręce** *przen.* give up, break down; **opuścić nos na kwintę** lose heart. **2.** (= *obniżać cenę*) lower, reduce; **opuścić 5 złotych na kilogramie** lower *l.* reduce the price by 5 zlotys per kilo. **3.** (= *porzucać kogoś, coś*) leave, abandon, desert; **nie opuszczać łóżka** be bedridden *l.* laid up; **opuścić szkołę** (= *ukończyć naukę*) leave school, graduate; (= *przerwać naukę*) not complete education, drop out of school; **opuścić świat** depart this life, breathe one's last; **szczęście mnie opuszcza** my luck is running out; **odwaga mnie opuściła** my courage failed *l.* abandoned *l.* deserted me; **siły go opuściły** he lost his strength, his strength gave up (on him); **nie opuszczać kogoś** stand by sb. **4.** (= *odjeżdżać, od-*

chodzić) leave. **5.** (= *pomijać coś, nie uczestniczyć w czymś regularnie*) skip, leave out; **opuszczać lekcje** cut *l.* miss *l.* skip *l.* blow off class, play truant *l.* hooky; **opuszczać strony** skip pages; **opuszczać przypisy** skip the footnotes. ~ **się** *ipf.* **1.** (= *kierować się w dół*) (*np. o chmurach*) lower; (= *zjeżdżać*) go down. **2.** (= *tracić samodyscyplinę*) slacken, neglect sth, grow remiss; **opuszczać się w nauce** neglect one's studies, lower one's standards, slack off.

opuszczenie *n.* **1.** (= *zniżenie*) lowering. **2.** (= *wyjazd; odejście*) leaving, abandoning. **3.** (*cen*) reduction. **4.** (= *osamotnienie*) solitude. **5.** (= *zaniedbanie*) neglect. **6.** (= *pominięty fragment*) omission.

opuszczony *a.* -eni **1.** (= *zniżony*) lowered. **2.** (= *pozostawiony*) abandoned. **3.** (*o cenach*) reduced. **4.** (= *osamotniony*) lonely, forlorn, desolate; deserted. **5.** (= *zaniedbany*) neglected, derelict. **6.** (= *niechlujny*) untidy, neglected, slovenly.

opuszka *f. Gen.pl.* -ek **1.** (*palca*) fingertip. **2.** *anat.* (digital) pulp.

opuścić *pf. zob.* **opuszczać**. ~ **się** *pf. zob.* **opuszczać się**.

opychać się *ipf. pot.* (= *zjeść zbyt dużo*) stuff o.s., pig out, pork out.

opylacz *mi Gen.* -a *roln.* duster.

opylać *ipf.*, **opylić** *pf.* **1.** *leśn., roln., ogr.* dust. **2.** *sl.* (= *sprzedać*) move, push, drum.

oracja *f.* **1.** *lit.* (= *przemówienie*) oration. **2.** *rz.-kat.* (*modlitwa*) solemn prayer.

oracz *mp* plowman, *Br.* ploughman.

orać *ipf.* **1.** *roln.* plow; **każdy orze, jak może** you do what you can. **2.** *pot.* (= *harować*) sweat.

oralny *a.* oral; **tradycja oralna** oral tradition; **seks oralny** oral sex.

orangutan *ma zool.* orangutan, orangutang, orangoutang (*Pongo pygmaeus*).

oranż *mi* orange color; **oranż metylowy** *chem.* methyl orange.

oranżada *f. kulin.* orangeade.

oranżeria *f. Gen.* -ii orangery.

oranżeryjny *a.* orangery, greenhouse, hothouse; **rośliny oranżeryjne** greenhouse *l.* hothouse plants.

oranżysta *mp polit.* Orangeman.

orator *mp lit.* orator.

oratorium *n. sing. indecl. pl.* -ria *Gen.* -riów *muz.* **1.** oratorio. **2.** *rel.* oratory.

oratorski *a.* oratorical; **po oratorsku** oratorically.

oratorstwo *n.* oratory, eloquence.

oratoryjny *a. muz.* oratorio; **muzyka oratoryjna** oratorio music; **kompozycja** *l.* **utwór oratoryjny** oratorio.

oraz *conj.* and, as well as, not to mention.

orbita *f.* **1.** *astron.* orbit; **orbita okołosłoneczna** circumsolar orbit; **umieścić na orbicie** launch *l.* put into orbit. **2.** *anat.* orbit, eye socket; **oczy mu wychodzą z orbit** his eyes are popping out of his head.

orbitalny *a. astron.* orbital.

orbitować *ipf.* **1.** (*o pojeździe kosmicznym*) orbit. **2.** (*o astronaucie*) walk in space.

orchidea *f. Gen.* **-ei** *pl.* **-ee** *bot.* orchid (*Orchis*).

orczyk *mi Gen.* **-a 1.** *lotn.* rudder bar. **2.** *roln.* whiffletree, whippletree, singletree. **3.** *sport* trapeze. **4.** (*wyciąg narciarski*) ski tow.

orczykowy *a.* **koń orczykowy** leader; **wyciąg orczykowy** ski tow.

orda *f. hist.* **1.** (*plemiona*) horde. **2.** (*obóz*) Tartar military camp. **3.** (*armia*) Tartar army, horde.

ordalium *n. sing. indecl. pl.* **-lia** *Gen.* **-liów** *hist.* ordeal.

order *mi* decoration, medal; **zasłużyłeś sobie na order** *przen.* you deserve praise *l.* recognition *l.* a medal.

ordowik *mi geol.* the Ordovician, the Ordovician Period.

ordynacja *f.* **1.** *prawn.* (= *przepisy*) regulations; **ordynacja wyborcza** electoral regulations *l.* law. **2.** *hist.* (*majątek ziemski*) estate, manor.

ordynans *mp arch., wojsk.* orderly.

ordynaria *f. Gen.* **-ii** *hist.* allowance in kind.

ordynariat *mi kośc.* office of an ordinary, bishopric.

ordynariusz *mp kośc.* (*biskup*) ordinary.

ordynarnie *adv.* **1.** (= *grubiańsko*) vulgarly; rudely. **2.** (= *pospolicie*) simply; cheaply.

ordynarność *f.* **1.** (= *grubiaństwo*) vulgarness; rudeness. **2.** (= *prostactwo*) simpleness; cheapness.

ordynarny *a.* **1.** (= *grubiański*) vulgar; rude; crude; **ordynarny sposób bycia** rude behavior; **ordynarne słowa** vulgar language; **ordynarne kłamstwo** outright lie. **2.** (= *prostacki*) simple, ordinary; cheap; **ordynarne jedzenie** simple food; **ordynarny tytoń** cheap tobacco.

ordynat *mp hist.* lord, landowner.

ordynator *mp med.* head of a hospital department *l.* ward.

ordynować *ipf. zwł. med.* (= *być ordynatorem*) act as a head of a hospital department *l.* ward; (= *leczyć*) see patients, treat patients; (= *przepisywać leki, kurację*) prescribe medications *l.* treatment.

ordynus *mp pog. pl.* **-y** boor, lout, oaf.

Orestes *mp mit.* Orestes.

orędować *ipf. przest.* plead, advocate.

orędownictwo *n. przest.* pleading, advocacy.

orędowniczka *f. Gen.pl.* **-ek, orędownik** *mp lit.* advocate, supporter, champion.

orędzie *n. Gen.pl.* **-i** *zwł. polit.* address; **orędzie o stanie państwa** *US* State of the Union Address.

oręż *mi Gen.* **-a 1.** *lit.* (*broń*) arms, weapon; *przen.* weapon, measure; **wytrącić komuś oręż z ręki** disarm sb, render sb helpless *l.* defenseless. **2.** *lit.* (= *siły zbrojne*) army. **3.** *myśl.* antlers.

orężny *a. lit.* armed.

Orfeusz *mp mit.* Orpheus.

orficki *a. hist.* Orphic.

orfik *mp hist.* Orphist.

orfizm *mi* **1.** *hist.* Orphism. **2.** *sztuka* orphism, orphic cubism.

organ *mi* **1.** *anat.* organ; **organ chwytny** pre-

hensile organ; **organ szczątkowy** vestigial *l.* rudimentary organ; **organ wegetatywny** vegetative organ; **organ słuchu** hearing organ; **organ mowy** organ of speech; **organ wzroku** organ of vision *l.* sight. **2.** *pl.* **-y** *l.* **-a** (*jednostka administracji*) organ, authority; **organ administracyjny** organ of administration; **organ sądowy** court of law; **organ ścigania** law enforcement authority. **3.** (*czasopismo, dziennik*) organ.

organdyna *f. tk.* organdy, *Br.* organdie.

organelle *pl. Gen.* **-i** *biol.* organelles, cell organs; **organelle komórkowe** cell organelles, plastids.

organicyzm *mi fil., socjol.* organicism.

organicznie *adv.* **1.** organically; **organicznie nie cierpieć kogoś** feel an innate *l.* inborn aversion to sb. **2.** organically, inherently; **coś organicznie powiązane z czymś** sth inherently linked with sth.

organiczny *a.* **1.** (*właściwy roślinom i zwierzętom*) organic; **choroba organiczna** *pat.* organic disease; **chemia organiczna** organic chemistry; **kwas organiczny** *chem.* organic acid; **nawóz organiczny** *chem., roln.* organic fertilizer; **związek organiczny** *chem.* organic compound; **praca organiczna** *hist.* Organic Work (*social and economic development approach in 19th century Poland*). **2.** (= *nierozerwalny*) organic, inherent; **organiczna całość** organic whole.

organista *mp muz.* organist.

organizacja *f.* **1.** (*zrzeszenie*) organization. **2.** (*sposób przeprowadzania czegoś*) organization; system.

organizacyjnie *adv.* organizationally.

organizacyjny *a.* organization, organizational; organizing; **komitet organizacyjny** organizing committee.

organizator *mp,* **organizatorka** *f. Gen.pl.* **-ek** organizer.

organizatorski *a.* organizing.

organizm *mi biol.* **1.** organism; **organizm żywy** living organism; **organizm roślinny** plant; **organizm zwierzęcy** animal; **mieć silny organizm** have a strong constitution; **to był wstrząs dla jego organizmu** it was a shock to his system. **2.** *przen.* organism, system; **organizm państwowy** state; **organizm polityczny** political system.

organizować *ipf.* **1.** (*bal, wycieczkę itp.*) organize; (*komitet, spółkę itp.*) set up, establish; (*spotkanie*) arrange. **2.** (= *uporządkować, wprowadzić ład*) arrange. **3.** *pot.* (= *zdobywać coś na pół legalnie*) fix up. **~ się** *ipf.* **1.** (= *zrzeszać się*) organize. **2.** (= *być zakładanym*) be set up, be established.

organki *pl. Gen.* **-ów** *muz.* harmonica, mouth organ; *pot.* harp.

organogeneza *f. zool.* organogenesis.

organogeniczny *a. geol.* organogenous; **skały organogeniczne** organogenous rocks.

organoleptyczny *a.* organoleptic.

organoleptyka *f.* organoleptics.

organopreparat *mi med.* preparation made from organs.

organoterapia *f. Gen.* **-ii** *med.* organotherapy.

organowy *a. muz.* organ; **muzyka organowa** organ music; **piszczałka organowa** organ pipe.

organum *n. indecl. muz.* organum.

organy *pl. Gen.* **-ów** *muz.* (pipe) organ.

orgazm *mi fizj.* orgasm, climax.

orgia *f. Gen.* **-ii 1. orgie** *hist.* orgies. **2.** (*rozwiązła zabawa*) orgy. **3.** *przen.* (= *bogactwo*) riot, abundance.

orgiastyczny *a.* orgiastic.

orgiazm *mi* **1.** *hist.* orgies. **2.** *psych.* orgasm.

orgietka *f. Gen.pl.* **-ek** *pot.* sex party, gang bang.

Orient *mi geogr., hist.* the Orient.

orientacja *f.* **1.** (*w przestrzeni*) orientation; **zmysł orientacji** sense of direction; **bieg na orientację** *sport* orienteering; **tracić orientację** lose one's bearings. **2.** (*ogólna wiedza*) grasp, knowledge; **wykazać się doskonałą orientacją w zagadnieniu** demostrate a very good grasp of the problem; **okazać brak orientacji** demostrate lack of knowledge. **3.** (*skłonność*) orientation, leaning, tendency; **orientacja lewicowa** *l.* **prawicowa** left- *l.* right-wing leanings; **orientacja seksualna** sexual preferences; **orientacja homoseksualna** homosexual preferences.

orientacyjnie *adv.* approximately, roughly.

orientacyjny *a.* **1.** (= *przybliżony*) approximate, rough. **2.** (= *pozwalający orientować się w przestrzeni*) reference, landmark.

orientalista *mp uniw.* Orientalist.

orientalistyczny *a. uniw.* Oriental; **studia orientalistyczne** Oriental studies.

orientalistyka *f. uniw.* Orientalism, Oriental studies.

orientalizm *mi* **1.** *jęz.* (*wyraz*) Orientalism. **2.** (*cecha typowa dla Wschodu*) Orientalism.

orientalnie *adv.* orientally.

orientalny *a.* oriental, Oriental; **orientalna kuchnia** Oriental cuisine; **orientalna sztuka** Oriental art.

orientować *ipf.* inform, brief, introduce to. ~ **się** *ipf.* **1.** (*w terenie*) orient o.s., get one's bearings. **2.** (= *mieć rozeznanie*) have a good grasp (*w czymś* of sth); be at home (*w czymś* in sth); **o ile się orientuję** as far as I know, as far as I am aware, to my knowledge. **3.** *rzad.* show tendency towards, have a leaning towards.

orka[1] *f. tylko sing.* **1.** *roln.* plowing, *Br.* ploughing; **orka płytka** shallow plowing; **orka głęboka** deep plowing; **orka średnia** mean plowing; **orka jesienna** fall plowing; **orka wiosenna** spring plowing. **2.** *przen.* (= *harówka*) drudgery, bone-breaker, bull-work.

orka[2] *f. Gen.pl.* **-ek** *zool.* killer whale (*Orcinus orca*).

orkan *mi meteor.* hurricane.

orkiestra *f. muz.* orchestra; band; **orkiestra dęta** brass band; **orkiestra kameralna** chamber orchestra; **orkiestra symfoniczna** symphony orchestra; **orkiestra taneczna** dance band.

orkiestracja *f. muz.* orchestration.

orkiestrion *mi muz.* orchestrion.

orkiestrować *ipf. muz.* orchestrate.

orkiestrowy *a.* orchestra, orchestral; **fosa or-**

kiestrowa orchestra pit; **muzyka orkiestrowa** orchestral music; **zespół orkiestrowy** orchestra.

orkisz *mi bot.* **1.** (*jęczmień*) two-rowed barley (*Hordeum distichon*). **2.** (*pszenica*) spelt (*Triticum spelta*).

Orkus *mp mit.* Orcus.

orli *a.* eagle's, eagle; aquiline; **orli dziób** eagle's beak; **orle gniazdo** aerie, *Br.* eyrie; **orli nos** aquiline nose; **orli wzrok** eagle eye.

orlica *f.* **1.** (*samica orła*) female eagle. **2.** *bot.* bracken (*Pteridium aquilinum*).

orlik *ma* **1.** (= *młody orzeł*) eaglet. **2.** *orn.* **orlik krzykliwy** lesser spotted eagle (*Aquila pomarina*); **orlik stepowy** tawny eagle (*Aquila rapax*); **orlik grubodzioby** greater spotted eagle (*Aquila clanga*). – *mi bot.* columbine (*Aquilegia*).

orłosęp *ma orn.* **orłosęp brodaty** lammergeier, bearded vulture (*Gypaetus barbatus*).

Ormianin *mp pl.* **-anie** *Gen.* **-an, Ormianka** *f. Gen.pl.* **-ek** Armenian.

ormiański *a.* Armenian.

ornament *mi* **1.** *sztuka* ornament, adornment, embellishment; **ornament roślinny** floral ornament, vignette. **2.** *muz.* ornament, embellishment, grace note. **3.** *druk.* ornament.

ornamentacja *f. sztuka, teor.lit.* ornamentation.

ornamentacyjny *a.* ornamental; **motyw ornamentacyjny** ornamental motif.

ornamentować *ipf.* ornament, embellish, decorate.

ornamentyka *f.* **1.** *teor.lit., muz.* ornamentation. **2.** (= *zdobnictwo; = ornamenty*) ornamentation.

ornat *mi rel.* chasuble, vestment.

ornitofauna *f. orn.* avifauna.

ornitolog *mp pl.* **-dzy** *l.* **-owie** ornithologist.

ornitologia *f. Gen.* **-ii** ornithology.

ornitologiczny *a.* ornithological, ornithologic.

ornitoza *f. wet.* ornitosis, psittacosis.

orny *a. zwł. roln.* arable, cultivable, farmable; **grunt orny** arable, arable land *l.* acreage.

orogen *mi geol.* orogen.

orogeneza *f. geol.* orogeny, orogenesis.

orogeniczny *a. geol.* orogenic, orogenetic.

orografia *f. Gen.* **-ii** *geol.* orography, orology.

orograficzny *a. geol.* orographic, orographical; **orograficzne zjawisko atmosferyczne** *meteor.* orographic atmospheric phenomenon.

oronim *mi jęz.* oronym.

oronimia *f. Gen.* **-ii** *jęz.* oronymy.

oronimiczny *a. jęz.* oronymous, oronimic.

orszak *mi* (= *świta*) retinue, cortege; (= *procesja*) procession, train, cortege; **orszak weselny** wedding procession; **orszak żałobny** funeral procession *l.* cortege.

ortalion *mi* **1.** (*tkanina*) Ortalion, type of polyamide fabric. **2.** (*płaszcz*) coat made of polyamide fabric.

ortalionowy *a.* Ortalion, polyamide.

ortocentrum *n. sing. indecl. pl.* **-ra** *Gen.* **-rów** *mat.* orthocenter.

ortochromatyczność *f. fot.* orthochromatic properties.

ortochromatyczny *a. fot.* orthochromatic.

ortodoks *mp* orthodox person.

ortodoksja *f.* orthodoxy.

ortodoksyjność *f.* orthodoxness, orthodoxy.

ortodoksyjny *a.* orthodox; żyd ortodoksyjny Orthodox Jew; Kościół ortodoksyjny *rel.* Orthodox Church.

ortodoncja *f. dent.* orthodontics, orthodontia.

ortodonta *mp dent.* orthodontist.

ortodontyczny *a. dent.* orthodontic, orthodontal.

ortodroma *f. geogr.* great circle.

ortoepia *f. Gen.* -ii *jęz.* orthoepy.

ortoepiczny *a. jęz.* orthoepic, orthoepical.

ortofonia *f. Gen.* -ii *jęz.* orthophony.

ortofoniczny *a. jęz.* orthophonic.

ortogonalny *a. geom.* orthogonal, perpendicular; trajektoria ortogonalna orthogonal trajectory.

ortografia *f. Gen.* -ii 1. (*zbiór zasad*) orthography. 2. (*pisanie*) spelling; błędna ortografia incorrect *l.* wrong spelling, misspeling.

ortograficznie *adv.* (potrafić) pisać ortograficznie be a good speller.

ortograficzny *a.* spelling; reguła *l.* norma ortograficzna spelling rule; błąd ortograficzny spelling mistake, misspeling; zrobić błąd ortograficzny misspell (*a word*).

ortoklaz *mi min.* orthoclase.

ortopeda *mp med.* 1. (*lekarz*) orthopedist, *Br.* orthopaedist. 2. (*protetyk*) orthopedic technician.

ortopedia *f. Gen.* -ii *med.* orthopedics, *Br.* ortopaedics.

ortopedyczny *a. med.* orthopedic, *Br.* orthopaedic; oddział ortopedyczny orthopedic ward.

ortostat *mi bud.* orthostat, orthostates.

ortowodór *mi* -o- *chem.* orthohydrogen.

ortyl *mi Gen.* -a *Gen.pl.* -i *l.* -ów *hist., prawn.* verdict, judgment.

Orygenes *mp hist.* Origen.

oryginalnie *adv.* originally.

oryginalność *f.* 1. (= *osobliwość*) originality. 2. (= *niezwykłość*) uniqueness.

oryginalny *a.* 1. (= *autentyczny*) genuine, original; oryginalna pisownia original spelling; oryginalny scyzoryk szwajcarski genuine Swiss army knife. 2. (= *samodzielny*) original; oryginalny utwór original work; oryginalny poeta original poet. 3. (= *niezwykły*) unique; oryginalny sposób bycia unique behavior.

oryginał *mi Gen.* -u original; oryginał dokumentu original document; oryginał świadectwa original certificate. – *mp Gen.* -a *pl.* -y eccentric.

orzec *pf.* -knę -kniesz, -knij, -kł *zob.* orzekać.

orzech *mi Gen.* -a 1. (*owoc i nasiono*) nut; orzech włoski walnut; orzech laskowy hazelnut; orzech kokosowy coconut; orzech ziemny peanut; orzech galasowy gallnut; dziadek do orzechów nutcracker; twardy orzech do zgryzienia hard *l.* tough nut to crack. 2. *bot.* orzech laskowy hazel (*Corylus avellana*); orzech włoski walnut (*Juglans regia*); orzech wodny water chestnut, water caltrop (*Trapa natans*); orzech ziemny peanut (*Arachis hypogaea*); orzech amerykański *l.* brazylijski brazil *l.* Brazil nut (*Bertholettia*). 3. (*drewno*) walnut. 4. (*węgiel*) chestnut coal, nut coal.

orzechowate *pl. Gen.* -ych *bot.* the walnut family (*Juglandaceae*).

orzechowy *a.* nut; czekolada orzechowa nut chocolate; orzechowe oczy nut-brown eyes; podłoga orzechowa walnut floor; kolor orzechowy nut-brown color.

orzechówka *f. Gen.pl.* -ek 1. (*wódka*) walnut-flavored vodka. 2. *orn.* Eurasian nutcracker (*Nucifraga caryocatactes*).

orzeczenie *n.* 1. (= *opinia*) judgment, opinion; orzeczenie lekarskie medical certificate. 2. *gram.* predicate. 3. *prawn.* (= *postanowienie*) ruling; (= *wyrok*) sentence.

orzecznictwo *n.* 1. *prawn.* body of rulings, judicial decisions. 2. *med.* certification.

orzecznik *mi Gen.* -a *gram.* orzecznik przymiotnikowy predicate adjective; orzecznik rzeczownikowy predicate nominative.

orzekać *ipf.* 1. (= *stwierdzić*) decide, state. 2. *prawn.* rule, adjudicate, adjudge; orzec o winie (= *uznać winnym*) adjudge sb guilty; (= *zdecydować o winie / niewinności*) determine sb's guilt or innocence.

orzekający *a. gram.* indicative; tryb orzekający indicative mood.

orzeł *ma* orł- 1. *orn.* eagle (*Aquila*). 2. *przen.* ace, whiz, mavin, high-flier; nie taki z niego orzeł he's not that clever. 3. (*godło*) eagle; orzeł czy reszka? heads or tails?

orzełek *ma* -łk- (*godło*) eagle.

orzeszek *mi* -szk- *Gen.* -a nutlet, (small) nut; orzeszek ziemny peanut.

orzesznica *f.* 1. orzesznica wyniosła *bot.* brazil *l.* Brazil nut (*Bertholletia excelsa*). 2. *zool.* common dormice (*Muscardinus avellanarius*).

orzesznik *mi Gen.* -a *bot.* hickory (*Carya*).

orzeźwiać *ipf.* refresh. ~ się *ipf.* refresh o.s.

orzeźwiający *a.* refreshing; kąpiel orzeźwiająca invigorating bath; napój orzeźwiający refreshing drink.

orzeźwić *pf.* -ij *zob.* orzeźwiać. ~ się *pf.* -ij *zob.* orzeźwić się.

orzęski *pl. zool.* ciliates (*Ciliata*).

orżnąć *pf.* -ij 1. *pot.* (= *oszukać*) clip, cheat, swindle. 2. *pot.* (= *wygrać dużo w karty*) skin.

osa *f.* 1. wasp; cięty jak osa waspish; jest cienka w pasie jak osa she's wasp-waisted, she's got an hour-glass figure. 2. *przen.* toughie, bitch.

osaczać *ipf.*, osaczyć *pf.* 1. (= *okrążać*) beset, corner. 2. *przen.* haunt. 3. *myśl.* (*o psie*) hold at bay.

osad *mi* 1. sediment; (*z kawy, herbaty*) dregs; (*z napojów alkoholowych*) lees. 2. *geol.* sediment.

osada *f.* 1. (*miejscowość*) settlement. 2. *sport* (*załoga łodzi, bobsleja*) team.

osadnictwo *n.* 1. (= *kolonizacja*) settlement, colonization. 2. (= *zespół osad*) settlements.

osadniczka *f. Gen.pl.* **-ek** *zob.* **osadnik[1]**.
osadniczy *a.* settler's *l.* settlers', settlement; **teren osadniczy** settlement area.
osadnik[1] *mp pl.* **-cy** settler.
osadnik[2] *mi Gen.* **-a** *pl.* **-i** *techn.* sedimentation tank.
osadowy *a.* sedimentary.
osady *pl. Gen.* **-ów** *geol.* sediments.
osadzać *ipf.*, **osadzić** *pf.* **1.** (= *osiedlać*) settle. **2.** (= *nanosić coś*) deposit. **3.** (= *przytwierdzać*) fix, secure. **4.** (= *oprawiać*) set. **5.** *chem.* precipitate. **6.** *tylko pf.* (*o koniu*) (= *zatrzymać w miejscu*) halt, stop. **7.** *tylko pf.* (= *umiejscowić*) place. ~ **się** *ipf.*, **osadzić się** *pf.* **1.** (= *osiedlać się*) settle. **2.** *chem.* precipitate. **3.** *tylko pf.* (*o koniu*) (= *zatrzymać się*) halt, stop.
osamotnienie *n.* solitude, loneliness; **żyć w osamotnieniu** live a solitary life, lead a lonely life.
osamotniony *a.* **-eni** lonely; forlorn.
osąd *mi lit.* judgment, judgement.
osądzać *ipf.*, **osądzić** *pf.* **1.** *prawn.* adjudge, judge. **2.** (= *wydawać opinie*) judge, pass judgment.
oschle *adv.* dryly, drily, coldly.
oschłość *f.* dryness, coldness.
oschły *a.* dry, cold, indifferent.
oscylacja *f.* **1.** *fiz.* oscillation. **2.** (= *wahanie*) oscillation, fluctuation.
oscylacyjny *a. fiz.* oscillatory, oscillating.
oscylator *mi Gen.* **-a** *fiz.* oscillator.
oscylograf *mi fiz.* oscillograph.
oscylografia *f. Gen.* **-ii** *fiz., med.* oscillography.
oscylograficzny *a. fiz.* oscillographic.
oscylogram *mi fiz.* oscillogram.
oscylometria *f. Gen.* **-ii** *med.* oscillometry.
oscyloskop *mi fiz.* oscilloscope.
oscyloskopowy *a. fiz.* oscilloscopic; **lampa oscyloskopowa** cathode-ray oscilloscope.
oscylować *ipf.* **1.** oscillate. **2.** (= *wahać się*) oscillate; **oscylować pomiędzy jedną a drugą partią** oscillate between the two parties; **temperatura oscylowała między 3 a 5 stopniami Celsjusza** the temperature varied from 3 to 5 degrees centigrade.
osełka *f. Gen.pl.* **-ek** **1.** (*do ostrzenia*) whetstone. **2.** (*masła*) pat (of butter).
osesek *mp* **-sk-** suckling.
oset *mi* **ost-** *bot.* thistle (*Carduus; Cirsium*).
osetnik *ma ent.* painted lady (*Vanessa cardui*).
osiadać *ipf.* **1.** (= *osiedlać się*) settle. **2.** (= *pokrywać coś*) cover. **3.** (= *osuwać się, pogrążać się*) sink, subside; **osiąść na mieliźnie** *żegl.* run aground.
osiadły *a.* **1.** settled. **2.** *zool.* resident, sedentary; **ptactwo osiadłe** resident birds.
osiągać *ipf.* **1.** (= *uzyskiwać*) attain, achieve, gain; **osiągać rozgłos** gain publicity; **osiągać sukces** achieve *l.* attain success; **osiągać zaszczyty** win honors; **osiągać wysoką cenę** fetch *l.* command a high price. **2.** (= *zbliżać się do celu*) reach; **osiągać szczyt** reach a summit; **osiągać cel** achieve one's aim; **osiągać punkt kulminacyj-**

ny come to *l.* reach a climax; **osiągać zawrotną liczbę sprzedanych egzemplarzy** sell in great numbers.
osiągalny *a.* attainable; **osiągalny cel** attainable aim.
osiągi *pl. Gen.* **-ów** *techn.* performance.
osiągnąć *pf.* **-ij** *zob.* **osiągać**.
osiągnięcie *n.* achievement; **osiągnięcie artystyczne** artistic achievement.
osiąść *pf.* **osiądę osiądziesz osiadł osiadła osiedli** *zob.* **osiadać**.
osiec *ma* **ośc-** **osiec korówkowy** *ent.* woolly apple aphid (*Aphelinus mali*).
osiedlać *ipf.* settle. ~ **się** *ipf.* settle.
osiedle *n. Gen.pl.* **-i** development; *Br.* estate; **osiedle mieszkaniowe** housing development, *Br.* housing estate.
osiedleniec *mp* **-ńc-** *pl.* **-y** settler; colonist.
osiedlić *pf. zob.* **osiedlać**. ~ **się** *pf. zob.* **osiedlać się**.
osiedlowy *a.* housing development, *Br.* housing estate; local; community; **klub osiedlowy** community center; **szkoła osiedlowa** local school.
osiem *num.* **ośmi-** *Ins.* **-oma** *l.* **-u** eight; **ośmiu studentów czekało na egzamin** eight students were waiting for the exam; **osiem studentek odbyło praktykę w szkole** eight students had (teaching) practice at a school; **osiem słowników stało na półce** there were eight dictionaries on the shelf.
osiemdziesiąt *num.* **-ęci-** *Ins.* **-oma** *l.* **-u** eighty.
osiemdziesiątka *f. Gen.pl.* **-ek** **1.** (*liczba*) eighty. **2.** (*autobus, tramwaj nr 80*) number eighty. **3.** *pot.* (*wiek*) eighty (years of age); **stuknęła mu osiemdziesiątka** *pot.* he turned eighty.
osiemdziesiąty *a.* eightieth; **osiemdziesiąte urodziny** eightieth birthday; **lata osiemdziesiąte** the eighties, the 80s.
osiemdziesięciolecie *n. Gen.pl.* **-i** **1.** (*okres*) period of eighty years. **2.** (*rocznica*) eightieth anniversary; **osiemdziesięciolecie urodzin** eightieth birthday.
osiemdziesięcioletni *a.* eighty-year-old.
osiemnastka *f. Gen.pl.* **-ek** **1.** (*liczba*) eighteen. **2.** (*tramwaj, autobus, dom*) number eighteen. **3.** *pot.* (*dziewczyna*) sweet eighteen. **4.** *pot.* (*urodziny*) eighteenth birthday. **5.** (*przyjęcie*) sweet eighteen party.
osiemnastolatek *mp* **-tk-** *pl.* **-i**, **osiemnastolatka** *f. Gen.pl.* **-ek** eighteen-year-old person.
osiemnastoletni *a.* eighteen-year-old.
osiemnastowieczny *a.* eighteenth century, 18th century.
osiemnasty *a.* eighteenth.
osiemnaście *num.* **-st-** *Ins.* **-oma** *l.* **-u** eighteen; **osiemnaście po pierwszej** eighteen past one; **trzynasta osiemnaście** eighteen past one, one eighteen.
osiemset *num.* **osiem-** *decl. like num.*, **-set** *indecl.* eight hundred.
osiemsetny *a.* eight hundredth.
osierdzie *n. Gen.pl.* **-i** *anat.* pericardium.

osierdziowy *a. anat.* pericardial, pericardiac; **worek osierdziowy** heart sac, pericardial sac.

osierocić *pf.* **1.** *rzad.* (*dzieci*) orphan; (*bliskich*) bereave. **2.** *przen.* (= *opuścić*) desert.

osika *f.* **1.** *bot.* aspen (*Populus tremula*). **2.** (*drewno*) aspen wood.

osikowy *a.* aspen.

osiłek *mp* **-łk-** *żart.* bruiser, muscleman.

osiodłać *pf.* saddle; **osiodłać kogoś** bring sb to heel, get sb under control.

osioł *ma* **osł-** **1.** *zool.* ass, donkey (*Equus asinus*); **uparty jak osioł** as obstinate *l.* stubborn as a mule; **harować jak dziki osioł** *pot.* work one's hands to the bone, work like a dog *l.* monkey. **2.** *przen.* (= *głupiec*) ass, airbrain, jerk.

osiołek *ma* **łk-** **1.** (*zwierzę*) ass, donkey; **osiołkowi w żłoby dano** like a donkey between two budles of hay. **2.** (= *głuptas*) silly-billy; **ale z ciebie osiołek!** you silly!

osiowość *f.* axiality.

osiowy *a.* axial.

osiwieć *pf.* gray, turn gray.

oskalpować *pf.* scalp.

oskard *mi Gen.* **-a** pick, pickax, *Br.* pickaxe.

oskarżać *ipf.* **1.** (= *obwiniać*) accuse; **oskarżać kogoś o coś** accuse sb of sth. **2.** *zwł. prawn.* charge, indict, accuse; **oskarżać kogoś przed sądem o coś** charge sb with sth, indict sb for sth; (*w języku potocznym*) accuse sb of sth. **3.** *tylko ipf. prawn.* (= *być oskarżycielem w procesie sądowym*) prosecute. **~ się** *ipf.* **1.** (= *obwiniać siebie*) accuse o.s. **2.** (= *obwiniać jeden drugiego*) accuse each other.

oskarżenie *n. zwł. prawn.* accusation, charge; **bezpodstawne oskarżenie** groundless *l.* unfounded accusation; **akt oskarżenia** indictment; **wnieść akt oskarżenia przeciw komuś** indict sb; **świadek oskarżenia** witness for the prosecution; **postawić kogoś w stan oskarżenia** indict sb, charge sb; **wnieść oskarżenie przeciw komuś** bring *l.* make an accusation against sb, press charges against sb; **zrzec się oskarżenia** drop *l.* withdraw a charge.

oskarżona *f. Gen.* **-ej**, **oskarżony** *mp prawn.* (the) defendant, (the) accused.

oskarżyciel *mp*, **oskarżycielka** *f. Gen.pl.* **-ek** *prawn.* prosecutor; **oskarżyciel posiłkowy** auxiliary prosecutor (*usu. a member of the public, often a friend or relative of the wronged party*); **oskarżyciel prywatny** private prosecutor; **oskarżyciel publiczny** public prosecutor, prosecuting attorney.

oskarżycielski *a.* accusatory, accusative; **oskarżycielskie spojrzenie** accusatory look.

oskarżyć *pf. zob.* **oskarżać**. **~ się** *pf. zob.* **oskarżać się**.

oskoła *f. bot.* sap.

oskórek *mi* **-rk-** *Gen.* **-a** *zool.* epidermis.

oskrobać *pf.* **-ę -esz**, **oskrobywać** *ipf.* scrape; **oskrobać ziemniaki/marchew** peel potatoes/carrots; **oskrobać rybę** scale a fish; **oskrobać starą farbę** scrape *l.* peel old paint off.

oskrzela *pl. Gen.* **-i** *anat.* bronchi, bronchia, bronchial tubes.

oskrzelik *mi Gen.* **-a** *anat.* bronchiolus, bronchiole.

oskrzelowy *a. anat., pat.* bronchial; **dychawica oskrzelowa** bronchial asthma.

oskrzydlać *ipf.*, **oskrzydlić** *pf. wojsk.* outflank.

oskubać *pf.* **-ę -esz**, **oskubywać** *ipf. kulin.* (*kurczaka, kaczkę*) pluck; **oskubać kogoś z pieniędzy** fleece sb.

osłabiacz *mi Gen.* **-a** *fot.* reducer.

osłabiać *ipf.*, **osłabić** *pf.* **1.** (= *czynić mniej intensywnym*) reduce, lessen; **osłabić tempo** reduce pace, slow down; **poduszka powietrzna osłabiła siłę uderzenia** air bag reduced the impact. **2.** (= *czynić słabszym, mniej sprawnym*) weaken, enfeeble; **grypa osłabia serce** flu weakens the heart; **zmęczenie osłabiło moją zdolność koncentracji** fatigue reduced my ability to concentrate. **3.** (= *nadwerężyć*) weaken; **powódź osłabiła fundamenty** flood weakened *l.* undermined the foundations. **4.** (= *złagodzić*) soften, cushion. **~ się** *ipf.*, **osłabić się** *pf.* weaken.

osłabienie *n.* **1.** (= *zmniejszenie*) reduction, lessening. **2.** (= *utrata sił*) weakness, feebleness; **ogólne osłabienie organizmu** general weakness, asthenia.

osłabiony *a.* **-eni** weak, weakened; **osłabiony wzrok** weakened eyesight.

osłabnąć *pf.* **-ij**, **-ł** *l.* **-nął -ła -li** **1.** (= *stać się mniej aktywnym*) weaken, grow weaker; **osłabnąć ze zmęczenia** grow weaker with fatigue. **2.** (= *stracić na sile, zmniejszyć się*) diminish, decline; die down; **osłabnąć w swoich zapędach** lose interest; **zapał osłabł** enthusiasm faded; **burza osłabła** storm died down.

osładzać *ipf. t. przen.* sweeten.

osłaniać *ipf.*, **osłonić** *pf.* **1.** (= *okrywać, chronić*) shelter, protect. **2.** (= *bronić w walce*) cover. **3.** *pot.* (= *kryć*) cover up (*kogoś* for sb); **osłania go sam dyrektor** the director himself covers up for him. **~ się** *ipf.* **1.** (*samego siebie*) shelter o.s., protect o.s. **2.** (*jeden drugiego*) cover up for each other.

osławiony *a.* **-eni** renowned, famous, famed; **osławiona piękność** famous beauty.

osłoda *f.* comfort; **na osłodę** as a comfort.

osłodzić *pf.* **-odź** *l.* **-ódź** **1.** *zob.* **osładzać**. **2.** (= *dodać cukru*) sweeten, sugar.

osłomuł *ma zool.* hinny.

osłona *f.* **1.** (= *okrycie*) cover, shield; (= *zabezpieczenie*) protection; **pod osłoną nocy** under cover of darkness; **osłona biologiczna** (*w reaktorze jądrowym*) biological shield. **2.** *wojsk.* cover; **osłona z powietrza** fighter cover, air support; **osłona ogniem** fire cover.

osłonek *adv.* **bez osłonek** openly, straightforwardly.

osłonice *pl. Gen.* **-c** *zool.* tunicates (*Tunicata*).

osłonić *pf. zob.* **osłaniać**. **~ się** *pf. zob.* **osłaniać się**.

osłonka *f. Gen.pl.* **-ek** **1.** cover, shield; protection; **mówić bez osłonek** speak bluntly. **2.** *kulin.* casing.

osłonowy *a.* protective; **drzewa osłonowe** shelter trees; **ściana osłonowa** *bud.* curtain *l.* panel wall; **ogień osłonowy** *wojsk.* cover fire; **oddział osłonowy** *wojsk.* covering party.

osłuchać *pf. zob.* **osłuchiwać.** ~ **się** *pf. zob.* **osłuchiwać się.**

osłuchany *a.* **1.** (= *zorientowany, zaznajomiony z czymś, co się słucha*) familiar, acquainted, conversant (*w czymś* with sth); **osłuchany w muzyce barokowej** familiar with Baroque music. **2.** (= *spowszedniały przez częste słuchanie*) heard too often, hackneyed; **osłuchany przebój** an overplayed hit.

osłuchiwać *ipf. med.* **1.** auscultate. **2.** *techn.* sound. ~ **się** *ipf.* **1.** (= *słuchając, zaznajomić się z czymś, przywyknąć do czegoś*) get a feel (*z czymś* for sth); familiarize o.s. (*z czymś* with sth). **2.** (*spowszednieć*) be heard too often.

osłuchiwanie *n. med.* auscultation.

osłuchowo *adv. med.* by auscultation; **badać osłuchowo** examine by auscultation.

osłuchowy *a. med.* ausculatory, auscultative.

osłupieć *pf.* be stunned, be bewildered, be confounded.

osłupienie *n.* **1.** (= *zdumienie*) bewilderment; **wprawić kogoś w osłupienie** bewilder sb, confound sb. **2.** *psych., pat.* stupor, stupefaction.

osm *mi chem.* osmium.

osmagać *pf.* lash, flog, whip.

Osman *mp Gen.* **-a** *hist.* Ottoman.

osmarować *pf.,* **osmarowywać** *ipf.* **1.** (*zabrudzić*) smear, smudge. **2.** *pot.* (= *zniesławić*) smear, bismirch, run down.

osmologia *f. Gen.* **-ii** *med.* osmology.

osmometr *mi fiz.* osmometer.

osmoregulacja *f. fizj.* osmoregulation.

osmotyczny *a. fiz.* osmotic; **ciśnienie osmotyczne** osmotic pressure.

osmoza *f. chem., fiz.* osmosis.

osnowa *f. Gen.pl.* **-ów** **1.** *tk.* warp; **osnowa opony** *mot.* tire carcass, *Br.* tyre carcass; **osnowa stopu** *metal.* matrix. **2.** *teor.lit.* (= *kanwa*) fabric, structure.

osnuć *pf.* **1.** (= *opleść*) weave around; *przen.* envelop, (en)shroud. **2.** *teor.lit.* base; **powieść osnuta na motywach ludowych** novel based on *l.* interwoven with folk motifs.

osnuja *f. Gen.* **-ui osnuja czerwonogłowa** *ent.* pine false webworm (*Acantholyda erythrocephala*).

osoba *f. Gen.pl.* **osób 1.** (= *człowiek*) person, individual, personage; **osoba fizyczna** *zwł. prawn.* natural person; **osoba prawna** *zwł. prawn.* legal person, artificial person, juristic person; **osoba prywatna** private person; **osoba urzędowa** (government) official, civil servant; **osoba króla** His Majesty the King; **osoba postronna** outsider; **bez obecności osób trzecich** without third parties; **prezydent we własnej osobie** the President himself; **nie pozwolę pomiatać swoją osobą** I won't be ordered about *l.* around. **2.** *jęz.* person. **3.** *teor.lit.* (= *postać dramatu*) persona, personage; **osoby** (*lista postaci w dramacie, powieści*) dramatis personae.

osobistość *f.* personage; celebrity, personality.

osobisty *a.* (= *prywatny*) personal; private; **bagaż osobisty** carry-on luggage; **rzeczy osobiste** personal belongings; **sekretarz osobisty** private secretary; **dowód osobisty** identity card, ID card; **komputer osobisty** *komp.* personal komputer, PC; **majątek osobisty** personal property; **rewizja osobista** body search; **robić osobiste wycieczki pod czyimś adresem** make personal remarks about sb; **to mój osobisty wkład** that is my personal contribution.

osobiście *adv.* personally, in person; **przyjść osobiście** appear in person; **znać osobiście** know personally; **osobiście uważam, że...** I personally think that...

osobliwość *f.* **1.** curiosity; oddity. **2.** (*czyjegoś zachowania, krajobrazu, spojrzenia*) peculiarity.

osobliwy *a.* curious, odd, peculiar; **osobliwy sposób bycia** peculiar behavior; **nie ma w tym nic osobliwego** there's nothing peculiar about that.

osobniczy *a. biol.* ontogenetic, ontogenic; **cechy osobnicze** ontogenetic traits; **rozwój osobniczy** ontogenetic development.

osobnik *ma pl.* **-i** *biol.* (= *okaz*) specimen, individual organism. – *mp pl.* **-cy** *uj.* character, individual; **podejrzany osobnik** suspicious character.

osobno *adv.* separately, individually, apart; (*mieszkać, płacić*) separately; (*poinformować*) individually, separately.

osobności *adv.* **na osobności** in private, privately, aside; **trzymać się na osobności** keep to o.s., live in seclusion; **pomówić z kimś na osobności** have a quiet word with sb, talk to sb in private, take *l.* draw sb aside (*to talk to them*).

osobny *a.* separate, individual, distinct; (*o wejściu, wykładzie*) separate, independent; (*o stoliku*) individual, separate; (*o domu*) detached; **wszem wobec i każdemu z osobna** *przest.* all and sundry.

osobowość *f.* **1.** personality, selfhood, personhood, individuality; (= *imponująca osoba*) presence, personality; **silna osobowość** strong *l.* assertive *l.* type A personality; **zaburzenia osobowości** *psych.* personality disorder; **rozdwojenie osobowości** dual personality; **typ osobowości** personality type; **rozszczepienie osobowości** *pat.* multiple *l.* split personality. **2.** *prawn.* personality; **osobowość prawna** legal personality; **nadanie/uzyskanie osobowości prawnej** incorporation; **posiadający osobowość prawną** (*o firmie, spółce*) incorporated.

osobowy *a.* personal, personnel; passenger; (*o samochodzie*) passenger; (*o dziale*) human resources, personal, personnel; **osobowy fundusz płac** personnel wage fund; **dział osobowy** personnel/human resources department; **ochrona danych osobowych** personal data protection; **pociąg osobowy** slow train; **końcówka osobowa** *gram.* personal ending; **forma osobowa czasownika** *gram.* finite form; **zaimek osobowy** *gram.* personal pronoun. – *mi* slow train; **jechać do Szczecina osobowym** take a slow train to Szczecin.

osocze *n. biol.* plasma; **osocze krwi** *fizj.* blood plasma.

osolić *pf.* **-ól** salt, season with salt.

osowate *pl. Gen.* **-ych** *zool.* vespids (*Vespidae*).

osowaty *a.* wasp-like, vespine.

osowiały *a.* dejected, despondent, mopish, glum, mopy, morose, lethargic, listless, inert; (*o chłopaku*) mopy, glum, morose, apathetic; (*o spojrzeniu*) dejected, depressed, long-faced.

osóbka *f. Gen.pl.* **-ek** *żart.* young lady.

ospa *f. pat.* smallpox; **wietrzna ospa** chicken-pox, water pox, varicella; **czarna ospa** black smallpox.

ospale *adv.* drowsily, groggily, sluggishly, lethargically; (*pracować, obsługiwać*) drowsily, languidly; (*odpowiadać*) languidly, indifferently, lifelessly; (*poruszać się*) slowly, sluggishly, lazily.

ospałość *f.* drowsiness, grogginess, lethargy, dullness, listlessness; (*ociężałość*) sluggishness, heaviness.

ospały *a.* drowsy, groggy, sleepy, dull, lethargic, draggy; (*o studencie*) drowsy, sleepy; (*o ekspedientce*) phlegmatic, slow, drowsy, half-awake *l.* half-asleep.

ospowatość *f.* pockmarks; (*śliw, ziemniaków*) surface blowholes, pitted skin.

ospowaty *a.* pockmarked, pocked; (*o twarzy*) pockmarked, (pock) pitted, cratered; (*chory na ospę*) pocky.

osprzęt *mi* **1.** *techn.* equipment; fitting; gear; accessories. **2.** *żegl.* rigging, sailing gear.

ostać się *pf.* **ostoję ostoisz, ostój** *przest.* **1.** (= *pozostać*) remain, stay, continue. **2.** (= *przetrwać, ocaleć*) survive, endure, prevail.

ostaniec *mi* **-ńc-** *Gen.* **-a** *geol.* (*zwł. na wybrzeżu*) inlier, monadnock, stack.

ostatecznie *adv.* **1.** (= *definitywnie*) decisively, conclusively, ultimately. **2.** (= *w końcu*) finally, in the end, at last, eventually. **3.** (= *w ostateczności*) as a last resort; (= *w końcu*) after all.

ostateczność *f.* extremity, necessity, extreme; **doprowadzić kogoś do ostateczności** drive sb to extremes *l.* the limit, push sb to *l.* past *l.* beyond his/her limit, push *l.* press sb's buttons, make sb's blood boil; **w ostateczności** as a last resort, in the last resort, in a pinch, when *l.* if push comes to shove; **wpadać z jednej w drugą ostateczność** go from one extreme to the other; **posuwać się do ostateczności** go to great *l.* any lengths.

ostateczny *a.* **1.** (= *definitywny*) ultimate, decisive, conclusive; **ostateczny dowód** conclusive proof; (= *końcowy*) final, ultimate, terminal, eventual, overall; (*o decyzji, wyniku, zwycięstwie*) final; (*o terminie*) closing, cut-off, final; (*o argumencie*) concluding, final; **ostateczny rezultat** final *l.* net *l.* end result, upshot; **ostateczny rezultat był taki, że...** the upshot of it all was that...; **ostateczny cios** finisher, finishing stroke; **dzień ostateczny** *Bibl.* Judgement day; **sąd ostateczny** *Bibl.* last Judgement, last doom; **do ostatecznych granic** to extremes, to the limit;

w ostatecznym razie if need be, in a pinch, as a last resort. **2.** (= *krańcowy*) extreme, utmost, supreme; (*o nędzy*) utmost, extreme; **środek ostateczny** extremity.

ostatek *mi* **-tk-** *Gen.* **-a** remainder, remnant, remains, residue; (*pieniędzy, chleba, zboża na polu*) rest; **ostatki** (*jedzenia*) leftovers, the leavings; **gonić ostatkiem sił** be at the end of one's tether *l.* rope, be on one's last legs; **do ostatka** to *l.* till the bitter end, to *l.* till the last; **walczyć do ostatka** throw *l.* fling away the scabbard, fight to *l.* till the bitter end; **na ostatku** in the end, eventually, finally.

ostatki *pl. Gen.* **-ów** Shrovetide; (*wtorek przed środą popielcową*) Mardi Grass, Shrove Tuesday.

ostatni *a.* **1.** (= *końcowy*) last, final, endmost, hindmost; (*o pociągu, autobusie*) last; (*z rzędu*) latter; (*o seansie, lekcji*) last, previous; **ostatnie słowo** the last word; **mieć ostatnie słowo** have the final say (in sth); **ostatnie namaszczenie** *rel.* extreme unction, last rites; **ostatnia instancja** *prawn.* last instance; **ostatnia wieczerza** *Bibl.* the Last *l.* Lord's Supper; **ostatnia deska ratunku** last resort, sheet anchor; **ostatnia godzina** the end; **wybiła ostatnia godzina** the end has come; **ostatnia posługa** (= *chrześcijański pochówek*) last rites; **odłożony na ostatnią minutę** (*o decyzji*) postponed *l.* left until *l.* to the eleventh hour; **na ostatnią chwilę** at the last minute; **z ostatniej chwili** (*o informacji*) just-in, (late-)breaking, up-to-the-minute; **w ostatnim momencie** in the nick of time; **ostatnia szansa** last chance *l.* opportunity; **ostatni grosz** bottom dollar, the *l.* sb's last penny; **stawiać ostatni grosz na coś** bet one's bottom dollar; **być spłukanym do ostatniego grosza** be down to one's last dollar; **ostatni krzyk mody** the latest fad *l.* thing *l.* trend *l.* craze, dernier cri, all the rage go, high style; **ostatni toast** grace cup; **po raz ostatni** for the last time; **ostatnim razem** last time; **ostatni raz widziałem go...** I last saw him...; **śmiać się ostatni** have the last laugh; **ostatnia wola** last will; *prawn.* will, last will and testament; **ostatnie życzenie** dying wish *l.* request; **ostatnia odsłona** the final curtain; **ostatnia kropla (goryczy)** the last straw; **ostatnia prosta** home stretch; **ostatnia poprawka** finishing stroke; **ostatnimi czasy** *l.* **w ostatnich czasach** recently, in recent years, lately; **walczyć do ostatniej kropli krwi** fight to *l.* till the very end, fight to the death; **być na ostatnich nogach** *pot.* be on one's last legs; **jest na ostatnich nogach** (*przed rozwiązaniem*) she is far along on in her time; **sala wypełniona do ostatniego miejsca** full house; **Adam jest ostatnią osobą, do której bym się zwrócił** Adam is the last person I'd ask *l.* approach; **zapięta na ostatni guzik** dressed (up) to the nines, in perfect trim; **dopiąć na ostatni guzik** stitch sth up, sew sth up; **oddałby ostatnią koszulę** he'd give you *l.* away the shirt off his back; **nasz konkurent nie powiedział jeszcze ostatniego słowa** our rival still has the last word *l.* final say; **rzucić ostatnie spojrzenie** look one's last; **wydać ostatnie tchnienie** breathe one's last;

do ostatniego tchu to one's dying death, to *l*. till the last. **2.** (= *najgorszy*) meanest, out-and-out, last; (*o miejscu, uczniu*) last; **zwymyślać od ostatnich** revile sb in the grossest *l*. coarsest of terms, throw *l*. sling mud at sb, pull sb to pieces.

ostatnio *adv*. lately, recently, of late.

ostemplować *pf*. stamp, seal.

ostentacja *f*. brashness, ostentation; (*demonstracja uczuć*) demonstrativeness.

ostentacyjnie *adv*. brashly, flauntingly, ostentatiously.

ostentacyjny *a*. ostentatious, showy, brash, glitzy; (*o grzeczności, przepychu*) demonstrative, showy, ostentatious.

osteoblast *mi fizj*. osteoblast.

osteocyt *mi fizj*. osteocyte.

osteoklast *mi* **1.** *biol*. osteoclast. **2.** *chir*. osteoclast.

osteologia *f. Gen*. -ii *med*. osteology.

osteon *mi biol*. osteon(e).

osteopatia *f. Gen*. -ii *med*. osteopathy.

ostępnować *pf*. quilt round.

ostęp *mi* **1.** (= *gęsty las*) backwoods. **2.** *leśn*. (*jednostka podziału lasu*) section.

ostnica *f. bot*. esparto (grass) (*Stipa tenacissima*).

ostoja *f. Gen*. -oi **1.** *lit*. mainstay, anchorage, support, bulwark, bastion; **tylko w tobie mogę mieć ostoję** you are my only support, you are the only person I can rely *l*. count *l*. depend on; **matka jest dla mnie ostoją** my mother is a real source of strength *l*. support to me, my mother is my anchorage; (*konserwatyzmu*) stronghold. **2.** *biol*. fothergilla (*Fothergilla*). **3.** *leśn*. refuge, refugium. **4.** *tech*. underframe.

ostracyzm *mi* **1.** *hist*. ostracism. **2.** (= *wykluczenie, bojkot*) ostracism, exclusion, the cold shoulder, boycotting.

ostrakodermy *pl. Gen*. -m *paleont*. ostracoderms.

ostrężyna *f. bot*. blackberry, bramble (*Rubus plicatus*).

ostrężynowy *a*. blackberry; (*o soku*) blackberry, bramble.

ostro *adv*. **1.** (= *spiczasto*) sharply; (= *stromo*) steeply, abruptly; (*wznosić się*) abruptly, steeply, rapidly. **2.** (= *mocno*) severely; **dać komuś ostro popalić** *pot*. give sb hell, make sb's life a living hell, make it *l*. things hot for sb, ride roughshod over sb. **3.** (= *wyraziście*) sharply, acutely. **4.** (= *energicznie*) briskly, sharply, resolutely, vigorously; (*hamować*) rapidly, suddenly; **ostro zakręcić** make a tight *l*. sharp turn; **ostro wziąć się do roboty** put *l*. set one's shoulder to the wheel, wade into sth, get cracking *l*. weaving, pull up one's socks, go roundly to work. **5.** (= *gniewnie*) sharply; (*odpowiedzieć*) sharply, harshly, brusquely; **ostro zareagować** put one's foot down, lower the boom on sb; **potraktować kogoś ostro** be sharp with sb, take sth out on sb, give sb a hard time, give sb a hell of a time. **6.** (= *intensywnie*) strongly, intensely; **podać coś na ostro** serve sth hot *l*. spicy.

ostrobok *ma* **ostrobok pospolity** *icht*. Atlantic

horse mackerel (*Trachurus trachurus l. Caranx trachurus*).

ostrodziób *ma orn*. sharpbill (*Oxyruncus cristatus*).

ostroga *f. Gen.pl*. -óg **1.** (*jeździecka*) spur; **spiąć ostrogi** set spurs to a horse; **zdobyć ostrogi** gain *l*. win one's spurs; **spinać ostrogami** spur, rowel. **2.** *orn*. (*u niektórych ptaków*) carina, calcar. **3.** *bot*. (*u niektórych kwiatów*) spur. **4.** (*na rzece*) wing dam, groin, groyne.

ostrogocki *a. hist*. Ostrogothic.

ostrogony *pl. Gen*. -ów *zool*. horseshoe crabs (*Xiphosura*).

ostrokątny *a*. sharp-angled; **trójkąt ostrokątny** *geom*. acute triangle.

ostrokół *mi* -o- palisade, fraise; *wojsk*. stockade.

ostrokrzew *mi bot*. ilex, holly (*Ilex*); **ostrokrzew kolczasty** holly (*Ilex aquifolium*).

ostrołuk *mi bud*. ogive, pointed *l*. lancet arch, gothic arch.

ostrołukowy *a. bud*. ogival, pointed, lanceted; (*o sklepieniu, oknie*) ogival; (*o stylu, kształcie okien*) lanceted.

ostromlecz *mi Gen*. -a *Gen.pl*. -y *l*. -ów *bot*. euphorbia, spurge (*Euphorbia*).

ostronos *ma zool*. coati, coatimondi, coatimundi (*Nasua*).

ostropest *mi* **ostropest plamisty** *bot*. milk thistle (*Silybum marianum*).

ostrosłup *mi Gen*. -a *geom*. pyramid; **ostrosłup ścięty** truncated pyramid.

ostrość *f*. **1.** (*szlifu*) sharpness; (*zbocza*) abruptness, steepness. **2.** (= *intensywność*) acuteness, sharpness; (*światła*) sharpness; **tracić na ostrości** (*o kolorze*) grow dim *l*. pale, fade, bleach; (*o uczuciach*) decline, die away, fade away. **3.** (= *wrażliwość*) keenness; (*węchu*) acridity, pungency; (*słuchu, wzroku*) acuity, keenness, quickness; (*smaku, zapachu*) acridity, pungency. **4.** (= *wyrazistość*) sharpness, clearness; (*widzenia*) acuity, clearness; (*konturów, obrazu*) definition, acutance, sharpness; **głębia ostrości** *fot., opt*. depth of focus *l*. field; **nastawić ostrość czegoś** bring sth into focus. **5.** (= *surowość*) stringency, strictness; (*klimatu*) severity, harshness; **przedstawiłem sytuację z całą ostrością** I gave *l*. presented a sharp *l*. clear *l*. vivid picture of the facts. **6.** (*potrawy*) spiciness.

ostrowłosy *a*. wire-haired; **terier ostrowłosy** *kynol*. wire-haired terrier.

ostrożeń *mi* -żni- *Gen*. -a *bot*. thistle (*Cirsium*); **ostrożeń polny** creeping thistle (*Cirsium arvense*).

ostrożna *adv*. **z ostrożna** carefully, warily, attentively, watchfully; **wszystko można, byle z ostrożna** there is a limit to everything.

ostrożnie *adv*. carefully, cautiously, charily, warily; (*w poleceniu*) watch *l*. look out!, steady!; (*na paczce*) handle with care; **ostrożnie podchodzić do czegoś** be chary of *l*. about sth *l*. doing sth; **iść ostrożnie** watch *l*. mind one's steps.

ostrożność *f*. caution, prudence, wariness; **za-**

chować środki ostrożności take precautions, take protective measures; zachować ostrożność exercise caution; daleko idąca ostrożność utmost care; zalecać ostrożność urge *l.* advise caution; ostrożność nie zawadzi better safe than sorry, you can't be too careful.

ostrożny *a.* careful, cautious, wary, prudent; (*o kierowcy*) careful, safe; (*o pukaniu do drzwi*) discreet; (*o prognozach, oszacowaniach*) conservative, cautious; (*o słowach*) guarded; przesadnie ostrożny overcareful, gun-shy, behaving *l.* acting with exaggerated care.

ostróg *mi* -o- *hist.* black house, donjon, keep.

ostrów *mi* -o- *lit.* holm, islet, ait, isle.

ostróżka *f. Gen.pl.* -ek *bot.* larkspur, delphinium (*Delphinium*).

ostruda *f. bot.* wild rice, Indian rice, water rice, water oats (*Zizania aquatica*).

ostrugać *pf.* (*o warzywach, owocach*) peel, pare; (*o kiju, gałęzi*) strip, whittle.

ostrużyny *pl. Gen.* -n peelings, parings, shavings.

ostry *a.* 1. (= *tnący*) sharp, sharp-edged, cutting; (*o nożu, siekierze*) sharp; (*o żarcie*) incisive, caustic; (*o języku*) caustic, biting, sharp; ostry nabój ball cartridge, war head; ostry język sharp tongue; ostre pióro sharp style, sharp pen *l.* tongue; ostry dowcip spicy joke; ostry jak brzytwa sharp as a razor. 2. (= *kłujący*) rough, crude; (*o piasku, trawie*) rough, crude; (*o powierzchni*) unpolished, crude, rough; kąt ostry *geom.* acute angle. 3. (= *surowy*) strict, severe, sharp; (*o szefie, nauczycielu*) strict, demanding, tough; (*o słowach*) brusque, curt, harsh; (*o krytyce*) harsh, caustic, severe; (*o psie*) quick. 4. (= *trudny*) hard, tight; (*o zakręcie, podejściu*) tight, sharp. 5. (= *intensywny*) sharp, acute, pungent, intense; (*o przyprawie*) hot, spicy; (*o zapachu*) pungent, acrid, burning; (*o smaku*) pungent, tangy, acid, piquant; (*o głosie*) piercing, shrill, strident; (*o świetle*) intense, sharp, dazzling; (*o kolorach*) vivid, glaring, intense; (*o bólu*) acute, piercing, intense; (*o słuchu, wzroku*) sharp, keen; (*o mrozie*) severe, hard; (*o wietrze, chłodzie*) sharp, bitter, cutting; (*o potrawie*) spicy, hot; (*o współzawodnictwie*) stiff, tough, keen; ostra wymiana zdań heated discussion. 6. (= *wyrazisty*) sharp, clear-cut, distinct; (*obraz*) sharp, clear; *fot.* in focus; (*o konturach*) clear-cut; o ostrych rysach with sharp *l.* angular features, hatchet-faced. 7. (= *surowy*) stringent, sharp, severe. 8. (= *gwałtowny*) sudden, abrupt, rapid; wybuchnąć gwałtownymi słowami launch into strong language; kilka ostrych słów a few choice words; (*o tempie, grze*) rough, quick; ostra piłka piłka nożna quick ball; ostry kurs *żegl.* close to the wind. 9. ostry dyżur emergency; ostre pogotowie constant readiness, highest state of readiness; ostre zapalenie wyrostka robaczkowego *pat.* severe appendicitis; ostry nieżyt żołądka *pat.* severe gastritis.

ostryga *f. zool.* oyster (*Ostrea*); muszla ostrygi oyster shell; młoda ostryga seed oyster, spat.

ostrygojad *ma orn.* oystercatcher (*Haematopus ostralegus*).

ostryż *mi Gen.* -a *bot.* curcuma (*Curcuma*); ostryż długi turmeric (*Curcuma longa*).

ostrzał *mi* firing, shelling, cannonade; (*artyleryjski*) bombardment, shelling; pole ostrzału field of fire; być pod ostrzałem be *l.* come under fire.

ostrzarka *f. Gen.pl.* -ek *tech.* sharpener, tool grinder, sharpening machine.

ostrze *n. Gen.pl.* -y blade, edge, point; (= *szpic*) spike, point, nib; (*strzały*) arrowhead; (*krzywej, łuku*) cusp; stawiać sprawę na ostrzu noża bring sth *l.* matters to a head, back sb into a corner; *Br.* give sb Hobson's choice.

ostrzec *pf.* -gę -żesz -gł *zob.* ostrzegać.

ostrzegacz *mi Gen.* -a *techn.* alarm box.

ostrzegać *ipf.* warn, caution (*kogoś przed czymś l. zrobieniem czego*) sb against (doing) sth); (*przed niebezpieczeństwem*) alarm, alert, caution; (*z góry*) forewarn (*przed czymś of l.* about *l.* against sth).

ostrzegawczo *adv.* warningly; trącić kogoś ostrzegawczo give sb a warning nudge, nudge sb warningly.

ostrzegawczy *a.* warning, cautionary, monitory, admonitory; (*o spojrzeniu, świetle*) warning; sygnał *l.* znak ostrzegawczy warning sign, red flag, beacon; petarda ostrzegawcza torpedo, beacon; strajk ostrzegawczy token strike.

ostrzelać *pf.*, ostrzeliwać *ipf.* 1. (*pociskami*) shell, shoot, fire on, play guns; (*z ciężkiej artylerii*) bombard, bomb; (*z dział*) cannonade. 2. (= *wypróbować broń*) test, try out. ~ się *pf.*, ostrzeliwać się *ipf.* 1. fire *l.* shoot back, play guns. 2. (= *nabrać wprawy w strzelaniu*) train *l.* practice shooting.

ostrzelany *a.* 1. *wojsk.* shot, fired, shelled; (*o karabinie*) tested. 2. *myśl.* (*o psie*) shooting trained, used *l.* accustomed to shots.

ostrzeń *mi Gen.* -a *bot.* hound's-tongue (*Cynoglossum*).

ostrzeżenie *n.* warning, premonition, caution, notice; (*sztormowe*) gale *l.* storm warning; (*nagłe*) wake-up call; bez ostrzeżenia without notice.

ostrzyc *pf.* -gę -żesz -gł cut; (*o owcy*) shear; (*o drzewach*) trim, clip. ~ się *pf.* 1. (*samego siebie*) cut one's hair, have a haircut. 2. (*zostać ostrzyżonym*) have *l.* get a haircut, have one's hair cut.

ostrzyć *ipf.* sharpen, whet, grind, edge; ostrzyć sobie zęby na kimś badmouth sb, run sb down, backbite sb; ostrzyć sobie apetyt na coś have designs upon sth, set one's sights on sth, set one's heart on sth.

ostudzać *ipf.*, ostudzić *pf.* 1. (= *obniżać temperaturę*) cool down, chill. 2. (= *uspokajać*) quieten, appease, chill; ostudzić czyjś zapał damp down *l.* dampen sb's spirit *l.* zeal *l.* enthusiasm, put a damper on sth; (*nadzieję, plany*) pour *l.* throw water on sth; (*uczucia, stosunki*) cool off, damp down, moderate. ~ się *pf.* 1. (= *obniżyć swoją temperaturę*) cool, chill. 2. (= *uspokoić się, ochłonąć*) calm down, settle, quieten down.

ostukać *pf.*, ostukiwać *ipf.* sound, tap.

ostygnąć *pf.* -ij, -ł *l.* -nął -ła -li **1.** (= *stać się zimnym*) chill. **2.** (*o uczuciach*) (= *stracić intensywność*) cool off, lessen, abate.

osunąć się *pf. zob.* **osuwać się.**

osuszacz *mi Gen.* -a *techn.* drier, dehumidifier; (*do żywności*) desiccator.

osuszać *ipf.*, **osuszyć** *pf.* **1.** (= *usuwać wilgoć*) dry, dehumidify; (= *odwadniać*) drain; **osuszyć butelkę** *żart.* crack a bottle. **2.** (= *wycierać*) dry away, mop; **osuszać łzy** wipe *l.* dry (away) tears; *przen.* comfort sb, cheer sb up, sympathize with sb. ~ **się** *pf.*, **osuszyć się** *pf.* dry one's clothes; (= *wytrzeć się do sucha*) wipe o.s. dry, towel off, pat o.s. dry.

osuwać się *ipf.* **1.** (= *opadać, ześlizgiwać się*) subside, slide down, lower; (*o ziemi, brzegu*) slide; (*o nodze*) slip. **2.** (*o człowieku*) (= *upadać*) slump, collapse, fall.

osuwisko *n.* landslide, landslip; (*skalne*) rockslide, rockfall.

oswabadzać *ipf. zob.* **oswobadzać.** ~ **się** *ipf. zob.* **oswobadzać się.**

oswajać *ipf.*, **oswoić** *pf.* -ój **1.** (= *przyzwyczajać*) accustom, habituate (*kogoś do czegoś* sb to sth) acquaint (*kogoś do czegoś* sb with sth). **2.** (*o zwierzętach*) domesticate, tame. ~ **się** *ipf.*, **oswoić się** *pf.* **1.** (= *przyzwyczajać się*) grow *l.* get accustomed, get used (*z czymś* to sth); get acquainted (*z czymś* with sth). **2.** (*o zwierzętach*) become tamed *l.* domesticated.

oswobadzać *ipf.*, **oswobodzić** *pf.* -odź *l.* -ódź **1.** (= *wyzwalać*) free, liberate; affranchise; *wojsk.* relieve. **2.** (= *uwalniać od jakiejś konieczności*) free, deliver (*kogoś z czegoś* sb from sth) relieve (*kogoś z czegoś* sb of sth). ~ **się** *ipf.*, **oswobodzić się** *pf.* **1.** (= *odzyskiwać wolność*) liberate, free o.s., set o.s. free. **2.** (= *odzyskiwać swobodę ruchów*) extricate o.s., free o.s. **3.** (= *pozbywać się jakiejś przykrej konieczności*) get rid *l.* shot *l.* free of sth, extricate *l.* disentangle o.s. from sth.

oswobodzenie *n.* liberation, deliverance; affranchisement.

oswobodziciel *mp lit.* liberator, rescuer, savior.

oswobodzić *pf.* -odź *l.* -ódź *zob.* **oswobadzać.** ~ **się** *pf.* -odź *l.* -ódź *zob.* **oswobadzać się.**

oswoić *pf.* -ój *zob.* **oswajać.** ~ **się** *pf.* -ój *zob.* **oswajać się.**

oswojony *a.* -eni familiar, acquainted (*z czymś* with sth) accustomed (*z czymś* to sth); (*o psie, kocie*) domesticated, pet, tame; (*o niedźwiedziu*) tame; **na pół oswojony** semi-domesticated.

osyfiony *a. pot.* yucky, skanky, rank, putrid; (*o pokoju, materiale*) skanky, rank, putrid.

osypka *f. Gen.pl.* -ek coarse flour.

oszacować *pf.* estimate, evaluate, appraise; (*straty, zyski, koszty*) estimate; **oszacować coś na sto dolarów** assess sth at $100; **dający się oszacować** estimable; **niedający się oszacować** (*o skutkach*) imponderable.

oszalały *a.* crazed, crazy, out of one's wits *l.* mind, mad, frantic; **oszalały z bólu** wild with

pain; **oszalały z miłości** crazy *l.* mad with love; **jak oszalały** like mad, frantically.

oszaleć *pf.* go mad *l.* crazy *l.* nuts; **Adam oszalał na punkcie Ewy** Adam has gone crazy over Eve, Adam has gone mad *l.* nuts about Eve.

oszalować *pf.* timber, plank, board.

oszałamiać *ipf.* **1.** (= *pozbawiać przytomności*) daze, stun, stupefy. **2.** (= *wprowadzać w zachwyt*) bewilder, stun, boggle, devastate.

oszałamiająco *a.* stunningly, breathtakingly, devastatingly; (*wyglądać*) stunning, devastating.

oszałamiający *a.* stunning, bewildering, breathtaking, overwhelming; (*o karierze, sukcesie*) roaring, dazzling, impressive; (*o wyglądzie, urodzie*) devastating, stunning, ravishing, gorgeous; (*o tempie*) dizzy; (*o szczerości*) staggering, shocking.

oszczekać *pf.*, **oszczekiwać** *ipf.* **1.** (*o psie*) bark (*kogoś* at sb). **2.** *pot.* (= *oczerniać*) badmouth sb, run sb down, put a slur on sb, throw *l.* sling mud *l.* dirt at sb.

oszczenić się *pf.* whelp, pup, have pups.

oszczep *mi* **1.** *hist.* (= *broń*) spear, javelin, gig. **2.** *sport* (*do rzucania*) javelin; **rzut oszczepem** javelin throw. **3.** *sport* (= *dyscyplina*) javelin.

oszczepniczka *f. Gen.pl.* -ek *sport zob.* **oszczepnik** 2.

oszczepnik *mp* **1.** *hist.* spearman. **2.** *sport* javelin thrower.

oszczerca *mp* slanderer, calumniator, mudslinger, backbiter, muck-raker.

oszczerczy *a.* slanderous, backbiting, defamatory, slurring; (*o wypowiedzi*) defamatory, calumnious, backbiting.

oszczerstwo *n.* slander, calumny; **rzucać na kogoś oszczerstwa** cast aspersions on sb, throw *l.* sling mud *l.* dirt at sb, drag sb through the mud.

oszczędnie *adv.* economically, sparingly, charily, prudently; (*żyć, budować*) economically, sparingly; **żyć oszczędnie** scrimp and save; **gospodarować oszczędnie** tighten one's belt, be frugal *l.* thrifty, cut costs *l.* expenditure(s), draw in one's horns.

oszczędności *pl. Gen.* -i **1.** (= *to, co zostało zaoszczędzone*) savings, nest egg; (*materiałowe, paliwa*) reserves, resources. **2.** (= *pieniądze*) savings, funds; **dobrze ulokować swoje oszczędności** invest one's savings well, manage one's money *l.* savings wisely *l.* prudently; **kupić coś z własnych oszczędności** buy sth with one's savings *l.* own money, draw on one's savings, spend one's savings on sth; **robić oszczędności** make savings, lay money by, save up, put *l.* set aside; **wyciągnąć oszczędności** draw out *l.* withdraw one's savings.

oszczędnościowy *a.* economical, saving; (*o książeczce*) saving; (*o względach, budownictwie*) economical; (*o budżecie*) stripped-down; **rachunek oszczędnościowy** savings account.

oszczędność *f.* **1.** (= *bycie oszczędnym*) frugality, chariness, thriftiness; **oszczędnością i**

pracą ludzie się bogacą by saving comes having, spare well and have to spend. **2.** (= *racjonalne zużywanie czegoś*) economy, saving; (*węgla, energii elektrycznej*) economy; **oszczędność czasu/pracy** time/labor saving.

oszczędny *a.* **1.** (= *nierozrzutny*) thrifty, frugal, prudent; (*o gospodyni*) thrifty, prudent; **oszczędny w słowach** (a man) of few words, thrifty *l.* economical *l.* sparing with words. **2.** (= *racjonalny w zużyciu czegoś*) economical, sparing; (*o gospodarce paliwowej, trybie życia*) efficient; (*o stylu*) economical; (*o pochwałach, wydatkach*) sparing; (*o dekoracjach*) sparse; **przesadnie oszczędny** cheeseparing, stingy; (*o gospodarce*) lean. **3.** (= *niekosztowny*) low-cost.

oszczędzać *ipf.*, **oszczędzić** *pf.* **1.** (= *zbierać pieniądze*) save up, lay money by, set *l.* put aside; **oszczędzać na czarną godzinę** save for a rainy day; **oszczędzać na jedzeniu** economize on food, scrimp on food. **2.** (= *ochraniać kogoś*) spare; **choroba nie oszczędza nikogo** illness doesn't spare anyone. **3.** (*bólu, szczegółów*) spare, save; **oszczędzać siły na coś** save o.s. for sth; **oszczędzać komuś kłopotu/bólu** save sb trouble/pain; **nie oszczędzać wysiłku** spare no pains; **oszczędzać słów** be (a man) of few words, be thrifty *l.* economical *l.* sparing with words. **4.** *tylko ipf.* (= racjonalnie *zużywać coś*) save, conserve; (*o gazie, węglu, energii elektrycznej, paliwie*) conserve. **~ się** *ipf.*, **oszczędzić się** *pf.* **1.** (= *ochraniać swoje zdrowie*) take care of o.s. **2.** (= *mieć wzgląd na siebie*) spare o.s., take it easy; **nie oszczędzać siebie** pull one's weight, pay one's way, earn one's keep.

oszkalować *pf.* backbite, slander, defame, calumniate.

oszklić *pf.* **-ij** glaze in.

oszlifować *pf.* polish.

oszołom *mp pl.* **-y** *uj.* freak, buff, nut.

oszołomić *pf. zob.* **oszałamiać.**

oszołomienie *n.* bewilderment, stun, daze, giddiness; **w oszołomieniu** dizzily.

oszołomiony *a.* in a daze, dizzy (*czymś* from sth) staggered, bewildered (*czymś* by *l.* at sth); (= *upojony sukcesem, powodzeniem itp.*) giddy (*czymś* with sth).

oszpecać *ipf.*, **oszpecić** *pf.* mar, deform, disfigure; (*wizerunek, rzeźbę*) deface. **~ się** *ipf.*, **oszpecić się** *pf.* deface, deform, disfigure.

oszronić się *pf.* frost, be frosted, be covered with hoarfrost.

oszroniony *a.* frosted, hoary, rimy.

oszukać *pf. zob.* **oszukiwać.** **~ się** *pf. zob.* **oszukiwać się.**

oszukańczy *a.* crooked, underhand, cheating; (*o procederze, wykrętach*) deceitful, crooked, deceptive; (*o transakcji*) fraudulent, underhand; **oszukańcze praktyki** fraudulent practices, fraudulence.

oszukaństwo *n. pot.* trickery, cheat, double-dealing, leg-pull.

oszukiwać *ipf.* **1.** cheat, swindle, chisel; **oszukiwać kogoś** take sb in, take sb for a ride; **oszukiwać na wadze** give short weight; **oszukał mnie**

na dziesięć dolarów he swindled me out of $10; he overcharged me $10; **oszukiwać głód** beguile one's hunger. **2.** (*dla żartu*) hoax, trick, take sb for a ride, pull sb's leg. **~ się** *ipf.* **1.** (= *dać się oszukiwać*) be led down the garden path, be taken in, be taken for a ride, be caught with chaff. **2.** (*siebie samego*) kid o.s., delude o.s. **3.** (*jeden drugiego*) pull the wool over each other's eyes, deceive *l.* cheat each other.

oszust *mp*, **oszustka** *f. Gen.pl.* **-ek** scamp, swindler, crook, con; (*karciany*) palmer; (*matrymonialny*) bigamist.

oszustwo *n.* trickery, take-in, fake, imposture; **oszustwo finansowe** swindle; **oszustwo podatkowe** tax fraud.

oszwabić *pf. pot.* stiff, chisel, spoof, con.

oś *f. pl.* **-e 1.** *geom.* axis; **oś Ziemi** *geogr.* axis; **oś biegunowa** polar axis; **oś optyczna** *fiz.* optic axis; **oś liczbowa** *mat.* axis; **oś liczb rzeczywistych** real axis; **oś współrzędnych** *mat.* coordinate axis; **oś odciętych** *l.* **zmiennej X** axis of abscissae, X-axis; **oś rzędnych** *l.* **zmiennej Y** axis of ordinates, Y-axis; **oś symetrii** *geom.* axis of symmetry, symmetry axis; **oś krystalograficzna** *min.* crystallographic axis; **oś kwiatowa** *bot.* rachis; **państwa osi** *hist.* the Axis. **2.** (*koła*) axle. **3.** *tech.* pivot, swivel, arbor. **4. oś systemu politycznego** *przen.* keystone.

ościenny *a.* neighboring, adjacent, contiguous; (*o państwie, województwie*) adjacent.

oścień *mi Gen.* **-a** *ryb.* leister, fishing spear *l.* goad, gig.

oścież *adv.* **na oścież** wide open.

ościeże *n. Gen.pl.* **-y** *bud.* reveal, jamb.

ościeżnica *f. bud.* casing, case; **ościeżnica drzwiowa** door casing.

ościeżyna *f. bud.* door trim *l.* lining.

ościęgna *f. Gen.* **-ej** *anat.* epitendineum, peritendineum, tendon sheath.

ościsty *a.* **1.** (*o rybie, mięsie rybim*) bony. **2.** (*o roślinie*) husky. **3.** (*o chlebie*) husky.

ość *f.* **1.** (*ryby*) fishbone; **z ością** *kulin.* (*o rybie*) unboned; **stanąć komuś ością w gardle** stick in one's throat *l.* craw. **2.** *bot.* husk, awn.

ośka *f. Gen.pl.* **-ek** axle, swivel.

ośle *ma zob.* **osioł.**

oślep *adv.* blindly; **na oślep** blindfold, headlong; (*o strzale*) hit-or-miss; (*o pytaniu, strzale*) wild; **walić kogoś na oślep** hit sb with wild abandon, pummel sb, lash at sb, hit *l.* strike *l.* flail out at sb.

oślepiać *ipf.* **1.** (*o blasku*) dazzle, blind, glare. **2.** (*o uczuciach, miłości, nienawiści*) blind, dazzle, delude.

oślepiający *a.* dazzling, glaring; (*blask*) dazzling; **oślepiające światło** dazzle; **oślepiająca jasność** garishness.

oślepić *pf. zob.* **oślepiać.**

oślepnąć *pf.* **-ij**, **-ł** *l.* **-nął -ła -li** go blind, lose one's eyesight.

ośli *a.* **1.** donkey, asinine; **ośli upór** mulishness; **z oślim uporem** mulishly; **z oślimi uszami** well-thumbed, dog-eared; **ośla łączka** *narty* bunny hill, nursery slope; **ośla ławka** *szkoln. przest.*

dunce's bench; **posadzić kogoś w oślej ławce** put sb on the dunce's bench; **ośle uszy** dog ears; **ośla głowa** dimwit. **2. ośli ogórek** *bot.* squirting cucumber (*Echallium elaterium*).

oślica *f.* jenny, she-ass.

ośliczka *f. Gen.pl.* **-ek 1.** (= *mała oślica*) jennet. **2.** *zool.* water louse, asellus (*Asellus aquaticus*).

oślinić się *pf.* slaver, dribble, slobber *l.* wet with saliva.

ośliniony *a.* slobbered; (*o niemowlęciu*) dribbled, slavered.

ośliz(g)ły *a.* oozy, slimy, mucous; (*o kamieniu, drewnie*) slippery, slimy; (*o mięsie*) slimy; (*o człowieku*) slimy, greasy.

ośmielać *ipf.*, **ośmielić** *pf.* embolden, encourage (*kogoś* sb) egg sb on; (*pozbawić kogoś nieśmiałości*) put *l.* set sb at his/her ease. **~ się** *ipf.*, **ośmielić się** *pf.* **1.** dare (*coś zrobić* do sth) venture, have the nerve (*coś zrobić* to do sth) take the liberty (*coś zrobić* of doing sth). **2.** (*nabierać odwagi*) pluck up *l.* muster (up) courage.

ośmieszać *ipf.*, **ośmieszyć** *pf.* ridicule, deride, stultify (*kogoś* sb) make fun *l.* a mockery *l.* a fool (*kogoś* of sb) poke fun, laugh (*kogoś* at sb); (*publicznie*) gibbet. **~ się** *ipf.*, **ośmieszyć się** *pf.* make a fool of o.s.

ośmioboczny *a.* octagonal; (*o figurze, dziedzińcu, kolumnie*) octagonal; (*o bryle*) octahedral.

ośmiobok *mi geom.* octagon.

ośmiogodzinny *a.* eight-hour; (*podróż*) eight-hour long; **mieć ośmiogodzinny dzień pracy** work an eight-hour day.

ośmiokąt *mi Gen.* **-a** *geom.* octangle.

ośmiokątny *a.* octangular.

ośmioklasista *mp*, **ośmioklasistka** *f. Gen.pl.* **-ek** *szkoln.* eight-grader, eighth-grade pupil; *zwł. Br.* eight-former, eighth-form pupil.

ośmioklasowy *a. szkoln.* eight-grade; *zwł. Br.* eight-form.

ośmiokrotny *a.* eightfold, octuple, eight-time; (*o zysku*) eightfold.

ośmiolatek *mp* **-tk-** *pl.* **-i** eight-year-old boy, boy of eight.

ośmiolatka *f. Gen.pl.* **-ek** eight-year-old girl, girl of eight.

ośmioletni *a.* eight-year-old, of eight, octennial; (*o domu, samochodzie*) eight-year-old; (*o dziecku*) (kid) of eight.

ośmioraczki *pl.* octuplets.

ośmiornica *f. zool.* octopus, devilfish (*Octopus*).

ośmioro *num. decl. like n.* **-rg-** eight.

ośmiu *num. zob.* **ośmiem**.

ośnieża *f. bot.* silverbell tree, snowdrop tree (*Halesia*); **ośnieża czteroskrzydła** Carolina silverbell (*Halesia carolina*).

ośnieżać *ipf.* snow (*coś* on sth).

ośnieżony *a.* snow-covered; snow-clad; (*o drzewie, górach, polach*) snowy; (*o wierzchołku*) snow-capped.

ośnieżyć *pf. zob.* **ośnieżać**.

ośnik *mi Gen.* **-a** *techn.* spokeshave, drawknife, drawshave.

ośrodek *mi* **-dk-** *Gen.* **-a 1.** (= *punkt centralny, centrum, instytucja*) center; *t. przen.* hub; (*wypoczynkowy*) resort; **ośrodek korowy/oddechowy/odruchowy** *anat.* cortical/respiratory/reflex center; **ośrodek mowy/snu/wzwodu** *anat.* speech/sleep/erection center; **ośrodek kultury** (*lokalna instytucja*) community center; (*kraj, miasto*) culture center; **ośrodek zdrowia** clinic; **ośrodek badawczy/naukowy/przemysłowy/sportowy/telewizyjny** research/scientific/industrial/sports/TV center; **ośrodek wczasowy** holiday center *l.* resort. **2.** *meteor.* area; **ośrodek niskiego/wysokiego ciśnienia** low/high pressure area. **3.** *fiz.* medium.

ośrodkowy *a.* central; **ośrodkowy układ nerwowy** *anat.* central nervous system.

ośródka *f. przest.* crumb; core.

oświadczać *ipf.* declare, profess; (= *ogłaszać*) announce; (=*stwierdzać*) state; *t.* affirm; (= *orzekać*) pronounce (*że coś jest czymś* sth sth). **~ się** *ipf.* propose (*komuś* to sb); *pot.* pop the question.

oświadczenie *n.* (*t. majątkowe, podatkowe*) declaration; (= *ogłoszenie*) announcement; **oświadczenie prasowe** press release; **oświadczenie woli** *prawn.* assent, declaration; **oficjalne oświadczenie** official statement; **złożyć oświadczenie w sprawie...** give *l.* make a statement concerning...; **uzyskać oświadczenie** get *l.* take a statement.

oświadczyć *pf. zob.* **oświadczać**. **~ się** *pf. zob.* **oświadczać się**.

oświadczyny *pl. Gen.* **-n** proposal (of marriage).

oświata *f.* education; school system; **oświata środowiskowa/zdrowotna** environmental/health education; **być pracownikiem oświaty** work in education; **ministerstwo oświaty** ministry of education.

oświatowy *a.* (= *służący oświacie*) educational; (= *związany z oświatą*) education; **film/program oświatowy** educational film/program; **placówka oświatowa** educational institution *l.* establishment; seat of learning; **władze oświatowe** education authorities.

oświecać *ipf.* **1.** (= *informować*) enlighten (*kogoś co do czegoś* sb on sth); illuminate, illumine; **oświeciło go** it dawned on him; *pot.* it clicked with him. **2.** (= *szerzyć wiedzę*) educate.

oświecenie *n.* **1.** enlightenment; illumination; **doznać oświecenia** *rel.* see the light. **2.** *hist.* Enlightenment (period); (*angielskie, francuskie*) Age of Reason.

oświeceniowy *a.* Enlightenment; **hasła/idee oświeceniowe** slogans/ideas of the Enlightenment period.

oświecić *pf. zob.* **oświecać**.

oświecony *a. pl.* **-eni** enlightened; **oświecony absolutyzm** enlightened absolutism; **Jaśnie Oświecony** His Grace; (*przy zwracaniu się*) Your Grace; **oświeceni** illuminati.

oświetlacz *mi opt.* illumination.

oświetlać *ipf.* light, lighten; illuminate;

(*punktowo*) spotlight; (*reflektorami*) floodlight; **jasno oświetlony** brightly lit *l.* illuminated.

oświetlenie *n.* lighting; illumination; **oświetlenie awaryjne** emergency *l.* safety lighting; **oświetlenie elektryczne/gazowe/uliczne** electric/gas/street lighting; **oświetlenie kabiny** *mot.* courtesy light; **oświetlenie tylne** *fot.* contre, jour.

oświetleniowiec *mp film, teatr* lighting engineer, lighting man.

oświetleniowy *a.* (*o instalacji, sprzęcie*) lighting.

oświetlić *pf. zob.* **oświetlać.**

Oświęcim *mi* -mi- *Gen.* -a *hist., geogr.* Auschwitz.

ot *particle* **ot co!** and that's that!; **ot tak** just like that; for no reason at all.

otaczać *ipf.* **1.** surround (*coś czymś* sth by *l.* with sth); encompass; (= *ogradzać*) encircle, enclose (*coś czymś* sth by sth); **dom otoczony był lasem** the house was surrounded with a forest; **otaczała go aura tajemnicy** there was an air of mystery about him; **otaczać fosą/palisadą/rowem/siatką/wałem/żywopłotem** moat/stockade/(en)trench/net/mound/hedge. **2.** (= *okazywać*) lavish (*czymś kogoś* sth (up)on sb); **otaczać kogoś miłością/opieką** lavish affection/attention on sb; **być otoczonym czcią** be hallowed; **być otoczonym szacunkiem** be held in respect. **3.** *kulin.* coat (*coś czymś* sth in sth). ~ **się** *ipf.* (= *gromadzić wokół siebie*) surround o.s. (*kimś / czymś* with sb/sth).

otaklować *pf. żegl.* rig.

otaklowanie *n. żegl.* rigging.

otaksować *pf.* (= *ocenić wartość*) appraise; (*np. wzrokiem*) size up.

otarcie *n.* **1.** (*skóry*) graze, abrasion. **2. na otarcie łez** *przen.* to soften the blow; **- Na otarcie łez!** - To cheer you up!

otaria *f. Gen.* -ii *zool.* eared seal (*Otaria*).

otąg *ma bot.* cereus, torch thistle (*Cereus*).

otchłanny *a.* abysmal.

otchłań *f. pl.* -e chasm; *przen., t.* piekielna abyss; **otchłań piekielna** *Bibl.* the pit (of hell); **otchłań wód** the deep, the depths of the ocean.

otczestwo *n.* patronymic.

otępiać *ipf.* numb; (*np. zmysły*) dull.

otępiały *a.* (*o człowieku*) numbed; listless, torpid; **patrzeć otępiałym wzrokiem** gaze listlessly, look numbly.

otępić *pf. zob.* **otępiać.**

otępieć *pf.* become *l.* grow numb, become *l.* grow listless.

otępienie *n.* **1.** (= *apatia*) listlessness, torpidity; stupor, stupefaction; **wpaść w otępienie** become listless *l.* torpid. **2.** *psych., pat.* dementia; **otępienie starcze** senile dementia.

otiatria *f. Gen.* -ii *med.* otology.

otłuszczenie *n. med.* lipomatosis, adiposity, fat deposition; **otłuszczenie serca** cardiac adiposis; fatty heart.

otłuszczony *a.* fatty; *pat.* adipose.

oto *particle* **1.** here (is *l.* are); **oto on/ona (we własnej osobie)** here he/she is (as large as life). **2.** (= *mianowicie*) here; **ten/te oto** this/these...

here; **nabyłem tę papugę w tym oto sklepie** I purchased that parrot from this very shop.

otocjon *ma zool.* bat-eared fox, cape fox, big-eared fox, motlosi (*Otocyon megalotis*).

otocysta *f. zool.* otocyst.

otoczak *mi Gen.* -a *geol.* (*mały*) pebble; (*duży*) cobble, boulder.

otoczenie *n.* **1.** (= *okolica*) surroundings; **bezpośrednie otoczenie** immediate surroundings. **2.** (= *atmosfera miejsca*) ambience. **3.** (= *środowisko*) environment; milieu; **zmiana otoczenia** change of scene. **4.** (= *świta*) entourage. **5.** (= *sztafaż*) mise-en-scène; setting.

otoczka *f. Gen.pl.* -ek **1.** integument; encasement; **mistyczna otoczka** mystique. **2.** *anat.* areola. **3.** *biol.* sheath. **4.** *astron., geol.* aureola; **otoczka metamorficzna** contact *l.* metamorphic aureola.

otoczyć *pf. zob.* **otaczać.** ~ **się** *pf. zob.* **otoczyć się.**

otok *mi Gen.* -u *l.* -a (= *obrzeże*) rim; (*czapki*) cap band.

otolaryngolog *mp pl.* -dzy *l.* -owie *med.* otolaryngologist, otologist.

otolaryngologia *f. Gen.* -ii *med.* otolaryngology.

otolit *mi anat.* otolith.

otologia *f. Gen.* -ii *med.* otology.

otomana *f.* divan, ottoman.

otomański *a. hist.* Ottoman; **Porta Otomańska** Sublime Porte.

otorbiać się *ipf.*, **otorbić się** *pf. pat.* encyst.

otorbienie *n. pat.* encystment.

otorbiony *a. pat.* encysted.

otoskleroza *f. pat.* otosclerosis.

otoskop *mi med.* otoscope, auriscope.

otoskopia *f med.* otoscopy.

otóż *particle* **1.** (= *oto*) here is/are. **2. otóż to!** quite so!, precisely!, exactly!, that's it!

otręby *pl. Gen.* -ów *kulin.* bran.

otruć *pf.* poison. ~ **się** *pf.* poison o.s.

otrzaskać się *pf. pot.* get the feel, get the hang (*z czymś* of sth); learn the ropes.

otrzaskany *a. pot.* **być z czymś otrzaskanym** know the ropes, be no stranger to sth.

otrząsać *ipf.*, **otrząsnąć** *pf.* shake (*coś z czegoś* sth off sth). ~ **się** *ipf.*, **otrząsnąć się** *pf.* **1.** (= *odzyskiwać równowagę psychiczną*) shake off (*z czegoś* sth); get over (*z czegoś* sth). **2.** (= *wzdrygać się*) shudder.

otrzeć *pf.* **otrę otrzesz, otrzyj, otarł** *zob.* **ocierać.** ~ **się** *pf. zob.* **ocierać się.**

otrzepać *pf.* -ę -esz, **otrzepywać** *ipf.* brush (*coś z czegoś* sth off sth). ~ **się** *pf.*, **otrzepywać się** *ipf.* (*z kurzu, pyłu*) dust o.s. off; (*np. po upadku*) *US* brush o.s. off; *Br.* brush o.s. down.

otrzewna *f. Gen.* -ej *anat.* peritoneum; **zapalenie otrzewnej** *pat.* peritonitis.

otrzewnowy *a. anat., med.* peritoneal.

otrzeźwiać *ipf.*, **otrzeźwić** *pf.* -wij *l.* -w sober (up).

otrzeźwieć *pf.* sober (up).

otrzęsiny *pl. Gen.* -n *szkoln., uniw.* hazing; **poddawać otrzęsinom** haze.

otrzymać *pf.*, **otrzymywać** *ipf.* receive; (*pozwolenie, szlachectwo itp.*) obtain, be granted; (*tytuł*) be conferred; (*pensję, zasiłek*) draw; (*nagrodę, odszkodowanie, odznaczenie, stypendium naukowe*) be awarded.

otucha *f.* courage; **dodać komuś otuchy** hearten sb, lift *l.* raise sb's spirits; *pot.* buck sb up, buck up sb's spirits *l.* morale; **nabrać otuchy** take heart.

otulać *ipf.*, **otulić** *pf.* wrap (*kogoś/coś czymś* sth around *l.* about sb/sth). ~ **się** *ipf.*, **otulić się** *pf.* wrap o.s. (*czymś* in sth); gather (*czymś* sth around one).

otulina *f.* **1.** *bud.* lagging; covering. **2.** *techn.* jacket. **3.** *ekol.* protection zone.

otumaniać *ipf.*, **otumanić** *pf.* **1.** (= *ogłupić*) addle; stupefy. **2.** (= *odurzyć*) intoxicate.

otumanienie *n.* wooziness.

otumaniony *a.* addled; (*t. alkoholem*) woozy, muzzy, hazy; (*narkotykiem*) dopey.

otwarcie[1] *n.* **1.** (= *inauguracja*) opening; **uroczystość otwarcia** opening ceremony. **2.** (= *bycie czynnym*) **godziny otwarcia** opening hours; **godziny otwarcia banku** banking hours; **kurs** *l.* **notowanie otwarcia** *fin.* starting price *l.* quotation; **opóźnione otwarcie (spadochronu)** delayed drop.

otwarcie[2] *adv.* (= *wprost, szczerze*) openly, plainly, straightforwardly.

otwartość *f.* openness.

otwarty *a.* **1.** (= *dostępny, jawny, rozległy*) open; **otwarty na oścież** open wide; **otwarta gruźlica** *pat.* open tuberculosis; **otwarta przestrzeń** open space; **otwarta rana** gaping wound; **otwarte morze** the open sea, high sea; **otwarty umysł** open mind; **grać z kimś w otwarte karty** *przen.* be open with sb, play fair with sb; **mieć oczy szeroko otwarte** *przen.* keep one's eyes (wide) open; **na otwartym powietrzu** outdoors, in the open (air); **ogłaszać coś za otwarte** declare sth open; **polityka otwartych drzwi** open door (policy); **witać kogoś z otwartymi ramionami** *przen.* greet *l.* welcome sb with open arms; **dom otwarty** open house; **drzwi otwarte** *uniw., szkoln. US* open house; *Br., Austr.* open day; **konkurs otwarty** open competition; **list otwarty** open letter; **przedział/zbiór otwarty** *mat.* open interval/set; **samogłoska/sylaba otwarta** *fon.* open vowel/syllable; **złamanie otwarte** *med.* open *l.* penetrating fracture. **2.** *przen.* (*o człowieku*) (= *elastyczny*) open, flexible; **być otwartym na coś** be open to sth. **3.** *przen.* (= *szczery*) honest, straightforward, candid.

otwieracz *mi Gen.* **-a** opener; (*do butelek*) bottle opener; (*do puszek*) *US* can opener; *Br.* tin opener.

otwierać *ipf.* **1.** (*coś przymkniętego/zamkniętego, np. drzwi, granicę, list, oczy, puszkę; t. rozpoczynać, inicjować, inaugurować, np. olimpiadę, rachunek*) open; **otwierać do kogoś ogień** *t. wojsk.* open fire on sb; **otworzyć komuś oczy na coś** *przen.* open sb's eyes to sth; **otworzyć przed kimś duszę** *przen.* bare one's soul to sb, unbosom o.s. to sb; **otworzyć przed kimś serce** *przen.* open one's heart to sb. **2.** (*w rozkazach*) open up;

otwierać, policja! open up, this is the police! **3.** (*o firmie, sklepie*) open; **o której otwierają biura?** what time do the offices open?; **na naszej ulicy otworzyli nową stację benzynową** a new gas station has opened on our street. **4.** (*coś zamkniętego na klucz l. zamek*) unlock. ~ **się** *ipf.* (= *być otwieranym, rozchylać się*) open (up); **okno otwiera się do wewnątrz** window opens in-(wards); **sezamie, otwórz się** open sesame. **2.** (= *zacząć mówić*) open up.

otworek *mi* small hole, pinhole.

otwornica *f. techn.* fret saw; (*ręczna*) keyhole saw, compass saw.

otwornice *pl. Gen.* **-c** *zool.* foraminifers (*Foraminifera*).

otworzyć *pf.* **-órz** *zob.* **otwierać**. ~ **się** *pf.* **-órz** *zob.* **otwierać się**.

otwór *mi* **-o-** **1.** opening; hole; **otwór gębowy** *zool.* mouth opening; **otwór okienny** *bud.* window opening; **stać otworem** be open; *przen.* stand open. **2.** *techn.* hole; **otwór strzałowy** *górn.* shot hole; **otwór strzelniczy** *wojsk.* port(hole); **otwór szpuntowy** (*w beczce*) bunghole; **otwór wentylacyjny** *l.* **odpowietrzający** (extraction) vent, ventilation hole *l.* slit; **otwór wiertniczy** *górn.* borehole; **otwór wlotowy/wylotowy** *techn.* inlet/outlet; (*po kuli*) entrance/exit hole; **otwór zapałowy** *wojsk.* touchhole. **3.** *form.* orifice. **4.** *anat.* orifice; (*w złożeniach*) foramen, aperture.

otyłość *f.* obesity; *pat.* adiposity.

otyły *a.* obese.

otynkować *pf.* plaster.

owa *a.* that.

owacja *f.* (hearty) round of applause, applause, ovation; **owacja na stojąco** standing ovation; **gorąca owacja** thunderous applause *l.* ovation; **zgotować komuś owację** cheer sb, give sb an ovation, give sb a big hand.

owacyjnie *adv.* enthusiastically; **być przyjętym owacyjnie** meet with (loud) applause, receive (an ecstatic) ovation.

owacyjny *a.* enthusiastic; **owacyjne przyjęcie** thunderous applause, ecstatic ovation.

owad *ma* insect; **owad domowy** household insect; **owady dwuskrzydłe** *ent.* dipterans (*Diptera*); **owady prostoskrzydłe** *ent.* orthopterans.

owadobójczy *a.* insecticidal; **środek owadobójczy** insecticide.

owadopylność *f. biol.* entomophily.

owadopylny *a. biol.* entomophilous.

owadożerne *pl. Gen.* **-ych** *zool.* insectivores.

owadożerny *a. biol.* insectivorous, entomophagous.

owady *pl. Gen.* **-ów** *ent.* insects (*Insecta*).

owadziarki *pl. Gen.* **-rek** *zool.* terebrantia (*Terebrantes*).

owak *adv.* **tak czy owak** anyhow, either way, in any case; one way or the other, be that as it may, just the same, all the same.

owaki *a.* **w taki czy owaki sposób** one way or another; either way; **taki owaki** so-and-so.

owal *mi Gen.pl.* **-i** *l.* **-ów** oval.

owalny *a.* (*np. o twarzy, lustrze*) oval; **Gabinet Owalny** *polit.* the Oval Office.

owca *f. Gen.pl.* **owiec** sheep; **owca perska** broadtail; **stado owiec** flock *l.* herd of sheep; **czarna owca** *przen.* black sheep; **i wilk będzie syty, i owca cała** *Bibl.* we can have the best of best worlds.

owczarek *ma* -**rk**- *kynol.* sheepdog, shepherd (dog); **owczarek niemiecki** German shepherd, Alsatian; **owczarek podhalański** Polish shepherd; **owczarek staroangielski** Old English sheepdog; **owczarek szetlandzki** Shetland sheepdog, sheltie; **owczarek szkocki** collie.

owczarnia *f. Gen.pl.* -**i** *l.* -**ń** (*pomieszczenie*) sheepshed; (*zagroda, stado*) sheepfold.

owczarstwo *n. roln.* *US* sheep ranching; *Br.* sheep farming.

owczarz *mp* shepherd.

owczy *a.* ovine; (*o serze, wełnie*) sheep's; **owczy pęd** following the crowd, moving with the crowd; **wilk w owczej skórze** *przen.* wolf in sheep's clothing; **Wyspy Owcze** *geogr.* Faroe Islands, Faeroe Islands, Faroes.

owdowiały *a.* (*o kobiecie*) widowed; (*o mężczyźnie*) widowered.

owdowieć *pf.* be widowed; (*o kobiecie*) become a widow; (*o mężczyźnie*) become a widower.

owego *itd. a. zob.* **ów**.

owerlok *mi Gen.* -**a** *techn.* electric knitting machine.

owędy *adv.* **tędy i owędy** hither and thither.

owiać *pf.* -**eję** -**ejesz** *zob.* **owiewać**.

Owidiusz *mp* Ovid.

owieczka *f. Gen.pl.* -**ek** lamb; **łagodny jak owieczka** meek as a lamb; **zbłąkana owieczka** lost sheep.

owies *mi* ows- *Gen.* -**a** **1.** *bot.* oat (*Avena*); **owies bizantyjski** red oat (*Avena byzantina*); **owies głuchy** wild oat (*Avena fatua*); **owies krótki** little oat (*Avena brevis*); **owies nagoziarnowy** *l.* **nagi** naked oat (*Avena nuda*); **owies szorstki** lopsided oat (*Avena strigosa*); **owies wodny** wild *l.* Indian rice (*Zizania aquatica*); **owies zwyczajny** common oat (*Avena sativa*). **2.** (= *ziarno, nasiona*) oats.

owiewać *ipf.* **1.** (*o wietrze*) (= *pieścić*) stroke, caress. **2.** (= *spowijać*) envelop, embrace, enshroud, engulf; **owiany tajemnicą** *przen.* shrouded *l.* cloaked in secrecy; **łąki owiane mgłą** meadows enveloped in mist.

owiewka *f. Gen.pl.* -**ek** *lotn.* fairing; *pot.* (= *osłona kabiny*) canopy.

owijacze *pl wojsk.* puttees.

owijać *ipf.*, **owinąć** *pf.* wrap (up) (*w coś* in sth); *t. przen.* envelop (*w coś* in sth); **owinąć kogoś dookoła palca** *przen.* wrap sb around one's little finger; **nie owijał niczego w bawełnę** *pot.* he didn't beat around *l.* about the bush, he got right to the point, he made no bones about it. ~ **się** *ipf.*, **owinąć się** *pf.* wind (*wokół czegoś* around sth).

owijanie *n. med.* pack; **owijanie w mokre prześcieradło** wet pack.

owładnąć *pf.* -**ij** (*o uczuciu, nastroju*) pervade, overwhelm; (*o smutku, strachu*) overwhelm,

grip; (*o chorobie, uczuciach*) invade; (*o myśli*) prepossess.

owłosienie *n.* **1.** (*włosy*) growth of hair; **owłosienie łonowe** pubic hair, pubes; **nadmierne owłosienie** hirsuitism. **2.** *biol.* (*t. na roślinach*) pilosity, pubescence; *zool.* coat.

owłosiony *a.* **1.** hairy; *t. bot.* (*zwł. silnie*) hirsute. **2.** *biol.* (*t. o roślinach*) pilose, pubescent. **3.** *bot.* piliferous.

owo *a.* that; **to i owo** this and that; **wiedzieć to i owo** know a thing or two.

owoc *mi t. przen.* fruit; **owoce cytrusowe/kandyzowane/pestkowe** citrus/candied/stone fruit; **owoce morza** *kulin.* seafood; **owoc czyichś lędźwi** *Bibl.* the fruit of sb's loins; **owoc czyichś starań** *l.* **wysiłków** *przen.* the fruit of sb's labor; **po owocach poznacie ich** *Bibl.* by their fruits ye shall know them; **przynosić owoce** *przen.* (*np. o planie*) bear fruit; **zakazany owoc** *przen.* forbidden fruit.

owocek *ma bot.* acinus.

owocnia *f. Gen.pl.* -**i** *bot.* pericarp.

owocnie *adv.* fruitfully; (*np. obradować*) successfully, effectively.

owocnik *mi Gen.* -**a** *bot.* (*grzyba*) fruiting body.

owocny *a.* fruitful; (*o spotkaniu, dyskusji, pracy*) rewarding; successful, effective, productive.

owocolistek *mi* -**tk**- *Gen.* -**a** *bot.* carpel.

owocolistkowy *a. bot.* carpellary.

owoconośny *a. bot.* fructiferous.

owocostan *mi bot.* fructification.

owocować *ipf.* **1.** *bot.* fructify; *pot.* be in fruit. **2.** *przen.* (= *dawać rezultaty*) bear fruit.

owocowanie *n. bot.* fructification, fruiting.

owocowo-warzywny *a.* fruit and vegetable; **stragan owocowo-warzywny** fruit and vegetable stall; **sklep owocowo-warzywny** greengrocer.

owocowy *a.* (*np. o drzewie, sałatce, soku, winie*) fruit; (*o posmaku, zapachu*) fruity; **cukier owocowy** *chem.* fruit sugar, fructose; **deser owocowy** fruit cup; **muszka owocowa** *ent.* drosophila, fruit fly (*Drosophila melanogaster*); **sok owocowy** fruit juice.

owocożerny *a.* fruit-eating; *zool.* frugivorous.

owocówka *f. Gen.pl.* -**ek** *ent., pot.* fruit fly (*Drosophila*); **owocówka jabłkóweczka** (apple) codling moth (*Cydia pomonella*); **owocówka śliwóweczka** plum fruit moth (*Cydia funebrana*).

owodnia *f. Gen.pl.* -**i** *biol.* amniotic sac, amnion.

owodniowce *pl. Gen.* -**ów** *zool.* amniotes (*Amniota*).

owodniowy *a. biol.* amniotic; **płyn owodniowy** amniotic fluid.

owręże *n. żegl.* midship bend *l.* section.

owrężenie *n. żegl., bud.* body plan; framing; **owrężenie łukowe/poprzeczne/wzdłużne** arch/transverse/longitudinal framing.

owrzodzenie *n. pat.* ulceration.

owrzodzony *a.* -**eni** *pat.* ulcerated, ulcerating.

owsianka *f. Gen.pl.* -**ek** **1.** *kulin.* porridge. **2.** (*słoma*) oat straw.

owsiany *a.* oat; **płatki owsiane** rolled oats; *kulin.* oatmeal.

owsica *f.* **1.** *bot.* blue oat grass, ornamental oats (*Helictotrichon*). **2.** *pat.* oxyuriasis, enterobiosis.

owsik *mp Gen.* **-ów 1.** *zool.* **owsik ludzki** pinworm, seat worm, threadworm (*Enterobius l. Oxyuris vernicularis*); **owsik koński** horse pinworm (*Oxyuris equi*). **2.** oat grass (*Arrhenatherum, Danthonia*); **owsik pastewny** *l.* **wyniosły** *bot.* tall oat grass (*Arrhenatherum elatius*).

owszem *part.* **1.** (= *istotnie*) indeed. **2.** *lit.* (= *wręcz przeciwnie*) on the contrary.

owulacja *f.* *fizj.* ovulation.

owulacyjny *a.* *fizj.* ovulatory.

oz *mi geol.* esker.

ozalid *mi druk.* Ozalid.

ozdabiać *ipf.* **1.** (= *upiększać*) adorn, embellish, ornament (*czymś* with sth). **2.** *lit.* (= *być ozdobą*) adorn. **~ się** *ipf.* adorn o.s.

ozdoba *f. Gen.pl.* **-ób 1.** (= *dekoracja*) ornament, (decorative) embellishment, decoration; (*ubioru*) trimming, accessory; **dla ozdoby** for ornament; **ozdoby świąteczne** Christmas decorations. **2.** *przen.* (= *chluba*) ornament, adornment; **stanowić ozdobę** adorn (*czegoś* sth); be an ornament (*czegoś* to sth).

ozdobić *pf.* **-ób** *zob.* **ozdabiać. ~ się** *pf. zob.* **ozdabiać się.**

ozdobnie *adv.* ornately, decoratively; elaborately.

ozdobnik *mi Gen.* **-a 1.** *sztuka* ornament, decorative detail. **2.** *muz.* grace (note), ornament.

ozdobność *f.* ornateness; elaborateness; (= *kwiecistość*) floridity.

ozdobny *a.* decorative; ornamental; (*zwł. nadmiernie*) ornate, elaborate; *pot.* fancy.

ozdóbka *f.* (= *błyskotka*) trinket, bauble, trifle, knickknack, kickshaw.

ozdrowieć *pf.* recover, get well.

ozdrowieniec *mp* **-ńc-** *pl.* **-y** convalescent.

ozębna *f. Gen.* **-ej** *anat.* periodontium, periodontal membrane.

oziębiać *ipf.* cool (down); chill; *techn.* refrigerate; *metal.* quench. **~ się** *ipf.* cool (down); chill; (*do normalnej temperatury*) cool off.

oziębiający *a.* (*np. o kompresie*) cooling.

oziębianie *n.* cooling; *techn.* refrigeration.

oziębić *pf. zob.* **oziębiać. ~ się** *pf. zob.* **oziębiać się.**

oziębienie *n.* cooling; *techn.* refrigeration; **oziębienie klimatu** climate cooling.

ozięble *adv.* coldly, lovelessly; **potraktować kogoś ozięble** give sb the cold shoulder, cold-shoulder sb.

oziębłość *f.* **1.** (= *obojętność*) coldness, chilliness. **2.** *pat.* (sexual) frigidity.

oziębły *a.* (= *wrogi*) chilly; (*np. o spojrzeniu*) frigid; *pat.* (sexually) frigid; *pot.* undersexed.

ozimina *f. roln.* winter crop *l.* corn.

ozimy *a. roln.* winter; **pszenica ozima** winter wheat.

ozłacać *ipf.*, **ozłocić** *pf.* (= *pozłacać*) gild; **ozłocę cię** *przen.* I'll cover *l.* bury you in gold.

oznaczać *ipf.* **1.** *tylko ipf.* (= *znaczyć*) mean; *form.* denote; (= *wskazywać*) indicate; **co oznacza ten napis?** what does this inscription mean? **2.** (= *zaznaczać*) mark. **3.** *t. chem.* (= *ustalać*) determine. **4.** *mat.* define.

oznaczanie *n.* **1.** *log.* designation. **2.** *chem.* determination; **oznaczanie ilościowe/jakościowe/objętościowe/wagowe** quantitative/qualitative/volumetric/gravimetric determination.

oznaczenie *n.* **1.** (= *symbol, znak*) marking. **2.** *zob.* **oznaczanie.**

oznaczony *a.* marked; (*o czasie, terminie*) appointed; (*np. o trasie*) predetermined, preset; **całka oznaczona** *mat.* definite integral.

oznaczyć *pf. zob.* **oznaczać.**

oznajmiać *ipf.*, **oznajmić** *pf.* **-ij** *lit.* announce; declare.

oznajmujący *a.* *gram.* indicative; **tryb oznajmujący** indicative mood; **zdanie oznajmujące** declarative sentence.

oznaka *f.* **1.** (*np. choroby, słabości, zmęczenia, życia*) (= *symptom*) sign; indication; **oznaki zatrucia** poisoning symptoms; **oznaki życia** signs of life. **2.** (= *emblemat*) sign, emblem; (= *symbol*) token; **oznaka godności/władzy** badge of office/authority.

oznakować *pf.* mark; (*etykietą*) label.

oznakowanie *n.* marking, marks; (*etykietą*) labeling; *wojsk.* markings; **oznakowanie nawigacyjne** *żegl.* buoyage, navigational aids; **oznakowanie toru wodnego** *żegl.* fairway *l.* channel markings, clearing marks; **oznakowanie trasy** *sport* course marking; **bez oznakowań** (*np. o samochodzie*) unmarked.

ozokeryt *mi chem.* ozocerite, mineral wax; **ozokeryt oczyszczony** ceresin.

ozon *mi chem.* ozone.

ozonizacja *f. chem.* ozonization.

ozonizator *mi Gen.* **-a** *chem.* ozonizer.

ozonki *pl. Gen.* **-ów** *chem.* ozonides.

ozonometr *mi techn.* ozonemeter.

ozonosfera *f. meteor.* ozonosphere, ozone layer.

ozonować *ipf. techn.* ozonize.

ozonowy *a.* ozonic, ozonous; **dziura/warstwa ozonowa** ozone hole/layer.

ozorek *mi* **-rk-** *Gen.* **-a 1.** (= *mały ozór*) little tongue. **2.** *kulin.* tongue. **3.** *bot.* **ozorek pospolity** ox-tongue, beef-steak fungus (*Fistulina hepatica*).

ozorka *f. bot.* **ozorka zielona** green-bracted orchid, long-bracted orchid, frog orchid (*Coeloglossum viride*).

ozór *mi* **-o-** *Gen.* **-a 1.** *pot.* (= *język*) clapper; **chlapnąć ozorem** blab; **latać z ozorem** spill the beans about; **latać z wywieszonym ozorem** bustle about *l.* around; **mleć ozorem** wag one's tongue; **rozpuścić ozór** start gabb(l)ing *l.* jabbering. **2.** *kulin.* tongue; **ozór wołowy** ox tongue.

Ozyrys *mp mit.* Osiris.

oźrebić się *pf.* foal.

ożaglowanie *n. żegl.* rig; **ożaglowanie łacińskie/rejowe/sztakslowe/topowe** lateen/square/staysail/masthead rig.

ożanka *f. bot.* germander (*Teucrium*); **ożanka nierównozabkowa** wood sage (*Teucrium scorodonia*); **ożanka właściwa** germander (*Teucrium chamaedrys*).

ożebrować *pf.* rib.

ożebrowanie *n. bud., techn.* ribbing; **ożebrowanie sklepienia** vault ribbing.

ożenek *mi* **-nk-** *lit.* marriage, wedlock, matrimony.

ożenić *pf.* marry (off); *przest.* wive. **~ się** *pf.* get married (*z kimś* with sb); marry; *przest.* wive (*z kimś* sb).

ożędka *f. bot.* ball mustard (*Neslia*).

ożóg *mi* **-o-** *Gen.* **-a 1.** (*pogrzebacz*) poker. **2.** (= *tląca się głownia*) brand.

ożyć *pf.* **-ję -jesz, ożywać** *ipf.* **-am -asz** come alive; **jego twarz ożyła** his face came alive.

ożywczy *a.* invigorating, restorative; (*o podmuchu, deszczu, powietrzu*) bracing, stimulating.

ożywiać *ipf.*, **ożywić** *pf.* **1.** (= *reanimować*) revive; *med.* resuscitate. **2.** (= *pobudzać, urozmaicać*) enliven, liven up; perk up. **~ się** *ipf.*, **ożywić się** *pf.* come to life; liven up, perk up.

ożywienie *n.* liveliness; animation; **mówić z ożywieniem** talk animatedly *l.* excitedly.

ożywiony *a.* **-eni** (*o ruchu, handlu, dyskusji, działalności, rozmowie, korespondencji*) lively, animated; (*o materii, przyrodzie*) animate, living.

Ó, ó *n. indecl.* (*litera*) Ó, ó.

ósemka *f. Gen.pl.* **-ek 1.** (*osiem osób lub rzeczy*) eight; **cyfra osiem** the figure of eight; (*coś, np. tramwaj, o numerze osiem*) the eight; (*elementów*) octad. **2.** *druk.* (*format książki*) octavo. **3.** *muz.* US eighth note; *Br.* quaver. **4.** *sport* (*ewolucja, łódź*) eight; *bilard* eight ball. **5.** *żegl.* (*węzeł*) figure of eight, figure-eight knot; (*zwój liny*) figure-eight fake.

ósmoklasista *mp*, **ósmoklasistka** *f. Gen.pl.* **-ek** US eighth grader; *Br.* eighth former.

ósmy *a.* eighth; **godzina ósma** eight o'clock;

jedna ósma one eighth; **ósmy cud świata** eighth wonder of the world; **ósmy krzyżyk** one's seventies. – *mi* (*ósmy dzień miesiąca*) the eighth.

ów *a.* **ow- 1.** *lit.* (= *właśnie ten*) this here; this very; that there. **2.** (= *inny*) some other. **3.** *pot.* **ten czy ów** someone or other; **ten i ów** some; **ni z tego, ni z owego** out of the blue; **ni to, ni owo** neither fish nor fowl; neither one thing nor the other.

ówczesny *a.* the then.

ówdzie *adv.* (= *nie tutaj*) elsewhere; **tu i ówdzie** here and there.

P

P, p *n. indecl.* (*litera*) P, p; **P jak Paweł** P is for Papa; P as in Papa.

p.[1] *abbr.* (= *patrz*) s. (*see*).

p.[2] *abbr.* **1.** (= *pan*) Mr. (*mister*). **2.** (= *pani*) Mrs. (*missis*).

p.[3] *abbr.* (*przy wyliczaniu*) (= *punkt*) point, item.

p.[4] *abbr.* (= *piętro*) floor, story; *Br.* storey.

pa *int.* bye.

pac *int.* flop.

paca *f. bud.* long float.

pacan *mp pl.* **-y** *pog.* moron.

pach *int.* pop.

pacha *f.* **1.** (*u człowieka, zwierzęcia*) armpit, underarm; *anat.* axilla; **pod pachą** under one's arm. **2.** (*między rękawem a resztą ubrania*) armpit, underarm.

pachnidło *n. Gen.pl.* **-eł** *przest.* scent, perfume.

pachnieć *ipf.* **-nę -niesz, -nij** smell, scent; **pachnieć ładnie/brzydko** smell nice/bad; **pachnieć różą** smell of roses; **ta sprawa pachnie mi kłopotami** it savors of trouble; **groszek pachnący** *bot.* sweet pea (*Lathyrus odoratus*); **fiołek pachnący** *l.* **wonny** *bot.* sweet violet (*Viola odorata*).

pachnotka *f. Gen.pl.* **-ek** *bot.* perilla (*Perilla*).

pachołek *mi Gen.* **-a** *pl.* **-i 1.** (*na remontowanej drodze*) cone. **2.** *żegl.* bollard, makefast; **bitt. –** *mp pl.* **-ki** *l.* **-cy** *l.* **-owie 1.** *hist.* menial, servant. **2.** *pog.* (= *sługus*) menial, lackey.

pachwina *f.* **1.** (*u człowieka, zwierzęcia*) groin. **2.** *bot.* axil.

pachwinowy *a.* **1.** (*u człowieka, zwierzęcia*) inguinal; **przepuklina pachwinowa** *pat.* bubonocele. **2.** *bot.* (*o pączku*) axillary.

pacierz *mi Gen.* **-a 1.** prayer; **zmówić pacierz** say one's prayers; **nie ucz księdza pacierza** *przen.* don't teach your grandmother to suck eggs; **jak amen w pacierzu** sure as eggs are eggs. **2.** *przest.* spine, backbone.

pacierzowy *a. przest.* spinal; **stos pacierzowy** spine, backbone.

paciorecznik *mi Gen.* **-a** *bot.* canna (*Canna*).

paciorek *mi* **-rk-** *Gen.* **-a 1.** (= *koralik*) bead; **oczy jak paciorki** beady eyes. **2.** *emf.* (= *pacierz*) prayer.

paciorkowiec *ma* **-wc-** *med., biol.* streptococcus (*Streptococcus*).

pacjent *mp* patient; **pacjent ambulatoryjny** *l.* **dochodzący** outpatient; **pacjent hospitalizowany** inpatient; (*szpitala psychiatrycznego*) inmate.

pacjentka *f. Gen.pl.* **-ek** *zob.* pacjent.

packa *f. Gen.pl.* **-ek 1.** (*na muchy*) (fly) swatter. **2.** *bud.* float.

pacnąć *pf.* **-ij** *pot.* flap; (*zwł. muchę, komara*) swat.

pacyficzny *a.* Pacific; **typ pacyficzny** *antrop.* Pacific Islander.

Pacyfik *mi geogr.* the Pacific (Ocean).

pacyfikacja *f.* pacification.

pacyfikacyjny *a.* pacificatory.

pacyfikał *mi rz.-kat.* pax.

pacyfikator *mp* pacificator, pacifier; (*o rewolwerze, okręcie wojennym*) peacemaker.

pacyfikować *ipf.* pacify.

pacyfista *mp* pacifist.

pacyfistka *f. Gen.pl.* **-ek** *zob.* **pacyfista**.

pacyfistyczny *a.* pacifistic.

pacyfizm *mi* pacifism.

pacykarz *mp pog.* dauber.

pacykować *ipf. pog.* daub. ~ **się** *ipf.* lay it on thick, try to compensate for all that missed beauty sleep.

pacynka *f. Gen.pl.* **-ek** hand puppet.

paczka *f. Gen.pl.* **-ek 1.** (= *pakunek*) package. **2.** (*na poczcie*) parcel. **3.** (= *opakowanie*) packet, package; (*papierosów*) pack; (*banknotów*) wad; (*gazet*) batch. **4.** *pot.* (= *grupa koleżeńska*) pack, crowd, gang.

paczkować *ipf.* package, prepackage.

paczula *f. Gen., Dat., Loc.* **-li** *bot.* coleus (*Coleus*).

paczuszka *f. Gen.pl.* **-ek 1.** (*na poczcie*) packet. **2.** (*opakowanie*) (small) package *l.* packet.

paczyć *ipf.* distort. ~ **się** *ipf.* become distorted.

paćka *f. Dat., Loc.* **-će** *pot.* mash, pulp.

paćkać *ipf. pot.* smear, smudge. ~ **się** *ipf. pot.* smear one's face/hands/clothes.

pad *mi sport* fall, drop; **wykonać pad** hit the deck, take a tumble.

padaczka *f. pat.* epilepsy, falling sickness; **mieć padaczkę** be epileptic.

padaczkowy *a. pat.* epileptic; **mały napad padaczkowy** petit mal.

padać *ipf.*, **paść** *pf.* **padnę padniesz, padnij, padł 1.** (= *przewracać się*) fall, drop, tumble down; **padać na wznak** fall *l.* land on one's back; **padać na kolana** *l.* **klęczki** fall on *l.* drop to one's knees; **padać plackiem** fall flat on the ground; **padam z nóg** I'm dead tired, I'm on my last legs, I'm done in; **padać ze zmęczenia** flake out; **padać na twarz** prostrate; *przen.* be done in; **padać komuś w ramiona** fall into sb's arms; **padam do**

nóg! at your service!, your humble servant!; **padnij!** *wojsk.* hit the deck *l.* dirt!, hit it! **2.** die violently; **padać jak muchy** (= *gwałtownie ginąć*) be dropping like flies; **padać ofiarą czegoś** fall victim *l.* prey to sth; **padać trupem** fall dead; **niech trupem padnę** strike me dead. **3.** (= *zostać zdobytym*) be captured; **miasto padło po długim oblężeniu** town *l.* city was captured after a long siege. **4.** (= *spadać*) fall, drop; *meteor.* precipitate; **padać przelotnie** shower; (*o deszczu*) rain; (*o śniegu*) snow; **pada** (*deszcz*) it's raining; (*śnieg*) it's snowing; **podejrzenie pada na ciebie** you're under suspicion, you fall under suspicion; **padł na nich lęk** *l.* strach they were seized with fear; **najwięcej głosów padło na twoją kandydaturę** you received the majority of votes, majority of votes were cast for you; **akcent pada na przedostatnią sylabę wyrazu** stress falls on the penultimate syllable; **niedaleko pada jabłko od jabłoni** like father, like son. **5.** (= *trafiać na coś*) fall; **wzrok zwiedzających pada na obraz Picassa** visitors' eyes *l.* gaze fell on the Picasso; **na mózg ci padło?** *pot.* have you lost your marbles?, are you off your rocker?, are you losing it?; **los padł na mnie** the lot fell (up)on me; **pada rozkaz** order is given; **pada strzał** shot is fired; **nie padło ani słowo** not a word was uttered; **pada bramka** *sport* goal is scored; **pada rekord** *zwł. sport* record is broken.

padalec *ma* **-lc-** *pl.* **-e** *zool.* blindworm, slowworm (*Anguis fragilis*). – *mp* **-lc-** *pl.* **-y** *pog.* crawler.

padanie *n. fiz.* incidence; **kąt padania** angle of incidence.

padlina *f.* carrion; (*na szosie*) roadkill; **żywić się padliną** *zool.* scavenge.

padlinożerca *ma zool.* scavenger.

padlinożerny *a. zool.* necrophagous, scavenging.

padnę *itd. pf.* zob. **paść**[1].

padnięty *a. pot.* dead tired, done in; **po całym dniu pracy jestem padnięty** I'm on my last legs after working all day.

padok *mi* paddock.

padół *mi* **-o-** *przest.* valley; **padół łez** *l.* **płaczu** *lit.* (this) vale of tears *l.* misery; **na tym padole** here below.

padyszach *mp pl.* **-owie** Padishah.

paf *int.* bang, pop.

pagaj *mi Gen.* **-a** *żegl.* paddle.

pager *mi Gen.* **-a** pager; **wywołać kogoś pagerem** page sb.

pagina *f. druk.* page number, folio; **żywa pagina** running head *l.* title.

paginacja *f. druk.* pagination; **bez paginacji** unpaged.

paginować *ipf. druk.* paginate, page.

pagoda *f. Gen.pl.* **-ód** *rel.* pagoda.

pagon *mi* shoulder board.

pagórek *mi* **-rk-** *Gen.* **-a** hill, hillock, hummock, mound, knoll.

pagórkowaty *a.* hilly, hummocky.

pagrus *ma icht.* common seabream, red porgy (*Pagrus pagrus*).

pajac *mp* **1.** (= *błazen*) clown. **2.** *pog.* buffoon. – *ma* (*zabawka*) puppet.

pajacować *ipf. pot.* clown.

pajacowaty *a.* clownish.

pajacyk *ma* (*zabawka*) jumping jack. – *mi Gen.* **-a** (*ubranie dziecięce*) **1.** rompers, crawlers. **2.** (*ćwiczenie*) jumping jack, star jump.

pająk *ma zool.* spider (*Araneae*). – *mi Gen.* **-a 1.** (= *żyrandol*) chandelier (*with many arms, resembling a spider*). **2.** (*ozdoba ludowa*) folk ornament made of straw hanging from the ceiling.

pajda *f. pot.* slice (*of bread*).

pajdocentryczny *a. szkoln.* pedocentric.

pajdocentryzm *mi szkoln.* pedocentrism.

pajęczak *ma zool.* arachnid (*Arachnida*).

pajęczarz *mp* **1.** *pot.* (= *złodziej okradający strychy*) attic thief. **2.** (= *osoba korzystająca z radia l. telewizora bez uiszczenia opłat*) subscription fee dodger (*person illegally listening to radio stations and / or watching TV channels for which subscription fee is required*).

pajęczy *a.* spidery; (*o koronce*) gossamer; **opona pajęcza** *anat.* arachnoid.

pajęczyna *f.* **1.** (= *sieć pajęcza*) cobweb, spiderweb. **2.** (= *splątane linie*) tangle, knot, snarl. **3.** (= *spisek*) plot.

pajęczynówka *f. Gen.pl.* **-ek** *anat.* arachnoid.

pak[1] *mi chem.* pitch.

pak[2] *mi geogr.* pack ice, ice pack.

paka *f.* **1.** (= *skrzynia*) crate, case. **2.** (= *paczka*) (big) package. **3.** *pot.* (= *więzienie*) can, cooler, stir. **4.** *pot.* (= *grupa koleżeńska*) gang, crowd, pack.

pakamera *f. pot.* storage.

pakiet *mi* **1.** (= *paczka*) packet. **2.** (= *zestaw*) set; **pakiet informacyjny** (*dla mediów*) press kit; **pakiet ustaw** *parl.* set of laws, legislation package; **pakiet socjalny** benefit package; **pakiet programów** *komp.* suite; **pakiet danych** *komp.* batch. **3.** *ekon.* shareholding; **kontrolny pakiet akcji** controlling interest.

Pakistan *mi geogr.* Pakistan.

Pakistanka *f. Gen.pl.* **-ek** zob. **Pakistańczyk**.

Pakistańczyk *mp* Pakistani.

pakistański *a.* Pakistani.

paklon *ma Gen.* **-u** *Loc.* **-ie** *bot.* hedge maple, field maple (*Acer campestre*).

pakowacz *mp* packer; (*worków*) sacker.

pakowaczka *f. Gen.pl.* **-ek 1.** zob. **pakowacz**. **2.** (*maszyna*) packing machine.

pakować *ipf.* **1.** (= *układać w czymś*) pack; (= *zawijać*) wrap (up); (*do puszek*) can; (*w kartony*) carton; (*na prezent*) gift-wrap; (*próżniowo*) shrink-wrap; (*w skrzynki, kontenery*) crate; **pakować komuś coś łopatą do głowy** *pot.* spoonfeed sb, drive sth home; **pakować kulę w kogoś** lodge a bullet in sb. **2.** *pot.* (= *upychać*) cram, crowd, ram, stuff; **pakował do buzi duże kawały mięsa** he stuffed large chunks of meat into his mouth. **3.** *pot.* (= *dużo inwestować w coś*) pump *l.* pour money into; **wszystkie oszczędności pakują w dom** they pour all their savings into their house. **4.** *pot.* (= *ograniczać wolność*) clap; **pakować ko-**

goś do więzienia clap sb in prison; **pakować kogoś do wojska** press sb into the army. **5.** *pot.* (= *ćwiczyć mięśnie*) pump iron. ~ **się** *ipf.* **1.** (*swoje rzeczy*) pack up, pack one's things. **2.** *pot.* (= *wchodzić niepotrzebnie*) barge, push one's way; **pakować się w tarapaty** *l.* **kłopoty** get o.s. into trouble, be asking *l.* heading for trouble.

pakownia *f. Gen.pl.* **-i** packing shop, packing department.

pakowność *f.* capaciousness.

pakowny *a.* capacious, roomy, spacious.

pakowy *a.* wrapping; **papier pakowy** brown paper.

pakt *mi* pact, agreement, compact; **pakt o nieagresji** non-aggression pact; **pakt Ligi Narodów** *hist.* Covenant of the League of Nations; **Pakt Północnoatlantycki** *polit.* North Atlantic Treaty.

paktować *ipf.* negotiate.

pakuły *pl. Gen.* -ł *l.* -ów *tk.* hards, hurds, tow.

pakunek *mi* -nk- **1.** (= *paczka*) pack, package. **2.** *techn.* caulk, caulking.

pal *mi Gen.* -a *Gen.pl.* -i *l.* -ów **1.** (= *słup*) post, pale, stake. **2.** (*narzędzie tortur*) stake; **wbicie na pal** impalement; **wbić kogoś na pal** impale sb.

palacz *mp* **1.** (*w kotłowni*) stoker; (*zwłok*) cremator. **2.** (*nałogowiec*) smoker, nicotine addict; (*palący jednego papierosa za drugim*) chain-smoker; **nałogowy palacz marihuany** pot head.

palaczka *f. Gen.pl.* -ek *zob.* palacz.

paladyn *mp hist.* paladin.

palant *mi* **1.** *Acc.* -a (*gra*) stickball. **2.** *Acc.* -t *pl.* -y (*kij*) bat. – *mp pl.* -y *uj.* (= *głupiec*) conehead, jerk.

palarnia *f. Gen.pl.* -i *l.* -ń **1.** (*tytoniu*) smoke *l.* smoking room. **2.** (*kawy*) coffee-roasting plant.

palatalizacja *f. jęz.* palatalization.

palatalizować *ipf. jęz.* palatalize. ~ **się** *ipf. jęz.* undergo palatalization.

palatalność *f. jęz.* palatalism, palatality.

palatalny *a. jęz.* palatal.

palatografia *f. Gen.* -ii *fon.* palatography.

palatograficzny *a. fon.* palatographic.

palatogram *mi fon.* palatogram.

palatyn *mp hist.* palatine; count *l.* earl palatine; (*w Niemczech*) palsgrave.

palatynat *mi hist.* **1.** palatinate. **2.** *hist.* (*w Niemczech*) the Palatinate; **Palatynat Dolny** *l.* **Nadreński/Górny** the Lower *l.* Rhine/Upper Palatinate.

paląca *f. Gen.* -ej smoker.

palący *a.* **1.** (= *istotny, pilny*) urgent. **2.** (= *trudny*) complex, difficult; **palący problem** burning *l.* thorny issue. **3.** (= *gorący*) hot, scorching; **palące słońce** blazing sun. **4.** (*papierosy*) smoking. – *mp* smoker; **przedział dla palących** smoking compartment.

palcować *ipf. muz.* finger.

palcowanie *n. muz.* fingering.

palcówka *f. Gen.pl.* -ek **1.** *muz.* fingering exercise. **2.** *obsc.* fingerfucking; **robić komuś palcówkę** fingerfuck sb.

palczak *ma* **1.** *icht.* fingerling. **2.** *zool.* palczak

madagaskarski aye-aye (*Daubentonia madagascariensis*).

palec *mi* -lc- *Gen.* -a **1.** (*u ręki*) finger, digit; **palec serdeczny** ring finger; **palec wskazujący** index finger; **palec środkowy** middle finger; **mały palec** little finger, pinkie; **pokazywać coś palcem** point a finger at sth; **szeroki na palec/dwa palce** one finger/two fingers wide; **liczyć na palcach** tick sth off on one's fingers; **móc coś policzyć na palcach jednej ręki** be able to count sth on (the fingers of) one hand; **bębnić palcami** drum one's fingers; **przebierać palcami** twiddle one's thumbs; **pstrykać palcami** click *l.* flip one's fingers; **zrobiłbym to z palcem w nosie** I could do it standing on my head; **pogrozić komuś palcem** wag one's finger at sb; **kiwnąć na kogoś palcem** beckon sb; **podróżować palcem po mapie** *żart.* daydream a vacation; **palec boży** the hand of God, divine intervention, an act of God; **sam jak palec** all alone; **maczać w czymś palce** have a hand in sth, meddle with sth; **mieć coś w małym palcu** know sth inside out; **nawet cię palcem nie tknąłem** I didn't even touch you; **owinąć kogoś wokół małego palca** have sb on a leash, twist sb round one's little finger; **palce lizać!** finger-licking good!, yummy!; **plany palcem na wodzie pisane** everything's still up in the air; **nie kiwnąć palcem** not lift *l.* raise a finger; **patrzeć na coś przez palce** wink at sth, turn a blind eye to sth; **wytykać kogoś palcami** point one's finger at sb; **pieniądze przeciekają mu przez palce** money flows like sand through his fingers, his paycheck is burning a hole in his pocket; **te brednie wyssałeś z palca** it's a trumped-up story, you fabricated this story; **mieć lepkie palce** have sticky fingers, be light-fingered; **poparzyć sobie palce** burn one's fingers. **2.** (*u nogi*) toe, digit; **wspinać się na palce** stand on one's toes; **chodzić na palcach** walk on tiptoe, tiptoe; *przen.* treat sb in kid gloves, be overconsiderate; **nie kiwnąć palcem w bucie** not lift *l.* raise a finger. **3.** (*rękawiczki*) finger; **rękawiczka z jednym palcem** mitten, mitt; **rękawiczka z pięcioma palcami** glove. **4.** *techn.* finger, pin; **palec rozdzielacza** distributor rotor arm.

palenie *n.* **1.** burning; **palenie tytoniu** smoking; **palenie zwłok** cremation; **palenie śmieci** incineration. **2.** (= *uczucie pieczenia*) burning; **palenie w żołądku** *med.* heartburn, pyrosis; **palenie się do robienia czegoś** eagerness to do sth.

palenisko *n.* hearth; grate; **palenisko kowalskie** *techn.* forge hearth.

paleniskowy *a.* hearth; grate; (*o komorze*) firebox.

paleoamerykański *a. antrop.* Paleo-American.

paleoantropologia *f. Gen.* -ii *antrop.* paleoanthropology.

paleoantropologiczny *a. antrop.* paleoanthropological.

paleoazjatycki *a. antrop.* Paleo-Asiatic.

paleobiologia *f. Gen.* -ii *paleont.* paleobiology.

paleobiologiczny *a. paleont.* paleobotanical.

paleobotanik *mp paleont.* paleobotanist.

paleobotanika *f. paleont.* paleobotany.

paleocen *mi geol.* the Paleocene (Epoch).
paleogen *mi geol.* the Paleogene (Period).
paleogeografia *f. Gen.* -ii paleogeography.
paleografia *f. Gen.* -ii paleography.
paleograficzny *a.* paleographic, paleographical.
paleoklimat *mi meteor.* paleoclimate.
paleoklimatologia *f. Gen.* -ii paleoclimatology.
paleoklimatyczny *a. meteor.* paleoclimatic; paleoclimatological, paleoclimatologic.
paleolit *mi archeol., geol.* Paleolithic.
paleolityczny *a. archeol., geol.* paleolithic.
paleomagnetyczny *a. geol.* paleomagnetic.
paleomagnetyzm *mi geol.* paleomagnetism.
paleontolog *mp pl.* -dzy *l.* -owie paleontologist.
paleontologia *f. Gen.* -ii paleontology.
paleontologiczny *a.* paleontologic, paleontological.
paleotypy *pl. hist., druk.* incunabula.
paleozoiczny *a.* Paleozoic.
paleozoik *mi* the Paleozoic (Era).
paleozoologia *f. Gen.* -ii *paleont.* paleozoology.
paleozoologiczny *a. paleont.* paleozoological, paleozoologic.
palestra *f.* **1.** (= *adwokatura*) the bar. **2.** *Gen.pl.* -tr *hist.* palaestra, palestra.
Palestyna *f. geogr.* Palestine; **Organizacja Wyzwolenia Palestyny** *polit.* Palestine Liberation Organization (*PLO*).
Palestynka *f. Gen.pl.* -ek *zob.* **Palestyńczyk.**
Palestyńczyk *mp* Palestinian.
palestyński *a.* Palestinian.
paleta *f.* **1.** *sztuka* (*malarza*) (painter's) palette. **2.** (*barw*) spectrum of colors. **3.** (*platforma*) pallet.
paletka *f. Gen.pl.* -ek **1.** *sztuka* (*malarza*) (small) palette. **2.** *pot.* (= *rakieta do badmintona, tenisa stołowego itp.*) racket.
paletowy *a.* pallet.
paletyzacja *f. Gen., Dat., Loc.* -cji *techn.* palletization.
paliatyw *mi med.* palliative (medicine).
paliatywny *a. med.* palliative.
palić *ipf.* **1.** (= *rozniecać ogień*) build *l.* light a fire. **2.** (= *ogrzewać*) heat; (*pod kotłami*) stoke; **w starym piecu diabeł pali** there's life in the old dog yet. **3.** (= *oświetlać*) light. **4.** (= *niszczyć ogniem*) burn (down); (*zwłoki*) cremate; (*śmieci*) incinerate; **palić się gwałtownie** deflagrate; **palić za sobą mosty** burn one's boats *l.* bridges (behind one); **palić kogoś żywcem** burn sb alive; **pal licho!** *l.* **pal sześć!** never mind! **5.** (= *opiekać, przypiekać, wypalać*) (*kawę*) roast; (*cegły*) burn; (*wapno*) slake; **palić kadzidło** incense. **6.** (*papierosa, fajkę, cygaro*) smoke; **palić coś** puff on/at sth; **palić heroinę** chase the dragon; **palić skręty** roll one's own. **7.** (*o samochodzie, silniku*) (= *zużywać benzynę l. ropę*) consume, use up. **8.** (= *parzyć, piec*) burn; (*o słońcu*) scorch, burn, blaze down. **9.** (*o bólu*) burn, sting; **pali mnie wstyd** I'm burning with shame. **10.** (= *strzelać*) fire, shoot; **cel! pal!** *wojsk.* ready! aim! fire! **~ się** *ipf.* **1.** (= *spalać się*) burn, be on fire; **ogień się pali** fire is lighted, there is a fire in the stove; **robota**

pali mu się w rękach he is a demon for work, he works like a house on fire; **ziemia** *l.* **grunt pali mi się pod nogami** he is burning to leave; **pali się!** fire!; **nie pali się** *przen.* there's no hurry *l.* rush; **niech się pali, niech się wali** I couldn't care less. **2.** (= *świecić*) be alight, shed light; **światło się pali** light is on. **3.** *przen.* (*o uczuciu*) inflame, burn; **palę się ze wstydu** I'm burning with shame; **palić się do kogoś** be infatuated with sb, burn with desire for sb; **palić się do zrobienia czegoś** be burning *l.* keen to do sth.
palik *mi Gen.* -a picket, pale, stake, pin, peg.
palikować *ipf.* picket, stake.
palimpsest *mi* palimpsest.
palindrom *mi* palindrome.
palingeneza *f. biol., fil., geol.* palingenesis.
palinodia *f. Gen.* -ii *teor.lit.* palinode.
palisada *f.* **1.** *wojsk.* stockade, palisade. **2.** *techn.* piling.
palisander *mi* -dr- *Gen.* -a **1.** *bot.* (*drzewo*) rosewood (*Dalbergia*). **2.** (*drewno*) rosewood, palisander.
palisandrowy *a.* rosewood.
paliwo *n.* fuel; *mot.* gasoline, gas; *Br.* petrol; **paliwo bezołowiowe** unleaded gasoline; **paliwo jądrowe** nuclear fuel; **paliwo kopalne** fossil fuel; **paliwo stałe** solid fuel; **uzupełniać zapas paliwa** *zwł. lotn.* refuel; **stacja paliw** gas station, filling station; *Br.* petrol station.
paliwomierz *mi Gen.* -a *techn.* fuel gauge.
paliwowy *a.* fuel; **pompa paliwowa** *zwł. mot.* fuel pump.
pallad *mp chem.* palladium.
palma *f.* **1.** *bot.* palm (*Palmae*); **palma daktylowa** date palm (*Phoenix dactylifera*). **2.** (*ozdobna gałązka*) palm; **palma pierwszeństwa** the (victor's) palm; **dzierżyć palmę zwycięstwa** bear the palm; **oddać palmę pierwszeństwa** yield the palm; **palma męczeństwa** the palm of martyrdom; **święcić palmy** *rz.-kat.* bless the palms; **palma komuś odbiła** *pot.* sb's losing his marbles.
palmeta *f. sztuka* palmette.
palmiarnia *f. Gen.pl.* -i *l.* -ń palm house.
palmityna *f. chem.* palmitin.
palmitynowy *a. chem.* palmitic; **kwas palmitynowy** palmitic acid.
palmowy *a.* palmy, palm; *bot.* palmaceous; **Niedziela Palmowa** *rz.-kat.* Palm Sunday.
palnąć *pf.* -ij **1.** *pot.* (= *uderzyć*) bang, biff, hit, strike; **palnąć pięścią w stół** bang one's fist on the table; **palnąć kogoś w głowę** give sb a rap *l.* crack on the head. **2.** *pot.* (= *strzelić*) shoot, fire; **palnąć sobie w łeb** blow one's brains out. **3.** *pot.* (= *powiedzieć bez namysłu*) blunder, blurt out; **palnąć głupstwo** blunder, goof; **palnąć gafę** drop a brick, put one's foot in one's mouth. **~ się** *pf.* -ij bang (o *coś* against sth); **palnij się w głowę!** are you out of your mind!?
palnik *mi Gen.* -a **1.** (*w kuchence gazowej*) burner. **2.** *techn.* (*do podgrzewania*) burner; (*do spawania*) torch.
palność *f.* combustibility, flammability.
palny *a.* combustible, flammable; **broń palna** firearms.

palony *a.* burnt, burned; (*o kawie*) roasted; (*o wapnie*) burnt, quick, unslaked.

palować *ipf.* **1.** (= *przymocowywać*) stake, picket. **2.** (= *umacniać*) pile.

palowy *a.* stake, pale; **korzeń palowy** *bot.* taproot.

palpitacja *f. pat.* palpitation, throbbing of the heart.

palto *n.* overcoat, coat.

paluch *mi Gen.* **-a 1.** *emf.* (= *palec*) finger; **Tomcio Paluch** Tom Thumb. **2.** *anat.* hallux, big toe.

paluszek *mi* **-szk-** *Gen.* **-a 1.** *emf.* (= *palec*) finger; **paluszki lizać!** finger-licking good!; yummy!; **2.** *kulin.* stick, finger; **słone paluszki** salt sticks; **paluszki rybne** fish sticks; *Br.* fishfingers.

paluszník *ma Gen.* **-a** *Ins.* **-iem** *bot.* crabgrass, finger grass (*Digitaria*).

pała *f.* **1.** (= *pałka*) club; *pog.* (= *pałka policyjna*) billy (club), truncheon, club. **2.** *szkoln., pot.* fail, F. **3.** *pot.* (= *głowa*) dome, pate; **zalać pałę** booze it up; **łysa pała** baldhead, baldie *l.* baldy; **coś się w pale nie mieści** sth blows one's mind, sth is mind-blowing *l.* boggling; **ostrzyc na pałę** *l.* **do gołej pały** shave one's head clean; **przeginać pałę** go too far, lay it on thick. **4.** *pog.* (= *głupiec*) blockhead, woodenhead, clunk, muttonhead.

pałac *mi* palace; château, mansion; **pałac ślubów** civil registry office; **Pałac Kultury i Nauki w Warszawie** Palace of Culture and Science in Warsaw; **wart Pac pałaca, a pałac Paca** tarred with the same brush.

pałacowy *a.* palatial, palatine, palace; **przewrót pałacowy** *polit.* palace revolution.

pałacyk *mi* (little) palace.

pałać *ipf. lit.* (= *błyszczeć*) be afire, glow; **policzki mi pałają** my cheeks are flushed, I feel the blood in my cheeks; **pałać nienawiścią** *przen.* be burning with hate.

pałasz *mi Gen.* **-a** *Gen.pl.* **-y** *l.* **-ów 1.** *hist.* broadsword. **2.** *icht.* cutlass fish (*Trichurus lepturus*).

pałaszować *ipf. pot.* chow, scarf, scoff.

pałąk *mi Gen.* **-a 1.** (= *kabłąk*) bail, bow; **zgiąć się w pałąk** arch one's back. **2.** (= *pantograf*) pantograph. **3.** (= *garda*) (hilt-)guard.

pałąkowatość *f.* arching.

pałąkowaty *a.* arched, bow-shaped, bowed; **z pałąkowatymi nogami** bandy-legged.

pałeczka *f. Gen.pl.* **-ek 1.** (= *kijek*) stick; (*dyrygencka*) baton; *sport* baton; (*do gry na bębnie itp.*) drumstick; **przejąć pałeczkę** *przen.* take over the reins; **magiczna pałeczka** magic wand. **2.** (= *przedmiot w takim kształcie*) stick; **pałeczka do spawania** *techn.* welding *l.* filler rod; **pałeczka higieniczna** cotton swab. **3.** (*do jedzenia*) chopstick; **jeść pałeczkami** eat with chopsticks. **4.** *biol.* (= *bakteria*) bacillus.

pałętać się *ipf. pot.* (= *włóczyć się, kręcić się*) putter around, hang around.

pałka *f. Gen.pl.* **-ek 1.** (= *kij*) club, bat; **pałka policyjna** billy (club), truncheon; **nie kijem go, to pałką** swings and roundabouts; **bić pałką** club, bludgeon, cudgel, bat. **2.** *szkoln., pot.* fail, F. **3.**

bot. cattail, bulrush, reed mace (*Typha*); **pałka wąskolistna** narrow-leaf cattail (*Typha angustifolia*); **pałka szerokolistna** common cattail (*Typha latifolia*).

pałować *ipf. pot.* club; *Br. t.* truncheon.

pamflecista *f.* lampooner.

pamflet *mi teor.lit.* lampoon.

pamiątka *f. Gen.pl.* **-ek 1.** (*przedmiot*) souvenir; (*po kimś*) keepsake; **sklep z pamiątkami** souvenir shop; **pamiątka rodowa** heirloom. **2.** (*symbol, znak*) token, memento; **na pamiątkę czegoś** in token of sth; **na pamiątkę** for a keepsake, in remembrance.

pamiątkarski *a.* (*o przemyśle, rzemiośle*) souvenir.

pamiątkarstwo *n.* souvenir manufacturing.

pamiątkowy *a.* memorial, commemorative; **tablica pamiątkowa** commemorative plaque; **księga pamiątkowa** (*wydana na cześć kogoś l. czegoś*) commemorative book; (*z podpisami gości*) visitor's book.

pamięciowo *adv.* (= *na pamięć*) by heart; (= *z pamięci*) from memory; **rachować pamięciowo** calculate mentally, do mental arithmetic.

pamięciowy *a.* mnemonic; (*o metodzie, rachunku*) mental; **rachunek pamięciowy** mental arithmetic; **ślad pamięciowy** *psych.* engram; **portret pamięciowy** *kryminologia* composite sketch; *Br.* identikit picture.

pamięć *f.* **1.** (*zdolność psychiczna*) memory, mind; **pamięć wzrokowa** visual memory; **mieć dobrą/krótką pamięć** have a good/short memory; **mieć kurzą/doskonałą pamięć** have a memory like a sieve/an elephant; **zanik pamięci** amnesia; memory loss, loss of memory; **pamięć absolutna** total recall; **pamięć asocjacyjna/skojarzeniowa** associative/content-addressable memory; **pamięć długotrwała** *psych.* long-term memory; **pamięć operacyjna** *psych.* working memory; **pamięć proceduralna** *psych.* procedural memory; **uczyć się na pamięć** learn by heart, memorize; **znać coś na pamięć** know sth (off) by heart; **wytężać pamięć** rack one's brains; **liczyć w pamięci** calculate mentally; **odświeżać komuś pamięć** refresh *l.* jog sb's memory; **wymazać kogoś/coś z pamięci** put sb/sth out of one's mind; **zakochać się bez pamięci** fall head over heels in love; **przywodzić komuś na pamięć** bring sth back to mind; **przebiegać pamięcią** retrace in one's memory; **wracać do czegoś pamięcią** look back on sth; **utkwić w pamięci** *l.* **wryć** *l.* **wbić się komuś w pamięć** be imprinted on sb's mind, be etched *l.* stamped on sb's mind, be engraved in sb's memory; **zachować (kogoś/coś) w pamięci** keep (sb/sth) in memory; **zachować coś w miłej pamięci** treasure sth in one's memory; **za ludzkiej pamięci** in *l.* within living *l.* human memory; **mieć coś świeżo w pamięci** sth is fresh in sb's mind; **mam słabą pamięć do nazwisk** I have a bad memory for names; **jeżeli mnie pamięć nie myli** if my memory serves me; **pamięć mi nie dopisuje** *l.* **pamięć mnie zawodzi** my memory is failing me, my memory is playing tricks on me; **wypadło mi to zupełnie z pamięci** it eluded me. **2.** (= *wspomnie-*

nie) memory, remembrance; **świętej pamięci** late; **nieodżałowanej pamięci** the late lamented; **błogosławionej pamięci** of blessed memory; **ku pamięci** (*osoby zmarłej*) in memoriam; **ku czyjejś pamięci** in memory *l.* remembrance of sb; **pamięć o kimś pozostaje żywa** sb's memory lives on; **dziękuję za pamięć** thank you for your remembrance; **czcić pamięć** memorialize, remember; **uczcić pamięć** commemorate. 3. *el., komp.* memory, storage; **pamięć buforowa** *komp.* buffer; **pamięć podręczna** *komp.* cache storage; **bank pamięci** memory bank; **funkcja pamięci** (*w telefonie*) memory facility; **pamięć numeru** (*w telefonie*) speed dial.

pamiętać *ipf.* 1. (= *nie zapominać*) remember ((*żeby*) *coś zrobić* to do sth); **dobrze/wyraźnie pamiętać** remember well/clearly; **pamiętam jak dziś** I remember quite clearly; **pamiętam babcię jak przez sen** *l.* **mgłę** I have a dim *l.* vague recollection of my granny; **niezupełnie pamiętam** I don't quite remember; **prawie nie pamiętać** scarcely remember; **pamiętać o czymś** bear sth in mind; **nie pamiętam, żebym o tym wspominał** I don't remember mentioning it; **w czasach, których nie pamiętasz** before your time; **o ile pamiętam** if I remember correctly, if my memory serves me right; **będę pamiętał, żeby wysłać ten list** I'll remember to send this letter; **należy pamiętać, że...** (*przy wprowadzaniu nowej myśli*) now, we have to remember that... 2. (= *troszczyć się*) be mindful, be careful; **pamiętać o innych** be mindful of others; **pamiętaj o zdrowiu** be careful about your health. 3. (= *mieć żal, urazę*) remember; **pamiętać komuś doznaną krzywdę** harbor rancor against sb. 4. (= *brać pod uwagę*) bear in mind. 5. (*o rzeczach*) (= *być starym*) have witnessed (*dawne czasy* distant times); **pałac pamięta czasy rewolucji** the palace witnessed the revolution; **to futro pamięta lepsze czasy** *żart.* this fur has seen better days; **pamiętać króla Ćwieczka** be as old as the hills.

pamiętliwość *f.* unforgiveness, unforgivingness.

pamiętliwy *a.* grudge-bearing, unforgiving.

pamiętnik *mi Gen.* -a 1. (*dziennik*) diary, journal. 2. *teor.lit.* memoirs. 3. (*sztambuch*) album.

pamiętnikarka *f. Gen.pl.* -ek *zob.* **pamiętnikarz**.

pamiętnikarski *a.* 1. diarist's. 2. memoirist's; (*o zapisie, charakterze, materiale*) autobiographic.

pamiętnikarstwo *n.* 1. keeping a diary. 2. *teor.lit.* memoirism, the writing of memoirs.

pamiętnikarz *mp* 1. diarist. 2. memoirist.

pamiętny *a.* memorable.

pampa, pampas *f. geogr.* pampas.

pampers ® *mi Gen.* -a 1. (*pielucha*) diaper; *Br.* nappy. 2. *pot. uj. l. żart.* (= *osoba z małym doświadczeniem zawodowym*) Johnny-come-lately, greenhorn, rookie.

PAN *abbr.* (= *Polska Akademia Nauk*) Polish Academy of Sciences.

pan *mp Dat. i Loc.* -u *pl.* -owie 1. (= *bliżej nieznany mężczyzna*) gentleman; (*przy bezpośrednim zwracaniu się*) you; **pan w średnim wieku** a middle-aged gentleman; **jakichś dwóch panów** some two gentlemen. 2. (*władca*) lord; **pan lenny** *l.* **feudalny** *hist.* liege; **najjaśniejszy pan** His Highness; **być panem sytuacji** be the master of the situation; **być panem życia i śmierci** be the master of life and death; **być panem siebie** be one's own man *l.* boss; **być panem własnego losu** be the captain of one's soul; **być panem u siebie** be one's own master; **mój pan i władca** *żart.* my lord and master; **(co) pan każe, sługa musi** the servant follows his master's orders; **pan na włościach** lord of the manor; **znaj pana** know your master. 3. (= *Bóg*) God, Lord; **Pan Bóg** God; **nasz Pan** Our Lord; **zasnąć w Panu** rest in peace; **Pan zastępów** *rel.* Lord of Hosts; **chwalcie Pana** *rel.* exhalt ye the Lord; **na chwałę Pana** *rel.* to the glory of God; **wzywać imię Pana nadaremnie** *rel.* take the Lord's name in vain; **strzeżonego Pan Bóg strzeże** forewarned is forearmed; an ounce of prevention is worth a pound of cure; **(świecić) Panu Bogu świeczkę, a diabłu ogarek** run with the hare and hunt with the hounds. 4. *szkoln.* (= *nauczyciel*) master; **pan od polskiego** Polish teacher. 5. (*gospodarz*) master; **pan domu** master of the house; **jaki pan, taki kram** like master, like man. 6. (*oficjalna forma grzecznościowa*) you; **pan Jan Kowalski** Mr Jan Kowalski; **pan Kowalski** Mr Kowalski; **pan Jan** Jan; **pan profesor** Professor; **pan Kowalski** (= *nieokreślona osoba*) Mr. Smith, Joe Public; **niejaki pan Kowalski** a certain Mr Kowalski, one Mr Kowalski; **pan profesor Kowalski** Professor Kowalski; **proszę pana,...** sir...; **czym mogę panu służyć?** (how) can I help you, sir?; **to pana samochód?** it that your car, sir?; **pan pozwoli** allow me; **panie dyrektorze, telefon do pana** Manager, a phone call for you; **panie prezydencie** Mr President!; **panie przewodniczący** Mr Chairman!; **pan młody** the bridegroom; **być z kimś za pan brat** be on familiar terms with sb, be palsy-walsy with sb; **być z kimś na pan** not address sb by his first name, not be on intimate terms with sb; **nagi jak go Pan Bóg stworzył** in his birthday suit; **Pan Bóg nierychliwy, ale sprawiedliwy** God comes with leaden feet, but strikes with iron hands; **pan władza** *pot.* officer; **Piotruś Pan** (*w bajce*) Peter Pan.

panaceum *n. sing. indecl. pl.* -ea *Gen.* -eów 1. *med.* panacea. 2. *przen.* (= *środek zaradczy*) cure-all, panacea; **panaceum na wszelkie zło** cure for *l.* to all evil, panacea to all evil.

panafrykanizm *mi* Pan-Africanism.

panafrykański *a.* Pan-African.

Panama *f.* Panama.

panama *f.* (*kapelusz*) Panama hat, Panama, panama.

panamerykanizm *mi* Pan-Americanism.

panamerykański *a.* Pan-American.

panamski *a.* Panamanian; **Kanał Panamski** Panama Canal; **Przesmyk Panamski** Isthmus of Panama; **Zatoka Panamska** Gulf of Panama.

pancerfaust *mi hist.* bazooka, anti-tank rocket (*used in World War II*).

pancerniak *mp pot.* tanker.

pancernik *mi Gen.* **-a** (*okręt*) battleship. – *ma zool.* armadillo (*Dasypodidae*).

pancerny *a.* armored, ironclad; **pancerny wóz bojowy** armored fighting vehicle; **blacha pancerna** armorplate; **koszulka pancerna** (*noszona pod kolczugą*) habergeon; **pojazd pancerny** *wojsk.* armored vehicle; **skarbiec pancerny** *l.* **kasa pancerna** safe-deposit, strongbox; **szyba pancerna** armor glass; **tarcza pancerna** *wojsk.* mantelet; **wojska pancerne** armor, armored troops; **towarzysz pancerny** *hist.* cuirassier; **ryby pancerne** *icht.* armored fish. – *mp* (*żołnierz*) cuirassier.

pancerz *mi Gen.* **-a** **1.** *hist.* armor, cuirass; **pancerz łuskowy** scale armor. **2.** (*osłona z blachy*) armorplate; (*czołgu*) armor; (*pocisku*) hull. **3.** (*u zwierząt*) crust, armor, shield; (*u żółwia, homara t.*) mail.

pancerzowce *pl. Gen.* **-ów** *zool.* malacostracans (*Malacostraca*).

pancerzownica *f. wojsk.* bazooka.

panchromatyczność *f. fot.* panchromatism.

panchromatyczny *a. fot.* panchromatic.

panczenista *mp*, **panczenistka** *f. Gen.pl.* **-ek** *sport* speed skater.

panczenlama *mp rel.* Panchen Lama.

panczeny *pl. Gen.* **-ów** *l.* **-n** *sport* speed skates.

panda *f. zool.* panda (*Procyonidae l. Ailuropodadae*); **panda wielka** panda, giant panda (*Ailuropoda melanoleuca*); **panda mała** lesser panda, red panda (*Ailurus fulgens*).

pandan *mi bot.* screw pine (*Pandanus*).

pandemia *f. Gen.* **-ii** pandemic.

pandemiczny *a.* pandemic.

pandemonium *n. indecl. lit.* **1.** (*piekło*) Pandemonium. **2.** *przen.* (= *chaos*) pandemonium, tumult; **kiedy wyszedłeś, rozpętało się prawdziwe pandemonium** real pandemonium broke out when you left.

pandit *mp* pundit.

Pandora *f. mit.* Pandora; **otworzyć puszkę Pandory** open Pandora's box, open a can of worms.

pandora *f. muz.* bandore, pandore, pandora.

panegiryczny *a.* panegyrical, encomiastic.

panegiryk *mi* panegyric, eulogy, encomium.

panegirysta *mp* panegyrist, encomiast, eulogist.

panegiryzm *mi* panegyrizing.

panegiryzować *ipf.* panegyrize, eulogize.

panel *mi* **1.** (*dyskusja*) (*eksperci*) panel; **panel ekspertów** panel of experts. **2.** *techn.* panel; **panele drewniane** wood panelling, wainscoting.

panelowy *a.* **dyskusja panelowa** panel discussion.

paneuropejski *a. polit.* Pan-European.

panew *f.* **-nwi** *pl.* **-e** **1.** (*naczynie*) pan. **2.** *techn.* bearing bush, bearing shell.

panewka *f. Gen.pl.* **-ek** **1.** *anat.* (*stawu*) socket; (*zwł. stawu biodrowego*) acetabulum. **2.** *hist.* (*w dawnej broni palnej*) pan; **spalić na panewce** fall flat, go down like a lead baloon. **3.** *techn. zob.* **panew** 2.

pangeneza *f. biol.* pangenesis.

pangermanizm *mi hist.* Pan-Germanism.

pangermański *a. polit.* Pan-Germanic.

pangolin *ma zool.* pangolin (*Pholidota*); **pangolin olbrzymi** giant pangolin (*Manis gigantea*).

panhellenizm *mi hist.* Panhellenism.

panhelleński *a. polit.* Panhellenistic.

pani *f. Acc.* **-ą** **1.** (= *bliżej nieznana kobieta*) lady; **pani w średnim wieku** middle-aged lady; **jakieś dwie panie** some two ladies. **2.** (*władczyni*) mistress; **najjaśniejsza pani** My Lady, Her Ladyship; **pani dziedziczka** lady of the manor; **pani domu** lady of the house; **łaskawa pani!** my dear lady!; **pani sytuacji** mistress of the situation; **być panią siebie** be one's own mistress; **być panią swej woli** be the mistress of one's life; **pani mojego serca** my mistress. **3.** *rz.-kat.* (*Matka Boska*) Our Lady. **4.** *szkoln.* (= *nauczycielka*) mistress; **pani od polskiego** Polish teacher. **5.** (= *żona*) wife, lady. **6.** (*oficjalna forma grzecznościowa*) you; (*przed nazwiskiem, niezależnie od stanu cywilnego*) Ms.; (*przed nazwiskiem kobiety niezamężnej*) Miss; (*przed nazwiskiem kobiety zamężnej*) Mrs.; (*przed nazwiskiem zamężnej Francuzki*) madame; **pani Kowalska** Ms. Kowalska; **pani Janina** Janina; **pani profesor** Professor; **proszę pani,...** madam, ma'am; **proszę pani!** (*do nauczycielki*) miss!; **czym mogę pani służyć?** (how) can I help you, madam?; **czy to pani samochód?** it that your car, madam?; **pani przewodnicząca, telefon do pani** Madam Chairman, a phone call for you; **być z kimś na pani** not address sb by her first name, not be on intimate terms with sb.

panicz *mp* **1.** *przest.* the young master; **panicz Edward** Master Edward. **2.** *iron.* dandy, fop.

panicznie *adv.* **bać się panicznie (kogoś/czegoś)** be terrified (of sb/sth).

paniczny *a.* (*pełen paniki*) panic-struck; (*o lęku*) deadly; **rzucić się do panicznej ucieczki** flee in panic.

panienka *f. Gen.pl.* **-ek** **1.** *przest.* (= *dziewczyna*) young lady, girl; *pot.* (= *młoda kobieta*) miss, missy. **2.** *pot.* (= *prostytutka*) hooker, hustler.

panieński *a.* girlish, maiden; **nazwisko panieńskie** maiden name; **panieński rumieniec** maiden blush; **wieczór panieński** hen party, hen night.

panieństwo *n.* girlhood, maidenhood.

panier *mi*, **panierka** *f. Gen.pl.* **-ek** *kulin.* (*z tartej bułki*) breadcrumb; (*z mleka, mąki i jajek*) batter.

panierować *ipf. kulin.* (= *obtaczać w jajku i tartej bułce*) egg and breadcrumb; (= *obtaczać w cieście z mleka, mąki i jajek*) batter.

panierowany *a. kulin.* (*w tartej bułce*) breaded; (*w cieście*) battered.

panika *f.* panic; **szerzyć panikę** spread panic; **ulec panice** give in to panic; **wpaść w panikę** start to panic; **bez paniki!** don't panic!, stay cool!; **ogarnięty paniką** panic-stricken.

panikara *f.*, **panikarz** *mp pot.* panicmonger.

panikarka *f. Gen.pl.* **-ek** = **panikara**.

panikarski *a.* alarmist, panicky; (*szerzący panikę*) panic-mongering.

panikarstwo *n.* panic-mongering.

panikarz *mp zob.* **panikara**.

panikować *ipf.* panic (*z powodu czegoś* about sth); **nie panikuj!** don't panic!

panislamizm *mi hist.* Pan-Islam, Pan-Islamism.

panislamski *a. polit.* Pan-Islamic.

paniusia *f. Voc.* **-u** *iron.* Lady Muck.

panklastyt *mi chem.* panclastite.

pankreozymina *f. biol.* pancreozymin.

panna *f. Gen.pl.* **-nien 1.** (= *kobieta niezamężna*) miss, maiden; **panna młoda** bride; **panna na wydaniu** marriageable girl, eligible bachelorette; **stara panna** old maid, spinster; **panna służąca** lady's maid, maidservant. **2.** (= *sympatia*) girlfriend. **3.** (*forma grzecznościowa; wychodzi z użycia*) Miss; **panna Janina Nowakówna** Miss Janina Nowak; **panno Janko!** Janka! **4. Panna Święta** *l.* **Najświętsza Maria Panna** *rz.-kat.* the Blessed Virgin Mary. **5.** (*znak zodiaku*) Virgin, Virgo.

panneau *n. indecl. sztuka* panel.

pannica *f. uj.* miss.

Panonia *f. Gen.* **-ii** *hist.* Pannonia.

panoplia *f. Gen.* **-ii** *hist., sztuka* panoply.

panoptikum *n. sing. indecl. pl.* **-ka** *Gen.* **-ków 1.** (= *muzeum osobliwości*) curiosity museum. **2.** (= *muzeum figur woskowych*) waxworks exhibition.

panorama *f.* **1.** (*widok*) panorama. **2.** (*zagadnień, problemów*) panorama. **3.** *sztuka* cyclorama, panorama; **panorama firm** classified directory, yellow pages ®.

panoramiczny *a.* panoramic; (*o obrazie*) cycloramic; **film panoramiczny** widescreen movie; **zdjęcie panoramiczne** panoramic picture.

panoszyć się *ipf.* **1.** *pot.* (= *szerzyć się*) spread. **2.** (= *rządzić się*) throw one's weight about *l.* around. **3.** (= *grasować*) be rampant.

panować *ipf.* **1.** (*rządzić*) rule, reign. **2.** (= *przewodzić komuś*) dominate. **3.** (= *kontrolować coś*) control (*coś* sth); be in control of sth (*coś* of sth); have control (*coś* over *l.* of sth); **panować nad sytuacją** have the situation in hand; **panować nad sobą** be in control, exercise self-control *l.* self-restraint; **panować nad namiętnościami** control one's emotions. **4.** (*o błędnym poglądzie, wierzeniu*) persist, prevail. **5.** (*w jakimś miejscu, na jakimś obszarze*) (*np. o pogodzie*) pervade. **6.** (= *górować nad okolicą*) dominate; **wieża kościoła panuje nad miasteczkiem** the church tower dominates the town.

panowanie *n.* domination, prevalence; (*króla*) rule, reign; **pod czyimś panowaniem** under sb's rule; **stracić panowanie nad sobą** lose one's temper, blow a fuse; **zachować panowanie nad sobą** keep *l.* maintain one's composure; **rozciągnąć panowanie nad czymś** (*nad jakimś obszarem*) have *l.* hold dominion over sth; **kierowca stracił panowanie nad samochodem** the car went out of control.

panpsychizm *mi fil.* panpsychism.

panseksualizm *mi* pansexualism.

panseksualny *a.* pansexual.

panslawista *mp polit.* Pan-Slavist.

panslawistyczny *a. polit.* Pan-Slavic.

panslawizm *mi polit.* Pan-Slavism.

pantagrueliczny *a.* Pantagruelian.

pantaleon, pantalon *mi muz.* pantaleon, pantalon.

pantalony *pl. Gen.* **-ów 1.** *żart.* pantaloons. **2.** *hist.* loose trousers worn by peasants.

pantałyk *mi* **zbić kogoś z pantałyku** throw sb off his *l.* her balance, put sb off his *l.* her stride.

pantarka *f. Gen.pl.* **-ek** *orn.* guinea fowl (*Numida meleagaris*).

panteista *mp* pantheist.

panteistyczny *a.* pantheistic.

panteizm *mi fil.* pantheism.

panteon *mi* **1.** (*świątynia*) (*mauzoleum*) (*ogół bóstw*) pantheon. **2.** *mit.* Pantheon. **3.** (= *grupa znakomitości*) (*pisarzy, aktorów itp.*) pantheon.

pantera *f. zool.* leopard, panther (*Panthera l. Felis pardus*); **śnieżna pantera** snow leopard, ounce (*Panthera l. Felis uncia*).

panterka *f. Gen.pl.* **-ek** *pot.* (*kurtka*) camouflage jacket.

pantofel *mi* **-fl-** *Gen.* **-a** (*but*) shoe; (*bez napiętka*) mule; (*ranny*) slipper; **być pod pantoflem żony** be henpecked, be a henpecked husband; be uxorious; **trzymać pod pantoflem** henpeck. – *mp żart.* henpecked husband.

pantofelek *ma* **-lk-** *zool.* paramecium, slipper animalcule (*Paramecium*).

pantofelnik *mi Gen.* **-a** *bot.* calceolaria, slipperwort (*Calceolaria*).

pantoflarski *a.* **1.** (*obuwniczy*) shoe; (*o pracowni*) slipper-making. **2.** *żart.* henpecked husband's; (*zachowanie*) uxorious.

pantoflarstwo *n.* **1.** (*rzemiosło*) slipper-making. **2.** *pog.* (*uległość*) uxoriousness, henpeckedness.

pantoflarz *mp* **1.** (*rzemieślnik*) slipper maker. **2.** *żart.* henpecked husband.

pantoflowy *a.* **poczta pantoflowa** bush telegraph, moccasin telegraph; the grapevine; **coś doszło do kogoś pocztą pantoflową** sb heard about sth on *l.* through the grapevine.

pantograf *mi* (*lokomotywy*) (*do kopiowania*) pantograph.

pantografia *f. Gen.* **-ii** pantography.

pantomima *f.* (*widowisko*) pantomime, dumb show.

pantomimiczny *a.* pantomimic.

pantomimika *f.* pantomime.

pantomimista *mp* pantomimist.

pantotenowy *a. chem.* panthothenic; **kwas pantotenowy** panthothenic acid.

panujący *a.* predominant, ruling, prevailing; **panująca królowa** regnant queen; **panujące poglądy** prevailing views, tide of opinion; **klasa panująca** ruling class; **religia panująca** dominant religion; **rodzina panująca** ruling family, ruling house. – *mp* ruler.

panzootia *f. wet.* panzootic.

pański *a.* **1.** (*właściwy panu - mężczyźnie*) your, yours; **pański list otrzymałem 10 lipca** I received your letter on July 10; **proszę pozdrowić pańskiego ojca** please, give my best regards to your father; **czy to pański długopis?** is that your pen, sir?; **zapoznałem się z pańską sytuacją** I'm familiar with your situation. **2.** (= *arystokratyczny*) lordly, master; (*o manierach*) lordlike; **na pańskie usługi** at your service; **po pańsku** in a lordly manner; **łaska pańska na pstrym koniu jeździ** being in your master's good graces doesn't last forever; your good fortune can be changed by a twist of fate; **pańskie oko konia tuczy** looking after your possessions brings good results; the eye of a master does more work than both his hands. **3.** (= *Boży*) Lord's; **Anioł Pański** *rz.-kat.* Angelus; **Męka Pańska** *rel.* the Passion; **modlitwa Pańska** *rel.* the Lord's Prayer, Our Father; **stacja Męki Pańskiej** *rz.-kat.* Station (of the Cross); **Przemienienie Pańskie** *rel.* Transfiguration; **Wniebowstąpienie Pańskie** *rel.* Ascension Day; **Objawienie Pańskie** *rel.* Epiphany; **Narodzenie Pańskie** *rel.* the Nativity; **wieczerza Pańska** *rel.* the Lord's Supper; **stół Pański** (*w kościele protestanckim*) the Lord's Table; **roku Pańskiego** *arch.* Anno Domini, in the year of our Lord; **mam z tobą krzyż pański** you're a heavy cross to bear.

państwo *n. Dat. i Loc.* **-wie** (= *kraj*) state, nation; **państwo członkowskie** member state; **państwo demokratyczne** democracy, democratic state; **państwo lenne** *hist.* vassal state; **państwo opiekuńcze** welfare state; **państwo prawa** the rule of law (*in a state*); state of law; **państwo w państwie** a state within the state; **Rada Państwa** *hist.* State Council; **zarządzany przez państwo** (*o przedsiębiorstwie*) state-controlled, state-operated. – *n. Dat. i Loc.* **-u** **1.** (= *pan i pani*) Mr. and Mrs.; **państwo Kowalscy** Mr. and Mrs. Kowalski, the Kowalskis; **czy to państwa samochód?** is that your car?; **szanowni państwo!** Ladies and Gentlemen!; **państwo młodzi** newlyweds, the Bride and Groom. **2.** (*forma grzecznościowa używana wobec bliżej nieznanych osób*) you; **proszę państwa, proszę o chwilę uwagi** Ladies and Gentlemen, may I have your attention, please. **3.** *przest.* (= *gospodarze wobec służby*) the master and mistress; **państwo wyszli do teatru, proszę zadzwonić za godzinę** the master and mistress are at the theater, could you call in an hour, please?

państwowość *f.* statehood.

państwowotwórczy *a* state-building.

państwowy *a.* national, state, public; (*o sektorze*) state-owned, public; **hymn państwowy** national anthem; **święto państwowe** national holiday; **urzędnik państwowy** public servant, civil servant; **sprawy wagi państwowej** matters of the state.

pańszczyzna *f.* **1.** *hist.* corvée. **2.** *pot.* (= *harówka*) drudgery.

pańszczyźniany *a.* (of) corvée; **chłop pańszczyźniany** serf, villein; **praca pańszczyźniana** corvée.

papa¹ *f.* (*do krycia dachu*) asphalt roofing, roofing paper.

papa² *f. pot.* (= *gęba*) muzzle, mug; **nie drzyj papy!** shut up!; **dać komuś w papę** slap sb in the face; **brać komuś do papy** *wulg.* suck sb off.

papa³ *mp pl.* **-owie** *przest.* (= *ojciec*) papa, dad.

papaja *f. bot.* papaya (*Carica papaya*).

paparazzi *mp indecl. l. decl. like a. sing. t. indecl.* **paparazzo** paparazzi.

papaweryna *f. chem.* papaverine.

papeć *mi* **-pci-** *Gen.* **-a** *pot.* slipper.

papeteria *f. Gen.* **-ii** stationery; **papeteria firmowa** letterhead.

papier *mi* **1.** (*do pisania, drukowania, pakowania itp.*) paper; **papier biblijny** Bible paper; **papier ciągły** continuous paper; **papier czerpany** handmade paper; **papier firmowy** letterhead; **papier kreślarski** drawing paper; **papier milimetrowy** graph *l.* plotting paper; **papier nutowy** music paper; **papier pergaminowy** parchment; **papier ścierny** sandpaper, abrasive paper; **papier toaletowy** toilet paper; **szary papier** brown paper; **papier maché** papier-mâché; **biały** *l.* **blady jak papier** white as a sheet; **cienki jak papier** wafer-thin; **papier jest cierpliwy** paper is patient, paper has patience; **przelać myśli na papier** commit sth to paper *l.* writing; **mam to na papierze** I have it in black-and-white; **budowa szpitala pozostaje tylko na papierze** the construction of the hospital is only on paper. **2.** *pot.* (*dokument*) document; **składać papiery na studia** send an application to college; **papiery wartościowe** *ekon.* securities; **lewe papiery** fake *l.* forged documents; **giełda papierów wartościowych** *ekon.* stock exchange.

papierek *mi* **-rk-** *Gen.* **-a** **1.** (= *skrawek papieru*) piece of paper; **papierek lakmusowy** *chem.* litmus paper; **papierek wskaźnikowy** *chem.* indicator paper, test-paper. **2.** *iron.* (= *dokument*) document, paper, record.

papierkowy *a.* paper; **papierkowa robota** *iron.* paperwork.

papiernia *f. Gen.pl.* **-i** *l.* **-ń** paper mill.

papiernica *f. techn.* paper machine.

papiernictwo *n.* paper industry.

papierniczy *a.* paper; **artykuły papiernicze** stationery; **sklep papierniczy** stationer's.

papiernik *mp* paper manufacturer.

papieroch *mi Gen.* **-a** *uj.* cancer stick, sickerette.

papieros *mi Gen. i Acc.* **-a** cigarette; **pudełko papierosów** pack of cigarettes; **zapalić papierosa** smoke a cigarette, light up a cigarette.

papierosowy *a.* cigarette; **bibułka papierosowa** cigarette paper; **dym papierosowy** cigarette smoke.

papierośnica *f.* cigarette case.

papierowość *f.* unnaturalness, artificiality.

papierowy *a.* **1.** (*z papieru*) paper. **2.** (*podobny do papieru*) paperlike; **książka w papierowej okładce** paperback; **ręcznik papierowy** kitchen roll; **waga papierowa** *boks* light flyweight. **3.** (*o obietnicach, planach*) paper. **4.** (*o postaci w książce*) unnatural.

papierówka *f. Gen.pl.* **-ek** **1.** (*jabłoń i owoc*) greening. **2.** (*drewno*) pulpwood.

papierzysko *n. uj.* **1.** (= *kawałek papieru*) a piece of paper. **2.** (= *dokument*) paper, document.

papieski *a.* papal; **legat papieski** *rz.-kat.* papal legate; **list papieski** *rz.-kat.* papal brief.

papiestwo *n.* papacy, popedom.

papież *mp* pope, pontiff; **świętszy od papieża** more royalist than the king, holier-than-thou; **być w Rzymie i nie widzieć papieża** be in Rome and not see the Pope.

papilarny *a.* papillary; **linie papilarne** papillary ridges.

papiloty *pl. Gen.* **-ów** curlpapers, papillotes.

papirolog *mp pl.* **-owie** *l.* **-dzy** papyrologist.

papirologia *f. Gen.* **-ii** papyrology.

papirologiczny *a.* papyrological.

papirus *mi* **1.** (*do pisania*) papyrus. **2.** *bot.* papyrus (*Cyperus papyrus*).

papirusowy *a.* papyrus; **zwój papirusowy** papyrus scroll; **cibora papirusowa** *bot.* papyrus (*Cyperus papyrus*).

papista *mp* papist, ultramontane.

papizm *mi hist.* (*system rządów*) papacy.

papka *f. Gen.pl.* **-ek** (*masa*) mash, mush; (*jako pokarm*) pap; **rozgotować coś na papkę** boil *l.* cook sth to a pulp.

papkowaty *a.* mushy, pappy.

papla *mp l. f.* chatterbox.

paplać *ipf. pot.* babble, prattle; **paplać jak najęty** talk one's head off.

paplanina *f. pot.* babble, prattle.

papowy *a.* asphalt paper; **gwóźdź papowy** roofing nail.

paprać *ipf.* **-rzę -rzesz 1.** *pot.* (= *brudzić*) mess up, smear. **2.** *pot.* (= *robić niechlujnie*) make a mess, do a messy job (*coś* of sth). **~ się** *ipf. pot.* **1.** (= *brudzić się*) mess o.s. up, smear. **2.** (= *wykonywać nieprzyjemną pracę*) do a messy job. **3.** (= *nie goić się*) (*o ranie, skaleczeniu*) fester.

papranina *f. pot.* mess.

paproch *mi Gen.* **-a** fluff.

paprociowe *pl. Gen.* **-ych** *bot.* ferns (*Filicinae*).

paproć *f. pl.* **-e** *bot.* fern (*Filix*); **liść paproci** fern frond; **kwiat paproci** *przen.* the crock of gold.

paprotka *f. Gen.pl.* **-ek** *bot.* polypody (*Polypodium*).

paprotkowate *pl. Gen.* **-ych** *bot.* the polypody family (*Polypodiaceae*).

paprotnik *mi Gen.* **-a** *bot.* pteridophyte (*Pteridophyta*).

papryka *f.* **1.** (*roślina*) *bot.* pepper, capsicum (*Capsicum annuum*). **2.** (*warzywo*) (*przyprawa*) (*słodka*) paprika; (*ostra*) pepper; **czerwona papryka** red pepper; **zielona papryka** green pepper; **papryka chili** chili pepper.

paprykarz *mi kulin.* a pepper, fish and rice pâté.

paprykowy *a.* (*ostry*) paprika, seasoned with paprika; (*słodki*) pepper, seasoned with pepper.

papu *n. indecl.* **1.** *dziec.* me want eat! **2.** *żart.* tucker.

Papua *f.* Papua; **Terytorium Papui** Territory of Papua.

Papuas *mp* Papuan.

papuaski *a.* Papuan.

papuć *mi Gen.* **-a** *pot.* slipper.

papuga *f.* **1.** *orn.* parrot (*Psittaciformes*). **2.**

uj. parrot, copycat; **powtarzać jak papuga** repeat parrot-fashion, parrot.

papugi *pl. Gen.* **-g** *orn.* parrots (*Psittaciformes*).

papugoryba *f. icht.* parrot fish (*Scaridae*).

papugować *ipf. pot.* parrot.

papuzi *a.* parrot, parrot's; (*w języku fachowym*) psittacine; **choroba papuzia** *med.* psittacosis, parrot fever.

papużka *f.* small parrot; **papużka falista** budgerigar (*Melopsittacus undulatus*).

par *mp pl.* **-owie** peer; **par dożywotni** (*w Izbie Lordów*) life peer.

par. *abbr.* (= *paragraf*) *prawn.* art.

para¹ *f.* **1.** (= *skroplony gaz*) steam, vapor; **zamieniać się w parę** evaporate; **para nasycona** *fiz.* saturated vapor; **para nienasycona** *fiz.* superheated vapor; **gotować na parze** steam; **żelazko na parę** steam iron; **być pod parą** (*o statku, parowozie*) be under steam; **pełną parą** at full speed *l.* steam; **pracować pełną** *l.* **całą parą** work at full speed; **praca idzie pełną parą** the work is in full swing; **mieć parę** (= *dużo sił*) have power. **2.** (= *tchnienie*) breath; **nie puścić pary z ust** *l.* **gęby** not breathe a word; **ani pary z ust** *l.* **gęby!** don't breathe a word!

para² *f.* **1.** (= *dwa przedmioty*) pair, couple; **nie do pary** odd; **para spodni/rękawiczek/skrzydeł** pair of trousers/gloves/wings; **łączyć się w pary** *zool.* mate; **inwestycje idą w parze ze zwiększonymi przychodami** investments go hand in hand with increased revenues; **nieszczęścia zawsze chodzą parami** misfortunes never come alone, it never rains but it pours; **to inna para kaloszy** *żart.* that's a horse of a different color. **2.** (= *dwie osoby*) couple; **iść parami** go in pairs *l.* twos; **młoda para** bride and groom; **dobrać się w pary** pair up.

parabellum *n. indecl.* (*pistolet*) parabellum.

parabola *f.* **1.** *geom.* parabola. **2.** *teor.lit.* parable.

paraboliczny *a.* parabolic.

paraboloida *f. geom.* paraboloid.

parać się *ipf.* dabble (*czymś* at *l.* in sth).

parada *f.* **1.** (*widowisko*) parade, show; **ubranie od parady** one's Sunday best; **dyrektor od parady** manager just for show; **nie od parady** not merely for show; **masz głowę nie od parady** your head is screwed on the right way; **wchodzić komuś w paradę** cross sb's path, put sb's nose out of joint. **2.** (*defilada*) parade, review of troops. **3.** *szermierka* parry, ward. **4.** *piłka nożna* dive.

paradentoza, parodontoza *f. pat.* periodontitis.

paradnie *adv.* **ubrać się paradnie** wear one's Sunday best.

paradny *a.* **1.** (= *galowy*) gala; **paradne ubranie** one's Sunday best. **2.** (= *zabawny*) hilarious.

paradoks *mi* **1.** (*sprzeczność*) paradox, contradiction; **to brzmi jak paradoks** that sounds like a paradox. **2.** *log.* contradiction, paradox.

paradoksalnie *adv.* paradoxically.

paradoksalny *a.* paradoxical.

parodontoza *f. pat. zob.* **paradentoza**.

paradować *ipf. pot.* parade; **paradować w czymś** (*np. w modnym ubraniu*) sport sth.

paradygmat *mi jęz.* paradigm.

paradygmatyczny *a. jęz.* paradigmatic.

parafa *f.* initial; **postawić parafę (na dokumencie)** initial (a document).

parafia *f. Gen.* -ii *kośc.* parish; **parafia ewangelicko-augsburska** Lutheran parish; **ewangelicko-reformowana** Calvinist parish; **prawosławna** Orthodox parish; **rzymskokatolicka** Roman Catholic parish; **objąć parafię** become a parish priest; **każdy z innej parafii** *przen. pot.* each of a different kind; **to nie moja parafia** *przen. pot.* this is not my cup of tea.

parafialny *a.* parish, parochial; **kościół parafialny** parish church; **księga parafialna** parish register; **święto parafialne** parish holiday; **szkoła parafialna** parochial school.

parafianin *mp pl.* -anie *Gen.* -an, **parafianka** *f. Gen.pl.* -ek parishioner.

parafiańszczyzna *f. przest., uj.* parochialism.

parafina *f. chem.* paraffin.

parafinować *ipf.* paraffin.

parafinowy *a.* paraffin; **olej parafinowy** paraffin oil, paraffin; **świeca parafinowa** paraffin candle.

parafka *f. Gen.pl.* -ek initials; **postawić na czymś parafkę** initial sth.

parafować *ipf.* **1.** (*przyjąć, zatwierdzić*) initial. **2.** (*zabezpieczyć, zapieczętować*) seal.

parafraza *f.* (*omówienie*) *muz., teor.lit.* paraphrase.

parafrazować *ipf.* paraphrase.

paragon *mi* receipt.

paragraf *mi* **1.** (*przepis*) article, section. **2.** (= *akapit*) (= *znak*) paragraph.

Paragwaj *mi geogr.* Paraguay.

Paragwajczyk *mp*, **Paragwajka** *f. Gen.pl.* -ek Paraguayan.

paragwajski *a.* Paraguayan.

paralaksa *f. astron., fiz.* parallax.

paralaktyczny *a. astron.* parallactic; **trójkąt paralaktyczny** astronomical triangle.

paralela *f. Gen.pl.* -i *l.* -l (= *porównanie*) parallelism, parallel; (*rzecz l. cecha podobna*) parallel; **przeprowadzać paralelę** draw a parallel.

paralelizm *mi* (*jednoczesność*) *teor.lit.* parallelism.

paralelnie *adv.* parallelly.

paralelny *a.* parallel; **rozwój paralelny** parallel development.

paralityczka *f. Gen.pl.* -ek, **paralityk** *mp* paralytic.

paraliż *mi* **1.** *pat.* paralysis, palsy; **paraliż dziecięcy** poliomyelitis; **paraliż postępujący** general paraplegia, general paresis; paralytic dementia; **dotknięty paraliżem** paralyzed. **2.** (*brak zdolności funkcjonowania*) paralysis.

paraliżować *ipf.* **1.** *pat.* paralyze. **2.** *przen.* (= *hamować czyjeś działanie*) paralyze; frustrate; **być sparaliżowanym strachem** be petrified, be seized by fear; **śnieżyce paraliżują ruch na autostradach** blizzards bring all freeway traffic to a stop, blizzards make driving impossible.

paraliżująco *adv.* paralyzingly.

paraliżujący *a.* paralyzing; **paraliżujący strach** overpowering fear.

paralogizm *mi log.* paralogism.

paralotnia *f. lotn.* paraglider.

paramagnetyczny *a. fiz.* paramagnetic.

paramagnetyk *mi fiz.* paramagnet.

paramagnetyzm *mi fiz.* paramagnetism.

parametr *mi mat., techn.* parameter; **optymalne parametry odbioru** optimum reception parameters; **niskie/wysokie parametry** poor/good performance.

paramilitarny *a.* paramilitary.

paranoiczka *f. Gen.pl.* -ek, **paranoik** *mp pat. psych.* paranoid, paranoiac.

paranoiczny *a.* **1.** *pat., psych.* paranoid, paranoidal. **2.** *przen.* crazy, absurd; **paranoiczny pomysł** crazy idea, absurd idea; **paranoiczny plan** crazy plan.

paranoidalny *a. pat., psych.* paranoid, paranoidal.

paranoik *mp zob.* **paranoiczka**.

paranoja *f. Gen.* -oi **1.** *pat., psych.* paranoia. **2.** *pot.* (= *obłęd*) bedlam; **to, co tu się dzieje, to jakaś paranoja** what's happening here is utter bedlam.

paranormalny *a.* paranormal; **zjawisko paranormalne** paranormal phenomenon.

parantele *pl. Gen.* -i *lit.* (*związki*) relationships; (*krewni*) relations, relatives.

parapet *mi* sill; **parapet okienny** windowsill; **parapet zewnętrzny/wewnętrzny** external/internal sill.

parapetówa *f. pot.* (*przyjęcie*) housewarming.

parapetówka *f. Gen.pl.* -ek = **parapetówa**.

paraplegia *f. Gen.* -ii *pat.* paraplegia.

parapsycholog *mi pl.* -dzy *l.* -owie parapsychologist.

parapsychologia *f. Gen.* -ii parapsychology.

parapsychologiczny *a.* parapsychological.

parasol *mi Gen.* -a (*przeciwdeszczowy*) umbrella; (*przeciwsłoneczny*) parasol, sunshade; **parasol kawiarniany** bar *l.* cafe umbrella; **parasol ogrodowy** garden umbrella; **parasol plażowy** beach umbrella.

parasolka *f. Gen.pl.* -ek *zob.* **parasol**.

parasolnik *mp* umbrella maker.

parasympatyczny *a. anat.* parasympathetic; **parasympatyczny układ nerwowy** parasympathetic nervous system.

parataksa *f. jęz.* parataxis.

parataktycznie *adv. jęz.* paratactically.

parataktyczny *a.* paratactic.

parathormon *mi med.* parathormone, parathyroid hormone.

paratyfus *mi pat.* paratyphoid fever.

paratyfusowy *a. pat.* paratyphoid fever.

parawan *mi* **1.** (*zasłona*) screen. **2.** *przen.* front, screen; **ta inwestycja jest parawanem dla ich kombinacji finansowych** this investment is just a front *l.* screen for their shady financial dealings.

parawodór *mi* -o- *chem.* parahydrogen.

parazytolog *mp Gen.* **-dzy** *l.* **-owie** *med., wet.* parasitologist.

parazytologia *f. Gen.* **-ii** *med., wet.* parasitology.

parazytologiczny *a. med., wet.* parasitological.

parazytoza *f. pat., wet.* parasitosis, parasitism.

parcela *f. Gen.pl.* **-i** *l.* **-l** lot; *zwł. Br.* plot.

parcelacja *f. zwł. polit. t. hist.* lotting; plotting.

parcelować *ipf.* lot; plot.

parch *mi Gen.* **-u** *l.* **-a** **1.** *pot. pat.* mange. **2.** *roln. bot.* scab. **3.** *pog.* ragamuffin.

parciany *a.* sackcloth, sacking; **pas parciany** sackcloth belt; **torba parciana** sackcloth bag.

parcie *n.* **1.** (= *napór*) pressure, thrust; **parcie korzeniowe** *bot.* root pressure. **2.** *fizj., med.* tenesmus; **parcie na pęcherz** urgency; **parcie porodowe** uterine pressure.

pardon *mi* **bez pardonu** unceremoniously.

pardwa *f. Gen.pl.* **-dw** *l.* **-dew** *orn.* willow ptarmigan, willow grouse (*Lagopus lagopus*).

pareczniki *ma zool.* centipedes (*Chilopoda*).

paremiograf *mp Gen.* **-owie** paroemiographer.

paremiografia *f. Gen.* **-ii** paroemiography.

paremiograficzny *a.* paroemiographic.

paremiolog *mp pl.* **-dzy** *l.* **-owie** paroemiologist.

paremiologia *f. Gen.* **-ii** paroemiology.

paremiologiczny *a.* paroemiologic.

parenchyma *f. bot., zool.* parenchyma.

parenchymatyczny *a. bot., zool.* parenchymal, parenchymatous.

parenetyczny *a.* parenetic, paraenetic; **literatura parenetyczna** parenetic literature, paraenetic literature.

parenetyka *f. teor.lit.* parenetic literature, paraenetic literature.

parenteza *f. gram.* parenthesis.

parę *num. Ins.* **-oma** *l.* **-u** a few, several; **parę dni temu** a few days ago; **od paru godzin** for a few hours; **parę osób** a few people; **parę słów** a few words; **ona ma ze czterdzieści parę lat** she's over forty; **mam parę groszy** I've got a little money; **ładne parę złotych** quite a lot of money; **napisać do kogoś parę słów** drop sb a line.

parędziesiąt *num.* **-ęci-** *Ins.* **-oma** *l.* **-u** a score or so; **parędziesiąt kilometrów** a score or so kilometers.

paręnaście *num.* **parunast-** *Ins.* **-oma** *l.* **-u** a dozen or so; **paręnaście kilometrów** a dozen or so kilometers.

paręset *num.* **parę-** *decl. like num.,* **-set** *indecl.* several hundred; **paręset złotych** several hundred zlotys *l.* zloty.

parias *mp* **1.** *Ind.* Pariah. **2.** *przen.* pariah, outcast.

park *mi* **1.** (*dla rekreacji*) park; **park narodowy** national park; **park angielski** *l.* **krajobrazowy** romantic style park, English garden; **park francuski** *l.* **włoski** Italian park, baroque park, architectural garden; **park krajobrazowy** (national) scenic park; **park rozrywki** amusement park, theme park. **2.** (*baza maszyn*) equipment, machinery; **park autobusowy** bus fleet, fleet of buses; **park tramwajowy** streetcar fleet; *Br.* tram

fleet; **park komputerowy** computers (*in a company, institution, etc.*); **park maszynowy** machinery (*in a company, factory, etc.*). **3.** *wojsk.* park.

parka¹ *f. Gen.pl.* **-ek** **1.** (*o narzeczonych, młodożeńcach itd.*) couple, pair; (*o dzieciach*) (= *dwoje*) two. **2.** (*o zwierzętach*) pair.

parka² *f. Gen.pl.* **-ek** (*kurtka*) parka.

parkan *mi* fence; (*tymczasowy, np. wokół placu budowy*) hoarding.

parkiet *mi* **1.** (*posadzka*) parquet. **2.** (*do tańca*) dance floor. **3.** *ekon., giełda* floor.

parkietowy *a.* parquet.

parking *mi* parking lot; *Br.* car park; **parking niestrzeżony** unattended parking lot *l.* car park; **parking strzeżony** attended parking lot *l.* car park.

parkingowy *a.* parking; **miejsce parkingowe** parking space. – *mp* parking lot attendant.

parkinsonizm *mi pat.* Parkinson's disease.

parkocić się *ipf. myśl.* couple.

parkometr *mi* parking meter.

parkoty *pl. Gen.* **-ów** *myśl.* rut.

parkować *ipf.* park.

parkowanie *n.* parking; **miejsce do parkowania** parking space; **parkowanie zabronione** (*napis*) no parking.

parkowy *a.* park; **alejka parkowa** park alley, park avenue.

parlament *mi* **1.** *polit.* parliament; **obrady parlamentu** parliamentary session, parliamentary debates; **parlament dwuizbowy** bicameral parliament; **izba niższa parlamentu** lower chamber of the parliament; **izba wyższa parlamentu** upper chamber of the parliament; **wybory do parlamentu** parliamentary election; **zasiadać w parlamencie** be a member of parliament; **rozwiązać parlament** dissolve parliament. **2.** (*budynek*) parliament building, parliament.

parlamentariusz *mp polit.* parliamentary.

parlamentarno-gabinetowy *a.* *polit.* parliamentary-cabinet.

parlamentarny *a.* **1.** *polit.* parliamentary; **frakcja parlamentarna** parliamentary faction; **komisja parlamentarna** parliamentary committee; **monarchia parlamentarna** constitutional monarchy; **odpowiedzialność parlamentarna** parliamentary responsibility. **2.** *przen.* (= *taktowny*) civil, polite; parliamentary; **odezwać się w sposób niezbyt parlamentarny** say sth uncivil *l.* impolite.

parlamentaryzm *mi* parliamentarism, parliamentary government.

parlamentarzysta *mp* member of parliament; *rzad.* parliamentarian.

parlando *n. muz.* parlando.

parlatorium *n. sing. indecl. pl.* **-ria** *Gen.* **-riów** *kośc.* parlor, locutorium.

parmezan *mi kulin.* Parmesan, Parmesan cheese.

parnas *mi mit., przen.* Parnassus.

parnasista *mp teor.lit.* Parnassian.

parnasizm *mi teor.lit.* Parnassianism, Parnassism.

parnik *mi Gen.* **-a** *roln.* steamer.

parnikowy *a.* steaming.

parno *adv.* sultrily; **jest parno** it's sultry.

parność *f.* sultriness.

parny *a.* sultry; **parny dzień** sultry day.

parobek *mp* -bk- *pl.* -owie *l.* -cy *l.* -i *hist.* farmhand, farm hand.

paroch *mp* *kośc.* (Greek Catholic) parish priest.

parochia *f. Gen.* -ii *kośc.* (Greek Catholic) parish.

parodia *f. Gen.* -ii parody, travesty; **parodia sprawiedliwości** travesty of justice; **ten związek to parodia małżeństwa** *pot.* this relationship is a parody *l.* travesty of marriage.

parodiować *ipf.* parody.

parodiowy *a.* parodic, parodical; **wykonanie parodiowe** parodic performance.

parodniowy *a.* a few days'; **parodniowa kuracja** treatment lasting a few days; **parodniowy wyjazd** a few days' trip.

parodontoza *f. med. zob.* **paradentoza.**

parodysta *mp*, **parodystka** *f. Gen.pl.* -ek (= *autor(ka) parodii*) parodist; (*zwł. znanych osób*) impressionist.

parodystyczny *a.* parodic, parodical.

parogodzinny *a.* a few hours'; **parogodzinna dyskusja** discussion lasting a few hours; **parogodzinna podróż** a few hours' journey.

parokilometrowy *a.* a few kilometers'; **parokilometrowa przejażdżka** a few kilometers' ride *l.* drive.

parokrotnie *adv.* repeatedly, several times.

parokrotny *a.* repeated; **parokrotny mistrz świata** several times world champion.

paroksyton *mi jęz.* paroxytone.

paroksytoneza *f. jęz.* paroxytonic accentuation.

paroksytoniczny *a. jęz.* paroxytonic.

paroksyzm *mi* paroxysm, spasm; **paroksyzm bólu** spasm of pain; **paroksyzm gniewu** paroxysm of rage; **paroksyzm śmiechu** paroxysm of laughter.

parol *mi* **1.** *przest.* (= *hasło*) password, parole. **2.** *przest.* (= *słowo honoru*) word of honor, parole; **zagiąć parol na kogoś** have designs on sb.

parolatek *mp* a few-year old.

paroletni *a.* a few years'; a few-year old; **paroletni samochód** a few-year old car; **paroletni pobyt za granicą** a few years' residence abroad.

parometrowy *a.* a few meters'.

paromiesięczny *a.* a few months'.

parominutowy *a.* a few minutes'.

paronim *mi jęz.* paronym.

paronomazja *f. jęz.* paronomasia, pun.

parostatek *mi* -tk- steamship, steamer.

parostki *pl. Gen.* -ów *myśl.* spikes.

parostopniowy *a.* of a few degrees; **parostopniowy mróz** several degrees below zero; **parostopniowe eliminacje** qualification procedure consisting of several stages.

parotomowy *a.* of a few volumes.

parotonowy *a.* of a few tons; **parotonowy ciężar** load weighing a few tons; **parotonowy podnośnik** hoist of a few tons' capacity.

parotygodniowy *a.* a few weeks'; **parotygodniowy pobyt** a few weeks' stay.

parotysięczny *a.* of a few *l.* several thousand; **parotysięczny tłum** crowd of several thousand.

parować[1] *ipf.* **1.** (= *zamieniać się w gaz*) evaporate, vaporize. **2.** (= *wydzielać parę*) evaporate. **3.** (= *poddać działaniu pary*) steam.

parować[2] *ipf.* (*w szermierce l. boksie*) parry, ward off; **parować zarzuty** refute accusations.

parowanie[1] *n.* evaporation, vaporization; **ciepło parowania** *fiz.* heat of vaporization, heat of evaporation.

parowanie[2] *n.* parry, parrying.

parowiec *mi* -wc- *Gen.* -a steamer, steamship.

parowiekowy *a.* of several centuries; several centuries old; **parowiekowa budowla** several centuries old building.

parownica *f. chem.* evaporating dish, vaporizer.

parownik *mi Gen.* -a **1.** *techn.* (= *wymiennik ciepła*) evaporator. **2.** *techn., tk.* ager.

parowozownia *f. Gen.pl.* -i *kol.* steam engine depot, steam engine barn.

parowozowy *a.* steam engine; **maszynista parowozowy** steam engine driver.

parowóz *mi* -o- *kol.* steam engine.

parowy *a.* steam; **kocioł parowy** steam boiler; **maszyna parowa** steam engine; **młot parowy** steam hammer; **silnik parowy** steam engine; **statek parowy** steamship; **turbina parowa** steam turbine.

parów *mi* -o- ravine.

parówa *f. pot.* (= *upał*) **1.** heat. **2.** *wulg.* (= *penis*) meat. **3.** *wulg.* (= *homoseksualista*) fag.

parówka *f. Gen.pl.* -ek **1.** (*kiełbasa*) hot dog, frankfurter. **2.** *pot.* (= *łaźnia, t. kąpiel parowa*) steam bath. **3.** (= *gorące powietrze*) heat.

parówkowy *a.* hot dog, frankfurter.

parsek *mi Gen.* -a *astron.* parsec.

parskać *ipf.*, **parsknąć** *pf.* -ij (*o zwierzęciu, człowieku, silniku*) snort; **parskać śmiechem** burst out laughing.

parszywiec *mp* -wc- *pl.* -y *obelż.* ragamuffin.

parszywieć *ipf.* **1.** *pot.* (*o ludziach, zwierzętach*) be affected with mange. **2.** *bot.* scab.

parszywy *a.* **1.** (*pokryty parchami*) mangy; scabious, scabby; (*o psie, koniu*) mangy, scabby; (*o ziemniaku*) scabby; **parszywa owca** *przen.* black sheep. **2.** *pot.* (= *podły*) lousy, rotten; **parszywy nastrój** lousy mood; **parszywa pogoda** lousy weather.

partacki *a.* (*rzemieślnik*) bungling; (*robota*) bungled, botched; **po partacku** bunglingly.

partactwo *n.* bungled work.

partacz *mp* bungler, botcher.

partaczyć *ipf.* bungle, botch.

partanina *f.* botched work.

partenogenetyczny *a. biol.* parthenogenetic.

partenogeneza *f. biol.* parthenogenesis.

partenokarpia *f. Gen.* -ii *bot.* parthenocarpy.

parter *mi* **1.** (= *pierwsza kondygnacja*) first floor; *Br.* ground floor. **2.** (*w sali widowiskowej, kinie, teatrze*) (*z przodu sali*) stalls; *Br.* orchestra; (*z tyłu sali*) parquet circle, parterre. **3.** *ogr.*

parterre. **4.** *zapasy* par terre position, down position, on-the-ground position; **sprowadzenie przeciwnika do parteru** takedown; **walka w parterze** on-the-ground wrestling.

parterowy *a.* **1.** (*o budynku*) one-story, *Br.* one-storey; **dom parterowy** one-story house; **zabudowa parterowa** one-story buildings. **2.** (= *znajdujący się na parterze*) first floor; **okna parterowe** first floor windows; **akrobatyka parterowa** *sport* floor exercise. **3.** (*o miejscach*) orchestra; **loże parterowe** orchestra boxes.

partia *f. Gen.* **-ii 1.** *polit.* party; **partia chadecka** christian-democratic party; **partia chłopska** peasants' *l.* people's party; **partia demokratyczna** democratic party; **partia komunistyczna** communist party; **partia konserwatywna** conservative party; **partia liberalna** liberal party; **partia pracy** labour party; **partia robotnicza** workers' party; **partia socjaldemokratyczna** social democratic party; **partia opozycyjna** opposition party; **partia rządząca** ruling party; **Polska Zjednoczona Partia Robotnicza** *hist.* Polish United Workers' Party; **Partia Demokratyczna/Republikańska** (*w USA*) Democratic/Republican Party; **Partia Konserwatywna/Pracy** (*w Wielkiej Brytanii*) Conservative/Labour Party; **wstąpić do partii** join a party. **2.** (*zespół osób*) team, group; **gracze podzielili się na dwie partie** players split into two teams; **kolejna partia uchodźców z Kosowa przekroczyła granicę Albanii** another group of Kosovar refugees crossed the Albanian border. **3.** (*część*) part, portion; (*seria produktów, część towaru*) lot, batch; (= *fragment, ustęp*) fragment; **partia towaru** batch *l.* lot of goods; **wysyłać zboże partiami** send grain in several shipments; **przeczytać partię opracowania naukowego** read a fragment of a scientific study. **4.** (*część gry*) game, round; **partia szachów** game of chess; **partia brydża** round of bridge; **zrobić partię** *brydż* win a game. **5.** (*do zaśpiewania, zagrania*) part; **partia solowa** solo part; **partia tytułowa** leading part. **6.** *przest.* (= *kandydat do małżeństwa*) match; **być dobrą partią** be a good match; **zrobić dobrą partię** marry well.

partita *f. muz.* partita, suite.

partner *mp*, **partnerka** *f. Gen.pl.* **-ek 1.** partner; **partner do rozmowy** conversation partner; **partner do tańca** dancing partner; **partner do tenisa** tennis partner; **partner życiowy** partner; (= *małżonek*) spouse. **2.** *prawn., handl., kino, teatr* partner.

partnerować *ipf.* partner; *kino, teatr* (*w jednej z ról głównych*) co-star (*komuś* with sb); (*w roli drugoplanowej*) support.

partnerski *a.* based on partnership.

partnersko *adv.* **traktować kogoś po partnersku** treat sb like a partner.

partnerstwo *n.* partnership.

partolić *ipf. pot.* botch, bungle.

Partowie *pl. Gen.* **-ów** *hist.* Parthians.

party *n. indecl.* party.

partycypacja *f.* (= *uczestnictwo*) participation; (*w kosztach, wydatkach*) sharing; **partycypacja w kosztach** cost sharing.

partycypować *ipf.* (= *uczestniczyć*) participate; (*w kosztach, wydatkach*) share, have a share in.

partyjka *f. pot.* (*w grze*) game, round; *karty* rubber.

partyjniak *mp uj.* party member.

partyjny *a.* party; **dyscyplina partyjna** party discipline; **działacz partyjny** party activist/militant; **towarzysz partyjny** party comrade; **zebranie partyjne** party meeting. – *mp* party member.

partykularny *a.* (= *prowincjonalny*) provincial; **partykularny interes** vested interest, particularist interest.

partykularyzm *mi* particularism.

partykularz *mi Gen.* **-a** *przest.* the sticks, boondocks.

partykuła *f. gram.* particle; **partykuła deiktyczna** deictic particle, deictic; **partykuła modyfikująca** modifying particle, modifier; **partykuła poprzedzająca** prepositive.

partytura *f.* **1.** *muz.* score. **2.** *teatr* script.

partyzancki *a.* guerrilla, guerilla; partisan; **oddział partyzancki** guerrilla squad; **działania partyzanckie** guerrilla warfare.

partyzant *mp* **1.** (= *żołnierz podziemia*) guerrilla, guerilla; partisan. **2.** *hist.* partisan.

partyzantka *f.* **1.** (*walka*) guerrilla warfare. **2.** (*grupy żołnierzy*) guerrilla forces, underground army. **3.** *przen.* swimming against the tide; **uprawiać partyzantkę dziennikarską** engage in partisan journalism. **4.** *Gen.pl.* **-ek** (*kobieta żołnierz*) guerrilla.

paru *itd. num. zob.* **parę**.

parusetletni *a.* a few hundred years'; several hundred years old; **parusetletni dąb** several hundred year old oak.

paruzja *f. rel.* parousia.

parweniusz *mp* parvenu.

parweniuszka *f. Gen.pl.* **-ek** parvenue.

parweniuszostwo *n.* parvenuism.

parweniuszowski *a.* parvenu; **parweniuszowskie zachowanie** parvenu behavior.

paryski *a.* Parisian; **bułka paryska** French loaf *l.* bread; **błękit paryski** Paris blue; **zieleń paryska** Paris green; **moda paryska** Parisian fashion; **Komuna Paryska** *hist.* Paris Commune.

parytet *mi ekon.* **1.** parity; **parytet złota** gold standard *l.* parity. **2.** *prawn.* equality before the law.

parytetowy *a. ekon.* parity, par.

Paryż *mi Gen.* **-a** *geogr.* Paris.

paryżanin *mp*, **paryżanka** *f.* Parisian.

parzonka *f. Gen.pl.* **-ek** *roln.* mash.

parzyć *ipf.* **1.** (*o czymś gorącym*) burn, scorch; (*o cieczy*) scald. **2.** (= *podrażnić*) (*np. o pokrzywie*) sting, prick. **3.** (= *zalewać wrzątkiem*) scald, blanch. **4.** (= *zaparzać*) brew. **~ się**[1] *ipf.* **1.** (= *oparzyć się*) burn, scald. **2.** (= *podrażnić*) be stung. **3.** (= *zaparzać się*) brew.

parzyć się[2] *ipf. myśl.* (= *odbywać gody*) mate.

parzydełko *n. Gen.pl.* **-ek** *zool.* nematocyst.

parzystokopytne *pl. Gen.* **-ych** *zool.* even-toed ungulates, artiodactyls (*Artiodactyla*).

parzysty *a.* **1.** (*o liczbie*) even. **2.** (*w parze*) paired, coupled; *biol.* geminate, binate.

pas¹ *mi Gen.* **-a 1.** (*przy ubraniu*) belt; **oberwać pasem** get belted; **pas do pończoch** garter belt; **pas ratunkowy** life belt; **pas przepuklinowy** truss; **pas rycerski** *hist.* knight's belt; **pas słucki** *hist.* sash; **brać nogi za pas** show a clean pair of heels; **popuszczać pasa** loosen sb's belt; **zaciskać pasa** tighten sb's belt; **poniżej pasa** below the belt; **wiosna za pasem** spring is near, spring is coming. **2.** (*materiału, skóry*) strip, belt, band; **pas napędowy** *l.* **transmisyjny** transmission belt; **pas bezpieczeństwa** seat belt, safety belt. **3.** (*powierzchnia*) strip, zone; **pas pola** strip of land; **pas graniczny** border zone; **pas ochronny** *leśn.* shelter belt; **pas przybrzeżny** coastal waters; **pas rozdzielczy** *mot.* median (strip); **pas ruchu** lane; **pas startowy** runway, airstrip; **pas zieleni** green belt; **pasy dla pieszych** pedestrian crossing; **w pasy** striped. **4.** (= *talia*) waist; **rozebrać się do pasa** undress from the waist up; **od pasa w dół** from the waist down; **po pas** waist-deep, waist-high; **kłaniać się komuś w pas** make a low bow to sb. **5.** *anat.* girdle; **pas barkowy** shoulder girdle; **pas miednicowy** pelvic girdle.

pas² *n. indecl.* **1.** (*krok w tańcu*) step. **2.** (*w szermierce*) pass.

pas³ *mi indecl. l. Gen.* **-u** *karty* (*w brydżu*) no bid; (*w pokerze*) pass.

pasać *ipf.* shepherd, graze; **tobie świnie pasać!** *pot.* you are a good-for-nothing; **świń z tobą nie pasałem** *pot.* I don't think I know you, I don't recall being on first-name terms with you.

pasat *mi meteor.* trade wind.

pasaż *mi* **1.** (*przejście*) passageway; **pasaż handlowy** shopping arcade. **2.** *muz.* passage.

pasażer *mp pl.* **-owie**, **pasażerka** *f. Gen.pl.* **-ek** passenger; **pasażer na gapę** fare-dodger; (*ukrywający się na pokładzie statku, samolotu itd.*) stowaway.

pasażerski *a.* passenger; **samolot pasażerski** airliner, passenger aircraft; **statek pasażerski** liner.

Pascha *f. rel.* Passover; Pesach, Pesah.

pascha *f. kulin.* paschal dish.

paschalny *a. rel.* paschal.

paschał *mi kośc.* paschal candle.

pasek *mi* **-sk-** *Gen.* **-a 1.** (*przy ubraniu*) belt. **2.** (*do pończoch*) garter belt. **3.** (*materiału, skóry*) strap, belt, band; **pasek do zegarka** watch strap; **pasek klinowy** *mot.* fan belt; **on chodzi na pasku (u) żony** he crouches before his wife. **4.** (*deseń na ubraniu*) strip; **koszulka w paski** striped T-shirt. **5.** (*naszywka na mundurze*) stripe.

pasemka *pl. Gen.* **-ek** (*fryzura*) highlights, streaks.

pasemko *n. Gen.pl.* **-ek 1.** (*nici*) strand. **2.** (*dymu*) wisp. **3.** *światła* beam.

paser *mp*, **paserka** *f. Gen.pl.* **-ek** fence.

paserski *a.* fencing, fence.

paserstwo *n.* fencing.

pasę *itd. ipf. zob.* **paść**.

pasiak *mi Gen.* **-a 1.** (*strój ludowy*) (traditional) striped folk costume. **2.** (*w obozie koncentracyjnym*) concentration camp stripes.

pasiasty *a.* striped.

pasibrzuch *mp pl.* **-y** *żart.* guzzler.

pasieka *f.* apiary.

pasierb *mp pl.* **-owie** *l.* **-y** stepson.

pasierbica *f.* stepdaughter.

pasikonik *ma ent.* (long-horned) grasshopper (*Tettigoniidae*); **pasikonik zielony** great green bush cricket (*Tettigonia viridissima*).

pasja *f.* **1.** (= *zamiłowanie*) passion; love; **pracować z pasją** work passionately; **zapasy są moją pasją** wrestling is my passion; **lubić coś pasjami** love sth, be crazy about sth. **2.** (= *furia*) rage, fury; **wpadać w pasję** fly into a fury *l.* rage; **doprowadzasz mnie do pasji!** you're driving me mad!; **ogarnęła go szewska pasja** he was quivering with rage. **3.** *muz., rel., sztuka* Passion.

pasjans *mi Gen.* **-a** *l.* **-u** *Acc.* **-a** *pl.* **-e** *l.* **-y** solitaire; *Br.* patience.

pasjonat *mp*, **pasjonatka** *f. Gen.pl.* **-ek 1.** (= *choleryk*) impulsive person, hothead. **2.** (= *entuzjasta*) lover, enthusiast (*czegoś* of sth).

pasjonować *ipf.* (= *fascynować*) fascinate; (= *pochłaniać*) absorb. **~ się** *ipf.* be keen on, be into (*czymś* sth).

pasjonująco *adv.* fascinatingly; **zapowiadać się fascynująco** sound *l.* look *l.* seem exciting.

pasjonujący *a.* fascinating, exciting.

paskal *mi Gen.* **-a** *fiz.* pascal.

paskarka *f. Gen.pl.* **-ek** *zob.* **paskarz**.

paskarski *a.* profiteering, profiteer.

paskarstwo *n.* profiteering.

paskarz *mp Gen.pl.* **-y** *l.* **-ów** profiteer.

paskówka *f. Gen.pl.* **-ek** *zool.* natterjack (*Bufo calamita*).

paskuda *f. l. mp decl. like f. Gen.pl.* **-d** *l.* **-ów** *pot.* **1.** (*osoba*) nasty, ugly person. **2.** *przest.* (= *zło*) evil; (= *szkoda*) harm.

paskudnie *adv.* uglily, nastily.

paskudny *a.* (= *brzydki*) ugly; (= *nieznośny*) nasty; **paskudny chłopak** nasty boy; **paskudna grypa** bad flu; **paskudna sprawa** nasty business; **paskudna rana** nasty wound; **paskudny zapach** foul smell.

paskudzić *ipf.* **1.** *pot.* (= *zanieczyszczać*) foul. **2.** *pot.* (= *partaczyć*) botch, bungle. **~ się** *ipf.* **1.** *pot.* (= *brudzić się*) become dirty, soil. **2.** *pot.* (*o ranach*) fester.

paskudztwo *n. pot.* **1.** (*coś ohydnego*) abomination; **ten obraz to paskudztwo!** this picture is abominable! **2.** (= *nieczystości*) filth, muck.

pasmanteria *f. Gen.* **-ii 1.** (*dodatki*) notions; *zwł. Br.* haberdashery. **2.** (*sklep*) haberdashery.

pasmanteryjny *a.* **sklep pasmanteryjny** haberdasher's shop, haberdashery; **wyroby pasmanteryjne** haberdashery.

pasmo *n. Loc.* **pasmie** *l.* **paśmie** *Gen.pl.* **pasm** *l.* **pasem 1.** (*radiowe, telewizyjne*) band; **pasmo częstotliwości** frequency band. **2.** (*nici, przędzy*) strand, ply; **pasmo włosów** strand of hair. **3.** (*powierzchnia*) strip; **pasmo gór** *l.* **pasmo górskie** mountain range; **pasmo lądu** strip of land; **pasmo jezdni** lane. **4.** *przen.* (= *ciąg*) series, streak; **pasmo klęsk** losing streak; **pasmo zwycięstw** winning streak.

pasować¹ *ipf.* **1.** (*części czegoś do siebie*) fit, adjust. **2.** (= *dobrze leżeć, przylegać*) fit; **ta sukienka nie pasuje na ciebie, jest za ciasna** this dress does not fit you, it's too tight; **pasuje jak ulał** it fits like a glove. **3.** (= *harmonizować*) match, go together, suit; **kapelusz nie pasuje do płaszcza** the hat does not match the coat; **trwała nie pasuje mi do twarzy** the perm does not suit me; **coś pasuje jak wół do karety** sth is *l.* feels like a square peg in a round hole.

pasować² *ipf. l. pf.* **pasować kogoś na kogoś** appoint sb (to be *l.* as) sb; **pasować kogoś na rycerza** knight sb, dub sb.

pasować³ *ipf. karty* **1.** pass. **2.** *przen.* (= *wycofywać się z czego*) back out. **~ się** *ipf. l. pf.* **1.** (*na kogoś*) appoint o.s. **2.** (= *zmagać się*) wrestle, struggle.

pasowanie *n.* (*na kogoś*) appointment; **pasowanie na rycerza** knighting, dubbing.

pasowy *a.* belt, strip, strap; **koło pasowe** *techn.* pulley; **przekładnia pasowa** *techn.* belt transmission; **siew pasowy** *roln.* strip cropping.

pasożyt *ma* **1.** *biol.* parasite. **2.** (*człowiek*) *pog.* sponger, parasite.

pasożytnictwo *n.* **1.** *biol.* parasitism. **2.** (*tryb życia*) sponging.

pasożytniczy *a.* parasitic, parasitical; **pasożytniczy tryb życia** *t. przen.* parasitic mode of existence.

pasożytować *ipf.* **1.** *biol.* parasitize. **2.** *pog.* (*o człowieku*) sponge (*na kimś* on *l.* off sb).

passa *f.* spell, streak, run; **mieć dobrą passę** be on a winning streak, have a run of good luck; **mieć złą passę** be on a losing streak, have a run of bad luck.

passacaglia *f. muz.* passacaglia.

passe-partout *n. indecl.* (*bilet*) (*ramka*) passepartout.

passus *mi lit.* passage.

pasta *f.* paste; (*do szorowania*) polish; (*do jedzenia*) spread; **pasta do butów** shoe polish; **pasta do podłóg** floor polish; **pasta do zębów** toothpaste; **pasta rybna** fish spread.

pastel *mi Gen.pl.* -i *l.* **-ów** (*farba, technika malarska, obraz*) pastel.

pastelowo *adv.* in pastel colors.

pastelowość *f.* pastelness.

pastelowy *a.* pastel.

pastereloza *f. pat., wet.* pasteurellosis.

pasterka *f. Gen.pl.* -ek **1.** (*owiec*) shepherdess; (*gęsi*) gooseherd; (*krów*) cowherd. **2.** *kośc.* (*msza*) Christmas midnight mass. **3.** (*kapelusz*) *przest.* lady's broad-brimmed straw hat.

pasternak *mi Gen.* -a *bot.* parsnip (*Pastinaca sativa*); **figa z makiem, z pasternakiem** *przest.* nothing doing.

pasterski *a.* **1.** (*o pastuchu*) shepherd's, shepherds', pastoral; **pies pasterski** shepherd dog; **życie pasterskie** pastoral life. **2.** *rel.* pastoral; **list pasterski** pastoral, pastoral letter.

pasterstwo *n.* grazing; (*owiec*) shepherding.

pasteryzacja *f.* pasteurization.

pasteryzator *mi Gen.* -a pasteurizer.

pasteryzować *ipf.* pasteurize.

pasteryzowany *a.* pasteurized.

pasterz *mp* (*bydła*) herder; *Br.* herdsman; (*owiec*) shepherd; (*gęsi*) gooseherd.

pastewnik *mi Gen.* -a *roln.* pasture, grazing ground.

pastewny *a.* fodder, forage; **burak pastewny** fodder beet; mangel-wurzel, mangold-wurzel; **mieszanka pastewna** fodder mixture; **rośliny pastewne** forage crops.

pastisz *mi Gen.pl.* -y *l.* **-ów** pastiche.

pastiszowy *a.* pastiche.

pastor *mp pl.* -rzy *l.* **-owie** *rel.* parson, pastor.

pastoralny *a.* (*o poezji, widowisku*) *rel.* pastoral.

pastorał *mi kośc.* crosier, crozier; pastoral, pastoral staff.

pastorałka *f. Gen.pl.* **-ek 1.** (*kolęda*) carol. **2.** *teor.lit.* pastoral.

pastorski *a.* pastoral, ministerial.

pastować *ipf.* polish; (*woskiem*) wax.

pastuch *mp pl.* **-y** (*koni, bydła*) herder; *Br.* herdsman; (*owiec*) shepherd.

pastuszek *mp* -szk- *pl.* -i *l.* **-owie** *zob.* **pastuch.**

pastwa *f.* **paść pastwą powodzi** be destroyed by flood; **wydać kogoś na pastwę losu** leave sb to their own fate.

pastwić się *ipf.* torment (*nad kimś* sb).

pastwisko *n.* pasture, grazing land.

pastylka *f. Gen.pl.* -ek (*do połknięcia*) pill, tablet; (*do ssania*) lozenge; pastille, pastil.

pasy *pl. Gen.* **-ów** (= *przejście dla pieszych*) pedestrian crossing; *Br.* zebra crossing; **zwolnić na pasach** slow down at *l.* on a pedestrian crossing; **potrącić staruszkę na pasach** run an elderly woman down in a pedestrian crossing.

pasygrafia *f. Gen.* **-ii** pasigraphy.

pasyjny *a. rel.* passion, Passion; **widowisko pasyjne** Passion play.

pasynkować *ipf. ogr.* prune, trim.

pasywa *pl. Gen.* **-ów** *ekon.* liabilities; **aktywa i pasywa** assets and liabilities.

pasywacja *f. techn.* passivation.

pasywizm *mi lit.* (= *bierność*) *polit.* passivism.

pasywnie *adv.* passively.

pasywność *f.* passivity, passiveness.

pasywny *a.* passive; **pasywne zachowanie** passive behavior; **pasywny bilans płatniczy** *ekon.* balance of payments deficit; **pasywny bilans handlowy** *ekon.* balance of trade deficit.

pasza¹ *f. pl.* **-e** fodder, forage; **pasza kiszona** ensilage; **pasza objętościowa** bulky feed, roughage; **pasza treściwa** concentrate, nutritive fodder; **pasza zielona** green fodder.

pasza² *mp pl.* **-owie** (*w imperium osmańskim*) pasha, pacha.

paszarnia *f. Gen.pl.* -i *l.* **-ń** *roln.* food *l.* fodder store.

paszcza *f.* **1.** (*u zwierząt*) mouth; **lwia paszcza** *bot.* (common) snapdragon (*Antirrhinum majus*); **wilcza paszcza** *pat.* cleft palate, palatoschisis. **2.** *żart.* (*u człowieka*) mouth; **wydrzeć coś komuś z paszczy** take sth by force from sb; **leźć komuś w paszczę** go out on a limb, stick sb's neck out.

paszczęka *f. lit.* mouth.

paszkot *ma orn.* mistle thrush (*Turdus viscivorus*).

paszkwil *mi Gen.pl.* **-i** *l.* **-ów** lampoon; pasquinade, pasquil.

paszkwilancki *a.* pasquilic.

paszkwilant *mp* lampooner, lampoonist.

paszoł *int. przest., pot. wulg.* **paszoł won** get the fuck out of here.

paszowy *a.* fodder, forage.

paszoznawstwo *n. roln.* forage science.

paszport *mi* passport; **paszport dyplomatyczny** diplomatic passport; **paszport konsularny** consular passport; **paszport maszynowy** *techn.* machine data sheet; **paszport przedsiębiorstwa** *prawn.* information memorandum.

paszportowy *a.* passport; **kontrola paszportowa** passport control; **wydział paszportowy** passport office.

pasztecik *mi Gen.* **-a** 1. (*pasztet*) small pâté. 2. (*do zup*) patty, pasty.

pasztet *mi* 1. *kulin.* pâté. 2. *pot.* (= *kłopotliwa sytuacja*) nuisance, mess; **ładny pasztet!** what a mess!

pasztetowa *f. Gen.* **-ej** liverwurst; *Br. zwł.* liver sausage.

pasztetowy *a.* pâté; **kiszka pasztetowa** *zob.* **pasztetowa**.

pasztetówka *f. Gen.pl.* **-ek** *dial.* = **pasztetowa**.

paść¹ *pf.* **padnę padniesz, padnij, padł** 1. *zob.* **padać**. 2. (= *zostać zdobytym*) be captured; (= *poddać się*) surrender.

paść² *ipf.* **pasę pasiesz, pasł** 1. (= *wypasać*) graze, pasture. 2. (*zwierzęta*) (= *tuczyć*) fatten; (= *karmić*) feed (*czymś* on sth). 3. *żart.* (= *karmić człowieka*) feed; **paść czymś oczy** feast one's eyes on sth. **~ się** *ipf.* 1. (= *wypasać się*) graze, pasture. 2. (*o zwierzętach*) (= *przybierać na wadze*) fatten. 3. (*o ludziach*) *żart.* (= *przybierać na wadze*) put on weight.

paśnik *mi Gen.* **-a** 1. *roln.* (= *pastwisko*) pasture. 2. (*karmnik dla dzikiej zwierzyny*) feeding rack.

pat *mi Gen.* **-a** *szachy* stalemate; (= *sytuacja bez wyjścia*) stalemate, deadlock.

patafian *mp pl.* **-y** *pot. żart.* moron.

patałach *mp pl.* **-y** *pot.* sucker.

patat, batat *mi Gen.* **-u** *l.* **-a** *bot.* sweet potato (*Ipomoea batatas*).

patataj *int.* giddyup horsey *l.* horsie.

patefon *mi* phonograph; *Br.* gramophone.

patelnia *f. Gen.pl.* **-i** 1. (*do smażenia*) frying pan; **wyłożyć coś jak na patelni** explain very clearly. 2. *pot.* (= *upał*) heat; **prażyło jak na patelni** it was scorching.

patena *f. kośc.* paten.

patent *mi* 1. (*na wynalazek*) patent. 2. (= *drobne usprawnienie*) *pot.* improvement. 3. *przen., iron.* (= *sposób*) way (*na coś* to do sth); **on ma patent na nieomylność** he always knows better, he thinks he's infallible. 4. (= *uprawnienia*) certificate, license; (= *nominacja*) commission; *żegl.* certificate of competence; **patent żeglarza jachtowego** inland skipper's certificate of com-

petence; **patent sternika jachtowego** coastal skipper's certificate of competence; **patent oficerski** commission. 5. *pot.* (*zamek do drzwi*) Yale lock.

patentować *ipf.* (*wynalazek*) *techn.* patent.

patentowany *a.* 1. (*o wyrobie*) patented. 2. *pot.* total, complete, utter; **patentowany dureń** blithering idiot; **patentowany leń** utter layabout.

patentowy *a.* patent; **Urząd Patentowy** Patent and Trademark Office; **zamek patentowy** Yale lock; **prawa patentowe** patent rights; **kotwica patentowa** *żegl.* patent anchor, stockless anchor.

patera *f.* epergne.

paternalistyczny *a.* paternalistic.

paternalizm *mi* paternalism.

patetycznie *adv.* pompously, bombastically.

patetyczność *f.* pomposity, pompousness.

patetyczny *a.* pompous, bombastic.

patio *n. indecl. l. Gen.pl.* **-ów** patio.

patison *mi Gen.* **-a** *bot.* (summer) squash, pumpkin (*Cucurbita pepo patissonia*).

patka *f. Gen.pl.* **-ek** tab.

patofizjologia *f. Gen.* **-ii** *med.* pathophysiology, physiopathology.

patofizjologiczny *a. pat.* pathophysiological, pathophysiologic; physiopathological, physiopathologic.

patogen *mi biol.* pathogen, pathogene.

patogenetyczny *a. pat.* pathogenic.

patogeneza *f. pat.* pathogenesis, pathogeny.

patogeniczność *f. pat.* pathogenicity.

patoka *f.* strained honey.

patol *mi Gen.* **-a** *pot.* (= *tysiąc*) grand; **dwa/trzy (itd.) patole** two/three (etc.) grand.

patolog *mp pl.* **-dzy** *l.* **-owie** *med.* pathologist.

patologia *f. Gen.* **-ii** *med., pat.* pathology; **patologia społeczna** *socjol.* social pathology.

patologiczny *a.* pathological, pathologic.

patomorfologia *f. Gen.* **-ii** *med.* pathomorphology.

patos *mi* 1. (= *podniosłość*) pathos; **dzieło pełne patosu** work full of pathos. 2. (*styl*) grandiloquence; **mówić z patosem** speak in a lofty *l.* pompous manner.

patowy *a.* stalemate; **sytuacja patowa** stalemate, deadlock.

patriarcha *mp pl.* **-owie** *rel.* (= *starzec*) (= *senior rodu*) patriarch.

patriarchalność *f.* patriarchal character *l.* nature *l.* quality.

patriarchalny *a.* patriarchal, patriarchic; **ustrój patriarchalny** patriarchal system.

patriarchat *mi* 1. *rel.* patriarchate. 2. *polit.* patriarchy.

patriota *mp*, **patriotka** *f. Gen.pl.* **-ek** patriot.

patriotycznie *adv.* patriotically.

patriotyczny *a.* patriotic; **literatura patriotyczna** patriotic literature; **uczucia patriotyczne** patriotic feelings.

patriotyzm *mi* patriotism; **patriotyzm lokalny** regionalism, localism.

patrochy *pl. Gen.* **-ów** *myśl.* entrails, guts.

patrol *mi* 1. (*grupa żołnierzy, policjantów*) patrol; **patrol policji** police patrol; **lotny patrol** flying squad. **2.** *wojsk.* (= *zwiad*) patrol; **nocny patrol** night patrol; **być na patrolu** scout, reconnoiter. **3.** *sport* patrol.

patrologia *f. Gen.* **-ii** *teol.* patrology.
patrolować *ipf.* patrol.
patrolowiec *mi* **-wc-** *pl.* **-y** (*samolot*) patrol plane; (*okręt*) patrol boat.
patrolowy *a.* patrol; **okręt patrolowy** patrol boat; **radiowóz patrolowy** squad car; *Br.* patrol car; **samolot patrolowy** patrol plane.
patron[1] *mp Gen.* **-a** *pl.* **-owie** *l.* **-i 1.** (= *protektor*) patron, protector. **2.** (*w starożytnym Rzymie*) patron. **3.** *prawn.* supervisor. **4.** *rel.* patron saint, patron.
patron[2] *mi Gen.* **-u** *pl.* **-y** (*wzornik*) stencil.
patronacki *a.* patronly; **sklep patronacki** factory outlet.
patronat *mi* **1.** (= *protektorat*) patronage, support; **pod patronatem** under the auspices. **2.** (*w starożytnym Rzymie*) patronage.
patronimiczny *a.* *jęz.* patronymic.
patronimik *mi* = **patronimikum**.
patronimikum *n. sing. indecl. pl.* **-ka** *Gen.* **-ków** *jęz.* patronymic, patronym.
patronka *f. Gen.pl.* **-ek** *rel. zob.* **patron**[1] 4.
patronować *ipf.* support, patronize.
patroszyć *ipf.* gut, disembowel; (*zwł. ryby*) gut; (*zwł. drób*) draw.
patrycjat *mi* (*w starożytnym Rzymie: arystokracja*) (*w starożytnym Rzymie: godność*) (*w średniowieczu: mieszczanie*) patriciate.
patrycjusz *mp Gen.pl.* **-y** *l.* **-ów**, **patrycjuszka** *f. Gen.pl.* **-ek** (*w Rzymie*) (= *mieszczanin*) patrician.
patrycjuszowski *a.* patrician.
patrystyka *f. teol.* patristics.
patrzałki *pl. Gen.* **-ek** *żart.* **1.** (= *oczy*) eyes. **2.** (= *okulary*) glasses.
patrzeć *ipf.* **-ę -ysz 1.** (= *spoglądać*) look; **patrzeć badawczo** scrutinize, observe attentively; **patrzeć bezmyślnie** look blankly; **patrzeć ukradkiem** look furtively; **patrzeć wstecz** *l.* **w przyszłość** look back *l.* ahead; **patrzeć komuś prosto w oczy** look sb squarely in the eye; **patrzeć śmierci w oczy** face death; **śmierć patrzy komuś w oczy** sb is facing death; **patrzeć komuś na ręce** keep a watchful eye on sb; **patrzeć na coś przez różowe okulary** see sth through rose-colored spectacles; **patrzeć wilkiem** look askance; **patrzeć na coś z boku** be unbiased *l.* impartial; **patrzeć na kogoś/coś jak sroka w gnat** gaze at sb/sth; **patrzeć na kogoś/coś jak cielę na malowane wrota** gape at sb/sth; **coś jest zrobione jak się patrzy** sth is well done; **patrzeć na księżą oborę** *przest.* have one foot in the grave, be about to kick the bucket *l.* buy the farm; **dobrze/źle ci z oczu patrzy** you have kind/mean eyes; **nie mogę na ciebie patrzeć** I can't bear the sight of you; **aż żal na ciebie patrzeć** you are a pity to behold; **tylko patrzeć, jak śnieg spadnie** winter is near; **tylko patrzeć, jak zacznie padać śnieg** it'll start snowing any moment; **patrzcie państwo!** (*dla zwrócenia uwagi*) look!; *iron.* fancy that! **2.** (= *mieć pogląd na coś*) view; **patrzeć na coś optymistycznie** view sth

with optimism, take an optimistic view of sth; **patrzeć na coś trzeźwo** view sth with objectivity; **patrzeć w przyszłość** think ahead. **3.** (= *obserwować*) watch, observe; **już od dłuższego czasu patrzę na wasze zachowanie** I have been watching you for quite some time. **4.** (= *traktować coś, kogoś w jakiś sposób*) regard, treat; **patrzeć (na kogoś) z góry** look down on (sb); **patrzeć na coś przez palce** turn a blind eye to sth; **patrzeć na coś życzliwym okiem** regard sth with favor; **patrzeć na kogoś** *l.* **coś krzywym okiem** look askance at sb *l.* sth. **5.** *pot.* (= *zważać na coś*) mind, take care; **patrz tylko, żebyś się nie spóźnił** just make sure you're not late; **patrz swego nosa** mind your own business. **6.** *pot.* (= *dbać o swoje*) seek; **patrzał tylko, żeby być sławnym** he sought fame.
patrzyć *ipf. zob.* **patrzeć**.
patyczaki *ma ent.* walking sticks; *zwł. Br.* stick insects (*Phasmidae*).
patyczkować się *ipf. pot.* **patyczkować się z kimś** handle sb with kid gloves.
patyk *mi Gen.* **-a** (= *kijek*) stick; **ona ma nogi jak patyki** she's spindle-legged.
patykowaty *a.* spindly, lanky.
patyna *f.* (= *nalot*) patina; (= *śniedź*) verdigris.
patynować się *ipf.* take on patina.
paulin *mp rz.-kat.* Paulite, Paulinite.
pauperyzacja *f.* pauperization.
pauperyzować się *ipf. form.* pauperize.
pauza *f.* **1.** (= *przerwa*) pause, interval. **2.** *szkoln.* break; **wielka** *l.* **duża pauza** *szkoln.* playtime. **3.** (*w interpunkcji*) dash. **4.** *muz.* rest.
pauzować *ipf.* pause; **pauzować za kartkę** *pot. sport* miss a game (*for being booked*).
paw *ma* **-wi- 1.** *orn.* peafowl (*Pavo cristatus*). **2.** (= *samiec pawia*) peacock; **dumny jak paw** as proud as a peacock; **puścić pawia** *pot.* puke, throw up.
pawana *f. muz.* pavane, pavan.
pawi *a.* (*o ogonie, krzyku, piórach*) peacock's; (*w języku fachowym*) pavonine; **pawie oczko** (*na piórach*) eye of a peacock's tail; *icht.* guppy (*Lebsites reticulatus*); **stroić się w pawie piórka** put on airs.
pawian *ma zool.* baboon (*Papio*).
pawik *ma ent.* peacock butterfly (*Inachis io*).
pawilon *mi* **1.** (*budowla*) pavilion; **pawilon handlowy** shopping center; **pawilon wystawowy** exhibition hall, exhibition pavilion. **2.** (*skrzydło budowli*) extension, annex.
pawlacz *mi Gen.* **-a** storage place (*under the ceiling*).
pazerność *f. pot.* voracity, rapacity.
pazerny *a. pot.* voracious, rapacious.
paznokciowy *a. anat.* nail; (*w języku fachowym*) ungual, ungular.
paznokieć *mi* **-kci-** *Gen.* **-a** nail; **paznokieć u ręki** fingernail; **paznokieć u nogi** toenail; **obcinać/piłować paznokcie** clip/file one's nails; **malować paznokcie** varnish one's nails; **obgryzać paznokcie** bite one's nails.
pazucha *f.* breast pocket; **za pazuchą** in one's breast pocket; **zza pazuchy** out of one's breast

pocket, from under one's jacket; **schować coś za pazuchę** put sth into one's breast pocket.

pazur *mi Gen.* **-a 1.** (*u zwierząt*) claw; **bazgrać jak kura pazurem** *pot.* scrawl, scribble. **2.** *uj.* (= *paznokieć*) claw; **ostrzyć sobie na kogoś/coś pazury** set one's sights on sth/sb; **pokazać pazury** show one's claws; **schować pazury** draw in one's claws; **skakać z pazurami do oczu** fly into sb's face, fly at sb's throat; **trzymać się czegoś pazurami** claw to sth, clutch at sth; **wpaść w czyjeś pazury** fall into sb's clutches; **bronić czegoś zębami i pazurami** fight tooth and nail for sth. **3.** (*w maszynach, urządzeniach*) claw, fang. **4.** (*do wyciągania gwoździ*) nail claw.

pazurczatka *f. zool.* marmoset (*Callithricidae*).

pazurek *mi* **-rk-** *Gen.* **-a** (*u zwierzęcia*) claw; **z górki na pazurki** *dziec.* as fast as one's legs will carry one.

pazurki *pl. Gen.* **-ów** *ogr.* three-pronged cultivator.

paż *mp pl.* **-owie** *Gen.* **-ów** *hist.* page; **paź królowej** *ent.* swallowtail (*Papilo machaon*).

październik *mi Gen.* **-a** October.

październikowy *a.* October; **rewolucja październikowa** *hist.* October Revolution.

paździerze *pl. Gen.* **-y** harl of flax.

paździerzowy *a.* **płyta paździerzowa** flaxboard.

pączek *mi* **-czk-** *Gen.* **-a 1.** (= *zawiązek*) bud; (*liścia*) leafbud. **2.** (*kwiatu*) flowerbud. **3.** (*ciastko*) donut, *Br.* doughnut; **żyć jak pączek w maśle** live in the lap of luxury, be in clover. **4.** *biol.* gemma.

pączkować *ipf.* **1.** (*o roślinach*) bud. **2.** *biol.* (*o komórkach*) gemmate.

pączkowanie *n. biol.* gemmation; **rozmnażanie przez pączkowanie** reproduction by budding, gemmation.

pąk *mi Gen.* **-a** bud.

pąkle *pl. Gen.* **-i** *zool.* barnacles (*Balanus*).

pąkowie *n.* blossom; **drzewa pokryte pąkowiem** trees in blossom.

pąs *mi* **1.** (*kolor*) bright red, poppy. **2.** (*rumieniec*) blush; **stanąć w pąsach** blush all over.

pąsowieć *ipf.* **1.** (*o kolorze*) redden. **2.** (*o twarzy, policzkach*) blush.

pąsowy *a.* bright red, poppy.

pątnik *mp hist.* pilgrim.

PC *komp.* PC.

pchacz *mi Gen.* **-a** *żegl.* pusher-tug, pushboat.

pchać *ipf.* **1.** (= *przesuwać*) push, shove; **Pchać** (*napis na drzwiach*) Push; **pchnąć sprawę** push ahead with a case, push on with a case. **2.** *pot.* (= *zmuszać*) urge, prod (*kogoś do czegoś* sb to do sth); **bieda pchnęła go do kradzieży** he was driven to theft by poverty. **3.** (= *wpychać*) stuff, cram; **pchać nos w nie swoje sprawy** *pot.* poke one's nose into other people's business. **~ się** *ipf.* **1.** (= *tłoczyć się*) crowd. **2.** (= *przepychać się*) push one's way; **pchać się drzwiami i oknami** throng; **pchać się w ręce** be for the asking. **3.** *pot.* (= *zabiegać o coś*) strive for; **pchać się w górę** (*na wyższe stanowisko*) push one's way upwards.

pchełka *f. Gen.pl.* **-ek 1.** *dimin. zob.* **pchła. 2.** (*do gry*) tiddlywink.

pchełki *pl.* (*gra*) tiddlywinks.

pchli *a.* flea's; **pchli targ** flea market.

pchła *f. Gen.pl.* **pcheł** *ent.* flea (*Siphonaptera*).

pchnąć *pf.* **-ij 1.** *zob.* **pchać. 2.** (= *ugodzić*) stab; **pchnąć sztyletem/nożem** stab with a dagger/knife. **3.** (= *wysłać*) dispatch. **4.** *wulg.* (= *przelecieć*) poke. **~ się** *pf.* **1.** *zob.* **pchać się. 2.** (= *zadać sobie pchnięcie*) stab o.s.

pchnięcie *n.* push, thrust, shove; **pchnięcie kulą** *sport* shot put.

pchor., podchor. *abbr.* (= *podchorąży*) officer cadet.

PCK *abbr.* (= *Polski Czerwony Krzyż*) Polish Red Cross.

pean *mi teor.lit.* paean.

pecet *mi pot.* (*komputer*) PC.

pech *mi Gen.* **-a** bad luck; **mieć pecha** be unlucky; **a to pech!** tough luck!, worse luck!; **to przynosi pecha** it brings bad luck.

pechowiec *mp* **-wc-** *pl.* **-y** unlucky person.

pechowo *adv.* unluckily, unfortunately; **a to pechowo!** tough luck!

pechowy *a.* unlucky, unfortunate.

pedagog *mp pl.* **-dzy** *l.* **-owie 1.** (= *nauczyciel*) teacher. **2.** (= *wychowawca*) educator. **3.** (= *teoretyk nauczania i wychowania*) educationalist.

pedagogiczny *a.* pedagogical, pedagogic; educational; **rada pedagogiczna** teaching staff meeting; **ciało pedagogiczne** teaching staff.

pedagogika *f.* pedagogy.

pedalizacja *f. muz.* pedalling.

pedalstwo *n. pot. pog.* faggotry.

pedał *mi Gen.* **-u 1.** (*dźwignia*) pedal, footlever; **pedał gazu** accelerator; **pedał hamulca** brake pedal. **2.** *druk.* treadle-press. **–** *mp Gen.* **-a** *pl.* **-y** *pot. pog.* fag, faggot, homo; *Br.* queer.

pedałować *ipf.* (*t. na rowerze*) *muz.* pedal.

pedałowy *a.* pedal, treadle.

pedant *mp,* **pedantka** *f.* pedant.

pedanteria *f. Gen.* **-ii** pedantry.

pedantka *f. Gen.pl.* **-ek** *zob.* **pedant.**

pedantyczny *a.* pedantic.

pederasta *mp uj.* pederast.

pediatra *mp* pediatrician, *Br.* paediatrician.

pediatria *f. Gen.* **-ii 1.** (*nauka*) pediatrics; *Br.* paediatrics. **2.** (*oddział*) children's ward.

pediatryczny *a.* pediatric; *Br.* paediatric; (*o szpitalu, oddziale*) children's.

pedicure, pedikiur *mi* pedicure.

pedicurzysta, pedikurzysta *mp,* **pedicurzystka, pedikiurzystka** *f.* pedicurist.

pedofil *mp Gen.pl.* **-ów** pedophile; *Br.* paedophile; pedophiliac, *Br.* paedophiliac.

pedofilia *f. Gen.* **-ii** pedophilia; *Br.* paedophilia.

pedologia *f. Gen.* **-ii** *psych.* pedology; *Br.* paedology.

pedologiczny *a.* pedological; *Br.* paedological.

pedryl *mp pot. pog.* fag; *Br.* queer.

pedzio *mp Gen.pl.* **-ów** *pot. pog. zob.* **pedał.**

peeling *mi* (*zabieg*) peeling; (*krem*) scrub.

peem *mi pot.* (*broń*) submachine gun.

peerel *mi* Polish People's Republic.

peeselowiec *mp* -wc- *pl.* -y *polit.* member of the Polish Peasant Party.

peeselowski *a. polit.* Polish Peasant Party.

Pegaz *ma mit.* Pegasus; **dosiąść Pegaza** *przen.* mount one's Pegasus.

pegeer *mi* state-owned farm (*in communist Poland*).

pegmatyt *mi geol.* pegmatite.

pejcz *mi Gen.* -a *Gen.pl.* -y *l.* -ów whip.

pejoratyw *mi jęz.* pejorative.

pejoratywny *a.* pejorative, deprecatory.

pejotl *mi chem.* peyote, peyotl.

pejs *mi Gen.* -a sideburn, sideboard.

pejsachówka *f. Gen.pl.* -ek (*wódka*) plum brandy.

pejzaż *mi* (*krajobraz*) (*tematyka malarstwa*) landscape.

pejzażowy *a.* landscape.

pejzażysta *mp*, pejzażystka *f. Gen.pl.* -ek landscape painter, landscapist.

pekaes *mi* public road transport (*in Poland*); **pojechałem pekaesem** I went by coach *l.* bus.

pekari *ma indecl. zool.* peccary (*Tayassuidae*).

Pekin *mi* Beijing, Peking.

pekińczyk *mp pl.* -cy, pekinka *f.* Pekingese, Pekinese. – *ma pl.* -i *kynol.* Pekingese, Pekinese; *pot.* peke.

pekiński *a.* Beijing, Pekingese, Pekinese; **kapusta pekińska** *bot., kulin.* Chinese cabbage, petsai cabbage (*Brassica pekinensis*).

peklować *ipf.* pickle, corn.

pektorał *mi* **1.** *rel.* (= *krzyż*) pectoral cross, pectoral. **2.** *hist.* (= *napierśnik*) pectoral.

pektyna *f. chem.* pectin.

pektynowy *a. chem.* pectic, pectinous.

pekuniarny *a. lit.* pecuniary.

pelagial *mi geogr.* pelagial.

pelagiczny *a. geogr.* pelagic, pelagial; **strefa pelagiczna** pelagic zone.

pelagra *f. pat.* pellagra.

pelargonia *f. Gen.* -ii *bot.* geranium, pelargonium (*Pelargonium*).

peleng *mi lotn., żegl.* bearing.

pelengator *mi Gen.* -a *lotn., żegl.* bearing-finder, course and bearing indicator.

pelengować *ipf.* take the bearings (*coś* of sth).

peleryna *f.* **1.** (*płaszcz*) cloak. **2.** (*część płaszcza*) cape.

pelerynka *f. Gen.pl.* -ek (*płaszcz*) cloak; (*kobieca*) pelerine.

peleton *mi* (*w kolarstwie*) main group of cyclists.

pelikan *ma zool.* pelican (*Pelecanus*).

pelisa *f.* pelisse.

pellikula *f. zool.* pellicle.

peloponeski *a.* Peloponnesian; **wojna peloponeska** *hist.* Peloponnesian War.

Peloponez *mi* the Peloponnese, Peloponnesus.

pelota *f.* pelota.

peluga *f. icht.* peled (*Coregonus peled*).

pelur *mi* (*papier*) onionskin paper.

peluszka *f. Gen.pl.* -ek field pea.

pełen *a. indecl. zob.* pełny.

pełł *itd. ipf. zob.* pleć.

pełnia *f.* **1.** (*Księżyca*) full moon; **twarz jak księżyc w pełni** moon face. **2.** (= *obfitość*) fulness; (= *szczyt*) peak; **pełnia lata** full summer, height of summer; **pełnia sezonu** peak season; **pełnia szczęścia** complete happiness; **pełnia morza** open sea, high seas; **w pełni rozkwitu** in full swing; **w pełni sił** sound in body; **w pełni władz umysłowych** of sound mind; **zasługiwać na coś w pełni** fully deserve sth; **w pełni się z tobą zgadzam** I agree with you entirely.

pełnić *ipf.* -ij *l.* -ń perform, fulfil; **pełnić obowiązki** fulfil one's duties, perform one's duties; **pełnić służbę** be on duty; **pełnić wartę** keep guard; **pełniący obowiązki (kierownika)** acting (manager).

pełnik *mi Gen.* -a *bot.* globeflower (*Trollius*).

pełno *adv.* **1.** (= *po brzegi*) to the brim; **nalać pełno wody do szklanki** fill the glass to the brim; **mam pełno wody w butach** my boots are full of water. **2.** (= *pod dostatkiem*) in abundance, in plenty; **pełno wody/ludzi** plenty of water/people; **wszędzie go pełno!** he is everywhere!; **w pociągu było pełno (ludzi)** the train was full, the train was crowded. **3.** *tylko w stopniu wyższym i najwyższym* (= *najlepiej*) fully, to the highest degree.

pełnoetatowy *a.* full-time.

pełnogłos *mi jęz.* pleophony.

pełnokrwisty *a.* thoroughbred, purebred.

pełnoletni *a.* of age; **być pełnoletnim** be of age.

pełnoletność *f.* majority; **osiągnąć pełnoletność** come of age.

pełnometrażowy *a.* **film pełnometrażowy** feature film.

pełnomocnictwo *n.* **1.** (*prawo*) power of attorney, proxy; **pełnomocnictwo procesowe** power of attorney ad litem; **nieograniczone pełnomocnictwo** unlimited authority; **udzielić komuś pełnomocnictwa (do zrobienia czegoś)** invest sb with a power of attorney (to do sth), authorize sb (to do sth); **odwołać pełnomocnictwo** revoke the power of attorney. **2.** (*dokument, zaświadczenie*) letter of attorney, letter of authority; **pełnomocnictwo handlowe** commercial representation; **pełnomocnictwo ogólne** general powers of attorney.

pełnomocnik *mp* attorney, holder of a proxy; (*zwł. dyplomata*) plenipotentiary; **pełnomocnik handlowy** commercial representative; **przez pełnomocnika** by proxy.

pełnomocny *a.* endowed with full powers, having full powers, plenipotentiary; **pełnomocny wysłannik** *polit.* plenipotentiary envoy.

pełnomorski *a.* (*o statku oceanicznym*) ocean-going; (*o statku morskim*) seagoing; **rejs pełnomorski** offshore cruise; **żegluga pełnomorska** offshore sailing.

pełnopłatny *a.* full-price, full-pay; **pełnopłatny urlop** full-pay leave.

pełnoprawny *a.* rightful, with full rights; **pełnoprawny członek/właściciel** rightful member/owner.

pełnorejowiec *mi* -wc- *Gen.* -a *żegl.* full-rigged ship.

pełnorogi *a.* solid-horned; **przeżuwacz pełnorogi** solid-horned ruminant.

pełnotłusty *a.* full, full-cream; **pełnotłuste mleko** full-cream milk.

pełnowartościowy *a.* whole, balanced; **pełnowartościowy jadłospis** balanced diet; **pełnowartościowa żywność** whole food.

pełnoziarnisty *a.* wholemeal, whole wheat; **chleb pełnoziarnisty** wholemeal bread.

pełny, pełen *a.* **1.** (= *wypełniony czymś*) full (*czegoś* of sth); filled with sth (*czegoś* with sth); **tramwaj pełen ludzi** tram full of people; **pokój pełen kwiatów** room filled with flowers; **pełen etat** full-time employment; **czerpać z czegoś pełną garścią** *l.* **pełnymi rękami** take sth by the handful; **mieć pełne ręce roboty** have one's hands full; **do pełna** up to the brim. **2.** (= *przepełniony czymś*) brimming, teeming (*czymś* with sth); **oczy pełne łez** eyes brimming with tears. **3.** (= *obfitujący w coś*) full (*czegoś* of sth); abundant (*czegoś* in sth); **droga pełna zakrętów** road full of bends. **4.** (= *zupełny, absolutny*) complete, total, absolute; **pełne szczęście** complete happiness; **pełne utrzymanie** full board; **pełne poparcie** whole-hearted support; **pełne morze** high seas; **pełny wiatr** *żegl.* quartering wind; **pod pełnym żaglem** *żegl.* at full sail; **mówić pełnym głosem** speak freely; **odetchnąć pełną piersią** breethe deeply; **darzę cię pełnym zaufaniem** I trust you entirely; **mam pełną władzę nad nimi** I've got absolute power over them; **on ma pełną swobodę wyboru** he is free to choose. **5.** (= *zupełny, doskonały*) full, high; **pełną parą** *l.* **na pełnych obrotach** at full blast; **w pełnym toku** in full swing; **koń pełnej krwi** thoroughbred horse, purebred horse. **6.** (= *kompletny*) complete, unabridged; **w pełnym brzmieniu** without omissions, unabridged; **komisja w pełnym składzie** committee at full strength; **rycerz w pełnej zbroi** fully-armored knight; **pełne mleko** full-cream milk; **kąt pełny** *geom.* round angle; **w pełnym tego słowa znaczeniu** in the full sense of the word. **7.** (= *lity*) solid, massive. **8.** (= *zaokrąglony, tłusty, gruby*) round, plump; (*o kształtach*) curvy. **9.** (*o kwiatach*) (= *rozwinięty*) full.

pełzacz *ma orn.* tree-creeper (*Certhia*).

pełzać *ipf.* **1.** (*o płazach, gadach, owadach, roślinach*) creep. **2.** (*o ssakach*) crawl. **3.** (*o mgle, dymie*) drift. **4.** (= *płaszczyć się*) kowtow (*przed kimś* to sb).

pełzak *ma zool.* ameba; *Br.* amoeba (*Amoeba*).

pełzakowaty *a. biol.* amebic; *Br.* amoebic; **ruch pełzakowaty** amebic movement.

pełzakowica *f. pat.* amebiasis; *Br.* amoebiasis.

pełzakowy *a.* **czerwonka pełzakowa** = **pełzakowica**.

pełznąć *ipf.* -ę -zniesz *l.* -źniesz, -ij, -zł *l.* -znął -zła -zli *l.* -źli *zob.* **pełzać**.

penalizacja *f.* penalization.

penaty *pl. Gen.* -ów *mit.* penates; **lary i penaty** (= *sprzęty domowe*) lares and penates.

peneplena *f. geol.* peneplain, peneplane.

penetracja *f.* **1.** (= *przenikanie*) penetration; (*dżungli, tajemnic*) penetration, exploration; **penetracja rynku** penetration of a market. **2.** (= *stosunek płciowy*) *form.* penetration.

penetracyjny *a.* penetrative.

penetrować *ipf.* **1.** (= *przenikać*) penetrate. **2.** (= *eksplorować*) penetrate, explore. **3.** (*o penisie*) penetrate.

penicylina *f. med.* penicillin.

penis *mi Gen.* -a *anat.* penis.

penitencjarny *a.* penitentiary; **system penitencjarny** penitentiary system.

penitent *mp*, **penitentka** *f. Gen.pl.* -ek *rz.-kat.* penitent.

peniuar *mi* (*podomka*) dressing gown.

penologia *f. Gen.* -ii *prawn.* penology.

pens *mi Gen.* -a penny; **pięć pensów** five pence.

pensja *f.* **1.** (*miesięczna dla pracowników umysłowych*) salary; (*godzinna, dzienna, tygodniowa dla pracowników fizycznych*) wage. **2.** *przest.* (*szkoła żeńska*) girls' boarding school.

pensjonariusz *mp*, **pensjonariuszka** *f. Gen.pl.* -ek **1.** (*w pensjonacie*) guest. **2.** (*w domu opieki społecznej*) inmate.

pensjonarka *f. Gen.pl.* -ek *przest.* schoolgirl (*in a girls' boarding school*).

pensjonat *mi* boardinghouse; (*w Europie kontynentalnej*) pension.

pensum *n. sing. indecl. pl.* -sa *Gen.* -sów obligatory teaching hours.

pentagon *mi* pentagon; **Pentagon** *US wojsk.* the Pentagon.

pentagonalny *a.* pentagonal.

pentagram *mi geom.* pentagram; (*w magii, astrologii*) pentagram; pentacle, pentangle.

pentametr *mi teor.lit.* pentameter.

Pentateuch *mi Bibl.* Pentateuch.

pentatlon *mi hist.*, *sport* pentathlon.

pentatonika *f. muz.* pentatonic scale.

pentoda *f. techn.* pentode.

pentoza *f. biochem.* pentose.

peon *mp* (*robotnik*) *Gen.* -a peon. – *mi teor.lit. Gen.* -u paeon.

peonia *f. bot.* = **piwonia**.

pepeerowiec *mp* -wc- *pl.* -y *hist.* member of the Polish Workers' Party.

pepeerowski *a. hist.* Polish Workers' Party.

pepeesowiec *mp* -wc- *pl.* -y *hist.* member of the Polish Socialist Party.

pepeesowski *a. hist.* Polish Socialist Party.

pepegi *pl. Gen.* -ów *pot.* (= *tenisówki*) sneakers.

pepesza *f. pot.* (*karabin*) pepesha (*Soviet submachine gun used in World War II*).

Pepiczek *mp* -czk- *pl.* -i *pog.* (= *Czech*) Czech.

Pepik *mp pl.* -i *pog.* (= *Czech*) Czech.

pepitka *f. Gen.pl.* -ek shepherd'(s) check, shepherd'(s) plaid; **spódnica w pepitkę** shepherd's check skirt.

peplos *mi hist.* peplos, peplus.

peplum *n.* = **peplos**.

pepsyna *f. biol.* pepsin, pepsine.

pepton *mi biol.* peptone.

peptyd *mi chem.* peptide.

peptydazy *pl. Gen.* **-z** *chem.* peptidases.

peptydowy *a. chem.* peptide; **wiązanie peptydowe** peptide bond.

peptyzacja *f. chem.* peptization.

per *prep.* per, by; **per procura** *prawn.* by proxy; **per se** per se; **mówić do kogoś per ty** be on first name terms *l.* first name basis with sb; **mówić do kogoś per pan/pani** mister/madam sb; **traktować kogoś per noga** turn one's nose up at sb.

percepcja *f. psych.* perception; **percepcja podprogowa** subliminal perception; **percepcja zmysłowa** sense perception.

percepcyjny *a. psych.* perceptional, perceptual; (*o zdolnościach*) perceptive.

perceptywność *f. psych.* perceptivity, perceptiveness.

percypować *ipf.* perceive.

perć *f. pl.* **-i** *l.* **-ie** *Gen.* **-i** *dial.* steep mountain footpath.

peregrynacja *f. lit.* peregrination.

perełka *f. Gen.pl.* **-ek** **1.** (= *mała perła*) small pearl. **2.** *przen.* (= *coś nadzwyczajnego*) gem; **to jest prawdziwa perełka muzyki barokowej** it's a real gem of baroque music.

perełki *pl. Gen.* **-ek** *sztuka, bud.* bead molding, chaplet, astragal.

perełkowiec *mi* **-wc-** *Gen.* **-a** *bot.* **perełkowiec** *l.* **szupin japoński** Japanese pagoda tree, Chinese scholartree (*Sophora japonica*).

peremptoryczny *a.* peremptory.

perfekcja *f.* perfection; **doprowadzić coś do perfekcji** make sth perfect, bring sth to perfection; **osiągnąć w czymś perfekcję** reach perfection in sth; **dojść do perfekcji** reach perfection; **chodząca perfekcja** the cat's meow *l.* pyjamas.

perfekcjonista *mp* perfectionist, precisionist.

perfekcjonistka *f. Gen.pl.* **-ek** *zob.* **perfekcjonista**.

perfekcjonizm *mi* perfectionism.

perfekcyjny *a.* perfect.

perfekt *adv.* very well, perfectly; **mówić perfekt po angielsku** speak perfect English. – *a.* perfect; **ona jest perfekt w tym, co robi** she's great at what she does.

perfektum *n. indecl. jęz.* perfect tense.

perfektywność *f. jęz.* perfectiveness, perfectivity.

perfektywny *a. jęz.* perfective.

perfidia *f. Gen.* **-ii** perfidy.

perfidnie *adv.* perfidiously.

perfidny *a.* perfidious; **perfidne kłamstwo** perfidious lie; **perfidny kochanek** treacherous lover.

perforacja *f. t. pat.* (= *dziurkowanie; dziurki*) perforation.

perforator *mi Gen.* **-a** *techn.* punch, perforator.

perforatorka *f. Gen.pl.* **-ek** *techn.* perforating machine.

performance *mi* **-nce'-** *Loc.* **-nsie** *sztuka, teatr* performance.

performer *mp sztuka, teatr* performer.

perforować *ipf.* perforate.

perforowany *a.* perforated; **karta perforowana** punch card.

perfumeria *f. Gen.* **-ii** perfumery.

perfumeryjny *a.* perfume; **stoisko perfumeryjne** perfume stand *l.* stall; **przemysł perfumeryjny** perfume industry; **wyroby perfumeryjne** perfumery.

perfumować *ipf.* perfume. ~ **się** *ipf.* perfume o.s., spray o.s. with perfume.

perfumy *pl. Gen.* **-um** perfume.

pergamin *mi* **1.** (*papier*) parchment. **2.** (*skóra*) parchment, sheepskin. **3.** (*rękopis*) parchment.

pergaminowy *a.* pergameneous, parchmentlike; **cera pergaminowa** pallid *l.* parchmenty complexion; **papier pergaminowy** parchment paper, vegetable parchment; **zwój pergaminowy** parchment scroll.

Pergamon *mi hist.* Pergamum, Pergamon.

pergola *f. Gen.pl.* **-i** pergola.

perhydrol *mi chem.* peroxide.

perillus *ma ent.* perillus, stink bug (*Perillus circumcinctus*).

perintegracja *f. jęz.* reanalysis.

period *mi fizj.* menstruation; *pot.* period.

periodyczność *f.* periodicity.

periodyczny *a.* periodic, periodical; **wydawnictwo periodyczne** periodical; **ruch periodyczny** *l.* **okresowy** *mech.* periodic movement.

periodyk *mi* (= *czasopismo*) periodical.

periodyzacja *f.* periodization.

periodyzować *ipf. rzad.* periodize.

perkal *mi Gen.pl.* **-i** *l.* **-ów** *tk.* percale.

perkalowy *a. tk.* percale; **perkalowa zasłona** percale curtain.

perkaty *a.* snub, stubby, puggish; **perkaty nos** pug nose.

perkotać *ipf.* **1.** (*przy gotowaniu*) bubble. **2.** (*np. o silniku*) rattle.

perkoz *ma orn.* grebe (*Podideps*).

perkozek *ma* **-zk-** *orn.* little grebe, dabchick (*Tachybaptus ruficollis*).

perkusista *mp muz.* drummer.

perkusja *f. muz.* percussion; *pot.* drums.

perkusyjny *a. muz.* percussion; **instrumenty perkusyjne** percussion instruments.

perl *mi druk.* pearl.

perlak *mi Gen.* **-a** **1.** (*maszyna*) barley pearler, pearler. **2.** (*kasza*) pearl barley. **3.** *pat.* cholesteatoma.

perlakowy *a. med.* cholesteatomic; **perlakowe zapalenie ucha środkowego** chronic otitis media.

perlica *f. orn.* guinea fowl (*Numida meleagris*).

perliczka *f. Gen.pl.* **-ek** *zob.* **perlica**.

perlić się *ipf.* bead (up).

perlisty *a.* **1.** (*o pocie*) beady; **perlisty pot** beads of perspiration. **2.** *przen.* (*o śmiechu*) rippling; **perlisty śmiech** rippling laughter.

perlit *mi* **1.** *chem.* perlite, pearlite. **2.** *metal.* pearlite.

perlokucja *f. jęz.* perlocution.

perlokucyjny *a. jęz.* perlocutionary; **akt perlokucyjny** perlocutionary act.

perła *f. Gen.pl.* **pereł** **1.** (= *wytwór perłopławów*) pearl; **perła hodowlana** cultured *l.* culture pearl; **sztuczne perły** imitation *l.* simulated pearls; **poławiacz pereł** pearler; **rzucać perły przed wieprze** cast pearls before swine. **2.** *przen.* (= *ktoś/coś nadzwyczajnego*) gem, jewel, pearl; **perła w koronie** jewel in the crown; **perły muzyki renesansowej** pearls of the Renaissance music.

perłopław *ma zool.* pearl oyster (*Avicula l. Pinctada*); **perłopław perłorodny** great pearl oyster (*Pinctada margaritifera*).

perłoródka *f. Gen.pl.* **-ek** *zool.* pearl mussel (*Margaritifera margaritifera*).

perłowiec *ma* **-wc-** *zool.* fritillary (*Argynnis*).

perłowo *adv.* pearl-like, pearly; **zrobić kogoś na perłowo** *pot.* dress sb down, give sb a dressing down.

perłowy *a.* pearly; **kasza perłowa** pearl barley; **masa** *l.* **macica perłowa** mother-of-pearl; **proso perłowe** *bot.* pearl millet (*Pennisetum glaucum*).

perły *pl. Gen.* **pereł 1.** (= *naszyjnik z pereł*) pearls. **2.** *myśl.* pearls.

perm *mi geol.* the Permian, the Permian Period.

permaloj *mi metal.* Permalloy.

permanentnie *adv. lit.* perpetually, permanently.

permanentny *a. lit.* perpetual, permanent; **permanentny deszcz** unceasing rain; **permanentna niechęć** permanent aversion.

permisywny *a.* permissive; **permisywne społeczeństwo** permissive society.

permski *a. geol.* Permian.

permutacja *f. mat.* permutation.

peron *mi kol.* platform; **pociąg ekspresowy z Gdyni do Radomia gotowy do odjazdu z toru pierwszego przy peronie drugim** express train from Gdynia to Radom is ready to depart from platform two.

peronista *mp polit.* Peronist.

peronistka *f. zob.* **peronista.**

peronizm *mi polit.* Peronism.

peronowy *a. kol.* platform; **bilet peronowy** platform ticket; **dyżurny peronowy** platform attendant.

peronówka *f. Gen.pl.* **-ek** *kol., pot.* platform ticket.

perora *f. lit.* harangue.

perorować *ipf. lit.* perorate, harangue.

perpetuum mobile *n. indecl.* perpetuum mobile.

Pers *mp pl.* **-owie** Persian.

pers[1] *mi pl.* **-y** *pot.* (= *dywan perski*) Persian carpet *l.* rug.

pers[2] *ma pl.* **-y** *pot.* (= *kot perski*) Persian cat.

Persefona *f. mit.* Persephone.

Perseusz *mp mit.* Perseus.

perseweracja *f.* **1.** *fon.* perseverance. **2.** *pat., psych.* perseveration.

Persja *f. hist., geogr.* Persia.

Persjanka *f. zob.* **Pers.**

perski *a.* Persian; **bez perski** *bot.* Persian lilac (*Syringa persica*); **dywan** *l.* **kobierzec perski** Persian carpet *l.* rug; **kot perski** Persian cat; **proszek perski** Persian insect powder, pyrethrum; **Zatoka Perska** *geogr.* the Persian Gulf; **wojna w**

Zatoce Perskiej *hist.* the Gulf War (*1991*); **zrobić** *l.* **puścić do kogoś perskie oko** wink at sb.

persona *f.* personage; **ważna persona** big shot, bigwig, VIP; **persona non grata** persona non grata.

personalia *pl. Gen.* **-ów** personal data.

personalista *mp fil., psych.* personalist.

personalistyczny *a. fil., psych.* personalistic.

personalizm *mi* **1.** *fil.* personalism, personal idealism. **2.** *psych.* personalism.

personalna *f. Gen.* **-ej** *zob.* **personalny**[2].

personalnie *adv.* personally.

personalny[1] *a.* personal; **akta personalne** personnel records; **dane personalne** personal data; **dział personalny** personnel department, human resources *l.* HR department; **unia personalna** *polit., hist.* personal union.

personalny[2] *mp* personnel officer, human resources *l.* HR manager *l.* director.

personel *mi* personnel, staff, human resources; **personel dydaktyczny** teaching staff; **personel medyczny** health professionals; **personel naziemny** ground crew; **tylko dla personelu** (*napis na drzwiach*) staff *l.* employees only.

personifikacja *f. teor.lit.* personification.

personifikować *ipf.* personify.

perspektywa *f.* **1.** *sztuka* perspective; **bez perspektywy** (*np. o obrazie*) flat. **2.** (= *panorama*) perspective, vista, prospect; **spojrzeć na coś z innej perspektywy** view sth from a different angle. **3.** *przen.* (= *widoki na coś*) prospect, vista, view; **perspektywa zrobienia czegoś** prospect of doing sth; **mieć coś w perspektywie** have sth in prospect *l.* view; **mamy przed sobą perspektywę owocnej współpracy** we're looking forward to the prospect of fruitful cooperation; **dobre perspektywy zawodowe** good professional prospects; **otwierać nowe perspektywy** open up new vistas; **praca bez perspektyw** dead-end job. **4.** (= *dystans czasowy*) retrospective view, distance; **z perspektywy czasu** in retrospect; **oceniać coś z perspektywy lat** assess sth in retrospect. **5.** *geom.* perspective; **perspektywa zbieżna** linear perspective.

perspektywiczność *f. rzad.* perspectivity.

perspektywiczny *a.* **1.** *sztuka* perspective; **malarstwo perspektywiczne** scenography; **skrót perspektywiczny** foreshortening. **2.** (= *przyszły*) prospective; **plan perspektywiczny** long-term plan; **myślenie/planowanie perspektywiczne** forward thinking/planning.

perswadować *ipf.* persuade (*komuś coś* sb to do sth).

perswazja *f.* persuasion; **łagodna perswazja** gentle persuasion; **z łagodną perswazją w głosie** coaxingly.

persyflaż *mi teor.lit.* persiflage.

persymona *f. bot.* Oriental persimmon, kaki (*Diospyros kaki*).

persz *mi Gen.* **-a** *cyrk* perch.

perszeron *ma* (*rasa koni*) Percheron.

perta *f. żegl.* footrope.

pertraktacje *pl. Gen.* **-ji** negotiations; (*np. w*

sprawie rozejmu) parley; **prowadzić pertraktacje** negotiate; (*np. w sprawie rozejmu*) parley.

pertraktować *ipf.* negotiate; (*np. w sprawie rozejmu*) parley.

perturbacje *pl. Gen.* **-ji 1.** (= *zakłócenie*) perturbation. **2.** (= *zamieszanie*) perturbation, commotion. **3.** *astron.* perturbation.

perturbacyjny *a. astron.* perturbational.

perturbować *ipf. astron.* perturb.

Peru *mi indecl. geogr.* Peru.

peruka *f.* **1.** (= *sztuczne włosy*) wig. **2.** *myśl.* peruque (*osseous growth covered with velvet on the head of a deer during the growth of its antlers*).

perukarka *f. Gen.pl.* **-ek** *zob.* **perukarz.**

perukarnia *f. Gen.pl.* **-i** *l.* **-ń** wigmaker's shop.

perukarz *mp* wigmaker, wigger, peruker. – *ma zool.* a breed of domesticated pigeon (*with rich feather on the neck*).

perukowiec *mi* **-wc-** *Gen.* **-a** *bot.* smoke tree (*Cotinus*).

Peruwiańczyk *mp,* **Peruwianka** *f. Gen.pl.* **-ek** Peruvian.

peruwiański *a.* Peruvian; **balsam peruwiański** Peru balsam, balsam of Peru, Peruvian balsam, black balsam, China oil, Indian balsam.

perwersja *f. pat.* perversion; (= *wynaturzenie*) perversion, perversity.

perwersyjność *f.* perversity.

perwersyjny *a.* perverse; **perwersyjny obraz** obscene painting; **perwersyjne skłonności** perverse tendencies *l.* predilections.

peryderma *f. bot.* periderm.

peryferie *pl. Gen.* **-ii** (= *część zewnętrzna*) periphery; (= *obrzeża miasta*) outskirts, suburbs.

peryferyjność *f.* peripherality, marginality.

peryferyjny *a.* **1.** (= *zewnętrzny*) peripheral; **stacja robocza peryferyjna** *komp.* satellite; **urządzenie peryferyjne** *komp.* peripheral (device). **2.** (= *znajdujący się na peryferiach*) suburban; **dzielnice peryferyjne** (*zwł. wielkich miast, posiadające własny styl życia*) suburbia; **kino peryferyjne** suburban movie theater. **3.** (= *marginalny*) peripheral, incidental, marginal.

peryfrastyczny *a. jęz.* periphrastic.

peryfraza *f. teor.lit.* periphrasis, periphrase.

peryfrazować *ipf. teor.lit.* periphrase.

perygeum *n. sing. indecl. pl.* **-ea** *Gen.* **-eów** *astron.* perigee.

peryglacjalny *a. geogr.* periglacial; **utwór peryglacjalny** periglacial formation.

peryglacjał *mi geogr.* periglacial area.

peryhelium *n. sing. indecl. pl.* **-lia** *Gen.* **-liów** *astron.* perihelion.

perykarp *mi bot.* pericarp.

peryklaz *mi min.* periclase.

peryklejski *a. hist.* Periclean.

Perykles *mp hist.* Pericles.

peryklina *f. geol., min.* perycline.

perykopa *f. rz.-kat.* (= *czytanie z Biblii*) lection, pericope.

perymetr *mi med.* perimeter.

perypatetyczny *a. fil.* Peripatetic.

perypatetyk *mp fil.* Peripatetic.

perypatetyka *f. fil.* Peripateticism.

perypetie *pl. Gen.* **-ii 1.** (= *trudności*) trials and tribulations. **2.** *teor.lit.* peripeteia, peripetia, peripety.

perypter *mi bud.* peripteros.

peryskop *mi opt., wojsk., żegl.* periscope.

peryskopowy *a. opt., wojsk., żegl.* periscopic, periscopical; **głębokość peryskopowa** periscope depth.

perysperm *mi bot.* perisperm.

perystaltyczny *a. fizj.* peristaltic; **ruchy perystaltyczne** peristalsis.

perystaltyka *f. fizj.* peristalsis.

perystom *mi bot., zool.* peristome.

perystyl *mi Gen.pl.* **-i** *l.* **-ów** *bud.* peristyle, peristylium.

perz *mi bot.* quitch, couch grass (*Agropyron*); **perz właściwy** couch grass, quack grass, quick grass, quitch grass, scutch grass, twitch grass, witchgrass (*Agropyron repens*); **kłącze perzu** couch grass rootstalk *l.* rhizome.

perzyna *f. lit.* ashes; **obrócić coś w perzynę** reduce sth to rubble *l.* ashes.

PESEL *mi* personal identification number on Polish IDs.

peseta *f.* (*waluta*) peseta.

peso *n. indecl.* (*waluta*) peso.

pestka *f. Gen.pl.* **-ek 1.** (*jabłka, pomarańczy*) pip; (*wiśni, śliwki, brzoskwini*) stone, pit; (*dyni, słonecznika*) seed; **zalać się w pestkę** get blind drunk; **zalany w pestkę** three *l.* four sheets to the wind. **2.** *pot.* (= *nic trudnego*) piece of cake, cinch, walkaway; **to pestka!** it's a piece of cake!, it's a cinch!

pestkowiec, pestczak *mi* **-wc-** *Gen.* **-a** *bot.* drupe; *pot.* stone fruit.

pestkowy *a.* **1.** stone; *bot.* (= *wytwarzający pestki*) drupaceous, drupiferous; **owoc pestkowy** = **pestkowiec. 2.** *kulin.* **nalewka pestkowa** = **pestkówka.**

pestkówka *f. Gen.pl.* **-ek** *kulin.* persico, persicot (*cordial flavored with fruit kernels*).

pestycyd *mi chem.* pesticide.

pesymista *mp* pessimist.

pesymistka *f. Gen.pl.* **-ek** *zob.* **pesymista.**

pesymistycznie *adv.* pessimistically; **pesymistycznie nastawiony do świata** having a pessimistic attitude to life.

pesymistyczny *a.* pessimistic; **pesymistyczny nastrój** pessimistic mood; **przedstawiać pesymistyczny obraz czegoś** paint a gloomy picture of sth.

pesymizm *mi* pessimism.

peszyć *ipf.* abash, disconcert, baffle, confound; **peszyć kogoś** put sb off their stride. **~ się** *ipf.* get abashed; **łatwo się peszyć** be easily disconcerted.

pet *mi Gen.* **-a** *pot.* dog-end, fag end.

petarda *f.* (= *typ dawnego ładunku wybuchowego*) petard; (= *rodzaj fajerwerku*) petard, firecracker, squib.

petent *mp* applicant, petitioner, supplicant, inquirer.

petentka *f. Gen.pl.* **-ek** *zob.* **petent.**

Petersburg *mi Gen.* **-a** *geogr.* St. Petersburg.

petersburski *a.* St. Petersburgian.

petit *mi druk.* brevier.

Petrarca *mp (poeta)* Petrarch (*1304-74*).

petrochemia *f. Gen.* **-ii** *chem., geol.* petrochemistry.

petrochemiczny *a.* petrochemical; **przemysł petrochemiczny** petrochemical industry.

petrochemik *mp* petrochemist.

petrodolary *pl. fin.* petrodollars.

petrogeneza *f. min.* petrogenesis.

petroglif *mi archeol.* petroglyph, petrograph.

petrograf *mp min.* petrographer.

petrografia *f. Gen.* **-ii** *min.* petrography.

petrograficzny *a. min.* petrographic, petrographical; **prowincja petrograficzna** petrographic province.

petrolog *mp min.* petrologist.

petrologia *f. Gen.* **-ii** *min.* petrology.

petrologiczny *a. min.* petrologic, petrological.

petryfikacja *f.* **1.** *lit.* petrification. **2.** *geol., bud.* petrification.

petryfikować *ipf.* **1.** *lit.* petrify. **2.** *geol., bud.* petrify. **~ się** *ipf.* **1.** *lit.* become petrified. **2.** *geol., bud.* become petrified.

petting *mi* petting; **uprawiać petting** pet.

petunia *f. Gen.* **-ii** *bot.* petunia (*Petunia*).

petycja *f.* petition; **wnieść petycję do władz** petition the authorities.

pewien[1], **pewna, pewne** *a.* a *l.* an, one, certain; **pewien pan** a man; **pewien mój znajomy** a friend of mine; **pewna moja znajoma** a woman I know; **pewnego dnia** (*w przyszłości*) one day, some day, one of these days; **pewna doza czegoś** (*np. swobody*) a measure of sth; **pewnego razu** (= *kiedyś*) once; (*w bajkach*) once upon a time; **w pewnym sensie** in a sense; **w pewnym stopniu** to some extent, to a certain extent; **w pewnym wieku** at a certain age; **w pewnej odległości** at a (certain) distance; **koniec pewnej epoki** the end of an era; **pewna część ciała** *euf.* the backside; **przez pewien czas** for some time.

pewien[2] *a. por.* **pewny.**

pewniacha *f. l. mp decl. like f. Gen.pl.* **-ch** *l.* **-ów** *pot.* sb very self-confident.

pewniak *mp pl.* **-cy** *pot.* dependable person; **na pewniaka** for sure, surely; **wygramy na pewniaka** we're sure to win; **zda egzamin na pewniaka** she's sure to pass the exam. – *ma pl.* **-i** *pot.* **1.** (*w sporcie*) (= *pewny zwycięzca*) favorite, sure thing; **Kowalski to pewniak** Kowalski is sure to win, Kowalski is a sure thing, it's a safe bet Kowalski will win. **2.** (*koń*) (dead) cert.

pewnie *adv.* (= *zdecydowanie*) confidently, resolutely; **czuć się pewnie** (= *być pewnym siebie*) be confident, feel sure of o.s.; (= *czuć się bezpiecznie*) feel secure. – *particle* (= *prawdopodobnie*) probably; **pewnie przyjadą dopiero jutro** they probably won't come until tomorrow, I guess they won't come until tomorrow; **ty pewnie jesteś Tom** you must be Tom; **pewnie, że...** surely,...; **(no) pewnie!** you bet!; **pewnie, że lubię lody** of course I like ice-cream.

pewnik *mi Gen.* **-a 1.** (= *oczywistość*) certain-

ty; **brać coś za pewnik** take sth for granted. **2.** *log.* axiom.

pewno *particle* (= *prawdopodobnie*) probably; (= *pewnie*) surely; **pewno chce ci się pić** you must be thirsty; **pewno już to masz** you surely have already got it; **na pewno** sure, sure thing.

pewność *f.* **1.** (= *przekonanie*) certainty, certitude, confidence; **z całą pewnością** undoubtedly; **nabrałem pewności, że...** I'm now absolutely sure that...; **nie mam pewności co do godziny odjazdu pociągu** I'm not sure about the time of the train's departure; **dla pewności** to be on the safe side, just in case; **z pewnością go spotkamy** we're sure to meet him; **pewność siebie** self-confidence; **nabrać pewności siebie** gain self-confidence; **natchnąć kogoś pewnością siebie** breathe confidence into sb, instil confidence in sb; **stracić pewność siebie** (*np. w trudnej sytuacji*) lose one's self-confidence; **odebrać komuś pewność siebie** deflate sb, set sb back on their heels; **zachwiać czyjąś pewność siebie** shake sb's self-confidence; **z pewnością** for certain. **2.** (= *zdecydowanie*) sureness, firmness, steadiness; **pewność ręki** sure *l.* steady hand, sureness of touch. **3.** (= *prawdziwość*) reliability.

pewny *a.* **1.** (= *niechybny*) sure, certain; **pewna śmierć** certain death; **pewne zwycięstwo** certain *l.* sure victory. **2.** (= *godny zaufania*) sure, dependable, reliable; **zostawić kogoś/coś w pewnych rękach** put sb/sth in safe hands. **3.** (= *niewątpliwy*) sure, certain, reliable; **pewna informacja** reliable information; **pewne źródło informacji** reliable source of information; **z pewnego źródła** (*o informacjach*) straight from the horse's mouth; **to pewne, że...** it's a sure thing that... **4.** (= *niezawodny*) sure, certain, unfailing; **pewna ręka** steady hand; **pewny krok** firm step. **5.** (= *przekonany o czymś*) confident, sure, certain; **musisz być tego pewien** *l.* **pewny** make no mistake about it; **nie jestem pewien** I'm not sure, I don't know exactly; **jestem pewien zwycięstwa** I'm sure *l.* certain of victory *l.* winning; **nie jestem tego taka pewna** I'm not so sure; **nie jesteśmy pewni jutra** there's no telling what the future *l.* tomorrow holds *l.* will bring; **jestem absolutnie pewny Adama** I have complete confidence in Adam; **jesteś zbyt pewny siebie** you're overconfident. **6.** (= *bezpieczny*) secure, safe; **tylko tutaj mogę czuć się pewna** this is the only place I feel safe.

pezetpeerowiec *mp* **-wc-** *pl.* **-y** *polit.* member of the Polish United Workers' Party.

pezetpeerowski *a. polit.* of or related to the Polish United Workers' Party.

pęcherz *mi Gen.* **-a 1.** (*po oparzeniu, otarciu*) blister; **pęcherz żywiczny** *leśn.* pitch pocket. **2.** *anat.* bladder; **pęcherz moczowy** urinary bladder; **pęcherz płodowy** amniotic sac, bag of waters; **pęcherz pławny** *icht.* air *l.* swim bladder; **latać jak kot z pęcherzem** *pot.* run *l.* rush around like a chicken with its head cut off. **3.** *metal.* blowhole.

pęcherzowy *a.* **1.** blistery. **2.** bladder; **wziernik pęcherzowy** *med.* cystoscope.

pęcherzyca *f.* **1.** *bot.* bladder cherry, Chinese lantern, ground cherry, winter cherry (*Physalis alkekengi*). **2.** *pat.* pemphigus.

pęcherzyk *mi Gen.* -a **1.** *zwł. pat.* (= *chorobowa zmiana skórna*) blister, bleb. **2.** *anat.* sac, follicle, cyst, vesicle; **pęcherzyk Graafa** Graafian follicle; **pęcherzyk jajnikowy** ovarian follicle; **pęcherzyk nasienny** *zool.* seminal vesicle; **pęcherzyk oskrzelowy** bronchial sac; **pęcherzyk płucny** alveolus; **pęcherzyk żółciowy** gall bladder; **pęcherzyk żółtkowy** *zool.* yolk sac. **3.** (= *bąbelek*) bubble. **4.** *metal.* blowhole.

pęcherzykowy *a.* **1.** bubble, bubble-like. **2.** vesicular, follicular.

pęcina *f.* fetlock.

pęczak *mi* **1.** (*kasza*) hulled barley. **2.** *tk.* off-cuts, scraps, snatches.

pęczek *mi* -czk- *Gen.* -a bunch, bundle; **pęczek rzodkiewek** a bunch of radishes; **mieć czegoś na pęczki** have heaps *l.* (shit)loads *l.* oodles of sth.

pęcznieć *ipf.* bloat, swell; **pęcznieć z dumy** swell *l.* be puffed up with pride.

pęd *mi* **1.** (= *bieg*) dash, rush, scurry, impetus; **pęd powietrza** rush of air; **pęd wody** rush of water; **pęd pociągu** rush of a train; **owczy pęd** craze, stampede; **robić coś w pędzie** do sth in a rush, do a rush job of sth; **w te pędy** *pot.* right away, at once; **puścić się pędem** break into a rush. **2.** (= *potrzeba wewnętrzna*) hunger, urge, rush, yearning, craving; **pęd do czegoś** drive for sth; **pęd do wiedzy** hunger for knowledge. **3.** *bot.* shoot, sprout; **pęd boczny** offshoot; **pęd główny** leader; **pęd kwiatonośny** flowering shoot. **4.** *fiz.* momentum; **zasada pędu i popędu** equation of momentum and impulse; **zasada zachowania pędu** principle of conservation of momentum.

pędnia *f. techn.* shafting.

pędny *a.* driving; **oś pędna** driving axle; **materiał pędny** fuel.

pędrak *ma* **1.** *ent.* grub. **2.** *żart.* (= *dziecko*) tot, kid.

pędzel *mi* -dzl- *Gen.* -a brush; **pędzel ławkowiec** paintbrush; **pędzel do golenia** shaving brush; **pędzel z włosia** hair pencil; **obraz pędzla...** a picture by...

pędzelek *mi* -lk- *Gen.* -a **1.** (= *mały pędzel*) small brush; (*do nakładania kolorów*) pencil. **2.** (*na uszach niektórych zwierząt*) tuft.

pędzić *ipf.* **1.** (= *szybko się poruszać*) rush, scurry, shoot, speed; **pędzić co sił *l.* co tchu** go full-tilt *l.* full-speed; **pędził jak na skrzydłach** he rushed as if he had wings on his feet; **pędzić na łeb na szyję** rush headlong. **2.** (= *poganiać*) drive; **pędzić bydło** drive cattle. **3.** (= *spędzać*) lead, spend; **pędzić marny żywot** lead a life of misery. **4.** (= *zmuszać kogoś*) force, push; **pędzić kogoś do nauki** push sb to learning. **5.** *pot.* (*alkohol*) produce, distil (*moonshine*). **6.** *ogr.* (= *przyśpieszać dojrzewanie*) force.

pędziwiatr *mp pl.* -y *pot.* harum-scarum; **Struś Pędziwiatr** (*postać z kreskówki*) Roadrunner.

pędzlak *mi Gen.* -a *bot.* penicillium (*Penicillium*).

pędzlować *ipf.* (*gardło*) swab, paint.

pęk *mi* **1.** (= *wiązka*) bunch, bundle, cluster; **pęk chrustu** fagot; **pęk kluczy** bunch of keys; **pęk kwiatów** bunch of flowers; **pęk rózg** (*do bicia*) a bunch *l.* bundle of switches. **2.** *geom.* pencil; **pęk płaszczyzn** pencil of planes; **pęk prostych** pencil of lines.

pękać *ipf.* **1.** (*o szybie, lodzie*) crack; (= *zarysować się*) flaw; (= *rozłupać się*) rift, cleave; (*o desce, pniu*) split; (*o farbie*) check, crack; (*o sznurku, strunie, strąkach*) burst; (*o wrzodzie*) burst (open); (*o ubraniu, tkaninie*) rip; **uszy mi pękają od tego hałasu** this noise is ear-splitting; **głowa mi pęka** I've got a splitting headache, my head is splitting; **choćbym pękł, to...** not even if I had all the power in the world...; **pękać z ciekawości** burn *l.* burst with curiosity; **pękać z dumy** swell with pride, be puffed up with pride; **pękać z zazdrości** be burning with envy, be eating one's heart out; **pękać ze śmiechu** laugh one's head off, split one's sides; **pękać w szwach** burst *l.* split at the seams; **sala pęka w szwach** the house is full to bursting. **2.** (= *rozrywać się*) snap, break, split, rip; **pękły mi spodnie** my pants split. **3.** (= *wybuchać*) burst, explode; **co chwila pękały granaty** grenades would explode now and again; **bomba pęka** *pot.* the shit hit the fan, the curtains parted. **4.** (*o wydaniu, konsumpcji*) crack, blow, pop; **pękło parę butelek** *pot.* we cracked a few; (*o piwie, winie*) we popped a few; (*o wódce*) we tossed back *l.* killed a few; **pękło tysiąc złotych** *pot.* we blew a grand. **5.** (= *bać się*) pussyfoot, chicken out; **nie pękaj!** don't be such a chicken.

pękaty *a.* **1.** (= *zaokrąglony*) squab, round, rounded; (*o ludziach*) stocky, thickset, stubby. **2.** (= *wypchany*) bulging; **pękaty portfel** bulging wallet.

pęknąć *pf.* -ij, pękł *zob.* **pękać**.

pęknięcie *n.* crack, rift, burst, cleft, split, fissure; **pęknięcie kości** bone fracture; **pęknięcie naczynia krwionośnego** blood vessel burst; *zob. t.* **pęknąć**.

pępawa *f. bot.* pygmy hawk's beard (*Crepis pygmaea*).

pępek *mi* -pk- *Gen.* -a navel; *pot.* bellybutton; *anat.* umbilicus; **być pępkiem świata** be the navel *l.* hub of the universe.

pępkowaty *a.* umbilicate, umbilical; **zagłębienie pępkowate** *biol.* umbilicus.

pępkowy *a. anat.* umbilical; **sznur pępkowy** (= *pępowina*) umbilical cord.

pępowina *f. anat.* umbilical cord, umbilical; *pot.* navel string; **przeciąć pępowinę** (= *usamodzielnić się*) cut the cord.

pęseta *f.* (*kosmetyczna, zecerska, zegarmistrza*) tweezers; *chir.* forceps; **pęseta anatomiczna** surgeon's tourniquet; **pęseta naczyniowa** artery forceps.

pęsetka *f. Gen.pl.* -ek tweezers, pincers.

pęta *pl. Gen.* pęt (*dla zwierząt*) hobble, hopple, trammels; (= *więzy*) fetters, shackles; **pęto kiełbasy** sausage ring, ring of kielbasa; **pęta niewoli** *przen.* yoke of captivity.

pętać *ipf.* **1.** (*konie, bydło*) hobble, hopple. **2.** (= *krępować*) fetter, shackle. ~ **się** *ipf.* **1.** (= *krępować siebie wzajemnie*) fetter each other *l.* one another. **2.** *pot.* (= *wałęsać się*) hang around; **pętać się pod nogami** get in people's way.

pętak *mp pl.* **-i 1.** *pot.* (= *mały chłopiec*) tyke, tike. **2.** *pot.* (= *ktoś niepoważny*) sucker.

pętelka *f. Gen.pl.* **-ek** loop; **guzik z pętelką** zilch; *Br.* nought, naught.

pętelkowy *a.* loop, loopy; *tk.* terry; **dzianina pętelkowa** terry cloth; **ścieg pętelkowy** terry stitch *l.* weave.

pętla *f. Gen.pl.* **-i 1.** (*ze sznura*) noose, loop; **pętla na szyję** hangman's halter. **2.** (= *odcinek drogi, rzeki itp.*) loop. **3.** *lotn.* loop; **robić pętlę** *lotn.* loop the loop. **4.** (= *miejsce, w którym zawracają tramwaje, autobusy*) loop; (= *przystanek końcowy*) terminus. **5.** *myśl.* snare. **6.** *żegl.* loop knot. **7.** *komp.* loop.

pęto *n. zob.* **pęta**.

pfe *int.* yuk, yuck, bah; **pfe, ale brudno!** yuk, that's dirty!

pfu *int.* yuck, ooh, eew; **pfu, ale ohyda!** yuck, that's disgusting *l.* gross!

pfuj *int.* whew, phew, yuck, pooh; **pfuj, jak tu śmiedzi!** phew, what a stench!

PGR *abbr.* (= *Państwowe Gospodarstwo Rolne*) state-owned farm (*in former Poland*).

phi *int.* gosh; **phi, co mi mogą zrobić?!** gosh, what can they do to me?!

pi[1] *int.* wow; **pi, niezły w tym jesteś!** wow, you're good at this! – *ipf. indecl.* tweet, peep; **ptaszek pi, pi, bo było mu zimno** poor birdie went tweet-tweet because it was cold.

pi[2] *n. indecl.* (*litera grecka*) pi; **pi razy oko** *pot.* something like, more or less, somewhere in the neighborhood of.

piach *mi* sand; **iść do piachu** *pot.* bite the dust.

piać *ipf.* **pieję piejesz 1.** (*o kogucie*) crow. **2.** *pot.* (= *mówić piskliwie*) pipe. **3.** *pot.* (= *wygłaszać pochwały*) cry up, praise, extol; **piać nad kimś/czymś z zachwytu** fawn over sb/sth; **piać z radości** cry out with joy, let out a whoop.

piana *f.* foam, froth; (*z mydła*) lather; (= *szumowina*) scum; (*na powierzchni piwa*) head, froth; **ubijać pianę z białek** *kulin.* whip egg whites to a froth; **ubijać na sztywno pianę** *kulin.* beat until stiff; **z pianą na ustach** (= *ze wściekłością*) frothing at the mouth; **toczyć pianę z ust** *pat. t. pot.* froth *l.* foam at the mouth.

pianino *n. muz.* (upright) piano; **grać na pianinie** play the piano; **brzdąkać na pianinie** tickle *l.* tinkle the ivories; **ćwiczyć grę na pianinie** practice on the piano.

pianissimo *adv. muz.* pianissimo.

pianista *mp,* **pianistka** *f. Gen.pl.* **-ek** pianist, piano player.

pianistyczny *a.* pianistic; **konkurs pianistyczny** piano competition; **talent pianistyczny** talent for the piano.

pianistyka *f.* **1.** (*sztuka gry*) pianism. **2.** (= *pianiści i pianistki*) pianists; **w konkursie wystąpiły największe nazwiska polskiej pianistyki** competition featured Poland's greatest pianists.

pianka *f. Gen.pl.* **-ek 1.** (*piwa, mleka*) froth, foam; (*piwa*) head, foam, froth; **piwo z (dużą) pianką** beer with (e.g. two inches of) head. **2.** *kulin.* (*deser*) mousse. **3.** (*w kosmetyce*) foam, mousse; **pianka do golenia** shaving foam; **pianka do włosów** styling mousse. **4.** *min.* meershaum, sea foam. **5.** *techn.* foam; **pianka poliuretanowa** polyurethane foam. **6.** *pot.* (= *kostium surfera, windsurfera, czasami nurka*) wet suit.

piano *adv. muz.* piano.

pianobeton *mi bud.* foam *l.* foamed concrete.

pianogips *mi bud.* foam plaster, plaster foam.

pianoguma *f. techn.* foam rubber.

pianola *f. Gen.pl.* **-i** *l.* **-l** *muz.* player piano, Pianola.

pianotwórczy *a. zw. chem.* foaming; **środek pianotwórczy** foaming agent.

pianowy *a.* foam; **gaśnica pianowa** foam extinguisher.

piarg *mi* scree, talus.

piarżysko *n.* scree-covered area.

piasawa *f.* (*włókno*) piassava, piasaba.

piasek *mi* **-sk- 1.** (*skała*) sand; **piasek formierski** *techn.* molding sand; **piasek moczowy** *med.* urinary sand; **piasek roponośny** *geol.* oil sand; **piasek krzemionkowy** *l.* **szklarski** *techn.* silica, quartz sand; **lotne piaski** *geogr.* shifting sands; **ruchome piaski** *geol.* quicksand; **budować zamki na piasku** build castles in the air *l.* in Spain; **chować głowę w piasek** bury *l.* hide one's head in the sand; **chowanie głowy w piasek** ostrich policy; **kręcić bicz z piasku** try to make a silk purse out of a sow's ear, try to turn a sow's ear into a silk purse; **mam piasek w oczach** my eyes are burning, my eyes are on fire. **2.** (*gleba*) sand(s); **piaski gliniaste** clay sands.

piaskarka *f. Gen.pl.* **-ek** sand spreader; *Br.* gritter.

piaskołaz *mi zool.* soft-shell clam (*Mya arenaria*).

piaskować *ipf.* **1.** (*drogi*) sand; *Br.* grit. **2.** *techn.* (= *czyścić strumieniem piasku*) sandblast.

piaskowiec *mi* **-wc-** *Gen.* **-a 1.** (*skała*) sandstone. **2.** *bot.* (*grzyb*), bolete (*Gyroporus*). **3.** *bot.* (*chwast*) sandwort (*Arenaria*). **4.** *orn.* sanderling (*Crocethia alba*).

piaskownia *f. Gen.pl.* **-i** *górn.* sandpit.

piaskownica *f.* **1.** (*dla dzieci do zabawy*) sandbox; *Br.* sandpit. **2.** *bot.* beach grass (*Ammophila*); **piaskownica zwyczajna** European beachgrass, marram grass (*Ammophila arenaria*). **3.** *techn.* sandblaster. **4.** *kol.* (*w lokomotywie*) sandbox.

piaskowy *a.* **1.** (= *z piaskiem*) sandy, sand; **burza piaskowa** sandstorm; **dolarek piaskowy** *bot.* sand dollar (*Echinarachnius parma*); **dziadek piaskowy** (*w wierzeniach ludowych*) sandman; **efa piaskowa** *zool.* saw-scaled viper (*Echis carinatus*); **gleba piaskowa** *l.* **piaszczysta** sandy soil; **pchła piaskowa** *ent.* chigoe, sand flea (*Tunga penetrans*); **roślina piaskowa** arenicolous plant; **wydmuchrzyca piaskowa** *bot.* lyme grass, beach rye (*Elymus arenarius*); **zegar piaskowy** (= *klepsydra*) hourglass. **2.** (*o kolorze*) sandy; **piasko-**

we spodnie sandy trousers; **babka piaskowa** *kulin.* pound cake.

piaskówka *f. zool.* **1.** (*wieloszczet*) lugworm, blow lug (*Arenicola marina*). **2.** (*szczur*) fat sand rat (*Psammomys obesus*).

piasta *f. techn.* hub.

piastować *ipf.* **1.** *lit.* (*dziecko*) nurse. **2.** *lit.* (= *sprawować*) hold; **piastować urząd** hold office; **piastować władzę** wield power.

piastr *mi* (*moneta*) piaster, piastre.

piastunka *f. Gen.pl.* **-ek** *przest.* nursemaid, nursery maid.

piaszczarka *f. techn.* sandblaster.

piaszczysty *a.* sandy, sand; **piaszczysta gleba** sandy soil; **łacha** *l.* **ławica piaszczysta** (= *mielizna na rzece*) sandbank.

piącha *f. pot.* **1.** (= *pięść*) duke. **2.** (= *cios zadany pięścią*) sock; **przywalić komuś z piąchy** punch sb, give sb a sock, sock sb.

piąć się *ipf.* **pnę pniesz, -ij 1.** (= *wchodzić z trudem*) climb, climb along, work one's way up; **piąć się w górę po schodach** climb up the stairs, work one's way up the stairs. **2.** (*o roślinach*) climb, creep. **3.** (*o drodze*) climb, slope upwards; **droga pięła się pod górę** road sloped upwards. **4.** (= *awansować*) climb; **piąć się po szczeblach kariery** work one's way to the top.

piąstka *f. Gen.pl.* **-ek** little fist; **twarz jak piąstka** tiny face, baby face.

piąstkować *ipf.* piłka nożna fist (*the ball*).

piąta *f. Gen.* **-ej** (*godzina*) five (o'clock); **jest piąta rano** it's five a.m.; **będę piętnaście po piątej** I'll be there at a quarter past five; **kończę za piętnaście piąta** I finish at a quarter to five; **mam pociąg o wpół do piątej** my train leaves at half past four.

piątak *mi Gen.* **-a** *pot.* (= *banknot l. moneta o nominale pięć*) fiver.

piątal *mi Gen.* **-a** *pot.* zob. **piątak**.

piątek *mi* **-tk-** Friday; **Wielki Piątek** *rel.* Good Friday; **w piątek i świątek** seven days a week; **jaki piątek, taki świątek** the holiday will turn out to be however your workdays go, Friday makes your weekend.

piątka *f. Gen.pl.* **-ek 1.** (*cyfra*) five. **2.** *szkoln.* (*ocena*) A. **3.** (= *tramwaj, autobus nr 5*) five; **do szpitala dojedziesz piątką** take a five to get to the hospital. **4.** (= *dom, mieszkanie, pokój nr 5*) number five; **mieszkamy pod piątką** we live at number five. **5.** (= *grupa pięciu osób*) group *l.* party of five. **6.** *karty* five, cinque; **piątka pik** five of spades. **7.** *pot.* (*moneta, banknot*) fiver. **8.** (*sposób przywitania*) high-five; **przybij piątkę!** gimme five!

piątkowy¹ *a.* Friday; **piątkowe zebranie o 18** the Friday meeting at 6 p.m.; **piątkowy wieczór** Friday night.

piątkowy² *a.* (= *dotyczący liczby 5*) of or related to five; (= *dotyczący oceny bdb*) A; **uczeń piątkowy** an A student; **układ piątkowy** *mat.* quinary *l.* quintuple system.

piątoklasista *mp szkoln.* fifth-grader; *zwł. Br.* fifth-former.

piątoklasistka *f. Gen.pl.* **-ek** zob. **piątoklasista**.

piąty *a.* fifth; **piąta klasa** *szkoln.* fifth grade; *Br.* fifth form; **piąte dziecko w rodzinie** fifth child in the family; **jedna piąta** *t. mat.* one *l.* a fifth; **piąta część** one *l.* a fifth; **piąte koło u wozu** fifth *l.* third wheel; **cztery kąty i piec piąty** four walls and a roof; **brak mu piątej klepki** he's one *l.* a brick short of a load, he has a screw *l.* tile loose; **rozumiałem go piąte przez dziesiąte** I only understood bits and pieces of what he said; **umiesz to piąte przez dziesiąte** you've only just scratched the surface, there's much more to it than that. — *mi* fifth (*day of a month*); **umówić się z kimś na piątego czerwca** arrange a meeting with sb on the fifth of June; **skończyć pracę do piątego** finish work by the fifth.

pic *mi pot.* puffery; **pic na wodę** (*fotomontaż*) puffery, fakery, sth bogus.

picer *mp pot.* phony, faker.

pichcić *ipf. żart.* concoct (*a meal*).

picie *n.* **1.** (*czynność*) drinking; **zdatny do picia** fit to drink, fit for drinking, potable. **2.** *pot.* (*napój*) drink; **podaj no mi picie!** gimme a drink, will you?

picować *ipf. pot.* dupe, con, humbug.

picuś *mp pot.* fop, dandy.

picza *f. wulg.* slit, slot, scar.

piczka *f. Gen.pl.* **-ek** *wulg.* pussy, muff, mink.

pić¹ *ipf.* **piję pijesz 1.** (*jakikolwiek napój*) drink; **pić coś przez słomkę** drink sth through the straw. **2.** (*alkohol*) drink; **pić na umór** drink like a fish; **pić bez umiaru** drink hard; **pić nałogowo** be addicted to alcohol; **pić jak szewc** *l.* **jak stary** *l.* **jak ryba** *l.* **jak świnia** drink like there's no tomorrow, drink like a sailor, drink like prohibition is coming back, drink like it's going out of style, booze it up, hit the bottle; **pić strzemiennego** have one for the road; **pić za czyjeś zdrowie** drink to sb's health; **pić toast za kogoś** toast sb; **pić z kimś bruderszaft** drink to close friedship with sb (*after which the parties agree to be on first name terms*); **pić z kimś brudzia** *pot.* zob. **pić z kimś bruderszaft**; **pić do lustra** drink with the flies; **przestać pić** (*o alkoholiku*) dry out; **zacząć pić** (= *wpaść w nałóg*) take to drink; **nie pić** (*o alkoholiku*) be on the wagon; **znów zacząć pić** (*o alkoholiku*) fall off the wagon; **do kogo pijesz?** who are you referring to?, what are you trying to say?, who are you bad-mouthing this time?

pić² *ipf.* **pije** pinch; **buty mnie piją** my shoes pinch.

pidżyn *mi jęz.* pidgin.

pidżynowy *a. jęz.* pidgin; **język pidżynowy** pidgin language.

piec¹ *mi Gen.* **-a** *Gen.pl.* **-ów 1.** (*do ogrzewania, w kuchni*) stove; **piec akumulacyjny** accumulation heater *l.* stove; **piec chlebowy** bread oven; **piec kaflowy** tile stove; **piec kuchenny** kitchen stove; **prosto z pieca** hot and hot; **cztery kąty i piec piąty** four walls and a roof; **żyć jak u Pana Boga za piecem** be as snug as a bug in a rug; **z niejednego pieca chleb jadłem** (*o człowieku światowym*) I'm a graduate of the University of Life; (*o człowieku boleśnie doświadczonym*) I went to the School of Hard Knocks; (*o człowieku,* *który wiele podróżował*) I've been around, I've slept in many beds. **2.** *techn.* furnace, kiln, oven; **piec ceramiczny** ceramic kiln; **piec do wypalania cegieł** brick kiln; **piec emalierski** enamel kiln; **piec hutniczy** metallurgical furnace; **piec kremacyjny** crematory, crematorium; **piec martenowski** open hearth furnace; **piec piekarski** baking oven; **piec szybowy** shaft furnace.

piec² *ipf.* **-kę -czesz, -kł 1.** (*chleb, ciasto*) bake; (*mięso*) roast; **piec chleb** bake bread; **piec ciasto** bake a cake; **piec mięso** roast meat; **piec ziemniaki na ognisku** bake *l.* roast potatoes on the bonfire *l.* campfire coals; **piec na ruszcie** barbecue, grill; **pieczone gołąbki nie lecą same do gąbki** no pain, no gain, no reward without toil. **2.** (= *parzyć*) burn, smart; **słońce dziś strasznie piecze** it's a real burner today, you could fry an egg on the pavement today, hot enough for you? **3.** (= *sprawiać ból*) burn, smart, sting; **twarz mnie piecze** my face is burning; **oczy mnie pieką** my eyes are smarting *l.* stinging *l.* burning; **zgaga mnie piecze** I've (a) heartburn; **ta brandy strasznie piecze w gardło** this brandy burns your throat. **~ się** *ipf.* **1.** (= *być pieczonym*) (*o chlebie, cieście*) be baking; (*o mięsie*) be roasting; **ciasto się piecze** the cake is baking. **2.** (= *odczuwać ciepło*) bake; **piec się na słońcu** bake in the sun.

piechociarz *mp wojsk., pot.* infantryman, doughboy.

piechota *f. wojsk.* infantry; **piechota morska** Marine Corps, Marines; **pułk piechoty** infantry regiment; **piechota łanowa** *l.* **wybraniecka** *hist.* infantry troops whose members were recruited from among the nobility, clergy and town dwellers; **piechotą** *l.* **na piechotę** on foot; **drałować piechotą** *pot.* pad it; **zasuwać piechotą** *pot.* hoof it; **to tylko dziesięć minut piechotą** it's just a ten-minute walk, it's just ten minutes on foot; **można tam dojść na piechotę** it's within walking distance; **muszę iść tam, gdzie król piechotą chodzi** *przen.* I have some business to attend to, I'll be in my office if you need me.

piechtą, na piechtę *adv. dial.* on foot.

piechur *mp* **1.** (= *człowiek idący pieszo*) walker, hiker, pedestrian. **2.** *wojsk.* infantryman.

piecowy *a.* stove; furnace; **ogrzewanie piecowe** stove *l.* furnace heating; **lakier piecowy** *techn.* stoving lacquer *l.* varnish. – *mp* furnace *l.* kiln *l.* stove operator.

piecuch *mp pot.* sb who likes to be snug; **mój pies to straszny piecuch** my dog just loves to be snug and cosy.

piecuszek *mi orn.* willow warbler (*Phylloscopus trochilus*).

piecyk *mi Gen.* **-a 1.** stove. **2.** *pot.* (= *piekarnik*) oven. **3.** (*do ogrzewania*) heater; (*zwłaszcza w łazience*) hot-water heater; *Br.* geyser; **piecyk elektryczny** electric heater; **piecyk gazowy** gas heater.

piecza *f. lit.* care; **otaczać kogoś/coś pieczą** have charge of sb/sth, be responsible for sb/sth; **powierzyć kogoś/coś czyjejś pieczy** entrust sb/sth with the care of sb; **sprawować pieczę nad czymś** be in charge of sth.

pieczara *f.* cave, cavern.

pieczarka *f. Gen.pl.* **-ek** *bot., kulin.* agaric, mushroom, champignon (*Agaricus*); **pieczarka polna** meadow mushroom (*Agaricus campestris*); **pieczarka polowa** horse mushroom (*Agaricus arvensis*).

pieczarkarnia *f. Gen.pl.* **-i** *l.* **-ń** mushroom farm.

pieczarkarz *mp* mushroom grower *l.* farmer.

pieczarkowy *a.* mushroom; **zupa pieczarkowa** (meadow) mushroom soup.

pieczątka *f. Gen.pl.* **-ek 1.** (*przyrząd*) (rubber) stamp; **poduszka do pieczątek** ink pad. **2.** (*znak*) stamp; **postawić pieczątkę na dokumencie** stamp a document.

pieczeniarz *mp pot., przest.* sponger, hanger-on, leech.

pieczenie *n.* **1.** (*czynność*) baking; **blacha do pieczenia** baking tray; **proszek do pieczenia** baking powder. **2.** (= *piekący ból*) burning (sensation); **pieczenie w żołądku** burning sensation in the stomach.

pieczeniowy *a. kulin.* roasting; **mięso pieczeniowe** roasting meat; **sos pieczeniowy** gravy.

pieczeń *f. pl.* **-e** *kulin.* roast; **pieczeń rzymska** meatloaf; **pieczeń wieprzowa** roast pork; **pieczeń wołowa** roast beef; **pieczeń z rusztu** barbecue; **upiec dwie pieczenie przy jednym ogniu** kill two birds with one stone; **upiec własną pieczeń przy czyimś ogniu** warm o.s. at sb else's fire, cash in on sb else's efforts.

pieczęciowy *a.* sealing; **lak pieczęciowy** sealing wax.

pieczęć *f. pl.* **-e 1.** (*lakowa*) seal; (*gumowa*) (rubber) stamp; **przystawić pieczęć** affix a seal *l.* stamp; **odcisnąć pieczęć** *prawn.* impress a seal; **potwierdzić** *l.* **poświadczyć coś pieczęcią** put one's seal on sth; **złamać pieczęć** *l.* **plombę** break a seal. **2.** (*odcisk, znak*) stamp; **akt** *l.* **dokument opatrzony pieczęcią** *prawn.* specialty.

pieczętować *ipf.* seal, stamp. **~ się** *ipf.* (= *używać herbu*) bear (*a lion, a horse etc. in one's coat of arms*).

pieczołowicie *adv.* assiduously, painstakingly.

pieczołowitość *f.* assidousness, painstakingness.

pieczołowity *a.* assidous, painstaking; **pieczołowite badania** painstaking research; **pieczołowita opieka** great care.

pieczony *a.* (*o pieczywie, cieście*) baked; (*o rybie, mięsie, warzywach*) roast; **pieczony na ruszcie** grilled; **pieczone ziemniaki** roast potatoes; **kurczę pieczone** *l.* **kurczak pieczony** roast chicken.

pieczyste *n. Gen.* **-ego** *kulin.* roast.

pieczywo *n.* bread, breadstuff; **pieczywo chrupkie** crispbread; **koszyk na pieczywo** bread basket.

piedestał *mi* pedestal; **postawić kogoś na piedestale** put *l.* set sb on a pedestal; **spaść z piedestału** fall off the *l.* one's pedestal; **strącić kogoś z piedestału** knock sb off his/her pedestal.

piegi *pl. Gen.* **-ów** freckles.

piegowaty a. freckled; **piegowaty nos** freckled nose.

piegus mp pl. **-y** pot. freckle-face.

pieguska f. Gen.pl. **-ek** zob. **piegus**.

piegża f. Gen.pl. **-y** l. **-ż** orn. lesser whitethroat (Sylvia curruca).

pieję itd. ipf. zob. **piać**.

piekarnia f. Gen.pl. **-i** l. **-ń** (wytwórnia, sklep) bakery; (sklep) baker's.

piekarnictwo n. baker's trade.

piekarniczy a. baking; **piec piekarniczy** industrial l. bread oven; (o wyrobach) = **piekarski**.

piekarnik mi Gen. **-a** oven; **piekarnik elektryczny** electric oven; **piekarnik gazowy** gas oven.

piekarski a. (= dotyczący piekarstwa) baking; (= dotyczący piekarzy) bakers'; (= dotyczący piekarza) baker's; **tłuszcz piekarski** (dodawany do ciasta dla kruchości) shortening; **wyroby piekarskie** zob. **wyroby piekarnicze**.

piekarz mp baker.

piekący a. **1.** (= gorący) scorching, searing; **piekące słońce** scorching sun; **piekące spojrzenie** przen. scorching look. **2.** (o bólu, zazdrości) smarting, scorching; **piekący ból** smarting pain.

piekielnica f. **1.** zob. **piekielnik**. **2.** icht. schneider, chub (Alburnoides bipunctatus).

piekielnie adv. awfully, dreadfully, devilishly; **piekielnie gorąco** boiling hot; **piekielnie trudny** wretchedly difficult, the devil's own; **piekielnie trudne pytanie** (np. na egzaminie) fiendish question; **piekielnie zdolny** damn gifted.

piekielnik mp pot. scold, shrew, spitfire, nag.

piekielny a. **1.** lit. (= z piekła) hellish, infernal; **piekielny upał** devilish heat; **machina piekielna** infernal machine; **moce piekielne** infernal powers, the powers of darkness; **ogień piekielny** hellfire; rel. fire and brimstone. **2.** (= intensywny) awful, dreadful, devilish; **piekielny ból** excruciating pain; **piekielny hałas** a hell of a noise; **piekielna robota** a devil of a job; **piekielny strach** crazy l. hellish fear; **zrobić piekielną awanturę o coś** raise hell about sth. **3.** (= zły) hellish, wicked; **co za piekielne babsko!** what a damn shrew!; **miałem piekielny dzień** I had a hell of a day.

pieklić się ipf. pot. rampage, rage; **pieklić się o coś** raise hell about sth; **pieklił się przez cały dzień** he rampaged for the whole day.

piekło n. Gen.pl. **-kieł** hell, the Inferno; **z piekła rodem** fiendish, ungodly, contemptible; **robić l. urządzać komuś piekło** give sb hell; **tłukłeś się wczoraj jak Marek po piekle** I thought you were going to wake the dead last night; **pójść za kimś do piekła** go through fire and water for sb, go through hell and high water for sb; **istne piekło** sheer l. pure hell; **rozpętało się piekło** all hell broke lose, the fur began l. started to fly; **zamieniać czyjeś życie w piekło** make sb's life a living hell; **piekło na ziemi** hell on earth; **piekło rewolucji** the hell of revolution; **piekło wojny** the hell of war; **ciekawość to pierwszy stopień do piekła** curiosity killed the cat; **dobrymi chęciami piekło wybrukowane** the road to hell is paved with good intentions; **wstąpił do piekieł, po drodze mu było**

iron. he just happened to be in the neighborhood.

pielesze pl. Gen. **-y** lit. the home; **pielesze domowe** l. **rodzinne** the home.

pielęgnacja f. care; (chorych) nursing; (roślin) nurturing; (zwierząt) tending; **pielęgnacja włosów** hair care; **krem do pielęgnacji twarzy/rąk** face/hand cream.

pielęgnacyjny a. of or related to looking after l. taking care of; **krem pielęgnacyjny** beauty cream; **zabiegi pielęgnacyjne** (t. roślin) looking after, nurturing.

pielęgniarka f. Gen.pl. **-ek** nurse; **pielęgniarka szkolna** school nurse; **pielęgniarka środowiskowa** visiting nurse.

pielęgniarski a. nursing; **czepek pielęgniarski** nurse's cap; **opieka pielęgniarska** nursing; **szkoła pielęgniarska** nursing school.

pielęgniarstwo n. nursing.

pielęgniarz mp (male) nurse.

pielęgnice pl. Gen. **-c** icht. cichlids (Cichlidae).

pielęgnować ipf. (np. chorych, rannych) nurse, tend; (np. młode) foster; (np. przyjaźń, język, tradycje) cultivate; (np. rośliny) look after, cultivate; (np. pamięć o czymś) cherish.

pielgrzan mi Gen. **-u** l. **-a** bot. traveler's palm (Ravenala madagascariensis).

pielgrzym mp pilgrim; **Ojcowie Pielgrzymi** hist. Pilgrim Fathers.

pielgrzymi a. pilgrim's; **kij pielgrzymi** pilgrim's staff.

pielgrzymka f. **1.** (wędrówka) pilgrimage; **pójść z pielgrzymką** l. **na pielgrzymkę** make a pilgrimage. **2.** (grupa ludzi) pilgrims.

pielgrzymować ipf. pilgrimage, make a pilgrimage.

pielić ipf. zob. **pleć**.

pielografia f. med. pyelography.

pielucha f. diaper; Br. nappy.

pieluszka f. Gen.pl. **-ek** zob. **pielucha**.

piemoncki a. Piedmontese.

Piemont mi geogr. Piedmont.

pieniacki a. barratrous, barretrous; **pieniackie usposobienie** barratrous disposition.

pieniactwo n. barratry, barretry.

pieniacz mp barrator, barrater, barretor.

pieniądz mi Gen.pl. **-ędzy** Ins.pl. **-ędzmi** money; **ciężkie** l. **grube** l. **duże pieniądze** pots of money; **drobne pieniądze** small change; **fałszywe pieniądze** counterfeit money; **małe** l. **marne** l. **psie pieniądze** pittance, chicken feed; **łatwe pieniądze** easy money; **papierowe pieniądze** paper money; **wartość pieniądza** value of money; **być pazernym na pieniądze** have an itching palm; **jest krucho z pieniędzmi** money is tight; **kosztować masę pieniędzy** cost a bundle; **kupić coś za psie pieniądze** buy sth dirt cheap; **leżeć na pieniądzach** be rolling in money; **mieć dużo pieniędzy** have a lot of money, have deep pockets; **mieć nosa do pieniędzy** have a scent for money; **mieć pieniędzy jak lodu** have money to burn; **możemy się pożegnać z pieniędzmi** we can whistle for our money; **nie chodzi tu o pieniądze** money's not the issue, money doesn't come into it; **nie żałować na coś**

pieniędzy not stint money on sth; **pakować** *l.* **ładować** *l.* **pompować w coś pieniądze** pump *l.* inject money into sth; **obracać pieniędzmi** put money to profit; **pieniądze nie grają roli** (*nie stanowią problemu*) money is no object; **pieniądze się kogoś nie trzymają** money is burning a hole in sb's pocket; **podejmować pieniądze z banku** take money out of the bank, withdraw money from one's bank account; **pożyczać od kogoś pieniądze** borrow money from *l.* off sb; **prać brudne pieniądze** launder money *l.* funds; **robić pieniądze** make money; **stawiać na coś pieniądze** put money on sth; **szastać pieniędzmi na prawo i lewo** chuck one's money around *l.* about; **ulokować pieniądze w banku** put *l.* deposit money in a bank; **wydawać pieniądze lekką ręką** spend money like water *l.* like it grows on trees *l.* like it's going out of style; **wypuszczać pieniądze w obieg** issue money; **wyrzucać pieniądze w błoto** throw money down the drain; **pieniądze i sława** fame and fortune; **zapłacić za coś furę** *l.* **pieniędzy** pay through the nose for sth; **za żadne pieniądze** not for love or money, not for all the world; **czas to pieniądz** time is money; **nie mam przy sobie pieniędzy** I have no money on me.

pieniążek *mi* -żk- *Gen.* -a **1.** (= *drobna moneta*) small coin. **2.** *żart.* (*zwykle pl.*) money.

pienić się *ipf.* **1.** (= *wytwarzać pianę*) foam, froth. **2.** *pot.* (= *być wściekłym*) froth *l.* foam at the mouth.

pienie *n. lit.* **1.** (= *pieśń*) descant, warble. **2.** (= *pochwała*) eulogy, plaudit.

pieniek *mi* -ńk- *Gen.* -a **1.** (= *pniak*) stump; **mieć z kimś na pieńku** be at daggers drawn with sb, have a bone to pick with sb, have *l.* put a rod in pickle for sb. **2.** *dent.* snag.

pieniężnik *mi bot.* moneywort, creeping Jennie, creeping Charlie (*Lysimachia nummularia*).

pieniężny *a.* money; (*finansowy*) financial; (*kara*) pecuniary; (*zasoby*) monetary, pecuniary; **kara pieniężna** fine, mulct; **pomoc pieniężna** financial aid; **odszkodowanie pieniężne** financial compensation; **przekaz pieniężny** money order; *Br.* postal order; **rynek pieniężny** money market; **zasoby pieniężne** financial resources *l.* means; **względy pieniężne** financial *l.* pecuniary reasons; **Rada Polityki Pieniężnej** Monetary Policy Council (*in Poland*).

pienny *a. bot.* standard; **róża pienna** standard rose.

pień *mi* pni- *Gen.* -a (*żywego drzewa*) **1.** trunk; **sprzedać coś na pniu** (*o zbożach*) sell standing crops; (*np. powieść, scenariusz*) sell a half-baked manuscript, sell the promise of sth; **głuchy jak pień** (as) deaf as a post, stone-deaf; **wyciąć w pień** kill everybody. **2.** (*po ścięciu drzewa*) stump, stub. **3.** (= *ul z pnia*) bee gum. **4.** *gram.* stem. **5.** *myśl.* pedicel.

pieprz *mi* **1.** *bot.* (*roślina*) pepper (*Piper*); **uciekać, gdzie pieprz rośnie** cut and run, head South (of the border). **2.** (*przyprawa*) pepper; **pieprz angielski** allspice, pimento, Jamaica pepper; **pieprz biały** white pepper; **pieprz cayenne**

cayenne pepper; **pieprz czarny** black pepper; **pieprz mielony** ground pepper; **pieprz turecki** capsicum, red pepper; **pieprz ziołowy** herb pepper; **suchy jak pieprz** *l.* **wiór** as dry as a bone, bone-dry.

pieprzenie *n. pot.* **1.** (= *gadanie głupot*) bullshitting. **2.** (= *stosunek płciowy*) screwing.

pieprznąć *pf.* -ij *pot.* **1.** (= *rzucić*) chuck. **2.** (= *uderzyć*) sock. ~ **się** *pf.* -ij *pot.* **1.** sock o.s. **2.** (= *pomylić się*) get sth damn wrong, get sth fucked up; **pieprznąłem się w obliczeniach** I fucked up these sums.

pieprzniczka *f. Gen.pl.* -ek pepperbox, pepper shaker, pepper pot.

pieprznięty *a. pot.* nuts; **ten koleś jest zupełnie pieprznięty** this dude is completely nuts *l.* out of his gourd.

pieprznik¹ *mi Gen.* -u *pot.* (= *bałagan*) pigsty; **o Jezu, jaki tu pieprznik!** Jesus, what a pigsty!

pieprznik² *mi Gen.* -a *bot.* chanterelle (*Cantharellus cibarius*).

pieprzny *a.* **1.** (*z pieprzem*) peppery; **pieprzna zupa** peppery soup. **2.** (= *nieprzyzwoity*) spicy; **pieprzna anegdota** spicy anecdote *l.* joke.

pieprzojad *mi zob.* **tukan.**

pieprzony *a.* -eni *pot.* frigging, freaking, fucking, pissy; *Br.* bloody; **to pieprzone życie!** this frigging life!; **ty pieprzony głupku!** you fucking idiot!

pieprzowy *a.* pepper; **mięta pieprzowa** *bot.* peppermint (*Mentha piperita*); **wódka pieprzowa** *zob.* **pieprzówka** 1.

pieprzówka *f. Gen.pl.* -ek **1.** (*wódka*) pepper-flavored vodka. **2.** *bot.* peperomia (*Peperomia*).

pieprzyć *ipf.* **1.** (= *dodawać pieprzu*) pepper. **2.** *pot.* (= *mówić bez sensu, głupoty*) talk bullshit; **pieprzyć głupoty** *l.* **jak potłuczony** talk through one's ass; **przestań pieprzyć!** cut the crap! **3.** *wulg.* screw; *Br.* shag; **ja pieprzę!** *l.* **cię pieprzę!** holy shit!; **pieprz się!** fuck you! ~ **się** *ipf. wulg.* **1.** (= *odbywać stosunek*) have a screw; *Br.* have a shag, have it away *l.* off; **pieprzyć się z każdym** *l.* **kim podleci** screw around, sleep around. **2.** (= *spadać*) take a hike, beat it; **pieprz się, debilu!** beat it, you moron! **3.** (= *mylić się*) get freaking confused, muddle up; **pieprzy mi się to wszystko** I can't work the damn thing out. **4.** (= *nie udawać się*) go freaking wrong; **wszystko mi się pieprzy w tym cholernym życiu** every freaking thing goes wrong in my damn life.

pieprzyk *mi Gen.* -u *l.* -a (*na twarzy, na skórze*) mole, nevus.

pierdel *mi* -dl- *Gen.* -a *pot.* can, clink, cooler.

pierdnąć *pf.* -ij *zob.* **pierdzieć.**

pierdolec *mi* -lc- *Gen.* -a *wulg.* obsession, insanity, bug in the head; **mieć pierdolca** be fucked in the head, be fucked up.

pierdolenie *n. wulg.* (= *stosunek, t. głupie gadanie*) fucking; **pierdolenie kotka za pomocą młotka** whacking off; - **co było wczoraj na zebraniu?** - **jak zwykle, pierdolenie kotka za pomocą młotka** - how was the meeting yesterday? - oh, just the usual whacking off.

pierdolić *ipf. wulg.* **1.** (*o mężczyźnie*) fuck. **2.**

(= *lekceważyć*) fuck, not give a fuck; **pierdolę to!** fuck that!, I don't give a fuck about that! **3.** (= *mówić bez sensu, głupoty*) talk fucking bullshit; **nie pierdol!** stop this fucking bullshit, will you? **4. ja pierdolę!** *l.* **cię pierdolę!** fucking hell!, fuck me! ~ **się** *ipf. wulg.* **1.** (= *odbywać stosunek*) fuck, have a fuck; **pierdolić się z każdym** *l.* **z kim podleci** fuck around; **pierdolić się jak króliki** *l.* **norki** fuck like rabbits *l.* bunnies; **pierdol się!** up yours! **2.** (= *obchodzić się z kimś/czymś delikatnie*) handle with kid gloves, be walking on eggshells with; **nie pierdol się z nim!** to hell with him!, fuck him! **3.** (= *mylić się*) get fucking confused, muddle up; **wszystko mi się pierdoli** I can't work this fucking thing out.

pierdolnąć *pf.* **-ij** *wulg.* **1.** (= *uderzyć*) hit; **pierdolnąć kogoś** *l.* **komuś w głowę** hit sb in their fucking head. **2.** (= *powiedzieć*) say; **pierdolnąć frachę** say sth fucking stupid. ~ **się** *pf.* **-ij** *wulg.* **1.** (= *uderzyć się*) hit o.s.; **kurwa, pierdolnąłem się w łokieć!** fuck, I hit my freaking elbow! **2.** (= *pomylić się*) get sth fucking wrong; **znowu się pierdolnąłem w obliczeniach** I got my fucking sums wrong again.

pierdolnięty *a. wulg.* fucking nuts; **ten koleś jest zupełnie pierdolnięty!** this dude is just fucking nuts!

pierdolony *a.* **-eni** *wulg.* fucking; **pierdolona dziwka** fucking bitch; **to pierdolone życie** this fucking life; **ty chuju pierdolony!** you fucking prick!

pierdoła *f. l. mp decl. like f. pog. Gen.pl.* **-ów** fart; **ten stary pierodoła znowu o tym ględzi** the old fart's gabbing about it again *l.* rehashing it.

pierdołki *pl. Gen.* **-ek** *pot.* gibberish, rubbish.

pierdoły *pl. Gen.* **-ł** *pot.* **1.** (= *bzdury*) bullshit, crap; **co on tu za pierdoły gada?** what is this crap he's talking about? **2.** (= *rzeczy nieistotne*) trifles; **daj spokój, życia szkoda na pierdoły** come on, don't sweat the small stuff.

pierdykać *ipf.,* **pierdyknąć** *pf.* **-ij** *pot.* hit, punch; **ja pierdykam!** holy cow!, I'll be damned!

pierdzieć *ipf.* **-dzę -dzisz** *pot.* fart; **pierdzieć w stołek** (= *obijać się*) fart around.

pierdzielić *ipf. pot.* talk shit; **pierdzielić głupoty** talk shit.

pierestrojka *f. Gen.pl.* **-ek** *polit., hist.* perestroika.

piernat *mi. Gen.* **-ów** **1.** (= *materac z pierzem*) feather bed *l.* mattress. **2.** (*zwykle pl.*) (= *pościel*) bedding.

pierniczek *mi* **-czk-** *Gen.* **-a** *kulin.* small ginger bread.

pierniczyć *ipf. pot.* **1.** (= *bredzić*) talk rubbish. **2.** (= *olewać*) not give a damn (*coś* about sth); **pierniczę to!** I don't give a damn about it!; **ja pierniczę!** holy cow! ~ **się** *ipf. pot.* **1.** (= *mylić się*) muddle up. **2.** (= *psuć się*) break down; **cholera, znów mi się komputer pierniczy** damn, the computer's on the fritz again.

piernik *mi Gen.* **-a** **1.** *kulin.* (*ciast(k)o*) gingerbread; **co ma piernik do wiatraka?** what's that got to do with the price of tea in China? **2.** *pog.* (= *stary mężczyzna*) old buffer, old fart.

pierogi *pl. Gen.* **-ów** *kulin.* pierogi, pirogi, piroshki, pirogen; **pierogi z mięsem** meat pierogi; **leniwe pierogi** dumplings made from flour, cottage cheese and eggs; **ruskie pierogi** pierogi with potato and cottage cheese filling.

pieróg *mi* **-o-** *Gen.* **-a** **1.** *kulin.* pirog. **2.** *hist.* (*kapelusz*) tricorne, tricorn.

pierrot *mp* (= *pajac*) Pierrot.

piersiasta *f. Gen.* **-ej** *pot.* busty, chesty, top-heavy, buxom.

piersiowy *a.* pectoral; **głos piersiowy** chest voice; **klatka piersiowa** *anat.* ribcage, chest; **kręg piersiowy** *anat.* dorsal *l.* thoracic vertebra; **mięsień piersiowy** *zwł. orn.* pectoral muscle; **płetwa piersiowa** *icht.* pectoral fin.

piersiówka *f. Gen.pl.* **-ek** *pot.* hip/chest flask.

pierś *f.* **1.** (*u człowieka, u zwierząt*) chest, breast; **owłosiona pierś** hairy chest; **uderzać się w piersi** beat one's breast; **biec co tchu w piersiach** run like a flash, bolt; **braknie mi tchu w piersiach** I'm breathless; **żyć pełną piersią** live one's life to the fullest; **zapierać komuś dech w piersiach** take one's breath away. **2.** (*u kobiety*) breast; **karmić piersią** breast-feed; **odstawić dziecko od piersi** wean a baby; **rak piersi** *pat.* breast cancer. **3.** *kulin.* (*mięso drobiowe*) breast.

pierścienice *pl. Gen.* **-c** *zool.* annelids, annelidans (*Annelida*).

pierścieniopłat *mi lotn.* coleopter.

pierścieniowaty *a.* **1.** (= *mający kształt pierścienia*) annular, ring-shaped; **chrząstka pierścieniowata** *anat.* cricoid. **2.** (= *mający ciało z pierścieni*) annelid, annelidan.

pierścieniowy *a.* **1.** (*o kształcie pierścienia*) annular, ring-shaped; **mgławica pierścieniowa** *astron.* annular nebula; **związek pierścieniowy** *chem.* cyclic compound. **2.** (*z pierścieniami*) ringed; **wał pierścieniowy** *roln.* cultipacker, corrugater roller.

pierścień *mi Gen.* **-a** **1.** *lit.* (*na palcu*) ring; **gonić do pierścienia** *hist.* tilt at the ring. **2.** (= *pukiel włosów*) ringlet. **3.** (*np. utworzony przez ludzi, przedmioty*) ring. **4.** *chem.* ring. **5.** *fiz.* halo. **6.** *techn.* ring, collar; **pierścień tłokowy** piston ring. **7.** *leśn.* annual *l.* tree ring. **8.** *zool.* segment.

pierścionek *mi* **-nk-** *Gen.* **-a** **1.** (*na palcu*) ring; **pierścionek zaręczynowy** engagement ring; **pierścionek z brylantem** diamond ring; **wymienić pierścionki** exchange rings, get engaged. **2.** (= *pukiel włosów*) ringlet.

pierwiastek *mi* **-tk-** *Gen.* **-a** **1.** (= *element*) element. **2.** *chem.* element; **pierwiastek czysty** *l.* **prosty** pure *l.* simple element; **pierwiastek dwuwartościowy** dyad; **pierwiastek izotopowy** isotopic element; **pierwiastek jednowartościowy** monad; **pierwiastek mieszany** mixed element; **pierwiastek niemetaliczny** non-metal; **pierwiastek promieniotwórczy** radioactive element; **pierwiastek śladowy** trace element; **pierwiastek wskaźnikowy** tracer (element), label; **układ okresowy pierwiastków** periodic table. **3.** *mat.* root; **pierwiastek kwadratowy/sześcienny z dwóch**

square/cube root of two; **pierwiastek równania** root of an equation. **4.** *jęz.* root.

pierwiastka *f. Gen.pl.* **-ek** primipara.

pierwiastkować *ipf. mat.* extract the root of a number.

pierwiastkowanie *n. mat.* evolution.

pierwiastkowy *a. jęz. mat.* radical.

pierwiosnek *mi* **-nk-** *Gen.* **-a** *bot.* primrose, primula (*Primula*); **pierwiosnek lekarski** cowslip (*Primula officinalis l. veris*). — *ma* **-nk-** *orn.* chiffchaff (*Phylloscopus collybita*).

pierwociny *pl. Gen.* **-n** *lit.* **1.** (= *zalążki*) origins, inception. **2.** (= *pierwsze utwory*) early writings.

pierwodruk *mi* (= *pierwsze wydanie*) first edition.

pierwokup *mi prawn.* preemption; **prawo pierwokupu** preemption, right of preemption.

pierwopis *mi* original manuscript.

pierworodny *a.* firstborn; **syn pierworodny** firstborn son; **grzech pierworodny** *teol.* the original sin.

pierworódka *f. zob.* **pierwiastka**.

pierworództwo *n. prawn.* primogeniture.

pierworys *mi* original sketch *l.* outline.

pierwotniak *ma zool.* protozoan (*Protozoa*).

pierwotnie *adv. lit.* originally, primarily, initially.

pierwotny *a.* **1.** (= *dawny*) primordial, primeval, primal; **las pierwotny** primeval forest. **2.** (= *prymitywny*) primitive; **człowiek pierwotny** primitive man; **narzędzia pierwotne** primitive tools; **kultura pierwotna** primitive culture. **3.** (= *początkowy*) initial, original, incipient. **4.** (= *wcześniejszy, ważniejszy*) primary; **funkcja pierwotna** *mat.* primitive.

pierwowzór *mi* **-o-** **1.** (= *prototyp*) prototype. **2.** (*o utworze literackim*) (= *oryginał*) original.

pierwsza *f. Gen.* **-ej** (*godzina*) one o'clock, one; **o pierwszej** at one; **punkt pierwsza** one sharp; **przed pierwszą** before one; **po pierwszej** after one; **o wpół do pierwszej** at half past twelve.

pierwszak *mp pl.* **-i** *szkoln., pot.* first-grader, first-grade student; *zwł. Br.* first-former.

pierwszeństwo *n.* **1.** priority, precedence; **zdobyć** *l.* **zyskać palmę pierwszeństwa** bear the palm, carry off the palm; **bezwzględne pierwszeństwo** top priority; **dawać pierwszeństwo rzeczom najważniejszym** put first things first; **mieć pierwszeństwo przed kimś/czymś** take precedence over sb/sth, have priority over sb/sth. **2.** (*w przepisach drogowych*) right of way; **wymusić pierwszeństwo przejazdu** violate the right of way; **ustąpić pierwszeństwa przejazdu** yield the right of way.

pierwszoklasista *mp zob.* **pierwszak**.

pierwszoklasistka *f. Gen.pl.* **-ek** *zob.* **pierwszak**.

pierwszoligowy *a. sport* first-league.

pierwszomajowy *a.* May-Day; **pochód pierwszomajowy** May-Day celebration.

pierwszoplanowy *a.* **1.** (= *bardzo ważny*) crucial, vital, of utmost importance, of paramount importance. **2.** (= *odgrywający główną rolę*) leading; **pierwszoplanowy aktor** leading role;

pierwszoplanowy bohater main protagonist. **3.** (= *na pierwszym planie*) foreground.

pierwszoroczny *a. uniw., szkoln.* first-year.

pierwszorzędnie *adv.* splendidly, excellently, exquisitely.

pierwszorzędny *a.* splendid, first-rate, superb, excellent; **pierwszorzędna jakość** top quality; **pierwszorzędny pomysł** brilliant idea; **pierwszorzędna restauracja** top-class restaurant.

pierwszy *a.* **1.** first; **pierwsza rocznica** first anniversary; **pierwsza klasa** *szkoln.* first grade; *zwł. Br.* first form; **pierwszy raz** first time; **pierwsze piętro** second floor; *Br.* first floor; **pierwszy września** the first of September; **pierwsza wojna światowa** *hist.* World War One, the First World War; **pierwsza pomoc** first aid; **pierwsze śniadanie** breakfast; **forma w pierwszej osobie liczby pojedynczej** *gram.* first person singular; **pisać w pierwszej osobie** write in the first person; **równanie pierwszego stopnia** *mat.* linear equation; **pierwszy oficer** *żegl.* first mate, first officer; **Pierwsza Dama** *polit.* First Lady; **pierwsze skrzypce** *muz.* first violin; **pierwszy bieg** *mot.* first gear; **stawiać pierwsze kroki** take one's *l.* the first steps; **zrobić pierwszy krok** make the first move; **pierwszy lepszy** *l.* **z brzegu** any (old) one, whichever, random; **na pierwszy rzut oka** at first glance, on the face of it; **w pierwszej chwili** at first, in the first moment; **z pierwszej ręki** firsthand; **relacja z pierwszej ręki** inside story; **po pierwsze** firstly, first of all, first and foremost; **grać pierwsze skrzypce** play the first fiddle; **posłać kogoś na pierwszy ogień** send sb to the frontline; **miłość od pierwszego wejrzenia** love at first sight; **pierwsze wrażenie** first impression; **ciekawość - pierwszy stopień do piekła** curiosity killed the cat; **kto pierwszy, ten lepszy** first come, first served; **pierwsze koty za płoty** the first try doesn't count, the first attempt is just for practice. **2.** (= *taki, przed którym nie było innych podobnych*) first, fresh, new; **nie pierwszej młodości** past one's prime, well on in years; **nie pierwszej czystości** soiled; **przełamać pierwsze lody** break the ice; **zaspokoić pierwszy głód** take the edge off one's appetite; **pani pierwsza!** after you! **3.** (= *zasadniczy, główny*) main, chief, primary, principal; **pierwszy plan** *film* foreground; **artykuły pierwszej potrzeby** necessities; **liczba pierwsza** *mat.* prime number; **wysuwać coś na pierwszy plan** put sth first. **4.** (= *najlepszy*) top, finest, first-rate; **wagon pierwszej klasy** *kol.* first-class car; **zająć pierwsze miejsce** *zwł. sport* come in first, be the first; **pierwsza liga** *sport* first league; **lody - pierwsza klasa!** *pot.* delicious ice-cream!; **pierwsza nagroda** first prize. — *mi* first (*day of a month*); **umówić się z kimś na pierwszego czerwca** arrange a meeting with sb on the first of June; **skończyć pracę do pierwszego** finish work by the first.

pierwszyzna *f. arch.* novelty, thing happening for the first time; **dla mnie to nie pierwszyzna** *pot.* I've been through that before, I've done this before, that's nothing new to me, this isn't the first time.

pierzastodzielny *a. bot.* pinnate.

pierzasty *a.* **1.** (= *z piórami*) fledged, feathered. **2.** (= *z piór*) feather; **wachlarz z piór** feather fan. **3.** (= *podobny do piór*) feathery; **chmura** *l.* **obłok pierzasty** *meteor.* cirrus. **4.** *bot.* pinnate; **liść pierzasty** pinnate leaf.

pierzchać *ipf.* **1.** (= *zmykać*) (*o ludziach*) take (to) flight; (*o zwierzętach*) scamper away, flee. **2.** *przen.* (= *rozwiać się*) dissipate, dispel.

pierzchliwy *a.* jittery, jumpy; (*o zwierzynie, zwierzętach*) skittish.

pierzchnąć *pf.* -**ij 1.** *zob.* **pierzchać. 2.** (*o skórze, cerze*) chap.

pierze *n.* **1.** *orn.* plumage, feathers. **2.** (*w kołdrze, poduszce*) feather; **skubać pierze** strip feathers.

pierzeja *f. bud.* frontage.

pierzga *f. pszczelarstwo* beebread.

pierzyć się *ipf. orn.* molt.

pierzyna *f.* **1.** (*do przykrycia*) eiderdown. **2.** *przen.* (= *pokrywa*) cover, layer; **pierzyna świeżego śniegu** layer of fresh snow.

pies *ma* **ps-** *Dat.* -**u** *zool., kynol.* dog (*Canis familiaris*); **pies pokojowy** pet dog; **pies podwórzowy** bandog; **pies gończy** *myśl.* hound; **pies myśliwski** *myśl.* hunting dog; **pies pasterski** sheep dog; **pies rasowy** pedigree dog; **pies latający** *zool.* Malayan *l.* large flying fox (*Pteropus vampyrus*); **pies morski** *zool.* common seal (*Phoca vitulina*); **wierny jak pies** as faithful as a dog; **żyć jak pies z kotem** fight like cats and dogs; **to wszystko zda się psu na budę** it's all of no use; **pogoda jest pod psem** wretched weather; **czuję się jak zbity pies** I feel like I've been (put) through the wringer; **jak psu z gardła wyjęte** *pot.* crumpled, spindled and mutilated; **pies na kobiety** ladykiller, scorer, playboy; **ni pies, ni wydra** neither fish nor fowl; **pies z kulawą nogą nie przyjdzie** not a soul is coming; **wieszać na kimś psy** run sb down, slander sb; **zdechł pies!** *pot.* it's a lost cause!, it's a total loss!; **zejść na psy** go to the dogs; **łżesz jak pies** you're lying like a dog, you lie like a dog; **pies ci mordę lizał** *pot.* take a hike, get lost; **nie dla psa kiełbasa** this is too good for the likes of you; **ty parszywy psie!** you dirty dog!

piesek *ma* -**sk-** doggy, little dog; **piesek preriowy** *l.* **stepowy** *zool.* prairie dog (*Cynomys*); **francuski piesek** coddle.

piesiec *ma Gen.* **pieśca** *zool.* arctic fox, white fox (*Alopex lagopus*).

pieski *a. pot.* darn, damn, shitty; **pieskie życie** shitty life.

piestrzenica *f. bot.* **piestrzenica kasztanowata** false morel (*Gyromitra esculenta*).

pieszczoch *mp pl.* -**y** pet.

pieszczota *f.* caress.

pieszczotka *f. Gen.pl.* -**ek** (= *pieszczota*) caress.

pieszczotliwie *adv.* tenderly, caressingly, gently.

pieszczotliwość *f.* tenderness.

pieszczotliwy *a.* tender, gentle, cuddly, cuddlesome; **pieszczotliwy dotyk** tender touch; **pieszczotliwy głos** gentle voice; **pieszczotliwa nazwa** pet name.

pieszo *adv.* on foot; **iść pieszo** go on foot, walk.

pieszy *a.* **1.** (= *idący piechotą*) pedestrian; **pieszy turysta** hiker, backpacker; **piesza wycieczka** hike. **2.** *wojsk.* (= *związany z piechotą*) infantry; **pieszy żołnierz** infantryman. **3.** (= *do chodzenia, nie jeżdżenia*) foot, pedestrian. – *mp* pedestrian; **przejście dla pieszych** pedestrian crossing.

pieścić *ipf.* -**szczę** -**ścisz** fondle, caress, cuddle. ~ **się** *ipf.* **1.** (= *okazywać czułość*) pet, caress, cuddle; **nie pieścić się z kimś** be hard on sb. **2.** (= *oszczędzać się*) pamper o.s. **3.** (= *mówić jak dziecko*) use baby talk.

pieśniarka *f. Gen.pl.* -**ek** *zob.* **pieśniarz.**

pieśniarstwo *n.* singing.

pieśniarz *mp* **1.** (= *śpiewak*) songster, singer. **2.** (= *kompozytor pieśni*) songster, song writer.

pieśń *f.* **1.** (*do śpiewania*) song; **pieśń ludowa** folk song. **2.** (*wiersz*) song.

Pieta, pieta *f. rel., sztuka* Pietà.

pieter *mi* -**tr-** **mieć pietra** be shit-scared; **dostać pietra** get the wind up; **napędzić komuś pietra** scare sb shitless.

pietruszka *f. Gen.pl.* -**ek** *bot.* parsley (*Petroselinum sativum*); **natka pietruszki** parsley.

pietyzm *mi* reverence; **robić coś z pietyzmem** do sth with reverence.

piewca *mp lit.* **1.** eulogist. **2.** (= *poeta*) poet singer.

piewik *ma ent.* cicada (*Cicada*).

pieza *f. fiz.* pieze.

piezoelektryczność *f. fiz.* piezoelectricity.

piezoelektryczny *a. fiz.* piezoelectric.

piezoelektryk *mi Gen.* -**a** *fiz.* piezoelectric crystal.

piezometr *mi fiz.* piezometer.

pięcioaktowy *a.* five-act; **sztuka pięcioaktowa** five-act play.

pięcioboczny *a.* pentagonal.

pięcioboista *mp sport* pentathlete.

pięciobok *mi* pentagon.

pięciobój *mi* -**o-** *Gen.pl.* -**ów** *sport* pentathlon; **pięciobój nowoczesny** modern pentathlon.

pięciodniowy *a.* **1.** (= *trwający pięć dni*) five-day; **pięciodniowa konferencja** five-day conference. **2.** (= *w wieku pięciu dni*) five-day-old; **pięciodniowe dziecko** five-day-old baby.

pięciodrzwiowy *a.* five-door.

pięciogodzinny *a.* five-hour; **pięciogodzinne zebranie** five-hour meeting.

pięciogroszowy *a.* five-groszy; **moneta pięciogroszowa** five-groszy coin.

pięciogroszówka *f. Gen.pl.* -**ek** five-groszy coin.

pięciogwiazdkowy *a.* five-star; **pięciogwiazdkowy hotel** five-star hotel.

pięciokąt *mi Gen.* -**a** pentagon; **pięciokąt gwiaździsty** pentagram, pentacle, pentangle.

pięciokątny *a.* pentagonal.

pięciokilogramowy *a.* five-kilogram.

pięciokilometrowy *a.* five-kilometer.

pięciokilowy *a. pot.* five-kilo.

pięcioklasowy *a. szkoln.* five-grade; *zwł. Br.* five-form; **pięcioklasowa szkoła** five-grade school.

pięciokondygnacyjny *a.* five-floor, five-story.

pięciokrotnie *adv.* five times.

pięciokrotny *a.* fivefold, quintuple, five-times; **kwiat pięciokrotny** *bot.* pentamerous flower.

pięcioksiąg *mi* -ę- *Bibl.* Pentateuch.

pięciolatek *mp* -tk- *pl.* -i (= *pięcioletni chłopiec*) five-year-old (boy). – *ma* -tk- (= *pięcioletnie zwierzę*) five-year-old (animal).

pięciolatka *f. Gen.pl.* -ek **1.** *zob.* **pięciolatek**. **2.** five years, five-year period.

pięciolecie *n. Gen.pl.* -i **1.** (*okres*) five years, five-year period. **2.** (*rocznica*) fifth anniversary.

pięcioletni *a.* **1.** (= *trwający pięć lat*) five-year; **studia pięcioletnie** five-year (course of) studies; **pięcioletni okres spłat kredytu** five-year loan repayment period. **2.** (= *w wieku pięciu lat*) five-year-old; **pięcioletnia dziewczynka** five-year-old girl; **pięcioletni pies** five-year-old dog.

pięciolinia *f. Gen.* -ii *muz.* staff, stave.

pięciometrowy *a.* five-meter.

pięciomiesięczny *a.* **1.** (= *trwający pięć miesięcy*) five-month; **pięciomiesięczny urlop** five-month leave. **2.** (= *w wieku pięciu miesięcy*) five-month-old; **pięciomiesięczne dziecko** five-month-old baby.

pięciominutowy *a.* five-minute; **przerwa pięciominutowa** five-minute break.

pięciooodcinkowy *a.* (*o serialu*) five-episode; (*o powieści*) five-part; (*o podróży*) five-stage.

pięciopalcowy *a.* five-fingered, pentadactyl.

pięciopalczasty *a.* five-fingered, pentadactyl; **pięciopalczasta rękawica** five-fingered glove.

pięciopiętrowy *a.* five-floor, five-story.

pięciopokojowy *a.* five-room; **mieszkanie pięciopokojowe** five-room apartment.

pięcioraczki *pl. Gen.* -ów quintuplets.

pięcioramienny *a.* five-arm; **gwiazda pięcioramienna** five-pointed star.

pięciornik *mi Gen.* -a *bot.* cinquefoil, five-leaf (*Potentilla*).

pięcioro *num. decl. like n.* -rg- five.

pięciostopniowy *a.* **1.** (= *liczący pięć stopni w jakiejś skali*) five degrees'; **skala pięciostopniowa** *muz.* pentatonic scale. **2.** (= *mający pięć etapów, członów itp.*) five-grade; five-tier; five-part; five-stage.

pięciozłotowy *a.* five-zloty; **moneta pięciozłotowa** five-zloty coin.

pięciozłotówka *f. Gen.pl.* -ek five-zloty coin.

pięciusetzłotowy *a.* five-hundred-zloty; **banknot pięciusetzłotowy** five-hundred-zloty bill.

pięć *num. Ins.* -oma *l.* -u **1.** (= *liczba 5*) five; **za pięć dwunasta** at five to twelve; *przen.* at the eleventh hour; **ni w pięć, ni w dziewięć** a propos of nothing in particular. **2.** *szkoln., uniw.* (= *ocena bdb*) A; **zdać na pięć** pass *l.* come through with flying colours, get an A, ace (*a test, exam, etc.*).

pięćdziesiąt *num.* -ęci- *Ins.* -oma *l.* -u fifty.

pięćdziesiątka *f. Gen.pl.* -ek **1.** (= *zbiór 50 egzemplarzy*) fifty, collection of fifty, batch of fifty. **2.** *pot.* (*moneta, banknot*) fifty-zloty coin *l.* bill. **3.** *pot.* (= *pięćdziesiąt lat*) fifty (years of age). **4.**

(*pokój, autobus, tramwaj itp. nr 50*) fifty, number fifty.

pięćdziesiąty *a.* fiftieth; **pięćdziesiąta rocznica** fiftieth anniversary; **lata pięćdziesiąte** the fifties.

pięćdziesięciogroszówka *f. Gen.pl.* -ek fifty-groszy coin.

pięćdziesięciokilkuletni *a.* **1.** (= *w wieku pięćdziesięciu kilku lat*) fifty-odd-year-old, fifty something; **pięćdziesięciokilkuletni człowiek** fifty-something-year-old man, man in his fifties. **2.** (= *trwający pięćdziesiąt kilka lat*) fifty-odd-year(-long).

pięćdziesięciolecie *n. Gen.pl.* -i **1.** (*rocznica*) fiftieth anniversary. **2.** (*okres*) fifty years.

pięćdziesięcioletni *a.* **1.** (= *w wieku pięćdziesięciu lat*) fifty-year-old; **pięćdziesięcioletni mężczyzna** fifty-year-old man. **2.** (= *trwający pięćdziesiąt lat*) fifty-year(-long).

pięćdziesięcioro *num. decl. like n.* -rg- fifty.

pięćdziesięciozłotowy *a.* fifty-zloty; **banknot pięćdziesięciozłotowy** fifty-zloty bill.

pięćdziesięciozłotówka *f. Gen.pl.* -ek fifty-zloty bill.

pięćset *num.* pięć- *decl. like num.,* -set *indecl.* five hundred.

pięćsetka *f. Gen.pl.* -ek five-hundred(-zloty/dollar/etc.) bill.

pięćsetlecie *n. Gen.pl.* -i **1.** (*rocznica*) five-hundredth anniversary, quincentenary. **2.** (*okres*) five hundred years.

pięćsetletni *a.* **1.** (= *w wieku 500 lat*) five-hundred-year-old. **2.** (= *trwający 500 lat*) five-hundred-year(-long).

pięćsetny *a.* five-hundredth.

pięćsetzłotowy *a.* five-hundred-zloty; **banknot pięćsetzłotowy** five-hundred-zloty bill.

pięćsetzłotówka *f. Gen.pl.* -ek five-hundred-zloty bill.

piędź *f. pl.* -e *l.* -i inch of ground; **bronić każdej piędzi ziemi** defend every single inch of ground; **walczyć o każdą piędź ziemi** fight for every single inch of ground.

pięknie *adv.* **1.** beautifully, gorgeously, prettily; **wyglądać pięknie** look beautiful, look gorgeous; **pięknie dziękuję** thanks a lot, thanks so much, thanks a bunch; **wszystko pięknie, ale...** well and good, but... **2.** *iron.* great; **no pięknie!** now, that's just great!; **pięknie się spisałeś!** that's just great!, you couldn't have done a worse job of it! **3.** (= *idealnie*) perfectly, ideally.

pięknieć *ipf.* grow pretty, become more and more *l.* increasingly beautiful *l.* lovely.

piękniś *mp pog.* fop, dandy, popinjay.

piękno *n.* beauty.

piękność *f.* **1.** (= *bycie pięknym*) beauty. **2.** (= *piękna osoba, zwł. kobieta*) beauty; **salon piękności** beauty parlor; **konkurs piękności** beauty contest *l.* pageant.

piękny *a.* **1.** (= *urodziwy*) beautiful, gorgeous; **piękny dzień** beautiful day; **piękna pogoda** nice weather, fine weather; **literatura piękna** belles-lettres; **sztuki piękne** fine arts; **akademia sztuk pięknych** academy *l.* school of fine arts;

płeć piękna the fair sex; **pewnego pięknego dnia** one fine day; **zrobić coś na piękne oczy** do sth just for sb's good looks; **odpłacić komuś pięknym za nadobne** give sb tit for tat, pay sb back in kind. **2.** (= *najlepszy*) excellent, finest, superb; **piękny wynik** excellent result; **piękny wiek** venerable age. **3.** *iron.* fine, great; **piękne rzeczy!** fine!, beautiful!, just great!

pięściarski *a. sport* boxing; **pojedynek pięściarski** boxing match.

pięściarstwo *n. sport* boxing.

pięściarz *mp sport* boxer.

pięść *f. pl.* **-i** *l.* **-e** fist; **walka na pięści** fistfight; **uderzyć pięścią w stół** thump the table; **zacisnąć pięści** clench one's fists; **prawo pięści** might is right, law of the jungle; **pasuje jak pięść do nosa** it doesn't fit here, it won't work here.

pięta *f.* **1.** (*część stopy*) heel; **pięta achillesowa** *l.* **Achillesa** Achilles' heel; **deptać komuś po piętach** be hot on sb's heels, trail hard on sb's heels; **nie dorastać komuś do pięt** be no match for sb; **poszło mu w pięty** it cut him to the quick; **obrócić się na pięcie** turn on one's heel. **2.** (*w bucie, skarpecie, pończosze*) heel. **3.** *żegl.* heel.

pięterko *n. Gen.pl.* **-ek** mezzanine.

piętka *f. Gen.pl.* **-ek** (*u stopy*) heel; **gonić w piętkę** be losing it, be becoming unhinged *l.* unglued.

piętnasta *f. Gen.* **-ej** (*godzina*) three p.m.

piętnastka *f. Gen.pl.* **-ek 1.** (= *liczba 15*) fifteen. **2.** (= *tramwaj, autobus, dom, pokój nr 15*) fifteen, number fifteen; **do szpitala dojedziesz piętnastką** the fifteen takes you to the hospital, streetcar/bus, etc. number fifteen takes you to the hospital; **mieszkamy pod piętnastką** our house *l.* apartment number is fifteen. **3.** *pot.* (*dziewczyna*) fifteen. **4.** *pot.* (*urodziny*) fifteenth birthday. **5.** (*wielkość czcionki*) fifteen-point font; **pisać piętnastką** write using a fifteen-point font.

piętnastodniowy *a.* **1.** (= *trwający piętnaście dni*) fifteen-day, fifteen days'; **piętnastodniowy urlop** fifteen-day holiday. **2.** (= *mający piętnaście dni*) fifteen-day-old; **piętnastodniowy osesek** fifteen-day-old baby.

piętnastolatek *mp* **-tk-** *pl.* **-i** (= *piętnastoletni chłopiec*) fifteen-year-old (boy). – *ma* **-tk-** (= *piętnastoletnie zwierzę*) fifteen-year-old (animal).

piętnastolatka *f. Gen.pl.* **-ek** *zob.* **piętnastolatek.**

piętnastolecie *n. Gen.pl.* **-i 1.** (*okres*) fifteen years, fifteen-year period. **2.** (*rocznica*) fifteenth anniversary.

piętnastoletni *a.* **1.** (= *mający piętnaście lat*) fifteen-year-old. **2.** (= *trwający piętnaście lat*) fifteen-year, fifteen years'; **piętnastoletni wyrok** fifteen years in prison.

piętnastomiesięczny *a.* **1.** (= *trwający piętnaście miesięcy*) fifteen-month, fifteen months'. **2.** (= *mający piętnaście miesięcy*) fifteen-month-old; **piętnastomiesięczne dziecko** fifteen-month-old baby.

piętnastominutowy *a.* fifteen-minute, fifteen

minutes'; **przerwa piętnastominutowa** fifteen-minute break.

piętnastowieczny *a.* fifteenth-century; **piętnastowieczny kościół** fifteenth-century church, church from the fifteenth century.

piętnasty *a.* fifteenth; **godzina piętnasta** three p.m.

piętnaście *num.* **-st-** *Ins.* **-oma** *l.* **-u** fifteen.

piętnaścioro *num. decl. like n.* **-rg-** fifteen.

piętno *n.* **1.** (= *znak*) brand, stamp. **2.** (= *cecha charakterystyczna*) stamp, imprint; **wycisnąć/odcisnąć na kimś/czymś swoje piętno** leave one's stamp *l.* mark on sb/sth. **3.** (= *znamię*) birthmark.

piętnować *ipf.* **1.** (= *potępiać, ganić*) stigmatise, brand, condemn. **2.** (= *znakować*) brand, mark; **znakować zwierzęta** brand animals.

piętowy *a. anat.* heel; **kość piętowa** calcaneus.

piętro *n. Gen.pl.* **-er 1.** (= *kondygnacja*) story, floor; **pierwsze piętro** second floor; *Br.* first floor. **2.** *bot., leśn.* belt, layer, zone. **3.** *geol.* stage. **4.** *górn.* level, stage.

piętrowy *a.* storied; **piętrowy dom** storied house; **pięciopiętrowy dom** five-story house; **autobus piętrowy** double-decker; **łóżko piętrowe** bunk beds; **ułamek piętrowy** *mat.* complex fraction.

piętrus *mi Gen.* **-a** *pot.* (= *autobus piętrowy*) double-decker.

piętrzyć *ipf.* pile up; **piętrzyć wodę** dam up, bank up; **piętrzyć trudności** pile up difficulties. **~ się** *ipf.* **1.** tower, rise; **piętrzą się przeszkody** difficulties are piling up. **2.** (= *nawarstwiać się*) accumulate, heap up, pile up.

pif-paf *int.* bang bang.

Pigmej *mp Gen.pl.* **-ów 1.** Pygmy, Pigmy. **2.** (= *niski człowiek*) pygmy, pigmy.

pigment *mi biol., chem.* pigment.

pigmentacja *f. biol.* pigmentation.

pigmentacyjny *a. biol.* pigmentary.

pigmentowy *a. biol.* pigmentary.

piguła *f.* **1.** ball; **śniegowa piguła** snowball. **2.** *pot.* (= *pielęgniarka*) nurse.

pigułka *f. Gen.pl.* **-ek 1.** pill; **pigułka antykoncepcyjna** contraception pill, the pill; **brać pigułki antykoncepcyjne** be on the pill; **pigułka nasenna** sleeping pill; **przełknąć gorzką pigułkę** *przen.* swallow a bitter pill. **2.** (= *kulka*) (small) ball.

pigwa *f. bot.* **1.** (*krzew, drzewko*) quince (*Cydonia oblonga*). **2.** (*owoc*) quince.

pigwowiec *mi* **-wc-** *Gen.* **-a** *bot.* Japanese flowering quince (*Chaenomeles japonica*).

pijacki *a.* drunken, boozy; **pijacka impreza** bender, bash, guzzle.

pijaczek *mp* **-czk-** *pl.* **-i** *pog.* boozer, wino, lush.

pijaczka *f. Gen.pl.* **-ek** *zob.* **pijak.**

pijaczyna *mp pog.* boozer, guzzler, stiff.

pijać *ipf.* drink; **zwykle pijamy kawę na śniadanie** we usually have coffee for *l.* with breakfast.

pijak *mp pl.* **-cy** *l.* **-i** drunkard, boozer, lush, chain-drinker; **prowadzić po pijaku** *pot.* drive drunk, drive under the influence, drink and drive.

pijalnia *f. Gen.pl.* **-i** *l.* **-ń** (*w uzdrowisku*) pump room; **pijalnia piwa** beer house, brew-pub, beer hall.

pijanica *mp pog.* guzzler, wino, lush.

pijany *a.* drunk, boozed up, loaded, buzzed; **pijany jak bela** plastered, tight as a drum; **po pijanemu** under the influence (of alcohol); **robić coś po pijanemu** do sth while drunk, do sth while boozed up; **jazda po pijanemu** drunk driving; **pijany sukcesem/szczęściem** *przen.* drunk with success/happiness.

pijaństwo *n.* **1.** (= *opilstwo*) alcoholism, alcohol addiction. **2.** (= *libacja*) boozing, drinking, chain-drinking, binge, drinking spree.

pijar *mp rz.-kat.* Piarist.

pijarski *a. rz.-kat.* Piarist.

pijatyka *f.* bash, drinking spree.

pijawka *f. Gen.pl.* **-ek 1.** *zool.* leech (*Hirudo medicinalis*). **2.** *przen.* bloodsucker, leech.

piję *itd. ipf. zob.* **pić**.

pijus *mp pl.* **-y** *pot.* boozer, wino, loadie.

pik¹ *mi Gen.* **-a** *karty* spade; **as pik** ace of spades.

pik² *mi Gen.* **-a** *l.* **-u** *żegl.* peak (*of sail*).

pik³ *int. indecl.* (*o sercu*) beat; (*o urządzeniu*) beep.

pika¹ *f. tk.* piqué, pique.

pika² *f. hist.* (*broń*) pike, lance.

pikać *ipf.* **1.** (*o ptakach*) chirp; (*o urządzeniach*) beep; **ani piknął** he didn't (even) say a word. **2.** *pot.* (*o sercu*) beat.

pikador *mp* picador.

pikanteria *f. Gen.* **-ii** spice; **dodawać czemuś pikanterii** spice sth up.

pikantność *f.* piquancy, spiciness, zest.

pikantny *a.* **1.** (*o zupie, sałatce*) (= *ostry*) hot, spicy, piquant. **2.** (= *nieprzyzwoity*) spicy, bawdy, risqué; **pikantny dowcip** bawdy *l.* dirty *l.* off-color joke; **pikantna historia** risqué story.

pikap *mi mot.* pick-up.

Pikardia *f. Gen.* **-ii** *hist., geogr.* Picardy.

pikfał *mi żegl.* peak halyard.

pikielhauba *f. hist.* spiked helmet.

pikieta *f.* **1.** *hist.* (*straż*) picket, sentry. **2.** (= *demonstracja*) demonstration, picket.

pikietować *ipf.* (= *demonstrować*) picket.

pikle *pl. Gen.* **-i** *kulin.* pickles.

pikling *ma kulin.* bloater.

piknąć *pf.* **-ij** *zob.* **pikać**.

piknik *mi* picnic.

piknikowy *a.* picnic; **kosz piknikowy** picnic basket.

piknometr *mi fiz.* pycnometer.

pikolo *n. Gen.pl.* **-i** *muz.* piccolo.

pikować *ipf.* **1.** (= *obszywać*) quilt. **2.** (*o samolocie*) nosedive, nose-dive. **3.** *ogr.* plant out.

pikowany *a.* (*o kołdrze*) quilted.

pikowy *a. karty* spade; **as pikowy** ace of spades; **walet pikowy** knight of spades.

pikrynowy *a. chem.* picric; **kwas pikrynowy** picric acid.

piktografia *f. Gen.* **-ii** picture writing, pictography.

piktograficzny *a.* pictographic.

piktogram *mi* pictograph, pictogram.

pilak *ma icht.* black-mouthed dogfish (*Pristiurus melanostomus*).

pilarka *f. techn.* sawing machine.

pilarz *mp* (*robotnik*) sawer, sawman. – *ma ent.* sawfly (*Tenthredinidae*).

pilaster *mi* **-tr-** *Gen.* **-u** *l.* **-a** *bud.* pilaster.

pilastrowy *a. bud.* pilaster.

pilaw *mi Gen.* **-u** *kulin.* pilaf, pilaff, pilau.

pilchowate *pl. Gen.* **-ych** *zool.* dormice (*Gliridae*).

pilić *ipf. pot.* press, rush.

pilniczek *mi* **-czk-** *Gen.* **-a** file; **pilniczek do paznokci** nail file.

pilnie *adv.* **1.** (= *z uwagą*) attentively, carefully, intently; **uczyć się pilnie** study hard, study dilligently. **2.** (= *niezwłocznie*) urgently; **pilnie poszukiwany** urgently needed.

pilnik *mi Gen.* **-a** file; **pilnik do paznokci** nail file.

pilno *adv.* **pilno mi do czegoś** I'm in a hurry to do sth, I'm eager to do sth; **dokąd ci tak pilno?** what's your hurry?, where are you hurrying off to?; **wcale mi nie pilno wracać do pracy** I'm in no great hurry to go back to work.

pilność *f.* diligence, care.

pilnować *ipf.* **1.** (= *strzec, czuwać*) watch, keep an eye on, watch over, take care of, keep tabs on; **pilnować dzieci** watch over the kids, look after the kids; **pilnować domu** mind the house; **pilnować psa** mind the dog; **pilnować porządku** maintain order; **pilnować studentów na egzaminie** supervise students during an exam; **pilnuj swego nosa!** mind your own business! **2.** (= *przestrzegać*) maintain, abide, obey; **pilnować przepisów** abide by the rules. ~ **się** *ipf.* **1.** (= *czuwać nad sobą, uważać na siebie*) take care of o.s., look after o.s.; (= *kontrolować się*) watch o.s. **2.** (= *pilnować jeden drugiego*) look after each other *l.* one another.

pilny *a.* **1.** (= *niezwłoczny*) urgent, pressing; **pilna sprawa** pressing matter, matter of great urgency. **2.** (= *pracowity*) dilligent, industrious, hard-working. **3.** *przest.* attentive; **słuchać czegoś z pilną uwagą** listen attentively, listen carefully.

pilocik *mi Gen.* **-a** *lotn.* **pilocik spadochronu** auxiliary parachute, pilot parachute.

pilot *mp pl.* **-ci 1.** *lotn.* pilot; **pilot doświadczalny** *l.* **oblatywacz** test pilot; **pilot automatyczny** *l.* **samoczynny** automatic pilot, autopilot; **drugi pilot** co-pilot. **2.** *żegl.* (harbor) pilot; **wziąć na pokład pilota** take on the pilot. **3.** (= *osoba zajmująca się wycieczką*) guide, tourist guide. **4.** *sport* (= *osoba przekazująca kierowcy rajdowemu informacje nt. trasy*) co-driver. – *ma pl.* **-y** *icht.* pilotfish (*Naucrates ductor*). – *mi Gen.* **-a** *pl.* **-y 1.** *el.* (= *zdalne urządzenie do uruchamiania sprzętu radiowo-telewizyjnego*) remote control. **2.** *techn.* guide pin, aligning pin. **3.** *film, telew.* pilot.

pilotaż *mi* **1.** *lotn.* pilotage. **2.** *żegl.* piloting, pilotage. **3.** *meteor.* use of pilot balloons.

pilotażowy *a.* piloting, pilot.

pilotka *f. Gen.pl.* -ek *zob.* **pilot** 1, 2. – *f. (czapka)* (leather) flying cap.

pilotować *ipf.* **1.** *lotn., żegl.* pilot. **2.** *(wyciecz-kę)* guide.

pilotowy *a.* piloting, pilot; **mapa pilotowa** pilot chart; **statek pilotowy** *żegl.* pilot boat; **balonik pilotowy** pilot balloon.

pilśniarka *f. Gen.pl.* -ek *tk.* fulling mill, fuller.

pilśniarz *mp tk.* fuller.

pilśnić *ipf.* -ij *tk.* full.

pilśniowy *a. tk.* felt; **kapelusz pilśniowy** felt hat; **płyta pilśniowa** *bud.* fiberboard, millboard; **konstrukcyjna płyta pilśniowa** *bud.* panel board.

pilśń *f. tk.* felt; **pilśń mineralna** *techn.* rock cork.

pilzner *mi Gen.* -a *kulin. (piwo)* Pilsner, Pilsener.

piła *f.* **1.** *(= narzędzie do przecinania)* saw; **piła ręczna** hand saw; **piła przenośna elektryczna** saber saw; **piła mechaniczna** power saw, sawing machine; **piła do drewna** woodworking saw; **piła do metalu** hacksaw; **piła tarczowa** circular saw, buzz saw; **piła łańcuchowa** chain saw; **piła ramowa** frame saw; **piła taśmowa** band saw; **piła do drzew** felling saw; **piła do szkła** slitting disk. **2.** *muz.* musical saw. **3.** *icht.* sawfish *(Pristis)*. **4.** *przen. (= wymagający nauczyciel)* slave driver.

Piłat *mp hist., Bibl.* Pilate, Pontius Pilate.

piłeczka *f. Gen.pl.* -ek *(do gry)* ball; **piłeczka pingpongowa** table tennis ball, Ping-Pong ball; **odbić piłeczkę** *przen.* pass the buck.

piłka[1] *f. Gen.pl.* -ek *(do gry)* ball; **piłka lekarska** medicine ball; **krótka piłka** fast ball; **ścięta piłka** smash; **wysoka piłka** lob; **piłka setowa** set ball; **piłka meczowa** match ball; **grać w piłkę** play ball; **piłka nożna** soccer; **piłka ręczna** handball; **piłka wodna** water polo; **piłka siatkowa** volleyball.

piłka[2] *f. Gen.pl.* -ek *techn.* saw; **piłka do metalu** hacksaw.

piłkarka *f. Gen.pl.* -ek *zob.* **piłkarz**.

piłkarski *a. sport (= dotyczący piłki nożnej)* soccer, football; **drużyna piłkarska** soccer team, football team; *(= dotyczący piłki ręcznej, wodnej, etc.)* (hand)ball/water polo/etc.

piłkarstwo *n. sport (= gra w piłkę nożną)* soccer, football; *(= gra w piłkę ręczną, wodną itp.)* handball/water polo/etc.

piłkarz *mp sport (= gracz w piłkę nożną)* soccer player, football player, footballer; *(= gracz w piłkę)* (handball/water polo/etc.) player.

piłować *ipf.* **1.** *(= przecinać)* saw. **2.** *(= wygładzać)* file; **piłować paznokcie** file nails. **3.** *żart. (= zanudzać)* bore.

piłowate *pl. Gen.* -ych *icht.* sawfishes *(Pristidae)*.

piment *mi bot.* allspice, pimento.

pimentowy *a. bot.* allspice, pimento; **drzewo pimentowe** allspice *(Pimenta diocia l. officinalis)*; **olejek pimentowy** allspice oil.

PIN *abbr.* PIN *(Personal Identification Number)*.

pinakiel *mi* -kl- *Gen.* -u *l.* -a *bud.* pinnacle.

pinakoteka *f. Gen.pl.* -ek *hist., sztuka* pinacotheca.

pinceta *f.* tweezers.

pinczer *ma kynol.* pinscher.

pinda *f. wulg.* **1.** *(= srom)* cunt, pussy, beaver. **2.** *(= kobieta źle się prowadząca)* slut, bitch, broad.

pindrzyć się *ipf. pot.* get *l.* doll o.s. up, dress o.s. to the nines.

pineska, pinezka *f. Gen.pl.* -ek thumbtack.

ping-pong *mi Gen.* -a *sport* table tennis, Ping-Pong.

pingpongista *mp sport* table tennis player, Ping-Pong player.

pingpongistka *f. Gen.pl.* -ek *zob.* **pingpongista**.

pingpongowy *a. sport* table-tennis, Ping-Pong.

pingwin *ma orn.* penguin *(Sphenisciformes)*.

pinia *f. Gen.* -ii *bot.* stone pine *(Pinus pinea)*.

piniowy *a.* stone-pine; **orzeszki piniowe** stone-pine seeds.

pinocytoza *f. biol.* pinocytosis.

piołun *mi bot.* wormwood *(Artemisia absinthium)*.

piołunowy *a.* wormwood, absinth(e); *(o wódce, likierze)* absinth(e).

piołunówka *f. Gen.pl.* -ek *kulin.* absinth(e).

pion[1] *mi Gen.* -u **1.** *(= linia prostopadła do powierzchni ziemi)* perpendicular, vertical; **ustawić kogoś do pionu** *przen.* give sb a dressing down. **2.** *(przyrząd)* plumb-line; **pion żyroskopowy** *lotn.* gyroscopic vertical. **3.** *(= pionowy odcinek instalacji)* riser; **pion wentylacyjny** vent stack. **4.** *(= dział, resort)* division.

pion[2] *mi Gen.* -a *szachy* pawn.

pionek *mi* -nk- *Gen.* -a **1.** *(w grze planszowej)* pawn; *(w warcabach)* checker. **2.** *(= człowiek, który wykonuje polecenia innych)* puppet.

pionier *mp* **1.** *(= osadnik)* pioneer. **2.** *(= prekursor)* pioneer. **3.** *(w byłym Związku Radzieckim)* Pioneer. **4.** *wojsk. (= żołnierz wojsk inżynieryjnych)* pioneer.

pionierka *f. Gen.pl.* -ek *zob.* **pionier**.

pionierski *a.* pioneering; **pionierska praca** pioneering work.

pionować *ipf. bud.* plumb.

pionowo *adv.* **1.** vertically; **pionowo w górę** rise sheer; **pionowo w dół** descend sheer; **ustawić pionowo** set *l.* put upright. **2.** *(w krzyżówce)* down.

pionowy *a.* vertical, perpendicular; **start pionowy** vertical takeoff; *(o postawie)* upright.

pionowzlot *mi lotn.* vertical takeoff and landing aircraft, VTOL (airplane), vertiplane.

piorun *mi Gen.* -a *l.* -u thunderbolt, thunder; **piorun kulisty** ball lightning; **burza z piorunami** thunderstorm; **runąć jak piorun z jasnego nieba** strike like a lightning; **do pioruna!** holy shit!, holy hell!, hell!; **niech to (jasny) piorun trzaśnie** *l.* **strzeli!** damn!, dammit!, holy shit!

piorunem *adv.* in a jiffy, like a shot.

piorunian *mi chem.* fulminate.

piorunochron *mi* lightning conductor *l.* rod.

piorunować *ipf. (= występować przeciw)* fulminate, inveigh; *(= kląć, przeklinać)* swear, curse;

piorunować wzrokiem give sb a withering *l.* fierce glare.

piorunowy *a.* lightning, thunder; **kwas piorunowy** *chem.* fulminic acid.

piorunujący *a.* electrifying, thunderbolt; **piorunująca wiadomość** electrifying news, thunderbolt; **piorunujący wzrok** withering glare; **robić piorunujące wrażenie** act like a thunderbolt.

pioruński *a. pot.* goddamn, darn, damn.

piosenka *f. Gen.pl.* **-ek** song; **piosenka ludowa** folk song; **piosenka miłosna** love song; **stara *l.* ta sama piosenka** *l.* **śpiewka** same old story.

piosenkarka *f. Gen.pl.* **-ek** *zob.* **piosenkarz.**

piosenkarstwo *n.* **1.** (= *śpiewanie piosenek*) singing. **2.** (= *pisanie piosenek*) song-writing.

piosenkarz *mp* **1.** (= *wykonawca piosenek*) singer. **2.** (= *autor piosenek*) composer.

piotrosz *ma icht.* John Dory (*Zeus faber*).

Piotruś *mi* (*gra karciana*) old maid.

piórko *n. Gen.pl.* **-ek 1.** (*u ptaka*) feather; **lekki jak piórko** as light as a feather; **podnieść kogoś/ coś jak piórko** lift sb/sth as if they/it were as light as a feather; **obrosnąć w piórka** feather one's nest; **stroić się w cudze piórka** deck o.s. out in borrowed plumes. **2.** *bud.* feather. **3.** *bot.* blade. **4.** (*do gry np. na gitarze*) plectrum, pick. **5.** *sztuka* (*do robienia szkiców*) drawing pen. **6.** *sztuka* (*technika szkicu*) pen-and-ink drawing.

piórkowy *a.* **1.** (*o rysunku, szkicu*) pen-and-ink. **2.** feather; **waga piórkowa** *boks* featherweight.

piórnik *mi Gen.* **-a** pencil case.

pióro *n.* **1.** *orn.* feather. **2.** (= *narzędzie do pisania*) pen; **gęsie pióro** quill; **wieczne pióro** fountain pen; **człowiek pióra** man of letters; **zarabiać piórem** live by one's pen. **3.** *techn.* (*wiosła, wycieraczki*) blade; (*klucza*) bit; (*resoru*) spring leaf *l.* plate. **4.** *bud.* tongue, feather.

piórolotek *ma* **-tk-** *ent.* (= *motyl z rodziny Pterophoridae*) plume moths.

pióropusz *mi Gen.* **-a 1.** plume; **pióropusz dymu** plume of smoke. **2.** (= *pióropusz na hełmie*) crest.

pióropusznik *mi Gen.* **-a** *bot.* ostrich fern (*Matteuccia*).

piórowy *a.* feather; **resor piórowy** *techn.* leaf spring.

pipa *f. wulg.* **1.** (= *srom*) pussy, cunt, beaver. **2.** (= *wredna kobieta*) slut, bitch, cunt; **ty stara pipo!** you old cunt!

pipeta *f.* pipette.

pipetka *f. Gen.pl.* **-ek** *zob.* **pipeta.**

pipidówka *f. Gen.pl.* **-ek** *uj.* dump, jerkwater town, ass-end of nowhere.

piracki *a.* pirate; **statek piracki** pirate ship; **pirackie nagranie/płyta/CD** bootleg recording/ record/CD, pirated recording/record/CD; **piracka radiostacja** pirate radio station; **pirackie oprogramowanie komputerowe** warez.

piractwo *n.* piracy; **piractwo komputerowe** cracking, hacking; **piractwo drogowe** roadhogging.

piramida *f.* **1.** *hist.* pyramid. **2.** (= *stos*) pile, pyramid, heap; (= *kupka kamieni na szczycie gó-*

ry) cairn. **3.** (*ćwiczenie gimnastyczne*) pyramid. **4.** *mat.* pyramid.

piramidalny *a.* **1.** (= *przypominający piramidę*) pyramidal, pyramid-shaped, pyramidic, pyramidical. **2.** *pot.* (= *kolosalny*) colossal, gigantic, massive; **piramidalne kłamstwo** monstrous *l.* blatant *l.* barefaced lie; **piramidalna bzdura** sheer nonsense, total rubbish; **piramidalna głupota** sheer stupidity, the height of stupidity.

pirania *f. Gen.* **-ii** *icht.* piranha (*Serrasalmus*).

pirargiryt *mi min.* pyrargyrite, ruby silver.

pirat *mp* **1.** (*na morzu*) pirate. **2.** (*komputerowy*) cracker, hacker. **3.** (*nielegalnie coś produkujący*) pirate; **pirat drogowy** road hog, speeder.

Pireneje *pl. Gen.* **-ów** *geogr.* the Pyrenees.

pirenejski *a. geogr.* Pyrenean; **Półwysep Pirenejski** Pyrenean Peninsula.

piroelektryczność *f. fiz.* pyroelectricity.

pirofyllit *mi min.* pyrophyllite.

piroga *f.* (= *długa łódź wiosłowa*) pirogue.

pirogen *mi pat.* pyrogen.

pirografia *f. Gen.* **-ii** *sztuka* pyrography.

piroklastyczny *a. geol.* pyroclastic; **skała piroklastyczna** pyroclastic rock.

piroksen *mi min.* pyroxene.

piroksenit *mi geol.* pyroxenite.

piroksylina *f. chem.* guncotton.

piroliza *f. chem.* pyrolysis, thermal decomposition.

piroluzyt *mi min.* pyrolusite, battery manganese.

piroman *mp* pyromaniac.

piromania *f. Gen.* **-ii** pyromania.

pirometalurgia *f. Gen.* **-ii** *metal.* pyrometallurgy.

pirometr *mi techn.* pyrometer.

pirop *mi min.* pyrope.

pirotechniczny *a.* pyrotechnic; **pokaz pirotechniczny** firework show *l.* display, fireworks.

pirotechnik *mp* pyrotechnician.

pirotechnika *f.* pyrotechnics.

pirs *mi żegl.* pier.

piruet *mi Gen.* **-u** *l.* **-a** (*w tańcu, t. obrót konia*) pirouette.

pirydoksyna *f. chem.* pyridoxin(e), vitamin B6.

pirydyna *f. chem.* pyridine.

pirymidyna *f. chem.* pyrimidine.

pirymidynowy *a. chem.* pyrimidine; **zasada pirymidynowa** pyrimidine base.

piryt *mi min.* pyrite, iron pyrite(s).

pirytowy *a. min.* pyritic, pyritical.

pisać *ipf.* **piszę piszesz 1.** (= *stawiać znaki na papierze*) write; **pisać jak kura pazurem** scrawl, scribble; **coś jest palcem *l.* widłami na *l.* po wodzie pisane** sth is written in the water *l.* sand *l.* air; **pisać na maszynie** type; **pisać drukowanymi literami** print; **to było mu pisane** it was his destiny; **jak to się pisze?** how do you spell it?; **to się pisze przez...** it is spelled with...; **długopis nie chce pisać** pen won't write, pen doesn't want to write; **prawo pisane** *prawn.* statute law; **język pisany** written language. **2.** (= *tworzyć na piśmie*) write; **pisać artykuł** write an article. **3.** (= *informować na piśmie*) report, notify; **gazety piszą, że...** the papers say that...; **pisz do mnie na Berdyczów** *przest.* I'm through with you. **~ się** *ipf.* **1.** *pot.* (= *opowiadać się za czymś, zgadzać się*) be on for sth, be game for sth; **nie piszę się na to** I am out, count me out. **2.** (= *być pisanym*) be spelled, be written; **jak się pisze po angielsku koń?** how do you spell horse in English? **3.** *przest.* (= *podpisywać się*) write one's name, sign one's name.

pisak *mi Gen.* **-a 1.** (= *flamaster*) felt-tip pen, felt tip. **2.** (*w urządzeniu*) pen.

pisanie *n.* writing; **maszyna do pisania** typewriter.

pisanina *f. pog.* **1.** (= *redagowanie tekstu*) penpushing. **2.** (= *bezwartościowy tekst*) trash, rubbish.

pisanka *f. Gen.pl.* **-ek** (= *malowane jajko*) Easter egg.

pisarka *f. Gen.pl.* **-ek** *zob.* **pisarz** 1.

pisarski *a.* **1.** (= *odnoszący się do pisarza*) writer's, literary; **talent pisarski** literary talent; **spuścizna pisarska** literary heritage. **2.** (= *odnoszący się do pisania*) writing; **znaki pisarskie** punctuation marks.

pisarstwo *n.* writing.

pisarz *mp* **1.** (= *autor utworów prozatorskich*) writer, novelist, man of letters. **2.** *hist.* (= *sekretarz*) clerk, secretary.

pisemnie *adv.* in writing; **odpowiedzieć pisemnie** respond in writing, provide a written reply.

pisemny *a.* written; **zadanie pisemne** written assignment; **egzamin pisemny** written exam(ination); **pisemne upomnienie** written reminder; **pisemne dowody** evidence in writing.

pisk *mi* (*dzieci, myszy*) squeak, squeal; (*opon, hamulców*) screech.

pisklak *ma pot. zob.* **pisklę**.

pisklę *n.* **-lęci-** *pl.* **-lęt-** *Gen.* **-ąt** nestling.

piskliwie *adv.* shrilly, squeakily.

piskliwy *a.* squeaky, shrill.

piskorz *ma icht.* weatherfish (*Misgurnus fossilis*); **wykręcać** *l.* **wywijać się jak piskorz** dodge around.

pismak *mp pl.* **-i** *l.* **-cy** *pog.* hack, newshawk, newshound.

pismo *n.* **1.** (= *szereg liter*) writing; (= *alfabet*) alphabet; **pismo maszynowe** type; **pismo (od)ręczne** handwriting; **pismo obrazkowe** picture writing, pictography; **pismo klinowe** cuneiform; **pismo runiczne** runic alphabet; **pismo gotyckie** Gothic lettering; **pismo techniczne** lettering; **pismo nutowe** *l.* **muzyczne** musical notation; **pismo hieroglificzne** hieroglyphics, hieroglyphic writing; **pismo drukowane** print; **pismo pochyłe** italics; **pismo pogrubione** boldface; **pismo stenograficzne** shorthand (writing); **pismo czytelne** legible handwriting; **zawrzeć umowę na piśmie** *zwł. prawn.* conclude a contract in writing; **władać angielskim w mowie i piśmie** have good command of both written and spoken English; **na piśmie** in writing. **2.** (= *charakter pisma*) hand

writing; **mieć ładny charakter pisma** have good handwriting. **3.** (= *tekst pisany*) letter, note, document; **pismo urzędowe** official letter; **pismo okólne** circular letter; **pismo procesowe** *prawn.* pleading; **pismo poufne** confidential letter; **pismo uwierzytelniające** credentials; **zwąchać pismo nosem** find out that there's sth in the air; **pisma** *l.* **dzieła wszystkie** (*autora*) complete writings *l.* works; **Pismo Święte** *rel.* the Holy Bible, the Scriptures; **uczony w piśmie** *żart.* learned *l.* erudite person. **4.** (= *gazeta codzienna*) paper, daily; (= *czasopismo*) magazine. **5.** (= *dzieło*) work.

pisnąć *pf.* **pisnę piśniesz, -ij** *zob.* **piszczeć**.

pisownia *f. Gen.pl.* **-i** spelling, orthography; **poprawna pisownia** correct spelling; **pisownia fonetyczna** phonetic spelling.

pistacja *f.* **1.** *bot.* pistachio (*Pistacia vera*). **2.** (= *orzech tego drzewa*) pistachio (nut).

pistacjowy *a.* **1.** (= *odnoszący się do drzewa l. orzechu pistacjowego*) pistachio; **drzewo pistacjowe** *bot.* pistachio (*Pistacia vera*). **2.** (*kolor*) pistachio, pistache.

pistolet *mi* (*broń*) gun, pistol; **pistolet maszynowy** submachine gun, machine gun; **pistolet natryskowy** *techn.* spray gun, airbrush.

piston *mi* **1.** *muz.* (*w instrumencie dętym*) piston. **2.** *hist.* (*w dawnej broni palnej*) percussion cap.

pisuar *mi* urinal.

pisywać *ipf.* **1.** (= *tworzyć od czasu do czasu*) write; **pisywać do gazety/czasopisma** contribute to a paper/magazine. **2.** (= *pisać listy*) write, drop a line.

piszczałka *f. Gen.pl.* **-ek 1.** *muz.* (*instrument*) pipe. **2.** *muz.* (= *część składowa instrumentu*) pipe; (*w organach*) organ-pipe; **piszczałka stroikowa** reed pipe. **3.** (*do wabienia ptaków*) decoy pipe.

piszczałkowy *a. muz.* pipe; **mechanizm piszczałkowy** pipework.

piszczeć *ipf.* **-ę -ysz 1.** (*o człowieku i niektórych zwierzętach*) squeal, sqeak; **nie pisnąć słówka** not to breathe a word; **piszczeć z radości** squeal with delight; **u nich bieda, że aż piszczy** they can't make both ends meet; **on wie, co w trawie piszczy** he knows which way the wind is blowing. **2.** (*o piszczałkach*) pipe. **3.** (*o kole, drzwiach*) screech, squeak.

piszczel *f. l. mi Gen.pl.* **-i** *l.* **-ów** *anat.* tibia, shinbone.

piszczelowy *a. anat.* tibial; **kość piszczelowa** tibial bone.

piśmidło *n. Gen.pl.* **-eł** *pog.* (= *bezwartościowy utwór literacki*) trash; (= *marne czasopismo*) tabloid.

piśmiennictwo *n. teor.lit.* literature.

piśmienny *a.* **1.** (*o materiałach*) stationery. **2.** (*o człowieku*) literate.

PIT *abbr. mi Loc.* **Picie** tax return form (*in Poland*).

pita *f. kulin.* pita (bread).

pitagoreizm *mi fil.* Pythagoreanism.

pitagorejczyk *mp fil.* Pythagorean.

pitagorejski *a. fil.* Pythagorean.

pitekantrop *mp pl.* **-y** *antrop.* pithecantrope (*Pithecanthropus*).

pitny *a.* drinking, drinkable, potable; **woda pitna** drinking *l.* drinkable water; **miód pitny** mead.

pitolić *ipf. pot.* grate, rasp.

pitrasić *ipf.* **-szę -sisz** *pot.* whip up, fix, rustle up.

piure *n. indecl. kulin.* purée, puree, mash. – *a. indecl.* purée, puree, mashed; **ziemniaki piure** mashed potatoes.

piuska *f. Gen.pl.* **-ek** *rz.-kat.* zucchetto, calotte.

piwiarnia *f. Gen.pl.* **-i** *l.* **-ń** pub, beer house, beer hall.

piwiarniany *a.* beer-house.

piwko *n. Gen.pl.* **-ek** *pot.* beer, brew, brewski, cold one; **dwa piwka!** two cold ones!

piwnica *f.* **1.** (= *pomieszczenie pod budynkiem mieszkalnym*) cellar, basement. **2.** (= *zapas win*) wine cellar; **mieć dobrze zaopatrzoną piwnicę** keep a good cellar.

piwniczka *f. Gen.pl.* **-ek 1.** (= *pomieszczenie pod budynkiem mieszkalnym*) (small) cellar. **2.** (= *zapas win*) wine cellar.

piwniczny *a.* cellar.

piwny *a.* beer; **bar piwny** pub, beer house, beer hall; **piwne oczy** hazel eyes; **ogródek piwny** beer garden.

piwo *n.* **1.** (*napój*) beer, brew; **piwo jasne** lager; **piwo ciemne** brown *l.* dark ale; **piwo imbirowe** ginger beer; **piwo beczkowe** draught beer; **piwo słodowe** malt beer; **postawić komuś piwo** stand sb a brew, spring for it, buy sb a cold one; **nawarzyć sobie piwa** get o.s. into hot water. **2.** (= *porcja piwa*) pint, brew; **małe piwo** *przen.* piece of cake, cinch.

piwonia *f. Gen.* **-ii** *bot.* peony (*Paeonia*).

piwosz *mp* beer lover *l.* af(f)icionado.

piwowar *mp* brewer.

piwowarski *a.* brewery, brewing; **przemysł piwowarski** brewing industry; **drożdże piwowarskie** beer yeast.

piwowarstwo *n.* brewing.

pizda *f. wulg.* **1.** (= *srom*) cunt, pussy, beaver; **idź w pizdu!** fuck off!, go fuck yourself! **2.** (= *wredna kobieta*) cunt, slut, cooze; **ty głupia pizdo!** you stupid cunt! **3.** (= *wredny mężczyzna*) fuck, fuckhead, dickface.

pizza *f. kulin.* pizza.

pizzeria *f. Gen.* **-ii** pizzeria, pizza parlor.

piździć *ipf.* **piździ** *wulg.* (*o wietrze*) blow fucking hard; **piździ jak w Kieleckiem (na przystanku autobusowym)!** the wind is blowing fucking hard!

piździelec *mp* **-lc-** *pl.* **-y** *wulg.* motherfucker, fucker, dickface.

piżama *f.* pajamas; *Br.* pyjamas.

piżmaczek *ma bot.* **piżmaczek wiosenny** muskroot (*Adoxa moschatellina*).

piżmak *ma zool.* muskrat, musquash (*Ondatra zibethica*).

piżmo *n.* musk.

piżmoszczur *ma zob.* **piżmak.**

piżmowiec *ma* **-wc-** *zool.* musk deer (*Moschus moschiferus*).

piżmowół *ma* **-o-** *Gen.* **-u** *zool.* muskox, musk ox (*Ovibos moschatus*).

piżmowy *a.* musk, musky; **kaczka piżmowa** *orn.* Muscovy duck, musk duck (*Carina moschata*); **szczur piżmowy** *zob.* **piżmak**; **wół piżmowy** *zob.* **piżmowół.**

PKOl *abbr.* (= *Polski Komitet Olimpijski*) Polish Olympic Committee.

PKP *abbr.* (= *Polskie Koleje Państwowe*) Polish National Railways.

PKS *abbr.* (= *Państwowa Komunikacja Samochodowa*) National Coach Transport Company.

pkt *abbr.* (= *punkt*) pt. (*point*).

pl. *abbr.* (= *plac*) sq. (*square*).

plac *mi Gen.pl.* **-ów 1.** (*przestrzeń w mieście*) square; **plac budowy** building site; **plac zabaw** playground; **plac defilad** parade ground; **plac sportowy** sports field. **2.** *przest.* (= *działka budowlana*) building lot. **3.** *przest.* (= *pole walki*) battlefield, battle ground; **dotrzymać placu** *lit.* stand one's ground, stand up to; **ustąpić z placu** give up the struggle; **zostać na placu** win, defeat one's rivals.

placebo *n. indecl. med.* placebo.

placek *mi* **-ck-** *Gen.* **-a 1.** *kulin.* (= *płaskie, słodkie ciasto*) cake, tart, pie; **placek ze śliwkami/z jabłkami/drożdżowy** plum/apple/yeast cake; **masz babo placek!** now you've done it!, you're in it now! **2.** *kulin.* (*z mąki i ziemniaków*) potato pancake; **leżeć plackiem** lie flat; **padać** *l.* **leżeć plackiem przed kimś** *przen.* prostrate o.s. before sb. **3.** (= *niewielka przestrzeń*) patch.

placenta *f. anat., bot., med.* placenta.

plackowaty *a.* cake-like; **łysienie plackowate** *pat.* alopecia areata, alopecia cumscripta.

placowe *n. Gen.* **-ego** (= *opłata za użytkowanie placu*) yardage.

placówka *f. Gen.pl.* **-ek 1.** (= *przedstawicielstwo*) post; **placówka dyplomatyczna** diplomatic agency *l.* post; **placówka handlowa** agency, sales *l.* branch office. **2.** (= *instytucja*) institution, establishment; **placówka handlowa** business establishment; **placówka naukowa** *l.* **badawcza/kulturalna/służby zdrowia** research/cultural/health-care institution. **3.** *wojsk.* outpost; **wysunięta placówka** far-flung outpost.

plafon *mi bud.* plafond.

plafonowy *a. bud.* plafond.

plaga *f.* plague, scourge; (*pasożytów, robactwa*) infestation; **plaga egipska** the plagues of Egypt.

plagiat *mi* plagiarism, crib; **popełniać plagiat czegoś** plagiarize sth.

plagiator *mp* plagiarist, cribber.

plagiatorski *a.* plagiaristic.

plagiatorstwo *n.* plagiarizing.

plagioklaz *mi min.* plagioclase.

plajta *f. pot.* (= *bankructwo*) bankruptcy.

plajtować *ipf. pot.* go broke, go bankrupt, go to the wall.

plakacista *mp sztuka* poster-designer.

plakat *mi* poster.

plakatować *ipf.* post, put up, hang (*posters*).

plakatowy *a.* poster; **farby plakatowe** poster paints *l.* colors.

plakatówka *f. Gen.pl.* **-ek** *pot.* (*farba*) poster paint *l.* color.

plakietka *f. Gen.pl.* **-ek** **1.** (= *identyfikator*) badge, name tag. **2.** *sztuka* plaque.

plama *f.* **1.** (*zabrudzenie*) stain, blot; **plamy słoneczne** *astron.* sunspots. **2.** (= *niesława*) blemish, stain, blot; **plama na czyimś honorze** stain on sb's honor, blot on one's escutcheon; **dać plamę** *pot.* blow it, screw up. **3.** *sztuka* patch, splash.

plamiak *ma icht.* haddock (*Melanogrammus aeglefinus*).

plamica *f. wet.* purpura, peliosis.

plamić *ipf.* **1.** (= *brudzić*) stain, soil, besmirch, sully. **2.** (= *hańbić*) stain, tarnish, sully. **~ się** *ipf.* **1.** (= *brudzić się*) soil. **2.** (= *zniesławiać się*) tarnish (one's reputation).

plamiec *ma Gen., Acc.* **-mca** *ent.* **plamiec agreściak** currant moth, magpie moth (*Abraxas grossulariata*).

plamistość *f.* **1.** (= *pokrycie plamami*) spottiness, mottle. **2.** *ogr.* black spot.

plamisty *a.* spotted, mottled; (*o cerze, rumieńcu*) splotchy, blotchy; **dur** *l.* **tyfus plamisty** *pat.* typhus fever; **salamandra plamista** *zool.* spotted salamander (*Salamandra salamandra*).

plamka *f. Gen.pl.* **-ek** spot, mottle; **plamka światła** speck of light; **plamka ślepa** *anat.* blind spot; **plamka żółta** *anat.* yellow spot, macula.

plan *mi* **1.** (= *zamiar*) intention; (*działania*) scheme; **pokrzyżować czyjeś plany** upset the *l.* sb's applecart, thwart sb's plans; **mieć w planie** plan; **według planu** *l.* **zgodnie z planem** according to the plan, as planned. **2.** (= *rozkład zajęć, czynności*) schedule, timetable; **plan podróży** itinerary; **plan działania** action plan; **plan inwestycyjny** investment plan; **plan perspektywiczny** long-term plan. **3.** (= *zarys*) blueprint, design; (*wypracowania, wykładu*) outline. **4.** (= *rysunek*) plan, map; **plan miasta** street map; **na planie prostokąta** of rectangular plan; **plan badań naukowych** research project; **plan sytuacyjny** *l.* **działki** site plan. **5.** *film, telew.* (= *odległość od kamery, oka widza*) ground; **drugi plan** background; **pierwszy plan** foreground; **być na pierwszym planie** be in the foreground *l.* forefront; **wysuwać się na pierwszy plan** come to the fore; **zejść na drugi** *l.* **dalszy plan** recede *l.* fade into the background *l.* distance. **6.** *film* (*poza studiem*) location; (*w studiu*) set; **na planie filmowym** on location.

plandeka *f.* tarp(aulin), canvas.

planet *mi roln.* planet, wheel hoe.

planeta *f. astron.* planet.

planetarium *n. sing. indecl. pl.* **-ria** *Gen.* **-riów** planetarium.

planetarny *a. astron.* planetary; **układ** *l.* **system planetarny** planetary system.

planetoida *f. astron.* asteroid, planetoid.

planetować *ipf. roln.* planet.

planigloby *pl. Gen.* **-ów** *geogr.* planispheres.

planimetr *mi geom.* planimeter.

planimetria *f. Gen.* **-ii** *geom.* planimetry.

planimetrować *ipf. geom.* measure by a planimeter.

planimetryczny *a. geom.* planimetric.

planisfera *f. geogr.* planisphere.

planista *mp* planner.

planistyczny *a.* planning.

plankton *mi biol.* plankton.

planktonowy *a. biol.* planktonic; **siatka planktonowa** plankton net.

planktonożerny *a.* planktonophagous, feeding on plankton.

plano *n. indecl. druk.* broadside.

planować¹ *ipf.* **1.** (= *układać plany*) plan, draft, scheme. **2.** (= *projektować budowle*) design, plan. **3.** *techn.* face. **4.** (= *wyrównywać grunt*) surface, level.

planować² *ipf. lotn.* plane.

planowanie *n.* planning; **planowanie przestrzenne** *bud.* town (and country) planning.

planowo *adv.* as planned, according to the plan; (*zakończyć, odjechać*) on time.

planowy *a.* planned; (*o odjeździe, przyjeździe*) on time *l.* schedule, as scheduled.

plansza *f.* **1.** (= *tablica, ilustracja*) chart; (*w grach planszowych*) board. **2.** *szermierka* piste; *gimnastyka artystyczna* floor.

planszowy *a.* chart; board; **gra planszowa** board game.

plantacja *f. roln.* plantation.

plantator *mp* planter, grower.

plantować *ipf.* **1.** (= *wyrównywać grunt*) level, surface. **2.** *roln., ogr.* (= *uprawiać rośliny*) grow.

planty *pl. Gen.* **-t** (= *zieleńce publiczne*) commons.

planula *f. zool.* planula.

plask *mi* (*odgłos*) smack, slap. – *int.* smack.

plaskać *ipf.*, **plasnąć** *pf.* **-snę -śniesz, -ij** smack, slap.

plasować się *ipf. rzad.* settle o.s.; **plasować się na pierwszej/drugiej pozycji** come in first/second.

plastelina *f.* modeling clay; *Br.* Plasticine.

plaster *mi* **-tr-** *Gen.* **-a** **1.** (*opatrunek*) Band-Aid, adhesive bandage. **2.** (= *kawał czegoś*) (*wędliny, mięsa, cytryny*) slice; **pokroić coś w plastry** slice sth. **3.** *pszczelarstwo* (*miodu*) honeycomb.

plasterek *mi* **-rk-** *Gen.* **-a** *zob.* **plaster**.

plastik *mi* = **plastyk²**.

plastikowy *a.* plastic; **plastikowe pieniądze** *fin.* plastic, credit card(s).

plastomer *mi techn.* thermoplastic.

plastron *mi Gen.* **-u** *sport, t. zool.* plastron.

plastyczka *f. Gen.pl.* **-ek** *zob.* **plastyk¹**.

plastycznie *adv.* **1.** (= *artystycznie*) artistically. **2.** (= *przestrzennie, trójwymiarowo*) plastically, in relief. **3.** (= *barwnie*) vividly, graphically.

plastyczność *f.* **1.** (= *wyrazistość*) vividness. **2.** *sztuka* plasticity. **3.** *biol.* plasticity. **4.** *techn.* plasticity, ductility, malleability.

plastyczny *a.* **1.** (= *wyrazisty*) (*o opisie, opowiadaniu*) vivid, graphic. **2.** *sztuka* plastic;

sztuki plastyczne fine arts. **3.** (= *przestrzenny*) relief; **mapa plastyczna** relief map. **4.** *techn.* plastic, ductile, malleable. **5.** *med.* (*o chirurgii, operacji*) plastic.

plastydy *pl. Gen.* **-ów** *bot.* plastids.

plastyfikatory *pl. Gen.* **-ów** *chem.* plasticizers.

plastyk[1] *mp sztuka* artist.

plastyk[2] *mi* **1.** plastic. **2.** *pot.* plastic explosive, plastique.

plastyka *f.* **1.** (= *sztuki piękne*) fine arts. **2.** (= *obrazowanie*) plasticity, vividness. **3.** (= *przestrzenność*) plasticity, relief. **4.** *szkoln.* (= *wychowanie plastyczne*) art(s), art classes. **5.** *chir.* plastic surgery; **plastyka naczyń** angioplasty.

plastykowy *a. zob.* **plastikowy; bomba plastykowa** *wojsk.* plastic bomb.

platan *mi bot.* plane (tree) (*Platanus*); *US* sycamore (*Platanus occidentalis*).

platana *f. zool.* platanna (*Xenopus laevis*).

platanowate *pl. Gen.* **-ych** *bot.* the plane-tree family (*Platanaceae*).

plateau *n. indecl. geogr.* plateau.

plater *mi* **1.** (*zwł. naczynie*) platter, plate; (*pokryty złotem*) gold plate; (*pokryty srebrem*) silver plate. **2.** (= *warstwa metalu*) plate.

platerować *ipf.* **1.** *metal.* plate. **2.** *tk.* make unions.

platerowanie *n.* **1.** *metal.* plating. **2.** *tk.* making of unions.

platforma *f.* **1.** *kol.* (*kolejowa, do przewozu towarów*) railway truck, lorry. **2.** *kol.* (= *pomost w wagonie osobowym*) platform. **3.** (= *płaszczyzna*) plane; **platforma wiertnicza** *górn.* drilling rig *l.* platform. **4.** *geol.* platform; **platforma kontynentalna** continental shelf. **5.** *polit., przen.* platform. **6.** (*typ podeszwy*) platform. **7.** *komp.* platform; **platforma programowa** software platform; **platforma sprzętowa** hardware platform.

platfus *mi Gen.* **-a** *pl.* **-y** *pat.* flatfoot, splayfoot. – *mp pl.* **-i** *l.* **-y** *pog.* flatfoot.

platoniczny *a.* (*o miłości, marzeniach, idei*) platonic.

platonik *mp fil.* Platonist.

platonizm *mi fil.* Platonism.

platoński *a.* (*o filozofii, nauce, systemie, dialogu*) Platonic, Plato's.

platyna *f. chem.* platinum.

platynit *mi metal.* platinoid.

platynować *ipf. techn.* platinize.

platynowce *pl. Gen.* **-ów** *chem.* platinoids, platinum elements.

platynowy *a.* **1.** (= *z platyny*) platinum, platinic; **czerń platynowa** *chem.* platinum black. **2.** (*o kolorze, włosach, blondynce*) platinum; **platynowa płyta** (= *album, który sprzedał się w co najmniej milionie egzemplarzy*) platinum album record.

playback *mi* playback; **odtwarzać z playbacku** play back; **śpiewać z playbacku** lip-sync.

plazma *f. biol., fiz., min.* plasma, plasm.

plazmatyczny *a. biol.* plasmatic, plasmic; **komórki plazmatyczne** plasma cells, plasmacytes.

plazmidy *pl. Gen.* **-ów** *biol.* plasmides.

plazmodium *n. sing. indecl. pl.* **-dia** *Gen.* **-diów**

1. *biol.* plasmodium. **2.** *zool.* plasmodium (*Plasmodium*).

plazmoliza *f. biol.* plasmolysis.

plazmotron *mi techn.* plasma torch *l.* gun *l.* burner.

plazmowy *a.* plasma; **palnik plazmowy** *techn.* plasma torch *l.* gun *l.* burner.

plaża *f.* beach; **dzika plaża** unguarded beach; **plaża strzeżona** guarded beach.

plażować *ipf.* sunbathe, lie on the beach.

plażowicz *mp Gen.pl.* **-ów** sunbather.

plażowiczka *f. Gen.pl.* **-ek** *zob.* **plażowicz**.

plażowy *a.* beach; **strój plażowy** beachwear.

plażówka *f. Gen.pl.* **-ek** *pot.* (*sukienka*) sundress.

plądrować *ipf.* **1.** (= *grabić*) plunder, loot. **2.** (= *szperać*) ransack.

pląsać *ipf. żart.* dance; romp (about).

pląsawica *f. pat.* chorea.

pląsy *pl. Gen.* **-ów** dancing, capers.

plątać *ipf.* **-czę -czesz 1.** (*włosy, nici*) (= *gmatwać*) tangle (up). **2.** *pot.* (= *mylić*) mix up, confuse. **~ się** *ipf.* **1.** (*o włosach, niciach*) (= *gmatwać się*) tangle, become entangled. **2.** (= *mylić się*) mix up, confuse; **język mu się plącze** he can't find his tongue; **nogi mu się plączą** he falters; **wszystko mi się plącze** I'm all confused, I can't think straight. **3.** (= *kręcić się niepotrzebnie*) hang around; **plątać się komuś pod nogami** *pot.* get in sb's way, get under one's feet. **4.** *pot.* get involved.

plątanina *f.* (*myśli*) tangle; (*ulic*) maze.

plebania *f. Gen.* **-ii** *kośc.* parsonage, presbytery; *rz.-kat.* rectory.

plebejski *a. przest.* plebeian.

plebejskość *f. przest.* plebeianism.

plebejusz *mp Gen.pl.* **-y** *l.* **-ów** *t. hist.* (= *człowiek z plebsu*) plebeian.

plebiscyt *mi t. hist.* (= *głosowanie*) plebiscite.

plebiscytowy *a.* plebiscite.

plebs *mi* **1.** (= *gmin*) common people, mob, plebeians, plebs. **2.** *hist.* plebs.

plecak *mi Gen.* **-a** rucksack, backpack, knapsack; **podróżować z plecakiem** backpack.

plecha *f. bot.* thallus.

plechowce *pl. Gen.* **-ów** *bot.* thallophytes (*Thallophyta*).

plecionka *f. Gen.pl.* **-ek** braiding, plaiting.

plecionkarski *a.* braided, plaited.

plecionkarstwo *n.* braiding, plaiting; basketmaking.

pleciuch *mp pl.* **-y** *pot., pog.* (= *gaduła*) chatterbox; (= *plotkarz*) gossip.

pleciuga *f. l. mp decl. like f. Gen.pl.* **-g** *l.* **-ów** *pot.* (= *gaduła*) chatterbox; (= *plotkarz*) gossip.

plecowy *a. lotn.* (*o locie*) inverted.

plecy *pl. Gen.* **-ów 1.** (*u człowieka*) back, shoulders; **mieć plecy** *pot.* have friends in high places, know the right people; **chować się za czyimiś plecami** hide behind the skirts of sb; **robić coś za czyimiś plecami** do sth behind sb's back; **odwrócić się plecami do kogoś** turn one's back on sb; **pokazać komuś plecy** show one's back to sb; **cios w plecy** stab in the back; **wbić**

komuś nóż w plecy stab sb in the back. **2.** (*w ubraniu*) back.

pleć *ipf.* **pielę pielisz** weed (out).

pled *mi* blanket.

plejada *f.* **1.** (= *grupa ludzi wybitnych*) pleiad. **2. Plejady** *mit.* Pleiades.

plejstocen *mi geol.* the Pleistocene (Epoch).

plejstoceński *a. geol.* Pleistocene.

pleksiglas, plexi *mi techn.* Plexiglas.

plektron *mi muz.* pick, plectrum.

plemienny *a.* (*o związku, państwie, ustroju, wodzu*) tribal.

plemię *n.* **-mieni-** *pl.* **-mion-** **1.** tribe, band. **2.** *przest.* (= *pokolenie*) generation; (= *potomstwo*) offspring; (= *ród*) kin; **ludzkie** *l.* **człowiecze plemię** humankind; **szatańskie plemię** hellhound.

plemnia *f. Gen.pl.* **-i** *bot.* antheridium.

plemnik *mi Gen.* **-a** *biol.* spermatozoon, sperm (cell).

plemnikobójczy *a.* spermicidal; **krem plemnikobójczy** spermicide.

plenarny *a.* plenary; **sesja plenarna** plenary (session).

plener *mi* **1.** *sztuka* open air. **2.** *film* location.

plenerowy *a.* (*o malarstwie, zdjęciach, imprezie*) open-air.

pleneryzm *mi sztuka* plein-airism.

plenerzysta *mp sztuka* plein-airist.

plenić się *ipf.* **1.** (*o zwierzętach*) multiply, proliferate. **2.** (*o roślinach*) spread.

pleniówka *f. Dat., Loc.* **-wce** *ent.* **ziemiórka pleniówka** fungus gnat, mushroom fly (*Sciara militaris*).

plenipotencja *f. prawn., przest.* plenipotentiary power, power of attorney.

plenipotent *mp prawn., przest.* plenipotentiary.

plenność *f. zwł. roln.* prolificacy.

plenny *a. zwł. roln.* prolific.

plenum *n. sing. indecl. pl.* **-na** *Gen.* **-nów** *zwł. polit.* plenum, general assembly.

pleochroizm *mi fiz.* pleochroism.

pleonastyczny *a. jęz.* pleonastic.

pleonazm *mi jęz.* pleonasm.

pleszka *f. Gen.pl.* **-ek** *orn.* redstart (*Phoenicurus phoenicurus*).

pleść *ipf.* **plotę pleciesz plótł plotła pletli** **1.** (= *splatać*) braid, plait, weave. **2.** *pot.* (= *mówić bez sensu*) blab, blabber; **pleść trzy po trzy** talk baloney, bullshit. **~ się** *ipf.* **plotę pleciesz plótł plotła pletli** (= *wić się, przeplatać się z czymś*) twine.

pleśniak *mi Gen.* **-a** *bot.* phycomycete.

pleśniawki *pl. Gen.* **-wek** *pat.* thrush, aphthous fever.

pleśnieć *ipf.* **1.** mold, get *l.* grow moldy. **2.** *przen.* grow musty.

pleśniowy *a.* moldy; **grzyb pleśniowy** mold, mildew; **ser pleśniowy** *kulin.* blue cheese.

pleśń *f. pl.* **-e** (*nalot*) mold, mildew.

pletyzmograf *mi med.* plethysmograph.

pleura *f. anat.* pleura.

pleuritis *n. pat.* pleurisy.

pleuropneumonia *f. pat.* pleuropneumonia.

pleuston *mi biol.* pleuston.

plewić *ipf. dial.* weed (out).

plewka *f. Dat., Loc.* **-wce** *bot.* **plewka dolna** lemma; **plewka górna** palea.

plewy *pl. Gen.* **-w** *roln.* chaff; **brać kogoś na plewy** sell sb a bill of goods; **odróżniać** *l.* **oddzielać ziarno od plew** separate the wheat *l.* grain from the chaff.

plezjozaur *ma paleont.* plesiosaur (*Plesiosauria*).

plik *mi* **1.** (*pieniędzy, dokumentów, banknotów*) roll, wad, bundle. **2.** *komp.* file.

pliocen *mi geol.* the Pliocene (Epoch).

plioceński *a. geol.* Pliocene.

plisa *f.* **1.** (= *naszyta wstęga tkaniny*) trimming; (= *listwa podszyta od spodu*) list, salvage. **2.** (= *fałd*) pleat.

plisować *ipf.* pleat.

pliszka *f. Gen.pl.* **-ek** *orn.* wagtail (*Motacilla*).

plomba *f.* **1.** (*zabezpieczenie*) seal; **coś jest pod plombą** sth is sealed. **2.** *dent.* filling; inlay. **3.** *bud.* infill construction.

plombować *ipf.* **1.** (= *zakładać zabezpieczenie*) seal. **2.** *dent.* fill.

plombownica *f. techn.* sealing-tongs.

plon *mi* **1.** (*z pola, ogrodu, sadu*) crop, yield; (= *żniwo*) harvest. **2.** *przen.* (= *efekt działania*) fruit.

plonować *ipf.* (= *wydawać plon*) yield.

ploter *mi Gen.* **-a** *komp.* plotter.

plotę *itd. ipf. zob.* **pleść.**

plotka *f. Gen.pl.* **-ek** gossip, rumor.

plotkarka *f. Gen.pl.* **-ek** *zob.* **plotkarz.**

plotkarski *a.* gossipy, gossip.

plotkarstwo *n.* gossip.

plotkarz *mp* gossip, rumormonger.

plotkować *ipf.* gossip.

plucha *f.* wet weather.

pluć *ipf.* spit; **pluć krwią** spit *l.* cough up blood; **pluć na kogoś/coś** not give a damn about sb/sth; **plunąć na coś** be through with sth; **pluć sobie w brodę** be kicking o.s. (in the teeth).

plugastwo *n.* filth, obscenity.

plugawić *ipf.* befoul, defile.

plugawiec *mp pl.* **-wcy** *Gen.pl.* **-wców** abominable person.

plugawość *f.* filth.

plugawy *a.* filthy, foul, obscene.

plujka *f. Gen.pl.* **-ek** **1.** *ent.* bluebottle (fly) (*Calliphora*). **2.** *komp., pot.* (= *drukarka atramentowa*) ink-jet printer.

plumbago *n. bot.* leadwort (*Plumbago*).

plunąć *pf. zob.* **pluć.**

pluralista *mp fil.* pluralist.

pluralistyczny *a. fil.* (*o poglądzie, systemie*) pluralistic, pluralist.

pluralizm *mi fil.* pluralism.

plus *mi Gen.* **-a** **1.** *mat.* plus (sign); **plus minus** more or less; **jest plus dwa stopnie** it's (plus) two degrees; **dostałem trójkę z plusem** I got a C plus. **2.** *Gen.* **-u** (= *zaleta*) plus (point), advantage; **jedyny plus czegoś** saving grace of sth; **plusy i minusy życia w mieście** pros and cons of city life; **masz u mnie plus!** I like that!; **zmieniać się na**

plus change for the better; **być na plusie** *pot.* (= *mieć dodatnie saldo na koncie, nie być w długach*) be in the black. – *adv.* plus, additionally; **mam pole plus duży sad** I've got a field plus a big orchard.

plusk¹ *mi* **1.** (*odgłos*) splash; (*deszczu*) patter. **2.** *myśl.* (= *ogon bobra*) beaver's tail; (= *płetwa ogonowa ryb*) tail fin.

plusk² *int.* splash; **ryba plusk do wody i już jej nie widać** splash goes the fish into the water and disappears.

pluskać *ipf.* **-am** *l.* **-szczę -asz** *l.* **-szczesz 1.** (*wydawać odgłos*) splash; (*o deszczu*) patter. **2.** (= *uderzać*) splash, dabble. ~ **się** *ipf.* (= *kąpać się*) splash, dabble.

pluskiewka *f. Gen.pl.* **-ek** thumbtack; *Br.* drawing pin.

pluskolec *ma* **-lc-** *ent.* boat-fly, water boatman (*Notonecta glauca*).

pluskwa *f. Gen.pl.* **-kiew 1. pluskwa** *l.* **pluskwa domowa** *ent.* bedbug (*Cimex lectuarius*). **2.** *pot.* (= *ukryte urządzenie podsłuchowe*) bug. **3.** *komp., pot.* (= *błąd w programie*) bug.

pluskwiak *ma ent.* bug, true bug (*Hemiptera*).

plusnąć *pf.* **-snę -śniesz, -ij** *zob.* **pluskać.**

plusowy *a.* (= *dodatni*) (*o temperaturze*) above zero, above freezing; (*o wartości*) positive.

plusz *mi Gen.pl.* **-ów** *tk.* plush.

pluszcz *ma Gen.pl.* **-y** *l.* **-ów** *orn.* dipper, water ouzel (*Cinclus*).

pluszowy *a.* *tk.* plush; **pluszowa zabawka** stuffed animal, soft toy; **pluszowy miś** teddy bear.

plut. *abbr.* = **plutonowy.**

plutokracja *f.* **1.** (*ustrój*) plutocracy. **2.** (*warstwa społeczna*) plutocracy.

plutokrata *mp* plutocrat.

plutokratyczny *a.* plutocratic.

Pluton *mi Gen.* **-a** *astron., mit.* Pluto.

pluton¹ *mi wojsk.* platoon; **pluton egzekucyjny** firing squad.

pluton² *mi chem.* plutonium.

plutonit *mi geol.* pluton.

plutonizm *mi geol.* plutonism.

plutonowy¹ *mp wojsk.* sergeant; *US* (sergeant) specialist 5.

plutonowy² *a. chem.* plutonium.

pluwiograf *mi meteor.* pluviograph.

pluwiometr *mi meteor.* pluviometer, rain gauge.

plwocina *f.* expectoration, sputum; spittle, spit.

płaca *f.* pay; (*godzinowa, dzienna, tygodniowa*) wage; (*miesięczna*) salary; **lista płac** payroll; **płaca akordowa** piecework pay; **płaca minimalna** minimum wage; **płaca na czysto** *l.* **na rękę** take-home *l.* in-hand pay; **płaca podstawowa** *l.* **zasadnicza** basic wage; **płaca realna** real *l.* actual wage; **fundusz płac** (*pracowników nieprodukcyjnych*) salary fund; (*pracowników produkcyjnych*) wage fund; **podwyżka/obniżka płac** pay raise/cut.

płachta *f.* (*materiału*) cloth; (*papieru*) sheet; **jak płachta na byka** like a red rag to a bull.

płacić *ipf.* **1.** (*pieniędzmi*) pay; **kelner, płacić!** check please!; **płacić gotówką/czekiem/kartą kredytową** pay in cash/by check/by credit card; **płacić frycowe** *przen.* pay one's dues; **płacić pięknym za nadobne** *przen.* pay back in kind. **2.** (= *ponosić konsekwencje*) pay; **płacić za coś życiem/zdrowiem** pay for sth with one's life/health.

płacz *mi Gen.pl.* **-ów** cry; **komuś jest do płaczu** sb is on the brink of tears; **powstrzymywać się od płaczu** fight back tears; **wybuchnąć płaczem** burst into tears.

płaczek *mp* **-czk-** *pl.* **-i 1.** (= *beksa*) crybaby. **2.** (*na pogrzebie*) weeper.

płaczka *f. Gen.pl.* **-ek** *zob.* **płaczek.**

płaczliwy *a.* (*o dziecku*) weepy, tearful; (*o głosie*) tearful.

płakać *ipf.* **-czę -czesz 1.** (= *ronić łzy*) cry (*nad czymś l. z jakiegoś powodu* over/about sth); weep; **nie warto płakać** it's no use crying; **płakać jak bóbr** cry like a baby *l.* child; **płakać krokodylimi łzami** shed crocodile tears; **płakać z bólu/ze złości** cry with pain/anger; **płakać z radości** cry for joy. **2.** (= *lamentować*) mourn; **płakać nad swoim smutnym losem** bemoan one's fate, bewail one's lot; **płakać mi się chce, gdy pomyślę...** I feel like crying when I think...; **siąść i płakać** sit and weep. **3.** (= *skarżyć się*) complain; **płakać na męża pijaka** complain of one's heavy- *l.* hard-drinking husband.

płaksa *f. l. mp decl. like f. Gen.pl.* **-s** *l.* **-ów 1.** (= *osoba często płacząca*) crybaby. **2.** *zool.* New World monkey (*Cebidae*).

płaski *a.* flat; **bieg płaski** *sport* flat race; **fala płaska** *fiz.* plane wave; **figura płaska** *geom.* plane figure; **płaska stopa** *pat.* flatfoot; **płaski dowcip** dry *l.* flat *l.* insipid joke; **płaski film** shallow movie; **płaski jak stół** flat as a pancake *l.* board; **węzeł płaski** *żegl.* carric bend; **siad płaski** *sport* L-seat; **szkło płaskie** *techn.* sheet glass; **talerz płaski** dinner plate.

płaskonos *ma orn.* shoveler (*Spatula clypeata*).

płaskorzeźba *f. sztuka* bas-relief, low relief.

płaskostopie *n. Gen.pl.* **-i** *pat.* flatfoot.

płaskownik *mi Gen.* **-a** *techn.* flat (bar).

płaskowyż *mi Gen.pl.* **-ów** *geogr.* plateau, tableland.

płastuga *f. icht.* plaice (*Pleuronectes platessa*); **płastugi** flatfishes (*Pleuronectiformes*).

płaszcz *mi Gen.* **-a 1.** (*ubranie*) coat, overcoat; **płaszcz kąpielowy** bathrobe; **płaszcz przeciwdeszczowy** raincoat; **powieść płaszcza i szpady** cloak-and-dagger novel. **2.** *techn.* jacket; mantle; casing; **płaszcz reaktora** (nuclear) reactor blanket. **3.** *zool.* (*u mięczaków*) mantle.

płaszczka *f. Gen.pl.* **-ek** *icht.* ray (*Raja*).

płaszczowina *f. geol.* nappe.

płaszczowy *a.* (*o kroju, fasonie*) coat; **materiał płaszczowy** coating; **jama płaszczowa** *zool.* mantle cavity.

płaszczyć *ipf.* flatten (out). ~ **się** *ipf.* **1.** (= *stawać się płaskim*) flatten (out). **2.** *pot.* (= *poniżać się przed kimś*) crawl, cringe (*przed kimś* to sb).

płaszczyk *mi Gen.* **-a** (= *mały płaszcz*) **1.** coat.

2. (= *pozór*) cloak, guise; **robić coś pod płaszczykiem czegoś** do sth under the cloak *l.* guise of sth, do sth under the pretense of sth.

płaszczyzna *f.* **1.** (= *równa powierzchnia*) plane, level; **wspólna płaszczyzna** *przen.* common ground. **2.** *geom.* plane; **płaszczyzna symetrii** symmetry plane; **płaszczyzna odbicia** *min.* reflection plane.

płat *mi Gen.* **-u** *l.* **-a 1.** (*materiału*) piece; (*metalu, szkła*) sheet; (*farby*) flake; *mot.* panel; **płat nośny** *lotn.* airfoil. **2.** (= *kawał czegoś*) piece, slice; (*szynki, łososia*) slice. **3.** *anat.* lobe; **płaty mózgowe** cerebral lobes.

płatać *ipf. przest.* **1.** do; **płatać komuś figle** play tricks on sb. **2.** slice.

płatek *mi* **-tk-** *Gen.* **-a 1.** (*kwiatu*) petal. **2.** (= *kawałek czegoś*) (*szynki, sera*) slice; (*mydła, śniegu*) flake; (*złota*) leaf; **płatki kukurydziane** *kulin.* cornflakes; **płatki owsiane** *kulin.* oatmeal; **płatek małżowiny (usznej)** *anat.* earlobe; **coś idzie jak z płatka** sth is going smoothly.

płatew *f. Gen., Dat., Loc.* **-twi** *bud.* purlin, purline.

płatkowy *a.* flaky; **złoto płatkowe** gold leaves.

płatnerski *a. hist.* armorer's.

płatnerstwo *n. hist.* armorer's trade *l.* craft.

płatnerz *mp hist.* armorer.

płatniczy *a.* of payment; **bilans płatniczy** balance of payments; **karta płatnicza** debit card; **środek płatniczy** legal tender; **zdolność płatnicza** solvency.

płatnik *mp* payer; **płatnik podatków** taxpayer.

płatność *f.* (= *płacenie*) payment; **płatność czekiem** payment by check; **płatność gotówkowa** *l.* **gotówką** cash payment; **płatność zaległa** overdue payment; **sposób płatności** method of payment; **termin płatności** date *l.* term of payment; **warunki płatności** payment terms (and conditions).

płatny *a.* **1.** (= *wynagradzany*) paid, salaried; **dobrze/nisko płatny** well/low paid; **płatny morderca** *l.* **zabójca** hit man, contract killer; **pracownik nisko płatny** poorly paid worker. **2.** (= *opłacany*) paid; **urlop płatny** paid leave. **3.** (= *taki, za który trzeba płacić*) paid; **płatne gotówką/z góry** paid in cash/advance; **płatne przy odbiorze** cash on delivery. **4.** (= *do zapłacenia*) due, payable.

płatowiec *mi* **-wc-** *Gen.* **-a** *lotn.* airframe.

płatowy *a.* lobar; **płatowe zapalenie płuc** *pat.* lobar pneumonia.

pława *f.* **1.** *żegl.* (= *boja*) buoy; floating beacon. **2.** *ryb.* (*przy sieci rybackiej*) float.

pławić *ipf.* duck; (*konia, bydło*) swim. **~ się** *ipf.* **1.** (= *zanurzać się*) bathe; **pławić się we krwi** bathe *l.* wallow in blood. **2.** (= *rozkoszować się*) wallow; **pławić się w luksusie/bogactwie** wallow in luxury/riches; **pławić się w słońcu** bask in the sunshine, soak up the sun.

pławik *mi Gen.* **-a 1.** *ryb.* (= *spławik*) float, cork, bobber, (fishing) bob. **2.** = **pława** 2.

pławnica *f. ryb.* drift net.

pławny *a.* (= *ułatwiający pływanie, służący do pływania*) natatorial, natatory; **błona pławna** *l.*

pływna web; **pęcherz pławny** *icht.* air *l.* swim bladder.

płaz *ma Gen.* **-a 1.** *zool.* amphibian (*Amphibia*). **2.** (*broni siecznej*) flat; **puścić coś komuś płazem** let sb get away with sth; **to ci nie ujdzie płazem!** you won't get away with it! – *mi Gen.* **-u** *bud.* deal.

płaziniec *ma* **-ńc-** *zool.* platyhelminth, flatworm (*Platyhelminthes*).

płciowo *adv.* sexually; **dojrzały/dojrzewający płciowo** pubescent.

płciowy *a.* (*o stosunku, dojrzałości, popędzie itd.*) sexual; genital; sex; **choroba przenoszona drogą płciową** sexually transmitted disease; **dyskryminacja płciowa** sex discrimination; **gruczoł płciowy** sex gland, gonad; **przedwczesny rozwój płciowy** sexual precocity; **rozmnażanie płciowe** sexual reproduction; **stosunek płciowy** (sexual) intercourse, coitus; **dojrzałość płciowa** sexual maturity; **komórki płciowe** gametes; **narządy płciowe** *l.* **rozrodcze** sex organs, genitals; **popęd płciowy** sex drive.

płd. *abbr.* **1.** (= *południowy*) s. (*southern*). **2.** (= *południe*) S. (*south*).

płeć *f.* **płci-** (*męska, żeńska, biologiczna*) sex; (*kulturowa*) gender; **obojga płci** of both sexes *l.* genders; **płeć piękna** fair *l.* gentle sex; **płeć brzydka** sterner sex; **płeć przeciwna** opposite sex; **słaba płeć** weaker sex.

płetwa *f.* **1.** *zool.* (*ryby*) fin; (*foki, pingwina*) flipper, paddle; **płetwa brzuszna/grzbietowa/ogonowa** pelvic/dorsal/caudal fin; **płetwa steru** *l.* **sterowa** *żegl.* rudder. **2.** (*do nurkowania*) flipper, fin.

płetwal *ma Gen.pl.* **-i** *l.* **-ów** *zool.* rorqual, finback (*Balaenoptera*).

płetwonogie *pl. Gen.* **-ich** *zool.* pinnipeds (*Pinnipedia*).

płetwonurek *mp* **-rk-** *pl.* **-owie** (scuba) diver, frogman.

płetwonurkowy *a.* diving.

płk *abbr.* (= *pułkownik*) Col. (*Colonel*).

płn. *abbr.* **1.** (= *północny*) n. (*northern*). **2.** (= *północ*) N. (*north*).

płocha *f. tk.* reed.

płochacz *ma* **1.** *myśl.* hound. **2.** *orn.* accentor (*Prunella*).

płochliwy *a.* (*o człowieku*) timid, shy; (*o zwierzęciu*) skittish.

płochość *f. przest.* frivolousness.

płochy *a. przest.* frivolous; (*o dziewczynie*) flighty.

płoć *f.* **-ci-** *pl.* **-e** *icht.* roach (*Rutilus rutilus*).

płodność *f.* fertility, fecundity; *przen.* productivity, prolificacy.

płodny *a.* **1.** (= *plenny*) fertile, fecund, prolific. **2.** *przen.* productive; (*o pisarzu, umyśle*) prolific, fecund.

płodowy *a.* fetal; **błony płodowe** fetal membranes; **wody płodowe** amniotic fluid, waters.

płodozmian *mi roln.* crop rotation.

płodu *itd. mi zob.* **płód.**

płody *pl. Gen.* **-ów** (*rolne*) (= *dobra natury*) produce, crop; **płody ziemi** fruits of the earth.

płodzić *ipf.* 1. (= *zapładniać*) beget, breed. 2. *przen.* produce.

płomienisty *a.* fiery, blazing; (*o czerwieni*) flaming; fiery.

płomiennorudy *a.* (*chłopak, dziewczyna*) with fiery red hair; (*włosy*) fiery red.

płomienność *f.* (*uczuć*) incandescence.

płomiennowłosy *a. lit.* red-headed.

płomienny *a.* fiery, incandescent; (*o miłości, zapale, spojrzeniu, pocałunku*) ardent, passionate; (*o mowie*) impassioned; (*o czerwieni*) flaming, violent; **piec płomienny** *metal.* reverberatory furnace.

płomień *mi Gen.* -a 1. (= *język ognia*) flame, blaze; **otwarty płomień** naked fire; **rzucić się w płomienie** jump into the flames; **stanąć w płomieniach** burst into flames. 2. *przen.* (= *błysk*) sparkle. 3. *przen.* (= *rumieniec*) blush, flush. 4. *przen.* (= *namiętność*) flame, passion. 5. *przen.* (= *zapał*) fire, ardor.

płomyk *mi Gen.* -a 1. (= *język ognia*) (little) flame; (*zapalniczki*) flame; (*piecyka*) pilot light. 2. *przen.* (= *błysk*) glimmer; **płomyk nadziei** flicker of hope. 3. *bot.* phlox (*Phlox*).

płomykówka *f. Gen.pl.* -ek *orn.* barn owl (*Tyto alba*).

płonąć *ipf.* 1. (*o ogniu*) burn, blaze. 2. (*o gwiazdach*) shine. 3. (= *rumienić się*) blush, flush; **płonąć ze wstydu** burn with shame. 4. (*o miłości, uczuciu*) burn, flame (*czymś* with sth); **płonąć chęcią zemsty** breathe revenge.

płonica *f. pat.* scarlet fever, scarlatina.

płoniczy *a. pat.* scarlatinal, scarlatinous.

płonić się *ipf. lit.* blush, flush.

płonnik *mi Gen.* -a *bot.* hair-cap moss, pigeon wheat (*Polytrichum*).

płonny *a.* 1. (= *daremny*) (*o nadziei, obawie, staraniach, zabiegach*) vain, futile; **skała płonna** *górn.* spoil. 2. *bot.* barren.

płoszyć *ipf.* scare away *l.* off, frighten away *l.* off. ~ **się** *ipf.* 1. (= *wpadać w popłoch*) get scared; (*o koniu*) shy. 2. (= *uciekać*) flee, take flight.

płot *mi* fence; (*wokół placu budowy itd.*) hoarding; **jestem sam jak kołek w płocie** I'm all alone; **trafić jak kulą w płot** miss by a mile, be off by a mile, be wide of the mark; **trzymać się czegoś jak pijany płotu** cling to sth like ivy *l.* grim death; **słowo się rzekło, kobyłka u płota** promise is a promise.

płotek *mi* -tk- *Gen.* -a 1. (= *niski płot*) (low) fence. 2. *sport* hurdle; **bieg przez płotki** hurdles.

płotka *f. Gen.pl.* -ek 1. = **płoć**. 2. (= *ktoś nieważny*) minnow, small potatoes.

płotkarka *f. Gen.pl.* -ek *zob.* **płotkarz**.

płotkarski *a. sport* hurdle.

płotkarz *mp sport* hurdler.

płowieć *ipf.* 1. (= *blaknąć*) fade, lose color; (*o włosach*) bleach. 2. (*o trawie, zbożu*) (= *żółknąć*) turn yellow, bleach.

płowowłosy *a.* tow-headed, flaxen-haired.

płowy *a.* fawn, fallow; (*o włosach, kłosach*) flaxen; **zwierzyna płowa** *myśl.* deer.

płoza *f. Gen.pl.* **płóz** *l.* **płoz** 1. (*u sanek, łyżwy*) runner; **płoza ogonowa** *lotn.* tail skid; **płozy wodowaniowe** *żegl.* sliding ways. 2. (*część narty*) runner.

płozić się *ipf.* -zi -żą (*o roślinie*) trail.

płożyć się *ipf.* (*o roślinie*) trail, creep; **rośliny płożące się** trailers, creepers.

płócienny *a.* (*o marynarce, worku, oprawie*) linen; flaxen; **splot płócienny** *tk.* plain weave.

płód *mi* -o- 1. (*ludzki*) fetus; **spędzić płód** procur *l.* produce an abortion. 2. (= *dzieło*) fruit, brainchild; **poroniony pomysł** stillborn idea.

płótno *n. Gen.pl.* -cien 1. *tk.* linen, cloth; (*żaglowe, namiotowe*) canvas; (*krawieckie*) wigan, buckram; (*tapicerskie*) scrim; **jesteś blady jak płótno** you're (as) white as a sheet *l.* ghost. 2. *sztuka* canvas; **przenieść coś na płótno** *lit.* reproduce sth on the canvas. 3. *sztuka* (= *obraz*) canvas; **wystawa płócien** painting exhibition.

płóz *mi* -o- *roln.* sole.

płucnica *f. bot.* lungwort (*Pulmonaria officinalis*); **płucnica islandzka** Iceland moss (*Cetraria islandica*).

płucny *a. anat.* pulmonic, lung; (*o tętnicy, krążeniu, żyle*) pulmonary; **pęcherzyk płucny** alveolus, air sac.

płuco *n. anat.* lung; **płaty płuc** lung lobes; **zapalenie płuc** *pat.* pneumonia; **rak płuc** *pat.* lung cancer; **sztuczne płuca** *med.* artificial lungs; **zrywać sobie płuca** *przen.* shout at the top of one's lungs; **płuca miasta** *przen.* lungs of the city.

płucodyszne *pl. Gen.* -ych *zool.* pulmonates (*Pulmonata*).

płucoserce *n. med.* heart-lung machine.

płucotchawka *f. Gen.pl.* -ek *zool.* trachea.

płuczka *f. Gen.pl.* -ek 1. *górn.* (*urządzenie*) washer, scrubber. 2. *górn.* (*ciecz*) drilling fluid. 3. *roln.* root cleaner. 4. (*w toalecie*) (toilet) cistern.

pług *mi Gen.* -a *roln.* 1. plow; **pług śnieżny** snowplow. 2. *Gen.* -u *narty* snowplow.

pługopiaskarka *f. Gen.pl.* -ek sand-spreading snowplow.

płukać *ipf.* -czę -czesz (*warzywa, naczynia, bieliznę, usta*) rinse; **płukać gardło** gargle.

płukanie *n.* rinse; (*gardła*) gargle; **płukanie żołądka** *med.* stomach pumping, gastric lavage; **płyn do płukania tkanin** fabric softener.

płukanka *f. Gen.pl.* -ek (*do gardła*) gargle; (*do włosów*) rinse.

płużny *a. narty* (*pozycja*) snowplow.

płużyć *ipf. narty* snowplow, stem.

płycej *adv. zob.* **płytko**.

płyciutki *a.* (very) shallow; (*o interpretacji, myśli*) skin-deep, trivial.

płycizna *f.* 1. shoal, shallows. 2. *przen.* shallowness, triviality.

płyn *mi* liquid, fluid; (*kosmetyczny, leczniczy*) wash; (*do soczewek kontaktowych*) solution; **mydło w płynie** liquid soap; **lekarstwo w płynie** liquid medicine; **mechanika płynów** *fiz.* fluid mechanics; **płyn nasienny** seminal fluid; **płyn hamulcowy** *mot.* brake fluid; **płyn do naczyń** washing-up liquid; **płyn do kąpieli** bubble bath; **płyn do płukania ust** mouthwash; **płyn do układania**

włosów setting lotion; **płyn mózgowo-rdzeniowy** *anat.* cerebrospinal fluid; **płyn po goleniu** aftershave lotion; **płyn przeciwmroźny** *zwł. mot.* antifreeze.

płynąć *ipf.* **1.** (*o płynie, prądzie*) flow; **czas/życie płynie** time/life goes by; **płynie we mnie irlandzka krew** I have *l.* there is Irish blood in my veins, Irish blood flows in *l.* through my veins; **pieniądze płyną jak woda** they spend/(s)he spends money like it grows on trees *l.* there's no tomorrow *l.* it's going out of style; **ziemia mlekiem i miodem płynąca** land of milk and honey. **2.** (*o dźwiękach*) flow. **3.** (= *przemieszczać się w wodzie*) swim; (*statkiem, jachtem*) sail; (*łodzią*) row; **płynąć pieskiem** dog-paddle; **płynąć żabką/ kraulem/na plecach/delfinem** swim breaststroke/ crawl/backstroke/butterfly; **płynąć pod prąd/z prądem** *przen.* swim *l.* go against/with the tide. **4.** (= *być następstwem czegoś*) follow from.

płynnie *adv.* (*mówić, czytać*) fluently; (*jechać, startować, poruszać się*) smoothly.

płynność *f.* **1.** (*substancji*) fluidity; liquidity. **2.** (*ruchów*) smoothness. **3.** (*wymowy*) fluency.

płynny *a.* **1.** (= *ciekły*) liquid, fluid; **spółgłoska płynna** *fon.* liquid. **2.** (*o poruszaniu się*) smooth. **3.** (*o stylu pisarskim*) flowing. **4.** (*o polszczyźnie, wymowie, czytaniu*) fluent. **5.** (= *niestały*) fluid.

płyta *f.* **1.** (= *tafla*) panel; plate; board; (*chodnikowa*) flagstone; (*szklana, metalowa*) sheet; (*pilśniowa, korkowa, paździerzowa*) board; (*kamienna, drewniana, metalowa*) slab; **płyta boiska** *sport* playing field; **płyta gipsowo-kartonowa** plasterboard, wallboard; **płyta paździerzowa** particle board; **płyta pilśniowa** fiberboard; **płyta lotniska** apron; **płyta nagrobkowa** tombstone; (*pozioma*) ledger; (*pionowa*) headstone, gravestone; **płyta pamiątkowa** memorial plaque; **płyta stropowa** *bud.* floor slab; **płyta pancerna** armour plate; **wielka płyta** *bud.* large concrete slab; **płyta fotograficzna** *fot.* plate. **2.** (*pieca kuchennego*) hot plate. **3.** (*z nagraniem, do słuchania*) record; **płyta kompaktowa** compact disk; **płyta długogrająca** long-playing record, LP; **zmień płytę** *t. przen.* change the record, put another record on. **4.** *komp.* board; **płyta główna** motherboard. **5.** *geol.* plate. **6.** *muz.* plate; **płyta rezonansowa** sounding board.

płytka *f. Gen.pl.* **-ek** plate; (*ceramiczna, podłogowa*) tile; **płytka nazębna** *dent.* plaque; **płytki krwi** *biol.* blood platelets.

płytkarz *mp* tiler, tile layer.

płytki *a.* **-tszy 1.** (*o oddechu, wodzie, naczyniu, orce*) (= *niegłęboki*) shallow; **płytki oddech** shallow breathing; **płytki sen** light sleep; **płytki talerz** dinner plate. **2.** (*o człowieku, umyśle, sądzie, filmie*) (= *powierzchowny*) shallow, superficial, surface.

płytko *adv.* **-cej 1.** (= *niegłęboko*) (*oddychać, orać, siać*) shallowly; (*zakopać, leżeć*) near the surface; **płytko spać** sleep lightly. **2.** (= *powierzchownie*) shallowly, superficially.

płytkość *f.* **1.** (= *niewielka odległość między powierzchnią a dnem*) shallowness. **2.** (= *powierzchowność*) shallowness, superficiality.

płytkowy *a.* plate; tile; **krwinka płytkowa** *biol.* blood platelet.

płytoteka *f.* record collection, record library.

pływ *mi geogr.* tide.

pływacki *a.* swimming; natatory; natatorial; **basen pływacki** swimming pool; natatorium; **czepek pływacki** bathing *l.* swimming cap; **spodenki pływackie** swimming trunks; **styl pływacki** stroke; **umiejętności pływackie** natatorial *l.* natatory skill.

pływacz *mi Gen.* **-a** *bot.* bladderwort (*Utricularia*). – *ma zool.* gray whale (*Eschrichtius robustus l. glaucus l. gibbosus*).

pływaczka *f. Gen.pl.* **-ek** *zob.* **pływak**[1].

pływać *ipf.* (*o ludziach, rybach*) **1.** swim; (*łódką*) row; (*jachtem, statkiem*) sail; (*na desce surfingowej*) surf; (*o korku, oliwie*) float; **dobrze pływać** be a good *l.* excellent *l.* strong swimmer; **pływać pieskiem** dog-paddle; **pływać żabką/kraulem/na plecach/delfinem** swim breaststroke/ crawl/backstroke/butterfly; **umieć pływać** know how to swim; **dok pływający** *żegl.* floating dock; **czołg pływający** *wojsk.* amphibious tank; **pływasz jak ryba** you swim like a fish. **2.** *pot.* (= *wykręcać się*) be evasive.

pływak[1] *mp pl.* **-cy** (= *ten, kto umie pływać*) swimmer.

pływak[2] *ma pl.* **-i** *orn.* (= *ptak pływający*) swimming *l.* natatorial bird, waterfowl.

pływak[3] *mi Gen.* **-a** *pl.* **-i 1.** (= *spławik*) float, bobber, (fishing) bob, cork. **2.** *ryb., żegl., lotn.* float.

pływakowy *a.* float; **wodnosamolot pływakowy** *lotn.* float seaplane; **komora pływakowa** *mot.* float chamber *l.* bowl.

pływalnia *f. Gen.pl.* **-i** swimming pool; **kryta pływalnia** indoor pool.

pływalność *f.* buoyancy; **pływalność statku** *żegl.* buoyancy.

pływanie *n.* swimming; *żegl.* navigation, sailing; (*na desce (z żaglem)*) (wind)surfing.

pływka *f. Gen.pl.* **-ek** *bot.* zoospore.

pływowy *a.* tidal; **elektrownia pływowa** tidal power plant.

pnący *a.* (*o roślinach*) climbing; **roślina pnąca** climber, climbing plant; **róża pnąca** rambler.

pnącze *n. Gen.pl.* **-y** *bot.* climber, climbing plant.

p.n.e. *abbr.* (= *przed naszą (nową) erą*) B.C., BC (*before Christ*).

pneumatofor *mi Gen.* **-a** *bot., zool.* pneumatophore.

pneumatoliza *f. geol.* pneumatolysis.

pneumatyczny *a.* pneumatic; (*o hamulcu, pistolecie, karabinku, kości*) air; **młot pneumatyczny** pneumatic drill; **silnik pneumatyczny** compressed-air engine.

pneumatyka *f. techn.* pneumatics.

pneumokoki *pl. Gen.* **-ów** *biol.* pneumococci (*Streptococcus pneumoniae*).

pnę *itd. ipf. zob.* **piąć**.

pnia *itd. mi zob.* **pień**.

PO *abbr. szkoln.* (= *przysposobienie obronne*) civil defence course.

po *prep.* + *Loc.* **1.** (*czas*) after; past; **dziesięć po trzeciej** ten past *l.* after three; **już po wszystkim** it's all over now; **mądry Polak po szkodzie** everybody's got 20/20 hindsight, (it's easy to be) wise after the event; **po chwili** after a while, a moment later; **po lecie przychodzi jesień** summer is followed by fall *l.* autumn; **po kilku latach** after a few years, (a) few years later; **po śniadaniu** after breakfast; **po zmroku** after dark; **przyjadę po świętach** I'll come after Christmas. **2.** (*kolejność*) after; **jeden po drugim** one after another. **3.** (*pochodzenie*) from, of; **butelka po winie** (empty) wine bottle; **garnek po mleku** dirty milk pot; **puszka po rybach** empty fish can; **rzeczy po kimś** hand-me-downs. **4.** (= *na podstawie*) by; **nie dać czegoś znać po sobie** not let sth show; **rozpoznać kogoś po akcencie/głosie** recognize *l.* tell sb by his *l.* her accent/voice. **5.** (*dziedziczenie*) after, from; **dostała imię po babce** she was named after her grandmother; **głos mam po ojcu** I get my voice from my father; **objąć stanowisko po kimś** take over from sb; **spadek po wujku** inheritance from one's uncle. **6.** (*hierarchia*) after, next to; **najważniejszy po prezydencie** next to president; **pierwszy po Bogu** next to God; **po Mickiewiczu** after Mickiewicz. **7.** (*przestrzeń, powierzchnia*) in, around, on, over, along; **całować kogoś po policzkach/rękach** kiss sb's cheeks/hand; **chodzić po linie** walk on a rope; **dreszcz przebiegł mi po plecach** chill ran down my spine; **głaskać kogoś po włosach** stroke sb's hair; **po drugiej stronie** on the other side; **po kładce** over the footbridge; **po korytarzu** in *l.* along the corridor; **po kraju** around the country; **po lesie/górach** in the forest/mountains; **po linii prostej** in a straight line; **po niebie** in the sky; **po mieście** around the city; **po okolicy** around the neighborhood; **po pokoju** around the room; **po trawie** on grass; **schodzić po schodach/drabinie** go down the stairs/ladder; **wchodzić po schodach/drabinie** go up the stairs/ladder; **wędrować po górach** walk *l.* hike the mountains. **8.** (*rozciągłość w przestrzeni*) around, round; **chodzić po ludziach** go from door to door; **przesiadywać po kawiarniach** sit around in cafes; **jeździć po sanatoriach** go from one sanatorium to another; **włóczyć się po sądach** drag o.s. from court to court. **9.** (*rozciągłość w czasie*) to, till, until; **pisać po całych dniach** write for days on end; **ślęczeć po nocach** sit up late. **10.** (*systematyczność*) by; **po kawałku** piece by piece, bit by bit; **po trochu** bit by bit; little by little. **11.** + *Acc.* (*zasięg*) (up) to; **stać w wodzie po kolana** stand knee-deep in water; **kufel wypełniony po brzegi** beer mug full to the brim; **uśmiać się po pachy** laugh one's head off. **12.** + *Acc.* (*kres*) till, until, to; **aż po wszystkie czasy** *przest.* till *l.* to the end of time; **po dziś dzień** *przest.* to this day. **13.** + *Acc.* (*cel*) for; **przyjść po poradę** come for advice; **dzwonić po lekarza** call a doctor; **sięgać po poradnik** reach for a handbook; **po co?** what for?; **po co to robisz?** what are you doing this for?; **nie pójdę tam, bo i po co?** I'm not going there, what's the use?; **po co o tym myślisz?** what's the use of thinking about it?;

nie wiem, po co to zrobiłem I don't know what I did it for; **licho wie po co** god knows why; **po co ta mowa?** *pot.* save your breath; **po jakie licho** *l.* **kiego grzyba?** *pot.* what the heck *l.* hell for? **14.** + *Acc.* (*określona, powtarzająca się ilość, liczba*) a, per; **po trzy złote za kilogram** three zloty a kilo; **po pięć sztuk w paczce** five items per pack. **15.** + *Acc.* (*wyliczanie*) **po pierwsze** firstly; **po trzecie** thirdly; **po wtóre** *l.* **drugie** secondly. **16.** + *Dat.* (*sposób*) in; **po angielsku/polsku** in English/Polish; **po bożemu** in a godly fashion; **po cichu** silently; **po góralsku** highlanders' fashion; **po koleżeńsku** friendly; **po ludzku** humanely; **po mistrzowsku** in a masterly way; **po nowemu** in a new way; **po ojcowsku** like a father; **po pijanemu** when drunk; **po prostu** just like that; **po staremu** in the (same) old way; **posuwać się po omacku** grope in the dark.

p.o. *abbr.* (= *pełniący obowiązki*) acting.

pobawić *pf.* **1.** (= *uprzyjemnić komuś czas*) (*dziecko*) take care of; (*gości*) entertain. **2.** *lit.* (= *pobyć gdzieś*) stay. ~ **się** *pf.* **1.** play. **2.** (= *uprzyjemnić sobie czas*) have fun *l.* a good time, enjoy o.s.

pobeczeć *pf.* **1.** (*o zwierzętach*) bleat. **2.** *pot.* blubber. ~ **się** *pf.* **-ę -ysz** *pot.* burst into tears, blubber.

pobekiwać *ipf.* **1.** (*o niektórych zwierzętach*) bleat. **2.** *pot.* (= *popłakiwać*) blubber.

pobiała *f.* **1.** (= *warstwa cyny*) tinning. **2.** (= *biel cynkowa*) zinc white. **3.** (= *wapno gaszone*) whitewash.

pobiałka *f. Gen.pl.* **-ek 1.** (= *wapno gaszone*) whitewash. **2.** *sztuka* (*glinka*) engobe. **3.** *sztuka* (*zaprawa*) ground.

pobić *pf.* **-biję -bijesz 1.** *zob.* **pobijać. 2.** (= *zwyciężyć*) defeat, beat; **pobić kogoś na głowę** smash sb; **pobić kogoś jego własną bronią** defeat sb with his own weapon, shoot sb with his own gun, give sb a taste *l.* dose of their own medicine; **pobić rekord** break the record. **3.** (= *zbić kogoś dotkliwie*) beat up. ~ **się** *pf.* have a fight.

pobiec *pf.* **-biegnę -biegniesz 1.** (= *pospieszyć dokąd*) run. **2.** (*o wzroku*) go; **moje spojrzenie pobiegło ku siostrze** I looked towards *l.* glanced at my sister.

pobiegać *pf.* run; **iść pobiegać** go for a run *l.* jog.

pobielić *pf.* **1.** (= *uczynić białym*) whiten; (*ściany, dom*) whitewash. **2.** *techn.* tin.

pobierać *ipf.* **1.** *form.* (= *brać*) (*rentę, wynagrodzenie, narzędzia*) collect; (*opłatę*) charge; (*energię*) consume; **pobierać naukę** study; **pobierać pieniądze z banku** draw money from the bank. **2.** (= *brać próbkę*) take; (*krew do analizy*) draw; **pobierać próbkę** sample. **3.** (= *czerpać*) take (in); (*tlen z powietrza*) take up. ~ **się** *ipf.* get married.

pobieżnie *adv.* cursorily; superficially; perfunctorily; **pobieżnie rzucić na coś okiem** have a cursory look at sth.

pobieżność *f.* cursoriness; superficiality; perfunctoriness.

pobieżny *a.* cursory; perfunctory; (*o ocenie, obliczeniu*) rough; **pobieżne spojrzenie** cursory glance.

pobijać *ipf.* (= *uderzając, wciskać*) hammer; hit.

pobijak *mi Gen.* **-a** (= *młotek drewniany l. do prostowania blachy*) mallet.

poblaknąć *pf.* **-kł** *l.* **-knął -kła** fade; **poblakła fotografia** faded photograph.

poblednąć, pobladnąć *pf.* **-ij, -bladł** *l.* **-blednął -bladła -bledli** 1. (= *stać się bladym*) (turn) pale. 2. (= *zblednąć*) fade.

pobliski *a.* nearby; neighboring.

pobliże *n. Gen.pl.* **-y** vicinity; **kręcić się w pobliżu** be around; **szkoła jest w pobliżu** school is nearby; **w pobliżu** nearby; **w pobliżu szkoły** in the vicinity of the school.

pobłażać *ipf.* be lenient (*komuś* with *l.* towards sb); be lax (*komuś* with sb); tolerate; (*dziecku*) spoil.

pobłażanie *n.* leniency.

pobłażliwie *adv.* (= *łagodnie*) leniently, indulgently; (= *ze zrozumieniem*) tolerantly; (= *z wyższością*) condescendingly.

pobłażliwość *f.* leniency; forbearance.

pobłażliwy *a.* lenient; indulgent; forgiving; tolerant.

pobłądzić *pf.* 1. (= *zabłądzić*) get lost. 2. (= *pobłąkać się*) roam around. 3. *lit.* (= *uczynić coś złego*) go astray.

pobłogosławić *pf.* bless; give one's blessing to; **niech Ci Bóg pobłogosławi** (may) God bless you.

pobłyskiwać *ipf.* glimmer.

pobocze *n. Gen.pl.* **-y** shoulder; **zjechać na pobocze** pull over.

poboczny *a.* collateral, secondary; (*o kwestii*) minor; **akcent poboczny** *jęz.* secondary stress; **morfem poboczny** *jęz.* affix; **wątek poboczny** subplot, underplot; **zdanie poboczne** *jęz.* subordinate clause.

pobojowisko *n.* shambles; **twój pokój wygląda jak pobojowisko!** your room is a shambles!

pobolewać *ipf.* ache (intermittently).

poborca *mp Gen.pl.* **-ów** collector; **poborca podatkowy** tax collector.

poborowy *a. wojsk.* (*o wieku*) conscriptable; **komisja poborowa** draft board; **w wieku poborowym** conscriptable. – *mp* conscript; draftee.

pobory *pl. Gen.* **-ów** salary; wages.

pobożnie *adv.* piously, devoutly.

pobożność *f.* piety, devotion.

pobożny *a.* pious, devout; (*o praktykach*) religious; **pobożne życzenie** wishful thinking.

pobór *mi* **-o-** 1. *wojsk.* conscription; draft. 2. (= *czerpanie czegoś*) (*tlenu, minerałów*) uptake; (*mocy, energii, gazu*) consumption. 3. (= *zbieranie należności*) collection.

pobóść *pf.* **-bodę -bodziesz, -bódź, -bodłem -bodła -bodli** gore, horn, butt.

pobrać *pf.* **-biorę -bierzesz** *zob.* **pobierać.** ~ **się** *pf. zob.* **pobierać się.**

pobratać się *pf.* fraternize.

pobratymczy *a. lit.* kin, kindred.

pobratymiec *mp* **-mc-** *pl.* **-y** *lit.* kin.

pobratymstwo *n. lit.* kinship.

pobrudzić *pf.* dirty, soil. ~ **się** *pf.* 1. (= *ubrudzić siebie*) get dirty, soil o.s. 2. (= *zostać pobrudzonym*) get dirty.

pobruździć *pf.* **-żdżę -ździsz** (*twarz, pole*) furrow.

pobrząkiwać *ipf.* 1. (= *grać na instrumencie niezobowiązująco*) strum, thrum. 2. (= *wydawać charakterystyczny dźwięk*) jingle; tinkle; **pobrząkiwać szabelką** *przen.* rattle the saber.

pobrzeże *n. Gen.pl.* **-y** 1. (= *wybrzeże*) littoral; (*morza*) seashore; (*rzeki*) riverside; (*jeziora*) lakefront. 2. (= *krawędź czegoś*) (*drogi, lasu*) edge; (*miasta*) outskirts.

pobrzmiewać *ipf. lit.* sound; **w twoich słowach pobrzmiewa nutka ironii** there's an undertone of irony in your words.

pobudka *f. Gen.pl.* **-ek** 1. (= *sygnał do wstawania*) reveille; **pobudka!** wake up! 2. (= *motyw działania, impuls*) impulse, motive; **robić coś ze szlachetnych/niskich pobudek** do sth out of noble/base motives; **mieć ukryte pobudki** have ulterior motives; **kierować się pobudkami osobistymi** be guided by personal motives, have an ax to grind.

pobudliwość *f.* (*emocjonalna*) excitability; (*nerwowa*) irritability; **próg pobudliwości** *fizj.* absolute *l.* sensitivity *l.* stimulus threshold.

pobudliwy *a.* excitable; hot-blooded.

pobudować *pf.* build. ~ **się** *pf.* (= *postawić sobie dom*) build o.s. a house.

pobudzać *ipf.* (= *wywoływać reakcję na coś*) stimulate; (*ciekawość, pragnienie, apetyt*) whet; **pobudzać kogoś do działania** spur sb to action, prompt sb to act, incite sb; **słowa pobudzające do myślenia** thought-provoking words.

pobudzający *a.* stimulating; **środki pobudzające** *med.* stimulants.

pobudzenie *n. fizj.* excitation; (*wzrostu, rozwoju*) stimulation; (*seksualne*) arousal.

pobudzić *pf.* 1. *zob.* **pobudzać.** 2. (= *obudzić*) wake up; **pobudzić wszystkich** wake everybody up. ~ **się** *pf.* 1. *zob.* **pobudzać się.** 2. (*o wielu osobach, zwierzętach*) wake up.

pobyczyć się *pf.* loaf around *l.* about (*for some time*).

pobyć *pf.* **-będę -będziesz, -bądź** stay, spend some time (*gdzieś* somewhere).

pobyt *mi* stay, sojourn; **pobyt stały/czasowy** permanent/temporary stay; **pobyt w sanatorium** sanatorium stay; **pobyt za granicą** stay abroad; **miejsce pobytu** place of residence.

pobytowy *a.* (of) stay, (of) sojourn; **wiza pobytowa** visitor's visa.

pocałować *pf.* kiss; **pocałować klamkę** find nobody in; **pocałuj mnie w nos** get stuffed; **pocałuj mnie w dupę** *wulg.* kiss my ass. ~ **się** *pf.* 1. (= *pocałować siebie wzajemnie*) kiss each other. 2. (= *zostać pocałowanym*) get a kiss; **nie pozwoliła się pocałować** she wouldn't let herself be kissed.

pocałunek *mi* **-nk-** kiss; **pocałunek z języczkiem** French kiss; **obsypać kogoś pocałunkami** shower sb with kisses; **przesłać komuś pocałunek** blow sb a kiss.

pocerować *pf.* **1.** (= *naprawić cerując*) darn. **2.** (= *spędzić jakiś czas cerując*) do some darning.

pochachmęcić *pf. pot.* make a mess (*coś* of sth).

pochewka *f. Gen.pl.* **-ek 1.** (= *mały futerał*) case. **2.** *bot.* capsule, theca.

pochlać *pf.* **-chlam** *l.* **-chleję -chlasz** *l.* **-chlejesz -chlali** *l.* **-chleli** *pot.* hit the booze, tank up.

pochlapać *pf.* **-pię -piesz** splash (*czymś* with sth). **~ się** *pf.* splash o.s.

pochlastać *pf.* slash. **~ się** *pf.* slash o.s.; **normalnie można się pochlastać przy tej robocie!** *pot.* this job really makes me puke!

pochlebca *mp* flatterer.

pochlebczy *a.* flattering, adulatory.

pochlebiać *ipf.*, **pochlebić** *pf.* flatter, adulate; **to mi bardzo pochlebia** it really flatters me; **pochlebiać sobie** flatter o.s.

pochlebnie *adv.* commendably, with praise, flatteringly; **wyrażać się o kimś/czymś pochlebnie** speak highly of sb/sth, hold sb/sth in high esteem.

pochlebny *a.* (= *schlebiający*) flattering, adultory; (= *pochwalny*) favorable; **pochlebna opinia/recenzja** favorable opinion/review; **pochlebne słowa** words of praise.

pochlebstwo *n.* flattery, adulation.

pochlipywać *ipf.* snivel.

pochlubić się *pf.* pride o.s. (*czymś* on sth).

pochłaniacz *mi Gen.* **-a 1.** *chem.* (= *absorbent*) absorbent. **2.** *techn.* (*urządzenie*) absorber. **3.** *wojsk.* (*część maski przeciwgazowej*) canister, cartridge.

pochłaniać *ipf.*, **pochłonąć** *pf.* **1.** (= *wchłaniać*) absorb; **pożar pochłonął tysiące ofiar** the fire took a heavy toll of thousands of victims; **remont pochłonął tysiące złotych** the redecoration soaked up several thousand zlotys; **jakby go ziemia pochłonęła** he simply vanished into thin air; **niech go piekło pochłonie!** to hell with him!; **on jest całkowicie pochłonięty pracą** he is completely immersed *l.* absorbed *l.* engrossed in his work. **2.** (= *zjadać dużo, łapczywie*) devour, gobble up; **pochłaniać kogoś oczami** gaze at sb with admiration; **pochłaniam ostatnio masę książek** *przen.* I've been devouring stacks of books recently. **3.** *chem., fiz.* (= *absorbować*) absorb.

pochmurnieć *ipf.* **-eję -ejesz** (*o niebie*) overcast; (*o osobie, twarzy*) become sullen.

pochmurno *adv.* cloudy, overcast; **było pochmurno** it was cloudy, the sky was cloudy; it was overcast, the sky was overcast.

pochmurny *a.* **1.** (*o pogodzie*) cloudy; (*o dniu, niebie, pogodzie*) overcast, cloudy. **2.** (= *posępny*) gloomy, sullen.

pochodna *f. Gen.* **-ej 1.** *mat.* derivative, differential coefficient. **2.** *chem.* derivative.

pochodnia *f. Gen.pl.* **-i** torch.

pochodnik *mi Gen.* **-a** *jęz.* derivative.

pochodność *f.* derivation.

pochodny *a.* derivative, derived; **wyraz pochodny** *jęz.* derivative.

pochodzenie *n.* origin, descent; **pochodzenie**

społeczne social class; **jestem Irlandczykiem z pochodzenia** I am of Irish descent; **Polak/Amerykanin francuskiego/niemieckiego pochodzenia** a Pole/American of French/German origin; **białko pochodzenia zwierzęcego** animal protein.

pochodzić *ipf.* (= *wywodzić się*) originate, descend. – *pf.* (= *pospacerować*) walk (*for some time*).

pochopnie *adv.* rashly, recklessly, hastily.

pochopność *f.* recklessness, hastiness.

pochopny *a.* rash, hasty; **wyciągać pochopne wnioski** jump to hasty conclusions.

pochorobowy *a.* (= *występujący po chorobie*) subsequent to a disease; (= *będący następstwem choroby*) disease-related; **komplikacje pochorobowe** disease-related complications.

pochorować się *pf.* be taken ill, fall ill.

pochować *pf.* **-am -asz 1.** (= *ukryć*) hide, stash away. **2.** (= *umieścić*) put; **pochować książki do szuflady** put one's books into the drawer. **3.** (= *pogrzebać*) bury. **~ się** *pf.* (= *ukryć się*) hide.

pochód *mi* **-o- 1.** (*manifestacja*) march, procession, parade; **pochód pierwszomajowy** *polit.* May Day parade; **otwierać pochód** head a procession; **zamykać pochód** bring up the rear. **2.** (= *przemarsz*) march; **tym zwycięstwem rozpoczął się tryumfalny pochód naszych wojsk** with this victory our army commenced its triumphal march.

pochówek *mi* **-wk-** burial.

pochrapywać *ipf.* **1.** (*o osobie*) snore. **2.** (*o koniu*) snort.

pochrzanić *pf. pot.* botch (*coś* sth); make a botch (*coś* of sth).

pochrząkiwać *ipf.* **1.** (= *chrząkać z lekka*) clear one's throat, hem. **2.** (*o świniach*) grunt.

pochrzyn *mi bot.* yam (*Dioscorea*).

pochrzynowate *pl. Gen.* **-ych** *bot.* the yam family (*Dioscoreaceae*).

pochwa *f. Gen.pl.* **pochew 1.** (= *futerał*) case, sheath; **wydobyć szablę z pochwy** unsheathe a saber. **2.** *anat.* vagina. **3.** *bot.* vagina, ocrea.

pochwalać *ipf.* approve (*coś* of sth).

pochwalić *pf.* praise, commend; **niech będzie pochwalony Jezus Chrystus!** *rel.* Lord be with you!, praised be Jesus Christ! **~ się** *pf.* boast (*czymś* of sth).

pochwalny *a.* laudatory, commendatory; **list pochwalny** letter of commendation.

pochwała *f.* praise, approval.

pochwica *f. med.* vaginismus, vaginal spasm.

pochwowy *a.* vaginal; **wziernik pochwowy** vaginal speculum; **rzęsistek pochwowy** *biol. pat.* vaginal trichomonad vaginalis (*Trichomonas vaginalis*).

pochwycić *pf.* **1.** (= *wziąć, złapać za coś*) catch, grasp; **pochwycić ster rządów** seize power. **2.** (= *wziąć do niewoli*) catch; **pochwycić kogoś** take sb captive; **pochwycić złodzieja/zbiega** catch a thief/fugitive. **3.** (= *zrozumieć*) grasp; **pochwycić czyjś wzrok** catch sb's eye; **pochwyciś sens czyichś słów** catch the meaning of sb's words.

pochylać *ipf.*, **pochylić** *pf.* incline, slant; (*cia-*

ło) bend; (*słup, drzewo*) tip, tilt; (*sztandar, flagę*) dip; **pochylać głowę przed kimś/czymś** bow down before sb/sth. ~ **się** *ipf.*, **pochylić się** *pf.* **1.** (*o człowieku, drzewie*) bend down; **pochylać się nad kimś/czymś** lean over sb/sth. **2.** (= *przechylić się*) tip, lean, incline.

pochylnia *f. Gen.pl.* **-i 1.** *żegl.* shipway, slipway. **2.** *bud.* ramp. **3.** *górn.* inclined drift.

pochylony *a.* oblique, slanting, sloping; (*o głowach*) bowed; (*o drzewach*) bent down; **samogłoska pochylona** *fon.* closed vowel.

pochyłomierz *mi Gen.* **-a** *techn.* inclinometer.

pochyłość *f.* inclination; (*zbocze*) slope.

pochyły *a.* inclined, oblique; (*o piśmie*) slanting; (*o drzewie*) leaning; (*o powierzchni*) sloping; **równia pochyła** *fiz.* inclined plane.

pociąć *pf.* **potnę potniesz, potnij 1.** (= *pokawałkować*) cut up; (*drewno*) chop; (*papier*) shred. **2.** (= *ponacinać*) incise. **3.** (*o owadach*) sting. ~ **się** *pf.* slash o.s.; **normalnie można się pociąć przy tej robocie!** *pot.* this job really makes you puke!

pociąg *mi* **1.** (= *lokomotywa i wagony*) train; **pociąg pasażerski** passenger train; **pociąg towarowy** freight *l.* cargo train; *Br.* goods train; **pociąg osobowy** slow train; **pociąg pospieszny** fast train; **pociąg ekspresowy** express train; **pociąg podmiejski** commuter train; **pociąg parowy** steam train; **pociąg elektryczny** electric train; **pociąg spalinowy** diesel train; **pociąg nocny** night train; **pociąg dalekobieżny** long-distance train; **pociąg okresowy** seasonal train; **pociąg specjalny** special train; **pociąg lokalny** *l.* miejscowy local train; **pociąg międzynarodowy** international train; **pociąg sanitarny** ambulance train; **pociąg pancerny** armored train; **pociąg opóźniony** delayed train; **pociąg InterCity** Intercity train; **pociąg InterRegio** InterRegio train; **pociąg EuroCity** EuroCity train; **planowy odjazd/ przyjazd pociągu** scheduled departure/arrival; **o której odjeżdża najbliższy pociąg do Szczecina?** what time does the next train to Szczecin leave?, what time is the next train to Szczecin?; **jechać pociągiem** go by train; **wyjść po kogoś na pociąg** meet sb at the (train) station, pick sb up from the (train) station; **spóźnić się na pociąg** miss one's *l.* the train. **2.** (= *skłonność*) penchant, liking (*do czegoś* for sth); **pociąg do alkoholu** weakness for drink; **mieć pociąg do kobiet** be attracted to women, be a womanizer.

pociągać *ipf.* **1.** (= *szarpać*) pull, tug (*za coś* at sth); **pociągać nosem** (= *wąchać*) sniff; (*płacząc*) snivel; (*przy katarze*) have a runny nose, snivel; **pociągnąć kogoś za język** milk sb for news; **nieźle pociągać z butelki** pull at the bottle, liquor up; **on już długo nie pociągnie** he won't last long; **pociągnąć kogoś do odpowiedzialności za coś** bring *l.* call sb to account for sth. **2.** (= *dotykać przesuwając*) pass (*czymś po czymś* sth over sth); **pociągać nogami** shuffle one's feet. **3.** (*o chłodzie, wietrze*) blow, gust; **pociągnęło chłodem** there was a gust of cold air. **4.** (= *spowodować*) cause, bring about. **5.** (= *malować*) coat. **6.** *tylko ipf.* (= *zaciekawiać*) appeal (*kogoś* to sb); **to**

mnie pociąga it appeals to me; **on pociąga dziewczyny swoim wysportowanym ciałem** he attracts girls with his athletic body, his athletic physique is a real magnet *l.* pull for the girls; **w całej tej opowieści najbardziej pociąga mnie wątek erotyczny** what appeals to me most of all in the story is the erotic plot.

pociągająco *adv.* (= *atrakcyjnie*) attractively; (= *podniecająco*) (*o osobie*) enticingly; **wyglądać pociągająco** look attractive, look enticing.

pociągający *a.* (= *atrakcyjny*) attractive; (= *przystojny*) good looking; (*o opowieści, książce, filmie*) captivating.

pociągły *a.* oblong; (*o twarzy*) oval.

pociągnąć *pf.* **1.** *zob.* **pociągać. 2.** (= *pomaszerować*) (*o grupie ludzi*) march; make for.

pociągnięcie *n.* draw, pull; (= *ruch, czyn*) move; **udane/nieprzemyślane/fatalne pociągnięcie** successful/not well thought out/disastrous move.

pociągowy *a.* **1.** (= *ciągnący*) pulling; **koń pociągowy** draft horse; **zwierzęta pociągowe** beast of burden; **siła pociągowa** *mech.* tractive force. **2.** (*związany z pociągiem*) train; **drużyna pociągowa** (train) onboard staff; **jednostka pociągowa** train unit.

pocić się *ipf.* **1.** (= *wydzielać pot*) sweat, perspire; **pocić się ze strachu/z gorąca** sweat from fear/the heat. **2.** (= *mozolić się*) slog away (*nad czymś* at sth). **3.** *pot.* (*o szkle*) steam up, fog up.

pociec *ipf.* **-cieknie** *l.* **-ciecze, -cieknij, -ciekł** *l.* **-cieknął -ciekła** drip, trickle.

pociecha *f.* **1.** (= *ukojenie*) comfort, consolation, solace. **2.** (= *radość*) joy, happiness; **będzie z ciebie jeszcze pociecha** you will still amount to sth; **mam z nim zawsze sto pociech** he is a riot; **mała z tego pociecha** it's cold comfort. **3.** *pot.* (= *dziecko*) kid; **mam dwie pociechy** I have two kids.

po ciemku *adv.* in the dark.

pociemnieć *pf.* darken, grow dark; **od uderzenia pociemniało mi w oczach** everything went black when I got hit.

pocierać *ipf.* rub.

pocierpieć *pf.* suffer.

pocieszać *ipf.* comfort, cheer up. ~ **się** *ipf.* console o.s.

pocieszająco *adv.* comfortingly; **wygląda/nie wygląda to pocieszająco** it looks/doesn't look comforting.

pocieszający *a.* consoling, comforting; (*o wiadomości, tonie*) encouraging.

pocieszenie *n.* consolation, comfort, solace; **na pocieszenie** by way of consolation.

pocieszny *a.* amusing, funny.

pocieszyciel *mp*, **pocieszycielka** *f.* consoler, comforter.

pocieszyć *pf. zob.* **pocieszać.** ~ **się** *pf. zob.* **pocieszać się.**

pociotek *mp* **-tk-** *pl.* **-i** *uj.* distant relative.

pocisk *mi* missile; (*strzelecki*) shell; (*zwł. rakietowy*) projectile; **pocisk artyleryjski** artillery shell; **pocisk balistyczny** ballistic missile; **pocisk dymny** smoke shell; **pocisk kierowany** guided missile; **pocisk nuklearny** nuclear missile; **pocisk odłamkowy** shrapnel missile; **pocisk przeciwlotniczy** air-defence missile; **pocisk przeciwpancerny** armor-piercing missile, APM; **pocisk świetlny** star shell; **pocisk zapalający** flare missile *l.* shell; **grad pocisków** volley of fire.

pocukrzyć *pf.* sweeten, sugar up.

pocwałować *pf.* gallop.

począć *pf.* **pocznę poczniesz, pocznij 1.** *zob.* **poczynać. 2.** *lit.* (= *zajść w ciążę*) conceive.

początek *mi* **-tk-** beginning, start, outset; **od początku** from the start, from the beginning; **z początku** at first, at the start; **z początkiem czegoś** at the beginning of sth; **od początku świata** from the beginning of things; **dać początek czemuś** give rise to sth; **brać z czegoś swój początek** originate from sth, rise from sth; **zrobić dobry początek** make a good start; **na początku było trudno** the beginning was hard *l.* tough; **na początek mogę panu zaproponować 1000 złotych miesięcznie** I can offer a starting salary of 1,000 zlotys a month; **jak na początek, poradził sobie nieźle** as for a start he did quite well, he did quite well just for starting; **od samego początku wszyscy byli nieżyczliwi** from the very beginning everybody was unfriendly; **uczę się niemieckiego od początku** I am a beginner in German; **urlop planujemy w początkach sierpnia** we're planning our vacation at the beginning of August; **z początkiem grudnia zaczęła się prawdziwa zima** early in December the real winter started; **zrób to jeszcze raz, od początku** do it again from the start; **miłe złego początki, lecz koniec żałosny** short pleasures, long lament.

początki *pl. Gen.* **-ów** (= *podstawy*) rudiments, the ABCs; **początki japońskiego** Japanese basics, rudiments of Japanese.

początkowo *adv.* at first, at the start, in the beginning; initially.

początkowy *a.* (= *stanowiący początek*) initial; (= *podstawowy, elementarny*) elementary; **kurs początkowy** elementary course, course for beginners.

początkujący *a.* novice; **początkujący nauczyciel/lekarz** novice teacher/physician. – *mp* beginner; **kurs dla początkujących** beginner's course.

począwszy *adv.* (*w przeszłości*) as early as; (*w przyszłości*) as of *l.* from, starting; **począwszy od wtorku, spotykać się będziemy popołudniami** starting Tuesday, we'll be meeting in the afternoons.

poczciwiec *mp* **-wc-** *pl.* **-y** good soul, kindhearted person.

poczciwina *f. l. mp decl. like f. Gen.pl.* **-n** *l.* **-ów** good soul, kind-hearted person.

poczciwy *a.* (= *dobroduszny*) kind-hearted; (= *zacny*) decent; **poczciwy dom** decent home; **on jest poczciwy z kościami** he's a good soul; **poczciwe psisko!** (*o psie*) there's a good boy!; (*o suczce*) there's a good girl!

Poczdam *mi* Potsdam.

poczdamski *a.* Potsdam.

poczekać *pf.* wait (*for a while*); **poczekaj, niech**

się zastanowię hang *l.* hold on, let me think; **poczekaj no ty!** you just wait!

poczekalnia *f. Gen.pl.* **-i** waiting-room.

poczekanie *n.* **na poczekaniu** (= *zaraz*) right off, right away; (*naprawić*) while you wait.

poczernieć *pf.* grow black, blacken.

poczerwienieć *pf.* redden, turn red; (= *dostać rumieńców*) blush.

poczesać *pf.* **-szę -szesz** comb.

poczesny *a.* prominent.

poczet *mi* **-czt-** *lit.* (= *zespół osób*) body, community; (= *świta*) retinue; **poczet sztandarowy** color guard; **poczet królów polskich** pictorial guide to the kings and queens of Poland; **zostać przyjętym w poczet członków organizacji** be admitted as member of an organization; **zaliczymy to na poczet wydatków przyszłorocznych** we'll put it on next year's budget *l.* account.

poczęcie *n. lit.* conception; **niepokalane poczęcie** *teol.* Immaculate Conception.

poczęstować *pf.* treat (*kogoś czymś* sb to sth). **~ się** *pf.* (= *przyjąć poczęstunek*) help o.s. (*czymś* to sth); **proszę się poczęstować owocami** help yourself to the fruit, please.

poczęstunek *mi* **-nk-** food and drinks.

poczłapać *pf.* **-pię -piesz** shuffle over (*to a place*).

poczta *f.* **1.** (*instytucja*) post office; **poczta lotnicza** air mail; **(wysłać) pocztą lotniczą** (send) by air mail; **poczta pneumatyczna** pneumatic mail; **poczta polowa** Army Postal Service, Army Post Office; **iść na pocztę** go to the post office; **załatwiać coś na poczcie** arrange sth at the post office; **wysłać coś pocztą** mail sth, send sth by post; **odpowiedzieć odwrotną pocztą** reply by return mail; **poczta pantoflowa** the grapevine; **poczta elektroniczna** *komp.* electronic mail, e-mail. **2.** (*listy, przesyłki*) mail; *Br.* post; **poczta poranna/popołudniowa** morning/afternoon mail; **przeglądać pocztę** look through the mail, go over the mail.

pocztowiec *mp* **-wc-** *pl.* **-y** post office employee. – *ma* **-wc-** *pl.* **-e** (*gołąb*) carrier pigeon, homing pigeon. – *mi* **-wc-** *Gen.* **-a** *pl.* **-e** mail boat.

pocztowy *a.* postal; **gołąb pocztowy** carrier pigeon, homing pigeon; **kartka pocztowa** postcard; **przekaz pocztowy** postal order; **skrzynka pocztowa** mailbox; **skrytka pocztowa** post-office box; **stempel pocztowy** postmark; **urząd pocztowy** post office; **wagon pocztowy** mail carriage; **znaczek pocztowy** postage stamp.

pocztówka *f. Gen.pl.* **-ek** postcard.

pocztówkowy *a.* postcard; (*o formacie zdjęcia*) postcard format.

poczucie *n.* sense, feeling; **poczucie bezpieczeństwa** sense of security, feeling of safety; **poczucie czasu** sense of time; **poczucie humoru** sense of humor; **poczucie obowiązku** sense of duty; **poczucie rzeczywistości** sense of reality; **poczucie taktu** sense of tact; **miał poczucie dobrze spełnionego obowiązku** he felt he had done his duty well.

poczuć *pf.* **1.** (= *odczuć*) feel, perceive; (*zapach*) smell. **2.** (= *doznać uczucia*) feel; **poczuć**

smutek/radość feel sadness/joy. **3.** (= *uświadomić sobie*) realize; **poczuć pismo nosem** smell a rat; **poczułem, że coś jest nie w porządku** I realized something was wrong. **~ się** *pf.* feel; **poczuć się dobrze/źle** feel well/unwell; **czuć się na siłach coś zrobić** feel able to cope with sth; **poczuć się w swoim żywiole** feel at home; **poczułem się Amerykaninem** I felt like an American, I felt American.

poczuwać się *ipf.* feel; **poczuwać się do odpowiedzialności/winy** feel responsible/guilty; **poczuć się w obowiązku coś zrobić** feel obliged to do sth.

poczwara *f. pot., uj.* eyesore.

poczwarka *f. Gen.pl.* **-ek** *biol.* chrysalis.

poczwórnie *adv.* four times as much; fourfold, quadruply; **złożony poczwórnie** (*o kartce, gazecie*) folded in four.

poczwórny *a.* four times as large; fourfold, quadruple; **poczwórna dotacja/pensja** fourfold subsidy/salary.

poczynać *ipf. lit.* commence; **śmiało sobie poczynać** act boldly; **co począć?** what to do?

poczynania *pl. Gen.* **-ń** actions, enterprises.

poczynić *pf. lit.* do, make; **poczynić zakupy do** shopping; **poczynić przygotowania** make preparations.

poczytać *pf.* **1.** *zob.* **poczytywać. 2.** (*długo czytać*) read (*for a while*); **poczytać komuś** read to sb; **poczytam sobie jeszcze z pół godziny** I'll read for about half an hour more.

poczytalność *f.* soundness of mind; **ograniczona poczytalność** *prawn.* diminished responsibility.

poczytalny *a.* of sound mind; **oskarżony w chwili popełnienia zbrodni był w pełni poczytalny** the accused was able in body and mind *l.* of sound mind and body at the time of the crime.

poczytność *f.* wide readership; **książka cieszyła się dużą poczytnością** the book was very popular, the book was a huge success.

poczytny *a.* widely-read, popular.

poczytywać *ipf. lit.* (= *uznawać za kogoś, coś*) consider, regard (*coś za coś* sth to be sth); **poczytywać coś sobie za zaszczyt** look upon sth as a great honor, consider sth to be one's honor. **~ się** *ipf.* (= *uznawać siebie za kogoś*) consider o.s. (*za kogoś* to be sb).

poćwiartować *pf.* quarter.

poćwiczyć *pf.* do some exercise, exercise. **~ się** *pf.* have some practice (*w czymś* in sth).

pod *prep.* + *Ins.* **1.** (= *poniżej*) under; **pod stołem** under the table; **pod ziemią** underground; **pod wodą** underwater; **pod spodem** below, underneath; **pod marynarką/płaszczem** under one's jacket/coat; **pod parasolem** under the umbrella. **2.** (= *tuż przy czymś*) by; **pod ścianą** by the wall; **pod drzwiami** at the door; **dom pod Londynem** a house near London; **bitwa pod Grunwaldem/Waterloo** the battle of Tannenberg/Waterloo; **pod ręką** at hand; **wszystkie potrzebne książki mam pod ręką** all the books I need are at hand. **3.** (*w zwrotach wyrażających przyczynę*) under; **pod przymusem** under pressure; **pod wpływem cze-**

goś under the influence of sth; **pod naciskiem** under duress; **pod zarzutem czegoś** on a charge of something; **ugiąć się pod ciężarem czegoś** be laden with sth, bend down under the load of sth; **pod pretekstem czegoś** under *l.* with the pretext of sth. **4.** (= *pod nadzorem, opieką*) under, in; **pod czyimś przewodnictwem** under the leadership of sb; **pod kontrolą** under control; **pod czyimś kierunkiem** under sb's supervision; **pod czyimś dowództwem** under sb's command; **pod okiem wychowawcy** under the tutor's supervision; **statek pod polską banderą** a ship under the Polish banner; **urodzić się pod szczęśliwą gwiazdą** be born under a lucky star. **5.** (*dla wyrażenia sankcji*) under, on; **pod groźbą czegoś** under threat of sth; **pod karą pozbawienia wolności** under threat of imprisonment; **zeznawać pod przysięgą** testify on *l.* under the oath. **6.** (*w zwrotach wyrażających nazwy*) kościół pod wezwaniem św. **Tomasza** St. Thomas Church, St. Thomas's Church, the Church of St. Thomas; **powieść pod tytułem...** novel entitled...; **lepiej znana pod panieńskim nazwiskiem** better known by her maiden name; **piszę pod pseudonimem Kulis** I write under the pen name of Kulis; **kino pod nazwą Paladium** Paladium movie-theater. **7.** (*w zwrotach wyrażających położenie*) **podpisać się pod listem/petycją** sign a letter/petition; **umieścić pieczęć pod umową** stamp the contract/agreement. **8.** (*w zwrotach wyrażających sposób*) **pod kątem prostym** at a right angle. **9.** + *Acc.* (*w zwrotach wyrażających kierunek*) under; **pod stół** under the table; **pod prąd** against the stream *l.* tide; **pod wiatr** against the wind; **pod górę** uphill; **wpaść pod tramwaj/samochód/pociąg** be hit by a streetcar/car/train, be run over by a streetcar/car/train. **10.** + *Acc.* (*w zwrotach wyrażających czas, okoliczności*) at, in; **pod koniec lipca** at the end of July; **pod wieczór** in the evening, towards (the) evening; **pod twoją nieobecność** in your absence; **mężczyzna pod pięćdziesiątkę** a man approaching *l.* nearing fifty. **11.** + *Acc.* (*w zwrotach wyrażających robienie czegoś na wzór czegoś*) **robić coś pod dyktando** do what one is told by sb; **dobrać zasłony pod kolor dywanu** match the curtains with the carpet; **malować pod kogoś** paint for sb. **12.** + *Acc.* (*w innych zwrotach*) **oddać propozycję pod dyskusję** submit the suggestion for discussion; **wziąć coś pod rozwagę** take sth into consideration; **oddać projekt ustawy pod głosowanie** submit the bill to a vote.

podać *pf.* **-dzą** *zob.* **podawać. ~ się** *pf. zob.* **podawać się.**

podagra *f. pat.* gout; (*palucha*) podagra.

podajnik *mi Gen.* **-a** *techn.* feeder.

podanie *n.* **1.** (*prośba urzędowa*) application. **2.** (= *legenda, opowieść*) legend, tradition. **3.** *sport* pass.

podarek *mi* **-rk-** gift, present.

podarować *pf.* **1.** (= *dać w prezencie*) give; **podarować coś komuś** give sth to sb as a present. **2.** (= *zrezygnować z jakiegoś należnego sobie świadczenia*) give up; (*dług*) remit; **podarować**

komuś karę pardon sb; **podarować coś komuś** forgive sb sth.

podarty *a.* torn, tattered.

podarunek *mi* -nk- gift, present.

podatek *mi* -tk- tax; **podatek dochodowy** income tax; **podatek katastralny** cadastral tax; **podatek obrotowy** sales tax; **podatek od darowizny** donation tax; **podatek od wartości dodanej** value added tax; **podatek od nieruchomości** real estate tax; **podatek spadkowy** inheritance tax; **podatek wyrównawczy** equalization tax, countervailing tax; **zwolnienie od** *l.* **z podatku** tax exemption; **obłożyć coś podatkiem** impose a tax on, levy a tax on sth; **ściągać podatki** collect taxes.

podatkowy *a.* tax; **polityka podatkowa** tax policy; **progresja/regresja podatkowa** tax progression/regression; **skala podatkowa** tax scale; **system podatkowy** tax system; **stopa podatkowa** rate of taxation; **ulga podatkowa** tax relief; **przepisy podatkowe** tax regulations.

podatnik *mp* taxpayer; **płacić za coś z kieszeni podatnika** pay for sth with taxpayers' money.

podatność *f.* (*na choroby*) susceptibility; (*na idee, wpływ*) receptivity (*na coś* to sth).

podatny *a.* (*na choroby*) susceptible; (*na idee, wpływ*) receptive (*na coś* to sth); **idea trafiła na podatny grunt** the idea has met with favorable conditions.

podawać *ipf.* -aję -ajesz, -awaj **1.** (= *dawać, wręczać*) give, hand; **podać piłkę** *sport* (*w tenisie, siatkówce*) serve; (*w piłce nożnej*) pass the ball; **podać komuś rękę** *l.* **podać sobie ręce** shake hands with sb; **podawać do stołu/herbatę** serve the meal/tea; **podać komuś ramię** give one's arm to sb; **podawać komuś pomocną dłoń** give a helping hand to sb; **podać komuś płaszcz** help sb put his/her coat on; **podawać dziecko do chrztu** (= *być rodzicem chrzestnym*) be godparent (*to sb's child*); (*w trakcie ceremonii*) hold the baby in the baptism ceremony. **2.** (= *ogłaszać, zawiadamiać*) announce; **gazety podają, że...** newspapers say that...; **podawać z ust do ust** pass by word of mouth; **podawać coś do wiadomości** announce sth; **podać coś do druku** submit sth for publication; **podać coś w wątpliwość** call sth into question; **podać kogoś do sądu** take sb to court; **czy może mi pani podać swoje nazwisko?** could you give me your name, please?; **za chwilę podamy wyniki dzisiejszego losowania totolotka** in a moment we will present the numbers drawn in today's lottery. ~ **się** *ipf.* profess o.s. (*za kogoś* as *l.* to be sb); pose (*za kogoś* as sb); **podać się do dymisji** hand in one's resignation.

podawarka *f. Gen.pl.* -ek *górn.* (loading) elevator.

podawczy *a.* **dziennik podawczy** mail register; **biuro podawcze** registry office.

podaż *f. ekon.* supply.

podążać *ipf.*, **podążyć** *pf. lit.* be on one's way (*dokądś* somewhere); **podążać za kimś** follow sb.

podbarwiać *ipf.*, **podbarwić** *pf.* give a slight coloring (*coś* to sth); **podbarwić opowiadanie** embellish the story.

podbiał *mi bot.* coltsfoot (*Tussilago farfara*).

podbicie *n.* **1.** (*stopy*) instep. **2.** (= *podpinka*) lining.

podbić *pf.* -biję -bijesz, -bij *zob.* **podbijać.**

podbiec *pf.* -gnę -gniesz, -gnij, -gł -gli **1.** *zob.* **podbiegać. 2.** (= *nasiąknąć*) get soaked up (*czymś* with sth); **oczy podbiegły mu krwią** his eyes were blood-shot.

podbieg *mi sport* ascent.

podbiegać *ipf.* (= *biegnąc, zbliżać się*) run up to; **podbiec do budynku/samochodu** run up to a building/car; **podbiegać krwią** (*o części ciała*) suffuse with blood; **podbiegać wodą** (*o piwnicy, lochu*) get flooded.

podbiegunowy *a.* subpolar, polar; **klimat podbiegunowy** subpolar climate; **koło podbiegunowe** polar circle; **noc podbiegunowa** polar night; **strefa podbiegunowa** subpolar zone.

podbierać *ipf.* (= *brać ukradkiem*) filch, pilfer; **podbierać zboże** *roln.* pick up, gather (*harvested cereal*); **podbierać miód** *l.* **ul** *pszczelarstwo* remove honey from a hive.

podbierak *mi Gen.* -a *ryb.* landing net.

podbijać *ipf.* **1.** (= *brać w posiadanie*) conquer, subjugate; **podbić kraj** conquer a country; **podbić czyjeś serce** *przen.* win *l.* captivate sb's heart; **podbić kogoś wdziękiem/dobrocią** win sb over with one's charm/kindness. **2.** (= *uderzać coś od spodu*) knock up; **podbić piłkę** toss the ball; **podbić komuś rękę** knock up sb's hand; **podbić komuś oko** give sb a black eye *l.* shiner; **podbijać cenę** push *l.* run up the price; **podbijać komuś bębenka** play up to sb. **3.** (= *wyściełać czymś od spodu*) line; **podbić płaszcz sztucznym futrem** line a coat with artificial fur.

podbijak *mi Gen.* -a **1.** *sport* bat. **2.** *techn.* tamper.

podbój *mi* -o- *Gen.pl.* -ów conquest; **podbój miłosny** love conquest.

podbramkowy *a.* **akcja podbramkowa** action near the goal; **sytuacja podbramkowa** *sport* (goal) scoring situation; *przen.* critical situation; **w sytuacji podbramkowej** when it comes to call.

podbródek *mi* -dk- *Gen.* -a chin; **drugi podbródek** double chin.

podbródkowy *a. anat.* genial; **cios podbródkowy** *boks* uppercut.

podbrzeźniak *mi Gen.* -a *bot.* birch bolete (*Leccinum scabrum*).

podbrzusze *n. Gen.pl.* -y **1.** (*u człowieka*) lower abdomen; (*w języku fachowym*) hypogastrium. **2.** (*u zwierzęcia*) underbelly.

podbudowa *f. Gen.pl.* -ów (= *fundament*) foundation; (*drogi, torów*) base course; *przen.* (= *podstawa*) basis; **mieć dobrą teoretyczną podbudowę** have a good theoretical basis.

podbudować *pf.*, **podbudowywać** *ipf.* underpin; **podbudowało mnie to, co powiedziałeś** what you said lifted my spirits. ~ **się** *pf.*, **podbudowywać się** *ipf. pot.* be reassured; **podbudowałem się tym, co powiedziałeś** what you said lifted my spirits.

podbudówka *f. Gen.pl.* -ek *bud.* substructure.

podburzać *ipf.*, **podburzyć** *pf.* instigate; **pod-**

burzać do buntu instigate rebellion. ~ **się** *ipf.*, **podburzyć się** *pf.* instigate one another.

podchmielony *a. pot.* tipsy, mellow.

podchody *pl. Gen.* **-ów 1.** (*gra*) stalking. **2.** *pot.* (= *knowania*) scheming; **robić pod coś podchody** have designs on sth. **3.** *myśl.* stalking (*game*).

podchodzić *ipf.* **1.** (= *idąc, posuwać się w jakimś kierunku*) approach (*do czegoś* sth); come up (*do czegoś* to sth); **podchodzić do egzaminu** take an exam; **samolot podchodzi do lądowania** the plane starts its landing approach; **ona potrafi życzliwie podejść do każdego ucznia** she has a friendly approach to every student; **może byśmy spróbowali podejść do tego zagadnienia naukowo** maybe we could try to tackle this issue scientifically. **2.** (= *wspinać się*) climb; **podchodzić pod górę** climb up a mountain, climb uphill; **serce podchodzi mi do gardła** I have my heart in my mouth; **żołądek podchodzi mi do gardła** I'm feeling sick. **3.** (= *nasiąkać*) seep. **4.** (= *zbliżać się ukradkiem*) steal up (*do kogoś / czegoś* to sb/sth).

podchor. *abbr.* (= *podchorąży*) = **pchor.**

podchorążówka *f. Gen.pl.* **-ek** *hist.* officer cadet school.

podchorąży *mp* cadet; **podchorąży rezerwy** officer cadet; **szkoła podchorążych** *hist.* officer cadet school.

podchwycić *pf. zob.* **podchwytywać.**

podchwyt *mi* **1.** *sport* snatch *l.* grip from underneath. **2.** *techn.* cage rest, fang.

podchwytliwy *a.* **podchwytliwe pytanie** trick question.

podchwytywać *ipf.* **1.** (= *chwytać*) snatch up, seize. **2.** (= *zauważać, spostrzegać*) spot; **podchwycić czyjeś spojrzenie** spot sb's glance; **podchwycić czyjś sekret** learn about sb's secret. **3.** (= *nawiązywać*) refer (*do czegoś* to sth); **podchwycić czyjeś słowa** refer to sb's words; **podchwycić śpiew/rozmowę** join in the singing/conversation.

podciąć *pf.* **podetnę podetniesz, podetnij, podciął podcięła podcięli** *zob.* **podcinać.**

podciąg *mi żegl.* buntline.

podciągać *ipf.*, **podciągnąć** *pf.* **-ij 1.** (= *wciągać*) pull up, draw up; **podciągnąć spodnie/rajstopy** pull up the pants/tights; **podciągnąć kolana pod brodę** draw up one's knees to one's chest. **2.** (= *ciągnąć*) pull; **podciągnąć stół do okna** pull the table to the window. **3.** (= *udoskonalać*) improve; **podciągnąć dyscyplinę** raise the discipline; **podciągnąć kogoś z fizyki** help sb improve his/her grades in physics. **4.** *pot.* (= *kwalifikować*) classify; **podciągnąć wszystko pod jedną kategorię** classify everything in the same category, put everything into the same category. ~ **się** *ipf.*, **podciągnąć się** *pf.* **1.** (= *unosić się*) pull o.s. up. **2.** (= *wciągać siebie nawzajem*) pull one another up. **3.** *pot.* (= *podnosić swój poziom wiedzy*) lift one's grades; **podciągnąć się z fizyki** improve in physics.

podcieniować *pf.* shade.

podcień *mi bud.* arcade.

podcierać *ipf.* wipe; **tym to możesz sobie dupę podetrzeć** *wulg.* I don't need that shit.

podcięcie *n.* **1.** (= *nacięcie*) incision. **2.** *geol.* washout.

podcięty *a.* (= *podpity*) sloshed, tipsy; (*o włosach*) trimmed.

podcinać *ipf.* **1.** (= *przycinać, skracać*) (*włosy*) trim; (*gałęzie, łodygi*) prune; **podciąć komuś skrzydła** clip sb's wings; **podciąć korzenie czegoś** strike at the root of sth. **2.** (*np. konia*) whip (*a horse*); **podciąć piłkę** slash the ball; **podciąć komuś nogę** trip sb up.

podciśnienie *n.* (= *niedobór ciśnienia*) negative pressure; **podciśnienie tętnicze** *pat.* arterial hypotension.

podczas *prep.* + *Gen.* during; **podczas gdy** *l.* **kiedy** (= *kiedy*) when, while; (= *natomiast*) whereas.

podczaszy *mp hist.* cupbearer.

podczepiać *ipf.*, **podczepić** *pf.* join, attach. ~ **się** *ipf.*, **podczepić się** *pf.* **podczepić się pod kogoś** *pot., przen.* band together with sb.

podczerwień *f. fiz.* infrared radiation.

podczerwony *a. fiz.* infrared; **promieniowanie podczerwone** infrared radiation.

podczołgać się *pf.*, **podczołgiwać się** *ipf.* crawl up (*do czegoś* to sth).

poddać się *pf.* **-dzą** *zob.* **poddawać się.**

poddany *mp hist.* subject.

poddaństwo *n.* **1.** *hist.* serfdom, bondage. **2.** *przest.* allegiance.

poddasze *n. Gen.pl.* **-y** loft, attic, garret.

poddawać *ipf.* **-aję -ajesz, -awaj 1.** (= *oddawać kogoś / coś pod obce panowanie*) surrender. **2.** (= *wystawiać na działanie czegoś*) expose; **poddawać coś pod dyskusję/rozwagę** submit sth to discussion/for consideration; **poddawać kogoś/coś próbie** put sb/sth to (the) test; **poddawać coś krytyce** subject sth to criticism; **poddawać kogoś przesłuchaniu/badaniu** put sb through an interrogation/examination; **poddawać coś pod głosowanie** put sth to the vote. **3.** (= *podsuwać*) suggest; **poddawać myśl/pomysł** suggest a thought/an idea; **poddawać projekt/wniosek** put forward *l.* propose a project/motion. ~ **się** *ipf.* **-aję -ajesz, -awaj 1.** (= *oddawać siebie pod obce panowanie, rezygnować z walki*) surrender (to), give in, yield. **2.** (= *wystawiać siebie na działanie czegoś*) expose; **poddawać się leczeniu/operacji** undergo treatment/operation; **poddawać się czyjejś woli** give in to sb, resign o.s. to sb's will.

poddostawca *mp* subcontractor.

poddusić *pf.* **-szę -sisz** *kulin.* stew awhile. ~ **się** *pf.* be choking.

poddźwiękowy *a. lotn.* subsonic; **prędkość poddźwiękowa** subsonic speed.

pode *prep. zob.* **pod.**

podebrać *pf.* **podbiorę podbierzesz** *zob.* **podbierać.**

podejmować *ipf. zob.* **podjąć.** ~ **się** *ipf. zob.* **podejmować się.**

podejrzana *f. Gen.* **-ej** *zob.* **podejrzany[2].**

podejrzany[1] *a.* suspicious; **podejrzany typ** shady character; **podejrzane zachowanie** suspicious behavior; **podejrzane towarzystwo** shady *l.* dubious company.

podejrzany² *mp zwł. prawn.* suspect.

podejrzeć *pf.* **-ę -ysz, -yj** *zob.* **podglądać**.

podejrzenie *n.* **1.** (= *posądzenie*) suspicion; **nieuzasadnione podejrzenie** unfounded *l.* groundless suspicion; **nabierać podejrzeń** become suspicious; **wzbudzać podejrzenia** arouse suspicion. **2.** (= *przypuszczenie*) assumption, suspicion; **podejrzenie zapalenia płuc** suspicion of pneumonia.

podejrzewać *ipf.* **1.** (= *posądzać*) suspect; **podejrzewać kogoś o coś** suspect sb of sth. **2.** (= *przypuszczać*) have an inkling, suspect; **lekarze podejrzewają zapalenie płuc** doctors suspect pneumonia. **~ się** *ipf.* suspect each other *l.* one another.

podejrzliwie *adv.* suspiciously.

podejrzliwość *f.* suspiciousness.

podejrzliwy *a.* suspicious, mistrustful, distrustful; **podejrzliwe spojrzenie** distrustful look; **podejrzliwy z natury** suspicious by nature; **podejrzliwy wobec** *l.* **w stosunku do kogoś** suspicious about sb, mistrustful of sb.

podejście *n.* **1.** (*pod górę*) climb. **2.** (= *nastawienie do kogoś, czegoś*) attitude (*do kogoś / czegoś* to *l.* towards sb/sth) approach (*do kogoś / czegoś* to sb/sth); **zrobić coś w pierwszym podejściu** *l.* **za pierwszym podejściem** do sth on the first attempt.

podejść *pf.* **podejdę podejdziesz podszedł podeszła podeszli** **1.** *zob.* **podchodzić**. **2.** *pot.* (= *oszukać kogoś*) outwit, overreach, trick.

podejźrzon *mi bot.* grape fern (*Botrychium*); **podejźrzon księżycowy** moonwort (*Botrychium lunaria*).

podekscytowany *a.* excited.

podenerwowany *a.* nervous.

podeń *adv. lit.* (= *pod niego*) under him *l.* it.

podeprzeć *pf.* **-prę -przesz, -przyj, -parł** *zob.* **podpierać**. **~ się** *pf. zob.* **podpierać się**.

podeptać *pf.* **-pczę -pcze** *l.* **-pcę -pce, -pcz** tread, trample (on); **podeptać trawnik** trample the lawn; **podeptać komuś nogi** tread *l.* trample on sb's toes *l.* feet; **podeptać czyjś honor** *przen.* trample on sb's honor; **podeptać przysięgę** *przen.* violate an oath.

poderwać *pf.* **-wę -wiesz, -wij** *zob.* **podrywać**. **~ się** *pf. zob.* **podrywać się**.

poderżnąć *pf.* **-ij** *zob.* **podrzynać**.

podeschnąć *pf.* **-ij, podsechł podeschła** *zob.* **podsychać**.

podesłać¹ *pf.* **-ślę -ślesz, -ślij** *zob.* **podsyłać**.

podesłać² *pf.* **-ścielę -ścielisz** *zob.* **podścielać**.

podesrać *pf. zob.* **podsrywać**.

podest *mi* **1.** (*przy schodach*) landing. **2.** (*dla mówcy*) podium.

podeszły *a.* old, ripe; **w podeszłym wieku** advanced in years, of advanced years *l.* age; **osoby w podeszłym wieku** the aged.

podeszwa *f. Gen.pl.* **-ew** **1.** (= *spód buta*) sole; **twardy jak podeszwa** (*zwł. o mięsie*) as tough as leather. **2.** (= *spód stopy*) sole. **3.** *techn.* footing.

podetknąć *pf.* **-ij** *zob.* **podtykać**.

podetrzeć *pf.* **-trę -trzesz, -yj, podtarł** *zob.* **podcierać**. **~ się** *pf. zob.* **podcierać się**.

podeżreć *pf.* **-ę -esz, -yj, podżarł** *zob.* **podżerać**.

podfrunąć *pf.*, **podfruwać** *ipf.* fly up, flutter up.

podfruwajka *f. Gen.pl.* **-ek** *żart.* giddy girl.

podgalać *ipf.* shave.

podganiać *ipf. pot.* catch up with; **podganiać robotę** catch up on one's work.

podgardle *n. Gen.pl.* **-i** **1.** *anat.* dewlap. **2.** *kulin.* (*część tuszy wieprzowej*) jowl.

podgatunek *mi* **-nk-** *biol.* subspecies.

podgiąć *pf.*, **podginać** *ipf.* **podegnę podegniesz, podegnij** tuck up, bend.

podgląd *mi* **1.** *techn.* monitoring; **być na podglądzie** be monitored. **2.** *komp.* (*dokumentu, strony*) view.

podglądacz *mp pot.* peeper, spier; voyeur.

podglądać *ipf.* spy on, watch, peep, snoop; **podglądać przez dziurkę od klucza/zza firanki** watch through the keyhole/from behind the lace curtain.

podglebie *n.* **1.** *geol.* subsoil, undersoil. **2.** *przen.* (= *podstawa, podłoże*) foundation.

podgłośniowy *a. med.* subglottis.

podgłówek *mi* **-wk-** *Gen.* **-a** bolster.

podgolić *pf.* **-ól** *l.* **-gol** *zob.* **podgalać**.

podgonić *pf. zob.* **podganiać**.

podgorączkowy *a. pat.* subfebrile; **stan podgorączkowy** subfebrile body temperature.

podgotować *pf.*, **podgotowywać** *ipf.* boil slightly, simmer. **~ się** *pf.*, **podgotowywać się** *ipf.* boil slightly, simmer.

podgórski *a.* piedmont, submontane.

podgórze *n. Gen.pl.* **-y** foothills, piedmont, submontane district.

podgrodzie *n. Gen.pl.* **-i** *hist.* borough.

podgromada *f. Dat.* **-adzie** *biol.* subphylum, subdivision.

podgrupa *f. Dat.* **-pie** subgroup.

podgryzać *ipf.*, **podgryźć** *pf.* **-zę -ziesz -zł -źli** **1.** (= *gryząc, niszczyć coś od spodu*) gnaw. **2.** *pot.* (= *działać ukradkiem na czyjąś niekorzyść*) undermine. **~ się** *ipf. pot.* (= *szkodzić sobie nawzajem*) scheme againt each other *l.* one another.

podgrzać *pf.* **-eję -ejesz** *zob.* **podgrzewać**. **~ się** *pf. zob.* **podgrzewać się**.

podgrzewacz *mi Gen.* **-a** **1.** (*do podgrzewania czegoś*) heater. **2.** *techn.* (*w silniku wysokoprężnym*) heater plug, glow plug.

podgrzewać *ipf.* heat; (*obiad, zupę*) heat up. **~ się** *ipf.* heat (up).

podgrzybek *mi* **-bk-** *Gen.* **-a** *bot.* bolete (*Xerocomus*); **podgrzybek brunatny** bay bolete (*X. badius*); **podgrzybek zajączek** yellow-cracked bolete (*X. subtomentosus*).

podgumowany *a.* rubber-lined; **podgumowany płaszcz przeciwdeszczowy** rubber-lined raincoat.

podhalański *a.* of the Polish Tatra Highlands; **owczarek podhalański** *kynol.* sheepdog.

podholować *pf.* tow.

podirytowany *a.* irritated, annoyed, exasperated.

podium *n. sing. indecl. pl.* **-dia** *Gen.* **-diów** **1.**

(= *podwyższenie*) podium. **2.** *sport* podium; **stanąć na podium** stand on the podium.

podiwanić *pf. pot.* (= *ukraść*) walk *l.* make off with, filch, lift.

podjadać *ipf.* **1.** (= *podgryzać coś od spodu*) fret, gnaw (*coś* at sth); (= *wyjadać ukradkiem*) eat furtively. **2.** (= *jeść po trochu przez długi czas*) munch on, chew on.

podjazd *mi* **1.** (= *dojazd do budynku*) driveway. **2.** (= *miejsce zadaszone przed budynkiem*) porch. **3.** *sport* uphill drive *l.* ride. **4.** *wojsk.* foray cavalry unit.

podjazdowy *a.* **1.** drive, driveway. **2.** *wojsk.* raid, foray; **wojna podjazdowa** guerila warfare.

podjąć *pf.* **podejmę podejmiesz, podejmij 1.** (= *unosić*) raise; **podjąć słuchawkę** pick up the receiver; **podjąć pieniądze z konta** withdraw money from one's account; **podjąć rękawicę** *przen.* accept the challenge. **2.** (= *przedsięwziąć coś*) take; (*podjąć pracę*) take up *l.* accept a job; **podjąć trud** make an effort; **podjąć decyzję** take *l.* make a decision; **podjąć uchwałę** make a resolution; **podjąć zobowiązanie** make a committment. **3.** (= *powracać do poruszanego już wątku, tematu*) return, go back; **podjąć dyskusję/temat** take up a discussion/topic. **4.** (= *gościć kogoś*) receive; **podjąć kogoś obiadem/kolacją/kawą** have sb over for dinner/supper/coffee; **podjąć kogoś bardzo serdecznie** be very hospitable. ~ **się** *pf.* (= *decydować się na coś, zobowiązywać się*) make a committment (*to do sth*), undertake (*sth l. to do sth*).

podjechać *pf.* **-jadę -jedziesz, -jedź** *zob.* **podjeżdżać**.

podjeść *pf.* **-jem -jesz, -jedz, -jadł -jedli 1.** *zob.* **podjadać. 2.** (= *zaspokoić głód*) eat one's fill, appease one's hunger, satisfy one's appetite; **czy podjadłeś sobie?** did you have *l.* get enough to eat?

podjeżdżać *ipf.* drive up to, draw up to; (*pod górę*) go uphill; **podjadę autobusem** I'll take a bus.

podjęzykowy *a. anat.* subglossal; **ślinianka podjęzykowa** sublingual gland; **nerw podjęzykowy** hypoglossal nerve.

podjudzać *ipf.*, **podjudzić** *pf.* instigate, incite. ~ **się** *ipf.*, **podjudzić się** *pf.* instigate each other *l.* one another.

podkanclerzy *mp hist.* Deputy Chancellor of the Treasury.

podkarmiać *ipf.*, **podkarmić** *pf.* feed.

podkarzeł *mi* **-rł-** *Gen. i Acc.* **-a** *astron.* subdwarf.

podkasać *pf.*, **podkasywać** *ipf.* **-szę -szesz** roll up, turn up.

podklasa *f.* subclass.

podkład *mi* **1.** (= *podłoże*) base, foundation, groundwork; **podkład pod farbę** undercoat; **podkład muzyczny** incidental music. **2.** (*kosmetyk*) foundation (cream). **3.** *kol.* tie; *Br.* sleeper.

podkładać *ipf.* **1.** (= *podsuwać*) put under; **podłożyć bombę** plant a bomb; **podłożyć ogień pod coś** set fire to sth; **podłożyć komuś nogę** trip sb (up). **2.** (= *podwijać coś przy szyciu*) turn up.

3. (= *kłaść ukradkiem*) put stealthily; plant. **4.** (= *harmonizować słowa z muzyką*) set words to music; (= *dodawać muzykę do filmu, programu itp.*) underscore. ~ **się** *ipf. pot.* put o.s. in an unfavorable position.

podkładka *f. Gen.pl.* **-ek 1.** (= *coś podłożonego*) rest, support; **podkładka pod talerz** mat; **podkładka pod kieliszek/szklankę/kufel** coaster. **2.** *ogr.* stock. **3.** *techn.* washer.

podkładowy *a.* base; (*o warstwie, warstwie makijażu*) foundation; **farba podkładowa** priming paint, undercoat.

podkochiwać się *ipf.* have a crush on, be infatuated with; **podkochiwać się w kimś** have a crush on sb, be sweet on sb.

podkolanówki *pl. Gen.* **-ek** knee-length socks.

podkomendny *a.* subordinate. – *mp* subordinate.

podkomisja *f.* subcommittee.

podkomorzy *mp hist.* chamberlain.

podkop *mi* tunnel.

podkopać *pf.* **-pię -piesz** *zob.* **podkopywać**. ~ **się** *pf. zob.* **podkopywać się**.

podkopywacz *mi Gen.* **-a** *roln.* excavator.

podkopywać *ipf.* **1.** (= *zrobić podkop, jamę itp.*) dig. **2.** (= *narażać na szwank, osłabiać*) undermine, impair; **podkopywać czyjeś zaufanie** undermine sb's confidence; **podkopywać czyjś autorytet** undermine sb's authority; **podkopywać zdrowie** undermine sb's health. ~ **się** *ipf.* tunnel one's way, dig a tunnel.

podkoszulek *mi* **-lk-** *Gen.* **-a, podkoszulka** *f. Gen.pl.* **-ek** undershirt.

podkowa *f. Gen.pl.* **-ków 1.** (*końska*) horseshoe. **2.** (*kształt*) horseshoe, semicircle. **3.** *myśl.* U shape.

podkowce *pl. Gen.* **-ów** *zool.* horseshoe bats (*Rhinolophidae*).

podkówka *f. Dat. i Loc.* **-ce** *Gen.pl.* **-ek 1.** (little) horseshoe. **2.** horseshoe, semicircle; **wyginać usta w podkówkę** pout. **3.** *pot.* (*portmonetka*) coin purse.

podkpiwać *ipf.* **-am -asz** tease; **podkpiwać z kogoś** poke fun at sb, pull sb's leg.

podkradać *ipf.*, **podkraść** *pf.* **-dnę -dniesz, -dnij, -dł** pilfer, steal. ~ **się** *ipf.*, **podkraść się** *pf.* creep up (on).

podkrążony *a.* dark-circled; **mieć podkrążone oczy** have dark circles under one's eyes.

podkreślać *ipf.* **1.** (= *rysować kreskę, linię pod czymś*) underline, underscore. **2.** (= *akcentować, uwydatniać*) emphasize, underscore, stress.

podkreślenie *n.* **1.** (*kreska, linia*) underline, underscore. **2.** (= *zaakcentowanie, uwydatnienie*) emphasis, stress; **podkreślenia wymaga fakt, że...** what needs underscoring is the fact that..., it is worth stressing that...

podkreślić *pf. zob.* **podkreślać**.

podkręcać *ipf.*, **podkręcić** *pf.* **1.** (= *kręcąc, nawinąć, wydłużyć, naciągnąć coś*) wind (up); turn up; **podkręcać wąsa** twist one's moustache. **2.** *pot.* (= *stymulować*) perk up, pep up. **3.** *pot.* (= *robić głośniej odtwarzaną muzykę*) turn up.

podkrzew *mi bot.* subshrub, suffrutex.

podkształcać się *ipf.*, **podkształcić się** *pf.* brush up on, study up, read up on.

podkuć *pf. zob.* **podkuwać**.

podkulać *ipf.*, **podkulić** *pf.* draw in (one's legs), bend (one's knees).

podkultura *f. socjol.* subculture.

podkupić *pf.*, **podkupywać** *ipf. pot.* outbid.

podkurczać *ipf.*, **podkurczyć** *pf.* draw in (one's legs), bend (one's knees).

podkurzacz *mi Gen.* **-a** *pszczelarstwo* smoker.

podkusić *pf.* **-szę -sisz** tempt.

podkuwać *ipf.* **1.** (*konia*) shoe. **2.** (*buty*) hobnail. **3.** *pot.* (= *poduczyć się*) cram.

podlać *pf.* **-leję -lejesz -lali** *l.* **-leli** *zob.* **podlewać**.

podlatywać *ipf.* **1.** (= *wznosić się w górę*) fly up, rise. **2.** *pot.* (= *biegnąc, zbliżać się*) run up to.

podle *adv.* **1.** (= *nikczemnie*) abjectly, despicably, vilely; **zachować się podle** behave despicably *l.* vilely. **2.** *pot.* (= *licho*) lousy; **czuć się podle** feel lousy *l.* rotten.

podlec[1] *mp Voc.* **-u** *pot.* (= *niegodziwiec*) scamp, rascal, mean person.

podlec[2] *pf. zob.* **podlegać**.

podlecieć *pf.* **-cę -cisz** *zob.* **podlatywać**; **jak** *l.* **co podleci** any (old) thing, whatever.

podleczyć *pf.* cure partly. **~ się** *pf.* cure partly, get (a little bit) better.

podlegać *ipf.* be subordinate; **podlegać prawu** be subject to the law, come under the law; **podlegać wpływom czegoś** be influenced by sth; **podlegać amnestii** be amenable to amnesty; **czyn podlega karze pozbawienia wolności do lat trzech** act is liable to a three-year imprisonment; **to nie podlega dyskusji** this is indisputable.

podległy *a.* subject, subordinate; **podległy komuś/czemuś** subordinate to sb/sth.

podlewać *ipf.* **1.** (*rośliny*) water. **2.** *kulin.* (*w czasie gotowania*) baste.

podleźć *pf.* **-lezę -leziesz -lazł -leźli** *zob.* **podłazić**.

podliczać *ipf.*, **podliczyć** *pf.* add up, count (up).

podlizać się *pf.* **-żę -żesz** *zob.* **podlizywać się**.

podlizuch *mp pl.* **-y** *pog.* toady, fawner, apple-polisher, brown-noser.

podlizywać się *ipf. pot.* suck up, toady (*komuś* to sb).

podlotek *mp* **-tk-** *pl.* **-i** teenage girl.

podłamywać się *ipf. pot.* get discouraged.

podłapać *pf.* **-pię -piesz** *pot.* **1.** (= *uzyskać coś korzystnego*) chance upon. **2.** (*chłopaka, dziewczynę*) pick up.

podłazić *ipf.* **-żę -zisz** *pot.* **1.** (*pod coś*) creep under. **2.** (*do czegoś*) come up to.

podłączać *ipf.*, **podłączyć** *pf. pot.* hook up. **~ się** *ipf.*, **podłączyć się** *pf.* **1.** *pot.* (= *przyłączać się do jakiejś instalacji*) hook up, get hooked up. **2.** *pot.* (= *włączać się do nieoczekiwanej zabawy*) join in.

podłoga *f. Gen.pl.* **-óg** floor.

podłogowy *a.* floor; **deski podłogowe** floor boards; **wykładzina podłogowa** fitted carpet; **pa**nele podłogowe floor panels; **pasta podłogowa** floor polish *l.* shine.

podłokietnik *mi Gen.* **-a** (*poręcz*) armrest.

podłość *f.* (= *bycie podłym*) meaness; (= *podły postępek*) mean trick.

podłoże *n. Gen.pl.* **-y** **1.** (= *podkład*) basis, groundwork; **choroba na podłożu nerwowym** nervous disease; **nie ukrywam, że u podłoża mojego działania leżą motywy osobiste** I don't deny that my behavior is driven by personal motives. **2.** (= *grunt, ziemia*) ground, soil; **podłoże piaszczyste/kamieniste/gliniaste** sandy/stony/clay ground. **3.** *biol.* substratum. **4.** *sztuka* ground.

podłożyć *pf. zob.* **podkładać**. **~ się** *pf. zob.* **podkładać się**.

podłubać *pf.* **-bię -biesz** **1.** (= *pogrzebać w czymś*) rummage; **podłubać w nosie** pick one's nose; **podłubać w zębach** pick one's teeth. **2.** (= *pomajstrować*) tinker, fiddle (*przy czymś* with sth).

podług *prep.* + *Gen. przest.* (= *według*) according to, in pursuance of, in conformity with.

podłużnie *adv.* longitudinally, lengthwise.

podłużny *a.* **1.** (= *wydłużony*) elongated. **2.** (= *ciągnący się wzdłuż*) longitudinal; **przekrój podłużny** *techn.* longitudinal cross-section.

podłużyć *pf.*, **podłużać** *ipf.* lengthen.

podły *a.* **1.** (= *niegodziwy*) mean; (*podły czyn*) mean *l.* base act. **2.** *pot.* (= *kiepski*) lousy; **podłe żarcie** disgusting food; **podłe warunki mieszkaniowe** abject *l.* shabby housing conditions.

podmalować *pf.*, **podmalowywać** *ipf.* (*oczy, twarz*) put on make-up, apply make-up. **~ się** *pf.*, **podmalowywać się** *ipf.* put on make-up, apply make-up.

podmiana *f. pot.* deceitful change.

podmiejski *a.* suburban; **pociąg podmiejski** commuter train.

podmieniać *ipf.*, **podmienić** *pf.* change (*sth for sth in a deceitful way*).

podminować *pf.*, **podminowywać** *ipf. wojsk.* mine.

podminowany *a.* mined; **być podminowanym** *przen.* be tense *l.* uptight.

podmiot *mi* **1.** *jęz.* subject; **podmiot bierny** passive subject; **podmiot czynny** active subject; **podmiot domyślny** understood subject; **podmiot logiczny** logical subject; **podmiot nierozwinięty** single subject; **podmiot rozwinięty** compound subject; **podmiot liryczny** *teor.lit.* lyrical I. **2.** *fil.* subject. **3.** *prawn.* entity; **podmiot gospodarczy** business entity.

podmiotowo *adv. fil.* subjectively.

podmiotowość *f. fil.* subjectivity.

podmiotowy *a.* **1.** *jęz.* subjective. **2.** *fil.* subjective. **3.** *prawn.* entitative.

podmokły *a.* boggy, marshy, wet.

podmorski *a.* submarine, undersea.

podmuch *mi* **1.** (*spowodowany wiatrem*) gust (*of wind*). **2.** (*w wyniku wybuchu*) blast.

podmurować *pf.*, **podmurowywać** *ipf. bud.* provide with a (brick) base *l.* foundation.

podmurówka *f. Gen.pl.* **-ek** *bud.* (brick) wall base, foundation.

podmyć *pf.* -ję -jesz, -yj, **podmywać** *ipf.* 1. (*o fali, rzece, morzu itp.*) undermine; wash away. 2. (*o higienie intymnej*) wash sb's private parts. ~ **się** *pf.*, **podmywać się** *ipf.* (*o higienie intymnej*) wash one's private parts.

podnająć *pf.* -mę -miesz, -mij *zob.* **podnajmować**.

podnajem *mi* -jm- *prawn.* sublease.

podnajemca *mp prawn.* sublessee.

podnajmować *ipf. prawn.* sublease.

podnawka *f. Gen.pl.* -ek *icht.* remora (*Echeneidae*).

podniebienie *n.* 1. *anat.* palate; **podniebienie twarde** hard palate; **podniebienie miękkie** soft palate, velum. 2. *przen.* (= *zmysł smaku*) palate, sense of taste; **wybredne podniebienie** choosy palate. 3. *bud.* intrados, soffit.

podniebienny *a.* palatal; **migdałki podniebienne** *anat.* tonsils; **głoska podniebienna** *fon.* palatal sound.

podniebny *a. lit.* soaring, sky-high.

podniecać *ipf.* 1. (= *pobudzać zmysły*) excite, thrill. 2. (*wyobraźnię, ambicję, apetyt*) (= *wzmagać intensywność czegoś*) stimulate, whet. 3. (= *pobudzać seksualnie*) excite, arouse. ~ **się** *ipf.* 1. (= *pobudzać swoje zmysły*) get excited, get thrilled; **podniecać się czymś** get excited about sth. 2. (= *ożywiać się*) get excited. 3. (= *pobudzać się seksualnie*) become excited *l.* aroused.

podniecająco *adv.* excitingly, stimulatingly.

podniecający *a.* exciting, stimulating.

podniecenie *n.* excitement; (*seksualne*) arousal.

podniecić *pf. zob.* **podniecać**. ~ **się** *pf. zob.* **podniecać się**.

podniecony *a.* -eni excited; (*seksualnie*) aroused, excited.

podniesienie *n. rz.-kat.* Elevation.

podnieść *pf.* -niosę -niesiesz -niósł -niosła -nieśli *zob.* **podnosić**. ~ **się** *pf. zob.* **podnosić się**.

podnieta *f.* 1. (= *zachęta*) stimulus, incentive, impulse. 2. *fizj.* stimulus, incentive, impulse.

podniosłość *f.* loftiness, sublimity.

podniosły *a.* lofty, elevated; (*o uroczystości, momencie*) solemn; (*o języku, uczuciach, utworze*) sublime.

podnosić *ipf.* -szę -sisz 1. (= *unosić, wznosić*) raise, lift, elevate; **podnieść kołnierz** stand up the collar; **podnieść słuchawkę** pick up the receiver; **podnieść kurtynę** raise the curtain; **podnieść kotwicę** *żegl.* weigh anchor; **podnieść żagle** *żegl.* set sail; **podnieść głos** raise one's voice; **podnieść głowę** *przen.* (= *nabrać otuchy*) take heart; (= *stać się zarozumiałym*) become conceited; **podnieść oczy** *l.* **wzrok** raise one's eyes; **podnieść rękę na kogoś** raise one's hand against sb; **podnieść kwestię/temat/problem** bring up *l.* raise an issue/a topic/problem; **kroczyć z podniesionym czołem** hold one's head high. 2. (= *wziąć coś, co upadło, przechyliło się, leży*) pick up; **podnieść kogoś na nogi** set sb (back) on their feet; **podnieść kogoś na duchu** cheer sb up, lift *l.* raise sb's spirits. 3. (= *podsuwać*) raise. 4. (= *wzniecać*) raise; **podnieść alarm** raise the alarm; **pod-**

nosić kurz raise dust; **podnosić krzyk** *l.* **wrzawę** raise a rumpus. 5. (= *wzrastać, podnosić poziom*) rise; **po ulewie rzeki się podniosły** after the downpour the rivers rose. 6. (= *wzmagać, poprawiać*) increase, augment, raise; **podnieść komuś pensję** raise sb's pay; **podnieść swoje kwalifikacje** raise one's qualifications; **podnieść wydajność** improve efficiency; **podnieść sprzedaż** increase sales; **podnieść liczbę do kwadratu/do sześcianu** *mat.* square/cube a number; **podnieść kogoś do godności biskupa** raise sb to the rank of bishop. ~ **się** *ipf.* 1. (= *unosić się z pozycji siedzącej lub leżącej*) stand *l.* get up, rise; **podnieść się z łóżka** get up; **podnieść się z nędzy/upadku** *przen.* raise from poverty/fall. 2. (= *być uniesionym*) rise, stand; **włosy mi się podniosły z wrażenia** my hair stood on end. 3. (= *podrywać się z ziemi*) take off, rise; **kurz się podniósł** dust rose; **samolot się podniósł** plane took off. 4. (= *wzmagać się, nasilać się*) rise, increase; **podniosła się sprzedaż** sales rose. 5. (*o głosie, o dźwięku*) erupt, resound. 6. (= *zerwać się*) start, break out; **wiatr się podniósł** wind started blowing.

podnoszenie *n.* lifting; **podnoszenie ciężarów** *sport* weightlifting.

podnośnik *mi Gen.* -a *techn.* jack; lift; elevator; hoist; **podnośnik widłowy** fork-lift truck.

podnośnikowy *a. techn.* jack; lift; elevator; hoist.

podnośny *a.* lifting; draw.

podnóże *n. Gen.pl.* -y foot; **u podnóża góry** at the foot of the mountain; **Zakopane leży u podnóża Tatr** Zakopane is located *l.* situated at the foot of the Tatras.

podnóżek *mi* -żk- *Gen.* -a 1. (*stołek*) footstool, footrest. 2. *przen.* (= *sługalec*) servant. 3. *bud.* tread.

podobać się *ipf.* be to sb's liking; **podobać się komuś** appeal to sb, sb likes sth; **podoba mi się ten pomysł** I like this idea, this idea appeals to me; **ona mi się podoba** I like her; **jak się komu żywnie podoba** as you like it.

podobieństwo *n.* similarity; (*wyglądu*) resemblance, likeness; **podobieństwo figur** *geom.* geometrical similarity; **na wzór i podobieństwo czegoś** in the likeness of sth; **na swoje podobieństwo** in one's image.

podobizna *f. przest.* likeness, image, effigy.

podobnie *adv.* (= *w podobny sposób*) similarly, alike, analogically; (= *równie*) as; **podobnie jak...** like..., similarly to...

podobno *part.* supposedly, allegedly, reportedly; **podobno jedziesz do Krakowa?** I've heard you're going to Cracow?; **mają podobno jeszcze jeden dom, w Zakopanem** they are said to have one more house in Zakopane.

podobny *a.* 1. (= *przypominający kogoś/coś*) similar; **podobna do ojca** similar to her father, like her father; **podobni jak dwie krople wody** as like as two peas in a pod; **być podobnym do ludzi** look quite attractive, be quite good-looking; **do czego to podobne!** how incongruous!, what is that supposed to be! 2. (= *taki, jak ten wspomniany*) like, alike, similar; **czytałem o podob-**

nym zdarzeniu I've read about a similar incident; **rzadko się spotyka dziewczynę podobnej urody jak ty** one seldom meets a girl as beautiful as you, one seldom meets a girl of your beauty; **i temu podobne** *l.* **i tym podobne** and the like; **coś podobnego!** it can't be!, really!

podobóz *mi* **-o-** subcamp.

podochocony *a.* **-eni** 1. (= *rozbawiony, podniecony*) merry, frisky, aroused, excited. 2. (= *podpity*) merry, tipsy; *Br.* tiddly.

podoczepiać *pf.* attach, tack on, hook on, hitch, fasten, pin.

pododawać *pf.* **-daję -dajesz, -dawaj** 1. (= *dołączyć*) add, append, attach, put on/in. 2. (= *dodać, zsumować*) add up, add together, sum up, count up, tot up.

pododdział *mi wojsk.* 1. subunit. 2. (*o instytucji*) subdivision.

pododmiana *f. biol.* subvariety.

podoficer *mp pl.* **-owie** *wojsk.* non-commissioned officer, non-com, NCO; (*w marynarce wojennej*) petty officer.

podoficerski *a. wojsk.* non-commissioned officer's.

podogonie *n. Gen.pl.* **-i** (*element uprzęży*) crupper.

podokiennik *mi Gen.* **-a** *bud.* (*zewnętrzny*) sill; (*wewnętrzny*) windowstool.

podoknie *n. Gen.pl.* **-i** *bud.* window ledge.

podoktorancki *a.* postdoctoral.

podolbrzym *mi Gen. i Acc.* **-a** *astron.* subgiant star.

podołać *pf. + Dat.* cope with (*sth*); manage, be up to (*sth*).

podomka *f. Gen.pl.* **-ek** housecoat, dressing gown.

podopieczna *f. Gen.* **-ej** ward, charge, protégée, tutee.

podopieczny *mp* ward, protégé, tutee; (*domu opieki, domu dziecka*) resident; (*zakładu opiekuńczego*) inmate.

podorać *pf.* **-rzę -rzesz, podorywać** *ipf. roln.* skim, give (*sth*) a first ploughing.

podorbitalny *a. astron., lotn.* suborbital.

podorędzie *n.* **na podorędziu** at hand, ready, within one's reach; **trzymać coś na podorędziu** keep *l.* have sth to hand.

podorywka *f. Gen.pl.* **-ek** *roln.* skimming, first ploughing.

podosiniak *mi Gen.* **-a** *bot.* (= *koźlarz czerwony*) red aspen bolete (*Leccinum aurantiacum*).

podoskopia *f. Gen.* **-ii** *kryminalistyka* podoscopy, foot-reading.

podostry *a. pat.* subacute.

podówczas *adv. lit.* then; at that time; on that occasion.

podpadać *ipf.* 1. *pot.* (= *mieścić się w jakiejś klasyfikacji*) come, fall (*pod coś* under sth); **to podpada pod ustawę** this comes within the provisions of the law. 2. **podpadać komuś** *pot.* (= *narażać się*) make oneself unpopular with sb; be in sb's black books; (= *budzić podejrzenia*) arose sb's suspicion.

podpadający *a. pot.* (= *budzący podejrzenia*)

suspicious; (*o zachowaniu, wyglądzie*) odd, strange, queer.

podpalacz *mp* 1. firebug, arsonist, fire-raiser, incendiary. 2. *przen.* (= *podżegacz wojenny*) warmonger.

podpalać *ipf.* 1. kindle, set fire to (*sth*); set (*sth l. sb*) on fire; *sl.* torch; **podpalać ogień** make *l.* light a fire. 2. (= *przypiekać*) burn. **~ się** *ipf.* set o.s. on fire.

podpalany *a.* (*o psie l. koniu*) bay, reddish-brown; **czarny podpalany** black-and-tan.

podpalenie *n.* arson, fire-raising; *sl.* torching.

podpalić (się) *pf. zob.* **podpalać (się)**.

podpałka *f. Gen.pl.* **-ek** fire-starter, kindling, firewood, splint.

podparcie *n.* 1. *sport* support. 2. (*wzmocnienie*) support, prop, shore, brace; **punkt podparcia** fulcrum.

podpaska *f. Gen.pl.* **-ek** (sanitary) napkin, sanitary pad.

podpasować *pf.* **podpasować komuś** *pot.* suit sb down to the ground; be right up sb's street.

podpaść *pf.* **-dnę -dniesz, -dnij, -dł** *zob.* **podpadać**.

podpatrywać *ipf.,* **podpatrzyć** *pf.* peep (*kogoś/coś* at sb/sth); spy (*kogoś/coś* on sb/sth); pry, peer, nose (*coś* into sth).

podpiąć *pf.* **-pnę -pniesz, -pnij** *zob.* **podpinać**.

podpiec (się) *pf.* **-piekę -pieczesz, -piekł** *zob.* **podpiekać (się)**.

podpiekać *ipf.* broil, roast, grill. **~ się** *ipf.* get broiled/roasted/grilled.

podpieprzyć *pf. sl.* (= *ukraść*) hook, hoist, rip off, stick up.

podpierać *ipf.* 1. (*podtrzymywać od dołu lub z boku*) support, carry, hold up, shore up, underpin; (*belkami*) timber; (*słupami*) stud; (*rośliną*) stick, pole; **przysiad podparty** *sport* crouch with front support; **podpierać ściany** *żart.* be a wallflower. 2. (= *przychodzić z pomocą*) support, give strength/support to, buoy up, bolster up. **~ się** *ipf. pot.* (= *powoływać się na kogoś, na coś*) 1. refer to; (*argumentami, autorytetem*) lean (*kimś/czymś* on sb/sth); **podpierać się dowodami** adduce evidence. 2. **podpierać się pod boki** hold one's arms akimbo.

podpierdolić *pf. wulg.* (= *ukraść*) heist, bag, snatch; *Br.* snitch (*sth*) (*komuś* from sb).

podpiłować *pf.,* **podpiłowywać** *ipf.* make a cut in (*sth*), saw (*sth*) across; (= *podciąć od spodu*) undercut; (= *zetrzeć pilnikiem*) file down.

podpinać *ipf.* 1. (= *przypinać coś od spodu*) pin, fasten; (*podgiąwszy zapiąć*) tuck up. 2. (*włosy*) pin up, sweep up.

podpinka *f. Gen.pl.* **-ek** detachable lining.

podpis *mi* 1. (= *własnoręcznie napisane imię i nazwisko*) signature. 2. (*na dokumentach urzędowych*) signature; **podpis na odwrocie** endorsement; **dołączony podpis** affixture; **wzór podpisu** specimen signature; **bez podpisu** unsigned, unlettered (*o nagrobku*); **sfałszowany podpis** forged *l.* counterfeited signature; **pieczątka z podpisem** signature stamp; **podpis w zastępstwie** proxy signature; **podpis in blanco**

blank signature; **wzory podpisów** signature book; **dać (komuś) dokument do podpisu** present *l.* submit a document to sb for signature, ask sb's signature; **złożyć podpis pod dokumentem** put a signature to a document, appose one's signature to a document; **dać na coś podpis** give one's consent to sth; **uwierzytelnić podpis** authenticate *l.* legalize *l.* attest a signature. **3.** (*objaśnienie pod rysunkiem, fotografią itp.*) legend, caption, underline. **4.** *prawn.* subscription. **5. podpisy** (*w telewizji*) subtitles.

podpisać (się) *pf.* **-szę -szesz** *zob.* **podpisywać (się).**

podpisywać *ipf.* **1.** (= *potwierdzać imieniem i nazwiskiem*) sign, autograph; ink (*coś* sth); put one's name *l.* signature (*coś* to sth); **podpisać umowę** sign an agreement; **podpisać na siebie wyrok śmierci** sign one's own death warrant; **podpisać coś na odwrocie** endorse sth. **2.** (= *pisać jedno pod drugim*) underwrite. **3.** (*objaśniać, komentować obrazek, zdjęcie itp.*) caption. **~ się** *ipf.* sign one's name, autograph; **podpisywać się pod czymś** (*wyrażając poparcie*) sign sth, subscribe one's name to sth; (= *uznawać za słuszne*) subscribe to sth, endorse sth; **pod tą propozycją mogę podpisać się obiema rękoma** I can subscribe to this proposal whole-heartedly.

podpity *a.* tipsy, boozed (up), on the booze.

podpiwek *mi* **-wk-** (*napój*) home brew.

podpiwniczenie *n.* basement.

podpiwniczyć *pf. bud.* build a basement.

podpiździć *pf.* **-żdżę -ździsz** *wulg.* = **podpierdolić.**

podpłomyk *mi* *Gen.* **-a** *kulin.* damper, crude biscuit.

podpłynąć *pf.*, **podpływać** *ipf.* **1.** (= *płynąc, zbliżyć się*) swim up; (*o statku*) sail up; (*o wioślarzu*) row up (*do czegoś* to sth). **2.** (= *płynąć, przebyć jakiś odcinek drogi*) swim, sail.

podpora *f. Gen.pl.* **-ór 1.** (= *wsparcie, wzmocnienie*) support, prop, buttress, shore; **podpora rodziny** *przen.* anchor, support, mainstay, comfort, crutch; **wnuki są podporą mojej starości** *przen.* the grandchildren are the comfort *l.* mainstay of my old age. **2.** *techn.* shore, stanchion; *bud.* abutment, cantilever, underpinning, bearing; *górn.* post, pillar, puncheon.

podporucznik *mp* *wojsk.* second lieutenant; *lotn. Br.* pilot officer; (*marynarki wojennej*) ensign; *Br.* sub-lieutenant.

podporządkować (się) *pf. zob.* **podporządkowywać (się).**

podporządkowany *a.* subordinate, ancillary, subservient, subject (*komuś / czemuś* to sb/sth); **droga podporządkowana** side road.

podporządkowywać *ipf.* subordinate, subjugate; (*sobie*) enslave, bring under manage, subject. **~ się** *ipf.* submit, conform, acquiesce (*komuś, czemuś* to sb/sth) abide (*komuś, czemuś* by sb/sth) knuckle (*komuś, czemuś* under sb/sth) toe the line, step into line.

podpowiadać *ipf.*, **podpowiedzieć** *pf.* **-wiem -wiesz, -wiedz** prompt (*komuś* sb, *coś* with sth); + *Dat.* give (*sb*) hints *l.* prompts *l.* a cue.

podpowiedź *f.* hint, prompt, suggestion, cue, clue.

podpór[1] *mi* **-o-** *sport* front support.

podpór[2] *f. zob.* **podpora.**

podpórka *f. Gen.pl.* **-ek 1.** (= *wzmocnienie*) support, prop, steady. **2.** (*w maszynie, urządzeniu*) bracket; (*na rękę, głowę*) rest; (*roweru, motocykla*) kickstand. **3.** *sport* front support. **4.** *muz.* bridge. **5.** *bud.* strut.

podprokurator *mp* *prawn.* deputy prosecutor.

podprowadzać *ipf.*, **podprowadzić** *pf.* **1.** (= *prowadząc, dochodzić gdzieś*) take *l.* bring (*sb l.* sth) near. **2.** (*idąc z kimś, przemierzać jakiś odcinek drogi*) accompany; see (*kogoś do czegoś* sb to sth). **3.** *pot.* (= *kraść*) hook (*coś komuś* sth from sb).

podpucha *f. pot.* frame up, put-on, set-up, fix-up.

podpułkownik *mp* lieutenant colonel; *lotn. Br.* wing commander.

podpunkt *mi* (*w tekście*) subsection.

podpuszczać *ipf.* **1.** (= *pozwalać się zbliżyć*) let (*sb*) approach *l.* come near, allow (*sb*) to approach. **2.** *pot.* (= *prowokować*) put *l.* lead sb on; drive *l.* egg sb on; **podpuszczać kogoś przeciwko komuś/czemuś** turn sb against sb/sth.

podpuszczka *f. Gen.pl.* **-ek** *biol., kulin.* rennet.

podpuszczkowy *f.* rennet.

podpuścić *pf.* **-szczę -ścisz** *zob.* **podpuszczać.**

podpylić *pf. sl.* (= *ukraść*) hook; *Br.* nick (*coś komuś* sth from sb).

podpytać (się) *pf. zob.* **podpytywać (się).**

podpytywać *ipf. pot.* sound (*sb*) out, probe, pump. **~ się** *pf. pot.* ask around, sound people out, probe.

podrabiać *ipf.* counterfeit, forge, falsify, fake.

podrabiany *a.* sham, fake, faked, forged.

podrajcowany *a. wulg.* turned on, horny, randy.

podrapać *pf.* **-pię -piesz 1.** (= *zrobić rany, rysy*) claw, tear, lacerate. **2.** (= *potrzeć*) scratch, rub, scrape. **~ się** *pf.* **1.** (*potrzeć*) scratch, rub, scrape. **2.** (= *być poranionym, porysowanym*) scrape, graze.

podrasować *pf. pot., mot.* soup up, hot up, beef up.

podrastać *ipf.* (*o dzieciach*) get older, get bigger; (*o roślinach*) grow, shoot up, sprout; (*o włosach*) grow.

podratować *pf.* **podratować kogoś** lend sb a helping hand, give sb a leg up; **podratować czyjąś karierę/czyjś prestiż** save sb's career/prestige.

podrażać *ipf.* rise the cost of sth, increase *l.* put up the price of sth.

podrażniać *ipf.*, **podrażnić** *pf.* **1.** (*uczulać, wywoływać stan zapalny*) irritate. **2.** (*irytować, denerwować*) irritate, annoy, vex, tease, gall.

podrażnienie *n.* **1.** *pat.* irritation; (*skóry*) chafe; **wywołujący podrażnienie** irritative; **powodować podrażnienie czegoś** irritate sth; **łagodzący podrażnienie** demulcent. **2.** (*zdenerwowanie, niepokój, irytacja*) irritation, vexation.

podrażniony *a.* **-eni 1.** *med.* irritated; (*o błonie śluzowej, spojówce*) irritated. **2.** (*poirytowany*) irritated, vexed, annoyed, aggravated, peeved; (*o głosie*) irritated, annoyed.

podregulować *pf.* (*silnik, komputer*) regulate, adjust; (*zegarek*) synchronize.

podreperować *pf.* (= *z grubsza naprawić*) (*zegarek, pralkę, telewizor, samochód*) fix, mend, repair, ; (*nadszarpniętą opinię*) *przen.* regain/restore one's reputation/good name; **podreperować zdrowie** repair one's health; **podreperować budżet** patch up a budget; **podreperować czyjeś ego** boost/bolster sb's ego.

podreptać *pf.* -pczę -pcze *l.* -pcę -pce, -pcz (= *drepcąc, pójść gdzieś*) trip along; (*o dziecku*) toddle, totter along.

podretuszować *pf.*, **podretuszowywać** *ipf. fot.* retouch (a photo).

podręcznik *mi Gen.* -a handbook, coursebook, manual, textbook.

podręcznikowy *a.* school-bookish; (*ujęcie, wykład, wiadomości*) bookish.

podręczny *a.* ready to hand, handy; (*biblioteczce*) reference; **apteczka podręczna** first aid kit; **bagaż podręczny** carry-on, hand luggage; **księgozbiór podręczny** reference library; **słownik podręczny** desk dictionary; **pamięć podręczna** *komp.* cache; **kasa podręczna** petty cash.

podrobić[1] *pf.* **1.** *zob.* **podrabiać. 2.** *pot.* (= *popracować jakiś czas nad czymś*) advance one's work, move on/forward with one's work.

podrobić[2] *pf.* (= *rozdrobnić*) crumble, crush, break up.

podrobiony *a.* sham, fake, faked, fictitious, dud; (*o paszporcie, prawie jazdy,*) fake(d), forged; (*o talii*) cold deck; (*o podpisie*) false, falsified, forged; (*o studolarówce*) counterfeit, dud.

podrobowy *a.* (*o konserwie, gulaszu, paszteciе*) offal, giblet.

podroby *pl. Gen.* -ów pluck, garbage, variety meat, offal; (*drobiowe*) giblets.

podrodzina *f. biol.* subfamily.

podrosnąć *pf.* -rosnę -rośniesz, -rośnij, -rósł -rosła -rośli *zob.* **podrastać.**

podrost *mi leśn.* brushwood, undergrowth.

podrostek *mp* -tk- *pl.* -i juvenile, youngster.

podrozdział *mi* subsection, cap section.

podrozjezdnica *f. kol.* switch sleeper.

podrożeć *pf.* rise/go up in price.

podrożyć *pf. zob.* **podrażać.**

podróbka *f. Gen.pl.* -ek *pot.* fake, sham, phony.

podróść *pf.* -rosnę -rośniesz, -rośnij, -rósł -rosła -rośli *zob.* **podrastać.**

podrównikowy *a.* equatorial; (*o klimacie, roślinności*) equatorial.

podróż *f. pl.* -e trip, journey, travel, voyage; (*morska*) voyage; (*powietrzna, lądowa*) journey; (*samochodem*) drive; **podróż zagraniczna** trip abroad; **podróż poślubna** honeymoon trip; **podróż służbowa** business trip; **cel podróży** destination; **towarzysz podróży** fellow traveler, traveling companion, fellow passenger; **szczęśliwej podróży!** have a nice trip!, bon voyage!, safe journey!; **biuro podróży** travel agency/bureau; **plan podróży** itinerary; **podróż krajoznawcza** ex-

cursion tour; **odbyć podróż** make a journey; **podróż tam i z powrotem** round trip; **podróż w nieznane** a journey into the unknown; **wyjechać w podróż** go on a trip; **w podróży** on one's journey.

podróżna *f. Gen.* -ej *zob.* **podróżny[2].**

podróżniczek *ma* -czk- *zool.* blue throat (*Luscinia svecica*). – *mi* -czk- *Gen.* -a *bot.* false champignon, fairy-ring champignon (*Marasmius oreades*).

podróżniczka *f. Gen.pl.* -ek *zob.* **podróżnik[1].**

podróżniczy *a.* travelers', travel; (*o literaturze*) adventure; (*o czasopiśmie*) travel.

podróżnik[1] *mp pl.* -cy (= *miłośnik podróży*) traveler, explorer.

podróżnik[2] *mi Gen.* -a *pl.* -i *bot.* chicory (*Cichorium*).

podróżny[1] *a.* (*o bagażu, torbie, ubraniu*) travel, traveling; **kufer podróżny** wardrobe trunk; **duża torba podróżna** carry-all, hold-all.

podróżny[2] *mp* traveler, voyager, tripper, passenger; **drzewo podróżnych** *bot.* traveler's palm/tree (*Ravenala madagascariensis*).

podróżować *ipf.* travel, voyage, go places, take a trip; (*samochodem, autobusem, pociągiem, statkiem, samolotem*) travel by car/bus/train/ship/plane; (*morzem*) travel by sea; **podróżować po morzach** sail the seas; **podróżować na gapę** stow away, jump a train (*pociągiem*); **podróżować z małym bagażem** travel light; **podróżować z plecakiem** backpack.

podrumienić *pf.* (*mięso, warzywa*) roast golden brown.

podrygi *pl. Gen.* -ów convulsions, twists; (*podskoki*) leaps, frisks, skips; **ostatnie podrygi** death pangs/throes/flurry.

podrygiwać *ipf.* dance about; (*podskakiwać*) skip, gambol, leap, prance.

podryw *mi pot.* (= *zaloty*) pick-up; **iść na podryw** go on the pull.

podrywacz *mp*, **podrywaczka** *f. Gen.pl.* -ek *pot.* woman/man-chaser, skirt chaser.

podrywać *ipf.* -am -asz **1.** (*unosić w górę*) raise, lift, hoist. **2.** (= *nadszarpywać coś*) undermine, weaken, damage; **poderwać czyjś autorytet** damage/undermine sb's authority. **3.** **podrywać do buntu** stir up. **4.** *pot.* (= *zainteresować sobą osobę płci przeciwnej*) pick up, chat up. ~ **się** *ipf.* (*podnieść się szybko*) start, spring, jump to one's feet; (*do działania*) bestir oneself; (*zerwać się do lotu*) raise from the ground, take flight, zoom (*o samolocie*).

podrywka *f. Gen.pl.* -ek *pot.* (= *zaloty*) **1.** pick-up. **2.** *ryb.* landing net, spoon-net.

podrząd *mi* -ę- *biol.* suborder.

podrzeć *pf.* -drę -drzesz, -drzyj, -darł **1.** (*na kawałki*) tear, tear up; (*list, papier*) tear to pieces, rip to shreds. **2.** (*o odzieży, butach itp.*) (*zniszczyć*) wear out. ~ **się** *pf.* (*o odzieży, butach itp.*) get worn out/tattered/threadbare.

podrzędnie *adv.* subordinately.

podrzędność *f.* subordination.

podrzędny *a.* **1.** (= *kiepski*) minor; (*o restauracji*) minor, second rate, secondary; (*o autorze*) insignificant, minor; (*o znaczeniu*) unimportant, minor. **2. droga podrzędna** back road; **podrzędna restauracja** greasy spoon, beanery; **podrzędne kino/teatr** fleapit. **3.** *jęz.* subordinate, dependent; (*o zdaniu*) subordinate, dependent; **o spójniku** subordinating (conjunction); **zdanie podrzędne** subordinate clause.

podrzucać *ipf.*, **podrzucić** *pf.* **1.** (*w górę*) throw up, fling up, joggle, jounce; (*dziecko na kolanach*) dance/bounce up and down. **2.** (*dokładać, dorzucać*) add; (*drewna do ognia*) feed the fire. **3.** (= *kłaść coś ukradkiem*) (*narkotyki, fałszywe dowody*) plant (*coś komuś* sth on sb); (*o dziecku*) abandon; **podrzucać komuś kwestię** feed lines to sb, prompt. **4.** *pot.* (= *dostarczać* (*przy okazji*)) deliver, drop off somewhere; **mogę cię podrzucić** I can give you a lift *l.* a ride; **podrzucił mnie pod dom** he let me down at my doorstep; **w piątek podrzucę ci te materiały** I'll get you the materials on Friday; **aż mnie podrzuciło** (*ze złości, oburzenia*) I was all wild with rage.

podrzut *mi* **1.** (*w górę*) jerk, toss. **2.** *sport* jerk with split.

podrzutek *mp* -tk- *pl.* -i foundling, waif; (*w baśniach*) changeling.

podrzynać *ipf.* cut; **podrzynać komuś gardło/ żyły** cut one's throat/veins.

podsadzać *ipf.* **1.** (= *podsuwać, podkładać*) put, place (*coś pod coś* sth under sth). **2.** (= *podnosić*) give (*sb*) a leg up *l.* a hoist, help (*sb*) up. **3.** *górn.* fill in. **4.** *leśn.* replant. ~ **się** *ipf.* **1. podsadzać się pod coś** (= *składać się do podniesienia*) put one's shoulder to sth. **2.** (= *unosić w górę siebie nawzajem*) help each other up.

podsadzka *f. Gen.pl.* -ek *górn.* filling, stowing, packing; **podsadzka płynna/sucha** hydraulic/ rock filling.

podsadzkowy *a. górn.* (*o piasku, materiale, robotach*) filling, stowing.

podsądna *f. Gen.* -ej, **podsądny** *mp* defendant, culprit, prisoner at the bar.

podscenie *n. Gen.pl.* -i *teatr* mezzanine.

podsekretarz *mp* undersecretary; **podsekretarz stanu** *polit.* undersecretary of state.

podsiew *mi leśn.* resow.

podsiębierny *a. techn.* undershot; **koło (wodne) podsiębierne** undershot waterwheel; **koparka podsiębierna** pull *l.* drag excavator.

podskakiwać *ipf.* **1.** (*w górę*) jump up, hop, frisk; (*o piłce*) bounce (up and down); (*o pojeździe*) bounce, joggle, jolt along; (*o koniu*) prance; **serce mi podskoczyło** my heart lept into my mouth; **podskakiwać z radości** jump for joy. **2.** *przen.* (= *wzrastać*) increase, go up; (*o cenach*) go up, shot up, soar; (*o temperaturze, pensji*) go up, increase. **3.** (= *podbiegać, zbliżać się bardzo szybko*) run up; **podskoczyć po coś** go fetch sth. **4.** (= *robić coś ryzykownego*) **nie podskakuj!** whoa!; you'd better be careful! **5.** + *Dat. pot.* (= *sprzeciwiać się, narażając się na przykre konsekwencje*) cross; hold out *l.* put up a fight against (*sb*); **nikt mu nie podskoczy** nobody's going to cross him.

podskarbi *mp hist.* undertreasurer.

podskoczyć *pf. zob.* **podskakiwać.**

podskok *mi* jump, hop, gambol; (*pojazdu*) jolt; (*konia*) prance; (*z przestrachu*) start; (*piłki*) bounce; **biec w podskokach** scamper; **uwijać się w podskokach** be on the hop; **zwiewać w podskokach** take a running jump; **sunąć w podskokach** leap along, bounce along.

podskórnia *f. Gen.pl.* -i *bot.* hypodermis, subcutis.

podskórny *a.* **1.** *med.* subdermic, hypodermic, subcutaneous; (*o zastrzyku*) hypodermic; (*o wylewie, tkance*) subcutaneous; **tkanka podskórna** *anat.* hypodermis; **woda podskórna** *geogr.* subsoil water. **2.** *ogr.* subsoil.

podsłuch *mi* **1.** (= *podsłuchiwanie*) eavesdropping; **być na podsłuchu** be bugged. **2.** *techn.* (*aparatura*) wire, tapping, bugging, tap; **zakładać komuś podsłuch** bug *l.* wire *l.* tap sb's phone; **usuwać skądś podsłuch** debug sth; **podsłuch elektroniczny** electronic surveillance; **podsłuch telefoniczny** phone tap.

podsłuchać *pf.*, **podsłuchiwać** *ipf.* overhear (*niechcący*); eavesdrop (*kogoś / coś* on sb/sth); listen in (*kogoś / coś* to sb/sth); (*za pomocą urządzenia*) tap, bug.

podsłuchowy *a.* overhearing, tapping; **instalacja podsłuchowa** overhearing plant, bugging; **urządzenie podsłuchowe** listening device, tapping device.

podsmażać *ipf.* fry (up), roast, sauté, stir-fry; **podsmażyć cebulkę do zrumienienia** sauté the onions until golden brown. ~ **się** *ipf.* fry (up), roast.

podsmażyć (się) *pf. zob.* **podsmażać (się).**

podsrywać *ipf.* -am -asz *wulg.* **podsrywać komuś** (= *bruździć*) put a spoke in sb's wheel, queer the pitch for sb, rock the boat.

podstacja *f. techn.* substation.

podstarości *mp hist.* subprefect.

podstarzały *a.* elderly, oldish, long in the tooth; **dobrze podstarzały** well on in years.

podstawa *f.* **1.** (*fundament*) base, basis, foundation; (*wieży, pomnika*) foundation, base; **podstawa czaszki** *anat.* the base of the skull; **podstawa erozji** *geol.* base level; **postawa chmur** *meteor.* cloud base. **2.** (*główne założenie*) principle, basis, foundation; (*naukowa*) framework; (*ekonomiczna, cywilizacji*) foundations; (*materialne, egzystencji, rozwoju*) basis; (*działania*) reasons; (*wykształcenia, wiedzy*) basics, rudiments, essentials, elements; (*systemu politycznego, filozoficznego*) keystone; (*teorii*) fundament; **podstawa prawna** legal basis; **podstawy utrzymania** source of income; **co leży u podstaw twojego rozumowania?** what's the basis for your reasoning?; **analiza opiera się na mocnej podstawie** the analysis is well founded; **na jakiej podstawie twierdzisz, że...** what makes you claim that..., on what ground do you assert that...; **mieć podstawy, by coś zrobić** be justified in doing sth; **nie bez podstaw** not without reason; **podstawa bytu** bread and butter; **podstawa pożywienia** staple diet; **podstawa programowa** core curriculum; **mam podstawy do podejrzeń** I have good reasons to be suspicious; **bez podstaw** unreasonably; **bez żadnych podstaw** groundlessly, without a leg to stand on; **być pozbawionym podstaw** lack substance, be unfounded; **leżeć u podstaw** underlie; **nie ma żadnych podstaw przypuszczać...** there's no reason to suppose...; **znajomość podstaw** grounding; **u podstaw** fundamentally (*np. wadliwy, błędny*); **solidna podstawa** firm footing; solid basis *l.* foundation; **na podstawie czegoś** on the basis *l.* ground of sth; by virtue of sth; based on sth; **mający dobre podstawy** well-grounded, well-founded. **3.** *gram.* **podstawa słowotwórcza** base (form). **4.** *mat.* radix; (*trójkąta, ostrosłupa, walca*) base; **podstawa potęgi** the base number. **5.** *techn.* footing, rest, bedplate. **6. podstawa dowodzenia** *log.* premise.

podstawczak *mi Gen.* **-a** *bot.* basidiomycete.

podstawek *mi* **-wk-** *Gen.* **-a 1.** *muz.* (*przy skrzypcach*) chin rest. **2.** *muz.* (= *mostek*) bridge. **3.** *dial.* = **podstawka** 2.

podstawiać *ipf.* **1.** (*podsuwać*) put, place; **podstawić komuś nogę** trip sb up. **2.** (= *dostarczać w jakieś miejsce*) bring round; (*autobus, pociąg*) put on. **3.** *pot.* (= *powoływać fałszywych świadków*) plant (a witness). **4.** *chem., fiz., mat.* substitute. **5.** *prawn.* substitute (*np. spadkobiercę*).

podstawianie *n.* substitution; **reakcja podstawiania** *chem.* (substitution) reaction, displacement reaction; **reguła podstawiania** *log.* rule of substitution.

podstawić *pf. zob.* **podstawiać**.

podstawka *f. Gen.pl.* **-ek 1.** support, pallet. **2.** (= *spodeczek*) saucer; (= *podkładka*) mat, coaster; (*pod garnek*) trivet. **3.** *techn.* stand, stillage. **4.** *bot.* (*część grzyba*) basidium.

podstawowy *a.* **1.** basic, fundamental, elemental, essential; (*o wykształceniu*) elementary, primary; (*o produkcie, surowcu*) staple; (*o założeniach, zasadach*) underlying; (*o składniku*) vital, essential; **podstawowe źródło utrzymania** primary source of income; **kwestia podstawowa** basic issue; **mieć podstawowe znaczenie** be of vital importance; **podstawowe dane** background; **podstawowe gałęzie przemysłu** key industries; **wynagrodzenie podstawowe** basic salary. **2.** *szkoln.* elementary, primary; **szkolnictwo podstawowe** elementary *l.* primary education; **szkoła podstawowa** elementary *l.* primary school. **3.** *gram.* base.

podstawówka *f. Gen.pl.* **-ek** *pot.* primary school.

podstemplować *pf.*, **podstemplowywać** *ipf.* **1.** (= *stawiać pieczątkę*) stamp. **2.** *bud.* pin, prop, underprop, underpin.

podsterowność *f. mot.* understeering, understeer.

podstęp *mi* trick; **uciekać się do podstępu** resort to deceit; **podstępem** under false pretences, by subterfuge; **zdobyć coś podstępem** get *l.* obtain sth deceitfully; **węszyć podstęp** smell the rat; **skłonić kogoś podstępem do zrobienia czegoś** trick *l.* beguile sb into doing sth; **podstępem**

pozbawić kogoś czegoś cheat *l.* trick *l.* do sb out of sth.

podstępnie *adv.* (*działać, niszczyć*) cunningly, insidiously, by subterfuge; (*knuć*) underhand, trickily.

podstępność *f.* craftiness, deceitfulness, cunning.

podstępny *a.* deceitful, scheming; (*o oszuście*) artful; (*o grze, zamiarach*) insidious; (*o praktykach*) underhand; (*o pytaniach*) nasty; (*o konstrukcji, urządzeniu*) tricky.

podstoli *mp hist.* steward.

podstrunnica *f. muz.* neck.

podstrzyc (się) *pf.* **-strzygę -strzyżesz -strzygł** *zob.* **podstrzygać (się)**.

podstrzygać *ipf.* **1.** (*skracać*) trim, even up, shear. **2.** (= *strzyc się*) have one's hair trimmed, trim one's hair. **~ się** *ipf.* have one's hair trimmed.

podstyczna *f. Gen.* **-ej** *mat.* subtangent.

podsufitka *f. Gen.pl.* **-ek** *bud.* soffit boards, ceiling; **podwieszona podsufitka** suspended ceiling.

podsumować *pf. zob.* **podsumowywać**; **podsumować kogoś** *pot.* (= *ocenić negatywnie*) sum sb up.

podsumowanie *n.* summary, recapitulation, afterword, synopsis; **podsumowanie wiadomości** news roundup.

podsumowywać *ipf.* **1.** (= *dodawać liczby*) add up, sum, total up. **2.** (*dyskusję, wyniki*) sum up, summarize, recapitulate; **podsumowując** to sum up; to make a long story short.

podsunąć (się) *pf. zob.* **podsuwać (się)**.

podsuszać *ipf.* dry up/off; (*o włosach*) dry up.

podsuszka *f. pat.* (*choroba zbóż*) corn mycosis.

podsuszyć *pf. zob.* **podsuszać**.

podsuwać *ipf.* **1.** (= *suwając, umieścić coś pod kimś, czymś*) push, shove, slip; (= *wkładać coś ukradkiem*) slip *l.* slide sth stealthily; **podsuwać coś komuś pod nos** put sth under sb's nose. **2.** (= *sugerować, proponować*) suggest, advance, set forth, put forward; **podsuwać komuś odpowiedź/właściwe słowo** prompt sb with an answer/the right word. **~ się** *ipf.* approach, move near, come closer, creep up to.

podsycać *ipf.*, **podsycić** *pf.* (= *wzmacniać, potęgować*) strengthen, fan, intensify, give a boost to; (*nastroje*) stir up, fuel; (*spekulacje*) fuel, refuel; (*niezgodę, nienawiść*) foment; **podsycać emocje** fan the flames; **podsycać czyjeś nadzieje** build up sb's hopes; **podsycać ogień** feed the fire, fan the flame/blaze, blow the coals.

podsychać *ipf.* dry out *l.* up; (= *więdnąć*) wither.

podsyłać *ipf.* send (*coś komuś* sth to sb).

podsypać *pf.* **-pię -piesz** *zob.* **podsypywać**.

podsypka *f. Gen.pl.* **-ek** *kol.* **1.** ballast. **2.** *bud.* filling; (*pod nawierzchnią drogi*) subcrust; **podsypka kamienna** rubble bed.

podsypywać *ipf.* + *Ins.* strew with (*sth*); (*cukrem, mąką, solą*) sprinkle with (*sth*).

podszczękowy *a. anat.* submaxillary, lower jaw.

podszczypywać *ipf.* pinch, nip, tweak.

podszedł *itd. pf. zob.* **podejść.**

podszepnąć *pf.* -ij *zob.* **podszeptywać.**

podszept *mi* suggestion, voice, prompt; **za czyimś podszeptem** at *l.* by sb's instigation, by *l.* under sb's advice.

podszeptywać *ipf.* (*szeptać na ucho*) whisper into sb's ear; (*sugerować*) insinuate, hint (*coś komuś* sth to sb); (*komuś odpowiedź*) prompt sb with an answer.

podszewka *f. Gen.pl.* **-ek** lining; **z podszewką** lined; **bez podszewki** unlined; **dać podszewkę pod płaszcz** line a coat; **dać nową podszewkę** re-line; **znać coś od podszewki** know sth inside out, have inside information of sth.

podszkolić *pf.* train, drill (*kogoś w czymś* sb in sth); **podszkolić kogoś (w czymś) błyskawicznie** give sb a crash course (in sth).

podszybie *n. Gen.pl.* **-i** *górn.* shaft station, shaft bottom, pit bottom; (*dźwigu*) lift-pit.

podszycie *n.* 1. (*odzieży*) lining. 2. (*w lesie*) brushwood, undergrowth, underbrush.

podszyć (się) *pf.* -ję -jesz, -yj *zob.* **podszywać (się).**

podszyt *mi* (*w lesie*) brushwood, underbrush, undergrowth.

podszywać *ipf.* -am -asz 1. (*o odzieży*) line (*czymś* with sth); (*wzmocnić czymś*) back (*czymś* with sth); **kurtka podszyta wiatrem** light/thin coat. 2. *przen.* **podszyty tchórzem** cowardly, spineless, chicken-hearted; **podszyty lisem** cunning, wily. 3. + *Ins. lit.* (= *charakteryzujący się*) fraught *l.* pregnant with (*sth*); full of (*sth*); **podszyty goryczą/groźbą** with bitter/threatening overtones. ~ **się** *ipf.* pretend (*pod kogoś / coś* to be sb/sth); impersonate (*pod kogoś* sb).

podścielać, podścielać *ipf.* (= *podsypywać, rozrzucać*) 1. spread. 2. (= *zaopatrywać w podściółkę*) litter (down), bed; **podścielać bydłu (słomą)** litter the cattle (with straw); **podścielać w stajni** litter down the stable.

podściółka *f. Gen.pl.* **-ek** 1. *roln.* bed; (*w stajni, oborze*) litter; **podściółka tłuszczowa** *anat.* fatty layer. 2. *żegl.* dunnage (*pod ładunek*). 3. *mot.* underfelt.

podśluzowy *a. anat.* (*o błonie, tkance*) submucous, submucosal.

podśmiewać się *ipf.* scoff, sneer (*z kogoś / czegoś* at sb/sth); mock (*z kogoś / czegoś* sb/sth); make fun (*z kogoś / czegoś* of sb/sth).

podśpiewywać *ipf.* hum, sing, croon.

podświadomie *adv.* subconsciously, unconsciously, intuitively.

podświadomość *f. psych.* subconsciousness, the subconscious; *psych.* preconscious, subliminal self; **psychologia podświadomości** depth psychology.

podświadomy *a.* subconscious, subliminal; (*o niechęci*) supressed; (*o lęku*) subconscious; (*o odruchu*) intuitive; (*o uczuciach, potrzebach*) unconscious; *psych.* preconscious, subliminal.

podświetlać *ipf.*, **podświetlić** *pf.* light from below, light up, illuminate, shed light on (*sth*).

podświetlony *a.* translucent, backlit (*od tyłu*).

podtatusiały *a.* (*o mężczyźnie*) of ripe years, past one's prime, oldish, over the hill.

podtatusieć *pf.* (*o mężczyźnie*) grow old, be getting on.

podtekst *mi* overtone, hidden *l.* implied meaning, implication; *teor.lit.* subtext, underlying theme.

podtlenek *mi* **-nk-** *chem.* suboxide; **podtlenek azotu** nitrous oxide.

podtorze *n. Gen.pl.* **-y** *kol.* trackbed.

podtrzymać (się) *pf. zob.* **podtrzymywać (się).**

podtrzymywać *ipf.* 1. (= *nie pozwalać osunąć się*) support, hold up, sustain, shore up. 2. (= *starać się, by coś nie skończyło się*) keep up, carry on, maintain, preserve; (*rozmowę, czynność, śpiew*) keep up; (*nadzieję, ogień*) keep alive; (*uczucie, zwyczaj*) nourish; **podtrzymywać ogień** feed the fire; keep the fire burning *l.* alive; **podtrzymywać tradycję** preserve *l.* uphold a tradition; keep a tradition alive; **podtrzymywać czyjąś uwagę** hold *l.* keep sb's attention; **podtrzymywać rozmowę** keep the ball rolling. 3. (= *dodawać otuchy*) support, buoy up, bolster up, comfort; **podtrzymywać kogoś na duchu** keep sb's spirits up; raise *l.* lift sb's spirits; **podtrzymuje mnie wiara, że wyzdrowieję** the hope of recovery keeps me alive; I am buoyed up by the hope of recovery. 4. (= *obstawać przy swoim*) maintain, stick to, insist on; (*słowo, opinię*) stand by; (*zarzut, twierdzenie*) affirm; **podtrzymać żądania** stand by one's claims; **podtrzymuję swoją wersję tego zdarzenia** I stick to my version of this event; **podtrzymać sprzeciw** *prawn.* sustain an objection; **podtrzymuję sprzeciw!** objection sustained! 5. *muz.* sustain. 6. *bud.* (*ścianę*) underpin; (*konstrukcję*) bear, support. ~ **się** *ipf.* 1. (= *chronić samego siebie przed upadkiem*) support o.s.; (= *chronić się wzajemnie przed upadkiem*) support each other, lean against each other. 2. (= *dodawać sobie wzajemnie otuchy*) comfort *l.* hearten (each other); give support *l.* strength (to each other); be a source of strength (to each other).

podtykać *ipf.* 1. *pot.* (= *podsuwać*) shove, press, thrust. 2. *pot.* (= *podawać coś do jedzenia, do picia*) force food, press (sb) to eat; **podtykać pod nos** put sth under sb's nose.

podtyp *mi bot., zool.* subtype.

podtytuł *mi* 1. subtitle, subheading; **o podtytule** subtitled; **nadawać podtytuł** subtitle, crosshead (*w tekście*). 2. *druk.* deck.

poduczać *ipf.* teach (*sb*) (a little); **poduczać kogoś z matematyki** help sb in maths. ~ **się** *ipf.* learn (a little).

poduczyć (się) *pf. zob.* **poduczać (się).**

podudzie *n. Gen.pl.* **-i** *crus*, shank.

podumać *pf. żart.* muse, meditate, reflect (*o czymś* over sth); (*zastanowić się*) consider (sth), give (sth) a thought.

podupadać *ipf.*, **podupaść** *pf.* **-dnę -dniesz, -dnij, -dł** 1. (= *tracić znaczenie, marnieć*) deteriorate, decline, fall into decay *l.* decline, go to the wall; (*finansowo*) go downhill, go to the wall; (*o poziomie usług*) lag; (*o gałęzi przemysłu*) be in the doldrums. **2.** (= *tracić zdrowie*) get sick, decline in health; **podupadł na zdrowiu** his health has deteriorated *l.* declined; **podupaść na duchu** break down, get depressed, lose heart; **podupadł na duchu** his spirit has sunk; **podupadły** impoverished, in strained circumstances, down-at-the-hill; (*o obiekcie*) deteriorated, dilapidated.

podusić *pf.* **-szę -sisz 1.** (= *udusić*) strangle, throttle, choke. **2.** (*mięso*) stew, simmer. **~ się** *pf.* **1.** (= *udusić się*) suffocate, choke. **2.** (*o mięsie*) stew.

poduszczać *ipf.*, **poduszczyć** *pf.* instigate, incite, egg (sb) on (*kogoś do czegoś* sb to do sth).

poduszeczka *f. Gen.pl.* **-ek 1.** (= *mała poduszka*) cushion; (*w łapie u kota, psa*) pad; **poduszeczka do igieł** pin cushion *l.* pad. **2.** (*palców*) pad; (*kciuka*) ball.

poduszka *f. Gen.pl.* **-ek 1.** (*do spania*) pillow; **poduszka elektryczna** warming cushion; **poduszka powietrzna** *mot.* aircushion; **lektura do poduszki** bedside reading; **czytać do poduszki** read in bed. **2.** (*palców*) pad; (*dłoni*) palm. **3.** (*do tuszu*) inkpad, stamp pad. **4.** *techn.* cushion, pad; *bud.* bolster; **poduszka fundamentowa** foundation mat; *bot.* (*liścia*) pulvinus.

poduszkowiec *mi* **-wc-** *Gen.* **-a** hovercraft, air-cushion-vehicle.

poduszkowy *a.* cushion; **rośliny poduszkowe** cushion plants; **materac poduszkowy** bolster.

podwajać *ipf.* double, duplicate, increase (sth) twofold, reduplicate; (*stawkę, dochody, płace, sprzedaż*) double; (*wysiłki*) redouble; (*litery*) double, geminate. **~ się** *ipf.* double, increase twofold, duplicate.

podwalina *f. bud.* ground beam, ground plate, groundsill, substructure.

podwaliny *pl. Gen.* **-n** (= *podstawy*) foundations, principles, rudiments, fundamentals, groundwork; (*wiedzy, pod nowoczesną mikrobiologię*) foundations; (*np. matematyki*) foundations, fundamentals, essentials; **położyć podwaliny pod coś** lay the foundations for sth; lay *l.* provide the ground for sth; **tworzyć** *l.* **stanowić podwaliny** underpin; **burzyć podwaliny czegoś** strike at the heart of sth.

podważać *ipf.*, **podważyć** *pf.* **1.** (*unosić coś*) lever up; (*wieko*) prize, pry; (*łomem*) jimmy. **2.** (= *kwestionować*) discredit, disprove, reject, question; (*opinię*) shake, challenge; (*autorytet*) impair; (*wiarę*) subvert; **podważać czyjeś dobre mniemanie o sobie** make a dent in sb's ego; **podważać słuszność czegoś** question the validity of sth; **nie do podważenia** (*o argumencie*) impregnable, irrefutable, flawless; (*o dowodach, teorii*) ironclad.

podwędzać *ipf.*, **podwędzić** *pf.* **1.** *pot.* (= *kraść*) nick, lift, pinch, snatch. **2.** (*ryby, ser*) smoke.

podwiać *pf.* **-eje** *zob.* **podwiewać**.

podwiatrowy *a. geogr.* windward; (*o stronie, kierunku*) windward.

podwiązać *pf.* **-żę -żesz** *zob.* **podwiązywać**.

podwiązanie *n. chir.* ligature; (*jajowodów*) tubal ligation; (*nasieniowodów*) vasectomy.

podwiązka *f. Gen.pl.* **-ek 1.** (*do pończoch*) garter, suspender; **Order Podwiązki** the Order of the Garter. **2.** *chir.* ligature.

podwiązywać *ipf.* **1.** (*wiązać*) suspend, bind up, tie up. **2.** *med.* ligate, secure.

podwieczorek *mi* **-rk-** *Gen.* **-u** *l.* **-a** tea, high tea; **pora podwieczorku** tea time.

podwiewać *ipf.* blow from below *l.* underneath, raise skirts; **podwiało mnie** I've caught a chill.

podwieźć *pf.* **-wiozę -wieziesz -wiózł -wiozła -wieźli** *zob.* **podwozić**.

podwięź *f. pl.* **-e** *żegl.* chainplate.

podwijać *ipf.*, **podwinąć** *pf.* **1.** (= *zwijając, skrócić*) tuck up; (*rękawy, spodnie*) turn up, roll up. **2.** (= *podkurczać*) tuck under; **podwijać nogi/ogon** tuck one's legs/tail under; **z podwiniętym ogonem** with its tail between its legs; **usiadł z podwiniętymi nogami** he tucked his knees under.

podwładna *f. Gen.* **-ej** *zob.* **podwładny**[2].

podwładny[1] *a.* subordinate, inferior, junior; (*o robotniku, pracowniku*) inferior, subordinate.

podwładny[2] *mp* subordinate, subaltern; **być czyimś podwładnym** be sb's inferior.

podwodny *a.* underwater, subaqueous; (*o skale*) sunken; (*o faunie i florze*) submersed, submerged; o łodzi, okręcie, submarine, U-boat (*o łodzi niemieckiej*); **prąd podwodny** undercurrent; **góra podwodna** seamount.

podwoić (się) *pf.* **-ję -isz, -ój** *zob.* **podwajać (się)**.

podwoje *pl. Gen.* **-ów** gate, door; **otwierać przed kimś swoje podwoje** open the door wide for sb.

podwozić *ipf.* **-wożę -wozisz, -woź** *l.* **-wóź** give sb a lift *l.* ride; **podwozić kogoś gdzieś** drop sb off somewhere; **podwozić kogoś do domu** drop sb at the doorstep; (*coś komuś*) supply *l.* provide sb with sth.

podwozie *n. Gen.pl.* **-i** *mot.* chassis; *lot.* landing gear, under-carriage; *kol.* running gear; **podwozie chowane/stałe** retractable/fixed undercarriage; **podwozie wolnonośne** cantilever undercarriage.

podwój *ma* **-o-** *zool.* aquatic crustacean (*Mesidotea entomon*).

podwójnie *adv.* **1.** twice, double, doubly, twofold; **płacić podwójnie** pay double; **sprawdzić podwójnie** double-check; **złożyć arkusz podwójnie** fold a sheet in two. **2.** (*dwojako*) twofold, in two different ways.

podwójny *a.* **1.** double, duplex; (*o numerze, oknie, sile ataku*) double; (*o porcji, dawce*) doubled, double; (*o znaczeniu*) dual, ambiguous; **gra podwójna** *tenis* doubles; **podwójny cios** *boks* one-two; **podwójne życie** double life; **podwójna moralność** double morality; **podwójny agent** double agent; **podwójna gra** double dealing; **gwiazda podwójna** *astron.* binary star; **podwójne przeczenie** *gram.* double negation; **podwójny rodzaj** common gender; **podwójna spółgłoska** *jęz.* geminate; **podwójna rezerwacja** double booking; **podwójne dno** double bottom; **podwójne zabezpieczenie** countercheck; **podwójny podbródek** double chin; **podwójne nieszczęście** double whammy; **podwójne obywatelstwo** dual citizenship; **podwójne szyby** double glazing; **osiągnąć podwójny cel** kill two birds with one stone; **za podwójną cenę** at twice the price. **2. liczba podwójna** *gram.* dual (number). **3.** (*wzmożony*) twofold, redoubled, twice as large. **4.** *mat.* binary. **5.** *zool., bot.* geminate, didymous.

podwórko *n. Gen.pl.* -ek court, courtyard; (*za domem*) backyard; **na podwórku** in the open air; **pokój** *l.* mieszkanie od podwórka back; **przyjść na czyjeś podwórko** *przen.* come to sb's way of thinking; **na własnym podwórku** in one's own backyard; within one's bailiwick; **robić porządki na własnym podwórku** set *l.* put one's own house in order.

podwórkowy *a.* courtyard; **grajek podwórkowy** street musician.

podwórze *n. Gen.pl.* -y courtyard, backyard, yard; (*gospodarskie*) farmyard, barnyard, poultry-yard; **mieszkam od podwórza** I live at the back.

podwórzec *mi* -rc- *Gen.* -a *lit.* court.

podwykonawca *mp* subcontractor.

podwykonawczy *a.* subcontract; (*o robotach, ekipie, przedsiębiorstwie*) subcontract.

podwymiar *mi techn.* subsize, sub-measurement.

podwyznacznik *mi Gen.* -a *mat.* minor.

podwyżka *f. Gen.pl.* -ek raise, increase, upsurge, increment; (*cen, kosztów*) rise; **podwyżka pensji** raise, increase; *Br.* rise; **domagać się podwyżki** demand a raise; **dostać podwyżkę** get a raise.

podwyższać *ipf.* **1.** (*podnosić*) raise, heighten, elevate, lift, uplift. **2.** (*zwiększać*) increase, raise, put up; (*ceny, podatki*) hike up, push up, scale up (*stopniowo*); **podwyższać czynsz** raise the rent; **podwyższać wymagania** raise one's demands; **podwyższać stawkę** upraise the ante; (*kwalifikacje*) improve, raise. **3.** (*nasilić się*) enhance, intensify. **4.** *muz.* inflect; **podwyższać o pół tonu** sharp. **~ się** *ipf.* **1.** (= *stawać się wyższym*) rise, go up, shift up. **2.** (= *zwiększać się*) increase, augment; (*o cenach*) soar, escalate, go up; (*o temperaturze*) heighten; (*o standardzie*) improve, go up, get higher. **3.** *muz.* inflect.

podwyższenie *n.* rise, increase, elevation; (*estrada*) platform, scaffold, dais; (*standardu*) upgrade; (*ceny, stawki, oferty*) advance, rise (*czegoś* in sth).

podwyższony *a.* increased, elevated; (*o ciśnieniu, temperaturze, terenie*) elevated.

podwyższyć (się) *pf. zob.* **podwyższać (się).**

podwzgórze *n. Gen.pl.* -y *anat.* hypothalamus.

podyktować *pf.* **1.** (*tekst do zapisania*) dictate, read out. **2.** (= *narzucić*) dictate, impose, lay down; **podyktować warunki** dictate terms; **podyktować rzut karny** *piłka nożna* order *l.* give a penalty; **moja decyzja podyktowana jest troską** my decision is motivated by concern; **sumienie mi podyktowało, żebym...** my conscience told me to...

podyluwialny *a. geol.* postdiluvial.

podyplomowy *a.* graduate; **szkoła podyplomowa** graduate school.

podyskutować *pf.* talk, have a conversation *l.* talk *l.* discussion, chat.

podzamcze *n. Gen.pl.* -y *hist.* homesteads lying at the foot of the castle.

podzastaw *mi prawn.* repledge.

podzbiór *mi* -o- *mat.* subset, subarray.

podzelować *pf.* (*buty*) sole, have one's shoes soled.

podzespół *mi* -o- *techn.* subassembly, component; **podzespoły** componentry.

podziać *pf.* -eję -ejesz -ali *l.* -eli *zob.* **podziewać. ~ się** *pf. zob.* **podziewać się.**

podział *mi* **1.** (*rozdzielenie*) division, partition, separation; (*spadku, dóbr, dochodu narodowego*) distribution; (*głosów*) split; **podział klasowy** class division; **podział pracy** division of labor; **podział dochodów** revenue sharing; **podział władzy** *polit.* separation of powers; **podział administracyjny** administrative division; **podział odcinka** *geom.* section; **podział na trzy części** tripartition. **2.** (*klasyfikacja*) classification, distribution, separation; (*głosek*) *jęz.* classification (of sounds); (*na sylaby*) *jęz.* syllabification. **3.** *biol.* fission; **podział komórkowy** cell division, cleavage; **rozmnażanie przez podział** schizogenesis.

podziałać *pf.* **1.** (= *wywierać wpływ*) exert an influence, produce an effect (*na coś / kogoś* on sb/ sth); **podziałać jak (czerwona) płachta na byka** act like a red rag to a bull. **2.** (*sprawdzić się*) do the trick. **3. podziałać czymś na coś** treat sth with sth.

podziałka *f. Gen.pl.* -ek **1.** (= *skala*) scale, gauge; **z podziałką** graduated, scaled; **podziałka wzorcowa** master scale; **linijka z podziałką** scale. **2.** *techn.* graduation; *mech.* pitch.

podzielać *ipf.* (*poglądy, uczucia*) share; **podzielać czyjąś troskę** *l.* **czyjeś obawy** share sb's concern (*o coś* about sth).

podzielić *pf.* **1.** (= *wspólnie doświadczyć czegoś*) share; **podzielić czyjś los** share sb's fate. **2.** (*na cząstki*) divide (*sth*) into parts, split up, cleave; **podzielić na pół** cut *l.* break in two; **zdania są podzielone** opinions vary *l.* differ; **dający się podzielić** divisible. **3.** (= *poklasyfikować*) classify, categorize, sort, group. **4.** *mat.* divide (*coś przez coś* sth by sth). **~ się** *pf.* **1.** (= *rozdzielić się*) separate, split; **podzielić się kosztami** split the costs. **2.** (= *powiadomić siebie nawzajem*) share *l.* exchange news, impart *l.* disclose *l.* convey a piece of news to sb. **3.** (= *rozdzielić między siebie*) share (*czymś z kimś* sth with sb) go shares (*czymś z kimś* in sth with sb); **podzielić się czymś po połowie** go fifty-fifty on sth; **podzielić się sprawiedliwie** (*np. pracą*) muck in together; **podzielić się opłatkiem** *rz.-kat.* share the wafer; **podzielić się jajkiem** *rz.-kat.* share the Easter egg. **4.** *mat.* be divisible.

podzielnik *mi Gen.* -a *mat.* divisor, common factor.

podzielność *f.* divisibility; (*uwagi*) divisibility, split; **podzielność liczby** *mat.* divisibility.

podzielny *a.* divisible; (*o kawałku ciasta*) divisible; (*o uwadze*) divided, multiple, split; (*o spadku*) partible; **liczba podzielna** *mat.* divident.

podziemie n. Gen.pl. **-i 1.** (*pod budynkiem, ulicą*) basement, vaults. **2.** (= *organizacja konspiracyjna*) the underground; **być w podziemiu** be in the underground; **zejść do podziemia** go underground. **3.** mit. the nether world. **4. podziemie gospodarcze** illegal traffic.

podziemny a. **1.** (= *pod ziemią*) underground, subterranean, below-ground, subterrestrial; (*o kolei, wykopie, przejściu*) underground; **przejście podziemne** underpass, tunnel (*na stacji*); **świat podziemny** the underworld; **pęd podziemny** bot. subterranean shoot. **2.** geol. hypogeal; **wody podziemne** geol. subsoil water. **3.** (= *konspiracyjny*) underground, secret; (*o armii, organizacji*) undercover.

podziewać ipf. **1. nie mam gdzie tego podziać** I don't know where to put it; I have nowhere to put it; **nie wiedzieć gdzie podziać oczy** not know where to look. **2.** (= *gubić*) mislay, lose, leave (*sth*) somewhere. **~ się** ipf. **1. nie mam gdzie się podziać** I have nowhere to go; **gdzie ja się podzieję?** where am I to go?; what shall I do with myself?; **gdzie się podziewałeś cały dzień?** where have you been all day long? **2.** (= *gubić się, zawieruszać się*) get lost, vanish, disappear; **gdzie się podziały moje okulary** where are my glasses?; where did I put l. leave my glasses?; **gdzie on się podziewa?** where's he gone?; what has become of him?

podzięka f. lit. thanks, gratitude; **słowa podzięki** acknowledgements; **w podzięce** to thank, to show gratitude.

podziękować pf. **1.** (= *wyrazić wdzięczność*) thank, show gratitude (*za coś* for sth). **2.** (= *zrezygnować z czegoś, odmówić czegoś*) thank, decline l. refuse kindly, reject with thanks.

podziękowanie n. thanks, gratefulness; (*na wstępie książki*) acknowledgements; **bez słowa podziękowania** without as much as a thank-you; **wyrazić swoje podziękowanie** extend thanks.

podziobać pf. **1.** (*o ptaku*) peck, strike. **2.** pot. (*o człowieku*) (= *zjeść trochę*) nibble, peck, pick (*jedzenie* at one's food).

podziurawić pf. pierce, puncture (*coś* sth) make holes (*coś* in sth); (*ziemię*) (*o deszczu, gradzie*) pit; (*kulami*) riddle with bullets, shoot up; (*o psie*) bite holes (*coś* in sth); **podziurawiony** full of holes, in holes; (*o ubraniu*) tattered; **w podziurawionej marynarce** out at elbows.

podziurkować pf. perforate, punch.

podziw mi admiration, approval, high regard; **godny podziwu** admirable, praiseworthy, laudable; **wprawić kogoś w podziw** impress sb; throw sb into raptures; carry sb away; carry l. sweep sb off his l. her feet; **wyrazić podziw dla kogoś** express admiration for sb; praise sb; **nie mogę wyjść z podziwu** I am lost in admiration; **nad podziw zdolna** admirably l. wonderfully talented; **budzący podziw** awe-inspiring; **wywołać czyjś podziw** fill sb with awe; **z podziwem** admiringly, with awe; **w niemym podziwie** in mute admiration; **być pełnym podziwu dla kogoś/czegoś** be full of praise for sb/sth; regard sb/sth with admiration, be l. stand in awe of sb/sth.

podziwiać ipf. admire (*kogoś za coś* sb for sth) wonder, marvel (*kogoś* at sb) look up (*kogoś* to sb).

podzwonne n. Gen. **-ego** death knell; **dzwonić podzwonne** ring the death knell.

podzwrotnikowy a. subtropical, semitropical; (*o lesie, burzy, klimacie*) tropical; **strefa podzwrotnikowa** subtropics; **kraje podzwrotnikowe** the tropics.

podźwięk mi lit. echo, after-sound.

podźwignąć pf. **-ij 1.** (*podnieść*) raise, lift, heave. **2.** (*zbudować*) restore, rebuild, reconstruct. **3.** (*dźwignąć z upadku*) przen. restore. **4.** (*uzdrowić*) bring back to health; (*podnieść na duchu*) revive sb's spirits. **~ się** pf. **1.** (*podnieść się*) pull oneself up, stagger to one's feet; (*z łóżka*) get up, get out of bed. **2.** (*wyzdrowieć*) recover. **3.** (*otrząsnąć się, nabrać na nowo sił*) recover one's spirits, get l. pull oneself together; (*z biedy, z upadku*) rise from one's ashes.

podżebrowy a. infracostal.

podżebrze n. Gen.pl. **-y** anat. hypochondrium.

podżegacz mp, **podżegaczka** f. Gen.pl. **-ek** instigator, inciter, fomenter, incendiary; **podżegacz wojenny** war-monger.

podżegać ipf. incite, instigate (*kogoś do czegoś* sb to do sth); (*do przestępstwa*) abet (*kogoś do czegoś* sb in sth); (*do buntu*) foment.

podżeganie n. incitement, instigation; (*namawianie do przestępstwa*) abetment; (*do wojny*) warmongering.

podżerać ipf. pot. (= *wyjadać po kryjomu*) eat out.

podżyrować pf. endorse.

poemat mi **1.** poem; (*epicki*) teor.lit. epic poem, epopee; (*heroikomiczny*) heroicomical poem; (*średniowieczny*) gest; (*symfoniczny*) muz. symphonic poem. **2.** (*arcydzieło*) masterpiece.

poeta mp poet, bard, minstrel; **marny z niego poeta** he's not much of a poet; **poeta liryczny** lyricist; **poeta narodowy** poet laureate; **urodzony poeta** a poet by birth.

poetka f. Gen.pl. **-ek** poetess.

poetycki a. poetic; (*o talencie, wyobraźni, języku*) poetic, creative, imaginative; **powieść poetycka** poetic novel; **proza poetycka** prose poetry.

poetycko adv. poetically; (*ująć, mówić*) poetically, in an inspired manner.

poetyckość f. poesy.

poetyczny a. poetic; (*o ujęciu, sposobie mówienia*) poetic.

poetyka f. **1.** (*teoria*) poetics. **2.** (*cechy dzieła literackiego*) poetics.

poetyzować ipf. **1.** poeticize. **2.** (*idealizować*) poetize, idealize.

poezja f. **1.** (*utwory literackie*) poetry, verse; **poezja liryczna** lyric poetry; **poezja epicka** epos, epopee, epic. **2.** (*nastrój*) poetry.

pofalowany a. wavy, undulate, creasy; (*o okolicy, polach*) undulate, ruffled; (*o włosach*) wavy; techn. corrugated.

pofałdować pf. (*spódnicę*) crease, pleat, rample; (*twarz zmarszczkami*) wrinkle; (*teren*) undulate. **~ się** pf. crease, pucker, ruckle up.

pofałdowany *a.* creasy, pleated, undulate; (*o okolicy, terenie, polach*) uneven, rugged, rough; (*o liściu*) undulate; *geol., biol.* plicate.

pofantazjować *pf.* dream, daydream, give reins to one's imagination; (*zmyślać*) indulge in fiction *l.* moonshine.

pofarbować *pf.* **1.** dye, stain, tincture; **trwale pofarbować** dye in grain, ingrain. **2.** (*puszczać kolor*) discolor, stain.

pofatygować się *pf.* take the trouble, troop down (*coś zrobić* to do sth).

pofiglować *pf.* frolic, mess.

pofilozofować *pf. pot.* play a philosopher.

poflirtować *pf.* flirt, toy, trifle (*z kimś* with sb) make eyes at sb.

pofolgować *pf.* **1.** *pot.* (= *okazać komuś pobłażanie*) indulge (*komuś* sb (in sth)) let off; (*sobie*) indulge oneself, treat oneself, give oneself a treat; (*dziecku*) pamper, indulge, mollycoddle. **2.** *pot.* (= *złagodnieć, zelżeć*) become *l.* grow milder, relent, subside, dwindle; (*o bólu*) abate.

pofrunąć *pf.* fly away.

pogadać *pf. pot.* chat, gossip, talk; (*z kimś*) have a word *l.* chat with sb, talk sth over with sb; **chciałbym z tobą o czymś pogadać** there's something I'd like to talk to you about; **on lubi sobie pogadać** he likes to have his say, he enjoys a chat.

pogadanka *f. Gen.pl.* **-ek** chat, talk, conversation, gossip.

pogaduszki *pl. Gen.* **-ek** chat, confab, rap.

pogalopować *pf.* **1.** gallop, canter, lope. **2.** (*pospieszyć*) hurry, hasten, dash.

poganiacz *mp* herdsman; (*bat*) whip.

poganiać *ipf.* **1.** (= *popędzać*) urge on, rush, egg on; (*krowy, owce*) whip on. **2.** (= *zmuszać do pośpiechu*) prod on, spur on, impel, encourage; **pogonić komuś kota** *pot.* put sb to rout *l.* to flight; **pogonić kogoś do roboty** *pot.* make sb get down to work, get sb to work.

poganin *mp pl.* **-anie** *Gen.* **-an, poganka** *f. Gen.pl.* **-ek** pagan, heathen.

pogański *a.* pagan, heathen, profane; (*o zwyczajach, obrzędach*) pagan.

pogaństwo *n.* paganism, heathendom; (*poganie*) heathenry.

pogarda *f.* contempt, disdain, scorn; **okazać komuś pogardę** show contempt *l.* scorn *l.* disrespect for sb; pour scorn at sb; sneer at sb; **mieć coś/kogoś w pogardzie** hold sth/sb in contempt; **dlaczego odnosisz się do mnie z pogardą?** why do you treat me with contempt?; **z pogardą** contemptuously, disdainfully; **godny pogardy** contemptible, despicable.

pogardliwie *adv.* with contempt *l.* scorn, contemptuously, disdainfully.

pogardliwy *a.* contemptuous, disdainful, scornful; (*o spojrzeniu*) contemptuous, condescending, sneering; (*o stosunku do czegoś*) disrespectful, insulting.

pogardzać *ipf.* despise, scorn, look down on (*kimś* sb) hold (sb) in contempt; (*tchórzami*) treat with disrespect, hold in contempt; (*śmier-*

cią, niebezpieczeństwem) ignore; (*radą, niebezpieczeństwem*) disregard.

pogardzenie *n.* contempt, disrespect, disdain; **to jest nie do pogardzenia** it's not to be despised *l.* sneezed at; it's worthwhile.

pogardzić *pf. zob.* **pogardzać; nie pogardziłbym tym** (= *nie odrzuciłbym*) I wouldn't reject it; I wouldn't say 'no' to it.

pogarszać *ipf.* worsen, make sth worse, exacerbate; **to tylko pogorszy sprawę** it will only make things worse. **~ się** *ipf.* worsen, get *l.* grow worse, deteriorate, take a turn for the worse; **pogoda się pogarsza** the weather is getting worse; **sytuacja z minuty na minutę się pogarszała** the situation was getting worse and worse with every single minute; **niestety, pogorszyło się jej** unfortunately she got worse; (*o standardzie*) decline, go downhill.

pogasić *pf.* **-szę -sisz** put out, extinguish, blow out, dampen, quench.

pogasnąć *pf.* **-snę -śniesz, -śnij, -sł** *l.* **-snął -sła -śli** (*o światłach*) go out, be extinguished; (*o blasku*) pale; (*o dźwięku*) die out.

pogawędka *f. Gen.pl.* **-ek** chat, chatter, chinwag, chit-chat; **uciąć sobie pogawędkę** have a chat (*z kimś* with sb).

pogawędzić *pf.* chat, have a chat (*z kimś* with sb).

pogderać *pf.* grumble, moan, groan, carp.

pogiąć *pf.* **-gnę -gniesz, -gnij** bend, twist; (*nadać kształt*) curve, bend, arch.

pogięty *a.* bent, curved, twisted, crooked; (*o drucie, korzeniu*) twisted.

pogląd *mi* opinion, view, outlook; **pogląd na świat** outlook upon life; **podzielać czyjeś poglądy** share sb's views *l.* opinions; **pozwalam sobie mieć inny pogląd** I beg to differ; **dominujący pogląd** prevailing view; **pogląd na coś** attitude towards; **reprezentować pogląd, że...** hold the view that...; **wyznawać pogląd** subscribe to a view *l.* belief; **zaryzykować pogląd** adventure an opinion; **zmieniać pogląd** shift one's ground; **liberalne poglądy** broad views; **szerokie poglądy** broadmindedness; **o liberalnych poglądach** broad minded; **o ciasnych poglądach** hidebound; **różnica poglądów** difference of opinion, dissent; **narzucać komuś swoje poglądy** inflict one's views on sb; **panujące poglądy** tide of opinion.

poglądowo *adv.* visually, demonstratively.

poglądowość *f.* demonstrative method.

poglądowy *a.* synoptic, demonstrative; (*o metodzie*) demonstrative; **lekcja poglądowa** object lesson.

pogładzić *pf.* stroke, give sb a stroke; **pogładzić po policzku** stroke sb's cheek. **~ się** *pf.* stroke.

pogłaskać *pf.* **-głaszczę** *l.* **-głaskam -głaszczesz** *l.* **-głaskasz, -głaszcz** *l.* **-głaskaj 1.** (*osobę, rękę*) stroke, fondle, caress. **2.** *przen.* (*dumę, próżność*) flatter sb, fawn upon sb.

pogłębiacz *mi Gen.* **-a 1.** *roln.* subsoil plow, chisel plow, subsoiler; **orać pogłębiaczem** subsoil. **2.** *techn.* countersink, counterbore.

pogłębiać *ipf.*, **pogłębić** *pf.* **1.** (= *czynić głęb-*

szym) deepen, dig deeper. **2.** *przen.* (= *czynić dokładniejszym*) deepen; (*np. trudności*) compound, intensify. **3.** *techn.* deepen. **4.** (*pole*) subsoil; (*wybierać muł*) dredge. ~ **się** *ipf.*, **pogłębić się** *pf.* **1.** (= *stawać się głębszym*) deepen. **2.** *przen.* (= *stawać się intensywniejszym*) intensify, become more intense.

pogłębiarka *f. Gen.pl.* **-ek** *techn.* dredge, drag; (*czerpakowa*) bucket dredge; *techn.* elevator dredge.

pogłos *mi* echo, distant sound, reverb; *muz.* reverberation; **z silnym pogłosem** (*o sali*) resonant.

pogłoska *f. Gen.pl.* **-ek** rumor, report, scuttlebutt, grapevine; **dowody oparte na pogłoskach** hearsay evidence; **krąży pogłoska, jakoby...** it is rumored *l.* whispered that...; **rozsiewać pogłoski** rumormonger.

pogłosowy *a.* reverb, reverberative; (*o magnetofonie, aparaturze*) reverb; **komora pogłosowa** echo chamber.

pogłowie *n. roln.* headage, stock, head.

pogłówkować *pf. pot.* rack *l.* cudgel one's brains about, think hard, puzzle.

pogłówne *n. Gen.* **-ego** *hist.* poll tax, capitation, headmoney.

pogłówny *a. roln.* (*o nawożeniu*) top dressing; **podatek pogłówny** capitation.

pogłupieć *pf.* lose one's mind *l.* wits, go haywire *l.* daft.

pogmatwać *pf.* entangle, complicate, muddle; **pogmatwany** entangled, confused, tangled up. ~ **się** *pf.* become *l.* get entangled; **sytuacja się pogmatwała** the situation got complicated.

pognać *pf. zob.* **poganiać, pogonić.**

pognębiać *ipf.*, **pognębić** *pf.* **1.** (*niszczyć moralnie i materialnie kogoś*) persecute, maltreat, oppress, repress. **2.** (= *przygnębiać, martwić*) sadden, cast down, weigh down, depress.

pognieść *pf.* **-gniotę** **-gnieciesz** **-gniótł** **-gniotła** **-gnietli** **1.** (= *zmiąć*) crumple, wrinkle, crease, rumple. **2.** (= *miażdżąc, zgnieść trochę czegoś*) smash, crumble, crush. ~ **się** *pf.* get rumpled *l.* wrinkled *l.* creased *l.* crumpled.

pogniewać się *pf.* **1.** (= *obrazić się*) get angry *l.* cross (*na kogoś* with sb, *o coś* about *l.* over sth). **2. pogniewać się z kimś** (= *pokłócić się*) fall out with sb, have a row *l.* fight with sb, quarrel with sb (*o coś* about *l.* over sth). **3.** (= *spędzić jakiś czas na gniewaniu się*) bicker about sth; be angry *l.* cross.

pogoda *f.* **1.** (= *aura*) weather; (*słoneczna*) sunny weather, sunshine; **deszczowa/upalna/mroźna/wietrzna pogoda** rainy/hot/frozy/windy weather; **niepewna pogoda** broken *l.* uncertain weather; **brzydka** *l.* **paskudna pogoda** dreadful *l.* nasty *l.* bad weather; **prognoza pogody** weather forecast *l.* outlook; **mapa pogody** weather map *l.* chart; **zmiana pogody** change of the weather; **pogoda pod psem** fine day for ducks; **pogoda w kratkę** changing weather; **z powodu złej pogody** due to bad weather. **2.** (*słoneczny dzień bez opadów*) fair weather; good *l.* nice *l.* fine weather; **jutro będzie pogoda** we'll have fine weather to-

morrow; the weather will be nice tomorrow; **idzie na pogodę** it seems good weather is coming; the weather bids fair to be fine; **jaka jest pogoda?** what's the weather like?; **pogoda nie dopisała** the weather fell short; the weather disappointed us; **bez względu na pogodę** regardless of weather conditions; in all weathers; **deszcz czy pogoda** rain or shine; **jeśli będzie ładna pogoda** weather permitting; **trafić na piękną/złą pogodę** make good/bad weather. **3. pogoda ducha** optimism, cheerfulness, buoyance, cheerful mood *l.* disposition.

pogodnie *adv.* (*uśmiechać się*) cheerfully, pleasantly, friendly; (*o pogodzie*) sunny, nice, fine; **na dworze jest pogodnie** it's nice outdoors, the weather is nice *l.* fine.

pogodny *a.* **1.** (= *ciepły i słoneczny*) sunny, fine; (*o dniu, ranku*) sunny, bright; (*o wakacjach, lecie*) sunny. **2.** (= *szczęśliwy, radosny*) cheerful, serene; (*o usposobieniu*) cheerful, serene; (*o nastroju*) agreable, merry, pleasant; (*o człowieku*) optimistic, cheerful, light-hearted.

pogodowy *a.* weather; (*o warunkach*) atmospheric, meteorological; **warunki pogodowe** weather conditions; **okienko pogodowe** weather window.

pogodynka *f. Gen.pl.* **-ek** weather information (phone service).

pogodzić *pf.* **-godzę** **-godzisz** **-gódź** reconcile; (*zwaśnione rodzeństwo*) reconcile, reunite, make peace between, bring together; **pogodzić pracę zawodową z obowiązkami domowymi** reconcile *l.* harmonize one's professional career with family life. ~ **się** *pf.* **1.** (= *wybaczyć sobie wzajemnie*) reconcile, make it up (*z kimś* with sb). **2.** (= *przestać się buntować przeciwko czemuś*) accept (*sth*); resign *l.* reconcile oneself to (*sth*); put up with (*sth*); **pogodzić się z losem** resign o.s. to (one's) fate; **musisz się z tym pogodzić** you have to grin and bear it; **niedający się pogodzić** incompatible (*z czymś* with sth).

pogonić *pf.* **1.** *zob.* **poganiać. 2.** (= *popędzić*) rush, hasten, dash, daft; (*ponaglić*) hurry (*sb*) up, urge *l.* prod *l.* egg (*sb*) on; (*zwierzę*) whip, hasten, goad on; (*konia*) spur.

Pogoń *f.* (*her.*) Vytis; the White Knight (*the Lithuanian coat-of-arms*).

pogoń *f. pl.* **-e 1.** (= *pościg*) chase, pursuit, hunt; **puścić się w pogoń za kimś** set off in pursuit of sb; make after sb. **2.** (= *ludzie goniący*) pursuers; **zmylić pogoń myśl.** outwit the hounds; (*o człowieku*) outwit the police. **3.** *przen.* search, quest; **w pogoni za czymś** in quest for sth *l.* after sth, searching sth.

pogorszenie *n.* worsening, deterioration, aggreviation; (*o warunkach, standardzie*) decline (*w czymś* in sth); **w nocy nastąpiło gwałtowne pogorszenie** there was a sudden breakdown *l.* crisis during the night.

pogorszyć *pf. zob.* **pogarszać.** ~ **się** *pf. zob.* **pogarszać się.**

pogorzelec *mp* **-lc-** *pl.* **-y** fire *l.* conflagration victim.

pogorzelisko *n.* fire *l.* conflagration site.

pogotowie *n.* **1.** (= *stan gotowości*) readiness, preparedness, alert; **pogotowie bojowe** action alert; **ostre pogotowie** instant readiness; **pogotowie wysokogórskie** mountain rescue service; **pogotowie lotnicze** air alert; **być w stałym pogotowiu** on the alert; on the look-out; on the qui vive; **pogotowie kasowe** *handl.* emergency fund; **mieć coś w pogotowiu** have sth ready; have sth at hand. **2.** (*doraźna pomoc*) emergency; (*gazowe, energetyczne, wodociągowe*) service, brigade; **pogotowie powodziowe** flood-watch, flood-warning service; **pogotowie drogowe** road service; **pogotowie techniczne** breakdown service; **pogotowie ratunkowe** emergency service; **karetka pogotowia** ambulance; **wezwać pogotowie** call the ambulance.

pogórze *n. Gen.pl.* **-y** *geogr.* plateau, highland, upland.

pograbić *pf.* **1.** (= *grabiąc, zgarnąć coś, wyrównać coś*) rake, even out, smooth. **2.** (= *spędzić jakiś czas na grabieniu*) rake. **3.** (= *dokonać wielu grabieży*) plunder, loot, pillage.

pograć *pf.* **1.** (*o grze sportowej*) play, have a game. **2.** (*o grze na instrumencie*) play.

pogranicze *n. Gen.pl.* **-y** borderland, frontier; **pogranicze kulturowe** cultural borderline; **być na pograniczu czegoś** fringe upon sth.

pogranicznik *mp* borderer, inhabitant of borderland.

pograniczny *a.* border, frontier; (*kulturze*) borderland; (*o dialektach, pasie*) borderline.

pogratulować *pf.* congratulate, compliment, felicitate (*komuś czegoś* sb on sth).

pogrążać *ipf.* **1.** (= *zanurzać w czymś*) sink, plunge, steep (*w czymś* in sth); (*w rozpaczy, w ruinie*) sink, plunge. **2.** (= *działać na czyjąś niekorzyść*) bring about the ruin, crush, ruin; **jej zeznania pogrążyły mnie zupełnie** her testimony brought about my ruin; **pogrążony w ciemnościach** plunged in darkness; **pogrążony w zadumie** lost *l.* engrossed in thought; **pogrążeni w ciemnocie** steeped in ignorance; **pogrążeni w smutku** *form.* the bereaved; **pogrążony w bólu** overcome with pain; **pogrążony w milczeniu** immersed in silence. **~ się** *ipf.* (= *zanurzać się w czymś*) sink, plunge, immerse; **pogrążać się w zadumie** *przen.* lose o.s. in thought, be engrossed *l.* absorbed in thought; (*w żałobie/smutku*) plunge in mourning/sorrow.

pogrążyć (się) *pf. zob.* **pogrążać (się)**.

pogrobowiec *mp* **-wc-** *pl.* **-y** posthumous child; *przen.* inheritor, successor, epigone.

pogrom *mi lit.* crushing defeat, rout; (= *rzeź*) slaughter; (*ludności żydowskiej*) pogrom.

pogromca *mp,* **pogromczyni** *f.* **1.** (= *zwycięzca*) conqueror, defeater, subjugator; **pogromca serc** lady killer. **2.** (*zwierząt*) tamer.

pogrozić *pf.* **-grożę -grozisz, -groź** *l.* **-gróź** threaten, make threats, intimidate; **pogrozić komuś palcem/pięścią** shake one's finger/fist at sb.

pogróżka *f. Gen.pl.* **-ek** threat, threatening *l.* intimidating remark, menace; **z pogróżkami** menacingly, minatorily; **list z pogróżkami** threatening letter; **sypać pogróżkami** bluster out threats.

pogrubiać *ipf.,* **pogrubić** *pf.* thicken, make thicker; **pogrubiać czcionkę** print *l.* set a type in boldface.

pogrubieć *pf.* **1.** (= *stać się grubszym*) thicken. **2.** (= *utyć*) fatten, grow *l.* become fatter. **3.** (*o skórze*) (= *stać się chropowatym*) coarsen. **4.** *pot.* (*o głosie*) roughen.

pogruchotać *pf.* **-czę** *l.* **-cę -czesz** *l.* **-cesz, -cz** crack, batter, break to pieces; **pogruchotać komuś kości** *pot.* give sb a thrashing.

pogrupować *pf.* group. **~ się** *pf.* group; **goście pogrupowali się przy stolikach** guests grouped at the tables.

pogruźliczy *a. pat.* post-tuberculotic.

pogrypowy *a. pat.* postinfluenzal.

pogrywać *ipf.* **-am -asz** *pot.* play a game (*with sb*); **nie pogrywaj sobie ze mną!** don't you try to play your game with me, will you!

pogryzać *ipf.* nibble (*coś* at sth).

pogryzmolić *pf. pot.* doodle, scribble (*all over one's books, notebooks, etc.*).

pogryźć *pf.* **-zę -ziesz -zł -źli** **1.** (= *skaleczyć zębami*) bite; **w zeszłym tygodniu pogryzł go własny pies** he was bitten by his own dog last week. **2.** (= *rozdrobnić zębami*) chew. **~ się** *pf.* **1.** (*o psach*) bite each other *l.* one another; **psy pogryzły się o kość** the dogs fought over a bone (*and bit one another*). **2.** *pot.* (= *pokłócić się*) have a fight *l.* row (*o kogoś/coś* over sb/sth).

pogrzeb *mi* **1.** (*ceremonia*) funeral, burial; **pogrzeb z honorami** honorable burial. **2.** (*kondukt*) funeral, funeral procession.

pogrzebacz *mi Gen.* **-a** poker.

pogrzebać *pf.* **-bię -biesz** **1.** (*zmarłego*) bury, inter. **2.** (*nadzieje*) bury, bid farewell to; **pogrzebać nadzieje** bury one's hopes, bid farewell to one's hopes. **3.** (= *poszukać tu i ówdzie*) rummage; **pogrzebać w kieszeniach** rummage one's pockets; **pogrzebać w szufladzie** rummage through one's drawer.

pogrzebowy *a.* funeral; **kondukt pogrzebowy** funeral procession, funeral cortege; **marsz pogrzebowy** funeral march; **mowa pogrzebowa** eulogy; **nabożeństwo pogrzebowe** *l.* żałobne funeral service; **obrzędy pogrzebowe** obsequies; **przedsiębiorca pogrzebowy** undertaker, funeral director; **stos pogrzebowy** funeral pyre, balefire; **uroczystość pogrzebowa** funeral ceremony; **zakład pogrzebowy** funeral parlor; **zasiłek pogrzebowy** survivors benefit; **mieć pogrzebową minę** wear a grave expression; **co masz taką pogrzebową minę?** you look like you just lost your best friend, who died?

pogubić *pf.* lose; **pogubiłem wszystkie długopisy** I've lost all my pens. **~ się** *pf.* **1.** (= *zginąć*) lose each other *l.* one another, go missing; **dzieci pogubiły się w lesie** children went missing in the forest. **2.** (= *nie rozumieć*) be *l.* get lost, get confused; **kompletnie** *l.* **zupełnie się pogubiłem** I'm completely confused; **kompletnie** *l.* **zupełnie się w tym pogubiłem** I'm completely lost (in it).

pogwałcać *ipf.* violate, infract (*coś* sth);

trench, infringe (*coś* on *l.* upon sth); **pogwałcić prawo** violate a law, infringe a law; **pogwałcić czyjeś uczucia** outrage *l.* offend sb's feelings.

pogwałcenie *n.* (*np. prawa*) infraction, violation; (*np. uczuć*) outrage, offence.

pogwałcić *pf. zob.* **pogwałcać**.

pogwar *mi* (*np. głosów*) murmur; (*np. ulicy, miasta*) drone, bustle.

pogwarka *f.* chat.

pogwarzyć *pf.* have a chat.

pogwizdać *pf.* -**gwiżdżę** -**gwiżdżesz** whiffle; **teraz możemy sobie pogwizdać** *pot.* all we can do now is wait.

pohamować *pf.* **1.** (= *powstrzymać*) contain, restrain, repress, suppress, bridle, check; **pohamować coś** keep *l.* hold sth in check; **pohamować czyjeś zapędy** stamp on sb; **pohamować gniew** contain one's anger, keep one's anger bottled up; **pohamować łzy** hold back one's tears; **pohamować wściekłość** hold one's rage in check; **pohamować zdumienie** suppress one's astonishment; **pohamować żądzę** supress a desire. **2.** (= *zahamować, zwolnić*) slow down. ~ **się** *pf.* check o.s., control o.s.

pohaniec *mp arch.* paynim.

pohańbić *pf.* disgrace, bring shame upon; (*kobietę*) defile. ~ **się** *pf.* disgrace o.s.

poharatać *pf.* **1.** *pot.* slash, gash, mangle; **poharatać kogoś nożem** slash *l.* gash sb with a knife. **2.** *pot.* (= *pociąć, zniszczyć*) slash. ~ **się** *pf. pot.* gash *l.* slice o.s.

pohukiwać *ipf.* **1.** (*na postrach*) boo. **2.** (*np. o armatach*) rumble. **3.** (*o ptakach*) hoot. **4.** (= *strofować*) scold.

pohybel *mi* -**bl**- *Gen.* -**a** death, annihilation; **wypić komuś na pohybel** drink to sb's death, misfortune, etc.; **na pohybel wrogom!** down with the enemies!

poić *ipf.* **poję poisz, pój 1.** (*bydło*) (= *dać pić*) water; **poić lekarstwem** *wet.* drench. **2.** *pot.* (*alkoholem*) ply, lubricate. ~ **się** *ipf.* **1.** (*o zwierzętach*) drink. **2.** (= *napawać się*) imbibe (*czymś* sth).

poidełko *n. Gen.pl.* -**ek** birdbath.

poidło *n. Gen.pl.* -**eł 1.** (*naczynie*) watering trough. **2.** (*karma płynna*) liquid fodder for cattle.

poinformować *pf.* inform; (*zwłaszcza oficjalnie*) notify; **poinformować kogoś o czymś** inform *l.* notify sb about sth, let sb know about sth, bring sth to sb's knowledge; *pot.* clue sb up on sth, put sb wise to sth. ~ **się** *pf.* inquire, request information (*o czymś* about sth).

poinformowany *a.* informed; **dobrze poinformowany** well-informed; **źle poinformowany** ill-informed; **być dobrze poinformowanym o czymś** be well-informed about sth, be well-posted on sth, be in the know about sth; **koła dobrze poinformowane** well-informed circles; **osoba dobrze poinformowana** insider; **wiadomości z dobrze poinformowanych źródeł** *zwł.* dzienn. news from reliable sources.

poinsecja *f. bot.* poinsettia (*Euphorbia pulcherrima*).

poinstruować *pf.* instruct.

pointa *f.* (*np. opowiadania*) (culminating) point, punch line; (*dowcipu*) punch line.

pointer *ma kynol.* pointer.

pointować *ipf.* deliver a punch line.

pointylista *mp sztuka* pointillist.

pointylistyczny *mi sztuka* pointillist, pointillistic.

pointylizm *mi sztuka* pointillism.

poirytować *pf.* irritate, annoy, vex, irk. ~ **się** *pf.* get irritated, get annoyed, get vexed, get irked.

poj. *abbr.* (= *pojemność*) vol. (*volume*).

pojadać *ipf.* (= *jeść powoli*) nibble (*coś* at sth); (*między posiłkami*) graze.

pojaśnieć *pf.* brighten up; **świat mu pojaśniał** his world brightened up.

pojawiać się *ipf.*, **pojawić się** *pf.* appear; (*na spotkaniu, przyjęciu*) show up, turn up; (= *wyłaniać się*) emerge; (= *stawać się widocznym*) come into view; (*o okazji, okoliczności*) come along, present itself; (*np. o trudnościach*) arise, crop up; (*np. o czyimś nazwisku w kontekście czegoś*) crop up; (*np. o zjawiskach w eksperymencie*) (= *wystąpić*) occur, surface; **pojawić się w czyimś życiu** enter one's life; **pojawić się ni stąd, ni zowąd** bob up; **pojawiać się i znikać** come and go.

pojazd *mi* vehicle, conveyance; **pojazd dwuśladowy** 4-wheeled vehicle; **pojazd gąsienicowy** tracked vehicle, caterpillar; **pojazd jednośladowy** 2-wheeled vehicle; **pojazd kosmiczny** spacecraft; **pojazd księżycowy** lunar module; **pojazd mechaniczny** motor vehicle; **pojazd pancerny** *wojsk.* armored car; **pojazd** *l.* **samochód terenowy** off-road vehicle, all-terrain vehicle; **pojazd szynowy** rail vehicle.

pojąć *pf.* **pojmę pojmiesz, pojmij** *zob.* **pojmować**.

pojebany *a. wulg.* (*o człowieku*) (= *nienormalny*) fucked in the head; **ten nauczyciel jest zupełnie pojebany!** this teacher is just fucked in the head!; (= *irytujący*) fucking; **co za pojebana robota!** what a fucking chore it is!; (= *pokręcony*) fucked up; **moje życie jest totalnie pojebane** my life is just totally fucked up.

pojechać *pf.* -**jadę** -**jedziesz** go (*dokąd* somewhere); **pojechać autobusem** go by bus, take a bus; **pojechać do Gdyni** go to Gdynia; **pojechać na studia do Krakowa** go to study in Cracow; **pojechać na wycieczkę** go on a trip; **pojechać na wymianę** *szkoln.* go on an exchange; **pojechać okrężną drogą** make a detour; **pojechać samochodem** go by car; **pojechać za granicę** go abroad; **pojechać do Rygi** *euf.* bow to the porcelain god, talk to Joan on the big white phone, abort a meal, laugh at the carpet, air one's belly.

pojednać *pf. zob.* **pojednywać**. ~ **się** *pf.* reconcile; **pojednać się z Bogiem** reconcile o.s. with God, make one's peace with God.

pojednanie *n.* (= *doprowadzenie do zgody*) conciliation; (= *zgoda*) reconciliation; **sakrament pojednania** *rz.-kat.* penance, sacrament of reconcilliation.

pojednawczo *adv.* conciliatingly, conciliatorily.

pojednawczy *a.* conciliatory, conciliative; **gest pojednawczy** conciliatory gesture; **krok pojednawczy** conciliatory measure *l.* step.

pojednywać *ipf.* conciliate, reconcile, bring to reconciliation.

pojedynczo *adv.* individually, singly, one by one, one at a time.

pojedynczy *a.* single, individual; **pojedyncze łóżko** single bed; **pojedynczy pokój** single room; **pojedyncze słowa** individual words; **liczba pojedyncza** *gram.* the singular (number); **gra pojedyncza** *tenis* singles.

pojedynek *mi* -nk- **1.** (*honorowy*) duel, single combat; **stoczyć pojedynek** fight a duel (*o kogoś / coś* over sb/sth); **wyzwać kogoś na pojedynek** challenge sb to a duel. **2.** *przen.* (= *rywalizacja*) duel, contest, competition; **pojedynek słowny** battle of words. **3.** *myśl.* rogue.

pojedynka *f. Gen.pl.* -ek **1.** (= *pokój jednoosobowy w hotelu*) sigle room; (*w więzieniu*) solitary confinement cell. **2.** (*strzelba*) single-barreled gun; **w pojedynkę** on one's own, single-handed, alone, by o.s.

pojedynkować *ipf. roln.* thin (*plants*).

pojedynkować się *ipf.* duel, fight a duel (*z kimś* with sb); **pojedynkować się z kimś na słowa** bandy words with sb.

pojemnik *mi Gen.* -a container, receptacle; (*zwłaszcza na ciecze*) vessel; (*np. na węgiel, ziarno*) bin; **pojemnik na pieczywo** breadbin; **pojemnik na popiół** ash can; **pojemnik na śmieci** trash *l.* garbage can; *Br.* rubbish bin, dustbin.

pojemnikowiec *mi* -wc- *Gen.* -a *żegl.* container ship.

pojemnościomierz *mi Gen.* -a *el.* capacitance meter.

pojemność *f.* **1.** (= *objętość*) capacity; **pojemność cieplna** *fiz.* heat capacity; **pojemność skokowa** *mot.* swept volume; **pojemność skokowa silnika** *mot.* engine cubic capacity; **pojemność statku** *żegl.* tonnage, tunnage; **pojemność pamięci** *komp.* storage capacity. **2.** *fiz.* capacitance, capacity; **pojemność akumulatora** battery capacity.

pojemny *a.* voluminous, capacious; **pojemny bagażnik** voluminous trunk; *Br.* voluminous boot; **pojemna walizka** voluminous suitcase; **pojemne pojęcie** *przen.* umbrella term.

pojeść *pf.* -jem -jesz -jedzą, -jedz, -jadł -jedli eat one's fill.

pojezierze *n. Gen.pl.* -y lake district, lakeland.

pojeździć *pf.* -jeżdżę -jeździsz (*np. rowerem*) have a ride; (*np. po świecie*) travel around *l.* about (*e.g. the world*).

pojęcie *n.* **1.** (= *myślowy odpowiednik nazwy*) concept, conception; (= *wyobrażenie ogólne*) notion; **pojęcie filozoficzne** philosophical concept; **pojęcie literackie** literary concept; **pojęcie z zakresu logiki** logical concept; **kojarzenie pojęć** *psych.* association of ideas. **2.** (= *wiedza, orientacja*) notion, idea, grasp; **masz pojęcie, czego oni ode mnie chcieli?** (do you have) any idea

what they wanted from me?; **to przechodzi ludzkie** *l.* **wszelkie pojęcie** that beats the Dutch, it's beyond belief; **nie do pojęcia!** it's unbelievable!, it's beyond belief!, it's beyond my grasp!; **nie mieć o czymś najmniejszego** *l.* **bladego** *l.* **zielonego pojęcia** not have the slightest *l.* faintest *l.* vaguest *l.* remotest idea, have no inkling of sth; **mieć dobre/marne pojęcie o czymś** have a good/ poor grasp of sth; **mieć o czymś ogólne pojęcie** have a general idea of sth; **zrobiony bez pojęcia** done in a foolhardy way, not well thought out.

pojęciowy *a.* conceptual, notional; **myślenie pojęciowe** conceptual thinking; **poznanie pojęciowe** conceptual *l.* notional cognition.

pojękiwać *ipf.* give an occasional groan.

pojętny *a.* bright, clever; **pojętny pies** clever dog; **pojętny uczeń** bright pupil.

pojkilotermia *f. biol.* poikilothermism, poikilothermy.

pojkilotermiczny *a. biol.* poikilothermal.

pojmać *pf.* -mę -miesz, -ij *przest.* (= *ująć, schwytać*) capture, take prisoner.

pojmować *ipf. lit.* comprehend, grasp, compass; **nie pojmuje ani słowa** he doesn't comprehend a single word; **wreszcie pojął, o co chodzi** he finally grasped it; **nic z tego nie pojmuję** I can't make anything of it; **pojąć kogoś za żonę** *przest.* take sb to wife.

pojutrze *adv.* the day after tomorrow.

pokajać się *pf.* repent.

pokalać *ipf. lit.* dishonor, defame.

pokaleczyć *pf.* cut, lacerate; **szkło pokaleczyło mu całą twarz** his face was cut all over by slivers of glass.

pokancerować *pf. pot.* scratch, scrape, scar.

pokapować się *pf. pot.* get the picture, get the hang (*w czymś* of sth).

pokarm *mi* **1.** (= *pożywienie*) food; **pokarm roślinny** vegetable food; **pokarm zwierzęcy** animal food; **pokarm bogaty w białko** protein-rich food; (*dla zwierząt*) feed, fodder, forage, provender; **pokarm dla ducha** *przen.* food *l.* nourishment for the spirit *l.* soul. **2.** (= *mleko matki*) milk.

pokarmowy *a.* alimentary, nutritional; **przewód pokarmowy** *anat.* alimentary canal *l.* tract, digestive tract; **treść pokarmowa** *fizj.* chyme; **zapotrzebowanie pokarmowe** *zwł. zootechnika* nutritional requirements; **zatrucie pokarmowe** food poisoning.

pokasływać *ipf.* cough (*every now and then*).

pokawałkować *pf.* split up, chop up, divide *l.* separate into pieces.

pokaz *mi* demostration, show, presentation; **pokaz lotniczy** air show; **pokaz mody** fashion *l.* couture show; **pokaz** *l.* **wystawa osobliwości** (*np. zwierząt z dwoma głowami itd.*) freak show; **pokaz pływacki** swimming gala; **pokaz przedpremierowy** (*np. filmu*) preview; **pokaz prywatny** *l.* **zamknięty** private view; **pokaz siły** show of force; *wojsk.* demonstration; **pokaz wojska** military parade; **pokaz sztucznych ogni** fireworks, pyrotechnic display; **pokaz „światło i dźwięk”** light show; **pokaz zamknięty** (*np. kolekcji mody dla dziennikarzy*) preview; **wystawiać coś na pokaz**

exhibit sth; (= *chcieć czymś zaimponować*) blazon sth abroad; **na pokaz** for show, for effect; **zrobić coś na pokaz** do sth for show.

pokazać *pf.* **-żę -żesz** *zob.* **pokazywać.** ~ **się** *pf.* *zob.* **pokazywać się.**

pokazowy *a.* **1.** (= *będący przedmiotem pokazu*) display, exhibition; **egzemplarz pokazowy** *l.* **demonstracyjny** (*np. dla celów reklamowych*) demonstration model; **lekcja pokazowa** object lesson; **proces pokazowy** *prawn., polit.* show trial; **mecz pokazowy** exhibition match. **2.** (= *wzorowy*) star; **pokazowa część czegoś** the star part of sth; **to jest pokazowa** *l.* **modelowa szkoła** this school is a showpiece.

pokazówka *f. Gen.pl.* **-ek** *pot.* dog and pony show.

pokazywać *ipf.* **1.** (= *demonstrować*) show; **pokazać figę** show sb one's fist with the thumb put between the index finger and the middle finger (*a gesture meaning 'it's no use', 'no go'*); **pokazywać fochy** fret and fume; **pokazać klasę** show class; **pokazać komuś drzwi** (= *wyprosić kogoś*) show sb the door; **pokazać komuś, gdzie (jest) jego miejsce** put sb in their place; **pokazać komuś, gdzie raki zimują** fix sb's wagon; **pokazać komuś gest Kozakiewicza** give sb two fingers; **pokazać komuś język** poke *l.* stick one's tongue out at sb; **pokazać komuś plecy** take to one's heels; **pokazać, na co kogoś stać** show *l.* prove one's mettle; **pokazać pazury** *l.* **rogi** *l.* **zęby** show one's teeth; **pokazać swoje prawdziwe oblicze** show one's true colors. **2.** (= *informować*) show; **zegar pokazuje pierwszą** clock shows one; **barometr pokazuje zmiany w pogodzie** barometer shows changes in the weather. **3.** (= *okazywać, przejawiać*) show; **nic po sobie nie pokazać** keep one's countenance; **nie pokazać czegoś po sobie** not show sth; **pokazać komuś** (= *dać nauczkę*) let sb have it; **ja ci jeszcze pokażę!** I'll teach you! ~ **się** *ipf.* **1.** (= *być widocznym, pojawiać się*) show up, turn up; (*np. na spotkaniu, przyjęciu*) put in *l.* make an appearance; **pokazywać się publicznie** be in the public eye. **2.** (= *odwiedzać*) come and see (*kogoś* sb); **nie pokazujecie się ostatnio u nas, dlaczego?** you haven't been too regular at our place recently, why's that? **3.** (= *dać się poznać*) show; **pokazał się jako dobry przywódca** he showed himself to be a good leader; **pokazać się z dobrej** *l.* **jak najlepszej strony** put one's best leg *l.* foot forward.

pokaźnie *adv.* substantially, considerably.

pokaźny *a.* **1.** (= *znaczny*) substantial, considerable, sizeable; **pokaźna biblioteka** (private) library of ample holdings; **pokaźny majątek** considerable fortune; **pokaźna** *l.* **imponująca sumka** princely sum. **2.** (= *okazały*) splendid, magnificent; **pokaźny dom** splendid house; **pokaźny pałac** magnificent palace.

pokąsać *pf.* (*np. o psie*) bite; (*np. o pszczołach*) sting.

pokątnie *adv.* illegally, illicitly; **sprzedawać coś pokątnie** sell sth under the counter.

pokątny *a.* illicit, illegal, backstreet; **pokątny handel alkoholem** illicit alcohol selling; **pokątny**

sprzedawca illegal seller; **pokątna aborcja** backstreet abortion.

poker *mi Gen.* **-a** *karty* poker; **poker królewski** *l.* **duży poker** (= *sekwens od 10 do asa w jednym kolorze*) royal flush; **poker rozbierany** strip poker.

pokerowy *a.* poker; **pokerowa twarz** poker face.

pokerzysta *mp* poker player; **wytrawny pokerzysta** demon poker player.

pokićkać *pf. pot.* (= *pomylić*) mix up, confuse; **pokićkać komuś w głowie** confuse sb. ~ **się** *pf. pot.* (= *pomylić się*) get mixed up, get confused; **wszystko mi się pokićkało** I'm all mixed up, I got confused.

pokiełbasić się *pf.* **-szę -sisz** *pot.* get muddled, get jumbled, get mixed up; **wszystko mi się pokiełbasiło** I'm all mixed up, I'm completely confused.

pokiereszować *pf.* mangle, savage, maul.

pokierować *pf.* **1.** (= *nadać kierunek*) direct. **2.** (= *zarządzić coś*) command. ~ **się** *pf.* follow; **pokierować się czyimiś wskazówkami** follow *l.* take sb's advice; **pokierować się własnym rozumem** use one's own judgement.

pokiwać *pf.* **-am -asz** (*ręką*) wave; (*głową*) shake; (*palcem*) wag; **pokiwać palcem w bucie** do sth useless.

poklask *mi lit.* acclaim, applause, éclat.

poklasyfikować *pf.* classify (*into types, groups, etc.*).

poklasztorny *a.* formerly belonging to a monastery *l.* convent; **budynki poklasztorne** buildings formerly belonging to a monastery *l.* convent.

pokląskwa *f. orn.* whinchat (*Saxicola rubetra*).

poklepać *pf.* **-pię -piesz**, **poklepywać** *ipf.* **1.** (= *uderzać dłonią*) pat, clap; **poklepać kogoś po plecach/ramieniu** give sb a pat *l.* clap on the back/shoulder. **2.** (*by naostrzyć coś*) planish. ~ **się** *pf.*, **poklepywać się** *ipf.* **1.** (= *uderzać siebie dłonią*) pat o.s., tap o.s.; **poklepać się po brzuchu** pat *l.* tap o.s. on the stomach. **2.** (= *uderzać dłonią siebie nawzajem*) pat each other *l.* one another, tap each other *l.* one another; **poklepali się po ramionach** they patted each other *l.* one another on the back.

pokład *mi* **1.** *żegl., t. lotn.* deck; **pokład dolny** lower deck; **pokład główny** main deck; **pokład górny** upper deck; **pokład spacerowy** promenade deck; **pokład startowy** (*lotniskowca*) flight deck; **pokład otwarty** weather deck; **pokład tylny** aft deck; **wchodzić na pokład** go on board *l.* aboard, embark (*a ship*); **wszyscy na pokład!** all hands on deck!; **witamy państwa serdecznie na pokładzie naszego samolotu** ladies and gentlemen, welcome aboard our plane; **na pokładzie (statku/samolotu)** on board (a ship/plane). **2.** (= *zalegająca warstwa czegoś*) layer; **pokłady tłuszczu** layers of fat, blubber. **3.** (= *zasób*) supply, reserve; **moje pokłady energii się powoli wyczerpują** my energy is flagging *l.* at an ebb; **moje pokłady cierpliwości się wyczerpują** my patience is wearing thin. **4.** *górn., geol.* bed, seam, stratum, layer; **pokład węgla** bed of coal.

pokładać *ipf.* (*np. zboża*) lodge, beat down; **pokładać nadzieje w kimś/czymś** pin *l.* lay *l.* set *l.* stake one's hopes on sb/sth; **pokładać zaufanie w kimś/czymś** place confidence *l.* trust in sb/sth. ~ **się** *ipf.* **1.** (= *kłaść się od czasu do czasu*) lie down (*usu. occasionally, because of an illness, tiredness, etc.*); **pokładać się ze zmęczenia** be dead on one's feet, be dog-tired, be done in. **2.** (= *zginać się*) bend down; (*np. o zbożach*) be lodged, be beaten down; **pokładać** *l.* **skręcać się ze śmiechu** be in convulsions *l.* hysterics, double up with laughter.

pokładełko *n. Gen.pl.* **-ek** *ent.* ovipositor, aculeus.

pokładowy *a.* deck; **dziennik pokładowy** *l.* **okrętowy** *żegl.* logbook, log; **dźwig pokładowy** deck crane; **karta pokładowa** boarding pass; **ładunek pokładowy** deck load; **oficer pokładowy** deck officer.

pokłaść *pf.* **-kładę -kładziesz -kładł** put; **pokładła dzieci do łóżek** she put the children to bed; **pokładł wszystkie książki na miejsce** he put all the books in order *l.* in their places. ~ **się** *pf.* **1.** (= *zająć pozycję leżącą*) lie down; **psy pokładły się przy ognisku** dogs lay down at the bonfire. **2.** (= *iść spać*) go to bed; **dzieci późno się pokładły** children went to bed late. **3.** (*o zbożu*) be lodged, be beaten down.

pokłon *mi lit.* bow; **bić pokłony** prostrate o.s.; **giąć się przed kimś w pokłonach** *l.* **bić komuś pokłony** (= *okazywać służalczość*) bow and scrape to sb.

pokłonić się *pf. lit.* bow; **pokłonić się w pas** bow at the waist (*komuś* to sb).

pokłosie *n. Gen.pl.* **-i 1.** *lit.* aftermath; **pokłosiem dyskusji było...** in the aftermath of the discussion... **2.** *roln.* gleanings.

pokłócić *pf.* bring to a quarrel; **pokłócił ze sobą siostry** he brought the sisters to a quarrel with each other *l.* one another. ~ **się** *pf.* have a quarrel, have a row, have a fight, fall out; **pokłócił się z matką** he had a quarrel *l.* a row *l.* a fight with his mother; **pokłócili się o pieniądze** they had a quarrel *l.* a row *l.* a fight over money, they fell out over money.

pokłuć *pf.* (*nożem, szpilką*) prick; (*o owadzie*) sting. ~ **się** *pf.* get pricked; **dzieci pokłuły się przy zbieraniu malin** children got pricked when picking raspberries.

pokłusować *pf.* (*o koniu, jeźdźcu*) set off at a trot, trot off.

pokochać *pf.* fall in love (*kogoś* with sb) come to love (*coś* sth); **pokochać kogoś jak brata/siostrę** start to love sb like a brother/sister; **pokochać kogoś/coś na zawsze** love sb/sth forever; **pokochałem ją bez wzajemności** my love for her was not requited; **pokochałem ją od pierwszego wejrzenia** it was love at first sight. ~ **się** *pf.* start to love each other *l.* one another, fall in love with each other; **pokochali się od pierwszego wejrzenia** it was love at first sight.

pokoik *mi* small room, cubbyhole.

pokojowiec *mp hist.* valet.

pokojowo *adv.* peacefully; **pokojowo nastawiony** with peaceful intentions; (*o narodzie, kraju*) peaceable.

pokojowy *a.* **1.** (= *nie wrogi*) peaceful, peace; **pokojowe współistnienie** *polit.* peaceful coexistence, concord; **pokojowe rozstrzygnięcie** peaceful settlement; **pokojowe zamiary** peaceful intentions; **inicjatywa pokojowa** peace initiative; **międzynarodowe siły pokojowe** *wojsk.* international peacekeeping forces; **misja pokojowa** *wojsk.* peace mission; **rokowania** *l.* **pokojowe** peace negotiations; **rozmowy pokojowe** peace talks; **traktat pokojowy** peace treaty; **wysłannik pokojowy** peace envoy. **2.** (= *dotyczący pokoju - pomieszczenia*) room; **malarz pokojowy** house painter; **piesek pokojowy** *l.* **salonowy** lap *l.* toy dog; **roślina pokojowa** house plant; **temperatura pokojowa** room temperature; **podawać w temperaturze pokojowej** *kulin.* serve at room temperature. **3.** *zob.* **pokojowiec.**

pokojówka *f. Gen.pl.* **-ek** chambermaid.

pokolenie *n.* **1.** (*potomstwo*) generation; **przemiana pokoleń** *biol.* alternation of generations. **2.** (*rówieśnicy*) generation; **dorastające pokolenie** the rising generation; **młode pokolenie** the younger generation; **konflikt** *l.* **różnica pokoleń** generation gap; **z pokolenia na pokolenie** from one generation to the next; **przekazywać coś z pokolenia na pokolenie** pass *l.* hand sth down; **w trzecim pokoleniu** third-generation; **Amerykanin w trzecim pokoleniu** third-generation American.

pokoleniowy *a.* generational; **różnica pokoleniowa** generation gap; **więź pokoleniowa** generational ties.

pokolonialny *a.* postcolonial; **gospodarka postkolonialna** postcolonial economy.

pokolorować *pf.* color.

pokombinować *pf.* **1.** *pot.* (= *wymyślić coś*) put together, think out. **2.** *pot.* (= *zrobić jakieś interesy*) wangle, contrive.

pokomplikować *pf.* complicate, make complicated. ~ **się** *pf.* become *l.* get complicated.

pokonać *pf. zob.* **pokonywać.**

pokonanie *n.* (*trudności*) overcoming; (*przeciwnika*) defeat; (*kraju*) conquest; (*odległości*) covering; **nie do pokonania** (*o trudnościach*) unsurmountable, insuperable; (*o graczu, drużynie*) unbeatable.

pokontrolny *a.* post-check, post-control, post-supervision; *zob. t.* **kontrola.**

pokonywać *ipf.* **1.** (= *zwyciężać*) (*wroga*) defeat; (*rywali*) beat; **pokonać kogoś jego własną bronią** beat sb at their own game. **2.** (= *podbić*) (*kraj*) conquer; (*naród*) subdue. **3.** (= *opanowywać*) overcome, surmount; (*np. inflację, chorobę*) conquer; (*np. strach, pragnienie, pokusę*) fight down; **pokonać przeszkodę** overcome an obstacle; **pokonać odległość** cover a distance; **pokonać zakręt** turn a corner.

pokończyć *pf.* **1.** (= *skończyć*) bring to an end, complete, finish (*doing sth*). **2.** die; **przestępcy pokończyli na szubienicy** criminals were hanged.

pokora f. humility, humbleness; **prosić o coś w pokorze** ask for sth humbly, ask for sth cap in hand; **w pokorze ducha** with all humility.

pokornie adv. humbly, cap in hand; **prosić kogoś pokornie** go to sb cap in hand.

pokornieć ipf. become l. grow humble.

pokorny a. humble, meek, submissive; **pokorny sługa** (your) humble servant; **pokorne cielę dwie matki ssie** the still sow eats up all the draff.

pokos mi roln. 1. (= pas skoszonej trawy lub zboża) swath. 2. (= plon jednych żniw) harvest, crop.

pokost mi oil varnish, boiled oil.

pokostować ipf. varnish, oil-finish.

pokot mi myśl. display of the game killed during a hunt; **leżeć pokotem** be lying in a row, be lying side by side.

pokój[1] mi -o- Gen.pl. -ów l. -oi 1. (= czas bez wojny) peace; **fajka pokoju** peace pipe, pipe of peace, calumet; **Korpus Pokoju** (organizacja amerykańska) Peace Corps; **gołąb pokoju** dove of peace. 2. (= traktat) Peace, peace treaty; **zawrzeć pokój** make peace; **zawrzeć l. podpisać pokój** polit. sign a peace treaty. 3. (= brak zmartwień) peace; **sędzia pokoju** prawn. justice of the peace, magistrate; **znak pokoju** kośc. pax; **przekażcie sobie znak pokoju** and now let us share with one another l. offer l. give one another a sign of Christ's peace; **idź w pokoju** peace be with you; **niech odpoczywa w pokoju** let him/her rest in peace.

pokój[2] mi -o- Gen.pl. -ów l. -oi (pomieszczenie mieszkalne) room; **pokój do pracy** study; **pokój dwuosobowy** (np. w hotelu) double room; **pokój dziecięcy** nursery; **pokój dzienny** living room; **pokój gościnny** guestroom, spare room; **pokój jadalny** l. **stołowy** dining room; **pokój jednoosobowy** (np. w hotelu) single room; **pokój przechodni** pass through room; **pokój nauczycielski** szkoln. staff room; **pokoje do wynajęcia** (napis) rooms to let; **wolny pokój** (w hotelu) vacancy; **dzielić z kimś pokój** share a room with sb; **kolega/koleżanka z pokoju** (np. w domu studenckim) roommate.

pokpić pf. -ij 1. (= zrobić coś źle) bungle, botch; **pokpić sprawę** flub it. 2. zob. **pokpiwać**.

pokpiwać ipf. (= żartować przez jakiś czas) banter.

pokracznie adv. grotesquely.

pokraczny a. grotesque, bizzare.

pokraka f. pog. freak, monster.

pokratkowany a. (= z narysowaną kratką) checked.

pokreślić pf. 1. (= pokryć liniami) cover with lines (e.g. a page). 2. (= skreślić) cross out, strike off, blue-pencil.

pokreślony a. covered with lines.

pokrewieństwo n. 1. (= więzi krwi) kinship, kindred, relation; **jest między nami bliskie/dalekie pokrewieństwo** we are closely/distantly related; **więzy pokrewieństwa** ties of kinship. 2. (języków) cognateness. 3. chem., biol. affinity; **pokrewieństwo skał** geol. consanguinity. 4. (= podobieństwo) affinity.

pokrewny a. related, similar, akin; **pokrewny charakter** similar character; **pokrewna** l. **bratnia dusza** kindred spirit, sb after one's own heart; **pokrewne gatunki** biol. allied species; **pokrewne języki** jęz. cognate languages; **pokrewny kierunek studiów** related studies; **nauki pokrewne** allied sciences; **osobnik pokrewny** biol. congener; **wyraz pokrewny** jęz. cognate, conjugate.

pokręcić pf. 1. (= obrócić) turn. 2. (np. włosy) curl. 3. (= zniekształcić, wygiąć) twist, distort; **żeby cię pokręciło!** bad cess l. scran to you! 4. (= pomylić) mess up. ~ **się** pf. 1. (= pokrzątać się) bustle around; **jeszcze się tu chwilę pokręcę** I'll stick around for a while. 2. (= poobracać się) turn round and round, spin; **pokręcić się na karuzeli** have a ride on the merry-go-round. 3. (o kończynach, drzewach itp.) (= powyginać się) get twisted, get distorted. 4. (= pomylić się) get messed up, get muddled up; **chyba coś mi się pokręciło** I think I've got it wrong. 5. (= postarać się) busy o.s.; **pokręcić się koło czegoś** hover about sth.

pokrętło n. Gen.pl. -eł crank; (np. do ustawiania stacji radiowej) dial.

pokrętnie adv. intricately, obscurely.

pokrętny a. 1. (= zagmatwany, niejasny) intricate, obscure, tortuous, labyrinthine, twisted; **pokrętna fabuła** intricate l. complicated plot; **pokrętne rozumowanie** obscure line of reasoning, labyrinthine reasoning, ambages; **pokrętne wyjaśnienie** (np. swego zachowania) song and dance (czegoś about sth). 2. techn. rotating.

pokroić pf. -krój 1. (na kawałki) cut up; (mięso) carve up; **pokroić coś w kostkę** dice sth; **pokroić coś na kawałki** cut sth to pieces; **pokroić coś na plasterki** slice sth. 2. (= skroić) tailor. 3. pot. (= zranić) cut up. 4. pot. (= zoperować) operate on; **tym razem będą musieli mnie pokroić** I'm gonna have to go under the knife this time.

pokropić pf. sprinkle; **dziś rano trochę pokropiło** it drizzled in the morning. ~ **się** pf. sprinkle o.s.

pokrowiec mi -wc- Gen. -a 1. (= futerał) case. 2. (= przykrycie) cover; **pokrowiec na garnitur** suit bag.

pokrój mi -o- Gen.pl. -oi l. -ów 1. (= typ) stamp, mold, cast; **człowiek tego pokroju co on** a man of his own cast; **zatrudniał tylko ludzi swojego pokroju** he would only employ people of his own stamp; **być osobą zupełnie innego pokroju** be cast in a completely different mold. 2. biol., geol. habit.

pokrótce adv. briefly, in short.

pokruszyć pf. crumble, crush. ~ **się** pf. crumble.

pokrwawić pf. 1. (= zranić) wound severely. 2. (= poplamić krwią) stain with blood.

pokrwawiony a. 1. (= poraniony) bleeding. 2. (= poplamiony krwią) blood-stained.

pokrycie n. 1. (materiał) cover, covering; **pokrycie dachu** roofing; **pokrycie ściany** facing. 2. ekon. cover, coverage; **czek bez pokrycia** dishonored check, dud check; pot. bouncer, rubber check; **wystawić czek bez pokrycia** float a check;

pot. fly a kite, kite; **brak pokrycia** (*adnotacja na czeku*) insufficient funds; **obietnice bez pokrycia** *przen.* empty promises; **słowa bez pokrycia** *przen.* empty words. **3.** (*zwierzęcia*) covering.

pokryć *pf.* -ję -jesz, -yj **1.** *zob.* **pokrywać. 2.** (= *pochować*) hide, conceal. ~ **się** *pf.* **1.** *zob.* **pokrywać się. 2.** (= *ukryć się*) hide.

po kryjomu *adv.* in secret.

pokrywa *f.* **1.** (= *wieko*) lid, cover. **2.** (= *warstwa*) cover; **pokrywa lądolodu** icecap; **pokrywa lodowa** ice cover *l.* sheet; **pokrywa śnieżna** snow cover *l.* mantle, layer of snow. **3.** *ent.* elytron, elytrum, wing case.

pokrywać *ipf.* -am -asz **1.** (*jakąś osłoną*) cover, coat (*czymś* with sth); **pokrywać farbą** coat with paint; **pokrywać deskami** board; **pokrywać metalem** metal; **pokrywać nawierzchnią** (*drogę*) surface; **pokrywać podłogą** floor; **pokrywać** *l.* **obijać skórą** leather. **2.** (= *płacić*) cover, defray; **pokrywać długi** settle one's debts. **3.** (*uczucia, emocje*) (= *ukrywać*) cover, conceal; **pokryć coś milczeniem** pass over sth in silence. **4.** (= *stać jeden za drugim*) form a single-file line. **5.** (= *zapłodnić*) cover. **6.** (= *być obiciem czegoś*) upholster, cover. ~ **się** *ipf.* **1.** (= *być pokrytym czymś*) become covered; **pokrywać się kurzem** dust over; **pokrywać się szronem** frost over. **2.** (= *być zbieżnym, podobnym*) agree, correspond; **teoria pokrywa się z faktami** theory agrees with *l.* corresponds to the facts.

pokrywka *f. Gen.pl.* -ek lid.

pokryzysowy *a.* post-crisis.

pokrzepiać *ipf.*, **pokrzepić** *pf.* **1.** (= *wzmacniać*) sustain. **2.** (= *orzeźwić*) refresh; (= *posilić*) refresh, nourish; **pokrzepić kogoś na duchu** lift *l.* raise sb's spirits. ~ **się** *ipf.*, **pokrzepić się** *pf.* have a refreshment, fortify o.s.

pokrzewka *f. Gen.pl.* -ek *orn.* warbler (*Sylvia*).

pokrzyczeć *pf.* -ę -ysz shout, cry (*for a while*).

pokrzyk *mi bot.* deadly nightshade, belladonna, dwale (*Atropa belladonna*).

pokrzykiwać *ipf.* **1.** (= *krzyczeć*) shout (*every now and then*). **2.** (*o ptakach*) call.

pokrzywa *f. bot.* nettle (*Urtica*).

pokrzywdzić *pf.* wrong, treat unjustly.

pokrzywdzona *f. Gen.* -ej *zob.* **pokrzywdzony.**

pokrzywdzony *a.* wronged, hard done by; **on czuje się pokrzywdzony przez los** he feels starcrossed. – *mp* sufferer, the aggrieved; **strona pokrzywdzona** *prawn.* the aggrieved party.

pokrzywiczny *a. pat.* post-rickets, rickets induced.

pokrzywić *pf.* bend, distort.

pokrzywka *f. Gen.pl.* -ek *pat.* urticaria; *pot.* hives, nettle rash.

pokrzywkowy *a. pat.* urticarial, urticarious.

pokrzywnik, rusałka pokrzywnik *ma Gen* -a *ent.* small tortoiseshell (*Vanessa urticae*).

pokrzyżować *pf.* **1.** (= *udaremnić*) foil, balk, thwart, frustrate; **pokrzyżować komuś szyki** *l.* **plany** put *l.* throw a spanner in the works, throw a monkey's wrench into the works *l.* sb's plans, rain on sb's parade. **2.** *rzad.* cross. ~ **się** *pf.* (=

pogmatwać się) become foiled, become thwarted, become frustrated.

pokumać się *pf. pot.* pal up (*z kimś* with sb).

pokupny *a.* (*o towarze*) marketable, sal(e)able.

pokupować *pf.* buy (*a number of things*); **pokupował dzieciom prezenty gwiazdkowe** he bought the children (all) their Christmas gifts.

pokurcz *ma l. mp Gen.pl.* -ów *pog.* **1.** (*pies*) (ugly) mongrel. **2.** (*człowiek*) eyesore, fright.

pokusa *f.* temptation; **wystawiać kogoś na pokusę** tempt sb; **wzięła mnie pokusa, żeby tam pójść** I succumbed to the temptation to go there.

pokusić się *pf.* -szę -sisz venture (*o coś* to do sth).

pokuszenie *n.* temptation; **wodzić** *l.* **wystawiać kogoś na pokuszenie** lead sb into temptation; **...i nie wódź nas na pokuszenie...** *rz.-kat.* (*wers z Ojcze nasz*)...and lead us not into temptation...

pokuśtykać *pf. pot.* totter along, dodder along.

pokuta *f.* penance, atonement; **sakrament pokuty** *rz.-kat.* penance; **odprawiać pokutę** do penance; **wyznaczyć** *l.* **zadać pokutę** impose a penance, shrive.

pokutnica *f. zob.* **pokutnik.**

pokutnik *mp zwł. rz.-kat.* penitent.

pokutny *a. zwł. rz.-kat.* penitential.

pokutować *ipf.* **1.** (= *odprawiać pokutę*) do penance. **2.** (= *cierpieć za coś*) suffer, pay for; **pokutować za błędy młodości** atone for *l.* do penance for the errors *l.* mistakes of one's youth. **3.** (= *trwać jako przeżytek*) linger on, persist; **to przeświadczenie ciągle jeszcze pokutuje w naszej świadomości** this conviction still lingers on *l.* persists in our awareness *l.* consciousness. **4.** *teol.* expiate one's sins in purgatory.

pokwapić się *pf. lit.* hasten, be eager (*by coś zrobić* to do sth); **nie pokwapić się, by coś zrobić** not be particularly eager to do sth.

pokwękać *pf.*, **pokwękiwać** *ipf.* grumble, whine.

pokwitać *ipf.* be pubescent.

pokwitanie *n. med.* pubescence.

pokwitować *pf.* acknowledge (*the receipt of sth*); **pokwitować odbiór czegoś** sign for sth.

pokwitowanie *n.* receipt.

Polaczek *mp* -czk- *pl.* -i *l.* -owie *pog.* Polack.

polać *pf.* -leję -lejesz -lali *l.* -leli *zob.* **polewać.** ~ **się** *pf.* **1.** *zob.* **polewać się. 2.** (= *popłynąć*) flow, shed; **krew się polała** blood was shed, there was bloodshed; **łzy się polały** tears flowed, tears were shed.

Polak *mp* Pole; **jestem Polakiem** I'm Polish; **mądry Polak po szkodzie** sadder but wiser.

polak *mi Gen.* -a *szkoln., pot.* a Polish lesson.

polakierować *pf.* (*paznokcie*) varnish; (*meble*) varnish; (*samochód*) paint.

polakować *pf.* (= *zakleić lakiem*) seal (*with sealing wax*).

polakożerca *mp* Pole-hater, Pole-eater.

polakożerczość *f.* polonophobia, anti-Polish sentiment.

polakożerczy *a.* polonophobic.

polana *f.* clearing, glade.

polano n. 1. (*kawałek drewna*) billet, log, block (*of wood*). 2. *myśl.* wolf's tail.

polar *mi pot.* 1. *tk.* fleece. 2. (= *bluza, kurtka z polaru*) fleece (jacket).

polarnictwo n. polar exploration.

polarnik *mp* polar explorer.

polarny a. polar; **dzień polarny** polar day; **front polarny** *meteor.* polar front; **krąg polarny** polar circle; **lis polarny** *zool.* arctic l. white fox (*Alopex lagopus*); **niedźwiedź polarny** *zool.* polar bear (*Thalarctos l. Ursus maritimus*); **noc polarna** polar night; **strefa polarna** polar (climatic) zone; **wyprawa polarna** polar expedition; **zorza polarna** aurora; (*widoczna na półkuli północnej*) aurora borealis, northern lights; (*widoczna na półkuli południowej*) aurora australis, southern lights; **Gwiazda Polarna** *astron.* Polaris, North Star, polestar.

polarografia f. Gen. -ii *chem., fiz.* polarography.

polaroid *mi fiz., fot.* Polaroid®.

polarymetr *mi fiz., chem.* polarimeter.

polaryzacja f. t. *fiz.* polarization; **polaryzacja światła** polarization of light.

polaryzacyjny a. *fiz.* polarizing; **błona polaryzacyjna** *fot.* Polaroid®; **mikroskop polaryzacyjny** *opt.* polarizing microscope.

polaryzator *mi Gen.* -a *chem., fiz.* polarizer.

polaryzować *ipf. fiz.* polarize. ~ **się** *ipf.* 1. (= *różnicować*) polarize, become polarized. 2. *fiz.* become polarized.

polatać *pf.* 1. (= *latać*) fly (*for a while*), spend some time flying. 2. *pot.* (= *pobiegać*) run (*for a while*).

polatucha f. *zool.* European flying squirrel (*Pteromys volans*).

polder *mi geogr.* polder.

pole n. *Gen.pl.* pól 1. *roln.* field; **pole jęczmienia/pszenicy** barley/wheat field, field of barley/wheat; **pole ryżowe** rice paddy l. field; **szukaj teraz wiatru w polu** you might as well try to catch l. chase the wind l. the sun l. the horizon; **wywieść** l. **wyprowadzić kogoś w pole** lead sb up the garden path. 2. (= *obszar*) field; **pole bitwy** battlefield; **pole firnowe** névé, firn; **pole lodowe** ice field; **pole kempingowe** campsite; **pole minowe** minefield; **pole naftowe** *górn.* oil field; **pole namiotowe** campsite; **pole rażenia** *wojsk.* field of fire; **martwe pole** *wojsk.* dead ground; **polec na polu chwały** die fighting l. with honor, go out in a blaze of glory, be killed in action; **dotrzymać komuś pola** *lit.* hold out, last out; **szczere pole** open field. 3. (= *dziedzina*) field, range, scope; **dać komuś pole do popisu** give sb room to display their talents; **pole działania** scope of activity; **na polu literatury** in the field of literature. 4. (= *tło herbu*) field. 5. *fiz.* field; **pole akustyczne** sound l. acoustic field; **pole elektryczne** electric field; **pole grawitacyjne** field of gravity, gravitational field; **pole magnetyczne** magnetic field; **pole siły** field of force; **pole widzenia** field of vision. 6. *geom.* area; **pole powierzchni** surface area; **pole powierzchni bocznej** lateral area. 7. *sport* field, area; **pole bramkowe** goal area; **pole**

golfowe golf course; **pole karne** penalty area. 8. (*na szachownicy*) square. 9. (= *boisko*) playing field. 10. *dial.* (= *dwór*) outside, outdoors; **wyjść na pole** go outside; **na polu dzisiaj zimno** it's cold outside today.

polec *pf.* -**legnę** -**legniesz**, -**legnij**, -**legł** *emf.* fall, perish.

polecać *ipf.* 1. (= *dawać pod opiekę*) entrust. 2. (= *rekomendować, zachwalać*) recommend, suggest; **polecać coś komuś** recommend sth to sb; **polecić kogoś na stanowisko...** suggest sb for the post of... 3. (= *nakazywać*) order, command, direct, instruct (*komuś coś zrobić* sb to do sth). ~ **się** *ipf.* (= *oddawać się, powierzać się*) commend o.s.; **polecam się na przyszłość** I hope to be of service in the future, keep me in mind for future reference.

polecający a. commending, recommending; **list polecający** letter of recommendation.

polecenie n. 1. (= *nakaz*) command, order; **wykonać polecenie** carry out an order; **na czyjeś polecenie** by order of sb; **stosować się do czyichś poleceń** follow sb's orders. 2. (= *rekomendacja*) recommendation; **godny polecenia** recommendable; **z czyjegoś polecenia** on sb's recommendation.

polecić *pf. zob.* **polecać**. ~ **się** *pf. zob.* **polecać się**.

polecieć *ipf.* -**cę** -**cisz** 1. (= *udać się dokądś drogą powietrzną*) fly; **polecieć do Londynu** fly to London. 2. (= *unieść się w powietrze*) fly in the air, go up in the air; **oczko jej poleciało** *pot.* (*w pończosze*) her stocking ran l. laddered; (*w rajstopie*) her tights ran l. laddered. 3. *pot.* (= *pobiec dokądś*) rush off, hasten off; **polecieć na coś** *pot.* go for sth; **polecieć na kogoś** *pot.* be head over heels for sb; **polecieć na skargę** l. **z gębą** *pot.* tattle, snitch, rat (*na kogoś* on sb); **polecieć komuś po premii** *pot.* cut l. trim sb's bonus; **polecą nam za to po premii** that's gonna come out of our bonus, that's gonna eat into l. take a bite out of our bonus.

polecony a. -**eni** recommended; **list polecony** certified letter, registered letter; **przesyłka** l. **poczta polecona** certified mail, registered mail; **wysyłać coś listem poleconym** send sth by certified l. registered mail.

polegać *ipf.* 1. (= *liczyć na kogoś*) rely, depend (*na kimś / czymś* on sb/sth); **polegać na sobie samym** be self-reliant; **można na nim całkowicie polegać** he's fully reliable; **polegać na kimś jak na Zawiszy** have complete confidence in sb. 2. (= *mieć w kimś oparcie*) lean (*na kimś* on sb); **dobrze jest mieć kogoś, na kim można polegać** it's good to have sb to lean on. 3. (= *zasadzać się na czymś*) consist (*na czymś* in sth); **na czym to polega?** what does it consist in?; **trudność polega na tym, że...** the problem is that...; **na czym polega sekret bycia dobrym lekarzem?** what's the secret of being a good doctor?

poległy¹ a. killed, fallen.

poległy² *mp* the fallen, the killed; **polegli na polu chwały** those who died fighting l. with honor.

polekowy *a. med.* drug-induced.

polemiczność *f.* (*artykułu, odpowiedzi*) polemic character.

polemiczny *a.* polemic, polemical; **artykuł polemiczny** polemic article.

polemika *f.* polemics.

polemista *mp* polemic, polemist, polemicist.

polemizować *ipf.* polemicize, polemize.

polenta *f. kulin.* polenta.

polepa *f. bud.* pugging, pug.

polepszać *ipf.* improve, ameliorate. **~ się** *ipf.* improve, ameliorate; (*o zdrowiu, koniunkturze*) pick up; **polepsza mu się** he's getting better.

polepszenie *n.* **1.** (= *zmiana na lepsze*) improvement, amelioration. **2.** (*o zdrowiu*) improvement.

polepszyć *pf. zob.* **polepszać. ~ się** *pf. zob.* **polepszać się; polepszyło mu się** (*o zdrowiu*) he's better now.

polerka *f. Gen.pl.* **-ek** polisher.

polerować *ipf.* **1.** (= *wygładzać*) polish, burnish; **polerować do połysku** *l.* **na wysoki połysk** shine. **2.** (= *udoskonalać*) polish, refine; **polerować przemówienie** polish *l.* refine one's speech.

poleśny *a. roln.* deforested.

poletko *n. Gen.pl.* **-ek 1.** (= *dziedzina zainteresowań*) field (*of interest*); **to, o czym mówisz, to nie moje poletko** what you're talking about is not my cup of tea. **2.** (= *małe pole*) plot (of land), small field; **poletko doświadczalne** experimental plot, trial plot; **poletko ryżowe** paddy field.

polewa *f.* **1.** (= *glazura, szkliwo; t. emalia*) enamel, glaze. **2.** *kulin.* topping, butter cream; **polewa lukrowa** icing, frosting.

polewaczka *f. Gen.pl.* **-ek 1.** (= *konewka*) watering can. **2.** (*samochód*) road sprinkler, street-cleaning truck.

polewać *ipf.* **1.** pour; **polewać coś wodą** pour water on *l.* over sth. **2.** (*wyroby ceramiczne*) glaze; (*wyroby metalowe*) enamel. **~ się** *ipf.* **1.** (= *oblewać się*) pour (*e.g. water on o.s.*). **2.** (= *oblewać siebie nawzajem*) pour (*e.g. water on each other l.* one another).

polewka *f. Gen.pl.* **-ek** *kulin.* type of soup (*prepared by thickening water, wine, broth, etc. with flour, yolk, etc., similar to brewis or caudle*); **czarna polewka** animal blood soup.

poleźć *pf.* **-lezę -leziesz -lazł -leźli 1.** *pot.* (= *pójść*) shuffle, shamble, trudge (*dokądś* somewhere). **2.** *pot.* (= *wpakować się, wepchnąć się gdzieś*) go (*dokądś* somewhere); **po co tam polazłeś?** what the hell did you go there for?

poleżeć *pf.* **-ę -ysz 1.** (= *leżeć jakiś czas*) lie down (*for a while*); **poleżeć sobie dłużej w łóżku** (*rano*) have a lie-in. **2.** (= *odleżeć jakiś czas, nie będąc używanym*) be kept (*somewhere for some time*), be shelved; **to mięso musi poleżeć w occie przed upieczeniem** this meat must be kept in vinegar before roasting.

polędwica *f.* (= *lędźwiowa część tuszy*) loin; *kulin.* sirloin, tenderloin, undercut.

poliamid *mi chem.* polyamide.

poliamidowy *a. techn.* polyamide.

poliandria *f. Gen.* **-ii** polyandry.

poliandryczny *a.* polyandrous.

polibuda *f. pot.* polytech, tech (school); **studiować na polibudzie** study at the polytech *l.* the tech.

policealny *a.* post-secondary; **policealne studium (marketingu)** (marketing) training college; **szkoła policealna** post-secondary school.

policentryczny *a.* polycentric.

policentryzacja *f.* creation of many centers (*e.g. cultural, economic, etc.*).

policentryzm *mi* polycentrism.

polichlorek *mi* **-rk-** *chem.* polychloride; **polichlorek winylu** polyvinyl chloride (*PVC*).

polichóralność *f. muz.* polychorality.

polichromatyczny *a. el.* polychromatic, polychromic.

polichromia *f. Gen.* **-ii** *sztuka* polychromy.

polichromiczny *a. sztuka* polychromous; **ołtarz polichromiczny** polychromous altar.

policja *f.* **1.** (*instytucja*) police, police force; **policja drogowa** traffic police; **policja konna** mounted police; **tajna policja** secret police; **granatowa policja** *hist.* police force organised by the Nazi occupants in the General Gouvernement; **komisariat policji** police station; **oddziały prewencyjne policji** (*do tłumienia zamieszek*) riot police; **zadzwonić na** *l.* **po policję** call the police; **zgłosić się na policję** *l.* **oddać się w ręce policji** (*o poszukiwanym*) turn o.s. in. **2.** *pot.* (*budynek*) police station; **iść na policję** report to the police, go to the police station.

policjant *mp* policeman, (police) officer; **policjant nieumundurowany** plain clothes detective.

policjantka *f. Gen.pl.* **-ek** policewoman, (police) officer.

policyjny *a.* police; **godzina policyjna** curfew; **kartoteka policyjna** police files; *sl.* rap sheet; **nieoznakowany samochód policyjny** unmarked police car; **mundur policyjny** police uniform; **odznaka policyjna** police badge; **pałka policyjna** baton; *Br.* truncheon; **państwo policyjne** *polit.* police state; **pies policyjny** police dog; **prowokacja policyjna** entrapment; **radiowóz policyjny** police *l.* patrol car; **rejestr policyjny** charge sheet.

policzalny *a.* countable, numerable; **rzeczownik policzalny** *jęz.* countable *l.* count noun.

policzek *mi* **-czk-** *Gen.* **-a 1.** (*część twarzy*) cheek; **nadstawić drugi policzek** turn the other cheek. **2.** (= *uderzenie w policzek*) slap on the face; **wymierzyć komuś policzek** slap sb on the face. **3.** (= *obraza*) slap in the face, cheek. **4.** *bud.* stringer. **5.** *zool.* cheek. **6.** (*część broni*) cheek.

policzkować *ipf.* slap in the face.

policzkowy *a.* cheek, buccal; **kość policzkowa** *anat.* zygomatic bone, cheekbone; **mięsień policzkowy** *anat.* buccinator; **torba** *l.* **worek policzkowy** *zool.* cheek pouch.

policzyć *pf.* **1.** (= *zsumować*) count, calculate, reckon; **móc policzyć na palcach jednej ręki** be able to count on (the fingers of) one hand; **jego dni są policzone** his days are numbered; **policzyć komuś kości** beat sb up, beat sb black-and-blue. **2.** (= *odliczyć kolejno*) count; **policzyć do**

stu count up to one hundred; **odwróć się, kiedy policzę do dziesięciu** turn around on the count of ten. **3.** (= *kazać sobie zapłacić*) charge; **policzyć sobie 100 dolarów za naprawę** charge 100 dollars for the repair. **4.** *przest.* (= *poczytać*) regard, reckon; **policzyć czyjeś zachowanie na karb czegoś** ascribe sb's behavior to sth, regard sb's behavior as resulting from sth; **będzie mu to policzone w niebie** he'll be rewarded for it in heaven. **~ się** *pf.* **1.** (= *rozliczyć się*) settle up, square up (*z kimś* with sb); **policzyć się z kimś** (= *zemścić się*) get even with sb. **2.** (= *policzyć siebie wzajemnie*) count one another.

polidaktylia *f. Gen.* **-ii** *med.* polydactyly, polydactylism.

polidyspersyjność *f. Gen.* **-ści** *chem.* polydispersity.

polielektrolit *mi chem., el.* polyelectrolyte.

poliembrionia *f. Gen.* **-nii** *biol.* polyembriony.

polien *mi chem.* polyene.

poliester *mi* **-tr-** *chem.* polyester.

poliestrowy *a. techn.* polyester; **włókno poliestrowe** polyester fiber; **żywica poliestrowa** polyester resin *l.* plastic.

polietylen *mi chem.* polyethylene.

polietylenowy *a. techn.* polyethylene.

polifag *ma zool.* polyphage, polyphagian.

polifagia *f. pat.* polyphagia.

polifagiczny *a. zool.* polyphagous; **owad polifagiczny** *ent.* polyphagous insect.

polifiletyzm *mi biol.* polyphyletism.

polifonia *f. Gen.* **-ii** *muz.* polyphony.

polifoniczność *f. muz.* polyphonicity.

polifoniczny *a. muz.* polyphonic.

polifonista *mp muz.* polyphonist.

poliformaldehyd *mi chem.* polyoxymethylene.

polifunkcyjność *f. muz.* polyfunctionality.

polifunkcyjny *a. muz.* polyfunctional.

poligamia *f. Gen.* **-ii** *bot., zool.* (*t. małżeństwo*) polygamy.

poligamiczny *a.* polygamous; **małżeństwo poligamiczne** polygamous marriage.

poligamista *mp* polygamist.

poligen *mi biol.* polygene.

poligenizm *mi antrop.* polygenesis.

poliginia *f. Gen.* **-ii** polygyny.

poliglota *mp,* **poliglotka** *f. Gen.pl.* **-ek** polyglot.

poliglotyzm *mi* polyglotism, polyglottism.

poligon *mi* **1.** *wojsk.* range, ground; **poligon doświadczalny** *przen.* testing ground. **2.** *miern.* traverse.

poligonowy *a.* military training ground; **strzelanie poligonowe** training ground firing.

poligraf[1] *mp pl.* **-owie** (= *poligrafik*) printer, typographer.

poligraf[2] *pl.* **-y** (= *wykrywacz kłamstw*) lie detector, polygraph.

poligrafia *f. Gen.* **-ii** printing, typography; **mała poligrafia** *komp.* desktop publishing, DTP.

poligraficzny *a.* printing; **przemysł poligraficzny** printing industry.

polihistor *mp pl.* **-rzy** *l.* **-owie** *lit.* polymath, polyhistor.

Polihymnia *f. Gen.* **-ii** *mit.* Polyhymnia.

polikarpiczny *a. bot.* polycarpic, polycarpous.

poliklinika *f. med.* policlinic, outpatients clinic.

polikondensacja *f. chem.* polycondensation, condensation polymerization.

polikondensat *mi chem.* polycondensate, condensation polymer.

polikrystaliczny *a. fiz.* polycrystalline.

Poliksena *f. mit.* Polyxena.

polimer *mi chem.* polymer.

polimeryzacja *f. chem.* polymerization.

polimeryzować *ipf. chem.* polymerize. **~ się** *ipf. chem.* polymerize.

polimorficzny *a. biol., chem.* polymorphic.

polimorfizm *mi biol., jęz., min.* polymorphism.

Polinezja *f. geogr.* Polynesia.

Polinezyjczyk *mp* Polynesian.

Polinezyjka *f. Gen.pl.* **-ek** *zob.* **Polinezyjczyk**.

polinezyjski *a.* Polynesian.

Polinik *mp mit.* Polynices.

poliniować *pf.* line, rule.

polinukleotyd *f. biochem.* polynucleotide.

polio *n. indecl. pat.* poliomyelitis, polio.

polip *mi Gen.* **-a 1.** *pat.* polyp, polypus. **2.** *zool.* polyp.

polipeptyd *mi chem.* polypeptide.

poliploid *mi biol.* polyploid.

poliploidalność *f. biol.* polyploidy.

poliploidalny *a. biol.* polyploid, polyploidic.

polipowatość *f. pat.* polyposis.

polipragmazja *f. pat.* polypragmasy.

polipropylen *mi chem.* polypropylene.

poliptyk *mi sztuka, rel.* polyptych.

polireakcja *f. chem.* polyreaction.

polirytmia *f. muz.* polyrhythm.

polis *n. hist.* polis.

polisa *f. ubezp.* policy; **polisa ubezpieczeniowa** insurance policy.

polisacharyd *mi chem.* polysaccharide, polysaccharose.

polisemantyczny *a. jęz.* polysemous, polysemantic.

polisemia *f. Gen.* **-ii** *jęz.* polysemy.

polisemiczny *a. jęz.* polysemous.

polispermia *f. Gen.* **-ii** *biol.* polyspermy.

polistyren *mi chem.* polystyrene.

polisylogizm *mi log.* polysyllogism.

polisyndeton *mi jęz.* polysyndeton.

polisyndetyczny *a. jęz.* polysyndetic.

polisyntetyczny *a. jęz.* polysynthetic, polysynthetical; **język polisyntetyczny** polysynthetic language.

poliszynel *mp Gen.pl.* **-i** *l.* **-ów** Punchinello; **tajemnica poliszynela** open secret.

politechniczny *a. uniw.* technical; **studia politechniczne** technical studies.

politechnika *f. uniw.* (uczelnia, budynek), technical university; institute of technology (*esp. in Poland*).

politechnizacja *f.* polytechnization.

politechnizować *ipf.* polytechnize.

politeista *mp rel.* polytheist.

699

politeistyczny *a. rel.* polytheistic, polytheistical.

politeizm *mi rel.* polytheism.

politolog *mp pl.* **-dzy** *l.* **-owie** political scientist.

politologia *f. Gen.* **-ii** political science.

politologiczny *a.* political science; **badania politologiczne** political science research; **studia politologiczne** political science studies.

politonalność *f. muz.* polytonality, polytonalism.

politonalny *a. muz.* polytonal.

politowanie *n.* (= *litość*) pity; (= *lekceważenie, pobłażliwość*) disdain; **godny politowania** pitiable; **spojrzeć na kogoś z politowaniem** (*z litością*) give sb a pitying look; (*z lekceważeniem*) look at sb with disdain, give sb a look of disdain.

polituk *mp pl.* **-i** *uj.* army officer in a communist state responsible for political indoctrination.

politura *f.* French polish.

politurować *ipf.* French-polish.

polityczny[1] *a.* political; **biuro polityczne** (*w krajach komunistycznych*) Politburo; **ekonomia polityczna** political economy; **klimat polityczny** (*np. w danym kraju*) political landscape; **mapa polityczna** political map; **partia polityczna** political party; **poglądy polityczne** political views; **poprawność polityczna** political correctness, PC; **proces polityczny** *prawn.* political trial; **przestępstwo polityczne** political crime; **represje polityczne** *l.* **ucisk polityczny** political repressions; **scena polityczna** political scene; **ustrój polityczny** political system; **więzień polityczny** political prisoner, prisoner of state; **względy polityczne** political considerations.

polityczny[2] *mp pl.* **-i** political prisoner.

polityk *mp* **1.** (*działacz*) politician; **polityk niezależny** independent; **polityk twardej ręki** strongman; **polityk zawodowy** career politician. **2.** *przen.* tactician, diplomat.

polityka *f.* (*o nauce l. sztuce rządzenia*) politics; (= *strategia działania*) policy; **polityka antyinflacyjna** disinflationary policy; **polityka dyskryminacji pozytywnej** affirmative action; **polityka firmy** company policy; **polityka gospodarcza** economic policy; **polityka kulturalna** cultural policy; **polityka mieszkaniowa** housing policy; **polityka nacisku** power politics; **polityka nieinterwencji** *l.* **wolnej ręki** *ekon.* laissez faire; **polityka otwartych drzwi** open-door policy; **polityka płacowa** payroll policy; **polityka równouprawnienia** equal opportunity; **polityka silnej ręki** power policy; **polityka socjalna** social policy, welfare policy; **polityka wewnętrzna** internal policy, domestic policy; **polityka zagraniczna** foreign policy; **strusia polityka** ostrich policy; **Rada Polityki Pieniężnej** Monetary Policy Council (*in Poland*).

politykier *mp pog.* politicaster, politician.

politykierski *a. pog.* politicizing, politicaster('s).

politykierstwo *n. pog.* politicking.

politykować *ipf.* politicize.

polityzacja *f. Gen.* **-cji** politicization.

poliuretan *mi chem.* polyurethane, polyurethan.

poliuria *f. Gen.* **-ii** *pat.* polyuria.

poliwęglan *mi chem.* polycarbonate.

poliwinyl *mi chem.* polyvinyl.

polizać *pf.* **-liżę** **-liżesz** (= *liznąć*) lick, give a lick; (= *posmakować liźnięciem*) have a lick.

Polka *f. Gen.pl.* **-ek** *zob.* **Polak.**

polka *f. Gen.pl.* **-ek** *muz.* polka.

polny *a.* field; **polna droga** dirt road; **bratek polny** *bot.* wild pansy, European field pansy (*Viola arvensis*); **koniczyna polna** *bot.* rabbit-foot (clover) (*Trifolium arvense*); **konik polny** *ent.* grasshopper (*Acrididae l. Tettigoniidae*); **kwiat polny** wild flower; **mak polny** *bot.* corn poppy, field poppy, Flanders poppy (*Papaver rhoeas*); **marszałek polny** *wojsk.* field marshal; **mysz polna** *zool.* striped field mouse (*Apodemus agrarius*).

polo[1] *n. indecl. sport* polo.

polo[2] *n. indecl.* (*koszulka*) polo shirt.

polodowcowy *a. geol.* postglacial.

polon *mi chem.* polonium.

polonez *mi Gen. i Acc.* **-a** (*taniec*) polonaise.

polonezowy *a. muz.* polonaise.

Polonia *f. Gen.* **-ii** Polish community (*abroad*); (= *Polacy na obczyźnie*) Polish diaspora; (*np. osoby narodowości polskiej w Kazachstanie, na Ukrainie*) ethnic Poles; **Polonia Amerykańska** Polish Americans.

polonijny *a.* Polish community; **działacz polonijny** Polish community activist; **ośrodek polonijny** Polish community center; **szkoła polonijna** Polish community school.

polonika *pl. Gen.* **-ów** documents, manuscripts, publications referring to Poland or Polish affairs.

polonista *mp* **1.** (*badacz, znawca*) Polish scholar, polonist. **2.** (*nauczyciel*) Polish teacher. **3.** (*student*) Polish student.

polonistka *f. Gen.pl.* **-ek** *zob.* **polonista.**

polonistyczny *a.* Polish; **studia polonistyczne** Polish studies.

polonistyka *f.* **1.** (*nauka*) Polish studies. **2.** (*wydział*) Polish faculty.

polonizacja *f.* Polonization.

polonizm *mi jęz.* Polonism.

polonizować *ipf.* Polonize. **~ się** *ipf.* Polonize.

polonofil *mp Gen.pl.* **-i** *l.* **-ów** polonophile.

polonofilski *a.* polonophile, polonophiliac, polonophilic.

polonofob *mp* polonophobe.

polonofobia *f.* polonophobia.

polonowy *a. chem.* polonium.

polonus *mp pl.* **-i** *l.* **-y** *l.* **-owie** typical old-fashioned Pole.

polopiryna *f.* type of aspirin.

polor *mi lit.* (= *dobre maniery*) polish, refinement.

polot *mi* flair, panache; **ubierać się z polotem** dress with flair; **bez polotu** artless.

polować *ipf.* **1.** (*o myśliwym*) hunt (*na coś* for sth). **2.** (*o zwierzęciu*) hunt (*na coś* for sth) prey (*na coś* on sth). **3.** *pot.* (= *starać się zdobyć coś*) hunt, be out (*coś* for sth); **polować na męża** hunt for a husband.

polowanie *n.* (*czynność*) hunting; (= *łowy*) hunting, hunt; **pójść na polowanie** go hunting; **polowanie na lisa** fox-hunting; **polowanie na ptactwo** fowling; **polowanie z nagonką** battue; **polowanie na czarownice** *zwł. polit.* witch-hunt; **okres polowań** open season.

polowy *a.* **1.** (= *polny*) field; **prace polowe** field works, work in the field. **2.** *wojsk.* (= *frontowy*) field, camp; **artyleria polowa** field artillery; **czapka polowa** forage cap; **kuchnia polowa** cookhouse; **łóżko polowe** cot, camp bed; **mundur polowy** fatigues; **poczta polowa** Army Postal Service; **sąd polowy** (*dla drobnych przewinień na okupowanych obszarach*) provost court; **sąd polowy** *l.* wojenny court-martial; **szpital polowy** field hospital, MASH (*Mobile Army Surgical Hospital*).

polówka *f. Gen.pl.* **-ek 1.** *pot.* (*łóżko*) camp bed. **2.** *pot.* (*czapka*) forage cap.

Polska *f. geogr.* Poland.

polski *a.* Polish; **język polski** the Polish language; **bracia polscy** *rel.* Polish Arians; **po polsku** in Polish; **mówić po polsku** speak Polish; **to jest napisane po polsku** this is written in Polish; **Rzeczpospolita Polska** Republic of Poland (*since 1989*); *hist.* Polish Republic; **Polska Rzeczpospolita Ludowa** *hist.* Polish People's Republic (*1945-1989*). – *mi* Polish, the Polish language.

polskojęzyczny *a.* Polish language, Polish speaking; **mniejszość polskojęzyczna** Polish speaking minority; **publikacja polskojęzyczna** Polish language publication, publication in Polish.

polskość *f.* Polishness.

polszczyć *ipf.* Polonize. **~ się** *ipf.* Polonize.

polszczyzna *f.* the Polish language.

polubić *pf.* get to like, take a liking to. **~ się** *pf.* get to like each other *l.* one another, take a liking to each other *l.* one another.

polubownie *adv.* amicably; *prawn.* out of court, amicably, arbitrally; **załatwić sprawę polubownie** *prawn.* settle a case out of court.

polubowny *a.* amicable; *prawn.* out of court, amicable, arbitral; **sąd polubowny** arbitration (court); **ugoda polubowna** out-of-court settlement.

polucja *f. fizj.* nocturnal emission; *pot.* wet dream.

polukrować *pf. kulin.* ice.

poluzować *pf.* loosen, slacken.

poluźnić *pf.* **-ij** loosen, slacken.

poła *f.* (*ubrania*) lap, flap.

połabski *a.* Polabian, Polabish.

połać *f.* (*ziemi, kraju, lasu*) stretch, tract.

połajanka *f. Gen.pl.* **-ek** *pot.* scolding, flite.

połakomić się *pf.* be tempted (*na coś* by sth).

połamać *pf.* **-mię -miesz** break; **można sobie na tym język połamać** it's a really hard tongue-twister; **połamać sobie zęby na czymś** knock *l.* wear o.s. out trying to do sth; **mało sobie nóg nie połamał** he was running at breakneck speed, he was rushing headlong. **~ się** *pf.* get broken.

połamaniec *mp Gen.* **-ańca** *pot.* cripple.

połamany *a.* broken; **jestem dziś strasznie połamany** I'm sore *l.* I ache all over today, I feel like *l.* as if I've been trampled by horses.

połapać się *pf.* **-pię -piesz** *pot.* twig, catch on, get it; **nie mogę się w tym połapać** I don't get it.

połaskotać *pf.* **-oczę -oczesz** *l.* **-ocę -ocesz, -ocz** tickle; **połaskotać czyjąś ambicję** *przen.* stir sb's ambition.

połaszczyć się *pf.* be tempted (*na coś* by sth).

poławiacz *mp* fisher; **poławiacz gąbek** sponge diver; **poławiacz pereł** pearl diver. – *mi Gen.* **-a** **poławiacz min** *wojsk.* minesweeper.

poławiać *ipf.* fish; (*nurkując*) dive (*coś* for sth).

połazić *pf.* **-żę -zisz** *pot.* knock around *l.* about, saunter.

połączenie *n.* **1.** (*złącze*) connection; joint. **2.** (*zespół elementów*) combination; **to zjawisko występuje w połączeniu z innym** this phenomenon occurs in combination with another one. **3.** (*łączność*) connection; **połączenie konferencyjne** conference call; **połączenie telefoniczne** phone connection. **4.** (*komunikacja*) connection, link; **połączenie autobusowe** bus *l.* coach connection; **połączenie kolejowe** train connection, rail link; **połączenie lotnicze** plane connection; **jakie mam rano połączenie do Krakowa?** what are the morning trains (coaches, planes, etc.) to Cracow?

połączyć *pf.* **1.** (= *zespolić*) connect, link; **naczynia połączone** *fiz.* communicating *l.* connected vessels; **połączyć węzłem małżeńskim** unite in marriage; **pobyt w Krakowie połączony był ze zwiedzaniem Wawelu** the stay in Cracow was combined with a Wawel tour; **połączyć siły** join forces. **2.** *tel.* (*rozmowę telefoniczną*) put through. **~ się** *pf.* **1.** (= *zespolić się*) connect, become linked; **połączyć się węzłem małżeńskim** contract marriage, enter into a marriage. **2.** *tel.* (= *dodzwonić się*) get through.

połechtać *pf.* **-chcę** *l.* **-chcę** *l.* **-chtam -chczesz** *l.* **-chcesz** *l.* **-chtasz, -chcz** *l.* **-chtaj 1.** (= *połaskotać*) tickle. **2.** *przen.* stir, excite; **połechtać czyjąś ambicję** stir sb's ambition; **połechtać czyjąś dumę** flatter sb.

połeć *mi* chunk (*of bacon*).

połknąć *pf.* **-ij** *zob.* połykać.

połogowy *a. med.* puerperal; **gorączka połogowa** *pat.* puerperal fever, childbed fever; **zakażenie połogowe** *pat.* puerperal sepsis.

połonina *f.* mountain pasture (*in the Carpathians*).

połowa *f. Gen.pl.* **-łów 1.** (= *jedna druga*) half; **do połowy pusty** half-empty; **moja druga** *l.* **lepsza połowa** *pot., żart.* my other *l.* better half; **jest w połowie Polakiem** he's half Polish; **to jest w połowie prawdą** it's only half the truth; **o połowę więcej** half as much; **o połowę mniej** half as much; **po połowie** fifty-fifty; **przeciąć na połowę** cut in half, halve; **za połowę ceny** half-price. **2.** (= *środek*) middle; **w połowie drogi** halfway, midway; **w połowie lipca** in the middle of July, in mid-July; **w połowie XVII wieku** in the middle of the 17th century, in the mid-17th century.

połowica *f. żart.* sb's other *l.* better half, wife.

połowiczność *f.* incompleteness.

połowiczny *a.* partial, limited, qualified; **połowiczny sukces** qualified success; **połowiczny środek** half measure, halfway measure; **okres połowicznego rozpadu** *chem., fiz.* half-life.

połowiczy *a.* **porażenie** *l.* **niedowład połowiczy** *pat.* hemiplegia.

połowinki *pl. Gen.* **-ek** *szkoln.* mid-school party (*a traditional party held in the middle of a given period of education; at high schools and at universities only*).

położenie *n.* **1.** (*miejsce, pozycja*) location, position; (*zwł. w stosunku do otoczenia*) situation; **położenie geograficzne** *geogr.* geographical position; **położenie martwe** *techn.* dead position *l.* center *l.* point; **położenie zerowe** *fiz.* zero position. **2.** (= *sytuacja, warunki*) situation, position; **ciężkie położenie** difficult position; **korzystne położenie** favorable position, fortunate situation; **przykre położenie** sorry plight; **gdybyś wszedł w moje położenie, nie mówiłbyś tego** if you were in my shoes, you would not be saying that.

położna *f. Gen.* **-ej** *zwł. med.* midwife.

położnica *f.* woman in childbirth, woman in puerperium.

położnictwo *n. med.* obstetrics.

położniczy *a. med.* obstetric, obstetrical; **oddział położniczy** maternity ward.

położnik *mp med.* obstetrician.

położony *a.* located, situated; **pałac położony jest nad jeziorem** the palace is situated on a lake.

położyć *pf.* **-łóż 1.** (*coś na czymś płaskim*) put, lay; **położyć nacisk na coś** lay *l.* place emphasis on sth; **położyć karty na stół** put *l.* lay sb's cards on the table; **położyć kres nienawiści** put an end to hatred; **położyć krzyżyk na czymś** give sth up; **położyć na czymś łapę** *pot.* lay one's hands on sth. **2.** (= *ułożyć*) lay; **położyć podłogę** lay a floor; **położyć tory tramwajowe** lay streetcar tracks; *Br.* lay tram tracks; **położyć kamień węgielny** lay a cornerstone; **położyć na kursie** *lotn., żegl.* set (*a plane, ship, boat*). **3.** (= *przewrócić*) lay down, knock down; **położyć kogoś do łóżka** put sb to bed; **położyć uszy po sobie** swallow sb's pride; **położyć kogoś na obie łopatki** *t. przen.* floor sb. **4.** *pot.* (= *zaprzepaścić coś*) ruin; **położyć sztukę** ruin a performance. **~ się** *pf.* **1.** (= *ułożyć się*) lie down; (= *iść spać*) go to bed; **położyć się na podłodze/kanapie** lie down on the floor/sofa; **położyć się spać** go to bed; **położył się i już nie wstał** *euf.* he died, he kicked the bucket. **2.** (= *pochylić się*) slant, slope.

połóg *mi* **-o-** *med.* puerperium.

połów *mi* **-o- 1.** (= *łowienie*) fishing. **2.** (= *to, co złowiono*) catch.

połówka *f. Gen.pl.* **-ek 1.** half. **2.** *pot.* a half liter bottle of vodka.

południca *f.* (*kobieta demon*) woman demon/ghost (*appearing at noon*).

południce *pl. ent.* nymphalids (*Nymphalidae*).

południe *n.* **1.** (= *środek dnia*) noon, midday; **przed południem** before noon, in the morning; **po**

południu in the afternoon; **od dziesiątej do południa** from 10 a.m. till noon; **w samo południe** at high noon *l.* midday (sharp). **2.** (*strona świata*) south; **jechać na południe** go *l.* head south; **jechać z południa** come *l.* arrive from the south; **Radom leży na południe od Warszawy** Radom is located south of Warsaw; **silny wiatr z południa** strong wind from the south. **3.** (*stany południowe w USA*) the South.

południk *mi Gen.* **-a** *geogr.* meridian; **południk zerowy** prime meridian, zero meridian; *pot.* Greenwich meridian; **południk niebieski** *astron.* (celestial *l.* astronomical) meridian.

południkowo *adv.* meridionally.

południowiec *mp* **-wc-** *pl.* **-y** southerner.

południowoafrykański *a. geogr.* South African.

południowoamerykański *a. geogr.* South American.

południowo-wschodni *a.* south-east, south east; south-eastern, southeastern; **wiatr południowo-wschodni** south-easterly wind.

południowo-zachodni *a.* south-west, south west; south-western, southwestern; **wiatr południowo-wschodni** south-westerly wind.

południowy *a.* **1.** (*około godziny 12*) noon, midday; **przerwa południowa** midday break. **2.** *geogr.* (= *charakterystyczny dla południa*) southern; south; southerly; **półkula południowa** southern hemisphere; **południowy wschód** southeast; **południowy zachód** southwest; **biegun południowy** the South Pole; **Korea Południowa** South Korea; **południowa Polska** southern Poland.

połykacz *mp* swallower; **połykacz ognia** fire-eater; **połykacz mieczów** sword swallower.

połykać *ipf.* swallow; (*gwałtownie*) gulp (down); **połknąć bakcyla** have got the bug; **połknąć haczyk** swallow bait, take the bait; **połykam ślinkę** my mouth waters; **połykać książkę** devour a book; **połykać łzy** gulp back one's tears; **na randce połykał ją oczami** he was devouring her with his eyes during the date.

połysk *mi* gloss, luster, sheen; **wysoki połysk** *zwł. techn.* full gloss; **zrobić coś na wysoki połysk** *przen.* do sth perfectly.

połyskiwać *ipf.* (*np. o tafli wody*) glisten; (*o lustrze, szybie, złocie*) glitter; (= *odbijać światło*) shine.

połyskliwość *f.* gloss; glitter; shine.

połyskliwy *a.* glossy; lustrous; glittering.

pomacać *pf.* (= *zbadać dotykiem*) **1.** feel, examine by touch. **2.** *pot., przen.* (= *zbić*) beat, bash.

pomachać *pf.* wave; **pomachać ręką** wave one's hand; **pomachać komuś na pożegnanie** wave sb goodbye; **pies pomachał ogonem** dog wagged its tail.

pomada *f.* (*do włosów*) pomade.

pomadka *f. Gen.pl.* **-ek 1.** (*do ust*) lipstick. **2.** (*cukierek*) fondant.

pomagać *ipf.* **1.** (= *udzielać pomocy*) help; **pomagać komuś w czymś** help sb with sth; **w czym mogę pomóc?** how can I help you? **2.** (= *poskutkować*) help; **pomagać na ból głowy** relieve a headache; **to lekarstwo mi nie pomaga** this medicine isn't working; **płacz tu nie pomoże** crying won't help (you); **jego propozycja pomoże mi jak umarłemu kadzidło** his proposal won't help me at all. **3.** (= *ułatwiać coś*) help, be helpful; facilitate; **znajomość angielskiego bardzo by mi pomogła w pracy** knowledge of English would be of great use in my work.

pomagier *mp żart.* helper.

pomaleńku *adv.* **1.** (= *wolno*) slowly. **2.** (= *nie najgorzej*) not bad.

pomalować *pf.* **1.** (*farbą, lakierem*) paint. **2.** (*o kosmetykach*) make up. ~ **się** *pf.* put on make-up, make up.

pomalutku *adv. zob.* **pomału.**

pomału *adv.* **1.** (= *wolno*) slowly. **2.** (= *nie najgorzej*) not bad.

pomarańcza *f. Gen.pl.* **-cz** *l.* **-y** *bot.* (*drzewo*) (*owoc*) orange (*Citrus sinensis*).

pomarańczarnia *f. Gen.pl.* **-i** *l.* **-ń** orangery.

pomarańczowoczerwony *a.* orange-red.

pomarańczowożółty *a.* orange-yellow.

pomarańczowy *a.* orange.

pomarszczony *a.* **-eni** wrinkled, creased; **pomarszczona twarz** wrinkled *l.* creased face; **pomarszczona sukienka** creased dress.

pomarszczyć *pf.* wrinkle, crease. ~ **się** *pf.* wrinkle, crease.

pomarznąć *pf.* **1.** (= *zginąć od mrozu*) freeze to death. **2.** (= *zziębnąć*) (= *zamarznąć*) freeze.

pomarzyć *pf.* dream, daydream; **o tym możemy tylko pomarzyć** we can only dream about it.

pomaszerować *pf.* march; **odwrócił się i pomaszerował do domu** he turned around and made for home.

pomaturalny *a.* postsecondary; **szkoła pomaturalna** community college.

pomawiać *ipf.* (= *oskarżać niesłusznie*) accuse unjustly; *prawn.* slander. ~ **się** *ipf.* unjustly accuse each other.

pomazać *pf.* **-żę -żesz 1.** (= *posmarować*) smear. **2.** (= *pogryzmolić*) scribble. **3.** (= *nadać godność*) *hist.* anoint (*kogoś* sb).

pomazaniec *mp* **-ńc-** *Voc.* **-cze** *pl.* **-y** *lit.* the anointed.

pomelioracyjny *a.* post-reclamation.

pomęczony *a.* **-ni** murdered.

pomęczyć *pf.* **1.** (= *utrudzić*) tire, exhaust, fatigue. **2.** (= *torturować*) torture. ~ **się** *pf.* **1.** (= *utrudzić się*) tire, become exhausted. **2.** (= *potrudzić się*) toil (*nad czymś* over sth).

pomiar *mi* measurement, measuring; **pomiary geodezyjne** survey.

pomiarowy *a.* measuring; surveying; **prace pomiarowe** measurements; **urządzenie pomiarowe** measuring *l.* surveying device.

pomiatać *ipf.* **1.** (= *lekceważyć*) hold in contempt; **pomiatać kimś** push sb around. **2.** *myśl.* litter, give birth.

pomidor *mi Gen.* **-a** *bot.* (*warzywo*) tomato (*Lycopersicon esculentum*).

pomidorowy *a.* tomato; **sos pomidorowy** tomato sauce; **zupa pomidorowa** tomato soup.

pomidorówka *f. Gen.pl.* **-ek** *pot.* (*zupa*) tomato soup.

pomierzwić *pf.* (= *potargać*) shag.

pomierzyć *pf.* **1.** (= *zmierzyć*) measure. **2.** (= *przymierzyć*) try on.

pomieszać *pf.* **1.** (= *zmieszać*) blend, mix. **2.** (= *mieszać jakiś czas*) stir. **3.** (= *wprowadzić zamęt*) mix up; **wódka pomieszała mu rozum** vodka drove him mad; **Adam próbuje pomieszać mi szyki** Adam is trying to upset my plans. ~ **się** *pf.* get mixed; **pomieszało się mu w głowie od wódki** vodka drove him mad; **wszystko mi się pomieszało** I got it all mixed up.

pomieszanie *n.* **1.** (= *zmieszanie*) blending. **2.** (= *zamieszanie*) stirring. **3.** (= *zamęt*) confusion; **pomieszanie zmysłów** *pot.* insanity; **pomieszanie z poplątaniem** *żart.* hodgepodge.

pomieszany *a.* **pomieszany na umyśle** *pot.* insane.

pomieszczenie *n.* room.

pomieścić *pf.* **-szczę -ścisz** (*o naczyniu, pomieszczeniu*) hold; (*o budynku*) house; (*o sali*) seat. ~ **się** *pf.* fit, have enough room; **nie chce mi się to w głowie pomieścić** it boggles my mind.

pomiędzy *prep. + Ins.* **1.** (= *między jednym a drugim obiektem, osobą*) between; **pomiędzy domem a chodnikiem był trawnik** there was a lawn between the house and the sidewalk; **pomiędzy tobą a mną nigdy nie będzie zgody** we'll never agree with each other. **2.** (*w jakimś okresie*) between; **przyjdę pomiędzy pierwszą a trzecią** I'll come between one and three. **3.** (*stadium przejściowe*) halfway through; **kolor pomiędzy żółtym a zielonym** color halfway between yellow and green. **4.** (= *wśród*) among; **dom stał pomiędzy jeziorami** the house was situated among lakes; **mam nadzieję, że to, o czym mówiliśmy, zostanie pomiędzy nami** I hope that what we talked about was only between you and me. **5.** + *Acc.* (= *pośród*) among; **premię rozdzielono pomiędzy pracowników** bonus was distributed among the employees. **6.** *por.* **między.**

pomijać *ipf.* **1.** (= *opuszczać*) omit; **pominę to milczeniem** I'll pass it over in silence, I won't comment on that. **2.** (= *nie uwzględniać*) pass over; **pominąwszy fakt, że...** except the fact that...

pomimo *prep. + Gen.* **1.** in spite of, despite; **pomimo to** all the same, nevertheless; **pomimo że...** even though, despite the fact that... **2.** *por.* **mimo.**

pominąć *pf. zob.* **pomijać.**

pomiot *mi* **1.** (*u zwierząt*) litter; (*u maciory*) farrow. **2.** (*potomstwo*) litter, offspring. **3.** (*poród u zwierząt*) birth, giving birth. **4.** (*kał*) dung, droppings.

pomknąć *pf.* **-ij** bolt; **pomknął do domu** he bolted home.

pomnażać *ipf.* **1.** (= *powiększać*) build up; **pomnażać majątek** amass a fortune; **pomnażać zbiory** build up crops. **2.** *zwł. mat.* multiply. ~ **się** *ipf.* build up.

pomnieć *pf.* **-nę -nisz, -nij** *lit.* remember; **nie pomnę, kiedy się to zdarzyło** I do not remember when it happened; **pomnij na tych, co odeszli** remember those who are no longer with us.

pomniejszać *ipf.*, **pomniejszyć** *pf.* diminish, lessen; *przen.* diminish, belittle. ~ **się** *ipf.*, **pomniejszyć się** *pf.* diminish, decrease.

pomniejszy *a.* 1. (= *mniejszy*) smaller, lesser. 2. *przen.* minor, lesser.

pomnik *mi Gen.* -a monument; **pomnik ku czci Chopina** monument to Chopin; **pomnik przyrody** nature monument; **pomnik kultury** cultural monument.

pomnikowy *a.* monumental.

pomnożyć *pf.* -**mnóż** 1. *zob.* **pomnażać**. 2. (= *skończyć mnożyć liczby*) multiply. ~ **się** *pf. zob.* **pomnażać się**.

pomny *a. lit.* mindful, remembering; **pomny na to, co razem przeszliśmy** mindful of what we have gone through together.

pomoc *f. pl.* -**e** 1. (= *wspieranie kogoś*) help, assistance, aid; **pomoc drogowa** emergency road service; **pomoc humanitarna** humanitarian aid; **pomoc lekarska** medical assistance, medical help; **pomoc natychmiastowa** immediate help, immediate assistance; **pomoc pieniężna** financial help, financial assitance; **pierwsza pomoc** first aid; **pomoc prawna** legal advice, legal assitance; **pomoc techniczna** (*produktu, oprogramowania*) technical support; **pomoce naukowe** teaching aids; **na pomoc!** help!; **wzywać pomocy** call for help; **przychodzić komuś z pomocą** *l.* **na pomoc** come to sb's aid *l.* rescue, help sb; **służyć komuś pomocą** be of help to sb; **pomoc nie nadeszła na czas** help *l.* rescue came too late; **przy pomocy** with the help *l.* aid of; **przy pomocy Adama** with Adam's help; **za pomocą tego klucza** by means of this key. 2. (*osoba*) help; **pomoc domowa** domestic help, domestic. 3. *piłka nożna, hokej* halfback.

pomocnica *f. zob.* **pomocnik** 1.

pomocniczy *a.* auxiliary.

pomocnik *mp* 1. (= *ten, kto pomaga*) helper. 2. *piłka nożna, hokej* halfback.

pomocny *a.* helpful; **podać komuś pomocną dłoń** give *l.* lend sb a helping hand; **czy mogę być dla ciebie w czymś pomocna?** can I be of any help to you?

pomocowy *a. form.* (*o organizacji, funduszu*) relief.

pomoczyć *pf.* 1. (= *zwilżyć*) wet. 2. (= *zanurzać jakiś czas*) soak. ~ **się** *pf.* 1. (= *stać się mokrym*) get wet. 2. (= *być w wodzie przez jakiś czas*) soak.

pomodlić się *pf.* -**módl** pray, say a prayer.

pomolog *mp pl.* -**dzy** *l.* -**owie** *ogr.* pomologist.

pomologia *f. Gen.* -**ii** *ogr.* pomology.

pomologiczny *a. ogr.* pomological.

pomordowany *a.* murdered; **pomordowani jeńcy** *l.* **więźniowie** murdered prisoners.

Pomorze *n. geogr.* Pomerania; **Pomorze Zachodnie** West Pomerania.

pomost *mi* 1. (*kładka*) platform; (*nad jeziorem, morzem*) pier, jetty. 2. (*w tramwaju*) platform.

pomóc *pf.* -**mogę** -**możesz**, -**móż**, -**mógł** -**mogła** -**mogli** *zob.* **pomagać**.

pomór *mi* -**o**- *wet., przest.* (= *zaraza*) plague.

pomówić *pf.* 1. *zob.* **pomawiać**. 2. (= *rozmawiać przez jakiś czas*) talk (*for a while*). ~ **się** *pf. zob.* **pomawiać się**.

pomówienie *n.* 1. (= *porozmawianie*) talk, word; **mam z wami do pomówienia** I've got to have a word with you. 2. *prawn.* (*ustne*) slander; (*pisemne*) libel.

pompa[1] *f.* 1. *techn.* pump; **pompa próżniowa** vacuum pump; **pompa ssąco-tłocząca** suction and force pump; **pompa wirowa** impeller pump, rotodynamic pump; **pompa olejowa** *mot.* oil pump. 2. *pot.* (*deszcz*) downpour.

pompa[2] *f.* (= *wystawność*) pomp; **z pompą** in grand style.

pompatycznie *adv.* pompously.

pompatyczność *f.* pomposity, pompousness.

pompatyczny *a.* pompous; **pompatyczna mowa** pompous speech.

pompka *f. Gen.pl.* -**ek** 1. (*do roweru*) (bicycle) pump. 2. *sport* push-up.

pompon *mi Gen.* -**a** *l.* -**u** pompom, pompon; bobble; **czapka z pomponem** bobble hat.

pompować *ipf.* (*ciecz, gaz*) pump (up); (*materac*) inflate; **pompować w coś pieniądze** *pot.* pump money into sth, inject money into sth.

pompownia *f. Gen.pl.* -**i** *techn.* pumping station, pumping plant.

pompowy *a.* pump; **elektrownia pompowo-szczytowa** *techn.* pumped storage power station.

pomroka *f. lit.* (= *zmierzch*) dusk; (= *mrok*) darkness, murkiness; **ginąć w pomroce dziejów** sink into oblivion, fade into the dusk of history.

pomruk *mi* murmur; (*kota*) purr; (*burzy*) rumble, growl; (*grzmotu, bębnów*) roll; (*lodówki*) humming.

pomrukiwać *ipf.* murmur; (*o kocie*) purr; (*o burzy*) rumble, growl; (*o grzmocie, bębnach*) roll.

pomsta *f. przest.* revenge; **ta niesprawiedliwość woła o pomstę do nieba** this injustice cries for vengeance.

pomstować *ipf.* execrate (*na kogoś/coś* sb/sth).

pomścić *pf.* -**mszczę** -**mścisz**, -**mścij** avenge (*kogoś/coś* sb/sth). ~ **się** *pf.* avenge o.s.

pomuchla *f. icht.* Atlantic cod (*Gadus morhua callarias*).

pomurnik *ma orn.* wall creeper (*Tichodroma muraria*). – *mi Gen.* -**a** *bot.* pellitory (*Parietaria*).

pomyć *pf.* wash (*a number of things*).

pomyje *pl. Gen.* -**j** swill; **wylewać pomyje na czyjąś głowę** *pot.* curse sb, run sb down.

pomyleniec *mp* -**ńc**- *pl.* -**y** *pot.* lunatic; looney, loony.

pomylić *pf.* 1. (*pokręcić, pomieszać*) confuse, mix up. 2. (= *wprowadzić kogoś w błąd*) mislead. ~ **się** *pf.* make a mistake; be wrong; **chyba coś ci się pomyliło** you must have got it wrong.

pomylona *f. Gen.* -**ej**, **pomylony** *mp pot.* lunatic; looney, loony.

pomyłka *f. Gen.pl.* **-ek 1.** (= *pomylenie się*) mistake; (= *błąd*) error; **przez pomyłkę** by mistake; **popełnić pomyłkę** make a mistake; **zatrudnienie go to była gruba pomyłka** employing him was a big mistake. **2.** *tel.* wrong number.

pomyłkowo *adv.* mistakenly, by mistake.

pomyłkowy *a.* (*o działaniu, telefonie*) wrong.

pomysł *mi* idea; **to dobry pomysł** (what a) good idea; **coś zrobione z pomysłem** *l.* **bez pomysłu** sth well *l.* badly designed; **człowiek z pomysłami** inventive *l.* resourceful person.

pomysłodawca *mp* originator.

pomysłowo *adv.* ingeniously, inventively.

pomysłowość *f.* ingenuity, inventiveness.

pomysłowy *a.* ingenious, inventive.

pomyślany *a.* conceived; **dobrze pomyślany** well designed; **coś jest pomyślane jako coś** sth is designed to be sth.

pomyśleć *pf.* **-ę -isz 1.** (= *myśleć chwilę*) think; **niech no tylko pomyślę** let me think. **2.** (= *wyobrazić sobie, uzmysłowić sobie*) imagine; **kto by pomyślał** who would have thought it; **i pomyśleć, że...** and one would think that... **3.** (= *zatroszczyć się*) think (*o kimś/czymś* of sb/sth).

pomyślenie *n.* **nie do pomyślenia** unthinkable.

pomyślność *f.* well-being, prosperity; **życzyć komuś pomyślności** wish sb luck.

pomyślny *a.* favorable, auspicious.

pomyślunek *mi* **-nk-** *pot.* cleverness; **robić coś bez pomyślunku** do sth without investing too much thought into it.

pomywacz *mp*, **pomywaczka** *f. Gen.pl.* **-ek** dishwasher.

pon. *abbr.* Mon. (= *Monday*).

ponad *prep.* **1.** (*na oznaczenie miejsca*) + *Ins.* above, over; **ponad domami** above houses; **ponad głowami** above heads. **2.** + *Acc.* (*na oznaczenie kierunku*) over. **3.** + *Acc.* (= *więcej niż*) above, over, more than; **ponad sto tysięcy osób** over one hundred thousand people; **pracuję tu ponad dziesięć lat** I have been working here for over ten years; **żyć ponad stan** spend more than sb has; **ponad miarę** excessively; **ponad wszystko** above all; **to jest już ponad moje siły** it's beyond me; **nie wiem wiele więcej ponad to, że...** I do not know more than...

ponadczasowość *f.* timelessness.

ponadczasowy *a.* timeless.

ponaddźwiękowiec *mi* **-wc-** *Gen.* **-a** *pot., lotn.* supersonic aircraft.

ponaddźwiękowy *a. lotn.* supersonic; **samolot ponaddźwiękowy** supersonic aircraft.

ponadnarodowy *a.* supranational, transnational.

ponadplanowy *a.* exceeding the planned quota *l.* level.

ponadpodstawowy *a. szkoln.* secondary; **szkoła ponadpodstawowa** high *l.* secondary school.

ponadprogramowy *a. szkoln.* extracurricular; **zajęcia ponadprogramowe** extracurricular activities.

ponadto *particle* furthermore, moreover.

ponaglać *ipf.* hurry, rush (*kogoś* sb); **ponaglać kogoś, żeby coś zrobił** press sb to do sth.

ponaglenie *n.* **1.** (= *zmuszenie do pośpiechu*) hurrying, rushing. **2.** (*pismo*) reminder.

ponaglić *pf.* **-ij** *zob.* **ponaglać**.

ponarzekać *pf.* complain; **lubi sobie ponarzekać** he likes to complain.

ponawiać *ipf.* (= *wznawiać*) renew; (= *powtarzać*) repeat, reiterate; **ponowić prośbę** repeat a request; **ponawiać próbę** retry. ~ **się** *ipf.* repeat; (*np. o bólach*) recur.

poncho *n. indecl. l. Gen.* **-a** poncho.

poncz *mi Gen.pl.* **-ów** *kulin.* punch.

ponderabilia *pl. Gen.* **-ów** *lit.* tangibles.

ponętnie *adv.* temptingly, enticingly.

ponętność *f.* allure, lure.

ponętny *a.* tempting, alluring, enticing.

poniechać *pf. lit.* abandon (*coś robić* doing sth).

poniedziałek *mi* **-łk-** Monday; **lany poniedziałek** Easter Monday; **szewski poniedziałek** Monday with a hangover after a weekend's binge.

poniedziałkowy *a.* Monday.

poniekąd *particle* in a way *l.* sense, to a certain *l.* some extent; **poniekąd masz rację** you're right, in a way.

ponieść *pf.* **-niosę -niesiesz -niósł -niosła -nieśli 1.** *zob.* **ponosić**. **2.** (*zanieść*) carry; (*o koniu*) bolt; **nosił wilk razy kilka, ponieśli i wilka** every fox must pay its skin to the furrier.

ponieważ *conj.* because, since; **wrócił, ponieważ wie, że go kocham** he came back because he knows that I love him.

poniewczasie *adv.* too late.

poniewierać *ipf.* slight, hold in contempt; **poniewierać kimś** treat sb badly. ~ **się** *ipf.* **1.** (= *tułać się*) knock about *l.* around. **2.** (*o rzeczach*) lie about *l.* around.

poniewierka *f. Gen.pl.* **-ek** (= *ciężkie chwile*) times of adversity; (= *tułaczka*) wandering.

poniżać *ipf.* humiliate. ~ **się** *ipf.* humiliate o.s., humble o.s.

poniżej *prep.* + *Gen.* (*niżej*) below, beneath, under; **jeśli temperatura spadnie poniżej pięciu stopni, trzeba będzie włączyć dodatkowe ogrzewanie** if the temperature falls below 5 degrees, we'll have to switch on additional heaters; **cios poniżej pasa** blow below the belt, low blow; **poniżej wszelkiej krytyki** beneath criticism; **to jest poniżej mojej godności** this is beneath my dignity; **nasi piłkarze zagrali poniżej swoich możliwości** our soccer team played not to the best of its ability. – *adv.* (= *dalej w tekście*) below; **poniżej przedstawiamy uzasadnienie** below we substantiate our claims; **poniżej przedstawione dane** data presented below; **patrz poniżej, na stronę 56** see below, page 56.

poniżenie *n.* humiliation.

poniższy *a.* mentioned below.

poniżyć *pf. zob.* **poniżać**. ~ **się** *pf. zob.* **poniżać się**.

ponoć *particle lit.* allegedly, apparently.

ponosić *ipf.* **-szę -sisz 1.** (= *doświadczać czegoś*) suffer; **ponosić fiasko** end in a fiasco; **ponosić karę** suffer punishment; **ponosić klęskę** meet *l.* suffer defeat; **ponosić odpowiedzialność za**

coś be responsible for sth; **ponosić ryzyko** assume *l.* take risk; **ponosić winę** be responsible, be guilty. **2.** (= *doznać, zostać obarczonym*) bear; **ponosić koszty** bear costs; **ponieść śmierć** be killed, meet sb's death. **3.** (*o silnym impulsie*) be carried away; **poszedł, gdzie go oczy poniosą** he went just anywhere. **4.** (*o silnym uczuciu*) be carried away; **poniosło go** he got carried away. **5.** (= *nosić przez jakiś czas*) carry (*for some time*). **6.** (= *pochodzić w ubraniu*) wear (*for some time*).

ponowić *pf.* **-ów** zob. **ponawiać.** ~ **się** *pf.* **-ów** zob. **ponawiać się.**

ponownie *adv.* again; **ponownie rozważyć** reconsider.

ponowny *a.* renewed, repeated.

ponowoczesność *f. sztuka* postmodernism.

ponowoczesny *a. sztuka* postmodern.

ponton *mi* pontoon.

pontonowy *a.* pontoon; **most pontonowy** pontoon bridge.

pontyfikalny *a. rel.* pontifical; **msza pontyfikalna** Pontifical Mass; **szaty pontyfikalne** pontificals.

pontyfikat *mi rz.-kat.* pontificate.

pontyjski *a.* **organizmy pontyjskie** *biol.* Pontic organisms; **Góry Pontyjskie** *geogr.* Pontic Mountains.

ponumerować *pf.* number.

ponuractwo *n.* gloom, cheerlessness.

ponurak *mp pl.* **-i** *l.* **-cy** gloomy *l.* cheerless person.

ponury *a.* (*o osobie, wiadomości*) gloomy; (*o wyglądzie*) bleak; (*o miejscu*) bleak, dreary; (*o myślach*) gloomy, dismal; **być ponurym jak noc** be as gloomy as a rainy day.

pony *ma indecl.* pony.

pończocha *f.* stocking; **chodzić w pończochach** wear stockings; **trzymać pieniądze w pończosze** *przen.* keep one's money stashed *l.* stuffed under the mattress.

pończosznictwo *n.* hosiery industry.

pończoszniczy *a.* hosiery; **ścieg pończoszniczy** garter stitch; **wyroby pończosznicze** hosiery.

poobiedni *a.* after-dinner; **drzemka poobiednia** after-dinner nap; **uciąć sobie poobiednią drzemkę** have a nap after one's dinner.

poobijać *pf.* **1.** (= *poobtłukiwać*) chip. **2.** (*np. skórą*) upholster.

pooglądać *pf.* watch (*for some time*).

po omacku *adv.* blindfold; **szukać czegoś po omacku** grope for sth.

poopalać się *pf.* sunbathe, (sun)tan (*for some time*).

pooperacyjny *a. med.* postoperative.

poorać *pf.* **-rzę -rzesz** (*ziemię, twarz, czoło*) plow (up), *Br.* plough (up).

pop¹ *mp pl.* **-i** *rel.* Orthodox priest.

pop² *mi tylko sing.* pop, pop art.

popadać¹ *ipf.* (= *pogrążać się w czymś*) fall; **popadać w nędzę** fall into poverty; **popadać w niełaskę** fall into disgrace; **popadać w ruinę** fall into ruin; **popadać w długi** fall *l.* get into debt; **popa-**

dać w chorobę nerwową go insane *l.* mad; **popadać w gniew** fly into a rage; **popadać w konflikt z prawem** violate the law; **popadać w tarapaty** get into trouble; **popadać w zadumę** be lost in meditation *l.* thought; **popadać w złość** lose temper *l.* nerve.

popadać² *pf.* **1.** (= *upaść jeden po drugim*) fall. **2.** (*o zwierzętach*) (= *zdechnąć*) die. **3.** (*o deszczu*) rain (*a little, for a while*); (*o śniegu*) snow (*a little, for a while*).

popakować *pf.* pack.

popalić *pf.* **1.** (= *spalić wiele czegoś, jedno po drugim*) burn; **popalić za sobą mosty** burn one's bridges *l.* boats. **2.** (= *sparzyć sobie coś w wielu miejscach*) burn. **3.** (= *spędzić jakiś czas na paleniu papierosa*) smoke; **ja ci dam popalić!** *pot.* I'll give you hell!

popamiętać *pf.* remember; **jeszcze mnie popamiętasz!** I'll show you!

poparcie *n.* support, backing; **udzielić komuś poparcia** give sb support, support sb; **szukać u kogoś poparcia** seek sb's support; **mieć** *l.* **znaleźć w kimś poparcie** have the support of sb; **zrobić coś na poparcie swoich słów/stanowiska** do sth to support sb's words/opinion.

popart *mi sztuka* pop art, Pop Art, pop.

popartowy *a. sztuka* pop art.

poparzenie *n.* burn; **poparzenie pierwszego/drugiego/trzeciego stopnia** *pat.* first-/second-/third-degree burn.

poparzyć *pf.* burn; (*o wrzątku, parze*) scald; (*o pokrzywach*) sting. ~ **się** *pf.* burn o.s.; be scalded; be stung.

popas *mi przest.* **1.** (= *postój*) (= *nakarmienie*) bait. **2.** (= *pastwisko*) pasture.

popaść¹ *pf.* **-padnę -padniesz, -padnij, -padł 1.** zob. **popadać. 2.** *pot.* (= *trafić się*) turn up, happen, occur; **co** *l.* **jak popadnie** at random, just anywhere, anyhow.

popaść² *pf.* **-pasę -pasiesz -pasł -paśli** (*w czasie przerwy w podróży*) bait.

popatrzeć *pf.,* **popatrzyć -ę -ysz 1.** (= *spojrzeć, rozejrzeć się*) look, have a look (*na coś/kogoś* at sth/sb). **2.** (= *przyjrzeć się uważnie*) take a close look (*na coś/kogoś* at sth/sb); **popatrz, to nie może być prawda, bo ona nigdy nie była w Warwick** look, this can't be true since she's never been to Warwick. ~ **się** *pf. emf.* **1.** (= *spojrzeć, rozejrzeć się*) have a look (*na coś/kogoś* at sth/sb). **2.** (= *przyjrzeć się*) take a close look (*na coś/kogoś* at sth/sb).

popatrzyć *pf.* zob. **popatrzeć.** ~ **się** *pf.* zob. **popatrzeć się.**

popchnąć *pf.* **-ij 1.** zob. **popychać. 2.** *pot.* (= *posłać kogoś*) send, dispatch. ~ **się** *pf.* zob. **popychać się.**

popegeerowski *a. roln.* post-state-owned farms, left after state-owned farms (*in pre-1990 Poland*).

popelina *f.* **1.** *tk.* poplin. **2.** *przen.* (*rzecz złej jakości*) (piece of) shit.

popelinowy *a. tk.* poplin; **popelinowy płaszcz** poplin coat.

popełniać *ipf.,* **popełnić** *pf.* **-nij** *l.* **-ń 1.** (= *zro-**

bić coś złego) commit; make; **popełniać błąd** make a mistake; **popełniać grzech** commit a sin; **popełnić przestępstwo** commit *l.* perpetrate a crime; **popełnić samobójstwo** commit suicide; **popełnić mezalians** marry below sb's station. **2.** *żart.* (= *stworzyć coś*) commit.

popęd *mi* **1.** (= *skłonność*) disposition, inclination; (= *pociąg*) drive, urge; **popęd siły** *fiz.* impulse of a force, time-effect. **2.** *psych.* drive, urge; **popęd płciowy** sexual drive.

popędliwość *f.* irritability, irascibility; impetuosity.

popędliwy *a.* irritable, irascible; impetuous.

popędzać *ipf.*, **popędzić** *pf.* **1.** (= *zmuszać do posuwania się do przodu*) drive. **2.** (= *nakłaniać do szybszego wykonania czynności*) hurry, rush (*do czegoś* to do sth). **3.** *pf.* (= *pobiec bez zwłoki*) rush, dash (off); **popędzić komuś kota** *pot.* scare the wits out of sb.

popić *pf.* **-iję -ijesz, -ij 1.** (= *wypić coś po połknięciu czegoś*) wash down. **2.** *pot.* (= *wypić dużo alkoholu*) booze, tank up; **on lubi sobie popić** he likes to guzzle.

popielato *adv.* grayly; **malować coś na popielato** paint sth gray.

popielaty *a.* gray, *zwł. Br.* grey.

popielcowy *a.* Ash Wednesday; **Środa Popielcowa** *rz.-kat.* Ash Wednesday.

Popielec *mi* **-lc-** *Gen.* **-a** *rz.-kat.* Ash Wednesday.

popielica *f.* **1.** *bot.* European dewberry (*Rubus caesius*). **2.** *zool.* common dormouse (*Glis glis*).

popielice *pl. Gen.* **-c** (*futro*) dormouse fur coat.

popielisko *n.* ashes, cinders.

popielnica *f.* **1.** *archeol.* urn. **2.** (= *duża popielniczka*) ashtray.

popielniczka *f. Gen.pl.* **-ek** ashtray.

popielnik *mi Gen.* **-a 1.** (*w piecu*) ashpit. **2.** *bot.* cineraria (*Senecio cruentus l. Cineraria cruenta*).

popieprzać *ipf. wulg.* **1.** (= *pracować intensywnie*) work like hell. **2.** (= *iść szybko*) scamper like hell.

popieprzony *a.* **-eni** *wulg.* bollixed up.

popieprzyć *pf.* **1.** (= *doprawić pieprzem*) pepper. **2.** *wulg.* (= *zrobić w czymś nieporządek*) screw up; (= *pomylić*) screw up. **3.** *wulg.* (= *odbyć stosunek płciowy*) fuck, screw. **~ się** *pf.* **1.** *wulg.* (= *skomplikować się*) get (all) screwed up; (= *pomylić się*) get (all) screwed up. **2.** *wulg.* (= *odbyć stosunek płciowy*) fuck, screw (*z kimś* sb).

popierać *ipf.* **1.** (= *pomagać komuś w działaniu*) support, back up; **popierać kandydata** support *l.* endorse a candidate; **popierać czyjąś prośbę** support sb's request; **popierać wniosek** second a motion. **2.** (= *uzasadniać*) corroborate, fortify. **~ się** *ipf.* support each other, support one another.

popierdalać *ipf. wulg.* **1.** (= *pracować bardzo intensywnie*) work like fucking hell. **2.** (= *szybko iść, jechać*) speed like fucking hell.

popierdolić *pf. wulg.* **1.** (= *zrobić nieporządek*) fuck up. **2.** (= *pomylić*) fuck up; **a ty co, popier-**

doliło cię czy jak? are you fucked in the head or something? **~ się** *pf. wulg.* **1.** (= *skomplikować się*) get (all) fucked up. **2.** (= *pomylić się*) get (all) fucked up. **3.** (= *odbyć stosunek*) fuck (*z kimś* sb).

popierdolony *a.* **-eni** *wulg.* fucked up; (= *nienormalny*) fucked in the head.

popierdzielić *pf. pot.* (= *zrobić nieporządek, pomylić*) make a hell of a mess (*coś* of sth).

popierniczać *ipf. pot.* (= *iść bardzo szybko*) scamper like hell.

popiersie *n. Gen.pl.* **-i** bust.

popijać *ipf.* **1.** (= *pić powoli*) sip. **2.** (= *pić od czasu do czasu*) hit the bottle, booze it up (*every now and then*). **3.** (= *pić po każdym kęsie, po jedzeniu*) wash down (*coś czymś* sth with sth).

popijawa *f. pot.* bash, tender, twister, drinking party.

popilnować *pf.* look after, mind (*kogoś/czegoś* sb).

popioły *pl. Gen.* **-ów** (= *prochy po umarłym*) ashes.

popiół *mi* **-o-** *Loc.* **-ele** ash; **nie zasypiać gruszek w popiele** use an opportunity, seize an opportunity *l.* occasion; **obrócić coś w popiół** reduce sth to ashes; **odradzać się (jak feniks) z popiołów** rise from the ashes; **popiół wulkaniczny** *geol.* volcanic ash.

popis *mi* show, display; **mieć pole do popisu** have an ideal setting to demonstrate sb's skills.

popisać się *pf.* **-szę -szesz** *zob.* **popisywać się**.

popiskiwać *ipf.* squeak.

popisowo *adv.* spectacularly, splendidly.

popisowy *a.* spectacular, splendid; **popisowy występ** showpiece performance.

popisywać się *ipf.* show off (*kimś/czymś* sb/sth); (*nowymi ubraniami*) sport (*coś* sth); **popisywać się odwagą** show off one's courage.

popitka *f. Gen.pl.* **-ek** *pot.* chaser.

popiwek *mi* **-wk-** (*podatek*) excessive income tax (*in Poland, paid by state-owned enterprises*).

poplamić *pf.* stain; (*drobnymi plamkami*) blot; (= *uwalać*) soil. **~ się** *pf.* get stained, stain; get blotted, blot; get soiled, soil.

poplątać *pf.* **-czę -czesz 1.** (= *splątać jedno z drugim*) tangle, snarl; **poplątać nici** tangle thread. **2.** (= *pomylić coś*) confuse, mix up; **poplątać komuś szyki** upset sb's plans. **~ się** *pf.* **1.** (= *splątać się*) tangle; **język mu się poplątał** he couldn't find his tongue. **2.** (= *zagmatwać się, skomplikować się*) confuse, mix up; **wszystko mu się poplątało** he got it all mixed up, he's all confused.

poplecznictwo *n.* **1.** (= *protekcja*) henchmanship, partisanship. **2.** *prawn.* rendering criminal assistance.

poplecznicza *f. Gen.pl.* **-ek, poplecznik** *mp* *pog.* henchman, partisan.

poplon *mi roln.* catch crop.

popłacać *ipf.* pay; **przestępstwo nie popłaca** crime doesn't pay; **uczciwość popłaca** honesty is the best policy.

popłakać się *pf.* sob, weep (*for a while*). **~ się** *pf.* **-czę -czesz** burst into tears.

popłakiwać *ipf.* weep, sob.

popłatny *a.* (= *dobrze płatny*) well-paid; (= *intratny*) profitable, lucrative.

popłoch *mi* **1.** (= *panika*) panic, scare; **wpaść w popłoch** panic. **2.** *bot.* thistle (*Onopordon*).

popłuczyny *pl. Gen.* **-n 1.** (*płyn*) washings, rinsings. **2.** *przen.* (= *pozostałości*) remnants, remains (*czegoś* of sth).

popłynąć *pf.* **1.** (= *zacząć płynąć*) (begin to) flow; **woda (gaz, prąd) popłynie w przyszłym miesiącu** water (gas, electricity) will be connected next month. **2.** (= *odpłynąć*) (*o statku*) sail away; (*o pływaku*) swim away. **3.** *pot.* (= *upić się*) booze it up.

popływać *pf.* **1.** (*w basenie, rzece, morzu*) have a swim, swim (*for some time*). **2.** (*jako marynarz*) be at sea (*for some time*).

popojutrze[1] *adv.* in three days' time.

popojutrze[2] *n.* the day three days from today.

popołogowy *a. med.* post puerperal; **okres popołogowy** post puerperal period.

popołudnie *n. Gen.pl.* **-i** afternoon.

popołudniowy *a.* afternoon; **popołudniowa drzemka** afternoon nap.

popołudniówka *f. Gen.pl.* **-ek** *pot.* **1.** (*dziennik, pismo*) evening paper. **2.** (*przedstawienie, seans*) matinée, matinee.

poporodowy *a. med.* postpartum, postnatal.

popracować *pf.* do some work, work (*for a while*); **długo tam nie popracował** he didn't work there for long.

poprać *pf.* **-piorę -pierzesz -prał** do some washing, wash (*for a while*); **poprałem trochę ubrań** I did some washing.

poprasować *pf.* do some ironing, iron (*for a while*); **poprasowałem trochę ubrań** I did some ironing.

poprawa *f.* **1.** (= *polepszenie*) improvement; (= *poprawienie czegoś, się*) betterment; (= *zmiana na lepsze*) change for the better; **nieznaczna/odczuwalna poprawa** small/significant improvement; **przyrzec poprawę** (*lepsze zachowanie*) promise to behave better; (*w nauce*) promise to study harder. **2.** (= *polepszenie stanu zdrowia*) improvement, recovery; **u chorego nastąpiła poprawa** the patient is recovering *l.* shows improvement.

poprawczak *mi Gen.* **-a** *pot.* reformatory, reform school; *Br.* youth custody centre.

poprawczy *a.* reformatory; **dom** *l.* **zakład poprawczy** reformatory, reform school; *Br.* youth custody centre.

poprawiać *ipf.*, **poprawić** *pf.* **1.** (= *doprowadzać do porządku, ładu*) tidy up; put straight, put in order; **poprawiać krawat** adjust one's tie; **poprawiać sobie makijaż** touch o.s. up; **poprawiać poduszki** fluff up the pillows. **2.** (= *ulepszać*) better (*coś* sth); improve (*coś* on *l.* upon sth); **poprawiać komuś/sobie humor** *l.* **nastrój** put sb/o.s. in a better mood; **poprawiać rekord świata** *sport* beat a world record. **3.** (= *reperować*) mend, repair. **4.** (= *usuwać błędy*) correct; (*rękopis, maszynopis*) proofread. **5.** (= *korygować czyjś błąd*) correct. **6.** (= *powtórzyć jakąś czyn-*

ność dla uzyskania lepszego efektu) improve (*coś* on *l.* upon sth). **~ się** *ipf.*, **poprawić się** *pf.* **1.** (= *korygować swoją wypowiedź*) correct o.s. **2.** (= *stawać się lepszym*) improve; **poprawić się z matematyki** improve at maths. **3.** (= *przybierać na wadze*) put on weight. **4.** (= *szukać najwygodniejszej pozycji do siedzenia, leżenia*) settle o.s. **5.** (= *o człowieku: zmieniać się na lepsze*) reform, mend one's ways.

poprawiny *pl. Gen.* **-n** wedding (baptism etc.) breakfast *l.* brunch; champagne breakfast *l.* brunch.

poprawka *f. Gen.pl.* **-ek 1.** (= *modyfikacja*) correction; (*wniosku, dokumentu*) amendment; (= *dostosowanie*) adjustment; **poprawki do ustawy** amendments to an act of parliament; **garnitur do poprawki** suit that needs a few adjustments. **2.** *pot.* retake exam, repeat exam. **3.** *techn.* correction, allowance; **brać poprawkę na coś** make allowances for sth.

poprawkowicz *mp*, **poprawkowiczka** *f.* (exam) retaker.

poprawkowy *a.* repeat, retake; **egzamin poprawkowy** retake examination, repeat examination.

poprawnie *adv.* correctly, properly.

poprawnościowy *a.* puristic; **reguły poprawnościowe** (*językowe*) correct usage rules.

poprawność *f.* correctness, correctitude; **poprawność polityczna** political correctness, PC; **kryteria poprawności językowej** correct language usage criteria, language accuracy criteria.

poprawny *a.* **1.** (= *prawidłowy*) correct; (= *bezbłędny*) faultless. **2.** (= *odpowiedni*) (*o stroju, manierach*) proper; (= *nienaganny*) impeccable.

popręg *mi jeźdz.* girth; **podciągnąć/rozluźnić popręg** tighten/loosen the girth.

poprodukcyjny *a.* **odpady poprodukcyjne** industrial waste; **wiek poprodukcyjny** retirement age.

popromienny *a. med.* postradiation, radiation-induced; **choroba popromienna** *pat.* radiation sickness.

poprosić *pf.* **1.** (= *zwrócić się z prośbą*) ask (*kogoś o coś* sb for sth *l.* sb to do sth); **poprosić o głos** ask for the floor, ask for permission to speak; **poprosić o pomoc** ask for help; **poprosić o pożyczkę** ask for a loan; **poprosić o ogień** ask for a light; **poprosić kogoś o rękę** propose to sb. **2.** (= *zaprosić*) invite; **poprosić kogoś do tańca** ask sb to dance. **3.** (= *wezwać*) call; **poprosić kogoś do telefonu** want sb on the phone; **czy mogę poprosić Adama do telefonu?** may I speak with Adam, please? **4.** (= *zażądać*) ask (*o coś* for sth); **poprosić o czyjś dowód osobisty** ask to see sb's ID, demand to see sb's ID.

poprowadzić *pf.* **1.** (= *zaprowadzić*) take; **poprowadzić kogoś do ołtarza** lead sb to the altar. **2.** (*np. linię*) draw, mark off. **3.** (= *pokierować kimś, czymś*) lead, direct; **poprowadzić oddział do ataku** lead the unit in the attack; **prowadzić rozmowę** have a conversation; **prowadzić samochód** drive a car; **prowadzić zebranie** chair a meeting.

popróbować *pf.* **1.** (= *przeprowadzić próbę czegoś*) try, test. **2.** (= *skosztować*) try, taste.

poprzeczka *f. Gen.pl.* **-ek 1.** *sport* (*w bramce*) (*w skoku wzwyż i o tyczce*) **strzelić w poprzeczkę** hit the bar; **przeskoczyć poprzeczkę** clear the bar; **strącić poprzeczkę** miss the bar, dislodge the bar. **2.** (*ścieżka polna*) crossroad. **3.** (*listwa, belka*) crossbar, crossbeam; **podnieść/obniżyć poprzeczkę** *przen.* raise/lower standards; **stawiać komuś wysoko poprzeczkę** *przen.* set very high standards for sb, set very ambitious targets for sb; **stawiać sobie wysoko poprzeczkę** *przen.* aim high.

poprzeczny *a.* crosswise, cross; transverse.

poprzeć *pf.* **-prę -przesz, -przyj** *zob.* **popierać**. ~ **się** *pf. zob.* **popierać się**.

poprzedni *a.* previous, preceding; (*np. właściciel, mąż, żona*) former.

poprzedniczka *f. Gen.pl.* **-ek, poprzednik** *mp* predecessor.

poprzednio *adv.* previously, before.

poprzedzać *ipf.* precede.

poprzedzający *a.* preceding; **dzień poprzedzający święto** day preceding a holiday.

poprzedzić *pf. zob.* **poprzedzać**.

poprzedzielać *pf.* divide, separate.

poprzeglądać *pf.* go *l.* look through, browse. ~ **się** *pf.* examine o.s. in the mirror.

poprzek *adv.* **w poprzek** across, crosswise, transversely.

poprzekładać *pf.* **1.** (= *zmienić miejsce, kolejność czegoś*) rearrange. **2.** (= *przełożyć czymś wielokrotnie*) layer; **poprzekładać tort kremem orzechowym** layer birthday cake with nut cream. **3.** (= *przetłumaczyć wiele tekstów*) translate.

poprzenosić *pf.* **-szę -sisz** (*książki, meble*) move; (*na inne stanowisko pracy*) transfer. ~ **się** *pf.* move; (*do innego domu, mieszkania*) move house.

poprzestać *pf.* **-stanę -staniesz, poprzestawać** *ipf.* **-aję -ajesz, -waj** confine o.s., limit o.s. (*na czymś* to sth); be satisfied (*na czymś* with sth).

poprzestawiać *pf.* (= *zmienić położenie*) (*np. mebli*) move, rearrange; (= *zmienić kolejność*) shift.

poprzewracać *pf.* **1.** (= *przewrócić jedno po drugim*) knock down *l.* over; **poprzewracać ubrania na drugą** *l.* **lewą stronę** turn clothes inside out. **2.** (= *zrobić nieporządek*) scatter, throw loosely about.

poprzewracać się *pf.* be knocked down *l.* over; **w głowach im się poprzewracało** it went to their heads.

poprzez *pron.* + *Acc.* **1.** (*przestrzeń*) through, across; **jechać poprzez las** go through *l.* across the wood *l.* forest. **2.** (*przeszkoda*) through; **próbowali zobaczyć coś poprzez mgłę** they were trying to see through the fog. **3.** (*czas*) for; **wiara trwająca niezmiennie poprzez wieki** faith lasting for ages. **4.** (*stadium rozwoju*) through; **poprzez kubizm aż do abstrakcji** through cubism to abstract painting. **5.** (*sposób*) by, through, thanks

to; **osiągnąć sukces poprzez intensywną pracę** achieve success thanks to hard work.

poprztykać się *pf. pot.* fall out (*z kimś* with sb).

poprzysiąc *pf.* **-sięgnę -sięgniesz, -sięgnij, -siągł -sięgła -sięgli, poprzysięgać** *ipf.* swear, vow; **poprzysiąc komuś wierność** swear fidelity to sb; **poprzysiąc komuś zemstę** vow vengeance to sb.

popsuć *pf.* **1.** (= *zepsuć*) break; **popsuć sobie oczy** *l.* **wzrok** ruin one's eyes; **popsuć sobie zdrowie** ruin one's health. **2.** (= *zmienić na gorsze*) spoil, ruin; **popsuć komuś humor** put sb in a bad mood; **popsuć zabawę** spoil the fun; **popsuć imprezę** spoil the party; **popsuć komuś szyki** upset sb's plans. ~ **się** *pf.* **1.** (= *zepsuć się*) (*o maszynie, urządzeniu*) break down; (*o jedzeniu*) go bad; *zwł. Br.* go off; **jabłko się popsuło** apple went bad; **samochód mi się popsuł** my car broke down. **2.** (= *pogorszyć się*) deteriorate, get worse; **pogoda się popsuła** weather got worse. **3.** (= *zdemoralizować się*) become depraved.

popukać *pf.* **1.** (*do drzwi*) knock; **popukaj się w głowę!** *pot.* are you nuts? **2.** (*z karabinu, strzelby*) shoot (*for a while*).

populacja *f. biol., socjol.* population.

populacyjny *a.* populational.

popularnonaukowy *a.* popular science; **czasopismo popularnonaukowe** popular science magazine.

popularność *f.* popularity; **osiągnąć szczyt popularności** be on top; **cieszyć się popularnością** enjoy popularity.

popularny *a.* **1.** (= *sławny*) popular, famous. **2.** (= *powszechnie znany*) well-known, famous. **3.** (= *przystępny*) popular; **muzyka popularna** *l.* **pop** popular *l.* pop music; **wykład przekazany w popularnej formie** lecture delivered in an accessible way.

popularyzacja *f.* popularization.

popularyzacyjny *a.* popularizing.

popularyzator *mp*, **popularyzatorka** *f. Gen.pl.* **-ek** popularizer.

popularyzatorski *a.* popularizing.

popularyzować *ipf.* popularize. ~ **się** *ipf.* become popular, become widely known.

populista *mp*, **populistka** *f. Gen.pl.* **-ek** populist.

populistyczny *a.* (*o hasłach, polityce*) populist.

populizm *mi* populism.

popuszczać *ipf.*, **popuścić** *pf.* **-szczę -ścisz 1.** (= *rozluźniać*) loosen, slacken; **popuścić cugle** *jeźdz.* slacken the reins. **2.** (= *darować komuś*) let off; **nie popuszczę ci** I won't let you get away with it. **3.** *pot.* (*mocz*) be incontinent; **popuścić w gacie** (*moczem*) wet one's pants; (*kałem*) shit one's pants.

popychacz *mi Gen.* **-a** *techn.* pusher, push rod; (*w silniku*) cam follower.

popychać *ipf.* **1.** (= *pchając, przesuwać*) push, shove; **popchnąć robotę** do most of the work. **2.** (= *skłaniać*) push (*kogoś do czegoś* sb into sth); **popychać kogoś do zbrodni** push sb into committing a crime; **popychać kogoś na złą drogę** lead sb astray. **3.** *wulg.* (= *odbywać stosunek* *płciowy*) (*o mężczyźnie*) fuck. ~ **się** *ipf.* push each other, push one another.

popychadło *n. Gen.pl.* **-eł** *pot.* doormat.

popyt *mi ekon.* demand (*na coś* for sth); **cieszyć się (dużym) popytem** be in (great) demand.

popytać *pf.* inquire, ask (*o coś* about sth). ~ **się** *pf.* inquire, ask (*o coś* about sth).

por[1] *mi Gen.* **-a** *bot.* (*warzywo*) leek; *rzad.* scallion (*Allium porrum*); **sałatka z porów** leek salad.

por[2] *mi Gen.* **-u** *l.* **-a** (*w skórze*) *chem., fiz.* pore.

por. *abbr.* 1. (= *porównaj*) cf. (= *compare*). 2. (= *porucznik*) Lt., Lieut. (= *lieutenant*).

pora *f. Gen.pl.* **pór** 1. (= *okres*) time, season; **pora obiadowa** dinnertime; **pora żniw** harvest time *l.* season; **późna pora** late; **wczesna pora** early; **o każdej porze dnia i nocy** at any time; **o tej porze** at this time; **pora roku** season; **pora deszczowa** rainy season. 2. (= *stosowna chwila*) time; **już pora na śniadanie** it's time for breakfast; **pora na nas** it's (high) time we went; **do tej pory** until now, so far; **od tej pory** from now on; **w samą porę** just in time; **nie w porę** inopportunely, untimely; **nie pora na...** this is no time for...; **najwyższa pora** (high) time.

porabiać *ipf.* do; **co porabiasz?** what are you up to (these days)?

porachować *pf.* count, calculate; **porachować komuś kości** beat sb up black and blue. ~ **się** *pf. przest.* settle up (*z kimś* with sb); **porachuję się jeszcze z wami** I'll get even with you.

porachunki *pl. Gen.* **-ów** matters to settle; **mieć z kimś porachunki** have a bone to pick with sb; **załatwić z kimś porachunki** settle an old score with sb.

porada *f.* advice, counsel; **porada lekarska** medical advice; **porada prawna** legal advice; **udzielić porady** give counsel *l.* advice; **za czyjąś poradą** on sb's advice; **zasięgać czyjejś porady** seek sb's advice.

poradnia *f. Gen.pl.* **-i** information *l.* counseling service; **poradnia lekarska** outpatient clinic; **poradnia małżeńska** marriage clinic.

poradnictwo *n.* guidance, counseling, clinic; **poradnictwo zawodowe** career counseling, job counseling.

poradnik *mi Gen.* **-a** guide, handbook.

poradnikowy *a.* guide, handbook.

poradzić *pf.* 1. (= *doradzić*) advise; **czy możesz mi coś poradzić?** could you give me some advice? 2. (= *podołać jakiemuś zadaniu*) cope, manage; **nie mogę sobie poradzić z tym zadaniem** I can't solve this problem, I can't cope with this task; **poradzić komuś/czemuś** overcome sb/sth; **poradzić sobie z czymś** manage sth. 3. (= *zaradzić czemuś*) help; **nic na to nie poradzę** I can't help it. ~ **się** *pf.* consult (*kogoś* sb); seek advice (*kogoś* from sb).

poranek *mi* **-nk-** *Gen.* **-u** *l.* **-a** 1. (= *ranek*) morning. 2. *kino, teatr* morning show; matinée, matinee.

poranić *pf.* wound, injure. ~ **się** *pf.* 1. (= *zostać zranionym*) wound o.s., injure o.s. 2. (= *za-*

dać sobie rany wzajemnie) wound each other *l.* one another, injure each other *l.* one another.

poranny *a.* morning; **gazeta poranna** morning paper; **gimnastyka poranna** morning exercise; **wiadomości poranne** morning news; **Gwiazda Poranna** *astron.* morning star, daystar.

porastać *ipf.* 1. (= *zarastać czymś*) overgrow (*czymś* with sth). 2. (= *zarastać coś*) overgrow. 3. (*o roślinach*) (= *puszczać kiełki w niewłaściwym momencie*) germinate, sprout.

poratować *pf.* help, lend a helping hand.

porazić *pf.* **-żę -zisz, porażać** *ipf.* 1. (= *sparaliżować*) paralyze; **porażony prądem** suffering from electric shock. 2. (= *oślepić*) dazzle; **porażony blaskiem reflektora** dazzled by the lights. 3. *ogr., roln.* (= *zostać zaatakowane chorobą*) attack, affect. 4. *lit.* (= *ugodzić kogoś*) strike, hit.

porażenie *n.* 1. shock, stroke; **porażenie prądem** electric shock; **porażenie słoneczne** sunstroke. 2. *pat.* paralysis, palsy; **porażenie dziecięce** polio, Heine-Medin disease; **porażenie połowicze** hemiplegia; **porażenie poprzeczne** paraplegia, transverse paraplegia; **porażenie postępujące** general paraplegia of the insane, general paresis (of the insane); paralytic dementia.

porażenny *a. pat.* paralytic; **drżączka porażenna** *l.* **poraźna** shaking palsy, paralysis agitans; Parkinson's disease; **porażenne zapalenie rogówki** neuroparalytic keratitis.

porażka *f. Gen.pl.* **-ek** 1. (= *klęska w bitwie*) defeat; **ponieść porażkę** *l.* **doznać porażki** *t. przen.* suffer defeat, be defeated. 2. (= *niepowodzenie*) failure.

porąbać *pf.* **-bię -biesz** 1. (= *rąbiąc, pokawałkować*) chop; **dałby się porąbać za swoje dzieci** he would die for his children. 2. (= *rąbać jakiś czas*) do some chopping, chop (*for some time*).

porąbany *a. pot.* stupid; crazy.

porcelana *f.* porcelain; (*zwł. wysokiej jakości*) china; **porcelana stołowa** table porcelain.

porcelanka *f. Gen.pl.* **-ek** *zool.* cowrie, cowry (*Cypraea*).

porcelanowy *a.* 1. (= *z porcelany*) china; porcelain, porcellaneous; **serwis porcelanowy** set of china; **glinka porcelanowa** *min.* white clay, kaolin. 2. *przen.* (= *biały jak porcelana*) chinawhite; (= *gładki jak porcelana*) china-smooth.

porcelit *mi techn.* semi-vitreous chinaware.

porcelitowy *a.* semi-vitreous chinaware.

porcja *f.* portion, helping; (= *racja żywnościowa*) ration; **porcja dzienna** *l.* **tygodniowa** daily *l.* weekly ration; **zamówić trzy porcje frytek** order three portions of French fries; **żelazna porcja** emergency ration; **zjesz jeszcze jedną porcję?** would you like another helping?

porcjować *ipf.* portion (out), ration (out).

porewolucyjny *a.* post-revolution, post-revolutionary.

poręba *f.* clear-cut, clear-cutting.

poręcz *f. pl.* **-e** 1. (*przy schodach*) guardrail, handrail. 2. (= *balustrada*) banister. 3. (*przy fotelu, krześle*) arm. 4. *pl. sport* parallel bars.

poręczać *ipf. prawn.* guarantee; **poręczać za**

kogoś/coś (= *zaręczyć*) vouch for sb/sth; (*za czy- jeś długi*) stand surety for sb/sth.

poręczenie *n. prawn.* guarantee; (*zwł. długu*) surety; (*zwł. słowne*) pledge; **poręczenie mająt- kowe** (*pieniężne*) bail; (*papierami wartościowy- mi*) appearance bond.

poręczny *a.* convenient; (*o bagażu, narzędziu*) handy.

poręczyciel *mp,* **poręczycielka** *f. Gen.pl.* **-ek** *fin.* guarantor, gurantee; security; (*zwł. długu*) surety.

poręczycielstwo *n.* **1.** (= *wystąpienie w roli po- ręczyciela*) provision of a guarantee. **2.** (= *gwa- rancja*) *zob.* **poręczenie.**

poręczyć *pf. zob.* **poręczać.**

poręka *f. prawn.* surety; (= *gwarancja*) guar- antee; **z czyjejś poręki** on sb's recommendation; **dać porękę za kogoś** vouch for sb.

porfir *mi geol.* porphyry.

porfirowy *a.* (= *z porfiru*) porphyritic; (*o skale, strukturze, budowie*) porphyritic, porphyrous.

porfiryna *f. geol.* porphyrin.

porfiryt *mi geol.* porphyrite.

porno *n. indecl. pot.* porn. – *a. indecl. pot.* porn; **sklep porno** sex shop; **film porno** porn film.

porno-biznes *mi* sex industry, porn business.

pornografia *f. Gen.* **-ii** pornography; **pornogra- fia miękka** soft-core pornography; **pornografia twarda** hard-core pornography.

pornograficzny *a.* pornographic; *pot.* blue.

pornos *mi Gen.* **-a** *pot.* porn movie, blue movie.

pornus *mi Gen.* **-a** *pot.* = **pornos.**

porobić *pf.* **1.** (= *wytworzyć*) make, do; **porobić notatki** make some notes; **porobić zakupy** do shopping. **2.** (= *popracować*) *pot.* do some work. **~ się** *pf.* **1.** (= *pojawić się w większej ilości*) ap- pear in large amounts; **na drogach porobiły się zaspy** the roads were covered with snowdrifts. **2.** (= *nabrać cech*) become; **porobili się z nich straszni nudziarze** they've become a bunch of terrible bores; **co się z tym/z nim porobiło!** what has become of it/him!

porodowy *a.* parturient; **sala** *l.* **izba porodowa** delivery room; **bóle porodowe** labor pains, pains of childbirth; travail.

porodówka *f. Gen.pl.* **-ek** *pot.* (*oddział*) mater- nity ward; (*sala*) delivery room.

porodzić *pf. rel.* bring forth. **~ się** *pf.* be born.

poronić *pf. pat.* miscarry, have a miscarriage.

poronienie *n. pat.* miscarriage; **poronienie na- wykowe** habitual miscarriage.

poroniony *a.* abortive; **poroniony pomysł** (*głu- pi*) foolish idea; (*nieudany*) abortive idea.

porosnąć *pf.* **-rosnę -rośniesz, -rośnij, -rósł -rosła -rośli** **1.** be overgrown. **2.** *zob.* **porastać.** **3.** (= *urosnąć*) grow.

porost *mi* **1.** (= *wzrost*) growth; **środek na po- rost włosów** hair growth stimulator. **2.** *bot.* lichen (*Lichenes*).

porostnica *f. bot.* liverwort (*Marchantia*); **po- rostnica wielokształtna** hepatica (*Marchantia polymorpha*).

porostowy *a. chem.* lichenic; **kwas porostowy** lichenic acid.

porośle *n. Gen.* **-i** *bot.* epiphyte.

porowatość *f.* porosity.

porowaty *a.* porous; *biol., geol.* poriferous.

porozbijać *pf.* **1.** (= *potłuc*) smash, shatter. **2.** (= *zranić*) smash. **3.** (= *rozstawić*) (*obóz, namio- ty*) pitch up.

porozbiorowy *a.* post-partition.

porozdawać *pf.* **-aję -ajesz, -waj** (*np. ulotki*) hand out; (*np. prezenty*) give out; (*np. role akto- rom*) distribute.

porozdzielać *pf.* **1.** (= *podzielić*) distribute. **2.** (= *przegrodzić*) separate.

porozmawiać *pf.* have a talk, have a word (*z kimś* with sb); **czy mogę z Panem porozmawiać?** can I have a word with you?; **już ja z tobą inaczej porozmawiam!** I will have a word with you!

poroznosić *pf.* **-szę -sisz** distribute.

porozpinany *a.* unbuttoned.

porozrzucać *pf.* scatter.

porozumieć się *pf.* **-em -esz, -miej** *l.* **-m** *zob.* **po- rozumiewać się.**

porozumienie *n.* **1.** (= *jednomyślność*) agree- ment, consensus; **dojść do porozumienia z kimś** reach an agreement with sb; **w porozumieniu z kimś/czymś** in consultation with sb/sth. **2.** (= *umowa*) agreement, understanding; (*zwł. mię- dzynarodowe*) accord; **zawrzeć** *l.* **podpisać poro- zumienie** enter into an agreement.

porozumiewać się *ipf.* **1.** (= *komunikować się*) communicate (*z kimś* with sb); **komunikować się na migi/po polsku** speak in sign language/Pol- ish. **2.** (= *dogadywać się*) reach an agreement.

porozumiewawczo *adv.* knowingly; **mrugnąć porozumiewawczo** wink meaningfully; **spojrzeć porozumiewawczo** look *l.* glance knowingly.

porozumiewawczy *a.* (*służący do porozumiewa- nia się*) agreement; **komisja porozumiewawcza** negotiating committee; (*o uśmiechu, spojrzeniu*) knowing.

porozwalać *pf.* shatter, demolish; **łby wam po- rozwalam!** *przen.* I will knock your brains out!

poroże *n. Gen.pl.* **-y** *myśl.* antlers.

poród *mi* **-o-** childbirth; *form.* parturition; *med.* delivery, labor, *Br.* labour; **poród kleszczo- wy** *med.* forceps delivery; **poród bezbolesny** *med.* anesthetic delivery.

porównać *pf. zob.* **porównywać.** **~ się** *pf. zob.* **porównywać się.**

porównanie *n.* **1.** (= *zestawienie*) comparison; **bez porównania lepszy/gorszy** incomparably better/worse; **w porównaniu z nim** in comparison with him *l.* to him; **dla porównania** for compari- son, per contra; **nie ma porównania** there is no comparison, nothing compares to (it); **drużyna z A nie wytrzymuje porównania z drużyną z B** the team from A compares unfavorably with the team from B; **porównanie dnia z nocą** equinox; **porównanie wiosenne/jesienne** vernal/autumnal equinox. **2.** *ret.* comparison.

porównawczy *a.* comparative; **językoznaw- stwo porównawcze** comparative linguistics; **ska-**

la **porównawcza** comparative scale; **wyrażenie porównawcze** comparative phrase.

porównywać *ipf.* **-nuję** *l.* **-nywam -nujesz** *l.* **-nywasz** compare (*kogoś/coś z kimś/czymś* sb/sth with *l.* to sb/sth); liken (*kogoś/coś z kimś/czymś* sb/sth to sb/sth); **nie można go porównać z innymi studentami** he cannot be compared with other students; **to nie da się z niczym porównać** nothing compares to this. **~ się** *ipf.* **1.** (= *zestawiać siebie z kimś, z czymś*) compare o.s. (*z kimś/czymś* with sb/sth). **2.** (= *być porównanym*) be compared.

porównywalność *f.* comparability.

porównywalny *a.* comparable (*z kimś/czymś l. do kogoś/czegoś* with sb/sth *l.* to sb/sth).

poróżnić *pf.* **-ij** set at variance; **poróżnić kogoś z kimś** set *l.* turn sb against sb else. **~ się** *pf.* quarrel (*z kimś* with sb).

port *mi* **1.** port; harbor, *Br.* harbour; **port lotniczy** airport; **port macierzysty** home port; **port morski** seaport; **port przywozowy** port of entry; **port wolnocłowy** *handl.* free port; **zawinąć do portu** call at the port. **2.** *przen.* haven; harbor, *Br.* harbour. **3.** *komp.* port.

portal *mi bud., komp.* portal.

portalowy *a.* (*o wnęce, rzeźbie*) *komp.* portal.

portatyw *mi muz.* portative organ.

porter *mi* (*piwo*) porter.

portfel *mi Gen.* **-a** *Gen.pl.* **-i** *l.* **-ów 1.** (*na pieniądze*) wallet, billfold. **2.** (= *pakiet*) portfolio; **portfel zamówień** backlog of orders. **3.** (*weksle, papiery wartościowe*) portfolio. **4.** (*wydatki z budżetu państwa*) budget funds (*assigned for financing particular types of expenses*).

portfenetr *mi bud.* port-fenetre.

portier *mp* porter.

portiera *f.* portière.

portierka *f. Gen.pl.* **-ek** portress.

portiernia *f. Gen.pl.* **-i** *l.* **-ń** (porter's) lodge.

portki *pl. Gen.* **-ek** *żart.* pants; *Br.* trousers; **chodzić bez portek** be in rags; **trząść portkami** *l.* **robić w portki** be in a blue funk.

portlandzki *a.* **cement portlandzki** *bud.* Portland cement.

portmonetka *f. Gen.pl.* **-ek** purse.

porto[1] *n. indecl. l. Gen.* **-a** *tylko sing.* (*wino*) port.

porto[2] *n. indecl. l. Gen.* **-a** *pl.* **-a** (*opłata za przesyłkę*) postage.

Portorykanka *f. Gen.pl.* **-ek**, **Portorykańczyk** *mp* Puerto Rican.

portorykański *a.* Puerto Rican.

Portoryko *n. indecl.* Puerto Rico.

portowiec *mp* **-wc-** *pl.* **-y** longshoreman, lumper; *zwł. Br.* docker.

portowy *a.* port; **basen portowy** port basin; **miasto portowe** port town; **robotnik portowy** = **portowiec.**

portrecista *mp*, **portrecistka** *f. Gen.pl.* **-ek** portraitist.

portret *mi* (*obraz*) (*charakterystyka*) portrait; **portret pamięciowy** *kryminologia* composite sketch; *Br.* identikit picture.

portretować *ipf.* (= *malować*) (= *opisywać,*

przedstawiać) portray. **~ się** *ipf.* have one's portrait painted.

portretowy *a.* portrait; **fotografia portretowa** portrait photography; **galeria portretowa** portrait gallery; **malarz portretowy** portrait painter.

Portugalczyk *mp*, **Portugalka** *f. Gen.pl.* **-ek** Portuguese.

Portugalia *f. Gen.* **-ii** Portugal.

portugalski *a.* Portuguese.

portulaka *f. bot.* purslane (*Portulaca*).

portwajn *mi* port.

portyk *mi bud.* portico.

poruczenie *n.* commission; **urzędnik do specjalnych poruczeń** officer-at-large, special task officer.

porucznik *mp* first lieutenant; *Br.* lieutenant.

porucznikostwo *f.* (*stopień*) (first) lieutenancy.

porucznikowski *a.* (first) lieutenant's.

poruszać *ipf.* **1.** (*ręką, głową, skrzydłami*) move; **poruszyć ręką** move one's hand. **2.** (= *wprawiać w ruch*) set in motion. **3.** (= *napędzać*) drive, propel; **poruszyć niebo i ziemię** move heaven and earth, leave no stone unturned. **4.** (= *zwracać uwagę na jakąś kwestię*) bring up. **5.** (= *wzruszać, podniecać*) move, touch; **poruszyć kogoś do żywego** cut sb to the quick. – *pf.* (= *ruszyć kilkakrotnie*) move (*several times*). **~ się** *ipf.* **1.** (= *przemieszczać się*) move; **poruszać się z trudem** move with difficulty; **poruszać się o kulach** walk on crutches; **poruszać się swobodnie w zagadnieniach dochodu narodowego** be knowledgeable about the national income issues. **2.** (= *ruszać swoimi kończynami, ciałem*) move, stir; **poruszył się przez sen** he stirred in his sleep; **flaga poruszała się na wietrze** the flag was fluttering in the wind. – *pf.* (= *ruszać się przez pewien czas*) spend some time moving; **muszę się trochę poruszać** *pot.* I need some exercise.

poruszenie *n.* agitation.

poruszony *a.* **-eni** agitated, moved; **jestem bardzo poruszony wiadomością o jej wypadku** I am very moved by the news about her accident.

poruszyć *pf. zob.* **poruszać. ~ się** *pf. zob.* **poruszać.**

poruta *f. sl.* (= *wstyd*) shame; (= *katastrofa, niepowodzenie*) disaster; **ale poruta!** what a shame!; what a disaster!

porwać *pf.* **-wę -wiesz, -wij 1.** *zob.* **porywać. 2.** (*podrzeć*) tear up. **3.** *lit.* (*popędzić*) speed. **~ się** *pf.* **1.** *zob.* **porywać się. 2.** (= *podrzeć się*) tear up, get torn.

porwanie *n.* kidnapping, abduction; **porwanie dla okupu** kidnapping for ransom.

poryblin *mi bot.* quillwort (*Isoetes*).

poryczeć się *pf.* **-ę -ysz** *pot.* blubber, start sobbing.

porysować *pf.* **1.** (= *spowodować powstanie rys*) scratch. **2.** (*przez jakiś czas*) draw (*for some time*), do a little drawing. **~ się** *pf.* get scratched; (= *popękać*) crack.

poryw *mi* **1.** (*wiatru*) gust; **wiatr w porywach osiągał prędkość 100 km/h** the wind was gusting up to 100 kph. **2.** (*uczuć*) flush; **w pierwszym porywie** on the spur of the moment.

porywacz *mp*, **porywaczka** *f. Gen.pl.* **-ek** kidnapper, abductor; (*samolotu*) hijacker.

porywać *ipf.* **1.** (= *uprowadzać*) kidnap; (*o samolocie*) hijack; **porwać kogoś dla okupu** kidnap sb for ransom; **niech cię diabli porwą!** *przest.* to the devil with you!, the deuce take you! **2.** (*o wietrze, wodzie*) (= *unosić*) sweep away, wash away. **3.** (= *chwytać, łapać gwałtownie*) snatch, grab. **4.** (*o uczuciu*) carry away; **porwać kogoś do walki (z kimś/czymś)** encourage sb to fight (against sb/sth); **przemówienie porwało tłumy** *przen.* the crowd was ecstatic about the speech. **~ się** *ipf.* **1.** (= *chwytać się gwałtownie*) clutch (*za coś* at sth). **2.** (= *gwałtownie wstawać*) spring, jump (*z czegoś* from sth); **porwać się na równe nogi** jump *l.* spring to one's feet. **3.** (= *atakować kogoś*) fall (*na kogoś* on sb); **porwać się na czyjeś życie** make an attempt on sb's life; **porywać się z motyką na słońce** try to square the circle, bite off more than one can chew. **4.** (= *chwytać się za coś nawzajem*) jump at one another.

porywająco *adv.* thrillingly, entrancingly.

porywający *a.* thrilling, entrancing; (*o uśmiechu, śpiewie, wyglądzie*) ravishing.

porywczość *f.* impetuosity, impulsiveness; quick temper.

porywczy *a.* impetuous, impulsive.

porywisty *a.* (*o wietrze*) gusty, boisterous; (*o tańcu*) boisterous.

porządek *mi* **-dk-** **1.** (= *ład*) order; (= *schludność*) tidiness, neatness; **porządek alfabetyczny** alphabetical order; **porządek prawny/publiczny** legal/public order; **przywołać kogoś do porządku** (*np. na zebraniu*) call sb to order; **utrzymywać porządek** *l.* **dbać o porządek** keep order; **zrobić z czymś porządek** put sth in order; **zrobić z kimś porządek** whip sb into line; **zrobić coś dla porządku** do sth just in case; **ładne porządki!** pretty *l.* fine state of affairs!; **to nie w porządku** it's not fair; **jesteś w porządku** you're OK; **w porządku, weź to** all right, take it; **w porządku** all right, OK; **w porządalu** *pot.* okee dokee. **2.** (*plan*) order; **porządek obrad** agenda; **porządek prac** worktime schedule; **porządek dzienny** order of the day; **naturalny** *l.* **przyrodzony porządek** natural order; **spóźnianie się jest u niego na porządku dziennym** being always late is typical of him; **przejść nad czymś do porządku dziennego** disregard sth, wave sth aside. **3.** *bud.* order; **porządek dorycki/joński/koryncki/toskański** Doric/Ionic/Corinthian/Tuscan order.

porządki *pl. Gen.* **-ów** (house)cleaning; **wiosenne/generalne porządki** spring/general housecleaning.

porządkowa *f. Gen.* **-ej** (*liczba*) ordinal.

porządkować *ipf.* (= *sprzątać*) clean up; (= *układać*) tidy up, put in order.

porządkowy *a.* **1.** (= *regulaminowy*) (of) regulation; **kara porządkowa** disciplinary penalty; **przepisy porządkowe** regulations. **2.** (= *kolejny*) serial; **numer porządkowy** serial number; **liczeb-nik porządkowy** *gram.* ordinal number. **– mp** security personnel member.

porządnie *adv.* **1.** (= *dokładnie, starannie*) carefully, thoroughly; (*ubrany, posprzątany*) neatly. **2.** (= *przyzwoicie*) decently. **3.** *pot.* (= *potężnie*) mighty, jolly well; **porządnie zmarznąć/zmęczyć się** get very cold/tired.

porządny *a.* **1.** (= *dokładny, staranny*) careful, thorough; (*o wyglądzie, ubraniu*) neat. **2.** (= *przyzwoity*) decent; **porządna rodzina** decent family. **3.** *pot.* (= *potężny*) strong, sound; **porządny kawał drogi** quite a distance; **porządny mróz** strong frost; **porządny obiad** hearty dinner; **porządna ulewa** heavy downpour.

porzeczka *f. Gen.pl.* **-ek** *bot.* (*owoc*) currant (*Ribes*); **czarna porzeczka** blackcurrant (*Ribes nigrum*); **czerwona porzeczka** redcurrant (*Ribes rubrum*).

porzeczkoagrest *mi bot.* jostaberry (*Ribes culverwellii Josta*).

porzeczkowy *a.* currant.

porzekadło *n.* saying.

porzucać *ipf.* **1.** (= *opuszczać kogoś, coś*) abandon, leave. **2.** (= *zarzucać, zaniedbywać coś*) quit, relinquish; **porzucić studia** quit one's studies; **porzucić pracę** (= *odejść z pracy*) quit work; (= *zastrajkować*) down tools. – *pf.* (= *rzucić coś wiele razy*) throw (*sth several times*).

porzucenie *n.* (= *pozostawienie*) abandonment, desertion; (= *zrezygnowanie*) relinquishment; **porzucenie mienia** *prawn.* abandonment of possessions.

porzucić *pf. zob.* **porzucać**.

porzygać się *pf. pot.* **1.** (= *zwymiotować*) puke. **2.** (= *wymiotując, pobrudzić się*) barf on o.s.

porżnąć *pf.* **1.** (*na części*) cut into pieces. **2.** (= *porysować*) scratch. **3.** (= *pozabijać, pomordować*) butcher, slaughter. **~ się** *pf.* (*siebie*) cut o.s.; (*nawzajem*) cut one another.

posada *f.* **1.** (= *stałe zajęcie*) post, position; **wolna posada** vacancy. **2.** *przest.* (= *podwalina*) foundation; **drżeć w posadach** *t. przen.* shake in its foundations.

posadka *f. zob.* **posada** 1; **ciepła posadka** plum job, sinecure.

posadzić *pf.* **1.** (*roślinę*) plant. **2.** (= *pomóc komuś usiąść*) seat, place. **3.** *pot.* (= *zamknąć kogoś w więzieniu*) send down, lock up.

posadzka *f. Gen.pl.* **-ek** floor; **posadzka drewniana** parquet floor; **posadzka kamienna** tile floor; **posadzka marmurowa** marble floor; **posadzka mozaikowa** inlaid floor.

posadzkarstwo *n.* floor laying.

posadzkarz *mp* floor layer, floorer.

posag *mi* dowry, marriage portion; **bez posagu** dowerless; **łowca posagów** fortune hunter.

posapywać *ipf.* puff, pant.

posażny *a.* having a good dowry, dowered.

posądzać *ipf.* suspect (*kogoś o coś* sb of sth); *form.* impute (*kogoś o coś* sth to sb). **~ się** *ipf.* suspect each other.

posądzenie *n.* imputation, suspicion; **niesłuszne posądzenie** unfair suspicion.

posądzić *pf. zob.* **posądzać**. ~ **się** *pf. zob.* **posądzać się**.

posąg *mi* statue, monument; **milczeć jak posąg** be as silent as the grave.

posągowość *f.* statuesqueness.

posągowy *a.* statuesque.

posążek *mi* -**żk**- *Gen.* -**a** statuette.

posegregować *pf.* (*na grupy, kategorie*) classify; (= *uporządkować*) sort out.

poselski *a.* parliamentary; **mandat poselski** seat in Parliament; **immunitet poselski** parliamentary privilege; **izba poselska** lower chamber of the Polish parliament; **klub poselski** parliamentary club.

poselstwo *n.* **1.** (*placówka dyplomatyczna*) legation. **2.** (*misja, zadanie*) legation. **3.** (= *posłowie*) legates, envoys.

poseł *mp* -**sł**- *pl.* -**owie 1.** (= *deputowany*) member of the Polish parliament. **2.** (*dyplomata*) legate, envoy. **3.** *pot.* (= *wysłannik*) messenger.

posesja *f.* estate, property.

posesywny *a. jęz.* possessive; **zaimek posesywny** possessive pronoun.

posezonowy *a.* off-season; **wyprzedaż posezonowa** clearance sale, summer (winter etc.) sale.

posępnie *adv.* sullenly, gloomily, dismally.

posępność *f.* (*o osobie*) gloominess, sullenness; (*o krajobrazie*) bleakness.

posępny *a.* (*o człowieku*) gloomy, sullen; (*o nastroju*) funereal, gloomy; (*o okolicy, krajobrazie*) bleak.

posiać *pf.* -**sieję** -**siejesz 1.** (*nasiona*) sow, seed; **posiać bakterie** inoculate bacteria; **posiać w kimś ziarno zwątpienia** plant a seed of doubt in sb's mind. **2.** *pot.* (= *zgubić coś*) lose, misplace; **gdzie posiałem moje okulary?** where did I ever put my glasses?

posiadacz *mp*, **posiadaczka** *f. Gen.pl.* -**ek** possessor.

posiadać[1] *ipf.* possess, own; **posiadać rozległą wiedzę** have a vast knowledge.

posiadać[2] *pf.* (= *usiąść kolejno*) sit down, take seats. ~ **się** *ipf.* **nie posiadać się (z radości/gniewu)** be beside o.s. (with joy/rage).

posiadanie *n.* possession, ownership; **brać** *l.* **wziąć** *l.* **objąć coś w posiadanie** take possession of sth; **być w posiadaniu czegoś** be in possession of sth; **po śmierci ojca dom przeszedł w moje posiadanie** after my father's death the house was turned over to me.

posiadłość *f.* estate, property; **posiadłość ziemska** landed estate.

posiadłości *pl. Gen.* -**i** (= *tereny należące do państwa*) dominion, domain; **posiadłości zamorskie** overseas dominion.

posiąść *pf.* -**siądę** -**siądziesz** -**siadł 1.** (= *przyswoić sobie*) master; **posiąść znajomość języka obcego** master a foreign language; **posiąść wszystkie rozumy** be a smart alec, be a know-all. **2.** (= *doprowadzić do stosunku płciowego*) take (*a woman*).

posiedzenie *n.* session, meeting, sitting; **posiedzenie plenarne** plenary session; **posiedzenie komisji** session of a committee, committee meeting; **posiedzenie rządu** government meeting, cabinet meeting; **posiedzenie sądu** court sitting; **posiedzenie zarządu** board meeting; **za jednym posiedzeniem** at one sitting.

posiedzieć *pf.* -**dzę** -**dzisz 1.** (= *siedzieć przez jakiś czas*) sit (*for a while*); **posiedzieć nad projektem** work at a project. **2.** (= *pobyć gdzieś*) stay (*somewhere for a while*). **3.** *pot.* (= *spędzić jakiś czas w więzieniu*) be jailed.

posiekać *pf.* chop up.

posiew *mi* **1.** *roln.* sowing. **2.** *biol.* inoculation.

posiewnica *f. orn.* bean goose (*Anser fabalis*).

posikać *pf. pot.* pee (*coś* on sth). ~ **się** *pf. pot.* pee; **posikać się w majtki** wet one's pants; **posikać się ze śmiechu** split one's sides (laughing).

posilać się *ipf.*, **posilić się** *pf.* have a meal (*czymś* of sth); **posilić się chlebem i mięsem** have a meal of bread and meat.

posiłek *mi* -**łk**- (*pożywienie*) meal.

posiłki *pl. Gen.* -**ów** (*ludzie*) reinforcements, relieving forces; **czekać na nadejście posiłków** wait for reinforcements.

posiłkować się *ipf. lit.* make use (*czymś* of sth).

posiłkowy *a.* auxiliary, ancillary; **słowo posiłkowe** *gram.* auxiliary verb; **oskarżyciel posiłkowy** *prawn.* auxiliary prosecutor (*usu. a member of the public, often a friend or relative of the wronged party*).

posiniaczony *a.* bruised.

posiusiać *pf. pot.* pee, wee-wee (*coś* on sth). ~ **się** *pf. pot.* wet one's drawers.

posiwieć *pf.* turn grey, go grey.

poskarżyć *pf.* denounce (*na kogoś* sb); *szkoln.* sneak. ~ **się** *pf.* **1.** denounce (*na kogoś* sb); *szkoln.* sneak. **2.** (= *wyżalić się*) complain (*na coś* of sth).

poskąpić *pf.* stint (*komuś czegoś* sb on sth); grudge (*komuś czegoś* sb sth).

posklejać *pf.* glue together. ~ **się** *pf.* get stuck together.

poskładać *pf.* **1.** (= *złożyć*) fold (*several things*). **2.** (= *odłożyć*) put (*several things in one place*). **3.** (= *zdeponować pieniądze w banku*) deposit.

poskramiacz *mp* tamer; **poskramiacz dzikich zwierząt** tamer of wild animals; **poskramiacz węży** snake tamer.

poskramiać *ipf.* **1.** (*gniew*) curb, suppress; (*ciekawość*) restrain, suppress. **2.** (*dzikie zwierzę*) tame.

poskręcać *pf.* **1.** (= *wygiąć*) bend, twist. **2.** (= *skręcając, złożyć w całość*) assemble. **3.** (= *zboczyć z drogi*) turn. ~ **się** *pf.* coil up.

poskromić *pf. zob.* **poskramiać**.

poskrom *mi* (*w lecznicy weterynaryjnej*) restraint module, vet rack.

poskutkować *pf.* have effect, work.

posłać[1] *pf.* **poślę poślesz, poślij** *zob.* **posyłać**.

posłać[2] *pf.* **pościelę pościelesz posłał 1.** (= *przygotować posłanie do spania*) make the bed; **jak sobie pościelesz, tak się wyśpisz** you must lie on the bed you have made for yourself. **2.** (= *zło-żyć pościel po spaniu*) do the bed.

posłanie¹ *n. lit.* **1.** (= *nauka*) message. **2.** *polit.* message. **3.** (= *zadanie*) mission.

posłanie² *n.* (= *miejsce do spania*) bed.

posłaniec *mp* **-ńc-** *pl.* **-y** messenger.

posłanka *f. Gen.pl.* **-ek** woman member of the parliament.

posłannictwo *n.* mission.

posłodzić *pf.* sweeten.

posłonek *mi* **-nk-** *Gen.* **-a** *bot.* rockrose (*Helianthemum*).

posłować *ipf.* **1.** (= *być posłem*) be a member of the parliament. **2.** (= *być wysłannikiem*) act as envoy.

posłowie *n. Gen.pl.* **-i** afterword.

posłuch *mi* **1.** (= *autorytet*) influence, authority; **mieć posłuch u podwładnych** gain the ear of one's subordinates; **dawać posłuch komuś** give ear to sb. **2.** (= *posłuszeństwo*) obedience; **ojciec zmusił go do posłuchu** his father forced him to obey.

posłuchać *pf.* **1.** (= *zrobić coś zgodnie z czyjąś wolą*) obey (*kogoś* sb); **posłuchać głosu serca** follow one's heart desire; **nie posłuchał mojej rady** he didn't take my advice. **2.** (= *słuchać czegoś przez jakiś czas*) listen (*for a while*) (*czegoś* to sth); **posłuchać muzyki** listen to music; **posłuchaj, może tam pójdziemy?** listen, why don't we go there?

posłuchanie *n.* (= *audiencja*) audience; **udzielić komuś posłuchania** give sb an audience.

posługa *f.* housework; **oddać komuś ostatnią posługę** pay one's last respects to sb; **chodzić na posługi** *przest.* do housework by the day.

posługacz *mp* attendant, menial.

posługaczka *f. Gen.pl.* **-ek** cleaning lady, *przest.* charwoman.

posługiwać *ipf.* **1.** (= *wykonywać dla kogoś prace domowe*) do housework, char. **2.** (= *być na służbie*) serve (*komuś* sb); **posługiwać w parafii** *rel.* (*o osobie duchownej*) serve in the parish; **posługiwać Bogu** serve God. **~ się** *ipf.* **1.** (= *wykorzystywać coś w jakimś celu*) use (*czymś* sth); (*encyklopedią, słownikiem, mapą*) refer (*czymś* to sth); (= *uciec się do czegoś*) resort (*czymś* to sth); **posługiwać się językiem obcym** speak a foreign language; **posłużył się kłamstwem, by uwolnić się od podejrzeń** he resorted to a lie to clear himself of suspicion. **2.** (= *wyręczać się kimś*) make use (*kimś/czymś* of sb/sth); **szef posługuje się sekretarką w kontaktach z klientami** the boss makes use of his secretary in contacts with the customers. **3.** (= *obsługiwać coś, obchodzić się z czymś*) operate; **nie umiem się posługiwać tym nowym programem komputerowym** I can't operate this new computer program.

posłuszeństwo *n.* obedience, submission; **bierne posłuszeństwo** passive obedience; **ślepe posłuszeństwo** unquestioning obedience; **zmusić kogoś do posłuszeństwa** force sb into submission; **odmówić komuś posłuszeństwa** *l.* **wypowiedzieć komuś posłuszeństwo** refuse sb obedience, fly in the face of sb; **język odmawia mi posłuszeń-**

-stwa my tongue is giving out; **nogi odmawiają mi posłuszeństwa** my feet are killing me; **silnik odmówił posłuszeństwa** the engine wouldn't start.

posłusznie *adv.* obediently, submissively; **melduję posłusznie** *przest. wojsk.* I duly report.

posłuszny *a.* obedient, submissive; **posłuszny woli ojca/prawu** obedient to his father's will/the law.

posłużyć *pf.* **1.** (= *zostać wykorzystanym w jakimś celu*) serve (*za l. jako coś* as sth); **cytat ten posłużył za l. jako motto** the quote served as a motto. **2.** (= *dać dobre rezultaty*) do good; **posłużył mi ten urlop w górach** the vacation in the mountains did me good. **3.** (= *przydać się do czegoś*) be of use; **stary płaszcz jeszcze mi posłuży** I can still use the old coat. **~ się** *pf. zob.* **posługiwać się**.

posmak *mi* **1.** (*odczucie smakowe*) aftertaste. **2.** (= *wrażenie, zabarwienie*) aftertaste, undertone; **sprawa ma posmak skandalu** this sounds like scandal; **po jego wyjeździe pozostał gorzki posmak niepowodzenia misji** his departure left a bitter aftertaste of a futile mission.

posmakować *pf. t. przen.* taste.

posmarować *pf.* **1.** (*coś, jakąś substancją*) smear; spread; (= *natłuścić, naoliwić*) lubricate, grease; **posmarować chleb masłem** butter one's bread; **posmarować chleb dżemem** spread jam on one's bread; **posmarować palec maścią** apply ointment to one's finger. **2.** *pot.* (= *ubrudzić*) soil; bedaub, (be)smear. **3.** *pot., uj.* (= *dać łapówkę*) grease (*sb's palm*), bribe. **~ się** *pf.* **1.** (*siebie jakąś substancją*) put on; **posmarować się kremem** put cream on. **2.** *pot.* (= *ubrudzić się*) get dirty, soil.

posmutnieć *pf.* become sad, sadden.

posnąć *pf.* **-ij 1.** (*o ludziach*) fall asleep. **2.** (*o rybach*) die.

posocznica *f. pat.* septic(a)emia.

posoczniczy *a. pat.* septic(a)emic.

posoka *f.* **1.** *myśl.* (= *farba*) gore, blood. **2.** *pat.* ichor, sanies.

posokowiec *ma* **-wc-** *myśl., kynol.* tracking dog, bloodhound.

posolić *pf.* **-sól** salt, sprinkle with salt.

posortować *pf.* sort; (*według wielkości, rozmiarów*) size.

pospacerować *pf.* **-ruję -rujesz, -ruj** walk, stroll (*for some time*).

pospać *pf.* **-śpię -śpisz, -śpij** sleep (*for some time*); nap, take *l.* have a nap.

pospierać się *pf.* argue (*o coś* about sth).

pospieszny *a. zob.* **pośpieszny**.

posplacać *pf.* **1.** (= *popłacić*) pay. **2.** (= *spłacić*) pay off, pay back, settle; **posplacać długi wobec kogoś** pay (back *l.* off) one's debts to sb.

pospolity *a.* **1.** (= *powszechny, częsty*) common, general; (= *codzienny*) everyday; **rzeczownik pospolity** *gram.* common noun. **2.** (= *przeciętny*) average; (= *zwyczajny, pospolity, banalny*) ordinary, common, commonplace. **3.** (= *prostacki*) boorish, coarse; (*o słowach, wyrażeniach*) (= *ordynarny*) vulgar, coarse. **4.** *lit.* (=

stanowiący ogół) common; **pospolite ruszenie** *hist.* mass levy, universal conscription.

pospołu *adv. przest.* together, jointly.

pospólstwo *n.* **1.** *hist.* commoners, common people, the rabble; *form.* populace. **2.** *pot.* mob, rabble.

posprzątać *pf.* **1.** (= *sprzątnąć*) clean (up). **2.** (= *uporządkować*) tidy up, clear (up); *t. przen.* arrange, set in order; **posprzątać ze stołu** clear the table. **3.** (= *zebrać plony z pola*) gather, harvest, reap (*crops*).

posprzeczać się *pf.* quarrel, fall out (*z kimś* with sb) (*z powodu czegoś* over sth).

posrebrzać *ipf.* **1.** (= *pokryć warstwą srebra*) silver, silver-plate. **2.** *przen.* (*o siwiźnie*) touch with gray *l.* grey; **siwizna/starość/wiek posrebrzyły komuś włosy** *l.* **głowę** sb's hair turned *l.* went gray *l.* grey.

posrebrzany *a.* silver-plated.

post *mi* fast; **ścisły post** *rel.* strict fast; **Wielki Post** *rz.-kat.* Lent; **zachowywać/złamać post** observe/break a fast.

postać[1] *f. pl.* **-i** *l.* **-e 1.** (= *kształt, wygląd*) shape, form; **postać stała/ciekła/gazowa** *zwł. fiz.* solid/liquid/gaseous state; **to zmienia postać rzeczy** it puts a different *l.* new complexion on things *l.* the matter, it changes *l.* alters the complexion of things *l.* the matter; **pod postacią czegoś** *l.* **w postaci czegoś** in the form of sth; **komunia pod dwiema postaciami** *rel.* wafer and wine (*holy communion in the form of consecrated bread and wine*). **2.** (= *sylwetka, figura*) figure; **barczysta postać** broad-shouldered figure. **3.** (= *osobowość; osobistość*) personality, personage, figure; **Adam to znana postać w kręgu literatów** Adam is a well-known figure among men of letters; **ciekawa postać** interesting personality; **wybitna** *l.* **znakomita postać** celebrity, celebrated personality; **psychologia postaci** *psych.* Gestalt psychology. **4.** (= *bohater utworu literackiego, filmu*) character, protagonist; **postać pierwszoplanowa** leading character; **postać drugoplanowa** supporting character; **postać historyczna/legendarna** historical/legendary figure; **odtwarzać/kreować/grać postać** play a character.

postać[2] *pf.* **-stoję -stoisz, -stój** (= *przetrwać jakiś czas, wytrwać, nie ustawać*) stand (*for some time*); **ten dom, choć już stary, postoi jeszcze z 50 lat** this house will stand about 50 years though it is already old.

postać[3] *pf.* **postanę, postaniesz** (= *zjawić się*) *przest.* appear; **ta myśl mi ani w głowie nie postała** I didn't even think about it, this idea did not even come to my mind, it didn't even occur to me; **niech twoja noga już tu nigdy nie postanie!** don't you dare set your foot in here again!

postanawiać *ipf.*, **postanowić** *pf.* decide on; **postanawiać o czymś** decide on *l.* about sth, take *l.* make one's decision on *l.* about sth; **postanowić coś zrobić** decide to do sth *l.* on doing sth; **postanowić czegoś nie robić** decide against doing sth; **postanowić, że...** decide that...

postanowienie *n.* **1.** (= *decyzja*) decision; (= *zamiar*) resolution, resolve; *prawn.* decision,

ruling. **2.** (= *zarządzenie*) regulation; resolution; provision; ordinance.

postarać się *pf.* **1.** (= *zwiększyć starania*) try, do one's best, make an effort; **postaram się to zrobić** I'll try to do this. **2.** (= *dostać, kupić, otrzymać coś, pokonując trudności*) obtain, manage to obtain *l.* get; **postarać się o dobrą posadę** find a good job.

postarzać *ipf.*, **postarzyć** *pf.* age, make look old *l.* older; **broda cię postarza** this beard makes you look old *l.* older. **~ się** *pf.* grow old *l.* older, age; **postarzał się od naszego ostatniego spotkania** he's aged since the last time we met.

postawa *f.* **1.** (= *pozycja, układ ciała*) posture, stance, bearing, position; **wada postawy** faulty posture; **postawa stojąca/siedząca/klęcząca** standing/sitting/kneeling position; **postawa niedbała** slouch; **przyjąć postawę obronną** *t. przen.* adopt a defensive posture. **2.** (= *poza*) pose, position; **postawa wyjściowa** *sport* starting position; **postawa zasadnicza** *wojsk.* attention. **3.** (= *nastawienie, opinia*) attitude, stance, posture; **nastawienie do kogoś** *l.* **czegoś** attitude to *l.* towards sb or sth; **postawa wobec problemu eutanazji** attitude towards euthanasia; (= *pogląd*) outlook, stance; **postawa wobec życia** outlook on life.

postawić *pf.* **1.** (= *ustawić coś*) put, place, set; **postawić żagle** set sail; **postawić komuś horoskop** cast sb's horoscope; **postawić komuś kabałę** tell sb's fortune by cards; **postawić pasjansa** play solitaire, *Br.* patience; **postawić wodę (na kawę** *l.* **herbatę)** put the kettle on; **postawić krok** take a step; **Piotr postawił swoją stopę w Ameryce pierwszy raz w 1990 roku** Peter set foot in America in 1990 for the first time; **postawić komuś ocenę** *l.* **stopień** *szkoln.* give sb a grade; *Br.* give sb a mark; **postawić przecinek** put *l.* place a comma; **postawić kropkę nad i** leave nothing unsaid, make things perfectly clear, lay *l.* put it *l.* everything on the line; **Ewa postawiła krzyżyk na Adamie** Ewa gave up Adam; **postawić problem na głowie** put the cart before the horse; **zawsze chcesz postawić na swoim** you just want to have everything your own way; **postawić kogoś w stan oskarżenia** *prawn.* indict sb, bring sb to trial; **postawić kogoś przed faktem dokonanym** confront sb with an accomplished fact; **postawić kogoś/coś w dobrym/złym świetle** show sb/sth in a good/bad light; **postawić kogoś w trudnej sytuacji** put sb in a difficult position; **postawić się w czyjejś sytuacji** put o.s. in sb's position; **postawić komuś drinka** *pot.* treat sb to a drink, stand sb a drink; **postawić komuś głos** *muz.* train sb's voice; *zob. t.* **stawiać**. **2.** (= *podnieść do pozycji pionowej*) raise, set upright; **poranna kawa postawiła mnie na nogi** a cup of coffee in the morning set me on my feet; **to lekarstwo wkrótce postawi cię na nogi** this medicine will soon have you back on your feet; **postawić uszy** (*gł. o psie*) prick up one's ears. **3.** (= *sformułować*) put forward, propose, suggest; **postawić pytanie** ask *l.* pose a question; **postawić problem** pose *l.* raise *l.* bring up a problem; **postawić tezę** put forward *l.* advance *l.* propose a thesis; **postawić diagnozę** *zwł. med.* make a diagnosis; **postawić warunek** impose *l.* set a condition; **postawić wniosek** *prawn., parl.* move; **postawić komuś** *l.* **przed kimś zadanie** assign sb a task; **postawić sobie coś za cel** set *l.* establish sth as an aim for o.s.; **postawić sobie coś za punkt honoru** make it a point of honor to do sth; **postawić kogoś za wzór do naśladowania dla kogoś innego** set sb as the example for sb else to follow. **4.** (= *zbudować, wznieść*) build, erect, construct. **5.** (*pieniądze w grze hazardowej*) stake, bet (*na coś* on sth); **postawić wszystko na jedną kartę** put all one's eggs in one basket; **postawić na złego konia** back the wrong horse. **6.** (= *umieścić na stanowisku, miejscu pracy*) appoint (*sb to a post*); **sierżant postawił dwóch ludzi przy drzwiach** sergeant put two people at the door. **~ się** *pf.* **1.** *pot.* (= *sprzeciwić się*) put one's foot down; **postawić się w czyimś położeniu** put o.s. in sb's position *l.* place. **2.** *pot.* (= *zrobić coś na pokaz, np. przyjęcie*) show off, do for show; **zastaw się, a postaw się** show off at any cost *l.* all costs.

postawny *a.* strapping.

postąpić *pf. zob.* **postępować.**

postdatować *pf.* postdate.

poste restante *n. indecl.* general delivery; *Br.* poste restante; **wysłać coś na poste restante** send sth general delivery; *Br.* send sth poste restante.

postemplować *pf.* stamp.

posterunek *mi* **-nk-** **1.** (= *wartownik*) sentry, sentinel, guard. **2.** (= *stanowisko, miejsce pełnienia warty*) *zwł. wojsk.* post; checkpoint. **3.** (= *siedziba jednostki policji*) police station; **posterunek straży pożarnej** fire station.

posterunkowy *mp* police officer of the lowest rank; *Br.* constable.

postękiwać *pf.* (= *stękać od czasu do czasu*) groan, moan (*from time to time*).

postęp *mi* **1.** (= *rozwój*) progress, advance, development; **postęp cywilizacyjny** civilization progress; **postęp nauki** *l.* **naukowy** scientific progress, advances in science; **postęp techniczny** technological progress; **iść z postępem** keep up *l.* move with the times, keep abreast of the times. **2.** (= *wzrost, osiągnięcie kolejnego stadium rozwoju*) development, growth; **postępy choroby** development of disease; **robić postępy w nauce niemieckiego** make progress in learning German, make headway in German; **postęp arytmetyczny** *mat.* arithmetic progression; **postęp geometryczny** *mat.* geometric progression. **3.** *górn.* progress, advance; **postęp ściany** wall advance.

postępek *mi* **-pk-** deed; **zły postępek** misdeed.

postępować *ipf.* **1.** (= *iść, postępować naprzód*) walk, go *l.* move forward. **2.** *przen.* (*o pracy*) proceed, progress, advance; **jak postępuje praca?** how is the work progressing *l.* going? **3.** *przen.* (*o chorobie, stanie fizycznym*) develop, progress; **choroba postępuje w zastraszającym tempie** disease develops *l.* progresses at an alarming rate. **4.** (= *robić postępy*) make

progress *l.* headway, advance (*w czymś* in sth). **5.** (= *zachowywać się w określonej sytuacji*) act, behave; **postępować należycie** act *l.* behave properly; **postępować ostrożnie** exercise caution; **źle/dobrze z kimś postępować** treat sb badly/well; **nie zamierzam postępować zgodnie z jego radami** I'm not going to act on his advice.

postępowanie *n.* **1.** (= *zachowanie*) conduct, behavior; **nienaganne postępowanie** irreproachable *l.* impeccable conduct; **właściwe/niewłaściwe postępowanie** appropriate/inappropriate conduct; **zasady** *l.* **normy postępowania** code *l.* rules *l.* standards of conduct. **2.** *prawn.* (legal) proceeding(s); **postępowanie sądowe** court proceeding(s); **postępowanie apelacyjne** appeal *l.* appellate proceeding(s); **postępowanie arbitrażowe** arbitration proceeding(s); **postępowanie cywilne** civil proceeding(s); **postępowanie karne** criminal proceeding(s); **postępowanie dowodowe** taking of evidence, hearing of evidence; **wszcząć postępowanie** institute *l.* initiate proceedings, take a legal action; **zawiesić/umorzyć/zamknąć postępowanie** suspend/discontinue/close proceedings.

postępowość *f. noncount* progressiveness; progressive views.

postępowy *a.* **1.** (*o pisarzu, artyście, haśle, ideach*) (= *nowoczesny*) progressive, advanced. **2.** (= *wzmagający się, stopniowy*) progressive; **upodobnienie postępowe** *fon.* progressive assimilation; **paraliż postępowy** *pat.* general paresis, paralytic dementia.

postglacjalny *a. geol., geogr.* postglacial.

postglacjał *mi geol., geogr.* postglacial period.

postimpresjonista *mp sztuka* postimpressionist.

postimpresjonistyczny *a. sztuka* postimpressionist, Postimpressionistic.

postimpresjonizm *mi sztuka* postimpressionism.

postindustrialny *a.* postindustrial.

postkolonialny *a.* postcolonial.

postkomuna *f. polit., pot.* (*ludzie*) postcommunists; (*system, rządy*) postcommunism.

postkomunista *mp polit.* postcommunist.

postkomunistyczny *a. polit.* postcommunist.

postludium *n. sing. indecl. pl.* **-dia** *Gen.* **-diów** *muz.* postlude.

postmodernistyczny *a.* **1.** *sztuka, teor.lit., fil.* postmodernist. **2.** *architektura* postmodern.

postmodernizm *mi sztuka, teor.lit., fil.* postmodernism.

postny *a.* **1.** *rel.* fast, fasting; *rz.-kat.* Lent; **postne dni** fast *l.* fasting days. **2.** (= *bezmięsny*) meatless, fast(ing).

postojowe *n. Gen.* **-ego** (= *opłata za postój, parkowanie*) parking fee.

postojowy *a.* parking, stopping; **karta postojowa** parking permit *l.* disk; **światła postojowe** *mot.* parking lights.

postój *mi* **-o-** *Gen.pl.* **-ów** *l.* **-oi** **1.** (= *przerwa w podróży*) stopover; **zrobić (sobie) postój** make a stop. **2.** (= *miejsce postoju*) stop; **postój taksó-**

wek cabstand; *Br.* taxi rank; **zakaz postoju** no waiting. **3.** (= *przerwa w produkcji*) stoppage.

postponować *ipf. lit.* slight.

postponowany *a. gram.* postposed; **przyimek postponowany** postposed preposition; **rodzajnik postponowany** postposed article.

postpozycja *f. gram.* postposition.

postrach *mi* **1.** (= *zastraszenie*) terror, fright, intimidation; **budzić postrach** inspire terror; **na postrach** as a deterrent; **strzelać na postrach** fire a warning shot. **2.** (= *osoba budząca strach*) terror; **matematyk był postrachem dla uczniów** maths teacher was the terror of his students.

postradać *pf.* lose; **postradać życie/majątek** lose one's life/possessions; **postradać zmysły** take leave of one's senses.

postraszyć *pf.* scare, frighten.

postronek *mi* -nk- *Gen.* -a cord, rope, string; **mieć nerwy jak postronki** have nerves of steel.

postronny *a.* (= *obcy, nienależący do danego środowiska*) outside; **osoba postronna** outsider, stranger.

postrzał *mi* **1.** (= *postrzelenie kogoś*) shooting, wounding with a shot; (= *rana od postrzelenia*) gunshot wound; **ptak dostał postrzał w skrzydło** bird was shot in the wing. **2.** *pat.* lumbago.

postrzałowy *a.* shot; **rana postrzałowa** gunshot wound.

postrzec *pf.* -strzegę -strzeżesz -strzegł, **postrzegać** *ipf.* perceive.

postrzegalność *f.* perceptibility.

postrzegalny *a.* perceptible.

postrzeganie *n.* perception.

postrzeleniec *mp* -ńc- *pl.* -y *pot.* madcap, daredevil.

postrzelić *pf.* shoot, wound with a shot; **postrzelić kogoś w nogę/rękę** shoot sb in the leg/arm. ~ **się** *pf.* **1.** (*wzajemnie*) shoot each other *l.* one another. **2.** (*samego/samą siebie*) shoot o.s., wound o.s. with a shot.

postrzelony *a.* -eni **1.** (= *zraniony*) shot, wounded (*with a shot*). **2.** *pot.* (= *narwany*) harum-scarum, madcap, daredevil; **Marek biegł jak postrzelony** Mark dashed like a madcap; **to postrzelony chłopak** this boy is a madcap.

postrzeżenie *n. psych.* perception, observation.

postrzępić *pf.* **1.** (= *poszarpać brzegi*) fray. **2.** (= *podrzeć na strzępy*) tear to pieces.

postrzępiony *a.* frayed, ragged, tattered.

postrzygacz *mp roln.* sheep-shearer.

postrzygalnia *f. Gen.pl.* -i *tk.* shearing department *l.* room.

postrzygarka *f. Gen.pl.* -ek *tk.* (rotary cloth-)shearing machine.

postrzyżyny *pl. Gen.* -n *hist.* hair cutting at the age of seven (*an ancient Slav rite*).

postscriptum *n. indecl.* postscript.

postsynchronizacja *f. film* postsynchronization.

postsynchronizacyjny *a. film* postsynchronization.

postukać *pf.* (= *popukać*) knock. ~ **się** *pf.*

knock o.s.; **postukaj się w głowę** *pot.* you must be crazy, are you right in the head?

postukiwać *ipf.* (*od czasu do czasu, z przerwami*) rattle (*from time to time*).

postulat *mi* **1.** (= *żądanie*) postulate, demand; **postulaty wyborcze** *polit.* electoral demands. **2.** *log., mat.* postulate.

postulować *ipf.* postulate.

postument *mi* plinth, pedestal.

postura *f. lit.* (= *wygląd l. pozycja ciała*) posture.

posucha *f. lit.* **1.** (= *susza*) drought, dry spell. **2.** *przen.* (= *brak*) scarcity, dearth, lack (*na coś* of sth); **posucha na wybitne dzieła literackie** dearth of outstanding literary works.

posunąć *pf. zob.* **posuwać**. ~ **się** *pf.* **1.** *zob.* **posuwać się**. **2.** (= *zestarzeć się*) *pot.* age, grow old.

posunięcie *n.* **1.** (= *ruch w niektórych grach*) move. **2.** (= *przemyślany krok w jakimś działaniu*) move; **dobre/złe posunięcie** good/bad move.

posunięty *a.* advanced; **posunięty w czasie/latach** advanced in time/years; **domysły zbyt daleko posunięte** farfetched guesswork; **dbałość o czystość posunięta do przesady** excessive cleanness.

posuwać *ipf.* **1.** (= *przesuwać z miejsca, do przodu*) move, shift; **posunąć pracę naprzód** move the job forward; **posuwać nogami** shuffle one's feet. **2.** *przen.* go too far; **posunąć żart za daleko** carry a joke too far. **3.** *wulg.* (= *odbywać stosunek płciowy*) fuck, screw (*kogoś* sb). ~ **się** *ipf.* **1.** (= *przemieszczać się naprzód*) move along *l.* forward, advance. **2.** (= *robić postępy w jakimś działaniu*) advance, progress; make progress (*in doing sth*); **budowa szkoły posuwa się w błyskawicznym tempie** construction of the school progresses very quickly. **3.** go too far; **posuwać się za daleko** go too far, carry *l.* take things too far; **tym żartem posunąłeś się za daleko** you carried this joke too far; **posuwać się do ostateczności** go to extremes; **nie posunąć się do czegoś** stop short of (doing) sth; **sądzę, że nie posunąłby się do szantażu** I believe he wouldn't resort to blackmail. **4.** (= *odsunąć się*) move. **5.** (= *postarzeć się*) age, grow old *l.* older; **posuwać się w latach** be getting on in years.

posuwistość *f.* ambling *l.* sliding *l.* gliding character (*usu. of movement*).

posuwisty *a.* **1.** (*o kroku, tańcu*) ambling, sliding, gliding; **posuwistym krokiem** at an amble, with long and easy strides. **2.** *techn.* moving, sliding; **ruch posuwisty** plane motion.

posyłać *ipf.* **1.** (= *wyprawić kogoś dokądś*) send; **posyłać kogoś po kogoś** *l.* **coś** send sb for sb/sth; **posyłać kogoś w jakimś celu** send sb to do sth; **posyłać kogoś dokądś** send sb somewhere; **posłać kogoś po lekarza/papierosy** send sb for a doctor/cigarettes; **matka posłała mnie do piekarni po chleb** my mother sent me to the bakery to get some bread; **posłać kogoś do szkoły/na kurs/na korepetycje** send sb to school/a course/private lessons; **posłać kogoś na urlop** give *l.* grant sb a leave (of absence), send sb on vacation *l.* holidays; **posłać kogoś na śmierć** sentence sb to death; **posłać kogoś na zieloną trawkę** fire sb, sack sb; **posłać kogoś do diabła** send sb to hell, send sb packing; **gdzie diabeł nie może, tam babę pośle** no one is proof against a woman's wiles. **2.** (= *przekazać za pośrednictwem poczty, posłańca itp.*) send, mail, post; **posyłać komuś list/paczkę** send sb a letter/parcel; **posłać komuś całusa** blow sb a kiss; **posłać komuś uśmiech** smile at sb, send sb a smile; **posłać komuś spojrzenie** look at sb. **3.** *pot.* (= *kierować coś w jakiś punkt*) send; **posłać piłkę do bramki** send the ball into the goal; **posłać łódź na dno** sink a boat; **posłać komuś kulę** shoot at sb.

posyłki *pl. Gen.* -ek errands; **chłopak na posyłki** errand boy; **chodzić na posyłki** run errands.

posypać *pf.* -pię -piesz, **posypywać** *ipf.* sprinkle, dredge (*coś czymś* sth with sth); **posypać ciasto cukrem** sprinkle a cake with sugar. ~ **się** *pf.*, **posypywać się** *ipf.* (*o pytaniach, listach, prośbach, groźbach*) pour in; (*o oklaskach*) ring out; (*o tynku, liściach itp.*) fall.

poszaleć *pf.* **1.** (= *szaleć jakiś czas*) revel, have fun. **2.** (= *oszaleć jeden po drugim*) go mad (*one by one*).

poszanowanie *n. lit.* **1.** (= *szacunek*) respect. **2.** (= *nienaruszenie czegoś*) observance; **poszanowanie prawa** observance of the law.

poszarpać *pf.* -pię -piesz **1.** tear, rend; **poszarpać na strzępy** tear *l.* rip to pieces *l.* shreds, shred. **2.** *rzad.* (= *potarmosić*) pull.

poszarpany *a.* (*o rzeczach, materiale*) torn, ragged, tattered; (*o skałach*) craggy; (*o powierzchni, brzegu*) jagged; (*o rozmowie, opowiadaniu*) disjointed.

poszarzeć *pf.* (= *zmienić kolor na szary*) grow *l.* turn gray *l.* grey; (*wieczorem*) grow dark.

poszatkować *pf.* (*np. kapustę*) shred.

poszczególny *a.* individual, particular, respective.

poszczekać *pf.* bark (*now and then*).

poszczekiwać *ipf. zob.* **poszczekać**.

poszczepienny *a. med.* postvaccinal.

poszczę *ipf. zob.* **pościć**.

poszczęścić się *pf.* (= *udać się*) come off, go off, turn out well; **(nie) poszczęściło mu się** he was (un)lucky, luck was(n't) on his side, he was in/out of luck.

poszczuć *pf.* set dogs on; **poszczuć kogoś psami** set dogs on sb.

poszczycić się *pf. lit.* boast (*czymś* sth); **mamy czym *l.* możemy czymś się poszczycić** we have sth to our credit, we have sth to boast *l.* be proud of.

poszedł *itd. pf. zob.* **pójść**.

poszerzać *ipf.*, **poszerzyć** *pf.* (*drogę, repertuar*) widen, broaden; (*ubranie, sukienkę*) let out. ~ **się** *ipf.*, **poszerzyć się** *pf.* widen, broaden, become *l.* grow wider.

poszewka *f. Gen.pl.* -ek pillowcase, pillowslip.

poszkodowana *f. Gen.* -ej *zob.* **poszkodowany**2.

poszkodowany1 *a.* suffering, injured; *zwł. prawn.* injured, aggrieved, wronged; **być poszkodowanym** be wronged; incur *l.* suffer damage; **być poszkodowanym przez los** be wronged

by fate; **być poszkodowanym w wypadku** be injured in an accident.

poszkodowany2 *mp* sufferer, victim; *prawn.* injured party, aggrieved party, wronged party.

poszlaka *f. prawn.* circumstantial evidence, indirect evidence, oblique evidence.

poszlakowy *a. prawn.* circumstantial; **dowody poszlakowe** circumstantial evidence; **proces poszlakowy** trial based on circumstantial evidence.

poszła *itd. pf. zob.* **pójść**.

poszperać *pf.* rummage, browse.

poszukać *pf.* look for; **poszukać kogoś/czegoś** look for sb/sth; **poszukać czegoś w pamięci** (= *przypomnieć sobie coś*) remember sth; **poszukać kogoś/czegoś wzrokiem** try to see sb/sth; **poszukał sobie nowej pracy** he found a new job.

poszukiwacz *mp* searcher; **poszukiwacz złota** gold-digger; **poszukiwacz przygód** adventure-seeker, adventurer.

poszukiwaczka *f. Gen.pl.* -ek *zob.* **poszukiwacz.**

poszukiwać *ipf.* search for; **poszukiwać kogoś/czegoś** search for sb/sth; **policja go poszukuje w związku z morderstwem** he's wanted by the police in connection with the murder.

poszukiwanie *n.* **1.** (*szczęścia, prawdy*) quest; (*zaginionej osoby, pracy*) search; (*zbiega, pracy*) hunt; (*złota*) digging; **bezowocne poszukiwanie** fruitless search; **prowadzić poszukiwanie** conduct *l.* make a search; **w poszukiwaniu czegoś** in search *l.* quest of sth; **wyruszył w góry w poszukiwaniu złota** he went to the mountains to dig for gold; **poszukiwania geologiczne** prospecting. **2.** *pl.* (= *badania naukowe*) research.

poszukiwany *a.* **1.** (= *mający popyt*) in-demand, sought-after; **poszukiwany na rynku** in great demand in *l.* on the market. **2.** (= *ceniony, wzięty*) sought-after, renowned. **3.** (= *ścigany*) wanted; **poszukiwany przez policję** wanted by the police.

poszukiwawczy *a.* (*o ekspedycji, oddziale, wierceniach, ekipie*) exploratory, explorative.

poszumieć *pf.* -ę -isz **1.** (*o falach, wietrze, wentylatorze*) hum. **2.** (= *pohulać*) revel.

poszwa *f. Gen.pl.* **poszew** (*na kołdrę*) quilt *l.* duvet cover, duvet case; (*na dużą poduszkę*) pillowcase.

poszybować *pf.* glide.

poszycie *n.* **1.** (*dachu*) roofing; (= *strzecha*) thatch. **2.** (*statku, samolotu*) plating, sheathing, planking. **3.** *rzad.* (= *runo*) undergrowth.

pościć *ipf.* **poszczę, pościsz 1.** (= *głodować*) starve, fast. **2.** *rel.* fast.

poście *m. zob.* **post**.

pościel *f. pl.* -e **1.** (= *bielizna pościelowa*) bed linen. **2.** (= *kołdry, poduszki wraz z bielizną pościelową*) bedding, bedclothes. **3.** (= *posłanie*) bed.

pościelić *pf. dial. zob.* **posłać**.

pościelowy *a.* bed; **bielizna pościelowa** bed linen; **muzyka pościelowa** *żart.* erotic music.

pościg *mi* **1.** (= *pogoń*) chase; *t. przen.* pursuit; **pościg policyjny** police chase; **pościg samo-**

chodowy car chase; **policja natychmiast wszczęła pościg** the police immediately gave chase; **przerwać pościg** give up *l.* abandon the chase; **ruszyć w pościg** set off in pursuit, give pursuit *l.* chase; **w pościgu za czymś** in pursuit of sth. **2.** (= *ścigający ludzie*) pursuers.

pościgowiec *mi* -wc- *Gen.* -a *lotn., wojsk.* pursuit airplane.

pościgowy *a.* pursuit, chase; **akcja pościgowa** chase, pursuit; **samolot pościgowy** *lotn., wojsk.* pursuit plane.

poślad *mi roln.* grain waste, siftings.

pośladek *mi* -dk- *Gen.* -a buttock.

pośladkowy *a. anat.* gluteal; **mięsień pośladkowy** gluteus; **położenie pośladkowe (płodu)** *pat.* breech presentation.

pośledni *a.* mediocre, inferior.

poślinić *pf.* moisten with saliva; (*nieświadomie*) drool; (*znaczek, kopertę*) lick.

poślizg *mi* **1.** (= *przesunięcie się po powierzchni*) slide, skid. **2.** (= *śliskość*) slipperiness. **3.** *techn.* slip, slide, skid; **poślizg kontrolowany** *mot.* power slide; **wpaść w poślizg** go into a skid. **4.** *pot.* (= *opóźnienie*) delay; **oddać dom do użytkowania z poślizgiem** put a house to use with a delay.

poślizgnąć się *pf.* -ij slip; **noga mu się poślizgnęła** his foot slipped.

poślubiać *ipf.,* **poślubić** *pf. lit.* wed.

poślubny *a.* postnuptial; **noc poślubna** wedding night; **podróż poślubna** honeymoon.

pośmiać się *pf.* -eję -ejesz -śmieli *l.* -śmiali laugh (*z czegoś* at sth) spend some time laughing *l.* joking.

pośmiertnie *adv.* (*odznaczyć kogoś, wydać książkę*) posthumously.

pośmiertny *a.* (*o odznaczeniu, hołdzie, wydaniu, dziełach*) posthumous; **maska pośmiertna** death mask; **stężenie pośmiertne** *med.* rigor mortis, cadaveric rigidity; **wspomnienie pośmiertne** obituary, necrology; **odprawa pośmiertna** survivors benefit, bereavement.

pośmiewisko *n.* **1.** (= *kpiny*) ridicule, mockery; **wystawić kogoś/coś na pośmiewisko** make a mockery of sb/sth, make a laughing stock of sb/sth, ridicule sb/sth. **2.** (= *przedmiot kpin*) object of ridicule; **być pośmiewiskiem** be an object of ridicule, be the laughing stock; **wystawić się na pośmiewisko** be exposed to ridicule, make a laughing stock of o.s.

pośniegowy *a.* (*o śliskości, gołoledzi, błocie*) occurring after snowfall.

pośpiech *mi* haste, hurry, rush; hurriedness; **nie ma pośpiechu** there's no hurry *l.* rush; **po co ten pośpiech?** what's the hurry?; **robić coś w pośpiechu** do sth in haste *l.* a hurry, do sth hurriedly; **robić coś bez pośpiechu** do sth without haste *l.* hurrying.

pośpiesznie *adv.* hurriedly, hastily.

pośpieszny *a.* **1.** (= *odbywający się w pośpiechu*) hurried, hasty. **2.** (= *szybszy niż inny*) fast; **pociąg pośpieszny** *kol.* fast train. **3.** (*o decyzji, wniosku, wyjeździe*) (= *przedwczesny*) premature; rash, precipitate, overhasty. **4.** (= *pobież-*

ny, niedbały) perfunctory, cursory. – *mi kol.* (= *pociąg pośpieszny*) fast train; **jechać pośpiesznym do Szczecina** take a fast train to Szczecin, go to Szczecin by fast train.

pośpieszyć *pf.* **1.** (= *udać się*) go, rush (*dokądś* somewhere); **pośpieszyć komuś z pomocą** rush to the aid of sb; **pośpieszyć na ratunek** go to the rescue. **2.** (= *zrobić coś bezzwłocznie*) hasten; **pośpieszył dodać, że bardzo dobrze zna angielski** he hastened to add that he knew English very well.

pośpieszyć się *pf.* **1.** hurry up, be quick; **pośpiesz się, bo się spóźnimy** hurry up, otherwise we'll be late. **2.** *iron.* (= *zrobić coś za wcześnie*) do prematurely, do too early; **pośpieszył się z tymi oświadczynami** he proposed to her too early.

pośredni *a.* **1.** (= *niebezpośredni*) intermediary; intermediate; **mieć na coś pośredni wpływ** have indirect influence on sth, influence sth indirectly; **pośredni związek** indirect connection; **podatek pośredni** *ekon.* indirect tax; **koszty pośrednie** *ekon.* indirect costs *l.* expenses; **wybory pośrednie** *polit.* indirect elections; **ogrzewanie pośrednie** *techn.* indirect heating. **2.** (= *przejściowy*) transitional, intermediate; **coś pośredniego między A i B** sth halfway *l.* intermediate between A and B.

pośredniak *mi Gen.* -a *pot.* job center, employment center.

pośrednictwo *n.* **1.** (= *mediacja*) mediation; **prosić kogoś o pośrednictwo** ask sb for mediation. **2.** (*w interesach*) agency; **za pośrednictwem kogoś/czegoś** through *l.* by the agency of sb/sth; **biuro pośrednictwa pracy** employment agency; **biuro pośrednictwa sprzedaży nieruchomości** real estate agency.

pośredniczka *f. zob.* **pośrednik.**

pośredniczyć *pf.* **1.** (= *prowadzić mediacje*) mediate. **2.** (*w interesach*) act as an agent, provide *l.* offer agency services, be an agent.

pośrednik *mp* **1.** (= *mediator*) mediator. **2.** (*w interesach*) agent; **pośrednik handlu nieruchomościami** real estate agent.

pośrednio *adv.* indirectly.

pośrodku *adv.* + *Gen.* in the middle of (*czegoś* sth).

pośród *pron.* + *Gen.* among(st), amid(st), in the midst of.

poświadczać *ipf.* authenticate, certify, attest.

poświadczenie *n.* **1.** (*czynność*) authentication, certification. **2.** (= *dokument poświadczający coś*) certificate; (= *pokwitowanie*) receipt; **poświadczenie odbioru** proof of receipt, receipt.

poświadczyć *pf. zob.* **poświadczać.**

poświata *f.* glow, glimmer, afterglow.

poświąteczny *a.* (*o dniach, okresie*) occurring after holidays.

poświecić *pf.* light the way, shine the light (*komuś* for sb); **poświeć (mi)!** shine the light for me!

poświerka *f.* **poświerka szponiasta** *orn.* Lapland longspur (*Calcarius lapponicus*).

poświęcać *ipf.* **1.** (= *składać w ofierze*) sacrifice (*coś komuś* sth to sb); (*spotkanie, wykład*) (=

podporządkować coś czemuś) devote (*coś komuś/czemuś* sth to sb/sth); (= *dedykować*) dedicate (*coś komuś* sth to sb); **poświęcić czas/wysiłki na coś** spend time/effort on sth; **konferencja była poświęcona energii atomowej** conference was devoted to nuclear energy; **poświęcać więcej uwagi czemuś** devote more attention to sth. **2.** *rel.* (= *dokonać obrzędu święcenia*) consecrate. ~ **się** *ipf.* **1.** (= *wyrzekać się czegoś*) sacrifice, make a sacrifice; **poświęcać się dla kogoś** make sacrifices for sb; **nie musisz się poświęcać** you don't have to make sacrifices. **2.** (= *zająć się czymś wyłącznie*) devote o.s., dedicate o.s. (*czemuś* to sth); **poświęcił się leksykografii** he devoted *l.* dedicated himself to lexicography.

poświęcenie *n.* **1.** (= *oddanie*) dedication, devotion; **robić coś z poświęceniem** do sth with dedication. **2.** (= *ofiara*) sacrifice; **być gotowym do największych poświęceń** be ready to make the greatest sacrifices. **3.** *rel.* consecration.

poświęcić *pf. zob.* **poświęcać.** ~ **się** *pf. zob.* **poświęcać się.**

poświętnik *ma ent.* scarab (*Scarabaeus*).

poświst *mi* whistle, whizz.

pot *mi* **1.** sweat, perspiration; **krople potu płynęły jej po twarzy** beads of perspiration *l.* sweat ran down her face; **pot leje się z niego** sweat is running off him; **pracować** *l.* **harować w pocie czoła** sweat blood; **siódme poty biją na mnie** I'm all sweaty; **w pocie czoła** by the sweat of one's brow; **wycisnąć z kogoś siódme poty** make sb sweat blood; **zlany potem** dripping with *l.* in sweat; **zlany zimnym potem** in (a) cold sweat. **2.** **poty** perspiration, sweating; **wziąć coś na poty** take a diaphoretic *l.* sudorific.

pot. *abbr.* (= *potocznie*) coll. (*colloquially*).

potajemnie *adv.* secretly, in secret, furtively.

potajemny *a.* *lit.* (*o spotkaniach, planach, związku*) secret, furtive.

potakiwacz *mp Gen.pl.* **-y** *l.* **-ów** *pot.* yes man, yes sayer, sycophant, toady.

potakiwać *ipf.*, **potaknąć** *pf.* **-ij** nod (*in agreement*); say yes; agree (*komuś* with sb).

potakująco *adv.* in assent; **skinąć głową potakująco** nod assent.

potanieć *pf.* cheapen, become cheap *l.* cheaper.

potańcówka *f. Gen.pl.* **-ek** *pot.* dance, dancing party, hop.

potargać *pf.* **1.** (*gł. włosy*) (= *splątać*) tousle. **2.** *przest.* (= *podrzeć*) tear, rend. ~ **się** *pf.* get tousled.

potargować się *pf.* bargain, haggle (*o coś* over sth).

potarmosić *pf.* **-szę -sisz** jostle, pull about.

potas *mi chem.* potassium; **cyjanek potasu** potassium cyanide; **nadmanganian potasu** potassium permanganate.

potasować *pf.* shuffle.

potasowce *pl. Gen.* **-ów** *chem.* alkali metals.

potasowy *a. gł. chem.* potassium.

potaż *mi chem.* potash, potassium carbonate; **potaż kaustyczny** *l.* **żrący** caustic potash.

potąd *adv.* up to here; **mam tego potąd** I've

had it up to here, I've had enough of this; **mam go potąd** I'm fed up with him, I can't take him any more.

potem *adv.* after, afterwards, then, next, later; **w chwilę potem** before long; **wkrótce** *l.* **niedługo potem** shortly after; **ani przedtem, ani potem** neither before nor after; **na potem** for later; **odkładać na potem** hive up *l.* away, lay away.

potencja *f.* **1.** *lit.* (= *moc*) potency, power. **2.** *fizj.* potency. **3.** *fil.* potentiality.

potencjalnie *adv.* potentially.

potencjalność *f.* potency, potential, potentiality.

potencjalny *a.* potential; (*o kliencie*) prospective, prospect; **energia potencjalna** *fiz.* potential energy.

potencjał *mi* **1.** (= *zasób możliwości*) potential; **potencjał wojskowy** *wojsk.* military potential; **potencjał ekonomiczny** *ekon.* economic potential. **2.** *fiz.* potential; **różnica potencjałów** potential difference; **potencjał bioelektryczny** biopotential.

potencjometr *mi fiz.* potentiometer; (= *pokrętło*) dial; **potencjometr oporowy** rheostat.

potencjometria *f. Gen.* **-ii** *fiz.* potentiometry.

potentat *mp* baron, magnate, potentate; (*finansowy, prasowy*) tycoon; (*o państwie l. osobie*) powerbroker; **potentat naftowy** oil magnate; **potentat przemysłowy** baron of industry.

potęga *f.* **1.** (= *siła, moc*) force, might, mightiness, potency; **miażdżąca potęga** steamroller; **na potęgę** a lot, in extreme amounts; **do entej** *l.* **n-tej potęgi** to the Nth degree *l.* power. **2.** (= *znaczenie, przewaga*) power, force; **rosnąć w potęgę** gain power. **3.** (= *mocarstwo*) power, superpower; **potęga morska** sea power; **potęga polityczna/militarna** political/military power. **4.** *mat.* power; **druga potęga** square; **trzecia potęga** cube; **czwarta potęga** biquadrate; **dwa do potęgi drugiej** two to the power of two *l.* to the second power; **dwa do potęgi trzeciej** two to the power of three *l.* to the third power; **podnieść trzy do potęgi czwartej** raise three to the fourth power; **wykładnik potęgi** *mat.* exponent, index.

potęgować *ipf.* **1.** (= *wzmagać*) intensify; (*np. barwę*) exalt; (*napięcie, negatywne skutki*) magnify; (*wrażenie*) enhance. **2.** *mat.* raise to a power. ~ **się** *ipf.* (= *wzmagać się*) intensify, strengthen; (*o odczuciu, emocjach*) swell, heighten.

potępiać *ipf.*, **potępić** *pf.* (= *uznać za złe*) condemn (*jako coś* as sth); denounce (*kogoś/coś jako kogoś/coś* sb/sth as sb/sth); dispraise; **potępiać kogoś za coś** condemn sb for sth; **potępiać z góry** foredoom.

potępiający *a.* castigatory, condemnatory, denunciatory, opprobrious.

potępienie *n.* **1.** (= *krytyka*) condemnation, castigation, censure, denouncement, denunciation. **2.** *rel.* damnation, perdition, reprobation; **skazać na wieczne potępienie** condemn to eternal damnation.

potępieniec *mp* **-ńc-** *pl.* **-y** *rel.* reprobate; **krzyczeć jak potępieniec** scream like one possessed.

potępiony *a. rel.* condemned, reprobate. – *mp lit.* reprobate.

potężnie *adv.* **1.** (= *z dużą siłą*) powerfully; **potężnie zbudowany** heavily built. **2.** (= *ogromnie*) mightily, powerfully.

potężnieć *ipf.* **-eję -ejesz** gain power *l.* might.

potężny *a.* **1.** (= *okazały*) huge, tremendous, voluminous; (*o mężczyźnie*) large, strapping. **2.** (= *wpływowy*) powerful, influential. **3.** (= *bardzo silny*) powerful, violent, forceful, hefty; **potężne cios** *l.* **potężne uderzenie** knock-down, pile driver. **4.** (= *donośny*) resounding, resonant. **5.** (= *intensywny*) intensive, potential.

potknąć się *pf.* **-ij** *zob.* **potykać się.**

potknięcie *n.* stumble, trip; (= *błąd, pomyłka*) stumble, slip-up, lapse.

potłuc *pf.* **-tłukę -tłuczesz -tłukł 1.** (= *rozbić na kawałki*) smash, shatter, break. **2.** (= *spowodować obrażenia*) hurt. **3.** *pot.* (= *zbić*) beat (up). **~ się** *pf.* **1.** (= *rozbić się*) get broken *l.* smashed. **2.** (= *odnieść obrażenia*) get hurt *l.* injured. **3.** *pot.* (= *pobić siebie nawzajem*) beat *l.* hurt each other *l.* one another.

potłuczenie *n.* bruise; injury.

potnę *itd. pf. zob.* **pociąć.**

potnica *f.* **1.** *pat.* dyshidrosis. **2.** *żegl.* sweat *l.* cargo batten.

potnieć *ipf.* **1.** (*o okularach, szybie*) sweat. **2.** (*o osobie, części ciała*) sweat, perspire.

potocznie *adv.* colloquially, informally.

potoczność *f.* colloquialism, informality.

potoczny *a.* (*o nazwie, rozmowie, sprawach*) colloquial, conversational; *biol.* (*o nazwie*) vernacular; **język potoczny** *jęz.* vernacular.

potoczyć *pf.* roll; (*kulę do gry*) bowl; **potoczyć (dookoła) spojrzeniem** look around. **~ się** *pf.* **1.** (= *tocząc się, przesunąć się naprzód*) roll (along). **2.** *przen.* (*o człowieku*) (= *iść ociężale*) waddle (along). **3.** (= *przesunąć się naprzód na kołach*) roll along. **4.** (*o łzach*) (= *popłynąć*) flow, roll. **5.** (*o czasie*) pass by, roll by. **6.** (= *przybrać tok*) take course; **potoczyć się innym torem** change course; **nie mam pojęcia, jak to się dalej potoczy** I don't know what's going to happen next.

potoczystość *f.* volubility.

potoczysty *a.* (*o języku, wierszu*) voluble; (*o nurcie, falach*) flowing.

potoczyście *adv.* (*pisać, mówić*) volubly, glibly; (*płynąć*) briskly.

potok *mi* **1.** (= *strumień*) stream, brook, creek; *geogr.* course, run; **potok górski** mountain stream; **wartki potok** running stream. **2.** (= *duża ilość cieczy*) flow, flood; (*łez, krwi*) stream, flow, gush; (*wyzwisk, pytań*) volley; *przen.* torrent; **potok wyzwisk** hail of abuse, torrent of invective; **wylewać potoki łez** gush with tears; **deszcz leje się potokiem** it's pouring down, it's raining cats and dogs; **potok słów** *przen.* flow *l.* roll *l.* flood of words; **nieprzerwany potok czegoś** constant *l.* steady stream of sth; **potok podróżnych** *przen.* flood of travelers. **3.** *bud.* stream, rivulet.

potomek *mp* **-mk-** *pl.* **-owie** descendant, offspring, issue, progeny.

potomność *f.* posterity, descendants, offspring; **przejść do potomności** be passed on *l.* handed down to posterity.

potomny *a.* **1.** *biol.* filial; **języki potomne** *jęz.* daughter languages. **2.** *przest.* following, next.

potomstwo *n.* offspring, brood, progeny; *Bibl.* seed; *zwł. prawn.* issue; **umrzeć nie pozostawiwszy potomstwa** *prawn.* die without issue; **płodzić potomstwo** procreate.

potop *mi* **1.** *rel.* the Flood, the Deluge. **2.** *dosł. przen.* deluge, flood; **potop szwedzki** *hist.* the Swedish Deluge.

potopowy *a.* diluvial, diluvian.

potowy *a. anat.* sudoriferous, sudoral, sweat, perspiratory; **gruczoł potowy** sweat gland.

potówka *f. Gen.pl.* **-ek** *pat.* prickly heat; **potówka czerwona** heat rash.

potracić *pf.* **-cę -cisz** lose.

potrafić *pf. l. ipf.* **1.** (= *być w stanie coś zrobić*) can, be able, manage; **pokaż, co potrafisz** show us what you can do, show your stuff; **nie bardzo potrafić coś zrobić** be at a loss as to how to do sth; **najlepiej jak potrafię** to the best of my ability; **potrafię się dogadać po hiszpańsku** I can get by in Spanish. **2.** (= *postępować ekstremalnie*) be capable of; **potrafił zasnąć przy stole** he could fall asleep at the table; **Ewa potrafiła mnie ignorować przez tydzień** Ewa could ignore me for a week.

potrajać *ipf.* triplicate, triple, treble. **~ się** *ipf.* triple, treble.

potraktować *pf.* **1.** (= *odnieść się do kogoś / czegoś*) treat; **potraktował to jako ostrzeżenie** he treated it as a warning; **ostro coś potraktować** make short shrift of sth; **potraktować kogoś łagodnie** let sb off lightly; **potraktować kogoś oschle** give sb the brush-off; **potraktować lekceważąco** snub. **2.** *chem.* treat. **3.** *przest.* treat to; **potraktować kogoś czymś** *przen.* (= *uderzyć*) hit sb with sth.

potransfuzyjny *a. med.* (*o wstrząsie, szoku*) posttransfusion.

potraw *mi zwł. roln.* rowen, aftermath.

potrawa *f. kulin.* dish, plate, course; **spis potraw** menu; **potrawa duszona** stew; **potrawa smażona** fry-up.

potrawka *f. Gen.pl.* **-ek** *kulin.* fricassee; **potrawka z zająca** jugged hare.

potrącać *ipf.* **1.** (= *niechcący uderzać*) jostle, jog, poke, push. **2.** (= *spowodować obrażenia u pieszego*) hit; **Tomek został potrącony przez ciężarówkę** Tomek was hit by a truck. **3.** (= *napomknąć*) touch upon, mention briefly. **4.** (= *odliczać jakąś sumę*) deduct; **potrącać z poborów** (*tytułem np. składki*) check off; (*tytułem kary*) dock sb's pay. **~ się** *ipf.* jog, jostle, nudge.

potrącenie *n.* **1.** (*wypadek*) accident involving a pedestrian. **2.** (= *potrącona suma*) (*jako kara*) deduction, dockage; (*jako składka*) check-off.

potrącić *pf. zob.* **potrącać. ~ się** *pf. zob.* **potrącać się.**

potrenować *pf.* practice, train.

potroić *pf.* **-ję -isz, -ój** *zob.* **potrajać. ~ się** *pf. zob.* **potrajać się.**

po trosze *adv. lit.* a little, bit by bit; **on jest po trosze prawnikiem** he is somewhat of a lawyer.

po troszeczku *adv.* a very little; **wszystkiego po troszeczku** just a very little bit of everything.

po troszku *adv. zob.* **po trosze.**

potrójny *a.* triple, threefold, triplex; **potrójny drink** *kulin.* triple; **potrójny podział** trichotomy.

potrudzić się *pf.* **1.** (= *wysilić się*) make an effort, take the trouble. **2.** *lit.* (= *pójść*) go; **czy zechciałaby się pani potrudzić do nas dziś po południu?** would you kindly come to see us this afternoon?, would you like to join us this afternoon?

potrwać *pf.* last, take; **to nie potrwa długo** it won't take long; **potrwać kilka lat** stretch over several years.

potrzask *mi myśl.* trap; **znaleźć się w potrzasku** *t. przen.* be trapped.

potrzaskać *pf.* **1.** (= *połamać*) smash, shatter, break to pieces. **2.** (= *popękać*) crack, break. **~ się** *pf.* (= *połamać się*) get smashed *l.* broken to pieces; (*w wypadku*) get injured *l.* hurt.

potrząsać *ipf.*, **potrząsnąć** *pf.* **-ij** (*głową, pięścią*) shake; (*szablą, kijem*) brandish; **potrząsnąć kiesą** spend (a lot of) money on sth.

potrzeba¹ *f.* **1.** (= *niezbędność*) need, necessity; **coś wykonane z potrzeby serca** a labor of love; **moja postawa wynika z głębokiej potrzeby niesienia pomocy** my approach stems from a profound need to give help; **nie ma potrzeby, aby...** there's no need to...; **jeśli zajdzie potrzeba, to...** if a need arises then...; **w miarę potrzeby możesz zadzwonić do mnie** if necessary you can call me; **zaspokajać czyjeś potrzeby** cater for sb's needs, satisfy *l.* serve sb's needs; **zabezpieczać czyjeś potrzeby** make provision for sb; **nagła potrzeba** emergency; **potrzeba chwili** expediency; **bez potrzeby** needlessly, unnecessarily; **potrzeba fizjologiczna** *l.* **naturalna** physiological need, need to relieve o.s.; **iść za (swoją) potrzebą** go relieve o.s.; **nie ma potrzeby się spieszyć** there's no need to hurry; **potrzeba jest matką wynalazku** necessity is the mother of invention. **2.** *pl.* (= *rzeczy, bez których trudno się obejść*) needs; **artykuły pierwszej potrzeby** necessities; **uprawa na własne potrzeby** subsistence crop. **3.** *przest.* (= *ciężkie położenie*) need; **w (pilnej) potrzebie** in (urgent) need; **opuścić kogoś w potrzebie** leave sb in the lurch, let sb down in his extremity.

potrzeba² *v. indecl.* need; **potrzeba mi pieniędzy na zakończenie budowy domu** I need money to finish the construction of the house; **czego ci potrzeba?** what do you need?; **nic mi więcej nie potrzeba** that's all I need *l.* want; **znów powiedziałaś więcej niż potrzeba** you said more than necessary again; **tego właśnie mi potrzeba** that's exactly what I need, that's the very thing I need.

potrzebny *a.* needed, necessary; **potrzebna kelnerka od zaraz** wait staff wanted, start immediately; **potrzebny jest mi spokój** I need peace *l.* quiet; **potrzebny jak dziura w moście** I need it like I need a hole in the head; **nie być komuś potrzebnym** be of no use to sb.

potrzebować *ipf.* need, want; **potrzebuje pie-**

niędzy na wakacje he needs money for vacation; **dziecko potrzebuje opieki** baby needs care; **nie potrzebujesz się spieszyć** you needn't hurry; **bardzo potrzebować czegoś** be badly off for sth; **nie potrzebujesz mi tego mówić** you don't need to tell me that.

potrzebująca *f. Gen.* **-ej** *zob.* **potrzebujący.**

potrzebujący *mp* needy, needful, in need; **pomoc dla najbardziej potrzebujących** help for the poor *l.* the needy.

potrzeć *pf.* **-trę -trzesz, -trzyj, -tarł** *zob.* **pocierać.**

potrzeszcz *ma Gen.pl.* **-y** *l.* **-ów** *orn.* corn bunting (*Emberiza l. Miliaria calandra*).

potrzos *ma Gen.pl.* **-y** *orn.* reed bunting (*Emberiza schoeniclus*).

potrzymać *pf.* **1.** (= *uchwycić na jakiś czas*) hold. **2.** (= *przechować przez jakiś czas*) keep. **3.** (*o mrozie, zimie*) (= *potrwać*) last. **~ się** *pf.* (= *trzymać siebie nawzajem przez jakiś czas*) hold each other; **potrzymali się przez chwilę za ręce** they held each other's hands for a while.

potulnie *adv.* acquiescently, docilely, meekly, tamely.

potulny *a.* acquiescent, biddable, docile, meek, sheepish; **potulny jak baranek** meek and mild, meek as a lamb.

potuptać *pf. dziec.* toddle.

poturbować *pf.* savage, rough up. **~ się** *pf.* **1.** hurt each other *l.* one antoher. **2.** get hurt.

poturlać się *pf.* roll.

potwarz *f. pl.* **-e** slander, defamation, calumny.

potwierdzać *ipf.* confirm, affirm; (*czek*) certify; (*opinię, wersję wydarzeń itp.*) bear out; (*teorię*) support, corroborate, verify; (*zarzut*) sustain, vindicate; (*zasadę, stwierdzenie*) validate; **potwierdzać odbiór czegoś** acknowledge (receipt of) sth. **~ się** *ipf.* be confirmed *l.* corroborated *l.* validated.

potwierdzenie *n.* confirmation, corroboration; validation, verification; **potwierdzenie odbioru** notice of receipt; **potwierdzenie spłaty** *fin.* acquittance.

potwierdzić *pf. zob.* **potwierdzać.** **~ się** *pf. zob.* **potwierdzać się.**

potwora *f. żart.* ugly person; **każda potwora znajdzie swego amatora** there is no goose so gray in the lake that cannot find a gander of her make.

potworniak *mi Gen.* **-a** *pat.* teratoma.

potwornie *adv.* **1.** (= *odrażająco*) monstrously, horribly. **2.** *pot.* (= *znacznie, bardzo*) terribly, awfully; **jestem potwornie głodny** I'm terribly hungry; **potwornie gorąco** boiling hot; **czuć się/wyglądać potwornie** feel/look like hell *l.* shit.

potworność *f.* **1.** (= *okropność*) abomination, atrociousness, atrocity, heinousness. **2.** (*np. o budowli, obrazie*) (= *coś budzącego grozę*) monstrosity. **3.** *pat.* monstrosity.

potworny *a.* **1.** (= *przerażający*) atrocious, monstrous; (*o zbrodni*) heinous. **2.** (= *wstrętny, brzydki*) horrible, hideous. **3.** *pot.* (= *silny, zna-*

czny) huge, terrible, stupendous, enormous; **potworny bałagan/hałas** a hell of a mess/noise.

potwór *mp* -o- *pl.* -y 1. (= *monstrum*) monster. 2. (= *zwyrodnialec*) monster.

potyczka *f. Gen.pl.* -ek 1. (= *utarczka*) skirmish, encounter, clash; **stoczyć potyczkę** engage in a skirmish *l.* fray. 2. (= *spór*) dispute, passage; **potyczka słowna** shouting match.

potykać się *ipf.* 1. (*tracąc równowagę*) trip, stumble (*o coś* over sth); falter. 2. (= *popełniać błąd*) slip, make a slip-up. 3. (= *w bitwie*) encounter; (*w turnieju*) tourney.

potylica *f. anat.* occiput.

potyliczny *a. anat.* occipital; **kość potyliczna** occipital (bone); **płat potyliczny** occipital lobe.

pouczać *ipf. Gen.pl.* (= *informować, tłumaczyć*) instruct. 2. (= *upominać*) admonish. 3. (= *prawić kazania*) patronize.

pouczający *a.* didactic, educative, informative; (*o przykładzie, książce*) instructive.

pouczenie *n.* 1. (= *wskazówka*) advice, hint, information. 2. (= *upomnienie*) admonishment.

pouczyć *pf. zob.* **pouczać**. ~ **się** *pf.* (= *uczyć się przez jakiś czas*) study for some time, study a bit.

poufale *adv.* familiarly, confidentially; (*zachowywać się*) intimately.

poufalić się *ipf.* take liberties, be familiar (*z kimś* with sb).

poufałość *f.* familiarity, intimacy, confidentiality; **pozwalać sobie na poufałość wobec kogoś** take liberties/freedoms with sb.

poufały *a.* familiar, confidential, hail-fellow-well-met; (*o stosunkach*) intimate; **zbyt poufały** overfamiliar.

poufnie *adv.* confidentially.

poufność *f.* confidentiality; **oświadczenie o zachowaniu poufności** *prawn.* confidentiality *l.* privacy statement.

poufny *a.* 1. (= *sekretny*) confidential; **ściśle poufne** strictly confidential; **poufne** (*na korespondencji*) confidential; **poufna informacja** tip, tip-off, confidence, privileged information. 2. (= *serdeczny*) friendly.

poukładać *pf.* arrange; **poukładać dzieci do snu** tuck children in; **poukładać sobie wszystko po kolei** get *l.* have all one's ducks in a row. ~ **się** *pf.* (*do snu*) go to bed.

pourazowy *a. med., pat.* post-traumatic; **stres pourazowy** post-traumatic stress disorder.

pourodzeniowy *a. med.* postnatal.

powab *mi lit.* allure, appeal, attraction, charm.

powabnie *adv.* charmingly, alluringly, attractively.

powabny *a.* charming, alluring, attractive.

powaga *f.* 1. (= *opanowanie, zrównoważenie*) seriousness, sobriety, solemnity; (*śmiertelna, całkowita*) earnestness; **zachować powagę** keep a straight face; **brak powagi** frivolity, levity. 2. (= *prestiż, t. ważność*) authority, prestige, high standing; (*sytuacji*) severity, gravity, graveness; (*chwili*) seriousness, importance; **nadawać sobie powagi** assume an air of importance.

powalać[1] *pf.* (= *zabrudzić, umazać*) soil.

powalać[2] *ipf.* 1. (= *przewracać*) knock down; **powalać kogoś ciosem** send sb sprawling; **powalać kogoś na deski** *boks* knock sb to the canvas; (*o chorobie*) strike down; **powalać kogoś na kolana** *przen.* bring the house down, blow sb's mind, knock sb out. 2. (= *uśmiercać strzałem*) cut down. ~ **się** *pf.* 1. get soiled *l.* smeared. 2. fall.

powalczyć *pf.* fight.

powalić *pf. zob.* **powalać**. ~ **się** *pf. pot.* (= *upaść*) fall.

powalony *a.* -eni 1. prostrate; **powalony chorobą** prostrated by illness; **drzewa powalone przez wichurę** trees blown down by the wind. 2. (= *szalony, głupi*) *pot.* crazy, nuts.

powała *f.* ceiling.

powałęsać się *pf. pot.* wander, roam.

powariować *pf.* 1. go crazy *l.* mad; **czyście powariowali?** are you crazy? 2. (*o dzieciach*) (= *pobawić się*) play around.

poważać *ipf.* esteem; **poważać kogoś** hold sb in (high) esteem, respect sb. ~ **się[1]** *ipf.* (= *szanować się*) respect each other *l.* one another.

poważać się[2] *ipf.* (= *mieć odwagę coś zrobić*) dare.

poważanie *n.* esteem, estimation, respect; **cieszyć się poważaniem wśród uczniów** be highly esteemed by one's students, be held in high esteem by one's students; **łącząc wyrazy poważania** *l.* **z poważaniem** truly *l.* faithfully yours; **darzyć kogoś poważaniem** respect sb, hold sb in high esteem *l.* repute.

poważany *a.* esteemed, held in (high) esteem, respectable, highly considered; **wielce poważany** *przen.* at a premium.

poważnie *adv.* 1. (= *z powagą*) in a dignified manner, with dignity, gravely; **wyglądać poważnie** (= *budzić szacunek*) look dignified; (= *wyglądać staro*) show one's age. 2. (= *na serio*) seriously, in earnest; **Adam myśli o Ewie poważnie** Adam is thinking seriously about Eve; **byłem tam, poważnie!** *pot.* I was there, no kidding *l.* honestly!; **poważnie?** *pot.* are you serious?; **całkiem na poważnie** in deadly earnest; **chłopak/dziewczyna na poważnie** steady boyfriend/girlfriend; **brać coś na poważnie** take sth seriously; **mówiąc poważnie** jokes apart; **porozmawiać poważnie** (*zwł. o interesach*) talk turkey. 3. (= *w sposób znaczący*) considerably, seriously, in great measure, greatly; **poważnie chory** seriously ill.

poważnieć *ipf.* become serious; (*o młodzieńcu*) settle down, grow up.

poważny *a.* 1. (= *pełen powagi*) serious, grave, solemn, dignified; (*o chorobie*) severe, serious; (*o kłopotach, zmartwieniach*) serious, deep, acute; (*o minie, twarzy*) sober; **mieć poważne zamiary wobec kogoś** be serious (about marrying sb); **muzyka poważna** *muz.* classical music; **poważny wiek** *l.* **poważne lata** respectable old age. 2. (*o firmie, organizacji, profesorze, uczonym*) (= *mający autorytet*) respectable. 3. (= *istotny*) important, weighty, grave; **poważny zabieg** *chir.* major surgery; **poważny związek** meaningful relationship; **to nic poważnego** it's only a pinprick; **ponieść poważne straty** (*o przedsiębiorstwie*) suffer heavy losses; **poważne przestępstwo** *prawn.* serious offense; **odgrywać poważną rolę w czymś** play an important part in sth.

poważyć się *pf. zob.* **poważać się.**

powąchać *pf.* smell, sniff; **nigdy nie powąchał prochu** *przen.* he never heard a shot fired. **~ się** *pf.* smell *l.* sniff at each other *l.* one another.

powątpiewać *ipf.* doubt, be dubious.

powątpiewanie *n.* doubtfulness, dubiousness; **z powątpiewaniem** doubtfully, doubtingly, dubiously.

poweseleć *pf.* cheer up, brighten (up).

powetować *pf.* (*stratę*) make up for, retrieve; **powetować sobie stratę** *fin.* indemnify o.s.

powędrować *pf.* **1.** (= *pójść dokądś*) go, wander; (*o wzroku, myślach*) wander; **powędrować do szpitala/więzienia** *pot.* go to hospital/prison; **powędrował dokądś wzrokiem/myślami** his glance/mind wandered. **2.** (= *być przekazanym*) be shipped, be sent; **węgiel powędrował z kopalni do Gdyni** the coal was shipped from the mine to Gdynia; **powędrować do kosza** *l.* **lamusa** (*o planach*) go by the board.

powiać *pf.* **-eję -ejesz** *zob.* **powiewać.**

powiadać *ipf. przest.* say, tell; **na spotkaniu, powiadam ci, było bardzo przyjemnie** I'm telling you, the meeting was very nice; **a więc powiada pan, że będzie ładna pogoda** so you're saying that the wheather will be nice; **jak powiada przysłowie** as the proverb has it; **powiada się, że...** they say...

powiadamiać *ipf.*, **powiadomić** *pf. lit.* inform (*kogoś o czymś* sb about *l.* of sth); notify (*kogoś o czymś* sb of sth); **mam zaszczyt powiadomić Pana** I have the honor to inform you; **powiadomić kogoś o czymś nieprzyjemnym** break the bad news to sb.

powiastka *f. Gen.pl.* **-ek** story, tale; **powiastka filozoficzna** philosophical tale.

powiat *mi* **1.** (*okręg administracyjny*) district. **2.** *pot.* (*władze tego okręgu*) district authorities.

powiatowy *a.* district.

powiązać *pf.* **-wiążę -wiążesz 1.** (= *związać*) tie, bind, join, connect, unite, link. **2.** (= *skrępować*) tie (up). **3.** (= *skojarzyć*) associate, colligate; **powiązać fakt z faktem** put two and two together.

powiązania *pl. Gen.* **-ń** relations.

powiązany *a.* interlinked, related, interrelated; **minister jest powiązany z tą sprawą** minister is involved in this affair.

powić *pf.* **-wiję -wijesz, -wij** *lit.* give birth, be brought to bed, usher into this world.

powidła *pl. Gen.* **-eł** plum confection, plum jam.

powiedzenie *n.* **1.** (= *komunikowanie*) saying; **mieć coś do powiedzenia** (= *chcieć coś wyjaśnić*) have sth to say; (*liczyć się*) have a say *l.* voice in sth. **2.** (= *aforyzm*) saying, adage; **utarte powiedzenie** byword.

powiedziany *a.* said; **nie jest powiedziane, że przyjedzie** it's not said *l.* certain that he/she will

come; **mało powiedziane!** that's an understatement!; **dobrze powiedziane** touché; **w regulaminie powiedziane jest, że...** it says *l.* is stated in the regulations that...

powiedzieć *pf.* **-wiem -wiesz -wiedzą, -wiedz 1.** (= *wyrazić coś słowami*) say, tell; **powiem ci w sekrecie** I'll tell you in secret; **powiedz mi wprost** give it straight to me; **co ty powiesz!?** you don't say (so)!, no kidding!, no shit!; **co powiesz na...** how about...; **ani słowa mi nie powiedziała** she didn't say a word; **prawdę** *l.* **szczerze powiedziawszy** frankly speaking; **powiedzieć prawdę w oczy** give sb a piece of one's mind; **powiedzieć komuś do słuchu** give sb an earful, send sb away with a flea in their ear; **powiedziałem sobie, że to już ostatni raz** I told myself that it was the last time; **powiedzieć coś w nieodpowiedniej chwili** say sth badly, say sth at an inopportune moment; **powiedzieć coś nie w porę** mistime sth; **powiedzieć coś przez łzy** weep sth out; **powiedzieć coś niewiele myśląc** say sth unguarded, blurt sth out; **powiedzieć, co się myśli** nail one's colors to the mast; **nie umiem powiedzieć** ask me another; **jak to powiedzieć** how shall I put it; **powiedzieć swoje** speak one's mind; **powiedzieć swoje zdanie** say sth out; **wystarczy powiedzieć, że...** suffice it to say that...; **powiedzieć jasno, że...** make it plain that...; **powiedzieć ostatnie słowo** say the last word; **powiedzieć komuś komplement** compliment sb, pay a compliment to sb; **powiedziałem do niej po imieniu** I addressed her by her first name; **łatwiej powiedzieć, niż zrobić** (it's) easier said than done; **chcę przez to powiedzieć, że...** what I mean is that...; **gdy się powiedziało A, trzeba powiedzieć B** in for a penny, in for a pound; **odszczekać** *l.* **odwołać to, co się powiedziało** eat *l.* swallow one's words; **tak mi się tylko powiedziało** I didn't mean it; **powiedzieć coś na kogoś** inform *l.* snitch *l.* rat *l.* tell on sb; **nic mi to nie powiedziało** it didn't ring a bell; **swoje powiedziałem** *pot.* I said what I had to say; **powiedział, co wiedział** *pot.* he said what he knew; **że tak powiem** so to say, if I may say so; **sam powiedz** *l.* **powiedz sam** wouldn't you agree?; **powiedzmy** (let's) say; **a jeśli to będzie, powiedzmy, piękna dziewczyna?** and if that's going to be, say, a beautiful girl? **2.** (= *oznajmić*) inform, announce, say; **co chcesz przez to powiedzieć?** what do you mean by that?; **to za mało/za dużo powiedziane** that's an understatement/overstatement; **nie można powiedzieć, by była zbyt miła** you can't say she's too nice; **kto by to powiedział?** who would have thought it?; **w Biblii powiedziane jest: Nie lękajcie się** the Bible says *l.* reads: Do not fear.

powiedzonko *n. Gen.pl.* **-ek** *pot.* tag, key phrase.

powieka *f.* eyelid, lid; **cień do powiek** eye shadow; **mrużyć powieki** squint; **bez zmrużenia powiek** without batting an eyelid; **spędzać komuś sen z powiek** loom large in sb's mind; **powieki mi się kleiły** I could barely keep my eyes open; **zamknąć komuś powieki** be at sb's deathbed; **zamknąć powieki** breathe one's last, die; **zatrze-**

potać powiekami (*zwłaszcza zalotnie*) bat one's eyelashes.

powiekowy *a. anat.* palpebral; **tarczka powiekowa** tarsus.

powielacz *mi Gen.* **-a** *techn.* duplicator, copier; *el.* multiplier.

powielać *ipf.*, **powielić** *pf.* copy, duplicate, reproduce; **powielać na ksero** xerox, photocopy; **powielać stereotyp** *socjol.* stereotype.

powiernica *f.* confidante.

powiernictwo *n.* **1.** *polit.* trust. **2.** *prawn.* trust.

powierniczka *f. Gen.pl.* **-ek** confidante.

powierniczy *a.* **1.** *polit.* trust; **terytorium powiernicze** trust territory. **2.** *prawn.* trust, fiduciary; **majątek** *l.* **fundusz powierniczy** trust fund; **zarząd powierniczy** trust.

powiernik *mp* **1.** (= *człowiek zaufany*) confidant, repository. **2.** *prawn.* trustee; fiduciary. **3.** *rel.* confessor, father confessor.

powierzać *ipf.* **1.** (= *zlecić coś*) entrust, commend, commit, consign; **powierzać coś komuś** entrust sb with sth; **powierzać komuś stanowisko** *admin.* appoint sb to a post, induct sb into a post. **2.** (= *zawierzyć*) trust, entrust, commit; **powierzać matce/ojcu opiekę nad dzieckiem** *prawn.* give *l.* grant *l.* award the mother/father custody of the child. **3.** (*tajemnicę*) (= *ujawniać*) confide. **~ się** *ipf.* confide to, put o.s. into sb's hands.

powierzchnia *f. Gen.pl.* **-i** **1.** (= *to, co na zewnątrz*) surface, plane, area; **dolna powierzchnia** underside, underneath; **górna powierzchnia** upside; **powierzchnia dachu** rooftop; **zniknąć z powierzchni ziemi** disappear *l.* vanish off the face of the earth; **utrzymać się na powierzchni** buoy; **zetrzeć coś z powierzchni ziemi** wipe sth out, wipe sth off the map; **wypłynąć na powierzchnię** rise *l.* float to the surface; **wydobyć na powierzchnię** bring to the surface; **zniknąć pod powierzchnią** bob below *l.* under; **nad powierzchnią ziemi** above ground; **nad powierzchnią morza** *geogr.* above sea level; **pod powierzchnią morza/oceanu** undersea. **2.** (= *obszar, przestrzeń*) area; **powierzchnia handlowa** commercial area; **powierzchnia mieszkalna** living space *l.* area; **powierzchnia kraju** area of a country; **powierzchnia tego kraju jest cztery razy większa niż Polski** this country's area is four times larger than Poland's; **powierzchnia ziemi** earth, ground; (*w akrach*) acreage. **3.** *geom.* area, plane. **4.** *górn.* surface.

powierzchniowo *adv.* superficially; **substancja powierzchniowo czynna** *chem.* surfactant.

powierzchniowy *a.* **1.** (= *dotyczący powierzchni*) surface, areal; **wody powierzchniowe** *geogr.* surface waters. **2.** (= *pracujący na powierzchni*) surface.

powierzchownie *adv.* superficially, perfunctorily; **robić coś powierzchownie** scratch the surface.

powierzchowność *f.* **1.** (*cecha*) exterior, appearance; **o miłej powierzchowności** clean-cut.

2. (= *niedokładność*) superficiality, perfunctoriness, shallowness.

powierzchowny *a.* **1.** (= *płytki*) surface, shallow; (*o ranie, oparzeniu*) slight, cutaneous. **2.** (= *pobieżny*) perfunctory, cursory; (*o wiedzy, obserwacji, znajomości czegoś*) surface, superficial.

powierzyć *pf. zob.* **powierzać**. **~ się** *pf. zob.* **powierzać się**.

powiesić *pf.* **-szę -sisz** **1.** (= *zawiesić*) hang up; **powiesić coś na kołku** (= *zakończyć działalność / karierę*) *pot.* hang sth up. **2.** (= *uśmiercić przez powieszenie*) hang, gibbet. **~ się** *pf.* (= *uśmiercić się przez powieszenie*) hang o.s.

powieścidło *n. Gen.pl.* **-eł** *uj.* literary trash, pulp fiction novel.

powieściopisarka *f. Gen.pl.* **-ek** *zob.* **powieściopisarz**.

powieściopisarski *a.* novelistic.

powieściopisarstwo *n.* fiction writing.

powieściopisarz *mp* novelist, fiction writer.

powieściowy *a.* fictional, novelistic.

powieść[1] *f. teor.lit.* novel; **krótka powieść** novelette; **powieść autobiograficzna/historyczna** autobiographical/historical novel; **powieść łotrzykowska** picaresque novel; **powieść kryminalna** detective novel; **powieść przygodowa** adventure novel; **powieść rzeka** saga (novel), roman-fleuve; **przerabiać na powieść** novelize.

powieść[2] *pf.* **-wiodę -wiedziesz -wiódł -wiodła -wiedli** **1.** (= *przesunąć czymś po czymś*) sweep, run; **powieść spojrzeniem po czymś** sweep one's eyes over sth; **powieść spojrzeniem za kimś** follow sb with one's gaze. **2.** *lit.* (= *poprowadzić*) lead, take; **ojciec powiódł córkę do ołtarza** father escorted *l.* took his daughter to the altar. **~ się** *pf.* succeed, become successful, come off; **chyba nam się tym razem powiedzie** we might succeed this time; **niestety nie powiodło się** unfortunately it didn't work; **powiodło mi się** I made it.

powietrze *n.* air, atmosphere; **ruch** *l.* **obieg powietrza** air flow; **na wolnym powietrzu** outdoors, in the open air; **teatr na wolnym powietrzu** open-air theater; **sporty na wolnym powietrzu** outdoor sports; **rozpłynąć się w powietrzu** vanish into thin air; **pocisk powietrze-powietrze** *wojsk.* air-to-air missile; **żyć powietrzem** *przen.* live on air; **coś wisi w powietrzu** sth is in the wind *l.* air; **wisieć w powietrzu** (*o kwestii, pytaniu*) loom up; **wisieć w powietrzu** (*o ptakach*) hover; **unosić się w powietrzu**, float; **w powietrzu** in midair; **traktować kogoś jak powietrze** cut sb dead, look through sb; **spuszczać powietrze** let down; **wysadzić w powietrze** blow up; **most wyleciał w powietrze** bridge was blown up; **wzbijać się w powietrze** take to the air, take off; **wypuszczać powietrze** exhale; **przenoszony przez powietrze** airborne; **zaczerpnąć świeżego powietrza** take a breath of fresh air; **odświeżacz powietrza** air freshener; **wilgotność powietrza** *meteor.* air humidity; **powietrze ciekłe** *chem.* liquid air.

powietrznodesantowy *a. wojsk.* airborne; **wojska powietrznodesantowe** airborne troops.

powietrzny *a.* aerial, air, airy; **pęcherzyk powietrzny** air bladder; **kąpiel powietrzna** *med.* air bath; **poduszka powietrzna** *lotn.* ground effect; *mot.* airbag; **komora powietrzna** air chamber; **obrona powietrzna** *wojsk.* air defense; **walka powietrzna** *wojsk.* aerial combat; **statek powietrzny** aircraft; **front powietrzny** *meteor.* front; **trąba powietrzna** *meteor.* funnel cloud, pendant cloud, whirlwind, twister; **most powietrzny** airlift; **ruch powietrzny** air traffic; **worek powietrzny** *biol.* air sac; **korzeń powietrzny** *bot.* aerial root.

powiew *mi* breath, puff; **lekki powiew** breath of air.

powiewać *ipf.* 1. (*o powietrzu*) (= *napływać*) blow; **powiało chłodem** a chill wind came; **powiał wiatr z innej strony** *euf.* wind blew from another quarter. 2. (= *łopotać*) fly. 3. (= *machać*) wave.

powiewnie *adv.* airily, ethereally.

powiewność *f.* airiness, etherealness.

powiewny *a.* airy, flowing.

powiększać *ipf.* (*obszar, teren*) expand; (*ilość, dostawy, deficyt*) increase; (*organizację, zespół*) enlarge; (*obraz*) magnify; *fot.* enlarge, blow up; **powiększać czyjeś zmartwienia** add to sb's worries; **powiększać maksymalnie** maximize. **~ się** *ipf.* (*o zasobach*) increase; (*o obszarze*) expand; (*o grupie*) grow; swell, grow larger.

powiększający *a.* augmentative; **szkło powiększające** magnifying glass.

powiększalnik *mi Gen.* -a *fot.* enlarger.

powiększenie *n.* 1. (= *wzrost, przyrost*) enlargement, increase, extension, amplification, growth. 2. *fot.* enlargement, blow-up.

powiększyć *pf. zob.* **powiększać.** **~ się** *pf. zob.* **powiększać się.**

powięź *f. pl.* -i *l.* -e *anat.* fascia.

powijaki *pl. Gen.* -ów swaddling clothes; **budowa jest ciągle w powijakach** construction is still in its infancy; **umrzeć w powijakach** (*o planach, projektach*) die aborning.

powikłanie *n.* 1. *med.* complication; **mogą wystąpić powikłania** complications are liable to occur; **grypa z powikłaniami** influenza *l.* flu with complications. 2. (= *komplikacja*) complication, intricacy.

powinąć się *pf.* **Adamowi noga się powinęła** Adam didn't succeed, Adam failed.

powinien, powinna, powinno *v.* should, ought to; **powinien zadzwonić do matki** he should call his mother; **nie powinnaś jej krytykować** you shouldn't criticize her; **powinienem to przewidzieć** I should have foreseen that; **powinieneś już spać** you should *l.* ought to be sleeping now; **powinien zaraz przyjechać** he ought to be here in a moment; **powinnam to zrozumieć** I should understand that; **woda powinna już się zagotować** the water should have boiled by now; **powinno się takich jak on natychmiast zwalniać** people like him should be fired immediately; **to powinno zadziałać** this should work; **to się nie powinno zdarzyć** this was not supposed to happen.

powinność *f. lit.* (= *obowiązek*) duty, obligation; **czyń swoją powinność** *żart.* do your duty, do what you have to do; **powinność małżeńska** *prawn.* conjugal duty.

powinowactwo *n.* kinship, relation; **bliskie po-**

winowactwo close relation; **powinowactwo dusz** *przen.* soul brothers/sisters, unity of souls; **powinowactwo chemiczne** *chem.* affinity.

powinowata *f. Gen.* -ej related, relative, kinswoman.

powinowaty *a.* (= *spowinowacony*) relative; **jestem z nim powinowaty** I'm related to him. – *mp* relative, kinsman.

powinszowanie *n. przest.* congratulations (*z okazji czegoś* on sth); **z powinszowaniem urodzin** happy birthday, many happy returns (of the day); **z powinszowaniem imienin** best wishes (*on one's patron's day*).

powitać *pf.* greet, welcome; **powitać kogoś z otwartymi ramionami** welcome sb with open arms; **powitać Nowy Rok** greet the New Year; **powitać kogoś skinieniem głowy** bob one's head to greet sb; **powitać kogoś ukłonem** bow sb in.

powitalny *a.* welcoming; *form.* salutatory; **ceremonia powitalna** welcoming ceremony; **komitet powitalny** welcoming committee.

powitanie *n.* greeting, welcome; **urządzić komuś królewskie powitanie** give sb royal welcome.

powlec *pf.* -wlokę *l.* -wlekę -wleczesz -wlókł *l.* -wlekł -wlokła *l.* -wlekła -wlekli 1. (= *zaciągnąć*) drag (*over somewhere*). 2. *zob.* **powlekać.** **~ się** *pf.* 1. (= *pójść z trudem, niechęcią*) drag o.s. 2. (= *zasnuć się*) be enshrouded (*czymś* with sth).

powleczenie *n.* bed linen.

powlekać *ipf.* (= *pomalować*) 1. coat (*czymś* with sth). 2. **powlekać pościel** change bed linen; **powlekać poduszkę** case a pillow; **powlekać galwanicznie** *techn.* plate. **~ się** *ipf. zob.* **powlec się** 2.

powlekarka *f. Gen.pl.* -ek *techn.* spreading machine, spreader, coater.

powłoczka *f. Gen.pl.* -ek 1. (*pościel*) pillowcase, pillowslip; (*dekoracyjna*) sham. 2. (*błonka*) integument.

powłoka *f.* 1. (*osłona*) cover; (*np. farby, lakieru*) coat; (= *błona*) film; (*np. śniegu, lodu*) mantle; (*czołgu, pocisku*) hull; **powłoka elektronowa** *fiz.* electron shell; **powłoka walencyjna** *chem.* valence shell. 2. (*pościel*) cover. 3. *bot., zool.* integument; (= *skorupa*) shell. 4. *myśl.* dragging bait.

powłóczyć[1] *ipf.* 1. (= *ciągnąć za sobą*) drag (*behind o.s.*); **powłóczyć nogami** scuff; drag *l.* scrape one's feet; **ledwo nogami powłóczył** *przen.* he was at the end of his tether. 2. (*pościel*) case.

powłóczyć[2] *pf. roln.* harrow. **~ się** *pf.* (= *pochodzić*) (*po sklepach, mieście*) hang around; (*po kraju, świecie*) wander.

powłóczystość *f.* **powłóczystość fałdów sukni** trailing folds; **powłóczystość spojrzenia** languishing glance.

powłóczysty *a.* trailing; (*o spojrzeniu*) languishing.

powodować *ipf.* 1. (= *wywoływać coś*) cause, bring about; (*zwł. przypadkowo*) occasion; (*zwł. coś nieprzyjemnego*) breed. 2. (*wpływać na kogoś*) induce, manipulate (*kimś* sb). **~ się** *ipf.* be driven, be motivated (*czymś* by sth).

powodowany *a.* driven, induced; **powodowany**

zazdrością, nie przyjął jej zaproszenia driven by jealousy he didn't accept her invitation.

powodowy a. prawn. plaintiff's, petitioner's.

powodzenie n. 1. (przedsięwzięcia) success; robić coś z powodzeniem/bez powodzenia do sth successfully/unsuccessfully; z powodzeniem to wszystko mogło odbyć się inaczej it could all well happen differently. 2. (szczęście) luck, fortune; życzę powodzenia! best of luck!, good luck! 3. (popularność) success, popularity; cieszyć się powodzeniem be successful; zapewnić komuś powodzenie make sb popular; X cieszy się wielkim powodzeniem ekon. X is in great demand.

powodzianin mp pl. -anie Gen. -an flood victim.

powodzić się ipf. thrive, prosper; (finansowo) be well off; dobrze/źle mu się powodzi (= ma się dobrze) he's doing well/badly; (finansowo) he's well/badly off.

powodziowy a. flood; klęska powodziowa flood disaster; komitet powodziowy flood relief committee.

powojenny a. postwar.

powojnik mi Gen. -a bot. clematis (Clematis); powojnik pnący traveler's joy; Br. traveller's joy; old man's beard (Clematis vitalba).

powojowate pl. Gen. -ych bot. bindweeds; the morning-glory family (Convolvulaceae).

powoli adv. slowly; powoli! easy!; śpiesz się powoli slow and steady wins the race.

powolność f. slowliness, tardiness.

powolny a. 1. (= wolny) slow, tardy. 2. przest. (= uległy) docile; być powolnym narzędziem w czyichś rękach be a tool in sb's hands.

powolutku adv. very slowly, at a snail's pace.

powołać pf. zob. powoływać. ~ się pf. zob. powoływać się.

powołanie n. 1. (wewnętrzny nakaz) calling, call; vocation; czuć l. mieć powołanie do robienia czegoś be l. feel called to do sth, be cut out for sth; minąć się z powołaniem miss one's vocation; nauczyciel z powołania a teacher by vocation, a born teacher. 2. (= wezwanie do odbycia służby wojskowej) call-up.

powołany a. 1. (= mający obowiązek) qualified, competent; (do wojska) called up; jedyny organ powołany do kontroli administracji the only body qualified to control administration. 2. (= wybrany) called; powołany do zrobienia czegoś called upon to do sth.

powoływać ipf. 1. (= wybrać) appoint; powołać kogoś na świadka summons sb; powołać do wojska call up; powołać pod broń muster in. 2. (= utworzyć) create; powołać do życia bring l. call into being. ~ się ipf. (= odwoływać się do kogoś, czegoś) refer (na coś to sth); (na przepis, precedens) invoke (na coś sth); prawn. plead (na coś sth); powoływać się na kogoś make reference to sb; powoływać się na chorobę psychiczną prawn. plead insanity.

powonienie n. olfaction.

powozić ipf. -żę -zisz, -oź l. -óź (zaprzęgiem konnym) team; Br. drive (a team). – pf. -żę -zisz,

-oź l. -óź (= wozić jakiś czas) drive (around) (for some time), spend some time driving (kogoś sb).

powozownia f. Gen.pl. -i coach-house.

powód mi -o- Gen. -u pl. -y 1. (= przyczyna) cause (czegoś of sth); reason (czegoś for sth); nie dać komuś powodu do gniewu give sb no reason to be angry; mieć powody do obaw have cause for concern; nieobecny z powodu choroby absent due to illness; mieć powody, by coś zrobić have just cause to do sth, be justified in doing sth. 2. (= uprząż) harness. – mp -o- Gen. -a pl. -owie prawn. plaintiff; Br. (zwł. w sprawie rozwodowej) petitioner.

powódka f. Gen.pl. -ek prawn. plaintiff; Br. (zwł. w sprawie rozwodowej) petitioner.

powództwo n. prawn. action, suit; powództwo cywilne civil action; wnieść l. wytoczyć powództwo przeciwko komuś/czemuś bring an action against sb/sth.

powódź f. -o- pl. -e 1. (= zalanie, wylew) flood, inundation; klęska powodzi flood disaster; obszary nawiedzone powodzią areas affected l. hit by flood. 2. przen. (= mnóstwo) multitude, shower, flood; powódź świateł flood of light.

powój mi -o- Gen.pl. -ów l. -oi bot. convolvulus (Convolvulus); powój żywiczny scammony (Convolvulus scammonia).

powóz mi -o- carriage; (zwł. zakryty) coach; (czterokonny) tallyho, four-in-hand.

powracać ipf. 1. (= wracać w jakieś miejsce) return, come back (skądś from sth); powrócić na stanowisko (w pracy, w organizacji) return to one's post; powracać tą samą drogą take the same root back; powracać do łask make/stage a comeback. 2. (= wznawiać jakąś przerwaną czynność) resume (do czegoś sth); powrócić do rozmowy resume one's conversation; powracać do zdrowia recover; powracać do przytomności regain consciousness, come round.

powrotny a. return; bilet powrotny return ticket, round-trip ticket; w drodze powrotnej on the way back; gorączka powrotna pat. relapsing fever, recurrent fever.

powroźnictwo f. rope making.

powroźnik mp ropemaker.

powrócić pf. zob. powracać.

powrósło n. Gen.pl. -eł roln. twine, binder.

powrót mi -o- 1. (do jakiegoś miejsca) return, comeback; powrót do domu home-coming; tam i z powrotem (o bilecie) return, round-trip. 2. (do stanu pierwotnego) restitution; powrót do zdrowia recovery, recuperation; na powrót (= znów) again; z powrotem (= znów) again.

powróz mi -o- binder, rope.

powrózek mi -zk- Gen. -a anat. funicle; powrózek nasienny spermatic cord.

powróżyć pf. foretell; powróżyć komuś tell sb's fortune.

powsinoga f. l. mp decl. like f. Gen.pl. -óg l. -ów żart. gadabout, loiterer.

powstać pf. -anę -aniesz zob. powstawać.

powstanie n. (zbrojne) uprising, insurrection; insurgence, insurgency; powstanie kościuszkowskie hist. Kosciuszko uprising l. insurrection;

powstanie listopadowe *hist.* Polish November Insurrection; **powstanie styczniowe** *hist.* Polish January Insurrection.

powstaniec *mp* -ńc- *pl.* -y insurgent; insurrectionary, insurrectionist.

powstaniowy *a.* insurrectional.

powstańczy *a.* insurgent.

powstawać *ipf.* -aję -ajesz, -waj **1.** (= *być tworzonym*) come into being, spring into existence; (*o trudnościach, problemach*) arise, emerge. **2.** (= *unosić się*) rise; **powstać z miejsca** rise from one's seat; **powstać z grobu** *l.* **z martwych** rise from the dead; **powstań!** *wojsk.* on your feet! **3.** (= *ruszać do walki*) stand up, revolt (*przeciw komuś/czemuś* agaist sb/sth).

powstrzymać *pf.*, **powstrzymywać** *ipf.* (= *zatrzymać*) stop; (*kogoś*) restrain; (*śmiech*) restrain, hold back; (*uczucie, pragnienie, chęć*) repress; **powstrzymywać płacz** restrain *l.* hold back one's tears; **powstrzymać upływ krwi** stanch *l.* staunch blood. ~ **się** *pf.*, **powstrzymywać się** *ipf.* (= *odmówić sobie*) abstain (*od czegoś* from sth); (= *pohamować się*) refrain (*od czegoś* from sth); **powstrzymywać się od śmiechu/od płaczu** restrain *l.* hold back one's laughter/tears.

powstydzić się *pf.* feel ashamed; **żadna firma nie powstydziłaby się takiego wzrostu obrotów** no company would consider such turnover increase a disgrace.

powszechnie *adv.* commonly, generally, popularly; (*stosowany, uznawany*) universally; **być osobą powszechnie znaną** be in the public eye; **być powszechnie wiadomym** be public knowledge; **powszechnie wiadomo, że...** it is common knowledge that...

powszechnik *mi Gen.* -a *fil.* universal.

powszechność *f.* commonness, generality; (*poglądu, wyrażenia*) currency, prevalence; (*zasady, obowiązku, nauczania*) universality.

powszechny *a.* (= *ogólny*) common, general; (= *publiczny*) popular, public; (*o opinii, poglądach*) prevailing; (*o praktyce*) prevalent; (*o zasadzie, zgodzie, obowiązku, nauczaniu*) universal; (*zwł. o podwyżce*) across-the-board; **powszechny obowiązek wojskowy** conscription, compulsory military service; **powszechna mobilizacja** general mobilization; **głosowanie powszechne** *polit.* general election; **historia powszechna** general history; **literatura powszechna** world literature; **sobór powszechny** *rel.* Ecumenical Council; **sąd powszechny** *prawn.* common court, court of common pleas; **szkoła powszechna** *hist.* elementary school; **artykuły powszechnego użytku** commodities.

powszedni *a.* (= *zwykły*) commonplace; (= *codzienny*) daily; **dzień powszedni** (*nieświąteczny*) weekday; **czyjś dzień powszedni** one's daily round; **chleb powszedni** daily bread, staple diet; **coś jest czyimś chlebem powszednim** sth is meat and drink to sb; **grzech powszedni** *rel.* venial sin.

powszednieć *ipf.* (= *pospolicieć*) become commonplace; (= *obojętnieć*) become indifferent.

powszedniość *f.* commonness.

powściągać *pf.* **1.** (*emocje, reakcje, osobę*) restrain, rein in; **powściągnąć język** hold one's tongue. **2.** (*lejce*) rein in. ~ **się** *pf.* restrain o.s., contain o.s.

powściągliwie *adv.* aloofly, reservedly, restrainedly.

powściągliwość *f.* (= *umiarkowanie*) restraint; (*zachowania*) discretion; (= *wyniosłość*) aloofness.

powściągliwy *a.* (= *wyniosły*) aloof; (= *pełen rezerwy*) reserved, undemonstrative; (*np. o wypowiedzi*) low-key; (*o krytyce, ocenie*) understated; (*o pochwale*) qualified; (*zwł. płciowo*) continent.

powściągnąć *pf.* -ij *zob.* **powściągać**. ~ **się** *pf. zob.* **powściągać się**.

powtarzać *ipf.* **1.** (= *robić powtórnie*) repeat; (*program, wyścig*) rerun; (*oblany egzamin*) retake, resit; (*rozgrywkę, mecz, fragment, sekwencję*) replay; (*eksperyment, badanie*) replicate, duplicate; (*obietnicę, groźbę*) restate; (*plotki*) retail; **powtórzyć trygonometrię/gramatykę** revise trigonometry/grammar; **powtarzać klasę/rok** repeat a class/year; **powtarzać w kółko** cuckoo, harp on one string. **2.** (*przekazywać*) repeat, retell; **nie powtarzaj tego nikomu** don't repeat it to anyone. ~ **się** *ipf.* **1.** (= *być powtarzanym*) recur. **2.** (= *mówić ciągle to samo*) repeat o.s.

powtarzający się *a.* recurring, repeating.

powtarzalność *f.* recurrence, repeatability.

powtarzalny *a.* repeating, cyclic; **broń powtarzalna** repeater, repeating firearm.

powtórka *f. Gen.pl.* -ek **1.** *pot.* (= *powtórzenie opanowanego materiału*) review, revision. **2.** (= *powtórzenie, ponowne zrobienie*) instant review; redoing, remaking; (= *powtórne przeczytanie*) rereading. **3.** *pot. telew.* (*programu, wyścigu*) rerun; (*ponowne odtworzenie części nagrania*) instant replay; (*w zwolnionym tempie*) action replay. **4.** (*rzutu wolnego itp.*) retake; **powtórka z... revisited.

powtórkowy *a.* (*o lekcji, programie*) revision; **egzamin powtórkowy** retake exam.

powtórnie *a.* again; **powtórnie napisać** rewrite; **powtórnie opowiedzieć** retell.

powtórny *a.* (= *wykonany po raz drugi*) second; (= *wykonany trzy lub więcej razy*) repeated.

powtórzenie *n.* **1.** (*słowa, słów, przemówienia*) repetition; (*ponowne powiedzenie lub zrobienie czegoś*) iteration; (*wyrazu l. zwrotu dla uzyskania efektu retorycznego*) gemination. **2.** (*egzaminu*) retake; *szkoln.* (*materiału*) revision. **3.** (*programu telewizyjnego*) rerun. **4.** *sport* (*ćwiczenia*) repetition, rep; (*rzutu wolnego itp.*) retake.

powtórzyć *pf. zob.* **powtarzać**. ~ **się** *pf. zob.* **powtarzać się**.

powulkaniczny *a.* volcanic.

powyborczy *a.* post-election.

powywracać *pf.* overturn, knock over. ~ **się** *pf.* (*o ludziach, drzewach*) fall; (*o przedmiotach*) overturn; (*o łodziach*) capsize.

powyżej *adv.* **1.** (= *wyżej niż*) above, over; **mam już tego powyżej uszu** I'm sick and tired of it. **2.** (= *w górę rzeki*) upstream. **3.** (= *na północ* *od*) North, northward. **4.** (= *więcej niż*) over, above; **powyżej trzech lat** over three years; **powyżej stu złotych** over PLN 100. **5.** (*o stanowisku*) above (*the rank of*); **powyżej pułkownika** above the rank of colonel. **6.** (*w tekście*) above; **powyżej wspomniane czynniki** above mentioned factors, foregoing factors.

powyższe *n. Gen.* **-ego** the foregoing; **wobec powyższego** in consideration of the above.

powyższy *a.* above, foregoing, preceding.

powziąć *pf.* **-wezmę -weźmiesz, -weźmij, -wziął 1.** (*postanowić*) reach, take; **powziąć decyzję** reach *l.* take *l.* arrive at a decision; **powziąć postanowienie** make a resolution. **2.** (*poczuć*) conceive; **powziąć podejrzenie** conceive a suspicion.

poz. *abbr.* (= *pozycja*) item.

poza[1] *f. Gen.pl.* **póz 1.** (= *układ postaci*) posture, pose; **przyjąć pozę** (*do zdjęcia*) (*o modelce, modelu*) strike a pose. **2.** (= *maniera*) pose, affectation.

poza[2] *prep.* + *Acc.* **1.** (*kierunek*) beyond, out of, outside; **poza horyzont** beyond the horizon; **wyjść poza granice dobrego smaku** go beyond the limits of good taste. **2.** + *Ins.* (*miejsce*) outside, out of; **być poza domem** be out; **poza godzinami pracy** outside working hours; **poza godzinami szczytu** off-peak, off-hour; **poza granicami kraju** (*np. o banku, inwestycjach*) offshore; **poza kadrem** *kino* off-screen; **poza kamerą** off camera; **poza kampusem** off-campus; **poza kimś/czymś** in addition to sb/sth; **poza kolejnością** out of turn; **poza miastem** out of town; **poza podejrzeniami/ krytyką** above suspicion/reproach; **poza protokołem** off-the-record; **poza sezonem** off-season, out of season; **poza rozkładem** (*o pociągu*) wildcat; **mam już to poza sobą** I'm through with it. **3.** + *Ins.* (*poszerzenie*) except for, in addition to; **ocaleli wszyscy poza kapitanem** everybody survived except for the captain; **poza tym** besides.

pozabijać *pf.* **1.** (*uśmiercić*) kill. **2.** (*przybić*) (*np. okna deskami*) board up. ~ **się** *pf.* **1.** (*jeden drugiego*) kill one another. **2.** (*o wielu: stracić życie*) kill.

pozagalaktyczny *a. astron.* extragalactic.

pozagrobowy *a.* **życie pozagrobowe** afterlife, life after death.

pozajelitowy *a. med.* parenteral.

pozaklejać *pf.* glue, paste.

pozakonkursowy *a.* non-competing.

pozalekcyjny *a.* extracurricular.

pozałatwiać *ipf.* settle.

pozamaciczny *a. pat.* extrauterine; **ciąża pozamaciczna** *pat.* ectopic pregnancy, extrauterine pregnancy.

pozamałżeński *a.* adulterous, extramarital; (*o dziecku*) illegitimate.

pozanaukowy *a.* non-scientific.

pozaotrzewnowy *a. med.* retroperitoneal, extraperitoneal.

pozapalny *a. med.* post-inflammatory.

pozarastać *pf.* overgrow.

pozaregulaminowy *a.* not provided for in regulations; (*np. o nagrodzie*) additional.

pozaszkolny *a.* extraschool.

pozauczelniany *a.* non-university.

pozawałowy *a. med.* post-infarctional.

pozazdroszczenie *n.* **godny pozazdroszczenia** enviable; **nie do pozazdroszczenia** unenviable, invidious.

pozazdrościć *pf.* **-roszczę -rościsz** envy (*komuś czegoś* sb sth).

pozaziemski *a.* extraterrestrial; **istota pozaziemska** extraterrestrial, alien.

pozbawiać *ipf.,* **pozbawić** *pf.* deprive, divest (*kogoś czegoś* sb of sth); **pozbawiać mocy prawnej** (*umowę, kontrakt*) outlaw; *Br.* invalidate; **pozbawiać prawa wykonywania zawodu** (*lekarza, prawnika*) strike off; **pozbawić kogoś życia** take sb's life; **pozbawiać kogoś obywatelstwa** *prawn.* revoke sb's citizenship. ~ **się** *ipf.,* **pozbawić się** *pf.* deprive o.s. (*czegoś* of sth); (= *odmówić sobie*) deny o.s. (*czegoś* sth); **pozbawić się życia** take one's own life.

pozbawienie *n.* deprivation, deprival; **pozbawienie wolności** *prawn.* deprivation of liberty; **pozbawienie praw obywatelskich** disfranchisement; **pozbawienie majątku** divestiture.

pozbawiony *a.* **-eni** devoid (*czegoś* of sth); **pozbawiony emocji** bland, unemotional; **pozbawiony mocy prawnej** *prawn.* invalid; **pozbawiony złudzeń** disenchanted.

pozbierać *ipf.* **1.** (= *zebrać*) gather, collect (*coś* sth); **pozbierać myśli** collect one's thoughts; **pozbierać siły** gather strength. **2.** (= *sprzątnąć*) gather up, pick up. ~ **się** *ipf.* **1.** (= *zgromadzić się*) gather. **2.** *pot.* (= *dojść do siebie*) get o.s. together, pick up the pieces; **po śmierci żony nie mógł się pozbierać** he couldn't get over his wife's death.

pozbyć się *pf.* **-będę -będziesz, -bądź, pozbywać się** *ipf.* **-am -asz** (*uwolnić się od czegoś*) dispose, get rid (*czegoś* of sth); (*uwolnić się od kogoś*) get rid (*kogoś* of sb); **pozbyć się nałogu** kick a habit, break o.s. of a habit.

pozdawać *pf.* **-aję -ajesz, -awaj 1.** (*egzaminy*) pass. **2.** (*jakieś rzeczy, przedmioty*) return.

pozdrawiać *ipf.,* **pozdrowić** *pf.* **-ów 1.** (*przy powitaniu*) greet; (*zwł. gestem*) salute. **2.** (= *przekazywać wyrazy szacunku*) give (*sb*) one's respects *l.* regards; (*listownie*) send (*sb*) one's greetings; **pozdrów ode mnie siostrę** remember me to your sister, give my regards to your sister. ~ **się** *ipf.,* **pozdrowić się** *pf.* **1.** (*przy powitaniu*) exchange greetings. **2.** (= *przekazywać sobie wyrazy szacunku*) exchange regards, exchange respects.

pozdrowienie *n.* **1.** (*przy powitaniu*) greetings. **2.** (= *wyrazy szacunku*) regards, respects.

pozer *mp pog.* poseur, poser.

pozerstwo *n. pog.* poseurism, attitudinizing.

pozew *mi* **-zw-** *prawn.* summons, petition; **wnieść pozew przeciwko komuś** bring *l.* file a suit against sb, institute an action against sb.

pozielenieć *pf.* turn green.

poziewnik *mi Gen.* **-a** *bot.* hemp nettle (*Galeopsis*).

poziom *mi* **1.** (*wysokość*) level, plane; **poziom morza** sea level. **2.** (*moralny, umysłowy*) standard; **być na poziomie** be up to scratch; **być na wysokim/niskim poziomie** be up to/below the mark; **być na jednym poziomie z kimś** be on a par with sb. **3.** *geol.* horizon. **4.** (*kierunek ustawienia papieru przy wydruku*) *komp.* landscape.

poziomica *f.* **1.** *techn.* = **poziomnica**. **2.** *geogr.* contour line, contour.

poziomka *f. Gen.pl.* -ek wild strawberry (*Fragaria vesca*).

poziomkowy *a.* wild strawberry.

poziomnica *f. techn.* level.

poziomo *adv.* horizontally, levelly.

poziomować *ipf. techn.* level; **śruba poziomująca** *bud.* leveling screw.

poziomy *a.* level, horizontal; **rzut poziomy** (*budynku*) ground plan.

pozjadać *pf.* eat up; **pozjadać wszystkie rozumy** *iron.* be a know-it-all.

pozjazdowy *a.* post-convention.

pozłacany *a.* gilt, gilded; gold plated.

pozłocić *pf.* gild, plate with gold.

pozłocisty *a. poet.* gilded.

pozłota *f.* gilding.

pozłotnictwo *mi* gilding.

pozłotnik *mp* gilder.

pozmieniać *pf.* change. ~ **się** *pf.* change, be changed.

pozmywać *pf.* -am -asz (*naczynia, podłogi*) wash up, do the dishes.

poznać *pf. zob.* **poznawać**. ~ **się** *pf. zob.* **poznawać się**.

poznanie *n.* **1.** (= *zapoznanie się*) acquaintance; **tracić/zyskiwać przy bliższym poznaniu** improve/lose on further *l.* closer acquaintance; **zmienił się nie do poznania** he has changed out of all recognition *l.* beyond recognition. **2.** *psych.* cognition; **poznanie zmysłowe** sense perception; **teoria poznania** *fil.* epistemology.

poznawać *ipf.* -aję -ajesz, -waj **1.** (= *zawrzeć znajomość*) meet; **miło mi panią poznać** nice to meet you. **2.** (= *przedstawić kogoś komuś*) introduce (*kogoś z kimś* sb to sb); acquaint (*kogoś z kimś* sb with sb); **poznałem Adama z Ewą** I introduced Adam to Eve. **3.** (= *zdobywać wiedzę*) acquaint o.s. (*coś* with sth); **poznać coś od podszewki** get to know sth like the back of one's hand; **poznawać arkana czegoś** learn the ropes of sth. **4.** (= *doznawać czegoś*) experience; **poznać biedę/strach/uczucie szczęścia** experience poverty/fear/happiness; **prawdziwych przyjaciół poznaje się w biedzie** a friend in need is a friend indeed. **5.** (= *domyślać się*) see, spot; **poznać się na kimś** see through sb, have sb taped; **kłamstwo można poznać po twojej minie** I can tell from your face that you're lying; **nie dał poznać po sobie, że się boi** he didn't let us feel that he was afraid; **można poznać, że jesteś zdenerwowany** you can tell that you're nervous. **6.** (= *identyfikować*) recognize; **poznać kogoś po krokach/głosie** recognize sb's footsteps/voice; **łatwo go poznać po...** he is easily recognizable by...; **nie poznajesz mnie?** don't you recognize me?; **udałem, że go nie poznaję** I pretended not to recognize him. ~ **się** *ipf.* **1.** (= *zawierać znajomość*) meet, get to know (*z*

kimś sb). **2.** (= *być sobie przedstawionym*) meet (*z kimś* sb); be introduced (*z kimś* to sb). **3.** (= *wiedzieć o sobie coraz więcej*) become closely acquainted (*z kimś* with sb). **4.** (= *doceniać, oceniać*) appreciate; **nareszcie poznałem się na nim** I finally appreciated him; **nie poznał się na żarcie** the joke was lost on him. **5.** (= *rozpoznawać się*) recognize one another; **poznaliśmy się po głosie** we recognized each other by the voice.

poznawalność *f.* cognizability.

poznawalny *a.* cognizable; (*rozumowo*) *fil.* intelligible.

poznawczy *a.* cognitional, cognitive; (*o psychologii*) cognitive.

pozorant *mp* **1.** *uj.* pretender. **2.** (*w szkoleniu psów policyjnych*) decoy.

pozornie *adv.* apparently, seemingly, ostensibly.

pozorność *f.* appearance.

pozorny *a.* apparent, seeming, ostensible; **pozorne słońce** *astron.* parhelion, mock sun; **obraz pozorny** *fiz.* virtual image.

pozorować *ipf.* simulate, feign.

pozostać *pf.* -stanę -staniesz *zob.* **pozostawać**.

pozostałość *f.* remnant, relic.

pozostały *a.* **1.** (*reszta*) remaining; **pozostałe dni urlopu** remaining days off. **2.** (*inny*) the other; **my poszliśmy pieszo, pozostali pojechali autobusem** we went on foot, the others took the bus; **nie wspominając nawet o pozostałych** not to mention the others.

pozostawać *ipf.* -aję -ajesz, -waj **1.** (*zostawać*) stay, remain; **pozostać w tyle** lag behind; **pozostać (na długo) w pamięci** be (long) remembered; **niech to pozostanie między nami** let's keep it for ourselves. **2.** (*tkwić w jakichś warunkach*) remain, continue to be; **pozostawać przy życiu** stay alive; **pozostawać na wolności** (*o przestępcy*) be at large; **pozostawać w ukryciu** remain in hiding; **pozostawać niezauważonym** go *l.* pass unnoticed; **pozostawać wiernym komuś** remain faithful to sb; **pozostawać w zapomnieniu** remain in oblivion. **3.** **pozostawać tym, kim** *l.* **czym się było** remain the same; **to nie pozostanie bez wpływu na jej psychikę** it won't be without influence on her psyche; **pozostanę waszym nauczycielem** I'll still be your teacher; **powodzianie pozostają bez dachu nad głową** flood victims continue to live without shelter; **pozostaje mi już tylko państwa przeprosić** now I can only apologize to you. **4.** (= *być tym, co zostało l. tym, kto został*) remain, be left over; **pozostaje ci jeszcze córka** you still have one daughter; **do końca miesiąca pozostało mi tylko 100 złotych** I have only 100 PLN left till the end of the month; **nie pozostaje mi nic do dodania** there's nothing to add.

pozostawiać¹ *ipf.*, **pozostawić** *pf.* **1.** (= *zostawiać*) leave (behind); **pozostawiać kogoś/coś za sobą** (= *minąć*) leave sb/sth behind; (= *wyprzedzić*) overtake sb/sth; **ewakuowani pozostawili cały swój majątek** the evacuees left all their belongings behind. **2.** (= *porzucać*) leave; **pozostawić sprawy własnemu biegowi** let things drift; **pozostawił żonę z małym dzieckiem** he left his wife and a small child. **3.** (= *opuścić, umierając*) leave; **pozostawiać komuś majątek** bequeath one's property to sb; **pozostawił żonę i troje dzieci** he left his wife and three kids, he is outlived by his wife and three kinds. **4.** (= *wywoływać*) leave; **pozostawić nieprzyjemny smak w ustach** leave a bad taste in one's mouth; **to pozostawia wiele do życzenia** it leaves much to be desired; **to nie pozostawia wątpliwości** it leaves no room for doubt. **5.** (= *wstrzymywać się*) leave; **pozostawili go w spokoju** they left him alone. **6.** (= *zdać się*) leave; **nie pozostawiać komuś wyboru** leave sb with no choice *l.* option; **pozostawiam ci decyzję w tej sprawie** I leave it to you to decide. **7.** (= *zatrzymywać, zachować*) keep; **pozostawiłem sobie dwa procent od transakcji** I kept two percent from the transaction for myself.

pozostawiać² *pf.* (= *zostawić wiele czegoś*) leave (behind) (*a number of things*).

pozować *ipf.* **1.** (*jako model, modelka*) model, strike a pose; **pozować do zdjęcia** pose for a photograph. **2.** (= *udawać*) affect (*na kogoś* sb); pose (*na kogoś* as sb).

pozowany *a.* **pozowane zdjęcie** portrait photo.

pozór *mi* **-o-** pretense; *Br.* pretence; false appearance; **stwarzać pozory czegoś** put on a show of sth; **zachowywać pozory** keep up appearances; **pozory mylą** appearances can be deceptive; beauty is but skin deep, don't judge a book by its cover; **na pozór** to *l.* by all appearances; **z pozoru** on the surface; **pod pozorem** under (the) pretence of sth, under color of sth; **pod żadnym pozorem** on no account *l.* consideration; **wbrew pozorom** contrary to *l.* against (all) appearances.

pozrywać *pf.* **-am -asz** **1.** (*zerwać*) tear off; (*owoce*) pick. **2.** (*np. negocjacje*) break; (*przyjaźnie, znajomości*) break up (*z kimś* with sb). **3.** (= *zakończyć*) put a stop (*z czymś* to sth). **~ się** *pf.* **1.** (= *popękać*) break. **2.** (= *powstać z miejsc*) jump to (one's) feet.

pozrzucać *pf.* **1.** (*coś na coś*) throw down. **2.** (*co gdzieś*) heap, pile. **3.** (*ubranie*) throw off.

pozwać *pf.* **-wę -wiesz, -wij** *zob.* **pozywać.**

pozwalać¹ *ipf.* **1.** (= *zgodzić się*) allow, permit; **pozwalać komuś na coś** allow sb to do sth; **za wiele sobie z kimś pozwalać** take freedoms with sb, make free with sb; **pozwolę sobie** allow me; **jeśli pan pozwoli** if you allow me; **pozwoliłem sobie go o to zapytać** I took the liberty to ask him about it; **nie pozwolę na takie traktowanie** I won't stand *l.* allow *l.* have such treatment; **nie możemy sobie pozwolić na nowy samochód** we can't afford to buy a new car. **2.** (= *dopuszczać do czegoś*) allow; **przyjdę, jeśli czas pozwoli** I'll come if the time allows; **okoliczności nie pozwalają na dłuższe dyskusje w tej sprawie** the circumstances do not allow further discussion of that matter.

pozwalać² *pf.* **1.** (*w jedno miejsce*) heap, pile. **2.** (*np. o koniach*) throw down. **3.** (*np. drzewa*) knock down, fell.

pozwalniać *pf.* **1.** (*pracowników*) dismiss, lay off. **2.** (*z obowiązku*) relieve, exempt (*kogoś z*

czegoś sb from sth). **3.** (*miejsca*) vacate. **~ się** *pf.* **1.** (*z obowiązków*) get released, be exempted (*z czegoś* from sth). **2.** (*miejsca*) be vacated.

pozwana *f. Gen.* **-ej**, **pozwany** *mp prawn.* defendant; (*w sprawie rozwodowej*) respondent.

pozwolenie *n.* permission; (*zwł. pisemne*) permit; **pozwolenie na budowę** construction permit; **pozwolenie na pracę** work permit; **bez pozwolenia** unauthorized; **za pozwoleniem** *przest.* by your leave; **prosić kogoś o pozwolenie (żeby coś zrobić)** ask sb's permission (to do sth).

pozwolić *pf.* **-ól** *zob.* **pozwalać.**

pozycja *f.* **1.** (= *położenie*) *t. przen.* position, location; **bronić straconej pozycji** fight for lost causes; **być na straconej pozycji** have the odds against o.s., be on a hiding to nothing; **stać na uprzywilejowanej pozycji** be on the inside track; **wyrobić sobie pozycję** make one's mark; **wysuwać się na czołową pozycję** vault into prominence. **2.** (*na liście*) point, item; *księgowość* entry, item. **3.** (= *miejsce w społeczeństwie*) status; **stracić pozycję społeczną** lose one's social standing. **4.** *sport* (= *miejsce w rankingu*) place; (*np. piłki*) lie; **zająć pierwszą/drugą pozycję** rank first/second. **5.** *wojsk.* position; *wojsk.* (*działa, baterii*) emplacement; **z góry upatrzone pozycje** fallback position; **utrzymać się na swoich pozycjach** stand one's ground. **6.** (*głowy, ramion itp.*) posture, position; **pozycja siedząca/stojąca/leżąca** sitting/standing/lying position; **zmienić pozycję** change one's *l.* the position.

pozycyjny *a.* position; **atak pozycyjny** *sport, wojsk.* positional attack; **język pozycyjny** *jęz.* isolating language; **światła pozycyjne** *mot.* running lights; **wojna pozycyjna** *wojsk.* positional warfare; **zapis pozycyjny** *komp.* positional notation.

pozyskać *pf.*, **pozyskiwać** *ipf.* gain, procure; (*fundusze*) leverage; (*pomoc, wsparcie*) enlist; **pozyskiwać czyjeś poparcie dla czegoś** *polit.* drum up sb's support for sth.

pozyton, pozytron *mi fiz.* positron.

pozytyw *mi* **1.** *fot.* positive. **2.** (= *strona dodatnia*) advantage, the positive aspect.

pozytywista *mp*, **pozytywistka** *f. Gen.pl.* **-ek** positivist.

pozytywistyczny *a. fil., teor.lit.* positivistic.

pozytywizm *mi fil., teor.lit.* positivism.

pozytywka *f. Gen.pl.* **-ek** music box, musical box.

pozytywnie *adv.* positively, favorably; **rozpatrzyć pozytywnie podanie** accept an application.

pozytywny *a.* **1.** (= *korzystny*) positive; (*o odpowiedzi*) affirmative; **dać wynik pozytywny** give a positive result. **2.** *pot.* (= *zarażony wirusem*) positive.

pozytywowy *a. fot.* positive.

pozywać *ipf.* **-am -asz** *prawn.* sue (*kogoś o coś* sb for sth); bring *l.* file a suit, institute an action (*kogoś* against sb).

pożalić się *pf.* **1.** (= *poskarżyć się*) cry one's heart out (*komuś* to sb); **śpiewak pożal się Boże** a pitiful singer. **2.** (= *ulitować się*) *przest.* take pity (*nad kimś* on sb).

pożałować *pf.* **1.** (= *poczuć żal*) regret; **gorzko**

tego pożałujesz! you'll bitterly regret it!, you will sweat for it! **2.** (= *współczuć*) feel sorry (*kogoś* for sb); take pity (*kogoś* on sb). **3.** (= *poskąpić*) grudge (*komuś czegoś* sb sth); stint (*komuś czegoś* sb on sth); **nie pożałować wysiłków, by...** spare no effort to...

pożałowanie n. **pożałowania godny** (= *budzący litość*) lamentable; (= *niestosowny*) regrettable.

pożar mi fire; **wzniecić pożar** (*przypadkowo*) start l. cause a fire (*czegoś* of sth); (*naumyślnie*) set fire (*czegoś* to sth); *prawn.* commit arson; **ugasić pożar** put out a fire, extinguish a fire; **pożar namiętności** *przen.* fire of passion.

pożarnictwo n. firefighting.

pożarniczy a. fire fighting; **sprzęt pożarniczy** fire fighting equipment; **samochód pożarniczy** fire engine.

pożarny a. fire; **straż pożarna** (*instytucja*) fire department; **ochotnicza straż pożarna** fire brigade.

pożarowy a. fire; **zagrożenie/bezpieczeństwo pożarowe** fire hazard l. risk/safety.

pożartować pf. joke (*for a while*); **pożartować z kogoś/czegoś** make fun of sb/sth.

pożądać ipf. **1.** (*fizycznie*) lust (*kogoś* after l. for sb); desire (*kogoś* sb). **2.** (*duchowo*) crave (*czegoś* for l. after sth); covet (*czegoś* sth).

pożądanie n. (= *żądza*) desire, lust; **obudzić w kimś pożądanie** arouse sb's desire.

pożądany a. coveted, desired; (*o gościu*) welcome; (*o skutku, działaniu*) desirable.

pożądliwie adv. (*chciwie*) greedily, hungrily; (*lubieżnie*) lustfully; **mój pies wpatrywał się pożądliwie w kanapkę z szynką i serem** my dog was staring hungrily at a ham and cheese sandwich.

pożądliwość f. (= *chciwość*) greed; (= *lubieżność*) lust, lewdness.

pożądliwy a. lustful, covetous; (*o spojrzeniu, ruchach*) lewd.

pożeglować pf. sail.

pożegnać pf. say goodbye (*kogoś* to sb). **~ się** pf. **1.** (= *powiedzieć „do widzenia"*) say goodbye (*z kimś* to sb); (= *rozstać się*) part (*z kimś* from sb); part company (*z kimś* with sb); **pożegnać się ze światem** euf. depart this life, quit this world. **2.** (= *zrezygnować*) give up, discontinue; **pożegnać się z planami/pracą** give up one's plans/job.

pożegnalny a. farewell, parting; **toast/gest pożegnalny** parting toast/gesture; **list/występ pożegnalny** farewell letter/performance; **przyjęcie pożegnalne** farewell l. going-away party.

pożegnanie n. **1.** (*słowa*) goodbye. **2.** (*moment*) farewell, parting; **pożegnanie zmarłego** memorial service; **uścisnąć komuś dłoń na pożegnanie** give sb a farewell handshake.

pożenić pf. marry off. **~ się** pf. marry.

pożeracz mp eater, devourer; **pożeracz serc** *żart.* lady-killer; **pożeracz książek** devourer of books; **pożeracz czasu/prądu** time/power eater.

pożerać ipf. **1.** (*o zwierzętach*) devour. **2.** (*o człowieku*) uj. devour (*coś* sth); gorge (*coś* on sth); **pożerać książki** devour books; **pożerać kogoś oczami** devour sb with one's eyes; **ciekawość mnie pożera** I am eaten up with curiosity. **3.**

przen. (= *niszczyć*) ravage (*coś* sth); wreak havoc (*coś* with sth); **ten piecyk pożera dużo prądu** this heater gobbles much electricity; **ogień co roku pożera wiele hektarów lasu** fire ravages many hectares of forest every year. **~ się** ipf. (*o zwierzętach*) devour each other; **pożerali się oczami** they were devouring each other with their eyes.

pożoga f. Gen.pl. **-óg** lit. conflagration.

pożółkły a. yellowed.

pożółknąć pf. **-ij** yellow, turn yellow.

pożreć pf. **-ę -esz, -yj, -żarł** zob. **pożerać. ~ się** pf. **1.** zob. **pożerać się. 2.** pot. (= *pokłócić się*) fall out (*z kimś* with sb).

pożycie n. life; **pożycie małżeńskie/seksualne** married/sex life.

pożyczać ipf. **1.** (*dać*) lend (*komuś coś* sth to sb). **2.** (*brać*) borrow (*coś od kogoś* sth from sb); **dobry zwyczaj nie pożyczaj** lend your money and lose your friend; **pożyczać coś sobie** (= *brać bez zgody*) appropriate sth; **słuchaj, pożyczyłem sobie twój długopis, dobra?** pot. by the way, I have borrowed your pen.

pożyczka f. Gen.pl. **-ek 1.** (*coś pożyczonego*) loan; **pożyczka pod zastaw** loan against security; **pożyczka bezzwrotna** non-returnable loan; **spłacać pożyczkę** pay off a loan; **udzielić komuś pożyczki** give sb a loan; **zaciągnąć pożyczkę w...** take out l. get a loan from...; **zaciągnąć pożyczkę w banku X** take out a loan with X bank. **2.** jęz. (*struktura składniowa, wyrażenie*) loan; (*słowo*) loanword.

pożyczkobiorca mp borrower.

pożyczkodawca mp lender, loaner.

pożyczyć pf. **1.** zob. **pożyczać. 2.** (= *złożyć życzenia*) wish (*komuś czegoś* sb sth); **pożyczyć komuś szczęścia** wish sb good luck.

pożyć pf. **-żyję -żyjesz, -żyj 1.** (*przez jakiś czas*) live (*for some time*); **już pewnie długo nie pożyje** he probably won't last much longer. **2.** (*w jakiś sposób*) live (*for some time*); **pożyć trochę w luksusie** spend some time in the lap of luxury; **pożyjemy, zobaczymy** let's wait and see.

pożytecznie adv. usefully.

pożyteczność f. usefulness, utility.

pożyteczny a. useful.

pożytek mi **-tk- 1.** (*korzyść*) benefit, advantage; **mieć z czegoś pożytek** benefit from sth; **z pożytkiem dla kogoś** to sb's benefit; **z pożytkiem dla czegoś** to the benefit of sth; **jest z tego pożytek** it is useful, it is beneficial. **2.** *prawn.* profit, benefit. **3.** *pszczelarstwo* bee nutrient (*nectar, honeydew and pollen*).

pożywienie n. food.

pożywka f. Gen.pl. **-ek 1.** biochem. culture medium. **2.** (*pożywienie*) nourishment, nutrient; **pożywka dla plotek** fuel for gossip.

pożywny a. nourishing, nutritious.

pójdźka f. Gen.pl. **-dziek** zool. little owl (*Athene noctua*).

pójść pf. **pójdę pójdziesz poszedł poszła poszli 1.** (= *skierować się*) go, head for; **pójść do kina/na spacer** go for a walk/to the movies; **pójść, gdzie oczy poniosą** go and never look back; **pójść w ślad za kimś** follow sb; **poszedł jak zmyty** pot. he buzzed off, he cleared out. **2.** (= *zacząć coś*) go; **pójść na studia** go to the university; **pójść do pracy** take a job; **pójść do łóżka** go to bed, go to sleep; **pójść do więzienia** go to prison *l.* jail; **pójść za kratki** *pot.* be sent down, be locked up; **pójść komuś na rękę** be accommodating with sb, do sb a favor; **pójść na emeryturę** retire; **pójść na kompromis** agree to a compromise; **pójść na pierwszy ogień** go over the top first; **pójść na swoje** start living on one's own; **pójść o zakład** make a bet; **pójść pod mur** be put against the wall; **pójść pod nóż** (*o zwierzętach*) be slaughtered; *pot.* (= *przejść operację*) go under the knife; **pójść pod młotek** come under the hammer; **pójść po rozum do głowy** turn (*sth*) over in one's mind; **pójść w czyjeś ślady** follow in sb's footsteps; **pójść w górę** go up; **pójść w świat** go in the world; **pójść za czyjąś radą** follow sb's advice; **poszło mu w pięty** he learnt a lesson; **pójść z kimś do łóżka** *pot.* go to bed with sb; **poszło z dymem** it went up in smoke; **pójść w kąt** be forgotten; **nie pójdę na to** *pot.* I'm not having it; **o co poszło?** what was the point?; **lekko przyszło, lekko poszło** easy come easy go; **nauka nie poszła w las** the lesson was not (has not been) forgotten. **3.** (= *zostać wysłanym*) be sent; **czy list już poszedł?** has the letter been sent yet? **4.** (= *potoczyć się*) go; **poszło jak po maśle** it went smooth, it went like a clockwork; **wszystko poszło po naszej myśli** everything turned out as we wished. **5.** *pot.* (= *zużyć*) be spent, be used up; **poszła opona** the tire is gone, the tire is flat; **żarówka poszła** the bulb is gone, the bulb is burnt; **wszystkie pieniądze poszły na remont domu** all the money has been spent on the redecoration of the house; **niech ci pójdzie na zdrowie!** much good may it do you; **praca całego życia poszła na marne** a lifetime's work has been wasted, a lifetime's work is gone; **kłótnia poszła w niepamięć** the quarrel has been forgiven and forgotten.

póki *conj.* as long as, while; **póki nie** until; **póki co** for the time being; **póki czas** before it's too late; **póki nie wrócę** until I come back; **idź, póki nie pada** go as long as it doesn't rain; **pracuję, póki sił starcza** I'll work as long as my strength does not fail; **korzystaj z życia, pókiś młody** enjoy life while you're young.

pół *num. indecl.* half; **trzy i pół metra** three and a half meters; **podzielić coś na pół** divide sth into two, halve sth; **przerwać komuś w pół słowa** cut sb short; **zawrócić w pół drogi** turn back half-way; **jest pół do drugiej** it's half past one, it's one thirty; **poproszę pół czarnej** half a cup of black coffee, please; **pół żartem, pół serio** half jokingly, half seriously; **z tym jest pół biedy** this is not much of a problem; **pół biedy, że..., ale...** the problem is not that..., but...; **na pół suche włosy** half dry hair.

półanalfabeta *mp* semi-illiterate person.
półanalfabetyzm *mi* semi-illiteracy.
półautomat *mi techn.* semi-automaton, semi-automatic machine.
półautomatyczny *a.* semi-automatic.
półbóg *mp* -o- *pl.* -owie *mit.* demigod.

półbut *mi Gen.* -a shoe, (*sznurowany*) oxford, tie shoe.
półcień *mi Gen.* -a *pl.* -e **1.** (= *słaby cień*) twilight. **2.** (*na obrazie*) half-tone.
półciężarówka *f. Gen.pl.* -ek light truck, pickup.
półciężki *a. sport* light heavyweight; *Br. t.* cruiserweight.
półdupek *mi* -pk- *Gen.* -a *pot.* buttock.
półdystans *mi sport* half-distance.
półdziki *a.* half-wild.
półetat *mi* part-time job; **pracować na półetacie** work part-time.
półfabrykat *mi* semi-finished product.
półfinalista *mp*, **półfinalistka** *f. Gen.pl.* -ek *sport* semi-finalist.
półfinał *mi sport* semi-final.
półfinałowy *a. sport* semi-final.
półgębkiem *adv.* in a mutter.
półgęsek *mi* -sk- *Gen.* -a half a roast goose.
półgłosem *adv.* in an undertone.
półgłówek *mp* -wk- *pl.* -i *pog.* half-wit, nitwit.
półgodzina *f.* half an hour; **wyjść po półgodzinie** leave after half an hour.
półgodzinny *a.* half an hour.
półgolf *mi Gen.* -u *l.* -a (*sweter*) mock turtleneck.
półgruby *a. druk.* druk półgruby semibold type.
półhurtowy *a.* half-wholesale.
półinteligencki *a.* half-educated.
półinteligent *mp*, **półinteligentka** *f. Gen.pl.* -ek half-educated person.
półinternat *mi* boarding and day school.
półjawa *f.* half-conscious state, half-consciousness.
półjawnie *adv.* half-secretly.
półjawny *a.* half-secret.
półka *f. Gen.pl.* -ek **1.** (*przy ścianie*) shelf; (*na książki*) bookshelf; (*na bagaż*) rack. **2.** (*skalna*) ledge.
półkilogramowy *a.* half-kilogram.
półkilometrowy *a.* half-kilometer.
półkoczowniczy *a.* half-nomadic.
półkoks *mi techn.* semi-coke.
półkole *n. Gen.pl.* -i (*zakręt*) *geom.* semicircle.
półkolem *adv.* in a half-circle.
półkolisty *a.* semicircular.
półkolonia *f. Gen.* -ii summer play center.
półkownik *mi Gen.* -a *żart.* film banned from screening (*usu. for political reasons*).
półkożuszek *mi* -szk- *Gen.* -a fur jacket.
półkrwi *f.* -rwi- half-breed; **Adam jest półkrwi Węgrem** Adam is half Hungarian; **koń półkrwi** half-bred horse.
półkruchy *a.* ciasto półkruche shortcrust pastry.
półkrzew *mi bot.* subshrub.
półksiężyc *mi Gen.* -a **1.** (= *fragment księżyca*) crescent moon, crescent. **2.** (*godło*) crescent; **Czerwony Półksiężyc** Red Crescent.
półkula *f.* (= *połowa kuli*) (*t. ziemskiej*) hemisphere; **półkula północna/południowa/wschodnia/zachodnia** northern/southern/eastern/west-

ern hemisphere; **półkula mózgowa** cerebral hemisphere.

póllegalny *a.* semi-legal.

półleżeć *ipf.* recline.

póllitrowy *a.* half-liter.

póllitrówka *f. Gen.pl.* **-ek** *pot.* half-liter bottle.

półmat *mi techn.* half-matt.

półmatowy *a.* half-matt.

półmetal *mi chem.* semi-metal.

półmetek *mi* **-tk-** *Gen.* **-a** halfway point; **osiągnąć półmetek** reach halfway point.

półmetrowy *a.* half-a-meter long.

półmilionowy *a.* half-million; **półmilionowe miasto** city of half a million inhabitants.

półmisek *mi* **-sk-** *Gen.* **-a** platter, dish; **szwedzki półmisek** Swedish platter.

półmrok *mi* twilight; (*zwł. w pomieszczeniu*) dimness.

półnagi *a.* half-naked.

półnago *adv.* half-nakedly.

północ *f.* **1.** (*pora nocy*) midnight; **wrócić o północy** come back at midnight, be back at midnight; **północ bije** the clock is striking midnight. **2.** (*strona świata*) north; **okna na północ** north windows, windows to the north; **jechać na północ** go northwards; **mieszkać na północy kraju** live in the north of the country. **3.** (*region świata*) the North; **na dalekiej północy** in the Far North.

północnoamerykański *a.* North-American.

północnoatlantycki *a.* North-Atlantic; **Pakt Północnoatlantycki** *polit.* North Atlantic Treaty Organization.

północno-wschodni *a.* north-east, northeast; north-eastern, northeastern.

północno-zachodni *a.* north-west, nortwest; north-western, northwestern.

północny *a.* (*klimat, półkula*) northern; (*wiatr, kierunek*) northerly; **północny wschód** north-east; **północny zachód** north-west; **północna Francja** northern France; **Ameryka Północna** North America; **Irlandia Północna** Northern Ireland.

północo-wschód *mi* **-o-** North-East.

północo-zachód *mi* **-o-** North-West.

półnuta *f. muz.* half-note; *Br.* minim.

półobrót *mi* **-o-** half-turn.

półoficjalny *a.* semi-official.

półokrąg *mi* **-ę-** (*łuk*) *geom.* semicircle.

półokrągły *a.* semicircular.

półokrągło *adv.* semicircularly.

półoswojony *a.* half-tame.

półoś *f. pl.* **-e** **1.** *geom.* semi-axis. **2.** *techn.* axle shaft, halfshaft.

półotwarty *a.* half-open; **spółgłoski półotwarte** *fon.* sonorants.

półpasiec *mi* **-śc-** *Gen.* **-a** *pat.* shingles.

półpasożyt *ma biol.* semi-parasite.

półpełny *a. geom.* **kąt półpełny** straight angle.

półpiętro *n. Gen.pl.* **-er** **1.** (*podest*) landing. **2.** (*kondygnacja*) mezzanine floor, mezzanine; entresol.

półpłaszczyzna *f. geom.* half plane.

półpłótno *n. Gen.pl.* **-cien** *introl.* half-cloth binding.

półpłynny *a.* semifluid, semifluidic; semiliquid.

półpokład *mi żegl.* half-deck.

półprawda *f.* half-truth.

półprodukt *mi* semi-finished product.

półprofesjonalny *a.* semiprofessional.

półprofil *mi* half-profile; **portret z półprofilu** portrait in half-profile.

półprosta *f. Gen.* **-ej** *geom.* ray.

półprzestrzeń *f. geom.* half space.

półprzewodnik *mi Gen.* **-a** *fiz.* semiconductor.

półprzezroczysty *a.* semitransparent, translucent.

półprzyczepa *f. techn.* semitrailer, semi.

półprzysiad *mi sport* half knee bend.

półprzytomny *a.* semiconscious, half-conscious; **być półprzytomnym ze zmęczenia** be dead tired.

półpustynia *f. Gen.pl.* **-i** *geogr.* semidesert.

półpustynny *a.* semidesert.

półrocze *n. Gen.pl.* **-y** **1.** (= *połowa roku*) half-year. **2.** *szkoln.* semester, term.

półroczny *a.* half-yearly, semi-annual; **półroczny pobyt** half-a-year stay, six-month stay; **półroczne dziecko** six-month-old baby.

półsamogłoska *f. fon.* **1.** semivowel. **2.** (= *samogłoska zredukowana*) reduced vowel.

półsen *mi* **-sn-** drowse.

półserio *adv.* half-seriously.

półsierota *f. l. mp decl. like f. Gen.pl.* **-t** *l.* **-ów** half-orphan.

półsłodki *a.* semi-sweet.

półsłówko *n. Gen.pl.* **-ek** **1.** (= *monosylaba*) monosyllable. **2.** (= *aluzja*) allusion; **mówić półsłówkami** make allusions.

półstały *a.* semisolid.

półstrunowce *pl. Gen.* **-ów** *zool.* hemichordates (*Hemichordata*).

półsurowiec *mi* semi-processed raw material.

półsurowy *a.* half-raw; (*o mięsie*) underdone; (*o cieście*) half-baked.

półsyntetyczny *a.* semisynthetic.

półszlachetny *a.* semi-precious.

półśredni *a. sport* welterweight.

półśrodek *mi* **-dk-** *Gen.* **-a** half-measure, stopgap measure; **stosować półśrodki** use *l.* apply stopgap measures.

półświadomie *adv.* semiconsciously.

półświadomy *a.* semiconscious.

półświatek *mi* **-tk-** *Gen.* **-a** **1.** (= *świat przestępczy*) underworld. **2.** (= *środowisko kobiet lekkiego prowadzenia się*) demimonde.

półświatło *n.* (*zwł. świtu, zmierzchu*) half-light.

półtłusty *a.* (*o mleku, twarogu*) semi-skimmed.

półton *mi* **1.** *muz.* semitone. **2.** (*odcień*) half-tone.

półtonowy[1] *a. muz.* semitonic, halftone.

półtonowy[2] *a.* (= *mający pół tony*) half a ton.

półtora, półtorej *num. indecl.* one and a half; **półtora litra** one and a half liters; **półtorej godziny** hour and a half, one and a half hours; **wyglą-**

dasz jak **półtora nieszczęścia** you look the very picture of misery.

półtoradniowy *a.* day and a half; **półtoradniowa podróż** day and a half long journey; **półtoradniowe dziecko** day and a half old baby.

półtoragodzinny *a.* one and a half hours', of an hour and a half.

półtorakilometrowy *a.* one and a half kilometer.

półtorametrowy *a.* one and a half meter.

półtoramiesięczny *a.* one and a half month; **półtoramiesięczne dziecko** one and a half month old baby; **półtoramiesięczna wycieczka** one and a half month trip.

półtoraroczny *a.* one and a half year; **półtoraroczne dziecko** one and a half year old baby; **półtoramiesięczny pobyt** one and a half year trip.

półtrampek *mi* sneaker.

półtusza *f. Gen.pl.* **-y** *roln.* side; **półtusza wieprzowa** side of pork.

półtwardy *a.* (*o stali, drucie*) semi-hard; (= *niedogotowany*) udercooked.

półuchem *adv.* **słuchać czegoś półuchem** listen with half an ear.

póługór *mi* **-o-** *roln.* semi-fallow.

półukłon *mi* half-bow.

półuśmiech *mi* half-smile.

półwalec *mi* **-lc-** *Gen.* **-a** *geom.* semicylinder.

półwiatr *mi żegl.* half-wind.

półwiecze *n. Gen.pl.* **-y** half-century.

półwiek *mi* half-century; **przed półwiekiem** half a century ago.

półwysep *mi* **-sp-** peninsula.

półwytrawny *a.* semi-dry.

półzwrot *mi sport żegl.* half-turn.

półżartem *adv.* half jokingly.

półżywy *a. pot.* half dead; **po całym dniu pracy jestem półżywy** after a whole day's work I am dead tired.

póty *conj.* till, until; **póty tu zostaniesz, póki nam wszystkiego nie powiesz** you will stay here until you have told us everything; **póty dzban wodę nosi, póki się ucho nie urwie** the pitcher goes so often to the well that it is broken at last.

póznawy *a. pot.* latish.

póznić się *ipf.* **-ij** (*o zegarze*) be late.

później *adv.* later; **prędzej czy później** sooner or later; **trzy dni później** three days later; **nie później niż w środę** no later than Wednesday; **odkładać coś na później** put sth off until *l.* till later; *por.* **późno**.

późniejszy *a.* subsequent, later; (*o żądaniach*) further.

późno *adv.* late; **wracać późno z pracy** come late from work; **kłaść się późno** go to bed late, turn in late; **robi się późno** it's getting late; **jest już późno** it's late; **lepiej późno niż wcale** better late than never; **do późna** till late; **pracować do późna** work till late; **siedzieć do późna** stay up late, sit up; **najpóźniej w przyszłym tygodniu** next week at the latest; **kto późno przychodzi, sam sobie szkodzi** first come first served.

póznobarokowy *a.* late baroque.

póznogotycki *a.* late Gothic.

póznorenesansowy *a.* late Renaissance.

póznoromański *a.* late Romanesque.

póznośredniowieczny *a.* late medieval, late Middle Ages.

późny *a.* **1.** (*o porze*) late; **późny wieczór** late evening; **późna wiosna** late spring; **późny barok/gotyk** late baroque/Gothic; **późny wiek** old age; **późna starość** advanced old age. **2.** (= *spóźniony*) late, delayed. **3.** (= *nowszy*) latest; **późne utwory** latest works. **4.** (= *późno dojrzewający*) (*o roślinach*) late.

ppłk *abbr.* Lt Col (= *lieutenant colonel*).

ppor. *abbr.* 2nd Lt (= *second lieutenant*).

prababka *f. Gen.pl.* **-ek** great-grandmother.

prabyt *mi fil.* original existence.

praca *f.* **1.** (*wytwarzanie*) work; labor; *Br.* labour; **praca fizyczna** physical work; **praca umysłowa** nonmanual work; **praca biurowa** office work; **praca dorywcza** odd jobs; **praca naukowa** research, researching; **praca twórcza** creative work; **praca sezonowa** seasonal work; **praca zawodowa** proffesional work; **praca zbiorowa** collective work; **praca zespołowa** team work; **praca zlecona** commissioned work; **pionierska praca** (*w jakiejś dziedzinie*) pioneering work; **praca nad kolejną powieścią** work on one's next novel; **bezpieczeństwo i higiena pracy** labor health and safety, health and safety at work; **dyscyplina pracy** work discipline, labor discipline; **karta pracy** work card; **podział pracy** division of labor; **prawo pracy** labor law; **organizacja pracy** labor organization; **wydajność pracy** productivity; **ludzie pracy** *przest.* working classe; **Święto Pracy** Labor Day, *Br.* Labour Day; May Day; **syzyfowa praca** a never-ending job; **bez pracy nie ma kołaczy** no pain no gain; **jaka praca, taka płaca** as you work, so you earn. **2.** (= *utwór, dzieło*) work, production; **praca pisemna z fińskiego** composition in Finnish; **praca poświęcona zagadnieniu bezrobocia** work on unemployment; **praca z zakresu teorii literatury** work on literary theory; **praca dyplomowa** diploma thesis; **praca licencjacka/magisterska** (*z zakresu nauk humanistycznych*) BA/MA thesis; (*z zakresu nauk ścisłych*) BSc/MSc thesis; **praca doktorska** doctoral *l.* PhD dissertation; **praca habilitacyjna** postdoctoral dissertation; **praca popularnonaukowa** popular science work. **3.** (= *proces*) work, function; **praca nóg** footwork; **prawidłowa praca serca** proper heart function; **bezawaryjna praca silnika** perfect engine functioning. **4.** (*etat*) job, post; **umowa o pracę** contract of employment; **dostać/stracić pracę** get/lose a job; **zwolnić kogoś z pracy** dismiss sb. **5.** *pot.* (= *miejsce zatrudnienia*) workplace; **być w pracy** be at work; **iść do/wrócić z pracy** go to/come back from work; **zakład pracy** place of employment; **kolega z pracy** colleague, co-worker, workmate. **6.** *fiz.* work; **jednostka pracy** unit of work.

prace *pl. Gen.* **-c** (*zadanie do wykonania*) task, work; **prace badawcze** research; **prace na wysokościach/polowe** high altitude/farm work.

pracobiorca *mp* employee.

pracochłonność *f. ekon.* labor consumption; *Br.* labour consumption; work consumption.

pracochłonny *a.* laborious.

pracodawca *mp* employer.

pracoholik *mp*, **pracoholiczka** *f. Gen.pl.* -ek workaholic.

pracować *ipf.* 1. (= *wykonywać pracę*) work; **pracować fizycznie** do physical work; **pracować umysłowo** do nonmanual work; **pracować zawodowo (jako...)** work professionally (as a...); **pracować naukowo** do research; **pracować dorywczo** do odd jobs; **pracować sezonowo** work seasonally; **pracować wydajnie** work efficiently; **pracować na akord** do piece work; **pracować na dniówkę** work by the day; **pracować na kawałek chleba** *l.* na utrzymanie work for a living, earn one's living; **pracować w pocie czoła** sweat and slave; **pracować jak mrówka** work hard; **pracować jak koń** work like a horse; **pracować jak dziki osioł** work one's head off; **pracuję na siebie** I make my own living; **pracuję dla tej firmy od dwóch lat** I've been working for this company for two years; **nad czym ostatnio pan pracuje?** what have you been working on recently?; **Marian pracuje nad sobą** Marian is working on himself; **czas pracuje na naszą niekorzyść** time is against us. 2. (= *być zatrudnionym*) work, be employed; **pracować w fabryce/w szkole** work in a factory/school; **pracuję jako nauczyciel** I work as a teacher. 3. (= *funkcjonować*) work, function; **serce pracuje prawidłowo** the heart works *l.* functions properly; **silnik pracował dotąd niezawodnie** the engine has been functioning unfailingly so far; **ta firma pracuje na eksport** *pot.* this company produces export goods; **linia produkcyjna pracuje pełną parą** the production line operates at full blast; **główka pracuje** *żart.* (*o sobie*) I have an idea! (*o kimś*) (*z podziwem*) that's a great idea! 4. *techn.* (*o materiale, konstrukcji*) (= *ulegać odkształceniom*) deform.

pracowicie *adv.* laboriously, diligently.

pracowitość *f.* laboriousness, diligence.

pracowity *a.* (= *pilny*) hard-working, laborious, diligent; (= *wypełniony pracą*) arduous; (= *staranny, wypracowany*) laborious.

pracownia *f. Gen.pl.* -i 1. (*artysty*) studio, atelier. 2. (*naukowca*) laboratory. 3. (= *warsztat*) workshop.

pracownica *f. zob.* **pracownik**.

pracowniczka *f. Gen.pl.* -ek (woman) worker.

pracowniczy *a.* worker's, employee's; **świadczenia pracownicze** labor benefits; *Br.* labour benefits; **wczasy pracownicze** company organized vacation (*often also subsidized by the company*).

pracownik *mp* worker, employee; **pracownik fizyczny** blue collar worker, physical worker; **pracownik biurowy** office worker; **pracownik dydaktyczny** teacher; **pracownik etatowy** full time employee; **pracownik naukowy** researcher, research worker; **pracownik sezonowy** seasonal worker; **pracownik techniczny** technical worker; **pracownik umysłowy** white-collar.

pracuś *mp Gen.pl.* -ów *żart.* workaholic.

pracz *mp* laundry worker; **szop pracz** *zool.* raccoon (*Procyon*).

praczas *mi* primeval times, remotest ages.

praczka *f. Gen.pl.* -ek washerwoman, laundress.

praczłowiek *mp* prehistoric man, ancient man.

prać *ipf.* **piorę pierzesz** 1. (= *usuwać brud*) wash, do the laundry; **prać chemicznie** dry-clean; **prać swoje brudy** *przen.* wash one's dirty linen in public; **prać brudne pieniądze** *przen.* launder money. 2. *pot.* (= *bić*) thrash, bash. 3. (*strzelać*) *pot.* shell, zap. ~ **się** *ipf.* 1. (= *być pranym*) wash. 2. *pot.* (= *bić się*) scuffle.

pradawny *a.* primeval.

pradolina *f. geogr.* proglacial stream valley.

pradziad *mp pl.* -owie great grandfather; **z dziada pradziada** from time immemorial.

pradziadek *mp* -dk- *pl.* -owie great grandfather.

pradzieje *pl. Gen.* -ów primeval history, prehistory.

Praga *f. geogr.* Prague.

pragmatycznie *adv.* pragmatically.

pragmatyczność *f.* pragmatism.

pragmatyczny *a.* pragmatic.

pragmatyk *mp* 1. (= *człowiek praktyczny*) pragmatist. 2. *fil.* pragmatist. 3. *prawn.* labor law specialist.

pragmatyka *f.* 1. (= *logiczność*) pragmatics. 2. *fil.* pragmaticism. 3. *prawn.* labor *l.* work regulations. 4. *jęz.* pragmatics.

pragmatysta *mp fil.* pragmatist.

pragmatystyczny *a. fil.* pragmatistic.

pragmatyzm *mi fil.* pragmatism.

pragnąć *ipf.* -ij (= *życzyć sobie*) desire, want; (= *pożądać*) lust for; **pragnąć coś zrobić** wish to do sth; **pragnąć czegoś gorąco** be anxious for, want in the worst (kind of) way; **pragnąć czegoś z całego serca** want sth with all one's heart; **pragnąć czegoś z całej duszy** want with all one's soul; **pragnę wyrazić swą wdzięczność** I wish *l.* would like to express my gratitude; **jak pragnę zdrowia/szczęścia** *pot.* I swear to God, honestly.

pragnienie *n.* 1. (= *chęć picia*) thirst; **mieć pragnienie** be thirsty. 2. (= *chęć osiągnięcia czegoś*) desire, anxiety, longing; **zaspokajać wszystkie pragnienia** satisfy all desires.

prahistoria *f. Gen.* -ii *hist.* prehistory.

prahistoryczny *a. hist.* prehistoric, prehistorical.

praindoeuropejski *a. hist.* primitive Indo-European, proto-Indo-European; **język praindoeuropejski** *jęz.* Proto-Indo-European (language).

prajęzyk *mi Gen.* -a *jęz.* protolanguage.

prakseolog *mp pl.* -dzy *l.* -owie *fil.* praxeologist, praxiologist.

prakseologia *f. Gen.* -ii *fil.* praxeology, praxiology.

prakseologiczny *a. fil.* praxeological, praxiological.

praktycysta *mp fil.* practicist.

praktycyzm *mi fil.* practicism.

praktycznie *adv.* practically, in practice; **sto-**

sować coś **praktycznie** use practically, make practical use of sth; **postępować praktycznie** act practically; **praktycznie rzecz biorąc** to all intents and purposes.

praktyczność f. practicality, practicalness.

praktyczny a. practical, useful; **umiejętności praktyczne** practical skills; **praktyczny człowiek** practical person.

praktyk mp (= osoba z doświadczeniem) experienced person; (= osoba zaradna) pragmatist, practian person; (= osoba wykonująca jakiś zawód, określoną czynność) practitioner; **prawnik praktyk** practicing lawyer.

praktyka f. **1.** (= doświadczenie) experience, practice; **zastosować coś w praktyce** put sth into practice; **praktyki religijne** religious practices; **nieuczciwe praktyki** dishonest practices. **2.** (= szkolenie, staż) training period; (u rzemieślnika) apprenticeship; **odbywać praktyki** undergo training; (u rzemieślnika) serve an apprenticeship; **praktyki szkolne** teacher training. **3.** (= wykonywanie zawodu) practice; **praktyka lekarska** medical practice.

praktykant mp (w firmie, w zawodzie) trainee, intern; (u rzemieślnika) apprentice; (w szkole) student l. practice teacher, intern.

praktykantka f. Gen.pl. -ek zob. **praktykant**.

praktyki pl. Gen. -k (czynności) practices, doings, dealings; **praktyki religijne/tajemne** religious/secret practices.

praktykować ipf. **1.** (= szkolić się) be in training; (u rzemieślnika) be an apprentice. **2.** (= wykonywać zawód) practice, pursue (a profession). **3.** (= stosować) apply, use; **tego się już nie praktykuje** it is not practiced any more. **4.** (= spełniać obowiązki religijne) be a practicing Christian/Baptist/etc.

praktykujący a. rel. church-going, practicing; **jestem praktykującym katolikiem** I am a practicing Catholic.

pralinka f. Gen.pl. -ek kulin. praline, chocolate cream.

pralka f. Gen.pl. -ek washing machine; **pralka automatyczna** automatic washing machine.

pralnia f. Gen.pl. -i **1.** (w domu) laundry. **2.** (zakład usługowy) laundrette, laundromat; **pralnia chemiczna** dry-cleaner's.

pralniczy a. laundering.

prałat mp rz.-kat. prelate.

pramatka f. Gen.pl. -ek lit. first mother.

pramonoteizm mi rel. primitive monotheism.

pranercze n. Gen.pl. -y anat. pronephros.

pranie n. **1.** (czynność) washing, laundering; **pranie brudów** muckraking; **pranie brudnych pieniędzy** money laundering; **pranie mózgów** brainwash, indoctrination; **oddać coś do prania** take sth to the laundry. **2.** (bielizna) laundry, washing.

praojciec mp -ojc- Dat. -u pl. -owie lit. forefather, ancestor.

praojczyzna f. lit. homeland.

prapłaziec ma -żc- icht. lungfish (Lepidosiren paradoxa).

prapolski a. primitive Polish, proto-Polish.

praprababka f. Gen.pl. -ek great-great-grandmother.

prapradziad mp pl. -owie great-great-grandfather.

prapradziadek mp pl. -dkowie great-great-grandfather.

prapraprzodek mp -dk- pl. -owie forefather, earliest ancestor.

praprawnuk mp pl. -owie l. -i great-great-grandson, great grandson's son.

prapremiera f. world premiere.

prapremierowy a. world premiere.

praprzodek mp -dk- pl. -owie primogenitor, protoplast.

prasa f. **1.** techn. (maszyna) press; **prasa drukarska** druk. printing press; **prasa hydrauliczna** hydraulic press; **prasa olejarska** oil press; **prasa ręczna** hand press. **2.** (czasopisma) press, papers; **prasa donosi, że...** papers report that...; **premier ma złą prasę** prime minister has bad publicity l. press; **przedstawiciele prasy** the Press, press representatives.

praser mp techn. presser.

prask int. crash!, bang!; **a ja prask go w pysk!** and then, I hit him in the face!

praski a. **1.** of Praga (a district in Warsaw). **2.** of Prague (in the Czech Republic); **praska wiosna** hist., polit. the Prague Spring.

prasłowiański a. proto-Slavonic, proto-Slavic; **język prasłowiański** Proto-Slavonic l. Proto-Slavic (language).

prasłowiańszczyzna f. **1.** jęz. Proto-Slavonic l. Proto-Slavic (language). **2.** (obszar) proto-Slavonic l. proto-Slavic areas; (ludność) Proto-Slavs.

prasować ipf. **1.** (= wyciskać pod prasą) press. **2.** (odzież) iron, press.

prasowalnia f. Gen.pl. -i ironing-room.

prasowalnica f. Gen.pl. -ic (do odzieży) (clothes) press; **prasowalnica do spodni** trouser press.

prasownia f. Gen.pl. -i techn. press shop, stamping plant.

prasownica f. (do odzieży) (clothes) press.

prasowniczy a. ironing; **manekin prasowniczy** ironing dummy.

prasowy a. (= odnoszący się do czasopism) **1.** press; **agencja prasowa** press l. news agency; **doniesienie prasowe** press report; **artykuł prasowy** press article; **prawo prasowe** prawn. press law; **rzecznik prasowy** spokesperson. **2.** techn. (= dotyczący prasy - maszyny) press.

prasoznawca mp press specialist l. expert.

prasoznawczy a. press, journalistic.

prasoznawstwo n. press science.

prasówka f. Gen.pl. -ek **1.** pot. press review, news briefing. **2.** techn. powder metallurgy compact.

prast int. crash!, bang!; **szast-prast!** in a trice!

prastary a. primeval, ancient; **prastary ród** ancient family; **prastary las** primeval forest.

praszczur mp pl. -owie **1.** lit. ancestor, forefather. **2.** great-great-grandson.

prawda f. truth; **szczera prawda** plain truth;

gorzka prawda bitter truth; **ziarno prawdy** grain of truth; **nie ma w tym, co mówisz, za grosz prawdy** there isn't a grain of truth in what you're saying, there isn't an iota of truth in what you're saying; **(to) prawda** it's true; **prawda!** true!; **jest ciepło, prawda?** it's warm, isn't it?; **lubisz go, prawda?** you like him, don't you?; **czy to prawda?** is that true?; **co prawda** as a matter of fact; **święta prawda** gospel truth; **prawdę mówiąc** to tell the truth, in truth, truth to tell; **mijać się z prawdą** depart from the truth; **powiedzieć prawdę w oczy** give sb a piece of one's mind; **dążyć do prawdy** aim at truth; **naga prawda** naked truth; **spojrzeć prawdzie w oczy** face the truth; **dać świadectwo prawdzie** *emf.* testify to the truth; **prawda w oczy kole** the greater the truth, the greater the libel; **zgodny z prawdą** truthful.

prawdomówność *f.* truthfulness.

prawdomówny *a.* truthful, veracious.

prawdopodobieństwo *n.* probability, likelihood; **według wszelkiego prawdopodobieństwa** in all likelihood *l.* probability; **istnieje małe prawdopodobieństwo, że...** it is (very) unlikely that...; **rachunek prawdopodobieństwa** *mat.* probability calculus, calculus of probability.

prawdopodobnie *adv.* **1.** (= *chyba*) probably; **prawdopodobnie przyjedzie w poniedziałek** he/she is likely to come on Monday; **to wygląda mało prawdopodobnie** it seems very unlikely. **2.** (= *autentycznie*) plausibly.

prawdopodobny *a.* **1.** (= *bliski prawdy*) probable. **2.** (= *możliwy*) probable, likely; **to jest mało prawdopodobne** it is very unlikely.

prawdziwek *mi* -**wk**- *Gen.* -**a** *bot.* king bolete, penny bun, cep (*Boletus edulis*).

prawdziwie *adv.* truthfully, truly, authentically; **dzień prawdziwie wiosenny** a truly spring day.

prawdziwość *f.* truth, truthfulness, authenticity, genuineness; **dowieść prawdziwości czegoś** prove the authenticity of sth.

prawdziwy *a.* (*o kłopocie, przyjemności*) real; (*o skórze, perle*) genuine; (*o opowieści*) true, truthful; (*o miłości*) true; (*o zdarzeniu*) authentic; (*o dokumencie*) original; **lekarz z prawdziwego zdarzenia** real medicine doctor; **to prawdziwa niespodzianka** it's a real surprise; **zdanie prawdziwe** *log.* true proposition.

prawica *f.* **1.** *polit.* the Right, right wing; **skrajna prawica** radical right, ultra-right. **2.** *emf.* (= *prawa ręka*) right hand; **po prawicy** on the right.

prawicowiec *mp* -**wc**- *pl.* -**y** *zwł. polit.* rightist, right-winger.

prawicowy *a. polit.* right-wing, rightist; **partia prawicowa** right-wing party.

prawiczek *mp* -**czk**- *pl.* -**i** *pot.* virgin, cherry.

prawiczka *f. Dat.* -**czce** *zob.* **prawiczek**.

prawić *ipf. przest.* talk, lecture; **prawić komuś kazania** *l.* **morały** sermonize sb; **prawić komuś komplementy** pay sb compliments, pay compliments to sb.

prawidło *n. Gen.pl.* -**deł 1.** (= *reguła*) rule, law;

trzymać się prawideł stick to the rules. **2.** (*szewskie*) shoetree.

prawidłowo *adv.* (= *należycie*) properly; (= *poprawnie*) correctly; (= *normalnie*) normally.

prawidłowość *f.* regularity; correctness.

prawidłowy *a.* (= *należyty*) proper; (= *poprawny*) correct; (= *normalny*) normal; **graniastosłup prawidłowy** *geom.* regular prism.

prawie *adv.* almost, nearly; **prawie jej nie znam** I hardly know her; **prawie skończyłem** I'm almost done, I've almost finished; **prawie nic** next to nothing; **prawie nigdy** hardly ever; **prawie nikt** scarcely anybody.

prawiek *mi lit.* time immemorial.

prawniczka *f. Gen.pl.* -**ek** *zob.* **prawnik**.

prawniczy *a.* (*zawód, wykształcenie*) legal; (*studia*) law.

prawnie *adv.* legally, lawfully; **Adamowi to się prawnie należy** Adam has a legal right to it.

prawnik *mp* **1.** (= *osoba z wykształceniem prawniczym*) lawyer. **2.** *pot.* (= *student prawa*) law student.

prawnuczek *mp* -**czk**- *pl.* -**owie** *l.* -**i** grandson.

prawnuczka *f.* granddaughter.

prawnuk *mp pl.* -**owie** *l.* -**i** grandson.

prawny *a.* (*radca, porada, moc, kodeks*) legal; (*akt*) legislative; (*właściciel*) lawful, rightful; **czynność prawna** legal act; **moc prawna** force and effect, legal efficacy; **osoba prawna** legal person, artificial person, fictitious person, juristic person, moral person; **osobowość prawna** legal personality; **radca prawny** attorney, attorney-at-law, lawyer; **środek prawny** legal remedy; **zdolność prawna** legal capacity.

prawo¹ *n.* **1.** (= *ogół przepisów*) law; **prawo rzymskie** Roman law; **prawo nowożytne** modern law; **prawo polskie** Polish law; **prawo amerykańskie** American law; **prawo angielskie** English law; **prawo administracyjne** administrative law; **prawo autorskie** copyright; **prawo cywilne** civil law; **prawo karne** criminal *l.* penal law; **prawo międzynarodowe** international law, law of nations; **prawo rodzinne** family law, domestic-relations law; **prawo rzeczowe** law of property; **prawo wyborcze** election law, right to vote; **prawo zwyczajowe** common law; **w imieniu prawa** in the name of law; **w obliczu prawa** in the eye of the law. **2.** (= *przepis*) law, rule, regulation; **naruszać literę prawa** violate the law; **wyjęty spod prawa** outlawed; **łamać prawo** break *l.* violate the law; **omijać prawo** flout the law; **prawo pięści** law of the fist; **prawem kaduka** *przest.* unlawfully, illegally. **3.** *uniw.* (= *nauka prawa*) law; **studiować prawo** study law; **ukończyć prawo** graduate with a degree in law, graduate in law; **absolwent prawa** law graduate; **wydział prawa** law faculty, faculty of law. **4.** (= *uprawnienie*) right; **prawo pierwokupu** preemption right; **prawa człowieka** human rights; **prawa obywatelskie** civil rights; **prawo jazdy** driver's license; *Br.* driving licence; **prawo pierwszeństwa przejazdu** *mot.* right of way; **prawo łaski** right to pardon; **dochodzić swoich praw** assert *l.* claim one's rights; **Adam nie ma prawa tak mówić** Adam has no right to talk like this; **Ewa nie ma prawa do tego domu** Eve has no right to this house, Eve is not entitled to this house; **jakim prawem?** by what right? **5.** (= *prawidłowość, zasada*) law, principle; **prawa naturalne/biologiczne/fizyczne** natural/biological/physical laws; **podlegać prawom przyrody** *l.* **natury** be subject to the laws of nature.

prawo² *adv.* right; **na prawo** (= *po prawej stronie*) on *l.* to the right; (= *w prawą stronę*) to the right; **w prawo** to the right; **na prawo i na lewo** on the right and on the left; **w prawo i lewo** right and left; **albo w prawo, albo w lewo** either right or left.

prawobrzeżny *a.* right-bank; **prawobrzeżny dopływ** right-bank tributary.

prawodawca *mp* (*osoba*) legislator; (*organ*) legislative body.

prawodawczy *a.* legislative, lawgiving, lawmaking; **organ prawodawczy** legislative body, legislature.

prawodawstwo *n.* **1.** (= *ogół praw*) legislation, law(s). **2.** (= *ustanawianie praw*) legislation, lawmaking.

prawomocnie *adv.* with legal validity.

prawomocność *f. prawn.* (legal) validity.

prawomocny *a. prawn.* (legally) valid; **wyrok prawomocny** final and binding sentence.

prawomyślność *f.* law-abidingness.

prawomyślny *a.* law-abiding; **prawomyślny obywatel** law-abiding citizen.

praworęczność *f.* right-handedness.

praworęczny *a.* right-handed.

praworządnie *adv.* legally.

praworządność *f.* law and order.

praworządny *a.* (= *postępujący zgodnie z prawem*) law-abiding; (= *zgodny z prawem*) legal; **praworządny obywatel** law-abiding citizen.

prawoskrętność *f.* dextrorotation, dextrogyration; (*śruby*) right-handedness.

prawoskrętny *a.* dextrorotatory, dextrorotary, dextrogyrate; (*o ruchu, śrubie*) right-handed.

prawoskrzydłowy *a.* right-wing. – *mp sport* right winger.

prawosławie *n. rel.* the Orthodox Church.

prawosławna *f. Gen.* **-ej** *rel.* (female) member of the Orthodox Church.

prawosławny *a. rel.* Orthodox; **cerkiew prawosławna** Orthodox church. – *mp rel.* (male) member of the Orthodox Church.

prawostronny *a.* right-hand, right-side; **ruch prawostronny** *mot.* right-side traffic.

prawość *f. emf.* integrity, rectitude, righteousness.

prawoślaz *mi bot.* althea, althaea (*Althaea*).

prawowierny *a. zob.* ortodoksyjny.

prawowitość *f. lit.* legality, legitimacy, lawfulness.

prawowity *a. zwł. prawn.* legal, lawful, legitimate; **prawowity spadkobierca** rightful heir; **prawowity właściciel** rightful owner; **prawowita małżonka** lawful wife.

prawoznawczy *a.* jurisprudential.

prawoznawstwo *n.* jurisprudence.

prawy *a.* **1.** (= *nie lewy*) right; **prawa noga** right leg; **prawa burta** *żegl.* starboard; **po prawej stronie** on the right-hand side; **z prawej strony** on the right-hand side; **w prawą stronę** to the right; **prawy prosty** *boks* right straight; **Adam jest prawą ręką szefa** Adam is the right hand of his boss. **2.** (= *wierzchni*) right-side; **prać coś prawą stroną do wewnątrz** wash sth inside out. **3.** *emf.* (= *uczciwy*) honest, righteous, honorable; **prawy człowiek** person of integrity; **prawy charakter** upright character. **4.** *polit. rzad.* right-wing; **prawe skrzydło partii** right wing of the party.

prawybory *pl. Gen.* **-ów** *polit.* primary election(s), primary *l.* primaries.

prawykonanie *n. muz.* world premiere.

praz *mi min.* prase.

prazeodym *mi chem.* praseodymium.

praźródło *n. Gen.pl.* **-deł** *lit.* origin(s).

prażony *a.* **1.** *kulin.* roasted; **prażone orzeszki** roasted peanuts; **prażona kukurydza** popcorn. **2.** *techn.* roasted; baked.

prażyć *ipf.* **1.** *kulin.* (= *przypiekać*) roast. **2.** swelter, beat down; **słońce dzisiaj praży** the sun is beating down today, it is a scorcher today, it is a sweltering day today. **3.** *techn.* roast; bake; torrefy; decrepitate; calcine. ~ **się** *ipf.* **1.** *kulin.* roast. **2.** swelter; **prażyć się na plaży** sunbathe on a beach, bask in the sun on a beach.

prażynki *pl. Gen.* **-ek** *kulin.* (potato) chips.

prącie *n. Gen.pl.* **-i** *anat.* penis.

prąd *mi* **1.** (= *nurt*) current; **prąd morski** sea current. **2.** *przen.* (= *ciąg ludzi, samochodów itp.*) stream; **iść pod prąd** go against the stream *l.* tide; **iść z prądem** go with the stream *l.* tide. **3.** (*gazu, powietrza*) current, flow, stream; **prądy powietrzne** *meteor.* air currents, currents of air. **4.** (*w sztuce, literaturze*) current, trend, tendency. **5.** *el.* (electric) current; (= *elektryczność*) electricity; **prąd indukcyjny** *l.* **indukowany** induced current; **prąd przemienny** alternating current; **prąd stały** direct current; **prąd zmienny** alternating current; **prądy błądzące** stray *l.* vagabond currents; **napięcie prądu** voltage; **natężenie prądu** current intensity *l.* strength.

prądnica *f. techn.* (current) generator; **prądnica prądu stałego** dynamo; **prądnica prądu zmiennego** alternator.

prądochłonny *a.* electricity-intensive; **urządzenie prądochłonne** electricity-intensive appliance.

prądomierz *mi Gen.* **-a** *techn.* current log.

prądotwórczy *a.* current-generating; **agregat prądotwórczy** current-generating unit.

prątek *mi* **-tk-** *Gen.* **-a** **1.** *pat.* bacillus. **2.** *ogr.* sprig, spray.

prątkować *ipf. pat.* be sputum-positive.

prążek *mi* **-żk-** *Gen.* **-a** stripe, line; **garnitur w prążki** striped suit.

prążkowany *a.* striped, lined; **mięśnie poprzecznie prążkowane** *anat.* striate muscles.

preambuła *f. prawn.* preamble.

precedens *mi* precedent; **bez precedensu** unprecedented, without precedent; **precedens są-dowy** *prawn.* (judicial) precedent.

precedensowy *a.* precedential.

precel *mi Gen.* **-cla** *kulin.* pretzel.

precelek *mi* **-lk-** *Gen.* **-a** *kulin.* (little) pretzel.

precesja *f. fiz.* precession.

precjoza *pl. Gen.* **-ów** valuables.

precypitacja *f. chem.* precipitation.

precypitat *mi chem.* precipitate.

precyzja *f.* precision, accuracy; **robić coś z aptekarską precyzją** do sth with surgical precision.

precyzować *ipf.* specify, state precisely. ~ **się** *ipf.* become specified.

precyzyjnie *adv.* precisely, exactly, with precision.

precyzyjność *f.* precision, accuracy, exactness.

precyzyjny *a.* **1.** (= *dokładny*) precise, exact, accurate. **2.** *pot.* (= *zajmujący się wyrobem narzędzi, instrumentów itp. precyzyjnych*) precision.

precz *adv.* away; **idź sobie precz!** go away!; **precz ode mnie!** go away from me!; **precz z łapami!** *pot.* keep your hands off!

predestynacja *f.* **1.** *lit.* (= *przeznaczenie*) fate, destiny, predestination. **2.** *rel.* predestination.

predestynować *ipf.* **1.** *lit.* (= *przeznaczać*) predestine. **2.** *rel.* predestinate.

predykacja *f.* **1.** *log.* predication. **2.** *jęz.* predication.

predykat *mi* **1.** *log.* predicate. **2.** *jęz.* predicate.

predykatywny *a. jęz.* predicative.

predylekcja *f. lit.* predilection (*do czegoś* for sth).

predysponować *ipf. lit.* predispose (*kogoś do czegoś* sb to sth).

predyspozycja *f. lit.* predisposition, predisposedness.

preenzym *mi chem.* zymogen, proenzyme.

prefabrykacja *f. bud.* prefabrication.

prefabrykat *mi bud.* prefabricated element *l.* unit, pre-cast element *l.* unit.

prefabrykować *ipf. bud.* prefabricate.

prefacja *f. rz.-kat.* preface.

prefekt *mp* **1.** *t. hist.* (*urzędnik*) prefect. **2.** *rel.* (= *ksiądz katecheta*) catechist, prefect.

prefektura *f.* **1.** (*jednostka administracyjna*) prefecture. **2.** (*urząd*) prefecture.

preferans *mi Gen. i Acc.* **-a** *karty* preference.

preferencja *f. lit.* preference; **preferencja celna** *ekon.* preferential tariff treatment.

preferencyjny *a.* preferential; **na preferencyjnych warunkach** on favorable conditions; **kredyt preferencyjny** *fin.* preferential loan.

preferować *ipf. lit.* prefer, favor.

prefiks *mi gram.* prefix.

prefiksacja *f. Gen.* **-cji** *gram.* prefixation, prefixion.

prefiksalny *a. gram.* prefixal.

preglacjalny *a. geol.* preglacial.

preglacjał *mi geol.* preglacial period.

prehistoria *f. Gen.* **-ii** *hist.* prehistory.

prehistoryczny *a. hist.* prehistoric, prehistorical.

prehistoryk *mp hist.* prehistorian.

prejotacja *f. fon.* preiotization.

prejudykat *mi prawn.* leading case.

prekambr *mi geol.* Pre-Cambrian (Era), Precambrian.

prekambryjski *a. geol.* Precambrian, Pre-Cambrian; **okres prekambryjski** Pre-Cambrian (Era), Precambrian.

prekluzja *f. prawn.* limitation (period).

prekluzyjny *a. prawn.* limitation; **okres prekluzyjny** limitation period.

prekolumbijski *a. hist.* pre-Columbian; **sztuka prekolumbijska** pre-Columbian art.

prekursor¹ *mp pl.* **-rzy** (= *ktoś, kto wyprzedza innych w danej dziedzinie*) precursor, predecessor; (= *zwiastun*) harbinger, forerunner.

prekursor² *mi Gen.* **-a** *pl.* **-y** *chem.* precursor.

prekursorka *f. zob.* **prekursor¹**.

prekursorski *a.* precursory.

prekursorstwo *n.* innovativeness.

prelegent *mp*, **prelegentka** *f. Gen.pl.* **-ek** speaker.

prelekcja *f. lit.* (public) lecture.

preliminaria *pl. Gen.* **-ów** *lit.* preliminary negotiations; **preliminaria pokojowe** *polit., prawn.* Preliminaries of Peace.

preliminarz *mi Gen.* **-a** **1.** *ekon.* estimate. **2.** *parl., ekon.* draft budget.

preliminować *ipf.* (= *układać preliminarz*) estimate, make an estimate.

preludium *n. sing. indecl. pl.* **-dia** *Gen.* **-diów** **1.** *muz.* prelude; **grać preludium** prelude, play a prelude. **2.** *przen.* prelude (*do czegoś* to sth).

premedytacja *f.* **1.** premeditation, deliberation. **2.** *prawn.* premeditation; (*w odniesieniu do zabójstwa, morderstwa*) malice aforethought, premeditated malice, preconceived malice, malice prepense, malitia praecogitata, premeditation; **morderstwo z premedytacją** premeditated killing *l.* murder; **dokonany z premedytacją** premeditated, prepense; **działać z premedytacją** act with premeditation.

premia *f. Gen.* **-ii** **1.** (*część pensji*) bonus, premium; **premia dla pracowników** employee bonus. **2.** (= *nagroda*) bonus, premium, reward, prize.

premier *mp polit.* prime minister, premier; **pełniący obowiązki premiera** acting *l.* caretaker prime minister; **urząd premiera** premiership; **ustępować ze stanowiska premiera** step down as prime minister; **Kancelaria Premiera** *l.* **Prezesa Rady Ministrów** Prime Minister's Office (*in Poland*).

premiera *f.* (*spektaklu, filmu, opery itd.*) premiere, première; (*zwł. spektaklu*) opening, first night; **mieć premierę** premiere, open; **premiera tej sztuki odbędzie się w sobotę** the play premieres *l.* opens on Saturday; **premiera prasowa** press premiere.

premierostwo¹ *n. Loc.* **-wie** *polit.* (= *urząd l. stanowisko premiera*) premiership.

premierostwo² *n. Loc.* **-wu** (= *premier z żoną*) prime minister and his wife.

premierowy *a.* first-night, opening, premiere; **publiczność premierowa** first-nighters.

premiować *ipf.* reward (*kogoś za coś* sb for sth); award a bonus (*kogoś* to sb).

premiowy *a.* bonus, premium; **pożyczka premiowa** *fin.* lottery *l.* premium loan; **system wynagrodzeń premiowych** bonus *l.* premium pay system; **fundusz premiowy** bonus fund.

prenatalny *a. biol., med.* prenatal, antenatal; **badanie prenatalne** prenatal examination.

prenumerata *f.* **1.** (= *prenumerowanie*) subscription (*czegoś* to sth); **zrezygnować z prenumeraty** cancel a subscription (*to a magazine, newspaper, etc.*); **opłaty za prenumeratę** subscription fees. **2.** (*kwota*) subscription (*za coś* to sth).

prenumerator *mp* subscriber.

prenumeratorka *f. Gen.pl.* **-ek** *zob.* **prenumerator.**

prenumerować *ipf.* subscribe (*coś* to sth); **prenumerować dziennik** subscribe to a daily.

preparacja *f. t. muz.* (= *przygotowanie*) preparation (*czegoś* of sth) (*na coś* for sth).

preparacje *pl. Gen.* **-i** *szkoln.* (= *objaśnienia*) annotations, explanatory notes.

preparat *mi* **1.** *chem.* preparation; **preparat farmaceutyczny** pharmaceutical; **preparat promieniotwórczy** radioactive preparation. **2.** (= *zakonserwowany organizm do badań*) specimen; **preparat mikroskopowy** section.

preparator *mp* preparator, laboratory assistant; preparer.

preparatyka *f. chem.* practical chemistry; **preparatyka chemiczna organiczna** practical organic chemistry.

preparować *ipf.* **1.** (= *przygotowywać do użytku*) prepare, make, concoct. **2.** *przen.* (*np. dane liczbowe, dokumenty*) cook, doctor; (*zarzuty, dowody*) fabricate, trump up; **preparować dowody** fabricate evidence. **3.** (= *sporządzać preparaty anatomiczne, zoologiczne itp.*) make a specimen of; (= *robić sekcję zwłok*) dissect.

prepozycja *mp jęz.* preposition.

prerafaelicki *a. sztuka* Pre-Raphaelite.

prerafaelita *mp sztuka* Pre-Raphaelite.

prerafaelityzm *mi sztuka* Pre-Raphaelitism.

preria *f. Gen.* **-ii** prairie; **Indianie Prerii (i Równin)** *US* the Plains Indians.

preriowy *a.* prairie; **piesek preriowy** *zool.* black-tailed *l.* Arizona prairie dog (*Cynomys ludovicianus*).

prerogatywy *pl. Gen.* **-w** *lit.* prerogatives.

preromantyczny *a. sztuka, teor.lit.* pre-Romantic.

preromantyk *mp sztuka, teor.lit.* pre-Romantic.

preromantyzm *mi sztuka, teor.lit.* pre-Romanticism.

presja *f.* pressure; **pod presją (kogoś)** under pressure (from sb); **pracować pod presją czasu** work against the clock; **wywierać nacisk** *l.* **presję na kogoś** put pressure on sb; **wywierać presję** *l.* **naciski na kogoś (żeby coś zrobił)** pressure *l.* pressurize sb (to do sth *l.* into doing sth).

pressing *mi sport, zwł. piłka nożna* pressing.

prestidigitator *mp* conjurer, conjuror, illusionist, prestidigitator.

prestidigitatorstwo *n.* prestidigitation, sleight of hand, legerdemain.

prestiż *mi* prestige, cachet, kudos; **cieszyć się dużym prestiżem** enjoy high prestige.

prestiżowy *a.* prestigious, of prestige.

presumpcja *f. prawn.* presumption.

presupozycja *f. jęz.* presupposition.

preszpan *mi techn.* pressed board.

pretekst *mi* pretext (*do l. dla czegoś* for sth); pretense; *Br.* pretence; excuse; **dać komuś/mieć/znaleźć pretekst do zrobienia czegoś** give sb/have/find an excuse to do sth; **wykorzystywać coś jako pretekst do czegoś** use sth as a pretext for sth *l.* to do sth; **pod fałszywym pretekstem** on *l.* under false pretenses; **pod pretekstem czegoś** under color of sth, on *l.* under the pretext of sth, under a show of sth; **pod pretekstem, że...** on the plea that...

pretendent *mp lit.* contender (*do czegoś* for sth); aspirant; (*do urzędu*) candidate; *zwł. sport* (*do tytułu*) challenger; **pretendent do tronu** pretender *l.* claimant to the throne.

pretendentka *f. Gen.pl.* **-ek** *zob.* **pretendent.**

pretendować *ipf.* (*o osobie, dziele*) aspire (*do czegoś* to sth); **nie pretenduję do roli geniusza** I don't profess *l.* pretend to be a genius; **pretendować do urzędu** (*w wyborach*) run for an office.

pretensja *f.* **1.** (= *roszczenie*) claim (*do czegoś* to sth); pretension (*do czegoś* to sth); **rościć (sobie) pretensje do czegoś** lay claim to sth; **rozpatrzenie pretensji** examination of a claim; **zaspokojenie pretensji** claim settlement; **uznawać pretensje (za uzasadnione)** recognise claims as justified. **2.** (= *żal*) resentment (*do kogoś o coś* against *l.* towards sb at *l.* of *l.* over sth); grievance (*do kogoś* against sb); rancour, grudge (*do kogoś* against sb); **mieć pretensję do kogoś** have a grievance against sb, have *l.* hold grudge against sb; **nie mieć do kogoś pretensji** have *l.* hold no grudge against sb. **3.** (= *wysokie mniemanie o sobie*) pretentiousness, affectation, pretense; *Br.* pretence; **osoba bez pretensji** unassuming *l.* unpretentious person; **z pretensjami** genteel.

pretensjonalnie *adv.* pretentiously; affectedly; **zachowywać się pretensjonalnie** be pretentious, put on airs, pose.

pretensjonalność *f.* (= *nacechowanie pretensją*) pretentiousness, pretense; (= *sztuczność*) affectation.

pretensjonalny *a.* pretentious, affected, arty, artsy.

pretor *mp hist.* pr(a)etor, pr(a)etorian.

pretorianin *mp pl.* **-anie** *Gen.* **-anów** *hist.* pr(a)etorian.

pretoriański *a. hist.* pr(a)etorian.

prewencja *f. prawn.* prevention; **oddziały prewencji (policji)** (*do rozpraszania demonstracji*) riot police.

prewencyjny *a. prawn.* preventive; **areszt prewencyjny** preventive custody.

prewenter, prewentormi *górn.* blow-out preventer.

prewentorium *n. sing. indecl. pl.* **-ria** *Gen.* **-riów** *med.* preventorium.

prewentoryjny *a. med.* preventorium; preventive.

prezbiter *mp* **-ter-** *l.* **-tr-** *pl.* **-rzy** *l.* **-owie** **1.** *rz.-kat.* priest, presbyter. **2.** *prezbiterianizm* presbyter, elder.

prezbiterialny *a. rel.* **1.** (= *dotyczący prezbiterium*) presbyterial. **2.** (= *dotyczący prezbitera*) presbyteral.

prezbiterianin *mp pl.* **-anie** *Gen.* **-anów** *rel.* Presbyterian.

prezbiterianizm *mi rel.* Presbyterianism.

prezbiterianka *f. Gen.pl.* **-ek** *rel.* *zob.* **prezbiterianin.**

prezbiteriański *a. rel.* Presbyterian.

prezbiterium *n. sing. indecl. pl.* **-ria** *Gen.* **-riów** *rel.* presbytery, sanctuary.

prezencja *f.* presence; **z dobrą prezencją** (*o osobie, t. w ofertach o pracy*) presentable.

prezent *mi* gift, present; **prezent urodzinowy** birthday gift *l.* present; **dać/dostać coś w prezencie** give/receive sth as a gift *l.* present; **to będzie dobre na prezent** it'll make a good gift; **obsypać kogoś prezentami** shower sb with gifts.

prezentacja *f.* **1.** (= *przedstawienie kogoś*) introduction; **dokonać (formalnej) prezentacji kogoś (komuś)** (formally) introduce sb (to sb); (*zwł. komuś wyższemu rangą*) present sb (to sb). **2.** (= *pokaz*) presentation, demonstration. **3.** (= *omówienie jakiegoś zagadnienia przez kogoś*) presentation; **prezentacja w Powerpoincie** *pot.* PowerPoint presentation.

prezenter *mp* **1.** *radio, telew.* announcer; *Br.* presenter; compere; (*zwł. wiadomości*) newscaster, anchor, news reader; (*zwł. na przedstawieniu, koncercie itp.*) master of ceremonies; *pot.* emcee; **prezenter radiowy** radio show host; **prezenter muzyczny** (*w TV*) video jockey, veejay, VJ; (*w radiu*) disc *l.* disk jockey, deejay, DJ. **2.** (fashion) model.

prezenterka *f. Gen.pl.* **-ek** *zob.* **prezenter.**

prezentować *ipf.* **1.** (= *pokazywać, demonstrować*) show (*coś komuś* sth to sb); present (*coś komuś* sth to sb); (*np. umiejętności*) display, exhibit; (*ubranie, kolekcję jako model*) model; (*urządzenie, produkt*) demonstrate; (*na wystawie, targach*) exhibit, display, show; **prezentować broń** *wojsk.* present arms; **prezentuj broń!** *wojsk.* port arms!, present arms! **2.** (= *przedstawiać*) introduce (*kogoś komuś* sb to sb); *form.* (*zwł. komuś wyższemu rangą*) present (*kogoś komuś* sb to sb). **~ się** *ipf.* (= *wyglądać*) look (*usu. attractively*); **dobrze się prezentować** look presentable; **marnie się prezentować** have a poor presence.

prezerwatywa *f.* condom, sheath.

prezes *mp US* president; *Br.* chairman; chairperson, chair; (*o kobiecie*) chairwoman; **Prezes Rady Ministrów** Prime Minister, Chairman of the Council of Ministers (*in Poland*); **prezes rady nadzorczej** *prawn. ekon.* president *l.* chairperson of the supervisory board (*in Poland*);

prezes zarządu *prawn. ekon.* president *l.* chairperson of the board of directors; **honorowy prezes** honorary president; **stanowisko prezesa** presidency, chairmanship; **pani prezes** Madam President *l.* Chairman.

prezeska *f. Gen.pl.* **-ek** *pot.* chairwoman.

prezesostwo[1] *n. Loc.* **-wie** (= *prezesura*) presidency, chairmanship.

prezesostwo[2] *n. Loc.* **-wu** (= *prezes z żoną*) president and his wife.

prezesować *ipf.* **1.** (= *być prezesem*) act as the president *l.* chairperson, be the president *l.* chairperson (*czegoś* of sth). **2.** (= *przewodniczyć*) preside (*czemuś* over sth); chair (*czemuś* sth).

prezesura *f.* presidency, chairmanship.

prezydencja *f. polit.* (= *przewodnictwo*) presidency (*in the EU*).

prezydencki *a. zwł. polit.* presidential; **kampania prezydencka** presidential campaign; **urząd prezydencki** presidency, office of a president; **orędzie prezydenckie** presidential address; **wybory prezydenckie** presidential election.

prezydent *mp* **1.** *polit.* (= *głowa państwa*) president; **były prezydent** former president, ex-president; **prezydent elekt** president-elect; **Prezydent Stanów Zjednoczonych** US President, Chief Executive; **wybrać kogoś na prezydenta** elect sb president; **kogoś wybrano na prezydenta** sb was elected president; **wystąpienie** *l.* **przemówienie** *l.* **orędzie prezydenta** presidential address; **ustępujący prezydent** outgoing president. **2.** (= *prezydent miasta, burmistrz większego miasta*) mayor. **3.** (= *prezes*) president, chairperson.

prezydentura *f.* presidency.

prezydialny *a.* presidium.

prezydium *n. sing. indecl. pl.* **-dia** *Gen.* **-diów** **1.** *polit.* presidium; **Prezydium Rządu** Cabinet. **2.** presiding officers; **prezydium zebrania** meeting board; **członek prezydium** member of presidium.

prezydować *ipf.* (= *przewodniczyć*) preside, chair, be the president *l.* chairman, act as the chairman; **prezydować zebraniu** chair a meeting, preside at *l.* over a meeting.

pręcik *mi Gen.* **-a** **1.** (= *laseczka*) rod, stick; *techn.* pin; **pręcik grafitowy** graphite, plumbago; **pręcik paliwowy** *fiz.* fuel pencil. **2.** *anat.* (*na siatkówce oka*) rod. **3.** *bot.* stamen.

pręcikowy *a.* **1.** rod, stick. **2.** *anat.* rod. **3.** *bot.* staminate; **kwiat pręcikowy** male *l.* staminate flower.

prędki *a.* **-dszy** **1.** (= *szybki*) fast, quick, swift. **2.** (= *natychmiastowy*) quick, immediate, instant, prompt. **3.** (= *popędliwy, gwałtowny*) hasty, rash, impulsive, impetuous, hot-headed.

prędko *adv.* **prędzej** **1.** (= *szybko*) quickly, fast, speedily, swiftly; **prędko!** quick(ly)!; **nie biegnij tak prędko** don't run so fast; **nie tak prędko!** not so fast!, hold on!, steady! **2.** (= *zaraz*) soon, shortly; **uporać się z czymś prędko** do sth quickly, do sth in the nick of time; (*z jedzeniem*) polish off; **czym prędzej coś zrobić** rush to do sth; **im prędzej, tym lepiej** the sooner the better; **prę-**

dzej czy później sooner or later; **prędzej kupiłbym samochód japoński niż koreański** I'd rather *l.* sooner buy a Japanese car than a Korean one; **prędzej się zabiję** I'll kill myself first.

prędkościomierz *mi Gen.* **-a** *techn.* speedometer, velocity meter, speed indicator, tachometer.

prędkość *f.* **1.** quickness, speed, swiftness. **2.** (*pojazdu*) speed; *fiz.* velocity; **nabierać prędkości** gather *l.* gain speed; **ograniczenie prędkości** speed limit; **jechać z nadmierną prędkością** speed, exceed the speed limit; **jechać (z prędkością) 60 km na godzinę** drive (at) 60 km an hour; *pot.* be doing 60 km an hour; **prędkość kątowa** angular velocity; **prędkość liniowa** linear velocity; **prędkość obrotowa** rotational speed; **prędkość dźwięku** speed of sound, acoustic velocity; **prędkość naddźwiękowa** supersonic speed; **prędkość poddźwiękowa** subsonic speed; **prędkość przydźwiękowa** transonic speed; **prędkość ucieczki** escape velocity; **prędkość światła** speed of light; **z dużą prędkością** at high speed; **z maksymalną prędkością** at full speed; *pot.* flat *l.* full out; **prędkość** *l.* **szybkość maksymalna** maximum speed.

prędzej *adv. zob.* **prędko.**

prędziutko *adv.* **1.** *emf.* quickly; **prędziutko!** quick(ly)!, hurry up! **2.** *zob.* **prędko.**

pręga *f.* **1.** (= *linia*) streak, stripe; (*od uderzenia*) wale, welt, wheal, weal; **krwawa pręga** bloody welt *l.* wheal. **2.** *kulin.* shin of beef.

pręgierz *mi Gen.* **-a** *hist.* pillory, whipping post; **stawiać pod pręgierzem** pillory; **postawić pod pręgierzem opinii publicznej** heap *l.* pour scorn on, hold up to shame, pillory, stigmatize.

pręgowany *a.* striped, striated, streaked.

pręt *mi Gen.* **-a 1.** (= *laska, drążek, tyczka*) rod, bar, stick. **2.** (*element konstrukcji*) bar; member; **pręty parasola** ribs; **pręt zbrojeniowy** *bud.* reinforced concrete bar, reinforcement bar, reinforcement rod, rebar. **3.** *techn.* bar; **pręt do spawania** welding rod; **pręt grzejny** *el.* heating rod, rod resistor; **pręt paliwowy** *fiz.* fuel rod. **4.** *bot.* twig.

prężnie *adv.* springily; (*rozwijać się*) resiliently, with resilience; (*działać*) vigorously; **prężnie rozwijająca się gospodarka** buoyant economy.

prężność *f.* **1.** (= *elastyczność*) resilience, suppleness, springiness. **2.** *przen.* (*umysłu, działania*) vigor. **3.** (*firmy, gospodarki*) (= *dynamiczność*) resilience, buoyancy. **4.** *fiz.* pressure; **prężność dysocjacji** dissociation pressure; **prężność gazu** gas pressure; **prężność pary** vapor pressure.

prężny *a.* **1.** (*np. o kroku, mięśniach*) (= *elastyczny*) resilient, springy. **2.** *przen.* (*np. o gospodarce*) (= *dynamiczny*) resilient, buoyant.

prężyć *ipf.* (*ramiona, grzbiet, mięśnie*) flex; **prężyć muskuły** *l.* **mięśnie** flex *l.* tense one's muscles; **kot prężył grzbiet** cat arched its back. **~ się** *ipf.* (= *napinać mięśnie*) flex one's muscles; (= *prostować się*) stand upright *l.* erect.

prima *a. indecl.* prime (quality). – *adv.* first-class, first-rate, prime; *pot.* hunky-dory.

prima aprilis *n. indecl.* April Fool's Day, All Fool's Day.

primabalerina *f.* prima ballerina.

primadonna *f.* prima donna; **odstawiać primadonnę** *pot.* put on airs.

primogenitura *f. lit.* primogeniture.

prion *mi pat.* prion.

priorytet *mi lit.* preference, priority; **wysoki priorytet** high priority; **najwyższy priorytet** top priority; **dawać czemuś priorytet** give priority to sth; **nadawać czemuś priorytet** prioritize sth.

priorytetowy *a. lit.* priority; preferred; **charakter priorytetowy** priority treatment; **traktować priorytetowo** prioritize.

PRL *abbr. hist.* (= *Polska Rzeczpospolita Ludowa*) the Polish People's Republic.

pro *prep.* **1.** *z przymiotnikami* pro-; **profrancuski** pro-French; **prokomunistyczny** pro-communist; **pro i kontra** pros and cons. **2.** (*w wyrażeniach pochodzenia łacińskiego*) pro; **pro forma** pro forma; **faktura proforma** *fin.* pro-forma invoice; **pro rata** pro rata.

proamerykański *a.* pro-American.

probabilistyczny *a.* **1.** *mat., stat.* probability. **2.** *fil.* probabilistic, probabilist.

probabilistyka *f. mat.* (= *rachunek prawdopodobieństwa*) probability calculus, calculus of probability.

probabilizm *mi fil.* probabilism.

probierca *mp* assayer.

probierczy *a.* test, testing; (*zwł. dotyczący badania zawartości metalu w rudzie lub zanieczyszczenia metali szlachetnych*) assay; **kamień probierczy** *techn.* touchstone; **urząd probierczy** assay office; **znak probierczy** hallmark, plate mark.

probiernia *f. Gen.pl.* **-i** *l.* **-ń 1.** (= *dział sprawdzania jakości*) quality (control) department. **2.** (= *lokal przeznaczony na degustację*) tasting room; **probiernia win** wine tasting room.

probierz *mi Gen.* **-a 1.** *lit.* touchstone, benchmark. **2.** *techn.* gauge; **probierz ciśnienia** pressure gauge.

problem *mi* (= *trudność*) problem, difficulty, complication; (= *zagadnienie*) problem, matter, question, issue; **bez problemu** without any problem; **nie ma problemu** *pot.* no problem, no pro; **problem polega na tym, że...** *l.* **problem w tym, że...** the problem *l.* thing is (that)...; **robić z czegoś problem** make an issue out of sth; **nierzadki problem** not an uncommon problem; **jedyny problem w tym, że...** the only thing is...; **pozostał nam tylko jeden problem do omówienia** there's only one more issue *l.* problem *l.* item on the agenda to be discussed *l.* dealt with; **odwieczny problem** perennial problem; **poruszono wiele problemów** many issues were raised; **problem delikatnej natury** sensitive issue; **problem natury technicznej** technical difficulty; **rozwiązać problem** solve a problem; **zająć się problemem** tackle a problem; **stanowić problem** pose a problem *l.* difficulty; **coś nie stanowi problemu** sth is not an issue; **to jego problem** that's his problem, that's his funeral; **to tylko w połowie rozwiązuje prob-**

lem it goes only halfway toward solving the problem; **w czym problem?** what's the problem?, what seems to be the problem?; **w tym cały problem!** that's the whole point!; **żaden problem!** no pro!; **przysporzyć komuś problemów** cause sb trouble; **sedno** *l.* **istota problemu** nub *l.* crux of the problem; **unikać podjęcia problemu** beg the problem; **problem poruszony przez mówcę...** issue raised by the speaker...; **mieć problemy z policją** be in trouble with the police; **mieć problemy ze zrobieniem czegoś/z czymś** have difficulties (in) doing sth/with sth; **mieć problemy z sercem** have a heart condition; **napotykać problemy** run into problems; **problemy osobiste** personal difficulties *l.* problems; **stwarzać problemy** cause *l.* create problems *l.* difficulties; **problem szachowy** *szachy* chess problem; **problem roku 2000** *komp.* year 2000 problem *l.* bug, Y2K problem *l.* bug, millenium bug.

problematyczny *a.* (= *budzący wątpliwości*) questionable, problematic, problematical, dubious; **zdanie problematyczne** *log.* problematic proposition.

problematyka *f.* issues, problems; *rzad.* problematique; **problematyka społeczna/polityczna** social/political issues.

problematyzacja *f. lit.* problematization.

problematyzować *ipf.* **1.** *lit.* (= *ujmować zagadnienie jako problem*) problematize. **2.** (= *czynić z czegoś problem*) make an issue (out) of sth.

problemowy *a.* (*o filmie, sztuce, literaturze*) problem.

probostwo *n.* **1.** *kość.* (= *parafia; urząd proboszcza*) cure; **nadawać komuś probostwo** institute sb. **2.** *rz.-kat.* (= *plebania*) rectory, parsonage.

proboszcz *mp pl.* **-owie** *Gen.* **-ów** *rz.-kat.* parish priest, curate; (*w kościele anglikańskim, protestanckim*) rector, parson.

proboszczowski *a. rz.-kat.* parish priest's, curate's; (*w kościele anglikańskim, protestanckim*) rector's, parson's.

probówka *f. Gen.pl.* **-ek** test tube; **dziecko z probówki** *pot.* test-tube baby.

probrytyjski *a.* pro-British.

proc. *abbr.* = *procent* pct. (*percent*); *Br.* p.c.

proca *f.* **1.** (*zabawka*) slingshot, sling. **2.** (*broń*) sling; **wylecieć** *l.* **wyskoczyć jak z procy** go like a shot, take off like a bat out of hell.

proceder *mi* dealings, trade, business; **niecny proceder** shady business *l.* dealings.

procedura *f.* **1.** (= *przebieg czegoś*) procedure; **skomplikowana/zawiła/złożona procedura** complex procedure; **stosować procedurę** follow a procedure. **2.** *prawn.* procedure, proceedings; **procedura apelacyjna** appellate procedure; **procedura arbitrażowa** arbitration procedure; **procedura cywilna** civil procedure; **procedura karna** criminal procedure; **procedura sądowa** court proceedings. **3.** *komp.* routine, procedure.

proceduralny *a. zwł. prawn.* procedural.

procent *mi* **1.** (= *odsetek*) percent; *zwł. Br.* per cent; percentage (*czegoś* of sth); **obniżyć się** *l.* **spaść o 20 procent** fall *l.* drop by 20 percent;

podwyżka cen o pięć procent five percent increase in prices; **pewien/duży procent** certain/high percentage; **w dziewięćdziesięciu procentach przypadków** nine times out of ten; **miasto zniszczone w 90 procentach** city *l.* town destroyed in 90 percent; **zgadzam się z tobą w stu procentach** I am *l.* agree with you a *l.* one hundred percent, I totally agree with you; **być pewnym (czegoś) na sto procent** be a *l.* one hundred percent sure (of sth). **2.** (= *odsetki*) interest; **procenty od kredytu** loan interest, interest on a loan; **na pięć procent** at five percent interest.

procentować *ipf.* (= *przynosić odsetki*) bear *l.* yield interest, pay dividends; *przen.* (= *przynosić korzyści*) pay (dividends).

procentowo *adv.* in percentage terms; percentage-wise.

procentowy *a.* (= *dotyczący procentów*) percentage; (= *przynoszący procenty*) interest-bearing; **punkt procentowy** *fin.* basis point; **stopa procentowa** *fin.* interest rate.

proces *mi* **1.** (= *przebieg zmian*) process, course of action; **procesy decyzyjne** decision-making processes; **bliskowschodni proces pokojowy** Middle East peace process; **proces chemiczny** *chem.* chemical process; **proces cieplny** *fiz.* thermal process; **proces ciśnieniowy** *fiz.* pressure process; **proces elementarny** *fiz., chem.* elementary process; **proces produkcyjny** manufacturing process; **proces technologiczny** technological process; **procesy życiowe** *fizj.* vital processes. **2.** *prawn.* (law)suit, process, trial; **proces cywilny** civil lawsuit; **proces karny** criminal lawsuit; **proces polityczny** political trial; **miał proces o zabójstwo** he was tried for murder; **proces przy drzwiach zamkniętych** in camera trial; **proces publiczny** public *l.* open trial; **rewizja procesu** retrial; **wytaczać komuś proces** bring *l.* take action against sb, bring *l.* file a suit against sb; **przegrać proces** lose a lawsuit *l.* case at law; **wygrać proces** win a lawsuit.

procesja *f.* **1.** *rel.* procession. **2.** *przen.* procession, train, cortege.

procesor *mi Gen.* **-a** *komp.* (= *jednostka obliczeniowa*) processor.

procesować się *ipf.* litigate (*z kimś* with sb); sue (*z kimś o coś* sb for sth); **procesować się (z kimś) (o coś)** fight (sb) in court (over sth).

procesowy *a.* **1.** *prawn.* lawsuit, trial, proceeding(s); **koszty procesowe** trial fees; **prawo procesowe** adjective law, procedural law. **2.** process.

procesualista *mp prawn.* specialist in matters of legal procedure.

procesualistyka *f. prawn.* science of legal procedure.

procesualny *a. prawn.* processual, procedural.

proch *mi* **1.** (*strzelniczy*) gunpowder; **proch bezdymny** smokeless powder; **proch czarny** black powder; **strzelać bez prochu** *przen.* make *l.* lay a false claim, lie; **wąchać proch** *wojsk.* see action; **prochu to on nie wymyśli** he won't set the world on fire; **beczka prochu** powder keg; **sie-**

dzieć na beczce prochu *przen.* (= *znaleźć się w bardzo niebezpiecznej sytuacji*) be sitting on a powder keg. **2. prochy** *lit.* (= *szczątki ludzkie*) remains, ashes. **3.** dust; **zetrzeć kogoś na proch** (= *zniszczyć doszczętnie*) pulverize sb; **rozpaść się w proch i w pył** crumble to dust, fall apart; **z prochu powstałeś** *l.* **jesteś i w proch się obrócisz** *rel.* ashes to ashes, dust to dust. **4. prochy** (= *narkotyki*) dope; **być na prochach** be on dope *l.* drugs; **branie** *l.* **łykanie prochów** pill popping.

prochowiec *mi* -wc- *Gen.* -a trench coat.

prochownia *f. Gen.pl.* -i *hist., wojsk.* powder magazine.

prochowy *a.* (gun)powder; **lont prochowy** blasting *l.* safety fuse; **Spisek Prochowy** *hist.* Gunpowder Plot.

prodiż *mi Gen.* -a *l.* -u *Gen.pl.* -y *l.* -ów electric baking tin.

producent *mp* **1.** (= *wytwórca*) manufacturer, producer, maker; **producent samochodów** car manufacturer, carmaker; **kupować coś bezpośrednio od producenta** buy sth directly from the manufacturer. **2.** (= *osoba finansująca nakręcenie filmu, wystawienie sztuki*) producer; **producent filmowy** movie *l.* film producer.

produkcja *f.* **1.** (= *wytwarzanie*) production, manufacture, making; **produkcja małoseryjna** low-volume production; **produkcja masowa** *l.* **seryjna** mass production, high-volume production; **produkcja krajowa** national production; **koszty produkcji** manufacturing *l.* production costs; **środki produkcji** means of production; **produkcja rolna** agricultural production; **produkcja zwierzęca** animal production. **2.** (= *wytwory*) production, output, manufacture. **3.** *film* production.

produkcyjny *a.* production, manufacturing; **linia produkcyjna** production line; **hala produkcyjna** workshop, shop; **zdolność produkcyjna** manufacturing capacity; **cykl produkcyjny** production cycle; **nadwyżka mocy produkcyjnych** manufacturing overcapacity; **spółdzielnia produkcyjna** *hist.* collective farm.

produkować *ipf.* **1.** (= *wytwarzać*) produce, manufacture, make; (*np. energię, elektryczność*) generate; **produkować masowo** mass-produce; **produkować w nadmiarze** overproduce; **przestać produkować** (*model, wzór wyrobu*) discontinue. **2.** *przen.* (*filmy, dzieła sztuki, informacje itp.*) produce. **3.** (= *wydzielać*) produce, generate; **produkować mleko** (*o samicach ssaków*) lactate. ~ **się** *ipf. zw. uj.* (= *występować*) perform.

produkt *mi* **1.** (= *wytwór*) product; **produkt końcowy** end product; **produkt uboczny** by-product, spinoff; **produkt wysokiej jakości** high quality product; **cykl życia produktu** product life cycle; **asortyment produktów** product range; **produkty krajowe** domestic products; **produkt krajowy brutto** *ekon.* gross domestic product; **produkt narodowy brutto** *ekon.* gross national product; **produkty rolne** farm produce; **produkty mleczarskie** dairy produce; **produkty pochodzenia zwierzęcego/roślinnego** animal/plant products; **pro-**

dukty spożywcze foodstuffs. **2.** *chem.* product; **produkt reakcji** (reaction) product; **produkt dyfuzji** diffusate; **produkt rozpadu promieniotwórczego** *chem., fiz.* decay *l.* disintegration *l.* daughter product; **produkt sublimacji** sublimate.

produktywnie *adv.* productively.

produktywność *f.* **1.** productivity, productiveness. **2.** *ekon.* productivity.

produktywny *a.* productive.

prodziekan *mp uniw.* deputy dean; **prodziekan do spraw studenckich** deputy dean for student affairs.

proenzym *mi chem.* zymogen, proenzyme.

prof. *abbr.* (= *profesor*) Prof. (*professor*).

profan *mp* layman, uninitiated person; dilettante, dabbler.

profanacja *f.* profanation, desecration, defilement.

profanator *mp* profaner, desecrator.

profanka *f. Gen.pl.* -ek *zob.* **profan.**

profanować *ipf.* profane, defile, debase.

profaszystowski *a.* pro-Fascist.

profaza *f. biol.* prophase.

profesja *f. lit.* profession, occupation, vocation.

profesjonalista *mp*, **profesjonalistka** *f. Gen.pl.* -ek professional.

profesjonalizm *mi* professionalism.

profesjonalnie *a.* professionally.

profesjonalny *a.* professional.

profesor *mp pl.* -owie *l.* -rzy **1.** *uniw.* professor; **emerytowany profesor** professor emeritus; **profesor kontraktowy** adjunct professor; **profesor nadzwyczajny** associate professor; **profesor zwyczajny** full professor; **profesor prawa** professor of law. **2.** *szkoln.* (= *nauczyciel*) teacher, professor; **profesor fizyki** physics teacher.

profesorek *mp* prof.

profesorka *f. Gen.pl.* -ek *pot. zob.* **profesor** 2.

profesorowa *f. Gen.* -ej professor's wife; **profesor Kowalski i profesorowa Kowalska** Prof. and Mrs. Kowalski.

profesorski *a.* professorial; **kadra profesorska** professors.

profesura *f.* **1.** (= *stanowisko, tytuł profesora*) professorship, professorate. **2.** *rzad.* (= *grono profesorskie*) professorate.

profeta *a. lit.* prophet.

profetyczny, profetycki *a. lit.* prophetic, prophetical.

profetyzm *mi lit.* prophetism, propheticism.

profil *mi Gen.pl.* -ów *l.* -i **1.** (*twarzy*) profile; **z** *l.* **w profilu** in profile. **2.** (= *kontur*) outline, contour; **profil rzeczny** *geogr.* river profile. **3.** (= *zakres, preferencje, charakterystyka*) profile, characteristics; **profil użytkownika** *komp.* user profile; **profil psychologiczny** *psych.* psychological profile. **4.** *geol.* profile; **profil glebowy** soil profile. **5.** *sztuka, bud.* molding. **6.** *techn.* (= *kształtownik*) section, shape.

profilaktycznie *adv.* prophylactically.

profilaktyczny *a.* preventive; *zwł. med.* prophylactic; **środek profilaktyczny** prophylactic.

profilaktyka *f. med.* prevention, prophylaxis, preventive treatment.

profilować *ipf.* **1.** *bud.* make moldings; mold, ornament *l.* decorate with moldings. **2.** *geol.* profile. **3.** *techn.* mold, form, shape.

profit *mi lit.* profit, benefit, gain.

pro forma *adv.* (= *dla formy, dla zachowania pozorów*) pro forma.

profrancuski *a.* pro-French.

progesteron *mi biochem.* progesterone, corpus luteum hormone.

prognatyzm *mi antrop.* prognathism, prognathy.

prognosta *mp* prognosticator, forecaster.

prognostyk *mi* **1.** (= *przepowiednia, zapowiedź*) prognostic, omen, portent, sign. **2.** (*osoba*) prognosticator, forecaster.

prognostyka *f.* forecasting, prognostication.

prognoza *f.* **1.** (= *przewidywanie*) forecast, projection; **prognoza pogody** weather forecast; **prognoza gospodarcza** economic forecast; **prognoza demograficzna** population forecast; **prognoza sprzedaży** sales forecast. **2.** *med.* prognosis.

prognozować *ipf.* forecast, predict, prognosticate, prophesy.

prognozowanie *f.* forecasting, prognostication; **prognozowanie popytu** *ekon.* demand forecasting.

progowy *a.* threshold; **dawka progowa** *med.* threshold dose.

program *mi* **1.** (= *założenia i wytyczne*) program; *Br.* programme; plan, schedule, scheme; **program wyborczy** *polit.* platform, manifesto; **program ubezpieczeń społecznych** social security scheme; **kompleksowy program** comprehensive program; **program rozwoju** development program; **program inwestycyjny** investment program; **program długoterminowy** long-term program. **2.** (= *plan zamierzonych czynności*) agenda, schedule, plan; **program działania** action plan; **program spotkania** agenda; **mieć coś w programie** have sth on the agenda. **3.** (= *zestawienie informacji o przedstawieniu, koncercie, pokazie itp.*) program, bill of fare; *Br.* programme; **program teatralny** playbill; **gwóźdź programu** highlight, main feature. **4.** *radio, telew.* (= *jedna audycja*) program; *Br.* programme, broadcast, show; (= *zestaw audycji*) (program) schedule; (= *kanał telewizyjny*) channel, station; **na pierwszym programie** on channel one; **program telewizyjny** (= *audycja telewizyjna*) TV program *l.* broadcast *l.* show; (= *opis, zestawienie audycji*) TV *l.* channel guide; **program dokumentalny** documentary. **5.** *szkoln., uniw.* curriculum, syllabus, program; *Br.* programme; **przewidziany programem** curricular. **6.** *komp.* program; **program antywirusowy** antivirus program, vaccine; **pakiet programów** software package, suite of programs.

programator *mi Gen.pl.* **-a** *techn.* control.

programista *mp komp.* (computer) programmer.

programistka *f. Gen.pl.* **-ek** *zob.* **programista**.

programować *ipf.* **1.** (= *planować*) program; *Br.* programme; plan, schedule. **2.** *komp.* program.

programowany *a.* programmed; **nauczanie programowane** *szkoln.* programmed instruction.

programowy *a.* **1.** (= *stanowiący, zawierający program*) (*artykuł, założenia*) manifesto, programmatic; (*działalność*) policy; **muzyka programowa** *muz.* program music; **mówca wygłaszający przemówienie programowe** keynoter speaker; **przemówienie programowe** keynote address. **2.** (= *odnoszący się do programu artystycznego*) program; *Br.* programme. **3.** *szkoln., uniw.* curricular. **4.** *telew., radio* programming. **5.** *komp.* programming, software.

progresja *f.* **1.** *lit.* progression; **progresja podatkowa** *ekon.* progressive tax(ation) system. **2.** *muz.* progression, sequence; **progresja melodyczna/harmoniczna** melodic/harmonic progression.

progresywizm *mi szkoln.* progressive education, progressivism.

progresywny *a.* progressive; **podatek progresywny** *ekon.* progressive tax; **progresywne opodatkowanie** *ekon.* progressive taxation; **asymilacja progresywna** *fon.* progressive assimilation.

prohibicja *f.* prohibition.

prohibicjonista *mp*, **prohibicjonistka** *f. Gen.pl.* **-ek** *ekon.* prohibitionist.

prohibicjonizm *mi ekon.* prohibitionism.

prohibita *pl. Gen.* **-ów** *bibl.* prohibited books, manuscripts, etc.

projekcja *f.* **1.** *kartogr., geom., psych.* projection. **2.** (*filmu, przeźroczy*) screening, projection; **mieć dobrą projekcję głosu** project one's voice well.

projekcyjny *a.* kino, psych. projective; **aparat projekcyjny** picture projector; **kabina projekcyjna** projection booth; **test projekcyjny** projective test.

projekt *mi* **1.** (= *plan działania*) project, plan; (= *zamiar*) intention, plan; **ambitny projekt** ambitious project, ambitious plan; **projekt małżeństwa** intention to marry; **mieć coś w projekcie** intend to do sth. **2.** (*szkic, schemat*) design, scheme; **projekt badawczy** research project; **projekt pilotażowy** pilot project *l.* scheme; **projekt racjonalizatorski** proposal for an improvement; **projekt budynku** design of a building; **projekt inwestycyjny** investment project; **kierownik projektu** project manager. **3.** *prawn.* draft; **projekt ustawy** bill; **projekt ustawy budżetowej** finance bill; **projekt umowy** draft (of a) contract; **sporządzić projekt budżetu/ustawy** draft a budget/bill.

projektant *mp*, **projektantka** *f. Gen.pl.* **-ek** designer; **projektant/ka mody** fashion designer; **projektant/ka odzieży** dress designer; **projektant/ka terenów zielonych** landscape architect; **projektant/ka wnętrz** interior designer.

projektodawca *mp* originator, initiator (*of a project, plan, etc.*).

projektor *mi Gen.* **-a** projector; (*do wyświetla-*

nia przezroczy) slide projector; **projektor kinowy** cine projector; **projektor filmowy** film projector.

projektować *ipf.* 1. (*zamierzać*) plan, intend. 2. (*opracowywać projekt*) design.

projektowanie *n.* planning, design; **projektowanie sieci** *komp.* network design, networking; **projektowanie terenów zielonych** landscape architecture; **projektowanie wnętrz** interior design.

projektowy *a.* 1. (= *dotyczący projektu*) design; **dokumentacja projektowa** design documentation; **prace projektowe** design works, designing. 2. (= *projektujący*) designing; **biuro projektowe** design company, design office.

prokarionty *pl. Gen.* **-ów** *biol.* prokaryotes, procaryotes.

proklamacja *f.* (*oświadczenie*) proclamation; **proklamacja niepodległości** proclamation of independence.

proklamować *ipf.* (*niepodległość, wiarę*) (= *ogłosić*) proclaim (*coś / kogoś czymś / kimś* sb/sth sb/sth). ~ **się** *ipf.* (*np. o państwie*) be proclaimed; (*np. o dyktatorze*) proclaim o.s. (*kimś* sb).

proklityka *f. jęz.* proclitic.

prokliza *f. jęz.* proclisis.

prokomunistyczny *a.* pro-communist.

prokonsul *mp pl.* **-owie** *Gen.* **-ów** *hist.* proconsul.

prokreacja *f.* procreation.

proksemika *f.* (*nauka*) proxemics.

proktolog *mp* proctologist.

proktologia *f. med.* proctology.

proktologiczny *a.* proctological.

prokura *f. prawn.* proxy.

prokurator *mp prawn.* prosecuting attorney, public prosecutor; (*hist.*) (*rzymski*) procurator; **prokurator generalny** general prosecuting attorney, public prosecutor general; **prokurator rejonowy/wojewódzki** district/province prosecuting attorney; **prokurator wojskowy** military prosecutor; **prokurator stanowy** *US* state prosecuting attorney.

prokuratorski *a.* prosecuting attorney's, public prosecutor's.

prokuratura *f. prawn.* public prosecution service; **prokuratura generalna** general prosecuting attorney's office, public prosecutor general's office; **prokuratura rejonowa/wojewódzka** district/province prosecution service; **prokuratura wojskowa** military prosecution service, army prosecuting authority.

prokurent *mp ekon.* proxy, agent; *prawn.* proxy, attorney.

prokurować *ipf. żart.* (= *przygotowywać*) prepare; **prokurować obiad/kolację** concoct dinner/supper.

prolaktyna *f. biol.* prolactin.

prolaminy *pl. Gen.* **-n** *chem.* prolamines.

prolegomena *pl. Gen.* **-ów** *lit.* prolegomena.

proletariacki *a.* proletarian; **internacjonalizm proletariacki** *polit.* proletarian internationalism.

proletariackość *f.* proletarianism.

proletariat *mi polit. t. hist.* (*w Rzymie*) prole-

tariat; **dyktatura proletariatu** *polit.* dictatorship of the proletariat.

proletariusz *mp polit. t. hist.* (*w Rzymie*) proletarian; **proletariusze wszystkich krajów, łączcie się** Workers of the World, Unite!

proliferacja *f.* (= *rozpowszechnianie*) *biol., zool.* proliferation.

prolina *f. chem.* proline.

prolog *mi* 1. (*część wstępna*) *muz., teatr, teor.lit.* prologue (*do czegoś* to sth). 2. *mp* (= *aktor wygłaszający ekspozycję dramatu*) = **prologista**.

prologista *mp* prologue.

prolongata *f.* prolongation; (*spłaty pożyczki, ważności dokumentu*) extension; (*płatności weksla, rachunku*) days of grace.

prolongować *ipf. l. pf.* (= *odraczać*) *fin.* prolong; (*spłatę odsetek, długu*) roll over; (= *przedłużać*) extend, prolong.

prom *mi* ferry, ferryboat; **prom kolejowy** train ferry; **prom motorowy** motor ferry; **prom samochodowy** car ferry; **prom kosmiczny** spaceshuttle; **przewozić coś promem** ferry sth.

promenada *f.* promenade; (*nadmorska z desek*) boardwalk.

promesa *f.* (*płatności*) promissory note.

promet *mi chem.* promethium.

prometeizm *mi teor.lit.* Prometheanism.

prometejski *a. teor.lit.* Promethean.

Prometeusz *mp mit.* Prometheus.

promienica *f.* 1. *zool.* radiolarian (*Radiolaria*). 2. *pat., wet.* actinomycosis; *pot.* lumpy jaw.

promienicowy *a.* 1. *zool.* radiolarian. 2. *pat., wet.* actinomycotic.

promienieć *ipf.* radiate (*czymś* sth); glow (*czymś* with sth); **promienieć radością** be bright with joy.

promienioczułość *f. med.* radiosensitivity.

promienionóżki *pl. Gen.* **-ek** *biol.* actinopods (*Actinopoda*).

promieniopłetwe *pl. Gen.* **-ych** *icht.* actinopterygians (*Actinopterygii*).

promieniotwórczość *f. chem., fiz.* radioactivity; **promieniotwórczość naturalna** natural radioactivity; **promieniotwórczość sztuczna/wzbudzona** artificial/induced radioactivity.

promieniotwórczy *a. chem., fiz.* radioactive; **odpady promieniotwórcze** radioactive waste; **opad promieniotwórczy** fallout; **rozpad promieniotwórczy** radioactive decay, radioactive disintegration.

promieniować *ipf.* (*energię*) (*uczucia*) (*o bólu*) radiate; **promieniowała z niego energia** he radiated energy; **promieniujący ból** radiating pain.

promieniowanie *n. astron., chem., fiz.* radiation, rays; **promieniowanie alfa/beta/gamma/delta** *fiz.* alpha/beta/gamma/delta rays, alpha/beta/gamma/delta radiation; **promieniowanie atmosfery** atmospheric radiation; **promieniowanie cieplne** heat radiation, thermal radiation; **promieniowanie kosmiczne** cosmic radiation, cosmic rays; **promieniowanie nadfioletowe** ultraviolet radiation; **promieniowanie rentgenowskie** X-radiation, X-rays.

promieniowce *pl. Gen.* **-ów** *biol.* actinomycetes (*Actinomycetales*).

promieniowy *a. geom.* radial; **kość promieniowa** *anat.* radius.

promienisty *a.* **1.** (*kształt, układ*) radial. **2.** (*światło, energia*) radiant.

promieniście *adv.* radially.

promiennie *adv.* brightly; **uśmiechać się promiennie** smile brightly.

promiennik *mi Gen.* **-a** *techn.* radiator.

promienny *a.* **1.** (*uśmiech*) radiant, beaming; (*poranek*) bright. **2.** *fiz.* (*o promieniach*) radiant.

promień *mi Gen.* **-a 1.** (*światło*) ray; **promień światła** ray of light; **promień słońca** ray of sunshine, ray of sunlight, sunbeam; **promień księżyca** moonbeam; **promień nadziei** *przen.* ray of hope, gleam *l.* glimmer of hope. **2.** *fiz.* (*światła, elektronów itp.*) ray, beam. **3.** *geom.* radius; **w promieniu 50 km** within 50 kilometres. **4.** *orn.* (*na stosinie pióra*) barb. **5.** *icht.* (*część płetwy*) ray.

promil *mi Gen.* **-a** per mill, per mil; **mieć dwa promile alkoholu we krwi** have a BAC of 0.20 per cent (*BAC = blood-alcohol concentration*).

prominencki *a.* (*o przywilejach, dzielnicy*) VIP; bigwig, big shot.

prominent *mp* VIP; bigwig, big shot.

prominentny *a.* (= *należący do elity*) elite; (= *ważny, znany*) prominent.

promocja *f.* **1.** *handl.* promotion, special offer; **promocja książki** book promotion; **w promocji** on special offer, on special; **promocja w sklepie** instore promotion; **promocja kończy się 31 stycznia** special offer closes January 31. **2.** (= *propagowanie*) (*idei, kultury*) promotion (*czegoś* of sth). **3.** (= *mianowanie*) promotion (*na coś/kogoś* to sth/sb); **otrzymać promocję do stopnia majora** be promoted major. **4.** *szkoln.* promotion. **5.** *szachy, warcaby* promotion (*of a pawn*).

promocyjny *a.* promotional.

promotor *mp pl.* **-rzy, promotorka** *f. Gen.pl.* **-ek 1.** *uniw.* (*pracy dyplomowej, magisterskiej, doktorskiej*) supervisor. **2.** (*inicjator*) promoter. – *mi Gen.* **-a** *pl.* **-y** *biochem.* promoter.

promować *ipf.* **1.** (*produkt*) (*ucznia*) (*ideę, kulturę*) promote. **2.** (*pracę dyplomową, magisterską, doktorską*) supervise. **3.** (= *mianować*) promote (*kogoś z czegoś/kogoś na coś/kogoś* sb from sth/sb to sth/sb). **4.** *szachy, warcaby* promote (*a pawn*).

promowy *a.* ferry; **komunikacja promowa** ferry services; **opłata promowa** ferriage; **przeprawa promowa** ferry crossing.

promulgacja *f. prawn.* promulgation.

promyk *mi Gen.* **-a** ray; **promyk nadziei** ray *l.* gleam of hope; **promyk słońca** ray of sunshine.

proniemiecki *a.* pro-German.

propagacja *f. biol., fiz.* propagation.

propaganda *f.* propaganda (*przeciw komuś/czemuś* against sb/sth) (*na rzecz kogoś/czegoś* for sb/sth); **propaganda sukcesu** *polit.* propaganda of success; **wroga propaganda** enemy propaganda; **spec od propagandy** *pot.* (*zwł. działa-*

jący na rzecz polityka l. partii politycznej) propaganda expert, *pot.* spin doctor.

propagandowy *a.* propagandist; **kampania propagandowa** propaganda campaign; **machina propagandowa** propaganda machine.

propagandysta *mp*, **propagandystka** *f. Gen.pl.* **-ek** propagandist.

propagator *mp*, **propagatorka** *f. Gen.pl.* **-ek** propagator; (*zwł. idei, sprawy*) exponent.

propagatorski *a.* propagation; **działania propagatorskie** propagation campaign.

propagować *ipf.* propagate, disseminate; (*pokój, współpracę, rozwój*) foster; (*wiedzę*) further; *fiz.* (*fale, drgania*) propagate.

propan *mi chem.* propane.

proparoksyton *mi jęz.* proparoxytone.

proparoksytoneza *f. jęz.* proparoxytonizing.

propedeutyczny *a.* propaedeutic, propaedeutical.

propedeutyka *f.* propaedeutics (*czegoś* of sth).

propinacja *f.* **1.** *hist.* (*prawo*) propination. **2.** (= *karczma*) inn.

propolis *mi* propolis; bee glue, hive dross.

propolski *a.* pro-Polish.

proponować *ipf.* **1.** (*działanie, rozwiązanie, kandydata*) suggest, propose (*komuś coś* sth to sb). **2.** (= *poczęstować, oferować*) offer (*coś komuś* sth to sb *l.* sb sth); **proponować kogoś na jakieś stanowisko** suggest sb for a post; **proponuję, żebyśmy porozmawiali o tym później** I suggest (that) we (should) talk about it later.

propos *adv. zob.* à propos.

proporcja *f.* (*stosunek*) *mat.* proportion, ratio (*czegoś do czegoś* of sth to sth); **o pięknych/dobrych proporcjach** beautifully/well proportioned; **zachować właściwe proporcje czegoś** keep the right proportions of sth; **zachować proporcje między czymś a czymś** *przen.* strike a balance between sth and sth.

proporcjonalnie *adv.* proportionately, commensurately; in proportion (*do czegoś* to *l.* with sth); **proporcjonalnie zbudowany** clean-limbed; **wprost/odwrotnie proporcjonalnie do czegoś** *mat.* in direct/inverse proportion to sth; **wzrastać/maleć proporcjonalnie** increase/decrease in proportion.

proporcjonalność *f.* **1.** (*harmonia*) proportionality. **2.** *mat.* proportion; **proporcjonalność prosta/odwrotna** direct/inverse proportion.

proporcjonalny *a.* **1.** (= *o określonym stosunku*) proportional, commensurate (*do czegoś* to sth); **proporcjonalny system wyborczy** *polit.* proportional electoral system; **reprezentacja proporcjonalna** *parl.* proportional representation. **2.** (= *harmonijny*) well-proportioned, proportionable. **3.** *mat.* proportional; **wprost/odwrotnie proporcjonalny** directly/inversely proportional (*do czegoś* to sth).

proporczyk *mi Gen.* **-a 1.** (*chorągiewka*) streamer, pennant. **2.** *żegl.* pennant.

proporzec *mi* **-rc-** *Gen.* **-a 1.** (= *chorągiew*) standard, banner. **2.** *żegl.* pendant.

propozycja *f.* (= *pomysł*) suggestion, proposal (*zrobienia czegoś* to do sth); (= *oferta*) offer (*zro-*

bienia czegoś to do sth); **propozycja małżeństwa** an offer *l.* proposal of marriage; **być otwartym na propozycje** be open to suggestions; **odrzucić propozycję** decline *l.* reject an offer *l.* proposal; **przedstawiać** *l.* **składać komuś propozycję** make sb a proposal, put forward a proposal to sb; **wyjść z propozycją** come up with a suggestion; **(no i) co powiesz na taką propozycję?** how's that for an offer?

propyleje *pl. Gen.* **-ów** *bud.* propylaeum.

proradziecki *a.* pro-Soviet.

prorektor *mp uniw.* vice-president; *Br.* pro-vice-chancellor.

proroctwo *n.* prophecy.

proroczo *adv.* prophetically.

proroczy *a.* prophetic.

prorok *mp rel.* prophet; **fałszywy prorok** false prophet; **obym był złym prorokiem** may my prediction never be fulfilled; **nikt nie jest prorokiem we własnym kraju** a prophet is without honor in his own country.

prorokować *ipf.* prophesy (*(komuś) coś /, że...* (sb) sth/that...).

prorządowy *a.* pro-government.

proscenium *n. sing. indecl. pl.* **-nia** *Gen.* **-niów** *hist., teatr* proscenium.

prosektor *mp* prosector.

prosektorium *n. sing. indecl. pl.* **-ria** *Gen.* **-riów** dissection room.

prosektoryjny *a.* dissection-room; **nóż prosektoryjny** dissecting knife.

proseminarium *n. sing. indecl. pl.* **-ria** *Gen.* **-riów** *uniw.* proseminar.

proseminaryjny *a. uniw.* proseminar.

prosiak *ma* **1.** (*świnia*) piglet. **2.** *pot.* (= *niechluj*) dirty pig.

prosić *ipf.* **-szę -sisz 1.** (*nakłaniać*) ask (*kogoś o coś* sb for sth *l.* sth of sb) (*kogoś, by coś zrobił* sb to do sth); **prosić o głos** ask for the floor; **prosić kogoś o przebaczenie** ask sb's forgiveness; **prosić kogoś o przysługę** ask sb a favor, ask a favor of sb; **prosić kogoś o radę/pomoc** ask *l.* seek sb's advice/help, seek advice/help from sb; **prosić kogoś o rękę** propose to sb; **prosić (kogoś) o pozwolenie** ask (sb's) permission, ask permission (from sb); **prosić o zadawanie pytań** (*o przewodniczącym, prelegencie*) invite questions; **prosić za kimś** put in a (good) word for sb; **czy mogę prosić o...** may *l.* can I trouble you for...; **czy mogę prosić o sól?** could you pass the salt?, may I trouble you for the salt?; **czy mogę prosić o uwagę?** may *l.* could I have your attention?; **czy mogę prosić Piotra?** (*do telefonu*) could I speak to Peter, please?; **uprzejmie prosimy pasażerów o przechodzenie do wyjścia** passengers are kindly requested to proceed to the exit; **proszę pozostać na miejscach podczas startu** (*samolotu*) you are requested to remain seated during takeoff; **proszę mi wierzyć** believe me; **proszę Pana/Pani** sir/madam; **proszę pana** (*do nieznanego mężczyzny*) mister; **proszę pani,... do nauczycielki** please miss,...; **proszę Państwa** ladies and gentlemen; **proszę (bardzo)** (*odpowiedź na „dziękuję"*) not at all, you're welcome, don't mention

it; (*podając l. wskazując coś*) here you are; (*wyrażając zgodę*) please do, go ahead; (*przepuszczając kogoś w drzwiach*) after you; **proszę!** (*wejść*) come in!; **no (i) proszę!** (well) what do you know!; **następny, proszę!** next please!; **proszę?** (*nalegając na powtórzenie*) pardon?, excuse me?; (= *czym mogę służyć?*) can I help you?; **proszę za mną** follow me, please; **proszę tędy** this way, please; **proszę wstać, sąd idzie** all rise, the court is in session; **proszę usiąść** *l.* **spocząć** please, be seated, please take a seat; **proszę o uśmiech!** (*do zdjęcia*) say cheese!; **proszę o wybaczenie** please accept my apologies; **proszę podać wiek, stan cywilny i zawód** please state your age, marital status and occupation; **proszę pozdrowić ode mnie siostrę/małżonka itp.** remember me to your sister/husband etc.; **proszę przyjść do mnie w piątek** come and see me on Friday. **2.** (*zapraszać*) invite (*kogoś na coś* sb to *l.* for sth); **prosić kogoś do pokoju/na herbatę** ask sb in/to tea. **~ się**[1] *ipf.* (= *błagać*) (*o osobie*) beg (*o coś* for sth); **sam się o to prosił** he asked for it; **prosić się o kłopoty** be asking for trouble; **(aż) prosić się o coś** (= *wymagać czegoś*) (*np. umycia, remontu*) be crying out for sth.

prosić się[2] *ipf.* (*o świni*) (= *rodzić prosięta*) farrow, pig.

prosię *n.* **-sięci-** *pl.* **-sięt-** *Gen.* **-ąt 1.** (*świnia*) piglet. **2.** (*niechluj*) dirty pig.

proskrypcja *f. hist.* proscription.

proso *n. bot., roln.* millet (*Panicum miliaceum*).

prosocjalistyczny *a.* pro-socialist.

prosówka *f. Gen.pl.* **-ek** *pat.* **prosówka potna** miliary fever; *pot.* sweating sickness; **prosówka ostra** serous tuberculosis.

prospekt *mi* prospectus, brochure; **prospekt emisyjny** (*przedsiębiorstwa*) prospectus.

prospektywny *a.* prospective.

prosperity *f. indecl. ekon.* economic boom.

prosperować *ipf.* flourish, prosper; **dobrze/źle prosperować** do well/badly.

prosta *f. Gen.* **-ej 1.** *geom.* straight line; **prosta prostopadła** perpendicular line, perpendicular; **prosta równoległa** parallel line, parallel. **2.** (= *prosty odcinek toru, drogi*) straightaway; (*Br.*) straight; **ostatnia prosta** *sport* (*przed metą*) home stretch; **wyprowadzić na prostą** (*np. spółkę z długów*) turn around.

prostacki *a.* coarse, boorish.

prostacko *adv.* coarsely, boorishly.

prostactwo *n.* **1.** (*zachowanie*) (*cechy*) coarseness, boorishness. **2.** (*ludzie*) boors, brutes.

prostaczek *mp* **-czk-** *pl.* **-owie** simpleton.

prostaglandyny *pl. Gen.* **-n** *chem.* prostaglandins.

prostaczka *f. Gen.pl.* **-ek**, **prostak** *mp pl.* **-cy** *l.* **-i** boor, churl; **prostak ze wsi** country bumpkin, hick.

prostata *f. anat.* prostate, prostate gland; **rak prostaty** prostate cancer.

prostnica *f.* **1.** *anat.* rectum. **2.** *bot.* orthostichy.

prosto *adv.* **1.** (= *na wprost*) straight, straight

ahead; **iść prosto przed siebie** go straight ahead; **spojrzeć komuś prosto w oczy** look sb straight in the eye; **śmiać się komuś prosto w twarz** laugh in sb's face; **prosto jak strzelił** *pot.* straight ahead. **2.** (= *pionowo*) upright, straight; **siedzieć/stać prosto** sit/stand upright *l.* straight; **trzymać się prosto** hold o.s. erect. **3.** (= *jasno*) clearly; **powiedzieć coś komuś prosto z mostu** tell sb sth straight from the shoulder. **4.** (= *bezpośrednio*) straight; **prosto z Paryża/ogrodu/piekarnika** straight from Paris/the garden/the oven; **prosto z serca** (*np. o życzeniach*) from the bottom of one's heart; **prosto spod prasy** (= *dopiero co wydany, napisany itp.*) hot off the press.

prostodusznie *adv.* simpleheartedly, guilelessly.

prostoduszność *f.* simpleheartedness, guilelessness.

prostoduszny *a.* simplehearted, guileless.

prostokąt *mi Gen.* **-a** *geom.* rectangle.

prostokątnie *adv.* rectangularly.

prostokątny *a.* rectangular; **trójkąt prostokątny** *geom.* right-angled triangle.

prostolinijnie *adv.* straightforwardly.

prostolinijność *f.* straightforwardness.

prostolinijny *a.* straightforward.

prostoliniowo *adv.* rectilinearly.

prostoliniowy *a.* rectilinear, straight-line.

prostopadle *adv.* perpendicularly (*do czegoś* to sth).

prostopadła *f. geom.* perpendicular line, perpendicular.

prostopadłościan *mi geom.* quadratic prism.

prostopadłościenny *a.* rectangular, cuboidal.

prostopadły *a.* perpendicular, orthogonal (*do czegoś* to sth); **prosta prostopadła** *geom.* perpendicular line, perpendicular; **rzut prostopadły** *geom.* orthogonal projection.

prostoskrzydłe *pl. Gen.* **-ych** *ent.* orthopterans (*Orthoptera*).

prostota *f.* simplicity.

prostować *ipf.* **1.** (= *czynić prostym, równym*) straighten; (*kończynę, organ*) protract; **prostować kości** stretch o.s.; **prostować plecy** straighten one's shoulders; **prostować prąd elektryczny** rectify electric current. **2.** (= *korygować*) (*sytuację*) straighten out; (*błąd*) rectify. **~ się** *ipf.* straighten up.

prostownica *f. techn.* straightener, flattener.

prostownik *mi Gen.* **-a 1.** *el.* rectifier. **2.** *anat.* extensor, protractor.

prostracja *f. psych.* prostration.

prostu *adv. zob.* **po prostu.**

prosty *a.* **-szy 1.** (= *niekrzywy*) (*o włosach, drodze*) straight; *geom.* (*o kącie*) right; (*o postawie, pozycji*) erect, upright; **po linii prostej** in a straight line; **krewny w linii prostej** direct descendant. **2.** (= *zwykły, przeciętny*) simple, common. **3.** (= *nieskomplikowany*) simple; (*np. o narzędziach*) crude; (*o narzędziach, metodach*) unsophisticated; (*o czynności, zadaniu*) straightforward, simple; (*o stroju*) simple, plain; **cukier prosty** *biol.* simple sugar; **prosty jak drut** (= *łatwy*) easy as pie; **rzecz prosta** obviously.

– *mi boks* straight; **lewy/prawy prosty** left/right straight.

prostytucja *f.* prostitution; **uprawiać prostytucję** prostitute o.s.

prostytutka *f. Gen.pl.* **-ek** prostitute; (*uliczna*) streetwalker; **męska prostytutka** male prostitute; **młodociana prostytutka** child prostitute.

prosylogizm *mi log.* prosyllogism.

prosząco *adv.* (*np. spojrzeć*) pleadingly.

proszący *a.* (*np. o tonie głosu*) pleading.

proszek *mi* **-szk- 1.** (*pył*) powder; **proszek do pieczenia** baking powder; **proszek do prania** washing powder; **proszek do zębów** tooth powder; **ciasto/zupa w proszku** cake/soup mix; **mleko w proszku** powdered milk; **mydło w proszku** (*do prania*) soap powder; **być w proszku** *przen.* be in pieces; **rozcierać coś na proszek** pulverize sth, powder sth; **posypywać coś proszkiem** sprinkle sth with powder, powder sth. **2.** *pot.* (*lekarstwo*) pill.

proszkować *ipf.* powder; *techn.* pulverize.

proszkownia *f. Gen.pl.* **-i proszkownia mleka** powdered milk factory.

proszony *a.* **1.** requested; **proszony obiad** dinner party. **2.** *zob.* **prosić.**

prośba *f. Gen.pl.* **próśb 1.** request; **na czyjąś prośbę** at sb's request; **chodzić po prośbie** beg one's bread; **godzić się na czyjąś prośbę** accede to sb's request; **odrzucić czyjąś prośbę** refuse *l.* deny sb's request; **przychylić się do czyjejś prośby** consent to sb's request; **spełnić czyjąś prośbę** grant sb's request; **zwracać się do kogoś z prośbą o coś** approach sb about *l.* for sth; **mam do ciebie prośbę** could I ask you a favor?, I have a favor to ask of you. **2.** (*urzędowa*) application; (*formalna*) petition; **prośba do władz** petition to the authorities; **prośba o ułaskawienie** *prawn.* petition for pardon; **wnieść prośbę** file an application, file a petition.

prościutki *a.* perfectly straight; *zob. t.* **prosty.**

prośna *a.* (*o maciorze*) in pig.

protagonista *mp teatr, teor.lit.* protagonist.

protaktyn *mi chem.* protactinium.

protegować *ipf.* pull strings, open doors (*kogoś* for sb).

protegowana *f. Gen.* **-ej** protégée.

protegowany *mp* protégé.

proteid *mi biochem.* proteid.

proteina *f. biochem.* protein.

protekcja *f.* favoritism; *Br.* favouritism.

protekcjonalnie *adv.* patronizingly, condescendingly; **traktować kogoś protekcjonalnie** patronize sb.

protekcjonalność *f.* condescension, patronage.

protekcjonalny *a.* patronizing, condescending.

protekcjonistyczny *a. ekon.* protectionist.

protekcjonizm *mi ekon.* protectionism, protection.

protekcyjny *a.* **1.** *ekon.* protective. **2.** (= *załatwiony przez protekcję*) preferential.

protektor *mp pl.* **-owie** *l.* **-rzy, protektorka** *f. Gen.pl.* **-ek** protector, patron. – *mi Gen.* **-a 1.** (= *bieżnik opony*) tread. **2.** (*podeszwa*) sole.

protektorat *mi* **1.** (*opieka*) patronage; **pod pro-**

tektoratem kogoś under the patronage of sb. **2.** *polit.* protectorate.

protektorka *f. zob.* **protektor.**

proteoliza *f. chem.* proteolysis.

proterozoiczny *a. geol., paleont.* Proterozoic.

proterozoik *mi geol., paleont.* Proterozoic.

protest *mi* (*sprzeciw*) protest (*przeciw l. przeciwko komuś/czemuś ze strony kogoś/czegoś* against sb/sth from sb/sth); **jako protest** *l.* **w proteście** *l.* **na znak protestu** in protest (*przeciw l. przeciwko komuś/czemuś* against sb/sth); **zgłosić protest** register a protest; **wystosować** *l.* **złożyć protest** lodge a protest; **bez protestów** without protest, without opposition; **protest song** protest song.

protestacyjny *a.* protest, remonstrative; **akcja protestacyjna** (*w zakładzie pracy*) industrial action; **list protestacyjny** letter of protest; **nota protestacyjna** note of protest; **marsz protestacyjny** protest march.

protestancki *a. rel.* Protestant; **kościół protestancki** Protestant Church.

protestant *mp*, **protestantka** *f. Gen.pl.* **-ek** *rel.* Protestant.

protestantyzm *mi rel.* Protestantism.

protestować *ipf.* (= *przeciwstawiać się*) protest (*przeciw l. przeciwko komuś/czemuś* against *l.* about sb/sth); (= *sprzeciwiać się*) object (*przeciw l. przeciwko komuś/czemuś* to sb/sth); **protestuję!** I object!

protetyczny *a.* **1.** (*dotyczący protetyki*) prosthetics; **pracownia protetyczna** prosthesis workshop. **2.** *fon.* prothetic.

protetyk *mp* prosthetist; **protetyk dentystyczny** *l.* **stomatologiczny** prosthodontist, prosthetic dentist.

protetyka *f.* prosthetics; **protetyka dentystyczna** *l.* **stomatologiczna** prosthodontics, prosthetic dentistry.

proteza *f.* **1.** *med.* (*ortopedyczna*) artificial limb, prosthesis; (*zębowa*) dentures, prosthesis. **2.** *fon.* prothesis, prosthesis.

protezownia *f. Gen.pl.* **-i** prosthesis workshop.

protokolant, protokólant *mp*, **protokolantka, protokólantka** *f. Gen.pl.* **-ek** reporter, recorder; *prawn.* (*sądowy*) court recorder.

protokolarny, protokólarny *a.* officially recorded.

protokołować, protokółować *ipf.* (*zebranie*) minutes, keep the minutes; (*rozprawę sądową*) record.

protokół *mi* **-o- 1.** (*sprawozdanie*) (*zebrania*) minutes; (*rozprawy sądowej*) record; (*negocjacji, zwł. międzynarodowych*) protocol; **poza protokołem** off the record. **2.** (*akt urzędowy*) report; **protokół akcesyjny** (*np. przy przyjęciu państwa do organizacji międzynarodowych*) protocol of accession; **protokół dyplomatyczny** diplomatic protocol; **protokół ekspertyzy** expert's report; **protokół oględzin** survey report. **3.** *komp.* protocol; **protokół transmisji plików** (*w Internecie*) File Transfer Protocol; **protokół przesyłu hipertekstu** (*w Internecie*) Hypertext Transfer Protocol.

protoma *f. bud.* protoma.

proton *mi fiz.* proton.

protoplasta *mp* ancestor, progenitor.

protoplazma *f. fiz.* protoplasm.

prototyp *mi* prototype.

prototypowość *f.* prototypicality.

prototypowy *a.* prototypical, prototypic; prototypal.

protozoologia *f. Gen.* **-ii** *biol.* protozoology.

protuberancja *f. astron.* prominence.

prowadnica *f. techn.* guide, runner.

prowadząca *f. Gen.* **-ej, prowadzący** *mp* (= *prezenter/ka*) host.

prowadzenie *n.* **1.** (*w lidze*) leading, lead; (*samochodu*) driving; (*interesu*) running; **prowadzenie (pojazdu) w stanie nietrzeźwym** driving while intoxicated; drunk *l.* drunken driving; *Br.* drink driving; **zdecydowane prowadzenie** comfortable lead; **być na prowadzeniu** be in the lead; **objąć prowadzenie** take the lead; **wyjść** *l.* **wysunąć się na prowadzenie** surge into the lead. **2.** (*także* **prowadzenie się**) (*sposób postępowania*) conduct; **złe prowadzenie się** misconduct; **kobieta lekkiego prowadzenia** woman of easy virtue.

prowadzić *ipf.* **1.** (= *wieść*) (*o drodze, korytarzu, drzwiach*) lead (*wzdłuż/przez/do czegoś* along/through/to sth); (*o drodze, ścieżce*) go, take; **furtka prowadzi do ogrodu** the gate opens into the garden; **wszystkie drogi prowadzą do Rzymu** all roads lead to Rome. **2.** (*określony styl życia*) live, lead; **prowadzić dostatnie życie** lead *l.* live a life of luxury; **prowadzić aktywny/zdrowy tryb życia** live an active/a healthy life; **prowadzić podwójne życie** lead a double life. **3.** (= *wywoływać coś*) lead, contribute (*do czegoś* to sth); conduce (*do czegoś* to *l.* towards sth); **jedzenie słodyczy prowadzi do otyłości** eating sweets leads to obesity. **4.** (*pojazd mechaniczny*) drive; (*samolot*) fly; (*statek*) sail; **prowadzić w stanie nietrzeźwym** drink and drive; **dobrze/źle prowadzić** (*samochód*) be a good/poor driver. **5.** (*w tańcu*) lead; **prowadzić partnera** lead one's partner. **6.** (= *nadzorować coś, kierować czymś*) conduct, run; **prowadzić dochodzenie** hold *l.* conduct an inquiry (*w sprawie czegoś* into sth); **prowadzić dom** keep *l.* run house; **prowadzić działalność gospodarczą** be in into business, have a business; **prowadzić firmę** run a business; **prowadzić księgi/księgowość** *fin.* keep the books/accounts; **prowadzić program** (*w radiu, telewizji*) host a show; **prowadzić rachunki/dziennik/spis** keep the accounts/a diary/a record; **prowadzić rozprawę sądową** conduct a trial; **prowadzić sprawę** (*o inspektorze policji itp.*) be on the case; **prowadzić śledztwo w sprawie czegoś** investigate sth; **prowadzić zebranie** *l.* **spotkanie** preside over *l.* chair a meeting; **prowadzić zajęcia** *szkoln.* tutor (*z czegoś* in sth). **7.** (= *kontynuować*) (= *realizować*) carry on, conduct, pursue; **prowadzić badania nad czymś** research sth; **prowadzić kampanię** campaign (*na rzecz czegoś/przeciw czemuś* for/against sth); **prowadzić korespondencję z kimś** carry on correspondence with sb; **prowadzić rozmowę** hold a conversation; **prowadzić zbiórkę pieniędzy na coś** collect money for sth; **prowa-**

dzić *l.* **toczyć wojnę z kimś/czymś** *l.* **przeciwko komuś/czemuś** *t. przen.* wage war on sb/sbth. **8.** (= *być na czele*) lead, be in the lead; **prowadzić dwoma punktami/dwiema bramkami** *sport* lead by two points/goals; **prowadzić stawkę** *sport* lead the field; **prowadzić pewnie** *l.* **z dużą przewagą** *polit.* hold a safe lead; **Anglia prowadziła z Niemcami 1:0** *sport* England led Germany 1 - 0; **firma prowadzi na rynku tanich komputerów** the company leads the market in cheap computers. **9.** *muz.* lead. **~ się** *ipf.* **1.** (= *postępować*) conduct o.s.; **dobrze/źle się prowadzić** conduct o.s. well/badly; **źle się prowadzić** misconduct o.s. **2.** (= *być prowadzonym*) be led; **dobrze się prowadzić** (*o samochodzie*) drive well.

prowansalski *a.* Provençal.

Prowansja *f.* Provence.

proweniencja *f. lit.* provenance.

prowiant *mi* provisions; **suchy prowiant** packed lunch.

prowincja *f.* **1.** (*jednostka administracyjna, kościelna*) province. **2.** (= *region na uboczu*) the provinces; **głucha** *l.* **zapadła prowincja** back country; **mieszkać na prowincji** live in the province.

prowincjał *mp pl.* **-owie** *kośc.* (*zakonu*) provincial.

prowincjonalizm *mi jęz.* (= *zaściankowość*) provincialism.

prowincjonalność *f.* provinciality, provincialism.

prowincjonalny *a.* **1.** (*regionalny*) (*o prasie, władzach, samorządzie*) provincial. **2.** (= *zaściankowy*) (*o guście, uprzedzeniach, modzie*) provincial; parochial; (*o miasteczku*) upcountry.

prowincjusz *mp*, **prowincjuszka** *f. Gen.pl.* **-ek** *uj.* provincial; *pot.* rustic, bumpkin.

prowitamina *f. biochem.* provitamin.

prowizja *f.* **1.** *ekon., handl.* commission; **prowizja maklerska** brokerage; **pięcioprocentowa prowizja** 5 per cent commission; **dostawać prowizję od sprzedaży** (*o przedstawicielu handlowym, akwizytorze*) work on commission. **2.** *kośc.* provision.

prowizorium *n. sing. indecl. pl.* **-ria** *Gen.* **-riów** (*ustalenie*) tentative arrangement, tentative provision; (*stan*) provisional state, temporary state; **prowizorium budżetowe** *ekon.* interim budget.

prowizorka *f. Gen.pl.* **-ek** *pot.* makeshift, quick fix.

prowizoryczność *f.* provisional character.

prowizoryczny *a.* provisional, makeshift; (*o umowie*) provisional; **prowizoryczne rozwiązanie** stopgap solution; **faktura prowizoryczna** *handl.* pro-forma invoice; **naprawa prowizoryczna** emergency repair; **scena prowizoryczna** *teatr* fit-up.

prowizyjny *a. ekon., handl.* comission; **list prowizyjny** *dyplomacja* consular patent.

prowodyr *mp pl.* **-owie** *l.* **-rzy** (*np. buntu*) instigator; (*zwł. działalności przestępczej*) ringleader.

prowokacja *f.* (*np. wywiadu*) provocation; (= *nakłonienie*) instigation, incitement; **prowokacja policyjna** entrapment; **prowokacja polityczna** political provocation.

prowokacyjnie *adv.* provokingly.

prowokacyjny *a.* provocative, provoking; (*o uśmiechu*) tempting, provoking; (*o przemówieniu, oświadczeniach*) provocative, inflammatory.

prowokator *mp*, **prowokatorka** *f. Gen.pl.* **-ek** provoker; *polit.* agent provocateur.

prowokować *ipf.* **1.** (*osobę, działanie*) provoke; (*kłótnie, konflikty, wspomnienia*) stir up; (*nieszczęścia, kłopoty*) invite; (*bunt, demonstracje*) instigate; (*dyskusję*) bring on *l.* about; **prowokować kogoś do zwierzeń** encourage sb to confess sth; **prowokować los** be asking *l.* heading for trouble. **2.** (= *wyzywać*) challenge, induce (*kogoś do czegoś* sb to do sth). **3.** (*o kobiecie w stosunku do mężczyzny*) make advances (*kogoś* to sb).

prowokująco *adv.* in a provocative way, provocatively.

prowokujący *a.* (*o wypowiedziach*) provocative, instigatory; (*o wyglądzie*) provocative, tempting.

proza *f.* **1.** *teor.lit.* prose; **pisany prozą** in prose; **utwór pisany prozą** prose work; **proza poetycka** poetry prose. **2.** (= *codzienność*) humdrum, monotony; **proza życia** humdrum of life.

prozachodni *a.* pro-Western.

prozaicznie *adv.* prosaically, banally.

prozaiczność *f.* prosaicness, banality.

prozaiczny *a.* **1.** *teor.lit.* (*o utworze, przekładzie*) prose, prosaic. **2.** (= *banalny*) mundane, pedestrian; (*o człowieku*) prosaic, uninspired; (*o zajęciu*) banal, commonplace.

prozaik *mp* prosaist, prose writer.

prozatorski *a.* (*o twórczości*) prose; (*o talencie*) prosaist's.

prozelita *mp rel.* **1.** (= *konwertyta*) proselyte. **2.** (= *krzewiciel*) promotor, apostle.

prozelityzm *mi rel.* proselytism.

Prozerpina *f. mit.* Proserpina, Proserpine.

prozodia *f. Gen.* **-ii** *jęz.* prosody.

prozodyczny *a.* prosodic.

próba *f.* **1.** (= *sprawdzenie*) test, trial; **próba charakteru** personality test; **próba sił** trial of strength, tug-of-war; **próba wytrzymałości** endurance test; **robić coś na próbę** do sth on a trial basis, do sth as an experiment; **wystawić kogoś na próbę** put sb through his/her paces, put sb on his/her mettle; **wystawić czyjąś cierpliwość/czyjeś nerwy na próbę** try *l.* strain *l.* stretch sb's patience/nerves; **wytrzymać próbę czasu** stand the test of time; **robić coś metodą prób i błędów** do sth by (the process of) trial and error; **poddać coś próbie** put sth to the test, put sth to the proof. **2.** (= *podjęty wysiłek*) attempt (*czegoś* at sth); trial (*czegoś* to do sth); **próba gwałtu** attempted rape; **próba samobójstwa** suicide *l.* suicidal attempt; **próba zamachu** assassination attempt; **podjąć próbę czegoś** make an attempt at sth. **3.** (= *sprawdzian*) test, tryout; **próba ogniowa** trial by fire, acid test; **ciężka próba** ordeal; **czas ciężkiej próby** hard time; **wytrzymać próbę**

stand a test. **4.** (*wynik*) attempt; **to są moje pierwsze próby pisarskie** these are my first literary attempts. **5.** (*przedstawienia*) rehearsal; **próba kostiumowa** full-dress rehearsal; **próba generalna** dress rehearsal; **próba chóru** choir practice. **6.** (= *zawartość metalu szlachetnego*) fineness. **7.** (= *znak probierczy*) hallmark. **8.** (*do badania*) sample; **próba krwi** blood sample; **próba tuberkulinowa** *med.* tuberculin test.

próbka *f. Gen.pl.* **-ek 1.** (*do badania*) sample, test piece; (*wody, gleby, moczu, krwi*) sample; (*pisma*) specimen; (*materiału, tkaniny, wykładziny*) swatch; **bezpłatna próbka** free sample; **wzorcowa próbka** standard sample; **pobrać próbkę** take a sample. **2.** (*umiejętności, przekładu, poetycka*) attempt.

próbnie *adv.* experimentally.

próbnik *mi Gen.* **-a** sampler, probe; *el.* testing set, tester; *tech.* trier; *med.* probe; **próbnik kosmiczny** *astron.* cosmic probe.

próbny *a.* test, probative; (*o locie*) test, experimental; **egzamin próbny** mock exam; **okres próbny** probation, trial period; **być zatrudnionym na okres próbny** be on probation; **zdjęcia próbne** screen test.

próbować *ipf.* **1.** (= *kosztować czegoś*) try, taste. **2.** (= *sprawdzać, testować*) try, test. **3.** (= *starać się coś zrobić*) try, attempt (*coś zrobić* to do sth); **próbować czegoś** (*wspinaczki, nurkowania, lotniarstwa itp.*) have *l.* take a shot at sth; **próbować coś zrobić** have a shot at doing sth; **próbować swoich sił w czymś** try one's hand at sth; **próbować szczęścia w czymś** try *l.* chance one's luck at sth; **próbować ze wszystkich sił** strain every nerve; **próbować wszystkiego** (*żeby coś zrobić, osiągnąć*) pursue *l.* explore every avenue; **nawet nie próbować czegoś zrobić** make no attempt to do sth. **4.** *teatr* rehearse.

próchnica *f.* **1.** *dent.* dental caries, decay. **2.** (*gleba*) humus.

próchniczy *a.* **1.** *dent.* (*o ubytku, zmianach*) carious, carietic. **2.** (*o glebie*) humus.

próchnieć *ipf.* (*o drewnie*) rot; (*o zębach*) decay.

próchno[1] *n. tylko sing.* (*produkt rozkładu drewna*) rotten wood; (*do zapalania*) touchwood, punk.

próchno[2] *n. Gen.pl.* **-chen** (*o człowieku*) old sack, old fogy; (*o samochodzie*) wreckage, wreck; (*o budynku*) ramshackle building; **próchno się z niego sypie** he is as old as the hills; **ten samochód to próchno** this car is a wreck.

prócz *prep.* + *Gen.* **1.** (*uzupełnienie*) apart from, besides; **prócz tego domu mam jeszcze mieszkanie w Nowym Jorku** apart from this house, I have a flat in New York. **2.** (*wyjątek*) except, but for; **nie zostało mi nic prócz wspomnień** I have nothing left but memories; **śpiewali wszyscy prócz Marii** everyone was singing except for *l.* but for Maria.

próg *mi* **-o- 1.** (*przy drzwiach*) threshold, doorsill; **próg bólu** pain threshold; **próg pobudliwości** *psych.* limen; **próg podatkowy** tax threshold; **próg słyszalności** *fiz.* audibility *l.* hearing threshold; **gościnne progi** open door; **domowe progi** one's own home and country; **już od progu** right from the door; **u progu wojny** at the brink of war; **u progu śmierci** at death's door; **zima za progiem** winter is coming *l.* is near; **przekroczyć próg czyjegoś domu** cross sb's threshold; **nie wyszedłem za próg przez trzy dni** I haven't been *l.* gone out for three days; I haven't left home for three days. **2.** *geol.* fault scrap, fault ledge; (*rzeczny*) chute, cataract. **3.** *muz.* (*gitary*) fret. **4.** *sport* (*w skoku*) take-off board.

prószyć *ipf.* (*o śniegu, popiele*) sift; **śnieg zaczął prószyć** snow began to sift down.

prósb *f. zob.* **prośba.**

próżne *n. Gen.* **-ego przelewać z pustego w próżne** (= *mówić bez treści*) talk for the sake of talking; argue the toss; **z próżnego i Salomon nie naleje** you cannot wring water from a flint.

próżnia *f.* **1.** (= *pustka*) void, emptiness; **mówić w próżnię** waste one's breath; **plan zawisł w próżni** the plan is deadlocked; **nasze argumenty padają w próżnię** our arguments fall on deaf ears *l.* on stony ground. **2.** *fiz.* vacuum; **próżnia graniczna** limit vacuum; **próżnia końcowa** ultimate vacuum; **próżnia kosmiczna** vacuum of space. **3.** *prawn.* vacuity. **4.** *lotn.* air-pocket.

próżniactwo *n.* idleness, slothfulness.

próżniaczy *a.* (*o trybie życia*) idle, slothful.

próżniaczyć się *pf.* laze away, idle away.

próżniak *mp pl.* **-i** *l.* **-cy** idler, dawdler.

próżniomierz *mi Gen.* **-a** *techn.* vacuum gauge.

próżniowy *a. techn.* vacuum; **hamulec próżniowy** vacuum brake; **komora próżniowa** vacuum chamber; **lampa próżniowa** vacuum tube; **opakowanie próżniowe** vacuum package; **pompa próżniowa** air *l.* vacuum pump.

próżno *adv.* vainly, in vain; futilely; **na próżno** in vain, to no avail; **strzępić sobie język na próżno** waste one's breath, whistle down the wind; **trudzić się na próżno** try in vain.

próżność *f.* vanity; **łechtać czyjąś próżność** tickle sb's vanity; **zaspokajać czyjąś próżność** feed sb's vanity.

próżnować *ipf.* idle, be idle; laze about, laze around.

próżny *a.* **1.** (= *pusty, niepełny*) void, empty; **odejść z próżnymi rękami** go empty-handed; **przelewać z pustego w próżne** argue the toss. **2.** (= *zarozumiały*) (*o osobie*) vain; (*o myśli*) haughty, vain. **3.** (= *niepotrzebny*) (*o wysiłkach*) futile, useless; (*o żalach, kłótniach*) to no purpose, fruitless.

prr *int.* whoa.

pruć *ipf.* **1.** (*rzecz z dzianiny*) unravel; (*rzecz uszytą, szwy*) unpick, unstitch. **2.** *przen.* (*fale, wodę*) plow; *Br.* plough; (*fale, powietrze*) cleave. **3.** *pot.* (*jechać*) tear along, rip. **4.** *pot.* (*strzelać*) fire away. **~ się** *ipf.* (*o dzianinie*) unravel; (*o czymś uszytym, szwach*) get unstitched.

pruderia *f. Gen.* **-ii** prudery.

pruderyjnie *adv.* prudishly.

pruderyjny *a.* prudish.

pruderyjność *f.* prudishness.

prukwa *f. pog.* cow.

prusactwo *n. uj.* (*charakter*) Prussianism; (*naród*) the Prussians.

prusak *ma pot., ent.* (= *karaluch*) German cockroach, crotonbug (*Blattella germanica*).

Prusak *mp* Prussian.

pruski *a.* Prussian; **błękit pruski** Prussian blue; **kwas pruski** prussic acid; **mur pruski** half-timbered wall.

Prus *mp pl.* **-owie** Prussian.

Prusy *pl. Gen.* **-s** Prussia; **Prusy Królewskie** *hist.* Royal Prussia; **Prusy Książęce** *hist.* Ducal Prussia.

prużyć *ipf.* (*na ogniu*) broil; (*w wodzie*) simmer.

prychać *ipf.*, **prychnąć** *pf.* **-ij** 1. (= *parskać*) snort; **prychnąć śmiechem** snort out with laughter. 2. (= *odpowiadać opryskliwie*) spit out. 3. (*o silniku*) wheeze.

prycza *f. Gen.pl.* **-cz** *l.* **-y** plank bed.

pryk *mp pl.* **-i** *pog.* **stary pryk** old fart.

prym *mi* predominance, leadership; **wieść prym w czymś** lead the way in sth, make all the running.

pryma *f.* 1. *muz.* (*interwał*) prime. 2. *muz.* (*dźwięk podstawowy*) prime tone; (*akordu*) root. 3. *rel.* prime.

prymarny *a.* (*o funkcji, wariancie, alofonie*) primary.

prymas *mp pl.* **-owie** *l.* **-i** *rz.-kat.* primate.

prymasostwo *n. rz.-kat.* primacy, primateship.

prymasowski *a. rz.-kat.* (*o urzędzie, godności*) primatial.

prymat *mi* primacy, predominance; **walczyć o prymat** fight for predominance.

prymicja *f. rz.-kat.* first mass.

prymityw *mi Gen.* **-u** *pl.* **-y** 1. (= *zacofanie*) primitiveness, backwardness. 2. *sztuka* primitive. – *mp.* 1. *pl.* **-y** *uj.* (= *prostak*) primitive, barbarian. 2. *pl.* **-i** *sztuka* (*twórca*) primitive.

prymitywista *mp sztuka* primitivist.

prymitywizm *mi* 1. (*niski poziom*) primitivism, crudity. 2. (= *pierwotność*) primitive state, primitiveness. 3. *sztuka* primitivism.

prymitywizować *ipf.* (*zagadnienie, problem*) primitivize.

prymitywnie *adv.* primitively.

prymitywność *f.* primitiveness, primitive character.

prymitywny *a.* 1. (= *pierwotny*) (*o ludzie, plemieniu, kulturze*) primitive; (*o narzędziach*) crude, unsophisticated; (*o emocjach, instynktach, formach życia*) primitive, primordial. 2. (= *zacofany*) primitive, backward; (*o człowieku*) coarse; (*o żarcie*) coarse, crude. 3. *sztuka* primitive.

prymka *f.* (*tytoń*) quid.

prymula *f. Gen.pl.* **-l** *l.* **-i** *bot.* primrose, primula (*Primula*).

prymus *mp pl.* **-i** *l.* **-y**, **prymuska** *f. Gen.pl.* **-ek** top student. – *mi* Primus®, Primus stove®.

pryncypał *mp Gen.* **-a** *pl.* **-owie** principal, chief. – *mi Gen.* **-u** *pl.* **-y** *muz.* principal.

pryncypat *mi hist.* principate.

pryncypializm *mi* adherence to principles, dogmatism.

pryncypialnie *adv.* uncompromisingly, in principle.

pryncypialność *f.* adherence to principles, dogmatism.

pryncypialny *a.* (*o człowieku*) of principles, principled; (*o postępowaniu, poglądach*) principled.

pryncypium *n. sing. indecl. pl.* **-pia** *Gen.* **-piów** fundamental, essential; **pryncypia polityki ekonomicznej** the fundamentals of economic policy.

pryskać *ipf.*, **prysnąć** *pf.* **-snę** **-śniesz**, **-ij** 1. (*np. rośliny wodą*) spray (*czymś* with sth). 2. (*o błocie, tłuszczu*) splatter, spatter. 3. (*znikać*) vanish, fade away; **czar prysnął** *l.* **prysł** the gilt is gone. 4. (= *kruszyć się*) shatter; (= *łamać się*) break. 5. *pot.* (= *uciekać*) do a bunk, scram.

pryszcz *mi Gen.* **-a** 1. (= *wyprysk*) spot, pimple. 2. *pot.* (= *coś łatwego*) kid's stuff, walk away; **to dla mnie pryszcz** it's a piece of cake for me.

pryszczarki *pl. Gen.* **-ek** *ent.* gall midges, cecidomyiids (*Cecidomyidae*).

pryszczaty *a.* spotty, pimply; **pryszczata twarz** pizza face; **wyciskać pryszcze** pick one's spots, squeeze one's pimples.

pryszczyca *f. wet.* foot-and-mouth disease, foot-and-mouth.

prysznic *mi Gen.* **-a** shower, douche; **wziąć prysznic** have *l.* take a shower; **zimny prysznic** *przen.* cold water.

prysznicowy *a.* shower; **kabina prysznicowa** shower cubicle.

prywaciarz *mp pot.* private entrepreneur.

prywata *f. lit.* jobbery.

prywatka *f. Gen.pl.* **-ek** *pot.* party.

prywatnie *adv.* in private, privately; **prywatnie uważam, że...** personally, I think that...

prywatność *f.* privacy; **naruszać czyjąś prywatność** intrude upon sb's privacy, invade *l.* disturb sb's privacy; **strzec własnej prywatności** guard one's privacy.

prywatny *a.* private, personal; (*o ocenach, odczuciach*) personal, intimate; (*o rozmowach*) (*np. między politykami*) unofficial, off-therecord; **prywatny detektyw** private eye, private investigator; private detective; **prywatny nauczyciel** private teacher, tutor; **adres prywatny** home address; **lekcje prywatne** private lessons; **oskarżyciel prywatny** *prawn.* private prosecutor; **osoba prywatna** *prawn.* private person; **praktyka prywatna** private practice; **prawo prywatne** *prawn.* private law; **przedsiębiorstwo prywatne** private company; **sektor prywatny** (*gospodarki*) private sector; **teren prywatny** private grounds; **własność prywatna** private property, personal property; **życie prywatne** private life; **na stopie prywatnej** on a personal level.

prywatyzacja *f. ekon.* privatization.

prywatyzować *ipf. ekon.* privatize. ~ **się** *ipf. ekon.* privatize.

pryzma *f.* 1. (= *usypisko*) pile, heap. 2. *geom.* prism. 3. *techn.* flitch.

pryzmat *mi fiz., geom.* prism; **patrzeć na coś przez pryzmat czegoś** look at sth through the prism of sth.

pryzmatoid *mi geom.* prismatoid.

pryzmatyczny *a. opt.* prismatic; **lornetka pryzmatyczna** prism binocular.

pryzmować *ipf.* 1. *roln., ogr.* pile, heap. 2. *techn.* flitch.

przaśny *a.* 1. (*o chlebie*) unleavened; (*o miodzie*) unfermented. 2. (*o żarcie, humorze, zachowaniu*) barnyard.

prządka *f. Gen.pl.* -ek 1. (*kobieta*) spinner. 2. **prządka pierścienica** *ent.* common lackey (*Malacosoma neustria*).

prząść *ipf.* **przędę przędziesz, przędź** *l.* **prządź, -ądł -ędła -ędli** spin; **cienko prząść** *pot.* live from hand to mouth.

przeanalizować *pf.* analyze, study.

przebaczać *ipf.* forgive (*komuś coś* sb sth); (*grzechy*) absolve (*komuś coś* sb from sth).

przebaczenie *n.* forgiveness; (*grzechów*) absolution.

przebaczyć *pf. zob.* **przebaczać.**

przebadać *pf.* examine.

przebarwiać *ipf.*, **przebarwić** *pf.* (= *nasycić barwą*) overcolor. **~ się** *ipf.*, **przebarwić się** *pf.* (= *zmienić barwę*) change color.

przebąblować *pf. pot.* fritter away.

przebąkiwać *ipf. pot.* hint (*o czymś* at sth); **przebąkiwać coś pod nosem** mutter sth.

przebicie *n.* 1. (*błony*) perforation; (*dętki*) puncture; (*włócznią, mieczem*) impalement. 2. *el.* breakdown. 3. *górn.* cut-through. 4. *pot.* (*zysk*) gain; **przebicie licytacyjne** overbid; **sprzedać coś z dwukrotnym przebiciem** sell sth at double price; **siła przebicia** push, wallop; **mieć siłę przebicia** pack a wallop.

przebić *pf.* -biję -bijesz, -bij *zob.* **przebijać.** **~ się** *pf. zob.* **przebijać się.**

przebiec, przebiegnąć *pf.* -biegnę -biegniesz, -biegnij, -biegł *zob.* **przebiegać.**

przebiedować *ipf.* (= *żyć przez jakiś czas w biedzie*) rough it; (= *przeczekać trudny okres*) weather the storm.

przebieg *mi* 1. (*tok*) course. 2. (*trasa*) route. 3. *mot.* mileage.

przebiegać *ipf.* 1. (= *przebyć biegiem*) run; **przebiec pięć kilometrów** run five kilometers; **czarny kot przebiegł mi drogę** a black cat crossed my way. 2. (= *szybko się przesunąć*) run, pass (*obok kogoś/czegoś* past *l.* by sb/sth); **przebiegać coś** *l.* **po czymś wzrokiem** run one's eyes over sth; **przebiegać coś myślą** *l.* **pamięcią** search one's memory for sth; **coś mi przebiegło przez myśl** sth crossed my mind; **wiadomość przebiegła kraj** the news spread across the country; **ironiczny uśmiech przebiegł po jej twarzy** an ironic smile ran across her face. 3. (= *ciągnąć się*) (*o drodze*) stretch, run; (*o rzece*) flow; **granica przebiega tamtędy** the border runs over there. 4. (= *odbywać się*) go, proceed; **przebiegać zgodnie z planem** go *l.* run according to plan; **operacja przebiegła bez trudności** the surgery proceeded

l. went without difficulties. – *pf.* (= *biegać przez jakiś czas*) run, spend some time running.

przebiegle *adv.* cunningly.

przebiegłość *f.* cunning; (*charakteru*) guile.

przebiegły *a.* (*o człowieku, oszuście*) cunning; (*o uśmiechu, minie*) sly, cunning; (*o planie*) tricky, crafty; (*o polityce, strategii*) shrewd, cunning; **przebiegły jak lis** cunning as a fox.

przebierać *ipf.* 1. (= *zmieniać ubranie*) change (*kogoś* sb's clothes); **przebierać kogoś za kogoś/coś** disguise sb as sb/sth, get sb up as sb/sth. 2. (= *sortować*) (*owoce*) sort out; (*ziarno*) sift; **przebierać do woli** pick and choose. 3. (= *poruszać*) tap; **przebierać palcami** tap one's fingers; **przebierać nogami** hop from one leg to the other. 4. *pot.* (= *grymasić*) be fussy, be fastidious; **nie przebierać w słowach** not mince one's words, talk turkey; **przebierać miarę** *l.* **miarkę** go over the top; **przebierać jak w ulęgałkach** pick and choose; **nie przebierając w środkach** by hook or by crook, by fair means or foul; **nie przebierać w środkach** be unscrupulous. **~ się** *ipf.* (= *zmieniać ubranie*) change, get changed (*w coś* into sth); **przebrać się za kogoś/coś** dress up as sb/sth, disguise o.s. as sb/sth; **przebrać się do obiadu** dress for dinner; **przebrała się miarka** this is way over the top, that was the last straw.

przebieralnia *f. Gen.pl.* -i dressing room.

przebieraniec *mp* -ńc- *pl.* -y masquerader; **bal przebierańców** costume party, costume ball; fancy-dress party.

przebieranka *f. pot.* masquerade.

przebieżka *f. pot.* jog.

przebijać *ipf.* 1. (= *przekłuwać*) (*deskę, skórę, rękę, nogę*) pierce; (*oponę*) puncture; (*kogoś nożem*) stab; (*kogoś mieczem, lancą*) impale. 2. (= *wywiercić*) bore; (= *przekopywać*) dig up; **głową muru nie przebijesz** what can't be cured must be endured. 3. (*konkurencję*) undersell, undercut; (*ofertę*) underbid, undersell; (*ceny*) underprice. 4. *karty* (*np. damę asem*) trump. 5. (= *prześwitywać*) show, be visible; **z jego listów przebija optymizm** optimism shows through his letters. **~ się** *ipf.* 1. (= *przekłuwać się*) (*o skórze, bucie*) be pierced; (*nożem*) stab o.s.; (*o oponie*) be punctured. 2. (= *przekłuć siebie nawzajem*) (*nożem, bagnetem*) stab one another; (*mieczem, lancą*) impale one another. 3. (= *przedzierać się*) (*przez gąszcz, śnieg*) break, fight one's way (*przez coś* through sth); (*przez książkę, trudne zadanie*) struggle, plow (*przez coś* through sth); **przebić się przez tłum** fight *l.* elbow one's way through the crowd; **przebić się przez oddziały wroga** fight one's way through enemy troops. 4. (= *prześwitywać*) show through, shine through; **w jej spojrzeniu przebijał się smutek** her look was full of sorrow.

przebijak *mi Gen.* -a punch.

przebijarka *f. Gen.pl.* -ek *techn.* punch press.

przebimbać *pf.* fritter away.

przebiśnieg *mi bot.* snowdrop (*Galanthus*).

przebitka *f. Gen.pl.* -ek 1. (*kopia*) carbon copy. 2. (*papier*) copying paper. 3. *karty* overtrumping, crossruff. **4.** (*księgowanie*) carbon recording. **5.** *pot.* (= *zysk*) gain, yield.

przebitkowy *a.* (*o papierze*) copying; (*o księgowaniu*) carbon.

przebłagać *pf.* (= *przejednać*) conciliate; (= *uspokoić*) appease, propitiate; **nie dać się przebłagać** be merciless.

przebłysk *mi* gleam, glimmer; **przebłysk geniuszu** stroke of genius; **przebłysk nadziei** glimmer of hope, ray of hope; **przebłysk słońca** sunburst; **przebłysk świadomości** *dosł. przen.* lucid interval; **przebłysk zrozumienia** flash of understanding, flash of comprehension; **przebłysk zainteresowania** spark of interest, gleam of interest.

przebłyskiwać *ipf.* glimmer; (*o świecy*) flicker.

przebogaty *a.* abundant.

przebojowość *f.* go-aheadness.

przebojowy *a.* **1.** (*o człowieku*) go-ahead. **2.** (*o piosence*) hit; (*o ubraniu, sukience*) all-the-rage. **3.** (= *przełomowy*) breakthrough.

przeboleć *pf.* get over; **przeboleć stratę** get over a loss; **jeszcze tego nie przebolał** he hasn't got over it yet, it is still rankling in his heart.

przebomblować *pf. pot.* fritter away.

przebój *mi* **-o-** *Gen.pl.* **-ów 1.** (*muzyczny*) hit, top song; (*kinowy*) blockbuster; **złoty przebój** golden oldie; **lista przebojów** (*spis utworów*) the charts; (*program*) hit parade; **przebój tygodnia/ miesiąca** (*najpopularniejszy l. najlepszy produkt*) the pick of the week/month. **2.** *sport* (*atak*) break through the defence; **iść przebojem** *przen.* force one's way; **zdobyć coś przebojem** (*zwł. stanowisko*) rocket to sth.

przebrać *pf.* **-biorę -bierzesz -brał** *zob.* **przebierać. ~ się** *pf. zob.* **przebierać się.**

przebranie *n.* disguise; (*na bal przebierańców*) fancy dress; **w przebraniu** in disguise.

przebrnąć *pf.* **-ij** (*przez bagno*) wade through; (*przez las, gęstwinę*) force one's way through; (*przez egzamin, eliminacje*) scrape through; **przebrnąć przez książkę** *przen.* wade through a book, plow through a book, *Br.* plough through a book; **przebrnąć przez trudności** (= *pokonać trudności*) tide over difficulties; **z trudem przebrnąć przez coś** stumble through sth, fumble through sth.

przebrzmiały *a.* (= *nieaktualny*) stale; (*o przeboju*) played-out; (*o sławie*) foregone; **przebrzmiała sprawa** dead and buried idea/matter.

przebrzmiewać *ipf.* (*o dźwięku*) die away; *przen.* (*o sławie*) wane, go with the wind; (*o twórczości*) fall *l.* pass into oblivion.

przebrzydły *a.* horrid; (*o leniu*) awful.

przebudowa *f.* **1.** *bud.* (*np. strychu na mieszkanie*) conversion (*na coś* into sth); (= *remont*) (*np. ulicy*) rebuilding. **2.** (*ulepszenie, zreformowanie*) (*systemu, państwa*) revamping, shake-up.

przebudować *pf.*, **przebudowywać** *ipf.* **1.** *bud.* (*np. strych na mieszkanie*) convert (*coś na coś* sth into sth); (= *wyremontować*) rebuild. **2.** (= *ulepszyć, zreformować*) (*system, państwo*) revamp, shake-up.

przebudzać *ipf.* rouse; (*uczucia, wspomnienia*) awaken; **przebudzić kogoś z marzeń** wake sb from their dreams; **przebudził go dzwonek do drzwi** the sound of the doorbell woke him up. **~ się** *ipf.* wake up, awaken; *przen.* wake; **przebudziła się w nim dusza artysty** he found himself to be a born artist.

przebudzenie *n.* awakening.

przebudzić *pf. zob.* **przebudzać. ~ się** *pf. zob.* **przebudzać się.**

przebyć *pf.* **-będę -będziesz, -bądź** *zob.* **przebywać.**

przebyty *a.* (*o drodze*) passed, traveled; (*o dystansie, odległości*) covered; (*o chorobie*) past.

przebywać *ipf.* **-am -asz 1.** (*być gdzieś*) stay; *form.* sojourn, tarry; **przebywać w Londynie/Waszyngtonie** stay in London/Washington; **przebywać poza domem** be out; **przebywać z kimś** spend time with sb; **przebywać na słońcu** (*dla zdrowia*) take the sun; **przebywać na wolności** be at large; **przebywać w areszcie** be in custody; **przebywać w szpitalu/więzieniu** be in hospital/prison; **przebywać za granicą** stay abroad. **2.** (*dystans, przestrzeń*) traverse, travel (*a distance*). **3.** (*granicę*) cross. **4.** (*trudny okres, chorobę*) go through, suffer.

przecedzać *ipf.*, **przecedzić** *pf.* (*przez sito*) strain; (*przez filtr*) filter.

przecena *f.* discount, reduction in prices; markdown; **towar z przeceny** cut-price goods; **kupić coś z przeceny** buy sth at a reduced price, buy sth at a discount.

przeceniać *ipf.*, **przecenić** *pf.* **1.** (= *obniżać cenę*) reduce (*the price of sth*), mark down; **przeceniać coś o 10%** reduce sth by 10%. **2.** (*czyjeś zdolności, wiedzę, znaczenie czegoś*) overestimate; **przeceniać swoje siły** overestimate one's strength, overplay one's hand; **przecenić swój apetyt** have eyes bigger than one's stomach; **trudno przecenić jego znaczenie** it's hard not to appreciate his role.

przeceniony *a.* (*o towarach*) discounted, on offer, overrated, markdown; (= *oceniony zbyt wysoko*) overestimated.

przechadzać się *ipf.* stroll, saunter.

przechadzka *f. Gen.pl.* **-ek** stroll, saunter; **iść na przechadzkę** go for a stroll.

przechera *mp l. f.* fox.

przechlać *pf. pot.* piss away, blow on boozing.

przechlapać *pf.* **-pię -piesz** *pot.* **przechlapać sobie u kogoś** get into sb's black books.

przechlapane *n. Gen.* **-ego** *pot.* **mieć u kogoś przechlapane** be in sb's black books; **no, to masz przechlapane** so, you're done for.

przechodni *a.* **1.** (*pokój*) connecting; **brama przechodnia** through-gate. **2.** *gram.* transitive; **czasownik przechodni** transitive verb.

przechodniość *f. gram.* transitivity.

przechodzić *ipf.* **1.** (= *przebyć idąc*) go, walk; **przechodzić obok kogoś/czegoś** go *l.* walk past *l.* by sb/sth; **przechodzić przez granicę** cross the border; **przechodzić przez most** go *l.* walk across the bridge; **przechodzić przez ulicę** *l.* **jezdnię** cross the street; **przejść do ogrodu/innego poko-**

ju go *l.* move to the garden/another room; **przejść przez coś suchą nogą** go through sth without wetting one's feet. **2.** (= *przesuwać się*) pass; **burza przeszła bokiem** the storm passed by. **3.** (= *przetoczyć się*) spread (*przez coś* across sth); **przez całą Europę przeszła zaraza** a plague spread across the whole of Europe. **4.** (= *zostać przekazanym*) be passed, be handed down; (*o obowiązkach, władzy*) devolve (*na kogoś* on *l.* upon sb); **przechodzić z rąk do rąk** be passed from hand to hand; **przechodzić z pokolenia na pokolenie** be handed down from one generation to another; **dom przeszedł na Adama** the house was inherited by Adam; **to wydarzenie przejdzie do historii** this event will go down in history; **wiadomość przechodziła z ust do ust** the news spread from mouth to mouth; **wszystkie listy przechodzą przez moje ręce** I handle all the letters. **5.** (= *przedostawać się przez coś*) get through; **przeszły mnie ciarki** I shivered down my spine; **słowa nie chcą mi przejść przez gardło** words stick in my throat; **ani przez myśl mi nie przeszło, że może go nie być w domu** it didn't even cross my mind that he might not be at home. **6.** (= *przebiegać, prowadzić dokądś*) run; **autostrada przejdzie tamtędy** the highway will run over there; **granica przechodzi wzdłuż rzeki** the border runs along the river. **7.** (= *mijać*) pass; **grypa nie chce mi przejść** I can't get rid of the flu; **koncert przeszedł bez echa** the concert passed by unnoticed; **nie martw się, to wkrótce przejdzie** don't worry, it will soon pass. **8.** (= *doświadczać*) experience, go through; (*szkolenie, operację*) undergo; **przechodzić kryzys** go through a crisis; **przechodzić piekło** go through hell; **przechodzić trudny okres** go through a difficult period; go through a rough patch; **wiele przeszłam w moim pierwszym małżeństwie** I went through a lot in my first marriage. **9.** (= *zmieniać stanowisko pracy, firmę*) change over (*z czegoś na coś* from sth to sth); **przejść na chrześcijaństwo** convert to Christianity; **przejść na emeryturę** retire; **przejść do następnej klasy** get *l.* be promoted; **przejść na wegetarianizm** turn vegetarian; **przejść nad czymś do porządku dziennego** disregard sth, wave sth aside; **przejść (z kimś) na ty** come to first name terms with sb; **przejdę do konkurencji** I will go over to our competition; **przejdźmy do sprawy** let's get down to business; **pozwolą państwo, że przejdę do następnego tematu** let me pass *l.* move on to the next topic, let me proceed to the next topic. **10.** (= *przekształcać się*) turn, develop (*w coś* into sth); **energia kinetyczna przechodzi w elektryczną** kinetic energy turns into electric energy; **kłótnia przeszła w bójkę** the quarrel developed *l.* turned into a fight. **11.** (= *zostać przyjętym, przegłosowanym*) be passed; **wniosek przeszedł** the motion was passed; **jego kandydatura nie przeszła** his candidacy was rejected. **12.** (= *przewyższać*) surpass, excel; **przechodzić siebie samego** surpass *l.* excel o.s.; **przechodzić czyjeś oczekiwania** exceed sb's expectations; **przechodzić czyjeś najśmielsze marzenia** be beyond one's wildest dreams; **to przechodzi ludzkie pojęcie** this all staggers the mind; **twoje zachowanie przechodzi granice mojej cierpliwości** your behavior is more than I can endure *l.* stand. — *pf.* (= *chodzić przez jakiś czas*) walk, spend some time walking; **przechodził całą noc** he spent the whole night walking.

przechodzień *mp* **-dni-** passer-by.

przechodzony *a.* (*o ubraniach*) worn-out; (*o samochodzie, kamerze*) run-down.

przechorować *pf.*, **przechorowywać** *ipf.* (= *chorować jakiś czas*) be sick; *Br.* be ill (*for some time*); **przechorował całe dwa tygodnie** he spent whole two weeks being sick.

przechować *pf.* **-am -asz** *zob.* **przechowywać**. ~ **się** *pf. zob.* **przechowywać się**.

przechowalnia *f. Gen.pl.* **-i** storage, storage room; **przechowalnia bagażu** checkroom; *Br.* left-luggage office.

przechowanie *n.* storage, storing; **oddać na przechowanie** (*okrycie, bagaż*) check; **oddać** *l.* **zostawić coś komuś na przechowanie** (*coś cennego*) leave sth in sb's trust, give sth to sb for safekeeping.

przechowywać *ipf.* **1.** (*magazynować*) store, stow; (*w lodówce*) refrigerate; (*w piwnicy*) cellar; (*w stanie zamrożenia*) deep-freeze; **przechowywać poniżej...** (*w temperaturze*) store below...; **przechowywać w chłodnym/suchym miejscu** store in a cool/dry place, keep cool/dry. **2.** (= *chronić przed zapomnieniem*) preserve, retain; **przechowywać w pamięci wspomnienie o...** nurse *l.* nurture the memory of...; **przechowywać w sercu wdzięczność** nurse *l.* cherish gratefulness. **3.** (= *ukrywać*) give shelter (*kogoś* to sb). ~ **się** *ipf.* **1.** (= *przetrwać*) be preserved; **przechowały się stare obyczaje** old traditions have been preserved. **2.** (= *zostać przechowanym*) be stored.

przechowywanie *n.* storage, storing; (*w lodówce*) refrigeration; *psych.* retention; **okres przechowywania** (*produktu*) shelf life; **na przechowanie** for safekeeping; **przechowanie krwi** blood preservation.

przechrzcić *pf.* **-chrzczę -chrzcisz -chrzcij 1.** (= *zmienić imię, nazwę*) rename. **2.** (= *zmienić wyznanie*) convert. ~ **się** *pf.* **1.** (= *zmienić swoje imię, nazwę*) change one's name. **2.** (= *zmienić swoje wyznanie*) convert (*na coś* to sth).

przechwalać *pf.* extol, exalt. ~ **się** *ipf.* brag (*czymś* of *l.* about sth).

przechwałka *f. Gen.pl.* **-ek** boast, brag; **czcze przechwałki** hot air.

przechwycić *pf.*, **przechwytywać** *ipf.* **1.** (= *przejąć*) (*posłańca*) seize; (*przesyłkę*) intercept. **2.** *lotn., wojsk.* intercept. **3.** *piłka nożna* (*podanie*) cut out, intercept.

przechylać *ipf.*, **przechylić** *pf.* tilt; (*do góry*) tip up; (*na dół*) bend down; **przechylić głowę na bok** tilt *l.* cock one's head to one side; **przechylić szalę na czyjąś korzyść** tip *l.* swing the balance *l.* scales in favor of sb. ~ **się** *ipf.*, **przechylić się** *pf.* tilt; (*o osobie*) lean over; (*o statku*) list; (*o samolocie*) bank; **przechylić się na czyjąś stronę** incline to sb's side; **szala zwycięstwa przechyla się na naszą stronę** the victory inclines to our side.

przechył *mi* **1.** (= *odchylenie od pionu*) tilt. **2.** *żegl.* list. **3.** *lotn.* bank.

przechytrzać *ipf.*, **przechytrzyć** *pf.* outwit, outsmart (*kogoś* sb); **przechytrzyć kogoś** steal a march on sb; **starać się kogoś przechytrzyć** match wits with sb, try to outwit sb.

przeciąć *pf.* -tnę -tniesz, -tnij *zob.* **przecinać.** ~ **się** *pf. zob.* **przecinać się.**

przeciąg *mi* **1.** (= *prąd powietrza*) draft; *Br.* draught. **2.** *przest.* (= *okres*) lapse, spell, span, stretch; **w przeciągu godziny** inside (of) an hour, within an hour; **w przeciągu trzech miesięcy** in *l.* within three months.

przeciągać *ipf.* **1.** (= *przewlekać*) (*nić*) thread; (*sznurek, żyłkę, rzemień itp.*) lace; (*sznur, linę*) reeve, pull through. **2.** (= *rozciągać między czymś*) stretch, extend; **przeciągać linię wysokiego napięcia** stretch high voltage wires. **3.** (= *ciągnąć, przesuwać*) drag, pull, haul; **przeciągać kogoś na swoją stronę** win sb over *l.* round, bring sb over to one's side; **przeciągać linę** play tug of war. **4.** (= *przesuwać po powierzchni*) rub, stroke, touch; **przeciągnąć ręką po czymś** run one's hand across sth; **przeciągnąć farbą po czymś** spread paint over sth, apply paint to sth. **5.** (= *pokonywać odległość*) pass; (*o ptakach*) fly overhead *l.* by; (*o wojsku*) march past; (*o pojazdach*) file past; **chmury przeciągają nad jeziorem** clouds are drifting above the lake. **6.** (= *przedłużać trwanie czegoś*) protract, prolong, draw out; **przeciągnąć debatę** wind up the debate. **7.** (= *naprężać*) stretch; **przeciągać strunę** overplay one's hand, stretch one's luck, overstep the mark; **nie przeciągaj struny** don't push it too far, don't push your luck. **8.** (= *wydłużać sylaby, słowa*) drawl, draw out. **9.** *techn.* pull, draw. ~ **się** *ipf.* **1.** (= *wydłużać swoje trwanie*) run over time, drag on *l.* out; (*w czasie*) stretch out, spin out, be protracted; **jej drzemka przeciągnęła się do dwóch godzin** her nap stretched to *l.* lasted two hours; **zebranie się przeciągnęło do późna** meeting lasted *l.* stretched till late in the evening. **2.** (= *rozciągać kończyny*) stretch (o.s.), have a stretch; **przeciągnął się i ziewnął** he stretched and yawned.

przeciąganie *n.* stretching; **przeciąganie liny** tug of war.

przeciągarka *f. Gen.pl.* -ek *techn.* **1.** (= *ciągarka*) drawing machine, drawing bench, drawbench. **2.** (= *obrabiarka do przeciągania*) broaching machine.

przeciągle *adv.* lingeringly, lengthily; **patrzeć na kogoś przeciągle** gaze at sb.

przeciągły *a.* lingering, lengthy; (*o wymowie*) drawly; (*o okrzyku*) prolonged; (*o dźwięku*) drawn out; (*o spojrzeniu*) lingering, languishing.

przeciągnąć *pf.* -ij *zob.* **przeciągać.** ~ **się** *pf.* -ij *zob.* **przeciągać się.**

przeciążać *ipf.* **1.** (= *obciążać*) overburden, overload, overtax, overweight (*kogoś czymś* sb with sth); **przeciążać kogoś pracą** overtask *l.*

overburden sb with work; **przeciążać kogoś obowiązkami** load sb down with duties; **przeciążać serce** overtax one's heart; (*zwierzę*) overburden, overload. **2.** *el.* (*o prądzie*) overload, overcharge. **3.** *techn.* (*o obciążeniu*) overload, overstress.

przeciążenie *n.* **1.** overburdening, overloading; **przeciążenie pracą** work overload, overwork. **2.** *techn.* overload, overcharge, excessive load; *el.* overload. **3.** *lotn.* gravity load, G-load.

przeciążony *a.* (*o sieci, maszynie*) overloaded; (*o zwierzęciu*) encumbered, overburdened; (*o rozkładzie pracy*) overburdened; **przeciążony pracą** overburdened with work, overworked.

przeciążyć *pf. zob.* **przeciążać.**

przeciec *pf.* -ciekne -ciekł *zob.* **przeciekać.**

przeciek *mi* **1.** (*cieczy*) leakage, leak; (*miejsce*) leak; (*substancji radioaktywnych*) spill. **2.** *przen. pot.* (= *nieoficjalne, nielegalne źródło czegoś*) leak, leakage; **przeciek informacji** information leak.

przeciekać *ipf.* **1.** (= *przepuszczać*) leak; **dach przecieka** roof leaks. **2.** (= *przenikać*) leak through, ooze, filter through; **pieniądze przeciekają mu przez palce** money runs through his fingers like water, he fritters money away. **3.** *przen.* (*o informacji, tajemnicy*) leak (out); **poufne informacje przeciekły wkrótce do prasy** secret information soon leaked to newspapers.

przecier *mi* zwł. *kulin.* purée, pomace; **przecier pomidorowy/jabłkowy** tomato/apple purée.

przecieraczka *f. Gen.pl.* -ek sieve, ricer.

przecierać *ipf.* **1.** (= *przesuwać po powierzchni*) wipe; (*kurze z mebli*) dust; (*buty*) polish; (*gąbką*) sponge; **przecierać drogę/szlak/ścieżkę** pave the way, blaze a trail; *przen.* blaze the way, pave the way; **przecierać czoło** rub one's forehead. **2.** (*przez sito*) sieve, rice. **3.** *techn.* saw. ~ **się** *ipf.* **1.** (= *dziurawić się*) wear through. **2.** (= *przejaśniać się*) clear up; **przeciera się** it's clearing up. **3.** (= *nabierać ogłady, kultury*) become polished *l.* refined.

przecierpieć *pf.* -pię -pisz **1.** (= *doznać cierpień*) suffer, endure. **2.** (= *znieść*) bear.

przecież *adv.* after all; (*przeciwstawiając*) but, yet, still, all the same, nevertheless; **przecież już ci mówiłem** I told you already, didn't I?; **zostaw go w spokoju, przecież on tego nie zrozumie** leave him alone, he won't understand it anyway; **wydaje się, że to niemożliwe, a przecież to prawda** it seems impossible but *l.* yet it's true; **musisz już iść, przecież czekają na ciebie** you've got to go, they're waiting for you, aren't they?; **przecież oni się kochają** they love each other, don't they?; **ale przecież** but then again, but; **przecież nie są biedni** it's not as if they're poor; **przecież to nie moja wina** it's hardly my fault; **przecież go nie znam** but I don't know him; **przecież to jasne** it's (rather) obvious, isn't it?, why, it's (rather) obvious.

przecięcie *n.* **1.** (= *otwór*) cut, slit. **2.** (= *skrzyżowanie*) crossing, cross; (*dróg*) intersection, crossing; **na przecięciu polityki i ekonomii** on the border *l.* verge of politics and economics.

przeciętna *f. Gen.* -ej **1.** zwł. *mat.*, *stat.* average, mean. **2.** (= *wartość zwykła, pospolita*) average, standard; **przeciętna długość życia** life expectancy; **powyżej/poniżej przeciętnej** above/below average.

przeciętniak *mp pl.* **-i** *l.* **-cy** *uj.* one of the boys, ordinary Joe, square John.

przeciętnie *adv.* (*wynosić, zarabiać*) on (the) average; (*wyglądać*) plain.

przeciętność *f.* mediocrity, ordinariness; **ponad przeciętność** out of the ordinary, above the ordinary.

przeciętny *a.* **1.** average, mean, run-of-the-mill. **2.** (= *zwykły, pospolity*) (*o pensji, człowieku*) average; (*o przedmiotach*) common, ordinary; (*o zdolnościach*) mediocre; (*o przedstawieniu, grze*) lackluster, mediocre, uninspired; **przeciętny człowiek** the man in the street, average man *l.* person.

przecinać *ipf.* **1.** (= *tnąc, rozdzielić coś*) cut; (*na plastry*) slice; **przeciął sobie palec** he cut his finger; **przecinać na pół** split into halves *l.* two; **przeciąć zakład** *pot.* seal a bet; **przeciąć plac/ulicę** cross a square/street; **przecinać komuś drogę** block sb's way. **2.** (= *znaleźć się w poprzek płaszczyzny*) cut across; (*o błyskawicy*) flash; (*o ptaku, samolocie*) (*powietrze*) knife through the air; (*niebo*) shoot across the sky. **3.** (= *przerywać, kończyć*) cut short, break off, interrupt; **przecinać kłótnię/dyskusję** cut a quarrel/discussion short; **przecinać jakąś sprawę** bring sth to an end, put an end to sth; **przecinać ciszę** break the silence. **~ się** *ipf.* (*o liniach, ulicach*) intersect, cross, decussate; *mat.* meet, intersect; **ich drogi się w końcu przecięły** they finally crossed each other's paths, their paths finally met.

przecinak *mi Gen.* **-a** *techn.* **1.** (*kowalski*) sett, sate. **2.** (*ślusarski*) cold chisel, engineer's chisel.

przecinarka *f. Dat.* **-rce** *techn.* cutting-off machine, cut-off machine.

przecinek *mi* **-nk-** *Gen.* **-a 1.** (*w interpunkcji*) comma. **2.** (*w ułamku dziesiętnym*) point; **przecinek dziesiętny** decimal point; **oddzielać przecinkiem** point off; **miejsce po przecinku** decimal place; **do trzech miejsc po przecinku** to three decimal places.

przecinka *f. Gen.pl.* **-ek 1.** (= *droga, ścieżka*) cut, glade. **2.** *leśn.* cutting. **3.** *górn.* cross-cut, cross heading.

przecinkowce *pl. Gen.* **-ów** *biol.* vibrios, comma bacilli (*Vibrio*).

przeciskać *ipf.*, **przecisnąć** *pf.* **-cisnę -ciśniesz, -ciśnij** squeeze, press, force (*coś przez coś* sth through sth); (*ziemniaki, warzywa*) rice; (*rozgnieść*) mash, pulp. **~ się** *ipf.*, **przecisnąć się** *pf.* scrape *l.* squeeze *l.* push through, push *l.* worm *l.* work one's way; **słowa nie chciały mu się przecisnąć przez gardło** words stuck in his throat, he couldn't utter a word; **przecisnąć się przez dziurę** work *l.* worm one's way through a hole; **przecisnąć się przez tłum** elbow *l.* shove one's way through the crowd.

przeciw *prep. + Dat.* **1.** (= *opozycja*) against, contra; **protestować przeciw rasizmowi** protest *l.* take a stand against racism; **być przeciw cze-**

muś be against sth, object to sth; **głosy przeciw** nays; **większość głosów jest przeciw** nays *l.* noes have it; **argumenty za i przeciw** pros and cons, for and against; **mieć coś przeciwko komuś/czemuś** mind sb/sth, have sth against sb/sth; **jeśli nie masz nic przeciw temu** if it's *l.* that's all right with you, if you don't mind; **nie mieć nic przeciw czemuś** have no objections to sth; **miałem okoliczności przeciw sobie** odds were against me, circumstances were very unfavorable; **przeciw kierunkowi wskazówek zegara** anticlockwise, counterclockwise; **jestem przeciw** I'm against, I disapprove, I object; **protestować przeciw czemuś** protest against sth, raise one's objections against sth; **w proteście przeciw czemuś** in protest against sth. **2.** (= *nieposłuszeństwo*) against; **działać przeciw prawu** act against the law. **3.** (= *środek*) against, anti-; **szampon przeciw łupieżowi** anti-dandruff shampoo.

przeciwalergiczny *a. med.* anti-allergic.

przeciwalkoholowy *a.* (*o kampanii*) antialcoholic; **poradnia przeciwalkoholowa** AA center.

przeciwatomowy *a.* antinuclear; **schron przeciwatomowy** fallout shelter.

przeciwbakteryjny *a.* antibacterial.

przeciwbólowy *a. med.* painkilling, analgesic; **środek przeciwbólowy** painkiller, analgesic.

przeciwciało *n. Loc.* **-ele** *biol.* antibody, immune body.

przeciwcierny *a. techn.* antifriction.

przeciwciężar *mi Gen.* **-u** *techn.* counterweight, counterbalance, counterpoise.

przeciwcukrzycowy *a. med.* (*o lekach*) antidiabetic; (*o poradni*) diabetic.

przeciwczołgowy *a. wojsk.* antitank, tank; **mina przeciwczołgowa** antitank mine; **blokada przeciwczołgowa** tank trap.

przeciwdesantowy *a. wojsk.* (*o obronie, patrolu*) antilanding.

przeciwdeszczowy *a.* rainproof; **płaszcz przeciwdeszczowy** raincoat.

przeciwdowód *mi* **-o-** *prawn.* evidence to the contrary.

przeciwdziałać *ipf.* counteract, act counter to, countercheck.

przeciwdziałający *a.* counteractive; **środek przeciwdziałający** counteractant; **siła przeciwdziałająca** counterforce.

przeciwdziałanie *mi* counteraction.

przeciwdźwiękowy *a.* soundproof.

przeciwepileptyczny *a. med.* antiepileptic; **poradnia przeciwepileptyczna** epileptic (outpatients) clinic.

przeciwgazowy *a. zwł. wojsk.* antigas, gas; **maska przeciwgazowa** gas mask; **schron przeciwgazowy** gas shelter.

przeciwgorączkowy *a. med.* febrifuge, antipyretic, refrigerant; **środek przeciwgorączkowy** febrifuge, antipyretic, refrigerant.

przeciwgruźliczy *a. med.* antituberculous; **poradnia przeciwgruźlicza** tuberculosis (outpatients') clinic.

przeciwgrypowy *a. zwł. med.* antiflu, anti-influenza; **szczepionka przeciwgrypowa** influenza vaccine, flu vaccine.

przeciwieństwo *n.* **1.** (= *sprzeczność*) contrast, conflict; **w przeciwieństwie do...** as opposed to..., in contrast to..., unlike..., contrary to...; **w przeciwieństwie do ciebie** unlike you, as opposed to you. **2.** (= *coś odwrotnego*) opposite, contradiction; **być przeciwieństwem kogoś/czegoś** be the opposite of sb/sth; **dokładne przeciwieństwo** exact *l.* direct opposite, antipode. **3.** (= *przeszkoda*) adversity, misfortune; **przeciwieństwa losu** life's adversities. **4.** *log., fil.* antithesis, opposition.

przeciwjad *mi biol.* antivenin, antivenom.

przeciwjadowy *a. zwł. med.* antivenin, antivenomous, anagotoxic; **surowica przeciwjadowa** antivenomous serum.

przeciwko *prep.* + *Dat.* **1.** zob. **przeciw. 2. iść z przeciwka** approach *l.* come from the opposite direction; **sąsiad z przeciwka** (*na osiedlu domów*) neighbor across the street, next-door neighbor; (*w bloku*) next-door neighbor; **nadjeżdżający z przeciwka** oncoming, coming from the opposite direction.

przeciwległy *a.* opposite; **przeciwległy budynek** building across the street; **budynek przeciwległy do poczty** building opposite *l.* facing the post office; **na przeciwległych krańcach czegoś** at opposite site ends of sth; **być przeciwległym** (*do boku, kąta*) *geom.* subtend; **na przeciwległym brzegu morza** on the other side of the sea.

przeciwlotniczy *a. wojsk.* antiaircraft; (*o ogniu*) fla(c)k; **działo przeciwlotnicze** antiaircraft gun, flak gun; **pocisk przeciwlotniczy** antiaircraft missile; **schron przeciwlotniczy** air-raid shelter.

przeciwmgielny, przeciwmgłowy *a. mot.* fog; **światła przeciwmgielne** fog lights.

przeciwmiażdżycowy *a. med.* antiatherogenic, antiarteriosclerotic.

przeciwmina *f. wojsk.* countermine.

przeciwnakrętka *f. Dat.* **-tce** *techn.* lock-nut, check nut, jam nut, pinch nut.

przeciwnatarcie *n. wojsk.* counterattack.

przeciwniczka *f. Gen.pl.* **-ek** zob. **przeciwnik** 2, 3.

przeciwnie *adv.* **1.** (= *na odwrót*) conversely, contrary, by *l.* in contrast; **wprost przeciwnie** on the contrary, just *l.* quite the opposite, quite the reverse; **przeciwnie do czegoś** contrary to sth, in opposition to sth. **2.** (= *w odwrotnym kierunku*) reversely, in the opposite direction; **przeciwnie do ruchu wskazówek zegara** counterclockwise, anticlockwise.

przeciwnik *mp* **1.** *wojsk.* (= *nieprzyjaciel*) enemy, adversary, foe. **2.** (= *oponent*) opponent, antagonist, adversary; **przeciwnik segregacji rasowej** anti-segregationist; **przeciwnik aborcji** anti-abortionist, pro-lifer; **znaleźć godnego przeciwnika** meet one's match; **być przeciwnikiem czegoś** be opposed to sth, be against sth. **3.** *sport* (= *rywal*) rival, opponent, competitor.

przeciwności *pl. Gen.* **-i** adversities, misfortunes; **przeciwności losu** life's adversities, reverses of fortune; **nie zrażać się przeciwnościami**

not get discouraged by adversities; **dzielnie stawić czoła przeciwnościom** face adversities with courage; **pogodzić się z przeciwnościami losu** take the bitter with the sweet.

przeciwny *a.* **1.** (= *przeciwległy*) opposite; **po przeciwnej stronie czegoś** on the other side of sth; **w przeciwną stronę** in the opposite direction; **wiatr przeciwny** headwind; **płeć przeciwna** opposite sex. **2.** (= *sprzeczny*) contrary, opposite; (*poglądy*) opposing, different, contrary; **jestem przeciwnego zdania** I hold a different opinion; **coś wręcz przeciwnego** quite the reverse *l.* opposite; **w przeciwnym razie** or else, otherwise. **3.** (= *wrogi*) antagonistic, hostile, opposed (*czemuś* to *l.* towards sth); (*o drużynie*) rival, competing; (*o obozie, stronie*) opposing, conflicting; (*segregacji rasowej, projektowi*) against, opposed to, anti-; **zdecydowanie przeciwny czemuś** dead set against sth; **być czemuś przeciwnym** oppose sth, be against sth; **nie byłbym temu przeciwny** I wouldn't mind it, I wouldn't have anything against it.

przeciwodblaskowy *a.* antireflection.

przeciwogniowy *a.* (= *ogniotrwały*) fireproof; (= *zapobiegający rozszerzaniu się ognia*) fire, fire-fighting.

przeciwpancerny *a. wojsk.* antitank, armor-piercing; **pocisk przeciwpancerny** antitank *l.* armor-piercing missile.

przeciwpiechotny *a. wojsk.* antipersonnel, anti-infantry; **mina przeciwpiechotna** antipersonnel *l.* anti-infantry mine.

przeciwpocisk *mi wojsk.* antimissile; **przeciwpocisk rakietowy** antimissile missile.

przeciwpoślizgowy *a.* antislip; antiskid, nonskid.

przeciwpowodziowy *a.* flood; **wał przeciwpowodziowy** levee; **tama przeciwpowodziowa** high water dam, flood detention dam; **zbiornik przeciwpowodziowy** flood control reservoir; **alarm przeciwpowodziowy** flood alert; **ochrona przeciwpowodziowa** flood control; **umocnienie przeciwpowodziowe** flood wall.

przeciwpożarowy *a.* (*o ochronie, przepisach, alarmie*) fire; (*o sprzęcie*) fire-extinguishing, fire-fighting; **ćwiczenia przeciwpożarowe** fire drill; **alarm przeciwpożarowy** fire alarm; **pas przeciwpożarowy** firebreak.

przeciwprostokątna *f. Gen.* **-ej** *geom.* hypotenuse.

przeciwpyłowy *a.* (*o filtrze, masce*) anti-dust, dust.

przeciwrakieta *f. wojsk.* antiballistic missile.

przeciwrakietowy *a. wojsk.* antimissile; **obrona przeciwrakietowa** antimissile defense; **pocisk przeciwrakietowy** antiballistic missile, ABM.

przeciwrakowy *a. med.* anticancer; **profilaktyka przeciwrakowa** cancer prophylaxis.

przeciwreumatyczny *a. med.* antirheumatic; **poradnia przeciwreumatyczna** rheumatic (outpatients) clinic.

przeciwskurczowy *a. med.* antispasmodic, spasmolytic.

przeciwsłoneczny *a.* sun; **okulary przeciw-**

słoneczne sunglasses, dark glasses; **osłona przeciwsłoneczna** *fot.* lens hood; *mot.* (*nad szybą*) sun visor; **daszek przeciwsłoneczny** (*na czoło*) sun visor; **krem** *l.* **filtr przeciwsłoneczny** sunblock, sunscreen.

przeciwstawiać *ipf.*, **przeciwstawić** *pf.* contrast, contrapose, set against; (= *skonfrontować*) confront; **przeciwstawić coś czemuś** contrast sth with sth. ~ **się** *ipf.*, **przeciwstawić się** *pf.* oppose, defy, counter; **przeciwstawiać się komuś** stand up to sb, oppose sb; **przeciwstawiać się czemuś** oppose sth.

przeciwstawienie *n.* contrast, opposition; **być przeciwstawieniem kogoś/czegoś** be the opposite of sb/sth; **w przeciwstawieniu do** contrary to, in contrast to; **przeciwstawienie się czemuś** opposition to sth.

przeciwstawność *f.* (*poglądów, teorii*) opposition.

przeciwstawny *a.* antithetic, contrary, opposed (*czemuś* to sth); opposite; (*o poglądach, teoriach*) opposing, contradictory, contrasting; **spójnik przeciwstawny** *gram.* adversative conjunction; **przeciwstawny cel** crosspurpose; **diametralnie przeciwstawny** antipodal, diametrically opposed; **znajdować się na przeciwstawnych biegunach** be poles apart.

przeciwślizgowy *a.* nonskid, antislip; **łańcuch przeciwślizgowy** *mot.* snow chain; **zabezpieczenie przeciwślizgowe** antislip protection.

przeciwśruba *f. Dat.* **-bie** *żegl.* contra-propeller.

przeciwtężcowy *a. med.* antitetanus, antitetanic; **surowica przeciwtężcowa** antitetanus serum.

przeciwuderzenie *n.* **1.** *sport* counterattack. **2.** *wojsk.* counterstroke, counterattack.

przeciwutleniacz *mi chem.* antioxidant.

przeciwwaga *f.* counterbalance, counterweight, counterpoise (*dla czegoś* to sth); **być przeciwwagą czegoś** *przen.* counterbalance sth, equipoise sth; **dla przeciwwagi** *przen.* to counterbalance, as a counterweight.

przeciwwskazanie *n. med.* contraindication.

przeciwwymiotny *a. med.* antiemetic, antemetic.

przeciwzakaźny *a. med.* anti-infectious.

przeciwzakłóceniowy *a. techn.* interference, anti-interference; **filtr przeciwzakłóceniowy** interference eliminator; **kondensator przeciwzakłóceniowy** interference suppressor capacitor.

przeciwzakrzepowy *a. med.* antithrombotic.

przeciwzapalny *a. med.* anti-inflammatory, antiphlogistic.

przeciwzawałowy *a. med.* anti-heart attack.

przecukrzenie *n. med.* **przecukrzenie krwi** hyperglyc(a)emia.

przeczący *a.* (*o zdaniu, odpowiedzi*) negative; (*o geście*) contradicting, refusing, denying; **odpowiedź przecząca** negative answer; **forma przecząca** *gram.* the negative; **zdanie przeczące** *gram.* negative sentence; **przedrostek przeczący** *gram.* privative prefix.

przeczekać *pf.*, **przeczekiwać** *ipf.* **1.** (= *spędzić czas na czekaniu*) wait (*for some time*); **przeczekał cały dzień na próżno** he waited the whole day in vain. **2.** (= *poczekać, aż coś się skończy*) wait out, ride out, wait for the end of; **przeczekać burzę** wait the storm out; (*w ukryciu*) lie low; **przeczekać sprawę** let it *l.* things lie.

przeczenie *n.* **1.** negation, denial. **2.** *gram.* negative; **podwójne przeczenie** double negation.

przeczesać *pf.* **-szę -szesz**, **przeczesywać** *ipf.* **1.** (= *gładzić grzebieniem, szczotką*) comb. **2.** (= *zmieniać fryzurę*) change (sb's) hair-do. **3.** (= *szukać*) comb (through), sweep (through) (*coś w poszukiwaniu kogoś/czegoś* sth for sb/sth); **policja przeczesuje teren w poszukiwaniu śladów** police are combing the area for clues.

przecznica *f.* **1.** (= *ulica*) turn, turning, street across; **pierwsza przecznica** the first street across; **trzy przecznice stąd** three blocks from here. **2.** *górn.* cross heading, crosscut, stone drift.

przeczołgać się *pf.*, **przeczołgiwać się** *ipf.* crawl, creep.

przeczucie *n.* feeling, hunch, intuition, premonition; **mieć przeczucie** have a hunch; **złe przeczucie** foreboding, presentiment; **mam złe przeczucia** I have bad feelings; **pełen złych przeczuć** full of apprehension; **mieć paskudne przeczucie, że...** have a nasty feeling that...

przeczuć *pf. zob.* **przeczuwać**.

przeczulenie *n.* oversensitivity, hypersensitivity.

przeczulica *f. pat.* hyper(a)esthesia; **przeczulica dotykowa** tactile hyper(a)esthesia; **przeczulica bólowa** hyperalgesia.

przeczulony *a.* **-eni** (= *przewrażliwiony*) oversensitive, touchy (*na punkcie kogoś/czegoś* about sb/sth); **być przeczulonym na punkcie czegoś** be oversensitive about sth.

przeczuwać *ipf.* sense, feel, have an inkling of; **przeczuwać kłopoty** smell trouble; **przeczuwać podstęp** smell a rat.

przeczyć *ipf.* (= *negować*) contradict, negate, deny, belie (*czemuś* sth); **przeczyć samemu sobie** contradict o.s.; **jego czyny przeczą słowom** his deeds go counter to *l.* belie his words; **fakty temu przeczą** the facts contradict it.

przeczysty *a. lit.* immaculate; **Przeczysta Dziewica** *rel.* Immaculate Virgin.

przeczyszczający *a. med.* laxative, purgative, cathartic; **środek przeczyszczający** laxative, aperient, purge.

przeczyszczenie *n. med.* purgation, catharsis; **dać/wziąć na przeczyszczenie** give/take a laxative.

przeczyszczać *ipf.*, **przeczyścić** *pf.* **-czyszczę -czyścisz 1.** (= *usuwać brud*) clean, cleanse; (*szmatką*) wipe; (*komin*) sweep. **2.** *med.* (= *powodować wypróżnienie*) purge.

przeczytać *pf.* read; (*dokładnie, szczegółowo*) peruse; **przeczytać coś od deski do deski** read sth from cover to cover; **przeczytać pobieżnie książkę** skim through a book.

przeć *ipf.* **prę przesz, przyj, parł 1.** (= *wywierać nacisk*) push, force, press. **2.** (= *skłaniać do cze-*

goś) drive; **ciekawość parła go do pójścia tam** he was driven by curiosity to go there; **przeć na kogoś (żeby coś zrobił)** pressure *l.* pressurize *l.* urge sb (to do sth). **3.** (= *zmierzać do czegoś*) press forward, strive for; **rodzice parli do ich ślubu** parents urged them to get married, parents insisted on their getting married; **przeć do czegoś** push for sth; **przeć naprzód** press on; **przeć przez tłum** work *l.* push *l.* elbow one's way through the crowd. **4.** *med.* push.

przećwiczyć *pf.* train, practice; (*materiał*) go *l.* run through; (*krok po kroku*) walk through; (*piosenkę, wystąpienie*) rehearse; **przećwiczyć kogoś** *pot.* teach sb a lesson.

przed *prep.* **1.** + *Ins.* (*miejsce*) in front of, outside; **przed kimś/czymś** in front of sb/sth; **spotkamy się przed bankiem** I'll meet you outside the bank; **stał przed domem** he stood in front of the house; **karetka jechała przed nami** ambulance was going in front of us; **ogródek przed domem** front garden; **prosto przed siebie** straight ahead; **stawić się przed** (*sądem, komisją itp.*) appear before *l.* in front of. **2.** (*moment*) before, ahead of; **przed południem** before midday, in the morning, a.m., ante meridiem; **przed końcem miesiąca** by the end of the month; **przed zapadnięciem zmroku** before (it gets) dark; **przed świętami** before holidays; **przed chwilą** a while *l.* moment ago; **przed czasem** ahead of time, in good time; (*o porodzie*) preterm; **samolot przyleciał przed czasem** plane arrived ahead of schedule; **krótko przed** shortly before; **przed czterdziestką** (*o wieku*) on the right side of forty *l.* the hill, approaching forty; **przed oczyma duszy** in one's mind's eye. **3.** (*okres*) ago, before; **przed trzema godzinami** three hours ago; **przed dwoma miesiącami** two months ago; **przed laty** years ago; **przed upływem tygodnia** before the week is over; **na długo przed czymś** long before; **coś nie ma przed sobą przyszłości** there's no future in sth; **przed Chrystusem** before Christ, B.C., before the Christian *l.* Common Era. **4.** (*obrona*) against, from; **uciekał przed policją** he was fleeing from the police; **bronił się przed ciosami napastnika** he defended himself from his rival's blows; **chronić kogoś przed czymś** protect sb against sth, keep sb from sth; **schronienie przed deszczem** shelter from the rain; **strach przed czymś** fear of sth. **5.** (*ocena*) to, before; **popisywał się przed dziewczyną** he showed off to impress the girl; **wyżaliła się przed przyjaciółką** she complained to her (girl)friend; **nic przede mną nie ukrywasz?** you're not hiding anything from me, are you? **6.** (= *kolejność*) before, above, previous to; **przybiegł na metę przed faworytami** he came to the finish line before the favorites, he finished before the favorites; **dała jej pierwszeństwo przed innymi** he gave her priority over the others; **przede wszystkim** first of all, first and foremost, above all; **daleko przed kimś** way ahead of sb; **mam to jeszcze przed sobą** (*w przyszłości*) it's still ahead of me. **7.** (= *szacunek*) to, before; **chylić głowę przed autorytetem** bow one's head to *l.* before sb; **chylić czoła przed kimś** take one's hat off to sb; **być od-**

powiedzialnym przed kimś be responsible to sb; **przed Bogiem** before God. **8.** + *Acc.* (= *kierunek*) before; **wyjść przed dom** go out; **ciężarówka wysunęła się przede mnie** truck passed me; **patrzyć przed siebie** look straight ahead; **iść przed siebie** walk straight on; **roztoczył się przed nami piękny widok** beautiful view opened before us; **iść/jechać przed kimś** go/drive before *l.* ahead of sb; **być dopuszczonym przed czyjeś oblicze** be admitted to sb's presence; **przed obliczem** in the presence; **zanieść prośbę przed majestat króla** present a request to the king.

przedagonalny *a. med.* preagonal.

przedakcentowy *a. fon.* pretonic.

przedarcie *n.* tear, hole.

przedawkować *pf. med.* (*t. narkotyki*) overdose (*coś* on sth).

przedawniać *ipf.*, **przedawnić** *pf.* **-ij** *rzad.* limit. **~ się** *ipf.*, **przedawnić się** *pf.* **-ij 1.** (*o legitymacji, paszporcie*) expire. **2.** *prawn.* become limited.

przedawnienie *n.* **1.** (*ważności*) expiration. **2.** *prawn.* limitation, limitation(s) period; prescription; **przedawnienie nabywcze** (acquisitive *l.* positive) prescription.

przedawniony *a.* expired; (*nieważny*) invalid, stale; (*o zbrodni, przestępstwie*) limited; prescribed.

przedbieg *mi Gen.* **-u** *sport* heat, qualifying race; **odpaść w przedbiegach** be eliminated in the heat.

przedchrześcijański *a.* (*o kulturze, okresie*) pre-Christian.

przeddzień *mi* **-dedni-** *Gen.* **-a** eve, the day before; **w przededniu** on the eve of, the day before; **w przededniu wojny** on *l.* at the brink of war.

przede *prep. zob.* **przed.**

przedefilować *pf. rzad.* march past, defile.

przedegzaminacyjny *a.* exam, examination, pre-examination; **przygotowania przedegzaminacyjne** preparations for the exam, exam preparations; **stres przedegzaminacyjny** pre-examination stress, pre-examination anxiety.

przedemerytalny *a.* pre-retirement, pre-pension.

przedeptany *a.* trodden; **przedeptane ścieżki** beaten tracks.

przedestylować *pf. techn.* distill.

przedfinałowy *a. zwł. sport* semi-final; **rozgrywki przedfinałowe** semi-finals.

przedgon *mi techn.* first running, forerunnings; heads.

przedgórze *n. Gen.pl.* **-y** *geol.* foreland, piedmont.

przedgwiazdkowy *a.* before Christmas; **przedgwiazdkowe zakupy** Christmas shopping.

przedhistoryczny *a.* (*o człowieku*) primitive, prehistoric; (*o epoce*) prehistoric.

przedimek *mi* **-mk-** *Gen.* **-a** *gram.* article; **przedimek określony/nieokreślony** definite/indefinite article.

przedkładać *ipf.* **1.** (= *przedstawiać coś komuś*) propose, submit, put forward (*coś komuś* sth to sb); lay (*coś komuś* sth before sb); bring forward; (*argumenty, racje*) present. **2.** (= *tłu-*

maczyć, argumentować) explain, expound; **przedkładał jej, że powinna odejść z firmy** he argued that she should leave the company *l.* firm. **3.** (= *preferować*) prefer (*coś nad coś* sth to sth); value, place, set (*coś nad coś* sth above sth).

przedlodowcowy *a. geol.* preglacial.

przedłożyć *pf.* -łóż *zob.* **przedkładać.**

przedłużacz *mi Gen.* -a **1.** (= *przewód*) extension cord. **2.** (*np. cyrkla*) lengthening bar, extension rod.

przedłużać *ipf.* **1.** (= *czynić dłuższym*) (*drogę, odcinek*) extend, lengthen; (*spodnie, sukienkę*) lengthen, let down, piece out. **2.** (= *przeciągać w czasie*) extend, prolong, protract; **przedłużać wizę/paszport** extend *l.* renew one's visa/passport. ~ **się** *ipf.* **1.** (= *stawać się dłuższym*) extend, lengthen, stretch. **2.** (= *przeciągać się w czasie*) stretch on, drag out; **spotkanie się przedłużyło** meeting dragged out.

przedłużenie *n.* lengthening; (*okresu*) prolongation; (*drogi*) extension; (*umowy*) renewal; **podlegający przedłużeniu** renewable.

przedłużony *a.* protracted, prolonged; extended; **rdzeń przedłużony** *anat.* medulla oblongata; **produkt o przedłużonej trwałości** long-life product.

przedłużyć *pf. zob.* **przedłużać.** ~ **się** *pf. zob.* **przedłużać się.**

przedmałżeński *a.* premarital, prenuptial; **umowa przedmałżeńska** *prawn.* prenuptial agreement, antenuptial agreement *l.* contract, premarital agreement *l.* contract, marriage settlement.

przedmiejski *a.* suburban.

przedmieście *n.* suburb; **rozległe przedmieście** sprawl; **przedmieścia** suburbs, environs, suburbia; **w kierunku przedmieść** uptown.

przedmiot *mi* **1.** (= *rzecz*) object, artifact; **traktować kogoś jak przedmiot** treat sb like an object; **przedmiot zbytku** luxury. **2.** (= *temat*) subject matter; (*dyskusji, sporu, badań*) topic, subject; **przedmiot prawa** *prawn.* subject of law; **odbiegać od przedmiotu** depart from the subject; **w przedmiocie czegoś** with regard to sth. **3.** (= *obiekt*) object; (*badań, obserwacji, zabiegów*) object; (*starań*) aim, target; **przedmiot pożądania** object of desire. **4.** *szkoln. uniw.* subject; course; **przedmiot nadobowiązkowy** extracurricular *l.* elective *l.* optional subject. **5.** *gram.* (= *dopełnienie*) object.

przedmiotowość *f.* objectivity, impartiality.

przedmiotowy *a.* **1.** (= *dotyczący przedmiotu*) object, product; **katalog przedmiotowy** *bibl.* subject catalogue; **szkiełko przedmiotowe** *chem., fiz.* microscopic *l.* micro slide. **2.** (= *rzeczowy*) objective; **sztuka przedmiotowa** *sztuka* imitative art. **3.** *gram.* object, objective. **4.** *prawn.* subject-of-law. **5.** *szkoln., uniw.* subject.

przedmowa *f. Gen.pl.* -ów preface, foreword.

przedmówca *mp* preceding speaker.

przedmówczyni *f. zob.* **przedmówca.**

przedmuchać *pf.*, **przedmuchiwać** *ipf.* (*coś*) blow through (*sth*).

przedmurze *n. Gen.pl.* -y **1.** *hist.* bulwark, rampant. **2.** *geol.* foreland.

przedni *a.* **1.** (= *na przodzie*) front, foremost, headmost; *anat.* anterior; **przednie siedzenie** *zwł. mot.* front seat; **przednia łapa** *zool.* forefoot, forepaw; **maszt przedni** *żegl.* foremast; **napęd przedni** *techn.* front-wheel drive; **samogłoska przednia** *fon.* front vowel; **orzeł przedni** *orn.* golden eagle (*Aquila chrysaëtos*). **2.** *lit.* (= *wyśmienity*) fine, exquisite, outstanding. **3.** *przest.* preceding, advance; **straż przednia** advance guard.

przedniojęzykowy *a. jęz.* front.

przednówek *mi* -wk- *Gen.* -a preharvest (period); **na przednówku** before the harvest.

przednutka *f. Gen.pl.* -ek *muz.* grace note, appoggiatura.

przedobiedni *a.* preceding dinner; **spacer przedobiedni** a walk before dinner.

przedobrzyć *pf.* -yj *pot.* gild the lily, overegg the pudding; **uważać, żeby nie przedobrzyć** leave well (enough) alone.

przedolimpijski *a. sport* (*o przygotowaniach, zgrupowaniu*) pre-Olympic.

przedostać się *pf.* -stanę -staniesz *zob.* **przedostawać się.**

przedostatni *a.* next to the last, penultimate; *Br.* last but one; **przedostatniej nocy** the night before last.

przedostawać się *ipf.* -aję -ajesz, -awaj **1.** (= *przemieszczać się mimo przeszkód*) force *l.* work one's way; **przedostawać się gdzieś** find one's way somewhere; **przedostawać się przez tłum** elbow *l.* squeeze *l.* thread one's way through the crowd; **przedostawać się na drugą stronę** get across, get to the other side. **2.** (= *przenikać, wnikać*) penetrate, get through, filter through, permeate; (*o wiadomości do prasy*) leak.

przedpiśmienny *a.* (*o okresie, polszczyźnie*) preliterate.

przedplon *mi roln., ogr.* forecrop, pioneer crop.

przedpłata *f.* prepayment, advance payment, down payment; **dokonać przedpłaty** prepay.

przedpoborowy *a. zwł. wojsk.* (*o wieku*) preconscription.

przedpokój *mi* -o- *Gen.pl.* -oi *l.* -ów hall, anteroom, foyer.

przedpole *n. Gen.pl.* -i **1.** outskirt(s). **2.** *sport* area in front of the goal. **3.** *wojsk.* foreground. **4.** *geol.* foreland, piedmont.

przedpołudnie *n. Gen.pl.* -i morning, forenoon.

przedpołudniowy *a.* (late) morning, forenoon.

przedporcie *n. Gen.pl.* -i *żegl.* outer harbor.

przedpotopowy *a. pot., żart.* ancient, antediluvian; (*o samochodzie, komputerze*) fossil, fossilized, obsolete; (*o ubraniu, uczesaniu*) old-fashioned; *Bibl.* from before the Flood.

przedramieniowy *a. anat.* antebrachial, forearm.

przedramię *n.* -mieni- *pl.* -mion- *anat.* antebrachium, forearm.

przedrenesansowy *a. sztuka* pre-Renaissance.

przedrewolucyjny *a.* pre-revolutionary, pre-revolution; (*o napięciu, nastrojach*) revolutionary.

przedromantyczny *a. teor.lit.* pre-romantic, pre-Romantic.

przedromański *a. sztuka* pre-Romanesque.

przedrostek *mi* -tk- *Gen.* -a *gram.* prefix.

przedrostkowy *a. gram.* prefixal.

przedrośle *n. Gen.pl.* -i *bot.* prothallium.

przedrozbiorowy *a. hist.* pre-partition (*of Poland*).

przedruk *mi druk.* 1. (= *reprint*) reprint. 2. (= *wznowienie*) new impression, reprint.

przedrukować *pf.*, przedrukowywać *ipf.* reprint.

przedrzeć *pf.* -drę -drzesz, -drzyj, -darł *zob.* przedzierać. ~ się *pf. zob.* przedzierać się.

przedrzeźniać *ipf.* mimic, mock.

przedsiębierny *a.* koparka przedsiębierna *techn.* push shovel, high shovel.

przedsiębiorca *mp* entrepreneur; przedsiębiorca budowlany building contractor; przedsiębiorca pogrzebowy funeral director, undertaker; przedsiębiorca prywatny private entrepreneur.

przedsiębiorczość *f.* (*cecha charakteru*) enterprise; (*działalność gospodarcza*) enterpreneurship.

przedsiębiorczy *a.* enterprising.

przedsiębiorstwo *n.* company, enterprise; przedsiębiorstwo budowlane construction company, building contractor; przedsiębiorstwo handlowe trading company; przedsiębiorstwo państwowe state-owned enterprise; przedsiębiorstwo prywatne private company *l.* enterprise; przedsiębiorstwo spółdzielcze cooperative, co-operative.

przedsiębrać *ipf.* -biorę, -bierzesz, przedsięwziąć *pf.* -wezmę -weźmiesz, -weźmij, -wziął -wzięła -wzięli undertake.

przedsięwzięcie *n.* undertaking, enterprise; (*zwł. ryzykowne*) venture.

przedsionek *mi* -nk- *Gen.* -a 1. (*w domu*) vestibule, entrance hall. 2. *anat.* (*serca*) atrium, auricle. 3. *anat.* (*w błędniku*) (labyrinthine) vestibule.

przedsionkowo-komorowy *a. anat.* atrioventricular.

przedsmak *mi* foretaste; mieć przedsmak czegoś have a foretaste of sth.

przedsprzedaż *f. pl.* -e advance sale; (*zwł. biletów*) pre-booking.

przedstawiać *ipf.* 1. (*z imienia i nazwiska*) introduce, present; pani pozwoli sobie przedstawić pana Adama Kowalskiego *l.* pani pozwoli, że przedstawię pani pana Adama Kowalskiego let me introduce to you Mr. Adam Kowalski; przedstawić kogoś do awansu recommend sb for promotion. 2. (*na scenie*) present. 3. (= *przedkładać*) put forward, present; przedstawić wniosek put forward *l.* present a motion; do końca miesiąca musimy przedstawić plan budżetu na następny rok we have to present a budget plan for the next year by the end of this month. 4. *tylko ipf.* (= *stanowić*) be; to nie przedstawia dla mnie żadnego problemu this is no problem for me; w

gruncie rzeczy ten jej nowy przyjaciel nic sobą nie przedstawia in fact, this new friend of hers is a good-for-nothing; przedstawiać wartość be of value. ~ się *ipf.* 1. (*z imienia i nazwiska*) introduce o.s. 2. (= *ukazywać się*) appear, show; z tarasu przedstawiał się jej piękny widok na jesienny park the terrace overlooked a beautiful fall park; from the terrace she had a beautiful view of a fall park.

przedstawiciel *mp*, przedstawicielka *f.* 1. *Gen.pl.* -ek (= *reprezentant*) representative; agent; przedstawiciel handlowy sales representative. 2. *prawn.* attorney; proxy.

przedstawicielski *a.* representational.

przedstawicielstwo *n.* 1. (= *reprezentowanie*) representation. 2. (= *pełnomocnictwo*) power of attorney. 3. (= *biuro, placówka*) agency, branch; przedstawicielstwo handlowe sales office, branch office. 4. (*placówka dyplomatyczna*) diplomatic post, diplomatic agency.

przedstawić *pf. zob.* przedstawiać. ~ się *pf. zob.* przedstawiać się.

przedstawienie *n.* 1. *teatr* show, performance; robić z czegoś przedstawienie put on a show of sth; nie rób z siebie przedstawienia! don't make a spectacle of yourself! 2. *psych.* representation.

przedstopie *n. Gen.pl.* -i *anat.* toes.

przedszkolak *mp pl.* -i *l.* -cy kindergarten pupil, preschooler.

przedszkolanka *f. Gen.pl.* -ek kindergarten teacher.

przedszkole *n. Gen.pl.* -i kindergarten.

przedszkolny *a.* kindergarten; preschool.

przedślubny *a.* premarital.

przedśmiertny *a.* deathbed; *zwł. med.* agonal, premortal.

przedświąteczny *a.* before a holiday.

przedświt *mi* 1. *poet.* daybreak, dawn. 2. *przen.* harbinger.

przedtakt *mi muz., teor.lit.* anacrusis.

przedtaktowy *a. muz., teor.lit.* anacrustic.

przedtem *adv.* (*wcześniej*) earlier, before; (*dawniej*) formerly, before; na krótko przedtem shortly before; przyjadę do was, ale przedtem muszę odwiedzić mamę I'll come to you but before I have to visit my mum.

przedterminowo *adv.* early, ahead of time.

przedterminowy *a.* early, ahead of schedule.

przedtytuł *mi druk.* half title.

przedtytułowy *a. druk.* half-title.

przedwczesny *a.* premature.

przedwcześnie *adv.* prematurely.

przedwczoraj *adv.* the day before yesterday; przedwczoraj rano the day before yesterday in the morning.

przedwczorajszy *a.* of the day before yesterday.

przedwieczny *a.* 1. (*np. o lesie*) primeval; (*np. o obyczaju*) ancient. 2. *rel.* eternal.

przedwiośnie *n. Gen.pl.* -i early spring.

przedwojenny *a.* prewar.

przedwrześniowy *a. hist.* pre-September 1939

(in Polish history, pertaining to the period before the outbreak of World War II).

przedwstępny *a.* preliminary.

przedwyborczy *a.* (*o zebraniu, wiecu*) election, electoral; (= *mający miejsce przed wyborami*) preelection.

przedyskutować *pf.*, **przedyskutowywać** *ipf.* **1.** (*omawiać*) discuss, talk over. **2.** (= *dyskutować przez jakiś czas*) discuss.

przedzawałowy *a. pat.* **stan przedzawałowy** imminent myocardial infarction.

przedział *mi* **1.** (*np. między ludźmi*) division. **2.** (*w wagonie*) compartment. **3.** *mat.* interval; **przedział cenowy** price range *l.* bracket. **4.** (*czasu*) period; **w przedziale wiekowym między 20. a 30. rokiem życia** between 20 and 30 (years of age).

przedziałek *mi* **-łk-** *Gen.* **-a** part, *Br.* parting.

przedziałowy *a.* **ściana przedziałowa** partition wall.

przedzielać *ipf.*, **przedzielić** *pf.* (*ścianą*) partition; (= *podzielić*) divide.

przedzierać *ipf.* (*częściowo*) tear, rend; (*całkowicie*) tear apart. ~ **się** *ipf.* **1.** (= *przedziurawić się*) tear. **2.** (= *iść, przedostawać się z trudem*) force one's way through, struggle through; **przedrzeć się przez zarośla** force one's way through the thicket *l.* bushes; **przedrzeć się przez problemy** struggle through problems; **słońce przedziera się przez chmury** the sun is breaking through the clouds.

przedzierzgać *ipf.*, **przedzierzgnąć** *pf.* **-ij** transform; *żart.* transmogrify (*kogoś / coś w kogoś / coś* sb/sth into sb/sth). ~ **się** *ipf.*, **przedzierzgnąć się** *pf.* **-ij** transform o.s.; *żart.* be transmogrified (*w kogoś / coś* into sb/sth).

przedzimie *n. Gen.pl.* **-i** early winter.

przedziurawiać *ipf.*, **przedziurawić** *pf.* pierce, puncture.

przedziurkować *pf.* perforate.

przedziwność *f.* bizarreness, strangeness.

przedziwny *a.* bizarre, strange, odd; **kobieta przedziwnej urody** woman of bizarre beauty.

przedzwaniać *ipf.*, **przedzwonić** *pf. pot.* give a ring, ring (up); **kiedy będę wiedziała, przedzwonię do ciebie** when I know I'll be calling you.

przedżołądki *pl.* **-dk-** *wet., zool.* rumen, reticulum and psalterium.

przeegzaminować *pf.* examine, test; **przeegzaminować kogoś z czegoś** test sb in sth.

przefaksować *pf.* fax, send by fax.

przefarbować *pf.* redye; **przefarbować coś na zielono/niebiesko** redye sth green/blue. ~ **się** *pf. pot.* **1.** (= *zmienić kolor włosów*) redye one's hair. **2.** (= *zmienić poglądy*) change one's colors.

przefiltrować *pf.*, **przefiltrowywać** *ipf.* filter.

przeflancować *pf.*, **przeflancowywać** *ipf. ogr.* transplant.

przeformułować *pf.*, **przeformułowywać** *ipf.* reformulate.

przeforsować *pf.*, **przeforsowywać** *ipf.* **1.** (*pomysł, kandydaturę*) push, press. **2.** (*nadwerężać*) strain. ~ **się** *pf.*, **przeforsowywać się** *ipf.* (= *przemęczać się*) strain o.s.

przefrunąć *pf.*, **przefruwać** *ipf.* fly (*nad czymś* over sth).

przegadać *pf.* **1.** *pot.* (= *gadać przez jakiś czas*) talk away; **przegadaliśmy całą noc** we talked the night away. **2.** *pot.* (= *być bardziej elokwentnym*) outtalk.

przegadany *a. pot.* wordy.

przeganiać *ipf.* **1.** (= *wyganiać, przepędzać*) chase away. **2.** (= *być szybszym*) outrun. **3.** (= *być lepszym*) surpass, outrun. **4.** (= *zmuszać do biegu, ruchu*) force to run, force to move.

przegapiać *ipf.*, **przegapić** *pf. pot.* miss, overlook.

przegiąć *pf.* **-gnę -gniesz, -gnij** *zob.* **przeginać.** ~ **się** *pf. zob.* **przeginać się.**

przegięcie *n. pot.* (= *przekroczenie granic*) going over the top; **to jest przegięcie** this is a bit over the top.

przeginać *ipf.* **1.** (= *przechylać*) bend; **kot przegiął głowę do tyłu** the cat bent its head back. **2.** *pot.* (= *przekraczać normy*) go over the top; **przegiąć pałę** go over the top. ~ **się** *ipf.* **1.** (= *wyginać się*) bend; **ogon kota przegina się do przodu** the cat's tail bends forward. **2.** (= *odkształcać się*) bend.

przegląd *mi* (= *kontrola*) inspection, review; (*literatury, materiałów na dany temat*) survey; **przegląd prasy** press review; **przegląd techniczny** service; **przegląd wiadomości** *l.* **wydarzeń** news roundup; **przegląd wojsk** parade.

przeglądać *ipf.* **1.** (= *oglądać*) look through, browse. **2.** (= *stawać się widocznym*) appear, become visible; **słońce przeglądało przez chmury** the sun was breaking through the clouds. ~ **się** *ipf.* (*oglądać się*) (*w lustrze*) examine o.s. in the mirror; (*w tafli wody, w szybie*) examine one's reflection.

przeglądarka *f. Gen.pl.* **-ek 1.** *fot.* viewer. **2.** *komp.* browser; **przeglądarka internetowa** Internet browser.

przeglądowy *a.* review; (= *ogólny*) general.

przegłębienie *n.* **1.** *geol.* overdeepening. **2.** *żegl.* trim.

przegłodzić *pf.* keep hungry. ~ **się** *pf.* (= *powstrzymać się od jedzenia*) refrain from eating food; (*dla celów zdrowotnych*) be on a strict diet.

przegłodzony *a.* **-eni** after being kept hungry; after a strict diet.

przegłos *mi jęz.* umlaut.

przegłosować *pf.*, **przegłosowywać** *ipf.* **1.** (*przyjąć w głosowaniu*) vote; **przegłosować ustawę** vote a bill into law. **2.** (*pokonać w głosowaniu*) vote down, outvote.

przegnać *pf. zob.* **przeganiać.**

przegnić *pf.* **-iję -ijesz, -ij** rot through, decay.

przegon *mi roln.* drive.

przegonić *pf. zob.* **przeganiać.**

przegotować *pf.*, **przegotowywać** *ipf.* **1.** (*ciecz*) boil. **2.** (= *gotować powtórnie*) boil *l.* cook again. **3.** (*zniszczyć smak*) boil for too long (*thus spoiling the taste*). ~ **się** *pf.*, **przegotowywać się** *ipf.* **1.** (= *zawrzeć*) boil. **2.** (= *stracić smak*) be boiled for too long.

przegrać *pf.* 1. *zob.* **przegrywać.** 2. (= *grać przez jakiś czas*) spend some time playing.

przegradzać *ipf.* (*ścianą, przegrodą*) partition; **przegrodził ich ocean** they were separated by the ocean.

przegrana *f. Gen.* **-ej** 1. (*stracona kwota*) loss. 2. (*klęska*) defeat; **nie boję się przegranej** I am not afraid to lose. 3. (*kobieta*) loser, defeated woman.

przegrany *a.* 1. (*o osobie*) defeated; **czuć się przegranym** feel defeated; **być przegranym u kogoś** *l.* **w czyichś oczach** be a loser in the eyes of sb. 2. (*o sprawie, pozycji*) lost. – *mp* (*mężczyzna*) loser, defeated man; **z przegranymi nie robię interesów** I don't do business with losers.

przegroda *f. Gen.pl.* **-ód** 1. (*to, co dzieli*) separation, division; (= *przepierzenie*) partition; **przegroda nosowa** *anat.* nasal septum; **przegroda serca** *anat.* interventricular septum. 2. (*wydzielone miejsce*) division, compartment; **skrzynia z przegrodami** box with divisions.

przegrodzić *pf.* **-grodź** *l.* **-gródź** *zob.* **przegradzać.**

przegródka *f. Gen.pl.* **-ek** compartment.

przegrupować *pf. zob.* **przegrupowywać.** **~ się** *pf. zob.* **przegrupowywać się.**

przegrupowanie *n.* 1. *wojsk.* redeployment. 2. *chem.* rearrangement.

przegrupowywać *ipf.* 1. (= *zmieniać układ*) regroup. 2. *wojsk.* redeploy. **~ się** *ipf. wojsk.* redeploy.

przegrywać *ipf.* **-am -asz** 1. (*w grze*) lose. 2. (= *doznawać porażki*) be defeated, lose; **przegrać wojnę** be defeated in a war; **przegrać zakład** lose a bet. 3. (= *próbować melodię*) play. 4. (= *kopiować*) copy.

przegryzać *ipf.*, **przegryźć** *pf.* **-zę -ziesz -zł -źli** 1. (*przerywać zębami*) bite through. 2. (= *zjeść naprędce*) have a snack, have a bite to eat. 3. (= *pijąc, jeść coś od czasu do czasu*) eat in between drinks *l.* sips. 4. *pot.* (= *niszczyć*) eat through, corrode. **~ się** *ipf.*, **przegryźć się** *pf. pot.* 1. (= *łączyć się w całość smakową*) mix well, blend well. 2. (*przez coś trudnego*) struggle through.

przegrzać *pf.* **-eję -ejesz -ali** *l.* **-eli** *zob.* **przegrzewać.** **~ się** *pf. zob.* **przegrzewać się.**

przegrzebek *ma* **-bk-** *zool.* scallop, pecten (*Pectinidae*).

przegrzewać *ipf.* overheat. **~ się** *ipf.* overheat.

przegub *mi* 1. *anat.* wrist; (*w języku fachowym*) carpus. 2. *techn.* joint, articulation. 3. *fot.* joint.

przegubowiec *mi* **-wc-** *Gen.* **-a** *pot.* (*autobus*) articulated bus.

przegubowy *a.* articulated.

przeholować *pf.*, **przeholowywać** *ipf.* 1. (*holować*) tow, haul. 2. *pot.* (= *przesadzać*) go too far, go over the top.

przehulać *pf.* 1. (= *stracić*) riot away, riot out. 2. (= *zabawić się przez jakiś czas*) riot.

przeinaczać *ipf.*, **przeinaczyć** *pf.* misrepresent, distort.

przeintelektualizowany *a.* excessively intellectual.

przeistaczać *ipf. lit.* metamorphose, transform. **~ się** *ipf.* metamorphose, transform o.s.

przeistoczenie *n. rel.* transsubstantiation.

przeistoczyć *pf. zob.* **przeistaczać.** **~ się** *pf. zob.* **przeistaczać się.**

przejadać *ipf. pot.* (*tracić pieniądze wyłącznie na jedzenie, utrzymanie*) waste money (*on one's food, keep, etc.*). **~ się** *ipf.* (= *jeść za dużo*) overeat.

przejaskrawiać *ipf.*, **przejaskrawić** *pf.* 1. (*malować*) paint in too bright colors. 2. (*przesadzać*) exaggerate; *pot.* (*zwłaszcza historię, opowieść*) lay it on thick.

przejaśniać się *ipf.*, **przejaśnić się** *pf.* (*o niebie*) clear up; **przejaśniło się** it's cleared up; **nareszcie przejaśniło mi się w głowie** *przen.* it finally dawned on me.

przejaśnienia *pl. Gen.* **-ń** *meteor.* sunny intervals, sunny spells.

przejaw *mi* manifestation, symptom (*czegoś of sth*).

przejawiać *ipf.*, **przejawić** *pf.* display, show; **przejawiać zainteresowanie czymś** show interest in sth. **~ się** *ipf.*, **przejawić się** *pf.* manifest itself (*w czymś* in sth).

przejazd *mi* 1. (*jazda*) ride; (*samochodem*) drive; **nie ma przejazdu!** (*napis*) no way through! 2. **być gdzieś przejazdem** be passing through a place; **opłata za przejazd** (*za bilet*) fare; (*przez most, płatną drogę*) toll. 3. (*kolejowy*) grade crossing; *Br.* level crossing.

przejażdżka *f. Gen.pl.* **-ek** ride; (*samochodem*) drive.

przejąć *pf.* **-jmę -jmiesz, -jmij** *zob.* **przejmować.** **~ się** *pf. zob.* **przejmować się.**

przejebane *n. Gen.* **-ego** *wulg.* fucked; **no to mamy przejebane** so, we're fucked.

przejechać *pf.* **-jadę -jedziesz** 1. *zob.* **przejeżdżać.** 2. (*np. pieszego*) run over; **przejechała go ciężarówka** he was run over by a truck. **~ się** *pf.* (= *jechać dla przyjemności*) go for a ride; **przejechać się po kimś** *pot.* run sb down; **przejechać się na czymś** *pot.* (= *stracić*) lose on sth; **przejechać się na tamten świat** *pot.* kick the bucket.

przejednać *pf.*, **przejednywać** *ipf.* conciliate.

przejedzenie *n.* overeating.

przejeść *pf.* **-jem -jesz, -jedz, -jadł -jedli** 1. *zob.* **przejadać.** 2. (= *zjeść wszystko*) eat up. **~ się** *pf.* 1. *zob.* **przejadać się.** 2. (= *sprzykrzyć się*) be fed up; **pieczeń wieprzowa już mi się przejadła** I am fed up with roast pork.

przejezdna *f. Gen.* **-ej**, *zob.* **przejezdny.**

przejezdność *f.* passableness; **utrzymać przejezdność** (*dróg*) keep *l.* maintain roads passable.

przejezdny *a.* 1. (= *goszczący przejazdem*) (*o gościach, turystach*) passing. 2. (= *dający się przejechać*) (*o drodze, szosie*) passable. – *mp* transient visitor.

przejeździć *pf.* **-żdżę -jeździsz, -jeźdź** 1. (= *jeździć przez jakiś czas*) ride *l.* drive for some time. 2. (= *wydać pieniądze na podróże*) spend (money) on travel.

przejeżdżać *ipf.* 1. (= *jadąc, przemieszczać*

się) travel; (*samochodem*) drive; **przejechać grzebieniem** run a comb through one's hair; **przejechać szmatką** wipe with a cloth; **przejechać coś wzrokiem** run one's eyes over sth. **2.** (= *przebyć*) travel over, cover; **przejechać pięć kilometrów** cover five kilometers. **3.** (= *przekraczać*) cross; **przejechać przez granicę** cross the border; **przejeżdżać przez miasto** be passing through a town. **4.** (= *mijać*) pass; **przejeżdżałem koło twojego domu** I passed your house, I drove *l.* rode past your house; **przejechać przystanek/stację** miss sb's stop/station.

przejęcie *n.* **1.** (= *podniecenie*) excitement. **2.** *ekon.* takeover; acquisition.

przejęty *a.* **1.** (= *podniecony*) excited; **jestem przejęta tymi wiadomościami** I am excited with the news. **2.** *ekon.* taken over; acquired.

przejęzyczać się *ipf.* make a slip (of the tongue).

przejęzyczenie *n.* slip of the tongue.

przejęzyczyć się *pf. zob.* **przejęzyczać się.**

przejmować *ipf.* **1.** (= *brać, odbierać*) take over; **przejąć władzę** take over the power; **przejąć piłkę** *sport* intercept the ball; **przejąć pałeczkę** *sport* take over the baton; *przen.* take over from sb, take over the baton. **2.** (= *chwytać*) (*posłańca*) seize; (*przesyłkę*) intercept. **3.** (= *przyswajać sobie*) adopt; **przejmować czyjś sposób mówienia** adopt sb's manner of speaking. **4.** (= *przenikać*) take hold of; **zimno przejmowało ją do szpiku kości** she was chilled to the bone; **przejął mnie smutek** grief took hold of me. **5.** (= *wzruszać*) move; **przejął mnie los tej bezrobotnej matki z trojgiem dzieci** I was moved by the plight of this unemployed mother with three children. **~ się** *ipf.* (= *wzruszać się*) be moved; (= *zaniepokoić się*) be concerned; **nie przejmuj się** don't worry.

przejmująco *adv.* (= *przenikliwie*) piercingly; (= *wzruszająco*) movingly.

przejmujący *a.* (= *przenikliwy*) piercing; (= *wzruszający*) moving.

przejrzały *a.* overripe.

przejrzeć[1] *pf.* **-ę -ysz, -yj 1.** *zob.* **przeglądać. 2.** (= *przeniknąć wzrokiem*) see through. **3.** (= *zacząć widzieć*) recover one's sight. **4.** (= *zrozumieć, zdać sobie sprawę*) see the light; **przejrzałem dopiero wtedy, kiedy mnie pobił** I only saw the light when he beat me up. **5.** (= *rozpoznać zamiary*) see through; **przejrzałem cię** I've seen you through; **Robert przejrzał zamiary konkurencji** Robert has seen through the plans of his competitors.

przejrzeć[2] *pf. zob.* **przejrzewać. ~ się** *pf. zob.* **przeglądać się.**

przejrzewać *ipf.* become overripe.

przejrzystość *f.* **1.** (*nieba, powietrza*) transparency. **2.** (*języka, wykładu*) clarity.

przejrzysty *a.* **1.** (= *przezroczysty*) transparent. **2.** (= *czytelny*) clear.

przejrzyście *adv.* **1.** (= *przezroczyście*) transparent. **2.** (= *czytelnie*) clear.

przejście *n.* **1.** (*czynność*) passage; **potrzebuję 10 minut na przejście na drugi peron** I need 10 minutes to get to the other platform. **2.** (*droga,*

ścieżka) passage; **przejście graniczne** border crossing; **przejście podziemne** underpass; *Br. zwł.* subway; **przejście przez jezdnię** *l.* **dla pieszych** pedestrian crossing; **stanąć w przejściu** stand in the way; **zróbcie mu przejście** make way for him; **przejścia nie ma!** (*napis*) no entry! **3.** (*stadium*) transition; **przejście muzyczne** interlude. **4.** (= *przykre przeżycie*) trial, ordeal; **kobieta po przejściach** woman who has gone *l.* been through a lot.

przejściowy *a.* **1.** (= *tymczasowy*) temporary; transitory, transient. **2.** (= *do przechodzenia*) connecting; **pokój przejściowy** connecting room. **3.** (= *pośredni*) transitional, transition.

przejść *pf.* **-jdę -jdziesz -szedł -szła -szli** *zob.* **przechodzić. ~ się** *pf.* (*na spacer*) go for a walk.

przekabacać *ipf.*, **przekabacić** *pf. pot.* talk (sb) around *l.* over. **~ się** *ipf.*, **przekabacać się** *pf. pot.* be talked around *l.* over.

przekalkować *pf.* transfer.

przekalkulować *pf.*, **przekalkulowywać** *ipf.* recalculate.

przekarmiać *ipf.*, **przekarmić** *pf.* overfeed.

przekartkować *pf.*, **przekartkowywać** *ipf.* leaf through.

przekaz *mi* **1.** (*blankiet*) money order form; **wypełnić przekaz** fill out a money order form. **2.** (*kwota*) remittance; **przekaz pocztowy** money order; *Br.* postal order; **wysłać pieniądze przekazem** remit money. **3.** (*źródło historyczne*) source; (= *legenda*) account. **4.** (= *sposób, proces przekazywania*) transmission; **środki (masowego) przekazu** mass media.

przekazać *pf.* **-żę -żesz,** **przekazywać** *ipf.* **1.** (= *powierzać*) hand over, transfer; **przekazywać majątek w spadku** bequeath; **przekazywać pieniądze** transfer *l.* send money; **przekazywać pieniądze na jakiś cel** donate money for sth; **przekazywać władzę/urząd** hand over power/office; **przekazywać komuś pałeczkę** *przen.* hand over to sb. **2.** (= *informować*) (*polecenie, wiadomość*) pass on. **3.** (*o narządach, urządzeniach*) (*sygnał, bodziec*) transmit; **przekazywać program telewizyjny** broadcast a TV program; **przekazać pieniądze na konto bankowe** transfer money to a bank account.

przekaźnik *mi Gen.* **-a 1.** *el.* relay. **2.** *radio, telew.* transmitter.

przekaźnikowy *a.* **1.** *el.* relay. **2.** *radio, telew.* transmitter; **stacja przekaźnikowa** relay station.

przekąs *mi* **z przekąsem** mockingly.

przekąsić *pf.* **-szę -sisz** (= *zjeść trochę*) have a bite to eat; **przekąsić czymś** (*pijąc alkohol*) eat sth to follow a glass of wine, vodka, etc.

przekąska *f. Gen.pl.* **-ek** (*podawana przed posiłkiem*) hors d'oeuvre; (*dla zaostrzenia apetytu*) appetizer; (*między posiłkami*) snack.

przekątna *f. Gen.* **-ej** *geom.* diagonal.

przeklasyfikować *pf.* reclassify.

przekląć *pf.* **-klnę -klniesz, -klnij** *zob.* **przeklinać.**

przekleństwo *n.* **1.** (= *wyraz obelżywy*) swearword; **obrzucić kogoś przekleństwami** swear at sb. **2.** *lit.* (= *klątwa*) curse; **ciąży na nim prze-**

kleństwo he is cursed; **coś jest dla kogoś prze-kleństwem** sth is a curse for sb.

przeklęty *a.* (god)damn, damned.

przeklinać *ipf.* **1.** (= *używać przekleństw*) swear, curse; **przeklinał na czym świat stoi** he was like a trooper; **przeklinać tak, że aż uszy więdną** swear like hell; swear so that sb's ears wither. **2.** (= *potępiać coś*) damn, curse; **przekli-nam dzień, w którym się urodziłem** I wish I had never been born. **3.** (= *rzucać klątwę*) curse.

przekład *mi* translation; **dosłowny przekład** literal translation; **swobodny przekład** free translation; **wierny przekład** faithful transla-tion; **dokonać przekładu** do a translation; **prze-kład z angielskiego na polski** translation from English into Polish.

przekładać *ipf.* **1.** (*z miejsca na miejsce*) rear-range; **przełożyć karty** *karty* cut the deck. **2.** (*coś nad czymś*) (*nogą*) step over; (*ręką*) reach over. **3.** (= *wkładać coś między warstwy czegoś innego*) sandwich; **przekładać tort kremem czekolado-wym** layer a birthday cake with chocolate cream. **4.** (= *zmieniać termin*) reschedule; **czy ty naprawdę nie możesz przełożyć tego spotkania na jutro?** can't you really reschedule this meet-ing for tomorrow? **5.** (*z jednego języka na drugi*) translate; **przełożyć coś z francuskiego na japoń-ski** translate sth from French into Japanese. **6.** *lit.* (= *preferować*) prefer; **Adam przekładał grę w piłkę nożną nad inne sporty** Adam preferred playing soccer to other sports.

przekładalny *a.* translatable.

przekładaniec *mi* -ńc- *Gen.* -a **1.** (*ciasto*) layer cake. **2.** *przen.* (= *to i owo*) this and that; (= *skła-danka, mieszanka*) (*np. utworów muzycznych w programie radiowym itp.*) mixture, variety.

przekładanka *f. Gen.pl.* -ek **1.** łyżwiarstwo choctaw, crossover. **2.** *rzut oszczepem* grapevine step.

przekładnia *f. Gen.pl.* -i **1.** *techn.* transmis-sion, gear. **2.** *ret.* anastrophe, inversion.

przekładnik *mi Gen.* -a *el.* transformer.

przekładowy *a.* translation, translational.

przekłamać *pf. zob.* **przekłamywać**.

przekłamanie *n.* distortion, misrepresenta-tion.

przekłamany *a.* distorted, misrepresented.

przekłamywać *ipf.* (*informacje, tekst, wiado-mość*) distort, misrepresent.

przekłuć *pf.*, **przekłuwać** *ipf.* (= *przedziurawić*) puncture; (= *skaleczyć się*) prick; (= *zrobić otwór na kolczyk*) pierce.

przekomarzać się *ipf.* banter (*z kimś* with sb).

przekomicznie *adv.* in an extremely funny manner.

przekomiczny *a.* extremely funny.

przekonać *pf. zob.* **przekonywać**. ~ **się** *ipf. zob.* **przekonywać się**.

przekonanie *n.* (= *przeświadczenie*) conviction; (= *wiara*) belief; **przekonania polityczne** political views, political beliefs; **przekonania religijne** re-ligious beliefs; **nabrać przekonania, że...** become convinced that...; **utwierdzić się w przekonaniu** become absolutely conviced; **bez przekonania**

halfheartedly; **z przekonaniem** wholeheartedly; **w moim przekonaniu** in my opinion; **to, co mó-wisz, nie trafia mi do przekonania** what you say does not appeal to me; **zrobiłem to w przekona-niu, że pojedziemy tam razem** I did it because I thought that we would go there together.

przekonany *a.* convinced, persuaded; *pot.* pos-itive; **jestem przekonana o słuszności decyzji dy-rektora** I am convinced that the director's deci-sion is right.

przekonsultować *pf.* consult, discuss (*coś z kimś* sth with sb).

przekonujący *a.* convincing; **mówić o czymś w przekonujący sposób** speak about sth convinc-ingly.

przekonywać *ipf.* -uję *l.* -ywam -ujesz *l.* -ywasz, -uj *l.* -ywaj convince (*kogoś o czymś* sb of sth); **przekonać kogoś do zrobienia czegoś** talk sb in-to doing sth. ~ **się** *ipf.* **1.** (= *upewnić się*) become convinced; **przekonywać się o czymś** (= *nabierać przeświadczenia*) become convinced that... **2.** (= *przezwyciężyć niechęć*) come to like (*do kogoś / czegoś* sb/sth).

przekonywający *a. zob.* **przekonujący**.

przekop *mi* **1.** (*odkryty*) cutting, ditch; (*pod-ziemny*) tunnel. **2.** *górn.* crosscut.

przekopać *pf.* -pię -piesz, **przekopywać** *ipf.* **1.** (*grunt, ziemię, rów*) dig. **2.** (*gazety, raporty*) wade through. ~ **się** *pf.*, **przekopywać się** *ipf.* **1.** (*przez wał, piasek*) dig through. **2.** (*przez gazety, raporty*) wade through.

przekora *f.* perversity, contrariness.

przekornie *adv.* perversely, contrariwise.

przekorność *f.* perversity, contrariness.

przekorny *a.* perverse, contrary; **Magda z natu-ry jest przekorna** Magda is perverse by nature.

przekoziołkować *pf.* **1.** (*przekręcić się w po-wietrzu*) somersault. **2.** (= *przewrócić kogoś*) knock over, overturn.

przekór *mi* **na przekór komuś/czemuś** in defi-ance of sb/sth.

przekraczać *ipf.* **1.** (*przechodzić przez granicę miejsca*) cross. **2.** (*osiągać większą liczbę l. wiel-kość*) exceed, surpass; **przekroczył pan dozwolo-ną prędkość o 20 kilometrów (na godzinę)** you have exceeded the speed limit by 20 kilometers (per hour); **temperatura zimą nie przekracza tu 0 stopni Celsjusza** the temperature here in winter is never more than 0 degrees centigrade. **3.** (*prawo, normy, zasady*) be in breach of, breach; transgress. **4.** (*wyjść poza granicę*) go *l.* be be-yond; **przekraczać wszelkie granice** *l.* **granicę przyzwoitości** go way too far; **przekroczyć Rubi-kon** *przen.* cross *l.* pass the Rubicon; **przekro-czyć stan konta** overdraw an account.

przekradać się *ipf.*, **przekraść się** *pf.* -kradnę -kradniesz, -kradnij, -kradł sneak (*koło czegoś* past sth) (*przez coś* through sth).

przekrawać *ipf.* cut (in half).

przekreślać *ipf.*, **przekreślić** *pf.* **1.** (*tekst*) cross out. **2.** (= *uznać za niebyłe*) write off. **3.** (= *ni-weczyć*) destroy, ruin.

przekręcać *ipf.*, **przekręcić** *pf.* **1.** (= *wykony-wać ruch obrotowy*) turn; (*o osobie*) (*z boku na* *brzuch itp.*) turn over; **przekręcić (mięso) przez maszynkę** mince (meat) in a mincer. **2.** (= *przesuwać coś, obracając*) twist. **3.** (= *mylić coś, przeinaczać*) twist, distort. ~ **się** *ipf.*, **przekręcić się** *pf.* **1.** (= *obracać się*) turn. **2.** (= *przekrzywić się*) twist. **3.** *tylko pf. pot.* (= *umrzeć*) kick the bucket.

przekręt *mi pot.* (= *oszustwo*) fiddle, wangle.

przekroczenie *n.* **1.** (*granicy, drogi*) crossing; **przekroczenie salda** overdraft. **2.** *prawn.* infringement; transgression; **przekroczenie prędkości** speeding.

przekroczyć *pf. zob.* **przekraczać**.

przekroić *pf.* -oję -oisz, -ój *zob.* **przekrawać**.

przekrojowy *a.* sectional; (*o opracowaniu*) cross-sectional.

przekrój *mi* -o- *Gen.pl.* -ów *l.* -oi *geom.* section; **przekrój poziomy/pionowy/poprzeczny** horizontal/vertical/transverse section; **przekrój społeczny** social cross-section.

przekrwienie *n. pat.* plethora.

przekrwiony *a. pat.* plethoric; **przekrwione oczy** bloodshot eyes.

przekrzyczeć *pf.* -ę -ysz, **przekrzykiwać** *ipf.* outshout. ~ **się** *pf.*, **przekrzykiwać się** *ipf.* outshout one another.

przekrzywiać *ipf.*, **przekrzywić** *pf.* tilt. ~ **się** *ipf.*, **przekrzywić się** *ipf.* tilt.

przekształcać *ipf.* **1.** (= *zmieniać*) transform; convert. **2.** *mat.* transform. ~ **się** *ipf.* (= *zmieniać się*) evolve (*w coś* into sth).

przekształcenie *n.* **1.** (= *zmiana, przeobrażenie się*) transformation; conversion; **minister przekształceń gospodarczych** minister of economic transformation. **2.** *mat.* transformation.

przekuć *pf. zob.* **przekuwać**.

przekupić *pf. zob.* **przekupywać**.

przekupień *mp*, **przekupka** *f. Gen.pl.* -ek peddler.

przekupność *f.* corruptibility; *form.* venality.

przekupny *a.* bribable; corruptible.

przekupstwo *n.* bribery; corruption.

przekupywać *ipf.* bribe; corrupt.

przekuwać *ipf.* **1.** (= *kując, przebijać się*) chip through, chisel through. **2.** (= *kując, nadawać czemuś nowy kształt*) hammer, forge (*na coś* into sth); **przekuć miecze na lemiesze** turn *l.* beat swords into plowshares.

przekwalifikować *pf.*, **przekwalifikowywać** *ipf.* retrain. ~ **się** *pf.*, **przekwalifikowywać się** *ipf.* retrain.

przekwitać *ipf.* **1.** *bot.* lose *l.* shed blossom. **2.** (*o kobiecie, urodzie*) wither.

przekwitanie *n. med.* climacterium; menopause.

przekwitnąć *pf.* -ij, -kwitł *l.* -kwitnął -kwitła *l.* -kwitnęła -kwitli *l.* -kwitnęli *zob.* **przekwitać**.

przelać *pf.* -leję -lejesz, -lał -lali *l.* -leli *zob.* **przelewać**. ~ **się** *pf. zob.* **przelewać się**.

przelatywać *ipf.*, **przelecieć** *pf.* -cę -cisz **1.** (*w powietrzu*) fly (*koło czegoś* by *l.* past sth) (*nad czymś* over sth). **2.** (= *szybko poruszać się*) speed (*koło czegoś* by *l.* past *l.* along sth); **przelatywać coś wzrokiem** *l.* **oczami** run one's eyes over sth;

pewna myśl przeleciała mi przez głowę a thought crossed my mind. **3.** (*o czasie*) fly; **jak ten czas leci** time does fly. **4.** (*o deszczu*) shower. **5.** (= *przedostawać się przez coś*) (*o wodzie, piasku*) seep; go through. **6.** *wulg.* (= *odbyć stosunek*) screw; *Br. t.* shag (*kogoś* sb). ~ **się** *pf.* **1.** (*w powietrzu*) fly. **2.** *pot.* (*pójść*) walk briskly; run; **przelecieć się po parku** have a brisk walk around the park.

przelew *mi* **1.** (= *przelewanie się*) overflow, spill; **przelew krwi** bloodshed. **2.** *fin.* transfer, remittance; **uregulować należność przelewem** transfer the payment, pay by transfer. **3.** *prawn.* cession. **4.** *techn.* overflow. **5.** *druk.* recasting.

przelewać *ipf.* **1.** (*z jednego naczynia do drugiego*) pour; **przelać krew za ojczyznę** spill blood for one's homeland; **przelać łzy** shed tears; **przelać myśli na papier** commit one's thoughts to paper; **przelewać z pustego w próżne** (= *mówić bez treści*) talk for the sake of talking; argue the toss; (= *robić coś bezcelowego*) spend time unproductively. **2.** (= *przepełnić naczynie*) overflow. **3.** (= *cedować*) transfer, cede; **przelewać wiedzę na kogoś** impart knowledge to sb. **4.** *fin.* transfer, remit. ~ **się** *ipf.* **1.** (*z miejsca na miejsce*) flow. **2.** (*o przepełnionym naczyniu*) overflow; **nie przelewało się u nich** they could barely make ends meet.

przelewki *pl. Gen.* -ek *pot.* **to nie przelewki** this is no joke.

przeleźć *pf.* -lezę -leziesz -lazł -leźli *zob.* **przełazić**.

przeleżeć *pf.* -ę -ysz **1.** (= *leżeć jakiś czas, odpoczywając*) lie (*for some time*). **2.** (*o przedmiotach*) remain hidden, lie unused; **moje podanie przeleżało miesiąc na biurku szefa** my application spent a month shelved on my boss' desk.

przelękły, przelękniony *a.* frightened.

przelęknąć się *pf.* -ij take a fright (*kogoś/czegoś* at sb/sth).

przelicytować *pf.*, **przelicytowywać** *ipf.* outbid; *przen.* outrun, surpass. ~ **się** *ipf. rzad.* outbid one another; *przen.* outrun one another, surpass one another.

przeliczać *ipf.* (= *policzyć*) count, calculate; (*np. walutę*) convert. ~ **się** *zob.* **przeliczyć się**.

przeliczalny *a. mat.* denumerable.

przeliczenie *n.* (= *policzenie*) count; (*np. waluty*) conversion; **w przeliczeniu na jednego mieszkańca** (as) per inhabitant.

przeliczeniowy *a.* conversion; **tabele przeliczeniowe** conversion tables; **kurs przeliczeniowy** (*walut*) *fin.* exchange rate.

przelicznik *mi Gen.* -a **1.** (*waluty*) conversion rate, exchange rate. **2.** *techn.* computer.

przelicznikowy *a.* conversion.

przeliczyć *pf. zob.* **przeliczać**. ~ **się** *pf.* **1.** (= *źle ocenić sytuację*) miscalculate. **2.** (= *pomylić się w liczeniu*) miscalculate, miscount.

przeliterować *pf.* spell; **przeliterować imię i nazwisko** spell one's name.

przelot *mi* **1.** (*samolotu*) flight; **być gdzieś przelotem** be passing through a place, be somewhere on a short visit; **zrobić coś w przelocie** do sth in passing. **2.** (*ptaków, owadów*) passage. **3.** *bot.* kidney vetch, ladies' fingers (*Anthyllis*). **4.** *techn.* (*wpływowy*) inlet; (*wypływowy*) outlet. **5.** *techn.* (*przestrzeń*) passage.

przelotnie *adv.* fleetingly.

przelotność *f.* fleetingness.

przelotny *a.* **1.** (= *krótkotrwały*) fleeting, short; **przelotne opady** *meteor.* occasional showers. **2.** (= *przemieszczający się*) passing; *orn.* visitant, migratory.

przelotowość, przelotność *f. mot., kol.* (traffic) capacity.

przelotowy *a.* arterial; **trasa/droga/ulica przelotowa** arterial highway/road/street, thoroughfare.

przeludnienie *n.* overpopulation.

przeludniony *a.* overpopulated.

przeładować *pf. zob.* **przeładowywać**.

przeładowany *a.* **1.** (= *wypełniony po brzegi*) (*pasażerami*) overcrowded. **2.** *pot.* (= *przepełniony*) (*o samochodzie, pociągu itd.*) overloaded.

przeładowywać *ipf.* **1.** (*z czegoś na coś*) reload, transship. **2.** (= *przeciążać ładunkiem*) overload. **3.** (*pamięć, umysł*) overburden; (*szczegółami, ozdobnikami*) (*o tekście, stroju, budowli*) overload.

przeładunek *mi* **-nk-** reloading, transshipment.

przeładunkowy *a.* reloading, transshipping.

przełaj *mi Gen.pl.* **-ów** *sport* (*bieg, wyścig*) cross-country; **iść na przełaj** take a shortcut.

przełaje *pl. Gen.* **-ów** *sport* cross-country races.

przełajowiec *mp* **-wc-** *sport* cross-country runner.

przełajowy *a. sport* cross-country.

przełamać *pf.* **-mię -miesz, przełamywać** *ipf.* **1.** (*na części*) break; **przełamać pierwsze lody** break the ice. **2.** (= *przezwyciężać*) overcome. **3.** *druk.* make up. **4.** (*kolor*) mix. **~ się** *pf.*, **przełamywać się** *ipf.* **1.** (*na części*) break. **2.** (= *podzielić się*) share; **przełamać się opłatkiem** share the wafer. **3.** (= *zwalczyć niechęć*) overcome one's reluctance; (= *zwalczyć obawy*) conquer one's fears; (= *pokonać słabość*) overcome one's weakness.

przełaz *mi* passage.

przełazić *ipf.* **-żę -zisz** *pot.* (*przez coś*) get through, get across; (*nad czymś*) climb over. *pf.* **-żę -zisz** *pot.* (= *spędzić jakiś czas na chodzeniu*) walk for some time, spend some time walking.

przełączać *ipf.* switch (over), change; **przełącz ten kanał!** change this channel!

przełącznik *mi Gen.* **-a** *techn.* switch.

przełączyć *pf. zob.* **przełączać**.

przełęcz *f. pl.* **-e** *geogr.* pass, col.

przełknąć *pf.* **-ij** *zob.* **przełykać**.

przełom *mi* **1.** (= *zwrot*) breakthrough; **na przełomie starej i nowej ery** at the turn of the old and new era. **2.** *geol.* gorge. **3.** *med., pat.* crisis, breakthrough.

przełomowość *f.* decisiveness.

przełomowy *a.* **1.** (= *doniosły*) crucial, critical; (= *znaczący*) (*film, utwór*) breakthrough; **przeło-**

mowy moment turning point, breakthrough. **2.** *geol.* gorge, gap.

przełożenie *n.* **1.** (*np. rzeczy na półkach*) rearrangement; (= *przesunięcie*) shift, move. **2.** (*spotkania*) rescheduling; (*na później*) postponement. **3.** (= *tłumaczenie*) translation. **4.** *techn.* transmission ratio; gear ratio.

przełożona *f. Gen.* **-ej** superior; **matka przełożona** *rz.-kat.* mother superior; **siostra przełożona** *med.* matron.

przełożony *mp* superior.

przełożyć *pf.* **-łóż** *zob.* **przekładać**.

przełupać *pf.* **-pię -piesz, przełupywać** *ipf.* split.

przełyk *mi anat.* esophagus; *Br.* oesophagus; *pot.* gullet.

przełykać *ipf.* **1.** (*o pokarmie*) swallow; **przełknąć gorzką pigułkę** swallow the bitter pill. **2.** *pot.* (= *zaakceptować*) swallow, buy; **szef tego rachunku nie przełknie** the boss won't swallow this bill.

przemaczać *ipf.* wet through, wet down; soak; **przemoczyć buty** get one's shoes soaked through. **~ się** *ipf.* get wet, get soaked.

przemagać *ipf.* **1.** (= *pokonywać*) overcome, defeat. **2.** (= *opanowywać*) overcome. **~ się** *ipf.* (= *przełamać niechęć*) overcome.

przemakać *ipf.* **1.** (= *zmoknąć*) get soaked, get drenched. **2.** (= *przemiękać*) let water through, leak; **kurtka zupełnie mi przemokła** my jacket is completely soaked.

przemakalny *a.* water-permeable.

przemalować *pf.*, **przemalowywać** *ipf.* paint over, repaint.

przemarsz *mi Gen.pl.* **-ów** *zwł. wojsk.* march-past.

przemarzać *ipf.*, **przemarznąć** *pf.* **-ij 1.** (= *ulegać działaniu mrozu*) freeze. **2.** *tylko pf.* (= *bardzo zmarznąć*) freeze.

przemarznięty *a.* frozen.

przemaszerować *pf.* march past.

przemawiać *ipf.* **1.** (= *wygłaszać mowę*) give *l.* make *l.* deliver a speech (*do kogoś* to sb); address (*do kogoś* sb). **2.** (= *mówić do kogoś*) appeal; **przemówić komuś do rozsądku** *l.* rozumu reason with sb; **przemówić komuś do serca** *l.* wyobraźni make an emotional appeal to sb; **przemówić komuś do kieszeni** grease the palm *l.* hand of sb; **wszystko przemawia za tym, żebyśmy podpisali tę umowę** there is every indication that we should sign this contract; **niestety, to do mnie nie przemawia** unfortunately, it doesn't appeal to me; **przemawia przez ciebie złość** you're burning with anger. **3.** (= *ujawniać się*) appear, manifest; **z twojego spojrzenia przemawia gniew** you have that angry look. **~ się** *ipf.* fall out (*z kimś* with sb).

przemądrzałość *f. pot.* bigheadedness.

przemądrzały *a. pot.* bigheaded; **nie bądź taki przemądrzały** don't be such a smart alec.

przemeblować *pf.*, **przemeblowywać** *ipf.* rearrange; **przemeblować pokój** rearrange one's room.

przemęczać *ipf.* (*pracą*) strain, overexert. **~**

się *ipf.* (*pracą*) strain, overexert; **nie przemęczaj się** take it easy.

przemęczenie *n.* exhaustion; overfatigue, overexertion; **zemdleć z przemęczenia** faint from (over)exhaustion.

przemęczony *a.* -eni exhausted, fatigued.

przemęczyć *pf.* 1. *zob.* **przemęczać.** 2. (= *wytrwać w niedogodnych warunkach*) survive, endure (*coś sth*). ~ **się** *pf.* 1. *zob.* **przemęczać się.** 2. (= *wytrwać w niedogodnych warunkach*) survive, endure; **przemęczyć się całe lato bez urlopu** endure the whole summer without a holiday.

przemiał *mi* 1. (*rozdrobnienie*) grinding, milling; **oddać coś na przemiał** give sth up for milling. 2. (*produkt*) meal.

przemiana *f.* transformation, change; (= *przeobrażenie się*) metamorphosis; **na przemian** alternatively; **przemiana duchowa** spiritual change; **przemiana chemiczna** chemical change; **przemiana ekonomiczna** *l.* **gospodarcza** economic transformation; **przemiana fizyczna** physical change; **przemiana materii** metabolism; **przemiana pokoleń** *biol.* alteration of generations; **przemiana polityczna** political transformation; **przemiana w myśleniu** change in the way of thinking.

przemianować *pf.*, **przemianowywać** *ipf.* rename.

przemieniać *ipf.*, **przemienić** *pf.* transform, change. ~ **się** *ipf.*, **przemienić się** *pf.* transform, change (*w coś* into sth).

przemiennie *adv.* alternatively.

przemienność *f.* 1. (= *zmienność*) alternation. 2. *mat.* commutativity.

przemienny *a.* alternating, changing; **prąd przemienny** *fiz.* alternating current.

przemierzać *ipf.*, **przemierzyć** *pf.* 1. (= *mierzyć jeszcze raz*) measure again. 2. (*np. kraj*) traverse; (= *przebyć*) (*dystans*) cover.

przemieszać *pf.* mix.

przemieszczać *ipf.* move; translocate. ~ **się** *ipf.* move.

przemieszczenie *n.* movement; translocation; **złamanie z przemieszczeniem** *pat.* displaced *l.* unaligned fracture.

przemieścić *pf.* -mieszczę -mieścisz *zob.* **przemieszczać.** ~ **się** *pf. zob.* **przemieszczać się.**

przemiękać *ipf.*, **przemięknąć** *pf.* -ij soak, get drenched.

przemijać *ipf.* (*o czasie, życiu*) go by, pass; *lit.* elapse; (*o urodzie*) fade; (= *kończyć się*) end.

przemijalność *f.* transitoriness, fleetingness.

przemilczać *ipf.*, **przemilczeć** *pf.* -ę -ysz 1. (= *zataić*) pass over (in silence). 2. *tylko pf.* (= *milczeć jakiś czas*) remain silent for some time, sit in silence for some time.

przemilczenie *n.* 1. passing over in silence; (= *zatajenie*) concealment. 2. *prawn.* (a method of) acquisition of a right which is not exercised by another.

przemiły *a.* (*o osobie*) awfully nice; lovable; (*o przedmiocie, miejscu itp.*) most enjoyable, delightful.

przeminąć *pf. zob.* **przemijać.**

przemknąć *pf.* -nę -niesz, -nij *zob.* **przemykać.** ~ **się** *pf.* -nę -niesz, -nij *zob.* **przemykać się.**

przemnażać *ipf.*, **przemnożyć** *pf.* -nóż multiply (*coś przez coś* sth by sth).

przemoc *f.* violence; **akt przemocy** act of violence; **przemoc w rodzinie** domestic violence; **przemocą** by force; **oprzeć się przemocy** resist violence; **uciec się do przemocy** resort to violence; **używać przemocy** use violence.

przemoczyć *pf.* 1. *pot.* (= *przegrać*) take a licking. 2. *zob.* **przemaczać.** ~ **się** *pf. zob.* **przemaczać się.**

przemoknąć *pf.* -ij 1. *zob.* **przemakać.** 2. (= *bardzo zmoknąć*) get soaked.

przemoknięty *a.* (*o ubraniu, osobie*) soaked (through), soaking wet.

przemowa *f. Gen.pl.* -ów speech; (*zwł. publiczna, formalna*) oration.

przemożnie *adv. lit.* overwhelmingly.

przemożny *a. lit.* overwhelming.

przemóc *pf.* -mogę -możesz, -móż, -mógł -mogła -mogli *zob.* **przemagać.** ~ **się** *pf. zob.* **przemagać się.**

przemówić *pf.* 1. *zob.* **przemawiać.** 2. (= *zacząć znów mówić*) speak.

przemówienie *n.* speech.

przemycać *ipf.*, **przemycić** *pf.* smuggle. ~ **się** *ipf.*, **przemycić się** *pf.* slip; **niezauważona przez nikogo przemyciła się do środka** she slipped inside without being seen.

przemyć *pf.* -myję -myjesz, -myj *zob.* **przemywać.**

przemykać *ipf.* shoot (*obok l. koło kogoś/czegoś* past sb/sth). ~ **się** *ipf.* weave (*przez coś* through sth).

przemysł *mi* industry; **przemysł budowlany** construction industry, building industry; **przemysł chemiczny** chemical industry; **przemysł ciężki** heavy industry; **przemysł drzewny** wood industry; **przemysł energetyczny** power industry; **przemysł lekki** light industry; **przemysł naftowy** oil industry; **przemysł odzieżowy** clothing industry; **przemysł papierniczy** paper industry; **przemysł poligraficzny** printing industry; **przemysł precyzyjny** precision industry; **przemysł samochodowy** automotive industry; **przemysł spożywczy** food industry; **przemysł włókienniczy** textile industry; **przemysł zbrojeniowy** armaments industry; **gałąź przemysłu** branch of industry; **robić coś własnym przemysłem** do sth on one's own.

przemysłowiec *mp* -wc- *pl.* -y industrialist.

przemysłowo-rolniczy *a.* (*o regionie, kraju*) industrial-agricultural.

przemysłowy *a.* industrial; **ośrodek/wywiad przemysłowy** industrial center/espionage.

przemyślany *a.* (*o wypowiedzi, decyzji*) considered; (*o planie*) well thought-out.

przemyśleć *pf.* -ę -isz, **przemyśliwać** *ipf.* -am -asz 1. (= *rozważyć*) think over, consider; **przemyśliwać nad czymś** reflect on sth, muse on/about sth. 2. *tylko pf.* (= *ponownie rozważyć*) rethink.

przemyślenie *n.* reflection.

przemyślność *f.* (= *spryt*) cleverness; (= *zaradność*) industriousness; (= *pomysłowość*) ingeniousness.

przemyślny *a.* (= *sprytny*) clever; (= *zaradny*) industrious; (= *pomysłowy*) ingenious.

przemyt *mi* **1.** (*czynność*) smuggling, contraband. **2.** (*towary*) contraband.

przemytnictwo *n.* smuggling.

przemytniczy *a.* smuggling, contraband; **szajka przemytnicza** band of smugglers.

przemytnik *mp*, **przemytniczka** *f.* smuggler; **przemytnik broni** gun runner.

przemywać *ipf.* bathe (*coś czymś* sth with sth).

przenajświętszy *a. rel.* most holy; **Przenajświętszy Sakrament** *rz.-kat.* the Blessed Sacrament.

przenicować *pf.* **1.** (*ubranie*) turn, reverse. **2.** (*wartości, idee*) twist, pervert.

przeniesienie *n.* **1.** (*pracownika*) transfer. **2.** *fin.* **do przeniesienia** to be carried forward; **z przeniesienia** carried forward, c/f.

przenieść *pf.* -niosę -niesiesz -niósł -niosła -nieśli *zob.* **przenosić.** ~ **się** *pf. zob.* **przenosić się.**

przenigdy *adv. emf.* never ever.

przenikać *ipf.* **1.** (= *przedostawać się*) penetrate, filter in. **2.** (= *przepełniać*) pervade, permeate. **3.** (= *zgłębiać*) fathom (*kogoś/coś* sb/sth). **4.** (= *przeszywać*) pierce; **przenikało mnie zimno** I shuddered with cold; **przeniknął mnie dreszcz** a tremor shook my body. ~ **się** *ipf.* (= *mieszać się*) intermingle.

przenikalność *f. fiz.* permeability; **przenikalność elektryczna** *l.* **dielektryczna** *el.* permittivity; **przenikalność magnetyczna** magnetic permeability.

przenikalny *a.* **1.** (= *zdolny do przenikania*) permeable, permeant. **2.** (= *dający się przenikać*) penetrable.

przenikliwie *adv.* (*patrzeć*) piercingly, intensely; (*brzmieć*) strident; **przenikliwie zimno** bitterly cold.

przenikliwość *f.* **1.** (= *bystrość*) acumen, perspicacity. **2.** (= *ostrość*) harshness. **3.** *fiz.* penetrability, penetrating power.

przenikliwy *a.* **1.** (= *dotkliwy*) harsh; (*o zimnie, bólu*) penetrating. **2.** (*o dźwiękach*) strident, piercing. **3.** (= *wnikliwy, bystry*) astute, perspicacious. **4.** (= *zdolny do przenikania*) penetrating.

przeniknąć *pf.* -ij *zob.* **przenikać.** ~ **się** *pf. zob.* **przenikać się.**

przenocować *pf.* put up (*u kogoś* with sb); **przenocować kogoś** put sb up for the night.

przenosić *ipf.* -szę -sisz **1.** (*z miejsca na miejsce*) move, shift; (*rękami*) carry; (*mechanicznie*) transport; (*chorobę*) transmit; (*termin, spotkanie*) move, switch; (*modę, obyczaj, siedzibę, pracownika*) transfer; (*wzrok*) shift; **komp.** (*zawartość schowka, tekst*) move. **2.** *druk., komp.* (= *złamać*) (*wyraz*) hyphenate, break. ~ **się** *pf.* **1.** (*przeprowadzać się, zmieniać miejsce pracy, studiów*) move. **2.** (= *zmieniać stanowisko*) transfer. **3.** (= *rozszerzać się*) spread.

przenosiny *pl. Gen.* -n *pot.* move.

przenośnia *f. Gen.pl.* -i *ret.* metaphor; **w przenośni** figuratively.

przenośnie *adv.* figuratively, metaphorically.

przenośnik *mi Gen.* -a **1.** *techn.* conveyor; **przenośnik taśmowy** conveyor belt; **przenośnik hydrauliczny/kubełkowy/pneumatyczny** hydraulic/bucket/pneumatic conveyor. **2.** *biol.* transmitter.

przenośny *a.* **1.** (= *dający się przenosić*) portable. **2.** (= *metaforyczny*) figurative, metaphorical. **3.** (= *podróżujący*) traveling, *Br.* travelling; **teatr przenośny** traveling theater company; **wystawa przenośna** traveling display.

przeobrazić *pf.* -żę -zisz, **przeobrażać** *ipf.* metamorphose, transform. ~ **się** *pf.*, **przeobrażać się** *ipf.* transform; *zool.* metamorphose.

przeobrażenie *n.* **1.** (= *przemiana*) transformation. **2.** *zool.* metamorphosis; **przeobrażenie zupełne/niezupełne** complete/incomplete metamorphosis.

przeobrażeniowy *a. zool.* metamorphic, metamorphotic.

przeoczenie *n.* oversight; (= *pominięcie*) omission.

przeoczyć *pf.* overlook, miss.

przeogromny *a. lit.* immense; *pot.* massive.

przeokropny *a. emf.* hideous.

przeor *mp pl.* -owie *l.* -rzy *rel.* prior.

przeorać *pf.* -oram *l.* orzę -orasz *l.* -orzesz **1.** *roln.* plow, *Br.* plough; (*w bruzdy*) furrow. **2.** (= *przeszukać*) (*archiwa, książki*) scour, rifle through. **3.** (= *zmienić*) (*myślenie, psychikę*) transform.

przeorganizować *pf.* reorganize.

przeorysza *f. rel.* prioress.

przepadać *ipf.* **1.** (= *gubić się*) disappear, vanish; **przepaść jak kamień w wodę** disappear *l.* vanish into thin air, disappear *l.* vanish without a trace. **2.** (= *unicestwiać się*) perish. **3.** (= *odpadać*) drop out. **4.** (*o okazji, majątku*) be lost; **wszystko przepadło** all is lost. **5.** *prawn.* (= *ulegać konfiskacie*) be forfeited. **6.** *tylko ipf.* be fond (*za kimś/czymś* of sb/sth).

przepadek *mi* -dk- *prawn.* forfeiture.

przepadły *a. prawn.* forfeited.

przepajać *ipf.*, **przepoić** *pf.* imbue (*kogoś/coś czymś* sb/sth with sth).

przepakować *pf.*, **przepakowywać** *ipf.* repack.

przepalać *ipf.* (*o ogniu, kwasie*) burn through. ~ **się** *ipf.* (*o żarówce, bezpieczniku*) blow.

przepalony *a.* (*o żarówce, bezpieczniku*) blown, burnt; (*o czajniku, żelazku*) burnt.

przepał *mi mot.* excessive fuel consumption; **mieć przepały** be heavy on gas.

przepasać *pf.* -szę -szesz *zob.* **przepasywać.** ~ **się** *pf. zob.* **przepasywać się.**

przepasiony *a.* -eni overfed.

przepaska *f. Gen.pl.* -ek band; **przepaska do włosów** hairband, fillet; **przepaska na biodra** loincloth; **przepaska na czoło** sweatband; **przepaska na oczy** blindfold.

przepastny *a. lit.* bottomless, abysmal.

przepasywać *ipf.* (= *przewiązać w pasie*) gird;

(*włosy*) bind. ~ **się** *ipf.* gird up; **przepasywać się czymś** wrap *l.* tie sth around one's waist.

przepaścisty *a.* bottomless, abysmal.

przepaść[1] *f. pl.* **-i** *l.* **-e** **1.** *geogr.* precipice, abyss. **2.** (*między ludźmi, kulturami*) chasm, gulf; **stać na skraju przepaści finansowej** be on the brink of ruin; **staczać się w przepaść** go downhill.

przepaść[2] *pf.* **-padnę -padniesz, -padnij, -padł** *zob.* **przepadać**.

przepatrywać *ipf.*, **przepatrzyć** *pf.* examine, inspect.

przepchać *pf. zob.* **przepychać**. ~ **się** *pf. zob.* **przepychać się**.

przepchnąć *pf.* **-ij** *zob.* **przepychać**. ~ **się** *pf. zob.* **przepychać się**.

przepełniać *ipf.*, **przepełnić** *pf.* **-ij** (*o osobach*) overcrowd; (*o rzeczach*) overfill; (*o uczuciach*) overflow. ~ **się** *ipf.*, **przepełnić się** fill (*kimś* with sb).

przepełnienie *n.* overcrowding.

przepełniony *a.* (*o autobusie, sali*) overcrowded; **serce przepełnione miłością** heart filled *l.* suffused with love.

przepędzać *ipf.*, **przepędzić** *pf.* **1.** (= *wyganiać*) chase away *l.* out; (= *odganiać*) chase off, drive off. **2.** (*bydło*) drive. **3.** (*życie*) live, spend.

przepicie *n. pot.* hangover; **chory z przepicia** hungover.

przepić *pf.* **-piję -pijesz, -pij** *zob.* **przepijać**. ~ **się** *pf. zob.* **przepijać się**.

przepieprzyć *pf.* **1.** *pot. obsc.* (= *zmarnować*) screw up, blow. **2.** *zob.* **przepieprzać**.

przepierka *f. Gen.pl.* **-ek** *pot.* hand wash.

przepierzenie *n.* **1.** *t. bud.* (= *ścianka*) partition. **2.** *górn.* stopping.

przepięknie *adv.* beautifully, gorgeously.

przepiękny *a.* beautiful, gorgeous.

przepijać *ipf.* **1.** (*pieniądze, czas*) waste on drink. **2.** (= *wznieść toast*) *pot.* toast (*do kogoś* sb). **3.** (= *spędzać czas na piciu*) drink, spend some time drinking; **przepić całą noc** spend the whole night drinking; *wulg.* piss the night away. ~ **się** *ipf. pot.* (= *przesadzić z piciem*) have had one too many.

przepikować *pf.*, **przepikowywać** *ipf.* **1.** *krawiectwo* quilt. **2.** *ogr.* prick out.

przepiłować *pf.*, **przepiłowywać** *ipf.* saw through.

przepiórka *f. Gen.pl.* **-ek** *orn.* quail (*Coturnix*).

przepis *mi* **1.** *kulin.* recipe; **przepis na kurczaka/ciasto** chicken/cake recipe. **2.** (= *reguła*) rule, regulation; **przepisy drogowe/bezpieczeństwa** traffic/safety regulations; **przepis prawny** precept *l.* rule of law.

przepisać *pf.* **-piszę -piszesz** *zob.* **przepisywać**.

przepisowo *adv.* **1.** (= *zgodnie z prawem*) legally. **2.** (= *zgodnie z regulaminem*) by the book.

przepisowy *a.* **1.** (= *legalny*) legal. **2.** (= *uczciwy*) clean. **3.** (= *zgodny z regulaminem*) regulation.

przepisywać *ipf.* **1.** (= *kopiować*) copy. **2.** (*lekarstwo*) prescribe. **3.** (= *przenieść tytuł własno-*

ści) make over; **przepisać coś na kogoś** make sth over to sb.

przepity *a.* hungover.

przeplatać *ipf.*, **przepleść** *pf.* **-plotę -pleciesz -plótł -plotła -pletli** **1.** (*nitki*) interlace, interweave. **2.** (*czynności*) (= *urozmaicać*) intermingle. ~ **się** *ipf.*, **przepleść się** *pf.* **1.** (*o nitkach*) interlace, interweave. **2.** (*o zdarzeniach*) intermingle.

przeplatanka *f. Gen.pl.* **-ek** **1.** (*coś poukładane na przemian*) medley. **2.** *łyżwiarstwo* crossover.

przepłacać *ipf.*, **przepłacić** *pf.* **1.** (= *za dużo zapłacić*) (*z powodu wygórowanej ceny*) be overcharged; (*przez pomyłkę*) overpay. **2.** (= *przekupywać*) *przest.* bribe.

przepłakać *pf.* **-płaczę -płaczesz, przepłakiwać** *ipf.* cry, spend some time crying; **przepłakać cały ranek/dzień itp.** spend the morning/day etc. crying; **przepłakać wiele godzin** cry for many hours.

przepławka *f. Gen.pl.* **-ek** *hydrol.* (*dla ryb*) fish pass.

przepłoszyć *pf.* scare off.

przepłukać *pf.* **-czę -czesz, przepłukiwać** *ipf.* rinse.

przepłynąć *pf. zob.* **przepływać**. ~ **się** *pf.* have a swim, have a dip.

przepływ *mi ekon., fiz., hydrol.* flow.

przepływać *ipf.* **1.** (*o cieczy, rzece, kapitale*) flow. **2.** (*o osobie, rybie*) swim (*przez coś* through sth); (*o przedmiocie*) float (*przez coś* through sth).

przepływomierz *mi Gen.* **-a** *techn.* flowmeter.

przepocić *pf.* sweat.

przepocony *a.* sweaty.

przepoczwarzać się *ipf.* **przepoczwarzyć się** *pf. zool.* metamorphose.

przepoić *pf. zob.* **przepajać**.

przepojony *a.* imbued (*czymś* with sth).

przepoławiać *ipf.*, **przepołowić** *pf.* **-ów** halve. ~ **się** *ipf.*, **przepołowić się** *pf.* break in two.

przepompować *pf. zob.* **przepompowywać**.

przepompownia *f. Gen.pl.* **-i** *techn.* pumping station; **przepompownia ścieków** sewage pumping station.

przepompowywać *ipf.* pump (over).

przepona *f. anat., techn.* diaphragm.

przeponowy *a.* diaphragmatic.

przepowiadać *ipf.* **1.** (= *przewidywać*) foretell, predict; (*pogodę*) forecast; **przepowiadać komuś przyszłość** tell *l.* read *l.* cast sb's fortune. **2.** *pot.* (= *powtórzyć*) repeat.

przepowiednia *f. Gen.pl.* **-i** prediction.

przepowiedzieć *pf.* **-wiem -wiesz -wiedzą, -wiedz** *zob.* **przepowiadać**.

przepracować *pf. zob.* **przepracowywać**. ~ **się** *pf. zob.* **przepracowywać się**.

przepracowanie *n.* overwork.

przepracowany *a.* **1.** (= *przemęczony*) overworked. **2.** (= *wypełniony pracą*) of work, (spent) working; **liczba przepracowanych godzin** number of hours worked.

przepracowywać *ipf.* (= *pracować jakiś czas*) serve, work; **przepracowałem tu 40 lat życia** I have worked 40 years of my life here. ~ **się** *ipf.* work too hard, overwork o.s.

przepraszać *ipf.*, **przeprosić** *pf.* **1.** (= *wyrażać winę*) apologize (*kogoś za coś* to sb for sth); **publicznie przeprosić za coś** apologize in public for sth; **nawet mnie nie przeprosił** he didn't even say he was sorry, he didn't even apologize; **chciałbym przeprosić państwa za wszelkie niewygody** I'd like to apologize for any inconvenience; **przeproś!** say you're sorry!, apologize! **2. przepraszam!** (*w zwrotach grzecznościowych: przeciskając się, zwracając uwagę, wtrącając się*) excuse me; **przepraszam, czy mogę przejść** excuse me, could I just slip through; **przepraszam, która godzina?** excuse me, what's the time?; **przepraszam, czy pan profesor Kowalski?** excuse me, are you Professor Kowalski?; **przepraszam, czy to pan profesor Kowalski?** excuse me, is this Professor Kowalski?; **przepraszam, muszę otworzyć drzwi** excuse me, I'm trying to open the door. **3. przepraszam!** (*w zwrotach grzecznościowych: gdy zrobiliśmy coś złego*) (I'm) sorry; **najmocniej przepraszam** I'm really (very) sorry; **przepraszam za spóźnienie** I'm sorry I'm late; **przepraszam, że przeszkadzam** sorry to interrupt. **4. przepraszam!** (*z oburzeniem*) excuse me!; **o, przepraszam, to nie moja wina** well, that's hardly my fault. **5. przepraszam!** (*korygując przejęzyczenie*) I mean, rather; **wyjedziemy o ósmej nie, przepraszam, o dziewiątej** we'll leave at eight, I mean nine; we'll leave at eight, nine, rather. **6.** (= *przerywać*) interrupt; **czy mogę przeprosić na chwileczkę?** could I interrupt for a second? **7.** (= *opuścić*) leave; **na chwilę państwa przeproszę** (you must) excuse me for a second, I'm afraid I'll have to leave for a little while. ~ **się** *ipf.*, **przeprosić się** *pf.* make up (*z kimś* with sb); **przeprosić się z czymś** *żart.* (have to) use sth after all.

przepraszająco *adv.* apologetically.

przepraszający *a.* apologetic.

przeprawa *f.* **1.** (= *przeprawianie się*) crossing. **2.** (*miejsce*) passage. **3.** (= *trudności*) trouble; **miała z nim przeprawę** she had a hard time with him.

przeprawiać *ipf.*, **przeprawić** *pf.* **1.** (*przez rzekę, jezioro, morze*) ferry (*kogoś przez coś* sb through sth). **2.** (*przez granicę, góry, las*) take (*kogoś przez coś* sb through sth). ~ **się** *ipf.*, **przeprawić się** *pf.* cross (*przez coś* sth).

przeprawowy *a. wojsk.* transporting.

przeprosić *pf.* **-szę -sisz** *zob.* **przepraszać.** ~ **się** *pf. zob.* **przepraszać się.**

przeprosiny *pl. Gen.* **-n** apology.

przeproszenie *n.* **za przeproszeniem** (= *przepraszam, że o tym mówię*) (*np. że ktoś jest głupcem*) with all due respect; (= *za pozwoleniem*) (*np. przed powiedzeniem brzydkiego wyrazu*) if you pardon the expression.

przeprowadzać *ipf.*, **przeprowadzić** *pf.* **1.** (= *przenosić*) move. **2.** (= *realizować*) (*plany*) carry out; (*eksperyment, ankietę, śledztwo*) conduct; (*operację, testy*) perform; (*testy, pomiary*) conduct, run; (*badania, doświadczenia*) do; (*linię kolejową, autostradę*) build. **3.** (= *wskazać dro-*

gę) lead (*kogoś przez coś* sb through sth); **przeprowadzać kogoś przez ulicę** help sb across the street. ~ **się** *ipf.*, **przeprowadzić się** *pf.* move.

przeprowadzka *f. Gen.pl.* **-ek** move, removal.

przeprowadzkowy *a.* removal; **firma przeprowadzkowa** removal company.

przepuklina *f. pat.* hernia.

przepuklinowy *a. med.* hernial; **pas przepuklinowy** truss.

przepust *mi* **1.** (*kanał*) culvert. **2.** (*otwór w ścianie*) penetration. **3.** (*otwór w przedmiocie*) pass.

przepustka *f. Gen.pl.* **-ek 1.** *wojsk.* (= *urlop*) furlough, pass; **na przepustce** on a pass, on furlough. **2.** (*dokument*) pass, permit; *wojsk.* furlough. **3.** *przen.* pass (*do czegoś* to sth).

przepustnica *f. mot.* throttle.

przepustowość *f. techn.* flow capacity.

przepuszczać *ipf.* **1.** (= *pozwalać przejść, przejechać, przepłynąć*) let through, let pass; (= *wpuścić*) let in; (= *pozwalać zdać*) pass sb; **przepuszczać kogoś do następnej klasy** *szkoln.* promote sb; **przepuszczać kogoś przodem** let sb go first; **przepuszczać przez coś prąd** run a current through sth; **nie przepuszczać wody** be water-resistant, keep the water out. **2.** *pot.* (= *trwonić*) blow (*coś* sth). **3.** (= *nie skorzystać*) let slip; **przepuścić okazję** miss an opportunity.

przepuszczalność *f. techn.* permeability.

przepuścić *pf.* **-puszczę -puścisz 1.** *zob.* **przepuszczać. 2.** (= *darować*) put up (*coś* with sth); **on nikomu nie przepuści** he won't spare anybody; **on nikomu nic nie przepuści** he won't let anybody get away with anything.

przeputać *pf. gł. dial.* (= *roztrwonić*) throw away.

przepych *mi* glamour; splendor; *Br.* splendour; **z przepychem** glamorously, lavishly.

przepychacz *mi Gen.* **-a** *techn.* force cup.

przepychać *ipf.* **1.** (= *przeforsować*) (*ustawę, kandydaturę*) force through; (*w pośpiechu*) rush through. **2.** (= *przeczyszczać*) unclog, unblock, clear. **3.** (= *przesuwać*) push (through). ~ **się** *ipf.* **1.** (= *torować sobie drogę*) push one's way (*przez coś* through sth). **2.** (= *popychać się*) jostle.

przepychanka *f. Gen.pl.* **-ek** (*fizyczna*) jostle; (*np. polityczna*) struggle.

przepysznie *adv.* **1.** (= *świetnie*) gorgeously, splendidly. **2.** (= *bardzo smacznie*) (*o jedzeniu*) deliciously, scrumptiously; **coś smakuje przepysznie** sth is delicious.

przepyszny *a.* **1.** (= *bardzo smaczny*) delicious, scrumptious. **2.** (= *okazały*) gorgeous, splendid.

przepytać *pf.*, **przepytywać** *ipf.* (*uczniów, studentów*) give (sb) an oral (*z czegoś* in sth). ~ **się** *pf.*, **przepytywać się** *ipf.* quiz each other.

przerabiać *ipf.* **1.** *szkoln.* (*materiał*) cover, do. **2.** (= *zrobić od nowa*) rework; (*film*) remake. **3.** (= *wprowadzać przeróbki*) remodel. **4.** (*na coś innego*) convert (*na coś* into sth). **5.** (= *przetwarzać*) process; **nieźle mnie przerobił!** *pot.* he made quite a fool of me!

przeradzać *ipf.* (= *zmienić*) transform (*kogoś* sb). ~ **się** *ipf.* turn; (*o człowieku, charakterze*) be transformed; **miłość przeradza się w nienawiść** love turns into hate.

przerastać *ipf.* 1. (= *prześcigać*) surpass; **to przerasta moje możliwości** it's beyond my capabilities. 2. (= *stawać się wyższym, większym*) overgrow; **przerastać kogoś o głowę** stand a head taller than sb. 3. (= *nadmiernie się powiększać*) overgrow; *pat.* hypertrophy.

przerazić *pf.* **-żę -zisz** *zob.* **przerażać.** ~ **się** *pf.* *zob.* **przerażać się.**

przeraźliwie *adv.* fearfully.

przeraźliwy *a.* fearful.

przerażać *ipf.* terrify, horrify; **dom przerażał pustką** the emptiness of the house was terrifying; **przeraziła mnie swoim wyglądem** her appearance was terrifying. ~ **się** *ipf.* be terrified; **przeraziłem się wczoraj na twój widok** I was terrified when I saw you yesterday.

przerażający *a.* terrifying.

przerażenie *n.* terror; **napawać kogoś przerażeniem** fill sb with terror; **patrzeć na kogoś/coś z przerażeniem** look on sb/sth with terror; **ku swemu przerażeniu** to sb's terror; **ogarnęło mnie przerażenie** I was filled with terror.

przerażony *a.* **-eni** terrified (*czymś* by sth).

przerąbać *pf.* **-bię -biesz** *zob.* **przerąbywać.**

przerąbane *indecl. pot.* **mieć przerąbane** be up a creek without a paddle, have one's ass in a sling; **masz u niej przerąbane** you're on her black books, you're on her crap-list.

przerąbywać *ipf.* chop; (*na dwie części*) chop in two; (*las, drzewa*) clear.

przerdzewieć *pf.* **-eję -ejesz** rust (through).

przeredagować *pf.*, **przeredagowywać** *ipf.* (*tekst, artykuł*) rewrite; (*zdanie, pismo*) rephrase, reword; (*umowę, dokument*) redraft.

przerejestrować *pf.* (*telefon, samochód*) transfer.

przereklamowany *a.* overhyped, overrated.

przerębel *mi* **-bl-** *Gen.* **-a, przerębla** *f.* **-bl-** *Gen.* **-li** air hole.

przerobić *pf.* **-rób** 1. *zob.* **przerabiać.** 2. *pot.* (= *oszukać*) dupe. ~ **się** *pf. pot.* (= *oszukać się*) be duped; **przerobić się na czymś** fall for sth.

przerobowy *a.* (*np. o surowcu*) processing; **moce** *l.* **zdolności przerobowe** output capacity.

przerodzić się *pf. zob.* **przeradzać się.**

przerosnąć *pf.* **-snę -śniesz, -śnij, -rósł -rosła -rośli** *zob.* **przerastać.**

przerost *mi* 1. (= *nadmiar*) excess; **przerost ambicji** excessive ambition; **przerost formy nad treścią** excess of form. 2. (= *nadmierny rozrost*) overgrowth, outgrowth. 3. *pat.* hypertrophy. 4. *leśn.* an overgrown tree.

przerośnięty *a.* 1. (= *nadmiernie wyrośnięty*) overgrown, outgrown. 2. (= *poprzerastany, porośnięty*) grown over (*czymś* with sth); **przerośnięty tłuszczem** (*o mięsie*) streaky. 3. (*o uczniu*) older.

przerób *mi* **-o-** 1. (*czynność*) processing. 2. (*produkt*) processed product. 3. (= *wydajność*) (*mierzony w produktach*) output; (*mierzony w*

wartości produkcji) turnover; **zwiększyć przerób o 7 procent** increase output by 7 percent.

przeróbczy *a.* processing; **zakład przeróbczy** processing plant.

przeróbka *f. Gen.pl.* **-ek** 1. (= *poprawka*) (*np. odzieży*) alteration. 2. (*np. strychu na mieszkanie*) conversion (*czegoś na coś* of sth into sth); (= *adaptacja*) (*filmu, utworu*) adaptation. 3. (= *przetwarzanie*) processing.

przeróżnie *adv.* in a variety of ways.

przeróżny *a. emf.* various, multifarious.

przerwa *f.* 1. (*w jakiejś czynności*) break; **przerwa na herbatę/kawę** coffee/tea break; **przerwa na papierosa** break for a cigarette; **przerwa obiadowa** lunch break *l.* hour; **przerwa na reklamę** *radio, telew.* commercial break. 2. (= *zakłócenie*) interruption; **przerwa w dopływie prądu** power cut, blackout. 3. *szkoln.* (*między lekcjami*) break; (= *wakacje*) break; **przerwa wiosenna** spring break. 4. *sport* (*w meczu*) half-time. 5. *prawn.* (*w rozprawie*) recess. 6. *kino, teatr* intermission; *Br.* interval. 7. (*luka*) gap; **bez przerwy** (*coś robić*) continually, nonstop; (*o czynności*) continual, nonstop; **z przerwami** on and off.

przerwać *pf.* **-wę -wiesz, -wij** *zob.* **przerywać.** ~ **się** *pf. zob.* **przerywać się.**

przerwanie *n.* 1. (= *zaprzestanie*) cessation. 2. (= *przerwa*) interruption. 3. (= *uszkodzenie*) rupture. 4. *komp.* interrupt; **przerwanie sprzętowe/programowe** hardware/software interrupt; **przerwanie ciągłości** discontinuity.

przerysować *pf.*, **przerysowywać** *ipf.* 1. (= *skopiować*) copy, transfer. 2. (= *wyolbrzymić*) exaggerate, overstate.

przerysowanie *n.* exaggeration, overstatement.

przerysowany *a.* exaggerated.

przerywacz *mi Gen.* **-a** *techn.* interrupter, breaker.

przerywać *ipf.* **-am -asz** 1. (= *rozrywać*) break. 2. (= *przystawać*) pause, interrupt. 3. (= *wtrącać się*) interrupt, interject; **przerywać komuś** interrupt sb; **proszę, nie przerywaj mi** please don't interrupt; **przerwać komuś w pół słowa** cut sb short. 4. (= *przeszkadzać w czymś*) interrupt. 5. (= *zakończyć*) (*ciążę, misję, wykonywanie programu*) abort; **przerywać ciążę** have an abortion. 6. (*czynność, rozmowę, transmisję*) interrupt. 7. (= *rozłączać*) disconnect. 8. *mot.* (*o silniku*) misfire, stall. 9. *roln., ogr.* (*grządkę, uprawę*) rogue. 10. *el.* (*obwód elektryczny*) open. ~ **się** *ipf.* 1. (= *rozrywać się*) break. 2. (= *być zakłóconym*) be interrupted.

przerywany *a.* interrupted, intermittent; **przerywany sen** broken sleep; **linia przerywana** dashed line; **stosunek przerywany** coitus interruptus.

przerywka *f. Gen.pl.* **-ek** *roln., ogr.* roguing.

przerywnik *mi Gen.* **-a** 1. (*wstawka w programie artystycznym*) interlude; (*zwł. muzyczny*) intermezzo. 2. *radio* jingle. 3. (= *krótkotrwała zmiana*) interlude. 4. *druk.* (= *ozdobnik*) ornament.

przerzedzać *ipf.*, **przerzedzić** *pf.* 1. (*las, upra-*

wę) thin out. **2.** (= *uszczuplać*) (*np. populację, pokolenie*) decimate; (= *zmniejszyć*) diminish. ~ **się** *ipf.*, **przerzedzić się** *pf.* **1.** (= *rozrzedzać się*) (*o lesie, mgle*) thin (out); (*o włosach*) thin, wear thin. **2.** (= *zmniejszać się*) diminish.

przerzucać *ipf.*, **przerzucić** *pf.* **1.** (= *odwracać*) (*kartkę*) flip over. **2.** (= *przeglądać*) (*książkę, gazetę*) flip through. **3.** *mot.* shift; **przerzucić bieg** shift gear; **przerzucić na jedynkę/dwójkę itp.** shift into first/second etc. **4.** (= *przewiesić*) throw over. **5.** *sport* (= *podawać*) lob. **6.** (*broń, narkotyki*) run (*przez granicę* across the border). **7.** (*zbudować*) (*most, kładkę*) put up, build; **przerzucić most przez rzekę** bridge a river. **8.** (= *przenosić*) (*pracownika*) transfer; (*odpowiedzialność*) shift; *wojsk.* (*siły*) redeploy. ~ **się** *ipf.*, **przerzucić się** *pf.* **1.** (= *zmieniać zainteresowanie, zajęcie*) switch over (*z czegoś na coś* from sth to sth). **2.** (= *rozprzestrzeniać się*) (*o ogniu, rdzy*) spread; *pat.* (*o raku*) metastasize.

przerzut *mi* **1.** *pat.* metastasis. **2.** (*pracowników, towarów*) transfer; *wojsk.* (*sił*) redeployment. **3.** (= *rzucenie*) throw. **4.** *sport* (= *podanie poprzeczne*) cross; (= *podanie ponad siatką, ponad przeciwnikiem*) lob. **5.** *zapasy* throw; *gimnastyka* flip; *skok wzwyż* (Fosbury) flop; *skoki do wody* (belly) flop.

przerzutka *f. Gen.pl.* **-ek** (*urządzenie*) derailleur; (= *biegi*) gears; **rower z przerzutką 21-biegową** 21-speed bicycle, 21-gear bicycle.

przerzutnia *f. Gen.pl.* **-i** *ret.* enjambment, enjambement.

przerzutowy *a.* **1.** (= *transportowy*) transfer; **punkt przerzutowy** transfer point; **trasa przerzutowa** transfer route. **2.** *pat.* metastatic. **3.** *skok wzwyż* **styl przerzutowy** (Fosbury) flop.

przerżnąć *pf.* **-nę -niesz, -nij 1.** (= *przekroić*) cut (in two). **2.** *pot.* (= *przegrać*) take a licking, lose. **3.** *pot.* (= *roztrwonić*) gamble away, blow. **4.** *pot. obsc.* (= *odbyć stosunek*) screw, hump (*kogoś* sb).

przesada *f.* exaggeration; **bez przesady!** come, come!, steady on!; **bez (żadnej) przesady** without (any) exaggeration; **do przesady** (*uczciwy, cierpliwy*) to a fault; **nie będzie w tym przesady, jeśli powiem, że...** you could safely say that...; **to (już) (lekka) przesada!** that's *l.* it's (a bit) much *l.* steep *l.* over the top!; this is stretching it (a bit)!

przesadnie *adv.* overly, excessively.

przesadny *a.* excessive, exaggerated; over-the-top.

przesadzać *ipf.*, **przesadzić** *pf.* **1.** (= *koloryzować*) exaggerate. **2.** (= *nie znać umiaru*) push it, overdo it; **przesadzać z czymś** overdo sth, carry sth too far. **3.** (*siedzącego*) move (*sb to another seat*). **4.** *ogr.* (*rośliny, sadzonki*) transplant, replant. **5.** (= *przeskakiwać*) clear (*przez coś* sth).

przesączać *ipf.*, **przesączyć** *pf.* filter. ~ **się** *ipf.*, **przesączyć się** *pf.* filter through.

przesąd *mi* **1.** (= *błędne przekonanie*) misconception. **2.** (= *zabobon*) superstition. **3.** (= *uprzedzenie*) prejudice. **przesądy** *pl. Gen.* **-ów 1.** (= *uprzedzenia*) prejudice; **hołdować przesą-**

dom be prejudiced. **2.** (= *zabobony*) superstition.

przesądny *a.* superstitious.

przesądzać *ipf.*, **przesądzić** *pf.* **1.** (= *decydować*) determine (*o czymś* sth); **przesądzić sprawę** settle an issue. **2.** (= *pochopnie oceniać*) prejudge.

przesądzony *a.* determined, prejudged; **jego zwycięstwo było przesądzone** his victory was a foregone conclusion.

przeschnąć *pf.* **-schnę -schniesz, -schnij, -schnął** *l.* **-sechł -schła -schli** *zob.* **przesychać.**

przesiać *pf.* **-sieję -siejesz -siał -siali** *l.* **-sieli** *zob.* **przesiewać.**

przesiadać się *ipf.* **1.** (*na inne siedzenie*) move; **przesiadł się** he moved to another seat. **2.** (= *zmieniać środek komunikacji*) change, transfer (*na coś* to sth).

przesiadka *f. Gen.pl.* **-ek** change, transfer; **mam przesiadkę w Kaliszu** I need to change in Kalisz; **połączenie bez przesiadki** direct connection.

przesiadywać *ipf.* (*u kogoś, w kawiarni*) hang out; **przesiadywać po nocach** stay up all night.

przesiąkać *ipf. zob.* **przesiąknąć.**

przesiąkliwy *a.* permeable, pervious.

przesiąknąć *pf.* **-ij 1.** (= *nasycić się wilgocią*) soak (through) (*czymś* with sth). **2.** (*obcą kulturą, ideologią*) absorb (*czymś* sth).

przesiąknięty *a.* (*cieczą*) soaked (*czymś* in sth); (*ideologią, obcymi zwyczajami*) imbued (*czymś* with sth); **przesiąknięty wodą** waterlogged; **przesiąknięty historią/tradycją** *itd.* steeped in history/tradition etc.

przesiąść się *pf.* **-siądę -siądziesz -siadł -siedli** *zob.* **przesiadać się.**

przesiedlać *ipf.* (= *wysiedlać*) displace. ~ **się** *ipf.* (= *emigrować*) emigrate; (= *przeprowadzać się*) move.

przesiedleniec *mp* **-ńc-** *pl.* **-y** (= *osoba wysiedlona*) displaced person; (= *imigrant*) immigrant.

przesiedleńczy *a.* (= *dotyczący przesiedlenia*) displacement; (= *dotyczący osób wysiedlonych*) displaced-persons; (= *dotyczący imigracji*) immigration; **prawo przesiedleńcze** immigration laws.

przesiedlić *pf. zob.* **przesiedlać.** ~ **się** *pf. zob.* **przesiedlać się.**

przesiedzieć *pf.* **-dzę -dzisz 1.** (= *pobyć*) spend some time; **przesiedział w więzieniu pięć lat** he spent *l.* did five years in prison. **2.** (= *spędzić na siedzeniu*) sit, spend some time sitting; **przesiedzieć trzy godziny** sit for three hours; **przesiedzieć cały dzień z książką** spend the whole day reading.

przesieka *f. leśn.* (= *polana*) clearing, opening.

przesiew *mi* **1.** (= *selekcja*) screening. **2.** (*przez sito*) sifting.

przesiewacz *mi Gen.* **-a** *roln., techn.* sifter, screen.

przesiewać *ipf.* **1.** (*kandydatów*) screen. **2.** (*przez sito*) sift, sieve.

przesiewowy *a. med.* **badania przesiewowe**

screening (*w kierunku czegoś* for sth), screen tests.

przesięk *mi med., pat.* (*proces*) transudation; (*substancja*) transudate.

przesilenie *n.* 1. (= *moment zwrotny*) turning point. 2. *pat.* (*w chorobie*) crisis. 3. *astron.* solstice; **przesilenie letnie/zimowe** summer/winter solstice.

przeskakiwać *ipf.*, **przeskoczyć** *pf.* 1. (= *skakać przez*) jump over, leap over. 2. (= *opuszczać*) skip. 3. (*z tematu na temat*) jump. 4. (= *wyprzedzić*) outdo (*kogoś* sb); do better (*kogoś* than sb); **nikt sam siebie nie przeskoczy** there's only so much you can do; **nie mów hop, póki nie przeskoczysz** do not halloo until you are out of the wood.

przesklad *mi druk.* resetting.

przeskok *mi* jump, leap (*przez coś* over sth).

przeskrobać *pf.* **-bię -biesz** *pot.* do something (bad); **znowu coś przeskrobałeś** you've been bad *l.* naughty again.

przesłać *pf.* **-ślę -ślesz, -ślij** *zob.* **przesyłać.**

przesładzać *ipf.* put too much sugar (*coś* in sth).

przesłaniać *ipf.* 1. (*widok*) shut out. 2. (= *utrudniać uświadomienie*) make blind (*coś* to sth); **praca przesłania mu cały świat** he is completely absorbed by his work.

przesłanie *n.* message.

przesłanka *f. Gen.pl.* **-ek** 1. (= *czynnik*) factor; **przesłanki ekonomiczne/społeczne** economic/social factors. 2. *log., prawn.* premise.

przesławny *a. emf.* illustrious.

przesłodzić *pf. zob.* **przesładzać.**

przesłodzony *a.* **-eni** *uj.* 1. (*o herbacie, dżemie itp.*) too sweet, with too much sugar in it. 2. (= *nadmiernie pozytywny*) pretty-pretty, sugary. 3. (= *nadmiernie sentymentalny*) cloying, syrupy.

przesłona *f.* 1. *fot.* (*nastawienie*) aperture; (*urządzenie*) diaphragm. 2. (= *zasłona*) screen. 3. *szachy* guard.

przesłonić *pf. zob.* **przesłaniać.**

przesłuchać *pf. zob.* **przesłuchiwać.**

przesłuchanie *n.* 1. *prawn.* (*podejrzanego*) interrogation; (*świadka*) examination. 2. (*przed komisją*) hearing. 3. (*kandydata*) interview; (*do roli, zespołu*) audition.

przesłuchiwać *ipf.* 1. (*podejrzanego*) interrogate; (*świadka*) examine. 2. (*kandydata*) interview; (*do roli, zespołu*) audition. 3. (*taśmę, płytę*) listen.

przesłużyć *pf.* serve (*for some time*).

przesłyszeć się *pf.* **-ę -ysz** mishear; **chyba się przesłyszałem** (= *musiałem cię źle zrozumieć*) I must have heard you wrong; (= *musiałem to źle zrozumieć*) I must have misheard it; (= *słyszałem coś dziwnego*) I must be hearing things; **chyba się nie przesłyszałem?** did I hear you right?

przesmażony *a. kulin.* overcooked.

przesmyk *mi geogr.* (*pas wody*) inlet; (*pas lądu*) isthmus.

przesmyknąć się *pf.* **-nę -niesz, -nij** slip through.

przesolić *pf.* **-sól** 1. (*zupę, mięso*) put too much salt (*coś* in sth). 2. *pot.* (= *przesadzić*) go over the top.

przesolony *a.* (*o zupie, ziemniakach*) too salty, with too much salt in it.

przespacerować się *pf.* go for a walk, take a walk.

przespać *pf.* **-śpię -śpisz, -śpij** 1. (= *śpiąc przegapić*) sleep (*coś* through sth). 2. *przen.* (= *przegapić*) miss (*coś* sth). 3. (= *spać jakiś czas*) sleep; **przespać całą noc/dwie godziny** sleep through the night/for two hours. ~ **się** *pf.* 1. (= *zdrzemnąć się*) take a nap. 2. (= *odbyć stosunek*) *euf.* sleep (*z kimś* with sb).

przesrać *pf. wulg. pot.* (*zmarnować*) screw up.

przesrane *indecl. wulg. pot.* **mieć u kogoś przesrane** be on sb's shitlist; **no, to mamy przesrane** so, we're done for.

przestać¹ *pf.* **-nę -niesz** *zob.* **przestawać.**

przestać² *pf.* **-stoję -stoisz, -stój** (= *stać jakiś czas*) stand, spend some time standing; **przestać trzy godziny** stand for three hours.

przestankowanie *n.* punctuation.

przestankowy *a.* punctuation; **znak przestankowy** punctuation mark.

przestarzałość *f.* antiquatedness, obsoleteness.

przestarzały *a.* 1. (*o maszynie, systemie*) antiquated, outdated, obsolete. 2. *jęz.* (*o wyrazie*) obsolete.

przestawać *ipf.* **-aję -ajesz, -waj** 1. **przestawać** (= *przerywać, zakończyć*) stop (*coś robić* doing sth); **przestań!** stop it!; **przestać istnieć** cease to exist. 2. *tylko ipf. lit.* (= *obcować*) associate (*z kimś* with sb); **kto z kim przestaje, takim się staje** he that lives with the wolves learns to howl. 3. *tylko ipf. przest.* (= *poprzestawać*) stop (*na czymś* at sth).

przestawiać *ipf.*, **przestawić** *pf.* 1. (= *przesuwać*) move. 2. (= *mieszać*) reorder. 3. (= *zamieniać miejscami*) switch. 4. (= *radykalnie zmieniać*) change (over). ~ **się** *ipf.*, **przestawić się** *pf.* (*np. na inną działalność*) change over (*na coś* to sth).

przestawka *f. Gen.pl.* **-ek** *jęz.* 1. (= *przesunięcie artykulacji*) sound shift. 2. (= *zamiana kolejności*) metathesis.

przestawnia *f. lit.* inversion.

przestawny *a.* (= *ruchomy*) portable; **szyk przestawny** *ret., gram.* inversion.

przestąpić *pf. zob.* **przestępować.**

przesterować *pf.* (*wzmacniacz*) overdrive.

przesterowanie *n.* overdrive.

przestęp *mi* 1. *bot.* bryony (*Bryonia*). 2. *myśl.* trot.

przestępca *mi*, **przestępczyni** *f.* (= *osoba oskarżona l. skazana*) criminal; (= *osoba łamiąca prawo*) offender; **młodociany przestępca** juvenile delinquent.

przestępczość *f.* crime; **wskaźnik przestępczości** crime rate.

przestępczy *a.* criminal; **czyn przestępczy** criminal act; **działalność przestępcza** criminal activity.

przestępny *a.* 1. *astron.* intercalary; **rok przestępny** leap year; **funkcja przestępna** *mat.* transcendental function. 2. *prawn.* criminal.

przestępować *ipf.* (= *przekroczyć*) step (*coś* over sth); **przestępować z nogi na nogę** shuffle one's feet; **przestąpić czyjś próg** *emf.* set foot in sb's house, darken sb's door.

przestępstwo *n.* (*zwł. groźne*) crime; (= *przekroczenie prawa*) offense; **przestępstwo gospodarcze/polityczne/wojenne** white-collar/political/war crime; **przestępstwo kryminalne** criminal offense; **popełnić przestępstwo** commit a crime; **przestępstwo nie popłaca** crime doesn't pay.

przestój *mi* -o- *Gen.pl.* -ów (= *okres braku aktywności*) (*w pracy*) stoppage; (*maszyny*) downtime, idle time; *handl.* (*środków transportu*) demurrage.

przestrach *mi* terror, fright.

przestrajać *ipf.* (*instrument, odbiornik*) retune.

przestraszać *ipf.* 1. (= *wywołać strach*) frighten, scare. 2. (= *zniechęcać, zrażać*) discourage, deter; **nie przestraszają go żadne przeciwności** he is undeterred by any opposition.

przestraszony *a.* -eni frightened, scared.

przestraszyć *pf. zob.* **przestraszać.** ~ **się** *pf.* get scared (*czegoś* of sth).

przestroga *f. Gen.pl.* -óg warning, caution; **ku przestrodze** as a warning.

przestroić *pf.* -stroję -stroisz, -strój *zob.* **przestrajać.**

przestronność *f.* spaciousness.

przestronny *a.* spacious.

przestrzał *mi* gun-shot wound; **na przestrzał** right through.

przestrzec *pf.* -strzegę -strzeżesz -strzegł, **przestrzegać** *ipf.* 1.(= *napominać*) warn, caution. 2. *tylko ipf.* (*reguł, przepisów*) obey (*czegoś* sth) abide (*czegoś* by sth); (*obyczaju*) observe (*czegoś* sth).

przestrzelać *pf.,* **przestrzelić** *ipf.* 1. *zw. ipf.* (*płuco, nogę*) shoot (*komuś coś* sb in sth). 2. *zw. pf.* (= *przetestować broń*) test-fire. 3. (= *nie trafić*) miss.

przestrzenny *a.* 1. (= *dotyczący przestrzeni*) spatial. 2. (= *trójwymiarowy*) three-dimensional; *geom.* (*o figurze*) solid; **kąt przestrzenny** solid angle; **sieć przestrzenna** *chem.* crystal lattice.

przestrzeń *f. pl.* -e 1. (= *trójwymiar*) space; **przestrzeń kosmiczna** (outer) space; **przestrzeń międzyplanetarna** interplanetary space; **przestrzeń mieszkalna** *l.* **życiowa** living space; **lęk przestrzeni** fear of open spaces, agoraphobia; **otwarta przestrzeń** open space. 2. (= *połać*) expanse. 3. (= *zakres*) space, distance; **od domu dzieli nas przestrzeń trzech kilometrów** we are three kilometers away from the house; **na przestrzeni...** (*czasu*) over a span of..., in *l.* within *l.* during the space of...; (*odległości*) within the range of...

przestudiować *pf.* study, go over (*coś* sth).

przestudzać *ipf.,* **przestudzić** *pf.* cool (down). ~ **się** *pf.* cool (down).

przestworza *pl. Gen.pl.* -y *lit.* 1. (= *przestrzeń*) expanses. 2. (= *powietrze*) air, skies.

przestwór *mi* -o- *lit.* expanse.

przestygnąć *pf.* -gnę -gniesz, -gnij, -gł *l.* -gnął -gła -gli cool (down).

przesunąć *pf. zob.* **przesuwać.** ~ **się** *pf. zob.* **przesuwać się.**

przesunięcie *n.* (= *przemieszczenie*) shift; (*niepożądane*) dislocation; **przesunięcie fazowe** *l.* **fazy** *l.* **w fazie** *el., fiz., opt.* phase shift; **wektor przesunięcia** *fiz.* displacement vector.

przesuszyć *pf.* 1. (= *wysuszyć*) dry. 2. (= *zbytnio wysuszyć*) overdry. ~ **się** *pf.* 1. (= *wysuszyć się*) dry. 2. (= *zbytnio się wysuszyć*) overdry.

przesuw *mi* advance; **przesuw taśmy** tape advance.

przesuwać *ipf.* 1. (= *przemieszczać*) (*przedmiot*) move, shift; (*dłoń, wzrok*) run (*po czymś* down *l.* along sth) (*przez coś* through sth); (*pracownika*) transfer. 2. (*np. spotkanie*) reschedule. 3. (= *zmieniać kolejność*) shift. 4. **przesunąć zegarek** *l.* **wskazówki do przodu/tyłu (o godzinę)** put the clock forward/back (by one hour). ~ **się** *ipf.* 1. (= *przemieszczać się*) move, shift. 2. (= *poruszać się*) travel.

przesuwny *a.* movable.

przesycać *ipf.* 1. (*substancją*) saturate; *chem.* supersaturate. 2. *przen.* (*np. kogoś ideami, wiersz liryzmem*) imbue. 3. (*np. rynek towarami*) saturate. ~ **się** *ipf.* 1. (*np. zapachem*) be saturated. 2. *chem.* supersaturate. 3. (= *doznać przesytu*) sate o.s., be satiated; **przesycić się słodyczami** have had enough sweets.

przesychać *ipf.* 1. (= *schnąć powoli*) dry out. 2. (= *schnąć nadmiernie*) overdry.

przesycić *pf. zob.* **przesycać.** ~ **się** *pf. zob.* **przesycać się.**

przesycony *a.* 1. (*substancją, zapachem*) saturated; *chem.* supersaturated; **roztwór przesycony** *chem.* supersaturated solution. 2. (= *syty*) satiated.

przesyłać *ipf.* 1. (*wiadomość, list, plik, pozdrowienia, pieniądze, całusa*) send; **przesyłać pocztą** mail; **przesyłać komuś wyrazy uszanowania** give *l.* send one's respects to sb. 2. (*energię, fale*) transmit.

przesyłka *f. Gen.pl.* -ek mailing; (*towarów*) shipment; **przesyłka polecona** registered mail; **przesyłką poleconą** by registered mail.

przesyłowy *a. techn.* transmission; **linia przesyłowa** transmission line; **energetyczna sieć przesyłowa** power grid.

przesympatyczny *a. emf.* delighful, lovable.

przesypać *pf.* -sypię -sypiesz *zob.* **przesypywać.** ~ **się** *pf. zob.* **przesypywać się.**

przesypiać *ipf. zob.* **przespać.** ~ **się** *ipf. zob.* **przespać się.**

przesypywać *ipf.* pour (*coś do czegoś* sth into sth). ~ **się** *ipf.* pour, sift (*do czegoś* into sth).

przesyt *mi* surfeit, satiety; **aż do przesytu** to (a) surfeit, to satiety; **odczuwać przesyt** be sated, have had enough.

przeszczep *mi chir.* (*organu*) transplant; **przeszczep kostny/skórny** bone/skin graft; **prze-**

szczep przyjął się the transplant took; **jej organizm odrzucił przeszczep** her body rejected the transplant.

przeszczepiać *ipf.*, **przeszczepić** *pf.* **1.** *chir.* (*organ*) transplant; (*zwł. skórę*) graft. **2.** *ogr.* graft. **3.** *przen.* (*idee, rozwiązania*) transplant.

przeszczepowy *a. chir.* transplant; **chirurgia przeszczepowa** spare-part surgery, transplant surgery.

przeszeregować *pf.* (*pracownika*) (= *przenosić*) transfer; (= *awansować*) promote.

przeszkadzać *ipf.* **1.** (= *rozpraszać*) distract, disturb (*komuś* sb); (= *przerywać*) interrupt (*komuś* sb). **2.** (= *utrudniać*) hamper, hinder (*w czymś* sth); (*o okolicznościach*) intervene; **czy mógłbym przeszkodzić na chwilę** could I interrupt for a second; **proszę sobie nie przeszkadzać** please don't let me disturb you; **komu to przeszkadzało!?** why couldn't things be the way they were?; **nie przeszkadzać** (*wywieszka, np. na drzwiach pokoju hotelowego*) do not disturb.

przeszkalać *ipf.* train. ~ **się** *ipf.* get training, train (*w czymś* in sth).

przeszklić *pf.* (*drzwi, okno*) glaze; (*pomieszczenie*) glass.

przeszklony *a.* (*o pomieszczeniu*) glassed-in; (*o drzwiach*) glazed.

przeszkoda *f. Gen.pl.* **-ód 1.** (= *trudność*) obstacle, hindrance, impediment; **natrafić na/napotkać przeszkodę** come across/encounter an obstacle; **przebiegać bez przeszkód** go unimpeded; **coś stoi na przeszkodzie czegoś** sth is in the way of sth; **usunąć wszelkie przeszkody na drodze do czegoś** clear the way for sth. **2.** *jeźdz.* fence; *Br. t.* obstacle; **bieg z przeszkodami** steeplechase, obstacle race; **tor przeszkód** obstacle course.

przeszkodzić *pf. zob.* **przeszkadzać.**

przeszkolenie *n.* training.

przeszkolić *pf.* **-szkol** *l.* **-szkól** *zob.* **przeszkalać.** ~ **się** *pf. zob.* **przeszkalać się.**

przeszło *adv.* over, more than; **ryba ważyła przeszło dwa kilogramy** the fish weighed over two kilograms; **nie byłem tu od przeszło trzech lat** I haven't been here for over three years.

przeszłość *f.* (the) past; **w przeszłości** in the past; **daleka** *l.* **odległa przeszłość** distant past; **czyjaś burzliwa przeszłość** sb's wild past; **należeć (już) do przeszłości** be a thing of the past; **żyć przeszłością** live in the past; **kobieta z przeszłością** *euf.* a woman with a past.

przeszły *a.* past; **czas przeszły** *gram.* the past tense, the past.

przeszmuglować *pf.* smuggle.

przeszpiegi *pl. Gen.* **-ów** *pot.* spying; **wysłać kogoś na przeszpiegi** send sb spying; **przyjść na przeszpiegi** come spying.

przeszukać *pf.*, **przeszukiwać** *ipf.* search.

przeszyć *pf.* **-szyję -szyjesz, -szyj, przeszywać** *ipf.* **-am -asz 1.** (= *przebić, przeniknąć*) pierce; **kula przeszyła mu ramię na wylot** the bullet went clean through his arm; **przeszyć kogoś wzrokiem** fix sb with a glance *l.* look. **2.** (= *przefastrygować*) tack.

prześcieradło *n. Gen.pl.* **-eł** sheet.

prześcigać *ipf.* **1.** (= *wyprzedzać*) (*np. samochodem*) overtake; (= *zostawiać w tyle*) (*np. w biegu*) outpace. **2.** (= *przewyższać*) outdo. ~ **się** *ipf.* (= *walczyć o prymat*) compete each other (*w czymś* in sth); **prześcigać się w komplementach/uprzejmościach** (*wzajemnych*) exchange compliments/courtesies.

prześcignąć *pf.* **-nę -niesz, -nij** *zob.* **prześcigać.**

prześladować *ipf.* **1.** (= *dyskryminować*) persecute. **2.** (= *narzucać się*) pester, hassle. **3.** (*o chorobach, nieszczęściach, niepowodzeniach*) plague, dog.

prześladowca *mp* persecutor.

prześladowczy *a.* persecutive; **mania prześladowcza** *pat.* persecution mania.

prześledzić *pf.* trace.

prześlicznie *adv.* beautifully, gorgeously.

prześliczny *a.* beautiful, gorgeous.

prześlizgiwać się *ipf.*, **prześlizgnąć się** *pf.* **-nę -niesz, -nij 1.** (= *przedostać się*) squeeze, slip (*przez coś* through sth). **2.** *pot.* (= *robić coś powierzchownie*) scratch the surface (*po czymś* of sth); **prześlizgnąć się przez studia** slide through college; **prześlizgnąć się wzrokiem po czymś** glance over sth.

prześmiewać się *ifp.* mock (*z czegoś* sth); scoff (*z czegoś* at sth).

prześmiewca *mp* mocker, scoffer.

przeświadczenie *n.* (= *przekonanie*) conviction; (= *wiara*) belief (*o czymś* that).

przeświadczony *a.* **-eni** convinced (*o czymś* of sth, *że...* that...).

przeświecać *ipf.* **1.** (= *prześwitywać*) show (*przez coś* through sth). **2.** (= *być półprzezroczystym*) be translucent. **3.** (= *prześwietlić, przebić światłem*) shine (*coś* through sth).

prześwietlać *ipf.* **1.** (= *przebić światłem*) shine (*coś* through sth). **2.** *med.* (*promieniami rentgenowskimi*) X-ray; (*skanerem*) scan. **3.** *fot.* overexpose. **4.** *ogr., leśn.* thin. **5.** *pot.* (= *starannie badać*) probe, scrutinize. ~ **się** *ipf.* **1.** *med.* (*promieniami rentgenowskimi*) get *l.* have an X-ray; (*skanerem*) get *l.* have a scan. **2.** *fot.* be *l.* get overexposed.

prześwietlenie *n. med.* (*promieniami rentgenowskimi*) X-ray (examination), X-ray (scan); (*skanerem*) scan.

prześwietlić *pf. zob.* **prześwietlać.** ~ **się** *pf. zob.* **prześwietlać się.**

prześwietny *a. emf.* (*o profesorze, trybunale*) eminent, distinguished.

prześwit *mi bud., mot., techn.* clearance; (*nad głową, dachem*) headroom, headway.

prześwitujący *a.* (*o materiale, bluzce*) see-through.

prześwitywać *ipf.* **1.** (*o materiale, bluzce*) be see-through. **2.** (= *być widocznym*) show through.

przetaczać *ipf.* **1.** *kol.* (*wagony*) shunt, switch. **2.** *med.* (*krew, plazmę, osocze*) transfuse; **przetaczać komuś krew** give sb a blood transfusion. **3.** (= *przesuwać*) roll. ~ **się** *ipf.* roll (by).

przetaczanie *n. med.* transfusion; **przetaczanie krwi** blood transfusion.

przetacznik *mi Gen.* -a *bot.* speedwell, veronica (*Veronica*).

przetak *mi Gen.* -a *l.* -u riddle.

przetańczyć *pf.* (*np. wieczór, noc*) dance away; przetańczyć całą noc dance the night away.

przetapiać *ipf.* (*metal*) melt down; (*rudę*) smelt; (*tłuszcz*) clarify; (*na nowo*) remelt. ~ się melt.

przetarcie *n.* abrasion; (*w ubraniu*) fray.

przetarg *mi prawn. ekon.* **1.** (= *wybór ofert*) tender; ogłaszać przetarg invite tenders; wygrać przetarg win a bid; stawać do przetargu (do czegoś) put in a bid (for sth), bid (for sth). **2.** (= *licytacja*) auction.

przetargi *pl. Gen.* -ów (= *negocjacje*) horse trading.

przetargowy *a.* bargaining; karta przetargowa bargaining chip; pozycja przetargowa bargain position.

przetasować *pf.* (*karty*) shuffle; (= *zmienić kolejność, układ, szyk*) reshuffle.

przetasowanie *n.* (*kart*) shuffle, shuffling; (*np. personalne*) reshuffle.

przetasowywać *ipf. zob.* przetasować.

przetchlinka *f. Gen.pl.* -ek **1.** *bot.* stoma; (*w łodydze*) lenticel. **2.** *ent.* spiracle.

przeterminować się *pf.* (*o żywności*) pass the expiration date; (*o dokumencie*) expire.

przeterminowany *a.* (*o żywności*) past the expiration date; (*o dokumencie*) expired; piwo przeterminowane o dwa lata beer two years past its expiration date.

przetkać *pf. zob.* przetykać.

przetłumaczalny *a.* translatable.

przetłumaczyć *pf.* **1.** (*na inny język*) translate; przetłumaczyć coś z niemieckiego/chińskiego na japoński/holenderski translate sth from German/Chinese into Japanese/Dutch. **2.** (= *wyjaśnić*) demonstrate; przetłumaczyć komuś, że... *pot.* get it into sb's head that...

przetłuszczać się *ipf.* (*o włosach*) be greasy; włosy mi się przetłuszczają I have greasy hair.

przetłuszczający się *a.* (*o włosach*) greasy; (*o cerze*) oily.

przetłuszczony *a.* **1.** (*o włosach*) greasy. **2.** *chem.* (*o mydle*) superfatted.

przeto *conj. arch. lit.* **1.** (= *a więc*) hence, thus; był już stary, przeto doświadczony he was old, thus experienced. **2.** (= *więc*) then.

przetoczyć *pf. zob.* przetaczać. ~ się *pf. zob.* przetaczać się.

przetoka *f.* **1.** *pat.* fistula. **2.** *geogr.* strait.

przetokowy *a.* **1.** *kol.* shunting. **2.** *pat.* fistular. – *mp kol.* switchman; *Br.* pointsman.

przetop *mi metal.* **1.** (*złomu metali*) melting. **2.** (*rudy*) smelting. **3.** (= *przetopienie na nowo*) remelting.

przetopić *pf. zob.* przetapiać.

przetranskrybować *pf.* transcribe.

przetransponować *pf. t. muz.* transpose.

przetransportować *pf.* transport.

przetrawiać *ipf.* **1.** (*w żołądku, umyśle*) digest. **2.** (*o ogniu*) consume. **3.** (*o środkach chemicznych*) corrode. ~ się *pf.* **1.** (*w żołądku*) be digest-

ed. **2.** (*pod wpływem środków chemicznych*) corrode.

przetrącić *pf. pot.* (= *złamać*) break; (= *zwichnąć*) sprain; (= *uderzyć*) bust; przetrącić coś *pot.* (= *zjeść coś*) catch a bite to eat.

przetrenować *pf.* overtrain. ~ się *pf.* overtrain.

przetrenowany *a.* overtrained.

przetrwać *pf.* survive, endure; przetrwać próbę czasu stand the test of time.

przetrwalnik *mi Gen.* -a *biol.* (resting) spore.

przetrwalnikowy *a. biol.* (*o zarodku*) resting.

przetrząsacz *mi Gen.* -a *roln.* tedder.

przetrząsać *ipf.*, przetrząsnąć *pf.* -nę -niesz, -nij **1.** (= *przeszukiwać*) (*kraj, las*) comb; (*kieszenie, szuflady*) rummage (through). **2.** (*skoszoną trawę, siano*) ted.

przetrzebić *pf.* (= *zniszczyć*) destroy; (= *zdziesiątkować*) decimate; (= *przerzedzić*) thin (out).

przetrzeć *pf.* -trę -trzesz, -trzyj, -tarł *zob.* przecierać. ~ się *pf. zob.* przecierać się.

przetrzepać *pf.* -pię -piesz, przetrzepywać *ipf.* **1.** (*dywan*) beat; przetrzepać komuś skórę *gł. przest.* give sb a hiding. **2.** *pot.* (= *przeszukać na granicy*) go over with a fine-tooth comb.

przetrzymać *pf.*, przetrzymywać *ipf.* **1.** (= *trzymać za długo*) keep overtime, hoard. **2.** (= *więzić*) detain, hold; (*jako zakładnika*) hold hostage. **3.** (= *przechowywać*) retain. **4.** (= *przetrwać*) endure, last out. **5.** (= *wytrzymać dłużej niż*) outlast (*kogoś/coś* sb/sth).

przetwarzać *ipf.* (= *obrabiać*) process; (*do innej postaci*) convert, transform (*na coś* into sth).

przetwornica *f. el.* converter.

przetwornik *mi Gen.* -a **1.** *muz.* (*przy gitarze*) pickup. **2.** *el., techn.* converter, transducer; przetwornik analogowo-cyfrowy analog-to-digital converter.

przetwory *pl. Gen.* -ów **1.** (= *wyroby*) products; przetwory mleczne dairy *l.* milk products. **2.** *kulin.* (= *dżemy, zaprawy*) preserves.

przetworzenie *n.* **1.** (= *przekształcenie*) transformation. **2.** *muz.* (= *druga część sonaty*) development.

przetworzyć *pf.* -órz *zob.* przetwarzać.

przetwórczy *a.* process, processing; przemysł przetwórczy processing industry.

przetwórnia *f. Gen.pl.* -i processing plant; przetwórnia owoców fruit processing plant.

przetwórstwo *n.* (= *przetwarzanie*) processing; (*dział przemysłu*) processing industry.

przetykać *ipf.* (= *udrażniać*) unclog, unblock.

przetykany *a. tk.* (*o materiale, taśmie*) shot (through) (*czymś* with sth).

przeuroczy *a. emf.* delightful.

przewaga *f.* (= *górowanie*) advantage; (= *wyższość*) superiority; (*liczebna*) majority; przewaga intelektualna intellectual superiority; przewaga techniczna technical advantage; mieć nad kimś przewagę hold an advantage *l.* edge over sb; przewaga 10 punktów *sport* a ten-point lead; zdobyć przewagę (nad kimś/czymś) gain *l.* get the upper hand (over sb/sth); z przewagą chrześcijan (*np. o społeczności*) with a Christian majority.

przewalać *ipf. pot.* **1.** (= *przewracać*) tip over. **2.** (= *przetaczać*) turn over. ~ **się** *ipf.* **1.** *pot.* (= *przewracać się*) tip over. **2.** (= *baraszkować*) horse around. **3.** *pot.* (= *przemieszczać się*) roll by.

przewalić *pf. zob.* **przewalać**. ~ **się** *pf. zob.* **przewalać się**.

przewał *mi*, **przewałka** *f. Gen.pl.* **-ek** *pot.* (= *oszustwo*) scam.

przewartościować *pf.*, **przewartościowywać** *ipf.* reevaluate.

przeważać *ipf.* **1.** (= *rozstrzygać*) prevail; (= *dominować*) dominate, predominate; **przeważa pogląd, że...** a belief prevails that...; **ten wzgląd przeważył** this factor prevailed; **wśród zebranych przeważała młodzież** most of the people assembled were teenagers and young adults. **2.** (= *odważać więcej towaru niż trzeba*) give a little extra. **3.** (= *zważyć po kolei*) weigh.

przeważający *a.* prevailing, dominant; **przeważająca większość** a vast majority.

przeważnie *adv.* predominantly, mostly.

przeważyć *pf. zob.* **przeważać**.

przewąchać *pf.*, **przewąchiwać** *ipf. pot.* (= *przeczuć*) sense (*coś* sth); **przewąchać coś** (*podstęp, coś podejrzanego*) smell a rat.

przewertować *pf.* leaf through.

przewędrować *pf.* **1.** (*przebyć*) travel; **przewędrować kawał drogi** travel a great distance. **2.** (*spędzić*) wander, spend some time wandering.

przewężenie *n.* narrowing; (*powodujące zator*) chokepoint, bottleneck.

przewiać *pf.* **-wieję -wiejesz** *zob.* **przewiewać**.

przewiązać *pf.* **-wiążę -wiążesz**, **przewiązywać** *ipf.* (*paczkę*) tie, strap; (*ranę*) bind, dress. ~ **się** *pf.*, **przewiązywać się** *ipf.* **przewiązać się czymś w pasie** tie sth round one's waist.

przewiązka *f. Gen.pl.* **-ek** *bud.* lacing.

przewidująco *adv.* foreseeingly.

przewidujący *a.* (*o osobie, polityce*) far-sighted.

przewidywać *ipf.* **1.** (= *zapowiadać*) predict; (= *oczekiwać*) anticipate; (= *wziąć w rachubę*) plan (*coś* for sth). **2.** (= *prognozować*) forecast, project; **przewidywać pogodę** tell weather. **3.** (= *precyzować*) (*o kontrakcie, przepisie*) stipulate, provide.

przewidywalny *a.* predictable.

przewidywanie *n.* **1.** (= *oczekiwanie*) anticipation; **w przewidywaniu czegoś** in anticipation of sth; **zgodnie z (czyimiś) przewidywaniami** as (sb) anticipated. **2.** (= *zapowiedź*) prediction. **3.** (= *prognoza*) forecast, projection.

przewidzenie *n.* (= *zapowiedź*) prediction; (= *prognoza*) forecast; **jak było do przewidzenia** predictably; **to było do przewidzenia** you could see it coming; **trudny do przewidzenia** unpredictable.

przewidziany *a.* **1.** (= *określony*) (*umową, ustawą*) provided for. **2.** (= *planowany*) planned; **coś jest przewidziane** (*w programie*) sth is on the agenda *l.* program.

przewidzieć *pf.* **-widzę -widzisz, -widzą** *zob.* **przewidywać**.

przewielebny *a.* **przewielebny Kowalski** *rel.* the Reverend Kowalski.

przewiercać *ipf.*, **przewiercić** *pf.* **1.** (*otwór*) bore, drill. **2.** (*deskę, ścianę*) drill through.

przewiercień *mi* **-tni-** *Gen.* **-a** *bot.* **wiciokrzew przewiercień** Italian honeysuckle, Italian woodbine (*Lonicera caprifolium*).

przewiesić *pf.* **-szę -sisz**, **przewieszać** *ipf.* **1.** (*torbę, płaszcz*) hang (*coś przez coś* sth over sth). **2.** (*na inne miejsce*) move. ~ **się** *pf.*, **przewieszać się** *ipf.* hang (o.s.) (*przez coś* over sth).

przewieszka *f. Gen.pl.* **-ek** *geogr.* overhang.

przewietrzać *ipf.*, **przewietrzyć** *pf.* (*pomieszczenie, rzeczy, glebę*) air; (*pomieszczenie*) ventilate. ~ **się** *ipf.*, **przewietrzyć się** *pf.* **1.** (*o rzeczach*) air. **2.** (*na spacerze*) get some fresh air.

przewiew *mi* draft, *Br.* draught.

przewiewać *ipf.*, **przewiać** *pf.* **1.** (*o wietrze*) (= *owiewać*) fan; (= *chłodzić*) chill; (*ubranie*) blow through. **2.** *roln.* (*ziarno*) winnow. **3.** (= *przegnać*) (*chmury*) blow away. **4.** *tylko pf. pot.* **przewiało mnie wczoraj na spacerze** the wind was so chilly when I went for a walk yesterday that I caught a cold.

przewiewność *f.* (*pomieszczenia*) airiness.

przewiewny *a.* **1.** (*o pomieszczeniu*) airy. **2.** (*o ubraniu*) (= *luźny*) loose-fitting.

przewieźć *pf.* **-wiozę -wieziesz -wiózł -wiozła -wieźli 1.** *zob.* **przewozić**. **2.** (= *zabrać na przejażdżkę*) take for a ride. ~ **się** *pf. pot.* (= *umrzeć*) check out, hop the twig.

przewijać *ipf.*, **przewinąć** *pf.* **1.** (*taśmę, film*) (*do tyłu*) rewind; (*do przodu*) fast-forward. **2.** (*dziecko*) change. **3.** *komp.* (*dokument, stronę*) scroll (through). **4.** *el.* (*cewkę, silnik, transformator*) rewind. ~ **się** *ipf.*, **przewinąć się** *pf.* **1.** (*o taśmie*) (*do tyłu*) rewind; (*do przodu*) fast-forward. **2.** (= *przechodzić kolejno*) (*o ludziach*) pass. **3.** (*o wątku, elemencie*) run (*przez coś* through sth).

przewinienie *n.* (= *występek*) offense, fault; *prawn., sport t.* violation.

przewlec *pf.* **-wlokę** *l.* **-wlekę -wleczesz -wlókł** *l.* **-wlekł -wlokła** *l.* **-wlekła -wlekli**, **przewlekać** *ipf.* **1.** (= *nawlec*) thread (*coś przez coś* sth through sth); **przewlec pościel** (= *zmienić pościel*) change sheets. **2.** (= *wydłużyć*) drag out; **przewlekać dyskusję/zebranie** drag out a discussion/meeting. ~ **się** *pf.*, **przewlekać się** *ipf.* (= *przedłużać się*) drag on.

przewlekle *adv.* **1.** (= *chronicznie*) (*chory*) chronically. **2.** (= *rozwlekle*) (*relacjonować*) at length.

przewlekłość *f.* **1.** (= *chroniczność*) (*choroby*) chronic character. **2.** (= *rozwlekłość*) lengthiness.

przewlekły *a.* **1.** (= *chroniczny*) (*o chorobie*) chronic. **2.** (= *rozwlekły*) lengthy, protracted.

przewodni *a.* leading; **duch przewodni** moving spirit; **motyw przewodni** leitmotif; **myśl przewodnia** guiding principle.

przewodnictwo *n.* **1.** (= *przewodzenie komuś, czemuś*) leadership, guidance; **pod czyimś przewodnictwem** under sb's leadership *l.* guidance. **2.** *fiz., el.* conductivity, conduction; **przewodnictwo elektryczne/cieplne** electric/thermal *l.* heat conductivity *l.* conduction; **przewodnictwo samoistne/niesamoistne** intrinsic/extrinsic conductivity *l.* conduction.

przewodnicząca *f. Gen.* -ej, **przewodniczący** *mp* chair, president.

przewodniczka *f. Gen.pl.* -ek 1. (*wycieczki*) (tour) guide. 2. (= *przywódczyni*) leader.

przewodniczyć *ipf.* preside (*czemuś* over sth); chair (*czemuś* sth).

przewodnik *mp pl.* -cy 1. (*wycieczki*) (tour) guide. 2. (= *przywódca*) leader. 3. *przen.* (= *doradca*) guide. – *ma pl.* -i (*stada*) leader; **pies przewodnik** seeing eye dog. – *mi Gen.* -a *pl.* -i 1. (*książka*) guidebook, guide. 2. *fiz.* conductor; **dobry/zły przewodnik** good/poor conductor.

przewodność *f. fiz.* conductivity, conductance.

przewodowy *a. el., tel.* (*o linii, telefonii*) wire; **znieczulenie przewodowe** *chir.* conduction anesthesia.

przewodzenie *n. el., fiz., fizj.* conduction.

przewodzić *ipf.* -ódź 1. (= *kierować*) lead, conduct (*komuś / czemuś* sb/sth). 2. *el., fiz., fizj.* conduct.

przewozić *ipf.* -żę, -zisz, -oź *l.* -óź transport.

przewozowy *a.* transport; *zwł. handl.* carriage, haulage; **list przewozowy** *handl.* bill of lading.

przewoźnik *mp* carrier.

przewód *mi* -o- 1. *techn.* line, conduit; (= *kabel*) wire, lead, cable; (= *kanał*) duct, shaft; (= *rura*) pipe; **przewód (główny** *l.* **zasilający) prądu/wody/gazu** power/water/gas main; **przewód sieciowy** *el.* power cord; **przewód wentylacyjny** ventilation duct. 2. *anat.* duct, canal; **przewód pokarmowy** alimentary canal; **przewód słuchowy** auditory canal. 3. (= *przywództwo*) lead; **pod czyimś przewodem** under sb's lead; **przewód doktorski/habilitacyjny** Ph.D./postdoctoral program; **otworzyć komuś przewód doktorski/habilitacyjny** admit sb into a Ph.D./postdoctoral program. 4. *prawn.* proceedings; **przewód sądowy** court proceedings. 5. (*w broni palnej*) bore.

przewóz *mi* -o- transport; *zwł. handl.* carriage, haulage; **przewóz pasażerów** passenger carriage *l.* transport; **przewóz towarów** carriage of goods; **wóz albo przewóz** neck or nothing; kill or cure.

przewracać *ipf.* 1. (= *wywracać*) tip over, overturn; (*uderzeniem*) knock over; **przewrócić coś do góry nogami** turn sth upside down. 2. (= *obracać*) (*kartkę*) turn over. 3. (= *przerzucać, przeszukiwać*) turn inside out; **przewrócić komuś w głowie** turn sb's head; **przewracać oczami** roll one's eyes. ~ **się** *ipf.* 1. (= *wywrócić się*) tip over, overturn; (= *upadać*) fall; **przewrócić się do góry nogami** turn upside down; **przewróciło mu się w głowie** he has grown too big for his boots; **przewróciłby się w grobie, gdyby to słyszał** he would turn in his grave if he heard this; **flaki mi się przewracają, gdy...** *pot.* my stomach turns when... 2. (*np. na drugi bok*) turn over; **przewracać się z boku na bok** (*w łóżku, nie mogąc zasnąć*) twist and turn.

przewrażliwienie *n.* oversensitivity, touchiness.

przewrażliwiony *a.* -eni oversensitive, touchy.

przewrotka *f. Gen.pl.* -ek 1. *piłka nożna* bicycle kick. 2. *gimnastyka* tumble, somersault.

przewrotnie *adv.* perversely, perfidiously.

przewrotność *f.* perversity, perfidiousness.

przewrotny *a.* perverse, perfidious.

przewrócić *pf. zob.* **przewracać.** ~ **się** *pf. zob.* **przewracać się.**

przewrót *mi* -o- 1. (= *przełom*) revolution. 2. *polit.* coup d'état, coup. 3. *gimnastyka* somersault, tumble. 4. *lotn.* wingover, stall turn.

przewyższać *ipf.,* **przewyższyć** *pf.* 1. (= *być większym*) exceed; **koszty przewyższają zyski** cost exceeds profit. 2. (= *dominować*) surpass; **przewyższać coś/kogoś (pod względem czegoś)** be superior to sth/sb (in sth). 3. (= *być wyższym*) be taller (*kogoś* than sb); **przewyższać kogoś o głowę** stand a head above sb.

przez *prep.* + *Acc.* 1. (= *poprzez*) (*śnieg, okno, bramę, ścianę*) through. 2. (= *w poprzek*) (*ulicy, rzeki*) across. 3. (*podróżować*) through, via; **lot przez Berlin** flight via Berlin. 4. (= *przy pomocy, za pomocą*) through, over; **przez Internet** through *l.* over the Internet; **przez kolegę** through a friend; **przez telefon/radio** over the phone/radio. 5. (= *nad*) (*przeskoczyć*) over; **przeskoczyć przez coś** jump *l.* leap over sth. 6. (= *w ciągu*) for, during, over; **przez minutę/tydzień/miesiąc** for a minute/week/month; **przez całą noc** throughout the night; **przez przerwę/weekend** during *l.* over the break/weekend. 7. **przez kogoś** (= *z powodu*) because of sb; (= *z winy*) through sb's fault; **to się stało przez niego** it happened because of him, it happened through his fault. 8. (*sprawca*) by; **napisany przez Kowalskiego** written by Kowalski; **dobrze traktowany przez nauczycieli** well treated by teachers. 9. (*w działaniach arytmetycznych*) by; **podziel to przez dwa** divide it by two; **trzeba pomnożyć powierzchnię podstawy przez wysokość** you need to multiply the area of the base by the height. 10. **przez przypadek** by accident; **mówić przez sen** speak in one's sleep; **co przez to rozumiesz?** what do you mean by this?; **to się pisze przez u** it's spelled with a „u".

przezabawny *a. emf.* hilarious.

przeze *prep. zob.* **przez.**

przezeń *adv. lit.* (= *przez niego*) because of him; because of it.

przezierać *ipf.* (*o słońcu, ukrytym uczuciu*) show, appear.

przeziernik *mi Gen.* -a 1. (= *wizjer*) peephole. 2. *opt.* (sight) vane. 3. *ent.* clearwing (*Sesia*).

przeziębiać *ipf.,* **przeziębić** *pf.* 1. (= *spowodować przeziębienie*) give a cold. 2. (= *wyziębić*) chill. ~ **się** *ipf.,* **przeziębić się** *pf.* catch *l.* get a cold.

przeziębienie *n. pat.* cold.

przeziębiony *a.* -eni **być przeziębionym** have a cold.

przezimować *pf.* 1. (= *spędzić zimę*) (*o zwierzętach, ludziach*) spend the winter; (*o rośli-*

nach) last through the winter. **2.** *pot. szkoln.* (= *zostać w tej samej klasie*) repeat the year.

przeznaczać *ipf.* **1.** (= *określać cel, obowiązki*) assign (*na coś* for sth); (*fundusze*) allot, allocate, earmark (*na coś* for sth); (*czas*) put aside (*na coś* for sth). **2.** (= *kierować*) (*słowa*) mean (*dla kogoś* for sb); **te słowa były przeznaczone dla ciebie** these words were meant for you. **3.** (= *planować*) intend (*coś dla kogoś / na coś* sth for sb/sth); **na co przeznaczysz wygraną?** what are you planning to do with the winnings? **4.** (= *poświęcać*) dedicate (*na coś* to sth). **5.** (= *wyznaczać*) designate (*coś na coś* sth for *l.* as sth). **6.** (*o losie*) destine; **los jej to przeznaczył** she was destined for this.

przeznaczenie *n.* **1.** (= *cel*) purpose; (= *użycie*) intended use; **miejsce przeznaczenia** destination. **2.** (= *los*) destiny.

przeznaczony *a.* **-eni 1.** (= *określony, przypisany*) assigned; (*o funduszach*) alloted, allocated, earmarked (*na coś* for sth); (*o czasie*) put aside (*na coś* for sth). **2.** (= *skierowany*) meant; **te słowa przeznaczone są dla ciebie** these words are meant for you. **3.** (= *zaplanowany*) intended, planned. **4.** (= *poświęcony*) dedicated (*na coś* to sth). **5.** (= *wyznaczony*) designated. **6.** (*przez los*) destined, fated; **oni są sobie przeznaczeni** they are destined for each other, thery are meant for each other.

przeznaczyć *pf. zob.* **przeznaczać**.

przezornie *adv.* **1.** (= *ostrożnie*) cautiously. **2.** (= *rozsądnie*) wisely.

przezorność *f.* **1.** (= *ostrożność*) caution. **2.** (= *przewidywanie*) foresight.

przezorny *a.* **1.** (= *ostrożny*) cautious. **2.** (= *rozsądny*) wise.

przezrocze *n. Gen.pl.* **-y** *fot.* slide.

przezroczystość *f.* transparency.

przezroczysty *a.* **-szy** (= *przepuszczający światło*) transparent; (= *przejrzysty*) see-through; (= *bezbarwny*) clear.

przezwać *pf.* **-wę -wiesz, -wij** *zob.* **przezywać**.

przezwajać *ipf.*, **przezwoić** *pf. techn.* rewind.

przezwisko *n.* nickname.

przezwoić *pf. techn. zob.* **przezwajać**.

przezwyciężać *ipf.*, **przezwyciężyć** *pf.* (*trudności, strach*) overcome. **~ się** *ipf.*, **przezwyciężyć się** *pf.* control o.s., contain o.s.

przezywać *ipf.* **-am -asz 1.** (= *nadać przydomek*) nickname. **2.** (= *ubliżać*) call (sb) names. **~ się** *ipf.* (= *ubliżać sobie wzajemnie*) call each other names; **proszę pani, on się przezywa!** Miss, he's calling me names!

przeżegnać *pf. kośc.* (*wiernych*) cross. **~ się** *pf. kośc.* cross o.s.

przeżerać *ipf.*, **przeżreć** *pf.* **-żrę -żresz, -żryj, -żarł 1.** (= *niszczyć*) eat (into/through), consume; **rdza przeżarła rury** rust has eaten through the pipes; **rak przeżarł mu płuca** cancer has consumed his lungs. **2.** *pot.* (= *przejadać*) (*pieniądze*) spend on food. **~ się** *ipf.*, **przeżreć się** *pf.* **1.** *uj. pot.* (= *przejadać się*) pig out, overeat. **2.** (= *penetrować*) eat (*do l. w głąb czegoś* into sth).

przeżuć *pf. zob.* **przeżuwać**.

przeżuwacz *ma zool.* ruminant.

przeżuwać *ipf.* **1.** (= *rozdrabniać pokarm*) chew. **2.** *tylko ipf.* (*o przeżuwaczach*) ruminate. **3.** *tylko ipf.* (= *rozmyślać*) ruminate (*coś* on *l.* upon sth).

przeżycie *n.* **1.** (= *doświadczenie*) experience; **bolesne/straszne przeżycie** painful/awful experience; **głębokie/niezapomniane przeżycie** profound/unforgettable experience. **2.** (= *przetrwanie*) survival.

przeżyć *pf.* **-żyję -żyjesz, -żyj 1.** *zob.* **przeżywać**. **2.** (= *przetrwać*) survive; (= *nie umrzeć*) stay alive, live. **3.** (= *żyć przez jakiś czas*) live; **przeżyć pięć lat za granicą** live abroad for five years. **4.** (= *pogodzić się z czymś*) get over; **nie mogę przeżyć jej wyjazdu** I can't get over her leaving. **5.** (= *doświadczać*) experience. **6.** (= *żyć dłużej niż*) outlive (*kogoś* sb). **~ się** *pf. zob.* **przeżywać się**.

przeżytek *mi* **-tk- 1.** (= *anachronizm*) anachronism. **2.** (= *relikt*) relic.

przeżywać *ipf.* **-am -asz 1.** (= *martwić się*) worry (*coś* about sth); **on bardzo to przeżywa** this is giving him a very difficult time. **2.** (= *przechodzić*) go (*coś* through sth); **przeżywać coś na nowo** relive sth. **~ się** *ipf.* go *l.* fall out of fashion, become outdated.

przeżywalność *f. med., biol.* survival rate.

przędny *a.* **1.** *biol.* spinning; **brodawka przędna** spinneret; **gruczoł przędny** spinning gland. **2.** *tk.* spinning; **włókno przędne** spinning fiber, staple.

przędza *f. tk.* yarn; **przędza szklana** *bud.* spun glass.

przędzalnia *f. Gen.pl.* **-i** *l.* **-ń** spinning mill; **przędzalnia bawełny** cotton mill.

przędzalnictwo *n.* spinning.

przędzalniczy *a.* spinning.

przędzarka *f. Gen.pl.* **-ek** spinning frame, spinner.

przędziwo *n.* spinning material.

przęsło *n. Gen.pl.* **-eł** *bud.* (*mostu*) span; (*kolumnady*) bay.

przodek *mp* **-dk-** *Gen.* **-a** ancestor. **– mi -dk-** *Gen.* **-u** *l.* **-a 1.** *górn.* coalface, mine face. **2.** *wojsk.* (*działa*) limber. **3.** (*wozu konnego*) fore-carriage.

przodem *adv.* **1.** (= *twarzą do przodu*) facing forward. **2.** (= *z przodu*) at the front; **iść przodem** lead the way; **puścić kogoś przodem** let sb go first.

przodkowy *a.* coalface; **górnik przodkowy** face miner.

przodomózgowie *n. Gen.pl.* **-i** *anat.* forebrain; (*w języku fachowym*) prosencephalon.

przodować *ipf.* lead the way (*w czymś* in *l.* at sth).

przodownica *f.*, **przodowniczka** *f.* leader; **przodownica pracy** shock worker.

przodownictwo *n.* leadership.

przodownik *mp* **1.** (= *lider*) leader; **przodownik pracy** shock worker. **2.** *hist.* police sergeant.

przodowy *mp górn.* foreman.

przodujący *a.* leading.

przód *mi* -o- front; **do przodu** forward, ahead; **na przodzie** at *l.* in the front; **do przodu i do tyłu** *l.* **w przód i w tył** forward and backward; **tyłem do przodu** *l.* tył na przód back to front; **patrz do przodu** look ahead; **wysunąć się na przód** take the lead, move ahead of the rest; **zrobić krok do przodu** take a step forward; **być 10 dolarów do przodu** *pot.* be $10 in pocket; **mieć coś do przodu** (*przedmiot*) *pot.*, *szkoln.*, *uniw.* get through sth, be through with sth.

prztyczek *mi* -czk- *Gen.* -a flick, fillip; **dać komuś prztyczka (w nos)** *dosł.* flick sb's nose; *przen.* take sb down a peg; **dostać prztyczka (w nos)** *dosł.* be flicked in the nose; *przen.* get a takedown.

prztykać *ipf.*, **prztyknąć** *pf.* -ij fillip, flick one's fingers; **prztykać w coś** flick *l.* fillip sth with one's fingers.

przy *prep.* + *Loc.* **1.** (= *w pobliżu*) by, near; **przy szosie/domu/oknie/rzece** by *l.* near the road/house/window/river; **przy ulicy X** on X street; *Br.* in X street; **przy biurku/stole** at the desk/table; **ramię przy ramieniu** side by side; **głowa przy głowie** head to head. **2.** (= *podczas*) at; **przy śniadaniu/pracy** at breakfast/work; **przy niedzieli** *gł.* *przest.* on Sundays. **3.** (= *w obecności*) in front, in the presence (*kimś/czymś* of sb/sth); **przy wszystkich/dzieciach** in front of everybody/the children. **4.** (= *z towarzyszeniem*) with; **przy odrobinie szczęścia** with a bit of luck; **przy muzyce** with music playing. **5.** (= *w porównaniu z*) next to, compared to *l.* with; **przy tym budynku nasz dom wydaje się mały** next to this building, our house seems small. **6.** (*obiekt czynności*) with; **nie grzeb przy tym komputerze** don't mess with this computer. **7.** (*w zwrotach*) **przy czym...** while...; **przy tym...** at the same time...; **być przy pieniądzach** *pot.* be loaded.

przybić *pf.* -biję -bijesz, -bij **1.** *zob.* **przybijać**. **2.** (= *zmartwić*) depress, upset.

przybiec *pf.* -biegnę -biegniesz, -biegnij, -biegł, **przybiegać** *ipf.* come running.

przybierać *ipf.* **1.** (*o wodzie, rzece*) rise; **przybierać na sile** gather strength; **przybrać na wadze** put on weight. **2.** (= *przyjmować*) (*nazwisko, postawę*) assume, adopt; (*pozę*) put on; **przybrać maskę (czegoś)** put on a mask (of sth); **sprawy przybrały zły obrót** things turned for the worse. **3.** (= *dekorować*) decorate, adorn; *kulin.* garnish.

przybijać *ipf.* **1.** (*gwóźdź, kołek*) drive in, hammer in; (*coś gwoździami*) nail; (*pieczęć*) affix. **2.** (= *dopłynąć, wylądować*) land, reach; **przybić do portu** *żegl.* reach port.

przybitka *f. Gen.pl.* -ek **1.** (*naboju*) wadding. **2.** (*w licytacji*) knockdown. **3.** *górn.* tamping.

przybity *a.* depressed (*czymś l. z powodu czegoś* about *l.* by *l.* over sth).

przyblaknąć *pf.* -nę -niesz, -nij (*o kolorze, blasku, wspomnieniach*) fade.

przyblednąć *pf.* -nę -niesz, -nij (*o osobie, twarzy, blasku, problemach*) pale.

przybliżać *ipf.* **1.** (= *skracać odległość l. różnicę*) bring closer, move closer (*do kogoś/czegoś* to

sb/sth). **2.** (*spotkanie, zwycięstwo*) bring nearer; **przybliżać kogoś do celu** take sb closer to the goal. **3.** (*o lunecie, szkle powiększającym*) magnify. **4.** (= *opisywać, wyjaśniać*) describe (*coś komuś* sth to sb); **przybliżyć komuś czyjąś sylwetkę** tell sb a few words about sb. **~ się** *ipf.* **1.** (= *zbliżać się*) move closer, get closer (*do kogoś/czegoś* to sth/sb). **2.** (= *nadchodzić*) be approaching. **3.** *mat.* approximate.

przybliżenie *n. mat.* approximation; **w przybliżeniu** approximately.

przybliżony *a.* approximate.

przybliżyć *pf. zob.* **przybliżać**. **~ się** *pf. zob.* **przybliżać się**.

przybłąkać się *pf.* (= *zostać znalezionym*) be found; (= *pojawić się*) turn up; **przybłąkał się do nich pies** they have found a stray dog.

przybłęda *f. l. mp decl. like f. Gen.pl.* -d *l.* -ów waif.

przyboczna *f.*, **przyboczny** *mp harcerstwo* assistant scout leader.

przyboczny *a. wojsk.* **oficer przyboczny** adjutant; **gwardia** *l.* **straż przyboczna** lifeguard.

przybojowy *a.* **fala przybojowa** *żegl.* surf (wave).

przybornik *mi Gen.* -a kit; **przybornik do szycia** sewing kit; **przybornik kreślarski** draftsman kit.

przybory *pl.* (*narzędzia*) implements; **przybory do pisania** (= *długopisy*) writing implements *l.* materials *l.* utensils; (= *papeteria*) stationery; **przybory toaletowe** toiletries, toilet articles.

przybój *mi* -o- *żegl.* surf.

przybór *mi* -o- **1.** (*narzędzie*) *zob.* **przybory**. **2.** (= *wzrost poziomu wody*) rise (*in water levels*); (*po opadach*) freshet.

przybrać *pf.* -biorę -bierzesz -brał *zob.* **przybierać**.

przybranie *n.* (*bukietu*) trimmings; *kulin.* garnish, trimmings.

przybrany *a.* **1.** (*o dziecku*) adopted; (*o rodzicach*) adoptive. **2.** (*o nazwisku, pseudonimie*) assumed; **pod przybranym nazwiskiem** under an assumed name. **3.** (= *udekorowany*) adorned. **4.** *kulin.* garnished.

przybrudzić *pf.* soil (*lightly*).

przybrudzony *a.* lightly soiled.

przybrzeże *n.* coastal waters.

przybrzeżny *a. żegl., geogr.* coastal; **pas przybrzeżny** coastal belt; **wody przybrzeżne** coastal waters.

przybudować *pf.* build an annex.

przybudówka *f. Gen.pl.* -ek *bud.* annex; *Br.* annexe; extension; (*mała*) lean-to.

przybycie *n.* arrival; **w chwili przybycia** on arrival.

przybyć *pf.* -będę -będziesz, -bądź *zob.* **przybywać**.

przybyły *a.* present; **nowo przybyły** newly arrived; **goście przybyli na spotkanie** guests present at the meeting.

przybysz *mp Gen.pl.* -ów **1.** (*człowiek*) newcomer, arrival. **2.** *ekol.* (*gatunek*) adventive, casual.

przybyszowy *a. bot.* adventitious; **pąk/korzeń przybyszowy** adventitious bud/root.

przybytek *mi* -tk- **1.** *lit.* (= *miejsce, budowla*) place, abode; **święty przybytek** *rel.* sanctum sanctorum. **2.** *euf.* (= *ubikacja*) powder room, convenience. **3.** (= *przyrost*) increase; **od przybytku głowa nie boli** plenty is no plague; store is no sore.

przybywać *ipf.* **1.** *form.* (= *przyjeżdżać*) arrive. **2.** (= *rosnąć*) increase, gain; **przybyło mi 5 kilogramów** I gained 5 kilograms; **przybyło nam pracy** we have more work now; **przybył nam kot** we have a new cat; **przybywa nam lat** we're getting older; **przybywa dnia** days are getting longer.

przychodnia *f. Gen.pl.* -i outpatient clinic; **przychodnia rejonowa** (community) health center.

przychodować *ipf. l. pf. fin.* credit.

przychodowość *f. fin.* **1.** (= *dochodowość*) profitability. **2.** (= *zysk*) profit.

przychodzić *ipf.* **1.** (= *przybywać*) (*o osobie*) come; (*o liście, pociągu, myśli*) arrive, come; **przyjść do kogoś** visit sb; **przyjść po kogoś** pick sb up; **przyjść do pracy/szkoły** come to work/school; **przyjść na spotkanie** come to a meeting; **przyjść za późno na dworzec/na spotkanie** be late at the station/for a meeting; **przyszła noc** night fell; **wreszcie przyszła wiosna** spring is here at last; **przyszła mi ochota na lody** I feel like having some ice cream; **burza przyszła z północy** the storm came from the north; **dzisiejsza poczta jeszcze nie przyszła** today's mail hasn't arrived yet; **przychodziły e-maile z wszystkich stron świata** emails were coming from all over the world; **co ci przyszło do głowy?** where did you get that idea?, what came into your head? **2.** (= *nastąpić, wyniknąć*) come (*z czegoś* of sth); **przyszła moda na coś** sth is in; **przyjdzie nam to poprawić** we'll have to fix that; **zwycięstwo przyszło łatwo** victory came easy; **co z tego przyjdzie?** what good will come of that?; **co mi z tego przyjdzie?** what do I get out of this?; **i na co nam przyszło?** *pot.* what good has it done us? **3.** (*w zwrotach*) **przychodzić do głowy** spring to mind; **przyjść do równowagi** contain o.s.; **przyjść do siebie** come to; **przyjść do zdrowia** recover, get better; **przyjść na świat** be born; **przyjść komuś z pomocą** come to sb's aid; **przyjść do kogoś z czymś** ask sb for help on sth; **łatwo przyszło, łatwo poszło** easy come, easy go; **przyjdzie koza do woza** I shall catch you some day carrying corn to our mill; you're going to need my help someday; **przyszła koza do woza!** so you've come (to beg) for my help, haven't you?; **kto późno przychodzi, ten sam sobie szkodzi** the early bird gets the late one's breakfast; **przyszła kryska na Matyska** the pitcher goes (once) too often to the well; sb's chickens have come home to roost.

przychód *mi* -o- *ekon., fin.* revenue, income.

przychówek *mi* -wk- *Gen.* -u *l.* -a **1.** (= *młode zwierzęta*) (the) young. **2.** *żart.* (= *dzieci*) fry.

przychrzaniać się *ipf.*, **przychrzanić się** *pf.* **przychrzaniać się do kogoś** *pot.* get on sb's back.

przychwycić *pf.* -cę -cisz catch. ~ **się** *pf.* (*na*

myśleniu, działaniu) catch o.s. (*na czymś* doing sth).

przychylać *ipf.*, **przychylić** *pf.* (= *przechylać*) tip; **przychylić szklankę do ust** lower the glass to one's lips; **przychyliłby jej skrawka nieba** he would do anything for her. ~ **się** *ipf.*, **przychylić się** *pf.* **1.** (= *pochylić się*) lean. **2.** (= *zgodzić się*) consent (*do czegoś* to sth); **przychylać się do czyjejś prośby** grant sb's request.

przychylnie *adv.* favorably.

przychylność *f.* favor; **okazać komuś przychylność** show one's favor to sb, look kindly on sb; **pozyskać czyjąś przychylność** win sb's favor.

przychylny *a.* (*o opinii, odpowiedzi, decyzji*) favorable; (*o osobie*) favorably disposed; **patrzeć na coś przychylnym okiem** look kindly on sth.

przyciasny *a.* (*o ubraniu*) (a little) tight.

przyciąć *pf.* -tnę -tniesz, -tnij *zob.* **przycinać**.

przyciągać *ipf.* **1.** (= *ciągnąc, przybliżać*) pull in. **2.** (= *wabić*) (*tłumy, klientów*) draw, attract, pull; **przyciągać uwagę** attract attention. **3.** *tylko ipf. astron., fiz.* attract, pull. ~ **się** *ipf. astron., fiz.* attract each other.

przyciągający *a.* attractive.

przyciąganie *n. astron., fiz.* attraction, pull.

przyciągarka *f. Gen.pl.* -ek *techn.* capstan.

przyciągnąć *pf.* -nę -niesz, -nij *zob.* **przyciągać**.

przycichnąć *pf.* -nę -niesz, -nij (*o dźwiękach*) quiet down; (*o sprawie*) calm down, settle down.

przyciemniać *ipf.*, **przyciemnić** *pf.* -ij **1.** (= *przygasić*) turn down. **2.** (= *uczynić ciemniejszym*) darken.

przycierać *ipf.* (*marchwi, ziemniaków*) grate some; **przytrzeć komuś rogów** take sb down a peg.

przycieś *f. pl.* -e *bud.* stringpiece.

przyciężki *a.* a little heavy, on the heavy side.

przycinać *ipf.* **1.** (= *skracać*) (*np. włosy*) clip, trim; (*gałęzie, krzewy, drzewa*) prune; **przycinać na wymiar** cut to size. **2.** (= *przygniatać*) catch; **przyciąć sobie język** bite one's tongue; **przyciąć sobie palec drzwiami** catch one's finger in the door. **3.** (= *dogryzać*) gibe (*komuś* at sb).

przycinek *mi* -nk- *Gen.* -a gibe.

przyciosać *pf.* hew (*to size*).

przycisk *mi* **1.** (= *klawisz*) (push *l.* press) button. **2.** (= *obciążnik*) weight; **przycisk do papieru** letter *l.* paper weight. **3.** *jęz.* (= *akcent*) stress. **4.** (= *podkreślenie*) emphasis.

przyciskać *ipf.*, **przycisnąć** *pf.* -snę -śniesz, -śnij **1.** (= *naciskać*) (*klawisz*) press, push; **przycisnąć kogoś do muru** drive *l.* push sb to the wall. **2.** (= *przygniatać*) press (*kogoś/coś* against sth/sb). **3.** (= *przytulać*) press, crush; **przycisnął ją do siebie** he crushed her to him. ~ **się** *ipf.*, **przycisnąć się** *pf.* **1.** (= *przywrzeć*) cling (*do czegoś* to sth). **2.** (= *przytulić się*) snuggle up (*do kogoś* to sb).

przyciszać *ipf.* (*muzykę, telewizor*) turn down; (*głos*) lower.

przyciszony *a.* (*o muzyce, telewizorze*) turned down low; (*o rozmowie, głosach*) hushed.

przyciszyć *pf. zob.* **przyciszać**.

przycumować *pf. żegl.* (= *mocować*) moor; (= *dokować*) berth.

przycupnąć *pf.* -nę -niesz, -nij crouch.

przyczadzić *pf.*, przyczadować *pf. pot.* (= *głośno grać*) pump up the volume, let it rip; (= *szybko jechać*) let it rip.

przyczaić się *pf.* -czaję -czaisz, -czaj, przyczajać się *ipf.* lurk; przyczaić się na kogoś lie in wait for sb.

przyczajony *a.* -eni lurking.

przyczep *mi anat.* attachment, insertion; przyczep mięśnia muscle attachment.

przyczepa *f. mot.* trailer; (*boczna do motocykla*) sidecar; przyczepa kempingowa trailer; *Br.* caravan.

przyczepiać *ipf.*, przyczepić *pf.* attach (*coś do czegoś* sth to sth); przyczepiać komuś etykietkę pin a label on sb; przyczepiać komuś łatkę have a dig at sb. ~ się *ipf.*, przyczepić się *pf.* 1. (= *przywrzeć, przylgnąć*) stick, attach (*do czegoś* to sth). 2. *pot.* (= *mieć nieuzasadnione pretensje*) pick (*do kogoś/czegoś* at sb/sth); (= *zmuszać ciągle do robienia czegoś*) pick (*do kogoś* on sb). 3. (= *narzucić swoją obecność*) tag along (*do kogoś* with sb); cling (*do kogoś* to sb); przyczepić się do kogoś jak rzep (do) psiego ogona cling to sb like a barnacle, stick to sb like a leech.

przyczepka *f. Gen.pl.* -ek 1. (= *mała przyczepa*) trailer; (*motocyklowa*) sidecar; na przyczepkę *przest.* in addition; poszli z nami na przyczepkę they tagged along with us. 2. *bot.* appendage.

przyczepność *f.* 1. *mot.* grip; mieć dobrą przyczepność have good grip. 2. *mech.* (*dynamiczna*) traction; (*statyczna*) adhesion.

przyczepny *a.* 1. (= *dający się przyczepić, dołączyć*) attached; (*o silniku*) outboard. 2. (= *czepny*) gripping. 3. *fiz.* adhesive.

przyczesać *pf.* -czeszę -czeszesz comb; przyczesać komuś/sobie włosy give sb's/one's hair a (quick) comb.

przyczłapać się *pf. pot.* drag o.s.; przyczłapać się do domu drag o.s. home.

przyczołgać się *pf.*, przyczołgiwać się *ipf.* come crawling, crawl (in).

przyczółek *mi* -łk- *Gen.* -a *l.* -u 1. *t. wojsk.* (*mostu*) bridgehead; (*wybrzeża*) beachhead. 2. *przen.* (= *ostoja*) stronghold, citadel.

przyczyna *f.* reason (*czegoś* for sth); cause (*czegoś* of *l.* for sth); przyczyna, dla której... the reason why... *l.* for which...; bez przyczyny for no reason; z tej przyczyny for that reason; nie bez przyczyny not without reason; z niewiadomych przyczyn for reasons unknown, for unknown reasons; z wiadomych przyczyn for known reasons; być przyczyną czegoś be the cause of sth, lie at the root of sth; wniknąć w przyczyny czegoś get at the root of sth; znaleźć przyczynę czegoś find the cause of sth.

przyczynek *mi* -nk- *form.* contribution.

przyczyniać się *ipf.*, przyczynić się *pf.* contribute (*do czegoś* to sth).

przyczynkarski *a. form.* contributory.

przyczynowo *adv. form.* causally.

przyczynowo-skutkowy *a. gł. form.* cause-and-effect, causal; związek przyczynowo-skutkowy cause-and-effect relationship, causal nexus.

przyczynowość *f. form.* causality, causation.

przyczynowy *a. gł. form.* causal; leczenie przyczynowe *med.* treating the cause; zdanie przyczynowe *gram.* causal sentence; związek przyczynowy causal connection *l.* relationship, causality.

przyćmić *pf.* -ij, przyćmiewać *ipf.* 1. (*lampę*) turn down; (*światło*) dim. 2. (= *przewyższyć, przytłumić*) overshadow, eclipse.

przyćmiony *a.* (*o kolorze*) dim; (*o świetle*) dull, dim.

przydać *pf. zob.* przydawać. ~ się *pf. zob.* przydawać się.

przydarzać się *ipf.*, przydarzyć się *pf.* happen (*komuś* to sb); *form.* befall (*komuś* sb).

przydatki *pl. Gen.* -ów *anat.* adnexa, appendages.

przydatność *f.* (= *użyteczność*) usability, usefulness; (= *odpowiedniość*) suitability (*kogoś na coś* of sb for sth, *czegoś do czegoś* of sth for sth); data przydatności do spożycia *handl.* best-before date, use-by date.

przydatny *a.* (= *użyteczny*) useful, helpful; (= *odpowiedni*) suitable (*na coś l. do czegoś* for sth); w czym mogę być ci przydatny? how can I help you? can I be of any use?

przydawać *ipf.* -aję -ajesz, -awaj *form.* lend; przydawać komuś powagi/czemuś wiarygodności lend authority to sb/credence to sth. ~ się *ipf.* come in useful, come in handy; be of use (*komuś* to sb, *na coś l. do czegoś* for sth); to na nic się nie przyda this is useless.

przydawka *f. Gen.pl.* -ek *gram.* attribute, noun modifier.

przydawkowy *a. gram.* attributive.

przydech *mi fon.* aspiration.

przydechowy *a. fon.* (*o spółgłosce*) aspirated.

przydenny *a.* bottom.

przydepnąć *ipf.*, przydeptać *pf.* tread (*coś* on sth).

przydługi *a.* lengthy, longish.

przydomek *mi* -mk- *Gen.* -u *l.* -a nickname.

przydomowy *a.* (*o ogrodzie, gospodarstwie*) adjoining to the house.

przydreptać *pf.* -pczę -pczesz *l.* -pcę -pcesz, -pcz toddle in, patter in.

przydrożny *a.* roadside; kapliczka przydrożna roadside shrine.

przyducha *f. ryb.* fish kills (*caused by an insufficient amount of oxygen*).

przydupas *mp pl.* -y *pog.* sidekick.

przydupić *pf. pot.* (= *złapać*) nail.

przydusić *pf.* -szę -sisz, przyduszać *ipf.* 1. (= *przygnieść*) crush. 2. (*płomień*) stifle. 3. (= *przyprzeć do muru*) push, press (*kogoś o coś* sb for sth).

przyduży *a.* slightly to big.

przydybać *pf.* catch (*kogoś na czymś* sb doing sth).

przydymić *pf.* (*np. szkiełko*) smoke.

przydymiony *a.* (= *przyćmiony*) dimmed; (= *przybrudzony dymem*) smoke-stained.

przydział *mi* **1.** (= *przydzielanie*) (*zadań*) assignment, allocation; (*osoby do grupy*) placement, assignment; *t. wojsk.* (*sprzętu, prowiantu*) issue. **2.** (= *działka*) allowance, share.

przydziałowy *a.* (= *przydzielony*) assigned; (= *standardowy*) standard-issue.

przydzielać *ipf.*, **przydzielić** *pf.* **1.** (= *przyznawać*) assign, allocate. **2.** (= *kierować*) assign, place.

przydźwięk *mi* hum.

przydźwiękowy *a.* (*o prędkości*) nearsonic.

przydźwigać *pf.* lug.

przyfastrygować *pf.* **1.** (= *przyszyć*) tack. **2.** *pot.* (= *uderzyć*) sock (*komuś* sb).

przyfrontowy *a.* frontline.

przyfrunąć *pf.* come flying.

przygadać *pf.*, **przygadywać** *ipf.* **1.** (= *docinać*) gibe, sneer (*komuś* at sb). **2.** (= *poderwać*) chat up. ~ **się** *pf.*, **przygadywać się** *ipf. pot.* sweettalk (*komuś* sb).

przygalopować *pf. dosł.*, *przen.* gallop.

przygana *f.* rap.

przyganiać *ipf.* **1.** (= *krytykować*) rap (*komuś* sb); **przyganiał kocioł garnkowi** (it's) the pot calling the kettle black, you're (he's etc.) a fine one to talk! **2.** (= *przypędzać*) drive in.

przygarbić się *pf.* stoop, slouch.

przygarnąć *pf.* **-ij**, **przygarniać** *ipf.* **1.** (= *przytulić*) clasp; **przygarnąć kogoś do serca** *l.* **do piersi** clasp sb in one's arms. **2.** (= *dać schronienie*) take in, take under one's roof.

przygarść *f. przest.* handful (*czegoś* of sth).

przygasać *ipf. zob.* **przygasnąć**.

przygasić *pf.* **-szę -sisz** (*światła*) dim, turn down; (*urodę, zapał*) dim, overshadow.

przygasły *a.* (*o wzroku, spojrzeniu*) lackluster; (*o blasku*) weak.

przygasnąć *pf.* **-nę -niesz, -nij** (*o światłach*) dim; (*o popularności*) wane.

przygaszony *a.* **-eni** subdued.

przygiąć *pf.*, **przyginać** *ipf.* bend. ~ **się** *pf.*, **przyginać się** *ipf.* **1.** (= *zgarbić się*) stoop. **2.** (*o krzewach, drzewach*) bend.

przyglądać się *ipf.* watch, observe (*komuś/czemuś* sb/sth); **przyjrzeć się sprawie** look into the matter.

przygładzać *ipf.*, **przygładzać** *pf.* (*włosy*) smooth (down); (*sukienkę*) smooth (out).

przygłuchy *a.* hard of hearing.

przygłup *mp pl.* **-y** *obelż.* butthead, dumbbell.

przygłupi *a. obelż.* (*o osobie*) dumb, braindead; *uj.* (*o filmie, historyjce*) inane.

przygnać *pf.* **1.** (= *przybiec*) come running. **2.** (= *przygonić*) drive in.

przygnębiać *ipf.* depress.

przygnębiająco *adv.* depressingly.

przygnębiający *a.* depressing; **coś sprawia przygnębiające wrażenie** sth is depressing.

przygnębienie *n.* depression; **otrząsnąć się z przygnębienia** get over one's depression; **ogarnęło mnie przygnębienie** I got depressed.

przygnębiony *a.* **-eni** depressed, cheerless (*czymś* about sth).

przygniatać *ipf.* **1.** (= *przyciskać*) crush. **2.** (= *obciążać*) weigh down. **3.** (= *przygnębiać*) bear hard (*kogoś* on sb).

przygniatający *a.* (*o uczuciu, ciszy, większości*) overwhelming.

przygnieść *pf.* **-gniotę -gnieciesz -gniótł -gniotła -gnietli** *zob.* **przygniatać**.

przygoda *f. Gen.pl.* **-ód 1.** (= *niecodzienne wydarzenie*) adventure; **przygody** adventure. **2.** (= *romans*) affair.

przygodny *a.* casual; **przygodna znajomość** passing acquaintance.

przygodowy *a.* (*o powieści, filmie*) adventure.

przygonić *pf. zob.* **przyganiać** 2.

przygotować *pf. zob.* **przygotowywać**. ~ **się** *pf. zob.* **przygotowywać się**.

przygotowanie *n.* preparation; **czynić przygotowania (do czegoś)** make preparations (for sth).

przygotowany *a.* prepared (*do czegoś* for sth).

przygotowawczy *a.* preparatory; **kurs przygotowawczy** preparation *l.* induction course.

przygotowywać *ipf.* prepare, get ready; **przygotowywać coś na czas** get sth ready on time; **przygotowywać kogoś na coś** *l.* **do czegoś** prepare sb for sth, get sb ready for sth. ~ **się** *ipf.* prepare (o.s.), get (o.s.) ready (*do czegoś* for sth); **przygotowywać się na najgorsze** prepare for the worst; **przygotowywać się do egzaminu** study for an exam.

przygraniczny *a.* frontier, border; **handel przygraniczny** frontier trade.

przygruby *a.* (*o osobie*) slightly too fat; (*o przedmiocie*) slightly too thick.

przygruchać *pf. pot.* chat up.

przygruntowy *a.* low-lying; **przygruntowe przymrozki** *meteor.* ground frost.

przygrywać *ipf.* **-am -asz** accompany (*komuś* sb); **przygrywać do tańca** play (some) dance music; **przygrywać na gitarze** play guitar.

przygrywka *f. Gen.pl.* **-ek 1.** *muz.* intro, introduction. **2.** (= *przedsmak*) prelude (*do czegoś* to sth); curtain-raiser (*do czegoś* for *l.* to sth).

przygryzać *ipf.*, **przygryźć** *pf.* **-gryzę -gryziesz -gryzł-gryźli 1.** (= *przyciąć zębami*) bite (*coś* into sth); **przygryzać wargi** bite one's lips; **przygryźć sobie wargę/język** bite one's lip/tongue. **2.** *pot.* (= *robić złośliwe uwagi*) gibe (*komuś* at sb).

przygrzać *pf.* **-grzeję -grzejesz -grzał -grzali** *l.* **-grzeli, przygrzewać** *ipf.* **1.** (= *odgrzać*) heat up. **2.** (*o słońcu*) beat down. **3.** *pot.* (= *uderzyć*) bang (*komuś* sb); **przygrzać głową w drzwi** bang one's head on the door.

przygważdżać *ipf.*, **przygwoździć** *pf.* **-żdżę -ździsz** (*argumentami*) crush; (*wzrokiem*) impale.

przygwożdżony *a.* **-eni przygwożdżony do łóżka** bed-ridden.

przyhamować *pf.*, **przyhamowywać** *ipf.* slow down, brake.

przyholować *pf.*, **przyholowywać** *ipf.* tow in.

przyimek *mi* **-mk-** *Gen.* **-a** *gram.* preposition.

przyimkowy *a. gram.* prepositional; **wyrażenie przyimkowe** prepositional phrase.

przyjaciel *mp pl.* **-e** *Acc. i Gen.* **-ół** *Dat.* **-ołom** *Loc.* **-ołach** 1. (= *bliska osoba*) friend; **bliski/prawdziwy przyjaciel** close/true friend; **przyjaciel domu** friend of the family, family friend; **prawdziwego przyjaciela poznaje się w biedzie** a friend in need is a friend indeed. 2. (= *protektor, wielbiciel*) friend, lover; **przyjaciel zwierząt** animal lover. 3. *euf.* (= *kochanek*) boyfriend; (*starszy i zamożny*) sugar daddy.

przyjacielski *a.* friendly.

przyjaciółka *f. Gen.pl.* **-ek** 1. (= *kobieta obdarzana zaufaniem, sympatią*) friend, girlfriend; **zaufana/najlepsza przyjaciółka** special/best friend. 2. (= *protektorka*) friend, lover; **przyjaciółka zwierząt** animal lover. 3. *euf.* (= *kochanka*) girlfriend.

przyjazd *mi Loc.* **-eździe** arrival; **planowy przyjazd pociągu o godzinie...** the train is due at...

przyjazdowy *a.* arrival; **hala przyjazdowa** arrival hall.

przyjazny *a.* friendly; **przyjazny dla środowiska/użytkownika** environment-/user-friendly; **podać komuś przyjazną dłoń** *l.* **rękę** lend sb a helping hand.

przyjaźnić się *ipf.* **-ij** *l.* **-ń** be friends (*z kimś* with sb).

przyjaźnie *adv.* in a friendly manner, amicably; **przyjaźnie usposobiony** *l.* **nastawiony (do kogoś/czegoś)** well-disposed (towards sb/sth).

przyjaźń *f. pl.* **-e** friendship; **darzyć kogoś przyjaźnią** be sb's friend; **nawiązywać przyjaźń (z kimś)** form a friendship (with sb); **żyć z kimś w przyjaźni** get along well with sb.

przyjąć *pf.* **-mę -miesz, -mij** *zob.* **przyjmować.** ~ **się** *pf. zob.* **przyjmować się.**

przyjechać *pf.* **-jadę -jedziesz** *zob.* **przyjeżdżać.**

przyjemniaczek *mp* **-czk-** *pl.* **-i** *uj.* sorehead.

przyjemnie *adv.* nicely, pleasantly; **przyjemnie spędzać czas** have a nice time; **jest przyjemnie** it is nice; **jak tu przyjemnie!** it is so nice here!; **byłoby mi bardzo przyjemnie** I'd be delighted; **przyjemnie jej się słucha** she's a joy to listen to.

przyjemność *f.* 1. (= *uczucie zadowolenia*) pleasure; **sprawiać komuś przyjemność** please sb; **podróżować dla przyjemności** travel for pleasure; **znajdować w czymś przyjemność** take pleasure in sth; **z przyjemnością** with pleasure; my pleasure; **cała przyjemność po mojej stronie** the pleasure is all mine; **miałem już przyjemność ją poznać** I've already had the pleasure of meeting her; **to nie należy do przyjemności** it's not particularly enjoyable; **to średnia przyjemność** *pot.* it's not all roses; **z kim mam przyjemność?** with whom do I have the pleasure?; **najpierw obowiązek, potem przyjemność** business before pleasure. 2. (= *to, co się podoba*) indulgence; pleasure; **uganiać się za przyjemnościami** seek pleasure; **używać przyjemności** indulge o.s.

przyjemny *a.* (*osoba, dzień*) nice; (*dzień, sytuacja*) pleasant; (= *zadowalający*) (*np. maniery, zachowanie*) agreeable; **łączyć przyjemne z poży-** tecznym combine business with pleasure; **przyjemny dla oka/ucha** pleasing to the eye/ear.

przyjezdna *f. Gen.* **-ej**, przyjezdny *mp* visitor.

przyjezdny *a.* visiting.

przyjeżdżać *ipf.*, przyjechać *pf.* arrive, come (over) (*czymś* by sth); **przyjechać samochodem/pociągiem** come by car/train; **przyjeżdżać z wizytą** (*gdzieś*) come on a visit; (*do kogoś*) come to visit (*do kogoś* sb); **przyjeżdżać po kogoś** come to pick sb up.

przyjęcie *n.* 1. (*spotkanie towarzyskie*) reception. 2. (*do szpitala; kandydata, studenta*) admission; (*pomysłu, wniosku*) adoption; (*prezentu*) acceptance; (*do pracy*) hiring; **godziny przyjęć** office hours; **izba przyjęć** admission room; **przyjęcie towaru** delivery; **spotkać się z chłodnym/gorącym przyjęciem** meet with a cold/warm reception *l.* welcome; **to jest nie do przyjęcia** this is unacceptable; **zgotować komuś serdeczne przyjęcie** give sb a warm welcome.

przyjęty *a.* (*o zwyczaju, praktyce*) established, customary; (*o kandydacie*) admitted.

przyjmować *ipf.* 1. (= *brać; nie odrzucać*) accept; (*lekarstwo*) take; (*meldunek, raport, skargę*) take note (*coś* of sth); (*nazwisko, nazwę*) assume; (*dostawę*) receive; (*postawę, rezolucję, wniosek*) adopt; (*protestantyzm, katolicyzm*) convert (*coś* to sth); (*sakrament, chrzest*) *rel.* receive; (*obywatelstwo*) assume; **przyjmować defiladę** review (troops); **przyjmować w zastaw** take in pawn. 2. (= *przygarniać kogoś*) take in; (*uchodźców, uciekinierów*) (*o kraju*) admit. 3. (= *podejmować się czegoś, zgadzać się na coś*) accept; (*wniosek, ustawę*) pass; **przyjąć coś do wiadomości** take note of sth; **przyjmować coś na wiarę** take sth on faith. 4. (= *angażować, wcielać kogoś*) (*do pracy*) engage, employ; (*do szkoły, do szpitala*) admit. 5. (= *podejmować*) (*gości*) entertain, receive; **przyjąć kogoś obiadem** treat sb to dinner. 6. (*petentów, interesantów, pacjentów*) see. 7. (= *reagować*) receive, take; **coś przyjęło zły/dobry obrót** sth took an unfavorable/a favorable *l.* good turn; **dobrze coś przyjmować** take sth well; **przyjąć coś za dobrą monetę** take sth at face value; **zostać entuzjastycznie przyjętym** *teatr* (*o przedstawieniu*) bring down the house. 8. (= *zakładać, że...*) assume. 9. (*w zwrotach*) **przyjmować kształt** take shape; **przyjmować podanie** *sport* take a pass; **przyjmować poród** deliver a baby; **przyjmować wartość** *mat.* (*o zmiennej*) take on a value. 10. (= *wchłaniać*) (*wodę, promieniowanie*) absorb. ~ **się** *ipf.* 1. (*o posadzonych roślinach*) take *l.* strike root. 2. (*o szczepionce*) take. 3. (= *upowszechniać się*) (*o modzie, zwyczajach, nazwie*) catch on.

przyjrzeć się *pf.* **-ę -ysz, -yj** *zob.* **przyglądać się.**

przyjść *pf.* **przyjdę przyjdziesz przyszedł przyszła przyszli** *zob.* **przychodzić.**

przykazać *pf.* **-każę -każesz** *zob.* **przykazywać.**

przykazanie *n.* 1. (= *polecenie*) command, order; (= *upomnienie*) injunction. 2. *rel.* commandment.

przykazywać *ipf.* command (*coś komuś* sb to do sth).

przyklaskiwać *ipf.*, **przyklasnąć** *pf.* **-snę -śniesz, -śnij** applaud (*czemuś* sth).

przyklasztorny *a.* (*o ogrodzie, bibliotece*) (*w klasztorze żeńskim*) convent; (*w klasztorze męskim*) monastery.

przykleić *pf.* **-eję -eisz, -ej, przyklejać** *ipf.* stick; (*klejem*) glue; (*taśmą*) tape; **przykleić komuś jakąś etykietkę** label sb as sth; **przykleić znaczek (na list)** put *l.* stick a stamp on (a letter); **uśmiech przyklejony do ust** glued-on smile. **~ się** *pf.*, **przyklejać się** *ipf.* **1.** (= *przylgnąć*) stick, get stuck. **2.** *pot.* (= *narzucić komuś swoją obecność*) tag along (*do kogoś* with sb).

przyklepać *pf.* (= *wygładzić*) pat, smooth; **przyklepać umowę** *pot.* seal a deal with a handshake.

przyklęk *mi* kneel; *kośc.* genuflection.

przyklękać *ipf.*, **przyklęknąć** *pf.* **-klęknę -klękniesz, -klęknij, -klęknął** *l.* **-kląkł -klękła -klęknęli** *l.* **-klękli** kneel; *kośc.* genuflect.

przykład *mi* **1.** (= *wzór*) example; **dla przykładu** (*np. ukarać kogoś*) as a warning; **brać z kogoś przykład** follow sb's example; **być typowym przykładem czegoś** be a typical example of sth, epitomize sth; **dawać dobry/zły przykład** set a good/bad example; **iść za czyimś przykładem** follow sb's lead; **świecić przykładem** set a good example; **przykład cnoty** model of virtue; **przykład idzie z góry** those in charge set the standards of conduct; you follow the example of your superiors. **2.** (= *ilustracja tezy*) example; **na przykład** for example, for instance; **dla przykładu** as an example, by way of example; **typowy/klasyczny/ najlepszy przykład** typical/classic/prime example (*czegoś* of sth); **stanowić przykład czegoś** exemplify sth; **daj choćby jeden przykład** give at least one example.

przykładać *ipf.* **1.** (= *stykać coś z czymś*) put (*coś do czegoś* sth against sth); (*kompres*) apply; (*pieczęć*) affix; **przyłożyć komuś nóż do gardła** put a knife to sb's throat; **ja nie przyłożę do tego ręki** *przen.* I won't have anything to do with it; **przykładać (dużą) wagę do czegoś** *przen.* attach (a lot of) importance to sth, put (much) stock in sth; **że do rany przyłóż** (as) nice as pie. **2.** (= *obciążyć*) weigh down (*czymś* with sth). **3.** (= *dołożyć*) give some more. **4.** *zw. pf. pot.* (= *zbić*) hit (*komuś* sb). **~ się** *ipf.* **1.** (= *starać się*) apply o.s.; (*do czegoś* to sth) do one's best. **2.** *pot.* (= *położyć się na spoczynek*) get to bed.

przykładnica *f.* (*narzędzie*) T-square.

przykładnie *adv.* properly; in an exemplary way; **żyć przykładnie** lead an exemplary life.

przykładny *a.* exemplary; (*o mężu, żonie*) model.

przykładowo *adv.* by way of example, as an instance; *pot.* (= *na przykład*) for example, for instance.

przykładowy *a.* (= *użyty jako przykład*) (*np. sytuacja*) hypothetical; (= *będący przykładem czegoś*) (*np. test, pytanie testowe*) sample; (= *typowy*) exemplary.

przykościelny *a.* church; **cmentarz przykościelny** churchyard.

przykręcać *ipf.*, **przykręcić** *pf.* **1.** (*śrubę, żarówkę*) screw in; (*półkę, osłonę*) screw; **przykręcać coś do czegoś** screw sth to sth; **przykręcić komuś śrubę** tighten the screws on sb. **2.** (= *zmniejszać dopływ*) (*wodę, gaz, światło*) turn down.

przykro *adv.* unpleasantly; **jest mi przykro, że...** I'm sorry that...; **(on) wygląda tak źle, że aż przykro patrzeć** (*o kimś chorym, w depresji*) he's a sorry sight; (*o kimś zaniedbanym, bezdomnym*) he's a pitiful sight.

przykrochmalać się *ipf.*, **przykrochmalić się** *pf.* **pot.** tag along (*do kogoś* with sb).

przykroić *pf.* cut to size.

przykrość *f.* **1.** (*uczucie*) distress; **mówię to z przykrością** I hate to say this; **z przykrością muszę stwierdzić, że...** I regret to conclude that...; **sprawiłeś mi wielką przykrość** you made me very sad. **2.** (= *to, co wywołuje to uczucie*) unpleasantness; trouble; **miałem przez ciebie mnóstwo przykrości** you caused me plenty of trouble; **nie chciałbym narazić cię na przykrości** I wouldn't like to get you into trouble.

przykrócić *pf.* curb; **przykrócić komuś cugli** whip sb into line.

przykrótki *a.* shortish.

przykry *a.* unpleasant; (*o szoku, niespodziance*) nasty; (*o osobie, tonie, wydarzeniu*) ugly; **przykry widok** (= *zasmucający*) sorry sight; (= *godny pożałowania*) pitiful sight; **przykry stan rzeczy** sad state of affairs; **przykre usposobienie** *l.* **przykry charakter** unpleasant *l.* nasty character; **być przykrym wobec kogoś** be nasty to sb; **powiedzieć komuś parę przykrych słów** give sb the rough side of one's tongue; **usłyszeć parę przykrych słów od kogoś** feel the rough side of sb's tongue.

przykrycie *n.* cover, covering; **gotować coś pod przykryciem** cook *l.* simmer sth in a covered pot.

przykryć *pf.* **-yję -yjesz, -yj** *zob.* **przykrywać. ~ się** *pf. zob.* **przykrywać się.**

przykrywa *f.* lid.

przykrywać *ipf.* **-am -asz** cover (up). **~ się** *ipf.* cover o.s. (up) (*czymś* with sth).

przykrywka *f. Gen.pl.* **-ek 1.** (*np. garnka*) lid. **2.** *przen.* cover-up; **być przykrywką dla czegoś** *przen.* be a cover-up for sth; **pod przykrywką czegoś** under the cover *l.* guise of sth.

przykrywkowy *a.* (*o szkiełku*) cover.

przykrzyć się *ipf.* **1.** (= *nudzić się*) be boring; **przykrzyło mi się czekać na niego** having to wait for him was so boring. **2.** (= *być znużonym*) be tired (*czymś* of sth); **przykrzy mi się ta praca** I'm sick of this work. **3.** (= *być uciążliwym*) be a nuisance (*komuś* to sb); **przykrzy mi się bezczynność** idleness is such a nuisance.

przykucać *ipf.*, **przykucnąć** *pf.* **-nę -niesz, -nij** squat, crouch down.

przykuć *pf. zob.* **przykuwać.**

przykurcz *mi Gen.pl.* **-y** *l.* **-ów** *med.* contracture.

przykuty *a.* (*łańcuchem*) chained (*do czegoś* to sth); **przykuty do łóżka** *przen.* bedridden.

przykuwać *ipf.* (*łańcuchem*) chain (*do czegoś*

to sth); **przykuwać czyjąś uwagę** rivet sb's attention; **przykuwać czyjś wzrok** catch sb's eye; **przykuwać kogoś do łóżka** *przen.* confine sb to bed; **stał przykuty do miejsca** he stood transfixed.

przylać *pf.* -leję -lejesz -lał -lali *l.* -leli **1.** *zob.* **przylewać. 2.** *pot.* (= *zbić*) beat up.

przylaszczka *f. Gen.pl.* -ek *bot.* hepatica (*Hepatica*).

przylatywać *ipf.* **1.** (*o ptakach, owadach*) fly in. **2.** (*o samolotach*) arrive. **3.** (= *przybywać dokądś samolotem*) fly in. **4.** *pot.* (= *przybiec*) come running. **5.** *zob.* **przylecieć.**

przylądek *mi* -dk- *Gen.* -a cape, headland; **Przylądek Dobrej Nadziei** Cape of Good Hope.

przylecieć *pf.* -cę -cisz **1.** *zob.* **przylatywać. 2.** *pot.* (= *przybiec*) come running.

przylegać *ipf.* **1.** (= *opinać, przywierać*) stick (*do czegoś* to sth); (*o ubraniu*) cling. **2.** (= *sąsiadować*) (*o pokoju*) adjoin (*do czegoś* sth); (*o polu, łące*) border (*do czegoś* on sth).

przylegający *a.* **1.** (= *opinający, przywierający*) (*o ubraniu*) close-fitting; (*o sukience*) clingy. **2.** (= *sąsiadujący*) adjacent (*do czegoś* to sth); (*o pokoju*) adjoing (*do czegoś* sth).

przyleganie *n. chem., fiz.* adhesion.

przyległości *pl. Gen.* -i outbuildings and adjacent land.

przyległy *a.* adjacent (*do czegoś* to sth); adjoining (*do czegoś* sth); **kąt przyległy** *geom.* adjacent angle.

przylepiać *ipf.*, **przylepić** *pf.* stick; (*klejem*) glue; (*taśmą*) tape; **przylepić komuś jakąś etykietkę** label sb as sth; **przylepić znaczek (na list)** put *l.* stick a stamp on (a letter); **uśmiech przylepiony do ust** glued-on smile. **~ się** *ipf.*, **przylepić się** *pf.* **1.** (= *przylgnąć*) stick, get stuck. **2.** *pot.* (= *narzucić komuś swoją obecność*) tag along (*do kogoś* with sb).

przylepiec *mi* -pc- *Gen.* -a **1.** (= *plaster*) Band-Aid®; *Br.* sticking plaster. **2.** (= *rzep przy odzieży, obuwiu*) Velcro®.

przylepka *f. Gen.pl.* -ek **1.** *żart.* (*dziecko*) sweetie. **2.** *dial.* (= *piętka chleba*) heel.

przylepność *f.* adhesiveness; stickiness.

przylepny *a.* **1.** (*o plastrze*) sticking; adhesive. **2.** (*o dziecku*) endearing.

przyleźć *pf.* -lezę -leziesz -lazł -leźli *zob.* **przyłazić.**

przylga *f.* **1.** *bud.* rabbet. **2.** *ent.* pad.

przylgnąć *pf.* -nę -niesz, -nij **1.** (= *przywrzeć*) cling (*do kogoś / czegoś* to sb/sth). **2.** (*o nazwie, przezwisku*) stick (*do kogoś* to sb).

przylistek *mi* -tk- *Gen.* -a *bot.* stipule.

przylizać się *pf.* -liżę -liżesz *zob.* **przylizywać się.**

przylizany *a.* (*o włosach, fryzurze*) *pot.* slicked (down).

przylizywać się *ipf. pot.* slick down one's hair.

przylot *mi* **1.** (*o samolocie*) arrival; **hala przylotów** arrival lounge. **2.** (*o ptakach*) coming.

przylutować *pf.*, **przylutowywać** *ipf.* **1.** (*przymocować*) solder on. **2.** (*uderzyć*) *pot.* wallop (*komuś* sb).

przyładować *pf. pot.* (= *uderzyć*) wallop (*komuś* sb).

przyłapać *pf.* -pię -piesz, **przyłapywać** *ipf.* catch (*kogoś na czymś* sb doing sth); **przyłapać kogoś na gorącym uczynku** catch sb red-handed *l.* in the act. **~ się** *pf.*, **przyłapywać się** *ipf.* catch o.s. (*na czymś* doing sth).

przyłazić *ipf.* -łażę -łazisz *pot.* come; show one's mug.

przyłączać *ipf.*, **przyłączyć** *pf.* **1.** attach (*coś do czegoś* sth to sth). **2.** (*budynek, komputer*) link; (*do instalacji wodociągowej, gazowej*) plumb in; (*do instalacji elektrycznej, telefonicznej*) connect. **3.** *chem.* bond. **~ się** *ipf.*, **przyłączyć się** *pf.* **1.** (*do jakiejś grupy*) join (in); (*do zbiórki pieniędzy, pracy, pomocy*) join in, pitch in. **2.** *chem.* bond.

przyłbica *f.* **1.** *hist.* visor; **robić coś z podniesioną przyłbicą** *pot.* do sth openly. **2.** *techn.* helmet shield; *Br.* visor.

przyłoić *pf.* -łoję -łoisz, -łój *pot.* beat up.

przyłożenie *n. rugby* try; **punkt przyłożenia siły** *fiz.* point of application of force.

przyłożyć *pf.* -łożę -łożysz, -łóż *zob.* **przykładać.** **~ się** *pf. zob.* **przykładać się.**

przymało *adv. pot.* somewhat too little; somewhat too few.

przymały *a.* smallish, a bit too small; (*o butach, spodniach*) a bit too tight.

przymarzać *ipf.*, **przymarznąć** *pf.* -nę -niesz, -nij, -marzną *l.* -marzł -marzła freeze (*do czegoś* to sth) (*do siebie* together).

przymaszerować *pf.* come marching.

przymiar *mi techn.* gauge.

przymiarka *f. Gen.pl.* -ek **1.** (*u krawca*) fitting. **2.** (= *próba*) trial run.

przymierać *ipf.* **przymierać głodem** starve.

przymierzać *ipf.* (*ubranie*) try on; (*jedną rzecz do drugiej*) compare (*coś do czegoś* sth with sth); **nie przymierzając** *przen.* if I may say so; if you'll excuse the comparison. **~ się** *ipf.* get ready (*do czegoś* for sth).

przymierzalnia *f. Gen.pl.* -i fitting room.

przymierze *n. Gen.pl.* -y alliance; *rel.* covenant; **Arka Przymierza** *rel.* Ark of the Covenant.

przymierzyć *pf. zob.* **przymierzać. ~ się** *pf. zob.* **przymierzać się.**

przymieszka *f. Gen.pl.* -ek (= *domieszka*) admixture.

przymilać się *ipf.* endear o.s. (*do kogoś* to sb).

przymilny *a.* (*o człowieku, uśmiechu*) ingratiating.

przymiot *mi* (= *zaleta*) virtue; (= *cecha*) attribute.

przymiotnik *mi Gen.* -a *gram.* adjective.

przymiotnikowy *a. gram.* adjectival; adjective.

przymiotny *a. gram.* adjectival.

przymknąć *pf.* -nę -niesz, -nij *zob.* **przymykać. ~ się** *pf.* **1.** *zob.* **przymykać się. 2.** *pot.* (= *zamilknąć*) shut one's trap, shut up.

przymocować *pf.*, **przymocowywać** *ipf.* fix, fasten (*coś do czegoś* sth to sth).

przymorze *n.* coastal regions.

przymrozek *mi* -zk- frost; **przygruntowy przymrozek** ground frost.

przymrużać *ipf.* narrow; **przymrużył oko** he winked; **przymrużył oczy** he squinted.

przymrużenie *n.* squint; **powiedzieć coś z przymrużeniem oka** say sth with tongue in cheek; **traktować coś z przymrużeniem oka** take sth with a pinch *l.* grain of salt.

przymrużyć *pf. zob.* **przymrużać.**

przymus *mi* (= *presja*) coercion; (*wewnętrzny, moralny*) compulsion; **przymus fizyczny** physical constraint; **robić coś bez przymusu** do sth without any constraint; **robić coś pod przymusem** do sth under compulsion *l.* coercion; *prawn.* do sth under duress; **środki przymusu** measures of coercion *l.* compulsion.

przymusić *pf.* -szę -sisz *zob.* **przymuszać.** ~ **się** *pf. zob.* **przymuszać się.**

przymusowo *adv.* (= *obowiązkowo*) compulsorily; (= *siłą*) forcedly.

przymusowy *a.* compulsory, obligatory; (*o lądowaniu, pracy*) forced.

przymuszać *ipf.* force (*kogoś do czegoś* sb to do sth); coerce (*kogoś do czegoś* sb into doing sth). ~ **się** *ipf.* force o.s. (*do czegoś* to do sth).

przymykać *ipf.* **1.** (= *zamykać niecałkowicie*) (*o drzwiach, oknie*) leave *l.* set ajar; **przymykać na coś oczy** turn a blind eye to sth. **2.** *pot.* (= *aresztować*) pinch. ~ **się** *ipf.* **1.** (*o drzwiach, oknie*) shut, close. **2.** (*o człowieku*) shut up; **przymknij się!** *pot.* keep your mouth shut!; pipe down!

przynaglać *ipf.*, **przynaglić** *pf.* -lę -lisz, -lij rush (*kogoś do czegoś* sb to do sth).

przynaglająco *adv.* pressingly.

przynajmniej *adv.* at least; **bądźcie przynajmniej godzinę przed odlotem** arrive at least an hour before the take-off time.

przynależności *pl. Gen.* -i *prawn.* fixtures.

przynależność *f.* affiliation; (*do partii, do organizacji*) membership; **przynależność etniczna** ethnicity; **przynależność państwowa** nationality; **związek przynależności** *gram.* collocation.

przynęcać *ipf.* entice.

przynęta *f.* bait; **stanowić przynętę** (*dla kogoś*) act as a decoy; **założyć przynętę na haczyk/do pułapki** bait a hook/trap.

przynieść *pf.* -niosę -niesiesz -niósł -niosła -nieśli, przynosił -noszę -nosisz **1.** (= *dostarczyć*) bring; **mówić, co ślina na język przyniesie** blabber; **co cię tu przyniosło?** what brought you here?; **diabli go przynieśli** what is he doing here? **2.** (= *przemieścić*) (*zapach, dźwięk*) bring, carry. **3.** (= *spowodować*) (*suszę, ulewę, ulgę, skutek, zmiany*) bring (about); **przynosić więcej szkody niż pożytku** bring more harm than good; **przynosić wstyd komuś/czemuś** be a disgrace to sb/sth. **4.** (= *poinformować, donieść*) (*sprawozdanie, opis, recenzje*) carry. **5.** (= *dać korzyści materialne*) bring in, generate.

przynosowy *a. anat.* paranasal; **zatoki przynosowe** nasal sinuses.

przynudzać *ipf. pot.* drone on (*o czymś* about sth).

przyoblec *pf.* -lekę -leczesz -lekł, **przyoblekać** *ipf.* array (*kogoś w coś* sb in sth). ~ **się** *pf.* array o.s. (*w coś* in sth).

przyodziać *pf.*, **przyodziewać** *ipf.* clothe (*kogoś w coś* sb in sth). ~ **się** *pf.*, **przyodziewać** *ipf.* clothe (*w coś* in sth).

przyozdabiać *ipf.*, **przyozdobić** *pf.* -dób adorn (*coś czymś* sth with sth). ~ **się** *ipf.*, **przyozdobić się** *pf.* adorn o.s. (*czymś* with sth).

przypadać *ipf.* **1.** (= *przywrzeć*) fall; **przypaść do ziemi** fall to the ground; **przypaść komuś do kolan** fall to sb's knees; **nie przypadł mi do gustu** I didn't take a liking to him. **2.** (= *dostać się komuś*) fall to; (*o nagrodzie, spadku*) go to; **ten wielki zaszczyt przypadł mi w udziale** this great honor falls to my lot; **to przypada na niedzielę/maj** it falls on Sunday/in May.

przypadkiem *mi* **1.** (= *zdarzenie*) coincidence, chance; **od przypadku do przypadku** from time to time; **przez przypadek** by accident *l.* chance; **to kwestia przypadku** it's a matter of chance; **w przypadku** in case of; in the event of. **2.** *med.* case; **nagły przypadek** emergency case; **szczególny przypadek** special case. **3.** *Gen.* -a *gram.* case.

przypadkiem *adv.* by chance *l.* accident; accidently; **czy nie widziałaś przypadkiem, gdzie położyłem kluczyki?** did you happen to see where I put my keys?; **nie masz przypadkiem jakichś drobnych?** you don't have any small change by any chance?

przypadkowo *adv.* by chance *l.* accident; accidently.

przypadkowość *f.* casualness; randomness.

przypadkowy *a.* **1.** (= *niezamierzony*) accidental; (*o próbce, ułożeniu*) random; (*o znajomości, spotkaniu*) chance; (*o kontaktach seksualnych*) casual; (*o zajęciu, pracy*) odd; (*o kuli, iskrze*) stray. **2.** *gram.* (*końcówka, forma*) case.

przypadłość *f.* (= *niedomaganie*) ailment; (= *choroba*) affliction.

przypalać *ipf.* **1.** (= *palić z wierzchu*) singe; (*o mięsie, mleku*) burn. **2.** *pot.* (= *palić*) smoke; **przypalić od kogoś papierosa** light one's cigarette off sb else's; *sl.* **przypalać gandzię** smoke ganja. ~ **się** *ipf.* (*na słońcu*) sunburn.

przypalenizna *f.* **1.** (= *przypalona warstwa*) burnt layer. **2.** (= *zapach czegoś przypalonego*) smell of sth burnt.

przypalić *pf. zob.* **przypalać.** ~ **się** *pf. zob.* **przypalać się.**

przypalony *a.* (*o mięsie, rybie, zupie*) burnt; (*od słońca*) sunburnt.

przypałętać się *pf. pot.* drag o.s. in.

przypasać *pf.* -szę -szesz *zob.* **przypasywać. przypasować** *pf.* fit.

przypasywać *ipf.* gird (on); **przypasać miecz** gird (on) one's sword.

przypaść *pf.* -padnę -padniesz, -padnij, -padł *zob.* **przypadać.**

przypatrywać się *ipf.*, **przypatrzeć się** *pf.* scrutinize (*komuś/czemuś* sb/sth); have a good look (*komuś/czemuś* at sb/sth).

przypełzać, przypełznąć *pf.* come crawling.

przypędzać *ipf.*, **przypędzić** *pf.* drive in.

przypętać się *pf. pot.* drag o.s. in.
przypiąć *pf.* -nę -niesz, -nij *zob.* **przypinać. ~ się** *pf. zob.* **przypinać się.**
przypiec *pf.* -piekę -pieczesz -piekł *zob.* **przypiekać. ~ się** *pf. zob.* **przypiekać się.**
przypieczętować *pf.*, **przypieczętowywać** *ipf.* seal.
przypiekać *ipf.* **1.** (*na ogniu*) roast; (*chleb, ser*) toast; (= *przyrumieniać*) brown. **2.** (*o słońcu*) beat down. **~ się** *ipf.* **1.** (*na ogniu*) roast; (*o chlebie, serze*) toast; (= *przyrumieniać się*) brown. **2.** *pot.* (*na słońcu*) suntan.
przypieprzać się *ipf. pot.* **przypieprzać się do kogoś** get on sb's back.
przypieprzyć *pf. pot.* **przypieprzyć komuś** beat the shit out of sb. **~ się** *pf. zob.* **przypieprzać się.**
przypierać *ipf.* pin (*kogoś do czegoś* sb against *l.* to sth); **przypierać kogoś do muru** drive *l.* push sb to the wall.
przypierdalać się *ipf. wulg.* **przypierdalać się do kogoś** get on sb's ass.
przypierdolić *pf. wulg.* **przypierdolić komuś** knock the living shit out of sb. **~ się** *pf. zob.* **przypierdalać się.**
przypierniczać się *ipf.*, **przypierniczyć się** *pf. pot.* **przypierniczać się do kogoś** hit on sb.
przypilać *ipf.*, **przypilić** *pf. pot.* hustle; **przypiliło go** he was taken short.
przypilnować *pf.* look after (*czegoś* sth); take care (*czegoś* of sth); **przypilnować, żeby coś zostało zrobione** see to it that sth is done.
przypinać *ipf.* (*szpiką*) pin; (*pinezką*) tack; (*pasami*) strap; (*broszkę*) pin; (*narty*) put on; **przypiąć komuś łatkę** have a dig at sb; **ni przypiął, ni przyłatał** without rhyme or reason. **~ się** *ipf. pot.* cling (*do czegoś* to sth).
przypis *mi* (*na dole strony*) footnote; (*na końcu tekstu*) endnote.
przypisać *pf.* -piszę -piszesz, **przypisywać** *ipf.* **1.** ascribe, attribute (*coś komuś* sth to sb); **nie jestem pewna, czemu to przypisać** I'm not sure how to account for it; **przypisywać sobie coś** claim credit for sth. **2.** (*do grupy, kategorii*) classify as. **3.** *hist.* (*o chłopie*) attach.
przypisaniec *mp* -ńc- *pl.* -y *hist.* bondman.
przypisek *mi* postscript.
przypisywać *ipf. zob.* **przypisać.**
przypłątać się *pf.* -ączę -ączesz, **przypłątywać się** *pf. pot.* (*o człowieku*) drag one's ass in; *Br.* drag one's arse in; (*o kocie, psie*) be found; **przypłątał się do nich pies** they have found a stray dog; **przypłątało mi się jakieś choróbsko** I caught a bug of some sort.
przypłacać *ipf.*, **przypłacić** *pf.* pay (*coś czymś* for sth with sth); **przypłacić coś życiem** pay for sth with one's life.
przypłynąć *pf. zob.* **przypływać.**
przypływ *mi* **1.** (= *wezbranie*) surge; (*gniewu, śmiechu, dumy*) flush, surge; (*ulgi, niepokoju, entuzjazmu*) gush; (*energii, entuzjazmu*) flush, spurt; (= *napływ*) (*ludzi, pomysłów*) influx; **w przypływie dobroci** in a flush of kindness; **w przypływie natchnienia/gniewu** in a flush of inspiration/anger. **2.** (*oceanu*) high tide.

przypływać *ipf.* -am -asz (*o statku, pasażerach*) arrive, come in; (*o pływaku*) swim up; **przypływać do brzegu** come ashore; (*o pływaku*) swim ashore.
przypochlebiać się *ipf.*, **przypochlebić się** *pf.* flatter (*komuś* sb).
przypodobać się *pf.* endear o.s. (*komuś* to sb); ingratiate o.s. (*komuś* with sb).
przypominać *ipf.*, **przypomnieć** *pf.* -nę -nisz, -nij **1.** remind (*komuś o czymś* sb about sth) (*komuś kogoś/coś* sb of sb/sth); **przypominać sobie** (*o kimś/czymś*) recall sb/sth; **przypominać komuś, żeby coś zrobił** remind sb to do sth; **nie przypominam sobie tego** I don't recall this. **2.** (= *wywołać w pamięci*) evoke. **3.** *tylko ipf.* (= *być podobnym do kogoś, czegoś*) resemble (*kogoś/coś* sb/sth); **podejrzanie coś przypominać** (*wyglądem*) look suspiciously like sth; (*brzmieniem*) sound suspiciously like sth; **w niczym nie przypominać czegoś** be a far cry from sth. **~ się** *ipf.*, **przypomnieć się** *pf.* **1.** (= *przychodzić na myśl*) come back (*komuś* to one); **teraz wszystko mi się przypomina** now I recall everything; **przypomniało mi się, że...** I remembered that... **2.** **przypomnieć się komuś** recall o.s. to sb's memory.
przypora *f. Gen.pl.* -ór **1.** *bud.* buttress. **2.** *górn.* sprag.
przyporządkować *pf.* assign (*coś czemuś* sth to sth).
przypowiastka *f. Gen.pl.* -ek (*z życia*) anecdote; (= *krótka przypowieść*) parable.
przypowieść *f. teor.lit.* parable.
przyprawa *f.* (*ziołowa*) seasoning; (*korzenna*) spice; (*dodatek, np. sól, sos, musztarda, keczup*) *form.* condiment.
przyprawiać *ipf.*, **przyprawić** *pf.* **1.** *kulin.* (= *dodać przyprawę*) season; (= *nadać aromat*) spice; (= *nadawać smak*) flavor, savor (*czymś* with sth); **przyprawiać do smaku** season to taste; **przyprawiać coś na ostro** make sth hot; **przyprawiać coś na słodko-kwaśno** make sth sweet and sour. **2.** (= *przymocować*) fix, attach, fasten; **przyprawiać sobie brodę** put on a false beard; **przyprawić komuś rogi** cuckold sb. **3.** (*np. opowieść*) (= *ubarwiać*) season. **4.** (= *doprowadzić do jakiegoś stanu*) make, cause, bring, give; **przyprawiać kogoś o chorobę** make sb sick; **przyprawiać kogoś o dreszcze** send a chill *l.* shivers down sb's spine; **przyprawiać kogoś o gęsią skórkę** give sb the creeps; **przyprawiać kogoś o mdłości** make sb nauseous, make sb sick, nauseate; **przyprawiać kogoś o obłęd** craze sb; **przyprawiać kogoś o zawroty głowy** make sb dizzy; **przyprawiać kogoś o zawał serca** give sb a heart attack.
przyprawiony *a. kulin.* spiced; (*ziołami, sosem*) seasoned; (= *o określonym smaku*) flavored, savored (*czymś* with sth).
przyprawowy *a. kulin.* flavoring, seasoning; **zioła przyprawowe** seasoning herbs.
przyprostokątna *f. Gen.* -ej *geom.* cathetus, leg.
przyprowadzać *ipf.*, **przyprowadzić** *pf.* **1.** (= *zabrać ze sobą*) bring; **przyprowadzić kogoś ze sobą** (*na przyjęcie*) bring *l.* take sb along (to a

party); **przyprowadzić dzieci ze szkoły** bring the children from school; **przyprowadź go ze sobą!** bring him around! **2.** (= *wprowadzić w stan*) cause, bring about, drive; **przyprowadzić kogoś do szaleństwa** drive sb mad; **przyprowadzić kogoś do śmierci** cause *l*. bring about sb's death; **przyprowadzić kogoś do porządku** put sb in their place, whip sb into line; (*zwłaszcza dzieci*) read sb the riot act.

przyprószony *a.* sprinkled, covered; **włosy przyprószone siwizną** hoary *l*. hoar *l*. frosty hair.

przyprószyć *pf.* **1.** (*o śniegu*) sprinkle, cover; **przyprószyć pyłem** cover with dust. **2.** (*włosy*) frost; **siwizna przyprószyła mu włosy** his hair turned *l*. went gray.

przyprzeć *pf.* -prę -przesz, -przyj, -parł *zob.* **przypierać.**

przypudrować *pf.* powder; **przypudrować twarz** powder one's face, dust one's face with powder; **przypudrować nosek** *pot.* (= *zażyć narkotyk przez nos*) powder one's nose. ~ **się** *pf.* powder (*one's nose, face, etc.*).

przypuszczać *ipf.* **1.** (= *mniemać, zakładać*) assume; (= *snuć domysły*) suppose; (= *zakładać*) presume; (= *wnioskować*) surmise; **przypuszczam, że tak** I suppose *l*. believe so; **przypuśćmy, że...** let's assume that...; **kto by przypuszczał, że...** who would ever assume that...; **mam powody przypuszczać, że...** I have reason(s) to believe that...; **jest gorzej, niż przypuszczałem** it's worse than I thought. **2.** (= *pozwalać zbliżyć się*) let approach *l*. come near (*e.g. an animal*); **przypuścić atak** launch *l*. let loose with an attack.

przypuszczający *a.* conditional; **tryb przypuszczający** *gram.* conditional mood.

przypuszczalnie *adv.* presumably, in all likelihood.

przypuszczalny *a.* presumable, likely.

przypuszczenie *n.* assumption, presumption, conjecture, guess; **to tylko przypuszczenie** it's just a guess, it's just an assumption; **gubić się w przypuszczeniach** be guessing o.s. dizzy; **snuć przypuszczenia** make conjectures; **nasuwa się przypuszczenie, że...** the assumption is that...

przypuścić *pf.* -szczę -ścisz *zob.* **przypuszczać.**

przypytać się *pf. pot.* push o.s. (*do kogoś* on sb).

przyrastać *ipf.* **1.** (= *zwiększać się*) increase (*in height, volume, length, etc.*); (*np. o zaległościach płatniczych*) accrue. **2.** (= *rosnąc, łączyć się z czymś*) accrete; **żołądek przyrósł mi do kręgosłupa** *pot.* I'm starving.

przyroda *f.* **1.** (= *natura*) nature; **dzika przyroda** wildlife; **ochrona przyrody** wildlife protection, nature conservation, environmental protection; **pomnik przyrody** natural monument; *zwł. Br.* nature monument; **rezerwat przyrody** nature reserve; **siły przyrody** powers of nature; **na łonie przyrody** in the open; **obcować z przyrodą** commune with nature. **2.** *szkoln. pot.* (*przedmiot*) natural science; (*lekcja*) natural science lesson *l*. class.

przyrodni *a.* step-, half; (*mający innego ojca*) uterine; **przyrodni brat** stepbrother, half brother.

przyrodniczka *f. Gen.pl.* -ek *zob.* **przyrodnik.**

przyrodniczy *a.* (*film*) nature; (*nauki*) natural; **książka przyrodnicza** nature book, book about nature; **film przyrodniczy** nature movie *l*. film *l*. documentary; **muzeum przyrodnicze** natural science(s) museum; **nauki przyrodnicze** natural science(s).

przyrodnik *mp* **1.** (*naukowiec*) naturalist. **2.** *szkoln.* (*nauczyciel*) natural science(s) teacher.

przyrodolecznictwo *n. med.* physical therapy, physiotherapy.

przyrodoleczniczy *a. med.* physiotherapeutic.

przyrodoznawstwo *n. przest.* natural history, natural science(s).

przyrodzenie *n. pot.* (= *zewnętrzne narządy płciowe*) private *l*. privy parts.

przyrodzony *a.* innate, inborn, inherent; **przyrodzony talent** natural talent (*do czegoś* for sth).

przyrosnąć *pf.* -rosnę -rośniesz, -rośnij, -rósł -rosła -rośli *zob.* **przyrastać.**

przyrost *mi* increase, growth, increment, gain; **przyrost funkcji** *mat.* increment in a function; **przyrost naturalny** population growth (rate); **przyrost objętości** volume increase; **przyrost produkcji** production growth; **przyrost wagi** weight gain.

przyrostek *mi* -tk- *Gen.* -a *jęz.* suffix.

przyrostkowy *a. jęz.* suffixal.

przyrostowy *a.* of or related to increase/growth/etc.; **pierścień** *l*. **słój przyrostowy** *leśn.* annual ring, tree ring.

przyrównać *pf.*, **przyrównywać** *ipf.* (= *porównać*) compare; (= *znajdować podobieństwo*) liken, equate (*kogoś/coś do kogoś/czegoś* sb/sth to sb/sth). ~ **się** *pf.*, **przyrównywać się** *ipf.* (= *porównać*) compare o.s.; (= *znajdować podobieństwo*) liken o.s., equate o.s. (*do kogoś/czegoś* to sb/sth).

przyrównikowy *a.* equatorial.

przyrumieniać *ipf.*, **przyrumienić** *pf.* brown. ~ **się** *ipf.*, **przyrumienić się** *pf.* brown; **mięso przyrumieniło się na patelni** the meat browned on the frying pan.

przyrząd *mi* appliance, device, instrument, apparatus; **przyrząd gimnastyczny** *sport* gymnastics apparatus; **przyrząd kontrolny** monitor; **przyrządy nawigacyjne** navigational aids; **przyrząd pomiarowy** measuring instrument, gauge; **przyrząd do mierzenia ciśnienia** *med.* tonometer.

przyrządzać *ipf.*, **przyrządzić** *pf.* prepare (*a meal, drink, etc.*).

przyrzec *pf.* -rzeknę -rzekniesz, -rzeknij, -rzekł *zob.* **przyrzekać.**

przyrzeczenie *n.* promise, pledge, vow; **złamać przyrzeczenie** break a promise, go back on one's word; **dotrzymać przyrzeczenia** keep a promise.

przyrzekać *ipf.* promise, make a promise.

przyrzynać *ipf.*, **przyrżnąć** *pf.* -nę -niesz, -nij **1.** (*np. deski*) cut to measure. **2.** *tylko pf. pot.* (= *uderzyć*) smack.

przysadka *f. Gen.pl.* -ek **1.** *bot.* stipule, stipel.

2. przysadka mózgowa *anat.* pituitary gland, hypophysis.

przysadkowy *a. anat., med.* pituitary.

przysadzisty *a.* chunky, stocky, podgy.

przysalać *ipf.* (= *dodawać soli*) add salt.

przysądzać *ipf.*, **przysądzić** *pf. prawn.* adjudge, award.

przyschnąć *pf.* -schnę -schniesz, -schnij, -schnął *l.* -sechł -schła *zob.* **przysychać.**

przysiad *mi* knee bend.

przysiadać *ipf.* **1.** (*gdzieś na chwilę*) sit down (*for a while*). **2.** (= *kucać*) squat, crouch down. **3.** (= *siedząc, przygniatać*) sit down (*on sth*); **przysiadł sobie płaszcz** he sat down on his coat (*while wearing it*); **przysiąść fałdów** buckle down, knuckle down. **4.** *myśl.* (*o ptaku*) alight (*na zdobyczy* on the prey). **~ się** *ipf.* join (sb); **czy mogę się przysiąść?** can I join you?

przysiąc *pf.* -sięgnę -sięgniesz, -sięgnij, -siągł -sięgła -sięgli *zob.* **przysięgać.**

przysiąść *pf.* -siądę -siądziesz, -siądź, -siadł -siedli *zob.* **przysiadać.** **~ się** *pf. zob.* **przysiadać się.**

przysięga *f.* oath, vow; **przysięga Hipokratesa** *med.* the Hippocratic oath; **przysięga małżeńska** marriage *l.* marital vows; **przysięga na wierność** oath of allegiance; **przysięga wojskowa** military oath of allegiance; **być związanym przysięgą** be under oath; **odbierać od kogoś przysięgę** administer an oath to sb; **składać przysięgę** take *l.* swear an oath; **zwolnić kogoś z przysięgi** relieve sb from their oath; **pod przysięgą** under oath; **jechać na przysięgę** *pot.* go to sb's military oath of allegiance.

przysięgać *ipf.* swear; (= *złożyć przysięgę*) take an oath; (= *zobowiązać się*) pledge; **przysięgać na Boga** swear by *l.* to God; **przysięgać na wszystkie świętości** swear by all that one holds dear; **przysięgać wierność** swear allegiance (*komuś/czemuś* to sb/sth); **mogę przysiąc, że...** I can swear that...; **przysiągł** *l.* **obiecał, że przestanie pić** he swore off drink.

przysięgać się *ipf. pot.* swear; **przysięgała się, że nigdy już tam nie pójdzie** she swore never to go there again.

przysięgły *a.* (= *zaprzysiężony*) sworn; **tłumacz przysięgły** (*słowa mówionego*) sworn *l.* certified interpreter; (*w sądzie*) court interpreter; (*słowa pisanego*) sworn *l.* certified translator; **sędzia przysięgły** *prawn.* juror. – *mp prawn.* juror, juryman, jurywoman; **ława przysięgłych** (= *zespół sędziów przysięgłych*) jury; (*część sali sądowej*) jury box.

przysiółek *mi* -łk- *Gen.* -a (= *mała wioska*) hamlet, wick; (= *skupisko domów poza wsią*) farm (*off a village*).

przyskakiwać *ipf.*, **przyskoczyć** *pf.* jump over *l.* up, spring over *l.* up (*do czegoś/kogoś* to sb/sth); **jednym susem przyskoczył do okna** he jumped over *l.* up to the window in one leap *l.* a single bound.

przyskrzynić *pf.* **1.** *rzad.* (= *przytrzasnąć*) jam, pinch, trap, catch (*e.g. one's finger in the door*). **2.** *pot.* pinch; **przyskrzynić kogoś na czymś** pinch

sb while they were doing sth, catch sb red-handed.

przysłać *pf.* -ślę -ślesz, -ślij, -słał *zob.* **przysyłać.**

przysłaniać *ipf.* (= *zasłaniać*) cover; **przysłaniać oczy/uszy** cover one's eyes/ears; (= *zasłaniać częściowo*) obscure, shade; (*dla ochrony*) shield; **wędkarstwo przysłoniło mu wszystkie obowiązki** he was so preoccupied with angling that he neglected all his duties.

przysłona *f.* **1.** *fot.* diaphragm, lens stop; aperture (stop). **2.** *techn.* (= *osłona*) cover, screen.

przysłonić *pf. zob.* **przysłaniać.**

przysłowie *n. Gen.pl.* -łów proverb, adage, byword; **jak mówi przysłowie** as the proverb has it.

przysłowiowy *a.* proverbial.

przysłowny *a. gram. zob.* **przysłówkowy.**

przysłówek *mi* -wk- *Gen.* -a *gram.* adverb.

przysłówkowy *a. gram.* adverbial; **imiesłów przysłówkowy** (*uprzedni*) perfect participle; (*współczesny*) present participle; (*w tradycji slawistów anglojęzycznych*) adverbial participle; **wyrażenie przysłówkowe** adverbial phrase; **zaimek przysłówkowy** *l.* **przysłowny** pronominal adverb.

przysłuchiwać się *ipf.* listen (*to sth attentively*).

przysługa *f.* favor, good turn; **niedźwiedzia przysługa** disservice; **ostatnia przysługa** *rel.* last rites *l.* offices; **przysługa za przysługę** you scratch my back and I scratch yours, one good turn deserves another; **prosić kogoś o przysługę** ask sb a favor, ask a favor of sb; **wyświadczyć komuś przysługę** do sb a favor *l.* good turn.

przysługiwać *ipf.* be vested (*komuś/czemuś* in sb/sth); **przysługuje mu urlop** he is entitled to a leave; **nie przysługuje jej do tego prawo** she doesn't have the right to do it, she's not entitled to do it.

przysłużyć się *pf.* be of service (*komuś/czemuś* to sb/sth); **źle się komuś przysłużyć** be of disservice to sb, do sb a bad turn.

przysmak *mi* delicacy, dainty, tidbit; *Br.* titbit.

przysmażać *ipf.*, **przysmażyć** *pf.* give a light fry (*coś* to sth); brown (*coś* sth). **~ się** *ipf.*, **przysmażyć się** *pf.* brown (*during frying*).

przysnąć *pf.* -snę -śniesz, -śnij *zob.* **przysypiać.**

przysolić *pf.* -sól **1.** *zob.* **przysalać. 2.** *pot.* (= *uderzyć*) bop (*komuś* sb); take a plug (*komuś* at sb).

przysparzać *ipf.* (= *powiększyć*) increase, add to, augment; (= *spowodować, sprowadzić*) cause, bring; **przysporzyło mi to dużo pieniędzy** I gained a lot of money thanks to it; **przysparzać chwały komuś/czemuś** reflect credit on sb/sth; **przysparzać komuś kłopotów** cause sb trouble; **przysparzać komuś sławy** make sb famous; **przysparzać komuś wstydu** (*o kimś*) be an embarrassment to sb; **przysparzać sobie przyjaciół/ wrogów** make friends/enemies.

przyspawać *pf.* fix by welding, weld on.

przyspieszacz *mi Gen.* -a *chem.* accelerator,

accelerant; **przyspieszacz zapłonu** *mot.* advance of spark device.

przyspieszać *ipf.* **1.** (= *zwiększać szybkość*) accelerate, speed up; (*np.* tempo prac) step up, push things ahead; (*np.* o samochodzie) pick up *l.* gather speed; **przyspieszyć kroku** quicken one's pace. **2.** (= *skracać czas oczekiwania na coś*) advance; (= *zwiększyć bieg wydarzeń*) precipitate, force ahead (*coś* sth); force the pace (*coś* of sth).

przyspieszenie *n.* **1.** acceleration, speeding up. **2.** *fiz.* acceleration; **przyspieszenie dośrodkowe** centripetal acceleration; **przyspieszenie grawitacyjne** gravitational acceleration, acceleration of gravity; **przyspieszenie liniowe** linear acceleration; **przyspieszenie ujemne** negative acceleration, deceleration, retardation; **przyspieszenie ziemskie** gravitational acceleration, acceleration of gravity (*of the Earth*); **przyspieszenie zapłonu** *techn.* advance of spark.

przyspieszeniomierz *mi Gen.* -a *fiz.* accelerometer.

przyspiesznik *mi Gen.* -a **1.** *mot.* accelerator. **2.** *ogr.* hotbed.

przyspieszony *a.* accelerated; **przyspieszony puls** frequent *l.* rapid pulse; **przyspieszony oddech** rapid *l.* quick breath; **autobus przyspieszony** limited (bus); **pociąg przyspieszony** limited (train); **tryb przyspieszony** *prawn.* summary procedure; **ruch (jednostajnie) przyspieszony** *fiz.* (uniformly) accelerated motion.

przyspieszyć *pf. zob.* **przyspieszać**.

przysporzyć *pf. zob.* **przysparzać**.

przysposabiać *ipf.*, **przysposobić** *pf.* -sób **1.** (= *uczynić zdatnym do czegoś*) adjust, adapt, accomodate. **2.** (= *wyszkolić*) train, coach. **3.** *prawn.* adopt. ~ **się** *ipf.*, **przysposobić się** *pf.* prepare (*na coś* for sth).

przysposobienie *n.* **1.** (= *dostosowanie*) adjustment, accomodation. **2.** (= *kurs*) training, preparation; **przysposobienie obronne** *szkoln.* civil defence training (*an obligatory course taught at high schools in Poland*); **przysposobienie zawodowe** vocational training. **3.** *prawn.* adoption.

przyssać *pf.* -ssę -ssiesz, -ssij *zob.* **przysysać**. ~ **się** *pf. zob.* **przysysać się**.

przyssawka *f. Gen.pl.* -ek **1.** *zool.* sucker; (*pijawki, tasiemca, głowonoga*) acetabulum. **2.** (*do mocowania*) sucker, suction *l.* vacuum cup.

przystać *pf.* -nę -niesz *zob.* **przystawać**[1].

przystanąć *pf. zob.* **przystawać**[2].

przystanek *mi* -nk- **1.** stop; **przystanek autobusowy** bus stop; **przystanek dla wsiadających** *pot.* pickup; **przystanek kolejowy** *gł. Br.* halt; **przystanek końcowy** terminus; **przystanek na żądanie** request stop; **przystanek tramwajowy** streetcar stop; **pojedź trzy przystanki** get off at *l.* on the third stop; **wysiąść na drugim przystanku** get off at *l.* on the second stop. **2.** (*w czasie podróży*) stop, rest stop; **zróbmy sobie przystanek, co?** let's stop for a while, shall we?

przystankowy *a.* of or related to a stop; **wiata przystankowa** bus shelter.

przystań *f. pl.* -e **1.** *żegl.* (inland) port, harbor; **przystań jachtowa** marina; **przystań rzeczna** levee; **przystań rybacka** fishing port. **2.** *przen.* haven; **przystań życiowa** safe haven (*in one's life*).

przystawać[1] *ipf.* -aję -ajesz, -awaj **1.** (= *przywierać*) adhere, cohere, cling; **okna nie przystają** the windows don't shut tight; **figury przystające** *geom.* congruent figures. **2.** (= *zgadzać się*) accede, consent; **przystał z ochotą na moją propozycję** he readily consented to my proposal; **przystać na czyjeś warunki** accede *l.* consent to *l.* accept sb's terms. **3.** *pot.* (= *przyłączać się do kogoś*) join; **przystać do kogoś na służbę** go to sb's service. **4.** (= *być odpowiednim*) befit, become; **jak przystało na człowieka honoru** as befits a man of honor; **to nie przystoi** it is improper, it is unbecoming.

przystawać[2] *ipf.* -nę -niesz -nął -nęła -nęli (= *zatrzymywać się*) stop (*for a while*).

przystawanie *n. geom.* congruence.

przystawiać *ipf.*, **przystawić** *pf.* **1.** (= *przysunąć*) move over; **przystaw krzesło do ściany, dobrze?** can you move the chair over to the wall?; **przystawić sobie krzesło** pull up a chair. **2.** (= *przyłożyć*) put against; **przystawił mu pistolet do głowy** he put the gun to *l.* against his head. ~ **się** *ipf. pot.* (= *podrywać*) make a pitch (*do kogoś* for sb), hit (*do kogoś* on sb).

przystawka *f. Gen.pl.* -ek **1.** *kulin.* starter, hors d'oeuvre, appetizer; **na przystawkę** for starters; **pieczeń/indyk pieczony z przystawkami** roast/roast turkey with trimmings. **2.** (= *urządzenie współpracujące z innym*) peripheral device, peripheral. **3.** *techn.* support.

przystąpić *pf. zob.* **przystępować**.

przystąpienie *n.* entry, joining, accession; **przystąpienie Polski do NATO** Poland's entry to NATO.

przystęp *mi* access; **nie mieć przystępu do kogoś/czegoś** have no access to sb/sth; **w przystępie radości** in a fit of joy.

przystępność *f.* accessibility, approachability, affordability; *zob. t.* **przystępny**.

przystępny *a.* (*np. styl, język, brzeg rzeki*) accessible; (*osoba*) approachable; (*cena*) affordable.

przystępować *ipf.* **1.** (= *podchodzić*) approach; **bez kija nie przystąp!** he/she/etc. will bite your head off!, he/she/etc. is so unaproachable! **2.** (= *rozpoczynać*) begin, start; **przystąpić do ataku** go on the attack; **przystąpić do działania** swing into action; **przystąpić do egzaminu** sit for an examination; **przystąpić do komunii/spowiedzi** go to communion/confession; **przystąpić do walki** (*o oddziałach wojskowych*) join battle; **przystąpmy do rzeczy** let's get down to business, let's come to the point. **3.** (= *przyłączyć się do kogoś*) join; **przystąpić do funduszu emerytalnego** join a pension fund; **przystąpić do spółki** enter a partnership.

przystojniaczek *mp* -czk- *pl.* -i *iron. l. żart. zob.* **przystojniak**.

przystojniak *mp pl.* -cy *l.* -i *iron. l. żart.* looker, hunk; **niezły z niego przystojniak** he's a hunk of a man.

przystojny *a.* handsome, good-looking.

przystopować *pf.*, **przystopowywać** *ipf. pot.* (*kogoś*) draw *l.* pull *l.* haul in one's horns; **przystopuj trochę, okej?** (= *daj spokój, nie wygłupiaj się*) gimme a break, will you?; (= *uspokój się*) cut it out, will you?, give it a rest, will you?, take a chill pill, will?

przystosować *pf. zob.* **przystosowywać.** ~ **się** *pf. zob.* **przystosowywać się.**

przystosowanie *n.* **1.** (= *dostosowanie*) adaptation, accomodation, adjustment. **2.** *biol.* adaptation. **3.** *psych.* adjustment.

przystosowany *a.* adjusted, adapted, accomodated; **przystosowany do nowych warunków** adjusted to new conditions; **przystosowany do użytku szkolnego** adapted for use in schools; **organizm przystosowany do życia pod wodą** organism adapted to living under water; **autobus przystosowany do przewozu niepełnosprawnych** bus accomodated for transportation of the handicapped.

przystosowawczość *f. biol.* adaptability.

przystosowawczy *a.* adaptive; **zdolność przystosowawcza** *biol.* adaptability.

przystosowywać *ipf.* adapt, adjust (*coś do czegoś* sth to sth). ~ **się** *ipf.* adapt, adjust; **przystosować się do nowych warunków pracy** adapt *l.* adjust to new working conditions.

przystrajać *ipf.*, **przystroić** *pf.* -**strój** (= *zdobić; stanowić ozdobę*) adorn, ornament (*czymś* with sth); (*np. ubranie dodatkiem*) perk up; **przystroiła sobie suknię czerwonym szalem** she perked up her dress with a red scarf.

przystrzyc *pf.* -**strzygę** -**strzyżesz** -**strzygł**, **przystrzygać** *ipf.* trim, clip; **przystrzyc coś** give sth a trim *l.* clip; **przystrzyc sobie brodę** trim *l.* clip one's beard.

przysunąć *pf.*, **przysuwać** *ipf.* **1.** push, move (*sth nearer to sth*); **przysunąć sobie krzesło** draw up a chair. **2.** *pot.* (= *uderzyć*) take a plug (*komuś* at sb). ~ **się** *pf.*, **przysuwać się** *ipf.* move closer, come closer.

przyswajać *ipf.* **1.** (= *opanowywać*) acquire; (*pomysł, metodę*) adopt; (*wartości, wiedzę*) internalize, absorb, learn. **2.** *biol.* assimilate.

przyswajalność *f. biol.* **1.** (= *zdolność przyswajania*) assimilativeness. **2.** (= *łatwość podlegania przyswajaniu*) assimilability.

przyswajalny *a. biol.* assimilable.

przyswoić *pf.* -**ję** -**isz**, -**ój** *zob.* **przyswajać.**

przysychać *ipf.* **1.** (= *przywierać*) get stuck (*to sth*); **język mi przyschnął do podniebienia** I'm completely parched. **2.** (= *stawać się suchym*) dry off (*a little*); **rana przysycha** the wound is healing over *l.* up; **poczekać, aż coś przyschnie** *przen.* wait for sth to become dead and buried.

przysyłać *ipf.* send (*coś* sth in) (*kogoś* sb a-round).

przysypać *pf.* -**pię** -**piesz** *zob.* **przysypywać.**

przysypiać *ipf.* doze off; **przysypiać za kierownicą** doze off at the wheel.

przysypywać *ipf.* **1.** (= *nasypać na wierzch*) (*piaskiem, liśćmi*) cover; (*gruzami, ziemią*) bury; (*mąką, posypką*) sprinkle. **2.** (= *dosypać*) add, put (*some more*); **przysypać węgla do pieca** put some more coal in the stove.

przysysać *ipf.* adhere, cling (*by suction*). ~ **się** *ipf.* cling; **przyssać się do kogoś** *pot.* stick to sb like glue; (= *łazić za kimś*) dog sb's steps.

przyszłoroczny *a.* next year's; **przyszłoroczny budżet** next year's budget.

przyszłościowy *a.* future, for the future; **przyszłościowe plany** plans *l.* designs for the future.

przyszłość *f.* future; **w niedalekiej przyszłości** in the near(est) *l.* immediate *l.* foreseeable future; **plany na przyszłość** plans for the future; **myśleć o przyszłości** think about the future; **wybiegać myślą w przyszłość** look to the future, think ahead; **mieć przyszłość** have a future; **zawód bez przyszłości** a job without future; **być przyszłością kogoś/czegoś** be the future of sb/sth; **przyszłość pokaże** the time will tell; **na przyszłość** for the future; **w przyszłości** in the future; **to jeszcze pieśń przyszłości** it's still a thing of the future; **być dobrze zabezpieczonym na przyszłość** have one's bread buttered for life; **czyjaś przyszłość nie wygląda różowo** it's a bad lookout for sb; **masz przed sobą wspaniałą przyszłość** you've got a great future ahead of you; **patrzeć w przyszłość** look forward *l.* look ahead *l.* to the future; **przepowiadać komuś przyszłość** (= *wróżyć*) tell *l.* read *l.* cast sb's fortune; **przyszłość należy do Internetu** the future lies in the Internet *l.* Web; **robić plany na przyszłość** look *l.* think ahead; **świetlana przyszłość** rosy future; **widoki na przyszłość** prospects, lookouts (*for the future*); **przenosić się myślami w przyszłość** project o.s. into the future.

przyszły *a.* future, coming, to be, next; **moja przyszła żona** my future wife; **przyszłe pokolenia** future generations; **przyszły rok** the coming year; **w przyszłym roku** next year; **przyszły lekarz** (*np. o studencie medycyny*) doctor-to-be; **czas przyszły** *gram.* the future tense, the future; **przyszłe życie** *rel.* the hereafter; **w przyszłym życiu** (= *po śmierci*) hereafter, in one's next life.

przyszpilać *ipf.*, **przyszpilić** *pf. pot.* (= *przypinać*) pin (*sth onto sth*); **przyszpilać kwiaty do włosów** pin flowers onto *l.* into one's hair; **przyszpilić kogoś wzrokiem** look daggers at sb.

przyszpitalny *a. med.* adjacent to or being located on a hospital premises; **apteka przyszpitalna** hospital drugstore *l.* pharmacy; **poradnia przyszpitalna** hospital outpatients' clinic.

przyszwa *f. Gen.pl.* -**szew** (*część buta*) vamp.

przyszyć *pf.* -**szyję** -**szyjesz**, -**szyj** *zob.* **przyszywać.**

przyszykować *pf.* prepare. ~ **się** *pf.* prepare o.s., get ready (*na coś* for sth).

przyszywać *ipf.* -**am** -**asz** stich, sew (*coś do czegoś* sth on(to) sth).

przyszywany *a.* **przyszywany wujek/przyszywana babcia** *itp. pot.* adopted *l.* adoptive uncle/granny (*a close friend considered to be a member of the family*).

przyścienny *a.* (*np. szafka, półka*) wall; (*np. filar*) engaged.

przyśnić się *pf.* **-ij** appear in one's dreams; **przyśniło mi się wczoraj, że...** I dreamt last night that..., last night I had this dream about...

przyśpieszacz *mi Gen.* **-a** *zob.* **przyspieszacz.**

przyśpieszać *ipf. zob.* **przyspieszać.**

przyśpieszenie *n. zob.* **przyspieszenie.**

przyśpieszeniomierz *mi Gen.* **-a** *zob.* **przyspieszeniomierz.**

przyśpieszony *a. zob.* **przyspieszony.**

przyśpieszyć *pf. zob.* **przyspieszać.**

przyśpiew *mi* **1.** (= *refren*) refrain, chorus. **2.** *fon., przest.* (= *akcent intonacyjny*) intonation.

przyśpiewka *f. Gen.pl.* **-ek** folk song (*usu. sung at traditional country weddings and festivals*).

przyśpiewywać *ipf.* croon, hum.

przyśrubować *pf.,* **przyśrubowywać** *ipf.* bolt (*sth down l. on*); screw (*sth down l. on*).

przyświadczać *ipf.,* **przyświadczyć** *pf.* **1.** (= *potwierdzić*) attest (*coś* to sth). **2.** (= *przytaknąć*) assent (*coś* to sth).

przyświecać *ipf.* **1.** (= *oświetlać*) light. **2.** (= *być źródłem światła*) shine; **słońce przyświecało** the sun was shining. **3.** (= *wskazywać kierunek działania*) beacon, guide; **przyświeca jej piękny cel** she has a noble purpose.

przytachać *pf. pot.* bring, drag (*sth along with o.s.*); **przytachał to wczoraj do domu** he dragged it home yesterday.

przytaczać *ipf.* **1.** (= *cytować*) quote, cite. **2.** (= *wyliczać*) (*np. przykłady*) mention, enumerate; (*np. argumenty*) set forth; (*np. dowody*) adduce; (*np. wymówki*) allege; **przytaczać źródło** refer to a source. **3.** (= *tocząc, przesuwać*) roll over (*to*); **do piwnicy przytoczono beczkę piwa** a barrel of beer was rolled over to the cellar.

przytakiwać *ipf.,* **przytaknąć** *pf.* **-ij** assent (*komuś* with sb) (*czemuś* to sth); **przytaknąć skinieniem głowy** nod one's assent.

przytakująco *adv.* in assent; **kiwnąć głową przytakująco** nod in assent.

przytarczyce *pl. Gen.* **-c** *anat.* parathyroid glands.

przytarczycowy *a. zob.* **przytarczyczny.**

przytarczyczny *a. anat.* parathyroid; **gruczoł przytarczyczny** parathyroid gland.

przytargać *pf. pot.* bring, drag (*sth along with o.s.*); **przytargał to wczoraj do domu** he dragged it home yesterday.

przytaszczyć *pf. pot. zob.* **przytargać.** ~ **się** *pf. pot.* drag o.s. along (*somewhere*); **przytaszczyliśmy się wczoraj do domu bardzo późno** we dragged ourselves home very late last night.

przytelepać się *pf.* **-pię -piesz** *pot.* shuffle, drag o.s. (*over somewhere*); **pociąg się spóźnił i przytelepaliśmy się do domu dopiero po północy** the train was late and we finally made it *l.* dragged ourselves home only after midnight.

przytępiać *ipf.,* **przytępić** *pf.* **1.** (*narzędzie*) blunt. **2.** (*wrażliwość, zmysły*) deaden, blunt, petrify; (*wzrok, słuch, ból*) dull. ~ **się** *ipf.,* **przytępić się** *pf.* **1.** (*o narzędziu*) become blunt. **2.** (*o wrażliwości, zmysłach*) deaden, become blunt.

przytępiony *a.* dull, blunt; **przytępiona pamięć** dimmed memory; **przytępiona uwaga** dulled attention; **mieć przytępiony słuch** be hard of hearing.

przytknąć *pf.* **-nę -niesz, -nij** *zob.* **przytykać.**

przytłaczać *ipf.* **1.** (= *przygniatać*) crush, press down. **2.** (= *przygnębiać*) (*o smutku, cierpieniu*) overwhelm, overweigh; (*o smutku, myślach, upale*) oppress; (*o obowiązkach, odpowiedzialności*) overwhelm (*kogoś* sb); press (*kogoś* on sb).

przytłaczający *a.* overwhelming; **przytłaczająca większość** overwhelming *l.* vast majority; **przytłaczająca atmosfera** oppressing atmosphere.

przytłoczyć *pf. zob.* **przytłaczać.**

przytłumiać *ipf.,* **przytłumić** *pf.* stifle, suppress, deaden; (*ogień*) damp; (*światło*) dim; (*odgłos*) muffle; (*pragnienie, namiętności*) subdue.

przytłumiony *a.* stifled, suppressed, subdued; **przytłumiony dźwięk** muffled *l.* dull *l.* muted sound; **przytłumione głosy** muffled voices; **przytłumione kolory** subdued colors; **przytłumione światło** dimmed light.

przytoczyć *pf. zob.* **przytaczać.**

przytomnie *adv.* **1.** (= *świadomie*) consciously, lucidly. **2.** (= *rozsądnie*) sensibly, soberly.

przytomnieć *ipf.* **-eję -ejesz** (= *odzyskiwać przytomność*) regain consciousness, come to *l.* around *l.* round.

przytomność *f.* consiousness; **przytomność umysłu** *t. prawn.* presence of mind; **leżeć bez przytomności** lie unconscious; **odzyskać przytomność** regain consciousness, come to *l.* around *l.* round; **pozbawić kogoś przytomności** (*np. ciosem*) knock sb out, knock sb unconscious; **stracić przytomność** lose consciousness, pass out; **zachować przytomność umysłu** keep a level head; **utrata przytomności** loss of consciousness.

przytomny *a.* **1.** (= *świadomy*) conscious. **2.** (= *rozsądny*) sensible, sober, astute; **przytomna odpowiedź** sensible answer; **przytomny umysł** lucid *l.* clear mind. **3.** *arch.* (= *obecny*) present.

przyton *mi muz.* aliquot tone.

przytrafiać się *ipf.,* **przytrafić się** *pf.* befall (*komuś* sb); happen (*komuś* to sb); **co ci się przytrafiło?** what happened to you?

przytroczyć *pf.* strap, buckle (*coś do czegoś* sth to sth).

przytrzaskiwać *ipf.,* **przytrzasnąć** *pf.* **-snę -śniesz, -śnij, -snął** jam (*e.g. one's coat/fingers in the door*). ~ **się** *ipf.,* **przytrzasnąć się** *pf.* jam; **płaszcz przytrzasnął mi się w drzwiach** my coat jammed in the door.

przytrzeć *pf.* **-trę -trzesz, -tryj, -tarł** *zob.* **przycierać.**

przytrzymać *pf.,* **przytrzymywać** *ipf.* **1.** (= *nie pozwolić się ruszyć*) hold down, keep down; **przytrzymywało go dwóch silnych mężczyzn** he was held down by two strong men. **2.** (= *nie pozwolić odejść*) detain, delay; **chciał już iść do domu, ale go przytrzymano** he wanted to go home but he was detained. **3.** (= *nie pozwolić upaść*) hold back; **możesz mi przytrzymać drabinę?** could you hold the ladder for me, please? **4.** (= *potrzymać*) hold (*for a while*); **przytrzymać kogoś za rękę** hold sb's hand for a while; **przytrzymać komuś miejsce** keep sb's seat, keep a seat for sb. **5.** (*np. złodzieja*) detain, apprehend. **~ się** *pf.*, **przytrzymywać się** *ipf.* hold on (*czegoś* to sth).

przytulać *ipf.*, **przytulić** *pf.* **1.** hug, cuddle; **przytulić kogoś** give sb a hug *l.* cuddle. **2.** *przest.* put up; **przytulić u siebie kogoś** take sb in *l.* under one's wings; **nie mieć gdzie głowy przytulić** have nowhere to lay *l.* rest one's head. **~ się** *ipf.*, **przytulić się** *pf.* cuddle up, snuggle up (*do siebie* together); **przytulać się do kogoś/czegoś** snuggle up to sb/sth, huddle up against sb/sth, cozy up to sb/sth.

przytulanka *f.* (*zabawka*) cuddly toy.

przytulia *f. bot.* bedstraw (*Galium*).

przytulisko *n. Loc.* **-kiem** shelter.

przytulnie *adv.* cozily; **przytulnie tu u ciebie** it's very cozy here.

przytulność *f.* coziness.

przytulny *a.* cozy, snug, homey; **przytulny kącik** snuggery, snuggerie.

przytułek *mi* **-łk-** **1.** (*zakład opieki*) shelter; **przytułek dla bezdomnych** homeless shelter. **2.** (*schronienie*) shelter, refuge, asylum.

przytup *mi pot.* stamp, stomp; **zatańczyć z przytupem** stomp during dancing.

przytupywać *ipf.* (*np. z zimna*) stamp one's feet; (*do rytmu*) beat time with one's foot.

przyturlać *pf.* roll over (*sth somewhere*); **przyturlać pod dom kulę śniegu i zbudować bałwana** roll a snowball over to the house and build a snowman. **~ się** *pf.* (*o rzeczy*) roll over (*somewhere*); **jabłko przyturlało się pod moje nogi** the apple rolled over to my feet.

przytwierdzać *ipf.*, **przytwierdzić** *pf.* **1.** (= *przymocować*) attach, fix, fasten (*coś do czegoś* sth to sth). **2.** (= *potwierdzić*) assent; **przytwierdzić coś skinieniem głowy** nod one's assent to sth.

przytyć *pf.* **-tyję -tyjesz, -tyj** put on weight.

przytyk *mi* (= *złośliwa uwaga*) dig (*pod czyimś adresem/do czegoś* at sb/sth).

przytykać *ipf.* **1.** (= *dotykać*) put (*coś do czegoś* sth against sth). **2.** *tylko pf.* (= *stykać się*) border, abut (*do czegoś* on sth).

przyuczać *ipf.*, **przyuczyć** *pf.* train (*kogoś do czegoś* sb in sth); (*zwierzę l. człowieka do wykonywania pewnych rzeczy, do obowiązków*) break in; **przyuczyć kogoś do zawodu murarza** train sb for the trade of a bricklayer. **~ się** *ipf.*, **przyuczyć się** *pf.* be trained, undergo training, learn.

przyusznica *f. anat.* parotid gland, parotid.

przyuszny *a. anat.* parotid; **ślinianka przyuszna** parotid gland.

przyuważyć *pf. pot.* spot, pick out, catch sight of (*kogoś/coś* sb/sth).

przywabiać *ipf.*, **przywabić** *pf.* lure; *przen.* attract.

przywalać *ipf.*, **przywalić** *pf.* **1.** (= *przygniatać*) crush, press down. **2.** *pot.* (= *dorzucić*) add, put some more. **3.** *tylko pf. pot.* (= *uderzyć*) give a whack (*komuś/czemuś* sb/sth). **~ się** *ipf. pot.* make a pitch (*do kogoś* for sb); hit (*do kogoś* on sb).

przywałęsać się *pf.* ramble over (*to a place*).

przywara *f.* vice.

przywdziać *pf.* **-wdzieję -wdziejesz -wdziali** *l.* **-wdzieli, przywdziewać** *ipf. lit.* don, array, endue; **przywdziać habit** take the habit; **przywdziać mundur** join the colors; **przywdziać sutannę** take the cloth; **przywdziać żałobę** go into mourning; **przywdziać maskę** *przen.* masquerade, dissemble.

przywiać *pf.* **-eję -ejesz** *zob.* **przywiewać**.

przywiązać *pf.* **-wiążę -wiążesz** *zob.* **przywiązywać.** **~ się** *pf. zob.* **przywiązywać się.**

przywiązanie *n.* attachment, adherence, devotion (*do kogoś/czegoś* to sb/sth); **okazać komuś przywiązanie** show sb one's devotion.

przywiązany *a.* (*do drzewa, do płotu*) tied; (*do rodziców, do przyjaciela*) attached, devoted.

przywiązywać *ipf.* **1.** (= *przymocowywać*) tie, bind (*kogoś/coś do kogoś/czegoś* sb/sth to sb/sth); **nie przywiązywać znaczenia** *l.* **wagi do czegoś** not to attach importance *l.* significance to sth, think little of sth; **przywiązywać wielką wagę** *l.* **wielkie znaczenie do czegoś** attach great importance *l.* significance to sth, set a high value on sth, set *l.* lay a great store by *l.* upon sth; **przywiązywać zbyt wielką wagę do czegoś** overemphasize sth, make too much of sth. **2.** (= *wywoływać sympatię*) attach (*kogoś do kogoś/czegoś* sb to sb/sth). **~ się** *ipf.* **1.** (= *przymocowywać się*) tie o.s., bind o.s. **2.** (*uczuciowo*) become (emotionally) attached.

przywidzenie *n.* illusion, hallucination; (= *omam wzrokowy*) trick of the light; **mieć przywidzenia** see things.

przywidzieć się *pf.* **-dzę -dzisz** appear (*komuś* to sb); **musiało ci się coś przywidzieć** you must have dreamt it, you must have been seeing things.

przywierać *ipf.*, **przywrzeć** *pf.* **1.** (= *przylegać*) adhere, cling. **2.** (*do garnka*) stick; **przywrzeć (ciałem) do ściany** flatten o.s. against the wall. **3.** (*drzwi, bramę*) (= *przymknąć*) leave ajar. **~ się** *ipf.* (= *przymykać się*) close.

przywiesić *pf.* **-szę -sisz, przywieszać** *ipf. rzad.* hang; fasten, attach.

przywieszka *f. Gen.pl.* **-ek** label, tag.

przywieść *pf.* **-wiodę -wiedziesz -wiódł -wiodła -wiedli** *zob.* **przywodzić.**

przywiewać *ipf.* **1.** (*liście, chmury*) blow, drift (*over to a place*); **co go tu przywiało?** *pot.* what brought him here? **2.** (*śniegiem*) (= *przykrywać*) cover.

przywieźć *pf.* **-wiozę -wieziesz -wiózł -wiozła -wieźli** *zob.* **przywozić.**

przywilej *mi Gen.pl.* **-ów** **1.** (= *uprawnienie*) privilege; **przywilej** *l.* **immunitet dyplomatyczny** diplomatic immunity. **2.** (*dokument*) charter; **przywilej erekcyjny** *hist.* building *l.* construction right *l.* privilege; **przywilej lokacyjny** *hist.* settlement grant; **nadać przywilej** grant a charter. **3.** *prawn.* lien.

przywitać *pf.* greet, welcome; **przywitać kogoś ciepło** roll out the welcome mat for sb; **przywitać kogoś oficjalnie** give sb red carpet welcome. **~**

się *pf.* exchange greetings, greet each other *l.* one another; **przywitać się z kimś serdecznie** give sb the glad hand.

przywitanie *n.* greeting, welcome; **zrobić coś na przywitanie** do sth by way of greeting.

przywlec *pf.* **-wlokę** *l.* **-wlekę -wleczesz -wlókł** *l.* **-wlekł -wlokła** *l.* **-wlekła -wlekli** drag (*kogoś/coś dokądś* sb/sth up to a place); **przywlec chorobę** bring in a disease; **mógłbyś wreszcie przywlec do mnie tyłek** you could finally drag your ass over to my place. ~ **się** *pf. pot.* drag o.s. (*over to a place*); **był tak słaby, że ledwo przywlókł się do domu** he was so weak that he barely made it *l.* dragged himself home.

przywłaszczać *ipf.* appropriate, purloin, arrogate; (*np. czyjeś ziemie*) appropriate, usurp; *prawn.* convert.

przywłaszczenie *n.* appropriation, arrogation; (*np. czyichś ziem*) appropriation, usurpation; *prawn.* conversion.

przywłaszczyciel *mp* appropriator, usurper, purloiner.

przywłaszczycielka *f. zob.* **przywłaszczyciel**.

przywłaszczyć *pf. zob.* **przywłaszczać**.

przywłoka *f. ryb.* trawl, dragnet (*usu. for lake fishing*).

przywodzący *a. anat.* adducent; **mięsień przywodzący** adductor.

przywodzenie *n. anat.* adduction.

przywodzić *ipf.* **-ódź** **1.** (= *przyprowadzić dokądś*) bring; **przywiedli go na policję** he was brought to the police station; **przywodzić (coś) na myśl** bring *l.* call (sth) to mind; **przywodzić (komuś) na myśl wspomnienia (czegoś)** bring back (in sb) memories (of sth); (*np. o otoczeniu, okolicznościach*) be suggestive of sth, suggest. **2.** (= *doprowadzić do czegoś*) drive, bring about; **przywieść kogoś do szaleństwa** *l.* **szału** drive sb mad; **przywieść kogoś do rozpaczy** drive sb to despair; **przywodzić kogoś do zguby** bring about sb's ruin *l.* downfall; **przywieść coś do ruiny** bring about the ruin of sth; **przywieść kogoś do ruiny** bring sb to ruin. **3.** *anat.* adduct.

przywołać *pf.*, **przywoływać** *ipf.* **1.** (= *zawołać*) call; **przywołać kogoś gestem** *l.* **skinieniem** beckon sb; (*np. psa, żeby kogoś zostawił*) call off; **przywołać kogoś do porządku** call sb to order, whip sb into line, bring sb to heel; (*zwłaszcza dzieci*) read sb the riot act. **2.** (= *przypomnieć sobie*) recall; **przywołać sen** recall a dream; **przywołać wspomnienia z dzieciństwa** recall (some memories of) one's childhood; **przywołać coś na pamięć** recall sth. **3.** *karty* call to rejoin (*on a player who passed*).

przywołanie *n.* (= *zawołanie*) call, calling; (= *przypomnienie sobie*) recall; **rozmowa z przywołaniem** person-to-person call.

przywozić *ipf.*, **przywieźć** *pf.* **-wożę -wozisz, -wóź** bring (over); **przywieźć kogoś/coś ze sobą** bring sb/sth along; (= *importować*) import; **przywozić** *l.* **sprowadzać coś samolotem** fly sth in.

przywozowy *a.* import; **cło przywozowe** import duty; **taryfa celna przywozowa** import tariff.

przywódca *mp* leader, captain; (*grupy przestęp-* *czej*) ringleader; **przywódca duchowy** spiritual leader, leading light; **przywódca związkowy** *polit.* labor leader; **marionetkowy przywódca** *polit.* figurehead; **nieudolny przywódca** *polit.* lame duck; **urodzony przywódca** born leader.

przywódczy *a.* leader's, leaders'; **zdolności przywódcze** leadership.

przywódczyni *f. zob.* **przywódca**.

przywództwo *n.* leadership; **pod czyimś przywództwem** under sb's leadership; **jednoczyć się pod czyimś przywództwem** unite under sb; **stanąć z kimś do walki o przywództwo** (*np. partii politycznej*) challenge sb for leadership.

przywóz *mi* **-o-** (= *przywiezienie*) delivery; (= *import*) import; (= *rzeczy importowane*) imports.

przywra *f. zool.* trematode, fluke (*Trematoda*).

przywracać *ipf.* restore (*kogoś/coś do* sb/sth to); **przywracać do stanu używalności** (*budynek, pomieszczenie*) rehabilitate; **przywrócić coś do dawnej świetności** restore *l.* return sth to its former glory; **przywrócić coś do porządku** put sth to rights; **przywrócić komuś prawo do czegoś/przywilej** reinvest sb with the right to do sth/with a privilege; **przywrócić komuś przywilej** reinvest sb with a privilege; **przywrócić komuś siły** put the roses back in sb's cheeks; **przywracać komuś wiarę w siebie** restore sb's confidence; **przywracać komuś zdrowie** restore sb's health; **przywracać komuś życie** bring sb back to life; **przywracać kogoś do pracy** *l.* **na stanowisko** reinstate sb; **przywracać kogoś do łask** return sb to one's good graces; **przywracać porządek** restore order; **przywracać równowagę** redress the balance; **przywrócić ruch** (*np. na linii kolejowej*) reopen.

przywrotnik *mi Gen.* **-a** *bot.* lady's mantle (*Alchemilla mollis*).

przywrócenie *n.* restoration; **przywrócenie do życia** revival; **przywrócenie kogoś do pracy** *l.* **na stanowisko** reinstatement; **przywrócenie mocy prawnej** *prawn.* revival; **przywrócenie ruchu** (*np. na linii kolejowej*) reopening.

przywrócić *pf. zob.* **przywracać**.

przywrzeć *pf.* **-wrę -wrzesz, -wrzyj, -warł** *zob.* **przywierać**.

przywspółczulny *a. anat.* parasympathetic; **przywspółczulny układ nerwowy** parasympathetic nervous system.

przywykać *ipf. zob.* **przywyknąć**.

przywykły *a.* accustomed (*do (robienia) czegoś* to (doing) sth); wont (*do (robienia) czegoś* to (do) sth); **przywykły do wczesnego wstawania** used *l.* accustomed to getting up early, wont to get up early.

przywyknąć *pf.* **-ij** get accustomed, get used (*do (robienia) czegoś/kogoś* to (doing) sth/sb); **przywyknąć do nowych warunków** get accustomed *l.* used to new conditions.

przyzakładowy *a.* (*przy fabryce*) factory; (= *firmowy*) company; **przychodnia przyzakładowa** factory *l.* company outpatients clinic; **stołówka przyzakładowa** factory *l.* company canteen; **szkoła przyzakładowa** vestibule school.

przyzębica *f. pat.* periodontosis, paradentosis.

przyzębie *n. Gen.pl.* **-i** *anat.* periodontium.

przyziemić *pf. lotn.* touch down.

przyziemie *n. bud.* ground floor.

przyziemność *f.* mundaneness, prosaicness, pedestrianism.

przyziemny *a.* **1.** (*przy ziemi*) ground; **izgrzyca przyziemna** *bot.* heath grass (*Sieglingia decumbens*); **liść przyziemny** *bot.* basal leaf; **mgła przyziemna** *meteor.* ground fog; **punkt przyziemny** *astron.* perigee. **2.** (= *bez polotu*) down-to-earth, earthbound, mundane; (*np. o stylu pisania*) pedestrian; **przyziemny człowiek** literal person; **przyziemne marzenia** mundane dreams; **przyziemne plany** down-to-earth plans; **przyziemne myśli** earthbound thoughts.

przyznać *pf.*, **przyznawać** *ipf.* **-znaję -znajesz, -znawaj 1.** (= *zgodzić się*) admit, acknowledge; **przyznać komuś rację** admit that sb is right; **przyznać, że...** acknowledge *l.* concede that...; **muszę przyznać, że...** I have to confess *l.* admit that...; **trzeba przyznać, że...** admittedly... **2.** (= *udzielić, wydać*) award, grant (*komuś coś* sb sth); (*tytuł naukowy*) confer (*komuś* upon sb); (= *przydzielić*) allocate; **przyznać coś komuś na drodze sądowej** adjudge sth to sb; **przyznać komuś odszkodowanie** award *l.* grant sb a compensation; **przyznać komuś nagrodę** award sb a prize; **przyznać komuś prawo stałego pobytu** grant sb the right of permanent residence; **przyznać komuś premię** award sb a bonus; **przyznać komuś stypendium** grant sb a scholarship. **~ się** *pf.*, **przyznawać się** *ipf.* confess, own up to (*do czegoś* to sth); admit; **przyznawać się do autorstwa czegoś** (*o mężczyźnie*) father sth; (*o kobiecie*) mother sth; **przyznać się do błędu** recognize one's error, own to a mistake; **przyznać się do bycia homoseksualistą** come out, come out of the closet; **przyznać się do czegoś** come clean about sth; (*np. do zamachu, zabójstwa*) claim responsibility for sth; **przyznać się do morderstwa** confess to murder; **przyznać się do porażki** admit *l.* acknowledge *l.* concede defeat, haul down the flag *l.* colors; **przyznać się do winy** confess one's guilt; **(nie) przyznać się do winy** *prawn.* plead (not) guilty; **muszę się do czegoś przyznać** I have sth to confess.

przyznanie *n.* (= *uznanie*) acknowledgement, admission; (= *udzielenie*) award, granting; (= *zasądzenie*) adjudication; (*stopnia naukowego*) conferment (*komuś* upon sb); (*np. funduszy*) allocation. **~ się** *n.* acknowledgement, confession, admission; **przyznanie się do błędu** recognition of one's error; **przyznanie się do porażki/niepowodzenia** admission of one's defeat/failure; **przyznanie się do winy** confession of one's guilt; *prawn.* plea of guilty.

przyzwać *pf.* **-zwę -zwiesz, -zwij** *zob.* **przyzywać.**

przyzwalać *ipf.*, **przyzwolić** *pf. lit.* consent, concede, acquiesce (*komuś na coś* to sb's doing sth).

przyzwalający *a.* **1.** permissive, acquiescent; **przyzwalający uśmiech** permissive *l.* acquiescent smile. **2.** *gram.* concessive, adversative;

zdanie przyzwalające concessive *l.* adversative clause, adverbial clause of concession.

przyzwoicie *adv.* (= *moralnie*) decently, properly, respectably; (= *odpowiednio*) decently, suitably; **przyzwoicie za coś wynagrodzić** offer a decent pay for sth; **wyglądać przyzwoicie** look decently; **zachowywać się przyzwoicie** behave properly; **zachowuj się przyzwoicie!** (*zwł. do dziecka*) behave yourself!; **żyć przyzwoicie** *l.* uczciwie keep to the straight and narrow, tread the straight and narrow path.

przyzwoitka *f. Gen.pl.* **-ek** chaperon, chaperone; **towarzyszyć dziewczynie w charakterze przyzwoitki** chaperon a girl, play propriety for a girl; **robić za przyzwoitkę** (= *towarzyszyć gdzieś parze jako osoba trzecia*) play gooseberry; **chyba nie chcecie, żebym z wami poszedł i robił za przyzwoitkę, co?** you don't really want me to go with you and play gooseberry, do you?

przyzwoitość *f.* decency, propriety, decorum; **dla przyzwoitości** for decency's sake, for the sake of appearances; **poczucie przyzwoitości** sense of decorum; **przyzwoitość nakazuje mi milczeć** I'll say nothing for decency's sake; **zdobyć się na tyle przyzwoitości, żeby...** have the grace to...; **zwykła przyzwoitość wymaga, żeby...** it's common decency to...

przyzwoity *a.* (= *moralny*) decent, respectable, proper; (*o dowcipie, języku*) clean; (*o ludziach*) nice; **przyzwoity człowiek** decent *l.* nice man; (= *odpowiedni*) decent, proper, suitable; (*np. o mieszkaniu, ubraniu*) presentable; **przyzwoite ubranie** decent *l.* presentable clothes; **przyzwoite zachowanie** proper behavior; **przyzwoity zarobek** decent pay; **na przyzwoitym poziomie** up to the mark.

przyzwolenie *n.* consent, concession, acquiescence; **bez przyzwolenia** without permission; **okolicznik przyzwolenia** *gram.* adverbial of concession.

przyzwolić *pf.* **-ól** *zob.* **przyzwalać.**

przyzwyczaić *pf.* **-czaję -czaisz, -czaj, przyzwyczajać** *ipf.* accustom, habituate (*kogoś do (robienia) czegoś* sb to (doing) sth). **~ się** *pf.*, **przyzwyczajać się** *ipf.* get used, get accustomed, accustom o.s. (*do kogoś / czegoś l. do (robienia) czegoś* to sb/sth *l.* to (doing) sth); (= *nabrać przyzwyczajenia*) fall into the habit (*do robienia czegoś* of doing sth); **do wszystkiego można się przyzwyczaić** one can get used to anything, you'll get used to it.

przyzwyczajenie *n.* habit; **mieć przyzwyczajenie robienia czegoś** be in the habit of doing sth; **nabrać przyzwyczajenia do robienia czegoś** fall into the habit of doing sth; **robił to z przyzwyczajenia** he did it out of habit *l.* as a matter of habit; **robić coś siłą przyzwyczajenia** do sth by *l.* from force of habit; **przyzwyczajenie jest drugą naturą człowieka** habit is *l.* becomes second nature; **niewolnik przyzwyczajeń** a creature of habit.

przyzwyczajony *a.* **-eni** used, accustomed (*do (robienia) czegoś* to (doing) sth); **przyzwyczajony do wstawania o szóstej rano** used *l.* accustomed to getting up at six (o'clock) in the morning; **nie**

jestem do tego przyzwyczajony I'm not used *l.* accustomed to this, I'm new to this.

przyzywać *ipf.*, **przyzwać** *pf.* **-am -asz** *lit.* summon; (*gestem*) beckon.

przyżegać *ipf.*, **przyżec** *pf. med.* cauterize.

przyżeglować *pf.* sail into.

przyżenić się *pf.*, **przyżeniać się** *ipf. pot.* marry into (*e.g. a family*).

przyżółknąć *pf.* grow *l.* become yellowish.

PS, P.S. *abbr.* (= *postscriptum*) P.S., p.s. (*postscript*).

psa *itd. ma zob.* **pies.**

psalm *mi Bibl.* Psalm; *teor.lit.* psalm; **psalm błagalny** psalm of supplication; **psalm dziękczynny** psalm of thanksgiving; **psalm pokutny** psalm of penance.

psalmista *mp* (*poeta; śpiewak*) psalmist.

psalmodia *f. Gen.* **-ii** (*zbiór psalmów; śpiewanie psalmów*) psalmody.

psalmograf *ma lit.* psalmograph, psalmist; psalmodist.

psalterion, psalterium *mi muz.* psaltery.

psałterz *mi Gen.* **-a** *Bibl.* Psalter.

psammit *mi miner.* arenite, psammite.

psammofit *mi bot.* psammophyte.

psammon *mi ekol.* psammon.

psefit *mi min.* psephite.

pseudo *n. pot.* (= *pseudonim*) pseudonym, alias.

pseudogotycki *a. gł. bud.* pseudo-Gothic.

pseudogotyk *mi bud.* pseudo-Gothic (style).

pseudointelektualizm *mi* pseudointellectualism.

pseudokibic *mp pog., sport* hooligan.

pseudoklasycyzm *mi teor.lit.* pseudoclassicism.

pseudoklasyczny *a. teor.lit.* pseudoclassic, pseudoclassical.

pseudoklasyk *mp teor.lit.* pseudoclassic.

pseudoludowość *f.* pseudo-folklore.

pseudonauka *f.* pseudoscience.

pseudonaukowy *a.* pseudoscientific.

pseudonim *mi* pseudonym; **pseudonim artystyczny** stage name; **pseudonim konspiracyjny** nom de guerre; **pseudonim literacki** pen name; **tworzyć pod pseudonimem** work pseudonymously.

pseudopodia *pl. Gen.* **-ów** *biol.* pseudopodia.

pseudopsychologiczny *f.* **żargon pseudopsychologiczny** psychobabble.

pseudouczony *mp iron.* pseudoscholar, sciolist.

psi *a.* dog's, doggish, doggy; (*w języku fachowym*) canine; **psia buda** kennel, doghouse; **psie figle** antics, capers; **psi grzyb** *pot.* inedible mushroom; **psi obowiązek** bounden duty; **psia pogoda** foul weather; **psia trawka** *bot.* matgrass (*Nardus stricta*); **psia wachta** *żegl.* dogwatch (*from midnight till four a.m.*); **psi węch** intuition, sixth sense; **psi zaprzęg** dog team; **kupić coś za psi grosz** buy sth dirt cheap; **psim swędem** by a fluke; **przyczepić się do kogoś jak rzep do psiego ogona** cling *l.* stick to sb like a leech, cling to sb like a barnacle; **psi synu!** *przest., obelż.* you son

of a bitch!; **Psia Gwiazda** *astron.* (= *Syriusz*) the Dog Star.

psiak *ma* doggy, doggie.

psiakość *int. pot.* damnation!, by jingo!

psiakrew¹ *int. pot.* damn!, hell!

psiakrew² *mi* (*zwykle pl., tylko jako wyzwisko*) scoundrel, rogue.

psiamać *int. wulg.* blast!

psianka *f. Gen.pl.* **-ek** *bot.* nightshade, solanum (*Solanum*); **psianka słodkogórz** bittersweet (*Solanum dulcamara*).

psiankowate *pl. Gen.* **-ych** *bot.* solanaceous plants (*Solanaceae*).

psiarnia *f. Gen.pl.* **-i 1.** (*pomieszczenie*) kennel(s); **zimno tu jak w psiarni** *pot.* it is colder than in a well *l.* grave here. **2.** (*sfora*) pack of hounds. **3.** (*psy*) doggery; **a to jest moja psiarnia** (= *a oto moje psy*) (*zwłaszcza pieszczotliwie*) and these guys here are my dogs.

psiątko *n.* pup, puppy.

psik *int.* **a psik!** ahchoo!

psikus *mi Gen.* **-a** lark, prank, trick; **spłatać komuś psikusa** *l.* **figla** play a trick on sb.

psina *f. emf.* doggy, doggie.

psioczyć *ipf. pot.* grumble (*na kogoś/coś* about *l.* at sb/sth); grouse (*na kogoś/coś* about sb/sth).

psipsi *n. indecl. dziec.* pee-pee, wee-wee.

psisko *n. emf.* great big dog; (*pieszczotliwie*) doggie; **moje kochane psisko!** (*do psa*) there's a good boy!, that's a good boy!

psocić *ipf.* play pranks (*komuś* on sb); (*o dzieciach*) be up to mischief.

psota *f.* prank; (*u dzieci*) mischief.

psotnica *f. zob.* **psotnik.**

psotnik *mp* prankster; (*zwłaszcza o dziecku*) mischief.

psotny *a.* prankish, impish, elfish; **psotne dziecko** mischievous *l.* impish *l.* elfish child; **psotny kotek/szczeniak** playful kitten/puppy.

psowate *pl. Gen.* **-ych** *zool.* canines, canids (*Canidae*).

pst *int. hist.*

pstrąg *ma icht.* trout (*Salmo l. Salvelinus*); **pstrąg potokowy** brown trout (*Salmo trutta*).

pstro *adv.* **1.** patchily, variedly; **mieć pstro w głowie** be light-headed, be a rattlebrain *l.* rattlehead *l.* rattlepate. **2.** *pot.* naught, zilch; **- No i co? - Pstro!** - And that? - Zilch!

pstrokacizna *f.* motley, medley, patchiness (*of light colors*).

pstrokaty *a.* patchy, motley; **pstrokaty koc** patchy blanket; **pstrokaty koń** dappled horse; (*o maści dwubarwnej, zwykle w czarno-białe kropki*) piebald horse.

pstruszka *f. orn.* **pstruszka szkarłatna** American redstart (*Setophaga ruticilla*).

pstry *a.* mottled, motley, patchy; **pstry koc** patchy blanket; **pstry tłum** motley crowd; **łaska pańska na pstrym koniu jeździ** being in your master's good graces doesn't last forever, your good fortune can be changed by a twist of fate, great men's favors are uncertain.

pstryczek *mi* -czk- *Gen.* -a *pot.* fillip; **dać komuś pstryczka w nos** take sb down a peg.

pstryk *int.* snap, click.

pstrykać *ipf.*, **pstryknąć** *pf.* -nę -niesz, -nij **1.** (*palcami, wyłącznikiem*) snap, click; **pstryknąć palcami** snap one's fingers. **2.** *pot.* (= *robić zdjęcia*) snap, take snapshots.

pstrzyć *ipf.* -yj fleck, dapple.

psubrat *mp pl.* -y *pot.* scoundrel.

psuć *ipf.* **1.** (= *uszkadzać*) break, damage; (= *powodować gnicie*) addle; (*zęby*) decay, rot; **psuć komuś krew** get under sb's skin, get sb's goat; **psuć** *l.* pokrzyżować **komuś szyki** upset sb's plans; *Br.* put a spoke in sb's wheel, queer one's pitch; **psuć sobie oczy** ruin one's eyesight, pore one's eyes out; **psuć sobie zdrowie/żołądek** ruin one's health/stomach; **psuć powietrze** *pot.* foul up the air, fart. **2.** (= *pogarszać, mącić*) spoil; (*efekt wizualny*) kill; (*stosunki między ludźmi*) sour; **psuć komuś humor** damp sb's spirits; **psuć zabawę** spoil *l.* kill the fun; **nie psuj innym** *l.* **ludziom zabawy** don't be such a spoilsport *l.* killjoy, don't be such a wet blanket; **osoba psująca innym zabawę** killjoy, sportspoil, wet blanket; **psuć widok** spoil the view; **psuć wrażenie** spoil the show. **3.** (= *rozpieszczać*) spoil; (*zwłaszcza dziecko*) pamper; (= *deprawować*) pervert, corrupt. **~ się** *ipf.* **1.** (= *uszkadzać się*) break down; **samochód znowu się zepsuł** the car's broken down again. **2.** (= *gnić*) (*o jedzeniu*) go bad; (*o zębach*) decay; **łatwo się psujący** perishable; **artykuły łatwo się psujące** perishables. **3.** (= *ulegać pogorszeniu*) deteriorate, worsen; **sprawy zaczęły się psuć** the rot has set in; **pogoda się psuje** so much for blue skies and sunshine, looks like we're in for it; **słuch/wzrok mi się psuje** my hearing/sight is going.

psuj *mp żart. zob.* **psuja.**

psuja *mp l. f. żart.* spoiler.

psychastenia *f. Gen.* -ii *pat.* psychasthenia.

psychasteniczny *a. pat.* psychasthenic.

psychastenik *mp pat.* psychasthenic.

Psyche *f. indecl. mit.* Psyche.

psyche *f. indecl.* psyche.

psychiatra *mp* psychiatrist; **biegły psychiatra sądowy** alienist.

psychiatria *f. Gen.* -ii psychiatry.

psychiatryczny *a.* psychiatric, psychiatrical; **klinika psychiatryczna** psychiatric *l.* mental clinic; **leczenie psychiatryczne** psychiatric *l.* mental treatment; **oddział psychiatryczny** psychiatric ward; **poradnia psychiatryczna** psychiatric outpatients' clinic; **szpital psychiatryczny** psychiatric *l.* mental hospital; **zakład psychiatryczny** mental asylum *l.* institution.

psychiczna *f. pot. zob.* **psychiczny².**

psychicznie *adv.* mentally, psychically; **chory psychicznie** mentally ill; (*pacjent*) mental patient; **niezrównoważony psychicznie** mentally *l.* emotionally disturbed; **skrzywiony psychicznie** mentally twisted; **przygotowywać się/kogoś psychicznie na coś** psych o.s./sb up for sth; **załamać się psychicznie** suffer a mental breakdown; *pot.* crack up.

psychiczny¹ *a.* mental, psychic, psychical; **choroba psychiczna** mental illness *l.* disease; **napięcie psychiczne** psychical *l.* mental tension; **rozwój psychiczny** psychical development; **uraz psychiczny** psychical *l.* mental trauma; **zaburzenia psychiczne** mental disorders; **zahamowanie psychiczne** mental inhibition; **załamanie psychiczne** mental breakdown; **przejść załamanie psychiczne** suffer a mental breakdown; *pot.* crack up.

psychiczny² *mi pot.* lunatic, mental; **a ty co, psychiczny jesteś?** are you mental or what?

psychika *f.* **1.** (= *cechy psychiczne*) psyche. **2.** (= *życie psychiczne*) mental make-up, mind, psychology (*e.g. of a criminal*).

psychoanalityczny *a.* psychoanalytic, psychoanalytical.

psychoanalityk *mp* psychoanalyst.

psychoanaliza *f. med., psych.* psychoanalysis; **poddawać psychoanalizie** psychoanalyze.

psychodeliczny *a.* psychedelic; **środek psychodeliczny** psychedelic (drug).

psychodrama *f. med., psych.* psychodrama.

psychofizjologia *f. Gen.* -ii psychophysiology.

psychofizyczny *a. psych.* psychophysical.

psychofizyka *f. psych.* psychophysics.

psychokineza *f.* telekinesis, psychokinesis.

psychol *mp pot.* (= *dziwak*) wacko, whacko; (= *chory psychicznie*) psycho.

psycholingwistyka *f. jęz.* psycholinguistics.

psycholog *mp pl.* -dzy *l.* -owie psychologist; **psycholog kryminalny** profiler; **psycholog szkolny** school psychologist.

psychologia *f. Gen.* -ii psychology; **psychologia funkcjonalna** functionalism; **psychologia głębi** depth psychology; **psychologia kliniczna** clinical psychology; **psychologia nauczania** educational psychology; **psychologia postaci** Gestalt psychology; **psychologia poznawcza** cognitive psychology; **psychologia rozwojowa** developmental psychology; **psychologia społeczna** social psychology; **psychologia stosowana** applied psychology; **psychologia zwierząt** animal psychology.

psychologiczny *a.* psychological; **wojna psychologiczna** psychological warfare.

psychologizacja *f.* psychologization.

psychologizm *mi* psychologism.

psychologizować *ipf.* psychologize.

psychometria *f. Gen.* -ii *psych.* psychometrics, psychometry.

psychomotoryczny *a.* psychomotor.

psychomotoryka *f.* psychomotion.

psychonerwica *f. pat.* neurosis, psychoneurosis.

psychopata *mp* psychopath, psychopathic person.

psychopatia *f. Gen.* -ii *pat., psych.* psychopathy.

psychopatka *f. Gen.pl.* -ek *zob.* **psychopata.**

psychopatologia *f. Gen.* -ii psychopathology.

psychopatyczny *a.* psychopathic.

psychosomatyczny *a.* psychosomatic.

psychosomatyka *f.* psychosomatics, psychosomatic medicine.

psychospołeczny *a. lit.* psychosocial.

psychotechniczny *a.* psychotechnical.

psychotechnika *f.* psychotechnics, psycho-technology.

psychoterapeuta *mp* psychotherapist, psy-chotherapeutist.

psychoterapeutyczny *a.* psychotherapeutic.

psychoterapia *f. Gen.* **-ii** psychotherapy; **psychoterapia grupowa** group psychotherapy *l.* therapy.

psychotoniczny *a. med.* psychotonic; **środek psychotoniczny** psychotonic drug.

psychotropowy *a. med.* psychotropic; **środek psychotropowy** psychotropic (drug).

psychotyczny *a.* psychotic.

psychotyk *ma* psychotic.

psychoza *f.* **1.** *pat.* psychosis; **psychoza maniakalno-depresyjna** manic-depressive disorder. **2.** *pot.* psychosis; **psychoza zbiorowa** mass psychosis.

psychrometr *mi fiz.* psychrometer, wet-and-dry-bulb thermometer.

psychrometria *f. Gen.* **-ii** *fiz.* psychrometry.

psyk *int.* hist. – *mi* hist.

psykać *ipf.*, **psyknąć** *pf.* **-nę -niesz, -nij** (*żeby uciszyć*) hush; (*żeby zwrócić uwagę*) psst.

psylofit *mi paleont.* psilophyte (*Psilophytopsida l. Psilophytinae*).

psyt *int.* hush, hist; ps(s)t.

pszczelarski *a.* apiarian.

pszczelarstwo *n.* beekeeping, apiculture.

pszczelarz *mp* beekeeper, apiculturist, apiarist.

pszczeli *a.* bee, bee's, bees'; (*w języku fachowym*) apian; **jad pszczeli** bee venom; **kit pszczeli** (= *propolis*) bee glue, hive dross; **mleczko pszczele** royal jelly; **miód pszczeli** bee honey; **wosk pszczeli** beeswax.

pszczelnik *mi Gen.* **-a** *bot.* dragonhead (*Dracocephalum*).

pszczolinka *f. ent.* andrena (*Andrena*).

pszczoła *f. Gen.pl.* **-ół** bee; **pszczoła miodna** *ent.* honeybee (*Apis mellifera*); **pszczoła robotnica** worker bee.

pszczołojad *ma orn.* honey buzzard, pern (*Pernis apivorus*).

pszczoły *pl. Gen.* **-ół** *ent.* bees (*Apoidea*).

pszczółka *f. Gen.pl.* **-ek** bee; **pracowity jak pszczółka** as busy as a bee.

pszenica *f. bot.* wheat (*Triticum*); **pszenica jara** spring wheat; **pszenica ozima** winter wheat; **obsiany pszenicą** *roln.* under wheat.

pszeniczny *a.* wheat, frumentaceous; **pole pszeniczne** wheat field, field of wheat.

pszenny *a.* wheat, wheaten; **chleb pszenny** wheat bread; **mąka pszenna** wheaten flour; **otręby pszenne** wheat bran.

pszenżyto *n. bot.* triticale (*Triticale*).

pt. *abbr.* **1.** (= *piątek*) Fri. (*Friday*). **2.** (= *pod tytułem*) entitled.

ptactwo *n.* fowl; **ptactwo domowe** domestic fowl, fowl; **ptactwo łowne** game fowl *l.* birds; **ptactwo ozdobne** decorative birds; **ptactwo wod-**

ne waterfowl, water birds; **dzikie ptactwo** wildfowl; **zwierzyna i ptactwo** fur and feather.

ptak *ma* bird; **ptak brodzący** wading bird, wader; **ptak drapieżny** bird of prey, raptor; **ptak hodowlany** domestic fowl; **ptak łowczy** *myśl.* hunting bird; **ptak łowny** game bird; **ptak nocny** nocturnal bird; **ptak przelotny** bird of passage; **ptak śpiewający** songbird; **ptak wędrowny** migratory bird; **ptak wodny** water *l.* aquatic bird, waterfowl; **ptak zimujący** wintering bird; **dziki ptak** wildfowl; **rajskie ptaki** *orn.* birds of paradise (*Paradisaeidae*); **niebieski ptak** (= *ktoś niezależny*) adventurer; (= *darmozjad*) sponger; **być niebieskim ptakiem** live by one's wits; **z lotu ptaka** from above; **widok z lotu ptaka** bird's eye view; **wolny jak ptak** (as) free as a bird; **zły to ptak, co swe gniazdo kala** it is an ill bird that fouls its own nest.

ptaki *pl. Gen.* **-ów** *zool.* birds (*Aves*); **(już) po ptakach** *pot.* it's all over (but the shouting).

ptasi *a.* bird's, birds'; (*w języku fachowym*) avian; **ptasie gniazdo** bird's nest; **ptasie mleko** *orn.* pigeon milk; **rdest ptasi** *bot.* knotgrass, birdgrass (*Polygonum aviculare*); **ptasie mleczko** *kulin.* chocolate-covered marshmallow; **ptasi móżdżek** *obelż.* birdbrain.

ptaszarnia *f. Gen.pl.* **-i** aviary.

ptaszek *ma* **-szk-** **1.** (= *mały ptak*) birdie; **ranny ptaszek** early bird; **jeść jak ptaszek** eat like a bird. **2.** *iron. l. żart.* good-for-nothing, rascal; **lepszy z niego ptaszek** he's some rascal; **ptaszek uciekł** *l.* **wyfrunął** (*zwykle o złodzieju*) the bird has flown. **3.** *pot.* (= *graficzny znak aprobaty*) check; *Br.* tick.

ptasznik *ma pl.* **-i** *zool.* bird spider (*Avicularia*). – *mp pl.* **-cy** (*hodowca*) bird breeder; (*łowca*) fowler.

ptaszory *pl. Gen.* **-ów** *icht.* flyingfishes (*Exocoetidae*).

ptaszyna *f.* **1.** (= *mały ptak*) (little) birdie. **2.** (= *dziecko l. kobieta*) darling; *Br.* ducky.

ptaszyniec *mi* **-ńc-** *Gen.* **-a** *bot.* (common) bird's-foot, bird-foot, French serradella (*Ornithopus sativus*). – *ma* **-ńc-** *zool.* red mite, chicken mite, roost mite (*Dermanyssus gallinae*).

pteranodon *ma paleont.* pteranodon (*Pteranodon*).

pterodaktyl *ma Gen.pl.* **-ów** *paleont.* pterodactyl (*Pterodactylus*).

pterozaur *ma paleont.* (= *gad z rzędu Pterosauria*) pterosaur.

ptialina *f. biol., chem.* ptyalin.

ptomaina *f.* (*zwykle pl.*) *chem.* ptomaine.

ptysiowy *a. kulin.* puff, chou; **groszek ptysiowy** puff pastry croutons.

ptyś *mi Gen.* **-a** *Gen.pl.* **-ów** *l.* **-i** *kulin.* cream puff, chou.

pub *mi* pub, saloon; *pot.* boozer; **rundka po pubach** pub-crawling.

publicity *f. indecl.* publicity.

public relations *pl. indecl.* (= *kreowanie pozytywnego wizerunku firmy, osoby, instytucji*) public relations.

publicysta *mp,* **publicystka** *f. Gen.pl.* **-ek** publicist, journalist.

publicystyczny *a.* journalistic; **program publicystyczny** political commentary program; **tekst publicystyczny** political commentary (text).

publicystyka *f.* (political commentary) journalism.

publiczka *f. Gen.pl.* **-ek** *iron.* the gallery; **grać pod publiczkę** play to the galley.

publicznie *adv.* publicly, in public; **ogłosić coś publicznie** announce sth publicly; **pokazywać się publicznie** appear in public, show o.s., be in the public eye; **ujawniać coś publicznie** divulge sth, blow the lid off sth; **publicznie prać brudy** wash one's dirty linen in public.

publiczność *f.* **1.** (= *widownia*) audience; **zelektryzować publiczność** (*o występie, artyście*) steal the show. **2.** (= *ogół*) the general public; **otwierać coś dla publiczności** open sth to the public; **zamknięty dla publiczności** (*posiedzenie, wykład*) closed-door, in camera.

publiczny *a.* public; **biblioteka publiczna** public library; **dobro publiczne** common good; **dom publiczny** brothel; *euf.* house of ill fame *l.* repute; **dług publiczny** *ekon.* public *l.* national debt; **droga publiczna** public road; **egzekucja publiczna** public execution; **finanse publiczne** public finance; **grosz publiczny** *l.* **kiesa publiczna** public funds, the public purse; **interes publiczny** public interest; **w interesie publicznym** in the public interest; **miejsce publiczne** public place; **w miejscu publicznym** in public; **obnażanie się w miejscu publicznym** *prawn.* indecent exposure; **opinia publiczna** the public opinion; **badanie opinii publicznej** (public) opinion poll; **oskarżyciel publiczny** *prawn.* public prosecutor, prosecuting attorney; **oskarżenie publiczne** *prawn.* public prosecution; **osoba publiczna** public figure; **być osobą publiczną** be a public figure, be in the public eye; **porządek publiczny** public order; *prawn.* peace; **naruszenie porządku publicznego** *prawn.* breach of the peace; **roboty publiczne** public works; **stanowisko publiczne** public office; **tajemnica publiczna** open secret; **telewizja publiczna** public television; **toaleta publiczna** public lavatory *l.* convenience; **własność publiczna** public property *l.* domain; **wróg publiczny** public enemy; **wystąpienie publiczne** (*przemówienie*) public speech; (*pokazanie się*) public appearance; **do użytku publicznego** for public use; **na widok publiczny** on public display; **wystawić coś na widok publiczny** put sth on public display.

publika *f. pot.* the gallery, the audience.

publikacja *f.* **1.** (= *opublikowanie*) publication, release. **2.** (= *utwór wydany drukiem*) publication.

publikatory *pl. Gen.* **-ów** mass media.

publikować *ipf.* (= *wydać drukiem*) publish; (= *podać do wiadomości*) release.

puch *mi* **1.** (*u ptaków, na twarzy, na roślinach*) down; **puch kielichowy** *bot.* pappus; **rozbić w puch** reduce *l.* smash sth to matchwood,

smash sth to smithereens. **2.** (= *meszek*) fluff. **3.** (= *śnieg*) powder snow.

puchacz *ma orn.* eagle owl (*Bubo bubo*).

puchar *mi* **1.** (= *kielich*) chalice, goblet; **między ustami a brzegiem pucharu** between the cup and the lip, 'twixt cup and lip there's many a slip. **2.** (= *nagroda; t. zawody*) cup; **puchar przechodni** challenge cup; **Puchar Davisa** *tenis* Davis Cup; **Puchar Polski** Polish Cup; **Puchar Świata** *piłka nożna* the World Cup; **Puchar UEFA** *piłka nożna* UEFA Cup; **Puchar Zdobywców Pucharów** *piłka nożna* Cup Winners' Cup (*discontinued*).

pucharek *mi* **-rk-** *Gen.* **-a** **1.** (*do wina*) (small) chalice, (small) goblet. **2.** (*do lodów*) cup.

pucharowy *a. sport* cup; **spotkanie pucharowe** cup tie; **system pucharowy** knockout system; **rozgrywki systemem pucharowym** knockout competition.

puchaty *a.* downy, fluffy; **puchate włosy** fluffy hair.

puchlina, puchlina wodna *f. pat.* edema, dropsy; **puchlina brzuszna** ascites.

puchlinowy *a. pat.* edematous, edematose, dropsical.

puchnąć *ipf.* **-nę -niesz, -nij, puchł** *l.* **puchnął puchła puchli** **1.** (= *nabrzmiewać*) swell; (*w języku fachowym*) intumesce; **głowa mi puchnie od tego hałasu!** this noise is ear-splitting!; **aż uszy puchną od tej muzyki** this music is ear-splitting; **uszy mi puchną od jej gadania** she talks my ears off; **bić kogoś i patrzeć, czy równo puchnie** give sb a sound thrashing. **2.** *pot.* (= *tracić kondycję*) burn out, flake out.

puchowiec *mi bot.* kapok (tree), silk-cotton (tree) (*Ceiba pentandra*).

puchowy *a.* **1.** (= *odnoszący się do puchu*) downy, fluffy; **piórko puchowe** *orn.* plumule. **2.** (= *zrobiony z puchu, wypchany puchem*) down; **kołdra puchowa** eiderdown; **kurtka puchowa** down jacket.

puchy *pl. Gen.* **puch** *pot.* emptiness; **Jezu, ale tu dziś puchy!** gee *l.* jeez, it's so empty here today!

pucołowaty *a.* chubby-cheeked.

pucować *ipf. pot.* (= *dokładnie czyścić*) rub (*sth clean*); (= *polerować*) polish, shine.

pucybut *mp pl.* **-ci** *l.* **-y** bootblack, shoeblack.

pucz *mi Gen.pl.* **-ów** *zwł. polit.* putsch; coup d'état.

pud *mi Gen.* **-a** *hist.* pood; **nudy na pudy** total snooze *l.* yawn; **- jak tam film? - nudy na pudy.** - how was the movie? - a total snooze *l.* yawn *l.* a snooze-o-rama.

pudding *mi kulin.* pudding.

pudel *ma* **-dl-** *kynol.* poodle.

pudełko *n. Gen.pl.* **-ek** (*pojemnik*) box; **pudełko od zapałek** matchbox; (*na lody, margarynę*) tub; (*zawartość*) box, boxful; **pudełko czekoladek** box of chocolates; **pudełko zapałek** box of matches.

pudełkowy *a.* (= *dotyczący pudełka*) box; (= *taki jak pudełko*) box-like.

puder *mi* **-dr-** powder; (*do twarzy*) face powder; **puder kosmetyczny** cosmetic powder; **cukier puder** *kulin.* caster sugar, confectioners' sugar; *Br.*

icing sugar; **puder w sztyfcie** powder stick; **puder formierski** *techn.* parting powder; **puszek do pudru** powder puff.

puderniczka *f. Gen.pl.* **-ek** (powder) compact.

pudło[1] *n. Gen.pl.* **pudeł 1.** (*opakowanie*) (large) box; **pudło na kapelusze** hatbox, bandbox; **pudło rezonansowe** *muz.* soundbox. **2.** (= *nadwozie*) body. **3.** *pot.* (*o samochodzie*) crate, jalopy. **4.** *pot.* (*o instrumencie*) old musical instrument; **czasem lubię trochę pobrzdąkać na moim starym pudle** (*o gitarze*) I sometimes like to give my old guitar a little strum. **5.** *pog.* (*kobieta*) frump; **stare pudło!** old frump! **6.** *pot.* (= *więzienie*) joint, stir, jug; **siedzieć w pudle** be in stir *l.* jug.

pudło[2] *n. pot.* (= *chybiony strzał*) miss; **bez pudła** (= *bezbłędnie, dokładnie*) spot-on.

pudłować *ipf. pot.* miss.

pudrować *ipf.* powder; **pudrować sobie twarz** powder one's face. **~ się** *ipf.* powder (*usu. one's face*).

pudu *ma zool.* pudu (*Pudu pudu*).

pueblo *n.* pueblo.

puenta *f.* (*np. opowiadania*) punch line, (culminating) point; (*dowcipu*) punch line.

puentować *ipf. lit.* (= *wyróżniać, akcentować*) highlight, stress, emphasize; (= *kończyć puentą*) deliver a punch line.

puentylizm *mi mal.* pointillism.

puf[1] *mi* (*mebel*) pouf, pouffe.

puf[2] *int.* chuff.

pugilares *mi przest.* wallet, billfold; *Br.* notecase.

puginał *mi hist.* dagger.

pukać *ipf.*, **puknąć** *pf.* **1.** (= *stukać, kołatać*) (*do drzwi*) knock; (*głośno*) rap; (*delikatnie*) tap; **pukać do drzwi** knock at *l.* on (sb's) door; **ktoś puka** there was a knock at *l.* on the door; **pukać palcem w czoło** hit *l.* slap o.s. on the forehead, tap one's forehead with disgust, roll one's eyes; **pukać do czyichś drzwi** *przen.* apply for sth. **2.** (= *zderzyć się*) (*tylko pf.*) bump; **puknąć komuś samochód** bump into sb else's car. **3.** *pot.* (= *strzelać*) shoot. **~ się** *ipf.* (*tylko w zwrocie*) **puknij się w czoło** *l.* **w głowę!** you must be nuts!

pukawka *f. Gen.pl.* **-ek 1.** (*zabawka*) popgun. **2.** *żart.* (*broń palna*) shooting iron.

pukiel *mi* **-kl-** *Gen.* **-a** *Gen.pl.* **-i** *l.* **-ów** lock (*of hair*); (= *kędzior*) curl.

puklerz *mi Gen.* **-a** *hist.* targe, target.

puknąć *pf.* **-nę -niesz, -nij** *zob.* **pukać. ~ się** *pf. zob.* **pukać się.**

puknięty *a.* **1.** (= *uderzony*) knocked, tapped, rapped; *zob. także* **pukać. 2.** (*o osobie*) *pot.* nuts. **3.** (*o pojeździe*) *pot.* dented.

puk-puk *int.* knock-knock.

pula *f.* **1.** (= *stawka*) pool, pot; jackpot; kitty; **zgarnąć całą pulę** (*w pokerze*) hit the jackpot; (*w kasynie*) sweep the board; **pula finałowa** pool of finalists, finalists' pool. **2.** (= *partia gry*) game. **3.** (= *ilość czegoś*) amount, supply; (*w loterii*) raffle prizes; **pula nagród** prizes (*available in a competition*).

pularda *f. roln., kulin.* poulard, poularde.

pulchność *f.* **1.** (*np. ciasta*) crumbiness, fluffiness; (*np. ziemi*) mellowness. **2.** (*np. ciała*) plumpness.

pulchny *a.* **1.** (*pieczywo*) crumby, fluffy; (*ziemia*) mellow. **2.** (*ciało*) plump; (*osoba*) podgy.

pulman *mi Gen.* **-a** *kol.* Pullman (car).

pulmanowski *a. kol.* Pullman; **wagon pulmanowski** Pullman (car).

pulmonologia *f. Gen.* **-ii** *med.* pulmonology.

pulmonologiczny *a. med.* pulmonary, pulmonic.

pulower *mi* pullover, slipover.

pulpa *f. techn.* pulp.

pulpet *mi Gen.* **-u** *l.* **-a 1.** *kulin.* meatball. **2.** *żart.* (= *grubas*) roly-poly.

pulpit *mi* (*na nuty*) music stand *l.* rest; desk top; (*do czytania*) reading desk; (*do pisania*) writing desk; *kośc.* (*t. wykładowcy*) lectern; **pulpit sterowniczy** *techn.* control panel.

puls *mi* pulse; **badać** *l.* **mierzyć komuś puls** take *l.* feel *l.* check sb's pulse; **trzymać rękę na pulsie** *przen.* keep *l.* have one's finger on the pulse.

pulsacja *f. astron., fiz.* pulsation.

pulsacyjny *a.* pulsational, pulsatory; **dźwięk pulsacyjny** pulsing *l.* pulsating sound; **hamowanie pulsacyjne** *mot.* pumping the brakes; *Br.* cadence braking; **światło pulsacyjne** pulsed light.

pulsar *mi Gen.* **-a** *astron.* pulsar.

pulsator *mi Gen.* **-a 1.** *techn.* pulsator. **2.** *el.* pulser.

pulsometr *mi techn.* pulsometer *l.* expulsor pump.

pulsować *ipf.* **1.** (*o krwi*) pulse; (*o naczyniach krwionośnych, żyłach*) pulsate, throb; (*o sercu*) beat, throb; *przen.* pulsate; **pulsować życiem** pulsate *l.* be throbbing *l.* be bustling with life. **2.** *astron., fiz.* pulsate.

pułap *mi* **1.** *bud.* (= *sufit*) ceiling; **ślepy pułap** false ceiling *l.* floor; **pułap przeciwdźwiękowy** sound boarding; **pułap chmur** *meteor.* cloud ceiling. **2.** *lotn.* ceiling; **pułap praktyczny** service ceiling; **pułap teoretyczny** absolute ceiling. **3.** *przen.* limit; **osiągnąć pułap swoich możliwości** reach the (upper) limits of one's abilities, exhaust one's potential; **(nieprzekraczalny) pułap kariery zawodowej** (*zwłaszcza wynikający z dyskryminacji*) glass ceiling.

pułapka *f. Gen.pl.* **-ek** (= *potrzask; zasadzka*) trap; (= *sidła*) snare; (= *podstęp*) setup, frame-up; **pułapka na myszy** mousetrap; **pułapka minowa** *wojsk.* booby trap; **wpaść w pułapkę** fall in a trap; **wietrzyć w czymś pułapkę** smell a rat in sth; **zastawiać na kogoś pułapkę** set a trap for sb; **złapać w pułapkę** ensnare, entrap; **złapać się w pułapkę** *l.* **sidła** (*o zwierzęciu*) spring a trap.

pułk *mi wojsk.* regiment; *lotn.* group; **pułk piechoty** infantry regiment.

pułkownik *mp zw. wojsk.* colonel.

pułkownikostwo *n.* **1.** (= *ranga pułkownika*) colonelcy, colonelship. **2.** *przest.* (= *pułkownik z żoną*) colonel and his wife.

pułkowy *a. wojsk.* regimental; **sztandar pułkowy** regimental standard.

puma *f. zool.* cougar, puma, mountain lion, panther (*Felis concolor*).

pumeks *mi* (*skała i do mycia*) pumice (stone).

pumeksowy *a.* pumiceous; **proszek pumeksowy** pounce.

pumpernikiel *mi* -kl- *Gen.* -a *l.* -u *kulin.* pumpernickel.

pumpy *pl. Gen.* **pump** *l.* **pumpów** (*spodnie*) plus fours.

punca *f.* 1. (*młotek, rylec*) punch, stamp. 2. (*znak*) maker's mark; *Br.* hallmark.

puncować *ipf.* stamp; *Br.* hallmark.

punicki *a. hist.* Punic; **wojny punickie** Punic Wars.

punk *mp pl.* -i (*osoba*) punker, punk; **punk rock** *muz.* punk rock.

punkcik *mi* speck, dot, spot; (*na ekranie radaru*) blip; **punkcik światła** pinprick *l.* pinpoint of light.

punkcja *f. med.* puncture; **punkcja rdzenia kręgowego** lumbar puncture.

punkt[1] *mi* 1. (*plamka, miejsce, kropka*) point; **patrzeć w jeden punkt** stare at one point; **martwy punkt** standstill, deadlock, stalemate; **utknąć** *l.* **stanąć w martwym punkcie** end in (a) stalemate; **negocjacje stanęły w martwym punkcie** negotiations have come to a standstill; **punkt odniesienia** point of reference; **punkt wyjścia** starting point; **znaleźć się (ponownie) w punkcie wyjścia** be back to square one; **punkt zwrotny** turning point; **czuły punkt** sore point *l.* spot, (soft) underbelly; **trafić w czyjś czuły punkt** hit sb where it hurts; **trafić w najczulszy** *l.* **najsłabszy punkt czegoś** strike at the very heart of sth, go for the jugular; **mocny/słaby punkt** strong/weak point; **to jest jego słaby punkt** it's his weak point, it's a chink in his armor; **w dobrym punkcie** well-situated; **Adam z punktu zmienił zdanie** Adam promptly changed his opinion; **punkt oparcia** point of support; **punkt zaczepienia** foothold; **punkt materialny** *fiz.* particle; **punkt potrójny** *fiz.* triple point; **punkt przegięcia** *mat.* point of inflection; **punkt równonocy** *astron.* equinoctial point; **punkt przyłożenia** *fiz.* point of application; **punkt topnienia** *fiz.* melting point; **punkt wrzenia** *fiz.* boiling point; **punkt wysokościowy** *geogr.* spot height; **punkt zamarzania** *fiz.* freezing point. 2. (*miejsce*) station, shop, outlet; **punkt apteczny** pharmacy; **punkt ksero** copy *l.* print shop; **punkt skupu butelek** bottle return; **punkt skupu makulatury** weigh and pay, waste paper drop; **punkt opatrunkowy** dressing station; **punkt sanitarny** *l.* **pomocy medycznej** dispensary; **punkt usługowy** service shop; **punkt zborny** rallying point; **czarny punkt** (*miejsce wielu wypadków*) black spot. 3. (*stanowisko*) point; **punkt dowodzenia** command headquarters; **punkt informacyjny** (*np. na lotnisku*) information desk; **punkt kontrolny** (*np. na granicy*) checkpoint; **punkt obserwacyjny** vantage point; **punkt oporu** point *l.* center of resistance, pocket of resistance; **punkt orientacyjny** landmark; **punkt strategiczny** strategic point; **punkt widzenia** point of view, viewpoint, standpoint. 4. (= *para-graf*) item; **punkt programu** item of the agenda; **punkt po punkcie** item by item. 5. (*kwestia*) point, matter, issue; **punkt honoru** point of honor; **punkt krytyczny** (= *kryzys*) critical point, crisis; (= *punkt zwrotny*) (*np. w czyichś losach*) tide; *fiz.* critical point; **punkt sporny** moot point, thorny issue; **punkt zapalny** flash point; *polit.* trouble spot; **newralgiczny punkt** (*źródło konfliktów*) pressure point; **w tym punkcie nie mogę się z tobą zgodzić** I can't agree with you in that *l.* on this point; **mieć bzika na punkcie kogoś/czegoś** go ape over sb/sth, be gaga over sb/sth, be mad keen on sb/sth, be wild about sb/sth; **on ma bzika na jej punkcie** he's mad about her; **mieć kompleks na punkcie czegoś** have a complex about sth. 6. (*granica*) point; **punkt kulminacyjny** *l.* **szczytowy** climax. 7. (*jednostka*) point, score; *szkoln., uniw.* mark; **punkt karny** (*za wykroczenie drogowe*) point; *sport* penalty point (*za coś* for sth); **punkt meczowy** *sport* match point. 8. *druk., geom.* point.

punkt[2] *adv.* sharp; **będę punkt piąta** *l.* **punkt o piątej** *pot.* I'll be there at five sharp, I'll be there at the dot of five.

punktacja *f.* 1. *sport* (*zasady*) scoring rules; *szkoln., uniw.* grading scale. 2. (*suma*) score, standings.

punktak *mi Gen.* -a *techn.* (center) punch.

punktować *ipf.* 1. (*oceniać*) award points. 2. *mal.* stipple. 3. *rzeźba* point. 4. *techn.* (center-)punch. 5. *pot.* (= *zdobywać punkty*) score (*points*).

punktowiec *mi* -wc- *Gen.* -a 1. (*budynek*) highrise, high-riser. 2. *teatr* (*reflektor*) spotlight.

punktowy *a.* of or related to (a) point; *geom.* punctual; **spawanie** *l.* **zgrzewanie punktowe** *techn.* spot welding; **oświetlenie punktowe** spot lighting; **reflektor punktowy** *teatr* spotlight; **sędzia punktowy** *sport* scorekeeper.

punktualnie *adv.* punctually, on time; (= *wg rozkładu jazdy*) on schedule; **punktualnie o piątej** at five (o'clock) sharp, on the strike *l.* dot of five.

punktualność *f.* punctuality.

punktualny *a.* punctual; (= *zgodny z rozkładem jazdy*) on schedule; **punktualny co do minuty** punctual to the minute; **on jest bardzo punktualny** he's very punctual, he's a good timekeeper.

pupa *f. euf.* bottom, derrière; **gładki jak pupa niemowlęcia** smooth as a baby's bottom.

pupil *mp Gen.pl.* -ów pet, favorite; (*zwłaszcza służalczy*) minion; (*nauczyciela*) teacher's pet; (*szefa*) fair-haired boy.

pupilek *mp Gen. pl.* -ów *zob.* **pupil**.

purchawka *f. Gen.pl.* -ek *bot.* puffball (*Lycoperdon*); **nadęty jak purchawka** full of o.s.

purée *n. indecl.* purée; **purée ziemniaczane** *l.* **kartofle purée** mashed potato.

purpura *f.* 1. (*kolor*) purplish red. 2. (*barwnik, materiał, ubiór*) purple; **purpura kardynalska** cardinal's red.

purpurat *mp lit.* cardinal.

purpurowy *a.* purple.

puryna *f. chem.* purine, purin.

purynowy *a. chem.* purine; **zasada purynowa** purine (base).

purysta *mp jęz.* purist.

purystyczny *a. jęz.* purist.

purytanin *mp pl.* **-anie** *Gen.* **-an** *rel.* Puritan; *przen.* puritan, precisian; *pot.* bluenose.

purytanizm *mi rel.* Puritanism; *przen.* puritanism.

purytanka *f. Gen.pl.* **-ek** *zob.* **purytanin**.

purytański *a. rel.* Puritan; *przen.* puritan.

puryzm *mi jęz., mal.* purism.

pustak *mi Gen.* **-a** *bud.* hollow brick *l.* block.

pustawo *adv.* with few people present *l.* about; **trochę tu pustawo** there's hardly anybody here.

pustawy *a.* emptyish, slightly empty; **grali przy pustawej sali** they played to a thin house.

puste *n. Gen.* **-ego przelewać z pustego w próżne** argue *l.* discuss *l.* dispute pointlessly.

pustelnia *f. Gen.pl.* **-i** hermitage; *przen.* solitude.

pustelnica *f.* hermit, anchoress.

pustelnictwo *n.*   hermitic   *l.*   anchoretic life(style).

pustelniczy *a.* hermitic, anchoretic.

pustelnik *mp* 1. hermit, anchorite, recluse; *przen.* recluse. 2. *zool.* hermit crab (*Pagurus*).

pustka *f. Gen.pl.* **-ek** 1. (= *puste miejsce*) void; (= *bycie pustym*) emptiness; **pustka w głowie** blank; **mam pustkę w głowie** my mind is a blank; **nagle poczułem zupełną pustkę w głowie** suddenly my mind went completely blank; **pustka intelektualna** vacuity; **pustka w sercu** void in one's heart; **pozostawić pustkę w czyimś życiu** leave a void in one's life; **trafić w pustkę** (*o propozycji*) fall on stony ground; **kino świeciło pustkami** the movie theater was (almost) empty; **ulice świeciły pustkami** the streets were deserted; **mieć pustki w kieszeni** be penniless. 2. (= *pustkowie*) void, desolation.

pustkowie *n. Gen.pl.* **-i** void, desolation.

pusto *adv.* emptily; **śmiać się pusto** laugh vacuously; **na ulicy było pusto** the street was deserted; **w mieszkaniu/pokoju było pusto** the apartment/room was empty; **mieć pusto w głowie** be lightheaded.

pustorożce *pl. Gen.* **-ów** *zool.* cavicorns, bovids (*Bovidae*).

pustosłowie *n.* (= *posługiwanie się zbędnymi słowami*) verbosity, empty rhetoric; (= *puste frazesy*) claptrap, bunkum.

pustostan *mi* uninhabited apartment; *Br.* uninhabited flat.

pustoszeć *ipf.* empty, become deserted.

pustoszyć *ipf.* lay (sth) waste, ravage, waste; (*zwłaszcza w czasie wojny*) harry.

pustota *f. przest.* frivolity, wantonness.

pustułeczka *f. Gen.pl.* **-ek** *orn.* lesser kestrel (*Falco naumanni*).

pustułka *f. Gen.pl.* **-ek** *orn.* kestrel (*Falco tinnunculus*).

pusty *a.* 1. (= *niepełny*) empty; (= *bezludny, opustoszały*) void, waste; (*o mieszkaniu, pokoju* = *bez sprzętów*) bare; *mat.* (*o zbiorze*) null; **pusty los** blank; **wyciągnąć pusty los** draw a blank; **mieć puste kieszenie** be penniless, be without a penny to one's name; **przyjść z pustymi rękami** (= *nie przynieść prezentu*) come empty-handed; **na pusty żołądek** on an empty stomach; **pusty przebieg** *techn.* deadhead run; **pusty wewnętrznie** empty *l.* crippled inside, not half the man one used to be. 2. (= *bezmyślny*) light-minded; **pusta głowa** rattlebrain; **pusty śmiech** vacuous laughter. 3. (= *czczy, próżny*) empty, vain; **puste frazesy** platitude; **pusta gadanina** empty *l.* idle talk; **pusta obietnica** empty promise.

pustynia *f.* 1. *geogr.* desert; **pustynia lodowa** ice desert; **pustynia piaszczysta** sand desert; **pustynia skalista** rocky desert; **Pustynia Gobi** the Gobi Desert; **Pustynia Kalahari** the Kalahari Desert; **Pustynia Nubijska** the Nubian Desert; (*zwłaszcza na Saharze*) hammada. 2. (= *pustkowie, odludzie*) desert, wilderness, wild, void; **pustynia intelektualna** intellectual desert, vacuity; **pustynia kulturalna** cultural desert.

pustynnieć *ipf.* **-eje** desertify.

pustynnik *ma orn.* Pallas's sand grouse (*Syrrhaptes paradoxus*).

pustynniki *pl. Gen.* **-ów** *orn.* sand grouse (*Pteroclididae*).

pustynny *a.* 1. (= *charakterystyczny dla pustyni*) desert, desertic; **pustynny klimat** *geogr.* desert *l.* desertic climate; **lakier pustynny** *geol.* desert varnish *l.* polish. 2. (= *bezludny*) desolate, barren; **pustynny kraj** desolate land.

puszcza *f.* primeval forest; **głos wołającego na puszczy** a voice (crying) in the wilderness.

puszczać *ipf.* 1. (= *nie trzymać*) let go (*coś* of sth); **puszczać wodze fantazji** allow full play to fantasy; **mróz puszcza** the frost is letting up, it's beginning to thaw; **lód puszcza** the ice is breaking; **puszczać w dzierżawę** rent *l.* let out. 2. (= *pozwalać na ruch*) let (*sb/sth go*), let off, let out; **puszczać gaz** turn the gas on; **puszczać komuś krew** bleed sb; **puszczać konia biegiem/galopem/kłusem** course/gallop/trot a horse; **puścić konia luzem** give a horse its head; **puszczać latawiec** fly a kite; **puszczać wodę** turn the water on; (*do wanny*) run one's bath; **nie puszczać kogoś na imprezę/do kina** not let sb go to a party/the movie theater; **puszczać w obieg** circulate, put into circulation; (*obligacje, banknoty*) issue; (*papiery wartościowe*) launch; (*fałszywe pieniądze*) utter; **puszczać w ruch pięści** let one's fists fly, let loose a barrage of punches; **puścić coś mimo uszu** let sth pass; **nie puszczać pary z ust** keep one's mouth shut, not breathe a word, keep mum; **puszczać coś komuś płazem** let sb get away with sth, let sth ride; **puszczać coś w niepamięć** commit sth to oblivion, forgive and forget sth, bury sth, put sth behind o.s.; **puścić coś z dymem** put sth to the torch, make a bonfire of sth, burn sth down; **puszczać oko do kogoś** ogle at sb, wink at sb; **puszczać kaczki** (*zabawa*) play ducks and drakes. 3. (= *uruchomić*) run (*a machine, etc.*); (*piosenkę, płytę*) play (*a song, record*); **puścić coś w ruch** set sth in motion, set sth going. 4. (= *pozwalać odejść*) let go; **puszczać kogoś wolno** set *l.* let sb free; **puszczać kogoś na wolność** release sb (*from prison, etc.*); **pu-**

ścić *l.* zwolnić kogoś za kaucją *zwł. prawn.* release sb on bail; **puszczać kogoś przodem** let sb go first; **puścić kogoś z torbami** eat sb out of house and home, take sb to the cleaner's; **puścić kogoś kantem** *pot.* sell sb down the river. **5.** (= *wydalać z siebie*) (*np. sok*) give off, ooze; (*pędy*) sprout, put forth, burgeon; (*o praniu - kolory*) bleed; **drzewa puszczają sok** trees are giving off *l.* oozing juice; **puścić farbę** *pot.* (= *wygadać (się)*) let the cat out of the bag, spill the beans; (= *zdradzić (się)*) let on; **puścić farbę** *myśl.* bleed; **puszczać wiatry** *pot.* break wind; **puścić pawia** *pot.* toss *l.* spill one's cookie, produce a liquid laugh, shout at the floor *l.* at the carpet *l.* one's shoes, air one's belly. **6.** (= *wytyczać przebieg*) build (*sth somewhere*); **puścić linię tramwajową tunelem** lay streetcar tracks in a tunnel. **7.** (= *ustępować pod naporem*) give way; (*o nerwach*) crack; **drzwi puściły** the door gave way; **oczko mi puściło** (*w pończosze*) my stocking ran; (*w rajstopie*) my tights ran. **8.** (*o brudzie, plamie*) come off. **9.** *pot.* (*trwonić*) squander (*money*); **puszczać pieniądze na dziwki** squander money on whoring. **~ się** *ipf.* **1.** start (*moving, running, etc.*), set off *l.* out; **puszczać się biegiem** break into run. **2.** *pot.* sleep around, fuck around, put out, put o.s. about.

puszczalska¹ *a. Gen.* **-ej** *pot.* sluttish, easy.

puszczalska² *f. Gen.* **-ej** *pot.* easy lay, slut.

puszczyk *ma orn.* tawny owl, brown owl, wood owl (*Strix aluco*).

puszek *mi Gen.sing.* **-szku 1.** (*u ptaków, roślin*) down; (*na twarzy*) fluff. **2.** *Gen.* **-szka** (*do pudrowania*) powder puff.

puszka *f. Gen.pl.* **-ek 1.** (*opakowanie*) can; *gł. Br.* tin; **puszka coli/groszku/piwa** can *l.* tin of coke/peas/beer; **puszka mózgowa** *anat.* cranium, braincase; **puszka Pandory** *mit.* Pandora's box; **otwieracz do puszek** can *l.* tin opener. **2.** (*skarbonka*) collection box; **puszka na pieniądze** money box. **3.** *pot.* (= *więzienie*) can, cooler, joint. **4.** *bot.* capsule. **5.** *rz.-kat.* pyx, pix.

puszkarnia *f. hist.* gunsmithy.

puszkarstwo *n. hist.* gunsmithing.

puszkarz *ma hist.* **1.** (*rzemieślnik*) gunsmith. **2.** (*kanonier*) cannoneer.

puszkować *ipf.* **1.** (*jedzenie*) can; *gł. Br.* tin. **2.** *pot.* (= *wsadzać do więzienia*) jug.

puszta *f. geogr.* puszta, Hungarian grassland steppe.

puszyć się *ipf.* **1.** (*o ptakach*) ruffle, puff up (*feathers*). **2.** (= *chwalić się*) puff o.s. with pride, blow one's own trumpet.

puszystość *f.* fluffiness, fleeciness, downiness.

puszysty *a.* **-szy** (*o włosach*) fluffy; (*o cieście*) fluffy, soufflé, souffléed, puffed up; (*o śniegu*) fleecy, flaky; (*o dywanie*) nappy; (*o futrze*) downy, furry; *euf.* (*o osobie*) well-padded.

puścić *pf.* **-szczę -ścisz** *zob.* puszczać. **~ się** *pf.* **1.** *zob.* puszczać się; **puścić się czegoś** (= *przestać się trzymać*) let go of sth. **2.** (= *zacząć iść, biec*) set off, break into; **puścić się biegiem/galopem/truchtem** break into run/gallop/trot; **puścić**

się na niebezpieczne wody run (a) risk *l.* take chances (*while trying to achieve sth*); **puścić się na szerokie wody** get serious about sth, think big; **puścić się w tany** begin to dance, join in the dance.

puścizna *f. przest.* legacy, heritage.

puślisko *n.* stirrup leather.

putrescyna *f. chem.* putrescine.

putto *n. sztuka* putto.

puzanek *mi icht.* shad (*Alosa*).

puzderko *n.* casket.

puzon *mi muz.* trombone.

puzonista *mp muz.* trombonist.

puzzle *mi Gen.* **-a** *pl.* puzzle puzzle.

puzzolana *f. geol., bud.* pozzuolana, pozzolana.

pych *mi pot.* (*tylko w zwrotach*) **płynąć na pych** punt, pole along; **uruchomić samochód na pych** push-start a car.

pycha *f.* pride, hubris, conceit; (*jako grzech*) pride. – *int.* sth great; **pycha** (= *świetnie*) *przest.* jolly good!; **to jest pycha!** this is yummy!

pychota *f. pot.* sth yummy; **pychota!** yummy!

pychówka *f.* (*łódź*) punt.

pykać *ipf.*, **pyknąć** *pf.* **-nę -niesz, -ij 1.** (= *palić*) puff; **pykać fajkę** *l.* **z fajki** puff on *l.* at one's pipe; **pyknąć sobie z fajki** have a puff on *l.* at one's pipe. **2.** (*o silnikach*) chug. **3.** (*o garnku*) bubble.

pykniczny *a. psych.* pyknic; **typ pykniczny** pyknic type.

pyknik *mp Gen.* **-a** *psych.* pyknic.

pyk-pyk *int.* puff-puff.

pylasty *a.* dusty.

pylica *f. pat.* pneumoconiosis, pneumonoconiosis; *pot.* black lung, dust disease; **pylica azbestowa** asbestosis; **pylica węglowa** anthracosis; *pot.* coal miner's lung.

pylić *ipf.* (= *wzniecać pył*) raise dust; (= *rozsiewać pył*) dust; (= *pokrywać pyłem*) cover with dust. **~ się** *ipf.* **1.** (*o kurzu*) cover with dust. **2.** *bot.* pollinate; give off *l.* release pollen.

pylnik *mi Gen.* **-a** *bot.* anther.

pylon *mi bud.* pylon.

pył *mi* dust; **pył kosmiczny** *l.* meteorowy *astron.* cosmic dust; **pył węglowy** coal dust; **pył wulkaniczny** volcanic dust; **gwiezdny pył** stardust; **rozpaść się w proch i pył** crumble to dust; **zetrzeć coś w pył** reduce *l.* smash sth to matchwood, smash sth to smithereens.

pyłek *mi* **-łk- 1.** (*kurz*) dust. **2.** (= *drobina*) speck, mote; **pyłek kurzu** speck of dust. **3.** *bot.* pollen; **stężenie pyłku** *l.* **pyłków (w powietrzu)** (*w prognozie dla alergików*) pollen count.

pyłkodajny *a. bot.* polliniferous.

pyłkowy *a.* pollinic, pollinical; **alergia pyłkowa** *pat.* pollinosis, pollenosis; *pot.* hay fever; **łagiewka pyłkowa** *bot.* pollen tube; **koszyczek pyłkowy** *ent.* pollen basket, corbicula.

pyłochłonny *a. techn.* dust-absorbing; **maska pyłochłonna** dust mask.

pyłomierz *mi techn.* dust counter.

pyłowaty *a.* powdery.

pyłowy *a.* dust, dusty; **burza pyłowa** *meteor.*

dust storm; **gleba pyłowa** dusty soil; **komora pyłowa** *techn.* dust chamber; **lawina pyłowa** powdery avalanche.

pypeć *mi* -pci- *Gen.* -a *Gen.pl.* -i *l.* -ów **1.** *pot.* (= *znamię*) blot (*on one's face*); **cholera, jakiś pypeć mi wyskoczył** damn, I've got this thing on my face. **2.** *wet.* pip.

pyra *f. dial.* spud, tater, murphy.

pyrgać *ipf.*, **pyrgnąć** *pf. dial.* chuck.

pyrheliometr *mi astron.* pyrheliometer.

pyrka *f. zob.* **pyra.**

pyrkać *ipf. dial.* whir(r), chug.

pyrkotać *ipf. pot.* bubble.

pyrofit *mi bot.* pyrrophyte.

pyrrusowy *a.* Pyrrhic; **pyrrusowe zwycięstwo** Pyrrhic victory.

pysk *mi Gen.* -a **1.** (*u zwierząt*) muzzle, snout; (*otwór gębowy*) mouth. **2.** *pot.* (= *twarz*) trap; **dać komuś w pysk** *l.* **po pysku** give it to sb right in the snout, punch sb in the face; **dostać** *l.* **oberwać po pysku** get it right in the snout, be punched in the face; **być mocnym w pysku** have the gift of the gab; **być mocnym tylko w pysku** be all mouth and no trousers; **mieć niewyparzony pysk** not to mince one's words; **nie mieć co do pyska włożyć** not have a crust of bread, not have a crumb to eat; **o suchym pysku** without food or drink; **siedzieć u kogoś o suchym pysku** be offered neither food nor drink (*while being sb's guest*); **padam na pysk ze zmęczenia** I'm dog tired, I'm dead beat, I'm done in; **rozpuścić** *l.* **rozedrzeć pysk** start bawling, start crying like a baby with 9-liter lung capacity; **wziąć kogoś za pysk** come down hard on sb, start ruling sb with an iron fist, crack the whip; **wylecieć na zbity pysk** be out on one's ear; **wyrzucić kogoś na zbity pysk** kick sb out; **zatkać komuś pysk** shut sb's mouth (*with a bribe, etc.*); **miękki/twardy w pysku** (*o koniu*) light/hard in mouth; **stul pysk!** shut your trap *l.* mouth!, shut up!; **daj pyska!** give us a kiss!

pyskacz *mp Gen.pl.* -ów *pot.* bawler, barker.

pyskaty *a. pot.* (= *arogancki*) cheeky, lippy; (= *skory do kłótni*) bawling.

pyskować *ipf. pot.* talk back (*komuś* to sb); (*zwłaszcza o dzieciach*) answer back (*komuś* to sb); **nie pyskuj mi tutaj!** none of your lip!, don't get fresh with me!

pyskówka *f. Gen.pl.* -ek *pot.* slanging *l.* shouting match, dust-up, sass.

pyszałek *mp* -łk- *pl.* -i braggart, jackanapes, swaggerer, coxcomb.

pyszałkowatość *f.* bumptiousness, prance.

pyszałkowaty *a.* bumptious, boastful, cocky.

pyszczek *mi* -szcz- *Gen.* -a **1.** (*u zwierząt*) snout. **2.** *żart.* (= *twarz*) darling little face.

pyszczyć *ipf. pot.* brawl, raise hell.

pysznić się *ipf.* -ij (= *szczycić się*) boast (*czymś* of *l.* about sth); brag (*czymś* of *l.* about sth); plume *l.* preen o.s. (*czymś* on *l.* upon sth); (= *wywyższać się*) put on airs, puff o.s. up.

pysznie *adv.* (= *smacznie*) deliciously; (= *świetnie*) gorgeously; **bawić się świetnie** have a whale of a time.

pysznogłówka *f. bot.* horsemint (*Monarda*).

pyszności *pl. Gen.* -i *pot.* dainties, delicacies, goodies, morsels; **ciasto - pyszności!** the cake's simpy delicious!

pyszny *a.* **1.** (= *dumny*) proud, haughty. **2.** (= *smakowity*) delicious, excellent. **3.** (= *wspaniały*) excellent, gorgeous; **pyszna zabawa!** what a whale of a good time!; **mieć się z pyszna** be in hot water, get into a scrape; **będziesz się miał z pyszna!** you'll be in for it!

pyt. *abbr.* (= *pytanie*) q., Q. (*question*).

pyta *f. dial.* (= *powróz*) rawhide, bullwhip.

pytać *ipf.* **1.** (= *zwracać się z pytaniem*) ask; **pytać o cenę czegoś** ask sb the price of sth; **pytać o drogę** ask sb the way, ask for directions; **pytać o godzinę** ask sb (for) the time; **pytać o kogoś** ask after sb; **pytać o pozwolenie** ask for permission; **pytać kogoś o radę** ask sb's advice; **pytał o ciebie dyrektor** the director has been asking about you; **kpisz, czy o drogę pytasz?** *pot.* did you just get off the boat? **2.** (= *egzaminować*) give an oral; **pytać kogoś z angielskiego** give sb an oral in English. **~ się** *ipf. zob.* **pytać** 1.

pytająco *adv.* questioningly, inquiringly; **spojrzeć na kogoś pytająco** look at sb questioningly.

pytający *a.* questioning, inquiring, interrogative; **pytające spojrzenie** *l.* **pytająca mina** questioning look; **pytający ton** interrogative tone; **zaimek pytający** *gram.* interrogative; **zdanie pytające** *gram.* interrogative sentence.

pytajnik *mi Gen.* -a question mark, interrogation mark.

pytajny *a. jęz.* interrogative.

pytanie *n.* **1.** (= *zapytanie*) question; **dobre pytanie!** (*gdy nie zna się odpowiedzi*) (that's a) good question!; **kłopotliwe pytanie** poser; **podchwytliwe pytanie** tricky question; **prowokować pytania** (*o decyzji, wydarzeniu*) invite questions; **zadać komuś podchwytliwe pytanie** lead sb on; **zadać pytanie** ask a question; **odpowiedzieć na pytanie** answer a question; **zwrócić się do kogoś z pytaniem** put a question to sb, address sb with a question; **zarzucić kogoś pytaniami** flood *l.* bombard *l.* besiege sb with questions, shoot questions at sb; **też pytanie!** what a question to ask!; **pytanie retoryczne** rhetorical question; **krzyżowy ogień pytań** cross-examination; **zrobić coś bez pytania** do sth without permission; **czy są jeszcze jakieś pytania?** are there any other questions?; **nie mam więcej pytań** (*w sądzie*) no further questions. **2.** (= *zagadnienie*) question; **to pytanie nurtuje mnie od dawna** this has been fretting *l.* nagging me for a long time; **nasuwa się pytanie, czy...** a question arises if...

pytel *mi* -tl- *Gen.* -a *Gen.pl.* -i *l.* -ów bolter.

pytia *f. Gen.* -ii **1.** *mit.* Pythia, pythoness. **2.** *przen.* pythoness.

pytlować *ipf.* **1.** (*mąkę*) bolt. **2.** *pot.* (= *gadać*) chatter.

pytlowy *a. kulin.* wholewheat.

pyton *ma zool.* python (*Python*).

pyuria *f. pat.* pyuria.

pyza *f.* **1.** *kulin.* potato dumpling. **2.** *pot.* (=

grubas) roly-poly. **3.** *myśl.* nose of bison *l.* moose.

pyzaty *a. pot.* chubby-cheeked.

PZPR *abbr. hist.* (= *Polska Zjednoczona Partia Robotnicza*) the Polish United Workers' Party.

PZU *abbr.* (= *Państwowy Zakład Ubezpieczeń*) the Polish State Insurance Company.

PŻM *abbr.* (= *Polska Żegluga Morska*) the Polish Steamship Company.

Q, q *n. indecl.* (*litera*) Q, q; **Q jak Quebec** Q is for Quebec; Q as in Quebec.

Q *abbr.* (= *znak najwyższej jakości*) top quality.

quantum *n. indecl. lit.* (= *wymagana ilość*) quantum, quantity; **niezbędne quantum wiedzy** necessary quantum of learning.

quasi- *a. i adv.* (*pisany łącznie z następnym wyrazem*) *zw. uj.* quasi-, para-, semi-; **quasi-religijny** quasi-religious; **quasi-nauka** parascience; **quasi-oficjalnie** semi-officially.

quasimodo *mp Gen.* **-a** *pl. rzad.* **-owie** (= *ktoś groteskowo brzydki*) gargoyle.

quattrocento *n. często indecl. sztuka* quattrocento.

Quebec *mi geogr.* Québec.

quebecki *a.* Québecois.

quebekijczyk *mp*, **quebekijka** *f. Gen.pl.* **-ek** Quebecer, Quebecker, Québecois.

quetzal *ma orn.* quetzal, quezal, resplendent trogon (*Pharomachrus mochinno*).

quickstep *mi Gen.* **-a** *taniec* quickstep.

qui pro quo *n. indecl.* comic misunderstanding.

quiz *mi* quiz.

quizowy *a.* quiz; **pytania quizowe** quiz questions.

quorum *n. indecl.* quorum.

R, r *n. indecl.* (*litera*) R, r; **R jak Roman** R is for Romeo; R as in Romeo.

r. *abbr.* (= *rok*) y. (*year*).

rab *mp lit., przest.* (= *niewolnik*) slave, servant.

rabacja *f. lit.* (= *bunt*) revolt.

raban *mi pot.* ruckus; **narobić rabanu** raise hell, kick up *l.* raise a ruckus.

rabarbar *mi bot.* rhubarb, pieplant (*Rheum*).

rabarbarowy *a.* rhubarb.

rabat *mi zwł. handl.* discount; **rabat detaliczny** trade discount; **stosować rabat** discount.

rabata, rabatka *f. Gen.pl.* **-ek** flowerbed.

rabatowy¹ *a.* (= *dotyczący rabatu*) discount.

rabatowy² *a.* (= *dotyczący rabaty*) flowerbed; **rośliny rabatowe** bedding plants.

rabbi *mp decl. like a.*, **rabin** *mp judaizm* rabbi.

rabinacki *a. judaizm* rabbinic.

rabinat *mi judaizm* rabbinate.

rabiniczny *a. judaizm* rabbinic.

rabować *ipf.* **1.** (= *łupić*) rob; (= *plądrować*) loot, plunder. **2.** *górn.* draw off, withdraw.

rabunek *mi* **-nk-** **1.** (= *grabież*) robbery; **dokonać rabunku** rob. **2.** *górn.* withdrawing, drawing off.

rabunkowo *adv.* wastefully.

rabunkowy *a.* (= *dotyczący grabieży*) predatory; **eksploatacja rabunkowa** *ekon.* predatory exploitation; **napad rabunkowy** holdup, robbery.

rabuś *mp Gen.pl.* **-siów** robber, mugger, plunderer; **rabuś kokosowy** *zool.* robber crab (*Birgus latro*).

raca *f.* flare, star shell; **wystrzelić racę** flare.

racemat *mi chem.* racemate.

rachatłukum *n. indecl. kulin.* Turkish delight *l.* paste.

rachitycznie *adv.* effetely.

rachityczny *a.* **1.** *pat., przest.* (= *krzywiczy*) rachitic. **2.** (= *wątły, wykrzywiony*) rickety, effete.

rachityk *mp* **1.** *przest.* (= *osoba chora na krzywicę*) person affected with rachitis *l.* rickets. **2.** (= *osoba słaba fizycznie*) effete person.

rachityzm *mi pat., przest.* (= *krzywica*) rachitis, rickets.

rachmistrz *mp* **1.** *przest.* (= *księgowy*) accountant. **2.** *lit.* (= *osoba biegła w rachunkach*) calculator. **3.** (*spisowy*) census representative.

rachować *ipf.* **1.** calculate, compute. **2.** *pot.* (= *spodziewać się*) figure, reckon; **rachować na kogoś/coś** rely on sb/sth, count on sb/sth. **~ się** *ipf.* **1.** (= *rozliczać się*) settle (accounts) (*z kimś* with

sb). **2.** *przest.* (= *liczyć się*) have regard (*z kimś* for sb).

rachuba *f. przest.* (= *liczenie*) calculation, count; **pomylić się w rachubach** *przen.* (= *przeliczyć się*) miscalculate, back the wrong horse; **stracić rachubę czegoś** lose count of sth; **nie wchodzić w rachubę** be out of the question; **wchodzić w rachubę** come into consideration.

rachunek *mi* **-nk-** **1.** (= *obliczanie*) calculation, count; **rachunek prawdopodobieństwa** *mat.* probability theory *l.* calculus; **rachunek całkowy** *mat.* integral calculus; **rachunek różniczkowy** *mat.* differential calculus; **rachunek zysków i strat** *ekon.* profit and loss account; **rachunek sumienia** *rel.* an examination of conscience. **2.** *fin.* (= *konto*) account; **rachunek bieżący** current account; **rachunek oszczędnościowy** savings account; **rachunek walutowy** foreign currency account; **rachunek depozytowy** deposit account; **rachunek rozliczeniowy** checking account; **obciążyć czyjś rachunek** debit sb's account; **(to) na mój rachunek** it's on me, it's my treat; **żyć na własny rachunek** live one's own life; **robić coś na własny rachunek** do sth on one's own. **3.** (= *należność do zapłacenia*) bill, check; *pot.* tab; **poproszę o rachunek** (can I have the) check, please; **rachunek za telefon/gaz** phone/gas bill; **wystawić rachunek** bill. **4.** *przen.* (*we frazach*) **mieć z kimś rachunki do wyrównania** have an old score to settle with sb; **stracić rachunek** lose count; **załatwić z kimś rachunki** get square with sb; **wyrównać z kimś rachunki** settle with sb; **zdać z czegoś rachunek** give an account of sth.

rachunkowość *f.* **1.** *fin.* (= *księgowość*) accountancy, accounting. **2.** (*dział instytucji*) accounting department.

rachunkowy *a.* **1.** (= *arytmetyczny*) arithmetic, arithmetical. **2.** (= *dotyczący rachunkowości*) accounting.

racica *f. zool.* (cloven) hoof.

raciczka *f. Gen.pl.* **-ek** *zool.* dewclaw.

raciczny *a.* (cloven-)hoof; (cloven-)hoofed.

racja *f.* **1.** (= *słuszność*) right, correctness; **(święta) racja!** absolutely right!; **mieć rację** be right, be right on, be in the right; **przyznać komuś rację** cede a point to sb, accept sb's argument; **udowodnić, że ktoś nie miał racji** prove sb wrong. **2.** (= *argument*) reason, argument; **trzymać się swoich racji** stick to one's guns. **3.** *lit.* (= *powód*) reason; **to nie ma racji bytu** there's no reason for its existence; **racja stanu** raison d'état; **racja bytu** raison d'être; **bez dania racji**

without giving any reasons; **nie bez racji** not without reason; **z jakiej racji?** by what right?; **z racji czegoś** on account of sth. **4.** (= *porcja*) ration; **racje żywnościowe** food rations; **racje na kilka dni** *wojsk.* compo rations.

racjonalista *mp* rationalist.

racjonalistycznie *adv.* rationalistically.

racjonalistyczny *a.* rationalistic, rationalistical.

racjonalizacja *f.* **1.** (= *usprawnienie*) improvement, streamlining. **2.** *psych.* rationalization.

racjonalizacyjny *a.* improvement, streamlining; **projekt racjonalizacyjny** improvement project.

racjonalizator *mp* inventor *l.* originator of improvement *l.* streamlining designs.

racjonalizatorski *a.* improvement, streamlining.

racjonalizm *mi t. fil.* rationalism.

racjonalizować *ipf.* **1.** (= *usprawniać*) improve. **2.** *psych.* rationalize.

racjonalnie *adv.* sensibly; **działać racjonalnie** act rationally *l.* reasonably, act in a reasonable *l.* sensible manner; *pot.* play with a full deck.

racjonalność *f.* **1.** efficiency. **2.** rationality, reasonableness.

racjonalny *a.* **1.** (= *przemyślany*) reasonable, sensible. **2.** (= *oparty na rozumie*) rational.

racjonować *ipf.* ration, allowance.

raczej *adv.* **1.** (= *właściwie*) rather; **jest raczej szczupły** he's rather thin. **2.** (= *lepiej, prędzej*) rather, sooner; **raczej nie** rather not; **raczej umrę, niż się poddam** I'd rather *l.* sooner die than give up; **raczej już tego nie zmieniaj** you'd rather keep it unchanged.

raczek *ma* **-czk-** (= *mały rak*) (small) crayfish; **spiec raczka** *przen.* turn crimson.

raczkować *ipf.* **1.** crawl. **2.** *przen.* (*w jakiejś dziedzinie*) be still in diapers, be still cutting one's teeth.

raczkujący *a.* (= *początkujący*) fledgling, green, unseasoned.

raczyć *ipf.* **1.** *lit.* (= *częstować*) regale (*kogoś czymś* sb with sth); treat (*kogoś czymś* sb to sth). **2.** *iron.* (= *chcieć*) condescend, deign (*coś zrobić* to do sth); **nie raczył nawet zadzwonić** he didn't even bother to call, he didn't even see fit to call; **Bóg raczy wiedzieć** God only knows, goodness *l.* heaven knows; it's anybody's guess. **~ się** *ipf. żart.* (= *jeść*) treat o.s. (*czymś* to sth).

rad[1] *a. tylko Nom.* **1.** *lit.* (= *zadowolony*) glad, happy; **rad jestem, że...** I'm happy to...; **czym chata bogata, tym rada** what's mine is yours, be my guest. **2.** *lit.* (= *chętny, przychylny*) glad; **rad bym ją poznać** I would be glad to meet her; **rad nierad** willy-nilly, whether you like it or not.

rad[2] *mi Gen.* **-u** *chem.* radium.

rad[3] *mi Gen.* **-a** *fiz.* rad, absorbed dose.

rada *f.* **1.** (= *porada*) advice, piece of advice; **dobra rada** tip, sound piece of advice; **zła rada** misguidance; **trudna rada** *l.* **nie ma rady** there's nothing we can do, there's no help for it; **nie da rady** *pot.* no can do, it's no go; **jest na to rada** there's a way, we'll figure sth out; **dawać sobie**

radę z czymś manage sth; **iść za czyjąś radą** follow sb's advice; **nie ma innej rady, tylko...** there's no other way (out *l.* around it) but to..., the only way (out *l.* around it) is to... **2.** (*grupa ludzi*) council; **Rada Bezpieczeństwa ONZ** *polit.* the UN Security Council; **Rada Ministrów** *polit.* the Council of Ministers; **rada miejska** city council; **rada nadzorcza** supervisory board; **rada pedagogiczna** *szkoln.* (= *zebranie*) staff *l.* teachers' meeting; (= *ciało decydujące np. o promocji do następnej klasy*) Board of Teachers; **rada wydziału** *uniw.* faculty council; **Rada Polityki Pieniężnej** *ekon., polit.* the Monetary Policy Council (*in Poland*); **rada starszych** *hist.* council of the elders; **rada wykonawcza** executive council; **Rada Europejska** *polit.* the European Council; **Rada Europy** *polit.* the Council of Europe.

radar *mi* radar; **radar meteorologiczny** weather radar; **tu często stoją z radarem** *pot.* this place is a speed trap.

radarowy *a.* radar.

radca *mp* counselor; **radca dworu** *hist.* Privy Councillor; **radca handlowy** commercial counselor; **radca prawny** *prawn.* attorney-at-law, attorney; lawyer.

radcostwo *n.* **1.** (= *stanowisko radcy*) counselorship. **2.** *przest.* (= *radca z żoną*) counselor with *l.* and his wife.

radełko *n. Gen.pl.* **-łek 1.** *roln.* shovel. **2.** *techn.* knurl, roulette.

radełkować *ipf. techn.* knurl, roulette.

radiacja *f. fiz.* radiation.

radiacyjny *a.* radiational; **chemia radiacyjna** *chem.* radiation chemistry.

radialny *a. lit.* radial; **opona radialna** *mot.* radial (tire).

radian *mi mat.* radian.

radiant *mi astron.* radiant.

radiator *mi Gen.* **-a** *techn.* radiator.

radiesteta *mp* dowser.

radiestezja *f.* dowsing.

radio *n. Loc.* **-u** *Gen.pl. not used* **1.** (= *odbiornik radiowy*) radio; *Br. t.* wireless; **radio tranzystorowe** transistor (radio); **radio CB** CB radio, citizens band radio; **radio z budzikiem** (alarm) clock radio; **w radiu** on the radio *l.* air; **słuchać radia** listen to the radio. **2.** (= *instytucja, rozgłośnia*) radio station, broadcasting corporation; **nadawać przez radio** broadcast.

radioabonent *mp* licensed listener.

radioaktywność *f. chem., fiz.* radioactivity.

radioaktywny *a.* radioactive; **opad radioaktywny** fallout; **odpady radioaktywne** nuclear *l.* atomic waste.

radioamator *mp* ham.

radioastronomia *f. Gen.* **-ii** radio astronomy.

radiobiologia *f. Gen.* **-ii** radiobiology.

radiochemia *f. Gen.* **-ii** radiochemistry.

radiochronologia *f. Gen.* **-ii** *fiz., techn.* radiodating.

radiodepesza *f.* radiotelegram.

radioelektronika *f.* radioelectronics.

radioelektryka *f.* radio engineering.

radiofonia *f. Gen.* **-ii 1.** (*dział radiokomunika-*

cji) radio broadcasting. **2.** (*instytucja*) broadcasting corporation.
radiofoniczny *a.* radio.
radiofonizacja *f.* development of radio services.
radiofonizować *ipf.* develop radio services.
radiogoniometr *mi* radiogoniometer.
radiogoniometria *f. Gen.* **-ii** radiogoniometry.
radiografia *f. Gen.* **-ii** *techn.* radiography.
radiogram *mi* **1.** (= *obraz rentgenowski*) radiograph. **2.** (= *radiotelegram*) radiogram, radiotelegram, wireless message.
radioizotop *mi chem.* radioisotope.
radiokompas *mi* radio compass, direction finder.
radiokomunikacja *f.* radiocommunications.
radiokomunikacyjny *a.* radiocommunication.
radiolatarnia *f. Gen.pl.* **-i** *l.* **-ń** radio beacon.
radioliza *f. Dat.* **-zie** radiolysis.
radiolog *mp pl.* **-dzy** *l.* **-owie** radiologist.
radiologia *f. Gen.* **-ii** radiology.
radiologiczny *a.* radiological, radiologic.
radiolokacja *f.* radiolocation.
radiolokacyjny *a.* radiolocation; **echo radiolokacyjne** radar echo *l.* return.
radiolokator *mi Gen.* **-a** radar.
radioluminescencja *f. fiz.* radioluminescence.
radiomagnetofon *mi* radio casette recorder.
radiomechanik *mp* radio technician.
radiometeorologia *f. Gen.* **-ii** radiometeorology.
radiometr *mi fiz.* radiometer.
radiometria *f. Gen.* **-ii** *fiz., techn.* radiometry.
radiometryczny *a.* radiometric.
radionadajnik *mi Gen.* **-a** radio transmitter.
radionadawczy *a.* broadcasting, radio-transmission.
radionamiar *mi* radio bearing.
radionamiernik *mi Gen.* **-a** radio (direction) finder.
radionamierzanie *n.* radio direction finding.
radionawigacja *f. żegl., lotn.* radionavigation.
radionawigacyjny *a.* radionavigation.
radionuklid *mi Gen.* **-u** radionuclide.
radioodbiornik *mi Gen.* **-a** radio, radio receiver.
radiooperator *mp* radio operator.
radiopajęczarstwo *n. pot.* unlicensed radio listening.
radiopajęczarz *mp pot.* unlicensed listener.
radiopeleng *mi* radio bearing.
radiopelengacja *f.* radio direction finding.
radiosekstans, radiosekstant *mi Gen.* **-u** radio sextant.
radioskopia *f. Gen.* **-ii** radioscopy.
radiosłuchacz *mp Gen.pl.* **-y** *l.* **-ów** (radio) listener.
radiosonda *f. meteor.* radiosonde.
radiostacja *f.* **1.** (*urządzenie*) radio transmitter and receiver. **2.** (*stacja nadawcza*) radio station.
radiotechnik *mp* radio engineer.
radiotechnika *f.* radio engineering.
radiotelefon *mi* radiotelephone.

radiotelegraf *mi* radiotelegraph.
radiotelegrafia *f. Gen.* **-ii** radiotelegraphy, wireless telegraphy.
radiotelegraficzny *a.* radiotelegraphic.
radiotelegrafista *mp* radiotelegraph operator; wireless operator, WO.
radiotelegrafistka *f. Gen.pl.* **-ek** *zob.* **radiotelegrafista.**
radiotelegram *mi* radiogram, radiotelegram, aerogram.
radiotelemechanika *f.* radio telemechanics.
radiotelemetria *f.* radio telemetry.
radioteleskop *mi astron.* radio telescope.
radioterapeuta *mp Gen.* **-ty** *med.* radiotherapist.
radioterapia *f. Gen.* **-ii** *med.* radiotherapy.
radiotoksyczny *a. chem.* radiotoxic.
radiowęglowy *a. fiz., chem.* radiocarbon; **metoda radiowęglowa** radiocarbon dating.
radiowęzeł *mi* **-zł-** *Gen.* **-a** radio center, wire broadcasting center, *Br.* radio centre.
radiowiec *mp* **-wc-** radio technician; (= *pracownik radia*) *pot.* person working at a radio station.
radiowóz *mi* **-o-** patrol car, radio car.
radiowy *a.* radio, wireless, broadcasting; **drogą radiową** by radio; **naprowadzać drogą radiową** (*samolot, pilota*) vector; **audycja radiowa** radio show; **fale radiowe** airwaves; **transmisja radiowa** broadcast, program, *Br.* programme; radio show.
radioźródło *n. Gen.pl.* **-deł** *astron.* radio source.
radlić *ipf.* **-lij** *l.* **-l** *roln.* hoe, ridge.
radlina *f. roln.* ridge.
radło *n. Gen.pl.* **-deł** *roln.* colter.
radna *f. zob.* **radny.**
radny *mp* councilor; councillor; **godność radnego** aldermancy, aldermanship.
radocha *f. pot.* ball; **mieć radochę z czegoś** have a ball doing sth.
radon *mi chem.* radon.
radosny *a.* joyful, cheerful; **przy radosnym biciu dzwonów** with all the joy-bells ringing; **radosny jak skowronek** happy as a lark.
radość *f.* happiness, joy, joyfulness; **radość życia** animal spirits, joie de vivre; **z radością** delightedly, joyfully; **przedwczesna radość** false dawn; **szaleć z radości** be delirious with joy; **skakać z radości** jump for joy; **płakać z radości** cry *l.* weep for joy; **nie posiadać się z radości** be in transports of joy, be beside o.s. with joy; **być przepełnionym radością** brim over with joy; **sprawić komuś radość** make sb happy; **z radością** with pleasure.
radośnie *adv.* merrily, joyfully; **śpiewać radośnie** sing joyously, carol.
radować *ipf. lit.* delight, elate, gladden; **radować czyjeś serce** gladden sb's heart. **~ się** *ipf. lit.* exult, rejoice (*czymś l. z czegoś* at *l.* in sth).
radowy *a. chem.* radium.
radyjko *n. Gen.pl.* **-jek** *pot.* mini radio.
radykalista *mp* radical, extremist.
radykalizacja *f.* radicalization.

radykalizm *mi t. polit.* radicalism, extremism.

radykalizować *ipf.* radicalize.

radykalnie *adv.* radically, dramatically, drastically.

radykalny *a.* (*o poglądach, metodach*) radical, dramatic; (*o reformach*) sweeping.

radykał *mp pl.* **-owie** radical, extremist.

radzić *ipf.* **1.** (= *zalecać*) advise, give advice, counsel; **radzę ci wyjechać** I advise you to leave; **nie radzę ci tego robić** I wouldn't do that, I wouldn't advise you to do that. **2.** (= *omawiać*) debate (*nad czymś* sth). **3.** look for a solution; **radzić sobie** (**z kimś/czymś**) handle (sb/sth). ~ **się** *ipf.* consult; **radzić się kogoś** ask sb for advice, seek sb's advice.

radziecki *a. hist.* Soviet; **Związek Radziecki** the Soviet Union.

radża *mp pl.* **-owie** rajah, raja.

rafa *f. geogr.* reef, ledge; **rafa koralowa** coral reef; **rafa przybrzeżna** coastal *l.* (off) shore reef; **Wielka Rafa Koralowa** *geogr.* the Great Barrier Reef.

rafia *f. Gen.* **-ii 1.** *bot.* raffia palm (*Raphia ruffia*). **2.** (*włókno*) raffia.

rafid *mi bot.* raphide, raphis.

rafinacja *f. chem.* refining.

rafinada *f. kulin.* refined sugar.

rafinat *mi chem.* raffinate.

rafineria *f. Gen.* **-ii** refinery; **rafineria cukru** sugar refinery; **rafineria ropy** (crude) oil *l.* petroleum refinery.

rafineryjny *a.* refining, refinery.

rafinować *ipf. chem.* refine.

rafinoza *f. chem.* raffinose.

rafiowy *a.* raffia.

raflezja *f. Gen.* **-zji** *bot.* rafflesia (*Rafflesia*).

rafowy *a.* reef.

raglan *mi* (*typ kroju*) raglan.

raić *ipf.* **raję raisz, raj** *pot.* act as a go-between.

raj *mi t. przen.* paradise; *Bibl.* Eden, the Garden of Eden; **raj na ziemi** earthly paradise, heaven on earth; **czuć się jak w raju** be in heaven, be on top of the world; **raj dla wędkarzy** paradise for anglers.

raja *f. Gen.* **rai** *icht.* skate, ray (*Raja*).

rajca *mp pl.* **-y** *l.* **-owie** *hist.* councilor, councillor.

rajcować *ipf.* **1.** *pot.* (= *gadać dużo, plotkować*) chatter. **2.** *pot.* (= *podniecać*) give sb a kick. ~ **się** *ipf. pot.* (= *podniecać*) get a kick (*czymś* from *l.* out of sth).

rajd *mi* (*samochodowy*) rally, road race; (*pieszy*) hike.

rajdowiec *mp* **-wc-** (*sportowiec*) (rally) racer; (*turysta*) hiker.

rajdowy *a.* (= *dotyczący wyścigu samochodowego*) rally, racing.

rajfur *mp przest.* procurer, pimp.

rajfurka *f. Gen.pl.* **-ek** *przest.* bawd, madam.

rajgras *mi bot.* **1.** tall oatgrass (*Arrhenatherum elatius*). **2.** ryegrass (*Lolium*).

rajski *a.* **1.** paradisiacal, paradisiac, paradisaical, paradisaic; **rajska jabłoń** *bot.* paradise apple (*Malus pumilla paradisiaca*); **rajski ogród**

the Garden of Eden; **rajski ptak** *orn.* bird of paradise (*Paradisaeidae*). **2.** (= *taki jak w raju*) heavenly, blissful.

rajstopy *pl. Gen.* **-p** pantyhose, tights.

rajtar *mp hist.* reiter, mercenary cavalryman.

rajtaria *f. Gen.* **-ii** *hist.* reiters, mercenary cavalry.

rajtuzy *pl. Gen.* **-ów** tights.

raju *int.* (**o**) **raju!** *pot.* (oh) gee *l.* jeez!.

rajza *f. pot.* (= *włóczenie się*) roaming, wandering.

rajzbret *mi techn.* drawing board.

rak *ma* **1.** *zool.* crayfish, crawfish, crawdad, crawdaddy (*Astacus*); **Rak** *astron.* Cancer; *pot.* the Crab; (= *osoba spod znaku Raka*) Cancerian; **zwrotnik Raka** *geogr.* the Tropic of Cancer; **pokazać komuś, gdzie raki zimują** *przen.* fix sb's wagon; **spiec raka** *l.* **raczka** *przen.* turn crimson; **chodzić rakiem** *przen.* crawl on all fours. **2.** *pat.* (= *nowotwór złośliwy*) cancer, carcinoma; **rak płuc** lung cancer; **rak wątroby** hepatoma. **3.** (*choroba roślin*) canker. **4.** *muz.* reverse canon, retrograde imitation.

rakarz *mp* dogcatcher.

raki *pl. Gen.* **-ów** **1.** (= *drzewołazy*) climbing irons, (climbing) spurs. **2.** *sport* (*do wspinaczki*) crampons, crampoons.

rakieta *f.* **1.** (*pojazd*) rocket; **rakieta kosmiczna** (space) rocket; **rakieta nośna** launch vehicle. **2.** *wojsk.* (*pocisk*) rocket, missile. **3.** (= *raca*) flare, signal rocket, Very lights. **4.** *sport* racket, racquet. **5.** (= *sprzęt ułatwiający poruszanie się w śniegu*) snowshoe.

rakietka *f. Gen.pl.* **-ek** *sport* racket; **rakietka do badmintona** badminton bat *l.* racket; **rakietka do ping-ponga** ping-pong bat *l.* paddle.

rakietnica *f.* flare pistol, Very pistol.

rakietoplan *mi Gen.* **-u** *wojsk.* rocket ship.

rakietowiec *mp Gen.* **-wca** *wojsk., pot.* missileman.

rakietowy *a.* **1.** (= *odnoszący się do statku, pocisku*) rocket; **napęd rakietowy** rocket propulsion; **silnik rakietowy** rocket (engine *l.* motor); **wyrzutnia rakietowa** rocket launcher; **baza rakietowa** *wojsk.* missile base *l.* installation. **2.** (= *dotyczący pocisków oświetlających*) flare. **3.** *sport* (= *dotyczący rakiet tenisowych itp.*) racket.

rakija *f. Gen.* **rakii** *kulin.* rakija, plum brandy.

rakoodporny *a.* **1.** *med.* cancer-resistant. **2.** *bot.* canker-resistant.

rakotwórczo *adv. pat.* carcinogenically.

rakotwórczy *a. pat.* carcinogenic.

rakowacieć *ipf. med.* cancerate, undergo malignant transformation.

rakowaty *a.* **1.** *pat.* cancerous. **2.** *bot.* cankerous.

rakowy *a.* **1.** (= *dotyczący skorupiaka*) crawfish, crawdad. **2.** (= *dotyczący nowotworu*) cancerous.

raksa *f. żegl.* hank, snap.

raksloty *pl. żegl.* parrels, parrals.

RAM *abbr. komp.* RAM (= *Random Access Memory*).

rama *f.* **1.** (= *obramowanie*) frame; **rama**

okienna *bud.* window frame, sash; **oprawić obraz w ramę** frame a picture. **2.** (= *przyrząd do rozpinania czegoś*) frame, rack; **rama na ubrania** coat rack. **3.** *techn.* (*część pojazdu*) frame.

ramadan, ramazan *mi rel.* Ramadan.

ramia *f. Gen.* **-ii 1.** *bot.* ramie (*Boehmeria nivea*). **2.** *techn.* (*włókno*) ramie.

ramiarz *mp Gen.* **-a** framer.

ramiączko *n. Gen.pl.* **-ek 1.** (= *taśma podtrzymująca stanik itp.*) shoulder strap. **2.** (= *wieszak*) hanger.

ramienionóg *ma* **-o-** *zool.* brachiopod (*Brachiopoda*).

ramieniowy *a.* shoulder, arm.

ramienny *a.* shoulder; **kość ramienna** *anat.* humerus; **staw ramienny** *anat.* shoulder joint.

ramię *n.* ramieni- *pl.* **-on- 1.** (= *bark*) arm, shoulder; **na ramię broń!** slope arms!, shoulder arms!; **ramię w ramię** *l.* **przy ramieniu** (= *razem, solidarnie*) arm in arm, shoulder to shoulder; **z duszą na ramieniu** with one's heart in one's mouth; **mieć duszę na ramieniu** have one's heart in one's mouth; **wzruszyć ramionami** shrug one's shoulders; **spojrzeć przez ramię** look back over one's shoulder. **2.** (= *kończyna górna*) arm; **z czyjegoś ramienia** on sb's behalf; **przyjąć kogoś z otwartymi ramionami** give sb a warm welcome, welcome sb with open arms; **wziąć kogoś pod ramię** take sb by the arm; **wziąć kogoś w ramiona** take sb in one's arms; **rzucić się komuś w ramiona** fling o.s. into sb's arms. **3.** (*część ubrania*) arm. **4.** (= *odnoga, rozgałęzienie*) branch; **ramię kąta** *mat.* arm of an angle; **ramię siły** *fiz.* arm of a force; **ramię kotwicy** *żegl.* arm. **5.** (*ruchomy element maszyny*) arm; **ramię wycieraczki** *mot.* wiper arm; **ramię dźwigu** jib. **6.** *zool.* (= *wypustka*) arm.

ramionko *n. Gen.pl.* **-ek** zob. **ramię** 1, 2.

ramka *f.* **1.** zob. **rama** 1, 2. **2.** *komp.* (= *prostokąt w tekście*) box.

ramol *mp pog.* old sack, old fart, (old) crock.

ramoleć *ipf. pog.* go crumb.

ramowy *a.* **1.** (= *mający kształt ramy*) frame; **konstrukcja ramowa** *bud.* frame. **2.** (= *szkicowy, schematyczny*) framework, blueprint.

ramówka *f. Gen.pl.* **-ek** pot. (= *schemat programu*) program framework.

rampa *f.* **1.** (= *miejsce do przeładunku*) loading platform, loading dock, delivery ramp. **2.** *teatr* footlights.

ramy *pl. Gen.* **ram** (= *zasięg, granice*) framework, confines; **w ramach czegoś** within the framework *l.* confines *l.* scope of sth; **w ramach normalnej działalności** in the ordinary course of business; **w ramach umowy** under the agreement.

rana *f.* (= *uszkodzenie ciała*) wound, injury; **rana postrzałowa** gunshot *l.* bullet wound; **rana cięta** cut; **opatrzyć ranę** dress a wound; **o rany (Julek)!** *l.* **rany boskie!** pot. holy smoke *l.* Christ *l.* hell!; **rozdrapywać rany** *przen.* open old wounds; **dobry, że do rany przyłóż** as nice as a pie; **czas leczy rany** time heals all wounds.

ranczo *n.* ranch.

randka *f. Gen.pl.* **-ek** date; **mieć randkę z kimś** have a date with sb, go out on a date with sb; **umówić się na randkę z kimś** make a date with sb; **randka w ciemno** blind date; **chodzić na randki z kimś** go out with sb, date sb.

randomizacja *f. nauk.* randomization.

ranek *mi* **-nk-** *Gen.* **-a** morning; **rankiem** in the morning.

ranga *f.* **1.** (= *stopień służbowy*) rank; **on jest wyższy rangą ode mnie** he's above me in rank, he outranks me; **być w randze majora** *gł. wojsk.* have the rank of major. **2.** *lit.* (= *znaczenie*) importance; **fachowiec najwyższej rangi** professional of the top *l.* first rank; **sprawa najwyższej rangi** a matter of (the) utmost importance; **urastać do rangi czegoś** develop into sth.

ranić *ipf.* **1.** (= *zadawać rany*) wound, injure; (= *kaleczyć*) cut, hurt; (*o kolcach itp.*) hurt. **2.** (= *sprawiać przykrość*) hurt; **ranić czyjeś uczucia** hurt sb's feelings. – *pf.* = **zranić**.

raniuszek *ma* **-szk-** *orn.* long-tailed tit (*Aegithalos caudatus*).

raniuteńko, raniutko *adv.* in the wee hours of the morning, in the small hours.

ranka *f. Gen.pl.* **-ek** (small) wound, cut.

ranking *mi* ranking.

rankingowy *a.* ranking; **lista rankingowa** *zwł. sport* ranking, standings.

ranny[1] *a.* (= *zraniony*) wounded, injured, hurt; **ciężko ranny** badly *l.* seriously wounded *l.* injured. – *mp* casualty.

ranny[2] *a.* (= *występujący rano*) morning; **ranna rosa** morning dew; **ranna mgła** morning mist; **ranne pantofle** slippers; **ranny ptaszek** early bird; **ranne wydanie gazety** morning issue.

rano *n.* (= *poranek*) morning; **nad ranem** in the wee *l.* small hours of the morning, early in the morning; **z rana** in the morning; **do białego rana** till dawn; **od rana do wieczora** from morning till night. – *adv.* (= *wcześnie*) in the morning; **jutro rano** tomorrow morning; **kto rano wstaje, temu Pan Bóg daje** the early bird catches the worm.

rant *mi przest.* edge, brim.

rap *mi muz.* rap (music).

raper *mp muz.* raper, rap singer.

rapier *mi Gen.* **-a** *hist.* (*broń*) rapier.

raport *mi* report; **raport biegłego** expert report *l.* opinion; **oficjalny raport rządowy** white paper; **raport karny** *wojsk.* reporting for disciplinary action; **stanąć do raportu** *wojsk.* report for disciplinary action, have disciplinary action taken against o.s.; **podać kogoś do raportu** *wojsk.* report sb for disciplinary action, take disciplinary action against sb; **składać komuś raport** give sb a report; **zdać komuś raport z czegoś** debrief sb on sth, report back to sb on sth.

raportować *ipf.* report.

raportowy *a.* report.

rapować *ipf. muz.* rap.

rapowy *a. muz.* rap.

rapsod *mi Gen.* **-u** *teor.lit.* rhapsody. – *mp Gen.* **-a** *hist.* (= *recytator*) rhapsodist.

rapsodia *f. Gen.* **-ii** *muz.* rhapsody.

rapsodyczny *a. teor.lit.* rhapsodic.

raptem *adv.* **1.** (= *nagle*) suddenly, all of a sudden, without warning. **2.** *pot.* (= *zaledwie*) barely, hardly; **znamy się raptem parę dni** we have only known each other for a couple of days; **miał raptem dwadzieścia lat** he was barely twenty; **przepracował raptem pół dnia** he barely worked half a day.

raptownie *adv.* suddenly, abruptly, unexpectedly.

raptowny *a.* **1.** (= *nagły*) sudden, abrupt, unexpected; **raptowna zmiana** abrupt *l.* sudden change; **raptowna zmiana planów** sudden change of plans. **2.** *rzad.* (= *porywczy*) impetuous, quick-tempered.

raptularz *mi Gen.* **-a** *hist.* tickler.

raptus *mp pl.* **-y** *przest.* (= *człowiek porywczy*) hothead.

raróg *ma* **-o-** *orn.* saker falcon (*Falco cherrug*); **patrzeć na kogoś jak na raroga** look at sb as if they were a freak.

rarytas *mi* **1.** (= *rzadkość*) rarity. **2.** (= *smakołyk*) delicacy, dainty.

rasa *f.* **1.** *antrop.* race; **rasa biała/czarna/żółta** the white/black/yellow race. **2.** (= *gatunek ludzki*) human race. **3.** *roln.* (= *grupa osobników jednego gatunku*) breed, variety.

rasista *mp*, **rasistka** *f. Gen.pl.* **-ek** racist.

rasistowski *a.* racist.

rasizm *mi* racism.

rasowy *a.* **1.** (= *dotyczący rasy ludzkiej*) racial; **dyskryminacja rasowa** racial discrimination, discrimination on the grounds of race; **segregacja rasowa** racial segregation; **przesądy rasowe** racial prejudice; **zamach na tle rasowym** racially motivated attack; **stosunki rasowe** race relations. **2.** (= *odnoszący się do zwierzęcia czystej krwi*) pedigree. **3.** *pot.* (= *wybitny*) outstanding; **rasowy artysta** an artist to the tips of his fingers.

rastafarianizm *mi rel.* Rastafarianism.

raster *mi* **-tr-** *Gen.* **-a** *l.* **-u** *druk.* screen; **raster telewizyjny** *telew.* raster.

raszka *f. Gen.pl.* **-ek** = rudzik.

raszpla *f. Gen.pl.* **-i 1.** *dial.* rasp. **2.** *icht.* angel shark, monkfish (*Squatina squatina*).

raszplować *ipf. dial.* rasp.

rata *f.* instalment, installment; **na raty** *przen.* (= *z przerwami*) intermittently, off and on, by fits and starts; **kupować coś na raty** buy sth on the instalment plan; *Br.* buy sth on hire purchase.

ratafia *f. Gen.* **-ii** *kulin.* ratafia.

ratalny *a.* instalment, installment **sprzedaż ratalna** instalment plan; *Br.* hire purchase.

ratler *ma kynol.* ratter.

ratlerek *ma* **-rk-** *zob.* **ratler**.

ratować *ipf.* (= *nieść pomoc*) save, rescue; (*nieprzytomnego*) resuscitate; **ratować honor** save one's face, salvage one's reputation; **ratować dobytek** salvage one's property; **ratować swoje małżeństwo** save one's marriage; **ratować komuś życie** save sb's life; **ratować swoją skórę** save one's skin *l.* neck *l.* bacon; **ratować sytuację** save the day; **ratować kogoś przed czymś** save *l.* rescue

sb from sth; **kiepski film ratowały tylko piękne zdjęcia** the only saving grace of that awful film was beautiful photography. **~ się** *ipf.* **1.** (= *ratować siebie*) save o.s., rescue o.s., save one's life; **ratować się ucieczką** run for one's life, run for dear life. **2.** (= *ratować siebie nawzajem*) save each other *l.* one another.

ratownictwo *n.* rescue, life-saving; **ratownictwo górskie** mountain rescue; **ratownictwo morskie** lifeboat service; **ratownictwo okrętowe** ship salvaging.

ratowniczy *a.* rescue; **akcja ratownicza** rescue operation *l.* mission, salvage operation; **ekipa ratownicza** rescue party *l.* team *l.* crew; **służby ratownicze** rescue *l.* emergency services.

ratownik *mp* (*na plaży*) lifeguard; (*górski itp.*) rescuer.

ratrak *mi Gen.* **-a** (*pojazd*) snow truck.

ratunek *mi* **-nk- 1.** (= *pomoc*) help; **ratunku!** help!; **pospieszyć komuś na ratunek** *l.* **z ratunkiem** come to sb's rescue. **2.** (= *wybawienie*) salvation, rescue; **ostatnia deska ratunku** last resort.

ratunkowy *a.* rescue; life-saving; **akcja ratunkowa** rescue operation; **ekipa ratunkowa** rescue party *l.* team; **kamizelka ratunkowa** life jacket; **koło ratunkowe** life buoy; **łódź ratunkowa** lifeboat; **tratwa ratunkowa** life raft; **pogotowie ratunkowe** ambulance *l.* emergency service.

ratusz *mi Gen.* **-a** town hall, city hall.

ratuszowy *a.* town-hall, city-hall.

ratyfikacja *f.* ratification.

ratyfikacyjny *a. gł. prawn.* ratification.

ratyfikować *ipf. gł. prawn.* ratify.

rausz *mi* high, buzz; **być na rauszu** be crocked, be tipsy.

raut[1] *mi Gen.* **-u** *form.* (= *przyjęcie*) reception.

raut[2] *mi Gen.* **-a** (= *mały diament*) rose-cut diamond.

rauwolfia *f. bot.* rauwolfia (*Rauwolfia*).

raz *mi* **1.** *pl.* blows. **2.** (*sytuacja, okoliczność*) time; **raz po raz** *l.* **za razem** time after time; **innym razem** some other time; **pewnego razu** once; **tym razem** this time; **na drugi raz** next time; **na razie** (= *tymczasem*) for the time being; **na razie!** *pot.* see you!; **na razie nie** not yet; **w każdym razie** in any case, at any rate; **w najlepszym razie** at best; **w najgorszym razie** at worst; **w przeciwnym razie** otherwise, or else; **w takim razie** so, well then, in that case; **w żadnym razie** no way, by no means; **w razie czego** just in case; **w razie pożaru** in the event *l.* case of fire; **w razie potrzeby** if need be; **w sam raz** just fine *l.* right; **przejść od razu do rzeczy** get straight to the point; **tak od razu** offhand, just like that; **trzeba było tak od razu mówić!** why didn't you say so in the first place?!. **3.** (*wielokrotność*) time; **(jeden) raz** once; **dwa razy** twice; **dwa razy dwa** two times two; **dwa razy więcej** (*policzalne*) two times more; (*niepoliczalne*) twice as much; **pierwszy raz** first time; **za pierwszym razem** on the first go, at the first attempt; **pierwszy raz słyszę** I've never heard that before; **raz na jakiś czas** from time to time; **raz na miesiąc/rok** once a month/year, monthly/

annually; **po raz pierwszy** for the first time; **raz na zawsze** for good, once and for all; **raz czy dwa** once or twice; **raz w życiu** once in a lifetime; **ani razu** not a single time; **choć raz** just once, just for once; **ile razy?** how many times?; **jeszcze raz** once again, once more; **na raz** at once; **zerknij na to jeszcze raz** take another look at it; **nie raz, nie dwa** many a time, more than once; **od razu** straightaway, at once; **za każdym razem** every time, each time, whenever. – *adv.* **1.** (= *kiedyś*) once; **raz go widziałem** I saw him once. **2.** (= *wreszcie*) at last. **3.** (= *ostatecznie*) eventually, finally. – *num. indecl. pot.* (= *jeden*) one; **raz, dwa, trzy...** one, two, three...; **raz dwa** (= *błyskawicznie*) in no time.

razem *adv.* **1.** (= *jednocześnie*) simultaneously, at the same time. **2.** (= *wspólnie*) together, jointly; **razem z kimś/czymś** along with sb/sth, together with sb/sth; **wszyscy razem** everybody; **wszystko razem** altogether; **to będzie razem sto złotych** it will be hundred zloty altogether.

razić *ipf.* **rażę razisz 1.** (= *sprawiać przykre wrażenie*) offend (*czymś* with sth); **raził wszystkich swoim zachowaniem** his behavior antagonized everybody. **2.** (= *oślepiać*) dazzle, blind; **raziło go ostre słońce** the blazing sun dazzled him. **3.** *lit.* (= *uderzać, ranić*) smite.

razowiec *mi* **-wc-** *Gen.* **-a** *kulin.*, *pot.* wholewheat bread.

razowy *a. kulin.* wholewheat; *Br.* wholemeal; **chleb razowy** wholewheat bread; **mąka razowa** wholewheat *l.* graham flour.

razówka *f. Gen.pl.* **-ek** *kulin.*, *pot.* (= *mąka razowa*) wholewheat *l.* graham flour.

raźnie, raźno *adv.* **1.** (= *żwawo*) briskly, jauntily, lively. **2.** (= *dobrze, zdrowo*) good; **poczuć się raźniej** feel better; **zrobiło mu się raźniej na duszy** his spirits lifted. **3.** (= *bezpiecznie*) safe; **poczuć się raźniej** feel safer.

raźny *a.* brisk, jaunty, lively.

rażąco *adv.* glaringly, strikingly, flagrantly.

rażący *a.* **1.** (*o świetle*) (= *oślepiający*) dazzling, blinding; (*o kolorach*) (= *jaskrawy*) bright, glaring. **2.** (= *wyraźny, bezsporny*) glaring, gross; **rażący kontrast** striking contrast; **rażąca niesprawiedliwość** flagrant *l.* glaring injustice; **rażący błąd** gross *l.* glaring error; **rażące zachowanie** gross *l.* crass *l.* offensive behavior; **rażące zaniedbanie** gross negligence; **rażąca głupota** crass stupidity.

rażenie *n. wojsk.* effective fire; **broń masowego rażenia** weapons of mass destruction; **pole rażenia** field of fire; **siła rażenia** firepower.

rażony *a.* **-eni** (= *obezwładniony, dotknięty*) afflicted, stricken, smitten; **rażony chorobą** afflicted *l.* stricken with (an) illness; **rażony nieszczęściem** grief-stricken, smitten by grief; **rażony piorunem** thunderstruck; **rażony prądem** victim of an electric shock.

rąb *mi* **1. -ę-** *leśn.* (= *wycinanie drzew*) tree cutting *l.* felling. **2.** *techn.* (*część młotka, siekiery*) peen.

rąbać *ipf.* **-bię -biesz 1.** (= *rozłupywać*) chop, hew. **2.** (= *robić wręby*) hack away, chop away.

3. *pot.* (= *uderzać*) hit, whack. **4.** *pot.* (= *jeść z apetytem*) chow, chow down. **5.** *pot.* (= *mówić bez ogródek*) give it straight; **rąbnąć komuś prawdę prosto w oczy** talk straight from the shoulder, tell sb to their face. **6.** *pot.* (= *strzelać*) bang away. **7.** *pot.* (= *grać hałaśliwie*) bang.

rąbanka *f. Gen.pl.* **-ek 1.** *kulin.* chopped meat. **2.** *pot.* (= *mechaniczna, głośna muzyka*) loud *l.* noisy music; **ścisz/wyłącz wreszcie tę rąbankę!** would you finally turn this noise down *l.* off?!

rąbek *mi* **-bk-** *Gen.* **-a** hem, hemline; **uchylić rąbka tajemnicy** lift the veil of secrecy.

rąbnąć *pf.* **-ij 1.** *zob.* **rąbać. 2.** *pot.* (= *ukraść*) pinch, hook. **3.** *pot.* (= *zabić*) bump off, blow away. **4.** *pot.* (= *rzucać, uderzać*) bang, hit; **rąbnąć pięścią w stół** bang one's fist on the table; **rąbnąć głową w sufit** bang one's head on the ceiling. **5.** (= *mieć wypadek, uderzyć samochodem w coś*) bump. **6.** *pot.* (= *wypić alkohol*) drink, swig. **~ się** *pf.* **1.** *pot.* (= *uderzyć się*) bang (*o coś* against *l.* into *l.* at sth); bump (*o coś* against sth); hit o.s.; **rąbnąć się w głowę** bang one's head; **rąbnąć się o ścianę** bang into the wall, bump against the wall. **2.** *pot.* (= *pomylić się*) screw up, blow it, goof up.

rączęta *pl. Gen.* **-ąt** (tiny little) hands.

rączka *f. Gen.pl.* **-ek 1.** (= *mała ręka*) (tiny) hand; **złota rączka** jack of all trades, Mr. Fix-it, handyman; **całuję rączki** *przest.*, *żart.* at your service; **prowadzić kogoś za rączkę** lead sb by the hand; **z rączki do rączki** from hand to hand. **2.** (= *uchwyt*) handle, grip.

rącznik *mi Gen.* **-a rącznik pospolity** *bot.* castor-oil plant, castor bean (*Ricinus communis*).

rączy *a. lit.* (= *chyży*) swift, fast.

rb. *abbr.* (= *roku bieżącego*) this year.

rdest *mi bot.* knotweed (*Polygonum*).

rdestnica *f. bot.* pondweed (*Potamogeton*).

rdza *f.* **1.** (*warstwa niszcząca*) rust. **2.** *Gen.pl.* **rdzy** *bot.* (*grzyb*) rust (*Puccinia*). **3.** *Gen.pl.* **rdzy** *roln.*, *ogr.* (*choroba*) wheat rust.

rdzawić się *ipf.* go rust.

rdzawo *adv.* rustily.

rdzawy *a.* rusty; (*o kolorze*) russet.

rdzeniarka *f. Dat.* **-rce** *metal.* coremaking machine.

rdzeniarnia *f. Gen.* **-ni** *metal.* core shop.

rdzeniarz *mp Dat.* **-a** *metal.* coremaker.

rdzeniowy *a.* **1.** *bot.* medullary, pithy; **promienie rdzeniowe** rays. **2.** *anat.* medullary; **nerwy rdzeniowe** spinal nerves.

rdzennica *f. Gen.* **-cy** *metal.* core box.

rdzennie *adv.* indigenously.

rdzenny *a.* **1.** = **rdzeniowy. 2.** *bot.* indigenous. **3.** *jęz.* root. **4.** (= *pierwotny, tubylczy*) indigenous; (*o ludności*) aboriginal, native, indigenous.

rdzeń *mi Gen.* **-a 1.** *bot.* medulla, pith. **2.** *anat.* medulla; (= **rdzeń kręgowy**) spinal cord. **3.** *przen.* (= *sedno*) core, heart; **rdzeń sprawy** heart *l.* core of the matter. **4.** *fiz.* core. **5.** *jęz.* root, stem. **6.** *metal.* core. **7.** *techn.* (= *środek*) core, center; *Br.* centre; **rdzeń kabla** central quad of cable. **8.** *techn.* (*element reaktora*) reactor core, atomic core *l.* kernel.

rdzewieć *ipf.* **1.** (= *pokrywać się rdzą*) rust. **2.** (*o umiejętnościach itp.*) (= *zanikać*) rust, grow rusty; **stara miłość nie rdzewieje** old flame dies hard. **3.** *lit.* (= *przybierać rdzawy kolor*) turn russet.

rdzoodporny *a.* rust-proof, rust-resistant.

re *mi indecl. muz.* re, D.

readaptacja *f.* readaptation.

readmisja *f.* readmission.

reagent *mi Gen.* **-a** *chem.* reacting substance, reagent.

reagować *ipf.* **1.** (= *odpowiadać działaniem*) react, respond (*na coś* to sth); **reagować zbyt emocjonalnie** overreact. **2.** *biol.* (= *odpowiadać na bodźce*) respond, react (*na coś* to sth). **3.** *chem.* react (*z czymś* with *l.* on sth).

reakcja *f.* **1.** (= *działanie w odpowiedzi na coś*) reaction, response (*na coś* to sth); **instynktowna reakcja** gut reaction. **2.** *biol., chem.* reaction; **reakcja jądrowa** nuclear reaction; **reakcja łańcuchowa** *t. przen.* chain reaction; **reakcja chemiczna** chemical reaction; **reakcja egzotermiczna** exothermic reaction; **reakcja endotermiczna** endothermic reaction. **3.** *polit.* reaction. **4.** *pot.* (= *reakcjoniści*) reactionaries.

reakcjonista *mp,* **reakcjonistka** *f. Gen.pl.* **-ek** reactionary.

reakcyjny *a.* **1.** *fiz., chem.* reactive; **turbina reakcyjna** *techn.* pressure *l.* reactive turbine. **2.** (= *wsteczny, konserwatywny*) reactionary, diehard, conservative.

reaktancja *f. Gen.* **-ji** *el.* reactance.

reaktor *mi Gen.* **-a** **1.** *chem.* reactor, reaction still. **2.** *fiz.* reactor; **reaktor atomowy** nuclear reactor, atomic pile *l.* reactor.

reaktywacja *f.* reactivation.

reaktywizacja *f.* (= *wznowienie*) reactivation.

reaktywność *f. chem.* reactivity, reactiveness.

reaktywny *a.* **1.** *chem.* reactive. **2.** *psych.* reactive; **depresja reaktywna** reactive depression.

reaktywować *ipf. lit.* (*instytucję, osobę*) reactivate.

realgar *mi min.* realgar.

realia *pl. Gen.* **-ów** (= *rzeczy realnie istniejące*) reality.

realista *mp,* **realistka** *f. Gen.pl.* **-ek 1.** (= *osoba trzeźwo myśląca*) realist, realistic person; **nie jesteś realistą** you are being unrealistic; **bądź realistą!** be realistic! **2.** *sztuka* realist.

realistycznie *adv.* realistically.

realistyczny *a.* **1.** (= *oparty na trzeźwym osądzie*) realistic, down-to-earth. **2.** *sztuka* realistic.

realizacja *f.* **1.** (= *urzeczywistnienie*) (*marzeń, celów*) realization; (*planu*) execution; (*projektu*) implementation; **realizacja filmu** production of a movie, movie production; **realizacja przedstawienia** *teatr* play production; **realizacja zamówienia** order processing; **realizacja recepty** prescription filling. **2.** *ekon.* cashing.

realizator *mp,* **realizatorka** *f. Gen.pl.* **-ek** ex-

ecutor, implementer *l.* implementor; *film, radio, telew.* producer.

realizm *mi* **1.** (= *trzeźwość poglądów*) realism. **2.** *fil.* realism. **3.** *teor.lit., sztuka* Realism.

realizować *ipf.* **1.** (= *urzeczywistniać*) realize, achieve, fulfill; **realizować swoje cele** realize one's objectives, achieve one's goals; **realizować swoje marzenia** make one's dreams come true, fulfill one's dreams; **realizować plan** execute a plan; **realizować projekt** implement a project; **realizować zadania** carry out *l.* execute tasks; **realizować postanowienia umowy** fulfill the terms and conditions of a contract; **realizować film** produce a movie; **realizować przedstawienie** *teatr* produce a play; **realizować receptę** fill a prescription. **2.** *ekon.* cash; **realizować czek** cash a check, *Br.* cash a cheque. **~ się** *ipf.* **1.** (= *być urzeczywistnianym*) come true, be implemented. **2.** *pot.* (= *spełniać się w jakiejś roli*) fulfill o.s.

realnie *adv.* **1.** (= *zgodnie z faktami, trzeźwo*) realistically, sensibly, rationally; **patrzeć na świat realnie** be realistic. **2.** (= *naprawdę, w rzeczywistości*) really, actually.

realność *f.* reality.

realny *a.* **1.** (= *faktyczny*) real, actual; **płaca realna** *ekon.* real pay; **dochody realne** *ekon.* real income; **nadawać czemuś realnych kształtów** put sth into shape. **2.** (= *osiągalny, wykonalny*) feasible, viable. **3.** (= *odznaczający się zdrowym rozsądkiem*) realistic, sensible.

Realpolitik *f. polit.* Realpolitik; practical politics, political realism.

reanimacja *f.* **1.** *med.* resuscitation. **2.** reanimation, revival, revivification.

reanimacyjny *a. med.* resuscitative, resuscitation; **karetka reanimacyjna** ambulance.

reanimować *ipf.* **1.** *med.* resuscitate. **2.** reanimate, revive, revivify.

reasekuracja *f. ubezp.* reinsurance.

reasekurator *mp ubezp.* reinsurer.

reasumować *ipf.* recapitulate, recap, sum up; **reasumując,...** to recap *l.* sum up...

rebelia *f. Gen.* **-ii** *przest.* rebellion.

rebeliancki *a. przest.* rebel.

rebeliant *mp przest.* insurgent, rebel.

rebus *mi* rebus, puzzle.

recenzent *mp,* **recenzentka** *f. Gen.pl.* **-ek** (*filmu, książki, pracy naukowej*) reviewer.

recenzja *f.* (*filmu, książki, pracy, projektu*) review; **film miał dobre recenzje** the movie got good reviews, the movie was well reviewed; **film miał złe recenzje** the movie got bad reviews.

recenzować *ipf.* review.

recenzyjny *a.* review; **egzemplarz recenzyjny** review copy.

recepcja *f.* **1.** (*pomieszczenie w hotelu*) reception *l.* front desk. **2.** *form.* (= *odbiór dzieła itp.*) reception. **3.** *form.* (= *przyjęcie galowe*) reception.

recepcjonista *mp,* **recepcjonistka** *f. Gen.pl.* **-ek** receptionist, desk clerk.

recepcyjny *a.* **1.** (= *dotyczący pomieszczenia*

hotelowego) reception. **2.** (= *dotyczący przyjęcia galowego*) reception.

recepta *f.* **1.** (= *pisemne zlecenie lekarskie*) prescription; **wypisać receptę na coś** make out a prescription for sth; **tylko na receptę** by prescription only; **bez recepty** nonprescription, over-the-counter; **dostać lek na receptę** obtain a drug on doctor's prescription. **2.** (= *sprawdzony przepis*) recipe (*na coś* for sth); **mieć na coś receptę** *przen.* (= *znać rozwiązanie*) have a cure for sth; **nie ma magicznej recepty** there's no magic formula.

receptariusz *mi Gen.* **-a 1.** (= *bloczek recept*) block of prescriptions; (= *zbiór recept*) formulary. **2.** (= *księga do zapisywania recept*) prescription book.

receptor *mi Gen.* **-a 1.** *fizj.* receptor; **receptor bólowy** nociceptor, pain receptor; **receptor czuciowy** sensory receptor. **2.** *komp.* receptor.

receptura *f.* **1.** (= *przepis*) recipe. **2.** *handl.* formula; **nowa, ulepszona receptura** new improved formula.

recepturka *f. Gen.pl.* **-ek** *pot.* (= *gumka*) rubber band.

receptywność *f. lit.* receptivity, receptiveness.
receptywny *a. lit.* receptive.

recesja *f.* **1.** (= *ustępowanie*) recession, withdrawal. **2.** *ekon.* recession, economic slump *l.* decline.

recesywny *a. lit.* recessive; **gen recesywny** *biol.* recessive gene.

rechot *mi* **1.** (= *odgłos wydawany przez żaby*) croak. **2.** (= *chrapliwy śmiech*) chortle, cackle.

rechotać *ipf.* **-choczę** *l.* **-chocę -choczesz** *l.* **-chocesz, -chocz 1.** (= *o żabach, wydawać głos*) croak. **2.** (= *śmiać się chrapliwie*) cackle.

rechotliwy *a.* cackling.

recital *mi muz.* recital.

recto *n. indecl. hist.* recto.

recydywa *f. prawn.* recidivism.

recydywista *mp,* **recydywistka** *f. Gen.pl.* **-ek** *prawn.* recidivist, repeat *l.* habitual offender.

recykling *mi* recycling.

recytacja *f.* recitation.

recytator *mp,* **recytatorka** *f. Gen.pl.* **-ek** reciter.
recytować *ipf.* **1.** (= *deklamować*) recite. **2.** *pot.* (= *wyliczać*) recite; **recytować lekcję** recite a lesson.

red. *abbr.* (= *redaktor*) ed. (= *editor*).

reda *f. żegl.* roadstead, roads.

redagować *ipf.* **1.** (= *opracowywać tekst*) edit, draw up. **2.** (= *kierować redakcją pisma, książki*) edit.

redakcja *f.* **1.** (= *opracowanie tekstu*) editing. **2.** (= *zespół redaktorski*) editorial staff. **3.** (= *kierowanie wydawaniem pisma, książki*) editing; **pod redakcją** edited by. **4.** (= *lokal redakcyjny*) editor's office.

redakcyjny *a.* editorial; **nota redakcyjna** editorial.

redaktor *mp,* **redaktorka** *f. Gen.pl.* **-ek 1.** editor. **2.** *dzienn.* editor; **redaktor naczelny** editor-in-chief. **3.** (*autor ustawy, zbioru przepisów itp.*) author. **4.** (= *osoba prowadząca program informacyjny*) newscaster.

redaktorski *a.* editorial.
redemptorysta *mp rz.-kat.* Redemptorist.
redentycyd *mi chem.* rodenticide.
redia *f. zool.* redia.
redisówka *f. Gen.pl.* **-ek** speedball pen.
reducent *ma biol.* decomposer.
redukat *mi techn.* asphaltum oil.
redukcja *f.* **1.** (= *zmniejszenie*) reduction, decrease, cutback; **redukcja chromosomów** *biol.* reduction, meiosis. **2.** (= *zwalnianie z pracy*) layoff, job cuts; *gł. Br.* redundancy; **redukcja wynagrodzenia** salary cut; **redukcja wydatków** cutback in spending, retrenchment. **3.** *chem.* reduction. **4.** *jęz.* syncope. **5.** *log.* reduction.

redukcjonizm *mi fil.* reductionism.

redukcyjny *a.* **1.** (= *ograniczający*) reduction; **podział redukcyjny komórek** *biol.* reduction division; **zawór redukcyjny** *techn.* pressure reducing valve. **2.** *chem.* reducing; **środek redukcyjny** reducing agent. **3.** *log.* reducing.

redukować *ipf.* **1.** (= *zmniejszać*) reduce, decrease, cut down on; **redukować bieg** *mot.* shift to a lower gear; **redukować wydatki** cut down on expenditures; **redukować koszty** cut costs, reduce costs. **2.** (= *ograniczać zatrudnienie*) lay off, downsize, cut jobs; *gł. Br.* make redundant. **3.** (= *upraszczać*) reduce. **4.** *chem.* reduce.

reduktor *mi Gen.* **-a 1.** *chem.* reducing agent, reducer. **2.** *techn.* reducer; **reduktor ciśnienia** reducing valve, pressure regulator; **reduktor prędkości** speed reducer, reduction gear.

redundancja *f. jęz., komp.* redundancy.
redundancyjny *a. komp.* redundant.
redundantny *a. jęz., komp.* redundant.
reduplikacja *f. t. jęz.* (= *podwojenie*) reduplication.

reduta *f. hist.* redoubt.
redyskonto *n. ekon.* rediscount.
redystrybucja *f.* redistribution; **redystrybucja towarów** *ekon.* redistribution of goods; **redystrybucja dóbr** *ekon.* redistribution of wealth.

redystrybucyjny *a.* redistributive.
reedukacja *f.* **1.** (= *ponowne uczenie*) reeducation. **2.** (= *wychowywanie przestępcy*) reeducation.

reedycja *f.* reprint, reimpression, reissue.
reeksport *mi ekon.* reexport.
reelekcja *f. gł. polit.* reelection.
reemigracja *f.* repatriation.
reemigrant *mp* repatriate.
ref *mi żegl.* reef.
refbant *mi żegl.* reef band.
refektarz *mi Gen.* **-a** *kośc.* refectory.
referat *mi* **1.** (= *pisemne opracowanie*) paper; report. **2.** (= *dział instytucji*) department.
referencje *pl. Gen.* **-i** references.
referendarz *mp hist.* (*urzędnik królewski*) referendary.
referendum *n. sing. indecl. pl.* **-da** *Gen.* **-dów** *polit.* referendum.
referent *mp,* **referentka** *f. Gen.pl.* **-ek 1.** (= *osoba referująca*) speaker. **2.** (*urzędnik*) clerk.
referować *ipf.* report (*coś* on sth); recount (*coś* sth).

refhals *mi żegl.* luff pendant.

refinansować *ipf. ekon.* refinance.

refinansowy *a. ekon.* refinancing; **kredyt refinansowy** refinancing loan.

reflacja *f. ekon.* reflation.

refleks *mi* 1. (= *zdolność szybkiego reagowania*) reflex; **mieć dobry refleks** have good reflexes; **mieć spóźniony refleks** *pot.* have slow *l.* bad reflexes. 2. (= *odbicie*) reflection.

refleksja *f.* 1. (= *głębsze zastanowienie*) reflection, contemplation. 2. (= *myśl na temat przeszłego zdarzenia*) afterthought, reflection. 3. *fil.* reflection.

refleksologia *f.* reflexology.

refleksyjnie *adv.* reflectively, thoughtfully.

refleksyjność *f.* reflectivity, thoughtfulness.

refleksyjny *a.* 1. (= *skłonny do refleksji*) reflective, thoughtful; (*o usposobieniu, nastroju*) thoughtful, reflective, pensive. 2. (= *będący efektem refleksji*) reflective.

reflektant *mp* (= *osoba ubiegająca się o kupno*) prospective buyer; (= *osoba ubiegająca się o pracę*) applicant.

reflektor *mi Gen.* **-a** 1. (*lampa*) lamp, light; **reflektor samochodowy** *mot.* headlight; **reflektor punktowy** spotlight. 2. *el.* reflector, repeller. 3. *astron.* reflecting telescope, reflector.

reflektować *ipf.* be interested (*na coś* in sth); be into (*na coś* sth). **~ się** *ipf.* think twice, come to one's senses.

reflina *f. żegl.* reef pendant.

refmaszynka *f. żegl.* worm gear.

reforma *f.* reform; **reforma gospodarcza** economic reform; **głęboka reforma** sweeping reform; **reforma szkolnictwa** educational reform.

reformacja *f. hist.* Reformation.

reformacyjny *a. hist.* Reformation, reformational.

reformator *mp* reformer.

reformatorski *a.* reformatory, reformative.

reforming *mi chem.* reforming (process).

reformista *mp polit.* reformist, reformer.

reformistyczny *a. polit.* reformist.

reformizm *mi polit.* reformism.

reformować *ipf.* reform.

reformowalny *a.* amendable.

reformowany *a. rel.* Reformed.

reformy *pl. Gen.* **-m** *pot.* (= *majtki damskie z nogawkami*) pantie briefs, undies.

refować *ipf. żegl.* reef.

refpatent *mi żegl.* roller reefing gear.

refrakcja *f. fiz., astron.* refraction.

refrakcyjny *a. fiz., astron.* refraction.

refraktometr *mi opt.* refractometer.

refraktometria *f. opt.* refractometry.

refraktor *mi Gen.* **-a** 1. *astron.* refracting telescope, refractor. 2. *fiz.* refractor.

refren *mi* 1. *teor.lit.* refrain. 2. *muz.* refrain, chorus.

refrenowy *a.* refrain, chorus.

refsejzing *mi żegl.* reef point.

refugium *n. Gen.* **-iów** *biol., geogr.* refuge (area).

refuler *mi Gen.* **-a** *techn.* dredger cutter.

refundacja *f.* 1. *ekon.* refund. 2. (= *zwrot kosztów*) reimbursement, refund.

refundować *ipf.* 1. *ekon.* refund. 2. (= *zwracać koszty*) reimburse, refund.

refutacja *f.* refutation, disproof.

regal *mi Gen.* **-u** *hist.* (= *przywilej królewski*) regality.

regalia *pl. Gen.* **-ów** (= *insygnia władzy królewskiej*) regalia.

regał *mi* (*na książki*) bookshelf; (*sklepowy*) rack, display cabinet.

regatowiec *mp* **-wc-** *pl.* **-y** *sport* regatta competitor.

regatowy *a. sport* regatta.

regaty *pl. Gen.* **-t** *sport* regatta.

regelacja *f. fiz., geogr.* regelation.

regencja *f.* 1. *hist.* (= *władza regenta*) regency. 2. *sztuka* Regency.

regencyjny *a.* regency.

regeneracja *f.* 1. *biol.* regeneration. 2. (= *powrót do sił*) recovery, recuperation. 3. *techn.* (= *remont*) reconstruction, renovation. 4. *techn.* (= *odzyskiwanie substancji*) reclamation.

regeneracyjny *a.* regeneration, reclamation.

regenerator *mi Gen.* **-a** *biol., techn.* regenerator; **regenerator ciepła** heat regenerator.

regenerować *ipf.* 1. *biol.* regenerate. 2. (= *odzyskiwać sprawność*) regenerate, recuperate, regain one's strength. 3. *techn.* regenerate, reclaim; recover. **~ się** *ipf.* regenerate, recover.

regenerujący *a.* regenerating; (*o kremie*) regenerating, rejuvenating.

regent *mp*, **regentka** *f. Gen.pl.* **-ek** 1. (= *osoba sprawująca regencję*) regent. 2. *hist.* (*urzędnik królewski*) regent.

reggae *n. indecl. muz.* reggae.

regiel *mi* **-gl-** *Gen.pl.* **-i** (= *stroma partia gór w Tatrach*) Tatra nappe; (= *las pokrywający regle*) subalpine forest.

regiment *mi hist.* regiment.

region *mi* region.

regionalista *mp* regionalist.

regionalizacja *f.* regionalisation, regionalism.

regionalizm *mi* 1. (*ruch społeczny*) localism. 2. (*kultura regionu*) regionalism, localism. 3. *jęz.* regionalism, localism.

regionalny *a.* regional, local.

regionizacja *f.* = **regionalizacja**.

register *mi* **-tr-** *druk.* register.

registratura *f.* 1. (= *zbiór dokumentów*) records. 2. (= *kancelaria*) records office, registry.

reglamentacja *f.* rationing.

reglamentacyjny *a.* rationing.

reglamentować *ipf.* ration.

reglan *mi* (= *rodzaj kroju*) raglan.

reglanowy *a.* raglan.

reglowy *a.* pertaining to the Tatra nappe; pertaining to subalpine forest.

regolit *mi geol.* regolith, mantle rock.

regres *mi* 1. *lit.* (= *cofanie się w rozwoju*) regress, regression. 2. *prawn.* recourse.

regresja *f.* 1. (= *regres, cofanie się*) regression,

regress. **2.** *biol.* regression, involution, degeneration. **3.** *geol.* regression.

regresywny *a. lit.* regressive.

regulacja *f.* **1.** (= *normowanie*) control; **regulacja należności/rachunków** settlement of one's dues/bills; **regulacja cen/płac** price/pay control; **regulacja urodzin** birth control. **2.** (= *nastawianie przyrządu*) tuning, adjustment; **regulacja automatyczna** automatic control; **regulacja ręczna** manual control; **regulacja zdalna** remote control; **regulacja siły głosu** volume control; **regulacja rzek** river engineering.

regulacyjny *a.* regulative, regulatory.

regulamin *mi* **1.** regulations, rules, rules and regulations; **regulamin pracy** work regulations; **zgodny z regulaminem** statutory, by the rulebook *l.* rules; **przestrzegać regulaminu** observe the rules, go by the rulebook *l.* rules. **2.** (= *zbiór przepisów*) rulebook.

regulaminowo *adv.* by the book, according to *l.* by the rules.

regulaminowy *a.* statutory; regulation.

regularnie *adv.* **1.** (= *według reguł, prawidłowo*) regularly, properly. **2.** (= *kształtnie, foremnie*) regularly, evenly. **3.** (= *systematycznie*) regularly, on a regular basis.

regularność *f.* **1.** (= *prawidłowość*) regularity. **2.** (= *kształtność*) regularity, evenness. **3.** (= *systematyczność*) regularity.

regularny *a.* **1.** (*o wierszu, formie, czasowniku*) (= *zgodny z regułami*) regular; **wojsko regularne** regular army. **2.** (= *kształtny, proporcjonalny*) regular, even; **regularne rysy** regular features, even features. **3.** (= *systematyczny*) regular; **prowadzić regularny tryb życia** keep regular hours; **w regularnych odstępach** at regular intervals; **regularna wojna** regular war. **4.** *pot.* (= *zwyczajny*) regular, usual, ordinary.

regulator *mi Gen.* **-a 1.** (*urządzenie*) regulator, adjustment; **na cały regulator** *pot.* at full blast. **2.** (*czynnik*) controller, control; **regulator wzrostu roślin** plant growth regulator; **regulator czasowy** timer.

regulować *ipf.* **1.** (= *normować*) regulate, control; **regulować rachunek** settle a bill; **regulować rachunki z kimś** *przen.* get even *l.* square with sb; **regulować ruch** control traffic; **regulować stosunki** normalize relations. **2.** (= *nastawiać przyrząd*) regulate, adjust; **regulować silnik** tune an engine. **3.** (= *wpływać na prawidłowość*) regulate; **regulować rzekę** engineer a river.

reguła *f.* **1.** (= *zasada*) rule, principle, norm; **reguły gramatyki** rules of grammar; **reguły gry** *t. przen.* rules of the game; **z reguły** as a rule; **trzymać się reguł** stick to the rules; **złamać reguły** break *l.* violate the rules; **naruszyć reguły** bend *l.* stretch the rules; **wbrew regułom** against the rules; **wyjątek od reguły** exception to the rule; **wyjątek potwierdza regułę** exception proves the rule; **stać się regułą** become the rule *l.* the norm. **2.** *rel.* observance.

rehabilitacja *f.* **1.** (= *przywrócenie praw*) rehabilitation, vindication. **2.** *med.* rehabilitation.

rehabilitacyjny *a.* rehabilitative; **ćwiczenia rehabilitacyjne** rehabilitative exercises.

rehabilitant *mp* rehabilitator.

rehabilitować *ipf.* **1.** (= *przywracać prawa*) rehabilitate, vindicate. **2.** *med.* rehabilitate. **~ się** *ipf.* rehabilitate o.s.

reifikacja *f. fil.* reification.

reifikować *ipf. fil.* reify.

reimport *mi Gen.* **-u** *ekon.* reimportation.

reinkarnacja *f. rel.* reincarnation.

reintegracja *f.* reintegration.

reinterpretacja *f.* reinterpretation.

rej *mi* **wodzić rej** call the tune.

rej. *abbr.* (= *rejon*) dist. (= *district*); (= *rejestracyjny*) registration.

reja *f. Gen. i Loc.* **rei** *Gen.pl.* **rei** *l.* **rej** *żegl.* yard.

rejent *mp prawn.* (= *notariusz*) notary public.

rejentalnie *adv. prawn.* notarially.

rejentalny *a. prawn.* notarial; **akt rejentalny** notarial deed.

rejestr *mi* **1.** (= *spis*) register; **rejestr handlowy** *prawn.* register of companies; **wpisać do rejestru** enter into a register, make a record in a register. **2.** *komp.* register. **3.** *muz.* (= *część skali dźwiękowej*) register. **4.** *muz.* (*część organów*) stop. **5.** *jęz.* register.

rejestracja *f.* **1.** (= *rejestrowanie*) registration. **2.** *muz.* registration. **3.** *techn.* (= *zapis*) record; **rejestracja danych** (data) logging *l.* recording. **4.** (= *nagranie dla radia, telewizji*) recording. **5.** (= *miejsce w przychodni, szpitalu*) reception. **6.** *pot.* (= *tablica rejestracyjna*) (license) plate.

rejestracyjny *a.* registration; **dowód rejestracyjny** *mot.* registration; **numer rejestracyjny** *mot.* registration number; **tablica rejestracyjna** *mot.* license plate; *Br.* numberplate.

rejestrator *mp* registrar. – *mi Gen.* **-a** *techn.* (= *urządzenie rejestrujące*) recorder, logger.

rejestratorka *f. Gen.pl.* **-ek** registrar; (*w przychodni, szpitalu*) receptionist.

rejestrować *ipf.* **1.** (= *wprowadzać do rejestru*) register, enter into a register; **rejestrować znak towarowy** register a trademark. **2.** *techn.* (= *utrwalać*) record, log; *radio, telew.* record. **~ się** *ipf.* register.

rejestrowy *a.* register, registration.

rejon *mi* (= *obszar*) district; region; (= *okolica*) area, neighborhood.

rejonowy *a.* district.

rejowiec *mi* **-wc-** *Gen.* **-a** *żegl.* square-rigged ship.

rejowy *a. żegl.* square-rigged.

rejs *mi* (= *podróż*) (*statkiem*) voyage; (*samolotem*) flight; **rejs turystyczny** cruise; **dziewiczy rejs statkiem** maiden voyage; **dziewiczy rejs samolotem** maiden flight; **rejs próbny** *l.* **ćwiczebny** shakedown voyage.

rejsowy *a.* scheduled; **lot rejsowy** scheduled flight; **samolot rejsowy** liner.

rejterada *f. przest., żart.* (= *ucieczka*) flight.

rejterować *ipf. przest., żart.* flee, run away.

rejwach *mi przest.* (= *rozgardiasz*) bustle, commotion.

rekalescencja *f. techn.* recalescence.

rekamiera *f. Gen.* **-erze** recamier, récamier.
rekapitulacja *f.* recapitulation.
rekapitulować *ipf.* recapitulate, recap.
rekcja *f. jęz.* government.
rekin *ma icht.* shark (*Squaliformes*); **rekin ludojad** great white shark (*Carcharodon carcharias*). – *mp pl.* **-y** *pot.* shark. – *mi żegl.* wind sail.
rekinek *ma* **-nk-** *icht.* lesser spotted dogfish (*Scyliorhinus caniculus*).
reklama *f.* **1.** (= *reklamowanie*) advertising; **reklama bezpośrednia** direct-mail (advertising); **reklama podprogowa** subliminal advertising. **2.** (= *ogłoszenie*) (*w gazetach, czasopismach*) advertisement, ad; (*w telewizji, radiu*) commercial; **przerwa na reklamę** commercial break, break for commercials; **reklama nowego filmu** trailer. **3.** (= *rozgłos*) publicity; **robić komuś/czemuś reklamę** *przen.* give sb/sth publicity, give sb/sth a good build-up. **4.** *pot.* (= *tablica reklamowa*) billboard; **reklama świetlna** neon sign.
reklamacja *f.* complaint; **wnieść** *l.* **złożyć reklamację** complain, make *l.* file *l.* lodge a complaint.
reklamacyjny *a.* complaint.
reklamodawca *mp* advertiser.
reklamować *ipf.* **1.** (= *zachwalać poprzez reklamę*) advertise, publicize. **2.** (= *składać reklamację*) make *l.* file *l.* lodge a complaint, complain (*coś* about sth).
reklamowy *a.* advertising; **agencja reklamowa** advertising agency, publicity bureau *l.* agency; **materiały reklamowe** advertising materials, publicity matter; **kampania reklamowa** advertising *l.* publicity *l.* promotion campaign; **ulotki reklamowe przesyłane pocztą** direct mail, *pot.* junk mail; **bezpłatna gazeta reklamowa** freesheet, giveaway; **ulotka reklamowa** flier *l.* flyer, handout, leaflet; **powierzchnia reklamowa** advertising space.
reklamówka *f. Gen.pl.* **-ek 1.** *pot.* (= *film reklamowy*) promo, promotional (video), infomercial (video). **2.** (= *ulotka reklamowa*) flier *l.* flyer, leaflet. **3.** (= *bezpłatna próbka towaru*) free sample. **4.** *pot.* (= *torba foliowa*) plastic bag (*with a print advertising a company, product, etc.*).
rekolekcje *pl. Gen.* **-ji** *rz.-kat.* retreat.
rekolekcyjny *a. rz.-kat.* retreat.
rekombinacja *f. genetyka* recombination.
rekomendacja *f. lit.* recommendation; **z czyjejś rekomendacji** on sb's recommendation.
rekomendować *ipf. lit.* recommend.
rekompensacyjny *a.* compensatory, indemnificatory.
rekompensata *f.* compensation, indemnity, indemnification; **dostać coś tytułem rekompensaty** *l.* **jako rekompensatę za coś** obtain sth in compensation for sth.
rekompensować *ipf.* compensate, indemnify; **rekompensować komuś straty** compensate *l.* indemnify sb for their loss *l.* losses.
rekonesans *mi t. wojsk.* reconnaissance.
rekonesansowy *a.* reconnaissance.
rekonstrukcja *f.* reconstruction; **rekonstrukcja**

zdarzeń reenactment; **rekonstrukcja rządu** *polit.* cabinet *l.* government reshuffle.
rekonstrukcyjny *a.* reconstructional, reconstructionary; restoration.
rekonstruować *ipf.* reconstruct; (= *przywracać dawny wygląd*) restore.
rekonwalescencja *f.* convalescence, recuperation.
rekonwalescencki *a.* convalescent, recuperative.
rekonwalescencyjny *a.* convalescent, recuperative.
rekonwalescent *mp*, **rekonwalescentka** *f. Gen.pl.* **-ek** convalescent.
rekord *mi* **1.** (= *najlepszy wynik*) record; **rekord świata/kraju** world/national record; **rekord życiowy** *sport* (one's) personal best; **pobić rekord** break a record; **poprawić rekord** improve (on) a record; **ustanowić rekord** set a record; **posiadać rekord świata** hold the world record. **2.** *komp.* record.
rekordowo *adv.* sumpremely; **w rekordowo krótkim czasie** at record speed.
rekordowy *a.* record; (*o wyniku, czasie*) record-breaking; **rekordowe zbiory** bumper crops; **rekordowy rok** peak year.
rekordzista *mp*, **rekordzistka** *f. Gen.pl.* **-ek** record holder; **rekordzista świata w czymś** world record holder in sth.
rekreacja *f.* (= *odpoczynek*) recreation; (= *rozrywka*) leisure; **centrum rekreacji** leisure center, *Br.* leisure centre.
rekreacyjny *a.* recreational; leisure.
rekrucki *a.* recruit.
rekrut *mp* recruit; *wojsk. t.* conscript.
rekrutacja *f.* **1.** (= *pobór do wojska*) draft; *Br.* conscription. **2.** (= *przyjmowanie do szkół lub do pracy*) enrollment, recruitment.
rekrutacyjny *a.* **1.** (= *dotyczący poboru wojskowego*) draft; *Br.* conscription. **2.** (*dotyczący przyjmowania do szkoły lub do pracy*) enrollment, recruitment.
rekrutować *ipf.* **1.** (= *przeprowadzać pobór do wojska*) draft; *Br.* conscript. **2.** (= *przyjmować do szkoły lub do pracy*) enroll, recruit. ~ **się** *ipf.* (= *pochodzić*) be recruited (*spośród* from).
rekrystalizacja *f. geol., techn.* recrystallization.
rektor *mp* **1.** *uniw.* (= *zwierzchnik uczelni*) president; *Br.* vice-chancellor; **pan rektor Kowalski** President Kowalski; Vice-Chancellor Kowalski. **2.** *kośc.* (= *przełożony seminarium*) rector.
rektorat *mi uniw.* president's office; *Br.* vice-chancellor's office.
rektorski *a.* president's; *Br.* vice-chancellor's; **dzień rektorski** class cancellation (*by the president's l. vice-chancellor's order, on a special occasion*); **godziny rektorskie** time off from lectures (*on a special occasion*).
rektoskopia *f. Gen.* **-ii** *med.* rectoscopy.
rektyfikacja *f. chem.* rectification, fractional distillation.
rektyfikacyjny *a. chem.* rectifying, rectification.
rektyfikat *mi chem.* (*spirytus*) rectified spirit.

rektyfikować *ipf. chem.* rectify.

rekultywacja *f.* (*terenów*) land reclamation; **rekultywacja terenów leśnych** reforestation.

rekultywować *ipf.* reclaim.

rekwiem *n. indecl. rel.* requiem.

rekwirować *ipf.* requisition; (*zwł. w czasie wojny*) commandeer.

rekwizycja *f.* **1.** (= *rekwirowanie*) requisition, commandeering. **2.** *prawn.* requisition.

rekwizycyjny *a.* requisitional.

rekwizyt *mi teatr* prop, property.

rekwizytor *mp teatr* propman, property man.

rekwizytorka *f. teatr* propwoman, property woman.

rekwizytornia *f. Gen.pl.* **-i** *teatr* prop room, property room.

relacja *f.* **1.** (= *sprawozdanie*) account, report (*z czegoś* of sth); **zdawać relację z czegoś** report sth, give an account of sth; **relacja z pierwszej ręki** firsthand account; (*zwł. dziennikarska*) inside story; **relacja na żywo** live report, live coverage. **2.** (= *zależność*) relation. **3.** *kol.* line; **relacja Lublin-Szczecin** Lublin-Szczecin line; **pociąg relacji Lublin-Szczecin** Lublin-to-Szczecin train.

relacjonizm *mi fil.* relationism.

relacjonować *ipf.* (= *zdawać sprawę*) report (*coś* on sth); relate (*coś* sth); give an account (*coś* of sth); (*w telewizji*) provide coverage (*coś* of sth); **relacjonować na żywo** provide live coverage of sth; **będziemy to dla państwa relacjonować na żywo** we'll be reporting it live for you.

relacyjny *a. komp.* relational.

relaks *mi* relaxation.

relaksacja *f.* (= *odprężenie*) *biol., techn.* relaxation.

relaksacyjny *a.* (*o muzyce, ćwiczeniach*) relaxing.

relaksować *ipf.* relax. ~ **się** *ipf.* relax, loosen up.

relaksowo *adv.* relaxingly.

relaksowy *a.* relaxing.

relaksujący *a.* relaxing.

relator *mi Gen.* **-a** *jęz.* relator.

relatywista *mp fil.* relativist.

relatywistyczny *a. fil.* relativistic.

relatywizacja *f. fil.* relativization.

relatywizm *mi* relativism.

relatywizować *ipf. fil.* relativize.

relatywnie *adv. lit.* relatively.

relatywność *f. lit.* relativity.

relatywny *a. lit.* relative.

relegacja *f. lit.* (*ucznia, studenta*) expulsion.

relegować *pf. l. ipf. lit.* (*ucznia, studenta*) expel.

relewantny *a. jęz.* relevant, distinctive.

relief *mi* **1.** *sztuka* relief; **relief płaski** bas-relief; **relief wypukły** high relief. **2.** *geogr.* relief.

reliefowy *a.* relief.

religia *f. Gen.* **-ii** religion; **nauka** *l.* **lekcje religii** religious instruction; **wyznawać religię** practise a religion.

religiancki *a.* religiose.

religianctwo *n.* religiosity.

religijnie *adv.* religiously.

religijność *f.* religiousness.

religijny *a.* **1.** (= *dotyczący religii*) religious; (*o muzyce, literaturze*) devotional; (*o szkole*) denominational. **2.** (= *pobożny*) religious.

religioznawca *mp* religious studies expert; specialist in the study of religion.

religioznawczy *a.* religious studies; related to the study of religion.

religioznawstwo *n.* religious studies; study of religion.

relikt *mi* **1.** (= *przeżytek*) relic. **2.** *biol., geol.* relict.

reliktowy *a.* relict.

relikwia *f. Gen.* **-ii** (= *szczątki świętych*) (= *cenna pamiątka*) relic.

relikwiarz *mi Gen.* **-a** *kość.* (*kapliczka*) (*zwł. przenośna*) feretory; (*pojemnik*) reliquary.

reling *mi żegl.* bulwarks.

REM *abbr. fizj.* REM (= *rapid eye movement*); **faza REM** (*stadium snu*) REM sleep.

rem *mi Gen.* **-a** *fiz. przest.* (*jednostka dawki skutecznej promieniowania*) rem.

remake *mi Gen.* **-'u** *kino* remake.

remanent *mi handl.* (= *spis okresowy*) stocktaking; (= *wykaz towarów*) inventory; **zrobić remanent** take stock.

remanentowy *a. handl.* stocktaking; inventory.

remburs *mi ekon.* reimbursement.

remedium *n. sing. indecl. pl.* **-ia** *Gen.* **-iów** **1.** *lit.* remedy (*na coś* for sth). **2.** *ekon.* (*tolerancja monety*) remedy, tolerance.

remik *mi Gen.* **-a** *karty* rummy.

remiks *mi* remix.

remilitaryzacja *f.* remilitarization.

reminiscencja *f.* (= *wspomnienie*) *sztuka* reminiscence.

remis *mi* draw; **uzyskać remis** draw.

remisja *f. med.* remission (*czegoś* from sth).

remisować *ipf.* draw.

remisowo *adv.* in a draw.

remisowy *a.* **wynik remisowy** draw.

remiz *ma orn.* Eurasian penduline-tit (*Remiz pendulinus*).

remiza *f.* **1.** (= *zajezdnia*) depot; **remiza strażacka** fire station, firehouse. **2.** *myśl.* preserve.

remont *mi* (*domu, mieszkania*) redecoration, refurbishment; (*ulicy*) repair; (*maszyny, statku*) repair; (*samochodu, maszyny*) overhaul; **kapitalny remont** (*samochodu, maszyny*) major overhaul; (*domu*) extensive redecoration; **przeprowadzić remont** redecorate, refurbish; repair; overhaul; **być w remoncie** be redecorated, be refurbished; be undergoing repairs; be overhauled.

remontować *ipf.* (*dom, mieszkanie*) redecorate, refurbish; (*ulicę*) repair; (*maszynę, statek*) repair; (*samochód, maszynę*) overhaul.

remontowiec *mp* repair worker.

remontownia *f. Gen.pl.* **-i** repair shop.

remontowy *a.* redecoration, refurbishment; repair; overhaul.

Ren *mi geogr.* the Rhine.

ren *ma Gen.* **-a** *zool.* (= *renifer*) reindeer (*Rangifer tarandus*). – *mi Gen.* **-u** *chem.* rhenium.
renacjonalizacja *f.* renationalization.
rencista *mp*, **rencistka** *f. Gen.pl.* **-ek** pensioner.
renegat *mp* renegate, turncoat.
renegocjacja *f.* renegotiation.
renegocjować *ipf. l. pf.* renegotiate.
renesans *mi* **1.** *hist., sztuka* the Renaissance. **2.** (= *odrodzenie*) renaissance, revival.
renesansowy *a.* Renaissance.
reneta *f. ogr.* pippin, russet.
renifer *ma zool.* reindeer (*Rangifer tarandus*).
reniferowy *a.* reindeer; **chrobotek reniferowy** *bot.* reindeer moss (*Cladonia rangiferina*).
renkloda *f. bot., ogr.* greengage (*Prunus domestica italica*).
renklodowy *a.* greengage.
renoma *f.* reputation, repute; **dobra/zła renoma** good/bad reputation, good/bad repute *l.* disrepute; **cieszyć się dobrą renomą** hold a good reputation; **mieć renomę wybitnego pisarza/lekarza** be reputed to be an outstanding writer/doctor; **zdobyć sobie renomę** make a reputation for o.s., win acclaim.
renomowany *a.* reputable.
renons *mi karty* renounce.
renowacja *f.* renovation, renewal.
renowacyjny *a.* renovation, renovating.
renowator *mp* restorer.
renta *f.* **1.** (= *świadczenie pieniężne*) pension; **renta inwalidzka** disability pension; **być na rencie** be a pensioner, draw a pension; **przejść na rentę** become a pensioner. **2.** *ekon.* (= *dochód*) (*z inwestycji kapitałowej*) rente; (*z majątku*) income from property.
rentgen *mi Gen.* **-a** **1.** *pot.* (= *aparat rentgenowski*) X-ray apparatus. **2.** *pot.* (= *prześwietlenie*) X-ray examination. **3.** *pot.* (= *zdjęcie rentgenowskie*) X-ray picture. **4.** *fiz.* (*jednostka promieniowania*) roentgen.
rentgenodiagnostyka *f. med.* X-ray diagnostics.
rentgenografia *f. Gen.* **-ii** *med.* roentgenography, X-ray photography.
rentgenogram *mi* roentgenogram.
rentgenolog *mp pl.* **-dzy** *l.* **-owie** roentgenologist.
rentgenologia *f. Gen.* **-ii** roentgenology.
rentgenologiczny *a.* roentgenological, roentgenologic.
rentgenoterapia *f. Gen.* **-ii** *med.* X-ray therapy.
rentgenowski *a.* X-ray; **aparat rentgenowski** X-ray apparatus; **badanie rentgenowskie** X-ray examination; **promienie rentgenowskie** X-rays; **zdjęcie rentgenowskie** X-ray picture.
rentier *mp* rentier.
rentierski *a.* rentier.
rentowność *f. ekon.* profitability.
rentowny *a. ekon.* profitable.
reński *a.* Rhenish; **wino reńskie** Rhenish wine.
reofil *ma Gen.pl.* **-i** *l.* **-ów** *zool.* rheophile.
reologia *f. Gen.* **-ii** *techn., med.* rheology.
reorganizacja *f.* reorganization.
reorganizacyjny *a.* reorganizational.

reorganizator *mp* reorganizer.
reorganizować *ipf.* reorganize.
reorientacja *f.* reorientation.
rep *mi Gen.* **-a** *fiz.* rep.
reparacje *pl. Gen.* **-ji** *polit.* reparations.
reparacyjny *a. polit.* reparation.
repartycja *f. lit.* repartition.
repasacja *f.* ladder-mending.
repatriacja *f.* repatriation.
repatriacyjny *a.* repatriation.
repatriancki *a.* repatriate, repatriate's.
repatriant *mp*, **repatriantka** *f. Gen.pl.* **-ek** repatriate.
repatriować *ipf.* repatriate.
repelent *mi chem.* repellent, repellant.
reper *mi Gen.* **-a** *geol.* bench mark, BM.
reperacja *f.* repair; **oddać coś do reperacji** have sth repaired; **kuchenka jest w reperacji** the cooker is being repaired.
reperkusja *f. lit.* repercussion.
reperować *ipf.* repair.
repertorium *n. sing. indecl. pl.* **-ia** *Gen.* **-iów** **1.** (= *rejestr*) index, repertory. **2.** *prawn.* register of cases.
repertuar *mi* repertoire; (*słów, zachowań*) stock-in-trade; **repertuar dowcipów/przekleństw** repertoire of jokes/curses; **żelazny repertuar** stock.
repertuarowy *a.* repertoire.
repeta *f. pot.* (= *dodatkowa porcja*) second helping.
repetent *mp pot.* repeater.
repetować *ipf.* **1.** *pot.* (*klasę*) repeat. **2.** *wojsk.* (*broń*) reload.
repetycja *f. muz., teor.lit.* repetition.
repetytorium *n. sing. indecl. pl.* **-ia** *Gen.* **-iów** **1.** (= *cykl wykładów*) revision course. **2.** (= *podręcznik*) repetition drills.
repetytoryjny *a.* revision; **zajęcia repetytoryjne** revision course.
replay *mi Gen.* **-a** *l.* **-u** *Gen.pl.* **-ów** action replay.
replika *f.* **1.** (= *odpowiedź*) reply; **ostra replika** counterblast. **2.** *sztuka* replica. **3.** *teatr* cue. **4.** *jęz.* (= *kalka*) calque.
replikować *ipf.* **1.** *lit.* reply. **2.** *biol.* (*DNA*) replicate.
repolonizacja *f.* re-Polonization.
repolonizacyjny *a.* re-Polonization.
repolonizować *ipf.* re-Polonize.
report *mi ekon.* carry-over, carry-forward.
reportaż *mi* report.
reportażowy *a.* report.
reportażysta *mp*, **reportażystka** *f. Gen.pl.* **-ek** reporter.
reporter *mp*, **reporterka** *f. Gen.pl.* **-ek** reporter.
reporterski *a.* reporter's.
repozycja *f. med.* reposition.
represalia *pl. Gen.* **-ów** *polit.* reprisals.
represja *f.* reprisal; **paść ofiarą represji** be victimized; **stosować represje wobec kogoś** victimize sb.
represjonować *ipf.* victimize.
represyjnie *adv.* repressively.

represyjny *a.* repressive.

reprezentacja *f.* **1.** (= *przedstawicielstwo*) representation, delegation; (*np. pielęgniarek na zjeździe związków zawodowych, mniejszości narodowych w parlamencie itp.*) contingent; **reprezentacja narodowa** *sport* national team; **reprezentacja szkoły** school team, varsity; **reprezentacja uniwersytetu** university team, varsity. **2.** *lit.* (*w sposobie bycia*) dignity.

reprezentacyjnie *adv.* presentably, elegantly; **wyglądać reprezentacyjnie** look presentable.

reprezentacyjność *f.* **1.** (*np. próbki*) representativeness. **2.** (= *wytworność*) elegance.

reprezentacyjny *a.* **1.** (= *służący reprezentacji*) representative; **fundusz reprezentacyjny** entertainment fund; **kompania reprezentacyjna** *wojsk.* guard of honor, *Br.* guard of honour. **2.** (= *okazały, wytworny*) presentable; (*o człowieku*) of good presence; **reprezentacyjna dzielnica/ sukienka** elegant district/dress.

reprezentant *mp*, **reprezentantka** *f. Gen.pl.* **-ek 1.** (= *przedstawiciel*) representative; **Izba Reprezentantów** *parl.* House of Representatives. **2.** *sport* team member; **reprezentant Polski/Anglii** (*w piłce nożnej, siatkówce itd.*) Poland/England international.

reprezentatywny *a.* representative (*dla czegoś* of sth).

reprezentować *ipf.* **1.** (*państwo, organizację, grupę ludzi*) represent; **godnie reprezentować drużynę** (*zwł. w sporcie*) keep the flag flying; **reprezentować pogląd, że...** hold the view that... **2.** (= *przedstawiać*) present.

reprint *mi druk.* reprint.

reprodukcja *f.* **1.** (= *kopia*) reproduction, copy. **2.** (= *wykonywanie kopii*) (= *rozmnażanie*) *ekon., psych.* reproduction.

reprodukcyjny *a.* reproductive.

reprodukować *ipf.* **1.** (= *robić kopie*) reproduce, copy. **2.** (= *odtwarzać*) (*opinie, wiadomości, poglądy*) copy. **3.** (= *rozmnażać*) (*zwierzęta, rośliny*) reproduce.

reproduktor *ma* breeder.

reprografia *f. Gen.* **-ii** reprography.

reprograficzny *a.* reprographic.

reprymenda *f. lit.* dressing-down, dusting down; earful; **dać komuś reprymendę** give sb a dressing down, dress sb down (*za coś* for sth).

reprywatyzacja *f.* reprivatization.

reprywatyzacyjny *a.* reprivatization.

reprywatyzować *ipf.* reprivatize.

repryza *f. muz.* reprise.

republika *f.* republic; **republika federacyjna** federative republic; **Republika Czeska** the Czech Republic; **Republika Federalna Niemiec** Federal Republic of Germany; **Chińska Republika Ludowa** People's Republic of China.

republikanin *mp*, **republikanka** *Gen.pl.* **-ek 1.** (= *zwolennik republikanizmu*) republican. **2.** (= *członek partii*) Republican.

republikanizm *f. polit.* republicanism.

republikański *a.* **1.** (= *dotyczący republiki*) republican. **2.** (= *dotyczący partii*) Republican.

repudiacja *f. ekon.* repudiation.

repulsja *f. psych.* repulsion.

reputacja *f.* reputation; **dbać o swoją/czyjąś reputację** guard one's/sb's reputation; **mieć złą/dobrą reputację** have a bad/good reputation; **psuć komuś reputację** damage sb's reputation.

requiem *n.* = **rekwiem**.

resekcja *f. med.* resection.

resentyment *mi lit.* disrelish.

resetować *ipf. komp.* reset.

reskrypt *mi hist.* rescript.

resocjalizacja *f.* rehabilitation.

resocjalizacyjny *a.* rehabilitative.

resocjalizować *ipf.* rehabilitate.

resor *mi* (suspension) spring; **resor piórowy** leaf spring; **bujda na resorach** *pot.* humbug.

resorbować *ipf. fizj.* resorb.

resorować *ipf.* spring.

resorowy *a.* spring.

resorpcja *f. fizj.* resorption.

resort *mi* department; **to nie mój resort** *pot.* it's outside my province.

resortowy *a.* departmental.

respekt *mi* respect; **budzić (czyjś) respekt** win *l.* gain the respect of sb; **czuć respekt przed kimś** be awed by sb; **mieć ogromny respekt dla kogoś** hold sb in the highest regard.

respektować *ipf. lit.* respect.

respirator *mi Gen.* **-a** *górn., med.* respirator.

respondent *mp*, **respondentka** *f. socjol.* respondent.

restauracja[1] *f.* (= *lokal gastronomiczny*) restaurant.

restauracja[2] *f.* (= *renowacja zabytków*) (= *przywrócenie dynastii, ustroju*) restoration.

restauracyjka *f. Gen.pl.* **-ek** bistro; (*zwł. tania*) brasserie.

restauracyjny *a.* restaurant; **wagon restauracyjny** dining car, restaurant car.

restaurator[1] *mp* (= *właściciel restauracji*) restaurateur.

restaurator[2] *mp* (= *konserwator zabytków*) restorer.

restauratorski *a.* restoration.

restaurować *ipf.* restore.

restrukturalizacja, restrukturyzacja *f.* restructuring.

restrukturyzacyjny *a.* restructuring.

restrukturyzować *ipf.* restructure.

restrykcja *f.* restriction.

restrykcyjny *a.* restrictive.

restytucja *f.* **1.** *lit.* (= *przywrócenie*) restitution; (= *odtworzenie*) restoration. **2.** *prawn.* (= *naprawienie szkody*) restitution.

restytuować *ipf. lit.* (= *przywrócić*) restitute; (= *odtworzyć*) restore.

résumé *n. indecl.* résumé.

resurs *mi lotn.* service life, overhaul life.

resuscytacja *f. med.* (= *reanimacja*) resuscitation.

reszka *f. Gen.pl.* **-ek** tails; **orzeł czy reszka?** heads or tails?

reszta *f.* **1.** (= *pozostałość*) rest, remainder; **bez reszty** (= *całkowicie*) completely; **do reszty** (= *doszczętnie*) completely. **2.** (*pieniądze*) change;

reszty nie trzeba! keep the change!; **wydać komuś za mało reszty** shortchange sb; **wydać resztę (z 10 złotych)** give change (for 10 PLN); **źle komuś wydać resztę** give sb the wrong change. **3.** *mat.* remainder.

resztka *f. Gen.pl.* **-ek 1.** (= *pozostałość*) remainder; (*ołówka*) stub; **resztki posiłku** leftovers; **gonić resztkami sił** be on one's last legs; be at the end of one's rope. **2.** (= *kawałek tkaniny*) remnant.

resztówka *f. Gen.pl.* **-ek** *prawn.* residue.

retabulum *n.* retable.

retardacja *f. biol., teor.lit.* retardation.

retencja *f. hydrol., pat., prawn.* retention.

retencyjny *a. hydrol.* retention; **zbiornik retencyjny** storage reservoir.

retman *mp* bargeman.

retor *mp* **1.** *lit.* rhetorician. **2.** *hist.* (*w starożytnej Grecji*) rhetor.

retorsja *f. prawn.* retorsion.

retorta *f. chem., metal.* retort.

retorycznie *adv.* rhetorically.

retoryczny *a.* rhetorical; **figura retoryczna** figure of speech; **pytanie retoryczne** rhetorical question.

retoryka *f.* rhetoric.

retransmisja *f.* rebroadcast.

retransmisyjny *a.* rebroadcast, rebroadcasting.

retransmitować *ipf.* rebroadcast.

retro *a. indecl.* retro; **meble w stylu retro** retro-style furniture.

retrospekcja *f.* **1.** (= *spojrzenie w przeszłość*) retrospection. **2.** *film, teor.lit.* flashback; *US t.* cutback.

retrospekcyjny *a.* **1.** (= *dotyczący przeszłości*) retrospective. **2.** *film, teor.lit.* flashback; *US t.* cutback.

retrospektywa *f.* **1.** (= *retrospekcja*) retrospection; (*w filmie, powieści*) flashback; *US t.* cutback; **w retrospektywie** in retrospect. **2.** (= *przegląd twórczości*) retrospective, retrospection.

retrospektywnie *adv.* retrospectively.

retrospektywny *a.* retrospective.

retrowirus *mi Gen.* **-a** *biol.* retrovirus.

return *mi tenis* return.

retusz *mi Gen.pl.* **-ów** *l.* **-y 1.** (= *poprawianie zdjęcia, obrazu*) retouch, touch-up. **2.** (= *poprawianie tekstu, zachowania*) touch-up.

retuszer *mp* retoucher.

retuszować *ipf.* **1.** (*zdjęcie, obraz*) retouch, touch up. **2.** (*tekst, zachowanie*) touch up.

rety *int. pot.* goodness gracious.

reumatolog *mp pl.* **-dzy** *l.* **-owie** rheumatologist.

reumatologia *f. Gen.* **-ii** *med.* rheumatology.

reumatologiczny *a. med.* rheumatological.

reumatyczny *a.* rheumatic.

reumatyk *mp,* **reumatyczka** *f.* rheumatic.

reumatyzm *mi* rheumatism.

rewa *f.* sandbank.

rewalidacja *f.* **1.** *med.* (= *rehabilitacja*) rehabilitation. **2.** *prawn.* revalidation.

rewalidować *ipf.* **1.** *med.* rehabilitate. **2.** *prawn.* revalidate.

rewaloryzacja *f.* **1.** *lit.* (= *przywrócenie wartości*) revalorization. **2.** (*zabytków*) restoration. **3.** *ekon.* (= *przywrócenie wartości zarobkom itp.*) indexation. **4.** *ekon.* (= *podniesienie kursu waluty*) revaluation.

rewaloryzacyjny *a.* compensation.

rewaloryzować *ipf.* **1.** *lit.* (= *przywracać wartość*) revalorize. **2.** (*zabytki*) restore. **3.** *ekon.* (= *przywracać wartość zarobkom itp.*) index. **4.** *ekon.* (= *podwyższać kurs waluty*) revaluate.

rewaluacja *f. ekon.* revaluation.

rewaluować *ipf. ekon.* revalue.

rewanż *mi Gen.pl.* **-ów 1.** (= *odwzajemnienie się*) return, reciprocation, requital; **dać komuś coś w rewanżu** give sb sth in return. **2.** (= *zemsta*) pay-off, revenge; **wziąć na kimś rewanż (za coś)** take revenge on *l.* upon sb (for sth). **3.** *sport* (= *powtórny mecz itp.*) return match, rematch.

rewanżować się *ipf.* repay (*komuś* sb, *czymś* with sth, *za coś* for sth).

rewanżowy *a.* return; **mecz rewanżowy** *sport* return match, rematch.

rewanżysta *mp polit.* revanchist.

rewanżyzm *mi polit.* revanchism.

rewelacja *f.* sensation; (*np. sezonu*) hit.

rewelacyjnie *adv.* sensationally.

rewelacyjność *f.* sensational character.

rewelacyjny *a.* sensational.

rewelator *mp lit.* revelator.

rewelersi *pl. Gen.* **-ów** *przest.* barbershop quartet, barbershop ensemble.

rewerencja *f. przest.* reverence (*dla kogoś / czegoś* for sb/sth).

rewers *mi* **1.** (= *odwrotna strona*) (*monety, medalu*) reverse, verso. **2.** *handl.* (= *pokwitowanie*) receipt. **3.** (= *formularz biblioteczny*) call slip.

rewia *f. Gen.* **-ii 1.** (*widowisko*) revue, review. **2.** (*pokaz*) show; **rewia mody** *t. przen.* fashion show; **rewia na lodzie** ice show. **3.** *wojsk.* review; parade.

rewident *mp,* **rewidentka** *f. Gen.pl.* **-ek** auditor; **biegły rewident** chartered auditor.

rewidować *ipf.* **1.** (= *przeprowadzać rewizję*) search; (= *przeszukiwać dłońmi po ciele*) frisk. **2.** *lit.* (= *zmieniać*) (*poglądy*) revise; (*politykę, strategię*) rethink. **3.** *fin., handl.* audit.

rewindykacja *f. prawn.* repossession.

rewindykacyjny *a. prawn.* repossession.

rewindykować *ipf. prawn.* repossess; **rewindykować czyjś majątek** repossess sb.

rewiowy *a.* review; **tancerka rewiowa** showgirl.

rewir *mi* **1.** (= *obszar pracy, nadzoru*) patch; (*policjanta*) beat. **2.** *myśl.* game range.

rewitalizacja *f. med.* revitalization.

rewizja *f.* **1.** (= *przeszukanie*) search; (*dłońmi po ciele*) frisk; **nakaz rewizji** search warrant; **rewizja osobista** body search; **przeprowadzać rewizję** conduct a search. **2.** (= *zmiana, modyfikacja*) review. **3.** (= *kontrola urzędowa*) inspection; (*ksiąg rachunkowych*) *fin.* audit. **4.** *polit.* (= *zmiana traktatów itp.*) revision. **5.** *prawn.* (=

zaskarżenie decyzji) review; **rewizja procesu** re- trial; **rewizja nadzwyczajna** extraordinary ap- peal; **wnieść rewizję od wyroku** appeal against a verdict. **6.** *druk.* clean proof, final proof.

rewizjonista *mp*, **rewizjonistka** *f. Gen.pl.* **-ek** re- visionist.

rewizjonistyczny *a. polit.* revisionist.

rewizjonizm *mi polit.* revisionism.

rewizor *mp* inspector; (*księgowy*) auditor.

rewizyjny *a.* **1.** (= *dotyczący kontroli*) revisory, revisional; *fin.* auditorial; **komisja rewizyjna** au- diting committee. **2.** *prawn.* review; **sąd rewi- zyjny** court of review.

rewizyta *f.* return visit; **złożyć komuś rewizytę** return sb's visit.

rewizytować *ipf.* return a visit.

rewokować *ipf.* (= *odwołać z urzędu*) revoke.

rewolta *f.* revolt (*przeciwko komuś/czemuś* against sb/sth).

rewolucja *f.* (= *obalenie ustroju*) (= *gwałtowna zmiana*) revolution; **Aksamitna Rewolucja** *hist.* Velvet Revolution; **rewolucja pałacowa** palace revolution.

rewolucjonista *mp*, **rewolucjonistka** *f. Gen.pl.* **-ek** revolutionary, revolutionist.

rewolucjonizm *f.* revolutionism.

rewolucjonizować *ipf.* revolutionize.

rewolucyjnie *adv.* in a revolutionary way.

rewolucyjność *f.* revolutionary nature *l.* char- acter.

rewolucyjny *a.* revolutionary.

rewolwer *mi* revolver; **rewolwer sześciostrza- łowy** six shot revolver.

rewolwerowiec *mp* **-wc-** *pl.* **-y** gunslinger.

rewolwerowy *a.* revolver; **tokarka rewolwero- wa** *techn.* turret lathe.

Reykjavik *mi geogr.* Reykjavik.

rezeda *f. bot.* reseda (*Reseda*).

rezedowy *a.* (*dotyczący rośliny*) reseda; (*kolor*) reseda green.

rezerwa *f.* **1.** (= *zapas*) reserve; **rezerwa fede- ralna** *US* federal reserve; **rezerwy walutowe** *ekon.* currency reserves; **czerpać z rezerw** draw on reserves; **mieć/trzymać coś w rezerwie** have/ keep sth in reserve. **2.** (= *powściągliwość*) re- serve; distance; **odnosić się do kogoś/czegoś z rezerwą** treat sb/sth with reserve. **3.** *sport* re- serve. **4.** *wojsk.* (= *ogół rezerwistów*) (= *odwód*) reserves; **iść do rezerwy** be transferred to the re- serve; **przenieść kogoś do rezerwy** transfer sb to the reserve.

rezerwacja *f.* reservation; *gł. Br.* booking; **zro- bić/potwierdzić/odwołać rezerwację** make/ confirm/cancel a reservation.

rezerwat *mi* **1.** (= *obszar krajobrazowy*) re- serve; (*zwł. dla ptaków*) sanctuary; **rezerwat przyrody** nature reserve; **rezerwat dzikiej przyro- dy** wildlife park, wildlife reserve. **2.** (= *obszar dla ludności autochtonicznej*) reservation.

rezerwista *mp* reservist.

rezerwować *ipf.* **1.** (= *dokonywać rezerwacji*) reserve; *gł. Br.* book. **2.** (= *trzymać w rezerwie*) (*pieniądze, czas*) set aside; **rezerwować sobie prawo do czegoś** reserve the right to do sth.

rezerwowy *a.* **1.** (= *zapasowy*) spare, reserve. **2.** *sport* reserve; **gracz rezerwowy** reserve play- er. **3.** *wojsk.* (= *odwodowy*) reserve. – *mp sport* substitute, reserve; **ławka rezerwowych** substi- tutes' bench.

rezerwuar *mi t. przen.* reservoir; **rezerwuar siły roboczej** workforce reservoir.

rezolucja *f.* resolution; **uchwalić/podjąć rezolu- cję** adopt/pass a resolution.

rezolutnie *adv.* (= *z pewnością siebie*) with self-assurance; (= *w bystry sposób, sprytnie*) cleverly.

rezolutność *f.* (= *pewność siebie*) self-assur- ance; (= *bystrość, spryt*) cleverness.

rezolutny *a.* (= *pewny siebie*) self-assured; (= *bystry, sprytny*) clever.

rezon *mi* self-assurance; **nie tracić rezonu** be undaunted.

rezonans *mi pl.* **-e** **1.** (= *pogłos*) *fiz., muz.* res- onance; **rezonans magnetyczny** *med.* magnetic resonance. **2.** (= *reakcja, oddźwięk*) response.

rezonansowy *a. fiz.* resonant; **płyta rezonanso- wa** *muz.* soundboard; **pudło rezonansowe** *muz.* soundbox.

rezonator *mi Gen.* **-a** *fiz., muz.* resonator.

rezoner *mp* **1.** *lit.* (= *człowiek lubiący rezono- wać*) reasoner; (*irytujący*) fault-finder. **2.** - *teor.lit.* raisonneur.

rezonować[1] *ipf. lit.* (= *mędrkować*) reason, ar- gue.

rezonować[2] *ipf. fiz.* resonate.

rezultat *mi* result; outcome; **w rezultacie** as a result (*czegoś* of sth); **bez rezultatu** without re- sult; **przynosić rezultaty** bring results; **ostatecz- ny rezultat tego był taki, że...** the upshot of it all was that...

rezurekcja *f. rz.-kat.* Resurrection service, Resurrection mass.

rezurekcyjny *a. rz.-kat.* Resurrection.

rezus *ma zool.* rhesus monkey (*Macaca mu- latta*).

rezydencja *f.* residence; (= *posiadłość*) man- sion.

rezydencjalny *a.* residentiary.

rezydent *mp* **1.** *hist.* (= *przedstawiciel dyplo- matyczny*) resident. **2.** *przest.* (= *ubogi krewny na utrzymaniu*) resident. **3.** (*w obcym kraju*) denizen.

rezydować *ipf. lit.* reside.

rezygnacja *f.* resignation; **z rezygnacją** re- signedly; **złożyć rezygnację** hand in one's resig- nation.

rezygnować *ipf.* **1.** (= *zrzekać się*) resign (*z czegoś* from sth); **rezygnować ze stanowiska** re- sign from one's post. **2.** (= *dawać za wygraną*) give up.

rezystor *mi Gen.* **-a** = **opornik**.

reżim, reżym *mi* **1.** *uj.* (= *system rządów*) regime. **2.** (= *rygor*) strict discipline.

reżimowy, reżymowy *a. uj.* **1.** (*dotyczący syste- mu rządów*) regime. **2.** (= *rygorystyczny*) rigor- ous.

reżyser *mp,* ‘ **1.** director; **asystent/ka reżysera** assistant director. **2.** *przen.* orchestrator.

reżyseria *f. Gen.* -ii **1.** direction; **w reżyserii...** directed by... **2.** *przen.* orchestration.

reżyserka *f. Gen.pl.* -ek **1.** *zob.* **reżyser. 2.** *pot.* (= *miejsce pracy reżysera*) control room.

reżyserować *ipf.* direct.

reżyserski *a.* director's; **wskazówki reżyserskie** stage directions.

rębacz *mp Gen.pl.* -y *l.* -ów *górn.* cutter.

rębajło *mp pl.* -y *Gen.* -ów *przest.* (= *sprawny szermierz*) swashbuckler.

rębnia *f. leśn.* felling.

ręce *pl. zob.* **ręka.**

ręczniczek *mi* -czk- *Gen.* -a cloth; small towel.

ręcznie *adv.* manually, by hand; **ręcznie malowany** hand-painted; **napisany ręcznie** handwritten; **robiony ręcznie** handmade, handcrafted.

ręcznik *mi Gen.* -a towel; **ręcznik kąpielowy/ plażowy/do rąk** bath/beach/hand towel; **ręcznik frotte** terry towel; **wieszak do ręczników** (*w łazience*) towel rail.

ręczny *a.* **1.** (= *wykonywany rękami*) manual, hand; **ręcznej roboty** hand-made; **broń ręczna** *wojsk.* hand-held weapon; **granat ręczny** *wojsk.* hand grenade; **piłka ręczna** *sport* handball; **robótki ręczne** (= *szycie*) needlework; (= *haft*) embroidery; (= *szydełkowanie*) crocheting; (*na drutach*) knitting; **sprawność ręczna** manual dexterity. **2.** (= *nieautomatyczny*) manual, hand-operated; **hamulec ręczny** emergency brake. **3.** (= *noszony na ręce l. w ręce*) hand-held; **kamera ręczna** hand-held camera; **zegarek ręczny** wrist watch.

ręczyć *ipf.* **1.** (= *gwarantować*) vouch (*za kogoś/coś* for sb/sth); **nie ręczę za siebie** I'm not sure I can control myself; **zamknij się, bo nie ręczę za siebie** shut up or else... **2.** (= *zapewniać*) give one's word.

rędzina *f. geol.* rendzina.

ręka *f. Loc.* **ręce** *l.* **ręku** *pl.* **ręce** *Gen.* **rąk** *Ins.* -ami *l.* -oma **1.** (= *dłoń*) hand; (= *wewnętrzna część dłoni*) palm; *pot.* (= *kończyna górna*) arm; **bronić się przed czymś rękami i nogami** resist sth with might and main; **być w dobrych rękach** be in good hands; **dać komuś wolną rękę** give sb a free hand; **dostać kogoś/coś w swoje ręce** get one's hands on sb/sth; **dostać się w czyjeś ręce** fall into the hands of sb; **dostarczyć coś do rąk własnych** deliver sth personally; **gołymi rękami** with one's bare hands; **grać z ręki** *karty* play from the hand; **iść komuś na rękę** be accommodating with sb; **jak ręką odjął** right away; **jeść komuś z ręki** eat out of sb's hand; **lekką ręką** (= *bezmyślnie*) recklessly; (= *bez wysiłku, bez problemu*) without batting an eyelid; **machnąć na coś ręką** let it go; **mieć czyste ręce** have clean hands; **mieć dwie lewe ręce** be all thumbs; **mieć pełne ręce roboty** have one's hands full; **mieć związane ręce** have one's hands tied; **na cztery ręce** *muz.* four-handed; **na rękę** (= *po opodatkowaniu*) net; **na własną rękę** on one's own; **niech ręka boska broni!** God forbid!; **od ręki** while you wait; **patrzeć komuś na ręce** breath down sb's neck; **po lewej/prawej ręce** on the left-/right-hand side; **podnieść rękę na kogoś** raise one's

hand against sb; **pod ręką** (close *l.* near) at hand; **prosić o czyjąś rękę** propose to sb; **przechodzić z rąk do rąk** change hands; be passed from hand to hand; **przyłożyć do czegoś rękę** have a hand in sth; **ręce do góry!** hands up!; **ręce przy sobie!** (keep your) hands off!; **ręce opadają** it's disheartening; **ręka boża** the hand of God; **rękę rękę myje** you scratch my back and I'll scratch yours; **siedzieć z założonymi rękami** sit on one's hands; **to jest mi (nie) na rękę** this is (in)convenient for me; **trzymać się za ręce** hold hands; **umywać (od czegoś) ręce** wash one's hands (of sth); **wszystko (jest) w twoich rękach** everything's in your hands; **wyjść z czegoś obronną ręką** (*z trudnej l. nieprzyjemnej sytuacji*) get out of sth; (= *mieć coś pod kontrolą*) have the upper hand; **wziąć coś w swoje ręce** take sth into one's hands; **zacierać ręce** rub one's hands; **(wiadomość) z pierwszej/drugiej ręki** first-/second-hand (news); **z pocałowaniem ręki** gladly; **z ręką na sercu** hand on heart; **żyć z pracy rąk** live off the labor of the hands; **brak rąk do pracy** labor shortage; **prawa ręka** right hand; **ręka sprawiedliwości** arm of the law. **2.** *sport* (= *niedozwolone zagranie ręką*) hand.

rękaw *mi Gen.* -a **1.** (= *część ubrania*) sleeve; **bez rękawów** sleeveless; **z krótkim rękawem** short-sleeved; **sypać (czymś) jak z rękawa** rattle (sth) off; **wyciągnąć asa z rękawa** play one's trump card; **zakasać rękawy** *t. przen.* roll one's sleeves up. **2.** *lotn.* (= *tunel między samolotem a halą*) airbridge. **3.** *lotn.* (= *wskaźnik wiatru*) windsock, wind sleeve, wind cone.

rękawek *mi* -wk- *Gen.* -a sleeve; **krótki rękawek** short sleeve; **z krótkim rękawkiem** short-sleeved; **rękawki do nauki pływania** water wings.

rękawica *f.* glove; (*rycerza*) gauntlet; (*z jednym palcem*) mitten; (*baseballowa*) mitt; **rękawica bokserska** boxing glove; **rękawica kuchenna** oven mitt; **rękawica ochronna** gauntlet; **podnieść** *l.* **podjąć rękawicę** *przen.* pick up the gauntlet; **rzucić (komuś) rękawicę** *przen.* throw down the gauntlet (to sb).

rękawiczka *f. Gen.pl.* -ek glove; (*z jednym palcem*) mitten; **w białych rękawiczkach** white-gloved; *przen.* in velvet gloves; **zmieniać jak rękawiczki** change like gloves.

rękawicznictwo *n.* glove-making.

rękawicznik *mp* glover.

rękoczyny *pl. Gen.* -ów fist fight; **doszło do rękoczynów** it came to blows.

rękodzielnictwo *n.* handicraft.

rękodzielniczy *a.* handicraft; **wyroby rękodzielnicze** handicraft.

rękodzielnik *mp* handicrafter.

rękodzieło *n.* handicraft.

rękojeść *f.* (= *uchwyt*) (*noża, łopaty*) handle; (*młotka, siekiery*) helve; (*pistoletu*) grip; (*miecza*) hilt.

rękojmia *f. Gen.pl.* -i **1.** *lit.* (= *poręczenie*) guarantee. **2.** *prawn.* implied warranty, statutory warranty.

rękopis *mi* manuscript.

rękopiśmienny *a.* handwritten.

RFN *abbr*. FRG (= *Federal Republic of Germany*).

Rh *abbr. med*. Rh; **Rh plus/minus** Rh positive/negative; **czynnik Rh** Rh factor.

rias *mi geol*. ria shoreline, rias.

richelieu *mi l. a. indecl*. cutwork.

riksza *f*. (*dwukołowa*) rickshaw; (*trzykołowa*) trishaw.

rikszarz *mp* rickshawman.

ring *mi sport* ring.

ringo *n. indecl*. (*gra*) deck tennis.

ringowy *a*. ring; **sędzia ringowy** referee.

riposta *f*. **1.** (= *cięta odpowiedź*) riposte, ripost; repartee. **2.** *szerm*. riposte, ripost.

ripostować *ipf*. riposte, ripost.

risotto *n. Loc*. **-tcie** risotto.

rittberger *mi Gen*. **-a** *sport* loop; Rittberger jump.

riuszka *f. Gen.pl*. **-ek** ruche, rouche.

Riwiera *f. geogr*. Riviera; **Riwiera Francuska** the French Riviera.

r-k *abbr*. a/c (= *account*).

rkm *abbr*. SMG (= *submachine gun*).

r.m. *abbr*. m., masc. (= *masculine*).

r.nij. *abbr*. n., neut. (= *neuter*).

roaming *mi tel*. roaming.

robactwo *n*. bugs, insects.

robaczek *ma* **-czk- 1.** (= *mały robak*) little worm; **robaczek świętojański** *ent*. firefly, lightning bug; *Br*. firefly, glow-worm (*Lampyridae*). **2.** (*pieszczotliwie o dziecku*) little dear, dearie. **3.** (*o piśmie*) (*zwł. pl*.) squiggle.

robaczkowy *a. fizj*. peristaltic; **ruchy robaczkowe** peristaltic movements; **wyrostek robaczkowy** *anat*. appendix; vermiform appendix, vermiform process; **usunięcie wyrostka robaczkowego** appendectomy; *Br*. appendicectomy; **zapalenie wyrostka robaczkowego** appendicitis.

robaczyca *f*. **1.** *med., wet*. helminthiasis. **2.** *zool*. ammocoete.

robaczywieć *ipf*. get worm-eaten.

robaczywy *a*. wormy, worm-eaten.

robak *ma* **1.** (*drobne zwierzę bezkręgowe*) worm; **zalewać robaka** *pot*. hit the bottle. **2.** *komp*. (= *program rozmnażający się w sieci*) worm. – *ma pl*. **-i** (= *pasożyt*) worm.

rober *mi* **-br-** *Gen*. **-a** *karty* rubber.

robić *ipf*. **rób 1.** (= *wytwarzać, przyrządzać*) make (*coś z czegoś* sth from sth *l*. sth (out) of sth); (*krok, spacer, notatki, zdjęcie*) take; **robić błędy ortograficzne** be a bad speller; **robić bokami** (= *oddychać ciężko*) pant; **robić długi** contract debts; **robić w majtki** *pot*. shit one's pants; **robić pieniądze** make money; **kaczki robią „kwa"** ducks go „quack". **2.** (= *czynić*) make, do; **robić swoje** (= *wykonywać swoją pracę*) do one's job; (= *nie wychylać się*) mind one's own business; **robić komuś kawały** play jokes on sb; **robić na kimś wrażenie** impress sb; **nie robić wrażenia** fail to impress; **zupełnie nie zrobiło to na nim wrażenia** it was completely lost on him; **robić plany na przyszłość** look ahead; **robić porządki** (*w domu*) clean house; **robić słodkie oczy do kogoś** make sheep's eyes at sb; **robić dobrą minę do złej gry** grin and bear it, put on a brave *l*. bold front; **robić (sobie) makijaż** make up; **robić coś na zamówienie** make sth to order; **robić (sobie) przerwę** take a break; **robić zakupy** do the shopping, shop; **dużo gadać, a mało robić** be all mouth and no action; **nic sobie nie robić z kogoś/czegoś** laugh at sb/sth, set sb/sth at naught; **robić sobie jaja** take the piss (*z kogoś/czegoś* out of sb/sth); **przestań robić sobie jaja!** cut the kidding!; **robić coś dla frajdy/zysku** *pot*. do sth for kicks/profit; **robić postępy w czymś** get on with sth, make headway in *l*. with sth; **robić kogoś w balona** take sb for a ride, take the mickey out of sb; **robić z czegoś dobry użytek** use sth to advantage; **robić z czegoś dramat** *l*. **tragedię** make a drama out of sth; **robić z igły widły** make a mountain out of a molehill; **robić wszystko z zegarkiem w ręku** live by the clock; **cóż on u licha robi?** what on earth is he doing?. **3.** (= *powodować*) (*zamieszanie, hałas, problemy*) make, cause; **robić alarm** raise the alarm; **robić komuś konkurencję** compete with sb; **robić trudności** raise difficulties; **robić z czegoś problem** *l*. **sprawę** make an issue out of sth; **robić komuś nadzieję** raise sb's hopes; **robić komuś krzywdę** harm sb, wrong sb; **robić z siebie głupka** make a fool of o.s.; **robić z siebie widowisko** make an exhibition *l*. a spectacle of o.s. **4.** (= *postępować, działać*) do, act; **to ci dobrze zrobi** it will do you good; **nie robi mi to różnicy** it's all the same to me, it doesn't make any difference to me. **5.** *pot*. (= *pracować zarobkowo*) work. ~ **się** *ipf*. **rób 1.** (= *być robionym*) be made; **robić się na bóstwo** doll o.s. up. **2.** (= *przeobrażać się, stawać się*) grow, become, turn, go; **robi się ciemno/zimno** it's getting dark/cold; **robi się go żal** one feels sorry for him; **robi mi się niedobrze** I'm beginning to feel sick; **robi mi się niedobrze już na samą myśl o tym** the very thought of it makes me sick; **już się robi** no sooner said than done; **już się robi!** I (we etc.) will get right down to it!; **na tym biurku robią się plamy** this desk stains easily; **tak się nie robi** (= *tak nie wolno*) it's not fair; **robiło się gorąco** *przen*. the situation was hotting up.

robinia *f. Gen*. **-ii** *bot*. locust tree, false acacia (*Robinia pseudoacacia*).

robinsonada *f*. **1.** *teor.lit*. robinsonade. **2.** *sport* flying save.

robiony *a. pot*. (= *udawany*) sham, fake.

robociarz *mp pog*. workman.

robocizna *f*. (= *praca*) labor; *Br*. labour; (= *koszt*) cost of labor.

roboczo *adv*. tentatively.

roboczodniówka *f. Gen.pl*. **-ek** man-day.

roboczogodzina *f*. man-hour.

roboczy *a*. **1.** (*związany z pracą*) working, labor; **dzień roboczy** (*nieświąteczny*) week day; **kombinezon roboczy** overall; *Br. t*. boiler suit; **mundur roboczy** fatigues; **siła robocza** workforce, labor force. **2.** (= *przygotowawczy, wstępny*) working, tentative; **obszar roboczy** *komp*. scratchpad; **plik roboczy** *komp*. scratch file.

robol *mp pog*. prole.

robot *mi Gen.* **-a** robot; **robot kuchenny** food processor.

robota *f. Gen.pl.* **-ót** 1. (= *praca*) work, job; (= *kradzież, włamanie itp.*) job; **dobra robota!** well done!, good job!, nice work!; **czarna robota** donkeywork; **głupiego robota** (= *bezsensowne przedsięwzięcie*) fool's errand; **mokra robota** (= *morderstwo*) rubout; **niewdzięczna robota** thankless task; **ręczna robota** handiwork, handwork; **robota papierkowa** paperwork; **domowej roboty** homemade; **mieć pełne ręce roboty** have one's hands full, have a lot of things to do; **odwalać za kogoś brudną robotę** do sb's dirty work (for them); **zabrać się do roboty** get down to business; **zrobili kawał dobrej roboty** they've done a fine job; **cała robota spadła na niego** he got all the work dumped in his lap. 2. *pot.* (= *posada, miejsce pracy*) job; **wylać kogoś z roboty** sack sb, give sb the sack; **rozglądać się za robotą** be looking for a job. 3. (= *jakość wykonania*) workmanship. 4. *pl.* (= *prace fizyczne*) works; **roboty drogowe** road repairs; *Br.* road works; **roboty przymusowe** forced labor, *Br.* forced labour; (*w obozach pracy, koncentracyjnych*) slave labor; *Br.* slave labour; **roboty ziemne** earthwork; **ciężkie roboty** hard labor; *Br.* hard labour; **5 lat ciężkich robót** 5 years hard labor; **roboty publiczne** public works.

robotnica *f.* 1. (*kobieta*) woman-worker, workwoman. 2. (*owad*) worker; **mrówka/pszczoła robotnica** worker ant/bee.

robotniczo-chłopski *a.* worker-peasant; **sojusz robotniczo-chłopski** worker-peasant alliance.

robotniczy *a.* workmen's, working; (*o etosie, wartościach, poglądach*) *pot.* cloth cap; **klasa robotnicza** working class; **hotel robotniczy** workers' hostel.

robotnik *mp* worker, workman; **robotnik budowlany** construction worker; **robotnik sezonowy** seasonal worker; **robotnik rolny** farm laborer, farmhand; **robotnik wykwalifikowany/niewykwalifikowany** skilled/unskilled worker.

robotny *a. pot.* hard-working.

roboty

robotyka *f.* robotics.

robotyzacja *f.* robotization.

robótka *f. Gen.pl.* **-ek** 1. *iron., żart.* (= *robota*) piece of work, job. 2. *przest.* (*szydełkowa*) crochet; (*wyszywana*) needlework; (*na drutach*) knitting.

rock *mi Gen.* **-a** *muz.* rock.

rock and roll *mi Gen.* **-a** (*tylko ostatni człon*) *muz.* rock and roll.

rockman *mp* rockman.

rockowy *a.* rock.

roczek *mi Gen.* **-czk-** year; **dziecko ma zaledwie roczek** the baby is barely one year old.

roczniak *ma* (*jeleń, koń*) yearling; *pot.* (*samochód*) one-year-old car.

rocznica *f.* anniversary; **rocznica ślubu/śmierci** wedding/death anniversary; **dziesiąta rocznica** tenth anniversary; decennial; **setna rocznica** hundredth anniversary; centennial, centenary.

rocznicowy *a.* anniversary; **obchody rocznicowe** anniversary celebrations.

rocznie *adv.* annually; per *l.* a year, per annum; **przyjmować dziesięciu studentów rocznie** take ten students a year; **uposażenie w wysokości 15 000 złotych rocznie** a salary of 15,000 PLN per annum *l.* p.a.; **zarabia 45 000 dolarów rocznie** he gets $45,000 a year.

rocznik *mi Gen.* **-a** 1. (= *zbiór wydań z jednego roku*) a year's issue. 2. (= *wydawnictwo wychodzące raz na rok*) annual; **rocznik statystyczny** statistical yearbook. 3. (= *annał*) *zob.* **roczniki**. 4. (*pokolenie*) generation (*people born in the same year*); *szkoln., uniw.* class; **rocznik 65** the class of 1965. 5. (*wina, samochodu*) vintage; **rocznik 1995** vintage 1995.

rocznikarz *mp* annalist, chronicler.

roczniki *pl.* (= *annały*) annals.

roczny *a.* 1. (= *trwający jeden rok*) year-long; **budżet roczny** *ekon.* annual budget. 2. (= *powtarzający się co roku*) annual, yearly; **bilans roczny** *ekon.* annual balance. 3. (= *mający jeden rok*) one-year-old; **słój roczny** (*drzewa*) *bot.* annual ring; **suchokwiat roczny** *bot.* immortelle (*Xeranthemum annuum*).

rod *mi chem.* rhodium.

rodaczka *f. Gen.pl.* **-ek** compatriot, fellow countrywoman.

rodak *mp* compatriot, fellow countryman.

rodał *mi rel.* Torah scroll.

reodencytyd *mi* rodenticide.

rodeo *n. indecl. l. decl. pl.* **-ea** *Gen.* **-eów** rodeo.

Rodezja *f. geogr., hist.* Rhodesia.

rodnia *f. Gen.pl.* **-i** *bot.* archegonium.

rodnik *mi chem.* radical; **wolny rodnik** free radical.

rodny *a.* **narząd rodny** *anat.* genital, reproductive organ.

rododendron *mi bot.* rhododendron (*Rhododendron*).

rododendronowy *a.* rhododendron.

rodopsyna *f. med.* rhodopsin, visual purple.

rodowity *a.* native, native-born; **rodowity nowojorczyk** native New Yorker.

rodowodowy *a.* (*o zwierzętach*) pedigree; **księga rodowodowa** (*psów, koni*) pedigree book; (*zwł. koni, bydła*) studbook.

rodowód *mi* **-o-** 1. (= *pochodzenie, początek*) (*dzieła, wyrazu, rodziny*) origin, descent; pedigree. 2. (= *genealogia*) genealogy, pedigree; **pies/kot z rodowodem** pedigree dog/cat.

rodowy *a.* (*o posiadłości, srebrach*) ancestral; **nazwisko rodowe** family name; **drzewo rodowe** family tree; **klejnot rodowy** *her.* family crest.

rodu *itd. mi zob.* **ród**.

rodzaj *mi Gen.pl.* **-ów** *l.* **-ai** 1. (= *gatunek, typ*) kind, type; (*wyrobu*) variety; **rodzaj ludzki** humankind; **tego rodzaju** of this kind; **tego samego rodzaju** of the same kind; **w rodzaju...** (= *podobny do*) on the order of...; **jedyny w swoim rodzaju** one of a kind, one-of-a-kind; (*o egzemplarzu, okazji*) unique; **wszelkiego rodzaju** of every description; **coś w tym rodzaju** something of that sort, something of the kind; **jakiego rodzaju praca Pan-a/ią**

interesuje? what kind of (a) job are you interested in?. **2.** *jęz.* (*gramatyczny*) gender; **rodzaj męski** masculine gender, masculine; **rodzaj nijaki** neuter gender, neuter; **rodzaj żeński** feminine gender, feminine; **Księga Rodzaju** *Bibl.* the Book of Genesis, Genesis. **3.** *biol.* genus. **4.** *film, sztuka, teor.lit.* genre.

rodzajnik *mi Gen.* -a *jęz.* article; **rodzajnik określony/nieokreślony** definite/indefinite article.

rodzajowy *a.* **1.** *biol.* generic. **2.** *jęz.* indicating gender. **3.** *sztuka* genre; **malarstwo rodzajowe** genre painting; **scena rodzajowa** genre scene.

rodzeństwo *n.* siblings, brothers and sisters; **cioteczne rodzeństwo** cousins; **stryjeczne rodzeństwo** cousins; **czy masz jakieś rodzeństwo?** do you have any brothers or sisters?.

rodzic *mp Gen.pl.* -ów parent; **rodzice chrzestni** godparents; **rodzice przybrani** stepparents; **rodzice zastępczy** foster parents; **zgoda rodziców** *gł. prawn.* parental consent.

rodzicielski *a.* parental; **komitet rodzicielski** *szkoln.* Parent-Teacher Association, PTA.

rodzić *ipf.* **1.** (= *wydawać potomstwo*) give birth (*kogoś* to sb); *med.* (= *przechodzić poród*) be in labor, *Br.* be in labour; (*o zwierzętach*) breed. **2.** (*o ziemi*) bear. **3.** (= *dawać początek*) give rise (*coś* to sth). **~ się** *ipf.* **1.** (= *przychodzić na świat*) be born. **2.** (= *powstawać*) be born, arise.

rodzimek *mi* -mk- *Gen.* -a *min.* nugget.

rodzimość *f.* native character.

rodzimy *a.* **1.** (= *macierzysty*) native; **rodzime strony** (one's) homeland; **rodzimy użytkownik języka** native speaker; **język rodzimy** mother tongue; **przemysł rodzimy** home industry. **2.** *chem.* native; **metal rodzimy** native metal.

rodzina *f.* **1.** (= *krewni*) family; **najbliższa rodzina** (one's) immediate family, (one's) next of kin; **pięcioosobowa rodzina** a family of five; **rodzina elementarna** *socjol.* nuclear family; **rodzina królewska** royal family; **rodzina niepełna** (= *bez jednego z rodziców*) one-parent family; **rodzina panująca** the ruling house; **rodzina trudna** *l.* **patologiczna** problem family; **rodzina zastępcza** foster family; **rozbita rodzina** broken family; **Święta** *l.* **Najświętsza Rodzina** *rel.* the Holy Family; **zakładać rodzinę** start a family; **przemoc w rodzinie** domestic violence. **2.** (= *ród*) family. **3.** *biol., jęz., muz.* family.

rodzinka *f. Gen.pl.* -ek *iron. żart.* (one's) folks, one's own flesh and blood.

rodzinny *a.* **1.** (= *dotyczący rodziny*) family; **dom rodzinny** (one's) home, (one's) house and home; **dodatek** *l.* **zasiłek rodzinny** family allowance; **firma rodzinna** family company; **lekarz rodzinny** general practitioner, family doctor; **kraj rodzinny** native land; **miasto rodzinne** home town; **sprawy rodzinne** family matters; **sąd rodzinny** family court, domestic relations court; **zjazd rodzinny** family reunion; **życie rodzinne** family life; **być cechą rodzinną** (*o zapalczywości, nieśmiałości, skłonności do alkoholu itp.*) run in

the family. **2.** (= *lubiący życie rodzinne*) family; **człowiek rodzinny** family man.

rodzony *a.* -eni (*o bracie, siostrze*) full, whole; **brat rodzony** brother-german; **mój rodzony brat** my own brother.

rodzynek[1] *mi* -nk- *Gen.* -a **1.** (*suszony owoc*) raisin; **rodzynek koryncki** sultana. **2.** (*coś atrakcyjnego*) plum.

rodzynek[2] *mp* (*jedyny mężczyzna w grupie kobiet*) the only male in a group of females.

rodzynka *f. Gen.pl.* -ek *pot.* = **rodzynek**[1] 1.

rodzynkowy *a.* raisin, sultana.

rogacizna *f.* horned cattle.

rogacz *ma* (= *dorosły jeleń*) stag. – *mp pot., żart.* (= *zdradzony mąż*) cuckold.

rogal *mi Gen.* -a *Gen.pl.* -i *l.* -ów *kulin.* crescent roll; (*z ciasta francuskiego*) croissant.

rogalik *mi Gen.* -a crescent roll; (*z ciasta francuskiego*) croissant.

rogatek *mi* -tk- *Gen.* -a *bot.* hornwort (*Ceratophyllum*).

rogatka *f. Gen.pl.* -ek **1.** (*brama*) tollgate; *hist.* (*przy której pobierano myto*) turnpike; (*do zbierania opłat na autostradzie*) toll booth. **2.** (*szlaban*) barrier.

rogaty *a.* **1.** (= *mający rogi*) horned; (*o jeleniu*) antlered; (*o czapce*) horned; **diabeł rogaty** the devil himself. **2.** *pot.* (= *zdradzany przez żonę*) deceived; **rogaty mąż** cuckold. **3.** (= *krnąbrny*) defiant, stubborn.

rogatywka *f. Gen.pl.* -ek four-cornered cap (*worn by the Polish Army*).

rogi *itd. mi zob.* **róg**.

rogowacieć *ipf.* become horny, become corneous.

rogowaty *a.* horny, corneous.

rogowiec *mi* **1.** *pat.* callus, callosity. **2.** *min.* chert, hornstone. **3.** *zool.* Baltic clam (*Macoma baltica*).

rogownica *f. bot.* mouse-ear chickweed (*Cerastium*).

rogowy *a.* **1.** (= *zbudowany z tkanki rogowej*) horny, ceratoid. **2.** (= *zrobiony z rogu*) horn; **okulary w rogowej oprawie** horn-rimmed spectacles.

rogoząb *ma icht.* Australian lungfish, Queensland lungfish (*Neoceratodus forsteri*).

rogoża *f. Gen.pl.* -y *l.* -góż **1.** *bot.* reed mace; *pot.* bulrush, false bulrush, cat's tail (*Typha latifolia*). **2.** (*mata*) doormat (*made of bulrush*).

rogówka *f. Gen.pl.* -ek *anat.* cornea.

rohatyna *f. hist.* spear (*with a hook near the spearhead*).

rohatyniec *ma ent.* European rhinoceros beetle (*Oryctes nasicornis*).

roić *ipf.* **roję roisz, rój** daydream (*o czymś* about sth). **~ się** *ipf.* **1.** (= *formować rój*) swarm. **2.** (= *występować gromadnie*) swarm, teem; **coś roi się od czegoś** sth is swarming with sth; **list roi się od błędów** the letter is full of mistakes; **w mieście roi się od szczurów** the city is infested with rats; **na trawniku roiło się od mrówek** the lawn was alive with ants. **3.** (= *marzyć się*) have dreams; **różne rzeczy roją mu się po głowie** he fancies all sorts of things.

rojalista *mp* royalist.

rojalistyczny *a.* royalist.

rojalizm *mi* royalism.

rojenia *pl. Gen.* -ń (= *mrzonki*) daydreaming.

rojnik *mi Gen.* -a *bot.* houseleek, hen-and-chickens (*Sempervivum*).

rojno *adv. lit.* **na ulicach było rojno** the streets swarmed *l.* teemed with people.

rojny *a. lit.* swarming, teeming (*e.g. with people*).

rojowisko *n.* **1.** (= *tłum*) hive, throng. **2.** (*miejsce*) hive, gathering place.

rok *mi pl.* **lata** *Gen.* **lat** year; **co rok(u)** every year, annually; **raz do roku** *l.* **raz na rok** once a year; **dwa razy do roku** twice a year; **ponad rok (temu)** over one *l.* a year (ago); **przez cały rok** all year long; **przez okrągły rok** all the year round; **rok temu** a year ago; **rok po roku** *l.* **z roku na rok** year in, year out; **pod koniec roku** at the end of the year, towards the end of the year; **przed upływem roku** before the year is out; **w lutym/ kwietniu zeszłego/przyszłego roku** last/next February/April; **w nadchodzącym roku** in the coming year; **w piętnastym roku życia** at fifteen (years old); **w połowie roku** at midyear; **dobry rok** (**dla czegoś**) vintage year (for sth); **rok akademicki** academic year; **rok budżetowy** budget year; **rok finansowy** *l.* **obrachunkowy** financial year; **rok kalendarzowy** calendar year; **rok podatkowy** tax year; **rok przestępny** leap year, bissextile; **rok szkolny** school year; **rok świetlny** *astron.* light year; **Rok Święty** Holy Year; **rok zwrotnikowy** astronomical year, solar year; **rok zwykły** (= *nieprzestępny*) common year; **nowy rok** (= *nadchodzący l. niedawno rozpoczęty*) New Year; **Nowy Rok** (*1 stycznia*) New Year's Day; **powitać nowy rok** see in the New Year; **Szczęśliwego Nowego Roku!** Happy New Year!; **Roku Pańskiego** Anno Domini, in the year of our Lord; **pora roku** season; **minął rok** a year passed; *por.* **lata.**

rokambuł *mi bot.* hardneck garlick (*Allium ophioscorodon*).

rokfor *mi Gen.* **-a** *l.* **-u** *kulin.* (*gatunek sera*) Roquefort.

rokita *f. bot.* rosemary willow (*Salix rosmarinifolia*).

rokitniczka *f. orn.* sedge warbler (*Acrocephalus schoenobaenus*).

rokitnik *mi Gen.* **-a** *bot.* sea-buckthorn (*Hippophae rhamnoides*).

rokoko *n. sztuka* rococo.

rokokowy *a.* rococo.

rokosz *mi Gen.pl.* **-ów** *l.* **-y** *hist.* rebellion (*of the nobility against the king*).

rokować *ipf.* (= *negocjować*) **1.** negotiate (*o coś* for sth). **2.** *lit.* (= *stanowić zapowiedź*) augur, presage; **rokować nadzieje** hold promise. **3.** *lit.* (= *przepowiadać*) betoken.

rokowania *pl.* (= *pertraktacje*) negotiations; (*zwł. między walczącymi państwami*) parley; **rokowania pokojowe** peace negotiations; **rokowania wstępne** preliminary negotiations; **drogą ro-**

kowań by negotiations; **ustalać w drodze rokowań** *ekon.* (*cenę, ulgę*) negotiate.

rokowanie *n. med.* prognosis.

rokrocznie *adv.* every year.

rola[1] *f. Gen.pl.* **ról** (= *pole uprawne*) soil; **uprawa roli** soil cultivation; **pracować na roli** farm; **osiąść na roli** settle down in the country; **Boża rola** (= *cmentarz*) *rel.* God's acre.

rola[2] *f. Gen.pl.* **ról** **1.** (*tekst*) part. **2.** (*postać*) role, part; **rola drugoplanowa** supporting role; **rola epizodyczna** walk-on part; **rola główna** leading role; **rola gościnna** (= *niewielka rola zagrana przez znanego aktora*) cameo; **rola tytułowa** title role; **w rolach głównych** (*napis*) starring; **grać** *l.* **odgrywać rolę** play a role; **obsadzić kogoś w roli kogoś** cast sb as sb. **3.** (= *udział, znaczenie*) role; **to nie gra roli** it doesn't matter; **odgrywać rolę** play a part, enter into the equation; **odgrywać zasadniczą/decydującą rolę w czymś** play a vital/decisive part *l.* role in sth; **spełniać rolę kogoś/czegoś** perform the function of sb/sth; **na czym polega moja rola?** where do I come in?; **role się odwróciły** the tables have turned; **koszty nie grają roli** (= *nie stanowią problemu*) money is no object. **4.** (= *duży zwój*) roll, scroll.

rolada *f.* **1.** (*wędlina*) roulade. **2.** (*ciasto*) jelly roll; *Br.* Swiss roll.

roleta *f.* roller blind.

rolka *f. Gen.pl.* **-ek 1.** *techn.* roll; **rolka filmu** roll of film, film pack; **rolka papieru toaletowego** toilet paper roll. **2.** *pot.* (= *łyżworolka*) skate; **jazda na rolkach** *l.* **łyżworolkach** roller-blading.

rolmops *mi Gen.* **-a** rollmop.

rolnica *f. bot.* field madder (*Sherardia arvensis*); **rolnica zbożówka** *ent.* turnip moth (*Euxoa segetum*).

rolnictwo *n.* (*nauka*) agriculture; (*dziedzina gospodarki*) agriculture, farming.

rolniczo *adv.* agriculturally.

rolniczy *a.* (*kraj, wystawa, produkt*) agricultural; (*spółdzielnia*) farming.

rolnik *mp* (= *osoba pracująca na roli*) farmer; (= *specjalista w dziedzienie rolnictwa*) agronomist.

rolny *a.* agricultural; **gospodarka rolna** farming, husbandry; **gospodarstwo rolne** farm; **płody rolne** farm produce; **reforma rolna** landowner reform; **robotnik rolny** farm laborer, *Br.* farm labourer; farmhand.

rolować *ipf.* **1.** (= *zwijać w rolkę*) roll. **2.** *pot.* (= *oszukiwać*) bamboozle.

ROM *mi komp.* ROM (= *Read Only Memory*); **pamięć ROM** Read Only Memory.

romadur *mi kulin.* (*gatunek sera*) Romadur.

romanca *f. muz., teor.lit.* romance.

romanista *mp*, **romanistka** *f. Gen.pl.* **-ek** Romance philologist, Romanist.

romanistyka *f.* Romance studies.

romanizacja *f.* Romanization.

romanizm *mi* **1.** *jęz.* (*przejęty z francuskiego*) Gallicism; (*przejęty z innego języka romańskiego*) borrowing from a Romance language. **2.** (= *sztuka romańska*) Romanism.

romanizować *ipf.* Romanise.

romans *mi pl.* **-e 1.** *muz., teor.lit.* romance; **romans łotrzykowski** *teor.lit.* picaresque romance; **romans rycerski** *teor.lit.* chivalry romance. **2.** (*książka, film*) love story. **3.** (= *miłostka*) (love) affair, romance; **burzliwy romans** whirlwind romance; **romans jak z bajki** storybook romance; **mieć romans z kimś** have an affair with sb; **mam do ciebie romans** *pot.* I want a word with you.

romansidło *n. Gen.pl.* **-deł** *uj.* tear-jerker.

romansować *ipf.* have an affair (*z kimś* with sb).

romansowy *a.* **1.** (*dotyczący romansu*) love-affair, romance. **2.** *żart.* (= *kochliwy*) flirtatious, amorous.

romantyczka *f. Gen.pl.* **-ek** romantic.

romantyczność *f.* romanticism.

romantyczny *a.* **1.** (*dotyczący romantyzmu*) Romantic. **2.** (= *poetyczny, marzycielski*) romantic, full of romance.

romantyk *mp* **1.** (= *przedstawiciel romantyzmu*) Romantic. **2.** (= *marzyciel*) romantic.

romantyka *f.* **1.** (*kierunek*) Romanticism. **2.** (*cecha*) romance.

romantyzm *mi* romanticism.

romański *a.* **1.** (*dotyczący starożytnego Rzymu*) Roman. **2.** (*język*) Romance; **języki romańskie** *jęz.* Romance languages. **3.** *sztuka* Romanesque; **styl romański** *bud.* Romanesque style.

romb *mi geom.* rhombus, diamond.

romboedr *mi* **1.** *geom.* rhombohedron. **2.** *min.* rhombohedral, trigonal.

romboedryczny *a.* rhombohedral.

romboid *mi geom.* rhomboid.

romboidalny *a.* rhomboid, rhomboidal.

rombowy *a.* rhombic.

romeo *mp Gen.* **-ea** *Loc.* **-eo** *żart.* Romeo.

rondel *mi* **-dl-** *Gen.* **-a 1.** (*naczynie*) saucepan. **2.** (*element fortyfikacji*) barbican.

rondelek *mi* **-lk-** *Gen.* **-a** saucepan.

rondo[1] *mi* **1.** (*część kapelusza*) brim. **2.** *muz.* roundel, roundelay. **3.** *teor.lit.* rondeau.

rondo[2] *n. mot.* traffic circle, rotary; *Br.* roundabout.

rondo[3] *n* (*rodzaj pisma*) round hand.

ronić *ipf.* **1.** *poet.* (= *tracić, gubić*) shed; **ronić łzy** shed tears. **2.** *pat.* miscarry. **3.** (*o zwierzętach*) (= *tracić sierść, skórę*) molt, *Br.* moult.

ropa *f.* **1.** *pat.* pus. **2.** *pot.* (*paliwo*) fuel oil; **ropa naftowa** *chem.* crude oil, petroleum; **rafineria ropy naftowej** oil refinery.

ropieć *ipf. pat.* suppurate, fester.

ropień *mi* **-pni-** *Gen.* **-a** *pat.* abscess.

ropniak *mi Gen.* **-a 1.** *pat.* (= *ropień*) abscess; (*zwł. opłucnej*) empyema. **2.** *pot.* (= *samochód na ropę*) diesel.

ropny *a.* **1.** (= *powodujący ropienie*) suppurative; (= *ropiejący*) purulent, pussy. **2.** (= *roponośny*) oil-bearing. **3.** (= *opalany ropą*) oil-fired; (= *napędzany ropą*) oil-fuelled; **silnik ropny** diesel engine.

ropociąg *mi techn.* oil pipeline.

ropodajny *a.* oil-bearing.

ropomocz *mi pat.* pyuria.

roponośny *a.* oil-bearing.

ropotok *mi pat.* pyorrhea, *Br.* pyorrhoea.

ropotwórczy *a. pat.* pyogenic, pus-forming.

ropowica *f. pat.* phlegmon.

ropucha *f.* **1.** *zool.* toad (*Bufo bufo*); **ropucha paskówka** natterjack (*Bufo calamita*). **2.** *pot.* (= *brzydka kobieta*) hag.

ropuszka *f. Gen.pl.* **-ek** *zool.* discoglossid (*Discoglossidae*).

roraty *pl. Gen.* **-ów** *l.* **-t** *rz.-kat.* early morning mass celebrated in Advent.

rosa *f.* dew; **krople rosy** dew-drops; **rosa miodowa** (*wydalana przez owady*) honey dew.

rosarium *n.* rosary.

rosiczka *f. Gen.pl.* **-ek** *bot.* sundew (*Drosera*).

rosić *ipf.* **roszę rosisz 1.** (*o deszczu*) (= *mżyć*) dizzle. **2.** *roln.* ret. **3.** *lit.* (= *zwilżać*) bedew, besprinkle.

Rosja *f. geogr.* Russia.

Rosjanin *mp pl.* **-anie** *Gen.* **-an, Rosjanka** *f. Gen.pl.* **-ek** Russian.

rosły *a.* (= *wysoki*) tall; (= *postawny*) robust, stalwart.

rosnąć *ipf.* **rosnę rośniesz, rośnij, rósł rosła rośli 1.** (*o organizmach*) grow; **rosnąć jak na drożdżach** *l.* **w oczach** shoot up; **serce rośnie** the heart swells. **2.** (*o roślinach*) (= *występować*) grow, vegetate; **rosnąć jak grzyby po deszczu** spring up like mushrooms; **rosnąć dziko** grow wild; *bot.* (*o roślinach uprawnych*) escape. **3.** (= *być wychowywanym*) grow up, be bred. **4.** (= *zwiększać się*) rise, grow; (*o cenach*) rise, climb. **5.** (= *potęgować się*) grow. **6.** (= *rozwijać się*) develop, rise. **7.** *kulin.* (*o cieście, podnosić się*) prove, rise.

rosocha *f.* **1.** (= *rozwidlony pień*) crotch, forked tree-trunk. **2.** *pl. myśl.* palmate antlers.

rosochaty *a. bot.* forked, furcate.

rosołowy *a.* broth; **kostka rosołowa** bouillon cube; *Br. t.* stock cube.

rosomak *ma zool.* wolverine; *Br. t.* glutton (*Gulo gulo*).

rosół *mi* **-o-** *kulin.* broth, consommé; **rosół w kostkach** stock cube; **rosół z kury** chicken broth; **rozebrać się do rosołu** *żart.* undress; *pot.* peel off.

rosówka *f. Gen.pl.* **-ek** dew-worm.

rostbef *mi* (*potrawa*) roast beef; (*część tuszy*) rump steak.

rosyjski *a.* Russian; **chart rosyjski** *kynol.* Russian wolfhound, borzoi; **rosyjska ruletka** Russian roulette. **–** *mi* (*język*) Russian.

roszada *f.* **1.** *szachy* castling; **robić roszadę** castle. **2.** *przen.* (= *przetasowanie*) reshuffle.

roszarnia *f. Gen.pl.* **-i** *l.* **-ń** rettery.

roszczenie *n. prawn.* claim; **roszczenia płacowe** wage claims, pay claims; **roszczenie ubezpieczeniowe** insurance claim; **roszczenie wzajemne** counterclaim; **zaspokoić czyjeś roszczenia** meet sb's claims; **zgłaszać roszczenia wobec czegoś** stake out a claim to sth; **zaspokoić roszczenie** settle a claim.

roszczeniowy *a.* (= *odnoszący się do roszczeń*)

claim; (= *wyrażający się w żądaniach*) demanding; **postawa roszczeniowa** demanding attitude.

roszponka *f. Gen.pl.* **-ek** *bot.* corn-salad, lamb's lettuce (*Valerianella*).

rościć *ipf.* **roszczę rościsz, rościć sobie prawo/ pretensję** set up claims/pretensions; **rościć sobie prawo do czegoś** claim a right to sth.

roścież *f.* **na roścież** wide; **otwarty na roścież** wide open; **otworzyć drzwi/okno na roścież** open the door/ window wide.

roślina *f. bot.* plant; **roślina doniczkowa** houseplant, potted plant; **roślina ozdobna** ornamental; **królestwo roślin** plant kingdom; **wzrost roślin** vegetation; **życie roślin** plant life; **mieć (dobrą) rękę do roślin** have a green thumb.

roślinka *f. Gen.pl.* **-ek** small plant; *rzad.* plantlet.

roślinność *f.* vegetation, flora.

roślinny *a.* (*barwnik, włókno*) vegetable; (*życie, wzrost*) vegetal; **tłuszcz/olej/wosk roślinny** vegetable fat/oil/wax.

roślinożerca *ma zool.* herbivore.

roślinożerny *a.* herbivorous; (*zwł. o owadach*) phytophagous; **zwierzę roślinożerne** herbivore.

rota[1] *f. hist.* (= *oddział piechoty*) troop, army unit; **roty** army; **roty aresztanckie** convict gangs.

rota[2] *f.* (= *tekst przysięgi*) (form of an) oath; the Rota (*anti-German anthem written by Maria Konopnicka and composed by Feliks Nowowiejski in 1910*).

rota[3] *f. muz.* (= *pierwowzór skrzypiec*) rote; (= *gęśle l. lira celtycka*) crwth.

rota[4] *f. kośc.* (= *sąd najwyższej instancji*) the Rota; **Rota Rzymska** *rz.-kat.* Rota.

rotacja *f.* 1. (= *wirowanie*) rotation (*wokół czegoś* about *l.* around sth); circulation; (*piłki*) twist, spin; *mat., fiz.* curl; (*zastępowanie*) rotation; **rotacja pracowników** staff rotation; **rotacja zapasów** (*w magazynie*) stock rotation. 2. *roln.* crop rotation.

rotacyjny *a.* rotational, rotary, rotatory; **maszyna rotacyjna** *druk.* rotary press *l.* machine; **prasa/pompa rotacyjna** rotary press/pump.

rotacyzm *mi jęz.* rhotacism.

rotmistrz *mp pl.* **-e** *l.* **-owie** *hist.* captain of horse.

rotmistrzowski *a. hist.* captain-of-horse.

rotograwiura *f. druk.* rotogravure.

rotor *mi Gen.* **-a** = **wirnik**.

rottweiler *ma kynol.* Rottweiler.

rotunda *f. bud.* rotunda.

rowek *mi* **-wk-** *Gen.* **-a** (= *mały rów*) (*w ziemi*) (small) ditch; (= *wyżłobienie*) groove; *anat.* groove sulcus; *biol.* vallecula; *mech.* spline; *stol.* coulisse; *bud.* (*w kolumnie*) flute, groove; (*płyty gramofonowej*) groove; *techn.* furrow; **rowek skorupy** *zool.* (*ślimaka*) varix; **rowek z boku toru** *kręgle* gully; **wyżłobić (rowek w czymś)** channel sth.

rower *mi* bicycle; *pot.* bike; *sl.* wheel; **mały** *l.* **lekki rower** minibike; **rower górski** mountain bike; **rower jednokołowy** unicycle; **rower terenowy** dirt bike; **rower treningowy** stationary bicycle, exercise bike; **rower trzykołowy** *l.* trójkołowy tricycle; **rower wodny** pedal boat, pedalo; **jechać rowerem** ride (on) a bike, bike, bicycle, cycle; **pas dla rowerów** cycle lane; **stojak na rowery** cycle rack; **jazda na rowerze** cycling.

rowerek *mi* **-rk-** *Gen.* **-a** *l.* **-u** bicycle; **rowerek trzykołowy** *l.* trójkołowy (*dla dziecka*) tricycle.

rowerowy *a. attr.* bicycle.

rowerzysta *mp*, **rowerzystka** *f. Gen.pl.* **-ek** cyclist, biker.

rowkować *ipf.* groove, channel, notch, furrow.

rowkowanie *n.* (= *wyżłobione rowki*) grooving, fluting.

rowkowaty *a.* grooved, furrowed, sulcate.

rowu *itd. mi zob.* **rów**.

rozanielać *ipf.* ravish, delight, enrapture. ~ **się** *ipf.* fall into raptures.

rozanielić (się) *pf. zob.* **rozanielać (się)**.

rozanielony *a.* **-eni** delighted, enraptured.

rozarium *n. sing. indecl. pl.* **-ia** *Gen.* **-iów** rosarium.

rozbabrać *pf.* **-brzę -brzesz** *l.* **-bram -brasz, rozbabrywać** *ipf. pot.* (= *rozgrzebywać*) make a muck (*coś* of sth); **rozbabrany** in a muck; (= *rozrzucać*) mess up, jumble, muddle; **rozbabrać pracę** bungle a piece of work.

rozbałamucać *ipf.* (*kogoś*) turn (*sb's*) head. ~ **się** *ipf.* triffle away one's time.

rozbałamucić (się) *pf. zob.* **rozbałamucać (się)**.

rozbawiać *ipf.* amuse, entertain; **umieć rozbawić towarzystwo** be a good laugh. ~ **się** *ipf.* cheer up, liven up.

rozbawić (się) *pf. zob.* **rozbawiać (się)**.

rozbawienie *n.* amusement, hilarity, mirth; **ku czyjemuś rozbawieniu** much to sb's amusement.

rozbawiony *a.* **-eni** amused (*czymś* at *l.* by sth).

rozbebeszyć *pf. pot.* jumble, tumble.

rozbeczeć się *pf.* **-ę -ysz** 1. (*o zwierzętach*) (= *zacząć beczeć*) start bleating. 2. *pot.* (= *rozpłakać się*) burst into tears.

rozbełtać *pf.*, **rozbełtywać** *ipf.* stir, churn, beat up.

rozbestwiać *ipf.* enrage, madden, brutalize. ~ **się** *ipf.* 1. (= *stawać się brutalnym*) go savage. 2. (= *stawać się niezdyscyplinowanym*) become unruly; get out of hand.

rozbestwić (się) *pf. zob.* **rozbestwiać (się)**.

rozbestwiony *a.* **-eni** (= *brutalny*) savage, brutal; (= *niezdyscyplinowany*) unruly, wayward.

rozbić *pf.* **-biję -bijesz, -bij** *zob.* **rozbijać**. ~ **się** *pf. zob.* **rozbijać się**.

rozbiec się *pf.* **-biegli** *zob.* **rozbiegać się**.

rozbieg *mi* 1. *lotn.* take-off. 2. *sport, skoki* run-up; *krykiet* run; *kręgle* approach; **skok z rozbiegu** running *l.* flying jump; **z rozbiegu** running; **wziąć rozbieg** to take a run-up. 3. *sport* (*część skoczni narciarskiej*) inrun.

rozbiegać się *ipf.* 1. (= *rozpierzchać się*) (*o ludziach*) disperse, run in all directions. 2. (*o drogach*) (= *rozchodzić się*) diverge; **nasze drogi się rozbiegły** we parted company.

rozbiegany *a.* 1. (= *śpieszący się*) running about; (*o palcach, czułkach*) flitting; **rozbiegane oczy** restless eyes. 2. (= *niespokojny*) uneasy, restless; **ktoś ma rozbiegane myśli** sb's thoughts are wandering.

rozbiegowy *a.* **pas rozbiegowy** *lotn.* runway.

rozbierać *ipf.* **1.** (= *zdejmować z kogoś ubranie*) undress, take (*sb's*) clothes off, strip (*sb*) (of his/her clothes); **rozbierać kogoś z czegoś** divest sb of sth. **2.** (= *rozkładać*) take apart, disassemble, dismantle; *jęz.* (*np. zdanie*) parse; (*urządzenie*) strip; (*kurczaka*) disjoint. **3.** (= *burzyć*) pull down. ~ **się** *ipf.* undress, strip, get undressed, take off one's clothes; **rozbierać się do bielizny** strip (down) to one's underwear; **rozbierać się do naga** strip naked.

rozbieralnia *f. Gen.pl.* **-i** changing-room.

rozbieralny *a. attr.* take-down; (*np. o meblach*) knock-down.

rozbieżnie *adv.* divergently.

rozbieżność *f.* (*linii, opinii*) discrepancy.

rozbieżny *a.* discrepant; *t. mat.* divergent; **ciąg rozbieżny** divergent sequence.

rozbijać *ipf.* **1.** (= *tłuc, rozłupywać na części*) break, shatter, break up; *fiz.* (*cząstkę, atom*) split; (*skałę*) spall; (*skorupkę*) (*zwł. o pisklętach*) chip; **rozbić coś w drobny mak** shaffer sth to smithereens, make a matchwood of sth; **rozbijać na ułamki** *mat.* fractionize. **2.** (= *roztrzaskiwać, niszczyć*) crush; **rozbić samochód** smash a car. **3.** (= *uszkadzać, ranić*) bruise, injure, hurt, mutilate; **rozbić komuś nos** smash sb's nose. **4.** (= *dezorganizować, skłócać*) disrupt, frustrate, throw into disarray; (*rodzinę, zespół, nadzieję*) break up; (*społeczeństwo, opozycję*) fragment; (= *powodować rozłam*) disunite, fraction; **rozbijać (na frakcje)** *polit.* factionalize, fraction. **5.** (= *ugniatać*) crush. **6.** (= *włamywać się*) break open; **rozbić bank** break the bank. **7.** (= *pokonać, rozgromić*) defeat, beat, crush; **rozbić kogoś w pył** *l.* **puch** pulverize sb, crush sb. **8.** (= *dzielić*) divide (*coś na coś* sth into sth). **9. rozbijać namiot** pitch a tent, set up a tent; **rozbijać obóz** set up camp, pitch a camp. ~ **się** *ipf.* **1.** (= *ulegać rozbiciu*) break, get broken, be shattered; (*o samochodzie, falach, dzbanku*) smash; (*o samolocie*) crash; **rozbijać się o coś** (*o kroplach deszczu*) splash against *l.* on *l.* over sth. **2.** (= *ranić się*) injure *l.* hurt o.s. **3.** (= *dzielić się*) divide, break up, separate. **4.** (= *nie dochodzić do skutku*) fall through (*o coś* because of sth); be thwarted (*o coś* by sth). **5.** *pot.* (= *hulać*) carouse, party; **rozbijać się samochodem po mieście** cruise around town.

rozbiorowy *a. hist.* partitioning; **państwa rozbiorowe** partitioning powers; **traktat rozbiorowy** treaty of partition.

rozbiór *mi* **-o- 1.** (= *analiza*) analysis; **rozbiór zdania** *jęz.* parsing. **2.** *hist.* partition.

rozbiórka *f. Gen.pl.* **-ek 1.** (= *burzenie budynku*) demolition; **dokonywać rozbiórki** pull down, demolish; **budynek przeznaczony do rozbiórki** building due for demolition. **2.** (= *demontaż*) disassembly.

rozbiórkowy *a. attr.* demolition.

rozbisurmaniać *ipf. pot.* let (*a child*) run wild, give (*a child*) a free rein. ~ **się** *ipf. pot.* run wild.

rozbisurmanić (się) *pf.* *zob.* **rozbisurmaniać (się)**.

rozbitek *mp* **-tk-** *pl.* **-owie** *l.* **-i** castaway; **życiowy rozbitek** *przen.* wreck, down-and-out, outcast.

rozbity *a.* (*o talerzu, rodzinie, domu*) broken; (*o samochodzie*) smashed; (*o nosie*) bruised; (*o partii*) factional.

rozbłysk *mi* flare; *astron.* flash; (*światła, płomienia*) flare-up.

rozbłyskiwać *ipf.*, **rozbłysnąć** *pf.* **-snę -śniesz, -śnij** shine, flare up, flash; **rozbłysnąć dumą** glow with pride.

rozboleć *pf.* **-boli** start aching.

rozbój *mi* **-o-** *Gen.pl.* **-ów** banditry, mugging; *prawn.* robbery; **rozbój w biały dzień** *t. prawn.* highway robbery; (= *zawyżona cena*) daylight robbery.

rozbójnik *mp przest.* (*napadający na podróżujących gościńcem*) highwayman; (*zwł. w górach i lasach*) brigand.

rozbrajać *ipf.* **1.** (= *odbierać broń*) disarm, unarm. **2.** (= *usuwać zapalnik bomby*) deactivate; **rozbroić minę** *itd.* remove the charge from a mine, etc., defuse *l.* defuze a mine. **3.** (= *uśmierzać złość, gniew*) disarm, appease. **4.** *fiz.* discharge. ~ **się** *ipf.* **1.** (= *demilitaryzować się*) disarm. **2.** *fiz.* discharge.

rozbrajający *a.* (*o uśmiechu, szczerości*) disarming.

rozbrat *mi lit.* disunity, breach; **wziąć rozbrat z czymś** give up sth.

rozbratel *mi* **-tl-** *Gen.* **-a** *kulin.* loin-chop.

rozbroić *pf.* **rozbroję rozbroisz, rozbrój** *zob.* **rozbrajać**.

rozbrojenie *n.* disarmament; **jednostronne rozbrojenie** unilateral disarmament; **rozbrojenie jądrowe** nuclear disarmament.

rozbrojeniowy *a. attr.* disarmament.

rozbrykać się *pf.* **1.** (*o zwierzętach*) (= *zacząć wierzgać*) bolt. **2.** (*o dziecku*) frolic, start frolicking.

rozbrykany *a.* **1.** (*o zwierzętach*) (= *wierzgający*) frisky, bouncy. **2.** (*o dziecku*) frisky, frolicsome, playful.

rozbryzgać (się) *pf. zob.* **rozbryzgiwać (się)**.

rozbryzgiwać *ipf.* splash (*sth*) about *l.* around. ~ **się** *ipf.* splash, scatter; (*o falach*) break.

rozbryznąć (się) *pf.* **-znę -źniesz, -źnij** *zob.* **rozbryzgiwać (się)**.

rozbrzmieć *pf.*, **rozbrzmiewać** *ipf.* **1.** (*o dźwiękach*) (= *rozlegać się*) sound, ring, resound, ring out. **2.** (= *napełniać się dźwiękiem*) resound (*czymś* with sth).

rozbuchać *pf. pot.* (= *wyolbrzymić*) exaggerate. ~ **się** *pf. pot.* (= *rozzuchwalić się*) grow impudent, start swaggering.

rozbuchany *a.* exaggerated.

rozbudowa *f.* **1.** (= *dobudowywanie*) extension; *komp.* upgrade. **2.** (= *rozwijanie potencjału gospodarczego*) development.

rozbudować (się) *pf. zob.* **rozbudowywać (się)**.

rozbudowywać *pf.* **1.** (= *powiększać, budując*) extend, enlarge, build up (*coś* sth); add (*coś to* sth); *komp*. upgrade. **2.** (= *rozwijać*) develop, expand. ~ **się** *ipf*. extend, expand, enlarge, grow.

rozbudzać *ipf*. **1.** (= *budzić*) wake (*sb*) up, arouse; **całkiem rozbudzony** (*ze snu*) wideawake. **2.** (= *wyrywać z apatii*) stir, rouse. **3.** (= *wzbudzać*) excite, arouse, waken; (*odwagę, entuzjazm*) get up; (*gniew*) rouse (*w kimś* in sb); (*zainteresowanie, emocje*) awake, arouse, kindle; **rozbudzać czyjeś nadzieje** build up sb's hopes; **rozbudzać (czyjeś) wątpliwości/podejrzenia** plant doubt/suspicion (in sb's mind). ~ **się** *ipf*. **1.** (= *budzić się*) wake up, awake. **2.** (*o uczuciach*) (= *pojawiać się*) awake, flare up.

rozbudzić (się) *pf. zob*. **rozbudzać (się)**.

rozbujać *pf*. swing, rock.

rozcapierzać (się) *ipf*. = **rozczapierzać (się)**.

rozcapierzyć (się) *pf*. = **rozczapierzyć (się)**.

rozcharakteryzować *pf*. remove (*sb's*) makeup. ~ **się** *pf*. remove one's makeup.

rozchełstany *a*. in loose attire, in untidy dress.

rozchichotać się *pf*. **-oczę** *l*. **-ocę -oczesz** *l*. **-ocesz, -ocz** giggle (unstrainedly).

rozchlapać *pf*. **-pię -piesz, rozchlapywać** *ipf*. (= *rozlewać*) spill, slop, splash; (= *rozdeptać, rozchodzić*) wear out.

rozchmurzać się *ipf*., **rozchmurzyć się** *pf*. **1.** (= *rozpogadzać się*) clear up. **2.** (= *rozweselać się*) cheer up, clear up; **rozchmurz się!** lighten up!.

rozchodnik *mi Gen*. **-a** *bot*. sedum, stonecrop (*Sedum*); **rozchodnik ostry** wall pepper (*S. acre*); **rozchodnik wielki** orpin, orpine, live-forever; *Br*. live-long (*S. telephium*).

rozchodować *pf*. spend.

rozchodowy *a. attr*. outgoing, outcoming.

rozchodowywać *ipf. zob*. **rozchodować**.

rozchodzić *pf*. **1.** *pot*. (= *poluźnić buty przez chodzenie*) break in, wear (*a pair of shoes*) comfortable; (*dolegliwość*) (= *wyleczyć spacerem*) walk off. **2.** (= *rozprzestrzeniać*) (*o chmurach*) lift; **rozchodzić się jak świeże bułeczki** go *l*. sell like hot cakes. ~ **się** *ipf*. **1.** (*o tłumie itp*.) (= *rozpraszać się*) disperse, scatter, melt away; (*piechotą*) trickle away *l*. out; (*zwł. na polecenie policji*) move on; (*o parze ludzi*) (= *rozstawać się*) part, split, break (up) (*z kimś* with sb); (*o parze ludzi*) (= *rozwodzić się*) divorce; **on się rozszedł z żoną** he divorced his wife. **2.** (*o dźwięku, świetle, wiadomościach itp*.) (= *rozprzestrzeniać się*) travel, spread; (*o informacjach, plotkach*) get around; (*o informacjach*) filter through. **3.** *fiz*. (*o falach*) propagate. **4.** *geom*. (= *tworzyć szeroki kąt*) divaricate; (*np. o mgle*) clear; (*np. o zapachu, głosie*) emanate (*skądś* from sth). **5.** (= *podzielić*) diverge, separate; (*o drogach*) (= *rozwidlać się*) split, diverge; (= *iść w różnych kierunkach*) split up. **6.** (*o pieniądzach*) (= *być wydawanym*) disappear; *handl*. (*o towarze*) move, sell. – *pf*. **1.** *pot*. (*o butach*) (= *ulec rozluźnieniu*) be comfortable, wear down. **2. rozchodzić się w szwach** (*o ubraniu*) gape at the seams. **3.** *pot*. (= *rozruszać się, chodząc*) stretch one's legs.

rozchorować się *pf*., **rozchorowywać się** *ipf*. fall ill, take to one's bed.

rozchód *mi* **-o-** outcoming, outgoing; **przychody i rozchody** incomings and outcomings.

rozchwiać *pf*. **-chwieję -chwiejesz -chwiali** *l*. **-chwieli, rozchwiewać** *ipf*. (= *rozkołysać*) set (*sth*) swinging; (*o wietrze*) toss (*sth*) to and fro.

rozchwytać *pf*., **rozchwytywać** *ipf*. (*chodliwy towar*) lap up; scramble (*coś* for sth).

rozchwytywany *a*. sought-after, like gold dust; **rozchwytywany towar** bestseller; **być rozchwytywanym** be much in demand.

rozchybotać *pf*. **-oczę -oczesz** *l*. **-ocę -ocesz** *l*. **-otam -otasz, -ocz** *l*. **-otaj** set (*sth*) swinging; (*o wietrze*) toss.

rozchylać *ipf*. part. ~ **się** *ipf*. part; **być szeroko rozchylonym** (*np. o koszuli*) gape.

rozchylić (się) *pf. zob*. **rozchylać (się)**.

rozciąć *pf*. **rozetnę rozetniesz, rozetnij** *zob*. **rozcinać**.

rozciągać *ipf*. **1.** (= *wydłużać*) (*sprężynę, mięśnie, sweter*) stretch; (*np. drut*) draw (out); (*ubranie*) bag (out). **2.** (= *wydłużać w czasie*) drag out, extend. **3.** (= *rozpościerać*) spread, expand; (*działalność, władzę, wpływy*) extend; **rozciągać władzę/opiekę nad kimś/czymś** extend one's authority/protection over sb/sth; **rozciągać panowanie** *l*. **zwierzchnictwo nad czymś** have *l*. hold dominion over sth. **4.** *pot*. (= *rozwlekać w różne miejsca*) scatter. ~ **się** *ipf*. **1.** (= *wydłużać się*) stretch, spread out. **2.** (= *wydłużać się w czasie*) stretch, extend. **3.** (= *rozprzestrzeniać się*) spread, stretch out; (*o dymie*) drift. **4.** (= *obejmować zasięgiem*) spread (*na jakiejś przestrzeni* over an area); (*o władzy, kontroli*) extend. **5.** (= *wyciągać się*) sprawl (out), stretch o.s.; **rozciągnięty (na całą długość)** (*np. o ciele*) outstreched; **rozciągać się nad** (*rzeką: o moście*) span; (*na dużą powierzchnię*) sheet; (*o obszarze, rzece*) extend; (*o równinie, morzu*) stretch (*aż do... to.../as far as...*); (*o widoku, dolinie*) spread out; (*o zabudowaniach, mieście*) sprawl; **rozciągający się w poprzek czegoś** astride of sth; **ćwiczenie rozciągające** *sport* stretch; **rozciągać się na długość czegoś** stretch the length of sth.

rozciągliwość *f*. extensibility.

rozciągliwy *a*. tensile, extendible, extensible.

rozciągłość *f*. stretch, reach, extent; *fiz*. (*ciała*) extension; **w całej rozciągłości** (= *na całą długość*) at full length; (= *w pełni*) in full, to the full extent; **zgadzam się w całej rozciągłości** I couldn't agree more.

rozciągnąć *pf*. **-ij 1.** *zob*. **rozciągać. 2.** (= *powalić*) knock (*sb*) down, fell (*sb*). ~ **się** *pf*. **1.** *zob*. **rozciągać się. 2.** (= *położyć się, rozprostowując ciało*) sprawl, spread; (= *upaść*) fall flat.

rozcieńczać *ipf*. dilute (*coś czymś* sth with sth); thin; (*napój*) water down; *techn*. (*roztwór*) reduce; (*alkohol, farbę*) cut (*czymś* with sth); **(środek) rozcieńczający** adulterant; **nierozcieńczony** (*o kwasie, alkoholu*) full strength.

rozcieńczalnik *mi Gen*. **-a** diluent, thinner; **rozcieńczalnik do farb olejnych** (*pokostowy*) megilp.

rozcieńczenie *n*. (= *stężenie roztworu*) dilution; **rozcieńczenie graniczne** dilution limit; **roz-**

cieńczenie nieskończenie wielkie infinite dilution.

rozcieńczyć *pf. zob.* **rozcieńczać.**

rozcierać *ipf.* **1.** (= *masować*) (*zwł. ręce dla rozgrzania*) chafe. **2.** (= *rozgniatać*) grind, triturate, pulverize; **rozetrzeć żółtka z cukrem** mix egg yolks with sugar; **rozcierać na miazgę** pulp; (*w moździerzu*) bray; **rozcierać na proszek** grind to powder, pulverize; **rozcierać na krem** cream. **3.** (= *rozmazywać*) (*krem, maść*) rub over.

rozcięcie *n.* (= *rozcięte miejsce*) cut, dissection, slit; (*w odzieży*) (*u dołu płaszcza, marynarki*) vent; (*na kieszonkę l. przy zapięciu*) placket; **robić rozcięcie w** vent.

rozcinać *ipf.* (= *rozdzielać, tnąc*) cut, cleave, sever; **rozciąć sobie głowę** cut one's head open.

rozczapierzać *ipf.* splay (*sth*) (out). ~ **się** *ipf.* (*o palcach*) splay (out).

rozczapierzyć (się) *pf. zob.* **rozczapierzać (się).**

rozczarować (się) *pf. zob.* **rozczarowywać (się).**

rozczarowanie *n.* disappointment; **przeżyć rozczarowanie** be disappointed (*co do kogoś/czegoś* in sb/sth).

rozczarowany *a.* disappointed (*kimś/czymś* with *l.* by sb/sth).

rozczarowywać *ipf.* disappoint, disillusion; let down. ~ **się** *ipf.* **rozczarować się** become disappointed *l.* disillusioned (*co do kogoś/czegoś* with sb/sth).

rozczepiać *ipf.* (= *rozłączać*) unfasten, detach, disconnect; (*wagony*) uncouple; (*sklejone elementy*) unstick. ~ **się** *ipf.* come unfastened *l.* unstuck.

rozczepić (się) *pf. zob.* **rozczepiać (się).**

rozczesać *pf.* **-szę -szesz,** **rozczesywać** *ipf.* comb, comb out.

rozczłonkować *pf.,* **rozczłonkowywać** *ipf.* divide up, dismember, segment, anatomize.

rozczochrać *pf.* dishevel, tousle, ruffle. ~ **się** *pf.* become disheveled, ruffle one's hair.

rozczochraniec *mp* **-ńc-** *pl.* **-y** *pot.* dishevelled fellow *l.* child.

rozczochrany *a.* (*o fryzurze, włosach*) unkempt, tousled, disheveled, wild; **rozczochrane włosy** tousle.

rozczulać *ipf.* move, touch, affect. ~ **się** *ipf.* melt; **rozczulać się nad kimś, czymś** take pity on sb; **rozczulać się nad sobą samym** wallow in self-pity; **rozczulić się do łez** melt into tears.

rozczulenie *n.* melting mood.

rozczulić (się) *pf. zob.* **rozczulać (się).**

rozczyn *mi* leaven.

rozczyniać *ipf.,* **rozczynić** *pf.* blend (*yeast with flour*).

rozczytać się *pf.,* **rozczytywać się** *ipf.* **1.** be able to decipher (*w czymś* sth). **2.** spend one's time reading (*w czymś* sth).

rozdać *pf. zob.* **rozdawać.**

rozdanie *n. karty* deal; **złe rozdanie** misdeal.

rozdarcie *n.* **1.** (= *uszkodzenie*) tear, rip. **2.** (*w grupie osób*) split. **3.** (= *rozterka*) dilemma, perplexity; **przeżywać wewnętrzne rozdarcie** be on the horns of a dilemma.

rozdarty *a.* (= *przedarty*) *t. przen.* torn.

rozdawać *ipf.* **-aję -ajesz, -awaj** (= *rozdzielać*) distribute, hand out *l.* around; (*np. nagrody*) give away; (*zwł. pieniądze, jedzenie*) dole (out); **rozdawać ulotki (w)** (*jakimś miejscu*) leaflet; **rozdawać na lewo i prawo** (*pieniądze, upominki*) ladle, dish out; **rozdawać karty** deal (out); **kto rozdaje?** whose deal is it?

rozdawnictwo *n.* (*posad przez rządzącą partię itp.*) patronage.

rozdąć *pf.* **rozedmę rozedmiesz, rozedmij** *zob.* **rozdymać.**

rozdeptać *pf.* **-pczę** *l.* **-pcę -pczesz** *l.* **-pcesz, -pcz, rozdeptywać** *ipf.* trample, crush, tread; (= *rozgniatać*) tread (*coś* on sth); **rozdeptać buty** (= *rozchodzić*) break in, get worn-down.

rozdmuchać *pf.,* **rozdmuchiwać** *ipf.* **1.** (= *rozwiewać*) blow about, scatter. **2.** (= *rozniecać ogień*) blow (*on the fire*). **3.** *pot.* (= *wyolbrzymiać*) amplify, fan.

rozdokazywać się *pf.* gambol, frolic.

rozdrabniacz *mi Gen.* **-a** *roln.* shredder, grinding machine; **kuchenny rozdrabniacz odpadków** grinder; **rozdrabniacz do pasz** feed mill; **rozdrabniacz złomu** fragmentizer.

rozdrabniać *ipf.* (= *dzielić na części*) (*chleb*) crumble; (*majątek*) break up; **rozdrabniać na proszek** powder, pulverize. ~ **się** *ipf.* **1.** (= *dzielić się*) crumble. **2.** *pot.* (= *rozpraszać swoje myśli*) get sidetracked *l.* distracted; **nie rozdrabniać się** hit the high spots; **nie rozdrabniaj się w szczegółach** don't get bogged down in details.

rozdrapać *pf.* **-pię -piesz, rozdrapywać** *ipf.* **1.** (= *rozdzierać, drapiąc*) scratch (raw); (*o kurze*) scratch. **2.** *pot.* (*przen. majątek, spadek*) snatch away, scramble (*coś* for sth).

rozdrażniać *ipf.,* **rozdrażnić** *pf.* **-ij 1.** (= *wywołać ból, drażniąc*) irritate. **2.** (= *irytować*) irritate, annoy.

rozdrażnienie *n.* irritation, annoyance, exasperation; **z rozdrażnieniem** waspishly, exasperatedly; **powód rozdrażnienia** annoyance; **przyczyna rozdrażnienia** irritant, gall.

rozdrażniony *a.* **-eni** irritated, annoyed, exasperated (*z powodu czegoś* about *l.* at *l.* with *l.* by sth).

rozdrobnić *pf.* **-ij** *zob.* **rozdrabniać.** ~ **się** *pf. zob.* **rozdrabniać się.**

rozdroże *n. Gen.pl.* **-y** cross-roads; **na rozdrożu** *t. przen.* at the crossroads; **stanąć na rozdrożu** *przen.* be in doubt.

rozdwajać *ipf.* divide into two, split. ~ **się** *ipf.* **1.** fork, branch; *form.* bifurcate; (= *dzielić się na dwoje*) split. **2.** *przen.* (= *dwoić się*) go out of one's way.

rozdwoić (się) *pf.* **-oję -oisz, -ój** *zob.* **rozdwajać (się).**

rozdwojenie *n.* division; **rozdwojenie jaźni** dissociated *l.* split personality.

rozdygotać się *pf.* **-ocę -ocesz** *l.* **-ocę -ocesz, -ocz** shake. ~ **się** *pf.* start shaking *l.* trembling.

rozdygotany *a.* (*ręce*) shaking; (*człowiek*) wobbly.

rozdymać *ipf.* **1.** (= *nadymać*) (*żagle*) puff out. **2.** (= *rozsadzać*) (*brzuch*) distend. **3.** (= *wyolbrzymiać*) (*incydent*) blow up; (*aferę, sprawę*) inflate; (*tekst, rachunki itp.*) pad. ~ **się** *ipf.*, swell; *pat.* (*o żołądku*) distend.

rozdysponować *pf.* dispense, allocate.

rozdziać *pf.* **-dzieję -dziejesz -dział -dziali** *l.* **-dzieli** *zob.* **rozdziewać.**

rozdzialik *mi* small chapter.

rozdział *mi* **1.** (*część książki, przen. t. życia*) chapter; *szkoln.* (*w podręczniku*) unit; **dzielić na rozdziały** chapter. **2.** (= *przydzielanie, dzielenie na części*) distribution; (*t. pieniędzy*) dispensation; **rozdział ról** *teatr* cast. **3.** (= *rozgraniczanie*) separation; **rozdział państwa od Kościoła** separation of Church and State; **rozdział majątku** *prawn.* partition of property; **trwały** *l.* **definitywny rozdział** divorce (*pomiędzy czymś a czymś* between sth and sth). **4.** (= *niezgoda*) discord, disagreement.

rozdziawiać *ipf.*, **rozdziawić** *pf.* *pot.* gape, gawk, goggle; **rozdziawiać gębę** (= *dziwić się*) gape; **rozdziawiony** *l.* **z rozdziawioną gębą** agape, gaping, open-mouthed.

rozdzielacz *mi Gen.* **-a 1.** (= *odcinek przewodu rurowego*) distributor, divider; **rozdzielacz rurowy (pożarowy)** dividing breeching. **2.** *techn., mot.* (= *rozdzielacz zapłonu*) (ignition) distributor.

rozdzielać *ipf.* **1.** (= *dzielić na części*) divide, break up, split; **rozdzielać na części składowe** decompose. **2.** (= *rozdawać, dzieląc*) distribute, deal out, dispense; **rozdzielać coś (po)między kogoś** distribute sth among sb. **3.** (= *oddzielać, rozłączać*) separate, divide. **4.** (= *przegradzać*) separate, divide. **5.** (= *skłócać*) set people at odds *l.* variance, disunite. **6.** (= *powodować rozłąkę*) separate. ~ **się** *ipf.* **1.** (= *dzielić się na części, grupy*) split up, divide. **2.** (= *rozgałęziać się*) fork, branch. **3.** (= *rozstawać się*) separate, part, go different ways.

rozdzielczość *f.* resolution; (*układu optycznego, teleskopu*) resolving power; *opt., fot.* definition; **rozdzielczość obrazu TV** *telew.* picture definition; **rozdzielczość liniowa TV** *telew.* line definition; *komp.* resolution; **duża/mała rozdzielczość** high/low resolution; **o dużej rozdzielczości** high-definition; **drukowanie z wysoką rozdzielczością** high resolution printing; **rozdzielczość optyczna/z przeplotem/interpolowana** optical/interlaced/interpolated resolution.

rozdzielczy *a.* distributive, distributing; *fiz.* separation; **deska rozdzielcza** *mot.* dashboard; **belka deski rozdzielczej** (*w nadwoziu samochodowym*) scuttle; **podświetlenie deski rozdzielczej** *mot.* dash light; **tablica rozdzielcza** control panel, instrument panel, switchboard.

rozdzielić (się) *pf. zob.* **rozdzielać (się).**

rozdzielnia *f. Gen.pl.* **-i** (= *pomieszczenie do sortowania*) distributing room; *kol.* switching station.

rozdzielnictwo *n.* distribution.

rozdzielnie *adv.* separately.

rozdzielnik *mi Gen.* **-a** distribution list; **rozdzielnik korespondencji** mailing list.

rozdzielnopłciowość *f. biol.* dioecism.

rozdzielnopłciowy *a. biol.* dioecious.

rozdzielność *f.* separation, divisibility; **prawo rozdzielności** (*mnożenia względem dodawania*) *mat.* distributive law.

rozdzielny *a.* separable.

rozdzierać *ipf.* (= *rozdzielać, drąc*) tear (apart); **rodzierać coś na kawałki** tear sth into pieces; **rozdzierać kopertę** tear *l.* rip open an envelope; **rozdzierać komuś serce** break sb's heart; **rozdzierać szaty** (*nad kimś, czymś*) *przen.* rend one's garments. ~ **się** *ipf.* **1.** (= *ulegać rozdarciu*) tear, rip. **2.** *pot.* (= *wydzierać się, krzyczeć*) start yelling.

rozdzierający *a.* (= *wstrząsający*) (*o bólu*) excruciating; (*o krzyku*) piercing.

rozdziewać *ipf. przest.* disrobe, disarray. ~ **się** *ipf. przest.* disrobe.

rozdziewiczyć *pf.* deflower.

rozdziobać *pf.* **-dziobię -dziobiesz, -dziob** *l.* **-dziób, rozdziobywać** *ipf.* peck to bits; (*skorupkę jajka*) (*o pisklęciu*) pip.

rozdzwaniać się *ipf.*, **rozdzwonić się** *pf.* **1.** (= *rozbrzmiewać*) (*o telefonie, dzwonku*) ring, start ringing; (*o budziku, alarmie*) go off. **2.** (= *wypełniać się dźwiękiem*) resound (*czymś* with sth).

rozdźwięczeć *pf.* **-ę -ysz** resound, ring (*czymś* with sth); **dom rozdźwięczał śmiechem** the house rang *l.* resounded with laughter.

rozdźwięk *mi* dissonance; (*między małżonkami, w rodzinie*) discord; (*między teorią a praktyką, faktami, liczbami*) discrepancy.

rozebrać *pf.* **rozbiorę rozbierzesz** *zob.* **rozbierać.** ~ **się** *pf. zob.* **rozbierać się.**

rozedma *f. pat.* (= *rozedma płuc*) emphysema, pulmonary emphysema.

rozednieć *pf.* dawn; **rozedniało** the day dawned, it dawned.

rozedrgać się *pf.* (*o osobie, głosie*) quiver; (*o strunie, głosie*) vibrate; **ziemia rozedrgała im się pod stopami** the earth trembled beneath their feet.

rozedrzeć *pf.* **-drę -drzesz, -drzyj, -darł** *zob.* **rozdzierać.** ~ **się** *pf. zob.* **rozdzierać się.**

rozegnać *pf. zob.* **rozganiać.**

rozegrać *pf. zob.* **rozgrywać.** ~ **się** *pf. zob.* **rozgrywać się.**

rozejm *mi wojsk.* armistice; (*zwł. tymczasowy*) *t. przen.* truce; **zawrzeć rozejm** call a truce.

rozejmowy *a.* armistice, truce; **układ rozejmowy** truce treaty.

rozejrzeć się *pf.* **-ę -ysz, -yj** *zob.* **rozglądać się.**

rozejść się *pf.* **rozejdę rozejdziesz rozszedł rozeszła rozeszli** *zob.* **rozchodzić się.**

rozemocjonować *pf.* (*o meczu, odkryciu, pomyśle*) excite, thrill; (*o kłótni, dyskusji*) agitate. ~ **się** *pf.* (*meczem, odkryciem*) be *l.* become excited, be *l.* become thrilled (*czymś* by sth); (*kłótnią, dyskusją*) be *l.* become agitated (*czymś* with sth).

rozemocjonowany *a.* (*meczem, odkryciem*) excited, thrilled; (*kłótnią, dyskusją*) agitated.

rozentuzjazmować *pf.* arouse enthusiasm (*kogoś* in sb). ~ **się** *pf.* become enthusiastic (*czymś* about sth).

rozentuzjazmowany *a.* enthusiastic (*czymś*

about sth); (*o tłumie, zwolennikach*) ecstatic, enthusiastic.

rozepchać *pf.*, **rozepchnąć** *pf.* **-ij** *zob.* **rozpychać.**

rozeprzeć *pf.* **-prę -przesz, -przyj, -parł** *zob.* **rozpierać.**

rozerwać *pf.* **-wę -wiesz, -wij 1.** *zob.* **rozrywać. 2.** *pot.* (= *zabawić*) entertain. ~ **się** *pf.* **1.** *zob.* **rozrywać się. 2.** *pot.* (= *zabawić się*) have some fun.

rozeschnąć się *pf.* **-schnij, -schnął** *l.* **rozsechł -schła -schli** *zob.* **rozsychać się.**

rozesłać¹ *pf.* **roześlę roześlesz, roześlij** *zob.* **rozsyłać.**

rozesłać² *pf.* **rozścielę rozścielesz** *zob.* **rozścielać.**

rozespać się *pf.* **-śpię -śpisz, -śpij** be heavy with sleep, be half asleep.

rozespany *a.* heavy with sleep, half asleep.

roześmiać się *pf.* **-śmieję -śmiejesz, -śmiali** *l.* **-śmieli** laugh (*z czegoś* at sth); **roześmiać się na głos** laugh out loud; **roześmiać się komuś w oczy** laugh in sb's face; **roześmiać się gorzko/szyderczo** laugh bitterly/sardonically; **nawet się nie roześmiał** he kept a straight face.

roześmiany *a.* laughing; (*o dziecku, twarzy, głosie*) cheerful.

rozeta *f.* **1.** (*ornament*) rosette, rosace. **2.** *bud.* rose window, rosace.

rozetka *f. Gen.pl.* **-ek 1.** (*ornament*) rosette, rosace. **2.** (= *wstążeczka orderowa*) rosette. **3.** *bot.* rosette. **4.** *techn.* (*w drukarce*) daisywheel, printwheel.

rozetkowy *a.* rosette; **drukarka rozetkowa** *komp.* daisywheel printer.

rozetnę *itd. pf. zob.* **rozciąć.**

rozetowy *a.* rosette; **okno rozetowe** *bud.* rose window.

rozetrzeć *pf.* **-trę -trzesz, -trzyj, roztarł** *zob.* **rozcierać.**

rozewrzeć *pf.* **-rę -rzesz, -rzyj, rozwarł** *zob.* **rozwierać.**

rozeznać się *pf. zob.* **rozeznawać się.**

rozeznanie *n.* (*w sytuacji, problemach*) grasp, understanding (*w czymś* of sth); (*w jakiejś dziedzinie*) command, knowledge (*w czymś* of sth); **mieć rozeznanie w czymś** be clued-in about sth; **tracić w czymś rozeznanie** lose touch with sth; **działać z rozeznaniem** *prawn.* act with discretion.

rozeznawać *ipf.* **-aję -ajesz, -awaj** discern. ~ **się** *ipf.* **1.** (*wiedzieć*) be well informed, be clued-in (*w czymś* about sth); **rozeznawać się w sytuacji** know where one stands. **2.** (*dowiedzieć się*) find one's way around (*w czymś* in sth); **rozeznać się w terenie** get one's bearings; **nie móc się w czymś rozeznać** not be able to tell what's what.

rozeźlić *pf.* **-ij** *pot.* exasperate, irritate. ~ **się** *pf. pot.* grow exasperated, get irritated.

rozfalować się *pf.* (*o tłumie, morzu*) surge; (*o morzu, zbożu na wietrze*) wave.

rozfanatyzowany *a.* fanatical, fanaticized.

rozformować *pf. wojsk.* disband.

rozgadać *pf.*, **rozgadywać** *ipf. pot.* (= *nie dochować tajemnicy*) babble out. ~ **się** *pf.*, **rozgadywać się** *ipf.* chatter away, start chattering away (*o czymś* about sth).

rozgadany *a.* babbling, chattering; garrulous.

rozgałęziacz *mi Gen.* **-a** *el.* adapter; **rozgałęziacz z 2/3/4 przyłączami** 2-/3-/4-way adapter.

rozgałęziać *ipf.*, **rozgałęzić** *pf.* branch. ~ **się** *ipf.*, **rozgałęzić się** *pf.* (*o krzewie, drzewie*) branch; (*o drodze*) branch, fork; (*w dwóch kierunkach*) bifurcate; (*w trzech kierunkach*) trifurcate.

rozgałęzienie *n.* **1.** (= *rozwidlenie*) (*drogi, rzeki*) fork. **2.** (= *miejsce rozgałęzienia*) fork, branch.

rozgałęziony *a.* (*o koronie drzewa*) furcate; (*o systemie dróg*) ramified.

rozganiać *ipf.* (*tłum, demonstrację*) disperse, scatter; (*chmury, mgłę*) disperse.

rozgardiasz *mi* hurly-burly; **w pokoju panował rozgardiasz** the room was in an uproar.

rozgarnąć *pf.* **-ij, rozgarniać** *ipf.* (*grabiami*) rake; (*włosy*) part, brush apart; **rozgarniać włosy palcami** comb one's hair with one's fingers; **rozgarnąć śnieg** clear a passage through the snow; (*łopatą*) shovel the snow aside.

rozgarnięty *a.* (= *bystry*) sharp-witted; **mało rozgarnięty** slow-witted.

rozgęszczać *ipf.*, **rozgęścić** *pf.* **-szczę -ścisz** dilute, thin.

rozgiąć *pf.* **rozegnę rozegniesz, rozegnij, rozgiął, rozginać** *ipf.* (*drut*) unbend; (*kratę*) pull apart, bend apart; (*palce*) spread, straighten out. ~ **się** *pf.* straighten out.

rozglądać się *ipf.* **1.** (*wokół siebie*) look around. **2.** (= *szukać*) look (*za kimś/czymś* for sb/sth); ask around (*za kimś/czymś* for sb/sth); **rozglądać się za pracą** be looking for a job.

rozgłaszać *ipf.* make known, make public; (*o mediach*) blazon; (*plotki, kłamstwa*) retail, spread; **rozgłaszać coś na cały świat** *przen.* shout sth from the rooftops; **rozgłaszać, że...** spread the word that...; **nie rozgłaszaj tego** keep it private, keep it to yourself.

rozgłos *mi* publicity; **bez rozgłosu** without publicity, in strict privacy; **cieszyć się rozgłosem** be famous *l.* popular; **nabrać rozgłosu** become famous, gain prominence; **nadać czemuś rozgłos** give sth a high profile, give publicity to sth; **zdobyć rozgłos** make a name for o.s., come to prominence; **unikający rozgłosu** low profile, self-effacing.

rozgłosić *pf.* **-szę -sisz** *zob.* **rozgłaszać.**

rozgłośnia *f. Gen.pl.* **-i** *radio* (= *stacja nadawcza*) broadcasting station; *pot.* (= *stacja radiowa, radio*) radio station.

rozgłośny *a. lit.* (*o śpiewie, echu*) resounding; (*o salwach*) loud.

rozgniatać *ipf.*, **rozgnieść** *pf.* **-gniotę -gnieciesz -gniótł -gniotła -gnietli** (*np. nogą*) crush; (*w moździerzu*) grind, pound; (*owoce*) squash; (*ziemniaki*) mash.

rozgniewać *pf.* make angry, anger (*kogoś*

czymś sb with sth). ~ **się** *pf.* get angry (*na kogoś/coś* with sb/sth).

rozgniewany *a.* angry (*na kogoś/coś* with sb/sth).

rozgonić *pf. zob.* **rozganiać.**

rozgorączkowany *a.* **1.** (= *trawiony gorączką*) feverish, hot. **2.** (= *podniecony, ożywiony*) feverish, frantic (*czymś* with sth).

rozgoryczać *ipf.* embitter, make bitter; **rozgoryczyła mnie jego postawa** I was embittered by his attitude. ~ **się** *ipf.* become embittered.

rozgoryczenie *n.* bitterness, embitterment; **ogarnęło go rozgoryczenie** he was overcome with bitterness.

rozgoryczony *a.* **-eni** embittered (*czymś* by sth).

rozgoryczyć *pf. zob.* **rozgoryczać.** ~ **się** *pf. zob.* **rozgoryczać się.**

rozgorzeć *pf.* **1.** (= *zapłonąć*) burst into flame, flare up; **emocje rozgorzały** emotions ran high; **rozgorzeć gniewem/miłością** be inflamed with rage/love. **2.** (= *wybuchnąć*) (*o walce, sporze*) flare up, break out.

rozgościć się *pf.* **-szczę -ścisz** make o.s. comfortable; **rozgościć się na dobre** be here to stay; **proszę się rozgościć!** make yourself at home!.

rozgotować *pf.*, **rozgotowywać** *ipf.* overcook; (*zwł. mięso*) overdo; **rozgotować coś na papkę** cook *l.* boil sth to a pulp. ~ **się** *pf.*, **rozgotowywać się** *ipf.* overcook; (*zwł. o mięsie*) be overdone.

rozgotowany *a.* overcooked; (*o mięsie*) overdone.

rozgrabiać *ipf.*, **rozgrabić** *pf.* **1.** (= *rozkradać*) steal away; (= *złupić*) (*np. miasto*) loot, pillage. **2.** (= *rozsuwać grabiami*) rake; (*na bok*) rake aside.

rozgradzać *ipf.* **1.** (= *rozbierać przegrodę*) remove railings, remove fence; **rozgrodzić ogród/park** remove the railings surrounding a garden/park. **2.** (= *rozdzielić*) divide, separate; **drzewa rozgradzały pole** trees ran across *l.* divided the field.

rozgramiać *ipf.*, **rozgromić** *pf.* rout.

rozgraniczać *ipf.* **1.** (= *wytyczać granicę*) mark the boundaries (*coś* of sth); demarcate (*coś* sth). **2.** (= *rozróżniać*) tell the difference (*między czymś a czymś* between sth and sth); separate (*między czymś a czymś* sth from sth). **3.** (= *przedzielać*) divide, separate.

rozgraniczenie *n.* boundary, border line; **dokonać rozgraniczenia między czymś a czymś** draw a line between sth and sth.

rozgraniczyć *pf. zob.* **rozgraniczać.**

rozgrodzić *pf. zob.* **rozgradzać.**

rozgromić *pf. zob.* **rozgramiać.**

rozgrymasić *pf.* spoil, pamper. ~ **się** *pf.* **-szę -sisz** (*o dziecku*) become fretful; (= *stać się wybrednym*) become fussy.

rozgrywać *ipf.* (= *prowadzić grę*) play; **rozgrywać bitwę** fight a battle; **rozgrywać partię szachów** play a game of chess; **dobrze coś rozegrać** *przen.* play one's cards well; **źle rozegrać sytuację** mishandle a situation. ~ **się** *ipf.* **1.** (= *dziać się*) take place, happen; **akcja rozgrywa się** the

action takes place, the scene is laid in; **bitwa rozegrała się w...** the battle was fought in... **2.** *pot.* (= *wpadać w zapał gry*) get into one's stride when playing, lose o.s. in playing.

rozgrywka *f. Gen.pl.* **-ek 1.** *sport* game; **rozgrywki wstępne** preliminaries; **rozgrywki finałowe** finals. **2.** (*taktyczne posunięcie*) game, tactics.

rozgryzać *ipf.* (= *gryząc rozdzielić*) bite in two; **rozgryzać pigułkę** crush a pill with one's teeth.

rozgryźć *pf.* **-gryzę -gryziesz -gryzł -gryźli 1.** *zob.* **rozgryzać. 2.** (= *poznać*) figure out; *Br. t.* suss out; **muszę to rozgryźć** I must get to the bottom of this; **nie mogę go rozgryźć** I can't figure him out.

rozgrzać *pf.* **-eję -ejesz** *zob.* **rozgrzewać.** ~ **się** *pf. zob.* **rozgrzewać się.**

rozgrzany *a.* **1.** (= *gorący*) hot; **rozgrzany do czerwoności/białości** red/white hot. **2.** *sport* warmed up.

rozgrzebać *pf.* **-bię -biesz**, **rozgrzebywać** *ipf.* **1.** (= *rozgarniać*) rake; (*ziemię*) dig up; *przen.* (*czyjąś przeszłość*) rake up; **rozgrzebywać brudne sprawki** dig the dirt. **2.** (= *wprowadzać nieład*) (*łóżko*) tumble. **3.** *pot.* (= *zaczynać i nie kończyć*) leave unfinished.

rozgrzeszać *ipf.* **1.** (= *darować winy*) absolve (*kogoś z czegoś* sb from sth); (= *wybaczyć*) forgive (*kogoś z czegoś* sb sth). **2.** *rz.-kat.* absolve (*kogoś z czegoś* sb from sth). ~ **się** *ipf.* (= *uwalniać się od skrupułów*) excuse o.s.

rozgrzeszenie *n. rz.-kat.* absolution; **udzielać (komuś) rozgrzeszenia** give *l.* grant (sb) absolution.

rozgrzeszyć *pf. zob.* **rozgrzeszać.** ~ **się** *pf. zob.* **rozgrzeszać się.**

rozgrzewać *ipf.* **1.** (= *ogrzewać*) heat up, warm up; (*piekarnik*) heat; (*o winie, gorącej herbacie*) warm up; (*nacierając np. maścią*) foment; **rozgrzać ręce przy grzejniku** warm one's hands on the radiator. **2.** (= *zachęcać do działania*) stimulate, encourage. ~ **się** *ipf.* **1.** (*o człowieku*) warm o.s. **2.** (= *stawać się cieplejszym*) (*o piecu, dachu*) heat up; (*o silniku*) warm up. **3.** (= *ożywiać się*) warm up, get heated. **4.** *sport* (*przed startem, meczem*) warm up.

rozgrzewka *f. Gen.pl.* **-ek 1.** (= *rozgrzanie się*) warming up; **przytupywać dla rozgrzewki** stamp one's feet to warm o.s. up; **wypić coś na rozgrzewkę** drink sth just to get warm. **2.** *sport* warm-up.

rozgwar *mi lit.* hubbub, uproar.

rozgwiazda *f. Dat. i Loc.* **-eździe** *zool.* starfish (*Asterias*).

rozgwieżdżony *a.* starlit, starry.

rozharatać *pf. pot.* (*ciało*) mangle; (= *rozerwać*) rip; (*ubranie*) rip, rend.

rozhartować *ipf.*, **rozhartowywać** *pf.* **1.** (= *pozbawiać stal itp. twardości*) unharden. **2.** (= *pozbawiać odporności*) make soft, unharden.

rozhermetyzować *pf.* depressurize, unseal.

rozhisteryzowany *a.* hysterical, frenzied.

rozhukany *a.* **1.** (= *rozbrykany*) (*o zwierzętach*) frisky; (*o dzieciach, uczniach*) frolicsom, frisky. **2.** (*o morzu*) stormy. **3.** (= *pędzący*) (*np. o koniach*) bolting.

rozhulać się *pf.* **1.** (= *rozbawić się*) let one's hair down, run riot. **2.** (*o wietrze, burzy*) rage.

rozhuśtać *pf.* rock, set swinging. **~ się** *pf.* swing, roll.

rozigrać się *pf.* (= *rozdokazywać się*) frolic.

rozindyczyć się *pf. pot.* flare up, fume (*na coś* over sth).

roziskrzać się *ipf.*, **roziskrzyć się** *pf.* (= *rozbłyskiwać*) sparkle; (*o ognisku, oczach, uczuciu*) kindle.

rozjarzać *ipf.*, **rozjarzyć** *pf.* light up, kindle. **~ się** *ipf.*, **rozjarzyć się** *pf.* (= *rozświetlać się*) shine, glow.

rozjaśniacz *mi Gen.* **-a** (*do włosów*) bleach, peroxide; **rozjaśniacz optyczny** *chem.* optical brightener, optical brightening agent.

rozjaśniać *ipf.*, **rozjaśnić** *pf.* **-ij 1.** (= *oświetlać*) illuminate, light up; **ogień rozjaśniał niebo** fire was lighting up the sky; **pochodnie rozjaśniają nocne niebo** the torches inflame the night. **2.** (= *uczynić jaśniejszym*) lighten, brighten; **rozjaśnić sobie włosy** bleach one's hair. **3.** (= *rozweselać*) jolly up, brighten; **kwiaty rozjaśnią to miejsce** flowers will brighten (up) this place; **uśmiech rozjaśnił mu twarz** a smile lit up his face. **4.** (= *wyjaśniać*) elucidate, clarify; **to mi rozjaśniło myśli** it clarified my mind; **rozjaśnić komuś w głowie** clear sb's head *l.* mind. **~ się** *ipf.*, **rozjaśnić się** *pf.* **1.** (= *stawać się jaśniejszym*) lighten, brighten up; **zaczyna się rozjaśniać** (*o porze dnia*) it's getting light, the day is dawning. **2.** (= *przejaśniać się*) (*o niebie*) clear up; **rozjaśnia się** it's clearing up. **3.** (= *rozpromieniać się*) brighten, light up; **twarz jej się rozjaśniła** her face lit up.

rozjazd *mi kol.* junction.

rozjazdy *pl. Gen.* **-ów** *pot.* (= *ciągłe wyjazdy*) tours, journeys; **być w rozjazdach** (= *podróżować*) be on the move; (= *być poza domem*) be out of town.

rozjazgotać się *pf.* **-oczę** *l.* **-ocę -oczesz** *l.* **-ocesz, -ocz** start yapping, start jabbering.

rozjątrzać *ipf.*, **rozjątrzyć** *pf.* **1.** (*ranę*) (= *podrażniać*) irritate; (= *powodować zapalenie*) cause inflammation; **rozjątrzać stare rany** *przen.* open old wounds. **2.** (= *wzbudzić gorycz*) embitter, fester (*kogoś* sb); (= *wzbudzić złość*) anger, irritate (*kogoś* sb). **~ się** *ipf.*, **rozjątrzyć się** *pf.* **1.** (*o ranie*) (= *zaogniać się*) inflame; (= *ropieć*) fester. **2.** (= *wpadać w gniew*) get irritated. **3.** (*o sporze*) (= *przybierać na sile*) exacerbate, aggravate.

rozjechać *pf.* **-jadę -jedziesz** (= *przejechać*) run over (*kogoś/coś* sb/sth). **~ się** *pf. zob.* **rozjeżdżać się.**

rozjemca *mp* (*sędzia*) arbitrator, arbiter; *polit.* peacemaker.

rozjemczy *a.* mediatory; **sąd rozjemczy** court of arbitration, arbitration court.

rozjeździć *pf.* **-jeżdżę -jeździsz** *zob.* **rozjeżdżać.**

rozjeżdżać *ipf.* **1.** (= *miażdżyć, jeżdżąc*) crush (*with wheels*). **2.** (= *robić koleiny*) make ruts. **~**

się *ipf.* **1.** (*o osobach*) (= *jechać w różne strony*) scatter away, travel away. **2.** (= *rozsuwać się*) (*o nartach, nogach itp.*) come apart.

rozjuszać *ipf.*, **rozjuszyć** *pf.* infuriate, enrage. **~ się** *ipf.*, **rozjuszyć się** *pf.* fly into a rage.

rozjuszony *a.* enraged, furious.

rozkaprysić *pf.* spoil, pamper. **~ się** *pf.* **-szę -sisz** (*o dziecku*) become fretful; (= *stać się wybrednym*) become fussy.

rozkapryszony *a.* **-eni** (= *wybredny*) fussy, choosy; (*o dziecku*) (= *rozpieszczony*) pampered; (= *zepsuty*) spoilt.

rozkasłać się, **rozkaszleć się** *pf.* **-lę -lesz, -l** *l.* **-laj, -lali** *l.* **-leli** (= *zacząć kaszlać*) start coughing; (= *dostać ataku kaszlu*) have a fit of coughing.

rozkaz *mi* **1.** (= *polecenie*) order; **rozkaz wymarszu** marching orders; **cofnąć rozkaz** revoke an order; **wydać rozkaz** give an order; **wykonać rozkaz** obey an order, carry out an order; **wykonywać czyjeś rozkazy** take orders from sb; **na czyjś rozkaz** *l.* **z czyjegoś rozkazu** by order of sb; **być na czyjeś rozkazy** be at sb's command; **być** *l.* **służyć pod czyimiś rozkazami** be under sb's command; **rozkaz to rozkaz** orders are orders, an order is an order; **twoje życzenie jest dla mnie rozkazem** your wish is my command; **rozkaz!** *wojsk.* (*do mężczyzny*) yes, Sir!; (*do kobiety*) yes, Ma-'am!; *żegl.* aye aye, Sir!. **2.** *komp.* instruction, command.

rozkazać *pf.* **-każę -każesz** *zob.* **rozkazywać.**

rozkazujący *a.* (*o tonie głosu*) imperative; **tryb rozkazujący** *gram.* imperative mood, the imperative.

rozkazywać *ipf.*, **rozkazać** *pf.* order; **rozkazać komuś, żeby coś zrobił** order sb to do sth; **rozkazywać komuś** (*niższemu rangą, będącemu niżej w hierarchii*) order sb about, pull rank on sb; **nikt mi nie będzie rozkazywał** I won't be dictated to.

rozkaźnik *mi Gen.* **-a** *jęz.* the imperative, imperative mood.

rozkaźnikowy *a. jęz.* imperative.

rozkiełznać 1. (*konia*) unbridle. **2.** (*wyobraźnię, emocje*) unbridle, unchain. **~ się** *pf.* (*o koniu*) unbridle; (*o wyobraźni, emocjach*) run wild.

rozkleić *pf.* **-kleję -kleisz, -klej, rozklejać** *ipf.* **1.** (= *rozlepić w wielu miejscach*) paste, put up; **rozkleić plakaty na ścianie** paste posters onto the wall. **2.** (= *oddzielić coś sklejonego*) unglue, unstick; **rozkleić kopertę nad parą** steam an envelope open. **~ się** *pf.*, **rozklejać się** *ipf.* **1.** (*na kawałki*) fall apart. **2.** (= *odkleić się*) (*od czegoś*) unglue, unstick. **3.** *pot.* (= *poddać się słabości, wzruszeniu*) go to pieces. **4.** (= *rozgotować się*) (*o kluskach, kaszy itp.*) boil to a pulp.

rozklekotany *a.* **1.** *pot.* (= *zniszczony*) (*o samochodzie*) clapped-out, cranky; (*o schodach, stole, krześle*) rickety. **2.** *pot.* (= *wyczerpany nerwowo*) unstable; **mieć rozklekotane nerwy** be an emotional wreck.

rozklepać *pf.*, **rozklepywać** *ipf.* hammer flat, flatten.

rozkloszowany *a.* bell-shaped; (*o spódnicy*) flaring.

rozkład *mi* **1.** (= *plan, porządek*) schedule, timetable; **rozkład jazdy** timetable, schedule; **rozkład zajęć** timetable; **mieć coś na rozkładzie** *przen.* have sth planned *l.* scheduled. **2.** (*mieszkania, miasta*) layout. **3.** (= *rozmieszczenie*) distribution, arrangement. **4.** *biol.* (= *gnicie*) decomposition, decay; **w rozkładzie** *l.* **w stanie rozkładu** in decay, decaying. **5.** (= *upadek, zniszczenie*) corruption; (*państwa*) collapse, disintegration; **rozkład małżeństwa** marriage breakdown, breakdown of marriage. **6.** *chem.* decomposition. **7.** (*na części składowe*) distribution; (*na czynniki*) *mat.* factoring; **rozkład prawdopodobieństwa** probability distribution. **8.** *myśl.* (= *pokot*) display of the trophies of a hunting expedition; kill.

rozkładać *ipf.* **1.** (= *rozpościerać*) spread, lay out; (*obrus, koc, palce*) spread; (*łóżko, gazetę*) unfold; (*parasol*) unfold, open; (*antenę, drabinę*) extend; (*ramiona*) spread out, stretch out; (*nogi*) sprawl, splay; **rozkładać obóz** make camp, camp down. **2.** (= *rozmieszczać*) lay out; **rozkładać pasjansa** play solitaire; *Br.* play patience. **3.** (= *rozdzielać, rozplanowywać*) (*pracę, obowiązki, siły, koszty*) distribute, divide; **rozkładać koszty na kilka osób** divide *l.* distribute the expenses among a number of people; **rozkładać płatność na raty** arrange instalments for a payment. **4.** (= *demontować, rozbierać na części*) take apart, take to pieces. **5.** (= *dokonywać analizy*) break down; *mat.* (*wektor*) resolve; *chem.* (*ropę na frakcje*) crack; **rozkładać na czynniki** factorize, factor; **rozkładać na czynniki pierwsze** (*teorię, wiersz*) dissect. **6.** *biol.* (= *powodować gnicie*) decompose, rot. **7.** *pot.* (= *działać niszcząco*) corrupt; **rozłożyła ją grypa** she came down with flu. **8.** *pot.* (= *powodować fiasko czegoś*) blow it, botch it. **9.** *pot.* (= *walcząc, przewracać kogoś*) knock down; **rozłożyć kogoś na łopatki** *dosł., przen.* floor sb. ~ **się** *ipf.* **1.** (= *kłaść się*) (*na kanapie, trawniku, w fotelu*) sprawl, lie down (*w/na czymś* in/on sth). **2.** (= *rozlokowywać się*) encamp; **rozkładać się obozem** make camp, camp down; **rozkładać się z towarem** spread one's wares. **3.** (= *rozpościerać się*) spread, extend. **4.** *biol.* (= *gnić*) decompose; decay, rot. **5.** (= *dzielić się na składniki*) *chem.* decompose. **6.** *pot.* (= *doznawać niepowodzenia*) fail, flunk; **rozłożył się na egzaminie** he failed *l.* flunked the exam.

rozkładany *a.* expandable; **stół rozkładany** drop-leaf table; **kanapa rozkładana** *l.* **łóżko rozkładane** sofa bed.

rozkładowy *a.* **1.** *biol.* decomposition, putrefactive. **2.** *chem.* decomposition; **destylacja rozkładowa** destructive distillation.

rozkładówka *f. Gen.pl.* **-ek** *druk.* centerfold; *Br.* centre spread.

rozkochać *pf. zob.* **rozkochiwać**.

rozkochany *a.* **1.** (= *kochający*) in love (*w kimś/czymś* with sb/sth); **rozkochany w sobie** self-loving, in love with o.s.; **osoba rozkochana w teatrze** lover of theater, theater enthusiast. **2.** (= *wyrażający miłość*) loving, full of love.

rozkochiwać *ipf.* enamor; *Br.* enamour; (*kogoś*

sb) inspire with love. ~ **się** *ipf.* **1.** fall in love (*w kimś/czymś* with sb/sth); **rozkochać się w kimś bez pamięci** fall for sb head over heels. **2.** (= *bardzo coś polubić*) develop a passion (*w czymś* for sth).

rozkodować *pf.*, **rozkodowywać** *ipf.* decode, uncode.

rozkojarzenie *n.* absent-mindedness, lack of concentration; (*zaburzenie toku myślenia*) incoherence.

rozkojarzony *a.* **-eni** absent-minded, distracted; (= *zaburzony*) incoherent.

rozkolportować *pf.* distribute, circulate; (*ulotki*) (= *rozdawać*) pass round, hand out.

rozkołysać *pf.* **-yszę -yszesz** set swinging, set rocking; **wiatr rozkołysał drzewa** wind tossed the trees. ~ **się** *pf.* rock, swing; (*o zbożu na wietrze*) wave; (*o morzu*) roll.

rozkołysany *a.* swinging, rocking; (*o tłumie, morzu*) surging.

rozkop *mi* excavation.

rozkopać *pf.* **-pię -piesz, rozkopywać** *ipf.* **1.** (= *robić dół*) (*ogród, ulicę*) dig up. **2.** (= *rozrzucać, uderzając nogami*) kick off; **rozkopać pościel** tumble the bedclothes. ~ **się** *pf.* tumble one's bedclothes, kick off one's bedclothes.

rozkorzeniać się *ipf.*, **rozkorzenić się** *pf.* (*o drzewie, krzewie*) take root, root.

rozkosz *f.* **1.** (= *przyjemność*) delight, bliss; **z rozkoszą** with delight, with pleasure; **doznawać rozkoszy** experience delight; **jęczeć z rozkoszy** moan in ecstasy; **znajdować w czymś rozkosz** indulge *l.* delight in sth; **zrobiłbym to z rozkoszą** I'd do it with atmost pleasure, I'd be more than happy to do it; **zemsta jest rozkoszą bogów** the best revenge is revenge. **2.** (= *to, co przyjemne*) delight; **rozkosz dla oka** a sight for sore eyes; **rozkosze miłości/stołu** the delights of love/the table; **to była rozkosz dla ucha/podniebienia** the music/food was a real treat.

rozkosznie *adv.* delightfully, delectably.

rozkoszny *a.* delightful, delectable.

rozkoszować się *ipf.* delight, take delight; revel (*czymś* in sth); **rozkoszować się myślą** relish the thought; **rozkoszować się pięknym widokiem** feast one's eyes on a beautiful view.

rozkraczać się *ipf.*, **rozkraczyć się** *pf.* **1.** *pot.* (= *rozsuwać nogi*) straddle. **2.** *pot.* (*o pojeździe*) (= *psuć się*) conk out, go kaput.

rozkradać *ipf.*, **rozkraść** *pf.* **-kradnę -kradniesz, -kradnij, -kradł** steal away.

rozkrawać *ipf. zob.* **rozkroić**.

rozkręcać *ipf.*, **rozkręcić** *pf.* **1.** (= *rozprostowywać*) untwist, unwind; (*nici*) unreel; **rozkręcić włosy** put the *l.* one's hair out of curl. **2.** (= *demontować*) (*mechanizm*) take to pieces; (*części mechanizmu*) unscrew. **3.** *pot.* (= *uaktywniać*) get moving; **rozkręcić sprawę** set the wheels in motion; **rozkręcić interes** start up a business, set up in a business. ~ **się** *ipf.*, **rozkręcić się** *pf.* **1.** (= *rozprostowywać się*) untwist, unwind; (*o szpulce*) unreel; (*o włosach*) go out of curl. **2.** *pot.* (= *robić coś z większą energią*) become animated. **3.** *pot.* (= *rozwijać się*) (*o zabawie, ryn-*

ku, produkcji) pick up steam; (*o interesie*) get going, start running at a profit; **zabawa rozkręciła się na dobre** the party was in full swing.

rozkrochmalić się *pf. pot.* thaw, come out of one's shell.

rozkroić *pf.* **-kroję -kroisz, -krój** (*na kawałki*) cut; (*na kromki, plasterki*) slice; **rozkroić na pół** cut in two.

rozkrok *mi* straddle; **stanąć w rozkroku** straddle, stand astride.

rozkruszać *ipf.*, **rozkruszyć** *pf.* (*chleb, skałę*) crumble; **rozkruszyć coś w drobny mak** crush sth to pieces.

rozkrwawiać *ipf.*, **rozkrwawić** *pf.* make bleed; **rozkrwawić komuś wargę/nos** make sb's lip/nose bleed.

rozkrzewiać *ipf.*, **rozkrzewić** *pf.* **1.** (= *propagować*) propagate, diffuse. **2.** *ogr.* (*rośliny*) layer. **~ się** *ipf.*, **rozkrzewić się** *pf.* **1.** (= *upowszechniać się*) propagate. **2.** (*o roślinach*) (= *rozrastać się*) develop, propagate.

rozkrzyczany *a.* (= *krzyczący*) shouting; (= *głośny*) noisy.

rozkrzyżować *pf.*, **rozkrzyżowywać** *ipf.* spread out.

rozkuć *pf.* **-kuję -kujesz** *zob.* **rozkuwać**.

rozkudłany *a.* (= *rozczochrany*) dishevelled, unkempt.

rozkulbaczać *ipf.*, **rozkulbaczyć** *pf.* unsaddle.

rozkupić *pf.* buy up.

rozkurcz *mi Gen.pl.* **-ów** *fizj.* relaxation; (*serca*) diastole.

rozkurczać *ipf.* (*mięśnie*) loosen; (*pięści*) unclench.

rozkurczowy *a. med.* diastolic; **lek** *l.* **środek rozkurczowy** relaxant.

rozkurczyć *pf. zob.* **rozkurczać**.

rozkurz *mi* **iść na rozkurz** *pot.* get wasted.

rozkuwać *ipf.* **1.** (= *rozbijać coś skutego*) unchain, unshackle; **rozkuć konia** unshoe a horse. **2.** (= *rozpłaszczać, kując*) hammer flat. **~ się** *ipf.* unchain one another, unshackle one another.

rozkwasić *pf.* **-szę -sisz** *pot.* (= *zranić*) smash; **rozkwasić komuś nos** smash sb's nose; **rozkwasić kogoś na kwaśne jabłko** smash sb's face in.

rozkwaterować *pf.*, **rozkwaterowywać** *ipf.* **1.** (= *rozlokowywać*) quarter, billet. **2.** (= *rozdzielać osoby mieszkające razem*) quarter separately. **~ się** *pf.*, **rozkwaterowywać się** *ipf.* (= *zająć mieszkanie*) settle down; (= *rozgościć się*) make o.s. at home.

rozkwiecony *a.* (= *kwitnący*) blooming; abloom.

rozkwilić się *pf.* **1.** (*o dzieciach*) (= *zacząć płakać*) start whimpering. **2.** (*o ptakach*) (= *zacząć ćwierkać*) start twittering.

rozkwit *mi* **1.** *bot.* (= *kwitnienie roślin*) flowering; bloom, blossom; **w rozkwicie** in bloom, in blossom. **2.** (= *rozwój*) *ekon.* heyday, prime; **w pełni rozkwitu** in its (his, her, etc.) prime.

rozkwitać *ipf.*, **rozkwitnąć** *pf.* **-tnij, -tł** *l.* **-tnął -tła 1.** (= *zakwitać*) bloom, blossom. **2.** (= *rozwijać się*) flourish, bloom. **3.** (= *stawać się widocz-*

nym) appear; (*o uśmiechu*) beam; (*o rumieńcu*) blush.

rozlać *pf.* **-leję -lejesz -lali** *l.* **-leli** *zob.* **rozlewać**. **~ się** *pf. zob.* **rozlewać się**.

rozlany *a.* **1.** (*o płynie*) spilt. **2.** (= *nieostry*) fuzzy, blurred. **3.** (= *nalany*) fat, obese.

rozlatany *a.* (= *rozdygotany*) shaky.

rozlatywać się *ipf.* **1.** (*o ptakach*) (= *lecieć w różne strony*) fly away (*in different directions*), scatter. **2.** (*o ludziach, zwierzętach*) (= *rozbiegać się*) scatter, disperse. **3.** (= *rozpadać się*) fall apart; (*o książce, dzbanku*) fall into pieces; (*o zespole*) fall apart.

rozlazły *a.* **1.** (= *miękki*) flabby, flaccid. **2.** *pot.* (= *niemrawy*) sluggish, slack.

rozlecieć się *ipf.* **-lecę -lecisz, -leć** *zob.* **rozlatywać się**.

rozlec się *pf.* **-legnę -legniesz, -legnij, -legł** *zob.* **rozlegać się**.

rozlegać się *ipf.* ring out, reverberate; **rozległo się pukanie do drzwi** there was a knock on *l.* at the door.

rozlegle *a.* **1.** (= *szeroko*) widely, broadly. **2.** (= *w dużym zakresie*) extensively.

rozległość *f.* **1.** (= *przestrzeń*) expanse; (= *obszar*) area. **2.** (= *zakres*) extent, range, scope.

rozległy *a.* **1.** (= *obszerny*) wide, broad, extensive. **2.** (= *mający szeroki zakres*) extensive.

rozleniwiać *ipf.*, **rozleniwić** *pf.* make lazy. **~ się** *ipf.*, **rozleniwić się** *pf.* become lazy.

rozlepiać *ipf.* **1.** (= *nalepiać w wielu miejscach*) post. **2.** (= *rozłączać coś sklejonego*) unstick.

rozlew *mi techn.* **1.** bottling; **rozlew krwi** bloodshed. **2.** *rzad.* flood waters.

rozlewać *ipf.* **1.** (= *powodować rozlanie cieczy*) spill. **2.** (= *wlewać do wielu naczyń*) pour; (*np. wino do butelek*) bottle; **rozlać wszystkim po kieliszku** pour everybody a drink. **3.** (*o wodzie*) (= *występować z brzegów*) overflow. **~ się** *ipf.* **1.** (*o cieczach*) (= *rozpływać się*) spill. **2.** (*o rzekach*) (= *występować z brzegów*) overflow, burst banks.

rozlewisko *n.* flood waters.

rozlewnia *f. Gen.pl.* **-i** *techn.* bottling plant.

rozlewny *a.* **1.** (= *rozpływający się*) broad, extensive. **2.** (= *powolny*) slow.

rozleźć się *pf.* **-lezę -leziesz, -leź, -lazł -leźli** *zob.* **rozłazić się**.

rozliczać *ipf.* balance, clear; **rozliczać kogoś** clear accounts with sb; **rozliczać coś** present an account of sth; **rozliczać z czegoś** account for sth. **~ się** *ipf.* settle, square up (*z kimś* with sb); account (*z czegoś* for sth).

rozliczenie *n.* settlement.

rozliczeniowy *a.* (= *dotyczący rozliczeń*) accounting; clearing; **rachunek oszczędnościowo-rozliczeniowy** checking account.

rozliczny *a. lit.* (= *wieloraki*) manifold, multifarious; (= *liczny*) numerous.

rozliczyć *pf. zob.* **rozliczać**. **~ się** *pf. zob.* **rozliczać się**.

rozlokować *pf.* (*osoby*) quarter; (*rzeczy*) place, put. **~ się** *pf.* settle.

rozlosować *pf.*, **rozlosowywać** *ipf.* distribute by lot (*usually prizes*).

rozluźniać *ipf.*, **rozluźnić** *pf.* **1.** (= *czynić luźniejszym*) loosen. **2.** (= *łagodzić*) relax. **3.** (*mięśnie*) relax. ~ **się** *ipf.*, **rozluźnić się** *pf.* **1.** (= *stawać się luźnym*) loosen. **2.** (*o atmosferze*) become relaxed. **3.** (= *odprężać się psychicznie*) relax, loosen up.

rozładować *pf.*, **rozładowywać** *ipf.* **1.** (*pojemnik, pojazd*) unload; **rozładować broń** unload a firearm. **2.** *fiz.* discharge; **rozładować akumulator** discharge a battery. **3.** (= *łagodzić*) relieve; **rozładować napięcie** relieve the tension. ~ **się** *pf.*, **rozładowywać się** *ipf.* **1.** *fiz.* discharge; **akumulator się rozładował** the battery went dead. **2.** *przen.* be defused; **napięcie szybko się rozładowało** the tension was defused quickly.

rozładunek *mi* -nk- unloading.

rozładunkowy *a.* unloading.

rozłam *mi* (= *podział*) split; (= *nieporozumienie*) dissension.

rozłamać *pf.* -łamię -łamiesz *zob.* **rozłamywać**.

rozłamowy *a.* dissenting, dissentient.

rozłamywać *ipf.* break; (*na pół*) split.

rozłazić się *ipf.* -łażę -łazisz **1.** *pot.* (= *rozchodzić się*) disperse, spread; (*o owadach*) crawl in various directions. **2.** *pot.* (= *rozpadać się*) fall apart; **rozłazić się w szwach** burst at the seams, gape at the seams.

rozłączać *ipf.* (= *oddzielać*) (*kable, elementy*) disconnect, disjoin; (*kable, sprzęt*) disengage; (*rozmowę telefoniczną*) disconnect, cut off; (*bijących się, rodzeństwo, kochanków*) separate. ~ **się** *ipf.* (= *oddzielać się*) (*o kablach, elementach*) disconnect, disjoin; (*o kablach, sprzęcie*) disengage; (*o rozmowie telefonicznej*) disconnect, be cut off; (*o bijących się, rodzeństwie, kochankach*) separate; **proszę się nie rozłączać!** please don't hang up!, please hold on!

rozłączenie *n.* **1.** (*rozmowy*) disconnection; (*kabli, elementów*) disjoining, disconnection. **2.** (= *rozłąka*) separation.

rozłącznie *adv.* separately.

rozłączny *a.* (= *oddzielny*) separate; disjunctive; *mat.* disjoint.

rozłączyć *pf. zob.* **rozłączać**. ~ **się** *pf. zob.* **rozłączać się**.

rozłąka *f.* separation.

rozłogowy *a. bot.* stoloniferous.

rozłożyć *pf.* -łożę -łożysz, -łóż *zob.* **rozkładać**.

rozłożysty *a.* (= *obszerny*) extensive; (= *rozległy*) vast; (*o drzewach*) branching, patulous.

rozłożyście *adv.* (= *rozległe*) vastly.

rozłóg *mi* -o- **1.** *poet.* (= *otwarta przestrzeń*) expanse. **2.** *bot.* stolon, runner.

rozłupać *pf.* -pię -piesz, **rozłupywać** *ipf.* (= *roztłuc*) (*np. orzechy, skałę*) crack; (= *rozdzielić, rozłamać*) (*np. gałąź*) split.

rozmach *mi* **1.** (= *impet*) force, momentum, impetus; **brać rozmach** take a swing. **2.** (= *dynamika, śmiałość*) momentum; **nabierać rozmachu** gather momentum; (**robić coś**) **z rozmachem** (do sth) with a flourish.

rozmaczać *ipf.* (= *nasączyć*) soak, sodden; (= *zamoczyć*) steep. ~ **się** *ipf.* soak, sodden.

rozmagnesować *pf.*, **rozmagnesowywać** *ipf. techn.* demagnetize, degauss. ~ **się** *pf.*, **rozmagnesowywać się** *ipf. techn.* become demagnetized, demagnetize; be degaussed.

rozmaicie *adv.* variously, in various *l.* different ways; **rozmaicie** *l.* **różnie (to) bywa** you never know (what you're gonna get); you can never tell.

rozmaitość *f.* **1.** (= *różnorodność*) variety. **2.** (= *odmiana, urozmaicenie*) change. **3.** (= *różności*) miscellany.

rozmaity *a.* (= *różny*) various, different; (= *zróżnicowany*) varied, diverse; (= *różnoraki*) miscellaneous; (= *różnorodny*) multiform; **rozmaite rzeczy** all sorts of things.

rozmakać *ipf.* get *l.* become soaked, get *l.* become sodden.

rozmamłany *a. pot.* (= *niechlujny*) unkempt, disheveled; (= *powolny, bez wyrazu*) sluggish, slothful.

rozmaryn *mi bot.* rosemary (*Rosmarinus officinalis*).

rozmarynowy *a.* rosemary.

rozmarzać *ipf.*, **rozmarznąć** *pf.* -marznij, -marzł thaw.

rozmarzać *ipf.*, **rozmarzyć** *pf.* make dreamy, put into a dreamy mood; *poet.* put into a reverie. ~ **się** *ipf.*, **rozmarzyć się** *pf.* fall into a reverie.

rozmarzenie *n.* reverie, dreaminess.

rozmasować *pf.* massage.

rozmawiać *ipf.* talk, speak, converse (*z kimś* with sb, *o czymś* about sth); **rozmawiać przez telefon** be *l.* talk on the phone; **nie rozmawiać ze sobą** (= *gniewać się na siebie*) not be on speaking terms; **rozmawiać z kimś na migi** speak to sb in sign language; **rozmawiać jak gęś z prosięciem** talk at cross-purposes.

rozmaz *mi med.* smear.

rozmazać *pf.* -mażę -mażesz, **rozmazywać** *ipf.* smear, smudge; (*obraz, pojęcie itp.*) blur. ~ **się** *pf.*, **rozmazywać się** *ipf.* **1.** (= *stawać się rozmazanym*) smudge. **2.** (= *tracić ostrość*) become blurred. **3.** *pot.* (= *rozpłakać się*) break into tears.

rozmiar *mi* **1.** (= *wielkość*) size, dimensions; **jaki rozmiar pan nosi?** what is your size?. **2.** (= *zakres*) extent, scope, range; **powódź nabrała rozmiarów klęski** the flood assumed disaster proportions.

rozmieniać *ipf.*, **rozmienić** *pf.* change, break; **czy możesz mi rozmienić sto złotych?** can you break a 100 zloty bill for me?. ~ **się** *ipf.*, **rozmienić się** *pf.* **rozmieniać się na drobne** focus on many unimportant things.

rozmieszać *pf.* mix, stir.

rozmieszczać *ipf.* (= *umieścić*) put, place; (*na miejscach siedzących*) seat; (= *ulokować*) locate, situate; (= *ustawić w określonej pozycji*) (*np. mebel*) position; *zwł. wojsk.* (*np. oddziały*) deploy.

rozmieszczenie *n.* (= *umieszczenie*) placement; (= *położenie*) location, position; (*np. oddziałów*) deployment; **rozmieszczenie rakiet bali-**

stycznych *wojsk.* deployment of ballistic missiles.

rozmieścić *pf.* **-mieszczę -mieścisz** *zob.* **rozmieszczać.**

rozmiękać *ipf.* (= *stać się miękkim*) soften; (= *przesiąknąć wilgocią*) get *l.* become soaked, get *l.* become sodden; sop.

rozmiękanie *n.* (*zmięknięcie*) softening; (*nasiąknięcie*) becoming soaked *l.* drenched; **rozmiękanie mózgu** *pat.* encephalomalacia.

rozmiękczać *ipf.*, **rozmiękczyć** *pf.* (= *czynić miękkim*) (= *roztkliwiać*) soften; **rozmiękczyć czyjeś serce** soften sb's heart.

rozmięknąć *pf.* **-knij, -kł** *l.* **-knął -kła -kli** *zob.* **rozmiękać.**

rozmigotać się *pf.* **-oczę -oczesz** *l.* **-ocę -ocesz, -ocz** start to flicker *l.* flickering; start to glimmer *l.* glimmering.

rozmijać się *ipf.* 1. (= *mijać się*) pass; **rozmijać się z prawdą** deviate from the truth; **rozmijać się z rzeczywistością** be different from reality; **teoria rozmija się z praktyką** theory differs from practice. 2. (= *nie spotykać się*) miss (*z kimś* sb).

rozmiłować *pf.*, **rozmiłowywać** *ipf. lit.* win affection *l.* love; inspire love *l.* fondness. ~ **się** *pf. lit.* 1. (= *stać się miłośnikiem*) become a great *l.* ardent lover (*w kimś/czymś* of sb/sth). 2. (= *zakochać się*) fall deeply in love (*w kimś* with sb).

rozmiłowany *a.* **być rozmiłowanym w czymś** be an ardent lover of sth; **być rozmiłowanym w kimś** be deeply in love with sb.

rozminąć się *pf. zob.* **rozmijać się.**

rozminować *pf.*, **rozminowywać** *ipf. zwł. wojsk.* clear of mines, sweep of mines.

rozmnażać *ipf.* 1. *biol.* reproduce, propagate; *pot.* breed. 2. (= *powiększać*) increase, multiply. ~ **się** *ipf.* 1. *biol.* reproduce, propagate; breed. 2. (= *zwiększać się liczebnie*) increase, multiply.

rozmnażanie *n.* 1. *biol.* reproduction, propagation; **rozmnażanie bezpłciowe** asexual reproduction; **rozmnażanie płciowe** sexual reproduction; **rozmnażanie przez pączkowanie** gemmation. 2. (= *powiększanie*) increase, multiplication.

rozmnożyć (się) *pf.* **-mnóż** *zob.* **rozmnażać (się).**

rozmoczyć *pf. zob.* **rozmaczać.**

rozmodlenie, rozmodlenie się *n.* ecstasy of prayer.

rozmodlić się *pf.* **-módl** become engrossed in prayer.

rozmodlony *a.* **-eni** engrossed in prayer.

rozmokły *a.* soaked, sodden, soggy.

rozmoknąć *pf.* **-mókł** *l.* **-moknął -mokła** *zob.* **rozmakać.**

rozmontować *pf.*, **rozmontowywać** *ipf.* disassemble, dismantle; (*na części*) take apart.

rozmotać *pf.*, **rozmotywać** *ipf.* 1. (= *rozplątywać*) unravel; disentangle, unentangle. 2. (= *odwijać*) unreel.

rozmowa *f. Gen.pl.* **-ów** conversation, talk; **rozmowa telefoniczna** phone call; **rozmowa międzymiastowa** long distance call; **rozmowa kwalifikacyjna** interview; **rozmowy** (= *negocjacje*) talks, negotiations; **prowadzić rozmowy** conduct *l.* hold negotiations *l.* talks; **przeprowadzić** *l.* **odbyć z kimś zasadniczą rozmowę** have a serious conversation *l.* talk with sb; **wdać się z kimś w rozmowę** strike up a conversation with sb.

rozmowny *a.* talkative.

rozmówca *mp*, **rozmówczyni** *f.* interlocutor.

rozmówić się *pf.* 1. (= *porozumieć się*) communicate (*z kimś* with sb); make o.s. understood. 2. (= *omówić*) have a word (*z kimś* with sb).

rozmówki *pl. Gen.* **-wek** phrase book; **rozmówki polsko-angielskie** Polish-English phrase book.

rozmównica *f.* 1. (= *pokój do rozmawiania*) parlor, *Br.* parlour; *rzad.* locutory, locutorium. 2. (= *kabina telefoniczna*) telephone booth.

rozmrażać *ipf.* defrost. ~ **się** *ipf.* defrost.

rozmrażalnia *f. Gen.pl.* **-i** *techn.* defrosting room.

rozmrozić *pf.* **-mrożę -mrozisz, -mróź** *l.* **-mroź** *zob.* **rozmrażać.** ~ **się** *pf. zob.* **rozmrażać się.**

rozmyć *pf.* **-myję -myjesz, -myj** *zob.* **rozmywać.** ~ **się** *pf. zob.* **rozmywać się.**

rozmydlać *ipf.*, **rozmydlić** *pf.* blur. ~ **się** *ipf.*, **rozmydlić się** *pf.* 1. (= *rozpuścić się w wodzie*) (*o mydle*) suds. 2. (= *rozmyć się*) blur.

rozmysł *mi* consideration; **z rozmysłem** with intent, intentionally.

rozmyślać *ipf.* meditate, ponder, cogitate (*o kimś/czymś* *l.* *nad kimś/czymś* on sb/sth).

rozmyślanie *n.* meditating, pondering; **rozmyślania** meditations.

rozmyślić się *pf.* change one's mind.

rozmyślnie *adv.* on purpose, deliberately.

rozmyślny *a.* deliberate, intentional.

rozmywać *ipf.* **-am -asz** 1. (= *rozpuścić, wypłukać*) (*o deszczu, powodzi*) wash out. 2. (*dźwięk, obraz*) blur. ~ **się** *ipf.* 1. (= *zostać rozmytym, wypłukanym*) (*przez deszcz, powódź*) be washed out. 2. (*o dźwięku, obrazie*) blur.

roznamiętniać *ipf.*, **roznamiętnić** *pf.* **-ij** impassion, inflame; **twoja piżamka w owieczki strasznie mnie roznamiętnia** your sheep-patterned pajamas really turns me on.

roznegliżować się *pf.* take off one's outer garments, undress.

roznegliżowany *a.* in a state of undress.

rozniecać *ipf.*, **rozniecić** *pf.* 1. (= *rozpalać*) start, kindle. 2. (= *wywoływać*) start, stir up; **rozniecić ciekawość** arouse *l.* excite *l.* whet curiosity; **rozniecić strajk** stage a strike; **rozniecić wojnę** start a war.

roznieść *pf.* **-niosę -niesiesz -niósł -niosła -nieśli** *zob.* **roznosić.** ~ **się** *pf. zob.* **roznosić się.**

roznosiciel *mp*, **roznosicielka** *f. Gen.pl.* **-ek** (*towarów, poczty*) deliverer; (*choroby*) carrier.

roznosić *ipf.* **-noszę -nosisz** 1. (= *nosić w różne miejsca*) deliver, distribute; **roznosić listy** deliver mail; **roznosić choroby** spread *l.* carry diseases. 2. (= *niszczyć*) (*budynek*) destroy; (*armię*) rout. 3. (= *rozpowszechniać*) spread; **roznosić plotki** spread gossip; **roznosić wiadomości** spread (the) news; **roznieść kogoś na językach** run sb down. 4. (= *przepełniać*) be full of, be bursting with; **roznosiła go duma** he was bursting with pride; **roznosiła go radość** he was overjoyed; **ale go roznosi!** *pot.* jeez, he's excited!. ~ **się** *ipf.* (*o dźwiękach, zapachach*) (= *rozchodzić się*) (*o wiadomościach*) (= *rozprzestrzeniać się*) spread.

rozochocić się *pf.* liven up, become animated *l.* lively.

rozochocony *a.* -eni animated, livened up.

rozogniać *ipf.*, **rozognić** *pf.* -ij 1. (= *rozżarzać*) heat (up); **rozognić ranę** make a wound fester. 2. (= *roznamiętniać*) heat, inflame, rouse.

rozogniony *a.* (= *w gorączce*) feverish; (= *podniecony*) excited, roused.

rozorać *pf.*, **rozorywać** *ipf.* 1. (= *przygotowywać ziemię, orząc*) plow; *Br.* plough. 2. (= *ryć, rozdrapywać*) plow up; *Br.* plough up; (= *dotkliwie zranić*) slash.

rozpacz *f.* despair; **czarna rozpacz** total *l.* utter despair; **obraz nędzy i rozpaczy** picture of despair; **doprowadzać kogoś do rozpaczy** drive sb to despair; **wpaść w rozpacz** fall *l.* sink into despair; **zrobić coś w przystępie rozpaczy** do sth out of despair.

rozpaczać *ipf.* (= *być w rozpaczy*) despair (*nad czymś* over sth); (= *opłakiwać*) mourn (*po kimś* sb).

rozpaczliwie *adv.* 1. (= *desperacko*) desperately, despairingly. 2. (= *strasznie*) terribly, awfully. 3. (= *bardzo*) hopelessly, totally.

rozpaczliwy *a.* 1. (= *desperacki*) desperate, despairing. 2. (= *zły, beznadziejny*) hopeless. 3. (= *straszny, okropny*) (*nieład, bałagan*) hopeless, total.

rozpaćkać *pf.* (*np. ziemniaki na talerzu*) pulp; (*np. farbę na ścianie*) smear, smudge.

rozpad *mi* 1. (= *rozkład*) disintegration, breakup; (= *upadek*) fall, collapse; **rozpad imperium** fall *l.* collapse of an empire; **rozpad małżeństwa** breakup of a marriage. 2. (= *gnicie*) decay. 3. *chem.*, *fiz.* disintegration, decay; **rozpad promieniotwórczy** radioactive disintegration *l.* decay; **okres połowicznego rozpadu** half-life.

rozpadać się[1] *ipf.* 1. (= *dzielić się na części*) disintegrate, fall (apart); (= *zawalić się*) collapse; (= *rozlecieć się*) break up; **ten budynek się rozpada** this building is falling apart, this building is on the verge of collapsing; **Związek Radziecki rozpadł się już jakiś czas temu** the Soviet Union collapsed some time ago. 2. *chem.*, *fiz.* disintegrate, decay.

rozpadać się[2] *pf.* (= *zacząć padać ciągle*) start raining for good.

rozpadlina *f.* cleft, crevice; (*w skale*) fissure; (*w lodowcu*) crevasse.

rozpadowy *a.* disintegration, decay.

rozpakować *pf.*, **rozpakowywać** *ipf.* 1. unpack. 2. *komp.* decompress, unzip. ~ **się** *pf.*, **rozpakowywać się** *ipf.* unpack.

rozpalać *ipf.*, **rozpalić** *pf.* 1. (= *rozniecać ogień*) start, kindle, light; **rozpalić ognisko** make *l.* build a fire; **rozpalić w piecu** light the stove. 2. (= *podsycać*) kindle, stir up; **rozpalać nadzieję** inspire *l.* stir up hope. 3. (= *rozżarzać*) heat up. 4.

(= *ożywiać*) excite, stir up; **rozpalać czyjąś wyobraźnię** fire sb's imagination. 5. (= *podniecić*) heat up, turn on. ~ **się** *ipf.*, **rozpalić się** *pf.* 1. (= *zapalać się*) start burning, catch (on) fire. 2. (= *wzmagać się*) flare up, flare out. 3. (= *rozżarzać się*) heat up. 4. (= *ożywiać się*) become excited, liven up; **dyskusja się rozpaliła** discussion became heated.

rozpalony *a.* -eni 1. (= *w gorączce*) feverish. 2. (= *gorący*) hot. 3. (= *rozżarzony*) red-hot. 4. (= *podniecony*) heated up, turned on.

rozpałka *f.* kindling; **drewno na rozpałkę** kindling (wood), lightwood.

rozpamiętywać *ipf.* brood (*coś* on *l.* over sth).

rozpanoszyć się *pf.* 1. (= *rządzić się*) throw about one's weight, be rampant. 2. (= *rozplenić się*) be rampant, proliferate.

rozpaplać *pf.* -lę -lesz *l.* -lam -lasz *pot.* babble (*sth*) out.

rozpaprać *pf.* -przę -przesz, -prz 1. (= *zrobić nieporządek*) mess up. 2. *pot.* (= *zacząć coś i nie skończyć*) leave (*a job*) unfinished.

rozparcelować *pf.*, **rozparcelowywać** *ipf.* parcel out.

rozpasanie *n.* debauchery, intemperance.

rozpasany *a.* (*o osobie*) debauched; (*o pysze*) unbridled.

rozpaść się[1] *pf.* -padnę -padniesz, -padnij, -padł *zob.* **rozpadać się**[1].

rozpaść się[2] *pf.* -pasę -pasiesz -pasł -paśli *pot.* (= *utyć*) become fat.

rozpatrywać *ipf.*, **rozpatrzyć** *pf.* (= *rozważyć*) consider; (= *zbadać*) examine, investigate; (= *przyjrzeć się*) look (*coś* into sth); **rozpatrywać podanie** examine an application; **rozpatrywać ponownie** reconsider; **rozpatrzeć negatywnie** (*np. podanie, wniosek*) turn down.

rozpełznąć się *pf.* -pełznę -pełzniesz *l.* -pełźniesz, -pełznij *l.* -pełźnij, -pełznął *l.* -pełzł -pełzła -pełzli *l.* -pełźli 1. (= *rozleźć się, pełznąc*) crawl in various directions; (*o ludziach*) disperse. 2. (= *rozpłynąć się*) disperse.

rozpęcznieć *pf.* (= *napęcznieć, nabrzmieć*) swell; (= *powiększyć się*) expand.

rozpęd *mi* momentum, impetus; **nabierać rozpędu** gather momentum; **wziąć rozpęd** take a running start, gather momentum; **zrobić coś z rozpędu** do sth because sb is on a roll.

rozpędowy *a.* accelerative.

rozpędzać *ipf.*, **rozpędzić** *pf.* 1. (= *zwiększać szybkość*) accelerate. 2. (= *rozganiać*) disperse, scatter; **rozpędzić na cztery wiatry** scatter to the four winds. 3. (= *usuwać, rozpraszać*) dispel. ~ **się** *ipf.*, **rozpędzić się** *pf.* (= *nabierać szybkości*) accelerate, speed up, pick up speed; **tylko się tak nie rozpędzaj!** *pot.* hey, hold it!

rozpęknąć się *pf.* -pęknij, -pękł (= *rozlecieć się*) fall apart; (= *rozpaść się na kawałki*) break into pieces; **granat rozpęknął się zaledwie o kilka metrów od nas** the grenade exploded only a few meters away from us.

rozpętać *pf.*, **rozpętywać** *ipf.* 1. (= *wyzwalać z pęt*) unfetter. 2. (= *wywoływać*) spark off, unleash; **rozpętać wojnę** start a war. ~ **się** *pf.*, **roz-**

pętywać się *ipf.* **1.** (= *wyzwalać się z pęt*) unfetter o.s., break loose. **2.** (= *rozhulać się*) start, blow up; (*o wojnie, kłótni*) break out.

rozpiąć *pf.* **rozepnę rozepniesz, rozepnij** *zob.* **rozpinać.** ~ **się** *pf. zob.* **rozpinać się.**

rozpić *pf.* **-piję -pijesz, -pij** *zob.* **rozpijać.** ~ **się** *pf. zob.* **rozpijać się.**

rozpieczętować *pf.*, **rozpieczętowywać** *ipf.* (= *otworzyć*) open; (= *zerwać pieczęć*) unseal.

rozpieprzać *ipf.*, **rozpieprzyć** *pf. wulg.* (= *rozwalać*) fuck up; **rozpieprzyć robotę** mess up a job, make a fucking mess of a job.

rozpieracz *mi Gen.* **-a** *techn.* expander.

rozpierać *ipf.* push from inside; expand; **duma go rozpiera** he's bursting with pride. ~ **się** *ipf.* sit back; **rozeprzeć się w fotelu** sit back in one's armchair.

rozpierdalać *ipf.*, **rozpierdolić** *pf. wulg.* (= *rozwalać, niszczyć*) fuck up, smash to fucking pieces; **totalnie mnie rozpierdolił** (= *zaskoczył, zdziwił*) I was fucking swept off my feet.

rozpierzchać się *ipf.*, **rozpierzchnąć się** *pf.* **-chnij, -chnął** *l.* **-chł -chła -chnęli** *l.* **-chli** scamper away, disperse.

rozpieszczać *ipf.* pamper, spoil.

rozpieszczony *a.* **-eni** pampered, spoiled; **rozpieszczony bachor** spoiled brat.

rozpieścić *pf.* **-pieszczę -pieścisz** *zob.* **rozpieszczać.**

rozpięcie *n.* (*w ubraniu*) opening, slit.

rozpiętość *f.* **1.** (= *odległość*) span; **rozpiętość skrzydeł** *lotn.* wingspan; *orn.* wingspread. **2.** (= *zakres*) range, scope; **rozpiętość cen** price range; **rozpiętość płac** wage differential. **3.** *fot.* contrast range.

rozpijać *ipf.* push into drinking. ~ **się** *ipf.* take to drink.

rozpiłować *pf.*, **rozpiłowywać** *ipf.* saw through.

rozpinacz *mi Gen.pl.* **-y** *l.* **-ów** *techn.* hanger.

rozpinać *ipf.* **1.** (= *odpinać*) unfasten; (*bluzkę, koszulę, marynarkę itp.*) unbutton; (*klamrę*) unbuckle; (*guziki*) undo; (*suwak*) undo, unzip. **2.** (= *rozpościerać*) spread; **rozpiąć namiot** pitch up a tent, put up a tent; **rozpinać** *l.* **stawiać żagle** set sail. ~ **się** *ipf.* **1.** (= *odpinać na sobie ubranie*) unbutton. **2.** (= *stawać się rozpiętym*) come undone. **3.** (= *rozpościerać się*) stretch.

rozpinany *a.* **to jest rozpinane z tyłu** it fastens at the back.

rozpisać *pf.* **-szę -szesz, rozpisywać** *ipf.* **1.** (= *ogłaszać*) announce; **rozpisać konkurs** announce a competition, invite entries for a competition; **rozpisać przetarg na coś** invite tenders for sth; **rozpisać wybory** call an election. **2.** (= *przepisywać role, głosy*) rewrite (*parts separately for each actor*). **3.** (*majątek*) convey, bequeath (*one's property among a few people*). ~ **się** *pf.*, **rozpisywać się** *ipf.* (= *pisać rozwlekle*) write at length.

rozpiska *f. Gen.pl.* **-ek** *pot.* schedule; **rozpiska zadań** work schedule.

rozplakatować *pf.* post, placard.

rozplanować *pf.*, **rozplanowywać** *ipf.* **1.** (= *sporządzać plan rozmieszczenia*) plan; (*wnętrze do-*

mu) design; (*układ ulic, miasto*) lay out. **2.** (= *sporządzać plan czynności*) plan (out).

rozplatać *ipf.* (*warkocz, sznurki*) unbraid, unplait; (*dłonie*) unclasp. ~ **się** *ipf.* (*o warkoczu, sznurkach*) become unbraided, become unplaited; (*o dłoniach*) unclasp.

rozplątać *pf.* **-plączę -plączesz, rozplątywać** *ipf.* **1.** (= *rozsuplać*) disentangle, untangle; unravel. **2.** (= *wyjaśnić*) solve, unravel.

rozpleniać się *ipf.*, **rozplenić się** *pf.* proliferate.

rozpleść *pf.* **-plotę -pleciesz -plótł -plotła -pletli** *zob.* **rozplatać.** ~ **się** *pf. zob.* **rozplatać się.**

rozplotkowany *a.* gossipy.

rozpłakać się *pf.* **-płaczę -płaczesz** burst into tears.

rozpłakany *a.* weeping, in tears, tearful.

rozpłaszczać *ipf.*, **rozpłaszczyć** *pf.* flatten out. ~ **się** *ipf.*, **rozpłaszczyć się** *pf.* (*np. na ziemi, podłodze*) flatten o.s.

rozpłaszczka *f. Gen.pl.* **-ek widliczka rozpłaszczka** *bot.* lesser club moss (*Selaginella selaginoides*).

rozpłatać *pf.* cleave.

rozpłodnik *ma* (= *reproduktor*) *roln.*, *wet.* breeder.

rozpłodowy *a. roln.*, *wet.* breeding; **bydło rozpłodowe** breeding cattle.

rozpłomieniać *ipf.*, **rozpłomienić** *pf.* inflame.

rozpłód *mi* **-o-** *roln.*, *wet.* breeding, reproduction.

rozpłynąć się *pf.*, **rozpływać się** *ipf.* **1.** (= *rozlać się*) spread out. **2.** (= *stopić się*) melt; **rozpływać się w ustach** melt in the mouth. **3.** (= *zniknąć*) melt away; **rozpływać się w mroku/we mgle** vanish in the dark/fog. **4.** (= *upajać się*) revel (*nad czymś* in sth); (= *zachwycać się*) go into ecstasies (*nad kimś / czymś* about *l.* over sb/sth); **rozpływać się w grzecznościach** be profuse in politeness; **rozpływać się we łzach** dissolve in tears, melt into tears.

rozpocząć *pf.* **-cznę -czniesz, -cznij** *zob.* **rozpoczynać.** ~ **się** *pf. zob.* **rozpoczynać się.**

rozpoczęcie *n.* beginning, start; **rozpoczęcie roku szkolnego** the beginning of the school year; **rozpoczęcie meczu piłkarskiego** kick-off.

rozpoczynać *ipf.* begin, start. ~ **się** *ipf.* begin, start.

rozpodobnienie *n. jęz.* dissimilation.

rozpogadzać się *ipf.* **1.** (*o niebie*) (= *wypogadzać się*) clear up; **rozpogodziło się** it cleared up. **2.** (*o człowieku*) (= *rozweselać się*) cheer up.

rozpogodzenie *n.* bright spell, sunny spell.

rozpogodzić się *pf.* **-ódź** *zob.* **rozpogadzać się.**

rozpolitykować się *pf.* start discussing politics.

rozpolitykowany *a.* eagerly discussing politics.

rozpoławiać *ipf.*, **rozpołowić** *pf.* **-ów** halve.

rozpora *f. Gen.pl.* **-ór** *bud.* tie beam, collar beam.

rozporek *mi* **-rk-** *Gen.* **-a** (*zamek, np. w spodniach*) fly; (*rozcięcie, np. w spódnicy*) slit.

rozporowy *a. bud.* stretcher; **belka rozporowa** *zob.* **rozpora.**

rozporządzać *ipf.* **1.** (= *zarządzać*) manage

(*czymś* sth); (= *zadysponować, rozdysponować*) dispose (*czymś* of sth); **rozdysponował swoim majątkiem w testamencie** his property was disposed of in his will. **2.** (= *mieć do dyspozycji*) have at one's disposal.

rozporządzenie *n.* **1.** (= *dekret*) decree; (= *przepis wykonawczy*) regulation; **agencję tę utworzono rozporządzeniem Rady Ministrów** this agency has been set up by the regulation of the Cabinet. **2.** (= *dyspozycja, polecenie*) order, instruction.

rozporządzić *pf. zob.* **rozporządzać**.

rozpostrzeć *pf.* **-trę -trzesz, -trzyj, -tarł, rozpościerać** *ipf.* spread, stretch. **~ się** *pf.*, **rozpościerać się** *ipf.* spread.

rozpowiadać *ipf.*, **rozpowiedzieć** *pf.* **-wiem -wiesz, -wiedz** put about, put around.

rozpowszechniać *ipf.*, **rozpowszechnić** *pf.* **-ij** diffuse, spread; (*film*) distribute. **~ się** *ipf.*, **rozpowszechnić się** *pf.* spread.

rozpowszechniony *a.* widespread.

rozpoznać *pf. zob.* **rozpoznawać**.

rozpoznanie *n.* **1.** (= *poznanie*) recognition; **rozpoznanie zwłok** body identification. **2.** *med.* diagnosis. **3.** *prawn.* examination (*of a case*). **4.** *wojsk.* reconnaissance, reconnoiter, *Br.* reconnoitre.

rozpoznawać *ipf.* **-aję -ajesz, -awaj 1.** (= *identyfikować*) recognize, identify. **2.** *prawn.* examine (*a case*). **~ się** *ipf.*, **rozpoznać się** *pf.* recognize one another.

rozpoznawalny *a.* recognizable.

rozpoznawczy *a.* distinctive; **hasło rozpoznawcze** password; **lot rozpoznawczy** *lotn.* reconnaissance flight; **znak rozpoznawczy** identification.

rozpożyczać *ipf.*, **rozpożyczyć** *pf.* lend (*sth to a number of people*).

rozpórka *f. Gen.pl.* **-ek** *bud.* strut.

rozpracować *pf.*, **rozpracowywać** *ipf.* **1.** (= *demaskować*) (*np. siatkę szpiegowską*) expose. **2.** (= *unieszkodliwić*) (*np. siatkę szpiegowską*) dismantle. **3.** (= *przemyśleć*) work out; *Br. t.* suss out.

rozprasować *pf.*, **rozprasowywać** *ipf.* **1.** (*żelazkiem*) iron out. **2.** (*prasą*) press out.

rozpraszać *ipf.* **1.** (= *roztaczać*) spread; (*zapach, światło*) diffuse. **2.** (= *rozganiać*) disperse, dissipate; (*tłum*) disperse, break up; (*wątpliwości*) dispel; (*ciemności*) disperse. **3.** (= *trwonić*) fritter away. **4.** (= *dekoncentrować*) distract. **~ się** *ipf.* **1.** (= *znikać*) (*np. o chmurach*) disperse; *przen.* (*np. o wątpliwościach*) vanish. **2.** (= *rozpierzchać się*) scatter, disperse. **3.** (= *dekoncentrować się*) get distracted. **4.** *chem.* dissolve. **5.** *fiz.* diffuse.

rozpraszanie *n.* (*światła, zapachu*) diffusion; (*tłumu, chmur*) dispersion; (*kogoś*) distracting, distraction; **rozpraszanie fal** *fiz.* wave dispersion.

rozprawa *f.* **1.** (= *dysputa*) debate, discussion. **2.** (= *rozstrzygnięcie*) settlement; (= *bitwa*) battle; (*np. z przestępczością*) crackdown (*z czymś* on sth). **3.** (= *dysertacja*) dissertation; (= *studium*) study; **rozprawa doktorska** doctoral the-

sis, doctoral dissertation; **rozprawa habilitacyjna** post-doctoral thesis, post-doctoral dissertation. **4.** *prawn.* trial, hearing; **rozprawa o kradzież/zabójstwo** theft/murder trial; **rozprawa przy drzwiach zamkniętych** in camera trial; **sala rozpraw** courtroom; **otworzyć/odroczyć/zamknąć rozprawę** open/adjourn/close a trial.

rozprawiać *ipf.* (= *omawiać*) speak at length (*o czymś* about sth); (= *dyskutować*) debate (*o czymś* sth). **~ się** *ipf.*, **rozprawić się** *pf.* (= *wyrównać rachunki*) get even (*z kimś* with sb); (*np. z przestępczością*) crack down (*z czymś* on sth).

rozprawka *f. Gen.pl.* **-ek** essay (*o czymś* on sth).

rozprażyć *pf.* heat up.

rozprątki *pl. bot.* schizophytes (*Schizophyta*).

rozprężać *ipf.* **1.** (= *rozciągać*) stretch (out), spread out. **2.** *fiz.* expand, decompress. **~ się** *ipf.* **1.** (= *relaksować się*) relax. **2.** *fiz.* expand, decompress.

rozprężliwy *a.* expansible.

rozprężyć *pf. zob.* **rozprężać**. **~ się** *pf. zob.* **rozprężać się**.

rozpromieniać *ipf.*, **rozpromienić** *pf.* **1.** *lit.* (= *rozjaśniać*) irradiate. **2.** (*np. twarz*) illuminate, radiate. **~ się** *ipf.*, **rozpromienić się** *pf.* brighten up.

rozpromieniony *a.* **-eni** radiant, beaming.

rozpropagować *pf.* propagate, disseminate.

rozprostować *pf.*, **rozprostowywać** *ipf.* (*ręce, nogi*) stretch; (*kartkę, drut*) straighten; **rozprostować kości** stretch one's legs. **~ się** *pf.*, **rozprostowywać się** *ipf.* **1.** (*stojąc*) stand erect; (*leżąc*) stretch. **2.** (*o przedmiotach*) (= *stawać się prostym*) straighten, unbend.

rozproszenie *n.* **1.** (= *rozsypka*) dispersion. **2.** (= *brak koncentracji*) distraction.

rozproszyć *pf. zob.* **rozpraszać**. **~ się** *pf. zob.* **rozpraszać się**.

rozprowadzać *ipf.*, **rozprowadzić** *pf.* **1.** (= *przesyłać*) (*energię, wodę*) supply. **2.** (= *rozdzielić*) (*bilety, prasę*) distribute. **3.** (= *nakładać cienką warstwą*) spread. **4.** (= *rozcieńczać*) dilute, thin (*coś czymś* sth with sth).

rozpróżniaczyć się *pf.* grow lazy.

rozprucie *n.* rip.

rozpruć *pf.*, **rozpruwać** *ipf.* **1.** (= *rozciąć*) (*np. rękaw, brzuch*) rip. **2.** (= *wypruć*) (*np. szew*) unpick. **3.** (= *rozbić*) (*np. kasę pancerną, sejf, zbroję*) crack.

rozprysk *mi* **1.** (*strumień cieczy*) splash. **2.** (= *rozerwanie się pocisku*) burst. **3.** (= *odłamek pocisku*) splinter.

rozpryskać *pf. zob.* **rozpryskiwać**.

rozpryskiwacz *mi Gen.* **-a** *techn.* sprayer, sprinkler.

rozpryskiwać *ipf.* (*błoto, wodę, np. idąc po kałużach*) splash; (*np. rozpryskiwaczem*) sprinkle.

rozpryskowy *a. wojsk.* (*o pocisku, granacie*) pre-fragmented.

rozprysnąć *pf.* **-snę -śniesz, -śnij, -snął** *l.* **-sł -snęła** *l.* **-sła -snęli** *zob.* **rozpryskiwać**.

rozprza *f. Gen.pl.* **-y** *żegl.* sprit.

rozprząc *pf.* **-przęgę -przężesz, -przяż** *l.* **-przęż, -przągł -przęgła -przęgli** *zob.* **rozprzęgać**.

rozprzedać *pf.*, **rozprzedawać** *ipf.* -aję -ajesz, -awaj sell out.

rozprzestrzeniać *ipf.*, **rozprzestrzenić** *pf.* 1. *lit.* (= *roztaczać, rozpościerać*) spread, diffuse. 2. (= *rozpowszechniać*) propagate, disseminate. ~ się *ipf.*, **rozprzestrzenić się** *pf.* 1. (= *zajmować nowy obszar*) spread, diffuse. 2. (= *rozpowszechniać się*) spread; **nowe poglądy szybko rozprzestrzeniały się wśród wykształconej młodzieży** new ideas spread quickly among the educated young people.

rozprzęgać *ipf.* 1. (= *odłączać od zaprzęgu*) unharness, unhitch. 2. *lit.* (= *niszczyć, dezorganizować*) disrupt, break up; **rozprząc dyscyplinę** relax the discipline.

rozprzężenie *n.* (= *brak dyscypliny*) disorder, anarchy; (= *chaos*) chaos; **rozprzężenie obyczajów** relaxation of morals, moral corruption.

rozpuk *mi* **śmiać się do rozpuku** roar with laughter.

rozpulchniacz *mi Gen.* -a *roln.* scarifier.

rozpulchniać *ipf.*, **rozpulchnić** *pf.* -ij (*ziemię*) loosen; (*ciasto*) leaven.

rozpusta *f.* 1. (= *rozwiązłość*) debauchery. 2. *pot.* (= *nadużywanie czegoś*) overindulgence; **zjedzenie pięciu batoników czekoladowych pod rząd to już lekka rozpusta** eating five chocolate bars one after another is overdoing it a bit *l.* a bit on the indulgent side.

rozpustnica *f.*, **rozpustnik** *mp* libertine, debauchee.

rozpustny *a.* 1. (= *rozwiązły*) licentious. 2. (= *niemoralny*) immoral; **(prowadzić) rozpustne życie** (live) a life of debauchery.

rozpuszczać *ipf.* 1. (= *sporządzać roztwór*) dissolve (*coś w czymś* sth in sth). 2. (= *roztopić*) melt. 3. (= *rozpościerać*) (*np. skrzydła*) spread, extend; **rozpuścić gębę na kogoś** *pot.* lash out at sb; **rozpuścić majątek** *przen.* squander one's fortune; **rozpuszczać włosy** let one's hair loose. 4. (= *rozwiązywać*) (*zespół, załogę*) disband, dissolve. 5. *pot.* (= *rozpieszczać*) spoil, pamper; **rozpuścić kogoś jak dziadowski bicz** turn sb into a spoiled brat; **chłopak jest rozpuszczony jak dziadowski bicz** the boy is just a spoiled brat. 6. (= *rozsyłać*) send (*in a number of directions*); **rozpuszczać plotki** spread gossip. ~ się *ipf.* 1. (= *tworzyć roztwór*) dissolve. 2. (= *topić się*) melt. 3. (*o włosach*) (= *rozplatać się*) come undone, come loose. 4. *pot.* (= *stawać się krnąbrnym*) become spoiled; **rozpuścić się jak dziadowski bicz** run riot.

rozpuszczalnik *mi Gen.* -a *techn.* (*do rozpuszczania, wywabiania plam*) solvent; (*do rozcieńczania*) thinner.

rozpuszczalność *f. chem.* solubility.

rozpuszczalny *a.* soluble; **kawa rozpuszczalna** instant coffee.

rozpuścić *pf.* -puszczę -puścisz *zob.* **rozpuszczać.** ~ się *pf. zob.* **rozpuszczać się.**

rozpychać *ipf.* 1. (*np. buty, spodnie*) stretch. 2. (= *roztrącać*) jostle. ~ się *ipf.* 1. (*np. o butach, spodniach*) be stretched, get stretched. 2. (=

pchać się) jostle; **rozpychać się łokciami** *dosł., przen.* push one's way.

rozpylacz *mi Gen.* -a 1. (*do lekarstw, kosmetyków*) atomizer. 2. *hist.* (= *pistolet automatyczny*) automatic pistol.

rozpylać *ipf.*, **rozpylić** *pf.* spray.

rozpytać *pf.*, **rozpytywać** *ipf.* ask around. ~ się *pf.*, **rozpytywać się** *ipf.* ask around.

rozrabiacz *mp*, **rozrabiaczka** *f. Gen.pl.* -ek *pot.* trouble-maker.

rozrabiać *ipf.* 1. (= *mieszać*) mix together, cream. 2. (= *rozcieńczać*) dilute. 3. *pot.* (= *awanturować się*) kick up a row, stir things up; **rozrabiać jak pijany zając (w kapuście)** *żart.* horse around.

rozrabiaka *mp pl.* -i *pot.* (*o małym chłopcu*) little rascal; (= *żartowniś*) prankster.

rozrachunek *mi* -nk- 1. *ekon.* reckoning, settlement; **być na własnym rozrachunku** be self-financing; **dokonać z kimś rozrachunku** square up with sb. 2. *lit.* (= *podsumowanie sukcesów i niepowodzeń*) final analysis; **w ostatecznym rozrachunku** in the final analysis; **rozrachunek z przeszłością** squaring up with the past.

rozrachunkowy *a. ekon.* clearance.

rozradować *pf.* rejoice, gladden. ~ się *pf.* rejoice.

rozradowany *a.* jubilant, delighted.

rozrastać się *ipf.* 1. (*o roślinach*) (= *krzewić się*) grow, expand. 2. (*o ludziach*) (= *mężnieć*) grow stronger. 3. (= *powiększać się*) (*o rodzinie, majątku*) increase; (*o mieście*) expand, grow bigger. 4. (= *wzmagać się*) increase, strenghten; (*o uczuciach, talencie*) develop.

rozrąbać *pf.* -bię -biesz, **rozrąbywać** *ipf.* cleave, chop up.

rozregulować *pf.*, **rozregulowywać** *ipf.* put out of order.

rozreklamować *pf.* publicize (*extensively*), advertise (*widely*).

rozrobić *pf.* -rób *zob.* **rozrabiać.**

rozrodczość *f.* reproduction capacity.

rozrodczy *a.* reproductive; **komórki rozrodcze** reproductive cells; **narządy rozrodcze** reproductive organs.

rozrosnąć się *pf.* -rosnę -rośniesz, -rośnij, -rósł -rosła -rośli *zob.* **rozrastać się.**

rozrost *mi* 1. (= *rozrastanie się*) growth, development. 2. (*tkanki, narządu*) hyperplasia.

rozrośnięty *a.* (*o człowieku*) sturdy, stalwart; (*o roślinności*) lush.

rozróba *f. pot.* brawl.

rozród *mi* -o- *biol.* reproduction.

rozróżniać *ipf.* distinguish, discern.

rozróżnialny *a.* distinguishable, discernable.

rozróżnić *pf.* -ij *zob.* **rozróżniać.**

rozróżnienie *n.* difference, distinction.

rozruch *mi* 1. (= *uruchomienie*) (*silnika*) starting; (*produkcji*) start. 2. *sport* (= *rozgrzewka*) warm up.

rozruchy *pl. Gen.* -ów (= *zamieszki*) riots.

rozruszać *pf.* 1. (= *przywrócić zdolność ruchu*) set in motion, set going; **rozruszać kości** *pot.* get some exercise. 2. (= *uruchomić*) start; (*silnik*) start, ignite. **3.** *pot.* (= *ożywić*) liven up, perk up. ~ **się** *pf.* **1.** (*rozluźnić rękę, nogę*) loosen up; (*po długim okresie bezczynności*) get some exercise. **2.** *pot.* (= *ożywić się*) liven up, perk up.

rozrusznik *mi Gen.* **-a** *mot.* starter; *med.* (= *rozrusznik serca*) pacemaker.

rozryczeć się *pf.* **-ę -ysz 1.** (= *zacząć ryczeć*) (*o byku*) start bellowing; (*o krowie*) start mooing; (*o lwie*) start roaring. **2.** *pot.* (= *rozpłakać się*) start blubbering.

rozryć *pf.* **-ryję -ryjesz** (= *rozkopać*) dig up; (= *rozorać, rozgrzebać*) turn up.

rozrysować *pf.*, **rozrysowywać** *ipf.* present on a picture, present pictorially.

rozrywać *ipf.* **1.** (= *rozdzierać*) tear apart, rip; (*opakowanie*) tear open; (*więzy*) break; (*tamę*) burst. **2.** *pot.* (= *rozchwytywać*) snatch away. **3.** (= *dostarczać rozrywki*) entertain. ~ **się** *ipf.* **1.** (= *rozdzierać się*) tear, get torn. **2.** (= *eksplodować*) explode, blow up. **3.** (= *zabawić się*) entertain o.s.

rozrywany *a. pot.* (= *rozchwytywany*) sought-after; **być rozrywanym** be much in demand, be sought-after.

rozrywka *f. Gen.pl.* **-ek** (= *zabawa*) entertainment; (= *zajęcie, hobby*) pastime; **rozrywki umysłowe** mental exercises; **park rozrywki** amusement park; **robić coś dla rozrywki** do sth for fun.

rozrywkowy *a.* entertainment, amusement; **muzyka rozrywkowa** light music; **program rozrywkowy** entertainment show; **przemysł rozrywkowy** entertainment industry, show business.

rozrząd *mi techn.* distribution; **wał rozrządu** camshaft.

rozrządowy *a.* **górka rozrządowa** *kol.* hump; **mechanizm rozrządowy** = **rozrząd**.

rozrządzać *ipf.*, **rozrządzić** *pf.* **1.** (= *dysponować*) administer. **2.** *kol.* marshal.

rozrzedzać *ipf.*, **rozrzedzić** *pf.* dilute, thin down. ~ **się** *ipf.*, **rozrzedzić się** *pf.* thin out.

rozrzedzony *a.* diluted.

rozrzewniać *ipf.*, **rozrzewnić** *pf.* **-ij** move, stir. ~ **się** *ipf.*, **rozrzewnić się** *pf.* be moved, be stirred.

rozrzewnienie *n.* emotion; **wspominać coś z rozrzewnieniem** have fond memories of sth.

rozrzucać *ipf.*, **rozrzucić** *pf.* **1.** (= *rzucać w różne strony*) throw about, scatter; **rozrzucać pieniądze garściami** squander money. **2.** (= *umieszczać w różnych miejscach*) (*np. zabawki po pokoju*) scatter, strew; (*nawóz*) spread; (*ulotki*) drop. ~ **się** *ipf.*, **rozrzucić się** *pf.* be scattered, be strewn.

rozrzut *mi* **1.** (= *rozrzucenie*) scattering, dispersion; (*nasion*) spread. **2.** (= *zróżnicowanie*) diversity. **3.** (= *rozmieszczenie*) placement. **4.** *wojsk.* (*pocisków*) dispersion.

rozrzutnica *f.* (= *utracjuszka*) spendthrift, squanderer.

rozrzutnie *adv.* extravagantly, wastefully.

rozrzutnik *mp pl.* **-cy** (= *utracjusz*) spendthrift, squanderer. — *mi Gen.* **-a** *pl.* **-i** *roln.* spreader.

rozrzutność *f.* extravagance, wastefulness.

rozrzutny *a.* extravagant, wasteful.

rozsada *f.* seedling.

rozsadnik *mi Gen.* **-a 1.** *ogr.* seedbed. **2.** *leśn.* nursery. **3.** (*choroby, zarazy*) carrier.

rozsadzać *ipf.*, **rozsadzić** *pf.* **1.** (*gości*) seat. **2.** (*np. niegrzecznych uczniów*) separate. **3.** (*rośliny*) plant out. **4.** (= *wysadzać w powietrze*) blow up; **rozsadza go duma/gniew** *przen.* he is bursting with pride/anger. **5.** (= *niszczyć od środka*) (*organizację, system*) disrupt.

rozsądek *mi* **-dk-** reason, sense; **zdrowy rozsądek** common sense, good judgment; **małżeństwo z rozsądku** marriage of convenience; **kierować się rozsądkiem** be guided by common sense; **przemawiać komuś do rozsądku** bring sb to their senses, talk some sense into sb; **to przekracza granice zdrowego rozsądku** (= *to niedorzeczne*) it is absurd; (*np. o cenie*) it is exorbitant.

rozsądnie *adv.* reasonably, sensibly.

rozsądny *a.* reasonable, sensible.

rozsądzać *ipf.*, **rozsądzić** *pf.* (= *rozstrzygnąć*) settle (*coś* sth); (= *wydać formalną decyzję*) adjudicate (*coś* upon sth).

rozsiać *pf.* **-sieję -siejesz** *zob.* **rozsiewać**.

rozsiadać się *ipf.*, **rozsiąść się** *pf.* **-siądę -siądziesz -siadł -siedli 1.** (= *siadać w wygodnej pozycji*) sit back. **2.** (= *rozlokowywać się*) sit down.

rozsiany *a.* **1.** (= *zasiany*) sown. **2.** (= *rozrzucony*) scattered; **stwardnienie rozsiane** *pat.* multiple sclerosis, disseminated sclerosis.

rozsiec *pf.* chop up; **rozsiec na kawałki** chop to pieces.

rozsierdzić *pf.* irritate, anger.

rozsiew *mi roln.* (*nasion*) sowing; (*nawozów*) spreading.

rozsiewacz *mi Gen.* **-a** *roln.* spreader.

rozsiewać *ipf.* **1.** (*nasiona*) sow; (*nawóz*) spread. **2.** (= *roztaczać, rozprzestrzeniać*) (*np. zapach, zarazki*) spread, diffuse. **3.** (= *rozpowszechniać*) disseminate, spread.

rozsiodłać *pf.* unsaddle.

rozsławiać *ipf.*, **rozsławić** *pf.* praise, glorify.

rozsmakować się *pf.*, **rozsmakowywać się** *ipf.* (= *nabrać upodobania*) acquire a taste (*w czymś* for sth).

rozsmarować *pf.*, **rozsmarowywać** *ipf.* spread.

rozsnuć *pf.*, **rozsnuwać** *ipf.* **1.** *lit.* (= *rozciągać nici*) unspin; **rozsnuć pajęczynę** (*o pająku*) spin its web. **2.** *lit.* (= *rozprzestrzenić*) (*np. o wietrze*) spread. **3.** *lit.* (= *roztaczać wizje*) unfold (*coś przed kimś* sth before sb).

rozstać się *pf.* **-anę -aniesz** *zob.* **rozstawać się**.

rozstaje *pl. Gen.* **-ów** *l.* **-ai** crossroads.

rozstajny *a.* crossroad; **rozstajne drogi** crossroads; **być na rozstajnych drogach** *przen.* be at the crossroads.

rozstanie *n.* parting.

rozstaw *mi* (= *odstęp*) span, distance; **rozstaw osi** *mot.* wheelbase.

rozstawać się *ipf.* **-aję -ajesz, -awaj 1.** (= *rozłączać się*) part (*z kimś* from sb); (*w danej chwili*) part company (*z kimś* with sth); (= *zerwać*) (*z narzeczonym, narzeczoną*) split up (*z kimś* with sth). **2.** (= *pozbywać się*) part (*z czymś* with sth); **rozstać się z życiem** (= *umrzeć*) depart from life, depart this life. **3.** (= *rezygnować*) give up (*z czymś* sth).

rozstawiać *ipf.*, **rozstawić** *pf.* **1.** (= *ustawiać w pewnym porządku*) arrange; **rozstawiać nogi** spread one's legs; **rozstawiać (kogoś) po kątach** *przen.* whip (sb) into line. **2.** *sport* (*zawodników*) line up. **3.** (= *rozkładać*) (*leżak, łóżko*) set up; (*np. talerze na stole*) lay out.

rozstawienie *n.* **1.** (= *ustawienie*) arrangement. **2.** *sport* (*zawodników*) line-up.

rozstawny *a.* **bieg rozstawny** relay; **konie rozstawne** relay horses.

rozstąpić się *pf.*, **rozstępować się** *ipf.* **1.** (= *usunąć się na boki*) step aside, draw aside. **2.** (= *pęknąć, utworzyć szczelinę*) come apart, open up.

rozstęp *mi* gap.

rozstępy *pl. Gen.* **-ów** *pat.* stretch marks.

rozstrajać *ipf.*, **rozstroić** *pf.* **-stroję -stroisz, -strój 1.** (*instrument*) put out of tune. **2.** (= *rozdrażniać*) upset, perturb.

rozstrojony *a.* **-eni 1.** (= *wydający nieprawidłowe dźwięki*) out of tune. **2.** (= *wytrącony z równowagi*) upset, perturbed; (*żołądek*) upset.

rozstrój *mi* **-o-** confusion, disorder; **rozstrój nerwowy** nervous breakdown; **rozstrój żołądka** stomach upset.

rozstrzelać *pf. zob.* **rozstrzeliwać¹**.

rozstrzelić *pf. zob.* **rozstrzeliwać²**.

rozstrzeliwać¹ *ipf.* (= *dokonywać egzekucji*) execute by firing squad, put before the firing squad.

rozstrzeliwać² *ipf. druk.* (= *wstawiać spacje*) space out.

rozstrzelony *a. druk.* spaced-out.

rozstrzygać *ipf.* **1.** (= *rozsądzać*) settle, decide; **rozstrzygnąć spór** settle a dispute. **2.** (= *być czynnikiem decydującym*) determine; **rozstrzygać o czyimś losie** determine sb's fate. **~ się** *ipf.* be determined, be decided.

rozstrzygający *a.* (= *decydujący*) decisive; **rozstrzygający głos** (*w głosowaniu, wyborach*) casting vote; (*czyjaś opinia w jakiejś sprawie*) final say; **rozstrzygający głos należy do ciebie** you have the final say.

rozstrzygnąć *pf.* **-ij** *zob.* **rozstrzygać.** **~ się** *pf. zob.* **rozstrzygać się.**

rozsunąć *pf. zob.* **rozsuwać.**

rozsupłać *pf.*, **rozsupływać** *ipf.* **1.** (= *rozwiązywać supły*) untangle, disentangle, untie, unravel. **2.** (= *rozwiązywać zagadki itp.*) solve, figure out, unriddle, unravel.

rozsuwać *ipf.* **1.** (= *rozdzielać*) separate, part; (*firanki*) draw (apart); (*kurtkę*) unzip. **2.** (= *wydłużać*) lengthen, elongate; (*stół, drabinę*) extend.

rozsuwany *a.* (*o drzwiach*) sliding; (*o stole*) extendable; (*o drabinie*) extension.

rozsychać się *ipf.* dry up *l.* out; **beczka się rozeschła** the barrel came unjointed.

rozsyłać *ipf.* send; (*ludzi*) dispatch; (*materiały, ulotki*) distribute.

rozsypać *pf.* **-pię -piesz** *zob.* **rozsypywać. ~ się** *pf. zob.* **rozsypywać się.**

rozsypka *f.* headlong flight; **biec** *l.* **uciekać w rozsypce** run *l.* flee helter-skelter; **iść** *l.* **pójść w rozsypkę** (= *rozproszyć się*) disperse; (= *ulec rozbiciu*) break up.

rozsypywacz *mi Gen.* **-a** (= *maszyna do posypywania ulic piaskiem i solą*) sand-and-salt spreader.

rozsypywać *ipf.* **1.** spill; **rozsypać wojsko w tyralierę** *wojsk.* order troops to form an extended line. **2.** (= *kruszyć*) crumble. **~ się** *ipf.* **1.** (= *być rozsypywanym*) spill; **mąka mi się rozsypała** I accidentally spilt the flour. **2.** (= *rozlatywać się*) fall apart, go to pieces; (*o skale*) crumble; (*o domu*) dilapidate; **rozsypać się w proch** molder (away), *Br.* moulder (away) **3.** (= *rozbiegać się*) scatter; *wojsk.* disperse.

rozszabrować *pf.*, **rozszabrowywać** *ipf. pot.* pillage, loot, plunder.

rozszalały *a.* **1.** (= *wzburzony*) (*o tłumie*) frenzied, hysterical; (*o ataku*) frenzied, uncontrolled; (*o zwierzęciu*) wild, mad. **2.** (= *gwałtowny*) (*o wietrze*) raging; (*o morzu*) stormy, foaming, raging.

rozszaleć się *pf.* **-eję -ejesz 1.** (= *wpaść w szał*) rage, run amok *l.* amuck, go wild; (*o zwierzętach*) go wild; (*o tłumie*) run riot; **rozszaleć się ze złości** be beside o.s. with anger *l.* fury. **2.** (= *rozpętać się*) (*o wojnie, zarazie, panice, burzy*) break out; **rozszalała się burza** storm broke out.

rozszarpać *pf.* **-pię -piesz** tear apart, rend; (*pazurami*) claw (*coś* at sth); **rozszarpywać rany** tear wounds open; **rozszarpać coś na kawałki** tear sth apart *l.* to pieces.

rozszczep *mi* cleft, split, cleavage; **rozszczep podniebienia** *pat.* cleft palate; **rozszczep wargi** *pat.* harelip, cleft lip; **rozszczep kręgosłupa** *pat.* rachischisis.

rozszczepiać *ipf.* **1.** (= *rozpoławiać*) split, cleave; (*na drzazgi, wąskie skrawki*) splinter; (*klinem*) wedge; **rozszczepione kopyto** *wet.* cloven hoof; **rozszczepiać** *l.* **dzielić włos na czworo** split hairs. **2.** *fiz.* disperse; **rozszczepiać światło** disperse light. **3.** *chem.* split, break. **~ się** *ipf.* **1.** (= *dzielić się*) split, cleave; (*na drzazgi*) splinter. **2.** *fiz.* disperse. **3.** *chem.* split, break.

rozszczepialny *a.* fissile, fissionable; **materiały rozszczepialne** *fiz.* fissile *l.* fissionable materials.

rozszczepić *pf. zob.* **rozszczepiać. ~ się** *pf. zob.* **rozszczepiać się.**

rozszczepienie *n.* **1.** split, cleft; **rozszczepienie osobowości** *pat.* multiple personality (disorder), personality split; **rozszczepienie warstw** delamination. **2.** *fiz.* fission; **rozszczepienie jądra** (*atomowego*) nuclear *l.* atomic fission; **rozszczepienie światła** dispersion of light. **3.** *chem.* split, break; **rozszczepienie tłuszczów** fat splitting.

rozszerzać *ipf.* **1.** (= *poszerzać*) expand, enlarge; (*szparę, otwór, źrenice*) dilate. **2.** (= *powiększać zakres*) broaden, widen, extend (*o coś* by sth); (*wypowiedź, temat*) expand, elaborate (*coś* on sth); amplify; (*dom, sklep*) extend, add on to; **rozszerzać horyzonty** broaden horizons; **rozszerzać czyjeś uprawnienia** extend sb's powers. ~ **się** *ipf.* **1.** (= *poszerzać się*) broaden (out), widen; (*o źrenicach*) dilate; (*o spodniach, rękawach*) flare. **2.** (= *rozprzestrzeniać się*) spread (out), extend, increase in scope; (*o epidemii, pożarze*) spread (*na coś* over *l.* across *l.* through sth); (*o konflikcie*) spill over, escalate; (*o wpływie, efektach postępowania*) extend (*na coś* (on)to sth). **3.** (= *powiększać się*) expand, grow larger; (*o wiedzy, zakresie*) increase, grow, develop; (*o naczyniach krwionośnych*) distend. **4.** *fiz.* (= *zwiększać objętość*) expand.

rozszerzalność *f.* dilatability; *fiz.* expansion; **rozszerzalność cieplna** thermal expansion; **współczynnik rozszerzalności** coefficient of expansion.

rozszerzalny *a.* expandable, dilatable, distensible, expansive.

rozszerzyć *pf. zob.* **rozszerzać**.

rozszlochać się *pf.* (begin to) sob *l.* weep, burst out sobbing *l.* weeping.

rozsznurować *pf.*, **rozsznurowywać** *ipf.* (*but, gorset*) unlace, undo. ~ **się** *pf.*, **rozsznurowywać się** *ipf.* come undone.

rozszumieć się *pf.* **-mię -misz 1.** (*o wietrze, drzewach*) sough; (*o morzu*) roar. **2.** *pot.* (*o osobie*) (= *oddać się zabawie*) become a party animal, start partying like crazy.

rozszyfrować *pf.*, **rozszyfrowywać** *ipf.* **1.** (= *odczytywać szyfr*) decipher, decode; **odczytywać niewyraźne pismo** decipher *l.* make out illegible handwriting. **2.** (= *odgadywać*) unravel, solve; (*zamiary, kogoś*) see through, figure out; **rozszyfrowałem ją** I saw her through; **nie mogę go rozszyfrować** I can't figure him out.

rozścielać *ipf.*, **rozścielić** *pf.* (*koc, dywan*) spread; **rozścielać łóżko** make the bed. ~ **się** *ipf.*, **rozścielić się** *pf.* spread, extend, stretch; **przed nami rozścielał się tylko ocean** all we could see was the large expanse of the ocean.

rozściełacz *mi Gen.* **-a** *bud.* spreader, paving machine.

rozśmieszać *ipf.* make laugh, amuse; **rozśmieszyć kogoś do łez** have sb in hysterics *l.* fits of laughter, leave sb in stitches; **nie rozśmieszaj mnie** *t. przen.* don't make me laugh.

rozśmieszająco *adv.* amusingly, comically.

rozśmieszyć *pf. zob.* **rozśmieszać**.

rozśpiewać *pf. rzad.* make sing, lead into singing. ~ **się** *pf.* (= *zacząć śpiewać*) start singing *l.* to sing.

rozśpiewany *a.* singing.

rozśrubować *pf.* unscrew.

rozświetlać *ipf.*, **rozświetlić** *pf.* **1.** (= *oświetlać*) light; (*ulice*) illuminate; **ogień rozświetlał niebo** fire was lighting up the sky. **2.** (= *rozpromieniać*) brighten up; **uśmiech rozświetlił mu twarz** his face lit up with a smile. **3.** (= *wyjaśniać*) explain, elucidate, clarify, illuminate; **rozświetlić mroki przeszłości** shed some light on the past.

roztaczać *ipf.* **1.** *lit.* (= *rozpościerać, rozwijać*) unfold, expand; (*skrzydła*) spread, unfold; **roztaczać opiekę nad kimś/czymś** take sb/sth under

one's wings, take care of sb/sth, protect sb/sth. **2.** (= *ukazywać*) display; **roztaczać wdzięki** display one's charms, turn on the charm. **3.** (= *rozsiewać*) spread; (*blask*) cast, shed; (*woń*) effuse; **roztaczała wokół siebie zapach francuskich perfum** she smelled of French scent *l.* perfume. **4.** *techn.* bore. ~ **się** *ipf.* (= *ukazywać się*) spread, extend; **roztoczył się przed nami piękny widok** a beautiful view spread *l.* stretched out *l.* opened before us.

roztajać *pf.* **-ę -esz** thaw, melt.

roztańczony *a.* **-eni** dancing.

roztańczyć się *pf.* start dancing; **goście roztańczyli się** guests started dancing for good.

roztapiać *ipf.* (*śnieg, masło, metal*) melt. ~ **się** *ipf.* **1.** melt. **2.** (= *topnieć*) thaw. **3.** (= *znikać*) fade away, vanish.

roztargnienie *n.* absent-mindedness, inattention; **w roztargnieniu** *l.* **z roztargnieniem** absent-mindedly, abstractedly; **słuchać w roztargnieniu** listen with (a) detached interest; **zrobić coś przez roztargnienie** do sth absent-mindedly.

roztargniony *a.* **-eni 1.** (*o uczniu, naukowcu*) (= *nieważny*) absent-minded, distracted, distrait. **2.** (= *machinalny*) (*o wzroku, spojrzeniu*) distracted, abstracted, absent; (*o ruchach*) distracted, awkward.

rozterka *f. Gen.pl.* **-ek** (= *brak zdecydowania*) indecision, irresolution; (= *problem, dylemat*) dilemma, quandary; **w rozterce** at a loss, in a dilemma *l.* quandary, irresolute, undecided; **jestem w rozterce** I have (my) doubts about it.

roztkliwiać się *ipf.*, **roztkliwić się** *pf.* be touched *l.* moved, sentimentalize, become *l.* get maudlin (*nad kimś/czymś* about *l.* over sb/sth); **roztkliwić się nad czyimś losem** feel sorry for sb, pity sb.

roztkliwienie *n.* sentimentality, mawkishness.

roztłuc *pf.* **-tłukę -tłuczesz -tłukł**, **roztłukiwać** *ipf.* (*wazon*) break; (*butelki, szybę*) smash; **roztłuc coś w drobny mak** break sth to pieces *l.* smithereens. ~ **się** *pf.* **-tłukę -tłuczesz -tłukł**, **roztłukiwać się** *ipf.* break.

roztocz *ma Gen.* **-a** *zool.* acarid (*Acarina*).

roztocze *n. Gen.pl.* **-y** *bot.* saprophyte.

roztoczek *mi Gen.* **-czka** *bot.* water mold; *Br.* water mould (*Saprolegnia*).

roztoczyć *pf. zob.* **roztaczać**. ~ **się** *pf. zob.* **roztaczać się**.

roztoka *f.* **1.** *geogr.* (= *dolina*) glen. **2.** (= *potok*) brook.

roztopić *pf. zob.* **roztapiać**. ~ **się** *pf. zob.* **roztapiać się**.

roztopy *pl. Gen.* **-ów** thaw.

roztrąbić *pf. pot.* noise (abroad *l.* about), blaze (abroad), blazon (abroad); (*plotki, kłamstwa*) spread, retail; **roztrąbić coś na cały świat** shout sth from the rooftops; **roztrąbić, że...** spread the word that...; **nie roztrąb tego** keep it private *l.* to yourself.

roztrącać *ipf.*, **roztrącić** *pf.* push (*kogoś* past *l.* between sb); jostle; **roztrącać tłum łokciami** elbow *l.* push one's way through the crowd.

roztropek *mp* **-pk-** *pl.* **-i** *pot.* **chłopek roztropek** smart aleck, smart alec; wise guy, wiseacre.

roztropnie *adv.* wisely, prudently, sensibly; **postąpiłbyś roztropnie/nieroztropnie, gdybyś...** you would be well/ill-advised to...; **postąpiłeś bardzo roztropnie** it was very thoughtful of you.

roztropność *f.* prudence, thoughtfulness, sagacity.

roztropny *a.* (*o człowieku*) prudent, sagacious; (*o decyzji, posunięciu*) prudent, thoughtful, well-advised.

roztruchan *mi Gen.* **-a** *l.* **-u** *hist.* wine goblet.

roztrwaniać *ipf.*, **roztrwonić** *pf.* (*pieniądze, fortunę*) squander, fool away, fritter away; (*uprawiając hazard*) gamble away; (*talent, czas*) waste, dissipate.

roztrzaskać *pf.*, **roztrzaskiwać** *ipf.* smash (up), dash, shatter; **roztrzaskać coś na kawałki** smash *l.* dash sth to pieces; **roztrzaskać komuś głowę** crack sb's head. ~ **się** *pf.*, **roztrzaskiwać się** *ipf.* shatter, get smashed *l.* dashed; (*o samolocie*) crash; **roztrzaskał się samochodem o drzewo** he crashed his car into a tree.

roztrząsacz *mi Gen.* **-a** *roln.* spreader.

roztrząsać *ipf.*, **roztrząsnąć** *pf.* **-snę -śniesz, -śnij** **1.** (= *rozrzucać*) spread, strew. **2.** (= *rozważać*) deliberate over, mull over, debate; **roztrząsać coś w myślach** ponder sth; **roztrząsać coś bez końca** belabor sth, *Br.* belabour sth; **rozważać możliwość zrobienia czegoś** deliberate whether or not to do sth; **roztrząsać przeszłość** rake in the past, brood on *l.* over the past.

roztrzepać *pf. zob.* **roztrzepywać**.

roztrzepanie *n.* scatterbrainedness, absentmindedness; **w roztrzepaniu** absent-mindedly, abstractedly; **zrobić coś przez roztrzepanie** do sth absent-mindedly.

roztrzepany *a.* **1.** (= *roztargniony*) scatterbrained, absent-minded. **2.** (*o włosach*) disheveled.

roztrzepywać *ipf.* (*jajka, śmietanę*) (= *mieszać trzepiąc*) whisk, whip, beat.

roztrzęsiony *a.* **-eni** (= *zdenerwowany*) (*o osobie*) jittery, trembling, shivering; distressed (*czymś* about sth); (*o głosie*) trembling; **był cały roztrzęsiony** he was in a dither *l.* all of a dither.

roztwór *mi* **-o-** *chem., fiz.* solution; **roztwór alkaliczny** alkaline solution; **roztwór Clarka** Clarke's soap solution; **roztwór fizjologiczny** *med.* physiological solution; **roztwór nasycony** saturated solution; **roztwór neutralny** neutral solution; **roztwór nienasycony** unsaturated solution; **roztwór właściwy** true solution; **roztwór wzorcowy** standard solution; **roztwór do zamaczania** soak.

roztyć się *pf.* **-tyję -tyjesz, -tyj** put on weight, grow *l.* get obese *l.* overweight.

rozum *mi* **1.** (= *umysł*) reason, mind, intelect; **czysty rozum** *fil.* pure reason; **niespełna rozumu** nuts, bats, crazy; **na mój (głupi) rozum** *pot.* in my (humble) opinion, as I see it; **mieć swój rozum** have one's wits about one, be in one's right senses; **kierować się własnym rozumem** use one's judgement *l.* own head; **postradać** *l.* **stracić rozum** loose one's marbles *l.* mind, be out of one's mind; **pójść po rozum do głowy** find a reason-

able solution to a problem, think of sth sensible; **mieć bystry rozum** have quick wits; **obdarzony rozumem** rational. **2.** (= *rozsądek*) judgement, wit(s), sense; **chłopski rozum** horse sense, common sense; **zdrowy rozum** common sense, native reason; **na chłopski** *l.* **zdrowy rozum** common sense suggests that...; **mieć więcej szczęścia niż rozumu** succeed by a fluke; **nauczyć kogoś rozumu** teach sb a lesson; **przemówić komuś do rozumu** make sb see sense *l.* reason, make sb listen to reason, bring sb to reason; **powinieneś mieć więcej rozumu w głowie** you should know better; **wydaje mu się, że posiadał wszystkie rozumy** he's such a smart alec *l.* aleck; **weź to na rozum** think it over, give it a reasonable thought.

rozumieć *ipf.* **-em -esz** **1.** (= *pojmować*) understand, comprehend, grasp, see; have an understanding (*coś* of sth); **rozumieć po angielsku** understand English; **nie rozumiesz po polsku?** (*napomnienie*) shall I make it clear *l.* spell it out for you?; **rozumiesz?** (*wzmocnienie rozkazu*) (do) you hear me?, (do) you understand?; **to rozumiem!** *pot.* that's more like it, that's better, now you're talking!, atta boy/girl!; **zaczynać rozumieć** get the idea, see daylight; **nic już z tego nie rozumiem** I can't make anything of this, beats me; **nie rozumieć czegoś** not understand sth, have no comprehension *l.* conception of sth; **niewiele z czegoś rozumieć** make little of sth, be unclear about sth; **nie rozumiem czemu (nie)** I don't see why (not); **nie rozumiesz istoty sytuacji** you miss the point, you can't see forest *l.* wood for the trees; **udawać, że się czegoś nie rozumie** pretend not to see sth, have a blind spot about *l.* for sth; **dobrze/źle coś rozumieć** have a good/poor understanding of sth; **rozumiem** (= *przyjmuję do wiadomości*) I see *l.* understand. **2.** (= *interpretować*) interpret, understand, take; **(nie) rozumiem (o co ci chodzi)** I (don't) know *l.* see what you mean, I (don't) get it, I (don't) follow *l.* get *l.* catch your drift; **rozumiem, że...** I gather *l.* understand that..., I take it that...; **co przez to rozumiesz?** what do you mean by that?; **nie tak rozumiałam przyjaźń** that's not my idea of friendship; **czy na pewno dobrze to rozumiem?** let me get this right *l.* straight; **rozumiem cię, ale...** I hear what you're saying, but...; **czy mam przez to rozumieć, że...** am I (supposed) to understand that...; **źle** *l.* **mylnie coś zrozumieć** misapprehend *l.* misinterpret *l.* misconstrue sth, mistake sth (*jako coś* for sth). **3.** (= *wykazywać zrozumienie*) (*sytuację, młodzież*) understand; relate (*kogoś / coś* to sb/sth); be understanding (*kogoś* towards sb). ~ **się** *ipf.* **1.** (= *rozumieć się nawzajem*) understand each other *l.* one another; **rozumieć się z kimś bez słów** be on the same wavelength with sb, speak the same language with sb; **dobrze się z kimś rozumieć** connect with sb, be tuned in with sb; **źle się z kimś rozumieć** be tuned out with sb; **nie rozumieć się nawzajem** be at cross-purposes. **2.** *pot.* (= *znać się*) understand (*na czymś* sth); have an understanding (*na czymś* of sth); **ma się rozumieć!** yes, of course; yes, that's right; **to się samo przez się ro-**

zumie it goes without saying, it is obvious by itself.

rozumienie *n.* understanding, comprehension; **w moim rozumieniu** in my opinion, to my mind, the way I see it; **błędne rozumienie** misconception; **(test na) rozumienie ze słuchu** *szkoln.* listening comprehension.

rozumnie *adv.* wisely, sensibly.

rozumny *a.* **1.** (= *mający rozum*) rational, thinking, intelligent; **istota rozumna** intelligent being; **człowiek rozumny** Homo sapiens. **2.** (= *świadczący o rozumie*) sensible, rational, wise, intelligent; (*o spojrzeniu, decyzji*) reasonable, rational.

rozumować *ipf.* reason.

rozumowanie *n.* reasoning, argumentation, intellection; **tok rozumowania** line of reasoning.

rozumowo *adv.* rationally, intellectually.

rozumowy *a.* rational; intellective, intellectual.

rozwadniać *ipf.* **1.** (= *rozcieńczać*) dilute, water down. **2.** (= *pozbawiać treści*) thin down *l.* out, weaken.

rozwaga *f.* **1.** (= *rozsądek*) mindfulness, prudence, sagacity, deliberation, judiciousness; **brać coś pod rozwagę** take sth into advisement *l.* consideration; **brak rozwagi** imprudence. **2.** (= *ostrożność*) caution, circumspection; **z rozwagą** deliberately.

rozwalać *ipf.*, **rozwalić** *pf.* **1.** *pot.* (= *niszczyć*) smash (up), shatter, break; (*ścianę, dom*) pull down, raze; (*system, małżeństwo*) smash, destroy, ruin; (*zwł. samochód*) total, wreck; **rozwaliło mnie to** *pot.* it swept me off my feet, it was smashing. **2.** *pot.* (*palec, kolano*) (= *skaleczyć*) cut; **rozwalić komuś głowę** crack sb's head open; **rozwalić komuś nos** set sb's nose bleeding. **3.** *pot.* (= *rozrzucać niedbale*) strew, scatter, throw about. **4.** *pot.* (= *zabić strzałem*) gun (down), blast, pop, hit. **~ się** *ipf.*, **rozwalić się** *pf.* **1.** *pot.* (= *rozlatywać się*) break down, get shattered, break into pieces, fall apart. **2.** *pot.* (= *rozbijać samochód w wypadku*) crash; **rozwalił się samochodem o drzewo** he crashed his car into a tree. **3.** *pot.* (= *rozsiadać się*) loll (*na czymś* on sth); lounge, sprawl (*na czymś* in *l.* on sth).

rozwałka *f. Gen.pl.* **-ek** *pot.* execution by a firing squad; **pójść na rozwałkę** be executed by a firing squad.

rozwałkować *pf.*, **rozwałkowywać** *ipf.* **1.** *kulin.* (= *rozpłaszczać*) roll (out). **2.** *pot.* (= *traktować rozwlekle*) dwell (*coś* on *l.* upon sth); debate over, drag; (*zagadnienie, problem*) talk *l.* write at length (*coś* on sth).

rozwarcie *n.* **1.** opening, gap, aperture; (*ust, pyska, kielicha*) rictus; **kąt rozwarcia** *geom.* angle; **rozwarcie szyjki macicy** *med.* dilation of the cervix; **rozwarcie zębów piły** *techn.* saw set. **2.** *fon.* release.

rozwarstwiać się *ipf.*, **rozwarstwić się** *pf.* **1.** (= *rozdzielać się na warstwy*) delaminate, foliate, layer; *geol.* (*o skale*) stratify. **2.** *socjol.* (*o społeczeństwie*) stratify, become *l.* get stratified.

rozwarstwienie *n.* **1.** *geol.* stratification. **2.** *so-*

cjol. stratification. **3.** *techn.* delamination, foliation.

rozwarty *a.* (*np. o oczach*) dilated, (wide) open; **kąt rozwarty** *geom.* obtuse angle.

rozważać *ipf.* **1.** (= *rozpatrywać*) consider, contemplate; ponder, reflect (*coś* on *l.* upon sth); **rozważać coś** take sth into consideration, debate sth in one's mind, ruminate on sth; **rozważać plany** *l.* zamierzenia go over *l.* through one's plans; **rozważyć wszystkie za i przeciw** consider all the pros and cons; **przez chwilę rozważaliśmy możliwość pójścia tam** we entertained the idea *l.* possibility of going there for a while; **nie całkiem poważnie rozważać jakiś pomysł/pomysł zrobienia czegoś** toy *l.* dally *l.* flirt with an idea of sth/of doing sth; **rozważać długofalowe skutki czegoś** take the long view of sth. **2.** (= *ważyć towar*) weigh out.

rozważanie *n.* **1.** *lit.* (= *zastanawianie się*) consideration, cogitation, deliberation; **snuć rozważania** ponder, muse, contemplate. **2.** *lit.* (= *wypowiedź*) reflections, ruminations (*o czymś* on sth).

rozważnie *adv.* judiciously, thoughtfully, mindfully, prudently.

rozważny *a.* **1.** (= *roztropny*) thoughtful, sagacious, prudent, sensible; (*o polityku*) clever. **2.** (*o decyzji, czynie*) (= *świadczący o roztropności*) prudent, thoughtful, considerate.

rozważyć *pf. zob.* **rozważać**.

rozweselać *ipf.*, **rozweselić** *pf.* cheer (up); **rozweselić kogoś** raise sb's spirits, put sb in good humor. **~ się** *ipf.* cheer up, brighten up, buck up.

rozwiać *pf.* **-eję -ejesz** *zob.* **rozwiewać**. **~ się** *pf. zob.* **rozwiewać się**.

rozwiązać *pf.* **-żę -żesz** *zob.* **rozwiązywać**. **~ się** *pf. zob.* **rozwiązywać się**.

rozwiązanie *n.* **1.** (*węzła*) unknotting, undoing. **2.** (= *likwidacja, unieważnienie*) dissolution, cancellation; (*parlamentu*) dissolution; (*umowy*) termination; (*małżeństwa*) dissolution, termination; (*spółki, firmy*) dissolution, liquidation. **3.** (= *rozstrzygnięcie*) solution (*czegoś* to sth); remedy (*czegoś* for sth); way out, course of action; (*sprawy, konfliktu*) resolution; (*zagadki*) unravelling, unfolding (*czegoś* of sth); **rozwiązanie problemu** solution *l.* answer to a problem; **nie do rozwiązania** (*o konflikcie, kwestiach*) unresolved, irreconcilable; (*o problemie*) intractable; (*o zagadce*) inextricable, insoluble; **pozostawać bez rozwiązania** remain unresolved; **możliwy do rozwiązania** soluble, solvable; **nie ma innego rozwiązania** there's no other solution; **rozwiązanie prowizoryczne** band-aid solution, quick fix, stopgap; **rozwiązanie doraźne** *polit.* interim measure; **rozwiązanie akcji** *teor.lit., film, teatr* denouement, finale. **4.** *bud.* (= *projekt i realizacja założeń*) solution; (= *wykonanie*) implementation. **5.** *med.* (= *poród*) delivery, childbirth, parturition; **bliska** *l.* **oczekująca rozwiązania** parturient. **6.** *mat.* solution, answer, result; **zbiór rozwiązań** solution set.

rozwiązłość *f.* promiscuity, loose morals, licentiousness, dissoluteness; **rozwiązłość obyczajów** libertinism.

rozwiązły *a.* promiscuous, licentious, dissolute, dissipated; **prowadzić rozwiązłe życie** live dissolutely.

rozwiązywać *ipf.* **1.** (= *usuwać supeł*) undo, untie, unknot; (= *rozplątać*) disentangle, unravel; (*gorset*) unlace; **rozwiązać kogoś** untie sb; **rozwiązywać paczkę** undo *l.* open a parcel; **alkohol rozwiązuje mu język** alcohol loosens his tongue; **rozwiązywać akcję** *teor.lit., film, teatr* resolve a plot. **2.** (= *unieważniać*) dissolve, cancel; (*umowę*) terminate; (*małżeństwo*) dissolve, terminate. **3.** (= *likwidować*) (*parlament*) dissolve; (*spółkę, firmę*) dissolve, liquidate; (*zgromadzenie*) dismiss; (*zespół, organizację*) disband. **4.** (= *odgadywać*) solve, figure out; (*zagadkę, tajemnicę*) unriddle, unravel; (*zadanie matematyczne*) work out; (*szyfr*) decipher, decode; (*problem*) solve; **rozwiązywać krzyżówkę** solve *l.* do a crossword puzzle; **rozwiązywać równanie** solve an equation. **5.** *bud.* (= *zaprojektować*) design; (= *zrealizować*) implement; **funkcjonalnie rozwiązane wnętrze** well-designed interior. ~ **się** *ipf.* **1.** (= *uwalniać się z więzów*) unstrap o.s., unbind o.s., free *l.* release o.s. from bonds. **2.** (= *rozsupływać się*) undo, unknot, come untied *l.* undone; **rozwiązał ci się but** your shoelace is undone; **język mu się rozwiązał po alkoholu** alcohol loosened his tongue. **3.** (= *ulegać likwidacji*) be dissolved, be terminated, be cancelled, be liquidated; (*o posiedzeniu*) be dismissed; (*o organizacji*) disband, dissolve. **4.** (= *rozstrzygać się*) resolve; **problem się sam rozwiązał** the problem found its solution.

rozwichrzony *a.* **1.** (= *potargany*) disheveled, disordered. **2.** (= *niezrównoważony*) crazy; (*o wyobraźni*) wild, lively.

rozwichrzyć *pf.* (*włosy*) dishevel, put in disorder.

rozwidlać się *ipf.* furcate, branch, ramify; (*w dwóch kierunkach*) bifurcate; (*w trzech kierunkach*) trifurcate; (*o drodze*) branch, fork.

rozwidlenie *n.* furcation, branching, branch; (*drogi, rzeki*) fork.

rozwidlić się *pf.* zob. **rozwidlać się**.

rozwidlony *a.* furcate, forked, branching; (*o systemie dróg*) ramified.

rozwidniać się *ipf.*, **rozwidnić się** *pf.* light up; **zaczyna się rozwidniać** (*o porze dnia*) the day is breaking *l.* dawning; **rozwidniło się zupełnie** it is broad daylight now.

rozwiedziony *a.* -dzeni divorced; **kobieta rozwiedziona** divorcée, divorcee, grass widow.

rozwielitka *f.* Gen.pl. -ek *zool.* daphnia (*Daphnia*).

rozwieracz *mi* Gen. -a **1.** *med.* dilator, dilater; **rozwieracz opon** *techn.* tire spreader. **2.** *anat.* dilator, dilater; **rozwieracz odbytu** dilator of anus.

rozwierać *ipf.* **1.** *lit.* (= *rozchylać*) (*oczy, usta*) open; (*drzwi, okna*) (throw) open. **2.** *techn.* pull apart, open out; **rozwierać zęby piły** set a saw. **3.**

lit. (= *rozpościerać*) spread; (*palce*) splay; (*ramiona*) spread, open.

rozwiercać *ipf.*, **rozwiercić** *pf.* (*otwór*) ream, drill, bore, enlarge; (*śrubę, plombę*) drill (*coś* into sth).

rozwiert *mi* górn. borehole.

rozwiertak *mi* Gen. -a *techn.* reamer, enlarging drill; **rozwiertak blokowy** block reamer; **rozwiertak kotlarski** boiler reamer; **rozwiertak ślusarski** diemakers' reamer.

rozwiesić *pf.* -szę -sisz, **rozwieszać** *ipf.* hang; (*sznurki, światełka*) suspend, string; (*pranie*) hang out; (*ogłoszenia, plakaty*) put up; **rozwiesić gdzieś ogłoszenia/ulotki** put up notices/fliers somewhere, paste up *l.* stick notices/fliers onto sth.

rozwieść się *pf.* **-wiodę -wiedziesz -wiódł -wiodła -wiedli** zob. **rozwodzić się**.

rozwiewać *ipf.* **1.** (*o wietrze*) (= *rozrzucać*) disperse, blow; **wiatr rozwiał dym** wind dispersed the smoke; **wiatr rozwiewał jej włosy** wind blew through her hair. **2.** (= *usuwać*) dispel, drive away; (*wątpliwości, obawy, smutek*) dispel, allay, resolve; (*nadzieje*) kill, extinguish, chill, put an end to; **rozwiać czyjeś obawy** put *l.* set sb's mind at ease *l.* rest, take sb's doubts away; **rozwiać złudzenia (w jakiejś sprawie)** prick *l.* burst the bubble *l.* baloon (of sth). ~ **się** *ipf.* **1.** (= *rozpraszać się na wietrze*) disperse; **włosy rozwiewały mu się na wietrze** his hair was blowing in the wind, wind blew through his hair. **2.** (= *znikać*) dissipate, disperse, disappear; (*o wątpliwościach*) dispel; (*o nadziejach, wspomnieniach*) be killed *l.* extinguished; **ich marzenia/nadzieje rozwiały się** their dreams/hopes have been shattered.

rozwieźć *pf.* **-wiozę -wieziesz -wiózł -wiozła -wieźli** zob. **rozwozić**.

rozwijać *ipf.* **1.** (= *rozpościerać*) unfold, unfurl, strech; (*kłębek wełny, zwój drutu, rulon*) uncoil, unreel, unroll, roll out; (*sprężynę*) unwind; (*flagę, sztandar*) unfold, unfurl; (*żagle, skrzydła*) spread; **rozwinąć pełne żagle** (*o statku*) be under *l.* in full sail; **rozwinąć skrzydła** przen. spread one's wings; **późno rozwinęła skrzydła** she's a late bloomer; **rozwinąć pasek menu** komp. pull the menu down. **2.** (= *rozpakowywać*) undo, open; (*kwiaty, śniadanie, paczkę*) unwrap. **3.** (= *kształtować*) develop; (*talent, zamiłowania*) cultivate; **rozwijać horyzonty myślowe** broaden one's mind *l.* horizons; **podróże rozwijają** travel broadens the mind; **rozwijać w dziecku zamiłowanie do czytania** instil(l) the love of reading in a child; **te ćwiczenia rozwinęły go fizycznie** these exercises enhanced his physical fitness. **4.** (= *rozbudowywać*) (*handel, gospodarkę*) develop, expand; **rozwinąć interes** set up *l.* establish a business; **rozwijać (dużą) prędkość** drive at great speed; **jego samochód rozwija prędkość do 250 km/h** his car is capable of reaching speeds of up to 250 kph; **rozwijać prędkość** żegl. log. **5.** (*wypowiedź, temat*) (= *omawiać szczegółowo*) expand, elaborate (*coś* on sth); **rozwijać plany na przyszłość** make plans for the fu ture. **6.** *bot.* (= *wykształcać kwiaty, pędy*) develop; **wiosna rozwinęła kwiaty** spring threw the flowers in bloom *l.* blossom. **7.** *wojsk.* (= *ustawiać w szyku*) deploy; **rozwijać wojsko w tyralierę** spread troops out in an extended line. ~ **się** *ipf.* **1.** (= *rozpościerać, rozkręcać się*) uncoil, unreel, unroll, roll out; (*o sztandarze*) unfurl, unfold; (*o taśmie, sznurku, sprężynie*) unwind. **2.** (*o roślinach*) (= *wzrastać*) develop, grow, sprout; (= *otwierać się, kwitnąć*) (*o kwiatach*) bloom, blossom, be in bloom *l.* blossom; (*o płatkach kwiatów*) expand; (*o liściach, kwiatach*) bud, open (out *l.* up). **3.** (= *przechodzić stadia rozwojowe*) develop, grow; emerge, evolve (*z czegoś w coś* out of *l.* from sth into sth); (*o chorobie*) develop; (*o talencie*) bud, flourish; **dziecko rozwijało się normalnie** the child was developing *l.* growing up properly; **Adam rozwija się wolniej od rówieśników** Adam is a late developer; **rozwijać się intelektualnie** develop intellectually; **kraje rozwijające się** developing *l.* underdeveloped countries. **4.** (= *toczyć się*) (*o sytuacji*) develop, progress; (*o wątku, fabule*) unfold; (*o konflikcie*) escalate. **5.** (= *nabierać rozmachu*) (*o rynku, produkcji*) grow, develop; (*o interesie*) thrive.

rozwikłać *pf.*, **rozwikływać** *ipf.* unravel, disentangle; *przen.* (*tajemnicę, zagadkę*) solve, figure out, unriddle, unravel; (*zadanie matematyczne*) work out.

rozwinąć (się) *pf. zob.* **rozwijać (się)**.

rozwinięcie *n.* development; **rozwinięcie akcji** *teor.lit.* development, unfolding; **rozwinięcie dziesiętne** *mat.* decimal; **rozwinięcie funkcji w szereg** *mat.* expansion of a function in a series.

rozwinięty *a.* **1.** (= *w pełni rozwoju*) developed; (*gospodarczo, cywilizacyjnie, intelektualnie*) developed, advanced; *biol.* fully-grown; *orn.* full-fledged; **wysoko rozwinięte społeczeństwo** highly developed society; **kraje rozwinięte** developed countries *l.* nations; **kraje słabo rozwinięte** underdeveloped countries *l.* nations; **nad wiek rozwinięte dziecko** precocious child. **2.** (*o pąku, o kwiecie*) (= *rozkwitnięty*) open, fully-blown. **3.** (= *pokaźny, wydatny*) developed; (*o mięśniach*) bulging; **nadmiernie rozwinięty** (*o poczuciu własnej wartości*) overdeveloped.

rozwlec *pf.* -wlokę *l.* -wlekę -wleczesz -wlókł *l.* -wlekł -wlokła *l.* -wlekła -wlekli, **rozwlekać** *ipf.* **1.** (= *roznieść, wlokąc*) scatter, spread. **2.** (= *przedłużyć, przeciągnąć*) drag out, protract; (*przemówienie*) string out, stretch out; (*sylaby, dźwięki*) drawl, draw out.

rozwlekle *adv.* **1.** (= *zbyt obszernie*) wordily, verbosely, lengthily, prolixly. **2.** in a drawl; **mówić rozwlekle** drawl, speak in a drawl.

rozwlekłość *f.* **1.** (= *zbytnia szczegółowość*) wordiness, verbosity, prolixity. **2.** (*sposób wymowy*) drawling.

rozwlekły *a.* **1.** (= *zbyt obszerny*) wordy, verbose, lenghty, prolix. **2.** (*o wymowie*) (= *przeciągany*) drawly.

rozwodnić *pf.* -ij *zob.* **rozwadniać**.

rozwodnik *mp* divorcé, grass widower.

rozwodowy *a. gł. prawn.* divorce; **sprawa rozwodowa** *l.* **postępowanie rozwodowe** divorce case *l.* proceedings; **prawomocny wyrok rozwodowy** decree absolute; **warunkowy wyrok rozwodowy** decree nisi.

rozwodzić się *ipf.* **1.** (= *mówić l. pisać szczegółowo*) talk *l.* write at length, dwell, descant, expatiate (*nad l. o czymś* (up)on sth); linger (*nad czymś* over *l.* on sth); **rozwodzić się nad czymś** labor the point, *Br.* labour the point; **rozwodzić się nad swoim ulubionym tematem** be on one's hobbyhorse. **2.** (= *uzyskiwać rozwód*) divorce (*z kimś* sb); get divorced *l.* a divorce (*z kimś* from sb).

rozwojowy *a.* **1.** (= *dotyczący rozwoju jako procesu zmian*) developmental, evolutionary, growth; **prace badawczo-rozwojowe** research and development. **2.** *biol.* developmental; **cykl rozwojowy** developmental cycle; **psychologia rozwojowa** developmental psychology; **wada rozwojowa** developmental anomaly. **3.** (= *rokujący nadzieje na rozwój*) progressive, developing; (*o inwestycji*) sound; (*o dziedzinie*) advanced.

rozwolnienie *n. pat.* diarrhea; *Br.* diarrhoea.

rozwora *f. Gen.pl.* -ór **1.** (*drąg w wozie*) perch. **2.** *bud.* (= *rygiel*) nogging.

rozwozić *ipf.* -wożę -wozisz, -woź *l.* -wóź deliver, distribute, transport; **rozwozić pocztę** deliver mail; **rozwozić nawóz** *roln.* spread manure.

rozwód *mi* -o- *zwł. prawn.* divorce; **wystąpić o rozwód** file for divorce; **wziąć z kimś rozwód** divorce sb, get divorced *l.* a divorce from sb; **rozwód bez orzekania winy** no-fault divorce.

rozwódka *f. Gen.pl.* -ek divorcée, divorcee; grass widow.

rozwój *mi* -o- **1.** (= *proces zmian*) development, advancement, progress, growth; **rozwój gospodarczy** economic progress *l.* growth; **kierunek rozwoju czegoś** development trend in sth; **niekontrolowany rozwój miast** urban sprawl *l.* expansion; **strategia rozwoju** *gł. ekon.* development strategy; **u szczytu rozwoju** in *l.* at one's prime; **wspierać rozwój** encourage *l.* support development *l.* growth. **2.** *biol.* development, growth, evolution; **rozwój psychiczny** *l.* **umysłowy** mental development; **rozwój emocjonalny/intelektualny** emotional/intellectual growth; **opóźniony w rozwoju** retarded, backward; **opóźnienie w rozwoju (umysłowym)** *psych.* (mental) retardation, backwardness; **przedwczesny rozwój umysłowy/płciowy** mental/sexual precocity; **wczesny rozwój** (*np. talentu*) precocity, early development. **3.** (= *tok*) progress, development; (*akcji, wydarzeń*) unfolding; (*wątku*) unravelling, unfolding, elaboration; **rozwój wypadków** turn of events; **w fazie rozwoju** (*o planach, pomysłach*) in gestation; **poczekać na rozwój sytuacji** wait and see which way the wind blows.

rozwrzeszczany *a. pot.* screaming, bawling; **rozwrzeszczany bachor** bawling brat.

rozwścieczenie *n.* fury, rage.

rozwścieczyć *pf.* infuriate, enrage; **mocno kogoś rozwścieczyć** make sb's blood boil. ~ **się** *inf.* fly into a rage, get mad, flare up.

rozwydrzenie *n.* *pot.* waywardness, unruliness.

rozwydrzony *a.* **-eni** *pot.* unruly, wayward; (*tłum*) rowdy.

rozwydrzyć *pf. pot.* spoil; **rozwydrzyć dzieci** let one's children become unruly *l.* wayward *l.* spoiled, spoil one's children.

rozziew *mi* **1.** discrepancy, dissonance, disparity; (*między osobami*) discord; (*między teorią a praktyką*) dichotomy. **2.** *fon.* hiatus.

rozzłoszczony *a.* angry, irritated, vexed.

rozzłościć *pf.* **-oszczę -ościsz** anger, irritate, vex, incense (*kogoś czymś* sb with sth); **rozzłościć kogoś** make sb angry *l.* irritated, get sb's dander up. **~ się** *pf.* get *l.* become angry *l.* irritated *l.* exasperated (*na kogoś/coś* with sb/sth); be *l.* become vexed *l.* incensed (*na kogoś/coś* at sb/sth).

rozzuchwalać *ipf.*, **rozzuchwalić** *pf.* embolden; **rozzuchwalić kogoś** encourage sb's impudence *l.* audacity, let sb get arrogant *l.* insolent. **~ się** *ipf.*, **rozzuchwalić się** *pf.* grow *l.* get *l.* become insolent *l.* arogant *l.* audacious *l.* impudent.

rozzuchwalony *a.* **-eni** insolent, audacious, arogant.

rozzuć *pf.*, **rozzuwać** *ipf. arch.* (= *zdjąć sobie obuwie*) take one's shoes off; (= *zdjąć komuś obuwie*) take sb's shoes off.

rozżalać się *ipf.* get *l.* become embittered.

rozżalenie *n.* embitterment, bitterness, chagrin, sorrow; **ogarnęło go rozżalenie** he was overcome with bitterness, he felt pity for himself; **z rozżaleniem** bitterly.

rozżalić się *pf. zob.* **rozżalać się**.

rozżalony *a.* **-eni** embittered; (*na los*) chagrin(n)ed (*czymś* by sth); bitter (*czymś* about sth).

rozżarzać *ipf.* (*żelazo, drucik*) incandesce; (*głownię, węgiel*) kindle, light. **~ się** *ipf.* (*o żelazie, drucie*) incandesce, become red *l.* white hot; (*o głowni, węglach*) glow, kindle.

rozżarzony *a.* (*o żelazie, druciku*) incandescent; **rozżarzony do czerwoności** red *l.* white hot; (*o węglach, głowni*) glowing, kindled; **siedzieć jak na rozżarzonych węglach** be on tenterhooks; **chodzenie po rozżarzonych węglach** (*zwł. jako rytuał*) fire walking.

rozżarzyć *pf. zob.* **rozżarzać**. **~ się** *pf. zob.* **rozżarzać się**.

rożek *mi* **-żk-** *Gen.* **-a 1.** *pl.* **rożki** *l.* **różki** (= *mały róg*) horn; (*sarny*) antler, horn; (*ślimaka, motyla*) horn, tentacle. **2.** (= *stożkowaty przedmiot*) cone, horn; **rożek na proch** powder horn; **rożek na atrament** inkhorn. **3.** *żegl.* fid. **4.** *muz.* horn; **rożek angielski** English horn; **rożek myśliwski** hunting horn. **5.** (= *brzeżek, narożnik*) (*chusteczki, kołnierzyka*) (*krzesła, szuflady*) edge. **6.** *kulin.* (*rodzaj ciastka*) croissant. **7.** *kulin.* (*wafel do lodów*) ice-cream cone.

rożen *mi* **-żn-** *Gen.* **-a** broach, (roasting) spit; (= *punkt gastronomiczny*) rotisserie; **kurczak z rożna** spitroasted chicken.

rożny *a.* **rzut rożny** *sport* corner kick, corner.

rób *itd. ipf. zob.* **robić**.

ród *mi* **-o- 1.** (*w społeczeństwie pierwotnym*) kin. **2.** family; (= *dynastia, linia*) house, line; **ród ludzki** *emf.* human race, mankind; **ród niewieści** *żart.* womankind; **historia rodu** genealogy; **rodem z Polski** of Polish origin *l.* descent; **z królewskiego rodu** of royal ancestry; **ktoś z piekła rodem** a (one) hell of a person. **3.** *pot.* (= *rodzina*) family; **zakała rodu** black sheep; **wywodzić się z rodu chłopskiego/szkockiego** be of peasant/Scottish stock.

róg *mi* **-o- 1.** (= *wyrostek*) horn; (*jelenia, łosia*) antler; (*ślimaka, owadów*) tentacle; **wziąć kogoś na rogi** (*o zwierzęciu*) gore sb; **chwytać byka za rogi** *przen.* take the bull by the horns; **pokazywać rogi** turn nasty, show one's true colors; **przyprawić komuś rogi** cuckold sb; **przytrzeć komuś rogów** teach sb a lesson; **zapędzić kogoś w kozi róg** show sb one's supremacy. **2.** (= *substancja rogowa*) horn; **grzebień z rogu** horn comb. **3.** (= *przedmiot w kształcie rogu*) horn; **róg obfitości** *mit.* cornucopia, horn of plenty; **ciemny jak tabaka w rogu** as thick as two short planks. **4.** *muz.* horn; **róg myśliwski** hunting horn. **5.** (= *brzeg, kąt*) corner; (*stołu*) edge; (*pokoju*) corner; (*kiężyca, sierpu*) crescent; **w prawym górnym rogu** (*kartki, zdjęcia*) in the top righthand corner. **6.** (= *zbieg ulic*) corner, intersection; **na rogu (ulicy) Wiejskiej i Polnej** at the intersection of Wiejska and Polna; **na rogu** on *l.* at the corner; **mieszkać za rogiem** live round the corner; **skręcić za róg** turn the corner; **ścinać róg** (= *iść na skróty*) cut corners. **7.** *sport* corner. **8.** *sport pot.* (= *rzut rożny*) corner, corner kick.

rój *mi* **-o-** *Gen.pl.* **-ów 1.** (= *rodzina pszczela*) swarm. **2.** (= *chmara, mrowie*) swarm, multitude, throng; **rój meteorów** *astron.* swarm of meteors.

ról *f. zob.* **rola**.

rólka *f. Gen.pl.* **-ek** *teatr, film* bit part, bit; **nie-ma rólka** walk-on.

rósł *ipf. zob.* **rosnąć**.

rów *mi* **-o- 1.** ditch; **rów melioracyjny** drainage ditch; **rów oceaniczny** *geogr.* oceanic trench; **Rów Mariański** *geogr.* Mariana Trench; **rów tektoniczny** *geol., geogr.* rift valley, fault rift; **przeskoczyć rów** take the ditch; **wpaść samochodem do rowu** ditch one's car. **2.** *wojsk.* (= *okop*) trench; **rów przeciwczołgowy** anti-tank trench.

rówieśnica, rówieśniczka *f. Gen.pl.* **-ek** *zob.* **rówieśnik**.

rówieśnik *mp Gen* **-a** peer; coeval, contemporary.

równać *ipf.* **1.** (= *niwelować*) level, even, smooth, flatten; (*drogę*) grade; **równać coś z ziemią** raze sth to the ground. **2.** (= *wyrównywać szereg*) keep ranks, dress; **równać w prawo/lewo** *wojsk.* dress right/left. **3.** (= *usuwać różnice*) equalize; (*prawa, obowiązki*) uniform, equalize; **równać w górę/dół** level up/down; **równać krok** *wojsk.* keep in step. **~ się** *ipf.* **1.** (= *być równym czemuś*) be equal (*z czymś* to *l.* with sth); add up, amount, be tantamount (*z czymś* to sth); **dwa plus dwa równa się cztery** two and two equals *l.* makes four; **niech x równa się zero** let x be *l.*

equal zero; **ten czyn równa się zdradzie** this act *l.* deed is tantamount to treason. **2.** (*o szeregu*) (= *prostować się*) fall into line; *wojsk.* dress. **3.** (= *dopędzać, zrównywać się*) level, catch up (*z kimś* with sb). **4.** (= *dorównywać*) equal (*z kimś/czymś* sb/sth); compare (*z kimś/czymś* to sb/sth); **nic nie może się równać z tobą** nothing compares to you; **nikt nie mógłby się z nim równać** there's no match for him.

równanie *n.* **1.** (*terenu*) leveling, evening, flattening. **2.** (*pracy, obowiązków*) equalization. **3.** *mat.* equation; **równanie kwadratowe/różniczkowe/logarytmiczne/macierzowe** quadratic/differential/logarithmic/matrix equation; **równanie pierwszego stopnia** linear equation; **równanie czasu/stanu** *fiz.* equation of time/state; **teoria równań kwadratowych** quadratics.

równia *f. Gen.pl.* **-i** *lit.* plane; **równia pochyła** *fiz.* inclined plane; **na równi z czymś** on a par with sth; **staczać się po równi pochyłej** *przen.* approach failure *l.* disaster, be going steadily downhill; **stać na równi z kimś/czymś** be on a par with sb/sth.

równiacha *mp pl.* **-y** *Gen.* **-ch** *l.* **-ów** *pot.* cool guy *l.* dude.

równiak *mi Gen.* **-a** *techn.* (*młot*) face hammer.

równiarka *f. Dat.* **-rce** *techn.* grader.

równie *adv.* equally; **równie szybki/bystry co...** as fast/smart as...; **every bit as fast/smart as...; nigdy w życiu nie widziałem nic równie pięknego** never in my life have I seen anything as beautiful; **równie dobrze możesz sobie iść** you might as well go.

również *adv.* also, as well, likewise; (*we frazach przeczących*) either, neither; **jak również...** and also..., as well as...; **to również nie powinno cię obchodzić** this shouldn't bother you either.

równik *mi Gen.* **-a** *geogr.* equator; **równik magnetyczny** magnetic equator, aclinic line; **równik świata** celestial equator.

równikowy *a.* equatorial; **las równikowy** rain forest.

równina *f. geogr.* plain; **równina błotna** mud flat.

równinny *a.* flat, even; **teren równinny** plain area *l.* country.

równiutki *a.* perfectly flat *l.* even; as flat *l.* even as can be.

równiutko *adv.* perfectly flat *l.* even; as flat *l.* even *l.* straight as can be.

równo *adv.* **1.** (= *gładko*) evenly, even (*z czymś* with sth); **równo przystrzyżony trawnik** evenly mowed *l.* trimmed lawn. **2.** (= *prosto*) straight; **równo z powierzchnią** flush with the surface. **3.** (= *jednakowo*) the same (way), equally; **traktować wszystkich równo** treat everybody the same way *l.* equally *l.* on a par; **dostać po równo** get equal shares; **dzielić się po równo** share equally. **4.** (= *miarowo*) regularly, evenly, steadily, uniformly. **5.** (= *dokładnie, akurat*) exactly; **skończyłem równo z nim** I finished at exactly the same time he did, I finished simultaneously with him; **jego córka miała rów-**

no trzy miesiące his daughter was exactly three months old.

równoboczny *a.* equilateral; **trójkąt równoboczny** *geom.* equilateral triangle.

równobrzmiący *a.* identical, verbatim; **dwa równobrzmiące teksty** two identical texts.

równoczesny *a.* simultaneous, concurrent (*z czymś* with sth); parallel (*z czymś* to sth).

równocześnie *adv.* **1.** (= *jednocześnie*) at the same time, simultaneously, concurrently, in parallel; **wydarzyć się równocześnie z czymś** synchronize *l.* co-occur with sth; **równocześnie z czymś** along with sth. **2.** *pot.* (= *zarazem, także*) at the same time; **może być zdenerwowany, ale równocześnie wie, jak zapanować nad stresem** he can be annoyed but at the same time he knows how to manage stress.

równokątny *a. geom.* equiangular; isogonic, isogonal.

równokierunkowy *a. fiz.* isotropic.

równokształtny *a.* isomorphic; (*o krysztale*) isomorphous.

równolatek *mp* **-tk-** *pl.* **-i** (= *człowiek w tym samym wieku co inny*) coeval, person of the same age (*czyjś/czyjaś* as sb). – *ma* **-tk-** *rzad.* (= *zwierzę w tym samym wieku co inne*) animal of the same age (*as some other animal*).

równolatka *f. Gen.pl.* **-ek** *zob.* **równolatek.**

równolegle *adv.* **1.** (*ułożony itp.*) parallel (*do czegoś* to *l.* with sth). **2.** *pot.* (= *jednocześnie*) simultaneously, concurrently.

równoległobok *mi geom.* parallelogram.

równoległościan *mi geom.* parallelepiped.

równoległy *a.* **1.** (= *jednakowo oddalony*) parallel (*do czegoś* to *l.* with sth); **połączenie równoległe** *el.* parallel connection. **2.** *pot.* (= *jednoczesny*) simultaneous, concurrent.

równoleżnik *mi Gen.* **-a** *geogr.* parallel (of latitude); **równoleżnik niebieski** *astron.* almucantar *l.* almacantar, parallel of altitude.

równomiernie *adv.* evenly.

równomierny *a.* even.

równonoc *f. pl.* **-e** *astron.* equinox; **równonoc jesienna** autumnal equinox; **równonoc wiosenna** vernal equinox.

równoprawny *a.* equal.

równoramienny *a.* even-armed; **trójkąt równoramienny** *geom.* isosceles triangle.

równorzędny *a.* equivalent; (*partner, przeciwnik*) equal; **to dla niego równorzędny przeciwnik** he's a match for him.

równość *f.* **1.** (= *identyczność*) equality, parity; **znak równości** *mat.* equal(s) sign; **stawiać znak równości między czymś a czymś** *przen.* equal sth with sth, put sth on a par with sth. **2.** (= *równouprawnienie*) equality (*of rights*); **równość wobec prawa** equality before the law; **równość rasowa** racial equality; **równość płci** equality of *l.* between the sexes; **równość traktowania** equality of treatment; **równość szans** equality of opportunities. **3.** (= *gładkość powierzchni*) smoothness, evenness.

równouprawnienie *n.* equality of rights; **rów-**

nouprawnienie kobiet women's rights, equal rights for women, equality of women.

równowaga *f.* **1.** (= *stała postawa*) balance; **równowaga umysłu** balance of mind, equanimity; **zaburzenie równowagi** balance disturbance; **zmysł równowagi** balance; **stracić równowagę** lose one's balance; **zachwiać równowagę** upset the balance; **przywrócić równowagę** redress *l.* restore the balance; **odzyskać równowagę** regain one's balance; **stworzyć równowagę** strike a balance. **2.** (= *opanowanie, spokój*) poise, composure, balance; **wyprowadzić** *l.* **wytrącić kogoś z równowagi** throw sb off balance; **wytrącony z równowagi** off balance. **3.** (= *zrównoważenie*) composure, poise. **4.** (= *równy układ sił*) balance, equilibrium; **równowaga gospodarcza** economic balance; **równowaga budżetowa** budget balance; **równowaga biologiczna** biological balance; **równowaga cenowa** price equilibrium. **5.** *fiz.* equilibrium; **równowaga chwiejna** *l.* **niestała** unstable *l.* labile equilibrium; **równowaga stała** stable equilibrium. **6.** *tenis* deuce.

równowartość *f.* equivalent; **stanowić równowartość czegoś** be equivalent to sth.

równoważnia *f. Gen.pl.* **-i** *sport* balance beam.

równoważnik *mi Gen.* **-a** equivalent; **równoważnik zdania** *gram.* verbless sentence, sentence fragment.

równoważność *f.* **1.** (= *równa wartość*) equivalence. **2.** *log.* equivalence.

równoważny *a.* equivalent (*z czymś* to sth).

równoważyć *ipf.* **1.** balance, counterbalance, counterpoise, offset; **równoważyć coś czymś** balance sth against sth. **2.** (= *rekompensować*) compensate, make up for. ~ **się** *ipf.* be in balance, balance.

równoznacznik *mi Gen.* **-a** *jęz.* synonym.

równoznaczność *f.* equivalence, synonymy.

równoznaczny *a.* equivalent, synonymous, tantamount.

równy *a.* **1.** (= *gładki*) even, smooth; (*o szosie, terenie*) flat; (= *prosty, niepowyginany*) flat; (*o szeregu, linii, zębach*) straight; **stopień równy** *jęz.* positive degree, the positive; **zerwać się na równe nogi** leap *l.* jump to one's feet. **2.** (= *jednakowy*) equal, identical; **w równych odstępach czasu** at regular intervals; **równo rozmieszczone** evenly spaced *l.* spread; **w równej mierze** equally; **na równej stopie** on equal footing; **jak równy z równym** on equal terms; **nie mieć sobie równego** have no match *l.* equal; **wszyscy są równi wobec prawa** everyone is equal before the law. **3.** (= *spokojny, zrównoważony*) steady, balanced; (*o usposobieniu*) balanced, poised. **4.** (= *miarowy, rytmiczny*) steady, even; (*o kroku, pracy silnika*) steady. **5.** *pot.* (= *sympatyczny*) cool, fab; **równy gość** cool dude *l.* guy. **6.** *pot.* (= *akurat tyle*) exactly, precisely; **równe dwa metry** two meters precisely *l.* exactly.

rózga *f. Gen.pl.* **1.** rózg *l.* rózeg rod, birch. **2.** *pl. przest.* (= *chłosta*) hiding, beating.

róż *mi Gen.pl.* **-ów 1.** (= *kolor różowy*) pink. **2.** (*kosmetyk*) blush, blusher.

róża *f.* **1.** *bot.* rose (*Rosa*); **róża chińska** hibis-

cus, China rose (*Hibiscus rosa-sinensis*); **róża jerychońska** rose of Jericho (*Anastatica hierochuntica*); **róża stulistna** rose absolute (*Rosa centifolia*); **dzika róża** wild rose, brier; **róża kompasowa** *żegl.* compass card; **róża wiatrów** *żegl.* wind rose; **życie usłane różami** bed of roses, all roses; **nie ma róży bez kolców** no rose without a thorn. **2.** *med.* erysipelas. **3.** *myśl.* coronet.

różanecznik *mi Gen.* **-a** *bot.* (= *rododendron*) rhododendron (*Rhododendron*).

różaniec *mi* **-ńc-** *Gen.* **-a** *rz.-kat.* (*modlitwa*) rosary; **odmawiać różaniec** tell one's beads; (= *sznur paciorków z krzyżykiem*) rosary, beads.

różanka *f. Gen.pl.* **-ek** *icht.* bitterling (*Rhodeus sericeus amarus*).

różany *a.* **1.** (= *dotyczący róży*) rose, rosy; **krzew różany** rosebush; **ogród różany** rosarium, rose garden. **2.** (= *rumiany*) rosy.

różańcowy *a. rz.-kat.* rosary.

różdżka *f. Gen.pl.* **-ek** (= *rozwidlony pręt*) divining rod, dowser; **czarodziejska różdżka** magic wand; **jak za dotknięciem czarodziejskiej różdżki** as if by magic.

różdżkarstwo *n.* divining, dowsing.

różdżkarz *mp* diviner, dowser; (*szukający wody*), water finder.

różnica *f.* **1.** (= *różność*) difference, disparity; **różnica czasu** time difference; **różnica zdań** difference of opinion, disagreement; **różnica pokoleń** generation gap; **bez różnicy** *pot.* (= *obojętnie*) doesn't matter; **a co za różnica?** what's the difference?, who cares?; **to mi nie robi różnicy** it doesn't make any difference to me, it makes no difference to me; **a to różnica** it makes all the difference; **z tą różnicą, że...** except that...; **różnica potencjałów** *fiz.* potential difference, voltage. **2.** *mat.* remainder.

różnicować *ipf.* (= *dzielić*) divide; (= *wyodrębniać według różnic*) differentiate. ~ **się** *ipf.* become different, differentiate.

różnicowy *a.* differential; **mechanizm różnicowy** *techn.* differential gear; **rachunek różnicowy** *mat.* calculus of differences.

różniczka *f. Gen.pl.* **-ek** *mat.* differential.

różniczkować *ipf. mat.* differentiate.

różniczkowy *a. mat.* differential; **rachunek różniczkowy** differential calculus.

różnić *ipf.* **-ij** distinguish, differ; **różnić kogoś/coś od kogoś/czegoś** distinguish sb/sth from sb/sth. ~ **się** *ipf.* differ, vary; **różnić się czymś** differ in sth; **różnić się od kogoś/czegoś** differ from sb/sth; **różnić się z kimś w jakiejś sprawie** disagree with sb on sth; **różnić się w poglądach na coś** have different views on sth, have divergent attitudes towards sth; **znacznie się różnić** differ considerably.

różnie *adv.* variously; **różnie bywa** there are ups and downs.

różnobarwny *a.* multicolored.

różnokierunkowy *a.* multidirectional; *fiz., biol.* anisotropic.

różnokolorowy *a.* colorful; *Br.* colourful; multicolored; *Br.* multicoloured.

różnokształtny *a.* having different shapes.

różnopostaciowy *a.* diversiform, multifarious; *biol.* heteromorphic.

różnoraki *a.* varied, diverse, diversified.

różnorodnie *adv.* diversely, variously, multifariously.

różnorodność *f.* diversity, variety.

różnorodny *a.* diverse, varied, multifarious.

różności *pl. Gen.* **-i** *pot.* (= *różne rzeczy*) odds and ends, sundries, various things/items/etc., miscellanea.

różność *f.* diversity, variety.

różnozarodnikowość *f. Gen.* **-ści** *bot.* heterospory.

różny *a.* **1.** (= *różnoraki*) various, different; **różne różności** miscellanea. **2.** (= *odmienny*) different, distinct.

różowawy *a.* rosy, pinkish.

różowić *ipf.* **-ów** make rosy (*in color*). ~ **się** *ipf.* turn *l.* become rosy; (*o policzkach*) glow.

różowo *adv.* **1.** (= *w kolorze różowym*) rosily. **2.** (= *optymistycznie*) in bright colors, *Br.* in bright colours; rosily.

różowy *a.* rose, pink; **patrzeć na coś przez różowe okulary** *l.* widzieć coś w różowych barwach see sth through rose-colored spectacles.

różyczka *f. Gen.pl.* **-ek 1.** (= *mała róża*) (small) rose. **2.** (= *przedmiot w kształcie róży*) rose. **3.** *pat.* rubella, German measles.

RP *abbr.* (= *Rzeczpospolita Polska*) the Republic of Poland.

RPA *abbr. geogr.* (= *Republika Południowej Afryki*) RSA (= *the Republic of South Africa*), *pot.* South Africa.

r. szkoln. *abbr.* (= *rok szkolny*) school year.

rtęciowy *a.* mercurial; **lampa rtęciowa** mercury discharge lamp, mercury-vapor tube.

rtęciówka *f. Gen.pl.* **-ek** *pot.* (= *lampa rtęciowa*) mercury discharge lamp, mercury-vapor tube.

rtęć *f. chem.* mercury, quicksilver.

rtg. *abbr.* (= *rentgen*) X-rays.

RTV *abbr.* (= *radio i telewizja*) radio and television.

Ruanda *f. geogr.* Rwanda.

Ruandyjczyk *mp*, **Ruandyjka** *f. Gen.pl.* **-ek** Rwandan.

ruandyjski *a.* Rwandan.

r. ub. *abbr.* (= *roku ubiegłego*) previous *l.* last year.

rubasznica *f. Gen.* **-cy** *bot.* stonecrop (*Crassula*).

rubasznie *adv.* coarsely, crudely.

rubaszny *a.* coarse, crude.

rubel *mi* **-bl-** *Gen.* **-a** (= *jednostka monetarna Rosji*) ruble.

rubensowski *a.* (*o obrazach, kształtach*) Rubenesque.

rubid *mi chem.* rubidium.

rubież *f. pl.* **-e** (= *pogranicze*) borderland, frontier.

Rubik *mp* **kostka Rubika** Rubik's cube.

Rubikon *mi hist., geogr.* Rubicon; **przekroczyć Rubikon** cross *l.* pass the Rubicon.

rubin *mi min.* ruby.

rubinowy *a.* **1.** (= *zrobiony z rubinu*) ruby. **2.** (= *barwy rubinu*) ruby.

rublowy *a. fin.* ruble.

rubryczka *f. Gen.pl.* **-ek** blank.

rubryka *f.* **1.** (= *pozycja w formularzu itp.*) blank, blank space. **2.** (= *stały dział w gazecie itp.*) column.

ruch *mi* **1.** (= *zmiana położenia*) movement, motion; **ruch jałowy** *techn.* dead movement; **ruch jednostajny** *fiz.* uniform motion; **ruch jednostajnie opóźniony** *fiz.* uniformly retarded motion; **ruch jednostajnie przyspieszony** *fiz.* uniformly accelerated motion; **ruch krzywoliniowy** *fiz.* curvilinear motion; **ruch obrotowy** *fiz.* rotary motion, rotation; **ruch prostoliniowy** *fiz.* (recti)linear motion; **ruch wahadłowy** *fiz.* swinging motion; **ruchy górotwórcze** *geol.* earth *l.* orogenic movements; **ruchy robaczkowe** *anat.* peristalsis; **być w ruchu** be on the run; **puścić** *l.* **wprawić coś w ruch** set sth in motion; **stać bez ruchu** stand still. **2.** (= *poruszanie się, gest*) movement, motion, move; **mieć swobodę ruchów** *t. przen.* have a free hand, have leeway; **zrobić pierwszy ruch** make the first move. **3.** (= *ćwiczenia fizyczne*) exercise; **zażywać ruchu** take exercise. **4.** (= *wzmożona aktywność, krzątanina*) commotion, bustle; **ruch w interesie** *pot.* hecticness; **być w ciągłym ruchu** live *l.* lead an active life. **5.** (= *poruszanie się pieszych i pojazdów*) traffic; **ruch drogowy** road *l.* vehicular traffic; **ruch prawostronny/lewostronny** *mot.* right-/left-side traffic; **ruch tranzytowy** transit traffic; **regulować ruch** control the traffic; **pas ruchu** lane. **6.** *polit., sztuka* movement; **ruch polityczny** political movement; **ruch oporu** Resistance. **7.** (= *posunięcie w grze planszowej*) move. **8.** *wojsk.* maneuver, *Br.* manoeuvre; movement.

ruchać *ipf. wulg.* **1.** (= *odbywać z kimś stosunek płciowy*) fuck, screw; **on rucha żonę swojego szefa** he fucks his boss's wife. **2.** (= *oszukiwać*) screw (*kogoś* sb). ~ **się** *ipf. wulg.* (= *odbywać stosunek płciowy*) fuck, screw; **ruchali się na morgi** they fucked like rabbits.

ruchawka *f. Dat.* **-wce** *pot.* riot, unrest.

ruchliwość *f.* **1.** (= *ruchomość*) mobility; **ruchliwość zawodowa** professional mobility. **2.** (= *ożywienie*) commotion, stir, agitation. **3.** (= *żwawość*) liveliness.

ruchliwy *a.* **1.** (= *ruszający się*) mobile; (*o rękach, oczach*) restless. **2.** (= *ożywiony*) animated, vigorous; (*o porcie, ulicy*) busy. **3.** (= *żwawy*) lively, active, vivacious; (*o dziecku*) lively, active. **4.** (= *rzutki*) active.

ruchomo *adv.* movably.

ruchomość *f.* **1.** (= *zdolność poruszania się*) movability, mobility. **2.** *prawn. zw. pl.* (= *majątek ruchomy*) personal property, movables.

ruchomy *a.* **1.** (= *będący w ruchu*) moving; **ruchome piaski** quicksand; **wydmy ruchome** migrating *l.* mobile dunes; **schody ruchome** escalator. **2.** (= *dający się ruszyć, przenośny*) movable; **majątek ruchomy** *prawn.* personal property, movables; **ruchomy czas pracy** flexible working hours, flexitime; **ruchome święto** *rel.* movable feast (day).

ruchowy *a.* (= *związany z ruchem*) locomotive, physical; **zabawy** *l.* **gry ruchowe** outdoor activities *l.* games; **nerwy ruchowe** *anat.* motor nerves; **afazja ruchowa** *pat.* motor aphasia.

ruczaj *mi poet.* brook, creek.

ruda *f. min., górn.* ore.

rudawy *a.* reddish, ginger.

rudbekia *f. Gen.* -**ii** *bot.* coneflower (*Rudbeckia*).

rudera *f.* ruin.

ruderalny *a. bot.* ruderal; **rośliny ruderalne** ruderals, ruderal plants.

rudowęglowiec *mi* -**wc**- *Gen.* -**a** *żegl.* coal(-and)-ore carrier.

rudowiec *mi* -**wc**- *Gen.* -**a** *żegl.* ore carrier *l.* vessel.

rudowłosy *a.* redheaded, red-haired, ginger-haired.

rudy *a.* red, ginger; **spocić się jak ruda mysz** *pot.* be all sweaty.

rudyment *mi* **1.** *lit.* (= *podstawa*) rudiment. **2.** *biol.* rudiment.

rudymentarny *a.* **1.** *lit.* (= *elementarny*) rudimentary, elementary. **2.** *lit.* (= *szczątkowy*) rudimentary.

rudzielec *mp* -**lc**- *pl.* -**y** *pot.* redhead, carrothead *l.* -top.

rudzik *ma orn.* (European) robin (*Erithacus rubecula*).

rufa *f. żegl.* stern; **na rufie** aft.

rufowy *a. żegl.* stern.

rugać *ipf. pot.* tell off.

rugbista *mp sport* rugby player.

rugby *n. indecl. sport* rugby.

rugować *ipf.* **1.** (= *wysiedlać*) displace. **2.** (= *usuwać, eliminować*) eliminate, eradicate.

ruina *f.* **1.** (= *stan zniszczenia, upadku*) decay, ruin, disrepair; **doprowadzić kogoś do ruiny** lead to sb's ruin, ruin sb, bring sb to ruin; **doprowadzić coś do ruiny** bring sth to ruin; **popaść w ruinę** fall into ruin *l.* disrepair, decay; **chylący się ku ruinie** run-down, tumble-down. **2.** (= *coś zniszczonego*) ruin; **ruina człowieka** *przen.* a wreck of a person.

ruiny *pl. Gen.* -**n** (= *rumowiska, gruzy*) ruins; **podnieść się z ruin** rise from the ruins.

ruja *f. Gen., Dat. i Loc.* **rui** *zool.* rut, heat.

rujnować *ipf.* **1.** (= *niszczyć*) ruin, devastate, destroy. **2.** (= *osłabiać*) ruin, spoil. ~ **się** *ipf.* go bankrupt; **musiałeś się zrujnować na ten prezent?!** you must have spent lots of money on that gift?!

ruletka *f. Gen.pl.* -**ek** roulette; **rosyjska ruletka** Russian roulette.

rulon *mi* **1.** (*materiału, papieru*) roll. **2.** (*monet*) roll, bunch.

rulonik *mi Gen.* -**a** roll.

rum *mi kulin.* rum.

rumak *ma lit.* steed.

rumb *mi żegl.* rhumb.

rumba *f.* (*taniec*) rumba.

rumianek *mi* -**nk**- *bot.* chamomile, camomile (*Chamaemelium nobile l. Anthemis nobilis*).

rumiankowy *a.* chamomile, camomile.

rumiany *a.* **1.** (= *mający rumieńce*) ruddy; (*o jabłkach*) red. **2.** (= *przypieczony do złocistego koloru*) gold, golden brown.

rumienić *ipf.* **1.** *kulin.* (= *przypiekać na złocisty kolor*) brown. **2.** *lit.* (= *zabarwiać na czerwono*) blush. ~ **się** *ipf.* **1.** (= *dostawać rumieńców*) blush. **2.** (= *przypiekać się na złocisty kolor*) get (golden) brown.

rumieniec *mi* -**ńc**- *Gen.* -**a** (= *zabarwienie policzków*) blush; **nabrać rumieńców** (= *dobrze wyglądać*) start looking good *l.* healthy; (= *nabierać życia*) become lively; **oblać się rumieńcem** blush, glow.

rumień *mi Gen.* -**a** *pl.* -**e** *pat.* erythema.

rumor *mi* (= *łoskot*) rumble; (= *zamieszanie*) turmoil, commotion.

rumosz *mi Gen.* -**u** *geol.* debris, rubble.

rumowisko *n.* **1.** (= *gruzy*) rubble. **2.** (= *odłamki skalne*) rubble, debris.

rumowy *a. kulin.* rum.

rumpel *mi* -**pl**- *żegl.* tiller.

rumsztyk *mi kulin.* rump steak.

Rumun *mp,* **Rumunka** *f. Gen.pl.* -**ek** Romanian; *rzad.* Rumanian, Roumanian.

Rumunia *f. Gen.* -**ii** *geogr.* Romania, *rzad.* Rumania, Roumania.

rumuński *a.* Romanian; *rzad.* Rumanian, Roumanian.

run *mi* **1.** *ekon.* (= *wycofywanie pieniędzy*) run. **2.** (= *wykupywanie towarów*) run (*na coś* on sth).

runąć *pf.* **1.** (= *upaść, zwalić się*) fall down, collapse, tumble down; (*o samolocie*) plummet. **2.** (= *zawalić się*) collapse, tumble down. **3.** (= *załamać się*) collapse, break down. **4.** (= *rzucić się gwałtownie*) plunge; (*o tłumie, armii*) pounce (*na kogoś/coś* on sb/sth); rush (*na kogoś/coś* at sb/sth); run (*na kogoś/coś* for sb/sth).

runda *f.* **1.** (= *faza, etap*) leg, stage, round. **2.** *sport* (= *cykl rozgrywek*) round; **runda finałowa** finals, final round. **3.** *sport* (*w boksie itp.*) round. **4.** *sport* (= *okrążenie bieżni itp.*) lap; **runda honorowa** victory lap; lap of honor, *Br.* lap of honour.

runiczny *a. jęz.* runic; **pismo runiczne** runic writing; **alfabet runiczny** futhark.

runo *n.* (= *skóra z wełną*) **1.** fleece; **runo owcze** lamb's wool; **złote runo** *mit.* the Golden Fleece. **2. runo leśne** underbrush, undergrowth.

runy *pl. Gen.* -**n** *jęz.* runes.

rupia *f. Gen.* -**ii** (= *jednostka monetarna Indii*) rupee.

rupieciarnia *f. Gen.pl.* -**i** lumber room.

rupieć *mi pl.* -**e** (piece of) junk, rubbish.

rura *f.* **1.** pipe; **rura wydechowa** *mot.* tailpipe, exhaust pipe; **walnąć** *l.* **wypalić z grubej rury** *pot.* say sth bluntly; **rura mu zmiękła** *pot.* he's come down a peg or two. **2.** *wulg.* (= *atrakcyjna kobieta*) piece of ass, chick; **niezła z niej rura** she's a fuckable chick. **3.** *wulg.* (= *pochwa*) slot.

rurka *f. Gen.pl.* -**ek** **1.** (= *mała rura*) pipe,

tube. **2.** (= *przedmiot w kształcie rurki*) tube; **zwinąć coś w rurkę** roll sth, make a roll of sth; *kulin.* (*makaron*) rigatoni.

rurkopław *ma Gen.* **-a** *zool.* siphonophore (*Siphonophora*).

rurkowaty *a.* pipelike, pipy; tubular.

rurociąg *mi techn.* pipeline.

rurociągowy *a. techn.* pipeline.

rurownia *f. Gen.* **-ni** *metal.* tube *l.* pipe works.

rurowy *a.* tube, pipe; **łącznik rurowy** *techn.* pipe coupling.

rusałka *f. Gen.pl.* **-ek 1.** (= *nimfa*) water sprite. **2.** *ent.* admiral (*Vanessa*); **rusałka admirał** red admiral (*Vanessa atalanta rubria*); **rusałka pawik** peacock butterfly (*Inachis io*).

Rusek *mp* **-sk-** *pl.* **-i** *pot.* (= *Rosjanin*) Russki.

ruski *a.* (*dotyczący Rusi*) Ruthenian; *pot.* (= *rosyjski*) Russian; **ruskie pierogi** *kulin.* cheese-and-potato-filled pierogi *l.* pirozhki.

rusofil *mp* Russophile.

rusofilstwo *n.* Russophilia.

rusofobia *f.* Russophobia.

rustykalny *a.* rustic.

rusycysta *mp*, **rusycystka** *f. Gen.pl.* **-ek 1.** (*uczony*) scholar in Russian studies; (*nauczyciel*) teacher of Russian, Russian teacher. **2.** (*student*) student of Russian; (*absolwent*) graduate in Russian, graduate of a Russian department.

rusycystyka *f. uniw.* **1.** (*dział nauki*) Russian studies. **2.** (*jednostka uniwersytetu*) Russian department.

rusycyzm *mi jęz.* Russian borrowing.

rusyfikacja *f.* Russification.

rusyfikować *f.* Russianize, Russify.

ruszać *ipf.* **1.** (= *wyruszać*) set off, start; (*o pojeździe*) pull out; **ruszać w drogę** set off, begin a journey; **co rusz** every second, again and again; **ruszać do ataku** charge, attack; **ruszać na kogoś/coś** pounce on sb/sth; **nie ruszaj się!** freeze!; **nie ruszaj się z miejsca!** stay where you are!, stand still!; **ruszyć z kopyta** (= *wystartować szybko*) shoot, tear. **2.** (= *poruszać*) move; **nawet nie ruszył palcem** he didn't even lift a finger; **ruszyć sprawy z miejsca** get things moving; **rusz głową!** use your head!; **rusz tyłek!** move your ass!; **rusz się!** get yourself moving!, get a move on!. **3.** (= *dotykać*) touch; **sumienie go ruszyło** his conscience began to nag him; **nie ruszaj tych spraw** *przen.* you'd better keep out of this thing!; **nie ruszaj tego!** keep your hands off (this thing)!, don't touch it!. **4.** *pot.* (= *wywoływać emocje*) move, touch; **mnie to nie rusza** I don't care. **5.** (= *zaczynać funkcjonować*) start, be launched; **ruszyliśmy z robotą w czerwcu** we got off the ground in June. **~ się** *ipf.* **1.** (= *wyruszać*) set off, get moving. **2.** (= *posuwać się*) get moving, be moving; **coś się ruszyło** (= *coś się zaczęło dziać*) things picked up; **tu nie ma gdzie się ruszyć** this place is so cramped. **3.** (= *być w ruchu*) move, keep moving, be on the move; **rusz się!** get a move on!, get yourself moving!; **nie ruszaj się!** freeze!; **ruszać się jak mucha w smole** move at a snail's pace. **4.** (= *chwiać się*) budge; (*o zębie*) be loose.

ruszenie *n. hist.* **pospolite ruszenie** mass levy, levy en masse.

rusznica *f. hist.* flintlock, matchlock; **rusznica przeciwpancerna** *wojsk.* anti-tank gun *l.* rifle.

rusznikarz *mp* gunsmith.

ruszt *mi* **1.** (*część paleniska*) grill; **mięso z rusztu** grilled meat; **wrzucić coś na ruszt** *pot.* (= *zjeść coś*) grab a bite, chow sth down. **2.** *bud.* (open) grillage, grid.

rusztowanie *n. zwł. bud.* scaffold, scaffolding.

ruszyć *pf. zob.* **ruszać**. **~ się** *pf. zob.* **ruszać się**.

Ruś *f. hist.* Ruthenia.

ruta *f. bot.* rue (*Ruta*).

ruten *mi chem.* ruthenium.

rutewka *f. Dat.* **-wce** *bot.* meadow rue (*Thalictrum*).

rutwica *f. Gen.* **-cy** *bot.* **rutwica lekarska** goat's-rue (*Galega officinalis*).

rutyl *mi min.* rutile.

rutyna *f.* **1.** routine, rut; **popaść w rutynę** move in a rut. **2.** (= *doświadczenie*) experience.

rutyniarz *mp* **1.** (= *człowiek skostniały*) old fog(e)y. **2.** (= *wyga, wyjadacz*) (old) stager, experienced person.

rutynowy *a.* **1.** (= *utarty*) routine, standard; **postępowanie rutynowe** routine procedure; **przesłuchanie rutynowe** routine questioning. **2.** (= *nudny*) menial, dull.

rwa *f.* **rwa kulszowa** *pat.* sciatic neuralgia, ischialgia.

rwać *ipf.* **rwę rwiesz, rwij 1.** (= *rozrywać*) tear (apart), rip; **porwać na strzępy** rip *l.* tear up, rip to shreds, tear to pieces; **cicha woda brzegi rwie** still water runs deep. **2.** (= *zrywać*) pick. **3.** (= *podrywać kobietę lub mężczyznę*) pick up. **4.** (= *wyrywać*) pull out; **rwać włosy z głowy** *przen.* tear one's hair (out). **5.** (*o zębie, stawach*) (= *sprawiać ból*) shoot; **ząb mnie rwie** I have a shooting pain in my tooth. **6.** (*o tkaninie*) tear, rip; **porwałam sobie rajstopy** I ripped my tights. **7.** (= *pędzić*) rush, dash, tear. **~ się** *ipf.* **1.** (= *pękać*) break, rip, burst. **2.** (= *przerywać się*) break; (*o rozmowie, głosie*) break off. **3.** *pot.* (= *mocno chcieć*) be dying (*do czegoś* for sth); **rwać się do walki** be spoiling for a fight.

rwanie *n.* **podnoszenie ciężarów** snatch.

rwący *a.* **1.** (= *wartki*) swift, rapid; (*o potoku*) torrential; **rwący potok** rapid torrent. **2.** (= *silny*) mighty, powerful; (*o bólu*) shooting, throbbing, acute.

RWE *abbr.* (= *Radio Wolna Europa*) RFE (= *Radio Free Europe*).

rwetes *mi pot.* ado, bustle, fuss.

RWPG *abbr.* (= *Rada Wzajemnej Pomocy Gospodarczej*) *hist.* COMECON (= *Council for Mutual Economic Assistance*).

ryba *f.* fish; **Ryby** *astrol.* Pisces; **gruba ryba** *przen.* bigwig, big shot; **zdrów jak ryba** (as) right as rain; **czuć się jak ryba w wodzie** feel like a fish in a pond; **jak ryba bez wody** like (a) fish out of water; **iść na ryby** go fishing; **pływać jak ryba** swim like a fish; **zimny jak ryba** as cold as a fish; **dzieci i ryby głosu nie mają** children should be seen and not heard.

rybacki *a.* fishing; **statek rybacki** fishing boat; **sieć rybacka** fishing net.

rybactwo *n.* fishery, fishing.

rybaczki *pl. Gen.* **-ek** (*spodnie*) pedal pushers.

rybak *mp* fisherman.

rybałt *mp hist.* minstrel.

rybi *a.* fishy, piscine.

rybik *ma Gen.* **-a** *ent.* **rybik cukrowy** silverfish (*Lepisma saccharina*).

rybitwa *f. orn.* tern (*Sterna*).

rybka *f. Gen.pl.* **-ek 1.** (= *mała ryba*) fish; **złota rybka** goldfish. **2.** (*pieszczotliwie*) (= *kochanie*) honey, darling, baby. **3.** *żegl.* king plank.

rybny *a.* **1.** (= *zrobiony z ryb*) fish; **zupa rybna** *kulin.* fish soup; **paluszki rybne** *kulin.* fish sticks *l.* fingers. **2.** (= *pełen ryb, dotyczący ryb*) fish; **staw rybny** fishpond; **sklep rybny** fishmonger's (shop); **targ rybny** fish market.

ryboflawina *f. chem.* riboflavin, vitamin B2.

rybołów *ma* **-o-** *orn.* osprey, fish hawk (*Pandion haliaetus*).

rybołówstwo *n.* fishery, fishing.

rybonukleaza *f. biochem.* ribonuclease, RNase, RNAse.

rybonukleinowy *a. biol.* **kwas rybonukleinowy** ribonucleic acid, RNA.

rybosom *mi biol.* ribosome.

rybostan *mi ryb.* fish stock.

ryboza *f. Dat.* **-zie** *chem.* ribose.

rybożerny *a.* piscivorous, fish-eating.

ryc. *abbr.* (= *rycina, rysunek*) fig. (= *figure*).

rycerski *a.* **1.** (= *dotyczący rycerza*) knight's; **turniej rycerski** knight's tournament; **zakon rycerski** order of knights; **zbroja rycerska** knight's armor, *Br.* knight's armour. **2.** (= *właściwy rycerzowi*) knightly; (*o honorze, odwadze, śmierci*) chivalrous. **3.** (= *bardzo uprzejmy*) courteous, chivalrous.

rycerskość *f.* **1.** (= *szlachetność postępowania*) chivalry. **2.** (= *kurtuazja*) courtesy, gallantry, civility.

rycerstwo *n.* knighthood.

rycerz *mp hist.* knight; **błędny rycerz** knight errant.

rychło *adv. lit.* **1.** (= *wkrótce*) soon; **rychło patrzeć jak...** any time now. **2.** (= *wcześnie*) early; **rychło w czas** (way) too late.

rychły *a. lit.* **1.** (= *niedaleki*) imminent, soon-to-be *l.* -happen. **2.** (= *wczesny*) early.

rycina *f.* print.

rycyna *f. pot.* (= *olej rycynowy*) castor oil.

rycynowy *a.* **olej rycynowy** castor oil.

ryczałt *mi fin.* (= *kwota niepodzielona*) lump sum; (= *ustalona stawka*) flat rate; **płacić coś ryczałtem** pay sth in a lump sum; **ryczałtem** *przen.* in the lump, en masse, wholesale.

ryczałtowy *a. fin.* undifferentiated; **oferta ryczałtowa** package deal; **stawka ryczałtowa** flat rate.

ryczeć *ipf.* **-ę -ysz 1.** (= *wydawać ryk*) (*t. o falach, tłumie, maszynach, pojazdach*) roar; (*zwł. o byku*) bellow; (*o krowie*) low; *myśl.* (*o jeleniu w okresie rui*) bell; (*o ośle*) bray; (= *wrzeszczeć, zawodzić*) bawl, yell; **ryczeć jak lew** roar like a lion;

ryczeć ze śmiechu/z bólu/z wściekłości roar with laughter/pain/rage; **ryczące czterdziestki** *żegl.* the roaring forties. **2.** *pot.* (= *płakać głośno*) howl; **przestań ryczeć** stop howling.

ryć *ipf.* **ryję ryjesz 1.** (= *kopać, drążyć ziemię*) dig (*za czymś l.* w poszukiwaniu czegoś for sth); (*o zwierzętach kopiących nory*) burrow. **2.** (*o świni*) root; **ryć ziemię w poszukiwaniu żołędzi** root (about *l.* around) for acorns; **ryć nory/korytarze w ziemi** burrow holes/tunnels in the ground; **ryć pod kimś** *przen.* (= *spiskować, szkodzić*) plot against sb. **3.** *techn., sztuka* (= *wyrzynać*) carve, engrave, incise; **ryć suchą igłą** drypoint. **4.** *pot.* (= *zaśmiewać się*) laugh out loud (*z kogoś* at sb). **5.** *pot.* (= *uczyć się, kuć*) grind.

rydel *mi* **-dl-** *Gen.* **-a** *przest.* spade.

rydwan *mi hist., jeździ.* chariot; **sztuka powożenia rydwanem** chariotry; **woźnica rydwanu** charioteer; **wyścig rydwanów** chariot race.

rydz *mi Gen.* **-a** *bot.* rufous milkcap, foxy milkcap (*Lactarius rufus*); **zdrów jak rydz** as sound as a bell; **lepszy rydz niż nic** half a loaf is better than no bread.

ryft *mi geol.* rift.

Ryga *f. geogr.* Riga; **jechać do Rygi** *żart., euf.* shoot the cat; lose *l.* abort one's lunch.

ryga *f.* **1.** (*liniowany papier*) sheet of ruled paper; **pisać przez rygę** write with the help of ruled paper. **2.** *bud.* ledger.

rygiel *mi* **-gl-** *Gen.* **-a 1.** (= *zasuwa*) bar, latch, bolt; (*w zamku broni palnej*) breechblock; bolt. **2.** *bud.* (= *rozwora*) nogging. **3.** *geol.* riegel, rock bar.

ryglować *ipf.* (= *blokować ryglem*) bolt; *przen.* (= *zamykać w potrzasku, uniemożliwiać manewrowanie*) shut off.

rygor *mi* **1.** (= *dyscyplina*) rigor, discipline; **rygor intelektualny** intellectual rigor; **utrzymywać rygor** maintain discipline. **2.** *prawn.* **rygor prawa** the rigor of the law; **pod rygorem czegoś** under pain *l.* penalty of sth.

rygorysta *mp*, **rygorystka** *f. Gen.pl.* **-ek** rigorist, pedant.

rygorystyczny *a.* rigorous, strict, pedantic.

rygoryzm *mi* rigorism, rigorousness.

ryj *mi Gen.* **-a 1.** (*część pyska*) snout. **2.** *wulg.* (= *gęba, morda*) mug; **co za ryj!** what an ugly mug!; **dać komuś w ryj** *l.* **w ryja** belt sb.

ryjek *mi* **-jk-** *Gen.* **-a 1.** *emf. zob.* **ryj** 1. **2.** (= *zwinięte wargi*) pursed lips; **zwinąć usta w ryjek** purse (up) one's lips. **3.** *żart.* (= *twarz, buzia*) kisser. **4.** *ent.* proboscis.

ryjkowiec *ma* **-wc-** *ent.* (= *chrząszcz z rodziny Curculionidae*) weevil.

ryjogłowy *a. zool.* **gad ryjogłowy** (= *z rzędu Rhynchocephalia*) rhynchocephalian.

ryjoskoczek *ma* **-czk-** *zool.* (= *ssak z rzędu Macroscelidea*) elephant shrew.

ryjówka *f. Gen.pl.* **-ek** *zool.* (= *ssak z rodziny Soricidae*) shrew, shrewmouse; **ryjówka aksamitna** common shrew (*Sorex araneus*).

ryk *mi* **1.** roar; (*byka*) bellow; (*krowy*) low, lowing, moo; *myśl.* (*jelenia w okresie rui*) bell; (*osła*) bray; (= *wrzask*) bawl, yell; **ryk lwa/tygrysa**

lion's/tiger's roar; **ryk morza** the roar of the sea; **ryk samochodów** the roar of traffic; **ryk śmiechu/ aplauzu/gniewu** roar of laughter/applause/rage. **2.** (*głośny płacz*) howl, boohoo; **wybuchnąć rykiem** burst out boohooing.

ryknąć *pf.* **-ij** *zob.* **ryczeć**.

rykoszet *mi wojsk.* ricochet; **odbić się rykoszetem** *t. przen.* ricochet, rebound.

rykowisko *n. myśl.* rutting area.

ryksza *f.* = **riksza**.

rykszarz *mp* = **rikszarz**.

rylcowaty *a. anat.* **wyrostek rylcowaty** styloid process.

rylec *mi* **-lc-** *Gen.* **-a 1.** *hist.* (*narzędzie skryby*) style. **2.** *techn.* graver. **3.** *archeol.* burin.

ryło *n. wulg.* = **ryj** 2.

rym *mi teor.lit.* **1.** rhyme (*do czegoś* for sth); **rym męski/żeński** masculine/feminine rhyme; **rym niedokładny** half-rhyme; **rym wewnętrzny** internal rhyme; **rym wzrokowy** eye-rhyme; **rym częstochowski** *pot.* doggerel rhyme; **mówić do rymu** speak in rhyme; **składać rymy** make rhymes; **ni do rymu, ni do taktu** *pot.* without rhyme or reason. **2.** *pl.* (= *poezja, mowa wiązana*) verse, rhymes.

rymarski *a.* saddler's; **warsztat rymarski** saddler's bench; **wyroby rymarskie** saddlery.

rymarstwo *n.* saddlery.

rymarz *mp* saddler.

rymnąć *pf.* **-ij** *pot.* (= *wywalić się*) come a cropper.

rymopis *mp iron.* rhymester, rimester; rhymer, rimer.

rymować *ipf.* rhyme (*sth*) (*z czymś* with sth). ~ **się** *ipf.* rhyme; **rymować się z czymś** rhyme with sth; be a rhyme for sth.

rymowanka *f. Gen.pl.* **-ek** ditty.

ryms *int.* wham!.

rymsnąć *pf.* **-ij** *pot.* = **rymnąć**.

rynek *mi* **-nk- 1.** (= *plac miejski*) market square; (*zwł. w krajach hiszpańskojęzycznych*) plaza; **Stary Rynek** the Old Town (Market) Square (*in Central European cities*). **2.** (= *targowisko*) market place, market. **3.** *ekon.* market; **rynek krajowy/światowy** home/world market; **rynki zagraniczne** foreign markets; **rynek mieszkaniowy** housing market; **rynek pracy** labor market, *Br.* labour market; **rynek zbytu** outlet; **czarny rynek** black market; **wolny rynek** free market; **Wspólny Rynek** (*w UE*) the Common Market; **dostępny na rynku** *handl.* on the market; **rzucać coś na rynek** put sth on the market; **udział w rynku** market share; **wchodzić na rynek** penetrate into the market; **wprowadzać produkt na rynek** launch a product; **zostać wypartym z rynku** (*wskutek konkurencji cenowej*) be priced out of the market.

ryngraf *mi* pectoral, breastplate.

rynienka, rynka *f. Gen.pl.* **-ek** (*rodzaj rondelka*) stewpan.

rynkowy *a. ekon.* market; **cena rynkowa** market price; **gospodarka rynkowa** market economy.

rynna *f. Gen.pl.* **rynien 1.** rainwater pipe; (*po-*

zioma) gutter; (*pionowa*) downspout, waterspout; *Br.* downpipe; **z deszczu pod rynnę** *przen.* out of the frying-pan into the fire. **2.** *techn.* (= *koryto transportowe*) trough; (= *zsyp*) chute. **3.** *geol.* gully; **rynna polodowcowa** glacial trough.

rynnowy *a. geol.* **jezioro rynnowe** finger lake.

rynsztok *mi Gen.* **-a** *l.* **-u 1.** (= *ściek uliczny*) gutter. **2.** *pot.* (= *margines społeczny*) the gutter; **stoczyć się do rynsztoka** end up in the gutter.

rynsztokowy *a. uj.* vulgar; **język** *l.* **słownik rynsztokowy** the language of the gutter; **prasa rynsztokowa** gutter press.

rynsztunek *mi* **-nk-** *hist., wojsk.* fighting gear; *zw. żart.* (= *wyposażenie*) equipment, gear; **w pełnym rynsztunku** in full gear.

rypać *ipf.* **-pię -piesz 1.** *zob.* **rypnąć** 1, 2. **2.** (*o części ciała*) (= *boleć uporczywie*) give (*sb*) pain. **3.** *wulg.* (*o mężczyźnie*) (= *kopulować*) screw, bang (*kogoś* sb). ~ **się** *ipf. wulg.* **rypać się z kimś** have a screw with sb.

rypnąć *pf.* **-ij** *pot.* **1.** (= *walnąć, przyłożyć*) thump, bang, whack. **2.** *przen.* **rypnąć coś komuś** (= *oznajmić szczerze*) tell sb sth bluntly *l.* in plain English; **rypnąć komuś mandat** (= *wlepić, kropnąć*) slap a ticket on sb *l.* on sb's car. **3.** (= *huknąć*) go bang. **4.** (= *wypić porcję alkoholu*) down (*coś* sth). **5.** = **rymnąć**. ~ **się** *pf. pot.* **1.** (= *uderzyć się*) **rypnąć się głową/kolanem w coś** bang one's head/knee on sth. **2.** *pot.* (= *pomylić się*) make a goof (*w czymś* in sth).

ryps *mi tk.* rep.

rypsowy *a. tk.* rep.

rys *mi* **1.** (= *właściwość*) feature, trait. **2.** *pl.* (= *cechy wyglądu twarzy*) features (*of sb's face*); **grube/delikatne rysy** coarse/delicate features. **3.** (= *streszczenie, notka*) sketch, note.

rys. *abbr.* (= *rysunek*) fig. (= *figure*).

rysa *f.* **1.** (= *zadrapanie*) scratch. **2.** (= *pęknięcie*) crack; (= *szczelina, rozpadlina*) crevice, fissure. **3.** (= *skaza, t. przen.*) flaw (*na czymś* in sth). **4.** (= *głęboka zmarszczka*) line.

rysi *a.* **1.** (= *dotyczący rysia*) lynx, lyncine; **rysi wzrok** *lit.* lyncean sight *l.* eyes. **2.** (= *zrobiony z futra rysia*) lynx, bobcat; *zob.* **ryś**.

rysik *mi Gen.* **-a 1.** *hist.* (*do pisania na tabliczce*) slate pencil. **2.** (= *wkład grafitowy*) lead. **3.** *techn.* scriber.

rysopis *mi* description; **odpowiadać rysopisowi** answer to a description.

rysować *ipf.* **1.** (= *robić rysunek*) draw; (*ołówkiem*) pencil; (= *szkicować*) sketch. **2.** *form., przen.* (= *przedstawiać w zarysie*) adumbrate, sketch. **3.** (= *robić zadrapania*) scratch. ~ **się** *ipf.* **1.** (= *uwidaczniać się*) appear, take shape; **rysować się wyraźnie** appear clearly *l.* distinctly; **widoki na przyszłość rysują się ponuro** the prospects for the future look gloomy. **2.** (= *pokrywać się rysami*) get scratched; (= *pokrywać się pęknięciami*) crack.

rysownica *f. techn.* drawing board.

rysownictwo *n.* draftsmanship, *Br.* draughtsmanship.

rysowniczka *f. Gen.pl.* **-ek 1.** drawer; *rzad.*

draftswoman, *Br.* draughtswoman. **2.** *zob.* **ry-sownik** 2.

rysownik *mp* **1.** drawer; draftsman, *Br.* draughtsman. **2.** (= *twórca komiksów l. rysunków humorystycznych*) cartoonist.

rysunek *mi* -**nk**- **1.** (= *to, co narysowane*) drawing; (*jako ilustracja*) figure, picture; (= *szkic*) sketch; (= *plan*) plan, design; **rysunek naskalny** *archeol.* rock drawing, petroglyph; **rysunek ołówkiem/piórkiem/węglem** pencil/pen/coal drawing; **rysunek roboczy** working drawing. **2.** *sztuka l. umiejętność* drawing; **rysunek artystyczny** artistic drawing; **rysunek techniczny** technical drawing, engineering drawing. **3.** (= *zarys, kontur*) outline. **4.** *pl. szkoln. pot.* (= *wychowanie plastyczne*) art class, art.

rysunkowy *a.* **1.** (*używany do rysowania*) drawing; **blok rysunkowy** drawing block; **papier rysunkowy** drawing paper; **przyrządy rysunkowe** drawing utensils. **2.** (= *w formie rysunku*) pictorial; **dowcip rysunkowy** cartoon; **film rysunkowy** (animated) cartoon, animation, cartoon film.

rysy *pl. Gen.* -**ów** (*twarzy*) *zob.* **rys.**

ryś *ma* **1.** *zool. lynx (Lynx)*; **ryś rudy** bobcat (*L. rufus*); **ryś europejski** (European) lynx (*L. lynx*); **bystry jak ryś** lynx-eyed. **2. Ryś** *astron.* (*gwiazdozbiór*) Lynx.

ryt *mi* **1.** *sztuka* engraving. **2.** *rel.* (= *obrządek*) rite; **ryt grecki/łaciński** the Greek/Latin rite.

rytm *mi* *t. muz., teor.lit.* rhythm; (= *tempo, puls*) pace; (= *taktowanie*) beat; **rytm okołodobowy** *biol.* circadian rhythm; **rytm synkopowany** *muz.* backbeat; **rytmy afrykańskie/latynoskie** *muz.* African/Latino rhythms; **wyczucie rytmu** sense of rhythm; **do rytmu** to the beat *l.* rhythm (*czegoś* of sth); **wybić kogoś z rytmu** put sb off his *l.* her rhythm.

rytmicznie *adv.* rhythmically.

rytmiczność *f.* (= *miarowość*) rhythmicity, regularity.

rytmiczny *a.* (= *miarowy*) rhythmic, rhythmical; (= *niezmienny, o stałym tempie*) steady, regular; **proza rytmiczna** rhythmic prose.

rytmika *f.* **1.** *muz.* rhythmic. **2.** (*ćwiczenia ruchowe*) eurhythmics; *szkoln.* fitness and dancing exercises.

rytownictwo *n. sztuka* engraving.

rytowniczka *f. Gen.pl.* -**ek**, **rytownik** *mp* engraver.

rytualizacja *f. biol.* ritualization.

rytualny *a.* ritual.

rytuał *mi* **1.** *rel., antrop.* (= *obrządek*) rite, ritual; **rytuał inicjacyjny** rite of passage; **rytuały płodności/pogrzebowe** fertility/burial rites. **2.** *przen.* (= *stale powtarzane czynności*) ritual; **przećwiczyć stały rytuał czegoś** go through the ritual of sth.

rywal *mp* (= *konkurent*) rival, competitor (*do czegoś* for sth) (*w czymś* in sth).

rywalizacja *f.* rivalry, competition.

rywalizować *ipf.* compete (*z kimś* with sb, *o coś* for sth) (*w czymś* in sth); contend (*z kimś* with *l.* against sb) (*o coś* for sth); vie (*z kimś* with sb, *o coś* for sth).

rywalka *f. Gen.pl.* -**ek** *zob.* **rywal.**

ryza *f.* **1.** (*miara papieru*) ream (*in Poland* = *125-500 sheets*); **zapisać ryzy papieru** *przen.* write reams. **2.** *leśn.* (*do spuszczania pni*) runway, chute. **3.** **trzymać kogoś/coś w ryzach** *l.* **wziąć kogoś/coś w ryzy** keep a tight rein on sb/sth.

ryzalit *mi* *bud.* break (*in a wall*).

ryzoid *mi* *bot.* rhizoid.

ryzosfera *f. ekol.* rhizosphere.

ryzykancki *a.* **1.** (= *śmiały*) daring, bold. **2.** (= *niepewny*) risky. **3.** *uj.* (= *podejmujący ryzyko*) reckless, foolhardy.

ryzykanctwo *n. uj.* recklessness.

ryzykant *mp* risk-taker.

ryzyk-fizyk *int. pot.* come what may.

ryzyko *n.* **1.** (= *możliwość niepowodzenia*) risk; **na własne ryzyko** at one's own risk; at one's peril; **podjąć ryzyko** take a risk. **2.** (= *potencjalne niebezpieczeństwo*) risk, jeopardy; hazard (*dla kogoś / czegoś* to sb/sth); **narażać się na ryzyko czegoś** run the risk of sth; **ryzyko dla zdrowia** health hazard; hazard to sb's health; **ryzyko zawodowe** occupational hazard; **zwiększone ryzyko czegoś** increased risk of sth. **3.** (= *niepewne przedsięwzięcie*) gamble, adventure.

ryzykować *ipf.* **1.** (= *podejmować ryzyko*) take risks; **ryzykować coś** *l.* **czymś** risk sth; hazard sth; **ryzykować głową** risk life and limb; **ryzykować życiem** hazard one's life. **2.** (= *decydować się na coś*) risk, venture, hazard (*sth*); **ryzykować pytanie/hipotezę** venture a question/hypothesis; **nie ryzykowaliśmy kolejnej próby** we didn't risk another attempt.

ryzykowny *a.* **1.** (= *niepewny, niebezpieczny*) risky, hazardous; **ryzykowna praca** hazardous work; **ryzykowne przedsięwzięcie** risky undertaking. **2.** (= *nieostrożny*) reckless; **ryzykowna jazda** reckless driving.

ryż *mi* *bot., kulin.* rice (*Oryza sativa*); *roln.* (*przed zbiorem l. w trakcie zbioru*) paddy; **ryż biały/brązowy** *kulin.* white/brown rice; **ziarnko ryżu** grain of rice.

ryżawy *a. pot.* reddish-headed.

ryżowy *a.* rice; **pudding ryżowy** *kulin.* rice pudding; **poletko ryżowe** paddy (field); **pole ryżowe** ricefield; **papier ryżowy** rice paper; **szczotka ryżowa** scrub brush.

ryży *a. pot.* red-headed.

rz. *abbr.* (= *rzeka*) R. (= *River*).

rzadki *a.* **1.** (= *nieczęsty, wyjątkowy*) rare, infrequent, uncommon; **rzadki gość** rare visitor; **rzadki okaz** rare specimen; (= *rarytas kolekcjonerski*) collector's item; **rzadkie widowisko** rare *l.* uncommon spectacle; **rzadkie zjawisko** rare phenomenon; **w rzadkich przypadkach** in rare *l.* isolated cases; **w rzadko spotykanym stopniu** to a rare degree; **z rzadkimi wyjątkami** with rare exceptions; **rzadki okaz** rare specimen. **2.** (= *rozrzedzony*) rare, rarefied, thin; **rzadka atmosfera** rare atmosphere. **3.** *kulin.* (*o cieście itp.*) runny. **4.** (= *rozproszony, niegęsty*) sparse; (*o splocie tkackim*) loose; **rzadkie włosy** sparse hair; **rzadkie zaludnienie** sparse population; **z rzadka** (= *nie* *gęsto*) sparsely; (= *tylko czasami*) rarely, seldom; **tylko z rzadka przychodzą tu obcy** only rarely do strangers come here. **5.** *pot.* **rzadka mina** puzzled *l.* bewildered look. **6.** *chem.* **ziemie rzadkie** rare earths.

rzadko *adv.* **1.** (= *nieczęsto*) rarely, seldom, infrequently; **rzadko u nas bywasz** you rarely *l.* seldom visit us; **rzadko się zdarza, żeby burza trwała tak długo** it's unusual for a storm to last so long. **2.** (*w utartych zwrotach*) **rzadko kto** few people; **rzadko kiedy** on rare occasions. **3.** (= *w rozproszeniu*) sparsely; **rzadko zalesione wzgórza** sparsely forested *l.* wooded hills.

rzadkoskurcz *mi med., pat.* bradycardia.

rzadkość *f.* **1.** (= *okaz, coś wyjątkowego*) rarity, rare specimen; **rzadkość nad rzadkościami** rarity of rarities; **to nie należy do rzadkości** it is not uncommon *l.* unusual. **2.** (= *nieczęstość występowania*) rarity, rare occurrence.

rzadzizna *f. metal.* (*wada odlewu*) shrinkage porosity.

rząd[1] *mi -ę-* **1.** (= *szereg*) row, line; **rzędem** *l.* **w rzędzie** in a row; **rzędami** *l.* **rząd za rzędem** in rows; row upon row. **2.** (*w utartych zwrotach dotyczących kolejności*) **w pierwszym rzędzie** (= *przede wszystkim*) first of all; first and foremost; in the first place; **z rzędu** in a row; **trzeci raz z rzędu** the third time in a row; **pod rząd** running; **dwa lata pod rząd** two years running. **3.** (= *zakres*) order; **rząd wielkości** order of magnitude; **coś rzędu...** *pot.* to the tune of...; **zapłaciłem coś rzędu stu dolarów** I paid to the tune of one hundred dollars; **pięć procent lub coś tego rzędu** five percent or something of that order. **4.** (= *kategoria*) **wartości wyższego rzędu** higher-order values; **w rzędzie...** in the ranks of...; **znaleźć się w rzędzie zwycięzców** join the ranks of winners. **5.** *biol.* (*jednostka systematyczna*) order; **rząd naczelnych** the order of primates, the order Primates, the primate order. **6.** *jeźdz.* set of horse tack; **konia z rzędem temu, kto... przen.** I'll eat my hat if anyone... **7.** *mat.* (*właściwość równania, funkcji*) order.

rząd[2] *mi -ą-* **1.** *polit.* (*władza, organ państwa*) government, administration; **rząd emigracyjny** *l.* **rząd na uchodźstwie** government in exile; **rząd koalicyjny** coalition government; **rząd marionetkowy** puppet government; **rząd tymczasowy** interim government; **prezydium rządu** the Cabinet; **rzecznik rządu** government spokesman; **szef rządu** head of government; **formować rząd** form a government. **2.** (= *sprawowanie władzy, t. przen.*) government, rule; **rządy liberalne/totalitarne** liberal/totalitarian government; **rządy parlamentarne** parliamentary government; **rządy silnej ręki** heavy-handed regime; **sprawować rządy** be in government; **ster rządów** the rein of government; **system rządów** regime. **3.** (*także związek rządu*) *gram.* (grammatical) government.

rządca *mp przest.* administrator, factor; **rządca majątku** estate manager.

rządek *mi -dk- Gen.* **-a** *emf. zob.* **rząd**[1] **1**; **rządkiem** *l.* **w jednym rządku** in a row.

rządny *a. przest.* orderly, well-governed.

rządowy *a.* governmental, administrative; **resort rządowy** government department.

rządzący *pl. decl. like a.* those in power, the government.

rządzić *ipf.* **1.** (= *władać*) rule; + *Ins. t. przen.* (= *panować nad*) control; **rządzić państwem/narodem** control a state/a nation; **rządzić nastrojami tłumu** control the emotions of the crowd; **rządzić żelazną ręką** rule with a rod of iron, rule with an iron hand; **dziel i rządź** divide and rule. **2.** (= *sprawować rządy*) be in government; (= *sprawować kontrolę*) *przen.* be in charge, be the boss; **kto tu rządzi?** who's in charge?; **kto w tym domu rządzi?** who's the boss in this house?; **ty tu rządzisz** (*oznacza zdanie się na czyjąś decyzję*) you are the boss *l.* doctor. **3.** + *Ins.* (= *kierować, zarządzać*) govern, manage, administer. **4.** + *Ins. jęz.* (= *wymuszać użycie danej formy*) govern. **5.** *sl.* (= *być górą*) rule. ~ **się** *ipf.* **1.** (= *sprawować władzę u siebie*) manage one's affairs. **2.** (= *panoszyć się*) boss the show; throw one's weight around *l.* about. **3.** + *Ins.* (= *kierować się*) let (*sth*) govern one's actions; **rządzić się w postępowaniu zdrowym rozsądkiem** act according to common sense.

rzec *pf.* **rzeknę rzekniesz, rzeknij, rzekł** *lit.* (= *powiedzieć*) say; **rzec (by) można, (że)...** *l.* **rzekłbym, (że)...** one could say (that)...; **jako się rzekło** as has been said.

rzecz *f.* **1.** (= *przedmiot*) thing, object. **2.** *pl.* (= *własność, dobytek, strój, wyposażenie*) things, belongings, property; **to są moje rzeczy** these are my things; **rzeczy osobiste** personal belongings *l.* possessions; **biuro rzeczy znalezionych** lost property office. **3.** (= *sprawa, dziedzina*) (*w wielu utartych wyrażeniach*) **ładne rzeczy!** a pretty kettle of fish!; **nic z tych rzeczy** nothing of the kind *l.* sort; **te rzeczy są mi obce** these things aren't up my street; **to moja rzecz** it's my business; **to nie moja rzecz** it's none of my business; **wielka mi rzecz!** *l.* **wielkie rzeczy!** big deal!; **wojsko to męska rzecz** army life is for men; **znać się na rzeczy** know one's stuff; be knowledgeable. **4.** *pl.* (= *naturalny bieg spraw*) things, affairs; **(zwykła) kolej rzeczy** the (ordinary) course of things; **stan rzeczy** the state of affairs; **siłą rzeczy** of course, naturally; **w gruncie rzeczy** essentially. **5.** (= *temat, treść, t. w licznych utartych zwrotach*) issue, matter, topic, point; **coś jest na rzeczy** there's something in it; **co to ma do rzeczy?** what does that have to do with the matter at hand?; **do rzeczy!** back to the point; **mówić do rzeczy/od rzeczy** talk sense/nonsense; **nazywać rzeczy po imieniu** call a spade a spade; **nie od rzeczy byłoby...** it would not be amiss to...; **ogólnie rzecz biorąc** generally speaking; **przystąpić do rzeczy** get to the point; address the issue; **rzecz w tym, że...** the problem is that...; **sedno/istota rzeczy** the heart/crux of the matter; **spis rzeczy** (= *spis treści*) contents; **to nie ma nic do rzeczy** that's neither here nor there; **to zmienia postać rzeczy** that makes a difference; **w rzeczy samej** indeed; **w tym (cała) rzecz** that's the whole point. **6.** *z przymiotnikami* (*tworzy równoważniki zdań* *okolicznikowych*) **rzecz dziwna...** strangely enough...; **rzecz jasna...** *l.* **rzecz oczywista...** of course..., needless to say..., it goes without saying that...; **rzecz prosta...** predictably (enough)... **7. na rzecz kogoś/czegoś** *prawn.* to *l.* for sb/sth; **przekazać darowiznę na rzecz instytucji** make a donation to *l.* for an institution; **zasądzić coś na czyjąś rzecz** adjudge sth to sb. **8.** *fil.* thing; **rzecz sama w sobie** thing-in-itself.

rzeczka *f. Gen.pl.* **-ek** rivulet, creek.

rzecznictwo *n.* advocacy.

rzeczniczka *f. Gen.pl.* **-ek 1.** (= *zwolenniczka*) *zob.* **rzecznik** 1. **2.** (= *osoba występująca w czyimś imieniu*) spokeswoman (*czyjaś/czegoś* for sb/sth); *zob.* **rzecznik** 2.

rzecznik *mp* **1.** (= *zwolennik*) advocate, supporter; **rzecznik rozbrojenia** advocate of disarmament. **2.** (= *osoba występująca w czyimś imieniu*) spokesman; (*bez względu na płeć*) spokesperson (*czyjś/czegoś* for sb/sth); **rzecznik prasowy** press spokesman; **rzecznik praw obywatelskich** ombudsman; *Br.* the Parliamentary Commissioner (for Local Administration); **rzecznik rządu** government spokesman.

rzeczny *a.* (= *dotyczący rzeki*) river; *form.* fluvial, riverine.

rzeczony *a.* **-eni** *przest. l. lit.* aforesaid, said.

rzeczownik *mi Gen.* **-a** *gram.* noun, substantive; **rzeczownik abstrakcyjny/konkretny** abstract/concrete noun; **rzeczownik odsłowny** deverbal noun; **rzeczownik policzalny/niepoliczalny** countable/uncountable noun; **rzeczownik pospolity** common noun; **rzeczownik rodzaju męskiego/żeńskiego/nijakiego** masculine/feminine/neuter noun.

rzeczownikowy, rzeczowny *a.* noun, nominal; substantival; **fraza rzeczowna** noun phrase; **rzeczownikowe końcówki odmiany** noun inflections.

rzeczowo *adv.* **1.** (= *zwięźle, konkretnie*) succinctly. **2.** (= *bez ulegania emocjom*) matter-of-factly, soberly.

rzeczowość *f.* matter-of-factness, soberness.

rzeczowy *a.* **1.** (= *dotyczący przedmiotów l. faktów, namacalny*) material, substantial, factual, tangible; **dowód rzeczowy** *prawn.* material proof; **świadectwa rzeczowe** substantial *l.* tangible evidence. **2.** (*o stylu, argumencie, dyskusji*) (= *zwięzły, solidny*) succinct, concrete, substantive. **3.** (*o tonie, podejściu*) (= *obiektywny, niezabarwiony emocjami*) matter-of-fact, businesslike; (*o człowieku*) sober, no-nonsense. **4. indeks** *l.* **skorowidz rzeczowy** (*w książce*) subject index.

rzeczoznawca *mp* expert.

rzeczoznawstwo *n.* expert's duties *l.* functions.

rzeczpospolita *f. decl. as one or two words: Gen.* **rzeczpospolitej** *l.* **rzeczypospolitej** *pl.* **rzeczpospolite** *l.* **rzeczypospolite** *arch.* (*z wyjątkiem użycia w odniesieniu do państwa polskiego*) commonwealth, republic; **Rzeczpospolita Polska** (*obecnie*) the Republic of Poland, *hist.* Polish Republic; **Rzeczpospolita Obojga Narodów** *hist.* the Commonwealth of Poland and Lithuania; **Polska Rzeczpospolita Ludowa** *hist.* the Polish People's Republic.

rzeczułka *f. Gen.pl.* **-ek** *emf. zob.* **rzeczka**.

rzeczywistość *f.* reality, fact; **rzeczywistość i fikcja** fact and fiction; **rzeczywistość wirtualna** *komp.* virtual reality; **naga rzeczywistość** stark reality; **w rzeczywistości** in reality, in fact; (*w sprostowaniach*) as a matter of fact, actually; **mieć poczucie rzeczywistości** have a sense of reality; **odpowiadać rzeczywistości** be the case, be factually true; **stać się rzeczywistością** come true, become reality.

rzeczywisty *a.* **1.** (= *istniejący*) real, existing. **2.** (= *faktyczny, prawdziwy*) real, true, actual; **rzeczywista przyczyna wypadku** the real cause of the accident; **rzeczywista wartość obrazu** the true value of the painting; **rzeczywisty koszt produkcji** the actual cost of production. **3.** (*w tytułach*) real; **członek rzeczywisty** real member. **4.** *mat.* **liczby/funkcje rzeczywiste** real numbers/functions.

rzeczywiście *adv.* (= *w rzeczy samej*) indeed, really.

rzednąć *pf.* **-dł** *l.* **-nął** **-dła** **-dli 1.** (= *tracić gęstość*) rarefy, liquefy; **mina komuś rzednie** sb's looking puzzled. **2.** (*o ruchu ulicznym, włosach, mgle, zaludnieniu*) (= *stawać się rzadkim l. rozproszonym*) thin (out).

rzednieć *ipf.* = **rzednąć**.

rzeka *f.* **1.** river; watercourse; *poet.* stream; **w górę/dół rzeki** up/down a river; **nad rzeką** on a river; **za rzeką** across a river; **obszar źródłowy rzeki** the headwaters *l.* headstreams of a river; **ujście rzeki** the mouth *l.* estuary of a river; **delta rzeki** river delta; **przejść rzekę w bród** ford a river. **2.** *przen.* **powieść rzeka** *teor.lit.* roman-fleuve; **rzeka krwi** bloodbath; **rzeka ludzi/samochodów** stream of people/cars.

rzekomo *adv.* allegedly; **ona jest rzekomo piękna** she's alleged *l.* supposed *l.* reputed *l.* purported to be a beauty; **rzekomo to on napisał ten list** this letter was allegedly written by him; **on był rzekomo chory** he alleged being sick.

rzekomy *a.* **1.** alleged, would-be. **2.** *anat., bot.* spurious; **owoc rzekomy** spurious fruit. **3.** *pat.* **ciąża rzekoma** phantom pregnancy, false pregnancy, pseudocyesis; **torbiel rzekoma** cystoid.

rzekotka *f. Gen.pl.* **-ek** *zool.* (*płaz nadrzewny, zwł. z rodziny Hylidae*) tree frog, tree toad; **rzekotka drzewna** green tree-frog (*Hyla arborea*).

rzemienica *f. bot.* leatherwood, wicopy (*Dirca palustris*).

rzemienny *a.* leather, leathern.

rzemień *mi Gen.* **-a** strap, thong; **rzemień bicza** whiplash; **rzemień strzemienia** stirrup leather.

rzemieślniczka *f. Gen.pl.* **-ek** craftswoman; *zob.* **rzemieślnik**.

rzemieślniczy *a.* **1.** handicraft, trade; **szkoła rzemieślnicza** school of arts and crafts. **2.** *pog.* (*o dziele literackim l. artystycznym*) mediocre, uninspired.

rzemieślnik *mp* **1.** (*mężczyzna*) craftsman, handicraftsman; (*bez względu na płeć*) artisan, craftsperson. **2.** *cz. pog.* (*o artyście l. pisarzu*) journeyman.

rzemiosło *n.* **1.** (= *rękodzielnictwo*) craftsmanship; **rzemiosło artystyczne** handicraft; **rzemiosła rękodzielnicze** arts and crafts. **2.** *cz. pog.* (= *umiejętności warsztatowe*) journeyman-work. **3.** *pot.* (= *fach, zawód*) craft, trade; **rzemiosło wojenne** *lit.* warfare.

rzemyk *mi Gen.* **-a** *emf. zob.* **rzemień.**

rzep *mi* **1.** (= *koszyczek łopianu*) bur, sticker; **przyczepić się do kogoś jak rzep do psiego ogona** *pot.* cling to sb like a barnacle. **2.** (*rodzaj zapięcia*) Velcro®.

rzepa *f. bot., roln.* turnip (*Brassica rapa*); **rzepa biała/pastewna** white/tankard turnip.

rzepak *mi bot., roln.* rape; cole, colza (*Brassica napus*); **nasiona rzepaku** rapeseed.

rzepakowy *a. kulin., techn.* **olej rzepakowy** rape oil, rapeseed oil, colza oil.

rzepicha *f. bot.* watercress (*Roripa*).

rzepik *mi bot.* agrimony (*Agrimonia*).

rzepka *f. Gen.pl.* **-ek 1.** *emf. zob.* **rzepa**; **każdy sobie rzepkę skrobie** *przen.* everybody has an ax to grind. **2.** *anat.* kneecap, patella.

Rzesza *f. hist.* the (German) Reich; **Trzecia Rzesza** the Third Reich.

rzesza *f. lit.* multitude, throng; **rzesza bezrobotnych** the host of the unemployed; **szeroka rzesza odbiorców** wide audience; **rzesze turystów** legions of tourists.

rzeszoto *n.* riddle; **podziurawiony jak rzeszoto** riddled with holes.

rześki *a.* brisk, fresh; (= *orzeźwiający, pełen świeżości*) crisp, bracing; (= *radosny, wypoczęty*) breezy, buoyant; **rześkim krokiem** at a brisk pace.

rześko *adv.* crisply, briskly, breezily; **wyglądasz dziś bardzo rześko** you look very breezy today.

rzetelnie *adv.* reliably, conscientiously.

rzetelność *f.* reliability, conscientiousness, probity.

rzetelny *a.* **1.** (= *sumienny, uczciwy*) reliable, dependable, conscientious; **rzetelny fachowiec** reliable specialist. **2.** (= *prawdziwy, autentyczny*) genuine; **rzetelna wiedza** genuine learning.

rzewień *mi Gen.* **-a** *bot.* = **rabarbar.**

rzewnie *adv.* plaintively; wistfully, nostalgically.

rzewny *a.* (= *smętny, melancholijny*) plaintive; (= *nostalgiczny*) wistful, nostalgic, maudlin; **rzewna piosenka** *żart.* torch song.

rzezimieszek *mp* **-szk-** *pl.* **-i** *przest.* **1.** (*rabuś*) cutpurse. **2.** (*bandyta*) cutthroat.

rzeź *f. pl.* **-zie 1.** (= *ubój zwierząt*) slaughter; **iść na rzeź** *t. przen.* go to the slaughter. **2.** (= *masowe zabijanie*) massacre, butchery, carnage; *przen.* (*o śmiertelnych wypadkach itp.*) massacre, slaughter; **rzeź niewiniątek** *rel.* Massacre of the Innocents (*przen.* massacre *l.* slaughter of the Innocents).

rzeźba *f.* **1.** (*dziedzina sztuki l. dzieło*) sculpture, carving; **rzeźba w drewnie** woodcarving. **2.** (= *ukształtowanie*) configuration, features; **rzeźba terenu** *l.* **krajobrazu** the features of the landscape; the lay of the land.

rzeźbiarka *f. Gen.pl.* **-ek** *zob.* **rzeźbiarz.**

rzeźbiarski *a.* sculptural.

rzeźbiarstwo *n.* sculpture, carving.

rzeźbiarz *mp* **1.** sculptor. **2. Rzeźbiarz** *astron.* (*gwiazdozbiór*) Sculptor.

rzeźbić *ipf.* **1.** (= *wykonywać rzeźby*) sculpt, carve; (*dłutem*) chisel. **2.** (= *kształtować powierzchnię, rysy*) form, mold, *Br.* mould; *geol.* sculpture.

rzeźnia *f. Gen.pl.* **-i** slaughterhouse.

rzeźnicki *a.* butcher's, butcherly; **hak rzeźnicki** butcher's hook; **tasak rzeźnicki** cleaver, meatax; **topór rzeźnicki** poleax.

rzeźnictwo *n.* butchery.

rzeźniczy *a.* = **rzeźnicki.**

rzeźnik *mp* (*t. pog.*) (= *oprawca, morderca*) butcher; **u rzeźnika** at the butcher's store.

rzeźny *a.* **bydło rzeźne** beef cattle.

rzeźwić *ipf.* energize, sober (*sb*) up.

rzeźwy *a.* = **rześki.**

rzeżączka *f. Gen.pl.* **-ek** *pat.* gonorrhea, *Br.* gonorrhoea.

rzeżączkowy *a. pat.* gonorrheal, *Br.* gonorrhoeal.

rzeżucha *f. bot.* cress (*Cardamine*); **rzeżucha łąkowa** lady's-smock, cuckooflower (*C. sativa*).

rzęch *mi Gen.* **-a** *pot.* (*samochód l. maszyna w bardzo złym stanie*) banger.

rzędna *f. Gen.* **-ej** *mat.* ordinate; *miern.* offset; **oś rzędnych** *mat.* the ordinate axis, the axis of ordinates.

rzędowy *a.* **siewnik rzędowy** *roln.* drill seeder; **silnik rzędowy** *mot.* inline engine.

rzędu *itd. mi zob.* **rząd¹.**

rzępolić *ipf. pot., żart.* grate (away), rasp (away) (*na czymś* on sth); saw *l.* scrape the fiddle.

rzępoła *f. l. mp decl. like f. Gen.pl.* **-ł** *l.* **-ów** *pog.* scraper.

rzęsa *f.* **1.** *anat.* eyelash; *form.* cilium. **2.** *przen.* **chodzić** *l.* **biegać na rzęsach** *żart.* romp around *l.* about; **stawać na rzęsach** *pot.* do one's utmost. **3.** *bot.* (*także* **rzęsa wodna**) duckweed (*Lemna*).

rzęsistek *mi* **-tk-** *Gen.* **-a** *biol.* (*pierwotniak*) trichomonad (*Trichomonas*).

rzęsistkowica *f. pat.* trichomoniasis; trich, trick.

rzęsisty *a. lit.* profuse; **rzęsiste brawa** rapturous applause; **rzęsiste łzy** profuse tears; **rzęsisty deszcz** pouring rain.

rzęsiście *adv. lit.* profusely; **rzęsiście oświetlony** floodlit, brilliantly illuminated.

rzęska *f. Gen.pl.* **-ek** *bot., zool.* cilium.

rzęskowy *a. anat.* ciliary; **mięsień/wyrostek rzęskowy** ciliary muscle/process.

rzęsorek *ma* **-rk-** *Gen.* **-a** water shrew (*Neomys*).

rzęśl *f. bot.* water-starwort (*Callitriche*).

rzęzić *ipf.* **-żę -zisz** (= *oddychać chrapliwie*) (*t. przen. o silniku itp.*) wheeze.

rzężenie *n.* wheeze; **rzężenie przedśmiertne** death rattle; *pat.* rhonchus, rale.

rzodkiew *f.* -kwi- *pl.* -e *bot.* (wild) radish (*Raphanus*).

rzodkiewka *f. Gen.pl.* -ek *bot., kulin.* (garden) radish (*Raphanus sativus*).

rzucać *ipf.* **1.** + *Acc. l. Ins.* (= *ciskać*) throw, cast; (*z dużą siłą*) fling, hurl; (*jak najdalej w danym kierunku*) project; (*piłkę baseballową, kamień*) pitch; (= *podrzucać*) toss; (= *zrzucać*) dash, dump, chuck (*sth somewhere*); **rzucać piłkę do kogoś** throw a ball to sb; **rzucać piłką w kogoś** throw a ball at sb; **rzucać karty na stół** (*kończąc grę*) chuck in one's hand; **rzucać kośćmi** cast *l.* roll dice; **rzucać monetą** toss *l.* flip a coin (*o coś* for sth); **rzucać kotwicę** *żegl.* cast *l.* drop anchor; **rzucać młotem** *sport* put the shot. **2.** *przen.* **rzucać cień na kogoś/coś** cast a shadow on sb/sth; **rzucać coś w kąt** (= *przestać się zajmować czymś*) cast sth aside; **rzucać gromy na kogoś/coś** thunder against sb/sth; **rzucać komuś kłody pod nogi** put a spoke in sb's wheel; **rzucać komuś rękawicę** fling *l.* throw down the gauntlet to sb; **rzucać (w kogoś) mięsem** *pot.* hurl abuse at sb; **rzucać obelgi** hurl insults; **rzucać światło na coś** cast *l.* throw *l.* shed light on sth; **rzucać snop światła na coś** project *l.* throw a beam of light on *l.* onto sth; **ten fakt rzuca (nowe) światło na sprawę** this fact sheds a new light on the issue; **rzucać przezrocze na ekran** project a slide on a screen; **rzucać komuś ukradkowe spojrzenie** cast a furtive glance at sb; **rzucać słowa na wiatr** speak idly; **rzucać myśl** *l.* **pomysł** come up with an idea. **3.** (= *wywoływać jakiś stan*) **rzucać na kogoś oskarżenia** throw accusations at sb; **rzucać na kogoś podejrzenie** throw suspicion on sb; **rzucać na kogoś oszczerstwa** cast aspersions on sb; **rzucać na kogoś czary** cast a spell on sb; **rzucać klątwę na kogoś** put a curse on *l.* upon sb; *rel.* pronounce an anathema upon sb; **rzucać pierwszy kamień** *Bibl.* (= *rozpocząć oskarżenia*) cast the first stone. **4.** (= *potrząsać, poruszać gwałtownie*) jerk, throw about, fling about, toss (about); (*o pojeździe*) (= *szarpać, trząść się*) jerk, jolt, bump; **rzucać głową** toss *l.* jerk one's head; **rzucać rękami** trash about with one's arms; **samochód rzucał na wyboistej drodze** the car jolted on the bumpy road. **5.** (= *przewracać, szarpać*) **rzucać kogoś na ziemię** fling *l.* hurl sb to the ground; **rzucać kimś o coś** fling *l.* hurl sb against sth; **rzucać kogoś na kolana** (*przen.* (= *upokorzyć, podporządkować sobie*)) bring sb to his *l.* her knees; **rzucać kogoś na głęboką wodę** (*przen.* (= *postawić przed kimś trudne zadanie*)) throw *l.* pitch sb in at the deep end; **fale rzucały statkiem na wszystkie strony** the waves tossed the ship to and fro. **6.** (= *wysyłać, wyprawiać*) **rzucać oddziały do walki** send troops into battle; **rzucać coś na rynek** launch sth on the market; **rzucać swój kraj w wir wojny** precipitate one's country into war. **7.** (= *porzucać*) abandon, forsake, desert; *pot.* drop, chuck (in), jack (in); **rzucić żonę/męża** abandon one's wife/husband; **rzucić rodzinę/przyjaciół** forsake one's friends/family; **rzuciła swojego chłopaka** she chucked her boyfriend; **rzuciłem robotę** I chucked in my job;

rzucę to wszystko w diabły *pot.* I'm going to jack it all in. **8.** (= *zrywać z nałogiem*) give (*sth*) up; *pot.* kick (*sth*); **rzucać palenie/picie** give up smoking/drinking. **9.** (= *wypowiadać krótko*) **rzucać uwagę** drop a remark; **rzucać rozkaz** snap out an order. **10.** (= *przerzucać*) throw; **rzucać most przez rzekę** throw a bridge across the river. **11.** *pot.* (= *podawać*) chuck; **rzuć mi gazetę** chuck me the paper. **~ się** *ipf.* **1.** (= *skakać w dół*) plunge, jump, throw o.s.; **rzucać się z urwiska do morza** plunge over a cliff into the sea. **2.** (= *kierować się gdzieś pędem*) dart, dash, rush, start, lunge, fling o.s., hurl o.s.; **rzucić się do ucieczki** bolt; dart away; make a bolt *l.* dash *l.* run for it; **rzucać się do walki** fling o.s. into battle; **rzucać się naprzód** leap forward, lunge forward; **rzucać się komuś na pomoc** rush to sb's rescue. **3.** **rzucać się w oczy** stand out; be conspicuous; *pot.* stick out (like a sore thumb); stick out a mile. **4.** (= *miotać się*) toss about *l.* around, jerk about *l.* around. **5.** (= *atakować*) throw o.s. *l.* one's weight (*na kogoś / coś* at sb/sth); go (*na kogoś / coś* at *l.* for sb/sth); (*o drapieżniku*) pounce (*na kogoś / coś* on *l.* upon sb/sth); **rzucać się komuś do gardła** go at sb's throat; **rzucił się na nią z nożem** he went for her with a knife; **rzucać się na wroga** go at the enemy; **rzucać się z motyką na słońce** *przen.* bite off more than one can chew. **6.** (= *padać, przypadać ciałem*) **rzucać się komuś w ramiona** fling o.s. into sb's arms; **rzucać się na kolana** go down on one's knees; **rzucać się do czyichś stóp** throw o.s. to sb's feet. **7.** *pot.* (= *sprzeciwiać się, awanturować się*) kick up a fuss *l.* row *l.* stink; **nie rzucaj się!** take it easy! **8.** *pot.* **rzucać się na coś** (= *oddawać się czemuś z zapałem*) pitch into sth; **rzuciliśmy się na jedzenie** we pitched into the food.

rzucawka *f. Gen.pl.* -ek **rzucawka porodowa** *pat.* eclampsia.

rzucić (się) *pf. zob.* **rzucać (się)**.

rzucik *mi Gen.* -a pattern.

rzut *mi* **1.** (= *rzucenie*) throw, cast, fling, hurl, toss; **celny/niecelny rzut** well-aimed/missed throw; **o rzut kamieniem** *l.* **beretem** a stone's throw away; **rzut monetą** (*przy losowaniu*) toss-up; **rzut kośćmi** throw *l.* cast of dice; **wynik rzutu** (*kością*) cast; **rzut kulą kręglową** bowl. **2.** *sport* (*w nazwach konkurencji*) **rzut młotem** the shot put; **rzut dyskiem** the discus; **rzut oszczepem** the javelin. **3.** *sport* (*stałe elementy gier zespołowych*) *piłka nożna, rugby* kick; *koszykówka* throw; **rzut karny** penalty kick; **rzut rożny** corner kick; **rzut wolny** *piłka nożna* free kick; *koszykówka* free throw. **4.** *judo, zapasy* (= *sposób przewrócenia przeciwnika*) throw; **rzut na łopatki** pin; **rzut na matę** (*z pozycji stojącej*) takedown. **5.** (= *energiczny ruch*) **rzut głową** toss of the head; **rzut oka** glance; **rzut oka na coś** *przen.* bird's-eye view of sth; **na pierwszy rzut oka** (= *na podstawie pierwszego wrażenia*) at first glance; at first blush; **zobaczyć na pierwszy rzut oka, że...** see at a (single) glance that...; **ocenić sytuację jednym rzutem oka** take in the scene at a glance. **6.** (= *etap, kolejna partia*) stage, instalment. **7.**

(= *kolejna wersja dzieła*) version. **8.** *wojsk.* (= *część ugrupowania bojowego*) echelon. **9.** *mat., kartogr.* (= *odwzorowanie*) projection; **rzut Merkatora** *geogr.* Mercator's projection; **rzut ortogonalny** *mat.* orthogonal projection. **10.** *bud., techn.* plan, view, projection; **rzut parteru** ground plan; **rzut poziomy/pionowy** floor/vertical projection.

rzutek *mi* **-tk-** *Gen.* **-a** *sport* (*cel wyrzucany w powietrze*) bird, clay pigeon; **strzelanie do rzutków** clay-pigeon shooting, trap shooting.

rzutka *f. Gen.pl.* **-ek 1.** *żegl.* messenger. **2.** (= *strzałka rzucana do tarczy*) dart.

rzutki *a.* enterprising, aggressive, go-ahead.

rzutkość *f.* enterprise.

rzutnia *f. sport* throwing area.

rzutnik *mi Gen.* **-a** *techn.* projector; **rzutnik obrazu z folii** overhead projector, *pot.* OHP; **rzutnik slajdów** slide projector.

rzutować *ipf.* **1.** *bud., mat., kartogr., fot.* project. **2.** *psych.* (= *przenosić*) project (*coś na kogoś* sth on *l.* onto sb). **3.** (= *wpływać*) influence (*na coś* sth); have an impact (*na coś* on *l.* upon sth).

rzutowy *a.* **1.** *mat.* **geometria/płaszczyzna rzutowa** projective geometry/plane. **2.** *roln.* **siewnik rzutowy** broadcaster.

rzygacz *mi Gen.* **-a** *bud.* (= *gargulec*) gargoyle.

rzygać *ipf.* + *Ins.* **1.** *pot.* puke (*sth*) (up), barf; **rzygać mi się chce od tego** it makes me puke. **2.** (= *chlustać*) spew, spout; **rzygać ogniem/lawą/ krwią** spew fire/lava/blood.

rzygi *pl. Gen.* **-ów** = **rzygowiny**.

rzygnąć *pf.* **-ij** *zob.* **rzygać**.

rzygowiny *pl. Gen.* **-in** *pot.* puke.

Rzym *mi geogr.* Rome; **wszystkie drogi prowadzą do Rzymu** all roads lead to Rome.

Rzymianin *mp pl.* **-anie** *Gen.* **-an**, **Rzymianka** *f. Gen.pl.* **-ek** Roman.

rzymski *a. hist., geogr.* Roman; **cesarstwo** *l.* **imperium rzymskie** the Roman Empire; **cesarz rzymski** Roman emperor; **cyfry rzymskie** Roman numerals; **łaźnia rzymska** Roman bath; **pieczeń rzymska** *kulin.* meat loaf.

rzymskokatolicki *a. rel.* Roman Catholic; **Kościół rzymskokatolicki** the Roman Catholic Church; **wyznanie rzymskokatolickie** Roman Catholicism.

rżeć *ipf.* **rżę rżysz, rżyj 1.** (*o koniu*) neigh; (*cicho l. radośnie*) whinny. **2.** *pot.* (= *śmiać się hałaśliwie*) guffaw, hee-haw.

rżenie *n.* **1.** (*konia*) neigh; **ciche rżenie** whinny. **2.** (= *śmiech, rechot*) hee-haw.

rżnąć *ipf.* **-ij 1.** (= *ciąć, przecinać*) cut; (*piłując*) saw; (*na plastry*) slice. **2.** (= *wyrzynać, rzeźbić*) carve, engrave. **3.** (= *zabijać, zarzynać*) butcher, slaughter. **4.** *pot.* (= *grać hałaśliwie*) bang away (*na czymś* on sth); **rżnąć na skrzypcach/ wiolonczeli** saw the violin/cello. **5.** *pot.* (= *udawać*) **rżnąć głupa** act the fool. **6.** *wulg.* (= *kopulować*) (*z kobietą*) screw, fuck (*sb*). **7.** *pot.* (= *robić coś zapamiętale*) **rżnąć w karty** play cards with gusto; **rżnąć z karabinów** shoot away like mad. **8.** *pot.* (= *boleć*) **rżnie mnie w brzuchu** *l.* **w kiszkach** I have a piercing bellyache. **9.** *wulg.* (= *oddawać kał*) crap; **rżnąć kupę** take a shit. **10.** *pf. pot.* (= *uderzyć*) punch. **11.** *pf.* + *Ins.* (= *rzucić, cisnąć*) fling, hurl, dash (*sth*) (*o coś* against sth) (*w coś* into sth). ~ **się** *ipf.* **1.** *pot.* (= *zabijać się*) butcher one another. **2.** *wulg.* (= *uprawiać seks*) screw, fuck.

rżnięty *a.* (*o krysztale itp.*) cut; **szkło rżnięte** cut glass.

rżysko *n.* stubble.

S

S, s *n. indecl.* (*litera*) S, s; **S jak Stanisław** S is for Sierra; S as in Sierra.

s *abbr.* sec. (= *second*).

s. *abbr.* **1.** (= *strona*) pg. (= *page*). **2.** (= *siostra*) *rel.* Sr (= *sister*).

SA, S.A. *abbr.* (= *spółka akcyjna*) (*polska, niemiecka*) joint-stock company; (*brytyjska l. amerykańska*) plc, PLC (= *public limited company*).

sabadyla *f. Gen.pl.* **-i** *l.* **-l** **1.** *bot.* sabadilla (*Sabadilla officinalis l. Schoenocaulon officinale*). **2.** (*wyciąg*) sabadilla extract.

sabadylowy *a.* sabadilla; **ocet sabadylowy** sabadilla extract.

sabat *mi rel.* Sabbath; **sabat czarownic** Sabbath, sabbat, witches' Sabbath.

sabot *mi Gen.* **-a** sabot.

sabotaż *mi* sabotage, subversive destruction; **mały sabotaż** small sabotage; **sabotaż pracy** absenteeism; **organizować sabotaż** sabotage.

sabotażowy *a.* sabotage.

sabotażysta *mp*, **sabotażystka** *f. Gen.pl.* **-ek** saboteur.

sabotować *ipf.* sabotage.

sacharoza *f. chem.* sucrose, saccharose.

sacharyd *mi biochem.* saccharide.

sacharymetr *mi techn.* saccharimeter.

sacharyna *f.* saccharin.

sacrum *n. indecl.* the sacred.

sad *mi* orchard; **sad wiśniowy/jabłoniowy** cherry tree/apple tree orchard.

sadło *n.* (*tkanka zwierzęca*) *żart.* (*człowieka*) fat; **obrastać w sadło** *dosł.* run to fat; *przen.* roll in money, feather one's nest; **wytapiać sadło** render fat; **zalać komuś sadła za skórę** make things hot *l.* lively for sb.

sadomasochizm *n. psych., med.* sadomasochism.

sadowić się *ipf.* **-ów** settle o.s.

sadownictwo *n.* fruit-growing, fruit-farming; orcharding, pomiculture.

sadowniczy *a.* fruit-grower's, fruit-growing; (*o roślinach, literaturze*) orchard; **maść sadownicza** grafting wax.

sadownik *mp* fruit grower, fruit farmer, fruiter; orchadist.

saduceusz *mp hist.* Sadducee.

sadyba *f.* (= *miejsce zamieszkania*) abode; (= *osiedle*) *hist.* settlement.

sadysta *mp*, **sadystka** *f. Gen.pl.* **-ek** sadist.

sadystyczny *a.* sadistic.

sadyzm *mi psych., med.* sadism.

sadz *mi* **1.** (*do hodowli*) fish cage; (*morski*) sea cage. **2.** (*na łodzi*) (fish) well.

sadza *f. Gen.pl.* **-y** soot; **sadza lampowa** lampblack.

sadzać *ipf.* seat (*kogoś* sb); **sadzać kogoś za kraty** *l.* **do więzienia** put sb behind the bars, put sb into prison; **sadzać kogoś do lekcji** make sb do his *l.* her homework; **sadzać kurę** *roln.* set a hen on eggs.

sadzarka *f. Gen.pl.* **-ek** *roln.* planter; **sadzarka ziemniaków** potato planter.

sadzawka *f. Gen.pl.* **-ek** pool, pond.

sadzeniak *mi Gen.* **-a** *ogr.* potato set, seed potato.

sadzić *ipf.* **1.** plant; (*w doniczce*) pot; (*w dołkach*) dibble. **2.** (= *używać*) use; **sadzić błędy** *pot.* make mistakes; **sadzić przekleństwami** hail down curses. **3.** *pot.* (= *biec*) bound, lope. **~ się** *ipf.* exert o.s., spare no effort (*na coś* to do sth); **sadzić się na dowcipy** try to be funny.

sadzonka *f. Gen.pl.* **-ek** **1.** (*pęd*) cutting. **2.** (= *rozsada*) seedling; (*drzewek*) sapling.

sadzonkowy *a.* cutting; seedling; **materiał sadzonkowy** seedlings.

sadzony *a.* (*o jajku*) sunny-side up.

sadź *f.* = **szadź**.

safandulstwo *n.* gawkiness, oafishness.

safanduła *f. l. mp decl. like f. Gen.pl.* **-ł** *l.* **-ów** *uj.* gawk, oaf.

safari *n. indecl.* (*polowanie*) (*ubranie*) safari; **jechać na safari** go on safari.

safian *mi* saffian.

safianowy *a.* saffian.

saficki *a. teor.lit.* Sapphic; **strofa saficka** Sapphic stanza.

safizm *mi* sapphism.

saga *f.* **1.** (*np. rodzinna*) *teor.lit.* saga. **2.** (*utwór epicki*) saga novel.

sagan *mi Gen.* **-a** cooking pot.

sago *n. indecl. kulin.* sago.

sagowiec *mi* **-wc-** *Gen.* **-a** *bot.* sago palm (*Metroxylon sagu*).

Sahara *f.* Sahara, the Sahara desert.

sahib *mp* sahib, saheb.

saintsimonizm *mi fil.* Saint-Simonianism, Saint-Simonism.

sak *mi Gen.* **-u** *l.* **-a** **1.** *ryb.* (*sieć*) purse seine. **2.** *przest.* (= *sidło*) snare.

sake *n. indecl.* sake.

sakiewka *f. Gen.pl.* **-ek** *przest.* pouch; **nabijać sobie sakiewkę** line one's pocket *l.* purse.

sakra f. **1.** rel. consecration; **sakra biskupia** consecration. **2.** hist. (króla) anointing.

sakralizacja f. rel. sacralization.

sakralny a. sacral; **muzyka sakralna** church music; **teksty sakralne** sacred texts.

sakramencki a. pot. (o draniu, oszuście, głupcu) cursed, goddamn.

sakrament mi rel. sacrament; **sakrament bierzmowania** confirmation; **sakrament chorych** anointing of the sick; **sakrament chrztu** baptism; **sakrament kapłaństwa** ordination; **sakrament komunii** the Eucharist; **sakrament małżeństwa** holy matrimony; **sakrament pokuty/pojednania** sacrament of penance/reconciliation; **ostatni sakrament** Last Sacrament, Viaticum; **Najświętszy** l. **Przenajświętszy Sakrament** the Holy l. Blessed Sacrament; **przyjmować sakrament** receive the sacrament; **udzielić sakramentu** give the sacrament.

sakramentalia pl. Gen. **-ów** sacramentals.

sakramentalny a. **1.** (= zwyczajowy) sacramental, time-honored, Br. time-honoured. **2.** kośc. sacramental.

sakshorn mi muz. saxhorn.

saksofon mi muz. saxophone.

saksofonista mp, **saksofonistka** f. Gen.pl. **-ek** saxophonist.

saksofonowy a. saxophone.

Saksonia f. Gen. **-ii** geogr. Saxony; **Dolna Saksonia** Lower Saxony; **Saksonia-Anhalt** hist. Saxony-Anhalt.

saksy pl. Gen. **-ów** pot. seasonal labor.

sakwa f. **1.** (przy siodle) przest. pannier, bag; (przy rowerze) pannier. **2.** (= sakiewka) przest. purse, scrip; **otwierać sakwę** have an open hand, be generous.

sakwojaż mi przest. traveling bag.

sala f. **1.** (duża) hall; (mała) room; **sala balowa** ballroom, dance hall; **sala gimnastyczna** gymnasium; **sala jadalna** dining room; **sala koncertowa** concert hall; **sala konferencyjna** conference room; **sala porodowa** delivery room; **sala posiedzeń** sessions chamber; **sala przesłuchań** interrogation room; **sala operacyjna** operating theater, operating room; **sala sądowa** courtroom; **sala szpitalna** (hospital) ward; **sala szkolna** school room; **sala tortur** torture chamber; **sala widowiskowa** auditorium; **sala widzeń** visitors' room; **sala wykładowa** lecture hall; **sala wystawowa** showroom. **2.** (publiczność) audience; (w kinie, teatrze) house; **pełna sala** full house; **pytania z sali** questions from the floor.

salamandra f. Gen.pl. **-er** zool. salamander (Salamandra).

salamandry pl. Gen. **-er** zool. salamanders (Salamandridae).

salami n. indecl. **1.** (kiełbasa) salami. **2.** (ser) mild hard cheese, usu. with mixed in bits of green and red pepper.

salaterka f. Gen.pl. **-ek** salad bowl.

salceson mi headcheese; Br. brawn.

saldo n. ekon. balance; **saldo debetowe** debit balance; **saldo dodatnie** active balance; **saldo gotówkowe** balance in l. on hand; **saldo odsetek** balance of interest; **saldo początkowe/końcowe** initial/final balance; **saldo ujemne** passive balance; **saldo zysków** profit balance; **wykazywać saldo w wysokości...** show a balance of...

saldować ipf. ekon. balance an account, strike the balance.

saletra f. nitrate; (jako środek konserwujący) saltpeter; **saletra amonowa** roln. ammonium nitrate; **saletra potasowa** potassium nitrate; **nawozić saletrą** nitrify.

saletrować ipf. **1.** roln. nitrify. **2.** (konserwować) preserve with saltpeter.

saletrzany a. roln. (o nawozie) nitrate.

salezjanin mp pl. **-anie** Gen. **-an** kośc. Salesian.

salezjański a. Salesian.

salicylan mi chem. salicylate.

salicylowy a. chem. salicylic; **kwas salicylowy** salicylic acid.

salina f. techn. saltern, salt works.

salka f. Gen.pl. **-ek** classroom, room; **salka katechetyczna** Sunday school classroom.

salmiak mi chem. ammonium chloride, sal ammoniac.

salmonella f. Gen.pl. **-i** biol. salmonella.

salmonelloza f. pat. salmonellosis.

salomonowy a. Solomonian, Solomonic; **Pieśń Salomonowa**, Bibl. Song of Solomon.

salon mi **1.** (= bawialnia) salon; (= duży pokój) living room. **2.** (towarzystwo) salon; **salon literacki** literary salon. **3.** (meble) suite. **4.** (sklep, zakład usługowy) salon; **salon fryzjerski** hair l. hairdressing salon; **salon piękności** beauty parlor; Br. beauty parlour; beauty salon. **5.** (wystawa) salon.

salonik mi (pokój) parlor; Br. parlour; salon.

salonka f. Gen.pl. **-ek** hist. parlor car; Br. saloon carriage.

salonowiec mp pl. **-y** man of the world.

salonowy a. (o rozmowie, grzeczności) cultivated, refined; (o towarzystwie, stylu mówienia) dignified, courtly; **piesek salonowy** lap dog.

salopa f. mantle.

salowa f. Gen. **-ej**, **salowy** mp orderly, ward-attendant.

salsefia f. Gen. **-ii** bot. salsify, oyster plant (Tragopogon porrifolius).

salto n. flip, somersault; **salto do tyłu/do przodu** backward/forward somersault; **salto mortale** double somersault.

salut mi salute; **salut bandery** żegl. dipping the colors; **salut honorowy** salute of honor; **oddać salut** give l. fire a salute.

salutować ipf. salute (komuś sb); (banderą) dip one's colors.

salwa f. burst; **salwa armatnia** wojsk. volley, salvo; **salwy śmiechu/braw** peals of laughter/applause; **salwa honorowa** salute; **oddać salwę honorową** fire a salute.

salwować ipf. żart. save. **~ się** ipf. save one's skin; **salwować się ucieczką** run for dear life.

sałata f. lettuce (Lactuca); **sałata głowiasta/liściasta** cabbage l. head/leaf lettuce; **sałata lodowa** iceberg lettuce; **sałata morska** sea lettuce (Ulva lactuca).

sałatka *f. Gen.pl.* -ek *kulin.* salad; **sałatka owocowa** fruit salad; **sałatka z pomidorów/ogórków** tomato/cucumber salad.

sałatkowy *a.* salad; **bar sałatkowy** salad bar; **sos sałatkowy** salad cream.

sam *a.* **1.** (= *opuszczony*) alone; **sam jeden** all alone; **całkiem sam** all alone, all by o.s.; **robić coś samemu** do sth o.s., do sth on one's own; **iść samemu** go alone; (*na imprezę*) stag it, come *l.* go stag; **zostać z kimś sam na sam** get sb to o.s.; **samemu podjąć decyzję** decide for o.s.; **chcę zostać sama** I want to be alone; **byłem sam w domu** I was alone at home; **zostaliśmy sami** we were left alone. **2.** (= *akurat*) just; **w sam raz** just fine *l.* right; **to mi wystarczy w sam raz** it'll be just fine; **w samą porę** just in time, (just) about time; (*jako komentarz*) just in time!, perfect timing!; (*zwł. sarkastyczny*) about time! **3.** (*przestrzeń*) right, very; **sam środek** the dead center; **w samym środku** right in the middle; **u samej góry** at the very top; **do samego dna** to the very bottom; **nad samym brzegiem rzeki** at the very bank of the river; **stanął pod samymi drzwiami** he stood right at the doorsteps. **4.** (*czas*) just; **do samej nocy** till late in the evening; **od samego rana** first thing in the morning. **5.** (= *wyłącznie*) nothing but; **same kłopoty** nothing but trouble; **dostawać same złe stopnie** get nothing but bad marks; **mówić same kłamstwa/samą prawdę** speak nothing but lies/the truth; **podać same tylko najważniejsze fakty** give nothing but the essentials. **6.** (*wyjątkowość*) myself (yourself etc.); **mszę odprawiał sam biskup** the mass was celebrated by the bishop himself. **7.** (*przyczyna*) mere, very; **na samą myśl o tym przechodzi mnie dreszcz** the very thought of it makes me shiver; **od samego zapachu robi mi się niedobrze** the mere smell makes me sick; **wystarczy sam jej widok** the mere *l.* very sight of her is enough. **8.** (= *nawet*) myself (yourself etc.); **zaśpiewał to tak, że nawet sam mistrz lepiej by nie mógł** he sang better than the master himself. **9.** (*wzmocnienie*) myself (yourself etc.); **sam z siebie** without being asked; **samo przez się** by itself; **to się rozumie samo przez się** it goes without saying, this is obvious by itself; **cel sam w sobie** an end in itself; **od samego początku** from the very beginning; **sam widzisz** there you go; **sam tak powiedział** he said so himself; **sam sobie jestem winien** I can only blame myself; **zobacz sam** see for yourself; **być pozostawionym samemu sobie** be left high and dry, be left stranded; **być sobie samemu panem** be one's own master; **dawać sobie samemu radę** fend for o.s.; **doświadczyć czegoś samemu** experience sth at first hand; **rumienić się/drżeć na samą myśl o czymś** blush/tremble at the mere thought of sth; **cyfry mówią same za siebie** the figures speak for themselves; **przychodzi mu to samo z siebie** it comes natural to him; **sama uroczystość zaczyna się o 9** the actual ceremony starts at 9 a.m.; **tym razem przeszedłeś samego siebie** you excelled *l.* surpassed yourself this time; **zostawmy go samemu sobie** let's leave him alone; **kochaj mnie dla mnie samej**

love me for who I am. **10.** (= *właśnie ten*) the (this, that) very, same, identical; **taki sam** the same, identical; **taki sam co do joty** mirror reflection; **jeden i ten sam** one and the same; **tak samo jak...** just as...; **tak samo jak wczoraj** just as yesterday; **tyle samo** the same amount; **tym samym** thus, thereby; **w ten sam sposób** (*zareagować, odpowiedzieć*) in the same way, by the same token; **kubek w kubek taki sam (jak)** the spitting image (of); **prawie taki sam jak...** much the same as...; **to jedna i ta sama osoba** they're one and the same person; **byłem chory i ona tak samo** I was ill and so was she; **jesteśmy w tym samym wieku** we're of the same age; **mam taką samą koszulkę** I have an identical T-shirt; **przyjedziemy tego samego dnia** we'll arrive on the same day; **to ten sam mężczyzna, który ci się ukłonił** it's the same man who said hello to you; **to to samo miejsce, w którym byliśmy w zeszłym roku** it's the same place we visited last year; **wracać tą samą drogą** retrace one's steps; **kto pod kim dołki kopie, sam w nie wpada** it's a case of the biter bit. – *mi* (*sklep*) supermarket, self-service store.

Samarytanin *mp pl.* -anie *Gen.* -an, **Samarytanka** *f. Gen.pl.* -ek Samaritan.

samarytanin *mp pl.* -anie *Gen.* -an, **samarytanka** *f. Gen.pl.* -ek Samaritan; **dobry Samarytanin** Good Samaritan.

samarytański *a.* Samaritan; (*o postępowaniu*) Samaritan, Good-Samaritan; **miłosierdzie samarytańskie** Samaritan kindness; **uczynek samarytański** (good) Samaritan deed.

samba *f.* samba.

samczy *a.* male; *uj.* (*o popędach, pewności siebie*) macho.

samczyk *ma* male.

samica *f.* **1.** (*zwierzę*) female; (*kozy*) she-goat; (*wilka*) she-wolf; (*dużych ssaków*) cow; (*zająca, królika, jelenia*) doe; (*psa, wilka*) bitch; (*niedźwiedzia, jeża, borsuka*) sow; (*ptaków, zwł. łownych*) hen. **2.** *pog.* (= *kobieta*) female.

samiczka *f. Gen.pl.* -ek female.

samiczy *a.* female, feminine; *uj.* (*o egocentryzmie itp.*) female.

samiec *ma* -mc- (*zwierzę*) male; (*psa i podobnych zwierząt*) dog; (*dużych zwierząt*) bull; (*owcy*) ram; (*ptaków*) cock. – *mp* -mc- *pog.* (= *mężczyzna*) macho.

samizdat *mi* (*hist.*) samizdat.

samo *a. zob.* **sam.**

samobiczowanie *n.* *hist.* self-flagellation; *przen.* self-flagellation, self-castigation.

samobieżny *a.* self-propelled; **działo samobieżne** self-propelled gun.

samobójca *mp* suicide; **zamachowiec samobójca** suicide bomber.

samobójczy *a.* suicidal; **bramka samobójcza** *sport* own goal; **próba samobójcza** suicide attempt, suicide bid; suicidal attempt; **skłonności samobójcze** suicidal tendencies; **zamach samobójczy** suicide bombing.

samobójczyni *f. zob.* **samobójca.**

samobójstwo *n.* suicide; **zbiorowe samobój-**

stwo mass suicide; **popełnić samobójstwo** commit suicide; **popchnąć kogoś do samobójstwa** drive sb to suicide; **usiłować popełnić samobójstwo** attempt suicide.

samochodowy *a.* car, auto, automotive; (*o przemyśle*) automotive, car; (*o sporcie*) motor; (*o wypadku*) car; **atlas samochodowy** road atlas; **fotelik samochodowy** car seat; **giełda samochodowa** car exchange; **mechanik samochodowy** car mechanic; **rajd samochodowy** road racing.

samochodziarz *mp pot.* motorist.

samochodzik *mi Gen.* **-u** *l.* **-a** **1.** (*zabawka*) toy-car; (*w wesołym miasteczku*) bumper car. **2.** *emf.* (= *samochód*) (little) car; **zasuwać jak mały samochodzik** *pot.* steam ahead, rip along; (*np. pracując*) work like crazy.

samochód *mi* **-o-** car, auto, automobile; **samochód bojowy** combat car; **samochód ciężarowy** truck; *Br.* lorry; **samochód małolitrażowy** low-powered car, small-engine car; **samochód opancerzony** armored car; *Br.* armoured car; **samochód osobowy** car, motor car; **samochód sportowy** sports car; **samochód terenowy** off-road vehicle, all-terrain vehicle; **samochód wyścigowy** racing car; **samochód kombi** station wagon; *Br.* estate car; **samochód patrolowy** squad car; **samochód służbowy** company car; **samochód-pułapka** booby-trap car; **samochód zabytkowy** veteran car; **samochód z automatyczną skrzynią biegów** automatic, self-shifter; **samochód z napędem na cztery koła** four-wheeler; **podrasowany samochód** hot rod; **wynajęty samochód** rent *l.* hire car; **fabryka samochodów** car factory; **oddać samochód do naprawy** get *l.* have one's car repaired; **jeździć samochodem** drive; **prowadzić samochód** drive a car; **przyjechać/pojechać samochodem** come/go by car; **uruchomić samochód** get the car started; **wsiadać do samochodu** get into the car, get inside the car; **wysiadać z samochodu** get off the car; **jesteś samochodem?** did you come by car?

samochwalstwo *n.* boastfulness, boastful talk.

samochwał *mp pl.* **-y** braggart, bragger; bigmouth.

samochwała *f. l. mp decl. like f. Gen.pl.* **-ł** *l.* **-ów** braggart, bragger; bigmouth.

samoczynnie *adv.* spontaneously; (*np. otwierać się*) automatically.

samoczynny *a.* automatic; self-starting; **zapłon samoczynny** spontaneous ingnition.

samodoskonalenie *n.* self-improvement, self-development.

samodyscyplina *f.* self-discipline, self-restraint.

samodział *mi* homespun.

samodziałowy *a.* homespun.

samodzielnie *adv.* (= *samemu*) alone, by oneself; (= *bez pomocy*) unaided, single-handedly; (= *odrębnie*) independently; (*mieszkać*) by oneself, alone; (*pracować, występować*) individually; **robić coś samodzielnie** do sth o.s., do sth on one's own.

samodzielność *f.* (= *niezależność*) independence; (= *poleganie na sobie samym*) self-re-

liance; **samodzielność finansowa** financial independence, self-sufficiency.

samodzielny *a.* (= *niezależny*) **1.** independent, self-reliant; (*finansowo*) self-sufficient, self-supporting; (*o państwie*) independent, sovereign; (= *oryginalny*) individual; (*o myśleniu*) individualistic, free; **samodzielny pracownik naukowy** independent academic. **2.** (= *bez pomocy*) unassisted, unaided. **3.** (= *samoistny*) independent; (*o mieszkaniu*) self-contained, separate.

samodzierżawca *mp polit.* autocrat.

samodzierżawie *n. polit.* autocracy.

samofinansować się *ipf.* provide for o.s., support o.s.

samofinansowanie *n.* self-financing, self-supporting.

samogłoska *f. fon.* vowel; **samogłoska długa/krótka** long/short vowel; **samogłoska niska/wysoka/średnia** low/high/mid vowel; **samogłoska przednia/tylna** front/back vowel; **samogłoska okrągła/płaska** round/non-round vowel; **samogłoska ustna/nosowa** oral/nasal vowel.

samogłoskowy *a.* vocalic, vowel; (*o temacie, rzeczowniku*) vocalic; **system samogłoskowy** vowel system; **przesuwka samogłoskowa** vowel shift.

samogłów *ma* **-ow-** *icht.* sunfish (*Mola mola*).

samogon *mi pot.* moonshine; (*w USA*) hooch; (*w Irlandii*) poteen.

samograj *mi Gen.pl.* **-ów** *pot., przen.* (*o sztuce, filmie, roli*) pushover.

samogwałt *mi przest.* masturbation, onanism.

samoindukcja *f. fiz.* self-induction.

samoistnie *adv.* intrinsically, spontaneously; (*występować*) naturally.

samoistny *a.* **1.** (= *istniejący samodzielnie*) spontaneous, intrinsic; *med.* idiopathic; **poronienie samoistne** spontaneous abortion; **powstawanie samoistne** autogeny; **reakcja samoistna** self-propagating reaction. **2.** (= *tworzący odrębną całość*) independent, self-contained; (*o dziele sztuki, utworze muzycznym*) autonomous.

samojezdny *a. techn.* self-propelled.

samokontrola *f.* self-control; self-restraint, self-discipline.

samokrytycyzm *mi* self-criticism.

samokrytycznie *adv.* (*np. podchodzić do czegoś*) with self-criticism.

samokrytyczny *a.* self-critical.

samokrytyka *f.* self-criticism, self-reproach; **ostra samokrytyka** self-flagellation; **złożyć samokrytykę** do a self-critique.

samokształcenie *n.* self-education, self-study.

samokształceniowy *a.* self-study, self-educative.

samolikwidacja *f.* self-liquidation, self-suppression.

samolocik *mi Gen.* **-u** *l.* **-a** **1.** (*zabawka*) toy-airplane. **2.** (= *mały samolot*) small plane.

samolot *mi* plane, aircraft, airplane; **samolot bombowy** bomber; **samolot czarterowy** charter plane; **samolot myśliwski** fighter plane, fighter; **samolot obserwacyjny** spotter; **samolot odrzuto-**

wy jet plane, jet-propelled aircraft; **samolot pasażerski** passenger plane; **samolot rejsowy** liner; **samolot transportowy** (*cywilny*) cargo plane; (*wojskowy*) troop carrier; **samolot wojskowy** warplane; **samolot zwiadowczy** scout; **przylecieć samolotem** come by plane; **polecieć samolotem** go by plane, fly.

samolotowy *a.* aircraft, airplane; **połączenia samolotowe** airway connections.

samolub *mp pl.* **-y** *l.* **-i** miser, self-seeker.

samolubnie *adv.* selfishly, in a selfish way; egoistically.

samolubny *a.* selfish, self-seeking; egoistic.

samolubstwo *n.* selfishness, selfhood; egoism.

samoładowanie *n. komp.* (*systemu operacyjnego*) bootstrap.

samoładowarka *f. Gen.pl.* **-ek** *techn.* self-loader.

samonaprowadzający *a. wojsk.* homing; **pocisk samonaprowadzający** guided missile, fire-and-forget missile.

samonaprowadzanie *n. wojsk.* homing guidance, target-homing.

samonośny *a. techn.* (*o nadwoziu*) self-supporting.

samoobrona *f.* **1.** (= *obrona samego siebie*) self-defense, self-protection; **w samoobronie** in self-defense. **2.** (= *cywilna obrona kraju*) civil self-defense.

samoobsługa *f.* self-service, help-yourself system.

samoobsługowy *a.* self-service; **pralnia samoobsługowa** Launderette®, Laundromat®; **restauracja samoobsługowa** self-service cafeteria.

samoocena *f.* self-assessment, self-evaluation.

samooczyszczenie *n.* self-purification, self-cleaning; **samooczyszczenie wód** self-purification of waters.

samookaleczenie *n. prawn.* self-mutilation.

samookreślenie *n.*, **samookreślenie się** *n. polit.* self-determination; **prawo do samookreślenia** the right to self-determination.

samoopalacz *mi* **-a** (*krem*) tanning foam, tanning cream.

samooskarżenie *n.* self-accusation.

samopał *m hist.* (*rodzaj broni*) arquebus, harquebus.

samopas *adv. przest.* **1.** (= *samemu*) on one's own. **2.** (= *bez opieki*) unheeded, uncared-for; **zostawić dzieci samopas** leave children unattended.

samopoczucie *n.* (*psychiczne*) frame of mind, mood; (*fizyczne dobre*) comfort; (*fizyczne złe*) discomfort; **dobre samopoczucie** (*psychiczne*) good mood *l.* disposition; **złe samopoczucie** (*psychiczne*) bad mood, bad frame of mind; **mieć dobre/złe samopoczucie** (*psychiczne*) be in a good/bad mood; (*fizyczne*) feel well/unwell *l.* badly; **jak samopoczucie?** how are you feeling?; **taka pogoda zawsze źle wpływa na moje samopoczucie** such weather always gets me down.

samopomoc *f.* self-help, mutual aid; **samopomoc społeczna** mutual aid society.

samopomocowy *a.* self-help, mutual aid.

samopowtarzalny *a. wojsk.* (*o broni*) self-loading.

samopoznanie *n.* self-analysis, introspection.

samoprzylepny *a.* self-adhesive, stick-on.

samopylność *f. bot.* self-pollination, autogamy.

samopylny *a. bot.* self-pollinating, autogamous.

samorealizacja *f.* self-fulfillment, self-realization.

samoregulacja *f.* self-regulation.

samorejestrujący *a.* (*o urządzeniu*) self-recording.

samorodek *mi* **-dk-** *Gen.* **-a** *min.* nugget.

samorodny *a.* autogenic, self-generating; (*o talencie*) natural, inborn.

samorództwo *n. biol., hist.* abiogenesis; autogenesis, autogeny; spontaneous generation.

samorząd *mi* self-government; **samorząd gospodarczy** economic local government; **samorząd miejski** municipal government; **samorząd studencki** student government; **samorząd terytorialny** local government; **samorząd uczniowski** student council; **wybory do samorządu** (*terytorialnego*) local government elections.

samorządność *f.* home rule.

samorządny *a.* autonomous, independent; (*o gminie, mieście*) autonomous, self-governed.

samorządowy *a.* self-government, council; (*o instytucji, subwencji*) local government; **okręg samorządowy** municipality.

samorzutnie *adv.* (= *spontanicznie*) spontaneously; (= *ochotniczo*) voluntarily.

samorzutny *a.* (= *spontaniczny*) spontaneous; (= *ochotniczy*) voluntary; **rozpad samorzutny** *chem.* autodecomposition.

samosąd *mi* (*zasada*) lynch law; (*działanie*) lynching.

samosia, Zosia samosia *f. Voc.* **-siu** *Gen.pl.* **-si** *l.* **-ś** *żart.* do-it-myself.

samosiejka *f. Gen.pl.* **-ek** *bot.* volunteer, volunteer plant; self-sown plant.

samosiew *mi bot.* **1.** (*roślina*) volunteer, volunteer plant; self-sown plant. **2.** (*wysiew*) self-seeding.

samosiewny *a.* self-sowing, self-seeding.

samospalenie *n.* self-immolation, self-burning.

samostanowienie *n. polit.* autonomy; (*narodów*) self-determination.

samoster *mi żegl.* self-steering gear.

samosterowny *a.* self-steering.

samosterujący *a. wojsk.* **pocisk samosterujący** guided missile.

samoświadomość *f.* self-awareness.

samotnia *f. Gen.pl.* **-i** retreat, hermitage.

samotnictwo *n.* (= *odosobnienie*) seclusion; (= *życie w odosobnieniu*) life in seclusion.

samotniczka *f. Gen.pl.* **-ek** loner, recluse.

samotniczy *a.* reclusive, lonely; **prowadzić** *l.* **pędzić samotniczy tryb życia** lead *l.* live a lonely life.

samotnie *adv.* **1.** (= *samodzielnie*) alone, on

one's own; **rodzic samotnie wychowujący dziecko** single parent. **2.** (= *w samotności*) lonely; **czuć się samotnie** feel lonely.

samotnik *mp* loner, recluse.

samotność *f.* (= *bycie opuszczonym*) loneliness; (= *przebywanie bez towarzystwa*) (*np. z wyboru, w jakimś miejscu*) solitude.

samotny *a.* (*np. o człowieku*) lonely; (*np. o domu, drzewie, skale*) solitary; **samotna kobieta/samotny mężczyzna** single *l.* unmarried woman/man; **samotna matka/samotny ojciec** single *l.* lone mother/father.

samouctwo *n.* self-education, self-instruction.

samouczek *mi* -czk- *Gen.* -a "teach-yourself" book.

samoudręka *f.* self-torment.

samouk *mp Nom.pl.* -ucy *l.* -uki self-taught person; autodidact; **historyk-samouk** self-taught historian, amateur historian.

samounicestwienie *n.* self-annihilation.

samouspokojenie *n.* self-appeasement.

samoutleniacz *mi Gen.* -a *chem.* autoxidator.

samoutlenianie *n. chem.* autoxidation.

samouwielbienie *n.* self-admiration, self-worship.

samowar *mi* samovar.

samowiedza *f.* self-knowledge.

samowładca *mp* autocrat.

samowładny *a.* autocratic.

samowola *f.* lawlessness.

samowolnie *adv.* without permission; **oddalić się samowolnie** go AWOL (= a*bsent without leave*).

samowolność *f.* lawlessness.

samowolny *a.* lawless; (*o decyzji, postępowaniu*) arbitrary; (*o człowieku*) willful.

samowyładowczy *a.* self-dumping; **wagon samowyładowczy** dump car.

samowystarczalność *f.* self-sufficiency; (*finansowa*) self-support.

samowystarczalny *a.* self-sufficient; (*finansowo*) self-supporting.

samowyzwalacz *mi Gen.* -a *fot.* self-timer, time releaser.

samowzbudzenie *n. fiz.* (*drgań, pola magnetycznego*) self-excitation.

samozachowawczy *a.* self-preservative, self-preserving; **instynkt samozachowawczy** instinct of *l.* for self-preservation.

samozadowolenie *n.* self-satisfaction.

samozagłada *f.* self-annihilation.

samozakażenie *n. med.* autoinfection.

samozamykacz *mi Gen.* -a self-closing mechanism.

samozapalenie się *n.* spontaneous ignition.

samozaparcie *n.* perseverance, persistence.

samozapłodnienie *n. biol.* autogamy, self-fertilization.

samozapłon *mi techn., wojsk.* self-ignition, spontaneous ignition.

samozapylenie *n. bot.* self-pollination, autogamy.

samozasiew *mi* self-seeding.

samozatrucie *n.* autointoxication.

samozwaniec *mp* -ńc- *pl.* -y usurper.

samozwańczo *adv.* usurpingly; **samozwańczo obwołać się królem** usurp the throne.

samozwańczy *a.* (*o królu, przywódcy*) self-proclaimed, self-appointed.

samożywność *f. biol.* autotrophy.

samożywny *a.* autotrophic.

samum *mi meteor.* simoom, simoon; samiel.

samuraj *mp pl.* -owie *l.* -e samurai.

sanacja *f. polit.* **1.** political reform; cleansing. **2.** *hist.* (*w przedwojennej Polsce*) (*działania*) moral cleansing policy; (*stronnictwo*) Piłsudski's followers.

sanacyjny *a.* reformatory.

sanatorium *n. sing. indecl. pl.* -ria *Gen.* -riów sanatorium.

sanatoryjnie *adv.* (*np. leczyć*) in a sanatorium.

sanatoryjny *a.* sanatorium.

sandacz *ma Gen.pl.* -y *l.* -ów *icht.* pikeperch (*Stizostedion l. Lucioperca*).

sandał *mi Gen.* -a sandal.

sandałek *mi* -łk- *Gen.* -a sandal.

sandałowiec *mi* -wc- *Gen.* -a *bot.* sandalwood (*Santalum*).

sandałowy *a.* sandalwood; **olejek sandałowy** sandalwood oil.

sandr *mi geol.* sandur.

sandwicz *mi Gen.* -a *Gen.pl.* -y *l.* -ów sandwich.

saneczkarka *f. Gen.pl.* -ek *zob.* **saneczkarz**.

saneczkarski *a.* toboggan; luge.

saneczkarstwo *n.* (*rekreacyjne*) tobogganing; *Br. t.* sledging; (*sportowe*) lugeing.

saneczkarz *mp* bobsledder; (*sportowiec*) luger.

saneczki *pl. Gen.* -ek toboggan; *Br. t.* sledge; (*sportowe*) luge.

saneczkowy *a.* toboggan; *sport* luge; **tor saneczkowy** toboggan run; (*sportowy*) luge chute.

sangwina *f.* (*kredka*) sanguine, red chalk.

sangwiniczka *f. Gen.pl.* -ek *zob.* **sangwinik**.

sangwiniczny *a.* sanguine.

sangwinik *mp* sanguine person; person of sanguine disposition.

sanhedryn *mi judaizm, hist.* the Sanhedrin.

sanie *pl. Gen.* -ń **1.** (*na śnieg*) sledge, sleigh. **2.** *żegl.* cradle.

sanitaria *pl. Gen.* -ów sanitary facilities.

sanitariat *mi* **1.** (*łazienka*) lavatory. **2.** (*urząd*) sanitary authorities.

sanitariusz *mp Gen.pl.* -y *l.* -ów **1.** (*w karetce*) paramedic. **2.** *wojsk.* medic; stretcher-bearer.

sanitariuszka *f. Gen.pl.* -ek nurse.

sanitarka *f. Gen.pl.* -ek ambulance.

sanitarny *a.* sanitary; (*o ekipie, inżynierii, przepisach*) sanitarian; **punkt sanitarny** first-aid station, dressing station; **świadectwo sanitarne** *żegl.* bill of health.

sankcja *f.* **1.** *prawn.* sanction; **sankcje gospodarcze** economic sanctions; **nakładać sankcje na kogoś/coś** impose sanctions on *l.* against sb/sth; **znieść sankcje** lift sanctions. **2.** (*zgoda, zatwierdzenie*) assent; *prawn.* sanction; **sankcja królewska** royal assent.

sankcjonować *ipf. prawn.* sanction, authorize; (*prawem*) legitimate.

sanki *pl. Gen.* **sanek** 1. toboggan; sled, sleigh. 2. *sport* luge.

sanktuarium *n. sing. indecl. pl.* **-ria** *Gen.pl.* **-riów** sanctuary.

San Marino *n. indecl.* San Marino.

sanna *f.* 1. (= *jazda saniami*) sleighing. 2. (= *zaśnieżona droga do jazdy saniami*) good sleighing conditions.

sanskrycki *a.* Sanskritic; (*o tekście, alfabecie*) Sanskrit.

sanskryt *mi* Sanskrit.

sanskrytolog *mp pl.* **-dzy** *l.* **-owie** Sanskritist.

sanskrytologia *f. Gen.* **-ii** Sanskrit studies.

sap *mi geol.* wet sandy soil.

sapać *ipf.* **sapię sapiesz** pant, puff; (*o silniku*) chug.

saper *mp wojsk.* (*rozbrajający miny itp.*) sapper; (*budujący mosty itp.*) engineer.

saperka *f. Gen.pl.* **-ek** 1. (*łopata*) camp shovel. 2. (*but*) boot.

saperski *a.* sapper; engineer.

sapka *f. Gen.pl.* **-ek** *med.* the snuffles.

sapnąć *pf.* **-ij** *zob.* **sapać**.

sapowaty *a. geol.* (*o glebie, gruncie, terenie*) boggy, marshy.

saprobiont *mi biol.* saprobe.

saprofag *mi Gen.* **-a** *zool.* saprophagan.

saprofit *mi bot.* saprophyte.

saprofityczny *a.* saprophytic.

sarabanda *f.* saraband, sarabande.

sardela *f. Gen.pl.* **-i** *icht.* anchovy (*Engraulis encrasicholus*).

sardonicznie *adv.* sardonically.

sardoniczny *a.* sardonic.

Sardynia *f. Gen.* **-ii** Sardinia.

sardynka *f. icht.* sardine (*Sardina pilchardus*); **sardynki w oleju** sardines in oil; **stłoczeni jak sardynki (w puszce)** packed like sardines.

sarenka *f.* small (roe) deer.

sarepski *a.* Sarepta; **gorczyca sarepska** *bot.* Sarepta mustard (*Brassica besseriana*).

sari *n. indecl.* sari.

sarkać *ipf.* 1. (= *narzekać*) repine (*na kogoś / coś* at sb/sth). 2. (= *burczeć*) snort.

sarkastycznie *adv.* sarcastically.

sarkastyczny *a.* sarcastic.

sarkazm *mi* sarcasm.

sarknąć *pf.* **-ij** *zob.* **sarkać**.

sarkofag *mi* sarcophagus.

sarkoma *f. med.* sarcoma.

sarmacki *a.* 1. (*o kulturze, literaturze, obyczajowości*) old-Polish; characteristic of the Polish gentry. 2. (*związany ze starożytnym plemieniem irańskim*) Sarmatian.

Sarmata *mp* 1. (= *polski szlachcic*) member of Polish gentry; (= *Polak starej daty*) old-Polish character. 2. (= *członek starożytnych plemion irańskich*) Sarmatian.

sarmatyzm *mi* backwardness.

sarna *f. Gen.pl.* **sarn** *l.* **saren** 1. *zool.* roe deer, roe (*Capreolus capreolus*). 2. *pot.* (*grzyb*) hedgehog mushroom (*Hydnum*).

sarni *a.* roe deer's.

sarnina *f.* venison.

sarong *mi* sarong.

sasanka *f. Gen.pl.* **-ek** *bot.* pasqueflower (*Pulsatilla vulgaris*).

saski *a.* Saxon; **saska porcelana** Dresden china.

saszetka *f. Gen.pl.* **-ek** 1. (*torba*) travel document organizer; (*przy pasie*) fanny pack. 2. (*zapachowa, ketchupu, cukru itp.*) sachet.

sataniczny *a.* (*o śmiechu, sekcie*) satanic.

satanista *mp* Satanist.

satanistyczny *a.* (*o kulcie, obrzędach, sekcie*) Satanist.

satanizm *mi* Satanism.

satelicki *a.* (*o państwie*) satellite.

satelita *mi astron., polit., techn.* satellite.

satelitarny *a.* satellite; **antena satelitarna** satellite dish; **transmisja satelitarna** satellite broadcast.

satem *a. jęz. indecl.* satem; **języki satem** satem languages.

satemowy *a. jęz.* satem.

satrapa *mp* 1. *hist.* satrap. 2. (*tyran*) tyrant; *rzad.* satrap.

saturacja *f. techn.* saturation; (*w cukrownictwie*) carbonation.

saturator *mi Gen.* **-a** 1. (*do wody sodowej*) soda fountain. 2. *techn.* saturator; (*w cukrownictwie*) carbonator.

satyna *f.* satin.

satynować *ipf. druk., tk.* calender.

satynowy *a.* satin.

satyr *mp pl.* **-owie** *l.* **-y** *mit., przen.* satyr.

satyra *f. t. teor.lit.* satire (*na kogoś / coś* on sb/sth); **zjadliwa/cięta satyra** scathing/biting satire.

satyrycznie *adv.* satirically; **przedstawić kogoś/coś satyrycznie** satirize sb/sth.

satyryczny *a.* (*o utworze*) satiric, satirical; (*o programie*) comedy.

satyryk *mp* satirist; (*występujący w krótkich monologach*) stand-up comic.

satysfakcja *f.* 1. (= *zadowolenie*) satisfaction; gratification; **dawać satysfakcję** (*np. o pracy*) be rewarding. 2. (= *rekompensata*) satisfaction; **dać komuś satysfakcję** *przest.* give satisfaction to sb.

satysfakcjonować *ipf.* satisfy.

satysfakcjonujący *a.* satisfying; (*o pracy*) rewarding.

sauna *f.* sauna.

sauté *adv.* sauté.

savoir-vivre *mi* savoir-vivre.

sawanna *f.* savanna, savannah.

sawannowy *a.* savanna, savannah.

sawantka *f. iron., uj.* bluestocking.

są *ipf. zob.* **być**.

sączek *mi* **-czk-** *Gen.* **-a** 1. *chem.* filter. 2. *med.* drain. 3. *techn.* drain pipe, drain.

sączkować *ipf. med.* drain.

sączyć *ipf.* 1. (*pić*) sip. 2. (*wlewać*) trickle. 3. (*wydzielać*) ooze. 4. (*filtrować*) strain, filter. ~ **się** *ipf.* 1. (*wyciekać*) ooze, trickle. 2. (*wylewać się*) leak.

sąd *mi* **1.** (*instytucja*) court; court of justice, court of law; **sąd apelacyjny** appellate court, court of appeal; **sąd boży** *hist.* ordeal; **sąd dla nieletnich** juvenile court; **sąd grodzki** magistrates' court; *hist.* borough court; **sąd honorowy** honor court, *Br.* honour court; **sąd karny** criminal court; **sąd koleżeński** peer tribunal; **Sąd Najwyższy** Supreme Court; **sąd okręgowy** district court; **sąd ostateczny** Last *l.* Final Judgement; **sąd pierwszej instancji** court of first instance; **sąd polowy** provost court; **sąd powszechny** court of law; **sąd pracy** labor court; *Br.* labour court; **sąd rejonowy** local court; **sąd rodzinny** family court, domestic relations court; **sąd wojenny** court martial; **sąd wojewódzki** provincial court; **nakaz sądu** court order; **obraza sądu** contempt of court; **orzeczenie sądu** court decision; **posiedzenie sądu** court sitting; **oddać sprawę do sądu** go to court; **podać kogoś do sądu** take sb to court; **postawić kogoś przed sądem** bring sb before court; **stawać przed sądem** appear before court; **stawić się w sądzie** appear in court; **proszę wstać, sąd idzie** all rise, the court is in session; **Wysoki Sądzie!** Your Honor! *Br.* Your Honour! **2.** (*rozprawa*) trial; **powiesić kogoś bez sądu** hang sb without trial. **3.** (*gmach*) courthouse, court. **4.** (*opinia*) judgment; **wydać sąd o kimś/czymś** pronounce judgment on *l.* upon sb/sth. **5.** *log.* proposition.

sądny *a.* **sądny dzień** *rel., przen.* doomsday.
sądownictwo *n.* judiciary, judicature.
sądowniczy *a.* (*o władzy*) judiciary.
sądownie *adv.* (*zająć lokal*) legally; (*dochodzić czegoś*) through legal action, in court; **dochodzić swoich praw sądownie** go to court; **ścigać kogoś sądownie** prosecute sb (*za coś* for sth).

sądowy *a.* court, judicial, legal; **dozór sądowy** probation; **kurator sądowy** probation officer; **koszty sądowe** legal fees; **medycyna sądowa** forensic medicine; **nakaz sądowy** court order; **pomyłka sądowa** miscarriage of justice; **procedura sądowa** legal procedure; **proces sądowy** lawsuit; **system sądowy** judicial system.

sądzić *ipf.* **1.** (*w sądzie*) try, judge. **2.** (= *oceniać*) judge; **nie sądzę** I don't think so; **sądzę, że tak** I think so; **sądzić po pozorach** judge by appearances. **3.** (= *być zdania*) suppose, think; **mam wszelkie powody, by sądzić, że...** I have every reason to believe that; **sądząc po...** judging by *l.* from...

sąg *mi* Gen. **-u** *l.* **-a** cord.
sąsiad *mp* Loc. **-edzie** *pl.* **-edzi, sąsiadka** *f.* Gen.pl. **-ek** neighbor; *Br.* neighbour; **najbliżsi sąsiedzi** immediate neighbors; **sąsiad z dołu/z góry** downstairs/upstairs neigbor; **sąsiad zza ściany** next door neighbor.

sąsiadować *ipf.* **1.** (*mieszkać*) live next door (*z kimś* to sb); be neighbors (*z kimś* with sb). **2.** (*graniczyć*) neighbor, *Br.* neighbour (*z czymś* on sth).

sąsiedni *a.* contiguous, adjacent; (*o kraju*) neighboring; *Br.* neighbouring; (*o mieszkaniu*) next-door; (*o pokoju*) adjoining; (*o stronie w książce*) opposite.

sąsiedzki *a.* (*o pomocy*) neighborly, *Br.* neighbourly; **mieszkać po sąsiedzku** live next-door (*z kimś* to sb); be neighbors (*z kimś* with sb).

sąsiedztwo *n.* **1.** (= *sąsiadowanie*) neighborhood, *Br.* neighbourhood. **2.** (= *okolica*) neighborhood, *Br.* neighbourhood; vicinity; **w sąsiedztwie czegoś** in the neighborhood *l.* vicinity of. **3.** (= *sąsiedzi*) neighbors, *Br.* neighbours.

sąsiek *mi* Gen. **-a** mow.
sążeń *mi* **-żni-** Gen. **-a** fathom.
sążnisty *a.* (*o liście, sprawozdaniu*) lengthy.
SB *abbr.* (= *Służba Bezpieczeństwa*) the Security Service (*secret police in communist Poland*).
s.c. *abbr.* (= *spółka cywilna*) general partnership.
scalać *ipf.* **1.** (= *łączyć*) integrate, consolidate. **2.** *komp.* (*pliki*) collate, merge. **~ się** *ipf.* unite, integrate.
scaleniowy *a.* (*o komisji, pracach*) integration.
scalić *pf. zob.* **scalać.** **~ się** *pf. zob.* **scalać się.**
scalony *a. el.* **układ** *l.* **obwód scalony** integrated circuit.
scałować *pf.*, **scałowywać** *ipf.* (*np. łzy*) kiss away.
scedować *pf.* cede.
scementować *pf.* **1.** (*cementem*) cement. **2.** (= *zjednoczyć*) (*np. przyjaźń*) solder, cement.
scena *f.* **1.** (*w teatrze*) stage; *przen.* arena, scene; **scena obrotowa** revolving stage; **scena otwarta** platform; **scena polityczna** *przen.* political arena, political scene; **zejść ze sceny** *przen.* (*o aktorze*) retire from the stage. **2.** (= *teatr*) stage; **występować na scenie** appear on (the) stage. **3.** (= *fragment dramatu*) scene. **4.** (= *epizod*) scene; **scena batalistyczna** battlepiece; **scena plenerowa/zbiorowa/miłosna** *kino, telew.* outdoor/crowd/love scene. **5.** (= *wydarzenie*) scene, episode; **dantejskie sceny** hair-raising scenes. **6.** *pot.* (= *kłótnia*) scene; **zrobić scenę** make a scene.
scenariusz *mi* Gen. **-a** **1.** *film, teatr* script; *film* screenplay. **2.** (= *przebieg wydarzeń*) scenario.
scenarzysta *mp,* **scenarzystka** *f.* Gen.pl. **-ek** scriptwriter; (*filmowy*) screenwriter.
sceneria *f.* Gen. **-ii** scenery.
sceniczność *f.* (*charakter*) stage character; (*przydatność*) stageability; *przen.* histrionics.
sceniczny *a.* (= *przeznaczony do wystawienia*) stage; (= *nadający się do wystawienia*) stageable; *przen.* histrionic; **wymowa sceniczna** stage pronunciation.
scenka *f.* Gen.pl. **-ek** scene.
scenograf *mp pl.* **-owie** *film, teatr* set designer.
scenografia *f.* Gen. **-ii** *film, teatr* set design.
scenograficzny *a.* *film, teatr* set-design.
scenopis *mi* *film, teatr* script.
scenopisarski *a.* *film, teatr* scriptwriting.
scenopisarstwo *n.* *film, teatr* scriptwriting.
scentralizować *pf.* centralize.
scentralizowany *a.* centralized.
scentrować *pf.* **1.** (*koło rowerowe*) twist,

warp. **2.** (*piłkę*) center, *Br.* centre. **3.** *techn.* align.

sceptycyzm *mi* skepticism, *Br.* scepticism.

sceptycznie *adv.* skeptically, *Br.* sceptically.

sceptyczny *a.* skeptical, *Br.* sceptical.

sceptyk *mp* skeptic, *Br.* sceptic.

schab *mi kulin.* pork loin, pork chine.

schaboszczak *mi pot.* pork chop.

schabowy *a. kulin.* pork loin, pork chine; **kotlet schabowy** pork chop. – *mi pot.* = **kotlet schobowy**.

schadzka *f. Gen.pl.* **-ek** (= *spotkanie*) rendezvous; (*potajemna*) tryst; **dom schadzek** house of ill fame.

schamieć *pf.* get rough, become boorish.

scharakteryzować *pf.* characterize.

scheda *f. lit.* (= *spadek*) heritage; (= *spuścizna*) legacy.

schemat *mi* **1.** (*zarys*) outline, scheme. **2.** (*rysunek*) schematic, diagram; **schemat blokowy** flow chart. **3.** (*wzór*) model.

schematycznie *adv.* (= *w uproszczeniu*) schematically; (= *nieoryginalnie*) conventionally.

schematyczność *f.* **1.** (*np. rysunku*) schematism. **2.** (= *brak oryginalności*) conventionalism.

schematyczny *a.* **1.** (= *uproszczony*) schematic. **2.** (= *nieoryginalny*) conventional, routine.

schematyzacja *f. form.* schematization.

schematyzm *mi form., uj.* orthodoxy, conformity.

schematyzować *ipf. form.* schematize.

scherzo *n. muz.* scherzo.

schizma *f.* **1.** *rel.* schism. **2.** *polit.* split, schism.

schizmatycki *a. rel.* (*o doktrynie, odłamie*) schismatic.

schizmatyk *mp gł. rel.* schismatic.

schizofrenia *f. Gen.* **-ii** *pat.* schizophrenia.

schizofreniczny *a. t. pat.* (*o obsesji, urojeniach*) schizophrenic.

schizofrenik *mp t. pat.* schizophrenic.

schizotymia *f. Gen.* **-ii** *psych.* schizothymia.

schizotymiczny *a. psych.* (*o typie, temperamencie*) schizothymic.

schizotymik *mp psych.* schizothymic.

schlać się *pf.* **-am -asz** *l.* **-eję -ejesz** *l.* **-ali -eli** *pot.* get loaded; **schlać się w trupa** *l.* **do nieprzytomności** get blind drunk, get stewed to the gills.

schlany *a. pot.* loaded, pissed.

schlapać *pf.* **-pię -piesz** splatter, splash. **~ się** *pf.* get splattered, get splashed.

schlastać *pf.* **1.** *pot.* (= *ochlapać*) splatter, splash. **2.** *pot.* (= *zbić*) whack. **~ się** *pf. pot.* (*np. nożem*) slash o.s.

schlebiać *ipf.,* **schlebić** *pf.* **1.** (= *pochlebiać*) flatter (*komuś* sb). **2.** (= *dogadzać*) indulge (*komuś* sb); (*zachciankom*) pander (*czemuś* to sth).

schludnie *adv.* neatly, tidily.

schludny *a.* neat, tidy.

schładzać *ipf.,* **schłodzić** *pf.* **-odzę -odzisz, -odź** *l.* **-ódź** (*coś gorącego*) cool down; (*poniżej normal-*

nej temperatury) chill; *handl., techn.* refrigerate.

schnąć *ipf.* **schnij, schnął** *l.* **sechł schła schli** **1.** (= *tracić wilgoć*) dry (out). **2.** (*o roślinach*) wither.

schodek *mi* **-dk-** *Gen.* **-a** step.

schodkowo *adv.* stepwise.

schodkowy *a.* stepwise.

schodowy *a.* stair; **klatka schodowa** staircase, stairway, stairwell.

schody *pl. Gen.* **-ów** **1.** *bud.* stairs; (*krótkie*) steps; (= *klatka schodowa*) staircase, stairway; **schody kręcone** spiral staircase; **schody kuchenne** backstairs; **schody pożarowe** fire escape; **ruchome schody** escalator; **spaść ze schodów** fall down *l.* off the stairs; **(i tu) zaczęły się schody** (this is where) things got tricky. **2.** *lotn.* echelon.

schodzić *ipf.* **1.** (*po drabinie, schodach*) go down, descend; *przen.* (*o lawinie*) strike; **schodzić po schodach** come down the stairs, descend the stairs; **schodzić po drabinie** climb down the ladder; **schodzić do lądowania** *lotn.* descend. **2.** (*na bok, z drogi*) step aside, move over; **zejdź mi z drogi!** off my way!; **schodzić komuś z drogi** get out of sb's way; **schodzić komuś z oczu** get out of sb's face; **schodzić z uczciwej drogi** *l.* **na manowce** stray (from the straight and narrow); **schodzić z kursu** *żegl., lotn.* deviate from the course; **schodzić z taśmy produkcyjnej** become available; **schodzić z tego świata** breathe one's last, pass away; **schodzić na drugi plan** take second place; **dyskusja schodzi na temat...** conversation steers in the direction of... **3.** (= *dawać się usunąć*) come off; **plama nie schodzi** the stain won't come off. **4.** (= *zsiadać*) (*z kanapy, fotela*) get off; (*z konia, roweru*) dismount. **5.** (*o czasie*) (= *wymagać*) take; (= *mijać*) go by, pass; **schodzi na tym sporo czasu** it takes a lot of time; **zawsze schodzi nam trochę czasu na przygotowaniach** preparation will always take (some) time; **tydzień schodzi zanim się obejrzysz** a week goes by before you know it. **6.** *handl.* (= *sprzedawać się*) sell. – *pf.* **1.** (= *przemierzyć*) walk; **schodzić całe miasto** walk all around town. **2.** (*buty*) wear thin. **~ się** *ipf.* **1.** (= *gromadzić się*) gather; (= *stopniowo nadchodzić*) trickle in. **2.** (= *stykać się*) touch. **3.** (= *odbywać się jednocześnie*) coincide. **4.** *pot.* (= *łączyć się w parę*) hit it off.

scholastycyzm *mi fil.* scholasticism.

scholastyczny *a. fil.* scholastic.

scholastyk *mp* scholastic.

scholastyka *f. fil., przen.* scholasticism.

schorowany *a.* sickly, ailing.

schorzenie *n. med.* ailment, condition; *przen.* malady; **schorzenie serca** heart condition.

schować *pf.* **-am -asz** *zob.* **chować. ~ się** *pf. zob.* **chować się.**

schowek *mi* **-wk-** *Gen.* **-a** **1.** (= *skrytka*) hiding place; (*w samochodzie*) glove compartment. **2.** *komp.* clipboard.

schron *mi wojsk.* shelter; **schron atomowy/przeciwlotniczy** air-raid/fallout shelter.

schronić *pf. zob.* chronić. ~ się *pf. zob.* chronić się.

schronienie *n.* shelter; dawać komuś schronienie *l.* udzielać komuś schronienia give sb shelter.

schronisko *n.* 1. (*turystyczne*) hostel; (*górskie*) hut, lodge; schronisko młodzieżowe youth hostel, hostel. 2. (= *przytułek*) shelter; schronisko dla bezdomnych zwierząt destitute animal shelter; schronisko dla bezdomnych (*ludzi*) homeless shelter. 3. (= *schronienie*) shelter.

schronowy *a. wojsk.* shelter.

schrupać *pf.* -pię -piesz *pot.* chow down.

schrypnąć *pf.* hoarsen; schrypł mu głos his voice grew hoarse.

schrypnięty *a.* (*o głosie, osobie*) hoarse.

schrystianizować *pf.* christianize. ~ się *pf.* christianize.

schrzaniać *ipf. pot.* (= *uciekać*) split, beat it.

schrzanić *pf. pot.* (= *zepsuć*) screw up, bungle. ~ się *pf. pot.* (= *zepsuć się*) go to pot *l.* hell.

schudnąć *pf.* -dnij, -dł *l.* -dnął -dła -dli *zob.* chudnąć.

schwycić *pf.* 1. (= *złapać*) grab (*coś* sth). 2. (= *zawładnąć*) catch, grasp; schwycił mróz frost came; schwycił ją smutek she was overcome by sadness; płacz schwycił ją za gardło (= *zachciało jej się płakać*) she felt like weeping; (= *stłumiła łzy*) she choked back her tears. ~ się *pf.* 1. (= *złapać się*) grab (*czegoś* onto sth). 2. (= *złapać jeden drugiego*) grab one another.

schwytać *pf.* (= *pojmać*) capture; schwytać kogoś na gorącym uczynku catch sb red-handed, catch sb in the (very) act.

schylać *ipf.*, schylić *pf.* bow; schylić głowę (*np. na powitanie*) bow one's head; (= *uchylić się*) duck one's head; schylić głowę *l.* kark przed kimś/czymś take one's hat off for sb/sth. ~ się *ipf.*, schylić się *pf.* stoop, bend.

schyłek *mi* -łk- decline; u schyłku życia *lit.* in the evening *l.* twilight of one's life.

schyłkowość *f.* decadence.

schyłkowy *a.* decadent.

science fiction *n. indecl.* science fiction.

scjentysta *mp fil.* scientist.

scjentystyczny *a. fil.* scientistic.

scjentyzm *mi fil.* scientism.

scukrzać *ipf.*, scukrzyć *pf.* saccharify. ~ się *ipf.*, scukrzyć się *pf.* saccharify.

scyntygrafia *f. Gen.* -ii *med.* scintiscanning.

scyntylacja *f. astron., fiz.* scintillation.

scypuł *mi myśl.* velvet.

scysja *f.* brush, run-in.

Scyta *mp hist., geogr.* Scythian.

Scytia *f. hist., geogr.* Scythia.

scyzoryk *mi Gen.* -a pocketknife, penknife.

sczepiać *ipf.*, sczepić *pf.* join, fasten together. ~ się *ipf.*, sczepić się *pf.* (*ramionami*) be locked; (= *zahaczyć*) hook, be locked.

sczernieć *pf.* turn black, blacken.

sczerstwieć *pf.* go stale.

sczerwienieć *pf.* redden, turn red.

sczesać *pf.* sczeszę sczeszesz, sczesywać *ipf.* comb; (*do tyłu*) comb back.

sczeznąć *pf.* -znę -źniesz, -źnij *arch., lit.* perish; bodajbyś sczezł perish you!

sczyszczać *ipf.*, sczyścić *pf.* sczyszczę sczyścisz clean; sczyszczać coś z czegoś get sth off sth.

sczytać *pf.*, sczytywać *ipf.* proofread.

SdRP *abbr.* (= *Socjaldemokracja Rzeczypospolitej Polskiej*) *polit.* Social Democratic Party of the Republic of Poland.

seans *mi pl.* -e *l.* -y 1. (*filmowy*) screening, show. 2. (*spirytystyczny*) séance.

secesja *f.* 1. *hist., lit.* (= *odłączenie*) secession. 2. *sztuka* Art Nouveau.

secesjonista *mp* 1. (= *zwolennik secesji*) *hist.* secessionist, seceder. 2. (*artysta*) Art Nouveau artist.

secesyjny *a.* 1. *hist.* secessionist; wojna secesyjna *hist.* Civil War. 2. *sztuka* Art Nouveau.

sedan *mi mot.* sedan.

sedes *mi* 1. (= *ubikacja*) toilet. 2. (= *muszla klozetowa*) toilet bowl. 3. (= *deska*) toilet seat.

sedesowy *a.* toilet; deska sedesowa toilet seat.

sedno *n.* (= *istota*) essence, crux; sedno sprawy heart *l.* crux of the matter; przejść do sedna (sprawy) come to the point; trafić w (samo) sedno hit the nail on the head.

sedymentacja *f. chem., geol.* sedimentation.

sedymentacyjny *a. chem., geol.* sedimentation, sedimentational.

segment *mi* 1. (= *moduł*) segment; (= *część*) section. 2. (*dom*) row house; segment dwupiętrowy triplex. 3. (*mebel*) unit, section.

segmentacja *f.* 1. *form.* (= *podział*) segmentation. 2. *biol.* (= *bruzdkowanie*) segmentation, cleavage. 3. *zool.* (= *metameria*) segmentation, metamerism.

segmentowy *a.* (= *dzielony*) split; (= *złożony z segmentów*) sectional, segmented.

segregacja *f.* 1. *socjol.* segregation; segregacja rasowa/etniczna racial/ethnic segregation. 2. (*sortowanie*) sorting, separation; segregacja śmieci *l.* odpadów waste separation, waste sorting.

segregacjonizm *mi polit.* segregation.

segregator *mi Gen.* -a 1. (*teczka*) binder. 2. (*mebel*) file cabinet.

segregować *ipf.* sort, separate.

sejf *mi* (*szafa*) (*t. w ścianie*) safe; (*skrzynka*) strongbox.

sejm *mi parl.* the Sejm (= *lower house of the Polish parliament*).

sejmik *mi* 1. *polit.* assembly; sejmik wojewódzki provincial assembly. 2. *hist.* diet.

sejmowy *a. parl.* (of the) Sejm; parliamentary.

sejsmicznie *adv. geol.* seismically.

sejsmiczny *a. geol.* seismic.

sejsmograf *mi techn.* seismograph.

sejsmolog *mp pl.* -dzy *l.* -owie *geol.* seismologist.

sejsmologia *f. Gen.* -ii *geol.* seismology.

sejsmologiczny *a. geol.* seismological.

sek. *abbr.* sec. (= *second*).

sekans *mi Gen.* -a *mat.* secant.

sekator *mi Gen.* **-a** pruning shears; *Br. t.* seca-teurs.

sekciarski *a. uj.* (*o poglądach, działalności*) sectarian.

sekciarstwo *n. polit., rel.* sectarianism.

sekciarz *mp polit., rel.* sectarian.

sekcja *f.* **1.** (= *oddział, dział*) section, division. **2.** *biol., chir.* dissection. **3.** (*zwłok*) *pat.* autopsy; *Br.* postmortem.

sekcyjny *a.* **1.** (= *w grupach*) section. **2.** *pat.* autopsy; *Br.* postmortem.

sekrecja *f. fizj.* (= *wydzielanie*) secretion.

sekret *mi* (= *tajemnica*) secret; **sekret powo-dzenia** the secret of success; **robić coś w sekrecie** do sth in secret.

sekretariat *mi admin.* (= *biuro sekretarek*) sec-retary's office; (= *oddział instytucji*) secretariat.

sekretarka *f. Gen.pl.* **-ek** *admin.* secretary; **automatyczna sekretarka** *tel.* answering *l.* voice machine.

sekretarz *mp* **1.** *admin., polit.* secretary; **se-kretarz generalny** secretary-general; **sekretarz stanu** secretary of state; **pierwszy sekretarz** (*hist.*) first secretary, secretary general. **2.** *orn.* secretary bird (*Sagittarius serpentarius*).

sekretarzyk *mi Gen.* **-a** writing desk; secre-tary.

sekretera *f. lit.* escritoire, secretaire; *Br. t.* bu-reau.

sekretnie *adv.* secretly.

sekretny *a.* secret.

seks *mi* sex; **bezpieczny seks** safe sex; **pełny seksu** sexy; **uprawiać seks (z kimś)** have sex (with sb).

seksagonalny *a. geom., arch.* (= *sześciokątny*) hexagonal.

seksapil *mi* sex appeal.

seksbomba *f. pot.* sex bomb.

seksizm *mi* sexism.

seksowny *a.* sexy.

seksta *f. muz.* sixth.

sekstans, sekstant *mi opt., żegl.* sextant.

sekstet *mi muz.* (*zespół, utwór*) sextet, sex-tette.

sekstylion *mi mat.* hendecillion (= *1 with 36 zeroes*).

sekstyna *f. wers.* sestine, sextina.

seksualizm *mi fizj., biol.* sexuality.

seksualnie *adv.* sexually.

seksualność *f. fizj., biol.* sexuality.

seksualny *a.* sexual; **wychowanie seksualne** sex education; **wykorzystywanie/życie seksualne** sexual abuse/life.

seksuolog *mp pl.* **-dzy** *l.* **-owie** sex therapist, sexologist.

seksuologia *f. Gen.* **-ii** sexology.

seksuologiczny *a.* sexologist.

sekta *f.* (*religijna, polityczna*) sect, cult.

sektor *mi Gen.* **-a** **1.** *geom., komp., ekon.* sec-tor; **sektor państwowy/prywatny** state/private sector. **2.** (*widowni, wystawy*) section.

sekularyzacja *f. form.* secularization.

sekularyzować *ipf. form.* secularize.

sekunda *f.* **1.** (*jednostka czasu, chwila*) sec-ond; **w ostatniej sekundzie** at the last minute; **w ułamku sekundy** in a split second. **2.** *geom., muz.* second.

sekundant *mp* (*w pojedynku*) *sport* second.

sekundarny *a. jęz.* (*o funkcji*) secondary.

sekundka *f.* second; **Sekundkę! Zaraz do pani podejdę!** Just a second! I'll be with you right away!

sekundnik *mi Gen.* **-a** (*w zegarku*) second hand.

sekundować *ipf. lit.* (= *pomagać*) *przest.* (*przy pojedynku*) second.

sekutnica *f. przest., obelż.* shrew, nag.

Sekwana *f. geogr.* the Seine.

sekwencja *f.* (= *fragment filmu*) (= *następstwo*) *muz.* sequence.

sekwens *mi karty* sequence.

sekwestr *mi prawn.* sequestration.

sekwestracja *f. prawn.* sequestration.

sekwestrator *mp prawn.* sequestrator.

sekwestrować *ipf. prawn.* sequester.

sekwoja *Gen.* **-oi** *f. bot.* sequoia (*Sequoia*); **se-kwoja wiecznie zielona** redwood (*Sequoia sem-pervirens*); **sekwoja olbrzymia** big tree, giant se-quoia (*Sequoiadendron giganteum*).

selcerski *a.* **woda selcerska** seltzer.

seledyn *mi* celadon, willow green.

seledynowy *a.* celadon, willow green.

selekcja *f. zwł. biol.* selection; **selekcja natural-na** natural selection; **selekcja kandydatów** screening; **selekcja rannych** (*do leczenia po bi-twie, wypadku*) triage.

selekcjoner *mp t. sport* selector; *piłka nożna* (team) manager.

selekcjonować *ipf. t. sport* select; (*kandyda-tów na stanowisko pracy*) screen.

selekcyjny *a.* selective, selection.

selektywnie *adv.* selectively.

selektywność *f. lit. t. techn.* (= *wybiórczość*) se-lectivity.

selektywny *a. lit.* selective; **selektywna uwaga** selective attention; **weto selektywne** *parl.* item veto.

selen *mi chem.* selenium.

selenawy *a. chem.* selenious; **kwas selenawy** selenious acid.

selenek *mi chem.* selenide.

selenian *mi chem.* selenate.

selenit *mi min.* selenite.

selenitowy *a. min.* selenitic.

selenofizyka *f.* selenophysics.

selenografia *f. Gen.* **-ii** selenography.

selenolog *mp pl.* **-dzy** *l.* **-owie** selenologist.

selenologia *f. Gen.* **-ii** selenology.

selenonautyka *f.* lunar exploration.

selenowy *a. chem.* selenic; **kwas selenowy** se-lenic acid.

seler *mi Gen.* **-a** *bot.* celery (*Apium graveo-lens*); **seler korzeniowy** celeriac (*Apium graveo-lens rapaceum*); **seler naciowy** celery (*Apium graveolens dulce*); **pęd selera** stick of celery.

selerowy *a.* (= *dotyczący selera korzeniowego*) celeriac; (= *dotyczący selera naciowego*) celery.

selskin *mi* (*rodzaj futra*) sealskin.

selwa *f.* (*las w Amazonii*) selva.

semafor *mi Gen.* -a *kol., żegl.* semaphore.

semaforowy *a.* semaphore.

semantem *mi jęz.* semanteme.

semantycznie *adv.* semantically.

semantyczny *a.* semantic; **teoria semantyczna** *jęz.* semantic conception *l.* theory.

semantyk *mp* semanticist, semantician.

semantyka *f. jęz., log.* semantics; **semantyka leksykalna** lexical semantics.

semazjologia *f. Gen.* -ii *jęz.* semasiology.

semazjologiczny *a. jęz.* semasiological.

semem *mi jęz.* sememe.

semestr *mi uniw., szkoln.* semester, term; **semestr letni** summer semester *l.* term; **semestr zimowy** winter semester *l.* term.

semestralny *a. uniw., szkoln.* semestral; **kolokwium semestralne** semester *l.* end-of-term test; **praca semestralna** semester *l.* term paper; **przerwa semestralna** semester *l.* term break; **test semestralny** semester *l.* end-of-term test.

semicki *a.* Semitic; **języki semickie** Semitic languages.

semickość *f.* (*np. rysów twarzy*) Semitism.

semikontenerowiec *mi* -wc- *Gen.* -a *żegl.* semi-container ship.

seminarium *n. sing. indecl. pl.* -ria *Gen.* -riów *uniw.* **1.** (*zajęcia dydaktyczne*) seminar. **2.** (*uczelnia*) seminary; **wyższe seminarium duchowne** seminary; **seminarium nauczycielskie** *przest.* teacher(s') training college. **3.** (*jednostka badawcza*) *przest.* research institute.

seminaryjny *a. uniw.* seminar; **sala seminaryjna** seminar room.

seminarzysta *mp uniw.* **1.** (*duchowny*) seminarian, seminarist. **2.** *przest.* (*student*) teacher(s') training college student, trainee teacher.

seminarzystka *f. Gen.pl.* -ek *zob.* **seminarzysta** 2.

semiolog *mp pl.* -dzy *l.* -owie semiologist.

semiologia *f. Gen.* -ii semiology.

semiotyczny *a.* semiotic.

semiotyk *mp* semiotician.

semiotyka *f.* semiotics.

Semita *mp*, **Semitka** *f. Gen.pl.* -ek Semite.

semitolog *mp pl.* -dzy *l.* -owie Semitist.

semitologia *f. Gen.* -ii Semitics.

semitysta *mp* Semitist.

semitystyka *f.* Semitics.

semteks, semtex *mi* (*materiał wybuchowy*) Semtex®.

sen[1] *mi* sn-, *Loc.* śnie **1.** (= *spanie*) sleep; **sen zimowy** *zool.* hibernation; **spać snem zimowym** *zool.* hibernate; **głęboki sen** deep *l.* sound sleep; **zapaść w głęboki sen** drop into a deep sleep; **pijacki sen** drunken stupor; **zapaść w pijacki sen** fall into a drunken stupor; **przerywany sen** broken sleep; **chodzić jak we śnie** moon about, be wandering with one's head in the clouds *l.* as if in a dream; **mieć lekki/mocny sen** be a light/heavy sleeper; **mówić przez sen** talk *l.* speak in one's sleep; **pamiętać coś jak przez sen** have a hazy recollection of sth; **położyć kogoś do snu** *l.* **spać** put sb to bed, tuck sb in; **spać snem spra-**

wiedliwego sleep the sleep of the just; **spać snem wiecznym** sleep the eternal sleep; **spędzać komuś sen z oczu** *l.* **powiek** (= *nie pozwolić zasnąć*) keep sb awake at night; (= *nękać*) loom large in sb's mind; **stracić apetyt i sen** loose one's appetite and one's night's rest; **wybiło mnie to ze snu** I couldn't get back to sleep after this; **zapadać w sen** lapse *l.* drift into sleep. **2.** (= *marzenie senne*) dream; **sen na jawie** daydream; **kraina snu** dreamland; **koszmarny sen** nightmare; **zły sen** bad dream; **wracać jak zły sen** (*np. o nieprzyjemnym wspomnieniu*) turn up like a bad penny, rear its ugly head.

sen[2] *mi* -a (*drobna moneta w Japonii, Kambodży*) sen.

senacki *a. parl.* Senate; **komisja senacka** Senate committee.

senat *mi* **1.** *parl.* (*izba parlamentu; t. w starożytnym Rzymie*) the Senate. **2.** *uniw.* (*szkoły wyższej*) senate.

senator *mp parl.* senator.

senatorski *a. parl.* senatorial; **godność senatorska** senatorship; **izba senatorska** Senate; **mandat senatorski** senatorial seat.

Senegal *mi geogr.* Senegal.

Senegalczyk *mp*, **Senegalka** *f. Gen.pl.* -ek Senegalese.

senegalski *a.* Senegalese.

senes *mi med.* senna.

senesowy *a. med.* senna; **liść senesowy** senna (leaf); **strączki senesowe** senna (pods).

senilizm *mi pat.* senility.

senior *mp* **1.** (= *najstarszy członek rodziny*) senior; **Kowalski senior** Kowalski senior; **John Smith senior** John Smith, Sr *l.* Sen. **2.** (*członek zespołu, grupy, organizacji itp.*) doyen. **3.** *sport* senior. **4.** *hist.* feudal lord; seignior, seigneur.

seniorat *mi hist.* **1.** (*dziedziczenie*) primogeniture. **2.** (*godność*) seigniory.

seniorka *f. Gen.pl.* -ek *zob.* **senior** 1, 2, 3.

sennie *adv.* sleepily, drowsily; **sennie mrużyć oczy** squint one's eyes sleepily *l.* drowsily.

sennik *mi Gen.* -a dream book.

senność *f.* sleepiness, drowsiness.

senny *a.* sleepy, drowsy; **senna atmosfera** torpid atmosphere; **senne marzenie** dream; **pogrążyć się w marzeniach sennych** fall adream; **senne miasteczko** sleepy town.

sens *mi* (= *znaczenie*) sens; (= *celowość*) point; (*gestu, słowa*) meaning; **bez sensu** pointless; **gadać bez sensu** talk gibberish; **to jest bez sensu** *l.* **to nie ma sensu** there's no point in it, this is pointless; **dalsze starania nie miały sensu** any further efforts were pointless; **nie ma sensu tego robić** there's no point in doing it; **to ma sens** this makes sense; **w pewnym sensie** in a sense; **coś w tym sensie** *pot.* something like that, something to this effect; **ogólny sens** effect (*czegoś* of sth); **ogólny sens jej listu był taki, że...** her letter was to the effect that...

sensacja *f.* sensation; **chwilowa** *l.* **krótkotrwała sensacja** a nine-days' wonder; **pogoń za sensacją** pursuit of the sensational; **wywołać** *l.* **wzbu-**

dzić **sensację** cause a sensation; (= *powiedzieć l. ogłosić coś zaskakującego*) drop a bombshell.

sensacje *pl. Gen.* **-i** (= *dolegliwości*) ailments, health problems; **sensacje żołądkowe** stomach upset *l.* trouble.

sensacyjnie *adv.* sensationally.

sensacyjność *f.* sensational character (*of news, events, etc.*).

sensacyjny *a.* sensational, thrilling; **sensacyjna wiadomość** sensational news; *dzienn.* scoop; **film sensacyjny** thriller, shocker; **powieść sensacyjna** thriller, shocker.

sensat *mp* **1.** (= *osoba dopatrująca się sensacji*) sensation seeker, rumor-monger. **2.** (= *osoba przesadnie poważna*) sobersides.

sensatka *f. Gen.pl.* **-ek** *zob.* **sensat**.

sensomotoryczny *a. psych.* sensorimotor, sensimotor, sensomotor.

sensomotoryka *f. psych.* sensorimotorics, sensomotorics.

sensor *mi Gen.* **-a** *gł. el.* sensor.

sensoryczny *a. psych.* sensory.

sensownie *adv.* sensibly, reasonably; **działać sensownie** *l.* **racjonalnie** act sensibly *l.* reasonably, play with a full deck; **to brzmi sensownie** it makes sense, it sounds reasonable, it adds up.

sensowność *f.* sensibleness, reasonableness.

sensowny *a.* sensible, reasonable.

sensualista *mp fil.* sensationalist, sensualist.

sensualistyczny *a. fil.* sensationalist, sensationalistic, sensualistic.

sensualizm *mi fil.* sensationalism, sensualism.

sensualny *a.* **1.** (= *odbierany przez zmysły*) sensory. **2.** (= *przyjemny dla zmysłów*) sensual.

sensu stricto *adv.* sensu stricto.

sensybilizacja *f. biol., fot.* sensitization.

sensybilizator *mi Gen.* **-a** *biol., fot.* sensitizer.

sentencja *f.* (= *aforyzm*) maxim, dictum, saying; **sentencja wyroku** *prawn.* sentence, legal conclusion.

sentencjonalny *a.* sententious.

sentyment *mi* **1.** (= *sympatia*) fondness; **czuć *l.* mieć do kogoś sentyment** have a fondness for sb, be fond of sb; **nie bawmy się w sentymenty** let's not get sentimental, this is hardly the time for nostalgia. **2.** *rzad.* (= *sentymentalizm*) sentimentality.

sentymentalista *mp,* **sentymentalistka** *f. Gen.pl.* **-ek** *gł. teor.lit.* sentimentalist.

sentymentalizm *mi* **1.** *teor.lit.* sentimentalism. **2.** (= *uczuciowość*) sentimentalism, schmaltz, schmalz.

sentymentalnie *adv.* sentimentally.

sentymentalność *f.* sentimentality.

sentymentalny *a.* **1.** *teor.lit.* sentimental. **2.** (= *uczuciowy*) sentimental; schmaltzy, gooey.

separacja *f. t. prawn.* (= *oddzielenie*) separation; **być w separacji** (*o małżeństwie*) be separated; *form., prawn.* live separate and apart.

separatka *f. Gen.pl.* **-ek** (*w szpitalu*) isolation room; (*w więzieniu*) solitary confinement cell.

separator *mi Gen.* **-a** *techn.* separator.

separatysta *mp* separatist.

separatystyczny *a.* separatistic.

separatyzm *mi* separatism.

separować *ipf. l. pf. t. prawn.* (= *oddzielać*) separate. **~ się** *ipf. l. pf.* separate.

sepia *f. Gen.* **-ii** **1.** (*barwnik, t. rysunek*) sepia. **2.** *icht.* cuttlefish, sepia (*Sepia*).

sepiolit *mi min.* meerschaum, sepiolite.

sepiowy *a.* sepia.

seplenić *ipf.* lisp, have a lisp.

seplenienie *n.* lisp.

septarium *n. sing. indecl. pl.* **-ria** *Gen.* **-riów** (*zwykle pl.*) *geol.* septarium.

septet *mi muz.* (*zespół, utwór*) septet.

septyczny *a. med.* septic.

septylion *mi Gen.* **-a** (*w USA i Kanadzie 1 i 24 zera*) septillion; *Br.* quadrillion; (*w Wielkiej Brytanii 1 i 42 zera*) septillion.

septyma *f.* **1.** *muz.* seventh. **2.** *szermierka* septime.

sepulkralny *a. sztuka* sepulchral.

ser *mi Gen.* **-a** *kulin.* cheese; **ser biały** cottage cheese; **ser chudy** lean cheese; **ser edamski** Edam; **ser ementalski** Emmenthal *l.* Emmental, Emmenthaler *l.* Emmental; **ser gouda** Gouda; **ser miękki** soft cheese; **ser owczy** goat cheese; **ser pleśniowy** blue cheese; **ser podpuszczkowy** rennet cheese; **ser szwajcarski** Swiss cheese; **ser tłusty** fat cheese; **ser topiony** processed *l.* process cheese; **ser twardy** hard cheese; **ser twarogowy** śmietankowy curd cheese; **ser żółty** hard cheese; **tarty ser** grated cheese; **śmiać się jak głupi do sera** laugh like stupid.

seradela *f. Gen.pl.* **-i** *bot.* serradella (*Ornithopus*); **seradela pastewna** *l.* **siewna** pink serradella (*Ornithopus sativus*); **seradela drobna** bird's-foot (*Ornithopus perpusillus*).

seraficzny *a. poet.* seraphic.

serafin *mp pl.* **-i** *l.* **-y** *rel.* seraph.

seraj *mi Gen.pl.* **-ów** *hist.* seraglio, serail.

serak *mi Gen.* **-a** *geol.* sérac.

Serb *mp pl.* **-owie** Serb, Serbian.

Serbia *f. Gen.* **-ii** *geogr.* Serbia.

Serbka *f. Gen.pl.* **-ek** *zob.* **Serb**.

serbski *a.* Serb, Serbian.

serbskochorwacki *a.* Serbo-Croatian, Serbo-Croat.

serce *n.* **1.** (*narząd; fragment piersi; natura człowieka; siedlisko uczuć; wyobrażenie serca, rysunek; odwaga; środek czegoś*) heart; **bratnie serce** a person after one's own heart; **Serce Jezusowe** *kośc.* the Sacred Heart; **serce miasta** the heart of the city; **sztuczne serce** *med.* artificial heart; **waleczne serce** brave heart; (*osoba*) a heart of oak; **niewydolność serca** *pat.* heart *l.* cardiac failure; **zawał serca** *l.* **mięśnia sercowego** *pat.* coronary thrombosis; *pot.* coronary, heart attack; **zatrzymanie akcji serca** *pat.* cardiac arrest; **bicie serca** heartbeat; **dama serca** ladylove; **dobroć serca** kind-heartedness, the milk of human kindness; **linia serca** (*na dłoni*) heartline; **operacja na otwartym sercu** *chir.* open-heart surgery; **przeszczep serca** *chir.* heart transplant; **przyjaciel od serca** bosom friend; **rozmowa od serca** heart-to-heart talk; **bez serca** (*o oso-*

bie) heartless; **całym sercem** *l.* **z całego serca** whole-heartedly, with all one's heart and soul; **chować w sercu urazę do kogoś** bear a grudge against sb; **chwytać za serce** tear at sb's heart; **co w sercu, to na języku** what the heart thinks, the mouth speaks; **co z oczu, to i z serca** out of sight, out of mind; **człowiek wielkiego serca** a person of great heart; **czego oczy nie widzą, tego sercu nie żal** what the eye sees not, the heart craves not; **drogi memu sercu** dear to my heart; **iść** *l.* **pójść za głosem serca** let one's heart rule one's head; **kamień spadł mi z serca** that's a load *l.* weight off my chest *l.* mind; **leżeć komuś na sercu** (*o problemie, sprawie*) press heavily on sb's mind; (*o winie*) lie heavy on sb; **mieć dobre serce** be kind-hearted, have one's heart in the right place; **mieć do czegoś serce** have one's heart in sth, have the heart to do sth; **nie miałem serca mu o tym powiedzieć** I didn't have the heart to tell him about it; **wiesz, jakoś nie mam do tego serca** (= *nie mam na to ochoty*) you know, I just don't have my heart in it; **mieć miękkie serce** be soft-hearted; **mieć miękkie serce dla kogoś** be an easy touch for sb, have a soft spot for sb; **mieć problemy z sercem** have a heart condition; **mieć serce na dłoni** wear one's heart on *l.* upon one's sleeve; **mieć serce z kamienia** have a heart of stone *l.* flint; **mieć złote serce** have a heart of gold; **miejże serce!** (= *okaż dobroć*) have a heart!, show mercy!; **nie mieć Boga w sercu** be heartless; **oddać komuś swe serce** (= *zakochać się*) give *l.* lose one's heart to sb; **od serca** *l.* **z serca płynące** (*np. o życzeniach*) from the bottom of one's heart, heart-felt; **okazać komuś serce** show kindness to sb; **otworzyć** *l.* **obnażyć przed kimś serce** open *l.* bare one's heart to sb; **podbić czyjeś serce** win sb's heart; **przyjąć kogoś z otwartym sercem** give sb a heart-felt welcome; **przypadł mi do serca** I got to like him; **radować czyjeś serce** gladden one's heart; **radujący serce** (*widok, historia*) heartwarming; **ranić czyjeś serce** make sb's heart ache; **rozdzierać komuś serce** rend one's heart, tear one's heart out; **rozpierać komuś serce** (*o uczuciu*) fill one's heart; **serce mi krwawi (z jej powodu)** my heart is bleeding (for her); **serce się kraje** my heart breaks *l.* bleeds; **serce mi się wyrywa** my heart is willing; **serce mi stanęło** (*ze strachu, podniecenia*) my heart missed *l.* skipped a beat; **serce mi zmiękło (z litości)** my heart melted (with pity); **serce nie sługa** the heart wants what it wants; **serce podchodzi mi do gardła** I've got my heart in my mouth *l.* throat; **serce zabiło mi mocniej** *l.* **skoczyło (z radości)** my heart leapt (with joy); **serce zaczęło mi bić szybciej** my heart quickened; **sercem jestem z tobą** my heart goes out to you; **skraść komuś serce** steal one's heart; **sprawić, że serce komuś szybciej zabije** stir sb's blood; **to balsam na moje serce** it warms the cockles of my heart; **to mi szkodzi na serce** it's bad for my heart; **w głębi serca** (*być kimś*) at heart; (*myśleć, czuć*) deep in one's heart, in one's heart of hearts; **wkładać w coś dużo serca** put one's heart to sth; **wziąć sobie coś do serca** take

sth to heart; **z biciem serca** with a beating *l.* pounding heart; **z całego serca** with all one's heart; (= *entuzjastycznie*) with heart and hand; (*kochać kogoś*) heart and soul; **z bólem serca** reluctantly; **z ciężkim/lekkim sercem** with a heavy/light heart; **zrobiłem to z ciężkim sercem** (*niechętnie*) it went very much against the grain with me; **z dobrego serca** out of the goodness of one's heart; **z głębi serca** from the bottom of one's heart; **złamać komuś serce** break sb's heart; **z ręką na sercu** hand on heart; **z ręką na sercu, nie wiem** cross my heart, I don't know; **żywiej zabiło mi serce** my pulse quickened. **2.** (*dzwonu*) tongue, clapper.

sercowaty *a.* heart-shaped, cordiform.

sercowiec *mp* -wc- *pl.* -y *pot.* cardiac.

sercowy *a.* **1.** (= *dotyczący serca*) cardiac; **mięsień sercowy** *anat.* myocardium. **2.** (= *miłosny*) romantic, of the heart; **sprawy sercowe** affairs of the heart. **3.** (= *chory na serce*) *pot.* cardiac; **nie stresuj go, jest sercowy** don't stress him, he's a cardiac one.

sercówka *f. Gen.pl.* -ek **1.** (*czereśnia*) heart cherry, bigarreau. **2.** (*łopata*) heart-shaped spade. **3.** *zool.* cockle (*Cardium*); **sercówka jadalna** edible cockle (*Cardium edule*).

serdaczek *mi* -czk- *Gen.* -a *zob.* **serdak**.

serdak *mi Gen.* -a jerkin (*usu. made of fur or padded*).

serdecznie *adv.* **1.** (= *z życzliwością*) warmly, cordially; **przywitać się z kimś serdecznie** greet sb warmly, give sb the glad hand; **witać kogoś serdecznie** welcome sb warmly. **2.** (= *z głębi serca*) from the bottom of one's heart. **3.** (= *z całego serca, bardzo, naprawdę*) heartily, really; **serdecznie** *l.* **bardzo dziękuję** thank you very much indeed; **serdecznie pozdrawiam** (*w zakończeniu listu*) kind *l.* best regards; **ściskam serdecznie** (*w zakończeniu listu*) love; **serdecznie się nie cierpią** there's no love lost between them; **mam tego serdecznie dosyć** I'm sick and tired of it, I've had just about enough of it; **uśmiać się serdecznie** have a jolly good laugh.

serdecznik *mi bot.* motherwort (*Leonorus*).

serdeczności *pl. Gen.pl.* -i warm, cordial words and gestures; (*w zakończeniu listu*) love.

serdeczność *f.* warmth, cordiality; **przyjąć kogoś z serdecznością** give sb a warm welcome.

serdeczny *a.* hearty, cordial, warm; **serdeczny przyjaciel** bosom friend; **serdeczny list** warm letter; **serdeczne pozdrowienia** (*w zakończeniu listu*) kind *l.* best regards; **palec serdeczny** ring finger.

serdelek *mi* -lk- *Gen.* -a frankfurter, hot-dog.

serdelowy *a. kulin.* **kiełbasa serdelowa** half-smoke.

serduszko *n. Gen.pl.* -ek *zob.* **serce**.

serek *mi* -rk- *Gen.* -a **1.** *kulin.* cheese; **serek biały kremowy** cream cheese; **serek homogenizowany** smooth cottage cheese (*similar to custard, usu. vanilla*); **serek topiony** processed *l.* process cheese; **serek wiejski** *l.* **ziarnisty** *l.* **grani** cottage cheese. **2.** (*rodzaj dekoltu*) V neck; **sweter w serek** V neck sweater.

serenada *f. muz.* serenade.

seria *f. Gen.* **-ii** (= *cykl*) series, sequence; (*antybiotyku, zastrzyków*) course; (*monet*) strike; (*takich samych wydarzeń*) line, succession; (*nieszczęść, wypadków*) train; (*strzałów z broni maszynowej*) round; **seria doświadczalna** *l.* **pilotażowa** pilot run; **seria nieszczęść** chapter of accidents; **seria ognia** burst of fire; **seria rozmów** (*w negocjacjach*) round of talks; **seria specjalna** (*produktu*) special series; **seria wydawnicza** book series; **seria wyrobów** product line; **seria znaczków** set of stamps; **film z serii...** another episode of...; **program z serii...** a program in the series...

serial *mi Gen.pl.* **-i** *l.* **-ów** *telew.* series, serial; **serial telewizyjny** TV series.

serialny *a. muz.* **muzyka serialna** dodecaphonic music.

serialowy *a. telew.* of or related to a (TV) series; **fabuła serialowa** (TV) series plot.

serigrafia *f. Gen.* **-ii** serigraphy.

serio[1] *adv.* (= *poważnie, bez żartów*) seriously, earnestly, really; **serio?** really?, no kidding?; **myśleć o czymś serio** think of sth seriously *l.* in earnest; **traktować kogoś na serio** treat sb seriously; **rozgniewać się na serio** get really angry; **pół żartem, pół serio** half seriously, half jokingly; (= *na dobre*) in earnest.

serio[2] *a. indecl.* (= *poważny*) serious; **praca serio** serious work; **człowiek serio** serious person.

sernik *mi Gen.* **-a** 1. *kulin.* cheesecake. 2. (= *kazeina*) casein.

sernikowy *a.* cheesecake.

serokonwersja *f. biol., med.* (= *wystąpienie przeciwciał po kontakcie z antygenem*) seroconversion.

serolog *mp pl.* **-dzy** *l.* **-owie** *biol., med.* serologist.

serologia *f. Gen.* **-ii** *biol., med.* serology.

serologiczny *a. biol., med.* serologic, serological; **konflikt serologiczny** serologic *l.* fetomaternal incompatibility; **odczyn serologiczny** serologic *l.* serological reaction.

seronegatywny *a.* seronegative.

seropozytywny *a.* seropositive.

serotonina *f. biol.* serotonin.

serowacenie *n. pat.* caseation.

serowacieć *ipf. pat.* caseate.

serowar *mp* cheese maker.

serowarnia *f. Gen.pl.* **-i** cheese dairy.

serowarski *a.* cheesemaker's, cheesemakers'.

serowarstwo *n.* cheese making.

serowaty *a.* cheesy, cheese-like; **serowate zapalenie płuc** *pat.* caseous pneumonia.

serowiec *mi* **-wc-** *Gen.* **-a** *kulin., dial.* (= *sernik*) cheesecake.

serowy *a.* cheese.

serpent *mi muz.* serpent.

serpentyn *mi min.* serpentine.

serpentyna *f.* 1. (*droga górska*) switchback, hairpin road. 2. (*taśma papierowa*) streamer. 3. (*szabla*) a type of saber. 4. (*działo*) serpentine, culverin.

serpentynowy *a.* hairpin; **serpentynowa droga** hairpin road.

serso *n.* (*gra rekreacyjna*) the graces; **grać w serso** play the graces.

serum *n. fizj.* serum.

serw *mi sport* service, serve.

serwal *ma zool.* serval (*Felis serval*).

serwantka *f. Gen.pl.* **-ek** glass *l.* glazed cabinet, glass case.

serwatka *f. Gen.pl.* **-ek** whey; *rzad.* serum.

serwer *mi komp.* server; **serwer lokalny** LAN server.

serweta *f.* tablecloth.

serwetka *f. Gen.pl.* **-ek** 1. (*do wycierania ust, rąk*) napkin, serviette; (*ozdobna, kładziona pod talerz*) doily; **serwetka papierowa** paper napkin. 2. (= *mały obrus*) (small) tablecloth.

serwilista *mp* yes-man, flunkey.

serwilistyczny *a.* servile.

serwilizm *mi* servility, servilism.

serwis *mi* 1. (*komplet naczyń*) set, service; **serwis do kawy/herbaty** coffee/tea set *l.* service; **servis obiadowy** dinner set *l.* service. 2. (*informacyjny*) news bulletin. 3. (*obsługa, konserwacja*) service. 4. (*punkt usługowy*) service station; **serwis RTV** radio and TV repair shop; **serwis samochodowy** garage, service station. 5. *sport* service, serve; **przełamać serwis (przeciwnika)** break (one's opponent's) service.

serwisowy *a.* 1. (= *naprawczy*) service; **punkt serwisowy** (*np. autoryzowanego przedstawiciela*) service station; (*prywatny*) repair shop; **umowa serwisowa** maintenance contract. 2. *sport* service; **as serwisowy** service ace; **błąd serwisowy** *tenis* fault; **linia serwisowa** service line; **przystanek serwisowy** (*w wyścigach samochodowych*) pit stop.

serwitut *mi hist.* servitude.

serwitutowy *a. hist.* servitude.

serwohamulec *mi* **-lc-** *Gen.* **-a** *techn.* servo brake.

serwolatka *f. Gen.pl.* **-ek** *kulin.* cervelat.

serwomechanizm *mi techn.* servomechanism.

serwomotor *mi techn.* servomotor.

serwować *ipf.* 1. *sport* serve (*do kogoś* to sb); **kto serwuje?** whose serve is it? 2. (= *podawać do stołu*) serve; **serwować obiad** serve dinner. 3. (= *dostarczać, sprzedawać*) do; **serwować śniadania** (*o lokalu*) do breakfasts. 4. (*wiadomości*) announce.

serwus *int. przest., pot.* howdy, hello.

serycyna *f. ent.* sericin.

serycyt *mi min.* sericite.

seryjnie *a.* serially, in series; **produkować seryjnie** mass produce.

seryjność *f.* seriality.

seryjny *a.* 1. (= *produkowany masowo*) mass-produced; **produkcja seryjna** mass production. 2. (= *jeden z serii*) serial, seriate; **seryjny morderca** *l.* **zabójca** serial killer; **film seryjny** *telew.* series, serial; **numer seryjny** *l.* **serii** serial number. 3. (= *kolejny*) consecutive; **seryjne niepowodzenia** consecutive failures.

seryna *f. chem.* serine.

sesja f. 1. (= *posiedzenie, okres posiedzeń*) session; (*sądu, ciała ustawodawczego*) session, assize; **sesja naukowa** symposium; **sesja wyjazdowa** *prawn.* out-of-court session; **sesja (egzaminacyjna)** *uniw.* end-of-term examinations. 2. *giełda* trading session; **sesja nagraniowa** *muz.* recording session, take; **sesja zdjęciowa** shoot.

sesterc *mi zob.* **sestercja**.

sestercja f. *hist.* sesterce.

seston *mi l. ma biol.* seston.

sestyna f. *teor.lit.* sestina, sextain.

Seszele *pl. geogr.* the Seychelles.

set *mi Gen.* **-a** *sport* set; **set przegrany do zera** love set.

seta f. *pot.* (*alkoholu*) shot (*usu. of vodka, of 100 ml*).

setbol *mi Gen.* **-a** *sport* set ball.

seter *ma kynol.* setter; **seter angielski** English setter; **seter irlandzki** Irish setter.

setka f. *Gen.pl.* **-ek** 1. (= *sto egzemplarzy*) hundred; **setki widzów** hundreds of spectators; **jechać setką** *pot.* hit *l.* top 100 km per hour, be doing 100 km per hour. 2. *pot.* (*banknot*) hundred zlotys/dollars/etc. bill *l.* note. 3. *tk., pot.* (= *czysta wełna*) pure wool; **garnitur z setki** pure wool suit. 4. *pot.* (*alkoholu*) *zob.* **seta**. 5. *sport* a *l.* one hundred meter race. 6. (*mapa*) map on *l.* to the scale of 1:100 000. 7. (= *autobus, tramwaj itp. nr 100*) the 100, number 100. 8. (= *mieszkanie, pokój, dom nr 100*) number 100; **mieszkam pod setką** I live at no. 100.

setna f. *Gen.* **-ej** one hundredth; **dwie setne procenta** two hundredths of a percent.

setnie *adv. przest.* splendidly; **bawić się setnie** have a whale of a time, have a jolly good time.

setnik *mp hist.* centurion.

setny a. 1. hundredth; **setna rocznica** centennial, a hundredth anniversary. 2. *przest.* great, jolly good; **setna zabawa** jolly good fun.

setowy a. *sport* set; **piłka setowa** set ball.

Seul *mi geogr.* Seoul.

Sewilla f. *geogr.* Seville.

sewrski a. **sewrska porcelana** Sèvres (ware).

sex appeal, seksapil *mi* sex appeal.

sex shop *mi* sex shop.

sexy a. sexy; **sexy lala** sexy chick.

sezam *mi* 1. *mit.* sesame; **sezamie, otwórz się!** open, sesame! 2. *bot.* sesame (*Sesamum indicum*).

sezamki *pl. Gen.* **-ów** *kulin.* (*ciasteczka*) sesame snaps.

sezamowate *pl. Gen.* **-ych** *bot.* sesame family (*Pedaliaceae*).

sezamowy a. sesame; **ziarno sezamowe** sesame seed.

sezon *mi* season; **sezon letni** summer season; **sezon na truskawki** strawberry season; **teraz jest sezon na truskawki** the strawberries are in now; **sezon piłkarski** football season; **sezon teatralny** theater season; *Br.* theatre season; **sezon turystyczny** tourist season; **szczyt sezonu** height of the season, high season; **w szczycie sezonu** at *l.* during high season; *sezon ogórkowy* (= *okres zastoju*) dog days; *dzienn.* silly season; **martwy se-**
zon off season, dead season; **w sezonie** in season; **moda w tym sezonie** this season's look; **gwiazda jednego sezonu** (*zawodnik, zespół*) a flash in the pan.

sezonować *ipf.* (*drewno*) season.

sezonowo *adv.* seasonally; **pracować sezonowo** work seasonally.

sezonowość f. seasonalness.

sezonowy a. seasonal; **praca sezonowa** seasonal labor; *Br.* seasonal labour; **owoce sezonowe** seasonal fruit; **robotnik sezonowy** seasonal; (*zwł. na farmie*) hired hand.

sęczek *mi* **-czk-** *Gen.* **-a** (*na pniu, desce*) small knot.

sędzia *mp Gen.* **-ego** *Ins.* **-ą** *Loc.* **-i** *pl.* **-owie** *Gen.pl.* **-ów** 1. *prawn.* judge; (*sądu wyższej instacji*) justice; **sędzia okręgowy** district judge; **sędzia pokoju** justice of the peace; **sędzia polubowny** arbitrator; **sędzia przysięgły** juror; (*mężczyzna*) juryman; (*kobieta*) jurywoman; **sędzia śledczy** examining magistrate, investigating judge. 2. (*w konkursie*) juror. 3. *sport* (*piłka nożna, koszykówka, boks*) referee; (*tenis, siatkówka*) umpire; **sędzia główny** referee; umpire; **sędzia liniowy** *l.* boczny linesman; **sędzia punktowy** scorekeeper; **sędzia techniczny** *piłka nożna* the fourth official.

sędzina f. *zob.* **sędzia** 1.

sędziostwo n. 1. (= *godność sędziego*) judgeship. 2. *przest.* (= *sędzia z żoną*) judge and his wife.

sędziować *ipf.* 1. *prawn.* judge. 2. *sport* (*piłka nożna, koszykówka, boks*) referee; (*tenis, siatkówka*) umpire.

sędziowski a. 1. *prawn.* judicial; **skład sędziowski** bench (of the court); **urząd sędziowski** judgeship. 2. *sport* referee's, umpire's; **rzut sędziowski** jump ball; **skład sędziowski** the referees, the umpires (*in a game*).

sędziwy a. gray, hoary, aged; **sędziwy wiek** (ripe) old age.

sęk *mi Gen.* **-a** 1. (*w desce, t. gałąź*) knot, knag, knar; **w tym sęk** that's where the shoe pinches, there's *l.* here's the rub. 2. *myśl.* (palmate antler) surroyal.

sękacz *mi Gen.* **-a** *Gen.pl.* **-y** *l.* **-ów** 1. *kulin.* baumkuchen, tree cake. 2. (*kij*) gnarled stick. 3. (*drzewo*) gnarled tree.

sękaty a. (*o drewnie*) gnarly, gnarled, knarry, knarred, knotty; *bot.* (*o cylindrycznej części rośliny*) torose.

sęp *ma orn.* vulture (*Vulturidae l. Cathartidae*); **sęp kasztanowaty** black *l.* monk *l.* cinereous vulture (*Aegypius monachus*); **sęp płowy** griffon vulture (*Gyps fulvus*). – *mp pl.* **-y** *przen.* (= *chciwiec*) cormorant, buzzard, predator.

sępi a. 1. (= *dotyczący sępa*) vulture's. 2. (= *taki jak u sępa*) vulturine, vulturous, vulture-like.

SF *abbr.* 1. (= *science fiction*) SF, s-f, sf (= *science fiction*). 2. (= *San Francisco*) SF (= *San Francisco*).

sf *abbr.* 1. (= *science fiction*) SF, s-f, sf (=

science fiction). **2.** *muz.* (= *sforzando*) sf (= *sforzando*).

sfabrykować *pf.* **1.** *pot.* (= *wytworzyć coś*) make, produce, fabricate. **2.** *pot.* (= *sfałszować dokumenty, dowody itp.*) fabricate, forge, fake; **sfabrykowany materiał** (*dowodowy l. obciążający*) plant.

sfabularyzować *pf.* fictionalize; **sfabularyzowany dokument** *telew., radio* docudrama.

sfajczyć *pf. pot.* burn. ~ **się** *pf. pot.* burn down.

sfalcować *pf. druk.* fold.

sfaleryt *mi min.* sphalerite, zinc sulfide.

sfalować *pf.* wave, undulate.

sfalowany *a.* wavy, waved; undulated, undulating.

sfałdować *pf.* **1.** (= *ułożyć w fałdy*) fold; (*spodnie, firanki, twarz*) crease; (*blachę, tekturę*) corrugate. **2.** (= *pokryć zmarszczkami*) wrinkle. **3.** *geol.* fold. ~ **się** *pf.* **1.** (= *ułożyć się w fałdy*) fold. **2.** (= *pokryć się zmarszczkami*) wrinkle. **3.** *geol.* fold.

sfałdowanie *n. geol.* folding; **sfałdowanie wgłębne** underthrust.

sfałszować *pf. zob.* **fałszować.**

sfałszowany *a.* (*księgi*) cooked, wangled; (*wyścigi, losowanie*) fixed, framed; (*wybory*) fixed, rigged; (*zarzuty, oskarżenie, dowody*) fabricated, trumped-up.

sfanatyzować *pf. zob.* **fanatyzować.**

sfastrygować *pf. zob.* **fastrygować.**

sfatygować *pf.* **1.** *zob.* **fatygować.** **2.** *żart.* (= *zniszczyć*) impair. ~ **się** *pf.* (= *zmęczyć się*) fatigue.

sfatygowany *a. żart.* slightly damaged, battered.

sfaulować *pf. zob.* **faulować.**

sfeminizować *pf.* feminize. ~ **się** *pf.* feminize, become *l.* get feminized.

sfera *f.* **1.** *astron.* sphere, firmament, atmosphere; **sfera niebieska** celestial sphere; **muzyka sfer (niebieskich)** music *l.* harmony of the spheres. **2.** (= *strefa, obszar*) zone, belt, area; **szara sfera** *przen.* gray area *l.* zone. **3.** (= *domena*) sphere, realm, area, domain, field; (*wpływów, zainteresowań*) orbit; **sfera materialna** material sphere; **sfera duchowa** the spiritual; **szeroka sfera wpływów** *przen.* wide circle of influence; **sfera działalności** sphere of activity; **sfera gospodarcza** economic sphere. **4.** (= *środowisko*) circles, class, world; **wyższe/niższe sfery** upper/lower classes; **z wyższych sfer** upper-class; (*o osobie l. sposobie mówienia*) refined, *uj.* posh; **kobieta/mężczyzna z wyższych sfer** man/lady of quality; **pochodzący z lepszych sfer** top drawer; **obracać się w wyższych sferach** rub shoulders with the upper classes; **ludzie (ze) wszystkich sfer** people from every walk of life. **5.** *geom.* sphere; **sfera opisana** circumsphere, circumscribed sphere; **sfera wpisana** insphere, inscribed sphere.

sfermentować *pf. zob.* **fermentować.**

sferoida *f. geom.* spheroid.

sferoidalny *a. geom.* spheroidal.

sferycznie *adv.* spherically.

sferyczny *a. geom., astron.* spherical, spheric, spheral; **aberracja sferyczna** *opt.* spherical aberration; **geometria** *l.* **trygonometria sferyczna** spherics; **trójkąt sferyczny** spherical triangle.

sfiksować *pf. zob.* **fiksować.**

sfilcować *pf.* felt. ~ **się** *pf.* felt.

sfilmować *pf. zob.* **filmować.**

sfinalizować *pf. zob.* **finalizować.**

sfinansować *pf. zob.* **finansować.**

sfingować *pf. lit.* fake; (*proces*) sham.

sfinks *ma* **1.** *sztuka* sphinx. **2.** *przen.* (= *tajemnicza osoba*) mystery, enigma.

sfinksowy *a.* **1.** (= *dotyczący l. podobny do sfinksa*) sphinxlike. **2.** (*o zagadce, minie, tajemnicy*) enigmatic, enigmatical.

sflaczały *a. pot.* (= *bez energii*) limp; (*np. o mięśniach, ramionach*) lax; (*o mięśniach, ciele*) flabby.

sflaczeć *pf. pot.* become limp *l.* lax *l.* flabby.

sfora *f.* **1.** *myśl.* (*psów*) pack (of hounds), cry, kennel. **2.** (*ludzi*) (= *zgraja*) gang, throng. **3.** *przest.* (= *smycz*) leash.

sformalizować *pf.* formalize.

sformatować *pf. zob.* **formatować.**

sformatowany *a. komp.* (*dysk, tekst*) formatted.

sformować *pf. zob.* **formować.** ~ **się** *pf. zob.* **formować się.**

sformułować *pf.* formulate, express, put into words; **niedający się sformułować** inarticulate; **niesformułowany wyraźnie** inexplicit; **jasno sformułowany** articulate.

sformułowanie *n.* expression, statement; (*dokumentu, umowy*) wording, phrasing; (*pojęcia, koncepcji*) conceptualization; **niefortunne sformułowanie** infelicity; **unikać jednoznacznego sformułowania** be suitably *l.* studiously vague.

sforsować *pf. zob.* **forsować.** ~ **się** *pf.* overstrain (o.s.).

sfotografować *pf. zob.* **fotografować.** ~ **się** *pf. zob.* **fotografować się.**

sfragistyka *f.* (= *nauka zajmująca się badaniem pieczęci*) sphragistics.

sfrajerować się *pf. pot.* make a proper *l.* complete fool *l.* ass of o.s., be taken for a ride; **dać się komuś sfrajerować** be bamboozled by sb, be fooled by sb, be taken in by sb.

sfrancuziały *a.* Frenchified.

sfrancuzieć *pf.* become Frenchified.

sfrunąć *pf. zob.* **sfruwać.**

sfrustrować *pf.* frustrate. ~ **się** *pf.* become *l.* get frustrated (*czymś* at *l.* with sth).

sfrustrowany *a.* frustrated (*czymś* at *l.* with sth).

sfruwać *ipf.* (*t. np. o liściach*) flutter down; (= *odlecieć*) fly away; (= *przylecieć*) come, flock.

sfukać *pf. pot.* reprimand, rebuke.

sfumato *n. Gen.pl.* **-ów** *sztuka* sfumato.

sfuszerować *pf. zob.* **fuszerować.**

sgraffito *n. Gen.pl.* **-ów** *sztuka, bud.* sgraffito.

sherry *n. indecl. kulin.* sherry.

shimmy *n. indecl.* (*taniec*) shimmy; **tańczyć shimmy** shimmy, dance the shimmy.

show *mi indecl.* show; **talk-show** *telew.* talk show.

show-biznes *mi* show business; *pot.* showbiz.

showman *mp* showman.

SI *abbr.* (= *międzynarodowy układ jednostek miar*) SI (= *Système International d'Unités*); **układ SI** International System of Units.

si[1] *a. arch.* **do siego roku!** Happy New Year!

si[2] *n. indecl. muz.* B, si, te, ti.

siać *ipf.* **sieję siejesz** (*ziarno*) **1.** sow, seed; (*zwł. ręcznie*) broadcast; **cicho, jak makiem siał** dead *l.* stony silence. **2.** (= *rozpowszechniać*) (*plotki, panikę*) spread; (*strach*) inspire, arouse; **siejący spustoszenie** (*np. o broni, huraganie*) devastating; **siać strach** arouse *l.* inspire fear. **3.** *pot.* (= *gubić*) lose. **4.** (= *przesiewać*) sift, sieve.

siad *mi sport* squat; **siad!** (*do psa*) sit!

siadać *ipf.* **1.** sit (down), take a seat, be seated; **siadać po turecku** sit cross-legged; **siadać wygodnie** sit comfortably; **siadać okrakiem na czymś** bestride sth; **siadać niedbale** sprawl; **siadać w kucki** squat, crouch, hunker down; **siadać do stołu/obiadu/kart** sit down to table/dinner/cards; **siadać na koń/rower** mount one's horse/bicycle; **proszę siadać!** take your seat, please!, please, be seated! **2.** (*o koniu, psie*) sit, come down *l.* sit on its haunches; (*o ptakach*) alight, light, perch, rest; **mucha nie siada!** *pot.* tiptop, topnotch; first-class, first-rate. **3.** *lotn.* land, touch down. **4.** (= *psuć się*) break down, conk out.

siadywać *ipf.* sit (*often l. from time to time l. sometimes*); **siadywał na ławeczce przed domem** he used to *l.* would often sit on the bench in front of his house.

siak *adv. arch.* differently; **tak czy siak** (= *w każdym wypadku*) in any case, anyway; **tak czy l. albo siak** (= *w ten czy inny sposób*) one way or the other, this or that way, either way; **ni tak, ni siak** neither one way nor the other, in no manner, in no shape or form, not at all; **(i) tak, i siak** by hook or by crook, by fair means or foul, by one means or another.

siaki *a. arch.* different, other; **(a)ni taki, (a)ni siaki** neither this nor that.

siamang *ma zool.* siamang (*Symphalangus syndactylus*).

siamto *pron. tylko Nom. i Acc. sing.* **bo tamto, bo siamto** now one thing then another.

sianko *n. dimin.* hay.

siano *n.* **1.** (= *skoszona trawa*) hay; **stóg siana** (*mały*) haycock; (*duży*) haystack, hayrick; **widły do siana** pitchfork; **szukać igły w stogu siana** look for a needle in a haystack; **wykręcić się sianem** get off lightly. **2.** *pot.* (= *pieniądze*) dough, bread, lettuce.

sianokosy *pl. Gen.* **-ów** haymaking.

siara *f.* **1.** *fizj.* colostrum. **2.** *sl.* (= *niepowodzenie, nieudana rzecz, próba itp.*) fuckup.

siarczan *mi chem.* sulfate; **siarczan amonowy** ammonium sulfate; **siarczan miedziowy** copper *l.* cupric sulfate; **siarczan sodowy** sodium sulfate.

siarczany *a.* sulfur; sulfuric, sulfurous; **źródło siarczane** sulfur spring.

siarczek *mi* **-czk-** *chem.* sulfide; **siarczek sodowy** sodium sulfide.

siarczyn *mi chem.* sulfite; **siarczyn sodowy** sodium sulfite.

siarczysty *a.* **1.** (= *silny*) strong, hard; (*o języku*) sulphurous; (*o uderzeniu*) powerful; (*o mrozie, o zadanym policzku*) hard, heavy; (*o mrozie*) biting, sharp. **2.** (= *żwawy*) spirited, lively.

siarczyście *adv.* **1.** (= *silnie*) violently, powerfully. **2.** (= *żwawo*) spiritedly, lively, briskly.

siarka *f. chem.* sulfur; *Br.* sulphur; *przest.* brimstone; **siarka bezpostaciowa** amorphous sulfur; **siarka krystaliczna** crystalline sulfur; **siarka organiczna** organic sulfur; **siarka rodzima** native sulfur, brimstone; **siarka rombowa** rhombic sulfur; **siarka strącona** lac of sulfur; **siarka sublimowana** sublimed sulfur; **dwutlenek siarki** sulfur dioxide.

siarkawy *a. chem.* sulfurous.

siarkonośny *a.* (*o złożu, pokładzie*) sulphur-bearing.

siarkować *ipf.* **1.** *chem.* sulfurize. **2.** *roln.* sulfitate.

siarkowodór *mi* **-o-** *chem.* hydrogen sulfide, sulfuretted hydrogen.

siarkowy *a.* sulfur; *chem.* sulfuric; **kwas siarkowy** sulfuric acid.

siateczka *f. Gen.pl.* **-ek** **1.** *zob.* **siatka. 2.** (*układ*) reticulation; (*np. naczyń krwionośnych, żył*) network; *bot.* reticulum.

siatka *f. Gen.pl.* **-ek** **1.** (*plecionka*) net, mesh; (*np. na okno, przeciw komarom*) screen; **siatka na motyle** butterfly net; **siatka na włosy** hair net; **siatka na zakupy** string bag, tote bag; **siatka druciana** wire net *l.* mesh; **siatka maskująca** *wojsk.* camouflage netting. **2.** (= *ogrodzenie*) wire fence; **otaczać siatką** net. **3.** (*układ*) network, grid, structure, web; **siatka płac** *ekon.* payroll; **siatka poligraficzna** *druk.* screen; **siatka geograficzna** *geogr.* geographical grid; **siatka kartograficzna** (*map*) graticule; **siatka wielościanu** *geom.* net. **4.** *sport* net. **5.** *sport, pot.* volleyball. **6.** (= *zorganizowana grupa*) ring; **siatka narkotykowa/szpiegowska** drug/spy ring.

siatkarka *f. Gen.pl.* **-ek** *zob.* **siatkarz**.

siatkarski *a. sport* volleyball.

siatkarz *mp sport* volleyball player, volleyballer.

siatkowy *a.* net, network; mesh; **piłka siatkowa** *sport* (*gra, piłka*) volleyball; **pończochy siatkowe** mesh stockings.

siatkówka *f. Gen.pl.* **-ek** **1.** *anat.* retina; **czopek siatkówki** cone; **uszkodzenie siatkówki** *pat.* retinal damage. **2.** *sport* volleyball; **piłka do siatkówki** volleyball.

siąkać *ipf.*, **siąknąć** *pf.* (*nosem*) sniffle, sniff.

siąpawica *f. pot.* drizzle.

siąpić *ipf.* (*o deszczu*) drizzle.

siąść *pf.* **siądę siądziesz siadł siedli** *zob.* **siadać**.

sic *int.* sic.

sidła *pl. Gen.* **sideł** snare, trap; *pl. t. przen.*

toils (*czegoś/kogoś* of sth/sb); *myśl.* (*w postaci pętli zaciskowej*) springe, noose; (*urządzenie mechaniczne*) trap; *t. przen.* (*uczuć, policji*) mesh, trap (*czegoś* of sth); **chwytać w sidła** ensnare; **wpaść we własne sidła** be hoist with *l.* by one's own petard.

siebie *pron. Acc.* **siebie** *l.* **się** *Gen.* **siebie** *Dat. i Loc.* **sobie** *Ins.* **sobą** **1.** (*identyczność, t. siebie samego*) oneself; **iść przed siebie** walk straight on *l.* ahead; **spojrzeć za siebie** look back; **spojrzenie za siebie** backward glance; **pozostawić** *l.* **zostawić coś za sobą** leave sth behind; **czuj się jak u siebie (w domu)** make yourself at home; **u siebie** *sport* (*o meczu*) home; **chodzą ze sobą od trzech miesięcy** they've been seeing each other for the past three months; **chodzić ze sobą** date; (*zwł. w okresie narzeczeństwa*) court; **zabierać kogoś/coś ze sobą** take sb/sth with sb *l.* along; **zabrała ze sobą wszystko, co tylko można sobie wyobrazić** she took along everything but the kitchen sink; **coś nie ma przed sobą przyszłości** there's no future in *l.* for sth; **masz przed sobą wspaniałą przyszłość** you've got a great future ahead of you; **chcę mieć to za sobą** I want to get it over; **mieć najgorsze za sobą** be over the hump; **mieć za sobą najtrudniejszą część czegoś** break the back of sth; **mieć najlepsze lata za sobą** be past one's prime, be over the hill; **mieć za sobą daleką drogę** (*bardzo się zmienić, dojrzeć itp.*) *t. dosł.* have come a long way; **nieść** *l.* **pociągać za sobą** involve, imply, entail; **porwać za sobą** (*zwł. tłum*) carry; **spalić za sobą mosty** burn one's bridges *l.* boats (behind one); **zamknij za sobą drzwi** shut *l.* close the door behind *l.* after you; **dochodzić do siebie po czymś** recover from sth; **brać coś do siebie** (*uwagi*) take sth personally; **przyciągnąć kolana do siebie** draw up one's knees; **przytulić kogoś do siebie** hug sb; **zapraszać kogoś do siebie** ask sb round, ask sb to come to one's place; **zrazić** *l.* **zniechęcać kogoś do siebie** antagonize sb, disaffect sb; **wyjść z siebie** blow *l.* pop one's cork, be beside o.s.; **wykrztuś** *l.* **wyrzuć** *l.* **wyduś to z siebie!** (= *powiedz to*) spit it out!; **wylewać z siebie żale** pour out one's sorrows; **wypruwać z siebie żyły** sweat blood, sweat one's guts out; **zadowolony z siebie** self-complacent, self-satisfied; **zrobić z siebie durnia** make an idiot *l.* ass of o.s.; **zrobić z siebie pośmiewisko** make o.s. a laughing stock; **być z siebie dumnym** be proud of o.s.; **robić z siebie głupka** play the fool; **robić z siebie widowisko** make an exhibition of o.s.; **a spectacle of o.s.; samemu z siebie** (*zrobić coś*) by o.s.; **samo z siebie** by itself, per se; **zostawiać coś po sobie** leave sth as one's legacy; **cel sam w sobie** an end in itself; **łączyć w sobie** (*zwł. cechy*) combine; **mieć w sobie to coś** (*trudną do zdefiniowania cechę, która dodaje atrakcyjności*) have this something; **mieścić w sobie** contain, hold; **ona ma w sobie trochę snobizmu** she's somewhat of a snob; **przemóc w sobie dumę** swallow one's pride; **rzecz sama w sobie** thing-in-itself, noumenon; **sprzeczność sama w sobie** a contradiction in terms; **zamknięty w sobie** indrawn, introvert, withdrawn; **ze-**

brać się w sobie pull o.s. together, get a grip on o.s.; **mieć coś przy sobie** have sth on *l.* about sb; **nie mam przy sobie pieniędzy** I have no money on me; **ręce przy sobie!** (keep your) hands off!; **sam sobie jesteś winien** it is your own fault, you only have yourself to blame; **sami sobie pieczemy chleb** we bake our own bread; **wmówić sobie, że...** kid o.s. (into believing) that... **2.** (*wzajemność, t. siebie wzajemnie*) each other, one another; **dzielić (pomiędzy siebie)** (*koszt, dochód*) split; **wyjaśnić sobie wszystko** get *l.* put *l.* set things straight; **wyjaśnijmy sobie jedną rzecz** let's have *l.* get one thing clear; **mówić sobie po imieniu** be on first name terms with each other; **przypadli sobie do gustu** they took (a) fancy *l.* liking to each other; **dalej od siebie** farther away from each other *l.* one another; **bliżej siebie** closer to each other *l.* one another.

siec *ipf.* **siekę sieczesz siekł** **1.** (= *ciąć*) hack, slash, gash. **2.** (= *bić*) lash, slash; (*o deszczu*) pelt.

sieciarka *f. ent.* (= *owad z rzędu Neuroptera*) neuropteran.

sieciowy *a.* **1.** net, mesh. **2.** *techn.* net, network; **odbiornik sieciowy** mains receiver; **gniazdko sieciowe** mains socket, wall plug; **skok napięcia sieciowego** *el.* power surge; **przewód sieciowy** *el.* power cord *l.* cable; **zasilacz sieciowy** alternating current *l.* AC adapter. **3.** *komp.* network; **etykieta sieciowa** (= *zasady poprawnego zachowania w sieci*) netiquette; **usługodawca sieciowy** network access provider; **karta sieciowa** network interface controller, network (adapter) card; **adres sieciowy** network address; **kabel sieciowy** network cable; **klient sieciowy** network client; **dysk sieciowy** network drive; **sterownik sieciowy** network driver; **otoczenie sieciowe** network neighborhood; **sieciowy system operacyjny** network operating system; **serwer sieciowy** network server; **usługi sieciowe** network services; **sieciowa stacja robocza** network workstation.

sieczka *f.* (= *pocięta słoma*) chaff; **zrobić z czegoś sieczkę** cut *l.* dash *l.* hack sth to pieces; **mieć sieczkę w głowie** be empty-headed.

sieczkarnia *f. Gen.pl.* **-i** *roln.* chaff-cutter.

sieczna *f. Gen.* **-ej** *geom.* secant.

sieczny *a.* **1.** cutting; edge; **broń sieczna** side arms. **2.** *geom.* secant. **3.** *anat.* incisive; **zęby sieczne** incisors.

sieć *f.* **1.** *gł. ryb.* (fishing) net; **zarzucać sieć** cast a net; **łapać w sieć** net; **sieć rybacka** fishing net. **2.** *przen.* (= *pułapka*) trap; **sieć intryg** web of intrigues. **3.** (*pajęcza*) web, cobweb. **4.** *techn.* net, network, grid; (*elektryczna, gazowa, wodna*) system; **sieć zasilająca** mains, supply network; **sieć telekomunikacyjna** telecommunications network; **sieć cyfrowa z integracją usług** *l.* **sieć ISDN** *tel., komp.* Integrated Services Digital Network; **włączać** *l.* **włączyć coś do sieci** plug sth in; **wyłączać** *l.* **wyłączyć coś z sieci** unplug sth; **sieć cieplna** *l.* **ciepłownicza** heat distribution network; **sieć drogowa** road system *l.* network; **sieć (elektro)energetyczna** power network;

ogólnokrajowa sieć (elektro)energetyczna power grid; **sieć kanalizacyjna** sewage *l.* sewerage system; **sieć kapilarna** *biol.* capillary network; **sieć jezdna** *kol.* contact system *l.* line; **sieć kolejowa** railway system; **sieć komunikacyjna** communication network; **sieć przewodów elektrycznych** wiring; **sieć rozdzielcza** distribution network; **sieć telefoniczna** telephone network; **sieć transmisji danych** teletransmission network; **sieć wodociągowa** water-supply system; **sieć wysokiego napięcia** high-voltage system; **sieć telefonii komórkowej** mobile network; **sieć bezprzewodowa** wireless network. **5.** *komp.* network, *pot.* (= *Internet*) the Web; **sieć komputerowa** computer network; **w** *l.* **podłączony do sieci** online; **surfować w** *l.* **po sieci** surf the Web *l.* net; **sieć rozproszona** distributed network; **łączyć w sieć** network; **nasza sieć oparta jest na Novellu** our LAN runs (on) Novell; **sieć lokalna** *l.* **wewnętrzna** intranet; **sieć lokalna** Local Area Network, *LAN*; **sieć miejska** Metropolitan Area Network, *MAN*; **sieć rozległa** Wide Area Network, *WAN*; **sieć szkieletowa** *l.* **bazowa** network backbone; **sieć danych** data network. **6.** chain, string; **sieć supermarketów** supermarket chain; **sieć restauracji fast food** fast food chain. **7.** *mat.* (*w teorii zbiorów i algebrze*) lattice; (*w topologii i teorii grafów*) network. **8.** *astron.* (*gwiazdozbiór*) Reticulum; *pot.* the Net. **9.** *anat.* omentum, reticulum.

siedem *num.* **-dmi-** *Ins.* **-oma** *l.* **-u** seven; **siedem cudów świata** the seven wonders of the world; **siedem grzechów głównych** seven deadly sins; **od siedmiu boleści** pitiable; **pocieszyciel od siedmiu boleści** Job's comforter; **złożony z siedmiu części** sevenfold; **siedmiu braci śpiących** (the) Seven Sleepers; **pięć plus dwa jest siedem** five and two make seven; **skrzywiony jak siedem nieszczęść** the very picture of misery; **zamknąć drzwi na siedem spustów** double-lock the door; **za siedmioma górami, za siedmioma lasami** (= *daleko*) far, far away (*jako początek bajki*) once upon a time...

siedemdziesiąt *num.* **-ęci-** *Ins.* **-oma** *l.* **-u** seventy; **jedna siedemdziesiąta** one *l.* a seventieth.

siedemdziesiątka *f. Gen.pl.* **-ek 1.** seventy. **2.** *pot.* (= *wiek 70 lat*) seventy years (of age); **osoba po siedemdziesiątce** septuagenarian; **on ma siedemdziesiątkę** he is seventy; **on ma siedemdziesiątkę na karku** he is getting on for seventy. **3.** *pot.* (= *autobus, tramwaj itp. nr 70*) the seventy, number seventy. **4.** (= *dom, mieszkanie nr 70*) number seventy; **mieszkamy pod siedemdziesiątką** we live at number seventy. **5.** *pot.* (*prędkość*) seventy kilometers *l.* miles per hour; **jechać siedemdziesiątką** be doing seventy, drive *l.* travel (at the speed of) seventy kilometers *l.* miles per hour.

siedemdziesiąty *a.* seventieth; **siedemdziesiąty pierwszy** seventy-first; **lata siedemdziesiąte** the seventies; **w latach siedemdziesiątych** in the seventies; **lata siedemdziesiąte dwudziestego wieku** the 1970s; **pod koniec lat siedemdziesiątych** (*dwudziestego wieku*) in the late 1970s.

siedemdziesięciolecie *n. Gen.pl.* **-i 1.** (*rocznica*) seventieth anniversary. **2.** (*okres*) (period of) seventy years.

siedemdziesięcioletni *a.* seventy-years-old; **człowiek siedemdziesięcioletni** man of seventy.

siedemnasta *f. Gen.* **-ej** (*godzina*) five (o'clock); **(godzina) siedemnasta** 5 p.m.; **jest (godzina) siedemnasta** it's 5 p.m.

siedemnastka *f. Gen.pl.* **-ek 1.** (= *cyfra l. liczba 17*) seventeen. **2.** (= *tramwaj, autobus nr 17*) the seventeen, number seventeen; **do szpitala dojedziesz siedemnastką** you take the seventeen to the hospital. **3.** (= *dom, mieszkanie, pokój nr 17*) number seventeen; **mieszkamy pod siedemnastką** we live at number seventeen. **4.** *pot.* (= *dziewczyna siedemnastoletnia*) girl of seventeen (years of age), seventeen-year-old (girl).

siedemnastolatek *mp* **-tk-** *pl.* **-i** boy of seventeen (years of age), seventeen-year-old (boy).

siedemnastolatka *f. Gen.pl.* **-ek** girl of seventeen (years of age), seventeen-year-old (girl).

siedemnastoletni *a.* (*o chłopaku, domu, stażu*) seventeen-year-old, seventeen years old, of seventeen (years of age).

siedemnastowieczny *a.* seventeenth-century, 17th century.

siedemnasty *a.* seventeenth. – *mi* seventeenth (*day of a month*); **umówić się z kimś na siedemnastego stycznia** arrange to meet sb on the seventeenth of January *l.* January 17.

siedemnaście *num.* **-st-** *Ins.* **-oma** *l.* **-u** seventeen.

siedemset *num.* **siedem-** *decl. like num.,* **-set** *indecl.* seven hundred.

siedemsetletni *a.* **1.** (= *mający 700 lat*) seven-hundred-year-old, seven hundred years old. **2.** (= *trwający 700 lat*) seven hundred years', seven-hundred-year.

siedemsetny *a.* seven-hundredth.

siedlisko *n.* **1.** *poet.* (*siedziba*) home, habitation, dwelling, abode. **2.** *biol.* habitat. **3.** *przen.* hotbed, nest; **siedlisko zarazy** pesthole.

siedliskowy *a.* *biol.* habitat.

siedmiobarwny *a.* seven-colored, *Br.* seven-coloured.

siedmiodniowy *a.* **1.** (= *trwający 7 dni*) seven-day, seven days'. **2.** (= *w wieku siedmiu dni*) seven-day-old.

siedmiogodzinny *a.* **1.** (= *trwający 7 godzin*) seven-hour, seven-hours'. **2.** (= *w wieku siedmiu godzin*) seven-hour-old.

siedmiokąt *f. geom.* heptagon.

siedmioklasowy *a.* *szkoln.* seven-grade; *Br.* seven-form.

siedmiokrotnie *adv.* seven times, sevenfold.

siedmiokrotny *a.* septuple, sevenfold; repeated *l.* iterated seven times.

siedmiolatek *mp* **-tk-** *pl.* **-i** (= *siedmioletni chłopiec*) seven-year-old (boy). – *ma* **-tk-** (= *siedmioletnie zwierzę*) seven-year-old (animal).

siedmiolatka *f. Gen.pl.* **-ek 1.** *zob.* **siedmiolatek. 2.** *szkoln.* seven-grade school; *Br.* seven-form school. **3.** (= *okres siedmiu lat*) septennium, (period of) seven years.

siedmiolecie *n. Gen.pl.* **-i 1.** (= *7 lat*) (period of) seven years, septennium. **2.** (= *siódma rocznica*) seventh anniversary.

siedmioletni *a.* **1.** (= *trwający siedem lat*) seven-year; **siedmioletni okres spłat kredytu** seven-year loan repayment period. **2.** (= *w wieku siedmiu lat*) seven-year-old, seven years old, of seven (years of age); **siedmioletni chłopiec** seven-year-old boy, boy of seven; **siedmioletnia dziewczynka** seven-year-old girl, girl of seven; **siedmioletni pies** seven-year-old dog. **3.** (*o okresie, planie*) seven-year, septennial.

siedmiomiesięczny *a.* **1.** (= *trwający siedem miesięcy*) seven-month, seven months'. **2.** (= *w wieku siedmiu miesięcy*) seven-month-old; **siedmiomiesięczne dziecko** seven-month-old child.

siedmiomilowy *a.* seven-league; **buty siedmiomilowe** (*w bajkach*) seven-league boots.

siedmiopiętrowy *a.* seven-story, seven-storey; **budynek siedmiopiętrowy** seven-story building.

siedmioraki *a.* sevenfold, of seven different kinds.

siedmioramienny *a.* seven-branched, seven-armed; **świecznik siedmioramienny** seven-branched candelabrum.

siedmioro *num. decl. like n.* **-rg-** seven.

siedmiozgłoskowiec *mi* **-wc-** *Gen.* **-a** *teor.lit.* heptastich.

siedmiozgłoskowy *a. teor.lit.* heptasyllabic, septisyllabic; **wers siedmiozgłoskowy** septenarius, septenary.

siedząco *adv.* sitting, sedentarily; **robić coś na siedząco** do sth sitting down.

siedzący *a.* **1.** (= *w pozycji siedzącej*) sitting; (*o postawie, zajęciu, trybie życia*) sedentary; (*o trybie pracy*) deskbound; *bot.* (*o organie*) sessile; **prowadzący siedzący tryb życia** (*o osobie*) sedentary. **2.** (= *przeznaczony do siedzenia*) sitting; **brak miejsc siedzących** (*wiadomość, ogłoszenie*) standing room only; **miejsce siedzące** seat; **liczba miejsc siedzących** seating capacity.

siedzenie *n.* **1.** (= *miejsce, na którym się siedzi*; *część krzesła, fotela itp.*) seat; **przednie/tylne siedzenie** front/back seat; **siedzenie kierowcy** driver's seat; **siedzenie dla pasażera** (*na motocyklu, skuterze*) pillion; **siedzenie rozkładane** reclining seat. **2.** *euf.* (= *pośladki*) bottom.

siedziba *f.* (*osoby*) (place of) residence, domicil, domicile; (*instytucji, spółki*) seat, registered *l.* statutory office; **siedziba główna** headquarters, head *l.* principal office; **stała siedziba** permanent residence; **z siedzibą w Chicago** based *l.* seated in *l.* at Chicago, Chicago-based.

siedzieć *ipf.* **-dzę -dzisz 1.** (= *nie stać, nie leżeć*) sit (*przy l. wokół czegoś* at *l.* around sth); (= *nie wstawać z miejsca*) remain seated; (*o ptakach*) perch (*na czymś* on sth); (*na grzędzie, drucie*) roost; (*o zwierzęciu*) sit, sit *l.* rest on its haunches; **siedzieć na jajach** (*o drobiu*) sit on eggs; **siedzieć do późnej nocy** sit up (*till late*); **siedzieć po turecku** sit cross-legged; **siedzieć komuś na kolanach** sit on sb's lap; **siedzieć na dwóch stołkach** *przen.* straddle the fence; **siedzieć bezczynnie** sit on one's hands; **siedzieć z**

założonymi rękami (= *nic nie robić*) sit on one's hands, twiddle one's thumbs; **siedzieć jak na szpilkach** be on pins and needles; **siedzieć cicho** be *l.* keep quiet, keep a low profile; **siedzieć cicho jak mysz pod miotłą** be as quiet as a mouse; **siedzieć cicho jak trusia** lie low; **siedź cicho!** be *l.* keep quiet!; **siedź spokojnie!** sit still!; **siedzieć u szczytu stołu** sit at the head of a table; **siedzieć w kucki** squat; **siedzieć w pierwszym rzędzie** sit in the front row; **siedzieć na pieniądzach** roll *l.* wade in money; **siedzieć z przodu** (*obok kierowcy*) sit in the front; **siedzieć na beczce prochu** *przen.* (= *być l. znaleźć się w bardzo niebezpiecznej sytuacji*) be sitting on a powder keg; **siedzieć komuś na ogonie** (= *ścigać drugi samochód trzymając się go bardzo blisko*) tailgate. **2.** *pot.* (= *przebywać*) stay, remain; **nie siedź długo** don't be long; **siedzieć za długo** (*o gościu*) overstay *l.* outstay one's welcome; **siedzieć w domu** stay *l.* be at home; **siedziałem tam jak na tureckim kazaniu** it was all Greek to me, I didn't get a word of it; **siedzieć pod pantoflem** be henpecked; **siedzieć u kogoś w kieszeni** *przen.* (= *być od kogoś zależnym finansowo*) be financially dependent on sb; **siedzieć w długach (po uszy)** be in debt up to one's eyeballs; **siedzieć komuś na głowie** *przen.* live off sb, inflict o.s. on sb. **3.** *pot.* (= *mieszkać*) live. **4.** *pot.* (= *zajmować się czymś*) do, work; (= *być zaabsorbowanym*) be engrossed; **siedzieć w komisji** sit on a committee; **siedzieć nad czymś** (*np. nad pracą*) work on sth; **siedzieć w czymś** *przen.* know sth inside out. **5.** *pot.* (*w więzieniu*) do time. **6.** *pot.* (= *tkwić*) sit; **gwóźdź dobrze siedzi** the nail sits tight. **7.** *szkoln.* (= *powtarzać rok*) repeat.

siedzisko *n.* (*krzesła, fotela, siodła*) seat.

siego *a. zob.* **si.**

sieja *f. Gen.* **siei** *icht.* common whitefish (*Coregonus lavaretus*).

sieję *itd. ipf. zob.* **siać.**

siekacz *mi Gen.* **-a 1.** *anat.* incisor. **2.** chopper, cutter.

siekać *ipf.* **1.** (*na kawałki*) chop (up), cut; (*w nieregularne kształty, szybko*) hack; (*drobno*) hash; (*bardzo drobno*) mince. **2.** (*o deszczu, śniegu*) pelt; (*o wietrze*) beat, lash.

siekaniec *mi* **-ńc-** *Gen.* **-a** (*pocisk z ołowiu*) lead shot.

siekanina *f.* **1.** *kulin.* hash. **2.** *pot.* (= *walka*) sword *l.* sabre fight.

siekanka *f. Gen.pl.* **-ek** *kulin., pot.* hash.

siekiera *f.* **1.** ax, *Br.* axe; **zaduch, że siekierę można powiesić** *przen.* it's so stuffy *l.* frowzy in here. **2.** *pot.* (= *mocna herbata l. kawa*) strong brew.

siekierka *f. Gen.pl.* **-ek** hatchet; **zamienił stryjek siekierkę na kijek** sb made a losing bargain; (*jako powiedzenie*) the cure is worse than the evil.

sielanka *f.* **1.** (= *beztroskie życie*) idyl, idyll; bed of roses. **2.** *Gen.pl.* **-ek** *teor.lit.* idyl, idyll; eclogue, bucolic.

sielankowo *adv.* idyllically.

sielankowy *a.* **1.** (= *szczęśliwy*) idyllic. **2.** *te-or.lit.* idyllic, pastoral, bucolic.

sielawa *f. icht.* vendace (*Coregonus albula*).

sielski *a. lit.* (= *wiejski*) rural, rustic, pastoral; (= *sielankowy*) idyllic.

siema, siemasz *int. pot.* howdy, hiya, hello.

siemię *n.* -mieni- birdseed, canary seed; **siemię lniane** flaxseed, linseed.

sienny *a.* hay; **katar sienny** *pat.* hay fever.

sień *f. pl.* -nie hall.

siepacz *mp Gen.pl.* -y *l.* -ów *lit.* myrmidon, oppressor, bravo.

siepać *ipf.* -pię -piesz **1.** (= *szarpać, targać*) pull. **2.** (= *smagać*) whip, lash; (*o deszczu*) pelt. ~ **się** *ipf.* (= *strzępić się*) fray.

siepnąć *pf.* -ij *zob.* **siepać.**

siermięga *f. hist.* homespun peasant's coat.

siermiężny *a.* **1.** (= *zgrzebny*) rough, coarse. **2.** (= *ubogi*) poor. **3.** (= *gburowaty*) boorish, uncouth.

sierociniec *mi* -ńc- *Gen.* -a *przest.* orphanage.

sieroctwo *n.* orphanhood, orphanage.

sierocy *a.* orphan; **choroba sieroca** *pat.* (*u dzieci z domów dziecka*) hospitalism; (*u dzieci niekochanych*) anaclitic depression.

sierota *f. l. mp decl. like f. Gen.pl.* -ot *l.* -ót **1.** orphan; **zostać sierotą** be orphaned. **2.** *pot.* (= *osoba niezdarna*) duffer, butterfingers. **3.** *pot.* (= *osoba łatwowierna l. potulna*) lamb, sop, dupe.

sierotka *f. Gen.pl.* -ek *zob.* **sierota.**

sierp *mi Gen.* -a **1.** *roln.* sickle; **żąć sierpem** cut with a sickle; **sierp Księżyca** *astron.* crescent. **2.** *boks* hook.

sierpień *mi* -pni- *Gen.* -a *Gen.pl.* -ów *l.* -i August; **w sierpniu** in August.

sierpniowy *a.* (*o urlopie, upale*) August.

sierpowaty *a.* sickle-shaped, crescent; *biol.* falcate, falcated, falciform; **lucerna sierpowata** *bot.* alfalfa, lucerne (*Medicago sativa*).

sierpowy *a.* **1.** sickle. **2.** *sport* hook; **cios sierpowy** hook; **lewy/prawy sierpowy** left/right hook. – *mi sport* (= *cios sierpowy*) hook.

sierpówka *f. orn.* Eurasian collared-dove (*Streptopelia decaocto*).

sierść *f.* fur, coat, pelage; **czyścić sierść** preen.

sierż. *abbr.* (= *sierżant*) Sgt. (= *sergeant*).

sierżant *mp gł. wojsk.* sergeant; **starszy sierżant** master sergeant, first class sergeant, gunnery sergeant; **sierżant sztabowy** senior master sergeant, first *l.* master sergeant; **starszy sierżant sztabowy** chief master sergeant, (command) sergeant major, master gunnery sergeant.

siew *mi roln.* sowing, seeding; **siew czysty** plain *l.* pure sowing; **siew mieszany** mixture seeding *l.* sowing; **siew rzędowy** drill seeding *l.* sowing, drilling; **siew rzutowy** broadcast sowing; **pora siewu** seedtime.

siewca *mp* **1.** *roln.* sower, seedsman. **2.** *przen.* propagator, disseminator.

siewka *f. Gen.pl.* -ek **1.** *bot.* seedling. **2.** *orn.* plover, dotterel (*Charadriidae*); **siewka złota** golden plover (*Pluvialis apricaria*).

siewnik *mi Gen.* -a *roln.* (*maszyna*) seeder, sower, drill; **siewnik nawozowy** fertilizer distributor; **siewnik ręczny** hand seed drill *l.* sower; **siewnik rzędowy** (seed) drill; **siewnik rzutowy** broadcast sower, broadcaster; **siewnik zbożowy** cereal *l.* grain drill.

siewny *a.* seed, sowing; **groszek siewny** *bot.* grass pea, chickling pea (*Lathyrus sativus*); **lnicznik siewny** *bot.* gold-of-pleasure (*Camelina sativa*).

siewruga *f. icht.* stellate sturgeon (*Acipenser stellatus*).

się *pron.* **1.** *zob.* **siebie. 2.** (= *siebie samego*) oneself; **widział/widzieli się w lustrze** he saw himself/they saw themselves in the mirror; **laska do podpierania się** a staff to support oneself with; **poddawać się czemuś** (*uczuciu, nastrojowi*) lend oneself over to sth; **przeistoczyć się w kogoś/coś** turn into sb/sth; **uważa się za artystkę** she fancies herself as an artist. **3.** (= *siebie nawzajem*) each other, one another; **X i Y znają się dobrze** X and Y know each other very well; **ci dwoje kochają się** those two love each other; **myślałem, że się rozumiemy** I thought we understood each other *l.* one another; **znamy się od lat** we have known each other *l.* one another for years. **4.** (*tworzy stronę zwrotną czasownika*) oneself; **skaleczyć się** hurt oneself; **czesać się** comb one's hair; **położyć się** lie down. **5.** (*jako odpowiednik strony biernej*) **ta książka sprzedaje się świetnie** this book sells very well; **to się dobrze nosi/pierze** it wears/washes well; **tak się tego nie robi** that's not the way to do it. **6.** (*bezosobowo*) you, one; **zrobiło się późno** it's got late; **idzie się prosto** one goes straight on *l.* ahead; **nigdy się nie wie** you never know, one never knows.

sięgać *ipf.*, **sięgnąć** *pf.* -ij **1.** (*wyciągać rękę itp.*) reach (*po coś l. do czegoś* (out) for sth); **mógłbyś mi sięgnąć po to pudło z szafy?** could you reach *l.* get me that box from the wardrobe?; **sięgnąć do kieszeni** reach into one's pocket; **sięgnąć do kieszeni** *l.* **portfela** *przen.* use one's own money; **sięgać do czyjejś kieszeni** (*przen.*) pick sb's pocket. **2.** (= *zbliżać się, docierać*) reach, come; extend (*czegoś* as far as sth); go (*od /do / aż do czegoś* from/to/up to sth); **straty sięgały milionów** losses ran into millions; **mamy długi sięgające...** our debt amounts to...; **sięgający w głąb duszy** heart-searching; **jego ambicje sięgają wysoko** he has high aspirations; **sięgać pamięcią do czegoś** go back in one's mind to sth; **jak okiem sięgnąć** as far as the eye can see. **3.** (= *zaglądać do*) refer (*do czegoś* to sth); consult (*do czegoś* sth); **sięgać do słownika/notatek** refer to a dictionary/one's notes. **4.** (= *starać się o coś*) strive; **sięgać po władzę** strive for power. **5.** (= *osiągać jakąś granicę*) reach; come (up *l.* down) (*(do) czegoś* to sth); **włosy sięgały jej do pasa** her hair came *l.* reached down to her waist; **sięgający do kolan** (*o płaszczu*) knee-length; (*o butach*) knee-high; **sięgający piersi** breast-high *l.* -deep; **woda**

sięgała mi do szyi the water came up *l.* reached to my neck; **sięgać zenitu** climax, reach a climax; **napięcie sięgało zenitu** tension was at fever pitch; **sięgnąć kresu** reach the end, reach the limit; **sięgnąć dna** hit rock-bottom. **6.** *tylko ipf.* (= *datować się*) go *l.* date back to; **nasza współpraca sięga roku 1980** our cooperation goes *l.* dates back to 1980.

sikacz *mi Gen.* **-a** *pot.* plonk, cheap wine.

sikać *ipf.* **1.** *pot.* (*cienkim strumieniem*) squirt, scoosh; (*silnym strumieniem*) spurt; (*silnym, obfitym i głośnym strumieniem*) gush. **2.** *pot.* (= *oddawać mocz*) piss.

sikawka *f. Gen.pl.* **-ek** *pot.* (hand-powered) fire pump.

Sikh *mp pl.* **-owie** Sikh.

sikhijski *a.* Sikh.

siki *pl. Gen.* **-ów** *pot.* piss.

siklawa *f. dial.* mountain waterfall.

siknąć *pf.* **-ij** *zob.* **sikać**.

sikora *f. orn.* titmouse; *Br.* tit (*Parus*); **sikora bogatka** great tit (*P. major*); **sikora czubatka** crested tit (*P. cristatus*); **sikora modra** tomtit (*P. caeruleus*); **sikora sosnówka** coaltit (*P. ater*); **sikora uboga** marsh tit (*P. palustris*).

sikorka *f. Gen.pl.* **-ek 1.** *orn.* = **sikora**. **2.** *żart.* (= *dziewczyna*) lass.

siksa *f. uj.* hussy.

siku *n. indecl. dziec.* pee; **zrobić siku** pee; **chce mi się siku** I want to pee.

silić się *ipf.* exert o.s., spare no effort (*na coś* to do sth); **sadzić się na dowcipy/uprzejmość** try to be funny/polite.

silikon *mi chem.* silicone.

silnia *f. Gen.pl.* **-i** *mat.* factorial; **cztery silnia** factorial four.

silniczek *mi* **-czk-** *Gen.* **-a** small motor.

silnie *adv.* **1.** (= *mocno*) strongly; (*np. uderzyć*) hard. **2.** (= *intensywnie*) intensely; (*np. odczuwać coś*) deeply; **silnie to przeżyła** she took it badly.

silnik *mi Gen.* **-a** *techn.* motor, engine; **silnik atomowy** atomic engine; **silnik cieplny** heat engine; **silnik elektryczny** electric motor; **silnik Diesla** diesel engine; **silnik jądrowy** nuclear engine; **silnik odrzutowy** jet engine; **silnik okrętowy** marine engine; **silnik parowy** steam engine; **silnik pneumatyczny** pneumatic engine, compressed-air engine; **silnik samochodowy** car engine, automobile engine; **silnik samolotowy** aeroplane engine; **silnik spalinowy** internal-combustion engine; **silnik tłokowy** piston engine; **silnik wodny** water engine; **silnik czterosuwowy** *l.* czterotaktowy four-stroke engine, four-cycle engine; **silnik dwusuwowy** *l.* dwutaktowy two-stroke engine, two-cycle engine.

silnikowy *a.* motor, engine; **olej silnikowy** motor oil, engine oil; **paliwo silnikowe** engine fuel, motor fuel.

silny *a.* strong; (*ból*) intense; (*lekarstwo*) strong, powerful; **rządy silnej ręki** heavy-handed rule; **prawo silniejszego** the rule of force.

silos *mi* **1.** (*na paszę, materiały budowlane*) silo. **2.** (*na ziarno*) grain elevator.

silosować *ipf. roln.* ensile.

silosowy *a.* silo; **roślina** *l.* zielonka silosowa silage, ensilage.

siła[1] *f.* **1.** (*energia*) power, strength; **siła nadprzyrodzona** supernatural force; **siła woli** willpower; **siły wytwórcze** *ekon.* production forces; **siła wyższa** *prawn.* force majeure, act of God; **siły przyrody** *l.* natury forces of nature; **siłą rzeczy** necessarily, perforce; **biec ile sił w nogach** run as fast as one's legs can carry one; **chodzić o własnych siłach** walk on one's own; **gonić resztkami sił** be at the end of one's rope *l.* tether; **leżeć bez sił** lie exhausted; **spróbować w czymś swoich sił** try one's hand at sth; **nie mam siły, by mu o tym powiedzieć** I can't bring myself to tell him about it; **nie czuję się na siłach, by to zrobić** this is too much for me, I don't feel fit to do it; **ojciec jest już w sile wieku** father is already in his prime; **opadam z sił** my strength is flagging; **to zadanie przerasta jego siły** this task is beyond his power; **ta praca jest ponad moje siły** this work is beyond my power. **2.** (*natężenie*) intensity; (*argumentów, rozumu, uczucia*) force, potency; **siła dźwięku** *muz.* volume of sound; **siła nabywcza (pieniądza)** *ekon.* purchasing power (of money), buying power (of money). **3.** (*pracownik*) employee, specialist; **siła fachowa** professional; **siła pociągowa** (= *zwierzęta pociągowe*) beast of burden; **(tania) siła robocza** (cheap) labor force, *Br.* (cheap) labour force. **4.** (*grupa społeczna*) forces; **siły postępu** forces of progress; **siły demokratyczne** forces of democracy. **5.** *fiz.* force; **siła bezwładności** force of inertia; **siła ciężkości** *l.* grawitacyjna gravity force, G-force; **siła dośrodkowa/odśrodkowa** centripetal/centrifugal force; **siła tarcia** friction force; **ramię siły** arm of a force. **6.** *wojsk.* force; **siły lądowe** ground *l.* land forces; **siły morskie** naval forces; **siły powietrzne** air force; **siły zbrojne** armed forces; **siły nieprzyjacielskie** enemy forces; **siły odwodowe** reserve forces; **siły szturmowe** assault forces. **7.** (= *przymus fizyczny*) force; **używać siły** use force. **8.** *wojsk.* (= *zdolność bojowa*) combat capacity.

siła[2] *num. indecl. przest.* much, many; **siła złego na jednego** too much evil for one man to cope with.

siłacz *mp* strongman.

siłaczka *f.* strongwoman.

siłą *adv.* by force.

siłomierz *mi Gen.* **-a** *techn.* dynamometer.

siłować się *ipf.* wrestle, struggle (*z kimś/czymś* with sb/sth).

siłownia *f. Gen.pl.* **-i 1.** *techn.* power plant; **siłownia parowa/wodna** steam/water power plant. **2.** *sport* gym.

siłownik *mi techn.* servomotor.

siłowy *a.* strength; **ćwiczenia siłowe** weight training; **sport siłowy** *sport* strength sport; **rozwiązanie siłowe** *polit.* settlement by force.

sinawy *a.* bluish.

Singapur *mi* Singapore.

singiel, singel *mi* **-gl-** *Gen.* **-a 1.** *sport* singles. **2.** *muz.* single. **3.** *karty* singleton.

siniak *mi Gen.* **-a 1.** (*na skórze*) bruise; *pat.* ecchymosis; (*pod okiem*) black eye; **nabić komuś siniaka** bruise sb. 2. *bot.* bluish bolete (*Boletus cyanescens*). – *ma orn.* stock dove (*Columba oenas*).

sinica *f.* 1. *pat.* cyanosis. 2. *bot.* blue-green alga (*Cyananophyta*).

siniec *mi* **-ńc-** *Gen.* **-a** bruise; **nabić komuś sińca** bruise sb; **mieć sińce pod oczami** (= *mieć podbite oczy*) have bruised eyes; (= *mieć podkrążone oczy*) have baggy eyes.

sinieć *ipf.* 1. (= *stawać się sinym*) become blue, become livid. 2. (= *być sinym*) be bluish.

sino *adv.* bluish; **w pokoju było sino od dymu** the room was bluish with smoke.

sinolog *mp pl.* **-dzy** *l.* **-owie** Sinologist, Sinologue.

sinologia *f. Gen.* **-ii** Sinology.

siność *f.* lividness, lividity.

sinto *n. indecl. rel.* (*religia japońska*) Shinto.

sintoizm *mi rel.* Shintoism.

sinus *mi Gen.* **-a** *mat.* sine.

sinusoida *f. mat.* sinusoid.

sinusoidalny *a. mat.* sinusoidal.

siny *a.* livid, bluish; **siny kamień** *chem.* bluestone; **patrzeć w siną dal** stare ahead dreamily; **pójść w siną dal** vanish into thin air.

sio[1] *int.* **a sio!** shoo!, pish!

sio[2] *pron.* **ni to, ni sio** neither fish nor fowl.

siodełko *n. Gen.pl.* **-ek** 1. (*roweru*) saddle. 2. *geogr.* saddle, col. 3. *żegl.* belaying cleat. 4. (*wyciągu*) seat.

siodełkowaty *a.* saddle-shaped.

siodełkowy *a.* **wyciąg siodełkowy** chair lift.

siodlarski *a.* saddler's.

siodlarstwo *n.* saddlery.

siodlarz *mp* saddler.

siodłać *ipf.* saddle.

siodło *n. Gen.pl.* **-eł** 1. (*do jazdy konnej*) saddle; **siedzieć mocno w siodle** *przen.* be in the saddle; **wysadzić kogoś z siodła** *dosł.* unsaddle sb; *przen.* unseat sb, knock sb off his *l.* her perch. 2. *geogr.* saddle.

sioło *n. Gen.pl.* **siół** *lit.* hamlet.

siorbać *ipf.* **-bię -biesz, siorbnąć** *pf.* **-ij** slurp.

siostra *f. Gen.pl.* **sióstr** 1. (*swojej siostry albo brata*) sister; **siostra cioteczna** *l.* **stryjeczna** cousin; **siostra mleczna** foster sister; **siostra przyrodnia** stepsister; **siostra rodzona** blood sister; **siostra syjamska** Siamese sister. 2. (*zakonnica*) sister; **siostra miłosierdzia** sister of mercy, sister of charity. 3. (*pielęgniarka*) nurse, sister; **siostra przełożona** matron; **siostra oddziałowa** ward sister.

siostrzany *a.* 1. (= *podobny*) twin. 2. (*o uczuciach, pocałunku*) sisterly.

siostrzenica *f.* niece.

siostrzeniec *mp* **-ńc-** *pl.* **-y** nephew.

siostrzyczka *f. Gen.pl.* **-ek** little sister.

siódemka *f. Gen.pl.* **-ek** 1. (*liczba*) seven. 2. (= *siedem egzemplarzy*) set of seven. 3. (*autobus, tramwaj*) the seven, number seven, service seven; (*budynek*) building number seven. 4. *karty* seven; **siódemka karo/kier** seven of diamonds/hearts.

siódma *f. Gen.* **-ej** (*godzina*) seven o'clock; **spotkajmy się o siódmej** let's meet at seven; **byłem w domu tuż po siódmej** I came home right after seven.

siódmoklasista *mp*, **siódmoklasistka** *f. Gen.pl.* **-ek** seventh-grade student; *Br.* seventh-form student.

siódmy *a.* seventh; **na stronie siódmej** on page seven; **być w siódmym niebie** be in seventh heaven; **siódme poty na mnie biją** I am bathed in sweat.

sir *mp indecl.* sir.

sirocco *n. Gen.* **-a** *l. indecl. meteor.* sirocco.

sitarski *a.* sieve maker's.

sitarz *mp* 1. *bot.* shallow-pored bolete (*Suillus bovinus*). 2. (*rzemieślnik*) sieve maker.

sitcom *mi film* sitcom, situation comedy.

siteczko *n. Gen.pl.* **-ek** 1. small sieve. 2. *pot.* (*mikrofon*) mike.

sitko *n. Gen.pl.* **sitek** small sieve, small strainer; **sitko do herbaty** tea strainer.

sitkowy *a.* sift; **chleb sitkowy** brown bread.

sito *n.* 1. (*do przesiewania*) sieve, strainer; **dziurawy jak sito** leaky like a sieve; **przesiewać przez sito** strain through a sieve; sieve, sift; **przejść przez sito eliminacji** *przen.* (*sportowych*) win a knockout competition. 2. *techn.* riddle.

sitodruk *mi druk.* screen process, silk-screen printing.

sitowie *n. bot.* bulrush (*Scirpus lacustris*).

sitowy *a.* sieve; **rurki sitowe** *bot.* sieve tubes.

sitwa *f. pot.* clique, cabal.

siup *int.* **no to siup!** (*toast*) down the hatch!, here's mud in your eye!

siurpryza *f. przest.* surprise.

siusiać *ipf. dziec., euf.* wee-wee, pee-pee.

siusiu *n. indecl. dziec., euf.* pee; **zrobić siusiu** pee; **chce mi się siusiu** I want to pee.

siwak *mi Gen.* **-a** earthen pot.

siwawy *a.* (*np. o włosach*) grayish, *Br.* greyish.

siwek *ma* **-wk-** gray, gray horse, *Br.* grey, grey horse.

siwieć *ipf.* gray, turn gray, *Br.* grey, turn grey.

siwizna *f.* gray hair, *Br.* grey hair; **włosy przyprószone siwizną** hoary hair.

siwowłosy *a.* gray-haired, *Br.* grey-haired.

siwy *a.* gray, *Br.* grey; **siwy mróz** hoarfrost, white frost; **czapla siwa** *orn.* grey heron (*Ardea cinerea*); **siwy jak gołąbek** snow-white.

sizal *mi techn.* sisal.

sizalowy *a.* sisal.

sjesta *f.* siesta.

s-ka, ska *abbr.* (= *spółka*) Co. (= *company*).

skabioza *f. bot.* scabious (*Scabiosa*).

skacowany *a. pot.* hungover.

skadrować *ipf. fot.* frame.

skafander *mi* **-dr-** *Gen.* **-a** 1. *kurtka* anorak. 2. (*strój ochronny*) protection suit; (*astronauty*) spacesuit; (*nurka*) diving suit; (*ciśnieniowy*) pressure suit.

skaj *mi* American cloth.

skajowy *a.* American cloth.

skakać *ipf.* **-czę -czesz** 1. (*w górę, w dół*) jump; **skakać koło kogoś** fawn on *l.* upon sb; **skakać z**

tematu **na temat** skip from one subject to another; **serce skoczyło mi do gardła** I have my heart in my mouth, my heart missed a beat. **2.** (*w jakimś kierunku*) jump towards; **skoczyć na drzewo/na konia** jump on a tree/horse; **skoczyć do wyjścia** make for the exit; **skoczyłby dla mnie w ogień** he would go through fire and water for me, he could go to the stake for me. **3.** (*odbijać się*) bounce; **obraz skacze** *telew.* the picture keeps jumping. **4.** (*trząść się*) tremble; **litery skaczą mi przed oczami** letters leap out at me. **5.** (*zaatakować*) set (*do kogoś* upon sb); **skakać komuś do oczu** *l.* **do gardła** fly at sb's throat. **6.** (*np. o cenach*) shoot up, jump.

skakanka *f. Gen.pl.* **-ek** jump rope; *Br.* skipping-rope.

skala *f. Gen.pl.* **-i** *l.* **-l 1.** (*do mierzenia*) scale; **skala Celsjusza** Celsius scale, centigrade scale; **skala Fahrenheita/Kelvina/Beauforta** Fahrenheit/Kelvin/Beaufort scale; **na małą/wielką skalę** on a small/large *l.* grand scale. **2.** (*mapy*) scale; **mapa w skali 1:25 000** map in the scale of 1:25000. **3.** (*radioodbiornika, przyrządów pomiarowych*) scale. **4.** *muz.* scale; **skala głosu** range of voice.

skalać *ipf. lit.* defile.

skalar *mi Gen.* **-u** *fiz.* scalar. – *ma Gen.* **-a** *icht.* angelfish, scalare (*Pterophyllum scalare*).

skalarny *a.* scalar.

skald *mp pl.* **-owie** skald, scald.

skaleczenie *n.* cut.

skaleczyć *pf.* cut. **~ się** *pf.* cut o.s.; **skaleczyć się w palec** cut one's finger; **skaleczyć się w rękę** hurt one's hand.

skaleń *mi Gen.* **-a** *min.* feldspar, felspar.

skalisty *a.* rocky; **Góry Skaliste** *geogr.* the Rocky Mountains, the Rockies.

skalkulować *pf.* calculate, compute.

skalnica *f. bot.* saxifrage (*Saxifraga*).

skalnik *mi pot.* rock garden, rockery.

skalny *a.* rocky; **odłamek skalny** chip of stone; **ogród skalny** rock garden, rockery; **roślinność skalna** rock plants; **rumowisko skalne** rubble of stone.

skalować *ipf.* calibrate.

skalp *mi* scalp.

skalpel *mi Gen.* **-a** *Gen.pl.* **-i** *l.* **-ów** scalpel.

skalpować *ipf.* scalp.

skała *f.* rock; **skała lita** solid rock; **skała magmowa** magmatic rock; **skała metamorficzna** metamorphic rock; **skała osadowa** sedimentary rock; **serce twarde jak skała** a heart of stone.

skałka *f. Gen.pl.* **-ek 1.** (*skała*) rock. **2.** (*w broni*) flint.

skałkowy *a.* **karabin skałkowy** flintlock.

skałodrzew *mi bud.* xylolith.

skamandrycki *a. teor.lit.* Skamander.

skamandryta *mp teor.lit.* member of the Skamander group of poets.

skamielina, skamieniałość *f. geol.* fossil.

skamieniały *a.* **1.** (*rośliny, zwierzęta*) fossilized. **2.** (*np. ze strachu*) petrified.

skamienieć *ipf.* **1.** (= *zamienić się w kamień*) fossilize, petrify. **2.** *przen.* be petrified; **skamienieć ze strachu** be petrified with fear.

skamlać *ipf.* **-lam** *l.* **-lę -lasz** *l.* **-lesz, -laj** *l.* **-l,** **skamleć** *ipf.* **-ę -esz 1.** (*o psie*) yelp, whine. **2.** *pot.* (= *prosić*) whimper.

skanalizować *pf.* provide with a sewer system.

skancerowany *a.* damaged.

skand *mi chem.* scandium.

skandal *mi Gen.pl.* **-i** *l.* **-ów** scandal.

skandalicznie *adv.* scandalously.

skandaliczny *a.* scandalous, shocking.

skandalista *mp,* **skandalistka** *f. Gen.pl.* **-ek** scandal.

skandalizować *ipf.* scandalize.

skandować *ipf.* chant.

skandowiec *mi* **-wc-** *Gen.* **-a** *chem.* scandium group element.

Skandynaw *mp pl.* **-owie,** **Skandynawka** *f. Gen.pl.* **-ek** Scandinavian.

Skandynawia *f. Gen.* **-ii** Scandinavia.

skandynawista *mp* Scandinavian scholar.

skandynawistyka *f.* Scandinavian studies.

skandynawski *a.* Scandinavian.

skaner *mi Gen.* **-a** *komp.* scanner.

skanować *ipf.* scan.

skansen *mi* open-air ethnographical museum, heritage park.

skapcanieć *pf. pot.* droop, sink.

skaperować *pf. pot.* win over.

skapitulować *pf.* **1.** *wojsk.* capitulate; **przed kimś/czymś** to sb/sth. **2.** (= *wycofać się*) give up, give in.

skapnąć *pf.* **-ij** (*np. o lzie*) drip; (*o pieniądzach*) come in.

skapotować *pf. lotn.* roll over, overturn.

skapować *pf. pot.* twig; **on chyba jeszcze nie skapował** it looks like he hasn't twigged yet. **~ się** *pf. pot.* = **skapować.**

skaptować *pf.* = **skaperować.**

skapywać *ipf.* drip.

skarabeusz *ma Gen.pl.* **-y** *l.* **-ów** *ent.* scarab (*Scarabaeus sacer*).

skarać *pf.* **-rzę -rzesz** *przest.* chasten.

skaranie *n.* **skaranie boskie z tym chłopakiem!** this boy is such a nuisance!

skarb *mi* **1.** (= *kosztowności*) (= *coś cennego*) treasure; **poszukiwacz skarbów** treasure hunter; **skarby kultury polskiej** treasures of the Polish culture; **za żadne skarby świata** for love or money; **nie zrobiłbym tego za żadne skarby świata** I wouldn't do it for love or money; **mój skarbie!** dearest!, my love! **2.** *ekon., hist.* **skarb państwa** the Treasury.

skarbiec *mi* **-bc-** *Gen.* **-a 1.** (*pomieszczenie*) vault, strong room. **2.** (*kosztowności*) treasure.

skarbnica *f.* **1.** *lit.* vault, strong room. **2.** *przen.* repository, storehouse; **skarbnica wiedzy** repository of knowledge, storehouse of knowledge.

skarbniczka *f. Gen.pl.* **-ek** (*np. stowarzyszenia*) *zob.* **skarbnik** 1.

skarbnik *mp* **1.** (*np. stowarzyszenia*) treasurer; (*w banku*) cashier; (*w sklepie*) teller. **2.** *hist.* (*urzędnik*) Lord Treasurer.

skarbonka *f. Gen.pl.* **-ek** money box; **świnka skarbonka** piggy bank.

skarbowość *f.* finances, financial matters.

skarbowy *a.* fiscal; **opłata skarbowa** stamp duty, stamp tax; **prawo skarbowe** fiscal law; **przepisy skarbowe** treasury regulations, fiscal regulations; **Urząd Skarbowy** *US* the Internal Revenue Service, IRS; *Br.* Inland Revenue, IR; **znaczek skarbowy** stamp, duty stamp.

skarcić *pf.* rebuke, scold.

skarga *f.* **1.** (*żalenie się*) complaint, grumble. **2.** (*obwinianie*) complaint (*na coś* about sth); **pójść na skargę do kogoś** complain to sb. **3.** (= *zażalenie*) complaint; **wnieść skargę na kogoś/coś** file *l.* lodge a complaint agaist sb/sth; **złożyć skargę z powodu czegoś** complain about sth, file *l.* lodge a complaint about sth.

skarleć *pf.* (= *stać się karłem*) become dwarfed; (= *zmaleć, zmniejszyć się*) dwindle.

skarłowacieć *pf.* = **skarleć**.

skarmiać *ipf.*, **skarmić** *pf.* feed.

skarpa *f.* **1.** (*urwisko*) slope; (*uformowana przez erozję*) escarpment, scarp. **2.** (*podpora*) buttress.

skarpeta *f.* sock.

skarpetka *f. Gen.pl.* -**ek** sock.

skarykaturować *pf.* caricature.

skarżyć *ipf.* **1.** (*do sądu*) sue (*kogoś o coś* sb for sth). **2.** (= *oskarżać, donosić*) tell (*na kogoś* on sb); *szkoln.* tell tales. ~ **się** *ipf.* complain (*na kogoś/coś* complain of sb/sth).

skarżypyta *f. l. mp decl. like f. Gen.pl.* -**t** *l.* -**ów** talltale.

skasować *pf.* (*bilet*) punch, cancel; (*plik, nagranie*) erase; (*instytucję*) close down; **skasować samochód** *pot.* wreck a car.

skat *mi Gen.* -**a** *karty* skat.

skatalogować *pf.* catalogue.

skatować *pf.* torture, beat mercilessly.

skaut *mp* boy scout.

skauting *mi* scouting.

skautowski *a.* scout.

skawalać *ipf.*, **skawalić** *pf.* clot. ~ **się** *ipf.*, **skawalić się** *pf.* lump.

skaza *f.* **1.** (= *wada*) flaw, defect; **bez skazy** flawless. **2.** *pat.* diathesis; **skaza krwotoczna** haemorrhagic diathesis; **skaza moczanowa** gout.

skazać *pf.* **skażę skażesz** *zob.* **skazywać**. ~ **się** *pf. zob.* **skazywać się**.

skazana *f. Gen.* -**ej** *zob.* **skazany**.

skazaniec *mp* -**ńc**- *pl.* -**y** convict.

skazany *mp* = **skazaniec**. – *a.* convicted; **skazany na niepowodzenie** doomed to failure; **być skazanym na własne siły** be thrown back on one's own resources.

skazić *pf.* **skażę skazisz** *zob.* **skażać**.

skazujący *a.* **wyrok skazujący** verdict of guilty.

skazywać *ipf.* **1.** *prawn.* sentence; **skazać na dwa lata w zawieszeniu** give *l.* deal a suspended sentence of two years; **skazać na pięć lat pozbawienia wolności** sentence to five years' imprisonment; **skazać na dożywocie** sentence to life imprisonment; **skazać na śmierć** sentence to death. **2.** (*przeznaczać*) be doomed, be fated; **być skazanym na zapomnienie** be doomed to

oblivion; **być skazanym na bezczynność** be fated to idleness. ~ **się** *ipf.* condemn o.s. (*na coś* to sth); **skazać się na wygnanie** condemn o.s. to exile.

skażać *ipf.* **1.** (= *zanieczyścić*) pollute. **2.** (= *zatruć*) contaminate. **3.** *lit.* taint, corrupt.

skażenie *n.* **1.** (= *zanieczyszczenie*) pollution. **2.** (= *zatrucie*) contamination.

skażony *a.* **1.** (= *zanieczyszczony*) polluted. **2.** (= *zatruty*) contaminated.

skąd *adv.* where from; **skąd jedziesz?** where are you coming from?; **powiedz, skąd to wiesz** tell me where you know that from?; **zanieś to tam, skąd to wziąłeś** take it to where you got it from. – *partykuła* **ależ skąd!** not at all!

skądinąd *adv.* (= *z innego źródła*) from another source; (= *z innego miejsca*) from another place. – *partykuła* (= *poza tym, zresztą*) otherwise.

skądkolwiek *adv.* no matter from where; **musisz mieć pieniądze, skądkolwiek byś je wziął** you must get the money, no matter where you get it from.

skądś *adv.* from somewhere, from some place or other; **my się chyba skądś znamy** I guess we know each other from somewhere; **skądś jednak dostała tę wiadomość** somehow she got this message.

skądże *adv.* where from, whence; **skądże przyjeżdżasz?** where are you coming from?; **skądże miałbym to wiedzieć?** where should I know it from? – *particle* **skądże znowu!** but of course not!

skąpać *pf.* -**pię** -**piesz** *lit.* bathe. ~ **się** *pf.* plunge (*w czymś* into sth) (*usu. accidentally*); **skąpać się we krwi** be bathed in blood.

skąpany *a. lit.* (*w słońcu, we łzach*) bathed (*w czymś* in sth).

skąpić *ipf.* (*zwł. jedzenia*) stint (*czegoś* on sth); (*pieniędzy*) pinch pennies (*na coś* for sth); **skąpić komuś czegoś** grudge sb sth; **nie skąpić wysiłków** spare no pains *l.* trouble.

skąpiec *mp* -**pc**- *pl.* -**y** *uj.* miser, niggard.

skąpiradło *n. Gen.pl.* -**eł** *uj.*, *pot.* skinflint, cheapskate.

skąpo *adv.* **1.** (*ubrany*) (= *prawie nagi*) scantily; (= *biednie*) poorly; (= *nędznie*) shabbily. **2.** (= *oszczędnie*) sparingly.

skąpomocz *mi pat.* oliguria.

skąposzczety *ma pl. zool.* oligochaetes (*Oligochaeta*).

skąpotchawce *pl. zool.* pauropods (*Pauropoda*).

skąpstwo *n.* stinginess, miserliness.

skąpy *a.* **1.** (*o człowieku*) stingy, miserly. **2.** (*o ubiorze, informacjach, świetle*) scant.

skecz *mi Gen.pl.* -**y** *l.* -**ów** skit.

skędzierzawić *pf.* (*o włosach*) curl.

skiba *f.* **1.** *roln.* ridge. **2.** *dial.* (*chleba*) slice.

skibka *f. Gen.pl.* -**ek** *dial.* (*chleba*) slice.

skibob *mi sport* skibob.

skierować *pf. zob.* **skierowywać**. ~ **się** *pf.* (= *zmierzać, zdążać*) head, make (*dokądś* for sth).

skierowanie *n.* **1.** (*do lekarza, szpitala*) referral; **dostałem skierowanie do specjalisty** I've been referred to a specialist. **2.** (*do pracy*) appointment.

skierowywać *ipf.* (= *wysyłać*) refer; (*krytykę, oskarżenie*) direct, level (*do kogoś/czegoś* at sb/sth); (*broń, cios, wysiłki*) aim (*na kogoś/coś* at sb/sth); (*wzrok, uwagę, kroki, wysiłki*) direct (*na kogoś/coś* at sb/sth); **skierować do kogoś pytanie** address *l.* put a question to sb; **skierować myśli ku przyszłości** direct one's thoughts towards the future; **skierować rozmowę na inny temat** switch the conversation to another topic *l.* subject; **skierować sprawę do sądu** bring the case into *l.* before the court; **skierować wysiłki w jakimś kierunku** direct one's efforts towards sth; **lekarz skierował pacjenta do szpitala** the doctor referred the patient to hospital; **czy może Pan skierować mnie na lotnisko?** (*pokazać drogę*) could you direct me to the airport?

skif *mi sport* skiff.

skifista *mp*, **skifistka** *f. sport* skiffer.

skikjöring *n. sport* skijoring.

skiksować *pf.* **1.** *sport* muff it. **2.** *pot.* sing out of tune.

skin *mp pl.* **-i** *l.* **-y** skinhead, skin.

skinąć *pf.* (*ręką*) beckon; (*głową*) nod; **skinąć na kogoś** beckon sb; **skinąłem, żeby wszedł** I beckoned him in.

skinienie *n.* (*ręką*) wave; (*głową*) nod; **być na (każde) czyjeś skinienie** be at sb's beck and call; **pojawić się jak** *l.* **jakby na skinienie czarodziejskiej różdżki** materialize *l.* appear out of nowhere.

skisnąć *pf.* **-snę -śniesz, -śnij, -snął** *l.* **-sł -sła -snęli** *l.* **-śli 1.** (*o mleku*) turn sour. **2.** (*o człowieku*) sink into sluggishness.

skit *mi sport* skeet, skeet shooting.

sklarować *pf.* **1.** (= *uczynić klarownym*) *t. chem.* clarify. **2.** *żegl.* clear. **~ się** *pf.* (= *ustać się*) settle.

sklasyfikować *pf.* **1.** classify. **2.** *szkoln.* (*ucznia*) award grades; *Br.* award marks.

sklasyfikowany *a.* classified, categorized; **sklasyfikowany na drugim miejscu** (*np. o zawodniku*) listed second.

skląć *pf.* **sklnę sklniesz, sklnij** curse.

sklecić *pf.* **-cę -cisz** rig up, throw together; **nic sensownego w tej chwili nie sklecę** *pot.* I won't get up anything sensible at the moment.

skleić *pf.* **skleję skleisz, sklejać** *ipf.* glue together, stick together. **~ się** *pf.*, **sklejać się** *ipf.* get stuck together; **oczy mi się sklejają ze zmęczenia** my eyes are heavy with sleep.

sklejarka *f. Gen.pl.* **-ek** (*do taśmy filmowej*) splicer.

sklejka *f. Gen.pl.* **-ek 1.** (*płyta*) plywood. **2.** *film* splice.

sklep *mi* store; *Br.* shop; **sklep mięsny** butcher's store *l.* shop; **sklep odzieżowy** clothes store *l.* shop; **sklep spożywczy** grocer's store *l.* shop, grocery; **prowadzić sklep** keep a store *l.* shop.

sklepać *pf.* **-pię -piesz** (= *spłaszczyć*) hammer flat, flatten; **sklepać komuś michę** *pot.* beat the living shit out of sb.

sklepiać *ipf.*, **sklepić** *pf. bud.* vault. **~ się** *ipf.*, **sklepić się** *pf. bud.* vault.

sklepienie *n.* **1.** *bud.* vault; **sklepienie beczkowe** *l.* **kolebkowe** barrel vault, wagon vault, tunnel vault; **sklepienie gwiaździste** *l.* **gwiazdowe** stellar vault; **sklepienie klasztorne** cloister vault; **sklepienie krzyżowe** groin vault; **sklepienie krzyżowo-żebrowe** rib vault; **sklepienie nieckowe** trough vault; **sklepienie sieciowe** net vault; **sklepienie wachlarzowe** fan vault; **sklepienie zwierciadlane** cavetto vault. **2.** *anat.* fornix; **sklepienie czaszki** calvaria, skullcap; **sklepienie stopy** arch of the foot. **3.** (*niebieskie*) firmament; *poet.* canopy of heaven.

sklepik *mi* small store; *Br.* small shop.

sklepikarka *f. Gen.pl.* **-ek** storekeeper; *Br.* shopkeeper.

sklepikarski *a.* storekeeper's; *Br.* shopkeeper's; (*o mentalności*) (= *chciwy*) mercenary.

sklepikarz *mp* storekeeper; *Br.* shopkeeper.

sklepowa *f. Gen.* **-ej** salesclerk; *Br.* shop assistant.

sklepowy *a.* (*o ladzie, wystawie, szyldzie*) store; *Br.* shop; **dzielnica sklepowa** shopping district; **wystawa sklepowa** shop window; **złodziej sklepowy** shoplifter.

sklepywać *ipf. zob.* **sklepać.**

sklerotyczny *a.* **1.** *pat.* sclerotic. **2.** *uj., obelż.* senile.

sklerotyk *mp* **1.** *pat.* patient with arteriosclerosis. **2.** *uj., obelż.* (= *ktoś zdziecinniały*) senile person; (= *ktoś roztargniony*) forgetful person.

skleroza *f.* **1.** *pat.* (= *stwardnienie*) sclerosis; (= *stwardnienie tętnic*) arteriosclerosis. **2.** *uj., obelż.* (= *zdziecinnienie*) senility; (= *roztargnienie*) forgetfulness.

skład *mi* **1.** (*budynek*) warehouse, storehouse; (*pomieszczenie*) storeroom, store; (*węgla, drzewa, opału*) yard; **skład amunicji** ammunition dump, ammunition depot; **mieć coś na składzie** have sth in store *l.* stock. **2.** (*składniki*) makeup, composition; (*drużyny*) lineup; (*komisji, delegacji*) makeup; **skład pociągu** train set; **Skład Apostolski** *rel.* Apostles' Creed; **w pełnym/niepełnym składzie** at full strength/below strength; **(robić coś) bez ładu i składu** (do sth) without rhyme or reason; **wchodzić w skład czegoś** be part of sth, be included in sth. **3.** *druk.* typesetting; **skład komputerowy** computer typesetting. **4.** *chem.* (*np. leku, krwi*) composition.

składacz *mp Gen.pl.* **-y** *l.* **-ów** *druk.* typesetter, compositor.

składać *ipf.* **1.** (*zginać*) (*kartkę, prześcieradło, ubranie, leżak, scyzoryk, parasol*) fold; (*parasol*) furl; (*ręce, np. do modlitwy*) clasp. **2.** (*zmontować*) (*silnik, mebel, model samolotu*) put together, assemble; (*złamaną rękę, nogę*) set, adjust. **3.** (*kłaść*) (*węgiel, towar*) store; **składać broń** lay down one's arms; **składać jaja** lay eggs; **składać kogoś do grobu** *lit.* consign sb to the grave; **złożyć pocałunek na czyichś ustach** seal sb's lips with a kiss. **4.** (*dawać, ofiarować*) submit; **składać coś w depozyt** deposit sth; **składać kaucję za kogoś** post *l.* put up *l.* stand bail for sb; **składać**

komuś hołd pay homage to sb; **składać komuś wizytę** pay sb a visit; **składać komuś życzenia** extend *l.* offer one's wishes to sb; **składać do druku** send to press; **składać kwiaty na czyimś grobie** put flowers on sb's grave; **składać wieniec** lay a wreathe; **składać meldunek** give a report; **składać ofertę** *ekon.* put in a tender (*na coś* for sth); **składać oświadczenie** make *l.* issue a statement; **składać wniosek o coś** apply for sth; **składać zeznania** testify, give evidence; **składać pieniądze na nowy samochód** save money *l.* save up for a new car; **składać pieniądze w banku** deposit money in a bank; **składać podpis** put *l.* affix one's signature; **składać podziękowania** express thanks, give one's thanks; **składać prośbę** file *l.* submit a request; **składać przysięgę** take *l.* swear an oath; **składać skargę** file *l.* lodge a complaint (*na kogoś / coś* against sb/about sth); **składać swój los w czyjeś ręce** put one's fate in sb's hands; **składać życie na ołtarzu ojczyzny** sacrifice one's life for one's homeland. **5.** *druk.* typeset. **~ się** *ipf.* **1.** (= *być elementem*) consist (*z kogoś / czegoś* of sb/sth); **dzisiejszy obiad składa się z dwóch dań** today's dinner consists of two courses; **na program koncertu złożą się utwory Mozarta i Bacha** the program of the concert will include compositions by Mozart and Bach; **składa się na to wiele przyczyn** many factors are involved here. **2.** (*np. o krześle, leżaku*) fold up, fold; **ten scyzoryk składa się z trudem** it's difficult to fold this penknife. **3.** (= *brać udział w składce*) *pot.* chip in. **4.** (= *przyjąć pozycję*) take position, get ready; **składać się do strzału** take aim. **5. dobrze/źle się składa, że...** it's fortunate/unfortunate that...; **tak się składa, że...** as it turns out...

składak *mi Gen.* **-a** *pot.* **1.** (*o rowerze*) folding bike. **2.** (*o kajaku*) inflatable kayak. **3.** (*o samochodzie*) (*wykonany samodzielnie*) self-made car; (*przerobiony*) customized car.

składanka *f. Gen.pl.* **-ek** *pot.* (*utworów*) medley, miscellany.

składankowy *a.* (*o programie, filmie*) miscellaneous.

składany *a.* **1.** (*o rowerze, fotelu, wędce*) folding, fold-up, collapsible; (*o łóżku*) foldaway. **2.** (*o programie widowiska l. słuchowiska*) miscellaneous.

składarka *f.* folding machine; *druk.* typesetting machine.

składka *f. Gen.pl.* **-ek 1.** (= *składanie się*) contribution, subscription; **składka członkowska** membership fee; **składka dobrowolna** voluntary contribution; **składka publiczna** public collection; **składka ubezpieczeniowa** insurance premium; **wybudowany ze składek publicznych** raised by public subscription. **2.** (= *zrzutka*) *pot.* whip-round.

składkowy *a.* subscription; **fundusz składkowy** subscription fund; **impreza składkowa** (*na którą każdy przynosi własne jedzenie*) *pot.* potluck party; (*na którą każdy przynosi coś do picia*) *pot.* BYOB party, bring-your-own-booze party; **przy-**

jęcie składkowe (*za wspólne fundusze*) subscription party.

składnia *f. Gen.pl.* **-i** *jęz.* syntax; **składnia czasownika** syntax of the verb.

składnica *f.* (= *skład, magazyn*) storehouse, depot; **składnica księgarska** book repository; **składnica złomu** scrapyard.

składnie *adv.* **1.** (= *porządnie*) neatly, in an orderly fashion. **2.** (= *sprawnie*) efficiently.

składnik *mi Gen.* **-a 1.** (*część, element*) component, constituent; (*potrawy*) ingredient; **składnik główny/uboczny** *chem.* major/minor constituent; **składnik pokarmowy** nutrient. **2.** *mat.* element.

składniowy *a. jęz.* syntactic, syntactical.

składny *a.* **1.** (= *porządny*) neat, orderly. **2.** (= *sprawny*) efficient.

składowa *f. Gen.* **-ej** *mat.* (*wektora, zbioru*) component; (*zbioru*) constituent.

składować *ipf.* store.

składowanie *n.* storing; **składowanie odpadów** waste disposal.

składowe *n.* (= *opłata za składowanie*) storage charges.

składowisko *n.* storage yard.

składowy *a.* **1.** (*o elemencie, części*) component, constitutive. **2.** (*o placu, powierzchni, pomieszczeniu*) storage.

składzik *mi Gen.* **-a** *l.* **-u 1.** (*budynek*) small storehouse. **2.** (*pomieszczenie*) storeroom.

skłamać *pf.* **-mię -miesz** tell a lie, lie; **żeby nie skłamać** to be honest, frankly speaking.

skłaniać *ipf.* **1.** (*wpływać*) induce, persuade (*kogoś do zrobienia czegoś* sb to do sth). **2.** *lit.* (*pochylać*) bow, lower; **skłaniać głowę przed kimś/czymś** *przen.* bow one's head before sb/sth; **nie mieć gdzie głowy skłonić** have nowhere to lay one's head, be homeless. **~ się** *ipf.* **1.** (= *przychylać się*) (= *mieć skłonność*) incline, lean (*do czegoś* to sth); **to nie skłania mnie do przyznania ci racji** that does not incline me to agree with you; **Robert skłania się ku materializmowi** Robert inclines towards materialism. **2.** (= *pokłonić się*) bow (*komuś* to sb). **3.** *lit.* (= *obniżać się*) lower; **słońce skłaniało się ku zachodowi** the sun was coming down.

skłębić się *pf.* billow.

skłon *mi* **1.** (*głowy*) nod; (= *ukłon*) bow. **2.** *sport* bend. **3.** (*nachylenie*) slope, declivity.

skłonić *pf. zob.* **skłaniać.** **~ się** *pf. zob.* **skłaniać się.**

skłonność *f.* **1.** (= *predyspozycja*) tendency (*do czegoś* to sth); inclination (*do czegoś* for *l.* to *l.* towards sth); **skłonność do tycia** tendency to get fat. **2.** (= *podatność*) susceptibility (*do czegoś* to sth); **skłonność do chorób** susceptibility to disease. **3.** (= *pociąg*) penchant (*do czegoś* for sth).

skłonny *a.* **1.** (= *podatny*) prone, susceptible; **skłonny do chorób** susceptible *l.* prone to disease. **2.** (= *chętny*) willing, inclined; **skłonny do bójki** ready to fight; **skłonny do gniewu** quick-tempered; **skłonny do kompromisu** willing to compromise; **skłonny do płaczu** given to crying; **skłonny do podejrzeń** open to suspicion; **skłonny do ustępstw** yielding, compliant; **być skłonnym coś zrobić** be willing to do sth; **nie być skłonnym czegoś zrobić** be unwilling *l.* reluctant to do sth; **jestem skłonny zgodzić się z tym, co mówiłeś na zebraniu** I'm inclined to agree with what you were saying at the meeting.

skłócać *ipf.*, **skłócić** *pf.* **1.** (= *antagonizować*) divide; **kwestia kary śmierci głęboko skłóciła członków partii** the issue of capital punishment deeply divided the party. **2.** (= *zmieszać*) stir; (= *wymieszać*) mix (*coś z czymś* sth with sth).

skłuć *pf.* (*nożem*) stab all over; (*igłą*) prick all over.

sknera *f. l. mp decl. like f. Gen.pl.* **-r** *l.* **-rów** *uj., pot.* scrooge, skinflint.

sknerstwo *n. uj., pot.* miserliness, stinginess.

sknocić *pf. pot.* botch up.

skobel *mi* **-bl-** *Gen.* **-a** staple.

skoczek *mp* **-czk-** *pl.* **-owie** *sport* jumper; **skoczek spadochronowy** parachutist. — *ma* **-czk-** *pl.* **-i** **1.** *zw. pl. ent.* leafhopper (*Cicadellidae l. Jassidae*). **2.** *zw. pl. zool.* jerboa (*Dipodidae*); **skoczek egipski** desert jerboa (*Jaculus jaculus*). — *mi* **-czk-** *Gen.* **-a** *pl.* **-i** *szachy* knight.

skocznia *f. Gen.pl.* **-i** *narciarstwo* **skocznia narciarska** hill, ski jump; **skocznia mamucia** flying hill; **Turniej Czterech Skoczni** the Four Hills Tournament.

skocznie *adv.* in a lively fashion.

skoczność *f.* **1.** (*tańca, muzyki*) liveliness. **2.** *sport* jumping ability.

skoczny *a.* **1.** (*o tańcu, muzyce*) lively. **2.** (*o zawodniku, koniu*) showing great ability to jump. **3.** (= *służący do skakania*) saltatorial, saltatory; **odnóża skoczne** *ent.* saltatorial legs.

skoczogonki *pl. ent.* collembolans (*Collembola*).

skoczyć *pf.* **1.** *zob.* **skakać. 2.** *pot.* (= *pobiec w jakimś celu, po coś*) pop out, nip out; **skoczyć po kogoś/coś** go and get sb/sth; **skoczyć na równe nogi** jump *l.* spring *l.* leap to one's feet; **skoczyć po rozum do głowy** use one's head; **możesz mi skoczyć!** *pot.* I don't give a damn!

skodyfikować *pf.* codify.

skojarzenie *n.* association; **wywoływać skojarzenia** call up associations.

skojarzeniowy *a. psych.* associative, association; **pamięć skojarzeniowa** associative memory; **test skojarzeniowy** association test; **uczenie skojarzeniowe** associative learning.

skojarzyć *pf.* **1.** (*fakty*) associate. **2.** (*małżeństwo*) match. ~ **się** *pf.* **1.** (*o faktach*) make think; **skojarzyło mi się to z...** it made me think of... **2.** (*w parę*) become a couple.

skok *mi* **1.** (*w górę, w dół*) jump, leap; (= *przeskok*) skip; **skok w dal** long jump; **skok wzwyż** high jump; **skok o tyczce** pole-vault; **skoki do wody** diving; **skoki narciarskie** ski-jumping; **skoki spadochronowe** parachuting; **skok w bok** one-night stand; **jednym skokiem** in a leap. **2.** (*nagła zmiana, np. cen*) (*w górę*) leap; (*w dół*) drop, slump; **wielkimi skokami** (*np. o postępie*) by leaps and bounds. **3.** *sl.* (= *napad rabunkowy*)

stick-up. **4.** *orn.* tarsus. **5.** *zw. pl. myśl.* hare's leg. **6.** *techn.* stroke, pitch; **skok gwintu** pitch of thread, lead of thread; **skok tłoka** piston stroke, piston travel.

skokietować *pf.* **skokietować kogoś** turn sb's head.

skokochron *mi* jumping sheet.

skokowy *a.* **1.** (= *dotyczący skoku*) jump; **narty skokowe** jumping skis; **kość skokowa** *anat.* astragalus, talus; *pot.* anklebone. **2.** (= *niejednostajny*) stepwise; **ruch skokowy** stepwise movement. **3.** *techn.* stroke; **pojemność skokowa silnika** engine cubic capacity.

skoksować *pf. chem.* coke.

skolacjonować *pf. form.* collate.

skolekcjonować *pf.* collect.

skolektywizować *pf.* collectivize.

skoligacony *a. przest.* connected by marriage.

skolioza *f. pat.* scoliosis.

skolonizować *pf.* colonize.

skołatany *a.* (*biedą, chorobą, kłopotami*) troubled, harassed.

skołowacieć *pf.* **1.** (= *zdrętwieć*) (*o języku*) stiffen; (*o kończynie*) go numb. **2.** *przen.* (*o człowieku*) be stupefied.

skołować *pf. pot.* **1.** (= *zdezorientować*) baffle. **2.** (= *zdobyć*) wangle.

skołowany *a.* (*np. sprzecznymi informacjami*) confused, baffled.

skołtunić *pf. pot.* (*włosy, sierść*) tangle, mat. ~ **się** *pf. pot.* (*o włosach, sierści*) get tangled, get matted.

skołtunieć *pf. pot.* become backward.

skomasować *pf.* integrate, consolidate.

skombinować *pf. pot.* (= *zdobyć, załatwić*) wangle.

skomentować *pf.* (= *zinterpretować*) (*np. dzieło literackie*) (= *zrobić przytyk*) comment (*coś* on sth).

skomercjalizować *pf. zw. uj.* commercialize. ~ **się** *pf. zw. uj.* become commercialized.

skomleć, skamlać *ipf.* **-lę -lisz** *l.* **-lesz, -lij** *l.* **-l, -leli** *l.* **-lali, skomlić** *ipf.* **-ij 1.** (*o psie*) whine; (*zwł. z bólu*) yelp. **2.** (*o osobie*) (= *prosić*) (= *skarżyć się, narzekać*) whine, moan (*o coś* for sth).

skompensować *pf.* **1.** *biol., fiz.* compensate (*coś* for sth). **2.** *lit.* compensate, make up (*coś* for sth); **skompensować stratę** compensate a loss.

skompilować *pf.* compile.

skompletować *pf.* (*listę*) compile; (*załogę*) assemble.

skomplikować *pf.* complicate. ~ **się** *pf.* complicate, get complicated.

skomplikowany *a.* **1.** (= *trudny do rozwiązania*) complicated; (= *zawiły*) complex; (= *wyszukany, wymyślny*) (*o mechanizmie, argumentach*) sophisticated. **2.** (*o złamaniu*) complicated.

skomponować *pf.* (*muzykę, obraz*) compose.

skompromitować *pf.* discredit. ~ **się** *pf.* compromise o.s., disgrace o.s.

skomputeryzować *pf.* computerize.

skomputeryzowany *a.* computerized.

skomunikować *pf.* (= *skontaktować*) put in

touch; **skomunikować kogoś z kimś** put sb in touch with sb. ~ **się** *pf.* (= *skontaktować się*) get in touch (*z kimś* with sb).

skomunikowany *a.* (*np. o pociągu*) connecting.

skomunizować *pf. polit.* communize.

skonać *pf. lit.* decease; **skonać ze śmiechu** die of laughter; **niech skonam!** I'll be damned!

skonany *a. pred. pot.* dog-tired, bushed.

skoncentrować *pf.* **1.** (= *skupić*) (*uwagę, wysiłki*) concentrate, focus; (= *zebrać*) (*myśli, siły*) collect, gather; **skoncentrował swoją uwagę na temacie** he focused *l.* concentrated his attention on the subject. **2.** (*rozmieścić*) (*wojsko*) gather, assemble; (*przemysł*) accumulate, concentrate. **3.** *biol., chem.* (= *zagęścić, skondensować*) condense, concentrate. ~ **się** *pf.* **1.** (= *być skupionym w jednym miejscu*) center, *Br.* centre (*gdzieś* around sth). **2.** (= *skierować całą uwagę na coś*) concentrate, focus. **3.** *biol., chem.* (= *zgęstnieć, skondensować się*) condense, concentrate.

skoncentrowany *a.* (= *skupiony*) concentrated.

skondensować *pf.* condense.

skondensowany *a.* **1.** (*np. o mleku*) condensed. **2.** (*o treści, tekście*) concise, succinct.

skonfiskować *pf.* confiscate.

skonfrontować *pf.* **1.** (= *zestawić, porównać*) confront. **2.** *prawn.* (*świadków*) confront.

skonkretyzować *pf.* specify. ~ **się** *pf.* take shape.

skonsolidować *pf.* consolidate. ~ **się** *pf.* consolidate.

skonstatować *pf. lit.* (= *odkryć*) discover; (= *dojść do wniosku*) conclude; (= *ustalić*) determine.

skonsternować *pf. lit.* disconcert, dismay. ~ **się** *pf.* (= *stropić się*) become disconcerted.

skonstruować *pf.* **1.** (= *wykonać*) construct, build; (*z części*) assemble. **2.** (= *zaprojektować*) design.

skonsultować *pf.* consult (*coś z kimś* sth with sb). ~ **się** *pf.* consult (*z kimś* sb).

skonsumować *pf. form.* consume.

skontaktować *pf.* put in touch; **skontaktować kogoś z kimś** put sb in touch with sb. ~ **się** *pf.* get in touch (*z kimś* with sb); contact (*z kimś* sb).

skontrastować *pf.* put in contrast; **skontrastować coś z czymś** contrast sth with sth.

skontrolować *pf.* (= *zrobić badanie kontrolne, zbadać*) check up, control; run a check; **skontrolować nowych pracowników** run a check on new employees.

skontrować *pf.* **1.** (*atak*) counter (*coś* sth); (*atak słowny*) retort (*coś* to sth). **2.** *karty* double. **3.** *boks, piłka nożna* counter.

skontrum *n. sing. indecl. pl.* **-ra** *Gen.* **-rów** *ekon.* audit.

skonwencjonalizować *pf.* conventionalize.

skończenie *n.* (= *koniec, kres*) end; **aż do skończenia świata** till the end of the world, till doomsday. – *adv.* absolutely, perfectly; **skończenie piękna kobieta** perfectly beautiful woman.

skończoność *f.* **1.** (*cecha*) *form.* finiteness. **2.** (= *doskonałość*) *przest.* perfection.

skończony *a.* **-eni 1.** (= *absolutny, całkowity*) absolute, perfect, utter; **skończone bzdury** sheer *l.* utter nonsense; **skończony głupiec** complete *l.* utter fool; **skończona piękność** absolute *l.* perfect beauty. **2.** (= *bez przyszłości*) finished; **jesteś skończony** *pot.* you're finished, you're a goner. **3.** (= *wykwalifikowany, dyplomowany*) (*o lekarzu, prawniku*) fully fledged, qualified.

skończyć *pf.* (= *zakończyć, ukończyć*) end, finish; **skończyć pracę** finish work; **skończyć studia** complete one's studies, finish one's studies; graduate from university *l.* college *l.* polytechnic; **skończyć szkołę** graduate from school; **skończyć w więzieniu** end up in prison; **skończyć z piciem** give up drinking; **skończyć z kimś** (= *zerwać z kimś*) be through with sb; (= *zabić kogoś*) *pot.* do sb in, do away with sb; **skończyć ze sobą** put an end to one's life, put an end to o.s.; **źle skończyć** *pot.* come to a sticky end *l.* bad end; **kłótnia skończyła się łzami** the argument ended in tears; **począwszy od..., skończywszy na...** from... down to...; **w tym roku skończyłem 35 lat** I turned 35 this year; **sprawa skończona!** it's over!, that's the end!; **skończyłaś już?** are you through yet? ~ **się** *pf.* **1.** (= *dobiec do końca*) end, finish; **skończyć się niepowodzeniem** end in failure; **jej cierpliwość się skończyła** her patience has given out; **jego małżeństwo skończyło się na niczym** his marriage has come to nothing; **wakacje się skończyły** holidays are over; **wszystko skończyło się tym, że zgodził się na nowy projekt** it ended up with his accepting the new project. **2.** (= *wyczerpać się*) run out; **skończyła nam się pasta do zębów** we've run out of toothpaste. **3.** (*o artyście, pisarzu*) wear o.s. out, be finished.

skoordynować *pf.* coordinate.

skop *ma roln.* wether.

skopać *pf.* **-pię -piesz 1.** *zob.* **skopywać**. **2.** *pot.* (*zbić*) kick repeatedly. **3.** (= *źle coś zrobić*) *pot.* botch up, bungle.

skopek *mi* **-pk-** *Gen.* **-a 1.** *hist.* (*naczynie*) pail. **2.** (*miara, zawartość naczynia*) pailful; **skopek mleka** pailful of milk.

skopiować *pf.* copy, reproduce.

skopywać *ipf.* **1.** (*ziemię*) dig; **skopywać ogród** dig one's garden. **2.** (*koc, kołdrę*) kick off.

skorcić *pf.* tempt.

skorek *ma* **-rk-** *ent.* (= *owad z rzędu Dermaptera*) earwig.

skoro *conj.* **1.** (= *ponieważ*) since, as; **skoro już jesteś tutaj,...** since you are here anyway,..., now that you are here,... **2.** (= *jeśli*) if; **skoro tak uważasz, nie będę cię już przekonywał** if that is your opinion I won't convince you any more. **3.** (= *gdy tylko*) as soon as; **skoro świt** at the break of the day, at daybreak.

skorodować *pf.* corrode.

skoroszyt *mi* file.

skorowidz *mi* **1.** (= *indeks*) index. **2.** (*notes*) indexed notebook.

skorpion *ma* **1.** *zool.* (= *pajęczak z rzędu Scorpionida*) scorpion. **2. Skorpion** *astron.* Scorpius, Scorpio; *astrol.* Scorpio; *pot.* the Scorpion; **ona jest spod znaku Skorpiona** she was born under

Scorpio; **ona jest typowym Skorpionem** she is a typical Scorpio.

skorumpować *pf.* bribe, corrupt.

skorumpowany *a.* (*o policjancie, polityku*) corrupt.

skorupa *f.* **1.** (*orzecha, ślimaka*) shell; (*śniegowa, lodowa*) crust; **skorupa lodowa** crust of ice; (*np. na lodowcu*) icecap; **skorupa pocisku** *wojsk.* shell case; **skorupa ziemska** *geol.* the earth's crust. **2.** *przen.* shell, crust; **schować się w skorupie** retreat *l.* withdraw into one's shell; **wyjść ze swej skorupy** come out of one's shell. **3.** (*kawałek naczynia*) potsherd, potshard. **4.** *pot.* (*naczynie*) pot. **5.** *bot., zool.* (*ślimaka, żółwia, orzecha*) shell; (*żółwia, kraba, homara*) carapace.

skorupiak *ma zool.* (= *stawonóg z gromady Crustacea*) crustacean.

skorupiakowy *a.* crustacean, crustaceous.

skorupka *f. Gen.pl.* **-ek 1.** (*np. jajka, orzecha*) shell; **skorupka jajka** eggshell; **skorupka orzecha** nutshell; **obrać ze skorupki** (*np. jajko*) shell. **2.** (*z rozbitego naczynia*) potsherd; **czym skorupka za młodu nasiąknie, tym na starość trąci** *przen.* what is bred in the bone will never come out of the flesh; what youth is used to, age remembers; the cask savors of the first fill.

skorupkowy *a.* **sąd skorupkowy** *hist.* ostracism.

skory *a.* (= *skłonny*) willing; (= *gotów*) ready; (= *chętny*) eager; **skory do gniewu** quick to anger, bad-tempered; **skory do nauki** willing to learn; **skory do ofiar** ready to make sacrifices; **skory do płaczu** given to crying; **skory do pomocy** willing to help.

skorygować *pf.* correct.

skorzonera *f. bot.* black salsify (*Scorzonera hispanica*).

skorzystać *pf.* (*z telefonu, łazienki*) use; (*z okazji, sytuacji, ładnej pogody*) take advantage (*z czegoś* of sth); (*z prawa*) exercise; **skorzystać z czyjejś rady** take sb's advice; **skorzystać z prawa do głosowania** exercise one's right to vote; **skorzystać z zaproszenia** accept an invitation; **czy mogę skorzystać z telefonu?** may I use your phone?

skos *mi* **1.** (*tkanina*) piece of fabric cut on the bias; (*linia cięcia*) bias; **ciąć tkaninę na skos** cut fabric on the bias. **2.** (*powierzchnia*) slant, bevel, cant; **na** *l.* **w skos at** *l.* on a slant.

skosić *pf.* **-szę -sisz 1.** (*trawę*) mow. **2.** (*ludzi z karabinu*) mow down. **3.** *sl.* (= *zdobyć*) wangle. **4.** *sl.* (= *ukraść*) sneak.

skostniały *a.* **1.** (= *zdrętwiały*) (*o człowieku, kończynie*) stiff, numb; **skostniały z zimna** numb with cold. **2.** *geol.* fossilized. **3.** *biol.* ossified. **4.** *przen.* (= *tradycyjny, utrwalony*) (*o poglądach, zwrotach*) fossilized, ossified.

skostnieć *pf.* **1.** (*o człowieku, kończynie*) grow stiff, grow numb; **skostnieć z zimna** grow numb with cold. **2.** *biol.* (*o tkance*) ossify, become ossified. **3.** *geol.* fossilize, become fossilized. **4.** *przen.* (*o poglądach, zwrotach*) fossilize, become fossilized; ossify, become ossified.

skostnienie *n.* **1.** (*człowieka, kończyny*) numb-

ness. **2.** *biol.* ossification. **3.** *geol.* fossilization. **4.** *przen.* fossilization, ossification.

skoszarować *pf.* barrack.

skosztować *pf. lit.* taste, try.

skośnie *adv.* aslant, at *l.* on a slant.

skośnooki *a.* slant-eyed.

skośny *a.* (*o powierzchni, suficie, podłodze*) slanting, inclined; (*o oczach*) slanting; (*o falbanie, rękawie*) bias-cut; **ożaglowanie** *l.* **żagle skośne** *żegl.* fore-and-aft sails; **splot skośny** *tk.* twill weave.

skotłować *pf. pot.* swirl, whirl. ~ **się** *pf. pot.* swirl, whirl; (*o cieczy*) seethe.

skowronek *ma* **-nk-** *orn.* lark (*Alaudidae*); **skowronek polny** skylark (*Alauda arvensis*).

skowronkowy *a.* skylark's.

skowyczeć *ipf.* yelp.

skowyczenie *n.*, **skowyt** *mi* yelp.

skóra *f.* **1.** (*człowieka, zwierząt*) skin; (*zwierząt gruboskórnych*) hide; (*u zwierząt futerkowych*) pelt; **skóra właściwa** *anat.* corium, derma; **skóra i kości** *przen.* bag of bones, skin and bones; **kolor skóry** (= *karnacja*) complexion; **zapalenie skóry** *pat.* dermatitis; **być w czyjejś skórze** *przen.* be in sb's shoes; **czuć coś przez skórę** feel sth in one's bones; **dać komuś w skórę** *l.* przetrzepać komuś skórę** tan sb's hide; **dobrać się komuś do skóry** (= *zbić*) tan sb's hide; *przen.* crack *l.* clasp down on sb; **dostać w skórę** have one's hide tanned, get a beating; **doświadczyć czegoś na własnej skórze** learn *l.* find out sth the hard way; **mieć cienką skórę** *przen.* have a thin skin, be thin-skinned; **mieć grubą** *l.* **twardą skórę** *przen.* have a thick skin, be thick-skinned; **obdzierać kogoś ze skóry** *przen., sl.* rip sb off; **ratować swoją skórę** save one's skin, save one's neck; **zdejmować skórę ze zwierzęcia** skin an animal; **krzyczy jakby go ze skóry obdzierali** he bawls as if he were flayed alive; **na wołowej skórze by nie spisał** it's too long a story; **nie chciałbym być w jego skórze** I wouldn't like to be in his shoes; **nie dziel skóry na niedźwiedziu** don't count your chickens before they are hatched; catch the bear before you sell his skin; **skóra mi cierpnie na myśl o nim** thinking of him gives me the creeps; **skóra mi schodzi z twarzy** my face peels; **tu chodzi o jego skórę** his life is at stake; **wyskakiwać** *l.* wychodzić *l.* wyłazić ze skóry, żeby coś zrobić** *przen.* bend over backwards to do sth; **zajść** *l.* zaleźć komuś za skórę** *przen.* get under sb's skin. **2.** (*po wygarbowaniu, wyprawieniu*) leather; **sztuczna skóra** artificial leather; *Br. t.* leatherette. **3.** (*owocu*) skin; (*chleba*) crust. **4.** *pot.* (*kurtka*) leather jacket; (*płaszcz*) leather coat.

skórka *f. Gen.pl.* **-ek 1.** (*u człowieka* l. *zwierzęcia*) skin; (*u zwierzęcia futerkowego*) pelt; **gęsia skórka** goose flesh, goose pimples, goose bumps, goose skin. **2.** (*przy paznokciu*) cuticle. **3.** (= *zadzior przy paznokciu*) hangnail, agnail. **4.** *bot.* epidermis. **5.** (*chleba*) crust; (*cytryny, pomarańczy, banana*) peel; (*winogrona, ziemniaka, banana*) skin; (*melona, pomarańczy, cytryny*) rind; **obierać ze skórki** peel, skin. **6.** (*po wygarbowa-*

niu, wyprawieniu) leather; (*np. na futro*) pelt; **skórka niewarta wyprawki** it's worth no efforts; **dostaję gęsiej skórki na myśl o nim** I get gooseflesh just thinking about him.

skórkowy *a.* (*np. o rękawiczkach, oprawie notesu*) leather.

skórnik *ma pl.* **-i** *ent.* dermestid (*Dermestes*). – *mp pl.* **-cy** 1. *pot.* (*lekarz*) dermatologist. 2. *przest.* (*= garbarz*) tanner.

skórny *a.* dermatological; skin.

skóropodobny *a.* leather-like, leatherette.

skórować *ipf. techn.* flay.

skórzany *a.* leather.

skórzasty *a. bot.* coriaceous; **liść skórzasty** coriaceous leaf.

skra *f. Gen.pl.* **skier** *poet.* spark.

skracać *ipf.* 1. (*długość*) shorten; **skrócić kogoś o głowę** *pot.* behead sb. 2. (*czas*) while (away). 3. (*= zredukować*) shorten; (*np. książkę, słownik*) abridge, abbreviate; **skrócić artykuł do 3 stron** shorten *l.* cut down the paper to 3 pages; **skrócić sobie drogę** take a short cut; **skrócić ułamek** *mat.* cancel a fraction. ~ **się** *ipf.* become shorter.

skradać się *ipf.* sneak, slink.

skraj *mi Gen.pl.* **-ów** (*= krawędź*) edge; (*= granica*) border; (*= brzeg*) brink, verge; **na skraju miasta** on the outskirts of the city; **być na skraju nędzy** be on the brink of poverty; **pójść za kimś na skraj świata** follow sb to the ends of the Earth.

skrajnie *adv.* extremely, radically; **skrajnie odmienny** radically different.

skrajnik *mi Gen.* **-a** *żegl.* **skrajnik dziobowy** forepeak; **skrajnik rufowy** lazarette, afterpeak.

skrajność *f.* extremity; **popadać z jednej skrajności w drugą** go from one extreme to the other.

skrajny *a.* (*= radykalny*) extreme, radical; (*= najdalszy*) utmost; **skrajna nędza** extreme poverty; **skrajne poglądy** radical views.

skrapiać *ipf.* (*= opryskiwać*) sprinkle.

skraplacz *mi Gen.* **-a** *techn.* liquefier, condenser.

skraplać *ipf.* liquefy, condense. ~ **się** *ipf.* liquefy, condense.

skraplarka *f. Gen.pl.* **-ek** *techn.* condensing unit.

skraść *pf.* **skradnę skradniesz, skradnij, skradł** steal (*coś komuś* sb sth).

skrawać *ipf. techn.* machine.

skrawanie *n. techn.* machine cutting, machining; **obróbka skrawaniem** machining.

skrawek *mi* **-wk-** *Gen.* **-a** (*kartki, tkaniny*) scrap; (*nieba, lądu*) patch.

skreślać *ipf.* 1. (*= przekreślać*) cross out, strike off; (*= usuwać*) delete. 2. *lit.* (*= pisać*) write; jot down, put down; (*= rysować*) draw.

skreślenie *n.* 1. (*= wykreślenie*) crossing out. 2. (*= usunięcie*) deletion.

skreślić *pf. zob.* **skreślać**.

skretynieć *pf. pot.* become a total moron *l.* idiot.

skrewić *pf. pot.* let down, fail.

skręcać *ipf.,* **skręcić** *pf.* 1. (*zespalać*) screw together. 2. (*pleść*) weave, twine. 3. (*zwijać*)

twist, roll; **skręcać papierosa** roll a cigarette. 4. (*noge*) sprain; **skręcić kark** break one's neck; **skręca mnie z głodu** I'm starving. 5. (*= zmienić kierunek*) turn; **skręcić w prawo/w lewo** turn right/left; **skręcić w drugą ulicę w prawo** take the second turn to the right. ~ **się** *ipf.,* **skręcić się** *pf.* 1. (*= zwijać się*) get twisted, get coiled; **kiszki mi się skręcają z głodu** I'm starving. 2. (*= wić się*) writhe, convulse; **skręcać się z bólu** writhe in pain; **skręcać się ze śmiechu** convulse with laughter; **skręcać się z ciekawości** *przen.* burn with curiosity; **skręcać się z zazdrości** *przen.* feel fierce jealousy.

skrępować *pf.* 1. (*= związać*) tie up. 2. *przen.* hamper.

skrępowanie *n.* 1. (*= ograniczenie*) restraint, hindrance. 2. (*= zakłopotanie*) embarrassment.

skrępowany *a.* 1. (*= związany*) tied up. 2. (*= ograniczony*) hampered, impeded. 3. (*= zakłopotany*) embarrassed.

skręt *mi* 1. (*ruch*) turn; (*miejsce*) turn, bend; **skręt w lewo/w prawo** left/right turn; **skręt jelit** *l.* **kiszek** *pat.* intestinal volvulus *l.* torsion; **łagodny skręt rzeki** gentle bend of a river. 2. (*= zwój*) coil. – *mi Gen.* **-a** *pot.* (*papieros*) roll-your-own; (*z marihuany*) joint.

skrętny *a.* torsional.

skrętoległy *a. bot.* alternate.

skrętoskłon *mi sport* side bend.

skrobaczka *f. Gen.pl.* **-ek** 1. *techn.* scraper. 2. *med.* raspatory, rasp; abrasor. 3. (*przed wejściem*) footscraper.

skrobać *ipf.* **-bię -biesz** 1. (*= zdrapywać*) scrape off; **skrobać rybę** scale a fish; **skrobać ziemniaki** scrape potatoes; **każdy sobie rzepkę skrobie** each *l.* every man for himself (and the devil take the hindmost). 2. (*= drapać*) scratch. 3. *żart.* (*= pisać*) scribble. ~ **się** *ipf.* 1. (*= drapać się*) scratch o.s. 2. *tylko ipf.* (*na coś wysokiego*) climb (*na coś* up sth).

skrobak *mi Gen.* **-a** *techn.* scraper.

skrobanka *f. Gen.pl.* **-ek** *pot.* abortion.

skrobia *f. biol., chem.* starch.

skrobiowy *a.* starchy.

skrobnąć *pf.* **-ij** *zob.* **skrobać**. ~ **się** *pf.* **-ij** *zob.* **skrobać się**.

skrofuloza *f. pat.* scrofula.

skroić *pf.* **skroję skroisz, skrój** 1. (*usunąć*) cut off, remove. 2. (*wyciąć*) tailor, cut; **skroić sukienkę** cut fabric for a dress. 3. (*pokroić*) cut up, cut into pieces. 4. (*zbić*) flog. 5. *pot.* (*= obrabować*) rob (*kogoś z czegoś* sb of sth).

skrojony *a.* tailored, cut; **dobrze skrojony** well-tailored; **cały chleb jest już skrojony** the whole loaf (of bread) has been already cut into slices.

skrom *mi myśl.* fat (*especially hare's*).

skromnie *adv.* 1. (*= nieśmiało*) shyly, modestly; **skromnie się zachowywać** behave modestly, behave shyly. 2. (*= nie dbając o rozgłos*) modestly, unassumingly; **skromnie podziękować za zaszczyt** thank modestly for an honor. 3. (*= prosto, niewyszukanie*) simply, plainly; **ubierać się**

skromnie wear simple clothes. **4.** (= *niepokaź-nie, niewiele*) modestly, not much; **skromnie za-rabiać** not earn too much, have a meager income.

skromnisia *f. Voc.* **-u** *Gen.pl.* **-i** *l.* **-ś** *iron.* prissy woman *l.* girl.

skromniś *mp Gen.pl.* **-ów** *iron.* prissy man *l.* boy.

skromność *f.* **1.** (*w zachowaniu*) modesty, shyness. **2.** (= *brak zarozumiałości*) modesty, unassumingness; **nie mówić o swoim sukcesie przez skromność** not mention one's success out of modesty; **skromność posiłków** simplicity *l.* plainness of meals; **nie grzeszyć skromnością** be boastful.

skromny *a.* **1.** (= *nieśmiały*) shy, modest. **2.** (= *niedbający o rozgłos*) modest, unassuming; **skromny z natury** modest by nature. **3.** (= *prosty, niewyszukany*) simple, plain; **skromna uroczystość** simple *l.* quiet ceremony. **4.** (= *niezamożny*) poor; **skromny urzędnik państwowy** ordinary civil servant. **5.** (= *niepokaźny, niewielki*) meager, *Br.* meagre; not too big; **skromne zarobki** meager income.

skroniowy *a. anat.* temporal; **kość skroniowa** temporal bone; **płat skroniowy** temporal lobe.

skroń *f. pl.* **-e** temple; **mieć siwe skronie** have gray hair.

skropić (się) *pf. zob.* **skrapiać (się)**.

skroplić (się) *pf. zob.* **skraplać (się)**.

skrócić *pf. zob.* **skracać**.

skrócony *a.* shortened; abbreviated, a-bridged; **skrócona nazwa** abbreviated name; **skrócona sukienka** shortened dress; **skrócona wersja** (*encyklopedii, słownika itp.*) abridged version (*czegoś* of sth).

skrót *mi* **1.** (= *streszczenie*) summary; (= *skró-cenie, opuszczenie*) cut; **skrót myślowy** brachylo-gy; **skrót (najważniejszych) wiadomości** the headlines; **w (błyskawicznym** *l.* **telegraficznym) skrócie** in short. **2.** (= *krótsza droga*) short cut; **iść na skróty** *t. przen.* take a short cut. **3.** *jęz.* abbreviation. **4.** *tenis, badminton, piłka* drop shot. **5.** *sztuka* foreshortening.

skrótowiec *mi* **-wc-** *Gen.* **-a** *jęz.* acronym.

skrótowo *adv.* in short, in brief; **przedstawić coś skrótowo** present a summary of sth.

skrótowość *f.* brevity.

skrótowy *a.* brief, short; **skrótowy opis** brief *l.* short description, summary; **skrótowa relacja** brief *l.* short report, summary (*of facts l. events*).

skrucha *f.* repentance; **okazać skruchę za coś** repent of sth.

skrupiać się *ipf.*, **skrupić się** *pf.* **to się na mnie skrupi** I'll be the scapegoat; I'll bear the brunt.

skrupulant *mp*, **skrupulantka** *f. Gen.pl.* **-ek** scrupulous *l.* meticulous person.

skrupulatnie *adv.* (= *pedantycznie*) meticu-lously, scrupulously; (= *szczegółowo*) precisely, in detail.

skrupulatność *f.* (= *pedantyczność*) meticu-lousness, scrupulousness; (= *szczegółowość*) pre-cision.

skrupulatny *a.* **1.** (= *pedantyczny*) meticulous, scrupulous. **2.** (= *szczegółowy*) detailed, precise.

skrupuły *pl. Gen.* **-ów** scruples; **pozbawiony skrupułów** unscrupulous; **robić coś bez skrupu-łów** not have scruples about doing sth.

skruszeć *pf.* **1.** (*o murze, kamieniu, skale*) crumble. **2.** (*o mięsie*) become tender. **3.** (*o oso-bie*) soften; **jej opór skruszał** her resistance soft-ened.

skruszony *a.* **-eni** **1.** (*sypki*) crumbled. **2.** (= *wyrażający skruchę*) apologetic; **skruszona mina** apologetic look.

skruszyć *pf.* **1.** (= *rozdrobnić*) crush. **2.** (= *obudzić sumienie*) make show repentance. **~ się** *pf.* **1.** (= *być rozdrobnionym*) crumble, be crushed. **2.** (= *poczuć skruchę*) repent.

skrutacyjny *a.* **komisja skrutacyjna** *polit.* re-turning committee.

skrwawić *pf.* cover with blood; **skrwawić ko-muś serce** *przen.* make sb's heart bleed.

skryba *mp pl.* **-y** **1.** *hist.* scribe. **2.** *żart.* (*lite-rat*) scribe; (*urzędnik*) clerk, civil servant.

skrycie *adv.* secretly.

skryć (się) *pf.* **skryję skryjesz, skryj** *zob.* **skry-wać (się)**.

skrypt *mi* **1.** (*podręcznik*) textbook. **2.** *przest.* (= *pismo urzędowe*) official document; **skrypt dłużny** *handl., prawn.* (= *potwierdzenie zaciąg-nięcia długu*) debenture, debenture note; (= *obietnica zapłaty*) promissory note, note of hand.

skryptorium *n. sing. indecl. pl.* **-ria** *Gen.* **-riów** *hist.* scriptorium.

skrystalizować *pf. chem.* (= *sprecyzować*) crys-tallize. **~ się** *pf. chem.* (= *skonkretyzować się*) crystallize.

skrytka *f. Gen.pl.* **-ek** hiding place; *mot.* glove compartment; **skrytka głosowa** voice mail box; **skrytka pocztowa** post office box, P.O. box.

skrytobójca *mp lit.* assassinator.

skrytobójczo *adv.* **skrytobójczo zamordowany** *lit.* assassinated.

skrytobójczy *a. lit.* treacherous; **skrytobójczy mord** assassination; **skrytobójcza śmierć** death by assassination.

skrytobójstwo *n. lit.* assassination.

skrytopączkowy *a.* cryptophytic; **roślina skry-topączkowa** *bot.* cryptophyte.

skrytość *f.* secretiveness; **w skrytości serca** *l.* **ducha** in one's heart of hearts.

skryty *a.* **1.** (*o charakterze, człowieku*) secre-tive. **2.** (*o planach, zamiarach*) secret, clandes-tine; **najskrytsze marzenia** wildest dreams.

skrytykować *pf.* criticize.

skrywać *ipf.* **-am -asz** **1.** (= *ukrywać*) hide, con-ceal. **2.** (= *zasłaniać*) conceal, obscure. **3.** (= *za-tajać*) conceal, keep secret. **~ się** *ipf.* **1.** (= *ukry-wać się*) hide (out). **2.** (= *być zasłoniętym*) be concealed, be obscured; **słońce skryło się za ho-ryzontem** the sun passed below the horizon, the sun set.

skrzat *mp pl.* **-y** **1.** (*w bajkach*) brownie. **2.** *żart.* (= *dziecko*) sprat, tot.

skrzeczeć *pf.* -ę -ysz 1. (*o zwierzętach*) croak. 2. (*o człowieku*) screech.

skrzek *mi* 1. (*głos*) croak; screech. 2. *zool.* spawn.

skrzekliwy *a.* croaky, screechy.

skrzele *n. pl.* -a *l.* -e *Gen.* -i 1. *zool.* gill. 2. *lotn.* slat.

skrzelotchawka *f. Gen.pl.* -ek *zool.* spiracle.

skrzelowy *a. zool.* branchial.

skrzep *mi* 1. *med.* clot, coagulum. 2. *metal.* skull, bear.

skrzepnąć *pf.* -pnij, -pł *l.* -pnął -pła -pli 1. (= *stwardnieć*) set. 2. (= *zakrzepnąć*) (*o krwi*) clot, coagulate. 3. (= *zsiąść się*) curdle; (= *ściąć się*) set, curdle.

skrzepowy *a.* skrzepowe zapalenie żył *pat.* thrombophlebitis.

skrzesać *pf.* -szę -szesz (*ogień*) strike fire; (*iskry*) strike sparks.

skrzętnie *adv.* (= *zapobiegliwie*) providently; (= *sumiennie*) assiduously.

skrzętny *a.* (= *zapobiegliwy*) provident; (= *sumienny*) assiduous.

skrzyczeć *pf.* -ę -ysz scold, chide.

skrzyć się *pf.* -yj sparkle; rozmowa skrzyła się humorem *przen.* the conversation was full of humor.

skrzydełko *n. Gen.pl.* -ek 1. (= *małe skrzydło*) winglet; skrzydełko nosa *anat.* ala of a nose. 2. *techn.* blade, wing. 3. (*obwoluty*) flap. 4. *bot.* (*wyrostek na nasionach*) wing. 5. *bot.* (*u motylkowatych*) wing.

skrzydełkowy *a. techn.* blade; wing; nakrętka skrzydełkowa wing *l.* butterfly *l.* ear nut; pompa skrzydełkowa vane *l.* semi-rotary pump.

skrzydlak *mi Gen.* -a *bot.* samara, key fruit. – *ma icht.* eagle ray (*Myliobatis aquila*).

skrzydlaty *a.* winged.

skrzydło *n. Gen.pl.* -eł 1. *orn.* wing; być pod czyimiś skrzydłami be under sb's wing; dodawać komuś skrzydeł lend wings to sb; pędzić jak na skrzydłach run like the wind; podciąć *l.* spętać komuś skrzydła discourage sb, restrict sb's freedom of action; rozwinąć skrzydła (*do lotu*) spread one's wings; zwichnąć sobie skrzydła suffer a defeat; wziąć kogoś pod swoje skrzydła take sb under one's wing; skrzydła ci już opadły? you've already lost your heart? 2. *lotn.* wing. 3. *techn.* blade. 4. *bud.* (*budynku*) wing. 5. (*część składowa*) wing; skrzydło drzwi door leaf; skrzydło okna sash; skrzydło ołtarza altar wing. 6. *polit.* wing; skrzydło konserwatywne conservative wing, the conservatives; lewe/prawe skrzydło left/right wing. 7. *hist.* (*część zbroi husarskiej*) wing. 8. *sport* (*boiska*) wing; skrzydło królewskie *szachy* the king's side. 9. *wojsk.* (*w szyku bojowym*) wing, flank. 10. *wojsk.* (*oddział lotniczy*) wing.

skrzydłowiec *mi* -wc- *Gen.* -a *lotn.* ornithopter, orthopter.

skrzydłowy *a.* 1. *zool.* wing, alar. 2. *sport* wing. 3. *wojsk.* flank. – *mp* 1. *sport* winger, wing. 2. *myśl.* (*myśliwy*) wing hunter; (*naganiacz*) wing beater.

skrzykiwać *ipf.*, skrzyknąć *pf.* -ij muster, call

together. ~ się *ipf.*, skrzyknąć się *pf.* muster, get *l.* come together.

skrzynia *f.* 1. (*pudło*) chest, crate; skrzynia biegów *mot.* gear box; automatyczna skrzynia biegów *mot.* automatic transmission; pięciobiegowa skrzynia biegów *mot.* five-speed transmission; skrzynia gimnastyczna *sport* box; skrzynia inspektowa *ogr.* hotbed; skrzynia ładunkowa *mot.* loading platform. 2. (= *kufer*) chest, coffer.

skrzyniowy *a.* box.

skrzynka *f. Gen.pl.* -ek 1. (*pudło*) box; skrzynka na kwiaty window box; skrzynka na listy letter box. 2. *techn.* box, chest; czarna skrzynka *lotn.* black box, flight recorder.

skrzyp *mi* 1. (*odgłos*) creak. 2. *bot.* horsetail, scouring rush (*Equisetum*). – *int.* creak.

skrzypaczka *f. Gen.pl.* -ek *zob.* skrzypek.

skrzypce *pl. Gen.* -piec violin; pierwsze/drugie skrzypce *muz.* first/second violins; grać pierwsze skrzypce play first fiddle.

skrzypcowy *a.* vilion; klucz skrzypcowy *l.* wiolinowy treble *l.* violin clef.

skrzypek *mp* -pk- *pl.* -owie violinist; pierwszy skrzypek first violinist.

skrzypieć *ipf.* -ę -isz, skrzypnąć *pf.* -ij creak, squeak.

skrzywdzić *pf.* wrong, harm.

skrzywić *pf.* bend; (*prawdę, słowa*) twist; (*rzeczywistość, prawdę*) distort; skrzywić usta *l.* twarz make *l.* pull a face. ~ się *pf.* 1. (= *wykrzywić się*) bend. 2. (= *robić grymasy*) make *l.* pull a face. 3. (= *obruszyć się*) bridle (*na coś* at sth).

skrzywienie *n.* 1. (*wygięcie*) bend; skrzywienie zawodowe *pot.* professional bent. 2. *pat.* curvature; skrzywienie kręgosłupa curvature of the spine; boczne skrzywienie kręgosłupa lateral curvature of the spine, scoliosis. 3. (= *grymas*) wry face.

skrzyżny *a. sport* cross-legged.

skrzyżować *pf.* 1. (= *złożyć na krzyż*) cross; skrzyżować z kimś miecze *t. przen.* cross swords with sb. 2. *biol.* cross. ~ się *pf.* 1. cross, intersect; ich spojrzenia skrzyżowały się they exchanged glances. 2. *biol.* cross.

skrzyżowanie *n.* 1. (*rąk, nóg*) cross, crossing. 2. (*ulic*) intersection, junction. 3. (*prądów, kierunków*) intersection; na skrzyżowaniu cywilizacji at a point where two civilizations meet.

skserować *pf. zob.* kserować.

skubać *ipf.* -bię -biesz 1. (*wyrywać*) pluck; skubać kurczaka pluck a chicken; skubać kogoś z pieniędzy *pot.* (= *wyłudzać*) fleece sb. 2. (*chleb, trawę*) nibble. 3. (*szarpać*) pluck; skubać kogoś za rękaw pluck sb's sleeve. ~ się *ipf.* (*szarpać sobie coś*) pluck; skubał się po brodzie he was plucking his beard.

skubaniec *mp* -ńc- *pl.* -y *pot.* sun of a gun.

skubany *a. pot.* damn.

skubnąć *pf.* -ij *zob.* skubać. ~ się *pf. zob.* skubać się.

skucha *f. pot.* miss, error.

skuć *pf.* 1. *zob.* skuwać. 2. *pot.* (= *zbić*) beat up; skuć komuś mordę beat the shit out of sb. ~ się *pf. pot.* (= *upić się*) get stoned.

skudlić, skudłacić *pf.* (*włosy*) ruffle.

skulić *pf.* (*o głowie*) duck; (*o ramionach*) hunch, bend; **ze skulonym ogonem** (*o psie, kocie*) with its tail between its legs. **~ się** *pf.* shrink, cringe.

skumać się *pf. pot.* make friends (*z kimś* with sb).

skumbria *f. Gen.* **-ii** canned mackerel in tomato sauce.

skumulować *pf. zob.* **kumulować**.

skunks *ma zool.* striped skunk (*Mephitis mephitis*). *– mp pl.* **-y** *pog.* skunk.

skup *mi* **1.** (*kupowanie*) purchase, buying. **2.** (*miejsce*) purchasing center; **skup butelek** bottle return.

skupiać *ipf.*, **skupić** *pf.* **1.** (= *gromadzić*) assemble, gather; **soczewka skupiająca** *opt.* converging lens, focusing lens. **2.** (= *koncentrować*) concentrate, focus; **skupiać myśli** collect one's thoughts; **skupiać uwagę na czymś** focus on sth; **skupiać na sobie czyjąś uwagę** attract sb's attention. **~ się** *ipf.*, **skupić się** *pf.* **1.** (= *gromadzić się*) assemble, gather. **2.** (= *koncentrować się*) concentrate. **3.** (= *ogniskować się*) concentrate, focus.

skupić *pf.* **1.** *zob.* **skupiać**. **2.** *zob.* **skupować**.

skupienie *n.* **1.** *chem., fiz.* concentration; *min.* aggregate; **stan skupienia** state of aggregation. **2.** (*zbiorowisko*) gathering; concentration. **3.** (= *koncentracja*) concentration; **głębokie skupienie** deep concentration.

skupiony *a.* **-eni** (*o człowieku*) concentrated, focused; (*o wyrazie twarzy*) intent; (*o zabudowie*) dense.

skupisko *n.* cluster.

skupować *ipf.* (= *kupować*) buy, purchase; (= *odkupować*) buy back.

skupsztina, skupsztyna *f. polit.* the Skupstina.

skurcz *mi Gen.pl.* **-ów 1.** *fizj.* (= *ściągnięcie*) contraction; (*bolesny*) cramp; **skurcz mięśnia** muscular contraction; **skurcz serca** myocardial contraction, cardiac contraction; **skurcze porodowe** labor pains, *Br.* labour pains. **2.** *techn.* contraction, shrinkage.

skurczowy *a. med.* (*o ciśnieniu*) systolic; (*o leku*) contractile.

skurczybyk *mp pl.* **-i** *żart.* son of a gun.

skurczyć *pf.* shrink, contract. **~ się** *pf.* **1.** shrink, contract. **2.** *przen.* shrink, drop.

skurwysyn *mp pl.* **-y** *wulg.* son of a bitch.

skurwysyństwo *n. wulg.* roguery, sth despicable; **to, co jej zrobił, to prawdziwe skurwysyństwo** what he did to her is fucking despicable.

skusić *pf.* **skuszę skusisz 1.** (= *zwabić*) tempt; **skusiło mnie, żeby...** I was *l.* felt tempted to... **2.** *dziec.* (= *pomylić się*) make a mistake; (= *nie trafić*) miss. **~ się** *pf.* yield to the temptation; **skusiłem się na kawałek ciasta** I decided to eat a piece of cake.

skutecznie *adv.* efficiently, effectively, successfully.

skuteczność *f.* effectiveness, efficacy.

skuteczny *a.* effective, efficacious.

skutek *mi* **-tk-** result, effect; **skutek prawny** *prawn.* legal effect; **pożądany/niepożądany skutek** desired/adverse effect; **aż do skutku** to the bitter end; **bez skutku** to no effect; **na skutek czegoś** as a result of sth; **ze skutkiem** effectively, successfully; **doprowadzić coś do skutku** bring sth about; **dojść do skutku** come into effect; **nie dojść do skutku** not come into effect, come to nothing; **spotkanie nie doszło do skutku** the meeting didn't take place; **odnosić piorunujący skutek** have a dramatic effect; **ponosić skutki czegoś** bear the consequences of sth.

skuter *mi Gen.* **-a** motor scooter.

skutkować *ipf.* **1.** (= *być skutecznym*) work; be effective, be efficacious. **2.** *prawn.* take effect, lead to.

skutkowy *a.* **zdanie skutkowe** *gram.* consecutive clause.

skuwać *ipf.* **1.** (*łączyć w całość*) forge together, hammer together. **2.** (*o więźniu*) (*w kajdanki*) handcuff; (*w łańcuchy*) chain.

skuwka *f. Gen.pl.* **-ek** tip; (*metalowa*) ferrule; (*np. na sznurowadle*) aglet.

skwapliwie *adv.* (= *z zapałem*) eagerly; (= *z gotowością*) readily, willingly.

skwapliwość *f.* (= *zapał*) eagerness; (= *gotowość*) readiness, willingness.

skwapliwy *a.* (= *pełen zapału*) eager; (= *pełen gotowości*) ready, willing.

skwar *mi* heat, swelter.

skwarek *mi* **-rk-** *Gen.* **-a**, **skwarka** *f. Gen.pl.* **-ek** *kulin.* crackling.

skwarno *adv.* swelteringly, torridly.

skwarny *a.* sweltering, torrid.

skwasić *pf.* **skwaszę skwasisz** sour, put in a bad mood; **był jakiś taki skwaszony** he was in a bad mood or something.

skwaszony *a.* **skwaszona mina** sour face; **zrobić skwaszoną minę** pull a sour face.

skwaśnieć *pf.* **1.** (*o mleku i żywności*) go sour, turn sour; sour. **2.** (= *stać się ponurym*) sour.

skwer *mi* square.

skwierczeć *ipf.* **-ę -ysz** sizzle, frizzle.

skwitować *pf.* **1.** (= *pokwitować*) sign (*coś* for sth); acknowledge the receipt (*coś* of sth). **2.** (*podsumować*) react, reply; **skwitować coś uśmiechem** greet sth with a wry smile.

slab *mi metal.* slab.

slabing *mi metal.* **1.** (= *walcarka, zgniatacz*) slab mill. **2.** (= *walcownia*) slabbing mill.

slajd *mi* slide.

slalom *mi sport* slalom; **slalom gigant** giant slalom; **slalom specjalny** special slalom; **slalom równoległy** parallel slalom; **slalom kajakowy** kayak slalom, K-slalom.

slalomista *mp*, **slalomistka** *f. Gen.pl.* **-ek** *sport* Alpine skier.

slalomowy *a. sport* slalom, Alpine.

slang *mi jęz.* slang.

slangowy *a. jęz.* slang; **wyraz/powiedzenie slangowe** slang word/expression.

slawista *mp*, **slawistka** *f. Gen.pl.* **-ek** Slavicist.

slawistyczny *a.* Slavic.

slawistyka *f.* Slavic studies.

slawizm *mi jęz.* Slavism.

sliping *mi kol.* sleeping car.

slipy *pl. Gen.* **-ów** briefs.

slogan *mi* **1.** (*w reklamie, propagandzie*) slogan. **2.** (= *komunał*) commonplace, platitude.

sloganowy *a.* **1.** (*w reklamie, propagandzie*) slogan. **2.** (= *zawierający komunały*) commonplace, platitude.

slow-fox *mi Gen. i Acc.* **-a** (*taniec*) slow-fox.

slumsy *pl.* slums; **dzielnica slumsów** shantytown.

slup *mi żegl.* sloop.

słabeusz *mp Gen.pl.* **-ów** *pot.* weakling.

słabizna *f. pot.* **1.** (*rzecz*) poor stuff; **jego ostatnia powieść to słabizna** his last novel was really lousy. **2.** (*osoba*) loser; **słabizna z niego jako pisarz** he's a lousy writer. **3.** (= *słaba strona*) weak side, Achilles heel. **4.** (= *pachwina*) groin.

słabnąć *ipf.* **-nij, -bł** *l.* **-nął -bła -bli 1.** (= *tracić siły*) weaken, grow weak *l.* feeble; droop, flag. **2.** (= *tracić na sile*) decline, diminish, be on the decline, ebb; (*o burzy*) moderate, let up; (*o energii, zainteresowaniu, tendencji*) flag, sag; (*o nadziei, ochocie, więziach*) wither; (*o deszczu*) take off, let up; (*o wierze, uczuciu*) waver; (*o dźwięku*) die out; (*o świetle*) dim, die out; (*o wietrze, ruchu*) die down; (*o bólu, trudnościach*) ease off.

słabo *adv.* **1.** (= *niemocno*) weakly, feebly, faintly; **czuję się słabo** *l.* **słabo mi** I feel faint; **zrobiło mi się słabo** I came over dizzy *l.* giddy. **2.** (= *ledwie*) poorly, barely; **słabo słyszeć** *l.* **niedosłyszeć** be hard of hearing; **słabo widzieć** *l.* **niedowidzieć** have poor eyesight. **3.** (= *marnie*) poorly; **słabo oświetlony** poorly lit *l.* lighted; **słabo przygotowany** ill-equipped (*do (robienia) czegoś* to (do) sth); **słabo** *l.* **ledwie widoczny** (*linia, zarys*) faint; (*kształt, postać*) obscure; **słabo rozwinięty** (*kraj, region*) underdeveloped; **słabo zaludniony** (*kraj, region*) underpopulated; **słabo mówić po angielsku** speak English badly, speak poor English; **on słabo mówi po angielsku** his English is quite poor; **słabo orientować się w czymś** have a poor grasp *l.* understanding of sth; **słabo się uczyć** be a poor student, be a slow learner; **słabo znać się na czymś** have a poor knowledge of sth; **główka coś słabo pracuje** *pot.* not a lot happening upstairs.

słabostka *f. Gen.pl.* **-ek** foible, weakness.

słabość *f.* **1.** (= *osłabienie*) weakness, feebleness, frailty. **2.** (= *brak mocy*) weakness, impotence. **3.** (= *uległość*) weakness, frailty; **w chwili słabości** in a moment of weakness; **wykorzystać czyjąś słabość** take advantage of *l.* capitalize on sb's moment of weakness. **4.** (= *skłonność*) weakness, weak *l.* soft spot; **mieć słabość** have a weakness, have a weak *l.* soft spot (*do kogoś / czegoś* for sb/sth). **5.** (= *wada*) weakness; **nie tolerować czyichś słabości** not tolerate sb's weaknesses.

słabowity *a.* weakly, feeble, frail.

słaby *a.* **1.** (= *wątły*) weak, feeble, frail; **słabe zdrowie** ill *l.* poor health; **być słabego zdrowia** be of ill *l.* poor health; **słaba płeć** the weaker sex; **mieć słabe nerwy** be of a nervous disposition;

słaba głowa (= *brak zdolności*) feeble-mindedness; (*osoba*) thickhead; **mieć słabą głowę** (= *łatwo się upijać*) be weakheaded. **2.** (= *uległy*) weak, frail, lacking character; **słaba wola** weak will; **człowiek o słabym charakterze** man of straw. **3.** (= *mało intensywny, nieznaczny*) (*o dźwięku, zapachu, podmuchu*) faint; (*o świetle*) faint, wan; (*o widoczności*) poor; (*o pamięci*) poor, irretentive; (*o leku, proteście*) mild; (*o dowodach, demokracji, nadziei*) frail; (*o konstrukcji, argumencie*) vulnerable; (*o świetle, blasku*) dull, dim; (*o wymówce*) lame; (*o argumencie, dowodzie, wymówce, teorii*) flimsy; (*o napoju*) weak; **mieć słabe pojęcie o czymś** have a remote idea of sth; **prąd słaby** *fiz.* weak current. **4.** (= *nietrwały*) weak, flimsy; **słaby punkt** (*w rozumowaniu*) flaw; (*w strategii*) blot; **czyjś słaby punkt** sb's weak spot, a chink in sb's armor; **czyjaś słaba strona** sb's weak side. **5.** (= *niedostateczny*) bad, poor; **słaby słuch** poor hearing; **mieć słaby słuch** be hard of hearing; **słaby uczeń** poor student, slow learner; **słaba** *l.* **miękka waluta** *fin.* soft currency; **słaby wzrok** weak eyes, bad eyesight; **jest słaby z geografii** *szkoln.* he's bad at geography, he fares poorly in geography. **6.** *jęz.* (*o czasowniku*) weak.

słać¹ *ipf.* **ślę ślesz, ślij** *lit.* send; **ślę wyrazy szacunku** (*w zakończeniu listu*) kind regards.

słać² *ipf.* **ścielę ścielesz 1.** (= *rozściełać*) spread, strew; **słać łóżko** (= *rozkładać na noc*) make the bed; (= *składać na dzień*) do the bed. **2.** (*słomę*) litter (*straw for cattle, etc.*). **~ się** *ipf.* **ścielę ścielesz** spread, stretch; (*np. o mgle, dymie*) float; **trup ściele się** *l.* **pada gęsto** people are dropping like flies; **ścielę się do nóg** *żart.* humbly yours.

słaniać się *ipf.* stagger.

sława *f.* **1.** (= *rozgłos*) fame; **muzyk światowej sławy** world-famous musician; **być u szczytu sławy** be at the height of one's fame; **zdobyć sławę** rise *l.* vault to fame, win fame; **pieniądze i sława** fame and fortune. **2.** (= *reputacja*) reputation, repute; **cieszyć się dobrą sławą** have a good name; **cieszyć się złą sławą** be ill-reputed, be in disrepute; **cieszyć się sławą uczciwego człowieka** have a reputation of honesty, be reputed honest; **zła sława** disrepute, ill fame, notoriety; **okryty złą sławą** ill-famed, ill-reputed. **3.** (= *ktoś sławny*) celebrity; **światowa sława w dziedzinie inżynierii genetycznej** world-famous genetic engineering expert.

sławetny *a. lit.* famous.

sławić *ipf.* extol, extoll, exhalt; (*Boga*) praise; **sławić kogoś pod niebiosa** praise sb to the skies, sing sb's praises.

sławny *a.* (= *chwalebny*) glorious; (= *znakomity*) illustrious; (= *znany*) famous, renowned, famed (*z czegoś* for sth).

sławojka *f. Gen.pl.* **-ek** *rzad., pot.* outhouse, outdoor privy.

słodkawy *a.* sweetish.

słodki *a.* **-dszy** (*o smaku, zapachu, dźwięku, zemście*) sweet; (*zwł. o dźwiękach*) honeyed, dulcet, mellifluous; **słodka idiotka** bimbo; **słodka ka-**

pusta non-fermented cabbage; **słodkie mleko** sweet milk; **słodkie słówka** endearments; *iron.* sweet talking, (soft) sawder; **słodkie wino** sweet wine; **słodka woda** (*nie morska*) fresh water; **ten tort jest za** *l.* **zbyt słodki** this cake is too sweet; **to moja słodka tajemnica** that's for me to know and for you to find out, it's my own sweet secret; **robić do kogoś słodkie oczy** make sheep's eyes at sb; **zobacz, jaki słodki!** (*o psie, kocie itd.*) isn't he/she/it a sweetie *l.* cute?

słodko *adv.* sweetly, sweet; **pachnieć/brzmieć/smakować/wyglądać słodko** smell/sound/taste/look sweet; **potrawa na słodko** sweet dish; **przyjęcie na słodko** sweets-only party.

słodko-gorzki *a.* bitter-sweet.

słodkogórz *mi bot.* **psianka słodkogórz** woody nightshade, bittersweet (*Solanum dulcamara*).

słodko-kwaśno *adv.* sweet and sour; **wieprzowina na słodko-kwaśno** sweet-and-sour pork.

słodko-kwaśny *a.* sweet-and-sour.

słodkości *pl. Gen.* -**i** (= *słodycze*) sweets.

słodkość *f.* sweetness.

słodkowodny *a.* freshwater.

słodlin *mi bot.* wisteria (*Wisteria*).

słodować *ipf.* malt.

słodownia *f. Gen.pl.* -**i** malting, malt house.

słodownik *mp* maltster.

słodowy *a.* malt; **cukier słodowy** malt sugar, maltose; **whisky słodowa** malt whiskey.

słodu *itd. mi zob.* **słód.**

słodycz *f. tylko sing.* **1.** (*smak, łagodność*) sweetness; **sama słodycz** (*o smaku*) sugar and spice; (*w zachowaniu*) all sweetness and light. **2.** (= *rozkosz*) sweetness, bliss.

słodycze *pl. Gen.* -**y** sweets, sweetmeats, confectionery; **sklep ze słodyczami** candy store, confectioner's; *Br.* sweet-shop; **przepadać za słodyczami** have a sweet tooth.

słodzić *ipf.* **słodzę słodzisz, słodź** *l.* **słódź** sweeten; **słodzić kawę/herbatę** (*wykonywać czynność*) put sugar in one's coffee/tea; **dziękuję, nie słodzę herbaty** I don't take sugar in my tea, thank you.

słodzik *mi Gen.* -**a** sweetener.

słodziny *pl. Gen.* -**n** draff.

słodziutki *a.* (*o osobie*) sweetie, cutesy; (*o potrawie*) very sweet.

słoi *mi zob.* **słój.**

słoiczek *mi* -**czk**- *Gen.* -**a** (small) jar.

słoik *mi Gen.* -**a** jar; (*na maść*) gallipot.

słoisty *a.* (*o drewnie*) ringed.

słoja *itd. mi zob.* **słój.**

słojować *ipf. stol.* (= *mazerować*) grain.

słojowanie *n. stol.* graining.

słoma *f.* straw; **dach kryty słomą** thatched roof; **słoma mu wychodzi z butów** *przen.* he's such a country yokel, he's a straw-sucker.

słomianka *f. Gen.pl.* -**ek** doormat (*made of straw*).

słomiany *a.* straw; **słomiany dach** *l.* **słomiana strzecha** thatched roof; **słomiany kapelusz** straw hat; **słomiana mata** straw mat; **słomiana wdowa** grass widow; **słomiany wdowiec** grass widower; **słomiany zapał** short-lived enthusiasm.

słomka *f. Gen.pl.* -**ek** (= *źdźbło; t. słomka do napojów*) straw; **pić przez słomkę** drink through the straw.

słomkowożółty *a.* straw-colored; *Br.* straw-coloured.

słomkowy *a.* straw; **kapelusz słomkowy** straw hat; **kolor słomkowy** straw color; *Br.* straw colour.

słonawy *a.* saltish; (*o wodzie*) brackish.

słoneczko *n.* **1.** (*słońce*) sun. **2.** *el.* electric heater. **3.** (*osoba ukochana*) sweetheart; (*pieszczotliwa forma zwracania się*) sunshine, sugar.

słonecznie *adv.* sunnily; **było wczoraj bardzo słonecznie** it was a very sunny day yesterday.

słonecznik *mi Gen.* -**a** **1.** *bot.* sunflower (*Helianthus*). **2.** (*ziarna*) sunflower seeds.

słonecznikowy *a.* sunflower; **olej słonecznikowy** sunflower (seed) oil.

słoneczny *a.* (= *dotyczący słońca*) solar; (*o dniu, niebie*) sunny; (*o ścianie, pokoju*) sunward; **słoneczny** *l.* **promienny uśmiech** radiant smile; **bateria słoneczna** solar battery *l.* cell; **doba słoneczna** solar day; **energia słoneczna** solar power *l.* energy; **kąpiel słoneczna** sunbath; **łuk słoneczny** *meteor.* fog bow; **okulary słoneczne** *l.* **przeciwsłoneczne** sunglasses, shades; **pokład słoneczny** *żegl.* sundeck; **porażenie słoneczne** *pat.* sunstroke; **splot słoneczny** *anat.* solar plexus; **światło słoneczne** sunlight, sunshine; **Układ Słoneczny** *astron.* solar system; **zegar słoneczny** sundial.

słoniątko *n.* baby elephant.

słonica *f.* female *l.* cow elephant.

słonik *ma* **1.** *zob.* **słoniątko. 2.** *ent.* weevil, snout beetle (*Curculio*).

słonina *f.* **1.** (*wieprzowa*) fatback, pork fat. **2.** (= *tworzywo do produkcji podeszew*) crepe (rubber).

słoniowatość, słoniowacizna *f. pat.* elephantiasis.

słoniowaty *a.* elephantine.

słoniowy *a.* elephant's; **kieł słoniowy** elephant's tusk; **kość słoniowa** ivory; **wieża z kości słoniowej** *przen.* ivory tower.

słonka *f. Gen.pl.* -**ek** *orn.* woodcock (*Scolopax rusticola*).

słonko *n. Gen.pl.* -**ek** *zob.* **słoneczko.**

słono *adv.* saltily; **słono jadać** eat salty foods (*as a habit*); **słono za coś zapłacić** pay a pretty penny for sth; **to cię będzie słono kosztowało** this is going to cost you dear.

słonogorzki *a.* bitter-salt.

słonorośl *f. bot.* halophyte.

słoność *f.* saltiness.

słonowodny *a.* saltwater.

słony *a.* salty; **słona woda** salt water; **ta zupa jest za** *l.* **zbyt słona** the soup is too salty; **słona cena** steep price; **słony dowcip** spicy joke, salt wit.

słoń *ma zool.* (= *ssak z rodziny Elephantidae*) **1.** elephant; **słoń afrykański** African elephant (*Loxodonta africana*); **słoń indyjski** Indian elephant (*Elephas maximus*); **słoń-albinos** white elephant; **jak słoń w składzie porcelany** like a bull in a china shop; **słoń mu nadepnął na ucho** he's tone-deaf. **2. słoń morski** elephant seal, sea elephant (*Mirounga*).

słońce *n.* **1.** *astron.* sun; (*pisane wielką literą przy określaniu słońca w naszym układzie słonecznym*) the Sun; **wschód słońca** sunrise; **zachód słońca** sunset; **słońce wschodzi** the sun is rising; **słońce zachodzi** the sun is setting; **zaćmienie słońca** solar eclipse; **sztuczne słońce** *pot.* (= *kwarcówka*) sunlamp; **to jasne jak słońce** it's crystal clear; it's as plain *l.* clear as crystal *l.* day; it's as plain as the nose on your face; **porywać się z motyką na słońce** try to square the circle; bite off more than one can chew; try to hitch one's wagon to the stars; **wstać ze słońcem** rise with the sun; **najlepszy pod słońcem** the best under the sun, the best ever; **najmądrzejszy człowiek pod słońcem** the wisest man alive; **najładniejsze dziecko pod słońcem** the prettiest child imaginable. **2.** (*blask, światło*) sun, sunshine; **patrzeć na coś pod słońce** look at sth with the sun in one's eyes; **wygrzewać się w** *l.* **na słońcu** bask in the sun, soak up the sun; **poparzony słońcem** *pat.* sunburned; **spieczony słońcem** (*np. o ziemi*) sunbaked; **zalany słońcem** sundrenched.

słota *f.* (a period of) rainy weather.

słotny *a.* (= *deszczowy*) rainy, drizzly; (= *wilgotny, mokry*) wet, damp.

Słowacja *f. geogr.* Slovakia; **na Słowację** to Slovakia; **na Słowacji** in Slovakia.

słowacki *a.* Slovak, Slovakian.

Słowaczka *f. Gen.pl.* **-ek, Słowak** *mp* Slovak, Slovakian.

Słowenia *f. Gen.* **-ii** *geogr.* Slovenia.

Słoweniec *mp* **-ńc-** *pl.* **-y, Słowenka** *f. Gen.pl.* **-ek** Slovene, Slovenian.

słoweński *a.* Slovene, Slovenian.

Słowianin *mp pl.* **-anie** *Gen.* **-an, Słowianka** *f. Gen.pl.* **-ek** Slav.

słowianizm *jęz.* Slavism, Slavicism.

słowianofil *mp Gen.pl.* **-ów** Slavophile, Slavophil.

słowianofilski *a.* Slavophilic.

słowianofilstwo *n.* Slavophilism.

słowianoznawczy *a.* of or related to Slavonic studies; **studia słowianoznawcze** Slavonic studies.

słowianoznawstwo *n.* Slavonic studies.

słowiański *a.* Slavonic, Slavic.

słowiańszczyzna *f.* **1.** (*ziemie, narody*) Slavdom. **2.** (= *języki słowiańskie*) Slavonic languages. **3.** (= *kultura słowiańska*) Slavonic culture. **4.** (= *literatura słowiańska*) Slavonic literature.

słowiczy *a.* nightingale's.

słowik *ma orn.* nightingale (*Luscinia*); **słowik rdzawy** (common) nightingale (*Luscinia megarhynchos*); **słowik szary** thrush nightingale (*Luscinia luscinia*).

słownictwo *n.* (*języka l. użytkownika języka*) vocabulary; (*danego języka, osoby, grupy osób l. dyscypliny*) lexicon; **ograniczone/szerokie słownictwo** *l.* **ograniczony/szeroki zasób słownictwa**

limited/wide (range of) vocabulary; **poszerzyć swoje słownictwo** *l.* **swój zasób słownictwa** expand *l.* widen one's vocabulary.

słowniczek *mi* **-czk-** *Gen.* **-a 1.** (= *mały słownik*) mini-dictionary. **2.** (= *wykaz terminów, np. na końcu książki*) glossary.

słownie *adv.* in words; **słownie: dwieście dolarów** (the amount) in words: two hundred dollars; **napisać sumę słownie** write the amount in words.

słownik *mi Gen.* **-a 1.** (*książka*) dictionary; **słownik dwujęzyczny** bilingual dictionary; **słownik języka polskiego** Polish dictionary; **słownik matematyczny** dictionary of mathematics; **słownik obrazkowy** pictorial dictionary; **słownik ortograficzny** spelling dictionary; **słownik polsko-angielski** Polish-English dictionary; **słownik poprawnej polszczyzny** Polish usage dictionary; **słownik psychologiczny** dictionary of psychology; **słownik tematyczny** thematic dictionary; **słownik wyrazów obcych** dictionary of foreign words; **sprawdzić coś w słowniku** look sth up in a dictionary, consult a dictionary. **2.** (= *zasób słownictwa*) vocabulary, lexicon; **bogaty słownik** wide (range of) vocabulary; **ograniczony** *l.* **ubogi słownik** limited vocabulary. **3.** *komp.* glossary.

słownikarski *a.* lexicographic.

słownikarstwo *n.* lexicography.

słownikarz *mp* lexicographer.

słownikowy *a.* dictionary; **układ słownikowy** dictionary layout.

słowno-muzyczny *a.* music-and-word.

słowny *a.* **1.** (= *wiarygodny*) reliable, dependable; **być słownym** be as good as one's word; **on jest bardzo słowny** he's a man of his word. **2.** (= *wyrażony mową*) verbal.

słowo *n. Gen.pl.* **słów 1.** (= *wyraz*) word; **brzydkie słowo** four-letter word, swearword; **cierpkie** *l.* **gorzkie słowa** bitter words; **dobre słowo** kind word; **mocne słowa** blunt words; **ostre** *l.* **szorstkie słowa** harsh words; **próżne** *l.* **puste słowa** empty words, hot air; **święte** *l.* **złote słowa** gospel truth; **wielkie słowa** big words; **Słowo Boże** *rel.* God's Word, the Word of God; **słowa prawdy** naked truth; **to moje ostatnie słowo** this is my last word; **mieć ostatnie słowo** (*w jakiejś sprawie*) have the final say (*w czymś* in sth); **jednym słowem** in a *l.* one word; **innymi słowy** in other words; **w krótkich słowach** in short *l.* brief; **gra słów** wordplay, play on words; (*żart słowny*) pun; **szkoda słów** it's a waste of breath, it's no use (*talking to him, trying to convince them, etc.*); **od słowa do słowa, zaczęli rozmawiać o...** while chatting, they moved on to...; **w dosłownym tego słowa znaczeniu** in the literal sense of the word, literally; **połykać słowa** swallow words; **ważyć słowa** weigh one's words; **nie mogę znaleźć słów** (= *jestem zbyt wzruszony, zdenerwowany itp.*) words fail me; **słowo w słowo** word for word; **powtórzyć coś słowo w słowo** repeat sth verbatim; **cytować coś słowo w słowo** quote *l.* cite sth chapter and verse *l.* verbatim; **mam do pana dwa słowa** could I have a word with you?; **nie pisnąć ani słowa** not breathe a word; **nie po-**

wiem o nim złego słowa I won't say a word against him, I'll never speak ill of him; **wspomnisz moje słowo** you'll remember my words; **opowiedzieć coś swoimi słowami** tell sth in one's own words; **powiedzieć coś w dwu słowach** put sth in a nutshell; **przerwać komuś w pół słowa** cut in on sb; **chwytać kogoś za słowa** catch sb in their words; **nie przebierać w słowach** not mince one's words; **licz się ze słowami!** watch your mouth *l.* language!; **nie dał/dała/dali mi dojść do słowa** I couldn't get a word in edgewise; *Br.* I couldn't get a word in edgeways; **brak mi słów** I'm at a loss for words; **muzyka do słów Mickiewicza** music to the lyrics by Mickiewicz; **wymiana słów** verbal exchange; **nie móc wykrztusić słowa** not be able to speak a word, be dumbstruck; **słowa więzną mi w gardle** I'm choked up; **słowa, które padły z twoich ust, są dla nas bardzo bolesne** the words you said are very painful to us. **2.** *(wypowiedź)* word, utterance; **słowo drukowane** the printed word; **słowo mówione** the spoken word; **słowo pisane** the written word; **słowo wiążące** lead-in; **słowo wstępne** foreword, introductory remarks; **wolność słowa** freedom of speech; **ostatnie słowo** *prawn.* last word; **wpadać komuś w słowo** cut in on sb; **wypluj to słowo!** perish the thought! **3.** *(= obietnica)* word, promise; **dać słowo** give one's word; **dotrzymać słowa** keep one's word; **nie dotrzymać słowa** go back on one's word; **ręczyć za kogoś/coś słowem** give one's word for sb/sth, vouch for sb/sth; **poprzeć słowo czynem** suit the action to the word; **słowo honoru** word of honor; *Br.* word of honour; *(jako wykrzyknik)* on my honor! *Br.* on my honour! **rzucać słowa na wiatr** give empty promises; **słowo daję** *l.* **daję słowo** I swear to God!, no kidding!; **trzymać kogoś za słowo** hold sb to their word; **uwierzyć komuś na słowo** give sb the benefit of the doubt; **być po słowie** be bethroted; **słowo?** promise?; **możesz mi wierzyć na słowo** take my word for it; **słowo się rzekło, kobyłka u płota** delivered as promised. **4.** *przest., jęz.* verb; **słowo posiłkowe** auxiliary verb. **5.** *tylko pl.* *(= tekst piosenki)* lyrics.

słowotok *mi psych.* logorrhea; *pot.* talkarrhea, verbal diarrhea.

słowotwórczo *adv. jęz.* derivationally, of or related to word-formation; **podzielny/niepodzielny słowotwórczo** morphologically analyzable/unanalyzable.

słowotwórczy *a. jęz.* derivational, of or related to word-formation; **analiza słowotwórcza** word-formation *l.* morphological analysis; **budowa słowotwórcza** morphological structure; **podstawa słowotwórcza** derivational base.

słowotwórstwo *n. jęz.* word-formation.

słód *mi* -o- malt.

słódź *itd. ipf. zob.* słodzić.

słój *mi* -o- Gen. -a Gen.pl. -ów *(naczynie)* **1.** jar; *(= pojemność l. zawartość)* jarful. **2.** Gen. -u *l.* -a *bot.* ring; **słój roczny** *l.* **słój przyrostu rocznego** annual *l.* tree ring.

słów *n. zob.* słowo.

słówka *pl. Gen.* -ek *(języka obcego)* vocabulary (items), words *(of a foreign language)*; **ucz się słówek!** learn your words!

słówko *n. Gen.pl.* -ek word; **czułe słówka** sweet nothings, terms of endearment; **szepnąć za kimś słówko** put in a good word for sb.

słuch *mi* **1.** *(= słyszenie)* hearing; **mieć słaby słuch** be hard of hearing; **stracić słuch** lose one's hearing ability; **wytężyć słuch** strain one's ears; **zamieniam się w słuch** I'm all ears; **słuch po nim zaginął** he disappeared without trace, he wasn't heard of any more; **powiedzieć komuś do słuchu** give sb a piece of one's mind; send sb off *l.* away with a flea in their ear; give sb an earful; **w zasięgu/poza zasięgiem słuchu** within/out of earshot. **2.** *muz.* pitch; **słuch muzyczny** a good ear for music; **słuch absolutny** absolute *l.* perfect pitch; **grać ze słuchu** play by ear; **nie mieć słuchu** have a bad ear for music.

słuchacz *mp,* **słuchaczka** *f. Gen.pl.* -ek **1.** *(= słuchający)* listener; **być wdzięcznym słuchaczem** be a good listener. **2.** *(student)* student; *(= kursant)* course participant; **wolny słuchacz** auditor.

słuchać *ipf.* **1.** *(= chcieć słyszeć)* listen to; **słuchać głosu sumienia** follow one's conscience; **słuchaj uważnie, bo nie będę powtarzać** listen carefully, I won't say it again; **słuchaj, jak do ciebie mówię** would you listen to me when I'm talking to you?; **słuchaj, zmień temat** look, why don't you change the topic?; **słucham, tu Kowalski** *tel.* Kowalski speaking; **słucham?** *(prośba o powtórzenie)* pardon?, sorry?, how's that?; *(z zaskoczeniem)* what?, I beg your pardon?; **słuchajcie, co to było?** I say, what was that?; **słuchać spowiedzi** *rel.* hear confession; **słuchać jednym uchem** listen with half an ear. **2.** *(= być posłusznym)* obey; **słuchać rozkazów/rodziców** obey one's orders/parents. **~ się** *ipf.* obey.

słuchawka *f. Gen.pl.* -ek **1.** *(telefonu)* receiver, handset; **odłożyć słuchawkę** hang up the phone, hang up; **podnosić słuchawkę** pick up *l.* answer the phone; **rzucić słuchawką** hang up on sb, put the phone down on sb; **źle odłożyć słuchawkę** leave the phone off the hook; **proszę nie odkładać słuchawki** please hold the line! please don't hang up! **2.** *(zakładana na głowę)* headphones; *(wkładana do ucha)* earphones, earpiece. **3.** *med.* stethoscope.

słuchowiec *mp* -wc- *pl.* -y audile.

słuchowisko *n. radio* drama *l.* play.

słuchowy *a. (dotyczący organu słuchu)* aural, auricular; *(dotyczący funkcji narządu słuchu)* auditory; **aparat słuchowy** *med.* hearing aid; **kosteczki słuchowe** *anat.* auditory ossicles; **nerw słuchowy** *anat.* acoustic nerve; **pamięć słuchowa** *psych.* auditory memory; **przewód słuchowy** *anat.* auditory canal *l.* meatus; **trąbka słuchowa** *l.* **Eustachiusza** *anat.* Eustachian tube, syrinx.

słuchy *tylko pl.* **1.** *(= pogłoski)* rumor; *Br.* rumour; **chodzą słuchy, że...** it is rumored that..., there is rumor that...; **chodzą o nim słuchy, że...** he is rumored to... **2.** *(uszy)* hare's *l.* rabbit's *l.* boar's ears.

sługa *f. l. mp decl.* like *f. pl.* -i *l.* -dzy Gen. -g *l.*

-ów servant; **sługa boży** rel. servant of God; **sługa pańszczyźniany** bondservant, serf; **Pański uniżony sługa** (np. żartobliwie w zakończeniu listu) your humble l. obedient servant.

sługus mp pl. **-y** l. **-i** pog. minion, lackey, flunkey.

słup mi **1.** (pal) pole, post, pylon; **słup graniczny** boundary marker, landmark; **słup elektryczny** l. **wysokiego napięcia** electric pylon; **słup latarni** lamppost; **słup ogłoszeniowy** bill-post, kiosk; **słup telefoniczny** telephone pole; **słup totemiczny** totem pole; **słup trakcyjny** utility pole; **postawić oczy w słup** look with a fixed stare. **2.** przen. (= pionowa smuga) (ognia, dymu, pyłu) pillar; (wody) spout. **3.** (np. rtęci) (= słupek) column. **4.** geol. pillar, column. **5.** **zmienić się w słup soli** przen. be petrified, turn into a pillar of salt.

słupek mi **-pk-** Gen. **-a 1.** (= mały słup) post, pole; (bramy) gatepost; (bramki) goalpost; **słupek startowy** pływanie starting block; **słupek mety** winning post; **stanąć słupka** (o zającu, króliku) sit up, stand on hind legs. **2.** (w termometrze) column; **słupek rtęci** mercury column. **3.** zw. pl. (ścieg szydełkowy) bride, bar. **4.** anat. peduncle, stalk; **słupek oka** (u skorupiaków) eyestalk. **5.** bot. pistil. **6.** mat. column; **dodawać/odejmować w słupkach** do one's sums in columns.

słupkowy a. **1.** (= mający cechy słupka) pillar-like; **wykres słupkowy** bar chart l. graph. **2.** bot. (o kwiecie) pistillate.

słupnik mp rz.-kat. stylite.

słupołaz mi Gen. **-a** techn. (zwykle pl.) climbing-irons.

słusznie adv. **1.** (= zgodnie z prawdą) rightly, justly; **słusznie zauważyć, że...** point out rightly that...; **słuszniej byłoby powiedzieć, że...** to be more exact... **2.** (= sprawiedliwie) rightly, fairly, justly; **słusznie spodziewać się nagrody** be rightly expecting a reward. **3.** (jako przyznanie racji) (that's) right!; **całkiem słusznie** quite rightly (so); **słusznie, mieliśmy iść do teatru** that's right, we were (supposed) to go to the theater.

słuszność f. **1.** (= racja, prawda) rightness; **mieć słuszność** be right; **nie mieć słuszności** be wrong; **przyznawać komuś słuszność** admit that sb is right. **2.** (= sensowność) (postępowania) advisibility; (roszczenia, rozumowania, wniosku, zarzutu) legitimacy; (argumentu, decyzji, krytyki) validity.

słuszny a. **1.** (= trafny) right, correct. **2.** (= sprawiedliwy, uzasadniony) just, fair, due; (obawy, podejrzenia) justified; (argument, krytyka) valid; (gniew, decyzja) righteous; (skarga, wniosek) rightful; (wniosek, rozumowanie, zarzut) legitimate. **3.** (= pokaźny) przest. substantial; **mężczyzna słusznego wzrostu** lit. man of substantial height; **słusznych rozmiarów** (ciało, osoba) generously proportioned.

służalczo adv. servilly, obsequiously.
służalczość f. servility, obsequiousness.
służalczy a. servile, obsequious.

służalec mp **-lc-** pl. **-y** flunkey, cringer.
służąca f. Gen. **-ej** servant, maid.
służący mp manservant, servant.

służba f. **1.** (= praca dla dobra publicznego) service; (religijna) ministry, ministration; **służba czynna** wojsk., policja active service l. duty; **służba drogowa** public roads maintenance service; **służba dyplomatyczna** the Diplomatic Service; **służba meteorologiczna** weather service; **służba patrolowa** patrol duty; **służba ruchu** kol. rail traffic control; policja traffic police; **służba wojskowa** military service; **zasadnicza służba wojskowa** compulsory l. obligatory military service; **odbywać służbę wojskową** do one's military service; **niezdolny do służby wojskowej** unfit for military service, noneffective; **służba wywiadowcza** intelligence service; **(państwowa) służba zdrowia** (national) health service; **publiczna służba zdrowia** public health service; **państwowa służba cywilna** the Civil Service; **tajna służba** secret service; **mieć za sobą 25 lat służby** be a veteran of 25 years' service; pot. (w wojsku, policji itp.) have clocked 25 years in the force; **zaciągnąć się na służbę** enter service; **w służbie narodu** in the line of duty. **2.** (dyżur) duty; **na/po służbie** on/off duty; **iść na służbę** go into service; **meldować się na służbę** report for duty. **3.** (= poświęcenie się jakiejś sprawie) service (dla idei to a cause). **4.** (= służący) servants. **5.** (= praca służącego) service; **być u kogoś na służbie** be in the service of sb, be in sb's employ; **wstąpić do kogoś na służbę** take service with sb; **wypowiedzieć komuś służbę** quit sb's employ.

służbista mp, **służbistka** f. Gen.pl. **-ek** disciplinarian, martinet, jack-in-office, bureaucrat.

służbisty a. rzad. formal, stiff.

służbowo adv. (= urzędowo) officially; (= w związku z wykonywaną pracą) on business; **wyjechać służbowo** be away on business.

służbowy a. (= urzędowy) official; (= związany z wykonywaną pracą) business, office; (= związany ze służbą) service; **broń służbowa** service gun; **czapka służbowa** service cap; **godziny służbowe** business l. office hours; **mieszkanie służbowe** company apartment; Br. tied flat; **notatka służbowa** memorandum, memo; **obowiązki służbowe** one's business duties; **samochód służbowy** company car; **stopień służbowy** rank; **stanowisko służbowe** position, post; **tajemnica służbowa** confidential information; **wyjazd służbowy** business trip; **służbowy lunch** business l. working lunch; **drogą służbową** through official channels.

służbówka f. Gen.pl. **-ek** duty room.

służebnica f. emf. servant.

służebny a. **1.** (= związany ze służeniem) menial; **panna służebna** maid servant; **roboty służebne** menial tasks. **2.** (= pomocniczy) ancillary, subsidiary.

służyć ipf. **1.** (= pełnić posługi) serve (komuś to sb); **służyć pod bronią** bear arms; **służyć w wojsku** serve in the army; **służyć do mszy** kość. serve at Mass; **dobrze komuś służyć** serve sb well, stand sb in good stead. **2.** (= być gotowym *do pomocy*) serve, be of service; **służyć komuś pomocą** offer one's help to sb, lend support to sb; **służyć komuś pożyczką** accommodate sb with a loan; **służyć komuś przykładem** give sb a lead; **czym mogę służyć?** how can I help you?; **służę panu!** (I am) at your service! **3.** (= *pracować dla idei*) serve; **służyć ojczyźnie** serve one's (home) country; **służyć ludzkości/ludziom** serve the humankind *l.* humanity/people; **służyć dwóm panom** serve two masters. **4.** (= *być używanym jako coś*) serve, do duty; (*o osobie*) act; **służyć jako coś** serve as sth, do duty as *l.* for sth, serve *l.* fulfill the function of sth; **służyć za przewodnika** act as a guide. **5.** (= *wpływać dodatnio*) do good (*komuś* sb); agree (*komuś* with sb); **klimat górski mi nie służy** the mountain climate doesn't agree *l.* disagrees with me. **6.** (= *być w dobrym stanie*) work well; **pamięć mi nie służy tak jak dawniej** my memory is failing me these days, my memory is not as good as it used to be. **7.** (*w czymś domu*) serve; **służyć u kogoś** be in the service of sb. **8.** (*o psie*) beg.

słych *mi* (*tylko w wyrażeniu*) **ani widu, ani słychu** neither hide nor hair (*o kimś / czymś* of sb/ sth).

słychać *ipf. indecl.* **1.** (= *coś daje się słyszeć*) be heard, be audible; **słychać było muzykę** music could be heard; **ledwo go było słychać** he was hardly audible. **2.** (= *mówi się o czymś*) they say, there is news; **co słychać?** what's up?, what's new?, how are things?, what's the crack?; **(i) co tam u ciebie słychać?** (so,) what have you been up to?; **jak zewsząd słychać** by *l.* from all accounts; **nic nie słychać o ich ślubie** there is no news about their wedding.

słynąć *ipf.* be famous (*z czegoś* for sth); be remarkable (*z czegoś* for sth); **ta okolica słynie ze swoich jezior** the area is famous for its lakes.

słynny *a.* famous, famed (*z czegoś* for sth); **słynny na cały świat** world-famous.

słyszalność *f.* audibility; **próg słyszalności** audibility threshold.

słyszalny *a.* audible; **dobrze słyszalny** clearly audible, as clear as a bell; **ledwie słyszalny** barely audible; **źle słyszalny** (*o dźwięku*) obscure.

słyszeć *ipf.* **-ę -ysz 1.** (= *odbierać dźwięki*) hear; **móc słyszeć** be within earshot; **odeszła, żeby nie słyszeć** she went away to get out of earshot; **słabo** *l.* **źle słyszeć** be hard of hearing; **słyszałem to na własne uszy** I've heard it with my own ears; **nie chcę o tym słyszeć** I won't hear of it, I won't have any of this; **miło/przykro mi to słyszeć** I'm delighted/sorry to hear that; **słyszysz?** can you hear it?; **pierwsze słyszę!** that's a new one on me!, it's the first time I've heard of it!; **co ja słyszę!** that's impossible!; **słyszeliście, co się stało?** have you heard what's happened?; **nie słyszę własnych myśli** I can barely hear myself think; **słyszał, że dzwonią, ale nie wie, w którym kościele** in the right church but in the wrong pew; **kto to słyszał!** that's incredible! **2.** (= *dowiadywać się*) hear; **słyszałem, że się żenisz** I heard you were getting married; **słyszałem, że pani wyjeżdża** I understand you are leaving. ~

się *ipf.* hear each other *l.* one another; **dać się słyszeć** (*o dźwięku*) be heard.

słyszenie *n.* hearing; **wiem o tym ze słyszenia** I know about it from hearsay; **znam go ze słyszenia** I have heard about him.

smaczek *ma Gen.* **-ów 1.** (= *posmak*) (faint) taste, relish, flavor; *Br.* flavour. **2.** (= *osobliwość*) curiosity.

smacznie *adv.* **1.** (= *w smaczny sposób*) tastily, appetizingly; **wyglądać smacznie** look tasty; **smacznie gotować** cook tasty food. **2.** (= *ze smakiem*) with relish; **zajadać coś ze smakiem** eat sth with relish; **spać smacznie** *przen.* be sound *l.* fast asleep.

smaczny *a.* tasty, tasteful; savory; *Br.* savoury; **smacznego!** enjoy!, bon appétit!; (*kelner do gościa*) enjoy your meal!; **smaczny kąsek** *przen.* tidbit; *Br.* titbit.

smagać *ipf.* whip, flog; (*o deszczu, wietrze*) lash; **wiatr smagał jej twarz** cutting wind lashed her face. ~ **się** *ipf.* whip each other *l.* one another, flog each other *l.* one another.

smagliczka *f. Gen.pl.* **-ek** *bot.* alyssum (*Alyssum*).

smagławy *a.* swartish.

smagły *a.* swarthy, dusky.

smagnąć *pf.* **-ij** *zob.* **smagać.**

smagnięcie *n.* (*biczem*) whip, flog; (*wiatru*) lash.

smak *mi* **1.** (*zmysł*) taste; **przypaść komuś do smaku** (= *zasmakować*) relish, savor; *Br.* savour (*a meal*); (= *spodobać się*) appeal; **trochę mi to nie w smak** it's a bit against the grain with me. **2.** (*właściwość pożywienia*) taste, flavor; *Br.* flavour; **czuć smak czegoś** can taste sth; **mieć smak czegoś** taste of sth; **coś jest gorzkie w smaku** sth tastes bitter; **ta pieczeń jest bez smaku** this roast is tasteless; **dodać sól do smaku** add salt to taste; **pozostawić nieprzyjemny smak w ustach** leave a bad taste in one's mouth; **smak sukcesu** *przen.* taste of success; **obejść się smakiem** fail to achieve sth. **3.** (= *apetyt*) appetite, relish; **jeść coś ze smakiem** eat sth with relish. **4.** (= *przyprawa*) flavoring; *Br.* flavouring; **smaki do ciast** cake flavorings. **5.** (= *gust*) taste; **ubierać się ze smakiem** dress tastefully; **mieszkanie urządzone ze smakiem** tastefully decorated flat.

smakołyk *mi Gen.* **-u** *l.* **-a** delicacy, tidbit; *Br.* titbit.

smakosz *mp Gen.pl.* **-y** *l.* **-ów** gourmet, gastronome; **jedzenie/wino/restauracja dla smakoszy** gourmet food/wine/restaurant.

smakoszostwo *n.* gourmandise.

smakować *ipf.* (= *próbować; być smacznym*) taste; **dobrze/świetnie/wyśmienicie/źle smakować** taste nice/excellent/delicious/bad; **smakować czymś** taste of sth; **jak to smakuje?** what does it taste like?; **jak ci smakuje?** do you like it?, any good?; **obiad bardzo mi smakował** I enjoyed my dinner a lot; **pokazać komuś, jak smakuje ciężka praca** show sb the taste of hard work.

smakowanie *n.* (= *próbowanie*) tasting; (= *degustacja*) tasting.

smakowicie *adv.* **1.** (= *smacznie*) deliciously,

appetizingly; **pachnieć/wyglądać smakowicie** smell/look delicious. **2.** (= *ze smakiem*) with relish *l.* gusto; **zajadać coś smakowicie** eat sth with relish *l.* gusto.

smakowitość *f.* **1.** (= *smaczność*) deliciousness, daintiness. **2.** (= *smakołyk*) dainty, delicacy.

smakowity *a.* delicious, dainty, mouth-watering; **smakowity kąsek** dainty morsel.

smakowy *a.* **1.** (*dotyczący zmysłu smaku*) gustatory; **kubki smakowe** *anat.* taste buds. **2.** (= *dotyczący smaku potraw*) of taste; **dodatek smakowy** flavor enhancer; *Br.* flavour enhancer.

smalec *mi* -lc- *kulin.* lard; (*do smarowania pieczywa*) dripping.

smalić *ipf.* (*tylko w wyrażeniu*) **smalić cholewki do kogoś** *przest.* court sb.

smalta *f. chem.* smalt.

smaltyn *mi min.* smaltite.

smar *mi* (*stały*) grease; (*ciekły*) lubricant; **smar grafitowy** graphite grease; **smar maszynowy** machine grease; **smar narciarski** *l.* **do nart** ski wax.

smard *mp hist.* serf, villein.

smardz *mi Gen.* -a *Gen.pl.* -ów *bot.* morel (*Morchella*).

smark *mi Gen.* -u *pot.* (*z nosa*) snot. – *mp Gen.* -a *pl.* -i *pog. zob.* **smarkacz.**

smarkacz *mp Gen.pl.* -y *l.* -ów *pog.* snot; whippersnapper, whipster.

smarkać *ipf. pot.* blow one's nose.

smarkata *f.* (*dziewczyna*) chit.

smarkateria *f. Gen.* -ii *pog.* whippersnappers, whipsters.

smarkaty *a. pog.* wet behind the ears; **badał mnie jakiś smarkaty doktorzyna** I was examined by this wet-behind-the-ears medico.

smarknąć *pf.* -ij *zob.* **smarkać.**

smarkula *f. pog.* chit.

smarność *f. techn.* lubricity.

smarowacz *mp* greaser; lubricator.

smarować *ipf.* **1.** (= *powlekać smarem*) grease; lubricate. **2.** (= *rozprowadzać masło, dżem*) spread; **smarować chleb masłem** spread butter on one's bread, spread bread with butter. **3.** (*maścią*) rub, smear, bedaub (*coś czymś* sth with sth); **smarować komuś plecy maścią** apply ointment to sb's back; **smarować twarz kremem** put cream on one's face, cream one's face. **4.** *pot.* (= *pisać*) scribble, doodle. **5.** *pot.* (= *brudzić*) blot, stain, soil. **6.** *pot.* (= *biec*) dash; **smaruj do domu!** off you go home! **7.** *pot.* (= *dawać łapówkę*) grease sb's palm *l.* hand. ~ **się** *ipf.* put on (*cream, oil, ointment, etc. on one's face, body, etc.*).

smarowanie *n. techn.* lubrication.

smarowidło *n. Gen.pl.* -eł *pot.* **1.** (= *smar*) lubricant; grease. **2.** (= *maść*) ointment, unguent.

smarownica *f. techn.* lubricator; **smarownica kapturowa** grease cup; **smarownica tłokowa** *l.* **ciśnieniowa** (*ręczna*) grease gun.

smarowniczka *f. Gen.pl.* -ek *techn.* grease nipple.

smarowniczy[1] *a.* lubricating; **oliwa smarownicza** lubricating oil.

smarowniczy[2] *mp zob.* **smarowacz.**

smarowy *a.* lubricating.

smażalnia *f. Gen.pl.* -i fried food stand; (*ryb i frytek*) fish-and-chips shop.

smażenina *f. pot.* (= *potrawa smażona*) fry, fried food; *Br.* (= *smażone jajka, boczek, kiełbaski, pomidory i ziemniaki jadane na śniadanie*) fry-up.

smażony *a.* fried.

smażyć *ipf.* fry; (*bez panierki*) sauté; **smażyć w** *l.* **na głębokim tłuszczu** deep-fry. ~ **się** *ipf.* **1.** (*na ogniu*) be fried. **2.** *pot.* (*od gorąca*) fry; (*w słońcu*) bake (*in the sun*).

smecz *mi Gen.pl.* -y *l.* -ów *tenis* smash.

smeczować *ipf. tenis* smash.

smęcić *ipf. pot.* (= *ględzić*) nag.

smętek *mi lit.* wistfulness, dolefulness.

smętnie *adv.* **1.** *lit.* (= *melancholijnie*) wistfully, dolefully; (= *smutno*) cheerlessly. **2.** *pot.* (= *marnie*) sadly, shabbily; **smętnie wyglądać** have a long face.

smętnieć *ipf. lit.* become wistful.

smętny *a.* **1.** *lit.* (= *melancholijny*) wistful, doleful; (= *smutny*) cheerless; **smętna mina** long face. **2.** *pot.* (= *marny*) sad, sorry, shabby. **3.** *pot.* (*o osobie*) (= *nudny, nijaki*) dull, sad.

smitsonit *mi min.* smithsonite.

smoczek *mi* -czk- *Gen.* -a **1.** (*do ssania*) pacifier, comforter; *Br.* dummy. **2.** (*na butelkę*) teat. **3.** *zool.* (*u minogów*) sucking *l.* suctorial mouth. **4.** *ent.* proboscis.

smoczkouste *pl. icht.* jawless fishes, cyclostomes (*Cyclostomata*).

smocznik *ma icht.* **smocznik kolczak** greater weever (*Trachinus draco*).

smoczy *a.* dragon's; **smocza jama** dragon's den; **smocze drzewo** *l.* **smokowiec** *l.* dracena *bot.* dragon tree (*Dracaena draco*).

smog *mi* smog.

smok *ma* (*w bajkach*) dragon; **smok latający** *zool.* flying dragon, flying lizard (*Draco volans*). – *mi Gen.* -a **1.** *astron.* Draco, Dragon. **2.** *techn.* oil strainer; *Br.* sump filter.

smoking *mi* tuxedo; *Br.* dinner jacket.

smokowiec *ma zob.* **smocze drzewo.**

smolarz *mp arch.* pitch burner.

smolić *ipf.* smól *l.* smol *pot.* soil (*usu. with soot, tar, etc.*), tar; **przygania kocioł garnkowi, a sam smoli** the pot is calling the kettle black.

smolik *ma ent.* pine weevil (*Pissodes*).

smolisty *a.* **1.** (= *zawierający smołę*) pitchy, tarry; **blenda smolista** *l.* **uranowa** *min.* pitchblende, uraninite; **substancje smoliste** (*w papierosach*) tar; **o niskiej zawartości substancji smolistych** low-tar. **2.** (= *czarny jak smoła*) pitchblack.

smolny *a.* pitchy, tarry.

smolt *ma icht.* smolt.

smoluch *mp pl.* -y *pog.* sloven.

smoła *f. Gen.pl.* smół tar, pitch; **smoła drzewna** wood tar; **smoła węglowa** coal tar; **ruszać się**

jak mucha w smole move at a snail's pace; czarny jak smoła as black as pitch, pitch-black.

smołobeton *mi bud.* tar concrete.

smołować *ipf.* tar, pitch; (*łódkę*) pay.

smołowiec *mi* 1. (= *płynna smoła*) (liquid) tar. 2. *min.* pitchstone.

smółka *f. Gen.pl.* -ek 1. (*żywica*) galipot, gallipot. 2. *bot.* viscaria (*Viscaria*). 3. *med.* meconium.

smrek *mi Gen.* -a *dial.* spruce.

smrodek *mi* (*woń*) slight stench. − *mp* (*chłopiec*) little stinker, little bugger.

smrodliwie *adv.* reekingly, stinkingly.

smrodliwy *a.* reeking, stinking.

smrodzić *ipf. pot.* 1. (= *wydawać smród*) give off a stench. 2. (= *puszczać wiatry*) foul up the air.

smrodzieniec *mi* (*rodzaj żywicy*) asafoetid, asafetida.

smród *mi* -o- *Gen.* -u 1. (= *fetor*) stench, stink. 2. (*nieprzyjemna atmosfera*) stench. − *mp* -o- *Gen.* -a *pl.* -y *pog.* whippersnapper.

smucić *ipf.* sadden, grieve; smucić kogoś (*o wydarzeniu*) make sb sad. ~ się *ipf.* be sad; nie smuć się! don't be (so) sad!, cheer up!

smuga *f.* streak, trail; (*światła, koloru*) bar; (*zapachu*) waft; smuga kondensacyjna *lotn.* condensation trail.

smugowaty *a.* streaky.

smugowy *a.* pocisk smugowy *wojsk.* tracer.

smukły *a.* slender.

smutas *mp pot.* sourpuss; (= *osoba psująca dobry nastrój*) wet blanket.

smutek *mi* -tk- 1. (= *stan psychiczny*) sadness; (*zwłaszcza po śmierci osoby bliskiej*) grief; pogrążony w smutku grief-stricken. 2. (= *zmartwienie*) sorrow; topić smutki w kieliszku drown one's sorrows.

smutnawy *a.* saddish.

smutnieć *ipf.* become sad, sadden.

smutno *adv.* sadly; robi mi się smutno I'm starting to feel sad; wyglądać smutno look sad.

smutny *a.* 1. (= *pogrążony w smutku*) sad, sorrowful; smutne myśli sad thoughts; jesteś smutna? are you sad? 2. (= *opłakany*) sad, sorry; smutny koniec (*kogoś l. czegoś*) sticky end; smutny widok sorry sight.

smużka *f. Gen.pl.* -ek (little) streak, (little) trail.

smycz *f. pl.* -e 1. (*rzemień*) leash, lead; prowadzić psa na smyczy walk a dog on a leash; spuścić psa ze smyczy unleash a dog; pies zerwał się ze smyczy the dog broke the leash; obowiązek prowadzenia psów na smyczy leash law. 2. *myśl.* (= *para chartów*) brace of greyhounds.

smyczek *mi* -czk- *Gen.* -a *muz.* bow; *pot.* fiddlestick.

smyczki *pl. Gen.* -ów *muz.* (*część orkiestry*) the strings.

smyczkowy *a. muz.* string, stringed; instrument smyczkowy stringed instrument; kwartet smyczkowy (*utwór; zespół*) string quartet; orkiestra smyczkowa string orchestra; zespół smyczkowy string band.

smyk *mp pl.* -i *żart.* kid, shaver. − *int.* whoosh; pies smyk za kotem off rushed the dog after the cat.

smykać *ipf.* 1. *pot.* (= *biec*) whoosh, whisk (away). 2. *pot.* (= *skubać*) pluck, nibble (*coś at* sth).

smykałka *f. Gen.pl.* -ek *pot.* flair, knack; mieć smykałkę do czegoś have a flair for sth, have a knack for *l.* of sth.

smyknąć *pf.* -ij 1. *zob.* smykać. 2. *pot.* (= *ukraść*) nick.

smyrgać *ipf.*, smyrgnąć *pf.* -ij 1. *pot.* (= *biec*) whisk, whoosh (away). 2. *pot.* (= *rzucać*) chuck.

snadnie *adv. arch., lit.* facilely, easily.

snadź *adv. arch., lit.* peradventure, apparently.

snajper *mp pl.* -rzy (= *strzelec wyborowy*) sniper, marksman; *pot.* deadeye. − *mi Gen.* -a *pl.* -ry *pot.* (*karabin*) sniper rifle.

snajperski *a.* sniper's; karabin snajperski sniper rifle.

snąć *ipf.* śnie (*o rybach*) die.

snob *mp pl.* -i *l.* -y, snobka *f. Gen.pl.* -ek snob; *pot.* high-hat.

snobistyczny *a.* snobbish; *pot.* high-hat, clubby.

snobizm *mi* snobbery.

snobować się *ipf.* (= *interesować się*) do (sth) out of (sheer) snobbery; (= *zachowywać się*) behave like a snob; snobować się muzyką współczesną be interested in modern music out of (sheer) snobbery.

snobowaty *a.* toffee-nosed.

snop *mi Gen.* -a 1. (*zboża, słomy*) sheaf. 2. (*trawy*) (= *wiązka*) sheaf, bundle. 3. (*światła*) beam, shaft; (*światła, iskier*) shaft. 4. *wojsk.* sheaf.

snopek *mi* -pk- *Gen.* -a (*zboża*) sheaf; (= *wiązka*) sheaf, bundle.

snopienie *n. el.* brush discharge.

snopowiązałka *f. Gen.pl.* -ek *roln.* (reaper) binder.

snowalnia *f. Gen.pl.* -i *tk.* warping shop.

snowarka *f. Gen.pl.* -ek *tk.* warping machine, warper.

snowboard *mi sport* snowboard.

snowboardowy *a. sport* deska snowboardowa snowboard.

snowboardzista *mp*, snowboardzistka *f. Gen.pl.* -ek *sport* snowboarder.

snu *itp. mi zob.* sen.

snuć *ipf.* 1. (= *prząść*) spin; snuć domysły speculate (*o czymś l. na temat czegoś* on *l.* about sth); snuć opowieść tell a story; (*zwłaszcza długą i pełną niesamowitych zdarzeń*) spin a yarn; snuć plany devise plans; snuć wspomnienia reminisce (*o czymś* about sth). 2. (= *rozwijać nitkę*) unreel. 3. (*pajęczynę*) spin; snuć pajęczynę spin a web; snuć intrygi intrigue (*przeciw komuś* against sb). 4. *tk.* (*osnowę*) warp. ~ się *ipf.* 1. (*o opowieści*) be spun out, be told. 2. (= *rozwijać się*) unreel. 3. (= *być przędzionym*) be spun. 4. (*o drodze, ścieżce*) wind. 5. (= *przesuwać się w powietrzu*) float; (= *ciągnąć się*) trail; co ci się snuje po głowie? what's in your head?, what's going on in there? 6. (= *włóczyć się*) moon about, mope about, lallygag.

snycerka *f. zob.* snycerstwo.

snycerski *a.* woodcarver's, woodcarving.

snycerstwo *n.* woodcarving.

snycerz *mp* woodcarver.

sob. *abbr.* (= *sobota*) Sat. (= *Saturday*).

sobaczyć *ipf. pot.* cuss, turn the air blue.

sobą *pron. zob.* siebie.

sobek *mp* -bk- *pl.* -owie *l.* -i *pot.* egoist, self-seeker.

sobie *adv.* (*przy przymiotnikach*) quite; (*przy czasownikach*) just; był sobie zwykłym, przeciętnym człowiekiem he was just a usual, average man; podjadł sobie jak nigdy he's had the feed of his life, he's had his biggest feed ever; szedł sobie ulicą he was quitely walking down the street; dawno, dawno temu był sobie król once upon a time there was a king; czy Adam już sobie poszedł? is Adam gone yet?; co ty sobie myślisz? who do you think you are?, what the hell were you thinking?; idź sobie! go away!; ręce przy sobie! hands off!; żartujesz sobie! you must be joking!; ach, róbcie sobie, co chcecie oh, just do whatever you want *l.* please; taki sobie so-so; dobry sobie *l.* dobre sobie *iron.* yeah, whatever; niczego sobie quite all right; - Co robisz? - Ot tak sobie siedzę i myślę - What are you doing? - Just sitting and thinking. – *pron. zob.* siebie.

sobiepanek *mp iron.* self-seeker.

sobiepański *a.* cavalier, high-handed.

sobiepaństwo *n.* high-handedness.

sobkostwo *n. pot.* egoism, self-seeking, selfishness.

sobkowski *a. pot.* egoist, self-seeking, selfish.

sobole *pl. Gen.* -i (*futro*) sable fur *l.* coat.

soboli *a. zob.* sobolowy.

sobolowaty *a.* (*o maści konia*) chestnut.

sobolowy *a.* sable.

soborowy *a. rel.* conciliar.

sobota *f. Gen.pl.* -ót Saturday; Wielka Sobota *rel.* Holy Saturday; wolna sobota Saturday off work (*introduced in Poland in the early 1980s*).

sobotni *a.* Saturday; sobotni wieczór Saturday night.

sobowtór *mp pl.* -y double, lookalike, twin; *pot.* (dead) ringer.

soból *ma* -o- *zool.* sable (*Martes zibellina*).

sobór *mi* -o- 1. *rz.-kat.* council; sobór powszechny *l.* ekumeniczny ecumenical council; Sobór Nicejski the Nicene Council (*325, 787*); Sobór Trydencki the Council of Trent (*1545-1563*); Sobór Watykański Pierwszy the First Vatican Council (*1869-70*); Sobór Watykański Drugi the Second Vatican Council (*1962-75*). 2. *rel.* (= *rada biskupów prawosławnych*) council. 3. *rel.* (*świątynia prawosławna*) cathedral (*in the Orthodox Church*).

sobótka *f. Gen.pl.* -ek 1. (*obrzędy*) Midsummer *l.* Midsummer's Day feast. 2. (*ognisko*) Midsummer Day bonfire (*lit up during the feast*).

sobótkowy *a.* Midsummer Day (*feast, traditions, etc.*).

socha *f. hist., roln.* ard, wooden plow.

socjaldarwinizm *mi socjol.* Social Darwinism.

socjaldemokracja *f. polit.* 1. (*kierunek polityczny*) Social Democracy. 2. (*partia*) Social Democratic Party; Socjaldemokracja Rzeczypospolitej Polskiej Social Democratic Party of the Republic of Poland.

socjaldemokrata *mp polit.* Social Democrat.

socjaldemokratyczny *a. polit.* Social Democratic.

socjaldemokratyzm *mi polit.* Social Democracy, Social Democratic movement.

socjalista *mp*, socjalistka *f. Gen.pl.* -ek *polit.* socialist.

socjalistyczny *a. polit.* socialist; realizm socjalistyczny *sztuka* socialist realism.

socjalizacja *f. psych.* socialization.

socjalizm *mi polit.* socialism; socjalizm naukowy scientific socialism; socjalizm utopijny utopian socialism; narodowy socjalizm national socialism.

socjalizować *ipf.* 1. *ekon., psych.* socialize. 2. (= *skłaniać się ku socjalizmowi*) favor socialism.

socjalny *a.* (= *społeczny; bytowy*) social; dział socjalny employee affairs department; fundusz socjalny social fund; minimum socjalne poverty line; pokój socjalny common room (*for employees*); pracownik socjalny social worker; świadczenia socjalne social services; warunki socjalne living conditions.

socjeta *f. przest.* high society.

socjobiologia *f. Gen.* -ii *socjol.* sociobiology.

socjocentryczny *a. socjol.* sociocentric.

socjogeografia *f. Gen.* -ii *socjol.* sociogeography.

socjografia *f. Gen.* -ii *socjol.* sociography.

socjolingwistyka *f. jęz.* sociolinguistics.

socjolog *mp pl.* -dzy *l.* -owie sociologist.

socjologia *f. Gen.* -ii sociology; socjologia roślin *bot.* plant sociology, phytosociology; socjologia zwierząt *zool.* animal sociology; socjologia literatury *teor.lit.* sociology of literature.

socjologiczny *a.* sociological.

socjometria *f. Gen.* -ii *socjol.* sociometry.

socjopata *mp psych.* sociopath.

socjopatia *f. Gen.* -ii *psych.* sociopathy.

socjopatologia *f. Gen.* -ii *socjol.* sociopathology.

socjopsychologia *f. Gen.* -ii *psych.* social psychology.

socjotechniczny *a. socjol.* social engineering; badania socjotechniczne social engineering research.

socjotechnika *f. socjol.* social engineering.

socrealistyczny *a. sztuka* socialist realism; literatura socrealistyczna socialist realist *l.* realism literature.

socrealizm *mi sztuka* socialist realism.

socynianin *mp rel.* Socinian.

socynianizm *mi rel.* Socinianism.

soczewica *f. bot., kulin.* lentil (*Lens culinaris l. esculenta*); sprzedać coś za miskę soczewicy sell sth for a mess of pottage.

soczewka *f. Gen.pl.* **-ek** **1.** *fiz.* lens; **soczewka elektronowa** electron lens; **soczewka kontaktowa** contact lens; **płyn do soczewek kontaktowych** soaking solution; **soczewka optyczna** optical lens; **soczewka skupiająca** converging *l.* focusing *l.* positive lens; **soczewka rozpraszająca** diverging lens; **soczewka wklęsła** concave lens; **soczewka wypukła** convex lens. **2.** *anat.* (crystalline) lens.

soczewkowaty *a.* lenticular, lentoid.

soczewkowy *a.* lens, lenticular; **luneta soczewkowa** lens telescope.

soczystość *f.* **1.** (= *obfitość soku*) juiciness, sappiness; succulence, succulency; (*barw*) richness, mellowness. **2.** (= *dosadność*) pithiness. **3.** (= *rubaszność*) coarseness.

soczysty *a.* **1.** (= *pełen soku*) juicy, sappy, succulent; (*barwa*) rich, mellow. **2.** (= *dosadny*) pithy, terse. **3.** (= *rubaszny*) coarse, brutish.

soda *f. chem.* soda; **soda do pieczenia** baking soda; **soda do prania** washing soda; **soda kaustyczna** *l.* żrąca caustic soda; **soda krystaliczna** sal soda; **soda oczyszczona** saleratus; **soda rodzima** natron.

sodalicja *f. rz.-kat.* sodality; **Sodalicja Mariańska** Marian Sodality.

Sodoma *f. Bibl.* Sodom.

sodoma *f.* Sodom; **sodoma i gomora!** Sodom and Gomorrah!

sodomia *f. Gen.* **-ii** **1.** (= *zoofilia*) bestiality, zoophilia. **2.** *przest.* (= *pederastia*) pederasty.

sodomita *mp* **1.** (= *zoofil*) a person who practices bestiality. **2.** *przest.* (= *pederasta*) pederast.

sodowy[1] *a. chem.* sodium; **lampa sodowa** sodium *l.* sodium-vapor lamp; **ług sodowy** sodium lye.

sodowy[2] *a. kulin.* soda; **woda sodowa** soda water; **woda sodowa uderzyła mu do głowy** he has grown too big for his boots *l.* breeches; he has a swelled *l.* swollen head; his brains went to his head.

sodu *itp. mi zob.* **sód.**

sofa *f.* sofa, settee.

Sofia *f. Gen.* **-ii** *geogr.* Sofia, Sofiya.

sofista *mp fil. t. przen.* sophist.

sofistyczny *a. fil.* sophistic.

sofistyka *f.* **1.** (*ruch umysłowy*) sophistry. **2.** (*argumentacja*) sophistry, sophism.

sofizmat *mi* (*rozumowanie, argument*) sophism, sophistry.

Sofokles *mp* Sophocles.

software *mi Gen.* **-e'u** *komp.* software.

softwarowy *a. komp.* software.

soja *f. Gen.* **soi** *bot.* (*roślina, ziarno*) soybean; *Br.* soya bean (*Glycine max l. soja*).

sojowy *a.* soy; *Br.* soya; **olej sojowy** soybean oil; *Br.* soya oil; **sos sojowy** soy *l.* soya sauce.

sojusz *mi Gen.pl.* **-y** *l.* **-ów** alliance; **wejść z kimś w sojusz** ally o.s. with sb; **zawrzeć z kimś sojusz** contract an alliance with sb.

sojuszniczy *a.* allied; **mocarstwo sojusznicze** *polit.* friendly power; **państwo sojusznicze** ally; (*w czasie wojny*) cobelligerent; **układ sojuszniczy** alliance; **podpisano układ sojuszniczy pomiędzy Polską i USA** an alliance between Poland and the USA was signed; **wojska sojusznicze** allied forces.

sojusznik *mp* ally.

SOK *mi* (= *Straż Ochrony Kolei*) Polish railway police.

sok *mi* **1.** (*do picia*) juice; **sok cytrynowy** lemon juice; **sok owocowy** fruit juice; **sok pomarańczowy** orange juice; **sok pomidorowy** tomato juice; **herbata z sokiem malinowym** tea with raspberry juice; **wycisnąć z kogoś ostatnie soki** bleed sb dry. **2.** *bot.* sap; **sok komórkowy** cell sap; **krążenie soków** circulation of sap. **3.** *fizj.* juice; **sok jelitowy** intestinal juice; **sok trawienny** digestive juice; **sok trzustkowy** pancreatic juice; **sok żołądkowy** gastric juice.

sokista *mp* (*strażnik*) railway policeman.

sokoli *a.* falcon's, falconine; **sokoli wzrok** eagle eye; **mieć sokoli wzrok** be eagle-eyed *l.* hawk-eyed.

sokolnictwo *n.* falconry, hawking.

sokolniczy *a.* falconer's, hawker's.

sokolnik *mp* falconer, hawker.

sokoły *pl. Gen.* **-ów** *zool.* falcons (*Falconidae*).

sokora *f. Dat.* **-orze** *bot.* black poplar (*Populus nigra*).

sokowirówka *f. Gen.pl.* **-ek** juicer; *Br.* juice extractor.

sokół *ma* **-o-** *orn.* falcon (*Falco*); **sokół wędrowny** peregrine falcon (*Falco peregrinus*).

Sokrates *mp* Socrates.

sokratyczny *a. fil.* Socratic; maieutic, maieutical; **metoda sokratyczna** Socratic method.

sol[1] *n. indecl. muz.* sol, so.

sol[2] *mi* (= *jednostka monetarna Peru*) sol.

sola *f. Gen.pl.* **-i** *icht.* sole (*Solea solea*).

solanina *f. chem.* solanine.

solanka *f. Gen.pl.* **-ek** **1.** (*spożywcza*) brine. **2.** (*lecznicza*) saline. **3.** (*słona woda*) salt water; (*morska*) salt water, brine. **4.** *bot.* saltwort (*Salsola*). **5.** *dial.* (*bułka*) salted bread roll.

solankować *ipf.* brine.

solankowy *a.* briny, saline; **kąpiel solankowa** saline bath, brine bath; **źródło solankowe** salt spring.

solarium *n. sing. indecl. pl.* **-ria** *Gen.* **-riów** solarium.

solarka *f.* salt spreader.

solarnia *f.* saltery, salting shop *l.* room.

solarny *a.* solar.

solarymetr *mi meteor.* solarimeter.

solaryzacja *f. fot.* solarization.

solarz *mp* salter.

sold *mi hist.* (*moneta włoska*) soldo.

soldateska *f.* (= *rozpasane wojsko*) bestial soldiery.

solecyzm *mi gram.* solecism.

solenizant *mp,* **solenizantka** *f. Gen.pl.* **-ek.** person celebrating their birthday *l.* nameday.

solennie *adv.* solemnly, earnestly; **obiecać solennie** give a solemn promise.

solenny *a.* solemn.

solenoid *mi fiz.* solenoid.

solfatara *f. geol.* (= *ujście gazów*) solfatara.

solfeż *mi Gen.pl.* **-y** *l.* **-ów** *muz.* solfeggio, solfège.

soli *itp. f. zob.* **sól** *l.* **solić.**

solić *ipf.* **sól** (*podczas gotowania, konserwowania*) salt (*coś* sth); corn (*coś* sth); (*danie na talerzu, kanapkę*) put some salt (*coś* on sth).

solidarnie *adv.* solidarily, jointly and severally, in sympathy (*with others*).

solidarnościowy *a.* sympathetic; **strajk solidarnościowy** sympathy strike; *polit.* (= *dotyczący NSZZ „Solidarność"*) Solidarity.

solidarność *f.* **1.** (= *wsparcie*) solidarity (*z kimś* with sb); **poczucie solidarności** (*w zespole*) team spirit; **Niezależny Samorządny Związek Zawodowy „Solidarność"** the Independent Self-Governing Trade Union "Solidarity". **2.** *prawn.* joint and several liability.

solidarny *a.* solidary, solid; *prawn.* joint and several; **solidarne działanie** solidary *l.* unanimous action; **związkowcy byli solidarni w tej kwestii** the unionists were solid on this issue; **dług solidarny** joint debt; **dłużnik solidarny** joint debtor; **wierzyciel solidarny** joint creditor.

solidaryzm *mi polit., ekon.* solidarism.

solidaryzować się *ipf.* sympathise (*z kimś* with sb); **(całkowicie) solidaryzować się z kimś** be behind sb (all the way).

solidnie *adv.* (= *rzetelnie*) solidly, reliably; (= *mocno*) solidly, sturdily; (= *tęgo*) soundly; **solidnie wykonać pracę** do one's work well; **solidnie zbudowany dom** a well-built house; **solidnie oberwać** get a sound thrashing.

solidność *f.* (= *rzetelność*) solidity, reliability; (= *masywność, trwałość*) solidity, sturdiness.

solidny *a.* (= *mocny, pokaźny, uczciwy*) solid; (*o budowie ciała*) sturdy, compact; (*o budynku*) solid, foursquare; (*o gałęzi*) stout; (*o konstrukcji, budowie*) solid, staunch; (*o meblu, butach, zabezpieczeniach*) robust; (*o opakowaniu, przedmiocie*) sturdy; (*o osobie, fachowcu, firmie, usłudze*) solid, reliable; (*o szafie, domu, posiłku*) substantial; (*o posiłku*) square; (*o osobie, obywatelu*) stalwart.

soliflukcja *f. geol.* creep; solifluction, solifluxion.

solilokwium *n. teor.lit., teatr* soliloquy.

solipsysta *mp fil.* solipsist.

solipsystyczny *a. fil.* solipsistic.

solipsyzm *mi fil.* solipsism.

soliród *mi bot.* glasswort (*Salicornia*).

solista *mp*, **solistka** *f. Gen.pl.* **-ek 1.** *muz.* soloist. **2.** *sport* individual, soloist.

soliter *ma zool.* (= *tasiemiec uzbrojony*) pork tapeworm; tenia, *Br.* taenia (*Taenia solium*); *pot.* (= *tasiemiec*) tapeworm. – *mi Gen.* **-a 1.** *jubilerstwo* solitaire. **2.** *ogr.* solitary bush or tree (*esp. in a park or garden*).

solmizacja *f. muz.* solmization.

solmizacyjny *a. muz.* solmization.

solnictwo *n. górn.* salt mining.

solniczka *f. Gen.pl.* **-ek** (*do przechowywania soli*) saltcellar; (*do posypywania solą*) saltshaker.

solniczki *pl. anat.* (*zagłębienia przy kościach obojczykowych*) saltcellars.

solny *a.* salt, saline; **kąpiel solna** *metal.* salt bath; **kwas solny** *chem.* hydrochloric acid; **zalewa solna** brine; **złoże solne** *górn.* saliferous *l.* saline deposit; **źródło solne** salt spring; **żupa solna** *górn.* salt mine.

solo *n. indecl.* **1.** (*utwór*) solo; **solo na skrzypce** violin solo. **2.** (*walka*) *pot.* fist fight (*usu. one to which a teenager challeges another*). – *a. indecl.* solo; **śpiewać solo** sing solo; **sonata na wiolonczelę solo** sonata for cello solo.

solodajny *a.* saliferous.

solomierz *mi Gen.* **-a** *techn.* salinometer, salimeter.

Solon *mp* Solon.

solonka *f.* salted vegetables *l.* meat (*usu. pork*).

solonośny *a.* saliferous; **złoże solonośne** saliferous deposit.

solony *a.* salted.

solowy *a.* **1.** *muz.* solo; **partia solowa** solo part. **2.** *sport* individual, solo.

solówka *f. Gen.pl.* **-ek** *zob.* **solo.**

solstycjum *n. astron.* solstice.

soluks *mi med.* sunlamp.

solwat *mi chem.* solvate.

sołdat *mp pog.* soldier (*usu. Russian*); **pójść w sołdaty** be press-ganged, be drafted.

sołecki *a. admin.* of or related to the elected chair of a village council.

sołectwo *n. admin.* **1.** (*siedziba*) the seat of the village council chair (*usu. their house*). **2.** (*stanowisko*) the office of the village council chair. **3.** (*jednostka terytorialna*) the smallest administrative unit in Poland.

sołtys *mp admin.* (elected) chair of a village council.

soma *f. biol. t. lit.* soma.

Somalia *f. Gen.* **-ii** *geogr.* Somalia.

Somalijczyk *mp*, **Somalijka** *f. Gen.pl.* **-ek** Somali, Somalian.

somalijski *a.* Somali, Somalian.

somatologia *f. biol.* physical anthropology, somatology.

somatycznie *adv.* somatically.

somatyczny *a. biol.* somatic; **choroba somatyczna** somatic disease; **komórki somatyczne** somatic cells.

sombrero *n. Gen.* **-a** *l. indecl.* sombrero.

somit *mi biol.* somite.

somnambulicznie *adv.* somnambulistically.

somnambuliczny *a.* somnambulistic, somnambulic, somnambular.

somnambulik *mp* somnambulist, somnambule.

somnambulizm *mi psych.* somnambulism, sleep walking.

sonant *mi fon.* sonant.

sonantyczny *a. fon.* sonant, sonantal, sonantic; **spółgłoska sonantyczna** sonant.

sonar *mi techn.* sonar.

sonata *f. muz.* sonata; **sonata na skrzypce** violin sonata.

sonatina *f. muz.* sonatina.

sonatowy *a. muz.* sonata; **forma sonatowa** sonata form.

sonda *f.* **1.** *techn.* probe; **sonda akustyczna** echo sounder; **sonda głębinowa** deep-sea lead; **sonda kosmiczna** space probe. **2.** *meteor.* sonde; **balon sonda** sounding balloon. **3.** *med.* sound, probe; **sonda żołądkowa** stomach tube; **zapuścić sondę do rany** probe a wound. **4.** (= *sondaż*) opinion poll.

sondaż *mi Gen.pl.* -y *l.* -ów **1.** (*opinii publicznej*) opinion poll. **2.** *techn.* probing, sounding.

sondażowy *a.* **1.** (= *dotyczący sondażu*) opinion poll; **ankieta sondażowa** opinion poll questionnaire; **badanie sondażowe** opinion poll. **2.** (= *dotyczący sondowania*) probing, sounding; **balon sondażowy** sounding balloon; **łódź sondażowa** sounding boat.

sondolina *f. żegl.* sounding line.

sondować *ipf.* **1.** *techn.* probe; **sondować kogoś** (= *badać czyjąś opinię*) sound sb out, feel sb's pulse. **2.** *med.* (*narząd, ranę*) probe; (*żołądek, jamę*) sound. **3.** (*opinię publiczną*) sound; (*zwł. przed wyborami*) canvass.

sonet *mi teor.lit.* sonnet; **sonet szekspirowski** Shakespearean sonnet; **sonet włoski** Italian *l.* Petrarchan sonnet.

song *mi* **1.** *jazz* song. **2.** *kabaret* (cabaret) song (*usu. with elements of satire*); **protest song** protest song.

sonometr *mi fiz.* objective noise meter, sound level meter.

sonorność *f. fon.* sonority.

sonorny *a. fon.* sonorous; **spółgłoska sonorna** sonorant.

sopel *mi* -pl- *Gen.* -a (*lodu*) icicle; **zmarznąć na sopel lodu** be frozen through *l.* solid; **mieć ręce jak sople** have hands like ice; **zmarznąć na sopel** *l.* **zamienić się w sopel lodu** freeze to the bone.

sopelek *mi* -lk- *Gen.* -a (*lodu*) icicle.

sopran *mi Gen.* -u *muz.* (*głos*) soprano; **sopran dramatyczny** dramatic soprano; **sopran koloraturowy** coloratura soprano, coloratura; **sopran liryczny** lyric soprano. – *f. l. mp decl. like mp Gen.* -a *pl.* -y (*śpiewaczka*) soprano.

sopranista *mp*, **sopranistka** *f. Gen.pl.* -ek *muz.* soprano.

sopranowy *a. muz.* soprano.

sorabistyczny *a. jęz.* Wendish, Sorbian; **studia sorabistyczne** *uniw.* Wendish *l.* Sorbian studies.

sorabistyka *f. uniw.* Wendish *l.* Sorbian studies.

sorbent *mi chem.* sorbent.

sorbet *mi napój* sorbet, sherbet.

sorbit *mi chem.* sorbitol.

sorbować *ipf.* absorb.

sorboza *f. chem.* sorbose.

sorek *ma zool.* shrew (*Sorex*).

sorgo *n. bot.* sorghum, sorgo (*Sorghum*).

sorpcja *f. chem.* sorption.

sort *mi* sort, kind, type; **sorty mundurowe** kit issue; **prima sort** *pot.* first class, A1.

sortowacz *mp*, **sortowaczka** *f. Gen.pl.* -ek sorter.

sortować *ipf.* sort; segregate.

sortowanie *n.* sorting; **sortowanie danych** *komp.* data sorting; **sortowanie śmieci** *l.* **odpadów** waste separation, waste sorting.

sortownia *f. Gen.pl.* -i sorting plant; (*na poczcie*) sorting office; **sortownia listów** (*maszyna*) letter-sorting installation.

sortowniczy *a.* sorting; **maszyna sortownicza** sorting machine, sorter.

sortownik *mi Gen.* -a *techn.* sorter.

sortyment *mi handl.* assortment, range, line (*of goods*).

soryt *mi log.* sorites.

SOS *abbr. lotn., żegl.* (*komunikat radiotelegraficzny*) SOS; (*komunikat słowny*) Mayday.

sos *mi kulin.* sauce; (*do sałatek*) dressing; (*do polewania potrawy*) topping; (*do zamaczania zakąsek*) dip; **sos pieczeniowy** gravy; **sos pomidorowy** tomato sauce; **sos tatarski** tartare *l.* tartar sauce; **sos winegret** vinaigrette (sauce); **być nie w sosie** *przen.* be out of sorts.

sosjerka *f. Gen.pl.* -ek gravy boat, sauce boat.

sosna *f. Gen.pl.* sosen **1.** *bot.* (*drzewo*) pine (*Pinus*). **2.** (*drewno*) pine wood, pine.

sosnowate *pl. bot.* pines (*Pinaceae*).

sosnowaty *a.* pinaceous.

sosnowy *a.* pine; (*o zapachu*) piney, piny; **las sosnowy** pine wood; **tarcica sosnowa** red deal, deal.

sosnóweczka *f. ent.* **zwójka sosnóweczka** pine shoot moth (*Evetria buoliana*).

sosnówka *f.* **1.** *orn.* **sosnówka czarna** *l.* **sikora sosnówka** coal tit (*Parus ater*). **2.** *ent.* **barczatka sosnówka** pine-tree lappet (*Dendrolimus pini*).

sośnina *f.* **1.** (*las*) pine grove. **2.** (*gałęzie*) pine twigs. **3.** (*drewno*) pine (wood).

sotern *mi kulin.* Sauternes, sauternes.

sotnia *f. hist.* sotnya (*a troop of 100 Cossacks*).

sou *mi l. n. indecl.* (*moneta francuska*) sou.

soul *mi indecl. muz.* soul music, soul.

soulowy *a. muz.* soul; **muzyka soulowa** soul music.

souvenir *mi* souvenir, memento.

sowa *f. Gen.pl.* sów *orn.* (= *ptak z rzędu Strigiformes*) owl; **mądry jak sowa** as wise as an owl.

sowchoz *mi hist.* sovkhoz (*a state-owned farm in the former USSR*).

sowi *a.* owlish.

sowicie *adv.* amply, lavishly, generously; **być** *l.* **zostać sowicie wynagrodzonym** be richly *l.* amply rewarded.

sowiecki *a. uj.* Soviet; **rząd sowiecki** Soviet goverment; **władza sowiecka** Soviet rule; **Związek Sowiecki** *hist.* the Soviet Union.

sowietolog *mp pl.* -dzy *l.* -owie Sovietologist, Kremlinologist.

sowietologia *f. Gen.* -ii Sovietology, Kremlinology.

sowiety *pl. hist.* (= *rady rewolucyjne*) soviets.

sowietyzacja *f.* Sovietization.

sowity *a.* (*zapłata, napiwek*) generous; (*posiłek*) lavish.

sowizdrzalski *a.* mischievous, scatterbrained;

literatura sowizdrzalska *teor.lit.* picaresque literature.

sowizdrzał *mp pl.* **-y** 1. (= *trzpiot*) scatterbrain. 2. *teor.lit.* picaro, rogue.

sowy *pl. Gen.* **sów** *orn.* owls (*Strigiformes*); **sowy właściwe** typical owls (*Strigidae*).

sozologia *f. Gen.* **-ii** environmental protection science.

sód *mi* **-o-** *chem.* sodium; **chlorek sodu** sodium chloride.

sójka *f. Gen.pl.* **-ek** 1. *orn.* Eurasian jay (*Garrulus glandarius*). 2. (= *kuksaniec*) punch, rap; **dać komuś sójkę w bok** *pot.* rap sb on the side.

sól *f.* **-o-** *pl.* **-e** 1. (*w kuchni*) salt; **sól jadalna** *l.* **kuchenna** domestic salt, table salt; **sól kamienna** rock salt, halite; **sól ziemi** the salt of the earth. 2. *przen.* **być komuś solą w oku** be a thorn in sb's side *l.* flesh; **zamienić się w słup soli** be dumbfounded, be astonished; **zjadłem z nim beczkę soli** I've been through thick and thin with him; we go a long way. 3. *chem.* salt; **sól angielska** *l.* **gorzka** bitter salt; **sól fizjologiczna** *med.* normal *l.* physiological saline, isotonic salt solution; **sól kwaśna** acid salt; **sól obojętna** neutral salt; **sól trzeźwiąca** smelling *l.* volatile salt; **sól zasadowa** basic salt.

sów *f. zob.* **sowa**.

sóweczka *f. orn.* pygmy owl (*Glaucidium passerinum*).

sówka *f. Gen.pl.* **-ek** 1. (= *mała sowa*) owlet, small owl. 2. **sówka choinówka** *ent.* pine beauty moth (*Panolis flammea*).

sówki *pl. Gen.* **-ek** *ent.* noctuids (*Noctuidae*).

sp. *abbr.* (= *spółka*) Co. (= *company*).

spacer *mi* walk; **iść na spacer** go for a walk, take a walk; **wyprowadzić psa na spacer** take the dog out, walk the dog.

spacerek *mi* **-rk-** walk; **iść spacerkiem** walk slowly.

spacerniak *mi Gen.* **-a** prison yard.

spacerować *ipf.* walk, stroll; **spacerować po pokoju** pace up and down the room.

spacerowicz *mp Gen.pl.* **-ów** *pot.* stroller, walker.

spacerowy *a.* walking; **statek spacerowy** excursion boat; **wózek spacerowy** stroller; *Br.* pushchair.

spacerówka *f. Gen.pl.* **-ek** (*wózek*) stroller; *Br.* pushchair.

spacja *f.* 1. *druk.* (= *odstęp*) (= *rozstrzelenie druku*) space. 2. *pot.*, *komp.* (*klawisz*) space bar; **wciśnij spację** press space.

spacjować *ipf. druk.* space, space out.

spacyfikować *pf.* pacify.

spaczyć *pf.* 1. (*podłogę, okno*) warp, distort. 2. (*charakter, osobowość*) warp. ~ **się** *pf.* warp, distort.

spać *ipf.* **śpię śpisz, śpij** sleep; **on śpi** he's asleep, he's sleeping; **on nie śpi** he's awake; **iść spać** go to bed; **spać jak suseł** *l.* **zabity** sleep like a log, be sound asleep; **spać jak zając** sleep lightly; **spać snem sprawiedliwego** sleep the sleep of the just; **spać snem wiecznym** sleep the eternal sleep; **kłaść się spać z kurami** (= *wcześnie*) go to bed early; (= *o zmierzchu*) go to bed at dusk; **coś nie daje komuś spać** sth keeps sb awake; sth bothers sb; sth is on sb's mind; **chce mi się spać** I'm sleepy; **licho nie śpi** one has to be on the lookout all the time; **spać z kimś** *pot.* sleep with sb.

spad *mi* 1. (*nachylenie*) slope, tilt. 2. *ogr.* windfall.

spadać *ipf.* 1. (*z góry na dół*) fall, fall down; **spadać na ziemię** fall on the ground; **spadać z dachu** fall off the roof; **spaść na cztery łapy** land on one's feet; **spaść komuś na kark** *l.* **głowę** (*np. o niespodzianych gościach*) descend on sb; **cios spadł na kogoś** a blow came down on sb; **kamień spadł mi z serca** it was a load *l.* weight off my mind; **korona z głowy ci nie spadnie** you won't die if you do it, it will do you no harm; **spadło na mnie wielkie nieszczęście** a great misfortune befell me; **spadło to na mnie jak grom z jasnego nieba** it was like a bolt from the blue; **odpowiedzialność (za to) spadła na dyrektora** the director was held responsible (for that); **z byka spadłeś?** are you out of your mind?, are you crazy?; **spadasz mi z nieba!** you are a godsend!; **jak spaść, to z dobrego konia** one may *l.* might as well be hanged *l.* hung for a sheep as a lamb. 2. (= *zmniejszać się*) fall, drop, go down; **spadać gwałtownie** plummet, fall *l.* drop sharply; **spaść na wadze** lose weight; **dolar spadł** the dollar exchange rate went down; **temperatura spadła do minus trzech stopni** the temperature fell to minus three degress. 3. *tylko ipf.* (= *obniżać się*) descend; **droga spada ku rzece** the road descends towards a river. 4. *tylko ipf.* (= *osuwać się*) hang down; **włosy spadały jej na ramiona** her hair hung down to her shoulders. 5. *tylko ipf.* (= *uciekać*) *pot.* split; **spadaj!** get lost!, take a hike!

spadek *mi* **-dk-** 1. (= *obniżenie*) slope, tilt. 2. (= *zmniejszenie się*) (*temperatury, ciśnienia, cen, napięcia*) fall, drop; (*gospodarczy*) decline; (*np. liczby zabójstw, wypadków*) decrease; (*do niższej ligi*) relegation. 3. *prawn.* inheritance, bequest, devise; **zostawić** *l.* **zapisać coś komuś w spadku** bequeath *l.* leave *l.* devise sb sth. 4. *teor.lit.* cadence. 5. *fiz.* fall; **spadek swobodny ciała** free fall.

spadkobierca *mp prawn.* heir, inheritor; (*zwł. nieruchomości*) devisee.

spadkobierczyni *f. prawn.* heiress; inheritress, inheritrix; (*zwł. nieruchomości*) devisee.

spadkobranie *n. prawn.* inheriting.

spadkodawca *mp prawn.* testator.

spadkodawczyni *f. prawn.* testator, testatrix.

spadkowy *a.* 1. *prawn.* inheritance; **masa spadkowa** inheritance; **prawo spadkowe** law of succession. 2. (= *malejący*) declining; (*o tendencji*) downward.

spadochron *mi* parachute; **skoki ze spadochronem** parachuting; **pilocik spadochronu** pilot parachute.

spadochroniarski *a.* parachuting.

spadochroniarstwo *n.* parachuting.

spadochroniarz *mp* parachuter; *wojsk.* paratrooper.

spadochronowy *a.* parachuting.

spadowy a. **młot spadowy** techn. drop hammer.

spadziowy a. **miód spadziowy** honeydew honey.

spadzisto adv. steeply.

spadzistość f. 1. (terenu) fall, tilt. 2. (= spadek, stok) slope.

spadzisty a. (= stromy) steep; (= nachylony) sloping, tilting.

spadź f. bot. honeydew.

spaghetti n. indecl. spaghetti.

spajać¹ ipf. (= łączyć) (strukturę, zjawiska, elementy, grupę osób) join, unite; (np. o moście) connect. **~ się** ipf. (= łączyć się) join, unite.

spajać² ipf. (= upijać) make drunk. **~ się** ipf. (= upijać się) get drunk.

spakować pf. pack. **~ się** pf. pack, pack up.

spalać ipf. zob. **spalić**. **~ się** ipf. zob. **spalić się**.

spalanie n. 1. fizj. oxidization. 2. techn. combustion.

spalatalizować pf. fon. palatalize. **~ się** pf. fon. become palatalized.

spalenizna f. sth burnt; **czuję spaleniznę** I can smell sth burning.

spalić pf. 1. (ogniem) burn, burn down; **spalić za sobą mosty** burn one's boats l. bridges (behind one); **pomysł spalił na panewce** the idea didn't go off. 2. (o przemianie materii) oxidize. 3. mot. (paliwo) consume, use. 4. (= przypiec) (np. skórę, pieczeń) burn, scorch. 5. pot. (= opalić na słońcu) sunburn. 6. (chemikaliami) burn. 7. techn. burn (out); blow. 8. sport foul out, cut. **~ się** pf. 1. (pod wpływem ognia) burn down; **spalić się ze wstydu** be ashamed; **dom się spalił** the house burnt down. 2. (pod wpływem temperatury) burn, scorch. 3. (pod wpływem słońca) sunburn. 4. (o przemianie materii) oxidize. 5. (= tracić siły witalne) burn out. 6. pot. (= zdekonspirować się) expose o.s., uncover o.s.

spalinowy a. techn. combustion; **gazy spalinowe** combustion gases; **lokomotywa spalinowa** kol. diesel engine; **silnik spalinowy** internal combustion engine.

spaliny pl. Gen. **-n** fumes, exhaust.

spalony a. 1. (ogniem) burnt, burnt down. 2. (= spieczony) burnt, scorched. 3. (= opalony) sunburnt; **spalone wargi** chapped lips. 4. (= uszkodzony) damaged. 5. sport disqualified (jump, throw, etc.). 6. pot. (= zdekonspirowany) exposed, uncovered. **– mi** sport offside.

spałaszować pf. pot. wolf down, gobble up.

spałować pf. pot. zob. **pałować**.

spamiętać pf. remember; **trudno to wszystko spamiętać** it's hard to memorize all this.

spanie n. 1. (czynność) sleeping. 2. (miejsce) bed; pot. sack; **wagon z miejscami do spania** kol. sleeping car.

spaniel ma kynol. spaniel; **cocker spaniel** cocker spaniel.

spanikować pf. pot. panic.

spanikowany a. panicky, panicked.

spaprać pf. **-przę -przesz** pot. mess up, louse up.

sparafrazować pf. zob. **parafrazować**.

sparaliżować pf. pat., przen. paralyze; **sparaliżować komunikację** paralyze transport; **sparaliżować ruch uliczny** bring traffic to a stop l. halt; **strach go sparaliżował** he was paralyzed with fear.

sparcieć pf. wilt, get flabby.

sparing mi boks sparring; **piłka nożna** training match, test match.

sparingowy a. sport sparring; **piłka nożna** training, test.

sparmania f. bot. African hemp (Sparmannia africana).

sparodiować pf. parody.

sparować pf. szermierka parry.

sparszywieć pf. 1. (o zwierzęciu, człowieku) become mangy; (o roślinach) scab. 2. przen. become lousy.

Sparta f. geogr., hist. Sparta.

spartaczyć pf. pot. botch, bungle.

spartakiada f. sports games.

Spartanin mp, **Spartanka** f. Gen.pl. **-ek** Spartan.

spartanin mp, **spartanka** f. Gen.pl. **-ek** Spartan.

spartański a. Spartan.

spartolić pf. pot. = **spartaczyć**.

sparzyć¹ pf. 1. (gorącem) burn. 2. (substancją drażniącą) burn; (pokrzywą) sting. 3. (mięso, warzywa) blanch. **~ się¹** pf. 1. (gorącem) get burnt, burn o.s. 2. (substancją drażniącą) get burnt, burn o.s.; (pokrzywą) sting. 3. (= rozczarować się) become disappointed (czymś by l. with sth); **kto się gorącym sparzył, ten na zimne dmucha** once bitten, twice shy.

sparzyć² pf. (zwierzęta) mate. **~ się²** pf. (o zwierzętach) mate.

spasać ipf. roln. pasture, graze.

spasiony a. **-eni** pot. (o zwierzęciu) fattened; (o człowieku) fat.

spaskudzić pf. pot. botch, bungle.

spasły a. pot. fat.

spasować pf. 1. karty pass. 2. (= wycofać się) give up.

spastyczny a. pat. spastic.

spaść¹ pf. **spadnę spadniesz spadnij, spadł** zob. **spadać**.

spaść² pf. **spasę spasiesz spasł spaśli** zob. **spasać**. **~ się** pf. pot. get fat.

spatałaszyć pf. pot. bungle, botch.

spatynowany a. patinated.

spauperyzowany a. pauperized.

spauzować pf. pot. pause.

spaw mi techn. 1. (spoina) weld. 2. (= spawanie) welding.

spawacz mp techn. welder.

spawać ipf. 1. zwł. techn. weld. 2. wulg. (= wymiotować) barf, puke.

spawalnia f. Gen.pl. **-i** l. **-ń** techn. welding shop.

spawalnictwo n. techn. welding technology.

spawalniczy a. techn. welding.

spawalność f. techn. weldability.

spawanie n. techn. welding; **spawanie acetyle-**

nowe acetylene welding; **spawanie łukowe** arc welding.

spawarka *f. Gen.pl.* **-ek** *techn.* welder, welding machine.

spazm *mi* spasm.

spazmować *ipf.* (= *łkać*) sob.

spazmy *pl.* (= *płacz*) sobbing.

spazmatyczny *a.* spasmodic, spasmodical.

spąg *mi górn.* floor.

spąsowieć *pf. zob.* **pąsowieć**.

spec *mp pot.* whiz, expert; **spec od komputerów** computer whiz.

specjalista *mp*, **specjalistka** *f. Gen.pl.* **-ek** **1.** (*fachowiec*) expert, specialist. **2.** (*lekarz*) specialist.

specjalistyczny *a.* specialist; **badania specjalistyczne** (*naukowe*) specialist research, specialized research; **książki specjalistyczne** subject books, specialist books; **literatura specjalistyczna** specialist literature, subject literature.

specjalizacja *f.* specialization, specialty; *med.* specialty.

specjalizacyjny *a.* specialty, subject.

specjalizować się *ipf.* specialize (*w czymś* in sth).

specjalnie *adv.* especially, on purpose; **to nie jest specjalnie miłe** *pot.* this is not particularly nice; **zrobiłeś to specjalnie!** you did it on purpose!

specjalność *f.* **1.** (*wiedza*) specialty; métier, metier; **magister filologii angielskiej ze specjalnością nauczycielską** M.A. in English with a teaching major. **2.** (*umiejętność*) specialty, special skill; **sprzątanie to moja specjalność** cleaning is my specialty, I specialize in cleaning. **3.** (= *specjał*) specialty; **torty urodzinowe to moja specjalność** birthday cakes are my specialty; **specjalność zakładu** *kulin.* specialty of the house.

specjalny *a.* special; **korespondent specjalny** special correspondent; **pedagogika specjalna** special education; **służby specjalne** special services; **szkoła specjalna** special school; **wysłannik specjalny** special envoy; **dziecko specjalnej troski** *szkoln.* child with special needs, learning-disabled child; **to nic specjalnego** it's nothing special.

specjał *mi* delicacy.

specyficznie *adv.* (= *właściwie, charakterystycznie*) specifically; (= *szczególnie*) peculiarly.

specyficzność *f.* (= *właściwość, bycie charakterystycznym*) specificity; (= *swoistość, szczególność*) peculiarity.

specyficzny *a.* (= *właściwy, charakterystyczny*) specific; (= *szczególny*) peculiar.

specyfik *mi med.* patent medicine, proprietary drug.

specyfika *f.* (= *właściwość, bycie charakterystycznym*) specificity; (= *swoistość, szczególność*) peculiarity.

specyfikacja *f. handl.* specification; *techn.* specifications; **specyfikacje techniczne** technical specifications.

spedycja *f. handl.* shipping, forwarding; **spedycja kolejowa** railway shipping.

spedycyjny *a. handl.* shipping, forwarding; **przedsiębiorstwo spedycyjne** shipping company.

spedytor *mp handl.* shipping agent, shipper; forwarding agent, forwarder.

spektakl *mi Gen.pl.* **-i** *l.* **-ów** *teatr* performance, show.

spektakularnie *adv.* spectacularly.

spektakularny *a.* spectacular; **spektakularne zwycięstwo** spectacular victory.

spektralny *a. fiz.* spectral; **analiza spektralna** spectroscopic analysis.

spektrograf *mi fiz.* spectrograph; **spektrograf akustyczny** sound spectrograph.

spektrografia *f. Gen.* **-ii** *fiz.* spectrography.

spektrograficzny *a. fiz.* spectrographic.

spektrometr *mi fiz.* spectrometer.

spektrometria *f. Gen.* **-ii** *fiz.* spectrometry.

spektroskop *mi fiz.* spectroscope.

spektroskopia *f. Gen.* **-ii** *fiz.* spectroscopy.

spektroskopowy *a. fiz.* spectroscopic, spectroscopical.

spektrum *n. sing. indecl. pl.* **-ra** *Gen.* **-rów** **1.** (*zakres*) range, scope, spectrum; **szerokie spektrum działania leku** wide range of drug application. **2.** *fiz.* spectrum.

spekulacja *f.* **1.** (*myślenie*) speculation; **opierać się na spekulacjach** base on speculations. **2.** (*transakcja*) speculation, profiteering.

spekulacyjny *a.* speculative.

spekulancki *a.* speculative.

spekulant *mp*, **spekulantka** *f. Gen.pl.* **-ek** speculator, profiteer.

spekulować *ipf.* **1.** (= *przeprowadzać nieuczciwe transakcje*) speculate, profiteer; **spekulować na czymś** speculate in sth. **2.** (*myślowo*) speculate.

speleolog *mp pl.* **-dzy** *l.* **-owie** speleologist.

speleologia *f. Gen.* **-ii** speleology.

speleologiczny *a.* speleological.

spelunka *f. Gen.pl.* **-ek** *pot.* dive.

spełniać *ipf.*, **spełnić** *pf.* **spełnij** *l.* **spełń** **1.** (= *wypełnić, wykonać*) fulfill, *Br.* fulfil; meet; **spełniać obietnicę** fulfill *l.* keep a promise; (*zwł. wyborczą, polityczną*) deliver on a promise; **spełniać oczekiwania** live up *l.* come up to the expectations, meet expectations; **spełniać prośbę** act on a request; **spełniać życzenie** fulfill *l.* realize a wish; **spełniać równanie** *mat.* satisfy an equation. **2.** (= *wypijać*) drink up; **spełnić czyjeś zdrowie** drink a toast to sb. **~ się** *ipf.*, **spełnić się** *pf.* **1.** (*o prognozie, marzeniach, miłości*) come true. **2.** (*o człowieku*) fulfill o.s. (*w czymś* in sth).

spełnienie *n.* fulfillment; (**dawać/mieć poczucie spełnienia** (give/have) a sense of fulfillment.

spełznąć *pf.* **-znę -zniesz** *l.* **-źniesz, -znij** *l.* **-źnij, -zł** *l.* **-znął -zła -zli** *l.* **źli** **1.** (= *osunąć się*) creep down, crawl down; **dziecko spełzło z tapczanu** the child crawled off the couch; **spełznąć na niczym** come to nothing. **2.** (= *spłowieć*) fade.

spencer *mi Gen.* **-a** (*ubiór*) (*damski i męski*) spencer.

spenetrować *pf. zob.* **penetrować.**

sperma *f. biol.* sperm, semen.

spermatogeneza *f. biol.* spermatogenesis.

spermatozoid *mi* (*u człowieka, zwierząt*) spermatozoon; (*u roślin*) spermatozoid.

speszony *a.* **-eni** abashed, off balance, disconcerted; **był speszony widokiem swojego rywala** he was put off balance at the sight of his rival, he lost countenance at the sight of his rival.

speszyć *pf.* disconcert, put off balance. **~ się** *pf.* get disconcerted, lose countenance.

spetryfikować *pf. bud.* reinforce (*a wall, foundation etc. with cement injections*). **~ się** *pf.* **1.** *bud.* petrify. **2.** *lit.* (= *utrwalić się*) fossilize.

spetryfikowany *a. lit.* fossilized.

spęcznieć *pf.* bloat, swell.

spęd *mi roln. t. iron.* (*ludzi*) roundup.

spędzać *ipf.*, **spędzić** *pf.* **1.** (= *przepędzać*) drive away; **spędzać płód** *med.* procure *l.* produce an abortion; **spędzać psa z łóżka** shoo the dog off the bed; **myśl o budowie domu spędza mi sen z powiek** the thought of building a house keeps me awake at night; I shiver at the thought of building a house. **2.** (*gromadzić*) round up, gather. **3.** (*czas*) spend; **spędziliśmy miło czas** we had a good time; **wakacje spędziliśmy nad morzem** we spent the holidays at the seaside.

spękać *pf.* **1.** (= *popękać*) crack, rift. **2.** *pot.* (= *stchórzyć*) chicken out.

spękany *a.* **1.** (= *popękany*) cracked; **spękana skóra** chapped skin; **spękane wargi** chapped lips; **spękana ziemia** parched land. **2.** *pot.* (= *przerażony*) scared out of his *l.* her wits.

spętać *pf.* **1.** (*zwierzę*) hogtie; (*człowieka*) tie. **2.** *przen.* hogtie, trammel.

spętany *a.* **1.** (= *związany*) (*o zwierzęciu*) hogtied; (*o człowieku*) tied. **2.** *przen.* hampered; **mieć spętane ręce** have one's hands tied.

spiąć *pf.* **zepnę zepniesz, zepnij** *zob.* **spinać. ~ się** *pf. zob.* **spinać się.**

spichlerz *mi Gen.* **-a** *Gen.pl.* **-y** *l.* **-ów** granary.

spichrz *mi Gen.* **-a** *Gen.pl.* **-y** *l.* **-ów** *zob.* **spichlerz.**

spichrzowy *a.* **organy spichrzowe** *bot.* storage organs.

spiczasty *a.* pointed, spiky, peaked.

spić *pf.* **spiję spijesz, spij** *zob.* **spijać. ~ się** *pf. zob.* **spijać się.**

spiec *pf.* **spiekę spieczesz spiekł** *zob.* **spiekać. ~ się** *pf. zob.* **spiekać się.**

spieczony *a.* burnt; **spieczony chleb** crusty bread; **spieczona twarz** sunburnt face, chapped face.

spiek *mi techn.* sinter.

spiekać *ipf.* **1.** (= *przypiekać*) burn; **spiec raka** blush deeply. **2.** *techn.* sinter. **~ się** *ipf.* **1.** (= *przypiekać się*) burn. **2.** *techn.* become sintered.

spiekota *f.* searing heat.

spieniać *ipf.*, **spienić** *pf.* foam, froth. **~ się** *ipf.*, **spienić się** *pf.* **1.** (= *stawać się pianą*) foam, froth. **2.** *pot.* (= *denerwować się*) steam, burn with anger.

spieniężać *ipf.*, **spieniężyć** *pf.* cash, cash in.

spieniony *a.* **-eni** **1.** (*np. woda*) foamy, frothy. **2.** *pot.* burning with anger.

spieprzać *ipf.*, **spieprzyć** *pf. pot.* **1.** (= *uciekać*) buzz off. **2.** *tylko pf.* (= *zepsuć*) screw up. **~ się** *pf. pot.* (= *zepsuć się*) get screwed up.

spierać *ipf.* (*brud*) wash out.

spierać się *ipf.* (= *dyskutować*) argue (*o coś* over *l.* about sth).

spierdalać *ipf.*, **spierdolić**[1] *pf. wulg.* **1.** (= *uciekać*) get the fuck out; **spierdalamy stąd!** let's get the fuck out of here! **2.** (= *odczepić się*) fuck off; **spierdalaj!** fuck off!; *Br. t.* piss off!

spierdolić[2] *pf. wulg.* (*sprawę*) (= *zepsuć*) fuck up, screw up. **~ się** *pf. wulg.* (= *zepsuć się*) get fucked up.

spierzchnąć *pf.* (*o wargach, rękach*) chap, roughen, crack.

spierzchnięcie *n.* chap, chapped skin.

spierzchnięty *a.* (*o skórze, wargach*) chapped, sore; (*o rękach*) rough.

spierzesz *itd. pf. zob.* **sprać.**

spieszczać *ipf.* use baby-talk; (= *zdrabniać*) use diminutive forms.

spieszczenie *n. gram.* hypocoristic, diminutive.

spieszyć *ipf. zob.* **śpieszyć.**

spieścić *pf.* **spieszczę spieścisz** *zob.* **spieszczać.**

spietrać się *pf. pot.* chicken out.

spięcie *n.* **1.** (*połączenie*) clip, clasp, brace; **krótkie spięcie** *el.* short circuit; (= *spowodowane przez burzę*) weather contact. **2.** *przen.* clash, argument.

spiętrzać *ipf.* pile (up), heap; accumulate; (*rzekę*) dam up; **spiętrzone wody** rough waters. **~ się** *ipf.* (*o wodzie*) back up; (*o krze, trudnościach*) accumulate, tower, pile up.

spiętrzenie *n.* **1.** (*tama*) dam. **2.** (*trudności, robót*) pile-up, accumulation.

spiętrzyć *pf. zob.* **spiętrzać. ~ się** *pf. zob.* **spiętrzać się.**

spięty *a.* **1.** (= *połączony*) clasped, braced, clipped; (*o włosach*) cued, swept; (*o dokumentach*) clipped. **2.** (= *zestresowany*) tense, stressed-out, nervous; **być spiętym** be tense, be keyed up. **3.** (*o mięśniach*) tense, taut.

spijać *ipf.* **1.** (*śmietankę*) drink off; **spijać sukcesy** reap the fruits; **spijać słowa z czyichś ust** hang on to sb's words. **2.** *pot.* (= *upijać kogoś*) get *l.* make drunk, liquor up.

spiker *mp telew.*, *radio* announcer, presenter, newsreader; (*w programach na żywo*) anchor; anchorman *l.* anchorwoman; (*osoba mówiąca wprost do kamery*) talking head.

spikerka *f.* **1.** *Gen.pl.* **-ek** *zob.* **spiker. 2.** *Gen.pl.* **-ek** *pot.* (*studio*) presenter's room *l.* studio.

spikerski *a.* (*o studio, dyżurze*) presenter's.

spiknąć *pf.* **-ij** *pot.* set up, fix up (*kogoś z kimś* sb with sb). **~ się** *pf. pot.* get together, become as thick as thieves; be in cahoots.

spilśniać *ipf.*, **spilśnić** *pf.* **-ij** **1.** *tk.* (*wełnę*) full, felt. **2.** *techn.* (*masę papierniczą*) felt.

spiłować *pf.*, **spiłowywać** *ipf.* **1.** (= *ścinać*) saw off *l.* up. **2.** (*pilnikiem*) (= *ścierać*) file off *l.* up.

spin *mi fiz.* spin; **spin połówkowy** half-integral spin; **wektor spinu** spin vector.

spinacz *mi Gen.* **-a 1.** (*biurowy*) clip, paperclip. **2.** (*do bielizny*) clothespin. **3.** *żegl.* clip, clamp, lug piece.

spinać *ipf.* (= *łączyć*) clasp, fasten together *l.* up *l.* in; (*papiery, dokumenty*) clip; (*włosy*) pin, sweep back, cue; (*na sprzączkę*) buckle (up); (*klamrą*) brace; **spiąć konia** set spurs to one's horse. ~ **się** *ipf.* **1.** (= *obejmować się*) clasp, embrace, cuddle. **2.** *pot.* (= *mobilizować się*) pull one's socks up, brace o.s. up.

spinaker *mi żegl.* (*typ żagla*) spinnaker.

spinka *f. Gen.pl.* **-ek** pin, clip, stud; (*do włosów*) bobby pin, hairclip, hairgrip; (*do krawata*) tie clasp; (*do mankietów*) cuff link.

spinning *mi sport* (*wędka*) spinning rod; (*sposób łowienia*) spinning, spin casting *l.* fishing; **łowić na spinning** spin.

spinningowy *a. sport* (*o zawodach*) spinning; **sprzęt spinningowy** spinning tackle *l.* gear.

spiorę *itd. pf. zob.* **sprać**.

spiorunować *pf.* paralyze, render motionless, stun, stagger; **spiorunować kogoś wzrokiem** cast a withering glance at sb.

spirala *f.* **1.** spiral, volute; (*dymu*) curl; **spirala agresji** *przen.* spiral of aggression. **2.** *techn.* helix; **spirala grzejna** (heating) coil; **spirala inflacyjna** *ekon.* inflationary spiral. **3.** *lotn.* spin, tailspin; **opadać spiralą** spin; **spirala śmierci** *łyżwiarstwo* death spiral; **skręcić w spiralę** curl, coil. **4.** *mat.* spiral. **5.** *med.* intrauterine device, IUD; loop, contraceptive coil. **6.** *sztuka* vermiculation.

spiralnie *adv.* spirally, spiral-like; (*skręcony, spawany*) curled up, whorled; (*zwinięty*) involute; **skręcać się spiralnie** curl up.

spiralny *a.* spiral, helical, involute, volute, corkscrew; (*o drucie, wiertle*) spiral; **galaktyka spiralna** *astron.* spiral galaxy; **spiralna zjeżdżalnia** (*w wesołym miasteczku*) spiral slide; *Br.* helter-skelter; **muszla spiralna** turbinate; **w oprawie spiralnej** spiral-bound; **ornament spiralny** scrollwork.

spirant *mi fon.* fricative, spirant.

spirituals *pl. indecl. muz.* spirituals.

spirometr *mi med.* spirometer.

spirula *f. zool.* spirula (*Spirula*).

spirytualia *pl.* (= *napoje alkoholowe*) alcohols, liquors.

spirytualista *mp fil.* spiritualist.

spirytualistyczny *a. fil.* (*o systemie, poglądach*) spiritualistic.

spirytualizm *mi fil.* spiritualism.

spirytus *mi* spirits, spirit; *chem.* spirit; (*do dezynfekcji i nacierania*) rubbing alcohol; **spirytus rektyfikowany** rectified *l.* proof spirit; **spirytus salicylowy** surgical spirit; **spirytus kamforowy** spirits of camphor; **spirytus denaturowany** denatured alcohol; **spirytus drzewny** wood spirit; **spirytus skażony** denatured spirit.

spirytusowy *a.* (*o przemyśle, monopolu, ma-*

szynce) spirit; **lampka spirytusowa** spirit lamp; **lakier spirytusowy** spirit varnish.

spirytysta *mp,* **spirytystka** *f. Gen.pl.* **-ek** spiritualist, spiritist.

spirytystyczny *a.* spiritualistic, spiritistic; **seans spirytystyczny** seance, séance.

spirytyzm *mi* spiritualism, spiritism.

spis *mi* **1.** (= *rejestr*) register, list; (*instytucji, mieszkańców*) directory; (*urzędowy*) file, record; (*alfabetyczny*) index; (*rzeczy do kupienia, zrobienia*) list; (*wyczerpujący*) laundry list; **spis inwentarza** *handl.* inventory; **spis potraw** menu, bill of fare; **spis treści** (table of) contents; **prowadzić spis** keep a record; **spis podatkowy** tax roll; **figurować w spisie** be on the list. **2.** (= *spisywanie*) registration; (**powszechny**) **spis ludności** census.

spisa *f. hist.* spear.

spisać *pf.* **spiszę spiszesz** *zob.* **spisywać**. ~ **się** *pf. zob.* **spisywać się**.

spisek *mi* **-sk-** plot, conspiracy, cabal; (*przeciw królowi*) confederacy; **uknuć spisek** engineer *l.* hatch a plot; **teoria spisku** conspiracy theory.

spiskować *ipf.* conspire, plot, scheme (*przeciwko komuś* against sb); be in conspiracy (*z kimś* with sb).

spiskowiec *mp* **-wc-** *pl.* **-y** conspirator, conspirer, plotter, cabalist; **grupa spiskowców** cabal.

spiskowy *a.* (*o organizacji*) conspiratorial; **teoria spiskowa** conspiracy theory.

spisowy *a.* (*o komisji*) registration; **rachmistrz spisowy** census representative.

spisywać *ipf.* **1.** (= *tworzyć spis*) list, make a list, inventory; (*w kolejności wydarzeń*) chronicle; (*z taśmy*) transcribe; **spisać coś/kogoś na straty** write sb/sth off, give sb/sth up; **spisywać coś na karb czegoś** put sth down to, charge sth off to sth, chalk sth up to. **2.** (= *tworzyć tekst na podstawie wspomnień, notatek*) write down, note down; **spisać testament** make one's last will. **3.** (= *przepisywać skądś*) copy; *szkoln.* (= *odpisywać*) cheat, crib, copy. **4.** (*osobę zatrzymaną przez policję*) book. ~ **się** *ipf.* (= *wypełniać zadanie*) perform well, do well; **spisać się na medal** do an outstanding *l.* excellent job, deserve a medal; **spisywać się dobrze/źle** do well/badly; (*o samochodzie, maszynach itp.*) run good/badly; **dzielnie się spisywać** keep *l.* hold one's end up.

spity *a.* (*o osobie*) drunk, drunken; tanked (up), juiced; **spity do nieprzytomności** dead *l.* blind drunk, drunk as a lord.

spiż *mi* **1.** (*stop*) red bronze; (*armatni*) ordnance bronze. **2.** *Gen.pl.* **-y** *l.* **-ów** *przen.* (*działo*) red-bronze cannon; (*dzwon*) red-bronze bell.

spiżarnia *f. Gen.pl.* **-i** pantry, larder, buttery.

spiżowy *a.* (*o dzwonie, bramie*) bronze; (*o dźwięku*) booming; (*o charakterze*) indomitable, invincible, steadfast.

splajtować *pf. pot.* go broke *l.* bankrupt, go to the wall.

splamić *pf. lit.* maculate, stain; (*ręce krwią, honor*) stain, tarnish, blemish; **splamić czyjąś opinię** tarnish *l.* soil sb's reputation; **splamić czyjeś dobre imię** sully sb's good name, drag sb through the mud; **ręce splamione krwią** blood-stained hands. ~ **się** *pf. lit.* bring shame upon o.s., tarnish *l.* sully one's good name; (*kłamstwem, tchórzostwem*) be tainted by.

splamiony *a.* maculate, tainted (*czymś* by *l.* with sth); **splamiony korupcją** corrupt; **splamiony krwią** *t. przen.* bloodstained.

splantować *pf. zob.* **plantować.**

splatać *ipf.* enlace, braid; (*włosy*) cue, plait, braid; (*liny*) splice; (*sznurek*) twist, twine; (*ręce*) clasp; (*palce*) interlock, lace; (*kosz, gniazdo, wikline*) weave. ~ **się** *ipf.* **1.** interlace, intertwist. **2.** (*o dwóch cechach itp.*) intermingle, interweave, mix; (*w uścisku*) hug, embrace.

splądrować *pf.* **1.** (= *ograbić*) plunder, pillage; (*grobowiec, grób*) devastate, despoil. **2.** (= *przeszukać*) ransack.

splątać *pf.* (*włosy*) tangle, entangle; **wiatr splątał jej włosy** the wind tangled her hair; (*wełnę*) knot. ~ **się** *pf.* get *l.* become tangled, knot.

splątany *a.* entangled, tangled; knotted; (*o linie*) foul.

splendor *mi lit.* splendor; *Br.* splendour; glamor, *Br.* glamour; glitter; luster; *Br.* lustre; **dodawać czemuś splendoru** add luster to sth; **pełen splendoru** lustrous.

spleść *pf.* **splotę spleciesz splótł splotła spletli** *zob.* **splatać.** ~ **się** *pf. zob.* **splatać się.**

spleśniały *a.* mildewed; (*o chlebie, serze*) moldy; *Br.* mouldy; (*o jabłkach*) rotten; (*o kompocie, piwie*) musty.

spleśnieć *pf.* go moldy, *Br.* mouldy; go mildew.

splin *mi lit.* spleen, blues, low spirits, gloom.

splot *mi* **1.** (= *splecenie*) braid, cord, twine; (*gałęzi*) tangle; (*włosów*) plait, braid; (*liny*) coil; **splot okoliczności** chain of circumstances; **splot wydarzeń** concourse *l.* chain of events, concatenation. **2.** *anat.* plexus; **splot lędźwiowy** lumbar plexus; **splot słoneczny** solar plexus. **3.** *żegl.* (*lin*) splice. **4.** *tk.* weave, structure; (*różnych nici*) intertexture; (*w robocie na drutach*) knit.

splugawić *pf.* defile, taint, besmirch, cast a slur on; **splugawić czyjeś dobre imię** tarnish *l.* sully sb's good name *l.* reputation.

splunąć *pf. zob.* **spluwać.**

spluwa *f. pot.* piece, gat, heater.

spluwaczka *f. Gen.pl.* -ek cuspidor, spittoon.

spluwać *ipf.* spit, expectorate; **spluwać krwią** spit blood; **splunąć komuś w twarz** spit sb in the eye *l.* face, trample on *l.* upon sb.

spłacać *ipf.*, **spłacić** *pf.* (*pożyczkę, dług*) pay off, repay; (*długi*) square, clear, acquit; **spłacać ratami** *l.* **w ratach** pay back in installments; **spłacić kogoś** buy sb off; **spłacić wierzycieli** get square with one's creditors; **spłacić dług hipoteczny** pay off *l.* redeem a mortgage; **spłacić dług wdzięczności** repay sb's kindness, return a favor; *Br.* return a favour; **spłacić dług innym długiem** rob Peter to pay Paul.

spłakać się *pf.* **spłaczę spłaczesz** weep, sob; **spłakać się jak bóbr** cry *l.* weep one's heart *l.* eyes out; **spłakać się z radości/śmiechu** cry with joy/laughter.

spłakany *a.* (*o wdowie, sierocie*) all in tears, weeping, crying; **spłakane oczy** tear-swollen eyes; **spłakany głos** tearful voice.

spłaszczać *ipf.*, **spłaszczyć** *pf.* (*rzecz*) flatten (out), level (out); compress; (*problem*) trivialize, simplify, downplay. ~ **się** *ipf.*, **spłaszczyć się** *pf.* go flat, flatten out; compress.

spłata *f.* repayment, settlement; (*długu, zobowiązania*) quittance, discharge; (*kredytu, długu*) repayment; **spłata ratalna** installment plan; **rozłożyć spłatę na raty** arrange installments for a payment; **ostateczna spłata** pay-off; **warunki spłaty** terms of repayment; **żądać spłaty** demand a repayment.

spłatać *pf.* make; **spłatać komuś figla** play a trick *l.* joke on sb, play hob with sb.

spław *mi* (*drewna*) floating (of timber), rafting.

spławiać *ipf.*, **spławić** *pf.* **1.** (*towary*) float, raft; (*kanałem*) flume. **2.** *pot.* (*osobę*) get rid of, kiss off, shake off.

spławik *mi Gen.* -a *ryb.*, *sport* bob, cork, float.

spławikowy *a.* float; **wędka spławikowa** float (fishing) rod.

spławny *a.* (*o rzece, kanale*) navigable, negotiable; (*np. dla tratw*) floatable; **droga** *l.* **kanał spławny** waterway.

spłodzić *pf.* **spłodzę spłodzisz, spłódź 1.** *lit.* (*dziecko*) beget, sire, father. **2.** *żart.* (*wiersz, tekst*) compose, produce.

spłonąć *pf.* **1.** (*od ognia*) burn down, go down in flames; **spłonąć doszczętnie** burn to ashes *l.* the ground, be burned to the ground; **spłonąć na stosie** be burned at the stake, go to the stake. **2.** *przen.* (*rumieńcem*) blush, flush, redden; **spłonąć gniewem** flash with anger; **spłonąć z zakłopotania** redden in embarrassment.

spłonić się *pf. lit.* rouge, blush.

spłonka *f. Gen.pl.* -ek (percussion) cap, priming, primer; (*bomby*) fuze; (*rozsadzająca*) detonator; **detonacja spłonki** percussion.

spłonkowy *a.* (*o naboju*) percussion; **mechanizm spłonkowy** percussion lock.

spłoszony *a.* -eni frightened; (*o zającu*) flushed; (*o złodzieju*) scared away; (*o spojrzeniu*) embarrassed; (*o oczach*) frightened; (*o twarzy*) abashed.

spłoszyć *pf.* frighten, scare, spook; (*zwierzęta*) flush, scare off *l.* away.

spłowiały *a.* faded, washed out.

spłowieć *pf.* fade, become pale *l.* bleached.

spłuczka *f. Gen.pl.* -ek (*w toalecie*) (toilet) cistern.

spłukać *pf.* -uczę -uczesz, **spłukiwać** *ipf.* (*toaletę*) flush; (*włosy, naczynia*) rinse; (*brud, błoto*) wash away, rinse away *l.* off. ~ **się** *pf.*, **spłukiwać się** *ipf.* **1.** (= *obmywać się*) have a quick shower *l.* bath, wash o.s. **2.** *pot.* (= *stracić pieniądze*) go broke *l.* bust, blow all one's money.

spłukany *a. pot.* broke, hard up, strapped; **spłukany do cna** stone *l.* flat broke; **być spłukanym** be on one's *l.* the beam-ends.

spłycać *ipf.*, **spłycić** *pf.* **1.** (= *czynić płytkim*) shallow. **2.** (*problem, zagadnienie, sprawę*) (=

trywializować) shallow, oversimplify, trivialize, downplay.

spłynąć *pf. zob.* **spływać.**

spływ *mi* **1.** (= *spływanie wody*) runoff, flow; **średni roczny spływ** *hydrol.* mean annual runoff. **2.** (= *zbieg rzek*) confluence. **3.** (= *wycieczka szlakiem wodnym*) rafting trip; **spływ kajakowy** canoeing trip.

spływać *ipf.* **-am -asz 1.** (= *ściekać*) flow, run down; (*o łzach, pocie*) roll, stream; **pot z niego spływał** his entire body poured with sweat; (*o strumyku, cieczy, wodzie*) run, trickle; (*o zarzutach, krytyce*) flow over; **całe miasto spływało krwią** the whole town ran with blood; **moje słowa spłynęły po nim jak po kaczce** my words rolled off him like water off a duck's back; **zdenerwowanie spłynęło z niej w końcu** her excitement finally ebbed away *l.* waned *l.* died out; **spłynął na nią spokój** she was overcome *l.* overwhelmed with peace, she calmed down; **łzy spływały mu po policzkach** tears were running down his cheeks. **2.** (*o danych, listach, wiadomościach itp.*) trickle in, pour in; **dane o zniszczeniu spływały do redakcji** reports on the devastation poured in to the editor's office. **3.** (= *płynąć z prądem*) flow, drift, float; (*o wodach rzeki*) tumble, flow, run. **4.** (*o włosach, szatach*) (= *opadać*) fall; **włosy spływały jej na ramiona** her hair fell to her shoulders. **5.** *pot.* (= *odchodzić*) split; **spływaj!** beat it!, buzz off!, get lost!

spochmurnieć *pf.* **1.** (*o niebie*) cloud up *l.* over, darken, grow dim *l.* dark. **2.** (= *stać się ponurym*) cloud (over), grow troubled *l.* gloomy; **jego twarz spochmurniała** his face clouded over *l.* darkened.

spocić się *pf.* sweat, break out in a sweat, get sweaty; (*z wysiłku*) work up a sweat; **spocił się jak (ruda) mysz** he was sweating like a bullock.

spocony *a.* **-eni** in a sweat, sweaty; (*o biegaczu, robotniku*) sweating; (*o skórze, rękach*) clammy, sweaty.

spocząć *pf.* **-cznę -czniesz, -cznij 1.** *zob.* **spoczywać. 2.** (*siadać*) sit down; **proszę spocząć** do sit down, please be seated, please take a seat. **3.** (= *zostać pochowanym*) be laid to rest; **niech spoczywa w pokoju** may he *l.* she rest in peace; **tutaj spoczywa...** (*inskrypcja na nagrobku*) here lies... **4.** *wojsk.* **spocznij!** at ease!; **stać na spocznij** stand at ease.

spoczynek *mi* **-nk- 1.** (= *wytchnienie*) rest, repose, leisure; **udać się na spoczynek** retire, have a rest; **podczas** *l.* **w spoczynku** in repose, at rest; **w stanie spoczynku** (*o generale, oficerze*) retired, inactive; **przejść w stan spoczynku** retire; **okres spoczynku** *biol.* state of repose, resting state; **miejsce wiecznego spoczynku** resting place; **złożyć na wieczny spoczynek** lay to rest. **2.** (= *sen*) sleep; **iść** *l.* **udać się na spoczynek** go to bed. **3.** *fiz.* state of rest. **4.** *wojsk.* retirement.

spoczynkowy *a.* rest, resting; **spoczynkowa przemiana materii** *biol.* resting metabolism; **kuracja spoczynkowa** rest cure; **okres spoczynkowy** state of repose; **masa spoczynkowa** *fiz.* rest mass.

spoczywać *ipf.* **-am -asz 1.** *lit.* (= *kłaść się*) lie (down); (= *siadać*) sit (down); **spocząć sobie** take a rest; **spocząć na laurach** rest *l.* sit on one's laurels; **on nie spocznie dopóki...** he will not rest until... **2.** *lit.* (= *leżeć*) lie, rest; **spoczywać na kimś** (*o odpowiedzialności, obowiązku*) lie *l.* rest with sb; (*o uprawnieniach*) be vested in; **władza wykonawcza spoczywa w rękach prezydenta** the executive power is vested in the President; **mój los spoczywa w twoich rękach** my fate rests with you *l.* is in your hands; **wszystkie dokumenty spoczęły w sejfie** all documents were deposited in the safe; **spoczywać na czyichś barkach** rest on sb's shoulders; **cała odpowiedzialność spoczywa na nim** all responsibility rests upon him, the buck stops with him; **spoczywać na czymś** (*o spojrzeniu, głowie*) rest upon *l.* on sth.

spod *prep.* + *Gen.* **1.** (*wskazuje na ruch od miejsca pod czymś ku górze, na boki*) from under, from below; **spod nóg** from under the feet; **grunt obsuwał mu się spod nóg** he was losing ground, ground was cut from under his feet; **spod podłogi** from under the floor; **spod drzewa** from below the tree; **spod krzaka** from under the bush; **spod lady** (*o towarze*) under-the-counter; **patrzeć na kogoś spode łba** give sb black looks, look daggers at sb; **typ spod ciemnej gwiazdy** shady character; **usunąć komuś grunt spod nóg** cut the ground from under sb's feet; **rzeźba wyszła spod dłuta Fidiasza** the sculpture was carved *l.* chiseled by Phidias; **jak spod igły** (*eleganckie, czyste*) spick-and-span; (*nowe*) brand-new; **być spod znaku Ryb** be a Pisces. **2.** (*okolica*) from somewhere around, from the area; **był spod Warszawy** he came from somewhere around *l.* from the area of Warsaw. **3.** (*poza*) out; **wyjęty spod prawa** outlaw; **wyjęcie spod prawa** *hist.* ban; *prawn.* outlawry; **uwolnić się spod przemocy/tyranii** shake o.s. free from violence/tyranny, free o.s. from abuse/tyranny; **wymykać się spod kontroli** get out of control *l.* hand, spin out of control; (*o demonstracji, myślach*) run riot.

spode *prep.* + *Gen. zob.* **spod.**

spodeczek *mi* **-czk-** *Gen.* **-a** (small) saucer.

spodek *mi* **-dk-** *Gen.* **-a 1.** (*pod filiżankę*) saucer; **latający spodek** flying saucer. **2.** *górn.* (*wyrobiska*) bottom, sole. **3.** *geom.* (*prostopadłej*) foot.

spodem *adv.* **pod spodem** under, underneath; **mam pod spodem koszulę** I have a shirt underneath; **sąsiedzi mieszkający pod spodem** downstairs neighbors; **leżący pod spodem** subjacent.

spodenki *pl. Gen.* **-ek 1.** (*małe spodnie*) trousers, pants. **2.** (*sportowe*) shorts; **spodenki kolarskie** (*sportowe*) shorts; **spodenki kąpielowe** bathing trunks; **spodenki bokserskie** shorts, trunks; **krótkie spodenki** shorts, short trousers.

spodleć *pf. pot.* turn vile *l.* mean *l.* abject, become vile *l.* mean *l.* abject.

spodlić *pf.* **-ij** debase; **wojna spodliła ludzi** war debased people. **~ się** *pf.* turn vile *l.* mean *l.* abject, become vile *l.* mean *l.* abject.

spodni *a.* bottom; (*o warstwie*) underneath;

(*strona*) bottom, back; **warstwa spodnia** underside.

spodniarstwo *n.* trouser tailor industry, trouser tailoring.

spodniarz *mp* trouser tailor.

spodnie *pl. Gen.* -**i** trousers, pants; (*luźne*) slacks; (*dżinsowe*) jeans, denims; (*lekkie, letnie*) summer slacks; (*obcięte*) cutoffs; (*robocze*) dungarees; **spodnie narciarskie** salopettes; **spodnie rybaczki** toreador pants; **spodnie dresowe** *l.* **od dresu** sweatpants; **długie spodnie** longs; **spódnica-spodnie** culottes; **spuścić spodnie** drop one's pants *l.* trousers.

spodnium *mi Gen.* -**u** *l. indecl. pot.* trouser suit.

spodobać się *pf.+Dat.* take (sb's) fancy; (*o pomyśle*) click (*komuś* with sb); appeal (*komuś* to sb); **spodobała mi się ta dziewczyna** I liked that girl; **spodobał im się nowy nauczyciel** they took to the new teacher; **spodobał mi się twój pomysł** I liked your idea, your idea appealed to me; **spodobało mi się pójście do kina** I enjoyed going to the cinema; **nie spodobać się** receive a thumbsdown.

spodu *itd. mi zob.* **spód.**

spodziewać się *ipf.* **1.** (= *przypuszczać*) expect; hope (*czegoś* for sth); **spodziewamy się, że zda wszystkie egzaminy** we expect him to pass all the exams, our expectation is that he will pass all the exams; **kto by się spodziewał!** surprise, surprise!, that's a turn-up for the books!; **nie spodziewać się czegoś** not bargain for *l.* on sth, be unprepared for sth; **nie spodziewałem się tego po tobie** I didn't expect that of you; **nie spodziewałem się tego usłyszeć** I was surprised to hear this; **prędzej bym się śmierci spodziewał niż ciebie** you are the last person I'd expect, seeing you is the last thing I'd expect; **jak można się było spodziewać,...** sure enough,...; as was expected,...; as you could expect,...; **poniekąd się tego spodziewałem** I half expected that; **można się było tego spodziewać** it *l.* that figures, it was only to be expected; **można się tego po nim spodziewać** that's just like him, you would expect that of him; **spodziewać się awansu/podwyżki** be due for promotion/a raise; **spodziewam się, że tak/nie** I hope so/not; **dostałam więcej niż się spodziewałam** I got more than I had expected. **2.** (= *oczekiwać kogoś*) expect, await; **spodziewać się gości** be expecting guests *l.* visitors; **spodziewać się dziecka** be expecting (a baby), *pot.* be in the family way; **spodziewam się zobaczyć cię wkrótce** I'm looking forward to seeing you soon.

spodziewany *a.* (*o zdarzeniu, gościu*) expected, anticipated; (*o zdarzeniu*) due; (*o rezultatach*) hoped-for; **w najmniej spodziewanym momencie** in the least expected moment.

spoglądać *ipf.* look, have *l.* take *l.* cast a look *l.* glance (*na kogoś/coś* at sb/sth); (*w górę*) look up; (*za siebie*) look round; (*wstecz*) look back; (*posępnie*) lower (*na kogoś/coś* at *l.* on *l.* upon sb/sth); (*w zamyśleniu*) muse (*na kogoś/coś* at *l.* on sb/sth); **spoglądać na zegarek** look at one's watch; **spoglądać w lustro** look in the mirror;

spoglądać po sali look round the room; **spoglądać z góry na kogoś/coś** look down on *l.* upon sb/sth, look down one's nose at sb/sth; **spoglądać na kogoś jako na...** view *l.* consider sb as...; **spoglądać przez ramię** look over one's shoulder; **spoglądać na coś niechętnie** squint at sth; **spoglądać na kogoś wrogo** look daggers at sb, give sb a hostile look; **Adam nie śmiał spojrzeć Ewie w oczy** Adam didn't dare look Eve straight *l.* square in the eyes; **spoglądać sobie w oczy** look each other in the eyes; **spójrz prawdzie w oczy** wake up and smell the coffee, face the truth; **spojrzeć śmierci w oczy** look death in the face; **spojrzeć komuś prosto w oczy** look sb straight in the eyes; **spojrzałem z dystansem na tę sprawę** I looked at this matter without emotions; **spójrz poważnie na ten problem** give it a serious consideration; **spojrzeć na kogoś znacząco/życzliwie/pogardliwie** give sb a meaningful/friendly/scornful look; **spojrzeć na coś z innej perspektywy** view sth from a different angle; **spojrzeć na coś we właściwym świetle** get *l.* put sth in the right perspective; **spojrzeć w przyszłość** look to the future.

spoić[1] *pf.* **spoję spoisz, spój** *zob.* **spajać**[1].

spoić[2] *pf.* **spoję spoisz, spój** *zob.* **spajać**[2]. ~ **się** *pf. pot.* (= *upić się*) liquor up, get drunk.

spoiler, spojler *mi Gen.* -**a** *lotn., mot.* spoiler.

spoina *f.* **1.** *bud.* joint. **2.** *techn.* weld, seam.

spoinowy *a. bud.* joint.

spoistość *f.* **1.** cohesion, cohesiveness, compactness; (*skały*) solidity. **2.** (*rodziny*) unity, close family ties.

spoisty *a.* cohesive; (*o glebie*) solid, compacted; (*o substancji*) cohesive, dense; (*o tekście, strategii*) coherent; (*o stylu*) succinct, concise.

spoiwo *n.* bind, binder; *chem.* binding agent; *spawanie* filler metal; **spoiwo ceramiczne** vitrified bond; **spoiwo farby** paint vehicle; **spoiwo hydrauliczne** *bud.* hydraulic binding agent.

spojenie *n. techn.* joint, weld, seal; (*za pomocą węzła, kleju*) bond; *anat.* symphysis; **spojenie łonowe** pubic symphysis.

spojler *mi Gen.* -**a** *zob.* **spoiler.**

spojówka *f. Gen.pl.* -**ek** *anat.* conjunctiva; **zapalenie spojówek** *pat.* conjunctivitis, pinkeye; (*wiosenny*) **nieżyt spojówek** *pat.* spring *l.* vernal conjunctivitis.

spojówkowy *a. anat.* conjunctival; **worek spojówkowy** conjunctival sac; **spojówkowe zapalenie oka** *pat.* conjunctival ophthalmia.

spojrzeć *pf.* **spojrzę spojrzysz, spójrz** *l.* **spojrzyj** *zob.* **spoglądać.**

spojrzenie *n.* look, stare, glance; (*uporczywe*) gaze; (*drwiące*) fleer; (*groźne*) lower; (*przelotne*) glimpse, fugitive glance; **nieobecne spojrzenie** faraway look; **badawcze spojrzenie** scrutiny; **bezradne spojrzenie** helpless look; **życzliwe spojrzenie** sympathetic look; **czarujące spojrzenie** charming look; **zdumione spojrzenie** astounded *l.* surprised look; **pożądliwe spojrzenie** leer; **jednym spojrzeniem** at a glance; **obrzucić kogoś badawczym spojrzeniem** stare *l.* look sb up and down; **unikać czyjegoś spojrzenia** avoid sb's look; **czuć na sobie czyjeś spojrzenie** feel sb's look on o.s.; **wyczytać coś w czyimś spojrzeniu** read sth in sb's eyes; **ich spojrzenia się skrzyżowały** their eyes met; **zatopić spojrzenie w czymś** feed *l.* fasten one's eyes on sth; **mieć trzeźwe spojrzenie na sprawę** have a sober attitude towards the issue *l.* matter; **rzucić spojrzenie na kogoś/coś** cast *l.* dart a glance *l.* look at *l.* towards sb/sth, shoot a glance at sb/sth; **zmierzyć kogoś spojrzeniem** measure sb with one's eye; **przeszyć kogoś spojrzeniem** give sb a piercing look, shoot a glance at sb; **odwracać spojrzenie od czegoś** avert one's gaze from sth; **odwzajemnić czyjeś spojrzenie** meet sb's eye *l.* gaze *l.* glance; **spojrzenie na coś** *przen.* perspective *l.* outlook on sth; **wytrzymać czyjeś spojrzenie** outstare sb; **o łagodnym spojrzeniu** dove-eyed; **uciszać kogoś spojrzeniem** stare sb into silence.

spoko *int. pot.* (= *spokojnie*) (*w odpowiedzi na pytanie*) cool, sure; (*uspokajająco*) be cool, take it easy *l.* slow.

spokojnie *adv.* at ease, calmly; *form.* composedly, placidly; (*upływać*) slowly; (*spędzać czas, płynąć*) at leisure, relaxedly; (*mówić*) levelly, at ease; (*spać, żyć*) peacefully; (*żyć*) humbly, quietly; **spokojnie** (*pocieszając, upominając kogoś*) now, now; **mógłbym spokojnie iść tam pieszo** I might just as well walk there; **najspokojniej w świecie zrobił sobie kawy** he made himself some coffee, as if nothing had happened; **można spokojnie powiedzieć...** one can safely say...; **spokojnie! cool it!**, (just) calm down!, keep your hair *l.* shirt on!; **tylko spokojnie!** steady!, cut the rough stuff!; **był tam spokojnie pół godziny** *pot.* (= *przynajmniej*) he was there at least half an hour if not more.

spokojny *a.* (*o głosie*) quiet, gentle; (*o charakterze, usposobieniu*) placid; (*o nastroju, atmosferze*) relaxed; (*o osobie*) composed, collected, good-tempered; (*o śnie, wodach*) tranquil, serene; (*o morzu*) still; (*o morzu, atmosferze, twarzy*) calm; (*o okolicy, miejscu, dzielnicy, czasach*) peaceful, quiet; (*o barwach*) restrained, sober; (*o kolorze, świetle*) mellow; **być z natury spokojnym** be calm *l.* peaceful by nature; **możesz być spokojny, że...** rest assured that...; **o Adama możesz być spokojny** don't worry about Adam, make your mind easy about Adam; **mieć spokojne sumienie** have a clear *l.* good conscience; **idealnie spokojny** cool as a cucumber; **spokojnym głosem** in a soft voice, levelly; **przybrać spokojny wyraz twarzy** compose one's features; **spokojna głowa!** *pot.* easy, don't worry about it; **Ocean Spokojny** *geogr.* the Pacific Ocean; **dom spokojnej starości** home for the elderly, old peoples' home, residential home.

spokornieć *pf.* draw *l.* pull in one's horns, come down a peg or two.

spokój *mi -o-* **1.** (*równowaga*) calmness, quiet; (*ducha, sumienia*) ease, placidity; **spokój ducha** peace of mind; **błogi spokój** serenity; **stoicki** *l.* **olimpijski spokój** stoical calmness; **mieć z kimś/czymś spokój** have sb/sth off one's head; **zachować spokój** stay calm *l.* quiet, keep one's cool;

dla świętego spokoju for the sake of peace of one's mind; **daj mi (święty) spokój** *l.* **zostaw mnie w spokoju** leave me alone, stop bothering me, get out of my face; **dać sobie z czymś spokój** let sth drop *l.* rest, give sth up; **daj sobie z nim spokój** forget about him; **daj spokój!** come on!, drop it!, knock it off!, let it ride!; **ta myśl nie daje mi spokoju** this thought is haunting me all the time; **niedający spokoju** (*o wspomnieniu*) haunting; (*o myśli*) uneasy; **w spokoju** at leisure; **zostawić coś w spokoju** let sth *l.* it rest, ease up on sth; **dla spokoju sumienia** for conscience's sake; **zostawić kogoś w spokoju** leave *l.* let sb alone, go easy on *l.* with sb; **zakłócać komuś spokój** invade *l.* disturb sb's privacy, intrude upon sb's privacy; **dać całej sprawie spokój** drop the thing *l.* matter; **przyjąć coś ze spokojem** be stoical about sth. **2.** (= *cisza*) calm, rest, tranquility; **proszę o spokój!** quiet, please!, order!; **nie dawać komuś spokoju** (*o myśli, wątpliwościach*) nag sb, prey on sb's mind; **nie dawać komuś chwili spokoju** keep bothering *l.* pestering *l.* bugging sb. **3.** *rel.* **niech spoczywa w spokoju** (may he *l.* she) rest in peace; **msza za spokój duszy Adama** a mass for the repose of the soul of Adam. **4.** (= *ład*) order, peace; **spokój publiczny** public order; **spokój! order!**; **na świecie panowałby większy spokój, gdyby...** the world would be a better place if...

spokrewniony *a.* **-eni** cognate, connected; kin, kindred; (*z ojcem, z rodziną królewską*) related (*z kimś* to sb); (*w linii męskiej*) agnate; (*o językach*) cognate, akin to; **blisko spokrewniony** next of kin.

spolaryzować *pf. fiz.* polarize.

spolaryzowany *a. fiz.* (*o świetle*) polarized.

spolegliwość *f.* **1.** (*ustępliwość*) obsequiousness, submissiveness. **2.** (*rzetelność*) trustworthiness, reliability.

spolegliwy *a.* **1.** (= *ustępliwy*) obsequious, subservient, submissive. **2.** (= *wzbudzający zaufanie*) trustworthy, reliable.

spoliczkować *pf.* slap in the face.

spolonizować *pf.* Polonize. **~ się** *pf.* become Polonized.

spolszczać *ipf.*, **spolszczyć** *pf.* **1.** (= *spolonizować*) Polonize. **2.** (*przetłumaczyć*) translate into Polish. **~ się** *ipf.*, **spolszczyć się** *pf.* become Polonized.

społeczeństwo *n.* society, community, public; **społeczeństwo klasowe/bezklasowe** class/classless society; **społeczeństwo wielorasowe** multiracial society; **społeczeństwo demokratyczne** democratic society; **społeczeństwo kapitalistyczne** capitalist society; **społeczeństwo socjalistyczne** socialist society; **społeczeństwo burżuazyjne** bourgeois society; **społeczeństwo feudalne** feudal society; **społeczeństwo masowe** mass society; **społeczeństwo obywatelskie** civic *l.* citizen society; **społeczeństwo prymitywne** primitive *l.* primeval *l.* primordial society; **społeczeństwo konsumpcyjne** consumer society; **społeczeństwo niepiśmienne** oral society; **dobro społeczeństwa** social welfare; **ogół społeczeństwa**

the general public, the community *l.* society *l.* public at large; **wyrzutek społeczeństwa** outcast, down-and-out; **struktura społeczeństwa** social fabric, structure *l.* fabric of society; **być poza nawiasem społeczeństwa** be outside *l.* beyond the pale of society; **na marginesie społeczeństwa** on the margin of society; **sfery społeczeństwa** sectors of society; **społeczeństwo uprzemysłowione** industrial society; **społeczeństwo owadów** *ent.* insect community.

społecznie *adv.* (*szkodliwy, użyteczny, myśleć*) socially; (*w obrębie danej społeczności*) communally; **społecznie akceptowany** (*o zwyczaju, zachowaniu*) socially acceptable; (*o korupcji, wyzysku, przemocy*) institutionalized; **pracować społecznie** do community work; **społecznie awansujący** upwardly mobile; **upośledzony społecznie** (*o grupach*) underprivileged; **myślący społecznie** socially-minded; **napiętnowany społecznie** socially stigmatized; **zdegradowany społecznie** déclassé.

społecznik *mp* social activist.

społecznikostwo *n.* social activism.

społecznikowski *a.* (*o zapale, tendencjach*) (of a) social activist.

społeczność *f.* community, society; **społeczność lokalna** local community, populace; **społeczność uniwersytecka** academic community.

społeczny *a.* social, communal; (*o więzi, reformach, polityce*) social; (*o własności, poparciu*) public; (*o konfliktach*) civil; (*o organizacji*) voluntary; (*o pracy, pracowniku - bez wynagrodzenia*) voluntary, volunteer; **drabina społeczna** social ladder; **klasa społeczna** social class; **choroba społeczna** social disease; **nauki społeczne** social sciences, social science, social studies; **zasiłek społeczny** welfare benefit; **pozycja społeczna** social standing, social status, station; **warstwa społeczna** social stratum; **pochodzenie społeczne** social background; **margines społeczny** lowlife, scum; **niziny społeczne** the gutter; **wyżyny społeczne** upper crust; **niższe warstwy społeczne** the lower orders, lower classes; **wysoka/niska pozycja społeczna** high/low standing *l.* social status; **wymiar społeczny** social dimension; **awans społeczny** social advancement; **działalność społeczna** community work, social activism; **fundusz społeczny** social fund; **społeczny podział pracy** social division of labor; **mit społeczny** urban myth *l.* legend; **wrażliwość społeczna** social conscience; **awans społeczny** upward mobility; **nastroje społeczne** climate of opinion; **względy społeczne** social considerations; **ubezpieczenie społeczne** social security *l.* insurance; **świadczenia społeczne** social *l.* welfare services; **pomoc społeczna** public *l.* social assistance; **praca społeczna** community work; **opieka społeczna** social welfare *l.* service, social work, casework; **pracownik opieki społecznej** *l.* **społeczny** social worker; **niepokoje społeczne** social unrest, civil disorder; **szkoła społeczna** *szkoln.* community school; **reklama społeczna** public service announcement; **dom opieki społecznej** residential home; **w interesie społecznym** in the

public interest; **obniżyć swój status społeczny** come down in the world; **u szczytu/dołu drabiny społecznej** at the top/bottom of the social ladder.

spomiędzy *prep.* + *Gen.* from between; from among; **spomiędzy drzew** from between the trees; **spomiędzy wybijających się studentów** from among outstanding students.

sponad *prep.* + *Gen.* (= *znad*) from above; **sponad dachów/chmur** from above the roofs/clouds; **sponad okularów** from behind one's glasses.

spondej *mi Gen.* -**a** *Gen.pl.* -**ów** *teor.lit.* spondee.

sponiewierać *pf.* (*kogoś*) oppress, maltreat; (*coś*) batter, treat badly; *przen.* (*znieważyć*) offend, abuse; (*słowami*) insult.

sponiewierany *a.* (*o samochodzie, kapeluszu, walizce*) battered, shabby; (*o osobie*) abused, maltreated.

sponsor *mp* sponsor, patron.

sponsoring *mi* sponsorship, patronage.

sponsorować *ipf.* (*osobę, imprezę*) sponsor, be a patron of, provide funds for; (*przedsięwzięcie*) underwrite.

sponsorowanie *n.* sponsorship.

spontanicznie *adv.* spontaneously; (*pomagać*) voluntarily, unasked for; (*reagować*) naturally.

spontaniczność *f.* spontaneity; naturalness.

spontaniczny *a.* spontaneous; (*o śmiechu*) involuntary, instinctive, natural; (*o reakcji*) spontaneous, spur-of-the-moment; (*o darach, pomocy*) unasked for, unsolicited; (*o uwadze, spostrzeżeniu*) casual, off-the-cuff; (*o działaniach*) unprompted, voluntary; (*o występie, wystąpieniu*) unrehearsed, impromptu, extemporaneous.

spopielać *ipf.* **1.** (= *zamienić w popiół*) incinerate, burn to ashes. **2.** (= *nadać barwę popiołu*) make *l.* render ash-gray; **słońce spopieliło ziemię** the sun made the soil ash-gray. ~ **się** *ipf.* burn to ashes.

spopieleć *pf.* burn to ashes, be burned to ashes; (*o ziemi*) turn ash-gray.

spopielić *pf. zob.* **spopielać.** ~ **się** *pf. zob.* **spopielać się.**

spopularyzować *pf.* popularize, propagate, promote; (*miasto, miejsce*) (*w sensie turystycznym*) put on the map. ~ **się** *pf.* become popular, become widespread; gain ground.

spora *f. Dat.* **sporze** *bot.* spore.

sporadycznie *adv.* (*odbywać się, zdarzać się*) sporadically, spasmodically, episodically; (*bywać, widywać się*) occasionally, on and off.

sporadyczność *f.* occasionality, rarity, sporadic character.

sporadyczny *a.* sporadic; (*o błędach*) infrequent, scattered; (*o zjawiskach*) episodic, occasional.

sporangium *n. bot.* sporangium.

sporawy *a.* sizeable; pretty big, fairly large.

sporny *a.* arguable, contestable; (*o kwestii, sprawie*) disputable, divisive, moot, debatable; *prawn.* litigious, contentious; **punkt sporny** moot *l.* sticking point; **sporny charakter** divisiveness; **w sposób sporny** contestably, arguably;

sporne zagadnienie contentious question *l.* issue; **sporne twierdzenie** contestation; **postępowanie sporne** *prawn.* litigation.

sporo *adv.* a good *l.* great deal (*czegoś* of sth); (*zjeść, powiedzieć, mieć*) quite a lot; **to zabierze sporo czasu** it'll take time; **sporo ludzi** a considerable number of people, quite a lot of people, a good few *l.* many people; **sporo czasu** a good while; **sporo trudności** a certain amount of difficulty; **wkładać w coś sporo wysiłku** put a lot of effort into sth.

sporofil *mi Gen.pl.* -i *l.* -ów *bot.* sporophyl, sporophyll.

sporofit *mi bot.* sporophyte.

sporogon *mi bot.* sporogonium.

sporogonia *f. bot.* sporogony.

sporowiec *ma zool.* sporozoan.

sporozoit *ma zool.* sporozoite.

sport *mi* sport, sports; **sport motorowy** motorsports; **sport narciarski** skiing; **sport piłkarski** soccer, association football; **sport spadochronowy** parachuting; **sport amatorski** amateur sport; **sport zawodowy** *l.* **wyczynowy** professional sport; **sporty walki** combat sports; **sporty zręcznościowe** skill sports; **sport rekreacyjny** recreational sport; **sporty wodne** aquatic *l.* water sports; **sporty zimowe/letnie** winter/summer sports; **sporty terenowe** field sports; **sport kontaktowy** contact sport; **sport widowiskowy** spectator sport; **dyscyplina sportu** (a) sport, sports discipline; **sporty ekstremalne** extreme sports; **sport strzelecki** shooting; **sport urazowy** high-injury sport; **uprawiać sport** practice sports; **królowa sportu** track and field; *Br.* athletics; **robić coś dla sportu** *przen.* do sth for fun; **dzień sportu** *szkoln.* field *l.* sports day; **ośrodek sportów zimowych** winter sports resort.

sportowiec *mp* -wc- *pl.* -y athlete, sportsman.

sportowo *adv.* athletically, sportily; (*ubierać się*) casually; **ubrany sportowo** casually dressed, wearing sports clothes.

sportowy *a.* athletic; (*o klubie, dyscyplinie*) sports; (*o samochodzie*) sports, sporty; (*o ubraniu*) casual; **zawody sportowe** sports competition; **dyscyplina sportowa** (a) sport, sports discipline; **klub sportowy** athletic *l.* sports club; **boisko sportowe** sports ground *l.* field; **sprzęt sportowy** sports equipment; **obiekty sportowe** sports facilities; **sportowe zachowanie** sportsmanship; **sprawozdanie sportowe** sportscast; **sprawozdawca sportowy** sportscaster; **bluza sportowa** sweatshirt; **wydarzenie sportowe** sports event; **odzież sportowa** sportswear; **totalizator sportowy** lottery; *US* Lotto; *Br.* National Lottery.

sportretować *pf. zob.* **portretować**.

sportsmen *mp przest.* athlete, sportsman.

sportsmenka *f. przest.* athlete, sportswoman.

sporu *itd. mi zob.* **spór**.

spory[1] *a.* (*o ilości*) substantial, considerable, fair, sizeable; (*o domu, pakunku, tłumie*) (quite) large, (quite) big; (*o dochodzie, zysku*) handsome, tidy; (*o porcji, kawałku ciasta*) generous; (*o podwyżce*) significant; **spora chwila** quite a while; **przebyć spory kawał drogi** travel quite a

long way, cover a lot of ground; **w sporej odległości** a good distance away.

spory[2] *pl. Gen.* -ów *bot.* spores, agametes.

sporysz *mi bot.* ergot.

sporządnieć *pf.* grow decent, become honest.

sporządzać *ipf.*, **sporządzić** *pf.* make, prepare; (*lekarstwo*) make up, dispense; (*testament, notatkę*) make, draw up; (*projekt, umowę*) prepare, draw up; (*wykres*) plot, chart; **sporządzić protokół z czegoś** take minutes of sth; **sporządzić kosztorys** prepare an estimate; **sporządzić projekt budżetu** draft a budget.

sposępnieć *pf.* sadden, gloom, turn gloomy; (*o twarzy*) cloud over.

sposobić *ipf.* -ób **1.** *przest.* (= *przygotowywać*) prepare, prime. **2.** *przest.* (= *uczyć*) teach, train. ~ **się** *ipf.* -ób **1.** *przest.* (= *przygotowywać się*) get ready, prepare (o.s.) (*do czegoś* for sth); **sposobić się do drogi** get ready for the journey; **sposobić się do sezonu turystycznego** gear o.s. up for the tourist season. **2.** *przest.* (= *uczyć się*) study, train.

sposobność *f.* opportunity, chance, occasion (*do czegoś* for sth); **przy sposobności** by the way, incidentally, while we are about it; **skorzystać ze sposobności** take the chance *l.* opportunity, seize a chance *l.* opportunity, avail o.s. of an opportunity; **przy najbliższej sposobności** at sb's earliest convenience; **przy każdej/pierwszej sposobności** at every/the earliest occasion *l.* opportunity; **nadarzyła się sposobność** an opportunity presented itself *l.* occurred; **czekać na dogodną sposobność** bide one's time; **dać komuś sposobność zrobienia czegoś** give sb a chance *l.* an opportunity to do sth.

sposób *mi* -o- (*metoda*) way, manner (*robienia czegoś* of *l.* for doing sth); method (*na coś* for sth); (*środek*) means; (*działania, postępowania*) mode, method; **sposób użycia** usage, directions for use; **sposób mówienia** turn of phrase, locution, manner of speaking; **sposób myślenia** way of thinking, habit of thought *l.* mind; **sposób rozumienia** understanding; **sposób bycia** manners; **w ten sposób** this *l.* that way, like this *l.* that; **nie mów do mnie w ten sposób** don't talk to me like that; **nie lubię sposobu, w jaki on się uśmiecha** I don't like the way he smiles; **tym sposobem** thus, thereby; **jakimś sposobem** somehow; **w inny sposób** otherwise, in a different way; **nie ma innego sposobu** there's no other way; **w dowolny sposób** whichever way, any way; **w jakikolwiek** *l.* **żaden sposób** by any possibility, anywise, at all; **w następujący sposób** in the following way *l.* manner; **w podobny sposób** in like manner, along similar lines; **w prosty sposób** simply, straightforwardly; **w taki czy inny sposób** one way or the other *l.* another, by hook or by crook; **w podziwu godny sposób** admirably; **robić coś na sposób francuski/amerykański** do sth the French/American way *l.* fashion; **zrobię to swoim sposobem** I'll do it my way; **na wszystkie sposoby** *l.* **wszelkimi sposobami** by all means, using all methods; **w żaden sposób** nohow, noway, by no means; **w żaden sposób nie**

mogę sobie na to pozwolić I can't possibly afford it; **wziąć się na sposób** resort to an expedient; **mam na niego sposób** I have a way to deal with him; **na to nie ma sposobu** there's no help *l.* remedy for it; **znaleźć sposób** find a way; **to najlepszy sposób na nudę** it's the best remedy *l.* cure for boredom; **ujmować coś w inny sposób** rephrase *l.* paraphrase sth, put sth in a different way; **nie sposób odmówić** there's no refusing; **był na swój sposób miły** he was nice in his own way; **nie sposób jej dogodzić** she is impossible *l.* hard *l.* difficult to please; **w tradycyjny sposób** in the traditional way *l.* manner, in the old ways; **na sposób wiejski** country style; **we właściwy sposób** fitly, in the right way; **wykorzystać wszystkie sposoby** use every trick in the book; **znaleźć sposób na zrobienie czegoś** find a way to do sth, contrive to do sth; **domowym sposobem** home-made; **sposób płatności** method of payment; **sposób podania** *kulin.* presentation; **sposobem** (= *sprytem*) by a trick; **zrobić coś sposobem** find a way around the problem; **okolicznik sposobu** *gram.* adverbial *l.* adjunct of manner.

spospolicieć *pf.* lose attractiveness, become commonplace *l.* ordinary; pall, cloy; **wkrótce przyjemności doczesne spospoliciały** the earthly pleasures soon palled.

spospolitować się *pf.* have mixed with socially inferior people.

spostponować *pf. zob.* **postponować.**

spostrzec *pf.* **-egę -eżesz -egł, spostrzegać** *ipf.* **1.** (= *zauważyć*) spot, catch sight of; notice, observe, discern. **2.** (= *uświadomić sobie*) become aware *l.* conscious of, realize, see. ~ **się** *pf.,* **spostrzegać się** *ipf.* realize, become aware, notice; **zanim się spostrzegłem...** before I noticed..., the next thing I knew...

spostrzegawczość *f.* perceptiveness, acuteness, astuteness; **wykazać się dużą spostrzegawczością** be very insightful *l.* perceptive.

spostrzegawczy *a.* perceptive, observant; insightful, astute; **mało spostrzegawczy** imperceptive, unobservant.

spostrzeżenie *n.* **1.** (= *obserwacja*) perception, observation. **2.** (= *uwaga*) remark, observation, comment; **dzielić się z kimś spostrzeżeniami** share one's observations with sb. **3.** *psych.* perception.

spośród *prep.* + *Gen.* from among; **spośród tłumu** from amidst the crowd; **spośród najlepszych prac wybrana zostanie jedna** out of best projects only one will be chosen; **wyróżniać kogoś spośród innych** (*np. o cechach charakteru*) make sb stand out.

spotęgować *pf. zob.* **potęgować.** ~ **się** *pf. zob.* **potęgować się.**

spotężnieć *pf. zob.* **potężnieć.**

spotkać *pf. zob.* **spotykać.** ~ **się** *pf. zob.* **spotykać się.**

spotkanie *n.* **1.** (*umówione*) meeting, appointment, engagement (*z kimś* with sb); (*przypadkowe*) encounter; (*towarzyskie*) get-together, party; **spotkanie pożegnalne** farewell party; **spotka-**

nie powitalne welcome(-home) party; **przypadkowe spotkanie** chance encounter *l.* meeting; **miejsce spotkania** rendezvous, meeting place; **spotkanie informacyjne** orientation meeting; **spotkanie integracyjne** mixer party; **spotkanie robocze** working meeting; **spotkanie na szczycie** summit meeting; **wyjść komuś na spotkanie** go to meet sb; *przen.* meet sb halfway; **co za spotkanie!** fancy meeting you!; **przyjść/nie przyjść na spotkanie** keep/miss an appointment; **być obecnym na spotkaniu** attend a meeting; **umówić się z kimś na spotkanie** make an appointment with sb; **odwołać spotkanie** cancel an appointment. **2.** *sport* (sports) meeting *l.* meet; (= *mecz*) match; **spotkanie eliminacyjne** qualifying match; **spotkanie pucharowe** cup tie; **spotkanie rewanżowe** return match; **spotkanie towarzyskie** friendly.

spotnieć *pf.* **1.** (*o człowieku*) sweat, get sweaty, break out in a sweat. **2.** (*o szybach, okularach*) mist over; (*o ścianach*) sweat.

spotulnieć *pf.* grow meek *l.* tame; draw in one's horns, come down a peg or two.

spotykać *ipf.* **1.** (= *natykać się na kogoś*) meet, encounter, stumble *l.* run across *l.* on; **miło, że cię spotkałem** it was nice to see you, I'm glad to see you; **spotkać swoje przeznaczenie** meet one's doom *l.* destiny; **spotykaliśmy go od czasu do czasu** we used to *l.* would see him from time to time. **2.** (= *poznawać kogoś nowego*) meet, make acquaintance. **3.** (= *stawać się czyimś udziałem*) happen; **spotkało mnie nieszczęście** a misfortune has befallen me; **spotkał ich ten sam los** they suffered the same fate, the same fate befell them; **spotkało mnie rozczarowanie** I got disappointed; **nie może cię nic złego spotkać** nothing bad can happen to you; **spotkała go miła niespodzianka** he had a nice surprise; **śmierć spotyka wszystkich, którzy...** death comes to all who... **4.** (= *znaleźć, odkryć*) come across, discover, find. ~ **się** *ipf.* **1.** meet (*z kimś* with sb); get together; **spotkać się na drinka** meet for a drink; **spotkać się z czyjąś aprobatą/życzliwością** meet with sb's approval/kindness; **spotkać się z kimś przypadkowo** stumble across *l.* on sb, come *l.* run across sb; **spotkać się z kimś twarzą w twarz** meet sb face to face; **ich spojrzenia spotkały się** their eyes met; **spotkać się z czyimś wzrokiem** catch *l.* meet sb's eye; **spotykam się dziś z nim na lunchu** I'm seeing *l.* meeting him today for lunch; **nasz plan spotkał się z trudnościami** our plan was faced with *l.* met with *l.* encountered difficulties; **nie spotkałem się z tym** I am unfamiliar with this, I haven't come across it; **to się rzadko spotyka** it's unusual, this is (rather) rare; **spotkać się z ogólnym uznaniem** meet with general acceptance *l.* approval; **spotkać się z silnym sprzeciwem** meet with *l.* face strong *l.* fierce opposition. **2.** (*o drogach, rzekach, przewodach*) meet, cross, converge; **ich drogi się spotkały** their paths crossed.

spotykany *a.* occurring, found; **rzadko spotykany gatunek** rare *l.* scarce species; **często spotykany** common, popular, frequently occurring; **powszechnie spotykany** common, commonly found.

spoufalać *ipf.*, **spoufalić** *pf.* encourage (sb) to be on familiar terms; **spoufalać wychowanków** establish close relationship with the pupils, get on close terms with the pupils. ~ **się** *ipf.*, **spoufalić się** *pf.* get close (*z kimś* to sb); become intimate (*z kimś* with sb); **nie spoufalać się z kimś** keep sb at arm's length, keep sb at a distance.

spowalniacz *mi Gen.* **-a** *fiz.* moderator; **spowalniacz ognia** fire retardant.

spowalniać *ipf.* slow down, moderate, decelerate; (*akcję*) detain, delay; (*reakcję*) inhibit; **spowalniać neutrony** *fiz.* moderate neutrons.

spowalniany *a.* inhibited, moderated; **spowalniane neutrony** *fiz.* moderated neutrons.

spoważnieć *pf.* (*o młodzieży, niepoważnym człowieku*) grow up, settle down; (*o twarzy*) turn grave, become serious *l.* straight.

spowiadać *ipf. rel.* confess, hear confession. ~ **się** *ipf.* **1.** *rel.* confess. **2.** *przen.* (= *zwierzać się*) confide (*komuś* in sb)(*komuś z czegoś* sth to sb); unburden o.s. (*komuś* to sb); **spowiadała mu się z wszystkich trosk** she revealed all her worries to him.

spowić *pf.* **-wiję** **-wijesz**, **-wij**, **spowijać** *ipf. lit.* (*o ubraniu, szacie*) cloak; (*o mroku, mgle, nocy*) envelop, enwrap, swathe; (*o chmurach*) shroud, wreathe; **mrok spowił ziemię** the earth was shrouded *l.* covered in darkness.

spowiednik *mp rel.* confessor, father confessor.

spowiedź *f. rel.* confession, shrift; **iść do spowiedzi** go to confession; **przystąpić do spowiedzi** be to confession; **nie była u spowiedzi od roku** she hasn't been to confession for a year; **spowiedź powszechna** general confession; **spowiedź wielkanocna** Easter duty; **pod tajemnicą spowiedzi** under the seal of confession; **wysłuchać czyjejś spowiedzi** hear sb's confession.

spowinowacać *ipf.*, **spowinowacić** *pf.* relate by marriage, make affine. ~ **się** *ipf.*, **spowinowacić się** *pf.* become related by marriage.

spowinowacony *a.* affine, related by marriage.

spowity *a.* (*chmurami, tajemnicą, mgłą*) enveloped, cloaked, shrouded; **spowity dymem** wreathed in smoke.

spowodować *pf.* **1.** (*wypadek, powódź, wybuch*) cause; (*konsekwencje*) bring about, produce; (*śmiech, określoną reakcję*) provoke; (*szkody*) inflict; (*nieporozumienie, konflikty*) give rise to, trigger; **spowodować, że ktoś coś zrobi** make sb do sth; **spowodować, że coś się stanie** make sth happen; **spowodować śmierć** cause *l.* lead to death; **spowodować kłopoty** cause trouble; **jego lekkomyślność spowodowała śmierć wielu ludzi** his carelessness resulted in the death of many people. **2.** (= *pociągnąć za sobą*) result (*coś* in sth); entail, involve.

spowodowany *a.* triggered, caused, effected (*czymś* by sth); related, due, owing (*czymś* to sth); **spowodowany stresem** stress-related, due to stress; **pożar spowodowany zaniedbaniem** fire caused by neglect *l.* negligence; **zniszczenia spowodowane powodzią** flood damage; **być spowodowanym czymś** be due to sth, stem from sth.

spowszedniały *a.* (*powszechny*) commonplace, common; (= *zwykły*) ordinary; (*powiedzenie*) hackneyed.

spowszednieć *pf.* lose attractiveness *l.* charm, become commonplace *l.* hackneyed.

spoza *prep.* + *Gen.* **1.** (= *zza*) from behind, from beyond; **słońce wyszło spoza chmur** the sun appeared from behind the clouds. **2.** (= *nie stąd*) from outside; **dziewczyna spoza środowiska akademickiego** a girl from outside the academic community; **osoba spoza towarzystwa** outsider.

spożycie *n.* consumption; (*witamin, tłuszczów itp.*) intake; **wzrost/spadek spożycia** increase/decrease in consumption; **data** *l.* **termin przydatności do spożycia** best-before date, use-by date, expiry date; **nadający/nienadający się do spożycia** fit/unfit for consumption; **wskaźnik spożycia** consumption index; **dzienne spożycie** daily intake; **dzienne dopuszczalne spożycie** acceptable *l.* allowable daily intake, ADI; **w stanie wskazującym na spożycie** (*być, prowadzić samochód*) under the influence, over the (legal) limit.

spożyć *pf.* **-żyję** **-żyjesz**, **-żyj** zob. **spożywać**.

spożytkować *pf.* make use of, use; (*zwł. z pożytkiem*) turn *l.* put to good account *l.* use.

spożywać *ipf.* **-am** **-asz** *lit.* consume; partake (*coś* of sth).

spożywca *mp* consumer.

spożywczy *a.* food; **artykuły spożywcze** groceries, foods; comestibles, edibles; **sklep spożywczy** grocery (store), the grocer's; **przemysł spożywczy** food industry; **folia spożywcza** cling film; **barwnik spożywczy** food coloring, *Br.* food colouring.

spód *mi* **-o-** bottom, foot, base, underside; (*butów*) sole; (*pizzy, ciasta*) base; (*chleba*) crust; (*spódnicy*) foundation; **na spodzie** at the bottom; **na spodzie szafy** at the bottom of a wardrobe; **pod spodem** underneath, down below; **od spodu** from the bottom, from below; from under; **u spodu** at the foot; **suknia na atłasowym spodzie** a dress with satin foundation.

spódnica *f.* skirt; **spódnica do ziemi** full-length skirt; **spódnica-spodnie** culottes; **trzymać się matczynej spódnicy** be tied to one's mother's apron strings; **złej tanecznicy zawadza i rąbek u spódnicy** a bad workman always quarrels with *l.* blames his tools.

spódniczka *f. Gen.pl.* **-ek** skirt; **spódniczka baletnicy** tutu; **spódniczka mini** miniskirt; **spódniczka szkocka** kilt; **latać za spódniczkami** *pot.* chase girls *l.* women.

spójka *f. Gen.pl.* **-ek** *gram.* copula, linking verb.

spójnia *f. Gen.pl.* **-i** bond, link, tie (*czegoś z czymś* between sth and sth); **spójnia nauki z techniką** the union of science and technology.

spójnik *mi Gen.* **-a** *gram.* conjunction, connective; **spójnik współrzędny** coordinating conjunction.

spójnikowy a. gram. conjunctional, conjunctive.

spójność f. 1. (= zwartość) (tekstu) coherence; (systemu) cohesion, uniformity; (argumentu, teorii) consistency; **brak spójności** incoherence. 2. fiz. cohesion. 3. mat. connectivity.

spójny a. (o tekście, argumencie, teorii) coherent, consistent; (o systemie) uniform, organized; (o stylu, tekście) succinct; fiz. cohesive; mat. (o zbiorze) connected.

spółdzielca mp cooperative (society) member.

spółdzielczość f. (pracy, mieszkaniowa, produkcyjna) cooperative movement.

spółdzielczy a. 1. (= dotyczący spółdzielni) cooperative, collective; **sklep spółdzielczy** cooperative store. 2. (= będący własnością spółdzielni) cooperative; **mieszkanie spółdzielcze** cooperative apartment, housing association apartment.

spółdzielnia f. Gen.pl. -i 1. (zrzeszenie) cooperative, cooperative society l. association; **spółdzielnia mieszkaniowa** cooperative apartment corporation, housing association; **spółdzielnia produkcyjna** producer's cooperative; **spółdzielnia rolna** agricultural cooperative; **spółdzielnia lekarska** (medical) group practice. 2. pot. (sklep) coop, cooperative store.

spółgłoska f. Gen.pl. -ek fon. consonant; **spółgłoska dźwięczna/bezdźwięczna** voiced/voiceless consonant; **spółgłoska zwarta** stop consonant, stop; **spółgłoska szczelinowa** fricative; **spółgłoska zwarto-szczelinowa** affricate; **spółgłoska wargowa** labial consonant; **spółgłoska zębowa** dental consonant.

spółgłoskowy a. fon. consonantal; **przesuwka spółgłoskowa** consonant shift; **zbitka spółgłoskowa** consonantal cluster.

spółka f. Gen.pl. -ek ekon. 1. company, corporation, partnership; **spółka akcyjna** (w Polsce) joint-stock company; (w krajach anglosaskich) public limited company; **spółka holdingowa** holding company; **spółka jawna** unlimited company; **spółka kapitałowa** company; **spółka komandytowa** limited liability partnership; **spółka osobowa** partnership; **spółka cywilna** general partnership; **spółka z ograniczoną odpowiedzialnością** limited liability company; **spółka joint venture** joint venture; **spółka zależna** daughter company; **kapitał spółki** equity; **statut spółki** articles of association l. incorporation; **umowa spółki z o.o.** (w Polsce) deed of association; **dyrektor spółki** company director; **wejść do spółki** join a company; **utworzyć spółkę** establish l. set up l. form a company; **zlikwidować spółkę** dissolve l. liquidate a company. 2. przest. joint action; **robić coś na spółkę** l. **do spółki z kimś** do sth together with sb; **zapłacić na spółkę** split the bill, share the costs, go Dutch; **wynajmować z kimś pokój/mieszkanie na spółkę** share a room/an apartment with sb.

spółkować ipf. copulate, couple.

spółkowanie n. copulation, coitus.

spór mi -o- argument (o coś about sth); dispute, controversy (o coś over sth); **zażarty spór** heated argument; **spór prawny** prawn. legal dis-

pute; **strony sporu** prawn. parties to a dispute; **toczyć** l. **wieść spór** dispute, argue, contend; **być przedmiotem sporu** be in l. under dispute, be an object at issue; **będący przedmiotem sporu** in contention; **rozstrzygnąć spór** settle a dispute; **zażegnać spór** prevent l. avert l. ward off l. stave off a dispute.

spóźniać się ipf. come l. be late; (o płatności, przelewie itp.) be overdue; (o zegarze) lose; **spóźniać się z czymś** be late l. behindhand with sth; **spóźnić się na coś pięć minut** be five minutes late for sth; **spóźnić się na zebranie** be late for a meeting; **spóźnić się z obiadem** be late with dinner; **obiad spóźnia się** dinner is late; **pociąg się spóźnił** the train was late l. delayed; **dlaczego on się tak spóźnił?** what made him so late?; **spóźniać się na pociąg/samolot** miss one's l. a train/plane; **zegar się spóźnia** the clock is slow; **zegarek spóźnia się o pięć minut** my watch loses five minutes.

spóźnialska f. Gen. -iej, **spóźnialski** mp decl. like a. pot. latecomer.

spóźnić się pf. -ij zob. **spóźniać się**.

spóźnienie n. 1. (= zbyt późne przybycie) lateness, late-coming; **mieć spóźnienie** be running late; **przepraszam za spóźnienie** I'm sorry I'm late, I'm sorry for being late; **pociąg ma godzinę spóźnienia** the train is one hour late. 2. (= zaległość) delay.

spóźniony a. -eni (o osobie) late; (o środku komunikacji) late, delayed; (o wpłatach, płatnościach) overdue, in arrears; (o wiośnie, żalu, życzeniach, korespondencji) belated; (o odpowiedzi) delayed; (o zegarku) slow; **spóźniony refleks** slow reaction l. reflexes; **spóźnieni goście** latecomers; **być spóźnionym** be running late; **lecę, bo jestem już spóźniony** I've got to go because I'm (already) late.

spracować się pf. tire o.s. out, exhaust o.s.

spracowany a. exhausted, tired out; (o rękach) toilworn.

sprać pf. spiorę spierzesz 1. zob. **spierać**. 2. pot. (= zbić) work over, wallop; **sprać kogoś na kwaśne jabłko** beat l. knock the tar out of sb, beat sb to a pulp. ~ **się** pf. 1. zob. **spierać się**. 2. pot. (= zbić się) wallop l. clout l. clobber each other.

spragniony a. -eni thirsty, dry; **spragniony czegoś** avid l. eager for sth; **spragniony miłości** craving l. starving for love; **spragniony krwi** blood-thirsty; **być spragnionym czegoś** przen. long for sth.

sprasować pf., **sprasowywać** ipf. techn. press, compress.

spraszać ipf. (gości) invite; (oficjalnie) gather, summon.

sprawa f. 1. (fakt) affair, matter; **sprawy rodzinne** family matters; **sprawy zawodowe** business; **sprawy codzienne** everyday concerns; **sprawy państwowe** public affairs; **nie wtrącaj się do cudzych spraw** mind your own business; **jak się mają sprawy?** where l. how do things stand?; **ruszyć sprawę z miejsca** get things going; **gorsza sprawa, że...** what's worse...; **niepokojąca sprawa**

matter of concern; **delikatna sprawa** touch-and-go; **niezałatwiona sprawa** loose end; **pilna sprawa** urgent matter; **przegrana sprawa** lost cause; **nieczysta sprawa** shady business; **omawiana sprawa** issue *l.* matter under discussion; **inna sprawa, że...** not to mention that...; **to załatwia sprawę** that settles it; **sprawa jest oczywista** no doubt about it, it's (pretty) straightforward; **sprawa honoru** matter of honor; **sprawa wagi państwowej** matter of the state, pressing issue; **sprawa urzędowa** official business; **sprawa otwarta** open question; **sprawy sercowe** affairs of the heart; **na dobrą sprawę** as a matter of fact, strictly speaking, to tell the truth; **zdać sprawę z czegoś** render an account of sth, report on sth; **zdać sobie jasno sprawę z...** take sth in, be well aware of sth, awake to sth; **zdałem sobie sprawę, że...** I realized that..., it occurred to me that...; **władze zdały sobie w końcu sprawę z rozmiaru problemu** authorities finally awoke to the extent of the problem; **nie zdawać sobie sprawy z czegoś** be unaware *l.* unconscious *l.* ignorant of sth; **pokpić sprawę** blow it; **przeczekać sprawę** let things lie, lie low; **zakończyć sprawę** call it quits; **zaciemniać sprawę** fog *l.* cloud *l.* confuse the issue; **zajmować stanowisko w sprawie** take a stand on an issue; **to jego sprawa** it's his problem *l.* business; **to nie twoja sprawa** (it's) none of your business, mind your own business; **to nie moja sprawa** it's not my business *l.* concern; **to sprawa kilku dni** it's a matter *l.* question of a few days; **to poważna sprawa** this is no laughing matter; **to sprawa przesądzona** there's nothing I (you etc.) can do about it; **sprawa życia i śmierci** a matter of life and death; **to całkiem inna sprawa** that's a different kettle of fish, it's an altogether different matter; **zająć się sprawą...** address the issue of...; **komplikować sprawę** make things difficult; **pogarszać sprawę** make things *l.* matters worse, rub salt into the wound; **to przesądza sprawę** that settles it; **załagodzić sprawę** pour oil on the waters *l.* on troubled waters; **stawiać jasno sprawę** be clear about sth; **nie dostrzegać istoty sprawy** miss the point; **zostawić sprawę w spokoju** drop the matter, let the matter rest; **porządkować swoje sprawy** set *l.* put one's own house in order, order *l.* settle one's affair przejść do sedna sprawy get down to the point; **sedno sprawy** the heart *l.* crux of the matter; **sprawy nie układają się najlepiej** things are not going right. **2.** (*interes*) business; **mam do pana sprawę** I have a favor to ask of you; **nie mam do niego żadnej sprawy** I have no business with him; **zwracać się do kogoś w jakiejś sprawie** approach *l.* turn to sb about sth; **sprawa niecierpiąca zwłoki** urgent matter; **zrób coś w tej sprawie** do sth about it; **kilka spraw do załatwienia** a few things to attend to; **wziąć sprawę w swoje ręce** take matters into one's hands; **mieć mnóstwo spraw na głowie** have a lot on one's mind, have many things to take care of; **przedyskutować wiele spraw** cover a lot of ground, discuss many issues; **doprowadzić sprawę do końca** tie up the loose ends, bring the matter to an issue; **mam**

jeszcze kilka spraw do załatwienia I still have a few errands to do *l.* run; **mieć inne/ważniejsze sprawy na głowie** have other/bigger fish to fry; **nie ma sprawy** *pot.* no problem, (it's) no big deal, forget it, it's no trouble at all; **Ministerstwo Spraw Zagranicznych** the Ministry of Foreign Affairs; *US* the Department of State; *Br.* the Foreign Office; **Ministerstwo Spraw Wewnętrznych** the Ministry of Internal Affairs; *US* the Department of Homeland Security; *Br.* the Home Office; **sprawy wewnętrzne/zagraniczne** home/foreign affairs. **3.** *lit.* (= *wzniosły cel*) cause; **sprawa wielkiej wagi** matter of great importance; **poświęcić się dla sprawy** sacrifice o.s. for the cause; **walczyć o wspólną sprawę** fight for the common cause; **słuszna sprawa** fair cause; **bronić słusznej sprawy** defend a good cause; **zrobić coś dla dobra sprawy** do sth towards promoting the cause. **4.** *prawn.* case; **sprawa cywilna** civil case; **sprawa karna** criminal case; **sprawa rozwodowa** divorce case; **prowadzić sprawę** (*o inspektorze policji*) be on the case; **wygrać/przegrać sprawę** win/lose a case; **umorzyć sprawę** discontinue proceedings; **załatwić sprawę polubownie** settle a case out of court; **oddać sprawę do sądu** go to court; **wytoczyć komuś sprawę** take legal action against sb, bring an action against sb.

sprawca *mp* (*czynu*) doer, author, performer; (*przestępstwa*) perpetrator; (*uprowadzenia*) abductor; **on jest sprawcą mojej niedoli** he is the cause of my misfortune; **sprawca wypadku** the guilty party.

sprawczy *a.* instrumental, ministerial; (*o czynniku*) causative.

sprawczyni *f. zob.* **sprawca**.

sprawdzać *ipf.* check, examine; (= *przeprowadzać kontrolę*) inspect; (*rachunki*) audit; (= *weryfikować*) verify; (*w słowniku*) look up; (*pisownię*) spell-check; (*drugi raz*) double check; (= *upewniać się*) make sure; **sprawdzać listę obecności** call the roll; **sprawdzać czyjś stan** (*o lekarzu*) check on sb; **sprawdzać kogoś** (*potajemnie*) check up on sb, run a check on sb. **~ się** *ipf.* (= *urzeczywistniać się*) come true, prove correct; **wszystko sprawdza się w praniu** the proof of the pudding is in the eating; (= *wykazać się*) prove o.s.; (= *okazać się przydatnym*) turn out to be useful.

sprawdzalność *f.* verifiability, testability; **sprawdzalność prognoz meteorologicznych** reliability of weather forecasts.

sprawdzalny *a.* (*o teorii, hipotezie*) verifiable, confirmable; (*o efekcie*) provable.

sprawdzian *mi* **1.** (= *miernik*) measure; (*uczciwości, wytrwałości*) touchstone; (*umiejętności*) test. **2.** *szkoln.* test, quiz. **3.** *techn.* gauge; **sprawdzian kontrolny** inspection *l.* check gauge.

sprawdzić *pf. zob.* **sprawdzać**. **~ się** *pf. zob.* **sprawdzać się**.

sprawdzony *a.* (*o leku*) tested; (*o skuteczności, sposobie*) proven; (*o zawodniku, taktyce*) sure, dependable, reliable.

sprawiać *ipf.*, **sprawić** *pf.* **1.** (= *powodować*) cause, bring about; **sprawiać kłopot** cause trouble, be a nuisance; **sprawiać ból** hurt, cause pain; **sprawiać komuś przykrość** make sb sorry; **sprawiać komuś radość** make sb happy; **sprawiać dobre/złe wrażenie** make a good/bad impression; **sprawiać komuś zawód** let sb down, disappoint sb, be a disappointment to sb; **sprawić komuś niespodziankę** spring *l.* uncork a surprise on sb; **sprawić niespodziankę** come as a surprise; **sprawiać trudności** cause trouble; **sprawić, że coś się stanie** make sth happen; **sprawić, że ktoś coś zrobi** make sb do sth; **sprawiać komuś frajdę** give sb a buzz; **przypadek sprawił, że...** it was only a pure chance that...; **czy sprawiłoby ci to kłopot?** would it cause you any trouble?, would it put you out?; **sprawić komuś lanie** *l.* **baty** give sb a drubbing *l.* thrashing; **nie sprawiać kłopotu** be no trouble; **sprawiać wrażenie czegoś** make *l.* give the impression of (being) sth. **2.** *przest.* (= *kupować*) buy, purchase. **3.** *kulin.* (= *oprawiać*) dress. ~ **się** *ipf.*, **sprawić się** *pf.* perform *l.* do well; **spraw się dobrze!** do your best!; **samochód dobrze się sprawia** the car is working properly.

sprawiedliwie *adv.* (*osądzić, oceniać*) fairly, justly, rightly; (*postępować*) righteously.

sprawiedliwość *f.* **1.** justice, fairness, equity; (= *bezstronność*) impartiality; **sprawiedliwość społeczna** social justice; **poczucie sprawiedliwości** sense of justice; **wymiar sprawiedliwości** the judiciary; **wymierzać sprawiedliwość** administer justice; **wymierzyć komuś sprawiedliwość** bring sb to justice; **uczynić zadość sprawiedliwości** do justice; **oddać kogoś w ręce sprawiedliwości** hand sb over to justice, bring sb to justice; **oddając komuś sprawiedliwość** in all fairness to sb, in justice to sb; **po sprawiedliwości** *pot.* giving credit where credit's due, in all justice; **oddać komuś sprawiedliwość** give sb their due, do justice to sb; **wymierzyć samemu sprawiedliwość** take the law into one's own hands; **stało się zadość sprawiedliwości** justice has been done *l.* served; **sprawiedliwość zwycięży** justice will prevail; **sprawiedliwość wymaga, by...** it's only fair *l.* just that...; **żądać sprawiedliwości** demand justice. **2.** (= *sądownictwo*) the judiciary; **karząca ręka sprawiedliwości** the long arm of the law; **ramię sprawiedliwości cię dosięgnie** you will be brought to justice; **minister sprawiedliwości** Minister of Justice; *US* Attorney General; **Ministerstwo Sprawiedliwości** the Ministry of Justice; *US* the Department of Justice.

sprawiedliwy *a.* (*o człowieku*) just, upright; (*o wyroku, sądzie, ustawie*) just, fair; (*o sędzim, oceniającym*) impartial, unbiased; (*o podziale, ocenie, czynie, postępowaniu*) fair; (*o karze*) deserved; (*o krytyce*) justified; **Pan Bóg nierychliwy, ale sprawiedliwy** punishment is lame, but it comes; God comes with leaden feet, but strikes with iron hands. – *mp lit.* the just; **spać snem sprawiedliwego** sleep the sleep of the just.

sprawka *f. Gen.pl.* **-ek** (*wybryk, psota*) doing, trick, prank; **to jego sprawka** this is his doing; **ujawniać brudne sprawki** muckrake.

sprawnie *adv.* ably, deftly, skillfully; (*pracować*) efficiently; (*obsługiwać klientów*) competently; **szybko i sprawnie** with dispatch; **sprawnie działający** efficient.

sprawnościowy *a.* **1.** fitness; **test sprawnościowy** fitness test; **ćwiczenia sprawnościowe** fitness *l.* agility exercises. **2.** *techn.* efficiency.

sprawność *f.* **1.** (= *zdolność*) ability, capability; (= *zręczność*) dexterity, adroitness, skillfulness; **sprawność fizyczna** fitness; **sprawność umysłowa** mental *l.* intellectual ability; **sprawność bojowa** *wojsk.* combat proficiency *l.* efficiency; **sprawność seksualna** potency, sexual prowess; **sprawność urządzenia** efficiency. **2.** (= *wiedza, umiejętności*) proficiency, competence, skill. **3.** (*w harcerstwie*) scout proficiency. **4.** *fiz., techn.* efficiency.

sprawny *a.* able, deft; (*o umyśle*) agile, nimble; (*o ruchach, rękach*) dexterous, adroit; (*o samochodzie, statku*) in running order; (*o zarządzaniu, administracji, pisarstwie*) competent, efficient, skillful; (*o osobie, działaniu*) expeditious; (*o pracowniku, maszynie*) efficient; (*o urządzeniu*) functional, running; (*manualnie*) dexterous, deft; **sprawny fizycznie** physically fit; **niesprawny/sprawny umysłowo** mentally handicapped/healthy.

sprawować *ipf.* (*urząd*) hold; (*władzę, rządy, kontrolę*) wield, exercise; **sprawować urząd ministra** serve as a minister; **sprawować mandat poselski** be a Member of Parliament; **sprawować kontrolę** be in control, control; **sprawować władzę** wield power; **sprawować wysoki urząd** hold a high office; **sprawować nadzór nad czymś** supervise sth; **sprawować opiekę nad kimś/czymś** care for sb/sth; **sprawować rządy twardej ręki** rule with a heavy *l.* firm hand. ~ **się** *ipf.* behave; **sprawuj się dobrze!** be a good boy *l.* girl!; **samochód sprawuje się bez zarzutu** the car is working properly; **sprawować się źle** misbehave, misconduct (o.s.).

sprawowanie *n.* *szkoln.* conduct; **dobre/złe sprawowanie** good/bad conduct.

sprawozdanie *n.* report (*z czegoś* on sth); account (*z czegoś* of sth); rundown (*z czegoś* on sth); **sprawozdanie prasowe** media coverage; **sprawozdanie sportowe** sportscast; **sprawozdanie radiowe** radio coverage; **sprawozdanie finansowe** finacial report *l.* statement; **sprawozdanie z procesu** trial report; **sprawozdanie z meczu** game coverage *l.* commentary; **sprawozdanie urzędowe** official report; **sprawozdanie o postępie prac(y)** progress report; **sprawozdanie miesięczne/roczne** monthly/annual report; **sporządzić sprawozdanie** draw up *l.* make *l.* prepare a report; **składać sprawozdanie z czegoś** render an account of sth, report on sth.

sprawozdawca *mp* reporter; **sprawozdawca telewizyjny/radiowy** TV/radio commentator; **poseł sprawozdawca** *parl.* rapporteur (deputy); **sprawozdawca sportowy** sportscaster, sports commentator; **sprawozdawca zagraniczny** foreign correspondent.

sprawozdawczość *f.* **1.** (= *pisanie sprawo-*

zdań) reporting. **2.** (*dział przedsiębiorstwa, instytucji*) reporting department *l.* division.

sprawozdawczy *a.* report, reporting; (*o dziale, okresie*) reporting; **okres sprawozdawczy** *ekon.* accounting period.

sprawunek *mi* **-nk-** purchase, buy; **robić sprawunki** do the shopping; **iść po sprawunki** go shopping; **chodzić za sprawunkami** *pot.* go about shopping.

spray *mi Gen.pl.* **-ów** spray, aerosol; **spray na owady** insect spray; **perfumy/dezodorant w sprayu** spray *l.* aerosol perfume/deodorant; **lakier do włosów w sprayu** hair spray; **malować sprayem** spray.

sprecyzować *pf.* (*program, stanowisko, oczekiwania*) specify.

spreparować *pf.* **1.** (*coś fikcyjnego*) cook up; (*dowody*) fabricate, trump up; (*wymówkę*) concoct; (*historię, opowiadanie*) make up. **2.** (*miksturę*) make up, concoct, prepare. **3.** (= *zrobić preparat biologiczny*) make a specimen (*coś of* sth).

sprezentować *pf. przest.* present, show, display; **sprezentować broń** *wojsk.* present arms.

sprężać *ipf.* **1.** (= *naprężyć*) tense. **2.** *fiz.* (*gaz, powietrze*) compress. **3.** *bud.* prestress. **~ się** *ipf.* **1.** (= *napinać mięśnie*) pull tight, tense up, tighten (*the muscles*). **2.** (= *kondensować się pod wpływem ciśnienia*) compress, undergo compression. **3.** *pot.* (= *mobilizować się*) get o.s. together, pull up one's socks.

sprężarka *f. Gen.pl.* **-ek** *techn.* compressor.

sprężarkowy *a. techn.* compression; **chłodziarka sprężarkowa** compression refrigerator.

sprężony *a.* (*o gazach*) compressed; (*o betonie*) prestressed.

sprężyć *pf. zob.* **sprężać.** **~ się** *pf. zob.* **sprężać się.**

sprężyna *f.* **1.** (*z drutu*) spring; **sprężyna zegarka** mainspring; **przekręcić sprężynę w zegarku** overwind. **2.** (= *czynnik sprawczy*) mainspring; **być główną sprężyną czegoś** be the prime mover *l.* mainspring of sth; **poruszyć wszystkie sprężyny** pull all the strings, move heaven and earth.

sprężynka *f. Gen.pl.* **-ek** (small) spring.

sprężynować *ipf.* **1.** (*być elastycznym*) spring back. **2.** *roln.* harrow (*with a spring (tooth) harrow*).

sprężynowiec *mi* **-wc-** *Gen. i Acc.* **-a** *Gen.pl.* **-ów** *pot.* switchblade (knife); *Br.* flick knife.

sprężynowy *a.* (*o napędzie, zegarze, wadze*) spring; **nóż sprężynowy** switchblade (knife); *Br.* flick knife; **materac sprężynowy** inner-spring *l.* interior-sprung mattress; **zamek sprężynowy** springlock; **brona sprężynowa** *roln.* spring (tooth) harrow.

sprężynujący *a.* (*o materacu*) springing, springy, bouncy; (*o mechanizmie*) spring-loaded.

sprężystość *f.* **1.** (*materaca*) springiness, bounce; **materac stracił już sprężystość** there's little elasticity left in the mattress. **2.** (*ruchów*) nimbleness, elasticity, agility. **3.** *mech.* re-

silence. **4.** *fiz.* elasticity; **granica sprężystości** elastic limit.

sprężysty *a.* **1.** (= *elastyczny, giętki*) elastic; (*o materacu*) bouncy, springy. **2.** (= *gibki, zwinny*) nimble, agile; **chodzić sprężystym krokiem** walk with a spring in one's step. **3.** (= *sprawny, energiczny*) efficient. **4.** *mech.* resilient.

sprint *mi sport* sprint; **pobiec sprintem** sprint.

sprinter *mp,* **sprinterka** *f. Gen.pl.* **-ek** *sport* sprinter.

sprinterski *a. sport* (*o biegu, dystansie*) sprint, short-distance.

sprofanować *pf. zob.* **profanować.**

sprofilować *pf. zob.* **profilować.**

sprokurować *pf. zob.* **prokurować.**

sprolongować *pf. zob.* **prolongować.**

sprosić *pf.* **sproszę sprosisz** *zob.* **spraszać.**

sprostać *pf.* **1.** (= *dorównać komuś/czemuś*) equal, be a match for, be equal *l.* level with; **nikt mu nie sprosta** there's no match for him. **2.** (= *podołać*) manage; (*obowiązkom, trudnościom*) cope with; (*żądaniom, wyzwaniu*) meet; **sprostać czyimś oczekiwaniom** live up to *l.* measure up to *l.* meet sb's expectations.

sprostować *pf.* (*błędy*) correct, rectify; (*fakty, informacje*) straighten out, set right.

sprostowanie *n.* correction, démenti; **żądać sprostowania** demand that sth be straightened out *l.* corrected.

sproszkować *pf. zob.* **sproszkowywać.** **~ się** *pf. zob.* **sproszkowywać się.**

sproszkowany *a.* pulverized, powdery; (*o mleku*) powdered, dried.

sproszkowywać *ipf.* pulverize, grind to powder, triturate. **~ się** *ipf.* turn to powder.

sprośnie *adv.* obscenely, lewdly, bawdily.

sprośność *f.* obscenity, lechery, lewdness.

sprośny *a.* obscene, lubricious; (*o żarcie*) dirty, spicy; (*o opowiadaniu, książce*) salacious; (*o wyrazie twarzy*) lecherous; **sprośna mowa** bawdy; **mieć sprośne myśli** have dirty thoughts.

sprowadzać *ipf.,* **sprowadzić** *pf.* **1.** (= *przyprowadzać, dostarczać*) bring, fetch, get; (*np. towary z zagranicy*) import; **sprowadzać lekarza** call in *l.* fetch *l.* get a doctor; **sprowadzać samolot na ziemię** land a plane; **co panią tu sprowadza?** what brings you here?; **sprowadzić kogoś na złą drogę** lead sb astray; **sprowadził wszystkich swoich kolegów** he brought all his friends with him; **sprowadzić kogoś na ziemię** bring sb down to earth; **sprowadźcie pomoc!** (go) get (some) help!; **sprowadził go tutaj jakiś interes** some sort of business brought him here. **2.** (= *powodować, wywołać*) cause, bring about, give rise to; **wiatr sprowadził ochłodzenie** the wind brought about colder weather; **sprowadzić na kogoś nieszczęście** bring a misfortune on sb. **3.** (= *zmieniać tok*) switch, turn away; **sprowadzić rozmowę na inny temat** change topic. **4.** (*kogoś z góry*) lead (sb) downstairs *l.* down, help (sb) down. **5.** (= *ograniczać*) reduce; **więc sprowadzasz miłość do seksu?** so you equal love to sex, then?; **sprowadzić ułamki do wspólnego mianownika** *mat.* reduce fractions to a common denominator. **~ się**

ipf., **sprowadzić się** *pf.* **1.** (= *osiedlać się*) move in, settle. **2.** (= *ograniczać się*) boil down to, amount to, be equal to; **to wszystko sprowadza się do jednego** it all comes down *l.* amounts to the same thing; **dla niego wychowanie sprowadza się do zakazów i nakazów** according to him, upbringing boils down to do's and don'ts; **to sprowadza się do powiedzenia...** it's as good as saying...

sprowokować *pf. zob.* **prowokować.**

spróbować *pf.* **1.** (*jak coś smakuje*) taste. **2.** (*coś zrobić*) try, attempt; **spróbować czegoś** have a go *l.* try *l.* shot at sth; **spróbuj sam** try (for) yourself; **spróbuj poszukać tutaj** try looking here; **nie zaszkodzi spróbować** it's worth a try; **spróbować czegoś nowego/innego** try sth new/different. **3.** *pot.* dare; **tylko spróbuj!** *pot.* don't you dare!, don't even think about it! **4.** *przest.* try, test; **spróbować szczęścia** take a chance, try one's luck; **spróbować w czymś sił** try one's hand at sth, take a crack at sth; **choćby po to, by spróbować** if only to try.

spróchniały *a.* (*o desce, dachu, podłodze*) rotten; (*o zębie*) decayed, carious.

spróchnieć *pf.* **1.** (*o drewnie*) rot. **2.** (*o zębie*) decay.

spruć *pf.* undo, unstitch, unseam.

spryciarka *f. Gen.pl.* **-ek** *pot. zob.* **spryciarz.**

spryciarz *mp pot.* (smooth) operator, wheeler-dealer, smart cookie.

sprymitywizować *pf. uj.* (*problem, zagadnienie*) simplify, trivialize, downplay.

spryskać *pf. zob.* **spryskiwać.** ~ **się** *pf. zob.* **spryskiwać się.**

spryskiwacz *mi Gen.* **-a** *ogr.* sprinkler; *mot.* (*do szyb*) windscreen washer.

spryskiwać *ipf.* (*wodą, perfumami*) spray, sprinkle, spritz (*czymś* with sth); (*strumieniem*) jet; (*rośliny, pole*) spray; **spryskała szyję perfumami** she spritzed her neck with perfume; **spryskać rośliny pestycydami** spray plants with pesticides. ~ **się** *ipf.* **1.** (*siebie*) spray, spritz. **2.** (*jeden drugiego*) splash; **chłopcy spryskiwali się wodą** boys splashed each other with water.

spryt *mi* cunning, artfulness, shrewdness; **brak ci sprytu** you lack cunning; **wykazać się sprytem** be cunning.

sprytnie *adv.* cunningly; (*pomyślane*) shrewdly, cleverly; (*zorganizowane*) cannily, artfully, smartly; **sprytnie to sobie wymyślił** that was pretty smart of him.

sprytny *a.* (*o osobie*) shrewd, smart, artful; (*o uśmiechu, minie, urządzeniu, rozwiązaniu*) cunning; (*o pomyśle, urządzeniu, kryjówce*) clever, ingenious, tricky; (*o złodzieju*) cunning, crafty, wily; **sprytny pomysł** clever idea.

sprywatyzować *pf. zob.* **prywatyzować.** ~ **się** *pf. zob.* **prywatyzować się.**

sprząc *pf.* **-ęgę -ężesz, -aż** *l.* **-ęż, -ągł** *zob.* **sprzęgać.** ~ **się** *pf. zob.* **sprzęgać się.**

sprzączka *f. Gen.pl.* **-ek** buckle, clasp.

sprzątacz *mp* cleaner.

sprzątaczka *f. Gen.pl.* **-ek** cleaner, cleaning lady, charwoman.

sprzątać *ipf.* **1.** (= *robić porządki*) clean; (*pokój*) clean, tidy up; (*jakieś przedmioty skądś*) clear; **sprzątać po kimś/sobie** clean after sb/o.s.; **sprzątnąć ze stołu** clear the table; **sprzątnąć bałagan** clear out the mess. **2.** *roln.* gather crop, harvest. **3.** *pot.* (*zabierać*) knock off, clear out; **sprzątnąć komuś coś sprzed nosa** take sth from under sb's nose; **sprzątnęła swojej koleżance chłopaka** she stole her friend's boyfriend, she took her friend's boyfriend away. **4.** *pot.* (= *zajadać*) put away, polish off, scoff.

sprzątanie *n.* cleaning; (*zbóż*) harvest, harvesting.

sprzątnąć *pf.* **-ij 1.** *zob.* **sprzątać. 2.** *pot.* (= *zabić*) erase, rub out, wipe out; do in *l.* away with. **3.** *pot.* (= *zjeść*) polish off, put away, scoff; **sprzątnęli wszystkie kiełbaski z lodówki** they polished off all the sausages from the fridge.

sprzeciw *mi* **1.** (*opór*) objection (*przeciwko czemuś* to *l.* against sth); opposition (*przeciwko czemuś* to sth); (*społeczny*) resistance; **powszechny sprzeciw** public outcry; **zgłaszać sprzeciw** raise *l.* voice an objection; **spotkać się z silnym sprzeciwem** meet with fierce *l.* strong opposition; **bez sprzeciwu zrobiła, co jej kazali** she did what she was told without any objections; **ton nieznoszący sprzeciwu** assertive *l.* imperious tone; **bez sprzeciwu** without demur; **jako wyraz sprzeciwu wobec czegoś** in opposition to sth; **głos sprzeciwu** dissenting *l.* dissentient voice. **2.** *prawn.* objection; **wnosić sprzeciw** object; **sprzeciw!** objection!; **odrzucać/podtrzymywać sprzeciw** overrule/sustain an objection; **podtrzymuję sprzeciw** (objection) sustained.

sprzeciwiać się *ipf.*, **sprzeciwić się** *pf.* **1.** (= *nie zgadzać się*) oppose, stand against (*komuś/czemuś* sb/sth); object, stand opposed (*komuś/czemuś* to sb/sth); **zdecydowanie sprzeciwić się** put one's foot down, be dead against, stand firm *l.* fast against. **2.** (= *być niezgodnym z czymś*) contradict, counter; be contrary to, run counter to, clash with; **sprzeciwiać się czyimś interesom** run against sb's interests; **to sprzeciwia się zasadom mojej wiary** this contradicts *l.* is contrary to my faith. **3.** *przest.* (= *dokuczać*) tease.

sprzeczać się *ipf.* have an argument, argue, bicker (*o coś* about sth); fight, quibble (*o coś* about *l.* over sth); **nie sprzeczaj się ze mną** don't argue with me.

sprzeczka *f. Gen.pl.* **-ek** quarrel, row, squabble, argument (*o coś* about *l.* over sth); (*między mężem i żoną, narzeczonymi itp.*) falling-out; **wywołać sprzeczkę z kimś** pick a quarrel with sb; **wdawać się w sprzeczkę** get into an argument.

sprzecznie *adv.* incongruously, inconsistently; (*z zasadami, z nakazami, z zaleceniami*) contrary to, in opposition to.

sprzeczność *f.* **1.** (= *niezgodność*) contradiction; discrepancy (*pomiędzy czymś a czymś* between sth and sth); inconsistency (*z czymś* with sth); **sprzeczność interesów** conflict of interests; **wewnętrzna sprzeczność** self-contradiction; **być w sprzeczności z czymś** run counter to sth, contradict sth; **być w sprzeczności z konwenansami** run counter to conventions; **stać w sprzeczności z czymś** be out of line with sth, be at variance with sth, be in contradiction to sth. **2.** *log.* contradiction, contrariety; **prawo sprzeczności** law of contradiction.

sprzeczny *a.* contradictory, contradictive; (*o opiniach, zeznaniach, interesach, uczuciach*) conflicting; (*o interesach*) competing; (*o informacjach*) contradictory, inconsistent, discrepant; **sprzeczny z konstytucją** *prawn., polit., parl.* unconstitutional; **sprzeczny z etyką zawodową** unprofessional; **sprzeczne wersje** contradictory versions *l.* accounts; **mieć sprzeczne zamiary** be at cross purposes; **sprzeczne z prawem** against the law; **być sprzecznym z czymś** be at variance with sth, conflict with sth, go against sth; (*o poglądach, opiniach*) collide; **zdanie sprzeczne** *log.* contradictory sentence; **sprzeczny układ równań** *mat.* contradictory system of equations.

sprzed *prep. + Gen.* **1.** (*miejsce*) from in front of; **zabrać komuś coś sprzed nosa** take sth from under sb's nose. **2.** (*czas*) from before; **wspomnienia sprzed lat** years-old memories; **sprzed wojny** prewar; **sprzed rewolucji francuskiej** from before the French Revolution; **wiadomość sprzed godziny** news received an hour ago; **historia sprzed dwóch lat** a two-year old story; **fotografia sprzed dwóch lat** a photo taken two years ago.

sprzedać *pf. zob.* **sprzedawać.** ~ **się** *pf. zob.* **sprzedawać się.**

sprzedająca *f. Gen.* **-ej** *zob.* **sprzedający.**

sprzedający *mp* (= *sprzedawca, ekspedient*) salesclerk, shop assitant; *prawn.* seller, vendor.

sprzedajny *a.* venal, corruptible.

sprzedany *a.* sold.

sprzedawać *ipf.* **-aję -ajesz, -awaj 1.** (*za pieniądze*) sell; (*narkotyki*) peddle; (*o maszynie, sprzedawcy ulicznym*) vend; **sprzedawać coś detalicznie/hurtem/na sztuki/na raty** sell sth at retail/wholesale prices/by the item/on installments; **sprzedawać coś z zyskiem/stratą** sell sth at a profit/loss; **sprzedać duszę diabłu** sell one's soul *l.* o.s. to the devil; **drogo sprzedać swe życie** sell one's life dear; **tanio sprzedawać swój talent** prostitute one's talent; **on potrafi sprzedać swoją wiedzę/umiejętności** he can turn his knowledge/skills to good account. **2.** *tylko ipf.* (= *być sprzedawcą*) sell (*coś* sth); deal (*coś* in sth). ~ **się** *ipf.* **1.** (*o towarze*) sell; **dobrze/źle się sprzedawać** sell well/badly. **2.** (*o osobie*) sell out; (*swoje ciało*) prostitute o.s.

sprzedawca *mp* (= *handlowiec*) salesman; (*w sklepie*) salesclerk; *Br.* shop assistant; *prawn.* seller, vendor; **sprzedawca detaliczny** retailer.

sprzedawczyk *mp Nom.pl.* **-i** *uj., lit.* renegade; traitor.

sprzedawczyni *f.* (= *kobieta handlowiec*) saleswoman; (*w sklepie*) salesclerk; *Br.* shop assistant.

sprzedaż *f. pl.* **-e** sale; **akt kupna-sprzedaży** sale contract; **dział sprzedaży** sales department;

sprzedaż detaliczna retail; **sprzedaż hurtowa** wholesale; **sprzedaż ratalna** installment plan; **sprzedaż wysyłkowa** mail order; **sprzedaż z zyskiem/ze stratą** sale at a profit/loss; **umowa sprzedaży** sale contract; **wysokość sprzedaży** *handl.* sales figures; **(być) na sprzedaż** (be) for sale; **wystawić coś na sprzedaż** put sth up for sale.

sprzedażny *a.* (*o cenie, wartości*) salable; **umowa sprzedażna** sale contract.

sprzeniewierzać *ipf.*, **sprzeniewierzyć** *pf.* embezzle. ~ **się** *ipf.*, **sprzeniewierzyć się** *pf.* betray (*komuś / czemuś* sb/sth).

sprzęgać *ipf.* (= *zespalać*) couple; *el.* link; *komp.* interface. ~ **się** *ipf. mech.* engage.

sprzęgło *n. Gen.pl.* **-gieł 1.** *mot.* clutch; **wcisnąć/puszczać sprzęgło** engage/disengage the clutch. **2.** *techn.* clutch, coupling.

sprzęgłowy *a. mot., techn.* clutch.

sprzęgnąć *pf.* **-ij** *zob.* **sprzęgać.** ~ **się** *pf. zob.* **sprzęgać się.**

sprzęt *mi* **1.** (= *mebel*) piece of furniture. **2.** (*wyposażenie*) equipment, gear; **sprzęt gospodarstwa domowego** domestic appliances; **sprzęt elektroniczny** home electronics; **sprzęt sportowy/laboratoryjny/budowlany** sports/laboratory/construction equipment; **sprzęt do wspinaczki** climbing equipment, climbing gear; **sprzęt wędkarski** fishing tackle, fishing equipment. **3.** (*narzędzia*) kit; **sprzęt komputerowy** computer hardware, hardware. **4.** *roln.* (= *koszenie*) harvest.

sprzętowy *a.* equipment; **wymagania sprzętowe** *komp.* hardware requirements.

sprzężenie *n. techn.* coupling; interlock; **sprzężenie indukcyjne** *fiz.* inductive coupling; **sprzężenie magnetyczne** *fiz.* magnetic coupling; **sprzężenie zwrotne** feedback.

sprzężony *a. techn.* coupled; *muz.* (*o drganiach, strunie*) sympathetic; **liczba sprzężona** conjugate number.

sprzyjać *ipf.* **1.** (= *być przychylnym*) be sympathetic (*komuś / czemuś* towards sb/sth). **2.** (= *stworzyć dobre warunki do czegoś*) be conducive (*czemuś* to sth); (*o pogodzie*) be favorable, *Br.* be favourable.

sprzyjający *a.* conducive (*czemuś* to sth); (*o warunkach, pogodzie, klimacie, okolicznościach*) favorable, *Br.* favourable; **jeśli będzie sprzyjająca pogoda** weather permitting.

sprzykrzyć się *pf.* tire of; **sprzykrzyło mi się...** I'm tired of...

sprzymierzać się *ipf.* ally o.s. (*z kimś* with sb).

sprzymierzeniec *mp* **-ńc-** *Voc.* **-cze** *l.* **-u** *pl.* **-y** ally.

sprzymierzony *a.* (*o państwach, wojskach*) allied; **siły sprzymierzone** *wojsk.* allied forces.

sprzymierzyć *pf. zob.* **sprzymierzać.** ~ **się** *pf. zob.* **sprzymierzać się.**

sprzysiąc się *pf.*, **sprzysięgnąć się** *pf.* **-sięgnę -sięgniesz, -sięgnij, -siągł -sięgła -sięgli, sprzysięgać się** *ipf.* conspire (*przeciwko komuś / czemuś* against sb/sth); **wszystko sprzysięgło się prze-**

ciwko nim they have all the odds stacked against them.

sprzysiężenie *n.* conspiracy (*przeciw komuś / czemuś* against sb/sth).

spsocić *pf. zob.* **psocić.**

spuchnąć *pf.* **spuchnij, spuchł** *l.* **spuchnął spuchła spuchli** **1.** (= *nabrzmieć*) swell, swell up; (*w języku fachowym*) intumesce. **2.** *pot.* (= *stracić siły*) (start to) feel the pace, run out of steam.

spuchnięty *a.* (*o nodze, stawie*) swollen; (*o oczach, ciele*) puffy.

spudłować *pf. pot.* miss, miss the mark.

spuentować *pf.* (*dowcip*) drive home the point; (*podsumować*) sum up.

spulchniacz *mi Gen.* **-a** **1.** *kulin.* leavening *l.* rising agent. **2.** *roln.* cultivator.

spulchniać *ipf.*, **spulchnić** *pf.* **-ij** **1.** (*glebę*) loosen; cultivate. **2.** (*pieczywo*) leaven.

spust *mi* (*mechanizm*) release; (*pistoletu*) trigger; (*migawki*) shutter release; **spust żużla** *hutn.* slag escape; **mieć spust** *pot.* (= *jeść dużo*) be a heavy eater; **zamknąć coś na cztery spusty** lock sth up.

spustoszenie *n.* devastation; **czynić spustoszenie** wreak havoc.

spustoszyć *pf.* ravage, devastate.

spustowy *a.* trigger; **język spustowy** *wojsk.* trigger; **rynna spustowa** *metal.* tapping spout *l.* runner.

spuszczać *ipf.*, **spuścić** *pf.* **spuszczę spuścisz** **1.** (*z góry*) drop; (*flagę, oczy, głos*) lower; (*statek na wodę*) launch; **spuścić komuś (porządne) lanie** give sb a (sound) thrashing; **spuścić nos na kwintę** pull a long face; **spuścić oczko** *tk.* drop a stitch; **spuścić psa ze smyczy** unleash a dog; **spuścić z tonu** come down a peg or two; **nie spuszczać kogoś/czegoś z oczu** keep an eye on sb/ sth. **2.** (*wodę, powietrze*) let out; **spuszczać wodę** (*w toalecie*) flush the toilet. **3.** *pot.* (*cenę*) bring down. **4.** *pot.* (= *sprzedać*) sell. ~ **się** *ipf.*, **spuścić się** *pf.* **1.** (*z góry*) come down; (*o słońcu*) be coming down, be setting. **2.** (*o mężczyźnie*) *wulg.* shoot off one's load.

spuścizna *f.* **1.** (= *dziedzictwo*) inheritance, heritage. **2.** (*wojny, literacka*) legacy; **spuścizna kulturowa** cultural heritage.

sputnik *mi Gen.* **-a** *astron.* sputnik.

spychacz *mi Gen.* **-a** **1.** *bud.* bulldozer. **2.** *żegl.* push block.

spychać *ipf.* **1.** (*w dół*) push down; (*na bok*) push aside; **spychać na kogoś odpowiedzialność** shift responsibility onto *l.* upon sb; **spychać coś na drugi plan** marginalize sth. **2.** (= *zmusić do wycofania się*) drive back. ~ **się** *ipf.* push one another, push each other (*z czegoś* off sth).

spycharka *f. Gen.pl.* **-ek** *bud.* bulldozer.

spytać *pf.* **1.** ask (*kogoś o coś / czy... sb* about sth/if...); **spytać kogoś o drogę/godzinę** ask sb the way/time; **spytać kogoś o radę** ask sb's advice. **2.** (= *egzaminować*) give (sb) an oral (*z czegoś* in *l.* on sth). ~ **się** *pf.* ask.

spytki *pl.* **brać na spytki** *pot.* cross-examine, pump.

spytlować *pf. zob.* **pytlować.**

sp. z o.o. *abbr.* (= *spółka z ograniczoną odpowiedzialnością*) Ltd. (= *limited liability company*).

sracz *mi Gen.* **-a** *wulg.* shit-house.

sraczka *f. Gen.pl.* **-ek** *wulg.* the runs.

srać *ipf. wulg.* shit, crap; **srać na kogoś/coś** *wulg.* not to give a shit about sb/sth.

sreberko *n. Gen.pl.* **-ek** tinfoil.

srebrnik *mi Gen.* **-a** silver coin; **trzydzieści srebrników** *Bibl.* thirty pieces of silver; **Judaszowe srebrniki** blood money, thirty pieces of silver.

srebrny *a.* silver; (= *w kolorze srebra*) silvery; **srebrne wesele** *l.* **gody** silver wedding anniversary; **srebrny lis** *zool.* silver fox (*Vulpes argenteus*).

srebro *n. Gen.pl.* **-er** **1.** (*metal*) silver; **srebro standardowe** sterling silver; **nowe srebro** German silver, nickel; **bromek srebra** *chem.* bromic silver; **chlorek srebra** *chem.* silver chloride; **kolczyki ze srebra** silver earrings; **związki srebra** silver compounds; **żywe srebro** (= *rtęć*) quicksilver; *przen.* live wire; **mowa jest srebrem, a milczenie złotem** speech is silver, silence is golden. **2.** (*kolor*) silver; **srebro księżyca** silver moon. **3.** (*zastawa*) silverware.

srebrowy *a. chem.* argentic; (*o tlenku, siarczku*) silver.

srebrzyć *ipf.* silver. ~ **się** *ipf.* (= *błyszczeć*) glitter; (= *świecić jak srebro*) shine like silver.

srebrzystobiały *a.* silvery-white.

srebrzystoszary *a.* silvery-gray, *Br.* silverygrey.

srebrzystość *f.* silveriness.

srebrzysty *a.* (*o kolorze, śniegu, dźwięku, śmiechu*) silvery.

srebrzyście *adv.* silverly; (*mienić się*) with a silvery luster; (*śmiać się*) with a silvery sound.

sroczy *a.* (*o gnieździe, ogonie*) magpie's.

srodze *adv. lit.* (*zawieść się, zmarznąć*) badly; (*mylić się*) gravely.

srogi *a.* **-ższy** (*o władcy*) stern; (*o karze, prawie, mrozie*) severe.

srogo *adv.* **-żej** harshly; (*ukarać*) severely.

sroka *f. orn.* magpie (*Pica pica*); **gapić się (na kogoś/coś) jak sroka w gnat** *pot.* stare (at sb/sth) like a stuck pig; **trzymać kilka srok za ogon** have *l.* keep several irons in the fire; **nie wypadłem sroce spod ogona** *pot.* I'm not a mere nobody.

srokaty *a.* (*o koniu*) piebald.

srokosz *ma* **1.** (*koń*) piebald. **2.** *orn.* great grey shrike (*Lanius excubitor*).

srom *mi* **1.** *anat.* vulva, pudenda. **2.** *lit.* (= *wstyd*) ignominy, disgrace.

sromotnie *adv.* (*przegrać*) ignominiously.

sromotnik *mi Gen.* **-a** *bot.* stinkhorn (*Phallus*).

sromotny *a.* (*np. o klęsce*) ignominious.

sromowy *a. anat.* vulvar, pudendal; **wargi sromowe** labia.

srożyć się *ipf.* (*o zimie, burzy, człowieku*) rage.

ssać *ipf.* **ssę ssiesz, ssij** **1.** (*mleko*) suck; (*pierś matki*) nurse at; **ssać mleko matki** (*o dziecku, szczeniaku*) suckle. **2.** (*cukierek, palec, fajkę*) suck (*coś* on sth); **ssie mnie w dołku** (*z głodu*)

I feel pangs of hunger; (*ze zdenerwowania*) I've got a sinking feeling (in my stomach). **3.** *techn.* suck; **pompa ssąca** suction pump.

ssak *ma zool.* mammal (*Mammalia*). – *mi Gen.* -a *med.* aspirator.

ssanie *n.* **1.** (*tabletki, cukierka, palca*) sucking; **ssanie w żołądku** (*z głodu*) pangs of hunger; (*ze zdenerwowania*) sinking feeling. **2.** *mot.* choke. **3.** *techn.* suction.

ssawka *f. Gen.pl.* -ek **1.** *bot.* sucker. **2.** *ent.* proboscis.

ssawny *a. techn.* aspiration; (*o rurze, przewodzie*) suction.

ssący *a. techn.* (*o pompie*) suction.

SS-man *mp hist.* SS man.

st. *abbr.* **1.** (= *stacja*) sta. (= *station*). **2.** (= *starszy*) Sr (= *senior*).

stabilizacja *f.* stabilization; **brak stabilizacji ekonomicznej/politycznej** economic/political instability.

stabilizator *mi Gen.* -a *t. chem., el., lotn., techn.* stabilizer.

stabilizować *ipf. t. techn.* stabilize. ~ **się** *ipf.* stabilize.

stabilnie *adv.* stably.

stabilność *f.* stability.

stabilny *a.* stable.

staccato *n. Gen.* -a *l. indecl. muz.* staccato.

stachanowiec *mp* -wc- *pl.* -y *iron.* Stakhanovite.

stacja *f.* **1.** (*dworzec*) station; **stacja autobusowa** bus depot; *Br.* bus station; **stacja kolejowa** railroad station; *Br.* railway station; **stacja końcowa** terminal station, terminus; **wysiadać na następnej stacji** get off at the next stop. **2.** *komp.* drive; **stacja dysków** disc drive. **3.** (*placówka*) station; **stacja badawcza** research station; **stacja benzynowa** gas station; *Br.* filling *l.* petrol station; **stacja kosmiczna** space station; **stacja meteorologiczna** weather station; **stacja obsługi** service station; **stacja pomp** pumping station; **stacja telewizyjna/radiowa** TV/radio station. **4.** *rz.-kat.* (*drogi krzyżowej*) station (*of the Cross*).

stacjonarny *a.* stationary; **komputer stacjonarny** *komp.* desktop computer; **orbita stacjonarna** *astron.* stationary orbit; **stan stacjonarny** stationary condition; **studia stacjonarne** full-time studies.

stacjonować *ipf. wojsk.* be stationed, be garrisoned.

stacyjka *f. Gen.pl.* -ek **1.** *mot.* ignition; **kluczyk od stacyjki** ignition key; **przekręcić kluczyk w stacyjce** turn the ignition key. **2.** (= *mała stacja*) minor station.

stacyjny *a.* (*o budynku, urządzeniach*) station.

staczać *ipf.* **1.** (*w dół*) roll down. **2.** (*walkę, pojedynek*) fight. ~ **się** *ipf.* **1.** (= *spadać*) roll down, tumble down. **2.** (*o osobie*) *przen.* go downhill; **stoczyć się na samo dno** *przen.* hit rock bottom.

stać *ipf.* **stoję stoisz, stój** **1.** (= *utrzymywać się w pionie*) stand; **stać na głowie** stand on one's head; **stanąć na głowie** do a headstand; *przen.* bend *l.* lean over backwards; **stanąć na rękach**

do a handstand; **stać na palcach** stand on tiptoe; **stać prosto** stand upright; **stój, bo strzelam!** freeze (or you're dead)! **ledwie stoję ze zmęczenia** I'm dead tired; **stać!** halt! **2.** (*w miejscu, bez ruchu*) stand still; **stać na warcie** keep guard *l.* watch; **stać w kolejce** stand in a line; *Br.* stand in a queue; **stać po coś** (*w kolejce*) line up for sth; *Br.* queue up for sth; **stać za ladą** stand behind the counter; **stać na czele czegoś** spearhead sth; **stać nad kimś** (*w hierarchii*) be superior to sb; **stać nad grobem** *przen.* have one foot in the grave; **stać ponad prawem** stand above the law; **stać na stanowisku, że...** be of the opinion that...; **stać nad przepaścią** *przen.* be on the brink of ruin; **stać na własnych nogach** *przen.* stand on one's own (two) feet; **stać pod znakiem zapytania** (*o losach, przyszłości*) be on a knife edge; **stać otworem** be wide open; **drzwi naszego domu zawsze stoją dla was otworem** you're always welcome in our house; **kariera stoi przed tobą otworem** you've got a glamorous career ahead you; **stać przy kimś murem** *przen.* stand firmly behind sb; **stać w gotowości** stand ready; **stać w miejscu** (= *nie ruszać się*) stand still; (= *nie rozwijać się*) be at a standstill; **stać w obliczu klęski** face defeat; **stać w ogniu** be on fire; **stać ramię w ramię** stand shoulder to shoulder; **dobrze/źle stać** (*o interesach*) be going well/badly; **armia stoi pod bronią** the army is under *l.* in arms; **coś stoi na przeszkodzie** sth stands in the way; **kto za tym stoi?** *przen.* who's behind it?; **nie wiem, na czym stoję** I don't know where I stand; **umowa stoi** you got a deal. **3.** (*znajdować się*) stand; **kląć na czym świat stoi** curse and swear; **dom stał pod lasem** the house stood on the edge of the forest; **zboże stoi w polu** corn stands *l.* is in the field. **4.** (= *nie działać*) (*o fabryce*) be at a standstill; **mój zegarek stoi** my watch has stopped. **5.** *pot.* (= *mieć wartość*) be rated; **jak stoi dzisiaj dolar/euro?** what's the dollar/euro today?; **stoi?** *pot.* (*o umowie, zakładzie*) is it a deal? **6.** (*o sierści, włosach*) bristle; *obsc.* (*o członku*) be erect; **włosy stały mu (dęba) na głowie** his hair stood on end. **7.** *przest.* (= *kwaterować*) be quartered. **8.** **nie stać mnie na kupno tego domu** I can't afford to buy this house; **stać mnie na taksówkę** I can afford a taxi.

stać się *pf.* **stanę staniesz 1.** *zob.* **stawać się**. **2.** (= *zdarzyć się*) happen; **coś się stało?** what happened?; **co mu się stało?** what's up *l.* the matter with him?; **co się stało, to się nie odstanie** what's done cannot be undone; **gdyby coś mi się stało...** if anything should happen to me...; **nie wiemy, co się z nim stało** we don't know what happened to him; **tak się musiało stać** it was meant to happen; **sprawiedliwości stało się zadość** justice has been done *l.* served; **stało się!** the damage is done!; **stało się jasne, że...** it became clear that...

stadialny *a. geol.* stadial.

stadiał *mi geol.* stadial.

stadion *mi sport, hist.* stadium.

stadium *n. sing. indecl. pl.* -dia *Gen.* -diów **1.**

(= *faza*) stage, phase; *pat.* (*choroby*) stadium. **2.** *hist.* stadium.

stadko *n. Gen.pl.* **-ek** (*dzieci w rodzinie*) flock; (*kuropatw, ludzi*) covey.

stadło *n. Gen.pl.* **-eł** *żart.* wedlock.

stadnik *ma roln.* stud.

stadnina *f.* **1.** (*hodowla*) stud farm, stud. **2.** (*zwierzęta*) stud.

stadny *a.* (*o zwierzętach*) gregarious, social; **instynkt stadny** *zool.* herd instinct.

stado *n.* (*bydła, słoni*) herd; (*wilków, psów*) pack; (*ptaków, owiec*) flock; (*lwów*) pride; **chodzić stadami** *przen.* flock together; **odłączyć się od stada** stray; **stado turystów/dzieci** *uj.* gaggle of tourists/children.

stagflacja *f. ekon.* stagflation.

stagnacja *f. t. ekon.* stagnation.

stajać *pf.* **-e** melt, thaw.

stajenka *f. Gen.pl.* **-ek** stable.

stajenny *a.* (*o chłopaku, boksie*) stable. – *mp* stableboy.

stajnia *f. Gen.pl.* **-i** (*budynek*) (*konie*) *t. przen.* (= *zawodnicy, drużyna*) stable; **stajnia Augiasza** *mit.* the Augean stables.

stal *f. Gen.pl.* **-i** steel; **stal budowlana** *l.* **konstrukcyjna** structural steel; **stal damasceńska** Damascus steel, damask; **stal nierdzewna** stainless steel; **huta stali** steelworks; **walcownia stali** steel mill; **ostrze ze stali** steel edge; **ktoś jest twardy jak stal** sb is hard as nails; **spojrzenie zimne jak stal** chilly look.

stalag *mi hist.* stalag.

stalagmit *mi geol.* stalagmite.

stalagmitowy *a.* stalagmitic.

stalagnat *mi geol.* column.

stalaktyt *mi geol.* stalactite.

stalaktytowy *a.* stalactitic.

stale *adv.* constantly, always; **stale się spóźniasz** you are always late.

stalinizm *mi hist.* Stalinism.

stalinowiec *mp hist.* Stalinist.

stalinowski *a. hist.* (*o rządach*) Stalin's; (*o okresie*) Stalinist.

staliwny *a. techn.* cast steel; **odlew staliwny** steel casting.

staliwo *n. techn.* cast steel.

stalle *pl. Gen.* **-i** *l.* **-ll** *sztuka* stalls.

staloryt *mi sztuka* (*technika*) (*rysunek*) steel engraving.

stalorytnictwo *n.* steel engraving.

stalorytniczy *a.* steel-engraver's.

stalorytnik *mp* steel engraver.

stalować *ipf. pot.* order.

stalownia *f. Gen.pl.* **-i** *hutn.* steelworks.

stalowniczy *a. metal.* steelmaking; **piec stalowniczy** steelmaking furnace.

stalownik *mp* steelworker.

stalowo *adv.* (*np. błyszczeć*) like steel.

stalowoniebieski *a.* steel-blue.

stalowoszary *a.* steel-gray; *Br.* steel-grey.

stalowy *a.* **1.** (*ze stali*) steel; **blacha stalowa** steel sheet. **2.** (*jak stal*) steely; **stalowe nerwy** nerves of steel; **stalowy uścisk dłoni** viselike grip; *Br.* vicelike grip; **twardy jak stal** hard as

steel; *przen.* hard as nails. **3.** (*w kolorze stali*) steel blue; (*t. o niebie*) steely.

stalówka *f. Gen.pl.* **-ek 1.** (*do pisania*) nib. **2.** (*lina*) wire rope.

stała *f. Gen.* **-ej** *chem.*, *fiz.*, *mat.* constant.

stałocieplność *f. zool.* homoiothermy, homothermy; endothermy; *pot.* warm-bloodedness.

stałocieplny *a. zool.* (*o zwierzętach*) homoiothermic, homothermal; endothermic, endothermal; *pot.* warm-blooded; **zwierzę stałocieplne** warm-blooded animal, endotherm.

stałopalny *a.* **piec stałopalny** *techn.* slow-combustion stove.

stałość *f.* (*uczuć, charakteru*) constancy; (*zatrudnienia, dochodów*) permanence; (*celu*) fixity.

stały *a.* **1.** (= *nieciekły, nielotny*) solid; **ciało stałe** solid; **stały ląd** mainland. **2.** (*o mieszkańcach, pracy, pobycie*) permanent; (*o kliencie*) regular; (*o cenie, opłacie*) fixed; (*o czasie, kursie*) set; **akcent stały** *fon.* fixed stress accent; **gwiazdy stałe** *astron.* fixed stars; **koszty stałe** overheads, fixed costs; **prąd stały** *el.* direct current; **równowaga stała** *fiz.* stable equilibrium; **stała prędkość** *fiz.* constant velocity *l.* speed; **podróżować ze stałą prędkością** travel at a steady pace; **stała rubryka** (*w prasie*) column; **teatr stały** stock company, repertory company *l.* theater; *Br.* repertory company; **zęby stałe** *anat.* permanent teeth. **3.** (= *nieprzerwany*) constant; (*o ekspozycji, wystawie*) permanent; (*o komisji, zaproszeniu*) standing; (*o postępie*) steady; **na stałe** permanently; **stałe siły zbrojne** *wojsk.* standing army. **4.** (= *niezachwiany*) (*o uczuciach, charakterze*) constant; (*o poglądach*) set.

stamtąd *adv.* from there; **stamtąd było już niedaleko do Bydgoszczy** from there it was just a short way to Bydgoszcz; **pojechałem do Szczecina, a stamtąd do Koszalina** I went to Szczecin, and then to Koszalin; **otworzył sejf i wyjął stamtąd plik banknotów** he opened the safe and took a wad of notes out of it.

stan *mi* **1.** (*sytuacja*) state; (= *kondycja*) condition; **stan cywilny** marital status; **stan konta** *fin.* balance of account; **stan nieważkości** *fiz.* state of weightlessness; **stan podgorączkowy** *med.* subfebrile body temperature; **stan rzeczy** state of affairs; **stan skupienia** *chem.*, *fiz.* state of matter, phase; **zmiana stanu skupienia** *chem.*, *fiz.* phase transition; **stan wody** *meteor.* water level; **stan wojenny** *prawn.* martial law; **stan wyjątkowy** *prawn.* state of emergency; **w ciężkim stanie** in critical condition; **w dobrym/złym stanie** (*zdrowia*) in good/poor condition; **w stanie surowym** (*o domu*) in the rough; **urząd stanu cywilnego** registry office; **być w stanie (coś zrobić)** be able (to do sth), be capable (of doing sth); **niestety, nie będę w stanie ci pomóc** unfortunately, I won't be able to help you; **być stanu wolnego** be single; **być w stanie wskazującym na spożycie** *pot.* be under the influence; **być w poważnym** *l.* **odmiennym stanie** (*o kobiecie*) be expecting, be in the family way; **przejść w stan spoczynku** retire from active service *l.* duty; **generał w stanie**

spoczynku retired general; **mieć coś na stanie** *pot.* have sth in stock; **postawić kogoś w stan oskarżenia (pod zarzutem morderstwa)** *prawn.* indict sb (on murder charges); **żyć ponad stan** live beyond one's means. **2.** (*nastrój*) state; **stan ducha** frame of mind; **stan lękowy** *psych.* anxiety state; **być w stanie apatii/podniecenia/depresji** be apathetic/excited/depressed. **3.** (= *talia*) waist. **4.** (*część sukni*) bodice. **5.** *kraj, prowincja* state; **stan Oregon** the state of Oregon; **Stany Zjednoczone (Ameryki)** the United States (of America), *pot.* the US; **mieszkać w Stanach** *pot.* live in the States, live in the US. **6.** (= *warstwa społeczna*) estate, estate of the realm; class; **stan średni** middle class; **stan ziemiański** gentry; **trzeci stan** *hist.* third estate. **7.** *lit.* (= *zawód*) occupation; **stan nauczycielski/wojskowy** teaching/military profession. **8.** *polit.* state; **mąż stanu** statesman; **podsekretarz stanu** undersecretary of State; **racja stanu** raison d'état, reasons of State; **sekretarz stanu** secretary of State; **więzień stanu** political prisoner; **zamach stanu** coup d'état, coup; **zdrada stanu** high treason.

stanąć *pf.* **1.** *zob.* **stawać. 2.** (= *być wzniesionym*) be erected; **na placu stanął pomnik** a statue was erected in the square; **staną tu nowe domy** new houses will be built here. **3.** (= *dojść do skutku*) be decided; **stanęło na tym, że...** it was decided that...; the upshot of it all was that... **4.** (*o wodzie*) (= *zamarznąć*) freeze; (*o galarecie*) (= *stężeć*) set.

stancja *f. Gen.pl.* **-i** lodgings; *pot. Br. t.* digs; **mieszkać na stancji** live in lodgings.

standard *mi fin., muz.* standard; **standard złota/srebra** gold/silver standard; **wysoki/niski standard** high/low standard; **produkt o standardzie europejskim** European-quality product; **osiągnąć wymagany standard** reach the required standard, make the grade.

standardowo *adv.* in a standard way.

standardowy *a.* (*o wyrobie, wyposażeniu*) standard; (*o sposobie myślenia*) conventional.

standaryzacja *f.* standardization.

standaryzacyjny *a.* (*o przepisie, normie*) standardization.

standaryzować *ipf.* standardize.

stangret *mp* coachman.

stanica *f.* **1.** (*turystyczna*) campsite (*on a river or lake*). **2.** (*osiedle kozackie*) stanitsa, stanitza. **3.** *przest., wojsk.* borderland watchtower.

staniczek *mi* **-czk-** *Gen.* **-a** bra.

stanieć *pf.* get cheaper.

stanik *mi Gen.* **-a 1.** (= *biustonosz*) bra, brassiere; **nosić stanik rozmiaru D** wear a D cup. **2.** (*górna część sukni*) (*ozdobny kaftanik*) bodice. **3.** (= *gorset*) corset.

staniol *mi* tinfoil.

stanowczo *adv.* firmly; (*odmówić, odrzucić, zaprzeczyć*) flatly, categorically; **stanowczo najważniejszy** by far the most important; **stanowczo zbyt wysoki/niski** unacceptably high/low.

stanowczość *f.* firmness; (= *zdecydowanie*) determination; (*odmowy, zaprzeczenia*) flatness.

stanowczy *a.* firm; (*o odmowie, zaprzeczeniu*) flat.

stanowić *pf.* **-ów 1.** (*tworzyć, być*) make; (*problem, zagrożenie*) present; (*wyjątek*) constitute; (*punkt zwrotny*) mark; **nie stanowić wyjątku** be no exception; **stanowić przykład czegoś** exemplify sth; **stanowić część czegoś** be part of sth; **coś nie stanowi problemu** sth is not an issue; **to nie stanowi dla mnie różnicy** it doesn't make any difference to me; **książka ta stanowi miłą lekturę** the book makes pleasant reading. **2.** (*decydować*) determine, decide; **sprawność podejmowania decyzji stanowi o powodzeniu akcji** efficiency of the decision-making process determines the success of the action. **3.** *lit.* (*ustanawiać*) make, institute; **stanowić prawa** make law; **prawo stanowi, że...** law specifies that...; **stanowić o czymś** determine sth. **4.** *myśl.* (*o psie*) bar the way (*of an escaping animal*). **5.** *roln.* have (*a female*) covered.

stanowisko *n.* **1.** (*miejsce*) position; (*produkcyjne, archeologiczne, pomiarowe*) site; (*badawcze, obserwacyjne, pracy*) station; **zająć stanowisko** take a position. **2.** (= *peron dla autobusów*) bay. **3.** (= *posada*) position, post; **człowiek na stanowisku** person of rank; **być na wysokim stanowisku** hold a high-ranking position; **zwolnić kogoś ze stanowiska** remove sb from the post. **4.** (= *pogląd*) stance, standpoint; **stać na stanowisku, że...** take the position *l.* view that...; **zająć stanowisko w jakiejś sprawie** take a stand on sth. **5.** *myśl.* post, stand. **6.** *wojsk.* position; (*np. strażnika*) post; **stanowisko bojowe** battle station; **być na stanowisku** be on post.

stanowy *a.* **1.** (*dotyczący kraju, prowincji*) state; (= *w całym stanie*) statewide; **gubernator stanowy** state governor. **2.** (*dotyczący klasy społecznej*) estate, class; **społeczeństwo stanowe** class society.

Stany *pl. pot.* (= *USA*) the US, the States; **pojechać do Stanów** go to the States.

Stany Zjednoczone Ameryki *pl. Gen.* **Stanów Zjednoczonych Ameryki** the United States of America.

stapelia *f. bot.* stapelia (*Stapelia*).

stapiać *ipf.* **1.** (= *roztapiać*) melt. **2.** (= *topiąc spoić*) fuse. **~ się** *ipf.* **1.** (= *roztapiać się*) melt. **2.** (= *spoić się*) fuse.

stara *f. Gen.* **-ej 1.** *pot.* (= *koleżanka*) old girl. **2.** *pot.* (= *matka*) old lady *l.* woman. **3.** *pot.* (= *żona*) the missus, the missis. **4.** *pot.* (= *szefowa*) the boss.

starać się *ipf.* **1.** (= *zabiegać o coś*) try (*o coś* to do sth); **starać się o pożyczkę** apply for a loan; **starać się o pracę** be looking for a job; **starać się nie zwracać na siebie uwagi** make o.s. inconspicuous; **starać się o czyjąś rękę** court sb. **2.** (= *robić jak najlepiej*) do one's best; **starać się czegoś nie zrobić** take care not to do sth.

staranie *n.* effort, care; **dołożyć wszelkich starań, aby...** do one's best to...; **nie szczędzić starań, aby...** spare no pains to...

starannie *adv.* carefully; (*pakować, kłaść*)

neatly; **starannie dobrany** well-chosen; **starannie dobierać słowa** pick one's words.

staranność *f.* care; *prawn.* diligence; **z należytą starannością** *prawn.* with due diligence.

staranny *a.* careful; (*o uczniu*) studious; (*o badaniu*) searching.

staranować *pf.* ram down; *żegl.* (*statek*) run down.

starawo *adv.* **wyglądać starawo** look oldish.

starawy *a.* oldish.

starcie *n.* **1.** (*bitwa*) scuffle; (*krwawe, gwałtowne*) clash. **2.** (*sprzeczka*) squabble. **3.** (= *obtarcie skóry*) abrasion. **4.** *boks* round.

starczać *ipf.* be enough, be sufficient; (*do końca miesiąca, na długo*) last; **ledwie starczyło miejsca** there was just enough room; **na dziś starczy** we'll call it quits for the day; **nie dla wszystkich starczyło** there wasn't enough for everyone; **(ledwo) starcza nam do pierwszego** we've got (just) enough money to live through the month; **starczy!** that's enough!; **starczy tego dobrego!** enough is enough!

starczo *adv.* senilely.

starczość *f.* senility.

starczowzroczność *f.* *pat.* presbyopia.

starczowzroczny *a.* *pat.* presbyopic.

starczy *a.* senile; **zniedołężnienie starcze** *l.* **uwiąd starczy** senility.

starczyć *pf. zob.* **starczać.**

stare *n.* *Gen.* **-ego** the old; **walka starego z nowym** the struggle of the old and the new.

stareńki *a.* (*o osobie*) very very old.

stargać *pf.* **1.** (*nerwy*) fray; (*zdrowie*) undermine. **2.** (*włosy*) tangle. **~ się** *pf.* **1.** (*o nerwach*) get frayed; (*o zdrowiu*) be undermined. **2.** (*o włosach*) get tangled.

starka *f.* *Gen.pl.* **-ek 1.** (*wódka*) mature rye vodka. **2.** *myśl.* brood hen.

staro *adv.* old.

staro-cerkiewno-słowiański *mi* Old Church Slavonic. – *a.* Old Church Slavonic.

starochrześcijański *a.* early Christian.

staroć *f.* *Nom.pl.* **-cie 1.** (= *antyk*) antique. **2.** (= *grat*) piece of junk. **3.** (*o piosence, filmie*) oldie.

starodawny *a.* antique; (*o zwyczajach, pieśni*) old-time.

starodruk *mi* old print.

starodrzew *mi leśn.* old-growth forest.

starokatolicki *a. rel.* Old Catholic.

starokatolik *mp rel.* Old Catholic.

starokawalerski *a.* confirmed-bachelor.

starokawalerstwo *n.* confirmed bachelorhood.

staromiejski *a.* old town.

staromodnie *adv.* old-fashionedly.

staromodny *a.* old-fashioned; (*o człowieku*) behind the times; **osoba staromodna** mossback.

staropanieński *a.* old-maidish.

staropanieństwo *n.* spinsterhood.

staropolski *a.* (*t. o języku*) Old Polish.

staropolszczyzna *f.* **1.** (*język*) Old Polish. **2.** (*zwyczaje*) old Polish way of life.

starorzecze *n.* *Gen.pl.* **-y** *hydrol.* oxbow, oxbow lake; cutoff.

starosłowiański *a.* Old-Slav; (*o języku*) Old-Slavic *l.* -Slavonic.

starosta *mp pl.* **-owie 1.** *admin.* district governor. **2.** *hist.* starost.

starostwo *n.* **1.** *admin.* district, county. **2.** *hist.* starosty.

staroszlachecki *a.* of the ancient nobility.

starościna *f. hist.* starost's wife.

starość *f.* **1.** (= *sędziwy wiek*) old age; **zdziwaczeć na starość** be going soft in the head; **na starość** in the latter years of sb's life, in one's old age; **starość nie radość** old age has its problems; **czym skorupka za młodu nasiąknie, tym na starość trąci** the child is father to the man. **2.** (= *dawność*) age, antiquity; **spłowiały ze starości** faded with age.

staroświecczyzna *f.* old-fashionedness.

staroświecki *a.* antiquated, archaic, mossgrown, old-fashioned; (*o osobie, poglądach*) stuffy; (*w atrakcyjny sposób*) old-world; **po staroświecku** after the old fashion.

staroświeckość *f.* fogyism, stuffiness.

starotestamentowy *a.* *Bibl.* Old Testament.

starować *pf. zob.* **tarować.**

starowin *mi kulin.* well-matured vodka.

starowina *f. l. mp decl. like f. Gen.pl.* **-n** *l.* **-ów** *emf.* old gentleman *l.* lady.

starowinka *f. l. mp decl. like f. Gen.pl.* **-nek** *l.* **-nów** *emf.* old granny.

starozakonny *a.* **1.** *Bibl.* (= *odnoszący się do Starego Testamentu*) Old Testament. **2.** *rel.* (= *wyznający religię mojżeszową*) Orthodox Jew.

starożytność *f.* **1.** *hist.* antiquity. **2.** (= *dawność*) antiquity.

starożytny *a.* ancient, antique, old.

starówka *f.* *Gen.pl.* **-ek** old town.

starsi *pl.* *Gen.* **-szych 1.** the aged, the elderly. **2.** *pot.* (= *rodzice*) (one's) folks.

starszak *mp pl.* **-i** senior kindergarten pupil.

starszawy *a.* oldish.

starszeństwo *n.* seniority, eldership; **prawo starszeństwa** precedence.

starszy *a.* **1.** *zob.* **stary. 2.** (*o panu, pani, małżeństwie*) older; (*o synu, córce, bracie, siostrze*) elder; **Adam jest o trzy lata starszy od Ewy** Adam is three years older than Eve; Adam is Eve's elder by three years; **starszy sierżant** *wojsk.* sergeant first class, master sergeant; *Br.* staff sergeant; **starszy szeregowiec** *wojsk.* private first class; *Br.* lance corporal; **starszy bosman sztabowy** *wojsk.* master chief petty officer; **starszy rangą** superior; **starszy kelner** head waiter; **starszy wykładowca** *uniw.* senior lecturer. **3.** (*o kolorze w kartach*) majority (suit). – *mp* **1.** (= *mędrzec*) elder, senior; **rada starszych** council of the elders. **2.** *pot.* (= *ojciec*) (one's) old man.

starszyzna *f.* the elders.

start *mi* **1.** *sport* start; **start lotny** flying start; **start niski** block starting; **start wysoki** standing start; **na miejsca, gotowi, start!** on your marks, get set, go! **2.** *lotn.* takeoff, liftoff; (*rakiety*) blastoff, liftoff. **3.** (= *początek*) beginning, start; **zapewnić wszystkim równy start** give everybody an equal chance.

starter *mp pl.* **-rzy** *sport* starter. – *mi Gen.* **-a** *pl.* **-ry** (= *rozrusznik*) starter.

startować *ipf.* **1.** *sport* start; **startować w wyścigu** run in a race. **2.** *lotn.* take off. **3.** *pot.* (= *rozpoczynać*) start; **startować w wyborach** *polit.* stand for election, run in an election.

startowy *a.* *sport* starting; **blok startowy** starting block; **pas startowy** *lotn.* runway. – *mp lotn.* air traffic controller.

staruch *mp pl.* **-y** *uj.* geezer.

starucha *f. uj.* crone; carline, carlin.

staruszek *mp* **-szk-** *pl.* **-owie** **1.** (*mężczyzna*) gaffer, old man; **dziarski staruszek** valetudinarian. **2.** *pot.* (= *ojciec*) old man.

staruszka *f. Gen.pl.* **-ek** **1.** (*kobieta*) gammer, old lady. **2.** *pot.* (= *matka*) old lady.

staruszkowie *pl. Gen.* **-ów** **1.** (*małżeństwo*) old couple; (= *starsze osoby*) old folks. **2.** *pot.* (= *rodzice*) (one's) folks.

stary *a.* **1.** (= *niemłody*) old; (*o domu, samochodzie*) long-lived; (*o anegdocie, argumencie*) stale; (*o przyjaźni, znajomości*) long-standing; **stary kawaler** confirmed bachelor; **stara panna** old maid, spinster; **stary jak świat** as old as the hills; **stary, ale jary** hale and hearty in old age; **stary, ale dobry** oldie but goldie; **Adam jest dla Ewy za stary** Adam is too old for Eve; **stary cap** *przen.* old goat; **stary ramol** *pot.* old fogy, fuddy-duddy; **stary pryk** *pot.* old fart; **stary pierdoła** *pot.* old buffer; **stary wyga** old hand, old soldier; **stary wyjadacz** old stager, war horse; **stary gruchot** (*o samochodzie*) old crock; **w starym piecu diabeł pali** there's life in the old dog yet; **Stary Świat** the Old World. **2.** (*o adresie, wiadomości, tygodniku*) (= *nieaktualny*) old; **człowiek starej daty** an old-fashioned man; (*z uznaniem*) he is one of the old school; **stara miłość nie rdzewieje** you never forget an old flame. **3.** (= *ponadczasowy*) old, ancient; **stare dobre czasy** good old days; **stary kawał** stale joke; **stare dzieje** ancient history; **czuć się/wyglądać po staremu** feel/look like one's old self; **po staremu** same old story. **4.** (*o chlebie*) (= *nieświeży*) stale. – *mp pot.* **1.** (= *kolega*) mate; **stary!** my man! **2.** (= *ojciec*) (one's) old man. **3.** (= *szef*) boss, the old man.

starzec *mp* **-rc-** *pl.* **-y** old man, whitebeard. – *mi* **-rc-** *Gen.* **-a** *pl.* **-e** *bot.* groundsel (*Senecio*).

starzeć się *ipf.* **1.** (= *mieć więcej lat*) be getting old, get l. grow old, age; (*o społeczeństwie, teorii*) grow old, age. **2.** (= *psuć się, tracić świeżość*) go bad *l.* stale.

starzy *pl. Gen.pl.* **-ych** *pot.* (= *rodzice*) (one's) folks.

starzyzna *f. pot.* junk, rubbish, rummage; **sklep ze starzyzną** junk shop.

statecznik *mi Gen.* **-a** *lotn.* stabilizer.

stateczność *f.* **1.** (*charakteru*) steadiness. **2.** *żegl., lotn.* stability.

stateczny *a.* **1.** (= *spokojny*) sedate, staid, steady. **2.** *żegl., lotn.* stable.

statek *mi* **-tk-** **1.** *żegl.* ship; *pot.* boat; *form.* vessel, craft; **statek dostawczy** *wojsk.* supply ship; **statek eskortujący** *zw. wojsk.* consort; **statek handlowy** merchantman, trader; *arch.* ship

of burden; **statek rybacki** fishing boat; **statek kaperski** *l.* **korsarski** privateer; **statek parowy** steamship; **statek ratowniczy** salvage ship; **statek oceanograficzny** oceanographic research ship; **statek pasażerski** liner; **statek piracki** rover, pirate, corsair; **statek przetwórnia** factory ship; **statek spacerowy** pleasure boat; **statek towarowy** cargo ship *l.* vessel; **statek wielorybniczy** whaler; **wodować statek** launch a ship; **płynąć statkiem** go *l.* travel by sea; **na pokładzie statku** on board, aboard a ship; **umieszczać na statku** ship; **załoga statku** ship's company. **2.** *lotn.* aircraft, craft; **statek powietrzny** aifcraft; **statek kosmiczny** spaceship. **3.** *pl. przest.* (*naczynia, sztućce*) dishes; **myć statki** do the dishes.

statoskop *mi lotn.* statoscope.

statua *f. Gen.* **-ui** *l.* **-uy** *Gen.pl.* **-ui** monument, statue; **Statua Wolności** the Statue of Liberty.

statuetka *f. Gen.pl.* **-ek** figurine, statuette.

status *mi* position, status; **status prawny** *prawn.* legal status; **status cudzoziemca** *prawn.* alienage, alienism; **status kobiety zamężnej** *prawn.* coverture; **status quo** status quo.

statut *mi* (= *przepisy*) statute, constitution, articles; **statut spółki** *prawn.* articles of association.

statutowy *a.* statutory; **kapitał statutowy** *l.* **zatwierdzony** *prawn.* authorized capital.

statyczność *f.* stability.

statyczny *a.* **1.** static. **2.** stable.

statyka *f.* **1.** *fiz.* statics. **2.** (= *równowaga*) equilibrium.

statysta *mp*, **statystka** *f. Gen.pl.* **-ek** dummy; *balet* figurant; *film* extra; *teatr* super, supernumerary, walk-on; (*obserwator*) onlooker, spectator.

statystować *ipf. teatr, film* play walking parts.

statystycznie *adv.* statistically; **statystycznie znaczący** *stat.* statistically significant.

statystyczny *a.* statistic; **błąd statystyczny** *stat.* probable error, PE.

statystyk *mp* statistician.

statystyka *f.* (*nauka, dane*) statistics.

statyw *mi fot.* tripod; (*mikrofonu*) stand.

staw *mi* **1.** (*akwen*) pond; **staw rybny** fishpond; **wedle stawu grobla** cut one's coat according to the cloth; the Lord tempers the wind to the shorn lamb. **2.** *anat.* joint; **staw kolanowy** knee joint; **staw biodrowy** hip joint; **zapalenie stawów** *pat.* arthritis.

stawać *ipf.* **staję stajesz, stawaj 1.** (= *wstawać*) stand up, rise; **stawać na baczność** stand to attention; **stawać na nogi** be up and about, get on to one's feet; **stawać okoniem** stand pat; **stanąć przed czymś** confront sth; **stanąć w miejscu** come to a dead stop; **stanąć w obliczu wyzwania** face a challenge; **stawać na głowie, żeby coś zrobić** lean over backwards to do sth, stand on one's head to do sth. **2.** (*o przedmiotach*) (= *prostować się*) rise; **stawać dęba** (*o koniu*) rear; (*o włosach*) stand on end; **język stanął mu kołkiem** he was speechless; **stanął mi na jej widok** *wulg.* I had a hard-on when I saw her. **3.** (= *zatrzymywać się*) stop, come to a halt *l.* standstill; **pociąg staje na wszystkich stacjach** the train calls *l.* stops at all stations; **stanął mi zegarek** my watch stopped; **stanął jak wryty** he froze in his tracks; **negocjacje stanęły w martwym punkcie** negotiations ended in a stalemate; **słowa stanęły mi w gardle** the words stuck in my throat; **te pieniądze staną ci kością w gardle** *pot.* this money will stick in your gizzard; **ruch uliczny stanął** the traffic ground to a halt; **statek stanął na kotwicy** the ship came to anchor. **4.** (= *pojawiać się*) turn up, come, appear; **stanąć przed sądem** be on *l.* go on *l.* stand trial; **stanąć z kimś oko w oko** confront sb; **noga ludzka tu nigdy nie stanęła** no human foot has ever trodden on this land; **łzy stanęły komuś w oczach** tears stood in sb's eyes; **stanąć na czele** take the lead, head; **stanąć na wysokości zadania** rise to the emergency *l.* occasion *l.* challenge; **stawać w czyjejś obronie** defend sb, stand up for sb, stick up for sb; **hotel stanął w ogniu** the hotel went on fire; **sprawa stanęła na ostrzu noża** matters were brought to a head. **5.** *przest.* (= *wystarczać*) have enough; **nie staje mu odwagi/sił** he doesn't have enough courage/energy; **tak krawiec kraje, jak mu materii staje** cut one's coat according to one's cloth. **6.** *przest.* (= *kwaterować*) quarter, lodge; **wojsko stanęło we wsi** soldiers were quartered in the village.

stawać się *ipf.* **staję stajesz, stawaj 1.** (= *zostawać kimś, czymś, jakimś*) become; **stawać się czyimś przyjacielem** become sb's friend; **zaniedbanie stało się przyczyną pożaru** the fire was caused by negligence; **stawać się kimś** *pot.* become somebody. **2.** (= *zdarzyć się*) happen; **sprawiedliwości stało się zadość** justice was done.

stawiacz *mi Gen.* -a *Gen.pl.* -y *l.* -ów *wojsk.* **stawiacz min** mine layer.

stawiać *ipf.* **1.** (= *umieszczać*) put, place, set; **stawiać sidła** set a trap; **stawiać horoskop** cast a horoscope; **stawiać kropkę nad i** leave nothing unsaid; **stawiać coś na głowie** turn *l.* stand sth on its head; **stawiać coś pod znakiem zapytania** cast doubts on sth, put sth in question; **stawiać kogoś w trudnej sytuacji** put sb in an awkward position, put *l.* place sb at a disadvantage; **stawiać kogoś na piedestale** put *l.* place sb on a pedestal; **stawiać kogoś za przykład komuś** set sb as an example for sb; **stawiać komuś duże wymagania** make heavy demands on sb; **stawiać pierwsze kroki** get one's feet wet (*w czymś* in sth); **stawiać znak równości pomiędzy A i B** make the equation between A and B; **stawiać opór** resist, offer resistance, make a stand; *prawn.* (*o zatrzymanym*) resist arrest; **stawiać sobie ambitne cele do osiągnięcia** set ambitious goals for o.s.; **stawiać klocka** *wulg.* (= *oddawać kał*) take a dump. **2.** (*w górę, pionowo*) raise, put upright *l.* up; **stawiać żagle** *żegl.* set sail. **3.** (= *wznosić*) erect, construct, build. **4.** (= *przedstawiać*) present, put forward; **stawiać warunki** lay down *l.* impose conditions; **stawiać trudne warunki** drive a hard bargain; **stawiać jasno sprawę** be clear on sth. **5.** (*pieniądze w grze*) bet, place a bet; (*na konia*) back; **stawiać wszystko na jedną kartę** put

all one's eggs in one basket. **6.** *pot.* (= *fundować*) buy, stand; **ja stawiam** it's on me, it's my treat. **~ się** *ipf.* **1.** (= *zgłaszać się osobiście*) turn up, appear; **stawiać się do pracy** report for work *l.* duty. **2.** *tylko ipf. pot.* (= *sprzeciwiać się*) sauce, spurn. **3.** (= *ustawiać się*) place o.s.; **stawiać się wysoko** have a high regard for o.s.

stawić *pf.* **stawić komuś/czemuś czoło/czoła** stand up to sb/sth, meet sb/sth head-on; **stawić opór** resist. **~ się** *pf. zob.* **stawiać się.**

stawidło *n. Gen.pl.* -eł water gate.

stawiennictwo *n. prawn.* appearance; **nakaz stawiennictwa** summons.

stawka *f. Gen.pl.* -ek **1.** (*jednostka*) rate; **stawka akordowa** piece rate. **2.** (*w grze*) stake, bet, wager; (*w pokerze*) ante; **gra o wysoką stawkę** play for high stakes; **podwoić stawkę** parlay; **zgarnąć całą stawkę** sweep the board. **3.** *pot., sport* (*zawodnicy*) field; **doborowa stawka zawodników** (world's, Europe's, country's etc.) best athletes. **4.** *pot., jeźdz.* (*konie*) field.

stawonóg *ma* -o- *zool.* arthropod (*Arthropoda*).

stawowy *a.* **1.** *ryb.* pond; (*o gospodarstwie*) fish-breeding. **2.** *anat.* articular; **maź stawowa** synovia; **torebka stawowa** synovial capsule. **3.** *pat.* arthral; **gościec stawowy** rheumatic arthritis.

staż *mi Gen.pl.* -y *l.* -ów **1.** (= *praktyka*) internship, training; **odbywać staż** intern, undergo training; **staż specjalizacyjny** (*w szpitalu*) residency. **2.** seniority; **staż pracy** (job) seniority; **pracownik z dużym stażem** senior worker.

stażysta *mp,* **stażystka** *f. Gen.pl.* -ek (= *praktykant/ka*) trainee, intern.

stąd *adv.* (= *z tego miejsca*) from here; **nie pochodzę stąd** I'm not from here, I'm a stranger here; **pięć kilometrów stąd jest jezioro** there's a lake five kilometers away; **stąd na dworzec jest już niedaleko** it's not far from here to the station; **nie oddalaj się stąd** don't go away; **ni stąd, ni zowąd** out of the blue, apropos of nothing, without rhyme or reason; **zabieraj się stąd!** get out of here!; **kawał drogi stąd** miles away. – *conj.* (= *z tej przyczyny*) hence; **jego matka pochodzi z Austrii, stąd jego zainteresowanie językami niemieckim** his mother comes from Austria, hence his interest in German.

stągiew *f.* -gwi- *pl.* -e *przest.* vat.

stąpać *ipf.,* **stąpnąć** *pf.* -ij tread, step; **stąpać ostrożnie** pick one's steps; **stąpać po cienkim lodzie** sail close to the wind, skate on thin ice; **mocno stąpać po ziemi** have one's feet (firmly) on the ground.

stąpnięcie *n.* footfall, tread, step.

stchórzyć *pf.* chicken out, show the white feather.

stearyna *f.* stearin, stearine, paraffin wax.

stearynowy *a. chem.* stearic; **kwas stearynowy** stearic acid.

stebnować *ipf. zob.* **stębnować.**

stebnowanie *n. zob.* **stębnowanie.**

stebnówka *f. Gen.pl.* -ek *zob.* **stębnówka.**

stechnicyzować *pf.* technicalize.

stek¹ *mi* **1.** *anat.* cloaca, vent. **2.** (= *nagromadzenie*) load; **stek kłamstw** pack of lies; **stek bzdur** a load of crap *l.* rubbish; **stek wyzwisk** a stream *l.* torrent of abuse.

stek² *mi kulin.* steak.

stekowiec *ma* **-wc-** *zool.* (= *ssak z rzędu Monotremata*) monotreme.

stela *f. bot., sztuka* stele, stela.

stelaż *mi Gen.* **-a** *l.* **-u** **1.** (*podstawka*) stand; (*podstawa*) framework; *bud.* support frame. **2.** (*półka*) rack. **3.** (*plecaka*) backpack frame.

stelefonizować *pf. zob.* **telefonizować**.

stelmach *mp arch.* wheelwright.

stempel *mi* **-pl-** *Gen.* **-a** **1.** (= *pieczęć*) stamp, seal; **data stempla pocztowego** postmark date. **2.** *górn.* prop, shore. **3.** *techn.* punch, die, stamping-machine.

stempelek *mi* **-lk-** *Gen.* **-a** (= *pieczątka*) stamp.

stemplować *ipf.* **1.** (= *pieczętować*) stamp. **2.** *górn.* prop, shore.

stemplowanie *n. górn.* propping, shore.

stemplowy *a.* **1.** *górn.* prop, shore. **2.** (= *związany ze stemplem skarbowym*) statutory-fee, stamp; **opłata stemplowa** stamp duty.

sten *mi Gen.* **-a** *wojsk., hist.* Sten gun.

stenga *f. żegl.* topmast.

steniczny *a. psych.* sthenic.

stenograf *mp pl.* **-owie** stenographer.

stenografia *f. Gen.* **-ii** shorthand, stenography.

stenograficzny *a.* stenographic, shorthand.

stenografować *ipf.* take sth down in shorthand, stenograph.

stenogram *mi* stenographic record.

stenotypia *f. Gen.* **-ii** typed shorthand, stenotypy.

stenotypista *mp,* **stenotypistka** *f. Gen.pl.* **-ek** shorthand typist.

stentorowy *a.* (*o głosie*) stentorian.

step *mi* steppe, grassland.

stepować *ipf.* tap-dance.

stepowieć *ipf.* turn into a steppe.

stepowy *a.* steppe; (*o klimacie*) semiarid.

stepówka *f. orn.* sand grouse (*Pterocles*).

ster *mi* **1.** *żegl.* helm, rudder. **2.** *lotn.* rudder; **być sobie sterem, żeglarzem, okrętem** *przen.* paddle one's own canoe. **3.** *przen.* (= *kierownictwo*) leadership.

sterać *pf. pot.* ruin, wear out.

steradian *mi geom.* steradian.

sterburta *f. żegl.* starboard side, starboard.

stercz *mi Gen.* **-a** *anat.* prostate gland, prostate.

sterczeć *ipf.* **-ę -ysz** **1.** (= *odstawać*) protrude, jut *l.* poke out, stand out, project; (*o psich uszach*) perk; **sterczeć na wszystkie strony** (*o włosach*) straggle. **2.** *pot.* (= *stać*) stand like a post.

stereo *a. indecl.* stereo; **nagrać w stereo** record in stereo. – *n. indecl.* stereo.

stereochromia *f. Gen.* **-ii** *sztuka* stereochromy.

stereofon *mi techn.* stereo player *l.* recorder.

stereofonia *f. Gen.* **-ii** *fiz.* stereophony.

stereofoniczny *a.* stereo; (*o nagraniu*) stereophonic.

stereofotografia *f. Gen.* **-ii** *fot.* stereophotography.

stereofotograficzny *a. fot.* stereophotographic.

stereokardiograf *mi med.* stereocardiograph.

stereokardiografia *f. Gen.* **-ii** *med.* stereocardiography.

stereokardiograficzny *a. med.* stereocardiographic.

stereometria *f. Gen.* **-ii** *geom.* stereometry, solid geometry.

stereometryczny *a. geom.* stereometric.

stereoskop *mi fot.* stereoscope.

stereoskopia *f. Gen.* **-ii** *fot.* stereoscopy.

stereoskopowy *a. fot.* stereoscopic.

stereotyp *mi* **1.** *socjol., psych.* stereotype; **powielać stereotypy** stereotype. **2.** *druk.* stereotype.

stereotypia *f. Gen.* **-ii** *druk., psych.* stereotypy.

stereotypowo *adv.* stereotypically.

stereotypowy *a.* stereotypic, stereotypical.

sterlet *ma icht.* sterlet (*Acipenser ruthenus*).

stermaszt *mi żegl.* mizzenmast.

sternik *mp żegl.* helmsman, steersman, wheelsman; **sternik automatyczny** *l.* **samoczynny** automatic pilot.

sterol *mi chem.* sterol.

sterolotka *f. lotn.* elevon.

sterować *ipf.* **1.** *żegl.* helm. **2.** *lotn.* pilot. **3.** (= *kierować*) steer, drive; (*gospodarką*) control, regulate; (*opinią publiczną*) govern; (*skomplikowanym przedsięwzięciem*) mastermind; (*urządzeniem*) control.

sterowanie *n. żegl.* steering, steerage; **sterowanie numeryczne/zdalne** *techn.* numerical/remote control; **sterowanie popytem** *ekon.* demand management.

sterowany *a.* driven, controlled; **zdalnie sterowany** remote-controlled; **sterowany głosem** (*o urządzeniu*) voice-activated; **gospodarka sterowana centralnie** state-controlled economy, central economy.

sterowiec *mi* **-wc-** *Gen.* **-a** *lotn.* airship, dirigible, zeppelin.

sterownia *f. Gen.pl.* **-i** **1.** *techn.* control room. **2.** *żegl.* pilothouse, wheelhouse.

sterowniczy *a.* control; **pulpit sterowniczy** control panel; **drążek sterowniczy** control lever.

sterownik *mi Gen.* **-a** *komp.* driver.

sterowność *f. żegl., lotn.* navigability, controllability, steerability.

sterowny *a. żegl., lotn.* navigable, controllable, steerable.

sterowy *a.* steering; **drążek sterowy** control column, joystick, stick; **koło sterowe** steering wheel.

sterówka *f. Gen.pl.* **-ek** **1.** = **sterownia** 2. **2.** *orn.* rectrix.

sterroryzować *pf. zob.* **terroryzować**.

sterta *f.* **1.** (= *stos*) pile, stack, heap, mound; (*śmieci, gnoju*) midden. **2.** *roln.* mow.

steryd *mi biochem.* steroid; **steryd anaboliczny** anabolic steroid.

sterydowy *a. biochem.* steroidal.

sterylizacja *f.* 1. (*narzędzi, rany, produktów*) sterilization. 2. *wet., med.* sterilization.

sterylizacyjny *a.* sterilizing, sterilization.

sterylizator *mi Gen.* **-a** *med.* (= *aparat do niszczenia zarazków*) sterilizer.

sterylizować *ipf.* 1. (*narzędzia, ranę, produkty*) (= *wyjaławiać*) sterilize. 2. *wet., med.* sterilize, neuter, castrate; (*samicę*) spay.

sterylnie *adv. med.* aseptically, sterilely.

sterylność *f. biol.* (= *niepłodność*) sterility, sterileness, infertility.

sterylny *a.* aseptic, sterile.

stetoskop *mi med.* stethoscope.

stetryczeć *pf.* become grumpy, become bilious.

stewa *f. żegl.* stern; **stewa rufowa** sternpost.

steward *mp pl.* **-owie** *l.* **-dzi** (*na statku*) steward; (*w samolocie*) steward, flight attendant.

stewardesa *f.* (*na statku*) stewardess; (*w samolocie*) stewardess, flight attendant.

stębnować *ipf.* quilt.

stębnowanie *n.* quilting.

stębnówka *f. Gen.pl.* **-ek** quilted work, quilting.

stęchlizna *f.* dankness, moldiness, *Br.* mouldiness; must, mustiness.

stęchły *a.* musty; (*o powietrzu*) stale; (*o zapachu*) moldy; *Br.* mouldy.

stęchnąć *pf.* **-chnij, -chł** grow musty.

stękać *ipf.*, **stęknąć** *pf.* **-ij** 1. (= *pojękiwać*) groan, moan. 2. *tylko ipf. pot.* (= *uskarżać się*) whine, complain. 3. *tylko ipf. pot.* (= *jąkać się*) stutter out. 4. *myśl.* troat.

stęp *mi Gen.* **-a** *jeźdz.* walk; **jechać stępa** walk.

stępak *ma* carthorse.

stępiać *ipf.*, **stępić** *pf.* 1. (= *czynić nieostrym*) blunt, take the edge off. 2. (= *czynić niewrażliwym*) grow dull. ~ **się** *ipf.*, **stępić się** *pf.* get blunt, lose one's edge.

stępieć *pf.* 1. get blunt. 2. *przen.* grow dull.

stępka *f. Gen.pl.* **-ek** *żegl.* keel.

stępor *mi Gen.* **-a** stamp, stamper.

stęsknić się *pf.* **-ij** miss (*za kimś/czymś* sb/sth); long (*za kimś/czymś* for sb/sth); hanker (*za kimś/czymś* after sb/sth).

stęskniony *a.* **-eni** longing, nostalgic; (*za domem*) homesick.

stężać *ipf.* concentrate.

stężeć *pf.* harden.

stężenie *n.* 1. *fizj.* **stężenie pośmiertne** rigor mortis. 2. *chem.* concentration; strength.

stężony *a. chem.* concentrated; **roztwór stężony** concentrated solution.

stężyć *pf. zob.* **stężać**.

stiuk *mi bud.* stucco.

stiukarz *mp bud.* stuccoer.

stiukowy *a. bud.* stuccoed.

stlić się *pf.* burn to cinders.

stłaczać *ipf.* cram, stuff, crowd. ~ **się** *ipf.* crowd together, herd together, coop up.

stłamsić *pf.* **-szę -sisz** 1. (= *zgnieść*) crush. 2. (= *zdusić*) strangle, suppress.

stłoczyć *pf. zob.* **stłaczać**. ~ **się** *pf. zob.* **stłaczać się**.

stłuc *pf.* **stłukę stłuczesz stłukł** 1. (= *rozbić*) break; (*na drobne kawałki*) shatter; (*głośno i gwałtownie*) smash. 2. (= *ulec kontuzji*) bruise, contuse; **cholera, stłukłem sobie łokieć** damn, I've hit *l.* hurt my elbow. 3. *pot.* (= *zbić*) batter, beat up; **stłuc kogoś na kwaśne jabłko** beat sb to a pulp, beat *l.* knock the hell *l.* (living) daylight out of sb. ~ **się** *pf.* get broken, break.

stłuczenie *n. pat.* (*rodzaj obrażenia*) contusion; (*stłuczone miejsce*) bruise.

stłuczka *f. Gen.pl.* **-ek** 1. (*samochodowa*) fender-bender, bump. 2. (= *złom szklany*) cullet. 3. (*przedmiot*) breakages; *tylko pl.* seconds.

stłumić *pf.* (*dźwięk*) muffle; (*kaszel*) stifle; (*ogień*) damp down; (*ogień, uczucie, śmiech, chichot*) smother; (*bunt*) suppress; (*gniew*) suppress, repress, choke; **stłumić** *l.* **zdusić coś w zarodku** nip sth in the bud.

stłumienie *n. polit.* suppression.

stłumiony *a.* suppressed; **stłumiony dźwięk** muffled sound; **powiedzieć coś stłumionym głosem** say sth in a hushed voice.

stłuszczenie *n. pat.* fatty degeneration, steatosis.

sto *num. Ins.* **stoma** *l.* **stu** hundred; **sto osiem** a *l.* one hunded and eight; **sto studentek** a *l.* one hundred students; **sto kilometrów na godzinę** a *l.* one hundred kilometers an *l.* per hour; **jechać autobusem sto dwanaście** go with the hundred and twelve bus *l.* service a hundred and twelve; **na sto procent** surely, for sure; **w stu procentach** completely; **na sto dwa** first-rate, A-one; **udać się na sto dwa** (*np. o przyjęciu*) go off with a bang; **firma działa już od ponad stu lat** the company has been on the market for over one hundred years; **powtarzałem ci już sto razy** I've told you a million times; **chyba sto lat się nie widzieliśmy!** we haven't seen each other for donkey's years!; **do stu diabłów!** for heaven's sake!; **zły jak sto diabłów** angry as hell; **sto lat!** (*jako życzenie urodzinowe*) many happy returns (of the day)!; **sto lat** (*piosenka urodzinowa*) Happy Birthday; (*piosenka śpiewana na urodzinach, jubileuszach itp.*) For She's *l.* He's a Jolly Good Fellow.

stoa *f. indecl.* 1. *bud.* portico; (*zwłaszcza w starożytnej Grecji*) stoa. 2. *hist., fil.* the Stoa, the Porch.

stochastyczny *a. mat.* stochastic.

stocze *n. zob.* **stok**.

stoczek *mi* 1. *metal.* wax vent, strum. 2. *zob.* **stok**.

stocznia *f. Gen.pl.* **-i** shipyard; **stocznia produkcyjna** shipbuilding yard; **stocznia remontowa** repair shipyard; **stocznia marynarki wojennej** navy yard, dockyard.

stoczniowiec *mp* **-wc-** *pl.* **-y** shipyard worker.

stoczniowy *a.* shipyard; **przemysł stoczniowy** shipyard industry.

stoczyć *pf.* 1. *zob.* **staczać**. 2. (*zniszczyć*) gnaw (*coś* at *l.* upon sth); eat away; **korniki stoczyły dom** woodworms have eaten away the house. ~ **się** *pf. zob.* **staczać się**.

stodoła *f. Gen.pl.* **-ół** *t. uj. l. żart.* barn.

stoicki *a. fil.* Stoic; (= *spokojny*) stoical, stoic.

stoicyzm *mi fil.* Stoicism; **powiedzieć coś ze stoicyzmem** say sth stoically.

stoik *mp fil.* (= *zwolennik stoicyzmu*) Stoic; (= *człowiek spokojny i opanowany*) stoic.

stoisko *n.* 1. (= *dział sklepu*) department; stoisko meblowe furniture department. 2. (*w sklepie*) counter; stoisko z pieczywem/mięsne bread/meat counter. 3. (*na kiermaszu, lotnisku, ulicy*) stand, stall; stoisko z gazetami newsstand; stoisko z prasą i książkami bookstall.

stoisz *itp. ipf.* zob. stać.

stojak *mi Gen.* -a rack; (= *wieszak*) stand; stojak na dokumenty *komp.* copyholder; stojak na kapelusze hat rack; stojak na nuty music stand; stojak na parasole umbrella stand; stojak na ręczniki towel horse; stojak na rowery cycle rack; na stojaka *pot.* standing.

stojan *mi Gen.* -a *techn.* stator.

stojąco *adv.* standing (up); jeść na stojąco have a standup meal; posiłek na stojąco standup meal; owacja na stojąco standing ovation.

stojący *a.* (*o osobie, pozycji, wodzie*) standing; (*o kołnierzu*) standup; (*o wodzie, powietrzu*) dead; lampa stojąca floor lamp; *Br.* standard lamp; miejsca stojące (*w autobusie, pociągu*) standing room; pozycja stojąca standing posture, erect stance; woda stojąca stagnant water, ditchwater; zegar stojący grandfather clock; wolno stojący (*mebel, lampa*) freestanding; (*dom, budynek*) detached house.

stoję *itp. ipf.* zob. stać.

stok *mi* slope; stok górski mountain slope, mountainside; stok kontynentalny *geogr.* continental slope; stok narciarski ski run; stok zjazdowy piste.

stoker *mi techn.* stoker.

stokłosa *f. bot.* bromegrass (*Bromus*).

stokroć *adv.* 1. (= *sto razy*) a hundred times; (= *wielokrotnie*) a million times; mówiłem ci po stokroć, żebyś tam nie szedł I've told you a million times not to go there. 2. (= *bardzo, znacznie*) hundredfold; (po) stokroć lepiej a hundredfold better.

stokrotka *f. Gen.pl.* -ek *bot.* daisy (*Bellis perennis*); wianek ze stokrotek daisy chain.

stokrotnie *adv.* hundredfold; stokrotnie dziękuję thank you ever so much; stokrotnie przepraszam I'm terribly *l.* awfully sorry.

stokrotność *f.* hundredfold, centuplicate.

stokrotny *a.* hundredfold, centuplicate; stokrotny zysk hundredfold gain; stokrotne dzięki thanks a million *l.* bunch.

stola *f. hist.* (*rzymska*) stole.

stolarka *f.* (*rzemiosło; wyroby*) woodwork, carpentry.

stolarnia *f. Gen.pl.* -i *l.* -ń carpenter's *l.* joiner's (work)shop.

stolarski *a.* carpenter's, joiner's; warsztat stolarski *zob.* stolarnia; (= *stół stolarski*) woodworker's bench; zakład stolarski *zob.* stolarnia.

stolarstwo *n.* carpentry, woodwork.

stolarz *mp* carpenter, joiner; stolarz meblowy cabinet-maker.

stolcowy *a. anat.* fecal, rectal; kiszka stolcowa rectum.

stole *mi zob.* stół.

stolec *mi* -lc- *Gen.* -a *Gen.pl.* -ów 1. (= *odchody*) stool; oddać stolec defecate; zaparcie stolca *pat.* constipation. 2. *arch.* (= *tron; stanowisko*) stool.

stolica *f.* (*państwa, regionu*) capital; Stolica Apostolska *rz.-kat.* the Holy See.

stoliczek *mi* -czk- *Gen.* -a small table.

stolik *mi Gen.* -a 1. small table; (*niemający określonego zastosowania*) occasional table; stolik do gry *karty* gaming table; stolik nocny night *l.* bedside table. 2. (*w restauracji*) table; zarezerwować stolik book *l.* reserve a table.

stoliwo *n. geogr.* tableland.

stolnica *f.* molding board, *Br.* moulding board.

stolon *mi* 1. *bot.* stolon, runner. 2. *zool.* stolon.

stołeczek *mi* -czk- *Gen.* -a 1. (*do siedzenia*) (small) stool. 2. (*splecione dłonie*) lady chair.

stołeczny *a.* capital; miasto stołeczne capital city.

stołek *mi* -łk- *Gen.* -a 1. stool. 2. *przen.* berth, billet; siedzieć na dwóch stołkach straddle the fence, run with the hare and hunt with the hounds; bić się o stołki fight for one's position; spaść ze stołka lose one's job.

stołować *ipf.* board. ~ się *ipf.* board (*u kogoś* with sb); tu się stołuję this is where I go for *l.* eat my meals.

stołowniczka *f. Gen.pl.* -ek, stołownik *mp* boarder.

stołowy[1] *a.* table; łyżka stołowa tablespoon; pokój stołowy dining room; meble stołowe dining room furniture; musztarda stołowa table mustard; tenis stołowy *sport* table tennis; wino stołowe table wine; zastawa stołowa tableware.

stołowy[2] *mi* (= *pokój stołowy*) dining room.

stołówka *f. Gen.pl.* -ek canteen; (*zwł. szkolna*) lunchroom; (*dla bezdomnych l. ubogich*) soup kitchen.

stołówkowy *a.* canteen; jedzenie stołówkowe canteen food.

stołp, stołb *mi hist.* donjon, dungeon.

stołu *itp. mi zob.* stół.

stomatolog *mp pl.* -dzy *l.* -owie *dent.* dentist, dental surgeon.

stomatologia *f. Gen.* -ii *dent.* dentistry, stomatology.

stomatologiczny *a. dent.* dental, stomatological; badanie stomatologiczne (*kontrolne*) dental checkup; chirurgia stomatologiczna dental surgery; gabinet stomatologiczny dentist's (surgery); leczenie stomatologiczne dental treatment; poradnia stomatologiczna dental clinic.

stonka, stonka ziemniaczana *f. Gen.pl.* -ek *ent.* Colorado (potato) beetle, potato bug *l.* beetle (*Leptinotarsa decemlineata*).

stonkowate *pl. ent.* chrysomelids (*Chrysomelidae*).

stonkowaty *a.* chrysomelid.

stonoga f. Gen.pl. **-óg** zool. pill bug, wood louse, sow bug (Oniscus).

stonować pf. **1.** (barwy) tone down. **2.** (= osłabić) tone down, soften.

stonowany a. (= zharmonizowany; osłabiony) toned down, moderated; (o kolorze) sober, subdued; (o kolorze, świetle) subdued, mellow; (o wypowiedzi) low-key.

stop[1] mi metal. alloy; **stop drukarski** druk. printer's metal.

stop[2] mi **1.** mot. (światło) stoplight, brake light; **znak stopu** stop sign; **przejechać znak stopu** (nie zatrzymać się) run a stop sign. **2.** (= autostop) pot. hitchhiking. **3.** (= zatrzymanie) stop, halt; **stop! - ani kroku dalej!** stop! - don't move an inch!; **silniki stop!** all engines stop!, stop all engines! **4.** (w telegramie) stop.

stopa f. Gen.pl. **stóp 1.** (część nogi) foot; **od stóp do głów** from head to foot; **leżeć u czyichś stóp** lie at sb's feet; **stopa ludzka tu nie stanęła** no man has set his foot here before, no human foot has ever trodden on this land; **nietknięty ludzką stopą** untrodden by man; **grunt pali mu się pod stopami** ground burns under his feet, he's being dogged; **na stopie prywatnej** on a personal level; **jestem z nim na stopie koleżeńskiej** I'm on friendly terms with him; **żyć na wysokiej stopie** have a high living standard, lead the life of Riley; **wieś leżąca u stóp gór** a village at the feet of the mountains; **moja stopa nigdy więcej tu nie postanie** I'll never set foot in this house again; **stopa procentowa** ekon. interest rate; **stopa życiowa** ekon. living standard; **stopa zysku** ekon. profit rate; **stopa inflacji** ekon. inflation rate; **odpowiadać z wolnej stopy** prawn. be released pending trial; (w prawie anglosaskim, za kaucją) appear on bail; (bez kaucji) be released on one's own recognizance. **2.** (skarpetki, pończochy) sole. **3.** teor.lit. foot; **stopa metryczna** metric foot. **4.** miern. foot; **stopa mennicza** the content of noble ore in a coin. **5.** techn. foot, base.

stoper mi Gen. **-a** pl. **-ry** (czasomierz) stopwatch. – mp pl. **-rzy** piłka nożna center halfback; Br. centre half l. back.

stopić pf. zob. **stapiać**. ~ **się** pf. zob. **stapiać się**.

stopień mi **-pni-** Gen. **-a 1.** (schodów) step, stair; **uwaga, stopień!** (napis ostrzegawczy) mind the step!; **stopień wodny** bud. barrage. **2.** (hierarchia) rank; **stopień naukowy** (university) degree; **stopień wojskowy** military rank; **nagroda pierwszego stopnia** first degree award; **awansować do stopnia majora** be promoted to a major; **stopień doktora** doctorate; **przyznać komuś stopień doktora** confer the doctoral degree on l. upon sb; **uzyskać stopień doktora** be awarded one's doctoral degree; **stopień pokrewieństwa** genealogia degree; **oparzenie pierwszego stopnia** pat. first-degree burn; **ciekawość to pierwszy stopień do piekła** curiosity killed the cat. **3.** szkoln. grade; Br. mark. **4.** (na skali) degree; **mam trzydzieści osiem stopni gorączki** I('ve) got a fever of thirty and eight; **pięć stopni Celsjusza** five degrees centigrade l. Celcius; **siedemdzie-**

siąt stopni Fahrenheita seventy degrees Fahrenheit; **stopień długości/szerokości geograficznej** degree of longitude/latitude; **stopień równania** mat. degree. **5.** geom. degree; **kąt ma trzydzieści stopni** the angle has thirty degrees. **6.** mat. (pierwiastka) index. **7.** (intensywności) degree; (np. zniszczeń) extent; **do pewnego stopnia** l. w pewnym stopniu to some degree l. extent; **w dużym stopniu** to a large extent; **do tego stopnia go nienawidził, że...** he hated him so much that...; **to jest w najwyższym stopniu zabronione** it is strictly prohibited. **8.** jęz. degree; **stopień równy** positive degree, the positive; **stopień wyższy** comparative degree, the comparative; **stopień najwyższy** superlative degree, the superlative; **okolicznik stopnia** adverbial of degree. **9.** muz. degree.

stopięćdziesięciolecie n.   sesquicentennial, one hundred and fiftieth anniversary.

stopka f. Gen.pl. **-ek 1.** druk. footer. **2.** (karabinu) butt plate. **3.** techn. (= następ) treadle. **4.** (do dociskania tkaniny w maszynie do szycia) (presser) foot. **5.** (= mała stopa) little foot; **kurza stopka** (zmarszczka) crow's foot.

stop-klatka f. Gen.pl. **-ek** film freeze frame.

stopnieć pf. **1.** (o lodzie, śniegu) melt (down), thaw; (o metalu) melt. **2.** przen. (o pieniądzach) dwindle away; (o siłach) ebb away.

stopniować ipf. **1.** (= zwiększać stopniowo) gradate, graduate. **2.** jęz. compare.

stopniowanie n. **1.** (zwiększanie) gradation. **2.** jęz. comparison.

stopniowo adv. gradually, by degrees, bit by bit, step by step; **stopniowo coś obniżać** (np. ceny, podatki) scale sth down; **stopniowo coś podwyższać** (np. ceny, podatki) scale sth up; **stopniowo przestać funkcjonować** (np. o gospodarce) grind to a standstill; **wprowadzać coś stopniowo** phase sth in; **wycofywać coś stopniowo** phase sth out.

stopniowy a. gradual.

stopochodny a. zool. plantigrade; **zwierzę stopochodne** plantigrade (animal).

stopować ipf. (osobę, proces, urządzenie) (= hamować) halt, stop; **stopować piłkę** sport stop the ball.

stopowy[1] a. metal. alloy; **stal stopowa** alloy steel.

stopowy[2] a. teor.lit. foot, footed.

stora f. drape, (thick) curtain.

storczyk mi Gen. **-a** bot. orchid (Orchis).

storczykowate pl. Gen. **-ych** bot. orchids, the orchid family (Orchidaceae).

storczykowaty a. bot. orchidaceous.

stornia f. icht. European flounder (Platichthys flesus).

storno n. ekon. correcting entry.

stornować ipf. ekon. correct (entries).

storpedować pf. **1.** wojsk. torpedo. **2.** (= uniemożliwić) torpedo, thwart.

storturować pf. zob. **torturować**.

stos mi **1.** (= sterta) pile; (= kupa) heap; (poukładany, równy) stack; **stos atomowy** fiz. atomic pile, nuclear reactor; **stos pacierzowy**

anat., przest. vertebral *l.* spinal column. **2.** (*do spalenia*) pile; (*zwł. ofiarny l. pogrzebowy*) pyre; **stos pogrzebowy** funeral pyre; *rzad.* balefire. **3.** (*rodzaj kary*) the stake; **spalić kogoś na stosie** burn sb at the stake; **skazać na stos** sentence sb to the stake; **zginąć na stosie** perish at the stake. **4.** *górn.* crib, cribwork. **5.** *komp.* stack. **6.** *leśn.* stack of logs.

stosina *f. orn.* rachis.

stosować *ipf.* **1.** (= *wprowadzać w życie*) put into practice *l.* operation; (*metody, przepisy, siłę*) apply; (*zasady*) observe; **stosować ogólnie przyjęte zasady** (*postępowania w jakiejś sprawie*) follow the usual practice. **2.** (= *używać*) use, apply; (*leki*) administer. **3.** (= *odnosić do kogoś*) apply; **stosować bojkot towarzyski wobec kogoś** ostracize sb. ~ **się** *ipf.* **1.** (= *przestrzegać czegoś*) comply (*do czegoś* with sth); adhere (*do czegoś* to sth). **2.** (= *odnosić się do kogoś*) apply (*do kogoś* to sb); hold (good) (*do kogoś* for sb).

stosowalny *a.* applicable.

stosowany *a.* **1.** (= *służący potrzebom praktycznym*) applied; **nauka stosowana** applied science. **2.** (= *będący w użyciu*) in use.

stosownie *adv.* **1.** (= *odpowiednio*) appropriately, suitably, befittingly. **2.** (= *przyzwoicie*) properly. **3.** (= *według czegoś*) accordingly; **stosownie do czegoś** according *l.* pursuant to sth.

stosowność *f.* **1.** (= *odpowiedniość*) appropriateness, suitability. **2.** (= *przyzwoitość*) properness. **3.** (= *zgodność*) accordance.

stosowny *a.* **1.** (= *odpowiedni*) appropriate, suitable, befitting. **2.** (= *przyzwoity*) proper. **3.** (= *zgodny*) in accordance (*z czymś* with sth); **uznać za stosowne (coś zrobić)** see *l.* think fit (to do sth).

stosunek *mi* -nk- **1.** (= *relacja, proporcja*) ratio, proportion; **w stosunku 3 do 5** in the ratio of 3 to 5; **w stosunku do wielkości sprzedaży w ubiegłym roku w tym roku sprzedaż rośnie** in relation to last year this year's sales are on the increase. **2.** (= *relacja, zależność*) relation; **stosunek pokrewieństwa** consanguinity, kinship; **stosunek powinowactwa** affinity, relationship by marriage; **stosunek prawny** privity. **3.** (= *nastawienie wobec kogoś/czegoś*) attitude; **stosunek do zwierząt** attitude to animals. **4.** (= *związek*) relation; **w stosunku do** (= *w porównaniu z*) in *l.* with relation to; (= *w odniesieniu do*) with reference to; **zerwać z kimś stosunki** part company with sb; *form.* break *l.* sever relations with sb; **stosunki dyplomatyczne/handlowe** diplomatic/business relations; **zerwać z kimś stosunki dyplomatyczne** sever diplomatic relations with sb; **pozostawać z kimś w bliskich** *l.* **zażyłych stosunkach** be on intimate terms with sb; **utrzymywać z kimś stosunki przyjacielskie** be on friendly terms with sb; **stosunki między państwami są napięte** the relations between the states are tense. **5.** (= *warunek*) condition; **stosunki społeczne** social conditions *l.* relations; **stosunki produkcji** *ekon.* labor relations. **6.** (= *znajomości*) connections; **mieć rozległe stosunki** be well-connected, be a person of wide connections. **7.** (*płciowy*) in-

tercourse; coitus, coition. **8.** *mat.* quotient, ratio; **stosunek jednokładności** *geom.* scale factor.

stosunkowo *adv.* relatively, comparatively.

stosunkowy *a.* **1.** (= *względny*) relative. **2.** (= *proporcjonalny*) proportional.

stotinka *f.* (*moneta bułgarska*) stotinka.

stowarzyszać się *ipf.* **1.** (= *utworzyć stowarzyszenie*) associate. **2.** (= *przyłączyć się do stowarzyszenia*) affiliate o.s.

stowarzyszenie *n.* association; **stowarzyszenie wyższej użyteczności** charitable *l.* philanthropic organization (*any humanitarian organization such as the Red Cross whose goals entitle it (in Poland) to certain privileges, e.g. financial*).

stowarzyszeniowy *a.* association.

stowarzyszona *f. Gen.* -ej *zob.* **stowarzyszony**.

stowarzyszony *a.* associated, affiliate; **członek stowarzyszony** (*np. organizacji naukowej*) associate member. – *mp* association member.

stowarzyszyć się *pf. zob.* **stowarzyszać się**.

stożek *mi* -żk- *Gen.* -a **1.** (= *coś spiczastego*) cone; **stożek wzrostu** *bot.* growing point. **2.** *geom.* cone; **stożek obrotowy** circular cone; **stożek ścięty** frustum of a cone, truncated cone. **3.** *geol.* talus; **stożek wulkaniczny** volcanic cone.

stożkowa *f. geom.* conic (section).

stożkowaty *a. geom.* conoid, conoidal; (= *w kształcie stożka*) cone-like, cone-shaped.

stożkowy *a.* (= *w kształcie stożka*) conic, conical; *geom.* conoid; **powierzchnia stożkowa** *geom.* conical surface.

stóg *mi* -o- stack, rick; **stóg siana** haystack *l.* hayrick; **szukać igły w stogu siana** look *l.* search for a needle in a haystack.

stój *itp. ipf. zob.* **stać**.

stójka *f. Gen.pl.* -ek **1.** (*kołnierzyk*) stand-up collar. **2.** *myśl.* (*o psie*) stand, dead set. **3.** *gimnastyka* stand.

stójkowy *mp hist.* constable, peeler.

stół *mi* -o- **1.** (*mebel*) table; **stół kuchenny** kitchen table; **stół konferencyjny** conference table; *przen.* the conference; **Stół Pański** *rel.* the Lord's Table; **usługiwać przy stole** wait at the table; **siedzieć przy stole** sit at the table; **usiąść do stołu** sit down to table; **wstać od stołu** stand down from the table; **nakryć do stołu dla sześciu osób** lay the table for six (people); **podać do stołu** serve food; **podano do stołu** (*informacja udzielana przez lokaja*) dinner (breakfast etc.) is *l.* has been served; **zapraszać do stołu** invite to the table; **stół uginał się od jedzenia** the table was piled with food; **szczyt stołu** the head of the table; **rozkosze stołu** the pleasures of the table; **droga równa jak stół** the road as level as a floor; **wyłożyć karty na stół** put *l.* lay *l.* set one's cards on the table; **wyłożyć pieniądze na stół** pay down in hard cash; **uderz w stół, a nożyce się odezwą** if the cap fits wear it, the hit dog howls. **2.** *techn.* table, bench; **stół kreślarski** drawing table; **stół montażowy** *film, radio* cutting *l.* editing table *l.* bench. **3.** *med.* table; (*operacyjny*) operating table; **umrzeć na stole** die on the (operating) table.

stóp *f. zob.* **stopa**.

stówa *f. pot.* C-note, a hundred.

str. *abbr.* **1.** (= *strona*) p., pg. (= *page*). **2.** (= *strony*) pp. (= *pages*).

stracenie *n.* **1.** (= *utrata*) loss; **nie mam nic do stracenia** I've got nothing to lose; **nie ma chwili do stracenia** there's no time to spare; **nie ma czasu do stracenia** there's no time to lose. **2.** (= *egzekucja*) execution; **miejsce straceń** place of execution.

straceniec *mp* -ńc- *pl.* -y desperado.

straceńczy *a.* desperate; **straceńcza odwaga** desperate bravado.

strach *mi Gen.* -u (= *przerażenie*) fear; **strach przed nieznanym** fear of the unknown; **strach przed śmiercią** fear of death; **strach o dzieci** fear for one's children; **blady** *l.* **śmiertelny strach** mortal fear; **blady ze strachu** white *l.* pale with fear, shuddering with fear; **spocony ze strachu** sweat with fear; **ze strachem myślę o przyszłości** I dread to think about the future; **na wieś padł blady strach** the villagers were petrified with fear; **zimno dziś, że aż strach** it's awfully cold today; **aż strach pomyśleć, co to będzie za rok** I shudder to think what's going to happen in a year's time; **mieć stracha** have cold feet; **najeść się strachu** get *l.* have the wind up; **napędzić komuś strachu** frighten sb out of their wits *l.* the wits out of sb, give sb a fright; **umierać ze strachu** be scared stiff; **skończyło się (u niej) na strachu** she was more scared than hurt; **robić w portki ze strachu** *pot.* shit one's pants with fear; **nie ma strachu** *pot.* never fear; take it easy; **strach ma wielkie oczy** fear has big eyes, fear makes cowards of us all. – *ma Gen.* -a **1.** (= *duch*) ghost; **nie wierzę w strachy** I don't believe in ghosts. **2.** (*na wróble*) scarecrow.

strachajło *mp pl.* -y *Gen.pl.* -ów *pog.* fraidy-cat, chicken.

strachliwie *adv.* timidly, faint-heartedly.

strachliwość *f.* timidity, faint-heartedness, cowardice.

strachliwy *a.* timid, faint-hearted.

stracić *pf.* **1.** (= *nie mieć już więcej*) lose; **stracić cierpliwość do kogoś** lose one's patience with sb; **stracić cnotę/dziewictwo** lose one's cherry/virginity; **stracić energię** *l.* **zapał** run out of gas; **stracić głowę dla kogoś** be swept off one's feet by sb, fall for sb; **stracić z czymś kontakt** lose touch of sth; **stracić matkę** lose one's mother; **stracić posadę** lose one's job; **stracić liście** (*o drzewie na jesieni*) shed leaves; **stracić na wadze** lose weight; **stracić orientację** lose one's bearings; **stracić panowanie nad sobą** blow a fuse, go off at the deep end; **stracić panowanie nad samochodem** lose control of the car; **kierowca stracił panowanie nad samochodem** the car went out of control; **stracić równowagę** lose one's balance; **stracić życie** lose one's life; (= *polec*) perish; **stracić rachubę czasu** lose the track of time; **stracić twarz** lose one's face; **stracić urodę** lose one's looks; **stracić wątek** lose one's train of thought; **stracić grunt pod nogami** have the ground taken *l.* cut from under one's feet; **stracić kogoś z oczu** lose track of sb; **stracić pokarm** stop *l.* cease

milking; **stracić rozum** *l.* **głowę** lose one's head; **stracić władzę** fall from power. **2.** (= *nie zarobić*) lose; **stracić na akcjach** sink capital *l.* money in shares; **niech stracę!** my loss!, never mind (the loss)!, what the hell! **3.** (= *nie wykorzystać*) waste; (= *roztrwonić*) squander; **stracić okazję/ szansę** waste an opportunity/a chance. **4.** (= *stać się gorszym*) lose; **stracić na sile** (*np. o burzy*) abate; **stracić na atrakcyjności** lose in attractiveness, become less attractive; **stracić w czyichś oczach** come down in sb's opinion. **5.** (*skazanego na śmierć*) execute, put to death. ~ **się** *pf.* **1.** disappear, vanish; **stracić się z oczu** (= *przestać się widzieć*) lose sight of each other *l.* one another. **2.** (= *przestać się kontaktować*) lose track of each other *l.* one another.

stracony *a.* -eni **1.** (= *zgubiony, zaginiony*) lost. **2.** (= *zmarnowany*) wasted; **stracone pokolenie** *t. teor.lit.* the Lost Generation; **być** *l.* **stać na straconej pozycji** be on a hiding to nothing; **nadrabiać stracony czas** make up for lost time; **stracony bezpowrotnie** lost beyond retrieval; **nic straconego** all is not yet lost. **3.** (= *zabity*) executed, put to death.

stradivarius, stradivari *mi Gen.* -a *muz.* Stradivarius; *pot.* Strad.

stragan *mi* (market) stall.

straganiarka *f. Gen.pl.* -ek, **straganiarz** *mp* stallholder.

straganik *mi Gen.* -u *l.* -a (market) stall.

straganowy *a.* **1.** (= *sprzedawany na straganie*) (market) stall. **2.** (= *niskiej jakości*) lowbrow; **literatura straganowa** pulp fiction, dime novels; *Br.* penny dreadfuls.

strajk *mi* strike; **strajk generalny** *l.* **powszechny** general strike; **strajk głodowy** hunger strike; **strajk okupacyjny** sit-in *l.* sit-down (strike); **strajk ostrzegawczy** token strike; **strajk protestacyjny** protest strike; **strajk solidarnościowy** sympathy strike; **strajk włoski** go-slow; **grozić strajkiem** threaten with a strike; **ogłosić strajk** call a strike; **przyłączyć się do strajku** join in a strike; **rozpocząć strajk** go on strike.

strajkować *ipf.* strike (*o coś* for sth); be on strike.

strajkowy *a.* strike; **akcja strajkowa** industrial *l.* strike action; **komitet strajkowy** strike committee; **zasiłek strajkowy** (*związku zawodowego*) strike pay.

strapić *pf.* distress, worry. ~ **się** *pf.* be distressed, be worried, be anxious.

strapienie *n.* heartache, heartsore; worry.

strapiony *a.* -eni distressed, worried.

straponten *mi Gen.* -u *l.* -a (*siedzenie w pociągu, autobusie, teatrze*) tip-up seat, folding seat.

stras *mi* (*szkło*) paste, strass.

Strasburg *mi geogr.* Strasbourg.

strasburski *a.* Strasbourg; **pasztet strasburski** *kulin.* pâté de foie gras.

straszak *mi Gen.* -a **1.** (= *imitacja pistoletu*) toy gun. **2.** (= *coś, co ma przestraszyć*) deterrent, bugaboo; **straszak jądrowy** *polit., wojsk.* the nuclear deterrent; **akcja strajkowa jest straszakiem**

dla rządu the purpose of the industrial action is to intimidate the government.

straszliwie *adv*. **1.** (= *przerażająco*) horrendously, horrifyingly; **straszliwie zagrzmiało** there was a horrifying clap of thunder. **2.** (= *bardzo*) awfully.

straszliwy *a*. **1.** (= *przejmujący lękiem*) horrifying. **2.** (= *bardzo zły, straszny*) horrible; **straszliwa chała** (*o książce, filmie*) a load *l*. bunch of crap. **3.** (= *wielki, bardzo duży*) awful.

strasznie *adv*. **1.** (= *groźnie*) terrible, horrible; **nagle zrobiło mi się strasznie** suddenly I felt a pang of fear. **2.** (= *okropnie*) horribly, badly; **strasznie kogoś traktować** treat sb terribly; **wyglądać strasznie** look horrible. **3.** *pot*. (= *niezmiernie*) awfully, dreadfully, horribly, dead; **jest mi strasznie zimno** I'm freezing cold; **strasznie tu gorąco** it's baking in here; **strasznie dziękuję** thanks a lot; **strasznie się cieszę** I'm awfully happy; **jest już strasznie późno** it's dead late; **strasznie boli mnie łokieć** my elbow hurts so bad; **strasznie mi jej żal** my heart bleeds for her; **strasznie się nudziłem** I was bored stiff.

straszność *f*. horribleness, terribleness.

straszny *a*. **1.** (= *przerażający*) terrible, horrible; **straszny sen** terrible dream, nightmare; **straszny widok** horrible sight; **straszna śmierć** awful death; **nie taki diabeł straszny, jak go malują** the devil is not so black as he is painted. **2.** (= *okropny*) horrible, terrible, awful; **straszna dzisiaj pogoda** the weather's so awful today. **3.** *pot*. (= *wielki*) terrible, awful, a hell of a; **straszny ból** awful pain; **straszny smutek** terrible sorrow; **straszne pieniądze** a hell of a lot of money; **straszna odległość** a hell of a distance; **straszny z niego dzieciuch** he's such a child; **w pokoju jest straszny bałagan** the room is a mess; **być w strasznym dołku** (*w depresji*) be in a blue funk.

straszyć *ipf*. **1.** (= *wzbudzać strach*) frighten, terrify, scare. **2.** (= *grozić*) threaten. **3.** (*o duchach*) haunt; **w tym domu straszy** this house is haunted. **~ się** *ipf*. frighten each other *l*. one another, scare each other *l*. one another.

straszydło *n*. *Gen.pl*. **-deł 1.** *pot*. (= *czupiradło*) scarecrow, fright; (*np. o budynku szpecącym okolicę*) eyesore. **2.** *przest*. (= *duch*) ghost.

strata *f*. **1.** (= *ubytek, szkoda*) loss, waste; **strata czasu/pieniędzy** waste of time/money; **to żadna strata** that's not much of a loss; **to niewielka strata** that's not much of a waste; **ponieść niepowetowaną stratę** suffer an irreparable harm, suffer a dead loss; **narażać kogoś na straty** run the risk of sb incurring losses; **strata najbliższych** the loss of one's dearest ones; **spisać kogoś/coś na straty** write sb/sth off; **zadać nieprzyjacielowi dotkliwe straty** inflict substantial losses on the enemy; **oszacować straty** estimate the losses; **straty w ludziach** casualties; **bez strat w ludziach** without casualties. **2.** *ekon*. loss; **rachunek zysków i strat** profit and loss account; **ponieść milionowe straty** incur *l*. suffer a loss running to millions; **sprzedać ze stratą** sell sth at a loss *l*. below par; **wykazywać stratę** show a loss;

moja strata *pot*. my loss, never mind (the loss), what the hell.

strateg *mp pl*. **-dzy** *l*. **-owie 1.** (*wojskowy, ekonomiczny*) strategist. **2.** *hist*. strategus.

strategia *f*. *Gen*. **-ii** strategy; **strategia inwestycyjna** *ekon*. investment strategy; **strategia przedsiębiorstwa** *ekon*. company strategy; **strategia rozwoju** *ekon*. development strategy.

strategicznie *adv*. strategically; **strategicznie ważny** (*o obiekcie, posunięciu*) of strategic importance *l*. significance, strategic.

strategiczny *a*. strategic; **broń strategiczna** *wojsk*. strategic arms *l*. weapons; **manewr strategiczny** strategic maneuver; *Br*. strategic manoeuvre.

stratny *a*. out; **być stratnym 100 złotych** be out 100 PLN; **niech będę stratny** my loss, never mind (the loss), what the hell.

stratocumulus *mi Gen*. **-a** *meteor*. stratocumulus.

stratosfera *f*. *meteor*. stratosphere.

stratosferyczny *a*. *meteor*. stratospheric, stratospherical.

stratować *pf*. (= *podeptać*) trample; (*w tłumie*) crush *l*. squeeze to death.

stratowizja *f*. *Gen.pl*. **-ji** *tel*. Stratovision.

stratus *mi meteor*. stratus.

stratyfikacja *f*. *geol*., *meteor*., *roln*., *socjol*. stratification.

stratygrafia *f*. *Gen*. **-ii** *geol*. stratigraphy.

stratygraficzny *a*. *geol*. stratigraphic, stratigraphical; **przekrój stratygraficzny** *archeol*. stratigraphy.

strawa *f*. *lit*. repast, pabulum; **strawa dla ducha** food for thought, pabulum.

strawestować *pf*. travesty.

strawić *pf*. **1.** (*pokarm*) digest; **nie móc strawić czegoś** not be able to digest sth. **2.** (= *zniszczyć*) consume, destroy; **pożar strawił wieś** the fire consumed *l*. destroyed the village; **rdza strawiła dach** the rust consumed *l*. ate the roof. **3.** (*metal*) etch (away). **4.** *lit*. (= *spędzić*) spend; **strawić życie na podróżach** spend one's life traveling.

strawność *f*. digestibility.

strawny *a*. digestible; **ciężko strawny** heavy, stodgy; **lekko strawny** light.

straż *f*. *pl*. **-e** (*nadzór, strażnicy*) guard; **straż graniczna** border guard; **straż honorowa** guard of honor; *Br*. guard of honour; **straż obywatelska** home guard; **straż pałacowa** palace guard; **straż pożarna** fire brigade; **straż przyboczna** personal guard; **straż przednia** *wojsk*. advance guard, vanguard; **straż tylna** *wojsk*. rear guard; **być pod (silną) strażą** be under (heavy) guard; **pełnić straż** be on guard; **stać na straży** (= *pełnić straż*) be on guard; (= *strzec*) safeguard, uphold; **trzymać straż** stand sentinel; **wystawiać straże** set guards; **zaciągnąć straż** mount guard (*przy czymś* at sth).

strażacki *a*. fireman's, firefighter's; **orkiestra strażacka** firemen's band; **remiza strażacka** fire station; **wóz strażacki** fire engine, fire truck.

strażak *mp* fireman, firefighter.

strażnica *f*. (= *wieża strażnicza*) watchtower.

strażniczka *f. Gen.pl.* **-ek** (*w instytucji*) security guard; (*więzienna*) prison guard, wardress; **strażniczka leśna** forest ranger.

strażniczy *a.* guard's, watchman's; **budka strażnicza** sentry box.

strażnik *mp* guard, watchman; (*w wojsku*) sentry; (*w instytucji*) security guard; (*więzienny*) prison guard, warder; (*wartości, praw*) upholder; **strażnik leśny** forest ranger; **strażnik przyrody** conservator.

strącać *ipf.*, **strącić** *pf.* **1.** (= *zrzucać*) knock off; (= *strząsać*) shake off. **2.** (*strzałem*) shoot down, bring down. **3.** (= *odliczać*) deduct. **4.** *chem.* precipitate. ~ **się** *ipf.*, **strącić się** *pf. chem.* precipitate.

strącanie *n. chem.* precipitation.

strączek *mi* **-czk-** *Gen.* **-a** (small) pod, (small) legume.

strączkowy *a.* leguminous; **rośliny strączkowe** *bot.* leguminous plants, legumes.

strączyniec *mi bot.* cassia (*Cassia*).

strąk *mi Gen.* **-a 1.** *bot.* pod, legume. **2.** *pl.* stringy hair.

strąkowy *a.* leguminous; **rośliny strąkowe** *bot.* leguminous plants, legumes.

streamer *mi komp.* (= *pamięć taśmowa*) streamer.

strefa *f.* zone, area; belt; **strefa niskiego ciśnienia** *l.* **niżu** *meteor.* area of low pressure; **strefa buforowa** *wojsk.* buffer zone; **strefa ciszy** *geogr.* (*przy równiku*) the doldrums; **strefa czasowa/dolarowa/erogenna** time/dollar/erogenous zone; **Strefa Gazy** *admin.* the Gaza Strip; **strefa klimatyczna** climatic zone; **strefa międzyzwrotnikowa** *geogr.* the tropics; **strefa ograniczonego parkowania** *mot.* restricted parking zone; **strefa podzwrotnikowa** *geogr.* the subtropics, the subtropical region(s); **strefa przygraniczna** border zone; **strefa wolnego ognia** free fire zone; **strefa wolnoclowa** (duty) free zone; **strefa zakazu lotów** *wojsk.* no-fly zone; **strefa zdemilitaryzowana** *wojsk.* demilitarized zone; **szara strefa** *ekon.* black economy, economic twilight zone; **Specjalna Strefa Ekonomiczna** *ekon.* Special Economic Zone.

strefowy *a.* zonal, zonary; zonate, zonated; **czas strefowy** zonetime.

strelicja *f. bot.* **strelicja królewska** bird of paradise (*Strelitzia reginae*).

stremować *pf.* make nervous. ~ **się** *pf.* become nervous, be affected with stage fright.

strepet *ma orn.* little bustard (*Otis tetrax*).

streptokok *ma biol.* streptococcus (*Streptococcus*).

streptomycyna *f. med.* streptomycin.

stres *mi* **1.** *psych.* stress, pressure; **w stresie** (*np. o pracy*) under pressure. **2.** *geol.* stress.

stresor *mi Gen.* **-a** *psych.* stressor.

stresować *ipf. psych.* stress.

stresowy *a. psych.* stressful, stress-related.

stresujący *a. psych.* stressful.

streszczać *ipf.* summarise, give the main points of; **streścić coś komuś** give sb the gist of

sth. ~ **się** *ipf.* be brief, speak *l.* write briefly; **streszczaj się!** *pot.* keep it short!, be brief!

streszczenie *n.* summary; (*wydarzeń*) résumé; (*odcinka serialu, akcji filmu*) synopsis; (*tekstu pisanego*) epitome; (*publikacji naukowej, dokumentu, przemówienia*) abstract; **streszczenie w języku angielskim** abstract in English.

streścić *pf.* **-szczę -ścisz** *zob.* **streszczać.** ~ **się** *pf. zob.* **streszczać się.**

stretch *mi tk.* stretch fabric; **ze stretchu** stretch.

stręczyciel *mp* procurer; *pot.* pimp, panderer.

stręczycielka *f. Gen.pl.* **-ek** procuress; *pot.* panderer.

stręczycielstwo *n.* procuration, pimping.

stręczyć *pf.* pimp, pander; **stręczyć do nierządu** *prawn.* procure.

striptiz *mi* striptease, strip show; **robić striptiz** do a strip, strip, perform a striptease.

striptizer *mp*, **striptizerka** *f. Gen.pl.* **-ek** stripteaser; *pot.* peeler.

striptizowy *a.* striptease; **tancerka striptizowa** striptease dancer.

strit *mi karty* straight.

strobila *f. zool.* strobila.

stroboskop *mi med., techn.* stroboscope.

stroboskopowy *a.* stroboscopic.

stroczek *mi bot.* dry rot (*Merulius*).

strofa *f. teor.lit.* **1.** (= *zwrotka*) stanza, stave. **2.** (*w dramacie antycznym*) strophe.

strofant *mi bot.* strophantus (*Strophantus*).

stroficzny *a. teor.lit.* stanzaic, stanzaed; strophic, strophical.

strofika *f. teor.lit.* **1.** the study of stanzaic forms *l.* strophic structure. **2.** stanzaic forms *l.* strophic structure (*characteristic of l. employed by a given poet*).

strofka *f. Gen.pl.* **-ek** stanza; *pot.* verse.

strofować *ipf.* scold, rebuke (*kogoś za coś* sb for (doing) sth); admonish (*kogoś za coś* sb for (doing) sth).

stroiciel *mp* tuner; **stroiciel fortepianów** piano tuner.

stroiczka *f. bot.* lobelia (*Lobelia*).

stroić *ipf.* **stroję stroisz, strój 1.** (= *ubierać*) dress up. **2.** (= *zdobić*) adorn. **3.** (= *wyprawiać, wyrabiać*) make; **stroić figle** play pranks; **stroić miny** pull *l.* make faces; **stroić sobie żarty** make fun (*z kogoś/czegoś* of sb/sth). **4.** (*instrument, radio*) tune; **stroić instrumenty** (*o orkiestrze*) tune up. ~ **się** *ipf.* dress up, preen o.s., primp, prink, deck out; **stroić się w cudze piórka** sail under false colors.

stroik *mi Gen.* **-a 1.** (= *czółko*) headdress (*usu. in regional folk costume*). **2.** *muz.* reed; (*w oboju, organach*) tongue. **3.** (*z gałązek*) spray; **stroik świąteczny** (*na Boże Narodzenie*) Christmas wreath.

stroikowy *a. muz.* reed; **instrumenty stroikowe** the reeds, reed instruments; **piszczałka stroikowa** (*w organach*) reed pipe.

strojnie *adv.* smartly, dressily, chicly; **strojnie ubrany** smartly dressed.

strojnisia *f. Voc.* -**u** *iron.* fashion victim, snappy dresser, glamorpuss.

strojniś *mp Gen.pl.* -**ów** *iron.* dandy, clotheshorse.

strojny *a.* smart, dressy, chic; **choinka strojna w świecidełka** Christmas tree adorned with trinkets.

strojowy *a. muz.* tuning; **widełki strojowe** tuning fork.

stromizna *f.* 1. (= *stromość*) steepness. 2. (= *strome zbocze*) steep slope, (the) steep.

stromo *adv.* steeply; *geol.* abruptly.

stromy *a.* steep; *geol.* abrupt.

strona *f.* 1. (= *bok; skraj; aspekt*) side; **strona „ma"** *ekon.* credit side; **strona „winien"** *ekon.* debit side; **z jednej strony...**, **z drugiej strony...** on (the) one hand..., on the other hand...; **przejść na drugą stronę ulicy** cross the street; **pod drugiej stronie ulicy** across the street; **po prawej/lewej stronie** on the right/left (hand side); **racja jest po twojej stronie** you're right; **mieć kogoś po swojej stronie** have sb on one's side; **być po czyjejś stronie** be on sb's side, side with sb; **stanąć po czyjejś stronie** take sides with sb; **przejść na czyjąś stronę** come over to sb's side, take one's stand at sb's side; **przejść na stronę wroga** defect to the enemy; **przeciągnąć kogoś na swoją stonę** gain sb over; **walczyć po czyjejś stronie** fight on the side of sb, fight side by side with sb; **z mojej strony** on *l.* for my part; **to ładnie z twojej strony** it is kind of you; **druga strona medalu** the other side of the coin; **pomoc finansowa ze strony rodziców** financial help on the part of one's parents; **krewny ze strony matki** a relative from one's mother's side; **poszli każdy w swoją stronę** everybody went his/her own way; **włożyć sweter na lewą stronę** put on the sweater inside out; **po lewej stronie znajduje się pomnik...** on our left we *l.* you can see the monument of...; **patrzył w moją stronę** he was looking my way; **rozważyć coś ze wszystkich stron** consider sth in all its aspects; **pokazać się z najlepszej strony** put one's best leg forward; **nie należy oczekiwać pomocy z tej strony** there's no help to be looked for in that quarter; **cztery strony świata** the four cardinal points; **rozglądać się na wszystkie strony** look around; **rozjechać się w różne strony** set off in different directions; **pójść na stronę** go to the restroom *l.* toilet; **z której strony wieje wiatr?** which way is the wind from?; **wziąć kogoś na stronę** take sb aside; **strona równania** *mat.* member *l.* side of an equation. 2. (*np. książki*) page; **strona domowa** *l.* **główna** *komp.* home page; **strona internetowa** web page; **strona tytułowa** title page. 3. (*cecha*) aspect, angle, bearing; **jasne i ciemne strony życia** the rough and the smooth; **znać czyjeś dobre** *l.* **złe strony** know the length of sb's foot; **tłumaczenie nie jest moją mocną stroną** translation is not one of my strong points; **ta praca ma też swoje dobre/złe strony** there are also good/bad aspects of this job; **znać kogoś z dobrej strony** know the good side of sb. 4. (*okolica, kraj*) parts; neighborhood; *Br.* neighbourhood; **nie znam tych stron** I don't know these parts; **z jakich stron pani po-**

chodzi where(abouts) do you come from?; **to są moje rodzinne strony** this is my homeland, that's where I come from; **tęsknię do stron ojczystych** I miss my homeland. 5. (= *uczestnik sporu*) party; **walczące strony** the warring parties; **te propozycje nie mogą być zaakceptowane przez stronę polską** these proposals cannot be accepted by the Polish delegation. 6. *prawn.* party; **być stroną w czymś** be a party to sth; **nakłonić strony do ugody** persuade the parties to reach an amicable agreement; **pełnomocnik strony** a party's attorney(-in-fact); **wysokie układające się strony** the high contracting parties. 7. *gram.* voice; **strona bierna** passice voice, the passive; **strona czynna** active voice, the active; **strona zwrotna** the reflexive, middle voice.

stronica *f. t. przen.* page; **piękne stronice historii** fine pages of history.

stronicowy *a.* paginal.

stroniczka *f. Gen.pl.* -**ek** page.

stronić *ipf.* shun (*od kogoś /czegoś* sb/sth); **on stroni od alkoholu** he never touches liquor; **nie stronić od czegoś** (= *lubić coś*) be partial to sth.

stronnictwo *n. zwł. polit.* party; **stronnictwo polityczne** political party.

stronniczka *f. Gen.pl.* -**ek** *zob.* **stronnik**.

stronniczo *adv.* partially, one-sidedly.

stronniczość *f.* partiality, one-sidedness, bias; **zarzucać komuś stronniczość** accuse sb of partiality.

stronniczy *a.* partial, biased, one-sided; (*o artykule, reportażu*) unbalanced.

stronnik *mp* backer, supporter, partisan; **mieć wielu stronników** *l.* **zwolenników** have a great following.

stront *mi chem.* strontium; *rzad.* strontian.

strop *mi* 1. *bud.* structural ceiling, floor; (= *sklepienie*) vault; (*korytarza, tunelu*) roof. 2. *geol., górn.* roof.

stropić *pf. przest.* abash, disconcert. ~ **się** *pf.* become abashed, become disconcerted.

stropiony *a.* -**eni** abashed, disconcerted; **umilkł stropiony** abashed, he fell silent.

stropodach *mi bud.* flat roof.

stropowy *a.* 1. *bud.* ceiling, floor; **belka stropowa** joist, ceiling beam. 2. *geol.* roof. 3. *górn.* roof; **calizna stropowa** layer *l.* body of coal (*over a roof in a coalmine*).

stroskany *a.* troubled, distressed, vexed.

stroszyć *ipf.* bristle, ruffle; **stroszyć pióra** (*o ptakach*) ruffle feathers. ~ **się** *ipf.* bristle up, ruffle up.

strój *mi* -**o**- *Gen.pl.* -**ów** 1. (*ubranie*) dress; (*do wykonywania określonej pracy*) outfit; (*charakterystyczny dla danej profesji*) attire; (*charakterystyczny dla danej epoki; t. kostium*) costume; **strój błazna** jester's costume; **strój galowy** full dress; **strój historyczny** historical costume; **strój ludowy** folk costume; **strój narodowy** national dress; **strój plażowy** beachwear; **strój roboczy** working outfit *l.* clothes; **strój sportowy** sportswear; **strój wieczorowy** evening dress *l.* wear; **obowiązuje strój wieczorowy** (*informacja na zaproszeniu*) evening dress (is) de rigueur;

strój wizytowy formal dress; strój do jazdy konnej riding clothes; w stroju adamowym wearing *l.* in one's birthday suit. **2.** *muz.* (= *skala*) pitch. **3.** *muz.* key.

stróż *mp Gen.pl.* -ów (= *strażnik*) guardian; (= *wartownik*) watchman; (= *dozorca, gospodarz domu*) caretaker, janitor; *Br.* porter; anioł stróż *rel.* guardian angel; stróż nocny night watchman; stróż moralności/demokracji guardian of morality/democracy; stróż prawa law enforcement officer; odstawić się jak stróż na Boże Ciało *l.* pochód pierwszomajowy be done *l.* got up like a dog's dinner.

stróża *f. hist.* watch, guard (*the obligation, on the part of a master's subjects, to guard his castle, mansion, etc.*).

stróżostwo *n.* functions *l.* duties of a caretaker, janitor, etc.

stróżować *ipf.* **1.** (= *strzec*) guard, watch, keep watch. **2.** (= *pracować jako stróż*) work as a watchman.

stróżowski *a.* caretaker's, watchman's, janitorial.

stróżówka *f. Gen.pl.* -ek (*przy wejściu, bramie wjazdowej*) gatehouse; (*przy wejściu na teren majątku ziemskiego*) lodge.

struchleć *pf.* **1.** (= *bardzo się przestraszyć*) be terrified. **2.** (= *zdrętwieć z przerażenia*) be petrified, be paralysed with fear.

strucla *f. Gen.pl.* -i *kulin.* stollen.

struć *pf.* **1.** (= *wywołać chorobę*) poison. **2.** (= *zmartwić*) dishearten, daunt. ~ się *pf.* **1.** (= *ulec zatruciu*) get poisoned. **2.** (= *zmartwić się*) become disheartened, become daunt.

strudel *mi* -dl- *Gen.* -a *kulin.* strudel; strudel z jabłkami apple strudel.

strudzić się *pf.* weary, fatigue, become prostrated.

strudzony *a.* fatigued, prostrated, wearied.

strug *mi Gen.* -a *techn.* plane.

struga *f.* stream, trickle; strugi deszczu sheets of rain; wino lało się strugami the wine flowed freely *l.* like water.

strugaczka *f.* (= *temperówka*) pencil sharpener.

strugać *ipf.* strugam *l.* strużę strugasz *l.* strużesz, strugaj *l.* struż **1.** (*nożem*) whittle. **2.** (= *heblować*) plane. **3.** (*ołówek, kredkę*) point, sharpen. **4.** (*rzeźbić*) carve; strugać wariata act *l.* play the fool; strugać ważniaka be too big for one's boots. **5.** *dial.* (= *obierać warzywa*) scrape, peel.

strugarka *f. Gen.pl.* -ek *techn.* planer.

struktura *f.* (= *układ*) structure; (= *budowa*) make-up; struktura danych *komp.* data structure; struktura języka language structure; struktura głęboka *jęz.* deep structure; struktura powierzchniowa *jęz.* surface structure; struktura społeczna the social fabric, the fabric of society; struktura kryształu *fiz.* crystal structure; język jako struktura language as structure.

strukturalista *mp fil., jęz., sztuka, teor.lit.* structuralist.

strukturalistycznie *adv. fil., jęz., sztuka, teor.lit.* structurally.

strukturalistyczny *a. fil., jęz., sztuka, teor.lit.* structuralist.

strukturalizacja *f.* structuralization.

strukturalizm *mi fil., jęz., sztuka, teor.lit.* structuralism.

strukturalizować *ipf.* structuralize.

strukturalnie *adv.* structurally.

strukturalny *a.* structural; zmiany strukturalne structural changes; wzór strukturalny *chem.* structural formula; analiza strukturalna *fiz.* structural *l.* structure analysis.

strumienica *f. techn.* jet pump.

strumieniomierz *mi Gen.* -a *fiz.* fluxmeter.

strumieniowy *a. icht.* stream, brook; minóg strumieniowy European brook lamprey (*Lampetra planeri*); prąd strumieniowy *meteor.* jet stream.

strumień *mi Gen.* -a **1.** (= *rzeczka*) stream, brook. **2.** (= *potok, struga*) stream, flux; (*wody, pary, gazu*) jet; strumień cząsteczek *fiz.* particle beam; strumień lawy *geol.* flow of lava, coulee; strumień piasku *techn.* sandblast; wylewać strumienie łez be in floods of tears; krew lała się strumieniami blood was gushing in spurts; stać w strumieniach *l.* strugach deszczu be standing in the pouring rain; strumień świetlny *fiz.* luminous flux.

strumyczek *mi* -czk- *Gen.* -a streamlet, rivulet.

strumyk *mi Gen.* -a **1.** (= *strumień*) brooklet. **2.** (= *potok, struga*) trickle; krew ściekała mu strumykiem po twarzy blood trickled down his face.

struna *f.* string; przeciągać strunę stretch one's luck, overstep the mark; uderzyć w czyjąś czułą strunę strike a deep chord with sb, touch *l.* hit *l.* strike a raw nerve with sb; wyprostować się jak struna stand as stiff as a poker; struny głosowe *anat.* vocal cords *l.* folds; struna grzbietowa *zool.* notochord.

strunnik *mi Gen.* -a *muz.* tailpiece.

strunowiec *ma* -wc- *zool.* chordate (*Chordata*).

strunowy *a.* **1.** *zool.* chordal. **2.** *muz.* stringed; instrumenty strunowe stringed instruments, the strings.

strup *mi Gen.* -a scab, crust.

strupek *mi* -pk- *Gen.* -a scab, crust.

strupieszałość *f.* decrepitude, decay.

strupieszały *a.* decrepit, decayed.

strusi *a.* ostrich's; strusia ferma ostrich farm; strusia polityka *przen.* ostrich policy; mieć strusi żołądek have a stomach made of lead.

strusie *pl. Gen.* -i *orn.* ratites (*Struthioniformes*).

strusiowaty *a.* struthious.

struś *ma orn.* ostrich (*Struthio camelus*); Struś Pędziwiatr (*postać z kreskówki*) Roadrunner.

struty *a.* (= *zatruty*) poisoned; chodzić jak struty be disheartened.

strużka[1] *f. Gen.pl.* -ek (= *strumień*) trickle.

strużka[2] *f. Gen.pl.* -ek *techn.* shavings.

strużyny *pl. Gen.pl.* -n shavings.

strwonić *pf.* waste; (*pieniądze*) squander; **strwonić życie** waste one's life.

strwożony *a.* -eni *lit.* affrightened.

strwożyć *pf.* -óż *lit.* affright. ~ **się** *pf.* -óż *lit.* take fright.

strych *mi* attic, loft.

strycharstwo *n. przest.* brickmaking.

strycharz *mp przest.* brickmaker.

strychnina *f.* strychnine.

strychulec *mi* -lc- *Gen.* -a **1.** (*deszczułka*) strickle, strike. **2.** *jeźdz.* leather *l.* rubber strap used as padding for a horse's pastern.

stryczek *mi* -czk- *Gen.* -a **1.** (*sznur*) halter, noose, the rope. **2.** *pot.* (*kara*) halter, the noose, the rope; **zadyndać na stryczku** dance on air; **skazać kogoś na stryczek** sentence sb to the gallows; **to mi pachnie stryczkiem** it looks like a hanging matter to me.

stryj *mp pl.* -owie *Gen.* -ów (paternal) uncle.

stryjeczny *a.* **babka stryjeczna** great-aunt *l.* grandaunt; **dziadek stryjeczny** great-uncle *l.* granduncle; **brat stryjeczny** first cousin, cousin-german, full cousin; **siostra stryjeczna** first cousin, cousin-german, full cousin.

stryjek *mp* -jk- *pl.* -owie *emf.* (paternal) uncle; **zamienił stryjek siekierkę na kijek** sb made a losing bargain; (*jako powiedzenie*) the cure is worse than the evil.

stryjenka *f. Gen.pl.* -ek (paternal) uncle's wife.

stryjostwo *n.* (paternal) uncle and his wife.

stryjowski *a.* avuncular.

stryszek *mi* -szk- *Gen.* -u *l.* -a cockloft, garret.

strywializować *pf.* **1.** (= *zbanalizować*) trivialize. **2.** (= *uczynić wulgarnym*) vulgarize, debase.

strzał *mi* **1.** (*z broni*) shot; (*z broni palnej*) gunshot; **celny strzał** hit; **chybiony strzał** miss; **broń gotowa do strzału** weapon ready to fire; **zabić jednym strzałem** kill with one shot; **ślepy strzał** blank shot; **ostry strzał** live shot; **strzał w ciemno** a shot in the dark; **podejść kogoś/coś na strzał** come within the shooting distance of sb/sth; **poza zasięgiem strzału** out of shooting distance; **oddać strzał** fire a shot; **oddać coś bez strzału** (*fortecę, twierdzę, miasto przeciwnikowi*) surrender sth without one shot being fired; **strzał w dziesiątkę** bull's eye. **2.** *górn.* shot. **3.** *sport* shot; (*w piłce nożnej, rugby*) kick; **strzał do bramki** shot on goal; **strzał samobójczy** own goal; **oddać strzał** take a shot; **niezły strzał!** good shot! **4.** (= *wybuch spalin l. paliwa w silniku*) backfire. **5.** *sl.* (= *porcja alkoholu*) shot. **6.** *sl.* (= *wstrzyknięcie narkotyku*) shot, fix.

strzała *f.* **1.** (*do łuku*) arrow; (*do kuszy*) quarrel; **zatruta strzała** poison *l.* poisoned arrow; **strzała Amora** Cupid's arrow; **prosty jak strzała** straight as an arrow; **pędzić jak strzała** whizz by; **wystrzelić strzałę** shoot an arrow. **2.** *leśn.* spire-shaped tree-trunk (*e.g. of a pine*).

strzałka *f. Gen.pl.* -ek **1.** (*znak graficzny*) arrow; *komp.* pointer; (*na jezdni*) lane arrow; **iść za strzałkami** follow the arrows; **strzałka wodna** *bot.* arrowhead (*Sagittaria sagittifolia*). **2.** (*wskaźnik*) pointer. **3.** (*na głowie konia*) blaze.

4. (*na kopycie konia*) frog. **5.** *anat.* fibula. **6.** *mot.* (*dla skręcających*) green arrow signal; *Br.* filter. **7.** *pl. bot.* sagittoideans (*Sagittoidea*). **8.** (*gra*) darts; **grać w strzałki** *l.* rzutki play darts. **9.** (*pocisk*) dart.

strzałkowaty *a. bot.* sagittate, sagittiform.

strzałkowy *a. anat.* fibular, peroneal; **kość strzałkowa** fibula; **mięsień strzałkowy** peroneus longus, long peroneus.

strzałowy *a.* **1.** *górn.* blasting, shot; **górnik strzałowy** shot-firer; **otwór strzałowy** shot hole. **2.** *sport* shooting; **pozycja strzałowa** shooting position. – *mp górn.* shot-firer.

strzaskać *pf.* shatter; **strzaskać na kawałki** shatter to pieces; **strzaskać w drobny mak** shatter to smithereens. ~ **się** *pf.* shatter, get shattered; **strzaskać się na kawałki** shatter to pieces, get shattered to pieces; **strzaskać się w drobny mak** shatter to smithereens, get shattered to smithereens.

strząsać *ipf.*, **strząsnąć** *pf.* -snę -śniesz, -śnij shake off, flick off *l.* away; **strząsać gruszki z drzewa** shake pears from a tree; **strząsać popiół z papierosa** flick the ash off one's cigarette.

strzebla *f. icht.* minnow (*Phoxinus*).

strzec *ipf.* **strzegę strzeżesz strzegł 1.** (= *pilnować*) guard (*kogoś / czegoś przed kimś / czymś* sb/ sth against sb/sth); be on one's guard (*kogoś / czegoś* over sb/sth); keep watch (*z kimś / czymś* with sb/sth); **strzec tajemnicy** keep a secret; **strzec kogoś/czegoś jak oka w głowie** keep *l.* guard sb/sth like the apple of one's eye, look after sb/sth like it was your own; **strzeżonego Pan Bóg strzeże** forewarned is forearmed, an ounce of prevention is worth a pound of cure. **2.** (= *opiekować się*) protect (*kogoś / czegoś* sb/sth). ~ **się** *ipf.* **1.** (= *mieć się na baczności*) beware (*kogoś / czegoś* of sb/sth); **strzeż się pociągu!** beware of the train! **2.** (= *unikać*) keep away (*kogoś / czegoś* from sb/sth).

strzecha *f.* thatch, thatched roof; **dom kryty strzechą** thatched cottage; **strzecha włosów** shock (of hair).

strzelać *ipf.* **1.** (*z broni*) shoot, fire (*do kogoś / czegoś* at sb/sth); **strzelać z działa** fire a cannon; **strzelać z łuku** shoot a bow; **strzelać z pistoletu/ karabinu** fire a gun; **strzelać z procy** catapult; **strzelać w powietrze** shoot in the air; **strzelać na wiwat** fire a salute; **strzelić sobie/komuś w łeb** blow one's/sb's brains out; **strzelać oczami** give sb the glad eye; **prosto jak strzelił** straight ahead, as the crow flies; **co ci strzeliło do głowy** *l.* **łba?** *pot.* what came over you?; **strzelić byka** *l.* **głupstwo** *pot.* drop a brick; **strzelić sobie** *sl.* (= *napić się alkoholu*) have a shot (*of an alcoholic drink*); **strzelić sobie działkę** *sl.* (= *wstrzyknąć narkotyk*) shoot up; **człowiek strzela, pan Bóg kule nosi** man proposes, God disposes. **2.** (= *trzaskać*) crack; **strzelać z bata** crack one's whip; **strzelać obcasami** click one's heels; **strzelać palcami** snap one's fingers; **tłuszcz strzela na patelni** the fat is sizzling in the pan; (**coś minęło) jak z bicza strzelił** *l.* **trzasł** sth was over in a flash; **jakby go piorun strzelił** he was flabbergasted; **strze-**

lić kogoś w twarz (*pięścią*) punch sb in the face; (*otwartą dłonią*) slap sb in the face; **strzelają korki od szampana** champagne bottles are being popped open. **3.** (= *sięgać wysoko; wyrastać*) shoot up. **4.** *górn.* fire. **5.** *sport* shoot; **strzelić bramkę** score a goal. **6.** *myśl.* shoot (*game*); go shooting *l.* hunting; **strzelać ptactwo** (*w locie*) flight fowl. **7.** (*o paliwie, spalinach*) backfire. ~ **się** *ipf.* **1.** (*do siebie*) shoot o.s. **2.** (= *pojedynkować się*) duel with pistols.

strzelanie *n.* shooting, firing; **ostre strzelanie** *wojsk.* live fire training; **ćwiczenia w strzelaniu** target practice; **strzelanie do rzutków** *sport* trap-shooting, clay pigeon shooting.

strzelanina *f.* fusillade; (*między dwiema osobami*) gunfight; (*zwł. między przestępcami*) gunplay.

strzelba *f.* shotgun.

strzelczyk *ma icht.* archerfish (*Toxotes jaculator*).

Strzelec *mp* -lc- *pl.* -y *astrol.* Sagittarius; **urodzić się pod znakiem Strzelca** be born under Sagittarius; **osoba urodzona pod znakiem Strzelca** Sagittarius *l.* Sagittarian.

strzelec *mp* -lc- *pl.* -y **1.** (= *ten, kto strzela*) shooter, rifleman; **wolny strzelec** freelancer. **2.** (*żołnierz*) rifleman; **strzelec wyborowy** marksman, deadeye; **oddział strzelców** rifles; **strzelec pokładowy** aerial *l.* air gunner. **3.** *hist.* (= *szeregowiec*) private; **starszy strzelec** private first class; *Br.* lance corporal. **4.** (*sportowiec*) shooter; (*rzutów karnych*) kicker. **5.** *sport* (*bramki*) scorer.

strzelecki *a.* shooting; **broń strzelecka** shotguns (*esp. sports shotguns treated collectively*); **dół strzelecki** *wojsk.* rifle pit; **klub** *l.* **związek strzelecki** rifle club *l.* association; **oddział strzelecki** *wojsk.* rifles; **rów strzelecki** *wojsk.* fire trench; **umiejętności strzeleckie** marksmanship; **wieżyczka strzelecka** *wojsk.* gun turret.

strzelectwo *n.* the art of shooting, shooting; **strzelectwo sportowe** rifle shooting.

strzelić *pf. zob.* **strzelać; strzelić głupstwo** put one's foot in it.

strzelistość *f.* slenderness, steeple-shapedness (*e.g. of a Gothic building*).

strzelisty *a.* tapering, spiry, aerial.

strzeliście *adv.* in a spiry manner; **wznosić się strzeliście** (*np. o wzgórzu, budowli*) spire up.

strzelnica *f.* **1.** (*na wolnym powietrzu*) target range, shooting range, rifle range, butts; (*w pomieszczeniu, w wesołym miasteczku*) shooting gallery. **2.** (= *otwór strzelniczy*) embrasure; (*w blankach*) crenel, crenelle.

strzelniczy *a.* shooting; **bawełna strzelnicza** *chem.* guncotton; **proch strzelniczy** gunpowder; **otwór strzelniczy** (*w murze*) porthole; **tarcza strzelnicza** target, butt.

strzemiączko *n. Gen.pl.* -czek **1.** (*przy spodniach*) strap. **2.** *anat.* stirrup. **3.** *ogr.* hoe. **4.** *roln.* (*część pługa*) bridle.

strzemienne *n. Gen.* -ego one for the road; (*przed wsiadaniem na konia*) stirrup cup; **wypić strzemiennego** have one for the road.

strzemię *n.* -mieni- *pl.* -mion- **1.** *jeźdz.* stirrup. **2.** *techn.* (*uchwyt*) shackle, stirrup, clevis.

strzepnąć *pf.* -nij, -nął -nęła -nęli, **strzepywać** *ipf.* **1.** (= *strząsnąć*) shake off; (*popiół*) flick off; **strzepnąć popiół z papierosa** flick the ash off one's cigarette. **2.** (= *zatrzepotać*) shake; **strzepnąć skrzydła** (*o ptaku*) flutter, flap the wings; **strzepnąć termometr** shake the thermometer.

strzeżony *a.* guarded, protected; **parking strzeżony** attented parking lot; *Br.* attented car park; **dobrze strzeżony** well-guarded; **strzeżonego Pan Bóg strzeże** forewarned is forearmed, an ounce of prevention is worth a pound of cure.

strzęp *mi* scrap, shred; **podrzeć coś na strzępy** tear to shreds *l.* pieces; **rozerwać kogoś na strzępy** tear sb limb to limb; **został z niego strzęp człowieka** he's a shadow of his former self, he's a wreck of a man; **w strzępach** in rags, in tatters; **strzępy rozmowy** snatches of conversation.

strzępek *mi* -pk- *Gen.* -a **1.** (= *strzęp*) scrap, shred. **2.** *bot.* slime mold (*Arcyria*).

strzępiasty *a.* (= *o nierównych brzegach*) jagged, ragged; (*o liściu*) lacerate; (*o chmurze*) fringed, jagged.

strzępić *ipf.* (= *robić strzępy*) fray; (= *wydzierać*) shred; (= *wyskubywać*) jag, pick; **strzępić sobie język** *l.* **jęzor** *pot.* waste one's breath; **szkoda sobie języka strzępić** (= *daj spokój, nie ma sensu o tym mówić*) save your breath. ~ **się** *ipf.* (= *przecierać się*) tatter, fray; (= *dzielić się na włókna*) (*o tkaninie*) unravel.

strzępka *f. Gen.pl.* -ek *bot.* hypha.

strzępkowy *a. bot.* hyphal.

strzyc *ipf.* **strzygę strzyżesz strzygł** (*człowieka*) cut sb's hair, barber; (*owcę*) shear, fleece; (*krzewy*) trim, prune; (*trawę*) mow; **strzyc uszami** (*o zwierzęciu*) prick its ears. ~ **się** *ipf.* have one's hair cut; **strzyc się raz na miesiąc** have one's hair cut once a month; **strzyc się na jeża** have *l.* get a crew cut; **strzyc się na krótko** have *l.* get one's hair cropped *l.* cut short.

strzyga *f.* lamia, vampire (*in folk beliefs, a soul of a child assuming different forms as a demon*).

strzygadło *n. roln.* shears, shearer.

strzygonia *f. ent.* pine beauty moth (*Panolis flamea*).

strzyk *mi zootechnika* teat.

strzykać *ipf.* **1.** (= *tryskać*) spurt, squirt. **2.** (*o bólu*) twinge, crick; **strzyknęło go w karku/plecach** he felt a crick in his neck/back.

strzykawka *f. Gen.pl.* -ek syringe; **strzykawka (do) jednorazowego użytku** disposable syringe.

strzyknąć *pf.* -ij *zob.* **strzykać.**

strzykwa *f. zool.* (= *szkarłupień z rzędu Holothuroidea*) holothurian.

strzyża *f. roln.* **1.** (*strzyżenie*) shearing, fleecing. **2.** (*wełna*) fleece. **3.** (= *ilość wełny nastrzyżonej w danym miejscu l. okresie*) clip. **4.** (*okres*) shearing season, fleecing season.

strzyżenie *n.* (*człowieka*) cutting, haircut; (*owiec*) shearing, fleecing; (*trawnika*) mowing.

strzyżyk *ma orn.* wren (*Troglodytidae*); **strzy-**

żyk woleoczko winter wren (*Troglodytes troglodytes*).

stu *itd. num. zob.* **sto.**

stubarwny *a.* multicolored.

studencki *a.* students', student; **legitymacja studencka** student ID card; **dom studencki** dormitory; *Br.* hall of residence; **klub studencki** student union; **życie studenckie** student life.

student *mp uniw.* student; (*przed otrzymaniem tytułu licencjata*) undergraduate; (*na uzupełniających studiach magisterskich*) graduate student; (*specjalizujący się w jakimś kierunku*) major; **student pierwszego roku** first year student, fresher, freshman; **student drugiego roku** second year student, sophomore; **student trzeciego roku** third year student, junior; **student prawa/medycyny** law/medical student; **wieczny student** *żart.* eternal student.

studenteria *f. Gen.* **-ii** *żart.* studentfolk.

studentka *f. Gen.pl.* **-ek** *zob.* **student.**

studia *pl. Gen.* **-ów 1.** *uniw.* studies; **studia dzienne** full-time studies; **studia zaoczne** part-time studies, extramural studies; **studia eksternistyczne** auditing students' academic program; **studia wieczorowe** evening studies (program); **iść na studia** (*licencjackie l. trzyletnie*) go to college; (*magisterskie l. pięcioletnie*) go to university; **skończyć studia** graduate. **2.** (*badania*) research.

studialny *a.* study, research; **etap studialny** research stage.

studio *n. Gen.pl.* **-ów 1.** studio; **studio filmowe** film studio; **studio radiowe** (broadcasting) studio; **studio nagrań** recording studio; **studio telewizyjne** (broadcasting) studio. **2.** (= *pracownia artysty*) studio, atelier.

studiować *ipf.* **1.** (= *badać; uczyć się*) study; *Br. rzad.* read; **studiować prawo** read law; **studiować na uniwersytecie** study at university. **2.** (= *czytać*) peruse. **3.** (= *zapoznawać się*) study; **studiować mapę** study a map.

studium *n. sing. indecl. pl.* **-dia** *Gen.* **-diów 1.** (*rozprawa*) study (*czegoś* of *l.* into sth). **2.** (*szkoła*) college; **studium pedagogiczne** teacher(s') training college. **3.** (*dział szkoły wyższej*) department; **studium języków obcych** foreign languages department. **4.** *sztuka* study.

studnia *f. Gen.pl.* **-i** *l.* **-dzien 1.** (*z wodą*) well; **studnia abisyńska** driven well; **studnia artezyjska** artesian well; **wykopać studnię** sink *l.* dig a well; **studnia bez dna** *przen.* black hole (*sth insatiable*); **czuć się** *l.* **użyć jak pies w studni** be in trouble; **lać w siebie jak w studnię** drink like there's no tomorrow, drink like prohibition is coming back. **2.** *lotn., meteor.* air pocket.

studniarz *mp* well sinker.

studniówka *f. Gen.pl.* **-ek** *szkoln.* pre-graduation ball (*a traditional party organized for high school students a hundred days before the final exams*).

studyjny *a.* studio; **teatr studyjny** studio theater; **nagranie studyjne** studio recording.

studzić *ipf.* cool down *l.* off; **studzić czyjś zapał** damp one's ardor. **~ się** *ipf.* cool down *l.* off.

studzienka *f. Gen.pl.* **-ek 1.** (= *mała studnia*) well; **studzienka przeciwpożarowa** pit hydrant. **2.** *bud.* manhole; **studzienka rewizyjna** inspection chamber; **studzienka ściekowa** drain.

studzienny *a.* well; **pompa studzienna** well pump.

stugębny *a.* **stugębna plotka/wieść** rumor/news spread *l.* repeated by many people.

stugłowy *a.* with a hundred heads.

stugramowy *a.* hundred gram.

stuhektarowy *a.* hundred hectare.

stuk¹ *mi* (= *stukanie*) clatter; (= *stuknięcie*) rap, knock.

stuk² *int.* knock; **stuk-puk** *l.* **stuk-stuk** rat-tat, ratatat.

stukać *ipf.* **1.** (= *uderzać*) knock; **stukać do drzwi** knock on *l.* at the door; (= *kołatać*) clatter; **stukać na maszynie** clatter (away) at the typewriter; **stukać palcem w czoło** tap one's forehead with disgust, roll one's eyes; **stuknęła mi pięćdziesiątka** I'm past the magic fifty. **2.** (*o silniku*) knock, pink. **~ się** *ipf.* **1.** (= *uderzać się*) hit o.s.; **stuknąć się w kolano** hit one's knee; **stuknij się (w czoło)!** get wise! **2.** (= *uderzać jeden drugiego*) knock (against) each other *l.* one another; **stukać się kieliszkami/szklankami** clink glasses.

stukaratowy *a.* hundred carat.

stukartkowy *a.* of one hundred sheets *l.* pages.

stukilometrowy *a.* hundred kilometer; *Br.* hundred kilometre.

stuknąć *pf.* **-ij 1.** *zob.* **stukać. 2.** *pot.* (= *walnąć*) hit, bump into. **3.** *pot.* (= *zastrzelić*) bump off, knock off. **~ się** *pf.* **-ij 1.** *zob.* **stukać się. 2.** *pot.* (= *zderzyć się*) run into each other *l.* one another; (*o samochodach*) bump into each other *l.* one another.

stuknięty *a.* **1.** (= *uderzony*) bumped. **2.** (= *nienormalny*) bonkers, dotty, nutty, nuts.

stukonny *a. techn.* one hundred HP *l.* h.p.

stukot *mi* clatter, patter.

stukotać *ipf.* **-oczę** *l.* **-ocę -oczesz** *l.* **-ocesz, -ocz** clatter, patter.

stulać *ipf.* (= *zamknąć*) close up; (= *zewrzeć*) press tightly together; **stulić ogon** *t. przen.* put one's tail between one's legs; **stulić uszy** draw one's horns; **stul gębę!** *pot.* shut your trap! **~ się** *ipf.* close up.

stulatek *mp* **-tk-** *pl.* **-i** (*mężczyzna*) centenarian. **— ma -tk-** (*zwierzę*) a centenary animal. **— mi -tk-** *Gen.* **-a** (*roślina*) a centenary plant.

stulatka *f. Gen.pl.* **-ek** *zob.* **stulatek.**

stulecie *n. Gen.pl.* **-i 1.** (= *wiek*) century. **2.** (*rocznica*) centenary, centennial.

stulejka *f. pat.* phimosis.

stuletni *a.* centenarian, centenary, centennial; **wojna stuletnia** *hist.* Hundred Years' War (*1337-1453*).

stulić *pf. zob.* **stulać. ~ się** *pf. zob.* **stulać się.**

stulitrowy *a.* hundred liter; *Br.* hundred litre.

stuła *f. rel.* stole.

stułbia *f. Gen.pl.* **-i** *zool.* hydra (*Hydra*).

stułbiopław *ma zool.* hydrozoan (*Hydrozoa*).

stumanieć *pf. pot.* become a moron; **zupełnie**

stumaniał w tej szkole he became a complete moron in this school.

stumarkowy *a.* (= *o wartości stu marek jako waluty niektórych krajów*) hundred mark.

stumetrowy *a.* hundred meter; *Br.* hundred metre.

stupor *mi psych.* stupor.

stuprocentowy *a.* **1.** (= *czysty, bez domieszki*) (*wełna, frekwencja*) one hundred per cent; pure. **2.** (= *całkowity, kompletny*) complete; **stuprocentowe zaufanie** complete confidence; **stuprocentowy mężczyzna** complete man.

stutonowy *a.* a hundred ton.

stutysięczny *a.* (*w kolejności*) one hundred thousandth; (= *liczący sto tysięcy*) (*o armii, nakładzie*) one hundred thousand; **stutysięczne miasto** town of one hundred thousand inhabitants.

stuzłotowy *a.* hundred zloty; **banknot stuzłotowy** a hundred zloty bill; *Br.* a hundred zloty note.

stuzłotówka *f. Gen.pl.* **-ek** (*banknot*) a hundred zloty bill; *Br.* a hundred zloty note; (*moneta*) a hundred zloty coin.

stwardnieć *pf.* (*o rękach, ziemi, charakterze, spółgłosce*) harden.

stwardnienie *n. t. jęz.* hardening; *pat.* callus, callosity; **stwardnienie rozsiane** multiple sclerosis; **stwardnienie tętnic** hardening of the arteries, arteriosclerosis.

stwarzać *ipf.* create; (*warunki, możliwości*) offer; **stwarzać pozory czegoś** (*o osobie*) (= *udawać coś*) put on a show of sth; (*o rzeczy*) (= *wyglądać jak coś*) look like sth; **takim go Pan Bóg stworzył** God created him this way; **jak go Pan Bóg stworzył** in his birthday suit. ~ **się** *ipf.* be created, be in the making.

stwierdzać *ipf.* (*uznać*) affirm, ascertain; (*mówić*) state, note; **stwierdzać autentyczność/tożsamość** establish authenticity/identity; **lekarz stwierdził zgon** doctor pronounced him *l.* her dead; **stwierdziłem, że...** I satisfied myself that...

stwierdzenie *n.* (*wypowiedź*) statement; (*poświadczenie*) assertion.

stwierdzić *pf. zob.* **stwierdzać**.

stworek *ma* **-rk-** little creature.

stworzenie *n.* **1.** (*istota*) creature; **wyglądać jak nieboskie stworzenie** look slovenly; **wyglądasz jak nieboskie stworzenie!** just look at you! **2.** (*czynność*) creation, formation; **od stworzenia świata** since the beginning of the world.

stworzonko *n.* little creature.

stworzony *a.* **-eni** created; **być stworzonym dla kogoś** be meant for sb; **być stworzonym do czegoś** (*np. do jakiejś pracy*) be cut out for sth.

stworzyć *pf.* **stwórz** *zob.* **stwarzać**. ~ **się** *pf.* come into being.

stwór *ma* **-o-** (*istota*) creature; (*potwór*) monster.

Stwórca *mp rel.* the Creator.

stwórczy *a.* creative; **akt stwórczy** act of creation; **siła stwórcza** creative power.

styczeń *mi* **-czni-** *Gen.* **-a** *Gen.pl.* **-ów** January; **do końca stycznia** till the end of January; **przed**

pierwszym stycznia by January the first, before the first of January.

styczna *f. Gen.* **-ej** *geom.* tangent.

stycznie *adv.* contiguously.

stycznik *mi Gen.* **-a** *el.* contactor.

styczniowy *a.* January.

styczność *f.* **1.** (= *kontakt*) contact; **mieć styczność z kimś/czymś** be in contact with sb/sth, be in touch with sb/sth. **2.** *geom.* tangency; **punkt styczności** point of contact.

styczny *a. geom.* tangent; **punkt styczny** *przen.* sth in common.

stygmat *mi lit., rel.* stigma.

stygmatyczka *f. Gen.pl.* **-ek**, **stygmatyk** *mp rel.* stigmatic, stigmatist.

stygmatyzm *mi rel.* stigmatism.

stygnąć *ipf.* **-ij** cool down; **krew stygnie komuś w żyłach** (*z przerażenia*) blood freezes in sb's veins.

styk *mi* **1.** (= *przyleganie*) adjacency; (*np. ściany z sufitem*) point of contact; **na styku dwóch linii** at the meeting point of two lines; **łączyć coś z czymś na styk** butt sth against sth. **2.** (= *kontakt*) contact; **na styku dwóch kultur** where two cultures meet, at the meeting point of two cultures. **3.** *el.* (*połączenie*) (*przewód*) contact.

stykać *ipf.* (*np. przewody*) connect; **stykać kogoś z kimś** put sb in touch *l.* contact with sb; **po wojnie los ich znowu zetknął** after the war fate joined them again. ~ **się** *ipf.* **1.** (= *dotykać się*) touch (*z czymś* sth). **2.** (= *przylegać*) adjoin (*z czymś* sth). **3.** (= *spotykać się*) encounter (*z kimś / czymś* sb/sth).

stykowy *a.* contact; **zdjęcie stykowe** *fot.* contact print.

Styks *mi mit.* the Styx.

styksowy *a. mit.* Stygian.

styl *mi Gen.pl.* **-ów** **1.** (*mówienia, pisania, w muzyce, malarstwie*) style; **styl artystyczny** artistic style; **styl literacki** literary style; **styl mówiony** spoken style, conversational style; **styl naukowy** scientific style; **styl pisany** written style; **styl potoczny** colloquial style; **styl publicystyczny** journalistic style; **styl telegraficzny** telegraphese; **styl urzędowy** official style. **2.** *sztuka* style; **styl barokowy/renesansowy** baroque/Renaissance style. **3.** (*zachowania się*) style; **styl bycia** conduct; **styl życia/pracy/ubierania się** life/work/dress style; **to nie w twoim stylu** it's not like you, it's unlike you; **zwyciężyć w pięknym stylu** win in great style. **4.** *sport* (*np. pływacki, tenisowy*) stroke; (*np. skoków narciarskich*) style; **styl wolny** free style; **styl klasyczny** breast stroke; **styl grzbietowy** backstroke; **styl motylkowy** butterfly stroke. **5.** (*kalendarz*) style; **25 grudnia według nowego/starego stylu** 25th of December according to the New/Old Style. **6.** *hist.* stylus.

stylisko *n.* handle.

stylista *mp*, **stylistka** *f. Gen.pl.* **-ek** (*pisarz*) (*projektant*) (*mody, samochodów itd.*) stylist.

stylistycznie *adv.* stylistically.

stylistyczny *a.* stylistic; **analiza stylistyczna** stylistic analysis; **błąd stylistyczny** stylistic error; **figura stylistyczna** figure of speech; **wariant stylistyczny** stylistic variant; **redaktor stylistyczny** style editor.

stylistyka *f.* **1.** (= *badania nad stylem*) stylistics. **2.** (= *styl*) (*np. dzieła literackiego*) style.

stylita *mp hist.* stylite.

stylizacja *f.* stylization; **stylizacja wnętrz** interior decoration.

stylizacyjny *a.* stylization.

stylizować *ipf.* **1.** (= *nadawać cechy jakiegoś stylu*) stylize; **stylizować tekst na coś** adapt a text to a certain style. **2.** (= *formułować*) formulate. ~ **się** *ipf.* pose (*na kogoś* as sb).

stylowo *adv.* as regards style; (*ubierać się*) stylishly.

stylowość *f.* **1.** (= *styl*) style. **2.** (= *cechy stylu*) conformance to a style.

stylowy *a.* **1.** (= *stylistyczny*) (*niezgodność, różnorodność*) of style, stylistic. **2.** (= *mający cechy stylu*) (*budynek, uczesanie*) in (a given) style. **3.** (= *estetyczny*) (*uczesanie, ubranie, budynek, ubiór*) stylish. **4.** (= *właściwy pewnemu okresowi w sztuce, literaturze*) (*kostiumy, meble, budynki*) period.

stymulacja *f.* stimulation.

stymulacyjny *a.* stimulation; **czynnik stymulacyjny** stimulating factor.

stymulator *mi Gen.* **-a** **1.** (*bodziec*) (*np. wzrostu roślin*) stimulator; **stymulator wzrostu** *biol.* growth stimulator. **2.** (*rozwoju, wzrostu gospodarczego*) stimulus. **3.** (*służący do wytwarzania bodźców, np. w celach badawczych*) stimulus. **4.** *med.* (*pobudzający organ*) stimulant.

stymulować *ipf.* (*wzrost, pracę mózgu, rozwój gospodarczy*) stimulate.

stynka *f. icht.* smelt (*Osmerus eperlanus*).

stypa *f.* funeral banquet; *lr.* wake.

stypendialny *a.* scholarship.

stypendium *n. sing. indecl. pl.* **-dia** *Gen.* **-diów** **1.** (*pieniądze*) scholarship. **2.** (*pobyt*) (*w trakcie studiów*) study period; (*w ramach badań naukowych*) research visit.

stypendysta *mp,* **stypendystka** *f. Gen.pl.* **-ek** **1.** (= *otrzymujący stypendium*) scholarship holder. **2.** (= *przebywający na stypendium*) (*student*) visiting student; (*naukowiec*) visiting researcher.

styrakowcowate *pl. Gen.* **-ych** *bot.* Styracaceae (*Styracaceae*).

styrakowcowaty *a. bot.* styracaceous.

styrakowiec *mi* **-wc-** *Gen.* **-a** *bot.* styrax (*Styrax*).

styranizować *pf.* tyrannize.

styren *mi chem.* styrene.

styropian *mi techn.* polystyrene foam, Styrofoam®.

styropianowy *a.* polystyrene foam, Styrofoam®.

suahili *n. indecl. jęz.* Swahili.

subantarktyczny *a. geogr.* subantarctic, subpolar.

subarktyczny *a. geogr.* subarctic, subpolar.

subdiakon *mp rel.* subdeacon.

subdominanta *f. muz.* subdominant.

subendemiczny *a. bot., zool.* subendemic.

subglacjalny *a. geol.* subglacial.

subiekt *mi Gen.* **-u** *pl.* **-y** *jęz.* subject. – *mp Gen.* **-a** *pl.* **-ci** salesclerk; *Br.* shop assistant.

subiektywista *mp* subjectivist.

subiektywistyczny *a.* subjectivistic.

subiektywizm *mi* **1.** (= *stronniczość*) subjectivity, subjectiveness; partiality. **2.** *fil.* subjectivism.

subiektywnie *adv.* subjectively.

subiektywność *f.* subjectivity, subjectiveness.

subiektywny *a. t. fil.* subjective.

subkonto *n. fin.* subaccount.

subkontynent *mi geogr.* subcontinent.

subkultura *f. socjol.* subculture.

sublimacja *f. chem., fiz., psych.* sublimation.

sublimat *mi chem.* sublimate, mercury chloride.

sublimować *ipf.* **1.** *chem., fiz.* sublime. **2.** *psych.* sublimate, sublime.

sublokator *mp pl.* **-rzy** *l.* **-owie,** **sublokatorka** *f. Gen.pl.* **-ek** subtenant.

sublokatorski *a.* subtenant.

submikron *mi fiz.* submicron.

subnordyczny *a. antrop.* sub-Nordic.

subordynacja *f.* discipline.

subregion *mi geogr.* subregion.

subskrybent *mp* subscriber.

subskrybować *ipf.* subscribe (*coś* to sth).

subskrypcja *f.* subscription (*na coś* to sth).

subskrypcyjny *a.* subscription; **talon subskrypcyjny** subscription coupon.

substancja *f.* **1.** *chem., fiz.* substance; **substancja stała** solid substance; **substancja płynna** fluid substance; **substancja gazowa** gaseous substance; **substancja prosta** simple substance; **substancja złożona** compound substance; **substancja białkowa** protein substance; **substancja tłuszczowa** fatty substance; **substancja odżywcza** nutrient; **substancja pokarmowa** nutritious substance; **substancja biała** *anat.* white matter; **substancja szara** *anat.* gray matter; *Br.* grey matter. **2.** *fil., prawn.* substance.

substancjalizm *mi fil., psych.* substantialism.

substantywizacja *f. jęz.* substantivization.

substrat *mi* **1.** *lit.* (= *podstawa*) *fil.* substratum. **2.** *chem.* substrate.

substytucja *f. lit.* (= *zastąpienie*) *jęz., prawn.* substitution.

substytuować *ipf. lit.* (= *zastępować*), *prawn.* substitute.

substytut *mi Gen.* **-u** *pl.* **-y** substitute. – *mp Gen.* **-a** *pl.* **-owie** *prawn.* substitute.

subsydiować *ipf.* subsidize.

subsydium *n. sing. indecl. pl.* **-dia** *Gen.* **-diów** subsidy.

subtelnie *adv.* subtly.

subtelnieć *ipf.* become subtle.

subtelność *f.* **1.** (= *delikatność*) (*człowieka*) delicacy; (*zachowania*) refinement; (*rysów*) subtlety. **2.** (*zapachu, dźwięku; analizy, umysłu; żartu, uwagi*) subtlety. **3.** (*sprawy*) (= *drażliwość*) touchiness.

subtelny *a.* **1.** (*zachowanie, człowiek*) (= *delikatny*) delicate; (*rysy*) subtle. **2.** (*zapach,* *dźwięk*) (= *nieznaczny*) subtle; **subtelna różnica** fine distiction. **3.** (*analiza, umysł*) (= *wnikliwy*) subtle. **4.** (*żart, uwaga*) (= *wyszukany*) subtle, refined. **5.** (*sprawa*) (= *drażliwy*) touchy.

subtropikalny *a. geogr.* subtropical.

suburbium *n. sing. indecl. pl.* -**bia** *Gen.* -**biów** suburbs.

subwencja *f.* subsidy, subvention; **udzielić subwencji** grant a subsidy; **otrzymać subwencje** receive a subsidy.

subwencjonować *ipf.* subsidize.

subwencyjny *a.* subventionary.

suchar *mi Gen.* -**a** (*pieczywo*) biscuit.

sucharek *mi* -**rk-** *Gen.* -**a** (*pieczywo*) rusk.

suche *n. Gen.* -**ego** dry; **wytrzeć się do sucha** wipe o.s. dry.

sucho *adv.* dryly, drily; **było sucho i słonecznie** it was dry and sunny; **zrobiło się sucho** it dried up; **jeść na sucho** eat on an empty stomach; **mam sucho w gardle/ustach** my throat/mouth is dry; **powiedzieć coś sucho** say sth dryly; **nie ujdzie ci to na sucho** you won't get away with it!

suchodrzew *mi bot.* fly honeysuckle (*Lonicera xylosteum*).

suchorośle *n. Gen.pl.* -**i** *bot.* xerophyte.

suchoryt *mi sztuka* dry-point engraving.

suchorytniczy *a. sztuka* dry-point.

suchość *f.* dryness; **czuję suchość w gardle/ustach** my throat/mouth is dry.

suchotnica *f.,* **suchotnik** *mp przest.* consumptive.

suchotniczy *a. przest.* consumptive.

suchoty *pl. Gen.* -**t** *pat.* pulmonary consumption; **galopujące suchoty** galloping consumption, pulmonary tuberculosis.

suchy *a.* **1.** (= *niemokry*) dry; **sucha destylacja** *chem.* destructive distillation, dry distillation; **suchy dok** *żegl.* dry dock; **suchy kaszel** dry cough; **suchy lód** *chem.* dry ice; **suchy prowiant** packed lunch; **suchy tynk** *bud.* plasterboard; **sucha sterylizacja** *med.* autoclaving; **sucha zaprawa** *sport* dry training, dry practice; **suchy jak pieprz** *l.* wiór as dry as a bone, bone-dry; **przejść przez coś suchą stopą** walk across sth dry-shod; **siedzieć u kogoś o suchym pysku** be offered neither food nor drink (*while being sb's guest*); **żyć o suchym chlebie** live on dry bread; **zmoknąć do suchej nitki** be dripping *l.* soaking wet; get soaked *l.* drenched to the skin; **nie zostawiłem na nim suchej nitki** I picked him to pieces. **2.** (*klimat, region*) dry. **3.** (*ton, rozmowa, wykład, fakty*) dry. **4.** (= *sttumiony*) muted, muffled. **5.** (= *chudy*) lean, lank; **suchy jak szczapa** as thin as a lath *l.* rake.

suczka *f. Gen.pl.* -**ek** (*zwł. pieszczotliwie*) she dog.

Sudan *mi geogr.* Sudan.

Sudanka *f. Gen.pl.* -**ek, Sudańczyk** *mp* Sudanese.

sudański *a.* Sudanese.

sudecki *a.* Sudeten, Sudetic.

Sudety *pl. Gen.* -**ów** *geogr.* the Sudetes, the Sudeten Mountains.

sueski *a.* Suez; **Kanał Sueski** *geogr.* the Suez Canal.

sufiks *mi gram.* suffix.

sufiksalny *a. gram.* suffixal.

sufit *mi* ceiling.

sufitowy *a.* ceiling.

sufler *mp* prompter; **budka suflera** prompt box.

suflerka *f. Gen.pl.* -**ek 1.** (*kobieta*) *zob.* **sufler. 2.** (*zawód*) prompting.

suflerować *ipf.* prompt, be a prompter.

suflerski *a.* prompter's; **budka suflerska** prompt box.

suflet *mi kulin.* soufflé.

sufragan *mp rel.* suffragan.

sufrażystka *f.* suffragette.

sugerować *ipf.* suggest (*coś komuś* sth to sb); **sugerować, że...** suggest that... **~ się** *ipf.* be influenced (*czymś* by sth).

sugerowany *a.* (*np. o cenie*) recommended.

sugestia *f. Gen.* -**ii** *t. psych.* suggestion; **sugestia zbiorowa** collective suggestion; **przyjąć czyjąś sugestię** accept sb's suggestion; **ulegać sugestii** yield to a suggestion; **wysunąć sugestię** put forward a suggestion.

sugestywnie *adv.* suggestively.

sugestywność *f.* suggestiveness.

sugestywny *a.* suggestive.

suhak *ma zool.* saiga antelope (*Saiga tatarica*).

suita *f. muz.* suite.

suka *f.* **1.** (*pies*) *t. wulg.* (*kobieta*) bitch. **2.** *pot.* (*samochód policyjny*) Black Maria.

sukces *mi* success; **pasmo sukcesów** series of success; **występ uwieńczony sukcesem** successful performance; **odnieść sukces** be a success; **odnosić sukcesy jako** be successful as; **to połowa sukcesu** that's half the battle.

sukcesja *f.* **1.** (*tronu*) succession. **2.** *przest.* (= *spadek*) inheritance.

sukcesor *mp* **1.** (= *następca*) successor; (*tronu*) heir to the throne. **2.** *przest.* (= *spadkobierca*) heir.

sukcesorka *f.* **1.** (= *następczyni*) successor; (*tronu*) heiress to the throne. **2.** *przest.* (= *spadkobierczyni*) heiress.

sukcesyjny *a. hist.* **wojna sukcesyjna** war of succession.

sukcesywnie *adv.* (= *kolejno*) successively; (= *stopniowo*) gradually.

sukcesywny *a.* (= *kolejny*) successive; (= *stopniowy*) gradual.

sukienka *f. Gen.pl.* -**ek** dress; **sukienka do kolan** knee-length dress; **sukienka przed/za kolana** above-/below-the-knee dress; **sukienka z długimi/krótkimi rękawami** long-/short-sleeved dress; **sukienka bez rękawów** sleeveless dress; **lekka/letnia sukienka** light/summer dress.

sukienkowy *a.* dress.

sukiennice *pl. Gen.* -**ic** *hist.* cloth hall.

sukinsyn *mp pl.* -**y** *wulg.* son of a bitch.

sukmana *f. hist.* russet coat (*worn by peasants*).

suknia *f. Gen.pl.* **sukni** *l.* **sukien 1.** (*strój*) dress; **suknia balowa** ball dress; **suknia ciążowa** maternity dress; **suknia ślubna** wedding dress; **suknia wieczorowa** evening *l.* party dress; **suknia wizytowa** dinner dress; **suknia do kostek/kolan** ankle-/knee-length dress; **suknia z długimi/krótkimi rękawami** long-/short-sleeved dress; **suknia bez rękawów** sleeveless dress. **2.** *myśl.* coat.

sukniowy *a.* dress.

sukno *n. Gen.pl.* **sukien** cloth.

sukulent *mi bot.* succulent.

sukurs *mi* succor; *Br.* succour; **przyjść komuś w sukurs** come to sb's aid.

sulfon *mi chem.* sulfone; *Br.* sulphone.

sulfonamid *mi chem.* sulfonamide; *Br.* sulphonamide.

sulfonowy *a. chem.* sulfonic; *Br.* sulphonic.

sulki *pl.* (*pojazd*) sulky.

sułtan *mp pl.* **-owie** *l.* **-i** sultan.

sułtanat *mi* sultanate.

sułtanka *f. Gen.pl.* **-ek 1.** (*kobieta*) sultana, sultaness. **2.** (*winogrono*) sultana.

sułtański *a.* sultan's.

sum *ma icht.* catfish; **sum europejski** European catfish, sheatfish (*Silurus glanis*).

suma *f.* **1.** (*kwota*) amount, sum of money; **bajońskie sumy** mind-boggling sums of money; **grubsza** *l.* **okrągła suma** substantial amount of money; **zainwestować pewną sumę** invest some money. **2.** (*wynik*) sum, total; **suma logiczna** *log.* logical sum; **suma częściowa** *mat.* partial sum. **3.** (*ogół*) whole; **suma doświadczeń** the whole of experiences; **w sumie** *pot.* all things considered, all in all. **4.** *kośc.* High Mass, high mass.

sumaryczny *a.* (= *podsumowujący*) summary; (= *skrócony*) concise.

sumator *mi Gen.* **-a 1.** *komp.* digital adder. **2.** (*kalkulator*) calculator.

sumiasty *a.* **sumiasty wąs** bushy mustache, *Br.* bushy moustache.

sumienie *n.* conscience; **czyste/nieczyste sumienie** clear/guilty conscience; **z czystym sumieniem** with a clear conscience; **rachunek sumienia** *rel.* examination of conscience; **wolność sumienia** freedom *l.* liberty of conscience; **wyrzuty sumienia** remorse; pangs of conscience, qualms of conscience; **brać coś na swoje sumienie** take sth on o.s.; **mieć kogoś/coś na sumieniu** have sb/sth on one's conscience; **uśpić swoje sumienie** hush the voice of one's conscience; **gryzie mnie sumienie** my conscience pricks me; **jesteś bez sumienia** you have no scruples; **sumienie go ruszyło** his conscience spoke up.

sumiennie *adv.* conscientiously.

sumienność *f.* conscientiousness.

sumienny *a.* conscientious.

sumka *f. Gen.pl.* **-ek** sum; **grubsza** *l.* **niezła** *l.* **okrągła sumka** substantial amount of money.

summa *f. hist., teol.* summa.

sumować *ipf.* **1.** (= *dodawać*) add up, sum up, total up. **2.** (= *uogólniać*) summarize. **~ się** *ipf.* add up, sum up.

sumowate *pl. icht.* silurids, catfishes (*Siluridae*).

sumpt *mi* **własnym sumptem** at one's own expense.

sunąć *ipf.* **1.** (*przesuwać się*) glide (*po czymś* over sth). **2.** (*przesuwać*) push, move (*coś po czymś* sth along sth).

Sunna *f. rel.* Sunna.

sunnita *mp rel.* Sunnite, Sunni.

supeł *mi* **-pł-** *Gen.* **-a** knot, tangle; **związać coś na supeł** knot sth.

supełek *mi* **-łk-** *Gen.* **-a** knot, tangle; **związać coś na supełek** knot sth.

super *a. indecl. pot.* super; **super film** excellent movie; **super wakacje** great vacation; *Br.* fantastic holiday; **etylina super** premium gasoline. – *adv. pot.* greatly, wonderfully; **super się bawiłem** I had a great time.

superarbiter *mp* **-tr-** *pl.* **-rzy** *l.* **-owie** *prawn.* umpire.

superata *f. handl.* surplus.

superciężki *a. sport* **waga superciężka** super heavyweight.

superego *n. indecl.* superego.

superekspres *mi* **1.** (*pociąg*) express train. **2.** *handl.* (*tempo*) express.

superekspresowy *a.* express.

superfilm *mi film* superproduction.

superforteca *f. lotn.* superfortress.

superfosfat *mi roln.* superphosphate.

superfosfatowy *a. roln.* superphosphate.

supergigant *mi Gen.* **-a** *narty* super giant slalom.

supergwiazda *f. Dat. i Loc.* **-gwieździe**, **supergwiazdor** *mp* superstar.

superheterodyna *f. el.* superheterodyne receiver, superhet.

superintendent *mp rel.* superintendent.

superlatiwus *mi Gen.* **-wu** *jęz.* superlative.

superlatywy *pl. Gen.pl.* **-ów** **wyrażać się o kimś w samych superlatywach** speak highly of sb.

superman *mp* superman.

supermarket *mi* supermarket.

supermocarstwo *n.* superpower.

supernowoczesny *a.* ultramodern; (*o rozwiązaniach, sprzęcie*) high-tech, state-of-the-art.

superprodukcja *f. kino* superproduction.

superrewizja *f. druk.* revised proof.

supersam *mi* supermarket.

suplement *mi* supplement.

supletywizm *mi jęz.* suppletion.

supletywny *a. jęz.* suppletive.

suplika *f. hist.* supplication.

suplikacja *f. Gen.* **-i** *rel.* supplication.

supłać *ipf.* knot, tangle.

suponować *ipf. lit.* (= *zakładać*) suppose.

suport *mi* **1.** *techn.* (*część obrabiarki*) slide. **2.** (*część roweru*) bottom bracket. **3.** *pot.* (*zespół grający przed głównym występem*) the support.

supozycja *f. lit.* (= *założenie*), *log.* supposition.

supraporta *f. bud.* fronton, frontal.

suprema *f. bud.* insulating board.

supremacja *f.* supremacy.

suprematysta *mp sztuka* suprematist.

suprematyzm *mi sztuka* suprematism.

sura *f. rel.* sura.

surdopedagogika *f.* education of the deaf and dumb.

surdut *mi Gen.* **-a** frock-coat.

surdyna *f. muz.* sordino, sourdine.

surf *mi Gen.* **-a** 1. *sport* water skiing. 2. (*taniec*) surf.

surfing *mi sport* surfing.

surfingowy *a. sport* surfing; **deska surfingowa** surfboard.

surfować *ipf. pot.* (*na desce, po Internecie*) surf; **surfować po sieci/Internecie** surf the Web/ Internet.

surma *f.* trumpet.

surogat *mi* substitute, surrogate.

surojadka *f. Gen.pl.* **-ek** *bot.* russula (*Russula*).

surowcowy *a.* raw material; **zasoby surowcowe** raw material resources.

surowica *f.* 1. (*osocze*) blood serum, serum. 2. (*preparat*) serum.

surowiczy *a.* serous, serumal; **płyn surowiczy** serous fluid.

surowiec *mi* **-wc-** *Gen.* **-a** raw material; **surowce** (*do produkcji*) raw materials; (= *zasoby*) resources; **surowce energetyczne** energy resources; **surowce mineralne** mineral resources; **surowce naturalne** natural resources; **surowce wtórne** recyclable materials.

surowizna *f. pot.* (*warzywa*) raw vegetables; (*owoce*) raw fruit; (*mięso*) raw meat.

surowo *adv.* (= *kategorycznie*) harshly, severely, strictly; (*urządzony*) austerely; **jeść coś na surowo** eat sth raw; **surowo ukarać** punish severely; **surowo wzbroniony** strictly prohibited; **palenie surowo wzbronione** (*napis*) no smoking.

surowość *f.* 1. (*potraw, materiałów*) rawness. 2. (*osoby, przepisów*) strictness; (*wyroku, kary*) harshness, strictness; (*miny, twarzy*) sternness; **z całą surowością** with all severity; **z całą surowością prawa** (*ukarać*) to the full extent of the law, with all severity of the law. 3. (*wnętrza, stroju, budynku*) austerity. 4. (*klimatu, zimy*) harshness, severity. 5. (*losu, warunków życia*) severity, austerity.

surowy *a.* 1. (= *niegotowany*) raw. 2. (= *nieprzetworzony*) raw, unprocessed; (*drewno*) unseasoned; **surowa cegła** adobe; **budynek w stanie surowym** shell of a building. 3. (= *bezwzględny*) (*osoba, przepisy*) strict; (*wyrok, kara*) harsh, strict; (*mina, twarz*) stern. 4. (= *bez ozdób*) (*wnętrze, strój, budynek*) austere. 5. (*klimat, zima*) harsh, severe. 6. (*los, warunki życia*) severe, austere.

surówka *f. Gen.pl.* **-ek** 1. (*potrawa*) salad. 2. (*płótno*) unbleached linen. 3. *bud.* adobe. 4. *hutn.* pig-iron.

surrealista *mp*, **surrealistka** *f. Gen.pl.* **-ek** surrealist.

surrealistycznie *adv.* surrealistically.

surrealistyczny *a.* surrealist, surrealistic.

surrealizm *mi* surrealism.

sus *mi Gen.* **-a** leap; **dać susa** take a leap; **jednym susem** in one leap.

suseł *ma* **-sł-** *zool.* ground squirrel, gopher (*Citellus*); **spać jak suseł** sleep like a log.

suspendować *ipf. rel.* suspend.

suspens *mi* suspense.

suspensa *f. rel.* suspension.

suspensorium *n. sing. indecl. pl.* **-ria** *Gen.* **-riów** 1. *med.* suspensory. 2. *sport* jockstrap, athletic support.

susz *mi* 1. (*owoce*) dried fruit; (*warzywa*) dried vegetables. 2. (= *chrust*) dry brushwood.

susza *f.* drought.

suszarka *f. Gen.pl.* **-ek** dryer; **suszarka do włosów/rąk** hair/hand dryer; **suszarka do naczyń** dish drainer.

suszarnia *f. Gen.pl.* **-i** *l.* **-ń** (*pomieszczenie*) drying room; (*budynek*) drying plant.

suszarnictwo *n. techn.* dehydration industry.

suszarniczy *a.* dehydrating.

suszka *f. Gen.pl.* **-ek** 1. (*owoc*) dried fruit; (*kwiat*) dried flower. 2. *leśn.* dried up tree. 3. (*do atramentu*) blotter.

suszony *a.* dried; **suszona śliwka** prune.

suszyć *ipf.* dry; **suszyć komuś głowę o coś** pester sb about sth; **suszyć sobie głowę nad czymś** rack one's brains over sth; **ale mnie suszy!** *pot.* I'm dying for a drink! **~ się** *ipf.* 1. (= *schnąć*) dry, get dry. 2. (= *osuszać się*) dry o.s.

sutanna *f. rel.* cassock; (*w kościele rzymskokatolickim*) soutane.

sutasz *mi* soutache.

sutek *mi* **-tk-** *Gen.* **-a** *anat., zool.* nipple; mamilla, papilla.

sutener *mp* pimp; *Br. t.* ponce.

sutenerstwo *n.* pimping.

suterena *f.* basement.

sutkowy *a. anat.* mammary, mastoid; **gruczoł sutkowy** mammary gland.

suto *adv.* abundantly, richly; **suto zastawiony stół** table laden with food.

suty *a.* (*posiłek*) sumptuous; (*napiwek*) generous.

suw *mi techn.* stroke.

suwać *ipf.* push, shove (*czymś po czymś* sth across sth). **~ się** *ipf.* (= *przesuwać się*) slide.

suwak *mi Gen.* **-a** 1. (= *zamek błyskawiczny*) zipper; *Br.* zip, zip fastener. 2. *muz., techn.* slide; **suwak logarytmiczny** *mat.* slide rule.

suwakowy *a. muz., techn.* slide.

suweren[1] *mp pl.* **-owie** (*władca*) sovereign.

suweren[2] *mi pl.* **-y** (*moneta*) sovereign.

suwerennie *adv.* sovereignly; (*panować*) independently.

suwerenność *f.* (*państwa, władcy*) sovereignty.

suwerenny *a.* (*państwo, władca*) sovereign.

suwmiarka *f. Gen.pl.* **-ek** caliper gage; *Br.* vernier calliper gauge; *pot.* vernier.

suwnica *f. techn.* gantry.

suwnicowy *a.* gantry. *– mp* gantry operator.

suzeren *mp pl.* **-owie** *l.* **-i** *hist.* suzerain.

swa *a. zob.* **swój**.

swada *f.* 1. (= *elokwencja*) eloquence, fluency;

mówić ze swadą speak eloquently, speak volubly. **2.** (*temperament*) zest.

swarliwie *adv.* quarrelsomely.

swarliwość *f.* quarrelsomeness.

swarliwy *a.* (*ton, dyskusja*) quarrelsome; (*kobieta, przekupka*) shrewish.

swary *pl. Gen.* **-ów** quarrels, squabbles; **swary rodzinne** family feuds.

swastyka *f.* (*symbol religijny*) (*hitlerowska*) swastika.

swat *mp pl.* **-owie** *l.* **-ci** matchmaker; **ani mi on brat, ani swat** he is nothing to me.

swatać *ipf.* **swatać kogoś z kimś** arrange for sb to marry sb.

swatka *f. Gen.pl.* **-ek** *zob.* **swat**.

swaty *pl. Gen.* **-ów** matchmaking; **słać kogoś w swaty** send sb as a matchmaker.

swawola *f. Gen.pl.* **-i** **1.** (= *dokazywanie*) frolicking. **2.** *przest.* (= *nieposłuszeństwo*) license; *Br.* licence.

swawolić *ipf.* frolic.

swawolnie *adv.* playfully.

swawolny *a.* **1.** (= *figlarny*) (*osoba*) rollicking; (*żart, uśmiech*) playful. **2.** (= *samowolny, niesforny*) (*np. szlachta*) dissolute.

swąd *mi* **-ę-** smell of burning; **psim swędem** by fluke.

swe *a. zob.* **swój**.

sweter *mi* **-tr-** *Gen.* **-a** sweater; *Br. t.* jumper; **sweter rozpinany** cardigan.

sweterek *mi* **-rk-** *Gen.* **-a** sweater.

swędzenie *n.* itching.

swędzić *ipf.*, **swędzieć** *ipf.* **-i** itch; **swędzi mnie oko** my eye is itchy; **język kogoś swędzi** sb is dying to say sth; **ręka kogoś swędzi** *przen.* sb is dying to punch sb.

swing *mi muz.* (*rytm*) (*taniec*) swing.

swingować *ipf. muz.* swing.

swingowy *a. muz.* swing.

swoboda *f. Gen.pl.* **-ód** **1.** (= *wolność*) liberty, freedom; **swoboda działania** freedom of action; **mieć swobodę działania** have a free hand; **swoboda ruchów** liberty of movement; **swoboda poruszania się** freedom of movement; **swobody obywatelskie** civil liberties; **żyć na swobodzie** live in freedom. **2.** (= *łatwość*) ease; **mieć swobodę w nawiązywaniu kontaktów** make friends easily. **3.** (= *obycie*) familiarity (*w czymś* with sth).

swobodnie *adv.* freely; (*czuć się*) at ease, comfortable; (*decydować, wybierać*) freely; (*ubierać się*) casually, informally; (*zachowywać się*) freely, without restraint; **oddychać swobodnie** breathe freely; **odetchnąć swobodnie** breathe a sign of relief.

swobodny *a.* **1.** (= *wolny*) free; **swobodny oddech** *med.* free breath; **swobodny przekład** *teor.lit.* free translation; **swobodne ręce** free hands; **swobodny wybór** free choice; **mieć swobodną głowę** be untroubled. **2.** (= *luźny, ruchomy*) free, loose; **akcent swobodny** *jęz.* free accent; **rytm swobodny** *muz.* free rhythm; **swobodny spadek** *fiz.* free fall. **3.** (*strój, rozmowa, na-*

strój) casual, informal. **4.** (= *frywolny*) (*osoba, zachowanie, żarty*) uninhibited.

swoistość *f.* peculiarity.

swoisty *a.* (= *specyficzny, wyróżniający się*) peculiar; (= *charakterystyczny*) characteristic (*dla kogoś / czegoś* of sb/sth).

swoiście *adv.* (= *specyficznie, w wyróżniający się sposób*) peculiarly; (= *w charakterystyczny sposób*) characteristically (*dla kogoś / czegoś* of sb/sth).

swoja *itd. a. zob.* **swój**. – *f.* **swoj-** *l.* **sw-** (= *rodaczka, krajanka*) fellow countrywoman; (= *przyjaciółka*) friend; **ona jest swoja** she's one of us.

swojak *mp* fellow countryman.

swoje *a. zob.* **swój**. – *n.* **swoj-** *l.* **sw-** one's own; **dbać o swoje** take care of one's own interests; **dopiąć swego** accomplish one's ends; **oberwać za swoje** be taught a lesson; **pić za swoje** drink for one's own money; **pracować na swoim** be self-employed, work in one's own company; **mieszkać na swoim** live in one's own home; **robić swoje** do one's job; **wyjść na swoje** come out on top; **jakoś wychodzę na swoje** somehow I pay my way; **zrobię to po swojemu** I'll do it my way.

swojski *a.* **1.** (= *znajomy*) familiar. **2.** (= *domowej roboty*) home-made.

swojsko *adv.* familiarly; **czuć się gdzieś swojsko** feel at home somewhere.

swołocz *f. pl.* **-e** *uj.* **1.** (= *łajdak*) rascal, scoundrel. **2.** (= *hołota*) the rabble.

sworzeń *mi* **-rzni-** *Gen.* **-a** *Gen.pl.* **-i** *l.* **-ów** *techn.* pivot.

swój *a.* **swoj-** *l.* **sw-** **1.** (*zaimek dzierżawczy*) one's, one's own; (= *mój*) my; (= *twój*) your; (= *jego*) his; (= *jej*) her; (= *nasz*) our; (= *wasz*) your; (= *ich*) their; **kochać swoją żonę** love one's wife; **kocham swoją żonę** I love my wife; **lubić swoją pracę** like one's job; **on lubi swoją pracę** he likes his job; **spakować swoje rzeczy** pack one's things; **spakowali swoje rzeczy** they packed their things; **swoją drogą,...** still,...; **na swój sposób** in a way; **w swoim czasie** in due course. **2.** (= *swojski*) home-made; **kiełbasa/wino swojej roboty** home-made sausage/wine; **to swój chłop** he is one of us. – *mp* **swoj-** *l.* **sw-** *pot.* (= *rodak, krajan*) fellow countryman; (= *przyjaciel*) friend; **swoi** (= *rodzina*) one's folk; **swój swego zawsze znajdzie** birds of a feather flock together.

sybaryta *mp* sybarite.

sybarytyzm *mi* sybaritism.

Syberia *f. Gen.* **-ii** *geogr.* Siberia.

syberyjski *a.* Siberian.

sybiliński *a.* Sibylline; **księgi sybilińskie** *hist.* the Sybilline Books.

Sybilla *f. mit.* Sybil, Sibyl.

sybirak *mp* **1.** (= *mieszkaniec Syberii*) Siberian. **2.** (= *zesłaniec na Syberię*) person deported to Siberia.

sycić *ipf.* **1.** (= *czynić sytym*) satiate; **sycić czymś oczy** *l.* **wzrok** feast one's eyes on sth; **sycić głód** satisfy one's hunger. **2.** (= *napełniać, przenikać*) fill; **sycić miód** ferment honey (*to produce mead*). **~ się** *ipf.* **1.** (= *nasycać się*) sate o.s.

(*czymś* on sth). **2.** (= *upajać się*) take delight (*czymś* in sth).

syciwo *n. techn.* impregnant.

Sycylia *f. Gen.* **-ii** *geogr.* Sicily.

sycylijski *a.* Sicilian; **mafia sycylijska** the Mafia, the Maffia.

syczący *a. fon.* sibilant; **spółgłoska sycząca** *fon.* sibilant consonant, sibilant.

syczeć *ipf.* **-ę -ysz 1.** (= *wydawać syk*) hiss; (*o tłuszczu*) sizzle; **syczeć z bólu** hiss with pain. **2.** (*mówić*) *tylko pf.* hiss.

syderyczny *a. astron.* sidereal; **miesiąc syderyczny** sidereal month.

syderyt *mi* **1.** *min.* siderite, chalybite. **2.** (*meteoryt*) siderite.

syf *mi* **1.** *pot.* (= *bałagan*) mess; **ale tu syf!** look at this mess! **2.** *Gen.* **-a** *wulg.* (= *syfilis*) syph; **złapać syfa** catch syph. **3.** *wulg.* (= *tandeta*) shit; **naprawdę kupiłeś ten syf?** did you really buy this shit?; **ja pierdzielę, ale syf!** (*o kiepskim filmie, książce itp.*) jeez, this sucks big time! **4.** *wulg.* (= *problemy*) fuckup; **mamy teraz w pracy niezły syf** we're really fucked at work now. **5.** *wulg.* (= *pryszcz*) zit; **zrobił mi się syf na twarzy** I've got a zit on my face.

syfiasty *a.* crappy, shitty.

syfilis *mi pot.* (= *kiła*) syphilis.

syfilityczny *a.* syphilitic.

syfilityk *mp* syphilitic.

syfon *mi* **1.** (*z wodą sodową*) siphon bottle; *Br.* soda siphon, siphon. **2.** (*przy umywalce*) U-bend. **3.** *geol.*, *zool.* siphon.

sygnalista *mp* signalman.

sygnalizacja *f.* **1.** (= *przekazywanie sygnałów*) signaling; *Br.* signalling. **2.** (*urządzenia*) signaling equipment; *Br.* signalling equipment; **sygnalizacja świetlna** *l.* **uliczna** traffic lights.

sygnalizacyjny *a.* signaling; *Br.* signalling.

sygnalizator *mp pl.* **-rzy** (= *sygnalista*) signalman. *– mi Gen.* **-a** *pl.* **-ry** (*urządzenie*) signalling equipment.

sygnalizować *ipf.* **1.** (= *dawać sygnał*) signal. **2.** (= *informować*) indicate.

sygnalny *a. druk.* **egzemplarz sygnalny** advance copy.

sygnał *mi* signal; (*w słuchawce*) tone; **sygnał radiowy** (*np. zapowiadający audycję*) signature tune; **jechać na sygnale** drive with the siren going; **zatrzymać się pod sygnałem** *kol.* stop at the signal.

sygnałowy *a.* signal.

sygnatariusz *mp Gen.pl.* **-y** *l.* **-ów** signatory.

sygnatura *f.* **1.** *bibl.* catalog number; *Br.* catalogue number. **2.** *druk.*, *sztuka* (= *podpis*) signature.

sygnaturka *f. Gen.pl.* **-ek** *kośc.* ave-bell.

sygnet *mi* signet ring; **sygnet drukarski** *druk.* publisher's imprint.

sygnować *ipf.* sign.

Syjam *mi geogr.* Siam.

syjamski *a.* Siamese; **bracia** *l.* **siostry syjamskie** Siamese twins; **kot syjamski** Siamese cat.

syjonista *mp* Zionist.

syjonistyczny *a.* Zionist, Zionistic.

syjonizm *mi* Zionism.

syk *mi* hiss, hissing.

sykać *ipf.* **1.** *zob.* **syczeć. 2.** (= *psykać*) hush.

syknąć *pf.* **-ij 1.** *zob.* **syczeć. 2.** *zob.* **sykać.**

sykomora *f. bot.* sycamore (*Ficus sycomorus*).

sylaba *f. fon.* syllable; **sylaba otwarta/zamknięta** open/close syllable.

sylabiczność *f.* **1.** *jęz.* syllabicity. **2.** *teor.lit.* syllabification.

sylabiczny *a. jęz.*, *teor.lit.* syllabic.

sylabizm *mi teor.lit.* syllabism.

sylabizować *ipf.* read letter by letter.

sylabotoniczny *a. teor.lit.* syllabotonic.

sylabotwórczy *a. jęz.* syllabic.

sylabowiec *mi* **-wc-** *Gen.* **-a 1.** *jęz.* syllabic abbreviation, acronym. **2.** *teor.lit.* syllabic verse.

sylabowy *a. jęz.* syllabic.

sylen *mp pl.* **-owie** *mit.* silenus.

sylf *ma* (*duch*) sylph.

sylikat *mi bud.* calcium silicate brick.

sylikatowy *a. bud.* calcium silicate.

sylikon *mi bud.* silicon.

sylikonowy *a. bud.* silicon.

sylogistyczny *a. log.* syllogistic, syllogistical.

sylogistyka *f. log.* syllogistic.

sylogizm *mi log.* syllogism.

sylur *mi geol.* Silurian period, the Silurian.

sylurski *a. geol.* Silurian.

sylwester *mi* **-tr-** *Gen.* **-a** (*dzień*) New Year's Eve; (*zabawa*) New Year's Eve party; **co robisz w tym roku w sylwestra?** what are you up to for the New Year's Eve this year?

sylwestrowy *a.* New Year's.

sylwetka *f. Gen.pl.* **-ek 1.** (= *figura*) figure. **2.** (= *cień*) silhouette. **3.** (= *zarys postaci*) silhouette, profile. **4.** (= *charakterystyka*) profile. **5.** (*obraz*) silhouette. **6.** (*w strzelaniu*) bobbing target.

symbiotycznie *adv. biol.* symbiotically; (*współżyć*) in symbiosis.

symbiotyczny *a. biol.* symbiotic, symbiotical.

symbioza *f. biol.* symbiosis.

symbol *mi Gen.pl.* **-i** *l.* **-ów** (*znak*) (*t. w matematyce, chemii, muzyce itp.*) symbol; **być symbolem czegoś** be the symbol of, represent sth.

symbolicznie *adv.* **1.** (*przedstawiać, rozumieć, opisywać*) symbolically. **2.** (*płacić, wynagradzać*) nominally.

symboliczność *f.* **1.** (*postaci, wiersza*) symbolicalness. **2.** (*upominku, wynagrodzenia*) nominal value.

symboliczny *a.* **1.** (*postać, znaczenie, powieść*) symbolic. **2.** (*wynagrodzenie, upominek*) nominal; **symboliczna złotówka** token dollar; *Br.* token penny.

symbolika *f.* **1.** (= *system znaków*) symbols. **2.** (= *ogólne znaczenie*) symbolism.

symbolista *mp* Symbolist.

symbolistyczny *a.* symbolist, symbolistic.

symbolizm *mi* **1.** (= *symboliczny charakter*) symbolism. **2.** *teor.lit.*, *sztuka* Symbolism.

symbolizować *ipf.* symbolize, represent.

symetralna *f. Gen.* **-ej** *geom.* bisector, bisectrix.

symetria *f. Gen.* **-ii** *biol.*, *geom.* (= *proporcjo-*

nalność, harmonia) symmetry; **symetria dwuboczna** dissymmetry; **oś/płaszczyzna symetrii** axis/ plane of symmetry.

symetrycznie *adv.* symmetrically.

symetryczność *f.* symmetricalness.

symetryczny *a.* symmetrical.

symfonia *f. Gen.* **-ii** *muz., przen.* symphony; **symfonia barw/zapachów** symphony of colors/ smells; *Br.* symphony of colours/smells.

symfoniczny *a. muz.* symphonic; **koncert symfoniczny** symphony concert; **muzyka symfoniczna** symphonic music; **orkiestra symfoniczna** symphony orchestra.

symfonik *mp* symphonist.

symonia *f. Gen.* **-ii** *kośc.* simony.

sympatia *f. Gen.* **-ii** **1.** (*uczucie*) liking (*do kogoś* for sb); **cieszyć się sympatią u kogoś** be liked by sb; **nie cieszyć się czyjąś sympatią** be in sb's bad books; **czuć sympatię do kogoś** feel attracted to sb; **poczuć do kogoś sympatię** take a fancy to sb, get to like sb; **darzyć kogoś sympatią** feel affinity for sb. **2.** *pot.* (= *chłopak*) boyfriend; (= *dziewczyna*) girlfriend.

sympatyczka *f. Gen.pl.* **-ek** *zob.* **sympatyk**.

sympatycznie *adv.* pleasantly, nicely; **wyglądać sympatycznie** look nice.

sympatyczny *a.* pleasant, nice, likeable; **atrament sympatyczny** invisible sink; **układ sympatyczny** *anat.* sympathetic system.

sympatyk *mp* sympathizer.

sympatyzować *ipf.* sympathize (*z kimś / czymś* with sb/sth).

symplifikacja *f. log.* simplification.

symplistyczny *a. form.* simplistic.

sympozjum *n. sing. indecl. pl.* **-zja** *Gen.* **-zjów** *t. hist.* symposium.

symptom *mi med. l. przen.* symptom.

symptomatyczny *a.* symptomatic.

symulacja *f. techn., komp., mat.* (= *modelowanie, imitowanie*) **1.** simulation; **symulacja komputerowa** computer simulation. **2.** (= *udawanie*) feigning.

symulacyjny *a.* simulative.

symulanctwo *n.* malingering.

symulant *mp*, **symulantka** *f. Gen.pl.* **-ek** *zwł. wojsk., żegl.* malingerer.

symulator *mi Gen.* **-a** *techn., komp.* simulator; **symulator lotu** *lotn.* flight simulator.

symulować *ipf.* **1.** (= *imitować*) simulate. **2.** (= *udawać*) feign; (= *udawać chorego*) malinger.

symultana *f. szachy* simultaneous play.

symultanicznie *adv.* simultaneously.

symultaniczny *a.* simultaneous; **szachy symultaniczne** simultaneous chess; **tłumaczenie symultaniczne** simultaneous interpreting.

symultanista *mp sztuka, teor.lit.* simultaneist.

symultanizm *mi sztuka, teor.lit.* simultaneism.

symultanka *f. Gen.pl.* **-ek** *szachy* = **symultana**.

syn *mp Loc. i Voc.* **-u** *pl.* **-owie** *t. przen.* **1.** son; **młodszy syn** younger son; **starszy syn** elder *l.* older son; **przybrany syn** foster-son; **syn z prawego/nieprawego łoża** legitimate/illegitimate son; **syn chrzestny** godson; **syn marnotrawny** prodigal

son; **jaki ojciec, taki syn** like father, like son; **Syn Boży** *rel.* the Son of God; **Syn Człowieczy** *rel.* the Son of Man; **synowie i córki Ameryki** *przen.* the sons and daughters of America. **2.** *Voc.* **synu** (*do jakiegokolwiek młodego człowieka*) son, sonny. **3.** *pl.* **-y** *pot. euf.* **taki syn** son-of-a-gun.

synagoga *f. rel.* synagogue.

synagogalny *a.* synagogical, synagogal.

Synaj *mi geogr.* Sinai; **góra Synaj** *Bibl.* Mount Sinai.

synalek *mp iron.* daddy's boy.

synantropia *f. Gen.* **-ii** *biol.* synanthropy.

synantropijny *a. biol.* synanthropic.

synapizm *mi med., przest.* mustard plaster.

synapsa *f. anat.* synapse.

synaptyczny *a. fizj.* synaptic, synaptical; **przekaźnictwo synaptyczne** synaptic transmission; **szczelina synaptyczna** synaptic cleft.

synchronia *f. Gen.* **-ii** **1.** (= *jednoczesność*) synchronism. **2.** *jęz.* synchrony.

synchronicznie *adv.* synchronically.

synchroniczny *a.* (= *dotyczący jednoczesności*) synchronic, synchronical; (= *jednoczesny, zsynchronizowany*) synchronous, synchronized (*z czymś* with sth); **językoznawstwo synchroniczne** *jęz.* synchronic linguistics; **orbita synchroniczna** *astron., lotn.* synchronous orbit; **pływanie synchroniczne** *sport* synchronized swimming.

synchronizacja *f.* synchronization.

synchronizacyjny *a. techn.* **błąd synchronizacyjny** synchronization error.

synchronizator *mi Gen.* **-a** *techn.* synchronizer.

synchronizować *ipf.* synchronize.

synchrotron *mi fiz.* synchrotron.

synchrotronowy *a. fiz.* synchrotronic; **promieniowanie synchrotronowe** synchrotronic radiation; **wiązka synchrotronowa** synchrotronic beam.

syndrom *mi med. l. przen.* syndrome (*czegoś* of sth); **syndrom napięcia przedmiesiączkowego** premenstrual syndrome; **syndrom wietnamski** *przen., polit.* Vietnam syndrome.

syndyk *mp* **1.** (*urzędnik publiczny*) syndic (*in some European countries*). **2.** *prawn.* receiver; **syndyk masy upadłości** receiver in bankruptcy.

syndykalista *mp polit.* syndicalist.

syndykalizm *mi polit.* syndicalism.

syndykat *mi ekon.* syndicate.

synek *mp* **-nk-** *pl.* **-owie** *emf.* sonny; *zob.* **syn**.

synekdocha *f. teor.lit.* synecdoche.

synekura *f. zw. iron.* sinecure.

synergetyczny *a. med.* synergic, synergistic, synergetic.

synergizm *mi* **1.** *med.* synergism, synergy. **2.** *rel.* synergism.

synestezja *f. psych.* synesthesia, synaesthesia.

syningia *f. bot.* gloxinia (*Sinningia*).

synklina *f. geol.* syncline.

synkopa *f. muz.* syncopation; *fon.* syncope.

synkopować *ipf. muz.* syncopate.

synkopowany, synkopowy *a. muz.* syncopated; **rytm synkopowany** backbeat.

synkretyczny *a. form.* syncretic; **religia synkretyczna** syncretic religion.

synkretyzm *mi form.* syncretism.

synod *mi kośc.* synod, council; **synod biskupi** synod of bishops.

synodalny *a. kośc.* synodal.

synodyczny *a. astron.* synodic; **miesiąc/obieg synodyczny** synodic month/period.

synogarlica *f. orn.* ringed turtledove (*Streptopelia risoria*).

synonim *mi jęz.* synonym.

synonimia *f. Gen.* **-ii** *jęz.* synonymy.

synonimiczność *f. jęz.* synonymity.

synonimiczny *a. jęz.* (= *dotyczący synonimii*) synonymic; (= *równoznaczny*) synonymous (*z czymś* with sth).

synonimika *f. jęz.* = **synonimia**.

synoptyczny *a.* synoptic; **mapa synoptyczna** *meteor.* synoptic chart, weather map; **ewangelie synoptyczne** *Bibl.* the Synoptic Gospels, the Synoptics.

synoptyk *mp meteor.* weather-man.

synoptyka *f. meteor.* weather forecasting.

synostwo *n.* filiality; *rzad.* sonhood.

synowa *f. Gen.* **-ej** daughter-in-law.

synowski *a.* filial, son's; **obowiązki synowskie** filial duties.

syntagma *f. jęz.* syntagm.

syntagmatyczny *a. jęz.* syntagmatic.

syntaksa *f. jęz.* (= *składnia*) syntax.

syntaktycznie *a. jęz.* syntactically.

syntaktyczny *a. jęz.* syntactic.

syntetycznie *adv.* synthetically.

syntetyczny *a.* synthetic; *fil., log. t.* synthetical; **produkt syntetyczny** synthetic product; **tworzywo syntetyczne** synthetic (material); **włókno syntetyczne** synthetic fiber; **żywica syntetyczna** synthetic resin.

syntetyk *mp Gen.* **-ka** *pl.* **-cy** (*człowiek*) synthetist. – *mi Gen.* **-ku** *pl.* **-ki** (*produkt*) synthetic.

syntetyzować *ipf. t. chem.* synthesize.

synteza *f. chem., teor.lit., fil.* synthesis; *fiz.* fusion; **synteza jądrowa** *fiz.* (nuclear) fusion; **synteza mowy** *komp.* speech synthesis; **synteza dialektyczna** *fil.* dialectical synthesis; **synteza pojęć/przeciwieństw** synthesis of ideas/opposites.

syntezator *mi Gen.* **-a** *techn.* synthesizer; **syntezator elektroniczny** *muz.* (electronic) synthesizer; **syntezator dźwięków/mowy** *el., komp.* sound/speech synthesizer.

syntonia *f. Gen.* **-ii** *psych.* syntony.

sypać *ipf.* **sypię sypiesz** **1.** + *Acc. l. Ins.* (*piasek, ziarno, proszek*) pour (*sth*) (*na coś* on *l.* onto sth) (*do czegoś* into sth); (*kwiaty, kawałki papieru itp.*) strew (*sth*) (*na coś* on *l.* over sth); (*przyprawę*) sprinkle (*sth*) (*na coś* on *l.* over sth); (= *rozrzucać*) scatter (*sth*) (*po czymś* on *l.* over *l.* around sth); (= *rzucać czymś sypkim*) throw (*sth*) (*w coś/kogoś* at sb/sth); (*pociskami*) shower *l.* hail (*sth*) (down) (*w kogoś/coś* on *l.* upon sb/sth); **sypać cukier do kawy/herbaty** put sugar into one's coffee/tea; **sypać iskrami** send (out) sparks; spark. **2.** (*o zjawiskach przyrody*) **śnieg sypie** it's snowing; **sypało cały dzień** it snowed

all day; **sypało nam piaskiem w twarze** the wind blew sand in our faces. **3.** *przen.* **sypać dowcipami jak z rękawa** crack jokes all the time; **sypać pieniędzmi** scatter one's money around; **sypać pochwałami/komplementami** be lavish with praises/compliments; **sypać przekleństwami/obelgami** hurl curses/insults. **4.** *pot.* (= *zdradzać, donosząc*) squeal on (*sb*); **sypać kolegów na policji** squeal on one's friends to the police; squeak. **5.** *tylko ipf.* (= *usypywać*) heap up, build, raise; **sypać szańce** build ramparts. **~ się** *ipf.* **1.** (= *opadać*) fall, pour down; (= *spadać masowo*) shower (down), hail (down); (*o śniegu*) snow (*na kogoś/coś* on sb/sth). **2.** *tylko ipf.* (= *rozpadać się*) crumble, fall apart, fall to pieces. **3.** (*o iskrach*) fly. **4.** (= *napływać w dużej ilości*) flow in, come streaming. **5.** (*o wąsie, zaroście, brodzie*) sprout. **6.** (*o brawach, okrzykach*) come. **7.** (*o komplementach, nagrodach, pochwałach*) shower down (*na kogoś* on sb); (*o karach, naganach*) fall (*na kogoś* on sb). **8.** *pot.* (= *obciążać samego siebie mimowolnie*) betray o.s. **9.** *pot.* (= *pomylić się*) goof; **sypnąć się z czegoś** *szkoln.* (= *oblać coś*) flunk sth.

sypiać *ipf.* **1.** sleep. **2.** *pot. euf.* **sypiać z kimś** do it with sb; **oni sypiają ze sobą** they're lovers.

sypialnia *f. Gen.pl.* **-i** *l.* **-ń** bedroom.

sypialny *a.* sleeping; **pokój sypialny** bedroom; **sala sypialna** dormitory, dorm; **wagon sypialny** *kol.* sleeping car. – *mi* **1.** (*pokój*) bedroom. **2.** (*wagon*) *kol.* sleeping car.

sypki *a.* loose; **towary sypkie** *handl.* dry goods; **skała sypka** *geol.* detached rock.

sypko *adv.* **na sypko** *kulin.* loose.

sypnąć (się) *pf.* **-ij** *zob.* **sypać (się)**.

Syrakuzy *pl. Gen.* **-z** *geogr.* Syracuse.

syrena *f.* **1.** *mit.* mermaid; (*w mitach greckich*) siren. **2.** (*sygnalizator, dźwięk*) siren; **syrena fabryczna** factory siren *l.* horn; *Br.* hooter; **syrena okrętowa** *żegl.* foghorn. **3.** *zool.* (= *ssak z rzędu Sirenia*) sirenian. **4.** *zool.* (= *płaz z rodziny Sirenidae*) siren.

syreni *a. mit.* **syreni śpiew/urok** siren song/charm; **syrenie głosy** siren voices.

Syria *f. Gen.* **-ii** *geogr.* Syria.

syringa *f. muz.* syrinx.

Syriusz *mi Acc.* **-a** *astron.* Sirius.

syriuszowy *a. astron.* Sirian.

syrop *mi* syrup, sirup; **w syropie** *kulin.* in syrup; **syrop klonowy/malinowy** maple/raspberry syrup; **syrop na kaszel** *med.* cough syrup.

syropowaty *a.* syrupy, sirupy.

Syryjczyk *mp,* **Syryjka** *f. Gen.pl.* **-ek** Syrian.

syryjski *a.* **1.** Syrian. **2.** *zool.* **chomik syryjski** golden hamster (*Mesocricetus auratus*).

system *mi* **1.** system; **system ekonomiczny/filozoficzny/prawny/społeczny** economic/philosophical/legal/social system; **system polityczny** political system, régime; **system wierzeń** system of beliefs; **system komputerowy/operacyjny** *komp.* computer/operating system; **system dwójkowy/dziesiętny** *mat., komp.* the binary/decimal system; **system metryczny** *miern.* the metrical system; **system odwadniający** *roln.*, *techn.* drainage system; **system rozpoznawania mowy** *komp.* speech recognition system; **globalny system lokalizacji** *techn.* global positioning system, GPS; **administrator systemu** *komp.* system administrator; *pot.* admin. **2.** (= *metoda, plan, sposób*) system, method, plan; **system pucharowy** *sport* knock-out system *l.* principle; **system ratalny** *handl.* installment plan; **pracować według systemu** work methodically.

systematycznie *adv.* (= *metodycznie*) systematically, methodically; (= *stale, regularnie*) regularly, steadily.

systematyczność *f.* method.

systematyczny *a.* **1.** (= *uporządkowany*) systematic, methodical, ordered. **2.** *biol.* (= *taksonomiczny*) systematic, taxonomic; **nazwa systematyczna** systematic name; **jednostka systematyczna** taxonomic unit, taxon.

systematyk *mp biol.* systematician.

systematyka *f. biol.* systematics.

systematyzacja *f.* systematization.

systematyzować *ipf.* systematize.

systemowy *a.* system, systems, systemic; **analiza systemowa** systems analysis; **podejście systemowe** systems approach; **oprogramowanie systemowe** *komp.* system software.

syt *a. attr.* + *Gen. lit. l. arch.* **1.** not in want of (*sth*); (= *nieco znużony*) tired of (*sth*); **syt już jestem pochlebstw** I have heard enough flattery. **2. do syta** to satiety, to the full, to one's heart's content; **najeść/napić się do syta** eat/drink one's fill; **cieszyć się życiem do syta** enjoy life to the full.

sytość *f.* satiety, repletion, fulness; **uczucie sytości** feeling of fulness.

sytuacja *f.* (= *położenie, okoliczności*) situation, position, circumstances; **znaleźć się w głupiej/trudnej/żenującej sytuacji** find o.s. in a stupid/difficult/embarrassing situation; **wykaraskać się z trudnej sytuacji** get out of a difficult situation; **sytuacja kryzysowa** crisis situation; **być w ciężkiej sytuacji finansowej** *pot.* be in dire straits; **być w lepszej/gorszej sytuacji niż ktoś** be better/worse off than sb; **sytuacja bez wyjścia** dead end, cul-de-sac; **postaw siebie w mojej sytuacji** put yourself in my position *l.* in my shoes; **wprowadzać kogoś w sytuację** put sb in the picture; **rozeznać się w sytuacji** find one's bearings; learn one's way around *l.* about; **w tej sytuacji...** in these circumstances...; under the circumstances...; **pogorszyć sytuację** make matters worse; **być panem sytuacji** control the situation; **uratować sytuację** save the day.

sytuacyjny *a.* situation; *form.* situational; **komedia sytuacyjna** situation comedy, sitcom; **kontekst sytuacyjny** situational context; **plan sytuacyjny** general layout; *bud.* site plan.

sytuować *ipf.* situate, place, locate. **~ się** *ipf.* be situated, be located.

sytuowany *a.* **dobrze/źle/lepiej/gorzej sytuowany** well/badly/better/worse off.

syty *a.* **1.** (= *niegłodny*) satiated, full, replete; **i wilk syty, i owca cała** this will make everybody

happy. **2.** (*o posiłku*) (= *sycący*) nourishing, satisfying.

syzyfowy *a.* Sisyphean; **dźwigać syzyfowy kamień** roll Sisyphean stones; **syzyfowy trud/wysiłek** Sisyphean toil/labor.

syzygijny *a. astron.* syzygial, syzygal, syzygetic; **pływy syzygijne** *hydrol.* spring tides.

syzygium *n. indecl. in sing. Gen.pl.* **-iów** *astron.* syzygy; **być w syzygium** be at syzygy.

sza *int.* hush!, s-s-sh!; **o tym (cicho) sza** don't breathe a word of it.

szabas *mi rel.* Sabbath.

szabasowy *a. rel.* Sabbath; **świeca szabasowa** Sabbath candle.

szabat *mi rel. zob.* **szabas.**

szabelka *f. Gen.pl.* **-ek** *emf.* **1.** = **szabla** 1. **2.** *przen.* **potrząsać szabelką** rattle the saber; flex one's muscles; **wymachiwanie** *l.* **potrząsanie szabelką** saber-rattling.

szaber *mi* **-br-** *pot.* looting.

szabla *f. Gen.pl.* **-bli** *l.* **-bel** **1.** *broń* (*t. sportowa*) saber; *Br.* sabre; (*nieściśle*) sword; **szabla marynarska** cutlass; **nosić szablę** carry a saber; **władać szablą** wield a saber. **2.** *myśl.* (= *kieł dzika*) tusk.

szablastozębny *a.* = **szablozębny.**

szablista *mp*, **szablistka** *Gen.pl.* **-ek** *sport* saber-fencer.

szablodziób *ma* **-dziob-** *orn.* avocet (*Recurvirostra avosetta*).

szablon *mi* **1.** (*z literami itp.*) stencil; (= *wzornik*) template, templet; (= *forma do kopiowania*) model, pattern. **2.** *przen.* (= *bezmyślnie stosowany schemat*) routine, stereotype.

szablonowo *adv.* routinely, stereotypically.

szablonowy *a.* routine, stereotypical, hackneyed.

szablozębny *a.* **tygrys szablozębny** *paleont.* saber-toothed cat.

szabrować *ipf. pot.* loot.

szabrownictwo *n. pot.* looting.

szabrowniczy *a. pot.* looting.

szabrownik *mp pot.* looter.

szach *mp pl.* **-owie** *hist.* (= *władca perski*) shah. **–** *int. i mi Gen.* **-u** *l.* **-a** *tylko sing. szachy* check; **szach i mat** checkmate; **szach z odsłony** discovered check; **podwójny szach** double check; **dać szacha (królowi)** check (the king); **trzymać kogoś w szachu** *przen.* get *l.* have sb over the barrel.

szachista *mp*, **szachistka** *f. Gen.pl.* **-ek** chessplayer; **mieć refleks szachisty** *żart.* be slow-witted.

szachować *ipf.* **1.** *szachy* check. **2.** (= *uniemożliwiać działanie*) keep *l.* hold (*sb*) in check.

szachownica *f.* **1.** (*do gry w szachy*) chessboard; (*do gry w warcaby*) checkerboard. **2.** (= *układ dwukolorowych kwadratów*) checker; **pole szachownicy** square. **3.** *bot.* fritillary (*Fritillaria*); **szachownica cesarska** crown imperial (*F. imperialis*).

szachowy *a.* chess; **turniej szachowy** chess tournament; **stolik szachowy** chess table; **figura**

szachowa chess piece; **notacja szachowa** chess notation; **koń** *l.* **konik szachowy** knight.

szachraj *mp Gen.pl.* **-ów** *l.* **-ai** *pot.* swindler, crook.

szachrajstwo *n.* swindling.

szachrować *ipf. pot.* swindle, cheat.

szachy *pl. Gen.* **-ów 1.** chess; **szachy błyskawiczne** lightning chess; **grać w szachy** play chess; **komplet szachów** chess set. **2.** (= *bierki szachowe*) chessmen.

szacować *ipf.* estimate, assess, evaluate; **szacować wartość czegoś na...** value *l.* rate sth at...; **szacować kogoś/czyjś charakter** gauge sb/sb's character.

szacowny *a.* esteemed, worthy.

szacunek *mi* **-nk- 1.** (= *poważanie*) respect, esteem, high regard; **bez szacunku** disrespectfully; **z całym szacunkiem** with all due respect, respectfully; **żywić do kogoś duży szacunek** have high regard for sb; **otaczać kogoś nabożnym szacunkiem** hold sb in awe. **2.** (= *oszacowanie wartości*) evaluation, estimate; **według szacunków** according to estimates; **przybliżony szacunek** rough approximation; **zawyżony szacunek** overestimate.

szacunkowo *adv.* approximately.

szacunkowy *a.* estimated, approximate; **szacunkowe koszty** estimated cost.

szadź *f. meteor.* rime(-frost); **pokryty szadzią** rime-frosted.

szafa *f.* (*zwł. z półkami*) **1.** cupboard; (*na ubrania*) wardrobe; **szafa wnękowa** built-in wardrobe; **szafa ścienna** closet; **szafa pancerna** strongbox; **szafa grająca** jukebox. **2. szafa gra!** *pot.* all right!

szafarka *f. Gen.pl.* **-ek** *przest.* housekeeper.

szafarz *mp* **1.** *hist.* (*urząd tytularny*) steward. **2.** *lit.* (= *rozdawca*) giver, dispenser.

szafir *mi min.* (*t. kolor*) sapphire.

szafirek *mi* **-rk-** *Gen.* **-a** *bot.* grape hyacinth (*Muscari botryoides*).

szafirowy *a.* (= *wykonany z szafiru, barwy szafiru*) sapphire.

szafka *f. Gen.pl.* **-ek** cabinet, cupboard; **szafka na akta** file cabinet; **szafka na książki** bookcase; **szafka łazienkowa/kuchenna** bathroom/kitchen cabinet; **szafka nocna** bedside table; **szafka w szatni** locker; **oszklona szafka** glass case.

szafkowy *a.* **umywalka szafkowa** vanity unit; **zegar szafkowy** grandfather clock, longcase clock.

szaflik *mi Gen.* **-a** *przest.* wooden tub.

szafot *mi* scaffold; **trafić na szafot** go to the scaffold.

szafować *ipf. + Ins.* be free *l.* liberal *l.* lavish with (*sth*); **szafować czasem/pieniędzmi/oszczędnościami** squander time/money/one's savings.

szafran *mi* **1.** *kulin.* saffron. **2.** *bot.* crocus (*Crocus*); **szafran barwierski** safflower (*Carthamus tinctorius*).

szafranowy *a.* saffron.

szajba *f. pot.* madness; **chyba ci szajba odbiła!** you must be off your nut!

szajbus *mp pl.* **-y** *pot.* crank, nut.

szajka *f. Gen.pl.* **-ek** gang; **szajka przemytników** gang *l.* ring of smugglers.

szakal *ma zool.* jackal; **szakal złocisty** golden jackal (*Canis aureus*); **szakal czaprakowy** black-backed jackal (*C. mesomelas*).

szakla *f. Gen.pl.* **-i** *żegl.* = szekla.

szakłak *mi bot.* buckthorn (*Rhamnus*).

szal *mi Gen.* **-a** *Gen.pl.* **-i** *l.* **-ów** (*na szyję*) scarf; (= *chusta zarzucana na ramiona*) shawl.

szala *f.* **1.** (= *miseczka wagi*) scale, pan. **2.** *przen.* (= *wyrok losu*) **położyć wszystko na jednej szali** put everything at stake; **przeważyć szalę na czyjąś stronę** tip the balance *l.* scale in favor of sb; **ważyć się na szali** be *l.* hang *l.* tremble in the balance.

szalbierczy, szalbierski *a. przest.* fraudulent.

szalbierstwo *n. przest.* imposture, quackery, fraud.

szalbierz *mp przest.* mountebank, quack, fraud.

szaleć *ipf.* **1.** (= *wariować*) go mad *l.* crazy *l.* insane. **2.** (= *być w furii*) rage, run wild, run amok *l.* amuck, go berserk. **3.** *przen.* (*o siłach przyrody, epidemiach, bitwie itp.*) rage; **szalejący sztorm** raging storm; **rozszalało się prawdziwe piekło** all the hell broke loose. **4.** *przen.* (= *ulegać silnym emocjom*) **szaleć z zachwytu nad kimś/czymś** rave about sb/sth; be mad about sb/sth; **szaleć za kimś/czymś** be crazy about sb/sth; **szaleć z miłości do kogoś** be madly in love with sb; **szaleć z gniewu** fly into a rage; fly off the handle. **5.** *przen.* (= *bawić się, dokazywać*) frolic about, romp about; (= *zabawiać się hałaśliwie*) revel; **jak szaleć, to szaleć** (one) might as well be hanged for a sheep as a lamb.

szalej *mi Gen.pl.* **-ów** *l.* **-ei** *bot.* cowbane, water hemlock (*Cicuta*); **najadłeś się szaleju?** are you mad?

szalenie *adv.* exceedingly, mighty, most; **szalenie się cieszę** I'm most delighted; **szalenie miła osoba** exceedingly nice person.

szaleniec *mp* **-ńc-** *pl.* **-y** madman, lunatic.

szaleńczo *adv.* madly.

szaleńczy *a.* mad, insane; **szaleńczy plan** mad scheme; **gnać z szaleńczą prędkością** run at breakneck speed.

szaleństwo *n.* **1.** (= *szał, skrajne emocje*) madness, fury; **do szaleństwa** crazily, madly. **2.** (= *lekkomyślność, ryzykanctwo*) lunacy, madness, recklessness; **popełnić szaleństwo** do something foolish; **to czyste szaleństwo** it's sheer madness *l.* lunacy.

szalet *mi* outdoor toilet.

szalik *mi Gen.* **-a** scarf.

szalikowiec *mp* **-wc-** *Voc.* **-u** supporter of a soccer team.

szalka *f. Gen.pl.* **-ek** scale, pan; **szalka Petriego** (*naczynie laboratoryjne*) Petri dish.

szalkowy *a.* **waga szalkowa** *techn.* pan scales.

szalona *f. Gen.* **-ej** madwoman.

szalony *a.* **-eni 1.** (= *zwariowany, nieobliczalny*) mad, crazy, insane; **jak szalony** like mad; **on jest kompletnie szalony** he's raving mad; **szalona głowa** hothead; **choroba szalonych krów** *wet.*

mad cow disease. **2.** (= *zawrotny*) breakneck. **3.** (= *gwałtowny*) frantic, raging. **4.** *pot.* (= *nadzwyczajny*) extraordinary, enormous. – *mp* (= *wariat*) madman.

szalotka *f. Gen.pl.* **-ek** *bot., kulin.* shallot, scallion (*Allium ascalonicum*).

szalować *ipf. bud.* board.

szalowanie *n. bud.* boarding formwork; *Br.* shuttering.

szalowy *a. ubiór* **kołnierz szalowy** shawl collar.

szalunek *mi* **-nk-** *bud.* = **szalowanie**.

szalunkowy *a. bud.* (*o desce, konstrukcji*) boarding.

szalupa *f. żegl.* shallop, dinghy, pinnace, ship's boat; (= *mała łódź okrętowa*) cockboat; **szalupa ratunkowa** lifeboat.

szał *mi* (= *szaleństwo*) madness, folly; (= *furia*) fury, rage; (= *gorączkowa aktywność*) frenzy, orgy; **szał bitewny** battle fury; **szał namiętności** frenzy of passion; **szał zakupów** shopping binge; **doprowadzać kogoś do szału** drive sb mad; **wpaść w szał** *l.* **dostać szału** fly into a fury *l.* rage; throw a fit.

szałaput *mp pl.* **-y** = **szaławiła**.

szałas *mi* shelter, shanty, lean-to, hut; (*indiański*) lodge.

szaławiła *mp* scatterbrain.

szałowy *a. pot.* awesome, cool.

szałwia *f. Gen.* **-ii** *bot., kulin.* sage (*Salvia*).

szałwiowy *a.* (*kolor*) sage-green.

szaman *mp antrop.* shaman, medicine man, witch doctor.

szamanizm *mi antrop.* shamanism.

szamanka *f. Gen.pl.* **-ek** *antrop.* medicine woman.

szamański *a. antrop.* shamanic.

szambelan *mp pl.* **-owie** *l.* **-i** *hist.* chamberlain.

szambelański *a. hist.* chamberlainship.

szambo *n.* cesspool, sump.

szamerować *ipf.* trim with galloon-lace.

szamerowanie *n.*, **szamerunek** *mi* **-nk-** galloon trimming.

szames *mp judaizm* beadle, shammes.

szamot *mi ceramika* chamotte.

szamotać się *ipf.* **-oczę -oczesz** *l.* **-ocę -ocesz, -ocz** tussle (*z kimś/czymś* with sb/sth) (*o coś* for *l.* about *l.* over sth); struggle (*z kimś/czymś* with sb/sth) (*o coś* for sth); scuffle (*z kimś* with sth).

szamotanina *f. pot.* tussle (*o coś* for *l.* about *l.* over sth); struggle, scramble (*o coś* for sth).

szamotowy *a. ceramika* **osłona szamotowa** saggar, sagger; **cegła szamotowa** *bud.* chamotte brick.

szampan *mi Gen.* **-a** *Acc.* **-a** *l.* **-n** champagne.

szampanka *f. Gen.pl.* **-ek** champagne flute.

szampański *a.* sparkling.

szampańsko *adv.* **bawić się szampańsko** have a sparkling good time.

szampon *mi* (*do włosów*) shampoo; **szampon do karoserii/obić tapicerskich/dywanów** car/upholstery/carpet shampoo; **myć szamponem** shampoo.

Szanghaj *mi geogr.* Shanghai.

szaniec *mi* **-ńc-** *Gen.* **-a** *wojsk.* rampart, earthwork.

szankier *mi* **-kr-** *Gen.* **-a** *pat.* chancre.

szanować *ipf.* **1.** (= *poważać, traktować serio*) respect; **szanować czyjąś wolę** respect sb's will; **szanować prawo** respect the law; **szanować starszych** respect one's elders; **ogólnie szanowany** widely respected. **2.** (= *cenić*) value, esteem; **szanować czyjąś przyjaźń** value sb's friendship. **3.** (= *oszczędzać*) spare, protect; be careful with (*sth*); **szanować czyjeś uczucia** spare sb's feelings; **szanować książki** treat books with care; **szanuj zieleń** keep off the grass. ~ **się** *ipf.* **1.** (= *dbać o siebie*) take care of o.s. *l.* of one's health. **2.** (= *mieć godność*) have respect for o.s.; carry o.s. with dignity.

szanowny *a.* (*w zwrotach grzecznościowych*) **czego sobie szanowny pan życzy?** how can I help you, sir?; **Szanowna Pani/Szanowny Panie** Dear Madam/Sir; **szanowni państwo!** ladies and gentlemen!

szansa *f. pl.* **-e** chance, odds (*czegoś l. na coś* of sth); **szansa na zwycięstwo** chance of victory; **szanse wygrania meczu** the odds of winning the match; **jedna szansa na milion** a chance in a million; **mieć (niezłą) szansę na coś** stand a (fair *l.* good) chance of sth; **nie mieć cienia szansy** not have a snowball's chance in hell; **dawać komuś drugą szansę** give sb another chance; **i już po szansie!** there goes our chance!; **nie ma szans** (there's) no chance; **równość szans** equal opportunity; **to twoja ostatnia szansa** this is your last chance; **życiowa szansa** the chance of a lifetime.

szansonista *mp*, **szansonistka** *f. Gen.pl.* **-ek** *przest. l. żart.* cabaret singer.

szanta[1] *f. żegl.* shanty, chanty, chantey.

szanta[2] *f. bot.* horehound (*Marrubium vulgare*).

szantaż *mi Gen.pl.* **-y** *l.* **-ów** blackmail; **uciekać się do szantażu** resort to blackmail; **ulegać szantażowi** yield to blackmail.

szantażować *ipf.* blackmail.

szantażysta *mp*, **szantażystka** *f. Gen.pl.* **-ek** blackmailer.

szantrapa *f. pog. l. żart.* strumpet.

szantung *mi tk.* shantung.

szanujący się *a.* self-respecting, self-respectful.

szapoklak *mi Gen.* **-a** *przest.* opera hat, crush hat.

szaraczkowy *a.* **szlachta szaraczkowa** *hist.* small freeholders (*formerly in Poland*).

szarada *f.* **1.** (*rymowana zagadka*) charade. **2.** *przen.* (= *enigmatyczna wypowiedź*) conundrum. **3.** *przest.* (*gra salonowa*) charades.

szaradzista *mp*, **szaradzistka** *f. Gen.pl.* **-ek** author of charades.

szarak *ma* **1.** *zool., myśl.* common hare (*Lepus timidus*). **2.** (= *osoba mało ważna*) a nobody, man in the street.

szarańcza *f. Gen.pl.* **-y** *ent.* locust; **szarańcza wędrowna** migratory locust (*Locusta migratoria*).

szarańczak *mi ent.* acridoid grasshopper.

szarańczyn *mi bot.* carob(-tree), St. John's bread (*Ceratonia siliqua*).

szarawary *pl. Gen.* **-ów** *strój, hist.* galligaskins.

szarawy *a.* grayish; *Br.* greyish, grizzled; *form.* griseous.

szarfa *f.* sash; (= *przepaska*) girdle.

szargać *ipf.* decry, disparage, attack; **szargać świętości** profane sacred things; **szargać czyjeś dobre imię** tarnish sb's good name; drag sb's name through the mud.

szariat *mi islam* sharia, shariat, shari'at.

szarlatan *mp* charlatan, quack, mountebank.

szarlataneria *f.* charlatanry, charlatanism, quackery.

szarlatanka *f. zob.* **szarlatan**.

szarlatański *a.* charlatan, charlatanic, quackish; **szarlatańskie praktyki** charlatan practises, charlatanry.

szarlotka *f. Gen.pl.* **-ek** *kulin.* layered apple cake.

szarłat *mi bot.* amaranth (*Amaranthus*).

szarmancki *a.* gallant, chivalrous.

szarmanteria *f. przest.* gallantry.

szaro *adv. zob.* **szary**; **zrobić kogoś na szaro** frame sb.

szarobury *a.* dirty brown.

szarogęsić się *ipf.* **-szę -sisz** *pot.* boss the show.

szarość *f.* **1.** (*kolor*) gray, *Br.* grey. **2.** = **szarzyzna**. **3.** = **szarówka**.

szarota *f. bot.* cudweed (*Gnaphalium*).

szarotka *f. Gen.pl.* **-ek** *bot.* edelweiss (*Leontopodium alpinum*).

szarówka *f. Gen.pl.* **-ek** dusk, twilight; **szarówka świtu** the gray *l.* grayness of the dawn.

szarpać *ipf.* **-pię -piesz** **1.** (= *pociągać gwałtownie*) pull, tug, twitch (*za coś* at sth); jerk, tweak (*sth*); (*strunę*) pick, pluck. **2.** (*rwać*) tear (*sth*) (up) (*na kawałki* into pieces); (*o psie*) (= *łapać zębami, podrzucać*) worry (*sth*). **3.** *przen.* (*o kaszlu*) rack (*sb*); **szarpać komuś nerwy** jar on sb's nerves. **~ się** *ipf.* **1.** (= *wyrywać się, wierzgać, robić gwałtowne ruchy*) flinch (back); struggle (*z czymś* with *l.* against sth); (*o koniu*) buck. **2.** (= *walczyć chaotycznie*) struggle, tussle (*z kimś / czymś* with sb/sth).

szarpanina *f.* struggle, tussle.

szarpie *pl. Gen.* **-i** *med., przest.* lint.

szarpnąć *pf.* **-ij** **1.** *zob.* **szarpać**. **2.** (= *ruszyć gwałtownie*) tug, start, jerk, lunge. **~ się** *pf.* **1.** *zob.* **szarpać się**. **2.** *pot.* (= *wydać dużo*) spend a fortune (*na coś* on sth).

szarpnięcie *n.* pull, twitch, tweak; *żegl.* (*w celu uwolnienia liny*) hitch; (= *gwałtowny ruch pojazdu itp.*) tug, jerk, jolt.

szaruga *f.* foul weather, rainy day.

szary *a.* **1.** (*o kolorze*) gray, *Br.* grey; (*o sierści, włosach*) grizzle; **rządzić się jak szara gęś** *przen.* boss the show. **2.** (= *pogrążony w cieniu, t. przen.*) gray, shadowy, twilight; **szara eminencja** gray eminence, éminence grise; **szara strefa** gray area. **3.** *przen.* (= *nudny, przeciętny, nierzucający się w oczy*) drab, humdrum, ordinary,

run-of-the-mill; **szara egzystencja** drab existence; **szary człowiek** everyman, ordinary man, the man in the street; **szary koniec stołu** the bottom of a table; **na szarym końcu** at the very end. **4.** (*w terminologii naukowej i technicznej*) **ciało szare** *fiz.* gray body; **istota szara** *anat.* gray matter; **szare komórki** gray cells; *przen.* (= *intelekt*) gray matter; **szara maść** *med., przest.* blue ointment, mercurial ointment; **szare mydło** green soap, soft soap. **5.** (*w nazwach gatunków*) **niedźwiedź szary** *zool.* grizzly bear (*Ursus arctos horribilis*); **orzech szary** *bot.* white walnut (*Juglans cinerea*); **wal szary** *zool.* gray whale (*Eschrichtius glaucus*); **wiewiórka szara** *zool.* gray squirrel (*Sciurus carolinensis*); **wilk szary** *zool.* (*odmiana północnoamerykańska*) gray wolf, timber wolf (*Canis lupus occidentalis*); **żarłacz szary** *icht.* tope (*Galeorhinus galeus*).

szarytka *f. Gen.pl.* **-ek** **1.** *rz.-kat.* sister of charity. **2.** *orn.* (= *sikora uboga*) marsh tit (*Parus palustris*).

szarzeć *ipf.* **1.** (= *stawać się szarym*) gray, grizzle, turn gray; **szarzeje** (= *zmierzcha się*) it's getting dusky. **2.** *lit.* (= *majaczyć w półmroku*) loom, darkle.

szarzyzna *f.* drabness, monotony.

szarża *f. wojsk.* **1.** (= *atak*) charge; **szarża konna** cavalry charge. **2.** (= *ranga*) rank; **wysoka szarża** *pot.* brass hat.

szarżować *ipf.* **1.** *gł. wojsk.* (= *przypuszczać atak*) charge (*na coś* (at) sth). **2.** (= *przesadzać*) exaggerate; *teatr* overact; ham (it up).

szast *int.* swish, swoosh; **szast-prast i po krzyku** *l.* **po robocie** *l.* **po ptokach** *żart.* wham-bamdone.

szastać *ipf.* + *Ins.* **1.** (= *wydawać, pozbywać się szybko*) chuck (*sth*) about *l.* around; **szastać pieniędzmi (na prawo i lewo)** be careless with one's money. **2. szastać nogą/nogami** shuffle one's foot/feet. **~ się** *ipf.* + *Ins.* = **szastać 1**.

szaszłyk *mi Gen.* **-a** *kulin.* shish kebab, shashlik.

szaszłykarnia *f. Gen.pl.* **-i** shish-kebab restaurant.

szata *f.* **1.** vestment, garment; *pl.* garb, clothes; **szaty duchownego** *kośc.* clerical garb; *pot.* clericals; (*symbol stanu duchownego*) the cloth; **szata liturgiczna** *kośc.* liturgical vestment; **rozdzierać szaty** *przen.* tear one's clothes. **2.** *przen.* **szata graficzna** *druk.* layout; **szata roślinna** *ekol.* plant cover; **szata letnia/zimowa** *orn.* (= *barwy upierzenia*) summer/winter dress.

szatan *mp pl.* **-i** *l.* **-y** **1.** *rel.* Satan, the Devil. **2.** (= *zły duch; t. przen.*) devil, fiend, demon; **istny szatan (z piekła rodem)** *żart.* fiend out of hell; **szatan wcielony** devil incarnate; **wypędzać diabła szatanem** use the devil to cast out the devil. – *mi Gen.* **-a** *pl.* **-y** **1.** *bot.* (*grzyb*) Satan's bolete (*Boletus satanas*). **2.** *pot.* (= *mocna czarna kawa*) mud.

szatański *a.* satanic, devilish, fiendish; **szatańskie nasienie** the spawn of Satan; **grzyb** *l.* **borowik szatański** *bot.* = **szatan**.

szatkować *ipf.* shred; **szatkowana kapusta** shredded cabbage.

szatkownica *f.* shredder.

szatnia *f. Gen.pl.* **-i 1.** (*na wierzchnie okrycia*) cloakroom. **2.** (= *przebieralnia, zwł. sportowa*) locker room, changing room.

szatniarka *f. Gen.pl.* **-ek, szatniarz** *mp* cloakroom attendant.

szatny *mp hist.* valet.

szatyn *mp,* **szatynka** *f. Gen.pl.* **-ek** brownhaired *l.* chestnut-haired person.

szczać *ipf. wulg.* piss.

szczapa *f.* chip (of wood); **chudy jak szczapa** as thin as a lath.

szczaw *mi* **-wi-** *bot., kulin.* sorrel, dock (*Rumex*).

szczawian *mi chem.* oxalate.

szczawik *mi bot.* oxalis (*Oxalis*); **szczawik zajęczy** wood sorrel (*O. acetosella*); **szczawik bulwiasty** oca (*O. tuberosa, O. crenata*).

szczawiowy *a.* **1.** *kulin.* sorrel; **zupa szczawiowa** sorrel soup. **2.** *chem.* oxalic; **kwas szczawiowy** oxalic acid.

szczątek *mi* **-tk-** *pl.* **-i 1.** (= *częściowa pozostałość*) fragment, rudiment, vestige, residue (*czegoś* of sth). **2.** *pl.* (= *resztki, t. zwłoki, prochy*) remains, relics, remainders (*kogoś / czegoś* of sb/ sth); **szczątki doczesne** mortal remains; **szczątki wraku** *żegl.* flotsam.

szczątkowo *adv.* fragmentarily, rudimentarily.

szczątkowy *a.* fragmentary, rudimentary, vestigial, residual; **szczątkowe ślady** residual traces (*czegoś* of sth); **narząd szczątkowy** *biol.* rudimentary *l.* vestigial organ; **promieniowanie szczątkowe** *astron.* background radiation.

szczebel *mi* **-bl-** *Gen.* **-a 1.** (*drabiny*) rung; (*płaski*) ladder step; **piąć się po szczeblach kariery** *przen.* move *l.* go up the ladder. **2.** (= *poziom*) level, grade.

szczebiot *mi* (*ptaka*) chirp, chirrup, warble, twitter; *t. przen.* (= *głos dziecka itp.*) chattering.

szczebiotać *ipf.* **-czę -czesz** *l.* **-cę -cesz, -cz** (= *ćwierkać*) chirp, chirrup; (= *o ptakach*) warble, twitter, tweet; (*t. przen. o ludziach*) chatter.

szczebiotliwy *a.* chirpy, chirrupy, chatty.

szczecina *f.* **1.** (*zwierzęcia*) bristles; *orn.* (*na dziobie ptaka*) beard. **2.** (= *krótki, kłujący zarost*) stubble.

szczeciniasty *a.* bristly, stubbly.

szczecinka *f. Gen.pl.* **-ek** *bot., ent.* (*część kłosa l. czułka*) arista; *zool.* = **szczeć** 3.

szczeciogonki *pl. Gen.* **-ów** *ent.* (*rząd owadów*) bristletails, thysanurans (*Thysanura*).

szczecioszczękowce *pl. zool.* (*typ*) arrowworms, chaetognaths (*Chaetognatha*).

szczeć *f. pl.* **-cie** *l.* **-ci 1.** = **szczecina**. **2.** *bot.* teasel (*Dipsacus*). **3.** *zw. pl. zool.* (*chitynowy włosek u stawonogów i pierścienic*) chaeta, seta.

szczególnie *adv.* **1.** (= *zwłaszcza, specjalnie*) particularly, especially, in particular; **szczególnie ładny/interesujący** particularly *l.* especially fine/interesting; **nie było szczególnie gorąco** it wasn't particularly hot; **szczególnie lubię róże** I

like roses in particular; I especially like roses; **szczególnie że...** especially because... **2.** (= *osobliwie*) extraordinarily; *uj.* (= *dziwnie, dziwacznie*) oddly; **zachowywał się szczególnie** he behaved oddly.

szczególność *f.* **w szczególności** in particular.

szczególny *a.* **1.** (= *specjalny*) particular, special, especial; **szczególna okazja** special occasion; **szczególna teoria względności** *fiz.* special (theory of) relativity; **to rzecz szczególnej wagi** it's a matter of especial *l.* special *l.* particular importance; **to nic szczególnego** (= *nic takiego*) it's nothing special; **nie miałem na myśli nikogo szczególnego** (= *nikogo w szczególności*) I meant nobody in particular. **2.** (= *osobliwy, nadzwyczajny*) extraordinary; **to człowiek o szczególnych talentach** he's a man of extraordinary talents. **3.** *uj.* (= *dziwny, dziwaczny*) odd, strange, queer.

szczegół *mi* detail; *pl. t.* specifics, minutiae; **szczegóły praktyczne** nuts and bolts; **przejść do szczegółów** get down to specifics; get down to brass tacks; **oszczędź mi szczegółów** spare me the details; **to naprawdę szczegół** it's really just a detail; **wchodzić w szczegóły** go into details; **w każdym szczególe** in every detail; **w (najdrobniejszych) szczegółach** in (minute) detail; **diabeł tkwi w szczegółach** *przen.* the devil's in the details.

szczegółowo *adv.* in detail, accurately.

szczegółowość *f.* minuteness, accuracy.

szczegółowy *a.* = *zawierający szczegóły*) detailed; (= *precyzyjny*) accurate, precise; (*szczegółowa lista / analiza*) detailed list/analysis; (*szczegółowy opis*) detailed *l.* accurate description; (*szczegółowy plan*) detailed *l.* precise plan.

szczekacz *mp pot., pog.* barker.

szczekaczka *f. Gen.pl.* **-ek 1.** *pot.* (= *głośnik*) loudspeaker (*in a public place*). **2.** *pot., pog. zob.* **szczekacz.**

szczekać *ipf.* (*o psie, myśl. o lisie*) bark (*na kogoś / coś* at sb/sth); *onomat.* woof, bow-wow; (= *ujadać, t. przen.*) bay (*na kogoś / coś* at sb/sth); **psy szczekają, karawana idzie dalej** *przen.* dogs bark but the caravans move on.

szczekliwy *a.* barking.

szczeknąć *pf.* **-ij** *zob.* **szczekać.**

szczekuszka *f. Gen.pl.* **-ek** *zool.* (= *zajęczak z rodziny Ochotonidae*) pika; *pot.* cony.

szczelina *f.* **1.** (= *odstęp*) gap, cleft; *techn.* aperture, clearance (*między... a...* between... and...); *fon.* (*przy artykulacji*) constriction. **2.** (= *pęknięcie*) crack, chink, fissure, crevice; (*w lodowcu, wale przeciwpowodziowym*) crevasse.

szczeliniak *mi Gen.* **-a** *techn.* (*narzędzie*) nicker, tracer.

szczelinomierz *mi Gen.* **-a** *techn.* gap gage, clearance gage.

szczelinowaty *a. geol.* fissured, crevassed.

szczelinowy *a.* **1.** *fon.* **głoska szczelinowa** fricative. **2.** *bud.* **mur szczelinowy** cavity wall.

szczelnie *adv.* tight; (*przed imiesłowem biernym*) tightly; **szczelnie zapakowany** tightly packed; packed tight.

szczelność *f*. tightness.

szczelny *a*. tight; (= *nieprzepuszczający powietrza*) airtight; (= *wodoszczelny*) watertight; (= *nieprzenikalny, nieprzepuszczalny*) impermeable, impenetrable.

szczeniacki *a. pot., pog*. infantile.

szczeniactwo *n. pot., pog*. infantility.

szczeniak *ma* (= *piesek*) pup, puppy, doggie. – *mp pl*. -i *pot., uj*. (= *chłopak*) whelp; *gł. Br*. young pup *l*. puppy.

szczenić się *ipf*. pup, whelp, have puppies; **nasza suka będzie się szczenić** our dog is in pup.

szczenię *n*. -nięci- *pl*. -niąt- *Gen*. -niąt *zool*. (*psa, foki, wilka, lisa*) pup; (*lisa, wilka, lwa, niedźwiedzia*) cub; *arch*. whelp.

szczenięctwo *n. żart*. puppy years.

szczenięcy *a. żart*. cubbish; **szczenięca miłość** puppy-love, calf-love; **szczenięce lata** puppy years, cub years.

szczenna *a*. (*o suce*) in pup.

szczep *mi* 1. *antrop*. tribe; **członek/członkini szczepu** tribesman/tribeswoman. 2. *harcerstwo* scout company; scout group (*in certain Boy Scout organizations*). 3. *biol*. strain. 4. *ogr*. graft.

szczepić *ipf*. 1. *med*. vaccinate, inoculate, immunize (*sb*) (*czymś* with sth) (*na coś l. przeciw czemuś* against sth). 2. *ogr*. graft (*sth*) (*na czymś* on *l*. onto sth). ~ **się** *ipf. med*. get vaccinated *l*. inoculated (*czymś* with sth) (*na coś l. przeciw czemuś* against sth).

szczepienie *n. med*. vaccination, inoculation, immunisation.

szczepionka *f. Gen.pl*. -ek *med*. vaccine; **szczepionka przeciwko ospie/wściekliźnie** smallpox/rabies vaccine.

szczepowa *f. Gen*. -ej *harcerstwo* zob. **szczepowy**.

szczepowy *a*. tribal; **starszyzna szczepowa** the elders of the tribe. – *mp harcerstwo* company leader, group leader.

szczerba *f*. 1. (= *wyszczerbienie*) chip; (= *nacięcie*) nick, notch. 2. (= *luka w uzębieniu*) gap; (= *brak zęba*) missing tooth; *przen*. (*w murze itp*.) gap, breach.

szczerbak *ma zool*. (= *ssak z rzędu Xenarthra*) xenarthran; *przest*. edentate.

szczerbaty *a*. 1. (= *nadttuczony*) chipped. 2. (= *z lukami w uzębieniu*) gap-toothed.

Szczerbiec *mi* -bc- *Gen*. -a *hist*. the Kings of Poland's coronation sword.

szczerbina *f*., **szczerbinka** *f. Gen.pl*. -ek *broń* (*część celownika*) aperture, backsight.

szczerk *mi roln*. gravelly soil.

szczerklina *f. ent*. caterpillar hunter (*Ammophila*).

szczerość *f*. frankness, candor, honesty, earnestness; **szczerość za szczerość** since you've been frank with me, I'll be frank with you too.

szczerozłoty *a*. (made of) pure gold.

szczery *a*. 1. frank, honest, candid (*z kimś l. wobec kogoś* with sb); (= *prostolinijny*) straight (*wobec kogoś* to sb); (= *naprawdę odczuwany*) earnest; **szczera nadzieja/obietnica** earnest hope/promise; **szczere podziękowania** heartfelt thanks; **jeśli mam być (z tobą) szczery...** to be honest (with you)... 2. (*o kruszcach*) pure; **szczere złoto** pure gold. 3. **szczere pole** the open.

szczerze *adv*. frankly, candidly, honestly; **szczerze mówiąc...** frankly (speaking)...; to be honest...; to be frank...; honestly...; frankly...

szczerzyć *ipf*. **szczerzyć zęby/kły** show *l*. bare one's teeth/fangs; **szczerzyć zęby do kogoś** *pot*. grin at sb. ~ **się** *ipf*. grin; show *l*. bare one's teeth.

szczeżuja *f. zool. Gen*. -ui *Gen.pl*. -ui *l*. -uj swan mussel (*Anodonta cygnea*).

szczędzić *ipf. rzad. bez przeczenia* spare; **nie szczędzić sił/czasu/pieniędzy** *lit*. spare no effort/time/money.

szczęk *mi* clash, clang, clank, jangle, clatter, rattle; **szczęk mieczy/oręża** the clash of swords/arms; **szczęk noży i widelców** the clatter of knives and forks.

szczęka *f*. 1. *anat*. (*u człowieka i większości kręgowców*) jaw; (*zwł. górna*) maxilla; (*zwł*. = *żuchwa*) mandible; (*u człowieka*) jowl; **sztuczna szczęka** (dental) plate; (set of) dentures; false teeth; **zaciskać szczęki** clench one's teeth *l*. jaws; **zadać komuś cios w szczękę** punch sb on the jaw. 2. *zool*. (*część narządów gębowych stawonogów*) maxilla. 3. *techn*. (*część imadła, uchwytu, szczypiec l. klucza nastawnego*) jaw; **szczęka hamulcowa** brake shoe.

szczękać *ipf*., **szczęknąć** *pf*. -ij 1. (+ *Ins*.) clang, clank; *gł. ipf*. clatter, jangle, rattle; **szczękać garnkami** clatter pots and pans; **szczęknąć mieczami** clash swords. 2. *tylko ipf*. (*o zębach*) chatter (together); **szczękała zębami** her teeth chattered.

szczękościsk *mi pat*. lockjaw.

szczękowce *pl. Gen*. -ów *zool*. gnathostomes (*Gnathostomata*).

szczękowy *a. anat*. mandibular, maxillary, gnathic; **kość szczękowa** jawbone; **chirurgia szczękowa** *chir*. oral surgery; **hamulec szczękowy** *mot*. shoe brake; **łamacz szczękowy** *techn*. jaw breaker.

szczęściara *f. pot*. lucky woman.

szczęściarz *mp* lucky man; *pot*. lucky beggar *l*. dog *l*. devil.

szczęścić *ipf. tylko imp*. **szczęść Boże** God speed (you). ~ **się** *ipf. tylko 3 os. sing*. **komuś się szczęści** sb is lucky; **komuś się nie szczęści** sb is down on his *l*. her luck; **niech ci się szczęści** I wish you good luck.

szczęście *n*. 1. (= *powodzenie*) luck (*w czymś* in sth *l*. at sth) (*do kogoś/czegoś* with sb/sth); good luck, (good) fortune; **na szczęście...** *l*. **szczęściem...** *l*. **szczęście, że...** fortunately...; luckily...; happily...; by a stroke of luck *l*. good fortune...; **całe szczęście, że ciebie tam nie było** it was fortunate that you weren't there; **szczęście, że nikt nie zginął** mercifully, nobody was killed; **mieć szczęście** be in luck; **nie mieć szczęścia** be down on one's luck; **mieć szczęście w czymś** be lucky in sth; **nie mam szczęścia do ko-**

biet I have no luck with women; **szczęście w nie-szczęściu, że...** the only lucky thing is that...; **przynosić komuś szczęście** bring sb luck *l.* good fortune; **próbować szczęścia (w czymś)** try one's luck *l.* fortune (at sth); **dziecko szczęścia** *przen.* minion of fortune; **łut szczęścia** a little bit of luck; **uśmiech szczęścia** smile of fortune; **kto nie ma szczęścia w kartach, ten ma szczęście w miło-ści** (*przysłowie, często odwracane*) unlucky at cards, lucky in love. **2.** (= *błogość, radosne sa-mopoczucie*) happiness, felicity, bliss; **szczęście małżeńskie** marital bliss; **nic mi więcej do szczę-ścia nie potrzeba** this is all I need to make me happy; **dać komuś szczęście** make sb happy.

szczęśliwie *adv.* **1.** (= *błogo, radośnie*) happi-ly. **2. ...i żyli razem szczęśliwie** (*w zakończeniu bajki*) ...and they lived happily ever after. **3.** (= *z powodzeniem*) luckily, fortunately, happily.

szczęśliwiec *mp* -**wc**- *Voc.* -**cze** *l.* -**u** = szczę-ściarz.

szczęśliwość *f. lit.* = szczęście 2.

szczęśliwy *a.* **1.** (= *mający szczęście l. powo-dzenie, przynoszący powodzenie*) lucky, fortu-nate; **dziękować swojej szczęśliwej gwieździe** thank one's lucky stars. **2.** (= *udany*) good, hap-py, felicitous, prosperous; **szczęśliwej podróży!** have a safe journey; **szczęśliwego Nowego Ro-ku!** Happy New Year!; **szczęśliwy wybór** felici-tous choice. **3.** (= *odczuwający szczęście*) happy, blissful.

szczęt *mi* **do szczętu** completely, every last *l.* single one; **kłusownicy wybili do szczętu jelenie w tych lasach** poachers have killed every single deer in these woods.

szczmiel *mi bot.* China grass (*Boehmeria ni-vea*).

szczodrobliwość *f. przest.* = szczodrość.

szczodrobliwy *a. przest.* = szczodry.

szczodrość *f. lit.* generosity.

szczodry *a. lit.* generous, openhanded, lavish, profuse; **rozdawać coś szczodrą ręką** give sth out freely.

szczodrze *adv. lit.* freely, liberally, generous-ly; **szczodrze obdarowany (przez naturę)** (*o wro-dzonych talentach l. zaletach*) well-endowed (*czymś* with sth).

szczodrzeniec *mi* -**ńc**- *Gen.* -**a** *bot.* broom (*Cy-tisus*).

szczoteczka *f. Gen.pl.* -**ek** **1.** brush; **szczotecz-ka do rąk** *l.* **paznokci** nailbrush; **szczoteczka do zębów** toothbrush. **2.** *ent.* (*na odnóżach owa-dów*) scopula.

szczotka *f. Gen.pl.* -**ek** **1.** brush; (*na kiju, do zamiatania*) broom; **szczotka do butów** shoe-brush; **szczotka do ubrań** clothesbrush; **szczotka do włosów** hairbrush; **szczotka ryżowa** scrub-bing brush; **kij od szczotki** broomstick. **2.** *el.* (collecting) brush. **3.** *druk.* galley proof.

szczotkarski *a.* brushmaking.

szczotkarstwo *n.* brushmaking.

szczotkować *ipf.* brush (down).

szczotkowaty *a.* brushlike; (*o zaroście*) stub-bly.

szczotkowy *a.* **1.** *druk.* **odbitka szczotkowa**

galley proof. **2.** *el.* **wyładowanie szczotkowe** brush discharge.

szczuć *ipf.* **1.** *gł. myśl.* (*szczuć psa na kogoś l. coś l. szczuć kogoś l coś psem*) set a dog on sb/sth; **szczuć psami** (*schwytane zwierzę*) bait. **2.** *myśl.* (= *popędzać okrzykami*) (*psy l. zwierzynę*) hal-loo, tally-ho. **3.** *przen.* (= *podjudzać*) **szczuć ko-goś przeciwko komuś** turn sb against sb.

szczudłak *ma orn.* stilt, longshanks (*Himan-topus himantopus*).

szczudło *n. Gen.* -**deł** *zw. pl.* stilt; **para szczu-deł** pair of stilts; **chodzić na szczudłach** walk on stilts.

szczudłowaty *a.* stilty.

szczupaczek *ma* -**czk**- *icht.* **szczupaczek żywo-rodny** pike killifish (*Belonesox belizanus*).

szczupak *ma* **1.** *icht.* pike, luce (*Esox lucius*); **szczupak morski** (= *belona*) garpike, garfish, sea-pike (*Belone*). **2. dać szczupaka** *l.* skoczyć szczupakiem *pot.* plunge, jump headlong.

szczupieńczyk *ma icht.* killifish (*Aplocheilus*).

szczupleć *ipf.* -**eję** -**ejesz** **1.** (= *chudnąć*) lose weight, grow thin *l.* slim. **2.** *lit.* (= *zmniejszać się*) diminish, get reduced.

szczupło *adv.* **wyglądać szczupło** look slim *l.* thin.

szczupły *a.* **1.** (= *niegruby*) slim, thin; **szczu-pła w talii** slim-waisted. **2.** *lit.* (= *nieliczny, skromny*) meager, short; **szczupła racja żywno-ściowa** short ration; **szczupłe zasoby** meager means.

szczur *ma* **1.** *zool.* rat (*Rattus*); **szczur śniady** black rat (*R. rattus*); **szczur wędrowny** brown rat, Norway rat (*R. norvegicus*). **2. szczur piż-mowy** *zool.* muskrat (*Ondatra zibethica*). **3.** *pog.* (*o człowieku*) rat; **szczur lądowy** *żart.* land-lubber; **szczur pustynny** (= *weteran kampanii w Afryce 1941-42*) desert rat.

szczurołap *mp* ratcatcher.

szczurzy *a.* ratlike; (*o zapachu itp.*) ratty.

szczutek *mi* -**tk**- *Gen.* -**a** fillip; **dać komuś szczutka** give a fillip to sb.

szczwany *a.* cunning, sly, wily, clever; **szczwa-ny lis** *przen.* cunning old fox.

szczycić się *ipf.* **1.** + *Ins.* (= *mieć prawo do du-my z posiadania czegoś*) boast (*czymś* sth). **2.** (= *być dumnym*) (+ *Ins.*) be proud of (*sth*); **szczycić się (tym), że...** be proud that...

szczygieł *ma* -**gł**- *orn.* goldfinch (*Carduelis carduelis*); **wesoły jak szczygieł** *l.* szczygiełek *przen.* (as) merry as a lark.

szczyl *mp pog.* brat.

szczyny *pl. Gen.* -**n** *wulg.* piss.

szczypać *ipf.* -**pię** -**piesz** **1.** (*palcami*) pinch; (*wykręcając l. pociągając*) tweak; **szczypać ko-goś w policzek/ramię** pinch sb's cheek/arm; give sb a pinch on the cheek/arm; **szczypać kogoś w ucho** tweak sb's ear; give sb's ear a tweak. **2.** (= *powodować pieczenie*) bite, nip, sting; **mróz szczypał nas w policzki** the frost nipped our cheeks. **3.** (*o skórze, oczach, ranie, języku*) (= *piec*) prickle, sting; **oczy mnie szczypią od dymu** my eyes are stinging from the smoke. **4.** (*o zwie-rzęciu*) (= *skubać zębami*) nibble, crop; **szczypać**

trawę (*o przeżuwaczach*) browse. ~ się *ipf.* **1.** (= *szczypać samego siebie*) pinch o.s.; **szczypać się w ucho** tweak one's own ear. **2.** *pot.* (= *krępować się, zwlekać*) pussyfoot (about *l.* around); **nie szczyp się i mów, czego chcesz** stop pussyfooting around and say what you want.

szczypawka *f. Gen.pl.* **-ek** *pot.* (*popularna nazwa różnych owadów*) **1.** (= *biegacz*) ground beetle. **2.** (= *skorek*) earwig.

szczypce *pl. Gen.* **-piec 1.** *techn.* (*narzędzie do chwytania o ramionach połączonych pośrodku zawiasem*) (pair of) pincers; (*o ramionach połączonych na jednym końcu*) (pair of) tongs; **szczypce do cukru/węgla** sugar/fire tongs; **szczypce do cięcia drutu** wire-cutters, nippers; **szczypce z wysięgnikiem** lazy tongs; **szczypce uniwersalne** (= *kombinerki*) (pair of) pliers. **2.** *med., chir.* forceps; **szczypce dentystyczne** tooth forceps. **3.** *zool., anat.* (*narząd chwytny niektórych zwierząt*) pincers, forceps; (*u krabów, raków*) nipper, claw.

szczypczyki *pl. Gen.* **-ków** (*narzędzie*) (pair of) tweezers.

szczypior *mi kulin.* spring onion (leaves), green onion, scallion.

szczypiorek *mi* **-rk- 1.** *pot., kulin.* = **szczypior. 2.** *bot., kulin.* chive, cives (*Allium schoenoprasum*).

szczypiorkowy *a.* chive.

szczypiorniak *mi Gen.* **-a** *sport* handball.

szczypiornista *mp*, **szczypiornistka** *f. Gen.pl.* **-ek** *sport* handball player.

szczypta *f. kulin. t.* pinch; *kulin. t.* sprinkle, dash (*czegoś* of sth); *przen.* (= *mała ilość*) grain, scintilla; **szczypta zdrowego rozsądku** grain of common sense.

szczyr *mi bot.* **szczyr trwały** dog's mercury (*Mercurialis perennis*).

szczyt *mi* **1.** (= *wierzchołek, t. przen.*) top; (*góry*) summit, peak, top; (= *czubek*) tip, apex; **szczyt budynku** *bud.* gable; **szczyt dachu** *bud.* rooftop; **szczyt masztu** masthead; **szczyt schodów** stairhead. **2.** *przen.* **szczyt stołu** the head of a table; **szczyt płuca** *anat.* the apex of a lung. **3.** *polit.* (= *wysoki szczebel*) **szczyt polityczny** political summit; **spotkanie na szczycie** summit meeting. **4.** *przen.* (= *maksimum, zwieńczenie*) climax, apex, culmination, peak; **godziny szczytu** rush hours; **szczyt kariery** the climax of one's career; **szczyt możliwości** the best one can do; **szczyt sezonu** high season; **szczyt złego smaku** the extreme of bad taste; **to jest szczyt wszystkiego!** this is the end!

szczytny *a. lit.* lofty, high, noble; **szczytne cele** noble ends; **szczytne ideały** lofty ideals.

szczytować *ipf. fizj.* climax, reach an orgasm.

szczytowanie *n. fizj.* climax, orgasm.

szczytowy *a.* **1.** top, highest; **pąk szczytowy** *bot.* terminal bud; **pęd szczytowy** *bot.* shoot apex, terminal shoot; **kręg szczytowy** *anat.* atlas; **ściana szczytowa** *bud.* gable. **2.** (= *maksymalny*) highest, maximum; (*wartość szczytowa*) *fiz.* peak.

szedł *itd. ipf. zob.* **iść.**

szef *mp pl.* **-owie 1.** boss, head, chief. **2.** *Voc. pot.* (*sposób poufałego zwracania się do obcych*) chief, boss, mister. **3.** (*w utartych zwrotach*) **szef rządu** *l.* **gabinetu** *polit.* prime minister, *pot.* PM; **szef kompanii** *wojsk.* first sergeant; **szef kuchni** chef; **szef orkiestry** bandleader; **szef policji** police chief; **szef sztabu** *wojsk.* chief of staff.

szefostwo *n. pot.* exec, chiefdom, (the) top brass.

szefowa *f. Gen.* **-ej** *zob.* **szef** 1.

szejk *mp pl.* **-owie** *polit., rel.* sheik.

szejkanat, szejkat *mi polit.* sheikdom.

szekla *f. Gen.pl.* **-i** *żegl.* shackle.

szekspirolog *mp pl.* **-dzy** *l.* **-owie** *teor.lit.* Shakespearian (scholar).

szekspirologia *f. Gen.* **-ii** *teor.lit.* Shakespearology, Shakespearian studies.

szekspirologiczny *a. teor.lit.* Shakespearological.

szelak *mi techn.* shellac.

szeląg *mi Acc. i Gen.* **-a 1.** *hist.* (*rodzaj monety w różnych krajach*) shilling. **2.** *przen.* **nie mieć złamanego szeląga** not have a penny; **znam go jak zły szeląg** he turns up like a bad penny.

szelest *mi* rustle.

szeleścić *ipf.* **-szczę -ścisz** rustle.

szelf *mi geol.* shelf; **szelf kontynentalny** *geogr.* continental shelf.

szelfowy *a.* shelf.

szelki *pl. Gen.* **-lek 1.** (*do spodni*) suspenders; *Br.* braces. **2.** (*dla dzieci do nauki chodzenia*) baby's harness. **3.** (*uprząż*) harness.

szelma *f. l. mp decl. like f. Gen.pl.* **-m** *l.* **-ów** rogue, rascal.

szelmostwo *n.* roguery, rascality.

szelmowski *a.* **1.** (= *łotrowski*) roguish, rascally. **2.** (= *figlarny*) skittish.

szemrać *ipf.* **-mrzę -mrzesz** *l.* **-mram -mrasz, -mrz** *l.* **-mraj 1.** (= *szumieć*) (*np. o strumyku*) (= *szeptać*) murmur. **2.** (*narzekać*) murmur (*na coś* at sth).

szemranie *n.* murmur; **bez szemrania** without a murmur.

szemrany *a. pot.* (*o towarzystwie, osobie*) shady, lowlife; (*o interesach, sprawach*) shady.

szepnąć *pf.* **-ij** *zob.* **szeptać.**

szept *mi* whisper; **szepty** (= *plotki, pogłoski*) whispering; **mówić szeptem** whisper, speak in a whisper; **powiedzieć coś szeptem** say sth in a whisper; **słyszałem jakieś szepty w korytarzu** I heard somebody whispering in the corridor.

szeptać *ipf.* **-pczę -pczesz** *l.* **-pcę -pcesz 1.** (= *mówić szeptem*) whisper; **szepnij za mną słówko szefowi** put in a good for me to the boss. **2.** (*plotkować*) whisper.

szer. *abbr.* **1.** (= *szeregowy*) Pvt. (= *private*). **2.** (= *szerokość*) w. (= *width*).

szereg *mi* **1.** (= *rząd*) row; **szeregi** (*wojskowe*) ranks; **służyć w szeregach piechoty** serve in the infantry; **ustawić się w szeregu** line up; **stanąć z kimś w jednym szeregu** line up with sb. **2.** (= *duża liczba*) (a) number, (an) array (*czegoś* of sth); **szereg zdarzeń/dni** a number of incidents/days;

szereg informacji a lot of information; **przez szereg lat** many years in a row. **3.** *mat.* series.

szeregować *ipf.* rank, range.

szeregowiec *mp* **-wc-** *pl.* **-y** *wojsk.* private; **starszy szeregowiec** *US* private first class; *Br.* lance corporal. – *mi* **-wc-** *pl.* **-e** (*dom*) row house; *Br.* terraced house, terrace house.

szeregowo *adv.* in series.

szeregowy *a.* **1.** (= *w szeregu*) arranged in rows; *el.* serial; **dom szeregowy** row house; *Br.* terraced house, terrace house; **połączenie szeregowe** serial connection. **2.** (= *zwykły*) rank and file; **szeregowy członek** (*partii, związku itp.*) rank and file member. – *mp wojsk. zob.* **szeregowiec.**

szermierczy *a.* fencing; **zawody szermiercze** fencing competition; **plansza szermiercza** piste.

szermierka *f.* fencing; **szermierka słowna** verbal sparring, sword-play.

szermierz *mp* **1.** (*sportowiec*) fencer. **2.** (= *bojownik*) champion (*czegoś* of sth).

szermować *ipf.* **1.** (*słowami, argumentami*) bandy. **2.** (*białą bronią*) fence.

szeroki *a.* **-rszy 1.** (*rzeka, brama, rękaw, ekran*) wide; (*uśmiech, widok, czoło*) broad; **szeroki ekran** wide screen; **szeroki uśmiech** broad smile; **szeroki na trzy metry** three meters wide. **2.** *przen.* (*plany, zakres, horyzonty*) broad; (*publiczność, grono*) wide; **jak kraj długi i szeroki** all across the country; **mieć szeroki gest** be open-handed; **mieć szerokie horyzonty myślowe** be broad-minded; **odbić się szerokim echem** have far-reaching consequences; **wypłynąć na szerokie wody** rise to prominence.

szeroko *adv.* **-rzej 1.** (= *rozciągle*) widely; (= *na wszystkie strony*) broadly; **szeroko na centymetr** one centimeter wide; **mieć oczy szeroko otwarte** keep one's eyes peeled *l.* skinned; **rozstaw nogi szeroko** spread your legs wide; **zostaw okno szeroko otwarte** leave the window wide open; **otworzył szeroko oczy ze zdumienia** he opened his eyes wide in amazement. **2.** (*opowiadać, opisywać*) at large; **wieść o tym rozeszła się szeroko** the news about it spread far and wide.

szerokoekranowy *a. kino* wide-screen.

szerokokątny *a. fot.* **obiektyw szerokokątny** wide-angle lens.

szerokonosy *a.* broad-nosed; **małpy szerokonose** *zool.* platyrrhines, platyrrhinians (*Cebidae*).

szerokość *f.* **1.** (*wymiar*) width, breadth; **szerokość geograficzna** latitude; **pod każdą szerokością geograficzną** (= *wszędzie*) the world over; **szerokość toru** *kol.* gauge; **mieć pięć metrów szerokości** be five meters wide; **otworzyć coś na całą szerokość** open sth wide. **2.** (*opisu*) extensiveness; **szerokość zainteresowań** wide range of interests.

szerokotorowy *a. kol.* broad-gauge.

szerszeń *ma ent.* hornet (*Vespa crabro*).

szeryf[1] *mp Gen.* **-a** *pl.* **-owie 1.** (*w USA*) sheriff. **2.** *hist.* (*w Anglii*) sheriff.

szeryf[2] *mi Gen.* **-u** *pl.* **-y** *druk.* serif.

szerzyciel *mp* propagator, promulgator.

szerzyć *ipf.* **1.** (= *propagować*) (*oświatę, idee*) propagate, promulgate. **2.** (= *wzmagać, nasilać*) (*plotki, informacje, choroby*) spread; (*postrach*) cause; **szerzyć zniszczenie** play havoc, wreak havoc. ~ **się** *ipf.* spread.

szesnasta *f. Gen.* **-ej** (*godzina*) four p.m., sixteen hours.

szesnastka *f. Gen.pl.* **-ek 1.** (*liczba*) sixteen. **2.** (= *zbiór szesnastu elementów, osób*) a group of sixteen. **3.** (= *autobus, tramwaj 16*) (service) sixteen. **4.** (= *mieszkanie, dom nr 16*) number sixteen; **mieszkam pod szesnastką** I live at number sixteen. **5.** (= *jedna szesnasta*) a *l.* one sixteenth (*czegoś* of sth). **6.** *druk.* sixteenmo, sextodecimo. **7.** *muz.* sixteenth note; *Br.* semiquaver. **8.** *pot.* (*dziewczyna*) sixteen year old girl.

szesnastolatek *mp* **-tk-** *pl.* **-i** (*chłopak*) boy of sixteen.

szesnastolatka *f. Gen.pl.* **-ek** (*dziewczyna*) girl of sixteen.

szesnastoletni *a.* **1.** (= *mający szesnaście lat*) sixteen-year-old. **2.** (= *trwający szesnaście lat*) sixteen-year-long, sixteen years long; **szesnastoletni staż** work experience of sixteen years.

szesnastowieczny *a.* sixteenth-century.

szesnasty *a.* sixteenth; **być szesnastym na liście** be sixteenth on the list; **mieszkać pod szesnastym** live at number sixteen. – *mi* (*dzień*) the sixteenth; **dziś mamy szesnastego marca** it is the sixteenth of March today.

szesnaście *num.* **-st-** *Ins.* **-oma** *l.* **-u** sixteen.

sześć. *abbr.* (= *sześcienny*) cu., c. (= *cubic*).

sześcian *mi geom., mat.* cube; **sześcian liczby** cube of a number; **podnieść do sześcianu** cube.

sześcienny *a.* cubic; **metr/centymetr sześcienny** cubic meter/centimeter, *Br.* cubic metre/centimeter; **pierwiastek sześcienny** *mat.* cube root.

sześcioboczny *a.* hexagonal.

sześciobok *mi geom.* hexagon.

sześciodniowy *a.* **1.** (= *mający sześć dni*) six-day-old. **2.** (= *trwający sześć dni*) six-day-long, six days long.

sześciogodzinny *a.* **1.** (= *mający sześć godzin*) six-hour-old. **2.** (= *trwający sześć godzin*) six-hour-long, six hours long.

sześciokąt *mi Gen.* **-a** *geom.* hexagon; **sześciokąt foremny** regular hexagon, symmetrical hexagon.

sześciokątny *a.* hexagonal.

sześciokonny *a.* drawn by six horses.

sześciokrotnie *adv.* six times; sixfold, sextuple; **zwyciężyć sześciokrotnie** win six times.

sześciokrotny *a.* (*zwycięzca*) six-time, six times; (*podwyżka, obniżka, wzrost, spadek*) sixfold, sextuple.

sześciolatek *mp* **-tk-** *pl.* **-i 1.** (*chłopiec*) six-year-old boy. **2.** (*zwierzę*) six-year-old animal. **3.** *pot.* (*samochód*) six-year-old car.

sześciolatka *f. Gen.pl.* **-ek 1.** (*dziewczynka*) six-year-old girl. **2.** (*klacz*) six-year-old mare. **3.** *hist.* (*plan*) six-year plan.

sześcioletni *a.* **1.** (= *mający sześć lat*) six-year-old. **2.** (= *trwający sześć lat*) six-year-long, six years long; **plan sześcioletni** *hist.* six-year plan.

sześciomiesięczny *a.* **1.** (= *mający sześć miesięcy*) six-month-old. **2.** (= *trwający sześć miesięcy*) six-month-long, six months long.

sześcioodcinkowy *a.* six-episode.

sześciopiętrowy *a.* six-floor; six-story, *Br.* six-storey.

sześciopokojowy *a.* six-room.

sześcioprocentowy *a.* six per cent.

sześcioraczki *pl. Gen.* **-ów** sextuplets.

sześcioro *num. decl. like n.* **-rg-** six; **sześcioro dzieci** six children.

sześciostrzałowy *a.* six shot.

sześciotygodniowy *a.* **1.** (= *mający sześć tygodni*) six-week-old. **2.** (= *trwający sześć tygodni*) six-week-long, six weeks long.

sześciowiersz *mi Gen.* **-a** *teor.lit.* sestina, sextain.

sześć *num. Ins.* **-oma** *l.* **-u** six; **pal sześć!** *pot.* never mind!

sześćdziesiąt *num.* **-ęci-** *Ins.* **-oma** *l.* **-u** sixty.

sześćdziesiątka *f. Gen.pl.* **-ek 1.** (*liczba*) sixty. **2.** (*wiek*) sixty; **być po sześćdziesiątce** be in sb's sixties; **mam sześćdziesiątkę na karku** *pot.* I am sixty years old; **stuknęła mi sześćdziesiątka** *pot.* I have turned sixty. **3.** (*prędkość*) sixty; **jechać sześćdziesiątką** be driving sixty kilometers per hour, be doing sixty. **4.** (*żarówka*) sixty-watt bulb. **5.** (= *autobus, tramwaj 60*) service sixty. **6.** (= *mieszkanie, dom nr 60*) number sixty; **mieszkam pod sześćdziesiątką** I live at number sixty.

sześćdziesiąty *a.* sixtieth; **lata sześćdziesiąte** the sixties.

sześćdziesięciolecie *n. Gen.pl.* **-i** sixtieth anniversary.

sześćset *num.* **sześć-** *decl. like num.,* **-set** *indecl.* **sześciuset** six hundred.

sześćsetlecie *n. Gen.pl.* **-i** sexcentenary.

sześćsetletni *a.* sexcentenary.

sześćsetny *a.* six hundredth.

szetland *mi* (*wełna*) **1.** Shetland wool. **2.** *Gen.* **-u** *l.* **-a** (*sweter*) Shetland.

Szetlandy *pl. Gen.* **-ów** *geogr.* Shetland Islands.

szetlandzki *a.* Shetland.

szew *mi* **szw-** **1.** (= *zszycie kawałków materiału*) seam; **pękać w szwach** be bursting at the seams. **2.** *med.* suture, seam. **3.** *anat.* suture. **4.** *techn.* seam.

szewc *mp* shoemaker, cobbler; **kląć jak szewc** swear like a trooper; **szewc bez butów chodzi** the cobbler's wife is the worst shod; the shoemaker's son always goes barefoot.

szewiot *mi* **1.** *roln., zool.* (*rasa owiec*) Cheviot. **2.** *tk.* cheviot.

szewski *a.* shoemaker's; **szewska pasja** towering rage; **szewski poniedziałek** *pot.* absence from work on a Monday due to Sunday night's partying.

szewstwo *n.* shoemaking.

szezlong *mi* chaise longue.

szkalować *ipf.* vilify, malign.

szkapa *f. iron., żart.* hack, nag.

szkaplerz *mi rel.* (*część stroju zakonnego*) (*medalik*) scapular, scapulary.

szkaradnie *adv.* **1.** (*zachowywać się, być ubranym*) hideously; **wyglądać szkaradnie** look hideous. **2.** (*nudno, dokuczliwie*) terribly.

szkaradny *a.* **1.** (*widok, kolor, człowiek, postępek*) hideous. **2.** (*sytuacja, pogoda*) terrible.

szkaradzieństwo *n.* eyesore, atrocity.

szkarlatyna *f. pat.* scarlet fever; (*w języku fachowym*) scarlatina.

szkarłat *mi* (*kolor*) (*tkanina*) purple.

szkarłatnica *f. bot.* Porphyra (*Porphyra*).

szkarłatny *a.* dark red.

szkarłupień *ma* **-pni-** *zool.* echinoderm (*Echinodermata*).

szkatuła *f. lit.* **1.** (*skrzynia*) chest, coffer. **2.** (*fundusze*) coffers.

szkatułka *f. Gen.pl.* **-ek** casket.

szkic *mi* **1.** (*literacki, naukowy, publicystyczny*) *t. sztuka* sketch. **2.** (= *plan, projekt*) draft.

szkicować *ipf.* **1.** (*rysować*) sketch. **2.** (= *przedstawiać w zarysie*) sketch out.

szkicownik *mi Gen.* **-a** sketchbook.

szkicowy *a.* (*plan, rysunek*) draft; (*opis*) sketchy.

szkielet *mi* **1.** *anat.* skeleton. **2.** *techn.* framework. **3.** *przen.* (*spalonego budynku*) shell. **4.** *przen.* (*utworu, dzieła*) basis, foundation.

szkieletowy *a.* **1.** *anat.* skeletal; **grób szkieletowy** inhumation grave. **2.** *techn.* framework.

szkiełko *n. Gen.pl.* **-ek** **1.** (*np. od zegarka*) glass; **szkiełko mikroskopowe** slide. **2.** (*odprysk, drzazga*) piece of glass. **3.** (= *imitacja biżuterii*) gewgaw.

szklanica *f. lit.* large glass (*usu. decorated*).

szklanka *f. Gen.pl.* **-ek** **1.** (*naczynie*) glass; (*zawartość*) glass, glassful; **szklanka wody** glass of water; **burza w szklance wody** storm in a teacup. **2.** *kulin.* (*jako miara*) cup, cupful; **szklanka cukru** cup of sugar, cupful of sugar. **3.** *pot.* (= *gołoledź*) glaze; *Br.* glaze ice, glazed frost. **4.** *żegl.* bell.

szklany *a.* **1.** (= *ze szkła*) glass; **wata szklana** glass wool; **włókno szklane** glass fiber; *Br.* glass fibre; **szklany ekran** the small screen. **2.** (= *podobny do szkła*) glass-like; **szklane oczy** *l.* **szklany wzrok** glassy eyes.

szklarka *f. ent.* downy emerald (*Cordulia aenea*).

szklarnia *f. Gen.pl.* **-i** greenhouse; (*ogrzewana*) hothouse.

szklarniowy *a.* greenhouse; hothouse.

szklarski *a.* glazier's; **piasek szklarski** silica sand.

szklarstwo *n.* glaziery.

szklarz *mp* **1.** (*rzemieślnik*) glazier. **2.** *pot.* = szklarka.

szklić *ipf.* **-ij** (= *wprawiać szyby*) **1.** glaze. **2.** *pot.* (= *oszukiwać*) lie. **~ się** *ipf.* (= *lśnić*) glitter.

szklisty *a.* glassy; **ciałko szkliste** *anat.* vitreous body.

szkliście *adv.* glassily.

szkliwić *ipf.* glaze.

szkliwo *n.* **1.** (*w ceramice*) glaze. **2.** *anat.* enamel.

szkło *n. Gen.pl.* szkieł **1.** (*tworzywo*) glass; szkło alabastrowe *l.* mleczne milk glass; szkło bezpieczne *l.* bezodpryskowe safety glass; szkło budowlane architectural glass; szkło czeskie optical flint, flint glass; szkło hartowane toughened glass; szkło kryształowe *l.* ołowiowe lead glass; szkło kwarcowe silica glass, quartz glass; szkło optyczne optical glass; szkło organiczne organic glass; szkło wodne water glass; szkło zbrojone wire glass; huta szkła glassworks; uprawiać coś pod szkłem grow sth under glass; trzymać kogoś pod szkłem *przen.* be overprotective towards sb. **2.** (*naczynia*) glassware; szkło artystyczne artistic glass; szkło laboratoryjne laboratory glassware; szkło stołowe table glass. **3.** *zwykle pl. pot.* (= *soczewka optyczna*) glasses; szkła kontaktowe contact lenses.

Szkocja *f. geogr.* Scotland.

szkocki *a.* Scottish, Scotch.

szkoda *f. Gen.pl.* -ód **1.** (= *strata*) damage; szkoda majątkowa damage to property; szkody górnicze mining damage; działać na szkodę kogoś/czegoś be detrimental to sb/sth; ze szkodą dla kogoś/czegoś to the detriment of sb/sth; bez szkody dla kogoś/czegoś without any detriment to sb/sth; na czyjąś szkodę to the detriment of sb; mądry Polak po szkodzie sadder but wiser. **2.** *roln.* damage; szkoda łowiecka hunting damage. – *adv.* too bad; szkoda, że... it's a pity that...; szkoda, że nie możesz przyjść what a pity you can't come!; szkoda czasu/pieniędzy it is a waste of time/money; szkoda twoich słów/twojego czasu you're wasting your breath/time; szkoda mi stąd odchodzić I wish I could stay here; szkoda tego budynku na rozbiórkę it would be a pity to pull down this building; szkoda każdej minuty let's not waste a single minute; jaka szkoda! what a pity!; szkoda gadać! what can I say?

szkodliwie *adv.* harmfully; działać *l.* wpływać na coś szkodliwie be harmful to sth; wpływać szkodliwie na zdrowie be detrimental to one's health.

szkodliwość *f.* harmfulness; szkodliwość społeczna *prawn.* social harm, damage to society.

szkodliwy *a.* harmful, damaging (*dla czegoś* to sth); szkodliwy dla zdrowia detrimental to one's health.

szkodnictwo *n.* **1.** (= *szkodzenie, powodowanie strat*) harmful activity, injurious activity. **2.** (= *szkody wyrządzone przez zwierzęta*) pest damage.

szkodnik *mp pl.* -cy spoiler. – *ma pl.* -i pest.

szkodzić *ipf.* be harmful, do harm (*komuś/czemuś* to sb/sth); (*np. reputacji*) (= *niszczyć*) damage (*czemuś* sth); (*na żołądek, wątrobę*) be bad (*czemuś* for sth); palenie szkodzi smoking is bad for you; palenie szkodzi zdrowiu (*ostrzeżenie na papierosach*) smoking can (seriously) damage your health; co ci szkodzi (zobaczyć się z nim)? what's the harm (of meeting him)?; czosnek mi szkodzi garlic disagrees with me; nic nie szkodzi! never mind!; kto późno przychodzi, sam sobie szkodzi first come, first served.

szkolenie *n.* training; szkolenie zawodowe professional training.

szkoleniowiec *mp* -wc- *pl.* -y (*sportowy*) coach; (*zawodowy*) instructor, trainer.

szkoleniowy *a.* training, instruction; materiały szkoleniowe training aids; obóz szkoleniowy training camp; ośrodek szkoleniowy training center; *Br.* training centre; samolot szkoleniowy training aircraft.

szkolić *ipf.* -ol *l.* -ól train. ~ się *ipf.* -ol *l.* -ól train.

szkolnictwo *n.* (*system*) educational system; (*nauczanie*) education; szkolnictwo niemieckie/francuskie German/French educational system; szkolnictwo podstawowe elementary education; szkolnictwo średnie secondary education; szkolnictwo wyższe higher education; szkolnictwo specjalne special education; szkolnictwo zawodowe vocational education and training; pracować w szkolnictwie (= *być nauczycielem*) have a teaching job.

szkolny *a.* school; autobus szkolny school bus; boisko szkolne school playground; budynek szkolny school building; dziecko w wieku szkolnym schoolchild; kolega szkolny schoolmate; kolega ze szkolnej ławy old school friend; legitymacja szkolna student ID; pomoce szkolne teaching aids; rok szkolny school year.

szkoła *f. Gen.pl.* -ół **1.** (*instytucja*) school; szkoła podstawowa *US* elementary school; *Br.* primary school; szkoła średnia *l.* ponadpodstawowa *US* high school; *Br.* secondary school; szkoła pomaturalna college of further education, further education college; szkoła policealna post-secondary school; (*zawodowa*) vocational college; szkoła wyższa tertiary-level school; szkoła integracyjna integration school (*both for normally developing and special needs children*); szkoła specjalna special school; szkoła społeczna community school; szkoła korespondencyjna correspondence school; distance learning center; *Br.* distance learning centre; szkoła wieczorowa night school, evening school; szkoła zawodowa vocational school; szkoła zbiorcza consolidation school; szkoła morska naval college; szkoła oficerska Military College; szkoła przetrwania survival school; chodzić do szkoły go to school. **2.** (*budynek*) school, school building. **3.** (*uczniowie i nauczyciele*) school; cała szkoła pojechała na wycieczkę the whole school went on a trip. **4.** (= *doświadczenie, wiedza*) schooling, training; być po dobrej szkole be well-trained; szkoła życia school of life; dać komuś szkołę *pot.* teach sb a lesson; zostać po szkole (*np. by się pouczyć*) stay after school; zaraz po szkole poszedł do pracy he went to work straight after school. **5.** (= *metoda*) school; szkoła Arystotelesa/flamandzka Aristotelian/Flemish school. **6.** *muz.* (= *podręcznik*) manual, handbook.

szkop *mp pl.* -y *pog.* Kraut.

szkopuł *mi* hitch; **szkopuł w tym, że...** the hitch is that...

szkorbut *mi pat.* scurvy.

Szkot *mp* Scotsman.

Szkotka *f. Gen.pl.* **-ek** Scotswoman.

szkółka *f. Gen.pl.* **-ek 1.** *leśn.* nursery. **2.** (*kurs*) course; **szkółka narciarska** ski school; **szkółka niedzielna** Sunday school.

szkółkarstwo *n. leśn.* arboriculture.

szkrab *mp pl.* **-y** tot.

szkuner *mi Gen.* **-a** *żegl.* schooner.

szkuta *f. żegl.* barge.

szkutnictwo *n.* boatbuilding.

szkutniczy *a.* boatbuilder's, shipwright's.

szkutnik *mp* (*budujący łodzie*) boatbuilder; (*budujący statki*) shipwright.

szkwał *mi żegl.* squall.

szkwałowy *a.* squall.

szlaban *mi* barrier; **mieć szlaban** *pot.* be grounded.

szlachcianka *f. Gen.pl.* **-ek** noblewoman.

szlachcic *mp* nobleman; **szlachcic na zagrodzie równy wojewodzie** a man's home is his castle.

szlachecki *a.* noble; **dwór szlachecki** manor house; **demokracja szlachecka** *hist.* democracy of nobles; **stan szlachecki** the nobility.

szlachectwo *n.* nobility; **nadać komuś szlachectwo** ennoble sb; (*współcześnie w Wielkiej Brytanii*) knight sb.

szlachetnie *adv.* nobly; **szlachetnie urodzony** of noble birth.

szlachetnieć *ipf.* **1.** (= *stawać się szlachetnym*) become noble. **2.** (= *pięknieć*) become beautiful. **3.** (= *polepszać się*) acquire refinement.

szlachetność (*urodzenia*) nobility; (*człowieka, czynu, charakteru*) nobleness; (*rysów, kształtów*) refinement.

szlachetny *a.* **1.** (*człowiek, czyn, charakter, urodzenie*) noble. **2.** (= *wysokiej jakości*) quality; **gaz szlachetny** noble gas; **kamień szlachetny** precious stone; **metal szlachetny** noble metal.

szlachta *f.* nobility.

szlachtować *ipf.* (*ludzi, zwierzęta*) slaughter.

szlafmyca *f.* nightcap.

szlafrok *mi Gen.* **-a** dressing gown; **szlafrok kąpielowy** bathrobe.

szlag *mi pot.* **szlag mnie trafia** it gets my goat; **drukarkę/telewizor szlag trafił** the printer/TV (has) conked out; **zaraz szlag mnie trafi!** I'm gonna go bonkers in a sec!; **niech to/cię szlag trafi!** damn it/you!

szlagier *mi pot.* **1.** (*piosenka*) hit. **2.** (*książka*) bestseller. **3.** (*film*) blockbuster.

szlajać się *ipf. pot.* roam; **gdzie się do diabła szlajałeś?** where the hell have you been?

szlak *mi* **1.** (*droga*) track, trail; (*trasa*) route; **szlak turystyczny** tourist trail, hiking trail; **szlak handlowy** trade route; **szlak bursztynowy** *hist.* amber route. **2.** (*dekoracja*) border. **3.** *myśl.* trail.

szlaka *f.* clinker.

szlam *mi* silt, ooze.

szlamnik *ma orn.* godwit (*Limosa*).

szlamować *ipf.* **1.** (*zbiornik wodny*) remove silt *l.* ooze from (*sth*). **2.** (*jelita ubitych zwierząt*) remove mucus from (*sth*).

szlara *f. orn.* facial disk; *Br.* facial disc.

szlauch *mi Gen.* **-u** *l.* **-a** rubber hose.

szlem *mi Gen. i Acc.* **-a** *karty* grand slam.

szlemik *mi Gen. i Acc.* **-a** *karty* little slam, small slam.

szli *ipf. zob.* **iść.**

szlichta *f. bud.* finishing coat.

szlif *mi* **1.** (= *oszlifowanie*) cut. **2.** (= *ogłada*) polish.

szlifierka *f. Gen.pl.* **-ek** *techn.* grinding machine, grinder.

szlifiernia *f. Gen.pl.* **-i** *l.* **-ń** polishing shop.

szlifierski *a.* grinding, polishing; **kamień szlifierski** grindstone; **proszek szlifierski** grinding powder.

szlifierz *mp* grinder.

szlifować *ipf.* **1.** (= *poddawać obróbce*) grind; (*kamień szlachetny, kryształ*) cut. **2.** (= *polerować*) polish. **3.** (= *doskonalić*) polish up; **szlifować swój angielski** polish up on one's English.

szlify *pl.* epaulets; *Br.* epaulettes; **szlify generalskie** the rank of general; *US* generalis stars.

szloch *mi* sob.

szlochać *ipf.* sob.

szlufka *f. Gen.pl.* **-ek 1.** (*spódnicy, spodni*) belt carrier; *Br.* belt loop. **2.** (*na pasku*) carrier; *Br.* keeper.

szlus *mi pot.* end; **mam już szlus z robotą** I'm done with my work at last; **no to szlus!** this is it!

szlusować *ipf.* catch up (*do kogoś* with sb).

szła *itd. ipf. zob.* **iść.**

szmaciaki *pl. Gen.* **-ów** (*obuwie*) carpet slippers.

szmaciany *a.* rag; **szmaciana lalka** rag doll.

szmaciarz *mp pot.* **1.** (*handlarz*) rag-and-bone man, ragman. **2.** loser.

szmal *mi pot.* dough.

szmaragd *mi* emerald.

szmaragdowozielony *a.* emerald green.

szmaragdowy *a.* emerald.

szmat *mi* a good bit; **szmat czasu/drogi** a long time/way; **szmat ziemi** tract of land.

szmata *f.* **1.** (*tkanina*) rag. **2.** *pog.* (= *niegodziwiec*) bastard. **3.** *pog.* (*o kobiecie*) (= *dziwka*) slut. **4.** *pog.* (*gazeta*) rag; *zob. t.* **szmaty.**

szmatka *f. Gen.pl.* **-ek** (= *ścierka*) cloth.

szmatławiec *mi* **-wc-** *Gen.* **-a** *pog.* (*gazeta*) rag.

szmatławy *a. pog.* lousy.

szmaty *pl. pot.* (= *zniszczone ubranie*) rags.

szmelc *mi pot.* **1.** (= *złom*) scrap; **wyrzucić coś na szmelc** bin sth. **2.** *pot.* (= *śmieć, coś bezużytecznego*) (piece of) junk; **tym szmelcem nie dojadę nawet na drugi koniec miasta** I won't even get to the other side of town in this piece of junk.

szmer *mi* **1.** (= *szelest*) murmur; (*rozmów*) hum; (*np. wysypywanej mąki, cukru*) swoosh; **szmer niezadowolenia** murmur of discontent. **2.** *pat.* murmur, bruit; **szmer płucny** pulmonary murmur, pulmonic murmur; **szmer sercowy** cardiac murmur, heart murmur.

szmergiel *mi* **-gl-** *Gen.* **-a** *l.* **-u 1.** (*skała*) emery.

2. (*papier*) emery paper; **mieć/dostać szmergla** *pot.* be/go mad *l.* crazy.

szmerglowy *a.* emery.

szminka *f. Gen.pl.* **-ek** (*do ust*) lipstick; (*do charakteryzacji*) greasepaint.

szminkować *ipf.* (*usta*) put on lipstick; (= *charakteryzować twarz*) paint. ~ **się** *ipf.* (*usta*) put on lipstick.

szmira *f.* trash, rubbish.

szmirowaty *a.* trashy, rubbishy.

szmizjerka *f. Gen.pl.* **-ek** chemise.

szmonces *mi* Jewish quip.

szmugiel *mi* **-gl-** **1.** (= *przemycanie*) smuggling, contraband. **2.** (= *przemycone towary*) smuggled goods, contraband.

szmugler *mp*, **szmuglerka** *f. Gen.pl.* **-ek** smuggler.

szmuglerski *a.* smuggling, contraband.

szmuglować *ipf.* smuggle.

sznaps *mi Gen.* **-a** *pot.* schnapps, schnaps; vodka.

sznaucer *ma kynol.* schnauzer.

sznur *mi Gen.* **-a** **1.** (= *cienki powróz*) string; (= *lina*) rope; **sznur do bielizny** clothes line; **sznur naramienny** *wojsk.* fourragère, aiguillette; **sznur korali** string of beads; **sznur pereł** pearl necklace; **sznur pępowiny** *anat.* umbilical cord, navel string; **jak pod sznur** straight; **za mundurem panny sznurem** all the nice girls like a sailor. **2.** (= *szereg*) line; **sznur samochodów** line of cars. **3.** *el.* cord, lead.

sznureczek *mi* **-czk-** *Gen.* **-a** **1.** (= *sznurek*) string. **2.** (*ścieg*) stem stitch.

sznurek *mi* **-rk-** *Gen.* **-a** string; **chodzić jak na sznurku** toe the line; **chodzić u kogoś jak na sznurku** be kept on a tight rein by sb; **trzymać kogoś na sznurku** keep sb on a string; **pociągać za sznurki** (= *mieć władzę, kontrolę*) pull the strings; **pociągnąć za sznurki** (= *wywrzeć wpływ*) pull strings; **ułożyć pod sznurek** arrange *l.* put in a straight line.

sznurkowy *a.* string.

sznurować *ipf.* **1.** (*buty, gorset*) lace. **2.** *myśl.* trot.

sznurowadło *n. Gen.pl.* **-eł** shoelace, shoestring.

sznurowanie *n.* lacing.

sznurowany *a.* laced; **buty sznurowane** laced shoes, lace-ups.

sznurowy *a.* rope, string; **drabinka sznurowa** rope ladder; **ceramika sznurowa** *archeol.* string pottery, linear pottery; linear ceramics.

sznurówka *f. Gen.pl.* **-ek** shoelace, shoestring.

sznycel *mi* **-cl-** *Gen.* **-a** *kulin.* **1.** (*panierowany i usmażony plaster mięsa*) schnitzel; **sznycel wiedeński** Wiener schnitzel. **2.** *dial.* (= *kotlet siekany*) rissole.

sznyt *mi* **1.** (= *szyk*) chic, elegance; (= *fason, styl*) style. **2.** *sl.* (*nacięcie*) cut.

sznytka *f. dial.* (= *kromka*) slice; (= *kanapka*) sandwich.

szodon *mi kulin.* (*napój*) caudle.

szofer *mp pot.* driver.

szoferka *f. pot. Gen.pl.* **-ek** **1.** (*kabina*) cab. **2.** *pot.* (*zawód*) driving.

szoferski *a. pot.* driver's; driving.

szogun *mp pl.* **-owie** *l.* **-i** *hist.* shogun.

szok *mi* **1.** (= *wstrząs*) shock; **być w szoku** be in shock; **przeżyć szok** *l.* **doznać szoku** get a shock; **szok kulturowy** culture shock. **2.** *pat.* shock; **szok anafilaktyczny** anaphylactic shock; **szok pooperacyjny** postoperative shock, surgical shock.

szokować *ipf.* shock.

szokowy *a.* shock; **terapia szokowa** *t. przen.* shock therapy, shock treatment.

szokująco *adv.* shockingly, outrageously.

szokujący *a.* shocking, outrageous.

szop *ma zool.* raccoon; *pot.* coon (*Procyon*); **szop pracz** North American racoon; *pot.* coon (*Procyon lotor*).

szopa *f.* **1.** (*budynek*) shed. **2.** *pot.* (*fryzura*) mop.

szopka *f. Gen.pl.* **-ek** **1.** (*schowek*) shed. **2.** *rel.* crib. **3.** *rel., teatr* nativity play. **4.** *pot.* (= *heca*) carry-on, performance; **robić szopkę** put on a show; **nie rób szopek!** stop being ridiculous!; cut that crap, will you?

szopkarz *mp Gen.pl.* **-y** *l.* **-ów** **1.** (= *osoba wykonująca szopki*) crib-maker. **2.** (= *kolędnik*) caroler with a crib.

szopowate *pl. zool.* the Procyonidae family (*Procyonidae*).

szor *mi*, **szory** *pl.* breast harness.

szorować *ipf.* **1.** (*myć*) scrub, scour. **2.** (= *ocierać*) rub (*o coś* against sth). **3.** *pot.* (= *spieszyć się dokądś*) run; **szoruj do łazienki** off you go to the bathroom; **szoruj stąd!** beat it!

szorstki *a.* **1.** (*o powierzchni*) rough; (*o materiale*) coarse. **2.** (= *opryskliwy*) curt, brusque, coarse. **3.** (*o dźwięku, głosie*) harsh.

szorstko *adv.* **1.** (= *niegładko*) roughly, coarsely. **2.** (*traktować, odpowiedzieć*) curtly, brusquely, coarsely. **3.** (*brzmieć*) harshly.

szorstkolistne *pl. bot.* the Boraginaceae family (*Boraginaceae*).

szorstkość *f.* **1.** (= *chropowatość*) roughness, coarseness. **2.** (= *opryskliwość*) curtness, brusqueness. **3.** (*dźwięku*) harshness.

szorstkowłosy *a.* wirehaired, wire-haired; **jamnik szorstkowłosy** *kynol.* wirehaired dachshund.

szorty *pl. Gen.* **-ów** shorts.

szosa *f.* road, highway.

szosowiec *mp* **-wc-** *pl.* **-y** *kolarstwo* road cyclist.

szosowy *a.* road.

szot *mi żegl.* sheet.

szowinista *mp*, **szowinistka** *f. Gen.pl.* **-ek** chauvinist.

szowinistyczny *a.* chauvinistic.

szowinizm *mi* chauvinism.

szósta *f. Gen.* **-ej** (*godzina*) six; **dziesięć po szóstej** ten past six.

szóstka *f. Gen.pl.* **-ek** **1.** (*cyfra*) six. **2.** (= *grupa sześciu osób*) group of six. **3.** (*sześć koni w zaprzęgu*) team of six horses. **4.** *karty* six; **szóstka pik/trefl** six of spades/clubs. **5.** (*punkty na kostce*) six (spots); **wyrzucić szóstkę** get a six. **6.** (=

autobus, tramwaj nr 6) (service) six. **7.** (= *dom, mieszkanie nr 6*) six; **mieszkać pod szóstką** live at number six. **8.** *szkoln.* outstanding (*highest grade in up to secondary school; corresponds to an A +*).

szóstoklasista *mp*, **szóstoklasistka** *f. Gen.pl.* **-ek** *szkoln.* sixth-grader; *Br.* sixth-former.

szósty *a.* sixth; **szósty zmysł** the sixth sense; **szósty krzyżyk** fifty to sixty years of age; **niedługo stuknie mu szósty krzyżyk** he's approaching sixty. – *mi* **1.** (*dzień*) the sixth; **urodziny mam szóstego marca** my birthday is on the 6th March *l.* March 6th. **2.** (= *dom, mieszkanie nr 6*) six; **mieszkam pod szóstym** I live at number six.

szpachelka *f. Gen.pl.* **-ek** *bud.* = **szpachla** 1.

szpachla *f. Gen.pl.* **-i** *bud.* **1.** (*narzędzie*) (*do skrobania*) scraper; (*do zatykania*) putty knife, filling knife; *mal.* palette knife, pallet knife. **2.** (*masa*) (*do wypełniania*) filler; (*do wygładzania*) putty.

szpachlować *ipf. bud.* **1.** (*trzeć, zdzierać*) scrape. **2.** (*zalepiać*) stop. **3.** (*wygładzać, wyrównywać*) putty.

szpachlowy *a. bud.* **gładź szpachlowa** *l.* **tynkarska** finishing coat; **masa szpachlowa** putty.

szpachlówka *f. Gen.pl.* **-ek** *bud.* (*do wypełniania*) filler; (*do wygładzania*) putty.

szpada *f.* **1.** (*broń*) sword; (*w języku fachowym*) épée; (*matadora*) estoque; **szpada dworska** dress sword, court sword; **skrzyżować z kimś szpady** *t. przen.* cross swords with sb. **2.** *sport* (*broń*) (*konkurencja*) épée.

szpadel *mi* **-dl-** *Gen.* **-a** spade.

szpadzista *mp*, **szpadzistka** *f. Gen.pl.* **-ek** épéeist.

szpagat *mi* **1.** *sport* splits; **robić szpagat** do the splits. **2.** (*sznurek*) cord, twine.

szpak *ma orn.* common starling; *pot.* starling (*Sturnus vulgaris*).

szpaki *pl. Gen.* **-ów** *orn.* starlings (*Sturnidae*).

szpakowacieć *ipf.* grizzle.

szpakowaty *a.* (*t. o maści konia*) grizzled.

szpaler *mi* line, row.

szpalta *f. druk.* **1.** (*kolumna*) column; **na szpaltach prasy** in newspapers *l.* magazines. **2.** (*odbitka*) galley proof.

szpaltowy *a. druk.* column; galley.

szpan *mi pot.* swank.

szpaner *mp pot.* swank, swanky person.

szpanerski *a.* swanky, showy.

szpanerstwo *n. pot.* swank, showing off.

szpanować *ipf. pot.* swank, show off.

szpara *f.* **1.** (*np. w niedomkniętych drzwiach*) gap, opening; (= *szczelina*) slit; (= *rozpadlina*) crevice; (= *pęknięcie*) rift, crack. **2.** *wulg.* slit, crack.

szparag *mi Gen.* **-a 1.** *bot.* asparagus (*Asparagus*). **2.** (*danie*) asparagus.

szparagowy *a.* asparagus; aspariginous; **zupa szparagowa** asparagus soup; **fasola szparagowa** string bean.

szpargały *pl. Gen.* **-ów** old documents, old papers.

szparka *f. Gen.pl.* **-ek** *zob.* **szpara**; **szparki oddechowe** *bot.* stomata *l.* stomas.

szpatułka *f. Gen.pl.* **-ek** *med.* spatula.

szpecić *ipf.* (*wygląd*) mar; *przen.* blemish.

szperacki *a.* rummaging.

szperactwo *n.* rummaging disposition.

szperacz *mp* **1.** *pot.* (= *badacz*) rummager; explorer, searcher. **2.** *wojsk.* scout. – *ma myśl.* coursing dog. – *mi* (*reflektor*) searchlight.

szperać *ipf.* rummage, browse; **szperać po kieszeniach** rummage through one's pockets.

szpetnie *adv.* uglily.

szpetny *a.* ugly, unsightly.

szpetota *f.* ugliness, unsightliness.

szpic[1] *mi Gen.* **-a** (= *czubek*) point, tip; **bródka w szpic** Vandyke beard.

szpic[2] *ma kynol.* spitz.

szpica *f. wojsk.* point; (*czołowa*) picket, picquet.

szpicel *mp* **-cl-** *Gen.pl.* **-i** *l.* **-ów** *pog.* snoop, snooper.

szpiclować *ipf. pog.* snoop.

szpicruta *f.* horsewhip.

szpiczak *mi Gen.* **-a** *pat.* myeloma, plasmocytoma. – *ma myśl.* spike buck.

szpiczasty *a.* pointed, peaked.

szpieg *mp* spy.

szpiegostwo *n.* espionage, spying.

szpiegować *ipf.* spy (*kogoś* on sb).

szpiegowski *a.* spy, spying; **siatka szpiegowska** spy network; **film szpiegowski** spy movie.

szpik *mi* marrow; **szpik kostny** *anat.* bone marrow; **przemarznąć do szpiku kości** be chilled to the bone; **zepsuty do szpiku kości** rotten to the core.

szpikować *ipf.* **1.** (*mięso*) lard. **2.** (*wypowiedź, tekst*) interlard, lard.

szpikulec *mi* **-lc-** *Gen.* **-a** skewer, spit.

szpila *f.* **1.** (*szpilka*) pin; **wsadzać** *l.* **wbijać komuś szpilę** make biting remarks about sb. **2.** *myśl.* dewclaw.

szpilka *f. Gen.pl.* **-ek 1.** (*do spinania*) pin; **siedzieć jak na szpilkach** be on tenterhooks; **ciasno, że nie da się szpilki wetknąć** it's jam packed, there's not enough room to swing a cat; **wbijać komuś szpilkę** make biting *l.* caustic remarks about sb. **2.** (*do włosów*) hairpin, bodkin. **3.** (*ćwieczek szewski*) peg. **4.** (*obcas*) stiletto heel, stiletto; spike heel.

szpilki *pl. Gen.* **-ek** (*buty*) stiletto shoes.

szpilkować *ipf.* (*przybijać do buta*) peg.

szpilkowy *a.* **1.** *bot.* coniferous. **2.** (*o obuwiu*) pegged.

szpinak *mi bot., kulin.* spinach (*Spinacia oleracea*).

szpinet *mi muz.* spinet.

szpital *mi Gen.* **-a** hospital; **szpital miejski** municipal hospital; **szpital ogólny** general hospital; **szpital polowy** field hospital; **szpital zakaźny** infectious diseases hospital; (*zwł. dla trędowatych*) lazaretto, lazaret; **leżeć w szpitalu** be in hospital; **zabrać kogoś do szpitala** take sb to hospital.

szpitalik *mi Gen.* **-a** infirmary.

szpitalniany *a.* hospital.

szpitalnictwo *n.* **1.** (*kraju, regionu*) hospital system. **2.** (*organizacja*) hospital management. **3.** (*leczenie*) hospital treatment.

szpitalny *a.* hospital.

szpon *mi Gen.* **-a** *l.* **-u** talon, pounce, claw; **być w czyichś szponach** be in sb's clutches.

szponder *mi* **-dr-** *Gen.* **-a** *kulin.* (*część przednia*) flat rib; (*część tylna*) thin flank.

szponiasty *f.* claw-like.

szpotawość *f. pat.* varus deformity.

szpotawy *a. pat.* varus, bent inwards; **stopa szpotawa** talipes varus.

szprot *ma icht.* sprat (*Sprattus sprattus*); *zwł. kulin.* brisling.

szprotka *f. Gen.pl.* **-ek** *icht. zob.* **szprot**; **szprotki w oleju/pomidorach** sprats in oil/tomato sauce.

szpryca *f.* **1.** (*narzędzie*) syringe. **2.** *sl.* (*dawka narkotyku*) shot.

szprycer *mp pot.* spritzer.

szprycha *f.* **1.** (*przy rowerze*) spoke. **2.** *sl.* (*dziewczyna*) chick, tail; **niezła z niej szprycha** she's a nice piece of tail.

szprycować *ipf.* syringe; (= *wstrzykiwać*) inject; (=*spryskiwać*) sprinkle. ~ **się** *ipf. pot.* shoot up.

szpula *f.* (*rolka*) spool, reel. – *adv. przest., pot.* (= *prędko*) lickety-split.

szpulka *f. Gen.pl.* **-ek** bobbin, spool; **szpulka nici** spool of sewing thread.

szpulowy *a.* reel-to-reel; **magnetofon szpulowy** reel-to-reel tape recorder.

szpunt *mi* bung, plug.

szpuntować *ipf.* bung up, plug.

szrama *f.* scar.

szranki *pl. Gen.* **-ów** **1.** *hist.* lists. **2.** *przest.* contest; **stanąć w szranki z kimś** enter the lists against sb.

szrapnel *mi Gen.* **-a** *hist., wojsk.* (= *pocisk*) *pot.* (= *odłamek pocisku*) shrapnel.

szreń *f. meteor.* névé, firn.

szron *mi* hoarfrost, white frost.

szt. *abbr.* (= *sztuka*) pc. (= *piece*); (= *sztuk, sztuki*) pcs. (= *pieces*).

sztab *mi* staff; **sztab doradców** board of advisors; **sztab ekspertów** panel of experts; **sztab generalny** *wojsk.* general staff.

sztaba *f.* (*na drzwi, złota*) bar; **złoto w sztabach** gold bullion.

sztabka *f. Gen.pl.* **-ek** bar; **sztabka złota** bar of gold.

sztabowiec *mp* **-wc-** *wojsk.* staff officer.

sztabowy *a. wojsk.* staff; **mapa sztabowa** military map; **oficer sztabowy** staff officer; **sierżant sztabowy** staff sergeant.

sztabówka *f. Gen.pl.* **-ek** *wojsk., pot.* military map.

sztachać się *ipf. pot.* toke.

sztacheta *f.* pale.

sztachetka *f. Gen.pl.* **-ek** pale.

sztachnąć się *pf.* **-ij** *zob.* **sztachać się.**

sztafaż *mi Gen.pl.* **-ów** *sztuka* staffage.

sztafeta *f. sport* relay, relay race; **sztafeta cztery razy czterysta (metrów)** 4 by 400 meters relay.

sztafetowy *a. sport* relay; **bieg sztafetowy** relay race.

sztag *mi żegl.* stay; headstay, forestay.

sztaksel *mi* **-sl-** *Gen.* **-a** *żegl.* staysail.

sztaluga *f. Gen.pl.* **-g** *zwł. sztuka* easel.

sztalugowy *a.* **malarstwo sztalugowe** *sztuka* easel painting.

sztama *f. pot.* good understanding, friendship; **trzymać z kimś sztamę** cotton with sb, be as thick as thieves with sb.

sztambuch *mi Gen.* **-a** *l.* **-u** *przest.* album.

sztampa *f.* (*sposób robienia czegoś*) set pattern; (= *maniera*) manner.

sztampowy *a.* run-of-the-mill.

sztanca *f. techn.* die.

sztancować *ipf. techn.* die.

sztandar *mi* standard, banner; **pod sztandarem czegoś** under the banner of sth.

sztandarowy *a.* **1.** (= *dotyczący sztandaru*) standard, banner; **poczet sztandarowy** color guard; *Br.* colour guard. **2.** (= *reprezentacyjny; główny*) leading, major, flagship; **sztandarowy przykład** flagship example. – *mp* standard *l.* banner bearer.

sztanga *f.* **1.** (= *sztaba*) bar. **2.** *sport* weight.

sztangista *mp sport* weightlifter.

szterling *mi Gen.* **-a funt szterling** *Br.* pound sterling.

sztok *mi arch.* log, trunk; **zalany w sztok** *pot.* pie-eyed, dead drunk.

sztokfisz *mi Gen.* **-a** stockfish.

Sztokholm *mi geogr.* Stockholm.

sztolnia *f. Gen.pl.* **-i** *l.* **-ń** *górn.* drift, adit.

szton *mi Gen.* **-a** *l.* **-u** (*do gry*) chip, counter; (*do automatu*) token.

sztorc *mi przest.* edge; **na sztorc** on end; **stawać sztorcem** (= *sprzeciwiać się*) stand up to.

sztorcować *ipf. pot.* scold.

sztorm *mi* storm, gale.

sztormiak *mi Gen.* **-a** oilskins.

sztormowy *a.* stormy; **sztormowa pogoda** stormy weather; **lina sztormowa** *żegl.* lifeline; **zapałka sztormowa** fusee, fuzee.

sztormówka *f. Gen.pl.* **-ek** *żegl.* **1.** (*ubranie*) oilskins. **2.** (*lampa*) hurricane lamp.

sztormtrap *mi żegl.* jack ladder, Jacob's ladder.

sztruks *mi tk.* corduroy.

sztruksowy *a. tk.* corduroy; **spodnie sztruksowe** corduroys.

sztruksy *pl. pot.* cords, corduroys.

sztubacki *a. pot., przest.* schoolboy's, school kid's; immature, childish.

sztubak *mp pot., przest.* high *l.* secondary school student.

sztucer *mi Gen.* **-a** *myśl.* hunting rifle.

sztuczka *f. Gen.pl.* **-ek** **1.** (*popis*) trick; **pokazywać sztuczki** show tricks. **2.** (= *wybieg, fortel*) ploy, trick; **nie próbuj ze mną żadnych sztuczek** don't try anything funny with me, don't play any tricks on me, don't play games with me.

sztucznie *adv.* artificially.

sztuczność *f.* artificiality.

sztuczny *a.* **1.** (= *nienaturalny*) artificial;

sztuczna biżuteria imitation jewelry; **sztuczne kwiaty** artificial flowers; **sztuczne lodowisko** artificial rink; **sztuczna nerka** *med.* artificial kidney; **sztuczne oddychanie** *med.* artificial respiration *l.* ventilation; **sztuczne oddychanie z masażem serca** *med.* cardiopulmonary resuscitation, CPR; **sztuczne odżywianie** *med.* artificial feeding *l.* nutrition; **sztuczne ognie** fireworks; **sztuczne płuco** *med.* artificial lung, pulmotor; **sztuczny satelita** artificial satellite; **sztuczne serce** *med.* artificial heart; **sztuczne światło** artificial light; **sztuczne zapłodnienie** *med.* in vitro fertilization; **sztuczne zęby** false teeth; **język sztuczny** artificial language; **nawozy sztuczne** artificial *l.* chemical fertilizers; **tworzywo sztuczne** plastic; **włókno sztuczne** synthetic fiber; *Br.* synthetic fibre. **2.** (= *wymuszony*) artificial; **sztuczny uśmiech** artificial smile; **sztuczne zachowanie** stilted behavior.

sztuczydło *n. pog.* paltry play.

sztućce *pl. Gen.* -**ćców** cutlery.

sztufada *f. kulin.* stewed beef.

sztuka *f.* **1.** (= *wytwory o charakterze estetycznym*) art; **sztuka abstrakcyjna** abstract art; **sztuka barokowa** Baroque art; **sztuka filmowa** cinematic art, the cinema; **sztuka ludowa** folk art; **sztuki piękne** fine arts; **sztuki plastyczne** plastic arts; **sztuka realistyczna** realistic art; **sztuka renesansowa** Renaissance art; **sztuka sakralna** sacred art; **sztuka starożytna** ancient art; **sztuka stosowana** (the) applied arts; **sztuka średniowieczna** medieval art; **sztuka użytkowa** craft; **sztuka współczesna** modern art; **sztuka zdobnicza** artisanship, craftsmanship; **dzieło sztuki** work of art; **historia sztuki** history of art; **sztuka dla sztuki** art for art's sake. **2.** *teatr* play. **3.** (= *kunszt*) art; **sztuki walki** martial arts; **sztuki wyzwolone** *hist.* liberal arts; **to nie sztuka tak śpiewać** there's nothing to singing like that; **(cała) sztuka w tym, że...** the (whole) trick is to...; **do trzech razy sztuka** third time lucky; **wielka (mi) sztuka!** (= *to żadne osiągnięcie*) and you call this an achievement?; (= *to dla mnie nic trudnego*) sounds like a piece of cake to me! **4.** (= *pojedyncza rzecz*) piece; **płacić od sztuki** pay by the piece; **po pięć złotych sztuka** *l.* **za sztukę** five zloty apiece; **sprzedawać na sztuki** sell by the piece; **sztuka mięsa** piece of meat. **5.** (*człowiek*) dude; **niegłupia z niego sztuka** he's a clever dude. **6.** (= *bela tkaniny*) bolt.

sztukas *mi hist., lotn.* Stuka.

sztukateria *f. Gen.* -**ii** *bud.* stucco, stuccowork.

sztukator *mp bud.* stucco-worker.

sztukatorski *a. bud.* stucco.

sztukatorstwo *n. bud.* stucco work.

sztukmistrz *mp Gen.pl.* -**ów** *przest.* (= *magik*) conjurer.

sztukować *ipf.* piece out, piece up.

szturchać *ipf.* nudge. ~ **się** *ipf.* nudge each other.

szturchaniec *mi* -**ńc-** *Gen.* -**a** nudge; **dać komuś szturchańca** give sb a nudge, nudge sb.

szturchnąć *pf.* -**ij** *zob.* **szturchać.** ~ **się** *pf.* -**ij** *zob.* **szturchać się.**

szturm *mi* storm, assault, onslaught; **przypuścić szturm do miasta** storm *l.* assault a town, launch an assault on a town; **odeprzeć szturm** repel an assault; **wziąć szturmem** take by storm *l.* assault.

szturmować *ipf.* storm, assault; **szturmować do drzwi** pound *l.* bang on the door.

szturmowiec *mi* -**wc-** *Gen.* -**a** *wojsk., lotn.* (= *samolot szturmowy*) strafer, strike *l.* attack aircraft.

szturmowy *a. wojsk.* assault; **oddział szturmowy** shock troops; **samolot szturmowy** strafer, strike *l.* attack aircraft.

szturmówka *f. Gen.pl.* -**ek** flag, banner.

sztyblety *pl. Gen.* -**ów** gaiters.

sztych *mi* **1.** (*rycina*) engraving, etching. **2.** (*ostrze*) point. **3.** (*pchnięcie*) thrust. **4.** *ogr.* spade; **(dół) głęboki na dwa sztychy** *pot.* two spades deep (hole).

sztyft *mi* **1.** (*gwóźdź*) sparable; (= *ćwiek*) pin; **dezodorant w sztyfcie** stick deodorant, deodorant stick. **2.** *orn.* outer feather.

sztygar *mp górn.* foreman.

sztygarski *a.* (*o egzaminie, uprawnieniach*) foreman, foreman's.

sztylet *mi* **1.** (*broń*) dagger, poniard. **2.** *druk.* (*zecerski*) bodkin, spike. **3.** *orn.* outer feather.

sztyletować *ipf.* dagger, poniard, stab; **sztyletować kogoś wzrokiem** *przen.* look daggers at sb.

sztywniak *mp pl.* -**cy** *l.* -**i** *pot.* (*o osobie wyniosłej, nieboszczyku*) stiff.

sztywnieć *ipf.* **1.** stiffen, get *l.* become stiff; **szyja mi zesztywniała** I have a stiff neck; **ręka mi zesztywniała** my hand is numb *l.* asleep. **2.** (= *stawać się oschłym*) become reserved *l.* stiff.

sztywnik *mi Gen.* -**a** (*butów, kołnierzyka*) stiffener; (*w tkaninie*) wigan.

sztywno *adv.* (*sterczeć, chodzić, zginać się*) stiffly, inflexibly; (*traktować przepisy*) rigidly, inflexibly; (*zachowywać się*) stiffly, formally; **sztywno chodzić** stalk.

sztywność *f.* **1.** (= *nieelastyczność*) (*kołnierzyka, materiału*) stiffness, starkness; (*rąk, nóg*) stiffness; (*włosów*) wiriness; **sztywność mięśni** *pat.* rigor. **2.** (= *niezmienność*) (*przepisów, obyczajów*) rigidity; (*cen*) fixedness. **3.** (*kroku, ruchów*) (= *brak gracji*) stiffness. **4.** (= *oschłość*) stiffness, buckram, starch, formality. **5.** *techn.* rigidity, stiffness; **sztywność sprężyny** spring rate; **sztywność akustyczna** acoustic stiffness; **sztywność rozciągania/zginania** longitudinal/bending rigidity.

sztywny *a.* **1.** (= *nieelastyczny*) inflexible, rigid; (*o kołnierzyku, oprawie*) stiff; (*o włosach*) wiry; **ciało sztywne** *fiz., chem.* rigid body. **2.** (= *stały*) inflexible; (*o cenie*) fixed; (*o przepisach*) rigid; (*o pianie*) stiff. **3.** (*o palcach, nodze, karku*) (= *bezwładny*) stiff, numb. **4.** (= *bez gracji*) wooden; (*o ruchach*) angular; **sztywny krok** stalk; **sztywny jakby kij połknął** *l.* **jak manekin** as stiff as a poker. **5.** (= *oschły*) (*o sposobie bycia, uśmiechu*) constrained, starchy; (*o atmosferze, nastroju*) stiff; (*o osobie*) starchy, stiff, offish; (*o języku, stylu*) stilted.

szubienica *f.* **1.** (*narzędzie*) gallows. **2.** (*kara*) gallows; **posłać kogoś na szubienicę** send sb to the gallows; **za to grozi szubienica** it's a hanging matter; **wykręcić się od szubienicy** cheat the gallows.

szubrawiec *mp* -wc- *pl.* -y scoundrel, blackguard.

szubrawstwo *n. przest.* villainy.

szufelka *f. Gen.pl.* -ek (*do śmieci*) dustpan; (*do węgla*) shovel.

szufla *f. Gen.pl.* -i **1.** (*łopata*) shovel; **szufla piachu** shovelful of sand; **szufla do odgarniania śniegu** snow shovel. **2.** *druk.* (slip) galley.

szuflada *f.* drawer; (*w ladzie, kasie*) till; **pisać do szuflady** pigeonhole one's writing, not get one's writings published, write (just) for writing's sake.

szufladka *f. Gen.pl.* -ek (small) drawer.

szufladkować *ipf.* (*dane, informacje*) pigeonhole, compartmentalize; *przen.* (*ludzi*) pigeonhole.

szufladkowy *a.* drawer; **komódka szufladkowa** drawer case; **pamięć szufladkowa** *psych.* mechanical memory.

szuflować *ipf.* shovel.

szuja *f. l. mp decl. like f. Gen.pl.* -j *l.* -ów *obelż.* rat, scum(bag).

szukać *ipf.* **1.** (= starać się znaleźć) (*książki, złodzieja, postoju taksówek*) look for; search (*kogoś/coś* for sb/sth); (*słówka w słowniku, pociągu w rozkładzie*) look up; **szukać czegoś po omacku** feel around *l.* fumble for sth; **szukać czegoś w internecie** search the Internet for sth; **wszędzie czegoś/kogoś szukać** hunt *l.* search high and low for sth/sb; **szukałem wszędzie** I looked everywhere; **szukać po kieszeniach** search *l.* rummage through one's pockets; **szukać w pamięci** rack one's brain(s) for sth; **szukać słów** be at a loss for words; **takich ludzi ze świecą szukać** such people are few and far between; **szukać dziury w całym** find fault in everything; **szukać igły w stogu siana** look for a needle in a haystack; **szukaj wiatru w polu** it's a wild goose chase, gone with the wind. **2.** (= usilnie dążyć) seek, look for (*czegoś* sth); (*okazji, sposobności*) hunt for; (*przyjemności*) be bent on, seek; (*rozwiązania, słów*) grope (*czegoś* after *l.* for sth); **szukać schronienia** seek sanctuary *l.* refuge, run for shelter *l.* cover (*przed czymś/kimś* from sth/sb); **szukać szczęścia** seek one's fortune; **szukać w czymś pocieszenia** seek solace in sth; **szukać zapomnienia w alkoholu** seek oblivion in alcohol; **szukać guza** be looking for trouble; **szukać zaczepki** be spoiling for a fight, pick a quarrel. ~ **się** *ipf.* look for each other *l.* one another.

szuler *mp* cardsharp(er), card shark, rook.

szulerka *f. Gen.pl.* -ek **1.** cardsharping. **2.** *zob.* **szuler.**

szulerski *a.* (*o grze, sztuczkach*) cardsharper's, rooking.

szum *mi* **1.** (= szmer) buzz; (*ruchu ulicznego, maszyn, głosów, fal*) hum; (*wentylatora, skrzydeł*) whir; (*drzew*) rustle, sough; (*deszczu*) spatter; **szum w głowie/uszach** buzzing in the head/

ears. **2.** (= rozgłos) hype, publicity; **narobić szumu wokół czegoś** hype sth (up), make fuss about sth; **narobić szumu wokół jakiejś sprawy** (*zwł. w mediach*) give sth a high profile. **3.** *fiz., el., radio* noise; **biały szum** white noise; **szum informacyjny** information noise; **szum syczący** hiss; **szumy** (*w radiu*) static.

szumek *mi* -mk- hype.

szumieć[1] *ipf.* -i buzz; (*o drzewach, liściach*) rustle, sough; (*o falach, morzu, ruchu ulicznym, maszynach*) hum; (*o strumyku*) murmur; (*o wentylatorze*) whir; **szumi mi w głowie/uszach** my head/ears is/are buzzing.

szumieć[2] *ipf.* -i **1.** (= musować) sparkle, effervesce; (= pienić się) foam, froth; **wino szumi mi w głowie** the wine has gone to my head. **2.** *przen.* live it up; **szumieć za młodu** *pot.* sow one's (wild) oats.

szumnie *adv.* **1.** (= górnolotnie) bombastically, boisterously. **2.** (= wystawnie) pompously, sumptuously; **szumnie świętować** celebrate sumptuously *l.* with pomp.

szumny *a.* **1.** (= hałaśliwy) noisy, loud. **2.** (= górnolotny) (*o odezwie, deklaracjach*) bombastic, grandiloquent, high-sounding; (*o języku, frazesach*) high-flown; (*o mowie, stylu*) sonorous. **3.** (*o imieninach, przyjęciu, zabawie*) (= wystawny) sumptuous, showy, grand.

szumować *ipf.* scum, skim.

szumowiny *pl. Gen.* -n **1.** (*na płynie*) scum. **2.** *pot., uj.* scum, dreg.

szur *int.* scrape.

szurać *ipf.* **1.** make a scraping sound *l.* noise; **szurać nogami** scuff *l.* shuffle one's feet. **2.** *pot.* (= zmykać) rush, scamper; **szuraj stąd!** (= zmykaj) off you go!, off with you! **3.** *tylko ipf. pot.* (= być zaczepnym) be spoiling for a fight, be cheeky.

szurgot *mi* shuffling.

szurnąć *pf.* -ij **1.** *zob.* **szurać. 2.** (= rzucić, posunąć) fling, hurl, throw.

szurnięty *a. pot.* bananas, nuts.

szus *mi Gen.* -u *l.* -a *narty* schuss; **zjeżdżać szusem** schuss.

szusować *ipf. narty* schuss.

szusowy *a. narty* schuss.

szuter *mi* -tr- *bud.* road metal, ballast.

szutrować *ipf. bud.* ballast, furnish with road metal.

szutrowy *a.* (*o drodze, alejce*) ballast, road-metal.

szuwary *pl. Gen.* -ów rushes.

szwa *f. fon.* schwa, shwa.

Szwab *mp pl.* -i *hist.* (= mieszkaniec Szwabii) Swabian. – *mp pl.* -y *pog.* (= Niemiec) Kraut, Fritz.

szwabacha *f. druk.* Schwabacher type.

Szwabia *f. Gen.* -ii *hist., geogr.* Swabia, Schwaben.

Szwabka *f. Gen.pl.* -ek *zob.* **Szwab.**

szwabski *a.* **1.** *hist.* (= dotyczący Szwabii) Swabian. **2.** *pog.* (= niemiecki) Kraut, Fritz.

szwaczka *f. Gen.pl.* -ek *tk.* seamstress.

szwadron *mi wojsk.* squadron; **szwadron śmierci** death squad.

szwadronowy *a. wojsk.* squadron.

szwagier *mp* -gr- *pl.* -owie brother-in-law.

szwagierka *f. Gen.pl.* -ek sister-in-law.

Szwajcar *mp* Swiss, Switzer, Helvetian; **on jest Szwajcarem** he's Swiss.

szwajcar *mp* commissionaire, doorman.

Szwajcaria *f. Gen.* -ii *geogr.* Switzerland.

Szwajcarka *f. Gen.pl.* -ek *zob.* **Szwajcar.**

szwajcarski *a.* Swiss, Helvetian, Helvetic; **ser szwajcarski** *kulin.* Swiss (cheese).

szwalnia *f. Gen.pl.* -i *l.* -ń *tk.* sewing room, tailor's shop.

szwalniczy *a. tk.* (*o maszynie, oddziale, przemyśle*) sewing.

szwank *mi* harm, injury, scathe; **narażać kogoś/coś na szwank** jeopardize sb/sth; **wyjść z czegoś bez szwanku** escape unharmed *l.* unscathed *l.* without injury.

szwankować *ipf.* be failing, be deficient, be defective; (*o urządzeniu*) act up; **szwankować na zdrowiu** feel *l.* be unwell; **szwankować na umyśle** *żart.* be (a bit) lacking.

szwarccharakter *mp* villain, bad guy.

szwargot *mi* jabber, gibberish.

szwargotać *ipf.* -czę -czesz jabber, gibber.

Szwecja *f. geogr.* Sweden.

Szwed *mp,* **Szwedka** *f. Gen.pl.* -ek Swede; **on jest Szwedem** he is Swedish.

szwedzki *a.* Swedish; **szwedzki stół** (*w restauracji*) all-you-can-eat buffet; (*na przyjęciu*) buffet lunch (dinner, banquet, etc.); (*na przyjęciu w domu, prywatce itp.*) help-yourself-table; **szwedzki klucz** adjustable spanner.

szwendać się *ipf. pot.* hang around *l.* about, gad around *l.* about.

szwie *itd. mi zob.* **szew.**

szwindel *mi* -dl- *Gen.pl.* -i *l.* -ów *pot.* swindle, fiddle, fraud.

szwindlować *ipf. pot.* swindle, fiddle, cheat.

szwoleżer *mp pl.* -owie *hist., wojsk.* light cavalryman.

szwoleżerski *a. hist., wojsk.* light cavalryman('s).

szyb *mi* **1.** *górn.* shaft, well; **szyb solny** salt well; **szyb naftowy** oil well, oiler. **2.** *bud.* shaft, well; **szyb dźwigowy** elevator shaft; **szyb klatki schodowej** stairwell; **szyb wentylacyjny** air *l.* ventilating shaft. **3.** *metal.* shaft.

szyba *f.* **1.** (glass) pane; (*okna*) (window) pane; **przednia szyba samochodu** *mot.* windshield, windscreen; **szyba pancerna** armor glass; (*w samochodzie*) bulletproof windshield. **2.** *przen.* (*wody*) sheet.

szyber *mi* -br- *Gen.* -a **1.** (= *zasuwa w kanale kominowym*) baffle. **2.** (= *łopata piekarska*) peel.

szyberdach *mi mot.* sunroof.

szybka *f. Gen.pl.* -ek small (glass) pane.

szybki *a.* -bszy **1.** (= *prędki*) fast, quick, speedy, rapid; (*o spojrzeniu*) quick, cursory; **szybki jak błyskawica** quick as a flash; **nie bądź taki szybki Bill** *przest., pot.* haste makes waste;

szybki Bill *żart.* Johnny on the spot; **szybki krok** scuttle; **szybki ruch** scoot; **szybki rzut okiem** look-see, once-over; **szybkie tempo** celerity; **w zastraszająco szybkim tempie** at an alarming rate; **pas szybkiego ruchu** *mot.* fast *l.* express lane; **droga szybkiego ruchu** *mot.* expressway; **bardzo szybki** (*o tempie*) cracking, double-quick; **mieć szybki refleks** have quick reflexes; **szybkie czytanie** speed reading; **łyżwiarstwo szybkie** *sport* speed skating. **2.** (= *bezzwłoczny*) (*np. o reakcji*) instant, immediate, prompt; (*o decyzji*) quick.

szybko *adv.* **1.** (= *prędko*) (*jechać, biec, mówić, oddychać*) fast, quickly, rapidly; (*płynąć, toczyć się*) swiftly; **za szybko** too quickly *l.* fast *l.* swiftly, with too much hurry; **jak szybko?** (*kiedy*) how soon?; **jak szybko jedziemy?** how fast are we going?, what speed are we doing?; **szybko schnąca farba** quick-dry paint; **szybko działający środek** quick-acting remedy. **2.** (= *bezzwłocznie*) at a short notice, with speed; (*odpowiedzieć, zdecydować się, zareagować*) promptly, right away, in short *l.* soon order; **szybko odpowiadać** be quick to answer; **szybko załatwiać** (*sprawy*) expedite; **szybko i sprawnie** with dispatch; **szybko zapomniany** soon forgotten; **szybko robić postępy w czymś** make good *l.* quick progress at sth. – *int.* **szybko!** hurry!, hurry up!, quick!; **nie tak szybko!** not so fast, easy (does it)!

szybkobiegacz *mp,* **szybkobiegaczka** *f. Gen.pl.* -ek *sport* sprinter.

szybkobieżny *a.* (*o tramwaju, windzie, turbinie, pompie*) high-speed; **silnik szybkobieżny** high-speed engine.

szybkonogi *a.* fleet of foot, swift-footed.

szybkoobrotowy *a.* high-speed; **silnik szybkoobrotowy** high-speed engine.

szybkostrzelny *a.* (*o karabinie, pistolecie, dziale*) quick-firing, QF.

szybkościomierz *mi Gen.* -a speedometer; tachometer.

szybkościowy *a.* high-speed; *sport* (*o treningu*) speed.

szybkość *f.* **1.** (= *prędkość*) (*pociągu, samochodu*) speed, velocity; (*wystrzałów*) rapidity; **szybkość działania** (*komputera, programu*) performance; **szybkość obiegu** (*pieniądza*) *ekon.* velocity of circulation; **szybkość czytania** reading speed; **zwiększać/zmniejszać szybkość** *mot.* accelerate/decelerate; **maksymalna szybkość** *mot.* speed limit; **z szybkością 20 km/h** at (the speed of) 20 kph; **z dużą/małą szybkością** at high/low speed; **dostać mandat za przekroczenie szybkości** be fined for speeding; **punkt kontroli szybkości** speeding trap; **nabierać szybkości** pick up *l.* gather speed. **2.** (*decyzji, odpowiedzi, reakcji*) (= *natychmiastowość*) promptness, quickness.

szybkowar *mi Gen.* -u *l.* -a pressure cooker.

szybować *ipf.* **1.** (*o ptakach*) soar; (*o chmurach*) float. **2.** *lotn.* (*o szybowcu*) glide.

szybowcowy *a. lotn.* (*o klubie, lotnisku, zawodach, kursie*) gliding; (*o hangarze*) glider.

szybowiec *mi* -wc- *Gen.* -a *lotn.* glider; (*wyczynowy*) sailplane.

szybownictwo *n. lotn.* gliding.

szybownik *mp lotn.* glider pilot.

szybowy *a. górn.* shaft, well; **piec szybowy** *metal.* shaft furnace. – *mp górn.* shaftsman.

szych *mi tk.* (*nić*) tinsel.

szycha *f. pot.* big shot, bigwig, fat cat.

szychta *f.* **1.** *górn.* shift. **2.** *przest.* (= *warstwa*) course (*of stone, bricks, etc.*).

szycie *n.* sewing, needlework; **maszyna do szycia** sewing machine; **kurs szycia** sewing course; **komplet przyborów do szycia** sewing kit.

szyć *ipf.* -**ję** -**jesz** **1.** (*odzież*) sew; (= *zszywać*) stitch; (*igłą*) needle; (*kapę, kołdrę*) quilt; **szyć na okrętkę** sew overhand. **2.** *med.* suture, stitch.

szydełko *n. Gen.pl.* -**ek** crochet hook *l.* needle; **szalik zrobiony na szydełku** *l.* **szydełkiem** crochet scarf.

szydełkować *ipf.* crochet.

szydełkowy *a.* crochet.

szyderca *mp* scoffer, jeerer, sneerer.

szyderczo *adv.* derisively, scoffingly, jeeringly, in a jeering way; **uśmiechać się szyderczo** sneer (*do kogoś* at sb).

szyderczy *a.* derisive, scoffing; (*o uśmiechu*) sneering; (*o wypowiedzi*) venomous.

szyderstwo *n.* scoff, sneer, jeer, derision.

szydło *n. Gen.pl.* -**deł** awl; **szydło zecerskie** *druk.* bodkin; **wyszło szydło z worka** murder is out, the truth has come out.

szydzić *ipf.* scoff, sneer, jeer (*z kogoś/czegoś* at sb/sth).

szyfon *mi tk.* chiffon.

szyfonowy *a. tk.* chiffon, made of chiffon.

szyfr *mi* code, cipher; (*w zamku, sejfie*) combination; **zapisać szyfrem** encipher, encrypt, encode, cipher; **wysłać szyfrem** send in code *l.* cipher; **złamać szyfr** break a code *l.* cipher.

szyfrant *mp* cryptographist, coder.

szyfrantka *f. Gen.pl.* -**ek** *zob.* **szyfrant**.

szyfrarka *f. Gen.pl.* -**ek** *techn.* cryptograph.

szyfrator *mi Gen.* -**a** *techn.* coder, encoder.

szyfrogram *mi* code message, cryptogram.

szyfrować *ipf.* code, cipher.

szyfrowy *a.* code; (*o zapisie, kluczu*) cipher; **zamek szyfrowy** combination lock.

szyicki *a. rel.* Shi'itic.

szyita *mp rel.* Shi'ite, Shiite, Shi'ah.

szyizm *mi rel.* Shi'ism.

szyja *f. Gen.* **szyi** **1.** *anat.* (*człowieka, zwierzęcia*) neck; **po szyję** up to the chin, up to one's neck; **rzucić się komuś na szyję** fling one's arms around sb; **objęła go za szyję** she threw her arms round his neck; **zapiąć się pod szyją** button one's coat *l.* shirt under one's chin; **miał koszulę rozpiętą pod szyją** his shirt was open at the neck; **chustka na szyję** neckerchief; **na łeb, na szyję** *pot.* headlong, headfirst; **wyciągać szyję** crane one's neck; **być komuś kamieniem (młyńskim) u szyi** be a millstone around sb's neck. **2.** *przen. przest.* **dać szyję (pod topór)** lay one's head on the block; **ocalić szyję** save one's neck.

szyjka *f. Gen.pl.* -**ek** **1.** (*butelki*) neck; **szyjka słupka** *bot.* style. **2.** *anat.* (*zwł. macicy*) cervix; **zapalenie szyjki macicy** *pat.* cervicitis. **3.** *muz.* neck.

szyjny *a. anat.* cervical; **tętnica szyjna** carotid (artery); **żyła szyjna** jugular (vein).

szyk¹ *mi* **1.** (= *porządek*) order, arrangement, array; **pokrzyżować komuś szyki** thwart sb's plans. **2.** *wojsk.* line, formation; **ustawiać się w szyku** fall into line; **szyk bojowy** line of battle; **ustawiać w szyk bojowy** (*wojsko przed bitwą*) embattle. **3.** *gram.* word order; **szyk przestawny** inversion; **szyk stały** fixed word order.

szyk² *mi* (= *wytworność*) chic, smartness, flair, style; **ubierać się z szykiem** dress in *l.* with style; **zadać szyku (czymś)** *pot.* be dressed to kill (in sth); **Ewa zadała szyku na wczorajszym przyjęciu** *pot.* Eve stunned everyone at the party last night with her new dress.

szykanować *ipf.* persecute, oppress, harass. ~ **się** *ipf.* persecute each other *l.* one another, harass each other *l.* one another.

szykany *pl. Gen.* -**n** **1.** (= *prześladowania*) persecution, oppression, harassment; **narażać się na szykany** be exposed to persecution *l.* harassment. **2.** *żart.* (= *luksus*) luxury; **ceremonia z wszystkimi szykanami** a lavish *l.* sumptuous ceremony.

szyki *pl. Gen.* -**ów** **1.** *lit.* (*wojsko*) lines. **2.** (= *plany*) plans; **mieszać komuś szyki** upset sb's apple cart, put a spoke in sb's wheel, throw the spanner in the works, thwart sb's plans.

szykować *ipf.* **1.** *pot.* prepare, get ready; **szykować komuś niespodziankę** prepare a surprise for sb. **2.** *przest.* (*wojsko*) array, embattle. ~ **się** *ipf. pot.* get ready, prepare (o.s.) (*do czegoś* for sth); **szykuje mi się wyjazd do Krakowa** I am in for a trip to Cracow; **szykować się do czegoś** *l.* **na coś** gear up to *l.* towards *l.* for sth, have one's mind set on sth; **szykować się na kogoś** be after sb.

szykownie *adv.* nattily, stylishly, with taste; (*ubrać się*) smartly, elegantly, fashionably; (*wyglądać*) smart, stylish, elegant.

szykowny *a.* chic, elegant, smart; (*o marynarce, sukni, wyglądzie*) elegant, smart, classy.

szyld *mi* signboard; **działać pod szyldem...** operate behind the facade of...

szyling *mi Gen.* -**a** **1.** (*w Austrii*) schilling. **2.** (*w Wielkiej Brytanii*) shilling, twelve pence.

szylkret *mi* tortoiseshell.

szylkretowy *a.* (*o grzebieniu, masie*) tortoiseshell; **żółw szylkretowy** *zool.* hawksbill (turtle) (*Eretmochelys imbricata*).

szympans *ma zool.* chimpanzee (*Pan*).

szyna *f.* **1.** *kol.* rail; **szyny kolejowe** rail tracks. **2.** *komp.* bus; **szyna danych** data bus. **3.** (= *prowadnica*) guide. **4.** (*do firanek*) (curtain) rod. **5.** *med.* splint. **6.** *dent.* (= *aparat na zęby*) braces.

szynel *mi Gen.* -**a** *l.* -**u** *zwł. wojsk.* greatcoat.

szynion *mi* chignon.

szynk *mi Gen.* -**u** *przest.* tavern.

szynka *f. Gen.pl.* -**ek** *kulin.* (*surowa, gotowana*) ham; (*wędzona, peklowana*) gammon; (*suszona*) prosciutto; (*konserwowa, mielona*) Spam.

szynkowy *a. kulin.* ham.

szynowy *a.* rail; **komunikacja szynowa** railway transport.

szynszyla *f. Gen.pl.* **-i** *zool.* chinchilla (*Chinchilla laniger*).

szynszyle *pl. Gen.* **-i** (*futro*) chinchilla (fur coat).

szynszylowate *pl. Gen.* **-ych** *zool.* chinchillas (*Chinchillidae*).

szynszylowy *a.* (*o futrze*) chinchilla.

szyper *mp* **-pr-** *pl.* **-owie** *żegl.* skipper.

szyperski *a.* (*np. o uprawnieniach*) skipper's.

szypszyna *f. Gen.pl.* **-yn** *bot.* dog rose (*Rosa canina*).

szypułka *f. Gen.pl.* **-ek** *bot.* pedicel; (*truskawki*) hull; **bez szypułek** (*o owocu, kwiecie*) stemmed.

szypułkowy *a. bot.* pedicellate; **dąb szypułkowy** English oak (*Quercus robur*).

szyszak *mi Gen.* **-a** *l.* **-u** *hist.* casque, helmet. – *ma Gen.* **-a** *orn.* t(o)uraco (*Musophagiformes*).

szyszka *f. Gen.pl.* **-ek** **1.** *bot.* cone, strobile; **szyszka chmielowa** hop cone. **2.** *żart. l. iron.* (= *osobistość*) bigwig, big shot, fat cat.

szyszkojagoda *f. Gen.* **-ód** *bot.* berry-like cone.

szyszkowy *a. bot.* cone.

szyszynka *f. Gen.pl.* **-ek** *anat.* pineal gland *l.* body.

szyty *a.* sewn; **szyte grubymi nićmi** thinly disguised, perfectly obvious; **szyty na zamówienie** bespoke; **szyty na miarę** made-to-measure, tailor-made; **szyty ręcznie** handsewn; **szyty maszynowo** machine-sewn.

Ś, ś *n. indecl.* (*litera*) S with an accent, s with an accent; S acute, s acute.

ściana *f.* **1.** (= *mur*) wall; **ściana boczna/frontowa** side/front wall; **ściana działowa** partition wall; **ściana nośna** load-bearing wall; **ściana przeciwpożarowa** firewall; **ściana szczytowa** (*w domu*) gable wall; (*w bloku*) side wall; **ściana ślepa** windowless wall; **blady jak ściana** white as a sheet; **jak groch o ścianę** *pot.* like water off a duck's back; **gadać jak do ściany** *pot.* it's like talking to a brick wall; **mieszkać z kimś przez ścianę** live next door to sb; **podpierać ściany** *pot.* (*na potańcówce*) be a wallflower; **postawić kogoś pod ścianą** put sb up against a wall; **wbić gwóźdź w ścianę** drive a nail into the wall; **ściany mają uszy** walls have ears. **2.** (= *płaszczyzna*) wall; (= *bok*) side; **ściana komórkowa** *bot.* cell wall. **3.** (= *zbocze*) wall; **wejść na szczyt południową ścianą** reach the top from the south. **4.** *górn.* (= *wyrobisko*) face. **5.** (= *przeszkoda*) barrier; **ściana deszczu** sheet of rain; **ściana ognia** wall of fire; **ściana milczenia** wall of silence. **6.** *geom.* face, side.

ścianka *f. Gen.pl.* **-ek 1.** (= *przepierzenie*) partition. **2.** (= *bok*) side.

ściąć *pf.* **zetnę zetniesz, zetnij** *zob.* **ścinać. ~ się** *pf.* **1.** *zob.* **ścinać się. 2.** *pot.* (= *pokłócić się*) fall out (*z kimś* with sb).

ściąga *f. szkoln.* crib, crib sheet.

ściągacz *mi Gen.* **-a** *Gen.pl.* **-y** *l.* **-ów** welt; (*przy rękawie*) ribbed cuff.

ściągaczka *f. Gen.pl.* **-ek** *zob.* **ściąga.**

ściągać *ipf.* **1.** (= *zsuwać*) (*np. flagę z masztu*) take down; (*np. obrączkę z ręki*) take off, pull off. **2.** (*buty, koszulę*) take off; **ściągać ubranie** take off one's clothes. **3.** (= *mocno związywać*) pull tight, tighten. **4.** (= *schodzić się*) come flocking. **5.** (= *skupiać*) draw; **ściągać na siebie uwagę/podejrzenie** draw attention/suspicion upon o.s.; **ściągnął na siebie gniew rodziców** he incurred his parents' anger. **6.** (= *zbierać*) gather, collect; **ściągać podatki** levy taxes, collect taxes; **ściągać długi** collect debts. **7.** (= *sprowadzać*) bring, get; **ściągnął z zagranicy najlepszych lekarzy** he brought the best doctors from abroad; **ściągnij go tu najszybciej jak się da** get him over here as quickly as possible. **8.** (= *odprowadzać, wypompowywać*) (*ciecz*) draw off. **9.** (= *kurczyć*) shrink; **ściągać brwi** knit one's eyebrows, frown; **ściągać usta** tighten one's lips. **10.** *pot.* (= *kraść*) pinch, nick. **11.** *szkoln.* cheat, crib. **12.** *komp.* (*pliki, dane*) download. **~ się** *ipf.* **1.** (= *kurczyć się*) *jęz.*

contract. **2. ściągnąć się paskiem** tighten one's belt.

ściągający *a. med.* astringent; **tonik ściągający** astringent lotion.

ściągawka *f. Gen.pl.* **-ek** *szkoln.* crib, crib sheet.

ściągnąć *pf.* **-ij** *zob.* **ściągać.**

ściągnięty *a.* **1.** (= *skurczony*) shrank; (*o twarzy*) pinched, drawn; (*o brwiach*) knitted; (*o ustach*) tightened. **2.** *jęz.* contracted; **forma ściągnięta** contracted form.

ścichapęk *mp pl.* **-i** *żart.* the silent type.

ściec *pf.* **ścieknie, ścieknij, ściekł** *zob.* **ściekać.**

ścieg *mi* stitch; **ścieg prawy/lewy** right/left stitch; **ścieg jodełkowy** chevron stitch; **ścieg krzyżykowy** cross stitch; **ścieg łańcuszkowy** chain stitch; **ścieg płaski** flat stitch; **ścieg ryżowy** staggered tuck stitch; **ścieg węzełkowy** knot stitch.

ściek *mi* (*kanał*) sewer; **ściek uliczny** gutter.

ściekać *ipf.* trickle, trickle down.

ścieki *pl. Gen.* **-ów** sewage; **ścieki przemysłowe** industrial sewage.

ścieknąć *pf.* **ścieknie, ścieknij, ściekł** *l.* **ścieknął ściekła** *zob.* **ściekać.**

ściekowy *a.* sewage; **kanał ściekowy** (*otwarty*) drainage ditch; (*podziemny*) sewer; **rura ściekowa** waste pipe; **studzienka ściekowa** drain.

ścielić *ipf. dial.* **ścielić łóżko** (= *rozkładać na noc*) make the bed; (= *składać na dzień*) do the bed.

ściemniacz *mi el.* dimmer.

ściemniać *ipf.*, **ściemnić** *pf.* **-ij 1.** (*np. lampę, światło*) darken. **2.** *pot.* (= *zmyślać, oszukiwać*) **ściemniać komuś** pull the wool over sb's eyes; **nie ściemniaj mi tu, dobra?** stop playing your tricks on me, will you? **3.** *pot.* (= *podrywać kogoś*) chat up (*kogoś* sb); (= *starać się o kogoś*) work (*kogoś* on sb); **ściemniłem ją na mój nowy samochód** she fell for me when she saw my new car; **udało mi się ją ściemnić dopiero kiedy zaproponowałem, że pójdę z jej psem na spacer, kiedy musiała zostać w pracy** I finally won her over when I proposed to take her dog for a walk when she had to stay at work; **chyba ciągle ją ściemnia** I think he's still working on her. **~ się** *ipf.*, **ściemnić się** *pf.* get dark; **ściemnia się** it's getting dark.

ściemnieć *pf.* **1.** (*o kolorze*) darken. **2.** (*o obrazie, niebie*) go dark, darken. **3.** (*o świetle*) dim.

ścienny *a.* wall; **gazetka ścienna** wall newspaper; **malowidło ścienne** mural.

ściera f. pot. rag.

ścierać ipf. **1.** (= usuwać z powierzchni) wipe off, wipe away; **ścierać kurz z mebli** dust furniture; **ścierać tablicę** wipe the board. **2.** (napis, rysunek) rub off; (skórę) scrape, abrade. **3.** (np. warzywa na tarce) grind; **ścierać nieprzyjaciela w proch** pulverize the enemy. **~ się** ipf. **1.** (o tkaninie, dywanie) get worn, weat thin; (o butach) wear out. **2.** (o armiach, poglądach, osobach) clash (z kimś/czymś with sb/sth).

ścieralność a. techn. grindability.

ściereczka f. Gen.pl. **-ek** (small) cloth; **ściereczka do naczyń** dishcloth.

ścierka f. Gen.pl. **-ek 1.** (do wycierania) cloth; **ścierka do naczyń** dishcloth; **ścierka do podłogi** floor cloth. **2.** wulg., pog. (o kobiecie) slut.

ściernisko n. roln. **1.** (pole) stubble field. **2.** (= ścierń) stubble.

ścierny a. techn. abrasive; **materiał ścierny** abrasive; **papier ścierny** sandpaper.

ścierń f. pl. **-e** roln. stubble.

ścierpieć pf. **-ę -isz** stand, suffer; **nie ścierpię tego dłużej** I can't stand it anymore.

ścierpnąć pf. **-pnij, -pł** l. **-pnął -pła -pli** grow numb, become numb; **nogi mi ścierpły** my legs grew numb; **skóra mi ścierpła, gdy to zobaczyłem** it made my flesh creep.

ścierpnięty a. numb, asleep.

ścierwo n. **1.** (= padlina) carcass, carrion. **2.** wulg., obelż., fucker, dick-face; **ty ścierwo!** you motherfucker!

ścierwojady pl. orn. cathartines (Cathartes).

ścieśniać ipf., **ścieśnić** pf. **-ij** (np. pismo) squeeze together; **ścieśniać szeregi** move in closer. **~ się** ipf., **ścieśnić się** pf. **1.** (np. o ulicy) (= zwężać się) narrow. **2.** (= zwierać się) huddle up, huddle together.

ścieżka f. Gen.pl. **-ek** t. komp. path; **ścieżka dostępu** komp. access path; **ścieżka dźwiękowa** film soundtrack; **ścieżka rowerowa** bicycle path; **ścieżka zdrowia** fitness trail; **być z kimś na wojennej ścieżce** be on the warpath with sb; **chodzić własnymi ścieżkami** be independent; **kroczyć utartymi ścieżkami** follow the beaten track, tread the beaten path.

ścieżyna f. zob. **ścieżka.**

ścieżynka f. Gen.pl. **-ek** zob. **ścieżka.**

ścięcie n. **1.** (= egzekucja) beheading; **szedł tam jak na ścięcie** (niechętnie) he would rather die than have to go there; (świadomy, co go czeka) he went there sensing the imminent disaster. **2.** (= przejście w stan stały) setting, coagulation. **3.** sport smash.

ścięgno n. Gen.pl. **-gien** anat. tendon; **zerwane/naderwane/nadwyrężone ścięgno** broken/torn/strained tendon; **ścięgno Achillesa** Achilles tendon.

ścięty a. **1.** (= spiczasty) pointed. **2.** t. geom. truncate, truncated. **3.** (= zabity przez ścięcie) beheaded; **marzenie ściętej głowy** wishful thinking, pie in the sky.

ścigacz mi Gen. **-a** wojsk. fast attack craft; **ścigacz rakietowy** missile-firing fast attack craft.

ścigać ipf. **1.** (= gonić) chase, pursue; (o policji) hunt (kogoś for sb); **ścigać się z czasem** work against the clock. **2.** prawn. prosecute; **ścigać kogoś listem gończym** issue an arrest warrant on sb. **~ się** ipf. race (z kimś against sb).

ściganie n. pursuit, hunt-down; **organy ścigania** law enforcement agencies.

ścinać ipf. **1.** (= oddzielić) cut off; (trawę) mow; (włosy) cut; (drzewo) cut down, fell; **ścinać kogoś z nóg** knock sb sideways. **2.** (= wygładzać) smooth; **ścinać zakręty** cut corners. **3.** (= powodować krzepnięcie) set; **strach ściął mu krew w żyłach** fear curdled his blood. **4.** (= dokonywać egzekucji) behead. **5.** sport smash. **6.** pot. (= oblewać na egzaminie) fail, flunk. **~ się** ipf. **1.** (= krzepnąć) set. **2.** pot. (= pokłócić się) fall out (z kimś with sb). **3.** pot. (= nie zdać) fail, flunk; **ściąć się na egzaminie** fail an exam.

ścinek mi **-nk-** Gen. **-a** offcut.

ściółka f. Gen.pl. **-ek 1.** leśn. forest bed, litter. **2.** (dla zwierząt) bedding, litter.

ścisk mi **1.** (= tłok) crowd, crush. **2.** (= zwarcie) jam.

ściskać ipf. **1.** (= gnieść) squeeze, clench; **ściska mnie w żołądku** I have butterflies in my stomach; **smutek ściska mi serce** it grieves my heart; **płacz ścisnął mnie za gardło** I felt a lump in my throat. **2.** (= przewiązać, opasać) band. **3.** tylko pf. (= pochwycić) (np. ręką, imadłem) grip. **4.** zw. ipf. (= trzymać mocno, pewnie) clasp tightly; **ściskać coś w dłoni** clasp sth in one's hand; **ścisnąć zęby** set one's teeth, clench one's teeth. **5.** (= obejmować serdecznie) hug, embrace; **ściskać czyjąś rękę** squeeze sb's hand; **ściskać kogoś w objęciach** clasp sb in one's arms; **ściskać kogoś po bratersku** give sb a brotherly hug. **~ się** ipf. **1.** (= zaciskać się) tighten; (o pięściach, zębach) clench; **pięści/zęby mu się ścisnęły** he clenched his fists/teeth; **serce mi się ściska** my heart grieves. **2.** (= obejmować się) hug; (o żołądku) knot; **ściskać się za ręce** shake hands.

ścisłość f. **1.** (= dokładność) exactness; (= trafność) accuracy; **jeśli chodzi o ścisłość** to be precise, as a matter of fact. **2.** (np. tkaniny) compactness, denseness.

ścisły a. **1.** (= zwarty) compact, dense; (o piśmie, druku) condensed. **2.** (o związkach, kontaktach) close, tight. **3.** (= bezpośredni) direct; (o zależności, związku teorii z praktyką) close. **4.** (= dokładny) exact; (= trafny) accurate; (o danych, informacjach) precise, correct; (o umyśle) scientific, exact; **nauki ścisłe** the sciences; **w ścisłym znaczeniu tego słowa** in the strict sense of the word. **5.** (= surowy) strict, severe; (o diecie, areszcie, rezerwacie) strict, rigid. **6.** (= elitarny) top; **ścisłe grono** one's l. the inner circle; **ścisła czołówka** the leading edge.

ścisnąć pf. **ścisnę ściśniesz, ściśnij 1.** zob. **ściskać. 2.** (= stłoczyć) cram, crowd. **~ się** pf. **1.** zob. **ściskać się. 2.** (= stłoczyć się) crowd, flock.

ściszać ipf., **ściszyć** pf. **1.** (radio, telewizor itp.) turn down, turn the volume down. **2.** (głos) lower one's voice. **~ się** ipf., **ściszyć się** pf. **1.** (= milknąć) fall silent. **2.** (o wietrze, burzy) subside.

ściszony *a.* (*głos*) lowered; (*barwy, kolory*) toned down.

ściśle *adv.* **1.** (= *zwarcie*) tightly. **2.** (= *dokładnie*) precisely, exactly; (*wyrazić się, określić*) precisely, accurately; **ściśle rzecz biorąc** as a matter of fact; **ściśle mówiąc** strictly speaking, to be precise; **zmierzać do ściśle określonego celu** pursue a clearly defined goal. **3.** (= *rygorystycznie*) strictly, rigorously; **ściśle tajny** top secret, strictly confidential; **ściśle przestrzegać** observe rigorously.

ściśliwość *f. fiz.* compressibility.

ściśliwy *a. fiz.* compressible.

Śl. *abbr.* (= *Śląski*) Silesian.

ślad *mi* **1.** (= *trop*) trace; (*zwierzęcia*) track; (*stopy*) footprint, footmark; (*kopyta*) hoof-print; **ślad na ciele** mark; **ślad torowy** *żegl.* wake, dead water; **fałszywy ślad** false track; **iść śladem kogoś/czegoś** follow sb/sth; **iść w czyjeś ślady** follow in sb's footsteps; **nosić ślady czegoś** bear the traces of sth, show signs of sth; **naprowadzić kogoś na ślad kogoś/czegoś** lead sb to sb/sth. **2.** (= *pozostałość*) trace, remnant; (*łez*) tearstain; **ślady dawnej świetności** remnants of the former glory; **przepaść bez śladu** disappear without trace, vanish without trace; **zacierać za sobą ślady** cover one's tracks; **zostawić po sobie jakiś ślad** leave one's trace; **ani śladu kogoś/czegoś** no trace of sb/sth, neither hide nor hair of sb/sth; **ani śladu strachu** no trace of fear; **ani śladu ironii** no hint of irony.

śladowy *a.* minute, vestigial; **śladowe ilości (czegoś)** trace quantities (of sth); **pierwiastki śladowe** *chem.* trace elements.

ślamazara *f. l. mp decl. like f. Gen.pl.* **-r** *l.* **-ów** *uj.* sluggard.

ślamazarnie *adv.* sluggishly.

ślamazarność *f.* sluggishness.

ślamazarny *a.* sluggish, flabby.

ślaz *mi bot.* mallow (*Malva silvestris*).

ślazowate *pl. Gen.* **-ych** *bot.* the Malvaceae family (*Malvaceae*).

ślazowy *a.* mallow; **cukierki ślazowe** marshmallows.

Śląsk *mi Gen.* **-a** *geogr.* Silesia; **Dolny/Górny Śląsk** Lower/Upper Silesia.

śląski *a.* Silesian.

Ślązaczka *f. Gen.pl.* **-ek**, **Ślązak** *mp* Silesian.

śledczy *a.* investigation; **areszt śledczy** (*nałożony na kogoś*) custody; (*miejsce*) detention facility; **oficer śledczy** investigating officer. – *mp pot.* investigating officer.

śledzić *ipf.* **1.** (= *tropić*) follow. **2.** (= *obserwować*) (*np. akcję filmu, najnowsze wydarzenia kulturalne*) follow; (*np. ruchy wojsk*) monitor; (*o radarze*) track.

śledzik *ma* (small) herring. – *mi Gen. i Acc.* **-a** *dial.* (= *przyjęcie*) Shrove Tuesday party.

śledziona *f. anat.* spleen.

śledziowy *a.* herring.

śledztwo *n.* investigation; **śledztwo w sprawie... *l.* w związku z...** inquiry into...; **śledztwo w toku** investigation in progress; **prowadzić śledztwo** carry out an investigation, conduct an investigation; **wszcząć śledztwo** launch an investigation.

śledź *ma icht.* herring (*Clupea harengus*). – *mi Gen. i Acc.* **-a** (= *kołek*) tent peg.

ślemię *n.* **-mieni-** *pl.* **-mion-** *bud.* transom.

ślepak *mi pl.* **-i** *pot.* (*pocisk*) blank. – *ma zool.* horse fly; (*afrykański*) mango fly; (*amerykański*) deerfly (*Chrysops*).

ślepia *pl. Gen.* **-ów** **1.** (*u zwierzęcia*) eyes. **2.** *pot.* (*u człowieka*) optics, peepers.

ślepić *ipf. pot.* strain one's eyes.

ślepiec *mp* **-pc-** *Voc.* **-cze** *l.* **-u** *pl.* **-y** blind man.

ślepnąć *ipf.* **-ij** go blind.

ślepo *adv.* (= *bezkrytycznie*) blindly; **na ślepo** blindly, randomly.

ślepota *f. pat.* blindness; **ślepota barw** color blindness, *Br.* colour blindness; **kurza ślepota** *l.* **ślepota zmierzchowa** night blindness, moon blindness.

ślepowron *ma orn.* night heron (*Nycticorax nycticorax*).

ślepy *a.* **1.** (= *niewidzący*) *t. przen.* blind; **ślepa furia** blind fury; **ślepa kiszka** *anat.* appendix, vermiform appendix; **ślepy pilotaż** blind flying; **ślepa uliczka** cul-de-sac, dead end; **ślepy zaułek** blind alley, dead end; **ślepy nabój** blank cartridge, blank; **ślepy na jedno oko** blind in one eye; **być ślepym na czyjeś błędy** be blind to sb's mistakes; **być ślepym narzędziem w czyichś rękach** be a tool in sb's hands. **2.** (= *przypadkowy*) blind; **ślepy traf** blind chance. – *mp* blind person; **ślepi** the blind.

ślę, ślesz *itd. ipf. zob.* **slać**.

ślęczeć *ipf.* **-ę -ysz** (*nad aktami, książką*) pore over; (*nad szyciem*) labor over; *Br.* labour over; **ślęczeć nad czymś po nocach** burn the midnight oil.

ślicznie *adv.* prettily, nicely; **ślicznie wyglądać** look lovely; **ślicznie dziękuję** thank you so much.

śliczność *f.* beauty; **moje ty śliczności!** my little cutie!

ślicznotka *f. Gen.pl.* **-ek** pretty face.

śliczny *a.* **1.** (= *piękny, uroczy*) lovely. **2.** *przen.* pretty; **śliczny bałagan!** here's a pretty mess!

ślimaczek *ma* **-czk-** (small) snail.

ślimacznica *f.* **1.** *bud.* volute, helix. **2.** *techn.* wormwheel.

ślimaczy *a.* snail's; **w ślimaczym tempie** at a snail's pace.

ślimaczyć się *ipf.* **1.** (= *wlec się*) drag along, move at snail's pace. **2.** (*o ranie*) fester.

ślimak *ma zool.* snail; (*bez skorupy*) slug (*Helicidae*); **iść jak ślimak** move at snail's pace. – *mi* **1.** (= *pętla drogowa*) cloverleaf. **2.** *sztuka* scroll, helix. **3.** *muz.* (*na instrumencie*) scroll. **4.** *anat.* cochlea. **5.** *techn.* worm.

ślimakowy *a. techn.* worm; **przekładnia ślimakowa** worm gear.

ślina *f.* saliva, spit; **mówić co ślina na język przyniesie** *pot.* talk off the top of one's head.

śliniaczek *mi* **-czk-** *Gen.* **-a** bib.

śliniak *mi Gen.* **-a** *zob.* **śliniaczek**.

ślinianka *f. Gen.pl.* **-ek** *anat.* salivary gland.

ślinić *ipf.* moisten (*with saliva*). ~ **się** *ipf.* **1.** (= *wydzielać ślinę*) dribble. **2.** *przen.* drool (*na coś* over sth).

ślinka *f. Gen.pl.* **-ek** spit; **ślinka mi leci na samą myśl** it makes my mouth water.

ślinotok *mi pat.* salivation.

ślinowy *a.* salivary; **gruczoł ślinowy** *anat.* salivary gland.

śliski *a.* **1.** (*o jezdni, posadzce*) slippery; (*o tkaninie*) smooth. **2.** *pot.* (= *niepewny, podejrzany*) (*o sprawie, temacie*) dodgy; (*o człowieku*) slippery.

ślisko *adv.* slipperily; **na drogach jest ślisko** the roads are slippery.

śliskość *f.* **1.** (*jezdni*) slipperiness. **2.** (*tematu, sprawy*) dodginess.

śliwa *f.* **1.** *bot.* (*owoc*) plum (*Prunus*). **2.** (= *siniak*) *pot.* shiner.

śliwka *f. Gen.pl.* **-ek** (*owoc*) (*drzewo*) plum.

śliwkowy *a.* plummy; (*o dżemie, powidłach, sadzie*) plum.

śliwowica *f.* slivovitz.

ślizg *mi* **1.** *lotn.* side-slip. **2.** *sport* run; **ślizg lodowy** (= *bojer*) iceboat. **3.** *techn.* slide block. **4.** *żegl.* = **ślizgacz.**

ślizgacz *mi Gen.* **-a** *żegl.* hydroplane, speedboat.

ślizgać się *ipf.* **1.** (*np. na śliskim chodniku*) slither; (*o samochodzie na jezdni*) skid. **2.** (*na łyżwach*) skate; (*na butach*) slide. **3.** *przen.* (= *przesuwać się*) slide (*po czymś* over sth).

ślizgawica *f.* icy roads conditions.

ślizgawka *f. Gen.pl.* **-ek** slide.

ślub *mi* **1.** (= *zawarcie małżeństwa*) wedding; **ślub cywilny** civil marriage; **ślub kościelny** church wedding, white wedding; **akt ślubu** marriage certificate; **brać ślub** get married; (*pot.*) tie the knot; **udzielać ślubu** officiate at a wedding. **2.** *lit.* (= *przyrzeczenie*) vow; **śluby zakonne** holy orders; **złożyć śluby zakonne** take vows.

ślubna *f. żart.* the missus.

ślubny *a.* wedding; **obrączka ślubna** wedding ring; **suknia ślubna** wedding dress; **ślubne dziecko** legitimate child; **ślubny orszak** wedding procession; **stanąć na ślubnym kobiercu** get married; *pot.* walk down the aisle. – *mp żart.* old man.

ślubować *ipf.* (*miłość*) pledge; (*zemstę*) swear; **ślubować sobie wierność** vow loyalty to each other; **ślubować komuś wierność** swear allegiance to sb.

ślubowanie *n.* oath, vow.

śluby *pl. Gen.* **-ów** (= *przysięga zakonna*) holy orders; **złożyć śluby** take vows.

ślusarski *a.* locksmith's; **zakład ślusarski** locksmith's shop, forge.

ślusarstwo *n.* locksmithery, locksmithing.

ślusarz *mp* locksmith.

śluz *mi fizj.* mucus.

śluza *f.* (= *zapora*) sluice; (*na szlaku wodnym*) lock; **śluza portowa** tidelock.

śluzowaty *a. fizj.* mucous, mucose; **obrzęk śluzowaty** *pat.* myxedema; *Br.* myxoedema.

śluzowy[1] *a. anat.* mucous; **błona śluzowa** mucous membrane.

śluzowy[2] (*o systemie, komorze*) lock.

śluzówka *f. Gen.pl.* **-ek** *anat.* mucosa.

śmiać się *ipf.* **śmieję śmiejesz** laugh (*z czegoś / kogoś* at sb/sth); **śmiać się do rozpuku** laugh one's head off; **śmiać się komuś prosto w nos** laugh in sb's face; **śmiać się przez łzy** laugh through tears; **śmiać się w duchu** laugh in one's sleeve; **ten się śmieje, kto się śmieje ostatni** he laughs best who laughs last.

śmiałek *mp* **-łk-** *pl.* **-owie** daredevil.

śmiało *adv.* **śmielej 1.** (= *bez obaw*) boldly; (= *zdecydowanie*) resolutely; **śmiało!** come on!, go ahead! **2.** (= *łatwo*) easily; **można śmiało powiedzieć, że...** it is safe to say that...; **możesz śmiało zdążyć na ten pociąg** you can easily catch that train.

śmiałość *f.* boldness; **nie mieć śmiałości do dziewcząt** be shy with girls; **mieć śmiałość coś zrobić** have the cheek to do sth.

śmiały *a.* **śmielszy** bold, daring.

śmichy-chichy *pl. Gen.* **-ów -ów** *pot.* the giggles; **to nie żadne śmichy-chichy** this is no laughing matter.

śmiech *mi* laughter; **wybuch śmiechu** burst of laughter; **parskać śmiechem** burst out laughing; **pękać ze śmiechu** laugh one's head off; **sikać ze śmiechu** *pot.* piss o.s. laughing; **zanosić się śmiechem** rock with laughter; **zrobić coś dla śmiechu** do sth for a laugh; **zrywać boki ze śmiechu** burst one's sides with laughter; **śmiechu warte** it's ludicrous!, that's a laugh!

śmieci, śmiecie *pl. Gen.* **-ci** (= *odpadki*) garbage; *Br.* rubbish; (*zwł. leżące na ulicy*) litter; **kosz na śmieci** garbage can; *Br.* dustbin; **wysypisko śmieci** (*małe*) dump; (*duże, komunalne*) landfill site; **wywóz śmieci** garbage disposal; *Br.* waste disposal; **wyrzucić coś do l. na śmieci** throw sth into a waste bin; *pot.* bin sth.

śmieciarka *f. Gen.pl.* **-ek** (*pojazd*) garbage truck; *Br.* dustcart.

śmieciarz *mp* **1.** *pot.* (= *wywożący śmieci*) garbage collector; *Br.* dustman. **2.** (= *ubogi człowiek przeszukujący śmietniki*) junkman; *Br.* rag-and-bone man.

śmiecić *ipf.* litter, throw litter about.

śmiecie *pl. Gen.* **-ci** = **śmieci.**

śmieciuszka *f. orn.* crested lark (*Galerida cristata*).

śmieć[1] *mi pl.* **-i** *l.* **-e** *pog.* (= *rzecz bezwartościowa*) **1.** rubbish, junk. **2.** (= *odpadek*) piece of litter, piece of junk; *zob. t.* **śmieci.** – *mp pl.* **-e** *pog.* (= *człowiek godny pogardy*) piece of shit.

śmieć[2] *ipf.* **śmiem śmiesz, śmiej** dare; **jak śmiesz!** how dare you!; **nie śmiałem podnieść oczu** I didn't dare to raise my eyes.

śmiercionośny *a. lit.* lethal, deadly; **śmiercionośna broń** lethal weapon; **śmiercionośny cios** deadly blow.

śmierć *f.* **1.** (= *zgon*) death; **śmierć biologiczna** biological death; **śmierć głodowa** starvation, death of starvation; **śmierć kliniczna** clinical death; **śmierć naturalna** natural death; **umrzeć**

naturalną śmiercią die of natural causes, die a natural death; śmierć mózgu brain death; śmierć męczeńska martyrdom; umrzeć śmiercią męczeńską die the death of a martyr; śmierć samobójcza suicidal death; śmierć z przyczyn naturalnych death of natural causes; śmierć tragiczna (*w wypadku, wskutek morderstwa*) violent death; zginąć śmiercią tragiczną die a violent death; nagła śmierć sudden death; przedwczesna śmierć premature death; anioł śmierci angel of death; cela śmierci death row, death house; kara śmierci capital punishment, death penalty; obóz śmierci death camp; rocznica śmierci anniversary of death, deathday; szwadron śmierci death squad; bliski śmierci close to death, nearing death; pod groźbą śmierci under pain of death; otrzeć się o śmierć have a brush with death; oszukać śmierć cheat death; podpisać na siebie wyrok śmierci sign one's own death warrant; ponieść śmierć be killed; ujść śmierci escape death; wykrwawić się na śmierć bleed to death; wystraszyć kogoś na śmierć scare the living daylights out of sb; zanudzić kogoś na śmierć bore sb stiff; zatłuc na śmierć beat to death; sprawa życia i śmierci matter of life and death; pan życia i śmierci master of life and death, lord of life and death; walka na śmierć i życie life and death struggle, mortal combat; aż do śmierci to one's dying day; (*w przysiędze małżeńskiej*) till death do us part; na łożu śmierci on one's deathbed; raz kozie śmierć a man can die but once; come what may!; na śmierć zapomniałem I clean forgot; nie wybaczę ci tego aż do śmierci I won't forgive you to my dying day; grozi ci śmierć you're in danger of death. **2.** (= *kościotrup z kosą*) Death, the grim reaper; taniec śmierci *sztuka* dance of death, danse macabre.

śmierdnąć *ipf. pot.* start to stink, start stinking.

śmierdzący *a.* stinking; **śmierdzący leń** stinker, lazy bones; **śmierdząca sprawa** fishy business.

śmierdzieć *ipf.* -dzę -dzisz stink (*czymś* of sth); **śmierdzi tutaj** this place stinks; **coś mi tu śmierdzi** (= *coś podejrzewam*) I smell a rat here; **nie śmierdzę groszem** *pot.* I'm broke.

śmierdziel *mp obelż.* stinker, stinky.

śmiertelniczka *f.* mortal.

śmiertelnie *adv.* (*blady, zimny*) deathly; (*chory*) terminally; (*ranny*) fatally, mortally; **śmiertelnie nudny** deadly dull, deadly boring; **śmiertelnie poważny** deadly serious; **śmiertelnie przerażony** scared to death, scared stiff; **śmiertelnie zmęczony** dead beat; **śmiertelnie znudzony** bored to death, bored stiff.

śmiertelnik *mp* mortal.

śmiertelność *f.* **1.** (*organizmów*) mortality. **2.** (*w statystykach*) mortality rate, death rate; **śmiertelność noworodków** infant mortality rate.

śmiertelny *a.* (*istota, organizm; wróg, niebezpieczeństwo*) mortal; (*bladość, cisza*) deathly; (*rana*) fatal, mortal; **śmiertelna choroba** fatal illness, terminal illness; **śmiertelna dawka** lethal dose; **śmiertelny cios** mortal blow, death blow;

śmiertelny strach mortal fear; **grzech śmiertelny** *rel.* mortal sin, deadly sin; **ofiary śmiertelne** fatalities; **wypadek śmiertelny** fatality; **człowiek jest istotą śmiertelną** man is a mortal being.

śmieszek *mi* -szk- *Gen.* -u *pl.* -i (= *śmiech*) giggle. – *mp* -szk- *Gen.* -a *pl.* -owie (= *wesołek*) joker, giggler.

śmieszka *f. Gen.pl.* -ek giggler; **mewa śmieszka** *orn.* black-headed gull (*Larus ridibundus*).

śmiesznie *adv.* comically, funnily; **śmiesznie tani** ridiculously cheap.

śmieszność *f.* ridiculousness; **narazić się na śmieszność** become the butt of ridicule.

śmieszny *a.* **1.** (= *zabawny*) funny, amusing; **śmieszna mina** funny face. **2.** (= *żałosny, absurdalny*) ridiculous, laughable; **nie bądź śmieszny!** *pot.* don't be ridiculous!

śmieszyć *ipf.* amuse.

śmietana *f. kulin.* cream; **śmietana kremówka** rich cream; *Br.* double cream; **bita śmietana** whipped cream; **kwaśna śmietana** sour cream; **śledź w śmietanie** creamed herring.

śmietanka *f. Gen.pl.* -ek **1.** (*do kawy*) cream; **kawa ze śmietanką** coffee with cream. **2.** *przen.* (= *elita*) cream, crème de la crème; **śmietanka towarzyska** cream of society. **3.** (*kosmetyczna*) cleansing cream.

śmietankowy *a.* cream, creamy.

śmietniczka *f. Gen.pl.* -ek **1.** (= *pojemnik*) litter bin. **2.** (= *szufelka*) dustpan.

śmietnik *mi Gen.* -a **1.** (*miejsce*) the bins; (*zbiornik*) dumpster; *Br.* skip. **2.** *pot.* (= *bałagan*) mess; (*miejsce*) pigsty.

śmietnisko *n.* garbage dump; *Br.* rubbish dump.

śmigać *ipf.* **1.** (= *przelatywać*) whoosh, whizz; **śmigaj stąd!** *pot.* get gone!, fade out! **2.** (= *machać*) swish. **3.** (= *wznosić się*) rocket.

śmigło *n. Gen.pl.* -gieł *lotn.* propeller.

śmigłowiec *mi* -wc- *Gen.* -a *lotn.* helicopter; *pot.* chopper.

śmignąć *pf.* -ij *zob.* **śmigać**.

śmigus *mi Gen.* -a *l.* -u **śmigus-dyngus** the custom of sprinkling each other with water on Easter Monday; (*zwł. na wsi*) the custom of dousing women with water on Easter Monday.

śniadanie *n.* breakfast; (= *kanapki do szkoły, pracy itp.*) bag lunch; *Br.* packed lunch; **śniadanie kontynentalne** continental breakfast; **drugie śniadanie** midmorning snack; *Br.* elevenses.

śniadaniowy *a.* breakfast; **papier śniadaniowy** sandwich paper; **płatki śniadaniowe** breakfast cereal.

śniadanko *n. emf. Gen.pl.* -ek breakfast.

śniadość *f.* tawniness.

śniady *a.* tawny.

śnić *ipf.* -ij **1.** (*w czasie snu*) dream; **śnić o ukochanej** dream about one's love; **śnił, że jest królem plemienia afrykańskiego** he dreamed that he was a king of an African tribe. **2.** (= *marzyć*) dream (*o czymś* fo sth); **śnić na jawie** daydream. **~ się** *ipf.* (*we śnie, w marzeniach*) appear in a dream; **śniłaś mi się dziś w nocy** I dreamed about you last night; **śniło mi się, że...** I dreamed that...; **nic mi się nie śni** I don't dream about anything; **co ci się śniło?** what did you dream about?; **śnią mi się wielkie pieniądze** I dream about big money; **nowy samochód nawet mu się nie śni** he wouldn't even dream about a new car; **ani mi się śni!** no way!; **ani mi się śni z nim rozmawiać!** I don't have the slightest intention of talking to him!

śnie *mi zob.* **sen**.

śnieć *f.* **1.** *bot.* smut (*Tilletia*). **2.** *pat.* bunt; **śnieć cuchnąca** stinking smut, bunt; **śnieć karłowata** dwarf bunt.

śniedzieć *ipf.* gather patina, become patinated.

śniedź *f.* patina, patine; verdigris.

śnieg *mi* snow; **śnieg z deszczem** sleet; **wieczny śnieg** permanent snow; **opady śniegu** snowfall; **pada śnieg** it's snowing; **biały jak śnieg** (as) white as snow; **obchodzi mnie to tyle, co zeszłoroczny śnieg** I couldn't care less about it.

śniegowiec *mi* **-wc-** *Gen.* **-a** overshoe, galosh.

śniegowy *a.* snow; **gaśnica śniegowa** *techn.* carbon-dioxide extinguisher; **pleśń śniegowa** *bot.* snow mold; *Br.* snow mould.

śnieguliczka *f. Gen.pl.* **-ek** *bot.* snowberry (*Symphoricarpos albus*).

śnieżek *mi* **-żk-** light snow.

śnieżka *f. Gen.pl.* **-ek** snowball; **bitwa na śnieżki** snowball fight; **rzucać się śnieżkami** throw snowballs at each other; **Królewna Śnieżka** Snow White.

śnieżnobiały *a.* snow-white.

śnieżny *a.* snow; **koszula śnieżnej białości** snow-white shirt; **pług śnieżny** snowplow; *Br.* snowplough; **zamieć śnieżna** snowstorm, blizzard.

śnieżyca *f.* **1.** *meteor.* blizzard, snowstorm. **2.** *bot.* snowflake (*Leucoium*); **śnieżyca wiosenna** spring snowflake (*L. vernum*).

śnieżyczka *f. Gen.pl.* **-ek** *bot.* snowdrop (*Galanthus*).

śnieżynka *f. Gen.pl.* **-ek** snowflake.

śnieżysty *a.* (= *pełen śniegu*) (= *biały, puszysty jak śnieg*) snowy.

śnięty *a.* **1.** (*o rybie*) dead. **2.** (*o osobie*) sleepy, lethargic.

śp. *abbr.* (= *świętej pamięci*) abbreviation put before the name of a late Christian.

śpiąco *adv.* sleepily, drowsily; **mruczeć coś śpiąco pod nosem** muble sth in sb's sleep.

śpiący *a.* **1.** (= *pogrążony we śnie*) asleep, sleeping. **2.** (= *senny*) sleepy, drowsy; **chyba jesteś śpiący?** you are sleepy, aren't you?; **czuję się śpiący** I am *l.* feel sleepy; **Śpiąca Królewna** Sleeping Beauty.

śpiączka *f. Gen.pl.* **-ek** *pat.* **1.** coma; **śpiączka afrykańska** sleeping sickness, trypanosomiasis; **śpiączka cukrzycowa/wątrobowa** diabetic/hepatic coma. **2.** *pot.* sleepiness.

śpiesznie *adv.* *lit.* hurriedly, quickly.

śpieszno *adv.* *przest.* hurriedly; **śpieszno mi do domu** I am in a hurry to get home; **śpieszno mu do niej** he is dying to see her.

śpieszny *a.* *lit.* hurried; **śpiesznym krokiem** hurriedly.

śpieszyć *ipf.* *lit.* **1.** (= *podążać*) hurry; **śpieszyć komuś na ratunek** go to sb's rescue; **śpieszyć komuś z pomocą** rush to sb's aid, rush to the aid of sb; **śpieszę dodać, że...** I hasten to add that... **2.** (= *kwapić się*) be eager (*do czegoś* to do sth); **nie śpieszyłeś się za bardzo z odpowiedzią na mój list** you certainly took your time replying to my letter. **~ się** *ipf.* **1.** (= *nie zwlekać*) (be in a) rush, (be in a) hurry; **śpieszę się!** I am in a hurry!; **śpieszę się na pociąg** I am in a hurry to catch my train; **śpieszę się na wykład** I am in a hurry to make it to the lecture; **przepraszam, czy panu się śpieszy?** excuse me, are you in a hurry?; **nie śpieszę się do małżeństwa** I am in no hurry to get married, I am not that eager to get married; **nie śpiesz się!** take your time!; **śpiesz się powoli** more haste less speed; **gdy się człowiek śpieszy, to się diabeł cieszy** haste makes waste. **2.** (*o zegarze*) be fast; **ten zegar się śpieszy (o) pięć minut** this clock is five minutes fast.

śpiew *mi* **1.** (= *śpiewanie*) singing; **łabędzi śpiew** swan song. **2.** (*lekcja*) singing lesson, singing class. **3.** (*ptaków*) song, warble.

śpiewaczka *f. Gen.pl.* **-ek** *zob.* **śpiewak** 1.

śpiewaczy *a.* singing, choral.

śpiewać *ipf.* **1.** (= *wykonywać piosenkę*) sing; **śpiewać do snu** sing (a baby) to sleep; **śpiewać piosenkę** sing a song; **śpiewać przy akompaniamencie gitary** sing to a guitar accompaniment; **śpiewać w chórze** sing in a choir; **śpiewać na całe gardło** sing at the top of one's lungs; **cienko śpiewać** (= *żyć w biedzie*) live from hand to mouth, hardly make both ends meet; (= *spokornieć*) come down a peg or two. **2.** (*o ptakach*) warble, sing. **3.** *pot.* (= *zeznawać*) squeal, sing; **poczekamy, aż zacznie śpiewać** we'll wait till she starts talking.

śpiewające *pl. Gen.* **-ych** *orn.* songbirds (*Oscines*).

śpiewająco *adv.* easily, without any problems; **zdała egzamin śpiewająco** she passed the exam with flying colors; *Br.* she passed the exam with flying colours.

śpiewak *mp* **1.** (*artysta*) singer; **śpiewak operowy** opera singer. **2.** *pot.* *orn.* songbird.

śpiewka *f. Gen.pl.* **-ek** ditty, song; **stara śpiewka** the same old story.

śpiewnie *adv.* melodiously.

śpiewnik *mi Gen.* **-a** songbook; **śpiewnik kościelny** hymn-book, hymnal.

śpiewny *a.* (= *melodyjny*) melodious; (*wymowa*) singsong.

śpiewogra *f. Gen.pl.* **-gier** *teatr* vaudeville.

śpioch *mp pl.* **-y** sleepyhead, late riser.

śpiochy *pl. Gen.* **-ów** **1.** (*ubiór niemowlęcia*) rompers. **2.** *pot.* (*w oczach po przebudzeniu*) sand.

śpioszki *pl. Gen.* **-ów** = **śpiochy** 1.

śpiwór *mi* **-o-** *Gen.* **-a** sleeping bag.

śr. *abbr.* (= *średnio*) av. (= *average; on average*). **2.** (= *średnica*) d. (= *diameter*). **3.** (= *środa*) Wed. (= *Wednesday*).

średni *a.* **1.** (*między dużym a małym*) average; (*rozmiar*) medium; **średnie wykształcenie** secondary education; **klasa średnia** the middle class; **szkoła średnia** *US* high school; *Br.* secondary school; **fale średnie** *radio* medium wave; **waga średnia** *sport* middleweight; **biegi średnie** *sport* middle distance races; **Wieki Średnie** *l.* Średniowiecze *hist.* the Middle Ages; **w średnim wieku** middle-aged. **2.** (= *nienadzwyczajny*) mediocre, ordinary; **uczony średniej miary** mediocre scholar; **to raczej średnia przyjemność** *pot.* you wouldn't call it a pleasure. **3.** (= *przeciętny*) average.

średnia *f. Gen.* **-niej** (= *przeciętna*) average, mean; **średnia temperatury** mean of temperature; **średnia zarobków** average of earnings; **poniżej/powyżej średniej** below/above (the) average; *mat.* mean; **średnia arytmetyczna** arithmetic mean; **średnia geometryczna** geometric mean; **średnia harmoniczna** harmonic mean.

średniak *mp pl.* **-cy** *l.* **-i 1.** *pot.* average *l.* ordinary person. **2.** (*w przedszkolu*) a kindergarten pupil aged 5 to 6.

średnica *f.* **1.** *geom.* diameter; **mieć 15 cm średnicy** be 15 cm in diameter. **2.** *handl.* middlings.

średnicomierz *mi Gen.* **-a** *leśn.* caliper; *Br.* calliper.

średnicowy *a.* **1.** diametral, diametrical, diametric. **2. linia średnicowa** *kol.* crosstown railway line.

średnik *mi Gen.* **-a** semicolon.

średnio *adv.* on average; **średnio ciekawy** not very interesting; **średnio zdolny** of middling abilities, of average talents; **średnio na dzień wypada po 300 kilometrów do przejechania** on average, we have 300 kilometers to travel a day; **średnio na jeża** *żart.* so so.

średnioangielski *a. jęz.* Middle English.

średniodystansowiec *mp* **-wc-** *pl.* **-y** *sport* middle-distance runner.

średniodystansowy *a. sport* middle-distance.

średniofalowy *a.* **1.** (*np. odbiornik*) medium wave. **2.** (*np. plan rozwoju*) medium-term.

średniometrażowy *a.* **film średniometrażowy** medium-length movie *l.* film (*of 20 to 60 minutes*).

średniopłat *mi Gen.* **-a** *l.* **-u** *lotn.* mid-wing monoplane.

średniopolski *a. jęz.* Middle Polish.

średniopolszczyzna *f. jęz.* Middle Polish.

średnioroczny *a.* midyear.

średniorolny *a.* **gospodarstwo średniorolne** medium-sized farm (*of 4 to 6 hectares*).

średnioterminowy *a.* medium-term.

średniowiecze *n. hist.* Middle Ages.

średniowieczny *a.* medieval; *przest.* antiquated, old-fashioned; medieval.

średniozaawansowany *a.* intermediate.

średniówka *f. Gen.pl.* **-ek 1.** *teor.lit.* caesura; **średniówka męska** masculine caesura; **średniówka żeńska** feminine caesura. **2.** *żegl.* bridge house.

średniówkowy *a. teor.lit.* caesurial, caesuric.

środa *f. Gen.pl.* **śród** Wednesday; **środa popielcowa** *rz.-kat.* Ash Wednesday.

środeczek *mi* **-czk-** *Gen.* **-a** middle; center; *Br.* centre.

środek *mi* **-dk-** *Gen.* **-a 1.** (= *punkt centralny*) middle; center; *Br.* centre; **środek ciężkości** *fiz.* center of gravity; **środek symetrii** *geom.* center of symmetry; **złoty środek** the golden mean, the happy medium; **muzyka środka** middle-of-the-road music; **w środku** in the middle; **w samym środku filmu** in the middle of the movie; **na środku ulicy** in the middle of the street; **w środku tygodnia/miesiąca** *itd.* in the middle of the week/month etc., in midweek/midmonth etc. **2.** (= *wnętrze*) inside; **do środka** inward(s); **w środku** inside; **ze środka** from within; **poprosić kogoś do środka** ask sb in; **wejdź do środka** come in, come inside; **w środku było bardzo ciepło** it was very warm inside; **zamknięte od środka** locked from inside; **puste w środku** empty inside; **Adam gryzie się w środku** *pot., przest.* sth is eating *l.* bothering Adam. **3.** (*narzędzie*) medium, vehicle; **środek płatniczy** *ekon., prawn.* legal tender; **środek transportu** *l.* komunikacji means of transport *l.* transportation; **środki masowego przekazu** mass media. **4.** (*metoda*) means, measure; **środki bezpośredniego przymusu** force; **środek dowodowy** *prawn.* evidence; **środek prawny** *prawn.* legal remedy; **środki wychowawcze i poprawcze** *prawn.* corrective measures; **środki wyrazu** *l.* wysłowienia *teor.lit.* means of expression; **środki zapobiegawcze** *prawn.* preventive *l.* preventative measures; **uciekać się do jakichś środków** take certain measures *l.* steps; **nie przebierać w środkach** do sth by fair or foul means, use all means available; **cel uświęca środki** the end justifies the means. **5.** (*preparat*) *med.* medication, remedy; *chem.* agent; **środek antykoncepcyjny** *med.* contraceptive; **środek bakteriobójczy** bactericide; **środek nasenny** *med.* soporific drug, soporific; sleeping pill; **środek piorący** washing agent, detergent; **środek przeciwbólowy** *med.* painkiller, analgesic; **środek przeczyszczający** *med.* laxative; **środek uspokajający** *med.* tranquilizer.

środki *pl. Gen.* **-ów 1.** (= *pieniądze*) financial resources, financial means; funds; **dysponować ograniczonymi środkami** have limited financial resources at one's disposal; **mieć niewystarczające środki** have inadequate financial means; **zostać bez środków do życia** be left peniless, have nothing to live on; **nasze środki pozwalają nam na dostatnie życie** we are well-off, with our financial resources we can afford a comfortable life. **2.** *ekon.* means, assets; **środki obrotowe** current assets; **środki trwałe** fixed assets.

środkowa *f. Gen.* **-ej** *geom.* median.

środkować *ipf. techn.* center; *Br.* centre.

środkowoeuropejski *a. geogr., polit.* Central European.

środkowojęzykowy *a. fon.* palatal; **spółgłoska środkowojęzykowa** palatal consonant.

środkowy *a.* middle, central; **środkowy pas jezdni** middle lane; **środkowy tor bieżni** middle lane; **ucho środkowe** *anat.* middle ear; **napastnik/obrońca środkowy** *sport* center forward/defender; *Br.* centre forward/defender. – *mp sport* center; *Br.* centre.

środowisko *n.* **1.** (= *grupa ludzi*) circle, group; (= *społeczność*) community; **środowisko akademickie** academic community. **2.** *biol.* environment; (*miejsce występowania rośliny, zwierzęcia*) habitat; **środowisko naturalne** natural environment; **ochrona środowiska** environmental protection. **3.** *chem., fiz.* medium.

środowiskowy *a.* **1.** community; **pielęgniarka środowiskowa** *med.* community nurse; **wywiad środowiskowy** community interview. **2.** *biol.* environmental.

środowy *a.* Wednesday; **środowy wykład** Wednesday lecture.

śródbłonek *mi* -nk- *Gen.* -a *anat.* endothelium.

śródczaszkowy *a. med.* intracranial.

śródlądowy *a. żegl.* inland; **żegluga śródlądowa** inland navigation.

śródmiejski *a.* downtown; *Br.* central.

śródmieście *n. Gen.pl.* -i downtown; *Br.* city centre; **jak dojechać do śródmieścia?** how do I get downtown?; *Br.* how do I get to the city centre?

śródmózgowie *n. Gen.pl.* -i *anat.* mesencephalon; *pot.* midbrain.

śródmóżdże *n. Gen.pl.* -y *anat.* = **śródmózgowie.**

śródokręcie *n. Gen.pl.* -i *żegl.* waist; **na śródokręciu** amidships, midships.

śródpiersie *n. Gen.pl.* -i *anat.* mediastinum.

śródplon *mi roln.* companion crop, intercrop.

śródskórnie *adv. med.* intradermally, intracutaneously.

śródskórny *a. med.* intradermal, intracutaneous.

śródstopie *n. Gen.pl.* -i *anat.* metatarsus; *pot.* instep.

śródtytuł *mi druk.* caption.

śródwyrazowy *a.* **upodobnienie śródwyrazowe** *fon.* word-medial *l.* word-internal assimilation.

śródziemnomorski *a.* Mediterranean; **typ śródziemnomorski** *antrop.* Mediterranean type.

śródziemny *a.* inland, mediterranean; **Morze Śródziemne** *geogr.* Mediterranean Sea, the Mediterranean.

śruba *f.* **1.** (*do skręcania*) bolt; screw, screw bolt; **skok śruby** pitch; **dokręcić komuś śrubę** *pot.* put the screws on sb. **2.** *żegl.* propeller, screw. **3.** *sport* (*skok*) twist dive.

śrubka *f. Gen.pl.* -ek (*do skręcania*) screw, bolt.

śrubokręt *mi* screwdriver.

śrubować *ipf. przest.* screw, bolt; **śrubować ceny** jack up prices.

śrubowiec *mi* -wc- *Gen.* -a **1.** *żegl.* screw ship, screw- *l.* propeller-driven ship. **2.** *biol.* spirillum.

śrubowy *a.* **1.** (*dotyczący śruby*) screw, bolt; (*w kształcie śruby*) spiral, helical; **linia śrubowa** *mat.* helix. **2.** (*o statku*) screw, propeller; **statek**

śrubowy *żegl.* screw ship, screw- *l.* propeller-driven ship; **wał śrubowy** *techn.* propeller shaft.

śrut *mi* shot.

śruta *f. roln.* ground grain.

śrutować *ipf.* **1.** *roln.* grind. **2.** *techn.* (*oczyszczać*) shot-blast, shot-clean. **3.** *techn.* (*obrabiać*) shot-peen.

śrutownica *f. techn.* (*do oczyszczania*) shot-blasting machine, grit-blasting machine; (*do obrabiania*) shot peening machine.

śrutownik *mi Gen.* -a *roln.* grain mill, corn crusher.

śrutowy *a.* shot; **strzelba śrutowa** shotgun.

śrutówka *f.* shotgun.

śryż *mi meteor.* sludge, slush ice.

św. *abbr.* (= *święty*) St. (= *Saint*).

świadczenie *n.* **1.** (= *zeznawanie*) testifying. **2.** (= *pokazywanie, okazywanie*) showing, demonstrating. **3.** **świadczenia** (= *usługi*) services; (= *pomoc materialna*) benefit; **świadczenia emerytalne** retirement pension; **świadczenia medyczne** medical services; **świadczenia rentowe** disability pension; **świadczenia socjalne** welfare benefit; **otrzymywać świadczenia** get benefit. **4.** *prawn.* performance.

świadczyć *ipf.* **1.** (= *być dowodem*) show, prove; **o czym to świadczy?** what does this tell us?; **to bardzo dobrze o nim świadczy** this is to his credit. **2.** (= *składać zeznania*) testify (*za kimś /przeciw komuś* for/against sb). **3.** (= *czynić coś komuś*) provide; **świadczyć usługi dla ludności** provide services to the general public, provide public services; **świadczyć sobie grzeczności** (= *być uprzejmym*) be very nice to each other; (= *robić sobie przysługi*) do small favors to each other; *Br.* do small favours to each other.

świadectwo *n.* **1.** (*dokument*) certificate; **świadectwo dojrzałości** certificate of secondary education; *US* High School Diploma; *Br.* General Certificate of Secondary Education, GCSE; **świadectwo lekarskie** medical certificate; **świadectwo pochodzenia** certificate of origin; **świadectwo szkolne** *US* report card; *Br.* school report; **świadectwo ślubu** certificate of marriage, certified copy of an entry of marriage; **świadectwo urodzenia** certificate of birth, birth certificate; **świadectwo zgonu** death certificate, certified copy of an entry of death. **2.** (= *dowód*) testimony, evidence; **dać świadectwo męstwa** demonstrate one's bravery; **dawać świadectwo prawdzie** be a testimony to the truth, testify to the truth.

świadek *mp* -dk- *pl.* -owie **1.** *prawn.* witness; **świadek oskarżenia/obrony** witness for the prosecution/defense; **powołać** *l.* **wezwać na świadka** summon *l.* subpoena as a witness; **powołać** *l.* **wezwać świadka** call a witness; **być świadkiem w sprawie** (*jako świadek oskarżenia*) be a witness for the prosecution; (*jako świadek obrony*) be a witness for the defense. **2.** (= *obserwator*) witness; **naoczny świadek** eyewitness; **Świadkowie Jehowy** *rel.* Jehovah's Witnesses; **być świadkiem czegoś** witness sth; **rozmawiać przy świadkach** talk in the presence of witnesses; **chcę po-**

rozmawiać z tobą bez świadków I want to talk to you in private; **Bóg mi świadkiem** I swear to God.

świadom *a. indecl. tylko pred. zob.* **świadomy.**

świadomie *adv.* (= *w sposób świadomy*) knowingly; (= *celowo*) intentionally, deliberately.

świadomość *f.* consciousness, awareness; **świadomość klasowa** class consciousness; **próg świadomości** *psych.* threshold of consciousness; **mieć (pełną) świadomość czegoś** be (fully) aware of sth; **robić coś z całą świadomością** do sth knowingly *l.* deliberately; **dopiero teraz dotarło do mojej świadomości, że...** only now do I understand that..., only now has it dawned on me that...

świadomy *a.* (*o człowieku*) conscious, aware; (*o decyzji, działaniu*) conscious, deliberate; **był świadom niebezpieczeństwa** he was aware *l.* conscious of the danger; **świadomy praw i obowiązków** fully aware of my rights and duties *l.* obligations.

świat *mi Gen.* **-a** *Loc.* **-ecie 1.** (= *to, co otacza człowieka*) world; **Nowy Świat** the New World, Western Hemisphere; **Stary Świat** the Old World; **Trzeci Świat** the Third World; **tamten świat** the other *l.* next world; **ten świat** *l.* **świat doczesny** this world; **części świata** *geogr.* continents; **koniec świata** end of the world; **koniec świata!** this is unbelievable!; **mistrz świata** world champion; **możni** *l.* **wielcy tego świata** the most influential people in the world; **oś świata** *astron.* axis of the Earth; **obywatel świata** cosmopolitan, cosmopolite; **okno na świat** window on *l.* to the world; **ósmy cud świata** eigth wonder of the world; **pępek świata** *pot.* the most important person in the world; **rekord świata** world record; **strony świata** *geogr.* cardinal points; **do końca świata** till the end of time, till the end of the world; forever; **stary jak świat** (as) old as the hills *l.* time; **nikt/nic na świecie** absolutely nobody/ nothing; **ktoś/coś nie z tego świata** sb/sth unrealistic, sth strange/weird; **sb/sth not of this world; **ktoś nie wie, po jakim świecie chodzi** sb is a daydreamer; **bywały w świecie** (= *obyty*) well-mannered; (= *taki, który widział świat, dużo podróżował*) man of the world, worldling, worldly person; **(drań) jakiego świat nie widział** unheard-of (villain); **błagać** *l.* **prosić na wszystko w świecie** ask *l.* beg earnestly; **być dla kogoś całym światem** mean the world to sb; **być jedną nogą na tamtym świecie** have one foot in the grave; **być na świecie** live, exist; **być odciętym od świata** be cut off from the rest of the world; **być** *l.* **zostać samym na świecie** have no living relatives left; **chodzić po świecie** exist; **kląć na czym świat stoi** swear like a trooper; **nie wiedzieć o bożym świecie** know nothing, have never heard of anything; **podbić świat** be a success, become world-famous; **przyjść na świat** *lit.* come into the world; **puścić coś w świat** release sth, make sth public; **świata nie widzieć poza kimś** think the world of sb; **świat się nie kończy na kimś/czymś** there are people/things more important than sb/sth; there are plenty of fish in the sea; **świat stoi przed kimś otworem** *l.* **należy do kogoś** the world is sb's oyster; **umrzeć dla świata** isolate o.s. from the rest of the world; **używać świata** live it up; **wydać na świat** bring into the world; **wyprawić kogoś na tamten świat** *pot.* dispatch sb, do sb in; **zachowywać się, jakby świat do kogoś należał** be overly self-confident; **zapomnieć o całym świecie** forget about everything; **zejść ze świata** leave this world; **zobaczyć kawał świata** have seen a lot, have travelled a lot; **za żadne skarby świata** *l.* **za nic w świecie** not for the whole world, not for all the world; **cholerny świat!** *pot.* life sucks! **2.** (= *środowisko*) circles, community; world; **świat artystyczny** artistic circles; **świat literacki** literary circles; **świat muzułmański** the Muslim world; **świat naukowy** scholarly community. **3.** *biol.* world; **świat dzikiej przyrody** wildlife; **świat fauny i flory** animal and plant world, fauna and flora. **4.** (= *sfera*) world.

światek *mi* **-tk-** *Gen.* **-a** (= *mały świat*) small world; (= *środowisko*) circle, community.

światełko *n. Gen.pl.* **-ek** (= *płomień*) light, flame; (= *lampka*) lamp; (= *latarka*) torchlight; **światełko w tunelu** light at the end of the tunnel.

światło *n. Loc.* **świetle** *Gen.pl.* **świateł 1.** (= *świecenie*) light; **światło dzienne** daylight; **światło gwiazd** starlight; **światło księżyca** moonlight; **światło słoneczne** sunlight; **światło wiekuiste** *rel.* eternal life; **oglądać coś pod światło** hold sth up to the light; **przedstawić kogoś/coś w korzystnym/niekorzystnym świetle** present sb/sth in a good/bad light; **rzucić na coś światło** cast *l.* throw light on sth; **ujrzeć światło dzienne** come to light; **wydobyć coś na światło dzienne** unearth sth, bring to light; **w świetle tego, co powiedziano...** in the light of what has been said...; **światła pogasły** the lights went out; **razi mnie światło** light dazzles me. **2.** (= *źródło oświetlenia*) light; **światła awaryjne** *mot.* hazard lights; **światła cofania** *mot.* backup light; **światła drogowe** *l.* **długie** *mot.* high beams; **światła mijania** *l.* **krótkie** *mot.* dipped headlights, dippers; **światła pozycyjne** *l.* **postojowe** *mot.* parking lights; **światła odblaskowe** *mot.* reflectors; **światła stopu** *mot.* stoplights; **światła sygnalizacyjne** *mot.* traffic lights; **przejechać (skrzyżowanie) na czerwonym świetle** jump the red light, cross against the light; **zatrzymać się na światłach** stop at the (traffic) lights; **światła nawigacyjne** *żegl.* navigation lights; **zapalić/ zgasić światło** turn on/off the light; **zielone światło dla rolnictwa/drobnych przedsiębiorców** green light for agriculture/small business. **3.** (= *odblask*) glitter, sparkle. **4.** (= *średnica otworu*) bore, diameter. **5.** *fot.* light. **6.** *druk.* white distance.

światłocień *mi Gen.* **-a** *sztuka* chiaroscuro.

światłoczułość *f.* **1.** *fiz.* photosensitivity. **2.** *fot.* speed.

światłoczuły *a. fot.* photosensitive.

światłodruk *mi druk.* phototype.

światłodrukowy *a. druk.* phototypic.

światłokopia *f. Gen.* **-ii** *druk.* blueline copy, blue; diazo copy.

światłokopiarka *f. Gen.pl.* **-ek** *druk.* blue copy printer, diazo copy printer.

światłolecznictwo *n.* *med.* light therapy, phototherapy.

światłolubność *f.* *bot.* photophilia.

światłolubny *a.* *bot.* photophilic, photophylous.

światłomierz *mi* *Gen.* -a *fot.* exposure meter, light meter.

światłoodporny *a.* light-resistant, photostable.

światłość *f.* **1.** *lit.* light; **światłość wiekuista** *rel.* eternal life. **2.** *fiz.* luminous intensity.

światłowodowy *a.* *techn.* optical fiber; *Br.* optical fibre.

światłowód *mi* -o- *techn.* optical fiber; *Br.* optical fibre.

światłowstręt *mi* *pat.* photophobia, light intolerance.

światły *a.* *lit.* (= *mający szerokie horyzonty myślowe*) open-minded; (= *oświecony*) enlightened.

światoburca *mp* *lit.* world-shaking revolutionary; subversive.

światoburczy *a.* *lit.* world-shaking; subversive.

światopogląd *mi* outlook.

światopoglądowy *a.* concerning sb's outlook.

światowiec *mp* -wc- *pl.* -y man of the world; worldling, worldly person.

światowy *a.* world, global; world-wide; (*życie, towarzystwo*) high; **kryzys światowy** global crisis, world crisis; **rynki światowe** global market; **światowe życie** highlife; **wojna światowa** world war; **Światowa Organizacja Zdrowia** World Health Organization; **Światowa Rada Kościołów** World Council of Churches.

świąd *mi* *pat.* itch, pruritus.

świąt *mi* *zob.* **święta**.

świątecznie *adv.* festively; **świątecznie** *l.* **odświętnie ubrany** wearing one's Sunday best *l.* one's best clothes.

świąteczny *a.* festive, holiday; (*bożonarodzeniowy*) Christmas; (*wielkanocny*) Easter; **dzień świąteczny** holiday; **życzenia świąteczne** (*bożonarodzeniowe*) Season's *l.* Christmas greetings; **życzenia świąteczne** (*wielkanocne*) Easter greetings.

świątek *mi* -tk- *Gen.* -a *Gen.pl.* -ów **1.** (*wizerunek*) holy image (*produced by a folk artist*). **2.** *Gen.pl.* -tek *przest.* (= *święto*) holiday; **świątekpiątek** seven days a week; 24/7; **Zielone Świątki** *rel.* Pentecost, Whitsunday.

świątkarstwo *n.* *sztuka* carving holy images (*by folk artists*).

świątkarz *mp* *sztuka* folk sculptor *l.* artist making holy images.

świątobliwie *adv.* in a saintly manner, piously.

świątobliwość *f.* saintliness, piousness; **Jego Świątobliwość** *rz.-kat.* His Holiness.

świątobliwy *a.* saintly, pious.

świątynia *f.* temple, shrine; (*podniośle o kościele*) temple; **świątynia sztuki** *przen.* temple of the arts.

świder *mi* -dr- *Gen.* -a *techn.* drill.

świderek *mi* -rk- *Gen.* -a (small) drill; **oczy jak świderki** piercing eyes.

świderki *pl.* *pot.* (*makaron*) rotini pasta.

świdrować *ipf.* **1.** (= *wiercić*) drill; **świdrować kogoś wzrokiem** bore one's eyes into sb, penetrate sb with the eyes. **2.** (= *przenikać*) pierce, penetrate.

świdrowaty *a.* **1.** (= *spiralny*) spiral; **świdrowate oczy** piercing eyes. **2.** *pot.* squint.

świdrowce *pl.* *zool.* trypanosomes (*Trypanosoma*).

świdrująco *adv.* piercingly.

świdrujący *a.* piercing.

świdwa *f.* **dereń świdwa** *bot.* dogwood, midwinter fire (*Cornus sanguinea*).

świeca *f.* **1.** (*np. z wosku*) candle; **prosty jak świeca** (as) straight as a ramrod; **przy świecach** by candlelight; **ze świecą szukać takiego drugiego** search high and low to meet such a wonderful *l.* unique person. **2.** *mot.* spark plug. **3.** *wojsk.* flare; **świeca dymna** smoke pot. **4.** *lotn.* zoom. **5.** *piłka nożna* up and under. **6.** *gimnastyka* shoulder stand, shoulder balance.

świecący *a.* **1.** (*o lampie, słońcu*) shining. **2.** (=*połyskujący*) shiny; (*o tkaninie*) glossy, shiny. **3.** (=*fluorescencyjny*) luminous.

świecić *ipf.* **1.** (= *promieniować*) shine. **2.** (= *oświetlać*) light; **świecić oczami za kogoś** blush for sb, take the rap; **świecić przykładem** be a shining example. **3.** (= *błyszczeć*) gleam; (= *lśnić*) shine; (= *połyskiwać*) glisten; (= *migotać*) sparkle; **księżyc/słońce świeci** the moon/the sun is shining. **4.** (=*jaśnieć, bieleć*) be visible, show; **świecić pustkami** be half- *l.* almost empty; **świecić golizną** *pot.* wear scanty clothes. **~ się** *ipf.* **1.** (= *promieniować*) shine; **lampa się świeci** the lamp is on. **2.** (= *błyszczeć*) gleam; (= *lśnić*) shine; (= *połyskiwać*) glisten; (= *migotać*) sparkle; **oczy się komuś świecą do kogoś/czegoś** sb is looking avidly at sb/sth; **nie wszystko złoto, co się świeci** all that glitters is not gold, all is not gold that glitters. **3.** (= *jaśnieć, bieleć*) be visible, show.

świecidełko *n.* *Gen.pl.* -ek trinket, gewgaw.

świecie *mi* *zob.* **świat**.

świecki *a.* (*o osobie, kazaniu*) lay, laic, laical; (*o szkole, władzy, państwie*) secular; **duchowny świecki** *rz.-kat.* lay *l.* secular priest.

świeckość *f.* lay *l.* secular character.

świecowy *a.* candle; **kredki świecowe** crayons.

świeczka *f.* *Gen.pl.* -ek candle; **gra (nie) jest warta świeczki** the game is (not) worth the candle, it's (not) worth it; **świeczki mi stanęły w oczach** I saw the stars; **Panu Bogu świeczkę i diabłu ogarek** (try to) serve two masters; have one face to God and another to the devil; run with the hare and hunt with the hounds.

świecznik *mi* *Gen.* -a candlestick; **być na świeczniku** be in the spotlight.

świekra *f.* *arch.* mother-in-law.

świerczyna *f.* **1.** (*drewno*) spruce wood, spruce. **2.** (*gałązki*) spruce branches. **3.** (*las*) spruce forest.

świergolić *ipf.* *pot.* = **świergotać**.

świergot *mi* **1.** (*ptaków*) twitter. **2.** (*dzieci, kobiet*) twitter, chatter.

świergotać *ipf.* **-czę -czesz** *l.* **-cę -cesz, -cz 1.** (*o ptakach*) twitter; **wróble na dachu o tym świergocą** *przen.* everybody is already talking about it, everybody knows about it already. **2.** (*o dzieciach, kobietach*) twitter, chatter.

świerk *mi bot.* spruce (*Picea*); **świerk biały** white spruce (*P. glauca*); **świerk czarny** black spruce, spruce pine (*P. mariana*); **świerk pospolity** Norway spruce (*P. abies*); **świerk srebrzysty** *l.* **kłujący** blue spruce, balsam spruce (*P. pungens*).

świerkowy *a.* spruce.

świerszcz *ma ent.* cricket (*Gryllus*).

świerszcze *pl. Gen.pl.* **-y** *ent.* crickets (*Gryllidae*).

świerszczyk *ma ent.* small cricket. − *mi pot., żart.* (= *pismo pornograficzne*) porn magazine.

świerzb *mi pat., wet.* scabies.

świerzbiączka *f. Gen.pl.* **-ek** *pat.* prurigo, atopic dermatitis.

świerzbić *ipf.* itch; **język kogoś świerzbi** sb is dying to say sth, sb is dying to spill the beans; **ręka kogoś świerzbi** sb is itching to hit sb.

świerzbowiec *ma* **-wc-** *med., wet.* itch mite (*Sarcoptidae*).

świerzop *mi bot.* **1.** (*chwast*) charlock (*Sinapis arvensis*). **2.** (*rzodkiew*) wild radish, jointed charlock (*Raphanus raphanistrum*).

świetlany *a.* **1.** (= *świetlisty, jasny*) bright, shining. **2.** (= *nieziemski*) unearthly, heavenly; **świetlana przyszłość** bright future; **świetlanej pamięci** *emf.* the late.

świetle *n. zob.* **światło.**

świetlica *f. zwł. szkoln.* common room.

świetlicowa *f. Gen.* **-ej** *szkoln.* common room supervisor.

świetlicowy *a. zwł. szkoln.* common-room. − *mp zwł. szkoln.* common room supervisor.

świetliczanka *f. Gen.pl.* **-ek** *szkoln.* = **świetlicowa.**

świetlik *mi Gen.* **-a 1.** *bud.* skylight; (*zwł. półokrągły, nad drzwiami*) fanlight. **2.** *żegl.* porthole, portlight. **3.** *bot.* eyebright, euphrasy (*Euphrasia*). − *ma ent.* glowworm (*Lampyris noctiluca*).

świetliki *pl. Gen.* **-ów** *ent.* fireflies, lightning bugs (*Lampyridae*).

świetlistość *f.* (= *jasność*) brightness; (= *nasycenie światłem*) luminosity.

świetlisty *a.* (= *jasny*) bright; (= *jaśniejący*) shining; (= *pełen światła*) luminous.

świetlny *a.* (= *będący światłem*) light; (= *pełen światła*) luminous; **gaz świetlny** *techn.* illuminating gas, town *l.* city gas; **fale świetlne** *fiz.* light waves; **rok świetlny** *astron.* light-year; **strumień świetlny** *fiz.* luminous flux; **sygnalizacja świetlna** *mot.* traffic lights.

świetlówka *f. Gen.pl.* **-ek** fluorescent lamp.

świetnie *adv.* great, splendidly; **czuć się świetnie** feel great; **świetnie się bawić** have a great time, have a whale of a time; **świetnie wyglądać** look great; **świetnie cię rozumiem** I understand

you only too well; **świetnie nam idzie** we're doing great; **moja ciocia i wujek świetnie gotują** my aunt and uncle are excellent cooks; **świetnie!** great!; **no to świetnie!** *t. iron.* that's just great!

świetność *f. form.* **1.** (= *okazałość*) magnificence, splendor. **2.** (= *sława*) glory.

świetny *a.* **1.** (= *znakomity*) excellent. **2.** *form.* (= *okazały*) magnificent. **3.** *form.* (= *sławny*) glorious.

świeżo *adv.* (*przygotowany*) freshly; **wyglądać/ pachnieć świeżo** look/smell fresh; **świeżo malowane** (*napis ostrzegawczy*) wet paint; **ktoś ma coś świeżo w pamięci** sth is fresh in sb's mind; **świeżo po studiach** fresh from *l.* out of college *l.* university; **świeżo upieczony prawnik** freshly graduated lawyer.

świeżość *f.* freshness.

świeżutki *a.* (perfectly) fresh.

świeży *a.* (= *nowy, rześki, oryginalny*) fresh; **świeża krew** fresh *l.* new blood; **iść jak świeże bułeczki** sell *l.* go like hot cakes; **świeże owoce/warzywa** fresh fruit/vegetables; **łyk świeżego powietrza** breath of fresh air.

święcenia *pl. Gen.* **-ń** *rel.* (holy) orders.

święcić *ipf.* **1.** *rel.* consecrate. **2.** *lit.* (= *świętować*) celebrate. **3.** enjoy; **święcić triumfy** enjoy (great) success. ~ **się** *ipf.* **1.** (= *dziać się*) be in the wind; **coś tu się święci** there's something cooking *l.* in the wind. **2.** (= *być obchodzonym*) be celebrated.

święcie *n. zob.* **święto.** − *adv.* strongly; **święcie w coś wierzyć** swear by sth; **być święcie przekonanym** be absolutely sure.

święconka *f. Gen.pl.* **-ek, święcone** *n. Gen.* **-ego** *kość.* Easter meal (*blessed food eaten on Easter day*).

święcony *a. rel.* (= *poświęcony*) blessed.

święta *f. Gen.* **-ej** *zob.* **święty** *mp.*

święto *n. Gen.pl.* **świąt 1.** holiday; **Święto trzeciego Maja** Constitution Day (*May 3 in Poland*); **Święto Niepodległości** Independence Day; **Święto Pracy** *US* Labor Day; (*w Polsce*) May Day; **święto ruchome** *rel.* movable feast; **ubranie od święta** Sunday best; **od święta** (= *bardzo rzadko*) once in a blue moon. **2.** (= *dzień niezwykły*) red-letter day. **3.** *pl.* (*ogólnie*) holidays; **urządzać święta** celebrate holidays; **Wesołych Świąt!** Happy Holidays! **4.** *pl.* (= *Boże Narodzenie*) Christmas; **Święta Bożego Narodzenia** Christmas. **5.** *pl.* (= *Wielkanoc*) Easter; **Święta Wielkanocne** Easter (Holidays).

świętojański *a.* Midsummer (Day), St. John's (Day); **robaczek świętojański** *ent.* firefly, lightning bug (*Lampyris*); **chleb świętojański** *bot.* carob, Saint John's bread, algarroba (*Ceratonia siliqua*).

świętokradca *mp* sacrilegist, profaner.

świętokradczo *adv.* sacrilegiously.

świętokradczy *a.* sacrilegious.

świętokradztwo *n.* sacrilege.

świętopietrze *n. hist.* Peter('s) pence.

świętoszek *mp* **-szk-** *pl.* **-i** *l.* **-owie** *uj.* bigot, prude, goody-goody.

świętoszka *f. Gen.pl.* **-ek** *zob.* **świętoszek.**

świętoszkowato *adv. uj.* sanctimoniously, prudishly.

świętoszkowatość *f. uj.* sanctimony.

świętoszkowaty *a. uj.* sanctimonious, prudish.

świętość *f.* **1.** *rel.* sainthood, holiness, sacredness. **2.** (= *ważność*) sanctity. **3.** (= *to, co najdroższe*) sanctity; **zaklinam się na wszystkie świętości** I swear to the truth; **to dla mnie świętość** it's sacred to me.

świętować *ipf.* celebrate.

święty *a.* **1.** *gł. rel.* holy; **Duch Święty** Holy Spirit *l.* Ghost; **Trójca Święta** Holy Trinity; **Boże Święty!** Holy Father!; **na święty nigdy** *żart.* when hell freezes over; **Święty Boże nie pomoże** (you can) cry to heaven. **2.** (= *uświęcony*) holy, saint; **Ojciec Święty** *rz.-kat.* Holy Father; **Ziemia Święta** Holy Land; **msza święta** *kośc.* holy mass; **Pismo Święte** *Bibl.* (Holy) Bible, (Holy) Scripture, the Scriptures; **kościół (pod wezwaniem) Świętego Piotra** *kośc.* St. Peter's church; **Święty Mikołaj** Santa (Claus), Father Christmas. **3.** (= *cnotliwy, dobry*) saintly; **święty człowiek** angel of a man; **świętej pamięci...** the late...; **święte oburzenie** *często iron.* virtuous indignation; **święty spokój** peace and quiet; **daj mi święty spokój** leave me alone; **dla świętego spokoju** just in case, for peace of mind. **4.** (= *nienaruszalny*) sacred; **święta racja** *l.* **święte słowa!** amen (to that)!, well said! – *mp rel.* saint; **Wszystkich Świętych** All Saints' Day, Allhallows; **goły jak święty turecki** flat broke; **nie święci garnki lepią** a job is a job.

świnia *f.* **1.** *zool.* pig, hog, swine (*Sus domesticus*); **dzika świnia** (wild) boar; **świń z tobą nie pasałem!** I didn't know we were that close!, (are) you talking to me?; **upić się jak świnia** get roaring drunk; **podłożyć komuś świnię** *pot.* sell sb down the river, do sb dirty. **2.** *obelż.* (= *osoba niechlujna*) pig, hog; **brudny jak świnia** filthy. **3.** *obelż.* (= *kanalia*) scumbag; **ty świnio!** you pig *l.* scumbag!; **ale z ciebie kawał świni** you're such a scumbag!

świniak *ma roln.* pig, hog, swine.

świniarz *mp pot.* swineherd.

świnić *ipf. pot.* **1.** (= *zanieczyszczać*) muck (up). **2.** (= *robić świństwa*) do dirty; **świnić komuś** (= *knuć przeciw komuś*) do sb dirty, play sb foul.

świnina *f. kulin.* pork.

świniobicie *n. roln.* (home) slaugher of pigs *l.* swine.

świniopas *mp pog.* swineherd.

świnka *f. Gen.pl.* -ek **1.** *emf.* (= *mała świnia*) piggy, piglet; **świnka morska** *zool.* guinea pig (*Cavia porcellus*). **2.** (= *skarbonka*) piggy bank. **3.** *pat.* mumps. **4.** *icht.* nase (*Chondrostoma nasus*).

świntuch *mp pl.* -y *pot.* (o osobie) pig.

świntuszyć *ipf. pot.* talk dirty.

świński *a.* **1.** *pot.* (= *nieprzyzwoity, niemoralny*) dirty; **świński kawał** dirty joke; **postąpiłeś po świńsku** that was a rotten thing to do, that was a rotten trick. **2.** (= *ze świni*) pig; (o *mięsie*) pork; **świński blondyn** pale blond-headed guy; **świńskie oczka** piggy eyes; **ty świński ryju!** *obelż.* you shitface!

świństewko *n. Gen.pl.* -ek *pot.* dirty trick.

świństwa *pl. Gen.* -w *pot.* (= *obsceniczności*) smut.

świństwo *n.* **1.** *pot.* (= *podłość*) dirty trick, raw deal; **zrobić komuś świństwo** do *l.* play sb dirty. **2.** *pot.* (= *paskudztwo*) crap; **jeść jakieś świństwa** eat some crappy *l.* shitty stuff *l.* food.

świr *mp pl.* -y *pot., pog.* nut, psycho; **dostać świra** go nuts, crack up; **mieć świra** be nuts (*na punkcie czegoś / kogoś* about *l.* on *l.* over sth/sb).

świrować *ipf.* -ruję -rujesz, -ruj *pot.* **1.** (= *wariować, tracić rozum*) go nuts, go mad; **miał za dużo roboty i w końcu ześwirował** he had too much to do and he finally went nuts. **2.** (= *szaleć, wygłupiać się*) fool around; **nie świruj!, tak było naprawdę?** no shit? it actually happened?; **komputer mi świruje i ciągle się zawiesza** my PC is acting up and it crashes all the time.

świsnąć *pf.* -snę -śniesz, -śnij **1.** *zob.* świstać. **2.** *pot.* (= *ukraść*) lift, filch. **3.** *pot.* (= *uderzyć*) whack; **niech cię dunder świśnie!** damn you!

świst *mi* (*ptaka, wiatru*) whistle; (*pocisku, szpady*) swish, zip.

świstać *ipf.* -szczę -szczesz **1.** (o *ptaku, wietrze*) whistle; (o *kuli*) swish, zip. **2.** (= *machać*) swish.

świstak *ma zool.* Alpine marmot (*Marmota marmota*).

świstek *mi* -tk- *Gen.* -a *pot.* scrap (of paper).

świszczeć *ipf.* -ę -ysz whistle; **cisza aż w uszach świszczy** dead *l.* stony silence.

świt *mi* dawn, daybreak; **bladym świtem** *l.* **skoro świt** at the crack of dawn, at the break of day; **o świcie** at dawn; **od świtu do nocy** from dawn to dusk; **świt dziejów (ludzkości)** dawn of civilization.

świta *f.* entourage, retinue.

świtać *ipf.* dawn; **już świta** dawn is breaking; **zaczęło mi świtać (w głowie), że...** it dawned on me that...

świtanie *n. lit.* daybreak; **o świtaniu** at the break of day.

świtezianka *f. Gen.pl.* -ek **1.** *mit.* water nymph, undine. **2.** *ent.* **świtezianka modra** beautiful demoiselle (*Calopteryx virgo*); **świtezianka błyszcząca** banded demoiselle (*C. splendens*).

T

T, t *n. indecl.* (*litera*) T, t; **T jak Tadeusz** T is for Tango; T as in Tango.

t *abbr.* (= *tona*) t. (= *metric ton*).

t. *abbr.* (= *tom*) vol. (= *volume*).

ta *pron. Acc.* **tę** *zob.* **ten.**

tab. *abbr.* (= *tabela*) table.

tabaczkowy *a.* (*o kolorze*) snuffy.

tabaka *f.* snuff; **ciemny jak tabaka w rogu** thick as a brick.

tabakiera, tabakierka *f. Gen.pl.* **-ek** snuff box.

tabela *f.* table.

tabelarycznie *adv.* in tabular form.

tabelaryczny *a.* tabular.

tabelka *f. Gen.pl.* **-ek** table.

tabernakulum *n. sing. indecl. pl.* **-a** *Gen.* **-ów** *kośc.* tabernacle.

tabes *mi pat.* tabes.

tabetyczny *a. pat.* tabetic.

tabetyk *mp pat.* tabetic.

tabl. *abbr.* (= *tablica*) table.

tableau *n. indecl. fot.* photomosaic; *szkoln.* yearbook photo.

tabletka *f. Gen.pl.* **-ek** pill, tablet.

tabletkowy *a.* pill, tablet.

tablica *f.* **1.** (*informacyjna*) board; **tablica ogłoszeń** bulletin board. **2.** (= *płyta*) plate; (*także* **tablica pamiątkowa**) plaque; **tablica rejestracyjna** *mot.* license *l.* number *l.* registration plate. **3.** (*także* **tablica rozdzielcza**) *el.* (instrument) panel, switchboard. **4.** *szkoln.* board, blackboard. **5.** (= *tabela*) table. **6.** *druk.* plate.

tabliczka *f. Gen.pl.* **-ek 1.** (= *mała tablica*) plate; **tabliczka na drzwiach** doorplate. **2.** **tabliczka czekolady** chocolate bar, bar of chocolate; **tabliczka mnożenia** *mat.* multiplication table.

tabor *mi* **1.** (= *pojazdy*) (*także* **tabor kolejowy/ drogowy**) rolling stock. **2.** (= *grupa wędrujących ludzi*) train. **3.** (= *obóz*) camp. **4.** *hist.* (= *obóz z wozów*) corral.

taboret *mi* stool.

tabu *n. indecl.* **1.** (*zakaz*) taboo. **2.** *rel.* (= *nietykalna świętość*) taboo. **3. temat tabu** taboo subject, no-go area.

tabulator *mi Gen.* **-a** *komp.* (*w maszynie do pisania*) tab (key), tabulator (key).

tabulatura *f. muz.* tablature.

tabulogram *mi przest.* tabulation.

tabun *mi* (= *stado, tłum*) herd.

taca *f.* **1.** tray. **2.** *kośc.* (collection) plate; **zbierać na tacę** take collection.

tachać *ipf. pot.* (= *dźwigać*) haul.

tachometr *mi techn.* tachometer.

tachykardia *f. Gen.* **-ii** *pat.* tachycardia.

tachymetr *mi miern.* tachymeter.

tachymetria *f. Gen.* **-ii** *miern.* tachymetry.

tachymetryczny *a. miern.* tachymetric.

tacka *f. Gen.pl.* **-ek** tray.

tacy *a. zob.* **taki.**

Tacyt *mp hist.* Tacitus.

taczać *ipf. arch.* (= *kulać, obtaczać*) roll.

taczanka *f. Gen.pl.* **-ek** *hist., wojsk.* machine-gun cart.

taczka *f. Gen.pl.* **-ek** *zw. pl.* barrow, wheelbarrow.

tadżycki *a.* Tajik.

Tadżyjka *f. Gen.pl.* **-ek, Tadżyk** *mp pl.* **-cy** *l.* **-owie** Tajik.

Tadżykistan *mi geogr.* Tajikistan.

tafla *f. Gen.pl.* **-i 1.** (= *płyta*) plate, sheet; (*zwł. szkła*) pane. **2.** (= *lśniąca powierzchnia*) sheet.

taflowy *a.* sheet, plate.

tafta *f. tk.* taffeta.

Tahitanka *f. Gen.pl.* **-ek, Tahitańczyk** *mp* Tahitian.

tahitański *a.* Tahitian.

Tahiti *f. indecl. geogr.* Tahiti.

taić *ipf.* **taję taisz, taj** *gł. lit.* hide, conceal, keep secret; **nie tail, że...** he didn't hide the fact that...

Taj *mp pl.* **-owie** Thai.

tajać *ipf.* **-ę -esz** (= *topić się, łagodnieć*) *t. przen.* melt, thaw.

tajemnica *f.* **1.** (= *sekret*) secret. **2.** (= *niewiadoma*) mystery. **3. w tajemnicy** (*robić coś*) in secret; (*powiedzieć coś*) in confidence; **w tajemnicy przed kimś** unknown to sb; **publiczna tajemnica** *l.* **tajemnica poliszynela** open secret; **tajemnica handlowa/państwowa/wojskowa** trade/state/ military secret; **tajemnica korespondencji** privacy of correspondence; **tajemnica lekarska** doctor-patient privilege; **tajemnica spowiedzi** *rel.* seal of confession; **dochować tajemnicy** keep a secret; **trzymać coś w tajemnicy** keep sth secret, keep sth under cover; **uchylić rąbka tajemnicy** tip one's hand; **uchylić komuś rąbka tajemnicy** let sb in on a secret; **zgłębiać tajemnicę** unravel a mystery.

tajemniczo *adv.* mysteriously.

tajemniczość *f.* mysteriousness, mystery.

tajemniczy *a.* mysterious; **nie bądź taki tajemniczy** don't be so mysterious.

tajemnie *adv. lit.* furtively, secretly.

tajemny *a. lit.* furtive, secret.

tajfun *mi meteor.* typhoon.

tajga *f. ekol.* taiga.

Tajka *f. Gen.pl.* -ek *zob.* **Taj**.
Tajlandczyk *mp* Thai.
Tajlandia *f. Gen.* -ii *geogr.* Thailand.
Tajlandka *f. Gen.pl.* -ek *zob.* **Tajlandczyk**.
tajlandzki *a.* Thai.
tajniak *mp pot.* secret *l.* undercover agent.
tajnie *adv.* secretly.
tajniki *pl. Gen.* -ów *lit.* arcana.
tajność *f.* secrecy.
tajny *a.* secret; **ściśle tajne** strictly confidential; **tajna policja** secret police; **głosowanie tajne** (secret) ballot.
tajski *a.* Thai.
Tajwan *mi geogr.* Taiwan.
Tajwanka *f. Gen.pl.* -ek, **Tajwańczyk** *mp* Taiwanese.
tajwański *a.* Taiwanese.
tak *int.* (*potwierdzenie*) yes; **tak jest** *wojsk.* yes, Sir!; *marynarka wojenna* aye aye, captain!; **tak albo nie** yes or no; **i tak, i nie** yes and no; **zostaniesz tu, tak?** you're staying, aren't you? – *adv.* **1.** (*potwierdzenie*) **nie lubię chemii, ale fizykę tak** I don't like chemistry, but I do (like) physics. **2.** (= *w ten sposób*) so; **i tak dalej** and so on; and so forth; **tak a tak** so and so; **tak czy inaczej** anyway; **tak czy owak** *l.* **tak czy siak** in any case; **tak zwany** so called; **tak mi dopomóż Bóg** so help me God; **to było tak...** it went like this... **3.** (*nasilenie*) so; **tak bardzo** *l.* **tak dalece** so much; to such an extent; **tak sobie** (= *nie za bardzo*) so-so; (= *bez zastanowienia*) just like that; **tak bym się czegoś napił!** I really need a drink!; **jak go nie było, tak nie ma** still no sight of him. – *conj.* **1. tak on, jak i ona** he, as well as she. **2. tak że** (= *więc*) so (that), and; **nie padało, tak że mogłem iść na spacer** it wasn't raining, so (that) I was able to go for a walk.
taki *a.* **1.** (= *podobny*) such; **taki a taki** such and such, so-and-so; **taki czy owaki** such and such, so-and-so; **taki sam** same; **taki już jestem** that's just me; **w taki czy inny sposób** by hook or by crook; **w takim razie** (if so,) then; **taki bohater, jak ty** a hero like you; **tacy piłkarze, jak Deyna czy Boniek** players like Deyna or Boniek; **słońce jako takie** the Sun as such; **taki jakiś** *l.* **jakiś taki** (*osowiały*) sort of (glum), kind of (glum); **taki sobie** *pot.* so-so; **taki tam** *pot.* never mind; **nic takiego** (= *nic podobnego*) nothing of the sort; (= *nic się nie stało*) no big deal; **co takiego?** what's that?; **coś takiego!** no way!, no kidding! **2.** (*łączy zdania*) so; **jest taki upał, że...** it's so hot that...
takielunek *mi żegl.* rigging.
tako *adv.* **jako tako** so-so, after a fashion.
taksa *f. fin.* charge, fee, tax; **taksa klimatyczna** tourist fee *l.* supplement.
taksacja *f. fin.* appraisal.
taksator *mp fin.* appraiser.
taksiarz *mp pot.* cabbie.
taksja *f. biol.* taxis.
taksometr *mi* clock, taximeter.
taksonomia *f. Gen.* -ii *biol.* taxonomy.
taksonomiczny *a. biol.* taxonomic.
taksować *ipf. fin.* appraise; **taksować kogoś wzrokiem** eye sb up.

taksówka *f. Gen.pl.* -ek cab; **taksówka bagażowa** moving van.
taksówkarz *mp*, **taksówkarka** *f.* cab driver.
taksówkowy *a.* cab, taxi.
takt *mi* **1.** (= *maniery*) tact, finesse. **2.** *muz.* (= *główna jednostka metryczna*) bar, measure; (= *rytm*) time, beat, rhythm; **wybijać takt** beat time; **(klaskać) do taktu** (clap) to the beat. **3.** *mot., techn.* (= *suw*) stroke.
taktować *ipf. muz.* (= *dzielić na takty*) **1.** bar; mark (*sth*) off into bars. **2.** (= *wybijać rytm czegoś*) beat (*sth*) out. ~ **się** *ipf. muz.* (*o utworze*) **taktować się na trzy czwarte/cztery czwarte** be written in three/four-quarter time *l.* in three/four-four time.
taktowny *a.* tactful.
taktyczny *a. t. wojsk.* tactical.
taktyk *mp t. wojsk.* tactician.
taktyka *f. t. wojsk.* **1.** (= *droga postępowania*) tactic. **2.** (= *wiedza, umiejętność*) tactics.
także *particle* also, as well, too; **a także** and also, as well as; **nie tylko..., ale** *l.* **lecz także** not only..., but also.
tal *mi chem.* thalium.
talar *mi Gen. i Acc.* -a *hist., fin.* rix-dollar.
talarek *mi* -rk- *Gen.* -a *kulin.* round.
talent *mi* **1.** (= *uzdolnienie*) talent (*do czegoś* for sth). **2.** (= *człowiek uzdolniony*) talent, natural. **3.** *fin., hist.* talent.
talerz *mi Gen.* -a **1.** (*naczynie*) plate; **głęboki talerz** soup plate; **latający talerz** flying saucer; **płytki** *l.* **płaski talerz** dinner plate. **2.** (= *zawartość naczynia*) plateful. **3.** *muz.* cymbal. **4.** *myśl.* rump.
talerze *pl. Gen.* -y *muz.* cymbals.
talerzować *ipf. roln.* harrow.
talerzowy *a. techn.* disk.
talerzyk *mi Gen.* -a **1.** *kulin.* saucer. **2.** *techn.* disk.
talia *f. Gen.* -ii **1.** (= *kibić, t. sukni*) waist. **2.** **talia (kart)** *karty* deck *l.* pack (of cards). **3.** *żegl.* tackle.
Talib *mp pl.* -owie *islam polit.* member of the Taliban; **Talibowie** the Taliban.
Taliban *mi islam polit.* the Taliban.
talizman *mi* charm.
talk *mi* **1.** talcum powder. **2.** *min.* talc.
talkować *ipf.* powder.
Talmud *mi judaizm* Talmud.
talmudyczny *a. judaizm* Talmudic.
talmudysta *mp judaizm* Talmudist.
talmudyzm *mi judaizm* Talmudism.
talon *mi* coupon.
tałatajstwo *n. pot.* riffraff.
tałes *mi judaizm* tallith, prayer shawl.
tam *adv.* **1.** (*wskazuje miejsce, kierunek*) there; (*o podróży*) outward; **kto tam?** who's there?; **tam i z powrotem** there and back, up and down; **bilet tam i powrót** *l.* **z powrotem** round-trip ticket; **to tu, to tam** now here, now there; **tu i tam** here and there; **połóż to tam, skąd wziąłeś** put it back where you took it from; **kiedyś tam** some time or other *l.* another. **2.** (*wyraża lekceważenie*) **co (mi) tam!** what the heck!; **a** *l.* **e tam!** *pot.* tell

that to the marines!; **gdzie tam!** yeah, right!; **jak mu tam** what's his name; **kto go tam wie!** who knows what he's up to?; **tam do licha!** the hell with that!

tama *f. hydrol.* dam; **położyć tamę czemuś** *przen.* put a stop to sth.

tamaryszek *mi* -szk- *Gen.* -a *l.* -u *bot.* tamarisk (*Tamarix*).

tamborek *mi* -rk- *Gen.* -a hoop, tambour, taboret.

tamburyn *mi*, **tamburyno** *n. muz.* tambourine.

tamci *pron. zob.* **tamten.**

Tamil *mp pl.* -owie, **Tamilka** *f. Gen.pl.* -ek Tamil.

tamilski *a.* Tamil.

Tamiza *f. geogr.* the Thames.

tamować *ipf.* 1. (= *utrudniać*) block. 2. (= *powstrzymywać*) stem, stop; (*krew*) stem, staunch.

tampon *mi* tampon; *chir. t.* pack, packing.

tamponada *f. chir.* tamponade, packing.

tamponować *ipf. chir.* tampon, pack.

tamta *a. zob.* **tamten.**

tam-tam *mi muz.* tamtam, tomtom.

tamte *pron. zob.* **tamten.**

tamtejszy *a.* that; **tamtejsza ludność** people of that *l.* the country.

tamten *pron. decl. like* **ten** (*określa rzeczownik*) that; *arch.* yon, yonder; (*zastępuje rzeczownik*) that (one); the one over there; **tamten świat** (= *zaświaty*) kingdom come; **nie ten, tylko tamten** not this one, that one; **to i tamto** this and that; **tamto nigdy nie powinno się wydarzyć** that should never have happened (in the first place).

tamtędy *adv.* (down) that way.

tamto *pron. zob.* **tamten.**

tamże *adv.* 1. *emf.* that's (also) where, there; **wyemigrował do Stanów i tamże się ożenił** he went to the US and that's where he married. 2. *form.* (*odnośnik w tekście*) ibid., ibidem.

tan *mi lit.* **ruszyć w tan** trip the light fantastic, tread a measure.

tancbuda *f. pot., pog.* dance hall.

tancerka *f. Gen.pl.* -ek, **tancerz** *mp* dancer.

tandem *mi* 1. (= *rower dwuosobowy*) tandem (bicycle). 2. (*dwie osoby*) duo.

tandeta *f. pog.* trash.

tandetnie *adv.* cheaply, trashily.

tandetność *f.* cheapness, trashiness.

tandetny *a.* cheap, trashy.

taneczność *f.* (*ruchu*) grace.

taneczny *a.* 1. (= *odnoszący się do tańca*) dance; **krok taneczny** dance step; **muzyka taneczna** dance music. 2. (= *płynny*) flowing, graceful.

tangens *mi mat.* tangent.

tangensoida *f. mat.* tangent curve.

tango *n.* tango; **białe tango** lady's tango; **iść** *l.* **ruszyć w tango** *pot.* go (off) on a (drinking) spree.

tani *a.* 1. (= *niedrogi*) cheap; **tanim kosztem** cheaply, at small expense; **tani jak barszcz** dirt cheap. 2. (= *marny, powierzchowny*) cheap; **tani dowcip** cheap joke.

taniec *mi* -ńc- *Gen.* -a 1. dance; (*czynność*) dancing; **taniec klasyczny/ludowy/współczesny** classical/folk/modern dance; **taniec towarzyski**

ballroom dancing; **poprosić kogoś do tańca** ask sb to dance. 2. **taniec świętego Wita** *pat.* St. Vitus's dance, (Sydenham's) chorea.

tanieć *ipf.* get cheaper.

tanina *f. chem.* tannin.

tanio *adv.* cheaply.

taniocha *f. pot.* cheap stuff, cheapie.

tankietka *f. Gen.pl.* -ek *wojsk.* whippet (tank).

tankować *ipf.* 1. *mot.* (= *pobierać benzynę*) get gas; *techn.* (= *pobierać paliwo*) refuel, get fuel. 2. *pot.* (= *pić*) tank up, guzzle.

tankowiec *mi* -wc- *Gen.* -a *żegl.* (oil) tanker.

Tantal *mp mit.* Tantalus; **męki Tantala** tantalization.

tantal *mi chem.* tantalum.

tantiemy *pl. Gen.* -m 1. (= *wynagrodzenie autora*) royalty. 2. *film, telew.* residual. 3. (= *udział w zyskach*) profit share.

Tanzania *f. Gen.* -ii *geogr.* Tanzania.

Tanzanka *f. Gen.pl.* -ek, **Tanzańczyk** *mp* Tanzanian.

tanzański *a.* Tanzanian.

tańca *itd. mi zob.* **taniec.**

tańce *pl. Gen.* -ów (= *zabawa taneczna*) dance; **iść na tańce** go dancing.

tańcować *ipf. zwł. lit.* dance; **pies z tobą tańcował!** *obelż., pot.* go to hell!

tańczyć *ipf.* 1. (= *poruszać się w takt muzyki*) dance; **tańczyć polkę/sambę/walca** *itd.* polka/samba/waltz etc. 2. (= *chwiać się, kołysać*) swing. 3. (*o świetle*) (= *mrugać*) flicker. 4. *mot.* (= *ślizgać się*) skid.

tańszy *itd. a. zob.* **tani.**

taoista *mp rel.* Taoist.

taoizm *mi rel.* Taoism.

tapczan *mi Gen.* -u *l.* -a bed; (*składany*) futon, davenport.

tapczanik *mi Gen.* -u *l.* -a (= *łóżko jednoosobowe*) single bed; (*składany*) sofa bed.

tapeta *f.* wallpaper; **kłaść tapetę** wallpaper, paper; **na tapecie** on the tapis *l.* carpet; **wracać na tapetę** (*o temacie*) come back.

tapetować *ipf.* wallpaper, paper.

tapicer *mp* upholsterer.

tapicerka *f. Gen.pl.* -ek 1. *stol.* upholstery. 2. *mot.* trim, interior.

tapicerować *ipf.* upholster.

tapicerski *a.* upholstery; **zszywacz tapicerski** *techn.* staple gun.

tapicerstwo *n.* upholstery.

tapioka *f.* tapioca.

tapir *ma zool.* tapir (*Tapirus*).

tapirować *ipf.* (*włosy*) backcomb.

taplać się *ipf. pot.* splash about, wade, puddle about.

tara *f.* 1. *przest.* (*do prania*) washboard. 2. (*waga*) tare.

tarabanić się *ipf. pot.* (= *gramolić się*) clamber.

taran *mi Gen.* -a 1. *hist.* (= *machina oblężnicza*) (battering) ram. 2. *hist.* (= *belka na dziobie okrętu*) ram, beak. 3. *techn.* ram.

taranować *ipf.* ram.

tarantela *f. muz.* tarantella.

tarantula *f. ent.* tarantula (*Lycosa tarentula*).

tarapaty *pl. Gen.* **-ów** trouble; **wpaść w tarapaty** get into trouble; **wpakować się w tarapaty** land o.s. in trouble; **być w tarapatach** be in a fix *l.* jam *l.* stew.

taras *mi* **1.** terrace; (*przed domem*) porch; (*za domem*) deck; **taras widokowy** observation *l.* viewing deck. **2.** *geol.* terrace.

tarasować *ipf.* block, obstruct; **tarasować drogę** block the way *l.* path, be in the way.

tarasowaty *a.* terraced.

tarasowo *adv.* (*opadać*) in terraces.

tarasowy *a.* terraced.

tarcia *pl. Gen.* **-ć** *mech. i pot.* (= *nieporozumienia*) friction.

tarcica *f. leśn. US i Can.* lumber; *Br.* timber.

tarcie *n. mech.* friction.

tarcza *f.* **1.** (*broń*) shield. **2.** (= *cel do strzelania*) target. **3.** (*księżyca, słońca*) disk. **4.** (*zegara, kompasu*) face, dial. **5.** *techn.* (*szlifierska, hamulcowa*) disk. **6.** *szkoln.* badge. **7.** *geol.* shield. **8.** (= *płyta z herbem*) coat of arms.

tarczka *f. Gen.pl.* **-ek** *bot., zool.* scutellum.

tarcznik *ma ent.* scale (insect) (*Coccoidea*).

tarczowaty *a. form.* discoid; **chrząstka tarczowata** *anat.* thyroid cartilage.

tarczowy *a.* **1.** (= *okrągły*) circular; **piła tarczowa** buzz saw, circular saw. **2.** (*wykorzystujący działanie tarcz*) disk; **hamulce tarczowe** *mot.* disk brakes.

tarczówka *f. Gen.pl.* **-ek 1.** *techn.* buzz saw, circular saw. **2.** *ent.* (= *owad z rodziny Pentatomidae*) shield bug.

tarczyca *f. anat.* thyroid (gland).

tarczycowy *a. anat.* thyroid.

targ *mi* **1.** market; fair; **pchli targ** flea market. **2.** (= *targowanie się*) bargaining; **krakowskim targiem** by way of compromise; **dobić targu** strike a bargain. **3.** (= *spór, pertraktacje*) negotiations; bargaining; **(zgodził się) po długich targach** (he agreed) after long negotiations.

targać *ipf.* **1.** (= *potrząsać, tarmosić*) pull, jerk (*za coś* by sth); **targał nim niepokój** *przen.* anxiety tormented him, he was worried. **2.** (= *czochrać*) tousle, dishevel. **3.** *pot.* (= *nieść*) lug. **4.** *techn.* break bales. **~ się** *ipf.* **1.** (= *szarpać siebie*) pull; **targać się za brodę** pull one's beard. **2.** (= *szarpać się wzajemnie*) pull each other; **targać się za włosy** pull each other's hair. **3.** *lit.* (= *szamotać się*) struggle, tussle.

targi *pl. Gen.* **-ów** trade fair.

targnąć *pf.* **-ij** *zob.* **targać** 1, 2. **~ się** *ipf.* **1.** *zob.* **targać się**. **2.** (= *zaatakować*) attack, assault (*na kogoś* sb); **targnąć się na życie** make an attempt on one's life.

targować się *ipf.* bargain, haggle (*z kimś o coś* with sb over *l.* for sth).

targowisko *n.* market(place).

targowy *a.* market; **dzień targowy** market day; **plac targowy** marketplace.

tarka *f. Gen.pl.* **-ek 1.** (*narzędzie kuchenne*) grater. **2.** (*narzędzie do prania*) washboard. **3.** = **tarnina**.

tarlisko *n. icht.* spawning ground.

tarł *itd. ipf. zob.* **trzeć**.

tarło *n. icht.* spawning season; spawning.

tarmosić *ipf.* **-szę -sisz** *pot.* pull about.

tarnik *mi Gen.* **-a** *techn.* rasp.

tarnina *f. bot.* blackthorn, sloe (*Prunus spinosa*).

tarot *mi Gen. i Acc.* **-a** *karty* tarot.

tarować *ipf.* tare.

tarpan *ma zool.* tarpan (*Equus caballus gmelini*).

tartacznictwo *n. techn.* sawmilling; timber milling.

tartaczny *a. techn.* sawmill.

tartak *mi techn.* sawmill; timber mill.

tartan *mi* **1.** (*wzór szkocki*) tartan. **2.** *sport* synthetic surface (*of the race track*); *Br.* tartan.

tartanowy *a. sport* artificial, rubberized.

tartinka *f. Gen.pl.* **-ek** sandwich.

tarty *a. zwł. kulin.* grated; **bułka tarta** breadcrumbs.

taryfa *f.* **1.** (= *wykaz stawek*) rates; **taryfa celna** tariff of duties; **taryfa kolejowa** table of fares; **taryfa opłat** scale of charges; **taryfa ulgowa** *przen.* leniency; **stosować taryfę ulgową** *przen.* be lenient. **2.** *pot.* (= *taksówka*) cab.

taryfiarz *mp pot.* cabby *l.* cabbie, cab *l.* taxi driver.

taryfikacja *f.* rating.

taryfikator *mi Gen.* **-a** scale of charges; table of rates.

taryfowy *a.* rate; fare; tariff.

tarzać *ipf.* roll (*sb l. sth*) (*w czymś* in sth).

tarzać się *ipf.* wallow, roll (*w czymś* in sth); **tarzać się ze śmiechu** be in stitches, be convulsed with laughter; **tarzać się w pieniądzach** *przen.* be rolling (in money *l.* cash); wallow in money; **tarzać się w rozpuście** *przen.* indulge o.s. in debauchery.

tasak *mi Gen.* **-a** cleaver, chopper.

tasiemcowaty *a.* very long, lengthy; interminable.

tasiemcowy *a.* (= *długi*) very long, lengthy; interminable.

tasiemczyca *f. pat., wet.* cestodiasis, tapeworm infestation.

tasiemiec *ma* **-mc- 1.** *zool.* tapeworm, cestode; **tasiemiec nieuzbrojony** beef tapeworm (*Taenia saginata*); **tasiemiec uzbrojony** *l.* soliter pork tapeworm (*T. solium*). **2.** (= *coś długiego*) sth very long *l.* lengthy; sth interminable.

tasiemka *f. Gen.pl.* **-ek** ribbon; tape.

taskać *ipf. pot.* lug.

Tasmania *f. Gen.* **-ii** *geogr.* Tasmania.

Tasmanka *f. Gen.pl.* **-ek**, **Tasmańczyk** *mp* Tasmanian.

tasmański *a.* Tasmanian.

tasować *ipf. karty* shuffle.

taster *mi* **-tr-** *Gen.* **-a** *druk.* coding keyboard, code composing unit.

taszczyć *ipf. pot.* lug.

tasznik *mi Gen.* **-a** *bot.* shepherd's purse (*Capsella*).

taszysta *mp sztuka* tachist, tachiste.

taszyzm *mi sztuka* tachism, tachisme, action painting.

taśma *f.* 1. (= *wstęga*) tape; ribbon; band; belt; **taśma filmowa** film; **taśma izolacyjna** *techn.* insulating tape; **taśma klejąca** adhesive tape, Scotch tape; **taśma magnetofonowa** audiotape; **taśma maszynowa** (fabric *l.* carbon) ribbon. 2. *sport* tape; **wygrać rzutem na taśmę** win by lunging at the tape. 3. *techn.* (= *część przenośnika*) (conveyor) belt; **pracować przy taśmie** work at an assembly line. 4. *wojsk.* ammunition belt.

taśmociąg *mi techn.* belt conveyor flight.

taśmoteka *f.* tape collection, collection of tape recordings.

taśmowy *f.* tape; band; ribbon; belt; **produkcja taśmowa** *t. przen.* assembly line production, mass production.

tata *mp pl.* -owie dad, pop.

Tatar *mp* Tatar, Tartar.

tatar *mi Gen. i Acc.* -a *kulin.* tartar *l.* tartare steak.

tatarak *mi bot.* sweet rush, sweet flag (*Acorus calamus*).

tatarka *f. Gen.pl.* -ek *bot.* buckwheat (*Fagopyrum tataricum*).

tatarski *a.* (= *dotyczący Tatarów*) 1. Tatar, Tartar. 2. *kulin.* **befsztyk tatarski** *l.* **po tatarsku** tartar *l.* tartare steak; **sos tatarski** tartar *l.* tartare sauce, rémoulade.

taternictwo *n.* mountaineering, alpinism.

taterniczka *f. Gen.pl.* -ek, **taternik** *mp* mountaineer, alpinist.

tatko, tato *mp pl.* -owie = **tata**.

Tatry *pl. Gen.* -r *geogr.* the Tatra Mountains; the Tatras; **Tatry Wysokie** the High Tatras.

tatrzański *a.* Tatra; **Tatrzański Park Narodowy** Tatra National Park.

tatuaż *mi* tattoo.

tatuować *ipf.* tattoo.

tatuś *mp pl.* -owie *Gen.* -ów daddy.

tautogram *mi teor.lit.* tautogram.

tautologia *f. Gen.* -ii tautology.

tautologiczny *a.* tautological, tautologic.

tautologizm *mi* tautology, tautologism.

tawerna *f.* tavern.

tawuła *f. bot.* spirea (*Spiraea*).

taxi *n. indecl.* cab, taxi, taxicab.

tą *pron. zob.* **ten**.

tąpać *ipf.* **tąpie** *geol.* crump, bump.

tąpliwość *f. geol.* crumpability.

tąpnąć *pf. zob.* **tąpać**.

tąpnięcie *n. geol.* crump, bump.

tchawica *f. anat.* trachea, windpipe.

tchawiczny *a. anat.* tracheal.

tchawka *f. Gen.pl.* -ek *zool.* trachea.

tchem *itd. mi zob.* **dech**.

tchnąć *ipf. l. pf.* -ij 1. *lit.* (= *wydzielać zapach*) breathe; smell; feel; be; **mieszkanie tchnęło chłodem** the apartment was cold. 2. *lit.* (= *przejawiać*) be; feel. 3. *tylko pf. lit.* bring about a change; **tchnąć w coś (nowe) życie** breathe (new *l.* fresh) life into sth.

tchnienie *n.* 1. *lit.* (= *oddech*) breath; **wydać**

ostatnie tchnienie breathe one's last, die. 2. *lit.* (= *powiew*) breath *l.* waft (of air).

tchórz *mp Gen.pl.* -y *l.* -ów coward; **tchórzem podszyty** cowardly, chicken-hearted; **tchórz go oblecial** he got cold feet. – *ma Gen.pl.* -y *zool.* European *l.* common polecat, foul marten (*Mustela putorius*).

tchórzliwie *adv.* cowardly.

tchórzliwość *f.* cowardice.

tchórzliwy *a.* 1. (= *lękliwy*) cowardly. 2. (*świadczący o strachu*) cowardly; fearful, timorous.

tchórzostwo *n.* cowardice.

tchórzowski *a.* cowardly.

tchórzyć *ipf.* chicken out.

tchu *itd. mi zob.* **dech**.

te *pron. zob.* **ten**.

team *mi* 1. team, group of people. 2. *sport* (school, national, etc.) team.

teatr *mi* 1. (*dziedzina twórczości*) (the) theater; *Br.* theatre; **teatr lalkowy** *l.* **kukiełkowy** puppet theater; **teatr absurdu** theater of the absurd; **teatr cieni** shadow theater; **teatr muzyczny** musical theater. 2. (*instytucja, budynek, scena, t. przen.*) theater; *Br.* theatre; **teatr objazdowy** traveling theater; **teatr stały** repertory theater; **chodzić do teatru** go to the theater. 3. **teatr działań wojennych** theater of war.

teatralizacja *f. teatr* theatricalization.

teatralizować *ipf. teatr* theatricalize.

teatralnie *adv.* 1. (= *scenicznie*) theatrically, dramatically. 2. (= *nienaturalnie*) theatrically, histrionically.

teatralny *a.* 1. (= *sceniczny*) theatrical, dramatic; **krytyk teatralny** theater critic; **lornetka teatralna** opera glasses; **sezonowa grupa teatralna** stock company. 2. (= *nienaturalny*) theatrical, histrionic.

teatrolog *mi teatr* theatrologist.

teatrologia *f. Gen.* -ii *teatr* theatrology.

teatrologiczny *a. teatr* theatrological.

teatroman *mp*, **teatromanka** *f. Gen.pl.* -ek theatergoer.

teatroznawczy *a. teatr* = **teatrologiczny**.

teatroznawstwo *n. teatr* = **teatrologia**.

teatrzyk *mi* (small) theater.

Teby *pl. Gen.* **Teb** *hist.* Thebes.

technet *mi chem.* technetium.

technicyzacja *f.* introducing technological inventions, processes, methods, etc.; spreading technical knowledge.

technicznie *adv.* technically; technologically.

techniczny *a.* 1. (= *dotyczący techniki*) technical; technological; **rysunek techniczny** technical drawing. 2. (*dotyczący kreślarstwa*) drawing; **kalka techniczna** tracing paper; **pismo techniczne** lettering. 3. (*związany ze sposobem działania*) technical.

technik *mp* 1. (= *pracownik techniczny*) technician; **technik dentystyczny** *dent.* dental technician, dental prosthetist. 2. (= *osoba biegła w czymś*) technician.

technika *f.* 1. (= *ogół środków i umiejętności*

wytwórczych) technology. **2.** (= *metoda*) technique; **mieć dobrą technikę** have good technique.

technikolor *mi kino* Technicolor.

technikum *n. sing. indecl. pl.* **-ka** *Gen.* **-ków** vocational secondary school.

techno *n. indecl.* techno (music). – *a.* techno; **muzyka techno** techno music; **styl techno** techno style.

technokracja *f. fil., polit.* technocracy.

technokrata *mp fil., polit.* technocrat.

technokratyczny *a. fil., polit.* technocratic.

technolog *mp pl.* **-dzy** *l.* **-owie** *techn.* technologist.

technologia *f. Gen.* **-ii** *techn.* technology.

technologiczny *a. techn.* technological, technologic.

teczka *f. Gen.pl.* **-ek 1.** (*torba*) briefcase; portfolio. **2.** (*okładka na dokumenty*) folder; jacket. **3.** (*zbiór dokumentów*) file; dossier; **założyć teczkę** open a file.

teflon *mi techn.* Teflon®.

teflonowy *a. techn.* Teflon®; non-stick, Teflon-coated.

tego *pron. zob.* **ten, to.**

tegoroczny *a.* this year's.

teina *f. chem.* theine, caffeine.

teista *mp fil., rel.* theist.

teistyczny *a. fil., rel.* theistic, theistical.

teizm *mi fil., rel.* theism.

tej *pron. zob.* **ten.**

teka *f.* **1.** (= *duża teczka*) (large) briefcase; (large) portfolio; **teka ministerialna** *polit.* portfolio; **minister bez teki** *polit.* minister without portfolio. **2.** (= *zbiór prac*) portfolio; (= *zbiór dokumentów*) file; dossier.

tekowy *a.* teak; **drewno tekowe** teak, teakwood; **drzewo tekowe** *bot.* teak (*Tectona grandis*).

Teksanka *f. Gen.pl.* **-ek, Teksańczyk** *mp* Texan.

teksański *a.* Texan.

Teksas *mi geogr.* Texas.

teksas *mi tk.* jean(s); **teksasy** jeans.

tekst *mi* text; **tekst piosenki** lyrics.

tekstolog *mp pl.* **-dzy** *l.* **-owie** *teor.lit.* textual critic.

tekstologia *f. Gen.* **-ii** *teor.lit.* textual criticism.

tekstologiczny *a. teor.lit.* textual.

tekstowy *a.* textual; **plik tekstowy** *komp.* text file.

tekstura *f.* **1.** *druk.* (*pismo*) Textura Gothic, black letter, text. **2.** *geol.* texture. **3.** *komp.* (*element graficzny*) texture.

tekstylia *pl. Gen.* **-ów** *tk.* textiles.

tekstylny *a. tk.* textile.

tekściarz *mp pot.* songwriter.

tektoniczny *a. geol.* tectonic.

tektonika *f.* **1.** *geol.* tectonics, structural geology. **2.** *sztuka* tectonics.

tektura *f.* cardboard; **tektura falista** corrugated (card)board.

tekturka *f. Gen.pl.* **-ek** thin cardboard; small piece of cardboard.

tekturowy *a.* cardboard.

tel. *abbr.* (= *telefon*) tel., ph. (= *telephone*).

Tel-Awiw *mi geogr.* Tel Aviv.

telebim *mi telew.* big (broadcast) screen.

teledacja *f. tel.* data transmission.

teledetekcja *f. techn.* remote sensing.

teledysk *mi* (music) video.

teleelektronika *f. techn.* telecommunications electronic engineering.

teleelektryka *f. techn.* telecommunications engineering.

telefaks *mi* **1.** (*urządzenie*) facsimile, fax (machine). **2.** (*przesłany dokument*) facsimile, fax.

telefon *mi* **1.** (*urządzenie*) telephone, phone; **telefon bezprzewodowy** cordless phone; **telefon komórkowy** mobile *l.* cell(ular) (tele)phone; **telefon towarzyski** party line; **telefon zaufania** helpline; **przy telefonie!** speaking!; **rozmawiać przez telefon** be on the phone; **rozmawiać z kimś przez telefon** talk to sb on the phone; **wisieć na telefonie** be on the phone for hours; **być pod telefonem** be possible to reach under a phone number; **telefon się urywa** sb is swamped with phone calls, there's a deluge of phone calls. **2.** (= *rozmowa telefoniczna*) phone call; **odebrać telefon** pick up *l.* answer the phone; **telefon do ciebie!** there's a phone call for you!, it's for you! **3.** (= *numer telefonu*) phone number; **daj mi swój telefon** give me your phone number.

telefonia *f. Gen.* **-ii** *tel.* telephony, telecommunications.

telefonicznie *adv.* by (tele)phone; telephonically.

telefoniczny *a.* (tele)phone; telephonic; **budka telefoniczna** phone booth *l.* box; **automat telefoniczny** pay phone; **centrala telefoniczna** telephone exchange; **karta telefoniczna** phone card; **książka telefoniczna** (telephone) directory; telephone book, phone book; **linia telefoniczna** telephone line; **podsłuch telefoniczny** telephone tapping.

telefonista *mp*, **telefonistka** *f. Gen.pl.* **-ek** (switchboard) operator.

telefonizacja *f. tel.* installing telephone lines, devices, etc.

telefonogram *mi* message communicated and received by phone.

telefonować *ipf.* call, phone; make a phone call.

telefotografia *f. Gen.* **-ii** *techn.* phototelegraphy.

telegazeta *f. telew.* teletext.

telegraf *mi tel.* telegraph.

telegrafia *f. Gen.* **-ii** *tel.* telegraphy.

telegraficznie *adv.* by telegraph, by wire.

telegraficzny *a.* telegraph; telegraphic; **aparat telegraficzny** telegraph; **w telegraficznym skrócie** with telegraphic economy of words, in a telegraphic style.

telegrafista *mp* telegrapher, telegraphist.

telegrafować *ipf.* telegraph, wire.

telegram *mi* telegram, cable, cablegram.

telekineza *f. psych.* telekinesis, psychokinesis.

telekomunikacja *f. tel.* telecommunications.

telekomunikacyjny *a. tel.* telecommunications;

satelita telekomunikacyjny telecommunications satellite.

telekonferencja *f. tel.* teleconference.

teleks *mi* **1.** (*dalekopis*) telex; *Br.* teleprinter. **2.** (*przesłany tekst*) telex.

teleksować *ipf.* telex.

teleksowy *a.* telex.

telemark *mi narciarstwo* telemark.

telemechanika *f. techn.* telemechanics.

telemetria *f. Gen.* **-ii** *miern.* telemetry.

telenowela *f.* soap opera.

teleobiektyw *mi fot.* telephoto lens.

teleologia *f. Gen.* **-ii** *fil.* teleology.

teleologiczny *a. fil.* teleological, teleologic.

telepać *ipf.* **-pię -piesz** *pot.* (= *trząść*) shake, tremble. **~ się** *ipf.* **1.** *pot.* (= *trząść się*) shake, tremble, shimmy. **2.** *pot.* (= *podróżować powoli*) jolt along, joggle along.

telepajęczarstwo *n. pot.* unregistered viewing of TV programs, black viewing.

telepajęczarz *mp pot.* unregistered user of a TV set, black viewer.

telepatia *f. Gen.* **-ii** telepathy.

telepatycznie *adv.* telepathically.

telepatyczny *a.* telepathic.

telerekording *mi telew.* telerecording, television recording.

teleskop *mi* **1.** *opt.* telescope; **teleskop refrakcyjny/zwierciadlany** refracting/reflecting telescope. **2.** *techn.* (= *amortyzator*) shock absorber.

teleskopowy *a.* **1.** *opt.* telescopic. **2.** *techn.* telescopic; **amortyzator teleskopowy** telescopic shock absorber.

teletechniczny *a. techn.* telecommunications engineering.

teletechnik *mp techn.* telecommunications engineer.

teletechnika *f. techn.* telecommunications engineering, remote data communications and control.

teletekst *mi telew.* teletext.

teletransmisja *f.* **1.** *techn.* wire transmission; wireless transmission. **2.** *telew.* TV broadcast, telecast.

teletransmisyjny *a.* **1.** *techn.* transmission. **2.** *telew.* transmission; **wóz teletransmisyjny** mobile unit.

teleturniej *mi Gen.pl.* **-ów** quiz show.

telewidz *mp pl.* **-owie** viewer, TV watcher; **telewidzowie** (TV) audience.

telewizja *f.* **1.** (= *przekazywanie obrazów*) television, TV; **telewizja cyfrowa** digital television; **telewizja kablowa** cable television; **telewizja przemysłowa** closed-circuit television; **telewizja satelitarna** satellite television. **2.** (*instytucja*) television; **Telewizja Polska** *l.* **TVP** Polish TV. **3.** *pot.* (= *program telewizyjny*) (television) program, (television) broadcast; **co jest dzisiaj w telewizji?** what's on TV today?; **oglądać telewizję** watch TV. **4.** *pot.* (= *odbiornik telewizyjny*) television (set), TV (set).

telewizor *mi Gen.* **-a** television (set), TV (set).

telewizyjny *a.* television, TV.

tellur *mi chem.* tellurium.

tellurek *mi* **-rk-** *chem.* telluride.

telomer *mi biochem.* telomer.

temat *mi* **1.** (= *wątek*) subject, topic; **(nie) na temat** (not) to the point; **artykuł na temat...** article on the subject of..., article on...; **odbiegać od tematu** go off the topic, stray from the topic; **zmieniać temat** change the topic, change the subject; **co sądzisz na temat...?** how do you feel about...?; **what's your opinion about...?; przeskakiwać z tematu na temat** jump from one topic to another; **unikać tematu** avoid the issue; **trzymać się tematu** keep to the subject. **2.** *jęz.* stem. **3.** *muz.* theme.

tematowy *a.* **1.** (*dotyczący tematu*) subject, topic. **2.** *jęz.* theme.

tematycznie *adv.* thematically, in a thematic order.

tematyczny *a.* thematic.

tematyka *f.* subject matter.

temblak *mi Gen.* **-a** *l.* **-u** **1.** *med.* sling; **mieć rękę na temblaku** have an arm in a sling. **2.** *hist.* sword knot.

tembr *mi lit.* timbre.

Temida *f. mit. l. przen.* (= *personifikacja sprawiedliwości*) Themis; **Temida jest ślepa** justice is blind; **waga Temidy** the scales of justice.

temp. *abbr.* (= *temperatura*) temp. (= *temperature*).

tempera *f.* **1.** *sztuka* (*farba*) tempera. **2.** *sztuka* (*technika*) tempera.

temperament *mi* (= *usposobienie*) temperament.

temperamentny *a.* temperamental.

temperatura *f.* **1.** (*wielkość fizyczna*) temperature; **temperatura otoczenia** ambient temperature; **temperatura krzepnięcia** solidification point; **temperatura krytyczna** *fiz.* critical temperature; **temperatura pokojowa** room temperature; **temperatura wrzenia** boiling point; **temperatura spadła poniżej...** temperature dropped below... **2.** *pot.* (= *gorączka*) fever; **mieć temperaturę** have a fever, run down with a fever, run a fever.

temperaturowy *a.* temperature.

temperować *ipf.* **1.** (= *ostrzyć*) sharpen. **2.** (= *powściągać*) refrain, restrain.

temperowany *a.* **strój temperowany** *muz.* equal temperament.

temperówka *f. Gen.pl.* **-ek** sharpener.

templariusz *mp hist.* Templar knight.

tempo *n.* **1.** (= *szybkość*) pace; **żółwie tempo** snail's pace, snaillike pace; **tempo wzrostu** growth rate; **w zwolnionym tempie** in slow motion; **zwolnić tempo** slow down; **dyktować tempo** set the pace; **podkręcać tempo** speed up. **2.** (= *rytm*) rhythm; **w tempie walca** in the rhythm of waltz. **3.** *muz.* tempo, time.

temu *pron. zob.* **ten, to.**

temu *adv.* **dawno temu** long time ago, long ago; **dawno temu?** how long ago?; **parę dni temu** a couple of days ago; **rok temu** a year ago.

ten *pron.* **ta, to, t-** **1.** (*określa rzeczownik*) this; **coś w tym rodzaju** *l.* **guście** something like this; **tego roku** this year; **ten świat** this world; **mimo to** nevertheless, all the same; **poza tym** apart from this, except this; **ten sam** the same one; **tym razem** this time; **w tej chwili** at present, at the moment, in this very moment; **w te pędy** *pot.* straightaway, at once; **ta cała sprawa mi się nie podoba** *pot.* I don't like the whole thing. **2.** (*zastępuje rzeczownik*) this (one); **i ten zły i ten niedobry** both are no good; **ten i ów** this one and that one, this one and some other one; **ten i ten** this and that. **3.** (*nawiązuje do zdania podrzędnego*) **wobec tego** so; **w ten sposób** (in) this way; **ten, kto...** he who...

tendencja *f.* **1.** (= *skłonność*) tendency; **tendencja barometryczna** *meteor.* barometric tendency; **mieć tendencję do (robienia) czegoś** be inclined to (doing) sth. **2.** (= *trend*) trend, drift, run; **tendencja zwyżkowa** upward trend, rising trend; **tendencja zniżkowa** downward trend, downslide; **ogólna tendencja** general trend, underlying trend. **3.** *teor.lit.* trend.

tendencyjnie *adv.* in a biased way.

tendencyjność *f.* bias.

tendencyjny *a.* biased; *Br. t.* biassed.

tender *mi* **-dr-** *Gen.* **-a** *kol., żegl.* tender.

Teneryfa *f. geogr.* Tenerife.

tenis *mi Gen. i Acc.* **-a** *sport* tennis; **tenis stołowy** table tennis, ping-pong; **tenis ziemny** lawn tennis.

tenisista *mp,* **tenisistka** *f. Gen.pl.* **-ek** tennis player.

tenisowy *a.* tennis.

tenisówka *f. Gen.pl.* **-ek** tennis shoe, sneaker.

tenor *mi Gen.* **-u** *pl.* **-ry** *muz.* tenor. – *mp Gen.* **-a** *pl.* **-rzy** tenor; **tenor bohaterski** dramatic tenor, heroic tenor.

tenorowy *a.* (*o głosie, kluczu*) tenor.

teocentryczny *a. fil.* theocentric.

teodolit *mi miern.* theodolite, altometer.

teokracja *f.* theocracy.

teokratyczny *a.* theocratic.

teolog *mp pl.* **-dzy** *l.* **-owie** theologian.

teologia *f. Gen.* **-ii** theology.

teologiczny *a.* theological.

teoretycznie *adv.* theoretically, in theory.

teoretyczny *a.* theoretical.

teoretyk *mp* theoretician.

teoretyzować *ipf.* theorize.

teoria *f. Gen.* **-ii** theory; **teoria względności** relativity theory; **teoria poznania** epistemology; **teoria spisku** conspiracy theory; **w teorii** in theory, theoretically; **mam własną teorię na ten temat** I've got my own theory about it.

teownik *mi Gen.* **-a** *techn.* T-bar, tee bar.

teozofia *f. Gen.* **-ii** *fil.* theosophy.

ter *mi techn.* tar.

terakota *f.* terracotta.

terakotowy *a.* terracotta.

terapeuta *mp* therapist, counsellor.

terapeutyczny *a.* therapeutic.

terapia *f. Gen.* **-ii** therapy; **terapia grupowa** group therapy; **terapia wstrząsowa** shock therapy; **terapia zajęciowa** occupational therapy; **hormonalna terapia zastępcza** hormone replacement therapy.

terasa *f. geol.* bench.

teratologia *f. Gen.* **-ii** *biol. med.* teratology.

teraz *adv.* **1.** (= *w tej chwili*) now, at the moment; **i co teraz?** and what now? **2.** (= *współcześnie*) nowadays, now, these days; **teraz, gdy...** now that...; **nie teraz!** not now!; **teraz albo nigdy** now or never.

teraźniejszość *f.* the present.

teraźniejszy *a.* present, current; **czas teraźniejszy** *jęz.* present tense.

tercet *mi* **1.** *muz.* (*zespół*) trio. **2.** *muz.* (*utwór*) trio.

tercja *f.* **1.** *sport* (= *część meczu hokejowego*) period. **2.** *sport* (= *pozycja obronna w szermierce*) tierce. **3.** *muz.* third, terce.

tere-fere (kuku) *int. pot.* fiddlededee, fiddlesticks.

teren *mi* **1.** (= *część powierzchni ziemi*) ground, terrain, area; **teren budowy** construction site, building site; **teren fabryki** factory's premises, factory's confines; **teren szkoły** school grounds; **tereny zielone** green areas; **tereny rolnicze, wiejskie** rural area; **tereny leśne** woodland; **rzeźba terenu** *geol.* relief, land form; **uzbrajać teren** develop the ground. **2.** (= *obszar działań*) site, field, arena; **teren bitwy** the site of the battle; **teren działalności** *l.* **zainteresowań** domain, field. **3.** *pot.* (= *ośrodki prowincjonalne*) local branches, local offices; **pojechać w teren** go on a round; **być w terenie** be in the field, be on one's round; **mieć orientację terenu** have the sense of direction; **na swoim własnym terenie** on one's own ground.

terenowy *a.* **1.** (*odnoszący się do terenu*) ground, terrain; **samochód terenowy** off-road vehicle. **2.** (= *regionalny*) local; **władze terenowe** local government. **3.** (*o badaniach, pomiarach, praktyce*) field.

terenoznawstwo *n.* topography.

terenówka *f. Gen.pl.* **-ek** *pot.* (= *samochód terenowy*) off-road vehicle.

tergal *mi* Dacron®.

terier *ma kynol.* terrier.

terkot *mi* **1.** (= *warkot*) clatter, rattle. **2.** *pot.* (= *paplanina*) rattle.

terkotać *ipf.* **-czę -czesz** *l.* **-cę -cesz, -cz** **1.** (= *wydawać terkot*) clatter, rattle. **2.** *pot.* (= *paplać*) clatter, rattle.

terkotliwy *a.* clattering.

terlica *f.* tree.

terma *f.* **1.** (= *grzejnik*) heater. **2.** *geol.* thermal spring, hot spring.

termalny *a.* thermal.

termy *pl. Gen.* **-m** *hist.* (= *łaźnie*) baths.

termiczny *f.* thermal.

termika *f. meteor.* thermal air currents.

termin *mi* **1.** (= *wyznaczony czas*) time limit, deadline; **ostateczny termin** deadline, final deadline, closing date; **termin dostawy** delivery date, time of delivery; **(skończyć coś) w terminie** finish sth in time; **wyznaczyć termin** set a date; **zmieścić się w terminie** meet the deadline. **2.** (= *pojęcie o ustalonym znaczeniu*) term. **3.** *przest.* (= *nauka rzemiosła*) apprenticeship.

terminal *mi Gen.pl.* **-i** *l.* **-ów** **1.** (= *miejsce od-*

jazdów i przyjazdów) terminal. **2.** *komp.* terminal.

terminarz *mi Gen.* **-a 1.** (= *rozkład zajęć*) schedule. **2.** (= *kalendarz*) diary, organizer.

terminator *mp przest.* apprentice, trainee. – *mi Gen.* **-a** *astron.* terminator, circle of illumination.

terminatorski *a. przest.* apprentice.

terminologia *f. Gen.* **-ii** terminology.

terminologiczny *a.* terminological.

terminować *ipf. przest.* serve one's apprenticeship; **terminować u kogoś** be sb's apprentice.

terminowo *adv.* on time, punctually.

terminowy *a.* with a deadline; **lokata terminowa** deposit account.

termit *ma ent.* (= *owad z rzędu Isoptera*) termite. – *mi metal., techn., wojsk.* thermite.

termitowy *a. metal.* **spawanie termitowe** thermite welding.

termodynamiczny *a.* thermodynamic.

termodynamika *f. fiz.* thermodynamics.

termoelektryczność *f.* thermoelectricity.

termofor *mi* hot-water bottle.

termograf *mi techn.* thermograph, temperature recorder.

termografia *f. Gen.* **-ii** *techn.* thermography.

termogram *mi techn.* thermogram, thermal image.

termoizolacja *f.* thermal insulation.

termojądrowy *a.* thermonuclear.

termokatoda *f. techn.* thermionic cathode, hot cathode.

termometr *mi* thermometer.

termoplast *mi chem.* thermoplastic.

termoplastyczny *a.* thermoplastic.

termoreceptor *mi Gen.* **-a** *biol.* thermoreceptor.

termos *mi* thermos flask.

termostat *mi techn.* thermostat.

termostatyczny *a. fiz.* thermostatic.

termostatyka *f. fiz.* thermostatics.

termoterapia *f. Gen.* **-ii** *med.* thermal therapy.

termoutwardzalny *a. techn.* thermosetting, thermohardening.

termowentylator *mi Gen.* **-a** fan heater.

terpen *mi chem.* terpene.

terpentyna *f.* turpentine.

terpentynowy *a.* turpentine.

terrarium *n. sing. indecl. pl.* **-ria** *Gen.* **-riów** terrarium.

terror *mi* terror; **siać terror** inspire terror.

terrorysta *mp*, **terrorystka** *f. Gen.pl.* **-ek** terrorist.

terrorystyczny *a.* terrorist; **zamachy terrorystyczne** terrorist attacks.

terroryzm *mi* terrorism.

terroryzować *ipf.* terrorize.

terytorialnie *adv.* territorially.

terytorialny *a.* territorial; **wody terytorialne** territorial waters; **spory terytorialne** territorial disputes.

terytorium *n. sing. indecl. pl.* **-ria** *Gen.* **-riów** territory; **terytorium państwa** state territory.

test *mi* **1.** (= *próba, badanie*) test; **test ciążowy**

pregnancy test. **2.** (= *sprawdzian pisemny*) test; **test luk** cloze test; **test papierkiem lakmusowym** litmus test; **test osobowości** personality test.

testament *mi* will, last will, testament; **Stary, Nowy Testament** *rel.* Old, New Testament; **sporządzić testament** draw up a will, draw up a testament; **obalić testament** overturn a will; **zapisać coś komuś w testamencie** will sth to sb, bequeath sb sth.

testamentowy *a.* testamentary.

testator *mp prawn.* devisor, testator.

tester *mi Gen.* **-a** (= *próbka kosmetyku*) free sample. – *mp* (= *osoba testująca*) trier.

testosteron *mi biol.* testosterone.

testować *ipf.* **1.** (= *sprawdzać*) test, try out. **2.** *prawn.* put to a test.

testowy *a.* test.

teściowa *f. Gen.* **-ej** mother-in-law.

teściowie *pl. Gen.* **-ów** (= *teść i teściowa*) in-laws.

teść *mp pl.* **-owie** *Gen.* **-ów** father-in-law.

tetra *f.* **1.** *chem.* carbon tetrachloride. **2.** (*tk.*) diaper cloth.

tetraedr *mi geom.* (= *czworościan*) tetrahedron.

tetraedryt *mi min.* tetrahedrite.

tetragonalny *a.* **krystalografia** tetragonal.

tetralogia *f. Gen.* **-ii** *teor.lit.* **1.** (*cykl literacki*) tetralogy. **2.** (= *widowisko teatralne*) tetralogy.

tetrarcha *mp pl.* **-owie** *hist.* tetrarch.

tetroda *f. el.* tetrode.

tetryczeć *ipf.* go grumpy.

tetryk *mp* grump.

tetryl *mi chem.* tetryl.

Teutoni *pl. Gen.* **-ów** *lit.* (= *Germanie l. Niemcy*) the Teutons.

teutoński *a. hist. l. lit.* Teutonic.

teza *f.* **1.** (= *założenie*) thesis; **stawiać tezę** propose a thesis. **2.** *mat.* proposition.

tezaurus *mi Gen.* **-a** thesaurus.

też *particle* **1.** (= *również*) too, also, as well; **ja też nie** me neither; **ja też** me too; **ja wiem i on też** I know and he knows as well. **2.** *emf.* (*nadaje zabarwienie ujemne*) what?!; **też mi nowina!** that's nothing new for me!; **też pytanie!** what a question! – *conj.* **1.** too; also, as well. **2.** **nie tylko A, ale też B** not only *A* but also *B*; not only *A* but also *B* as well.

tę *pron. zob.* **ta.**

tęcza *f.* (*zjawisko optyczne*) rainbow; **mieniący się barwami tęczy** iridescent.

tęczanka *f. Gen.pl.* **-ek** *icht.* rainbowfish (*Melanotaenia*).

tęczowy *a.* iridescent, rainbow-colored; **pstrąg tęczowy** *icht.* rainbow trout (*Salmo gairdneri*).

tęczówka *f. Gen.pl.* **-ek** *anat.* iris.

tędy *adv.* this way; **tędy (i) owędy** this way or another; **nie tędy droga** *przen.* not (in) this way.

tęgi *a.* **tęższy 1.** (= *gruby*) stout. **2.** (= *krzepki, silny*) great, mighty. **3.** (= *intensywny*) mighty, great; (*o mrozie*) mighty; **tęga mina** bold face.

tęgo *adv.* **tężej** *pot.* (= *mocno*) mightily, greatly.

tęgość *f.* (= *otyłość*) obesity.

tępak *mp pot.* moron.

tępawy *a.* 1. (= *mało ostry*) blunt. 2. (= *dość głupi*) dull, obtuse.

tępić *ipf.* 1. (= *zwalczać*) combat, eradicate; (*o szkodnikach*) kill off, exterminate. 2. (= *nękać, dokuczać*) persecute. 3. (= *czynić tępym*) blunt. 4. (= *powodować osłabienie*) weaken. ~ **się** *ipf.* 1. (= *zwalczać się wzajemnie*) fight one another. 2. (= *stawać się nieostrym*) go blunt.

tępieć *ipf.* 1. (= *stawać się nieostrym*) go blunt. 2. (= *głupieć*) become stupid, become dull. 3. (= *słabnąć*) weaken.

tępo *adv.* 1. (= *nieostro*) bluntly. 2. (= *bezmyślnie*) dully. 3. (*o odgłosie, głucho*) hollowly.

tępota *f.* obtuseness.

tępy *a.* 1. (= *nienaostrzony*) blunt. 2. (= *ścięty, spłaszczony*) blunt, flat; **tępe spojrzenie** vacant stare. 3. (= *nieinteligentny*) dull, obtuse; (*o bólu*) dull; (*o odgłosie*) hollow.

tęsknić *ipf.* -**ij** 1. (= *odczuwać brak*) miss (*za kimś, czymś* sb, sth). 2. (= *bardzo chcieć*) long for, yearn for (*do kogoś, czegoś* sb, sth).

tęsknie *adv. lit.* longingly.

tęskno *adv.* **tęskno mi (do ciebie)** *lit.* I miss you.

tęsknota *f.* 1. (= *nostalgia*) longing, yearning (*do kogoś, czegoś l. za kimś, czymś* for sb, sth); **usychać z tęsknoty** pine for sth/sb. 2. (= *silne pragnienie*) crave (*za czymś l. do czegoś* for sth).

tęskny *a. lit.* longing.

tętent *mi* rattle, clatter; the drumming of hooves *l.* hoofs, hoofbeat.

tętniak *mi Gen.* -**a** *pat.* aneurysm.

tętnica *f. anat.* artery.

tętniczy *a.* arterial.

tętnić *ipf.* -**ij** 1. (*o podkowach itp.*) (= *stukać*) rattle, clatter, drum, beat. 2. (*o ziemi itp.*) (= *drżeć, dudnić*) rattle. 3. (*o krwi*) (= *pulsować*) pulsate. 4. (= *być pełnym odgłosów*) clatter, rattle; **tętnić życiem** be teeming with life.

tętno *n.* 1. (= *bicie serca*) heartbeat. 2. (= *rytm*) pulse.

tężec *mi* -**żc**- *Gen.* -**a** *pat.* tetanus.

tężeć *ipf.* 1. (= *ścinać się*) set, congeal, solidify. 2. (= *nieruchomieć*) freeze; (*o twarzy, mięśniach*) freeze. 3. (= *wzmagać się*) increase.

tężnia *f. Gen.pl.* -**i** (salt) graduation tower.

tężnik *mi Gen.* -**a** *techn.* brace.

tęższy *a. zob.* **tęgi**.

tężyzna *f.* fitness; **tężyzna fizyczna** physical fitness.

tfu *int.* 1. (*wyraża pogardę, wstręt*) yuck!, ugh! 2. *pot.* (*używany przy przejęzyczeniu*) oops!

thriller *mi Gen.* -**a** thriller.

tiamina *f. chem.* thiamine.

tiara *f. kośc.* tiara.

tie-break *mi sport* tie-break.

tik *mi* tic.

tik-tak *int.* tic-tac.

timbre *mi Gen.* -**re'u** *Loc.* -**rze** *Nom.pl.* -**re'y** = **tembr**.

tir *mi Gen.* -**a** *pot.* tractor-trailer truck; *Br.* TIR truck *l.* lorry (*in Europe*).

Tirana *f. geogr.* Tirana.

tiul *mi Gen.pl.* -**ów** *l.* -**i** *tk.* tulle.

tiulowy *a.* tulle.

tj. *abbr.* (= *to jest*) i.e.

tkacki *a.* loom; (*o warsztacie, krosnach*) loom.

tkactwo *n.* weaving, weaver's craft.

tkacz[1] *mp* weaver.

tkacz[2] *ma* 1. *orn.* (= *ptak z rodziny Ploceidae*) weaverbird, weaver finch. 2. *ent.* (*mrówka*) weaver ant (*Oecophylla, Polyrhachis*).

tkaczka *f. Gen.pl.* -**ek** *zob.* **tkacz**[1].

tkać *ipf.* weave.

tkanina *f.* fabric, cloth.

tkanka *f. Gen.pl.* -**ek** 1. *anat.* (= *system komórek*) tissue. 2. *przen.* (= *misterny układ*) tissue, network, web.

tkankowiec *ma* -**wc**- *zool.* eumetazoan.

tkankowy *a.* tissue.

tkany *a.* 1. (= *zrobiony na krosnach*) weaved. 2. (= *przetykany nitkami*) stitched.

tkliwość *f.* 1. (= *czułość*) affection, tenderness. 2. *med.* sensitivity.

tkliwy *a.* 1. (= *czuły, wyrażający czułość*) affectionate, loving, tender. 2. *med.* sensitive.

tknąć *pf.* -**ij** 1. *zob.* **tykać**. 2. (= *uderzyć, zrobić krzywdę*) strike, hit, harm; **spróbuj ją tknąć, a popamiętasz!** touch her and I'll show you! 3. (*o uczuciach*) (= *opanować*) seize, come over (*sb*); **tknęło mnie dziwne uczucie** I got an odd feeling; **coś mnie tknęło, żeby zajrzeć do środka** something prompted me to look inside. ~ **się** *pf. zob.* **tykać się**.

tkwić *ipf.* -**ij** 1. (= *być osadzonym*) be stuck *l.* embedded (*w czymś* in sth). 2. (= *być gdzieś przez dłuższy czas*) stick around. 3. (*o problemie itp.*) (= *mieć źródło*) lie, reside (*w czymś* in sth); **tu tkwi problem** there's the rub; therein lies the rub.

tlen *mi chem.* oxygen; **być pod tlenem** *med.* be in an oxygen tent.

tlenek *mi* -**nk**- *chem.* oxide.

tlenić *ipf.* bleach, oxidize. ~ **się** *ipf.* bleach one's hair; have one's hair bleached.

tleniony *a.* bleached; **tleniona blondynka** peroxide blonde.

tlenowiec *mi* -**wc**- *Gen.* -**a** 1. *biol.* aerobe, aerobic bacterium. 2. *chem.* oxygen group element.

tlenowy *a.* oxygen, oxygenic; **aparat/namiot tlenowy** oxygen respirator/tent; **maska tlenowa** oxygen mask.

tlić się *ipf.* 1. (= *żarzyć się*) glow, smolder. 2. (= *być mało intensywnym*) glimmer, flicker.

tłamsić *ipf.* -**szę** -**sisz** 1. (= *gnieść*) crumple, rumple. 2. (= *tłumić, gnębić*) suppress, oppress, strangle; (*łzy, uczucia*) hold back, suppress.

tło *n. Gen.pl.* **teł** 1. (= *dalszy plan*) background; **statek na tle morza** ship in the background of the sea; **na tle kolegów wypadał blado** he did poorly in comparison to other boys; **być (tylko) tłem dla czegoś** constitute the background of sth; **tło muzyczne** incidental music, background music. 2. (= *barwa, na której jest deseń*) background; **jasne prążki na zielonym tle** light stripes against a green background. 3. (= *podłoże*) background; **tło powieści** setting of the novel; **konflikt na tle etnicznym** ethnic conflict; **zabójstwo na tle rabunkowym** robbery murder.

tłocznia *f. Gen.pl.* -i *techn.* (= *prasa do wytłaczania soków itp.*) press; (= *prasa do obróbki plastycznej*) (embossing and coining) press.

tłoczno *adv.* **w pokoju jest tłoczno** the room is crowded *l.* packed.

tłoczny *a.* **1.** (= *zatłoczony*) crowded, packed, congested, filled to the brim. **2.** (= *tłoczący*) pressure; (*o pompie*) pressure pump.

tłoczyć *ipf.* **1.** (= *wpychać siłą*) press, force in; (*pod ciśnieniem*) press. **2.** *techn.* (= *wyciskać sok, olej itp.*) press. **3.** *techn.* (= *poddawać obróbce plastycznej*) imprint, impress. **4.** *druk.* print. ~ **się** *ipf.* crowd, swarm, flock, throng; (= *przybywać tłumnie*) arrive in swarms, swarm in.

tłok *mi* **1.** (= *ścisk*) crowd, rush; **ujdzie w tłoku** *przen., żart.* it'll pass in a crowd. **2.** *Gen.* -a *techn.* piston, plunger.

tłokowy *a. techn.* piston.

tłuc *ipf.* **tłukę tłuczesz 1.** (= *rozbijać*) break, smash, shatter. **2.** (= *miażdżyć, ubijać*) crush, grind, pestle; (*pieprz*) grind. **3.** (= *łomotać*) bang, hammer, batter; (*głową, pięścią*) bang (*w coś l. o coś* on *l.* against sth); **tłuc głową o mur** run one's head against a stone wall. **4.** *pot.* (= *bić*) beat, fight. **5.** *pot.* (= *zabijać*) kill, slaughter; (*muchy*) swat. **6.** *pot.* (= *robić długo i bezmyślnie*) drag on *l.* along, drone; (*na fortepianie, maszynie*) pound away; (*ten sam produkt*) mass-produce, knock out. ~ **się** *ipf.* **1.** (= *być tłuczonym*) break, get shattered. **2.** *pot.* (= *bić się wzajemnie*) fight. **3.** (= *uderzać, obijać się*) pound (*o coś* at sth). **4.** *pot.* (= *poruszać się, powodując hałas*) rattle. **5.** *pot.* (= *podróżować niewygodnie*) travel uncomfortably, bump along. **6.** *pot.* (= *wałęsać się*) roam, wander, ramble.

tłuczek *mi* -czk- *Gen.* -a pestle; (*do ziemniaków*) potato masher; (*do mięsa*) meat tenderizer; (*do maślniczki*) dasher.

tłuczeń *mi* -czni- *Gen.* -a rubble.

tłuczka *f. Gen.pl.* -ek (*ceramika*) chipped pottery; **tłuczka szklana** broken glass.

tłuk *mp pl.* -i **1.** (*narzędzie*) stamp. **2.** *pog.* moron, half-wit.

tłum *mi* **1.** (= *duża liczba ludzi*) crowd. **2.** (= *pospólstwo*) mob, herd, the hoi polloi; **gardzić tłumem** despise the crowd.

tłum. *abbr.* (= *tłumaczył/a*) translated by.

tłumacz *mp* (*pisemny*) translator; (*ustny*) interpreter; **tłumacz przysięgły** sworn translator.

tłumaczenie *n.* **1.** (= *tekst przekładu*) translation. **2.** (*czynność*) translation. **3.** (= *interpretacja*) interpretation. **4.** (= *wyjaśnienie*) explanation. **5.** (= *usprawiedliwienie*) excuse, justification.

tłumaczeniowy *a.* translator's, translational.

tłumaczka *f. Gen.pl.* -ek *zob.* **tłumacz.**

tłumaczyć *ipf.* **1.** (= *wyjaśniać*) explain, expound, explicate. **2.** (= *dokonywać przekładu*) translate (*na jakiś język* into..., *z jakiegoś języka* from...). **3.** (= *uzasadniać, usprawiedliwiać*)

justify, excuse; **to wszystko tłumaczy** that explains matters; *żart.* that accounts for the milk in the coconut. ~ **się** *ipf.* **1.** (= *usprawiedliwiać się*) explain/excuse oneself; **gęsto się tłumaczyć** apologize profusely. **2.** (= *znajdować uzasadnienie*) be explained, be accounted for; **to się tłumaczy samo przez się** it goes without saying.

tłumek *mi* -mk- mob.

tłumić *ipf.* **1.** (= *poskramiać, dusić*) restrain, curb, suppress; (*ogień*) smother; (*bunt*) suppress, quell, quash. **2.** (= *opanowywać*) contain, restrain; (*gniew, kaszel*) contain. **3.** (= *głuszyć*) muffle; (*hałas, dźwięki*) muffle.

tłumik *mi Gen.* -a **1.** *mot.* muffler; *Br.* silencer. **2.** *muz.* (*trąbki*) mute; (*fortepianu*) damper. **3.** (*do broni*) silencer.

tłumnie *adv.* in crowds, in swarms, in great numbers.

tłumny *a.* **tłumne przybycie** arrival in great numbers.

tłumok *mi Gen.* -a *pot.* (= *tobół*) bundle, pack. – *mp pl.* -i *pog.* (= *głupek*) moron, half-wit.

tłustawy *a.* **1.** (= *trochę tłusty*) fattish. **2.** (= *lekko natłuszczony*) lightly greased. **3.** (= *otyły*) fat, plump.

tłusto *adv.* **tłuściej 1.** (= *z dużą ilością tłuszczu*) with plenty of grease. **2.** (= *tak jak tłuszcz*) like fat.

tłustosz *mi Gen.* -a *bot.* butterwort (*Pinguicula*).

tłusty *a.* **tłustszy** *l.* **tłuściejszy 1.** (= *zawierający tłuszcz*) fat, oily, greasy; (*o mleku*) full-cream milk; (*o kremie*) oily cream; **tłusty druk** bold-faced print; **tłusty czwartek** last Thursday of carnival, the last Thursday before Lent; **tłusty wtorek** Shrove Tuesday; **tłusta ziemia** mellow earth/lands. **2.** (= *zaprawiony tłuszczem*) with fat/grease; **tłusty kąsek** *przen.* titbit; **tłuste lata** years of plenty. **3.** (= *zatłuszczony*) greasy, oily. **4.** (= *otyły*) obese, fat.

tłuszcz *mi Gen.pl.* -ów fat, grease; **tłuszcz roślinny/zwierzęcy** vegetable/animal fat; **obrastać w tłuszcz** grow fat.

tłuszcza *f. przest.* rabble, mob.

tłuszczak *mi Gen.* -a *med.* lipoma, fatty tumor. – *ma orn.* (= *ptak z rodziny Steatornithidae*) guacharo, oil-bird.

tłuszczowy *a. chem.* **1.** fatty, aliphatic; **kwasy tłuszczowe** fatty acids. **2.** *anat.* fat, adipose. **3.** **przemysł tłuszczowy** cooking oil industry.

tłuszczyk *mi* fat, grease.

tłuścić *ipf.* -szczę -ścisz **1.** (= *plamić tłuszczem*) stain *l.* smear (*sth*) with grease; leave greasy stains on (*sth*). **2.** (= *natłuszczać*) grease. ~ **się** *ipf.* get greasy.

tłuścieć *ipf. pot.* grow fat.

tłuścioch *mp pl.* -y *pot.* fatty; *obelż.* fatso.

tłuścioszek *mp* -szk- *pl.* -i *Gen.* -ów *pot., żart.* fatty.

to¹ *a. zob.* **ten.**

to² *pron. indecl.* **1.** (*zastępuje podmiot*) it; **to nic** it's nothing; **to prawda** it's true; **to tutaj** it's here; **to ty?** is that you?; **kto to?** who is it?, who's this?; (= *kto tam?*) who's that?; **to jest to!** this is it!; **otóż to!** exactly!; that's (just) it! **2.** (*zastępuje łącznik*) **delfiny to ssaki** dolphins are mammals; **to dobrze** it's good. – *conj.* **chcesz, to idź** go if you like; **jak skończysz, to posprzątaj** clean up when you finish; **co jeden, to głupszy** each one is more stupid than the other; **co kraj, to obyczaj** other countries other laws, every country has its habits/customs; **co wstał, to się przewrócił** every time he got up, he (instantly) fell; **co to, to nie!** no way!; **jak nie, to nie** if no, fine; **jeśli przyjdzie, to nie otwieraj** if he comes, don't open; **oglądała to jeden, to drugi palec** she was watching (now) one finger then another one; **przyszedł wieczorem, to jest około szóstej** he came in the evening, that is around six. – *particle* (*o charakterze ekspresywnym*) **to ci bezczelność!** what cheek!; **to ci (dopiero) pech!** bad *l.* tough luck!; **co to za łobuz!** what a rascal!; **no to co (z tego)?** so what?

toaleta *f.* **1.** (= *elegancki strój*) dress. **2.** (= *zabiegi higieniczne*) toilet. **3.** (= *ubikacja*) restroom, toilet; *Br.* lavatory; **toaleta damska/męska** the ladies'/men's (room). **4.** = **toaletka.**

toaletka *f. Gen.pl.* **-ek** dressing table.

toaletowy *a.* toilet; **przybory toaletowe** toilet set; **papier toaletowy** toilet paper.

toast *mi* toast; **wznosić/proponować toast** raise/propose a toast (*za kogoś l. na czyjąć cześć* to sb).

tobie *pron. zob.* **ty.**

tobogan *mi* toboggan.

tobołek *mi* **-łk-** *Gen.* **-a** bundle, pack.

tobół *mi* **-o-** (large) bundle.

toccata *f. muz.* toccata.

toczek *mi* **-czk-** *Gen.* **-a 1.** (*kapelusz*) (woman's) toque. **2.** *Gen.* **-a** *bot.* volvox (*Volvox*).

toczeń *mi* **-czni-** *Gen.* **-a** *med.* lupus.

toczny *a. techn.* rolling, turning; (*o części, łożysku*) rolling; **łożysko toczne** antifriction bearing.

toczony *a.* (= *krągły*) rounded.

toczyć *ipf.* **1.** (= *przesuwać, obracając*) roll; **toczyć wzrokiem** roll one's eyes (*po kimś / czymś* over sb/sth). **2.** (= *wieść*) wheel, draw; (*dyskusję*) conduct, carry on; (*wojnę*) conduct. **3.** *techn.* (= *skrawać*) turn. **4.** *techn.* (*z gliny*) shape, fashion. **5.** *lit.* (= *niszczyć*) eat, gnaw, canker; (*o raku, kornikach*) canker. **6.** *lit.* (= *gnębić*) rankle, fester; (*o smutku, zgryzocie*) trouble, disquiet. **7.** *lit.* (= *ściągać płyn*) draw; **rzeka toczy swe wody** the river rolls its waters. **~ się** *ipf.* **1.** (= *poruszać się ruchem obrotowym*) roll. **2.** (= *płynąć*) roll (on), flow. **3.** (= *dziać się*) go on, proceed. **4.** *pot.* (= *iść ociężale*) waddle.

toczydło *n. Gen.pl.* **-deł** grindstone, grinding stone.

toffi *n. l. mi indecl.* taffy.

toga *f. Gen.pl.* **tóg** gown, robe.

tojad *mi bot.* aconite, monk's hood (*Aconitum*).

tojeść *f. bot.* loosestrife (*Lysimachis vulgaris*).

tok *mi* (= *przebieg*) progress, course; **tok myśli** train of thought; **tok dyskusji** course of discussion; **(być) w toku** (be) in progress; **w toku czegoś** in the course of sth.

tokaj *mi Gen.pl.* **-ów** Tokay (wine).

tokarka *f. Gen.pl.* **-ek** *techn.* lathe.

tokarski *a.* lathe.

tokarstwo *n.* turnery.

tokarz *mp* turner.

toki *pl. Gen.* **-ów** *myśl.* toot.

Tokio *n. indecl. geogr.* Tokyo.

tokować *ipf.* **1.** (*o ptakach*) (= *wydawać dźwięki*) toot. **2.** (*o ludziach*) (= *mówić długo i z przejęciem*) toot one's horn.

toksoplazmoza *f. med.* toxoplasmosis.

toksycznie *adv.* toxically.

toksyczność *f.* toxicity.

toksyczny *a.* **1.** (= *trujący*) poisonous. **2.** (= *spowodowany działaniem toksyny*) toxic.

toksykolog *mp pl.* **-dzy** *l.* **-owie** toxicologist.

toksykologia *f. Gen.* **-ii** toxicology.

toksyna *f. biol.* toxin.

tolerancja *f.* **1.** (= *pobłażliwość*) tolerance, broadmindedness (*dla l. wobec kogoś, czegoś* towards/of/for sb/sth). **2.** *biol.* tolerance (*na coś* for sth). **3.** *techn.* tolerance.

tolerancyjnie *adv.* tolerantly.

tolerancyjność *f.* = **tolerancja** 1.

tolerancyjny *a.* tolerant (*dla kogoś / czegoś* towards sb/sth, *wobec kogoś / czegoś* of sb/sth).

tolerować *ipf.* **1.** (= *pobłażać*) tolerate. **2.** (= *dobrze znosić*) bear; *med.* tolerate.

tolos *mi hist., bud.* tholos.

Toltek *mp hist.* Toltec.

toluen *mi chem.* toluene.

toluidyna *f. chem.* toluidine.

toluil *mi chem.* toluyl.

tołpyga *f. icht.* silver carp (*Hypophthalmichthys molitrix*).

tom *mi* (*oprawiona książka l. część książki*) volume, book.

tomahawk *mi Gen.* **-a** tomahawk.

tombak *mi* tombac.

tombakowy *a.* tombac.

tomik *mi* little volume.

tomisko *n.* hefty volume.

tomista *mp* Thomist.

tomistyczny *a.* Thomistic.

tomizm *mi* Thomism.

tomograf *mi techn., med.* tomograph, CAT scanner.

tomografia *f. Gen.* **-ii** (*także* **tomografia komputerowa**) *techn., med.* (computer-aided) tomography, CAT scanning.

tomogram *mi techn., med.* tomogram, CAT image.

ton¹ *mi* **1.** *fiz., muz.* (= *dźwięk*) tone, sound; **cały ton** one tone; **mów o pół tonu ciszej!** speak quieter, please; **nadawać czemuś ton** *przen.* take the lead, lead the fashion; **spuścić z tonu** come down a peg or two, sing another tune. **2.** (= *sposób wypowiadania się*) tone (of voice); **nie mów do mnie takim tonem!** don't talk to me like that!; **uderzyć w podniosły ton** take on a solemn tone (of voice). **3.** (= *odcień*) tone, tint; **o ton jaśniejszy** one tone lighter. **4.** (= *etykieta, konwenans*) form; **w dobrym, złym tonie** it is good/bad form, it is the proper/improper thing to do; **to nie należy do dobrego tonu** it's not good form. **5.** *jęz.* tone.

ton² *mi chem.* (= *glinka kredowa*), potter's earth *l.* clay.

tona *f.* ton; **tona rejestrowa** *żegl.* metric (register) tone.

tonacja *f.* **1.** *muz.* key; **utwór w tonacji F-dur** piece in F major. **2.** (= *gama barw l. odcieni*) tone, tones; **w jasnej/ciemnej tonacji** in light/ dark tones.

tonalit *mi geol.* tonalite.

tonalność *f. muz.* tonality.

tonalny *a. muz.* tonal.

tonaż *mi* tonnage.

tonący *mp* drowning, sinking; **tonący brzytwy się chwyta** a drowning man clutches/catches at a straw.

tonąć *ipf.* **1.** (*o przedmiocie*) (= *iść na dno*) sink, go under; (*o człowieku*) (= *tracić życie*) drown. **2.** (= *zagłębiać się*) pore (*w czymś* over sth); **tonąć w długach** be sunk in debt, be up to one's ears in debt; **tonąć we łzach** be in floods of tears, cry one's heart/eyes out; **tonąć we mgle, w mroku** be enveloped in mist/darkness; **tonąć w niepamięci** fall into oblivion; **tonąć w zieleni** be smothered with flowers.

toner *mi Gen.* **-a** *techn.* toner.

toni *itd. f. zob.* **toń**.

toniczny *a.* **1.** (*dotyczący tonu*) tonal; (*o akcencie, wierszu*) tonic. **2.** *med.* tonic.

tonik *mi* **1.** (*napój*) tonic(water). **2.** (*kosmetyk*) (skin) tonic.

tonika *f. muz.* tonic, keynote.

tonizować *ipf. med.* tone up.

tonokilometr *mi Gen.* **-a** ton-kilometer.

tonować *ipf.* **1.** (= *zmniejszać odcień, intensywność*) tone down. **2.** *sztuka* gradate a color, tone down.

tonsura *f.* tonsure.

tonus *mi* tonus.

toń *f. pl.* **-e** *lit. l. ekol.* open waters; **(otwarta) toń wodna** the pelagic zone.

top¹ *mi* **1.** *techn.* (= *topienie metalu*) smelting. **2.** *techn.* (= *produkt topienia metalu*) alloy.

top² *mi* **1.** *żegl.* top, masthead. **2.** *pot.* (= *szczyt popularności*) top; **być na topie** be on top.

topaz *mi* topaz.

topić *ipf.* **1.** (= *powodować utonięcie*) drown, sink. **2.** *przen.* **topić w czymś pieniądze** sink money into sth; **topić troski (w alkoholu)** drown one's sorrows (in drink). **3.** (= *roztapiać*) melt.

~ się *ipf.* **1.** (= *tonąć*) drown. **2.** (= *grzęznąć*) get stuck (*w czymś* in sth). **3.** (= *roztapiać się*) melt.

topiel *f. pl.* **-e** deep water.

topielec *mp* **-lc-** *pl.* **-y**, **topielica** *f.* **1.** (= *zwłoki osoby utopionej*) drowned body. **2.** (*mit.*) (= *duch topiący ludzi*) water demon; *Scot.* kelpie.

topik *mi Gen.* **-a** *el.* fuse link, fusible element. **– ma** *zool.* water spider (*Argyoneta aquatica*).

topikowy *a. el.* **bezpiecznik topikowy** fuse.

toples, topless *mi* toplessness. **– a. i adv.** *indecl.* topless; **opalać się/występować topless** sunbathe/perform topless.

topliwość *f.* fusibility.

topliwy *a.* fusible, meltable.

topnieć *ipf.* **1.** (= *roztapiać się*) melt; (*o śniegu,*

lodzie, t. przen. o złych uczuciach) thaw. **2.** *przen.* (= *kurczyć się, maleć*) shrink, dwindle (away).

topnienie *n.* melting; **temperatura topnienia** *chem., fiz.* melting point.

topnik *mi Gen.* **-a** *techn., chem.* flux, fluxing agent.

topograf *mp pl.* **-owie** topographer.

topografia *f. Gen.* **-ii** **1.** (*dział geodezji*) topography. **2.** (= *ogół cech terenu*) topographic features.

topograficzny *a.* topographic, topographical.

topola *f. Gen.pl.* **-oli** *l.* **-ól** poplar (*populus*); **topola czarna/biała** black/white poplar (*P. nigra / alba*).

topolog *mp* topologist.

topologia *f. Gen.* **-ii** *mat.* topology.

topologiczny *a. mat.* topological.

topolowy *a.* poplar.

toponimia *f. Gen.* **-ii** *jęz.* toponymy.

toponimiczny *a. jęz.* toponymic, toponymical.

toponomasta *mp* toponymist.

toponomastyczny *a.* = **toponimiczny**.

toponomastyka *f.* = **toponimia**.

toporek *mi* **-rk-** *Gen.* **-a** hatchet, light ax; *Br.* chopper.

topornie *adv.* **1.** (= *z trudem*) hard, awkwardly, with difficulty. **2.** *zob.* **toporny**.

toporny *a.* (= *niekształtny, niezgrabny*) rough, rude, irregular, unwieldy.

topos *mi teor.lit.* topos.

topór *mi* **-o-** *Gen.* **-a** ax; **kłaść głowę pod topór** lay one's head on the block; **iść pod topór** *przen.* get the ax; be axed; **wykopać/zakopać topór wojenny** take up/bury the hatchet.

topsel *mi* **-sl-** *Gen.* **-a** *żegl.* topsail.

tor¹ *mi* **1.** (= *trasa*) path, route, course; (*pocisku*) trajectory; **tor wodny** fairway; **skierować coś/kogoś na nowe tory** give sth/sb a fresh start; **toczyć się swoim torem** take its normal course. **2.** *kol.* (= *szyny*) (railroad) track; **boczny tor** siding (track), sidetrack; **ślepy tor** *t. przen.* blind siding; **odsunąć kogoś/coś na boczny tor** sidetrack sb/sth. **3.** *sport* (*na bieżni, basenie*) lane; (*łyżwiarski*) track; **tor przeszkód** steeplechase track; **tor wyścigowy** racetrack; **tor żużlowy** cinder speedway track.

tor² *mi chem.* thorium.

Tora *f. judaizm* the Torah.

torakochirurgia *f. Gen.* **-ii** *med.* thoracosurgery.

torakochirurgiczny *a. med.* thoracosurgical.

torakoplastyka *f. med.* thoracoplasty.

torakotomia *f. Gen.* **-ii** *med.* thoracotomy.

torba *f. Gen.pl.* **toreb** **1.** bag; (*z paskiem na ramię*) satchel; **torba na zakupy** shopping bag; *Br.* carrier bag; **torba podróżna** traveling bag; **torba szkolna** schoolbag. **2.** *przen.* **pójść z torbami** be reduced to beggary; **puścić kogoś z torbami** make sb a beggar. **3.** *zool.* pouch, marsupium.

torbacz *ma zool.* marsupial.

torbiel *f. pl.* **-e** *med.* cyst.

torcik *mi* small cake.

toreador *mp* toreador.

torebka *f. Gen.pl.* **-ek 1.** (= *małe opakowanie*) bag, pack; *Br.* packet. **2.** (*damska*) purse; *zwł. Br.* handbag. **3.** *bot.* pouch, seed vessel. **4.** *anat.* **torebka stawowa** synovial capsule.

torf *mi* peat.

torfiasty *a.* peaty.

torfowiec *mi* **-wc-** *Gen.* **-a** *bot.* peatmoss (*Sphagnum*).

torfowisko *n.* peat bog.

torfowy *a.* peat, peaty.

torkretować *ipf. bud.* gunite, spray with concrete.

tornado *n. meteor.* tornado.

tornister *mi* **-tr-** *Gen.* **-a** backpack.

torować *ipf.* **torować drogę czemuś** (= *umożliwiać*) enable sth, pave the way for sth; **torować sobie drogę (przez tłum)** fight *l.* elbow one's way (through the crowd).

torowiec *mp* **-wc-** *pl.* **-y** *sport* track-racer.

torowisko *n.* rail line, trackway.

torowy[1] *a.* **1.** (*dotyczący szyn*) track; (*o pracach*) track works. **2.** *sport* track; (*o kolarstwie, wyścigach*) track racing.

torowy[2] *a. chem.* thorium.

torpeda *f.* **1.** (*pocisk*) torpedo; **żywa torpeda** live torpedo. **2.** *pot.* (= *bardzo szybki pojazd*) extremely fast vehicle.

torpedo *n. rower* hub brake.

torpedować *ipf.* **1.** (= *zatapiać torpedą*) torpedo. **2.** (= *utrudniać, utrącać*) torpedo, hamper, hinder.

torpedowiec *mi* **-wc-** *Gen.* **-a** *wojsk.* torpedoboat.

torpedowy *a.* torpedo.

torreador *mp* = **toreador.**

tors *mi* **1.** (= *górna część tułowia*) torso. **2.** (*rzeźba*) trunk.

torsje *pl. Gen.* **-ji** (a fit of) vomiting; (*odruchy wymiotne*) retching.

tort *mi* layer cake.

tortownica *f.* springform (pan), cake-pan.

tortowy *a.* cake.

tortura *f.* **1.** (= *cierpienia fizyczne*) torture; **narzędzia/sala tortur** instruments/chamber of torture; **to czysta tortura** *przen.* it's sheer torture. **2.** *lit.* (= *udręka*) torment, distress.

torturować *ipf.* **1.** (= *katować*) torture, put to torture. **2.** *lit.* (= *dręczyć, męczyć*) torment.

torus *mi Gen.* **-a** *geom.* torus.

torys *mp hist., polit., zw. pl.* Tory.

Toskania *f. Gen.* **-ii** *geogr.* Tuscany.

tost *mi* (piece *l.* slice of) toast.

toster *mi Gen.* **-a** toaster.

totalitarny *a.* totalitarian.

totalitaryzm *mi* totalitarianism.

totalizator *mi Gen.* **-a** (*na wyścigach*) parimutuel, totalizator, sweepstakes; **totalizator piłkarski** *Br.* the pools; **grać w totalizatora piłkarskiego** do the pools; *zob.* **totolotek.**

totalny *a.* **1.** (= *całkowity*) total, entire. **2.** (= *absolutny*) total, absolute.

totek *mi* **-tk-** *Gen.* **-a** *pot.* = **totolotek.**

totem *mi rel.* totem.

totemiczny *a. rel.* totemic.

totemizm *mi rel.* totemism.

toteż *conj. lit.* (and) so, which is why.

toto *pron. tylko 3 os. sing. żart.* the thing, the creature.

totolotek *mi* **-tk-** *Gen.* **-a** *pot. t. przen.* lottery.

totumfacki *mp przest.* factotum.

tournée *n. indecl.* tour.

Tow. *abbr.* (*w nazwach organizacji*) Soc. (= *Society*); Co. (= *Company*); Assoc. (= *Association*).

tow. *abbr. polit.* (*w partii lewicowej*) (= *towarzysz / ka*) comrade.

towar *mi* commodity, merchandise; **handel żywym towarem** *uj.* white-slave traffic, white slavery.

towarowy *a.* **1.** *handl.* (= *dotyczący towaru*) commodity, goods; **giełda towarowa** commodity exchange; **rynek towarowy** commodity market; **dom towarowy** department store; **wymiana towarowa** barter; **znak towarowy** trademark. **2.** *handl.* (= *dotyczący przewożenia towarów*) freight; **winda towarowa** freight elevator; **pociąg towarowy** freight train; *Br.* goods train. **3.** *sl.* (= *obiekt handlu l. zainteresowania*) it; the stuff.

towaroznawca *mp* commodity scientist.

towaroznawczy *a.* pertaining to commodity science.

towaroznawstwo *n.* commodity science.

towarzyski *a.* **1.** (= *nielubiący samotności*) sociable. **2.** (*dotyczący kontaktów między znajomymi*) social; **agencja towarzyska** escort agency; **gra towarzyska** parlor game; **mecz towarzyski** *sport* friendly match, friendly; **taniec towarzyski** social dance. **3.** (*należący do towarzystwa*) society; **śmietanka towarzyska** the cream of society; **kronika towarzyska** *dzienn.* gossip column *l.* section.

towarzysko *adv.* socially; **udzielać się towarzysko** socialize, go out.

towarzyskość *f.* sociability.

towarzystwo *n.* **1.** (= *towarzyszenie*) company, companionship; **być w czyimś towarzystwie** be in the company of sb, be in sb's company; **dotrzymywać komuś towarzystwa** keep sb company; **robić coś dla towarzystwa** do sth for the sake of company. **2.** (= *grono znajomych*) company, crowd; **dama do towarzystwa** companion; **towarzystwo wzajemnej adoracji** mutual admiration society; **wpaść w złe towarzystwo** fall in with a bad company. **3.** (= *organizacja*) society, company; **towarzystwo akcyjne** joint-stock company; **towarzystwo ubezpieczeniowe** insurance company; **towarzystwo naukowe** learned society. **4.** (= *elita*) society, elite, the world; **dobre towarzystwo** polite society.

towarzysz *mp* **1.** (= *osoba towarzysząca*) companion; **towarzysz broni** companion *l.* brother in arms; **towarzysz niedoli** companion of distress; **towarzysz podróży** traveling companion; **towarzysz życia** life companion. **2.** (= *członek partii lewicowej, gł. komunistycznej lub socjalistycznej*) comrade; **towarzysz Kowalski** comrade Kowalski.

towarzyszący *a.* accompanying, concurrent;

osoba towarzysząca escort; imprezy towarzyszące accompanying events.

towarzyszenie *n.* **z towarzyszeniem orkiestry/chóru** with the accompaniment of an orchestra/a choir.

towarzyszka *f. Gen.pl.* **-ek** *zob.* **towarzysz.**

towarzyszyć *ipf.* + *Dat.* **1.** (= *asystować*) attend upon, escort (*sb*). **2.** (= *występować jednocześnie z*) accompany (*sb l. sth*); **deszczom towarzyszyły wichury** the winds were accompanied by gales.

towot *mi techn.* cup grease.

toż *int.* **toż to** (**przecież**)...! why, it's...!

tożsamość *f.* identity; **dowód tożsamości** ID (card).

tożsamy *a.* identical (*z kimś/czymś* with sb/sth).

tóg *f. zob.* **toga.**

TPD *abbr.* (= *Towarzystwo Przyjaciół Dzieci*) Society of the Friends of Children.

TPN *abbr.* **1.** (= *Towarzystwo Przyjaciół Nauk*) Society of the Friends of Sciences. **2.** (= *Tatrzański Park Narodowy*) the Tatra National Park.

trabant *mp hist., wojsk.* lifeguard, trabant.

trach *int.* crash, bang.

tracheoskopia *f. Gen.* **-ii** *med.* tracheoscopy.

tracheotomia *f. Gen.* **-ii** *med.* tracheotomy.

tracić *ipf.* **1.** (= *przestawać mieć*) lose; **tracić głowę** *przen.* lose one's head; **tracić grunt pod nogami** lose one's footing, be out of one's depth; **tracić kogoś z oczu** lose sight of sb; **tracić nadzieję** abandon hope; **tracić miarę** know no measure in sth; **tracić pamięć/zdrowie/rozum** lose one's memory/health/mind; **tracić panowanie nad sobą** lose one's temper; **tracić przytomność** lose consciousness; **tracić wątek** lose one's thread; **tracić zainteresowanie** lose interest (*kimś/czymś* in sb/sth). **2.** (= *ponosić stratę*) lose out (*na czymś* on sth); **tracić bramkę** lose a goal; **tracić punkt** lose a point. **3.** (= *trwonić*) waste; **tracić czas** waste time; (*okazję, szansę*) miss. **4.** (*życie, bliską osobę*) lose. **5.** (= *doznawać uszczerbku*) **tracić na wadze/wartości/znaczeniu** lose weight/value/significance; **tracić w czyichś oczach** go down in sb's esteem *l.* opinion. **6.** *lit.* (= *zabijać*) execute; **zostać straconym** be executed.

Tracja *f. geogr.* Thrace.

tracz *mp pl.* **-e** sawyer. – *ma orn.* merganser, sawbill (*Mergus*); **tracz nurogęś** goosander (*M. merganser*).

tradycja *f.* tradition.

tradycjonalista *mp*, **tradycjonalistka** *f. Gen.pl.* **-ek** traditionalist.

tradycjonalistyczny *a.* traditionalistic.

tradycjonalizm *mi* traditionalism.

tradycyjnie *adv.* traditionally; *pot.* (= *jak zwykle*) as usual.

tradycyjny *a.* traditional.

traf *mi* chance; **ślepy traf** pure chance; **dziwnym trafem** oddly enough; **szczęśliwym trafem** by a stroke of luck, by a lucky chance; **traf chciał, że...** as luck would have it,...

trafiać *ipf.* **1.** (= *nie chybiać*) hit the target, hit one's mark; **trafić w dziesiątkę** hit the/a bull's-eye; **trafiać w sedno** hit the right spot, hit the nail on the head, hit home; **na chybił trafił** at random, hit-or-miss; **szlag mnie trafia!** *pot.* I'm furious, I'm livid with rage, I get pissed off. **2.** (= *znajdować drogę*) find one's way; **trafiać komuś do przekonania** bring sth home to sb; **trafiać na ślad czegoś** find the trace of sth; **trafiać w próżnię** miss one's aim. **3.** (= *dostawać się, docierać*) land (*do kogoś, czegoś* in sb/sth); **dobrze, źle trafić** fall on the right/wrong person; **trafić z deszczu pod rynnę** jump out of the frying pan into the fire. **4.** (= *natykać się*) run (*na kogoś, coś* into sb/sth). **~ się** *ipf.* **1.** *pot.* (= *przydarzać się*) happen. **2.** (= *występować gdzieniegdzie*) come up.

trafić (się) *pf.* = **trafiać (się).**

trafienie *n.* **1.** (= *celny strzał, uderzenie*) hit. **2.** (= *trafnie wytypowana liczba w totalizatorze*) lucky number.

trafika *f.* tobacconist, tobacco shop.

trafiony *a.* (= *trafny*) right; (*o zakupie, decyzji, inwestycji*) good.

trafnie *adv.* **1.** (= *poprawnie, dokładnie*) correctly, accurately. **2.** (= *stosownie*) aptly, pertinently. **3.** *przest.* (= *nie chybiając*) right on the mark.

trafny *a.* **1.** (= *poprawny, dokładny*) correct, accurate. **2.** (= *stosowny, celny*) apt, pertinent.

tragarz *mp* porter.

tragedia *f. Gen.* **-ii 1.** (*utwór dramatyczny*) tragedy. **2.** (= *nieszczęście*) tragedy, misfortune; **robić z czegoś tragedię** *pot.* dramatize sth.

tragediopisarz *mp* tragedian, tragic dramatist.

tragi *pl. Gen.* **-ów** handbarrow.

tragicznie *adv.* **1.** (= *dramatycznie*) tragically. **2.** *pot.* (= *źle, fatalnie*) terribly, awfully; **wyglądać tragicznie** look awful.

tragiczność *f.* tragicality.

tragiczny *a.* **1.** (*związany z tragedią teatralną*) tragic; **aktor tragiczny** tragic actor. **2.** (= *nieszczęśliwy, wstrząsający*) tragic, dismal, shocking, appalling; **tragiczna strata/pomyłka** tragic loss/mistake. **3.** *pot.* (= *bardzo zły, fatalny*) terrible, fatal, awful.

tragifarsa *f.* tragicomedy.

tragik *mp* (*autor tragedii l. aktor*) tragedian.

tragikomedia *f. Gen.* **-ii** tragicomedy.

tragikomiczny *a.* tragicomic.

tragizm *mi* tragicalness, tragedy.

tragizować *ipf.* take a tragic view of things.

trajektoria *f. Gen.* **-ii** trajectory.

trajkot *mi* **1.** (= *terkot*) chatter, rattle. **2.** *pot.* (= *paplanina*) jabber, gabble, chatter.

trajkotać *ipf.* **-oczę -oczesz** *l.* **-ocę -ocesz** *l.* **-otam -otasz, -ocz** *l.* **-otaj 1.** (= *terkotać*) chatter, rattle. **2.** *pot.* (= *paplać*) jabber, gabble, rattle.

trajlować *ipf. pot.* (= *blagować*) natter.

trak *mi Gen.* **-a** *techn.* saw gate.

trakcja *f.* traction.

trakcyjny *a.* traction; **słup trakcyjny** pylon; **sieć**

trakcyjna trolley wires; **silnik trakcyjny** traction engine.

trakt *mi* **1.** (= *droga, szlak*) track. **2.** *bud.* road. **3. w trakcie (robienia) czegoś** in the middle *l.* in the process of (doing) sth.

traktat *mi* **1.** *polit.* (= *umowa*) treaty. **2.** *nauk.* (= *rozprawa*) treatise.

traktatowy *a.* treaty.

traktor *mi Gen.* **-a** tractor.

traktorowy *a.* tractor.

traktory *pl. Gen.* **-ów** *pot.* (= *ciężkie buty*) hiking boots.

traktorzysta *mp* tractor driver.

traktować *ipf.* **1.** (= *obchodzić się*) treat, handle; (= *odnosić się*) treat, take; **traktować coś lekko** take sth lightly; **traktować kogoś jak psa** treat sb like a dog; **traktować kogoś/coś poważnie** take sb/sth seriously; **traktować kogoś jak powietrze** ignore sb; cut sb dead; **traktować kogoś z góry** patronize sb, treat sb condescendingly; look down on sb. **2.** *lit.* (= *omawiać*) treat (*o czymś* of sth). **3.** *chem.* treat (*sth*) (*czymś* with sth).

traktowanie *n.* treatment.

tralka *f. Gen.pl.* **-ek** *bud.* banister, baluster.

trał *mi żegl., wojsk.* trawl.

trałować *ipf.* **1.** (= *łowić trałem*) trawl. **2.** *wojsk.* minesweep, sweep for mines.

trałowiec *mi* **-wc-** *Gen.* **-a** *wojsk.* minesweeper.

tram *mi* **1.** *bud.* footing beam. **2.** *sport* beam.

tramp *mp pl.* **-owie** *l.* **-y** (= *włóczęga*) tramp, vagrant, hobo, bum. – *mi Gen.* **-a** *pl.* **-y** *żegl.* tramp.

trampek *mi* **-pk-** *Gen.* **-a** sneaker.

tramping *mi żegl., turystyka* tramping.

trampingowy *a. żegl., turystyka* tramping.

trampolina *f. sport* **1.** (= *deska do skoków do wody*) springboard, diving board. **2.** (= *deska do skoków gimnastycznych*) springboard, trampoline.

tramwaj *mi* **-ów** streetcar; *Br.* tram.

tramwajarz *mp* streetcar driver.

tramwajowy *a.* streetcar.

tran *mi* cod-liver oil.

trans *mi* (= *sen hipnotyczny*) trance; *przen.* (= *uniesienie, zapał*) trance, ecstasy; **wpadać w trans** go into a trance.

transakcja *f.* transaction; **transakcja wiązana** tie-in transaction; **dokonywać transakcji** make *l.* strike a deal.

transalpejski *a.* transalpine.

transarktyczny *a.* transarctic.

transatlantycki *a.* transatlantic.

transatlantyk *mi Gen.* **-a** (*statek*) transatlantic liner.

transcendencja *f. fil.* transcendence, transcendency.

transcendentalizm *mi fil.* transcendentalism.

transcendentalność *f. fil.* transcendentality.

transcendentalny *a. fil.* transcendental.

transcendentny *a. fil.* transcendent.

transept *mi bud.* transept.

transeuropejski *a.* trans-European.

transfer *mi* transfer.

transferowy *a.* **1.** *ekon.* transfer, transferable. **2.** *sport* transfer.

transfiguracja *f. lit.* transfiguration.

transfokator *mi Gen.* **-a** *fot.* transfocator.

transformacja *f.* transformation.

transformacyjny *a. jęz.* transformational.

transformator *mi Gen.* **-a** *el.* transformer, convertor.

transformatornia *f. Gen.pl.* **-i** *el.* transformer station.

transformatorowy *a. el.* transformer; **stacja transformatorowa** transformer station.

transfuzja *f. med.* (blood) transfusion.

transgresja *f. geol., biol.* transgression.

transkontynentalny *a.* transcontinental.

transkrybować *ipf.* transcribe.

transkrypcja *f.* transcription.

translacja *f.* translation.

translator *mp pl.* **-rzy** *lit.* (= *tłumacz*) translator. – *mi Gen.* **-a** *pl.* **-ry** *komp.* translator.

transliteracja *f.* transliteration.

transliteracyjny *a.* transliteration.

transliterować *ipf.* transliterate.

translokacja *f. lit.* translocation.

translokować *ipf. lit.* translocate.

transmisja *f.* **1.** *tel.* (= *przesyłanie na odległość*) transmission, broadcasting; **transmisja radiowa/telewizyjna** radio/TV broadcast; **transmisja bezpośrednia** *l.* **na żywo** live broadcast. **2.** *techn.* (= *pędnia*) overhead transmission.

transmisyjny *a.* **1.** *tel.* (= *dotyczący przesyłania*) broadcasting, transmitting; **wóz transmisyjny** mobile unit, outside broadcast van. **2.** *techn.* (= *napędowy*) driving; **pas transmisyjny** transmission belt.

transmitować *ipf.* transmit; (*mecz, sygnał*) broadcast (live); (*sygnał*) transmit.

transmutacja *f.* transmutation.

transoceaniczny *a.* transoceanic.

transparent *mi* banner.

transpiracja *f. bot.* transpiration.

transpirować *ipf. bot.* transpire.

transplantacja *f.* transplant, transplantation.

transplantacyjny *a. med.* transplantable.

transplantolog *mp pl.* **-dzy** *l.* **-owie** transplantologist.

transplantologia *f. Gen.* **-ii** *med.* transplantology.

transplantologiczny *a. med.* transplantological.

transplantować *ipf. med.* transplant.

transponować *ipf.* **1.** *lit.* (= *przystosowywać*) transpose. **2.** *muz.* transpose.

transport *mi* **1.** (= *przewóz*) transport, transportation; **transport bliski** materials handling; **transport dalekobieżny** long distance transport; **transport kołowy** road transport; **transport materiałów sypkich** mass transport; **transport rurociągowy** piping. **2.** (= *ładunek*) cargo, shipment.

transporter *mi Gen.* **-a** **1.** *techn.* conveyor. **2.** *wojsk.* armored personnel carrier.

transportować *ipf.* **1.** (= *przewozić*) transport, convey. **2.** (= *konwojować*) convoy, escort; (*więźniów*) convoy.

transportowiec *mp* **-wc-** *pl.* **-y** (*pracownik*)

transportation worker. – *mi* -**wc**- *Gen*. -**a** *pl*. -**e**
1. (*samolot*) cargo plane. **2.** (*statek*) freighter.

transportowy *a*. shipping.

transpozycja *f*. **1.** (= *przystosowanie*) transposition, rearrangement. **2.** *muz*. transposition.

transseksualista *mp* transsexual.

transseksualizm *mi* transsexualism.

transsyberyjski *a*. trans-Siberian.

transuranowiec *mi* -**wc**- *Gen*. -**a** *chem*. transuranium element.

transwestyta *mp* transvestite.

transwestytyzm *mi* transvestism.

transza *f*. *ekon*. tranche; **transza kredytu** tranche of a loan; **transza złota** gold tranche.

transzeja *f*. *Gen*. -**ei** *wojsk*. trench.

tranzystor *mi Gen*. -**a 1.** *el*. transistor. **2.** *pot*. (= *radio tranzystorowe*) transistor radio.

tranzystorowy *a*. *el*. transistor.

tranzyt *mi* transit; **przejazd, przewóz tranzytem** through a country.

tranzytowy *a*. transit.

tranzytywny *a*. *jęz*. transitive.

trap *mi* **1.** *żegl*. gangplank, gangway. **2.** *sport* trap.

traper *mp* trapper.

traperski *a*. trapper.

trapez *mi* **1.** *mat*. trapezoid. **2.** *sport* trapeze.

trapezoedr *mi krystalografia* trapezohedron.

trapezoid *mi mat*. trapezium.

trapić *ipf*. **1.** (= *niepokoić*) worry, bother; **co cię trapi?** what's bothering you?; what's eating you? **2.** *lit*. (= *nawiedzać, dotykać*) trouble, affect. ~ **się** *ipf*. *lit*. worry, fret.

trapista *mp rel*. Trappist.

trasa *f*. **1.** (= *szlak*) route, trail; *pot*. (= *droga, podróż*) the road; **być w trasie** be on the road. **2.** (= *droga do przebycia*) distance. **3.** (= *linia w terenie*) line, route; **wytyczać trasę** mark out the route.

trasant *mp handl*. payer (drawer).

trasat *mp handl*. drawee.

traseologia *f*. *Gen*. -**ii** *prawn*. traceology.

traser *mp* **1.** *techn*. tracer. **2.** *żegl*. mock-up maker.

trasować *ipf*. **1.** (= *wytyczać linię*) draw line, mark out. **2.** *techn*. (= *nanosić linie na elementy do obróbki*) lay out, loft. **3.** *handl*. make a draft.

trasowy *a*. route.

traszka *f*. *Gen.pl*. -**ek** *zool*. newt.

trata *f*. *handl*. draft.

tratować *ipf*. trample, tread down. ~ **się** *ipf*. trample (one another).

tratwa *f*. *Gen.pl*. -**tw** *l*. -**tew** raft, float; **tratwa ratunkowa** life raft.

trauma *f*. *med*. trauma.

traumatolog *mp pl*. -**dzy** *l*. -**owie** *med*. traumatologist.

traumatologia *f*. *Gen*. -**ii** *med*. traumatology.

traumatologiczny *a*. *med*. traumatic.

traumatyczny *a*. traumatic.

trawa *f*. grass; **mowa-trawa** *pot*. phony-baloney, gobbledygook; **hokej na trawie** *sport* field hockey; **wiedzieć, co w trawie piszczy** know which way the wind is blowing.

trawers *mi* **1.** (*rodzaj grobli*) dam. **2.** *bud*. cross-beam. **3.** *żegl*., *lotn*. traverse. **4.** *sport* traverse.

trawersować *ipf*. **1.** *żegl*., *lotn*. traverse. **2.** *sport* traverse.

trawestacja *f*. *teor.lit*. travesty.

trawestować *ipf*. travesty.

trawiasty *a*. **1.** (= *pokryty trawą*) grassy, covered with grass; **kort trawiasty** *sport* lawn/grass court. **2.** (= *koloru trawy*) grass-green.

trawić *ipf*. **1.** (= *przyswajać pokarm*) digest; **nie trawić kogoś/czegoś** *przen*. have no liking for sb/sth; not care for sb/sth. **2.** *lit*. (= *niszczyć*) consume, waste, wear away; (*o chorobie, pożarze*) consume; (*o niepokoju, nienawiści*) consume, devour. **3.** *chem*. corrode, eat into (*sth*). **4.** *techn*. sztuka (= *wytrawiać*) etch. **5.** (= *marnować*) waste.

trawienie *n*. **1.** *fizj*. digestion. **2.** *techn*. etching.

trawieniec *mi* -**ńc**- *Gen*. -**a** *zool*., *anat*. abomasum.

trawienny *a*. *fizj*., *anat*. digestive; **soki trawienne** digestive juices; **układ/przewód trawienny** digestive system/tract.

trawka *f*. *Gen.pl*. -**ek 1.** *emf*. (= *trawa*) grass; **posłać kogoś na zieloną trawkę** fire sb; *gł*. *Br*. sack sb; give sb the sack. **2.** *sl*. (= *marihuana*) pot, grass.

trawler *mi Gen*. -**a** *żegl*. trawler.

trawnik *mi Gen*. -**a** lawn, the green, the grass; **nie deptać trawników** (*ostrzeżenie w miejscu publicznym*) keep off the grass.

trawożerny *a*. *zool*. herbivorous, grass-eating.

trąba *f*. **1.** *muz*. horn. **2.** *meteor*. whirlwind, cyclone; **trąba powietrzna** whirlwind, twister. **3.** *zool*., *anat*. proboscis; (*słonia*) trunk. **4.** *pot*. (= *fajtłapa, naiwniak*) dupe, sucker; **zrobić** *l*. **puścić kogoś w trąbę** dupe sb.

trąbić *ipf*. **1.** (= *grać na instrumencie dętym*) blow (*sth*). **2.** (= *wydawać odgłos podobny do trąbki*) trumpet, blow, blare (out). **3.** (= *naciskać klakson*) honk *l*. sound the horn, hoot, toot. **4.** *pot*. **trąbić o czymś** (= *rozgłaszać*) spread the news of sth; *pot*. (= *mówić głośno*) roar, bellow, blare. **5.** *pot*. (= *czyścić nos głośno*) blow one's nose. **6.** *pot*. (= *pić dużo, zwł. alkoholu*) guzzle, soak, booze.

trąbka *f*. *Gen.pl*. -**ek 1.** *muz*. trumpet. **2.** (*coś w kształcie trąbki*) twist, cornet; **zwinąć coś w trąbkę** twist into a cone, roll sth up. **3.** *ent*., *anat*. proboscis. **4.** **trąbka Eustachiusza** *anat*. Eustachian tube.

trąbowiec *ma* -**wc**- *zool*. (= *ssak z rzędu Proboscidea*) proboscidean (*proboscidian*).

trącać *ipf*. (= *lekko uderzać*) nudge, jostle, tip; (= *potrącać w tłumie*) brush against *l*. past *l*. by (*sb l. sth*). ~ **się** *ipf*. **1.** (= *uderzać się lekko*) tip one another, jostle one another. **2.** *pot*. (= *stukać kieliszkiem o kieliszek*) clink *l*. chink one's glasses.

trącić¹ *pf*. *zob*. **trącać**.

trącić² *ipf*. **1.** (= *zalatywać*) smack of sth, reek of sth; (*stęchlizną, pleśnią*) be fusty, reek of mustiness/mold; **trącić myszką** be out of date, be going gray. **2.** (= *odznaczać się czymś*) savor of, border on.

trąd *mi pat.* leprosy.

trądzik *mi pat.* acne.

trefić *ipf. przest.* curl (one's hair).

trefl *mi Gen.* **-a** *karty* clubs; **dama/piątka trefl** queen/five of clubs.

treflowy *a. karty* of clubs.

trefniś *mp Gen.pl.* **-ów** *hist. l. przen.* jester, fool.

trefny *a.* **1.** *pot.* (= *podejrzany, nielegalny*) hot. **2.** *rel.* (= *niekoszerny*) not kosher, tref, ritually impure.

trel *mi Gen.pl.* **-i** *l.* **-ów** trill.

trele-morele *pl. Gen.* **treli-moreli** *pot.* tittle-tattle, fiddle-faddle.

trema *f.* stage fright, performance anxiety.

tremo *n. przest.* (*lustro*) pier glass.

tremolo *n. muz.* tremolo.

tremolować *ipf. muz.* (play) tremolo.

tremować *ipf.* fill (*sb*) with stage fright. **~ się** *ipf.* have stage fright.

tren[1] *mi teor.lit.* threnody.

tren[2] *mi* (= *ogon sukni*) train.

trencz *mi Gen.* **-a** *Gen.pl.* **-y** *l.* **-ów** trench coat.

trend *mi lit.* trend.

trener *mp sport* coach, trainer.

trenerski *a.* coach's, trainer's.

trening *mi* training, instruction.

treningowy *a.* training.

trenować *ipf.* **1.** (= *przygotowywać zawodników*) train, coach. **2.** (= *poddawać się treningowi*) practise; (*umiejętność*) practise, hone.

trep *mi Gen.* **-a** (= *chodak*) clog. – *mp pl.* **-y** **1.** *pog.* (= *żołnierz zawodowy*) jarhead. **2.** *obelż.* (= *osoba ograniczona*) half-witted, imbecile.

trepak *mi Gen.* **-a** *muz.* trepak (*Russian dance*).

trepan *mi med.* trepan; (*nowoczesna forma*) trephine.

trepanacja *f. med.* trepanation, trephination, trepan.

trepanować *ipf. med.* trephine, trepan.

treser *mp*, **treserka** *f. Gen.pl.* **-ek** trainer.

treserski *a.* trainer's.

treska *f. Gen.pl.* **-ek** hairpiece, female wig.

tresować *ipf.* train, tame; (= *uczyć dyscypliny*) break (*sb l. sth*) in.

tresowany *a.* trained.

tresura *f.* training, taming.

treściowy *a.* material.

treściwie *adv.* concisely, succinctly.

treściwy *a.* **1.** (= *pełen treści*) pithy, full of substance. **2.** (= *pożywny*) filling.

treść *f.* **1.** (= *fabuła, wątek*) plot; (*przemówienia, rozmowy*) content of the speech/conversation (talk); **spis treści** (table of) contents. **2.** (= *istota, sens*) essence, substance; **nabierać nowej treści** take on a new meaning. **3.** *biol.* matter.

trezor *mi Gen.* **-a** night safe.

trę *itd. ipf. zob.* **trzeć**.

trębacz *mp* trumpeter.

trędowaty *a.* leprous. – *mp* leper.

trędownik *mi Gen.* **-a** *bot.* figwort, scrophularia (*Scrophularia*).

triada *f.* triad.

triangel *mi* **-gl-** *Gen.* **-a** *muz.* triangle.

triangulacja *f. miern.* triangulation.

triangulacyjny *a. miern.* triangulating.

trias *mi geol.* the Triassic (period).

triasowy *a. geol., paleont.* Triassic.

triatlon *mi sport* triathlon.

triatlonista *mp*, **triatlonistka** *f. Gen.pl.* **-ek** *sport* triathlonist.

triennale *n. indecl.* triennial.

trik *mi* trick; **trik magiczny** conjuring trick; **posłużyć się trikami** resort to tricks.

trikowy *a.* trick.

trio *n. muz.* (*zespół, utwór*) trio.

trioda *f. el.* triode.

triumf *mi* **1.** (= *zwycięstwo, sukces*) triumph, success; **święcić triumfy** triumph, achieve triumphs. **2.** (= *duma, zadowolenie*) exultation, jubilation; **okrzyki triumfu** triumphant cheer; **spoglądać z triumfem** look with exultation *l.* triumphantly.

triumfalnie *adv.* triumphally, triumphantly.

triumfalny *a.* **1.** (= *uroczysty, wyrażający triumf*) triumphal, solemn; **marsz/pochód triumfalny** triumphal march/procession; **łuk triumfalny** triumphal arch. **2.** (= *zwycięski*) triumphant, victorious. **3.** (= *radosny, dumny*) triumphant, exultant, jubilant.

triumfator *mp lit.* (= *zwycięzca*) triumpher.

triumfować *ipf.* **1.** *lit.* (= *zwyciężać*) triumph, prevail (*nad kimś / czymś* over sb/sth). **2.** (= *cieszyć się*) exult, jubilate.

triumfujący *a.* triumphant.

triumwir *mp hist.* triumvir.

triumwirat *mi hist.* triumvirate.

trochaiczny, trocheiczny *a. teor.lit.* trochaic.

trochej *mi Gen.* **-a** *l.* **-u** *Gen.pl.* **-ei** *l.* **-ów** *teor.lit.* trochee.

trochę *adv.* **1.** (= *niewiele*) a little, a bit (*czegoś* of sth); **po trochu** little by little, bit by bit; **po trosze** *lit.* just a little; **w tym jest trochę racji** there is some truth in it. **2.** (= *w pewnym stopniu*) somewhat, a little; **ani trochę** not a bit. **3.** (= *przez krótką chwilę*) for a while, for a moment; **przyjdź trochę później** come a bit later.

trociczka *f. Gen.pl.* **-ek** pastille.

trocinobeton *mi bud.* sawdust concrete.

trociny *pl. Gen.* **-n** sawdust; **wypchaj się trocinami** *pot.* get stuffed.

trockista *mp polit.* Trotskyite.

trockizm *mi polit.* Trotskyism.

troczek *mi* **-czk-** *Gen.* **-a** strap.

troć *f. pl.* **-cie** *icht.* bulltrout (*Salmo trutta*).

trofeum *n. sing. indecl. pl.* **-ea** *Gen.* **-eów** trophy; **trofea myśliwskie** hunting trophies; **trofea sportowe** sports trophies; **trofea wojenne** the spoils of war.

troglodyta *mp t. przen.* cavedweller, caveman, troglodyte.

troić się *ipf.* **troję troisz, trój** triple; **troi mi się w**

oczach I see double; **dwoić się i troić** go out of one's way.

Troja f. Gen. -oi hist. Troy.

trojaczki pl. Gen. -ów (dzieci) triplets.

trojak mi Gen. i Acc. -a muz. trojak (Silesian dance).

trojaki a. threefold, of three kinds. – pl. Gen. -ów przest. (= potrójny garnek) stacked canteen, dinner-pail.

Trojanin mp pl. -anie Gen. -an, **Trojanka** f. Gen.pl. -ek hist. Trojan.

trojański a. hist., mit. Trojan; **Helena trojańska** Helen of Troy; **koń trojański** t. przen. Trojan horse.

troje num. decl. like n. -jg- three.

trojeść f. bot. milkweed (Asclepias).

trojka f. Gen.pl. -ek troika.

trok mi strap.

trokar mi med. trocar.

trolejbus mi trolley bus.

trolejbusowy a. trolley-bus.

troll mp troll.

trombina f. biol. thrombin.

trombita f. muz. alpenhorn, alphorn.

trombocyt mi biol. thrombocyte.

tron mi 1. (ozdobny fotel) throne. 2. (= władza monarsza) (the) throne; **następca tronu** heir (to the throne); **objąć tron** come to/ascend/ suceed to the throne; **zrzec się tronu** abdicate, give up the throne; **zrzucić z tronu** dethrone, depose.

tronowy a. throne; (o sali) throne room/hall; **mowa tronowa** speech from the throne, Queen's speech.

trop[1] mi (= ślad) track, trail; **być na tropie** be on the track (czymś, czegoś of sth/sb); **iść tropem, w trop za kimś** follow the track of sb; **być na właściwym/fałszywym tropie** be on the right/ wrong track; **iść jakimś tropem** follow the scent; **naprowadzać na trop** set on the trail (czyjś, czegoś of sb/sth); **świeży trop** hot scent; **zbić kogoś z tropu** throw sb off (their) balance, throw sb off the scent; **zgubić trop** be off the scent; **zmylić trop komuś** throw sb off the trail.

trop[2] mi 1. teor.lit. trope. 2. muz. trope.

tropiciel mp 1. (= myśliwy) hunter. 2. (= ktoś zajmujący się ściganiem) investigator. 3. (= badacz, poszukiwacz) explorer, researcher. – ma (= pies myśliwski) sleuth (hound).

tropić ipf. 1. (= ścigać zwierzynę) hunt, trail, track. 2. (= śledzić) follow, track; **tropić przestępców** hunt down criminals. 3. (= szukać uporczywie) search for (sb l. sth).

tropik mi 1. (obszar klimatyczny) the tropics. 2. (tkanina) tropical. 3. (= nakrycie namiotu) flysheet.

tropikalny a. 1. tropical. 2. **hełm tropikalny** pith helmet.

tropikowy a. tropical, equatorial.

tropizm mi biol. tropism.

troposfera f. meteor. troposphere.

tropowiec ma -wc- (pies) bloodhound, sleuthhound.

troska f. Gen.pl. -sk 1. (= zgryzota) worry,

care; **przyczyniać komuś trosk** make sb worry, cause sb worry. 2. (= opieka) concern (o kogoś/ coś for sb/with sth).

troskać się ipf. przest. care (o kogoś/coś for sb/ sth).

troskliwie adv. with care.

troskliwość f. care, consideration, thoughtfulness.

troskliwy a. 1. (= okazujący troskę) caring. 2. (= pieczołowity) careful, mindful, thoughtful.

troszczyć się ipf. 1. (= opiekować się) take care (o kogoś/coś of sb/sth). 2. (= martwić się) care (o kogoś / coś about sb/sth).

troszeczkę adv. = **trochę**.

troszkę adv. = **trochę**.

trotuar mi przest. sidewalk, pavement, trottoir.

trotyl mi chem., wojsk. trotyl, TNT.

trójbarwny a. three-colored, tricolor.

trójboista mp, **trójboistka** f. Gen.pl. -ek sport triathlonist.

trójbój mi -o- Gen.pl. -ów sport triathlon.

trójca f. 1. rel. Trinity; **Trójca Święta** rz.-kat. Holy Trinity. 2. lit. (= trzy osoby) trio, threesome.

trójdzielny a. triple, treble, threefold, tripartite; (o rytmie) triple; (o oknie) Venetian; (o nerwie) trifacial.

trójdźwięk mi muz. triad.

trójfazowy a. el. (o prądzie) three-phase.

trójgłowy a. tricephalic, tricephalous; (o smoku) three-headed; **mięsień trójgłowy** anat. triceps.

trójgraniasty a. triangular, three-cornered, three-sided.

trójka f. 1. (liczba) three. 2. pot. (= wejście, autobus, karta itp. oznaczone numerem trzecim) (the) number three; **wrzucić trójkę** mot. put the car in the third gears. 3. szkoln. C. 4. (to, co składa się z trzech jednostek) trio, threesome; **trójkami** in threes; **w trójkę** the three of us.

trójkąt mi Gen. -a 1. (kształt, figura) triangle; **trójkąt kreślarski** set square; **trójkąt równoboczny/równoramienny** geom. equilateral/isosceles; **trójkąt prostokątny/ostrokątny/rozwartokątny** geom. right/acute/obtuse(-angled) triangle; **trójkąt odblaskowy** l. **ostrzegawczy** mot. red warning triangle. 2. (= związek trzech osób) triangle, trio; **trójkąt miłosny** the eternal triangle. 3. muz. triangle.

trójkątny a. triangular.

trójkolorowy a. three-colored, trichromatic.

trójkołowy a. three-wheeled.

trójkombinacja f. sport alpine combined.

trójlistkowy a. bot. trifoliate.

trójmasztowiec mi -wc- Gen. -a three-master.

trójmasztowy a. three-mast.

trójmian mi mat. trinomial.

trójmiasto n. tricity.

trójniak mi Gen. -a l. -u quality mead.

trójnik mi Gen. -a techn. (three-way) adapter, tee.

trójnożny a. three-footed.

trójnóg *mi* -o- *Gen.* -a *l.* -u **1.** (*trójnożny mebel*) three-footed furniture. **2.** (= *statyw*) tripod.

trójpalczasty *a.* tridactyl.

trójpłatowiec *mi* -wc- *Gen.* -a *lotn.* triplane.

trójpolowy *a. roln.* three-field.

trójpolówka *f. Gen.pl.* -ek *roln.* three-field system, three-course system.

trójskoczek *mp* -czk- *pl.* -owie *sport* triple jumper.

trójskok *mi sport* triple jump.

trójstronny *a.* **1.** (= *mający trzy boki*) three-sided. **2.** (= *zawierany przez trzy strony*) tripartite, trilateral.

trójszereg *mi* three abreast.

trójścian *mi mat.* trihedron.

trójtlenek *mi* -nk- *chem.* trioxide.

trójwiersz *mi Gen.* -a triplet.

trójwymiarowy *a.* three-dimensional.

trójząb *mi* -ę- trident.

trójzębny *a.* tridentate.

trójzmianowy *a.* three-shift.

trubadur *mp hist.* troubadour.

truchleć *ipf. lit.* be terrified.

truchło *n. Gen.pl.* -cheł *przest.* corpse.

trucht *mi* trot, jog trot; **truchtem** trot.

truchtać *ipf.* trot.

truciciel *mp* poisoner.

trucicielski *a.* poisoning, poisoner's.

trucizna *f.* poison.

truć *ipf.* **1.** (= *niszczyć, zabijać trucizną*) poison, give poison to. **2.** *pot.* (= *podawać nieświeże jedzenie*) serve unfresh food. **3.** *pot.* (= *dręczyć, trapić*) worry, torment. **4.** *pot.* (= *ględzić*) gab, talk idly, babble, rattle. ~ **się** *ipf.* **1.** (= *zażywać truciznę*) take poison. **2.** *pot.* (= *dręczyć się, zamartwiać się*) worry oneself to death.

trud *mi* **1.** (= *wysiłek*) effort, trouble, pains; **bez trudu** with no difficulty *l.* trouble; **z trudem** with difficulty *l.* trouble; **zadać sobie wiele trudu** spare no pains; **zadać sobie trud zrobienia czegoś** take pains to do sth. **2.** (= *niedogodność*) inconvenience, hardship.

trudnić się *ipf.* -ij *lit.* do sth for a living.

trudno *adv.* (= *z trudnością*) with difficulty; (= *niełatwo*) hard; **trudno i darmo** *pot.* there is no getting out of it; **trudno o dobrego fachowca** a good specialist/expert/repairman is hard to find; **trudno (mi) powiedzieć** it's hard to tell; **jest nam trudno** we are up against difficulties, we are in difficulties; **(mówi się) trudno** tough luck.

trudność *f.* **1.** (= *utrudnienie, przeciwności*) difficulty, hardship; **z trudnością** with difficulty; **robić komuś trudności** cause difficulties for sb; **(cała) trudność w tym, że...** the crux of the matter lies in the fact that... **2.** (= *właściwość tego, co trudne*) difficulty, trickness; (*położenia*) difficulty.

trudny *a.* **1.** (= *wymagający wysiłku*) difficult, hard, tough; (*o życiu, czasach*) difficult; **trudna rada** *pot.* there is nothing to be done. **2.** (= *skomplikowany*) complicated, hard, stiff; (*o zadaniu*) tricky; (*o egzaminie*) stiff; **trudny orzech do zgryzienia** hard *l.* tough nut to crack. **3.** (*o człowieku* = *nieprzystępny*) difficult, difficile, unapproa-

chable, unaccomodating. **4.** (= *kłopotliwy*) akward, embarrassing.

trudzić *ipf. form.* trouble. ~ **się** *ipf. form.* take pains, bother.

trufla *f. Gen.pl.* -i truffle, earthnut (*Tuber*).

truflowy *a.* (*o smaku*) truffle-flavored.

truizm *mi* truism.

trujący *a.* poisonous, toxic.

trumienka *f. Gen.pl.* -ek *emf. zob.* **trumna**.

trumienny *a.* coffin.

trumna *f. Gen.pl.* -mien **1.** coffin, casket; *pot.* box; **gwóźdź do czyjejś trumny** *przen.* nail in one's coffin; **latająca trumna** *iron.* (= *stary l. zdezelowany samolot*) flying coffin. **2.** *techn.* (*rodzaj pojemnika*) casket, coffin.

trumniarz *mp* coffin-maker, casket-maker.

trunek *mi* -nk- alcoholic beverage.

trunkowy *a. pot.* hard-drinking, fond of drink.

trup *mp* corpse, dead body; *pot.* (= *stary samochód itp.*) wreck; **żywy trup** zombie; **trup na miejscu** *pot.* dead on the spot; **po moim trupie!** over my dead body!; **iść po trupach** give no quarter, claim one's pound of flesh; **kłaść kogoś/coś trupem** lay sb/sth dead; **paść trupem** fall dead, drop dead; **zalać się** *l.* **urżnąć się w trupa** *pot.* get boozed up, get smashed, get loaded; **trup w szafie** skeleton in the closet *l. Br.* in the cupboard.

trupa *f. przest.* theatrical company, troupe.

trupi *a.* cadaverous; (*o zapachu*) putrid; (*o bladości*) deadly; **trupia czaszka** skull; **trupia główka** *ent.* death's-head moth (*Acherontia atropos*).

trupiarnia *f. Gen.pl.* -i *l.* -ń *pot.* mortuary, deadhouse.

truposz *mp Gen.pl.* -y *l.* -ów *pot.* dead person, corpse.

trusia *f. Gen.pl.* -i *l.* -ś **1.** (= *człowiek bojaźliwy*) person meek as a lamb. **2.** *pot.* (= *królik*) bunny; **milczeć jak trusia** be as quiet as a mouse; **leżeć jak trusia** lie low.

truskawka *f. Gen.pl.* -ek *bot., kulin.* strawberry (*Fragaria*).

truskawkowy *a.* strawberry; (= *o smaku l. zapachu truskawek*) strawberry-flavored.

trust *mi ekon.* trust; **trust mózgów** *przen.* brain trust.

truteń *ma* -tni- *Gen.pl.* -i (= *samiec pszczoły*) drone. – *mp* -tni- *Gen.pl.* -i *l.* -ów *pot.* (= *darmozjad*) drone, sponger, parasite.

trutka *f. Gen.pl.* -ek poison (*na coś* for sth).

truwer *mp hist.* trouveur.

trwać *ipf.* **1.** (= *zajmować określony czas*) last, take; **jak długo to będzie trwać?** how long is it going to take?; **nic nie trwa wiecznie** nothing is eternal. **2.** (= *pozostawać, czuwać*) remain, stay, keep (on); **trwać w bezruchu/milczeniu** keep still/silent; **trwać na posterunku** remain at one's post; **trwać przy swoim zdaniu** stick to one's opinion. **3.** (= *istnieć nadal, nie zmieniać się*) persist, continue, remain, endure.

trwale *adv.* constantly, persistently.

trwała *f. Gen.* -ej (*fryzura*) perm.

trwałość *f.* durability.

trwały *a.* -lszy **1.** (= *trwający przez dłuższy czas*) constant, persistent, durable, permanent, long-lasting; (*o związku, przyjaźni*) lasting; **środki trwałe** *ekon.* capital assets, fixed assets. **2.** (= *odporny*) resistant; (*o kolorze, farbie*) fast.

trwanie *n.* duration.

trwoga *f. Gen.pl.* -óg fear, terror, fright; *arch.* affright.

trwonić *ipf. lit.* (*czas, zdolności*) waste; (*pieniądze*) squander, waste; (*zdrowie*) ruin.

trwożliwie *adv. lit.* fearfully.

trwożliwy *a. lit.* **1.** (= *bojaźliwy*) fearful. **2.** (= *niespokojny, zalękniony*) fearful, anxious, apprehensive.

trwożny *a. lit.* **1.** fearful. **2.** fearful, anxious, apprehensive.

trwożyć *ipf.* -óż *lit.* frighten, scare; *arch.* affright. ~ **się** *ipf. lit.* be frightened, be scared.

tryb *mi* **1.** (= *metoda*) mode, method, way; **tryb postępowania** course of action; **tryb życia** way of living, lifestyle; **prowadzić spokojny tryb życia** lead a quiet life; **siedzący tryb życia** sedentary life. **2. tryby** *techn.* gears; cogwheels. **3.** *jęz.* mood; **tryb oznajmujący/rozkazujący/łączący** the indicative/imperative/subjunctive (mood); **tryb przypuszczający** *l.* **warunkowy** the conditional (mood). **4.** *muz.* mode.

tryba *f. leśn.* vista.

trybik *mi techn.* gearwheel, cogwheel.

trybrach *mi teor.lit.* tribrach.

trybula *f.* **trybula ogrodowa** *bot.* chervil (*Anthriscus cerefolium*).

trybularz *mi Gen.* -a *kośc.* censer, thurible.

trybun *mp pl.* -i *l.* -owie **1.** (= *przywódca ludu*) tribune. **2.** *hist.* tribune.

trybuna *f.* **1.** (= *podwyższenie*) dais, platform; **trybuna honorowa** seats of honor. **2.** (= *mównica*) rostrum, tribune. **3.** (= *miejsca dla widzów*) stands, grandstand.

trybunalski *a. hist.* court (of last instance).

trybunał *mi* **1.** tribunal, court of justice. **2.** *hist.* court of last instance.

trybut *mi hist.* (= *danina, haracz*) tribute.

trychina *f. zool.* trichina (*Trichinella spiralis*).

trychinoskopia *f. Gen.* -ii *wet.* trichinoscopy.

trychinoza *f. wet.* trichinosis, trichinelliasis.

tryftong *mi jęz.* triphthong.

trygonometria *f. Gen.* -ii *mat.* trigonometry.

trygonometryczny *a.* *mat.* trigonometric, trigonometrical.

tryk *ma zwł. roln.* ram.

trykać *ipf.* horn, butt (*sb l. sth*) with one's horns. ~ **się** *ipf.* horn one another.

tryknąć (się) *pf.* -nij *zob.* **trykać (się)**.

trykot *mi* **1.** *tk.* tricot. **2.** (*kostium gimnastyczny*) leotard.

trykotaż *mi tk.* tricot clothing.

trykotowy *a.* tricot.

tryl *mi Gen.pl.* -i *l.* -ów *muz.* trill, shake.

tryliard *mi Gen.* -a *mat.* sextillion.

trylion *mi Gen.* -a *mat.* quintillion; *Br. t.* trillion.

trylogia *f. Gen.* -ii trilogy.

trym *mi żegl.* (= *przegłębienie*) trim.

trymestr *mi* trimester.

trynitarski *a. rel.* Trinitarian.

trynitarz *mp rel.* Trinitarian.

tryper *mi* -pr- *Gen.* -a *pat.* gonorrh(o)ea.

Trypolis *mi geogr.* Tripoli.

tryptyk *mi sztuka* triptych.

tryptykowy *a. sztuka* triptych.

tryskać *ipf.*, **trysnąć** *pf.* -snę -śniesz, -śnij **1.** (*o cieczach*) (= *wypływać obficie*) gush, spout. **2.** *tylko ipf.* (= *promieniować*) burst, beam; **tryskać energią** be bursting with energy; **tryskać radością** be bursting with joy, be overjoyed; **tryskać zdrowiem** be bursting with healt, enjoy good health.

tryt *mi chem.* tritium.

tryton[1] *ma zool.* (= *traszka*) newt (*Triturus*).

tryton[2] *mi muz.* tritone.

tryton[3] *mi chem.* triton.

tryton[4] *ma mit.* triton.

tryumf *mi* = **triumf**.

tryumfalnie *adv.* = **triumfalnie**.

tryumfalny *a.* = **triumfalny**.

tryumfator *mp* = **triumfator**.

tryumfować *ipf.* = **triumfować**.

trywializacja *f. lit.* **1.** vulgarization. **2.** trivialization.

trywializować *ipf. lit.* **1.** vulgarize. **2.** trivialize.

trywialnie *adv.* **1.** (= *prostacko*) vulgarly, coarsely, crudely. **2.** (= *banalnie*) trivially.

trywialność *f.* **1.** (= *prostactwo*) vulgarity, coarseness, crudeness. **2.** (= *banalność*) trivialism.

trywialny *a.* **1.** (= *prostacki*) vulgar, crude, coarse. **2.** (= *banalny*) trivial.

trzask[1] *mi* (*drzwi*) bang, slam; (*bata*) crack; (*gałęzi*) snap; (*ognia*) crackle.

trzask[2] *int.* bang, smack; **trzask prask** *pot.* suddenly, unexpectedly.

trzaskać *ipf.* **1.** (= *uderzać, powodując trzask*) hit, smack; **trzaskać batem** crack a whip; **trzaskać drzwiami** slam the door; **trzaskać pięścią w stół** bang one's fist on the table; **trzaskać obcasami** click one's heels; **jak z bicza trzasł** very quickly, in no time; **niech to piorun trzaśnie!** damn it! **2.** (= *wydawać trzask, pękając itp.*) burst; crack; snap. **3.** *pot.* (= *robić coś szybko*) do quickly. ~ **się** *ipf. pot.* (= *uderzać się*) hit o.s.

trzaskający *a.* **trzaskający mróz** hard *l.* heavy *l.* severe frost.

trzaski *pl. Gen.* -ów radio static.

trzasnąć (się) *pf.* -snę -śniesz, -śnij, -snął -snęła *l.* -sł -sła *zob.* **trzaskać (się)**.

trzaśnięty *a. pot.* (= *głupi*) cracked, touched.

trząchać *ipf.*, **trząchnąć** *pf.* -ij *pot.* (= *potrząsać*) shake.

trząść *ipf.* trzęsę trzęsiesz, trząś *l.* trzęś, trząsł trzęsła trzęśli **1.** (= *potrząsać*) shake; **trząść owoce** shake fruit from the tree; **trząść portkami** *pot.* be scared to death, be scared shitless; **trzęsie mnie** (= *jest mi zimno*) I'm shivering with cold; (= *jestem rozgniewany*) I'm burning with anger. **2.** (*o pojazdach*) (= *rzucać, huśtać*) toss. **3.** *pot.* (= *kierować despotycznie*) keep a firm grip on. ~ **się** *ipf.* **1.** (= *dygotać*) (*o człowieku, ziemi, głosie, rękach*) shake, tremble, quake; (*o głosie, ustach*) quiver; **trząść się jak galareta** *pot.* shake like jelly; **jadł, aż mu się uszy trzęsły** he was eating voraciously, he was eating as if he hadn't eaten for ages. **2.** (= *jechać, podskakując*) travel uncomfortably. **3.** *pot.* (= *być poruszonym*) be agitated, be angry; **trząść się nad kimś** be overly protective toward sb; **trząść się z oburzenia** feel (burning) indignation; **szkoła trzęsła się od plotek** rumors were going around the school.

trzcina *f.* **1.** *bot.* reed (*Phragmites*); **trzcina cukrowa** sugarcane (*Saccharum officinarum*). **2.** (= *łodygi tej rośliny*) reed.

trzciniak *ma orn.* great reed warbler (*Acrocephalus arundinaceus*).

trzcinka *f. Gen.pl.* **-ek** cane, reed.

trzcinowaty *a.* **mozga trzcinowata** *bot.* reed canary grass (*Phalaris arundinacea*).

trzcinowy *a.* reedy; reed; cane; **cukier trzcinowy** cane sugar.

trzeba *v. pred. indecl.* **1.** (= *należy*) one should, one ought to; **trzeba być głupcem, żeby...** one must be a fool to...; **trzeba ci wiedzieć, że...** you should know that...; **trzeba przyznać, że...** admittedly..., one has to admit that..., it should be admitted...; **trzeba mu pomóc** we *l.* sb should help him. **2.** (= *jest niezbędne*) it is necessary to *l.* that..., one needs to..., it is needed that...; **jeśli trzeba** if needed, if necessary; **nie trzeba go dwa razy prosić** you don't have to ask him twice; **trzeba wam czegoś?** do you need anything?; **dziękuję, nie trzeba** no, thanks; thank you, I am fine.

trzebić *ipf.* **1.** *leśn.* thin out. **2.** *myśl.* exterminate. **3.** *wet.* geld, castrate.

trzebież *f.* **1.** *leśn.* clearance, thinning. **2.** *myśl.* extermination.

trzech *num. zob.* **trzy.**

trzechsetny *a.* tree-hundredth.

trzeci *a.* third; **trzecia potęga** *mat.* third power, cube; **Trzecia Rzesza** *hist.* the Third Reich; **kraje Trzeciego Świata** *polit.* the Third World countries; **osoby trzecie** third parties; **jedna trzecia** a third, one third (*czegoś* of sth); **dwie trzecie** two thirds; **po trzecie** third, thirdly; **za trzecim razem** upon a third attempt. – *mi* (= *trzeci dzień miesiąca*) the third; **trzeciego lutego** on February (the) third; on the third of February.

trzecia *f. Gen.* **-ej** (= *godzina trzecia*) three o'clock.

trzecioklasista *mp*, **trzecioklasistka** *f. Gen.pl.* **-ek** *szkoln.* third-grader.

trzecioligowiec *mp* **-wc-** *pl.* **-y** *sport* third-division player *l.* athlete.

trzecioligowy *a. sport* third-division.

trzecioroczny *a.* remaining for the third year in a row; **uczeń trzecioroczny** *szkoln.* pupil *l.* student repeating the same grade for the third time.

trzeciorzęd *mi geol.* the Tertiary (period).

trzeciorzędny *a.* third-rate.

trzeciorzędowy *a. geol.* Tertiary.

trzeć *ipf.* **trę trzesz, trzyj, tarł** **1.** (= *pocierać*) rub. **2.** (= *rozdrabniać*) grate. **3.** (= *szlifować*) polish; grind; sand. **4.** (= *piłować*) saw. ~ **się** *ipf.*

1. (= *ocierać się*) rub, chafe against. **2.** *icht.* spawn.

trzej *num. zob.* **trzy.**

trzepaczka *f. Gen.pl.* **-ek 1.** (*narzędzie do trzepania dywanów*) carpet beater. **2.** (*przyrząd kuchenny*) whisk, egg beater.

trzepać *ipf.* **-pię -piesz 1.** (= *potrząsać*) beat; **trzepać ogonem** beat one's tail; **trzepać skrzydłami** beat one's wings, flutter the wings, flap the wings rapidly; **trzepać** *l.* **walić konia** *sl.* beat the meat, jerk off. **2.** (= *uderzać, usuwając kurz*) beat. **3.** *pot.* (= *bić*) hit, beat; **trzepać kogoś pasem** spank; **trzepnąć kogoś w głowę** hit sb on the head; **trzepnąć kogoś w ucho** give sb a thick ear. **4.** *tylko ipf. pot.* (= *trajkotać*) chatter; recite thoughtlessly; **trzepać językiem** wag one's tongue. **5.** *pot.* (= *wykonywać w dużych ilościach, trzaskać*) put out in large quantities, mass-produce. ~ **się** *ipf.* (= *uderzać siebie samego*) hit o.s.

trzepak *mi Gen.* **-a** carpet beating stand.

trzepnąć *pf.* **-ij** *zob.* **trzepać.** ~ **się** *pf. zob.* **trzepać się.**

trzepnięty *a. pot.* (*o osobie*) (= *nienormalny*) cracked, nuts.

trzepot *mi* flutter.

trzepotać *ipf.* **-oczę -oczesz** *l.* **-ocę -ocesz, -ocz** flutter; flap about, wave about; **ptak trzepotał skrzydłami** bird fluttered its wings; **sztandary trzepotały na wietrze** banners fluttered in the wind. ~ **się** *ipf.* flutter; toss, jerk about.

trzeszczeć *ipf.* **-ę -ysz 1.** (= *wydawać chrzęst*) crack; (= *skrzypieć*) creak; (*o ogniu*) crackle; **trzeszczeć w szwach** (*o ubraniu*) burst at the seams; (*o sali*) be packed, be full of people; **radio trzeszczy** there's a lot of static *l.* crackling *l.* interference on the radio. **2.** *pot.* (= *trajkotać, paplać*) jabber, chatter.

trzewia *pl. Gen.* **-i** intestines, guts; *anat., zool.* viscera.

trzewiczek *mi* **-czk-** *Gen.* **-a** ankle boot.

trzewik *mi Gen.* **-a** ankle boot.

trzewiowy *a.* visceral.

trzewny *a. anat.* visceral.

trzeźwiący *a.* **sól trzeźwiąca** smelling *l.* volatile salt.

trzeźwić *ipf.* bring round; sober (up).

trzeźwieć *ipf.* come round; sober (up).

trzeźwo *adv.* **1.** (= *nie będąc pijanym*) soberly; **na trzeźwo** when sober. **2.** (= *rozsądnie*) soberly, levelheadedly, sensibly; **trzeźwo oceniać** have sound judgement.

trzeźwość *f.* **1.** (= *trzeźwy stan*) sobriety; **badanie trzeźwości** breathalyzing. **2.** (= *rzeczowość*) sobriety, matter-of-factness.

trzeźwy *a.* **1.** (= *nie pijany*) sober. **2.** (= *rzeczowy*) sober, levelheaded, sensible; **mieć trzeźwe spojrzenie na coś** have a clear view of sth. **3.** (= *rozbudzony*) *rzad.* awake.

trzęsawisko *n.* swamp, quagmire, bog.

trzęsienie *n.* **trzęsienie ziemi** *geol.* earthquake.

trzmiel *ma ent.* bumblebee (*Bombus*).

trzmielina *f. bot.* cardinal's hat (*Evonymus*).

trznadel *ma* **-dl-** *orn.* bunting (*Emberiza*).

trzoda *f. Gen.pl.* **-ód** *przest.* herd; **trzoda chlewna** swine, pigs.

trzon *mi* **1.** (= *rdzeń*) core, nucleus, kernel; (*organizacji, grupy*) hard core; **trzon macicy** *anat.* body of the uterus. **2.** *bot.* stipe.

trzonek *mi* **-nk-** *Gen.* **-a 1.** (= *uchwyt*) handle. **2.** *bot.* hyphal branch, hypha.

trzonowy *a.* core, nuclear; **ząb trzonowy** *dent.* molar (tooth).

trzos *mi Gen.* **-a** *l.* **-u** pouch.

trzódka *f. Gen.pl.* **-ek 1.** (= *mała trzoda*) small herd, flock. **2.** (= *gromadka dzieci*) small group.

trzpień *mi Gen.* **-a 1.** *techn.* (= *walec do osadzania czegoś*) arbor, mandrel *l.* mandril. **2.** *techn.* (= *oś*) arbor, axle.

trzpiot *mp,* **trzpiotka** *f. Gen.pl.* **-ek** scatterbrain, featherbrain, flibbertigibbet, fribble.

trzpiotowaty *a.* scatterbrained, featherbrained.

trzustka *f. Gen.pl.* **-ek** *anat.* pancreas.

trzustkowy *a. anat.* pancreatic.

trzy *num. Nom. with mp* **trzej** *l.* **trzech** *Gen. i Loc.* **-ech** *Dat.* **-em** *Ins.* **-ema** three; **Święto Trzech Króli** *rz.-kat.* Epiphany, Twelfth Day; **trzy czwarte** three fourths; **do trzech razy sztuka** third time lucky; **po trzecie** third(ly); **nie umieć zliczyć do trzech** be slow-witted; **pleść trzy po trzy** talk nonsense; **pracować za trzech** work very hard; **wtrącać swoje trzy grosze** chip in one's penny's worth, chip in one's two pennies' worth *l.* two penn'orth, have a finger in every man's pie.

trzyaktowy *a. teatr* three-act, consisting of three acts.

trzycyfrowy *a.* three-digit.

trzyczęściowy *a.* three-part, consisting of three parts; three-piece.

trzydniowy *a.* **1.** (= *trwający trzy dni*) three-day, three-days'. **2.** (= *mający trzy dni*) three-day-old.

trzydrzwiowy *a.* three-door.

trzydziestka *f. Gen.pl.* **-ek 1.** (= *liczba trzydzieści*) thirty. **2.** (*wiek*) thirty years of age; **on jest po trzydziestce** he's over thirty, he's in his thirties. **3.** (*coś oznaczone cyfrą trzydzieści*) (number) thirty.

trzydziestolatek *mp* **-tk-** *pl.* **-owie** thirty-year-old (person). – *ma* **-tk-** *pl.* **-i** thirty-year-old (animal).

trzydziestolatka *f. Gen.pl.* **-ek** *zob.* **trzydziestolatek.**

trzydziestolecie *n. Gen.pl.* **-i 1.** (*okres*) period of thirty years. **2.** (*rocznica*) thirtieth anniversary.

trzydziestoletni *a.* **1.** (= *trwający trzydzieści lat*) thirty-year, thirty-years'. **2.** (= *mający trzydzieści lat*) thirty-year-old.

trzydziesty *a.* thirtieth. – *mi* (= *trzydziesty dzień miesiąca*) the thirtieth.

trzydzieści *num.* **-st-** *Ins.* **-oma** *l.* **-u** thirty.

trzydzieścioro *num. decl. like n.* **-rg-** thirty; **trzydzieścioro dzieci** thirty children.

trzygodzinny *a.* three-hour, three-hours'.

trzyizbowy *a.* **1.** three-room; **mieszkanie trzy-**izbowe three-room apartment. **2.** *polit.* tricameral.

trzykołowy *a.* three-wheel; **rower trzykołowy** tricycle.

trzykroć *adv.* (*także* **po trzykroć**) *lit.* thrice, three times; *zob.* **trzykrotnie.**

trzykrotka *f. Gen.pl.* **-ek** *bot.* spiderwort (*Tradescantia*).

trzykrotnie *adv.* threefold; three times.

trzykrotny *a.* threefold, triple, treble; three times; **trzykrotny mistrz świata** three-times world champion.

trzylatek *mp* **-tk-** *pl.* **-i** (= *trzyletni chłopiec*) three-year-old (boy). – *ma* **-tk-** (*trzyletnie zwierzę*) three-year-old (animal).

trzyletni *a.* **1.** (= *trwający trzy lata*) three-year, three-years'. **2.** (= *mający trzy lata*) three-year-old.

trzymać *ipf.* **1.** (= *nie wypuszczać*) hold, keep; **trzymać coś kurczowo** cling to sth; **trzymać kogoś do chrztu** be sb's godfather *l.* godmother, hold a child being baptized; **trzymać kogoś krótko** take a tight reign on sb; **trzymać kogoś w ryzach** keep a tight reign on sb; **trzymać kogoś za słowo** hold sb to sb's word *l.* promise; **trzymać nerwy na wodzy** keep one's temper in a leash, hold one's anger in check. **2.** (= *przetrzymywać, więzić*) hold, keep; **trzymać kogoś pod kluczem** lock sb up; **trzymać kogoś pod pantoflem** henpeck sb; **trzymać psa na smyczy** lead a dog on a leash. **3.** (= *utrzymywać pozycję, pozę itp.*) keep; **trzymać ręce w kieszeni** have one's hands in one's pockets; **trzymać język za zębami** hold one's tongue; **trzymać (za kogoś) kciuki** keep one's fingers crossed (for sb). **4.** (= *przechowywać*) keep; store; **trzymać coś pod kluczem** keep sth locked; **trzymać coś w sekrecie** keep sth secret. **5.** (= *utrzymywać w jakimś stanie*) keep; **trzymać kogoś na muszce** hold sb at gunpoint; **trzymać kogoś w niepewności** keep sb in suspense; **trzymać kogoś w szachu** keep sb in check; **trzymać rękę na pulsie** have *l.* keep one's finger on the pulse; **trzymać w napięciu** keep in suspense. **6.** (= *stanowić mocowanie, podtrzymywać*) hold; **trzymać ciepło** stay *l.* keep warm; **trzymać fason** keep up one's spirit; **mróz trzyma** frost lasts. **7.** *pot.* (= *hodować*) keep. **8.** *pot.* (= *sympatyzować*) be friends with, stick with; **trzymać z kimś** join up with sb, stick with sb. **~ się** *ipf.* **1.** (= *przytrzymywać się*) hold on to; **trzymać się czyjejś spódnicy** be tied to one's mother's *l.* wife's apronstrings; **głupstwa** *l.* **żarty się ciebie trzymają!** you are never serious!; **pieniądze się mnie nie trzymają** I never seem to have (enough) money. **2.** (= *być w jakimś stanie, być blisko*) stay, remain; **trzymać się na uboczu** stay away from, stay clear of; **trzymać się razem** stick together. **3.** (= *utrzymywać pozycję ciała*) stand; sit; **trzymać się prosto** keep o.s. erect; **ledwo trzymać się na nogach** be on one's last legs; **świetnie trzyma się w siodle** he *l.* she is a born *l.* great (horse-)rider. **4.** *pot.* (= *zachowywać kondycję*) be in good shape; **trzymać się przy życiu** stay alive; **świetnie się trzyma jak na swój wiek** he *l.* she is in good shape considering his *l.* her age. **5.** (= *nie upadać na duchu*) not lose one's heart, keep up; **trzymaj się (ciepło)!** (*forma pożegnania*) take care! **6.** (= *walczyć, nie poddawać się*) not give up, hang on. **7.** *pot.* (= *nie rozpadać się*) not fall apart, stick together; **trzymać się cudem** *l.* **na słowo honoru** hold together on a wing and a prayer; **to się nie trzyma kupy** this doesn't hang together. **8.** (= *przestrzegać*) (*przepisów, zasad*) keep to, stick to, adhere, observe. **9.** *pot.* (= *nie zmieniać się*) stay *l.* remain unchanged, not change. **10.** (= *nie zbaczać*) keep, follow; **trzymać się szlaku** *l.* **drogi** follow the path *l.* road. **11.** *pot., biol.* occur, belong to, be endemic to; live; grow.

trzymasztowy *a.* *żegl.* three-mast.

trzymetrowy *a.* three-meter.

trzymiesięczny *a.* **1.** (= *trwający trzy miesiące*) three-month, three-months'. **2.** (= *mający trzy miesiące*) three-month-old.

trzyminutowy *a.* three-minute, three-minutes'.

trzynasta *f.* *Gen.* **-ej** (= *godzina trzynasta*) one p.m.

trzynastka *f.* *Gen.pl.* **-ek 1.** (= *liczba trzynaście*) thirteen. **2.** (*zbiór trzynastu jednostek*) (group of) thirteen. **3.** (*coś oznaczone cyfrą trzynaście*) (number) thirteen. **4.** *pot.* (= *dodatkowa pensja*) annual bonus.

trzynastolatek *mp* **-tk-** *pl.* **-i** thirteen-year-old (boy).

trzynastoletni *a.* **1.** (= *trwający trzynaście lat*) thirteen-year, thirteen-years'. **2.** (= *mający trzynaście lat*) thirteen-year-old.

trzynastowieczny *a.* thirteenth century.

trzynasty *a.* thirteenth; **trzynasta pensja** annual bonus. – *mi* (= *trzynasty dzień miesiąca*) the thirteenth.

trzynaście *num.* **-st-** *Ins.* **-oma** *l.* **-u** thirteen.

trzynaścioro *num. decl. like n.* **-rg-** thirteen; **trzynaścioro dzieci** thirteen children.

trzynawowy, trójnawowy *a.* *kośc., bud.* three-nave; three-aisle.

trzyosobowy *a.* **1.** (= *przeznaczony dla trzech osób*) for three persons, three-person; threesome. **2.** (= *składający się z trzech osób*) of three persons, three-person.

trzypiętrowy *a.* three-story.

trzypokojowy *a.* three-room.

trzysta *num. Ins.* **-oma** *l.* **-u** three hundred.

trzystopniowy *a.* three-stage; three-tier.

trzytomowy *a.* three-volume.

trzytygodniowy *a.* **1.** (= *trwający trzy tygodnie*) three-week, three-weeks'. **2.** (= *mający trzy tygodnie*) three-week-old.

trzyzmianowy *a.* three-shift.

ts, tss *int.* shush.

tse-tse *f. indecl.* **mucha tse-tse** *ent.* tsetse fly (*Glossina*).

tu *adv.* (*wskazuje miejsce*) here; **tu i tam** *l.* **tu i ówdzie** here and there; **tu i teraz** here and now; **tu mówi Nowak!** this is Nowak speaking! – *particle* (*o charakterze ekspresywnym*) **co tu (dużo) gadać** there's nothing to talk about; **co tu robić?**

what to do (now)?; **tu trzeba działać szybko** we need to act quickly.

tuba *f.* **1.** (*opakowanie*) tube. **2.** (= *urządzenie do wzmacniania głosu*) bullhorn, bull horn; speaking tube. **3.** *muz.* tuba.

tubalnie *adv.* in a stentorian voice; with a stentorian sound.

tubalny *a.* stentorian.

tuberkulina *f.* *med.* tuberculin.

tuberkulinowy *a.* *med.* tuberculinic.

tuberoza *f.* *bot.* tuberose (*Polianthes tuberosa*).

tubka *f. Gen.pl.* **-ek** tube.

tubus *mi* *opt.* tube, barrel.

tubylczy *a.* native, indigenous, local, aboriginal.

tubylec *mp* **-lc-** *pl.* **-y** native, local, aborigine, autochthon.

tucz *mi* *roln.* fattening.

tuczarnia *f. Gen.pl.* **-i** *l.* **-ń** *roln.* fattening house.

tucznik *ma* *roln.* fattener, fattening pig.

tuczny *a.* *roln.* fattening.

tuczyć *ipf.* **1.** *roln.* fatten. **2.** (= *zbyt intensywnie karmić ludzi*) stuff, overfeed. **3.** (*o potrawach, powodować tycie*) be fattening, fatten, make fat; **kradzione nie tuczy** ill-gotten gains never prosper; ill-gotten, ill-spent; ill-gotten wealth never thrives. ~ **się** *ipf.* **1.** (*o zwierzętach*) (= *przybierać na wadze*) fatten. **2.** (*o ludziach*) (= *tyć*) fatten, grow fat, put on weight.

tuf *mi* *geol.* tuff.

tuja *f. Gen.* **tui** *Gen.pl.* **tui** *l.* **tuj** *bot.* arborvitae, thuja (*Thuja*).

tukan *ma* *orn.* toucan (*Ramphastos*).

tul *mi* *chem.* thulium.

tuleja *f. Gen.* **-ei 1.** *techn.* sleeve; quill. **2.** (= *tutka*) funnel, cornet, cone.

tulejka *f. Gen.pl.* **-ek 1.** *techn.* sleeve; quill. **2.** (= *tutka*) funnel, cornet, cone.

tulić *ipf.* **1.** hug, cuddle. **2.** snuggle, cuddle. **3.** hide; **tulić ogon pod siebie** hold its *l.* his *l.* her tail between its *l.* his *l.* her legs. ~ **się** *ipf.* (= *przyciskać*) nestle, cuddle (*do kogoś l. czegoś* up to sb *l.* sth).

tulipan *mi Gen.* **-a** *bot.* tulip (*Tulipa*).

tulipanowy *a.* tulip; tuliplike.

tułacz *mp* wanderer, drifter.

tułaczka *f. Gen.pl.* **-ek 1.** (= *poniewierka*) wandering. **2.** (= *kobieta tułacz*) *zob.* **tułacz.**

tułaczy *a.* wanderer's, wandering.

tułać się *ipf.* wander, drift, rove.

tułów *mi* **-owi-** *Gen.* **-a** trunk, torso.

tum *mi* *przest., kośc.* cathedral, minster.

tumak *ma* *zool.* pine marten (*Martes martes*).

tuman *mi Gen.* **-u** (= *chmura, kłąb*) cloud. – *mp* *Gen.* **-a** *pl.* **-y** *pot.* (= *matoł*) moron.

tumanić *ipf.* beguile.

tumba *f.* sarcophagus, tomb.

tumiwisizm *mi* *pot.* indifference, I-don't-care attitude, whatever attitude.

tumult *mi* tumult, uproar, turmoil.

tundra *f.* *geogr.* tundra.

tunel *mi Gen.pl.* **-i** *l.* **-ów 1.** (= *przejazd pod-*

ziemny) tunnel; **tunel aerodynamiczny** wind tunnel; **tunel foliowy** *ogr.* plastic tunnel, polyethylene greenhouse. **2.** *górn.* mine tunnel.

tunelowy *a.* tunnel; **zjawisko tunelowe** *fiz.* tunnel effect.

tuner *mi Gen.* **-a** *radio, telew.* tuner.

Tunezja *f. geogr.* Tunisia.

Tunezyjczyk *mp*, **Tunezyjka** *f. Gen.pl.* **-ek** Tunisian.

tunezyjski *a.* Tunisian.

tunika *f.* **1.** tunic. **2.** *hist.* tunic. **3.** *zool.* tunic.

tuńczyk *ma icht.* **1.** tuna (*Thunnus*). **2.** *kulin.* tuna; **kanapka/sałatka z tuńczykiem** tuna sandwich/salad.

tupać *ipf.* **-pię -piesz** tramp, stamp; **tupać nogami** stamp one's feet.

tupeciarz *mp pot.* cheeky *l.* impudent person.

tupecik *mi zob.* **tupet.**

tupet *mi* **1.** (= *zuchwałość*) cheek, impudence, effrontery; **z tupetem** cheekily, impudently; **mieć tupet** have a nerve. **2.** (*mała peruka*) toupee.

tupnąć *pf.* **-ij** *zob.* **tupać.**

tupot *mi* patter (of feet); pitapat (of feet).

tupotać *ipf.* **-czę -czesz** *l.* **-cę -cesz, -cz** patter.

tuptać *ipf. pot.* patter; (*zwł. o dziecku stawiającym pierwsze kroki*) paddle.

tur *ma zool.* aurochs (*Bos primigenius*); **silny jak tur** strong as an ox.

tura *f.* **1.** (= *faza*) (*rozgrywek, rozmów*) round; **druga** *l.* **ostateczna tura** *sport* runoff; **druga tura głosowania** *polit.* runoff; **druga tura rozmów/negocjacji** the second round of talks/negotiations. **2.** (= *grupa*) (*gości, wczasowiczów*) party.

turban *mi* turban.

turbina *f. techn.* turbine.

turbinowy *a. techn.* turbine.

turbogenerator *mi Gen.* **-a** *techn.* turbogenerator.

turboodrzutowy *a. lotn.* **samolot/silnik turboodrzutowy** turbojet aircraft/engine.

turbosprężarka *f. Gen.pl.* **-ek** *techn.* turbocompressor.

turbośmigłowiec *mi* **-wc-** *Gen.* **-a** *lotn.* propjet; turboprop.

turbośmigłowy *a. techn.* turboprop.

turbulencja *f. meteor., techn.* turbulence.

Turcja *f. geogr.* Turkey.

turcyzm *mi jęz.* Turkism.

Turczynka *f. Gen.pl.* **-ek** *zob.* **Turek.**

turecki *a.* Turkish; **goły jak święty turecki** poor as a church mouse; **kawa po turecku** Turkish coffee; **siedziałam jak na tureckim kazaniu** it was all Greek to me; **siedzieć po turecku** sit cross-legged.

Turek *mp* **-rk-** Turk.

turkawka *f. Gen.pl.* **-ek** *orn.* turtledove (*Streptopelia turtur*).

Turkmen *mp* Turkmen.

Turkmenia *f.* Turkmenistan.

Turkmenka *f. Gen.pl.* **-ek** *zob.* **Turkmen.**

turkmeński *a.* Turkmen.

turkologia *f. Gen.* **-ii** Turkish studies.

turkot *mi* rattle.

turkotać *ipf.* **-czę -czesz** *l.* **-cę -cesz, -cz** rattle.

turkuć (podjadek) *ma Gen.pl.* **-ów** *ent.* mole cricket (*Gryllotalpa gryllotalpa*).

turkus *mi Gen.* **-a** *l.* **-u** *min.* turquoise.

turkusowy *a.* turquoise.

turlać *ipf. pot.* wheel; roll. **~ się** *ipf. pot.* roll.

turmalin *mi min.* turmaline.

turnia *f. Gen.pl.* **-i** (mountain) peak.

turniej *mi Gen.pl.* **-ów** *sport, hist.* tournament.

turniejowy *a.* tournament.

turniura *f.* bustle.

turnus *mi* **1.** (= *okres wypoczynku*) period. **2.** *pot.* (= *grupa wypoczywających*) batch.

turoń *mp Gen.pl.* **-i** *l.* **-ów** Christmas mummer (*in Poland*) disguised as a horned animal.

turpista *mp teor.lit.* turpist.

turpistyczny *a. teor.lit.* turpist.

turpizm *mi teor.lit.* turpism.

Turyn *mi geogr.* Turin.

Turyngia *f. Gen.* **-ii** *geogr.* Thuringia.

turysta *mp*, **turystka** *f. Gen.pl.* **-ek** tourist; **turysta pieszy** hiker; backpacker; **turysta zmotoryzowany** motoring tourist.

turystycznie *adv.* touristically.

turystyczny *a.* touristic; (*o klasie, przewodniku, biurze, atrakcji*) tourist.

turystyka *f.* tourism; **turystyka górska** climbing; **turystyka piesza** hiking; backpacking; **turystyka rowerowa** cycling; **turystyka samochodowa** motoring.

turzyca *f. bot.* sedge (*Carex*).

tusz[1] *mi Gen.pl.* **-ów** **1.** (*farba wodna*) India ink; (*do drukarki, pieczątek, rysowania*) ink. **2.** (*kosmetyk*) mascara.

tusz[2] *mi Gen.pl.* **-ów** *przest.* (= *kąpiel pod prysznicem*) shower.

tusz[3] *mi Gen.pl.* **-ów** *muz.* fanfare.

tusz[4] *mi Gen.pl.* **-ów** *sport* touch.

tusza *f.* **1.** (= *figura l. masa ciała człowieka otyłego*) heavy frame; the weight of sb's body. **2.** (= *ubite zwierzę*) carcass.

tuszka *f. Gen.pl.* **-ek** *kulin.* carcass.

tuszować *ipf.* **1.** (= *rysować tuszem*) ink in. **2.** (= *zacierać*) (*błędy, różnice poglądów, winę*) paper over.

tutaj *adv. zob.* **tu.**

tutejszy *a.* local.

tutka *f. Gen.pl.* **-ek** **1.** (*coś zwinięte w rurkę, stożek*) roll; (*na słodycze*) cornet. **2.** *przest.* (= *gilza*) cigarette tube.

tutti-frutti *mi indecl. tylko pl.* tutti frutti.

tuz *mp pl.* **-y** *przen.* (= *osoba wybitna*) VIP. – *mi Gen.* **-a** *przest. karty* (= *as*) ace.

tuziemiec *mp* **-mc-** *pl.* **-y** native.

tuzin *mi Gen.* **-a** dozen.

tuzinkowy *a.* run-of-the-mill; unexceptional.

tuż *adv.* **1.** (*blisko w przestrzeni*) nearby; close by; **tuż obok kogoś/czegoś** right next to sb/sth. **2.** (*blisko w czasie*) close on; just; **lato tuż, tuż** summer's upon us.

tużurek *mi* **-rk-** *Gen.* **-a** frock coat.

TV *abbr.* (= *telewizja, telewizyjny*) TV.

TVP *abbr.* (= *Telewizja Polska*) Polish Television.

twa, twe *itd. a. zob.* **twój.**

twardawy *a.* hardish; toughish.

twardnieć *ipf.* **1.** harden; toughen; (*o cemencie*) set. **2.** *jęz.* dispalatalize.

twardo *adv.* **1.** (= *nie miękko*) hard; **jajko na twardo** hard-boiled egg; **spać twardo** be fast *l.* sound asleep. **2.** (= *surowo, ostro*) severely; (*wychowywać, traktować*) strictly. **3.** (= *kategorycznie*) (*żądać, upominać się*) firmly.

twardogłowy *mp* hard hat.

twardopodniebienny *a. jęz.* palatal.

twardość *f.* **1.** (= *bycie twardym*) toughness; (*materiału*) hardness; (*człowieka*) ruggedness. **2.** (= *surowość*) severity; strictness. **3.** (= *nieustępliwość*) firmness.

twardotematowy *a. jęz.* non-palatal-stem.

twardówka *f. Gen.pl.* **-ek** *anat.* sclera; sclerotic.

twardy *a.* **1.** (= *sztywny*) hard; (*o materacu*) firm; (*o mięsie, skórze*) tough; **twardy sen** sound sleep; **twarda woda** hard water; **twardy jak kamień** hard as a rock; **twardy orzech do zgryzienia** *przen.* tough *l.* hard nut to crack; **mieć twarde serce** have a hard heart. **2.** (= *wytrzymały*) tough; (*polityk, dziennikarz*) hard-bitten; (*charakter*) rugged; **twardy facet** tough guy. **3.** (= *ciężki, surowy*) rigid; firm; (*o życiu*) hard; **mieć twardą rękę** have a heavy hand. **4.** (= *ostry, nieprzyjemny*) stern.

twardziel *mp pot.* **1.** ballsy, tough guy, hard ass. **2.** *bot.* hardwood.

twardzioszek przydrożny *mi* **-szk-** *Gen.* **-a** *bot.* fairy ring mushroom (*Marasmius oreades*).

twarożek *mi* **-żk-** *zob.* **twaróg.**

twaróg *mi* **-o-** cottage cheese.

twarz *f. pl.* **-e 1.** (= *oblicze*) *t. przen.* face; **jest/nie jest ci w tym do twarzy** it becomes you/doesn't become you; **ktoś ma coś wypisane na twarzy** sth is written over sb's face; **mieć wiatr w twarz** have wind in one's face; **padać przed kimś na twarz** prostrate oneself before sb; **rysy twarzy** (facial) features; **roześmiać się/napluć komuś w twarz** laugh/spit in sb's face; **stracić/zachować twarz** *przen.* lose/save face; **twarz pokerzysty** poker face; **twarzą do kogoś/czegoś** facing sb/sth; **twarzą w twarz (z kimś/czymś)** face to face (with sb/ sth); **czyjś wyraz twarzy** expression on sb's face. **2.** (= *osoba*) face; **blada twarz** (= *człowiek białej rasy*) paleface; **znajome/nowe twarze** *przen.* familiar/new faces.

twarzoczaszka *f. Gen.pl.* **-ek** *med.* facial skeleton.

twarzowo *adv.* (*ubierać się*) becomingly.

twarzowy *a.* **1.** (*dotyczący twarzy*) facial. **2.** *pot.* (= *podkreślający urodę*) becoming.

twarzyczka *f. Gen.pl.* **-ek** little face.

tweed *mi* tweed.

tweedowy *a.* tweed; tweedy; **tweedowe ubranie** tweeds.

twierdza *f.* **1.** (= *forteca*) fortress; stronghold, citadel. **2.** *hist.* (= *więzienie w fortecy*) hold.

twierdząco *adv.* affirmatively.

twierdzący *a.* affirmative.

twierdzenie *n.* **1.** (= *zdanie*) statement. **2.** *log., mat.* theorem, proposition.

twierdzić *ipf.* maintain, claim, assert.

twist *mi Gen. i Acc.* **-a 1.** (*taniec*) twist. **2.** *Gen.* **-a** *l.* **-u** (*słoik*) twist-lid jar.

twoi, twoja *itd. a. zob.* **twój.**

twornik *mi Gen.* **-a** *techn.* armature.

tworzenie *n.* formation; creation.

tworzyć *ipf.* **-órz 1.** (= *pracować nad dziełem sztuki*) create; produce. **2.** (= *ustanawiać, formować*) form; create; (*plany, strategię*) formulate. **3.** (= *stanowić*) form; make up; (*parę*) make; **tworzyć całość** make a whole. **~ się** *ipf.* form; be formed, arise, take shape.

tworzywo *n.* material; **tworzywo sztuczne** plastic.

twój *a.* **twoj-** *lit.* **tw-** *pl. mp* **twoi** *attr.* your; *arch.* thy; *pred. l. bez rzeczownika* yours; *arch.* thine; **twoja książka** your book; **ta książka jest twoja** this book is yours; **czy to twoje?** is that yours?; **jedna z twoich książek** a book of yours.

twór *mi* **-o- 1.** (= *istota żywa*) creature. **2.** (*składnik przyrody*) formation. **3.** (= *wytwór pracy ludzkiej*) (*wynalazek, dzieło artystyczne*) creation; (*teoria*) construct. **4.** (*część organizmu, t. narośl, guz*) structure.

twórca *mp* creator; (*artysta*) artist; (*pisarz, autor*) author; (*muzyki*) composer; (*organizacji*) founder; (*pomysłu, planu, strategii*) generator; originator.

twórczo *adv.* creatively; artistically.

twórczość *f.* **1.** (= *tworzenie*) creation; production. **2.** (*ogół stworzonych dzieł*) (artistic) works; (*literackich danego autora*) oeuvre; **twórczość artystyczna** artistic *l.* creative activity.

twórczy *a.* (= *odkrywczy*) creative; (= *dotyczący twórców*) artistic; **zdolności twórcze** creativeness.

twórczyni *f. zob.* **twórca.**

ty *pron. Gen. i Acc.* **ciebie** *l.* (*nieakcentowane*) **cię** *Dat.* **tobie** *l.* (*nieakcentowane*) **ci** *Ins.* **tobą** *Loc.* **tobie** you; **być z kimś na ty** by on first-name terms with sb.

Tybet *mi geogr.* Tibet.

Tybetanka *f. Gen.pl.* **-ek, Tybetańczyk** *mp* Tibetan.

tybetański *a.* Tibetan.

tych *pron. zob.* **ci.**

tyci *a. pot.* tiny.

tycjanowski *a.* titian.

tyczka *f. Gen.pl.* **-ek 1.** (= *pręt*) stick. **2.** *sport* pole; **skok o tyczce** pole vault. **3.** *pot.* (*osoba wysoka*) beanpole.

tyczkarz *mp sport* pole-vaulter.

tyczkowaty *a.* spindly.

tyczkowy *a.* **fasola tyczkowa** scarlet runner (*Phaseolus vulgaris communis*).

tyczyć się *ipf. form.* concern; **co się tyczy...** as regards...

tyć *ipf.* **tyję tyjesz** put on *l.* gain weight; get *l.* grow fat.

tydzień *mi* **tygodni-** *Gen.* **-a** week; **co tydzień** weekly; every week; **Wielki Tydzień** *rel.* Holy Week; **(całymi) tygodniami** for weeks on end; **od**

dziś za tydzień a week from today; **za dwa tygo-dnie** in two weeks' time.

tyfus *mi med.* typhus (fever); **tyfus brzuszny** typhoid (fever); **tyfus plamisty** typhus fever.

tyfusowy *a. med.* typhous.

tygiel *mi* -gl- *Gen.* -a melting pot; crucible.

tygielek *mi* -lk- *Gen.* -a pot.

tygodnik *mi Gen.* -a weekly.

tygodniowo *adv.* weekly.

tygodniowy *a.* (*o zarobku*) weekly; (*o urlopie*) week-long.

tygodniówka *f. Gen.pl.* -ek *pot.* (weekly) wage.

Tygrys *mi geogr.* the Tigris.

tygrys *ma zool.* tiger (*Panthera tigris*).

tygrysi *a.* tiger('s); **tygrysie oko** *min.* tiger's-eye.

tygrysica *f.* tigress.

tygrysięta *pl. Gen.pl.* -siąt tiger cubs.

tykać[1] *ipf.* (= *dotykać*) touch; **nie tknąć jedze-nia** not to touch food. ~ **się[1]** *ipf.* **nie tykać się cze-goś** not to touch sth.

tykać[2] *ipf.* (*o zegarze*) (= *wydawać miarowy odgłos*) tick. ~ **się[2]** *ipf.* (= *mówić sobie po imie-niu*) be on first name terms.

tykać[3] *ipf. pot.* (= *mówić komuś po imieniu*) call by first name.

tyknąć *pf.* -ij *zob.* **tykać[2]**.

tykowaty *a.* spindly.

tykwa *f. bot.* bottle gourd (*Lagenaria vulga-ris*).

tylda *f. druk.* tilde.

tyle *pron. Ins.* -oma *l.* -u **1.** (*zastępuje liczeb-nik lub odnosi się do niego*) (*przed rzeczowni-kiem w l.mn.*) so *l.* this many; (*przed rzeczowni-kiem w l.poj.*) so *l.* this much; **dwa razy tyle** twice as many/much; **tyle a tyle** so many/much; **tyle sa-mo** as many/much (as); **tyle wystarczy** that (many/much) is enough; **mam dwa razy tyle lat, co ty** I'm twice as old as you are. **2. o tyle o ile** more or less; **ile osób, tyle opinii** as many opin-ions as people; **tyle co nic** *l.* **kot napłakał** next to nothing; **tyle że lepszy/tańszy** only better/cheap-er; **był na tyle rozsądny, że nie stawiał oporu** he was reasonable enough not to resist; **głupi jesteś i tyle!** *pot.* you're stupid, that's what you are; **i tyle go widziano** and so much he was seen; **twarz ma nie tyle ładną, ile interesującą** her face is not so much pretty as interesting; **tyle tylko, że** ex-cept that. **3.** (= *tak wiele, tak dużo*) (*przed rze-czownikiem w l.mn.*) so many; (*przed rzeczowni-kiem w l.poj.*) so much; **tyle lat cię nie widziałem** I haven't seen you for so many years; **tyle jest zła na świecie** there's so much evil in the world; **tyle o pierwszym zagadnieniu** so much for the first problem.

tylec *mi* -lc- *Gen.* -a back; (*gałęzi*) snag.

tylko *particle* only; just; **gdybym tylko wiedzia-ła** if only I had known; **kiedy tylko chcesz** when-ever you want; **tylko co** (= *przed chwilą*) just; **tyl-ko nie ja!** anybody but me!; **tylko patrzeć, jak...** *pot.* before long...; **tylko nie hałasujcie!** just make sure not to make any noise!; **tylko spokojnie!** stay calm!; **tylko tego brakowało!** that's the lim-it!, that beats all!; **tylko i wyłącznie** exclusively;

żebyś tylko się nie wygadał! just don't spill the beans!; **nic tylko śpiewa** he does nothing but sings. – *conj.* but; **nie jest głupi, tylko leniwy** he's not so much stupid as lazy; **wpadłbym, tylko że nie mogę** I'd drop in, but I cannot; **nie tylko ro-wery, ale i samochody** not only bikes, but also cars; **wtedy i tylko wtedy, gdy** when, and only when,...

tylnojęzykowy *a. jęz.* velar.

tylny *a.* **1.** (*znajdujący się z tyłu*) back; (*o kole, siedzeniu*) rear. **2.** *jęz.* back.

tylu *num. zob.* **tyle**.

tylżycki *a.* of Tilsit.

tył *mi* **1.** (*strona przeciwległa*) back; (*budyn-ku, samochodu*) rear; **tyłem do kogoś/czegoś** with one's back to sb/sth; **wejście od tyłu** back entrance; **na tyłach czegoś** in the back of sth; **iść tyłem** walk backwards; **jechać tyłem** reverse; **włożyć coś tył(em) na przód** put sth on back to front; **wystawić kogoś tyłem do wiatru** *pot.* leave sb out in the cold; **mieć tyły (w czymś)** *pot.* be be-hind (with sth); **mieć tyły u kogoś** *pot.* be in hock to sb. **2.** (*przestrzeń za kimś, czymś*) back; rear; **od tyłu** from behind; **do tyłu** backwards; **w przód i w tył** to and fro; **w tył zwrot!** about face!; **pozo-stawać w tyle (za kimś/czymś)** lag behind (sb/sth).

tyłek *mi* -łk- *Gen.* -a *pot.* rear (end); bottom; **dać komuś w tyłek** kick sb's butt; **dostać w tyłek** get kicked on the butt; **ratować czyjś tyłek** save sb's ass *l.* butt; **ruszyć tyłek** move one's ass; **wy-piąć na kogoś tyłek** leave sb high and dry; poop out on sb; **wziąć kogoś za tyłek** settle sb's hash.

tyłomózgowie *n. Gen.pl.* -i *anat.* rhombence-phalon; hindbrain.

tyłozgięcie *n. med.* retroflection.

tyły *pl. Gen.* -ów *wojsk.* rear; **na tyłach** behind the lines.

tym[1] *pron. zob.* **ten, to**.

tym[2] *particle* **im starszy, tym głupszy** the old-er, the stupider; **tym bardziej że...** especially that...; **tym gorzej/lepiej dla nas** it's all the worse/better for us; **tym samym** thereby; thus.

tymczasem *adv.* **1.** (= *w tym samym czasie*) meanwhile; in the meantime; **a tymczasem...** but at the same time... **2.** (= *obecnie*) mean-while, for the time being. – *conj.* (= *jednakże*) yet, however. – *int.* (*pożegnanie*) see you.

tymczasowo *adv.* temporarily.

tymczasowość *f.* temporariness.

tymczasowy *a.* temporary; (*o rządzie, decyzji*) provisional.

tymianek *mi* -nk- *Gen.* -u *l.* -a *bot.* thyme (*Thy-mus*).

tymotka *f. Gen.pl.* -ek *bot.* timothy (grass) (*Phleum*).

tympanon *mi* **1.** *bud.* tympan(um). **2.** *muz.* kettledrum.

tynf *ma hist.* Polish silver coin; **dobry żart tyn-fa wart** a good joke is worth a laugh.

tynk *mi* plaster.

tynkal *mi min.* tincal.

tynkarski *a.* plasterer's.

tynkarz *mp* plasterer.

tynkować *ipf.* plaster.

tynkowy *a.* plaster; **podkład tynkowy** rough coat.

tynktura *f.* tincture.

typ *mi Gen.* **-u** **1.** (= *model, wzór*) kind; type; pattern; **(nie) być w czyimś typie** (not to) be sb's type; **typ gospodarki** pattern of economy. **2.** (*człowiek określonej kategorii*) type; **typ naukowca/sportowca** scientific/sporting type. **3.** *pot.* (= *przewidywany zwycięzca*) bet. **4.** *biol., antrop., psych., teor.lit.* type. *– mp Gen.* **-a** *pot.* character; **typ spod ciemnej gwiazdy** shady character.

typek *mp* **-pk-** *pl.* **-i** *pot.* jerk.

typizacja *f.* typification.

typizować *ipf.* typify.

typograf *mp Gen.* **-a** *pl.* **-owie** *druk.* typographer. *– mi Gen.* **-u** *pl.* **-y** *druk.* typograph.

typografia *f. Gen.* **-ii** *druk.* typography.

typograficzny *a. druk.* typographic; (*o punkcie*) typography; **szata typograficzna** typography.

typologia *f. Gen.* **-ii** typology.

typologiczny *a.* typologic.

typować *ipf.* **1.** (= *wybierać*) select. **2.** (= *desygnować*) designate (*na coś* for sth). **3.** (= *przewidywać zwycięzcę*) (*na wyścigach*) put one's money on.

typowo *adv.* typically; characteristically.

typowość *f.* typicality.

typowy *a.* **1.** (= *charakterystyczny*) typical; characteristic (*dla kogoś/czegoś* of sb/sth); **być typowym przykładem czegoś** epitomize sth. **2.** (= *standardowy*) standard.

tyrać *ipf. pot.* grind.

tyrada *f. lit.* tirade.

tyraliera *f. wojsk.* extended order.

tyran *mp* tyrant; despot.

tyrania *f. Gen.* **-ii** *t. polit.* tyranny.

tyranizować *ipf.* tyrannize; oppress.

tyranozaur *ma paleont.* tyrannosaur (*Tyrannosaurus rex*); *pot.* T-rex.

tyrański *a.* tyrannical.

Tyrol *mi geogr.* Tyrol.

tyrolski *a.* Tyrolese.

tyrystor *mi Gen.* **-a** *techn.* thyristor.

tys. *abbr.* (= *tysiące*) thou.

tysiąc *num. i mi Gen.* **-siąca** *Gen.pl.* **-sięcy** **1.** thousand; (= *1000*) a thousand, one thousand; **pięć/sto/wiele tysięcy** five/a hundred/many thousand; **tysiące ludzi** thousands of people; **baśnie z tysiąca i jednej nocy** the tales of the Thousand and One Nights; Arabian Nights. **2.** *karty* thousand (*Eastern European card game*).

tysiąckroć *adv. lit.* (*także* **po tysiąckroć**) = **tysiąckrotnie**.

tysiąckrotnie *adv.* a thousand times, a thousandfold.

tysiąckrotny *a.* thousandfold; **tysiąckrotne dzięki** a thousand thanks.

tysiąclecie *n. Gen.pl.* **-i** millenium.

tysiączny, tysięczny *a.* **1.** (= *odpowiadający liczbie tysiąc*) thousandth. **2.** (= *niezliczony*) countless; **tysięczne dzięki** a thousand thanks.

tytan *mp Gen.* **-a** *pl.* **-i** *mit.* Titan; **tytan pracy** *przen.* demon for work. *– mi Gen.* **-u** *pl.* **-y** *chem.* titanium.

tytaniczny *a.* titanic.

tytanit *mi min.* titanite.

tytanowiec *mi* **-wc-** *Gen.* **-a** *chem.* titanium group element.

tytanowy *a. chem.* titanic.

tytłać *ipf. pot.* soil. **~ się** *ipf. pot.* make a mess of oneself.

tytoniowy *a.* (*o liściach, przemyśle*) tobacco.

tytoń *mi* **1.** *bot.* tobacco (*Nicotiana*). **2.** (*produkt*) tobacco.

tytularnie *adv.* nominally; titularly.

tytularny *a.* titular; nominal.

tytulatura *f.* **1.** titulature; (*panującego*) title. **2.** (*książki*) titulature.

tytuł *mi* **1.** (= *nazwa dzieła*) title; **film pod tytułem...** movie titled... **2.** (= *stopień, godność*) title; **obrońca tytułu** *sport* defending champion; **tytuł mistrzowski** championship; **tytuł szlachecki** knighthood. **3.** (= *uprawnienie*) title (*do czegoś* to sth); **tytuł własności** title deed; **tytułem próby** as an experiment; **tytułem rekompensaty** by way of compensation; **z tytułu dokonań** in recognition of achievements.

tytułować *ipf.* **1.** (= *nadawać tytuł dziełu itp.*) title. **2.** (= *używać tytułu danej osoby*) address (*sb*) (*kimś* as...). **~ się** *ipf.* **+** *Ins.* use the title of.

tytułowy *a.* title; (*o bohaterze*) eponymous; **strona/rola tytułowa** title page/role.

tzn. *abbr.* (= *to znaczy*) i.e.

tzw. *abbr.* (= *tak zwany*) so-called.

U

U, u *n. indecl.* (*litera*) U, u; **U jak Urszula** U is for Uniform; U as in Uniform.

u *prep.* + *Gen.* **1.** (*w pobliżu*) at; **u drzwi** at the door; **u stóp wzgórza** at the foot of the hill; **być u władzy** be in power; **znaleźć się u celu/mety** reach the destination/finishing line. **2.** (*część składowa, przynależność*) of; **rzemyk u hełmu** stap of one's helmet; **klamka u drzwi** doorhandle; **palce u nogi** toes; **palce u rąk** fingers; **szyja smukła jak u łabędzia** a neck as slender as a swan's; **u Szekspira** in Shakespeare. **3.** (*wskazuje na osobę*) at; **u Anny** at Anna's, at Anna's place; **wizyta u dentysty** a visit to the dentist; **(być) u siebie** (be) at one's own place; **czuć się jak u siebie w domu** feel at home; **mieszkać u przyjaciół** stay with one's friends; **pracować u szewca** work at shoemaker's; **co u was słychać?** how is it going?, how are things with you? – *int.* **1.** (*ból*) ooh. **2.** (*rozczarowanie*) doggone. **3.** (*zdziwienie*) oho.

uaktualniać *ipf.*, **uaktualnić** *pf.* **-ij** update, bring up to date.

uaktywniać *ipf.*, **uaktywnić** *pf.* **-ij** activate; *komp.* enable. **~ się** *ipf.*, **uaktywnić się** *pf.* be activated, become active.

UAM *abbr.* (= *Uniwersytet im. Adama Mickiewicza*) AMU (= *Adam Mickiewicz University*).

uatrakcyjniać *ipf.*, **uatrakcyjnić** *pf.* **-ij** make attractive.

UB *abbr. hist.* (= *Urząd Bezpieczeństwa*) secret political police (*in communist Poland*).

ub. *abbr.* (= *ubiegły*) last.

ubabrać *pf.* **-brzę -brzesz** *pot.* soil. **~ się** *pf. pot.* make o.s. dirty.

ubarwiać *ipf.*, **ubarwić** *pf.* **1.** *lit.* (= *nadawać barwę*) color, *Br.* colour. **2.** *przen.* (= *upiększać*) embellish.

ubarwienie *n.* (= *barwa skóry lub sierści*) coloration; coloring, *Br.* colouring; **ubarwienie ochronne** protective coloration *l.* coloring.

ubarwiony *a.* (*t. o relacji, opowieści*) colored, *Br.* coloured.

ubaw *mi* (= *wesoła zabawa*) *pot.* shindig, shindy; (= *coś śmiesznego*) riot; **niezły ubaw** great fun.

ubawić *pf.* amuse. **~ się** *pf. pot.* have fun.

ubecja *f. pog., hist.* secret political police (*in communist Poland*).

ubecki *a. pog., hist.* of secret political police (*in communist Poland*).

ubek *mp pog., hist.* secret police sleuth (*in communist Poland*).

ubezdźwięczniać *ipf.*, **ubezdźwięcznić** *pf.* **-ij** *jęz.* devoice.

ubezdźwięcznienie *n. jęz.* devoicing.

ubezdźwięczniony *a. jęz.* devoiced.

ubezpieczać *ipf.* **1.** (= *zawierać umowę o odszkodowanie*) insure (*kogoś/coś od czegoś* sb/sth against sth); **być ubezpieczonym na 200 tys. złotych** be insured for 200,000 zloty. **2.** (= *asekurować*) cover. **~ się** *ipf.* **1.** (= *ubezpieczać siebie lub mienie*) insure o.s. (*od czegoś* against sth). **2.** (= *asekurować się wzajemnie*) cover one another.

ubezpieczalnia *f. Gen.pl.* **-i** *pot.* insurance company, insurer.

ubezpieczenie *n.* **1.** (= *zabezpieczenie odszkodowania*) insurance; **ubezpieczenie na życie** life insurance; **ubezpieczenie od ognia/kradzieży/ nieszczęśliwych wypadków** fire/theft/accident insurance; **ubezpieczenie od odpowiedzialności cywilnej** third-party insurance; **ubezpieczenie społeczne** social security; **ubezpieczenie zdrowotne** health insurance; **wartość ubezpieczenia** insured value; **zakres** *l.* **pokrycie ubezpieczenia** coverage. **2.** (= *składka ubezpieczeniowa*) insurance premium. **3.** (= *zabezpieczenie, asekuracja*) *sport, wojsk.* protection.

ubezpieczeniowy *a.* insurance; **polisa ubezpieczeniowa** insurance policy; **składka ubezpieczeniowa** insurance premium.

ubezpieczony *a.* (= *objęty ubezpieczeniem*) insured.

ubezpieczyciel *mp* (= *firma ubezpieczeniowa*) insurer.

ubezpieczyć *pf. zob.* **ubezpieczać**. **~ się** *pf. zob.* **ubezpieczać się**.

ubezwłasnowolniać *ipf.*, **ubezwłasnowolnić** *pf.* **-ij** *prawn.* incapacitate.

ubezwłasnowolnienie *n. prawn.* incapacitation.

ubiczować *pf. zob.* **biczować**.

ubić *pf.* **ubiję ubijesz, ubij** *zob.* **ubijać**.

ubiec *pf.* **ubiegnę ubiegniesz, ubiegnij, ubiegł**, **ubiegać** *ipf.* **1.** (= *uprzedzić*) forestall; **chciałabym go w tym ubiec** I'd like to beat him to it. **2.** *lit.* (*o czasie*) (= *minąć*) go by. **3.** *tylko pf.* (= *przebiec jakiś dystans*) run, cover.

ubiegać się *ipf.* (= *starać się*) (*o pracę, pożyczkę*) apply (*o coś* for sth); **ubiegać się o pracę/wizę** apply for a job/visa; **ubiegać się o azyl/wybór** seek asylum/election; **ubiegać się o mandat poselski/prezydenturę** run for Parliament/President; **ubiegać się o czyjąś rękę** seek sb's hand in marriage.

ubiegłoroczny *a.* last year's.

ubiegłowieczny *a.* last century's.

ubiegły *a.* last; **w ubiegłym tygodniu/roku** last week/year.

ubiegnąć *pf.* **ubiegnę ubiegniesz, ubiegnij, ubiegł = ubiec.**

ubielić *pf.* whiten; (*ściany*) whitewash.

ubierać *ipf.* **1.** (= *zakładać komuś ubranie*) dress; **ubierać coś w słowa** *przen.* put sth into words. **2.** (= *sprawiać, szyć komuś odzież*) clothe. **3.** (= *ozdabiać*) (*choinkę, tort*) decorate. **~ się** *ipf.* **1.** (= *wkładać ubranie*) dress, get dressed; **dobrze/modnie się ubierać** dress well/fashionably; **nie mam w co się ubrać!** I have nothing to wear! **2.** (= *kupować odzież w określonej firmie*) buy one's clothes (*u kogoś* at sb's).

ubijacz *mi Gen.* **-a** (*przyrząd kuchenny*) whisk, beater.

ubijać *ipf.* **1.** (= *utwardzać*) compact, ram; **ubić interes** *przen.* strike a deal; **ubić na czymś złoty interes** make a great deal in sth. **2.** (= *zmieniać konsystencję*) (*śmietanę*) whip; (*jajko, białko*) whisk, beat; (*masło*) churn. **3.** (= *zabijać zwierzęta*) slaughter.

ubijak *mi Gen.* **-a 1.** (*przyrząd kuchenny*) masher. **2.** *techn.* rammer.

ubikacja *f.* toilet.

ubiorek *mi* **-rk-** *bot.* iberis, candytuft (*Iberis*).

ubiorę *itd. pf. zob.* **ubrać.**

ubiór *mi* **-o-** dress, clothing; **ubiór codzienny** *l.* **domowy** casual clothes.

ubliżać *ipf.* **1.** (= *obrażać*) insult (*komuś* sb). **2.** (= *naruszać*) (*np. czyjejś godności*) offend; **ubliżać obyczajom** offend custom; **nie ubliżając,...** no offence, but..., no disrespect, but...

ubliżająco *adv.* insultingly.

ubliżyć *pf. zob.* **ubliżać.**

ubłagać *pf.* **1.** (= *uprosić*) entreat; **dać się ubłagać** relent; **ubłagać kogoś, aby coś zrobił** beg sb into doing sth. **2.** (= *udobruchać*) appease.

ubłocić *pf.* soil with mud, muddy. **~ się** *pf.* get muddy.

ub.m. *abbr.* (= *ubiegłego miesiąca*) last month.

ubocze *n. Gen.pl.* **-y położony na uboczu** out-of-the-way, off the beaten track; **mieszkać na uboczu** live off the beaten track; **stać/mieszkać na uboczu** (*np. o domu*) be/live off the beaten track; **trzymać się na uboczu** keep o.s. in the background.

uboczny *a.* (*o kwestii*) extraneous (*dla czegoś* to sth); **skutek** *l.* **efekt uboczny** side effect; **działanie uboczne** *med.* side effect; **produkt uboczny** by-product.

ubodnąć *pf.* **-ij** *zob.* **ubóść.**

ubogi *a.* **uboższy 1.** (= *niezamożny; świadczący o ubóstwie*) poor; **ubogi duchem** poor in spirit; **ubogi krewny** *przen.* poor relation. **2.** (= *nieobfity*) meager, *Br.* meagre, scanty, poor (*w coś* in sth); (*o glebie*) hungry; (*o rudzie, złożu*) low-grade; (*o języku*) poor; **uboga mieszanka** *techn.* lean mixture. – *mp* poor person.

ubogo *adv.* **ubożej** poorly.

ubojnia *f. Gen.pl.* **-i** abattoir, slaughterhouse.

ubojowy *a.* **zakład ubojowy** abattoir; **zdolność ubojowa** slaughter capability.

ubolewać *ipf. lit.* regret (*nad czymś* sth); deplore (*nad kimś/czymś* sb/sth).

ubolewanie *n.* regret; **godny ubolewania** regrettable; **wyrazy ubolewania** condolences; **wyrażać ubolewanie z powodu...** express sorrow at..., regret that...

ubowiec *mp* **-wc-** *pl.* **-y** *pog., hist.* secret police sleuth (*in communist Poland*).

ubożeć *ipf. lit.* become impoverished.

ubożyć *ipf. lit.* impoverish.

ubój *mi* **-o-** *Gen.pl.* **-ów** slaughter; **ubój gospodarczy** home slaughter; **ubój przemysłowy** commercial slaughter; *Br. t.* industrial slaughter; **ubój rytualny** ritual slaughter.

ubóstwiać *ipf.* **1.** (= *bardzo lubić*) adore. **2.** (= *podnosić do godności boga*) idolize. **~ się** *ipf.* adore each other, adore one another.

ubóstwiany *a.* adored.

ubóstwić *pf.* **-ij** *zob.* **ubóstwiać 2.**

ubóstwienie *n.* **1.** (= *uwielbienie*) adoration. **2.** (= *podniesienie do godności boga*) idolatry.

ubóstwo *n.* poverty; **ubóstwo intelektualne** intellectual poverty; **ubóstwo roślin/zwierząt** floral/faunal poverty.

ubóść *pf.* **ubodę ubodziesz, ubódź, ubódł ubodła ubodli 1.** *zob.* **bóść. 2.** (= *sprawić przykrość, obrazić*) sting.

ub.r. *abbr.* (= *ubiegłego roku*) last year.

ubrać *pf.* **ubiorę ubierzesz** *zob.* **ubierać. ~ się** *pf. zob.* **ubierać się.**

ubranie *n.* **1.** (= *odzież*) clothing; **gotowe ubrania** off-the-rack clothes; *Br.* off-the-peg clothes; **ubranie ochronne** protective clothing; **ubranie robocze** work clothes *l.* suit. **2.** *pot.* (= *garnitur*) suit. **3.** *lit.* (= *ozdoba*) decoration.

ubraniowy *a.* **materiał ubraniowy** serge; (*na garnitury*) suiting.

ubranko *n. Gen.pl.* **-ek** (child's) clothes.

ubrany *a.* dressed; **być ubranym w coś** wear sth, be dressed in sth; **ubrany na żółto** dressed in yellow; **ubrany w piękne słowa** *przen.* couched in beautiful words.

ubrdać *pf.* **ubrdać sobie coś** *pot.* take sth into one's head. **~ się** *pf.* come into sb's head; **co ci się znowu ubrdało?** what did you get into your head this time?; *iron.* (*jako komentarz*) it's just your mind that's playing tricks on you.

ubrudzić *pf.* soil. **~ się** *pf.* get dirty.

ubyć *pf.* **ubędę ubędziesz, ubądź** *zob.* **ubywać.**

ubytek *mi* **-tk-** **1.** (= *utrata, ubywanie*) (*krwi, wagi, paliwa*) loss. **2.** *pat.* (*w zębie*) cavity; **ubytek kostny/tkanki** bone/tissue defect.

ubywać *ipf.* **-am -asz 1.** (*o ludziach*) (= *odchodzić, znikać*) go away, disappear; (= *umierać*) depart; **ubywa nam pracowników** we've got fewer and fewer workers. **2.** (= *zmniejszać się*) (*np. o ludności*) diminish; **ubywa dnia** the days are closing in; **ubyło mi lat** I feel years younger; **ubyło mi na wadze** I have lost weight; **ubywa księżyca** *t. astron.* the moon is waning; **w Polsce ubywa ludności** Poland's population is decreasing.

ubzdryngolić się *pf. pot.* get tight, get plastered.

ubzdryngolony *a.* **-eni** *pot.* tight, plastered.

ubzdurać *pf.* = **ubrdać**.

UC *abbr.* (= *Urząd Celny*) Customs Office.

ucałować *pf.* kiss; **ucałujcie od nas rodziców!** give our kisses to the parents!

ucałowanie *n.* **przesyłać ucałowania** send kisses.

ucapić *pf. pot.* (= *złapać*) grab (*kogoś za coś* sb by sth).

ucharakteryzować *pf. teatr* make up. **~ się** *pf. teatr* make o.s. up.

uchatka *f. Gen.pl.* **-ek** *zool.* sea lion, otarioid (*Otariidae*).

uchlać się *pf. pot.* (= *upić się*) get pissed.

ucho *n. pl.* **usz-** *Nom.* **-y** *Gen.* **-u** 1. (= *narząd słuchu*) ear; **ośle uszy** *przen.* dog-ears; **ból ucha** *pat.* earache; **zapalenie ucha** *pat.* inflammation of the ear, otitis; **zapalenie ucha środkowego** *pat.* inflammation of the middle ear, otitis media; **dostać po uszach** get a rap across the knuckles; **kłaść uszy po sobie** (*o zwierzęciu*) lay back its ears; *przen.* swallow one's pride; **mieć kogoś/czegoś po uszy** be fed up with sb/sth; **mieć muzykalne ucho** have an ear for music; **nadstawić ucha** *l.* **uszu** prick up one's ears; **natrzeć komuś uszu** *przen.* give sb a dressing-down; **nie wierzyć własnym uszom** not believe one's ears; **powiedzieć coś komuś na ucho** whisper sth to sb's ear; **puszczać coś mimo uszu** turn a deaf ear to sth; **słuchać jednym uchem** listen with half an ear; **strzyc uszami** *t. przen.* prick up one's ears; **tkwić w czymś po uszy** be up to one's ears in sth; **coś wychodzi komuś uszami** sb is fed up with sth; **od ucha do ucha** from ear to ear; **na własne uszy** with one's own ears; **zadłużony po uszy** up to his ears in debt; **zakochany po uszy** head over heels in love; **dzwoni mi w uszach** my ears are ringing; **hałas, od którego uszy puchną** ear-splitting noise; **uszy mi więdną od tego co mówisz** what you're saying makes me sick; **obiło mi się o uszy, że...** it's come to my ears that...; **ściany mają uszy** walls have ears; **uszy do góry!** cheer up! 2. (= *klapka u czapki*) flap. 3. *Nom.pl. i Acc.pl.* **ucha** *l.* **uszy** *Gen.* **uch** *l.* **uszów** *Dat.* **uchom** *l.* **uszom** *Ins.* **uchami** *l.* **uszami** *Loc.* **uchach** *l.* **uszach** (*uchwyt*) ear; **ucho igły** eye of a needle; **ucho holownicze** *techn.* towing lug; **póty dzban wodę nosi, póki mu się ucho nie urwie** the pitcher goes so often to the well that it is broken at last.

uchodzić *ipf.* 1. (*o cieczach, gazach*) (= *wydobywać się*) leak, escape. 2. *lit.* (= *uciekać, unikać*) abscond; **ujść kary** avoid punishment; **ujść śmierci** escape death; **ujść z życiem** save one's life; **zajście uszło jego uwagi** *l.* **uwadze** the incident escaped his attention; **to ci nie ujdzie płazem** *l.* **na sucho!** you won't get away with it! 3. *lit.* (*o rzekach*) (= *wpadać*) disgorge itself (*do czegoś* into sth). 4. (= *być uznanym, poczytywanym*) pass (*za kogoś/coś* as sb/sth). 5. (= *nadawać się*) be fit; **to nie uchodzi** (= *nie wypada*) it's

unseemly, it's not done; **ujdzie w tłoku** *l.* **od biedy** *pot.* it will just do.

uchodźca *mp* refugee.

uchodźstwo *n. lit.* exile; **(rząd) na uchodźstwie** (government) in exile.

uchować *pf.* **-am -asz** *lit.* (= *ustrzec*) preserve (*kogoś/coś przed kimś/czymś* sb/sth from sb/sth); **uchowaj Boże!** God forbid! **~ się** *pf.* 1. *lit.* (= *przetrwać*) remain untouched, be preserved; **nic się przed nią nie uchowa** nothing is safe from her. 2. *przest.* (= *przeżyć*) survive; **gdzieś ty się uchował?** which planet are you from?

uchronić *pf.* preserve (*kogoś/coś przed kimś/czymś* sb/sth from sb/sth). **~ się** *pf.* protect o.s. (*przed kimś/czymś* from sb/sth).

uchwalać *ipf.*, **uchwalić** *pf.* pass.

uchwała *f.* resolution.

uchwycić *pf.* 1. (= *złapać*) seize; **uchwycić moment** *l.* **sposobność** grasp the opportunity; **uchwycić ster rządów** seize the power. 2. (= *postrzec*) discern, perceive; (*sens, myśl*) grasp; (*dźwięk*) catch. 3. (= *trafnie przedstawić*) (*np. podobieństwo*) capture. **~ się** *pf.* 1. (= *złapać rękami*) catch hold (*czegoś* of sth). 2. *przen.* (= *uczepić się*) seize; (*nadziei, myśli*) cling (*czegoś* to sth).

uchwyt *mi* 1. (= *zaczep*) handle; (*na skale*) grip; (*w autobusie*) strap; (*do podnoszenia, holowania*) lug. 2. (= *rączka*) handle. 3. (= *uchwycenie się*) grip; **rozluźnić uchwyt** loosen one's grip *l.* hold.

uchwytny *a.* 1. (= *dostrzegalny*) noticeable, perceptible. 2. *pot.* (*o człowieku*) (= *osiągalny*) reachable.

uchybiać *ipf.*, **uchybić** *pf.* 1. *lit.* (= *naruszać normy*) transgress (*czemuś* sth). 2. *lit.* (= *obrażać*) offend (*komuś* sb).

uchybienie *n.* 1. (= *niedociągnięcie*) transgression. 2. (= *obraza*) offense, *Br.* offence. 3. (= *przeoczenie, błąd*) inadvertence.

uchylać *ipf.*, **uchylić** *pf.* 1. (= *nieznacznie otworzyć*) open slightly, set ajar; **uchylić okno/drzwi** open the window/door a crack. 2. (= *nieznacznie odsłonić*) draw (a little) aside; **uchylić firankę** pull the curtain a little to one side; **uchylać kapelusza** raise one's hat; **uchylić rąbka tajemnicy** lift the veil of secrecy. 3. *prawn.* (= *unieważniać*) (*przepis, ustawę*) repeal; (*decyzję*) reverse; (*wyrok*) quash; (*sankcje*) lift. **~ się** *ipf.*, **uchylić się** *pf.* 1. (= *otwierać się nieznacznie*) (*o oknie, drzwiach*) open slightly. 2. (= *odchylać się, unikając czegoś*) dodge; (= *przykucnąć*) duck. 3. (= *wymigiwać się*) evade (*od czegoś* sth).

uchylno *a.* **okno uchylno-rozwierane** turn-and-tilt window.

uchylny *a.* **okno uchylne** tilt window.

uchyłek *mi* **-łk-** *anat.* diverticulum.

uciąć *pf.* **utnę utniesz, utnij** *zob.* **ucinać**.

uciąg *mi techn.* towed weight.

uciągnąć *pf.* **-ij** lug.

uciążliwość *f.* inconvenience.

uciążliwy *a.* (*obowiązek, zadanie*) burdensome; (*człowiek, choroba*) troublesome.

ucichnąć *pf.* -**ij** **1.** (= *uciszyć się*) (*o człowieku*) fall silent; (*o bólu*) subside; (*o hałasie*) die away; **w pokoju nagle ucichło** suddenly the room fell silent. **2.** (= *uspokoić się*) die down; (*o burzy, pogłoskach, skandalu*) blow over.

uciec *pf.* **ucieknę uciekniesz, ucieknij, uciekł** *zob.* **uciekać.** ~ **się** *pf. zob.* **uciekać się.**

uciecha *f.* **1.** (= *radość*) joy, fun; **ale uciecha!** what a treat!; **ku uciesze widowni** to the amusement of the audience; **mieć dużo uciechy z kogoś/czegoś** have lots of fun with sb/sth; **sprawić komuś uciechę** make sb happy. **2.** (= *to, co sprawia radość*) pleasure; **drobne uciechy życia** life's little pleasures.

ucieczka *f. Gen.pl.* -**ek** **1.** (= *uciekanie*) escape; (*zwł. z więzienia*) breakout; (*kochanków*) elopement; **ucieczka kapitału** *ekon.* flight of capital; **ucieczka od rzeczywistości** *przen.* escape from reality; **ratować się ucieczką** run for one's life, run for dear life; **rzucić się do ucieczki** make a bolt for it; **zmusić kogoś do ucieczki** put sb to flight. **2.** (= *pociecha*) refuge. **3.** *sport* (*w czasie wyścigu*) breakaway. **4.** *fiz.* (*neutronów, gazu*) leakage.

uciekać *ipf.* **1.** (= *umykać*) escape; run away (*przed kimś / czymś l. od kogoś / czegoś* from sb/ sth); (*o kochankach*) elope; **uciec z domu** run away from home; **uciec z więzienia** break jail; **uciekać spojrzeniem** look away; **uciekać w marzenia** escape into fantasy; **uciekło mi to z pamięci** it slipped my mind; **uciekam, bo za chwilę mam zajęcia** *pot.* I have to run: my classes start in a minute; **to mi nie ucieknie** that can wait; **jak się dowie, ucieknie, gdzie pieprz rośnie** when he learns about it, you won't see him for dust; **uciekaj!** run!, run along! **2.** (*o czasie*) (= *mijać*) fly. **3.** (*o płynach, gazach*) (= *uchodzić*) leak. **4.** (= *odjechać*) (*o autobusie, pociągu*) leave; **uciekł mi autobus** *pot.* I missed the bus. ~ **się** *ipf.* **1.** (= *posługiwać się czymś*) resort (*do czegoś* to sth). **2.** (= *odwoływać się do kogoś l. czegoś*) seek help (*do kogoś / czegoś* from sb/sth).

uciekinier *mp*, **uciekinierka** *f. Gen.pl.* -**ek** runaway, fugitive; **uciekinier polityczny** defector.

ucieleśniać *ipf.*, **ucieleśnić** *pf.* -**ij** embody. ~ **się** *ipf.*, **ucieleśnić się** *pf.* materialize.

ucieleśnienie *n.* embodiment (*czegoś* of sth); **być ucieleśnieniem dobroci** be all heart.

uciemiężać *ipf. lit.* oppress.

uciemiężony *a.* -**eni** *lit.* oppressed.

uciemiężyć *pf. zob.* **uciemiężać.**

ucierać *ipf.* (*buraki, marchew*) grate; (*żółtka, ciasto*) mix.

ucierpieć *pf.* -**ę** -**isz** (= *ponieść szkodę, doznać uszczerbku*) suffer; be hard hit (*od czegoś l. wskutek czegoś* by sth); **kraj mocno ucierpiał wskutek powodzi** the country was severely affected by flood; **nie ucierpieliśmy na tym** we're none the worse for it; **ucierpiał wskutek wypadku** he suffered injuries in the accident.

ucieszny *a.* droll.

ucieszyć *pf.* delight, gladden; **ucieszyć oczy (czymś)** feast one's eyes (on sth); **ucieszy Panią**

wiadomość, że... you will be pleased to know that... ~ **się** *pf.* be delighted (*z czegoś* with sth).

ucinać *ipf.* **1.** (= *odcinać*) cut, cut off; **jak nożem uciął** abruptly; **dałbym sobie rękę uciąć za niego** I'd go through fire and water for him. **2.** (= *raptownie przerywać*) break off; (*dyskusję, rozmowę*) cut short. **3.** (*o owadach*) (= *kąsać*) sting. **4.** (= *zrobić coś*) have, do; **uciąć sobie drzemkę/pogawędkę** have a nap/chat.

ucisk *mi* **1.** (= *napór*) pressure. **2.** (= *gnębienie*) oppression. **3.** (= *ściskanie*) (*w gardle, piersiach*) constriction.

uciskać *ipf.* **1.** (= *ugniatać*) press. **2.** (= *uwierać*) (*o butach*) pinch; (*o pasku*) sqeeze. **3.** (= *ciemiężyć*) oppress.

uciskowy *a.* **opaska uciskowa** *med.* torniquet; **opatrunek uciskowy** *med.* pressure dressing.

ucisnąć *pf.* -**snę** -**śniesz**, -**śnij** *zob.* **uciskać.**

uciszać *ipf.*, **uciszyć** *pf.* silence, hush; (*ból, rozpacz*) suppress; **uciszyć kogoś spojrzeniem** stare sb into silence. ~ **się** *ipf.*, **uciszyć się** *pf.* **1.** (= *cichnąć*) (*o ludziach*) fall silent; (*o śmiechu*) subside. **2.** (= *uspokajać się*) (*o morzu, wietrze*) calm down.

uciśniony *a.* -**eni** oppressed, down-trodden. – *mp* an oppressed person; **ludzie uciśnieni** the oppressed, the down-trodden.

uciułać *pf. zob.* **ciułać.**

ucywilizować *pf. zob.* **cywilizować.** ~ **się** *pf. zob.* **cywilizować się.**

uczcić *pf.* **uczczę uczcisz, uczcij** *zob.* **czcić.**

uczciwie *adv.* **1.** (= *rzetelnie*) honestly; **zarobić uczciwie trochę grosza** earn *l.* turn an honest penny. **2.** *pot.* (= *porządnie*) properly; **uczciwie sobie pojeść** have a square meal; **uczciwie pracować** do a fair share of the work.

uczciwość *f.* honesty.

uczciwy *a.* **1.** (= *rzetelny*) honest; (= *sprawiedliwy*) fair; **uczciwy gość** *pot.* square shooter; **uczciwy układ** *pot.* fair deal; **uczciwe traktowanie** fair treatment; **w uczciwy sposób** by honest *l.* fair means. **2.** *pot.* (= *porządny*) good; (*o posiłku*) square.

uczelnia *f. Gen.pl.* -**i** higher education institution; (= *szkoła wyższa*) college; (= *uniwersytet*) university; (= *politechnika*) polytechnic.

uczelniany *a.* university; college; polytechnic.

uczennica *f. zob.* **uczeń.**

uczeń *mp* -**czni**- *pl.* -**owie** *Gen.* -**ów**, **uczennica** *f.* **1.** *szkoln.* student. **2.** (= *praktykant*) intern, trainee; (*zwł. rzemiosła*) apprentice. **3.** (= *kontynuator mistrza*) disciple.

uczepić *pf.* attach. ~ **się** *pf.* **1.** (= *chwycić się*) grab (*czegoś* sth); grab hold (*czegoś* of sth). **2.** *pot.* (= *być natrętnym*) hang on; **przyczepić się jak rzep do psiego ogona** stick *l.* cling to sb like a leech, cling to sb like a barnacle. **3.** *pot.* (= *złośliwie krytykować*) pick (*kogoś* on sb). **4.** *pot.* (= *obstawać przy czymś*) stick (*czegoś* to sth); (*myśli, nadziei*) cling (*czegoś* to sth).

uczernić *pf.* -**nij** *l.* -**ń** *zob.* **czernić.**

uczesać *pf.* -**eszę** -**eszesz** *zob.* **czesać.** ~ **się** *pf. zob.* **czesać się.**

uczesanie *n.* hairstyle, hairdo.

uczestnictwo *n.* participation (*w czymś* in sth).

uczestniczka *f. Gen.pl.* -ek *zob.* **uczestnik**.

uczestniczyć *ipf.* **1.** (= *brać udział*) participate (*w czymś* in sth); (*w konferencji, spotkaniu*) attend (*w czymś* sth). **2.** (= *mieć udział*) contribute (*w czymś* to sth).

uczestnik *mp*, **uczestniczka** *f. Gen.pl.* -ek participant; (*zawodów*) competitor.

uczęszczać *ipf. form.* attend; **uczęszczać do szkoły** attend school.

uczęszczany *a.* (*o miejscu*) frequented; (*o drodze, szlaku*) busy.

uczłowieczać *ipf.*, **uczłowieczyć** *pf.* humanize.

uczniak *mp pl.* -cy *l.* -i *uj.* kid.

uczniowski *a.* student, student's; **samorząd uczniowski** student council.

uczoność *f.* **1.** (= *erudycja*) erudition, learning. **2.** (= *naukowy charakter*) learnedness.

uczony *a.* -eni **1.** (= *wykształcony*) learned. **2.** (= *świadczący o wiedzy*) learned; (*o wykładzie, wywodzie*) erudite. – *mp* scholar; (*w naukach przyrodniczych i ścisłych*) scientist.

uczta *f.* **1.** (= *biesiada*) feast. **2.** (= *wielka przyjemność*) feast; **uczta duchowa** feast for the spirit *l.* soul, spiritual feast; **uczta dla oka** feast for the eye.

ucztować *ipf.* feast.

uczucie *n.* **1.** (= *doznanie, emocja*) emotion; (*samotności, strachu*) feeling; (*głodu, zimna*) sensation; **grać na czyichś uczuciach** play at sb's heart strings; **zrobić coś z uczuciem** do sth with feeling; **z mieszanymi uczuciami** with mixed feelings; **nie darzą się specjalnym uczuciem** *iron.* there's no love lost between them; **jakie to uczucie zostać zwycięzcą?** how does it feel to be the winner?; **mam uczucie, że...** I have the feeling that... **2.** (= *miłość*) affection; **darzyć kogoś uczuciem** feel affection for sb.

uczuciowo *adv.* emotionally.

uczuciowość *f.* emotionality.

uczuciowy *a.* emotional.

uczuć *pf.* (= *poczuć*) feel.

uczulacz *mi Gen.* -a *chem., fot.* sensitizer.

uczulać *ipf.* (*na piękno, lek, substancję*) sensitize (*kogoś na coś* sb to sth). ~ **się** *ipf.* **1.** (= *stawać się uczulonym*) become allergic (*na coś* to sth). **2.** (= *stawać się wrażliwym*) become sensitive (*na coś* to sth).

uczulenie *n.* allergy (*na coś* to sth); **mieć uczulenie na coś** be allergic to sth.

uczuleniowiec *mp* -wc- *pl.* -y allergic person.

uczuleniowy *a.* allergic.

uczulić *pf. zob.* **uczulać**. ~ **się** *pf. zob.* **uczulać się**.

uczulony *a.* -eni allergic (*na coś* to sth).

uczyć *ipf.* teach (*kogoś czegoś* sb sth); **uczyć w szkole** teach at school, be a teacher; **doświadczenie uczy, że...** experience teaches that...; **ja cię nauczę!** *pot.* I'll teach you a lesson!; **nie ucz ojca dzieci robić** *pot.* don't teach your grandmother to suck eggs. ~ **się** *ipf.* (= *przyswajać wiedzę*) learn, study; **uczyć się dobrze/źle** be a good/bad

student; **uczyć się do egzaminu** study for an exam; *Br. t.* revise for an exam; **uczyć się na piątki** be an A student; **uczyć się na trójki** be an average student, be a C student; **uczyć się na własnych/czyichś błędach** learn from one's/sb's mistakes; **uczyć się na kogoś** *pot.* study to be sb; **uczyć się na pamięć** learn by heart.

uczynek *mi* -nk- act, deed; **przyłapać kogoś na gorącym uczynku** catch sb red-handed; **zrobić dobry/zły uczynek** do a good/bad deed.

uczynić *pf. zob.* **czynić**. ~ **się** *pf. zob.* **czynić się**.

uczynniać *ipf.*, **uczynnić** *pf.* -ij *med.* activate.

uczynność *f.* obligingness, helpfulness.

uczynny *a.* obliging, helpful.

udać (się) *pf. zob.* **udawać (się)**.

udanie *adv.* successfully, with success.

udany *a.* **1.** sham, feigned, pretended. **2.** successful; **spotkanie było udane** the meeting was a success.

udar *mi* **1.** *pat.* (= *porażenie*) stroke, ictus; *przest.* apoplexy; **udar mózgu** (cerebral) stroke; **udar serca** heart stroke; **udar słoneczny** sunstroke. **2.** *techn.* stroke, percussion.

udaremniać *ipf.*, **udaremnić** *pf.* -ij foil, frustrate, thwart.

udarł *itd. pf. zob.* **udrzeć**.

udarowy *a. techn.* percussive; **wiertarka udarowa** hammer drill.

udatnie *adv. przest.* nicely, neatly; adequately; successfully.

udatność *f. przest.* nicety; adequateness; success, successfulness.

udatny *a. przest.* nice, neat; adequate; successful.

udawacz *mp pot.* pretender, fake *l.* faker.

udawać *ipf.* **udaję udajesz, udawaj 1.** (= *pozorować*) pretend, fake; **udawał, że nie pamięta** he pretended he didn't remember; **on tylko udaje** he's just pretending. **2.** (= *naśladować*) imitate; **udawać Greka** play ignorant, play dumb. **3.** (*o rzeczach*) (= *wyglądać jak coś innego*) imitate. ~ **się** *ipf.* **1.** (= *odbywać się pomyślnie*) be a success, succeed, go off; **nie udać się** fail, be a failure; **jemu zawsze się udaje** he's always lucky; **udało mi się ją przekonać** I managed to convince her; **udało się nam** we've been lucky. **2.** (*o roślinach*) (= *ładnie wyrastać*) thrive; bear a good crop. **3.** *form.* (= *podążać*) go; **udawać się na spoczynek** retire, go to bed.

udawany *a.* sham, pretended, false, fake *l.* faked.

udekorować *pf. zob.* **dekorować**.

udeptać *pf.* -pczę -pczesz *l.* -pcę -pcesz, -pcz, **udeptywać** *ipf.* trample, tread.

uderzać *ipf.* **1.** (= *zadawać cios*) hit, strike; **uderzać kogoś w coś** hit sb on *l.* in sth; **uderzyć kogoś pięścią** punch sb; **uderzać kogoś po kieszeni** hit sb in the pocket. **2.** (= *zaskakiwać*) strike; amaze; perplex; puzzle; **uderzyło mnie, że...** it struck me (as strange) that...; **uderzyła mnie uroda tego miejsca** the beauty of this place has really struck me. **3.** (= *walić, tłuc*) beat; (*pięścią*) bang; (*o zegarze*) strike; **uderzać na**

alarm sound the alarm; **uderzyć w czułą strunę** touch a nerve; **uderzać w gaz** *pot.* booze; **uderzyć w kimono** *pot.* hit the sack *l.* hay, turn in; **uderzyć w płacz** *l.* ryk burst into tears. **4.** (= *gwałtownie stykać się*) hit (*w coś l. o coś* sth); **uderzać komuś do głowy** (*o krwi*) rush to sb's head; (*o sławie, alkoholu*) go to sb's head; **woda sodowa uderzyła mu do głowy** his success, fame, fortune, etc. went to his head. **5.** (= *napadać*) *t. przen.* strike (*na kogoś/coś l. w kogoś/coś* at sb/sth); assail, attack. **6.** *pot.* (= *zwracać się*) address (*do kogoś* sb); **uderzać w konkury** *przest.* court. ~ **się** *ipf.* **1.** (= *trącać sobą coś*) hit o.s.; (*uderzać się wzajemnie*) hit each other; **uderzyć się w głowę** hit o.s. on the head, hit one's head. **2.** (= *uderzać jakąś część swego ciała*) slap, tap; clap; **uderzać się w piersi** beat one's breast.

uderzająco *adv.* strikingly.

uderzający *a.* striking.

uderzenie *n.* **1.** (= *cios*) blow, stroke, knock, hit; **uderzenie pioruna** thunderstroke; **uderzenie serca** heartbeat; **uderzenie zegara** strike, stroke. **2.** (= *zderzenie się*) clash, impact, collision. **3.** *sport* strike; kick; trow; hit; stroke. **4.** *muz.* touch. **5.** *wojsk.* strike, attack; **uderzenie w skorumpowanych polityków** strike against corrupt politicians.

uderzeniowy *a.* **1.** (*towarzyszący uderzeniu*) striking; **fala uderzeniowa** *fiz.* shock wave; **dawka uderzeniowa** *med.* (initial) loading dose. **2.** *wojsk.* striking, attacking; **grupa uderzeniowa** task force.

uderzyć (się) *pf. zob.* **uderzać (się)**.

udko *n. Gen.pl.* **udek** *kulin.* leg.

udławić się *pf.* choke to death; **udław się!** *przen.* damn you!

udo *n. t. anat.* thigh, upper leg; *zool.* thigh, the femoral region.

udobruchać *pf.* placate, mollify, appease. ~ **się** *pf.* be placated, be mollified.

udogadniać *ipf.*, **udogodnić** *pf.* **-ij** facilitate, improve.

udogodnienie *n.* **1.** convenience, help. **2.** improvement.

udoić *pf.* **udoję udoisz, udój** *zob.* **doić**.

udojowy *a. roln.* (milk-)flow, draw, drawing.

udokumentować *pf. zob.* **dokumentować**.

udokumentowany *a.* substantiated; documented.

udomawiać *ipf.*, **udomowić** *pf.* **-ij** domesticate.

udomowiony *a.* domesticated.

udoskonalać *ipf.* improve, refine.

udoskonalenie *n.* improvement.

udoskonalić *pf. zob.* **udoskonalać**.

udostępniać *ipf.*, **udostępnić** *pf.* **-ij** make *l.* render available; make public; **udostępniać coś komuś** make sth available to sb.

udowadniać *ipf.*, **udowodnić** *pf.* **-ij** prove; evidence; substantiate.

udowy *a. anat.* femoral, thigh; **kość udowa** femoral *l.* thigh bone; **tętnica udowa** femoral artery.

udój *mi* **-o-** *Gen.pl.* **-ów 1.** (= *dojenie*) milking. **2.** (= *ilość mleka*) milk yield, (milk) flow.

udramatyzować *pf.* dramatize.

udrapnąć *pf.* **-ij** scratch.

udrapować *pf. zob.* **drapować**.

udręczać *ipf.* torment, distress.

udręczenie *n.* torment, distress.

udręczony *a.* **-eni** tormented, distressed.

udręczyć *pf. zob.* **udręczać**.

udręka *f.* torment, distress.

udrożniać *ipf.*, **udrożnić** *pf.* **-ij** make passable, open a passage; *med.* restore patency.

udry *pl. indecl.* **iść z kimś na udry** *pot.* be at loggerheads with sb; oppose sb.

udrzeć *pf.* **udrę udrzesz, udrzyj, udarł** *zob.* **udzierać**.

uduchowiać *ipf.*, **uduchowić** *pf.* spiritualize.

uduchowiony *a.* **-eni** soulful.

udupić *pf. wulg.* fuck, do for (*sb*).

udusić *pf.* **-szę -sisz** *zob.* **dusić**. ~ **się** *pf. zob.* **dusić się**.

uduszenie *n.* strangulation; suffocation; asphyxiation.

udział *mi* **1.** (= *uczestnictwo*) participation; **brać udział w czymś** take part in sth, participate in sth. **2.** *ekon.* (= *wkład*) share; **udział członkowski** share, shareholder's share, member's share; **mieć udziały w spółce** hold shares in a company, own shares of a company; **mieć udział w czymś** (*sukcesie itp.*) have a privilege to participate in sth *l.* contribute to sth, contribute to sth; **być l. stać się czyimś udziałem** *przen.* participate in sth; deal with sth; go through *l.* undergo sth; **przypaść komuś w udziale** *przen.* fall to sb's lot to do sth; it is *l.* was sb's privilege to do sth.

udziałowiec *mp* **-wc-** *pl.* **-y** *zwł. ekon.* shareholder.

udziałowy *a. ekon.* share; shareholding; joint-stock; venture.

udziec *mi* **-dźc-** *Gen.* **-a** *kulin.* leg; haunch.

udzielać *ipf.* (= *dawać*) give; **udzielać informacji** furnish *l.* give *l.* provide information; **udzielać pomocy** give *l.* provide help; **udzielać pożyczki** *l.* **kredytu** grant a loan; **udzielać rabatu** grant a discount; **udzielać ślubu** marry, solemnize a marriage; **udzielać wsparcia** give *l.* lend *l.* provide support; **udzielać wywiadu** give *l.* grant an interview; **udzielić komuś głosu** give sb the floor; **udzielać komuś lekcji** *l.* **korepetycji** tutor sb. ~ **się** *ipf.* **1.** (*o emocjach*) (= *stawać się czyimś udziałem*) be infectious, pass on. **2.** (= *być aktywnym*) be active; be sociable.

udzielić (się) *pf. zob.* **udzielać (się)**.

udzielnie *adv. hist.* independently, sovereignly.

udzielny *a. hist.* independent, sovereign; **udzielny książę** *hist.* sovereign, independent ruler; *iron.* prima donna.

udzierać *ipf.* tear off.

udziobać *pf.* **-ię -iesz, udziob** *l.* **udzióib** take a peck at (*sth*).

udziwniać *ipf.*, **udziwnić** *pf.* **-ij** make strange *l.* bizzare.

udziwniony *a.* bizarre, outlandish.

udźwięczniać *ipf.*, **udźwięcznić** *pf.* **-ij** *jęz.* voice.

udźwięcznienie *n. jęz.* voicing.

udźwięczniony *a. jęz.* voiced.

udźwiękowiać *ipf.*, **udźwiękowić** *pf.* **-ij** *film* provide (a movie) with a soundtrack, record sound on a movie.

udźwig *mi techn.* (lifting *l.* carrying *l.* hoisting) capacity.

udźwignąć *pf.* **-ij** lift; **ledwo mogła to udźwignąć** she could barely carry it; **wziął tyle, ile mógł udźwignąć** he took as much as he could carry.

UE *abbr. polit.* (= *Unia Europejska*) EU (*the European Union*).

uelastyczniać *ipf.*, **uelastycznić** *pf.* **-ij** elasticize, make elastic; make flexible.

uf, uff *int.* whew; phew.

ufać *ipf.* trust (*komuś l. czemuś* sb *l.* sth); **ufam, że...** I thrust (that)..., I believe (that)...; **ufać we własne siły** be self-confident *l.* self-assured.

ufarbować (się) *pf. zob.* **farbować (się)**.

uff *int.* = **uf**.

ufnie *adv.* trustingly, trustfully; confidently.

ufność *f.* trust; **z ufnością** trustingly, trustfully; confidently; **pokładać ufność w kimś** *l.* **czymś** trust in sb *l.* sth, put sb's trust in sb *l.* sth.

ufny *a.* **1.** (= *pełen zaufania*) trustful (*w coś* in sth). **2.** (= *wyrażający zaufanie*) trusting.

UFO *abbr.* (= *unidentified flying object*) UFO.

ufolog *mp pl.* **-dzy** *l.* **-owie** ufologist.

ufologia *f. Gen.* **-ii** ufology.

ufologiczny *a.* ufological.

ufoludek *mp* **-dk-** *pl.* **-i** *żart.* alien, extraterrestrial, ET.

uformować (się) *pf. zob.* **formować (się)**.

ufortyfikować *pf. zob.* **fortyfikować**.

ufryzować *pf. zob.* **fryzować**.

ufryzowany *a.* with sb's hair done, coiffured.

ufundować *pf. zob.* **fundować**.

ugadać *pf.*, **ugadywać** *ipf.* win over, bring round; **ugadać kogoś** *pot.* win sb over.

ugałęziony *a. zwł. bot.* ramified, branched.

Uganda *f. geogr.* Uganda.

Ugandyjczyk *mp*, **Ugandyjka** *f. Gen.pl.* **-ek** Ugandan.

ugandyjski *a.* Ugandan.

uganiać się *ipf.* **1.** (= *biegać*) run around (*po czymś* sth). **2.** (= *gonić*) chase (*za kimś l. czymś* sb *l.* sth); **uganiać się za dziewczętami** chase girls, be a womanizer. **3.** *pot.* (= *zabiegać*) seek (*za czymś* sth).

ugarnirować *pf. zob.* **garnirować**.

ugasić *pf.* **ugaszę ugasisz** **1.** (= *stłumić ogień*) put out, extinguish. **2.** (= *zaspokoić*) quench, satisfy; **ugasić pragnienie** quench one's thirst.

ugaszczać *ipf.* entertain, have, treat; **ugościli nas serdecznie** they were hospitable; **ugościli nas obiadem** they treated us to dinner.

ugiąć (się) *pf.* **ugnę ugniesz, ugnij, ugiął ugięła** *zob.* **uginać (się)**.

ugier *mi* **-gr-** ocher *l.* ochre.

ugięcie *n.* bend; deflection; flexure; **ugięcie fali** *fiz.* diffraction of a wave.

uginać *ipf.* (= *pochylać, gnąć*) bend. **~ się** *ipf.* **1.** (= *pochylać się*) bend; give way (*pod kimś l. czymś* under sb's *l.* sth's weight); **nogi się pode**

mną ugięły my legs went from under me. **2.** (= *ulegać naciskowi*) bow, yield (*pod l. przed kimś / czymś* to sb/sth).

ugładzać *ipf.*, **ugładzić** *pf.* smooth (away *l.* out).

ugłaskać *pf.* **-aszczę -aszczesz**, **ugłaskiwać** *ipf.* **1.** placate, appease. **2.** stroke, caress; fondle.

ugniatacz *mi Gen.* **-a** *roln.* packer.

ugniatać *ipf.*, **ugnieść** *pf.* **ugniotę ugnieciesz, ugniótł ugniotła ugnietli** **1.** (= *uciskać, gniotąc*) press; **ugniatać ciasto** knead dough. **2.** (= *formować*) shape, mold. **3.** *tylko ipf.* (= *uwierać*) pinch.

ugnoić *pf.* **-oję -oisz, -ój** **1.** (= *pobrudzić gnojem*) soil with manure. **2.** *pot.* (= *pobrudzić*) soil, dirty.

ugoda *f. Gen.pl.* **ugód** compromise; *zwł. prawn.* settlement; **zawierać ugodę** reach *l.* arrive at a compromise; *zwł. prawn.* reach a settlement.

ugodowiec *mp* **-wc-** *pl.* **-y** advocate of conciliation.

ugodowo *adv.* amicably; conciliatingly; **była ugodowo nastawiona** her attitude was conciliatory; **załatwić sprawę ugodowo** settle the matter amicably.

ugodowość *f.* amicability; conciliatory *l.* conciliating attitude *l.* manner.

ugodowy *a.* **1.** (= *skłonny do ugody*) compromising. **2.** (= *oparty na ugodzie*) conciliatory, amicable.

ugodzić *pf.* **ugódź** **1.** *lit.* (= *trafić*) hit, strike. **2.** *pot.* hire. **~ się** *pf.* (= *dojść do porozumienia*) reach a compromise *l.* settlement.

ugościć *pf.* **-szczę -ścisz** *zob.* **ugaszczać**.

ugotować (się) *pf. zob.* **gotować (się)**.

ugór *mi* **-o-** *zwł. roln.* fallow.

ugrabić *pf.* rake.

ugrać *pf. karty* score.

ugrofiński *a.* Finno-Ugric.

ugruntować *pf. zob.* **ugruntowywać**.

ugruntowany *a.* established.

ugruntowywać *ipf.* establish, strengthen.

ugrupować *pf. zob.* **ugrupowywać**.

ugrupowanie *n.* **1.** (= *grupa ludzi*) group, grouping. **2.** *wojsk.* grouping.

ugrupowywać *ipf.* group.

ugryjski *a.* Ugrian, Ugric.

ugryźć *pf.* **-zę -ziesz -zł -źli** *zob.* **gryźć**; **nie mogę ugryźć tej sprawy** *pot.* I can't make head or tail of it; I can't solve this problem; **co go ugryzło?** *przen.* what came over him? **~ się** *pf. zob.* **gryźć się**.

ugrząźć *pf.* **-znę -źniesz, -źnij, ugrzązł ugrzęzła** **ugrzęźli** = **ugrzęznąć**.

ugrzeczniony *a.* obsequious; overly polite.

ugrzęznąć *pf.* **-znę -źniesz, -źnij, ugrzązł ugrzęzła ugrzęźli** *zob.* **grzęznąć**.

uhierarchizować *pf. zob.* **hierarchizować**.

uhm *int.* **1.** (*wyrażenie zgody*) hm. **2.** (*podtrzymanie rozmowy*) hm, oh, yeah.

uhonorować *pf.*, **uhonorowywać** *ipf.* honor.

uintensywniać *ipf.*, **uintensywnić** *pf.* **-ij** intensify.

uiszczać *ipf.*, **uiścić** *pf.* **uiszczę uiścisz** *form.* pay; settle.

UJ *abbr.* (= *Uniwersytet Jagielloński*) JU (*the Jagiellonian University*).

ujadać *ipf.* **1.** (*o psie*) (= *szczekać*) yap. **2.** *pot.* (= *kłócić się*) yap, argue, quarrel.

ujaić *pf.* **-ję -isz** *pot.* fuck, screw (*sb*) up, do for (*sb*).

ujarzmiać *ipf.*, **ujarzmić** *pf.* **-ij 1.** *lit.* (= *zniewalać*) conquer, subjugate. **2.** *lit.* (= *obłaskawiać*) (*zwierzę*) tame.

ujawniać *ipf.* **-ij** disclose, reveal. **~ się** *ipf.* **1.** (= *stawać się jawnym*) come to light, be disclosed *l.* revealed. **2.** (= *dekonspirować się*) come out.

ujawnić (się) *pf.* **-ij** *zob.* **ujawniać (się)**.

ujawnienie *n.* disclosure.

ująć *pf.* **ujmę ujmiesz, ujmij, ujął ujęła 1.** *zob.* **ujmować. 2.** (= *schwytać, aresztować*) arrest, apprehend; capture. **~ się** *pf. zob.* **ujmować się**.

ujdę *itd. pf. zob.* **ujść**.

ujechać *ipf.* **ujadę ujedziesz** travel (*a certain distance*).

ujednolicać *ipf.*, **ujednolicić** *pf.* standardize, (make) uniform.

ujednostajniać *ipf.*, **ujednostajnić** *pf.* **-ij** standardize, (make) uniform.

ujemnie *adv.* **1.** (= *szkodliwie*) negatively, harmfully. **2.** (*nie dodatnio*) negatively; **naelektryzowany ujemnie** negatively charged.

ujemny *a.* **1.** (= *niekorzystny*) negative, unfavourable. **2.** (= *nie dodatni*) negative; (*o liczbie*) negative; (*o temperaturze*) below zero, subzero; **bilans ujemny** *ekon.* negative *l.* adverse balance; **ujemny ładunek elektryczny** *fiz.* negative charge; **wynik ujemny** *med.* negative result.

ujeść *pf.* **ujem ujesz ujedzą, ujedz, ujadł ujedli** (= *zjeść trochę*) *rzad.* eat a little, nibble.

ujeździć *pf.* **-żdżę -ździsz, -źdź** *zob.* **ujeżdżać**.

ujeżdżacz *mp* roughrider.

ujeżdżać *ipf.* (*konia*) break.

ujeżdżalnia *f. Gen.pl.* **-i** arena, school, manege.

ujeżdżenie *n. sport* dressage; manege.

ujęcie *n.* **1.** (*forma opracowania*) depiction. **2.** *film* take. **3. ujęcie wody** *l.* **wodne** (water) intake.

ujędrniać *ipf.*, **ujędrnić** *pf.* **-ij** tone, make firmer.

ujma *f.* discredit, disgrace; **ujma dla honoru** stain on the scutcheon, stain on sb's reputation *l.* on the reputation of sb; **przynosić komuś ujmę** be a stain on sb's reputation.

ujmować *ipf.* **1.** *lit.* (= *brać*) take (away). **2.** *lit.* (= *przedstawiać*) express, formulate, present; **ujmować coś w słowa** express sth in words. **3.** *lit.* (= *zjednywać*) win, endear, captivate; **ujęła ludzi swoim zachowaniem** her behavior endeared her to everyone. **4.** *lit.* (= *odejmować*) lessen, diminish, retrench; **ujmować sobie lat** take a few years off one's age; **nic dodać, nic ująć** you got it right, exactly; **nie ujmując komuś czegoś** without prejudice to sb. **~ się** *ipf.* **1.** *lit.* (= *chwytać się*) hold; **ująć się za głowę** hold one's head in one's hands; **ujęli się za ręce** they

clasped hands; **ująć się pod boki** stand with arms akimbo. **2.** *lit.* (= *wstawiać się*) support, stand up for, defend; **ujmować się za kimś** plead sb's case, put in a good word for sb.

ujmująco *adv.* charmingly, winsomely.

ujmujący *a.* charming, winsome.

ujrzeć *pf.* **-ę -ysz, -yj** *lit.* see; **ujrzeć światło dzienne** be born; be published, come out; come to light.

ujście *n.* **1.** outlet, vent; **dać ujście czemuś** give vent to sth; **znajdować ujście w czymś** be expressed in *l.* by means of. **2.** (= *wylot*) outlet, vent; issue, escape, exit. **3.** *geogr.* estuary, mouth.

ujść *pf.* **ujdę ujdziesz uszedł uszła uszli 1.** *zob.* **uchodzić. 2.** (= *przebyć jakąś drogę, idąc*) go *l.* travel (*a certain distance*). **3.** *pot.* (= *nadać się*) pass, do; **od biedy ujdzie** this will do; **ta sukienka ujdzie (w tłoku)** this dress will just about do.

ukamienować *pf. zob.* **kamienować**.

ukarać *pf.* **ukarzę ukarzesz** *zob.* **karać**.

ukartować *pf.* plot, contrive, devise, plan, scheme.

ukatrupiać *ipf.*, **ukatrupić** *pf. pot.* dust off, rub out, blow off *l.* away, shove off.

ukaz *mi hist.* ukase, imperial edict (*in Tsarist Russia*).

ukazać (się) *pf.* **-żę -żesz** *zob.* **ukazywać (się)**.

ukazywać *ipf.* **1.** *lit.* (= *pokazywać*) show, present, display, reveal; **ukazać prawdziwe oblicze** show one's true colors; **ukazać zęby w uśmiechu** show one's teeth in a smile. **2.** *lit.* (= *przedstawiać*) present, demonstrate; **ukazywać kogoś w korzystnym świetle** show sb in a favorable light. **~ się** *ipf.* **1.** *lit.* (= *pokazywać się*) show (up), arise, appear, come into sight *l.* view; **ukazać się czyimś oczom** come into view, meet sb's eyes; **naszym oczom ukazał się piękny widok** a beautiful view opened *l.* unfolded before our eyes; **ukazać się na horyzoncie** heave into sight *l.* view; **ukazać się zza chmur** come out; **ukazać się komuś we śnie** show up in sb's dream; (*o duchu*) haunt sb. **2.** (= *być publikowanym*) appear (in print), come out; **poranna gazeta jeszcze się nie ukazała** the morning paper isn't out yet; **sztuka ukazała się na scenie w zeszłym tygodniu** the play was staged last week; **mający się ukazać** (*o książce, artykule*) forthcoming; **ukazujący się co dwa tygodnie** (*o audycji*) fortnightly.

ukąsić *pf.* **ukąszę ukąsisz** *zob.* **kąsać**.

ukąszenie *n.* **1.** (= *użądlenie*) bite, sting, prick; **ukąszenie owada** insect bite. **2.** (*rana*) bite.

UKF *abbr. radio* (= *ultrakrótkie fale*) UHF (= *ultra-high frequency*).

ukierunkować *pf. form.* direct, steer, guide; **ukierunkować czyjeś zainteresowania** guide sb's interests; **ukierunkować swoje badania na coś** direct *l.* guide one's research on sth.

ukierunkowanie *n. lit.* orientation, direction, inclination; (*np. humanistyczne*) specialization.

ukierunkowywać *ipf. form. zob.* **ukierunkować**.

ukisić (się) *pf.* **ukiszę ukisisz** *zob.* **kisić (się)**.

ukleja *f. Gen.* **-ei** *icht.* bleak (*Alburnus alburnus*).

uklepać *pf.* **-pię -piesz, uklepywać** *ipf.* (*ziemię*) pat down, flatten down, tap.

uklęknąć *pf.* **-ij** *zob.* **klękać.**

układ *mi* **1.** (= *ułożenie*) arrangement, ordering, structure, pattern, array; **układ graficzny** layout, make-up; **układ sceniczny** stage setting; **układ liter** lettering; **w takim układzie** *pot.* in this case. **2.** (= *system*) system; **układ współrzędnych** *mat.* coordinate system; **układ dziesiętny** decimal system; **układ dwójkowy** binary system; **układ molekularny** *chem.* molecular system *l.* orientation; **układ nerwowy** nervous system; **ośrodkowy/obwodowy układ nerwowy** central/ peripheral nervous system; **układ oddechowy** respiratory system; **układ odpornościowy** immune system; **układ pokarmowy** digestive system; **układ naczyniowy** vascular system; **układ moczowy** urinary system; **układ rozrodczy** reproductive system; **układ limfatyczny** lymphatic system; **układ krążenia** circulatory system; **okresowy układ pierwiastków** periodic table, the Mendeleeff system; **układ równań** *mat.* system of equations; **Układ Słoneczny** *astron.* the Solar System; **układ gwiazd** *astrol.* constellation; (*przy urodzeniu*) horoscopy; **układ niżowy/wyżowy** *meteor.* low/high-pressure weather system. **3.** (= *stosunek*) arrangement, proportion, rate; **układ sił** distribution *l.* composition of forces. **4.** (= *umowa*) agreement, contract, settlement, treaty, deal; **Układ Warszawski** *hist.* the Warsaw Pact; **układ powierniczy** trusteeship agreement; **zawierać układ** strike a deal (*z kimś w jakiejś sprawie* with sb over sth); **wchodzić w układy** enter negotiations, negotiate. **5.** *pot.* (= *powiązanie, zależność*) connection, link; **mieć dobre układy z kimś** be on good terms with sb; **uczciwy układ** square deal. **6.** *techn.* train, set; **układ kierowniczy** *mot.* steering (gear); **układ hamulcowy** braking system; **układ ABS** ABS, antilock braking system; **układ scalony** integrated circuit.

układacz *mp* stacker; **układacz spadochronów** *lotn.* parachute rigger.

układać *ipf.* **1.** (= *umieszczać, porządkować*) arrange, order, set, place; **układać pasjansa** play patience; **układać sobie życie** plan one's life; **ułożyć komuś życie** set sb up for life; **układać parami** pair, geminate; **układać pochyło** (*o dachu, dachówkach*) weather; **układać warstwami** stratify; **ułożyć w kolejności alfabetycznej** arrange in alphabetical order; *kulin.* layer; **układać według skali** graduate; **układać w tabelę** tabulate; **układać w stos** heap up, pile up, stack; **układać w kategorie/grupy/zespoły** sort into categories/ groups/teams. **2.** (= *tworzyć całość*) compose, arrange, put together; (*bukiet*) bunch (up), arrange (the flowers); (*podłogę, płytki, wykładzinę*) lay. **3.** (= *formować*) form, shape; (*włosy*) dress, coiffure, set; (*tkaninę, firankę*) drape; **ułożyć kwiaty** do the flowers; **układać sobie włosy** do one's hair. **4.** (= *umieszczać w pozycji leżącej*) lay down, put down; **układać do snu** put to bed, lay to sleep. **5.** (= *tworzyć*) compose; (*muzykę,*

wiersz) compose, make up; (*przemówienie*) prepare; (*list, pismo*) pen, phrase, draft, formulate; (*egzamin, pytania*) set; **układać horoskop** cast a horoscope. **6.** (= *ustalać*) plan, design, arrange, settle. **7.** (= *tresować zwierzęta*) school, train. ~ **się** *ipf.* **1.** (= *kłaść się*) lie, lie down, couch; **układać się w pozycji półleżącej** recline; **ułożyć się do snu** lie down to sleep, bed down; **ułożyć się wygodnie** snug, lie *l.* settle *l.* nestle comfortably; assume a comfortable position. **2.** (= *przybierać kształt*) assume a shape; (*o tkaninie*) drape, fall into folds (*w fałdy*); **moje włosy nie układają się** my hair doesn't set. **3.** (= *przebiegać*) occur, happen, pan out, turn out; **sprawy nie układają się najlepiej** things are not the way they should be, things are not doing fine; **wszystko się jakoś ułoży** it'll all come right, everything's going to be all right; **układać się (dobrze)** shape up, fall into place. **4.** (= *pertraktować*) negotiate, discuss terms (*z kimś* with sb).

układanka *f. Gen.pl.* **-ek** jigsaw puzzle, puzzle; **układanka chińska** tangram.

układnie *adv.* complaisantly, politely, urbanely, courteously.

układność *f.* complaisance, politeness, courtesy, urbanity.

układny *a.* **1.** (= *dobrze wychowany*) well-mannered, well-behaved, polite, courteous. **2.** (= *świadczący o uprzejmości*) accommodating, fair-spoken; (*o zachowaniu*) complaisant, urbane, agreeable.

układowy *a.* **1.** *med.* (*o objawach, infekcji*) *techn., roln.* systemic. **2.** (= *dotyczący traktatów*) pact, treaty. **3.** *pot.* (= *dotyczący powiązań, zależności*) shady, underhand.

układy *pl. Gen.* **-ów** (= *pertraktacje*) negotiations, talks, transactions; **prowadzić układy** negotiate, hold talks, discuss terms; **zerwać układy** break negotiations.

ukłon *mi* bow, greeting; **ukłon w czyjąś stronę** *l.* **pod czyimś adresem** a sign *l.* gesture of respect *l.* high regard toward sb; **niski** *l.* **głęboki ukłon** *lotn.* low bow; **złożyć ukłon** drop a bow, make *l.* drop obeisance, bend the knee; **ukłony dla rodziców!** my best regards to your parents!; **powitać/ pożegnać kogoś ukłonem** bow sb in/out; **ukłony** (*w zakończeniu listu*) compliments, greetings, kind regards; (*przed kurtyną*) call.

ukłonić się *pf. zob.* **kłaniać się.**

ukłucie *n.* **1.** (= *nakłucie*) sting, twinge, prod; (*strzykawką*) pinprick. **2.** (= *ślad po ukąszeniu*) prick. **3.** (= *kłujący ból*) pang, twinge, sharp pain; **ukłucie zazdrości** pang of jealousy.

ukłuć (się) *pf. zob.* **kłuć (się).**

uknuć *pf. zob.* **knuć.**

ukochać *pf.* **1.** *lit.* (= *umiłować*) grow very fond (*coś* of sth); become attached *l.* devoted (*coś* to sth); nurse *l.* feel affection (*kogoś* for sb); fall in love (*kogoś* with sb). **2.** (= *przytulić*) give (sb) a hug, hug.

ukochana *f. Gen.* **-ej 1.** beloved, love, sweetheart, truelove. **2.** *Voc. zob.* **ukochany.**

ukochany *a.* beloved, darling. – *mp* **1.**

beloved, love, sweetheart, truelove. **2.** *Voc.* honey, baby, darling, love.

ukoić *pf.* **ukój** *zob.* **koić.**

ukojenie *n. lit.* (*bólu, cierpienia*) consolation, assuagement, mollification, alleviation, solace; **znaleźć w czymś ukojenie** find solace *l.* assuagement in sth.

ukołysać *pf.* **-szę -szesz 1.** (= *uśpić kołysaniem*) rock sb asleep *l.* to sleep, lull, lullaby. **2.** *przen.* (*o wietrze, ciszy*) (= *uśpić*) lull, soothe, hush.

ukonkretniać *ipf.*, **ukonkretnić** *pf.* **-ij** (*wypowiedź, argumenty*) give substance to; (*wiedzę, zakres*) make concrete *l.* solid *l.* specific, specify.

ukonstytuować *pf. zob.* **konstytuować.** **~ się** *pf. zob.* **konstytuować się.**

ukontentować *pf. przest.* (*kogoś*) content, please, satisfy, gratify.

ukontentowany *a. przest.* contented, satisfied, pleased, gratified.

ukończenie *n.* completion, finish; (*studiów, szkoły*) graduation; **data ukończenia** completion date, target date; **świadectwo ukończenia szkoły średniej** high-school diploma; **być na ukończeniu** be nearing completion; **po ukończeniu czegoś** on completion of sth.

ukończyć *pf.* complete, finish, accomplish, go all the way, bring to an end; **ukończyć szkołę, kurs** complete; **ukończyć studia** graduate, take one's degree; **ukończyć studia z wyróżnieniem** graduate with honors; **ukończyć 18 lat** *form.* have one's eighteenth birthday; **ukończyć wyścig z piątą lokatą** finish the race in the fifth place *l.* position.

ukopać *pf.* **-pię -piesz** excavate, dig out.

ukoronować (się) *pf. zob.* **koronować (się).**

ukoronowanie *n.* **1.** (= *koronacja*) crowning, coronation. **2.** (= *szczytowe osiągnięcie*) culmination, crowning achievement; **ukoronowanie wszystkiego** the icing on the cake, the crown of sth, pièce de résistance.

ukorzeniać *ipf.* (*roślinę*) root. **~ się** *ipf.* strike *l.* take *l.* grow root, put down roots, root; **ukorzeniony** rooted; **silnie ukorzeniony** rooty.

ukorzenić się *pf. zob.* **ukorzeniać (się).**

ukorzyć *pf.* **ukórz** *lit.* (*kogoś*) humiliate, humble, bring low, disgrace; **ukorzyć się przed kimś** bow one's head to *l.* before sb, humble o.s. before sb. **~ się** *pf. zob.* **korzyć się.**

ukos *mi* (*muru itp.*) slant, incline, splay; *techn.* scarf; **na ukos** slantwise, aslant, diagonally, obliquely; **spojrzenie z ukosa** slantwise *l.* slanting *l.* oblique glance; **patrzeć na kogoś z ukosa** (*nie wprost*) squint at sb; *przen.* (*podejrzliwie*) look awry *l.* askance at sb, frown upon sb.

ukosem *adv.* **iść/posuwać się ukosem** go/move obliquely *l.* aslant.

ukosić *pf.* **-oszę -osisz** (*trawę*) mow, cut; (*kosą*) scythe.

ukośnie *adv.* askew, diagonally, at an angle, obliquely, slantwise; **skierowany ukośnie w tył** backswept; **wbijać ukośnie** (*gwóźdź*) toe; **łączyć ukośnie** *stol.* miter.

ukośnik *mi Gen.* **-a** slash, solidus, stroke; *mat.* rhombus; *druk.* diagonal, virgule; **ukośnik lewy** backslash.

ukośny *a.* oblique, sloping, slanting; (*o stożku, walcu*) scalene; **splot ukośny** latticework; **kreska ukośna** stroke; **linia ukośna** oblique.

ukracać *ipf.* (*niegrzeczne zachowanie, bezczelność*) suppress, stamp out, put an end to, keep a rein on, keep in check; (*kogoś*) teach sb a lesson, hold (sb) back.

ukradkiem *adv.* furtively, by stealth, under the table, surreptitiously, clandestinely; **zerkać na kogoś/coś ukradkiem** steal a glance at sb/sth, cast a furtive *l.* covert glance at sb/sth; **wyprowadzić kogoś ukradkiem** spirit sb away *l.* off; **wśliznąć się ukradkiem** steal in; **dosięgnąć kogoś ukradkiem** (*o starości, chorobie*) creep up on sb.

ukradkowy *a.* stealthy, surreptitious; (*o spojrzeniu*) furtive, covert, secretive; (*o spotkaniach*) secret, clandestine; **rzucać komuś ukradkowe spojrzenie** steal a glance *l.* look at sb.

Ukraina *f. geogr.* Ukraine; **Ukraina Zakarpacka** Ruthenia.

Ukrainiec *mp* **-ńc-** *pl.* **-y, Ukrainka** *f. Gen.pl.* **-ek** Ukrainian.

ukrainizm *mi jęz.* Ukrainism, Ruthenism, Ukrainian idiom.

ukraiński *a.* Ukrainian; **język ukraiński** Ukrainian.

ukrajać *pf.* **-ę -esz** cut off, slice (off); **ukrajać chleba** cut a slice of bread.

ukrasić *pf.* **-szę -sisz, ukraszać** *ipf. poet.* beautify, decorate, ornament, adorn.

ukraść *pf.* **ukradnę ukradniesz, ukradnij, ukradł** *zob.* **kraść.**

ukrawać *ipf.* = **ukrajać.**

ukręcać *ipf.* **1.** (= *mieszać, ucierać*) mix, whisk, stir. **2.** (= *łączyć, skręcając*) plait, twist, braid, weave; **ukręcić bicz na samego siebie** *przen.* shoot o.s. in the foot; make a rod for one's own back. **3.** (= *ułamywać*) tear off, wrench off, twist off, break off; **ukręcić łeb plotce/pogłosce** *przen.* suppress *l.* dispel a gossip/rumor; **ukręcić łeb sprawie** shelve an affair. **~ się** *ipf.* (*o kurku, gałce*) twist off; (*o guziku*) fall off; **krem się dobrze ukręcił** the cream is well mixed.

ukręcić (się) *pf. zob.* **ukręcać (się).**

ukrochmalić *pf. zob.* **krochmalić.**

ukroić *pf.* **ukrój** *zob.* **ukrajać.**

ukrop *mi* boiling water; **zwijać się jak w ukropie** work like billy-o, bustle about feverishly.

ukrócić *pf. zob.* **ukracać.**

ukruszyć *pf.* crumble, break off; **ukruszyć sobie ząb** break a tooth. **~ się** *pf.* splinter, crumble; (*o uszku od filiżanki*) break off.

ukrwienie *n.* blood-supply, blood flow.

ukrwiony *a.* blood-supplied.

ukrycie *n.* (= *kryjówka*) cover, hiding-place, shelter; **w ukryciu** undercover, on the quiet, in secret; **w ukryciu przed kimś** without sb's knowledge; **z ukrycia** (*atakować*) covertly; **wyjść z ukrycia** come out of the closet, break cover; **być w ukryciu** be in hiding, keep down *l.* low, keep out of sight; **nie mieć nic do ukrycia** have nothing to hide; **strzelać z ukrycia** snipe.

ukryć (się) *pf.* **ukryję ukryjesz, ukryj** *zob.* **ukrywać (się)**.

ukryty *a.* (= *niewidoczny*) hidden, invisible; (*o celu, wadzie*) hidden; (*o wielbicielu*) secret; (*o chorobie*) occult; (*o groźbie, znaczeniu*) implicit; (*miejscu, błędzie*) obscure; (*o zagrożeniu*) covert; (*o znaczeniu*) inner; (*o talencie*) latent; (*o kamerze*) concealed; **ukryty skarb** treasure-trove; **ukryty przed wzrokiem** hidden *l.* shielded from view; **ukryty mikrofon** bug; **ukryty cel/powód** ulterior *l.* underlying purpose/reason; **ukryte motywy** hidden agenda; **ukryte pobudki** ulterior motives; **ukryte zamiary** ulterior designs; „**ukryta kamera**" *telewizja* candid camera; **ukryta nuta goryczy/rasizmu** undercurrent of bitterness/racism; **ukryty w chmurach** wrapped *l.* shrouded in clouds.

ukrywać *ipf.* **-am -asz** 1. (= *chować*) conceal, cover up, hide, stash away (*coś przed kimś* sth from sb); (*zbiega*) harbor, give shelter to; **ukryć twarz w dłoniach** bury one's face in one's hands; **ukrywać w dłoni** palm. 2. (= *zatajać*) suppress, conceal, keep secret, hold back; (*ból, aferę*) conceal; (*chorobę, uczucia*) dissimulate; (*intencje*) mask, veil; (*prawdę*) cover up; (*błędy*) whitewash; (*wiek, fakty*) belie; (*uczucia, motywy*) disguise, dissemble; **ukrywać coś przed kimś** keep *l.* hold sth back from sb; **ukrywać coś pod maską** *l.* **płaszczykiem czegoś** hide sth under the pretense of sth, mask sth by the pretense of sth; **ukrywać swoje talenty, umiejętności** hide one's light under a bushel; **nie ukrywam, że...** I'm not denying that...; **nie da się ukryć, że...** there's no escaping the fact that...; **starać się coś ukryć** sweep sth under the carpet *l.* the rug; **nic się przed nim nie ukryje** he never misses a trick, nothing can be held back from him. 3. (= *mieścić w sobie*) harbor, house. ~ **się** *ipf.* hide (*przed kimś* from sb); be in hiding, take cover; (*o przestępcy*) be on the run, lie low; (*na statku, w samolocie*) stow away; **ukrywać się z czymś** keep sth secret.

ukrzywdzić *pf. przest.* harm, hurt; do harm (*kogoś* to sb); inflict pain (*kogoś* on sb).

ukrzyżować *pf.* crucify.

ukrzyżowanie *n.* crucifixion; *sztuka* the Cross, the Crucifixion.

ukształtować (się) *pf. zob.* **kształtować (się)**.

ukształtowanie *n.* shape, figure, formation; (*danego terenu, kraju*) geography, shape; **ukształtowanie terenu** *geol.* relief, the lay of the land, land form; **ukształtowanie charakteru** formation of personality.

ukuć *pf. zob.* **ukuwać**.

ukulele *n. indecl. muz.* ukulele.

ukulturalniać *ipf.*, **ukulturalnić** *pf.* **-ij** (*zachowanie*) cultivate, refine; civilize.

ukuwać *ipf.* 1. (= *formować, kując*) forge, hammer, beat into shape; (*monety*) mint. 2. (= *tworzyć*) produce, create, concoct; (*nową technologię*) mint; (*wyraz, termin*) coin; **nowo ukuty wyraz** coinage.

ukwasić *pf.* **-szę -sisz**, **ukwaszać** *ipf.* sour; (*ogórki, kapustę*) pickle.

ukwiał *ma Gen.* **-a** *l.* **-u** *zool.* sea anemone (*Actiniaria* (*rząd*)).

ukwiecać *ipf.*, **ukwiecić** *pf.* deck *l.* adorn with flowers.

ukwiecony *a.* strewn *l.* decked *l.* adorned with flowers; (*o stylu*) flowery.

ul *mi Gen.* **-a** beehive, hive; **w klasie wrzało jak w ulu** there was a great hubbub *l.* hurly burly *l.* uproar in the class; **gromadzić się w ulu** hive.

ul. *abbr.* (= *ulica*) St., Gds., Rd.

ulać *pf.* **-eję -ejesz ulali** *l.* **uleli** 1. *zob.* **ulewać**. 2. **leżeć jak ulał** fit like a glove, suit sb down to the ground; **suknia leży jak ulał** the dress fits perfectly *l.* to a T. ~ **się** *pf. zob.* **ulewać się**.

ulatniać się *ipf.* 1. (*o gazach itp.*) (= *rozchodzić się w powietrzu*) escape, leak, volatilize; **ulatniający się** leaking, volatile. 2. *pot.* (= *zapodziewać się*) vanish, disappear; **dokumenty ulotniły się z biurka** documents disappeared from the desk. 3. *pot.* (= *odchodzić niepostrzeżenie*) make o.s. scarce, make off, bunk off, evaporate, take wing; (*o obawach, wątpliwościach*) evaporate, melt away, pass away, vanish; **ulotnić się jak kamfora** vanish into thin air, disappear without a trace.

ulatywać *ipf.* 1. (*o ptakach itp.*) (= *odlatywać*) fly away, take wing, soar, take to the air; (*sen, uczucia*) pass, ebb, fade away; **uleciało mi to z pamięci** it slipped my memory. 2. (*o substancjach*) (= *wydobywać się*) evaporate, volatilize, escape, leak. 3. (*o czymś lekkim*) (= *wzbijać się w górę*) rise in the air.

ulać się[1] *pf.* **ulęknę ulękniesz, ulęknij, ulękł ulękła ulękli** = **ulęknąć się**.

ulać się[2] *pf.* **ulęgnie ulągł** *l.* **ulęgnął ulęgła ulęgły** = **ulęgnąć się**.

ulec *pf.* **ulegnę ulegniesz, ulegnij, uległ** *zob.* **ulegać**.

ulecieć *pf.* **-cę -cisz** *zob.* **ulatywać**.

uleczalność *f.* curability, recoverability.

uleczalny *a.* curable, healable, recoverable, medicable.

uleczyć *pf. lit.* (*chorobę, ranę*) heal, cure, remedy; (*pacjenta, chorego*) restore to health; **uleczyć kogoś z artretyzmu** heal *l.* cure sb of arthritis; (*sytuację*) rescue, cure; (*trędowatego*) cleanse; **czas uleczy rany/cierpienia** time will heal the wounds/pains; **uleczyć kogoś z czegoś** *t. przen.* get sth off sb's mind, put sth out of sb's head.

ulegać *ipf.* 1. (= *kapitulować*) succumb, surrender (*czemuś* to sth). 2. (= *podporządkowywać się*) surrender, submit; defer (*przez szacunek, grzeczność*) (*komuś* to sb); **ulec czyimś namowom** *l.* **czyjejś woli** yield to *l.* consent to sb's suggestions *l.* will; **ulegać naciskom** give in to pressure. 3. (= *znajdować się pod wpływem czegoś*) surrender, succumb (*czemuś* to sth); **ulegać wpływom/pokusie** succumb *l.* yield to influences/temptation; **ulec czyjemuś urokowi** be overcome *l.* overwhelmed with sb's charm; **ulec uczuciu** be seized with a feeling; **ulec zauroczeniu kimś** fall under sb's spell; **łatwo ulegać wpływom** be easily led on; **łatwo ulegający czemuś** vulnerable to sth; **nieulegający sentymentom** hard-boiled; **ulec wrażeniu** have an impression. **4.** (= *podlegać*) undergo; (*zniszczeniu*) be destroyed, suffer destruction; (*zepsuciu*) get spoiled, perish; (*awarii*) crash, break down; (*degeneracji*) degenerate; (*rozkładowi*) decay, rot; (*dezintegracji*) disintegrate, fray; (*likwidacji*) close down; (*modyfikacji*) modify; **ulec zmianom** undergo changes, be subject to change *l.* revision; **ulec wypadkowi** meet with an accident, have an accident; **ulec zakażeniu** become infected; **ulegać odwróceniu** (*o procesie, tendencji*) go into reverse; **ulegać przedawnieniu** *prawn.* prescribe, expire; **ulec złagodzeniu** relax; **to nie ulega wątpliwości** it is indisputable; it's beyond question; it stands to reason; **jego uczciwość nie ulega wątpliwości** his honesty admits of no question; **nieulegający wątpliwości** indisputable. **5.** *lit.* (*o kobiecie*) (= *oddawać się mężczyźnie*) give in (*komuś* to sb).

ulegle *adv.* compliantly, submissively, tamely, with docility, docilely.

uległość *f.* compliance, amenability, submissiveness, pliability (*wobec kogoś* to *l.* toward sb); **tchórzliwa uległość** craven submission; **zmusić kogoś do uległości** force sb into submission, reduce sb to submission; **zmusić kogoś głodem** *l.* **groźbami do uległości** starve *l.* frighten sb into submission.

uległy *f.* submissive, compliant, docile, obedient, dutiful.

ulegnąć *pf.* **ulegnij, uległ** = **ulec.**

ulem *mp pl.* **-i** *l.* **-owie** *rel.* Islamic theologian *l.* scholar, ulema; **Ulemowie** Ulema.

ulepek *mi* **-pk-** *rzad.* treacle, syrup; **słodki jak ulepek** sugary.

ulepić *pf.* mold, form; **ulepić coś z gliny** mold sth in clay; **ulepić bałwana ze śniegu** make a snowman; **być ulepionym z tej samej gliny** be cut from the same cloth, be cast in the same fold; **są ulepieni z tej samej gliny** they are two of a kind.

ulepszacz *mp pot., często iron.* reformer.

ulepszać *ipf.* (*stan, metody pracy, nauczania*) improve, perfect, better; ameliorate; (*konstrukcję, narzędzia*) modernize; **dający się ulepszyć** improvable; **ulepszona formuła** improved formula.

ulepszenie *n.* improvement, amelioration, betterment, reform; **małe** *l.* **drobne ulepszenie** tweak; **dokonywać ulepszeń w czymś** make improvements to sth, improve sth.

ulepszyć *pf. zob.* **ulepszać.**

ulewa *f.* downpour, rainstorm, heavy rain, deluge; **rzęsista ulewa** drenching rainfall; **ulewa z piorunami** thundershower; **ulewa świateł** *przen.* shower *l.* hail *l.* flood of lights; **ulewa oklasków** round *l.* storm of applause; *fiz.* (*cząstek, meteorów*) shower.

ulewać *ipf.* **1.** (= *wylewać trochę cieczy*) pour off *l.* out. **2.** (= *robić odlew*) cast, mold, teem. **~ się** *ipf.* brim over, slop over, overflow.

ulewnie *adv.* (*padać*) torrentially, in torrents *l.* sheets.

ulewny *a.* (*o deszczu*) pouring, torrential,

heavy; **padał ulewny deszcz** it rained heavily, it rained cats and dogs.

uleźć *pf.* **ulezę uleziesz ulazł uleźli** *pot.* plod one's way.

uleżeć *pf.* **-ę -ysz** lie (quiet *l.* still), stay quiet *l.* still; **nie mógł uleżeć w łóżku** he couldn't lie still in bed; **czekolada nie uleży u mnie długo** chocolate won't lie long in my cupboard. **~ się** *pf.* **1.** (*o ziemi*) (= *zespolić się*) settle. **2.** (*o owocach*) (= *dojrzeć*) mellow, ripen; **gruszki uleżały się w koszu** pears ripened *l.* got ripe in the basket.

ulęgać się *ipf.* **1.** (= *wykluwać się*) hatch out, be hatched. **2.** (*o pomyśle itp.*) (= *pojawiać się*) crop up, sprout *l.* mature in sb's mind.

ulęgałka *f. Gen.pl.* **-ek** wild pear; **przebierać w czymś jak w ulęgałkach** pick and choose.

ulęgnąć się *pf.* **ulągł** *l.* **ulęgnął ulęgła ulęgły** *zob.* **ulęgać się.**

ulęknąć się *pf.* **-ij, ulągł** *lit.* fear, take fright, be frightened.

ulga *f.* **1.** (= *odprężenie*) relief, release, ease; **westchnienie ulgi** sigh of relief; **uczucie ulgi** release; **odetchnąć z ulgą** heave a sigh of relief; **odczuwać ulgę** be *l.* feel relieved, feel relief; **przynosić ulgę** relieve, bring relief; (*w cierpieniu*) comfort; **przynieść ulgę w bólu** alleviate *l.* ease pain; **co za ulga!** what a relief!; **z wyraźną ulgą** visibly relieved. **2.** (= *zniżka*) discount, reduction; **dać komuś ulgę na coś** give sb a discount on sth; **ulga podatkowa** concession tax, privilege, tax allowance *l.* relief *l.* reduction.

ulgowo *adv.* preferentially, specially; **potraktować kogoś ulgowo** give sb a special treatment.

ulgowy *a.* **1.** (= *zniżkowy*) discount, reduced, low-rate; **bilet ulgowy** discount ticket; *przen.* preferential, special, privileged; **taryfa ulgowa** *przen.* preferential treatment. **2.** (= *niewymagający zaangażowania*) (*o okresie*) concessionary.

ulica *f.* **1.** (= *droga miejska*) street, road; (*w nazwach*) court, drive, lane; **ślepa ulica** dead end, cul-de-sac; **główna ulica** high street, main street; **ulica brukowana** cobbled street; **ulica jednokierunkowa/dwukierunkowa** one-way/two-way street; **ulica handlowa** shopping street; **ulica okrężna** circular street; **boczna ulica** by-street, side street; **pokój od ulicy** front room; **drzwi od ulicy** street door; **dziecko ulicy** street child, guttersnipe; **budynek po drugiej stronie ulicy** the building over *l.* across the street; **iść ulicą** walk down *l.* along the street; **na ulicy** on *l.* in the street; **przechodzić przez ulicę** cross the street *l.* road; **skręcać w boczną ulicę** turn off into a side street; **wyrzucić kogoś na ulicę** turn sb out into the street; **mieszkać na ulicy** be on the streets, be on the bum; **pracować na ulicy** walk the streets; **na ulicy Roosevelta** on Roosevelt street; **pieniądze leżą na ulicy** the streets are paved with gold; **spotkać kogoś na ulicy** meet sb in the street; **wyjść na ulicę** (= *demonstrować*) take to the streets; **skończyć na ulicy** *przen.* end up in the street; **biegać po ulicach** run the streets; **wałęsać się po ulicach** roam the streets; **ulice spłynęły krwią** the streets ran with blood; **muzyko-**

wać na ulicy busk; **na przeciwległym rogu ulicy** kitty-corner (from *l.* to sth). **2.** (= *tłum uliczny*) mob.

uliczka *f. Gen.pl.* **-ek** (= *wąska ulica*) lane, alley, row; **boczna uliczka** side street, by-street; **ślepa uliczka** blind alley, dead end, cul-de-sac; **znaleźć się w ślepej uliczce** *przen.* come to *l.* reach a dead end.

ulicznica *f. przest.* street walker, woman of the streets.

ulicznik *mp przest.* street urchin, guttersnipe, mudlark, gamin.

uliczny *a.* **1.** (= *dotyczący ulicy*) street; **handlarz uliczny** chapman, street vendor; **plakat uliczny** billboard; **targ uliczny** street market; **uliczny grajek** busker; **uliczni muzycy** street musicians; **uliczny rabuś** mugger; **żebrak uliczny** panhandler; **oświetlenie uliczne** street lighting; illumination (*kolorowe*); **światła uliczne** stoplights (*na skrzyżowaniu*); **latarnia uliczna** street lamp; **infrastruktura uliczna** street furniture. **2.** (= *pospolity*) (*język, wyrażenie, akcent*) of the gutter, coarse, vulgar.

ulik *ma* herring.

uliryczniać *ipf.*, **ulirycznić** *pf.* **-ij** make lyrical *l.* poetic.

ulistnienie *n. bot.* foliage, leafage.

ulistniony *a.* leaved, foliate; **silnie ulistniony** leafy.

ulitować się *pf.* take pity, have compassion, have mercy (*nad kimś/czymś* on sb/sth).

ulizać *pf.* **-iżę -iżesz** *pot.* (*włosy*) sleek; **ulizany** (*o włosach*) sleek, glossy. **~ się** *pf. pot.* sleek one's hair.

ulokować (się) *pf. zob.* **lokować (się)**.

ulotka *f. Gen.pl.* **-ek** leaflet, dodger, circular; (*reklamowa*) flysheet, flyer; (*informacyjna*) fact sheet, prospectus; **roznosić ulotki** leaflet, distribute leaflets.

ulotnić się *pf.* **-ij** *zob.* **ulatniać się**.

ulotnie *adv.* elusively, fugitively, fleetingly.

ulotność *f.* elusiveness, ephemerality, fugitiveness.

ulotny *a.* **1.** (= *ukazujący się nieregularnie*) (*o druku, pismach*) casual, irregular. **2.** (= *lotny*) (*o gazie, substancji*) volatile, vaporous, evaporative. **3.** (= *trwający krótko*) short-lived, transitory, ephemeral; (*o pomyśle, idei*) fugitive; (*o szczęściu*) elusive; (*o chwili*) fleeting; **pamięć ulotna** volatile memory; **ulotne chwile szczęścia** fleeting moments of happiness.

ulowy *a.* beehive.

Ulster *mi geogr.* Ulster; **Policja Królewska Ulsteru** Royal Ulster Constabulary; (*męski płaszcz wełniany*) ulster.

ulsterski *a.* Ulster.

ultimatum *n. indecl.* ultimatum; **postawić komuś ultimatum** give sb an ultimatum; **przedstawić komuś ultimatum** present sb with an ultimatum; **wystosować ultimatum** issue an ultimatum.

ultraakustyka *f.* ultrasonics, ultra-acoustics.

ultraczerwony *a.* ultra-red.

ultraczuły *a.* ultrasensitive.

ultrademokrata *mp*, **ultrademokratka** *f. Gen.pl.* **-ek** ultrademocrat.

ultradźwięk *mi fiz.* ultrasound.

ultradźwiękowy *a. fiz.* (*o czujniku, sondzie, częstotliwości*) ultrasonic, ultrasound; **oczyszczanie ultradźwiękowe** ultrasonic cleaning; **defektoskopia ultradźwiękowa** ultrasonic testing; *med.* (*o badaniu*) ultrasound.

ultraelement *mi* ultraelement.

ultrafiltr *mi* ultrafilter.

ultrafiolet *mi fiz.* ultraviolet, ultraviolet rays.

ultrafioletowy *a. fiz.* ultraviolet; **promieniowanie ultrafioletowe** ultraviolet radiation *l.* light.

ultraklerykalny *a.* (*przekonania*) ultraclerical.

ultrakonserwatysta *mp*, **ultrakonserwatystka** *f. Gen.pl.* **-ek** ultraconservative.

ultrakonserwatywny *a.* ultraconservative.

ultrakonserwatyzm *mi* ultraconservatism.

ultrakrótki *a. fiz., radio* ultra-short; **fale ultrakrótkie** ultra-short waves.

ultrakrótkofalowy *a.* (*nadajnik, łączność, terapia*) ultra-short wave.

ultralekki *a.* ultralight, ultra-lightweight.

ultralewica *f.* ultra-left wing, ultra-left.

ultralewicowy *a.* ultra-left, ultra-leftist.

ultraliberalny *a.* ultraliberal.

ultramaryna *f.* **1.** *chem.* ultramarine. **2.** *pot.* (*barwa*) ultramarine (blue).

ultramikroskop *mi* dark field microscope, ultramicroscope.

ultranowoczesny *a.* ultramodern, space-age.

ultraprawica *f.* ultra-right wing, ultra-right.

ultraprawicowy *a.* ultra-right, ultra-rightist; **ugrupowanie ultraprawicowe** ultra-right wing party.

ultraradykalizm *mi* ultraradicalism.

ultraradykalny *a.* ultraradical.

ultrareakcyjny *a.* ultrareactionary.

ultrarojalista *mp*, **ultrarojalistka** *f. Gen.pl.* **-ek** ultraroyalist.

ultras *mp* ultra, ultraist.

ultrasonograf *mi* ultrasonograph.

ultrasonografia *f. Gen.* **-i** ultrasonography.

ultrasonograficzny *a.* ultrasonographic.

ultrasonoterapia *f. Gen.* **-ii** ultrasonotherapy, ultrasound therapy.

ultrasowski *a.* ultrareactionary, extremist.

ultraszybki *a.* ultrafast, (of) ultra high speed.

ultratolerancyjny *a.* ultratolerant, ultraliberal.

ulubienica *f.*, **ulubieniec** *mp* **-ńc-** *pl.* **-y** favorite; *zw. iron. l. pog.* pet, fair-haired boy *l.* girl, golden boy *l.* girl, apple of one's eye; (*nauczyciela*) favorite; **ulubieniec losu** *przen.* fortune's darling; **ulubieniec pań** ladies' man; **ulubieniec publiczności** darling *l.* pet *l.* favorite of the public.

ulubiony *a.* **-eni** favorite, best-loved, favored, of choice; (*o potrawie, autorze*) favorite; (*o zwierzęciu*) pet; **ulubiona rozrywka** favorite pastime; **czyjeś ulubione miejsce** sb's favorite haunt, sb's stamping ground; **czyjś ulubiony temat** sb's pet subject, sb's hobbyhorse; **rozwodzić się na ulubiony temat** be *l.* ride on one's hobbyhorse; **czyjaś ulubiona teoria** sb's pet theory; **ulubiona ga-**

zeta/wino newspaper/wine of choice; **to moja ulubiona książka** this book is my favorite; **czyjaś ulubiona rzecz** sb's most prized possession; **czyjaś ulubiona kafejka** sb's hangout.

ululać *pf.* **1.** (= *uśpić*) lull *l.* rock to sleep, lullaby. **2.** *pot.* (= *upić*) souse, liquor up, soak up; **ululany** soused, sozzled, wiped, stiff. **~ się** *pf. pot.* (= *upić się*) get juiced-up; booze up, soak up, hit the sauce *l.* booze.

ulżyć *pf.* **-yj 1.** (= *pomóc, ułatwić*) unburden, help, ease; (*koniom*) unload. **2.** (= *sprawić ulgę*) relieve, ease, alleviate, lighten; **ulżyć czymś cierpieniom** ease *l.* alleviate sb's pain; **ulżyć komuś w smutku** ease *l.* relieve sb's distress; **ulżyć sercu** lighten one's heart; **ulżyło mi, kiedy...** I was relieved when...; **ulżyło mi, gdy usłyszałem...** I was relieved to hear...; **ulżyć sobie** *pot.* let *l.* blow off steam; get sth off one's chest; (*załatwić potrzebę*) ease o.s. *l.* nature, relieve nature.

uładzać *ipf.*, **uładzić** *pf.* put *l.* set things right *l.* straight, put *l.* set things in order; **uładzić dom** set one's house in order; **uładzić swoje sprawy** settle one's affairs.

ułagodzić *pf.* **-odź** *l.* **-ódź** (*osobę*) propitiate, placate, conciliate, appease; (*złość, gniew*) soothe, assuage, appease, ease; (*ból*) alleviate.

ułamać *pf.* **-mię -miesz** *zob.* **ułamywać**.

ułamek *mi* **-mk-** *Gen.* **-a 1.** *mat.* fraction; **ułamek dziesiętny** decimal fraction; **ułamek zwykły** common *l.* vulgar fraction; **ułamek właściwy/niewłaściwy** proper/improper fraction; **ułamek okresowy** circulating *l.* repeating *l.* recurring decimal; **o ułamek** fractionally. **2.** (= *kawałek*) fragment, bit, piece; (*szkła itp.*) sliver, chip. **3.** (= *urywek*) fragment, scrap; (*rozmowy*) part; **ułamek sekundy** flash, split second; **w ułamku sekundy** in a flash, within a second *l.* snap; **przez ułamek sekundy** for a fraction of a second, for a split second.

ułamkowy *a.* **1.** *mat.* fractional; **kreska ułamkowa** horizontal line. **2.** *lit.* (= *fragmentaryczny*) (*o badaniu, informacji*) fragmentary, incomplete, limited.

ułamywać *ipf.* break off.

ułan *mp wojsk.* uhlan, cavalryman.

Ułan Bator *mi indecl. geogr.* Ulan Bator; Urga (*until 1924*).

ułański *a.* uhlan's, of uhlans; **nogi ułańskie** bow *l.* bandy legs.

ułaskawiać *ipf.*, **ułaskawić** *pf. prawn.* pardon (*sb*); give *l.* grant (*sb*) a pardon.

ułaskawienie *n. prawn.* pardon, reprieve, amnesty; **wystąpić o ułaskawienie** ask for pardon; **otrzymać ułaskawienie** receive pardon; **ułaskawienie w ostatniej chwili** last-minute reprieve.

ułatwiać *ipf.*, **ułatwić** *pf.* facilitate, make easy *l.* easier; **ułatwiać coś komuś** aid sb with *l.* in sth; **ułatwić sprawę** make things easier; **ułatwiać komuś życie** make life easier for sb; **ułatwiać komuś zrobienie czegoś** make it easy for sb to do sth; **ułatwiać komuś drogę do czegoś** grease sb's path to sth.

ułatwienie *n.* facilitation, aid, shortcut; **dla uła-**twienia dodam, że... to make things simpler *l.* easier, I'd like to add...; **ułatwienia** amenities, conveniences, privileges; **korzystać z ułatwień** enjoy privileges; **to wielkie ułatwienie** it makes things much easier, that's a great help.

ułomek *mp* **-mk-** *pl.* **-i** *przest.* (= *okruch*) fragment, piece; (*skały*) chip; (*wspomnień*) scrap, fragment, shred; **nie być ułomkiem** *przen.* be no cripple.

ułomność *f.* **1.** (= *kalectwo*) handicap, disability, impairment. **2.** (= *wada*) defect, flaw, fault, imperfection; **ludzka ułomność** human imperfection; **ułomność fizyczna** physical defect *l.* handicap.

ułomny *a.* **1.** (= *kaleki*) handicapped, disabled. **2.** (= *niedoskonały*) defective, impaired; (*o charakterze, naturze*) faulty, imperfect, blemished; **czasownik ułomny** defective verb.

ułowić *pf.* **-ów ułowić jakiś dźwięk uchem** catch a sound; **ułowić coś okiem** get a glimpse of sth; catch sight of sth.

ułożenie *n.* **1.** (= *układ*) arrangement, setting, ordering; (*rąk, ramion*) position; **mycie i ułożenie** shampoo and set; **wadliwe ułożenie** (*np. płodu*) malposition. **2.** (= *grzeczność*) good manners, good conduct, politeness. **3.** (*o zwierzętach*) (= *tresura*) training.

ułożony *a.* arranged, ordered, set; **dobrze ułożony** well-mannered, well-bred, well-behaved; (*o psie*) amenable; **ułożony po kolei** seriate, arranged in order; **ułożony w kolejności alfabetycznej** arranged in alphabetical order; **z góry ułożony** preconcerted, prearranged; **wadliwie ułożony** (*zwł. o płodzie*) malposed.

ułożyć (się) *pf.* **ułóż** *zob.* **układać (się)**.

ułożyskować *pf. techn.* provide *l.* equip with bearings.

ułuda *f. lit.* delusion, phantom, illusion, fancy; **żyć ułudą** daydream, indulge in fancy *l.* woolgathering.

ułudny *a. lit.* deceptive, illusory.

ułupać *pf.* **-pię -piesz** chip off; (*np. drewno*) chop off.

UM *abbr.* (= *Urząd Miasta*) City Council.

umacniać *ipf.* **1.** (= *wzmacniać*) strengthen, bolster up, buttress; (*konstrukcję*) reinforce, fortify; (*walutę*) strengthen. **2.** (= *utrwalać*) solidify, add to (*sth*); (*przekonanie*) strengthen; (*przyjaźń*) cement; **umacniać kogoś w czymś** confirm sb in sth; **umocnić czyjeś postanowienie** stiffen sb's resolve, confirm sb's resolution; **umocnić swoją reputację** enhance *l.* bolster up one's reputation; **umocnić swoją pozycję na rynku** consolidate one's position on the market. **3.** *wojsk.* fortify, entrench. **~ się** *ipf.* **1.** (= *stawać się mocniejszym*) strengthen; (*konstrukcję*) consolidate, grow in strength; **umacniać się w czymś** stiffen in sth, become confirmed *l.* determined *l.* firm in sth; **umacniać się w wierze** be confirmed in one's faith *l.* beliefs. **2.** *wojsk.* fortify.

umaić *pf.* **umaję umaisz**, **umajać** *ipf. lit.* adorn *l.* deck with flowers; (*pokryć zielenią*) cover with verdure.

umalować *pf.* **1.** (= *zrobić makijaż*) (*twarz*)

make up; **umalować usta** put on lipstick. **2.** (*pokryć farbą*) paint (over). **~ się** *pf.* make up, put on makeup.

umarlak *mp pl.* **-cy** *l.* **-i** *pot.* stiff, goner.

umarł *itd. pf. zob.* **umrzeć**.

umarły *a.* dead. – *mp* deceased; **udawać umarłego** play possum; **wrzeszczał tak, że umarłego by obudził** he was screaming fit to wake the dead; **budzić umarłą przeszłość** bring up the dead past; **umarli** the dead; **żywi i umarli** the quick and the dead; **kraina umarłych** the nether world, the underworld, the realm of the dead.

umartwiać *ipf.* mortify. **~ się** *ipf.* mortify o.s. *l.* one's body.

umartwić (się) *pf. zob.* **umartwiać (się)**.

umartwienie *n.* mortification, restraint; **umartwianie się** self-mortification.

umarzać *ipf.* **1.** cancel; (= *likwidować zobowiązanie*) liquidate; (*dług, spłatę*) remit, extinguish, redeem; **umorzyć grzywnę** remit a fine; **umarzać pożyczkę** amortize a loan. **2.** *ekon.* (= *zmniejszać wartość*) amortize. **3.** *prawn.* (*postępowanie*) bar, discontinue (legal proceedings); (*karę, wyrok*) remit.

umarzalny *a.* cancelable.

umasawiać *ipf.*, **umasowić** *pf.* (*sport, turystykę*) popularize, propagate, give mass appeal to, disseminate.

umaszczenie *n.* color.

umawiać *ipf.* (*spotkanie*) arrange; **umówić kogoś z kimś** arrange a meeting with sb for sb; **umówić spotkanie z kimś** make an appointment with sb; **czy nadal jesteśmy umówieni na poniedziałek?** are we still on for Monday? **~ się** *ipf.* **1.** (= *ustalać*) arrange, make arrangements (*z kimś* with sb, *co do czegoś* about *l.* concerning sth); **umówię się w tej sprawie z moim adwokatem** I'll contact *l.* see my lawyer about it. **2.** *pot.* (= *ustalać spotkanie*) make a date (*z kimś* with sb); arrange to meet (*sb*).

umazać *pf.* **umażę umażesz** smear, smudge, soil; **umazać coś farbą** smear sth with paint. **~ się** *pf.* smear o.s. (*czymś* with sth); **umazać się atramentem** get smeared (all over) with ink.

umączyć *pf.* cover *l.* soil with flour; **umączyć kurzem** smother in dust.

umbra *f. min., mal.* umber; **umbra palona** burnt umber; **barwić umbrą** umber.

umeblować *pf. zob.* **meblować**.

umeblowanie *n.* furnishings, furniture.

umeblowany *a.* furnished; **skromnie umeblowany** barely furnished.

umęczyć *pf.* exhaust, tire out, wear out; **podróż go tak umęczyła** the journey tired him out completely; *kośc.* martyrize. **~ się** *pf.* frazzle o.s., exhaust o.s.; **umęczony** worn to a frazzle, exhausted, ragged, dead tired.

umiar *mi* moderation, restraint; (*w jedzeniu i piciu*) abstemiousness; **bez umiaru** immoderately, with abandon; **brak umiaru** immoderation, lack of restraint *l.* reserve; self-indulgence (*np. w jedzeniu i piciu*); **pić bez umiaru** drink hard; **z umiarem** in moderation; **nie mieć umiaru w**

czymś know no limits, indulge in sth; **okazywać/zachowywać umiar** show/exercise restraint.

umiarkować się *pf. zob.* **miarkować się**.

umiarkowanie *n.* = **umiar**. – *adv.* restrainedly, with restraint, with moderation; (*np. zainteresowany*) mildly; (*trudny*) moderately.

umiarkowany *a.* **1.** (= *powściągliwy, ostrożny*) (*o zachowaniu, osobie*) moderate, restrained, cautious; (*o zaskoczeniu, zainteresowaniu*) mild; (*o krytyce, poparciu, reakcji*) muted; (*żądania*) moderate; **umiarkowany optymizm** cautious optimism. **2.** (= *średni*) (*o cenie, klimacie*) moderate; (*o klimacie*) temperate, mild; **w cenie umiarkowanej** moderately priced. **3.** (*o poglądach*) (= *nie radykalny*) moderate, middle-of-the-road.

umieć *ipf.* **-em -esz, -ej 1.** (= *mieć wiedzę*) know; **umieć po polsku** *pot.* speak Polish; **nie umiem mówić po polsku** I can't speak Polish; **on nie umie zliczyć do trzech** he doesn't know how many beans make five; **umieć coś na pamięć/na wyrywki** know sth by heart/inside out. **2.** (= *potrafić*) can, be able; **umieć coś zrobić** know how to do sth; **ona nie umie kłamać** she cannot (tell a) lie; **nie umiem podjąć decyzji** I can't make a decision; **nie umieć przegrywać** be a bad *l.* poor loser; **to trzeba umieć robić** there's a knack to it; **umieć liczyć** be numerate; **umieć czytać i pisać** be literate; **umieć obsługiwać komputer** be computer-literate; **umieć odróżnić coś od czegoś** be able to tell sth from sth; **umieć pływać** know how to swim; **umieć słuchać** be a good listener.

umiejętnie *adv.* ably, skillfully, competently; **umiejętnie radzić sobie z trudnościami** roll with the punches.

umiejętność *f.* ability, competence, skill; **umiejętność czytania i pisania** literacy; **umiejętność przystosowania się** adaptability; **umiejętność obsługi komputera** computer literacy; **umiejętność prowadzenia rozmowy** conversational skills; **umiejętności jeździeckie** horsemanship; **umiejętności muzyczne** musicianship; **umiejętności żeglarskie** watercraft; **umiejętności kierownicze** executive skills; **umiejętności nawigacyjne** seamanship; **umiejętności komunikowania się** communication skills; **brak umiejętności** ineptitude; **brak umiejętności liczenia** innumeracy; **ukrywać swoje umiejętności** hide one's light under a bushel.

umiejętny *a.* (*o czynności*) skillful; (*o podejściu, wychowaniu*) competent, masterly, expert.

umiejscawiać *ipf.* **1.** (= *umieszczać*) locate, place, put; **umiejscawiać coś w czasie** locate sth in time; **umiejscowić akcję filmu w Paryżu** lay the scene of a film in Paris; **być umiejscowionym w czymś** reside in sth, be localized in sth. **2.** (= *ograniczać*) (*skutki czegoś*) localize. **~ się** *ipf.* (*o bólu*) be located (*in a given part of the body*).

umiejscowić (się) *pf. zob.* **umiejscawiać (się)**.

umierać *ipf.* **1.** (= *konać*) die (*z czegoś / na coś* from/of sth); pass away, decease; **umrzeć na raka/zapalenie płuc** die of cancer/pneumonia; **umrzeć nagle** die a violent death; **umrzeć z głodu** starve to death; **umierać z ciekawości/śmiechu/głodu** *przen.* be dying of curiosity/laughter/

hunger; **umrzeć jako bohater/żebrak** die a hero/ beggar; **umrzeć w nędzy** die destitute *l.* poor; **umarła na jego rękach** she died in his arms; **żyć nie umierać** heaven on earth, this is life!; **umrzeć młodo** die young; **umrzeć na posterunku** die with one's boots *l.* shoes on; **gdyby umarł** if he shall die; **umrzeć wcześniej od kogoś** predecease; **u-mrzeć za coś** die for sth; **umrzeć z zimna** die of exposure; **umrzeć za ojczyznę** die for one's country; **ona umiera** she's going; **pacjent nam umiera** we're losing the patient; **od tego jeszcze nikt nie umarł** this doesn't hurt; **prędzej bym umarł, niż...** I'd rather die than...; **o mało we umarłem** (*ze wstydu*) I nearly *l.* almost died; **umrzeć bezpotomnie** die without issue; **umrzeć nie pozostawiwszy testamentu** die intestate; **umrzeć przy porodzie** die in childbirth; **umrzeć śmiercią męczennika** die a saintly death, die a martyr; **u-mrzeć śmiercią naturalną** die a natural death, die of natural causes. **2.** (= *przestawać istnieć*) die out; (*o uczuciu, wspomnieniu, nadziejach*) melt away, fade (away).

umierający *mp* dying (*na coś* of sth); moribund; **czuwanie przy umierającym** deathwatch.

umieralność *f.* mortality, death *l.* mortality rate; **umieralność wśród noworodków** infant mortality.

umieszczać *ipf.* **1.** *form.* (= *lokować*) place, locate, position; (*gości*) put up; (*pieniądze*) lodge, locate, invest; (*ogłoszenie*) place; (*akcję filmu, książki*) set, lay; (*na stanowisku, posterunku*) post; (*między czymś a czymś*) interpose, sandwich; (*kogoś u kogoś*) lodge; **umieścić w nawiasie** parenthesize; **umieszczać w cudzysłowie** quote, put in inverted commas; **umieszczać coś na orbicie** inject sth into orbit, orbit; **umieścić w tekście** include in the text; **umieścić coś w internecie** put *l.* place sth on the Internet; **umieszczać na liście** list, post; **umieszczać na czarnej liście** blacklist; **umieszczać w kontekście** contextualize; **umieszczać w wykazie** schedule; **umieścić w internacie** board out; **umieścić artykuł** insert *l.* publish an article; **umieścić pieniądze** invest money; **umieścić swój podpis na dokumencie** subscribe a document; **umieścić w odosobnieniu** enisle. **2.** *form.* (= *osadzać*) put into; (*chorych*) commit; (*więźniów, przestępcę*) institutionalize; **umieszczać w obozie** encamp; **umieścić kogoś w szpitalu** put sb in a hospital, hospitalize sb. ~ **się** *ipf.* place o.s., settle o.s., plant o.s.; establish o.s.; **umieścić się wygodnie w fotelu** nestle comfortably in an armchair.

umieścić (się) *pf.* -eszczę -eścisz *zob.* **umieszczać (się).**

umiędzynarodowić *pf.* internationalize; **umiędzynarodowić osiągnięcia naukowe** internationalize scientific achievements; make scientific achievements international.

umiędzynarodowiony *a.* internationalized.

umięśnienie *n. anat.* musculature, brawn, muscle.

umięśniony *a.* muscled, muscular, brawny; **nadmiernie** *l.* **bardzo umięśniony** muscle-bound.

umilać *ipf.*, **umilić** *pf.* sugar, sweeten, render

pleasant; add charm (*coś* to sth); **umilać sobie czymś czas** amuse o.s. with sth, beguile the time doing sth; **umilać komuś życie** sweeten *l.* sugar sb's life.

umilknąć *pf.* **-ij** (*przestać mówić*) fall silent, cease talking, say no more; (*ucichnąć*) calm down, subside, die (away), quieten down; **śpiew ptaków umilkł** the sound of birds singing died away.

umiłować *pf. lit.* hold (*sth*) dear, set one's heart on (*sth*); fall for (*sth*); **umiłować sztukę** fall for arts; **umiłować kogoś** feel love *l.* affection for sb.

umiłowanie *n.* fondness, affection (*czegoś* for sth); love, liking (*czegoś* of *l.* for sth); **umiłowanie wiedzy/ziemi ojczystej** love of knowledge/of one's native land; *lit.* (= *przedmiot miłości*) love.

umiłowany *a. lit.* beloved, dear, dearest; **umiłowani bracia i siostry** dearly beloved; (*o zajęciu, rzeczy*) favorite, worshipped, adored.

umizgać się *ipf. zob.* **umizgiwać się.**

umizgi *pl. Gen.pl.* **-ów** *iron. l. żart.* courtship, wooing, love's labors.

umizgiwać się *ipf. iron. l. żart.* woo, court, spark (*do kogoś* sb); make sheep's eyes, play court (*do kogoś* to sb).

umknąć *pf. zob.* **umykać.**

umlaut *mi jęz.* umlaut, vowel mutation.

umłócić *pf.* (*żyto, pszenicę*) thresh, flail.

umniejszać *ipf.*, **umniejszyć** *pf.* lessen; (*czyjeś prawa, władzę*) diminish, take away; (*czyjś udział, zasługi*) understate, depreciate; (*powagę, znaczenie sytuacji*) underplay; (*wartość*) downgrade, devalue; (*znaczenie*) belittle, depreciate; (*winę, karę*) extenuate; **umniejszyć czyjeś zasługi** detract from *l.* belittle sb's merits.

umocnić (się) *pf.* **-ij** *zob.* **umacniać (się).**

umocnienie *n.* **1.** (= *uczynienie mocniejszym*) strengthening, solidification, reinforcement. **2.** *bud.* (= *konstrukcja umacniająca*) reinforcement, consolidation, bracing; (*budowli, muru*) revetment; (*brzegu*) bank protection. **3.** *wojsk.* fortification, fieldwork, defensive work; **linia umocnień** line of fortifications.

umocować *pf.*, **umocowywać** *ipf.* secure, fasten, fix (*sth*) (*do czegoś* to sth); (*łódź*) moor (*do czegoś* to sth); (*żagiel*) frap; **umocować w uchwycie** chuck; **dobrze umocowany** secure.

umoczyć *pf.* **1.** (= *zwilżyć*) dip, sop, immerse; **umoczyć usta** (= *wypić łyk*) take a sip; sip (*w czymś* at sth). **2.** *pot.* (= *popełnić błąd*) put a foot wrong.

umoralniać *ipf.* moralize, edify; **umoralniać młodzież własnym przykładem** set a good example to young people.

umoralniająco *adv.* elevatingly, moralizingly, edifyingly; **coś wpływa na kogoś umoralniająco** sth has a moralizing influence on sb.

umoralniający *a.* elevating, edifying, moralizing.

umoralnić *pf.* **-ij** *zob.* **umoralniać.**

umordować *pf. pot.* tire out, frazzle, exhaust, knock out, burn out; **podróż go umordowała** the journey tired him out. ~ **się** *pf. pot.* run o.s.

rugged, work o.s. into a frazzle; **umordował się treningiem** he was exhausted from the training.

umorusać *pf.* (*twarz, ręce, ubrania*) smear, soil, dirty, grime; **umorusał twarz węglem** he soiled his face with coal. ~ **się** *pf.* get soiled, get dirty; soil *l.* dirty one's face *l.* hands.

umorusany *a.* grimy, begrimed, smeared all over, smutty.

umorzenie *n.* **1.** *ekon.* extinguishment; (*przez spłatę*) amortization; (*długu*) remission, extinction; (*części zadłużenia*) abatement; **plan umorzenia** amortization schedule. **2.** *prawn.* discontinuance, discontinuation (of legal proceedings); (*kary*) remission, pardon.

umorzyć *pf. zob.* **umarzać.**

umościć (się) *pf.* **-szczę -ścisz** *zob.* **mościć (się).**

umotywować *pf. zob.* **motywować.**

umowa *f. Gen.pl.* **-ów** agreement, bargain, pact; *polit.* treaty, convention; *ekon.* contract; **umowa kupna, sprzedaży** sale contract; **umowa wydawnicza** publisher's agreement; **umowa maklerska** contract of brokerage; **umowa o pracę** contract of employment, employment contract; **umowa małżeńska** marriage contract; **umowa przedmałżeńska** prenuptial agreement; **umowa przedwstępna** precontract; **umowa najmu** *l.* dzierżawy lease, hiring contract; **umowa spółki** contract of partnership; **umowa kupna** contract of purchase; **umowa nieważna** void contract; **umowa zbiorowa** collective agreement; **projekt umowy** draft of a contract; **umowa społeczna** social contract; **pracować na umowę zlecenie dla kogoś** be under contract to sb; **zawierać umowę** contract, enter into a contract, conclude a contract; **sporządzić/podpisać umowę** draw up/sign a contract; **zerwać umowę** break a contract; **przedłużyć umowę** extend a contract; **być związanym umową** be bound by contract; **umowa jest umową** a bargain's a bargain; **postanowienia umowy** provisions of a contract; **naruszenie warunków umowy** breach of contract; **przestrzegać umowy** honor a contract; **zgodnie z warunkami umowy** by the terms of the agreement; **związany umową** bound by contract; **objęty umową** coming under contract; **umowa dwustronna** bilateral contract; **zawrzeć umowę o pracę** contract for work; **umowa stoi** *pot.* it's a deal!, done!

umownie *adv.* **1.** (= *w myśl umowy*) by contract, by mutual agreement. **2.** (= *nierealistycznie*) conventionally; **przedstawić coś umownie** present sth conventionally; **przyjmijmy umownie, że...** let's assume that...

umowność *f.* **1.** (= *zgodność z umową*) formality. **2.** (= *konwencjonalność*) conventionality, convention.

umowny *a.* **1.** (= *dotyczący umowy*) contractual, agreed upon. **2.** (= *konwencjonalny*) conventional, accepted; **to tylko kwestia umowna** it's just a matter of convention.

umożliwiać *ipf.,* **umożliwić** *pf.* facilitate, make (*sth*) possible; make easy *l.* easier; clear the way (*coś* for sth); (*o przepisie, prawie*) provide for;

umożliwiać komuś zrobienie czegoś enable sb to do sth, make it possible for sb to do sth.

umór *mi* **pić na umór** drink like a fish; **pijany na umór** stoned; **zakochać się w kimś na umór** be head over heels in love with sb.

umówić (się) *pf. zob.* **umawiać (się).**

umówiony *a.* **-eni** arranged, prearranged, agreed upon, scheduled; **jestem umówiony na czwartą** I have an appointment for 4 o'clock; **jesteśmy umówieni** it's a date; **umówione spotkanie** appointment, engagement; **sprawa umówiona** the business is settled; **jestem już z kimś umówiony** I have a prior *l.* previous engagement; **na umówiony sygnał** at a prearranged signal; **nie przyjść na umówioną godzinę** fail to keep an appointment.

umrzeć *pf.* **umrę umrzesz, umrzyj, umarł** *zob.* **umierać.**

umrzyk *mp pl.* **-i** *pot.* stiff, goner.

umundurować *pf. zob.* **mundurować.**

umundurowanie *n.* uniform, regimentals; **umundurowanie bojowe** riot gear.

umuzykalniać *ipf.,* **umuzykalnić** *pf.* **-ij** cultivate *l.* promote *l.* further the love of music (*kogoś* in sb).

umyć (się) *pf.* **umyję umyjesz, umyj** *zob.* **myć (się).**

umykać *ipf. lit.* (= *uciekać*) escape, slip away, get away, steal away (*przed czymś* from sth); elude (*przed czymś* sth); (*o czasie, marzeniach*) flee, fleet; **umykać czyjejś uwadze** escape sb's notice *l.* attention; **umykać wzrokiem** look away; **niewiele mu umyka** he doesn't miss much; **umknął nam** he gave us a slip.

umysł *mi* (= *intelekt*) mind, intellect, brain, intelligence; **trzeźwy umysł** clear *l.* cool head, wit; **chory umysł** twisted mind; **przenikliwy umysł** incisive mind; **jasność umysłu** lucidity; **przytomność umysłu** presence of mind; **ciasnota umysłu** narrowmindedness; **zachować przytomność umysłu** keep a level head; **zachować trzeźwość umysłu** keep one's wits about one; **być zdrowym na umyśle** be sane, be of sound mind; **to wciąż zaprząta jego umysł** it's still on his mind; **chory na umyśle** brain-sick, of unsound mind; **słaby na umyśle** feeble-minded, weak-minded; **ogarniać coś umysłem** encompass sth with one's mind; **wysilać** *l.* **wytężać umysł** beat one's brains out, think hard, exert one's mind; **coś przerasta ludzki umysł** the mind boggles at sth; **odświeżyć umysł** blow *l.* brush *l.* clear the cobwebs away; **zasiać podejrzenia w czyimś umyśle** plant a suspicion in sb's mind. – *mp* (*człowiek*) mind; **otwarty umysł** open mind; **wpływowe umysły** seminal minds; **wielkie umysły epoki** great minds of the day.

umysłowo *adv.* mentally, intellectually; **chory umysłowo** mentally ill, insane; **niedorozwinięty umysłowo** mentally retarded; **upośledzony umysłowo** mentally disabled *l.* handicapped; **szpital dla umysłowo chorych** mental hospital, insane asylum.

umysłowość *f.* **1.** (*sposób myślenia*) mentality, cast *l.* frame *l.* turn of mind, mental constitution, mental attitude. **2.** (*człowiek*) mind, personality; **twórcza/wszechstronna umysłowość** creative/versatile mind.

umysłowy *a.* (= *odnoszący się do intelektu*) (*o zajęciu, pracy, wysiłku*) intellectual; (*o chorobie*) mental; **w pełni władz umysłowych** compos mentis, of sound mind, in full possession of one's faculties *l.* senses; **nie w pełni władz umysłowych** of unsound mind; **pracownik umysłowy** white-collar worker; **praca umysłowa** mental work, brainwork; **niedorozwój umysłowy** mental retardation; **upośledzenie umysłowe** mental handicap *l.* defect *l.* deficiency; **choroba umysłowa** mental illness, insanity; **zaburzenia umysłowe** mental disturbance; **zdolność umysłowa** mental power; **gimnastyka umysłowa** mental gymnastics; **wysiłek umysłowy** mental exertion; **wiek rozwoju umysłowego** mental age; **lekarz chorób umysłowych** psychiatrist.

umyślić *pf. lit.* plan, think up, take (*sth*) into one's head; **umyślić sobie małżeństwo z kimś** set one's mind on marrying sb.

umyślnie *adv.* deliberately, intentionally, designedly, by design; on purpose, purposefully; **czy to było umyślnie zrobione?** was this intended?, was this done on purpose?

umyślny *a.* (*o działaniu*) intentional, deliberate, premeditated; **umyślnie działać na czyjąś szkodę** act intentionally to the detriment of sb; *prawn.* deliberate, voluntary. – *mp przest., żart.* (= *posłaniec*) special messenger; **wysłać coś przez umyślnego** send *l.* dispatch sth by special delivery.

umywać *ipf.* **-am -asz umywać ręce** *przen.* wash one's hands (*od czegoś* of sth). **~ się** *ipf.* **ktoś/coś nie umywa się do kogoś/czegoś** sb/sth can't hold a candle to sb/sth.

umywalka *f. Gen.pl.* **-ek** basin, washbasin; washstand, pedestal basin (*stojąca*); **szafka z umywalką** vanity unit.

umywalnia *f. Gen.pl.* **-i 1.** (*pomieszczenie*) washroom, bathroom. **2.** (*mebel*) washbasin, washstand.

unaczynienie *n. anat.* vascularity, vascularization, vascular supply; **unaczynienie tętnicze** arterialization, arterial vascularization; **nadmierne unaczynienie** venosity.

unaczyniony *a. anat.* vascularized.

unaoczniać *ipf.*, **unaocznić** *pf.* **-ij** visualize, demonstrate, manifest (*coś* sth); **unaoczniać słabe strony projektu** point to deficiencies of the project.

unaradawiać *ipf.*, **unarodowić** *pf.* **-ów** nationalize; (*upaństwowić*) put under State control.

unasawiać *ipf. jęz.* nasalize.

unasienniać *ipf.* inseminate.

unasiennianie *n. zool.* insemination; **sztuczne unasiennienie** artificial insemination; *med.* semination.

unasiennić *pf.* **-ij** *zob.* **unasienniać**.

unaukowiać *ipf.*, **unaukowić** *pf.* **-ów** make *l.* render scientific; **unaukowić metody pracy** make methods of work more scientific.

uncja *f. Gen.pl.* **-ji** (= *ok. 29 g*) ounce; **uncja aptekarska** (= *ok. 31 g*) ounce apothecary.

uncjalny *a. druk.* uncial; **pismo uncjalne** uncial.

uncjała *f. druk.* (*litera*) uncial letter; (*pismo*) uncial writing.

uncjowy *a.* ounce.

undecyma *f. muz.* undecime.

underground *mi sztuka, muzyka* underground.

undulacja *f. techn.* undulation.

undulator *mi Gen.* **-a** *techn.* undulator.

undyna *f. mit.* undine.

unerwiać *ipf.*, **unerwić** *pf.* innervate.

unerwienie *n.* **1.** *anat.* innervation, nervation. **2.** *bot.* (*liścia, skrzydła*) nervure, venation.

unerwiony *a.* nerved, innervated; *bot.* ribbed, nervate.

unia *f. Gen.* **-ii 1.** (= *związek*) union, consortium, coalition, confederation; **Unia Europejska** European Union; **unia personalna** *hist.* personal union; *ekon.* (*kilku przedsiębiorstw*) interlocking directorates; **unia realna** real union; **unia monetarna** monetary union; **unia gospodarcza** economic union; **unia celna** customs *l.* tariff union; **zawierać unię** enter a union. **2.** *rel.* (= *kościół unicki*) Uniate Church.

unicestwiać *ipf.*, **unicestwić** *pf.* (*niszczyć*) annihilate, destroy; (*gatunek, cywilizację*) extinguish, wipe out, exterminate; (*udaremnić*) frustrate, put an end to; (*szanse, nadzieje*) cancel, thwart; (*wysiłki*) baffle.

unicki *a. rel.* Uniate.

uniemożliwiać *ipf.*, **uniemożliwić** *pf.* make (*sth*) impossible, prevent, prohibit, hinder, thwart; **uniemożliwiać komuś zrobienie czegoś** bar *l.* keep *l.* prevent sb from doing sth; make it impossible for sb to do sth; **hałas na zewnątrz uniemożliwił zaśnięcie** the noise outside made falling asleep impossible; **uniemożliwić ucieczkę** prevent escaping, prevent an escape; **uniemożliwić kontynuację czegoś** pull the plug on sth.

unieruchamiać *ipf.*, **unieruchomić** *pf.* **1.** (= *czynić nieruchomym*) immobilize; **choroba zupełnie go unieruchomiła** the illness immobilized him totally *l.* rendered him totally immobile; **unieruchamiać kapitał** *ekon.* tie up *l.* lock capital; **unieruchomić ruch uliczny** hold up the traffic; **unieruchamiać kończynę** encase, immobilize; **unieruchomiony w śniegu/wśród lodów/we mgle/przez niepogodę** snow-/ice-/fog-/weather-bound; **unieruchomiony przez chorobę** bedridden; laid up with illness. **2.** (= *wstrzymywać funkcjonowanie*) (*fabrykę*) inactivate, bring to a standstill *l.* to a halt, render inactive; (*maszynę*) idle.

uniesienie *n.* **1.** (= *euforia*) ecstasy, rapture, elation, exultation; **w uniesieniu** extatically; **pełen uniesienia** extatic, rapturous, elated, exultant; **wpaść w uniesienie** go into a rapture. **2.** (= *poryw uczuć*) passion. **3.** (= *podniesienie*) lift; **uniesienie głowy** cock of the head.

unieszczęśliwiać *ipf.*, **unieszczęśliwić** *pf.* make (*sb*) unhappy *l.* miserable.

unieszkodliwiać *ipf.*, **unieszkodliwić** *pf.* (*prze-*

ciwnika) defang, render harmless; (*bombę itp.*) disable, defuse; (*truciznę*) neutralize.

unieść *pf.* **uniosę uniesiesz uniósł uniosła unieśli** 1. *zob.* **unosić.** 2. (= *móc udźwignąć*) carry, bear, lift; **unieść głowę** cock *l.* lift one's head; **unieść kogoś/coś w morze** sweep sb/sth out to sea. **~ się** *pf. zob.* **unosić się** 1, 2, 3, 4.

unieśmiertelniać *ipf.*, **unieśmiertelnić** *pf.* **-ij** immortalize; perpetuate, eternalize; **unieśmiertelnić swoje imię** make one's name immortal, immortalize one's name.

unieważniać *ipf.*, **unieważnić** *pf.* **-ij** invalidate, dissolve, abrogate; (*czek*) cancel; (*decyzję, rozkaz, przepis*) override; (*kontrakt, małżeństwo, umowę*) annul, dissolve, render *l.* declare null (and void) *l.* invalid; (*spisek*) defeat; (*kontrakt*) vitiate, invalidate; (*umowę*) void, abrogate; (*pełnomocnictwo, koncesję, dokument*) revoke; (*przepis, ustawę*) repeal, nullify; **unieważnić na mocy przedawnienia** prescribe; **unieważnić traktat** abrogate a treaty; **unieważnić proces** declare a mistrial.

unieważnienie *n.* (= *anulowanie*) abrogation, annulment, abatement; (*umowy*) voidance, defeasance; (*małżeństwa, wyroku, wyborów*) annulment; (*kontraktu, zapisu*) vitiation; (*pełnomocnictwa, koncesji, dokumentu*) revocation; **podlegający unieważnieniu** voidable; **proces o unieważnienie** *prawn.* nullity suit.

uniewinniać *ipf.*, **uniewinnić** *pf.* **-ij** exculpate, exonerate, absolve (*kogoś z czegoś* sb from sth); **uniewinnić z zarzutu** exculpate from a charge; *prawn.* acquit; **uniewinnić oskarżonego** acquit the accused; **wyrok uniewinniający** verdict of not guilty, (sentence of) acquittal; **uniewinniony** acquitted.

uniewinnienie *n.* exoneration, acquittal, absolution.

uniezależniać *ipf.* **-ij uniezależniać coś od czegoś** make sth independent of sth; **uniezależnić produkcję od importu** make production independent of import. **~ się** *ipf.* gain *l.* acquire independence, become independent (*od kogoś / czegoś* of sb/sth); (*o państwie*) become autonomous; (*od administracji lokalnej*) opt out; (*stać się samodzielnym*) strike out on one's own, come into one's own; (*o ludziach pozbawionych pełni praw*) emancipate o.s., liberate o.s.

uniezależnić (się) *pf. zob.* **uniezależniać (się)**.

unifikacja *f.* 1. *lit.* (= *ujednolicenie*) unification, standardization, normalization; **unifikacja polityczna** political unification; **unifikacja norm** unification of standards. 2. *lit.* (= *połączenie*) unification, union.

unifikacyjny *a.* 1. *lit.* (= *ujednolicający*) (*normy, przepisy*) unifying, standardizing. 2. *lit.* (= *zjednoczeniowy*) (*tendencje*) unification.

unifikować *ipf.* 1. *lit.* (= *ujednolicać*) unify, standardize, make uniform, normalize. 2. *lit.* (= *jednoczyć*) unite, bring together.

uniform *mi* uniform.

uniformizacja *f. lit.* uniformization, standardization, normalization.

uniformizm *mi lit.* uniformism.

uniformizować *ipf. lit.* make uniform, standardize, uniformize.

unijny *a.* union.

unik *mi* evasion, dodge; **zrobić unik** dodge, duck; **stosować uniki** *przen.* take evasive action; be evasive.

unikać *ipf.* 1. (= *zostać ominiętym*) escape, avert; (*niebezpieczeństwa, śmierci*) miss; (*śmierci, konfliktu*) escape; (*kary*) get off, walk free; (*ciosów*) dodge; **uniknąć śmierci** cheat death; **nie można tego uniknąć** it's unavoidable, it cannot be helped; **uniknąć nieszczęścia o włos** have a narrow escape, have a close shave, avoid sth by inches; **udało jej się uniknąć kary** she got off scotfree; **uniknąć pomyłki** avoid confusion; **zręcznie uniknąć** parry. 2. (= *stronić*) avoid, elude, eschew; sheer away (*czegoś* from sth); keep out, steer clear (*kogoś* of sb); (*osoby, ludzi, wysiłku*) avoid; (*problemu, kwestii*) evade, dodge; **unikać kłopotliwych pytań** dodge awkward questions; **unikać (robienia) czegoś** fight shy of (doing) sth; **unikać kogoś/czegoś jak ognia** avoid sb/sth like the plague; **unikać czyjegoś wzroku** avoid sb's look; **unikać zbędnych słów** waste no words; **unikać tematu** avoid *l.* dodge the issue; **unikać ryzyka** play for safety; **unikać alkoholu** stay dry; **unikać rozgłosu** keep a low profile.

unikalny *a.* = **unikatowy**.

unikat *mi* curiosity.

unikatowy *a.* unique; **unikatowy egzemplarz** unique specimen.

uniknąć *pf.* **-ij** *zob.* **unikać** 1.

unilateralny *a.* unilateral.

unionista *mp*, **unionistka** *f. Gen.pl.* **-ek** (*w wojnie secesyjnej*) Federal; (*zwolennik przynależności Irlandii Płn. do Wielkiej Brytanii*) Unionist.

unipolarny *a. fiz.* unipolar; **tranzystor unipolarny** unipolar transistor.

uniseks *mi* (*o strojach, fryzurze*) unisex.

uniseksowy *a.* unisex.

unisono *n. indecl.* unison. – *adv.* (*śpiewać*) in unison.

unita *mp* 1. *rel.* (= *grekokatolik*) Greek Catholic, Uniat. 2. *pot.* (= *członek jakiejkolwiek unii*) unionist.

unitarianizm *mi rel.* Unitarianism.

unitarny *a.* unitarian.

unitaryzm *mi* unitarianism.

unitka *f. Gen.pl.* **-ek** *zob.* **unita**.

uniwerbizacja *f. jęz.* lexical blending.

uniwerek *mi* **-rk-** *pot.* school; *Br.* varsity.

uniwersalia *pl. Gen.* **-ów** *fil.* universals; **jedno z uniwersaliów** a universal.

uniwersalizacja *f.* popularization, universalization.

uniwersalizm *mi* 1. (= *powszechność*) universality, universalism. 2. *fil.* universalism.

uniwersalnie *adv.* universally.

uniwersalność *f.* (= *powszechność*) 1. universality, catholicity. 2. (= *wszechstronność zastosowań*) versatility, universal applicability.

uniwersalny *a.* 1. (= *powszechny*) universal; **czas uniwersalny** universal time; **gramatyka uniwersalna** *jęz.* universal grammar. 2. (= *wszech-*

stronny) all-purpose, multipurpose, catholic, versatile; (*o rozmiarze*) universal; **ubrania o rozmiarze uniwersalnym** one-size-fits-all clothes; **uniwersalna płyta cyfrowa** *komp.* digital versatile disk, DVD; **uniwersalny dawca krwi** *med.* universal (blood) donor; **klucz uniwersalny** *techn.* master key, passkey; **prawdy uniwersalne** universal truths; **lekarstwo uniwersalne** universal remedy; panacea; **przegub uniwersalny** *mech.* Cardan joint, universal joint.
uniwersał *mi hist.* universal proclamation.
uniwersjada *f.* *sport* inter-university sports championships.
uniwersum *n. indecl. form.* universe.
uniwersytecki *a.* university, academic; **miasteczko uniwersyteckie** (university) campus; **profesor uniwersytecki** associate professor; **wykształcenie uniwersyteckie** university education; **studia uniwersyteckie** (*ukończone*) university diploma *l.* degree.
uniwersytet *mi* university; **uniwersytet otwarty** Open University; **uniwersytet trzeciego wieku** Third Age University.
unizm *mi sztuka* unism.
uniżenie *adv.* humbly, complaisantly, cap in hand; **zachowywać się uniżenie wobec kogoś** ingratiate o.s. with sb, kowtow to sb.
uniżoność *f.* obsequiousness, servility.
uniżony *a.* **-eni** servile, obsequious, complaisant; **sługa uniżony** *przest.* your humble servant.
unormować (się) *pf. zob.* **normować (się)**.
unormowany *a.* normalized, regularized, standardized; **unormowany tryb życia** stable life.
unosawiać *ipf. fon.* nasalize.
unosić *ipf.* **-szę -sisz** **1.** (= *podnosić*) lift, raise. **2.** *lit.* (*o wietrze, rzece itp.*) (= *porywać*) carry away *l.* off, sweep away *l.* along. **3.** *lit.* **unosić kogoś (w dal)** (= *zabierać*) (*o pojeździe, wierzchowcu*) carry sb away. **~ się** *ipf.* **1.** (= *podnosić się*) ascend, rise; **unosić się na palcach** *l.* **palce** stand on tiptoe. **2.** (= *być podnoszonym*) rise, be raised; (*o kurtynie*) be drawn up. **3.** (= *wznosić się*) (*o samolocie*) rise *l.* fly into the air, soar; (*o dymie, kurzu*) rise. **4.** (= *irytować się*) be vexed *l.* aggraviated *l.* irritated; **unosić się gniewem** fly into a rage; be transported with anger; (*emocjami*) vibrate (*czymś* with sth); **unosić się honorem, dumą** be too proud (to do sth); **nie unoś się!** calm down!, take it easy!, don't get excited! **5.** (= *utrzymywać się na pewnej wysokości*) float, drift, hover; **unosić się na wodzie/w powietrzu** float *l.* drift in the water/in the air; **unosić się na wietrze** blow in the wind; (*o helikopterze*) hover. **6.** (*o zapachu itp.*) (= *rozchodzić się*) rise, spread. **7.** *lit.* (= *zachwycać się*) rave (*nad kimś/czymś* about sb/sth).
unosowić *pf.* **-ów** *fon. zob.* **unosawiać**.
unosowienie *n. fon.* nasalization.
unowocześniać *ipf.*, **unowocześnić** *pf.* **-ij** modernize; (*sprzęt, system*) update, upgrade.
unurzać *pf. lit., t. przen.* steep, bathe (*sb l. sth*) (*w czymś* in sth); (= *zbrukać, skalać*) stain, soil, besmirch (*sth*) (*w czymś* with sth). **~ się** *pf.* **unu-**

rzać się w czymś be steeped *l.* bathed in sth; get stained *l.* soiled with sth.
unurzany *a.* (= *skąpany*) bathed, steeped (*w czymś* in sth); (= *zbrukany*) stained, soiled (*w czymś* with sth); **ostrze unurzane we krwi** blood-stained blade.
uobecniać *ipf.*, **uobecnić** *pf.* **-ij** *rzad., lit.* personalize, make (*sb l. sth*) present.
uodparniać, uodporniać *ipf. med.* **1.** immunize (*kogoś na coś* sb against sth). **2.** (= *czynić niewrażliwym*) toughen, harden (*sb*) (*na coś* to sth). **3.** *ogr.* **uodparniać młode rośliny** harden off young plants. **~ się** *ipf. med.* **1.** become immune *l.* immunized (*na coś* against sth). **2.** toughen, harden (*na coś* to sth).
uodpornić (się) *pf.* **-ij** *zob.* **uodparniać (się)**.
uogólniać *ipf.*, **uogólnić** *pf.* **-ij** generalize; **zbytnio uogólniać** overgeneralize.
uogólnienie *n.* generalization; **nadmierne uogólnienie** overgeneralization, sweeping generalization.
UOP *abbr. polit.* (= *Urząd Ochrony Państwa*) the Office of Homeland Security.
uosabiać *ipf.*, **uosobić** *pf.* **-sób** **1.** (= *reprezentować*) epitomize, typify. **2.** (= *personifikować*) personify, embody.
uosobienie *n.* embodiment, personification (*czegoś* of sth); **uosobienie miłości/piękna** love/beauty incarnate; **uosobienie cierpliwości/ignorancji/mądrości** patience/ignorance/wisdom personified; **uosobienie seksu** sex symbol; **być uosobieniem czegoś** typify sth.
UP *abbr.* (= *Urząd Pracy*) employment agency.
UPA *abbr. hist.* (= *Ukraińska Powstańcza Armia*) the Ukrainian Rebel Army.
upaćkać (się) *pf. zob.* **paćkać (się)**.
upad *mi geol.* dip; **upad warstwy** angle of dip.
upadać *ipf.* **1.** (= *przewracać się*) fall (down), drop (down), tumble (over), collapse; **upadł jak długi** he fell full length; **upaść na plecy** tumble backwards; **upaść z brzękiem** clatter down; **upaść z hukiem** *l.* **łomotem** collapse with a thud; **potknąć się i upaść** trip and fall; **upaść na kolana** fall to one's knees; throw o.s. on one's knees; **upadać na duchu** lose one's hope; **upadać pod ciężarem trosk/kłopotów** give in to worries/troubles; **upadać ze zmęczenia** be dead-beat *l.* exhausted; drop from exhaustion; **upaść na głowę** *pot.* lose one's mind *l.* one's senses; go nuts. **2.** (= *podupadać*) collapse, decline; (*o przedsiębiorstwie*) collapse, go under, go broke. **3.** (= *skończyć się fiaskiem*) fail; (*o powstaniu itp.*) break down. **4.** (*o wniosku, projekcie*) (= *nie przejść w głosowaniu*) be rejected, be voted down.
upadek *mi* **-dk-** **1.** (= *przewrócenie się*) fall, drop, tumble, collapse; **upadek na plecy** (*w zapasach*) backfall; **upadek na deski** *boks* dive. **2.** (= *spadnięcie*) fall; (*z konia, roweru*) spill. **3.** (= *podupadnięcie*) deterioration, decay, demise; (*obyczajów, miast*) decline; **chylić się ku upadkowi** be on the decline, be on the brink of ruin. **4.** (= *klęska*) downfall, fall, overthrow; **upadek gospodarczy** economic crash; **upadek komunizmu**

collapse of communism; **doprowadzić do czyje-goś/własnego upadku** engineer sb's/one's own downfall; **wzlot i upadek** rise and fall; **wzloty i upadki** ups and downs, highs and lows. **5.** (= *niemoralne postępowanie*) downfall; **upadek człowieka** *Bibl.* the Fall of Man.

upadlać *ipf.* **-ij** disgrace, debase, degrade; **upodliło go nadużywanie alkoholu** excessive drinking debased him. **~ się** *ipf.* disgrace o.s., debase o.s., lower o.s. (*czymś* by sth *l.* doing sth); **upodlił się kłamstwem** he lowered himself by telling a lie.

upadłościowy *a.* *prawn.* bankruptcy, insolvent's; **masa upadłościowa** insolvent's assets *l.* estate; **syndyk masy upadłościowej** trustee; **zarządca masy upadłościowej** receiver; **postępowanie upadłościowe** bankruptcy proceedings.

upadłość *f.* *prawn.* bankruptcy, insolvency, failure; **ogłaszać (swoją** *l.* **czyjąś) upadłość** declare o.s. *l.* sb insolvent, adjudge sb bankrupt.

upadły *a.* (= *zdegenerowany*) fallen; **upadły anioł** fallen angel; *prawn.* bankrupt; **dłużnik upadły** undischarged bankrupt; **do upadłego** *pot.* to the very end, to the hilt; **pracować do upadłego** work until one drops; **walczyć do upadłego** fight *l.* struggle to the bitter end.

upajać *ipf.* **1.** (= *odurzać alkoholem, narkotykami*) intoxicate, inebriate, drug. **2.** *przen.* (= *wywoływać euforię*) intoxicate, enchant, carry (*sb*) away. **~ się** *ipf.* **1.** (= *upijać się*) get intoxicated *l.* inebriated *l.* drunk. **2.** (= *napawać się*) revel, delight (*czymś* in sth) be carried away *l.* enchanted (*czymś* by sth); **upajać się zwycięstwem/świeżym powietrzem** be intoxicated with victory/fresh air.

upajająco *adv.* *przen. i dosł.* intoxicatingly.

upajający *a.* intoxicating.

upalać *ipf.*, **upalić** *pf.* **1.** (= *nadpalić*) singe, scorch. **2.** (= *uprażyć*) roast.

upalnie *adv.* **jest upalnie** it is sweltering *l.* scorching *l.* hot *l.* boiling.

upalny *a.* sweltering, scorching, boiling, hot.

upał *mi* the heat; **ale upał!** what a sweltering *l.* scorching *l.* hot day!

upamiętniać *ipf.* commemorate, immortalize; (= *uczcić*) celebrate, mark. **~ się** *ipf.* **-ij** be marked (*czymś* by sth).

upamiętnić (się) *pf.* **-ij** *zob.* **upamiętniać (się)**.

upaństwawiać *ipf.*, **upaństwowić** *pf.* nationalize, communize, put under state control.

upaństwowienie *n.* nationalization.

upaprać (się) *pf.* **-rzę -rzesz** *zob.* **paprać (się)**.

uparcie *adv.* persistently, stubbornly, obstinately, doggedly; **uparcie czemuś zaprzeczać** deny sth stubbornly; **uparcie twierdzić, że...** insist that...

uparciuch *mp pl.* **-y** mule.

uparł *itd.* *pf.* *zob.* **uprzeć się**.

uparty *a.* **1.** (= *nieustępliwy*) (*o człowieku*) stubborn, obstinate, dogged; (*zwł. w poglądach*) opinionated; **uparty jak osioł** (as) stubborn as a mule; mulish; (*w dążeniach, pracy*) persevering, persistent, tenacious, unyielding. **2.** (= *uporczywy*) (*o niechęci, walce*) stubborn, persistent.

upartyjniać *ipf.*, **upartyjnić** *pf.* **-ij** canvass for the party; encourage party membership among (*sb*).

upaść[1] *pf.* **upadnę upadniesz upadnij, upadł 1.** *zob.* **upadać. 2.** (= *zlecieć*) fall down, tumble; **upaść na głowę** *przen.* lose one's mind *l.* senses, go crazy. **3.** (= *zdemoralizować się*) degrade *l.* debase o.s.; **upaść nisko** cheapen o.s.

upaść[2] *pf.* **upasę upasiesz upasł upaśli** *pot.* (= *utuczyć*) (*zwierzę, człowieka*) fatten (up), feed up. **~ się** *pf.* *pot.* (= *utuczyć się*) grow fat; fatten up.

upatrywać *ipf.*, **upatrzyć** *pf.* **1.** *lit.* (= *wyszukiwać*) seek, look for (*kogoś/czegoś* sb/sth); **upatrzyć sobie kogoś/coś** choose sb/sth, single out sb/sth; **upatrzyłam sobie tę bluzkę** this blouse caught my eye; **upatrywać stosownej chwili** wait for the right moment. **2.** *lit.* (= *doszukiwać się*) suspect (*czego* sth); ascribe (*czegoś* sth, *w czymś* to sth); **w bólach głowy upatrywała symptomów poważnej choroby** she surmised that her headaches were symptoms of a grave illness.

upchać *pf.*, **upchnąć** *pf.* **-ij** *zob.* **upychać**.

upełnomocniać *ipf.*, **upełnomocnić** *pf.* **-ij** empower, authorize.

upełnoprawnić *pf.* **-ij** emancipate, give equal rights.

uperfumować (się) *pf.* *zob.* **perfumować (się)**.

upewniać *ipf.* assure, reassure (*kogoś* sb, *o czymś* of sth). **~ się** *ipf.* make sure *l.* certain (*o czymś* about sth); **upewnić się, że/czy wszystko jest w porządku** check *l.* make sure that/if everything is all right.

upewnić (się) *pf.* **-ij** *zob.* **upewniać (się)**.

upiąć *pf.* **upnę upniesz, upnij** *zob.* **upinać**.

upichcić (się) *pf.* *zob.* **pichcić (się)**.

upić (się) *pf.* **upiję upijesz, upij** *zob.* **upijać (się)**.

upiec *pf.* **-ekę -eczesz -ekł** *zob.* **piec; upiec dwie pieczenie przy jednym ogniu** kill two birds with one stone; eat the cake and have it too. **~ się** *pf.* *zob.* **piec się; upiekło ci się** you got off cheaply *l.* scott-free.

upieczony *a.* **-eni** baked, roasted; **świeżo upieczony chleb** new-baked bread; **świeżo upieczony student** *przen.* freshman.

upierać się *ipf.* insist, be firm (*przy czymś* on sth) persist (*przy czymś* in sth); **upierać się przy czymś** be bent on *l.* upon (doing) sth; **upiera się, żebyśmy to wzięli** he insists we (should) take it.

upierdliwy *a.* *pot.* bitchy; **być upierdliwym** be a pain (in the ass), be a pest.

upierścieniony *a.* (*o palcach*) adorned with rings, ringed.

upierzenie *n.* feathering, plumage; **upierzenie dorosłych ptaków** *orn.* definitive plumage.

upierzony *a.* feathered, plumed, plumy; **w pełni upierzony** full-fledged.

upięcie *n.* (*włosów*) hair dressing; (*zasłon, firanek*) fastening.

upiększać *ipf.* **1.** (= *przyozdabiać*) beautify, embellish, adorn, deck (out), decorate (*czymś* with sth). **2.** (= *idealizować*) embellish, glamorize, glorify; (*fakty, opowieść*) embroider, varnish; prettify. **~ się** *ipf.* deck o.s. out, dress up.

upiększenie *n.* beautification, embellishment, adornment; **bez zbędnych upiększeń** unadorned; *przen.* (*np. o opowieści*) unvarnished.

upiększyć *pf. zob.* **upiększać**. ~ **się** *pf. zob.* **upiększać się**.

upijać *ipf.* **1.** (= *wypijać trochę płynu*) sip; **upił trochę piwa z kufla** he drank a little beer from the glass. **2.** (= *odurzać alkoholem*) intoxicate, make drunk, inebriate.

upijać się *ipf.* get drunk, drink heavily.

upilnować *pf.* + *Gen.* (= *uchronić*) protect (*sb l. sth*) (*przed czymś* from *l.* against sth) (*przed kimś* from sb); take good care of (*sb*); keep (*sth*) safe.

upiłować *pf.,* **upiłowywać** *ipf.* (*piłą*) saw off; (*pilnikiem*) file off.

upinać *ipf.* fasten; (*materiał*) drape; (*włosy*) do up, pin up, dress; **upiąć włosy w kok** sweep back *l.* up one's hair into a bun.

upiornie *adv.* eerily; **wyglądać upiornie** look ghastly.

upiorny *a.* **1.** (= *wyglądający jak upiór*) spectral, ghostly. **2.** (= *okropny*) ghastly, horrible.

upiór *mi* -o- *Gen.* -a ghost, specter, revenant; (*zwł. w baśniach*) ghoul.

upitrasić *pf.* -szę -sisz *zob.* **pitrasić**.

uplasować (się) *pf. zob.* **plasować (się)**.

uplastyczniać *ipf.,* **uplastycznić** *pf.* -ij **1.** (= *czynić wyrazistym*) give prominence (*coś* to sth) bring out in (full) relief. **2.** *techn.* (= *czynić plastycznym*) plasticize.

uplatać *ipf.,* **upleść** *pf.* uplotę upleciesz uplótł uplotła upletli (*włosy, pasma*) plait, braid; (*koszyk, wianek*) weave.

upławy *pl. Gen.* -ów *pat.* leucorrhea, leukorrhoea; *pot.* whites.

upłaz *mi* (mountain) terrace.

upłynąć *pf. zob.* **upływać**.

upłynniać *ipf.,* **upłynnić** *pf.* -ij **1.** (= *rozpuszczać, topić*) flux, make fluid, melt. **2.** *pot.* (= *wyprzedawać*) clear stocks; *fin.* (*aktywa*) realize, liquidate.

upływ *mi* **1.** (= *minięcie czasu*) lapse, passage; **przed upływem miesiąca** within a month's time; before the month is out; **po upływie kilku lat** after a lapse of several years; **z upływem lat** as the years pass *l.* go by; **w miarę upływu czasu** as time goes on; (**szybki**) **upływ czasu** flight of time, passage of time; (*terminu*) expiry, expiration. **2.** flow, flux; **upływ krwi** loss of blood. **3. upływ prądu** *el.* leak.

upływać *ipf.* -wa **1.** (= *mijać*) (*o czasie*) lapse, elapse, pass, go by; (*o terminie*) expire, terminate. **2.** (*o cieczy*) (= *wypływać*) flow; **dużo wody upłynie, zanim...** it will take time before...

upływność *f. fiz.* leakage conductance, leakance.

upodabniać *ipf.* (= *czynić podobnym*) make alike, assimilate (*sth*) (*do czegoś* to sth); **upodabniać kogoś do kogoś/czegoś** make sb resemble sb/sth. ~ **się** *ipf.* **1.** (= *stawać się podobnym*) become similar (*do kogoś* to sb), imitate, become like (*do kogoś* sb); assimilate (*do kogoś* to *l.* with

sb). **2.** *fon.* assimilate, get assimilated (*do czegoś* to sth).

upodlać *ipf.* = **upadlać**.

upodlenie *n.* debasement, degradation, abjection.

upodlić *pf.* -ij *zob.* **upadlać**.

upodobać *pf.* **upodobać sobie kogoś/coś** take a liking for sb/sth; favor sb; set one's heart on sth.

upodobanie *n.* fondness, liking, predilection (*do czegoś* for sth); inclination (*do czegoś* for *l.* to *l.* toward sth); **mieć upodobanie do czegoś** have an affinity *l.* fondness for sth; **robić coś z upodobaniem** delight in doing sth; enjoy doing sth; **znajdować upodobanie w czymś** take pleasure *l.* delight in sth; **z upodobaniem** with gusto, delightedly.

upodobnić (się) *pf.* -ij *zob.* **upodabniać (się)**.

upodobnienie *n. jęz.* assimilation; *biol.* convergence.

upodrzędniać *ipf.,* **upodrzędnić** *pf.* -ij subordinate, subjugate.

upoetyczniać *ipf.,* **upoetycznić** *pf.* -ij *lit.* poeticize, poetize.

upoetyzować *pf. zob.* **poetyzować**.

upoić (się) *pf.* upoję upoisz, upój *zob.* **upajać (się)**.

upojenie *n.* (= *odurzenie*) intoxication, ecstasy; (*zwycięstwem, sukcesem*) intoxication; **upojenie alkoholowe** intoxication, drunkenness, inebration; **w rozkosznym upojeniu** in ecstasy of delight.

upojny *a. lit.* intoxicating, enchanting, inebriating.

upokarzać *ipf.* humiliate (*sb*) (*przed kimś* in front of sb *l.* before sb). ~ **się** *ipf.* humiliate o.s., abase o.s. (*przed kimś* in front of sb *l.* before sb).

upokarzający *a.* humiliating, humbling, shaming.

upokorzenie *n.* humiliation, abasment, indignity; **doznał upokorzenia, gdy dowiedział się, że...** he was humiliated when he heard that...

upokorzyć *pf.* -órz *zob.* **upokarzać**.

upolityczniać *ipf.,* **upolitycznić** *pf.* -ij politicize; arouse political consciousness among (*sb*).

upolować *pf.* **1.** (= *polując, złowić*) bag, shoot, kill. **2.** *pot.* (= *zdobyć*) hunt down, track down; (*rzadką książkę*) hunt; (*męża*) hook, reel in.

upominać *ipf.* rebuke, reprimand, reproach, admonish (*kogoś za coś/za zrobienie czegoś* sb for sth/for doing sth); **surowo upominać** chastise.

upominać się *ipf.* **1.** (= *dopominać się*) demand, claim (*o coś* sth); **upominać się o swoje prawa** assert one's rights; **upominać się o dług** demand payment of a debt; **upominać się o zwrot pożyczki** call in a loan. **2.** (= *wstawiać się*) speak up (*o kogoś* for sb); **upominał się o swoją krzywdę** he sought *l.* demanded redress of the wrong done to him.

upominek *mi* -nk- gift, present, souvenir; (*dodany do zakupu w ramach promocji*) giveaway; (*od firmy*) freebie, free gift; **drobny upominek** a little sth; **dać coś komuś w upominku** present sb with sth, give sb a souvenir.

upomnieć (się) *pf.* **-nę -nisz, -nij** *zob.* **upominać (się)**.

upomnienie *n.* **1.** (= *nagana*) rebuke, admonition, reprimand; *prawn.* (*od policjanta, sędziego*) caution; **upomnienie biskupie** *kośc.* monition. **2.** (= *pismo zawierające naganę*) reminder.

uporać się *pf.* handle, manage (*z kimś / czymś* sb/sth); deal, cope (*z kimś / czymś* with sb/sth); **uporać się ze zrobieniem czegoś** get sth done, get through sth.

uporczywie *adv.* insistently, persistently, stubbornly; (*zwł. wpatrywać się*) fixedly; **uporczywie do czegoś dążyć** set one's mind to sth; **uporczywie coś robić** persist in doing sth; **patrzeć uporczywie na coś/kogoś** stare *l.* gaze *l.* gape at sth/sb.

uporczywość *f.* **1.** persistance, stubbornness. **2.** (= *stałe naleganie*) insistence.

uporczywy *a.* persistent, pertinacious; (*o kaszlu*) obstinate; (*o bólach*) severe.

uporządkować *pf. zob.* **uporządkowywać**.

uporządkowany *a.* orderly, (well-)ordered.

uporządkowywać *ipf.* (= *porządkować*) **1.** put in order, arrange; (*dom*) tidy (up); (*myśli, wiadomości*) get right *l.* straight; (*dzieła, manuskrypty*) collate. **2.** (= *uregulować*) regulate, settle.

uposażać *ipf. przest.* endow.

uposażenie *n.* **1.** *przest.* endowment. **2.** salary, wages, pay; **wzrost uposażeń** salary increase; **dożywotnie uposażenie wdowy** dower.

uposażony *a.* **-eni dobrze/źle uposażony** well/badly paid.

uposażyć *pf. zob.* **uposażać**.

upostaciować *pf. zob.* **upostaciowywać**.

upostaciowanie *n. lit.* personification.

upostaciowywać *ipf. lit.* personify.

upośledzać *ipf.* handicap (*kogoś* sb), discriminate (*kogoś* against sb); impair (*coś* sth); *pat.* (*odporność*) suppress.

upośledzenie *n.* **1.** *med.* handicap, impairment, defect; **upośledzenie umysłowe/fizyczne** mental/physical handicap *l.* disability; **upośledzenie czucia** disesthesia; **upośledzenie słuchu/wzroku** auditory/visual impairment. **2.** (= *zaniedbanie, zacofanie*) (*ekonomiczne, społeczne*) disadvantage.

upośledzić *pf. zob.* **upośledzać**.

upośledzony *a.* **-eni 1.** handicapped, disabled; (*o wzroku, słuchu*) impaired; **upośledzony umysłowo/fizycznie** mentally/physically handicapped *l.* disabled. **2.** *ekon.* (*o grupach, regionach*) underpriviledged, disadvantaged.

upotocznić *pf.* **-ij** (*styl pisania, język*) colloqualize.

upoważniać *ipf.*, **upoważnić** *pf.* **-ij upoważniać kogoś do zrobienia czegoś** authorize sb to do sth.

upoważnienie *n.* authorization; **robić coś z czyjegoś upoważnienia** be authorized by sb to do sth.

upowszechniać *ipf.* **-ij** popularize, disseminate. **~ się** *ipf.* get popularized.

upowszechnić (się) *pf.* **-ij** *zob.* **upowszechniać (się)**.

upowszechniony *a.* widespread, widely spread, widely popularized.

upozorować *pf.*, **upozorowywać** *ipf.* simulate, fake.

upozować *pf. mal., fot.* pose, posture (*sb*). **~ się** *pf.* **1.** (= *przyjąć pozę*) posture, pose, assume a posture *l.* pose. **2. upozować się na kogoś/coś** *przen.* pose as sb/sth.

upozowywać (się) *ipf. rzad. zob.* **upozować (się)**.

upór *mi* **-o-** stubbornness, obstinacy; doggedness, cussedness; **ośli upór** mulishness, pigheadedness; **z uporem** stubbornly, obstinately; **robić coś z uporem** persist in doing sth; **przełamać czyjś upór** break sb's stubbornness; **robić coś z uporem maniaka** *l.* **godnym lepszej sprawy** do sth cussedly; **trwać w uporze** persist with one's cussedness *l.* obstinacy.

uprać (się) *pf.* **upiorę upierzesz** *zob.* **prać (się)**.

upragniony *a.* **-eni** longed-for, desired, coveted.

uprasować *pf. zob.* **prasować**.

upraszać *ipf. lit.* ask (*o coś* for sth) request (*o coś* sth); „**uprasza się o ciszę**" "silence, please"; „**uprasza się o niepalenie**" "smoking not allowed", "smoking prohibited"; **uprasza się kogoś o zrobienie czegoś** sb is (kindly) requested to do sth.

upraszczać *ipf.* **1.** (= *ułatwiać*) simplify; **uprościć komuś sprawę** make things easier for sb; **upraszczać ułamek** *mat.* reduce. **2.** (= *przedstawiać powierzchownie*) simplify, trivialise; **nadmiernie upraszczać** oversimplify.

uprawa *f.* **1.** (= *przygotowanie pod zasiew*) cultivation, tillage, farming; **wziąć ziemię pod uprawę** put *l.* bring land under cultivation; **uprawa roli** agriculture; **przydatność pod uprawę** arability; **gleba nadająca się pod uprawę** cultivable *l.* arable land; **gleba nienadająca się pod uprawę** uncultivable *l.* waste land. **2.** (= *opieka nad rozwojem roślin*) husbandry, cultivation; growing, raising (*czegoś* of sth); **uprawa leśna** forestry; **uprawa warzyw** cultivation of vegetables; **uprawa wstęgowa** strip cropping; **uprawa monokulturowa** one-crop culture, monoculture; **uprawa rynkowa** cash crop; **uprawa na własne potrzeby** subsistence crop. **3.** (= *uprawiane rośliny*) crop; **uprawy zbożowe** corn growing; **uprawa winorośli** viticulture; **uprawa drzew cytrusowych** citriculture; **uprawa mieszana** mixed crop; **uprawa wodna** aquiculture, hydroponics.

uprawdopodabniać *ipf.*, **uprawdopodobnić** *pf.* **-ij** make believable; give color to sth.

uprawiać *ipf.*, **uprawić** *pf.* **1.** (= *przygotowywać ziemię pod zasiew*) cultivate, till, farm; **uprawiać ogród** garden. **2.** *tylko ipf.* (= *hodować rośliny*) grow, raise. **3.** *tylko ipf.* (= *zajmować się*) practise (*czymś* sth); go in (*czymś* for sth); (*sport*) practise, do; (*zawód*) pursue; (*religię*) profess; (*sztukę*) cultivate; **uprawiać hazard** gamble;

uprawiać nierząd prostitute o.s.; **uprawiać alpinizm** mountaineer; **uprawiać jogging** jog; **uprawiać kłusownictwo** poach; **uprawiać magię** conjure; **uprawiać seks** have sex (*z kimś* to sb); make love (*z kimś* to sb).

uprawniać *ipf.*, **uprawnić** *pf.* **-ij 1.** (= *upoważniać*) authorize, entitle (*sb*) (*do czegoś* to do sth) (*do zrobienia czegoś* to do sth); qualify (*sb*) (*do czegoś* for sth) (*do zrobienia czegoś* to do sth). **2.** (= *legalizować*) legalize.

uprawnienie *n.* **1.** entitlement, power (*do zrobienia czegoś* to do sth); *prawn.* license, right, ability (*do robienia czegoś* to do sth); **brak uprawnień** ineligibility. **przekroczyć uprawnienia** act beyond one's capacities *l.* powers; **rozszerzyć czyjeś uprawnienia** strengthen sb's powers; **uprawnienia rządu** powers of the state. **2.** *pl.* (= *kwalifikacje*) qualifications, eligibility; **brak uprawnień** ineligibility.

uprawniony *a.* **-eni 1.** entitled, authorized (*do czegoś* to sth) (*do zrobienia czegoś* to do sth); *prawn.* able, licensed; **uprawniony do noszenia broni** licensed to carry firearms. **2.** eligible (*do czegoś* for sth).

uprawny *a.* *roln.* **1.** (*o glebie*) arable, cultivable, under crop; **ziemia uprawna** farmland; **warstwa uprawna ziemi** topsoil. **2.** (= *hodowany*) cultivated; **roślina uprawna** crop.

uprawomocniać *ipf.* legalize, legitimate, validate; (*dokument*) execute. **~ się** *ipf.* come into force, become valid *l.* operative.

uprawomocnić (się) *pf.* **-ij** *zob.* **uprawomocniać (się).**

uprawowy *a.* farming; **zabiegi uprawowe** tillage, cultivation.

uprażyć *pf. zob.* **prażyć.**

uproduktywnić *pf.* **-ij** make (*sth*) productive *l.* prolific.

uprosić *pf.* **-szę -sisz** *zob.* **upraszać.**

uproszczenie *n.* simplification; **zbytnie uproszczenie** oversimplification; *mat.* reduction; (*zagadnienia, problemu*) trivialization.

uproszczony *a.* simplified, basic; *media* (*o informacjach*) in brief, predigested; **nadmiernie uproszczony** simplistic.

uprościć *pf.* **-szczę -ścisz** *zob.* **upraszczać.**

uprowadzać *ipf.* lead (sb *l.* sth) away; (*osobę*) kidnap, abduct; (*samolot, pojazd*) hijack.

uprowadzenie *n.* kidnaping, abduction; (*samolotu itp.*) hijacking.

uprowadzić *pf. zob.* **uprowadzać.**

uprząść *pf.* **uprzędę uprzędziesz, uprządź** *l.* **uprzędź, uprządł uprzędła uprzędli** spin.

uprzątać *ipf.*, **uprzątnąć** *pf.* **-ij** tidy (up), clean up; remove.

uprząż *f.* **-ę-** *pl.* **-e** harness, gear; **zakładać koniowi uprząż** harness a horse; **uprząż spadochronu** *lotn.* harness.

uprzeć się *pf.* **uprę uprzesz, uprzyj, uparł** *zob.* **upierać się.**

uprzedmiotawiać *ipf.*, **uprzedmiotowić** *pf.* **-ów** objectify.

uprzedni *a. lit.* previous, prior.

uprzednio *adv. lit.* previously, earlier; (= *zawczasu*) beforehand.

uprzedniość *f. lit.* previousness, anteriority.

uprzedzać *ipf.* **1.** (= *wyprzedzać*) anticipate; **uprzedzać wypadki** anticipate events; **nie uprzedzajmy faktów** let's not speculate about it before it happens; let's wait and see what happens. **2.** (= *informować wcześniej*) warn (*kogoś o czymś* sb about *l.* of sth); advise (*kogoś o czymś* sb of sth); **z góry uprzedzam, że nie mogę pomóc** I am telling you in advance that I won't be able to help. **3.** (= *usposabiać nieprzychylnie*) prejudice (*kogoś do czegoś* sb against sth). **~ się** *ipf.* get prejudiced (*do kogoś l. czegoś* against sb *l.* sth).

uprzedzająco *adv.* **uprzedzająco miły/grzeczny** extremely nice/polite.

uprzedzający *a.* **uprzedzająca grzeczność** suavity.

uprzedzenie *n.* **1.** (= *zawiadomienie*) (advance) warning, notification; **przyjechał bez uprzedzenia** he came without telling us (about it) earlier; he came without warning. **2.** (= *negatywny stosunek*) prejudice, bias; **bez uprzedzeń** (= *bezstronnie*) impartially; **mieć uprzedzenie do kogoś** *l.* **czegoś** be prejudiced against sb *l.* sth; **nie mieć uprzedzeń** be free from prejudice.

uprzedzić (się) *pf. zob.* **uprzedzać (się).**

uprzedzony *a.* **-eni** prejudiced, biased (*do kogoś l. czegoś* against sb *l.* sth).

uprzejmie *adv.* politely, civilly, courteously; **dziękuję uprzejmie** thank you very much *l.* so much; **proszę uprzejmie** (it was) a pleasure, my pleasure; (*odpowiadając na podziękowania*) you're welcome; (*podając coś*) here you are.

uprzejmość *f.* **1.** (= *życzliwy stosunek*) politeness, civility, courtesy; **wymieniać z kimś uprzejmości** exchange courtesies with sb. **2.** (= *przysługa*) courtesy, favor; **dzięki uprzejmości pana Kowalskiego** (by) courtesy of Mr. Kowalski; **wyświadczyć komuś uprzejmość** do sb a favor.

uprzejmy *a.* **1.** (= *grzeczny*) polite, courteous. **2.** (= *świadczący o grzeczności*) polite.

uprzemysławiać *ipf.*, **uprzemysłowić** *pf.* **-ów** industrialize.

uprzemysłowienie *n.* industrialization.

uprzemysłowiony *a.* industrialized.

uprzyjemniać *ipf.*, **uprzyjemnić** *pf.* **-ij** make enjoyable.

uprzykrzać *ipf.* spoil; make unpleasant; **uprzykrzać komuś życie** be a pain in the neck, make sb's life unbearable *l.* miserable. **~ się** *ipf.* tire, weary; **uprzykrzyła mi się ta praca** I am sick of this job.

uprzykrzony *a.* **-eni** irritating, tiresome.

uprzykrzyć (się) *pf. zob.* **uprzykrzać (się).**

uprzystępniać *ipf.*, **uprzystępnić** *pf.* **-ij** make (*sth*) accessible, explain.

uprzytamniać, uprzytomniać *ipf.*, **uprzytomnić** *pf.* **-ij** make aware; **uprzytamniać coś komuś** make sb aware of sth; **uprzytomniłem sobie, że...** I realized that...

uprzywilejować *pf. zob.* **uprzywilejowywać.**

uprzywilejowanie *n.* privilege; preference; **klauzula najwyższego uprzywilejowania** *ekon.* most-favored-nation clause.

uprzywilejowany *a.* privileged; **akcje uprzy-**

wilejowane *ekon.* preferred stock; *Br.* preference shares; **pojazd uprzywilejowany** *mot.* emergency (services) vehicle.

uprzywilejowywać *ipf.* privilege.

upstrzony *a.* **1.** + *Ins.* (= *pokryty*) covered with, full of (*sth*); **upstrzony błędami** peppered *l.* riddled with errors; **upstrzony kleksami** blotted. **2.** (= *pobrudzony, poplamiony*) speckled; **u-pstrzony przez muchy** flyspecked.

upstrzyć *pf.* **-yj 1.** (= *poplamić*) speckle, blot. **2. upstrzyć coś błędami/uwagami/skreśleniami** pepper sth with errors/notes/cancellations.

UPT *abbr.* (= *Urząd Pocztowo-Telekomunikacyjny*) P.O. (*Post Office*).

upubliczniać *ipf.*, **upublicznić** *pf.* **-ij** make public, announce.

upudrować *pf. zob.* **pudrować.** ~ **się** *pf. zob.* **pudrować się.**

upupiać *ipf.*, **upupić** *pf. pot.* treat (*sb*) like a baby, make (*sb*) look like an idiot.

upust *mi* **1.** (= *odprowadzenie substancji*) bleeding; letting off; **upust krwi** *med.* bloodletting, phlebotomy; **dać czemuś upust** *przen.* give vent to sth. **2.** *techn.* sluice; sink; lock. **3.** *handl.* (= *obniżka*) discount, reduction.

upuszczać *ipf.*, **upuścić** *pf.* **-szczę -ścisz 1.** (= *wypuszczać z rąk*) drop; **uważaj, nie upuść tego!** be careful and don't drop it. **2.** (= *usuwać substancję*) let (off); drain; remove; **upuścić krwi** let blood.

upychać *ipf.* **1.** (= *pakować, wciskając*) stuff; crowd, cram. **2.** *pot.* (= *pozbywać się czegoś niepotrzebnego*) get rid of.

ur. *abbr.* (= *urodzony*) b., n. (= *born*).

urabiać *ipf.* **1.** (= *formować*) mold, shape, form; **urabiać ciasto** knead dough. **2.** *przen.* **urabiać kogoś/czyjś charakter** mold sb/sb's character; **urabiać opinię publiczną** mold public opinion. **3. urabiać sobie ręce po łokcie** work one's hands to the bone. **4.** *górn.* mine; (*rudy*) stope. ~ **się** *ipf.* (= *kształtować się*) **1.** be molded. **2.** *pot.* be done in.

uraczyć (się) *pf. zob.* **raczyć (się).**

uradować (się) *pf. zob.* **radować (się).**

uradowany *a.* joyful, overjoyed.

uradzać *ipf.*, **uradzić** *pf.* decide, resolve.

Ural *mi geogr.* the Ural Mountains, the Urals.

uralski *a. geogr.* Uralian; *jęz.* Uralic.

Uran *mi astron.* Uranus.

uran *mi chem.* uranium.

Urania *f. Gen.* **-ii** *mit.* Urania.

uranian *mi chem.* uranate.

uranina *f. chem.* uranine.

uraninit *mi min.* uraninite.

uranowce *pl. Gen.* **-ów** *chem.* uranoids, uranides.

uranowy *a. chem.* uranic.

urastać *ipf.* **1.** (= *rosnąć*) grow, increase, expand; **urastać do rangi** *l.* **rzędu** *l.* **rozmiarów czegoś** take on *l.* assume the proportions of sth. **2.** (= *gromadzić się*) pile up, accumulate, amass.

uratować (się) *pf. zob.* **ratować (się).**

urawniłowka *f. Gen.pl.* **-ek** *pot., uj.* one-size-fits-all policy.

uraz *mi* **1.** *pat.* injury, trauma; **liczne urazy** multiple injuries *l.* traumas. **2.** *psych.* trauma; **mieć uraz do kogoś za coś** bear sb a grudge for sth; **mieć uraz na punkcie czegoś** be sensitive *l.* oversensitive about sth.

uraza *f.* resentment, grudge; **żywić do kogoś urazę (o coś)** bear sb a grudge (for sth); **nie mam do ciebie urazy** I bear you no grudge; **zapomnijmy o wzajemnych urazach** let bygones be bygones.

urazić (się) *pf.* **-żę -zisz** *zob.* **urażać (się).**

urazowość *f. pat.* incidence of injuries *l.* traumas.

urazowy *a. pat.* traumatic.

urazówka *f. Gen.pl.* **-ek** *pot.*, *med.* emergency room, casualty ward.

urażać *ipf.* **1.** (= *uderzać w bolące miejsce*) hurt. **2.** (= *sprawiać przykrość*) offend, hurt, wound; **urazić czyjąś dumę** hurt sb's pride. ~ **się** *ipf.* **1.** (= *uderzać się w bolące miejsce*) hurt o.s. **2.** (= *obrażać się*) take offense, feel offended *l.* hurt.

urażony *a.* **-eni** (*człowiek*) offended; (*o dumie, ambicji*) hurt; **czuć się urażonym** feel offended.

urąbać *pf.* **-bię -biesz 1.** (= *narąbać*) chop. **2.** (= *rąbiąc, oddzielić*) chop off.

urągać *ipf.* + *Dat.* **1.** *pot.* (= *złorzeczyć, obrażać*) curse; offend, hurl abuse at (*sb*). **2.** *lit.* (= *wyszydzać*) mock, deride. **3.** *przen.* **urągać zdrowemu rozsądkowi** defy common sense; **to urąga wszelkim zasadom** it's against all rules.

urągliwy *a. lit.* derisive, sneering.

urągowisko *n. lit.* mockery; **jak na urągowisko** to make matters worse.

urbanista *mp*, **urbanistka** *f. Gen.pl.* **-ek** *bud.* urbanist, urban planner.

urbanistycznie *adv. bud.* of urban *l.* city planning.

urbanistyczny *a. bud.* **zagadnienia/rozwiązania urbanistyczne** urban planning issues/solutions.

urbanistyka *f. bud.* urban planning, city planning, urbanism.

urbanizacja *f.* urbanization.

urbanizować *ipf.* urbanize.

urealniać *ipf.*, **urealnić** *pf.* **-ij** (= *umożliwić*) enable, make (*sth*) viable; (= *urzeczywistnić*) realize, make (*sth*) real.

uregulować *pf. zob.* **regulować.**

uremia *f. Gen.* **-ii** *pat.* ur(a)emia.

urena *f. bot.* urena, aramina, bun ochra, Caesar weed, Congo jute (*Urena*).

urentownić *pf. ekon., handl.* make profitable.

urlop *mi* (*przerwa w pracy*) leave (of absence); (*wakacje*) vacation, holiday; **być na urlopie** be on leave *l.* vacation; **iść na urlop** go on leave; **wziąć urlop** take a leave; **urlop bezpłatny** unpaid leave; **urlop płatny** paid leave; **urlop dziekański** *uniw.* dean's leave; **urlop macierzyński** maternity leave; **urlop wychowawczy** (unpaid) parental leave; **urlop wypoczynkowy** vacation, holiday; **urlop zdrowotny** sick leave, sick days.

urlopować *ipf.* **1.** give *l.* grant sb a leave. **2.** be on leave; be on vacation.

urlopowicz *mp Gen.pl.* **-ów** vacationer, holiday-maker.

urlopowy *a.* vacation, holiday; **okres urlopowy** vacation *l.* holiday period.

URM *abbr. polit.* (= *Urząd Rady Ministrów*) the Office of the Council of Ministers.

urna *f.* **1.** (= *skrzynka do głosowania*) ballot box. **2.** (*naczynie, zwł. na prochy zmarłych*) urn.

urobek *mi* **-bk- 1.** *górn.* (= *wydobywanie kopalin*) winning. **2.** *górn.* (= *wydobyta kopalina*) output.

urobić *pf.* **-ób** *zob.* **urabiać.** ~ **się** *pf.* **1.** *zob.* **urabiać się. 2.** *pot.* (= *napracować się*) work one's hands to the bone, work very hard.

urobilina *f. biochem.* urobilin.

urobisko *n. górn.* borrow pit.

uroczy *a.* charming, adorable.

uroczysko *n.* **1.** *hist., rel.* sacred place (*deep in the woods*); (= *pustkowie*) waste. **2.** (*część terenu leśnego*) forest area.

uroczystość *f.* **1.** (= *święto*) ceremony; **uroczystość rodzinna** family occasion, family gathering; **uroczystości żałobne** funeral ceremony. **2.** (= *podniosłość*) solemnity.

uroczysty *a.* **-szy 1.** (= *odświętny*) special, formal. **2.** (= *podniosły*) solemn, formal, ceremonious.

uroczyście *adv.* **1.** (= *odświętnie*) formally. **2.** (= *podniośle*) solemnly, formally, ceremoniously.

uroda *f.* **1.** (= *piękność*) beauty; **nie grzeszyć urodą** be very ugly. **2.** (= *wdzięk, piękno*) beauty, charm, attraction.

urodzaj *mi Gen.pl.* **-ów 1.** (= *plony*) bumper crop. **2.** (= *obfitość*) abundance; **urodzaj na coś** abundance of sth, good year for sth.

urodzajność *f.* fertility.

urodzajny *a.* (= *żyzny*) fertile; **urodzajny rok** good year.

urodzenie *n.* (= *narodziny*) birth; **data i miejsce urodzenia** date and place of birth; **metryka urodzenia** certificate of birth, birth certificate; **wskaźnik urodzeń** birthrate; (**niewidomy**) **od urodzenia** (blind) since birth; **być Polakiem z urodzenia** be Polish by birth.

urodzić *pf.* **urodzę urodzisz, uródź** *l.* **uródź** *zob.* **rodzić.** ~ **się** *pf. zob.* **rodzić się.**

urodzinowy *a.* birthday.

urodziny *pl. Gen.* **-n 1.** (= *urodzenie się*) birth. **2.** (= *rocznica urodzin*) *birthday;* **wyprawiać urodziny** have *l.* organize *l.* throw a birthday party; **wszystkiego najlepszego w dniu urodzin!** happy birthday!, many happy returns!

urodziwie *adv.* prettily, nicely; **wyglądać urodziwie** look nice; be comely.

urodziwy *a.* pretty, nice; comely.

urodzony *a.* **-eni 1.** (= *zawołany*) born; **urodzony aktor** born actor. **2.** (= *rodowity*) born and bred, native; **urodzony nowojorczyk** New Yorker born and bred; **ktoś szlachetnie urodzony** sb of noble birth; **w czepku urodzony** born with a silver spoon in one's mouth.

urografia *f. Gen.* **-ii** *med.* urography.

urograficzny *a. med.* urographic.

urogram *mi med.* urogram.

uroić *pf.* **uroję uroisz, urój** fantasize, imagine; **uroić sobie coś** fantasize *l.* imagine sth.

urojenie *n.* **1.** (= *mrzonka*) fantasy, dream, illusion. **2.** *psych.* delusion; **mieć urojenia** suffer from delusions.

urojony *a.* imaginary.

urok *mi* **1.** (= *wdzięk*) charm, attraction. **2.** (= *siła magiczna*) spell; **być pod urokiem kogoś** *l.* **czegoś** be under the spell of sb *l.* sth; **rzucić na kogoś urok(i)** cast a spell on sb.

urokliwie *adv.* charmingly.

urokliwy *a.* charming.

urolog *mp pl.* **-dzy** *l.* **-owie** *med.* urologist.

urologia *f. Gen.* **-ii** *med.* urology.

urologiczny *a. med.* urologic, urological.

uromantycznić *pf.* **-ij** *rzad.* make romantic.

urometr *mi med.* urometer.

uronić *pf. zob.* **ronić.**

uronowy *a. chem.* uronic; **kwas uronowy** uronic acid.

uroskopia *f. Gen.* **-ii** *med.* uroscopy.

urosnąć *pf.* **urosnę urośniesz, urośnij, urósł urosła urośli** *zob.* **rosnąć, urastać.**

urostyl *mi zool.* urostyle.

urozmaicać *ipf.* vary; diversify.

urozmaicenie *n.* variety; diversity.

urozmaicić *pf. zob.* **urozmaicać.**

urozmaicony *a.* varied; diversified.

urób *pf. zob.* **urobić.**

uródź *pf. zob.* **urodzić.**

uróść *pf.* **urosnę urośniesz, urośnij, urósł urosła urośli** *zob.* **urosnąć.**

urson *ma zool.* North American porcupine (*Erethizon dorsatum*).

urszulanka *f. Gen.pl* **-ek** *rz.-kat.* Ursuline.

uruchamiać *ipf.,* **uruchomić** *pf.* **1.** (= *wprawiać w ruch*) start; set in motion; activate; **uruchamiać fabrykę** open a factory, render a factory operational; **uruchamiać silnik** start an engine. **2.** (= *czynić ruchomym*) make mobile, mobilize.

Urugwaj *mi geogr.* Uruguay.

Urugwajczyk *mp,* **Urugwajka** *f. Gen.pl.* **-ek** Uruguayan.

urugwajski *a.* Uruguayan.

urwać (się) *pf.* **urwę urwiesz, urwij** *zob.* **urywać (się).**

urwanie *n.* tearing (off); **urwanie głowy** hassle.

urwipołeć *mp* **-łci-** *Gen.pl.* **-ów** *żart.* rascal, scapegrace.

urwis *mp pl.* **-y** urchin.

urwisko *n.* precipice.

urwisty *a.* precipitous.

uryna *f.* urine.

urynał *mi przest.* urinal.

urywać *ipf.* **-am -asz 1.** (= *odrywać*) tear off. **2.** *lit.* (= *przerywać, nie kończyć*) stop, break off, discontinue; (*rozmowę*) cut short; **urwać w pół słowa** break off in mid-sentence. **3.** *pot.* (= *zmniejszać, uszczuplać*) reduce; take away; shorten; give *l.* put less. ~ **się** *ipf.* **1.** (*o czymś przytwierdzonym l. przyszytym*) (= *odrywać się*) come off; come unstuck; fall off; **ten guzik zaraz się urwie** this button will come off soon; **z choinki**

się urwałeś? *pot.* are you out of your mind?; **skąd on się urwał?** *pot.* is he from Mars?; **telefony się urywają** I am *l.* we are swamped with phone calls. **2.** (= *ulec przerwaniu*) tear, break apart. **3.** *przen.* (= *kończyć się nagle*) end, come to an end; (*o drodze*) end; (*o rozmowie, łączności*) break off; **film mu się urwał** *pot.* he got blind drunk. **4.** *pot.* (= *wychodzić niepostrzeżenie*) push off.

urywany *a.* interrupted; chopped.

urywek *mi* -**wk**- *Gen.* -**a** *l.* -**u** fragment; excerpt.

urywkowo *adv.* fragmentarily.

urywkowy *a.* fragmentary.

urząd *mi* -**ę**- **1.** (= *organ władzy*) office; agency; department; **Urząd Bezpieczeństwa** *hist.* the Security Service (*in communist Poland*); **urząd celny** customhouse, customs-house; **Urząd Ochrony Państwa** the State Security Office; **Urząd Patentowy** Patent Office; *US* the Patent and Trademark Office; **urząd pocztowy** post office; **Urząd Rady Ministrów** the Office of the Council of Ministers; **urząd skarbowy** *US* the Internal Revenue Service, IRS; *Br.* Inland Revenue; **urząd stanu cywilnego** (civil) registry office; **urząd wojewódzki** the Province Governor's Office; **urząd zatrudnienia** employment agency; **z urzędu** ex officio; **obrońca z urzędu** *prawn.* court-appointed attorney, assigned counsel. **2.** (= *biuro*) office. **3.** (= *oficjalna funkcja, stanowisko*) office, post; **piastować** *l.* **sprawować urząd** hold office; **pozostać na urzędzie** remain in office; **powołać kogoś na stanowisko dyrektora** appoint sb (to serve) as director, appoint sb director; **złożyć urząd** resign *l.* step down from office.

urządzać *ipf.* **1.** (= *wyposażać*) furnish. **2.** (= *organizować*) organize; **urządzać przyjęcie** throw a party; **urządzić komuś awanturę** have a row with sb, quarrel with sb, kick up a row. **3.** *pot.* (= *stwarzać odpowiednie warunki*) suit, be fine; **to mnie urządza** this suits me; **to mnie nie urządza** this doesn't suit me. **~ się** *ipf.* (= *zagospodarowywać się*) settle (down).

urządzenie *n.* **1.** (= *przyrząd*) device, appliance; **urządzenie alarmowe** alarm (device); **urządzenie pomiarowe** gauge, gage; **urządzenia przeciwpożarowe** fire-fighting equipment. **2.** *przest.* (= *umeblowanie*) furnishings; furniture.

urządzić *pf.* **1.** *zob.* **urządzać. 2.** *pot.* (= *wyrządzić krzywdę*) hurt; **nieźle mnie urządziłeś!** now, you got me into a pretty mess. **~ się** *pf.* **1.** *zob.* **urządzić się. 2.** *pot.* (= *zrobić sobie krzywdę*) get (o.s.) into a pretty mess.

urządzony *a.* -**eni 1.** (= *wyposażony*) furnished. **2.** *pot.* (= *zadomowiony*) settled (down). **3.** *pot.* (= *w fatalnej sytuacji*) in a mess.

urzec *pf.* -**eknę** -**ekniesz**, -**eknij**, -**urzekł** *zob.* **urzekać.**

urzeczony *a.* -**eni** enchanted, bewitched, charmed; fascinated.

urzeczowiać *ipf.*, **urzeczowić** *pf. fil.* objectify.

urzeczownikowiać *ipf.*, **urzeczownikowić** *pf. jęz.* nominalize.

urzeczywistniać *ipf.*, **urzeczywistnić** *pf.* -**ij** (*plany*) implement; (*marzenia*) realize, fulfil(l); **mo-**

je marzenia się urzeczywistniły my dreams have come true.

urzekać *ipf.* **1.** (= *zachwycać*) enchant, charm, fascinate, captivate. **2.** (= *rzucać czar*) bewitch.

urzekający *a.* enchanting, fascinating, captivating.

urzet *mi* (*także* **urzet barwierski**) *bot.* woad, dyer's-weed (*Isatis tinctoria*).

urzędas *mp pl.* -**y** *pog.* paper pusher.

urzędniczka *f. Gen.pl.* -**ek** clerk, office worker.

urzędniczy *a.* clerical; clerk's.

urzędnik *mp* clerk, office worker; **urzędnik państwowy** civil servant; **urzędnik stanu cywilnego** registrar.

urzędować *ipf.* work in an office.

urzędowanie *n.* **godziny urzędowania** office *l.* business hours.

urzędowo *adv.* **1.** (= *na mocy urzędu*) officially, formally, in (one's) official capacity. **2.** (= *zgodnie z przepisami*) in accordance with *l.* in pursuance of the regulations.

urzędowy *a.* **1.** (= *dotyczący urzędu*) official, formal. **2.** (= *zajmujący się czymś z urzędu*) official. **3.** (= *obowiązujący*) standard; national; official. **4.** (= *oficjalny, sztywny*) formal.

urzęsiony *a. zool.* ciliate, ciliated.

urzynać *ipf.* cut off. **~ się** *ipf. pot.* (= *upijać się*) get drunk, booze; **urżnąć się w trupa** get blind drunk, booze it up.

urżnąć (się) *pf.* -**ij** = **urzynać (się).**

urżnięty *a. pot.* (= *pijany*) drunk.

usadawiać *ipf.* seat. **~ się** *ipf.* sit comfortably down, settle (o.s.).

usadowić (się) *pf.* -**ów** *zob.* **usadawiać (się).**

usadzać *ipf.* **1.** (= *usadawiać*) seat. **2.** *pot.* (= *przywoływać do porządku*) curb, restrain, check. **3.** *pot., szkoln.* fail. **~ się** *ipf.* sit comfortably down, settle (o.s.).

usadzić (się) *pf. zob.* **usadzać (się).**

usamodzielniać *ipf.* make independent. **~ się** *ipf.* become self-dependent *l.* independent.

usamodzielnić (się) *pf. zob.* **usamodzielniać (się).**

usamowalniać *ipf.*, **usamowolnić** *pf.* -**ij** *przest.* make independent, give independence, emancipate.

usankcjonować *pf. zob.* **sankcjonować.**

usatysfakcjonować *pf. zob.* **satysfakcjonować.**

usatysfakcjonowany *a.* contented, satisfied, pleased (*czymś* with sth).

USC *abbr.* (= *Urząd Stanu Cywilnego*) public registrar's office (*in Poland*).

usceniczniać *ipf.*, **uscenicznić** *pf.* -**ij** adapt for the stage.

uschematyzować *pf. zob.* **schematyzować.**

uschły *a.* dry, dried-out.

uschnąć *pf.* -**ij** *zob.* **usychać.**

USG *abbr.* (= *ultrasonografia*) ultrasonography, ultrasound (scanning); **zrobić komuś USG** give sb an ultrasound.

usiać *pf.* **usieję usiejesz usiali** *l.* **usieli** strew, sprinkle, stud; (*kwiatami, gwiazdami*) spangle, speckle, set (*sth*) (*czymś* with sth); **usiać coś plamkami** fleck *l.* dot sth (over).

usiany *a.* (*gwiazdami*) studded, sown; (*kwiatami*) strewn; (*głazami, kraterami*) pitted; (*kropkami*) dotted; (*błędami, cytatami*) peppered; (*aluzjami, dowcipami*) sprinkled (*czymś* with sth); **niebo usiane gwiazdami** starlight *l.* starry *l.* star-spangled sky.

usiąść *pf.* **usiądę usiądziesz usiadł usiedli** *zob.* **siadać**.

usidlać *ipf.*, **usidlić** *pf.* **-ij** *t. przen.* ensnare, entrap.

usiec *pf.* **usiekę usieczesz usiekł** *przest.* (= *zabić l. zranić szablą*) saber.

usiedzieć *pf.* **-dzę -dzisz** sit; **nie móc usiedzieć** be unable to keep one's seat *l.* remain sitting; have ants in one's pants; get *l.* have the fidgets; **nie móc usiedzieć na wykładzie** have a hard time sitting out the lecture.

usiekać *pf.* (= *posiekać*) chop up, cut up; (*w kostkę*) dice.

usilnie *adv.* (= *wytrwale*) strenuously, persistently; **usilnie próbować** try hard; (= *natarczywie*) insistently, pressingly; **usilnie o coś zabiegać** be anxious for sth; **usilnie namawiać** exhort (*sb*) (*o zrobienie czegoś* to do sth); **usilnie prosić** entreat, beseech (*sb*) (*o zrobienie czegoś* to do sth).

usilny *a.* (= *wytrwały*) persistent; (*o wysiłkach*) strenuous; (*o prośbach, żądaniach*) insistent; (= *natarczywy*) insistent, pressing, urgent.

usiłować *ipf.* attempt, endeavour, strive, seek (*coś zrobić* to do sth); **usiłować pobić rekord** *sport* go after a record; make an attempt on a record; **usiłować popełnić samobójstwo** attempt suicide.

usiłowanie *n.* **1.** (= *wysiłek, dążność*) attempt, effort, endeavor. **2. usiłowanie morderstwa** *prawn.* attempt on sb's life, attempted murder.

uskakiwać *ipf.* dodge, duck, evade (*przed czymś* sth); **uskoczyć na bok** dodge out of the way.

uskarżać się *ipf.* complain, moan, grumble (*na kogoś / coś* of *l.* about sb/sth); **uskarżał się na ból w piersiach** he complained of a chest pain.

uskładać *pf.* save, put by, put aside, amass; **uskładać niezłą sumkę** amass a small fortune; **uskładał sobie na rower** he saved *l.* put aside enough money to buy a bike.

uskoczyć *pf.* *zob.* **uskakiwać**.

uskok *mi* **1.** (= *skok*) dodge, leap. **2.** (= *spadek terenu*) slope. **3.** *geol.* fault; **nachylenie płaszczyzny uskoku** hade; **uskok złożony** compound fault; **tworzyć uskok** fault. **4.** *bud.* (*w murze*) offset.

uskrzydlać *ipf.*, **uskrzydlić** *pf.* **-ij** *przen.* give wings to (*sb*); elevate (*sb's*) soul; **jej miłość uskrzydliła go** her love made him fly *l.* gave him wings.

uskrzydlony *a.* **-eni** **1.** *przen.* (= *pełen uniesienia l. zapału*) thrilled, excited. **2.** *orn.* alate, pennate.

uskubać *pf.* **-bię -biesz**, **uskubnąć** *pf.* **-ij** (= *skubiąc, oderwać*) (*chleba, ciasta*) snap off, tear off, brake off; (*pierza*) pluck; (*trawy*) nibble; **uskubnął ojcu trochę grosza** he lifted *l.* boosted some money from his father.

usłać *pf.* **uścielę uścielesz** *zob.* **uścielać**.

usłany *a.* covered, strewn, paved; **usłany różami** paved with roses.

usłojenie *n. stol.* figure.

usłonecznienie *n. meteor.* insolation.

usłuchać *pf.* listen, be obedient (*kogoś* to sb); **usłuchać czyjegoś nakazu** obey sb's command; **usłuchać czyjejś rady** follow *l.* take sb's advice.

usługa *f.* **1.** (= *przysługa*) service, favor; **być na czyichś usługach** be at sb's service, be sb's poodle; **wyświadczyć komuś usługę** do sb a favor; **(jestem) do usług** (I'm) at your service; **oddawać komuś usługi** be of service to sb. **2.** (= *świadczenie, wykonana praca*) service, duty; **usługa telefoniczna/internetowa** telephone/Internet service. **3.** *pl.* (*działalność gospodarcza na rzecz ogółu*) services, service; **usługi komunalne** public services; **usługi maklerskie** brokerage; **usługi pocztowe/transportowe/telekomunikacyjne** mail-delivery/transportation/telecommunication services; **świadczyć usługi dla kogoś** render services to sb.

usługiwać *ipf.* serve (*komuś* sb); attend (*komuś* to sb); be in attendance; (*o kelnerze, służącym*) wait (*komuś* on sb); fetch and carry (*komuś* for sb); **usługiwać do stołu** wait at table.

usługobiorca *mp ekon.* service receiver, client.

usługodawca *mp ekon.* service provider.

usługowy *a.* (= *świadczący usługi*) service; **punkt usługowy** service; **sektor usługowy** service industry.

usłużnie *adv.* attentively, with (great) attention; **podejmować kogoś usłużnie** lavish attention on sb.

usłużność *f.* attentiveness, complaisance.

usłużny *a.* attentive, obliging, complaisant.

usłużyć *pf.* be of service *l.* assistance (*komuś* to sb).

usłyszeć *pf.* **-ę -ysz** **1.** (= *posłyszeć*) hear; **usłyszeć kogoś** hear sb; **przypadkowo usłyszeć rozmowę** overhear *l.* pick up a conversation; **źle usłyszeć** mishear; **usłyszałem muzykę** music caught my ear; **usłyszeć coś na własne uszy** hear sth with one's own ears. **2.** (= *dowiedzieć się*) hear, find out, be told (*o czymś* about sth); **słyszę, że masz kłopoty** I hear (that) you are in trouble.

usmarkać *pf. pot.* besmear with snot. **~ się** *pf. pot.* get snotty.

usmarować *pf.* (= *pobrudzić*) besmear, smear, soil; **usmarować sobie ręce** besmear *l.* soil *l.* dirty one's hands. **~ się** *pf.* (= *pobrudzić się*) get besmeared *l.* soiled *l.* mucked; dirty one's face, hands.

usmażyć (się) *pf. zob.* **smażyć (się)**.

usmolić *pf.* **-ol** *l.* **-ól** *pot.* (= *ubrudzić*) smear, soil, dirty; **usmolić sobie kurtkę** besmear *l.* soil *l.* dirty one's coat. **~ się** *pf. pot.* (= *ubrudzić się*) get besmeared *l.* soiled *l.* dirty; besmear *l.* soil *l.* dirty one's face, hands.

usnąć *pf.* **usnę uśniesz, uśnij** *zob.* **usypiać**[1].

uspokajać *ipf.* **1.** (= *przywracać porządek, uciszać*) silence, pacify, calm (down), appease; (*tłum*) pacify; (*dziecko*) hush, lull. **2.** (= *koić*) soothe, settle down, reassure; (*nerwy, sumienie*) salve, ease; (*farmakologicznie*) tranquilize, sedate; **uspokoić kogoś** set sb's mind at rest *l.* ease; **uspokajać nerwy** settle *l.* steady one's nerves. **~ się** *ipf.* **1.** (= *stawać się spokojnym*) calm down, quiet down, grow quiet; (*o wietrze, hałasie*) lull, die down; (*o śmiechu*) subside; **uspokoiło się** (= *wypogodziło się*) it cleared up. **2.** (= *pozbywać się zdenerwowania*) calm down, relax, compose o.s., calm *l.* steady one's nerves. **3.** (= *ustatkować się*) settle down.

uspokajająco *adv.* reassuringly, soothingly; **krople działają uspokajająco** the drops have a sedative *l.* tranquilizing effect.

uspokajający *a.* (*o działaniu, słowach*) reassuring, soothing, pacificatory; (*o słowach*) placating; **środek uspokajający** sedative, tranquilizer.

uspokoić (się) *pf.* **-ję -isz, -ój** *zob.* **uspokajać (się)**.

uspokojenie *n.* **1.** (= *uciszenie*) silence, appeasement, pacification. **2.** (= *przywrócenie komuś spokoju*) reassurance; (*przez podanie środka uspokajającego*) sedation.

uspołeczniać *ipf.*, **uspołecznić** *pf.* **-ij 1.** (= *przysposabiać do życia społecznego*) socialize. **2.** (= *upaństwawiać*) communize, nationalize, socialize.

uspołeczniony *a.* nationalized, state-owned; **sektor uspołeczniony** public sector.

usportowić *pf. pot.* encourage (*sb*) to practise sports.

usposabiać *ipf.*, **usposobić** *pf.* **-ób 1.** (= *nastrajać*) dispose, incline (*sb*) (*do czegoś* to sth) (*do zrobienia czegoś* to do sth); **życzliwie kogoś usposabiać do kogoś/czegoś** dispose sb favourably to *l.* toward sb/sth; **usposabiać niechętnie** disincline, indispose (*do kogoś/czegoś* to *l.* toward sb/sth) bias, prejudice (*do kogoś/czegoś* against sb/sth). **2.** (= *wprowadzić w nastrój*) **to go usposobiło do żartów/płaczu** it put him in a mood to joke/cry.

usposobienie *n.* **1.** (= *natura, charakter*) disposition, nature, temper; **mieć pogodne usposobienie** have a cheerful *l.* sunny disposition; **mieć porywcze usposobienie** have a quick temper; **mieć łagodne usposobienie** be good-natured; **mieć przykre usposobienie** be ill-tempered; **z usposobienia** by nature, by disposition. **2.** (= *nastrój*) mood; **być w radosnym/złym/ponurym usposobieniu** be in a joyous/bad/gloomy mood.

usposobiony *a.* **-eni** disposed (*do czegoś* to sth); inclined (*do zrobienia czegoś* to do sth); **wrogo/przyjaźnie usposobiony** hostile/friendly (*do czegoś/kogoś* to *l.* toward sth/sb); in the mood (*do czegoś* for sth); **nie był usposobiony do rozmowy/żartów** he wasn't in the mood for talking/joking.

usprawiedliwiać *ipf.* **1.** (= *oczyścić z zarzutów*) exonerate, exculpate; justify; **to nie usprawiedliwia jego postępku** it doesn't justify his deed; **usprawiedliwiać swoje przestępstwo niewiedzą** plead ignorance in extenuation of one's crime. **2.** (= *uzasadniać*) justify, explain; **usprawiedli-**

wiać spóźnienie explain one's being late; **usprawiedliwiać swoje oskarżenia wobec kogoś** justify one's accusations against sb. **3.** (= *potwierdzać słuszność*) justify; (*działanie, motywy*) vindicate, warrant. **~ się** *ipf.* excuse o.s., explain o.s.; justify o.s. (*przed kimś* to sb); offer apologies (*z czegoś* for sth); **usprawiedliwiać się nieznajomością prawa** plead ignorance of the law.

usprawiedliwić (się) *pf. zob.* **usprawiedliwiać (się)**.

usprawiedliwienie *n.* **1.** (= *uzasadnienie, argument*) justification, explanation (*czegoś* for sth); (= *wymówka*) excuse; **co masz na swoje usprawiedliwienie?** how will you explain yourself?; **na usprawiedliwienie czegoś** in extenuation *l.* vindication of sth. **2.** *szkoln.* excuse note.

usprawiedliwiony *a.* **-eni** (*o prośbie, założeniu, konkluzji*) justified, legitimate; (*o nieobecności*) excused; **usprawiedliwione kłamstwo** white lie.

usprawniać *ipf.*, **usprawnić** *pf.* **-ij** (= *czynić sprawniejszym*) improve, rationalize, make more efficient; (*pracę, plan*) facilitate; (*organizację*) streamline; (*procedurę*) expedite.

usprawnienie *n.* improvement, rationalization, facilitation; **usprawnienia techniczne** technical improvements.

usta *pl.* mouth, lips; **oddychanie usta-usta** mouth-to-mouth resuscitation; **z ust do ust** from mouth to mouth; **być na ustach wszystkich** be on everyone's tongue *l.* lips; **nabrać wody w usta** shut up like a clam; **nie brać czegoś do ust** not touch sth; **nie mieć co do ust włożyć** have an empty cupboard; **nic nie miał w ustach od dwóch dni** he hasn't tasted food for two days, he hasn't eaten for two days; **nie mieć do kogo ust otworzyć** have nobody to talk to; **odejmować komuś chleb od ust** take the bread out of sb's mouth; **odejmować sobie od ust** crimp and save; **z ust mi to wyjąłeś** you took the words (right) out of my mouth; **zamknąć komuś usta** stop *l.* button *l.* shut sb's mouth; **nie puszczać pary z ust (o czymś)** breath not a word (of sth), keep mum (of sth); **nie schodzić ludziom z ust** be on everyone's tongue *l.* lips; **spijać słowa z czyichś ust** hang on sb's lips; **usta jej się nie zamykają** she talks her head off; **mówić z pełnymi ustami** talk with one's mouth full; **pocałować kogoś w usta** kiss sb on the mouth *l.* lips; **zaschło mi w ustach** my mouth is dry; **rozpływać się w ustach** melt in one's mouth; **z rozdziawionymi ustami** (open-)mouthed, agape; **wykrzywiać usta** grimace, curl one's lips; **pomadka do ust** lipstick; **błyszczyk do ust** lip gloss; **płyn do płukania ust** mouthwash.

ustabilizować *pf. zob.* **stabilizować**.

ustać[1] *pf.* **-anę -aniesz** *zob.* **ustawać**.

ustać[2] *pf.* **-oję -oisz, -ój** (= *wytrwać, stojąc*) keep standing, keep one's balance; **nie mógł ustać na nogach** he could hardly stand. **~ się** *pf.* **-oi się** (*o płynie*) (= *stać się klarownym*) settle, stand.

ustalać *ipf.* **1.** (= *określać*) set, establish, arrange; (*warunki pracy*) settle, describe; (*koszty*) tax; (*wysokość wypłaty*) adjust; (*cenę*) fix, settle, arrive at; (*szczegóły kontraktu*) firm up; (*war-*

tość) assess; (*czas*) set; **ustalać coś z góry** predetermine sth; **ustalić wstępnie** pre-establish; **ustalić, że...** establish that... 2. (= *stwierdzać, dociekając*) ascertain, determine, nail down; (*prawdę, fakty*) establish; **ustalić czyjeś ojcostwo** establish sb's fatherhood; **ustalać położenie czegoś** position sth, pinpoint; (*grupę krwi*) type; **niedający się ustalić** indeterminable; **ustalmy fakty** let's get things *l.* it straight. 3. (= *umacniać*) fix, establish; (*słup, glebę*) immobilize, fix, settle. ~ **się** *ipf.* 1. be *l.* become fixed *l.* settled, set; (*o zwyczaju*) to become established; **pogoda się ustaliła** the weather settled (down). 2. (= *ustatkować się*) settle down.

ustalenie *n.* 1. (= *dyrektywa*) directions; agreement, settlement. 2. (= *odkrycie*) ascertainment; (*faktów, przyczyny*) establishment, determination (*czegoś* of sth); **sprawa o ustalenie ojcostwa** paternity suit; *Br.* affiliation proceedings; **zgodnie z uprzednim ustaleniem** by prearrangement.

ustalić (się) *pf. zob.* **ustalać (się)**.

ustalony *a.* accepted, fixed, set; (*o stawce, terminie*) set, settled; (*o opinii*) fixed; (*o zwyczaju, praktyce*) established; (*o dacie, okolicznościach, faktach*) given; **z góry ustalony** predetermined; **to jeszcze nie jest ustalone** it is still undetermined *l.* in the vague; **orbita ustalona** *fiz., astron.* stable orbit; **stan ustalony** stationary state.

ustanawiać *ipf.*, **ustanowić** *pf.* **-ów** 1. (= *uchwalać*) establish, set (up); (*zasady, reguły*) lay down; (*prawo, ustawę*) pass, legislate; (*spadkobiercę*) institute; **ustanowić rekord** set a record; **ustanowić modę na coś** set the trend for sth; **ustanowić precedens prawny** establish *l.* set a legal precedent. 2. *prawn.* (= *powoływać*) appoint; **ustanawiać kogoś dyrektorem** appoint sb manager.

ustanku *mi* **bez ustanku** without cease, ceaselessly; **robić coś bez ustanku** keep on doing sth; **paplać bez ustanku** talk one's head off.

ustasze *pl. Gen.* **-y** *l.* **-ów** *hist.* the Ustase.

ustatkować się *pf.* settle down.

ustawa *f.* law, act, statute; **ustawa zasadnicza** constitution; **uchwalać ustawę** pass *l.* issue a law; **wnosić projekt ustawy** put forward a bill; **ustawa rolna** land law; **ustawa łowiecka** game act; **ustawa antyaborcyjna** antiabortion law; **ustawa o charakterze ogólnym** omnibus bill; **projekt ustawy** bill.

ustawać *ipf.* **ustaję ustajesz, ustawaj** 1. (= *kończyć się*) stop, cease; (*o ulewie, uczuciu*) subside; **nie ustawać** persist, go on, last; **ustać na chwilę** (*o gorączce, bólu, tętnie*) intermit. 2. *przest.* (= *opadać z sił*) be exhausted; **ustać z wyczerpania** be ready to drop, be overfatigued; **nie ustawać w staraniach** keep trying.

ustawiać *ipf.* 1. (= *umieszczać*) place, put (up). 2. (= *porządkować, rozstawiać*) arrange, place; **ustawiać coś na czymś** stand sth on sth; **ustawić książki na półce** put the books on the shelf; **ustawiać wojsko w szeregu** *wojsk.* draw up *l.* form a column of troops; **ustawiać w szyk bojowy** (*wojsko przed bitwą*) embattle, deraign; **ustawić ko-**

goś/coś w szeregu bring sb/sth into line; **ustawić w rzędzie** row; **ustawiać w snopki** shock. 3. (= *montować*) set, raise, erect; (*rusztowanie*) mount; (*namiot*) pitch; **ustawiać dekoracje** *teatr* set stage. 4. (= *regulować*) adjust, readjust; (*mechanizm, zegar*) set; **ustawiać ostrość lunety/ mikroskopu/kamery** focus a telescope/microscope/ camera; *chir.* (*złamanie*) reset; *mot.* (*rozrząd*) time. 5. *pot.* (= *komenderować, brać w karby*) curb, bring under control; **ustawić odpowiednio sprawę** angle the matter; **ustawiać kogoś finansowo** set sb up; **ustawić mecz** fix a match. ~ **się** *ipf.* 1. (= *stawać w określonym porządku*) range o.s., draw up in a line, form ranks. 2. *pot.* (= *urządzać się, stwarzać sobie odpowiednią sytuację życiową*) get settled in life.

ustawicznie *adv.* constantly, continually, incessantly, perpetually; **ustawicznie coś robić** keep on doing sth.

ustawiczność *f.* continuity.

ustawiczny *a.* constant, incessant, perpetual, endless; **ustawiczne kłopoty** endless problems.

ustawić (się) *pf. zob.* **ustawiać (się)**.

ustawienie *n.* (= *układ, porządek*) array, order; (*mebli, zawodników*) arrangement; (*kamery, ujęcia*) setup.

ustawiony *a.* **-eni** *pot.* (= *będący w dobrej sytuacji życiowej*) 1. well off. 2. **ustawiony mecz** fixed match.

ustawny *a.* (*o pomieszczeniu*) easy to furnish *l.* arrange.

ustawodawca *mp prawn.* legislator, lawmaker.

ustawodawczy *a. prawn.* legislative; **władza** *l.* **ciało ustawodawcze** legislature; **zgromadzenie ustawodawcze** parliament, legislative assembly.

ustawodawstwo *n. prawn.* 1. (= *ogół ustaw*) legislation, law. 2. (= *wydawanie ustaw*) legislation, legislative process.

ustawowo *adv.* legally, by law, statutorily.

ustawowy *a.* legal, statutory.

ustąpić *pf. zob.* **ustępować**.

ustąpienie *n.* 1. (= *rezygnacja, zrzeczenie się*) resignation, retirement. 2. (= *koniec, cofnięcie się*) (*wiatru, deszczu*) letdown; (*objawów choroby*) *med.* resolution, remission; **ustąpienie gorączki** defervescence.

usterka *f. Gen.pl.* **-ek** (= *niedociągnięcie*) defect (*w czymś* in sth), flaw, fault; *techn.* malfunction, failure; **pozbawiony usterek** faultless.

usterkowość *f.* defectiveness, proneness to failure.

usterkowy *a.* defect, fault; **protokół usterkowy** fault *l.* failure report.

usterzenie *n. lotn.* control surfaces; **usterzenie ogonowe** empennage, tail (assembly).

ustęp *mi* 1. (= *fragment tekstu*) passage, excerpt. 2. (= *ubikacja*) restroom, toilet; WC; *Br.* lavatory.

ustępliwość *f.* compliance.

ustępliwy *a.* permissive, compliant (*w sprawie czegoś* about sth); **rodzice ustępliwi wobec dzieci** permissive parents.

ustępować *ipf.* **1.** (= *cofać się*) withdraw, retire, retreat; **ustępować komuś z drogi** get off sb's way; **ustąpić pola (komuś/czemuś)** make room for sb/sth, be superseded by sb/sth; **ustąpić z pola** withdraw from the field; (*o wodzie*) recede, subside. **2.** (= *ulegać*) relent; yield, give in (*komuś/pod włymem czegoś* to sb/sth); make concessions; surrender; **nie ustąpić** stand firm (*w jakiejś sprawie* on sth); hold one's ground. **3.** (= *mijać*) pass, cease, go; (*o strachu, bólu*) subside, recede; **ból ustąpił** the pain has gone *l.* subsided; (*o złości*) melt away, subside; (*o mrozach, wietrze*) relent, abate; (*o mgle*) clear; (*o sztormie, burzy*) calm down, abate, die out. **4.** (= *zrzekać się*) resign, surrender (*z czegoś* sth); (*udziałów*) give up; **ustąpić komuś miejsca** give up one's seat to sb, surrender a seat to sb; **ustępować komuś pierwszeństwa** give way to sb; **ustępować pierwszeństwa przejazdu** *mot.* yield, give way; **deszcz ustąpił (miejsca) słońcu** after the rain came the sun. **5.** (= *rezygnować z pracy, stanowiska*) resign, step down (*z czegoś* from sth) give up (*z czegoś* sth); **król ustąpił z tronu** the king abdicated; **musiał ustąpić ze stanowiska premiera** he had to step down as prime minister. **6.** (= *być gorszym*) be inferior; **nie ustępować komuś ani na krok** match sb stride for stride; **nie ustępować nikomu w niczym** be second to none. **7.** (= *poddawać się naciskowi*) (*o drzwiach, zamku*) yield, give in. **8.** (= *obniżać cenę*) lower one's price (*o coś* by sth).

ustępstwo *n.* concession (*wobec kogoś l. na czyjąś rzecz* to sb); **robić** *l.* **iść na ustępstwa** make concessions, make an exception; **iść na ustępstwa wobec kogoś** meet sb half way; **nieskłonny do ustępstw** uncompromising, relentless; **polityka wzajemnych ustępstw** give and take policy.

ustępujący *a.* (*o urzędniku*) retiring; (*o rządzie, zarządzie*) outgoing; (*o technologii*) sunset; *biol.* (*o cesze*) recessive.

ustnie *adv.* orally, verbally, by word of mouth.

ustnik *mi Gen.* **-a 1.** (*część papierosa*) mouthpiece, filter; (*część fajki*) mouthpiece. **2.** *muz.* mouthpiece; (*zwł. instrumentów dętych*) fripple; (*zwł. instrumentu blaszanego*) embouchure. **3.** *techn.* mouthpiece.

ustny *a.* **1.** (*dotyczący ust*) oral, buccal; **jama ustna** *anat.* oral cavity; **zapalenie jamy ustnej** stomatitis; **harmonijka ustna** *muz.* mouth-organ, harmonica; **samogłoski ustne** *jęz.* oral vowels. **2.** (= *słowny*) oral, verbal, spoken; (*o egzaminie, tradycji, historii*) oral; **tłumaczenie ustne** interpretation.

ustosunkować się *pf.* *zob.* **ustosunkowywać się.**

ustosunkowany *a.* (= *mający dobre koneksje*) well-connected.

ustosunkowywać się *ipf.* issue an opinion, take a stance (*do kogoś, czegoś* on sb/sth); **pozytywnie/negatywnie się do czegoś ustosunkować** have a positive/negative attitude towards sth; **krytycznie/sceptycznie się do czegoś ustosunkować** be critical/skeptical of sth.

ustrajać *ipf.*, **ustroić** *pf.* **-rój** (= *stroić*) decorate, adorn, deck; **ustroić choinkę** decorate a Christmas tree; (*kwiatami*) deck (*czymś* with sth).

ustrojowy *a.* **1.** (*dotyczący ustroju państwa*) system; **zmiany ustrojowe** changes in the political system. **2.** (*dotyczący organizmu*) constitutional; **płyny ustrojowe** bodily *l.* body fluids.

ustrojstwo *n.* *żart.* (= *urządzenie*) contraption, gadget.

ustronie *n.* *Gen.pl.* **-i** retreat, seclusion, secluded spot *l.* place; **(mieszkać) na ustroniu** live in seclusion.

ustronny *a.* secluded, out of the way; (*o miejscu*) private.

ustrój *mi* **-o-** *Gen.pl.* **-ów 1.** (= *system organizacji państwa*) political system, form of government, establishment. **2.** (= *struktura, system*) system, organization, structure; (*prawny, szkolny*) system. **3.** *med.* (= *organizm*) organism.

ustrugać *pf.* **-gam** *l.* **-żę -gasz** *l.* **-żesz** *zob.* **strugać.**

ustrzec *pf.* **-egę -eżesz -egł** guard, protect (*kogoś* sb, *przed kimś/czymś* *l.* *od kogoś/czegoś* from *l.* against sb/sth), safeguard (*kogoś* sb, *przed kimś/czymś from l. against sb/sth*). **~ się** *pf.* avoid, escape (*kogoś, czegoś* *l.* *od kogoś, czegoś* *l.* *przed kimś, czymś* sth); **nie ustrzec się błędów** be unable to avoid mistakes.

ustrzelić *pf.* **1.** (= *zastrzelić*) (*zwł. zwierzę*) shoot, hit, kill. **2.** (= *odstrzelić*) shoot (*sth*) off.

ustylizować *pf.* *zob.* **stylizować.**

usunąć (się) *pf.* *zob.* **usuwać (się).**

ususzyć (się) *pf.* *zob.* **suszyć (się).**

usuwać *ipf.* **1.** (= *odsuwać, uprzątać*) remove; do away (*coś* with sth) get rid (*coś* of sth) clear (*kogoś/coś skądś* sb/sth from sth); **usunąć kogoś** (*np. z baru*) take sb away, get rid of sb; **usunąć kurz** remove dust, dust; **usunąć coś na bok** set sth aside; **usunąć kogoś z boiska** *sport* bench sb, send sb off the field; **usuwać kogoś/coś w cień** put sb/sth in the shade. **2.** (= *likwidować*) remove, do away with; (*plamę*) remove, get rid of; (*błędy*) delete, emend; (*usterkę*) repair; eliminate; (*z tekstu*) blank (out); (*program komputerowy*) uninstall; *techn.* (*zwł. wierzchnią warstwę czegoś*) ablate; (*niepożądane treści*) expurgate; (*złe nawyki*) weed out. **3.** (= *ewakuować*) remove, evacuate. **4.** (= *zwalniać, odprawiać*) dismiss, remove, oust (*sb*) (*z czegoś* from sth); (*z organizacji, ze szkoły*) expel; (*przeszkody*) sweep away; (*wątpliwości*) resolve. **5.** (= *wyciągać z organizmu*) remove; (*ząb*) pull, extract, draw; (*płód*) abort; **usuwać ciążę** have an abortion. **~ się** *ipf.* **1.** (= *odsuwać się*) step aside, draw back; **proszę się usunąć z drogi** clear the way, please; **usunąć się z drogi** get out of the way; withdraw (*skądś* from a place); leave (*skądś* a place). **2.** (= *zaprzestawać działalności, wycofywać się*) step down, retire; **usunąć się ze stanowiska** give up *l.* resign a post; **usunąć się w cień** take a back seat, efface o.s., keep a low profile. **3.** (= *osuwać się*) sink; **grunt usunął się komuś spod nóg** the ground gave way under sb's feet.

usychać *ipf.* (*o roślinach*) wither (away), wilt, droop, die; (*o owocach, nasionach*) shrivel, wither; **usychać z miłości, żalu** *przen.* be dying of love, grieve; **usychać z tęsknoty za kimś** pine for sb, languish for sb.

usynawiać *ipf.*, **usynowić** *pf.* **-ów** adopt, take as one's own son.

usypać *pf.* **-pię -piesz** *zob.* **usypywać.**

usypiać¹ *ipf.* (= *zapadać w sen*) fall asleep, drop off to sleep; **usnąć na wieki** go to one's last sleep *l.* rest; **nie mogę usnąć** I can't sleep.

usypiać² *ipf.* **1.** (= *powodować, że ktoś zapada w sen*) put sb to sleep; (*zwł. dziecko*) lull to sleep, send off to sleep; **usypiać sumienie** *przen.* cheat one's (guilty) conscience; **uśpić czyjąś czujność** *przen.* put sb's vigilance *l.* watchfulness to sleep. **2.** (= *czynić sennym*) make drowsy *l.* sleepy. **3.** *med.* (= *poddawać narkozie*) anaesthetize, put out; (*eterem*) etherize; (*chloroformem*) chloroform. **4.** *euf.* (= *uśmiercać zwierzę*) put to sleep.

usypiająco *adv.* drowsily, soporifically, sleepily; **działać usypiająco** have a soporific effect (*na kogoś* on sb) induce sleep (*na kogoś* in sb) make sleepy.

usypisko *n.* **1.** (= *hałda*) heap, pile, stack, mound; **usypisko śmieci** a heap of rubbish. **2.** *geol.* scree, talus.

usypywać *ipf.* **1.** (= *tworzyć kopiec*) build *l.* raise a heap *l.* mound of (*sth*); **usypać kopiec z kamieni/śniegu/buraków** heap up *l.* bank up stones/snow/beetroots; raise a mound *l.* heap of stones/snow/beetroots; **usypać szaniec** make a rampart; **usypać kopiec z piasku** bank up sand, pile sand into a moud. **2.** (= *odsypywać*) pour off.

usystematyzować *pf. zob.* **systematyzować.**

usytuować *pf. zob.* **sytuować.**

usytuowanie *n.* (= *położenie*) situation, location; **usytuowanie domu jest bardzo dogodne** the house is in a good location; the house is well situated *l.* located.

uszanka *f. Gen.pl.* **-ek** = **uszatka.**

uszanować *pf.* **1.** (= *okazać szacunek*) respect; show one's respect (*kogoś/coś* to sb/sth) show regard, show consideration (*kogoś/coś* for sb/sth); **uszanować czyjeś uczucia** respect *l.* spare sb's feelings. **2.** (= *nie naruszyć*) (*traktaty, czyjąś wolę*) respect, abide by, adhere to, comply with.

uszanowanie *n.* respect, esteem, (high) regard (*kogoś/czegoś* for sb/sth), appreciation (*czegoś* of sth); **mieć uszanowanie dla kogoś/czegoś** hold sb/sth in (high *l.* great) esteem; **moje uszanowanie** *form.* (*powitanie*) good morning *l.* afternoon *l.* evening; **przesyłać komuś wyrazy uszanowania** send one's respects to sb; **składać komuś wyrazy uszanowania** pay one's respects *l.* compliments to sb; **z uszanowaniem** (*w zakończeniu listu*) respectfully (yours).

uszargać *pf.* (= *pobrudzić*) besmear, soil, smear; **uszargać błotem** soil with mud.

uszarpać się *pf.* **-pię -piesz** *pot.* (= *namęczyć się*) tire, get tired, get exhausted; **uszarpał się za kierownicą** driving exhausted him *l.* wore him out.

uszatek *mp* **-tk-** *pl.* **-i** *pot., żart.* (*o osobie l. zwierzęciu z dużymi uszami*) bat ears.

uszatka *f. Gen.pl.* **-ek** (*czapka*) earflap cap.

uszaty *a.* **1.** (= *mający ucho l. ucha*) with ears *l.* flaps. **2.** (= *mający duże uszy*) big-eared.

uszczegółowić *pf.* **-ów** provide with details *l.* particulars.

uszczelka *f. Gen.pl.* **-ek** *techn.* gasket, washer, seal; (*gumowa*) rubber; **uszczelka dławikowa** gland.

uszczelniacz *mi Gen.* **-a** *techn.* sealing, sealant, sealing medium.

uszczelniać *ipf.*, **uszczelnić** *pf.* **-ij** seal, chink (up); (*od wody*) waterproof, make waterproof *l.* water-tight; (*od wiatru*) make windproof; (*np. granicę*) tighten; (*okna, kadłub łodzi*) caulk; **uszczelniać kitem** lute; **materiał uszczelniający** caulking.

uszczelnienie *n.* sealing, seal, gasket, packing, sealant; **uszczelnianie okien, drzwi (paskami)** weather stripping.

uszczerbek *mi* **-bk-** damage, harm, detriment, loss (*na czymś* to sth); **ciężki uszczerbek na zdrowiu** *prawn.* grievous bodily harm; **doznać uszczerbku (na czymś)** suffer a loss; **z uszczerbkiem (dla) kogoś/czegoś** to the prejudice of sb/sth; **bez uszczerbku (dla kogoś/czegoś)** without detriment *l.* prejudice (to sb/sth); **bez uszczerbku** safe, unharmed, without a scratch.

uszczęśliwiać *ipf.*, **uszczęśliwić** *pf.* make happy, delight; **to by go uszczęśliwiło** this would make him happy; **uszczęśliwiać kogoś na siłę** force someone to accept unwanted help.

uszczknąć *pf.* **-ij** + *Gen.* nip off *l.* tear off a bit of (*sth*); (= *skubnąć zębami*) nibble at (*sth*).

uszczuplać *ipf.*, **uszczuplić** *pf.* **-ij** diminish, reduce; (*zapasy, środki, zasoby*) deplete, eat into.

uszczypać *pf.* **-pię -piesz** = **uszczypnąć.**

uszczypliwość *f.* **1.** (= *bycie uszczypliwym*) acrimoniousness, acerbity. **2.** (= *uszczypliwa uwaga*) stinging remark.

uszczypliwy *a.* **1.** (= *złośliwy*) (*o człowieku*) sharp-tongued, astringent. **2.** (= *świadczący o złośliwości*) acerbic, pointed; (*o uwadze*) sharp, stinging.

uszczypnąć (się) *pf.* **-ij** *zob.* **szczypać (się).**

uszczypnięcie *n.* pinch, tweak, nip.

uszedł *itd. pf. zob.* **ujść.**

uszeregować *pf. zob.* **szeregować.**

uszkadzać *ipf.* damage, injure, impair; break; (*maszynę*) put out of order. **~ się** *ipf.* suffer damage, break down.

uszko *n. Gen.pl.* **uszek** **1.** *pl.* **-a** *l.* **-i** (= *małe ucho*) little ear. **2.** (*uchwyt*) ear, flap, eyelet; (*filiżanki*) ear; (*igły*) eye. **3.** *zw. pl. kulin.* (= *pierożki w kształcie ucha*) ravioli (*in Polish cooking*).

uszkodzenie *n.* **1.** (= *usterka*) damage (*czegoś* to sth), failure (*czegoś* in sth), impairment; **uszkodzenie konstrukcji** structural damage. **2.** *med.* (= *kontuzja*) damage, harm, injury; **uszkodzenie mózgu/wątroby** brain/liver damage; **ciężkie uszkodzenie ciała** *prawn.* grievous bodily harm.

uszkodzić (się) *pf. zob.* **uszkadzać (się).**

uszkodzony *a.* damaged, out of order, broken-down; *komp.* (*np. o pliku*) corrupt; **ciężko uszkodzony** severly disabled; **samochód/silnik nie został uszkodzony** the car/engine was intact *l.* undamaged.

uszlachcenie *n.* (= *nobilitacja*) ennoblement, nobilitation.

uszlachetniacz *mi Gen.* **-a** refiner.

uszlachetniać *ipf.*, **uszlachetnić** *pf.* **-ij 1.** (= *doskonalić moralnie*) ennoble, improve, elevate. **2.** *techn.* (= *poprawiać jakość czegoś*) improve; (*surowiec*) purify; (*olej, cukier*) refine. **3.** *hodowla* (= *krzyżować z odmianą l. rasą szlachetną*) grade.

uszła *itd. pf. zob.* **ujść.**

uszminkować (się) *pf. zob.* **szminkować (się).**

uszny *a.* aurical, ear; **małżowina uszna** auricle, pinna; **woszczyna uszna** earwax, cerumen; **specjalista chorób usznych** otologist, ear specialist.

usztywniacz *mi Gen.* **-a** stiffener, stiffening.

usztywniać *ipf.*, **usztywnić** *pf.* **-ij** (= *czynić sztywnym*) stiffen, toughen; (*krochmaląc*) starch; **usztywniać fiszbinami** bone; *krawiectwo* (*przez podszycie warstwą usztywniającą*) face; **usztywnić stanowisko** harden one's position.

uszy *itd. n. zob.* **ucho.**

uszyć *pf.* **-ję -jesz** *zob.* **szyć.**

uszykować *pf. zob.* **szykować.**

uścielać *ipf.* **1.** (= *robić posłanie*) make a bed. **2.** (= *rozpościerać*) strew; **usłać pole bitwy trupami** strew the battle-field with the dead; (*kwiatami*) strew, deck; (*fotel, krzesło*) cushion; **usłać sobie gniazdko** (*o ptaku*) build its nest.

uścisk *mi* **1.** (= *objęcie się*) embrace, hug; **uścisk dłoni** handshake, clasp; **czuły uścisk** warm *l.* tender embrace, cuddle; **przesyłać komuś uściski** send love to sb. **2.** (= *uchwyt*) clench, grip, holdfast; **rozluźnić uścisk** loosen one's grip; **trzymać kogoś w (żelaznym) uścisku** keep sb in a viselike grip.

uściskać *pf.* **1.** (= *objąć*) hug, embrace; **uścisnąć komuś rękę** (*na pożegnanie, powitanie*) shake hands with sb. **2.** (= *przekazać pozdrowienia*) give *l.* send love; **uściskaj swoich rodziców ode mnie** give my love to your parents. **~ się** *pf.* embrace, hug (*z kimś* with sb).

uścisnąć *pf.* **-snę -śniesz, -śnij, -snął 1.** = **uściskać. 2.** (= *ścisnąć*) squeeze; **uścisnąć komuś rękę** (*w przypływie uczuć*) squeeze sb's hand, give sb's hand a squeeze. **~ się** *pf.* = **uściskać się.**

uściślać *ipf.* specify, state precisely *l.* accurately; (*wypowiedź*) qualify; (= *czynić jednoznacznym*) disambiguate, clarify; be specific, be precise (*coś* about sth).

uściślenie *n.* specification, disambiguation; **proszę o uściślenie wypowiedzi** please be more specific.

uściślić *pf.* **-ij** *zob.* **uściślać.**

uściśnięcie *n.* squeeze, grip; **uściśnięcie dłoni** handshake.

uślizg *mi* skid, slide.

uśmiać się *pf.* **-eję -ejesz** laugh, have a good laugh, laugh heartily (*z kogoś* at sb); **uśmiać się do łez** cry with laughter; **koń by się uśmiał** it would make a cat laugh; **uśmiał się jak głupi** he laughed himself silly.

uśmiech *mi* smile; **głupawy, afektowany uśmiech** simper; **szyderczy uśmiech** sneer, fleer; **krzywy uśmiech** crooked smile; **promienny uśmiech** beam; **szeroki uśmiech** grin; **uśmiech przylepiony do twarzy** fixed smile; **uśmiech losu** lucky turn of fortune; **posyłać komuś uśmiech** send sb a smile; smile at sb; **proszę o uśmiech!** (*do zdjęcia*) smile please, say cheese; **zmusić się do uśmiechu** force a smile.

uśmiechać się *ipf.*, **uśmiechnąć się** *pf.* **-ij** smile (*do kogoś* at sb); **uśmiechnąć się do kogoś** give sb a smile; **uśmiechać się od ucha do ucha** smile *l.* grin from ear to ear; smile *l.* grin broadly; **uśmiechać się promiennie** beam; **uśmiechać się słabo** crack a smile; **uśmiechnąć się szyderczo** sneer; **szczęście się do nas uśmiechnęło** we are in luck; **to mi się nie uśmiecha** I don't like the idea.

uśmiechnięty *a.* smiling; **uśmiechnięta twarz** smiling face.

uśmiercać *ipf.*, **uśmiercić** *pf.* **1.** (= *zadawać śmierć*) put to death, do to death, kill (off); **pisarz uśmierca jednego z bohaterów w pierwszym rozdziale** the writer kills one of the characters in the first chapter. **2.** *żart.* (= *rozsiewać pogłoskę o czyjejś śmierci*) bury sb.

uśmierzać *ipf.* **1.** (= *łagodzić, koić*) relieve, alleviate, soothe. **2.** (= *uspokajać*) appease. **3.** (= *tłumić*) quell, suppress.

uśmierzająco *adv.* soothingly; **działać uśmierzająco** bring relief.

uśmierzający *a.* soothing, alleviative, lenitive; **lek uśmierzający ból** *med.* analgesic, pain-killer.

uśmierzyć *pf. zob.* **uśmierzać.**

uśmieszek *mi* **-szk-** (*drwiący*) sneer; (*pogardliwy, pełen wyższości*) smirk; (*głupawy*) simper.

uśnie *itd. pf. zob.* **usnąć.**

uśpić *pf.* **-ij** *zob.* **usypiać**[2].

uśredniać *ipf.*, **uśrednić** *pf.* **-ij** average (out).

uśredniony *a.* averaged.

uświadamiać *ipf.* (= *zaznajamiać*) educate, inform, enlighten; **uświadamiać coś komuś** make sb realize sth, alert sb to sth, make sb aware of sth; **uświadamiać młodzież** (*w sprawach seksu*) explain the facts of life to young people; **uświadomić dziecko** (*w sprawach seksu*) tell *l.* teach a child about birds and bees; **uświadamiać sobie coś** realize sth; **uświadamiać sobie, że...** realize that...; **uświadomić sobie swoje obowiązki** wake up to one's duties.

uświadczyć *pf.* **nie uświadczyć czegoś** *pot.* not see sth for dust, not find the remotest trace of sth (*somewhere*).

uświadomić *pf. zob.* **uświadamiać.**

uświadomienie *n.* consciousness, awareness, information; **uświadomienie sobie** realization; **uświadomienie klasowe** *l.* **polityczne** social consciousness; **uświadomienie seksualne** knowledge of sexual matters.

uświerknąć *pf.* **-ij** *pot.* (= *zmarznąć*) freeze; **Je-**

zu, można dzisiaj **uświerknąć** Jesus, it is damn freezing today.

uświetniać *ipf.*, **uświetnić** *pf.* -ij add splendor *l.* distinction to (*sth*); lend *l.* give luster to (*sth*); (*swoją obecnością*) dignify; **spotkanie było uświetnione obecnością prezydenta** the meeting was dignified by the President.

uświęcać *ipf.*, **uświęcić** *pf.* (= *uczynić świętym*) sanctify; (*tradycję, zwyczaj*) consecrate; **cel uświęca środki** the end justifies the means.

uświęcający *a.* sanctifying, consecrating; **łaska uświęcająca** *rel.* grace; **stan łaski uświęcającej** *rel.* state of grace.

uświęcony *a.* **uświęcony tradycją** *l.* zwyczajem time-honored.

uświnić *pf. zob.* **świnić**.

uświniony *a.* filthy.

utaić *pf.* **utaję utaisz**, **utajać** *ipf.* keep secret (*przed kimś/czymś* from sb/sth).

utajniać *ipf.*, **utajnić** *pf.* -ij (*informacje*) make classified; (= *wydać zakaz rozpowszechniania przez media*) black out.

utajony *a.* latent.

utalentowany *a.* talented, gifted.

utapirować *pf. zob.* **tapirować**.

utaplać *pf. pot.* (= *pobrudzić*) dirty, soil; **utaplać w błocie** muddy. **~ się** *pf. pot.* (= *pobrudzić się*) get dirty, dirty o.s., get soiled; **utaplać się w błocie** get covered with mud.

utarczka *f. Gen.pl.* -ek 1. *lit.* (= *sprzeczka*) squabble; **utarczka słowna** verbal sparring. 2. *lit.* (= *potyczka*) skirmish.

utarg *mi handl.* takings; **utarg dzienny** a day's takings.

utargować *pf.* 1. (= *zarobić*) make; **dziś utargowałem osiem funtów** I made eight pounds today. 2. (= *zbić cenę*) beat down; **utargowałem (od niego) pięć dolarów** I beat him down five dollars.

utarty *a.* (= *ogólnie przyjęty*) (= *powszechny*) widespread; (*o opinii*) accepted, common; (*o argumencie*) stock; **utarte wyrażenie** *l.* zwrot set phrase; **toczyć się** *l.* **iść utartym torem** go through the ordinary grind, follow a beaten track.

uteatralizować *pf. zob.* **teatralizować**.

utemperować *pf.* (*osobę*) pacify; (*temperament, zapędy*) curb; (= *złagodzić*) temper.

utensylia *pl. Gen.* -ów 1. (= *przybory*) implements, utensils. 2. (= *sprzęty domowe*) (household) utensils.

utęsknienie *n.* **z utęsknieniem** longingly.

utkać *pf. zob.* **tkać**, **utykać²**.

utknąć *pf.* -ij 1. *zob.* **utykać¹**. 2. (= *utkwić, wbić się*) get stuck; **utknąć w śniegu** get stuck in the snow; **utknąć w martwym punkcie** come to a standstill; (*np. o negocjacjach*) reach an impasse; **utknąć w gardle** (*o słowach*) stick in one's throat; **coś mi utknęło w gardle** (*o kawałku kości, jedzenia*) sth got stuck in my throat. 3. *pot.* (= *osiąść gdzieś wbrew woli*) get stuck (*somewhere*); **przyjechałem do tej dziury z dziesięć lat temu i chyba utknąłem na dobre** I came to this noplaceville some ten years ago and it looks like I got stuck here for good.

utkwić *pf.* -ij 1. (= *wbić się, utknąć*) stick; (*np. o pocisku*) lodge (*in a tree, wall*); **utkwić w pamięci** stick in sb's mind; **utkwić w kimś/czymś wzrok** fix one's eyes on sb/sth. 2. *pot.* (= *zatrzymać się gdzieś na dłużej*) get stuck; **ojciec utkwił na dobre przy telewizorze** father got glued to the TV for good.

utleniacz *mi Gen.* -a *chem.* oxidant; (*w paliwie silnika rakiety*) oxidizer.

utleniać *ipf. biol., chem.* oxidize; (*krew*) oxygenate, arterialize; **utleniać włosy** bleach one's hair. **~ się** *ipf.* oxidize.

utleniająco *adv.* **działać utleniająco** oxidize, have an oxidizing effect.

utlenialny *a.* oxidizable.

utlenić (się) *pf. zob.* **utleniać (się)**.

utleniony *a.* **woda utleniona** (hydrogen) peroxide, oxygenated water.

utłuc *pf.* **utłukę utłuczesz** 1. (= *pokruszyć*) crush, grind; (*w moździerzu*) pulverize, grind; (*ziemniaki*) mash. 2. (= *odkruszyć*) break off, chip off. 3. *pot.* (= *zabić*) do (*sb*) in.

utłuścić *pf.* -uszczę -uścisz smear with grease. **~ się** *pf.* get greasy.

utoczyć *pf.* 1. (*upuścić, ulać*) draw; **utoczyć komuś krwi** draw sb's blood; **utoczyć piwa z beczki** draw some beer from the barrel. 2. (*na tokarce*) lathe, turn. 3. (*np. kulę ze śniegu*) roll.

utonąć *pf. zob.* **tonąć**.

utonięcie *n.* (death by) drowning.

utopia *f. Gen.* -ii Utopia *l.* utopia; **świat utopii** cloud-cuckoo-land *l.* cloudland.

utopić *pf.* drown. **~ się** *pf.* (*wskutek wypadku*) drown; (*popełnić samobójstwo*) drown o.s.

utopijność *f.* Utopianism *l.* utopianism.

utopijny *a.* Utopian *l.* utopian; **socjalizm utopijny** utopian socialism.

utopista *mp*, **utopistka** *f.* Utopian *l.* utopian, Utopist *l.* utopist.

utorować *pf. zob.* **torować**.

utożsamiać *ipf.* identify (*kogoś/coś z kimś/czymś* sb/sth with sb/sth). **utożsamiać się** *ipf.* identify o.s. (*z kimś/czymś* with sb/sth); **utożsamiać się uczuciowo** empathize (*z kimś/czymś* with sb/sth).

utożsamić (się) *pf. zob.* **utożsamiać (się)**.

utracić *pf. zob.* **tracić**.

utracjusz *mp uj.* spendthrift, prodigal son, high roller.

utracjuszostwo *n.* prodigality, profligacy.

utracjuszowski *a.* prodigal, profligate.

utrafiać *ipf.*, **utrafić** *pf.* 1. (= *trafiać*) hit; **utrafić w czyjąś czułą strunę** touch the right chord with sb, strike a deep chord with sb, touch *l.* hit *l.* strike a raw nerve with sb; **utrafić (czymś) w czyjś gust** do (sth) to sb's liking; **utrafić w sedno** hit the nail on the head. 2. *pot.* (= *oddawać podobieństwo*) catch sb's likeness (*e.g. in a portrait*). 3. (= *przybywać w porę*) come at the right moment; **utrafić w samą porę** come *l.* arrive precisely at the right moment, have a good timing; **utrafić na obiad** come just at dinner time. 4. (= *odmierzyć dokładnie*) hit the correct measure.

utrakwista *mp rel.* Utraquist.

utrakwizm *mi* **1.** (*system szkolny*) bilingual school system. **2.** *rel.* Utraquism.

utrapienie *n.* nuisance, trouble; (*zwł. o dziecku*) menace; **być dla kogoś strasznym utrapieniem** be a great trial to sb; **mam z nią wieczne utrapienie** she's always causing me trouble; **utrapienie z tym kotem!** this cat is such a nuisance!; **ten dzieciak to wieczne utrapienie!** this kid is such a menace!

utrapieniec *mp* -ńc- *pl.* -y *pot.* menace, nuisance; **co za utrapieniec z ciebie!** what a menace *l.* nuisance (of a boy *l.* girl) you are!

utrapiony *a.* -eni trublesome, plaguey; **co za utrapiony chłopak!** what a nuisance of a boy he is!

utrata *f.* loss, deprivation; **utrata pamięci/przytomności** loss of memory/consciousness; **utrata praw obywatelskich** *prawn.* infamy; **utrata** *l.* **pozbawienie zdolności prawnej** *prawn.* disablement; **utrata tchu** breathlessness; **(upić się) do utraty przytomności** drink o.s. unconscious.

utrącać *ipf.*, **utrącić** *pf.* **1.** (= *odtłukiwać*) chip off, knock off. **2.** *pot.* (= *nie dopuścić do zajęcia stanowiska*) trip (*sb*) up; (= *spowodować usunięcie ze stanowiska*) unhorse, unsaddle (*sb*); (*projekt ustawy w parlamencie*) kill; **utrącić czyjąś kandydaturę** destroy sb's candidacy.

utrudniać *ipf.*, **utrudnić** *pf.* -ij make difficult, hamper, hinder, impede; **utrudniać coś komuś** make sth difficult for sb; **utrudniać komuś zrobienie czegoś** make it difficult for sb to do sth; **utrudniać komuś życie** make life difficult for sb; make it hot for sb.

utrudnienie *n.* difficulty, hindrance, holdback, impediment.

utrudzać *ipf. lit.* (= *męczyć*) fatigue, weary. ~ **się** *ipf. lit.* become fatigued, become weary.

utrudzenie *n. lit.* fatigue, weariness.

utrudzić (się) *pf. zob.* **utrudzać (się)**.

utrudzony *a.* -eni *lit.* fatigued, wearied, forspent (*arch.*), forworn (*arch.*).

utrwalacz *mi Gen.* -a **1.** *chem.* (*t. środek fryzjerski*) fixative. **2.** *fot.* fixer; (= *podsiarczyn sodu*) hypo. **3.** *sl., żart.* (= *piwo pite po mocniejszym alkoholu*) chaser.

utrwalać *ipf.*, **utrwalić** *pf.* **1.** (= *umacniać*) (*przyjaźń*) cement, solidify; (*pozycję*) strengthen. **2.** *sztuka* (= *upamiętniać*) preserve. **3.** (= *rejestrować*) record. **4.** (= *zapamiętać*) (*przed egzaminem*) revise; **utrwalić coś w pamięci** fix sth in one's mind. **5.** *fot.* fix.

utrwalać się *ipf.*, **utrwalić się** *pf.* become established, take root; **utrwalać się w pamięci** become fixed in sb's mind.

utrząsać *ipf.*, **utrząsnąć** *pf.* -snę -śniesz, -śnij, **utrząść** *pf.* utrzęsę utrzęsiesz, utrząś *l.* utrzęś, **utrząsł utrzęsła utrzęśli 1.** (= *układać, potrząsając*) shake down (*apples in a bag*). **2.** (= *strącać, potrząsając*) shake down (*apples from a tree*).

utrzeć *pf.* utrę utrzesz, utrzyj, utarł **1.** *zob.* **ucierać. 2. utrzeć komuś nosa** cut sb down to size, knock sb off their perch. ~ **się** *pf.* (= *wejść w zwyczaj*) become established; **utarło się wyrażenie** it has become a common saying.

utrzymać (się) *pf. zob.* **utrzymywać (się)**.

utrzymanek *mp* (*starszej od siebie kobiety*) gigolo; (*homoseksualisty*) catamite, pathic.

utrzymanie *n.* **1.** (= *środki do życia*) keep, maintenance; **koszty utrzymania** cost of living; **środki utrzymania** means of support, maintenance; **być na czyimś utrzymaniu** depend financially on sb, live off sb; **mieć rodzinę na utrzymaniu** have a family to provide for *l.* to keep; **zapewniać komuś utrzymanie** make provision for sb; **zarabiać na utrzymanie** earn *l.* make a living; (= *być żywicielem rodziny*) bring home the bacon; **jak zarabiasz na utrzymanie?** what do you do for a living?, how do you earn *l.* make your living? **2.** (= *wikt, wyżywienie*) board.

utrzymanka *f. Gen.pl.* -ek mistress, kept woman.

utrzymany *a.* **dobrze/źle utrzymany** well/badly kept; **list utrzymany w serdecznym tonie** a warm letter.

utrzymywać *ipf.* **1.** (= *trzymać*) hold. **2.** (= *podpierać, podtrzymywać*) bear, carry. **3.** (= *kierować, kontrolować*) hold, keep in hand; **utrzymać konia** keep a horse in hand, control a horse; **utrzymać kierownicę** control the steering wheel, not let go off the steering wheel; **utrzymać kogoś w ryzach** keep a tight hold on sb; **utrzymać coś w tajemnicy** keep sth secret; **utrzymywać kogoś w niepewności** keep sb in uncertainty, keep sb guessing; **utrzymywać kogoś w nieświadomości czegoś** keep sb in ignorance of sth; **nie potrafić utrzymać języka za zębami** not be able to hold one's tongue. **4.** (= *zachowywać*) keep, maintain; (*o cenach*) (= *nie pozwolić na zniżkę*) keep up; **utrzymywać dyscyplinę/formę** keep discipline/fit; **utrzymywać kurs** *żegl.* hold to a course; **utrzymać porządek** keep order; **utrzymać posadę** hold down a job; **utrzymać poziom** (*o szkole, uczelni itp.*) live up to the standard; **utrzymać spokój** keep calm; **utrzymać wagę** maintain one's weight; **utrzymywać coś w dobrym stanie/w czystości** keep sth in good condition/clean; **utrzymywać kontakt z kimś** be in touch with sb; **utrzymywać** *l.* **prowadzić z kimś korespondencję** carry on *l.* keep up a correspondence with sb; **utrzymywać kogoś przy życiu** keep sb alive. **5.** (= *zatrzymywać*) keep; **utrzymać kogoś na stanowisku** keep sb in their job; **utrzymać kogoś na miejscu** keep sb, not let sb go. **6.** (= *zapewniać byt*) provide for, support, maintain; **utrzymywać rodzinę** provide for one's family, support a family, bring home the bacon. **7.** (= *wynajmować, zatrudniać*) keep; **utrzymywać służbę** keep servants. **8.** (= *bronić*) hold, remain in possession of; **utrzymać twierdzę** hold a fortress. **9.** *lit.* (= *twierdzić*) maintain, hold, claim; **ona utrzymuje, że...** she will have it that... ~ **się** *ipf.* **1.** (= *nie zmieniać pozycji*) stay, remain; **utrzymywać się na nogach** be able to stand (*on one's own*), keep one's feet; **utrzymywać się na wodzie** float, rest on water, stay afloat; (*jako właściwość fizyczna*) be buoyant; **utrzymywać się na fali** *przen.* (manage to) stay on top. **2.** (= *nie tracić, pozostawać*) remain, keep; **utrzymać się na stanowisku** (*w pra-*

cy) remain at one's post; **utrzymać się w pracy** hold down one's job; **pozostać przy władzy** *l.* **u steru władzy** remain in power; **utrzymać się w lidze** stay in the league; **utrzymywać się przy życiu** stay alive. **3.** (= *trwać*) last, survive, persist, linger; (*o pogodzie*) hold; **utrzymywać się w dobrej formie** stay fit. **4.** (= *żyć*) make *l.* earn one's living, earn one's keep (*z czegoś* off sth); subsist (*dzięki czemuś* on sth); **utrzymywać się z pracy rąk** live by one's labor; **z czego się utrzymujesz?** what do you do for a living?; how do you make *l.* earn your living? **5.** (= *nie poddawać się*) hold one's ground, hold the line.

utuczyć (się) *pf. zob.* **tuczyć (się)**.

utulać *ipf.*, **utulić** *pf.* console, solace (*by hugging*); **utulić (czyjś) żal** assuage sb's grief; **utulić dziecko do snu** tuck a child in.

utwar *mi bot.* gum succory (*Chondrilla*).

utwardzacz *mi Gen.* **-a** hardener.

utwardzać *ipf.* harden. **~ się** *ipf.* harden, become hardened.

utwardzalny *a.* hardenable.

utwardzić (się) *pf. zob.* **utwardzać (się)**.

utwierdzać *ipf.* strengthen, confirm (*kogoś* sb, *w czymś* in sth). **~ się** *ipf.* strengthen o.s., confirm o.s. (*w czymś* in sth); **utwierdzać się w przekonaniu, że...** be strengthened in one's conviction that...

utwierdzić (się) *pf. zob.* **utwierdzać (się)**.

utworzyć (się) *pf.* **-órz** *zob.* **tworzyć (się)**.

utwór *mi* **-o-** **1.** (= *dzieło*) work, composition, production, piece; **utwór instrumentalny** *muz.* instrumental; **utwór liryczny** *teor.lit.* lyric; **utwór literacki** literary work; (*prozatorski*) work of fiction; **utwór muzyczny** piece of music; **utwór na życzenie** *radio* request; **utwór sceniczny** stage play; **utwór wokalny** *muz.* vocal; **utwory zebrane Szekspira** Shakespeare's collected works. **2.** (= *biol.*) part (*of an organ, developed for a certain purpose, e.g. the air bladder*). **3.** *geol.* formation.

utyć *pf.* **-yję -yjesz, -yj, -ył** *zob.* **tyć**.

utykać[1] *ipf.* **1.** (= *grzęznąć*) get stuck; **utknąć na mieliźnie** run aground; **utknąć w martwym punkcie** *przen.* come to a standstill *l.* deadlock. **2.** (= *urywać się*) stop, break off; **robota utknęła w miejscu** work has come to a standstill.

utykać[2] *ipf.* **1.** (= *zatykać, uszczelniać*) stuff up. **2.** (= *upychać, wciskać*) crowd, cram (*a room with furniture etc.*).

utykać[3] *ipf.* (= *lekko kuleć*) have a limp, limp, hobble; **utykać na prawą nogę** have a limp in one's right leg.

utylitarność *f.* utilitarianism.

utylitarny *a.* utilitarian.

utylitarysta *mp*, **utylitarystka** *f. Gen.pl.* **-ek** utilitarian.

utylitaryzm *mi fil.* utilitarianism.

utylizacja *f.* utilization; **utylizacja odpadów** waste management, recycling.

utylizator *mi Gen.* **-a** *techn.* sewage treatment appliance (*in a factory*).

utylizować *ipf.* utilize.

utyskiwać *ipf.* grumble (*na coś* about sth).

utyskiwanie *n.* grumbling.

utytłać (się) *pf. zob.* **tytłać (się)**.

utytłany *a.* mucky.

utytułować *pf.* (= *nadać tytuł*) grant a title.

utytułowany *a.* titled.

UW *abbr.* (= *Uniwersytet Warszawski*) Warsaw University.

uwadniać *ipf. chem.* hydrate.

uwaga *f.* **1.** (= *koncentracja*) attention, heed; **uwaga!** (= *ostrożnie!*) be careful!; (*w obliczu niebezpieczeństwa*) look out!, watch out!; (*w napisach*) caution!; **uwaga pasażerowie!** attention passengers!; **uwaga personel medyczny!** attention medical personnel!; „Uwaga! Mokra podłoga!" "Caution! Wet floor!"; „Uwaga! Stopień!" "Mind the step!"; „Uwaga! Strzeż się pociągu!" "Beware of the Train!"; „Uwaga! Świeżo malowane!" "Wet Paint"; „Uwaga! Wysokie napięcie!" "Danger! High voltage!"; „Uwaga! Zły pies!" "Beware of the dog!"; **brać coś po uwagę** take sth into consideration, take sth into account; **nie brać czegoś pod uwagę** leave sth out of account; **nie wziąłem pod uwagę, że mogę się spóźnić** I didn't allow for a delay; **mieć coś na uwadze** keep *l.* bear sth in mind; **mając na uwadze, że...** bearing in mind that...; **odwracać czyjąś uwagę** distract sb's attention; **odwrócić czyjąś uwagę od czegoś** draw sb's attention away from sth; **poświęcać komuś/czemuś uwagę** give one's attention to sb/sth; **poświęcać czemuś dużo uwagi** give a considerable amount of thought to; **przykuwać czyjąś uwagę** arrest sb's attention; **umykać** *l.* **uchodzić czyjejś uwadze** escape sb's notice; **starać się zwrócić na siebie uwagę** make a pitch for attention; **skupiać (na sobie) czyjąś uwagę** draw *l.* attract sb's attention (to o.s.); **ściągać na siebie** *l.* **przyciągać do siebie uwagę** attract notice; **zaprzątać czyjąś uwagę** absorb sb; **zasługiwać na uwagę** be noteworthy, deserve notice; **znaleźć się w centrum uwagi** become the focus of attention; **zwracać czyjąś uwagę na kogoś/coś** (= *zainteresować*) draw sb's attention to sb/sth; **zwracać uwagę na kogoś/coś** (= *dostrzegać*) pay attention to sb/sth; **zwracać komuś uwagę na coś** bring sth to sb's notice; **proszę o uwagę!** may I have your attention; **zwracam uwagę, że...** I'd like to draw your attention to the fact that...; **temu zagadnieniu poświęca się dużo uwagi** this problem is engaging a good deal of attention. **2.** (= *komentarz*) comment, remark, observation; **czynić uwagę** (*na jakiś temat* on sth), observe; **uwagi końcowe** (*część dokumentu*) closing remarks. **3.** (= *napomnienie*) reproof; *szkoln.* (*wpisana do zeszytu*) note to the parents; **robić komuś uwagi** reprove sb; **zwrócić komuś uwagę** admonish sb. **4. z uwagi na coś** owing to.

uwalać *pf.* soil, dirty; (*atramentem, tuszem*) smear.

uwalić się *pf.* **1.** *pot.* (= *położyć się*) throw o.s., sprawl o.s. (*on one's bed*); **uwalić się na wyro i zasnąć** hit the hay. **2.** *pot.* (= *upić się*) get sloshed, get blitzed.

uwalniać *ipf.* **1.** (= *zwracać wolność*) free, set free; (*niewolników*) enfranchise. **2.** (= *oswobo-*

dzić od kogoś l. czegoś) release, deliver (*od kogoś / czegoś* from sb/sth); **uwolnić kogoś od zarzutów** aquit sb. **3.** (= *zwalniać od obowiązku itp.*) exempt (*od czegoś* from sth); relieve (*od czegoś* from sth); free (*od czegoś* from sth). **4.** *chem.* release; (*zwł. gaz*) liberate; (*gaz*) outgas; (*reakcję*) unchain. **5.** (*ceny*) unpeg. ~ **się** *ipf.* **1.** (= *oswobadzać się*) free o.s. **2.** (= *pozbywać się*) rid o.s. (*od kogoś / czegoś* of sb/sth). **3.** (= *zwalniać się od obowiązków itp.*) be exempted, be relieved (*od czegoś* from sth). **4.** *chem.* be released; (*zwł. o gazie*) be liberated; (*gaz*) outgas.

uwalony *a.* *pot.* (= *pijany*) pissed.

uwapniać *ipf.*, **uwapnić** *pf.* **-ij** calcify.

uwarstwienie *n.* (= *ułożenie warstw; = zróżnicowanie społeczne*) stratification.

uwarunkować *pf.* *zob.* **uwarunkowywać.**

uwarunkowanie *n.* condition, circumstances.

uwarunkowywać *ipf.* condition (*coś czymś* sth on sth).

uwarzyć *pf.* *zob.* **warzyć.**

uważać *ipf.* **1.** (= *skupiać uwagę*) pay attention, be attentive; **uważaj!** (= *bądź ostrożny*) be careful; (*w obliczu niebezpieczeństwa*) look out!, watch out!, careful!; **uważaj, żebyś nie spadł** make sure you don't fall off *l.* down; **uważaj, co robisz** mind what you're doing. **2.** (= *obserwować*) be careful, mind; **uważaj na drogę!** watch the road!; **uważaj na stopień!** mind the step! **3.** (= *pilnować*) keep an eye (*na kogoś / coś* on sb/ sth); **uważaj na siebie!** take care of yourself! **4.** (= *doglądać*) look after. **5.** (= *traktować*) consider (*kogoś / coś* sb/sth, *za kogoś, coś* (to be) sb/sth); **uważać kogoś za przyjaciela** consider sb (to be) a friend; **uważać za stosowne coś zrobić** think *l.* see fit to do sth; **uważam to za obowiązek** I consider it (to be) my duty. **6.** (= *mniemać*) consider; (*rób*) **jak uważasz** (do) as you please *l.* wish. **uważać się** *ipf.* consider o.s. (*za kogoś / coś* sb/ sth); **uważał się za wielkiego eksperta w dziedzinie inżynierii genetycznej** he considered himself a great expert on genetic engineering.

uważanie *n.* *pot.* (= *szacunek*) respect, consideration; **po uważaniu** *pot.* at sb's discretion, as one pleases.

uważnie *adv.* (= *z uwagą*) attentively, carefully; **słuchaj uważnie!** listen carefully!, pin your ears back!; (= *ostrożnie*) carefully, cautiously.

uważny *a.* **1.** (= *skoncentrowany*) attentive, intent; **uważny kierowca** careful driver. **2.** (= *baczny*) watchful, alert. **3.** (= *świadczący o uwadze*) careful; **uważne spojrzenie** intent look.

uwertura *f.* *muz.* overture; **uwertura koncertowa** *muz.* concert overture.

uwędzić *pf.* *zob.* **wędzić.**

uwędzony *a.* smoked.

uwęglać *ipf.*, **uwęglić** *pf.* *geol.* carbonify.

uwęglać się *ipf.*, **uwęglić się** *pf.* *geol.* carbonify, become carbonified.

uwęglenie *n.* *geol.* carbonification.

uwiadamiać *ipf.*, **uwiadomić** *pf.* *przest.* advise (*o czymś* of sth) notify (*o czymś* about sth).

uwiarygodnić *pf.* **-ij** (*np. opowieść szczegółami*)

lend credence to sth, lend *l.* give color to sth; (*np. podpis*) authenticate.

uwiąd *mi* **1.** *biol., med.* atrophy; **uwiąd starczy** senility, decrepitude. **2.** (= *zanik, upadek*) decay, decline.

uwiązać *pf.* **-ążę -ążesz**, **uwiązywać** *ipf.* tie up; **uwiązać na łańcuchu** chain up.

uwić *pf.* **-iję -ijesz**, **-ij** *zob.* **wić.**

uwidaczniać *ipf.* (= *unaocznić*) demonstrate; **uwidocznić czyjeś wady** demonstrate sb's vices; (= *przedstawić w widoczny sposób*) show; **na mapie uwidoczniono główne miasta** the map shows major cities. ~ **się** *ipf.* (= *dać się widzieć*) become visible, appear; **w świetle lampy uwidoczniły się szczegóły obrazu** details of the picture appeared in the lamplight; (= *ujawnić się*) manifest o.s.; **uwidocznić swój talent** manifest one's talent.

uwidocznić (się) *pf.* *zob.* **uwidaczniać (się).**

uwieczniać *ipf.*, **uwiecznić** *pf.* **-ij** immortalize.

uwiedzenie *n.* seduction.

uwielbiać *ipf.* **1.** (= *ubóstwiać, wielbić*) adore, worship. **2.** (= *bardzo lubić*) adore, love.

uwielbienie *n.* worship, adoration; **w geście uwielbienia** in adoration.

uwielokrotniać *ipf.*, **uwielokrotnić** *pf.* **-ij** multiply.

uwieńczyć *pf.* **1.** (= *ozdobić wieńcem*) wreathe, crown with wreaths; (= *ozdobić kwiatami*) adorn, crown (*with flowers*). **2.** *lit.* (= *ukoronować*) crown.

uwierać *ipf.* (= *cisnąć*) pinch; **buty mnie uwierają** my shoes are pinching.

uwierzenie *n.* **nie do uwierzenia** that's unbelievable, that's beyond belief.

uwierzyć *pf.* *zob.* **wierzyć.**

uwierzytelniać *ipf.* authenticate; **uwierzytelniać notarialnie** notarize.

uwierzytelniający *a.* **listy uwierzytelniające** *polit.* credentials.

uwierzytelnić *pf.* **-ij** *zob.* **uwierzytelniać.**

uwierzytelnienie *n.* authentication; **uwierzytelnienie notarialne** *prawn.* notarization.

uwierzytelniony *a.* authenticated; **kopia uwierzytelniona** (*np. dokumentu*) certified copy.

uwiesić (się) *pf.* **-szę -sisz** *zob.* **uwieszać (się).**

uwieszać *ipf.* hang (*coś na czymś* sth on sth). ~ **się** *ipf.* hang (*na czymś* on sth); **uwiesić się na czyimś ramieniu** *l.* **u czyjegoś ramienia** hang on sb's arm.

uwieść *pf.* **uwiodę uwiedziesz uwiódł uwiodła uwiedli** *zob.* **uwodzić.**

uwieźć *pf.* **uwiozę uwieziesz uwiózł uwiozła uwieźli** *zob.* **uwozić.**

uwiędnąć *pf.* **-dnie uwiądł** *l.* **uwiędnął uwiędła uwiędli** *zob.* **więdnąć.**

uwięzić *pf.* **-żę -zisz** **1.** (= *pozbawić wolności*) confine, incarcerate; (= *osadzić w więzieniu*) imprison, incarcerate. **2.** (= *unieruchomić*) trap.

uwięzienie *n.* imprisonment, confinement, incarceration.

uwięziony *a.* **1.** (= *pozbawiony wolności*) confined, incarcerated; (= *osadzony w więzieniu*) imprisoned, incarcerated. **2.** (= *unieruchomiony*) trapped; **zostać uwięzionym** (*np. w płonącym* *pojeździe*) get trapped; **uwięziony przez burzę** stormbound; **uwięziony w lodach** (*o statku*) icebound.

uwięznąć *pf.* **uwięznę uwięźniesz, uwięźnij, uwiązł uwiązła uwięźli** *zob.* **więznąć; uwięznąć komuś w gardle** (*np. o słowach*) stick in one's craw *l.* throat.

uwięź *f.* tie; (= *smycz*) leash; (*łańcuch*) chain; (= *linka*) cord, rope; (= *pęta*) fetters, trammels; (= *linka do trenowania sokoła*) lune; (= *cuma*) stay, guy; **trzymać na uwięzi** hold on leash; **balon na uwięzi** *meteor.* captive baloon; **spuścić z uwięzi** (*o psie*) unleash, unchain.

uwijać się *ipf.* bustle about; **uwijać się jak w ukropie** work like a beaver.

uwikłać (się) *pf. zob.* **wikłać (się)**.

uwinąć się *pf.* make short work (*z czymś* of sth); **uwinąć się z robotą** toss off the work; **no dalej, uwijaj się!** come on, make it snappy!

uwłaczać *ipf. lit. + Dat.* (= *obrażać, ubliżać*) affront (*sb*); (= *przynosić ujmę*) discredit (*sb l. sth*); **uwłaczać czyjejś godności** be beneath sb; **uwłaczać czyjejś reputacji** blacken sb's name.

uwłaczający *a.* derogatory, discreditable.

uwłasnowolnić *pf.* **-ij** *prawn.* capacitate, restore sb's legal capacity.

uwłaszczać *ipf.* grant land *l.* property to (*sb*).

uwłaszczenie *n.* (= *przyznanie ziemi chłopom*) granting land to peasants; *polit.* (= *zmiana struktury własności*) ownership reform, enfranchisement.

uwłaszczeniowy *a.* **ustawa uwłaszczeniowa** *polit.* enfranchisement act.

uwłaszczyć *pf. zob.* **uwłaszczać**.

uwłosienie *n.* (*człowieka*) hair; (*zwierzęcia*) pelage.

uwodnić *pf. chem. zob.* **uwadniać**.

uwodnienie *n. chem.* hydration.

uwodniony *a. chem.* hydrated.

uwodorniać *ipf.,* **uwodornić** *chem.* hydrogenate.

uwodornienie *n. chem.* hydrogenation.

uwodziciel *mp* seducer.

uwodzicielka *f. Gen.pl.* **-ek** seductress.

uwodzicielski *a.* seductive; (= *kokieteryjny*) coquettish; **uwodzicielskie spojrzenie** seductive *l.* enticing look.

uwodzić *ipf.* **1.** (= *bałamucić*) seduce. **2.** (= *kokietować*) coquet. **3.** (= *mamić*) beguile.

uwolnić (się) *pf.* **-ij** *zob.* **uwalniać (się)**.

uwozić *ipf.* **-żę -zisz, uwoź** *l.* **uwóź 1.** (= *wywozić*) take away, carry away. **2.** *lit.* (*o pojazdach*) (= *przewozić*) take, convey.

uwrażliwiać *ipf.,* **uwrażliwić** *pf.* sensitize (*kogoś na coś* sb to sth).

uwrocie *n.* (= *niezaorany skraj pola*) headland.

uwspółcześniać *ipf.,* **uwspółcześnić** *pf.* **-ij** modernize, contemporize.

uwspółrzędniać *ipf.,* **uwspółrzędnić** *nauk.* co-ordinate, co-ordinate.

uwsteczniać się *ipf.,* **uwstecznić się** *pf.* **-ij** regress, suffer regress; *biol.* undergo reduction *l.* involution.

uwstecznienie *n. biol.* reduction, involution.

uwsteczniony *a. biol.* reduced.

uwularny *a. jęz.* uvular.

uwydatniać *ipf.* (= *czynić bardziej widocznym*) bring out; (= *podkreślać*) stress, emphasize, accentuate. **~ się** *ipf.* **-ij** stand out, be prominent.

uwydatnić (się) *pf.* **-ij** *zob.* **uwydatniać (się)**.

uwypuklać *ipf.* **1.** (= *podkreślać wypukłość*) emboss. **2.** (= *akcentować, podkreślać*) bring out, highlight, emphasize; **uwypuklić pewne fakty** bring out certain facts in full relief. **~ się** *ipf.* **1.** (= *stawać się wypukłym*) become embossed. **2.** (= *uwidaczniać się*) stand out in full relief.

uwypuklić (się) *pf.* **-ij** *zob.* **uwypuklać (się)**.

uwzględniać *ipf.,* **uwzględnić** *pf.* **-ij 1.** (= *brać pod uwagę*) take into consideration *l.* account, allow for. **2.** (= *spełniać*) comply (*coś* with sth) respect; **uwzględnić czyjąś prośbę** comply with sb's request; **uwzględnić czyjeś żądanie** meet sb's demand.

uwzględnienie *n.* **1.** (= *wzięcie pod uwagę*) consideration, allowance (*czegoś* for sth); **z uwzględnieniem czegoś** taking sth into consideration. **2.** (= *przychylenie się*) compliance (*czegoś* with sth).

uwziąć się *pf.* **uwezmę uweźmiesz, uweźmij 1.** *pot.* (= *zawziąć się*) set one's mind, be bent (*żeby coś zrobić* on sth). **2.** *pot.* (= *prześladować*) have it in (*na kogoś* for sb); be hard (*na kogoś* on sb).

uwznioślać *ipf.,* **uwznioślić** *pf.* **-ij** elevate, sublimate.

uzależniać *ipf.,* **uzależnić** *pf.* **-ij 1.** (= *czynić zależnym*) make dependent; **uzależniać swoją decyzję od czegoś** make one's decision dependent on sth, hang one's hat on sth. **2.** (*od leków, innych substancji*) addict (*od czegoś* to sth). **~ się** *ipf.,* **uzależnić się** *pf.* **1.** (= *stawać się zależnym*) become dependent (*od kogoś / czegoś* on sb/sth). **2.** (= *wpadać w nałóg*) become addicted, addict o.s. (*od czegoś* to sth).

uzależnienie *n.* **1.** (= *zależność*) dependence, dependency, subjection. **2.** (= *nałóg*) addiction, addictive disorder, substance abuse.

uzależniony *a.* **-eni 1.** (= *zależny*) dependent, conditional, contingent (*od czegoś* on *l.* upon sth); on the hook, hooked (*od czegoś* on sth). **2.** (= *mający nałóg*) addicted (*od czegoś* to sth). – *mp pot.* (= *nałogowiec*) addict, junkie.

uzans *mi handl.* usance.

uzasadniać *ipf.,* **uzasadnić** *pf.* **-ij** justify, substantiate; demonstrate, show; (*twierdzenie, teorię*) prove, validate.

uzasadnienie *n.* justification, substantiation; **uzasadnienie wyroku** *prawn.* (judicial) opinion; **racjonalne uzasadnienie** sensible justification.

uzasadniony *a.* justified, substantiated, well-founded; (*np. o obawach, podejrzeniach*) justified; (*o krytyce*) valid, just; **uzasadniona wątpliwość** reasonable doubt.

uzbecki *a.* Uzbek.

Uzbeczka *f. Gen.pl.* **-ek, Uzbek** *mp* Uzbek.

Uzbekistan *mi geogr.* Uzbekistan.

uzbierać *pf.* **1.** (= *nazbierać*) pick, collect; **uzbierać trochę grosza** scrape together some money. **2.** (= *zgromadzić*) gather. ~ **się** *pf.* **1.** (= *nagromadzić się*) gather, accumulate. **2.** (= *zgromadzić się*) gather, get together, assemble.

uzbrajać *ipf.*, **uzbroić** *pf.* **-oję -oisz, -ój 1.** (= *dostarczać broń*) arm; **uzbrajać bombę** fuse *l.* prime a bomb. **2.** (= *wyposażyć w narzędzia, przyrządy itp.*) equip, furnish (*w coś* with sth). **3.** (= *wyposażyć w maszyny, instalacje itp.*) fit, equip, furnish (*w coś* with sth); **uzbroić teren** *bud.* improve land, provide utilities *l.* service infrastructure. ~ **się** *ipf.*, **uzbroić się** *pf.* (= *zaopatrywać się w broń*) take up arms; **uzbroić się w cierpliwość** *przen.* arm o.s. with patience.

uzbrojenie *n.* **1.** *zwł. wojsk.* (= *broń*) weapons, armament, weaponry; **ciężkie uzbrojenie** hardware; **lekkie uzbrojenie** small arms. **2.** *techn.* (= *osprzęt*) fittings, fixtures, accessories, tooling. **3.** *bud.* utilities, service infrastructure.

uzbrojony *a.* **-eni 1.** (= *mający broń*) armed, up in arms; (*o bombie*) live; **uzbrojony po zęby** armed to the teeth; **tasiemiec uzbrojony** *zool.* pork tapeworm (*Taenia solium*). **2.** (= *wyposażony*) equipped, furnished (*w coś* with sth); **teren uzbrojony** *bud.* improved land, land provided with utilities *l.* service infrastructure.

uzda *f.* bridle.

uzdalniać *ipf.* = **uzdolniać**.

uzdatniać *ipf.*, **uzdatnić** *pf.* **-ij** *techn.* treat, condition; **uzdatniać wodę** treat *l.* condition water.

uzdolniać *ipf.*, **uzdolnić** *pf.* **-ij** capacitate, enable.

uzdolnienie *n.* ability, aptitude, talent (*do czegoś* for sth).

uzdolniony *a.* **-eni** talented, gifted, able, apt.

uzdrawiacz *mp* healer, curer.

uzdrawiać *ipf.* (= *leczyć*) cure, heal; **uzdrawiać stosunki** restore *l.* improve relations.

uzdrawiająco *adv.* restoratively.

uzdrowiciel *mp* curer, (faith) healer.

uzdrowicielski *a.* healing.

uzdrowić *pf.* **-ów** *zob.* **uzdrawiać**.

uzdrowienie *n.* cure, restoration to health.

uzdrowisko *n.* health resort, spa.

uzdrowiskowy *a.* spa.

uzewnętrzniać *ipf.*, **uzewnętrznić** *pf.* **-ij** manifest, show, demonstrate. ~ **się** *ipf.*, **uzewnętrznić się** *pf.* show, manifest o.s.

uzębienie *n.* **1.** (= *zespół zębów*) dentition. **2.** *techn.* teeth, toothing.

uzębiony *a.* **1.** (= *mający zęby*) toothed. **2.** *techn.* toothed, cogged.

uzgadniać *ipf.*, **uzgodnić** *pf.* **-ij** agree; (*treść, warunki*) negotiate; **uzgodniliśmy, że...** we have agreed that...

uzgodnienie *n.* agreement, arrangement; **do uzgodnienia** negotiable.

uziarnienie *n.* *techn.* graining, granulation.

uziemiać *ipf.*, **uziemić** *pf.* **1.** *el.* ground; *gł. Br.* earth. **2.** *pot.* (= *usadzić*) steamroll(er), flatten, quash. **3.** *pot.* (= *zabijać*) do in.

uziemienie *n.* *el.* ground; *gł. Br.* earth, earthing.

uziom *mi el.* ground; *gł. Br.* earth (electrode).

uzmysławiać *ipf.*, **uzmysłowić** *pf.* **-ów** demon-

strate; **uzmysławiać coś komuś** make sb aware of sth; **uzmysławiać coś sobie** realize.

uznać *pf. zob.* **uznawać**. ~ **się** *pf. zob.* **uznawać się**.

uznanie *n.* **1.** (= *akceptacja*) acceptance, approbation; **uznanie dziecka** *prawn.* fathering a child. **2.** (= *poważanie*) respect, esteem, regard; **w uznaniu zasług** in recognition of sb's merits; **cieszyć się (czyimś) uznaniem** command (sb's) respect, be well-thought-of; **zdobyć uznanie** gain recognition. **3.** (= *opinia*) acknowledgment, recognition; **według czyjegoś uznania** at sb's discretion; **pozostawić coś do czyjegoś uznania** leave sth to sb's discretion.

uznaniowy *a.* **1.** (= *przyznawany wedle własnego uznania*) arbitrary. **2.** (= *przyznawany w nagrodę*) bonus, special.

uznany *a.* recognized, established.

uznawać *ipf.* **-aję -ajesz, -awaj 1.** (= *akceptować*) recognize, acknowledge, accept; (*rząd, osiągnięcie*) recognize; (*błąd*) admit; **uznać dziecko** *prawn.* father a child. **2.** (= *poczytywać*) regard (*kogoś za kogoś/coś* sb as sb/sth); **uznawać kogoś za kłamcę** regard sb as a liar; **uznawać coś za konieczne** deem sth necessary; **uznawać coś za wiarygodne** give credit to sth; **uznawać coś za zaszczyt** deem sth an honor; **uznawać kogoś za niepoczytalnego** *prawn.* stultify; **uznawać za akt bezprawny** *prawn.* illegalize. ~ **się** *ipf.* **1.** feel, think of o.s. as; **uznawać się winnym** admit *l.* confess one's guilt. **2.** (= *poczytywać się za*) consider o.s.; **uznać się za przywódcę** consider o.s. (to be) the leader; **uznać się za pokonanego** admit one's defeat.

uznoić *pf.* **-oję -oisz, -ój** *przest.* (= *zmęczyć*) exhaust, fatigue. ~ **się** *pf. przest.* (= *zmęczyć się*) exhaust o.s., become fatigued.

uznojony *a.* **-eni** *lit.* exhausted, fatigued.

uzupełniać *ipf.* **1.** (= *kompletować*) (*wypowiedź, strój*) complete; (*zapasy*) replenish, refresh, restock; (*dietę, wyposażenie*) supplement; **uzupełniać braki** fill in the gaps, fill in the missing parts *l.* bits; **uzupełniać zapas wody** fill up with water. **2.** (= *stanowić dopełnienie*) complement. ~ **się** *ipf.* complement each other *l.* one another.

uzupełniający *a.* additional, complementary, supplemental; **wybory uzupełniające** *polit.* by-election.

uzupełnić *pf.* **-ij** *zob.* **uzupełniać**. ~ **się** *pf. zob.* **uzupełniać się**.

uzupełnienie *n.* **1.** (*diety, wyposażenia*) supplement; (*wypowiedzi, stroju*) completion; (*zapasów*) replenishment; **komenda uzupełnień** *wojsk.* Draft Board. **2.** (= *dodatek*) supplementation, supplement; (*do przepisu, ustawy*) rider.

uzurpacja *f.* usurpation.

uzurpator *mp* usurper, impostor *l.* imposter.

uzurpatorski *a.* usurping.

uzurpować *ipf.* usurp; **uzurpować sobie coś** usurp sth, arrogate sth to o.s.

uzus *mi lit.* custom.

uzwajać *ipf.*, **uzwoić** *pf.* **-oję -oisz, -ój** *techn.* wind, coil.

uzwojenie *n. techn.* winding; **uzwojenie pier-wotne** *el.* primary winding; **uzwojenie wtórne** *el.* secondary winding.

uzysk *mi Gen.* **-u** *techn.* yield, output.

uzyskać *pf.*, **uzyskiwać** *ipf.* (= *zdobyć*) (*przewa-gę, wynik*) gain; (*pomoc, stopień naukowy, zgo-dę*) get, obtain; (*stypendium*) receive, get; (*połą-czenie*) get through.

uździe *f. zob.* **uzda.**

użalać się *ipf.*, **użalić się** *pf.* **1.** (= *narzekać*) complain (*na coś* about sth). **2.** (= *współczuć*) bewail, pity (*nad kimś* sb); **użalać się nad sobą** pity o.s.

użąć *pf.* **użnę użniesz, użnij** reap, cut.

użądlić *pf. zob.* **żądlić.**

użebrać *pf.* **-brzę -brzesz** obtain by begging.

użebrować *pf. zob.* **żebrować.**

użeglownić *pf.* **-ij** (*jezioro, rzekę*) make naviga-ble.

użerać się *ipf. pot.* (= *wykłócać się*) quarrel (*z kimś* with sb); (= *przełamywać czyjś opór, zmu-szać*) wrangle (*z kimś* with sb).

użycie *n.* **1.** (= *stosowanie*) usage, use, appli-cation; **łatwy w użyciu** easy to use; **wychodzić z użycia** go out of use, obsolesce; **bez użycia siły** nonviolently; **sposób użycia** usage. **2.** *przest.* (= *rozkosz*) pleasure, enjoyment.

użyczać *ipf.*, **użyczyć** *pf.* **1.** *lit.* (= *pożyczać*) lend, spare, grant. **2.** *lit.* (= *udzielać*) accord; (*schronienia*) afford.

użyć *pf.* **użyję użyjesz** *zob.* **używać.**

użyteczność *f.* **1.** (= *przydatność*) usability, usefulness, utility. **2.** *form.* (= *używanie*) use, usage; **zakład użyteczności publicznej** public utility.

użyteczny *a.* **1.** (= *przydatny*) usable; **ciężar użyteczny** *gł. lotn.* payload; **kopalina użyteczna** *górn.* useful mineral. **2.** (= *pomocny*) useful (*dla kogoś* for sb).

użytek *mi* **-tk-** use; **do użytku wewnętrznego/zewnętrznego** *med.* for internal/external use; **zdatny do użytku** in working order, serviceable; **na użytek osobisty** for personal use; **jednorazo-**

wego użytku disposable; **wielokrotnego użytku** reusable; (*o zbiorniku, pojemniku*) refillable; **zrobić z czegoś użytek** make use of sth.

użytki *pl. Gen.* **-ów** (= *tereny uprawne*) arable land; **użytki leśne** forest products; **użytki zielone** grassland, pastures.

użytkować *ipf. lit.* (= *używać*) utilize, use; (*za-soby*) exploit.

użytkowanie *n.* **1.** (= *używanie*) exploitation. **2.** *prawn.* usufruct; **wspólne użytkowanie** com-monage; **użytkowanie wieczyste** perpetual lease *l.* usufruct.

użytkownik *mp* **1.** (= *osoba, instytucja posłu-gująca się czymś*) user; **użytkownik końcowy** end user; **użytkownik języka** *jęz.* speaker; **przyjazny dla użytkownika** (*o programie, interfejsie*) user-friendly. **2.** *prawn.* usufructuary, holder, ten-ant.

użytkowy *a.* utilitarian, useful, usable; **grunt użytkowy** *roln.* arable land; **program użytkowy** *komp.* application; **powierzchnia użytkowa** *bud.* usable area; **rośliny użytkowe** *roln.* crop plants; **sztuka użytkowa** applied art.

używać *ipf.* **-am -asz** **1.** (= *stosować*) use, em-ploy; (*autorytetu*) interpose; (*aplikacji*) *komp.* run. **2.** (= *wykorzystywać*) use (*do czegoś* for sth *l.* to do sth); **użyć uroku osobistego** turn on the charm; **użyć wpływów** pull strings *l.* wires; **użyć radykalnych środków** roll out the big guns. **3.** (= *zażywać*) use; (*leków*) take; **używać perfum** wear perfume. **4.** (= *korzystać z czegoś*) take advan-tage; **używać życia** live it up; **używać sobie** be on the loose, binge on sth.

używalność *f.* usability; **w stanie używalności** in working order, usable; **doprowadzić coś do stanu używalności** rehabilitate sth.

używalny *a.* in working order, usable.

używanie *n.* use, wear; **mieć używanie** *pot.* have a field day.

używany *a.* used, secondhand.

używka *f. Gen.pl.* **-ek** stimulant.

użyźniać *ipf.*, **użyźnić** *pf.* **-ij** fertilize.

V

V, v *n. indecl.* (*litera*) V, v; **V jak Violetta** V is for Victor; V as in Victor.

V *abbr. fiz., el.* (= *wolt*) V (= *volt*).

va banque *adv.* **zagrać va banque** put everything at stake.

vademecum *n. indecl.* reference book, handbook, vade mecum.

varia *pl. Gen.* **-iów** miscellany, miscellanea.

VAT *abbr. i mi Loc.* **Vacie** *ekon.* VAT (= *value added tax*); **podlegający opodatkowaniu VAT-em** *l.* **podatkiem VAT** liable to VAT; *pot.* VATable.

VAT-owski *a.* VAT; **faktura VAT-owska** VAT invoice.

vel *conj.* a.k.a. (= *also known as*); alias.

vendetta *f. Loc.* **-tcie** vendetta.

versus *conj. form.* versus, vs.

veto *n.* **1.** *polit.* = **weto**. **2.** *hist.* **liberum veto** right to suspend all parliamentary proceedings (*possessed by every member of parliament in 17th-18th c. Poland*).

via *prep.* + *Nom.* via; **polecę do Nowego Jorku via Frankfurt** I'll fly to New York via Frankfurt.

vice versa *adv.* vice versa.

vide *int. form.* see, cf., compare.

video *n. indecl.* = **wideo**.

viola *f. muz.* viola; **viola da gamba/d'amore** viola da gamba/d'amore.

VIP *mp pl.* **VIP-y** VIP (= *very important person*).

vis-à-vis *adv. i prep.* + *Gen.* opposite. – *n. indecl.* **moje/twoje/jego/jej vis-à-vis** the person opposite me/you/him/her.

vivace *adv. muz.* vivace.

voto *adv. lit.* (*przed nazwiskiem kobiety*) **primo/ secundo/tertio voto** first/second/third married name.

votum separatum *n. indecl.* **1.** *gł. polit.* note of dissent. **2. złożyć votum separatum** submit a note of dissent (*wobec czegoś* on sth *l.* regarding sth).

voucher *mi* tourist voucher.

vs. *abbr.* = **versus**.

W, w *n. indecl.* (*litera*) W, w; **W jak Wacław** W is for Whiskey; W as in Whiskey.

W *abbr. fiz.* W (= *watt*).

w *prep. + Loc.* **1.** (*miejsce, lokalizacja*) in, at, inside; **w domu** at home; **w pracy** at work; **w kinie** at the movie theater; *Br.* at the cinema; **w górach** in the mountains; **w lesie** in the forest; **w szklance** in a glass; **w samochodzie** in the car; **w pociągu** on the train; **w areszcie** in detention; **w biurze** at the office; **w odległości stu metrów** 100 meters away, within 100 meters; **w prasie** in the papers; **w radiu** on the radio; **w telewizji** on TV; **w wojsku** in the army; **w sądzie** in court; **w pamięci** in memory; **w wyobraźni** in one's imagination; **w sercu** in one's heart; **w duchu** in one's soul; **zimno mi w nogi** my feet are cold. **2.** (*okoliczności*) in; **w bójce** in fight; **w płomieniach** in flames; **w trzech tomach** in three volumes; **w dwóch egzemplarzach** in two copies; **w skrócie** in short; **w poszukiwaniu prawdy** in search for the truth; **w części (odnowiony)** partly (redecorated). **3.** (*stan*) in; **w chorobie** in illness; **w gorączce** in fever; **w miłości** in love; **w milczeniu** in silence; **w nędzy** in poverty; **w panice** in panic; **w budowie** under construction; **w blasku sławy** in a blaze of glory; **być w dobrym humorze** be in a good mood; **być w błędzie** be mistaken; **coś jest w modzie** sth is in vogue *l.* fashion. **4.** (*ograniczenie*) in; **w pasie** round the waist; **szorstki w dotyku** rough to the touch; **szczupła w biodrach** slim-hipped; **miły w kontaktach osobistych** pleasant in personal relations. **5.** (*ubiór lub jego część*) in; **w futrze** in a fur coat; **w okularach** wearing glasses; **w kapeluszu** with a hat on, in a hat; **kobieta w bieli** a woman in white. **6.** (*to, w czym się coś trzyma*) in; **w ręce** in hand; **w pułapce** in a trap; **trzymać kogoś w ramionach** hold sb in one's arms. **7.** (*postać*) in; **mydło w płynie** liquid soap; **cukier w kostkach** cube sugar; **rzeźba w marmurze** sculpture in marble; **milion dolarów w złocie** a million dollars in gold; **1000 zł w banknotach stuzłotowych** a thousand zlotys in one hundred zloty bills; *Br.* a thousand zlotys in one hundred zloty notes. **8.** (*typ działania*) in; **dostać (coś) w prezencie** get *l.* receive (sth) as a present; **płacić w gotówce/ratach** pay in cash/in installments. **9.** *+ Acc.* (*kierunek*) in, to; **w lewo/prawo** to the left/right; **w dół/górę** downwards/upwards; **patrzeć w niebo** look up in the sky; **pojechać w góry** go to the mountains; **wyjść w morze** set sail. **10.** (*kształt, właściwość*) in; **w kratkę** checked, checkered, *Br.* chequered; **w kwiaty**

flowered, millefleurs; **w paski** striped; **w parach** in pairs; **pokroić (coś) w kostkę** cut (sth) into cubes, cube (sth). **11.** (*przedmiot działania*) on, in; **bić w dzwony** ring the bells; **celować w serce** aim at the heart; **inwestować w swoją przyszłość** invest in one's future; **uderzyć się w palec** (*u nogi*) stub one's toe; (*u ręki*) hit one's finger; **uderzyć się w głowę** get a bang on the head; **walić w drzwi** bang on the door; **wdać się w bójkę** get into a fight; **wierzyć w Boga** believe in God; **wprawić w zdumienie** astonish, amaze; **puknij się w czoło** are you out of senses? **12.** *+ Acc.* (*całość*) in; **w całości** in full; **w pełni** to the full; **w całym słowa tego znaczeniu** par excellence; **układać fakty w logiczną całość** arrange facts logically. **13.** *+ Acc.* (*wyposażenie*) with; **uzbrojony w karabin** armed with a gun; **wyposażony w narzędzia** equipped with tools; **obfitować w ryby** swarm *l.* teem with fish; **zaopatrzyć w żywność** provide with food. **14.** *+ Acc.* (*sposób*) in; **rozumieć w lot** be quick on the uptake; **śmiać się w głos** laugh up *l.* in one's sleeve; **wyciąć w pień** kill every last one; **żyć w nędzy** live in poverty. **15.** *+ Acc.* (*cel*) in; **grać w karty** play cards; **pójść (do kogoś) w odwiedziny** pay (sb) a visit; **zapaść w sen** lapse into sleep, fall asleep. **16.** *+ Acc.* (*skutek*) into; **obrócić się w popiół** turn to dust; **rozpaść się w kawałki** fall into pieces; **śpiew przerodził się w krzyk** the singing turned into a scream. **17.** *+ Acc.* (*odczucia*) in; **być w dobrym humorze** be in a good mood; **leżeć w bólach** be lying in pains. **18.** *+ Acc. l. Loc.* (*czas*) at, on, in; **we wtorek** on Tuesday; **w dzień** during the day, by day; **w południe** at noon; **w nocy** at night; **w maju** in May; **w roku 1995** in 1995; **w lecie** in the summer; **w porze lunchu** at lunchtime; **w czasie urlopu** during the holiday; **w dniu ślubu** on the wedding day; **w wieczór wigilijny** on Christmas Eve; **w rok po spotkaniu** a year after the meeting; **w godzinę po twoim wyjściu** an hour after you left; **w ostatniej chwili** at the last minute *l.* moment, at the eleventh hour; **w ostatnich latach** in recent years; **w biały dzień** in broad daylight; **w młodości** in one's youth; **dzień w dzień** day after day.

w. *abbr.* c. (= *century*); **XX w.** the 20th c.; *pot.* C20.

wab *mi* -**bi-** *Gen.* -**a** *myśl.* decoy; **na wabia** as a decoy; **mieć wabia** be appealing.

wabić *ipf.* **1.** (= *nęcić*) allure, entice; **wabić kogoś zalotnym uśmiechem** lure sb with a tempting smile. **2.** (= *nazywać zwierzę*) call. **3.** *myśl.* decoy. **4.** (*o zwierzętach*) (= *przywoływać*) call.

~ **się** *ipf.* **1.** (*o zwierzęciu*) (= *mieć na imię*) be called; **pies wabił się Reksio** the dog was called Reksio, the dog's name was Reksio. **2.** (*o zwierzętach*) (= *przywoływać się*) call; **w zbożu wabiły się przepiórki** quails were calling one another in the corn.

wabik *mi Gen.* **-a 1.** (= *to co przyciąga uwagę*) *handl.* hook, come-on. **2.** *myśl.* decoy; (*dźwiękowy*) call.

wachlarz *mi Gen.* **-a 1.** (*do wachlowania*) fan; (*z liści palmy*) punkah. **2.** (= *różnorodność*) array; (*możliwości, propozycji, spraw, tematów*) range; **szeroki wachlarz zainteresowań** a vast array of interests. **3.** *myśl.* woodgrouse's tail.

wachlarzoskrzydłe *pl. ent.* strepsiterons, strepsiterans (*Strepsitera*).

wachlarzyk *mi Gen.* **-a** fan.

wachlować *ipf.* **1.** (= *chłodzić*) fan; **wachlować twarz chusteczką** fan one's face with a handkerchief. **2.** *przen.* (= *poruszać miarowo*) sway. ~ **się** *ipf.* fan o.s.

wachmistrz *mp pl.* **-e** *l.* **-owie** *Gen.* **-ów** *wojsk.* cavalry sergeant.

wachta *f. żegl.* (*warta*) (*załoga*) watch; **nocna/ poranna wachta** night/morning watch.

wachtowy *a. żegl.* (*o oficerze, służbie*) watch. – *mp* watch, sailor on watch.

waciak *mi Gen.* **-a** quilted jacket.

wacik *mi Gen.* **-a** cotton pad; (*do opatrywania ran*) pledget; *chir.* swab.

wada *f.* **1.** (= *przywara*) fault, vice; **nikt nie jest bez wad** nobody's perfect; **pomimo wszystkich swoich wad** for all his *l.* her faults. **2.** (= *cecha ujemna*) disadvantage, drawback (*czegoś* of sth); **zalety i wady mieszkania na wsi** advantages and disadvantages of living in the country, pros and cons of living in the country. **3.** (= *defekt fizyczny*) defect, flaw (*w czymś* in sth); **wada serca** cardiac defect; **wada słuchu** hearing impediment; **wada wymowy** speech defect, speech impediment; **wada wzroku/postawy** sight/posture defect; **wada genetyczna** genetic defect; **wada wrodzona** congenital defect. **4.** (= *usterka*) (*np. techniczna*) defect, fault; **wada ukryta** hidden flaw.

wademekum *n. indecl.* handbook, manual; *rzad.* vade mecum.

wadera *f. myśl.* she-wolf.

wadery *pl. Gen.* **-ów** (*spodnie*) waders.

wadialny *a.* (*o wypłacie, karze*) deposit.

wadis *mi geogr., geol.* wadi, wady.

wadium *n. sing. indecl. pl.* **-dia** *Gen.* **-diów** *handl.* bid bond, deposit.

wadliwie *adv.* defectively, faultily; **działać wadliwie** malfunction.

wadliwość *f.* (*artykułu, towaru*) defectiveness, faultiness; (*stylu*) inadequacy.

wadliwy *a.* (*postawa, wymowa*) defective; (*montaż*) faulty; (*styl*) inadequate.

wadzić *ipf. lit.* (= *być przeszkodą*) be in the way, hinder; **wadzić komuś swoją obecnością** be a nuisance to sb; **nie wadziłoby zapalić** it would do no harm to have a smoke.

wafel *mi* **-fl-** *Gen.* **-a** (*do lodów*) cone; *Br. t.* cornet; (*ciasto*) wafer.

wafelek *mi* **-lk-** *Gen.* **-a** wafer; (*w czekoladzie*) chocolate crispy bar.

waflowy *a.* (*np. o torcie*) wafer.

waga *f.* **1.** (*przyrząd*) scales, balance; **waga analityczna** analytical balance; **waga aptekarska** dispensing balance; **waga kuchenna/łazienkowa** kitchen/bathroom scales; **waga laboratoryjna/ elektroniczna/optyczna** lab/electronic/optic scales; **miary i wagi** weights and measures; **być języczkiem u wagi** tip the balance. **2.** (= *ważenie*) weight; **oszukiwać na wadze** give short weight; **sprzedawać na wagę** sell by weight. **3.** (= *ciężar*) weight; **waga netto** net weight; **waga brutto** gross weight; **przyrost wagi** weight gain; **utrata wagi** weight loss; **sto kilo żywej wagi** *żart.* Mr. Five-by-five; **woda jest na wagę złota** water is like gold; **tracić na wadze** *l.* **zrzucić wagę** lose weight; **przybrać na wadze** put on weight. **4.** (= *ważność*) importance, significance; (*problemu*) magnitude; **sprawy wagi państwowej** matters of state; **przywiązywać wagę do czegoś** assign *l.* attach importance to sth; **znikomej/wielkiej wagi** of little/great importance; **być dla kogoś sprawą pierwszorzędnej wagi** be high on sb's agenda. **5.** *sport* weight; **waga musza** flyweight; **waga piórkowa** featherweight; **waga lekka** lightweight; **waga półśrednia** welterweight; **waga półciężka** light heavyweight; *Br. t.* cruiserweight; **waga średnia** middleweight; **waga ciężka** heavyweight; **waga kogucia** bantamweight. **6.** *gimnastyka* arabesque. **7.** *astron.* Libra. **8.** *astrol.* Libra; the Scales, the Balance.

wagabunda *mp lit.* vagrant, vagabond.

wagant *mp hist.* goliard.

wagarować *ipf. szkoln.* play truant, play hooky.

wagarowicz *mp Gen.pl.* **-ów** *szkoln.* truant, hooky player.

wagary *pl. Gen.* **-ów** *szkoln.* truancy, hooky; **chodzić na wagary** play truant, play hooky.

wagon *mi* (*osobowy*) car; *Br.* carriage, coach; (*towarowy*) freight car; *Br.* wagon; **wagon bagażowy** baggage car; *Br.* luggage van; **wagon barowy** buffet car; **wagon bydlęcy** stock car; *Br.* cattle truck; **wagon chłodnia** refrigerator car; *Br.* refrigerator wagon; **wagon cysterna** tank car; *Br.* tank wagon; **wagon pocztowy** mailcar; *Br.* mailcoach; **wagon pulmanowski** Pullman car, Pullman; **wagon restauracyjny** dining car, restaurant car; **wagon silnikowy** railcar; **wagon sypialny** sleeping car.

wagonetka *f. Gen.pl.* **-ek** trolley.

wagonik *mi Gen.* **-a 1.** (*w kopalni*) trolley. **2.** (*kolei linowej*) cable railway car, cabin.

wagonownia *f.* carriage and wagon depot.

wagowy *a.* **1.** (*dotyczący przyrządu*) scale, balance; **mechanizm wagowy** scale work. **2.** (*dotyczący ciężaru*) (*o kategoriach*) weight. **3.** (*o odczycie*) gravimetric.

wahacz *mi Gen.* **-a** *techn.* rocker, rocker arm.

wahać się *ipf.* **1.** (= *poruszać się miarowo*) sway, rock. **2.** (= *oscylować*) (*np. o liczbie*) waver, fluctuate; **wahać się w granicach od... do...** run from... to...; **inflacja waha się w granicach 3%** inflation is hovering at 3%; **ich wiek waha się pomiędzy... a...** they range in age from... to... **3.** *tylko ipf.* (= *nie móc się zdecydować*) hesitate, waver; **nie wahając się** without hesitation, unhesitatingly; **nie wahać się czegoś powiedzieć** make no bones about saying sth. **4.** *techn.* oscillate (*pomiędzy czymś a czymś* between sth and sth).

wahadełko *n. Gen.pl.* **-łek** pendulum.

wahadło *n. Gen.pl.* **-deł 1.** (*np. zegara*) pendulum; **ruch wahadła** swing of the pendulum. **2.** *sport* swing. **3.** *pot.* (*pociąg, autobus kursujący tam i z powrotem*) shuttle.

wahadłowiec *mi* **-wc-** *Gen.* **-a** *lotn.* space shuttle.

wahadłowy *a.* (*o ruchu*) pendular, swinging; (*o locie, rejsie, przewozach*) shuttle; **drzwi wahadłowe** swing *l.* swinging door; **pociąg wahadłowy** shuttle train, down and up train; **zegar wahadłowy** pendulum clock.

wahanie *n.* **1.** (= *niezdecydowanie*) hesitation, wavering; **chwila wahania** a moment of hesitation; **z wahaniem** hesitantly, waveringly; **bez chwili wahania** without a moment's hesitation; **robić coś bez wahania** have no hesitation in doing sth, do sth without demur. **2.** (= *zmienność*) (*cen, kursu walut, temperatury*) fluctuation (*czegoś* in sth).

wahliwy *a.* swinging.

wahnięcie *n.* (*kursu walut, temperatury*) fluctuation.

wajcha *f. pot.* stick, shift.

wajdelota *mp hist.* Lithuanian bard.

wakacje *pl. Gen.* **-i** vacation, holidays; *Br.* holiday; **wakacje letnie** summer vacation, summer holiday; **wakacje zimowe** winter holidays; **wakacje podatkowe** tax holidays; **przez wakacje** over the holidays; **być na wakacjach** be on vacation; **wyjechać na wakacje** go on vacation.

wakacyjny *a.* vacation; *Br.* holiday; **kurs wakacyjny** vacation course, summer school; **praca wakacyjna** summer job; **sezon wakacyjny** holiday season; **szczyt wakacyjny** high summer season.

wakat *mi* **1.** (*posada*) vacancy, vacant post; **wypełnić wakat** fill a vacancy. **2.** *druk.* blank page.

wakcynacja *f. med.* vaccination.

wakcynoterapia *f. Gen.* **-ii** *med.* vaccination therapy, vaccinotherapy.

wakować *ipf. lit.* be vacant; **wakujące stanowisko** vacancy.

wakuola *f. biol.* vacuole.

wal[1] *ma* **wal biały** *zool.* white whale, beluga (*Delphinapterus leucas*); **wal grenlandzki** bowhead (*Balaena mysticetus*); **wal szary** gray whale (*Eschrichtius glaucus*).

wal[2] *chem.* gram equivalent.

walać *ipf. pot.* dirty; (*atramentem*) blot. **~ się** *ipf. pot.* **1.** (= *brudzić się*) soil (*one's hands*). **2.** (= *być brudzonym*) get dirty; **płaszcz walał mu się w błocie** his coat was getting smeared in mud. **3.** (= *poniewierać się*) lie about, be scattered.

walansjenka *f.* Valenciennes lace, Valenciennes.

walc *mi Gen. i Acc.* **-a** waltz; **walc angielski** hesitation waltz, boston; **walc wiedeński** quick waltz; **tańczyć walca** waltz, dance a waltz.

walcować *ipf.* **1.** (= *ugniatać*) roll, press. **2.** *metal.* roll, laminate.

walcownia *f. Gen.pl.* **-i** rolling mill.

walcowniczy *a.* (*o technologii, urządzeniach*) rolling mill.

walcownik *mp* mill operator.

walcowy *a.* cylindrical; **młyn walcowy** *techn.* roller mill; **sklepienie walcowe** *bud.* barrel vault, wagon vault, tunnel vault.

walcówka *f. metal.* billet.

walczyć *ipf.* **1.** (*bić się*) fight (*z kimś/czymś* against sb/sth); **walczyć do ostatniej kropli krwi** *l.* **do upadłego** fight to the bitter end; **walczyć na śmierć i życie** fight to the death; **walczyć o wolność/niepodległość** fight for freedom/independence; **walczyć w obronie ojczyzny** fight for one's country; **walczyć z wrogiem** fight the enemy; **walczyć zaciekle** fight tooth and nail; **walczyć jak lew** fight like a lion; **walczyć z kimś jego własną bronią** fight fire with fire; **walczyć z wiatrakami** tilt at windmills. **2.** *sport* (= *rywalizować*) compete, fight (*o coś* for sth). **3.** (*z uczuciami, siłami natury*) struggle, fight (*z czymś* with sth); (*z chorobą, pokusą, ze snem*) fight off (*z czymś* sth); (*ze łzami*) fight back, suppress (*z czymś* sth); **walczyć z czasem** (*np. pracując nad czymś*) work against the clock; **walczyć z przeciwnościami** grapple with difficulties; **walczyć ze śmiercią** be fighting with death. **4.** (= *zabiegać o coś*) (*o pokój, o wzrost wydajności pracy*) strive (*o coś* for sth); **walczyć o sprawę** fight for a cause; **walczyć o władzę** struggle for power.

walczyk *mi Gen.* **-a** quick waltz.

walec *mi* **-lc-** *Gen.* **-a 1.** *geom.* cylinder. **2.** (*maszyna drogowa*) roadroller; **walec parowy** steamroller. **3.** *techn.* roller.

walecznie *adv.* gallantly, bravely.

waleczność *f.* gallantry, bravery.

waleczny *a.* (*o żołnierzu, rycerzu*) gallant, brave; (*o czynie*) courageous, heroic; **Krzyż Walecznych** Cross of Valor, *Br.* Cross of Valour.

walenrodyzm *mi lit.* false loyalty towards the enemy of one's fatherland with the purpose of bringing them to ruin (*after Adam Mickiewicz's Konrad Wallenrod*).

walentynka *f. Gen.pl.* **-ek** (*kartka*) valentine, valentine card; **walentynki** Saint Valentine's Day.

waleń *ma zool.* (= *ssak z rzędu Cetacea*) cetacean.

waleriana *f.* **1.** *bot.* valerian, allheal (*Valeriana*). **2.** (*krople*) valerian.

walerianowy *a.* **krople walerianowe** valerian.

walet *ma karty* jack, knave; **walet kier/trefl** jack of hearts/clubs; **na waleta** *pot.* (= *nago*) in the altogether, stark naked; **spać na waleta** *pot.* sleep head to tail; **mieszkać na waleta** *pot.* crash out at sb's place.

waletować *ipf. pot.* crash out (*u kogoś* with sb *l.* at sb's place).

Walia *f. Gen.* **-ii** *geogr.* Wales; (*walijska nazwa kraju*) Cymru; **Nowa Południowa Walia** New South Wales.

walić *ipf.* **1.** *pot.* (= *uderzać*) hammer, lash (*w coś* at sth); (*np. o samochodzie*) bump (*w coś* into sth); (*o sercu*) pound, thump; (*w instrument*) pound away (*w coś* at sth); **walić głową w mur** *przen.* bang one's head against a brick wall; **walnąć pięścią w stół** bang one's fist on the table; **walić na oślep** hit with abandon, hit out; **walić konia** *obsc.* jerk off; *Br. t.* toss off; **serce mi waliło (jak młotem)** my heart was pounding, my heart was thumping; **wali mnie to!** *pot.* I don't give a damn! **2.** *pot.* (= *rzucić*) chuck, throw; **walnąć coś na podłogę** hurl sth on the floor. **3.** *pot.* (= *strzelać*) shower missiles, shell. **4.** *tylko ipf.* (= *burzyć*) knock down, tear down. **5.** *tylko ipf. pot.* (= *wydobywać się*) gush, stream; **para wali z rury** steam is gushing from the pipe. **6.** *tylko ipf. pot.* (= *padać*) (*o śniegu, deszczu*) fall; **śnieg wali płatami** snow is falling heavily, snow is coming in flakes. **7.** *tylko ipf. pot.* (= *iść*) tear along, go full blast; (*gromadnie*) crowd, stream. **8.** *tylko ipf. pot.* (= *mówić wprost*) speak bluntly; **walić prosto z mostu** talk straight from the shoulder, shoot from the hip. **9.** *wulg.* (= *odbywać stosunek*) fuck; **walić kogoś w dupę** *t. przen.* fuck sb in the ass. **~ się** *ipf.* **1.** *tylko ipf.* (= *rozpadać się*) collapse; (= *przewracać się*) fall down, collapse; **świat się wali** the world is falling apart, the world is collapsing; **walić się na głowę** (*o kłopotach, dużej ilości pracy*) weigh down; **praca mi się wali na głowę** I am snowed under with work, I am weighed down with *l.* by work. **2.** *pot.* (= *bić się wzajemnie*) hit one another. **3.** *pot.* (= *uderzać się*) hit o.s.; **walić się w piersi** beat one's chest; **walnął się w głowę** he hit himself on the head. **4.** *pot.* (= *spadać*) fall down, tumble down; **walnąć się do łóżka** *l.* spać hit the sack; **walić się z nóg** be ready to drop, be dog tired. **5.** *tylko ipf. pot.* (= *odpadać, spadać*) (*np. o tynku*) fall off, peel off. **6.** *wulg.* (= *kopulować*) fuck; **walić się jak króliki** fuck like rabbits.

waligóra *mp pl.* **-y** *l.* **-owie** fairy tale giant (*who could move mountains*).

Walijczyk *mp* Welshman, Cambrian.

Walijka *f. Gen.pl.* **-ek** Welshwoman, Cambrian.

walijski *a.* Welsh, Cambrian; **harfa walijska** Welsh harp.

walisneria *f. bot.* tape grass (*Vallisneria*).

walizka *f. Gen.pl.* **-ek** suitcase; **siedzieć na walizkach** live out of a suitcase.

walizkowy *a.* (*o maszynie do pisania, do szycia*) portable.

walka *f.* **1.** (*starcie*) fight (*z kimś / czymś* against sb/sth) (*o coś* for sth); (*np. o dobre miejsce, bilety*) scramble (*o coś* for sth); **walka o wolność/niepodległość/władzę** struggle for freedom/independence/power; **walka partyzancka** partisan struggle, guerilla war; **walka powietrzna** aerial combat; **walka zbrojna** armed combat; **walki we-**

wnętrzne *polit.* domestic conflicts; **walka na śmierć i życie** life-and-death struggle, mortal combat; **walka do upadłego** last-ditch battle; **czysta walka** clean fight; **nierówna walka** unequal fight; **odebrać komuś wolę walki** take the fight out of sb; **rwać się do walki** be spoiling for a fight; **stanąć do walki z kimś** draw one's sword against sb. **2.** (= *rywalizacja*) battle, competition; **walka ekonomiczna/polityczna/parlamentarna** economic/political/parliamentary battle; **walka o byt** fight for existence; **walka o przetrwanie** fight for survival; **walka klas** *polit.* class struggle. **3.** *sport* fight; **walka na pięści** fistfight; **walka byków** bullfighting; **walki kogutów** cockfighting; **walka psów** dogfight; **walka wręcz** unarmed combat. **4.** (= *zmaganie się*) struggle, fight (*z czymś* against *l.* sth); **walka ze zmęczeniem** struggle with fatigue; **walka ze złem** fight against the evil; **walka z przestępczością** crackdown on crime; **walka z wiatrakami** tilting at windmills.

walkiria *f. mit.* Valkyrie, Walkyrie.

walkman *mi Gen.* **-a** Walkman®, personal stereo.

walkower *mi sport* walkover; **wygrać walkowerem** walk over, win by a walkover; **przegrać walkowerem** lose by a walkover.

walnąć *ipf.* **-ij** *zob.* **walić**. **~ się** *ipf. zob.* **walić się**.

walnie *adv. lit.* significantly; **walnie przyczynić się do czegoś** (*o czymś*) be instrumental in (doing) sth; (*o kimś*) make a major contribution to sth.

walny *a.* **1.** (= *istotny*) significant, instrumental. **2.** (*o zgromadzeniu, zjeździe, zebraniu*) (= *ogólny*) general; **walne zgromadzenie** general assembly; **walne zgromadzenie akcjonariuszy** annual general meeting.

Walon *mp* Walloon.

Walonia *f. geogr.* Wallonia.

walonki *pl. Gen.* **-nek** felt boots.

walor *mi* **1.** (= *wartość*) value, virtue; (*filmu, powieści*) quality; **walory poznawcze/artystyczne** cognitive/artistic values; **walory smakowe** taste values. **2.** *fot., mal.* value.

walory *pl. Gen.* **-ów** *ekon.* (= *papiery wartościowe*) securities; (= *kosztowności*) valuables.

waloryzacja *f.* (*płac, podatków*) indexation.

waloryzować *ipf.* (*płace, podatki*) index.

waltornia *f. Gen.pl.* **-i** French horn.

waltornista *mp* French horn player.

waluciarstwo *n. pot.* black market currency trafficking.

waluciarz *mp pot.* black market currency trafficker.

waluta *f.* **1.** (*pieniądze*) currency; **koszyk walut** basket of currencies; **wymiana walut** foreign exchange; **kursy wymiany walut** foreign exchange rates. **2.** (*system pieniężny*) currency; **twarda/miękka waluta** hard/soft currency; **waluta wymienialna** convertible currency; **waluta złota/papierowa** gold/paper currency. **3.** *pot.* (= *pieniądze zagraniczne*) foreign money. **4.** *pot.* (= *gotówka*) cash, green.

walutowy a. (*o polityce, reformie*) monetary, currency; **kurs walutowy** foreign exchange rate; **kryzys walutowy** monetary crisis; **przepisy walutowe** currency regulations; **rynek walutowy** foreign exchange market; **system walutowy** currency standard; **Międzynarodowy Fundusz Walutowy** International Monetary Fund.

wał mi 1. (*usypisko*) embankment; (*przeciwpowodziowy*) levee; **wał kolejowy** railway embankment; **wał obronny** bulwark, rampart; **wał wysokiego ciśnienia** meteor. ridge of high pressure. 2. (= *walec*) roller. 3. techn. shaft; **wał przegubowy** cardan shaft; **wał korbowy** crankshaft; **wał napędowy** drive shaft, propeller shaft; **wał rozrządu** camshaft. 4. wulg. (= *penis*) rod, cock. – mp pl. -y obelż. asshole; **ty wale!** you asshole!

wałach ma gelding.

wałek mi -łk- Gen. -a 1. roller; (*tapczanu, kanapy*) bolster; (*do ciasta*) rolling pin. 2. mech. roller.

wałęsać się ipf. pot. rove about, roam about.

wałkonić się ipf. pot. loaf around.

wałkoń mp Gen.pl. -i l. -ów pot. loafer, idler.

wałkować ipf. 1. (= *rozpłaszczać*) (*ciasto*) roll out, flatten. 2. (= *zwijać w wałek*) (*np. plastelinę*) roll up. 3. pot. (= *omawiać wielokrotnie*) go over and over.

wałkowy a. techn. roller; **przenośnik wałkowy** roller conveyor; **łożysko wałkowe** pin bearing.

wałować ipf. roln. (*pole, boisko*) roll.

wałówka f. Gen.pl. -ek pot. (*na wycieczkę*) packed lunch; żart. (*np. przywieziona z domu*) care package.

wam pron. zob. **wy**.

wamp mp Nom.pl. i Acc.pl. -y vamp, vampire; **zrobiona na wampa** done up to kill.

wampir mp pl. -y 1. mit. vampire. 2. (= *seryjny morderca*) serial killer. – ma zool. vampire bat, vampire (*Desmodus*).

wampirzyca f. 1. mit. (woman) vampire. 2. (*kobieta demoniczna*) vamp, vampire.

wanad mi chem. vanadium.

wanadowiec mi -wc- Gen. -a chem. vanadium group element.

Wandal mp hist. Vandal.

wandal mp vandal.

wandalizm mi vandalism.

wandalski a. Vandalic; (*o czynie*) vandalistic, vandal.

wanienka f. 1. (*dla dzieci*) baby bath. 2. (*w laboratorium*) tub.

wanilia f. Gen. -ii bot. (*roślina*) (*owoc*) (*przyprawa*) vanilla (*Vanilla*); **laska wanilii** vanilla pod.

wanilina f. chem. vanillin.

wanilinowy a. chem. vanillin, vanillic.

waniliowy a. vanilla; **cukier waniliowy** vanilla sugar; **esencja waniliowa** l. **olejek waniliowy** vanilla essence; **lody waniliowe** vanilla ice-cream.

wanna f. Gen.pl. **wanien** 1. (*do kąpieli*) bath, bathtub; **wanna z hydromasażem** whirlpool bath. 2. techn. tank; **wanna elektrolityczna** cell;

wanna galwanizerska electroplating tank l. bath.

wannowy a. techn. bath; **piec wannowy** pot furnace.

wanta f. żegl. shroud.

wapiennik mi Gen. -a 1. (*kopalnia*) limestone quarry. 2. (*fabryka*) limestone plant. 3. (*piec*) limekiln.

wapiennolubny a. bot. calcicolous; **roślina wapiennolubna** calcicole.

wapienny[1] a. (*związany z wapieniem*) limestone; **skała wapienna** limestone.

wapienny[2] a. (*związany z wapniem*) calcium, calcic; (*o glebie*) lime; **farba wapienna** calcimine; **mleko wapienne** whitewash; **woda wapienna** limewater.

wapienny[3] a. (*związany z wapnem*) lime, calcic.

wapień mi limestone.

wapniak mi Gen. -a (*skała*) limestone; (*zmielony*) ground limestone. – mp pl. -i pot. (*człowiek starszy*) fossil, fogy.

wapnieć ipf. (*o naczyniach krwionośnych, tkankach, kościach*) calcify.

wapniowiec mi -wc- Gen. -a chem. calcium group element.

wapniowy a. calcium, calcic; **nawozy wapniowe** calcium fertilizers; **węglan wapniowy** chem. calcium carbonate.

wapno n. lime; **wapno gaszone** slaked lime; **wapno palone** l. **niegaszone** burnt lime, quicklime; **wapno nawozowe** lime.

wapnować ipf. 1. (*bielić*) whitewash. 2. (*nawozić*) lime.

wapń mi Gen. -a chem. calcium.

wapory pl. przest. the vapors, Br. the vapours.

war mi 1. przest. (*wrzątek*) boiling water. 2. przest. (*upał*) heat. 3. techn. gyle.

wara int. pot. hands off!, don't you dare!; **wara ode mnie!** stay away from me!

waran ma zool. monitor (*Varanus*).

warcaby pl. Gen. -ów checkers; Br. draughts.

warchlak ma roln. piglet.

warcholski a. rowdy.

warcholstwo n. rowdiness, brawling.

warchoł mp pl. -y (= *awanturnik*) brawler, rowdy; (= *wichrzyciel*) troublemaker.

warczeć ipf. -ę -ysz 1. (*o psie*) growl; (*obnażając zęby*) snarl (*na kogoś / coś* at sb/sth). 2. pot. (*o człowieku*) snarl (*na kogoś* at sb); **warknąć na kogoś** (= *odpowiedzieć komuś ze złością*) bite sb's head off. 3. tylko ipf. (*o silniku*) whirr.

Waregowie pl. hist. the Varangians.

warga f. 1. (*usta*) lip, labium; **górna warga** upper lip; **dolna warga** lower lip, nether lip; **zajęcza warga** pat. harelip; **wargi sromowe** anat. labia; **czytać z ruchu czyichś warg** read sb's lips; **wydymać wargi** pout; **wykrzywić wargi** (*na znak pogardy*) curl one's lip; **zaciskać wargi** press one's lips; **zagryzać wargi** bite one's lips; **z pobladłymi wargami** white-lipped. 2. bot. labium, labellum. 3. ent. labium.

wargowe pl. Gen. -ych bot. labiates (*Labiatae*).

wargowy *a.* **1.** *fon.* labial. **2.** *anat.*, *bot.* labiate.

wariacja *f.* **1.** *astron.*, *balet* variation. **2.** *pot.* (= *wybryk*) folly. **3.** *przest.* (= *choroba umysłowa*) insanity, lunacy; **wariacji można dostać!** this is driving me mad!

wariacje *pl. Gen.* **-i** *muz.* variations (*na temat* on the theme of).

wariacki *a.* crazy, mad; (*o pomyśle*) foolish, absurd; (*o planie*) madcap; (*o tempie, akcji*) crazy, breathtaking; **wariacka jazda** reckless driving; **po wariacku** helter-skelter; **mieć wariackie papiery** have a psychiatric record; **robić coś na wariackich papierach** (*bez przygotowania, po wariacku*) do sth helter-skelter.

wariactwo *n.* **1.** (= *szaleństwo*) lunacy, madness; (= *wybryk*) folly. **2.** *przest.* (= *choroba umysłowa*) insanity, lunacy.

wariacyjny *a. muz.* variation; **temat wariacyjny** variation theme.

wariant *mi* version; (*wymowy, pisowni*) variant; **opracować kilka wariantów czegoś** prepare a few versions of sth; **wybrać wariant optymalny** choose the best solution.

wariat *mp*, **wariatka** *f. Gen.pl.* **-ek** *pot.* freak, lunatic, schizo, madcap; **nieszkodliwy wariat** harmless lunatic; **dom wariatów** lunatic asylum; *t. przen.* (*o miejscu*) madhouse; **gra w wariata** piggy in the middle; **pędzić jak wariat** run like crazy *l.* mad; **robić coś na wariata** do sth helter-skelter; **robić z siebie wariata** make a fool of o.s.; **robić z kogoś wariata** make a fool of sb.

wariograf *mi el.* polygraph.

wariometr *mi* **1.** *el.* variometer. **2.** *lotn.* rate-of-climb indicator, variometer.

wariować *ipf.* **1.** *pot.* (= *tracić głowę*) go mad (*za kimś l. dla kogoś* about sb); (*ze zdenerwowania, niepokoju*) freak out (*z powodu czegoś* over sth); **wariować z radości** be mad with joy; **wariować z rozpaczy** go mad *l.* crazy with despair. **2.** *pot.* (= *bawić się hałaśliwie*) frolic about, romp about. **3.** *pot.* (= *tracić zmysły*) go mad, go insane. **4.** (*o obrazie telewizyjnym, urządzeniu*) go funny; (*o komputerze*) freak out.

warknąć *ipf.* **-ij** *zob.* **warczeć**.

warkocz *mi Gen.* **-a** **1.** (*fryzura*) plait, braid; **warkocz francuski** French plait; **warkocz komety** *astron.* tail of a comet; **warkocz dymu** trail of smoke. **2.** (*splot*) braid, twine.

warkoczyk *mi Gen.* **-a** pigtail.

warkot *mi* (*śmigła, silnika*) whirr; (*ciągły i wibrujący*) hum; (*głośny i rytmiczny*) throb; (*monotonny*) drone.

warkotać *ipf.* **-cze** (*o śmigle, silniku*) whirr; (*w sposób ciągły i wibrujący*) hum; (*głośno i rytmicznie*) throb; (*monotonnie*) drone.

Warna *f. geogr.* Varna.

warnik *mi Gen.* **-a** boiler.

warować *ipf.* **1.** (*o psie*) lie on guard; (*na komendę*) charge. **2.** *pot.* (*o człowieku*) keep guard, keep vigil; **warowała przy nim, gdy był w śpiączce** she kept vigil as he lay in a coma.

warownia *f. Gen.pl.* **-i** stronghold.

warowny *a.* fortified.

warstewka *f. Gen.pl.* **-ek** (*powłoka*) film, thin layer.

warstwa *f.* **1.** (*pokład*) layer; (*ochronna*) covering, coating; (*farby, lakieru*) coat; (*dekoracyjna*) overlay; (*cegieł*) course; (*tkaniny, sklejki, papieru toaletowego*) ply; **warstwa kulturowa** *archeol.* culture layer; **warstwa ozonowa** ozone layer; **warstwa podkładowa** *techn.* priming; **pokryty warstwą kurzu** coated with dust; **pokryty warstwą lodu** sheeted with ice; **górne warstwy atmosfery** upper atmosphere. **2.** *socjol.* stratum; **warstwa społeczna** social stratum; **warstwa wyższa** upper class; **warstwy średnie** middle classes; **niższe warstwy społeczne** the lower orders, lower classes. **3.** *geol.* stratum; **warstwa osadowa** horizon, deposit.

warstwowo *adv.* in layers; **układać warstwowo** stratify, arrange in layers.

warstwowy *a.* stratified, layered; (*o szkle*) laminated; *geol.* (*o skale*) stratiform; **chmura warstwowa** stratus; **struktura warstwowa** layered structure, lamination.

Warszawa *f. geogr.* Warsaw.

warszawiak *mp*, **warszawianin** *mp*, **warszawianka** *f. Gen.pl.* **-ek** Varsovian.

warszawka *f. pot.* a derogatory name for Warsaw and its inhabitants.

warszawski *a.* Warsaw, Varsovian; **Układ Warszawski** Warsaw Pact.

warsztat *mi* **1.** (*zakład, pracownia*) workshop; **warsztat artystyczny** *przen.* technique; **warsztat pracy** *przen.* field of activity; **warsztat samochodowy** garage; **warsztat naprawczy** repair shop. **2.** (*stół*) workbench, banker; **mieć coś na warsztacie** be working on sth; **wziąć coś na warsztat** set *l.* get to work on sth. **3.** (*spotkanie szkoleniowe*) workshop.

warsztatowy *a.* (*o wyposażeniu*) workshop; **braki warsztatowe** (*np. pisarza*) technical shortcomings; **stół warsztatowy** workbench.

wart *a. indecl. tylko pred.* **1.** (= *mający pewną wartość*) worth; **wart 50 dolarów** worth 50 dollars; **wart ryzyka** worth the risk; **być wartym starań** be worth the effort; **jeden wart drugiego** they are two of a kind, one is no better than the other; **nic niewart** not worth a damn; **nie jest wart złamanego grosza** *l.* **funta kłaków** not worth a hoot, not worth a crumpet; **śmiechu warte** it's ridiculous; **kobieta warta grzechu** dream boat, eyeful; **gra niewarta świeczki** the game is not worth the candle; **dobry żart tynfa wart** there's nothing like a good joke. **2.** (= *zasługujący na coś*) worthy, deserving (*czegoś* of sth); **coś warte zachodu** sth worth the trouble; **coś nie jest warte zachodu** sth is more trouble than it's worth.

warta *f.* **1.** (*posterunek*) guard, watch; **warta honorowa** guard of honor, *Br.* guard of honour; **zmiana warty** change of guard. **2.** (*służba*) guard, watch; **nocna warta** night watch; **stać na warcie** be on guard, be on sentry duty; *szkoln.* (= *pilnować czy nauczyciel nie idzie*) keep cave; **trzymać wartę** keep guard.

wartki *a.* (*o strumieniu, nurcie*) swift, brisk; (*o

rozmowie) lively, animated; **o wartkiej akcji** (*film, książka*) action-packed.

wartko *adv*. swiftly, briskly.

warto *adv. indecl.* worth; **warto spróbować** it's worth trying, it's worth a try; **warto to zobaczyć/ przeczytać** it's worth seeing/reading; **nie warto o tym wspominać** it's not worth mentioning; **warto było tu przyjechać** it was worth coming here; **warto było dożyć takiej chwili** it was worth living to see this.

wartościować *ipf.* value, appraise, evaluate.

wartościowo *adv.* according to the value.

wartościowość *f. biochem.* valence; *Br.* valency.

wartościowy *a.* **1.** (= *kosztowny*) (*o zegarku, przedmiocie*) valuable; **papiery wartościowe** securities; **przedmioty wartościowe** valuables. **2.** (= *pozytywny*) valuable; (*o pokarmie*) nutritious; (*o utworze*) worthwhile; (*o osobie*) worthy; **wartościowy człowiek** person of worth.

wartość *f.* **1.** (*cena*) value, worth; **wartość nabywcza** purchasing value; **wartość odżywcza** nutritional value; **wartość rynkowa/pieniężna** market/monetary value; **wartość ubezpieczenia** insured value; **wartość użytkowa** utility value; **wartość nominalna** *ekon.* face value; **wycena wartości** value assessment; **podatek od wartości dodanej** *ekon.* value added tax; **bez wartości** of no value; **towary wartości 100 dolarów** goods worth 100 dollars, 100 dollars' worth of goods. **2.** (*znaczenie*) value, significance; **wartość artystyczna** artistic merit; **wartość estetyczna** aesthetic value; **poczucie własnej wartości** self-esteem, self-consciousness; **mieć poczucie własnej wartości** have a high self-esteem; **szacować wartość czegoś (na)** estimate sth (at); **tracić na wartości** depreciate, lose value; **nie tracić na wartości** hold its value; **zyskiwać na wartości** increase in value, gain value; **umniejszać wartość czegoś/kogoś** (*np. czyichś osiągnięć*) belittle sth/sb; **znać swoją wartość** know one's value; **to nie przedstawia dla mnie żadnej wartości** this is of no value to me. **3.** *fiz., mat.* value; **wartość bezwzględna** absolute value; **wartość dodatnia** positive value; **wartość liczbowa** numerical value; **wartość średnia** mean *l.* average value; **wartość ujemna** negative value.

wartownia *f. Gen.pl.* **-i** (*budynek*) guardhouse; (*pomieszczenie*) guardroom.

wartowniczy *a.* guard, sentry; **budka wartownicza** sentry box; **kompania wartownicza** guard company; **służba wartownicza** sentry duty.

wartownik *mp* guard; (*wojskowy*) sentry; (*w budynku*) warden.

warunek *mi* **-nk-** **1.** (*zastrzeżenie*) condition (*czegoś* of *l.* for sth); **warunek konieczny** necessary condition; **warunek wstępny** prerequisite, precondition; **warunki umowy** terms (and conditions) of an agreement; **zgodnie z warunkami umowy** by the terms of the agreement, under the conditions of the agreement; **dotrzymać warunków** keep *l.* fulfill the terms; **dyktować/stawiać warunki** lay down/impose conditions; **stawiać twarde warunki** (*negocjując*) drive a hard

bargain; **uzgodnić warunki** settle the terms; **pod warunkiem, że...** on condition that..., provided that...; **pod jednym warunkiem** under *l.* on one condition; **pod pewnymi warunkami** on certain conditions; **pod żadnym warunkiem** on no account, in *l.* under no circumstance; **na dogodnych warunkach** on easy terms; **na równych warunkach** on equal terms; **zgodnie z ustalonymi warunkami** under the stated terms; **na jakich warunkach pracujesz?** what terms do you work on? **2.** *szkoln., uniw., pot.* condition; **mieć warunek (z czegoś)** *szkoln., uniw.* be conditionally promoted (in sth).

warunki *pl. Gen.* **-ów 1.** (*sytuacja*) circumstances; (*klimatyczne, do nauki, odpoczynku*) conditions; **warunki atmosferyczne** weather conditions; **warunki lokalowe** housing conditions; **warunki materialne** financial conditions; **warunki naturalne** (*danego terenu*) natural conditions; **warunki pracy** working conditions; **warunki życia** living conditions; **niesprzyjające warunki** adverse conditions; **sprzyjające warunki** friendly environment; **w obecnych warunkach** under the present circumstances, under existing conditions; **w warunkach laboratoryjnych** in *l.* under laboratory conditions; **w warunkach słabej widoczności** under poor *l.* low visibility conditions. **2.** (= *możliwości*) talents, aptness; **mieć warunki ku czemuś** be predisposed to do sth; **ma znakomite warunki na muzyka** he is cut out for *l.* to be a musician; **zawodnik ma świetne warunki** the contestant has what it takes; **dziewczyna z warunkami** *żart.* well-endowed girl.

warunkować *ipf.* condition, determine.

warunkowo *adv.* conditionally; **zwolnić kogoś warunkowo** parole sb; **zostać zwolnionym warunkowo** be released on parole.

warunkowy *a.* conditional; **bodziec warunkowy** *psych.* conditioned stimulus; **odruch warunkowy** *psych.* conditioned reflex *l.* response; **tryb warunkowy** *gram.* conditional mood, the conditional; **zdanie warunkowe** *gram.* conditional clause; **zwolnienie warunkowe** parole.

warząchew *f.* **-chwi-** *pl.* **-e** ladle.

warzelnia *f. Gen.pl.* **-i** (*soli*) salt works; (*piwa*) brewery.

warzelnictwo *n.* salt making.

warzęcha *f.* **1.** *bot.* horseradish (*Cochlearia armoracia*). **2.** *orn.* common spoonbill (*Platalea leucorodia*).

warzonka *f. Gen.pl.* **-ek** evaporated salt.

warzyć *ipf.* **1.** (*gotować*) boil; **warzyć piwo** brew beer; **warzyć sól** evaporate salt. **2.** *lit.* (= *powodować więdnięcie*) blast; (*o mrozie*) nip. **~ się** *ipf.* **1.** (*o mleku, śmietanie*) sour, turn sour. **2.** (*o piwie*) brew.

warzywniak *mi Gen.* **-a 1.** (*sklep*) greengrocery, greengrocer's. **2.** (*ogródek*) vegetable garden.

warzywnictwo *n.* truck farming, trucking; *Br.* market gardening.

warzywniczy *a.* **1.** (*o branży*) truck-farming, trucking; *Br.* market-gardening. **2.** (*o sklepie*) grocery, vegetable; **sklep warzywniczy** greengrocer('s).

warzywnik *mi Gen.* **-a 1.** (*część ogrodu*) vegetable garden. **2.** (= *osoba uprawiająca warzywa*) vegetable grower.

warzywny *a.* vegetal, vegetable; **ogród warzywny** vegetable garden; (*na własne potrzeby*) kitchen garden; **giełda owocowo-warzywna** fruit and vegetable market; **sklep warzywny** greengrocer('s).

warzywo *n.* vegetable.

was *pron. zob.* **wy**.

wasal *mp Gen.pl.* -*i l.* **-ów** *hist.* vassal, liege, feoffee.

wasi *pl. Gen.* **-ych** *pot.* (= *osoby z tej samej grupy co ktoś*) your folks.

wasz *a.* your; **Wasza Wielebność** Your Reverence; **Wasza Wysokość** Your Highness.

wasze *n. Gen.* **-ego** your stuff; **nie potrzebujemy waszego** we don't need your stuff.

waszmość *mp decl. like f. in sing. pl.* **-owie** *l.* -e *Gen.* **-ów** *arch.* m'lord; **waszmość pan** m'lord; **waszmość pani** m'lady, milady.

Waszyngton *mi geogr.* (*miasto*) Washington D.C.; (*stan*) Washington.

waśnić *ipf.* **-ij** *lit.* stir up discord (*kogoś* between *l.* among sb). ~ **się** *ipf.* **-ij** *lit.* brabble.

waśń *f. pl.* **-e** *lit.* discord, brabble, dissension.

wat *mi Gen.* **-a** *fiz.* watt.

wata *f.* (absorbent) cotton; *Br.* cotton wool; **wata cukrowa** cotton candy; *Br.* candyfloss; **wata szklana** glass wool; **ktoś ma nogi jak z waty** sb's legs have turned to jelly.

wataha *f. Dat. i Loc.* **-sze** *l.* **-że 1.** (= *zgraja*) rout, gang, band. **2.** *myśl.* (= *stado wilków*) throng *l.* rout *l.* pack of wolves; (= *stado dzików*) sounder *l.* drift *l.* clash *l.* brace of wild boar, throng of boars.

watażka *mp pl.* **-owie** *l.* **-i** *hist.* Cossack headman.

waterbaksztag *mi żegl.* bowsprit shroud.

waterpolista *mp sport* water polo player.

waterpolo *n. indecl. sport* water polo.

watersztag *mi żegl.* bobstay.

watka *f. Gen.pl.* **-ek** flock of cotton.

watolina *f. tk.* wadding.

watomierz *mi Gen.* **-a** *fiz.* wattmeter.

watować *ipf.* wad.

watowany *a.* wadded.

watowy *a.* watt; **żarówka 100 watowa** 100 watt bulb.

watówka *f. Gen.pl.* **-ek** *pot.* (*kurtka*) quilted jacket.

watra *f. dial.* bonfire, watch fire.

Watykan *mi geogr.* the Vatican.

wawrzyn *mi* **1.** *bot.* laurel, (sweet) bay (*Laurus nobilis*). **2.** (*laur*) laurel.

wawrzynek *mi bot.* daphne (*Daphne*).

waza *f.* **1.** *sztuka* vase. **2.** (*do zupy*) tureen.

wazelina *f.* **1.** (*substancja*) Vaseline, petrolatum. **2.** *pot.* (= *podlizywanie się*) brown-nosing. – *mp pot.* (= *lizus*) brown-noser.

wazeliniarski *a. pot.* brown-nosing, oily.

wazeliniarstwo *n. pot.* brown-nosing, taffy.

wazeliniarz *mp pot.* brown-noser.

wazelinować *ipf.* smear with Vaseline.

wazon *mi* (*na kwiaty*) vase, flowerpot.

wazonik *mi Gen.* **-a** (small) vase, (small) flowerpot.

wazowy *a.* **1.** *sztuka* vase; **malarstwo wazowe** vase painting. **2.** tureen; **łyżka wazowa** ladle.

ważka *f. Gen.pl.* **-ek** *ent.* (=*owad z rzędu Odonata*) dragonfly.

ważki *a. lit.* important, of substance, weighty.

ważkość *f. lit.* importance, weightiness, gravity.

ważniak *mp pl.* **-cy** *l.* **-i** *pot.* cockalorum; **zgrywać ważniaka** get too big for one's boots.

ważność *f.* **1.** (= *znaczenie*) importance, significance. **2.** (= *obowiązywanie*) validity; **data ważności** best-before date, expiry date, use-by date; **stracić ważność** run out, expire.

ważny *a.* **1.** (= *istotny*) important, crucial, vital, grave; **co ważniejsze** more importantly; **robić się ważnym** *pot.* throw one's weight about. **2.** (= *wpływowy*) important; **ważna osobistość** VIP; **ważna postać** person of consequence. **3.** (= *obowiązujący*) in force; (*o paszporcie*) valid; **ważny przez trzy lata** valid for three years.

ważyć *ipf.* **1.** (= *określać ciężar*) weigh. **2.** *lit.* (= *mieć znaczenie*) mean, be of importance. **3.** (= *rozpatrywać*) consider; **ważyć słowa** weigh one's words; **lekce sobie ważyć** ignore, disregard. ~ **się** *ipf.* **1.** (= *sprawdzać wagę*) weigh o.s. **2.** (= *być rozważanym*) hang in the balance; **moje losy właśnie się ważą** my future is on a knife edge. – *ipf. l. pf.* (= *mieć odwagę*) adventure (*na coś* on *l.* upon sth); venture; **ani (mi) się waż!** don't you dare!

wąchać *ipf.* smell; (*o psie*) sniff; **wąchać kwiatki od spodu** *pot.* (= *nie żyć*) push up the daisies, be six feet under.

wądół *mi* **-o- 1.** (= *wąwóz*) ravine. **2.** (= *wybój*) pit, rut.

wągier *mi* **-gr-** *Gen.* **-a 1.** (*larwa*) cysticertus, bladder worm. **2.** (= *zaskórnik*) blackhead.

wąglik *mi Gen.* **-a** *wet., pat.* anthrax, woolsorter's disease.

wągrzyca *f. pat., wet.* cysticercosis.

wąs *mi Gen.* **-a 1.** (*zarost*) mustache; *Br.* moustache; **śmiać się pod wąsem** laugh up one's sleeve; **podkręcić wąsa** twirl one's mustache; **wąs mu się sypie** he is sprouting a mustache. **2.** (*kłosa*) arista, awn, beard; (*koci, szczurzy, mysi*) whisker; (*rybi*) barbel.

wąsacz *mp Gen.pl.* **-y** *l.* **-ów** *pot.* mustached man.

wąsal *mp Gen.pl.* -*i l.* **-ów** *pot.* mustached man.

wąsaty *a.* **1.** (*o mężczyźnie*) mustached. **2.** (*o jęczmieniu, kukurydzy*) aristate, awned, bearded.

wąsik *mi Gen.* **-a** short mustache.

wąski *a.* **węższy 1.** narrow; (*o opiniach, rozumowaniu*) blinkered; **o wąskich horyzontach** (*o osobie*) narrow-minded; **wąskie gardło** *przen.* bottleneck. **2.** *druk.* condensed.

wąsko *adv.* **węziej** narrowly.

wąskonosy *a.* narrow-nosed, catarrhine; **mał-**

py **wąskonose** *zool.* Old World monkeys (*Cerco-pithecoidea*).

wąskotorowy *a. kol.* narrow-gauge; **lokomotywa wąskotorowa** dolly.

wąsy *pl. Gen.* **-ów 1.** (*u zwierząt*) whiskers. **2.** (*u pnączy*) tendrils.

wątek *mi* **-tk- 1.** (*myśli*) train; **stracić wątek** lose one's train of thought. **2.** (*wykładu, filmu, powieści*) thread; (*sztuki, książki*) plot, main story; **wątek poboczny** subplot, underplot. **3.** *tk.* filling, weft, woof.

wątły *a.* **1.** (= *o słabym zdrowiu*) weak; *pat.* asthenic. **2.** (= *słaby, cienki, wiotki*) (*o osobie*) fragile, frail, wispy; (*o roślinie*) frail. **3.** (= *nieznaczny, niedostrzegalny*) faint.

wątpiący *a.* doubting.

wątpić *ipf.* doubt; **wątpię, czy będę mógł was odwiedzić** I doubt I'll be able to visit you; **wątpić o czymś** be doubtful about sth; **wątpię** I doubt it.

wątpienie *n.* doubts; **bez wątpienia** undoubtedly, without question.

wątpliwie *adv.* dubiously, precariously.

wątpliwość *f.* doubt, dubiety; **budzić wątpliwości** be dubious *l.* questionable; **nie ma wątpliwości** there's no question; **ponad wszelką wątpliwość** beyond all doubt; **podawać w wątpliwość** call into question; **mieć wątpliwości (co do czegoś)** have one's doubts (about sth); **nie ulega wątpliwości, że...** it's beyond all doubt that...

wątpliwy *a.* (= *problematyczny*) questionable; (= *podejrzany*) doubtful, dubious; (= *mało prawdopodobny*) doubtful, debatable, disputable; (*honor, przyjemność*) dubious; **jest rzeczą wątpliwą, czy...** it's open to question if..., it is doubtful whether...; **wątpliwy przypadek** borderline case; **wątpliwy zaszczyt** dubious honor.

wątroba *f. Gen.pl.* **-ób 1.** *anat.* liver; **to mi leży na wątrobie** *pot.* it bothers *l.* bugs me; **zapalenie wątroby** *pat.* hepatitis; **marskość wątroby** *pat.* cirrhosis. **2.** *kulin.* liver.

wątrobianka *f. Gen.pl.* **-ek** *kulin.* liverwurst.

wątrobiany *a.* (*o bólu, atakach, potrawie*) liver.

wątrobowce *pl. Gen.* **-ów** *bot.* liverworts (*Hepaticae*).

wątrobowiec, wątrobiarz *mp* **-c-** *pl.* **-y** *pot.* person having *l.* suffering from a liver condition.

wątrobowy *a. anat., pat.* hepatic.

wątróbka *f. Gen.pl.* **-ek** *kulin.* liver.

wąwóz *mi* **-o-** gap, gorge, ravine.

wąziutki *a.* extremely *l.* very narrow.

wąż *ma* **-ę- 1.** *zool.* snake, serpent (*Serpentes*); **wąż morski** sea snake (*Hydrophidae*); **mieć węża w kieszeni** *pot.* be tight-fisted *l.* stingy. **2.** (*przewód*) hose; **wąż ogrodowy** garden hose.

wbetonować *pf.* cast *l.* set in concrete.

wbić *pf.* **wbiję wbijesz, wbij** *zob.* **wbijać.** **~ się** *pf. zob.* **wbijać się.**

wbiec *pf.* **wbiegnę wbiegniesz, wbiegnij, wbiegł, wbiegać** *ipf.* run (into); (*po schodach, na piętro*) run up.

wbijać *ipf.* **1.** (= *uderzając, osadzić*) hammer in, drive in; (*igły, pinezki*) stick; (*zęby, paznok-*

cie) sink; **wbić wzrok w kogoś/coś** stare at sb/sth; **wbić komuś nóż w plecy** *t. przen.* stab sb in the back; **wbijać gwóźdź do trumny** hammer *l.* drive a nail into sb's coffin; **wbić coś komuś/sobie do głowy** *pot.* get sth into sb's/one's head; **wbić dwa jajka do czegoś** add two eggs to sth; **wbić gola** *sport* score (a goal). **2.** (= *nasadzić*) put on; **wbić kogoś na pal** impale sb. **~ się** *ipf.* stick in; cut; **wbijać się w ciuchy** climb into clothes; **wbić się komuś w pamięć** be imprinted in sb's memory.

wbrew *prep.* + *Dat.* against, contrary to, in defiance of; **wbrew swojej/czyjejś woli** against one's/sb's will; **wbrew naturze** against nature; **wbrew pozorom** against all appearances; **wbrew powszechnemu przekonaniu** contrary to popular belief.

wbudować *pf.*, **wbudowywać** *ipf.* build (into).

WC *abbr. indecl.* (= *ubikacja*) WC, wc (*water closet*).

wcale *adv.* **1.** (*w sensie przeczącym*) (not) at all; **wcale się nie gniewam** I'm not angry at all; **wcale a wcale** not a whit; **lepiej późno niż wcale** better late than never; **wcale nie trudny** not at all difficult. **2.** (*w sensie częściowo pozytywnym*) quite; **teraz to wygląda wcale, wcale** *pot.* now it looks quite good.

wcelować *pf.* hit the target.

wcementować *pf.* cast *l.* set in cement *l.* concrete.

wchłaniać *ipf.* absorb, imbibe.

wchłanianie *n.* absorption; imbibition.

wchłonąć *pf. zob.* **wchłaniać.**

wchodzić *ipf.* **1.** (= *wkraczać*) enter, come in; **wejść bez pukania** enter without knocking; **wejdź do środka** come in; **wejść pod stół** get under the table; **wejść do łóżka** get into bed; **proszę wejść** come in; **wejść do rodziny** become a member of the family; **wejść do spółki** become a partner (*in a partnership*); become a shareholder (*in a company*); **wejść komuś w drogę** cross sb's path; **to nie wchodzi w zakres wykładu** that's not a part of the lecture; **wczesne wstawanie weszło mi w krew** I got into the habit of getting up early; **sprawa weszła pod obrady** the issue was put on the agenda; **to nie wchodzi w grę** that's out of the question; **wejść na ekrany** *film* be released; **wejść do finału** *sport* reach the final(s); **wejść do portu** *żegl.* put in *l.* into; **wchodzić na pokład** go on board, embark. **2.** (= *wspinać się*) climb, go up; **wejść na drabinę** climb up a ladder; **wejść komuś na głowę** keep sb under one's thumb. **3.** (= *zagłębiać się*) go in, sink; **gwóźdź wszedł głęboko w ścianę** the nail went deep into the wall. **4.** (= *włączać się*) come, go, enter; **wejść w konflikt** enter into conflict; **wchodzić w modę** come into fashion; **wejść na dobrą drogę** take the right path; **wejść w świat** go into society; **wejść na rynek** enter the market; **wejść w życie** come into effect *l.* force; **wchodzić do akcji** *wojsk.* come into operation *l.* action; **wejść do użytku** come into use. **5.** (= *mieścić się*) fit; **to już nie weszło do walizki** it didn't fit *l.* go into the suitcase; **szafa weszła na styk** the cupboard fitted snugly. **6.** (= *wnikać*) go; **wejść w szczegóły** go into detail(s);

spróbuj **wejść w moje położenie** try to put yourself in my place *l.* shoes. **7.** *tylko ipf.* (= *wrzynać się*) cut, pinch.

wciąć *pf.* wetnę wetniesz, wetnij *zob.* **wcinać.** ~ **się** *pf. zob.* **wcinać się.**

wciągać *ipf.* **1.** (= *ciągnąć*) pull (into); (*linę, żagiel, flagę*) hoist; **wciągać brzuch** pull in one's stomach. **2.** *pot.* (= *angażować kogoś*) engage, involve; **wciągać kogoś w zasadzkę** draw sb into a trap. **3.** (= *absorbować*) absorb, engross; **ta książka bardzo mnie wciąga** this book is a real page-turner. **4.** (= *zapisywać*) enter, register; **wciągnąć kogoś na listę** put sb on the list. **5.** (= *wdychać*) breathe in, inhale. **6.** (*spodnie, sweter, pończochy*) (= *założyć*) pull on. **7.** (= *wessać*) suck in *l.* down. ~ **się** *ipf.* **1.** (= *podciągnąć się*) pull o.s. up. **2.** *pot.* (= *przyzwyczajać się*) get into the swing. **3.** (*o pazurach, kłach*) retract, be drawn in.

wciągarka *f. Gen.pl.* **-ek** *techn.* winch.

wciągnąć *pf.* **-ij** *zob.* **wciągać.** ~ **się** *pf. zob.* **wciągać się.**

wciąż *adv.* still; **on ją wciąż kocha** he still loves her; **wciąż coś robić** keep (on) doing sth; **wciąż pada** it's still raining.

wciec *pf.* wcieknie, wciekł *l.* wcieknął wciekła, **wciekać** *ipf.* trickle in, ooze in.

wcielać *ipf.*, **wcielić** *pf.* **1.** (= *włączyć*) incorporate; **wcielić do wojska** enlist for the army. **2.** *lit.* (= *ucieleśniać*) incarnate, embody; **wcielić słowa w czyn** translate words into action. ~ **się** *ipf.*, **wcielić się** *pf.* **1.** (= *utożsamiać się*) impersonate. **2.** (= *urzeczywistniać się*) realize, come true.

wcielenie *n.* **1.** (= *uosobienie*) embodiment, image. **2.** *wojsk.* induction, enlistment; **karta wcielenia** draft card. **3.** *rel.* incarnation.

wcielony *a.* incarnate; **Bóg wcielony** *rel.* God Incarnate; **diabeł wcielony** the devil incarnate, holy terror.

wcierać *ipf.* rub in. ~ **się** *ipf.* be rubbed in.

wcięcie *n.* **1.** (= *zagłębienie*) indenture, cut, notch. **2.** (= *dekolt*) low-cut neck. **3.** *druk.* indentation.

wcięty *a.* **1.** (= *zwężony w pasie*) narrow in the waist. **2.** (= *szczupły*) slim. **3.** *pot.* (= *pijany*) tipsy.

wcinać *ipf.* **1.** (= *zagłębiać*) cut. **2.** *druk.* indent. **3.** *pot.* (= *jeść*) tuck into, muckamuck. ~ **się** *ipf.* **1.** (= *wchodzić w głąb*) cut into. **2.** (= *przerywać, wtrącać się*) cut in.

wcisk *mi* pressing (into); **zapięcie na wcisk** press stud, popper, snap fastener, snap-in.

wciskać *ipf.*, **wcisnąć** *pf.* **wcisnę wciśniesz, wciśnij** **1.** (= *wpychać*) press, push in, squeeze in, drive in; **wszędzie wciskać nos** be a prier; **wciskać komuś kit** *pot.* bullshit sb; **nie próbuj mi wciskać kitu!** cut the crap!; **wcisnąć coś komuś do ręki** press sth into sb's hand. **2.** (= *naciągać, nakładać*) cram, pull on; **wcisnąć czapkę na oczy** pull one's cap over one's eyes. **3.** (= *wyciskać*) squeeze; **wcisnąć cytrynę do herbaty** squeeze lemon into one's tea. **4.** *pot.* (*towar*) hustle, tout, oversell; **wciskać coś komuś** palm sth off on sb. **5.** *pot.* (= *lokować kogoś*) squeeze. ~ **się** *ipf.*,

wcisnąć się *pf.* **1.** *pot.* (= *dostać się gdzieś*) wedge in, squeeze in. **2.** (= *nałożyć na siebie*) squeeze into; **wcisnąć się w stare dżinsy** squeeze into old jeans.

wczasowicz *mp Gen.pl.* **-ów** vacationer; *gł. Br.* holidayer, holidaymaker.

wczasowiczka *f. Gen.pl.* **-ek** *zob.* **wczasowicz.**

wczasowy *a.* vacation; *gł. Br.* holiday; **dom** *l.* **ośrodek wczasowy** resort.

wczasy *pl. Gen.* **-ów** vacation; *gł. Br.* holiday; **jechać na wczasy** go on vacation *l.* holiday; **wczasy zorganizowane** package tour, prepackaged vacation *l.* holiday.

wczep *mi bud.* dovetail.

wczepiać *ipf.*, **wczepić** *pf.* sink, dig in. ~ **się** *ipf.*, **wczepić się** *pf.* cling, claw.

wczepiarka *f. Gen.pl.* **-ek** *bud.* dovetailing machine, dovetail jointer.

wczesny *a.* **1.** (= *niepóźny*) early; **wczesne godzinny poranne** small hours; **wczesnym rankiem** in the early morning; **wczesną wiosną/latem/jesienią/zimą** in early spring/summer/fall/winter. **2.** (= *poprzedzający*) previous; **wcześniejsze zeznanie** previous testimony; **wcześniejsze wydarzenia** earlier events. **3.** *bot.* early; **wczesna odmiana** early (maturing) variety.

wcześniactwo *n. med.* prematurity.

wcześniak *mp pl.* **-i** *med.* preterm, premature infant.

wcześnie *adv.* **1.** (= *niepóźno*) early; **pójść wcześnie spać** have an early night; **jak najwcześniej** as early as possible; **im wcześniej, tym lepiej** the sooner the better. **2.** (= *uprzednio*) before; **dwa dni wcześniej** two days before. **3.** (= *nie prędzej niż*) not sooner than; **najwcześniej za tydzień** in a week at the earliest; **o wiele za wcześnie** all too soon, way too early.

wcześniej *adv. zob.* **wcześnie.**

wcześniejszy *a. zob.* **wczesny.**

wczołgać się *pf.* crawl *l.* creep in.

wczoraj *adv.* yesterday; **wczoraj rano** yesterday morning; **wczoraj wieczorem** last night; **dopiero wczoraj** only yesterday; **nie urodziłem się wczoraj** I wasn't born yesterday. – *n. indecl.* yesterday; **od wczoraj** since yesterday.

wczorajszy *a.* yesterday; **szukać wczorajszego dnia** *pot.* look for a needle in a bottle of hay.

wczuć się *pf.*, **wczuwać się** *ipf.* get into the spirit of; **wczuwać się w sytuację/rolę** identify with a situation/role.

wczytać *pf.*, **wczytywać** *ipf. komp.* (= *wprowadzić dane*) enter; (= *odczytać dane*) load, read. ~ **się** *pf.*, **wczytywać się** *ipf.* pore over.

wdać się *pf.* **1.** *zob.* **wdawać się. 2.** *pot.* (= *wrodzić się w kogoś*) take after.

wdarł *itd. pf. zob.* **wedrzeć się.**

wdawać się *ipf.* **wdaję wdajesz, wdawaj, wdawdzą** **1.** (= *brać udział*) get involved; **wdać się w bójkę** get into a fight; **wdać się w romans z kimś** have an affair with sb; **wdać się w kłótnię** fall *l.* get into an argument. **2.** (= *wnikać*) go into; **nie wdając się w szczegóły** without going into detail(s). **3.** *pot.* (= *zadawać się*) associate *l.* mingle with; **wdać się w złe towarzystwo** fall into bad company, consort with shady people. **4.** (*o infek-cji*) set in.

wdech *mi* inhalation; **robić wdech** breathe in, inhale.

wdepnąć *pf.* **-ij 1.** (= *wejść w coś*) step into; **wdepnąć w błoto** step in mud; **wdepnąć w gówno** *pot.* get into deep shit. **2.** *pot.* (= *wstąpić gdzieś*) drop in.

wdeptać *pf.* **-pczę** *l.* **-pcę -pczesz** *l.* **-pcesz, -pcz, wdeptywać** *ipf.* tread into, trample on *l.* upon.

wdmuchać *pf.*, **wdmuchiwać** *ipf.*, **wdmuchnąć** *pf.* **-ij** insufflate.

wdowa *f. Gen.pl.* **wdów** widow; **słomiana wdowa** *żart.* grass widow.

wdowi *a.* widow's; **wdowi grosz** *l.* **grosik** widow's mite; **wdowia renta** dower.

wdowiec *mp* **-wc-** *pl.* **-y** widower; **słomiany wdowiec** *żart.* grass widower.

wdowieństwo *n.* widowhood.

wdówka *f. Gen.pl.* **-ek** widow; **ciepła wdówka** *żart.* richly dowered widow.

wdrapać się *pf.* **-pię -piesz, wdrapywać się** *ipf.* climb (up); **wdrapać się na dach** climb onto the roof.

wdrażać *ipf.* **1.** (= *przyzwyczajać, wprowadzać*) initiate, introduce. **2.** (= *wpajać*) inculcate. **3.** (= *podejmować działanie*) enter; **wdrożyć śledztwo** *prawn.* open *l.* start an inquiry; **wdrożyć postępowanie sądowe** *prawn.* institute (legal) proceedings. **4.** (= *wprowadzać w życie*) implement. **~ się** *ipf.* (= *przyzwyczajać się*) get accustomed.

wdrożenie *n.* implementation.

wdrożeniowy *a.* implementing, implementation.

wdrożyć *pf. zob.* **wdrażać**. **~ się** *pf. zob.* **wdrażać się**.

wdychać *ipf.* breathe in, inhale.

wdziać *pf.* **-eję -ejesz** *zob.* **wdziewać**.

wdzianko *n. Gen.pl.* **-nek** jacket.

wdzierać się *ipf.* **1.** (= *wchodzić siłą*) force one's way in, intrude. **2.** (= *wspinać się*) climb, ascend. **3.** (= *zagłębiać się*) penetrate; (*o morzu*) encroach.

wdziewać *ipf. przest.* put on, slip on; **wdziewać habit** *przen.* take the habit.

wdzięcznie *adv.* **1.** gracefully, charmingly. **2.** *lit.* (= *z wdzięcznością*) gratefully.

wdzięczność *f.* gratitude, appreciation, gratefulness; **mieć dług wdzięczności wobec kogoś** be indebted to sb, owe sb a debt of gratitude; **na dowód wdzięczności** as a token of gratitude; **w dowód wdzięczności za coś** in acknowledgment of sth; **serca przepełnione wdzięcznością** hearts overflowing with gratitude; **z wdzięcznością** gratefully.

wdzięczny *a.* **1.** (= *zobowiązany*) grateful, indebted; **być komuś wdzięcznym za coś** be indebted to sb for sth; **jestem bardzo wdzięczny za pańską pomoc** I deeply appreciate your assistance *l.* help. **2.** (= *uroczy*) graceful. **3.** (= *dający dobre wyniki*) rewarding; **wdzięczna praca** rewarding job; **być wdzięcznym słuchaczem** be a good listener.

wdzięczyć się *ipf.* simper; **wdzięczyć się do kogoś** flirt with sb.

wdzięk *mi* (= *urok*) charm, cuteness, grace; **z wdziękiem** gracefully; **pełen wdzięku** airy, lightsome.

wdzięki *pl. Gen.* **-ów** (= *kształty ciała*) charms, attractiveness; **obfite wdzięki** *żart.* (= *kształty ciała*) ample proportions.

we *prep. zob.* **w**.

weba *f. tk.* cambric.

weber *mi Gen.* **-a** *fiz.* weber (*Wb*).

wedle *prep.* + *Gen. przest.* according to, as per; **wedle instrukcji** as per instructions.

według *prep.* + *Gen.* according to, as per, by; **postępować według instrukcji** follow instructions; **według mnie** in my opinion; **według wzoru/faktury** per sample/invoice; **narysowany według skali** drawn to scale; **Ewangelia według Świętego Jana** *rz.-kat.* the Gospel according to John.

wedrzeć się *pf.* **wedrę wedrzesz, wedrzyj, wdarł** *zob.* **wdzierać się**.

weduta *f. sztuka* townscape.

wedyzm *mi rel.* Vedaism.

weekend *mi* weekend.

weekendowy *a.* weekend; **weekendowy gość** weekender.

wegetacja *f.* **1.** (= *przetrwanie*) vegetation, dull *l.* passive existence. **2.** *bot.* vegetation.

wegetacyjny *a.* **1.** vegetal, vegetative. **2.** *bot.* vegetative.

wegetarianin *mp pl.* **-anie** *Gen.* **-an** vegetarian.

wegetarianizm *mi* vegetarianism; **przejść na wegetarianizm** turn vegetarian.

wegetarianka *f. Gen.pl.* **-ek** *zob.* **wegetarianin**.

wegetariański *a.* vegetarian, veggie.

wegetatywnie *adv. bot.* vegetatively.

wegetatywny *a.* vegetative; **wegetatywny układ nerwowy** *anat.* autonomic nervous system; **rozmnażanie wegetatywne** *biol.* vegetative *l.* asexual reproduction.

wegetować *ipf.* **1.** (= *trwać*) vegetate, live a dull *l.* passive life; (*przed telewizorem*) veg out; (*np. o chorym*) linger (on). **2.** *biol.* vegetate.

wegnać *pf. zob.* **wganiać**.

wehikuł *mi żart.* vehicle; **wehikuł czasu** time machine.

wejmutka, sosna wejmutka *f. bot.* white pine (*Pinus strobus*).

wejrzeć *pf.* **-ę -ysz, -yj** *zob.* **wglądać**.

wejrzenie *n.* glance, look; **miłość od pierwszego wejrzenia** love at first sight; **polubić kogoś od pierwszego wejrzenia** take shine to sb.

wejście *n.* **1.** (*czynność*) entrance, entry. **2.** (*drzwi*) entrance; (*zwł. z ułatwieniami, np. dla inwalidów*) access; **wejście służbowe** service entrance; **mieć wejścia** *pot.* know the right people, be on the inside. **3.** (= *wstęp*) admission, entry. **4.** *el., komp.* input.

wejściowy *a.* entrance; (*drzwi*) front; (*dane, gniazdo*) input.

wejściówka *f. Gen.pl.* **-ek** *pot.* pass, entrance ticket *l.* card.

wejść *pf.* **wejdę wejdziesz wszedł weszła weszli** *zob.* **wchodzić**.

wek *mi Gen.* -a *l.* -u preserving jar.

wekować *ipf.* preserve, put up (*in a jar*).

weksel *mi* -sl- *Gen.* -a *fin.* bill (of exchange), note; **weksel ciągniony** drawn bill, bill of exchange; **weksel handlowy krótkoterminowy** commercial paper; **weksel skarbowy** Treasury bill; **weksel własny** promissory note.

wekslować *ipf. kol.* shunt.

wekslowy *a. fin.* exchange; **kredyt wekslowy** paper credit.

wektor *mi Gen.* -a *fiz., geom.* vector.

wektorowy *a. fiz., geom.* vector, vectorial.

welarny *a. fon.* velar.

welin *mi* (*skóra*) (*papier*) vellum.

welinowy *a.* vellum.

wellingtony *pl.* Wellington boots, wellingtons; *pot.* wellies.

welodrom *mi sport* velodrome.

welon *mi Gen.* -u (*woalka*) veil. – *ma Gen.* -a *icht.* goldfish.

welonik *mi Gen.* -a veil.

welur *mi tk.* (*skóra*) velour, velours.

welurowy *a.* velour.

welwet *mi tk.* velvet.

welwetowy *a. tk.* velvet.

wełna *f. Gen.pl.* **wełen 1.** (*sierść*) wool; **wełna angorska** angora wool; **wełna czesankowa** worsted; **wełna czysta** pure wool; **wełna drzewna** wood wool; **wełna szklana** glass wool; **wełna zgrzebna** carding wool. **2.** (*włóczka*) (*tkanina*) wool; **garnitur z wełny** wool suit.

wełniak *mi Gen.* -a **1.** (*tkanina*) woolen, *Br.* woollen. **2.** (*strój*) woolens, *Br.* woollens.

wełnianka *f. bot.* cotton grass (*Eriophorum*).

wełniany *a.* woolen, *Br.* woollen.

wełnisty *a.* wooly, *Br.* woolly; fleecy.

wemknąć się *pf.* sneak in.

wena *f. lit.* inspiration; **wena twórcza** creative inspiration; **wena mnie opuściła** my inspiration has abandoned me.

wendeta *f.* vendetta.

Wenecja *f. geogr.* Venice.

wenecki *a.* Venetian; **lustro weneckie** two-way mirror, see-through mirror; **okno weneckie** Venetian window, Palladian window.

wenerolog *mp pl.* -dzy *l.* -owie *med.* venereologist.

wenerologia *f. Gen.* -ii *med.* venereology.

weneryczny *a. pat.* venereal; **choroba weneryczna** venereal disease, sexually transmitted disease.

Wenezuela *f. geogr.* Venezuela.

Wenezuelczyk *mp*, **Wenezuelka** *f. Gen.pl.* -ek Venezuelan.

wenezuelski *a.* Venezuelan.

wentyl *mi Gen.* -a **1.** (*zawór*) valve; **wentyl bezpieczeństwa** *t. przen.* safety valve. **2.** *muz.* (*w instrumentach dętych*) valve; (*w organach*) pallet.

wentylacja *f.* (= *wietrzenie*) (*urządzenie*) ventilation.

wentylacyjny *a.* ventilation; ventilative, ventilatory.

wentylator *mi Gen.* -a fan, ventilator.

wentylować *ipf.* **1.** (= *wietrzyć*) air, ventilate. **2.** *med.* ventilate.

wentylowy *a.* valve.

Wenus *f. indecl. astron., mit.* Venus.

weń *pron.* (= *w niego*) *lit.* in him; into him; at him.

wepchać *pf. zob.* **wpychać.** ~ **się** *pf. zob.* **wpychać się.**

wepchnąć *pf.* -ij *zob.* **wpychać.** ~ **się** *pf. zob.* **wpychać się.**

weprzeć *pf.* **weprę weprzesz, weprzyj, wparł** *zob.* **wpierać.** ~ **się** *pf. zob.* **wpierać się.**

weranda *f.* veranda, verandah; porch.

werbalizm *mi* verbalism.

werbalizować *ipf. lit.* verbalize.

werbalny *a.* verbal; **komunikacja werbalna** verbal communication.

werbel *mi* -bl- *Gen.* -a **1.** *muz.* (*instrument*) snare drum, side drum. **2.** (*dźwięk*) drum roll.

werbena *f. bot.* vervain, verbena (*Verbena*).

werbenowate *pl. Gen.* -ych *bot.* verbena family, verbenas (*Verbenaceae*).

werbować *ipf.* **1.** (*do pracy, wojska*) recruit, enlist. **2.** (= *zjednywać*) canvass.

werbunek *mi* -nk- **1.** (*do pracy, wojska*) recruitment. **2.** (= *zjednywanie*) canvassing.

werbunkowy *a.* recruitment, recruiting.

werdiura *f. sztuka* verdure tapestry.

werdykt *mi* verdict; **ogłosić werdykt** return a verdict.

werk *mi* works of a watch.

wermiszel *mi kulin.* vermicelli.

wermut *mi kulin.* vermouth.

werniks *mi mal.* varnish, glaze.

werniksować *ipf. mal.* varnish, glaze.

wernisaż *mi sztuka* vernissage.

wers *mi teor.lit.* verse.

Wersal *mi geogr.* Versailles.

wersal *mi żart.* (*grzeczność*) courtesy, politeness.

wersalik *mi Gen.* -a *druk.* capital letter, capital; majuscule.

wersalka *f. Gen.pl.* -ek sofabed, sofa bed.

wersalski *a.* **1.** Versailles; **Traktat Wersalski** *hist.* the Treaty of Versailles. **2.** (= *wykwintny*) courteous, courtly.

werset *mi* verse.

wersja *f.* (*wariant*) (*odmiana*) version; **dwie różne wersje** two different versions.

wersyfikacja *f. teor.lit.* versification.

wersyfikacyjny *a. teor.lit.* versification.

wertepy *pl. Gen.* -ów rough *l.* bumpy terrain.

werterowski *adv. lit.* Wertherian, Werterian.

werteryzm *mi lit.* Wertherism.

wertować *ipf.* (*pobieżnie*) browse through; (*dokładnie*) pore over.

wertykalizm *mi sztuka* verticalism.

wertykalny *a. form.* vertical.

werwa *f.* verve; **pełen werwy** full of verve, spirited; **z werwą** with verve.

weryfikacja *f.* (*twierdzenia, teorii*) verification; (*kandydatów, pracowników*) vetting; **poddać kogoś weryfikacji** vet sb; **poddać coś weryfikacji** verify sth.

weryfikacyjny *a.* verifying; (*o komisji*) vetting.

weryfikator *mp* verifier.

weryfikować *ipf.* (*teorię, twierdzenie*) verify; (*kandydatów, pracowników*) vet.

werysta *mp teor.lit., sztuka* verist.

werystyczny *a. teor.lit., sztuka* veristic, verist.

weryzm *mi teor.lit., sztuka* verism.

werżnąć się *pf.* -ij *zob.* **wrzynać się.**

wesele *n.* **1.** (*przyjęcie*) wedding reception; *pot.* wedding; **diamentowe wesele** diamond wedding anniversary; **srebrne wesele** silver wedding anniversary; **złote wesele** gold wedding anniversary; **zaprosić kogoś na wesele** invite sb to one's wedding; **do wesela się zagoi** *żart.* don't worry, it will heal in no time. **2.** *lit.* (= *radość*) joy.

weselić się *ipf. lit.* rejoice.

weselnik *mp* wedding guest.

weselny *a.* wedding; **gość weselny** wedding guest.

wesołek *mp* -łk- *pl.* -i *l.* -owie *pot.* joker, jester.

wesoło *adv.* -elej cheerfully, joyfully, merrily; (*bawić się, spędzać czas*) happily; **brać coś na wesoło** take sth lightly; **było bardzo wesoło** there was a lot of fun; **zrobiło mi się weselej na duszy** sth *l.* sb lifted my spirits.

wesołość *f.* cheerfulness.

wesoły *a.* -elszy cheerful, joyful; **wesołe miasteczko** amusement park; *Br. t.* fun fair; **Wesołych Świąt!** (*Bożego Narodzenia*) Merry Christmas!; (*Wielkiej Nocy*) Happy Easter!; **wesołej zabawy!** have fun!

wesół *a.* *indecl. zob.* **wesoły.**

wespół *prep.* + *Ins. lit.* together with.

wesprzeć *pf.* **wesprę wesprzesz, wesprzyj, wsparł** *zob.* **wspierać.** ~ **się** *pf.* **wsparł** *zob.* **wspierać się.**

wessać *pf.* -ssę -ssiesz, -ssij *zob.* **wsysać.** ~ **się** *pf. zob.* **wsysać się.**

Westa *f. mit.* Vesta.

westalka *f. Gen.pl.* -ek *hist.* vestal virgin.

westchnąć *pf.* -ij *zob.* **wzdychać.**

westchnienie *n.* sigh.

western *mi* (*film, książka*) Western.

westernowy *a.* Western.

westybul *mi Gen.pl.* -i *l.* -ów vestibule.

wesz *f.* **wsz-** *ent.* louse (*Anoplura*); **wesz głowowa** head louse (*Pediculus capitis*); **wesz łonowa** pubic louse, crab louse (*Phthirius pubis*); **wesz odzieżowa** body louse (*Pediculus corporis*).

weszła *itd. pf. zob.* **wejść.**

wet *mi* **wet za wet** tit for tat.

weteran *mp,* **weteranka** *f. Gen.pl.* -ek (*żołnierz*) (*pracownik, działacz*) veteran; **weteran wojenny** war veteran.

weterynaria *f. Gen.* -ii *wet.* veterinary medicine.

weterynaryjny *a. wet.* veterinary.

weterynarz *mp wet.* veterinarian; *Br.* veterinary surgeon; *pot.* vet.

wetknąć *pf.* -ij *zob.* **wtykać.**

wetnę *itd. pf. zob.* **wciąć.**

weto *n. polit.* veto; **prawo weta** power of veto,

right to veto; **zgłaszać weto wobec czegoś** place a veto on sth, veto sth.

wetować *ipf. polit.* veto.

wetrzeć *pf.* **wetrę wetrzesz, wetrzyj, wtarł** *zob.* **wcierać.**

wew. *abbr.* (= *wewnętrzny*) ext. (= *extension*).

wewnątrz *prep.* + *Gen.* inside, within; **do wewnątrz** inward, *Br.* inwards; **od wewnątrz** from the inside, from within.

wewnątrzkomórkowy *a. biochem., biol.* intracellular.

wewnątrznaczyniowy *a. med.* intravascular.

wewnętrznie *adv.* internally; **zmienić się wewnętrznie** change inside.

wewnętrzny *a.* internal; (*okno, drzwi*) interior; (*spokój, dyscyplina*) inner; (*np. handel*) domestic; *zwł. polit.* home; **choroba wewnętrzna** *pat.* internal disease; **do użytku wewnętrznego** *med.* for internal use; (*o dokumentach itp.*) confidential; **Ministerstwo Spraw Wewnętrznych i Administracji** Ministry of the Interior *l.* Internal Affairs and Administration; *Br.* Home Office; **numer** *l.* **telefon wewnętrzny** extension; **ucho wewnętrzne** *anat.* internal *l.* inner ear; **wewnętrzna kieszeń** inside pocket; **wewnętrzna strona (czegoś)** the inside (of sth).

wezbrać *pf.* **wzbierze** *zob.* **wzbierać.**

wezbrany *a.* swollen; (= *rozlewający się*) overflowing; **wezbrana rzeka** river in spate; **piersi wezbrane mlekiem** breasts swollen with milk.

wezdmę *itd. pf. zob.* **wzdąć.**

wezgłowie *n. Gen.pl.* -i **1.** (*podpórka*) headrest. **2.** (*ścianka*) headboard.

wezmę *itd. pf. zob.* **wziąć.**

Wezuwiusz *mi Gen.* -a *geogr.* Vesuvius.

wezwać *pf.* -ę -iesz, -ij *zob.* **wzywać.**

wezwanie *n.* **1.** (*nakaz*) summons; (*lekarza, policji itp.*) call; **wezwanie do sądu** citation, subpoena; **wezwanie do wojska** draft. **2.** (= *odezwa*) appeal, address; **kościół pod wezwaniem Świętego Piotra** *rel.* St. Peter's Church.

wezyr *mp pl.* -owie vizier; **wielki wezyr** *hist.* grand vizier.

weź *itd. pf. zob.* **wziąć.**

weżreć się *pf.* **weżrę weżresz, weżryj** *zob.* **wżerać się.**

węch *mi* (sense of) smell; *przen.* nose; **mieć dobry węch** have a good sense of smell.

węchowy *a.* olfactory.

wędka *f. Gen.pl.* -ek fishing rod.

wędkarski *a.* angling, fishing.

wędkarstwo *n.* angling, fishing.

wędkarz *mp* angler.

wędkować *ipf.* angle, fish.

wędlina *f. kulin.* cured meat; (*wędzona*) smoked meat.

wędliniarski *a. kulin.* pertaining to cured *l.* smoked meat(s); (*sklep*) butcher's.

wędrować *ipf.* **1.** (*podróżować*) travel. **2.** (*z miejsca na miejsce*) wander, roam; (*pieszo*) hike, tramp. **3.** *pot.* (*chodzić*) walk, go; **wędrować za kratki** go to prison, get canned. **4.** (= *być przekazywanym*) be passed; **fotografia wędrowała z rąk do rąk** the photo passed from hand to hand.

wędrowiec *mp* -wc- *pl.* -y wanderer; (*turysta pieszy*) hiker.

wędrowny *a.* walking; (*lud*) nomadic; **obóz wędrowny** walking holiday, walking summer camp; **ptak wędrowny** *orn.* migratory bird, bird of passage; **teatr wędrowny** traveling theater, *Br.* travelling theatre.

wędrówka *f. Gen.pl.* -ek **1.** (*podróżowanie*) wandering, roaming; **wędrówka piesza** hike. **2.** (*przesuwanie się*) movement; **wędrówka ludów** *hist.* migration of peoples; **wędrówka dusz** transmigration of souls. **3.** *pot.* (*chodzenie*) walking, going.

wędzarnia *f. Gen.pl.* -i smokehouse.

wędzić *ipf.* smoke. ~ **się** *ipf.* **1.** (*konserwować się*) be smoked. **2.** *pot.* (= *przesiąkać dymem papierosów*) be enveloped in clouds of tobacco smoke.

wędzidło *n. Gen.pl.* -deł bit.

wędzisko *n.* (fishing) rod.

wędzonka *f. Gen.pl.* -ek *kulin.* smoked bacon.

wędzony *a.* smoked.

węgiel *mi* -gl- *Gen.* -a **1.** (*skała*) coal; **węgiel aktywny** active carbon; **węgiel brunatny** brown coal, lignite; **węgiel drzewny** charcoal; **węgiel kamienny** hard coal; **biały węgiel** *przen.* waterpower; **siedzieć jak na rozżarzonych węglach** be on tenterhooks. **2.** *chem.* carbon; **dwutlenek węgla** carbon dioxide; **tlenek węgla** carbon monoxide. **3.** *sztuka* charcoal.

węgielek *mi* -lk- *Gen.* -a small piece of coal; (*żarzący się*) ember.

węgielny *a.* **kamień węgielny** cornerstone.

węgieł *mi* -gł- *Gen.* -a *bud.* quoin, corner; **zza węgła** from round the corner.

Węgier *mp* -gr-, **Węgierka** *f. Gen.pl.* -ek Hungarian.

węgierka *f. Gen.pl.* -ek *bot., ogr.* plum (*Prunus domestica oeconomica*).

węgierski *a.* Hungarian.

węglan *mi chem.* carbonate.

węglarka *f. Gen.pl.* -ek *kol.* open freight car; *Br.* open goods wagon.

węglopochodne *pl. Gen.* -ych *chem.* carbon derivatives.

węglopochodny *a. chem.* carbon-derived; **produkt węglopochodny** carbon derivative.

węglowiec *mi* -wc- *Gen.* -a **1.** *żegl.* collier, coal carrier. **2.** *chem.* carbon group element.

węglowodan *mi chem.* carbohydrate.

węglowodór *mi* -o- *chem.* hydrocarbon; **węglowodory aromatyczne** aromatic hydrocarbons; **węglowodory nasycone** saturated hydrocarbons; **węglowodory nienasycone** non-saturated hydrocarbons.

węglowy *a.* **1.** coal; **epoka węglowa** *geol.* the Carboniferous; **górnictwo węglowe** coal mining; **przemysł węglowy** coal industry; **pylica węglowa** *pat.* anthracosis, coal miners' pneumoconiosis; **stal węglowa** carbon steel. **2.** *chem.* carbon; **kwas węglowy** carbonic acid.

węgorz *ma icht.* European eel (*Anguilla anguilla*).

Węgry *pl. Gen.* **Węgier** *Loc.* **Węgrzech** *geogr.* Hungary.

węgrzyn *mi Gen.* -a (*wino*) Hungarian wine.

węszyć *ipf.* **1.** (*o zwierzęciu*) sniff, nose. **2.** *pot.* (= *śledzić*) nose about *l.* around. **3.** *pot.* (= *doszukiwać się*) scent, smell; **węszyć coś podejrzanego** smell a rat.

węzeł *mi* -zł- *Gen.* -a **1.** (= *supeł*) knot; **węzeł gordyjski** the Gordian knot; **węzeł marynarski** reef knot, square knot; **węzeł chłonny** *anat.* lymph node. **2.** (*skrzyżowanie*) junction; **węzeł drogowy** junction; **węzeł kolejowy** railway junction. **3.** *bot.* node. **4.** *żegl.* knot. **5.** *techn.* center, *Br.* centre.

węzełek *mi* -łk- *Gen.* -a **1.** (= *supełek*) knot. **2.** (= *tobołek*) bundle.

węziej *adv. zob.* **wąsko**.

węzłowato *adv.* knottily; **krótko i węzłowato** briefly, to the point; **omówić coś krótko i węzłowato** give the long and the short of it.

węzłowaty *a.* knotty, knotlike; **krótki i węzłowaty** brief, to the point.

węzłowy *a.* **1.** junction; **stacja węzłowa** *kol.* junction station. **2.** *techn.* central. **3.** *przen.* key, vital; **węzłowe zagadnienie** key issue.

węzły *pl. Gen.* -ów (= *związki*) ties, bonds; **węzły rodzinne** family ties.

węża *itd. ma zob.* **wąż**.

węże *pl. Gen.* -y *zool.* snakes (*Serpentes*).

wężojad *ma orn.* secretary bird (*Sagittarius serpentarius*).

wężowate *pl. Gen.* -ych *zool.* colubrids (*Colubridae*).

wężowidło *n. zool.* ophiurid, ophiuroid (*Ophiura*).

wężowisko *n.* **1.** (= *kłąb węży*) brood of snakes. **2.** *przen.* tangle.

wężownica *f. techn.* coil pipe.

wężowy *a.* (*dotyczący węża*) snake; (*podobny do węża*) snakelike, serpentine.

węższy *a. zob.* **wąski**.

wężyk *mi Gen.* -a **1.** (= *młody wąż*) young snake. **2.** (= *zygzak*) wavy line; (*linia*) zigzag.

WF *mi szkoln.* (= *wychowanie fizyczne*) Phys.Ed.; *Br.* PE (= *physical education*).

wg *abbr.* acc. to (= *according to*).

wganiać *ipf.* drive in.

wgiąć *pf.* **wegnę wegniesz**, **wegnij** *zob.* **wginać**.

wgięcie *n.* dent.

wgięty *a.* dented.

wginać *ipf.* dent.

wgląd *mi* (= *wniknięcie*) insight (*w coś* into sth); (= *zbadanie*) inspection (*w coś* of sth); **do wglądu** available for inspection; **mieć wgląd do czegoś** have the right to inspect sth.

wglądać *ipf.* look into, inspect; **wejrzeć w czyjeś sprawy** look into sb's affairs.

wgłębiać się *ipf.*, **wgłębić się** *pf.* -ąb **1.** (*wciskać się*) sink into. **2.** (= *zgłębiać gruntownie*) go into.

wgłębienie *n.* **1.** (= *zagłębienie*) hollow, cavity. **2.** (*np. w murze*) niche, recess.

wgłębny *a.* (*np. o złożu*) subterranean.

wgniatać *ipf.* **1.** (= *robić wgłębienie*) dent. **2.** (= *wciskać*) press into, ram into.

wgniecenie *n.* dent.

wgnieść *pf.* **wgniotę wgnieciesz wgniótł wgniotła wgnietli** *zob.* **wgniatać.**

wgramolić się *pf. pot.* scramble (*na coś* onto sth).

wgryzać się *ipf.*, **wgryźć się** *pf.* **wgryzę wgryziesz wgryzł wgryźli 1.** (*przegryzać*) bite into. **2.** (= *dostawać się w głąb*) penetrate, get into. **3.** (= *wżerać się*) eat into, corrode; (*o dymie*) sting. **4.** *pot.* (= *poznawać szczegółowo*) go into, look into.

whisky *f. indecl. kulin.* whiskey, *Br.* whisky.

wiać *ipf.* **wieję wiejesz 1.** (*o wietrze*) blow; **mocno wieje** it's very windy; **wiał silny wiatr** there was a strong wind (blowing); **wiało całą noc** the wind was blowing all throughout the night; **wieje od drzwi** there is a draft from the door. **2.** (*o chłodzie*) waft; **wiało grozą** *przen.* it was scary; **wiało pustką** *przen.* it was empty. **3.** *roln.* winnow. **4.** *pot.* (= *uciekać*) take flight, scam; **wiać, gdzie pieprz rośnie** cut and run, head South (of the border).

wiaderko *n. Gen.pl.* **-rek** small bucket.

wiadomo *adv. indecl.* it is a well-known fact, it is common knowledge that...; **jak wiadomo** as everybody knows; **o ile wiadomo** as far as one can tell; **nie wiadomo, kto przyjedzie** I (we, etc.) don't know who is coming; **nie wiadomo co i jak** nobody knows anything; **nigdy nic nie wiadomo** you never know; **z szefem nigdy nie wiadomo** you never know with the boss; **nic mi o tym nie wiadomo** not to my knowledge, not that I know of; **wiadomo było, że...** it was known that...; **wiadomo, trzeba będzie to nadrobić** it's obvious that I (we, etc.) will have to make up for it.

wiadomości *pl. Gen.* **-i 1.** (*wiedza*) knowledge; **zakres wiadomości** breadth of sb's knowledge; **braki w wiadomościach** insufficient knowledge. **2.** *radio, telew.* news; **wiadomości z kraju i z zagranicy** national and foreign news.

wiadomość *f.* (= *informacja*) piece of news, piece of information; (*przekazana, przesłana*) (= *wieść*) message; **dobra/zła wiadomość** good/bad news; **czekać na wiadomość** be waiting for a message, be waiting for news; **podać coś do publicznej wiadomości** make sth publicly known; **przyjąć do wiadomości** take note *l.* cognizance of; **przyjąłem** *l.* **przyjmuję do wiadomości** point taken; **zostawić (komuś) wiadomość** leave (sb) a message; **do twojej wiadomości** for your information; **masz od niego jakieś wiadomości?** have you heard from him?

wiadomy *a.* known, well-known; **wiadoma osoba** you-know-who; **jest wiadomą rzeczą, że...** it is common knowledge that..., everybody knows that...

wiadro *n. Gen.pl.* **-der** (*naczynie*) bucket; (*zawartość*) bucketful.

wiadukt *mi* (*nad drogą*) overpass; *Br.* flyover; (*nad doliną, torami kolejowymi w wykopie itp.*) viaduct.

wialnia *f. Gen.pl.* **-i** *zwł. roln.* winnower, fan.

wianek *mi* **-nk-** *Gen.* **-a 1.** garland; (*stroik na głowę*) chaplet; **wianek ze stokrotek** daisy chain; **wianek czosnku/cebuli** rope of garlic/onions; **wianek panieński** *przen.* maidenhead. **2.** *żegl.* grommet, grummet.

wiano *n. przest.* dowry.

wiara *f. Dat. i Loc.* **wierze 1.** *rel.* faith; **wiara chrześcijańska/islamska/żydowska** the Christian/Muslim/Jewish faith; **wiara pogańska** pagan faith; **nawrócić się na wiarę chrześcijańską** be converted to the Christian faith; **akt/wyznanie wiary** act/confession of faith; **wiara jest silniejsza niż rozum** faith is stronger than reason; **wiara przenosi góry** faith moves mountains. **2.** (= *przeświadczenie, ufność*) faith, confidence, credence, reliance, trust; **dawać komuś/czemuś wiarę** give credence to sb/sth; **w dobrej wierze** in good faith, bona fide; **w złej wierze** in bad faith, mala fide; **wiara w siebie** self-confidence; **pokładać wiarę w kimś/czymś** put one's trust in sb/sth; rely on sb/sth; **przyjmować coś na wiarę** take sth on trust; **nie do wiary** incredible, unbelievable. **3.** (= *wierność*) faith; **dochować (komuś/czemuś) wiary** keep one's faith (with sb/sth); **nie dochować wiary** break one's faith; **odsądzać kogoś od czci i wiary** besmirch sb's reputation. **4.** *pot.* (= *ludzie*) folks.

wiarołomca *mp*, **wiarołomczyni** *f. lit.* renegade.

wiarołomny *a. lit.* forsworn, faithless, renegade.

wiarus *mp przest.* old campaigner; *sl.* old sweat.

wiarygodność *f.* credibility, reliability.

wiarygodny *a.* credible, reliable, trustworthy; **wiarygodne źródło informacji** reliable source of information; **uznawać coś za wiarygodne** give credit to sth.

wiata *f.* shelter; **wiata na przystanku autobusowym** bus shelter.

wiaterek *mi* **-rk-** light *l.* gentle breeze.

wiatr *mi* **1.** (*ruch powietrza*) wind; (*lekki*) breeze; (*porywisty*) gale; **wiatr of morza** see breeze; **wiatr boczny** *żegl.* crosswind; **wiatr zmienił kierunek** the wind shifted; **zmienne wiatry** variable winds; **północny wiatr** north *l.* northern *l.* northerly wind; **tchnienie/podmuch wiatru** breath/gust of wind; **pod wiatr** against the wind, into the wind, upwind; **z wiatrem** with the wind, downwind; *żegl.* off the wind; **na wiatr** *żegl.* on the wind, windward; **żeglować pod wiatr** *l.* **na wiatr** run *l.* sail to windward; **iść ostro pod wiatr** sail close to the wind; **żeglować z wiatrem** run *l.* sail before the wind; **pełny wiatr** *żegl.* full wind; **pomyślny wiatr** favorable wind; *żegl.* free wind; **chwycić wiatr w żagle** fill the sails. **2.** *przen.* **szukać wiatru w polu** go on a wild-goose chase; **wystawić kogoś do wiatru** *pot.* leave sb in the lurch. **3.** *myśl.* (*powonienie psa l. zwierzyny*) scent. **4.** *myśl.* (= *zapach niesiony przez wiatr*) wind; **złapać wiatr** get the wind. **5.** *pl. fizj.* wind, flatus; **puszczać wiatry** break wind.

wiatraczek *mi* **-czk-** *Gen.* **-a 1.** (*wentylator*) fan. **2.** (*zabawka*) pinwheel. **3.** *tk.* **wiatraczek motarski** swift.

wiatrak *mi Gen.* **-a 1.** windmill; **walczyć z wiatrakami** *przen.* tilt at windmills. **2.** = **wiatraczek** 1.

wiatrochron *mi roln.* windbreak.

wiatrołom *mi leśn.* windfall.

wiatromierz *mi Gen.* **-a** *techn.* anemometer, wind gage.

wiatropędny *a. med.* carminative.

wiatropylny *a. bot.* anemophilous, wind-pollinated.

wiatrował *mi leśn.* windfallen tree.

wiatrowy *a. techn.* **silnik wiatrowy** wind turbine.

wiatrówka *f. Gen.pl.* **-ek 1.** *broń* air gun, air rifle. **2.** (*kurtka*) field jacket, windbreaker; *Br.* windcheater.

wiatyk *mi rz.-kat.* viaticum.

wiącha *f. pot.* bunch of curses; **posłać** *l.* **puścić komuś wiąchę** curse sb up and down.

wiądł *itd. pf. zob.* **więdnąć**.

wiąz *mi bot., stol.* elm (*Ulmus*).

wiązać *ipf.* **-żę -żesz 1.** (= *łączyć, okręcając czymś*) tie, fasten, wrap (*sth*) (up *l.* together) (*czymś* with sth); **wiązać coś w pęczki** bundle sth up *l.* together; tie sth up in bundles. **2.** (= *krępować, ściskać*) bind, truss (*sb l. sth*) (up) (*czymś* with sth); (*osobę l. jej kończyny*) pinion; **wiązać komuś ręce i nogi** *t. przen.* bind *l.* tie sb hand and foot; **wiązać włosy wstążką** bind up one's hair with a ribbon. **3.** (= *zaplątywać w węzeł*) tie, knot; (= *łączyć węzłem*) knot (*sth*) together; **wiązać krawat/muszkę** knot a necktie/bow tie. **4.** *przest.* (= *organizować, zawiązywać*) contrive. **5.** (*o kleju, cemencie, zaprawie murarskiej*) (= *spajać*) bond; **ten klej wiąże szkło z metalem** this glue bonds glass to metal; this glue bonds glass and metal together; (= *twardnieć*) set. **6.** *przen.* (= *kojarzyć*) connect, associate; **ściśle związany z czymś** closely connected with sth; bound up with sth; (= *zaangażowany w coś*) bound up in sth; **wiązać koniec z końcem** make (both) ends meet; scrape a living; **wiązać z kimś/czymś (wielkie) nadzieje** have (high) expectations for sb/sth. **7.** *chem., biochem.* (= *wychwytywać, pochłaniać*) fix; **bakterie potrafią wiązać azot z atmosfery** bacteria are capable of fixing atmospheric nitrogen. **8.** *szachy* (*bierkę, ograniczając jej ruchy*) pin. **9.** *wojsk.* (*siły nieprzyjaciela*) engage. ~ **się** *ipf.* **1.** (= *przymocowywać się*) tie o.s., fasten o.s. (*do czegoś* to sth). **2.** *przen.* (= *tworzyć związek*) **wiązać się z kimś** (= *wybierać jako partnera*) engage into a relationship with sb; **wiązać się węzłem małżeńskim** be joined in matrimony; *pot.* tie the knot. **3.** **wiązać się z czymś** (= *przyłączać się*) affiliate *l.* associate o.s. with sth. **4.** *przen.* (*o skojarzeniach, zależnościach formalnych l. logicznych*) **wiązać się umową** *prawn.* be bound by an agreement; **z tym zezwoleniem wiąże się pewien warunek** there is a condition attached to this permission; **twoje nowe stanowisko wiąże się z większą odpowiedzialnością** your new post entails greater responsibility; **wiąże się z tym domem pewna opowieść** there is a story connected with this house. **5.** (*o rzeczach połączonych spoiwem*) *t. chem.* (*o atomach*) bond; **atomy węgla wiążą się w łańcuchy i pierścienie** carbon atoms bond to form chains and rings.

wiązadło *n. Gen.pl.* **-deł** *anat.* ligament.

wiązanie *n.* **1.** *chem., fiz.* bond; **wiązanie jonowe/wodorowe** ionic/hydrogen bond; **energia wiązania** binding energy. **2.** *bud.* (= *układ cegieł*) bond. **3.** *bud.* (= *twardnienie spoiwa*) setting. **4.** *narty* binding. **5.** *biochem.* fixation (*czegoś* of sth).

wiązanka *f. Gen.pl.* **-ek 1.** (= *pęk, bukiet*) bunch; (= *bukiecik kwiatów*) posy, bouquet. **2.** (= *wybór*) **wiązanka przebojów** selection of hits. **3.** *pot.* (= *seria przekleństw*) bunch of curses; *zob.* **wiącha**.

wiązany *a.* **1.** *handl.* (*o sprzedaży, umowie*) tie-in; **transakcja wiązana** package deal. **2.** *teor.lit.* **mowa wiązana** metrical language.

wiązar *mi Gen.* **-a** *bud.* truss.

wiązka *f. Gen.pl.* **-ek 1.** (= *pęk*) bundle; **wiązka siana/patyków** bundle of hay/sticks; **wiązka chrustu** fagot, *Br.* faggot. **2.** *anat., bot.* fascicle; **wiązka naczyniowa** *bot.* vascular bundle. **3.** *fiz.* beam; **wiązka światła/elektronów/laserowa** light/electron/laser beam.

wiązowiec *mi* **-wc-** *Gen.* **-a** *bot.* hackberry (*Celtis*).

wiązowy *a. stol.,bud.* elmwood; **drewno wiązowe** elm, elmwood.

wiążący *a. prawn.* (*o umowie, decyzji, uzgodnieniach*) binding.

wibracja *f.* **1.** vibration. **2.** *pl. pot.* (= *oddziaływanie osób l. miejsc na psychikę ludzką*) vibrations; *sl.* vibes.

wibracyjny *a.* (*o ruchu*) vibratory; **prostownik wibracyjny** *el.* vibrator.

wibrafon *mi muz.* vibraphone; *pot.* vibes.

wibrator *mi Gen.* **-a** vibrator.

wibrować *ipf.* vibrate.

wice *mp indecl. pot.* (= *zastępca*) vice; (= *wiceprezydent*) V.P., vp, veep.

wiceadmirał *mp pl.* **-owie** *wojsk.* vice-admiral.

wicedyrektor *mp* deputy director; *szkoln.* deputy (head).

wicegubernator *mp polit.* lieutenant governor.

wicehrabia *mp Acc.* **-ego** *l.* **-ę** *Gen.* **-ego** *l.* **-i** *Dat.* **-emu** *l.* **-i** *Ins.* **-ą** *Loc.* **-i** *l.* **-im** *Voc.* **-o** *pl.* **-owie** *Gen.* **-ów** viscount.

wicehrabina *f.* vicecountess.

wicekanclerz *mp uniw.* vice-chancellor.

wicekonsul *mp pl.* **-owie** *Gen.* **-ów** *polit.* vice-consul.

wicekról *mp pl.* **-owie** *Gen.* **-ów** *polit.* viceroy.

wicemarszałek *mp* **-łk-** *pl.* **-owie wicemarszałek Sejmu** Deputy-Speaker of the Sejm (*in Poland*).

wiceminister *mp* **-tr-** *pl.* **-owie** deputy minister.

wicemistrz *mp pl.* **-owie** *Gen.pl.* **-ów** *sport* vice-champion, runner-up.

wicemistrzostwo *n. sport* vice-championship.

wicemistrzowski *a. sport* (*o tytule*) vice-champion's.

wicepremier *mp polit.* deputy prime minister.

wiceprezes *mp pl.* **-i** *l.* **-owie** vice-president.

wiceprezydent *mp polit.* vice-president.

wiceprezydentura *f. polit.* vice-presidency.

wiceprzewodnicząca *f. Gen.* **-ej**, **wiceprze-wodniczący** *mp* vice-chair, viceperson; (*tylko o mężczyźnie*) vice-chairman.

wicher *mi* **-chr-** wind, gale; **pędzić jak wicher** run like the wind.

wichrzyciel *mp*, **wichrzycielka** *f. Gen.pl.* **-ek** troublemaker.

wichrzycielski *a.* troublemaking.

wichrzyć *md* **1.** (*włosy*) ruffle, muss up. **2.** stir up trouble; (= *podburzać*) stir (*sb*) up. **~ się** *ipf.* get ruffled.

wichura *f.* gale, storm wind.

wiciokrzew *mi bot.* woodbine (*Lonicera*).

wiciowiec *ma* **-wc-** *biol.* flagellate.

wić¹ *f.* **1.** (*gałązka*) with, twig. **2.** *pl. hist.* ban; summons to arms. **3.** *biol.* (*u jednokomórkow-ców*) flagellum. **4.** *zool., anat.* cirrus. **5.** *bot.* tendril.

wić² *ipf.* **wiję wijesz, wij** (*zwł. gniazdo*) weave. **~ się** *ipf.* **1.** (= *skręcać się*) writhe (about), wriggle, squirm, coil; **wić się z bólu/w męczarniach** writhe in pain/agony; **wić się z poczucia winy/wstydu** squirm with guilt/shame. **2.** (*o rzece, drodze*) wind (its way), meander, twist (and turn); (*o ścieżce, strumieniu, rozłogach rośliny*) ramble. **3.** (*o pnączu*) twine (*wokół czegoś* around *l.* about sth). **4.** (*o włosach, smużkach dymu*) curl.

wid *mi* (*w wyrażeniach idiomatycznych*) **ani widu, ani słychu o kimś/czymś** neither hide nor hair of sb/sth; **w pijanym widzie** in a drunken haze.

widać *ipf. tylko w formie bezosobowej* **widać kogoś/coś** sb/sth is visible; sb/sth can be seen; **widać, że...** it is evident that...; one can see that...; **to widać** it shows; **nie było cię widać** we couldn't see you; you were hidden from sight; **nigdzie ich nie widać** they're nowhere to be seen; **wciąż nie widać statku** the ship is still out of sight; **widać ci halkę** your petticoat is showing; **widać po nim, że pił** you can see he's been drinking; **widać, że jesteś przygotowany do egzaminu** you are evidently well prepared for the exam; **ze wzgórza będzie widać miasto jak na dłoni** the city will be plainly visible from the hill.

widelczyk *mi Gen.* **-a** small fork; **widelczyk de-serowy** dessert fork.

widelec *mi* **-lc-** *Gen.* **-a** *t. techn.* fork; **jeść no-żem i widelcem** eat with a knife and fork.

widełki *pl. Gen.* **-łek 1.** (*telefonu*) cradle; (*za-wieszonego pionowo*) hook. **2.** *muz.* **widełki stroi-kowe** tuning fork. **3.** (= *rozpiętość, zakres*) bracket.

wideo *n. indecl.* video, video (cassette) recorder, VCR; **gra wideo** video game; **kamera wideo** video camera, camcorder; **nagranie wideo** video recording; **taśma wideo** videotape; **nagra-ny na taśmę wideo** videotaped.

wideofon *mi* video phone.

wideokaseta *f.* videocassette.

wideoklip *mi* (music) video.

wideoteka *f.* video collection.

widlasty *a.* **1.** forked; *bot.* furcate. **2.** *techn.* **silnik widlasty** V-engine.

widliszek *ma* **-szk-** *ent.* malaria mosquito (*Anopheles*).

widłak *mi Gen.* **-a** *bot.* (= *roślina z rzędu Lyco-poda*) clubmoss, lycopod, wolf's-claw.

widły *pl. Gen.* **wideł 1.** fork, pitchfork; **robić z igły widły** make a mountain out of a molehill. **2.** (= *rozgałęzienie*) forking, branching; *form.* bi-furcation.

widmo *n.* **1.** (= *zjawa*) specter, phantom, ap-parition; **statek widmo** phantom ship. **2.** (= *przykre wyobrażenie l. wspomnienie*) ghost, specter; **widmo klęski/głodu** the specter of de-feat/famine. **3.** *fiz.* spectrum; **widmo elektro-magnetyczne** electromagnetic spectrum; **widmo Słońca** *astron.* solar spectrum.

widmowy *a.* **1.** (= *robiący wrażenie widma*) ghostly, ghostlike. **2.** *fiz.* spectral; **analiza wid-mowa** spectral analysis.

widnieć *ipf.* **-eję -ejesz 1.** (= *dawać się widzieć*) appear, be shown. **2.** *rzad.* (= *dnieć*) dawn; **już widnieje** it's dawning already.

widno *adv.* **1. jest widno** it's daylight. **2.** *arch.* = **widocznie**.

widnokrąg *mi* **-ę-** horizon.

widny *a.* light, full of light.

widoczek *mi* **-czk- 1.** (= *pejzaż*) landscape. **2.** (= *widokówka*) picture postcard.

widocznie *adv.* **1.** (= *sądząc po tym, co widać*) apparently; **widocznie nie ma go w domu** he's out, apparently; he seems to be out. **2.** (= *do-strzegalnie*) visibly, noticeably.

widoczność *f.* visibility; **dobra/zła/ograniczona widoczność** good/poor/low visibility.

widoczny *a.* visible, noticeable, evident; **po-mnik jest stąd widoczny** the monument can be seen from here.

widok *mi* **1.** view, prospect (*na coś* of sth); **wi-dok z lotu ptaka** bird's-eye view; **widok na morze** view of the sea; **pokój z widokiem na góry** room with a view of the mountains; **wystawić coś na widok publiczny** put sth on display; **mieć coś na widoku** (= *w planach*) have sth in view. **2.** (= *sce-na, rzecz do oglądania*) sight, scene; **co za wi-dok!** what a sight!; **niecіekawy widok** not a pret-ty sight; **przykry/przerażający widok** sore/appalling sight; **widok wart zobaczenia** sight worth seeing; **ujrzałem znajomy widok** I saw a fa-miliar scene. **3.** (= *pojawienie się w polu widze-nia*) sight (*kogoś / czegoś* of sb/sth); **nie cierpię wi-doku tego domu** I hate the sight of this house; **uciekłem na jego widok** I ran away at the sight of him. **4.** *mal.* (= *pejzaż*) landscape. **5.** *pl.* (= *perspektywy, szanse*) prospects, chance, expec-tation (*na coś* of sth); **widoki na błyskotliwą karie-rę** prospects of a brilliant career; **marne widoki na powodzenie** poor chance of success.

widokowy *a.* **okno widokowe** picture window; **punkt widokowy** beauty spot, overlook; **taras wi-dokowy** view terrace.

widokówka *f. Gen.pl.* **-ek** picture postcard.

widomy *a. lit.* visible, noticeable.

widowisko *n.* show, spectacle; **robić z siebie wi-dowisko** make an exhibition *l.* spectacle of o.s.

widowiskowo *adv.* spectacularly.

widowiskowość *f.* showiness.

widowiskowy *a.* **1.** (= *pokazany z rozmachem*) spectacular, impressive. **2.** *sport* **sporty widowiskowe** spectator sports.

widownia *f. Gen.pl.* **-i 1.** *teatr, kino* (*miejsca*) seats, house; (*widzowie*) audience; **pusta/pełna widownia** empty/full house. **2.** (= *miejsce zdarzeń*) stage, arena; **główna ulica była widownią strzelaniny** the main street was the stage of a shootout.

widywać *ipf.* see (occasionally). **~ się** *ipf.* see each other *l.* meet (occasionally).

widz *mp pl.* **-owie** spectator; (*przypadkowy*) onlooker; (= *świadek*) witness.

widzenie *n.* **1.** (= *wzrok*) sight, vision; **pole widzenia** *fiz.* field of vision; **punkt widzenia** point of view; **znać kogoś z widzenia** know sb by sight. **2.** (= *odwiedziny w więzieniu*) visit. **3.** (= *halucynacja*) vision, hallucination. **4. do widzenia** good bye.

widziadło *n. Gen.pl.* **-deł** apparition.

widzialność *f.* = **widoczność**.

widzialny *a.* visible; **widzialny gołym okiem** visible to the naked eye.

widziany *a.* seen; **mile widziany** welcome; **źle widziany** unwelcome.

widzieć *ipf.* **-dzę -dzisz 1.** (= *spostrzegać*) see (*że...* (that)...); notice (*że...* that...); catch sight of (*sb l. sth*); *arch.* espy; **widzę jak przez mgłę** I see as if through a mist; **widzieć kogoś/coś kątem oka** see sb/sth out of the corner of one's eye; **widziałem już ten film** I've seen this film before; **widziałem jakiś błysk w ciemnościach** I saw *l.* caught sight of a flash in the dark; **nie chcę cię więcej widzieć na oczy!** I don't want to set eyes on you again; **nikogo tam nie widziałem** I didn't see *l.* notice anyone there; **widziałem to na własne oczy** I saw it with my own eyes; **widzieć coś jak na dłoni** see sth plainly; **widzieć coś w ciemnych barwach** see sth in dark colors; **jak widzę, posprzątaliście pokój** I can see you've tidied up the room; **nic nie widzę** I can't see anything; **nie widzieć na jedno oko** I'm blind in one eye; **on świata poza nią nie widzi** he only has eyes for her; **to oszust, jakiego świat nie widział** he's a crook whose like the world hasn't seen; **tyle go widzieli** that was the last they saw of him; **co widzę!** what do I see?; **kogóż to widzę!** is it you I see?; **kto widział takie rzeczy!** who ever saw such a thing?; **sam widzisz** you can see for yourself. **2.** (= *spotykać*) see (*sb*) (*w sprawie czegoś* about sth); **miło mi znów cię widzieć** (it's) nice to see you again; **szef chce cię widzieć w sprawie tej umowy** the boss wants to see you about that contract. **3.** (= *wyobrażać sobie*) see, visualize; **nie widzę siebie w roli ojca** I can't visualize myself as a father. **4. widzieć w kimś coś** *l.* **widzieć kogoś jako coś** view sb as sth; look on *l.* upon sb as sth; **wszyscy widzą w nim bohatera** they all look on him as a hero. **5.** (= *pojmować, rozumieć*) see, understand; **a widzisz!** there you are!; **nie widzę w tym nic śmiesznego** I fail to see the funny side of it; **czy nie widzisz, że miałem rację?** can't you see I was right?; **wreszcie widzę, co masz na my-**

śli at last I see what you mean. **~ się** *ipf.* **1.** (= *oglądać siebie samego*) see o.s.; **widzę się w lustrze** I see myself in the mirror. **2.** (= *dostrzegać się nawzajem*) see one another *l.* each other. **3.** (= *wyobrażać sobie coś na własny temat*) see o.s., fancy o.s. (*czymś l. jako coś* as sth); **widział się laureatem Nagrody Nobla** he fancied himself as a Nobel Prize winner. **4.** (= *dostrzegać się nawzajem*) see one another *l.* each other; **nie widzieli się w tłumie** they couldn't see each other in the crowd. **5.** *pot.* (= *podobać się*) like; **jak ci się widzi moja marynarka?** how do you like my jacket? **6.** (= *spotkać się*) see, meet (*z kimś* sb) (*w sprawie czegoś* about sth) (*żeby coś zrobić* in order to do sth); **muszę się widzieć w tej sprawie z moim prawnikiem** I have to see my lawyer about it.

widzimisię *n. indecl.* whim, caprice.

wiec *mi* meeting, rally, gathering; **wiec wyborczy** electoral meeting; **wiec partyjny** party rally.

wiecha *f.* **1.** *bud.* perch. **2.** *bot.* tassel, panicle. **3.** *żegl.* sparable buoy.

wiecheć *mi* **-chci-** *Gen.* **-a** whisk, wisp; (*włosów na głowie*) mop.

wiecować *ipf.* meet, gather, hold a meeting.

wieczerza *f. Gen.pl.* **-y** *lit.* supper; **ostatnia wieczerza** *rel.* the Last Supper; **wieczerza wigilijna** Christmas Eve supper.

wieczerzać *ipf. przest.* have supper, sup.

wieczko *n. Gen.pl.* **-czek** lid, top.

wiecznie *adv.* eternally, endlessly, perpetually; always; **rośliny wiecznie zielone** *bot.* evergreen plants; **wiecznie jesteś głodny!** you're always hungry!

wieczność *f.* eternity.

wiecznotrwały *a.* everlasting.

wieczny *a.* **1.** (= *trwający bez końca*) eternal, everlasting, perpetual, undying, immortal; **wieczne prawdy** *fil.* the eternal truths; **życie wieczne** *l.* **żywot wieczny** *rel.* eternal life; **wieczny odpoczynek** eternal rest; **wieczna młodość** eternal youth; **wieczna miłość/przyjaźń** everlasting love/friendship; **wieczna sława** undying fame; **wieczny ruch** perpetual motion; **na wieczne czasy** forever, for all eternity; **wieczny student** *żart.* eternal student. **2. wieczne pióro** fountain pen. **3.** (= *istniejący nieprzerwanie, przez cały rok*) perennial; **wieczny śnieg** perennial snow; **wieczna zmarzlina** *geol.* permafrost. **4.** (= *nieustanny*) endless, unending, permanent; **wieczne kłopoty** endless troubles.

wieczorek *mi* **-rk-** evening party, soirée.

wieczorny *a.* evening; **gazeta wieczorna** evening paper; **wiadomości wieczorne** evening news.

wieczorowy *a.* **1.** evening; **suknia wieczorowa** evening dress. **2.** *szkoln.* **szkoła wieczorowa** night school.

wieczorówka *f. Gen.pl.* **-ek** *pot.* night school.

wieczorynka *f. Gen.pl.* **-ek** *TV* evening program for children.

wieczór *mi* **-o-** *Gen.* **-u** *l.* **-a 1.** (*część doby*) evening; (= *pora wieczornej aktywności*) night; **wieczorem** in the evening; **wieczorami** evenings;

of an evening; **co wieczór** every evening; nightly; **dziś wieczorem** tonight, this evening; **wczoraj wieczorem** last night; **tamtego wieczoru** that evening; **w piątek wieczór** Friday night *l.* evening; **od rana do wieczora** from morning till night; **co wieczór** every evening; **wieczór w kinie** night at the movies; **dobry wieczór!** good evening! **2.** (*impreza*) evening; **wieczór muzyczny/poetycki** musical/poetry evening; **wieczór kawalerski** bachelor party; *żart.* stag party.

wieczysty *a. prawn.* perpetual.

Wiedeń *mi* -**dni**- *Gen.* -**a** *geogr.* Vienna.

wiedeńczyk *mp* Viennese.

wiedeński *a.* Viennese.

wiedli *itd. pf. zob.* **wieść**.

wiedza *f.* knowledge; (*tradycyjna*) lore; (= *nauka*) learning; (= *uświadomienie sobie*) realization; **wiedza książkowa** book learning, booklore; **wiedza ogólna** general knowledge; **bez mojej wiedzy** without my knowledge; **dziedzina wiedzy** discipline of learning.

wiedzie *itd. ipf. zob.* **wieść**.

wiedzieć *ipf.* **wiem wiesz wiedzą** know (*o czymś* about *l.* of sth) (*że...* (that)...); **wiem o tobie wszystko** I know all about you; **wiem to na pewno** I know it for sure; **wiem, że byłeś w Detroit** I know (that) you've been to Detroit; **wiem, że ona jest niewinna** I know her to be innocent; **on dużo wie** he knows a lot; **wiedzieć, co w trawie piszczy** have *l.* keep one's ear to the ground; **czy ja wiem...** *l.* **bo ja wiem...** well, I don't know...; **niewiele wiem o Dublinie** I don't know much about Dublin; **nie wiem, co robić** I don't know what to do; **nie wie lewica, co czyni prawica** the left hand doesn't know what the right hand is doing; **o ile wiem** as far as I know; as far as I'm aware; **choćby nie wiem co** no matter what happens; **kto to wie?** who can say?; **kto wie, co nas czeka?** who knows what lies ahead?; **kto wie, co przyniesie przyszłość?** who knows what the future holds?; **skąd wiesz, że to prawda?** how do you know it's true?; **wiesz co?** (do) you know what?; **trzeba wam wiedzieć, że...** you must know that...; **a żebyś wiedział!** you bet!; **no wiesz!** (*wyraża zgorszenie*) how can you!; **Bóg jeden wie** God only knows; **diabli wiedzą co** the devil knows what.

wiedźma *f.* **1.** *mit.* witch. **2.** *pog.* (= *kobieta*) witch, hag, harridan.

wieję *itd. ipf. zob.* **wiać**.

wiejski *a.* village, country, rural; **życie wiejskie** country life; **ludność wiejska** rural population.

wiek *mi* **1.** (= *liczba przeżytych lat życia*) age, one's years; **w moim wieku** at my age; **w wieku pięciu lat** at (the age of) five; **osoba w twoim wieku** person of your age *l.* of your years; **młody/średni/podeszły wiek** young/middle/old age; **mężczyzna w średnim wieku** man of middle age, middle-aged man; **ona jest aktywna jak na swój wiek** she's active for her years; **wiek niemowlęcy** infancy; **wiek dziecięcy** childhood; **wiek pokwitania** adolescence; **wiek dojrzały** maturity; **wiek męski** manhood; **wiek kobiecy** womanhood; **wiek szkolny/przedszkolny** school/preschool age; **wiek**

odpowiedzialności prawnej *prawn.* the age *l.* years of discretion; **wiek emerytalny** retirement age; **wiek poborowy** the age of military service; **trudny wiek** the awkward age; **dożyć sędziwego wieku** live to a great age; **być nad wiek dojrzałym** be mature beyond one's years; **być w sile** *l.* **kwiecie wieku** be in one's prime; **dziecko nad wiek rozwinięte** precocious child; **(nie) wyglądać na swój wiek** (not) look one's age; **zachowuj się, jak na twój wiek przystało!** be *l.* act your age!; **wiek wyrębu** *leśn.* cutting age. **2.** (= *czas istnienia rzeczy nieożywionych*) **wiek Ziemi/Wszechświata** the age of the Earth/Universe; **smak wina poprawia się z wiekiem** the taste of wine improves with age. **3.** (= *epoka*) age; **złoty wiek** the golden age (*czegoś* of sth); **wiek brązu/żelaza** the Bronze/Iron Age; **wieki średnie** the Middle Ages; **ciemne wieki** the dark ages; **wiek oświecenia** the Enlightenment, the Age of Reason; **wiek atomowy** the nuclear age; **wiek komputerów osobistych** the age of personal computers. **4.** (= *stulecie*) century; **XXI wiek** the twenty-first *l.* 21st century; **na przełomie wieków** at the turn of the century; **w ubiegłym/przyszłym wieku** in the last/next century. **5.** *pl.* (= *wiele pokoleń l. stuleci; pot.* = *długi czas*) ages; **nie widziałem cię całe wieki** I haven't seen you for ages; **od wieków nie byliśmy w teatrze** it's (been) ages since we went to the theater; **na wieki** forever, for ever; **na wieki wieków** for ever and ever; **przed wiekami** ages ago.

wieko *n.* lid, top, cover.

wiekopomny *a. lit.* historic, immortal.

wiekowy *a.* ancient; (*o człowieku*) aged.

wiekuisty *a. rel.* eternal, everlasting; **światłość wiekuista** eternal light.

wielbiciel *mp*, **wielbicielka** *f. Gen.pl.* -**ek 1.** (= *miłośnik*) admirer, adulator, fan. **2.** (= *adorator*) adorer.

wielbić *ipf.* -**ij** adore, adulate.

wielbłąd *ma zool.* camel (*Camelus*); **wielbłąd jednogarbny** Arabian camel (*C. dromedarius*); **wielbłąd dwugarbny** Bactrian camel (*C. bactrianus*).

wielbłądzi *a.* camel('s); **wełna wielbłądzia** camelhair, camel's hair.

wielce *adv. lit.* very, greatly, highly; **wielce szanowny panie!** *przest.* (*w nagłówku listu*) Honored Sir.

wiele *num. Ins.* -**oma** *l.* -**u 1.** *count* many, a great many, a (great) number of (*sb l. sth*); *noncount* much, a great amount of, a great *l.* good deal of (*sth*); *pot.* (*bez względu na policzalność*) a lot, lots (*kogoś / czegoś* of sb/sth); **wielu studentów** many students; a (great) number of students; a lot of students; lots of students; **od wielu lat** for many years; **z wieloma przyjaciółmi** with many friends; **rodzina, jakich wiele** family like many others; **jeden z wielu** one of (a great) many; **pod wieloma względami** in many respects; in a number of respects; **wiele czasu** much time; a lot of time; lots of time; **wiele pieniędzy** a great amount of money; a good deal of money; a lot of money; lots of money; **zrobić wiele dobrego** do much good, do a lot of good; **wiele hałasu o nic**

much ado about nothing; **żeby to zrobić, trzeba wiele odwagi** it takes a lot of courage to do it. **2.** *przest.* (= *ile*) *count* how many; *noncount* how much; **wiele to kosztuje?** how much is it?; **wiele masz lat?** how old are you? – *adv.* **więcej** much, a lot, a good *l.* great deal; **wiele czytam/piszę** I read/write a lot; **o wiele lepszy** much better; far better; a lot better; a good deal better; **o wiele więcej** much more; **o wiele za dużo** *noncount* much too much; *count* much too many; **obsługa pozostawia wiele do życzenia** the service leaves much to be wished; **to wiele dla mnie znaczy** it means a lot to me; **tego już za wiele** that's too much.

wielebność *f.* **wasza/jego wielebność** Your/His Reverence.

wielebny *a. kośc.* **1.** reverend; (*skrót tytułu przed imieniem i nazwiskiem*) Rev.; **wielebny John Smith** the Reverend John Smith, Rev. J. Smith, Rev. Mr. Smith. **2.** (*tytuł archidiakona w kościele anglikańskim*) venerable. – *mp* (= *duchowny*) clergyman.

wielekroć *adv. lit.* many times, many a time.

wielgachny *a. pot.* whopping.

Wielka Brytania *f. Gen.* **Wielkiej Brytanii** *geogr.* Great Britain.

Wielkanoc *f. Gen.* **Wielkanocy** *l.* **Wielkiejnocy** *rel.* Easter; **na Wielkanoc** at Easter; **ferie wielkanocne** Easter break.

wielkanocny *a.* Easter; **jajko wielkanocne** Easter egg.

wielki *a.* **większy 1.** (= *duży według jakiejś skali*) big, large, huge; **wielki dom** big house; **wielkie drzewo** big tree; **wielkie litery** capital letters; **wielka liczba** large number; **wielka ryba** huge fish; **wielki majątek** large fortune; **wielkie straty** big losses; **wielki przemysł** big industry; **wielki palec u nogi** big toe; **wielki piec** *metal.* blast furnace. **2.** *w nazwach własnych* (*zw.* = *duży przez kontrast z małym*) Great; *rzad.* Big, Large, Grand; **Wielka Brytania** Great Britain; **Wielka Niedźwiedzica** the Great Bear; **Wielki Wóz** the Big Dipper; **Wielki Obłok Magellana** the Large Magellanic Cloud; **Wielki Kanion** the Grand Canyon. **3.** (= *silny, znaczny, emocjonujący, ambitny*) great; *pot. l. emf.* big; **wielkie cierpienie** great suffering; **wielka miłość** great love; **wielkie oczekiwania** great expectations; **wielka odpowiedzialność** great responsibility; **wielka pociecha** great comfort; **wielka przygoda** great adventure; **wielkie plany** great *l.* big plans; **zrobić na kimś wielkie wrażenie** make a great *l.* big impression on sb; **to nic wielkiego** it's nothing much; **wielka mi rzecz!** *iron.* big deal!; **Wielki Wybuch** *astron.* the Big Bang. **4.** (= *wyróżniający się, ważny, wybitny*) great; **wielki człowiek** great man; **wielkie odkrycie** great discovery; **wielki kryzys** *hist.* the (Great) Depression; **wielka wojna** *hist.* (= *I wojna światowa*) the Great War; **Aleksander Wielki** *hist.* Alexander the Great; **Piotr Wielki** *hist.* Peter the Great; **wielki Boże!** great God!, God almighty! **5.** (= *wysoki rangą*) grand; **wielki książę/wezyr/mistrz** Grand Duke/Vizir/Master; **Wielkie Księstwo Litewskie** *hist.* the

Grand Duchy of Lithuania; **wielka ława przysięgłych** *prawn.* grand jury. **6.** (= *imponujący; t. iron.*) grand; **wielka pani** grand lady; **wielki pan** grand lord; **na wielką skalę** on a grand scale; **w wielkim stylu** in grand style. **7.** *rel.* (= *związany z Wielkanocą*) **Wielki Tydzień** Easter week, Passion Week, Holy Week; **Wielki Czwartek** Maundy Thursday; *rz.-kat.* Holy Thursday; **Wielki Piątek** Good Friday; **Wielka Sobota** Holy Saturday; **Wielka Niedziela** Easter Saturday, Easter Day; **wielki post** Lent.

wielkoduszność *f.* magnanimity, generosity.

wielkoduszny *a.* magnanimous, generous.

wielkogłowie *n. pat.* megacephaly, megalocephaly.

wielkoksiążęcy *a.* grandducal.

wielkolud *mp pl.* **-y** *mit.* giant.

wielkomiejski *a.* urban, metropolitan.

wielkonakładowy *a.* high-circulation.

wielkopański *a. gł. uj.* lordly, grand.

wielkopłytowy *a bud.* system-built.

Wielkopolska *f. geogr., hist.* Great Poland.

wielkopostny *a. rel.* Lenten, Quadragesimal.

wielkoprzemysłowy *a.* industrial.

wielkoruski *a. hist.* Great Russian.

wielkość *f.* **1.** (= *rozmiary, gabaryty*) size; **naturalnej wielkości** life-size; **tej samej wielkości** of the same size; **drugi/trzeci co do wielkości** the second/third biggest *l.* largest. **2.** (= *ogrom*) greatness, largeness. **3.** (= *znaczenie, wybitność*) greatness, significance, grandeur; **mania wielkości** *psych., pat.* delusions of grandeur. **4.** *astron.* (*w skali jasności*) magnitude; **gwiazda pierwszej/drugiej wielkości** *t. przen.* star of the first/second magnitude. **5.** *mat.* quantity; **wielkość skalarna/wektorowa** scalar/vector quantity.

wielmożny *a.* **wielmożny pan** *l.* **wielmożna pani** *przest.* your *l.* his *l.* her honor.

wieloaspektowy *a.* multifaceted, many-sided.

wielobarwny *a.* colorful, multicolored, variegated.

wieloboczny *a. geom.* multilateral.

wielobój *mi* **-o-** *Gen.pl.* **-ów** *sport* (= *dziesięciobój*) decathlon; (= *pięciobój*) pentathlon.

wielobóstwo *n. rel.* polytheism.

wielocukier *mi* **-kr-** *chem.* polysaccharide.

wielocyfrowy *a.* multidigit.

wieloczęściowy *a.* multipartite, multiplex.

wielodostępny *a. komp.* multiaccess.

wielodyscyplinarny *a.* multidisciplinary.

wielodzietny *a.* with many children.

wieloetniczny *a. socjol.* multiethnic.

wielofunkcyjny *a.* multipurpose.

wielogłosowość *f. muz.* polyphony.

wielogłosowy *a. muz.* polyphonic.

wielogodzinny *a.* lasting many hours.

wieloguzkowiec *ma* **-wc-** *paleont.* (= *ssak z rzędu Multituberculata*) multituberculate.

wielojęzyczny *a.* multilingual.

wielokadłubowiec *mi* **-wc-** *Gen.* **-a** *żegl.* multihull.

wielokąt *mi Gen.* **-a** *geom.* polygon.

wielokątny *a. geom.* polygonal.

wielokierunkowy *a.* **1.** multidirectional. **2.** *uniw.* (*o studiach*) multidisciplinary.

wielokomórkowiec *ma* -wc- *biol.* multicellular organism.

wielokomórkowy *a. biol.* multicellular.

wielokrążek *mi* -żk- *Gen.* -a *mech.* pulley, block of pulleys.

wielokropek *mi* -pk- *Gen.* -a *druk.* suspension points.

wielokrotnie *adv.* many times, repeatedly, time and time again.

wielokrotność *f.*, **wielokrotna** *f. Gen.* -ej *mat.* multiple; **najmniejsza wspólna wielokrotność** the least common multiple.

wielokrotny *a.* **1.** multiple; **opakowanie wielokrotnego użytku** *handl.* reusable package; **złamanie wielokrotne** *pat.* multiple fracture. **2.** *gram.* iterative; **czasownik wielokrotny** iterative verb.

wielokształtny *a.* multiform.

wielokulturowy *a. socjol.* multicultural.

wielokwiatowy *a. bot.* multiflorous.

wieloletni *a.* **1.** of many years, of long standing; **wieloletnia współpraca** many years of collaboration. **2.** *bot.* perennial.

wielomęstwo *n. antrop.* polyandry.

wielomian *mi mat.* polynomial.

wielomiliardowy *a.* of several billion; **wielomiliardowy dług** debt of several billion.

wielomilionowy *a.* of several million.

wielomówny *a.* eloquent, loquacious.

wielonarodowościowy *a. polit., socjol.* multiethnic.

wielonarodowy *a. polit.* multinational.

wieloobwodowy *a. el.* multicircuit.

wieloosobowy *a.* **1.** (= *dla wielu osób*) for many people. **2.** (= *składający się z wielu osób*) numerous, of many people.

wieloowocowy *a.* (*o produktach spożywczych*) multifruit; *bot.* polycarpic.

wielopierścieniowy *a. chem.* polycyclic.

wielopiętrowy *a. bud.* multistory, highrise.

wielopłaszczyznowy *a.* multiplanar.

wielopłat *mi lotn.* multiplane.

wielopokoleniowy *a.* of many generations.

wielopostaciowy *f.* **1.** = **wielokształtny**. **2.** *min.* polymorphic.

wielopoziomowy *a.* multilevel.

wieloraczki *pl. Gen.* -ów multiplets.

wieloraki *a.* multiple; (*o barwach, argumentach*) manifold; **liczebnik wieloraki** *jęz.* distributive numeral.

wielorasowy *a.* multiracial; *kynol.* mixed breed.

wielorodzinny *a.* multi-family; **dom wielorodzinny** multi-family house.

wieloródka *f. Gen.pl.* -ek multipara.

wieloryb *ma zool.* whale.

wielorybi *a.* (*o mięsie, tłuszczu*) whale.

wielorybnictwo *n.* whaling; whale fishing.

wielorybniczy *a.* (*o harpunie, przemyśle*) whaling; (*o połowach*) whale.

wieloskładnikowy *a.* multicomponent; (*o nawozie*) mixed.

wielosłowie *n.* verbosity, wordiness.

wielostopniowy *a.* multistage; **rakieta wielostopniowa** multistage rocket.

wielostronny *a.* many-sided; multifaceted; (*o wykształceniu, zainteresowaniach*) versatile; (*o rokowaniach*) multilateral.

wieloszczet *ma zool.* polychaete (*Polychaeta*).

wielościan *mi geom.* polyhedron; **wielościan foremny** regular polyhedron.

wielościenny *a. geom.* polyhedral.

wielotomowy *a.* multivolume(d).

wielotonowy *a.* of many-tons.

wielotorowy *a.* **1.** (= *wielokierunkowy*) multifarious, multifaceted. **2.** (= *mający wiele torów*) multi-track.

wielotysięczny *a.* (*o tłumie, manifestacji*) of thousands.

wielowarstwowy *a.* multi-layered; multi-ply; **płyta wielowarstwowa** *techn.* sandwich board.

wielowartościowy *a. chem.* multivalent; polyvalent.

wielowarzywny *a.* mixed-vegetable; (*o mieszance*) vegetable; **sałatka wielowarzywna** *kulin.* mixed salad, cooked vegetable salad.

wielowątkowy *a.* varied; (*o powieści*) multiplot.

wielowiekowy *a.* of many centuries; (*o kulturze, tradycji*) centuries-old.

wielowymiarowy *a. t. mat.* multidimensional.

wielowypust *mi techn.* splines.

wielozakresowy *a. fiz., techn.* multirange.

wielozmianowy *a.* multishift; **praca wielozmianowa** shiftwork; **wielozmianowy system pracy** shiftwork system.

wieloznaczność *f.* ambiguity.

wieloznaczny *a.* ambiguous; equivocal.

wielożeństwo *n.* polygamy.

wielożerny *a. biol.* polyphagous.

wielu *num. zob.* **wiele**.

wieniec *mi* -ńc- *Gen.* -a **1.** (*wiązanka*) wreath; **wieniec laurowy** *przen.* laurels; **złożyć wieniec** lay a wreath. **2.** ring. **3.** *myśl.* antlers. **4.** *techn.* (*koła, koła zębatego*) rim.

wieńcowy *a. anat.* (*o naczyniach, tętnicy, krążeniu*) coronary; **choroba wieńcowa** *pat.* coronary heart disease.

wieńczyć *ipf.* **1.** *lit.* crown (*czymś* with sth); cap; **koniec wieńczy dzieło** the end crowns all; **wieńczyć wawrzynem** laurel. **2.** *bud.* surmount.

wieprz *ma Gen.pl.* -y *l.* -ów hog. – *mp Gen.pl.* -y *l.* -ów *obelż.* swine; **ty wieprzu!** you swine!; **rzucać perły przed wieprze** cast pearls before swine.

wieprzek *ma* -rzk- porker.

wieprzowina *f. kulin.* pork.

wieprzowy *a. kulin.* pork; **żeberka wieprzowe** spareribs.

wiercenie *n.* drilling.

wierch *mi dial.* peak, summit.

wiercić *ipf.* **1.** (= *świdrować*) drill, bore; **wiercić komuś dziurę w brzuchu** *pot.* badger sb; **wiercić w poszukiwaniu gazu/ropy/wody** drill for gas/oil/water. **2.** *przen.* (= *drażnić*) tingle; **wierci mnie w nosie** I'm feeling a tingle in my nose. ~ **się** *ipf.* (= *być niespokojnym*) fidget.

wiercipięta *f. l. mp żart.* fidget, fidgeter.

wiernie *adv.* faithfully.

wiernopoddańczy *a.* servile; (*o hołdzie*) abject.

wierność *f.* **1.** (= *oddanie*) faithfulness; **dochować wierności królowej** keep allegiance to the Queen; **przysięga wierności** oath of allegiance; **przysięgać/ślubować wierność (komuś/czemuś)** swear/pledge allegiance to (sb/sth). **2.** (*przekładu, adaptacji*) (= *zgodność*) faithfulness; **wierność odtwarzania** *techn.* fidelity (of reproduction); **wysoka wierność odtwarzania** high fidelity, hi-fi.

wierny *a.* faithful (*komuś/czemuś* to sb/sth). – *mp* (= *wyznawca*) believer, follower.

wiersz *mi Gen.* **-a** **1.** (= *utwór poetycki*) poem; **biały wiersz** blank verse. **2.** (= *wers*) verse. **3.** (= *linijka pisma*) line; **pisać od nowego wiersza** start a new line; **czytać między wierszami** read between the lines.

wierszokleta *mp pog.* versifier.

wierszowy *a.* **1.** (= *rymowany, wierszowany*) metrical. **2.** (= *dotyczący linijki tekstu*) line.

wierszówka *f. Gen.pl.* **-ek** *pot.* linage.

wierszyk *mi Gen.* **-a** rhyme; **wierszyk dla dzieci** nursery rhyme.

wiertarka *f. Gen.pl.* **-ek** drill; **wiertarka dentystyczna** *dent.* dental drill.

wiertło *n. Gen.pl.* **-teł** drill; bit.

wiertnia *f. Gen.pl.* **-i** *techn.* oil well surface installation.

wiertniczy *a.* drilling, boring; **otwór wiertniczy** borehole; **platforma wiertnicza** drilling rig *l.* platform; **wieża wiertnicza** derrick. – *mp* (*robotnik*) driller, borer.

wierutny *a.* (*o kłamstwie*) downright; (*o bzdurach*) utter; **to wierutne bzdury!** it's utter nonsense!

wierząca *f. Gen.* **-ej** *zob.* **wierzący.**

wierzący *mp rel.* believer, follower.

wierzba *f. bot.* willow (*Salix*); **wierzba płacząca** weeping willow (*Salix babylonica l. elegantissima*); **obiecywać gruszki na wierzbie** promise pie in the sky.

wierzbowy *a.* willow; **bazie wierzbowe** willow catkins.

wierzch *mi* **1.** (= *górna część*) top; (*dłoni*) back; (*ubrania*) outside; (*obuwia*) upper; **oczy wychodzą komuś na wierzch** *pot.* sb's eyes pop out; **nosić koszulę na wierzch** wear one's shirt over one's pants; **prawda wyjdzie na wierzch** the truth will out; **jeździć wierzchem** *jeźdź.* ride (on) horseback. **2.** (= *wieko*) lid.

wierzchni *a.* outer; top; **wierzchnia strona czegoś** the outside of sth; **wierzchnia warstwa (farby/lakieru)** overcoat (of paint/varnish); **odzież wierzchnia** outerwear.

wierzchołek *mi* **-łk-** *Gen.* **-a** **1.** (= *szczyt*) (*drzewa, masztu*) top; (*góry*) peak, summit, top; **wierzchołek góry lodowej** *przen.* tip of the iceberg. **2.** *geom.* vertex.

wierzchołkowy *a.* **1.** top. **2.** *geom., astron.* (*o kącie*) vertical.

wierzchowiec *ma* **-wc-** *lit.* mount, saddlehorse.

wierzchowy *a.* rid(e)able; (*o koniu*) riding, saddle; (*o jeździe*) (on) horseback.

wierze *f. zob.* **wiara.**

wierzeje *pl. Gen.* **-ei** *lit.* (= *brama*) gate; (= *drzwi stodoły*) barn door.

wierzenia *pl. Gen.* **-ń** (*religijne*) beliefs.

wierzgać *ipf.*, **wierzgnąć** *pf.* **-ij** kick.

wierzyciel *mp prawn., ekon.* creditor; *prawn.* obligee.

wierzycielski *a.* creditor's.

wierzyć *ipf.* **1.** *t. rel.* believe (*w coś* in sth); **nie wierzysz mi?** don't you believe me?; **przestać wierzyć w coś** lose faith in sth; **wierzyć święcie w kogoś/coś** swear by sb/sth. **2.** (= *ufać*) trust; **wierzę ci na słowo** I take your word for it, I take you at your word; **własnym oczom/uszom nie wierzę** I can't believe my eyes/ears; **wierzyć, że ktoś coś zrobi** trust sb to do sth.

wierzytelność *f. prawn.* liability.

wiesz *ipf. zob.* **wiedzieć.**

wieszać *ipf.* (*coś, kogoś*) hang; (*na stryczku*) halter; **Ewa psy na mnie wiesza** Eve is badmouthing me; **wieszać pranie bez wykręcania** drip-dry. **~ się** *ipf.* **1.** (= *czepiać się*) hang from, cling to; **wieszać się komuś na szyi** hang round sb's neck. **2.** (*popełniać samobójstwo*) hang o.s.

wieszak *mi Gen.* **-a** **1.** (= *przyrząd do wieszania ubrań*) (*stojący*) clothes *l.* coat tree; (*deska z kołkami*) (coat) rack; (*pojedynczy kołek*) peg. **2.** (*na ręczniki*) towel rail. **3.** (= *ramiączko*) (coat) hanger. **4.** (*pętelka*) loop.

wieszcz *mp pl.* **-owie** *l.* **-e** *Gen.* **-ów** **1.** (= *osoba przepowiadająca przyszłość*) seer, soothsayer. **2.** *lit.* (inspired) poet, bard.

wieszczek *ma Gen.* **-szczka** *orn.* yellow-billed chough (*Pyrrhocorax graculus*).

wieszczka *f. Gen.pl.* **-ek** *zob.* **wieszcz.**

wieszczy *a.* **1.** poetic. **2.** prophetic; mantic.

wieś *f. wsi-* *pl.* **-e** **1.** (= *osada; t. mieszkańcy osady*) village; **wieś zabita deskami** *l.* dechami backwoods, the sticks. **2.** (= *okolica poza miastem*) country, countryside; **jechać na wieś** go to the country(side); **na wsi** in the country(side).

wieścić *ipf.* **-szczę -ścisz** *lit.* prophesy.

wieść[1] *f.* news; **Adam zniknął bez wieści** Adam has disappeared without (a) trace; **wieść niesie, że...** rumor has it that...; **wieści ze świata** world news.

wieść[2] *ipf.* **wiodę wiedziesz wiódł wiodła wiedli** *lit.* **1.** (= *prowadzić*) lead; (*spór*) have. **2.** (= *przewodzić*) lead; **nie wódź mnie na pokuszenie** lead me not into temptation; **wieść prym** make the running. **3.** (*o drodze*) lead. **4.** (= *przeciągnąć czymś po jakiejś powierzchni*) run; **wieść za kimś oczyma** follow sb with one's eyes. **~ się** *ipf.* (= *powodzić się*) do; fare; **dobrze/źle mu się wiedzie** he's doing well/badly.

wieśniak *mp* peasant, villager.

Wietnam *mi geogr.* Vietnam.

Wietnamczyk *mp*, **Wietnamka** *f. Gen.pl.* **-ek** Vietnamese.

wietnamski *a.* Vietnamese.

wietrze *mi zob.* **wiatr.**

wietrzeć *ipf.* **1.** (= *tracić aromat*) (*o piwie*) go flat; (*o winie*) go off; (*o perfumach*) lose fragrance. **2.** *geol.* weather.

wietrznik *mi Gen.* **-a 1.** (= *wywietrznik*) vent. **2.** (= *lufcik*) window vent.

wietrzny *a.* windy; (*o erozji*) wind; **ospa wietrzna** *pat.* chickenpox, varicella.

wietrzyć *ipf.* **1.** (= *wentylować*) air. **2.** (*o zwierzęciu*) (= *t. wyczuwać*) smell; **wietrzyć podstęp** smell a rat. **~ się** *ipf.* air (out).

wietrzyk *mi Gen.* **-a** *l.* **-u** breeze.

wiewiórczy *a.* squirrel; sciurine.

wiewiórka *f. Gen.pl.* **-ek** *zool.* squirrel (*Sciurus*); **wiewiórka pospolita** red squirrel (*Sciurus vulgaris*); **wiewiórka szara** gray squirrel (*Sciurus carolinensis*).

wieźć *ipf.* **wiozę wieziesz wiózł wiozła wieźli** carry; transport.

wieża *f.* **1.** *bud.* tower; **wieża kościelna** steeple; **krzywa wieża w Pizie** the Leaning Tower of Pisa; **o dwóch wieżach** two-towered; **wieża hi-fi** hi-fi stack system; **Wieża Babel** (the tower of) Babel; **wieża ciśnień** water tower; **wieża kontrolna** *lotn.* control tower; **wieża triangulacyjna** *miern.* triangulation tower; **wieża strażnicza** watch tower. **2.** *szachy* rook, castle. **3.** *pływanie* diving tower. **4.** *wojsk.* (*czołgu, okrętu*) turret.

wieżowiec *mi* **-wc-** *Gen.* **-a** *pot.* high-rise(r).

wieżowy *a.* tower; (*o zegarze*) turret.

wieżyczka *f. Gen.pl.* **-ek 1.** *bud.* turret; (*ozdoba*) pinnacle; (= *strzelista wieża*) steeple; **zwieńczony wieżyczką** steepled. **2.** *wojsk.* turret.

więc *conj.* **1.** (*wynikanie*) so; thus; **jest ładna pogoda, więc wczasowiczów nie brakuje** the weather is nice, so there's no shortage of vacationers. **2.** (*wyliczenie*) namely; that is to say; **byli wszyscy moi znajomi, a więc Adam, Ewa, Basia i Tomek** all my friends were there, namely Adam, Ewa, Basia and Tomek. – *adv.* so; **a więc... well...; a więc to tak!** so that's how it is!; **więc jednak jedziesz** so you're going after all.

więcej *adv.* **1.** *zob.* **dużo. 2.** *zob.* **wiele. 3.** (*ilość, liczba, miara*) more; **będzie z tego więcej szkody niż pożytku** it will do more harm than good; **coraz więcej pijesz!** you've been drinking more and more!; **ani słowa więcej!** not a word more!; **to jest więcej niż głupie** it's more than silly; **on wie niewiele więcej od ciebie** he doesn't know a lot more than you; **a co więcej** what's more; **mniej więcej** more or less; **jak najwięcej skorzystać** benefit as much as possible; **mieć więcej szczęścia niż rozumu** be more lucky than wise, fortune favors fools; **im więcej, tym lepiej** the more, the better; **nikt więcej** nobody else; **nic więcej** nothing more; **więcej już nie przyszedł** he didn't come any more.

więcierz *mi Gen.* **-a** *ryb.* pot; **więcierz klatkowy** creel.

więdnąć *ipf.* **-ij 1.** wither, wilt; **nie da się słuchać, bo uszy więdną** *pot.* they're turning the air blue. **2.** *przen.* (*o urodzie*) fade; (*o chorym*) be wasted.

większość *f.* majority; **zwyciężyć większością głosów** win by a majority of votes; **znak większo-** ści *mat.* greater-than sign; **bezwzględna większość** *prawn.* absolute majority; **kwalifikowana większość** *prawn.* qualified majority; **mieć większość** be in the majority; **większość dnia** better part of the day; **większość ludzi** most people; **zwykła większość** *polit.* simple majority.

większy *a.* **1.** *zob.* **duży. 2.** *zob.* **wielki. 3.** (*samochód, część, objętość, rozmiar*) bigger; larger; (*doświadczenie, wysiłek, intensywność*) greater; (*gorączka*) higher; **dwa razy większy od kogoś/czegoś** twice as big as sb/sth; **mój brat jest znacznie większy ode mnie** my brother is much taller *l.* bigger than I am; **mam coraz większe trudności z oddychaniem** I've more and more problems breathing; **z największą przyjemnością** with utmost pleasure; **odgrywać większą rolę niż...** play a larger role than... **4.** (= *znaczny*) major; **mam większą gotówkę** *pot.* I've got a nice sum of money.

więzadło *n. Gen.pl.* **-deł** *anat.* ligament; **więzadła głosowe** true vocal cords, vocal folds.

więzić *ipf.* **-żę -zisz** keep prisoner *l.* in prison.

więzienie *n.* **1.** (*instytucja*) prison; jail; penitentiary; **być zwolnionym z więzienia** be released from prison; **siedzieć w więzieniu** be in prison; **uciec z więzienia** break jail; **ucieczka z więzienia** jailbreak; **więzienie o najwyższym rygorze** maximum security prison; **wtrącić kogoś do więzienia** cast *l.* put sb into prison; **zgnić w więzieniu** rot in jail. **2.** (*kara*) imprisonment; prison; **kara dożywotniego więzienia** life imprisonment.

więziennictwo *n.* **1.** (= *więzienia*) prison system. **2.** (= *zarządzanie więzieniami*) prison management.

więzienny *a.* prison; **dozorca więzienny** jailer; **izolatka więzienna** solitary confinement.

więzień *mp* **-źni-** *pl.* **-owie** *Gen.* **-ów** prisoner, inmate; **więzień sumienia** prisoner of conscience.

więznąć *ipf.* **więznę więźniesz, więźnij, wiązł więzła więźli** get stuck (*w czymś* in sth); (*w piasku, błocie*) sink (*w czymś* in sth); **głos więźnie mi w gardle** words stick in my throat.

więzy *pl. Gen.* **-ów 1.** (= *pęta*) fetters; bonds. **2.** (= *ograniczenia*) restrictions. **3.** (= *związki*) ties.

więź *f.* bond; ties; **więź społeczna** *socjol.* social bond.

więźba *f. bud.* roof truss.

więźniarka *f. Gen.pl.* **-ek 1.** *zob.* **więzień. 2.** (*samochód*) prison *l.* prisoner van.

WIG *mi ekon.* (= *Warszawski Indeks Giełdowy*) WIG (*Warsaw Stock Exchange Index*).

wigilia *f. Gen.* **-ii 1.** (*święto*) Christmas Eve. **2.** (*wieczerza*) Christmas Eve Supper. **3.** (= *przeddzień*) *lit.* eve; **wigilia Trzech Króli** *rel.* Twelfth Night.

wigilijny *a.* Christmas Eve; **wieczerza wigilijna** Christmas Eve Supper.

wigna *f. bot.* cowpea (*Vigna sinensis*).

wigoń *ma zool.* vicuna (*Vicugna vicugna*).

wigor *mi* vigor; **pełen wigoru** spirited.

wigwam *mi* wigwam.

wihajster *mi* **-tr-** *Gen.* **-a** *pot.* thingamajig, whatsit.

wij *ma zool.* myriapod, myriopod (*Myriapoda*).

wiję, wijesz *itd. ipf. zob.* **wić²**.

wikariusz *mp rz.-kat.* curate.

wikary *mp pl.* **-rzy** *Gen.* **-ych** = **wikariusz**.

wiking *mp pl.* **-owie** *hist.* Viking.

wiklina *f.* 1. *bot.* red osier (*Salix purpurea*). 2. (*surowiec*) wicker. 3. (*zarośla*) osier bed.

wikliniarski *a.* (*o przemyśle*) wickerwork; **wyroby wikliniarskie** wickerwork.

wikliniarstwo *n.* 1. (*uprawa*) osier growing. 2. (*przemysł*) wickerwork craft *l.* industry.

wiklinowy *a.* (*o koszu, fotelu*) wicker.

wikłacze *pl. orn.* weavers, weaver birds (*Ploceidae*).

wikłać *ipf.* 1. (= *splątywać*) tangle (up). 2. (= *mącić*) *przen.* entangle; complicate. 3. (= *wplątywać*) *przen.* embroil; involve (*kogoś w coś* sb in sth). ~ **się** *ipf.* 1. (= *gmatwać się*) tangle (up); (*o akcji, wątku, sytuacji*) become complicated. 2. (= *wplątywać się*) become embroiled (*w coś* in sth). 3. (= *mieszać się*) become confused; **wikłać się w sprzecznych wypowiedziach** entangle o.s. in contradictions.

wikt *mi przest.* board and lodging.

wiktoria *f.* 1. *bot.* victoria (*Victoria*). 2. *arch.* victory.

wiktoriański *a. hist.* Victorian.

wiktuały *pl. Gen.* **-ów** *żart.* victuals.

wilczarz *ma kynol.* wolfhound.

wilczomlecz *mi Gen.* **-u** *l.* **-a** *bot.* euphorbia (*Euphorbia*).

wilczur *ma pot., kynol.* German shepherd, Alsatian.

wilczy *a.* (*trop, futro*) wolf's; (*apetyt*) *przen.* wolfish, lupine; **(pokrzyk) wilcza jagoda** *bot.* belladonna, deadly nightshade (*Atropa belladonna*); **(wawrzynek) wilcze łyko** *bot.* mezereon (*Daphne mezereum*); **wilcze stado** pack of wolves; **wilczy dół** *myśl.* pitfall; **wilczy głód** *pat.* polyphagia; **wilcza paszcza** *pat.* cleft palate.

wilczyca *f.* she-wolf; **wilczyca kapitolińska** *hist.* the Capitoline wolf.

wilec *mi* **-lc-** *Gen.* **-a** *bot.* morning glory (*Ipomoea*).

wilga *f. orn.* golden oriole (*Oriolus oriolus*).

wilgoć *f.* (*gleby*) moisture; (*powietrza*) humidity; (*w piwnicy, na ścianie*) damp(ness); **czuć tu wilgoć** it smells of dampness in here; **odporny na wilgoć** moisture-proof; dampproof; **plamy wilgoci** patches of damp.

wilgotnawy *a.* dampish.

wilgotnieć *ipf.* (*o soli*) get damp; (*o oczach*) moisten.

wilgotność *f.* moistness; (*powietrza*) humidity; **bezwzględna/względna wilgotność** *meteor.* absolute/relative humidity; **stopień wilgotności** humidity degree.

wilgotny *a.* (*ubranie, ściana*) damp; (*powietrze, klimat*) humid, damp; (*oczy, gleba*) moist.

wilk *ma* 1. wolf; *zool.* (gray) wolf (*Canis lupus*); **wilk morski** *przen.* sea dog; **wilk w owczej skórze** a woolf in sheep's clothing; **patrzeć** *l.* **spoglądać wilkiem** glower (*na kogoś / coś* at sb/sth); **głodny jak wilk** (as) hungry as a wolf *l.* horse; **i**

wilk syty, i owca cała you can have your cake and eat it, too; **natura ciągnie wilka do lasu** the leopard can't change its spots; **nie wywołuj wilka z lasu** let sleeping dogs lie; **o wilku mowa (, a wilk tu)** speak *l.* talk of the devil (and he's sure to appear); **nosił wilk razy kilka, ponieśli i wilka** at length the fox is brought to the furrier. 2. *pot., kynol.* German shepherd. – *mi Gen.* **-a** 1. (*futro*) wolf pelt. 2. *bot.* sucker.

wilkołak *ma* werewolf.

willa *f. Gen.pl.* **-i** *l.* **will** (detached) house; *Br.* villa.

willowy *a.* **dzielnica willowa** residential area.

Wilno *n. geogr.* Vilnius.

wimpel *mi* **-pl-** *Gen.* **-a** *żegl.* pennant.

wina *f.* 1. (*wykroczenie*) fault; trespass; **ona nie jest bez winy** she's not without fault; **przypisywać komuś winę za coś** blame sb for sth, attribute the blame for sth to sb; **przyznać/nie przyznać się do winy** *prawn.* plead guilty/not guilty; **przyznanie się do winy** admission of guilt; **udowodnić komuś winę** prove sb guilty. 2. (*odpowiedzialność*) guilt; blame; **nie poczuwam się do winy** I don't feel guilty; **ponosić winę za spowodowanie wypadku** bear blame for the accident; **przyjmować winę za coś** take blame for sth; **zrzucać winę na kogoś** pin *l.* lay blame on sb. 3. (= *powód złego*) fault; **to moja wina** it's my fault; **rozwód z orzeczeniem winy** *prawn.* fault-based divorce; **rozwód bez orzekania winy** *prawn.* no-fault divorce.

winda *f.* elevator; *Br.* lift; **jedźmy windą!** let's take the elevator!

windować *ipf. pot.* (= *podnosić*) (*ceny*) hike; (*ciężary*) hoist. ~ **się** *ipf.* clamber.

windsurfing *mi sport* windsurfing, sailboarding.

windykacja *f. prawn.* recovery; **windykacja długów** debt collection.

windykować *ipf. prawn.* recover (*od kogoś* from sb); (*w prawie rzymskim i cywilnym*) vindicate.

windziarz *mp* elevator man.

winegret *mi kulin.* (*sos*) vinaigrette sauce; (*sałatka*) vinaigrette salad.

winiak *mi kulin.* brandy.

winiarnia *f. Gen.pl.* **-i** *l.* **-ń** 1. (*lokal*) wine bar. 2. (*wytwórnia*) winery.

winiarski *a.* (*o przemyśle*) winemaking.

winiarz *mp* vintner, winemaker.

winić *ipf.* blame (*kogoś za coś* sb for sth).

winidur *mi techn.* vinidur.

winien *pf. indecl.* owe; **ojcu jesteś winien szacunek** you owe respect to your father; **winnaś mi odpisać** you should write me back; **nikt nie jest winien** nobody's at fault. – *a. indecl.* 1. **jestem ci winien 50 zł** I owe you 50 zl. 2. *zob.* **winny¹**.

winieta *f.* 1. *druk., teor.lit.* vignette. 2. *mot.* (= *nalepka na szybie pojazdu potwierdzająca wniesienie opłat za korzystanie z płatnych dróg*) toll sticker *l.* label.

winkiel *mi* **-kl-** *Gen.* **-a** *Gen.pl.* **-i** *l.* **-ów** 1. *pot.* corner. 2. *miern.* square.

winna *f. Gen.* **-ej** *zob.* **winny¹**.

winnica *f.* vineyard.

winniczek *ma zool.* Roman snail (*Helix pomatia*).

winny[1] *a.* guilty (*czegoś* of sth); **on jest winny zaniedbań** he is guilty of negligence; **udowodniono, że jest winny** he was proved guilty; **Bogu ducha winien** innocent as a lamb *l.* dove; **sam sobie jesteś winien** you only have yourself to blame. – *mp* (*sprawca*) culprit; **ukarać winnych** punish the guilty.

winny[2] *a.* **1.** (= *dotyczący winorośli*) grapevine. **2.** (= *dotyczący wina*) (*smak, zapach*) vinous; (*drożdże, ocet, przemysł*) wine. **3.** *pot., karty* of spades.

wino *n.* **1.** (*napój*) wine; **wino musujące** sparkling wine; **wino słodkie/wytrawne/półwytrawne** sweet/dry/semidry wine; **lampka wina** glass of wine. **2.** *pot.* (*roślina*) (grape)vine; **dzikie wino** woodbine, American ivy; *Br.* Virginia creeper (*Parthenocissus quinquefolia*). **3.** *pot., karty* spades.

winobluszcz *mi bot.* creeper, ampelopsis (*Parthenocissus l. Ampelopsis*).

winobranie *n.* vintage.

winogrono *n.* **1.** (*owoc*) grape; **kiść winogron** bunch of grapes; **kwaśne winogrona** *przen.* sour grapes. **2.** *pot.* (= *winorośl*) grapevine.

winogronowy *a.* (*smak*) grapy, grapey; (*sok*) grape.

winorośl *f. pl.* **-e** *bot.* grapevine (*Vitis*).

winowajca *mp* culprit.

winowajczyni *f. zob.* **winowajca**.

winszować *ipf.* **1.** (= *życzyć*) wish (*komuś czegoś* sb sth). **2.** (= *gratulować*) congratulate (*komuś czegoś* sb on sth).

winyl *mi chem.* vinyl; **polichlorek winylu** polyvinyl chloride.

winyleum *n. indecl. techn.* vinoleum.

winylowy *a. chem.* vinyl.

wio *int.* (*do konia*) giddyup, giddyap; *Br.* gee up.

wiocha *f. pog.* the sticks.

wiodący *a.* leading.

wiodę, wiodła *itp. ipf. zob.* **wieść**[2].

wiola *f. muz.* viola.

wiolin *mi muz.* treble.

wiolinowy *a. muz.* treble; **klucz wiolinowy** treble clef.

wiolonczela *f. Gen.pl.* **-l** *l.* **-i** *muz.* cello, violoncello.

wiolonczelista *mp,* **wiolonczelistka** *f. Gen.pl.* **-ek** *muz.* cellist, violoncellist.

wiolonczelowy *a. muz.* cello, violoncello.

wionąć *pf. lit.* (= *nadlecieć*) (*o wietrze*) blow; (*o zapachu, cieple*) waft.

wiorsta *f. hist.* verst(e).

wiosennie *adv.* springlike; **na dworze jest wiosennie i ciepło** it's springlike and warm outside.

wiosenny *a.* vernal; (*o pogodzie, wietrze*) springlike; (*o słońcu, porządkach*) spring.

wioska *f. Gen.pl.* **-ek** village; **wioska olimpijska** *sport* Olympic Village.

wiosło *n. Gen.pl.* **-seł** (*do łodzi*) oar; (*do kajaka*) paddle; (*jednopiórowe*) scull.

wiosłować *ipf.* (*z łodzi*) row, oar; (*z kajaka*) paddle.

wiosłowy *a.* row, rowing; **łódź wiosłowa** rowboat.

wiosna *f. Gen.pl.* **-sen** **1.** (*pora roku*) spring; **na wiosnę** *l.* **wiosną (2002 roku)** in the spring (of 2002); **jedna jaskółka wiosny nie czyni** one swallow does not make a summer. **2.** *żart.* (= *rok życia*) summer; **liczył sobie pięćdziesiąt wiosen** he was 50 summers old.

wioślarka *f. Gen.pl.* **-ek** *zob.* **wioślarz**.

wioślarski *a. sport* rowing.

wioślarstwo *n. sport* rowing.

wioślarz *mp sport* rower, oarsman.

wiotczeć *ipf.* (*o skórze*) get slack; (*o mięśniach*) grow flabby.

wiotki *a.* **1.** (= *giętki*) (*o gałęzi*) pliant; (= *zwiotczały*) (*o skórze*) slack; (*o mięśniach*) flabby. **2.** (= *smukły*) willowy; (*o kibici*) slender.

wiotko *adv.* **1.** (= *szczupło*) willowy. **2.** (= *delikatnie*) delicately.

wiotkość *f.* **1.** (*o człowieku*) (= *szczupłość*) slenderness. **2.** (*o roślinie*) delicateness.

wiozę *itp. ipf. zob.* **wieźć**.

wiódł *ipf. zob.* **wieść**[2].

wiór *mi Gen.* **-a** (= *skrawek*) shaving; chip; **chudy jak wiór** (as) thin as a rake; **wyschnąć na wiór** become bone-dry; **gdzie drwa rąbią, tam wióry lecą** you can't make an omelette without breaking eggs.

wiórki *pl. Gen.* **-ów** chips; **wiórki czekoladowe** chocolate shavings; **wiórki kokosowe** desiccated coconut.

wiórkować *ipf.* **1.** (*podłogę, parkiet*) (= *czyścić*) scrub with metal shavings. **2.** *techn.* shave.

wiórować *ipf. techn.* shave.

wiórowy *a. techn.* **płyta wiórowa** chipboard; **obróbka wiórowa** machining.

wiózł *ipf. zob.* **wieźć**.

wir *mi* **1.** (= *lej wodny*) whirlpool. **2.** (= *wirowanie*) whirl. **3.** *przen.* merry-go-round (*czegoś* of sth); **rzucić się w wir walki/pracy** hurl o.s. into fight/work.

wiraż *mi Gen.pl.* **-y** *l.* **-ów** **1.** (= *zakręt drogi*) tight bend. **2.** (= *skręt*) turning.

Wirginia *f. Gen.* **-ii** *geogr.* Virginia.

wirki *pl. zool.* turbellarians (*Turbellaria*).

wirnik *mi Gen.* **-a** *techn.* rotor; (*w pompie, sprężarce odśrodkowej*) impeller.

wirnikowy *a. techn.* rotary; **pralka wirnikowa** impeller-type washing machine; **pług wirnikowy** snow cutter.

wirolot *mi lotn.* rotodyne, gyrodyne.

wiropłat *mi lotn.* rotorcraft.

wiroszybowiec *mi lotn.* gyroglider.

wirować *ipf.* **1.** (= *okręcać się*) whirl; (*o wodzie, tancerzu*) swirl; *mech.* rotate; **świat wirował mi przed oczami** my head swam. **2.** (= *odsączać*) (*mleko*) centrifuge; (*bieliznę*) spin-dry.

wirowy *a.* rotational; **ruch wirowy** *mech.* rotary motion.

wirówka *f. Gen.pl.* **-ek** **1.** (*do bielizny*) spin-dryer; *techn.* centrifuge. **2.** *lotn.* whirling arm; centrifuge.

wirtualny *a. komp.* virtual.

wirtuoz *mp pl.* -i *l.* -owie virtuoso.

wirtuozeria *f. Gen.* -ii virtuosity.

wirtuozowski *a.* (*o popisie, wykonaniu*) masterly, virtuosic.

wirulencja *f. biol.* virulence.

wirus *mi Gen.* -a **1.** *biol.* virus; *pot.* bug; **wirus grypy** flu virus. **2.** *komp.* virus.

wirusolog *mp pl.* -dzy *l.* -owie virologist.

wirusologia *f. Gen.* -ii virology.

wirusowy *a. med.* viral; virus; **wirusowe zapalenie wątroby** *pat.* viral hepatitis.

wirydarz *mi Gen.* -a *bud.* garth.

wirylizm *mi biol.* virilism.

wisieć *ipf.* -szę -sisz **1.** (= *być powieszonym*) hang; be suspended; **całymi godzinami wisisz na telefonie!** you're on the phone for hours on end!; **egzamin wisi nade mną jak miecz Damoklesa** the exam is hanging over my head like the sword of Damocles; **kłótnia wisi w powietrzu** quarrel is in the air *l.* wind; **marynarka wisi w szafie** the jacket is hanging in the wardrobe; **mój awans wisi na włosku** my promotion is hanging by a thread; **na drzwiach wisiała tabliczka** there was a plaque on the door; **to mi wisi!** *pot.* I don't give a damn (about it)! **2.** (= *źle leżeć*) (*o ubraniu*) hang loose (*na kimś* on sb); (*o tkaninie, skórze*) bag; **ta kurtka wisi na tobie jak worek** this jacket droops and sags. **3.** (= *unosić się w powietrzu*) hang (*nad kimś / czymś* over sb/sth); (*o helikopterze, ptaku*) hover (*nad kimś / czymś* over sb/sth); **mgła wisi nad łąkami** mist is hanging over the meadows. **4.** (= *być uśmierconym przez powieszenie*) hang; **co ma wisieć, nie utonie** if you're born to be hanged then you'll never be drowned.

wisielczy *a.* **wisielczy humor** *iron.* gallows humor.

wisielec *mp* -lc- *pl.* -y (*skazany*) hanged person; **grać w wisielca** play hangman.

wisiorek *mi* -rk- *Gen.* -a pendant; (*w kształcie zwierzątka, serduszka itd.*) charm.

wiskoza *f. tk.* viscose.

wiskozowy *a. tk.* viscose; **włókno wiskozowe** viscose rayon.

wiskozymetr *mi techn.* viscometer, viscosimeter.

Wisła *f. geogr.* the Vistula (River).

wist *mi Gen.* -a *karty* **1.** (*gra*) whist. **2.** (*zagrywka*) lead. **3.** (*licytacja*) bidding.

wistować *ipf. karty* lead.

wisus *mp pl.* -y *pot.* scamp.

wiszący *a.* (*t. o lampie*) hanging; (*o skórze*) loose; (*o gnieździe*) pensile; **most wiszący** suspension bridge; **ogrody wiszące** hanging gardens.

wiśnia *f. Gen.pl.* **wiśni** *l.* **wisien** **1.** (*owoc*) (sour) cherry. **2.** *bot.* (*drzewo*) cherry (tree); **wiśnia pospolita** sour cherry (*Prunus cerasus*).

wiśniak *mi* (*wódka*) cherry vodka.

wiśniowy *a.* **1.** (*o sadzie, soku*) (= *z wiśniami*) cherry. **2.** (= *taki jak wiśnia*) cherry-like; (*o kolorze, sukience*) cherry (red).

wiśniówka *f. Gen.pl.* -ek cherry liqueur.

witać *ipf.* (= *pozdrawiać*) greet; (*gości, zmia-*

ny) welcome; **witać kogoś chlebem i solą** greet with bread and salt; **witać kogoś na dworcu/lotnisku** meet sb at the station/airport; **witać kogoś z otwartymi ramionami** greet/welcome sb with open arms; **witaj!** welcome!; nice to see you!; greetings!; **witaj w domu** welcome home; **witamy w Londynie** welcome to London; **jej występ zawsze witano oklaskami** her performance was always greeted with applause. ~ **się** *ipf.* exchange greetings (*z kimś* with sb).

witalizm *mi fil., biol.* vitalism.

witalność *f.* vitality.

witalny *a.* vital; **siły witalne** vigor.

witamina *f. biochem.* vitamin; **bogaty w witaminy** rich in vitamins; **witamina C** vitamin C.

witaminizować *ipf.* add vitamins.

witaminizowany *a.* with added vitamins.

witaminowy *a.* vitamin; **preparat** *l.* **suplement witaminowy** vitamin supplement.

witka *f. Gen.pl.* -ek **1.** (= *gałązka*) twig; (*wiklinowa, łozinowa*) withe. **2.** *biol.* (*pierwotniaków, plemnika*) flagellum.

witlinek *ma Gen.* -nka *icht.* whiting (*Gadus merlangus*).

witraż *mi Gen.* -u *l.* -a *Gen.pl.* -y *l.* -ów **1.** (= *kompozycja z kolorowego szkła*) stained glass. **2.** *pot.* (= *okno z witrażem*) stained-glass window.

witrażowy *a.* stained-glass; **okno witrażowe** stained-glass window; **szkło witrażowe** stained glass.

witryna *f.* **1.** (*w sklepie*) window; (*w muzeum, na wystawie*) glass case *l.* cabinet. **2.** (= *oszklony mebel pokojowy*) display cabinet.

wiwarium *n. sing. indecl. pl.* -ria *Gen.* -riów *biol.* vivarium.

wiwat *mi* (*okrzyk*) cheer; **strzelać na wiwat** fire a salute; **dać komuś do wiwatu** *pot.* make sb's life hell. – *int.* long live; **wiwat młoda para!** long live the newlyweds!

wiwatować *ipf.* cheer; **wiwatować na czyjąś cześć** cheer sb.

wiwisekcja *f. Gen.pl.* -i **1.** *biol.* vivisection; **dokonywać wiwisekcji** vivisect. **2.** *przen.* (= *szczegółowa analiza*) dissection.

wiza *f.* visa; **odmówić komuś wydania wizy** refuse sb a visa; **wiza wjazdowa/turystyczna** entry/tourist visa.

wizerunek *mi* -nk- *lit.* picture; image; **wizerunek firmy** corporate image; **zmiana wizerunku** (*osoby, np. przy pomocy kosmetyczki l. firmy*) makeover.

wizja *f. t. telew.* vision; **jesteście na wizji** you're on the air; **wizja lokalna** *prawn.* scene-of-crime inspection; view.

wizjer *mi Gen.* -a **1.** *opt.* viewfinder. **2.** (= *wziernik w drzwiach*) peephole, eyehole. **3.** *wojsk.* sight.

wizjoner *mp* visionary.

wizjonerski *a.* visionary.

wizjonerstwo *n.* visionariness.

wizon *ma zool.* American mink (*Mustela vison*).

wizować *ipf.* visa.

wizowy *a.* visa; **formalności wizowe** visa formalities; **oddział/formularz wizowy** visa section/(application) form.

wizualizacja *f.* visualization.

wizualizm *mi sztuka* visualism.

wizualnie *adv. lit.* visually.

wizualny *a.* visual.

wizyjny *a.* 1. (= *wizjonerski*) visionary. 2. (= *wzrokowy*) visual; *telew.* (*o przekazie*) video.

wizyta *f.* 1. (= *odwiedziny*) visit (*u kogoś / gdzieś* to sb/sth); **pójść do kogoś z wizytą** call on sb; **wizyta oficjalna** *l.* **państwowa** state visit; **złożyć komuś wizytę** *form.* pay sb a visit. 2. (= *przybycie lekarza*) call; **umówiona wizyta lekarska** appointment; **wizyta domowa** house call; **zamówić wizytę** make an appointment.

wizytacja *f. admin., szkoln.* inspection.

wizytator *mp admin., szkoln.* inspector.

wizytatorka *f. Gen.pl.* **-ek** *zob.* **wizytator**.

wizytka *f. Gen.pl.* **-ek** *rz.-kat.* (*zakonnica*) Visitation Nun.

wizytować *ipf. admin., szkoln.* (= *odwiedzać służbowo*) inspect.

wizytowo *adv.* formally; **ubrać się wizytowo** wear formal clothes.

wizytowy *a.* (*o garniturze, sukni*) formal; **bilet wizytowy** calling card.

wizytówka *f. Gen.pl.* **-ek** 1. (business) card, calling card. 2. *przen.* showcase.

wjazd *mi Loc.* **-eździe** 1. (= *wjeżdżanie*) entering. 2. (= *dostęp*) entrance; (= *brama*) gate(way); (= *podjazd*) drive; **wjazd na parking** parking lot entrance; *Br.* car park entrance; **wjazd na autostradę** entrance ramp; **zakaz wjazdu** no entry. 3. *pot.* (= *opłata za wejście*) admission.

wjazdowy *a.* entry; **brama wjazdowa** gateway; **opłata wjazdowa** entry *l.* entrance fee; **wiza wjazdowa** entry visa.

wjechać *pf.* **wjadę wjedziesz, wjeżdżać** *ipf.* 1. (= *dostać się gdzieś*) (*o pociągu, autobusie*) come in; (*samochodem*) drive in; (*na stację*) pull in; **wjechać do miasta** drive into the city; **wjechać w rów** ditch, drive into a ditch; **pieczeń wjechała na stół** *żart.* the roast arrived at the table, the roast was served. 2. (= *dostać się wyżej*) go up; ascend; **wjechać windą na trzecie piętro** take the elevator to the third floor. 3. (= *najechać*) run into (*w kogoś / coś* sb/sth); **ktoś wjechał w tył mojego samochodu** I was rear-ended; **wjechał prosto w słup** he drove square into the post. 4. *pot.* (= *skrzyczeć*) jump on (*na kogoś za coś* sb for sth); **szef znów wjechał na mnie** boss jumped on me again.

wkalkulować *pf.,* **wkalkulowywać** *ipf.* 1. (= *wliczać*) include; **wkalkulować coś w cenę/koszt** include sth in the price/cost. 2. (= *brać pod uwagę*) factor in.

wkalkulowany *a.* 1. (= *wliczony*) included; **posiłki wkalkulowane w cenę** meals included in the price. 2. (= *wzięty pod uwagę*) taken into account; **wkalkulowane ryzyko** calculated risk.

wkleić *pf.* **-eję -eisz, wklejać** *ipf.* stick in.

wklejka *f. Gen.pl.* **-ek** *druk.* inset, insert.

wklepać *pf.* **-pię -piesz, wklepywać** *ipf.* 1. (*np.*

krem) (= *klepiąc wbić*) pat (in). 2. *pot.* (= *wpisać na klawiaturze*) key in; (*do komputera*) punch in.

wklęsłodruk *mi druk.* intaglio.

wklęsłość *f.* concavity; (*ziemi*) hollow.

wklęsły *a.* concave; (*o policzkach, brzuchu*) sunken; (*klatka piersiowa*) hollow; **zwierciadło wklęsłe** *fiz.* concave mirror; **kąt wklęsły** *geom.* reflex angle, re-entering *l.* re-entrant angle; **druk wklęsły** *druk.* intaglio.

wklęsnąć *pf.* **wklęśnie wklęsnął** *l.* **wkląsł** *l.* **wklęsł wklęsła** (*policzki, brzuch*) sink; (*dach*) cave in.

wklęśnięcie *n.* concavity.

wkład *mi* 1. *t. ekon.* input; contribution; **wkład w naturze** contribution in kind; **wkład artysty w kulturę narodową** artist's contribution to national heritage. 2. (= *pieniądze w banku*) deposit. 3. (*do długopisu*) (pen) refill; (*do ołówka*) refill lead; (*do termosu*) glass filler.

wkładać *ipf.* 1. (= *umieszczać*) put (*coś do czegoś* sth in *l.* into sth); insert; **wkładać słowa w czyjeś usta** *przen.* put words in sb's mouth; **włożył ręce do kieszeni** he put his hands into his pockets; **włożyć klucz do stacyjki** put the key in the ignition; **nie mam co do garnka włożyć** there's hardly enough food to go around; **wkładać coś komuś łopatą do głowy** spell sth out to sb; **możesz to między bajki włożyć** you can forget about it. 2. (= *ubierać się*) put on. 3. *pot.* (= *wpłacać*) pay in; **włożyć pieniądze na konto** put money into an account; **włożyć w coś pieniądze** put money into sth. 4. (= *angażować się*) put in; **wkładać w coś wiele wysiłku** put a lot of effort into sth.

wkładka *f. Gen.pl.* **-ek** 1. (*do czasopisma*) insert; (*do książki*) inset. 2. (*do butów*) insole; **wkładka higieniczna** pantyliner; **wkładka ortopedyczna** arch support; **wkładka wewnątrzmaciczna** intrauterine device. 3. *techn.* insert; pad; lining; **wkładka topikowa** *el.* fuse-element, fuselink.

wkłuć *pf.,* **wkłuwać** *ipf.* (*igłę*) insert. **~ się** *ipf.,* **wkłuwać się** *ipf. med.* insert a needle.

wkoło *prep.* + *Gen.* around; **siedzieć wkoło stołu** sit around the table.

wkomponować *pf. zob.* **wkomponowywać**.

wkomponowany *a.* incorporated (*w coś* into sth); **dom wkomponowany w otoczenie** house blending with its surroundings.

wkomponowywać *ipf.* incorporate (*w coś* into sth).

wkopać *pf.* **-pię -piesz, wkopywać** *ipf.* 1. (= *umieścić głęboko*) sink into the ground. 2. *tylko pf. pot.* (= *zdradzić*) rat on. 3. (= *postawić w trudnej sytuacji*) put on the spot. **~ się** *pf.,* **wkopywać się** *ipf.* 1. (= *kopiąc zagłębić się*) dig into. 2. *tylko pf. pot.* (= *zdradzić się*) give o.s. away. 3. *tylko pf. pot.* (= *znaleźć się w trudnym położeniu*) land o.s. in, get in trouble.

wkraczać *ipf.* 1. enter; (*o wojsku*) march *l.* move in; **wkraczać nielegalnie** *prawn.* trespass (*na coś* on/upon sth); **1 września armia niemiecka wkroczyła do Polski** on September 1 the German army invaded Poland; **wkroczyć na arenę dziejów** enter history; **wkroczyliśmy w XXI wiek** we entered the 21st century. **2.** (= *interweniować*) step in.

wkradać się *ipf.* (*o osobie*) sneak in; slip in; (*o błędzie*) *przen.* creep in; **wkraść się w czyjeś łaski** worm o.s. into sb's favor.

wkrajać *ipf.* cut into pieces and add.

wkrapiać *ipf.*, **wkraplać** *ipf.* (*np. krople do oczu*) instill.

wkraść się *pf.* **wkradnę wkradniesz, wkradnij, wkradł** *zob.* **wkradać się**.

wkrawać *ipf. zob.* **wkrajać**.

wkręcać *ipf.*, **wkręcić** *pf.* **1.** (= *umieszczać coś*) (*żarówkę, śrubę*) screw in; (*papier do maszyny*) load. **2.** *pot.* (= *umieszczać kogoś*) wangle into; **na to stanowisko wkręcił go ojciec** his father wangled him into this position. ~ **się** *ipf.*, **wkręcić się** *pf.* **1.** (= *być wkręcanym*) (*o śrubie*) screw; (*o materiale, włosach*) catch; get caught. **2.** *pot.* (= *próbować dostać się gdzieś*) wangle o.s. into.

wkręt *mi Gen.* **-a** *l.* **-u** *techn.* screw.

wkrętak *mi Gen.* **-a** *techn.* screwdriver; **wkrętak z grzechotką** ratchet screwdriver.

wkrętka *f. Gen.pl.* **-ek 1.** (= *mały kolczyk*) stud. **2.** *techn.* (screw) plug.

wkroczyć *pf. zob.* **wkraczać**.

wkroić *pf.* **wkroję wkroisz, wkrój** *zob.* **wkrajać**.

wkropić *pf.*, **wkroplić** *pf. zob.* **wkrapiać**.

wkrótce *adv.* soon; shortly; **wkrótce po jego przyjeździe** soon *l.* shortly after his arrival; **do zobaczenia wkrótce!** see you soon!; **ślub odbędzie się wkrótce** the wedding will take place soon; **wkrótce może być za późno** soon it can be too late.

wkuć *pf. zob.* **wkuwać**. ~ **się** *pf. zob.* **wkuwać się**.

wkupić się *pf.*, **wkupywać się** *ipf.* buy one's way (*do czegoś* into sth); **wkupić się w czyjeś łaski** *pot.* buy sb's favors.

wkurwiać *ipf.*, **wkurwić** *pf. wulg.* (= *denerwować*) piss off, drive fucking mad, make fucking angry; **nie wkurwiaj mnie!** don't piss me off!; (= *zamknij się*) shut the fuck up! ~ **się** *ipf.*, **wkurwić się** *pf. wulg.* (= *denerwować się*) get pissed off, get fucking angry, get fucking mad.

wkurzać *ipf.*, **wkurzyć** *pf. pot.* (= *denerwować*) get on one's nerves; **nie wkurzaj mnie!** don't get on my nerves!; **wkurza mnie twoje spóźnianie się** your being late really gets on my nerves. ~ **się** *ipf.*, **wkurzyć się** *pf. pot.* (= *denerwować się*) get angry.

wkuwać *ipf.* **1.** (= *kując, umieszczać coś*) drive (*coś w coś* sth into sth). **2.** *pot., szkoln.* cram (*do czegoś* for sth). ~ **się** *ipf.* (= *kując, dostać się gdzieś*) chisel in.

wlać *pf.* **wleję wlejesz wlali** *l.* **wleli 1.** *zob.* **wlewać**. **2.** *pot.* (= *zbić*) thrash. ~ **się** *pf. zob.* **wlewać się**.

wlatywać *ipf.* **1.** (= *dostawać się do środka*) (*o ptaku, owadzie*) fly in; (*o dymie, gazie*) pour in; get in; (*o piłce*) shoot in; **pieczone gołąbki nie wlecą same do gąbki** a fool expects that larks will fall ready roasted into his own mouth; **wlatywać**

jednym uchem, wylatywać drugim go in one ear and out the other. **2.** (= *wpadać w coś*) fall; **klucz wleciał mi w błoto** my key fell in the mud. **3.** *pot.* (= *wbiegać*) breeze in; **wleciał jak po ogień** he rushed in and out. **4.** *pot.* (= *wpadać na kogoś*) run (*na kogoś / coś* into sb/sth); bump (*na kogoś / coś* into sb/sth); **wleciał na mnie z całym impetem i nawet nie przeprosił** he rammed into me full force without even saying sorry.

wlazł *itd. pf. zob.* **wleźć**.

wlec *ipf.* **wlokę wleczesz wlókł wlokła wlekli 1.** (= *ciągnąć*) drag; haul; (= *wlec po ziemi*) draggle; **ledwie wlókł nogi za sobą** he could hardly drag one foot after the other. **2.** (= *prowadzić kogoś przemocą l. niepotrzebnie*) drag along. ~ **się** *ipf.* **1.** (= *poruszać się bardzo wolno*) drag along; **wlec się jak za pogrzebem** move at snail's pace; **wlec się w ogonie** lag behind; **wlekliśmy się przez miasto** we trailed through the city. **2.** (= *długo trwać*) drag; **czas się wlókł** time dragged on. **3.** (= *być ciągniętym*) drag. **4.** (= *przesuwać się wolno*) (*o pojeździe*) crawl; (*o dymie*) hang; **po niebie wlokły się chmury deszczowe** rain clouds were trailing over the sky.

wlecieć *pf.* **wlecę wlecisz** *zob.* **wlatywać**.

wlepiać *ipf.*, **wlepić** *pf.* **1.** (= *wklejać*) stick in; **wlepić w kogoś oczy** fix one's eyes on *l.* upon sb. **2.** *pot.* (= *ukarać*) give; **wlepić komuś mandat** give sb a ticket; **wlepić komuś dwóję** give sb an F, fail sb.

wlew *mi* **1.** (*otwór*) inlet; **wlew zbiornika** filler. **2.** *med.* infusion. **3.** *metal.* gate, runner.

wlewać *ipf.* (= *napełniać*) **1.** pour (*coś do czegoś* sth into sth); **wlewać kawę do filiżanek** pour coffee into cups; **wlewać w siebie wódkę** ply o.s. with vodka. **2.** *przen.* inspire; **wlać nadzieję w czyjeś serce** infuse sb with hope. ~ **się** *ipf.* **1.** (= *dostawać się*) pour in; flow in; **woda wlewała mi się do butów** water was getting into my shoes. **2.** *pot.* (= *upijać się*) get drunk.

wlewek *mi Gen.* **-wka** *metal.* ingot.

wlewka *f. Gen.pl.* **-ek** *med.* enema.

wleźć *pf.* **wlezę wleziesz wlazł wleźli** *zob.* **włazić**.

wliczać *ipf.* include; (= *uwzględniać*) count in; **wliczać coś w cenę/koszt** include sth in the price/cost.

wliczony *a.* included; **posiłki wliczone w cenę** meals included in the price.

wliczyć *pf. zob.* **wliczać**.

wlokę *itd. ipf. zob.* **wlec**.

wlot *mi gł. techn.* (*otwór*) inlet; (*wody, powietrza*) intake; (*tunelu, rury*) mouth; (= *początek ulicy*) entry.

wlotowy *a.* (*zawór, rura, kanał*) inlet; **otwór wlotowy** inlet; **szyb wlotowy** *górn.* downcast shaft.

włókł *ipf. zob.* **wlec**.

władać *ipf.* **1.** (= *rządzić*) (*o władcy*) rule; (*o władcy, anarchii*) reign. **2.** (= *posługiwać się biegle*) (*obcym językiem*) have a good command of; (*bronią, mieczem, narzędziem*) wield. **3.** (*nogą, ręką*) (= *móc poruszać*) have the use of.

władanie *n.* (*państwem*) rule; reign; (*językiem*)

command; **dostać** *l.* **objąć coś we władanie** *form.* come into *l.* take possession of sth; **mieć coś pod swoim władaniem** *form.* have sth under one's rule.

władca *mp* ruler; sovereign; (*t. feudalny*) lord; **władca absolutny** absolute ruler; **mój pan i władca** *żart.* my lord and master.

władczy *a.* imperious; (*o tonie, geście*) commanding.

władczyni *f. zob.* **władca**.

władny *a. lit.* competent; **nie jestem władny tego zrobić** I have no authority to do it.

władować *pf.* (= *załadować*) load. **~ się** *pf. pot.* clamber into; **władować się w kłopoty** *przen.* get in(to) trouble, land o.s. in trouble.

władyka *mp pl.* -cy *l.* -kowie *Gen.* -ków **1.** *hist.* lord. **2.** *rel.* vladyka.

władza *f.* **1.** (= *rządzenie*) rule; reign; **być u władzy** be in power; **dojść do władzy** rise to power; **odsunąć kogoś od władzy** remove sb from power; **odzyskać władzę** return to power; **sprawować władzę** yield *l.* exercise power; **walka o władzę** power struggle; **władza państwowa** state; **władza polityczna** political power. **2.** (= *organ rządzący*) authorities; **czwarta władza** (= *media*) fourth estate; **oddać się w ręce władz** surrender to authorities; **władza sądownicza** the judiciary; **władza ustawodawcza** the legislature; **władza wykonawcza** the executive. **3.** (= *moc*) authority; **mieć nad kimś nieograniczoną władzę** have unrestricted power over sb; **być w pełni władz umysłowych** be of sound mind; **stracić władzę w nogach** lose the use of one's legs.

włamać się *pf.* -mię -miesz *zob.* **włamywać się**.

włamanie *n.* **1.** burglary; **dokonać włamania** break in; **zabezpieczony przed włamaniem** burglar-proof. **2.** *komp.* hack.

włamywacz *mp* **1.** burglar. **2.** *komp.* hacker.

włamywać się *ipf.* **1.** break in; burglarize (*gdzieś* sth); **włamać się do mieszkania** break into an apartment. **2.** *komp.* hack.

własnoręcznie *adv.* (*zrobić, namalować*) with one's own hands; **ten problem został przez niego własnoręcznie stworzony** the problem is of his own making; **własnoręcznie napisany dokument** autograph.

własnoręczny *a.* made *l.* done with one's own (two) hands; (*o podpisie*) personal.

własnościowy *a.* ownership; **mieszkanie własnościowe** owner-occupied flat.

własność *f.* **1.** (= *mienie*) property; **dostać coś na własność** get sth for keeps; **mieć na własność** own; **własność osobista** personal *l.* private property; **coś przeszło na czyjąś własność** sth became sb's property; **stanowić czyjąś własność** belong to sb. **2.** *prawn.* ownership, property; **własność nieruchoma** real estate; *Br.* real property; **prawo własności** property *l.* proprietary right; **przekazanie praw własności** conveyance of property. **3.** (= *cecha charakterystyczna*) property, quality.

własny *a.* **1.** (= *należący do kogoś*) one's own; **być na własnym utrzymaniu** be self-supporting; **chodzić własnymi drogami** play a lone wolf; **dbać**

o **własną kieszeń** look to one's own interests; **do rąk własnych** (*adnotacja na przesyłce, dokumencie*) private; **dostosować coś do własnych potrzeb** tailor sth to one's needs; **kisić się we własnym sosie** keep to o.s.; **mieć wiarę we własne siły** be self-confident; **mieć własne zdanie** be one's own man *l.* woman; **mieć własny kąt** have a place of one's own; **mierzyć coś własną miarą** measure sth against one's own standards; **na własne ryzyko** at one's own risk; **na własny koszt** at one's own cost *l.* expense; **na własny użytek** for one's own use; **nazwa własna** *jęz.* proper noun; **nie wierzę własnym uszom/oczom** I can't believe my ears/eyes; **odczuć coś na własnej skórze** learn sth to one's cost; **opisać coś własnymi słowami** describe sth in one's own words; **o własnych siłach** unaided; on one's own; **ratować własny tyłek** *pot.* save one's own butt; **we własnej osobie** in person *l.* the flesh; **w imieniu własnym** on one's own behalf; **w obronie własnej** in self-defense; **z własnej kieszeni** out of one's own pocket; **z własnej woli** of one's free will; **znać coś jak własną kieszeń** know sth like the back of one's hand, know every nook and cranny of sth; **zrobić coś na własną rękę** do sth on one's own; **zrobić coś według własnego uznania** use one's own judgement. **2.** (= *własnej produkcji*) home-; **własne ciasto** home-made cake; **własne piwo** home-brewed beer.

właściciel *mp*, **właścicielka** *f. Gen.pl.* -ek owner; (*firmy*) proprietor; (*paszportu*) bearer; (*karty bibliotecznej*) holder; **mieć prywatnego właściciela** be privately owned; **właściciel pubu** publican; **właściciel sklepu spożywczego** grocer; **właściciel ziemski** landowner; **zmieniać właściciela** change hands.

właściwie *adv.* (= *należycie*) properly; (= *poprawnie*) correctly; (*wyposażony, przygotowany, ubrany*) suitably; **jeśli właściwie cię zrozumiałem...** if I understand you correctly...; **właściwie coś wykorzystywać** make good use of sth. – *adv.* (= *w gruncie rzeczy*) actually; as a matter of fact; **o co właściwie chodzi?** what is the matter anyway?; **właściwie nie mam już żadnych pieniędzy** I have practically no money left; **właściwie nie wiem** I don't know, actually; **właściwie (to) nie** not really.

właściwość *f.* **1.** (= *cecha charakterystyczna*) characteristic; (*materiału*) property, quality. **2.** (= *stosowność*) suitability. **3.** *prawn.* competence; **właściwość sądu** jurisdiction (of a court of law).

właściwy *a.* **1.** (= *stosowny, odpowiedni*) (*zachowanie, traktowanie*) proper; (*określenie, słowo*) suitable; (*człowiek, wybór*) right; (*odpowiedź*) correct; **we właściwym czasie** in due course *l.* time; **właściwa droga postępowania** right course of action; **właściwy człowiek na właściwym miejscu** right person for the job. **2.** (= *typowy*) characteristic (*czemuś* of sth); **robić coś z właściwą sobie energią** do sth with characteristic energy; **temperatura właściwa dla pory roku** seasonable temperature. **3.** (= *rzeczywisty*) actual; (*o nazwisku*) true; real; **ciepło właściwe** *fiz.*

specific heat; **ciężar właściwy** *fiz.* specific gravity; **ułamek właściwy** *mat.* proper fraction. **4.** *prawn.* competent; **właściwe władze** competent authorities.

właśnie *adv.* **1.** (= *istotnie*) indeed; precisely; **tego właśnie mi potrzeba** that's exactly what I need; **o to właśnie mi chodziło** that's what I meant. **2.** (= *dopiero co, akurat*) just; **właśnie miałam wyjść, kiedy...** I was (just) about to leave, when...; **właśnie nadchodzą** here they come; **właśnie się przejaśnia** it's clearing up right now; **właśnie widzę/słyszę** so I see/hear; **właśnie wstałem** I've just got up; **właśnie wtedy** just then; **właśnie w tym hotelu** in this very hotel. – *int.* **1.** (= *tak jest*) precisely; **no właśnie** quite (so). **2.** (= *jeszcze czego*) yeah, right; **właśnie, że nie** no way.

właz *mi* (*czołgu*) hatch; (*kanału*) manhole; (*na statku, na dachu*) scuttle; **właz ewakuacyjny** *l.* **ratunkowy** escape *l.* emergency hatch.

włazić *ipf.* **-żę -zisz 1.** *pot.* (= *wchodzić*) straggle in, barge in; (= *wczołgać się*) creep in; **gdzie włazisz!?** where do you think you're trying to get into?; **włazić do środka** *pot.* get inside; **włazić drzwiami i oknami** crowd into, throng into. **2.** *pot.* (= *wspinać się*) clamber up, climb up; **włazić komuś na głowę** walk over sb, keep sb under one's thumb. **3.** *pot.* (= *wdepnąć*) get, step (*w coś* into sth); **wleźć w błoto** get *l.* step into mud. **4.** *pot.* (= *wejść, nadepnąć*) step, tread (*w coś* on sth); **wleźć na mokrą podłogę** step *l.* tread on a wet floor; **wleźć komuś w drogę** get into sb's way; **wleźć komuś w oczy** crop up. **5.** *pot.* (= *dostawać się w głąb czegoś*) get (*w coś* into sth); **włazić komuś w dupę** *wulg.* (= *podlizywać się*) kiss sb's ass; **drzazga wlazła mi w nogę** a splinter stuck in my foot, I've got a splinter in my foot; **chemia nie włazi mi do głowy** chemistry just doesn't sink in with me. **6.** *pot.* (= *mieścić się w czymś*) go; **to pudło nie wlezie do bagażnika** the box won't go into the trunk; **ile wlezie** to one's heart content. **7.** *pot.* (= *ubrać się*) slip into, put on; **kiedy już wlezie w jakieś spodnie, nosi je potem miesiącami** once he slips into *l.* puts on a pair of trousers he won't change them for months.

włączać *ipf.*, **włączyć** *pf.* **1.** (= *uruchamiać*) turn on, switch on; **włączyć coś do sieci** *l.* **prądu** plug sth in; **włączyć radio/telewizor/światło** turn on *l.* switch on the radio/TV/light, turn *l.* switch the radio/TV/light on; **włączyć sprzęgło** *mot.* clutch; **włączyć** *l.* **wrzucić bieg** *mot.* put in *l.* into gear; **włączyć** *l.* **wrzucić wsteczny bieg** *mot.* put the car into reverse; **włączyć ssanie** *mot.* prime a carburettor; **włączyć zasilanie** turn the power on. **2.** (= *dołączać*) include, incorporate. **3.** (= *obejmować kogoś działaniem*) include. **~ się** *ipf.* **1.** (= *brać udział*) join (in) (*do czegoś l. w coś* sth); **włączyć się do dyskusji** join in the discussion; **włączyć się do ruchu** *mot.* (*z pobocza*) pull out. **2.** (*o urządzeniu*) come on; **jak to się włącza?** how do you turn *l.* switch it on?

włącznie *adv.* inclusively, inclusive (of), including; **od poniedziałku do środy włącznie** Monday to Wednesday inclusive; **włącznie z kosztami**

dowozu delivery included, including *l.* inclusive of the cost of delivery.

włączony *a.* (turned *l.* switched) on; **czy radio jest włączone?** is the radio on?; **zostawić włączone światło** leave the light on.

włączyć *pf. zob.* **włączać.** **~ się** *pf. zob.* **włączać się.**

Włoch *mp* Italian.

włochaty *a.* hairy; (*o psie*) shaggy; (*o ręczniku*) piled.

Włochy *pl. Gen.* **-ch** *Loc.* **-szech** *geogr.* Italy.

włodarz *mp* **1.** *lit.* ruler. **2.** *arch.* (= *zarządca*) steward, bailiff.

włogacizna *f. wet.* (bony) spavin.

włok *mi Gen.* **-a** *l.* **-u** *ryb.* trawl (net).

włos *mi Gen.* **-a 1.** (*na głowie*) hair; **o mały włos** by a hair's breadth *l.* hairbreadth, by the skin of one's teeth; **o (mały) włos od czegoś** within an ace of sth; **nie ustąpić ani na włos** not yield an inch; **pokonać kogoś o włos** nose sb out; **wygrać o włos** scrape home; (*o koniu na wyścigach*) win by a nose; **dzielić włos na czworo** split hairs; **włosy stanęły mu na głowie** *l.* **dęba** *l.* **włos mu się zjeżył na głowie** his hair rose *l.* stood on end; **ona ma więcej długów niż włosów na głowie** she owes more than she is worth; **prędzej mi włosy na dłoni wyrosną** *l.* **kaktus wyrośnie niż...** all hell will freeze over before..., it will be a cold day in August before...; **rwać sobie włosy z głowy** tear *l.* pull one's hair out; **jeśli choćby włos mu z głowy spadnie...** if you harm a hair on his head...; **farba do włosów** hair-dye; **kosmyk włosów** wisp of hair; **lakier do włosów** (*w aerozolu*) hair spray *l.* lacquer; **lokówka do włosów** hair-curler; **odżywka do włosów** hair-conditioner; **opaska do włosów** hair band; **pianka do (układania) włosów** (styling) mousse; **płukanka (koloryzująca) do włosów** rinse; **rozdwojone końcówki włosów** split ends; **spinka do włosów** bobby pin, hair clip; **suszarka do włosów** hairdryer; **środek na porost włosów** hair restorer; **wałek do włosów** curler; **wsuwka do włosów** hairpin; **żel do (układania) włosów** styling gel. **2.** (= *owłosienie ciała*) hair; **pies z długim włosem** dog with long hair; **pod włos** (*czesać, głaskać*) against the hair; **brać kogoś pod włos** rub sb the right way, give sb a pep talk. **3.** (*na tkaninie*) pile, nap; **dywan z długim włosem** long-pile carpet. **4.** *techn.* hairspring.

włosek *mi* **-sk-** *Gen.* **-a 1.** (= *delikatny, krótki włos*) hair; **wisieć na włosku** hang by a thread; **wojna wisiała na włosku** war hung by a (slender) thread, it was a touch-and-go whether there'd be a war. **2.** *bot.* trichome, hair; **włoski korzeniowe** root-hairs; **włoski parzące** stinging-hairs, stings. **3.** *zool.* hair.

Włosi *mp zob.* **Włoch.**

włosianka *f. Gen.pl.* **-ek** *tk.* haircloth.

włosiany *a.* hair.

włosie *n.* hair; (*np. szczotki, pędzla*) bristle.

włosiennica *f. rel.* hair shirt.

włosień *ma* **-śni-** *l.* **-sieni-** *Gen.* **-a** *zool.* trichina (*Trichinella spiralis*).

włoski *a.* Italian; **kapusta włoska** *bot., kulin.*

savoy cabbage (*Brassica oleracea sabauda*); **koper włoski** *bot., kulin.* fennel (*Foeniculum vulgare*); **makaron włoski** spaghetti; **orzech włoski** *bot., kulin.* English *l.* Persian walnut (*Juglans regia*); **sonet włoski** *teor.lit.* Petrarchan *l.* Italian sonnet; **strajk włoski** *polit.* go-slow; **topola włoska** *bot.* Lombardy poplar (*Populus nigra italica*).

włoskowatość *f. fiz.* capillarity.

włosogłówka *f. zool.* whipworm (*Trichocephalus trichiurus*).

włosowaty *a.* capillary; **naczynia włosowate** *anat.* capillary vessels.

włosowy *a.* hair; **cebulka włosowa** *anat.* hair bulb; **mieszek włosowy** *anat.* hair follicle.

włoszczyzna *f.* 1. (*warzywa*) a bunch of mixed vegetables (*usually carrot, leek, celeriac and parsley, used for cooking soups*). 2. (= to, co włoskie) (*o języku*) Italian language; (*o kulturze*) Italian culture; (*o charakterze*) Italian character (*of a book, film, etc.*).

Włoszka *f. Gen.pl.* **-ek** *zob.* **Włoch.**

włości *pl. Gen.* **-i** *hist. t. żart.* domain, demesne, manor; **pan na włościach** lord of the manor.

włościanin *mp pl.* **-anie** *Gen.* **-an, włościanka** *f. Gen.pl.* **-ek** peasant; *arch.* hind.

włościański *a.* peasant; **kapela włościańska** peasant (music) band.

włośniak *ma zool.* nemathelminth (*Nemathelminthes*).

włośnica *f.* 1. *bot.* foxtail (*Setaria*). 2. *pat., wet.* trichinosis, trichiniasis. 3. *techn.* fret saw.

włośniczka *f. Gen.pl.* **-ek** *anat.* capillary.

włożyć *pf.* **włóż** *zob.* **wkładać.**

włóczęga *f.* 1. (= wędrówka) roam, rove. 2. (= długa wycieczka) tramp, trek. – *mp pl.* **-i** *l.* **-dzy** (= obieżyświat) tramp, vagrant; (*zwł. żebrak*) vagabond.

włóczęgostwo *n.* vagrancy, vagabondage; **aresztować kogoś za włóczęgostwo** *gł. prawn.* (*świadczące o zamiarach przestępczych*) arrest sb for loitering with intent.

włóczęgowski *a.* vagrant, vagabondish; **prowadzić włóczęgowskie życie** live a vagabond life.

włóczka *f. Gen.pl.* **-ek** 1. (*nić*) crewel. 2. *myśl.* (= wleczenie po lesie kawałka padliny w celu pozostawienia zapachu; kawałek padliny użyty w tym celu) drag.

włóczkowy *a.* crewel.

włócznia *f. Gen.pl.* **-i** *hist.* spear.

włócznik *mp hist.* spearman, spear. – *ma icht.* swordfish, broadbill (*Xiphias gladius*).

włócznikowaty *a. icht.* xipioid.

włóczyć *ipf.* 1. (= wlec) trail, drag, haul; **włóczyć nogami** drag one's feet. 2. *pot.* (= ciągać ze sobą) lug about, drag; **włóczyć kogoś po sklepach** drag sb round the shops; **włóczyć kogoś po sądach** drag sb through the courts. 3. *roln.* drag (*a field*). – **się** *ipf.* 1. (= chodzić bez celu) roam, rove, ramble; **włóczyć się po nocy** roam through the night; **włóczyć się po knajpach** pub-crawl; **włóczyć się po sądach** (= procesować się) drag sb

through the courts. 2. (*o dymie, mgle*) drift, float.

włóczykij *mp Gen.pl.* **-ów** *pot.* knight of the road.

włóka *f.* 1. *roln.* drag (harrow). 2. *hist.* an area measurement unit of 16.8 ha.

włókienko *n. anat.* fibril; **włókienko mięśniowe** muscle fibril, sarcostyle.

włókiennictwo *n. tk.* textile industry.

włókienniczy *a. tk.* textile; **przemysł włókienniczy** textile industry; **technikum włókiennicze** textile industry secondary technical school.

włókiennik *mp tk.* textile engineer.

włókienny *a.* fibrous, made of fiber.

włókniak *mi Gen.* **-a** *pat.* fibroma.

włókniarz *mp Gen.* **-a** *tk.* textile worker.

włókniec *mp pat.* desmoid.

włóknieć *ipf.* become fibered.

włóknik *mi pat.* fibrin.

włóknikowy *a.* fibrinous.

włóknina *f. tk.* nonwoven *l.* unvowen fabric.

włóknisty *a.* 1. (= łykowaty) stringy, fibrous. 2. *biol., geol.* fibrous; **komórka włóknista** fibrous cell.

włókno *n. Gen.pl.* **-kien** *anat., bot., techn., tk., chem.* fiber; *Br.* fibre; (*przędzy, sznurka*) strand; (*fasoli, szparagu*) string; (*żarówki*) filament; **włókno akrylowe** acrylic fiber; **włókno azbestowe** asbestos fiber; **włókno jedwabne** floss; **włókno kokosowe** coir; **włókno mięśniowe** muscle fiber; **włókno nerwowe** nerve fiber; **włókno szklane** fiberglass, glass fiber; **włókno światłowodowe** optical fiber; **włókno wolframowe** (*w żarówce*) tungsten filament.

wmanewrować *pf. zob.* **wmanewrowywać.** ~ **się** *pf. zob.* **wmanewrowywać się.**

wmanewrowywać *ipf.* 1. *pot.* maneuver (*kogoś w coś* sb into sth). 2. (*np. samochód do garażu*) ease (*do czegoś* into sth). ~ **się** *ipf. pot.* be maneuvered (*w coś* into sth).

wmarznąć *ipf.* freeze in, get ice-bound.

wmasować *pf.*, **wmasowywać** *ipf.* rub in.

wmaszerować *pf.*, **wmaszerowywać** *ipf.* march in.

wmawiać *ipf.* make (sb) believe; **wmawiać coś komuś** lead sb to believe sth; **wmawiać coś w siebie** *l.* **sobie** get an idea into one's head; **wmawiać coś komuś jak w chorego jajko** *l.* **ciążę w brzuch** *pot.* try to sell an idea on sb.

wmeldować *pf.*, **wmeldowywać** register (*sb as a tenant*). ~ **się** *pf.*, **wmeldowywać się** *ipf.* register (*with the authorities as a tenant*).

wmiatać *ipf.*, **wmieść** *pf.* sweep into (*a room*); sweep under (*a carpet*); sweep onto (*a dustpan*).

wmieszać *pf.* 1. (= domieszać) mix in; **wmieszać cukier puder do ciasta** mix caster sugar into the dough. 2. *pot.* (= wplątać kogoś w coś) mix up. ~ **się** *pf.* 1. (= przyłączyć się) mix; **wmieszać się w tłum** mix with the crowd. 2. (= wplątać się) get mixed up (*w coś* in sth). 3. (= wtrącać się) meddle (*w coś* in sth).

wmieść *pf.* **wmiotę wmieciesz wmiótł wmiotła wmietli** *zob.* **wmiatać.**

wmontować *pf.*, **wmontowywać** *ipf.* build in.

wmontowany *a.* built-in; **radio z wmontowanym budzikiem** radio with a built-in alarm clock.

wmotać *pf.* 1. (= *zaplątać*) entangle. 2. *pot.* (= *wplątać*) entagle; **wmotać kogoś w cudze sprawy** entangle sb in sb else's affairs. ~ **się** *pf.* 1. (= *zaplątać się*) get entangled. 2. *pot.* (= *wplątać się*) get entangled, get mixed up; **wmotać się w podejrzane interesy** get entangled *l.* mixed up in shady deals.

wmówić *pf. zob.* **wmawiać**.

wmurować *pf.*, **wmurowywać** *ipf.* build in(to); (= *umieścić koniec cegły, belki itp. w ścianie*) tail in; **wmurować w ścianę tablicę pamiątkową** put up a commemorating plaque on the wall.

wmusić *pf.* **-szę -sisz, wmuszać** *ipf.* force (*coś w kogoś* sth upon sb); press (*coś w kogoś* sth upon sb).

wnerwiać *ipf.*, **wnerwić** *pf. pot.* get on sb's nerves. ~ **się** *ipf.*, **wnerwić się** *pf. pot.* 1. (= *zdenerwować się*) get worked up, get irked, get one's hackles up. 2. (= *skrzyczeć kogoś*) raise Cain *l.* hell.

wnet *adv. lit.* presently, soon, anon.

wnęka *f.* 1. *bud.* recess, alcove, bay. 2. *anat.* hilus.

wnękowy *a.* recessed, built *l.* placed in a recess; **szafa wnękowa** built-in closet.

wnętrostwo *n. pat.* cryptorchidism, cryptorchism.

wnętrzarz *mp pot.* interior designer.

wnętrze *n.* 1. (= *to, co nie jest na zewnątrz*) interior, the inside; **wnętrze** *l.* **głąb kraju** inland; **wnętrze Ziemi** the Earth's interior. 2. (*pomieszczenie*) interior; **architektura wnętrz** interior design; **dekorator wnętrz** interior decorator; **projektant wnętrz** interior designer.

wnętrzniak *ma zool.* endoparasite, internal parasite.

wnętrzniaki *pl. bot.* Gasteromycetes (*Gasteromycetes*).

wnętrzności *pl. Gen.* -i entrails; (= *narządy jamy brzusznej*) intestines; (*w języku fachowym*) viscera; *pot.* innards, guts.

wniebogłosy *adv. pot.* at the top of one's voice *l.* lungs; **drzeć się wniebogłosy** scream *l.* shout *l.* yell blue *l.* bloody murder; **wydzierać się wniebogłosy** shout *l.* scream one's head off.

wniebowstąpienie *n. rel.* ascension; **Wniebowstąpienie Pańskie** Ascension Day; **Wyspa Wniebowstąpienia** *geogr.* Ascension Island.

wniebowzięcie *n. rel.* assumption; **Wniebowzięcie Najświętszej Marii Panny** the Assumption.

wniebowzięty *a.* on cloud nine, rapturous; **być wniebowziętym** be tickled pink.

wnieść *pf.* **wniosę wniesiesz wniósł wniosła wnieśli** *zob.* **wnosić**.

wnikać *ipf.* 1. (= *przenikać*) penetrate, permeate; (*do wnętrza pomieszczenia, np. o świetle, dźwiękach*) filter in. 2. (= *zgłębiać*) go into, probe; **nie wnikając w szczegóły** without going into details; **wnikać w coś** probe into sth; **wniknąć w sedno sprawy** get to the core of an issue.

wnikliwie *adv.* 1. (= *dociekliwie*) penetratingly. 2. (= *przenikliwie*) piercingly, penetratingly.

wnikliwość *f.* penetration, insight; **badać coś z wnikliwością** inspect sth in great detail.

wnikliwy *a.* 1. (= *dociekliwy*) penetrating, searching; (*o obserwatorze*) shrewd; **wnikliwe pytanie** searching question. 2. (= *przenikliwy*) piercing, penetrating; **przenikliwe zimno** piercing cold.

wniknąć *pf.* **-ij** *zob.* **wnikać**.

wniosek *mi* **-sk-** 1. (= *propozycja*) proposal; (*na zebraniu, posiedzeniu*) motion; **odrzucić wniosek** reject a motion; **przyjąć** *l.* **przegłosować wniosek** pass a motion; **poprzeć wniosek** second a motion; **zgłosić wniosek** put forward *l.* propose a motion; **wolne wnioski** (*w porządku zebrania*) any other business. 2. (= *konkluzja*) conclusion; **dojść do wniosku, że...** arrive at the conclusion that...; **wyciągnąć wniosek** draw a conclusion; **dochodzić do pochopnych wniosków** jump to conclusions. 3. (= *podanie*) application; **złożyć wniosek o coś** apply for sth; **złożyć wniosek o odszkodowanie** (*od firmy ubezpieczeniowej*) claim *l.* make a claim on the insurance; **wniosek o pokój w akademiku** application for a room in a dorm; *Br.* application for a room in a hall of residence. 4. *log.* conclusion, inference. 5. *prawn.* petition.

wnioskodawca *mp* mover.

wnioskować *ipf.* conclude, gather; **wnioskować z czegoś, że...** conclude from sth that...

wnioskowanie *n.* 1. (= *wyciąganie wniosków*) inference. 2. *log.* conclusion.

wniwecz *adv.* **obrócić coś wniwecz** shatter sth.

wnosić *ipf.* **-szę -sisz** 1. (= *niosąc, dostarczać*) carry in, bring in; **wnieść kapitał** *fin.* contribute capital; **wnieść wkład do spółki** contribute shares to a company; **wnieść w aporcie** *ekon.* contribute in kind; **wnieść opłatę** pay a fee; **wnieść poprawki do czegoś** make amendments to sth. 2. *przen.* (= *uzupełniać*) contribute; **wnieść (swój) wkład w coś** make a contribution to sth, contribute to sth; **zeznanie nie wniosło nic znaczącego** his testimony didn't contribute anything of value. 3. (= *przedkładać*) file, submit; (*wniosek*) motion; **wnieść petycję** submit a petition; **wnieść podanie** apply (*o coś* for sth); **wnieść o zmianę premiera** motion for a change of prime minister. 4. *prawn.* petition, file; **wnieść akt oskarżenia** bring an indictment; **wnieść apelację** appeal (*od czegoś* against sth); **wnieść zażalenie** *l.* **skargę** complain (*do kogoś / czegoś* to sb/sth); lodge a complaint (*na czyjeś ręce* with (the hands of) sb); **wnosić oskarżenie** press charges (*przeciwko komuś* against sb); bring an accusation *l.* charges (*przeciwko komuś* against sb); prefer a charge *l.* charges (*przeciwko komuś* against sb); prosecute (*przeciwko komuś* sb); **wnosić sprawę do sądu** bring a case to court; **wnieść** *l.* **złożyć pozew o rozwód** file for divorce; **wnieść pozew** bring *l.* file (a) suit (*przeciwko komuś* against sb); institute an action (*przeciwko komuś* against sb); **wnieść sprzeciw** raise objections; demur. **5.** *tylko ipf. lit.* (= *wyciągać wnio-sek*) infer, gather; **stąd wnoszę, że...** therefore I gather that...

WNP *abbr.* (= *Wspólnota Niepodległych Państw*) CIS (*the Commonwealth of Independent States*).

wnuczek *mp* -czk- *pl.* -owie grandson.

wnuczka *f. Gen.pl.* -ek granddaughter.

wnuk *mp pl.* -owie (= *syn syna l. córki*) grandson.

wnuki *pl. Gen.* -ów (= *dzieci syna l. córki*) grandchildren.

wnykarz *mp* snarer.

wnyki *pl. Gen.* -ów *myśl.* snare.

woal *mi Gen.pl.* -i *l.* -ów **1.** (*szal*) veil. **2.** *tk.* voile.

woalka *f. Gen.pl.* -ek veil.

wobec *prep.* + *Gen.* **1.** (= *w obecności*) in the presence of; **powiedzieć coś wszem i wobec** announce sth to all and sundry. **2.** (= *w obliczu*) in the face of; **wobec niebezpieczeństwa** in the face of danger; **stanął wobec widma ruiny** ruin stared him in the face. **3.** (= *w stosunku do kogoś, do czegoś*) to, towards; **mieć zobowiązania wobec firmy** have duties *l.* obligations towards one's company; **mieć obowiązki wobec rodziny** have duties towards one's family. **4.** (= *w porównaniu*) in comparison with; **moje kłopoty są niczym wobec twoich zmartwień** my problems are nothing in comparison with your worries. **5.** (= *ze względu na coś*) because of; **wobec groźby ataku terrorystycznego zastosowano specjalne środki ostrożności** special security measures were taken because of the threat of a terrorist attack; **wobec tego** in that case.

wobła *ma icht.* Caspian roach (*Rutilus rutilus caspicus*).

woda *f. Gen.pl.* wód **1.** (*np. do picia*) water; **woda bieżąca** running water; **woda brzozowa** birch extract-based hair tonic; **woda deszczowa** rainwater; **woda gazowana** sparkling water; **woda gruntowa** ground water; **woda kolońska** eau de Cologne; **woda królewska** *chem.* aqua regia; **woda kwiatowa** flower-scented eau de Cologne; **woda letejska** Lethean water; **woda mineralna** mineral water; **woda ognista** (= *mocny alkohol, zwł. whisky*) firewater; **woda pitna** drinking water; **woda przegotowana** boiled water; **woda przemysłowa** industrial water; **woda różana** rosewater; **woda sodowa** soda water; **woda toaletowa** toilet water; **woda źródlana** spring water; **miękka/średnia/twarda woda** soft/medium/hard water; **słodka woda** fresh water; **słona woda** salt water; **czystej wody** (*diament, łgarz itd.*) first water; **warzywa/karp z wody** *kulin.* boiled vegetables/carp; **wody płodowe** *anat.* waters, amniotic fluid; **ciężka woda** *chem.* heavy water; **woda destylowana** *chem.* distilled water; **woda utleniona** hydrogen peroxide, peroxide; **woda święcona** *rel.* holy water; **woda wapienna** limewater; **woda z kranu** tap water; **ujęcie wody** *l.* **wodne** water intake; **nastawić wodę** (*na herbatę itp.*) put the kettle on; **burza w szklance wody** storm in a teacup; **jak ogień i woda** *przen.* like oil

and water; (**ci dwoje**) **są jak ogień i woda** never the twain shall meet; **krew nie woda** (*o kimś*) he/she is so hot-blooded; **o chlebie i wodzie** on bread and water; **spływać jak woda po gęsi** *l.* **kaczce** be like water off a duck's back; **wylać komuś kubeł zimnej wody na głowę** throw *l.* pour cold water on sb; **szło jak woda** it was selling like hot cakes; **nie bądź w gorącej wodzie kąpany** don't be such a hothead; **podobni do siebie jak dwie krople wody** as like as two peas (in a pod); **utopiłby mnie w łyżce wody** he'd like nothing better than see me perish; **nabrać wody w usta** keep one's mouth shut, not breathe a word (*about sth*); **chyba mu woda sodowa uderzyła do głowy** looks like he has a swollen head, looks like the brains he had went to his head; **bać się czegoś jak diabeł święconej wody** be afraid of sth like a vampire fears an olive stake; **lać wodę** *pot.* waffle; **póty dzban wodę nosi, póki się ucho nie urwie** the pitcher goes often to the well but it is broken at last. **2.** (*akwen*) water; **odpoczywać nad wodą** rest by the water; **wody stojące** stagnant waters; **wody terytorialne** territorial waters; **wody otwarte** open waters; **woda gruntowa** *geol.* ground water; **woda podskórna** subsurface water; **woda powierzchniowa** surface water; **cicha woda** *przen.* (*o osobie*) the silent type; **cicha woda brzegi rwie** still waters run deep; **zniknąć jak kamień w wodę** vanish into thin air; **to wszystko palcem po wodzie pisane** it's all like a castle in the air; **to woda na jego młyn** it's grist to his mill; **dziesiąta woda po kisielu** a (very) distant relative; **czuć się jak ryba w wodzie** be in one's element; **puszczać się na szerokie wody** go big (time); **dużo wody upłynie, zanim...** it will be a long time before..., a lot of water will run under the bridge before... **3.** *med.* water, serous liquid.

wodery, wadery *pl.* (= *gumowe wysokie spodnie l. buty używane przez wędkarzy*) waders.

wodewil *mi Gen.pl.* -i *l.* -ów vaudeville.

wodewilista *mp* vaudevillian, vaudevillist.

wodewilistka *f. zob.* **wodewilista**.

wodniacki *a.* aquatic.

wodniactwo *n.* aquatics.

wodniak *mp* lover of aquatics, water sports enthusiast.

wodniczka *f. Gen.pl.* -ek *bot.* vacuole; **wodniczka tętniąca** contractile vacuole.

wodnik *mp* **1.** (*w baśniach*) nix, water sprite. **2. Wodnik** *astron., astrol.* Aquarius; *pot.* the Water Bearer. **3.** *orn.* water rail (*Rallus aquaticus*). **4.** *zool.* (= *topik*) water spider (*Argyroneta aquatica*).

wodnisty *a.* watery; **wodniste oczy** watery *l.* insipid eyes.

wodnokanalizacyjny *a.* water-supply and sewage-disposal *l.* sewerage.

wodnopłat, wodnopłatowiec *mi lotn.* hydroplane, seaplane.

wodny *a.* **1.** (= *odnoszący się do wody l. akwenu*) water; **armatka wodna** water cannon; **bilans wodny** *biol., geogr.* water balance; **ciek wodny** watercourse; **droga wodna** waterway; **dział wodny** *geogr.* watershed, divide; **elektrownia wodna**

hydroelectric (power) plant *l*. station; **fajka wodna** hookah, water pipe; **farba wodna** water paint; **gospodarka wodna** water management; **łóżko wodne** waterbed; **młyn wodny** water mill; **narty wodne** *sport* water-ski; **nimfa wodna** *mit*. naiad, water nymph; **piłka wodna** *sport* water polo; **puchlina wodna** *pat*. dropsy; **rower wodny** pedalo; **roztwór wodny** *chem*. aqueous solution; **sporty wodne** water sports, aquatics; **stopień wodny** *bud*. barrage; **system wodny** (= *system zbiorników wodnych; system zaopatrzenia w wodę*) water system; **transport wodny** water transport; **ujęcie wodne** *l*. **wody** water intake; **zapora wodna** dam; **zbiornik wodny** water reservoir; **znak wodny** watermark. **2.** (= *żyjący w wodzie*) water, aquatic; **fauna/flora wodna** aquactic fauna/flora; **kurka wodna** *zool*. moor *l*. water hen (*Gallinula chloropus*); **lilia wodna** *bot*. water lily (*Nymphaea*); **ptactwo wodne** waterfowl; **strzałka wodna** *bot*. arrowhead (*Sagittaria sagittifolia*).

wodobrzusze *n. pat*. ascites.

wodochłonność *f*. (*substancji*) hygroscopicity.

wodochłonny *a*. (*o substancji*) hygroscopic; (*o fabryce, gałęzi przemysłu*) water-intensive, water-consuming.

wodociąg *mi* (*urządzenia*) water supply system.

wodociągi *pl. Gen*. **-ów** (*przedsiębiorstwo*) waterworks.

wodociągowy *a*. water supply; **rury wodociągowe** water (supply system) pipes; **sieć wodociągowa** water supply system *l*. network.

wododział *mi geogr*. watershed, divide.

wodogłowie *n. Gen.pl*. **-i** *pat*. hydrocephalus, hydrocephaly; *pot*. water on the brain.

wodogrzmot *mi lit*. waterfall.

wodolecznictwo *n. med*. hydrotherapy, hydrotherapeutics.

wodoleczniczy *a*. hydrotherapeutic; **zakład wodoleczniczy** hydropathic institute, water-cure establishment.

wodolejstwo *n. pot*. wordiness, verbiage.

wodolot *mi żegl*. hydrofoil.

wodolubny *a. bot*. hydrophilous.

wodołaz *ma kynol*. Newfoundland.

wodomierz *mi Gen*. **-a** water meter.

wodonercze *n. pat*. hydronephrosis.

wodonośność *f. geol*. water-bearing capacity.

wodonośny *a. geol*. water-bearing; **warstwa wodonośna** aquifer, water-bearing stratum.

wodoodporny *a*. (= *odporny na działanie wody*) water-resistant; (= *nieprzesiąkliwy*) waterproof, water-repellent; (= *niezmywalny*) (*barwnik, farba*) water-fast, indelible.

wodopój *mi* **-o-** *Gen.pl*. **-ów** waterhole, watering hole *l*. place.

wodopójki *pl. zool*. water mites (*Hydracarina*).

wodopylny *a. bot*. hydrophilous.

wodorek *mi* **-rk-** *chem*. hydride.

wodorokwas *mi chem*. hydracid.

wodorosiarczan *mi chem*. bisulfate.

wodorosiarczek *mi chem*. hydrosulfide.

wodorosiarczyn *mi chem*. bisulfite.

wodorosól *f*. **-o-** *pl*. **-e** *chem*. acid salt.

wodorost *mi bot*. waterweed; seaweed; hydrophyte.

wodorotlenek *mi* **-nk-** *chem*. hydroxide.

wodorotlenowy *a*. *chem*. hydroxyl; **grupa wodorotlenowa** hydroxyl group.

wodorowęglan *mi chem*. bicarbonate.

wodorowy *a*. hydrogen, hydrogenous; **bomba wodorowa** *wojsk*. hydrogen bomb, H-bomb; **wiązanie wodorowe** *chem*. hydrogen bond.

wodorzyg *mi bud*. gargoyle.

wodospad *mi* waterfall; **Wodospad Niagara** *geogr*. Niagara Falls.

wodostan *mi geogr*. water level.

wodoszczelny *a*. watertight; (*o zegarku*) water-resistant.

wodotrysk *mi* fountain.

wodować *ipf*. **1.** *żegl*. launch. **2.** *lotn*. splash down; **wodować przymusowo** ditch.

wodowanie *n*. **1.** *żegl*. launch, launching. **2.** *lotn*. splashdown; **wodowanie przymusowe** ditching.

wodowskaz *mi* water gauge *l*. glass.

wodowstręt *mi pat., wet*. hydrophobia; (= *wścieklizna*) rabies, hydrophobia.

wodór *mi* **-o-** *chem*. hydrogen; **ciężki wodór** heavy hydrogen, deuterium.

wodza *f*. **1.** (= *lejce*) (*zw. pl.*) reins; **trzymać nerwy na wodzy** keep one's temper; **puścić wodze czemuś** (*fantazji, wyobraźni, etc.*) give (full *l*. free) rein to sth; **puścić wodze fantazji** give *l*. allow full play to fantasy; **puścić wodze koniowi** give a horse the bridle. **2.** (= *przywództwo, dowództwo*) leadership, command; **pod czyjąś wodzą** under sb's command.

wodzian *mi chem*. hydrate.

wodzianka *f. Gen.pl*. **-ek** *kulin*. slops (*of bread and water*).

wodzić *ipf*. **wódź 1.** (= *prowadzić kogoś*) lead; **wodzić kogoś na pokuszenie** *lit*. lead sb into temptation; **wodzić kogoś za nos** lead sb by the nose; **wodzić prym** rule the roost, play first fiddle; **wodzić rej** hold sway. **2.** (*o samicy ptaka*) look after (*the hatchlings until they are ready to leave the nest*). **3.** (= *przesuwać czymś*) run, draw (*one's finger, etc. across sth*); **wodzić za kimś oczami** follow sb with one's eyes; **wodzić oczami po pokoju** sweep a room with one's eyes; **wodzić piórem po papierze** drive a pen across a sheet of paper; **wodzić smyczkiem (po strunach skrzypiec)** bow (violin strings). ~ **się** *ipf*. **1.** *pot*. walk, go. **2.** *przest*. wrestle; **wodzić się za łby** be at loggerheads; **w młodości ciągle wodzili się za łby** there was no love lost between them when they were young.

wodzidło *n*. **1.** *techn*. guide bar. **2.** *żegl*. jackstay.

wodzik *mi techn*. crosshead.

wodzirej *mp Gen.pl*. **-ów 1.** (*w tańcu*) dance leader. **2.** (*na zabawie*) Master of Ceremonies, MC. **3.** (= *herszt*) ringleader.

wodzostwo *n*. **1.** (*stanowisko*) chieftaincy. **2.** (*dowództwo*) chief command.

Wogezy *pl. geogr*. the Vosges.

woj *mp hist.* knight.

woj. *abbr.* (= *województwo*) prov. (*province*).

wojaczka *f. Gen.pl.* -ek *pot.* soldiering.

wojak *mp pl.* -cy *l.* -i *żart.* soldier, G.I.; *Br.* Tommy.

wojaże *pl. Gen.* -y travel (*usu. abroad*); **w swoim życiu odbył mnóstwo wojaży** he is a very well-travelled man.

wojażować *ipf.* travel (*usu. abroad*).

Wojciech *mp* **Święty Wojciech** *rz.-kat.* St. Adalbert.

wojenny *a.* (of) war; (= *czasów wojny*) wartime; (= *wojskowy*) martial; **barwy wojenne** (*u Indian*) war paint; **bohater wojenny** war hero; **działania wojenne** warfare; **inwalida wojenny** disabled war veteran; **jeniec wojenny** prisoner of war, POW; **kontrabanda wojenna** contraband of war; **kontrybucja wojenna** (*nakładana na zwyciężonego*) tribute; **korespondent wojenny** *dzienn.* war correspondent; **marynarka wojenna** navy; **narada wojenna** council of war; **okręt wojenny** warship, man-of-war; **podżegacz wojenny** warmonger; **port wojenny** naval base; **pożyczka wojenna** *hist., fin.* (*z czasów I wojny światowej*) liberty loan; **przemysł wojenny** (*czasów wojny*) war-time industry; (*produkujący na potrzeby wojska*) defense industry; **reparacje wojenne** reparation payments; **taktyka wojenna** war tactics; **sąd wojenny** court martial; **stan wojenny** martial law; **straty wojenne** (*w ludziach*) war losses; **ścieżka wojenna** warpath; **na wojennej ścieżce** (*t. przen.*) on the warpath; **zbrodnie wojenne** war crimes; **zbrodniarz wojenny** war criminal; **zniszczenia wojenne** war damage; **zakopać topór wojenny** bury the hatchet; **żyć z kimś na stopie wojennej** be on a war footing with sb, be at daggers drawn with sb.

wojewoda *mp pl.* -owie **1.** *admin.* province governor. **2.** *hist.* province governor, voivode (*used only as transliteration of the Polish term*); **szlachcic na zagrodzie równy wojewodzie** a man's home is his castle.

wojewódzki *a.* provincial; **miasto wojewódzkie** provincial capital, province capital (city); **sąd wojewódzki** provincial court; **sejmik wojewódzki** provincial assembly; **szpital wojewódzki** provincial hospital; **urząd wojewódzki** province governor's office.

województwo *n.* **1.** *admin.* province. **2.** *pot.* (*urząd*) province governor's office; **załatwiać swoje sprawy w województwie** take care of one's business in the province governor's office.

wojłok *mi tk.* low-quality felt.

wojna *f. Gen.pl.* wojen war, warfare; **wojna atomowa** *l.* **jądrowa** nuclear war; **wojna biologiczna** biological warfare; **wojna chemiczna** chemical warfare; **wojna celna** *ekon.* tariff war; **wojna domowa** civil war; **wojna elektroniczna** electronic warfare, e-warfare; **wojna gangów** gang warfare; **wojna na wyczerpanie** war of attrition; **wojna nerwów** war of nerves; **wojna pozycyjna** trench warfare; **wojna partyzancka** guerilla warfare; **wojna psychologiczna** psychological warfare; **wojna religijna** religious war; **wojna totalna**

total war; **dziwna wojna** *hist.* phony war (*1939*); **święta wojna** holy war; (*muzułmańska*) jihad; **wojna o pokój** *l.* **mająca położyć kres wszystkim wojnom** the war to end all wars; **zimna wojna** cold war; (*1945-89*) the Cold War; **I/II wojna światowa** *hist.* World War I/II, the First/Second World War; **wojna dwóch róż** *hist.* the War of the Roses (*1455-85*); **wojna secesyjna** *hist.* the Civil War (*1861-65*); **wojna stuletnia** *hist.* the Hundred Years' War (*1337-1453*); **okropności wojny** horrors *l.* atrocities of war; **pójść na wojnę** go to war; **toczyć wojnę** wage a war (*z kimś/czymś* against sb/sth); **wypowiedzieć wojnę** declare a war (*komuś/czemuś* on sb/sth); **na krawędzi wojny** at the brink of war; **w stanie wojny** at war (*z kimś/czymś* with sb/sth); **wybuchła wojna** war broke out.

wojować *ipf.* **1.** (= *zwalczać*) combat, fight (*z kimś/czymś* sb/sth). **2.** (= *prowadzić wojnę*) wage war (*z kimś/czymś* against sb/sth); **kto mieczem wojuje, od miecza ginie** he who lives by the sword shall perish by the sword.

wojowniczo *adv.* **1.** (= *zaczepnie*) aggressively, in a warlike spirit. **2.** (= *czupurnie*) belligerently, truculently.

wojowniczość *f.* **1.** (= *zaczepność*) warlike spirit, aggressiveness. **2.** (= *czupurność*) belligerence, truculence.

wojowniczy *a.* **1.** (= *skłonny do walki*) warlike, aggressive; **wojowniczy naród** warrior nation. **2.** (= *skłonny do zaczepek, agresji*) belligerent, truculent.

wojownik *mp* **1.** (= *żołnierz*) warrior. **2.** (*o sprawę*) fighter.

wojsko *n.* **1.** (= *siły zbrojne*) armed forces; **wojska lądowe** army, ground *l.* land forces; **wojska lotnicze** air force; **wojska przeciwlotnicze** air defense; **wojska ochrony pogranicza** Frontier Defense Force. **2.** (= *armia lądowa*) army. **3.** (= *wojskowi*) the military. **4.** (= *żołnierze*) soldiers. **5.** *pot.* (= *służba wojskowa*) military service; **iść do wojska** go to the army; **dostać powołanie do wojska** be called up *l.* conscripted; **powołać do wojska** call up, conscript; **służyć w wojsku** serve in the army; **wstąpić do wojska** join the army *l.* the colors; **zaciągnąć się do wojska** enlist, enroll; **zgłosić się do wojska na ochotnika** volunteer for the army; **chłopak po wojsku** a man who did his military service.

wojskowo *adv.* militarily; **dobrze wyszkolony wojskowo** of quality military training.

wojskowość *f.* (*wiedza*) military science; **historia wojskowości** military history; **specjalista w dziedzinie wojskowości** military expert.

wojskowy *a.* military; **attaché wojskowy** military attaché; **baza wojskowa** army *l.* military base; **ćwiczenia wojskowe** military exercise; **inżynieria wojskowa** military engineering; **jednostka wojskowa** military unit; **honory wojskowe** military honors; **obóz wojskowy** army *l.* military camp; **oddawać komuś honory wojskowe** pay military honors to sb, salute sb; **książeczka wojskowa** military service record and ID (*in the form of a booklet*); **manewry wojskowe** military maneuvers; **obiekt wojskowy** military installation; **odznaczenie wojskowe** military decoration; **orkiestra wojskowa** military band; **prokurator wojskowy** judge advocate; **regulamin wojskowy** service disciplinary code; **sąd wojskowy** court martial; **służba wojskowa** military service; **odbywać służbę wojskową** do one's military service; **obowiązkowa służba wojskowa** national service, compulsory military service; **ochotnicza służba wojskowa** volunteer military service; **niezdolny do służby wojskowej** unfit for military service; **niezdolny do czynnej służby wojskowej** unfit for active military service, noneffective; **podlegający służbie wojskowej** liable for military service; **tajemnica wojskowa** military secret; **teren wojskowy** military area *l.* zone; „**Teren wojskowy. Wstęp wzbroniony**" (*tablica informacyjna*) "No entry. Military area *l.* zone"; **wojskowa komenda uzupełnień** army recruiting command; **żandarmeria wojskowa** military police. – *mp* (= *żołnierz*) military man; **wojskowi w służbie ojczyzny** military men and women serving their country.

wojujący *a.* **1.** *dosł.* warring, militant. **2.** *przen.* militant; **wojujący ateizm** militant atheism; **wojujący ekolog** (*często stosujący nielegalne środki protestu*) ecowarrior.

wok *mi* (*patelnia*) wok.

wokabularz *mi Gen.* **-a** *lit., arch.* dictionary.

wokal *mi muz.* **1.** (= *partia śpiewana*) vocal. **2.** *pot.* (= *głos*) voice.

wokaliczność *n. fon.* vocality.

wokaliczny *a. fon.* vocalic.

wokalista *mp* (= *śpiewak*) vocalist; (*w zespole rockowym, jazzowym*) (*o mężczyźnie*) front man; (*o kobiecie*) front woman.

wokalistka *f. Gen.pl.* **-ek** *zob.* **wokalista**.

wokaliza *f. muz.* (exercise in) vocalization.

wokalizacja *f. fon.* vocalization; **wokalizacja jerów** vocalization of yers; **wokalizacja sonantów** vocalization of sonants.

wokalizm *mi fon.* vocalism.

wokalizować *ipf. fon.* vocalize. ~ **się** *ipf. fon.* vocalize.

wokalny *a. muz.* vocal.

wokanda *f. prawn.* docket; *Br.* cause list; **być na wokandzie** come to trial.

wokoło, wokół *prep.* + *Gen.* around, round; **chodzić wokoło domu** walk around *l.* round the house; **dyskusja wokół problemu zanieczyszczenia środowiska** discussion (centered *l.* focusing) on the problem of environmental pollution. – *adv.* all around; **rozejrzeć się wokoło** look around; **nie wiedziałem, co się wokoło mówiło** I didn't know what was being said all around.

wokółziemski *a.* circumterrestrial; **orbita wokółziemska** circumterrestrial orbit.

wola *f.* will; **silna/słaba wola** strong/weak will; **dobra wola** goodwill; **zła wola** ill will; **ostatnia wola** (= *testament*) last will; **wolna wola** free will; **wolność woli** freedom of will; **siła woli** willpower; **z własnej i nieprzymuszonej woli** of one's own volition, of one's own free will; **zgodnie z twoją wolą** according to your will; **podporządkować się czy-**

jejś woli comply with sb's will; **narzucić komuś swoją wolę** impose one's will on sb; **jeśli taka będzie wola boska** *l.* **nieba** God willing; **do woli** at will; **jeść/pić do woli** eat/drink to one's heart content, eat/drink one's fill; **mimo woli** involuntarily.

wolak *ma orn.* (*gołąb*) pouter.

wolant *mi Gen.* **-a 1.** (*pojazd*) cabriolet. **2.** *lotn.* control column *l.* stick. **3.** *sport* battledore *l.* battledore and shuttlecock. **4.** (*falbana*) flounce.

wolapik *mi jęz.* Volapük, Volapuk.

wole *n. Gen.pl.* **-i 1.** *zool.* crop, craw; (*u bydła*) dewlap. **2.** *pat.* goiter; *Br.* goitre.

woleć *ipf.* **wolę wolisz, wól** prefer; **wolę czytać niż pisać** I prefer reading to writing; **wolałbym ciastko** (**niż jabłko**) I'd rather have a cookie (than an apple); **wolałbym o niczym nie wiedzieć** (*o jakiejś nieprzyjemnej sprawie*) I'd rather not know about the whole thing; **wolałbym tego nie robić** I'd rather not do it; **wolałbym, żebyś tego nie robił** I'd rather you didn't do it.

wolej *mi Gen.* **-a** *Gen.pl.* **-ów** *sport* volley.

woleoczko *ma orn.* strzyżyk **woleoczko** winter wren (*Troglodytes troglodytes*).

wolfram *mi chem.* tungsten, wolfram.

wolframian *mi chem.* tungstate.

wolframit *mi min.* wolframite.

wolframowy *a. chem.* tungstenic, tungstic.

woli *a.* ox's; (*w języku fachowym*) bovine; **wole oczy** *sztuka* egg and dart, egg and tongue, egg and anchor; **wole oko** *bud.* bull's eye.

wolicjonalny *a. psych.* volitional.

woliera *f.* (= *ptaszarnia*) aviary.

wolina *f.* excelsior, woodwool.

wolkameria *f. bot.* glorybower (*Clerodendron*).

wolne *n. Gen.* **-ego** *pot.* (= *dzień wolny od pracy*) a day off; **wolnego!** take it slow!

wolno *adv.* **1.** (= *pomału*) slowly; **czas płynie wolno** the time is dragging on. **2.** (= *luźno*) loosely. **3.** (= *swobodnie*) freely; **puścić kogoś wolno** set sb free; **budynek wolno stojący** detached building. – *pf. indecl.* **czy wolno zapytać, jak pani godność?** may I have your name, please?; **jeśli wolno spytać** if I may ask; **nie wolno tak robić** you can't do that; **tu nie wolno palić** you can't smoke here; **nie wolno mu palić** he mustn't smoke; **tobie wszystko wolno** you are allowed to do everything; **wolnoć Tomku w swoim domku** my house is my castle.

wolnoamerykanka *f. sport* catch-as-catch-can.

wolnocłowy *a. ekon.* duty free; **sklep wolnocłowy** duty free shop; **strefa wolnocłowa** duty free zone.

wolnomularski *a.* freemasonic.

wolnomularstwo *n.* freemasonry.

wolnomularz *mp* freemason.

wolnomyśliciel *mp* freethinker.

wolnomyślicielski *a.* freethinking.

wolnomyślicielstwo *n.* freethinking.

wolnomyślność *f. fil.* freethinking.

wolnorynkowy *a. ekon.* free market; **cena wolnorynkowa** free market price; **gospodarka wolnorynkowa** free market economy.

wolnościowy *a.* freedom, liberation; **ruch wolnościowy** liberation movement.

wolność *f.* **1.** (= *niezawisłość*) freedom, liberty. **2.** (= *niezależność osobista*) freedom, independence; **wolność wyboru** freedom of choice; **wolności obywatelskie** civil liberties; **wolność osobista** personal freedom; **wolność słowa** freedom of speech; **wolność sumienia** freedom *l.* liberty of conscience; **wolność wyznania** freedom of religion; **wolność zgromadzeń** freedom of assembly; **złota wolność** *hist.* privileges of the nobility (*in the 17th-18th century Poland*); **kara pozbawienia wolności** *prawn.* (penalty of) imprisonment; **pozostawać na wolności** (*zwł. o przestępcy*) remain at large.

wolny *a.* **1.** (= *suwerenny*) free. **2.** (= *niepodporządkowany komuś*) free, independent; **wolny przekład** *teor.lit.* free translation; **wolny rynek** *ekon.* free *l.* open market; **wolny słuchacz** auditing student; **wolny wybór** free choice; **wolna wola** free will; **wolny zawód** freelance profession; **wolne wnioski** (*na zebraniu*) any other business; **rzut wolny** *sport* free throw *l.* kick; **wiersz wolny** *teor.lit.* free verse; **wstęp wolny** admission free; **wolny jak ptak** free as a bird; **wolne żarty!** you must be joking *l.* kidding!; **odpowiadać z wolnej stopy** *prawn.* be released pending trial; (*w prawie anglosaskim, za kaucją*) appear on bail; (*bez kaucji*) be released on one's own recognizance. **3.** (= *uwolniony od czegoś*) free, exempt; **droga wolna od zasp** road free of snowdrifts; **nie jestem wolny od wad** I also have to confess to my faults. **4.** (= *niezajęty*) free, spare; **czas wolny** spare time, free time; **dzień wolny od pracy** a day off; **dać komuś wolną rękę** give sb a free hand; **jesteś wolny?** are you free? **5.** (= *do zajęcia, wykorzystania*) free; (*etat, pokój*) vacant; (*przejazd, droga*) clear; (*taksówka*) off duty; **wolna droga!** do as you please!, do whatever you want!; **zostawić komuś wolne pole do popisu** give sb a free hand. **6.** (= *niezwiązany z kimś*) single; **wolna miłość** free love; **kobieta/mężczyzna stanu wolnego** single *l.* unmarried woman/man. **7.** (= *powolny*) slow; **z wolna** slowly; **gotować na wolnym ogniu** cook on a slow fire. **8.** *chem.* free; **wolny rodnik** free radical. **9.** (*o ubraniu*) (= *luźny*) loose. – *mp* **1.** (= *człowiek decydujący o sobie*) free *l.* independent person. **2.** *sport* (*np. w koszykówce*) free throw; (*np. w piłce nożnej*) free kick; **strzelić bramkę z wolnego** score a goal after a free kick.

wolontariat *mi* voluntary service.

wolontariusz *mp*, **wolontariuszka** *f. Gen.pl.* **-ek** volunteer.

wolt *mi Gen.* **-a** *fiz.* volt.

wolta *f.* **1.** (= *obrót ciała*) volt, volte; *przen.* volte-face, flip-flop, about-face. **2.** *jeźdz.* volt, volte.

woltametr *mi fiz.* voltameter, coulometer.

woltamper *mi fiz.* volt-ampere.

wolterianizm *mi fil.* Voltairianism.

woltomierz *mi Gen.* **-a** *fiz.* voltmeter.

woltyżer *mp pl.* **-owie** *cyrk* bareback rider.

woltyżerka *f. cyrk* **1.** (*kobieta jeździec*) bareback rider. **2.** (= *jazda*) bareback riding.

woltyżerski *a. cyrk* bareback riding, bareback rider's.

wolumen, **wolumin** *mi* volume.

woluntarny *a. psych.* voluntary.

woluntaryzm *mi fil.* voluntarism.

woluta *f. bud.* volute.

wołacz *mi Gen.* **-a** *gram.* vocative.

wołać *ipf.* **1.** (= *wzywać*) call; **wołać dzieci na kolację** call children home for supper. **2.** (= *prosić*) call, cry; **wołać o ratunek** cry for help; **to woła o pomstę do nieba** it's simply outrageous; **buty wołają jeść** *żart.* shoes are worn (down). **3.** *pot.* (= *nazywać kogoś*) call, name; **wołają go Marcin** they call him Marcin; **jak na ciebie wołają?** what is your name?; what do they call you?; what are you called?

wołający *a.* calling, crying; **głos wołającego na puszczy** a voice (crying) in the wilderness.

wołanie *n.* call, calling; (= *okrzyk*) cry, crying; **wołanie o pomoc** cry for help.

wołek *ma* **-łk-** *ent.* weevil, snout beetle (*Sitophilus*); **wołek zbożowy** grain weevil (*Sitophilus granarius*).

Wołga *f. geogr.* the Volga.

Wołoch *mp*, **Wołoszka** *f. Gen.pl.* **-ek** *hist.* Vlach, Wallachian, Walachian.

wołoski *a.* Vlach, Wallachian, Walachian.

Wołoszczyzna *f. hist.* Walachia, Wallachia.

wołowe *n. Gen.* **-ego** *kulin.* (*mięso*) beef.

wołowina *f. kulin.* beef.

wołowy *a.* beef; **dupa wołowa** *wulg.* ass, asshole; **pieczeń wołowa** roast beef; **na wołowej skórze by nie spisał** it's a neverending story.

wołu *itd. ma zob.* **wół.**

Wołyń *mi geogr.* Volhynia, Volynia.

won *int. pot.* (get) out!, (go) away!

wonieć *ipf. lit.* smell.

wonnie *adv.* fragrantly.

wonności *pl. Gen.* **-i** fragrances, perfumes.

wonny *a.* fragrant.

woń *f. pl.* **wonie** fragrance, scent; **nieprzyjemna woń** unpleasant odor; *Br.* unpleasant odour.

WOP *abbr.* (= *Wojska Ochrony Pogranicza*) *wojsk.* Border Guard *l.* Patrol.

wopista *mp wojsk.* border guard.

WOPR *abbr.* (= *Wodne Ochotnicze Pogotowie Ratunkowe*) Volunteer Lifeguards Association.

worać się *pf.* **1.** (= *zaorać*) filch (*some of one's neighbor land*); (*przypadkowo*) plow into; *Br.* plough into. **2.** (*wgryźć się*) cut into.

woreczek *mi* **-czk-** *Gen.* **-a 1.** (= *mały worek*) (small) bag, (small) sack. **2.** *anat.* sac; saccule, sacculus; **woreczek** *l.* **pęcherzyk żółciowy** gallbladder, gall bladder; *rzad.* cholecyst.

worek *mi* **-rk-** *Gen.* **-a 1.** (*opakowanie*) sack, bag; (*zawartość*) sack, sackful; **worek osierdziowy** *anat.* heart sac, pericardial sac; **worek treningowy** *sport* punching bag; **worek bez dna** (*o osobie*) maw; (*o czymś wymagającym bezustannych inwestycji*) black hole; **kupić kota w worku** buy a pig in a poke; **wrzucać wszystko do jednego worka** treat different things in the same way, make no difference between *l.* among; **wisi na nim jak worek** it's too loose for him; **wyszło szydło z worka** now it's all clear. **2.** (*fason sukni*) loose-fitting dress, baggy dress. **3.** (= *obwisła skóra pod okiem*) bag (*under the eye*); **mieć worki pod oczami** have bags under the *l.* one's eyes. **4.** *bot.* ascus.

workować *ipf.* sack.

workowaty *a.* baggy.

workowce *pl. bot.* ascomycetes (*Ascomycetes*).

workowy *a.* **zarodnik workowy** *bot.* ascus.

wosk *mi* wax; **wosk pszczeli** beeswax; **lać wosk** tell fortune by pouring hot wax into water; **miękki jak wosk** easily influenceable, pliable; **jej serce topnieje jak wosk** she's so emotional.

woskować *ipf.* wax.

woskowina *f. fizj.* cerumen; *pot.* earwax.

woskowy *a.* **1.** (= *z wosku*) wax; **gruczoły woskowe** *ent.* wax (secreting) glands. **2.** (= *podobny do wosku*) waxlike, waxy.

woszczyna *f.* (= *plaster pszczeli*) honeycomb.

wotum *n. sing. indecl. pl.* **-ta** *Gen.* **-tów 1.** *rel.* votive offering. **2.** *polit.* vote; **wotum nieufności** vote of no confidence; **wotum zaufania** vote of confidence.

wotywa *f. rz.-kat.* votive mass.

wotywny *a. rel.* votive.

wozak *mp* **1.** (*woźnica*) carter, driver. **2.** *górn.* car pusher, putter.

wozić *ipf.* **wożę wozisz, woź** *l.* **wóź 1.** (= *przewozić*) transport, carry. **2.** *pot.* (= *obwozić kogoś*) drive around. **~ się** *ipf.* **wozić się z czymś** take sth with one for one's journey.

woziwoda *mp* water carrier.

wozownia *f.* coach house.

wozu *itd. mi zob.* **wóz.**

woźna *f. Gen.* **-ej** janitor.

woźnica *mp* coachman, driver.

woźny *mp* **1.** (*w urzędzie, szkole*) janitor. **2.** *hist.* usher.

wód *f. zob.* **woda.**

wóda *f. pot.* booze.

wódka *f. Gen.pl.* **-ek 1.** (= *napój*) vodka; **wódka uderza komuś do głowy** vodka goes to sb's head. **2.** *pot.* (*kieliszek napoju*) shot, glass; **postawić komuś dużą wódkę** buy sb a double vodka.

wódz *mp* **-o-** *pl.* **-owie** (= *przywódca*) leader, chieftain; (*plemienia, indiański*) chief, chieftain; *wojsk.* commander; **wódz naczelny** commander-in-chief.

wódź *ipf. zob.* **wodzić.**

wójt *mp pl.* **-owie** (*na wsi*) commune head; **do wójta z tym nie pójdziemy** we won't quarrel about this, we'll reach an agreement.

wół *ma* **-o-** *Gen.* **-u** ox; **wół piżmowy** *zool.* musk-ox (*Ovibos moschatus*); **wół roboczy** drudge; **pracowity jak wół** extremely hardworking; **harować jak wół** work like a horse, work like a dog; **to pasuje jak wół do karety** it's like a square peg in a round hole; **jest tu jak wół napisane** it's all here down in black and white; **zapomniał wół, jak cielęciem był** the old cow thinks she was never a calf.

wór *mi* **-o-** *Gen.* **-a 1.** (*worek*) large bag, large

sack; (*zawartość*) sack, sackful. **2.** *pot.* (*pod okiem*) bag.

wówczas *adv. lit.* then.

wóz *mi* **-o- 1.** (*pojazd konny*) cart, wagon; **wóz drabiniasty** hayrack; **(albo) wóz, albo przewóz** it's either make or break; **(być) raz na wozie, raz pod wozem** have one's ups and downs; **piąte koło u wozu** the fifth wheel; **baba z wozu, koniom lżej** it is good riddance to bad rubbish; **przyjdzie koza do woza** I shall catch you some day carrying corn to our mill; you're going to need my help someday; **przyszła koza do woza!** so you've come (to beg) for my help, haven't you? **2.** (*ilość towaru*) cartload, wagonload. **3.** (*pojazd komunikacji miejskiej*) car; (= *tramwaj*) streetcar; *Br.* tramcar, tram; **na trasę nie wyjechało pięć wozów** five cars were not dispatched. **4.** *pot.* (= *samochód*) car, automobile. **5.** (*pojazd o specjalnym przeznaczeniu*) vehicle; **wóz bojowy** *wojsk.* armored car, *Br.* armoured car; **wóz meblowy** furniture truck; **wóz policyjny** patrol car; **wóz pogrzebowy** hearse; **wóz transmisyjny** *radio, telew.* outside broadcast vehicle *l.* van. **6. Mały/Wielki Wóz** (*gwiazdozbiory*) Little/Big Dipper.

wózek *mi* **-zk-** *Gen.* **-a 1.** (*dziecięcy głęboki*) baby carriage; *Br.* pram; (*dziecięcy spacerówka*) stroller; *Br.* pushchair. **2.** (*w supermarkecie*) cart; *Br.* trolley. **3.** (*pojazd*) cart, trolley, truck; **wózek inwalidzki** wheelchair; **jechać na jednym wózku** be in the same boat. **4.** *kol.* (*podwozie*) truck. **5.** *pot.* (= *samochód*) (*zwł. dobry*) wheels.

wózkarnia *f.*, **wózkownia** *f. Gen. pl.* **-i** *l.* **-ń** *a* room for keeping baby carriages and strollers in an apartment house.

WP *abbr.* (= *Wojsko Polskie*) the Polish Army.

wpadać *ipf.* **1.** (= *dostawać się do wnętrza*) fall; **wpaść w poślizg** go into a skid; **wpaść w pułapkę** be caught in a trap; **wpaść w niepowołane ręce** fall into the wrong hands; **wpaść w czyjeś ramiona** fall into sb's arms; **wpaść w wir pracy** threw o.s. into work; **wpaść w tarapaty** get into trouble; **wpaść w długi** fall *l.* get into debt; **wpaść komuś w oko** catch *l.* take sb's fancy; **wpadło mi coś do oka** sth has got into my eye; **to wpada w oczy** it catches attention; **wpaść komuś w słowo** interrupt sb; **wpaść z deszczu pod rynnę** fall out of the frying pan into the fire; **wpaść jak śliwka w kompot** get into serious trouble, *pot.* be in deep shit; **brać, co wpadnie w ręce** take whatever is available; **piłka wpadła do bramki** the ball went into the goal; **ta melodia wpadła mi w ucho** I like that tune; **samo mi wpadło w ręce** I found *l.* came across it by chance; **wpadł mi do głowy pomysł** I've hit upon an idea; **wpadło mi parę groszy** I earned some extra money; **kto pod kim dołki kopie, sam w nie wpada** he that mischief hatches, mischief catches; who digs a pit for another, falls into it himself; who makes a snare for another, falls into it himself. **2.** (= *wbiegać z impetem*) rush into, storm into; **wpadł do pokoju szukając Ewy** he rushed into the room in search of Eve. **3.** *pot.* (= *odwiedzać kogoś*) call on; **wpaść po kogoś** pick sb up; **wpaść jak po ogień** come and leave in a great hurry; **wpadnij do**

mnie wieczorem call on me tonight. **4.** (= *dostawać się pod coś*) get under, fall under; **wpaść pod samochód** be knocked down *l.* over by a car. **5.** (= *zderzać się*) run; **wpaść na drzewo** run into a tree. **6.** (= *mimowolnie natrafiać na kogoś, na coś*) bump into, come across; **wpaść na kogoś** bump into sb; **wpaść na ślad czegoś** find a trace of sth; **wpaść na pomysł** hit upon an idea. **7.** (= *być opanowanym przez uczucie*) be overcome, fall into; **wpaść w dobry humor** be in a good mood; **wpaść w gniew** fly into a rage; **wpaść w zachwyt** go into raptures over sth; **wpadać w panikę** start to panic; **wpaść w nałóg** fall *l.* get into a habit; **wpaść w przesadę** start exaggerating. **8.** (= *być zdekonspirowanym*) be exposed *l.* uncovered. **9.** *tylko ipf.* (= *uchodzić*) flow into; **rzeka wpada do morza** river flows into the sea. **10.** *tylko ipf.* (= *nabierać cech czegoś*) verge; **niebieski wpadający w szary** blue turning grey, blue verging on grey; *zob. t.* **wpaść**.

wpadka *f.* Gen.pl. -ek **1.** *pot.* (= *niepowodzenie*) slip-up. **2.** *pot.* (= *niechciana ciąża*) unwanted pregnancy. **3.** *karty* undertrick.

wpadnę *itd. pf. zob.* **wpadać**.

wpajać *ipf.* inculcate; **wpajać komuś coś** inculcate sth in sb.

wpakować *pf.* **1.** *pot.* (= *wcisnąć*) stuff, cram; **wpakować komuś kulę w łeb** pump a bullet into sb's head, blow sb's brains out; **wpakować w coś dużo pieniędzy** plow a lot of money into sth; *Br.* plough a lot of money into sth. **2.** *pot.* (= *umieścić kogoś*) put; **wpakować dziecko do łóżka** pack a child off to bed; **wpakować kogoś do więzienia** put sb away. ~ **się** *pf.* **1.** *pot.* (= *wejść*) get into; **wpakować się w kłopoty** get into trouble. **2.** *pot.* (= *znaleźć się gdzieś*) run into, get into; **wpakować się na drzewo** run into a tree; **wpakować się w błoto** get into mud.

wparować *pf. pot.* rush into, storm into.

wpasować *pf.*, **wpasowywać** *ipf.* fit in. ~ **się** *pf.*, **wpasowywać się** *ipf.* **1.** (= *wkomponować się*) fit in. **2.** *pot.* (= *dostosować się*) tune o.s. (*w coś* to sth). **3.** (= *zostać wpasowanym*) be fitted (*w coś* into sth).

wpaść *pf.* **wpadnę wpadniesz, wpadnij, wpadł 1.** *zob.* **wpadać**. **2.** *tylko pf. pot.* (= *zostać matką lub ojcem mimo woli*) conceive an unwanted child; (*o kobiecie*) become pregnant by accident.

wpatrywać się *ipf.*, **wpatrzyć się** *pf.* gaze, stare (*w coś* at sth).

wpatrzony *a.* -eni with one's eyes fixed on, looking intently at; **być wpatrzonym w kogoś jak w obrazek** *l.* **w tęczę** look up to sb, look at sb in awe and wonder.

wpełzać *ipf.*, **wpełznąć** *pf.* -znę -zniesz *l.* -źniesz, -znij *l.* -źnij, -znął *l.* -zł -zła -zli *l.* -źli crawl *l.* creep in.

wpędzać *ipf.*, **wpędzić** *pf.* drive in; **wpędzić kogoś do grobu** drive sb to an early grave; **wpędzać kogoś w chorobę** bring a disease on sb.

wpiąć *pf.* **wepnę wepniesz, wepnij** *zob.* **wpinać**.

wpić *pf.* **wpiję wpijesz, wpij** *zob.* **wpijać**. ~ **się** *pf. zob.* **wpijać się**.

wpierać *ipf.* **1.** (= *wciskać*) force, cram. **2.** (=

opierać się) press against. **3.** *tylko ipf. pot.* (= *wmawiać coś*) **wpierać coś komuś** try to make sb believe that... ~ **się** *ipf.* **1.** (= *wciskać się*) force one's way into. **2.** (= *zapierać się o coś*) push against (*w coś* against sth); lean heavily (*w coś* on sth).

wpierw *adv.* first, in the first place; **wpierw porozmawiam z ojcem, potem z matką** I'll talk to my father first and only then to my mother.

wpijać *ipf.* sink, bury (*coś w coś* sth into sth); **wpijać w kogoś oczy** stare at sb; **wpijać w coś paznokcie** sink *l.* bury one's nails into sth; **wpijać w coś zęby** sink one's teeth into sth. ~ **się** *ipf.* (= *zagłębiać się*) (= *wrzynać się*) sink (*w coś* into sth).

wpinać *ipf.* stick; (*szpilką*) pin; **wpiąć sobie/komuś kwiaty we włosy** put *l.* stick flowers in one's/sb's hair.

wpis *mi* **1.** (= *odnotowanie*) registration. **2.** *prawn.* entry. **3.** (= *wpisowe*) registration fee.

wpisać *pf.* -szę -szesz *zob.* **wpisywać**. ~ **się** *pf. zob.* **wpisywać się**.

wpisowe *n.* Gen. -ego (= *opłata rejestracyjna*) registration fee; (= *opłata za członkostwo*) membership fee.

wpisywać *ipf.* **1.** (= *umieszczać w rejestrze*) register, enter (*in a register*). **2.** (= *zapisywać w notatniku*) take down, write down. **3.** *geom.* inscribe. ~ **się** *ipf.* **1.** (= *umieszczać swoje nazwisko w rejestrze*) enroll; *Br.* enrol; register (o.s.). **2.** (= *umieszczać w czymś swoją notatkę*) write sth in sth; **wpisać się komuś do pamiętnika** put down one's name in sb's album.

wplatać *ipf.* braid, plait (*coś w coś* sth into sth); **wplatać wstążki we włosy** braid one's hair with ribbons; **wplatać do tekstu wyrazy łacińskie** *przen.* intersperse a text with Latin words, insert Latin words in a text.

wplątać *pf.* **wplączę wplączesz, wplątywać** *ipf.* **1.** (= *zaplątać*) tangle. **2.** *pot.* (= *wciągnąć kogoś w coś*) entangle (*kogoś w coś* sb in sth). ~ **się** *pf.*, **wplątywać się** *ipf.* **1.** (= *zaplątać się*) tangle. **2.** *pot.* (= *uwikłać się w jakąś sprawę*) become entangled *l.* embroiled (*w coś* in sth).

wpleść *pf.* **wplotę wpleciesz wplótł wplotła wpletli** *zob.* **wplatać**.

wpłacać *ipf.*, **wpłacić** *pf.* pay in; **wpłacić pieniądze na konto** deposit money in an account.

wpłata *f.* payment; **wpłata gotówkowa** cash payment; **dokonać wpłaty** make a payment; **dowód wpłaty** payment slip, voucher.

wpław *adv.* **przepłynąć (rzekę) wpław** swim across (the river).

wpłynąć *pf. zob.* **wpływać**.

wpływ *mi* (= *oddziaływanie*) influence, impact; **być pod czyimś wpływem** be under sb's influence; **być pod wpływem alkoholu** be under the influence of alcohol; **ulegać czyimś wpływom** come under sb's influence; *zob. t.* **wpływy**.

wpływać *ipf.* -am -asz **1.** *żegl.* sail in; **wpływać do portu** make port. **2.** (= *być dostarczanym*) come in. **3.** (= *oddziaływać*) influence, affect, exert influence; **nie chcę wpływać na jego decyzję** I don't want to influence his decision. **4.** (=

mieć odzwierciedlenie) influence, affect; **ta sytuacja wpływa negatywnie na moje życie rodzinne** this situation has a negative influence on my family life. **5.** *tylko ipf.* (= *znajdować ujście*) flow into; **rzeka wpływa do morza** the river flows into the sea.

wpływowy *a.* influential.

wpływy *pl. Gen.* **-ów 1.** (= *znaczenie*) influence; (= *znajomości*) influential friends; **używać wpływów** pull the strings. **2.** *fin.* receipts, takings.

wpoić *pf.* **wpoję wpoisz, wpój** *zob.* **wpajać**.

wpompować *pf.*, **wpompowywać** *ipf.* pump into; **wpompować w coś dużo pieniędzy** *przen.* pump a lot of money in sth.

wpół *adv.* **1.** (= *pośrodku*) half-way; **o wpół do trzeciej** at half past two; **trzymać kogoś wpół** hold sb round their waist; **zgiąć się wpół** bend double, double up. **2.** (= *nie do końca*) half, semi; **na wpół żywy** half-alive; **wpół uwierzyć w coś** half-believe sth.

wpółżywy *a.* half-alive.

wpraszać się *ipf.* invite o.s.

wprawa *f.* **1.** (= *biegłość*) proficiency, skill; **mieć w czymś wprawę** be adept at (doing) sth; **robić coś z wprawą** do sth skillfully. **2.** (= *wprawianie się*) practice; **dla wprawy** for practice; **wychodzić z wprawy** be out of practice.

wprawdzie *particle* admittedly, indeed; **wprawdzie zmarzł, ale się nie rozchorował** even though he had got cold he wasn't taken ill; **wprawdzie obiecywałem, że to zrobię na jutro, ale nie przewidziałem, że...** admittedly, I promised that I would do it for tomorrow but I didn't know that...

wprawiać *ipf.*, **wprawić** *pf.* **1.** (= *osadzać*) set, fix, mount. **2.** (= *wywoływać coś*) bring about; set, put; **wprawiać kogoś w dobry nastrój** put sb in a good mood; **wprawiać kogoś w zakłopotanie** embarrass sb; **wprawiać w ruch** set in motion. **3.** (= *przyzwyczajać*) train, accustom; **wprawiać dzieci do sprzątania po sobie** accustom children to cleaning up after themselves. **~ się** *ipf.*, **wprawić się** *pf.* **1.** (= *nabierać wprawy*) get practice (*w czymś* in sth). **2.** (= *doprowadzać się do jakiegoś stanu*) put o.s. in; **wprawiać się w dobry humor** put o.s. in a good mood.

wprawka *f. Gen.pl.* **-ek** *muz.* exercise.

wprawnie *adv.* (= *zręcznie*) skillfully, skilfully.

wprawny *a.* (= *wyćwiczony*) practiced; (= *doświadczony*) expert; (= *zręczny*) skillful, skilful, skilled.

wprosić się *pf.* **-szę -sisz** *zob.* **wpraszać się**.

wprost *adv.* **1.** (= *prosto*) straight ahead, straight on; **iść wprost przed siebie** go straight ahead *l.* on; **patrzeć na wprost** look straight ahead; **wprost proporcjonalny** *mat.* directly proportional. **2.** (= *bezpośrednio*) directly; **mleko wprost od krowy** milk directly from the cow; **zwrócić się wprost do prezesa** speak directly to the president. **3.** (= *otwarcie*) frankly, openly; (= *bez ogródek*) outright, point-blank; **mówić wprost, o co chodzi** speak one's mind frankly *l.* openly. **4.** (= *naprzeciw*) directly opposite; **sie-**

dzieć na wprost okna sit directly opposite the window. **–** *particle* (= *wręcz*) simply; **to wprost niemożliwe** this is simply impossible; **wprost przeciwnie** just the opposite.

wprowadzać *ipf.* **1.** (= *doprowadzać*) bring in, show in; **wprowadzić samochód do garażu** drive the car into the garage; **wprowadzić kogoś w życie** introduce sb to the world at large; **wprowadzić kogoś w błąd** mislead sb; **wprowadzić kogoś na tron** *hist.* enthrone sb. **2.** (= *umieszczać*) put, insert, introduce; **wprowadzić nabój do lufy** insert *l.* put the bullet into the barrel; **wprowadzić igłę do żyły** introduce the needle into a vein. **3.** (= *oddawać do użytku*) introduce, bring about; **wprowadzać coś w życie** *l.* **w czyn** put *l.* bring into effect; **wprowadzać do obiegu** bring into circulation; **wprowadzać zamęt** cause *l.* create confusion. **4.** (= *zapoznawać kogoś z czymś*) introduce (*kogoś w coś* sb to sth); **wprowadzać kogoś w arkana zawodu** introduce sb to the ins and outs of a profession. **5.** (= *wywoływać jakiś stan*) cause, put in; **wprowadzać kogoś w dobry nastrój** put sb in a good mood; **wprowadzać kogoś w zdumienie** amaze sb. **~ się** *ipf.* **1.** (*do domu, mieszkania*) move in. **2.** (= *popadać w jakiś nastrój*) put o.s. (*w coś* in sth); **wprowadzać się w dobry humor** put o.s. in a good mood; **wprowadzić się w stan upojenia alkoholowego** put o.s. in a state of drunken stupor.

wprowadzenie *n.* (= *wstęp*) introduction, preface.

wprowadzić *pf. zob.* **wprowadzać**. **~ się** *pf. zob.* **wprowadzać się**.

wprząc *pf.*, **wprzęgnąć** *pf.*, **wprzęgać** *ipf.* *t. przen.* harness.

wpust *mi* **1.** (*otwór*) inlet. **2.** *techn.* (*w desce, panelu*) rabbet, rebate.

wpustowy *a.* entry; **połączenie wpustowe** *stol.* tongue joint.

wpuszczać *ipf.*, **wpuścić** *pf.* **wpuszczę wpuścisz 1.** (= *pozwalać komuś l. czemuś dostać się do wnętrza*) let in, admit. **2.** (*np. ryby do stawu*) introduce; (*np. koszulę w spodnie*) put; (*np. wiadro do studni*) lower; (*np. słup w ziemię*) insert; (*krople do oczu*) apply; **wpuszczać kogoś w maliny** lead sb down *l.* up the garden path.

wpychać *ipf.* **1.** (= *wciskać coś*) shove in, cram in. **2.** *pot.* (= *zmuszać do przyjęcia*) force, ply; **wpychać** *l.* **wciskać coś komuś** push sth on sb, force sth on sb. **3.** *pot.* (= *umieszczać gdzieś*) install; **wepchnął swoją siostrę na sekretarkę szefa** he installed his sister as the boss' secretary. **~ się** *ipf.* **1.** (= *siłą przedostawać się dokądś*) push in; **wpychać się do kolejki** cut in line; *Br.* jump the queue. **2.** (= *wdzierać się*) get in, get into. **3.** *pot.* (= *brać w czymś udział bez zaproszenia*) barge in, be a gate-crasher. **4.** (= *popychać się*) push each other *l.* one another.

wrabiać *ipf.* **1.** *pot.* (= *wplątywać kogoś w coś*) frame; **wrabiać kogoś w coś** frame sb into sth. **2.** (= *wplatać nitki w tkaninę, dzianinę*) knit in.

wracać *ipf.* **1.** (= *przybywać z powrotem*) return, come back, get back; **wracać do łask** return to being in sb's favor *l.* good books, be in sb's favor *l.* good books again; **wrócić do żony/męża** return to one's wife/husband; **wrócić z kwitkiem** return empty-handed; **wraca mi apetyt** I am regaining my appetite. **2.** (= *zawracać*) turn back. **3.** (= *powracać*) (*np. o ziemiach do macierzy*) be returned, return. **4.** (= *robić coś ponownie*) go back to; **wracać do lektury** go back to reading, resume one's reading; **wracając do...** to return to...; **wróćmy do rzeczy** let's return to our subject, let's go back *l.* return to what we were talking about. **5.** (= *odzyskiwać stan poprzedni*) recover, regain; **coś wraca do normy** sth returns to normal, sth is back to normal; **wracać do zdrowia** recover, recuperate. ~ **się** *ipf.* **1.** (= *przybywać z powrotem*) return, come back. **2.** (= *zawracać*) turn back.

wradzać się *ipf.* take (*w kogoś* after sb).

wrak *mi Gen.* **-a** *l.* **-u** **1.** (*statek*) wreck, shipwreck. **2.** (*samochód*) wreck, carwreck. **3.** *pot.* (*człowiek*) wreck, ruin.

wrastać *ipf.* **1.** (= *zakorzeniać się*) grow into; (*korzeniami*) take root; **nogi mi wrastają w ziemię** my legs hurt from standing here for so long; **nogi wrosły mu w ziemię** he stood transfixed. **2.** (= *łączyć się w nierozerwalną całość*) blend into; **wrastać w nowe otoczenie** blend into the new surroundings; **wrastać w (czyjąś) pamięć** become rooted in (sb's) memory.

wraz *adv. lit.* together, along (*z kimś* with sb); **wraz z całym narodem** together with the whole nation.

wrażenie *n.* **1.** (= *reakcja na bodziec*) sensation. **2.** (= *odczucie*) impression, feeling; **mam wrażenie, że...** I have the impression that..., I get the feeling that...; **coś robi dobre wrażenie na kimś** sth makes a good impression on sb; **sprawia wrażenie zagubionej** she seems lost; **z wrażenia** in amazement.

wrażliwość *f.* **1.** (= *bycie wrażliwym*) sensitivity, sensibility. **2.** (= *brak odporności*) sensitivity, susceptibility.

wrażliwy *a.* **1.** (= *uczuciowy*) sensitive; **wrażliwy na krzywdę** compassionate. **2.** (= *czuły*) sensitive. **3.** (= *podatny*) susceptible, sensitive; **wrażliwy na ból** susceptible *l.* sensitive to pain; **wrażliwy na wstrząsy** sensitive to shocks; **wrażliwy na zmiany temperatury** sensitive to temperature changes.

wraży *a. lit.* inimical.

wrąb *mi* **-ę-** **1.** (= *wgłębienie*) notch, nick. **2.** (= *krawędź*) edge, brim; **po wrąb** *l.* **wręby** to the brim.

wrąbać *pf.* **-bię -biesz**, **wrąbywać** *ipf. pot.* (= *zjeść*) tuck in. ~ **się** *pf.* **1.** *pot.* (= *wbić się*) plow; *Br.* plough (*w coś* into sth). **2.** (*np. w las*) hew one's way (*do czegoś* into sth).

wre *itd. ipf. zob.* **wrzeć**.

wrednie *adv.* viciously, meanly.

wredny *a.* vicious, mean.

wreszcie *adv.* (= *nareszcie*) at last, finally; **wreszcie jesteś!** here you are at last! – *particle pot.* (= *ostatecznie*) after all; **co ty wreszcie sobie myślisz?** what are you thinking, after all?

wrę *ipf. zob.* **wrzeć**.

wręcz *a. indecl.* (= *bezpośredni*) direct, at a close distance; **walka wręcz** unarmed combat, hand-to-hand combat. – *adv.* **1.** (= *z użyciem rąk*) directly, from *l.* at a close distance; **walczyć wręcz** fight hand-to-hand. **2.** (= *bez ogródek*) plainly, straightforwardly; **powiedziała wręcz, w czym rzecz** she said straight what it was all about. – *particle* (= *wprost*) completely, totally; **to wręcz niemożliwe** this is simply impossible; **szedł szybko, wręcz biegł** he walked briskly or rather ran.

wręczać *ipf.*, **wręczyć** *pf.* (*dyplom, medal*) present (*komuś coś* sb with sth); (*kwiaty, prezent*) give (*komuś coś* sb sth *l.* sth to sb).

wręga *f.* **1.** (*kadłuba*) rib, frame. **2.** (*w desce*) rabbet, rebate.

wrobić *pf.* **wrób** *zob.* **wrabiać**.

wrodzić się *pf.* **wródź** *zob.* **wradzać się**.

wrodzony *a.* innate, inborn; *med., pat.* congenital.

wroga *itd. mp zob.* **wróg**.

wrogi *a.* (*o państwie, wojskach*) enemy; (*o zamiarach, milczeniu, spojrzeniu*) hostile, unfriendly.

wrogo *adv.* with hostility; **wrogo nastawiony** *l.* **usposobiony do kogoś** hostile to *l.* toward sb.

wrogość *f.* hostility, enmity.

wrona *f. orn.* (carrion) crow (*Corvus corone*); **kiedy wejdziesz między wrony, musisz krakać jak i one** when in Rome do as the Romans do, when in Rome do as Rome does.

wroni *a.* crow's; (*w języku fachowym*) corvine; **wronie gniazdo** crow's nest.

wrosnąć *pf.* **wrosnę wrośniesz, wrośnij, wrósł wrosła wrośli** *zob.* **wrastać**.

wrostek *mi* **-tk-** *Gen.* **-a** **1.** *jęz.* infix. **2.** *min.* included grain, endomorph.

wrośnięty *a.* **1.** (*o roślinie*) with roots grown deeply into ground. **2.** (*np. o elemencie krajobrazu*) blended into.

wrota *pl. Gen.* **wrót** gate, doors; **carskie wrota** *rel.* holy gates; **wrota do sukcesu** gateway to success; **patrzeć na coś jak cielę** *l.* **wół na malowane wrota** stare at sth blankly.

wrotka *f. Gen.pl.* **-ek** roller skate; **jeździć na wrotkach** roller-skate.

wrotkarski *a.* roller-skating, skating.

wrotkarz *mp* roller-skater.

wrotki *pl. zool.* rotifers, rotiferans (*Rotifera l. Rotatoria*).

wrotny *a. anat.* **żyła wrotna** portal vein.

wróbel *ma* **-bl-** *orn.* sparrow (*Passer*); **strach na wróble** scarecrow; **stary wróbel** *przen., żart.* experienced person, old stager; **lepszy wróbel w garści niż gołąb na dachu** a bird in the hand is worth two in the bush.

wróbli *a.* sparrow, sparrow's.

wróblowate *pl. orn.* passerines (*Passeriformes*).

wrócić *pf. zob.* **wracać**.

wróg *mp* **-o-** *pl.* **-owie** **1.** (= *nieprzyjaciel*) enemy, foe. **2.** (= *przeciwnik*) opponent (*czegoś* of sth).

wróść *pf.* **wrosnę wrośniesz, wrośnij, wrósł wrosła wrośli** *zob.* **wrosnąć.**

wróż *mp* = **wróżbiarz.**

wróżba *f.* **1.** (= *wróżenie*) prediction; **wróżby** fortune-telling. **2.** (= *prognostyk*) omen, sign.

wróżbiarka *f. Gen.pl.* **-ek** fortune-teller, soothsayer.

wróżbiarski *a.* fortune-telling, soothsaying.

wróżbiarz *mp* fortune-teller, soothsayer.

wróżbita *mp* = **wróżbiarz.**

wróżebny *a.* prophetic.

wróżka *f. Gen.pl.* **-ek 1.** (= *wróżbiarka*) fortune-teller, soothsayer. **2.** (*w bajkach*) fairy.

wróżyć *ipf.* **1.** (= *przepowiadać*) tell fortunes, soothsay; **na dwoje babka wróżyła** it's in the balance, it remains to be seen; **wróżyć komuś** tell sb's fortune; **wróżyć z kart/ręki** read the cards/palm. **2.** (= *przewidywać*) foretell, predict, forecast; **wróżyć komuś wielką karierę** foresee a brilliant career for sb. **3.** (= *zapowiadać coś*) herald, augur; **to nie wróży nic dobrego** it doesn't augur *l.* bode well.

wryć *pf.* **wryję wryjesz, wryj** *rzad.* dig into; **wryć sobie coś w pamięć** imprint sth on one's memory. **~ się** *pf.* (*o samochodzie*) get bogged; (*o pocisku*) sink; **wryć się komuś w pamięć** be engraved *l.* etched in sb's memory.

wrysować *pf.*, **wrysowywać** *ipf.* (*coś*) add an element to an existing drawing.

wryty *a.* dug into, sunk; **stanąć jak wryty** stop dead; stand nailed to the ground.

wrzask *mi* scream, yell; **podnieść wrzask** *l.* **narobić wrzasku** start to scream; *przen.* raise *l.* cause commotion *l.* a rumpus.

wrzaskliwie *adv.* (*bawić się, rozmawiać*) noisily.

wrzaskliwy *a.* **1.** (*goście, ulica*) noisy. **2.** (= *przenikliwy*) piercing.

wrzasnąć *pf.* **-snę -śniesz, -śnij** *zob.* **wrzeszczeć.**

wrzawa *f.* **1.** (= *gwar*) noise. **2.** (= *zamieszanie*) uproar, turmoil; **wywoływać wrzawę** create an uproar.

wrzątek *mi* **-tk-** boiling water.

wrzecionkowce *pl. zool.* fusobacteria (*Fusobacteria*).

wrzeciono *n.* **1.** *tk.* spindle. **2.** (*część wiosła*) grip.

wrzecionowaty *a.* spindle-shaped, fusiform.

wrzecionowy *a. techn.* spindle; **olej wrzecionowy** spindle oil.

wrzeć *ipf.* **wrę wrzesz wrze** *l.* **wre, wrzyj 1.** (= *kipieć*) boil. **2.** *przen.* rage; **praca wre** work is in full swing; **wszystko w nim wrzało** he was full of rage; **krew w nim wrzała** his blood boiled. **3.** (= *kłębić się*) seethe. **4.** (= *być podnieconym*) seethe, boil; **wrzeć z gniewu** be boiling with anger. **5.** (= *tętnić życiem*) bustle.

wrzenie *n.* **1.** (= *kipienie*) boiling; **temperatura wrzenia** *fiz.* boiling point. **2.** (= *wzburzenie*) turmoil.

wrzesień *mi* **-śni-** *Gen.* **-a** *Gen.* **-i** *l.* **-ów** September.

wrzeszczeć *ipf.* **-ę -ysz** scream, yell (*na kogoś*

at sb); **wrzasnąć z bólu** scream with pain; **wrzeszczeć wniebogłosy** *l.* **na całe gardło** scream bloody murder.

wrześniowy *a.* September.

wrzodowy *a. pat.* ulcerous; **choroba wrzodowa** peptic ulcer disease.

wrzodzieć *ipf.* **-eję -ejesz** *pat.* ulcerate.

wrzos *mi bot.* heather, ling, common heath (*Calluna vulgaris*).

wrzosiec *mi* **-śc-** *Gen.* **-a** *bot.* heath (*Erica*); **wrzosiec bagienny** cross-leaved heath (*E. tetralix*); **wrzosiec czerwony** winter heath (*E. carnea*); **wrzosiec popielaty** bell heath, bell heather (*E. cinerea*); **wrzosiec drzewiasty** briar, brier, tree heath (*E. arborea*); **korzeń wrzośca** (*do wyrobu fajek*) briarroot, briarwood.

wrzosowisko *n.* heath, moor, moorland.

wrzosowy *a.* (*kolor*) heather.

wrzoścowy *a.* briar; **fajka wrzoścowa** briar (pipe).

wrzód *mi* **-o-** *pat.* ulcer, sore; **wrzód trawienny/żołądka/dwunastnicy** peptic/stomach/duodenal ulcer; **wrzód weneryczny twardy** chancre; **wrzód weneryczny miękki** chancroid.

wrzucać *ipf.*, **wrzucić** *pf.* **1.** put, drop, throw (*sb l. sth*) (*do czegoś* in *l.* into sth); **wrzucać coś do kieszeni** slip sth into one's pocket; **wrzucać coś do ognia** throw *l.* chuck sth into the fire; **wrzucać monetę** (*do automatu*) insert a coin; **wrzucać wszystko do jednego worka** *przen.* lump things together. **2.** *pot.* (*różne czynności kojarzące się z wykonaniem ruchu ręką*) **wrzucać sprzęgło/jedynkę** *mot.* engage clutch/first gear; **wrzucać czwórkę** *mot.* kick into fourth; **wrzucać coś na siebie** slip sth on; **wrzucać coś na ruszt** have a snack.

wrzutowy *a.* **automat wrzutowy** slot machine.

wrzynać się *ipf.* cut, break, bite, penetrate, bore (*w coś* into sth); **sznur wrzynał mi się w skórę** the rope bit into my skin; **fiord wrzyna się w głąb lądu** the fjord penetrates far inland; **strumień wrzyna się pomiędzy skały** the stream cuts its way between the rocks.

wsad *mi techn.* batch, charge.

wsadowy *a.* **przetwarzanie wsadowe** *komp.* batch processing.

wsadzać *ipf.*, **wsadzić** *pf.* **1.** (= *wtykać*) stick, stuff, thrust, poke (*sth*) (*w coś l. do czegoś* in *l.* into sth) (*pod coś* under *l.* beneath sth) (*za coś* behind sth) (*przez coś* through sth); **wsadzać ręce do kieszeni** stuff one's hands in one's pockets; **wsadzić głowę przez okno** stick one's head in through the window; **wsadzić sobie ołówek za ucho** stick a pencil behind one's ear. **2.** (= *nasadzać, nakładać*) **wsadzać okulary na nos** set a pair of glasses on one's nose; **wsadzać czapkę (na głowę)** stick a cap on one's head. **3.** (= *pomagać przy wsiadaniu*) **wsadzać kogoś na konia/do samochodu/do pociągu** help *l.* put sb on a horse/into a car/on a train. **4.** (= *wysyłać kogoś w miejsce, w którym ograniczona jest swoboda*) put; **wsadzili mnie do szpitala** they put me in hospital; *pot.* (= *pozbawiać wolności*) lock (*sb*) up. **5.** *przen.* **wsadzać kij w mrowisko** put *l.* set a cat among the pigeons; stir up a hornets' nest; **wsadzać nos w nie swoje sprawy** poke *l.* stick one's nose into other people's affairs; **możesz to sobie wsadzić (w dupę)** *wulg.* you can stuff it (up your ass).

wsączać się *ipf.*, **wsączyć się** *pf. t. przen.* filter in, trickle in.

wsch. *abbr.* (= *wschodni l. wschód*) E (= *east, eastern*).

wschodni *a.* 1. eastern, east; (*o kierunku*) easterly; **wiatr wschodni** east *l.* eastern *l.* easterly wind; **wschodnie wybrzeże** the east coast; **czas strefowy wschodniego wybrzeża** (*Ameryki Północnej*) Eastern Standard Time; **wschodnie stany** eastern states; **Europa Wschodnia** Eastern Europe; **okna na wschodnią stronę** windows looking *l.* facing east; **w kierunku wschodnim** in an easterly direction; eastward; *Br.* eastwards; **10 stopni długości geograficznej wschodniej** *geogr.* longitude 10 degrees east. 2. *geogr., hist.* (*o części świata, kręgu kulturowym*) Eastern, oriental; **religie wschodnie** Eastern religions; **wschodnie stroje/obyczaje** oriental dress/customs. 3. *rel.* (*o podziale świata chrześcijańskiego*) Eastern; **Kościół/obrządek wschodni** the Eastern Church/rite.

wschodnioeuropejski *a.* East European.

wschodnio-południowo-wschodni *a.* *geogr., żegl.* east-southeast, east-southeastern, ESE.

wschodnio-południowo-wschód *mi* -o- *geogr., żegl.* the east-southeast.

wschodnio-południowo-zachodni *a.* *geogr., żegl.* west-southwest, west-southwestern, WSW.

wschodnio-południowo-zachód *mi* -o- *geogr., żegl.* the west-southwest.

wschodzący *a.* rising; **wschodząca gwiazda** *przen.* rising star.

wschodzić *ipf.* 1. (= *ukazywać się nad horyzontem*) (*o ciałach niebieskich*) rise, come up. 2. (= *kiełkować*) sprout, come up.

wschód *mi* -o- 1. (= *wzejście ciała niebieskiego*) rise; **wschód słońca** sunrise; **wschód księżyca** moonrise. 2. (*strona świata*) the east, the East; **na wschodzie** in the east; **ku wschodowi** eastward; *Br.* eastwards; **wiatr ze wschodu** wind from the east; **jechać na wschód** go east; **południowy/północny wschód** the southeast/northeast. 3. (*kraje Azji*) the East, the Orient.

wsi *itd. f. zob.* **wieś.**

wsiać *pf.* **wsieję wsiejesz wsiali** *l.* **wsieli** *zob.* **wsiewać.**

wsiadać *ipf.* 1. get (*do czegoś* into *l.* on sth) (*na pokład czegoś* aboard sth); (*o jeźdźcu, rowerzyście, motocykliście*) mount (*na coś* sth); get in; **wsiadł do samochodu** he got into the car; **wsiadaj!** get in!; **wsiadać do autobusu/pociągu** get on a bus/train; **wsiadać do samolotu/na statek** board an airplane/ship; get aboard an airplane/ship; embark (on an airplane/ship). 2. *przen.* **wsiąść komuś na głowę** *l.* **na kark** get on sb's back; **wsiąść na kogoś** (= *besztać, krytykować*) start in on sb; get down on sb; **wsiąść na swojego ulubionego konika** get onto one's favorite hobby horse.

wsiąkać *ipf.*, **wsiąknąć** *pf.* -ij 1. (*o cieczy*) (= *przenikać w głąb*) soak, filter (*w coś* into sth); soak in, infiltrate. 2. *żart.* (= *znikać*) evaporate, dematerialize.

wsiąść *pf.* **wsiądę wsiądziesz wsiadł wsiedli** *zob.* **wsiadać.**

wsierdzie *n. Gen.pl.* -i *anat.* endocardium.

wsierdziowy *a. anat.* endocardial.

wsiewać *ipf. roln.* sow (*sth*) as a companion crop.

wsiewka *f. Gen.pl.* -ek *roln.* companion crop.

wsiowy *a. pog.* hick, hillbilly.

wskakiwać *ipf.* 1. jump, hop, leap (*do czegoś* into sth); jump in, hop in, leap in; **wskakiwać do wody** dive *l.* plunge into the water; dive in, plunge in; take a plunge (into the water); **wskakiwać do pociągu** jump on a train. 2. *pot.* (= *wpaść z wizytą*) drop (*dokąd* into sth); drop in (*do kogoś* on sb).

wskazać *pf.* -żę -żesz *zob.* **wskazywać.**

wskazanie *n.* 1. (= *zalecenie*) prescription, indication, recommendation; **według wskazań lekarza** as indicated by the doctor. 2. *techn., miern.* (= *wartość odczytana z przyrządu pomiarowego*) indication; **odczytanie wskazań** reading. 3. (= *wytypowanie*) nomination.

wskazany *a.* (= *zalecany*) indicated, recommended, advisable.

wskazówka *f. Gen.pl.* -ek 1. *techn.* pointer, indicator; (*zegara*) hand; (*kompasu, miernika*) needle; **wskazówka sekundowa/minutowa/godzinowa** second/minute/hour hand. 2. (= *zalecenie*) direction, instruction; **udzielić komuś wskazówek** instruct sb; **wskazówki sceniczne** *teatr* stage directions. 3. (*w śledztwie, rozumowaniu*) clue, lead; (= *podpowiedź*) hint.

wskazujący *a.* **palec wskazujący** *anat.* index finger; **zaimek wskazujący** *gram.* demonstrative *l.* deictic pronoun.

wskazywać *ipf.* 1. (= *pokazywać*) indicate, point (*sb l. sth*) out (*komuś* to sb); **wskazać komuś drzwi** *przen.* show sb the door. 2. (= *świadczyć*) suggest, indicate; **nic nie wskazuje na to, że...** there's nothing to suggest that... 3. (= *typować kandydata*) nominate.

wskaźnik *mi Gen.* -a 1. *techn., chem.* (*sygnalizator, odczynnik*) indicator; (= *miernik*) gage; *Br.* gauge; **wskaźnik prętowy** (*np. poziomu oleju*) dipstick; **wskaźnik fluorescencyjny** *chem.* fluorescent indicator. 2. *stat.* index, rate (*czegoś* of sth); **wskaźnik giełdowy** *ekon.* stock exchange index.

wskoczyć *pf. zob.* **wskakiwać.**

wskórać *ipf. pot.* (= *osiągnąć*) achieve; **nic nie wskórać** cut no ice (*u kogoś* with sb); **niewiele zdołałem/nic nie zdołałem wskórać** there was little/nothing I could do (*w sprawie czegoś* about sth).

wskroś *adv. i prep.* + *Gen. lit.* across, through; **na wskroś** through (and through), thoroughly; **przejrzeć kogoś na wskroś** see through sb; **na wskroś uczciwy** honest to the backbone.

wskrzesić *pf.* -szę -sisz, **wskrzeszać** *ipf.* 1. (= *przywracać do życia*) raise (*sb*) from the dead, resurrect. **2.** *przen.* (= *wprowadzać na nowo*) revive, resuscitate.

wskutek *prep.* + *Gen.* because of (*sth*); as a result of (*sth*); owing to (*sth*); through; **wskutek tego** as a result; consequently.

wsławiać *ipf.* make (*sb l. sth*) famous. ~ **się** *ipf.* become famous (*czymś* for sth).

wsławić (się) *pf. zob.* **wsławiać (się)**.

wsłuchać się *pf.*, **wsłuchiwać się** *ipf.* listen attentively (*w coś* to sth).

wsobny *a.* **1.** **chów wsobny** *hodowla* inbreeding. **2.** **kojarzenie wsobne** *biol.* backcrossing.

wspak *adv.* backward; *Br.* backwards; **czytać coś wspak** *l.* **na wspak** read sth backward.

wspaniale *adv.* **1.** (= *doskonale*) gorgeously, wonderfully, excellently, brilliantly; **wyglądać/brzmieć wspaniale** look/sound gorgeous; **wspaniale!** great!, superb!, excellent!, wonderful!, marvelous! **2.** (= *okazale*) splendidly, magnificently, gorgeously.

wspaniałomyślność *f.* magnanimity, generosity.

wspaniałomyślny *a.* magnanimous, generous, great-hearted.

wspaniałość *f.* **1.** (= *doskonałość*) greatness, excellence. **2.** (= *okazałość, wystawność*) splendor, magnificence, gorgeousness, grandeur; **w całej swojej wspaniałości** in all its glory. **3.** (= *rzecz wyjątkowa, rarytas*) **podano same wspaniałości** gorgeous meals were served.

wspaniały *a.* **1.** (= *świetny, doskonały*) great, excellent, gorgeous, superb, wonderful, marvelous, brilliant; **wspaniała pogoda** gorgeous weather; **masz przed sobą wspaniałą przyszłość** you have a great future ahead of you; **wspaniałe wyniki** brilliant results. **2.** (= *okazały, wystawny*) grand, gorgeous, splendid, magnificent.

wsparcie *n.* support, backing; **otrzymać wsparcie** receive support (*od kogoś / skądś* from sb/sth).

wsparł *itd. ipf. zob.* **wesprzeć**.

wspiąć się *pf.* **wespnę wespniesz, wespnij** *zob.* **wspinać się**.

wspierać *ipf.* **1.** (= *podpierać*) back (*sth*) up, buttress (*sth*) (up), support (*sth*) (*czymś* with sth). **2.** (= *opierać*) prop (*sth*) (up), lean (*sth*) (*na czymś* on sth) (*o coś* against sth). **3.** (= *wzmacniać, np. argumenty*) support, bolster (up), reinforce. **4.** (= *wspomagać*) support (*sb l. sth*) (*czymś* with sth) (*za pomocą czegoś* by means of sth). ~ **się** *ipf.* **1.** (= *opierać się*) lean, support o.s., prop o.s. up (*na czymś* on sth) (*o coś* against sth); **wspierać się ręką/dłonią/głową o coś** rest one's arm/hand/head on sth. **2.** (= *podtrzymywać się wzajemnie*) lean against each other. **3.** (= *pomagać sobie wzajemnie*) provide mutual support.

wspinacz *mp* (rock-)climber.

wspinaczka *f. Gen.pl.* -**ek** **1.** *sport* (*czynność*) climbing; **uprawiać wspinaczkę** climb; **wybrać się na wspinaczkę** go climbing. **2.** (*osoba*) *zob.* **wspinacz**.

wspinać się *ipf.* **1.** (= *wdrapywać się, wchodzić*) climb (*sth*); climb up, ascend; (= *gramolić*

się) clamber, scramble (*na coś / po czymś* up/over sth). **2.** (= *unosić się na kończynach*) **wspiąć się na palcach** *l.* **na palce** stand on one's toes; **wspiąć się na tylnych łapach** rear (up).

wspomagać *ipf.* aid, back (*sb l. sth*) up, help (*sb l. sth*) (*czymś* with sth) (*za pomocą czegoś* by means of sth); **nauczanie wspomagane komputerowo** *szkoln.* computer-aided instruction, CAI; **projektowanie wspomagane komputerowo** *komp.* computer-aided design, CAD. ~ **się** *ipf.* provide mutual aid.

wspomaganie *n. mot.* **automatyczne wspomaganie kierownicy** power(-assisted) steering; **hamulce ze wspomaganiem** servo brakes, power brakes.

wspominać *ipf.* **1.** (= *przypominać sobie*) recall, recollect, bring (*sth*) back (to mind); **wspominać coś mile** have fond recollections *l.* memories of sth; **wspomnisz moje słowa** mark my words. **2.** (= *wzmiankować*) mention, refer to (*sb l. sth*); **nikomu o tym nie wspominałem** I didn't mention it to anyone; **nie wspominając (o)...** let alone...; not to mention...; never mind...; **wspominałeś, że go znasz** you mentioned that you knew him.

wspominki *pl. Gen.* -**ów** evening of recollections *l.* remembrances.

wspominkowy *a.* = **wspomnieniowy**.

wspomniany *a.* (= *wyżej wymieniony*) abovementioned, aforesaid; *prawn.* said, this same, that same.

wspomnieć *ipf.* -**nę** -**nisz**, -**nij** *zob.* **wspominać**.

wspomnienie *n.* **1.** (= *pamięć o tym, co było*) memory, recollection, remembrance, reminiscence; **wspomnienia z dzieciństwa** childhood memories; **wspomnienia młodości/czasów wojny** reminiscences of one's youth/of the war; **żyć wspomnieniami** live on memories (*czegoś* of sth). **2.** (= *tekst wspomnieniowy*) remembrance. **3.** (= *pamiątka*) memory, souvenir, remembrance. **4.** (= *napomknienie*) mention, reference; **ożywił się na samo wspomnienie o niej** he livened up at the very mention of her.

wspomnieniowy *a.* remembrance; **artykuł wspomnieniowy** remembrance article.

wspomożenie *n. arch.* help.

wspomóc *pf.* -**mogę** -**możesz**, -**móż**, -**mógł** -**mogła** -**mogli** *zob.* **wspomagać**.

wspornik *mi Gen.* -**a** **1.** support, prop; *bud.* cantilever; (= *przypora*) buttress. **2.** *techn.* bearer, bracket.

wspólnictwo *n.* **1.** (*w interesach*) partnership. **2.** (*w przestępstwie*) complicity.

wspólniczka *f. Gen.pl.* -**ek** *zob.* **wspólnik**.

wspólnie *adv.* together, collectively; (= *współpracując*) in collaboration.

wspólnik *mp* **1.** (*w przedsięwzięciu*) partner, copartner, associate; **wspólnik w interesach** business partner; **cichy wspólnik** secret partner; **starszy/młodszy wspólnik** senior/junior partner. **2.** (*przestępca*) accomplice, partner in crime.

wspólnota *f.* (= *wspólne posiadanie, więź społeczna l. polityczna*) community; **wspólnota interesów/celów** community of interests/purposes;

wspólnota społeczna social community; **wspólnota językowa** *polit.* speech community; **wspólnota narodów** *polit.* commonwealth (of nations); **wspólnota religijna** *rel.* communion; **duch** *l.* **poczucie wspólnoty** community spirit.

wspólny *a.* common, shared; (*w kilku utartych wyrażeniach*) mutual; **wspólne przekonanie** common *l.* shared belief; **wspólny pokój** shared room; **wspólny przodek/rodowód** common ancestor/descent; **wspólny przyjaciel** mutual friend; **wspólne zainteresowania** mutual interests; **wspólnymi siłami** by united effort; **najmniejszy wspólny mianownik** *mat.* the least common denominator; **największy wspólny podzielnik** *mat.* the greatest common divisor; **znajdować z kimś wspólny język** find common ground with sb; **mieć z kimś/czymś wiele wspólnego** have much *l.* a lot to do with sb/sth; **nie mieć z kimś/czymś nic wspólnego** have nothing to do with sb/sth; **co to ma wspólnego ze mną?** what does it have to do with me?; what's that to do with me?

współautor *mp*, **współautorka** *f. Gen.pl.* **-ek** coauthor.

współautorstwo *n.* coauthorship.

współbiesiadnik *mp* fellow reveler, table companion.

współbieżny *a. komp.* concurrent.

współbrzmiący *a. form.* consonant (*z czymś* with sth); harmonious.

współbrzmieć *ipf.* **-ię -isz, -ij** harmonize, be consonant (*z czymś* with sth).

współbrzmienie *n. muz.* consonance.

współczesność *f.* **1.** (= *dzisiejsze czasy*) modern times, the present time *l.* day. **2.** *zbiorowo* = **współcześni**. **3.** (= *jednoczesność*) contemporaneity, contemporariness.

współczesny *a.* **1.** (= *dotyczący obecnych czasów*) modern, contemporary, present-day; (*o dzisiejszym naśladownictwie czegoś z przeszłości*) latter-day; **literatura współczesna** modern literature; **człowiek współczesny** modern man; **współczesny rycerz** latter-day knight. **2.** (= *dotyczący tych samych czasów*) contemporaneous, contemporary. **3.** *gram.* **imiesłów współczesny** present participle.

współcześni *pl.* **1.** (= *ludzie żyjący obecnie l. w danych czasach*) contemporaries. **2. Szekspir i jego współcześni** Shakespeare and his contemporaries.

współcześnie *adv.* **1.** nowadays, in our times. **2.** (= *jednocześnie z czymś w przeszłości*) contemporaneously, contemporarily (*z kimś/czymś* with sb/sth).

współczucie *n.* sympathy, compassion (*dla kogoś* for sb); *form. l. żart.* commiseration (*z powodu czegoś* on *l.* over sth); **budzić czyjeś współczucie** arouse *l.* evoke sb's sympathy; **odczuwać/okazywać współczucie** feel/show sympathy *l.* compassion; **wyrazy współczucia** (*dla kogoś w żałobie*) condolences, sympathies; **proszę przyjąć wyrazy najgłębszego współczucia** (*dla kogoś w żałobie*) please accept my deepest sympathies.

współczuć *ipf.* sympathize, commiserate (*ko-*

muś with sb, *z powodu czegoś* on *l.* over sth); **współczuć komuś w kłopotach** sympathize with sb in trouble; pity (*sb*); feel pity (*for sb*); be *l.* feel sorry (*for sb*); **szczerze ci współczuję** I'm really sorry for you.

współczująco *adv.* sympathetically, compassionately.

współczulny *a. anat.* sympathetic; **układ nerwowy współczulny** sympathetic nervous system.

współczynnik *mi Gen.* **-a** *mat.* coefficient, factor; *stat.* rate.

współdziałać *ipf.* **1.** (= *współpracować*) cooperate, collaborate (*przy czymś* in sth). **2.** (= *wspólnie oddziaływać l. funkcjonować*) interact, concur (*z czymś* with sth).

współdziałanie *n.* **1.** (= *współpraca*) cooperation, collaboration. **2.** (= *funkcjonowanie w jakimś układzie, systemie*) interaction, concurrence.

współdzierżawca *mp prawn.* cotenant.

współgospodarz *mp* co-host; **być współgospodarzem programu** co-host a program.

współgrać *ipf.* (*o kolorze, kształcie*) match (*z czymś* sth); (*o kolorze*) blend, tone in (*z czymś* with sth).

współistnieć *ipf.* coexist (*z kimś/czymś* with sb/sth).

współistnienie *n.* **1.** coexistence; **pokojowe współistnienie** peaceful coexistence. **2.** *rel.* concomitance.

współistotny *a.* + *Dat. teol.* coessential with (*sb l. sth*).

współliniowy *a. geom.* collinear.

współlokator *mp*, **współlokatorka** *f. Gen.pl.* **-ek** cotenant, housemate; (*dzielący z kimś pokój*) roommate.

współmałżonek *mp* **-nk-** *pl.* **-owie** partner in marriage; *form. l. żart.* spouse.

współmierny *a. t. mat.* commensurate (*do czegoś* to sth) (*z czymś* with sth).

współmieszkaniec *mp* **-ńc-** *pl.* **-y 1.** = **współlokator**. **2.** = **współziomek**.

współobywatel *mp* fellow citizen, fellow countryman, compatriot.

współodpowiedzialność *f.* shared *l.* joint responsibility.

współodpowiedzialny *a.* jointly responsible (*za coś* for sth).

współorganizator *mp*, **współorganizatorka** *f. Gen.pl.* **-ek** co-organizer.

współorganizować *ipf.* co-organize, jointly organize.

współosiowy *a. mat., fiz.* coaxial.

współoskarżony *mp*, **współoskarżona** *f. Gen.* **-ej** *prawn.* codefendant.

współpasażer *mp pl.* **-owie** fellow passenger.

współpłaszczyznowy *a. geom.* coplanar.

współpraca *f.* cooperation, collaboration; **chęć** *l.* **gotowość do współpracy** cooperativeness; **we współpracy z kimś** in cooperation *l.* collaboration with sb.

współpracować *ipf.* (= *pracować wspólnie*) cooperate, collaborate, work together; (*o urządze-*

niach) (= *funkcjonować razem*) function together.

współpracowniczka *f. Gen.pl.* **-ek, współpracownik** *mp* co-worker, collaborator.

współredagować *ipf.* co-edit, jointly edit.

współredaktor *mp*, **współredaktorka** *f. Gen.pl.* **-ek** co-editor.

współrządzić *ipf.* share political power (*z kimś* with sb).

współrzędna *f. Gen.* **-ej** *mat.* coordinate; **oś/układ współrzędnych** axis/system of coordinates; **siatka współrzędnych** *kartogr.* grid.

współrzędny *a.* coordinate, coordinating; **spójnik współrzędny** *gram.* coordinating conjunction; **zdania współrzędnie złożone** *gram.* coordinated clauses.

współspadkobierca *mp*, **współspadkobierczyni** *f. prawn.* co-heir, distributee.

współsprawca *mp*, **współsprawczyni** *f. prawn.* accomplice, associate in crime.

współśrodkowość *f. geom.* concentricity.

współśrodkowy *a. geom.* concentric.

współtowarzysz *mp*, **współtowarzyszka** *f. Gen.pl.* **-ek** companion, partner, fellow.

współtowarzyszyć *ipf.* accompany.

współtworzyć *ipf.* **-twórz** jointly create, co-author.

współtwórca *mp* co-author.

współuczestniczyć *ipf.* take part (together) (*w czymś* in sth).

współuczestnik *mp*, **współuczestniczka** *f. Gen.pl.* **-ek** partner (*czegoś* in sth).

współudział *mi* partnership; (*w przestępstwie*) complicity.

współużytkowanie *n.* shared use, joint exploitation (*czegoś* of sth); **współużytkowanie pojazdów** (*w celu ograniczenia ruchu w mieście*) ridesharing.

współwięzień *mp* **-źni-** *pl.* **-owie** *Gen.* **-ów**, **współwięźniarka** *f. Gen.pl.* **-ek** fellow inmate *l.* prisoner.

współwina *f.* shared guilt.

współwinowajca *mp* fellow culprit.

współwłasność *f.* joint ownership, part-ownership; *prawn.* coparcenary.

współwłaściciel *mp*, **współwłaścicielka** *f. Gen.pl.* **-ek** joint owner, part-owner, coproprietor.

współwykonawca *mp*, **współwykonawczyni** *f.* 1. *prawn.* coexecutor. 2. *muz., teatr* fellow performer.

współwystępować *ipf.* cooccur, occur together.

współwystępowanie *n.* cooccurrence.

współwyznawca *mp*, **współwyznawczyni** *f. rel.* fellow believer, coreligionist.

współzależność *f.* interdependence, interrelation, correlation.

współzależny *a.* interdependent, interrelated, correlated.

współzawodnictwo *n.* competition, emulation, rivalry.

współzawodniczka *f. Gen.pl.* **-ek** *sport zob.* **współzawodnik**.

współzawodniczyć *ipf.* compete (*z kimś* with sb, *w czymś* in sth) (*o coś* for sth); emulate (*z*

kimś sb, *w czymś* at sth); vie (*z kimś* with sb, *o coś* for sth).

współzawodnik *mp sport* competitor, rival.

współziomek *mp* **-mk-** compatriot, fellow countryman.

współżycie *n.* 1. (= *wspólne życie społeczne*) coexistence, social intercourse. 2. (= *utrzymywanie stosunków płciowych*) intercourse. 3. *biol.* symbiosis.

współżyć *ipf.* **-żyję -żyjesz, -żyj** 1. (= *żyć w społeczeństwie*) coexist (*z kimś* with sb). 2. (= *utrzymywać stosunki płciowe*) have intercourse (*z kimś* with sb). 3. *biol.* live symbiotically; have a symbiotic relationship (*z czymś* with sth).

wstać *pf.* **wstanę wstaniesz, wstawać** *ipf.* **-aję -ajesz, -awaj** 1. (= *powstać*) rise, stand up; **wstać od stołu** rise from the table; **proszę wstać, sąd idzie!** all rise, the court is in session! 2. (*o słońcu*) (= *wzejść*) rise, come up. 3. (*o dniu*) (= *zacząć się*) begin, break; **wstaje nowy dzień** a new day begins. 4. (= *wychodzić z łóżka*) get up, get out of bed; **wstawaj!** get up!; **późno wstałem** I got up late; **wstać lewą nogą** *przen.* get up on the wrong side of the bed; **wstać razem z kurami** rise with the light; keep early hours; **kto rano wstaje, temu Pan Bóg daje** the early bird catches the worm; early to bed and early to rise makes a man healthy, wealthy and wise. 5. (= *móc się poruszać po wypadku l. chorobie*) leave one's bed, get about.

wstawiać *ipf.* 1. (= *umieszczać wewnątrz*) put, insert (*sth*) (*w coś l. do czegoś* in *l.* into sth) (*między coś* between sth); put (*sth*) in. 2. (= *wprawiać, instalować*) fit, insert, install, put (*sth*) in; **wstawiać sztuczne zęby** insert dentures; **wstawić wannę** put in a bath; **wstawić nową szybę w miejsce stłuczonej** replace a broken window pane. 3. *druk.* (= *dopisywać, dodawać do tekstu*) add, insert, interpolate; (= *umieszczać jako wstawkę*) inset, inlay; *komp.* paste (*sth*) in. 4. (= *rozpoczynać gotowanie*) put (*sth*) on; **wstawić wodę** put the kettle on. **~ się** *ipf.* 1. **wstawiać się za kimś** (= *brać w obronę*) put in *l.* say a good word for sb; intercede for sb *l.* on behalf of sb; plead sb's cause. 2. *pot.* (= *upijać się*) get tight.

wstawić (się) *pf. zob.* **wstawiać (się)**.

wstawiennictwo *n.* intercession.

wstawiony *a.* **-eni** *pot.* (= *pijany*) tight, soused, loaded.

wstawka *f. Gen.pl.* **-ek** 1. *druk.* (= *wstawiony tekst*) interpolation. 2. (*krawiectwo*) insertion, panel.

wstąpić *pf. zob.* **wstępować**.

wstążeczka *f. Gen.pl.* **-ek** ribbon.

wstążka *f. Gen.pl.* **-ek** 1. ribbon; (*do włosów*) fillet; (*do obszywania*) band; (*do zawiązywania czegoś*) tie. 2. *pl. kulin.* (*rodzaj makaronu*) tagliatelle.

wstecz *adv.* back, backward; *Br.* backwards; *żegl.* astern; **cała wstecz!** *żegl.* full speed astern!; **robić krok wstecz** *przen.* take a backward *l.* retrograde step; **patrzeć wstecz na coś** *przen.* (= *wspominać*) look back on sth; **patrząc wstecz** in retrospect; **prawo działające wstecz** *prawn.* retroactive law.

wstecznictwo *n. polit., uj.* reactionism.

wsteczniczka *f. Gen.pl.* **-ek, wstecznik** *mp polit., uj.* reactionary.

wsteczny *a.* **1.** *polit.* reactionary, obscurantist. **2.** (= *dotyczący cofania się*) retrograde, backward, regressive. **3.** *mot.* **bieg wsteczny** reverse gear; **lusterko wsteczne** rear-view mirror. **4.** (*w terminach naukowych*) **amnezja wsteczna** *jęz.* retrograde amnesia; **derywacja wsteczna** *jęz.* back-derivation; **kojarzenie wsteczne** *biol.* back-crossing; **ruch wsteczny** *astron.* retrograde motion; **upodobnienie wsteczne** *fon.* regressive assimilation. **5. moc wsteczna** *prawn.* retroactivity; **z mocą wsteczną (od...)** retroactive (to...).

wstęga *f.* **1.** ribbon, band; (*odznaczenia*) ribbon, riband; **przeciąć wstęgę** cut the ribbon; **uroczystość przecięcia wstęgi** ribbon-cutting ceremony. **2.** *meteor.* (= *pasmo zorzy polarnej*) streamer. **3.** *her.* (*z dewizą herbową*) scroll.

wstęgor *mi icht.* ribbonfish (*Trachypterus*); **wstęgor królewski** oarfish, king of the herrings (*Regalecus glesne*).

wstęp *mi* **1.** (= *pozwolenie wejścia*) entrance, admission; **bilet wstępu** entrance ticket; **opłata za wstęp** entrance fee, admission (fee); **wstęp wolny w poniedziałki** admission free Monday; **odmówiono im wstępu** they were refused entrance; **wstęp wzbroniony** no entry; no trespassing. **2.** (= *początek, wprowadzenie, t. tekst wstępny*) introduction (*do czegoś* to sth); **wstęp do teorii kwantów** introduction to quantum theory; **bez zbytecznych wstępów** without further ado; **na wstępie...** as an introduction..., as a preamble...; **po tym wstępie...** after this introduction..., after this overture...

wstępniak *mi Gen.* **-a** *pot., dzienn.* editorial.

wstępnie *adv.* **1.** (= *prowizorycznie*) provisionally. **2.** *techn.* (*w połączeniach z czasownikami i imiesłowami biernymi*) pre-; **wstępnie kształtować** preform; **wstępnie gotowany** precooked; **wstępnie podgrzewać** preheat; **wstępnie przetworzony** preprocessed.

wstępny *a.* **1.** (= *wprowadzający*) introductory, prefatory. **2.** (= *prowizoryczny*) provisional, preliminary, interim. **3.** *techn.* (= *przygotowawczy*) pre-; **badanie wstępne** pretest; **wstępne przetworzenie** preprocessing. **4.** *dzienn.* editorial.

wstępować *ipf.* **1.** (= *zachodzić*) call (in *l.* round), drop in (*do kogoś* on sb); **wstąpić na kieliszeczek** drop in for a quick one. **2.** (= *wchodzić, wkraczać*) step in *l.* into (*a place*); enter; go in; **diabeł w niego wstąpił** *przen.* something has possessed him. **3.** *lit.* (= *wspinać się*) ascend, climb; **wstępować po schodach** climb *l.* ascend the stair. **4.** *przen.* (= *rozpoczynać*) **wstępować w czyjeś ślady** follow in sb's footsteps; **wstąpić na nową drogę życia** embark on a new career; **wstąpić na tron** ascend the throne; **wstępować w szranki** enter the lists (*przeciw komuś / czemuś* against sb/sth). **5.** (= *przyłączać się do czegoś*) **wstąpić do wojska/marynarki/policji** join the

army/navy/police; **wstąpić do klubu** join a club; **wstąpić na uniwersytet** go to university.

wstężnica *f.* **1.** *bot.* (*zielenica*) mermaid's tresses (*Ulothrix*). **2.** *pl. zool.* (*t.* **wstężniaki**) (*typ*) ribbon worms (*Nemertini*).

wstręt *mi* **1.** (= *obrzydzenie*) disgust, repugnance, repulsion, revulsion, aversion; **przepełniony wstrętem** disgusted; **przemóc obrzydzenie** overcome one's repugnance. **2. spojrzała na mnie ze wstrętem** she looked at me with disgust; **mieć wstręt do czegoś** have a horror of sth. **3.** *przest.* (= *trudność*) **robić komuś wstręty** try to discourage sb.

wstrętny *a.* disgusting, repugnant, repulsive, revolting, loathsome; (*o smaku, zapachu*) foul, vile.

wstrząs *mi* **1.** (= *fizyczne wstrząśnięcie*) shock, impact; (*jadącego pojazdu*) jolt, bump, jerk; (*sejsmiczny*) shock, quake, tremor. **2.** (*emocjonalny*) shock, dismay, upheaval; **doznać wstrząsu** get a shock; **przeżyła wstrząs po śmierci męża** her husband death was a shock to her. **3.** *pat.* shock; **wstrząs elektryczny** electric shock; **wstrząs mózgu** concussion.

wstrząsać *ipf.* + *Ins* **1.** (= *potrząsać*) shake (*sth*) (up); **przed użyciem wstrząsnąć** shake before use. **2.** *przen.* (= *powodować gwałtowne skutki*) shake, convulse; **krajem wstrząsała wojna domowa** the country was convulsed by a civil war; **wstrząsany śmiechem** convulsed with laughter. **3.** (= *poruszać emocjonalnie*) shake, shock, distress, come as a shock to (*sb*). **~ się** *ipf.* shudder (*na widok kogoś / czegoś* at the sight of sb/sth) (*na myśl o kimś / czymś* at the thought of sb/sth).

wstrząsający *a.* shocking, distressing, harrowing.

wstrząsnąć (się) *pf.* **-snę -śniesz, -śnij** *zob.* **wstrząsać (się).**

wstrząsowy *a. med.* shock; **terapia wstrząsowa** shock therapy.

wstrząśnienie *n. pat.* **wstrząśnienie mózgu** concussion; **doznać wstrząśnienia** be concussed.

wstrząśnięty *a.* shocked, shaken, dismayed (*czymś* at sth).

wstrzelać (się), wstrzelić (się) *pf. zob.* **wstrzeliwać (się).**

wstrzeliwać *ipf.* **-wuję -wujesz** *bud.* (= *wbijać za pomocą specjalnego pistoletu*) drive in. **~ się** *ipf. wojsk.* straddle the target.

wstrzemięźliwość *f.* abstinence (*od czegoś* from sth); restraint; (*w jedzeniu, piciu*) abstemiousness; (*płciowa*) continence; **zachowywać wstrzemięźliwość od czegoś** abstain from sth.

wstrzemięźliwy *a.* abstinent, abstemious; (*w życiu płciowym*) continent.

wstrzykiwać *ipf.,* **wstrzyknąć** *pf.* **-ij** inject; **wstrzyknąć coś komuś** inject sth into sb; inject sb with sth.

wstrzymać (się) *pf. zob.* **wstrzymywać (się).**

wstrzymujący się *a.* (*o oddanym głosie*) abstaining.

wstrzymywać *ipf.* **1.** (= *powstrzymywać*) hold

(*sb l. sth*) back, keep (*sb l. sth*) back, restrain; **wstrzymywać oddech** hold one's breath. **2.** (= *przerywać*) stop, cease, discontinue; **wstrzymywać pomoc medyczną** cease medical aid; **wstrzymywać ogień** *wojsk.* cease fire. **3.** (= *opóźniać*) delay, suspend; *prawn.* (= *odraczać*) (*decyzję l. wykonanie wyroku*) stay, arrest. ~ **się** *ipf.* hold back, wait; **wstrzymać się od głosu** abstain (from voting *l.* from the vote); **wstrzymywać się z wydaniem sądu** reserve judgment.

wstyd *mi* shame, disgrace; **najeść się wstydu** be put to shame; **nie masz wstydu ani za grosz** you have no sense of shame; **ale wstyd!** what a disgrace!; **ze wstydem** with shame, shamefully; **bez wstydu** without shame, shamelessly; **jest mi wstyd (za siebie)** I'm ashamed (of myself); **nie wstyd ci?** aren't you ashamed?; **przynosić komuś/czemuś wstyd** be a disgrace to sb/sth; bring shame on sb/sth.

wstydliwość *f.* shyness, bashfulness, modesty.
wstydliwy *a.* **1.** (= *skrępowany*) bashful, shy, coy; (*w sposób afektowany*) demure. **2.** (= *żenujący, przynoszący wstyd*) shameful, embarrassing.

wstydzić się *ipf.* be ashamed; **wstydź się!** shame on you!

wsunąć *pf.*, **wsuwać** *ipf.* **1.** (= *zakładać*) put (*sth*) on, slip (*sth*) on. **2.** (= *wtykać*) **wsunąć komuś monetę do ręki** slip a coin in sb's hand; **wsunąć głowę przez okno** stuck one's head in through the window. **3.** (= *wkładać delikatnie*) slide, lower, ease (*sth*) (*do czegoś* into sth). **4.** *pot.* (= *zjeść*) tuck (*sth*) in *l.* away. ~ **się** *pf.*, **wsuwać się** *ipf.* **1.** (= *zakraść się*) steal in *l.* inside. **2.** (= *gładko wejść*) slide in.

wsuwka *f. Gen.pl.* **-ek** (*spinka*) hairpin, hairgrip.

wsypa *f.* **1.** *pot.* (= *wpadka*) give-away, gaffe, bad break. **2.** (*na pierze*) pillow-case, pillowslip.

wsypać (się) *pf.* **-pię -piesz** *zob.* **wsypywać (się)**.

wsypowy *a. techn.* of the chute; (*o urządzeniu*) chute.

wsypywać *ipf.* **1.** (= *sypiąc, wypełniać*) pour. **2.** *pot.* (= *dekonspirować*) make a bad break, give sb away, blow the whistle on sb. ~ **się** *ipf.* **1.** (= *dostawać się gdzieś*) get (into sth). **2.** *pot.* (= *dekonspirować się*) give o.s. away, make a bad break. **3.** *pot.* (= *dekonspirować jeden drugiego*) peach against one another.

wsysać *ipf.* suck in. ~ **się** *ipf.* **1.** (= *być wsysanym*) be sucked into. **2.** (= *przywierać*) suck on.

wszak *particle lit.* indeed, why.

wszakże *particle lit.* **1.** (= *jednak*) nevertheless, however; **dom duży, wszakże niewygodny** big house however uncomfortable. **2.** (= *przecież*) but; **wszakże to mój obowiązek** why, it's my duty.

wszarz *mp pl.* **-rze** *pot.* bum, louse, hobo.
wszawica *f. med.* pediculosis.
wszcząć (się) *pf. zob.* **wszczynać (się)**.
wszczepiać *ipf.* **1.** *med.* (= *zaszczepiać*) inoculate, vaccinate. **2.** *med.* (= *przeszczepiać*) graft,

implant. **3.** (= *wpajać coś komuś*) inculcate. **4.** *ogr.* inarch, graft. ~ **się** *ipf.* be grafted.

wszczepić (się) *pf. zob.* **wszczepiać (się)**.
wszczęcie *n.* begin, start, commence.
wszczynać *ipf.* begin, start, commence. ~ **się** *ipf.* arise, start, begin.

wszechmocny, wszechmogący *a. rel.* omnipotent, almighty; (*o Bogu*) the Almighty, the Omnipotent.

wszechnica *f.* university.
wszechobecny *a.* ubiquitous, omnipresent; (*o problemie*) omnipresent.
wszechogarniający *a. lit.* all-embracing, pervasive, all-pervasive; (*o strachu, zjawisku*) all-embracing, all-pervasive.
wszechpotężny *a. lit.* all-powerful, omnipotent, almighty; (*o władcy*) omnipotent, almighty; (*o sile*) all-powerful.
wszechstronnie *adv.* universally, comprehensively, extensively, versatilely; **wszechstronnie wykształcony** broadly educated, extensively educated.
wszechstronność *f.* versatility.
wszechstronny *a.* all-rounder, extensive, comprehensive, versatile; (*o wykształceniu*) broad; (*o artyście*) all-round; (*o badaniach*) extensive.
wszechświat *mi Gen.* **-a** universe, cosmos.
wszechwaga *f. boks* all-weight; **mistrz wszechwag** champion in all-weight classes.
wszechwiedza *f.* omniscience.
wszechwiedzący *a.* omniscient.
wszechwładny *a.* all-powerful; (*o monarsze*) sovereign.
wszechzwiązek *mi* **-zk-** all-union; **wszechzwiązek zjawisk** *fil.* interconnectedness of all phenomena.
wszedł *itd. pf. zob.* **wejść**.
wszego *a. przest.* all, every; **ze wszech stron** from all sides; **po wsze czasy** for all times; **ze wszech miar** in every respect, by all means; **wszem i wobec** all concerned.
wszelki *a.* **1.** (= *każdy*) all, every; (*o środkach, sposobach*) every possible means, all sorts of means; **wszelkiego rodzaju** of any kind; **wszelkie prawa zastrzeżone** *prawn.* all rights reserved; **wszelki duch Pana Boga chwali** God bless my soul. **2.** (= *jakikolwiek*) any; **za wszelką cenę** at any cost, at all cost; **na wszelki wypadek** just in case.
wszerz *adv.* broadways, broadwise, in breadth; **wzdłuż i wszerz** to and from, the length and breadth.
wszeteczeństwo *n. przest.* harlotry.
wszeteczny *a. przest.* meretricious, lecherous; (*o słowach, czynach*) lecherous.
wszędobylski *a.* ubiquitous; (*o dziennikarzu*) busybody, meddlesome; (*o dziecku*) ubiquitous.
wszędzie *adv.* everywhere, on all sides, far and near, far and wide, all over; **wszędzie cię pełno** I see you here, there and everywhere; **wszędzie dobrze, w domu najlepiej** there's no place like home; east or west, home is best.
wszyć *pf.* **wszyję wszyjesz, wszyj** *zob.* **wszywać**.

wszyscy *a. zob.* **wszystek.** – *pl.* **-stki-** *Gen.pl.* **-ich** all, everybody, everyone, all men; **jeden za wszystkich, wszyscy za jednego** one for all, all for one.

wszystek *a.* **-stki-** all, every; **ze wszystkich sił** with all one's might; **za wszystkie czasy** as never before; **po wszystkie czasy** for all times.

wszystkie *a. zob.* **wszystek.**

wszystko *a. zob.* **wszystek.** – *n.* **-tki-** *Gen.* **-ego** all, everything, anything, all this, things; **ktoś do wszystkiego** jack-of-all-trades; **zdolny do wszystkiego** he will do anything, he is apt to do anything; **już po wszystkim** it is all over now, it's too late; **przede wszystkim** first of all, in the first place; **wszystko gra** everything is in order; **mimo wszystko** after all; **nade wszystko** above all, most of all; **nie ze wszystkim** not altogether, not completely; **i to już wszystko** that's about all; **nie wszystko złoto, co się świeci** not all that glitters is gold.

wszystkoizm *mi iron.* know-all.

wszystkowiedzący *a.* omniscient; (*o rodzicach*) knowing.

wszystkożerny *a. zool.* omnivorous.

wszywać *ipf.* **-am -asz** sew in.

wścibiać *ipf.,* **wścibić** *pf. pot.* poke; **wścibiać nos w nie swoje sprawy** poke one's nose into other people's affairs.

wścibski *a.* meddlesome, inquisitive, snooping; **wścibska sąsiadka/teściowa** meddler neighbor/mother-in-law.

wściec się *pf.* **wścieknę wściekniesz, wścieknij, wściekł, wściekać się** *ipf.* **1.** (= *rozzłościć się*) rage, go mad; **wściec się ze złości** fly into a rage. **2.** *tylko pf.* (= *zachorować na wściekliznę*) become rabid.

wściekle *adv.* **1.** (= *zajadle*) madly, furiously, in a fit of rage; **wściekle krzyczeć** scream bloody murder; **wściekle szczekać** bark madly *l.* wildly *l.* savagely. **2.** *pot.* (= *mocno*) like mad; **jest wściekle gorąco** it is unbearably hot; **wściekle boli mnie głowa** I have a splitting *l.* pounding headache.

wścieklizna *f. pat., wet.* rabies.

wściekłość *f.* rage, fury.

wściekły *a.* **1.** (= *chory na wściekliznę*) rabid; (*o psie, lisie, wiewiórce*) mad. **2.** (= *gwałtowny*) mad (*na kogoś* at sb); (*o awanturze*) furious; (*o zazdrości*) furious, unrestrained. **3.** *pot.* (= *nie do zniesienia*) awful, terrible, damned, frightful; (*o bólu, upale, hałasie*) awful.

wślizgiwać się *ipf.,* **wślizgnąć się** *pf.* **-ij** slip in, dodge in, creep in.

wśród *prep.* + *Gen.* **1.** (= *w otoczeniu*) amidst, among, in the midst of; **wśród drzew** among trees. **2.** (= *w trakcie*) in the middle of, in the course of, during, amidst; **szukać schronienia wśród zamieci** look for a shelter amidst a blizzard, look for a shelter during a blizzard.

wtaczać *ipf.* roll in. ~ **się** *ipf.* **1.** (= *tocząc się, dostawać się*) roll in, run in. **2.** *pot.* (= *wchodzić gdzieś z trudem*) stagger in, totter in.

wtajemniczać *ipf.* initiate, acquaint; **wtajemniczać kogoś w coś** acquaint sb with sth, let sb

into sth, initiate sb into the secret of sth. ~ **się** *ipf.* become initiated, acquaint o.s.

wtajemniczenie *n.* initiation, mystagogicy; **dostąpić wtajemniczenia** attain an initiation.

wtajemniczony *mp* initiate, insider; **krąg wtajemniczonych** ring of initiates, circle of initiates.

wtajemniczyć (się) *pf. zob.* **wtajemniczać (się).**

wtapiać *ipf.* **1.** (= *harmonizować z otoczeniem*) interblend, melt, mingle, fuse. **2.** (= *topiąc, osadzać*) set. ~ **się** *ipf.* **1.** (= *być zharmonizowanym z otoczeniem*) interblend, melt, mingle. **2.** (= *być wtopionym*) be melted, be fused.

wtarabaniać się *ipf.,* **wtarabanić się** *pf.* **1.** (= *wspinać się z wysiłkiem*) get, clamber, climb with effort. **2.** *pot.* (= *wchodzić gdzieś bez zaproszenia*) barge in.

wtargnąć *pf.* **-ij** break; (*do czegoś*) break into sth; (*w jakieś terytorium*) make an irruption; (*do kraju*) invade.

wtargnięcie *n.* inroad, invasion.

wtarł *itd. pf. zob.* **wetrzeć.**

wtaszczać *ipf.,* **wtaszczyć** *pf.* lug in *l.* up.

wtedy *adv.* then, at that time; **wtedy mnie nie było w domu** I was not at home at that time; **zadzwonię do ciebie i wtedy wyjaśnię ci, o co chodzi** I'll call you and then I will explain; **zaczekaj jeszcze tydzień, a wtedy będzie po wszystkim** wait just another week, and then everything will be over.

wtem *adv.* suddenly.

wtłaczać *ipf.,* **wtłoczyć** *pf.* (= *z trudem wciskać*) **1.** force, pack, cram, ram. **2.** (= *wlewać coś pod ciśnieniem*) pour sth in under pressure.

wtoczyć (się) *pf. zob.* **wtaczać (się).**

wtopić (się) *pf. zob.* **wtapiać (się).**

wtopiony *a.* inwrought, melted, fused, blended in; **dom wtopiony w krajobraz** house blended in with the scenery.

wtorek *mi* **-rk-** Tuesday.

wtorkowy *a.* Tuesday's; (*o wykładzie, gościu*) Tuesday.

wtór *mi* accompaniment; **do wtóru** to the accompaniment.

wtórnie *adv.* secondarily, derivatively; (*przetworzony*) recycled.

wtórny *a.* **1.** (= *pochodny*) secondary, derivative, ectypal; (*o zjawisku, znaczeniu*) secondary; (*o analfabetyzmie*) functional; **surowce wtórne** recyclables. **2.** (= *uboczny*) secondary, incidental, side; **wtórne cechy płciowe** *biol.* secondary sexual features.

wtórować *ipf.* (= *śpiewać drugim głosem*) take second part; (= *akompaniować*) accompany; (= *towarzyszyć czemuś*) chime together.

wtóry *a.* second; **po wtóre** secondly.

wtranżalać *ipf. pot.* (= *jeść*) guzzle, dispatch. ~ **się** *ipf.* (= *wpychać się*) barge in.

wtranżolić (się) *pf. zob.* **wtranżalać (się).**

wtrącać *ipf.* **1.** (= *dodawać coś*) add; **wtrącić swoje trzy grosze** put in one's oar. **2.** (= *więzić*) thrust, clap, cast; **wtrącić kogoś do więzienia** cast sb into prison, fling sb in prison. ~ **się** *ipf.,* **wtrącić się** *pf.* **1.** (= *ingerować*) interfere, intrude, meddle, poke one's nose. **2.** (= *dopowia-dać*) break in, put in, chip in, interject.

wtrącenie *n*. (= *dopowiedzenie*) interjection.

wtrącić (się) *pf. zob*. **wtrącać (się)**.

wtrącony *a*. **1.** (*uwaga*) interpolated. **2.** *jęz*. parenthetical; **zdanie wtrącone** *gram*. parenthetical clause.

wtręt *mi* interpolation, intercalation; *med*. inclusion-body.

wtryniać *ipf*. **1.** *pot*. (= *kłaść byle gdzie*) mislay, misplace. **2.** *pot*. (= *sprzedawać coś na siłę*) palm sth off on sb. ~ **się** *ipf*. (= *wchodzić gdzieś bez zaproszenia*) slip in, steal in.

wtrynić (się) *pf. zob*. **wtryniać (się)**.

wtrysk *mi mot*. injection, gush.

wtryskarka *f. Gen.pl*. **-ek** *techn*. injection moulding machine.

wtryskiwacz *mi Gen*. **-a** *mot*. atomizing cone, injector. – *mp* (*robotnik*) injector.

wtryskiwać *ipf*. inject.

wtryskowy *a*. injection.

wtrysnąć *pf*. **-snę -śniesz, -śnij, -snął -snęła** *l*. **-sła -snęli** *zob*. **wtryskiwać**.

wtulać *ipf*. nestle. ~ **się** *ipf*. nestle down, burrow into, snuggle into.

wtulić (się) *pf. zob*. **wtulać (się)**.

wtyczka *f. Gen.pl*. **-ek 1.** *el*. plug, connector. **2.** *pot*. (= *donosiciel*) mole.

wtyczkowy *a. el*. plug-in; (*o gnieździe*) plug-in socket.

wtykać *ipf*. **1.** (= *wsuwać*) shove, stuff, tuck; (*do szafy, do szuflady, do kieszeni*) tuck away; **wetknąć kij w mrowisko** stir up a hornet's nest, put a cat among the pigeons. **2.** *pot*. (= *dawać do ręki*) slip. **3.** (= *kłaść byle gdzie*) tuck away, mislay, misplace; **gdzie to wetknęłaś?!** where did you tuck that away?!

wuef *mi szkoln. pot. zob*. **WF**.

wuefista *mp*, **wuefistka** *f. Gen.pl*. **-ek** *szkoln*. Phys.Ed. teacher; *Br*. PE teacher.

wuj *mp pl*. **-owie** *Gen*. **-ów** uncle.

wujeczny *a*. uncle's; (*o bracie, siostrze*) cousin.

wujek *mp* **-jk-** *pl*. **-owie** uncle; **Wuj Sam** Uncle Sam.

wujostwo *n*. auntie and uncle.

wulgarnie *adv*. vulgarly, coarsely, in vulgar terms; **wyglądać/zachowywać się/wyrażać się wulgarnie** be vulgar of appearance/manners/speech.

wulgarność *f*. vulgarity, coarseness.

wulgarny *a*. **1.** (= *nieprzyzwoity*) vulgar, crude; (*o słowach, piosence, dowcipie, wyglądzie*) vulgar. **2.** (= *uproszczony*) vulgar; **wulgarny materializm** vulgar materialism.

wulgaryzacja *f*. vulgarization.

wulgaryzm *mi jęz*. vulgarism.

wulgaryzować *ipf*. **1.** (= *czynić ordynarnym*) vulgarize. **2.** (= *upraszczać*) vulgarize.

wulkan *mi* volcano.

wulkaniczny *a*. volcanic.

wulkanizacja *f*. **1.** *mot*. vulcanization. **2.** *chem*. vulcanization.

wulkanizator *mp pl*. **-rzy** (*robotnik*) vulcanizer. – *mi Gen*. **-a** *pl*. **-ry** (*urządzenie*) vulcanizer.

wulkanizm *mi geol*. volcanism, volcanicity.

wulkanizować *ipf*. **1.** *mot*. vulcanize. **2.** *chem*. vulcanize.

wulkanolog *mp pl*. **-dzy** *l*. **-owie** vulcanologist.

wulkanologia *f. Gen*. **-ii** vulcanology.

ww. *abbr*. (= *wyżej wymieniony*) above-mentioned.

W-wa *abbr*. (= *Warszawa*) Warsaw.

wwalać *ipf. pot*. dump in, barge in. ~ **się** *ipf. pot*. (= *wpadać*) barge in, dump in.

wwalić (się) *pf. zob*. **wwalać (się)**.

wwieźć *pf*. **wwiozę wwieziesz wwiózł wwiozła wwieźli** *zob*. **wwozić**.

wwindować *pf. pot*. pull, lug. ~ **się** *pf. pot*. scramble up.

wwozić *ipf*. **wwożę wwozisz, wwoź** *l*. **wwóź** bring in, import.

wwóz *mi* **-o-** importation.

wy *pron. Gen., Acc. i Loc*. **was** *Dat*. **wam** *Ins*. **wami 1.** (= *ty i ty, ty i pozostali*) you; **u was** at your place; **do was** to your place. **2.** *dial*. (= *ty*) you. **3.** *polit*. (= *ty*) you.

wyabstrahować *pf. zob*. **abstrahować**.

wyakcentować *pf*. accentuate.

wyalienować (się) *pf. zob*. **alienować (się)**.

wyalienowany *a*. alienated.

wyartykułować *pf. zob*. **artykułować**.

wyasfaltować *pf*. asphalt.

wyasygnować *pf*. assign, allot, appropriate.

wybaczać *ipf*. forgive, pardon; **proszę mi wybaczyć** please, forgive me.

wybaczalny *a*. pardonable, excusable; *form*. venial; (*o błędzie*) pardonable, excusable.

wybaczenie *n*. forgiveness, pardon; **błąd nie do wybaczenia** an unforgivable error, an inexcusable mistake.

wybaczyć *pf. zob*. **wybaczać**.

wybadać *ipf*. investigate, explore, spy out, check out; **wybadać grunt** inquire into, spy out the land.

wybałuszać *ipf.*, **wybałuszyć** *pf*. stare, goggle, gape; **wybałuszać oczy na kogoś** gape at sb, stare at sb, goggle at sb.

wybawca *mp* rescuer, deliverer.

wybawiać *ipf*. redeem, deliver, rescue, save, disembarrass (*z kłopotu lub opresji*); **wybawić kogoś od śmierci** *l*. **zguby** rescue sb from death, ruin. ~ **się** *ipf*. (= *uwalniać się*) free, liberate.

wybawiciel *mp lit*. savior, rescuer, redeemer.

wybawić *pf. zob*. **wybawiać**. ~ **się** *pf*. **1.** *zob*. **wybawiać się**. **2.** (= *bawić się do syta*) enjoy o.s. to the full, have the time of one's life.

wybąkać *pf.*, **wybąknąć** *pf*. **-ij** *zob*. **wybąkiwać**.

wybebeszać *ipf.*, **wybebeszyć** *pf*. **1.** *pot*. (= *patroszyć*) disembowel, gut. **2.** *pot*. (= *opróżniać*) empty.

wybełkotać *pf*. **-oczę** *l*. **-ocę -oczesz** *l*. **-ocesz, -ocz** *zob*. **bełkotać**.

wybetonować *pf*. concrete, lay with concrete.

wybicie *n. sport* take-off.

wybić (się) *pf*. **-biję -bijesz, -bij** *zob*. **wybijać (się)**.

wybiec *pf*. **-biegnę -biegniesz, -biegnij, -biegł** *zob*. **wybiegać**.

wybieg *mi* **1.** (*dla zwierząt*) run, paddock (*zwł. dla koni*). **2.** (*dla modelek*) catwalk. **3.** (= *podstęp*) subterfuge, evasion, dodge. **4.** *lotn.* runway. **5.** *biegi* start. **6.** *skoki narciarskie* landing slope.

wybiegać *ipf.* run out; **wybiegać myślą naprzód** look ahead. **~ się** *pf.* run about, romp.

wybiegnąć *pf.* -biegnę -biegniesz, -biegnij, -biegł *zob.* **wybiegać**.

wybielacz *mi Gen.* -a bleach, bleaching substance, whitener.

wybielać *ipf.* **1.** (= *czynić białym*) bleach, whiten, (*wodą utlenioną*) peroxide. **2.** (= *oczyszczać z zarzutów*) clear of charges, exonerate from blame. **~ się** *ipf.* **1.** (= *stawać się białym*) bleach, whiten. **2.** (= *oczyszczać się z zarzutów*) clear o.s. of a demurrer.

wybieleć *pf.* whiten, bleach.

wybielić (się) *pf. zob.* **wybielać (się)**.

wybierać *ipf.* **1.** (= *typować*) make choice of, choose, select, pick out (*kandydata*); (*meble, książki*) choose; **wybrać kogoś na męża** choose sb for a husband; **jest w czym wybierać** there is a lot to choose from; **wybrać numer** *tel.* dial a telephone number. **2.** (= *usuwać*) take out; **wybierać kasztany z ognia** pull the chestnuts out of the fire. **3.** (= *wyjmować do końca*) take out; **wybrać pieniądze z konta** draw money from one's account. **4.** (= *powoływać kogoś poprzez głosowanie*) elect sb; **wybrać kogoś do rady nadzorczej** elect sb to the Supervisory Board; **wybrać kogoś na przewodniczącego** elect sb chairperson. **5.** *górn.* get. **6.** *żegl.* haul (in); **wybierać kotwicę** weigh anchor. **7.** *ryb.* haul in; **wybierać sieć** haul in a scoop-net. **~ się** *ipf.* (= *przygotowywać się do drogi*) prepare to go; **wybrać się na tamten świat** be at death's door; **wybierać się jak sójka za morze** delay one's trip repeatedly, keep putting one's trip off; **wybierać się za mąż** be going to get married.

wybierak *mi Gen.* -a *tel.* selector.

wybieralny *a.* (*o człowieku*) eligible, electable; (*o urzędzie, stanowisku, funkcji*) elective.

wybijać *ipf.* **1.** (= *uderzając, wypychać*) stave, break, knock; (*szybę, korek, gwóźdź*) break; **wybić komuś coś z głowy** put sth out of sb's head; **wybić klin klinem** take a hair of the dog that bit you; **wybić piłkę** *sport* clear. **2.** (= *przebijać*) knock through; (*dziurę, otwór*) make an opening. **3.** (= *odciskać*) impress; (*medal*) mint. **4.** (= *okładać*) stud, bind; (*pas ćwiekami*) stud a belt with nails. **5.** (= *wystukiwać*) beat; **wybijać rytm** beat time, tap the rhythm. **6.** (*o zegarze*) ring, strike; **wybiła godzina prawdy** the hour of truth struck; **wybiła jego ostatnia godzina** his sands are running out. **7.** (= *zabijać*) kill; **wybić do nogi** kill to a man. **8.** (= *niszczyć*) destroy; **grad wybił zasiewy** crops were destroyed by hail. **~ się** *ipf.* **1.** (= *wyróżniać się*) excel, distinguish o.s.; **wybić się na czoło** come to the top, come up. **2.** (= *wydostawać się*) free o.s.; **wybić się ze snu** *przen.* be unable to fall asleep again. **3.** *sport* take off.

wybiórczo *adv.* selectively.

wybiórczy *a.* selective.

wybitnie *adv.* **1.** (= *nieprzeciętnie*) notably, remarkably, markedly, prominently, preeminently, outstandingly, eminently; **wybitnie uzdolniony** brilliant, outstandingly talented, remarkably gifted. **2.** (= *wyraźnie*) markedly; **wybitnie trudne warunki do pracy** very hard working conditions.

wybitny *a.* **1.** (= *nieprzeciętny*) outstanding, eminent, brilliant, illustrious, prominent. **2.** (= *wyraźny*) marked; **wybitna zmiana postawy** marked change of attitude.

wyblakły *a.* faded, watery, colorless; (*o kolorze*) watery; (*o zdjęciu, rysunku*) faded.

wyblaknąć *pf.* -knie, -knij, -kł *l.* -knął -kła fade, discolor.

wyblednąć *pf.* -blednę -bledniesz, -blednij, -bladł *l.* -bladnął -bladła -bledli pale.

wybłagać *pf. form.* entreat, impetrate.

wyboisty *a.* rough, bumpy, uneven; (*o ścieżce*) bumpy.

wyboksować *pf. sport* box.

wyborca *mp* elector, voter, constituent.

wyborczy *a.* electoral, election; (*o lokalu, komisji, liście, kampanii, zebraniu, wiecu, prawie, ordynacji*) electoral; **okręg wyborczy** constituency; **bierne/czynne prawo wyborcze** passive/active voting rights.

wybornie *adv.* perfectly, splendidly, exquisitely; **bawić się wybornie** have a splendid time.

wyborny *a.* perfect, splendid, delicious; (*o okazji*) delightful; (*o zabawie*) splendid; (*o jabłkach*) delicious, exquisite.

wyborowy *a.* exquisite, excellent, perfect, first-class, choice; (*o towarzystwie*) perfect; (*o wódce*) first-class; **strzelec wyborowy** *wojsk.* marksman, sharpshooter.

wybory *pl. Gen.* -ów *polit.* election, elections; **wybory powszechne** general election; **wybory uzupełniające** special elections; *Br.* by-election; **kandydować w wyborach** stand/run for election; **wygrać wybory** win an election.

wybój *mi* -o- *Gen.pl.* -ów pothole.

wybór *mi* -o- **1.** (= *wybranie*) choice, selection, adoption, appointment; **trafny wybór** good choice; **bez wyboru** indiscriminately; **do wyboru** at choice; **nie masz wyboru** you have no choice; **do wyboru, do koloru** *pot.* in great variety. **2.** (= *zestaw*) assortment, selection. **3.** (= *wybieranie*) choice, selection, option, alternative.

wybrać (się) *pf.* -biorę -bierzesz *zob.* **wybierać (się)**.

wybrakować *pf.* reject; *przen.* scrap.

wybrakowany *a.* rejective, defective, faulty, deficient; (*o towarze, produkcie*) reject, scrap.

wybrana *f. Gen.* -ej (= *ukochana*) the girl of one's choice, ladylove.

wybraniec *mp* -ńc- *pl.* -y privileged, choice; **wybraniec losu** Fortune's darling, hotshot.

wybrany *mp* (= *ukochany*) the boy of one's choice; *iron.* (= *uprzywilejowany*) choice; **miejsce dla wybranych** place for the chosen few.

wybredny *a.* fastidious, squeamish, exacting, selective, choosy; (*o guście*) delicate palate; **wy-**

bredny w jedzeniu fastidious about food; **mało wybredny dowcip** unrefined joke.

wybrnąć *pf.* **-ij 1.** (= *poradzić sobie*) extricate o.s.; (*z kłopotów, z długów*) get out. **2.** (= *wydostać się z trudem*) find a way out, wade out; (*z zaspy, z błota*) wade out.

wybroczyna *f. pot.* ecchymosis, extravasation.

wybronić *pf.* exculpate, rescue, save; **wybronić kogoś przed czymś** rescue sb from sth.

wybrudzić *pf.* dirty, soil, stain. ~ **się** *pf.* dirty.

wybrukować *pf.* pave; **dobrymi chęciami jest piekło wybrukowane** the road to hell is paved with good intentions.

wybryk *mi* prank, frolic; **wybryk natury** freak of nature.

wybrzeże *n. Gen.pl.* -y sea-coast, sea-shore; **Wybrzeże Kości Słoniowej** *geogr.* the Ivory Coast.

wybrzuszać *ipf.* bulge, swell. ~ **się** *ipf.* bulge, swell out, balloon.

wybrzuszenie *n.* bulge, swelling, monticule.

wybrzuszony *a.* bulging.

wybrzuszyć (się) *pf. zob.* **wybrzuszać (się)**.

wybrzydzać *ipf.* fuss.

wybuch *mi* **1.** (= *eksplozja*) explosion; (*gazu, płomieni, wulkanu*) eruption. **2.** (= *początek czegoś*) explosion, outbreak; (*pożaru, wojny, powstania, kłótni*) outbreak. **3.** (*przejaw uczuć*) outburst; (*płaczu, śmiechu, radości*) peals. **4.** *fon.* explosion.

wybuchać *ipf.,* **wybuchnąć** *pf.* **-chnij, -chnął** *l.* **-chł -chnęła** *l.* **-chła -chnęli** *l.* **-chli 1.** (= *eksplodować*) explode; (*bomba, granat*) explode; (*wulkan*) erupt. **2.** (= *zaczynać się nagle*) break out; (*wojna, pożar, awantura, kłótnia*) outbreak. **3.** (= *gwałtownie reagować*) fume, flare-up; **wybuchać gniewem** fly into a passion; **wybuchać śmiechem** burst out laughing; **wybuchać płaczem** burst into tears.

wybuchowo *adv.* explosively; (*reagować*) vehemently, temperamentally, irritably.

wybuchowy *a.* **1.** (= *eksplodujący*) explosive; (*o substancji, mieszance, materiale*) explosive. **2.** (= *gwałtowny*) temperamental, vehement, bad-tempered; (*o człowieku*) bad-tempered, spiky; (*o temperamencie, usposobieniu*) peppery.

wybudować *pf.* build.

wybujać *pf.* overgrow; ((*o roślinach*) *wyrosnąć*) grow rank, straggle; *przen.* (*urosnąć nadmiernie*) become exuberant.

wybujałość *f.* (*rozrost*) overgrowth, rankness; *przen.* (*przerost*) exuberance, ebulience.

wybujały *a.* rank, rampant, exuberant; (*o trawie*) rank; (*o dziecku, temperamencie*) exuberant.

wybulić *pf. pot.* fork out; (*o pieniądzach*) cough up.

wyburzać *ipf.,* **wyburzyć** *pf.* demolish, tear down.

wybyć *pf.* **-będę -będziesz, -bądź, wybywać** *ipf.* **-am -asz** *pot.* leave, swan off.

wycałować *pf.* smother with kisses. ~ **się** *pf.,* **wycałowywać się** *ipf.* kiss each other.

wycedzić *pf. pot.* drawl out.

wycelować *pf.* aim, target, train.

wycena *f.* appraisal, assessment, valuation, quotation.

wyceniać *ipf.,* **wycenić** *pf.* price, appraise, valuate, value, quote.

wycharczeć *pf.* **-ę -ysz** wheeze out.

wychlać *pf.* **-chlam -chlasz** *l.* **-chleję -chlejesz -chlali** *l.* **-chleli** *pot.* guzzle, swill.

wychlapać *pf.* **-pię -piesz 1.** (= *rozlać*) splash. **2.** *pot.* (= *zużyć zbyt dużo*) (*farby*) drain. **3.** *pot.* (= *powiedzieć za dużo*) blab out.

wychlusnąć *pf.* **-snę -śniesz, -śnij, wychlustywać** *ipf.* sluice.

wychładzać *ipf.* cool, chill. ~ **się** *ipf.* cool off, become cool.

wychłeptać *pf.* **-pczę -pczesz** *l.* **-pcę -pcesz, -pcz, wychłeptywać** *ipf.* **1.** (*wypić*) lap up. **2.** (*powiedzieć*) snivel out.

wychłodzić (się) *pf.* **-chłodź** *l.* **-chłódź** *zob.* **wychładzać (się)**.

wychłostać *pf.* **-szczę -szczesz** *l.* **-stam -stasz, -szcz 1.** (= *zbić kogoś*) give (*sb*) a flogging. **2.** (*skrytykować*) castigate, lash (*sb*) with scathing criticism.

wychodek *mi* **-dk-** *Gen.* **-a** *pot.* outhouse.

wychodne *n. Gen.* **-ego** day off, day out.

wychodzić *ipf.* **1.** (= *opuszczać jakieś miejsce*) go out, come out; (*z domu*) leave (home), go out; **wychodzić po zakupy** go shopping; **wychodzić na spacer** go for a walk; **wychodzić naprzeciw kogoś** meet sb half-way; **wyjść kuchennymi drzwiami** go out backstairs; **wyjść na pierwsze miejsce** go into the lead; **wychodzić z roli** *pot.* go out of role; **wyjść na wolność** be released, regain one's liberty; **nie mogę wyjść z podziwu** I'm lost of admiration; **wyszedłem już z wprawy** I'm out of practice, I'm a bit rusty; **wyjść z obiegu** go out of use *l.* circulation, fall into disuse; **wychodzić z założenia, że...** assume that...; **wyjść za mąż** get married, marry; **wyjść z siebie** *pot.* be beside o.s., blow one's top *l.* stack; **nie może mi to wyjść z głowy** I can't get it out of my head. **2.** (*o statku*) (= *wypływać*) put to sea, launch out; **wyjść z portu** leave the port. **3.** (= *występować skądś*) leave. **4.** (= *wydostawać się z trudnej sytuacji*) free o.s., extricate o.s.; **wychodzić z kłopotów** free o.s. from difficulties; **wychodzić z długów** get out of debt; **wyjść z wypadku cało** get out of the accident unscathed, make it through the accident; **wychodzić z czegoś zwycięsko** come off victorious, come out top dog; **wychodzić z czegoś z honorem** come out of sth without loss of face; **wychodzić z czegoś bez straty** suffer no loss, come off well; **wychodzić z czegoś bez skazy** get off *l.* go unblemished; **wychodzić z czegoś bez szwanku** go *l.* get off scot-free; **wychodzić z czegoś obronną ręką** get the upper hand in sth, come off well in sth; **dobrze na tym wyszedł** he was all the better for it; **wyjść na czysto** *l.* **na swoje** break even; **wyjść na czymś jak Zabłocki na mydle** bring one's hogs *l.* pigs to a bad market. **5.** (= *brać początek*) descent, spring, start; **propozycja wyszła od prezesa** the suggestion came from the president. **6.** (= *dawać się zauważyć*) get out, come out; **oczy wychodzą komuś na wierzch** sb's eyes are popping; **wyszło na jaw** it came to light, it came out into the open; **łakomstwo wyjdzie ci bokiem** you'll be fed up with your greediness; **wyszło szydło z worka** he has shown the cloven foot. **7.** (= *być ogłoszonym*) come out; **wyszedł rozkaz/zakaz** the command/prohibition came out; **wyszło rozporządzenie** the ordinance came out. **8.** (= *być wydrukowanym*) issue from the press, come out; **w jakim nakładzie wyszła ta książka** what was print run of this book; **tygodnik wychodzi co środa** the weekly comes out every Wednesday; **powieść wyszła spod pras drukarskich** the novel came off the printing-press. **9.** (= *być uformowanym*) grow, turn out; **wyjść na człowieka** turn out a successful man; **wyjść na idiotę** make a fool of o.s.; **źle wychodzę na zdjęciach** I come out badly on photographs. **10.** (= *być zrealizowanym*) work out; **nie wyszło** it didn't work out; **nie chce mi wyjść to zadanie** I can't do this task, I can't solve this problem. **11.** *pot.* (= *być na wyczerpaniu*) run out, run short; **wyszedł nam chleb** we ran out *l.* short of bread. **12.** *pot.* (= *dawać jakiś rezultat*) yield a result; **na jedno wychodzi** it's all the same; **niech wyjdzie mu to na zdrowie** let it be all the better for him; **wychodzi na to, że...** it turns out that... **13.** (*o włosach*) (= *wypadać*) fall out. **14.** *karty* lead; **wyjść z asa** lead with an ace. **15.** *tylko ipf.* (= *być skierowanym*) face, look; **okna wychodzą na zachód** the windows face the west.

wychodźca *mp* emigrant.

wychodźstwo *n.* (= *emigracja*) emigration; (= *ogół emigrantów*) the emigrants.

wychować (się) *pf.* **-am -asz** zob. **wychowywać (się)**.

wychowanek *mp* **-nk-** *pl.* **-owie 1.** (= *absolwent*) alumnus. **2.** (= *dziecko pod opieką*) ward, foster-child.

wychowanie *n.* **1.** *szkoln.* education; **wziąć kogoś na wychowanie** adopt sb. **2.** (= *maniery*) manners.

wychowanka *f. Gen.pl.* **-ek 1.** (= *absolwentka*) alumna. **2.** (= *dziecko pod opieką*) ward, foster-child.

wychowany *a.* well-brought up; **jesteś źle wychowany** you're ill-mannered; **wychowany na najlepszych wzorach** brought up on the best examples.

wychowawca *mp* **1.** (= *nauczyciel*) home-room teacher; *Br.* form tutor. **2.** (= *opiekun*) (*na obozie, koloniach*) camp counselor; *Br.* camp counsellor; (*w domu dziecka*) housemaster; *Br.* house-father.

wychowawczy *a.* educational.

wychowawczyni *f.* **1.** (= *nauczycielka*) home-room teacher; *Br.* form tutor. **2.** (= *opiekunka*) (*na obozie, koloniach*) camp counselor; *Br.* camp counsellor; (*w domu dziecka*) housemistress; *Br.* house-mother.

wychowawstwo *n. szkoln.* home-room teacher's duties.

wychowywać *ipf.* **1.** (= *opiekować się*) bring

up, breed, rear; **wychować kogoś w szacunku do tradycji** bring up sb in respect of tradition, breed sb to the respect of tradition. **2.** (= *kształcić*) educate. **~ się** *ipf.* be brought up, be raised.

wychów *mi* **-o-** *roln.* raising; **zimny wychów** cold raising.

wychrypieć *pf.* **-pię -pisz** speak in a hoarse voice.

wychrzaniać *ipf. pot.* (= *znikać*) clear off; **wychrzaniaj stąd!** clear out!, beat it!

wychrzanić *pf. pot.* (= *wyrzucić*) chuck, boot.

wychrzcić *pf.* **-chrzczę -chrzcisz, -chrzcij** convert. **~ się** *pf.* be converted.

wychrzczony *a.* **-eni** convertive.

wychrzta *f. l. mp decl. like f. Gen.pl.* **-t** *l.* **-ów** convert, neophyte.

wychuchać *pf.* coddle up, nurse.

wychuchany *a.* coddled, hothouse, pampered; (*o dziecku*) coddled, pampered; (*o mieszkaniu*) spick-and-span.

wychudły *a.* emaciated, hollow-cheeked, pinched, scraggy, scrawny; (*o chłopaku, pacjencie*) emaciated.

wychudnąć *pf.* **-dnij, -dł** *l.* **-dnął -dła -dli** lose weight, emaciate; **wychudnąć z choroby** lose weight on account of sickness.

wychudzony *a.* **-eni** emaciated, hollow-cheeked, gaunt, pinched, scraggy; (*o dziecku, psie*) emaciated.

wychwalać *ipf.* praise, cry up, eulogize, extol, glorify. **~ się** boast.

wychwycić *pf. zob.* **wychwytać**.

wychwyt *mi* **1.** *techn.* escapement. **2.** *fiz.* capture. **3.** *biochem.* uptake.

wychwytać *pf.*, **wychwytywać** *ipf.* **1.** (= *wydobyć*) pull out. **2.** (= *wyłapać*) snatch. **3.** (= *zdemaskować*) catch.

wychylać *ipf.* bend, incline; **nie wychylać nosa z domu** not to stick one's nose out of the house; **wychylić kieliszek** toss back *l.* down a glass. **~ się** *ipf.* **1.** (= *odchylać się*) lean out; **wychylać się do przodu/tyłu** lean forward/back. **2.** (= *ukazywać się*) have sight, come into view. **3.** *pot.* (= *narażać się*) expose o.s.; **nie chciał się wychylać** he didn't want to stick his neck out.

wychylenie *n. fiz.* deflexion.

wychylić (się) *pf. zob.* **wychylać (się)**.

wychynąć *pf.* peep out.

wyciąć *pf.* **-tnę -tniesz, -tnij** zob. **wycinać**.

wyciąg *mi* **1.** *fin.* bank statement, compte rendu. **2.** (*skrót*) extract, excerpt; **wyciąg fortepianowy** piano score; (*aktu urodzenia*) copy. **3.** (*roztwór*) extract, essence. **4.** (*do jazdy w górę*) lift; **wyciąg narciarski** ski-lift; **wyciąg krzesełkowy** chair-lift; **wyciąg orczykowy** T-bar lift. **5.** *med.* extract, extension, traction.

wyciągać *ipf.* **1.** (= *wydobywać*) pull out, soak; **wyciągnąć od kogoś pieniądze** extort money from sb; **wyciągnąć konsekwencje w stosunku do kogoś** bring *l.* call sb to account; **wyciągnąć wnioski** draw conclusions; **wyciągać coś na światło dzienne** bring sth to light; **wyciągać z kogoś tajemnicę** worm a secret out of sb; **wyciągnąć pierwiastek** *mat.* extract the square root. **2.** (=

rozprostowywać) stretch; **wyciągać rękę po coś** hold out one's hand for sth; **wyciągnąć pomocną dłoń** lend a helping hand; **wyciągnąć rękę do zgody** extend *l.* offer an olive branch to sb; **wyciągnąć nogi** *pot.* (= *umrzeć*) turn up one's toes, peg out, hop the twig, pop one's clogs, kick the bucket. **3.** (= *rozciągać*) stretch; (*gumę*) draw; (*drut*) draw (out). **4.** *pot.* (= *nakłaniać do wyjścia*) draw out; **udało mi się wyciągnąć go do kina** I succeeded in persuading him to go to the movies; **wyciągnąć kogoś z łóżka** draw sb out of bed; **wyciągnąć kogoś na zwierzenia** draw sb out. **5.** (= *uwalniać*) get out; **wyciągnąć kogoś z więzienia** get sb out of prison; **wyciągnąć kogoś z biedy** lift sb out of poverty. **6.** *pot.* (= *uzyskiwać*) obtain, acquire, pull in; **wyciągam jakieś dwa tysiące miesięcznie** I pull in about two thousand a month; **ten samochód wyciąga nawet dwieście** this car makes even up to 200 kph. ~ **się** *ipf.* **1.** (= *rozprostowywać się*) stretch out; **wyciągnąć się jak długi** stretch out full length. **2.** (= *wysuwać się naprzód*) draw forward. **3.** (= *ulegać rozciąganiu*) stretch, extend; **sweter się wyciągnął** the sweater has stretched.

wyciągarka *f. Gen.pl.* **-ek 1.** *techn.* hoist. **2.** *lotn.* windlass.

wyciągnąć *pf.* **-ij** *zob.* **wyciągać.** ~ **się** *pf. zob.* **wyciągać się.**

wyciągnięty *a.* elongated, stretched; (*o swetrze*) stretched.

wyciągowy *a.* **1.** (*dotyczący wyciągu narciarskiego*) lift, lifting, winding, hauling; **maszyna wyciągowa** winding machine, winding engine, haulage engine; **lina wyciągowa** lifting rope, haulage cable; **wieża wyciągowa** hoist tower, lift pylon. **2.** exhaust; **wentylator wyciągowy** exhaust fan, extractive fan; **komin wyciągowy** exhaust *l.* vent chimney.

wycie *n.* **1.** (*zwierzęcia*) howl. **2.** *pot.* (*człowieka*) yell, scream. **3.** *pot.* (*urządzenia*) hoot, roar, whine.

wyciec *pf.* **-ciekie** *l.* **-ciecze -ciekł** *zob.* **wyciekać.**

wycieczka *f. Gen.pl.* **-ek 1.** (= *podróż turystyczna*) excursion, pleasure trip, outing, jaunt, junket, (*statkiem*) pleasure cruise. **2.** (= *grupa osób*) excursionists, holiday-makers, sightseeing group. **3.** *przest.* (= *atak*) sally, sortie; **robić osobiste wycieczki** make personal remarks.

wycieczkowicz *mp Gen.pl.* **-ów** tripper, hiker, excursionist, sightseer.

wycieczkowy *a.* excursional, excursionary, tourist; **trasa wycieczkowa** excursion route; **statek wycieczkowy** pleasure-boat.

wyciek *mi* **1.** (= *wypływ*) leak, leakage, outflow, seepage, escape, effluent; (*ze zbiornika*) effluent, escape; **wyciek ropy** oil *l.* petroleum spill *l.* leak, escape of oil *l.* petroleum. **2.** (= *wydzielina*) discharge; **wyciek z nosa** nasal discharge.

wyciekać *ipf.*, **wycieknąć** *pf.* **-knij, -kł** *l.* **-knął 1.** (= *wypływać*) leak (out), flow out, trickle, escape, dribble. **2.** *myśl.* scamper away.

wycielić się *pf. roln.* calve.

wycieniować *pf.*, **wycieniowywać** *ipf.* **1.** (*o*

włosach) layer. **2.** *sztuka* shade, grade. **3.** *muz.* modulate.

wycieńczać *ipf.* waste, weaken. ~ **się** *ipf.* waste away.

wycieńczenie *n.* emaciation, weakness; *pat.* atrophy, inanition, consumption, debility.

wycieńczony *a.* **-eni** wasted, emaciated; **wycieńczony organizm** wasted system; **wycieńczony chorobą/brakiem snu** wasted by disease/sleeplessness.

wycieńczyć (się) *pf. zob.* **wycieńczać (się).**

wycieraczka *f. Gen.pl.* **-ek 1.** (*do nóg*) doormat. **2.** *mot.* (windscreen) wiper.

wycierać *ipf.* **1.** (= *osuszać*) wipe; (*ręcznikiem*) towel; (*nos, buty*) wipe; **wycierać sobie kimś gębę** gossip about sb. **2.** (= *trąc, likwidować*) erase, rub out, scrape away, scuff. **3.** (= *zużywać*) wear out, fret; (*tkaninę*) fray; (*ubranie, buty, kanapę*) wear out. ~ **się** *ipf.* **1.** (= *osuszać się*) wipe, dry. **2.** (= *niszczyć się*) wear through.

wycierpieć *pf.* **-ę -isz** suffer. ~ **się** *pf.* go through a great deal of suffering.

wycięcie *n.* **1.** (= *nacięcie*) file cut, incision, notch, nick. **2.** (= *dekolt*) neck-line, V-neck.

wycinać *ipf.* **1.** (= *tnąc, usuwać*) cut out, carve out; (*niepożądane treści*) expurgate; (*las*) cut, deforest; (*ogłoszenie*) cut out. **2.** *chir.* excise. **3.** (= *tnąc, kształtować*) carve out; (*dziurę, otwór*) cut out. **4.** (= *skocznie grać*) play briskly. **5.** (= *mordować masowo*) cut down; **wyciąć w pień** cut down to a man.

wycinanka *f. Gen.pl.* **-ek** cutout.

wycinek *mi* **-nk-** *Gen.* **-a 1.** (= *kawałek*) sector; **wycinek koła/kuli** *geom.* segment of the circle/sphere. **2.** (*artykuł*) press cutting, clip; **zbierać wycinki na temat ochrony środowiska** gather press cuttings on environment preservation. **3.** *med.* segment, slice (of a tissue), section.

wycinka *f. Gen.pl.* **-ek** *leśn.* logging, forest clearance.

wycinkowo *adv.* fragmentarily.

wycinkowy *a.* fragmentary, sectorial; (*o relacji, wiadomościach*) fragmentary.

wycior *mi wojsk.* ramrod.

wyciosać *pf.* **-ciosam** *l.* **-cioszę -ciosasz** *l.* **-cioszesz, wyciosywać** *ipf.* chisel, cut out.

wycisk *mi* **1.** *pot.* (= *pobicie*) hiding; **dać komuś wycisk** beat sb black and blue, kick *l.* whip one's butt. **2.** (*wzór*) impression.

wyciskacz *mi Gen.* **-a** squeezer; **wyciskacz do cytryn** lemon squeezer.

wyciskać *ipf.*, **wycisnąć** *pf.* **-snę -śniesz, -śnij 1.** (= *wydobywać ciecz*) extract; (*ściereczkę, gąbkę*) press out; (*sok z cytryny*) squeeze; (*wodę z bielizny*) wring out; **coś wyciska komuś łzy** sth wrings tears from sb's eyes; **wycisnąć z kogoś siódme poty** sweat sb; **wycisnąć kogoś jak cytrynę** squeeze sb like a lemon. **2.** (= *wyduszać*) squeeze. **3.** (= *odcisnąć*) impress, leave an impression; **wojna wycisnęła na nim piętno** the war has left an impression on him. **4.** *pot.* (= *uzyskiwać*) (*pieniądze, zeznanie, prawdę*) extort.

wyciszać *ipf.* **1.** (= *ściszać*) turn down. **2.** (=

izolować) soften. ~ **się** *ipf.* (= *uspokajać się*) calm down, abate.

wyciszyć (się) *pf.* = **wyciszać (się)**.

wycofać (się) *pf. zob.* **wycofywać (się)**.

wycofanie *n. wojsk.* retreat, withdrawal.

wycofywać *ipf.* **1.** (= *odbierać*) withdraw, take sth off; (*podanie, poparcie, kapitał, pozew, oskarżenie*) withdraw; **wycofać z obiegu** withdraw from circulation. **2.** *wojsk.* retreat. ~ **się** *ipf.* **1.** (= *rezygnować z czegoś*) resign, scrap, withdraw; (*z interesów*) retire; (*z obietnic*) call off. **2.** *wojsk.* retreat.

wycwanić się *pf. pot.* become artful, become cunning.

wycyganiać *ipf.*, **wycyganić** *pf. pot.* coax, wheedle, gyp (*sth*) (*od kogoś* out of sb).

wycyzelować *pf.* **1.** (= *wygładzić*) chisel, carve. **2.** (= *szczegółowo opracować*) finish with meticulous care, elaborate.

wyczarować *pf.*, **wyczarowywać** *ipf.* conjure up, magic up.

wyczarterować *pf. zob.* **czarterować**.

wyczekać *pf.* expect, wait, be on the watch, anticipate. ~ **się** *pf.* wait indefinitely.

wyczekiwać *ipf. zob.* **wyczekać**.

wyczekująco *adv.* anticipatingly.

wyczekujący *a.* expectant, anticipatory, eager; (*o postawie*) anticipating.

wyczerpać *pf.* **-pię -piesz** *zob.* **wyczerpywać**. ~ **się** *pf.* run out, drain out, wear thin.

wyczerpanie *n.* **1.** (= *niedobór*) depletion, frazzle; **moja cierpliwość jest na wyczerpaniu** my patience wears thin. **2.** (= *osłabienie*) exhaustion, enervation, prostration; **padam z wyczerpania** I'm on my last legs, I feel washed out.

wyczerpany *a.* **1.** (= *zużyty*) running out, run down, frayed, depleted; (*o nakładzie książki*) out of print. **2.** (= *osłabiony*) exhausted, fagged; **jestem wyczerpany po całym tygodniu pracy** I'm exhausted after a whole week of work; **wyczerpany nerwowo** in a state of nervous prostration.

wyczerpująco *adv.* exhaustively, profoundly; (*omówić, przedstawić, odpowiedzieć*) exhaustively.

wyczerpujący *a.* **1.** (= *kompletny*) exhaustive, profound; (*o danych, omówieniu, referacie, odpowiedzi*) exhaustive. **2.** (= *osłabiający*) exhausting, harassing; (*o pracy, podróży*) exhausting.

wyczerpywać *ipf.* **1.** (= *zużywać*) exhaust, use up. **2.** (= *czerpiąc, usuwać*) scoop out; **wyczerpać temat** exhaust a subject. **3.** (= *osłabiać*) exhaust, weaken. ~ **się** *ipf.* **1.** (= *być zużywanym*) become exhausted, be low, run low, be used up; **baterie się wyczerpały** batteries have run out, batteries have gone flat; **moja cierpliwość się wyczerpała** my patience has run out. **2.** (= *osłabiać się*) become exhausted.

wyczesać *pf.* **-szę -szesz**, **wyczesywać** *ipf.* (*uczesać*) comb; (*wyczesać*) comb out.

wyczołgać się *pf.*, **wyczołgiwać się** *ipf.* crawl out, creep out.

wyczucie *n.* intuition, feeling, sense; **robić coś z wyczuciem** do sth tactfully; **bez wyczucia** tact-lessly; **na wyczucie** on a hunch; **brak ci wyczucia** you are tactless.

wyczuć *pf. zob.* **wyczuwać**.

wyczulony *a.* **-eni** sensitive, receptive; (*na krzywdę*) sensitive.

wyczuwać *ipf.* **1.** (= *uświadamiać sobie*) sense, scent, feel. **2.** (= *doświadczać zmysłami*) sense. **3.** (*o zwierzęciu*) (= *węszyć*) scent, sniff.

wyczuwalny *a.* perceptible, noticeable, (*o zdenerwowaniu, irytacji, podnieceniu, pulsie*) perceptible.

wyczyn *mi* **1.** (= *osiągnięcie*) achievement, feat, performance. **2.** (= *wybryk*) excess.

wyczyniać *ipf.* **1.** (= *wykonywać*) perform, produce. **2.** (= *wyprawiać*) **co ty wyczyniasz?** what on earth are you doing?

wyczynowiec *mp* **-wc-** *pl.* **-y** amateur *l.* professional athlete participating in competitions.

wyczynowo *adv.* **uprawiać sport wyczynowo** do sports for competition.

wyczynowy *a.* record-seeking, professional; (*o sporcie*) profession.

wyczyścić *pf.* **-szczę -ścisz** **1.** (= *usunąć brud*) clean up. **2.** (= *wypolerować*) polish. **3.** (= *dokonać korekty*) rectify; (*tekst z błędów*) proof-read. ~ **się** *pf.* (*być oczyszczonym*) be cleaned, be purified, be cleared; (= *uwolnić się*) purge o.s., be cleared.

wyczytać *pf.*, **wyczytywać** *ipf.* **1.** (= *dowiedzieć się*) read; **wyczytać między wierszami, że...** read between the lines that...; **wyczytać coś z czyjejś twarzy** read sth from sb's face; **wyczytać coś z gwiazd** read from the stars; **wyczytać coś z ręki** palm read. **2.** (= *odczytać nazwisko*) read out sb's name.

wyć *ipf.* **wyję wyjesz** **1.** (*o zwierzętach*) howl, ululate; **wyć z głodu** howl with hunger. **2.** (*o ludziach*) yell, howl. **3.** (*o urządzeniach*) hoot.

wyćwiczony *a.* trained, drilled; (*o mięśniach, ruchach*) trained.

wyćwiczyć *pf.* **1.** (= *wyszkolić*) school, train, drill. **2.** (= *zbić*) give (sb) a beating. ~ **się** *pf.* be schooled, be trained, be drilled.

wydać (się) *pf. zob.* **wydawać (się)**.

wydajnie *adv.* productively, efficiently; (*pracować*) efficiently.

wydajność *f.* productivity, efficiency, plenteousness; (*pracy*) productivity.

wydajny *a.* **1.** (= *obfity*) plenteous, efficient; (*o pracy, złożu*) efficient. **2.** (= *produktywny*) productive.

wydalać *ipf.*, **wydalić** *pf.* **1.** (= *zmuszać do opuszczenia*) expel; (*z kraju*) deport; (*ze szkoły*) expel; (*z pracy*) dismiss. **2.** *biol.* (= *usuwać*) extract; (*dwutlenek węgla*) evacuate.

wydalina *f. biol.* excretion.

wydalniczy *a. biol.* excretory.

wydanie *n.* **1.** (= *opublikowanie*) publication, edition; **wydanie zbiorowe** collected edition; **wydanie jubileuszowe** jubilee edition; **wydanie poprawione** revised edition; **wydanie kieszonkowe** pocket edition; **wydanie nadzwyczajne** special edition; **trzecie wydanie** third edition. **2.** *przest.*

(= *ożenek*) marriage, match; **panna na wydaniu** marriageable woman.

wydarzać się *ipf.* happen, occur.

wydarzenie *n.* 1. (= *zdarzenie*) event. 2. (= *osiągnięcie*) event; achievement.

wydarzyć się *pf. zob.* **wydarzać się**.

wydatek *mi* -tk- expense, outlay; **drobne wydatki** minor expenses; **pieniądze na drobne wydatki** pocket money; petty cash; **pokrywać wydatki** cover expenses.

wydatkować *ipf. lit.* expend.

wydatnie *adv.* considerably; significantly.

wydatny *a.* 1. (= *znaczny*) considerable; significant. 2. (= *okazały*) prominent.

wydawać *ipf.* -aję -ajesz, -awaj 1. (*pieniądze*) spend; **wydać na coś ostatni grosz** spend one's last dime on sth; **wydać pieniądze do ostatniego grosza** spend one's last dime; **wydać (komuś) resztę** give (sb) change. 2. (= *dawać*) give, issue; distribute; **wydać zaświadczenie** issue a certificate; **wydać bankiet** give a banquet; **wydać córkę za mąż** marry a daughter off. 3. (= *zdradzać*) give away; **wydać przestępcę w ręce policji** give a criminal over to the police. 4. (= *obwieszczać*) issue; **wydać opinię** give *l.* pass an opinion; **wydać polecenie** give an order; **wydać uchwałę** make a resolution; **wydać komuś wojnę** declare a war on sb; **wydać werdykt** return *l.* deliver a verdict; **wydać wyrok** pass *l.* pronounce a sentence. 5. (= *publikować*) publish. 6. (= *dawać plon*) yield; **wydać na świat** give birth to; **coś wydało rezultaty** sth produced results. 7. (= *wydobywać z siebie*) make, utter; **wydawać okrzyk** give a shout *l.* cry; **wydać ostatnie tchnienie** breathe one's last breath. ~ **się** *ipf.* 1. (= *być ujawnianym*) come out, be revealed; **wszystko się wydało** the secret is out. 2. (= *zdradzać się z czymś*) give o.s. away; **wydać się ze swoimi planami** give one's plans away. 3. *lit.* (= *wywoływać wrażenie*) seem, appear; **chwila wydała się całą wiecznością** moment seemed to last forever. 4. *pot.* (= *wychodzić za mąż*) marry.

wydawca *mp* 1. (*osoba*) publisher. 2. (*instytucja*) publishing house.

wydawnictwo *n.* 1. (*instytucja*) publishing house. 2. (*publikacja*) publication.

wydawniczy *a.* publishing; publisher's; **dom wydawniczy** publishing house; **arkusz wydawniczy** publisher's sheet; **korekta wydawnicza** editor's proof(reading).

wydąć (się) *pf.* -dmę -dmiesz, -dmij *zob.* **wydymać (się)**.

wydech *mi* 1. (*z płuc*) expiration, exhalation. 2. *techn.* exhaust.

wydechowy *a.* 1. (= *dotyczący oddychania*) expiratory; **akcent wydechowy** *fon.* expiratory stress. 2. exhaust; **rura wydechowa** *mot.* exhaust pipe.

wydedukować *pf. zob.* **dedukować**.

wydeklamować *pf. zob.* **deklamować**.

wydekoltować *pf.* make a décolleté *l.* low-cut.

wydekoltowany *a.* low-cut, décolleté, decollete.

wydelegować *pf. zob.* **delegować**.

wydelikacać *ipf.*, **wydelikacić** *pf.* make delicate, make fragile.

wydelikatniały *a.* delicate.

wydelikatnieć *pf.* become delicate, become fragile.

wydeptać *pf.* -pczę -pczesz *l.* -pcę -pcesz, -pcz, **wydeptywać** *ipf.* 1. (= *utorować*) tread; **wydeptać ścieżkę** wear a path. 2. (= *zniszczyć*) trample. 3. *pot.* (= *uzyskać usilnymi staraniami*) obtain by persistent endeavors.

wydestylować *pf. zob.* **destylować**.

wydezynfekować *pf. zob.* **dezynfekować**.

wydębić *pf. pot.* (= *uzyskać*) drum up.

wydęty *a.* (*o brzuchu*) bulging; (*o wargach*) pouted.

wydłubać *pf.* -bię -biesz, **wydłubywać** 1. (= *wydobyć*) pick. 2. (*wyciąć*) gouge out, dig out, force out.

wydłużać *ipf.* (*cykl, krok*) lenghten; (*czas, pobyt*) prolong, extend; (*podróż*) prolong, lengthen; **wydłużać piłkę** *tenis* play the ball deeper. ~ **się** *ipf.* lengthen, grow longer; **twarz się komuś wydłużyła** sb got a long face.

wydłużony *a.* elongated, extented, lengthened; prolonged.

wydłużyć (się) *pf. zob.* **wydłużać (się)**.

wydma *f.* (sand) dune; **ruchome** *l.* **wędrowne wydmy** shifting (sand) dunes.

wydmowy *a.* dune.

wydmuchać *pf.*, **wydmuchiwać** *ipf.*, **wydmuchnąć** *pf.* -ij 1. (= *usunąć*) exhale; puff away, blow out; **wydmuchać nos** blow one's nose. 2. (= *uformować*) blow. 3. *wulg.* lay, bang, ball.

wydmuchów *mi* -o- *Gen.* -a *pot.* middle of nowhere.

wydmuszka *f. Gen.pl.* -ek Easter egg shell.

wydobrzeć *pf.* -eję -ejesz recover, recuperate, get better.

wydobyć (się) *pf.* -będę -będziesz, -bądź *zob.* **wydobywać (się)**.

wydobywać *ipf.* 1. (= *wydostać*) get *l.* bring out; extract; **wydobyć kogoś z nędzy** get sb out of poverty; **nie mógł wydobyć z siebie głosu** he couldn't utter a sound; **wydobyć coś na jaw** bring sth to light. 2. *górn.* mine, extract. 3. (= *uwypuklić*) emphasize. 4. (= *uzyskać*) get, obtain, elicit; **wydobyć tajemnicę** ferret out a secret; **wydobyć zeznanie** extort a confession. ~ **się** *ipf.* 1. (= *wydzielić się*) get out, escape. 2. (= *wydostać się*) get out; **wydobyć się z nędzy** get out of poverty. 3. (= *dać się słyszeć*) come out; **wydobył się płacz** cry came out.

wydobywczy *a. górn.* mining.

wydoić *pf.* -dój 1. *roln.* milk. 2. *pot.* (= *wyłudzić*) milk, bleed. 3. *pot.* (= *wypić*) swill.

wydolność *f. fizj.* efficiency, fitness; (*zastawki*) competence.

wydolny *a. rzad., fizj.* efficient; competent.

wydołać *pf.* cope; manage; **nie wydołał obowiązkom** he couldn't *l.* didn't cope with his responsibilities.

wydoroślić *pf.* -eję -ejesz grow up, mature.

wydoskonalać *ipf.* perfect, bring to perfection; improve. ~ **się** *ipf.* become perfect; improve.

wydoskonalić (się) *pf. zob.* **wydoskonalać (się)**.

wydostać (się) *pf.* **-stanę -staniesz** = **wydostawać (się)**.

wydostawać *ipf.* **-staję -stajesz, -stawaj 1.** (= *wydobyć*) get out of; take out of; extract. **2.** (= *uzyskać z trudem*) get out of; obtain. **~ się** *ipf.* **1.** (= *wyjść z trudem*) get out; get away. **2.** (= *przeniknąć*) emerge; issue; flow.

wydra *f.* **1.** *zool.* (Eurasian) otter (*Lutra lutra*). **2.** *pot.* (*kobieta*) quarrelsome woman; provocatively dressed woman.

wydrapać *pf.* **-pię -piesz, wydrapywać** *ipf.* **1.** (= *usunąć*) scratch out, get out, force out; (*błąd*) scrape out; (*plamę*) scrub off; **wydrapać komuś oczy** scratch sb's eyes out. **2.** (= *wyryć*) carve, scratch.

wydrążać *ipf.* hollow (out); (*owoce pestkowe*) stone.

wydrążony *a.* hollow.

wydrążyć *pf. zob.* **wydrążać**.

wydreptać *pf.* **-pczę -pczesz** *l.* **-pcę -pcesz, -pcz, wydreptywać** *ipf. pot.* (= *załatwić z trudem*) obtain by persistent endeavors.

wydrowaty *a. pot.* quarrelsome; provocative-looking.

wydruk *mi* printout.

wydrukować *pf.* **1.** (= *powielić*) print. **2.** (= *opublikować*) publish.

wydrwić *pf.* **-ij, wydrwiwać** *ipf.* deride, mock, sneer.

wydrwigrosz *mp Gen.pl.* **-y** *l.* **-ów** *pot.* fraud.

wydrylować *pf. zob.* **drylować**.

wydrzeć (się) *pf.* **-drę -drzesz, -drzyj, -darł** *zob.* **wydzierać (się)**.

wydukać *pf. pot.* stutter (out), stammer (out).

wydumać *pf. żart.* imagine, invent.

wydumany *a.* invented.

wydusić *pf.* **-szę -sisz, wyduszać** *ipf.* **1.** (= *gniotąc, wydobyć*) squeeze, crush out, press; **wydusić z kogoś pieniądze** squeeze money out of sb, get out money from sb. **2.** *pot.* (= *zmusić do powiedzenia*) get out of, extort, squeeze; **wydusić z kogoś zeznanie** extort a confession from sb. **3.** *pot.* (= *powiedzieć z trudem*) stutter out; **nie mogła wydusić z siebie ani słowa** she was speechless, she couldn't utter a word. **4.** (= *dusząc, uśmiercić*) smother, stifle.

wydychać *ipf.* exhale, breathe out, expire.

wydymać *ipf.* **1.** (*usta*) pout; (*policzki*) puff out; **wiatr wydyma żagle** wind fills the sails. **2.** *wulg.* fuck, screw. **~ się** *ipf.* fill, swell.

wydział *mi* **1.** *uniw.* faculty; **rada wydziału** faculty council; **studiować na wydziale historii** study at the faculty of history. **2.** (*instytucji*) department; **naczelnik wydziału** department head.

wydziałowy *a.* **1.** *uniw.* faculty. **2.** departmental.

wydziedziczać *ipf.*, **wydziedziczyć** *pf.* disinherit, exclude from inheritance; **wydziedziczać kogoś z czegoś** disinherit sb from sth.

wydzielać *ipf.* **1.** (= *wyznaczać część*) ration out, dispense. **2.** (= *oddzielać*) assign, allot, apportion. **3.** *tylko ipf.* (= *wydawać z siebie*) emit, give off. **4.** *tylko ipf. biol.* secrete. **5.** *tylko ipf.*

fiz. emit, give off, release. **~ się** *ipf.* **1.** (= *wydobywać się*) be produced, be emitted; exude. **2.** *biol.* be secreted. **3.** *fiz., chem.* be emitted, be released; precipitate. **4.** (= *wyodrębniać się*) separate (*z czegoś* from sth).

wydzielanie *n. biol.* secretion; **gruczoły wydzielania wewnętrznego** endocrine glands.

wydzielić (się) *pf. zob.* **wydzielać (się)**.

wydzielina *f.* **1.** *biol.* secretion. **2.** *med.* secretion. **3.** *bot.* secretion.

wydzierać *ipf.* **1.** (= *szarpiąc, odrywać*) tear out; **wydzierać sobie włosy z głowy** tear one's hair (out), despair; **wydrzeć kogoś z czyichś rąk** save *l.* rescue sb; **wydrzeć kogoś śmierci** save sb's life. **2.** *pot.* (= *brać coś siłą*) snatch, grab; **wydzierać coś komuś** tear sth away from sb; **wydzierać sobie coś z rąk** scramble for sth. **3.** (*o ubraniu, obuwiu*) (= *niszczyć*) wear down. **~ się** *ipf.* **1.** (= *wydostawać się siłą*) wrench free, get out, get away. **2.** *pot.* (= *głośno krzyczeć*) holler. **3.** *pot.* (= *źle i głośno śpiewać*) scream a song out of tune. **4.** (*o ubraniu, obuwiu*) (= *niszczyć się*) be worn down.

wydzieranka *n. Gen.pl.* **-ek** *szkoln.* cut and paste picture, colored paper mosaic.

wydziergać *pf. zob.* **dziergać**.

wydzierżawiać *ipf.*, **wydzierżawić** *pf.* (= *brać w dzierżawę*) **1.** lease, rent (*sth*) (*od kogoś* from sb). **2.** (= *oddawać w dzierżawę*) lease, rent (*sth*) (out), let (*sth*) (out) (*komuś* to sb).

wydziobać *pf.* **-bię -biesz, wydziobywać** *ipf.* peck (up *l.* out).

wydziwiać *ipf. pot.* make a fuss about.

wydzwaniać *ipf.*, **wydzwonić** *pf.* **1.** (*o zegarze, kurancie*) (= *dzwoniąc, sygnalizować*) strike; ring, toll. **2.** *tylko ipf.* (= *często rozmawiać przez telefon*) make a lot of phone calls; gab a lot on the phone; **wydzwaniać do kogoś nieustannie** bug *l.* pester sb with phone calls; **wszyscy do mnie wydzwaniali przez cały dzień** my phone has been ringing off the wall all day.

wydźwięk *mi* overtone, undertone, implication.

wydźwignąć *pf.* **-ij 1.** (= *podnieść na wyższy poziom*) raise, lift, get out of; elevate, uplift. **2.** (= *odbudować*) rebuild, reconstruct. **~ się** *pf.* (= *odnaleźć równowagę ekonomiczną*) recover; (= *odnaleźć równowagę psychiczną*) recover, get out of.

wyedukować *pf. zob.* **edukować**.

wyegzekwować *pf. zob.* **egzekwować**.

wyeksmitować *pf. zob.* **eksmitować**.

wyekspediować *pf. zob.* **ekspediować**.

wyeksplikować *pf. zob.* **eksplikować**.

wyeksploatować *pf.* exploit completely, exhaust.

wyeksponować *pf. zob.* **eksponować**.

wyeksportować *pf. zob.* **eksportować**.

wyekwipować *pf. zob.* **ekwipować**.

wyelegantować się *pf. pot.* spruce up, dress up.

wyeliminować *pf. zob.* **eliminować**.

wyeliminowanie *n.* elimination.

wyemancypować się *pf.* *zob.* **emancypować się**.

wyemancypowany *a.* emancipated.

wyemigrować *pf.* *zob.* **emigrować**.

wyemitować *pf.* *zob.* **emitować**.

wyewoluować *pf.* evolve, develop (*z czegoś* out of sth).

wyfiokować się *pf.* *pot.* get a pretentious hairdo; rig o.s. out.

wyfiokowany *a.* *pot.* sporting a pretentious hairdo; rigged out.

wyfroterować *pf.* *zob.* **froterować**.

wyfrunąć *pf.*, **wyfruwać** *ipf.* **1.** (*o ptaku*) fly away. **2.** *przen.* (= *wjechać*) leave.

wyga *f.* *l.* *mp decl. like f. Gen.pl.* **-g** *l.* **-ów** *pot.* old stager.

wygadać *pf.* **1.** *pot.* (= *naopowiadać*) say, tell; **wygadała, co miała na sercu** she got it off her chest. **2.** *pot.* (= *zdradzić*) let slip, let out, blab. ~ **się** *pf.* **1.** *pot.* (= *naopowiadać się*) talk to one's heart content. **2.** *pot.* (= *zdradzić tajemnicę*) spill the beans, blab.

wygadany *a.* speaking, glib; **być wygadanym** have the gift of the gab.

wygadywać *ipf.* **1.** *pot.* (= *pleść bez sensu*) talk nonsense, talk rubbish; **co ty wygadujesz!** whatever on earth are you talking about!, what are you talking about!; **wygadywać bzdury** talk nonsense. **2.** *pot.* (= *obmawiać*) complain about; run down; **wygadywać na kogoś** *l.* **na coś** complain about sb *l.* sth; run sb *l.* sth down.

wyganiać *ipf.* drive out; chase away; **pogoda, że psa by nie wygnał** what a terrible weather, the weather is just terrible.

wygarbować *pf.* *techn.* tan; **wygarbować komuś skórę** tan sb's hide.

wygarnąć *pf.* **-ij**, **wygarniać** *ipf.* **1.** (= *wydostać*) get out, take out; rake (out). **2.** *pot.* (= *powiedzieć wprost*) give it straight; **wygarnąć komuś** give it to sb straight. **3.** *pot.* (= *strzelić*) shoot, fire.

wygasać *ipf.* **1.** (= *gasnąć*) go out, die out; (*świeca*) burn out; (*wulkan*) become extinct. **2.** (= *znikać, kończyć się*) fade, die away *l.* down *l.* out; (*epidemia*) subside. **3.** (= *tracić ważność*) expire.

wygasić *pf.* **-szę -sisz** *zob.* **wygaszać**.

wygasły *a.* extinguished, burnt out; (*o wulkanie*) extinct; (*o miłości, uczuciu*) extinguished, faded; (*o umowie*) expired.

wygasnąć *pf.* **-śnie, -śnij, -sł** *l.* **-snął -sła -śli** *zob.* **wygasać**.

wygaszać *ipf.* (*pożar, ogień*) put out, extinguish; (*światła*) turn off *l.* out.

wygaśnięcie *n.* (*wymarcie*) extinction; (*umowy*) expiry, termination.

wygenerować *pf.* *zob.* **generować**.

wygiąć (się) *pf.* **-gnę -gniesz, -gnij** *zob.* **wyginać (się)**.

wygibas *mi pot.* contortion.

wygięcie *n.* curve, bend.

wygięty *a.* curved, bent, crooked.

wygimnastykować *pf.* exercise. ~ **się** *pf.* become fit (*after a lot of exercise*).

wygimnastykowany *a.* supple.

wyginać *ipf.* **1.** (= *odkształcać*) bend, curve. **2.** (= *wychylać*) bend, incline. ~ **się** *ipf.* **1.** (= *odkształcać się*) bend, curve. **2.** (= *wychylać się*) bend, incline.

wyginąć *pf.* become extinct, die out.

wyginięcie *n.* extinction.

wygląd *mi* (*przedmiotu, zwierzęcia*) appearance; (*człowieka*) appearance, looks; **o wyglądzie kogoś** looking like sb; **przypominać kogoś z wyglądu** look like sb; **sądząc z wyglądu** judging by appearances.

wyglądać *ipf.* **1.** (= *wyzierać*) look out; **wyglądać przez okno** look out *l.* through the window. **2.** *przen.* (= *ukazywać się*) appear, emerge, be visible; **słońce wygląda zza chmur** sun appears from behind the clouds, clouds are clearing away. **3.** (= *dawać się widzieć*) be visible, appear; **wyglądać spod czegoś** appear from beneath sth. **4.** *tylko ipf.* (= *prezentować się*) look; **dobrze dzisiaj wyglądasz** you look good today; **wyglądać jak śmierć** look like death warmed up *l.* over; **on mi wygląda na złodzieja** he looks like a thief to me; **ładnie bym wyglądał** I would be in trouble; **jak to wygląda!** what is this!, what do you think this is!; **wyglądać jak półtora nieszczęścia** look the very picture of misery; **wyglądać świetnie** *l.* **źle** look great *l.* bad; **wyglądasz na zmęczonego** you look tired; **wyglądać blado** look pale; **wyglądać młodo (jak) na swój wiek** look young for one's age; **jak ona wygląda?** what does she look like?; **wygląda na to, że...** it looks as if...; **na to wygląda** so it would seem, so it seems. **5.** *tylko ipf.* (= *oczekiwać z tęsknotą*) look forward to, expect, await; **wyglądać kogoś** *l.* **czegoś jak kania dżdżu** crave (for) sth, long for sth, desire sth eagerly, crave to see, meet, etc. sb; be looking forward to meet, see, etc. sb, be looking forward to sth.

wyglądnąć *pf.* **-ij** *dial. zob.* **wyglądać**.

wygładzać *ipf.* **1.** (= *czynić gładkim*) smooth out. **2.** *przen.* (= *usuwać usterki*) iron out; improve, perfect. ~ **się** *ipf.* **1.** (= *stawać się gładkim*) smoothen, become smooth. **2.** *przen.* (= *udoskonalać się*) improve, get better.

wygładzić (się) *pf.* *zob.* **wygładzać (się)**.

wygłaszać *ipf.* deliver, make, give; **wygłaszać mowę** *l.* **przemówienie** deliver *l.* make *l.* give a speech; **wygłaszać hymny pochwalne na czyjąś cześć** give a hymn of praise to sb, praise sb.

wygłodniały *a.* ravenous, starving.

wygłodnieć *pf.* famish, be starving, be extremely hungry.

wygłodzić *się* *pf.* famish, be starving.

wygłodzony *a.* **-eni** ravenous, starving.

wygłos *mi fon.* (word- *l.* syllable-)final position, auslaut; **ubezdźwięcznianie w wygłosie** final devoicing.

wygłosić *pf.* **-szę -sisz** deliver, make, give; **wygłosić mowę** *l.* **przemówienie** deliver *l.* make *l.* give a speech.

wygłosowy *a.* *fon.* (word- *l.* syllable-)final.

wygłup *mi pot.* prank, caper, antics.

wygłupiać się *ipf.*, **wygłupić się** *pf.* **1.** (= *zacho-*

wywać się głupio) act *l.* play the fool; **nie wygłu- piaj się!** stop being silly, stop acting *l.* playing the fool. **2.** *tylko ipf.* (= *żartować*) fool *l.* play around.

wygłupy *pl. Gen.* -ów clowning, toomfoolery.

wygłuszać *ipf.*, **wygłuszyć** *pf.* **1.** soundproof, deaden; muffle. **2.** deaden, lessen, soothe.

wygnać *pf. zob.* **wygonić**.

wygnanie *n.* exile; **na wygnaniu** in exile.

wygnaniec *mp* -ńc- *pl.* -y exile.

wygniatać *ipf.* **1.** (= *cisnąc, odsączać*) squeeze. **2.** (= *robić ciasto*) knead. **3.** (= *odciskać wzór*) impress, imprint.

wygnić *pf.* -gnije **1.** (= *zgnić*) rot. **2.** (= *zgnić od środka*) rot through.

wygnieciony *a.* crumpled, wrinkled.

wygnieść *pf.* -gniotę -gnieciesz, -gniótł -gniotła -gnietli **1.** *zob.* **wygniatać**. **2.** (= *zmiąć*) crumple, wrinkle, rumple. ~ **się** *pf.* (= *zmiąć się*) crumple, wrinkle, rumple.

wygoda *f. Gen.pl.* -ód **1.** (*coś co dogadza*) com- fort; **dla własnej wygody** for one's own comfort; **mieć z kimś** *l.* **z czymś wygodę** find sb *l.* sth use- ful. **2.** (*udogodnienie*) convenience; **wygody** amenities.

wygodnicki *mp żart., iron.* person who likes to be comfortable, lazy person, loafer.

wygodnictwo *n. żart., iron.* avoidance of in- convenience, enjoying comfort, laziness.

wygodnie *adv.* comfortably.

wygodny *a.* **1.** (= *dający komfort*) comfort- able. **2.** (= *dogodny*) convenient. **3.** (= *dogadza- jący sobie*) lazy; self-indulgent; **jestem zbyt wy- godny, żeby tam iść pieszo** I am too lazy to walk there.

wygoić *pf.* -goję -goisz, -gój heal. ~ **się** *pf.* heal (up *l.* over).

wygolić *pf.* -gól (*zarost*) shave (off *l.* away). ~ **się** *pf.* (= *ogolić się*) shave.

wygolony *a.* -eni shaven, shaved; clean- shaven.

wygon *mi roln.* **1.** (*pastwisko*) common pas- ture(land). **2.** (*droga*) cattle path.

wygonić *pf. zob.* **wyganiać**.

wygospodarować *pf.*, **wygospodarowywać** *ipf.* save up.

wygotować (się) *pf.* = **wygotowywać (się)**.

wygotowywać *ipf.* boil. ~ **się** *ipf.* boil away.

wygódka *f. Gen.pl.* -ek *pot.* toilet.

wygórowany *a.* (*o sumie, cenie*) exorbitant, outrageous; (*o ambicjach, żądaniach*) excessive.

wygrabiać *ipf.*, **wygrabić** *pf.* rake.

wygrać *pf.* **1.** *zob.* **wygrywać**. **2.** *teatr* act.

wygramolić się *pf. pot.* clamber out.

wygrana *f. Gen.* -ej (*rzecz*) prize; (*pieniądze*) winnings; (*zwycięstwo*) victory; **główna wygrana** main prize; **dać za wygraną** give up.

wygrawerować *pf. zob.* **grawerować**.

wygrażać *ipf.* threaten; **wygrażać komuś pię- ścią** shake one's fist at sb.

wygrywać *ipf.* -am -asz **1.** (= *uzyskiwać nagro- dę*) win; **wygrać w totolotka** win the lottery; **wy- grać na wyścigach** win at the races; **wygrać za- kład** win a bet; **wygrać los na loterii** hit the jack-

pot; **nie wygrałem nóg na loterii** *pot.* I won't go there. **2.** (= *zwyciężać*) win, defeat. **3.** (*wykorzy- stywać*) exploit. **4.** *tylko ipf.* (*grać na instrumen- cie*) play.

wygrywająca *f. Gen.* -ej *zob.* **wygrywający**.

wygrywający *mp* winner. – *a.* winning.

wygryzać *ipf.*, **wygryźć** *pf.* -gryzę -gryziesz, -gryź, -gryzł -gryźli **1.** (= *gryząc, usuwać*) fret; **wygryzać dziurę** fret a hole. **2.** (= *gryząc, zjadać*) eat up. **3.** *pot.* (= *pozbawiać kogoś stanowiska*) drive out of office by intrigues.

wygrzać (się) *pf.* -eję -ejesz *zob.* **wygrzewać (się)**.

wygrzebać (się) *pf.* -bię -biesz *zob.* **wygrzeby- wać (się)**.

wygrzebywać *ipf.* **1.** (= *grzebiąc, wydostać*) dig out, dig up. **2.** (= *odszukać*) dig out, dig up. **3.** (= *zrobić dołek*) dig out. ~ **się** *ipf.* **1.** *pot.* (= *być gotowym*) be ready; **ciągle nie mogę się wy- grzebać na czas** I can never be ready on time. **2.** (= *wydostać się*) get out; *przen.* recover, get out.

wygrzewać *ipf.* warm, make warm. ~ **się** *ipf.* warm o.s.; **wygrzewać się na słońcu** bask in the sun.

wygrzmocić *pf. pot.* **1.** (= *uderzyć*) hit; **wy- grzmocić czymś w coś** hit sth on *l.* in sth. **2.** (= *zbić*) baste, thrash, cudgel; **wygrzmocić kogoś czymś** thrash sb with sth.

wygubić *pf. lit.* exterminate, wipe out.

wyguzdrać się *pf.* -dram *l.* -drzę -drasz *l.* -drzesz, -draj *l.* -drz stop dawdling.

wygwieździć *pf. poet.* star-spangle.

wygwieżdżony *a. poet.* starry; **wygwieżdżone niebo** star-spangled sky.

wygwizdać *pf.* -gwiżdżę -gwiżdżesz, **wygwizdy- wać** *ipf.* **1.** (= *zagwizdać coś*) whistle. **2.** (= *wy- razić dezaprobatę*) boo, hoot, hiss.

wygwizdów *mi* -o- *pot.* backwater, mudhole, middle of nowhere.

wyhaftować *pf. zob.* **haftować**.

wyhamować *pf.* (*pojazd*) bring to a stop.

wyhasać się *pf.* dance to one's heart content; gambol to one's heart content.

wyhodować *pf. zob.* **hodować**.

wyidealizować *pf. zob.* **idealizować**.

wyidealizowany *a.* idealized.

wyimaginować *pf.* imagine, dream up.

wyimaginowany *a.* imaginary.

wyimek *mi* -mk- *Gen.* -a (= *fragment*) excerpt.

wyimpasować *pf. brydż* finesse (*a card*).

wyizolować (się) *pf. zob.* **izolować (się)**.

wyjadacz *mp* **stary wyjadacz** *pot.* old stager.

wyjadać *ipf.* eat up; **kto wyjadł ciastka?** who ate up the cookies?

wyjadę *itd. pf. zob.* **wyjechać**.

wyjaławiać *ipf.*, **wyjałowić** *pf.* -ów **1.** (= *czynić nieurodzajnym*) impoverish. **2.** *med.* sterilize, render sterile. **3.** *przen.* (= *pozbawiać potrzeb intelektualnych*) impoverish, drain.

wyjałowieć *pf.* become impoverished; become sterile.

wyjałowiony *a.* **1.** (= *nieurodzajny*) impover- ished. **2.** *med.* sterilized, sterile, aseptic. **3.**

przen. (= *pozbawiony potrzeb intelektualnych*) impoverished, drained.

wyjaskrawiać *ipf.*, **wyjaskrawić** *pf.* exaggerate, bring to excess.

wyjaskrawiony *a.* exaggerated.

wyjaśniać *ipf.* **1.** (= *objaśniać*) explain. **2.** (= *uzasadniać*) justify; (*sprawę, nieporozumienie*) clear, straighten out. ~ **się** *ipf.* **1.** (= *stawać się zrozumiałym*) become clear, be cleared up. **2.** (= *stawać się jaśniejszym*) clear up; **wyjaśniło się na zachodzie** it's cleared up in the west.

wyjaśnić (się) *pf.* **-ij** *zob.* **wyjaśniać (się)**.

wyjaśnienie *n.* **1.** (= *objaśnienie*) explanation, clarification. **2.** (= *usprawiedliwienie*) explanation, justification.

wyjawiać *ipf.*, **wyjawić** *pf.* reveal, disclose.

wyjazd *mi Loc.* **-eździe 1.** (= *wyruszenie w drogę*) departure; **data wyjazdu** departure date. **2.** (= *podróż*) journey, trip, voyage; **wyjazd służbowy** business trip. **3.** (= *droga wyjazdowa, wyjście*) exit.

wyjazdowy *a.* travel(ing); departure; outgoing; exit; **mecz wyjazdowy** *l.* **na wyjeździe** *sport* away game *l.* match.

wyjąć *pf.* **-mę -miesz, -mij** *zob.* **wyjmować**.

wyjąkać *pf.* stutter (out), stammer (out); falter.

wyjątek *mi* **-tk- 1.** (= *odstępstwo od reguły*) exception; **wyjątek od reguły** exception to the rule; **zrobić dla kogoś wyjątek** make an exception for sb; **wszyscy bez wyjątku** nobody excepted; **z wyjątkiem kogoś** *l.* **czegoś** with the exception of sb *l.* sth; **z małymi wyjątkami** with some exceptions; **wyjątek potwierdza regułę** exception proves the rule; **w drodze wyjątku** by way of an exception. **2.** (= *ktoś, coś wyjątkowego, nadzwyczajnego*) sth *l.* sb exceptional; **on jest chlubnym wyjątkiem** he's a remarkable exception; **tego typu silniki należą do wyjątków** engines of that type are an exception. **3.** (= *fragment*) excerpt, fragment.

wyjątkowo *adv.* **1.** (= *szczególnie*) exceptionally, uniquelly. **2.** (= *w wyjątkowych okolicznościach*) unusually; **dziś wyjątkowo nie pada** quite unusually, it's not raining today; **w tym tygodniu wyjątkowo to ona ma dyżur** this week, quite unusually, she's is on duty.

wyjątkowość *f.* exceptionality, uniqueness.

wyjątkowy *a.* exceptional, unique, rare; **mieć wyjątkowe szczęście** be exceptionally lucky; **stan wyjątkowy** *prawn.* state of emergency.

wyjechać *pf.* **-jadę -jedziesz** *zob.* **wyjeżdżać**.

wyjednać *pf.*, **wyjednywać** *ipf.* obtain by persuasion.

wyjeść *pf.* **-jem -jesz -jedzą, -jedz, -jadł jedli** *zob.* **wyjadać**.

wyjeździć *pf.* **-jeżdżę -jeździsz 1.** (= *wyżłobić, zniszczyć jeżdżeniem*) rut. **2.** (= *jeżdżąc, zużyć l. nadwyrężyć*) wear (out *l.* down). ~ **się** *pf.* (= *zmęczyć się podróżowaniem*) do a lot of driving *l.* riding *l.* travelling.

wyjeżdżać *ipf.* **1.** (= *opuszczać jakieś miejsce*) (*w podróż, za granicę, do Wrocławia, do babci, z miasta, z kraju*) leave; (*z garażu, na drogę*) go *l.* drive out; **jutro wyjeżdżamy** we're leaving tomor-

row; **wyjechać do Kanady** leave for Canada; (*na stałe*) emigrate to Canada; **wyjechać na czymś** *pot.* take advantage of sth, use sth to one's benefit; **wyjechać na wakacje** go on vacation. **2.** *pot.* (= *zachowywać się nietaktownie*) make a rude remark; **wyjechać z pyskiem** bawl out.

wyjęty *a.* **wyjęty spod prawa** outlaw.

wyjmować *ipf.* **1.** (= *wyciągać*) take out, remove; get out; (*listy*) collect; **wyjmować coś z kieszeni** take sth out of one's pocket; **z ust mi to wyjąłeś** *pot.* you took the words out of my mouth. **2.** (= *wydzielić*) extract; separate; remove. **3.** *przest.* (= *wykluczać*) exclude; **wyjąwszy kogoś** *lit.* apart from sb, except sb, sb excepted.

wyjrzeć *pf.* **-ę -ysz, -yj** *zob.* **wyglądać**.

wyjście *n.* **1.** (= *wychodzenie*) departure; **punkt wyjścia** starting point; **po jego wyjściu** after he left. **2.** (= *miejsce, przez które się wychodzi*) exit, way out; **wyjście przeciwpożarowe** fire escape. **3.** (= *sposób przeprowadzenia sprawy*) solution, way out; **sytuacja bez wyjścia** dead end, blind alley; **jedynym wyjściem jest...** the only solution is...; **nie mamy wyjścia** we have no choice. **4.** *komp.* output. **5.** *techn.* outlet.

wyjściowy *a.* **1.** (= *służący do wychodzenia*) exit. **2.** (= *podstawowy*) initial. **3.** *pot.* (= *elegancki, odświętny*) special, best.

wyjść *pf.* **wyjdę wyjdziesz wyszedł wyszła wyszli** *zob.* **wychodzić**.

wyka *f. bot.* vetch, tare (*Vicia*).

wykadrować *pf.* film frame.

wykaligrafować *pf. zob.* **kaligrafować**.

wykalkulować *pf.* (= *dojść do wniosku*) **1.** figure out. **2.** *przest.* calculate.

wykałaczka *f. Gen.pl.* **-ek 1.** (*do zębów*) toothpick. **2.** (*do przekąsek*) toothpick.

wykantować *pf. pot.* gyp, con, rip off.

wykańczać *ipf.* **1.** (= *doprowadzać do końca*) complete, finish (up); put the finishing touches on. **2.** (= *zużywać całkowicie*) use up, finish (up *l.* off). **3.** *pot.* (= *niszczyć kogoś*) do in; finish (off); **wykańczać kogoś nerwowo** shatter sb's nerves; **wykończyła ją choroba** illness turned her into a wreck; illness did her in. ~ **się** *ipf.* **1.** *pot.* (= *doprowadzać się do złego samopoczucia*) ruin one's health; **wykańczać się nerwowo** become a nervous wreck. **2.** (= *zużywać się całkowicie*) be out of gas, be burned out.

wykańczalnia *f. Gen.pl.* **-i** *techn., zwł. tk.* finishing shop.

wykapany *a.* the picture, spit and image, spitting image, exact likeness; **wykapany ojciec** the picture of his father, the spitting image of his father.

wykaraskać się *pf.* **1.** *pot.* (= *wydostać się skądś*) get out. **2.** *pot.* (= *wybrnąć z kłopotów*) get out of trouble.

wykarczować *pf.* grub (up *l.* out).

wykarmić *pf.* **1.** (= *nakarmić własnym mlekiem*) feed. **2.** (= *utrzymać*) support, maintain.

wykasować *pf.* erase; delete.

wykastrować *pf.* castrate, emasculate, geld.

wykaszleć *pf.* **-lę -lesz, -l** *l.* **-laj** cough up *l.* out. ~ **się** *pf.* stop coughing.

wykaz *mi* list, listing, register, roll; statement, schedule, specification.

wykazać (się) *pf.* -żę -żesz *zob.* **wykazywać (się)**.

wykazywać *ipf.* 1. (= *pokazywać, unaoczniać*) show; reveal. 2. (= *dawać czemuś wyraz*) show, display. 3. (= *stwierdzać*) prove, demonstrate. ~ **się** *ipf.* (= *udowadniać*) prove o.s.; **wykazać się czymś** show sth.

wykąpać *pf.* -pię -piesz 1. (*umyć*) bathe. 2. *chem.* bathe, rinse, wash. ~ **się** *pf.* take a bath (*w wannie*), bathe (*w morzu*).

wykidajło *mp decl. like f. in sing. pl.* -y *l.* -owie *pot.* bouncer.

wykiełkować *pf. zob.* **kiełkować**.

wykierować *pf.* 1. (= *skierować*) direct. 2. *pot.* (= *pokierować*) guide, direct; **wykierować kogoś na człowieka** make a man (out) of sb. ~ **się** *pf. pot.* become.

wykipieć *pf.* -pię -pisz boil over.

wykitować *ipf. pot.* croak, kick the bucket, bite the dust.

wykiwać *pf.* -am -asz *pot.* (= *oszukać*) dupe, con, rip off.

wyklarować *pf.* 1. (= *uczynić przezroczystym*) clear, clarify, purify. 2. *pot.* (= *wyjaśnić*) clarify, explain. ~ **się** *pf.* 1. (= *stać się przezroczystym*) clear, clarify, purify. 2. (= *wyjaśnić się*) become clear, be cleared up.

wyklaskać *pf.* -klaszczę -klaszczesz *l.* -klaskam -klaskasz, **wyklaskiwać** *ipf.* 1. (= *wybić rytm*) clap (the rhythm). 2. *pot.* (*dać wyraz dezaprobaty*) give (sb) a slow handclap, jeer (sb) off the stage; (*wywołać ponownie na scenę*) call for an encore.

wykląć *pf.* -klnę -klniesz, -klnij, **wyklinać** *ipf.* 1. (= *wyrzec się kogoś*) curse. 2. *rel.* excommunicate.

wykleić *pf.* -eję -eisz, **wyklejać** *ipf.* (= *okleić*) line, stick *l.* glue paper, fabric, etc. to sth; **wykleić tapetą** hang wallpaper.

wyklejanka *f. Gen.pl.* -ek cut and paste picture, colored paper mosaic.

wyklejka *f. Gen.pl.* -ek *druk.* endpaper, end paper, end sheet.

wyklepać *pf.* -pię -piesz, **wyklepywać** *ipf.* 1. (= *klepiąc, nadać kształt*) hammer, beat out. 2. *tylko pf. pot.* (= *powiedzieć coś niepotrzebnie*) spill the beans, let out a secret. 3. *tylko pf. pot.* (= *powiedzieć coś bezmyślnie*) rattle off.

wykluczać *ipf.* (*ewentualność, możliwość*) exclude, rule out; (*o okolicznościach, przesłankach*) preclude; **wykluczyć kogoś z organizacji** expel sb from an organization; **wykluczyć zawodnika** *sport* send a player off; disqualify a player. ~ **się** *ipf.* be mutually exclusive.

wykluczony *a.* impossible; **to jest wykluczone!** it's out of the question.

wykluczyć *pf. zob.* **wykluczać**.

wykluć się *pf.*, **wykluwać się** *ipf.* 1. (*o pisklętach*) hatch. 2. *przen.* (= *powstać*) hatch, evolve, spring up; **nowy pomysł wykluł mi się w głowie** a new idea evolved in my head.

wykład *mi* 1. *uniw.* lecture; **prowadzić wykład**

z fizyki jądrowej lecture on nuclear physics; **cykl wykładów** series of lectures; **wykład fakultatywny** facultative *l.* elective *l.* optional lecture; **chodzić na wykłady** attend lectures; **rozumieć wykład** follow a lecture. 2. (= *sposób przedstawienia*) presentation.

wykładać *ipf.* 1. (= *wydobywać*) lay out, (put on) display, exhibit; **wyłożyć karty (na stół)** put *l.* lay one's cards on the table; **wyłożyć piłkę** *piłka nożna* pass the ball precisely to where you want it to be; **wyłożyć coś jak na patelni** *l.* **wyłożyć kawę na ławę** give sth to sb straight, spell sth out for sb. 2. (= *kłaść*) put, place. 3. (= *okładać*) cover; line; **wykładać podłogę dywanem** carpet the floor; **wykładać podłogę płytkami** tile the floor; **wykładać czymś szufladę** line a drawer with sth; **wykładać ścianę boazerią** panel the walls; **wykładać ścianę kafelkami** tile the walls; **wykładać ścianę tapetami** hang wallpaper (on the walls). 4. (= *płacić*) lay out. 5. (= *przedstawiać*) expound, set forth, present. 6. *tylko ipf. uniw.* lecture; **wykładać na uniwersytecie** work at a university; **wykładać gramatykę** lecture on grammar. ~ **się** *ipf.* 1. *pot.* (= *przewracać się*) fall (down). 2. *roln.* be lodged.

wykładnia *f. Gen.pl.* -i form. explanation, clarification; **wykładnia prawa** *prawn.* interpretation of the law.

wykładnik *mi Gen.* -a *mat.* exponent.

wykładowca *mp uniw.* lecturer.

wykładowy *a. uniw.* lecture; **język wykładowy** language of instruction; **sala wykładowa** lecture hall.

wykładzina *f.* fitted carpet; *zwł. techn.* lining.

wykłócać się *ipf.*, **wykłócić się** *pf.* argue; **wykłócać się z kimś o coś** argue with sb about sth.

wykłuć *pf.*, **wykłuwać** *ipf.* 1. (= *wyłupić*) gouge out; **ciemno, choć oko wykol** pitch dark; **kruk krukowi oka nie wykole** dog does not eat dog. 2. (= *wytatuować*) tatoo.

wykoleić (się) *pf.* -eję -eisz = **wykolejać (się)**.

wykolejać *ipf.* 1. *zwł. kol., t. transport miejski* derail; **wykoleić pociąg** derail a train. 2. *przen.* (= *zmienić czyjeś życie*) lead astray; ruin sb's life. ~ **się** *ipf.* 1. *zwł. kol., t. transport miejski* derail, become derailed. 2. (= *zmienić swoje życie*) be lead astray; ruin one's own life.

wykolejenie *n.* 1. *zwł. kol., t. transport miejski* derailment. 2. (= *odstępstwo od normy*) irregularity; error, erroneous form; **wykolejenie językowe** irregular *l.* erroneous form.

wykolejeniec *mp* -ńc- *pl.* -y derelict, outcast; *sl.* dreg.

wykolejony *a.* -eni 1. (= *zdeprawowany*) outcast, depraved. 2. (= *zdeformowany*) erroneous.

wykołować *pf.* 1. *pot.* (= *oszukać*) dupe, con, rip off. 2. *lotn.* taxi.

wykombinować *pf.* 1. (= *wymyślić*) think out. 2. *pot.* (= *postarać się*) come up with.

wykonać *pf. zob.* **wykonywać**.

wykonalność *f.* feasibility, practicability, workability.

wykonalny *a.* 1. (= *możliwy do realizacji*) feasible, practicable, workable, doable. **2.** *prawn.* enforceable.

wykonanie *n.* **1.** (= *doprowadzenie do skutku*) execution. **2.** (= *jakość*) workmanship, quality. **3.** *muz.* (= *interpretacja*) interpretation; performance, rendition.

wykonany *a.* done, executed; (*o utworze*) performed; **wykonany z drewna** made of wood.

wykonawca *mp* **1.** *bud.*, *techn.* contractor; executor; **wykonawca wyroku** executor; **wykonawcą rzutu wolnego będzie...** the free kick *l.* throw will be taken by... **2.** *muz.* performer, player. **3.** *teatr* performer, actor.

wykonawczy *a.* executive; **władza wykonawcza** executive power.

wykonawczyni *f.* **1.** *muz.* performer, player. **2.** *teatr* performer, actress.

wykonawstwo *n.* *bud.* contracting.

wykoncypować *pf.* *żart.* think out, work out.

wykonywać *ipf.* **1.** (*plan, polecenie, zadanie*) carry out, execute; (*doświadczenie, badania, operację, obowiązki*) carry out, perform; (*robotę, ćwiczenie*) do; (*odlew, otwór, obrót*) make; **wykonywać zawód nauczyciela** work as a teacher. **2.** (=*wytwarzać*) make; produce, manufacture, put out. **3.** *muz.* perform, play. **4.** *teatr* perform, play, act.

wykonywany *a.* **1.** (*o planie, poleceniu, zadaniu*) carried out, executed; (*o doświadczeniu, badaniach, operacji, obowiązkach*) carried out, performed; (*o robocie, ćwiczeniu*) done; (*o odlewie, otworze, obrocie*) made; **zawód wykonywany** occupation. **2.** (= *wytwarzany*) made. **3.** *muz.* performed, played, rendered. **4.** *teatr* performed, played, acted.

wykończać (się) *ipf.* = **wykańczać (się)**.

wykończenie *n.* **1.** (= *doprowadzenie do końca*) completion, finish; conclusion. **2.** (= *wystrój*) (*domu*) décor, decor; (*materiału, mebla*) finish; (*brzegu, krawędzi*) trim.

wykończeniowy *a.* *zwł.* *bud.*, *techn.* finishing.

wykończony *a.* **-eni** finished; completed; **jestem wykończony** I am exhausted.

wykończyć (się) *pf.* *zob.* **wykańczać (się)**.

wykop *mi* (*rów*) pit, excavation; trench, ditch.

wykopać (się) *pf.* **-pię -piesz** *zob.* **wykopywać (się)**.

wykopalisko *n.* *archeol.* **1.** (*zabytek*) find. **2.** (*miejsce*) excavation; *pl.* (*teren, prace archeologiczne*) excavations, excavation works.

wykopaliskowy *a.* *archeol.* excavation, excavating.

wykopcić *pf.* *pot.* puff, drag, pull; **wykopcić paczkę papierosów** smoke a pack *l.* packet of cigarettes.

wykopki *pl.* Gen. **-ów** **1.** *roln.* digging up, harvesting of root crops. **2.** *żart.* (*remont dróg*) roadworks.

wykopnąć *pf.* **-ij** kick.

wykopy *pl.* Gen. **-ów** (*roboty ziemne*) earthworks.

wykopyrtnąć się *pf.* **-ij** *pot.* fall.

wykopywać *ipf.* **1.** (= *kopiąc, robić dół*) dig. **2.** (= *kopiąc, wydobywać coś*) dig up *l.* out. **3.** *pot.*

(= *wyrzucać kogoś*) kick out. **~ się** *ipf.* dig one's way out.

wykorkować *pf.* *pot.* (= *umrzeć*) croak, kick the bucket, drop off.

wykorzeniać *ipf.* **1.** (= *usuwać*) root out, eradicate, uproot. **2.** *ogr.* root out, uproot. **~ się** *ipf.* be eradicated.

wykorzenić (się) *pf.* *zob.* **wykorzeniać (się)**.

wykorzystać *pf.*, **wykorzystywać** *ipf.* **1.** (= *osiągnąć korzyść*) take advantage of, avail o.s. of; **maksymalnie coś wykorzystać** make the most of sth; **nie wykorzystać okazji** *l.* **sposobności** waste an opportunity. **2.** (= *użyć*) use, make use of; **wykorzystać urlop** use one's vacation. **3.** (= *wyzyskać kogoś*) exploit; abuse.

wykosić *pf.* **-koszę -kosisz** **1.** (= *skosić*) mow. **2.** *pot.* (= *zabić*) mow down.

wykosztować się *pf.*, **wykosztowywać się** *ipf.* go to great expense; **wykosztować się na prezent** buy an expensive gift.

wykoślawiać *ipf.* twist, crook (*sth*). **~ się** *ipf.* twist, crook.

wykoślawić (się) *pf.* *zob.* **wykoślawiać (się)**.

wykpić (się) *pf.* **-ij** *zob.* **wykpiwać (się)**.

wykpiwać *ipf.* **-am -asz** ridicule, mock. **~ się** *ipf.* **1.** get out of doing; **wykpić się od wygłoszenia referatu** get out of delivering a paper. **2.** get away with; **wykpić się od kary** get away with one's crime *l.* offense.

wykraczać *ipf.* **1.** (= *dopuszczać się przewinienia*) violate, infringe, contravene, transgress; **wykroczyć przeciwko prawu** violate the law, be in breach of the law. **2.** (= *wychodzić poza zwyczajowe granice*) be *l.* go beyond, exceed; **zadanie wykracza poza moje obowiązki** this task goes beyond my responsibilities.

wykradać *ipf.* **1.** (= *brać po kryjomu*) steal, pilfer. **2.** (= *porywać kogoś*) abduct. **~ się** *ipf.* sneak out, steal out.

wykrajać *ipf.* *zob.* **wykrawać**.

wykrakać *pf.* **-czę -czesz** *pot.* croak, prophesy trouble.

wykraść (się) *pf.* **-kradnę -kradniesz, -kradnij** *zob.* **wykradać (się)**.

wykrawać *ipf.* **1.** (= *wycinać*) cut out. **2.** (*trochę wolnego czasu, pieniędzy*) set aside.

wykreować (się) *pf.* *zob.* **kreować (się)**.

wykres *mi* graph, chart, diagram; **przedstawić na wykresie** plot, chart.

wykreślać *ipf.*, **wykreślić** *pf.* **1.** (= *kreśląc, usuwać*) cross out, strike out; **wykreślić kogoś z pamięci** expunge sb from one's memory. **2.** (= *robić wykres*) plot, chart.

wykreślny *a.* *geom.* graphical; **geometria wykreślna** descriptive geometry.

wykręcać *ipf.* **1.** (= *kręcąc, odłączać*) (*śrubę, żarówkę*) unscrew; (= *demontować*) remove. **2.** (= *przekręcać*) (*szyję, rękę*) twist; **wykręcić komuś rękę** twist sb's arm. **3.** *tel.* (*numer*) dial. **4.** (= *osuszać*) (*bieliznę, pranie*) wring (out). **5.** *pot.* **wykręcić komuś numer** take sb for a ride. **~się** *ipf.* **1.** (*wymigać się*) cop out, weasel out (*od czegoś* of sth); **wykręcić się sianem** get off lightly.

2. (= *robić zwrot*) turn; **wykręcić się na pięcie** turn *l.* spin on one's heel.

wykręcić (się) *pf. zob.* **wykręcać (się)**.

wykręt *mi* excuse.

wykrętnie *adv.* (*odpowiadać, tłumaczyć*) evasively.

wykrętny *a.* (*o słowach, odpowiedzi*) evasive.

wykrochmalić *pf.* (*bieliznę*) starch.

wykroczenie *n. prawn.* (minor) offense; **wykroczenie drogowe** traffic violation; **kolegium do spraw wykroczeń** *hist.* magistrate court.

wykroczyć *pf. zob.* **wykraczać**.

wykroić *pf.* **-kroję -kroisz, -krój** *zob.* **wykrawać**.

wykrojnik *mi Gen.* **-a** *techn.* blanking die.

wykrok *mi sport* lunge.

wykropkować *pf.*, **wykropkowywać** *ipf.* (= *zastąpić kropkami*) prick out; (= *zaznaczyć kropkami*) dot; **wykropkowany** (*o słowie*) blanked.

wykrot *mi* **1.** (= *dziura*) pit, hole. **2.** *arch.* (= *zwalone drzewo*) fallen tree.

wykrój *mi* **-o-** *Gen.pl.* **-ów 1.** (*forma*) pattern; (*kształt*) shape. **2.** (= *otwór*) opening.

wykruszać *ipf.* **1.** (*niszczyć*) crumble. **2.** (*wydobywać*) (*ziarno*) shell. **~się** *ipf.* **1.** (= *odpadać*) drop out. **2.** (= *znikać*) vanish. **3.** (*niszczyć się*) crumble. **4.** (*o nasionach*) (= *wysypywać się*) shell.

wykruszyć (się) *pf. zob.* **wykruszać (się)**.

wykrwawiać się *ipf.*, **wykrwawić się** *pf.* (= *tracić krew*) *t. przen.* bleed (to death).

wykryć (się) *pf.* **-kryję -kryjesz, -kryj** *zob.* **wykrywać (się)**.

wykrystalizować *pf.*, **wykrystalizowywać** *ipf. chem.* crystallize. **~ się** *pf.*, **wykrystalizowywać się** *ipf.* **1.** (= *skonkretyzować się*) take shape, crystallize. **2.** *chem.* crystallize.

wykrywacz *mi Gen.* **-a** detector; **wykrywacz kłamstw/min** lie/mine detector.

wykrywać *ipf.* **-am -asz 1.** (= *badając, ustalać obecność czegoś*) (*wirus, pierwiastek, obecność ołowiu w wodzie*) detect. **2.** (= *wynajdować*) discover. **3.** (= *ujawniać*) uncover. **~ się** *ipf.* (= *wychodzić na jaw*) come out.

wykrywalność *n.* detection; **stopień wykrywalności przestępstw** crime detection rate.

wykrywalny *a.* (*o zmianie chorobowej, przestępstwie*) detectable.

wykrzesać *pf.* **-szę -szesz, wykrzesywać** *ipf.* **1.** (*także* **wykrzesać z siebie**) (*zapał, energię*) muster, summon (up). **2.** (*iskry, płomień*) strike.

wykrztusić *pf.* **-szę -sisz, wykrztuszać** *ipf.* **1.** (= *odkaszlnąć*) cough up, choke out. **2.** (*słowa*) cough out; **nie mogła wykrztusić słowa** she couldn't utter a word.

wykrztuśnie *adv.* (*działać*) as an expectorant.

wykrztuśny *a.* (*o leku*) expectorant.

wykrzyczeć *pf.* **-ę -ysz** shout out. **~ się** *pf.* shout it out.

wykrzykiwać *ipf.*, **wykrzyknąć** *pf.* **-ij** shout (out).

wykrzyknienie *n. gram.* (*część mowy*) interjection.

wykrzyknik *mi Gen.* **-a 1.** (*znak interpunkcyj-*

---

ny) exclamation mark *l.* point. **2.** *gram.* (*część mowy*) interjection.

wykrzyknikowy *a.* **zdanie wykrzyknikowe** *jęz.* exclamatory sentence.

wykrzywiać *ipf.* (*słup*) bend; (*deskę*) warp; (*twarz*) contort; **wykrzywić twarz** (= *skrzywić się*) screw (up) one's face. **~się** *ipf.* **1.** (= *skrzywiać się*) (*o słupie*) bend, get crooked; (*o belce*) warp. **2.** (= *robić grymas*) make a face.

wykrzywić (się) *pf. zob.* **wykrzywiać (się)**.

wykrzywiony *a.* (= *nie prosty*) crooked; (*o twarzy*) contorted.

wykształcać *ipf.* **1.** (= *rozwijać*) develop. **2.** (= *formować*) form. **~ się** *ipf.* **1.** (= *rozwijać się*) develop. **2.** (= *formować się*) form.

wykształcenie *n.* education; **wykształcenie podstawowe/średnie/wyższe** primary/secondary/higher education; **bez wykształcenia** uneducated; **zdobyć wykształcenie** get an education; **nauczyciel** *itd.* **z wykształcenia** teacher, etc. by profession.

wykształcić *pf.* **1.** *zob.* **wykształcać. 2.** (= *dać wykształcenie*) educate; **wykształcić kogoś na prawnika** educate sb to become a lawyer. **~ się** *pf.* **1.** *zob.* **wykształcać się. 2.** (= *zdobyć wykształcenie*) get an education, educate o.s.

wykształcony *a.* **1.** (= *wyedukowany*) educated. **2.** *t. biol.* (= *rozwinięty*) developed.

wykuć *pf. zob.* **wykuwać**.

wykup *mi* **1.** *ekon.* (*spółki*) buyout. **2.** *handl.* (*towarów*) buyup. **3.** (*obligacji*) buyback, redemption.

wykupić (się) *pf. zob.* **wykupywać (się)**.

wykupywać *ipf.* **1.** *handl.* (*zapas, towary*) buy up. **2.** *ekon.* (*spółkę, udziały*) buy out. **3.** (= *odkupić*) *zwł. ekon.* buy back, redeem. **4.** *handl.* (*abonament, subskrypcję*) take out. **5.** **wykupić kogoś z aresztu** bail sb out. **~ się** *ipf.* (= *wyswobadzać się*) buy o.s. out.

wykurować (się) *pf. pot. zob.* **wyleczyć (się)**.

wykurzać *ipf.*, **wykurzyć** *pf.* (= *wypłoszyć dymem, wyganiać*) smoke out.

wykusz *mi Gen.* **-a** *bud.* bay window.

wykuszowy *a.* **okno wykuszowe** *bud.* bay window.

wykuwać *ipf.* **1.** (*z metalu*) forge; (*z kamienia*) sculpt. **2.** (*otwór, tunel*) cut; (*zwł. z mozołem*) hammer. **3.** *gł. pf. szkoln.* cram.

wykwalifikowany *a.* (*o nauczycielu, kadrze, pracowniku*) qualified; **wykwalifikowana siła robocza** skilled labor.

wykwaterować *pf.*, **wykwaterowywać** *ipf.* evict.

wykwintnie *adv.* exquisitely, luxuriously.

wykwintność *f.* refinement.

wykwintny *a.* refined, exquisite.

wykwit *mi* **1.** *pat.* eruption, efflorescence. **2.** *geol., lit.* efflorescence. **3.** *bot.* slime mold (*Fuligo*).

wylać (się) *pf.* **-leję -lejesz -lali** *l.* **-leli** *zob.* **wylewać (się)**.

wylansować *pf. zob.* **lansować**.

wylatać *pf.* **1.** *lotn.* (*ileś godzin, kilometrów*) log. **2.** *pot.* (= *załatwić z trudem*) (finally) get one's hands on. **~ się** *pf.* **1.** (= *spędzić dużo cza-*

su w powietrzu) have one's fill of flying. **2.** *pot.* (= *pobiegać sobie*) run around to one's heart's content.

wylatywać *ipf.* **1.** (= *wzbijać się w powietrze*) take off, fly off. **2.** (= *wypadać*) fall out. **3.** (= *wydobywać się*) escape. **4.** *pot.* (= *wybiegać*) shoot out. **5.** *pot.* (= *być wyrzuconym*) get the boot. **6. wyleciało mi to z głowy** *pot.* it slipped my mind; **wylatywać w powietrze** blow up.

wyląc się *pf.* **-lęgnie -lągł -lęgła** *zob.* **wylęgać się**.

wylądować *pf.* **1.** (*o statku powietrznym*) land. **2.** *pot.* (= *znaleźć się gdzieś*) end up, land; **w domu wylądowaliśmy dopiero po północy** we didn't get home until after midnight, we got home only after midnight.

wyląg, wylęg *mi* **-ę-** *orn., zool.* **1.** (= *wykluwanie się*) hatching. **2.** (= *lęg*) hatch, brood.

wylec *pf.* **-legnie, -legnij, -legł** *zob.* **wylegać**.

wylecieć *pf.* **-cę -cisz** *zob.* **wylatywać**.

wyleczyć *pf.* **1.** (*chorego, chorobę*) cure; **wyleczyć kogoś z czegoś** cure sb of sth. **2.** *przen.* (= *odzwyczaić*) rid sb of sth. **~ się** *pf.* (= *odzyskać zdrowie*) recover; **wyleczyć się z czegoś** *t. przen.* get over sth.

wylegać *ipf.* **1.** (= *tłumnie wychodzić*) turn out; **wylegać na ulice** take to the streets. **2.** *roln.* (*o zbożu*) lodge.

wylegitymować *pf.* ID (*sb*); check (*sb's*) ID. **~ się** *pf.* (= *okazać dowód tożsamości*) show *l.* produce *l.* provide proof of identity, identify o.s.; **wylegitymować się czymś** (= *okazać coś*) show sth, produce sth.

wylegiwać się *ipf.* lie around, lounge.

wylepiać *ipf.*, **wylepić** *pf.* paste.

wyletniać się *ipf.*, **wyletnić się** *pf.* **-ij** dress too lightly.

wylew *mi* **1.** *pat.* stroke; **wylew krwi do mózgu** cerebral stroke *l.* hemorrhage. **2.** (= *podtopienie*) flooding, flood. **3.** (= *wylewanie*) outpour, outflow. **4.** *geol.* effusion.

wylewać *ipf.* **1.** (= *usuwać płyn*) pour out; (*niechcący*) (= *rozlewać*) spill. **2.** (*o rzece*) flood. **3.** *pot.* (= *usuwać*) (*ze szkoły, z organizacji*) flunk out, kick out; (*z pracy*) fire, sack. **4.** *bud.* (= *wypełniać*) (*szalunek*) fill; (= *pokrywać*) (*powierzchnię*) cover. **5. wylewać łzy** shed tears; **wylać wiele łez** gush tears; **wylać dziecko z kąpielą** throw the baby out with the bath (water); **wylać na kogoś kubeł zimnej wody** pour *l.* throw cold water on sb; **wylewać na kogoś swój gniew** vent one's anger on sb; **nie wylewać za kołnierz** (= *lubić wypić*) like to bend the elbow; **wylać na kogoś kubeł pomyj** flay sb; *US pot.* chew sb up. **~ się** *ipf.* **1.** (= *rozlewać się*) spill. **2.** (*o tłumie*) overflow.

wylewka *f.* **1.** *techn.* (*kranu*) spout, snout, nozzle. **2.** *bud.* (= *podłoga*) concrete floor.

wylewnie *adv.* (*żegnać się, dziękować*) effusively.

wylewność *f.* effusion, effusiveness.

wylewny *a.* **1.** (*o serdeczności, podziękowaniach*) effusive; (*o osobie*) expansive. **2.** *geol.* effusive.

wyleźć *pf.* **-lezę -leziesz -lazł -leźli** *zob.* **wylazić**.

wyleżeć *pf.* **-ę -ysz 1.** (= *wytrzymać w łóżku*) stay (in bed). **2.** (= *wygnieść*) nestle. **~ się** *pf.* *zob.* **wylegiwać się**.

wylęg *mi* = **wyląg**.

wylęgać się *ipf.* **1.** *orn., zool. t. przen.* hatch. **2.** *pat.* (*o zakażeniu*) incubate.

wylęganie *n.* **okres wylęgania** *pat.* incubation *l.* latent period.

wylęgarka *f. Gen.pl.* **-ek** *roln.* brooder, incubator.

wylęgarnia *f. Gen.pl.* **-i** *l.* **-ń 1.** *roln.* brooder, incubator. **2.** *przen.* hotbed (*czegoś* of sth).

wylęgnąć się *pf.* **-lęgnie -ląg -lęgła** *zob.* **wylęgać się**.

wylęgowy *a.* incubative; **aparat wylęgowy** *roln.* brooder, incubator.

wylękniony *a.* **-eni** *lit.* timorous, fearful.

wylicytować *pf. zob.* **licytować**.

wyliczać *ipf.* **1.** (= *wyszczególniać*) list. **2.** (= *obliczać*) calculate. **3.** (= *odliczać*) count. **4.** (= *wydzielać*) (*pieniądze*) control. **5.** *boks* (= *liczyć*) count. **~ się** *ipf.* (= *tłumaczyć się*) explain; **wyliczać się z czegoś** account for sth.

wyliczanka *f. Gen.pl.* **-ek** *dziec.* (who's it) chant *l.* rhyme, count, counting-out rhyme.

wyliczenie *n.* **1.** (= *lista*) listing. **2.** (= *obliczenie*) calculation.

wyliczyć (się) *pf. zob.* **wyliczać (się)**.

wyliniały *a.* (*o psie*) mangy; (*o futrze*) scruffy.

wylinieć *pf.* molt, shed hair.

wylizać (się) *pf.* **-liżę -liżesz** *zob.* **wylizywać (się)**.

wylizywać *ipf.* lick (*sth*) clean. **~ się** *ipf.* **1.** (= *liżąc, oczyszczać się*) lick o.s. clean. **2.** *pot.* (= *dochodzić do zdrowia*) pull through.

wylosować *pf. zob.* **losować**.

wylot *mi* **1.** (= *ujście*) exit, escape; (*spalin*) exhaust; (*rury, węża*) spout; (*lufy*) muzzle; (*jaskini, tunelu*) mouth, opening. **2.** *lotn.* (= *odlot*) departure; **wylot jest o trzeciej** the flight departs at three. **3. na wylot** right through; **znać kogoś/coś na wylot** know sb/sth inside out; **ktoś jest na wylocie** sb's days are counted.

wylotowy *a.* (= *ujściowy*) exit, escape; (= *spalinowy*) exhaust.

wyludniać *ipf.* depopulate. **~ się** *ipf.* depopulate.

wyludnić (się) *pf.* **-ij** *zob.* **wyludniać (się)**.

wyludnienie *n.* depopulation.

wyludniony *a.* **1.** (= *pozbawiony ludności*) depopulated. **2.** (= *pusty, opuszczony*) desolate.

wyluzować się *pf. pot.* chill out, cool out.

wyluzowany *a. pot.* cool, laid back, relaxed.

wyładnieć *pf.* get prettier.

wyładować (się) *pf. zob.* **wyładowywać (się)**.

wyładowanie *n. el., meteor.* discharge; **wyładowanie atmosferyczne** atmospheric discharge, lightning.

wyładowany *a.* **1.** (= *rozładowany*) (*o baterii, akumulatorze*) flat, dead; *el.* discharged. **2.** (= *pełny*) full; **wyładowany czymś** piled high with sth.

wyładowczy *a.* **1.** (= *dotyczący rozładunku*)

undloading; **prace wyładowcze** unloading; **urządzenie wyładowcze** unloader. **2.** *el.* discharge; **lampa wyładowcza** discharge lamp.

wyładowywać *ipf.* **1.** (*towar, ładunek, statek*) unload. **2.** (*napełniać*) fill, stuff; **wyładowywać coś czymś** stuff sth full of sth. **3.** (*baterię, akumulator*) drain; *el.* discharge. **4.** (= *dawać upust*) vent; **wyładować na kimś złość/gniew** vent one's anger on sb. ~ **się** *ipf.* **1.** (*o baterii, akumulatorze*) go dead *l.* flat; *el.* discharge. **2.** **wyładowywać się na kimś** take it out on sb.

wyładunek *mi* -nk- unloading, discharge.

wyładunkowy *a.* unloading, discharge; **rampa wyładunkowa** unloading dock *l.* ramp.

wyłamać (się) *pf.* -mię -miesz *zob.* **wyłamywać (się).**

wyłamywać *ipf.* **1.** (= *otwierać siłą*) (*drzwi, kraty*) force (open), break (down). **2.** (= *złamać*) break off. **3.** **wyłamywać palce** (= *strzelać palcami*) crack one's knuckles. ~ **się** *ipf.* **1.** (= *postąpić wbrew woli większości*) step *l.* get out of line. **2.** (= *złamać się*) break off.

wyłaniać *ipf. form.* (= *wybierać*) select. ~ **się** *ipf. lit.* emerge.

wyłapać *pf.* -pię -piesz, **wyłapywać** *ipf.* catch.

wyławiać *ipf.* **1.** (= *łapać*) catch, land. **2.** (= *wynajdować*) catch. **3.** (= *zidentyfikować*) spot, identify. **4.** (= *wydobywać z wody*) recover (from the water); (*na powierzchnię*) raise to the surface.

wyłaz *mi bud.* hatch; **wyłaz dachowy** roof hatch.

wyłazić *ipf.* -żę -zisz *pot.* **1.** (= *wydostawać się*) get out. **2.** (= *wystawać*) (*o koszuli, bieliźnie*) be showing, stick out. **3.** (= *wypadać*) (*o włosach*) come out. **4.** *dial. l. arch.* (= *wspinać się*) get up. **5. coś wyłazi komuś bokiem** sb is sick of sth; **oczy komuś wyłażą na wierzch** sb's eyes pop out; **wyłazić ze skóry** jump out of one's skin, bend over backward.

wyłączać *ipf.* **1.** (= *gasić*) switch off, turn off, shut down. **2.** (= *odcinać dopływ*) cut off, disconnect. **3.** (= *eliminować*) exclude; **nie wyłączając nikogo** excluding no-one. ~ **się** *ipf.* **1.** (= *przestawać działać*) (*o świetle*) go off, switch off; (*o urządzeniu*) shut down. **2.** (= *wykluczać się*) exclude each other, be mutually exclusive. **3.** (= *nie słuchać*) switch off, tune out. **4.** *tel.* (= *kończyć rozmowę telefoniczną*) hang up, disconnect; **proszę się nie wyłączać** please hold.

wyłączenie *n.* **1.** (*światła*) switching off; (*urządzenia*) shutdown. **2.** (*prądu*) cutoff, blackout; (*planowane*) brownout. **3.** (= *wykluczenie*) exclusion. **4.** *tel.* disconnection. **5. z wyłączeniem czegoś** excluding sth, exclusive of sth.

wyłącznie *adv.* exclusively, strictly, solely.

wyłącznik *mi Gen.* -a *el.* switch.

wyłączność *f. prawn.* exclusion, exclusive rights; **prawo wyłączności** exclusive rights.

wyłączny *a. t. prawn.* exclusive, sole.

wyłączony *a.* (= *zgaszony*) switched off, turned off; (= *odcięty*) cut off, disconnected; *zob. t.* **wyłączać.**

wyłączyć (się) *pf. zob.* **wyłączać (się).**

wyłgać się *pf.*, **wyłgiwać się** *ipf. pot.* get out, weasel out, cop out (*od czegoś* of sth).

wyłogi *pl. Gen.* -ów (*marynarki, płaszcza*) facings.

wyłoić *pf.* -łój **wyłoić komuś grzbiet** *przest.* flay sb's back.

wyłom *mi* **1.** (= *otwór*) (*szerszy*) gap; (*węższy*) crack. **2.** *lit.* (= *odstępstwo*) departure; (= *innowacja*) break; **zrobić wyłom w czymś** (*tradycji, praktyce*) break with sth.

wyłomotać *pf.* -oczę -oczesz *l.* -ocę -ocesz, -ocz *arch., pot.* (= *zbić*) clobber.

wyłonić (się) *pf. zob.* **wyłaniać (się).**

wyłowić *pf.* -łów *zob.* **wyławiać.**

wyłożony *a.* **wyłożony czymś** covered with *l.* in sth, laid with sth; **podłoga wyłożona kafelkami** tiled floor.

wyłożyć (się) *pf. zob.* **wykładać (się).**

wyłudzać *ipf.*, **wyłudzić** *pf.* **1.** (= *defraudować*) embezzle. **2. wyłudzać (coś od kogoś)** (*podstępem*) wheedle (sth out of sb), swindle (sb out of sth); (*szantażem*) extort (sth from sb).

wyłudzenie *n.* **1.** (*podstępem*) swindle; (*szantażem*) extortion. **2.** (= *defraudacja*) embezzlement.

wyługować *pf.*, **wyługowywać** *ipf. chem., tk.* leach.

wyłupać *pf.* -pię -piesz *zob.* **wyłupywać.**

wyłupiać *ipf. zob.* **wyłupić.**

wyłupiasty *a.* (*o oczach*) goggle, bulging, popping; **z wyłupiastymi oczami** goggle-eyed, with bulging eyes.

wyłupić *pf.* **wyłupić komuś oczy** gouge out sb's eyes.

wyłupywać *ipf.* **1.** (= *łuskać*) (*orzechy*) shell, hull. **2.** (= *wyrąbywać*) (*dziurę w ścianie*) knock out.

wyłuskać *pf.*, **wyłuskiwać** *ipf.* **1.** (*orzechy, owoce*) shell, hull. **2.** (= *wydobyć*) pick out.

wyłuszczać *ipf.* (*teorie*) enunciate, set out.

wyłuszczenie *n.* enunciation.

wyłuszczyć *pf. zob.* **wyłuszczać.**

wyłysieć *pf.* go bald.

wyłyżeczkować *pf. med.* curette.

wym. *abbr.* (= *wymawiaj, wymowa*) pron. (= *pronounced, pronunciation*).

wymacać *pf. zob.* **wymacywać.**

wymach *mi* swing.

wymachiwać *ipf.* wave; (*rękami*) flail; (*bronią*) brandish, flourish.

wymacywać *ipf.* (*przedmiot*) feel.

wymagać *ipf.* **1.** (= *żądać*) require; (*kategorycznie*) demand. **2.** (= *potrzebować*) require, need.

wymagający *a.* (*o nauczycielu, pracodawcy, zadaniu*) demanding.

wymaganie *n.* (= *żądanie*) demand, requirement; **wymagania** demands, requirements; **spełniać wymagania** meet demands *l.* requirements.

wymagany *a.* required.

wymaglować *pf.* **1.** (*pościel*) mangle. **2. wymaglować kogoś** *przen.* (= *przepytać*) grill sb, give sb the third degree.

wymalować *pf.* (*pokój*) paint; (*twarz*) make up;

wypisz wymaluj... a dead ringer for... ~ **się** *pf.* **1.** (= *zrobić makijaż*) make up. **2.** (= *ukazać się*) (*na twarzy*) show, appear.

wymamrotać *pf.* **-oczę -oczesz** *l.* **-ocę -ocesz, -ocz** mutter.

wymanewrować *pf.* **1.** *pot.* (= *oszukać*) manipulate, trick. **2.** (= *wykierować*) steer.

wymarcie *n.* extinction; **zagrożony wymarciem** *ekol.* threatened with extinction; **być na wymarciu** be on the way out.

wymarły *a.* **1.** (*o gatunku, roślinności*) extinct. **2.** (= *opustoszały*) (*o mieście, ulicach*) deserted.

wymarsz *mi* departure, start; **rozkaz wymarszu** *wojsk.* marching orders.

wymarzać *ipf.*, **wymarznąć -rznij, -rzł** *l.* **-rznął -rzła -rzli 1.** *ogr.* (= *ginąć od zimna*) freeze; (*przez zimę*) winterkill. **2.** *tylko pf.* (= *zmarznąć*) freeze.

wymarzony *a.* dream, perfect; **wymarzony dom** dream house; **wymarzony partner** perfect partner.

wymarzyć *pf.* **wymarzyć sobie coś** set one's heart on sth. ~ **się** *pf.* **wymarzyć się komuś** catch sb's fancy.

wymasować *pf.* massage, rub.

wymaszerować *pf.* set out.

wymawiać *ipf.* **1.** (= *artykułować*) pronounce. **2.** (= *wypowiadać*) (*wyraz, zaklęcie*) utter. **3. wymawiać coś komuś** (= *czynić wymówki*) reproach sb for sth. **4.** (*umowę, kontrakt*) terminate; **wymawiać (komuś) coś** (*mieszkanie, posadę*) give (sb) notice. ~ **się** *ipf.* **1.** be pronounced; **jak się to wymawia?** how do you pronounce that? **2. wymawiać się od czegoś** get *l.* weasel out of sth.

wymaz *mi med.* swab, smear (test); **wymaz z nosa/gardła** nasal/pharyngeal swab; **wymaz z szyjki macicy** cervical smear.

wymazać *pf.* **-ażę -ażesz, wymazywać** *ipf.* **1.** (= *ścierać*) erase, rub out. **2.** *przen.* (= *usuwać*) expunge, obliterate; **wymazać coś z pamięci** blot out the memory of sth. **3.** *tylko pf.* (= *ubrudzić*) smudge, soil, smear. ~ **się** *pf.* (= *ubrudzić się*) smudge, smear, get soiled.

wymądrzać się *ipf.*, **wymądrzyć się** *pf.* act a wise guy.

wymeldować *pf.*, **wymeldowywać** *ipf.* **wymeldować kogoś** report a change of address for sb. ~ **się** *pf.*, **wymeldowywać się** *ipf.* file *l.* report a change of address.

wymęczyć *pf.* **1.** (= *bardzo zmęczyć*) wear out, tire out. **2.** (= *zrobić z trudem*) force, turn out. ~ **się** *pf.* wear out, tire out.

wymiana *f.* **1.** (*zamiana*) exchange; **wymiana myśli/poglądów/ognia** exchange of ideas/views/fire; **wymiana walut** foreign exchange. **2.** (*zużytego na nowe*) replacement, change; **wymiana oleju** *mot.* oil change. **3.** *jęz.* alternation. **4.** *sport* substitution.

wymiar *mi* **1.** (= *wynik pomiaru*) measurement. **2.** (= *parametr, gabaryt*) dimension; **drugi/czwarty wymiar** second/fourth dimension; **wymiary liniowe** linear dimensions. **3. łagodny wymiar kary** *prawn.* lenient sentence; **wymiar spra-**

wiedliwości the judiciary; **pracować w pełnym/ niepełnym wymiarze godzin** work full-time/part-time; **wymiary** (*biust, talia, biodra*) measurements, vital statistics.

wymiatacz *mp piłka nożna* sweeper.

wymiatać *ipf.* sweep.

wymiąć *pf.* **-mnę -mniesz, -mnij** crease, crumple, wrinkle.

wymieniacz *mi* **wymieniacz jonowy** *chem., fiz.* ion exchanger.

wymieniać *ipf.* **1.** (= *zamieniać*) exchange; **wymieniać myśli/spojrzenia/pozdrowienia** exchange ideas/looks/greetings; **wymieniać pieniądze** change *l.* exchange money. **2.** (*stare na nowe*) replace, change. **3.** (= *wyliczać*) list. **4.** (= *wspominać*) mention. ~ **się** *ipf.* **1.** exchange; **wymieniać się czymś** exchange sth. **2.** *jęz.* alternate.

wymienialność *f. fin.* (*waluty*) convertibility.

wymienialny *a. fin.* (*o walucie*) convertible.

wymienić *pf. zob.* **wymieniać.** ~ **się** *pf. zob.* **wymieniać się.**

wymieniony *a.* mentioned; **wyżej wymieniony** *form.* aforementioned, said.

wymiennik *mi Gen.* **-a wymiennik ciepła** *techn.* heat exchanger.

wymienność *f.* interchangeability.

wymienny *a.* **1.** (= *zastępujący*) interchangeable. **2.** (= *wyjmowany*) (*o dysku*) removable. **3. handel wymienny** *handl.* barter.

wymierać *ipf.* die off, die out.

wymierny *a.* **1.** (= *zauważalny*) (*o zysku, efekcie*) measurable. **2.** (= *mierzalny*) quantifiable, measurable. **3. liczba wymierna** *mat.* rational number.

wymierzać *ipf.*, **wymierzyć** *pf.* **1.** (= *mierzyć*) measure (up). **2.** (*karę, sprawiedliwość*) measure out, mete out, dispense. **3.** (= *brać na cel*) take aim. **4.** (*cios, policzek*) land, deliver.

wymierzony *a.* aimed (*przeciw l. przeciwko czemuś/komuś* against sth/sb).

wymieszać *pf.* mix (together). ~ **się** *pf.* mix (together).

wymieść *pf.* **-miotę -mieciesz -miótł -miotła -mietli** *zob.* **wymiatać.**

wymię *n.* **-mieni-** *pl.* **-mion-** udder.

wymiękać *pf.*, **wymięknąć** *ipf. pot.* (= *słabnąć*) be going *l.* getting soft; (= *tchórzyć*) wimp out.

wymiętosić *pf.* **-szę -sisz** *pot.* crumple, crease. ~ **się** *pf. pot.* crumple, crease.

wymigać się *pf.*, **wymigiwać się** *ipf. pot.* **wymigać się (od czegoś)** duck out (of sth).

wymijać *ipf. zwł. mot.* pass. ~ **się** *ipf.* pass each other.

wymijająco *adv.* (*odpowiedzieć*) evasively.

wymijający *a.* (*o odpowiedzi*) evasive.

wyminąć (się) *pf. zob.* **wymijać (się).**

wymiociny *pl.* vomit.

wymiotny *a. med.* (*o środku*) emetic; **odruch wymiotny** *fizj.* gag reflex.

wymiotować *ipf.* vomit.

wymioty *pl. Gen.* **-ów** vomiting.

wymizerowany *a.* (*o osobie*) haggard, drawn; (*o twarzy*) pinched.

wymknąć się *pf.* **-ij** *zob.* **wymykać się.**

wymłócić *pf. roln.* thresh.
wymoczek *mp* -czk- *pl.* -i *pot., uj.* wimp.
wymoczyć *pf.* soak. ~ **się** *pf.* soak.
wymodelować *pf.* (= *ukształtować*) shape; (*włosy*) style.
wymodlić *pf.* -módl **wymodlić coś** *gł. rel.* (= *wyprosić*) have one's prayers for sth answered.
wymoknąć *pf.* -moknij, -moknął *l.* -mókł -mokła -mokli **1.** (= *zmoknąć*) get soaked. **2.** (= *zgnić*) rot.
wymontować *pf.*, **wymontowywać** *ipf.* remove.
wymordować *pf.* slaughter, kill off. ~ **się** *pf.* slaughter each other.
wymościć *pf.* -moszczę -mościsz line.
wymotać *pf. lit.* disentangle. ~ **się** *pf.* (= *wydostać się, wybrnąć*) disentangle o.s.
wymowa *f.* **1.** (= *wymawianie*) pronunciation. **2.** (= *znaczenie*) significance.
wymownie *adv.* meaningfully.
wymowność *f.* meaning.
wymowny *a.* **1.** (= *pełen znaczenia*) meaningful. **2.** *arch.* (= *elokwentny*) articulate, well-spoken.
wymóc *pf.* -mogę -możesz -mógł -mogła -mogli **wymóc coś na kimś** force *l.* pressure sb into sth.
wymóg *mi* -o- requirement; **spełniać wymogi** meet requirements.
wymówić (się) *pf. zob.* **wymawiać (się)**.
wymówienie *n.* notice; **dostać wymówienie** be given notice; **złożyć wymówienie** hand in one's notice.
wymówka *f. Gen.pl.* -ek **1.** (= *pretekst*) excuse. **2.** (= *wyrzut*) reproach.
wymruczeć *pf.* -ę -ysz mutter.
wymrzeć *pf.* -marł *zob.* **wymierać**.
wymurować *pf.* **1.** (*zbudować*) build. **2.** (= *obmurować*) line with brickwork *l.* bricks.
wymusić *pf.* -szę -sisz, **wymuszać** *ipf.* (= *narzucać*) force, impose (*coś na kimś* sth upon *l.* on sb); (= *wydobyć siłą*) (*obietnicę, zeznania*) extort (*coś na kimś* sth from sb).
wymuszenie *n.* **1.** *prawn.* extortion; **wymuszenie okupu** extortion. **2.** *mot.* **wymuszenie pierwszeństwa (przejazdu)** violation of the right of way, failure to yield (right of way). – *adv.* (*śmiać się*) constrainedly.
wymuszoność *f.* constraint.
wymuszony *a.* (*o uśmiechu, zachowaniu*) forced.
wymyć *pf.* -yję -yjesz, -yj *zob.* **wymywać**.
wymydlić *pf.* (*mydło*) use up.
wymyk *mi sport* back hip circle.
wymykać się *ipf.* slip out.
wymysł *mi* fabrication, invention.
wymyślać *ipf.*, **wymyślić** *pf.* **1.** (= *obmyślać*) think up. **2.** (= *odkrywać*) invent; **on/ona prochu nie wymyśli** he/she will never set the world on fire; *Br.* he/she will never set the Thames on fire. **3.** (= *zmyślać*) make up; **wszystko sobie wymyślił** he made it all up. **4.** *tylko ipf.* **wymyślać komuś** (= *obrzucać wyzwiskami*) hurl abuse at sb.
wymyślnie *adv.* fancifully.
wymyślny *a.* fanciful, fancy.

wymywać *ipf.* -am -asz (= *myć, drążyć*) wash.
wynagradzać *ipf.* reward.
wynagrodzenie *n.* **1.** (= *zapłata*) remuneration, pay; (*jednorazowa*) fee. **2.** (= *nagroda*) reward.
wynagrodzić *pf. zob.* **wynagradzać**.
wynająć (się) *pf.* -jmę -jmiesz, -jmij *zob.* **wynajmować (się)**.
wynajdować, wynajdywać *ipf.* **1.** (= *znajdować*) find. **2.** (= *wyszukiwać*) look for. **3.** (= *odkrywać*) invent.
wynajem *mi* -jm- rental, hire; **wynajem samochodów** car rental, rent-a-car.
wynajęcie *n.* rental, hire; **mieszkanie do wynajęcia** apartment for rent; *Br.* flat to let.
wynajmować *ipf.* **1.** (= *użytkować za opłatą*) rent, hire; (*mieszkanie*) lease. **2.** (= *użyczać za opłatą*) rent (out), hire out; (*mieszkanie*) let (out), lease (out). **3.** (= *zatrudniać czasowo*) hire. ~ **się** *ipf.* get hired.
wynajmujący *mp decl. like a. prawn.* lessor.
wynalazca *mp* inventor.
wynalazczość *f.* inventiveness.
wynalazczy *a.* inventive.
wynalazek *mi* -zk- invention; **potrzeba jest matką wynalazków** necessity is the mother of invention.
wynalezienie *n.* invention.
wynaleźć *pf.* -najdę -najdziesz -nalazł -naleźli *zob.* **wynajdywać**.
wynaradawiać *ipf.* -ów denationalize. ~ **się** *ipf.* -ów denationalize.
wynarodowić (się) *pf. zob.* **wynaradawiać (się)**.
wynaturzać *ipf.* pervert, distort. ~ **się** *ipf.* be perverted, be distorted.
wynaturzenie *n.* perversion, distortion.
wynaturzony *a.* -eni perverted, distorted.
wynaturzyć *pf. zob.* **wynaturzać**. ~ **się** *pf. zob.* **wynaturzać się**.
wynegocjować *pf. zob.* **negocjować**.
wynędzniały *a.* (*o osobie*) haggard, drawn; (*o twarzy*) pinched.
wynędznieć *pf.* languish.
wyniańczyć *pf.* nurse.
wynieść *pf.* -niosę -niesiesz -niósł -niosła -nieśli *zob.* **wynosić**. ~ **się** *pf. zob.* **wynosić się**.
wynik *mi* **1.** (= *efekt*) result; **osiągać (dobre) wyniki** get (good) results; **dawać wyniki** bring results; **być wynikiem czegoś** be a consequence *l.* result of sth; **w wyniku czegoś** as a result of sth. **2.** *sport.* score. **3.** (= *wniosek*) conclusion.
wynikać *ipf.* **1.** (= *powstawać jako następstwo*) result (*z czegoś* from sth). **2.** (= *rozwijać się*) develop (*z czegoś* from sth). **3.** *tylko ipf.* (= *okazywać się*) follow; **z tego wynika, że...** it folows that...
wynikanie *n. log.* implication, consequence.
wyniknąć *pf.* -nikł *l.* -niknął -nikła *zob.* **wynikać**.
wynikowy *a. form.* result.
wyniosłość *f. form.* **1.** (= *duma*) aloofness, haughtiness. **2.** (= *wzniesienie*) rising ground, rise.
wyniosły *a.* **wynioślejszy** **1.** (= *dumny*) aloof, haughty. **2.** *form.* (= *górujący*) towering.

wyniośle *adv.* haughtily.

wyniszczać *ipf.* 1. (= *poważnie uszkadzać*) devastate. 2. (= *unicestwiać*) destroy, eradicate, annihilate. 3. (= *rujnować*) (*zdrowie*) ruin. 4. (= *osłabiać, wyczerpywać*) deplete. ~ **się** *ipf.* 1. (= *rujnować zdrowie*) ruin o.s. 2. (= *niszczyć siebie wzajemnie*) destroy one another.

wyniszczyć (się) *pf. zob.* **wyniszczać (się)**.

wyniuchać *pf. pot.* ferret out.

wynocha *int. pot.* out!; **wynocha stąd!** get out of here!, beat it!

wynos *mi* **na wynos** *kulin.* to go, to take away; **dania na wynos** takeaway (food), takeout (food), carryout (food).

wynosić *ipf.* **-szę -sisz** 1. (= *niosąc, usuwać*) carry out *l.* away. 2. (= *być równym czemuś*) be, amount to; **rachunek wynosi 20 dolarów** the bill is $20. 3. *lit.* (= *podnosić*) raise; **wynosić kogoś pod niebiosa** praise sb to the skies; **wynieść kogoś na piedestał** put *l.* place *l.* set sb on a pedestal; **wynieść kogoś na tron** put sb on the throne, throne sb. ~ **się** *ipf.* 1. *pot.* (= *opuszczać jakieś miejsce*) get out; **wynoś się stąd!** get out of here! 2. *form.* (= *górować*) tower (*nad czymś* over sth). 3. **wynieść się na tamten świat** (= *u-mrzeć*) reach a better world, meet one's Maker. 4. *tylko ipf.* **wynosić się nad kogoś** (= *pogardzać kimś*) lord it over sb.

wynotować *pf.*, **wynotowywać** *ipf.* take down, put down, note down.

wynudzać *ipf.*, **wynudzić** *pf.* bore.

wynudzić się *pf.* get bored.

wynurzać *ipf.* show; (= *na powierzchnię*) bring to the surface; (= *nad powierzchnię*) raise above the surface. ~ **się** *ipf.* 1. (= *wydobywać się nad powierzchnię wody*) surface, emerge. 2. (= *wychodząc skądś, ukazywać się*) emerge. 3. *arch.* (= *zwierzać się*) confide (*przed kimś* in sb).

wynurzenie *n.* 1. (= *zwierzenie*) confession. 2. (*z wody*) emergence.

wynurzyć (się) *pf. zob.* **wynurzać (się)**.

wyobcować (się) *pf. zob.* **wyobcowywać (się)**.

wyobcowanie *n.* alienation.

wyobcowany *a.* alienated; (*z rodziny*) estranged.

wyobcowywać *ipf.* alienate. ~ **się** *ipf.* become alienated *l.* estranged.

wyobrazić *pf.* **-żę -zisz** *zob.* **wyobrażać**.

wyobraźnia *f.* imagination; **bez** *l.* **pozbawiony wyobraźni** unimaginative; **puszczać wodze wyobraźni** let one's imagination run riot; **to nie przemawia do mojej wyobraźni** it doesn't appeal to me; **wytwór (czyjejś) wyobraźni** figment of the imagination *l.* sb's imagination; **widzę to oczyma wyobraźni** I can see it with my mind's eye.

wyobrażać *ipf.* 1. (= *snuć przypuszczenia*) imagine; (= *przedstawiać w myśli*) picture; (= *myśleć*) think, believe; **wyobraź sobie, że...** guess what,...; **nie wyobrażaj sobie, że...** don't think that... 2. *lit.* (= *przedstawiać*) represent.

wyobrażalny *a.* imaginable, conceivable.

wyobrażenie *n.* 1. (= *stereotyp, podobizna*) image. 2. (= *przekonanie*) belief, idea. 3. (= *zdanie*) opinion; **mieć o kimś dobre/złe wyobrażenie**

have a good/bad opinion of sb; **to przechodzi wszelkie wyobrażenie** this is beyond all comprehension. 4. *fil.* notion.

wyodrębniać *ipf.* 1. (= *wyizolować*) isolate. 2. (= *wydzielać*) set apart. ~ **się** *ipf.* 1. (= *wyróżniać się*) stand out. 2. (= *wydzielać się*) stand apart.

wyodrębnić (się) *pf.* **-ij** *zob.* **wyodrębniać (się)**.

wyokrętować *pf. żegl.* disembark. ~ **się** *pf. żegl.* disembark.

wyolbrzymiać *ipf.*, **wyolbrzymić** *pf.* exaggerate, overrate.

wyorać *pf.* **-orzę -orzesz** *zob.* **wyorywać**.

wyostrzać *ipf.* 1. (*zmysły*) sharpen. 2. *żegl.* haul (up). ~ **się** *ipf.* sharpen.

wyostrzyć (się) *pf. zob.* **wyostrzać (się)**.

wypacać *ipf.* (*chorobę, toksynę*) sweat out; (*kilogramy*) sweat off. ~ **się** *ipf.* sweat it out.

wypacykować *pf. uj.* daub. ~ **się** *pf. uj.* put on heavy make-up.

wypacykowany *a.* (*o twarzy, osobie*) heavily made-up.

wypaczać *ipf.* 1. (= *zniekształcać*) distort. 2. *stol.* warp. 3. (= *demoralizować*) deprave. ~ **się** *ipf. stol.* warp.

wypaczyć (się) *pf. zob.* **wypaczać (się)**.

wypad *mi* 1. (= *wyprawa*) trip, outing. 2. *wojsk.* (= *wyprawa zbrojna*) sortie. 3. *sport* lunge.

wypadać *ipf.* 1. (= *wylatywać*) fall out; **przez okno** *l.* **z okna wypadła cegła** a brick fell out (of) the window; **samochód wypadł z trasy** the car went off track. 2. (= *być wyeliminowanym, znikać*) drop out; **autobus wypadł z rozkładu** the bus didn't run; **wypaść z roli** act *l.* drop out of character. 3. (= *wybiegać*) burst out. 4. (= *być w określonym czasie, miejscu*) fall, be; **wyjazd wypada w niedzielę** the departure falls on a Sunday. 5. (= *przytrafiać się*) come up, crop up; **coś mi/mu itp. wypadło** something has come up. 6. (= *powieść się*) go; **egzamin wypadł raczej źle** the exam went rather poorly. 7. (= *przypadać*) **na każdego wypada po dwa jabłka** everyone gets two apples. 8. *tylko ipf.* 3 os. *sing.* **coś komuś wypada** (= *przystoi, należy się*) it's right for sb to do sth; **coś komuś nie wypada** it's not right for sb to do sth, sth doesn't become sb; **cóż, wypada zgodzić się z panią** well, I can only agree with you; **to nie wypada** that's not done; **wypada, żeby...** it's only right that...

wypadek *mi* **-dk-** 1. (= *przypadek*) case; **na wszelki wypadek** just in case; **w tym wypadku** in this case; **ubezpieczony na wypadek śmierci/kradzieży** insured against death/theft; **w wypadku niezgłoszenia się pasażera...** should the passenger fail to report...; **jeszcze nie mieliśmy wypadku, by...** there hasn't been a single case of... 2. (= *nieszczęśliwe zdarzenie*) accident; **ulec wypadkowi** have an accident, meet with an accident; **wypadek losowy** chance accident; **wypadek drogowy** traffic accident; **wypadki chodzą po ludziach** accidents happen.

wypadkowa *f. Gen.* **-ej** 1. *fiz.* resultant. 2. (= *wynik*) product, result.

wypadkowość *f.* accident rate.

wypadkowy *a.* **1.** (= *związany z wypadkiem*) accident. **2.** *fiz.* (*o sile*) resultant.

wypadowy *a.* **baza wypadowa** (*do wycieczek*) staging area.

wypakować *pf.*, **wypakowywać** *ipf.* unpack.

wypalać *ipf.*, **wypalić** *pf.* **1.** (= *niszczyć ogniem*) burn down; (*trawę*) burn off. **2.** (= *paląc, zużywać*) burn. **3.** (= *ogrzewając, utwardzać*) (*rudę*) roast; (*cegły, naczynia*) fire. **4.** (*odciskać*) (*znak*) burn. **5.** *tylko pf. gł. pot.* (= *udać się*) work; **nie wypalić** misfire. **6.** *tylko pf.* (= *strzelić*) fire. **7.** *tylko pf.* (= *powiedzieć energicznie*) shoot.

wypaplać *pf.* **-lę -lesz** *l.* **-lam -lasz, -laj** *pot.* blab out, babble.

wyprać *pf.* **-prę -przesz** *pot.* **1.** (= *pobrudzić*) dirty, soil. **2.** (= *zużyć*) use up. ~ **się** *pf. pot.* (= *pobrudzić się*) dirty o.s.

wyparować *pf.*, **wyparowywać** *ipf.* (= *zmienić się w parę*) *t. żart.* (= *zniknąć*) evaporate.

wyparzać *ipf.*, **wyparzyć** *pf.* (*naczynie*) scald.

wypas *mi roln.* pasturing, grazing.

wypasać *ipf.* **-pasę -pasiesz -pasł -paśli** *roln.* **1.** (= *paść na pastwisku*) graze. **2.** (= *tuczyć*) feed. **wypasać się** *ipf. roln.* **1.** (= *paść się na pastwisku*) graze. **2.** (= *tuczyć się*) feed.

wypaść *pf.* **-padnę -padniesz, -padnij, -padł** *zob.* **wypadać**.

wypaść (się) *pf.* **-pasę -pasiesz -pasł** *zob.* **wypasać (się)**.

wypatroszyć *pf.* **1.** *kulin.* (*kurczaka, rybę*) dress. **2.** (= *wypruć flaki*) gut, degut.

wypatrywać *ipf.*, **wypatrzyć** *pf.* **wypatrywać czegoś/kogoś** look out for sth/sb; **wypatrywać oczy** strain one's eyes.

wypchać *pf. zob.* **wypychać**. ~ **się** *pf. pot.* get stuffed; **wypchaj się!** get stuffed!; *zob. t.* **wypychać się**.

wypchnąć *pf.* **-ij** *zob.* **wypychać**.

wypełniacz *mi Gen.* **-a** filling, filler.

wypełniać *ipf.* **1.** (= *napełniać*) fill. **2.** (= *spełniać*) satisfy, fulfill. **3.** (*formularz*) fill out, complete. ~ **się** *ipf.* fill up.

wypełnić (się) *pf.* **-ij** *zob.* **wypełniać (się)**.

wypełniony *a.* **1.** (= *pełny*) full. **2.** (= *spełniony*) fulfilled, satisfied. **3.** (= *o formularzu*) completed, filled out.

wypełzać *ipf.* crawl out.

wyperfumować *pf.* perfume, put perfume on. ~ **się** *pf.* put on perfume.

wyperfumowany *a.* perfumed.

wyperswadować *pf.* **wyperswadować coś komuś** get sth out of sb's mind, reason *l.* coax sb out of sth.

wypestkować *pf. kulin.* (*wiśnie*) stone.

wypędzać *ipf.*, **wypędzić** *pf.* **1.** (= *przepędzać*) drive out. **2.** (= *wydalać*) banish. **3. wypędzać bydło (na pastwisko)** *roln.* drive cattle (out) (to pasture).

wypiąć *pf.* **-pnę -pniesz, -pnij** *zob.* **wypinać**. ~ **się** *pf.* **wypiąć się na kogoś** *pot.* turn one's back on sb.

wypić *pf.* **-piję -pijesz, -pij 1.** *zob.* **wypijać**. **2.** (= *spożyć alkohol*) drink; **lubić wypić** like a drink, like to hit the bottle; **wypić za coś** drink to sth; **wypić (za) czyjeś zdrowie** drink (to) sb's health.

wypiec (się) *pf.* **-piekę -pieczesz -piekł** *zob.* **wypiekać (się)**.

wypieczony *a.* *kulin.* (*o steku*) well-done; (*o chlebie*) well-baked.

wypiek *mi kulin.* **1.** (= *pieczenie*) baking; (= *partia pieczywa*) batch, baking. **2.** *zob.* **wypieki**.

wypiekać *ipf.* bake. ~ **się** *ipf.* bake.

wypieki *pl. Gen.* **-ów 1.** (= *rumieńce*) blush, flush. **2.** *kulin.* baked goods.

wypielęgnować *pf.* cultivate.

wypielęgnowany *a.* well-groomed; (*o paznokciach*) manicured; (*o ogrodzie*) tended.

wypieprzać *ipf.*, **wypieprzyć** *pf. pot.*, *obsc.* **1.** (= *wyrzucać*) (*rzeczy*) boot, chuck (out); (*ludzi*) bounce, kick out. **2.** (= *uciekać*) fuck off, beat it.

wypierać *ipf. t. hydrol.* displace; (*technologię, obyczaj*) supplant, supersede; **wypierać kogoś/coś z rynku** *ekon.* squeeze sb/sth out of the market. ~ **się** *ipf.* **wypierać się czegoś** deny sth; **wyprzeć się czegoś w żywe oczy** deny sth flatly.

wypierdalać *ipf. pot.*, *obsc.* **1.** (= *wyrzucać*) (*rzeczy*) boot, chuck (out), shitcan; (*ludzi*) throw on the ass, bounce. **2.** (= *uciekać*) fuck off, get the fuck out, beat it. ~ **się** *ipf. pot.*, *obsc.* fall (over).

wypierdek *mp* **-dk-** *pl.* **-i** *pog.*, *sl.* jerk, shithead, scum.

wypierdolić (się) *pf. zob.* **wypierdalać (się)**.

wypierdzielać (się) *ipf.*, **wypierdzielić (się)** *pf. zob.* **wypierdalać (się)**.

wypierzać się *ipf.*, **wypierzyć się** *pf. orn.* fledge.

wypierzony *a. orn. l. przen.* fledged.

wypieszczony *a.* **-eni** (*o mieszkaniu*) shipshape.

wypieścić *pf.* **-pieszczę -pieścisz wypieścić coś** (*mieszkanie*) make (sth) shine.

wypięknieć *ipf.* grow pretty.

wypiętrzać *ipf. geol.* elevate, lift up. ~ **się** *ipf. geol.* elevate, lift up.

wypiętrzenie *n. geol.* uplift, elevation.

wypiętrzyć (się) *pf. zob.* **wypiętrzać (się)**.

wypijać *ipf.* **1.** (= *pić*) drink (up). **2.** (= *wchłaniać*) soak up.

wypiłować *pf.*, **wypiłowywać** *ipf.* cut out.

wypinać *ipf.* **1.** (= *wystawiać*) (*tyłek*) stick out; **wypinać dupę** *przen.* not to give a shit, not to give a rat's ass. **2.** (= *odpinać*) undo. **3.** (= *wyciągać*) remove. ~ **się** *ipf. zob.* **wypiąć się**.

wypindrzony *a. pot.* dolled up, dressed to the teeth.

wypis *mi* **1.** (= *wyciąg*) extract, excerpt. **2.** (= *odpis*) transcript. **3.** (*ze szpitala*) discharge.

wypisać *pf.* **-szę -szesz** *zob.* **wypisywać**. ~ **się** *pf. zob.* **wypisywać się**.

wypisany *a.* **ktoś ma coś wypisane na czole** sth stands out a mile.

wypisek *mi* **-sk-** *arch.* excerpt.

wypisy *pl. Gen.* **-ów** *gł. arch.* **1.** (= *podręcznik*) reader. **2.** (= *fragmenty*) excerpts.

wypisywać *ipf.* **1.** (= *wypełniać*) fill out; (*czek*) make out, write (out); **wypisać czek na 10 USD** write (out) a check for $10. **2.** (= *wynotowywać*) take down, copy (down). **3.** *emf.* (= *pisać*) write; **wypisywać brednie** write crap. **4. wypisywać kogoś** (= *wykreślać*) cancel sb's membership. **5.** (= *zużywać*) (*wkład*) use up. **6. wypisz wymaluj...** the picture of... ~ **się** *ipf.* **1.** (= *rezygnować*) quit, resign. **2.** (= *opuszczać szpital*) get discharged. **3.** (= *zużyć się*) (*o ołówku*) be (all) used up.

wyplamić *pf.* stain. ~ **się** *pf.* become stained.

wyplatać *ipf.* weave.

wyplątać (się) *pf.* -**plączę** -**plączesz** *zob.* **wyplątywać (się)**.

wyplątywać *ipf.* disentangle. ~ **się** *pf.* disentangle (o.s.), extricate (o.s.).

wypleniać *ipf.*, **wyplenić** *pf.* **1.** (= *zwalczyć*) eradicate, stamp out. **2.** *ogr.* (*chwasty*) kill.

wypleść *pf.* -**plotę** -**pleciesz** -**plótł** -**plotła** -**pletli** *zob.* **wyplatać**.

wypluć *pf. zob.* **wypluwać**.

wypluskać się *pf.* (= *wykąpać się w wannie*) soak.

wypluty *a.* dead-tired, pooped.

wypluwać *ipf.* spit out; **wypluj to słowo!** don't even think it!

wypłacać *ipf.* **1.** *fin.* (= *dawać*) pay out. **2.** *fin.* (= *pobierać*) withdraw. **3.** *lit.* (= *odwzajemniać się*) repay. ~ **się** *ipf. lit.* repay.

wypłacalność *f. fin.* solvency.

wypłacalny *a. fin.* solvent.

wypłacić *pf. zob.* **wypłacać**. ~ **się** *pf. zob.* **wypłacać się**.

wypłakać *pf.* -**aczę** -**aczesz** (= *powiedzieć płacząc*) weep out. ~ **się** *pf.*, **wypłakiwać się** *ipf.* have a good cry; **wypłakać się przed kimś** cry to sb.

wypłakiwać *ipf.* **wypłakiwać oczy** (= *tęsknić*) cry one's eyes out.

wypłaszać (się) *ipf. zob.* **wypłoszyć (się)**.

wypłata *f.* **1.** *fin.* (= *wycofanie pieniędzy*) withdrawal. **2.** *fin.* (= *wydanie pieniędzy*) payout. **3.** (= *pensja*) pay. **4.** (= *dzień wypłaty*) payday.

wypłoszyć *pf.* scare away *l.* off. ~ **się** *pf.* get scared off, scare away *l.* off.

wypłowiały *a.* faded.

wypłowieć *pf.* fade.

wypłukać *pf.* -**uczę** -**uczesz**, **wypłukiwać** *ipf.* **1.** *tylko pf.* (*naczynia, pranie*) rinse. **2.** (= *wyżłobić*) wash away.

wypłynąć *pf. zob.* **wypływać**.

wypływ *mi* **1.** (= *wypłynięcie*) (*gotówki, cieczy*) outflow. **2.** *pat.* (= *wydzielina*) discharge.

wypływać *ipf.* -**am** -**asz** **1.** (= *odpływać*) set out; *żegl.* set sail. **2.** (= *wynurzać się*) emerge, surface, rise *l.* come to the surface. **3.** (= *stawać się sławnym*) become known. **4.** (= *wychodzić na jaw*) come out. **5.** (= *wyciekać*) flow. **6. wypływać z czegoś** (= *wynikać*) rise out of sth, follow from sth. **7.** *tylko ipf.* (= *brać początek*) flow, spring; **ta rzeka wypływa z Tatr** the river flows from the Tatras. **8. wypłynąć na szerokie wody** spread *l.* stretch one's wings.

wypocić (się) *pf. zob.* **wypacać (się)**.

wypociny *pl. Gen.* -**n** *uj., pot.* garbage; (*o wypracowaniu*) scribble.

wypocząć *pf.* -**cznę** -**czniesz**, -**cznij** *zob.* **wypoczywać**.

wypoczęty *a.* refreshed, rested; **czuć się wypoczętym** feel refreshed.

wypoczwarzać się *ipf.*, **wypoczwarzyć się** *pf. ent.* pupate.

wypoczynek *mi* -**nk**- **1.** (= *odpoczynek*) rest. **2.** (= *relaks*) leisure, recreation.

wypoczynkowy *a.* recreational; **komplet wypoczynkowy** set of furniture (coffee table, couch and two armchairs); *Br.* three-piece suite; **miejscowość wypoczynkowa** (holiday) resort.

wypoczywać *ipf.* -**am** -**asz** **1.** (= *odpoczywać*) rest. **2.** (= *zażywać urlopu*) vacation.

wypogadzać się *ipf.*, **wypogodzić się** *pf.* -**ódź** **1.** *meteor.* clear up, brighten (up). **2.** (*o twarzy*) brighten (up).

wypolerować *pf.* polish (up).

wypomadować *pf. przest.* (*włosy*) pomade.

wypominać *ipf.* **wypominać coś komuś** rub sb's nose in sth.

wypominki *pl. Gen.* -**ów** *rz.-kat*, naming (*by the priest from the pulpit*) of the dead for whom prayers are requested (*esp. on All Saints' Day*).

wypomnieć *pf.* -**nę** -**nisz**, -**nij** *zob.* **wypominać**.

wypompować *pf.*, **wypompowywać** *ipf.* **1.** (*wodę*) pump out. **2.** *pot.* (= *zmęczyć*) poop out.

wypompowany *a. pot.* (= *zmęczony*) pooped out.

wyporność *f. żegl.* displacement.

wyporządnieć *pf.* **1.** (= *stać się uczciwym*) go straight. **2.** (= *stać się schludnym*) grow neater.

wyposażać *ipf.* **wyposażać coś w coś** fit sth with sth; **wyposażać kogoś w coś** equip sb with sth.

wyposażenie *n.* **1.** (= *oprzyrządowanie*) equipment. **2.** (= *umeblowanie*) furnishings. **3.** (= *akcesoria*) accessories.

wyposażony *a.* equipped, fitted (*w coś* with sth).

wyposażyć *pf. zob.* **wyposażać**.

wypościć się *pf.* -**poszczę** -**pościsz** go hungry.

wypośrodkować *pf.*, **wypośrodkowywać** *ipf.* (*opinię*) balance.

wypowiadać *ipf.* **1.** (= *wyrażać*) (*opinie*) express. **2.** (= *wymawiać*) (*słowa, zaklęcie*) utter. **3.** (= *zrywać*) (*umowę, kontrakt*) revoke; **wypowiadać coś komuś** (*mieszkanie, wynajem*) give sb notice. **4. wypowiedzieć (komuś/czemuś) wojnę** *t. polit.* declare war (on sb/sth); **wypowiedzieć posłuszeństwo** refuse to obey, renounce allegiance; **wypowiedzieć komuś posłuszeństwo** refuse to obey sb. ~ **się** *ipf.* (= *komentować*) comment; (= *odzywać się*) speak out.

wypowiedzenie *n.* **1.** *prawn.* (*najmu, pracy*) notice; (*umowy, kontraktu*) termination; **wypowiedzenie wojny** *polit.* declaration of war. **2.** *jęz.* utterance.

wypowiedzieć (się) *pf.* -**wiem** -**wiesz**, -**wiedz** *zob.* **wypowiadać (się)**.

wypowiedź *f.* statement, comment.

wypoziomować *pf. bud.* (*fundament, podłogę*) level, true.

wypożyczać *ipf*. **1.** (= *brać tymczasowo*) hire, rent; (= *użyczać tymczasowo*) hire out, lend, rent (out). **2.** *bibl*. (*książki, płyty*) (*z biblioteki*) check out, borrow. **3.** (*komuś*) lend.

wypożyczalnia *f*. *Gen.pl*. **-i 1.** rental service; **wypożyczalnia samochodów/wideo** car/video rental. **2.** *bibl*. lending library.

wypożyczony *a*. rented, hired; (*o książce*) checked out.

wypożyczyć *pf*. *zob*. **wypożyczać**.

wypór *mi* **-o-** *hydrol*. lift.

wypracować *pf*. *zob*. **wypracowywać**.

wypracowanie *n*. composition, essay.

wypracowywać *ipf*. (*zasady, system*) develop, work out; (*kompromis*) work out, achieve; **wypracować zysk** make a profit.

wyprać *pf*. **-piorę -pierzesz** wash.

wypraktykować *pf*. try out, test.

wypraska *f*. *Gen.pl*. **-ek** *techn*. molding.

wyprasować *pf*. (*ubranie*) iron, press.

wypraszać *ipf*. **1.** (= *nakazać wyjście*) ask to leave. **2.** (= *wybłagać*) wheedle out. **3.** **wypraszam sobie!** excuse me!, I beg your pardon!

wyprawa *f*. **1.** (= *podróż*) journey; (= *ekspedycja*) expedition; **wyprawa krzyżowa** *hist*. crusade. **2.** (= *posag*) trousseau. **3.** *techn*. (= *obróbka*) dressing.

wyprawiać *ipf*. **1.** *emf*. (= *wyrabiać*) do, be up to; **co ty wyprawiasz?** what are you doing?, what are you up to?; **wyprawiać awantury** kick up a fuss. **2.** (= *wysyłać*) send off; **wyprawić kogoś na tamten świat** *pot*. dispatch sb. **3.** (= *organizować*) do, throw; **wyprawiać urodziny** throw a birthday party. **~ się** *ipf*. set out.

wyprawić (się) *pf*. *zob*. **wyprawiać (się)**.

wyprawka *f*. *Gen.pl*. **-ek** (*dla niemowlęcia*) layette.

wyprażać *ipf*., **wyprażyć** *pf*. *techn*. roast.

wyprażyć się *pf*. (= *opalać się*) bake in the sun.

wyprężać *ipf*. (*mięśnie, grzbiet*) flex. **~ się** *ipf*. **1.** (= *napinać mięśnie*) flex one's muscles. **2.** (= *naciągnąć się*) (*o linie*) tighten. **3.** (= *wyprostować się*) draw o.s. up.

wyprężony *a*. tightened; (*o mięśniach*) flexed.

wyprężyć (się) *pf*. *zob*. **wyprężać (się)**.

wyprodukować *pf*. make, manufacture; (*film*) produce.

wyprofilować *pf*. (= *uformować*) shape, form; (*w opływowy kształt*) streamline.

wypromieniować *pf*., **wypromieniowywać** *ipf*. *fiz*. radiate.

wypromować *pf*. *handl*. (*nowy produkt*) launch, bring out, roll out; (*artystę, dzieło*) sell, spotlight.

wyprorokować *pf*. *gł*. *arch*. presage, forebode.

wyprosić *pf*. **-szę -sisz** *zob*. **wypraszać**.

wyprost *mi* *sport* extension; **wyprost nóg** leg extension.

wyprostować (się) *pf*. *zob*. **wyprostowywać (się)**.

wyprostowany *a*. straightened out; (= *prosty*) straight; *fizj*. (*o kończynie*) extended.

wyprostowywać *ipf*. **1.** (= *czynić prostym*) straighten (out). **2.** (= *wygładzać*) straighten (out), flatten. **~ się** *ipf*. **1.** (= *stawać się prostym*)

straighten (out). **2.** (= *wygładzać się*) straighten (out), flatten.

wyprowadzać *ipf*. **1.** (*z pomieszczenia*) (*osobę*) walk out, escort, take; (*pojazd*) take out; **wyprowadzać samochód z garażu** take a car out of the garage. **2.** (= *doprowadzać*) take. **3.** (= *przeprowadzać*) move out. **4.** (*wzór*) derive. **5.** **wyprowadzać samochód z poślizgu** regain traction, control a skid; **wyprowadzić kogoś z błędu** put sb straight *l*. right; **wyprowadzać wniosek** conclude. **~ się** *ipf*. move out.

wyprowadzenie *n*. **1.** (= *wywiezienie*) removal. **2.** (= *odprowadzenie*) escorting. **3.** *mat*. derivation.

wyprowadzić (się) *pf*. *zob*. **wyprowadzać (się)**.

wyprowadzka *f*. *Gen.pl*. **-ek** move, removal.

wypróbować *pf*. try out, test.

wypróbowany *a*. tried, tested.

wypróżniać *ipf*. (*kieszenie, szuflady*) empty. **~ się** *ipf*. *fizj*. evacuate.

wypróżnić (się) *pf*. **-ij** *zob*. **wypróżniać (się)**.

wypróżnienie *n*. *fizj*. evacuation.

wypruć *pf*., **wypruwać** *ipf*. **1.** (= *wyszarpnąć*, *wyrąbać*) rip out. **2.** (*nitkę*) unpick. **3.** **wypruwać z siebie żyły** *l*. **flaki** sweat one's guts out, work one's ass off.

wypruty *a*. **1.** (*nitka*) unpicked. **2.** *pot*. (= *zmęczony*) dead-tired, bagged.

wyprysk *mi* *pat*. eczema.

wypryskiwać *ipf*., **wyprysnąć** *pf*. **-snę -śniesz, -śnij, -snął** *l*. **-sł -snęła** *l*. **-sła -snęli 1.** (= *rozchlapywać się*) splash. **2.** *tylko pf*. (= *wybiec*) shoot out.

wyprząc *pf*. **-przęgnę -przęgniesz, -prząż** *l*. **-przęż, -przągł -przęgła -przęgli** *zob*. **wyprzęgać**.

wyprzeć *pf*. **-prę -przesz, -przyj, -parł** *zob*. **wypierać**. **~ się** *pf*. *zob*. **wypierać się**.

wyprzedać *pf*. *zob*. **wyprzedawać**.

wyprzedany *a*. *handl*. sold out.

wyprzedawać *ipf*. *handl*. **1.** (= *sprzedawać*) sell out. **2.** (*na wyprzedaży*) put on sale.

wyprzedaż *f*. *pl*. **-e** *handl*. sale.

wyprzedzać *ipf*. **1.** *mot*. (= *jechać szybciej niż*) pass; *Br*. overtake. **2.** (= *przewodzić*) be *l*. keep *l*. stay *l*. remain ahead of.

wyprzedzanie *n*. *mot*. passing; *Br*. overtaking; **manewr wyprzedzania** passing maneuver.

wyprzedzenie *n*. **1.** **z wyprzedzeniem** in advance, ahead of time; **z tygodniowym itp. wyprzedzeniem** a week, etc. in advance. **2.** (*przy planowaniu*) lead time. **3.** *myśl*., *wojsk*. (*przy strzelaniu*) lead.

wyprzedzić *pf*. **1.** *zob*. **wyprzedzać**. **2.** *mot*. pull ahead of. **3.** **wyprzedzić kogoś** (= *uprzedzić*) beat sb to it.

wyprzęgać *ipf*. **1.** *mot*. press *l*. engage the clutch. **2.** (*konia*) unharness; (*zwierzę pociągowe*) unyoke.

wyprztykać się *pf*. *pot*. **1.** **wyprztykać się z czegoś** (= *pozbawić się, wydać*) fritter sth away. **2.** (= *wyczerpać energię*) spend o.s.

wypsnąć się *pf*. **-ij** *pot*. **1.** **coś się komuś wypsnęło** sb let sth slip. **2.** **komu się wypsnęło?** (= *kto zanieczyścił powietrze?*) who cut the cheese?

wypstrykać *pf. pot. (kliszę)* use up.

wypucować *pf.* polish (up).

wypucowany *a. pot. (o mieszkaniu, samochodzie)* polished, spotless.

wypukać *pf.*, **wypukiwać** *ipf. pot., mot.* (= *wyklepać) (karoserię)* hammer out.

wypukłość *f.* 1. bulge, protrusion. 2. *techn.* convexity.

wypukły *a.* 1. (= *wystający*) bulging, protruding. 2. *techn., opt.* convex; **soczewka wypukła** convex lens. 3. **kąt wypukły** *geom.* salient angle. 4. *druk.* **druk wypukły** (= *metoda drukarska*) relief printing; (= *wydruk*) relief print.

wypunktować *pf.* 1. (= *wymienić*) list; (= *wyszczególnić*) itemize. 2. *boks* outpoint, defeat on points.

wypustka *f. Gen.pl.* **-ek** appendage; (*w ubraniu*) inset.

wypuszczać *ipf.* **-uszczę -uścisz** 1. (= *puszczać*) let go of. 2. (= *uwalniać*) (*zakładnika, więźnia*) let go, release. 3. (*z domu*) (*kota, psa*) put out. 4. (= *wydzielać*) let out, emit. 5. *fin.* (*obligacje*) issue. 6. *bot.* (*pędy, liście*) push out; (*o pędach, liściach*) shoot. 7. *szkoln.* (*absolwentów*) turn out. ~ **się** *ipf.* 1. (= *zapuszczać się*) stray. 2. (= *wyruszać*) set out.

wypuścić (się) *pf. zob.* **wypuszczać (się).**

wypychać *ipf.* 1. (= *wypełniać*) stuff. 2. (= *pchając wysuwać*) push out. 3. (*kolana, rękawy*) bag (out). ~ **się** *ipf.* (*o kolanach, rękawach*) bag (out).

wypytać (się) *pf. zob.* **wypytywać (się).**

wypytywać *ipf.* question. ~ **się** *ipf.* (= *podpytać*) ask around.

wyrabiać *ipf.* 1. (= *wykonywać*) complete; **wyrobić plan** carry out the plan. 2. **wyrabiać sobie** (= *nabywać*) (*opinię*) form; (*pozycję, reputację*) establish. 3. (*ciasto*) knead. 4. *tylko ipf.* (= *kombinować*) do, be (getting) up to; **co ty wyrabiasz?** what do you think you're doing?, what are you (getting) up to? ~ **się** *ipf.* 1. (= *zdobywać wprawę, umiejętności*) get better, improve. 2. (= *zdążyć*) make it; (= *zmobilizować się do pracy*) get one's act together; **nie wyrobię się przed ósmą** I won't make it before eight. 3. (= *zużywać się*) wear out. 4. *tylko ipf. pot.* (= *mieć miejsce*) **co tu się wyrabia?** what's going on here?

wyrachowanie *n.* calculation.

wyrachowany *a.* calculating.

wyradzać się *ipf.* 1. (= *być nieudacznikiem*) be a disgrace (*z rodziny* to one's family). 2. *bot.* (= *degenerować się*) degenerate.

wyrafinowanie[1] *n.* sophistication.

wyrafinowanie[2] *adv.* sophisticatedly.

wyrafinowany *a.* sophisticated.

wyrastać *ipf.* 1. (= *rosnąć, rozwijać się*) (*o osobie*) grow up (*na kogoś* to be sb); (*o roślinie*) grow; **wyrosnąć z czegoś** (*z ubrania, zabawek*) outgrow sth. 2. (= *pojawiać się*) pop up, show up. 3. *kulin.* (*o cieście*) rise.

wyratować *pf.* rescue, save. ~ **się** *pf.* save o.s.

wyraz *mi* 1. (*słowo*) *jęz.* word; **nieprzyzwoite wyrazy** dirty words, obscenities; **wyraz bliskoznaczny** synonym; **wyraz hasłowy** headword; **wy-**

raz pochodny derivative; **wyraz przestarzały** obsolete word. 2. (*przejaw*) expression; (*objaw*) sign; **bez wyrazu** expressionless, blank; **dać wyraz czemuś** give expression *l.* voice to sth; **pełen wyrazu** expressive; **środek wyrazu** medium; **siła wyrazu** expressiveness; **wyrazy szacunku** respect, regards; **wyrazy współczucia** (words of) sympathy; **wyraz twarzy** facial expression. 3. **nad wyraz** *form.* exceedingly. 4. *mat.* term.

wyraziciel *mp,* **wyrazicielka** *f. form.* mouthpiece (*czegoś* for sth).

wyrazić (się) *pf.* **-żę -zisz** *zob.* **wyrażać (się).**

wyrazistość *f. form.* 1. (=*jasność*) clarity; **z całą wyrazistością** with extreme clarity, emphatically. 2. (= *ekspresja*) expressiveness.

wyrazisty *a.* **-szy** 1. (= *wyraźny*) clear, pronounced. 2. (= *duży*) prominent. 3. (= *ekspresywny*) expressive.

wyraziście *adv.* 1. (= *wyraźnie*) clearly. 2. (= *ekspresywnie*) expressively.

wyrazowy *a. jęz.* word, lexical; **akcent wyrazowy** word *l.* lexical stress; **grupa wyrazowa** phrase.

wyraźnie *adv.* (= *jasno*) clearly; (= *charakterystycznie*) distinctly; (= *oczywiście*) obviously.

wyraźny *a.* (= *jasny*) clear; (= *charakterystyczny*) distinct; (= *oczywisty*) obvious.

wyrażać *ipf.* 1. (= *ujmować w słowa*) express, voice, communicate. 2. (= *przedstawiać opinię*) express. 3. (= *uzewnętrzniać*) show, indicate, express. 4. (= *odzwierciedlać*) reflect. ~ **się** *ipf.* 1. (= *wypowiadać się*) speak; **wyrażać się pochlebnie o kimś/czymś** speak highly of sb/sth; **wyrażać się jasno** make o.s. clear. 2. (= *znajdować odbicie*) be reflected *l.* expressed (*w czymś* in sth). 3. *tylko ipf. euf.* (= *kląć*) cuss, swear.

wyrażenie *n. mat., jęz.* expression; (= *zwrot*) phrase.

wyrąb *mi* **-ę** *leśn.* fell.

wyrąbać *pf.* **-bię -biesz,** **wyrąbywać** *ipf.* 1. (*otwór, przejście*) hew, cut, hack. 2. (*usunąć*) cut down. 3. *pot.* (= *powiedzieć wprost*) rap out.

wyrecytować *pf. zob.* **recytować.**

wyregulować *pf.* adjust.

wyrejestrować *pf.*, **wyrejestrowywać** *ipf.* deregister.

wyremontować *pf.* (*pomieszczenie*) redecorate, refurbish; (*pojazd*) repair; (*urządzenie*) repair, refurbish.

wyretuszować *pf.* retouch, airbrush, touch up.

wyreżyserować *pf.* 1. *film, teatr* direct. 2. (*przedsięwzięcie*) orchestrate, mastermind.

wyręczać *ipf.* **wyręczać kogoś (w czymś)** help sb (out) (with sth), relieve sb (at sth). ~ **się** *ipf.* **wyręczać się kimś** *uj.* take advantage of sb, use sb; **wyręczać się kimś w czymś** have sb do sth for sb, get sb to do sth for sb.

wyręczyć (się) *pf. zob.* **wyręczać (się).**

wyręka *f. form.* assistance.

wyrko *n. Gen.pl.* **wyrek** *pot.* (= *łóżko*) sack, hay.

wyro *n. pot.* (= *łóżko*) sack, hay, pad.

wyrobić (się) *pf.* **-rób** *zob.* **wyrabiać (się).**

wyrobienie *n.* (= *ogłada*) sophistication.

wyrobiony *a.* **1.** (= *doświadczony, wprawny*) sophisticated. **2.** (= *zużyty*) worn.

wyrobisko *n. górn.* pit.

wyrocznia *f. Gen.pl.* **-i 1.** (*autorytet*) arbiter, prophet; **wyrocznia w sprawie mody** arbiter of fashion *l.* taste. **2.** (= *przepowiednia*) prophecy. **3.** *hist., mit.* oracle.

wyrodek *mp* **-dk-** *pl.* **-i** *lit.* black sheep, rotten apple.

wyrodnieć *ipf. arch. l. form.* degenerate.

wyrodny *a. uj.* wayward.

wyrodzić się *pf.* **-rodzę -rodzisz, -rodź** *l.* **-ródź** *zob.* **wyradzać się.**

wyroić się *pf.* **-rój** *ent.* swarm.

wyrok *mi zwł. prawn.* sentence; (= *werdykt*) verdict; (= *decyzja*) ruling; **wyrok skazujący** sentence, conviction, verdict of guilty; **wyrok uniewinniający** verdict of not guilty, acquittal; **wyrok zaoczny** judgment by default; **wyrok w zawieszeniu** suspended sentence; **odsiadywać wyrok** serve a sentence, serve *l.* do time; **ogłosić wyrok** pronounce a sentence; **wydawać wyrok (na kogoś)** pass a sentence (on sb); **wykonać wyrok** execute a sentence; **zawieszenie wykonania wyroku** stay of execution.

wyroki *pl. Gen.* **-ów** *lit.* (= *przeznaczenie*) decrees; **niezbadane są wyroki boskie** *l.* **niebios** God moves in mysterious ways.

wyrokować *ipf.* **1.** (= *przewidywać*) cast *l.* make predictions, make a call. **2.** (= *decydować*) determine.

wyrolować *pf. pot.* take for a ride, stiff.

wyrosnąć *pf.* **-rosnę -rośniesz, -rośnij, -rósł -rosła -rośli** *zob.* **wyrastać.**

wyrost *mi* **robić coś na wyrost** do sth for future development.

wyrostek *mp* **-tk-** *pl.* **-i** *pot.* (= *nastolatek*) youngster, youth, teenager. – *mi Gen.* **-a** *anat.* appendix; (*zwł. kostny*) process; **wyrostek robaczkowy** vermiform appendix.

wyrośnięty *a.* grown.

wyrozumiale *adv.* with understanding.

wyrozumiałość *f.* understanding.

wyrozumiały *a.* understanding; **być wyrozumiałym (dla kogoś)** make allowances (for sb).

wyrozumować *pf. zob.* **wyrozumowywać.**

wyrozumowany *a. form.* reasoned.

wyrozumowywać *ipf. form.* reason out.

wyrób *mi* **-o- 1.** *form. l. handl.* (= *produkt*) product; **wyroby** goods; **wyroby ceramiczne** ceramics, ceramicware; **wyroby dziewiarskie** knitwear; **wyroby garncarskie** pottery; **wyroby gotowe** finished products, finished goods; **wyroby stalowe** finished steel; **wyroby szklane** glassware. **2.** *gł. form.* (= *wytwarzanie*) production, manufacture.

wyrój *mi* **-o-** *Gen.pl.* **-ów** *ent.* swarming.

wyrość *pf.* **-rosnę -rośniesz, -rośnij, -rósł -rosła -rośli** *zob.* **wyrastać.**

wyrównać (się) *pf. zob.* **wyrównywać (się).**

wyrównanie *n.* **1.** (*dopłata*) compensation. **2.** *sport* equalizer. **3.** *techn.* equalization, compensation. **4.** *lotn.* trim; (*z lotu nurkowego*) pull-out. **5.** *pat.* control, compensation.

wyrównany *a.* **1.** (*o poziomie*) even, close. **2.** (*o tempie*) steady. **3.** *druk., komp.* justified; **wyrównany do prawej/lewej** right/left-justified.

wyrównawczy *a.* **1.** *szkoln.* (*o zajęciach*) remedial, catch-up. **2.** (*o świadczeniu*) compensatory.

wyrównujący *a. sport* (*o bramce, zagraniu*) equalizing.

wyrównywać *ipf.* **1.** (= *czynić równym*) (*rachunki, obrus, mebel*) square, level. **2.** *sport* equalize, even the score. **3.** (= *rekompensować*) compensate for. **4.** *lotn.* (*o samolocie, pilocie*) level (out), flatten; (*o pilocie*) trim; (*z lotu nurkowego*) pull out. ~ **się** *ipf.* level (out *l.* off).

wyróżniać *ipf.* **1.** (= *faworyzować*) favor. **2.** (= *nagradzać*) honor. **3.** *form.* (= *wyodrębniać*) distinguish. ~ **się** *ipf.* stand out; **wyróżniać się czymś** be distinguished by sth; **wyróżniać się wśród** *l.* **spośród czegoś/kogoś** stand out above sth/sb.

wyróżniający *a.* (= *ponadprzeciętny*) above-average; (= *znakomity*) outstanding; **wyróżniający się** (= *ponadprzeciętny*) above-average; (= *znakomity*) distinguished, outstanding; (= *charakterystyczny*) distinctive.

wyróżnić (się) *pf.* **-ij** *zob.* **wyróżniać (się).**

wyróżnienie *n.* **1.** (= *dowód uznania*) distinction. **2.** (= *nagroda*) honorable mention. **3.** (= *oznaczenie*) identification.

wyróżnik *mi Gen.* **-a 1.** *form.* (= *cecha charakterystyczna*) distinguishing feature *l.* characteristic. **2.** *mat.* discriminant.

wyróżniony *a.* **1.** (= *nagrodzony*) honored. **2.** (= *wybrany*) singled out. **3.** (= *oznaczony*) (*o fragmencie tekstu*) highlighted, marked.

wyrugować *pf.* **1.** (= *usunąć*) oust. **2.** (= *wypędzić*) drive out.

wyruszać *ipf.,* **wyruszyć** *pf.* set out, start; **wyruszać w drogę** get on the road, hit the road.

wyrwa *f.* gap.

wyrwać (się) *pf.* **-wę -wiesz, -wij** *zob.* **wyrywać (się).**

wyrwidąb *mp* **-ę-** *pl.* **-y** *l.* **-owie** *mit.* giant; (*w bajkach*) Paul Bunyan.

wyryczeć *pf.* **-ę -ysz** *pot.* bawl out. ~ **się** *pf. pot.* (= *wypłakać się*) have a good cry.

wyryć *pf.* **-ryję -ryjesz, -ryj 1.** (= *napisać*) inscribe. **2.** (= *wyrzeźbić*) carve.

wyrypać *pf.* **-pię -piesz** *sl., obsc.* (= *odbyć stosunek z*) screw, fuck. ~ **się** *pf.* **-pię -piesz** *pot.* (= *wywrócić się*) take a spill.

wyrysować *pf.,* **wyrysowywać** *ipf.* sketch.

wyrywać *ipf.* **-am -asz 1.** (= *usuwać*) pull (out); (*pincetą*) pluck. **2.** (= *zabierać siłą*) snatch. **3.** **wyrywać kogoś ze snu/z odrętwienia** rouse sb from sleep/from torpor. **4.** *pot.* (= *znikać szybko*) bolt. **5.** **wyrwać kogoś do odpowiedzi** *pot., szkoln.* ask sb at random to answer a question. ~ **się** *ipf.* **1.** (= *wyswobadzać się*) break free. **2.** (= *wybierać się pozostawiając obowiązki*) get away. **3.** (= *mówić bez zastanowienia*) blurt out; **wyrwać się jak Filip z konopi** say sth beside the point; **komuś się coś wyrwało** sb spilled the beans.

wyrywki *pl. Gen.* **-ów na wyrywki** (*pytać*) at random; **znać/umieć coś na wyrywki** have/know sth down pat.

wyrywkowo *adv.* on-and-off, spottily, irregularly.

wyrywkowy *a.* on-and-off, spotty, irregular.

wyrządzać *ipf.*, **wyrządzić** *pf.* inflict; **wyrządzać szkodę** do damage; **wyrządzać krzywdę** harm.

wyrzec *pf.* **-rzeknę -rzekniesz, -rzeknij, -rzekł** *lit.* (= *wypowiedzieć*) utter. **~ się** *pf. zob.* **wyrzekać się.**

wyrzeczenie *n.* sacrifice; **gotowy do wyrzeczeń** prepared for sacrifice.

wyrzekać *ipf. arch. l. dial.* (= *narzekać*) wail. **~ się** *ipf.* **wyrzekać się czegoś/kogoś** renounce sth/sb, disown sth/sb.

wyrzekania *pl. Gen.* **-ń** *arch. l. dial.* wailing.

wyrzeźbić *pf.* **1.** (*rzeźbę*) sculpt, carve. **2.** (= *ukształtować*) shape.

wyrznąć *pf.* **-ij** *zob.* **wyrzynać.** **~ się** *pf. zob.* **wyrzynać.**

wyrzucać *ipf.*, **wyrzucić** *pf.* **1.** (= *ciskać*) throw, fling; **wyrzucać pieniądze** waste/squander money, throw money away; **wyrzucać ramiona, nogi** throw/fling up one's shoulders/legs. **2.** (= *pozbywać się kogoś*) throw away/out; (*z pracy*) fire/sack; (*ze szkoły*) expel; (*z mieszkania*) evict; **wyrzucić kogoś na bruk** throw sb on the street, turn sb into the street; **wyrzucić kogoś na zbity pysk** *pot.* throw sb out head first, kick sb out. **3.** *tylko ipf.* (= *robić wyrzuty*) reproach sb.

wyrzut *mi* **1.** (= *pretensja*) reproach; **robić komuś wyrzuty** reproach sb; **wyrzuty sumienia** pangs *l.* pricks of conscience, remorse, qualms. **2.** (= *rzucanie*) throw, cast, fling.

wyrzutek *mp* **-tk-** *pl.* **-i** outcast, castaway.

wyrzutnia *f. Gen.pl.* **-i 1. wyrzutnia rakietowa** *wojsk.* rocket launcher, launch pad. **2.** *jęz.* elision. **3.** *teor.lit.* ellipsis.

wyrzygać *pf.*, **wyrzygiwać** *ipf. pot.* puke, throw up, chuck up.

wyrzynać *ipf.* **1.** (= *tnąc, zrobić otwór*) carve (out). **2.** (= *tnąc, usuwać fragment*) cut off *l.* away. **3.** *pot.* (*mordować*) slaughter, massacre; **wyrżnąć w pień** *l.* **do nogi** put to the sword. **~ się** *ipf.* (*o zębach*) erupt; **wyrzynają jej się ząbki** she's teething.

wyrzynarka *f. Gen.pl.* **-ek** *techn.* **1.** (*piła*) fretsaw, jigsaw, scroll-saw. **2.** (*obrabiarka*) machine tool.

wyrżnąć *pf.* **-ij 1.** *zob.* **wyrzynać. 2.** (= *uderzyć mocno*) bash, bang; **wyrżnąć komuś prawdę w oczy** rap out the truth to sb's face, give sb a piece of one's mind. **3.** *wulg.* fuck, screw, lay. **~ się** *pf.* **1.** *zob.* **wyrzynać się. 2.** *pot.* (= *uderzyć się*) bang.

wys. *abbr.* (= *wysokość*) alt. (altitude).

wysadzać *ipf.* **1.** (*z pojazdu*) drop *l.* let off. **2.** (= *wysuwać*) put sth out. **3.** (= *wyłamywać*) push out. **4.** (= *niszczyć wybuchem*) blow up, explode; **wysadzić coś w powietrze** blow off *l.* out *l.* up, blast. **5.** *ogr.* plant out. **6.** (= *inkrustować biżuterię*) set sth with precious stones. **~ się** *ipf.* **1.** (= *powodować wybuch*) explode, blow up. **2.**

pot. (= *robić coś na pokaz*) show off, splurge, go all out for.

wysadzany *a.* (*o biżuterii*) (*kamieniami, szafirami, brylantami*) inset with sth, inlaid with sth.

wysadzić (się) *pf. zob.* **wysadzać (się).**

wysapać *pf.* **-pię -piesz** gasp out, get one's breath back.

wysączać *ipf.* (= *wylewać, wypływać*) ooze, trickle; (= *pić powoli*) sip. **~ się** *pf.* ooze out, drip away.

wysączyć (się) *pf. zob.* **wysączać (się).**

wyschnąć *pf.* **-schnij, -schnął** *l.* **-sechł -schła schli** *zob.* **wysychać.**

wyselekcjonować *pf.* select, make a selection, single out.

wysepka *f. Gen.pl.* **-ek 1.** (= *mała wyspa*) island. **2.** (*na przystanku*) safety island.

wysforować się *pf. pot.* take the lead, get ahead of the rest.

wysiać (się) *pf.* **-eję -ejesz, -siali** *l.* **-sieli** *zob.* **wysiewać (się).**

wysiadać *ipf.* **1.** (*z pojazdu*) get off *l.* out. **2. ja wysiadam** *pot.* (= *rezygnuję*) I give up *l.* quit. **3.** *pot.* (= *przestawać działać*) break down, crash; **wysiadła mi wątroba** I have a bad liver; **wysiadł silnik** the engine crashed *l.* went blooey.

wysiadka *f. Gen.pl.* **-ek** *pot.* time to get off.

wysiadywać *ipf.* **1.** (*o ptakach*) brood, incubate. **2.** *tylko ipf.* (= *przesiadywać gdzieś*) spend hours (sitting) somewhere.

wysiąkać *ipf.* ooze *l.* leak out.

wysiąść *pf.* **-siądę -siądziesz -siadł -siedli** *zob.* **wysiadać.**

wysiec *pf.* **-siekę -sieczesz -siekł 1.** (= *zabić*) slaughter, cut down *l.* out, cut (people) to pieces. **2.** (= *wychłostać*) flog, lash.

wysiedlać *ipf.* displace, resettle.

wysiedleniec *mp* **-ńc-** *pl.* **-y** displaced person.

wysiedlić *pf. zob.* **wysiedlać.**

wysiedzieć *pf.* **-dzę -dzisz 1.** *zob.* **wysiadywać. 2.** (= *wytrwać, siedząc*) sit out *l.* through sth.

wysiew *mi* **1.** *roln.* sowing, amount sown (in a given area). **2.** *biol.* seeding, inoculation.

wysiewać *ipf.* **1.** *roln.* (= *posiać*) sow. **2.** (= *zużyć ziarno*) sow out. **3.** *biol.* seed, inoculate. **~ się** *ipf.* **1.** (*o roślinach*) self-sow. **2.** (*o bakteriach*) plant, inoculate.

wysięgnik *mi Gen.* **-a** *techn.* exterior arm; **wysięgnik żurawia** crane jib.

wysięk *mi pat.* exudation, exudate.

wysiękowy *a. pat.* exudative.

wysilać *ipf.* exert, strain, force; **wysilać umysł** rack one's brains; **wysilać dowcip** plumb the depths to tell a joke; **wysilać wzrok/słuch** strain one's eyes/ears. **~ się** *ipf.* exert *l.* strain o.s.; **wysilić się na dowcip** try hard to tell a joke.

wysilić (się) *pf.* **= wysilać (się).**

wysiłek *mi* **-łk- 1.** effort, strain; **wysiłek fizyczny** physical effort. **2. wysiłek umysłowy** mental *l.* brain effort; **udaremniać czyjeś wysiłki** thwart *l.* foil one's efforts; **wkładać w coś wysiłek** put a lot of effort in sth, make great efforts; **robić coś bez wysiłku** do sth without any effort, do sth effortlessly; **zmusić się ostatnim wysiłkiem woli** put one last ounce of strength *l.* courage into sth, make a final effort to do sth.

wysiudać *pf. pot.* chuck *l.* kick sb out.

wyskakiwać *ipf.* **1.** (= *skacząc, wydostawać się*) jump out *l.* off; (*z pociągu*) jump off the train; **wyskakiwać z łóżka** jump out of bed; **wyskoczyć skądś jak z procy** take off like a shot; **o mało ze skóry nie wyskoczył** he almost leapt out of his skin; **przecież nie wyskoczył sroce spod ogona** but he didn't come out of the blue, but he didn't come out from nowhere. **2.** (= *pojawiać się nagle*) appear, show up, pop out; **wyskoczył zza rogu** he popped out from behind *l.* around the corner. **3.** (= *być wypychany*) be pushed off, come off; **pociąg wyskoczył z szyn** the train has come off the track; **serce mi o mało nie wyskoczyło z piersi** my heart almost leapt for joy; **oczy mu o mało nie wyskoczą z orbit** his eyes almost pop out. **4.** *pot.* (= *wychodzić na chwilę*) pop out, run over. **5.** *pot.* (= *mówić coś w nieodpowiednim momencie*) come out with sth.

wyskalować *pf. techn.* graduate, scale.

wyskalowany *a. techn.* graduated, calibrated.

wyskamlać *pf.* -mlam -mlę *l.* -mlasz -mlesz, -mlaj *l.* -ml *pot.* obtain by pestering people with one's whining, obtain by nagging others about it.

wyskandować *pf.* recite.

wysklepić (się) *pf. zob.* **wysklepiać (się)**.

wysklepiać *ipf.* arch. ~ **się** *ipf.* arch.

wysklepienie *n.* arching; **wysklepienie stopy** *anat.* arching of the foot.

wyskoczyć *pf. zob.* **wyskakiwać**.

wyskok *mi* **1.** (= *wybryk*) excess, fling. **2.** *pot.* (= *wypad dokądś*) outing, jaunt. **3.** *sport* jump.

wyskokowy *a. pot.* intoxicating, alcoholic; **napoje wyskokowe** booze, strong drinks.

wyskrobać *pf.* -bię -biesz *zob.* **wyskrobywać**.

wyskrobek *mp* -bk- *pl.* -i *żart. l. iron.* last-born child.

wyskrobywać *ipf.* **1.** (= *wydobywać, skrobiąc*) scrape up. **2.** (= *skrobiąc, usuwać*) scrape off. **3.** (= *skrobiąc, pisać*) scratch.

wyskubać *pf.* -bię -biesz, **wyskubywać** *ipf.* **1.** (= *skubiąc, usunąć*) pluck out. **2.** (*o zwierzętach*) nibble.

wysłać[1] *pf.* -ślę -ślesz, -ślij *zob.* **wysyłać**.

wysłać[2] *pf.* -ścielę -ścielesz, -ściel *zob.* **wyściełać**.

wysłanniczka *f. Gen.pl.* -ek, **wysłannik** *mp lit.* envoy.

wysławiać[1] *ipf. lit.* (= *nie szczędzić pochwał, zaszczytów*) glorify, praise.

wysławiać[2] *ipf.* (= *wyrażać słowami*) express. ~ **się** *ipf.* (= *wyrażać słowami*) express o.s.

wysłodki *pl. Gen.* -ów *roln.* beet pulp.

wysłody *pl. Gen.* -ów *roln.* sweatwater.

wysłowić (się) *pf.* -ów *zob.* **wysławiać (się)**.

wysłuchać *pf.*, **wysłuchiwać** *ipf.* **1.** (= *słuchając, przyjąć do wiadomości*) hear. **2.** *tylko pf.* (= *spełniać prośbę*) answer; **twoja modlitwa została wysłuchana** your prayer has been answered.

wysługa *f.* service; **wysługa lat** seniority.

wysługiwać *ipf.* (= *służąc, zapracowywać na coś*) obtain sth for one's service.

wysługiwać się *ipf.* **1.** *uj.* (= *służyć komuś*) serve sb; **wysługiwać się komuś za kawałek chleba** lackey sb for a piece of bread. **2.** (= *wyręczać się kimś*) make use of sb; **wysługiwać się kimś** use sb.

wysłużony *a.* well-worn; (*o samochodzie*) used car; (*o butach, ubraniu*) well-worn.

wysłużyć *pf.* **1.** *zob.* **wysługiwać**. **2.** (= *służąc, odpracować*) work off by service. ~ **się** *pf.* (= *zniszczyć się*) get worn out.

wysmagać *pf.* batter, beat, lash; (*batem*) flog.

wysmakowany *a.* refined, distinguished; (*o wystroju, stroju, kompozycji*) tasteful.

wysmarkać *pf. pot.* blow (one's nose). ~ **się** *pf. pot.* blow one's nose.

wysmarować *pf.* **1.** (= *smarując, pokryć powierzchnię*) smear, spread. **2.** (= *ubrudzić*) smear, stain. **3.** (= *smarując, zużyć coś*) use sth up for smearing. ~ **się** *pf.* **1.** (= *smarując, pokryć się czymś*) smear one's body/face (*czymś* with sth). **2.** (= *ubrudzić się*) get dirty.

wysmażać *ipf.* **1.** (= *smażyć dokładnie*) fry. **2.** *pot.* (= *pisać coś z trudem*) write with difficulty, put together. ~ **się** *ipf.* **1.** (= *smażąc, mocno się rumienić*) fry. **2.** (= *być wydalonym poprzez smażenie*) render.

wysmażony *a.* fried; **befsztyk dobrze/średnio/słabo wysmażony** well-done/medium/rare (beef)-steak.

wysmażyć (się) *pf. zob.* **wysmażać (się)**.

wysmołować *pf.* tar.

wysmuklać *ipf.*, **wysmuklić** *pf.* get slender.

wysmukły *a.* slender, slim; (*o chłopaku, dziewczynie, wieży*) slender.

wysnuć *pf.*, **wysnuwać** *ipf.* **1.** (= *wyciągnąć nić*) extract *l.* draw out. **2.** (= *rozwinąć z kłębka*) unravel. **3.** (= *dojść do przekonania*) deduce, infer, extrapolate; **wysnuć wniosek** draw a conclusion, conclude.

wysoce *adv. lit.* highly, extremely; **wysoce niestosowny/nietaktowny** highly inappropriate/intactful.

wysoczyzna *f. geogr.* upland, altitude.

wysoki *a.* **wyższy** **1.** (= *wyróżniający się wysokością*) tall; (*o chłopaku, dziewczynie, domu, kominie, górze*) tall; (*o fali*) tall, big; (*o obcasach*) high; **za wysokie progi na twoje nogi** you were born on the wrong side of the tracks. **2.** (= *mający wymiar od podstawy do wierzchołka*) tall; **wyższy ode mnie o dziesięć centymetrów** he's ten centimeters taller than me; **dom wysoki na trzy piętra** a three storey house. **3.** (= *położony powyżej czegoś*) high; (*o pułapie chmur, locie*) high; **wyższe partie gór** higher parts of the mountains; **spotkanie na najwyższym szczeblu** top-level meeting; **samogłoska wysoka** *fon.* high vowel; **wysoki poziom kandydatów** high level of knowledge of the candidates; **w najwyższym stopniu** in the highest degree; **wysokie mniemanie o sobie** good *l.* high opinion of o.s.; **dzieło wysokiego lotu** high-class work, high-standard work. **4.** (= *znaczny*) high, heavy; (*o cenach, stawkach, cłach,* *ciśnieniu*) high; **wysoka stawka** (*w grze hazardowej*) high stakes; (*o cłach*) heavy; **najwyższy wymiar kary** *prawn.* capital punishment; **wysokie napięcie** *el.* high voltage; **strefa wysokiego ciśnienia** *meteor.* high-pressure area; **najwyższy czas** it's high *l.* about time. **5.** (= *mający duże znaczenie*) high; (*o ocenie, nocie, gatunku, odznaczeniu, randze, urzędniku, instancji*) high; **wysoka stopa życiowa** *ekon.* high standard of living, high living standard; **Wysoki Sądzie!** Your Honor!; **Wysoka Izbo!** *polit.* Honorable Members!; **Wysoka Rado!** *uniw.* Honorable Members!; **szkoła wyższa** institution of higher learning; **wyższe wykształcenie** college *l.* university education; **stopień wyższy** *gram.* comparative; **stopień najwyższy** *gram.* superlative; **izba wyższa** *polit.* upper chamber *l.* house; **siła wyższa** force majeure; **to wyższa szkoła jazdy** it's the big league, that's a whole different ball game. **6.** (*o dźwięku, o głosie*) high(-pitched); (*o tonie, tenorze, sopranie*) acute. **7.** *lit.* (= *wzniosły*) superior, lofty, exalted; **instytucja wyższej użyteczności** high utility (institution); **powołany do wyższych celów** called for some higher purposes.

wysoko *adv.* **wyżej** **1.** (= *nie nisko*) high; (*skoczyć, rosnąć*) high. **2.** (= *powyżej*) higher; (*latać*) high; **wyżej wspomniany** the above mentioned; **co najwyżej** at (the) most; **najwyżej nie pojadę** in the worst case I won't go; **cenić kogoś wysoko** have a high opinion of sb, think highly of sb; **wysoko postawiony** *pot.* somebody high up, high-ranking official; **zajść wysoko** climb up, climb high (in the social scale). **3.** (= *znacznie*) highly; **wysoko ubezpieczony/płatny** highly-insured/paid; **grać wysoko** play high, play for high stakes; **wygrać wysoko z kimś** defeat sb crushingly. **4.** (*o dźwięku, o głosie*) high.

wysokociśnieniowy *a. techn.* high-pressure.

wysokogatunkowy *a.* high-class, high-grade, high-quality; (*o stali, wełnie, koniaku, wódce*) high-quality.

wysokogórski *a.* alpine; **klimat wysokogórski** alpine climate; **turystyka wysokogórska** mountaineering; **kurort wysokogórski** mountain resort; **klub wysokogórski** mountaineering club.

wysokokaloryczny *a.* high-calorie; (*o paliwie*) high-energy.

wysokoobrotowy *a. techn.* high-speed; (*o silniku*) high-revolution; (*o wiertarce*) high-speed.

wysokooktanowy *a.* high-octane.

wysokopienny *a.* standard; (*o lesie*) high forest.

wysokoprężny *a. techn.* **silnik wysokoprężny** diesel engine.

wysokoprocentowy *a.* high-grade; (*o alkoholu*) high-proof; (*o pożyczce*) high-interest.

wysokościomierz *mi Gen.* **-a** **1.** *techn.* height indicator, altimeter. **2.** *lotn.* altimeter.

wysokościowiec *mi* **-wc-** *Gen.* **-a** high-rise.

wysokościowy *a.* height, altitude; (*o locie, pomiarach*) high altitude.

wysokość *f.* **1.** (*wymiar*) height; (*domu, pokoju, wieży*) height; **drzewa do trzydziestu metrów**

wysokości trees as high as thirty meters. **2.** (*odległość*) altitude; **latać na dużej wysokości** fly at high altitude; **wznieść się na dużą wysokość** rise at high altitude; **widzieć coś z wysokości** see sth from high altitude; **jesteśmy na wysokości Gdyni** *żegl.* we're the same longitude as Gdynia; **nabierać wysokości** *lotn.* gain altitude; **wytracać wysokość** *lotn.* lose altitude; **stanąć na wysokości zadania** rise to the occasion. **3.** (= *wielkość*) height, amount, extent; **wysokość zarobków/renty** amount of earnings/pension; **wysokość temperatury** degree of temperature; **mandat w wysokości stu złotych** the fine in the amount of one hundred zloty; **wasza wysokość!** Your Highness; **jego wysokość** His Highness. **4.** (*o dźwięku*) pitch; **wysokość dźwięku/tonu/głosu** sound/tone/voice pitch. **5.** *geom.* height.

wysondować *pf.* **1.** (= *zbadać sondą*) probe, sound out. **2.** (= *zebrać informacje*) sound out.

wyspa *f.* island; **bezludna wyspa** desert island; **wyspa koralowa** coral island.

wyspać się *pf.* **-śpię -śpisz, -śpij** *zob.* **wysypiać się.**

wyspany *a.* well rested after a good sleep; **jestem wyspany** I (have) had a good night's sleep.

wyspecjalizować *pf.* specialize. **~ się** *pf.* (= *stać się specjalistą*) specialize in sth, become a specialist in sth.

wyspecjalizowany *a.* specialized; **wyspecjalizowany chirurg** specialist surgeon; **adwokat wyspecjalizowany w rozwodach** attorney specializing in divorces.

wyspiarski *a.* insular, island-living; (*o klimacie, plemieniu, zwyczajach*) insular.

wyspiarz *mp* islander.

wysportowany *a.* athletic.

wyspowiadać *pf. rel.* hear sb's confession, confess sb. **~ się** *pf.* **1.** *rel.* confess. **2.** (= *zwierzyć się*) confide sth to sb.

wyspowy *a.* insular; **szelf wyspowy** insular shelf.

wysprzątać *pf.* tidy up, clean up.

wysprzedać *pf. zob.* **wysprzedawać.**

wysprzedany *a.* sold out.

wysprzedawać *ipf.* **-aję -ajesz, -awaj** clear.

wysrać się *pf. wulg.* shit, take a shit.

wyssać *pf.* **-ssę -ssiesz, -ssij** *zob.* **wysysać.**

wystać *pf.* **-stoję -stoisz, -stój** **1.** (= *stojąc, wytrzymać*) stand for a long time. **2.** (= *stojąc, zdobyć coś*) obtain sth at the cost of long standing, get by standing and waiting. **~ się** *pf.* stand to the limit of one's patience.

wystający *a.* protruding, projecting; (*o kościach policzkowych*) protruding, pushed out; (*o belce*) sticking out.

wystarać się *pf.* arrange sth, fix up sth.

wystarczać *ipf.* suffice, be sufficient, be enough; **chleba nie wystarczy** there is not enough bread; **wystarczy, abyś...** it's enough to...; **wystarczy, jak zadzwonisz** just call.

wystarczająco *adv.* enough; (*zarabiać*) sufficiently.

wystarczający *a.* sufficient.

wystarczyć *pf. zob.* **wystarczać.**

wystartować *ipf.* **1.** *sport* take part. **2.** *lotn.* take off. **3.** *pot.* (= *rozpocząć*) go ahead, kick off.

wystawa *f.* **1.** (= *zbiór okazów*) exhibition, exhibit. **2.** (= *witryna*) shop window. **3.** (= *psów, kotów*) show.

wystawać *ipf.* **-aję -ajesz, -awaj 1.** (= *wysuwać się poza jakąś granicę*) protrude, stick out. **2.** (= *spędzać czas stojąc*) stand.

wystawca *mp* **1.** (*handlowiec*) exhibitor. **2.** (= *ten, kto wystawia zobowiązanie finansowe*) drawer.

wystawiać *ipf.*, **wystawić** *pf.* **1.** (= *wynosić na zewnątrz*) put *l.* take sth outside. **2.** (= *wysuwać coś poza obręb czegoś*) put *l.* take sth out of sth. **3.** (= *prezentować*) exhibit; **wystawić na sprzedaż** put sth up for sale *l.* auction; **wystawić kogoś na pośmiewisko** make a laughing stock of sb, make a fool (out) of sb. **4.** (= *poddawać działaniu czegoś*) expose to sth; **wystawić kogoś na próbę** put sb to the test; **wystawić piłkę** *sport* pass the ball. **5.** *teatr* put up, produce, stage. **6.** (= *proponować czyjąś kandydaturę*) put up sb. **7.** (= *wypisywać rachunek, czek*) make out, write out; **wystawić rachunek** make out the bill. **8.** *myśl.* point. **9.** *tylko pf.* (= *wznieść, zbudować*) raise, erect; (*pomnik*) erect.

wystawiać się *ipf.*, **wystawić się** *pf.* (= *czynić się widocznym*) show o.s.; **wystawić się na drwiny** expose o.s. to mockery.

wystawiennictwo *n.* the art of arranging exhibitions.

wystawienniczy *a.* **salon wystawienniczy** showroom.

wystawiony *a.* on display; (*o rachunku*) drawn; (*o przedstawieniu*) staged.

wystawnie *adv.* pompously, sumptuously; **podjąć gości wystawnie** treat the guests with a sumptuous feast.

wystawność *f.* lavishness, pomp.

wystawny *a.* sumptuous, pompous; (*o przyjęciu, życiu*) pompous; (*o obiedzie*) sumptuous.

wystawowy *a.* exhibition; **salon/teren wystawowy** showroom/showground; **okno wystawowe** shop window, window display.

wystąpić *pf. zob.* **występować**.

wystąpienie *n.* **1.** (= *przemowa*) speech. **2.** (= *pojawienie się*) appearance.

wysterylizować *pf.* sterilize.

występ *mi* **1.** (= *przedstawienie, popis*) performance, show. **2.** (= *wystająca część*) ledge, projection.

występek *mi* **-pk- 1.** (= *drobne wykroczenie*) misdemeanor. **2.** *prawn.* petty *l.* minor offense.

występny *a. lit.* wicked, criminal, vicious; (*o człowieku*) wicked; (*o czynie*) criminal.

występować *ipf.* **1.** *teatr* appear, star. **2.** (= *zabierać głos*) speak, take the floor. **3.** (= *pokazywać się, by wywołać wrażenie*) make an appearance, appear; **wystąpiła w sukni z głębokim dekoltem** she appeared in a low-cut dress. **4.** (= *przekraczać jakąś granicę*) step out; (*z szeregu, z brzegów*) drop out; **wystąpić z brzegów** overflow, burst its banks, flood; **wystąp!** *wojsk.* step out!, advance! **5.** (= *rezygnować z członkostwa*)

leave, retire; (*z partii, z organizacji*) leave. **6.** (= *ukazywać się na powierzchni*) surface; **objawy choroby występują po trzech dniach** the disease symptoms appear *l.* are visible after three days; **pot wystąpił mi na czoło** cold perspiration broke out *l.* started out on my forehead.

występowanie *n.* occurrence, appearance, incidence.

wystosować *pf. lit.* send in, submit.

wystraszyć *pf.* **1.** (= *przestraszyć*) scare, frighten. **2.** (= *odstraszyć*) scare *l.* frighten away. **~ się** *pf.* get scared *l.* frightened.

wystroić *pf.* **-strój** deck out, dress up. **~ się** *pf.* get dressed up, get spruced up.

wystrojony *a.* dressed up, spruced up; (*o dziewczynie*) dressed up; **wystrojony w nowe ubranie** dressed in a new outfit.

wystrój *mi* **-o-** *Gen.pl.* **-ów** *bud.* decor, interior decoration.

wystrugać *pf.* carve, whittle.

wystrychnąć *pf.* **-ij** let sb down; **wystrychnąć kogoś na dudka** make a fool of sb.

wystrzał *mi* **1.** (= *strzał z broni*) firing, (gun)-shot; **zdobyć miasto bez wystrzału** capture the city without a shot. **2.** (*huk*) report. **3.** *pot.* (= *sensacja*) sensation, scoop.

wystrzałowo *adv. pot.* sensationally; (*wyglądać*) snazzy, smart.

wystrzałowy *a. pot.* sharp, snazzy, flashy; (*o wyglądzie, samochodzie*) snazzy.

wystrzegać się *ipf.* beware (*kogoś / czegoś*) (of sb/sth).

wystrzelać *pf. zob.* **wystrzeliwać**. **~ się** *pf.* shoot each other *l.* one another (dead).

wystrzelić *pf. zob.* **wystrzeliwać**.

wystrzeliwać *ipf.* **-wuję -wujesz, -wuj 1.** (= *pozabijać*) shoot (dead). **2.** (= *strzelając, zużyć amunicję*) use up all one's ammunition. **3.** (= *strzelać z broni palnej*) fire, shoot; **wystrzelić rakietę** launch a rocket. **4.** (= *wznosić się w górę*) soar, rise.

wystrzępiać *ipf.* fray. **~ się** *ipf.* ravel, fray out.

wystrzępić (się) *pf. zob.* **wystrzępiać (się)**.

wystrzępiony *a.* frayed, fuzzy; (*o spodniach, sukience*) frayed pants/dress.

wystudiować *pf.* **1.** (= *zapoznać się z czymś*) study. **2.** (= *wypracować coś*) work out, develop.

wystudiowany *a.* worked out, developed; (*o pozie, roli*) studied, posing.

wystudzić *pf.* cool (down). **~ się** *pf.* cool.

wystukać *pf.*, **wystukiwać** *ipf.* tap, patter.

wystygnąć *pf.* **-gł** *l.* **-gnął -gła** cool (down).

wystylizować *pf.* stylize.

wysublimować *pf.* sublime, elevate. **~ się** *pf.* get sublimed.

wysublimowany *a.* sophisticated, sublime; (*o guście, teorii, dowcipie*) sophisticated.

wysubtelnieć *pf.* get refined.

wysunąć (się) *pf. zob.* **wysuwać (się)**.

wysunięty *a.* advance.

wysupłać *pf.*, **wysupływać** *ipf.* disentangle; (*pieniądze*) take out.

wysuszać *ipf.*, **wysuszyć** *pf.* dry, wither, parch.

wysuszyć się *pf.* dry up, get l. become dry.

wysuwać *ipf.* **1.** (= *sunąc, wystawiać coś poza jakąś granicę*) move out, push out, shove out; (*szufladę, stół, krzesło*) pull out; **wysunąć kandydaturę** put forward l. put up a candidate. **2.** (= *przedstawiać*) propose, put forward, set forward; (*zarzut, żądanie, propozycję, wniosek, postulat*) put forward. **3.** (= *wyjmować coś spod czegoś*) move out (of sth), take out (of sth); **wysunąć nogę spod koca** stick one's leg from under blanket. ~ **się** *ipf.* **1.** (= *ukazywać się*) appear, emerge; **wysunąć się na czoło** come out (at the) top (of), get ahead (of); **wysunąć się na pierwsze miejsce** l. **pierwszy plan** take the lead, come to the fore. **2.** (= *wypadać skądś*) slip. **3.** (= *wychodzić niepostrzeżenie*) leave unnoticed, sneak out, slip out.

wysuwalny *a. zool.* protractile; (*o języku*) protrusile.

wyswatać *pf.* match (sb with sb), marry sb off.

wyswobadzać *ipf.*, **wyswobodzić** *pf.* liberate, free.

wyswobodzić się *pf.* free o.s.

wysychać *ipf.* **1.** (= *tracić wilgoć*) dry; **wyschło mi w gardle** I feel dry. **2.** (*o cieczy*) (= *znikać pod wpływem temperatury*) dry up. **3.** *pot.* (= *chudnąć*) thin down.

wysyczeć *pf.* **-ę -ysz** hiss.

wysyłać *ipf.* **1.** send. **2.** (= *rzucać, kopać*) send, kick, shoot; (*piłkę do bramki*) kick. **3.** *tylko ipf.* (= *emitować*) send, emit; (*ciepło, światło*) emit.

wysyłka *f. Gen.pl.* **-ek** dispatch.

wysyłkowy *a.* mail order; (*o sprzedaży*) mail-order; **firma wysyłkowa** mail-order firm l. company.

wysyp *mi ogr.* bumper crop, good year for sth.

wysypać *pf.* **-pię -piesz** *zob.* **wysypywać**. ~ **się** *pf.* **1.** *zob.* **wysypywać się**. **2.** (= *pojawić się w dużej ilości*) break out, pour out; **krosty wysypały się jej na twarzy** pimples broke out on her face, she came out in spots l. pimples.

wysypiać się *ipf.* **1.** (= *śpiąc, wypoczywać*) get enough sleep. **2.** (= *spać długo*) sleep one's fill.

wysypisko *n.* dump, landfill (site).

wysypka *f. Gen.pl.* **-ek** *pat.* rash, eruption.

wysypywać *ipf.* **1.** (= *sypiąc, usuwać coś*) dump, spill l. pour out, empty; **wysypywać piasek z butów** pour l. take the sand out of the shoes; **wysypywać śmieci do pojemnika** dump the garbage into the garbage can. **2.** (= *sypiąc, pokrywać powierzchnię*) sprinkle, scatter, strew; **wysypywać alejkę żwirem** scatter an alley with gravel; **wysypywać blachę bułką tartą** scatter a baking tray with breadcrumbs. ~ **się** *ipf.* **1.** (= *sypiąc się, wydostawać się*) spill out. **2.** (= *wydostawać się skądś tłumnie*) pour out.

wysysać *ipf.* **1.** (= *ssąc, wyciągać substancję*) suck out; **wyssać coś z mlekiem matki** suck in with one's mother milk; **wyssać coś z palca** take sth out of the air, invent sth, fabricate sth. **2.** (= *wchłaniać coś*) suck up.

wyszabrować *pf.* loot.

wyszaleć się *pf.* have one's fling, sow one's (wild) oats.

wyszarpać *pf.* **-pię -piesz 1.** *zob.* **wyszarpywać**. **2.** (= *wytarmosić*) pull about. ~ **się** *pf. zob.* **wyszarpywać się**.

wyszarpnąć (się) *pf.* **-ij** *zob.* **wyszarpywać (się)**.

wyszarpywać *ipf.* tear, pull, wrench. ~ **się** *ipf.* **1.** (= *wyrywać się*) tear o.s. away. **2.** (= *być wyrwanym, podartym*) be l. get torn out.

wyszczebiotać *pf.* **-oczę -oczesz** l. **-ocę -ocesz, -ocz** chirp out.

wyszczególniać *ipf.*, **wyszczególnić** *pf.* **-ij** detail, specify.

wyszczególnienie *n.* detailed list, inventory.

wyszczekany *a. pot.* glib, big-mouthed, talky; (*o kobiecie, żonie*) big-mouthed.

wyszczerbić *pf.* chip. ~ **się** *pf.* get chipped.

wyszczerzać *ipf.*, **wyszczerzyć** *pf.* grin; (*zęby, kły*) bare.

wyszczotkować *pf.* brush.

wyszczuplać *ipf.* make sb look slimmer; **czarny mnie wyszczupla** black makes me look slimmer.

wyszczupleć *pf.* slim down, grow slimmer.

wyszedł *itd. pf. zob.* **wyjść**.

wyszeptać *pf.* **-pczę -pczesz** l. **-pcę -pcesz, -pcz, wyszeptywać** *ipf.* whisper.

wyszkolenie *n.* **1.** *sport* training. **2.** *wojsk.* training.

wyszkolić *pf.* **-kol** l. **-kól** train, educate. ~ **się** *pf.* get training, be educated.

wyszkolony *a.* trained.

wyszlachetnieć *pf.* become noble.

wyszli *itd. pf. zob.* **wyjść**.

wyszlifować *pf.*, **wyszlifowywać** *ipf.* polish.

wyszła *itd. pf. zob.* **wyjść**.

wyszmelcować *pf. pot.* wear (*sth*) out.

wyszmelcowany *a. pot.* grimy; (*o kurtce, siedzeniu*) worn out.

wyszorować *pf.* scrub. ~ **się** *pf.* wash up.

wyszperać *pf.* dig out, ferret out.

wyszpiegować *pf.* spy out.

wysztafirować się *pf. pot.* spruce up, primp, deck out.

wysztafirowany *a. pot.* spruced up, decked out; (*o sąsiadce, dziewczynie*) spiffed up.

wyszukać *pf. zob.* **wyszukiwać**.

wyszukanie *n.* search.

wyszukany *a.* sophisticated, fine; (*o projekcie, stroju, potrawach, grzeczności*) sophisticated.

wyszukiwać *ipf.* search out, look up.

wyszumieć *pf.* **-ę -isz** cease foaming. ~ **się** *pf.* have one's fling, sow one's wild oats.

wysumować *pf.* skim.

wyszyć *pf.* **-ję -jesz** *zob.* **wyszywać**.

wyszydzać *ipf.*, **wyszydzić** *pf.* scoff, deride.

wyszykować *pf. pot.* **1.** (= *przygotować*) prepare, get ready. **2.** (= *ubrać kogoś*) dress sb up.

wyszynk *mi* retail of alcoholic drinks, liquor license.

wyszywać *ipf.* **-am -asz** embroider; **wyszywać serwetę w kwiaty** embroider some flowers on a cloth.

wyszywanka *f. Gen.pl.* **-ek** embroidery.

wyszywany *a.* embroidered.

wyściełać *ipf.* line (*sth*) (*czymś* with sth).

wyścielany *a.* padded; (*o krześle*) upholstered *l.* cushioned.

wyścig *mi* **1.** *sport* race; **robić coś na wyścigi** vie with each another to do sth, race one another; **wyścig z czasem** race against time. **2.** *polit.* race; **wyścig zbrojeń** the arms race.

wyścigi *pl. Gen.* **-ów** (*teren*) race area; **grać na wyścigach** bet *l.* gamble on the horses.

wyścigowy *a.* race; **samochód/rower wyścigowy** racing car/bike; **koń wyścigowy** racehorse.

wyściółka *f. Gen.pl.* **-ek** lining, padding, stuffing.

wyściskać *pf.* hug, embrace. **~ się** *pf.* hug each other.

wyściubiać *ipf.*, **wyściubić** *pf. pot.* stick one's head out.

wyśledzić *pf.* track down.

wyślę *itd. pf. zob.* **wysłać**.

wyślizgać *pf.* (= *uczynić śliskim*) make slippery. **~ się** *pf.* (= *stać się śliskim*) become slippery.

wyślizgany *a.* slippery.

wyślizgiwać się *ipf.*, **wyślizgnąć się** *pf.* **-ij**, **wyślizgnąć się** *pf.* **-ij 1.** (= *wysuwać się*) slip (out). **2.** (= *wychodzić skądś niepostrzeżenie*) sneak *l.* slip out.

wyśmiać *pf.* **-śmieję -śmiejesz, -śmiali** *l.* **-śmieli** *zob.* **wyśmiewać**. **~ się** *pf.* **1.** *zob.* **wyśmiewać się**. **2.** (= *naśmiać się do woli*) be in stitches, laugh o.s. sick.

wyśmienicie *adv.* excellently.

wyśmienity *a.* excellent, stellar; (*o obiedzie*) delicious; (*o odpowiedzi, humorze*) excellent.

wyśmiewać *ipf.* jeer (*kogoś/coś* at sb/sth). **~ się** *ipf.* (= *szydzić*) deride, sneer, jeer (*z kogoś/czegoś* at sb/sth).

wyśnić *pf.* **-ij** imagine. **~ się** *pf.* **1.** (= *ukazać się we śnie*) appear in a dream. **2.** (*o śnie*) (= *urzeczywistnić się*) come true.

wyśniony *a.* dream; **wyśniony mąż/ideał** dream husband/ideal.

wyśpiewywać *pf.*, **wyśpiewywać** *ipf.* **1.** (= *odśpiewać*) sing. **2.** (= *wyrazić śpiewem*) sing, sound. **3.** *pot.* (= *powiedzieć bez zająknięcia*) say without a hitch. **4.** *pot.* (= *przyznać się*) give away. **5.** *tylko ipf.* (= *śpiewać z przejęciem*) sing with fervor.

wyśrodkować *pf.*, **wyśrodkowywać** *ipf. druk.* middle space.

wyśrubować *pf. zob.* **wyśrubowywać**.

wyśrubowany *a. pot.* inflated, steep; (*o normie*) exacting.

wyśrubowywać *ipf. pot.* inflate, raise.

wyświadczać *ipf.*, **wyświadczyć** *pf.* render; **wyświadczyć komuś przysługę, uprzejmość, grzeczność** do sb a favor.

wyświecać *ipf.* **1.** *przest.* (= *wygnać*) chase (away). **2.** *tylko pf.* (= *wypolerować*) polish. **3.** *tylko pf.* (*o ubraniu*) (*niszczyć*) wear (clothes) out. **~ się** *ipf.* (*o ubraniu*) wear out.

wyświechtać *pf. pot.* wear (*sth*) out. **~ się** *pf. pot.* wear out.

wyświechtany *a. pot.* shabby, threadbare, stale; (*o frazesach*) hackneyed platitudes.

wyświecić (się) *pf. zob.* **wyświecać (się)**.

wyświetlacz *mi Gen.* **-a** *techn.* display.

wyświetlać *ipf.* **1.** (*w kinie*) project, show. **2.** *techn.* display. **3.** (= *wyjaśniać*) clear up, elucidate. **~ się** *ipf.* get displayed.

wyświetlarka *f. Gen.pl.* **-ek** *techn.* projector.

wyświetlić (się) *pf. zob.* **wyświetlać (się)**.

wyświęcać *ipf.*, **wyświęcić** *pf.* **1.** *rel.* (*na kapłana*) ordain. **2.** *rel.* (= *poświęcić coś*) consecrate.

wytaczać *ipf.* **1.** (= *tocząc, wyciągać*) roll out, wheel out. **2.** (= *przedstawiać w wypowiedzi*) bring forward, present, set forth; (*argumenty, zarzuty, żale*) bring forward; **wytoczyć komuś proces** *prawn.* bring a lawsuit against sb, institution a suit against sb. **3.** *techn.* lathe. **~ się** *ipf.* **1.** (= *tocząc się, wysuwać się*) roll out. **2.** *pot.* (*o kimś grubym*) (= *wyjść*) roll *l.* waddle out.

wytapetować *pf.* paper, wallpaper.

wytapiać *ipf.* smelt, melt. **~ się** *ipf.* be smelted, be melted down.

wytargać *pf.* pull (out); **wytargać kogoś za uszy** pull sb's ears.

wytargować *pf.* beat down (price), obtain by haggling.

wytarmosić *pf.* **-szę -sisz** pull about.

wytarować *pf.* tare.

wytarty *a.* **1.** (= *zniszczony*) threadbare, shabby, worn out, frayed; (*o płaszczu, tapicerce*) threadbare; **wytarty banał, frazes** hackneyed banalities *l.* platitude, trite banalities *l.* platitude. **2.** *icht.* spent.

wytarzać *pf.* roll about, wallow. **~ się** *pf.* wallow.

wytaskać *pf.*, **wytaskiwać** *ipf.*, **wytaszczyć** *pf. pot.* (= *wynieść*) lug out.

wytatuować *pf.* tatoo. **~ się** *pf.* have o.s. tatooed.

wytchnąć *pf.* **-ij** pause (for breath).

wytchnienie *n.* pause, break, rest; **mieć kilka dni wytchnienia** have a couple of days off; **bez wytchnienia** without pausing for breath, without breathing spell.

wytępić *pf.* **1.** (= *zgładzić*) kill (off), exterminate. **2.** (= *wykorzenić*) eradicate.

wytęskniony *a.* longed-for, anxiously awaited.

wytężać *ipf.* strain; (*siły*) exert. **~ się** *ipf.* exert o.s.

wytężony *a.* strenuous; (*o pracy*) hard, intensive.

wytężyć *pf. zob.* **wytężać**. **~ się** *pf. zob.* **wytężać się**.

wytknąć *pf.* **-ij** *zob.* **wytykać**.

wytłaczać *ipf.* **1.** (= *wyciskać*) squeeze out, press; (*sok, oliwę, olej*) extract. **2.** (= *odciskać na powierzchni*) imprint, impress, emboss. **3.** *techn.* extrude.

wytłaczany *a.* embossed.

wytłaczarka *f. Gen.pl.* **-ek** *techn.* extruding machine, stamping-press.

wytłamsić *pf.* **-szę -sisz** *pot.* crumple.

wytłamszony *a. pot.* crumpled, rumpled, wrinkled.

wytłoczyć *pf. zob.* **wytłaczać.**

wytłoki *pl. Gen.* -ów (*odpadki*) pomace, waste; (*winogron*) marc.

wytłuc *pf.* -tłukę -tłuczesz -tłukł 1. *zob.* **wytłukiwać.** 2. *pot.* (= *zbić kogoś*) beat sb up, give sb a thrashing. 3. *pot.* (= *zamordować*) kill off, murder. ~ **się** *pf.* 1. (= *stłuc się doszczętnie*) get broken; **wszystkie talerze się wytłukły** all the plates got broken. 2. *pot.* (= *pozabijać się*) wipe out. 3. *pot.* (= *pobić się z wieloma*) beat sb up, give sb a thrashing.

wytłukiwać *ipf.* 1. (= *rozbijać*) break, smash. 2. (= *rozbijać wiele czegoś*) break up. 3. (*o gradzie*) ruin, spoil.

wytłumaczalny *a.* explicable, accountable; **naukowo wytłumaczalne zjawisko** scientifically explicable phenomenon.

wytłumaczenie *n.* explanation.

wytłumaczyć *pf.* 1. (= *wyjaśnić*) explain, explicate, elucidate. 2. (= *usprawiedliwić*) excuse, justify. ~ **się** *pf.* (= *usprawiedliwić się*) excuse o.s.

wytłumiać *ipf.*, **wytłumić** *pf.* sound-proof; (*o urządzeniu*) muffle.

wytłuszczać *ipf.*, **wytłuścić** *pf.* -tłuszczę -tłuścisz 1. (= *czynić tłustym*) grease. 2. *druk.* print in boldface; (*czcionkę*) boldface. ~ **się** *pf.* (= *zanieczyścić się tłuszczem*) soil o.s. with grease.

wytnę *itd. pf. zob.* **wyciąć.**

wytoczyć *pf. zob.* **wytaczać.** ~ **się** *pf. zob.* **wytaczać się.**

wytonować *pf.* tone (down).

wytop *mi hutn.* 1. (= *wytapianie*) smelting, melting. 2. (*metal*) cast.

wytopić (się) *pf. zob.* **wytapiać (się).**

wytracać *ipf.*, **wytracić** *pf.* 1. *lit.* (= *wyniszczać*) kill, put to death. 2. (= *redukować*) reduce, lose; **wytracać szybkość** lose speed.

wytransportować *pf.* transport, convey.

wytrasować *pf.*, **wytrasowywać** *ipf.* 1. (= *wytyczyć*) trace, lay out (a road). 2. *techn.* mark.

wytrawiać *ipf.*, **wytrawić** *pf.* 1. *chem.* etch. 2. *techn.* etch.

wytrawny *a.* 1. (= *doświadczony*) expert, master; (*o polityku, znawcy, obserwatorze*) experienced, master. 2. (= *niesłodki*) dry.

wytrąbić *pf. pot.* (= *wypić*) swill, gulp down.

wytrącać *ipf.* 1. (= *wybijać*) knock sth out; **wytrącać komuś rewolwer/szklankę/nóż z ręki** knock the gun/glass/knife out of sb's hand; **wytrącić komuś argumenty z ręki** take the wind out of sb's sails. 2. (= *wyrywać kogoś z jakiegoś stanu*) break, snatch away; **wytrącać kogoś ze snu** break sb's sleep. 3. *chem.* precipitate. ~ **się** *ipf. chem.* precipitate.

wytrącić (się) *pf. zob.* **wytrącać (się).**

wytrenować *pf.* train, coach. ~ **się** *pf.* train.

wytrenowany *a.* trained; **dobrze wytrenowany** well-trained.

wytresować *pf.* 1. (*zwierzę*) train (*an animal*). 2. *iron.* drill.

wytropić *pf.* 1. (*zwierzynę*) track down. 2. (*przestępcę*) run down, track down.

wytruć *pf.* poison, exterminate by poisoning. ~ **się** *pf.* 1. (= *otruć jeden drugiego*) poison one another. 2. (= *zostać wytrutym*) be exterminated by poisoning (*e.g. of vermin, insects*).

wytrwać *pf.* persevere (*w czymś* in sth), hold out; **wytrwać na posterunku** keep one's post (*till the very end*); **wytrwać w swoim zamiarze** stick to one's intention.

wytrwale *adv.* persistently, assiduously; **wytrwale dążyć do celu** pursue a goal persistently.

wytrwałość *f.* perseverance, persistence.

wytrwały *a.* persistent, assiduous.

wytrybować *pf.*, **wytrybowywać** *ipf.* 1. *kulin.* bone (and clean) (*meat before cooking*). 2. *sztuka* do a repoussé work.

wytrych *mi Gen.* -u *l.* -a picklock, skeleton key; **otworzyć zamek wytrychem** pick a lock.

wytrysk *mi* 1. (= *wypłynięcie*) gush, spurt. 2. *fizj.* ejaculation; **przedwczesny/opóźniony wytrysk** premature/retarded ejaculation.

wytryskać *ipf.*, **wytryskiwać** *ipf.*, **wytrysnąć** *pf.* -śnie -snął -snęła *l.* -sła 1. (*o wodzie, ropie*) gush, spurt (*z czegoś* from sth). 2. *fizj.* (*o nasieniu*) ejaculate.

wytrzasnąć *pf.* -snę -śniesz, -śnij *pot.* get hold (*coś* of sth) grab hold (*coś* of sth); **skąd to wytrzasnąłeś?** how did you get your hands on it?, how did you get hold of it?; **wytrzasnąć coś spod ziemi** go to the ends of the earth to get hold of sth; **jakimś cudem udało mu się wytrzasnąć trzy skrzynki piwa** he somehow managed to round up three cases of beer. ~ **się** *pf. pot.* (= *wystroić się*) doll up, put on one's glad rags.

wytrząsać *ipf.* 1. (= *trzęsąc, wysypywać*) shake (*coś z czegoś* sth out of sth). 2. *tylko ipf.* (= *wymachiwać*) (*kijem, mieczem*) brandish (*czymś* with sth); (*rękami*) flail (*one's arms, etc.*). ~ **się** *ipf. pot.* (= *wymyślać komuś*) **wytrząsać się nad kimś** tell sb off, take sb to task.

wytrząsnąć *pf.* -snę -śniesz, -śnij *zob.* **wytrząsać.**

wytrząść *pf.* -trzęsę -trzęsiesz -trząś *l.* -trzęś, -trząsł -trzęsła -trzęśli 1. *zob.* **wytrząsać.** 2. (= *zmęczyć kogoś drogą, jazdą*) jolt, jostle (*e.g. during a train ride*). ~ **się** *pf.* (= *zmęczyć się drogą, jazdą*) be jolted, be jostled (*e.g. during a train ride*).

wytrzebić *pf.* 1. (= *wykarczować*) grub out, stump; (= *pozbawić częściowo roślinności*) thin out, clear (*an area of trees, etc.*). 2. (= *usunąć*) extirpate. 3. (= *wybić*) exterminate. 4. (= *wykastrować*) geld.

wytrzeć (się) *pf.* -trę -trzesz, -trzyj, -tarł *zob.* **wycierać (się).**

wytrzepać *pf.* -pię -piesz, **wytrzepywać** *ipf.* beat; **wytrzepać komuś skórę** give sb a sound thrashing, give sb a good hiding. ~ **się** *pf. wulg.* jerk off.

wytrzeszcz *mi* 1. *pat.* exophthalmos *l.* exophthalmus *l.* exophthalmia. 2. *myśl.* (*zwykle pl.*) hare's *l.* rabbit's eye.

wytrzeszczać *ipf.*, **wytrzeszczyć** *pf. pot.* **wytrze-**

szczać gały *l.* **oczy** goggle (*na kogoś/coś* at sb/sth).

wytrzeźwić *pf.* -**ij** sober.

wytrzeźwieć *pf.* sober up.

wytrzeźwienie *n.* sobering up, return to the state of soberness.

wytrzymać *pf. zob.* **wytrzymywać**.

wytrzymałościowy *a.* **1.** endurance; **konkurencja wytrzymałościowa** (*np. maraton*) endurance competition; **trening wytrzymałościowy** endurance training. **2.** *techn.* (of) durability, (of) endurance; **test wytrzymałościowy** endurance *l.* durability test.

wytrzymałość *f.* **1.** (= *wytrwałość*) endurance (*na coś* of sth) resistance (*na coś* to sth); (*na przeciwieństwa losu, choroby*) resilience; **to przechodzi ludzką wytrzymałość!** it's more than flesh and blood can stand! **2.** *techn.* (= *graniczna wartość naprężenia*) strength; (= *trwałość*) durability, endurance.

wytrzymały *a.* **1.** (= *odporny*) resilient, tolerant; **wytrzymały na zimno/ból** tolerant of cold/pain. **2.** (= *nieniszczalny*) durable; (*o butach, odzieży, tkaninie*) heavy-duty.

wytrzymanie *n.* **to nie do wytrzymania!** this is unbearable!

wytrzymywać *ipf.* **1.** (= *znosić coś*) bear, withstand; **nie wytrzymywać krytyki** (*np. o teorii*) not hold water; **nie wytrzymywać porównania** not stand *l.* bear comparison (*z kimś/czymś* with sb/sth); **nie wytrzymywać próby czasu** not stand the test of time; **nie można z tobą wytrzymać!** you're the limit!, you're unbearable!; **nie wytrzymam!** (*reakcja na coś irytującego, zwł. głupotę*) give me strength! **2.** (= *przetrzymać*) hold out, endure; **musisz to wytrzymać!** you have to endure it!, you have to hold out!; **nie mogę już tego wytrzymać** *l.* **dłużej już nie wytrzymam** I can't stand it any longer *l.* more. **3.** (*o przedmiocie - nie ulec zniszczeniu*) hold; **mam nadzieję, że ta lina wytrzyma** I hope this rope will hold. **4.** (= *pozwolić czekać*) keep waiting; **wytrzymać kogoś pod drzwiami** keep sb waiting at the door.

wytupać *pf.* -**pię** -**piesz**, **wytupywać** *ipf.* (= *tupiąc, wystukiwać*) stamp; (*rytm*) mark time (*with one's feet*).

wytwarzać *ipf.* **1.** (= *produkować*) produce; (*np. ciepło, energię*) generate. **2.** (= *powodować*) create; **wytwarzać niepokój** create anxiety. **~ się** *ipf.* **1.** (= *tworzyć się*) be formed. **2.** (= *pojawiać się*) arise, spring up; **w pokoju wytworzyła się niemiła atmosfera** the atmosphere in the room became *l.* grew unpleasant.

wytwarzanie *n.* (*towarów, produktów*) production; (*ciepła, prądu*) generation; (*nastroju, uczucia, poczucia*) creation.

wytwornie *adv.* (*o sposobie ubrania, zachowania*) in a refined manner; (*o wystroju pokoju, mieszkania*) smartly, elegantly.

wytwornisia *f. iron.* woman of fashion, fashion slave.

wytworniś *mp iron.* dandy, swell.

wytworność *f.* refinement, elegance.

wytworny *a.* (*o osobie, manierach*) fine, refined; (*o mieszkaniu, pokoju*) smart, elegant.

wytworzyć (się) *pf. zob.* **wytwarzać (się)**.

wytwór *mi* -**o**- (*przemysłu*) product; (*kultury, wyobraźni*) creature, product; **wytwór** *l.* **produkt kultury masowej** product of mass culture; **wytwór wyobraźni** creature *l.* figment of sb's imagination; **wytwór chorej wyobraźni** product of a twisted mind.

wytwórca *mp* manufacturer, producer.

wytwórczość *f.* **1.** (= *wytwarzanie*) production, manufacture; **drobna wytwórczość** *ekon.* small-scale production. **2.** (= *wytwórcy*) producers, manufacturers.

wytwórczy *a.* (of) production; **zakład wytwórczy** manufacturing plant.

wytwórnia *f. Gen.pl.* -**i** (manufacturing) plant; **wytwórnia filmowa** film production company, motion-picture studio.

wytyczać *ipf.* (*linię kolejową, drogę*) (*w terenie*) mark out; (*na mapie*) trace out, plot out; (*kierunki działania*) lay out.

wytyczna *f. Gen.* -**ej** guideline (*dotycząca czegoś* on/for sth).

wytyczyć *pf. zob.* **wytyczać**.

wytyk *mi* reproach.

wytykać *ipf.* **1.** (= *wysuwać na zewnątrz*) stick out; **nie wytykać z domu nosa** not stick one's nose out of the house *l.* outdoors. **2.** (= *zarzucać komuś*) reproach (*komuś coś* sb for sth); **wytykać komuś błędy** point out sb's mistakes; **wytykać kogoś palcami** point a *l.* the finger at sb; **nie wytykając palcem** without naming names. **3.** (= *wyznaczać*) *zob.* **wytyczyć**.

wytypować *pf.* **1.** (= *wyznaczyć*) designate, select (*e.g. sb to do a job*). **2.** (*na wyścigach*) put one's money (*on a horse, greyhound, etc.*).

wyuczony *a.* (*o lekcji, roli*) learnt (by heart); **zachowanie wyuczone** *psych.* acquired behavior; **zawód wyuczony** trade.

wyuczyć *pf.* (= *nauczyć*) teach (*kogoś czegoś* sb sth); (*do zawodu*) train (*sb as an apprentice*). **~ się** *pf.* (= *nauczyć się*) learn (by heart); (*do zawodu*) be trained, train (*as an apprentice*).

wyuzdanie *n.* debauchery.

wyuzdany *a.* licentious, debauched.

wywabiacz *mi Gen.* -**a wywabiacz plam** stain remover.

wywabiać *ipf.*, **wywabić** *pf.* **1.** (= *nakłaniać do wyjścia*) lure, entice (*a person/animal to leave their hiding place*). **2.** (*plamę*) remove; **tej plamy chyba się nie da wywabić** I don't think this stain'll come out.

wywalać *ipf.* **1.** *pot.* (= *wyrzucać*) (*coś*) chuck away; (*kogoś*) bounce (*skądś* from somewhere); **wywalić coś do kosza** *l.* **do śmieci** bin sth; **wywalić gały** goggle (*na kogoś* at sb); **wywalić język** stick out one's tongue (*na kogoś* at sb); **wywalić kogoś na zbity pysk** *l.* **na łeb** kick sb out; (*z pracy*) give sb the kick; **wywalić kogoś za drzwi** kick sb out (*of a place*); **wywalić kogoś z pracy** give sb the sack. **2.** *pot.* (= *wyrwać*) break in, break open (*a door, window*); **wywalić bezpiecznik** (*o lampie, żelazku*) fuse. **~ się** *ipf. pot.* (= *przewra-*

cać się) fall over; **wywalić się jak długi** come a purler *l.* cropper.

wywalczać *ipf.*, **wywalczyć** *pf.* secure (*by fighting*), attain (*coś* to sth); **wywalczyć sobie prawo do (robienia) czegoś** win one's right to (do) sth.

wywalić (się) *pf. zob.* **wywalać (się)**.

wywar *mi* (= *ekstrakt*) decoction; (*z mięsa, warzyw, kości itp.*) stock; (*np. w kotle czarownicy*) concoction.

wywarzać *ipf.*, **wywarzyć** *pf.* decoct, extract, concoct.

wywatować *pf.* pad.

wyważać *ipf.*, **wyważyć** *pf.* **1.** (= *wybijać z podstaw*) force (open), break (open), pry open, prise; **wyważyć drzwi** force open *l.* prise the door; **wyważać otwarte drzwi** (try to) reinvent the wheel, hold the candle to the sun; **starannie wyważyć słowa** weigh one's words. **2.** (= *określić wagę*) *rzad.* weigh. **3.** *techn.* balance.

wywąchać *pf.*, **wywąchiwać** *ipf. zob.* **wywęszyć**.

wywczasować się *pf.* have a good rest (*e.g. during a holiday*).

wywczasowywać się *ipf.* be resting; (= *być na wakacjach*) be vacationing.

wywczasy *pl.* vacations, holidays.

wywdzięczać się *ipf.*, **wywdzięczyć się** *pf.* repay, return (*sb's kindness*); **wywdzięczyć się komuś za coś** repay sb for sth.

wywędrować *pf.* emigrate, migrate from; **wywędrować z domu** (*o dzieciach - rozpocząć samodzielne życie*) leave home.

wywęszyć *pf.* **1.** (= *wykryć węchem*) nose out, scent out. **2.** *pot.* (= *wykryć*) nose out; (*aferę, przestępcę*) ferret out.

wywiać *pf.* -wieję -wiejesz -wiali *l.* -wieli *zob.* **wywiewać**.

wywiad *mi* **1.** (= *rozmowa z dziennikarzem*) interview; **przeprowadzać wywiad** interview (*z kimś* sb); **udzielić wywiadu** give an interview. **2.** (= *szpiegowanie; = szpiedzy*) intelligence, secret service; **wywiad przemysłowy** industrial espionage. **3.** *med.* case history (*obtained through a conversation of a doctor with a patient*). **4.** *socjol.* survey, poll.

wywiadowca *mp* **1.** (= *pracownik wywiadu*) (secret) agent. **2.** *wojsk.* (= *zwiadowca*) scout.

wywiadowczy *a.* **1.** (= *dotyczący wywiadu*) intelligence; **siatka wywiadowcza** intelligence network; **służba wywiadowcza** intelligence service. **2.** *wojsk.* (= *zwiadowczy*) reconnoiter, *Br.* reconnoitre.

wywiadówka *f. Gen.pl.* -ek *szkoln.* parent-teacher conference.

wywiadywać się *ipf.* inquire (*o coś / kogoś* about sth/sb).

wywiązać się *pf.* -wiążę -wiążesz, **wywiązywać się** *ipf.* **1.** (= *być następstwem czegoś*) ensue, develop; **wywiązała się kłótnia** a quarrel ensued *l.* developed; (*o chorobie, gorączce*) set in, develop. **2.** (= *dotrzymywać obietnicy*) deliver; **wywiązać się z obowiązków** do one's duty, meet *l.* fulfil one's obligations; (= *spełnić swe obowiązki*) discharge one's duties; **wywiązać się z obietnicy** de-

liver on one's promise, deliver the goods; **dobrze/źle się z czegoś wywiązać** do a good/bad job of sth. **3.** *chem., fiz.* evolve.

wywiązanie *n.* performance (*of one's duties, tasks, etc.*); **wywiązanie się gazu** *chem., fiz.* gas evolution.

wywichnąć *pf.* -ij disjoint, dislocate, luxate; **wywichnąć sobie nogę w kostce** sprain one's ankle.

wywichnięty *a.* out of joint.

wywiedzieć się *pf.* -wiem -wiesz, -wiedz *zob.* **wywiadywać się**.

wywierać *ipf.* **1.** (= *wywoływać*) exert, make; **wywierać na kimś dobre/złe wrażenie** make a good/bad impression on sb; **wywierać pożądany skutek** have *l.* exert *l.* produce the desired effect. **2.** (= *działać na coś*) exert; **wywierać na kogoś presję** *l.* **nacisk** exert *l.* put pressure on sb, bring pressure to bear on sb; **wywrzeć na kogoś/coś wpływ** exert *l.* have influence on sb/sth.

wywiercać *ipf.*, **wywiercić** *pf.* drill, bore; (*studnię*) sink a well.

wywierzysko *n. geol.* karst *l.* rising spring.

wywiesić *pf.* -szę -sisz, **wywieszać** *ipf.* (*pranie, flagę*) hang out; (*plakaty, wyniki na tablicy*) put up, post up; (*język*) loll, stick out; **biegać z wywieszonym językiem** bustle about.

wywieszka *f. Gen.pl.* -ek (= *kartka z napisem*) notice; (*z informacją, ostrzeżeniem*) sign; (*lekarza, adwokata*) shingle.

wywieść (się) *pf.* -wiodę -wiedziesz -wiódł -wiodła -wiedli *zob.* **wywodzić (się)**.

wywietrzeć *ipf.* evaporate; (*o perfumach*) lose scent.

wywietrznik *mi Gen.* -a **1.** *techn.* ventilator. **2.** (= *lufcik*) window vent.

wywietrzyć *pf.* **1.** (= *przewietrzyć*) air. **2.** (= *zwietrzyć*) nose out, smell. ~ **się** *pf.* be aired.

wywiewać *ipf.* **1.** (= *wiejąc, usuwać*) blow away; **wiatr wywiał śnieg z podwórza** the wind blew the snow off the yard. **2.** *pot.* (= *uciekać*) do a bunk (*skądś* from somewhere).

wywieźć *pf.* -wiozę -wieziesz -wiózł -wiozła -wieźli *zob.* **wywozić**.

wywijać *ipf.* **1.** (= *wykładać na wierzch*) turn down, fold down; **wywijać mankiety** (*na rękawy marynarki*) shoot one's cuffs. **2.** (= *wymachiwać*) brandish (*czymś* sth); **wywinąć kozła** turn a somersault *l.* summersault. **3.** (*tańczyć*) spin, twirl (*esp. in dancing*); **wywinąć komuś numer** pull a fast one on sb. ~ **się** *ipf.* **1.** (= *nie dawać się złapać*) elude (*od czegoś* sth), wriggle out (*od czegoś* of sth); **wywinąć się śmierci** escape death. **2.** (= *wykręcać się od czegoś*) evade (*od czegoś* sth) shirk (*od czegoś* sth); **wywijać się od odpowiedzialności** evade *l.* shirk responsibility.

wywijas *mi Gen.* -a (= *zygzak*) flourish.

wywijasy *pl. Gen.* -ów (= *wymachiwanie*) waving (*one's hands*), twisting (*when dancing*).

wywikłać *pf.* disentangle, extricate (*e.g. sb from trouble*). ~ **się** *pf.* disentangle o.s., extricate o.s. (*e.g. from trouble*).

wywinąć (się) *pf. zob.* **wywijać (się)**.

wywindować *pf.* **1.** (= *wyciągnąć*) hoist (up).

2. (= *ustalić na wysokim poziomie*) hike; **wywindować ceny** hike prices. **3.** *pot.* (= *umieścić kogoś na wysokim stanowisku*) hoist up (*kogoś sb*). ~ **się** *pf.* clamber up; **wywindować się na parapet** clamber up *l.* over onto the window sill.

wywlec (się) *pf.* -wlokę *l.* -wlekę -wleczesz -włókł *l.* -wlekł -wlokła *l.* -wlekła -wlekli *zob.* **wywlekać (się).**

wywlekać *ipf.* **1.** (= *ciągnąć, wysunąć coś*) drag out. **2.** (= *ujawnić coś*) drag up; **wywlec coś na światło dzienne** let sth on, drag sth out. **3.** (= *wyprowadzić kogoś siłą*) drag out. ~ **się** *ipf.* shuffle out, scramble out.

wywłaszczać *ipf.* expropriate (*kogoś z czegoś sb of sth*) dispossess (*kogoś z czegoś sb of sth*); (*z ziemi*) oust (*kogoś z czegoś sb of sth*).

wywłaszczenie *n.* expropriation, dispossession, ouster.

wywłaszczyciel *mp* expropriator, dispossessor.

wywłaszczyć *pf. zob.* **wywłaszczać.**

wywłoka *f. pog.* trollop.

wywłócznik *mi bot.* water milfoil (*Myriophyllum*).

wywnętrzać się *ipf.* pour o.s. out, *pot.* spill one's guts.

wywnioskować *pf.* conclude, construe, induce.

wywodzić *ipf.* -wodzę -wodzisz, -wódź **1.** *lit.* take out, lead out; **wywieść kogoś w pole** lead sb up the garden path. **2.** *lit.* (*o drodze*) lead. **3.** (= *wysnuwać wnioski*) derive, deduce, infer; **wywieść wniosek z przesłanek logicznych** derive a conclusion from logical premises. **4.** (= *dowodzić*) reason, argue; **wywodzić swoje racje** prove one's point. ~ **się** *ipf.* (= *brać początek*) originate, trace back one's origin; **wywodzić się ze szlachty** descend from nobility, be of noble stock.

wywojować *pf.* secure (*by fighting*), attain (*coś* to sth).

wywołać *pf. zob.* **wywoływać.**

wywoławczy *a.* **1.** (= *dotyczący wywołania*) call; **sygnał wywoławczy** *radio* call sign; (*zwł. stacji komercyjnej*) call letters. **2.** (= *początkowy*) upset, reserve; **cena wywoławcza** asking price, reserve *l.* upset price.

wywoływacz *mi Gen.* -a *fot.* developer.

wywoływać *ipf.* **1.** (= *wzywać*) call; **wywołać kogoś z zebrania** call sb out of a meeting; **wywołać ucznia do tablicy** call a student to the board; **wywołać stację** *radio* call a station; **nie wywołuj wilka z lasu** let the sleeping dogs lie. **2.** (= *oznajmiać*) call out. **3.** (= *powodować coś*) bring about, cause; (*choroby*) cause; (*duchy*) call, invoke; (*niepokoje społeczne, rewolucję*) foment, stir up; (*np. podziw, zwł. mimowolny*) compel; (*powstanie, rozruchy, dyskusję*) trigger off; (*protesty*) spark; (*przerażenie, podziw*) evoke; (*sensację, pogłoski*) produce; (*skojarzenia, obrazy*) invoke; (*skutki uboczne leku*) cause; **wywołać bójkę** provoke a fight; **wywołać burzę oklasków** (*np. występem*) bring the house down; **wywoływać czyjś gniew** incur sb's wrath *l.* anger; **wywołać czyjeś zainteresowanie** evoke sb's interest;

wywołać panikę raise panic, give rise to panic; **wywołać poród** induce labor; **wywołać rewolucję/powstanie** trigger off a revolution/an uprising; **wywołać poruszenie** cause a stir; **wywoływać wojnę** trigger off a war; **wywołać zgorszenie** offend; **wywołać zainteresowanie** arouse interest (*czymś* in sth). **4.** *fot.* develop.

wywozić *ipf.* -wożę -wozisz, -woź *l.* -wóź **1.** (*ludzi*) take away; **wywiozłem dzieci na wieś na wakacje** I took the children to the country for the holidays. **2.** (= *usunąć*) remove, dispose of. **3.** *pot.* (= *eksportować*) export.

wywozowy *a.* **1.** (= *dotyczący wywożenia*) (of) removal, (of) disposal. **2.** (= *dotyczący eksportu*) (of) export; **cło wywozowe** export duty.

wywód *mi* -o- **1.** (*wypowiedź*) (= *prezentacja argumentów*) exposition; (= *sposób rozumowania*) (line of) reasoning, argument. **2.** (= *ukazywanie początków czegoś*) deduction. **3.** *hist.* (*rodowód*) pedigree. **4.** *rel.* (*obrzęd*) churching.

wywóz *mi* -o- **1.** (= *wywożenie*) removal, disposal; **wywóz śmieci** refuse collection, garbage disposal. **2.** (= *eksport*) exportation.

wywózka *f. Gen.pl.* -ek **1.** (= *wywożenie*) removal, disposal. **2.** *polit.* banishment, deportation.

wywracać *ipf.* **1.** (= *przewracać*) topple, overturn; (*statek, łódź*) capsize; **wywrócić koziołka** turn a somersault *l.* summersault; **wywracać** *l.* **przewracać oczami** roll one's eyes. **2.** (= *obracać lewą stroną na wierzch*) turn out; **wywrócić coś na drugą stronę** turn sth inside out; **wywrócić wszystko do góry nogami** turn everything upside down; **nie wywracaj kota ogonem!** don't move the goalposts. ~ **się** *ipf.* **1.** (*o człowieku*) tumble, trip over, fall down. **2.** (*o drzewie, słupie*) overturn. **3.** (*o łodzi*) capsize.

wywrotka *f. Gen.pl.* -ek **1.** (*samochód*) dump *l.* dumper truck, tipper *l.* tip truck *l.* lorry. **2.** (*wagonik*) tipping wagon *l.* truck. **3.** *pot.* (= *wywrócenie się*) tumble, fall; *pot.* cropper.

wywrotnica *f. techn.* tipple.

wywrotność *f.* (*łodzi, statku*) crankiness.

wywrotny *a.* crank, cranky.

wywrotowiec *mp* -wc- *pl.* -y subversive.

wywrotowy *a.* subversive, seditious; **działalność wywrotowa** subversion, sedition.

wywrócić (się) *pf. zob.* **wywracać (się).**

wywrót *mi* -o- **1.** *lotn.* bunt. **2.** *leśn.* (= *drzewo powalone wiatrem*) windfall.

wywróżyć *pf.* augur, foretell; **wywróżyć komuś przyszłość** tell sb's fortune; **wywróżyć komuś wielką karierę** foretell a brilliant career for sb.

wywrzaskiwać *ipf.* yell out.

wywrzeć *pf.* -wrę -wrzesz, -wrzyj, -warł *zob.* **wywierać.**

wywrzeszczeć *pf.* -ę -ysz *zob.* **wywrzaskiwać.** ~ **się** *pf.* let off steam by yelling.

wywyższać *ipf.* elevate, lift. ~ **się** *ipf.* put on airs.

wywyższyć *pf. zob.* **wywyższać.** ~ **się** *pf.* elevate o.s. (*ponad kogoś/coś above sb/sth*).

wyzbierać *pf.* pick, gather (*all the apples from an orchard, etc.*).

wyzbyć się *pf.* -będę -będziesz, -bądź, **wyzbywać się** *ipf.* -am -asz **1.** (= *pozbyć się czegoś*) divest o.s. (*czegoś* of sth) get rid (*czegoś* of sth); (*towaru*) sell out. **2.** (*nawyków, skrupułów, przyzwyczajeń*) overcome.

wyzdrowieć *pf.* get well, recover.

wyzdrowienie *n.* recovery.

wyzdychać *pf.* **1.** (*o zwierzętach*) die out *l.* off. **2.** *pog.* (*o ludziach*) die out *l.* off.

wyzgrabnieć *pf.* (*o kobiecie - stać się zgrabną*) become *l.* grow shapely; (*o mężczyźnie - zeszczupleć*) grow slim.

wyzierać *ipf.* **1.** (= *wyglądać*) peep out. **2.** (= *stawać się widocznym*) peep out, manifest itself; **wyzierać komuś z oczu** shine *l.* emanate from sb's eyes.

wyziewy *pl. Gen.* -ów (= *zapachy*) smells; (= *opary*) fumes; (*np. z rozkładającej się materii*) miasmata *l.* miasmas, effluvia *l.* effluviums.

wyziębiać *ipf.* cool off, chill. ~ **się** *ipf.* cool off, chill off.

wyziębić (się) *pf. zob.* **wyziębiać (się)**.

wyziębnąć *pf.* -ziębnij, -ziąbł *l.* -ziębnął -ziębła -ziębli **1.** (*np. o pomieszczeniu*) get cold. **2.** (= *zmarznąć*) freeze.

wyzionąć *pf.* emanate, exhale (*gas, fumes*); **wyzionąć ducha** give up the ghost, breathe one's last, draw one's terminal breath.

wyzłacać *ipf.*, **wyzłocić** *pf.* gild.

wyzłościć się *pf.* let off steam.

wyzłośliwiać się *ipf.*, **wyzłośliwić się** *pf.* jeer (*na kogoś/coś* at sb/sth).

wyznaczać *ipf.* **1.** (= *zakreślać granice czegoś*) mark out. **2.** (= *wytyczać granice*) demarcate, delimit; (*granice, zakres*) define. **3.** (= *wskazywać miejsce, czas, wielkość*) fix, set; **wyznaczyć cenę** set a prize; **wyznaczać cenę za czyjąś głowę** set a price upon one's head; **wyznaczyć nagrodę w konkursie** set a prize in a competition; **wyznaczyć termin spotkania** fix the date of the meeting. **4.** (= *powierzać komuś funkcję*) appoint, designate; **wyznaczyć kogoś na stanowisko prezesa spółki** appoint sb president of a company; **wyznaczyć kogoś na urząd** name sb to an office; **prezes wyznaczył mi tę pracę** the president designated me for the job. **5.** (= *określać coś poprzez obliczenia*) calculate, determine.

wyznacznik *mi Gen.* -a (= *wskaźnik*) *t. mat.* determinant.

wyznaczony *a.* **1.** (*o dacie, terminie, spotkaniu*) set, appointed; **o** *l.* **w wyznaczonym czasie** at the appointed time. **2.** (= *wydelegowany*) appointed, designated; **był wyznaczony do pracy w dziale marketingu** he was appointed for work in the marketing department.

wyznaczyć *pf. zob.* **wyznaczać**.

wyznać *pf. zob.* **wyznawać**.

wyznanie *n.* **1.** (= *zwierzenie*) confession, admission; **wyznanie miłosne** declaration of love. **2.** (= *religia*) denomination, religion; *rzad.* confession; **wolność wyznania** freedom of religion; **wyznanie wiary** confession *l.* profession of faith.

wyznaniowy *a.* denominational, religious; **państwo wyznaniowe** theocratic state, theocra-

cy; **różnice wyznaniowe** religious differences; **szkoła wyznaniowa** denominational school.

wyznawać *ipf.* -aję -ajesz, -awaj **1.** (= *wyjawić*) confess; (*miłość*) declare; **wyznać coś** make a clean breast of sth. **2.** (= *przyznawać się*) confess, admit, acknowledge. **3.** *tylko ipf. rel.* profess; **wyznawać religię** practice a religion; (*filozofię, pogląd*) subscribe to. ~ **się** *ipf. pot.* (= *orientować się w czymś*) have a grasp (*w czymś* of sth); **nie mogę się w tym wyznać** I can't make head or tail of it.

wyznawca *mp*, **wyznawczyni** *f.* **1.** *rel.* believer, follower. **2.** (= *zwolennik*) advocate, adherent.

wyzuć *pf.* divest (*kogoś z czegoś* sb of sth).

wyzuty *a.* divested (*z czegoś* of sth) barren (*z czegoś* of sth).

wyzwać (się) *pf.* -wę -wiesz, -wij *zob.* **wyzywać (się)**.

wyzwalacz *mi Gen.* -a **1.** *fot.* shutter release. **2.** *lotn.* ripcord.

wyzwalać *ipf.* **1.** (= *oswobadzać*) liberate (*od l. spod czegoś* from sth); (*niewolników*) enfranchise, manumit; (*w sensie politycznym l. obyczajowym*) emancipate (*od l. spod czegoś* from sth). **2.** (= *przywracać swobodę ruchów*) release. **3.** (= *wywołać jakieś działanie*) trigger off, spark off, release. **4.** *chem., fiz.* release; (*zwł. gaz*) liberate. ~ **się** *ipf.* **1.** (= *odzyskiwać wolność*) be liberated, free o.s.; **wyzwolić się spod jarzma niewoli** shake off the yoke of slavery. **2.** (= *odzyskiwać swobodę ruchów*) extricate o.s. (*e.g. from bonds, embraces, etc.*), be released. **3.** (= *gwałtownie się ujawniać*) be triggered off, be sparked off. **4.** *chem., fiz.* be released; (*zwł. o gazie*) be liberated.

wyzwanie *n.* challenge, defiance; **podjąć wyzwanie** accept a challenge, pick *l.* take up the gauntlet; **poradzić sobie z wyzwaniem** meet a challenge; **stanąć przed wyzwaniem zrobienia czegoś** face the challenge of doing sth; **rzucić komuś wyzwanie** issue a challenge to sb, bid defiance to sb.

wyzwisko *n.* term of abuse; **stek wyzwisk** volley *l.* hail of abuse; **obrzucić kogoś wyzwiskami** throw a volley of abuse at sb, hurl abuse at sb.

wyzwolenie *n.* **1.** (= *oswobodzenie*) liberation; (*niewolników*) emancipation, manumission; **ruch wyzwolenia kobiet** women's liberation movement. **2.** *chem., fiz.* release; (*np. gazów*) liberation.

wyzwoleńczy *a.* (= *oswobadzający*) liberating; **armia wyzwoleńcza** liberating army; (= *dążący do wyzwolenia*) liberation; **ruch wyzwoleńczy** liberation movement.

wyzwoliciel *mp* liberator.

wyzwolić (się) *pf.* -ól *zob.* **wyzwalać (się)**.

wyzwolony *a.* **sztuki wyzwolone** liberal arts.

wyzysk *mi* exploitation; **wyzysk ekonomiczny/społeczny** economic/social exploitation; **wyzysk człowieka przez człowieka** exploitation of man by man.

wyzyskać *ipf. zob.* **wyzyskiwać**.

wyzyskiwacz *mp* exploiter.

wyzyskiwać *ipf.* **1.** (= *korzystać ze sposobno-*

ści) take advantage (*coś* of sth); **wyzyskiwać pogodę/wolny czas** take advantage of the weather/one's free time (*and e.g. go for a walk*). **2.** (= *czerpać zyski cudzym kosztem*) exploit; *pot.* sweat.

wyzywać *ipf.* **-am -asz 1.** (= *obrzucać wyzwiskami*) call (*sb*) names. **2.** (= *wzywać do walki*) challenge, defy, dare; **wyzywać kogoś na pojedynek** challenge sb to a duel. **~ się** *ipf.* **1.** (= *obrzucać wyzwiskami siebie wzajemnie*) call one another names. **2.** (= *wzywać siebie wzajemnie do walki*) challenge one another.

wyzywająco *adv.* provocatively, defiantly.

wyzywający *a.* provocative, defiant.

wyż *mi Gen.pl.* **-ów 1.** *meteor.* high, anticyclone. **2.** (= *najwyższa wartość*) peak; **wyż demograficzny** population boom.

wyżalać się *ipf.*, **wyżalić się** *pf.* tell about one's grief (*komuś* sb); confide one's sorrows (*komuś* in sb); pour out all one's grief (*komuś* sb); **wyżalić się przed kimś** spill one's guts to sb.

wyżarzać *ipf.*, **wyżarzyć** *pf. techn.* anneal.

wyżąć[1] *pf.* **-żmę -żmiesz, -żmij** *zob.* **wyżymać**.

wyżąć[2] *pf.* **-żnę -żniesz, -żnij** *zob.* **wyżynać**.

wyżebrać *pf.* **-brzę -brzesz, wyżebrywać** *ipf. t. przen.* mooch; *Br.* cadge (sth) (od *kogoś l.* u *kogoś off* sb); **wyżebrał od ojca pięć dolarów na benzynę** he mooched five dollars for gas off his father.

wyżej *adv. zob.* **wysoko**.

wyżeł *ma* **-żł-** pointing dog; **wyżeł niemiecki krótkowłosy** German shorthaired pointing dog.

wyżerać *ipf.* **1.** (*o zwierzętach*) eat up. **2.** *pog.* (*o ludziach*) scoff, wolf down. **3.** (*o kwasie, korozji, chorobie*) eat away (*kogoś / coś* at sb/sth).

wyżerka *f. Gen.pl.* **-ek** *pot.* chow, scoff.

wyżlin *mi bot.* snapdragon (*Antirrhinum*).

wyżłabiać *ipf.* groove, furrow, gouge out. **~ się** *ipf.* groove, furrow.

wyżłobić (się) *pf.* **-ób** *zob.* **wyżłabiać (się)**.

wyżłobienie *n.* groove, furrow.

wyżłopać *pf.* **-pię -piesz** *pot.* gulp down.

wyżowy *a. meteor.* (of a) high, (of an) anticyclone; **klin wyżowy** wedge.

wyżreć *pf.* **-żrę -żresz, -żryj, -żarł** *zob.* **wyżerać**.

wyższość *f.* superiority; **kompleks wyższości** superiority complex; **poczucie wyższości** feeling of superiority; **traktować kogoś z wyższością** treat sb with superiority; **z wyższością** (*powiedzieć coś, zgodzić się na coś*) patronizingly, condescendingly.

wyższy *a. zob.* **wysoki**; **stopień wyższy** *gram.* comparative degree, the comparative.

wyżyć *pf.* **-żyję -żyjesz, -żyj 1.** (= *nie umrzeć*) survive; (*o rannym, ciężko chorym*) make it; **przykro mi, ale chyba nie wyżyje** I'm sorry but I don't think he'll make it. **2.** (= *utrzymać się*) get by (*z czegoś* on sth) survive (*z czegoś* on sth). **~ się** *pf. zob.* **wyżywać się**.

wyżyłować (się) *pf. zob.* **wyżyłowywać (się)**.

wyżyłowywać *ipf.* **1.** (= *usunąć żyły z mięsa*) trim (*meat before cooking*), remove veins (*from meat before cooking*). **2.** *pot.* (= *doprowadzić do maksimum*) escalate, raise; **wyżyłować ceny** hike prices. **3.** *pot.* (= *wyeksploatować*) sweat. **~**

się *ipf.* **1.** *pot.* (= *zmęczyć się*) become dead beat, become dog-tired. **2.** *pot.* (= *wydać wszystkie pieniądze*) blow all one's money (*na coś* on sth).

wyżymaczka *f. Gen.pl.* **-ek** mangle, wringer.

wyżymać *ipf.* wringle, mangle.

wyżyna *f. geogr.* upland.

wyżynać *ipf.*, **wyżąć** *pf.* mow down, cut down.

wyżynny *a.* upland; **roślinność wyżynna** upland vegetation.

wyżyny *pl. Gen.* **-n** (= *najwyższy poziom*) heights; **wznieść się na/osiągnąć wyżyny doskonałości** rise to/attain heights of perfection.

wyżywać się *ipf.* **-am -asz** find an outlet for one's energy (*w czymś* in sth); **wyżywać się na kimś** take out on sb.

wyżywić *pf.* feed. **~ się** *pf.* subsist, nourish o.s.

wyżywienie *n.* board; **nocleg** *l.* **zakwaterowanie z pełnym wyżywieniem** board and lodging, room and board; **pełne/niepełne wyżywienie** full/half board; **pokój z wyżywieniem** full board accomodation; **z własnym wyżywieniem** self-catering.

wzajemnie *adv.* **1.** (= *nawzajem*) mutually, reciprocally; **podziwiali się wzajemnie** they admired one another; **pomagamy sobie wzajemnie** we help each other. **2.** (= *tak samo*) likewise; **dziękuję, wzajemnie** thank you - (and the) same to you.

wzajemność *f.* reciprocation; *form.* reciprocity; **kocham ją bez wzajemności** I love her without being loved; **miłość bez wzajemności/z wzajemnością** unrequited/requited love.

wzajemny *a.* mutual; (*np. o przyjaźni, usługach, komplementach*) reciprocal; (*o stosunkach, współpracy, szacunku*) two-way; **towarzystwo ubezpieczeń wzajemnych** mutual insurance company; **towarzystwo wzajemnej adoracji** *iron., żart.* mutual admiration society.

w zamian *adv.* in return.

wzbić (się) *pf.* **wzbiję wzbijesz, wzbij** *zob.* **wzbijać (się)**.

wzbierać *pf.* **1.** (*o wodzie*) rise, swell. **2.** *lit.* (= *napływać*) rise, flow; **łzy wezbrały mu w oczach** tears were flowing to his eyes. **3.** *przen.* (= *potęgować się*) surge, well up; **powoli zaczął wzbierać w nim gniew** gradually anger surged *l.* welled up in him; **serce wezbrane radością** heart full of joy.

wzbierze *itd. pf. zob.* **wezbrać**.

wzbijać *ipf.* raise, stir, kick up; **wzbijać tumany kurzu** raise *l.* stir (clouds of) dust. **~ się** *ipf.* soar, rise.

wzbogacać *ipf.* **1.** (= *czynić bogatszym; = czynić różnorodniejszym*) enrich; **wzbogacać wiedzę/słownictwo** enrich one's knowledge/vocabulary; **wzbogacić pożywienie/glebę azotem/wapnem** enrich one's diet/the soil with nitrogen/calcium. **2.** *górn.* concentrate. **~ się** *ipf.* **1.** (= *stawać się bogatszym*) grow rich; (*o instytucji*) make new aquisitions, aquire; **biblioteka uniwersytecka wzbogaciła się ostatnio o 250 nowych publikacji** the university library acquired 250 new publications recently. **2.** (= *stawać się różnorodniejszym*) be enriched.

wzbogacić (się) *pf. zob.* **wzbogacać (się)**.

wzbraniać *ipf.* forbid (*komuś (robienia) czegoś*

sb (to do) sth). ~ **się** *ipf.* shrink (*przed czymś l. od czegoś* from sth).

wzbronić (się) *pf. zob.* **wzbraniać (się)**.

wzbroniony *a.* forbidden, prohibited; „**Palenie wzbronione**" "No smoking"; „**Palenie surowo wzbronione**" "Smoking strictly prohibited *l.* forbidden"; „**Wstęp wzbroniony**" (*do pomieszczenia, budynku*) "No entry", "No admittance"; (*na teren szkoły, budowy*) "Keep out"; „**Teren prywatny, wstęp wzbroniony**", (*pod groźbą kary*) "Tresspassers will be prosecuted"; „**Nieupoważnionym wstęp wzbroniony**", "Authorised personnel only"; „**Obcym wstęp wzbroniony**" (*napis na drzwiach*) "Private".

wzbudzać *ipf.*, **wzbudzić** *pf.* **1.** (= *wywoływać uczucia*) arouse, awake, move (*coś u kogoś* sb to sth); (*ciekawość*) excite; (*kontrowersje, niechęć*) ignite; (*nadzieje, wątpliwości*) raise; (*podziw, niezadowolenie*) stir up; (*strach, zaufanie*) inspire; (*sympatię, współczucie*) command; (*zainteresowanie*) attract. **2.** *fiz.* induce, induct, activate; (*drgania*) excite. ~ **się** *pf. fiz.* become excited *l.* activated.

wzbudzić (się) *pf. zob.* **wzbudzać się**.

wzburzać *ipf.* **1.** (*morze, jezioro*) agitate, trouble, ruffle. **2.** (= *rozjątrzyć*) agitate, whip up; **wzburzyć w kimś** *l.* **czyjąś krew** make sb's blood boil, make sb see red. **3.** (*włosy*) ruffle, fluff up. ~ **się** *ipf.* **1.** (= *pienić się*) be agitated, be troubled, be ruffled. **2.** (= *tracić równowagę*) be agitated, be whipped up. **3.** (*o włosach*) ruffle, fluff up.

wzburzenie *n.* **1.** (= *zdenerwowanie, podniecenie*) agitation. **2.** (*społeczne*) unrest, ferment. **3.** (*o morzu*) roughness, choppiness.

wzburzony *a.* **1.** (= *spieniony*) rough, choppy. **2.** (= *zdenerwowany*) agitated, whipped up; (*o opinii publicznej*) outraged; (*o tłumie*) turbulent, boisterous.

wzburzyć (się) *pf. zob.* **wzburzać (się)**.

wzdąć (się) *pf.* **wezdmę wezdmiesz, wezdmij** *zob.* **wzdymać (się)**.

wzdęcie *n.* **1.** *pat.* flatulence *l.* flatulency. **2.** *rzad.* (= *wybrzuszenie*) bulge.

wzdłuż *prep.* + *Gen.* along; **wzdłuż toru/rzeki/drogi** along the track/the river/the road; **iść wzdłuż ulicy** walk *l.* go down the street. – *adv.* lengthways; **wzdłuż i wszerz** (= *wszędzie*) all over; **8 kilometrów wzdłuż** (= *o długości 8 kilometrów*) 8 kilometers in length; **zmierzyć pokój wzdłuż i wszerz** measure the length and width of a room.

wzdłużać *ipf. fon.* lengthen.

wzdłużenie *n. fon.* lenghtening.

wzdłużnica *f.* **1.** *arch.* girder, stringer. **2.** *mot.* girder frame. **3.** *żegl.* buttock line.

wzdłużny *a. techn.* longitudinal.

wzdłużony *a. fon.* lengthened.

wzdłużyć *pf. zob.* **wzdłużać**.

wzdragać się *ipf.* flinch (*przed czymś* from sth).

wzdręga *f. icht.* rudd (*Scardinius erythrophthalmus*).

wzdrygać się *ipf.*, **wzdrygnąć się** *pf.* -ij flinch,

wince; **wzdrygnąć się na wspomnienie czegoś** wince at the very thought of sth (*that had happened*).

wzdychać *ipf.*, **westchnąć** *pf.* sigh; **westchnąć z ulgą** sigh with relief; **wzdychać za kimś** *l.* **do kogoś** pine for sb.

wzdymać *ipf.* (= *wydąć, nadąć*) inflate, swell; (*o żaglach*) swell, fill (*with air*); (*o policzkach*) puff out; (*o potrawie*) give wind, bloat; **wzdęło konia** the horse was bloated; **wzdęło mnie** I was *l.* felt bloated. ~ **się** *ipf.* **1.** (= *wydąć się, nadąć się*) inflate, distend, swell. **2.** (= *wzburzyć się*) (*o falach*) swell. **3.** (= *wybrzuszyć się*) bulge.

wzejść *pf.* **wzejdzie wzeszedł wzeszła** *zob.* **wschodzić**.

wzgarda *f.* disdain, scorn, contempt; **patrzeć na kogoś ze wzgardą** look at sb with contempt, give sb a scornful look, give sb a look full of disdain; **żywić wzgardę dla kogoś** hold sb in contempt.

wzgardliwie *adv.* disdainfully, scornfully, contemptuously, with contempt.

wzgardliwy *a.* disdainful, scornful, contemptuous, full of contempt.

wzgardzić *pf.* (= *odtrącić z pogardą*) spurn; (= *pogardzić*) scorn, disdain.

wzgardzony *a.* (= *odtrącony, np. o kochanku*) spurned.

wzgląd *mi -ę-* **1.** (= *liczenie się z kimś, z czymś*) regard, consideration; **bez względu na...** regardless of...; **bez względu na to, ile czasu to zabierze/ to będzie kosztować,...** no matter how much time it takes/it costs...; **mieć coś na względzie** take sth into account *l.* consideration; **mieć wzgląd na kogoś/na coś** take sb/sth into consideration; **ze względu na kogoś/coś** for the sake of sb/sth, for sb's/sth's sake; **z tego względu** for that reason; **ze względu na...** considering...; **mając na względzie...** with a view to...; **zrobiłem to (tylko) ze względu na ciebie** I did that (only) for your sake. **2.** (= *punkt widzenia*) respect, regard; **pod względem czegoś** as regards sth; **pod każdym względem** in every respect; **pod pewnym względem** in some respect; **pod tym względem** on that score; **pod wieloma względami** in many respects; **pod żadnym względem** in no respect; **w tym względzie** in that regard; **względem czegoś** with respect to sth; **z różnych względów** for various reasons.

względem *prep.* + *Gen.* **1.** (= *w stosunku do*) relative to, in relation to; **zarobki nieproporcjonalne względem wielkości produkcji** earnings unproportional relative to the production volume. **2.** (= *wobec*) towards, to; **obowiązki względem rodziny** duties towards *l.* to one's family.

względnie *adv.* **1.** (= *do pewnego stopnia*) relatively, fairly. **2.** *pot.* (= *do przyjęcia*) fairly, tolerably; **względnie dobrze** fairly well; **na wakacjach było względnie** the holidays weren't too bad. **3.** (= *lub*) or.

względność *f.* relativity; **(ogólna) teoria względności** *fiz.* (general) theory of relativity.

względny *a.* **1.** (= *relatywny*) relative; **liczba względna** *mat.* directed number; **prędkość**

względna *fiz.* relative velocity; **ruch względny** *fiz.* relative movement; **wartość względna** relative value; **wysokość względna** *geogr.* relative height; **zaimek względny** *gram.* relative pronoun; **zdanie względne** *gram.* relative clause. **2.** (= *umiarkowany, dość dobry*) comparative; **względny spokój** comparative calm. **3.** (= *znośny*) tolerable.

względy *pl. Gen.* **-ów 1.** (= *powody*) considerations, reasons; **względy bezpieczeństwa** safety reasons; **względy polityczne/społeczne/estetyczne** political/social/aesthetic considerations; **koncert odwołano ze względów bezpieczeństwa** the concert has been cancelled for safety reasons. **2.** (= *przychylność*) favors; *Br.* favours; **mieć u kogoś względy** be in sb's favor, be in sb's good graces; **okazywać komuś względy** show favor to sb; **zabiegać o czyjeś względy** make advances to sb; (*zwł. pochlebstwem, nadskakiwaniem*) favor curry with sb; **zaskarbić sobie czyjeś względy** find *l.* gain *l.* win favor with sb.

wzgórek *mi* **-rk-** *Gen.* **-a 1.** (= *niewielkie wzniesienie terenu*) hillock. **2.** *anat.* promontory, prominence; **wzgórek łonowy** mons veneris, mons pubis, pubic mound.

wzgórze *n.* hill; **Wzgórza Golan** *geogr.* the Golan Heights.

wziąć (się) *pf.* **wezmę weźmiesz, weź** *zob.* **brać (się).**

wziernik *mi Gen.* **-a 1.** *med.* endoscope, speculum; **wziernik brzuszny** laparoscope; **wziernik krtaniowy** laryngoscope; **wziernik oczny** ophthalmoscope; **wziernik odbytniczy** proctoscope; **wziernik oskrzelowy** bronchoscope; **wziernik pęcherzowy** cystoscope; **wziernik pochwowy** colposcope, vaginal speculum; **wziernik uszny** auriscope, otoscope, ear speculum. **2.** *techn.* (*np. palnika olejowego*) inspection window; (*np. pieca odlewniczego*) spyhole.

wziernikować *ipf. med.* examine with a speculum *l.* endoscope.

wziernikowanie *n.* endoscopy, specular examination.

wziewać *ipf.,* **wzionąć** *pf.* inhale.

wzięcie *n.* **1.** (= *zabranie*) taking, seisure, capture; **do wzięcia** (= *stanu wolnego*) marriageable, available; **jestem do wzięcia** I'm still to be had; **być do wzięcia** (*o posadzie, nagrodzie*) be up for grabs. **2.** (= *rozgłos*) popularity, fame; **mieć wzięcie** be popular, be in great demand, be much sought after; **on ma wielkie wzięcie u kobiet** he's very popular with women.

wzięty *a.* successful, popular, much sought after (*lawyer, doctor, etc.*).

wzionąć *pf. zob.* **wziewać.**

wzlatywać *ipf.* **1.** (= *wzbijać się w górę*) fly up, take wing. **2.** (= *być unoszonym w górę*) rise (*up in the air*).

wzlot *mi* (= *lot w górę*) rise, ascent.

wzloty *pl. Gen.* **-ów** (= *uniesienia*) flights; **wzloty i upadki** ups and downs.

wzmacniacz *mi Gen.* **-a 1.** *fiz.* amplifier. **2.** *fot.* intensifier. **3.** *muz.* resonator, amplifier.

wzmacniać *ipf.,* **wzmocnić** *pf.* **1.** (= *czynić*

mocniejszym) strengthen. **2.** (= *czynić trwalszym*) strengthen, reinforce; (*oddziały, straże itp.*) reinforce. **3.** (= *powiększać zespół o nowe osoby*) reinforce. **4.** (= *zwiększać intensywność*) *fiz.* amplify; *fot.* intensify; **wzmocnić ochronę** tighten up security. **~ się** *ipf.* **1.** (= *nabierać sił*) get stronger, gather (new) strength; (*o pacjencie*) recuperate. **2.** (= *powiększać się o nowe osoby*) be reinforced. **3.** (= *stawać się intensywniejszym*) (*o wietrze, barwie, dźwiękach*) get stronger; **wzmocniła się czujność załogi twierdzy** the fortress force became more vigilant. **4.** *fiz.* be amplified. **5.** *fot.* be intensified.

wzmagać *ipf.* increase, intensify; (*wysiłki*) step up; **wzmagać czujność** become more vigilant; **wzmagać represje** increase repression; **wzmagać terror** increase *l.* heighten terror. **~ się** *ipf.* (*o wietrze, burzy, deszczu*) strengthen, pick up; (*o upale, gniewie*) increase; (*o walce, ostrzale*) escalate; (*o podnieceniu*) rise; (*o napięciu, niepokoju, gniewie*) mount, compound; **napięcie w stosunkach dwustronnych wzmaga się od kilku miesięcy** the tension in the bilateral relations has been mounting for a few months; **jej rozpacz wzmogła niepokój rodziców** the parents' anxiety was compouded by her despair.

wzmianka *f. Gen.pl.* **-ek** mention (*o kimś / czymś* of sb/sth); reference (*na temat kogoś / czegoś* to sb/sth); (*w gazecie*) short paragraph (*na temat kogoś / czegoś* on sb/sth); **krótka wzmianka** passing reference.

wzmiankować *ipf.* mention (*o kimś / czymś* sb/sth); make a reference (*kogoś / coś* to sb/sth).

wzmocnić (się) *pf.* **-ij** *zob.* **wzmacniać (się).**

wzmocnienie *n.* **1.** (= *czynienie silniejszym*) strengthening; **coś na wzmocnienie** pick-me-up, restorative. **2.** *bud., techn.* reinforcement, bracing. **3.** *psych.* reinforcement. **4.** *fiz.* amplification. **5.** *fot.* intensification.

wzmożony *a.* increased.

wzmóc (się) *pf.* **wzmogę wzmożesz, wzmóż, wzmógł wzmogła wzmogli** *zob.* **wzmagać (się).**

wznak *adv.* **leżeć na wznak** lie supine; lie on one's back.

wznawiać *ipf.* (*dyskusję, rozprawę*) resume; (*obrady, sesję*) reopen, resume; (*serial, przedstawienie*) revive; (*publikację, książkę*) republish, reissue; (= *wykonać dodruk*) reprint.

wzniecać *ipf.,* **wzniecić** *pf.* **1.** (*ogień*) light, start; **wzniecić pożar** start a fire. **2.** (*uczucie*) incite; (*bunt, rewoltę*) raise; (*niepokoje społeczne, rewolucję*) foment. **3.** (= *powodować wzbijanie się w powietrze*) raise, stir up, kick up.

wzniesienie *n.* **1.** (= *zbudowanie*) erection. **2.** (= *wypukłość terenu*) rise, elevation, height; (= *wzgórze*) hill; **wzniesienie kontynentalne** *geogr.* (*dna morskiego*) continental rise; **wzniesienie nad poziom morza** altitude, elevation. **3.** (= *podwyższenie*) platform. **4.** *astron.* altitude.

wznieść (się) *pf.* **wzniosę wzniesiesz wzniósł wzniosła wznieśli** *zob.* **wznosić (się).**

wzniosłość *f.* loftiness.

wzniosły *a.* **-ślejszy** (*o celu, ideale*) lofty; (*o ję-*

zyku, prozie) rarefied; (*o uczuciach*) fine, finer; (*o zasadach, ideałach*) high.

wzniośle *adv.* loftily, in a sublime way.

wznos *mi sport* (*kończyn*) raising; (*przyrządów gimnastycznych*) lifting.

wznosić *ipf.* -**szę** -**sisz** 1. (= *podnosić*) raise; (*ramiona, ręce*) raise; **wznieść oczy** raise *l.* lift one's eyes, look up; **wznieść okrzyk** raise a shout; (*na czyjąś cześć*) give a cheer; **wznieść toast za kogoś/coś** raise a toast to sb/sth, raise a glass to sb/sth. 2. (= *budować*) erect, put up, raise. 3. (= *wzniecać kurz*) raise, stir up, kick up. ~ **się** *ipf.* 1. (= *być unoszonym*) be raised, be lifted; (*o falach*) surge; **wznieść się ponad przeciętność** rise above mediocrity. 2. (= *wzbijać się w górę*) rise, soar, ascend; (*o słońcu, samolocie*) climb. 3. (= *rozbrzmiewać*) resound; **wznosić okrzyki** (*na cześć kogoś*) cheer. 4. *tylko ipf.* (= *piąć się w górę*) rise, ascend. 5. *tylko ipf.* (= *sterczeć*) tower.

wznoszący *a.* **akcent wznoszący** *fon.* rising accent, rising pitch.

wznoszenie *n. lotn.* climbing.

wznowić *pf.* -**ów** *zob.* **wznawiać**.

wznowienie *n.* (*dyskusji, rozprawy*) resumption; (*obrad, sesji*) reopening, resumption; (*serialu, przedstawienia*) revival; (*publikacji, książki*) republication, reissue; (= *wykonanie dodruku*) reprint.

wzorcownia *f. Gen.pl.* -**i** 1. (= *biuro projektowe*) design office. 2. (= *oddział fabryki*) calibrating shop (*in a factory*).

wzorcowy *a.* 1. (= *modelowy*) model. 2. (= *normatywny*) standard; **kilogram/metr wzorcowy** standard kilogram/metre.

wzorek *mi* -**rk**- pattern; **sweter we wzorki** patterned sweater.

wzornictwo *n.* pattern-designing, model-making; **wzornictwo przemysłowe** industrial design.

wzornik *mi Gen.* -**a** 1. (*szablon*) mold, template *l.* templet (*for mass production*). 2. (*narzędzie*) template *l.* templet. 3. (*katalog*) pattern-book.

wzorować *ipf.* model (*coś na czymś* sth after sth); pattern (*coś na czymś* sth after sth). ~ **się** *ipf.* imitate (*na kimś/czymś* sb/sth); **wzorować się na kimś/czymś** take sb/sth as one's model; **wzorować się na kimś** model o.s. on sb, take a leaf from *l.* out of sb's book.

wzorowo *adv.* in exemplary fashion, excellently.

wzorowy *a.* model, exemplary; **wzorowa matka** exemplary mother; **wzorowy uczeń** *szkoln.* model *l.* exemplary student; **wzorowe sprawowanie** *szkoln.* exemplary conduct; **we wzorowym porządku** in apple-pie *l.* perfect order.

wzorzec *mi* -**rc**- *Gen.* -**a** 1. (= *schemat*) pattern. 2. (= *pierwowzór*) prototype. 3. (= *model*) model. 4. (*do naśladowania*) exemplar; **wzorzec osobowy** *socjol.* role model. 5. *techn.* standard.

wzorzysty *a.* patterned, figured.

wzorzyście *adv.* in patterned designs.

wzór *mi* -**o**- 1. (= *deseń*) pattern; (*do wyszywania, haftowania*) design. 2. (= *model, wzorzec*) model; „**wzór**" (*napis na czeku, banknocie itp.*)

"specimen"; **wzór podpisu** specimen signature; **na wzór francuski/angielski** after the French/English fashion. 3. (= *przykład do naśladowania*) paragon; **wzór cnót** paragon of virtue; **brać wzór z kogoś** follow sb's example; **robić coś na wzór kogoś/czegoś** do sth on the model of sb/sth; **stawiać kogoś za wzór** hold sb up as a model. 4. (= *formuła*) formula; **wzór chemiczny** chemical formula; **wzór cząsteczkowy** molecular formula; **wzór strukturalny** structural formula.

wzrastać *ipf.*, **wzrosnąć** *pf.* 1. (= *dorosnąć, wychować się*) grow up; **wzrastać w przekonaniu, że...** be growing up in the conviction that... 2. (= *powiększać się*) rise, be on the rise; **wzrasta deficyt budżetowy** the budget deficit is rising *l.* on the rise. 3. (= *wzmagać się*) grow, rise; **gorączka u dziecka wzrastała** the child's temperature rose; **hałas stopniowo wzrastał** the noise was gradually growing; **wzrosnąć w siłę** gather strength.

wzrastający *a.* rising, growing.

wzrok *mi* 1. (= *zmysł*) eyesight, sight, vision; **stracić/odzyskać wzrok** lose/recover *l.* regain one's sight; **badanie wzroku** (eye)sight checkup; **dobry/zły/krótki wzrok** good/bad *l.* poor/short sight; **mieć krótki wzrok** be short-sighted; **ostrość wzroku** sharpness of vision; **mieć sokoli wzrok** have eyes like a hawk. 2. (= *spojrzenie*) look, gaze, eyes; **wzrok bazyliszka** basilisk glance; **napawać** *l.* **sycić wzrok czymś** feast one's eyes on sth; **odprowadzić kogoś wzrokiem** follow sb with one's eyes; **odwrócić wzrok** rever one's eyes *l.* gaze, look away (*od kogoś / czegoś* from sb/sth); **podnosić wzrok** look up; **pożerać kogoś/coś wzrokiem** devour sb/sth with one's eyes; **przeszyć kogoś wzrokiem** look daggers at sb; **spuścić wzrok** *l.* oczy drop one's gaze *l.* eyes; **unikać czyjegoś wzroku** avoid sb's eyes; **utkwić wzrok** *l.* oczy w kimś/czymś fix one's gaze *l.* eyes on sb/sth; **wytężać wzrok** strain one's eyes; **zatrzymać wzrok na kimś/czymś** fasten one's eyes on *l.* upon sb/sth; **zmierzyć kogoś wzrokiem** look sb up and down; **jeśli mnie wzrok nie myli** unless my eyes deceive me.

wzrokowiec *mp* -**wc**- *pl.* -**y** *psych.* visualizer.

wzrokowo *adv.* visually.

wzrokowy *a.* 1. *anat.* optical; **nerw wzrokowy** optic nerve; **zaburzenia wzrokowe** visual disorders. 2. (= *wizualny*) visual; **kontakt wzrokowy** eye contact; **pamięć wzrokowa** visual memory; **wrażenia wzrokowe** visual sensation.

wzrosnąć *pf.* **wzrosnę wzrośniesz, wzrośnij, wzrósł wzrosła wzrośli** *zob.* **wzrastać**.

wzrost *mi* 1. (= *wysokość człowieka*) height; **być niskiego/średniego wzrostu** be of short/medium height; **być wysokiego wzrostu** be tall; **mieć prawie dwa metry wzrostu** be almost two meters tall; **ile masz wzrostu?** how tall are you?, what height are you? 2. (= *powiększanie się*) rise, growth, increase; **wzrost cen/płac** *ekon.* price/pay increase; **wzrost dochodów** growth of income; **wzrost gospodarczy** economic growth; **wzrost obrotów** *ekon.* increase in turnover; **wzrost wydatków** increase in spending. 3. (= *rośnięcie*) growth; **stożek wzrostu** growing point.

wzróść *pf.* wzrosnę wzrośniesz, wzrośnij, wzrósł wzrosła wzrośli *zob.* wzrastać.

wzruszać *ipf.*, wzruszyć *pf.* 1. (= *rozczulać*) move, touch; wzruszać kogoś czymś move sb by sth; wzruszyć kogoś do głębi move sb deeply; wzruszyć kogoś do łez move sb to tears; to mnie nie wzrusza I couldn't care less about it, it leaves me cold. 2. (= *spulchniać*) (*ziemię*) loosen; (*poduszki*) shake up; wzruszać ramionami shrug one's shoulders. ~ się *ipf.* (= *rozczulać się*) be moved, be touched; wzruszać się czyjąś tragedią be moved *l.* touched by sb's misfortune; wzruszać się do łez be moved to tears.

wzruszająco *adv.* movingly, touchingly.

wzruszający *a.* moving, touching.

wzruszenie *n.* emotion; ogarnęło mnie wzruszenie I was overcome with emotion; nie umiał ukryć swojego wzruszenia he couldn't hide his emotion; wzruszenie ścisnęło ją za gardło her throat was tight with emotion; słuchałem jego opowieści ze wzruszeniem I was deeply moved *l.* touched by his story.

wzruszony *a.* moved, touched.

wzruszyć (się) *pf. zob.* wzruszać (się).

wzuć *pf.*, wzuwać *ipf. przest.* put on (*one's shoes, boots, slippers, etc.*).

wzwód *mi* -o- *fizj.* erection; *pot.* hard-on.

wzwyż *adv.* upwards; skok wzwyż high jump; skoczek wzwyż high jumper; od trzech wzwyż three and over.

wzywać *ipf.* -am -asz, wezwać *pf.* 1. (= *przywoływać*) call; wzywać pomocy *l.* ratunku call for help; wezwać pod broń call to arms; wzywać pogotowie/policję call an ambulance/the police; wezwać do sądu summon sb to appear before a court of law, cite sb; wzywać imię Boga nadaremnie *Bibl.* take God's name in vain. 2. (= *apelować do kogoś*) call; wzywać kogoś do zrobienia czegoś call on sb to do sth; wezwać do pojednania call for reconciliation.

wżarł *itd. pf. zob.* weżreć.

wżdy *particle arch.* (= *przecież, jednak*) however, notwithstanding.

wżenić się *pf.* marry into.

wżer *mi techn.* pit (*caused by corrosion*).

wżerać się *ipf.* 1. (= *trawiąc, niszczyć*) eat into; rdza wżarła się głęboko w karoserię samochodu rust has eaten deeply into the body of the car. 2. (*o zwierzętach*) (= *wbijać zęby w coś*) bite, sink teeth into; weżreć się w pamięć be imprinted on one's mind.

wżyć się *pf.* wżyję wżyjesz, wżyj, wżywać się *ipf.* -am -asz become a part of, familiarize o.s., identify o.s. with; wżyć się w atmosferę czegoś enter into the spirit of sth.

X, x *n. indecl.* (*litera*) X, x; **X jak Xantypa** X for X-ray; X as in X-ray; **promienie X** X-rays; **pan/ pani X** (*o osobie niewiadomego nazwiska*) Mr./ Mrs. X; *zob.* **iks.**

xenia *f. Gen.* **-ii** distichal epigram.

Y, y *n.* (*litera*) Y, y; **Y jak Ygrek** Y is for Yankee; Y as in Yankee; **pan/pani Y** (*o osobie niewiadomego nazwiska*) Mr./Mrs. Y; *zob.* **igrek.**
  yacht club *mi żegl.* (= *jachtklub*) yacht club.
  yachting *mi żegl.* (= *jachting*) yachting.

yale *mi indecl.* (*typ zamka*) Yale lock.
  yeti *mp indecl.* yeti; the Abominable Snowman.
  yo-yo *n.* yo-yo; **efekt yo-yo** the yo-yo effect.
  ypsilon *mi Gen.* **-a** upsilon.

Z

Z, z *n.* (*litera*) Z, z; **Z jak Zygmunt** Z is for Zulu; Z as in Zulu.

z[1], **ze** *prep.* + *Gen.* **1.** (*punkt wyjścia*) from; **z domu** from home. **2.** (*źródło informacji*) from; **z gazet/książki/doświadczenia** from newspapers/ the book/experience. **3.** (*czas*) from, of; **z dziesiątego wieku** from the 10th century; **z rana** in the morning; **list z drugiego maja** a letter of 2nd May. **4.** (*surowiec, składnik*) of, from; **zrobiony z drewna** made of wood; **stół z drewna** wooden table. **5.** (*przynależność, zbiorowość*) of, from; **jeden z nas** one of us; **kolega ze szkoły** a friend from school, school friend; **z domu Janowska** *née l.* nee Janowska. **6.** (*przyczyna*) (out) of; **z bólu/ nudów/radości** (out) of pain/boredom/joy; **z jakiej racji?** for what reason?, how come?; **ni z tego, ni z owego** all of a sudden. **7.** (*zmiana stanu*) of; **co z nami będzie?** what's going to become of us? **8.** (*nasilenie*) with; **z całych sił** with all one's might; **z całego serca** with all one's heart, wholeheartedly. **9.** (*wzór, model*) from; **wyrecytować z pamięci** recite from memory. **10.** (*ograniczenie zakresu*) at, by, in; **podobny z wyglądu** similar-looking; **egzamin z angielskiego** examination in English; **ona jest dobra z biologii** she's good at biology; **on jest z zawodu leksykografem** he's a lexicographer by profession. **11.** (*tworzy wyrażenia przysłówkowe*) **z grubsza** roughly; **z lekka** lightly, delicately; **z rzadka** rarely. **12.** + *Ins.* (*towarzyszenie*) with; **jedź z nami** come with us; **deszcz ze śniegiem** sleet. **13.** + *Ins.* (*element, składnik*) and, with; **chleb z masłem** bread and butter; **bułka z dżemem** bread roll with jam; **kawa ze śmietanką/mlekiem** coffee with cream/ milk; **sklep z zabawkami** toy store *l.* shop. **14.** + *Ins.* (*stan*) with; **z wysiłkiem** with effort; **z uwagą** attentively. **15.** + *Ins.* (*obiekt podlegający działaniu, stanowi*) **co z nim?** how is he? **16.** + *Ins.* (*cel*) **przyjść z pomocą** come to sb's aid; **przyjść do kogoś z wizytą** pay sb a visit. **17.** + *Ins.* (*skutek*) with; **z dobrym skutkiem** with a good result; **z powodzeniem** successfully.

z[2], **ze** *adv. pot.* (= *około*) about; **z godzinę** about an hour.

za[1] *prep.* **1.** + *Gen.* (*okres*) during, in; **za króla Jana** during the reign of king John; **za młodu** in one's youth. **2.** + *Acc.* (*upływ, miara czasu*) in; **za godzinę/rok** in an hour/a year; **za pięć piąta** five to five. **3.** + *Acc.* (*miejsce*) out (of); **wyrzucić kogoś za drzwi** kick sb out. **4.** + *Acc.* (*obiekt trzymany l. chwytany*) by; **trzymać kogoś za rękę** hold sb by the hand. **5.** + *Acc.* (*cel*) for, to; **umie-** rać **za ojczyznę** die for one's country; **wypić za czyjeś zdrowie** drink to sb's health. **6.** + *Acc.* (*zastępstwo*) **pracować za pięciu** do five people's work. **7.** + *Acc.* (*przedmiot transakcji, kary, nagrody itp.*) for, at; **za darmo** for free; **za nic** *pot.* not for love or money; **za wszelką cenę** *przen.* at any price; **order za zasługi** order of merit; **być za (czymś)** be for *l.* in favor of (sth); **odpowiadać za kradzież** be charged with theft. **8.** + *Acc.* (*funkcja*) as; **mieć kogoś za wariata** consider sb (to be) a madman; **uchodzić za gbura** pass as a boor. **9.** + *Ins.* (*następstwo*) after; **jeden za drugim** one after another; **raz za razem** time after time; **iść za kimś** follow sb. **10.** + *Ins.* (*miejsce z tyłu, poza czymś*) behind, beyond; **za miastem** out of town; **za burtą** overboard; **za oknem** behind the window. **11.** + *Ins.* (*czas*) after; **dzień za dniem** day after day; **za każdym razem** every *l.* each time. **12.** + *Ins.* (*cel*) of, for; **przepadać za kimś/czymś** be fond of sb/sth; **chodzić za pracą** *pot.* be looking for work. **13.** + *Ins.* (*przyczyna*) at, with; **za czyjąś namową** at sb's insistence; **za czyjąś zgodą** with *l.* (up)on sb's consent *l.* approval.

za[2] *adv.* **1.** (= *zbyt*) too; **za późno/wcześnie** too late/early; **tego już za wiele!** enough is enough!, that's too much!; **co za dużo, to niezdrowo** (*jako uwaga do kogoś*) you can have too much of a good thing. **2.** (*o charakterze ekspresywnym*) what; **co za czasy!** what times!; **co za film!** what a film!

zaabonować *pf. zob.* **abonować.**

zaabsorbować *pf. zob.* **absorbować.** ~ **się** *pf. zob.* **absorbować się.**

zaabsorbowany *a.* engrossed (*czymś* in *l.* with sth); preoccupied (*czymś* with sth).

zaadaptować *pf. zob.* **adaptować.**

zaadoptować *pf. zob.* **adoptować.**

zaadresować *pf. zob.* **adresować.**

zaadresowany *a.* addressed (*do kogoś / czegoś* to sb/sth).

zaaferowany *a.* wrought-up, worked up; **był tak zaaferowany rozmową przez telefon ze swoją dziewczyną, że nie zauważył wejścia szefa** he was so wrought-up talking to his girlfriend on the phone that he didn't see the boss come in.

zaagitować *pf. zob.* **agitować.**

zaakcentować *pf. zob.* **akcentować.**

zaakceptować *pf. zob.* **akceptować.**

zaaklimatyzować *pf. zob.* **aklimatyzować.** ~ **się** *pf. zob.* **aklimatyzować się.**

zaalarmować *pf. zob.* **alarmować.**

zaambarasować *pf. zob.* **ambarasować**. ~ **się** *pf. zob.* **ambarasować się**.

zaanektować *pf. zob.* **anektować**.

zaangażować *pf. zob.* **angażować**. ~ **się** *pf. zob.* **angażować się**.

zaangażowany *a.* **1.** (= *zatrudniony*) engaged, employed. **2.** (= *związany emocjonalnie*) involved, concerned; (*o sztuce, literaturze*) committed; **literatura zaangażowana społecznie** socially committed literature.

zaanimować *pf. zob.* **animować**.

zaanonsować *pf. zob.* **anonsować**.

zaapelować *pf. zob.* **apelować**.

zaaplikować *pf. zob.* **aplikować**.

zaaportować *pf. zob.* **aportować**.

zaaprobować *pf. zob.* **aprobować**.

zaaranżować *pf. zob.* **aranżować**.

zaaresztować *pf. zob.* **aresztować**.

zaasekurować *pf. zob.* **asekurować**. ~ **się** *pf. zob.* **asekurować się**.

zaatakować *pf. zob.* **atakować**.

zaawansowany *a.* advanced; **zaawansowane prace badawcze** advanced research; **w zaawansowanej ciąży** heavily pregnant, at an advanced stage of pregnancy; **być w zaawansowanej ciąży** be heavy with child. – *mp* advanced learner; **kurs angielskiego dla zaawansowanych** advanced English course, course in English for advanced learners.

zaawizować *pf. zob.* **awizować**.

zababrać *pf.* **-brzę -brzesz** *pot.* (= *ubrudzić*) smear, dirty.

zabagniać *ipf.* **1.** (*teren*) turn into a marsh. **2.** *pot.* (= *gmatwać*) muddle up. ~ **się** *ipf.* **1.** (*o terenie*) turn into a marsh, become marshy. **2.** *pot.* (= *gmatwać*) get muddled up.

zabagnić (się) *pf.* **-ij** *zob.* **zabagniać (się)**.

zabagniony *a.* **1.** (= *bagnisty*) marshy. **2.** *pot.* (= *zagmatwany*) muddled up.

zabajtlować *pf. zob.* **bajtlować**.

zabalować *pf. zob.* **balować**.

zabalsamować *pf. zob.* **balsamować**.

zabałaganić *pf. zob.* **bałaganić**.

zabandażować *pf. zob.* **bandażować**.

zabarwiać *ipf.*, **zabarwić** *pf.* **1.** (= *nadać barwę*) tinge, dye; **zabarwić coś na zielono** tinge sth green. **2.** (*opowiadanie, historię*) (= *koloryzować*) embroider, embellish. ~ **się** *ipf.*, **zabarwić się** *pf.* turn, become; **zabarwić się na zielono** turn *l.* become green.

zabarwienie *n.* **1.** (= *barwa*) tinge, tint. **2.** (= *charakter*) overtone. **3.** (= *brzmienie głosu*) tone.

zabarykadować *pf. zob.* **barykadować**. ~ **się** *pf. zob.* **barykadować się**.

zabawa *f.* **1.** (*np. dziecięca*) play; (= *gra*) game; **plac zabaw** playground; **towarzysz zabaw** playmate; **dla zabawy** for fun; **miłej zabawy!** have fun!, have a good time!; **ale zabawa!** this is fun!, what fun!; **to taka świetna zabawa!** this is such great *l.* good fun!; **zapowiada się dobra zabawa!** this sounds like fun!; **popsuć całą zabawę** take the gilt off the gingerbread; **nie psuj ludziom za-**bawy don't be such a spoilsport. **2.** (= *potańcówka*) dance; **urządzać zabawę** organize a dance.

zabawiać *ipf.* **1.** (= *dostarczać rozrywki*) entertain (*kogoś czymś* sb with sth); **zabawiać** *l.* bawić **gości** entertain one's guests. **2.** *lit.* (= *spędzać czas*) stay; **zabawić przejazdem u krewnych** stay with one's relatives for a couple of days *l.* hours (*on one's way somewhere else*). ~ **się** *ipf.* **1.** (= *uprzyjemniać sobie czymś czas*) amuse o.s.; **wczoraj cały wieczór zabawiali się opowiadaniem dowcipów** they spent the whole of last night amusing themselves by telling jokes. **2.** (= *bawić się*) have (good) fun, have a good time, enjoy o.s.; **kiedy wróciłem do domu, całe towarzystwo zabawiało się w najlepsze** when I came back home the whole company were having a jolly good time *l.* were enjoying themselves greatly; **chciałem pójść na tę imprezę i trochę się zabawić, ale miałem zbyt dużo do zrobienia** I wanted to go to that party and have some good fun but I had too much work to do; **zabawiać się cudzym kosztem** make jokes at sb else's expense. **3.** (= *trudnić się*) play at; **czasem z nudów zabawiam się w ogrodnika** sometimes I play at being a gardener when I'm bored.

zabawić (się) *pf. zob.* **zabawiać (się)**.

zabawka *f. Gen.pl.* **-ek 1.** (= *przedmiot do zabawy*) toy; (*t. o osobie*) plaything; **sklep z zabawkami** toy store; **zabrać swoje zabawki i iść do domu** *przen.* (= *obrazić się*) pick up one's marbles and go home. **2.** *pot.* (= *błahostka*) child's play; **wojna to nie zabawka** war is not child's play, war is not for children; **to dla mnie (dziecinna) zabawka!** it's a piece of cake for me!

zabawkarski *a.* toy, toymaking; **sklep zabawkarski** toy store.

zabawkarstwo *n.* toymaking.

zabawkowy *a.* **1.** toy; **zabawkowy pistolet** toy gun. **2.** toymaking.

zabawnie *adv.* amusingly, funnily.

zabawny *a.* amusing, funny.

zabawowy *a.* **1.** *pot.* (*dotyczący zabawy*) (of) play, (of) amusement. **2.** *pot.* (*lubiący zabawę*) fun-loving; **on jest strasznie zabawowy** he's such a party animal.

zabazgrać *pf.* **-grzę -grzesz, -grz** *l.* **-graj** *pot.* (= *pokryć bazgrołami*) scribble (all) over.

zabeczany *a. pot.* boohooed.

zabeczeć *pf.* **-ę -ysz 1.** (*o kozie itp.*) (= *wydać głos*) bleat, baa. **2.** *pot.* (= *zapłakać*) blubber, boohoo. **3.** *pot.* (= *zaśpiewać fałszywie*) bleat, bellow.

zabejcować *pf. zob.* **bejcować**.

zabełkotać *pf.* **-oczę -oczesz** *l.* **-ocę -ocesz, -ocz** mumble, mutter; (*zwł. po pijanemu*) slur.

zabełtać *pf. zob.* **bełtać**.

zabetonować *pf. zob.* **betonować**.

zabezpieczać *ipf.* **1.** (= *ochraniać*) protect (*przed kimś/czymś* from sb/sth); guard (*przed kimś/czymś* against sb/sth); **zabezpieczać tyły/odwrót** *wojsk.* cover the rear/withdrawal. **2.** (= *czynić bezpiecznym*) secure; **zabiezpieczyć broń** put a gun on safety, secure a gun. **3.** (= *wzmacniać*) secure, reinforce (*with concrete, boards,* *etc.*). **4.** *fin., prawn.* secure; **zabezpieczać dług/ pożyczkę hipoteką** secure a debt/loan by mortgage. **~ się** *ipf.* **1.** (= *zapewniać sobie bezpieczeństwo*) protect o.s. (*przed czymś* from sth); guard o.s. (*przed czymś* against sth). **2.** (= *zapewniać sobie dobra itp.*) secure, make provisions; **zabezpieczyć się na przyszłość** secure one's future; **zabezpieczyć się finansowo na starość** make financial provisions for one's old age. **3.** (= *stosować środki antykoncepcyjne*) use protection, use contraceptives.

zabezpieczyć (się) *pf. zob.* **zabezpieczać (się)**.

zabezpieczenie *n.* **1.** (= *ochrona*) protection (*przed kimś / czymś* from sth/sth); **zabezpieczenie antykorozyjne** *techn.* rustproofing. **2.** *fin., prawn.* (= *gwarancja, rękojmia*) warranty, guarantee; (*pożyczki*) security; **zabezpieczenie majątkowe** collateral. **3.** *wojsk.* protection (*of a military operation, etc.*).

zabezpieczyć *pf. zob.* **zabezpieczać**. **~ się** *pf. zob.* **zabezpieczać się**.

zabębnić *pf.* **-ij 1.** (= *uderzyć w bęben*) drum, beat a drum. **2.** (= *uderzyć, zastukać*) drum (*one's fingers, etc.*).

zabicie *n.* **dla zabicia czasu** to kill time, to pass the time.

zabić[1] *pf.* **-biję -bijesz, -bij** *zob.* **zabijać**. **~ się** *pf. zob.* **zabijać się**.

zabić[2] *pf.* **-biję -bijesz, -bij** (*o dzwonie itp.*) (= *wydać dźwięk*) strike, beat; **serce jej zabiło mocno** her heart started to pound.

zabiec *pf.* **-biegnę -biegniesz, -biegnij 1.** *zob.* **zabiegać. 2.** (= *biegnąc, dotrzeć na miejsce*) run right up to (*a place*).

zabiedzić *pf.* emaciate.

zabiedzony *a.* **-eni** (= *niedożywiony*) emaciated; (= *wynędzniały*) haggard, gaunt.

zabieg *mi* **1.** (= *interwencja*) procedure, measure. **2.** *med., chir.* procedure; (*operacja*) minor surgery, surgical intervention; **zabieg korygujący** corrective surgery; **zabieg leczniczy** therapy; **zabieg operacyjny** *l.* **chirurgiczny** surgery (*czegoś* on sth). **3.** *pot.* (= *przerwanie ciąży*) abortion.

zabiegać *ipf.* **1.** run up to; **zabiegać komuś drogę** bar sb's way. **2.** (= *starać się*) strive (*o coś* for sth); exert o.s. (*o coś* to achieve sth); (*o głosy wyborców, zamówienia*) canvass (*o coś* for sth); (*np. wybór na stanowisko*) make a bid (*o coś* for sth); **zabiegać o czyjeś względy** make advances to sb; (*zwł. pochlebstwem, nadskakiwaniem*) favor curry with sb.

zabiegany *a.* bustling, busy as a bee.

zabiegi *pl. Gen.* **-ów** (= *starania*) endeavors; *Br.* endeavours; **czynić zabiegi o coś** strive for sth, make efforts to achieve sth; **zabiegi dyplomatyczne** démarche.

zabiegnąć *pf.* **-biegnę -biegniesz, -biegnij** *zob.* **zabiec , zabiegać**.

zabiegowy *a. med., chir.* surgical; **gabinet zabiegowy** surgery.

zabielać *ipf.*, **zabielić** *pf.* (*mlekiem*) add milk (*to soup, coffee, etc.*); (*kawę śmietanką*) cream.

zabierać *ipf.* **1.** (= *odbierać*) take (*coś komuś* sth away from sb); **nie zabieraj mu tego!** don't

take it away from him!; **złodzieje zabrali mi portfel** the thieves have taken my wallet. **2.** (= *unieść*) sweep away; **powódź zabrała ze sobą wszystkie mosty** the flood swept away all the bridges. **3.** (= *brać ze sobą*) take; **nie zapomnij zabrać ze sobą parasolki** don't forget to take your umbrella; **zabrać dzieci na spacer** take children for a walk; **zabrać tajemnicę do grobu** carry one's secret to the grave, take one's secret with one. **4.** (= *przyprowadzić ze sobą*) bring (along); **zabierz go ze sobą na przyjęcie, dobra?** bring him (along) to the party, will you? **5.** (*ładunek, pasażerów*) pick up; **autobus był pełen i nie zabrał nas z przystanku** the bus was full and didn't pick us up from the stop. **6.** (= *mieścić*) (*o statku, autobusie*) take; **ten autobus nie może zabrać więcej pasażerów** this bus can't take more passengers. **7.** (= *usuwać, przenosić*) take; **zabrano go do szpitala** he was taken to hospital; **śmierć go zabrała** death took him. **8.** (= *zajmować*) take up; **zabierać komuś czas** take up sb's time; **nie powinno mi to zabrać więcej niż 5 minut** it shouldn't take more than 5 minutes. **9.** speak; **zabierać głos** (*na zebraniu, konferencji*) take the floor. **~ się** *ipf.* **1.** (= *rozpoczynać*) get down (*do czegoś* to sth); **zabierać się do wyjścia** be getting ready to leave, be about to leave. **2.** *pot.* (= *zaczynać stosować jakieś środki*) get around (*do kogoś / czegoś* on sb/sth). **3.** *pot.* (= *przyłączać się*) come along (*z kimś* with sb) (*somewhere*); join (*z kimś* sb) (*going somewhere*); **mogę się z wami zabrać na dworzec?** will you give me a ride *l.* lift to the station? **4.** *pot.* (= *wychodzić*) get out; **zabieraj się stąd!** get out of here!; **zabieraj tyłek!** move *l.* shift your ass *l.* carcass!

zabierak *mi Gen.* **-a** *techn.* lifter.

zabijać *ipf.* **1.** (= *pozbawiać życia; niszczyć*) kill; **zabić w kimś radość** kill joy in sb; **zabijać czas** kill time; **zabijać zapach/zarazki** kill a smell/germs. **2.** (*np. okno, skrzynię*) nail up; **zabijać deskami** board up *l.* over; **dziura zabita deskami** the sticks, Godforsaken village *l.* small town; **zabić komuś ćwieka** *l.* **klina** put sb on the spot, stump sb; **a toś** *l.* **aleś mi zabił ćwieka!** you've stumped me here! **3.** *karty* beat. **4.** (= *uderzać*) beat, hit; **zabijać rękami** (*na rozgrzewkę*) beat goose. **~ się** *ipf.* **1.** (= *popełniać samobójstwo*) kill o.s., commit suicide. **2.** (= *ginąć*) die; **jego syn zabił się w wypadku samochodowym** his son died in a car crash; **zabić się na miejscu** (*np. w wypadku samochodowym*) die on the spot. **3.** (= *mordować się wzajemnie*) kill each other *l.* one another. **4.** *pot.* (= *zamęczać się*) burn o.s. out; **od lat zabija się ciężką pracą** he's been burning out with hard work for years. **5.** *pot.* (= *zabiegać*) knock o.s. out (*o coś* over sth); **nie mam zamiaru zabijać się o parę groszy więcej** I'm not gonna knock myself out over a few pennies extra.

zabijaka *mp pl.* **-i** *pot.* brawler.

zabity *mp* killed; **spać jak zabity** sleep like a log.

zabliźniać *ipf.* (= *pokryć się blizną*) cicatrize, scar (up); *pot.* (= *goić*) heal (over). **~ się** *ipf.*

zabliźnić (się) *pf.* **-ij** *zob.* **zabliźniać (się)**.
zablokować *pf. zob.* **blokować**.
zabłądzić *pf.* **1.** (= *zmylić drogę*) get lost, lose one's way. **2.** (= *trafić dokądś przypadkiem*) wander over (*to a place*), stray.
zabłąkać się *pf.* **1.** (= *zmylić drogę*) *zob.* **zabłądzić**. **2.** (= *trafić dokądś przypadkiem*) stray. **3.** (= *zawieruszyć się*) make way, find way; **między papiery zabłąkały się jakieś stare zdjęcia** some old pictures somehow made *l.* found their way into *l.* among the papers.
zabłąkany *a.* stray, lost; **zabłąkany pies** stray dog; **zabłąkana kula** *przen.* stray bullet.
zabłocić *pf.* muddy, dirty with mud. **~ się** *pf.* get soiled with mud, muddy.
zabłysnąć *pf.* **-snę -śniesz, -śnij, -snął -snęła** *l.* **-sła -snęli** **1.** (= *zalśnić*) glitter, flicker; (*o oczach*) twinkle. **2.** (*o latarce, ostrzu miecza w ciemności*) (= *wydać błysk*) flash. **3.** (*o światłach*) (= *zaświecić się*) come on. **4.** (*o nadziei itp.*) (= *pojawić się nagle*) flash. **5.** (= *zrobić wrażenie*) shine; **zabłysnąć elokwencją** shine with eloquence.
zabłyszczeć *pf.* **-ę -ysz** *zob.* **zabłysnąć** 1, 2, 4.
zabobon *mi* superstition, old wives' tale.
zabobonnie *adv.* superstitiously.
zabobonność *f.* superstitiousness.
zabobonny *a.* superstitious.
zaboleć *pf.* **-li -lał** **1.** (= *zacząć boleć*) hurt, ache. **2.** (= *urazić*) hurt; **zabolało mnie to** it hurt; **zabolało mnie serce, kiedy to powiedziałeś** it cut me to the quick when you said it.
zaborca *mp* partitioner, annexationist.
zaborczo *adv. przen.* possessively.
zaborczość *f. t. przen.* possessiveness.
zaborczy *a.* **1.** (= *dotyczący zaborów l. zaborcy*) (of) partition, (of) annexation; **władze zaborcze** occupation authorities (*authorities representing the partitioner country's authorities*). **2.** (= *żądny, zachłanny*) possessive.
zabój *mi arch.* murder, killing; **kochać się w kimś na zabój** be in love with sb head over heels.
zabójca *mp* killer, murderer; (= *zamachowiec*) assassin; **seryjny zabójca** *l.* **morderca** serial killer.
zabójczo *adv.* **1.** (= *śmiercionośnie*) lethally, fatally; **działać zabójczo** have a lethal effect; **zabójczo nudna książka** *przen.* killingly boring book. **2.** *pot.* (= *świetnie*) killingly, smashingly; **zabójczo wyglądać** look smashing; (= *być świetnie ubranym*) be dressed to kill. **3.** (= *zalotnie*) seductively.
zabójczy *a.* **1.** (= *śmiercionośny*) lethal, fatal. **2.** (= *dotkliwy*) killing; **ta nuda jest po prostu zabójcza** this boredom is killing me. **3.** (= *szkodliwy*) destructive; (= *męczący*) killing; **zabójczy tryb życia** destructive life style; **zabójcze tempo** killing pace. **4.** *pot.* (= *zalotny*) seductive.
zabójczyni *f. zob.* **zabójca**.
zabójstwo *n.* (= *czynność zabijania*) killing; (*z premedytacją*) murder; (= *zabicie człowieka*) homicide; (*zwł. polityczne*) assassination; (*zwł. na zlecenie*) hit; **usiłowanie zabójstwa** *prawn.* attempted murder; **proces o zabójstwo** murder

trial; **być sądzonym za zabójstwo** be tried for murder; **popełnić zabójstwo** commit murder; **postawić komuś zarzut zabójstwa** charge sb with murder.
zabór *mi* **-o-** **1.** (= *przywłaszczenie*) annexation; **zabór mienia** *prawn.* larceny. **2.** *hist.* (= *kraj okupowany*) annexed territory (*of a partitioned country*); **pod zaborem pruskim** under Prussian partition *l.* rule. **3.** *hist.* (= *okres okupacji*) the period of partitions (*of Poland*).
zabrać *pf.* **-biorę -bierzesz -brał** *zob.* **zabierać**. **~ się** *pf. zob.* **zabierać się**.
zabradziażyć *pf. pot.* tarry, linger; **wczoraj wieczorem zabradziażył w jakieś podłej knajpie do trzeciej nad ranem** last night he tarried *l.* lingered in some squalid bar until 3 a.m.
zabraknąć *pf.* **-nie -kło** run out; **zabrakło mi proszku do prania** I've run out of laundry detergent, the laundry detergent has run out; **kiedy zabrakło nam ojca** when our father was no longer with us; **zabrakło mi odwagi** I lacked courage, my courage failed me.
zabraniać *ipf.*, **zabronić** *pf.* forbid, prohibit (*czegoś* sth); **zabraniać komuś coś robić** forbid sb to do sth, prohibit sb from doing sth; **zabrania się wstępu do lasu** no entry (*to the forest*), keep out (*of the forest*).
zabrnąć *pf.* **-ij** **1.** (= *brnąc, zajść*) wade (*somewhere*), work *l.* labor one's way (*somewhere*). **2.** (= *zawędrować*) wander (*somewhere*). **3.** (= *uwikłać się*) fall, get (*w coś* into sth); **zabrnąć w długi** fall *l.* get into debts; **zabrnąć w ślepą uliczkę** (*w sytuację bez wyjścia*) come to *l.* reach a dead end.
zabronić *pf. zob.* **zabraniać**.
zabroniony *a.* forbidden, prohibited.
zabronować *pf. zob.* **bronować**.
zabrudzić *pf. zob.* **brudzić**. **~ się** *pf. zob.* **brudzić się**.
zabrudzony *a.* dirty, filthy, mucky.
zabrukować *pf. zob.* **brukować**.
zabryzgać *pf.*, **zabryzgiwać** *ipf.* spatter (*with mud, etc.*).
zabrząkać *pf.* **1.** (= *wytworzyć brzęk*) clink, jangle. **2.** (*o instrumencie*) (= *wydać dźwięk*) twang.
zabrzdąkać *pf.* (= *zagrać od niechcenia*) tinkle; (*na gitarze, mandolinie*) twang; **zabrzdąkać coś na pianinie** tinkle the ivories.
zabrzęczeć *pf.* **-ę -ysz** **1.** (= *zadźwięczeć*) (*o metalach*) clang; (*o telefonie*) jangle; (*o szkle*) clink; (*o strunie*) twang. **2.** (= *spowodować brzęk*) clink (*e.g. one's keys, glasses, etc.*).
zabrzękać *pf.* = **zabrząkać**.
zabrzmieć *pf.* **-ij** **1.** (= *rozlec się*) resound. **2.** (*o słowach itp.*) (= *wyrazić*) sound; **jego słowa zabrzmiały bardzo ostro** his words sounded *l.* were very harsh. **3.** (= *wypełnić się*) resound (*z czymś* with sth). **4.** (= *wydać dźwięk*) sound; **zabrzmiały fanfary** the fanfares sounded.
zabuczeć *pf.* **-ę -ysz** **1.** (*np. o syrenie alarmowej*) boot, hoot. **2.** (= *głośno zapłakać*) boohoo.
zabudowa *f. Gen.pl.* **-ów** **1.** (= *zabudowywanie*) development (*of a plot of land*); **działka do**

zabudowy plot for development. **2.** (= *budynki na określonym terenie*) buildings.

zabudować *pf. zob.* **zabudowywać**.

zabudowania *pl. Gen.* -ń buildings.

zabudowany *a.* **teren zabudowany** built-up area.

zabudowywać *ipf.* **1.** (= *wznosić budowle*) develop (*an area, a track of land*). **2.** (*kuchnię, łazienkę*) furnish.

zabujać się *pf. pot.* (= *zakochać się*) fall (*w kimś* for sb).

zabujany *a. pot.* (= *zakochany*) in love (*w kimś* with sb); **on jest w niej kompletnie zabujany** he's head over heels in love with her.

zabukować *pf. zob.* **bukować**.

zabuksować *pf. zob.* **buksować**.

zabulgotać *pf.* -ocze *l.* -oce **1.** (= *zacząć bulgotać*) gurgle, bubble. **2.** (*o indykach*) gobble.

zabulić *pf. zob.* **bulić**.

zaburczeć *pf.* -ę -ysz **1.** (*o brzuchu*) (= *wydać charakterystyczny odgłos*) rumble; **zaburczało mu w brzuchu** his stomach rumbled. **2.** *pot.* (= *odezwać się burkliwie*) grunt.

zaburzać *ipf.* **1.** (*równowagę, oddychanie*) upset. **2.** (*spokój*) disturb. **3.** *astron., fiz.* perturb.

zaburzenie *n. Gen. pl.* -ń (*np. psychiczne*) disturbance; (*np. żołądkowe, mowy*) disorder; *astron.* perturbation; *geol.* dislocation; **zaburzenia emocjonalne** *psych.* affective disorders; **zaburzenia łaknienia** *pat.* (*np. bulimia, anoreksja*) eating disorders; **zaburzenia mowy** *pat.* speech impediments *l.* disorders; **zaburzenia procesu myślowego** *pat.* thought disorder; **zaburzenia psychiczne/emocjonalne/snu** *pat.* mental/emotional/sleep disorder; **zaburzenie czynności** dysfunction; **zaburzenie osobowości** *pat.* personality disorder; **zaburzenie pola geomagnetycznego** *meteor.* magnetic disturbance.

zaburzyć *pf. zob.* **zaburzać**.

zabytek *mi* -tk- (*kultury, przyrody*) monument; (*języka; przedmiot pochodzący z przeszłości*) relic; **zabytek przyrody** natural monument; **zabytek narodowy** national monument.

zabytkowy *a.* (*budynek*) historic; (*przedmiot, mebel*) antique.

zabzykać *pf.* buzz.

zacałować *pf.*, **zacałowywać** *ipf.* shower with kisses, smother with kisses.

zacementować *pf. zob.* **cementować**.

zacentrować *pf. zob.* **centrować**.

zacerować *pf. zob.* **cerować**.

zach. *abbr.* (= *zachodni*) W (= *western*).

zachachmęcić *pf. pot.* **1.** (= *zagmatwać*) muddle up (*coś* sth); spread confusion (*coś* about sth). **2.** (= *zgubić*) lose.

zacharczeć *pf.* -ę -ysz wheeze.

zachcianka *f. Gen.pl.* -ek *pot.* whim, fancy; **spełniać czyjeś zachcianki** pander to sb's whims, pander to the whims of sb.

zachcieć się *pf.* -chce -chciało **zachciewać się** *ipf.* **zachciało jej się iść na spacer** she felt like going for a walk; **zachciało mi się spać** (= *zrobiłem się senny*) I felt drowsy; **dziwnych rzeczy ci się zachciewa!** you've got strange fancies!; **czego to im się zachciewa!** and what fancies they have!

zachciewajka *f. Gen.pl.* -ek *pot., żart.* (= *krosta*) pimple, zit.

zachęcać *ipf.* (= *usposabiać*) encourage (*kogoś do czegoś* sb to do sth); (= *nakłaniać*) urge (*kogoś do czegoś* sb to do sth); (= *dawać impuls*) prompt (*kogoś do czegoś* sb to do sth). ~ **się** *ipf.* **1.** (= *zachęcać się wzajemnie*) encourage one another *l.* each other. **2.** (= *nabierać ochoty*) become keen (*coś zrobić* on doing *l.* to do sth).

zachęcająco *adv.* encouragingly; (*spojrzeć*) invitingly.

zachęcający *a.* encouraging; (*spojrzenie*) inviting.

zachęcić *pf. zob.* **zachęcać**. ~ **się** *pf. zob.* **zachęcać się**.

zachęta *f.* encouragement, incentive (*do czegoś* to do sth); **być dla kogoś zachętą** be an incentive for sb.

zachichotać *pf.* -ocze -oczesz *l.* -ocę -ocesz, -ocz (*nerwowo*) giggle; (*cicho*) chuckle; (*ukradkowo*) snigger.

zachlać się *pf. pot.* (= *upić się*) get sloshed, get soaked; **zachlać się w trupa** get blind drunk.

zachlany *a. pot.* (= *pijany*) sloshed, soaked.

zachlapać *pf.* -pię -piesz, **zachlapywać** *ipf.* splash. ~ **się** *pf.*, **zachlapywać się** *ipf.* get splashed.

zachlipać *pf.* -pię -piesz snivel, whimper.

zachlupotać *pf.* -ocę -oczesz *l.* -ocę -ocesz, -ocz squelch.

zachłannie *adv.* (= *chciwie*) rapaciously; (*jeść, czytać*) voraciously; (*zgarniać pieniądze*) greedily, avariciously; (*kochać*) possessively.

zachłanność *f.* (= *chciwość*) rapacity, rapaciousness; (*np. na jedzenie, czytanie*) voracity, voraciousness; (*na pieniądze*) avarice, avariciousness; (*na czyjąś miłość*) possessiveness.

zachłanny *a.* (= *chciwy*) rapacious; (*np. na jedzenie, czytanie*) voracious; (*na pieniądze*) greedy, avaricious; (*na czyjąś miłość*) possessive.

zachłysnąć się *pf.* -snę -śniesz, -śnij, **zachłystywać się** *ipf.* **1.** (= *zakrztusić się*) choke. **2.** (= *silnie coś przeżyć*) relish (*czymś* sth); revel (*czymś* in sth); **zachłysnąć się wolnością** revel in one's freedom; **zachłysnąć się z przerażenia** give a gasp of horror.

zachmurzać *ipf.* **1.** (= *pokrywać chmurami*) overcast, overcloud. **2.** (= *zasępić*) gloom, sadden, overcast. ~ **się** *ipf.* **1.** (= *pokrywać się chmurami*) cloud over, overcast, overcloud; **zachmurzyło się** the sky has clouded over. **2.** (= *zasępiać się*) become gloomy, overcast.

zachmurzenie *n. pot.* clouds; *meteor.* state of the sky; **zachmurzenie małe** fair (state of the sky); **zachmurzenie umiarkowane** partly cloudy (state of the sky); **zachmurzenie duże** cloudy (state of the sky); **zachmurzenie całkowite** overcast (state of the sky); **przewiduje się na dziś zachmurzenie umiarkowane z przejaśnieniami** today it will be partly cloudy with sunny intervals.

zachmurzony *a.* **1.** (= *pokryty chmurami*) clouded, overcast. **2.** (= *zasępiony*) gloomy, overcast.

zachmurzyć *pf. zob.* **zachmurzać.** ~ **się** *pf. zob.* **zachmurzać się.**

zachodni *a.* **1.** *geogr.* (= *dotyczący kierunku i strony świata*) western, west; **Indie Zachodnie** the West Indies; **Zachodni Brzeg Jordanu** the West Bank; **zachodnia Polska** western Poland, the west of Poland. **2.** (= *dotyczący kierunku wiatru*) westerly, west; **wiatr zachodni** westerly (wind). **3.** (= *dotyczący Zachodu*) Western, Occidental; **Berlin Zachodni** West Berlin; **Europa Zachodnia** Western Europe; **półkula zachodnia** western hemisphere.

zachodzić *ipf.* **1.** (= *docierać*) reach (*do jakiegoś miejsca* a place); get (*do jakiegoś miejsca* to a place); **zajść wysoko** *przen.* get ahead (in life); **zachodzić w głowę** rack one's brains. **2.** (= *wstępować, odwiedzać*) drop by, drop in, pop in. **3.** (= *podchodzić cichaczem*) surprise; **zachodzić komuś drogę** bar sb's way. **4.** *form.* (= *zdarzać się*) occur; **zaszła pomyłka w obliczeniach** there was a mistake in the calculations, a mistake occurred in the calculations; **zachodzi konieczność, żeby...** there is a necessity to..., it is necessary to...; **zajść w ciążę** become pregnant. **5.** (*o słońcu, księżycu*) set, descend. **6.** (= *powlekać się*) cover (*czymś* with sth); **zachodzić parą** mist *l.* film over; **zachodzić łzami** fill with tears. **7.** (= *pokrywać*) overlap (*na coś* sth); reach (*na coś* beyond *l.* above sth); **buty zachodziły jej za kostkę** her shoes reached above the ankle; **listwy zachodziły na siebie** the battens overlapped.

zachomikować *pf. pot.* (= *schować*) stash away.

zachorować *pf.* **1.** (= *stać się chorym*) be taken ill (*na coś* with sth); fall ill; come *l.* go down (*na coś* with sth). **2.** *pot.* (= *bardzo pragnąć*) be mad (*na coś* about sth); **mój ojciec zachorował na nowy samochód** my father is mad about buying a new car.

zachorowalność *f. med., pat.* incidence; **wysoka zachorowalność na grypę** high incidence of flu.

zachować *pf. zob.* **zachowywać.** ~ **się** *pf. zob.* **zachowywać się.**

zachowanie *n.* **1.** (= *sposób bycia*) behavior; *Br.* behaviour. **2.** (= *maniery*) manners, bearing. **3.** *fiz.* conservation; **zachowanie energii** conservation of energy. **4.** *ekol.* (*zasobów naturalnych, środowiska*) conservation; preservation.

zachowawczo *adv.* conservatively.

zachowawczość *f.* conservatism.

zachowawczy *a.* **1.** (= *mający na celu zachowanie*) preservative, conservative; **instynkt zachowawczy** *psych.* the instinct for self-preservation; **leczenie zachowawcze** *med.* conservative treatment; **układ zachowawczy** *fiz.* conservative system. **2.** (= *konserwatywny*) conservative.

zachowek *mi* -**wk**- *Gen.* -**a** *l.* -**u** *prawn.* legitime, forced *l.* legal *l.* legitimate portion.

zachowywać *ipf.,* **zachować** *pf.* **1.** (= *przechowywać*) keep, retain; **zachowywać kogoś/coś w pamięci** keep sb/sth in memory; **zachować coś dla potomności** preserve sth for posterity. **2.** (= *przestrzegać*) observe, stick to; **zachować dietę** stick to one's diet; **zachować post** (*jako rytuał religijny*) observe a fast; (= *nie jeść*) refrain from excessive eating. **3.** (= *utrzymywać*) keep, maintain; **zachować coś dla siebie** keep sth for o.s.; **zachowywać miarę** *l.* **umiar w czymś** do sth in moderation; **zachować milczenie** (= *milczeć*) keep one's tongue, remain silent; (= *nie zdradzić tajemnicy*) not breathe a word; **zachowywać pozory** keep up appearances; **zachować twarz** save face; **zachować (szczupłą) sylwetkę** stay slim; **zachować zdrowie** stay healthy; **zachowywać zwyczaj** keep a custom alive. **4.** (= *trwać w jakimś stanie*) keep; **zachować panowanie nad sobą** keep *l.* maintain one's composure; **zachować pewność siebie** keep one's countenance; **zachować przytomność umysłu** keep a level head; **zachować spokój** *l.* **zimną krew** keep one's calm *l.* cool; **zachować trzeźwość umysłu** keep one's wits about one. ~ **się** *ipf.,* **zachować się** *pf.* **1.** (= *postępować*) behave, act; **dobrze się zachowywać** (*zwł. o dzieciach*) behave o.s.; **zachowywać się jak dziecko/dama** behave *l.* act like a child/lady. **2.** (= *przetrwać, przechowywać się*) (*np. o budowlach*) remain, survive; **niewiele zachowało się ze średniowiecznych budowli w tym mieście** not much has remained of the medieval buildings in this city; **ze średniowiecznego zamku zachowała się do dziś tylko jedna ściana** only one wall of the medieval castle has survived till the present day. **3.** (*o dokumentach, tradycji, legendzie*) survive; **zachować się przy życiu** stay alive, survive.

zachód *mi* -**o**- **1.** *astron.* setting, set; **zachód księżyca** moonset; **zachód słońca** sunset; **o zachodzie słońca** at sunset; **dzień chyli się ku zachodowi** the sun is coming down. **2.** (*strona świata*) west; **północny zachód** North-West; **na zachód od Londynu** west of London. **3.** (= *kraje zachodnie*) the West, the Occident; **Dziki Zachód** the Wild West. **4.** *pot.* (= *trud, fatyga*) trouble; **to jest niewarte zachodu** it isn't worth the trouble, it's more trouble than it's worth; **to jest warte zachodu** it's worth the trouble; **to wymaga wiele zachodu** it takes a lot of trouble.

zachrapać *pf.* -**pię** -**piesz** **1.** (= *wydać chrapliwy dźwięk podczas snu*) snore. **2.** (*o koniu*) (= *wydać odgłos przez chrapy*) snort.

zachrobotać *pf.* -**oczę** -**oczesz** *l.* -**ocę** -**ocesz,** -**ocz** scrape.

zachrypieć *pf.* -**ę** -**isz** **1.** (= *powiedzieć coś zachrypniętym głosem*) croak out, say sth in a hoarse voice. **2.** (= *ochrypnąć*) hoarsen.

zachrypły *a.* hoarse; **powiedzieć coś zachrypłym głosem** say sth in a hoarse voice.

zachrypnąć *pf.* -**pnij,** -**pł** -**pnęli** *l.* -**pli** hoarsen.

zachrypnięty *a.* hoarse; **powiedzieć coś zachrypniętym głosem** say sth in a hoarse voice.

zachrzęścić *pf.* -**szczę** -**ścisz** grit, grate; **piasek**

zachrzęścił jej pod stopami sand gritted under her feet.

zachwalać *ipf.* praise; **zachwalać swój towar** (*o przekupniach*) ply *l.* cry one's wares. **~ się** *ipf.* vaunt, brag.

zachwaszczać *ipf.*, **zachwaścić** *pf.* **1.** (*o chwastach*) (= *rozrastać się*) grow over, spread; **perz zachwaścił cały ogród** couch grass has grown over *l.* spread all over the whole garden. **2.** (= *pozwolić chwastom rosnąć*) let weeds grow. **3.** (= *wprowadzać obce zwroty do języka*) corrupt (*a language with foreign words*).

zachwaszczenie *n.* weediness, amount of weeds.

zachwaścić *pf.* **-szczę -ścisz** *zob.* **zachwaszczać**.

zachwiać *pf.* **-wieję -wiejesz -wiali** *l.* **-wieli 1.** (= *zakołysać*) shake; **wybuch zachwiał budynkami** the explosion shook the buildings. **2.** (= *zakłócić*) shake, upset; **zachwiać czyjąś pewność siebie/wiarę** shake sb's confidence/faith; **zachwiać czyjąś wiarą w coś** shake sb's belief in sth; **zachwiać** *l.* **zatrząść czymś w posadach** shake *l.* rock sth to its foundations; **zachwiać równowagę** shake the balance. **~ się** *pf.* **1.** (= *stracić równowagę*) totter; **zachwiać** *l.* **zatrząść się w posadach** be shaken to foundations. **2.** (= *zawahać się*) falter, stagger; **jego odwaga zaczęła się chwiać w przeddzień bitwy** his courage started to stagger the day before the battle.

zachwycać *ipf.* delight, enchant, enrapture; **zachwycać urodą/wdziękiem** delight with beauty/grace; **zachwyciła mnie jego opowieść** I was delighted by his story. **~ się** *ipf.* be delighted, be enchanted, be enraptured.

zachwycić (się) *pf. zob.* **zachwycać (się)**.

zachwycająco *adv.* delightfully, admirably.

zachwycający *a.* delightful, admirable.

zachwycenie *n.* rapture.

zachwycić *pf. zob.* **zachwycać**. **~ się** *pf. zob.* **zachwycać się**.

zachwycony *a.* **1.** (= *oczarowany*) enchanted (*kimś/czymś* by sb/sth). **2.** (= *niezwykle zadowolony*) delighted (*czymś* at *l.* by sth). **3.** (= *uradowany*) overjoyed (*czymś* at sth). **4.** (= *podekscytowany*) thrilled (*czymś* with sth).

zachwyt *mi* (= *podziw*) admiration; (= *uniesienie*) delight, rapture; **cielęcy zachwyt** uncritical *l.* blind admiration (*dla kogoś/czegoś* for sb/sth); idolatry (*dla kogoś/czegoś* of sb/sth); **budzić zachwyt** enrupture, throw into ecstasies; **piać z zachwytu nad kimś/czymś** *pot.* cry sb/sth up, fawn over sb/sth; **wpaść w zachwyt** go into raptures (*nad kimś/czymś* over sb/sth); **nie posiadać się z zachwytu** be transported with delight.

zachybotać *pf.* **-oczę -oczesz** *l.* **-ocę -ocesz, -ocz** *zob.* **chybotać**. **~ się** *pf. zob.* **chybotać się**.

zachyłek *mi* **-łk-** *Gen.* **-a** *anat.*, *med.* recess.

zaciąć *pf.* **zatnę zatniesz, zatnij** *zob.* **zacinać**. **~ się** *pf. zob.* **zacinać się**.

zaciąg *mi* **1.** (= *werbunek*) (*do wojska*) enlist-

ment, recruitment; (*do pracy*) recruitment. **2.** *ryb.* (= *połów*) catch.

zaciągać *ipf.* **1.** (= *wlec*) drag (*sth over somewhere*); **zaciągnąć dług** incur a debt; **zaciągać długi** run up *l.* incur debts; **zaciągnąć pożyczkę w banku** raise a loan with a bank; **zaciągnąć wartę** mount guard (*przy czymś* at sth). **2.** (= *zasłaniać*) draw; **zaciągnąć zasłony** draw curtains. **3.** (= *zaciskać*) tighten; **zaciągnąć pasek** tighten one's belt. **4.** *pot.* (= *nakłaniać do pójścia gdzieś*) drag (*kogoś gdzieś* sb somewhere); **zaciągnął mnie wczoraj wieczorem ze sobą do jakiegoś dziwnego baru** he dragged me to some weird bar last night. **5.** (= *smarować, powlekać*) coat (*with paint, glue, etc.*); **zaciągnąć zupę żółtkiem** thicken soup with egg-yolk. **6.** (*o chłodzie, zapachu itp.*) (= *zawiewać*) blow; **od lasu zaciągnęło chłodem** there was a cold gust of wind from the forest; **w pokoju zaciągało amoniakiem** there was a smell of ammonia in the room. **7.** *pot.* (= *mówić, rozciągając głoski*) speak with a drawl (*characteristic of eastern Poland*). **~ się** *ipf.* **1.** (= *wstępować*) enlist (*do czegoś* with sth); enroll (*do czegoś* with sth). **2.** (= *wciągać dym w płuca*) inhale; **zaciągać się papierosem/cygarem** draw on a cigarette/cigar; **palić, nie zaciągając się** smoke without inhaling. **3.** (*o niebie*) (= *pokrywać się chmurami*) overcloud, overcast.

zaciągnąć (się) *pf.* **-ij** *zob.* **zaciągać (się)**.

zaciążyć *pf.* **1.** (= *stać się ciężkim*) weigh heavily; **plecak zaciążył mu po paru godzinach marszu** the rucksack weighed heavily on him after a few hours of marching. **2.** (= *stać się nie do zniesienia*) weigh heavily; **zaciążyło na nim wspomnienie ojca** the memory of his father weighed heavily on him. **3.** (= *odbić się negatywnie*) have a negative impact (*na czymś* on sth); **na jego złym zachowaniu zaciążyło nieodpowiednie towarzystwo** what contributed to his misbehavior was inappropriate company.

zaciec *pf.* **-ciekniе -ciekł** *zob.* **zaciekać**.

zaciek *mi* water stain, patch of damp (*usu. on a wall l. ceiling*).

zaciekać *ipf.*, **zaciec** *pf.* **1.** (= *przeciekać*) leak. **2.** (*o wodzie*) (= *tworzyć zaciek*) leak through, run down to; **deszcz zaciekał na parapet** the rain was falling on the window sill through the open window.

zaciekawiać *ipf.* arouse (sb's) interest (*kimś/czymś* in sb/sth); intrigue; **zaciekawiła mnie ta sprawa, Watsonie** I'm intrigued by this case, Watson. **~ się** *ipf.* become interested (*kimś/czymś* in sb/sth); be intrigued (*kimś/czymś* by sb/sth).

zaciekawić (się) *pf. zob.* **zaciekawiać (się)**.

zaciekawienie *n.* **1.** (= *zainteresowanie*) interest; **wzbudziło to we mnie zaciekawienie** it aroused my interest. **2.** (= *ciekawość*) curiosity.

zaciekle *adv.* fiercely, ferociously.

zaciekłość *f.* (*debaty, kłótni, pojedynku, walki*) heatedness, furiousness; (*konkurencji*) fierceness; (*wroga*) bitterness.

zaciekły *a.* (*o debacie, kłótni, pojedynku, wal-*

ce) heated, furious; (*o konkurencji*) fierce; (*o wrogu*) bitter; **zaciekły opór** stout resistance.

zacieknąć *pf.* -cieknie -ciekł *l.* -cieknął -ciekła *zob.* **zaciekać**.

zacielić *pf.* impregnate, service (*a cow, female roe deer, etc.*).

zaciemniać *ipf.*, **zaciemnić** *pf.* -ij **1.** (*np. pokój*) darken; (*miasto, budynek przed nalotem*) black out. **2.** *przen.* (*sprawę, prawdę, krajobraz*) obfuscate, becloud; **zaciemniać sprawę** fog the issue.

zaciemnieć *pf.* appear as a dark patch; **las zaciemniał na horyzoncie** a dark patch of forest appeared on the horizon.

zaciemnienie *n.* **1.** (= *zasłanianie okien w czasie wojny*) blackout. **2.** (= *ciemna plama*) dark patch.

zacieniać *ipf.*, **zacienić** *pf.* shade, shadow; **wysokie drzewa zupełnie zacieniały wąską uliczkę** the narrow street was completely shadowed by the high *l.* tall trees.

zacieniować *pf.*, **zacieniowywać** *ipf.* shade (*a part of a*) picture).

zacier *mi techn.* mash.

zacierać *ipf.* **1.** (= *wymazywać*) (*np. napis na tablicy*) wipe out, rub out; (*np. ślady na śniegu*) blot out; (*np. o mgle - kontury*) blur; **zacierać ręce** (*z zimna*) rub one's hands (together); (*z zadowolenia*) lick one's lips. **2.** (= *tuszować*) cover up; (*wrażenie, wspomnienia*) efface; (*różnice*) obliterate; **zacierać ślady za sobą** cover one's tracks. **3.** (*ściany gipsem, gładzią szpachlową*) (= *wygładzać*) float; (= *zatykać pęknięcia, dziury*) putty up. **4.** *techn.* (*np. silnik*) seize up. ~ **się** *ipf.*, *pf.* **1.** (= *zamazywać się*) (*np. o napisie*) be wiped out; (*np. o śladach*) be blotted out; (*np. o wspomnieniach*) fade away. **2.** *techn.* (*np. o silniku*) seize up.

zacierka *f. Gen.pl.* **-ek** *kulin.* hasty pudding (*with small, hard flour dumplings*).

zacieśniać *ipf.* **1.** (= *ścieśniać*) tighten; **zacieśniać pętlę** tighten a noose. **2.** (= *zagęszczać*) make denser, compact. **3.** (= *czynić ściślejszym*) tighten; **zacieśniać więzy przyjaźni** tighten bonds of friendship; **zacieśnić kontrolę nad czymś** tighten one's grip on sth. **4.** (= *zawężać*) confine, restrict, narrow down; **zacieśnić zakres badań** confine *l.* narrow down the scope of one's research. ~ **się** *ipf.* **1.** (= *ścieśniać się*) narrow; **krąg tańczących zacieśnił się** the circle of dancers narrowed. **2.** (= *stawać się ściślejszym*) tighten; **kontakty między nami zacieśniają się od miesięcy** contacts between us have been tightening for months. **3.** (= *zawężać się*) be confined, be restricted, be narrowed down.

zacieśnić (się) *pf.* -ij *zob.* **zacieśniać (się)**.

zacietrzewiać się *ipf.*, **zacietrzewić się** *pf.* flare up (*z powodu kogoś/czegoś* at sb/sth); boil over (*z powodu kogoś/czegoś* at sb/sth).

zacietrzewienie *n.* heat, frenzy, wrongheadedness.

zacietrzewiony *a.* heated, frenzied, wrongheaded.

zacięcie *n.* **1.** (= *nacięcie*) cut. **2.** (= *rowek*)

groove. **3.** (= *predyspozycja*) bent (*do czegoś* for sth); flair (*do czegoś* for sth). **4.** *pot.* (= *zapał*) verve; (**robić coś**) **z zacięciem** (do sth) with verve. – *adv.* (= *zawzięcie*) relentlessly, persistently.

zaciętość *f.* (= *upór*) stubbornness; (= *zawziętość*) relentlessness; (= *zajadłość*) fierceness.

zacięty *a.* (= *uparty*) stubborn; (= *zawzięty*) relentless; (= *zajadły*) fierce.

zaciężny *a. hist.* mercenary.

zacinać *ipf.* **1.** (= *ranić czymś ostrym*) cut. **2.** (= *smagać*) whip, lash. **3.** (= *ściskać*) clench, set; **zacinać zęby** *przen.* clench *l.* set one's teeth. ~ **się** *ipf.*, **zaciąć się** *pf.* **1.** (= *kaleczyć się*) cut o.s. **2.** (*o zamku, karabinie, drzwiach*) jam; (= *utknąć, nie dać się otworzyć, poruszyć*) (*np. o drzwiach, szufladzie*) get *l.* be stuck, stick. **3.** *pot.* (= *jąkać się*) stumble (*na czymś* over sth). **4.** (= *upierać się*) persist (*w czymś* in sth); **zaciąć się w gniewie** persist in one's anger.

zacios *mp* **1.** *stol.* dovetail, dap. **2.** *leśn.* blaze (*on a tree that is to be cut down*).

zaciosać *pf.*, **zaciosywać** *ipf.* **1.** (= *zaostrzyć*) sharpen (*usu. with an ax*). **2.** (= *oznakować drzewo do wycięcia*) blaze (*a tree that is to be cut down*).

zacisk *mi* **1.** (= *zaciśnięcie*) grip. **2.** *techn.* clamp, clip. **3.** *el.* terminal. **4.** *chir.* clamp.

zaciskać *ipf.* tighten; **zaciskać pasa** tighten one's belt; **zacisnąć pięści** clench one's fists; **zacisnąć zęby** (= *nie wydać głosu*) grit one's teeth, bite the bullet; (= *zawziąć się*) grit one's teeth. ~ **się** *ipf.* tighten.

zaciskowy *a. el.* terminal; **śruba zaciskowa** clamping screw.

zacisnąć *pf.* -snę -śniesz, -śnij *zob.* **zaciskać**. ~ **się** *pf. zob.* **zaciskać się**.

zacisze *n. Gen.pl.* **-y 1.** (= *miejsce osłonięte od wiatru*) shelter, sheltered spot. **2.** (= *miejsce ustronne*) refuge, secluded spot; **domowe zacisze** domesticity; **w zaciszu domowym** in the privacy of one's home, at one's fireside.

zacisznie *adv.* **1.** (= *bezwietrznie*) quietly, windlessly. **2.** (= *przytulnie*) cosily, snugly.

zaciszny *a.* **1.** (= *osłonięty od wiatru*) quiet, windless. **2.** (= *ustronny*) secluded. **3.** (= *przytulny*) cosy, snug.

zaciukać *pf. pot.* (= *zabić*) butcher, cut down.

zacmokać *pf.* smack.

zacnie *adv. lit.* (= *w sposób prawy*) righteously; (= *w sposób przyzwoity*) respectably.

zacność *f. lit.* (= *prawość*) righteousness; (= *przyzwoitość*) respectability.

zacny *a. lit.* (= *prawy*) righteous; (= *przyzwoity*) respectable.

zacofanie *n.* backwardness.

zacofaniec *mp* -ńc- *pl.* -y *pot.* stick-in-the-mud, fogy.

zacofany *a.* backward.

zacukać się *pf. pot.* (= *zaniemówić*) get tongue-tied, be dumbstruck.

zacumować *pf. zob.* **cumować**.

zacytować *pf. zob.* **cytować**.

zacz *pron. indecl. lit.* **kto (on) zacz?** who is he?

zaczadzić *pf.* asphyxiate, poison with a noxious gas (*usu. carbon monoxide*). ~ **się** *pf. zob.* **zaczadzieć.**

zaczadzieć *pf.* asphyxiate, be poisoned with a noxious gas (*usu. carbon monoxide*).

zaczaić się *pf.* -**aję** -**aisz, zaczajać się** *ipf.* lie in ambush (*na kogoś/coś* for sb/sth).

zaczajony *a.* -**eni** lying in ambush (*na kogoś/ coś* for sb/sth).

zaczarować *pf.* **1.** (= *rzucić urok*) put *l.* cast a spell (*kogoś/coś* on sb/sth). **2.** *pot.* (= *olśnić, urzec*) cast a spell (*na kogoś/coś* for sb/sth); bewitch (*na kogoś/coś* sb/sth).

zaczarowany *a.* **1.** (= *pod działaniem czarów*) bewitched; **być zaczarowanym kimś** be under sb's spell. **2.** (= *czarowny*) magic, enchanting.

zaczarterować *pf. zob.* **czarterować.**

zacząć *pf.* -**cznę** -**czniesz, -cznij** *zob.* **zaczynać.** ~ **się** *pf. zob.* **zaczynać się.**

zaczątek *mi* -**tk-** *lit.* beginning, germ; incunabulum; **zaczątki państwa polskiego** the beginnings of the Polish state; **zaczątki rewolucji** the germs of revolution.

zaczątkowy *a.* **1.** incipient; **zaczątkowe stadium rozwoju** incipient stage of development. **2.** *biol.* (*o organie*) rudimentary; **liście zaczątkowe** *bot.* rudimentary leaves.

zaczekać *pf.* wait (*na kogoś/coś* for sb/sth); (*przy telefonie*) hold on, hold the line; **zaczekaj no!** (*groźba*) you just wait!

zaczep *mi* fastener, hitch, catch.

zaczepiać *ipf.* **1.** (= *przyczepiać*) hitch, fasten. **2.** (= *zahaczać, zawadzać*) catch (*czymś o coś* sth on sth); **zaczepiłem rękawem o gwóźdź** I caught my sleeve on a nail. **3.** (= *zatrzymywać, zagabywać kogoś*) accost; **wczoraj zaczepił mnie na ulicy jakiś facet** I was accosted by some dude in the street yesterday. **4.** (= *zachowywać się agresywnie wobec kogoś*) try to pick up *l.* look for a fight (*kogoś* with sb); provoke (*kogoś* sb). ~ **się** *ipf.* **1.** (= *zahaczać się*) be caught (*o coś* on sth); **latawiec zaczepił się o drzewo** the kite was caught on a tree. **2.** (= *chwytać się*) catch hold (*o coś* of sth); **zaczepił się o gałąź** he caught hold of a branch. **3.** (= *sczepić się*) be locked together; **gałęzie drzew zaczepiały się o siebie na wietrze** the branches of the trees were locking together in the wind. **4.** *pot.* (= *znajdować pracę, mieszkanie*) get a foothold (*w czymś* in sth).

zaczepić (się) *pf. zob.* **zaczepiać (się).**

zaczepienie *n.* **punkt zaczepienia** foothold; **znaleźć punkt zaczepienia** get *l.* gain a foothold (*w czymś* in sth).

zaczepka *f. Gen.pl.* -**ek** (= *sprowokowanie*) provocation; (= *zaczepne słowa*) gibe, taunt; **szukać zaczepki** be spoiling for a fight.

zaczepnie *adv.* **1.** (= *napastliwie*) aggressively. **2.** (= *prowokująco*) provocatively, provokingly.

zaczepność *f.* **1.** (= *napastliwość*) aggressiveness. **2.** (= *prowokowanie*) provocativeness.

zaczepny *a.* **1.** (= *napastliwy*) aggressive. **2.** (= *prowokujący*) provocative, provoking. **3.** *wojsk.* (= *ofensywny*) offensive; **broń zaczepna** arms *l.* weapons of offense; **działanie** *l.* **działania zaczepne** offensive.

zaczepowy *a.* **wyciąg zaczepowy** *l.* orczykowy surface lift.

zaczerniać *ipf.*, **zaczernić** *pf.* -**ń** *l.* -**nij** blacken. ~ **się** *pf.* = **zaczernieć.**

zaczernieć *pf.* appear as a black patch; **las zaczerniał na horyzoncie** a black patch of forest appeared on the horizon.

zaczerpnąć *pf.* -**ij, zaczerpywać** *ipf.* **1.** (= *nabrać*) (*np. wody ze studni*) draw; (*piasku, mąki*) scoop; (*np. łyżką wazową*) ladle; **zaczerpnąć powietrza** take a breath (of fresh air). **2.** (= *wziąć, zdobyć*) gather; **zaczerpnąć informacji** gather information (*o kimś/czymś* on *l.* about sb/sth); **zaczerpnąć informacji u kogoś** ask sb for information (*o kimś/czymś* on *l.* about sb/sth); **zaczerpnąć sił** gather strength; **zaczerpnąć rady u kogoś** ask sb for (a piece of) advice (*o kimś/czymś* on *l.* about sb/sth).

zaczerwieniać *ipf.* redden. ~ **się** *ipf.* **1.** (= *stawać się czerwonym*) turn red, redden. **2.** (= *dostawać rumieńców*) blush, flush; **zaczerwienić się jak burak** *l.* **po uszy** blush to the roots of one's hair. **3.** *tylko pf. zob.* **zaczerwienieć.**

zaczerwienić (się) *pf. zob.* **zaczerwieniać (się).**

zaczerwienieć *pf.* **1.** (= *pojawić się jako czerwona plama*) appear as a red patch; **czapeczka dziecka zaczerwieniała na końcu ulicy** the red patch of the child's cap appeared at the end of the street. **2.** (= *poczerwienieć*) turn red, redden.

zaczerwienienie *n.* (*np. oczu*) redness; (*na skórze*) red mark.

zaczerwieniony *a.* -**eni** (*o oczach, skórze*) red.

zaczesać *pf.* -**czeszę** -**czeszesz, zaczesywać** *ipf.* comb; **zaczesać do tyłu** comb back. ~ **się** *pf.*, **zaczesywać się** *ipf.* comb one's hair; **zaczesać się do tyłu** comb one's hair back.

zaczłapać *pf.* -**pię** -**piesz** **1.** (= *zaszurać*) shuffle; **zaczłapać butami** shuffle one's feet. **2.** (= *doczłapać*) shuffle over (*to a place*).

zaczołgać się *pf.* crawl over (*to a place*).

zaczopować *pf.*, **zaczopowywać** *ipf.* **1.** (= *zatkać czopem*) bung (up). **2.** *pat.* (= *spowodować niedrożność*) (*żyły*) clot; (*inne przewody*) block. ~ **się** *pf.*, **zaczopowywać się** *ipf. pat.* (*o żyłach*) become clotted; (*o innych przewodach*) be blocked.

zaczyn *mi* **1.** *kulin.* (= *zakwas*) leaven, leavening. **2.** *lit.* (= *zaczątek*) germ; *lit.* incunabulum. **3.** *biochem.* ferment. **4.** (= *zaprawa*) mortar.

zaczynać *ipf.* **1.** (= *rozpoczynać*) begin, start; **zaczynać od nowa** make a new start, start over; *lit.* start from anew; **zaczynać życie od nowa** make a new start in one's life; **zaczynać od zera** start from scratch; **zacząć od powiedzenia...** start by saying...; **wcześnie zaczynać** (*karierę, działalność*) start young, make an early start; **zaczynać dzień od filiżanki herbaty** start (off) the day with a cup of tea; **zaczynać od końca** (= *robić coś niewłaściwie*) put the cart before the horse. **2.** (= *wchodzić w początkowy etap czegoś*) begin, start; **zacząć coś robić** begin *l.* start doing sth;

zacząć od samego początku start at the very beginning; **dobrze/źle zacząć** make a good/bad start; **zacząć tracić cierpliwość** start getting *l*. be growing short of patience; **zaczyna nam brakować pieniędzy** we're running out of money; **zaczyna wyglądać na to, że...** it's beginning to look as if... **3.** (= *napoczynać*) open; **zaczynać butelkę/paczkę papierosów** open a new bottle/packet of cigarettes. **4.** (= *zaczynać mówić, pisać*) start, begin; **Szanowni Państwo! – zaczął.** "Ladies and Gentlemen!" – he started *l*. began; **zacząć z innej beczki** change the topic; **zacznijmy z innej beczki** let's change the topic; **nie wiem od czego zacząć** I don't know where *l*. how to start. **5.** *pot.* (= *zaczepiać*) provoke; **lepiej z nim nie zaczynaj!** you'd better not provoke him!; **znowu zaczynasz!** there you go again! **~ się** *ipf.* start, begin; **zaczyna się!** *(pretensja do kogoś)* there you go again!; **wyraz zaczyna się na literę S** the word starts with an S; **zaczęły się schody** *pot.* that's where the trouble starts.

zaczyniać *ipf.*, **zaczynić** *pf.* **1.** *kulin.* (= *dodać zakwasu*) leaven. **2.** (= *rzucić urok*) cast a spell.

zaczytać (się) *pf. zob.* **zaczytywać (się)**.

zaczytywać *ipf. pot.* (= *zniszczyć częstym czytaniem*) wear (*a book by frequent reading*). **~ się** *ipf.* **1.** (= *zagłębić się w czytaniu*) be engrossed in reading. **2.** *zw. ipf.* (= *czytać z zamiłowaniem*) delight in reading (*a particular book l. type of literature*).

zaćma *f. pat.* cataract.

zaćmić *pf.* **-ij 1.** *zob.* **zaćmiewać. 2.** (= *zaboleć*) ache; **zaćmił mnie ząb** I felt a (slight) toothache. **3.** *pot.* (= *zapalić papierosa, fajkę*) light (*a cigarette, pipe, etc.*). **~ się** *pf. zob.* **zaćmiewać się**.

zaćmienie *n.* **1.** *astron.* eclipse; **zaćmienie Księżyca/Słońca** lunar/solar eclipse; **zaćmienie obrączkowe** annular eclipse; **całkowite/częściowe zaćmienie** total/partial eclipse. **2.** (= *zamroczenie*) haze, obfuscation.

zaćmiewać *ipf.* **1.** (= *przesłaniać*) obscure, dim, darken; **zaćmiło mnie na egzaminie** *przen.* my mind went completely blank during the exam. **2.** *lit.* (= *przewyższać, przyćmiewać*) outshine (*czymś* with sth); overshadow (*czymś* by sth). **~ się** *ipf.* **1.** (= *przesłaniać się*) darken, become dim; **zaćmiło mi się w oczach** I'm seeing spots before my eyes, things went dark before my eyes. **2.** (*o lampie*) (= *przygasać*) dim.

zaćpać *pf. pot.* have a hit; **w tym tygodniu zaćpał już dwa razy** he's had two hits already this week. **~ się** *pf. pot.* get high; **zaćpać się na śmierć** overdose, OD.

zaćpany *a. pot.* (= *pod wpływem narkotyku*) high; (*pod wpływem marihuany*) stoned; (*pod wpływem heroiny*) strung-out.

zaćwiczyć *pf.* flog to death.

zaćwierkać *pf.* chirp.

zad *mi* **1.** (= *pośladki u dużych ssaków*) rump. **2.** *pot.* (= *grube pośladki u człowieka*) rump, buttocks.

zadać *pf.* **-dadzą** *zob.* **zadawać. ~ się** *pf. zob.* **zadawać się**.

zadanie *n.* **1.** (= *to, co należy wykonać*) task, assignment; **zadanie bojowe** *wojsk.* combat mission; *żart.* mission; **twoje zadanie bojowe na dziś to sprzątnąć wreszcie mieszkanie** your mission today is to finally clean up the apartment; **dać komuś zadanie** set *l*. give sb a task; **postawić komuś/sobie zadanie zrobienia czegoś** set sb/o.s. the task of doing sth; **powierzyć komuś zadanie** assign sb a task; **spełniać swoje zadanie** (*o urządzeniu*) serve its purpose; **stanąć na wysokości zadania** rise to the occasion; **wykonać zadanie** perform a task; **mam za zadanie to zrobić** it is my task to do it. **2.** *szkoln.* task, exercise; (= *problem do samodzielnego przestudiowania, opracowania*) assigment; (*zwł. matematyczne*) problem; **rozwiązać zadanie z matematyki** solve a maths problem; **zadanie domowe** *l*. **praca domowa** homework; **odrobić zadanie domowe** *l*. **pracę domową** do one's homework. **3.** (= *zagadnienie do rozwiązania*) problem. **4.** *szachy* problem.

zadaniowy *a.* (of a) task, (of an) assignment.

zadanko *n.* *Gen.pl.* **-ek** *dimin.* (small) task, (small) assignment; (small) problem.

zadarty *a.* snub, turned up, upturned; **z zadartym nosem** (*o osobie*) snub-nosed.

zadaszenie *n.* (= *dach*) roofing; (*na przystanku autobusowym*) (bus) shelter.

zadatek *mi* **-tk-** (= *zaliczka*) (*za wykonanie umowy, usługi*) advance payment, earnest; (*na zakup samochodu, czegoś na raty*) down payment; **dawać komuś zadatek** advance money to sb; **wpłacić zadatek na coś** put down a deposit on sth, make a down payment on sth.

zadatki *pl. Gen.* **-ów** (= *zaczątki*) makings; **on ma zadatki na dobrego aktora** he's got the makings of a good actor, he'll make a good actor.

zadatkować *ipf. l. pf.* (= *wpłacić zadatek na coś*) put down a deposit (*coś* on sth); make a down payment (*coś* on sth).

zadawać *ipf.* **-aję -ajesz, -awaj 1.** (= *wyznaczać zadanie*) assign, set; **zadawać pytanie** ask a question; **zadać komuś zagadkę** give sb a riddle to solve. **2.** (= *sprawiać*) inflict; **zadać klęskę wrogowi** defeat the enemy; **zadać komuś ból** inflict pain on sb; **zadać komuś śmierć** deal out death to sb, take the life of sb; **zadać pokaźne straty** cause severe losses; **zadawać komuś cios** deal a blow to sb; **zadawać kłam komuś/czemuś** give the lie to sb/sth, belie sb/sth; **zadać sobie trud, żeby coś zrobić** take the trouble to do sth, take pains to do sth; **zadać sobie wiele trudu, żeby coś zrobić** go to great pains to do sth, go out of one's way to do sth; **zadać sobie/komuś gwałt, żeby coś zrobić** force o.s./sb to do sth; **zadać komuś czymś szyku** dazzle sb with sth (*usu. one's clothes*). **3.** (= *zaprawiać*) treat. **4.** (= *dawać pokarm zwierzętom*) give, feed (*fodder to animals*). **5.** (= *podnosić i zakładać komuś ciężar*) put (*a sack etc. on sb's shoulders*). **~ się** *ipf. pot.* hang around, mix (*z kimś* with sb); **z nikim się nie zadawać** keep o.s. to o.s.

zadawniony *a.* (*np. o urazie*) inveterate; **zadawnione poczucie wrogości** an inveterate feeling of hostility; (*o urazie, konflikcie*) deep-rooted, long-standing; **zadawniony konflikt mię-**

dzy rodzinami deep-rooted *l.* long-standing conflict between the families.

zadąć *pf.* **-dmę -dmiesz, -dmij 1.** (*o wietrze*) (= *dmuchnąć*) blow. **2.** (= *zagrać na instrumencie dętym*) blow (*a trumpet, etc.*); **zadąć w gwizdek** blow one's whistle.

zadąsany *a.* sulky, sulking.

zadbać *pf. zob.* **dbać.**

zadbany *a.* (*człowiek*) well-groomed; (*dom, ogród*) well-groomed, neat and tidy; (*o trawniku*) (= *przycięty*) manicured.

zadebiutować *pf. zob.* **debiutować.**

zadecydować *pf. zob.* **decydować.**

zadedykować *pf. zob.* **dedykować.**

zadek *mi* **-dk-** *Gen.* **-a** *pot.* buttocks, butt.

zadeklamować *pf. zob.* **deklamować.**

zadeklarować *pf. zob.* **deklarować.** ~ **się** *pf. zob.* **deklarować się.**

zadekować *pf. zob.* **dekować.** ~ **się** *pf. zob.* **dekować się.**

zadekretować *pf. zob.* **dekretować.**

zademonstrować *pf. zob.* **demonstrować.**

zadenuncjować *pf. zob.* **denuncjować.**

zadepeszować *pf. zob.* **depeszować.**

zadeptać *pf.* **-pczę** *l.* **-pcę -pczesz** *l.* **-pcesz, zadeptywać** *ipf.* **1.** (= *rozdeptać*) trample; **zadeptać na śmierć** trample to death. **2.** (*np. papierosa*) stamp out. **3.** (= *zabrudzić, depcząc*) soil.

zadeszczony *a.* rainy.

zadęcie *n.* **1.** (*dźwięk*) blast. **2.** *pot.* (= *pretensjonalność*) swank, pretentiousness. **3.** *pot.* (= *zacięcie*) bent (*do czegoś* for sth).

zadiektywizowany *a. jęz.* adjectivized.

zadiustować *pf. zob.* **adiustować.**

zadławić *pf.* choke. ~ **się** *pf.* choke (*na czymś* on sth).

zadłużać *ipf.* incur debts; (*np. przedsiębiorstwo*) put into debt; (*konto*) debit. ~ **się** *ipf.* incur debts, get into a debt (*u kogoś* to sb); **zadłużać się na 100 tysięcy dolarów** get into a debt of 100 thousand dollars.

zadłużenie *n.* debt; indebtedness.

zadłużony *a.* **-eni** indebted; **być zadłużonym** be in debt.

zadłużyć *pf. zob.* **zadłużać.** ~ **się** *pf. zob.* **zadłużać się.**

zadni *a. przest.* hind; **zadnie nogi** hind legs.

zadokumentować *pf. zob.* **dokumentować.**

zadołować *pf. zob.* **dołować.**

zadomawiać się *ipf.*, **zadomowić się** get settled.

zadomowiony *a.* **1.** feeling (completely) at home. **2.** (*o zwierzęciu*) domesticated.

zadość *adv.* **czynić zadość czemuś** satisfy sth, fulfill sth; **czynić zadość prośbie/wymaganiom** satisfy a request/demands; **stało się zadość czemuś** sth was complied with; **sprawiedliwości stało się zadość** justice was done, justice was served; it was poetic justice.

zadośćuczynić *pf.* **1.** *lit.* (= *sprostać wymaganiom*) satisfy. **2.** *lit.* (= *wynagrodzić*) (*finansowo*) reimburse.

zadośćuczynienie *n.* **1.** (= *spełnienie wymagań, zaspokojenie*) satisfaction, gratification. **2.**

(= *rekompensata*) compensation; (*finansowe*) reimbursement.

zadowalać *ipf.* satisfy, please. ~ **się** *ipf.* make do (*czymś* with sth); settle (*czymś* for sth).

zadowalająco *adv.* satisfactorily.

zadowalający *a.* satisfactory.

zadowolenie *n.* satisfaction; **z zadowoleniem** with satisfaction, contendedly.

zadowolić *pf. zob.* **zadowalać.** ~ **się** *pf. zob.* **zadowalać się.**

zadowolony *a.* **-eni** (= *szczęśliwy*) glad, pleased; (= *usatysfakcjonowany*) satisfied, contended; **zadowolony z kogoś/czegoś** pleased with sb/sth; **zadowolony z siebie** complacent, self-satisfied.

zadra *f.* splinter; **nosić zadrę w sercu** *przen.* bear sb a grudge.

zadrapać *pf.* **-pię -piesz** *zob.* **zadrapywać.** ~ **się** *pf. zob.* **zadrapywać się.**

zadrapanie *n.* scratch.

zadrapnąć *pf.* **-ij** *zob.* **zadrapywać.** ~ **się** *pf. zob.* **zadrapywać się.**

zadrapnięcie *n.* scratch.

zadrapywać *ipf.* scratch. ~ **się** *ipf.* scratch o.s.

zadrasnąć *pf.* **-snę -śniesz, -śnij 1.** (= *skaleczyć*) scratch, graze. **2.** (= *urazić*) *przen.* hurt. ~ **się** *pf.* scratch o.s.

zadraśnięcie *n.* scratch, graze.

zadrażniać *ipf.*, **zadrażnić** *pf.* **-ij** exacerbate.

zadrażnienie *n.* friction.

zadręczać *ipf.* **1.** (= *nagabywać*) pester, badger (*kogoś o coś* sb for sth). **2.** (= *zakatować*) torture to death. ~ **się** *ipf.* torture o.s., torment o.s. (*czymś* with sth).

zadręczyć (się) *pf. zob.* **zadręczać (się).**

zadrgać *pf.* **1.** (= *zadrżeć*) tremble, quiver; (*o świetle*) flicker, twinkle. **2.** (*o głosie*) (= *załamać się*) quaver, tremble.

zadruk *mi druk.* **1.** (= *miejsce zadrukowane*) printed space *l.* area. **2.** (= *gęstość druku*) print density.

zadrukować *pf.*, **zadrukowywać** *ipf.* print.

zadrwić *pf.* **-ij** *zob.* **drwić.**

zadrzeć *pf.* **-drę -drzesz, -drzyj, -darł** *zob.* **zadzierać.** ~ **się** *pf. zob.* **zadzierać się.**

zadrzewiać *ipf.*, **zadrzewić** *pf. leśn., roln.* afforest.

zadrzewienie *n. leśn., roln.* afforestation.

zadrzewiony *a.* wooded.

zadrżeć *pf.* **-ę -ysz, -yj 1.** (= *zadrgać*) shake, tremble; (*o świetle*) flicker. **2.** (*o głosie*) (= *załamać się*) tremble, quaver. **3.** (= *przestraszyć się*) *przen.* shudder; **zadrżał na myśl, że...** he shuddered at the thought that...

zaduch *mi* stuffy air, stuffiness; **straszny tu zaduch!** it's so stuffy here!

zadudnić *pf.* **-ij** rumble.

zadufanie *n.* overconfidence, presumptuousness.

zadufany *a.* overconfident, presumptuous; **zadufany w sobie** self-assured.

zaduma *f.* reflection, meditation; **pogrążyć się w zadumie** sink into meditation.

zadumać się *pf. lit.* muse (*nad czymś* on *l.* about sth); reflect (*nad czymś* over sth).

zadumany *a. lit.* reflective, pensive.

zadupie *n. Gen.pl.* **-i** *wulg.* shithole, jerkwater town.

zadurzony *a.* **-eni** *pot.* infatuated (*w kimś* with sb).

zadurzyć się *pf. pot.* become infatuated (*w kimś* with sb); fall (*w kimś* for sb).

zadusić *pf.* **-szę -sisz** *zob.* **dusić.** ~ **się** *pf. zob.* **dusić się.**

Zaduszki *pl. Gen.* **-szek** *rz.-kat.* All Souls' Day.

zaduszkowy *a. rz.-kat.* All Souls' Day.

zaduszny *a. rz.-kat.* All Soul's Day; related to prayers for the dead; **Dzień Zaduszny** All Souls' Day.

zadygotać *pf.* **-oczę** *l.* **-ocę -oczesz** *l.* **-ocesz** tremble, start trembling; shake, start shaking.

zadyma *f. pot.* (= *zamieszki*) riot, turmoil; (= *zamieszanie, awantura*) fuss (*o coś* over sth).

zadymiać *ipf.* **1.** (= *wypełnić dymem*) fill with smoke; (= *przesłonić dymem*) obscure *l.* screen with smoke. **2.** (= *wydzielić dym*) smoke; (= *buchnąć dymem*) steam. ~ **się** *ipf.* **1.** (= *wydzielić dym*) smoke; (= *buchnąć dymem*) steam. **2.** (= *wypełnić się dymem*) be filled with smoke; (= *okopcić się*) be blackened with smoke.

zadymiarski *a. pot.* rowdyish.

zadymiarz *mp pot.* rowdy, troublemaker.

zadymić *pf.* **1.** *zob.* **zadymiać. 2.** (= *wydzielić dym*) smoke; (= *buchnąć dymem*) steam. ~ **się** *pf. zob.* **zadymiać się.**

zadymiony *a.* smoky.

zadymka *f. Gen.pl.* **-ek** *zwł. meteor.* snowstorm, blizzard.

zadyndać *pf.* **1.** *pot.* (= *zakołysać się*) swing. **2.** *pot.* (= *zostać powieszonym*) be stringed up, be hanged.

zadysponować *pf. zob.* **dysponować.**

zadyszany *a.* breathless, out of breath.

zadyszeć *pf.* **-ę -ysz** pant, gasp. ~ **się** *pf.* run short *l.* out of breath.

zadyszka *f. Gen.pl.* **-ek** breathlessness; **dostać zadyszki** lose one's breath, be out of breath.

zadziałać *pf.* **1.** *pot.* (*o mechanizmie*) (= *zacząć działać*) work, start working. **2.** *pot.* (= *podziałać*) have an effect; (*o leku*) work, start working; **to powinno zadziałać** this should do the job *l.* trick. **3.** *pot.* (= *przystąpić do działania*) take action.

zadzierać *ipf.* **1.** (= *naddzierać*) tear. **2.** (= *podnosić*) pull up, lift up; (*spódnicę*) pull up; **zadzierać głowę** crane one's neck; **zadzierać nosa** put on airs. **3.** *pot.* (= *kłócić się*) mess (*z kimś* with sb). ~ **się** *ipf.* **1.** (= *naddzierać się*) get torn. **2.** (= *zaginać się ku górze*) turn up.

zadzierzgnąć *pf.* **-ij** *przest.* tie up; **zadzierzgnąć węzły** *l.* **więzy przyjaźni** *lit.* develop the bonds of friendship, make *l.* strike up a friendship.

zadzierzgnięcie *n. pat.* (= *niedrożność jelit*), *prawn.* (= *uduszenie przez ucisk pętlą*) strangulation.

zadzierzystość *f. lit.* truculence, truculency; cantankerousness.

zadzierzysty *a. lit.* truculent, cantankerous.

zadzierzyście *a. lit.* truculently, cantankerously.

zadziobać *pf.* **-bię -biesz** peck to death.

zadzior *mi Gen.* **-a** *l.* **-u** splinter, sliver.

zadziora *f.* **1.** *pot.* (= *awanturnik*) blusterer, brawler. **2.** (= *zadzior, drzazga*) splinter, sliver.

zadziornie *adv.* contentiously, quarrelsomely.

zadziorność *f.* contentiousness, quarrelsomeness.

zadziorny *a.* contentious, quarrelsome.

zadziwiać *ipf.* (= *wywołać podziw*) win admiration, arouse admiration; (= *zdumieć*) astonish, amaze.

zadziwiająco *adv.* astonishingly, amazingly.

zadziwiający *a.* astonishing, amazing.

zadziwić *pf. zob.* **zadziwiać.** ~ **się** *pf.* be astonished, be amazed (*czymś* by sth).

zadzwonić *pf.* **1.** (= *nacisnąć dzwonek*) ring the bell; **zadzwonić na służbę** ring for the servant. **2.** (*o dzwonku, telefonie*) (= *wydać dźwięk*) ring. **3.** (= *zabrząkać*) (*o kluczach*) jangle; (*o szybie, szklankach*) clink. **4.** (= *zatelefonować*) ring up; call, call up (*do kogoś* sb); **zadzwonić na policję** call the police.

zadźgać *pf. pot.* (= *zabić nożem*) stab (*sb*) to death.

zadźwięczeć *pf.* **-ę -ysz** **1.** (= *wydać metaliczny dźwięk*) resound; (*o dzwonku*) ring; (*o szybie*) clink; (*o kluczach*) jangle. **2.** (= *zabrzmieć*) sound.

zadżumiony *a.* **-eni** plagued, plague-stricken.

zafajdać *pf.* **1.** *pot.* (= *zabrudzić kałem*) muck up. **2.** *pot.* (= *zepsuć*) screw up, botch; **zafajdać sobie/komuś opinię** ruin *l.* tarnish one's/sb's reputation.

zafajdany *a. pot.* (= *marny*) shitty.

zafalować *pf.* wave.

zafałszować *pf. zob.* **fałszować.**

zafarbować *pf. zob.* **farbować.**

zafascynować *pf. zob.* **fascynować.** ~ **się** *pf. zob.* **fascynować się.**

zafascynowanie *n.* fascination.

zafascynowany *a.* fascinated.

zafasować *pf. pot., dial.* (= *dostać*) draw, collect; (= *zdobyć*) get hold (*coś* of sth).

zafastrygować *pf. zob.* **fastrygować.**

zafiksować *pf. pot., dial.* (= *ustalić*) fix, set.

zaflegmiony *a.* **-eni** *zwł. pat.* phlegmy.

zafrapować *pf. zob.* **frapować.**

zafrasować *pf. zob.* **frasować.** ~ **się** *pf. zob.* **frasować się.**

zafrasowany *a. lit.* troubled, worried.

zafundować *pf. zob.* **fundować.**

zagabnąć *pf.* **-ij**, **zagabywać** *ipf.* (= *zacząć rozmowę*) strike up a conversation (*kogoś* with sb); (= *zagadnąć*) address (*kogoś* sb); (= *spytać*) ask (*kogoś o coś* sb about sth).

zagadać *pf.* **1.** *zob.* **zagadywać. 2.** *pot.* (= *zacząć mówić*) start talking (*do kogoś* to sb). **3.** *pot.* (= *mówić dużo*) talk down, outtalk. ~ **się** *pf. pot.* become lost in conversation.

zagadany *a.* engrossed in conversation.

zagadka *f. Gen.pl.* **-ek** **1.** (= *zadanie do odgad-*

nięcia) riddle, puzzle; **mówić zagadkami** speak in riddles, riddle; **rozwiązać zagadkę** solve a riddle *l.* puzzle; **zadać zagadkę** propound a riddle. **2.** (= *tajemnica*) mystery; **ona jest/pozostaje dla mnie zagadką** she is/remains a mystery to me.

zagadkowo *adv.* mysteriously, enigmatically.

zagadkowość *f.* mysteriousness.

zagadkowy *a.* (= *tajemniczy*) mysterious, enigmatic; (= *zadziwiający*) puzzling.

zagadnąć *pf.* -**ij** *zob.* **zagadywać**.

zagadnienie *n.* (= *problem*) problem; (= *kwestia*) issue, question.

zagadywać *ipf.* **1.** (= *zwracać się*) speak (*do kogoś* to sb); (= *zapytać*) ask (*kogoś o coś* sb about sth). **2.** (= *tuszować mówieniem*) talk down.

zagaić *pf.* -**ję** -**isz**, **zagajać** *ipf. form.* open; **zagaić zebranie/dyskusję** open a meeting/discussion; **zagajać rozmowę** *pot.* strike up a conversation.

zagajenie *n. form.* opening address.

zagajnik *mi Gen.* -**a** *zwł. leśn.* copse, coppice.

zagalopować się *pf.*, **zagalopowywać się** *ipf. pot., przen.* go too far, overstep the mark.

zaganiacz *ma orn.* icterine warbler (*Hippolais icterina*).

zaganiać *ipf.* **1.** (= *zapędzać*) drive in. **2.** *pot.* (= *zmuszać*) drive, force; **zaganiać kogoś do robienia czegoś** force sb to do sth.

zaganiany *a. pot.* busy; (= *zapracowany*) overworked; **byłem dziś strasznie zaganiany** I had a hectic day.

zagapić się *pf.* **1.** *pot.* (= *zapatrzyć się*) stare, gape (*na kogoś / coś* at sb/sth). **2.** *pot.* (= *wykazać się nieuwagą*) fail to pay attention, miss; **zagapiłem się** I wasn't paying attention.

zagapiony *a.* -**eni** *pot.* **1.** (= *zapatrzony*) staring, gaping (*na kogoś / coś* at sb/sth). **2.** (= *nieuważny*) inattentive.

zagarnąć *ipf.* -**ij**, **zagarniać** *pf.* **1.** (= *zebrać, zsunąć*) gather; (*o koparce, spychaczu*) move (*to one place*), heap up. **2.** (= *przywłaszczyć*) seize.

zagarnięcie *n. prawn.* (unlawful) appropriation.

zagasać *ipf. lit.* **1.** (= *gasnąć*) die down. **2.** (= *ciemnieć*) dim, pale.

zagasić *pf.* -**szę** -**sisz** *zob.* **zagaszać**.

zagasnąć *pf.* -**snę** -**śniesz**, -**śnij**, -**sł** *l.* -**snął** -**sła** -**śli** *zob.* **zagasać**.

zagaszać *ipf.* **1.** (= *gasić*) put out, extinguish. **2.** (= *przyciemniać*) dim, obscure.

zagazować *pf.*, **zagazowywać** *ipf.* **1.** (= *skazić gazem*) contaminate with gas. **2.** (= *uśmiercić gazem*) gas.

zagdakać *pf.* cackle, start cackling.

zagęgać *pf.* gaggle, start gaggling.

zagęszczać *ipf.* **1.** (= *czynić gęstym*) thicken, condense. **2.** (= *przeludniać*) overcrowd, congest. ~ **się** *ipf.* **1.** (= *gęstnieć*) thicken, condense. **2.** (= *przeludniać się*) overcrowd.

zagęszczenie *n.* **1.** (*substancji*) thickening, condensation. **2.** (*zaludnienia*) density; **zagęszczenie ludności** population density. **3.** (= *nagromadzenie, skupisko*) concentration.

zagęszczony *a.* **1.** (*płyn, substancja*) congest-

ed, concentrated; (*o mleku*) condensed; (*o soku*) concentrated. **2.** (= *zatłoczony*) crowded.

zagęścić *pf.* -**szczę** -**ścisz** *zob.* **zagęszczać**. ~ **się** *pf. zob.* **zagęszczać się**.

zagiąć *pf.* -**gnę** -**gniesz**, -**gnij** *zob.* **zaginać**. ~ **się** *pf. zob.* **zaginać się**.

zagięcie *n.* fold, bend.

zaginać *ipf.* **1.** (= *wykrzywiać, załamywać*) crook, curve; (*drut*) bend; (*kartkę*) fold. **2.** (= *podwijać*) fold up, turn up; (*rękawy*) roll up. **3.** *pot.* (= *zaskakiwać kłopotliwym pytaniem*) beat; **a to mnie zagiąłeś!** you've got me here!; (it) beats me!

zaginąć *pf.* go missing, disappear; **chłopak zaginął trzy dni temu** the boy has been missing for three days; **ślad po** *l.* **słuch o niej zaginął** there is no trace left of her.

zaginiony *a.* missing. – *mp* missing person.

zagipsować *pf. zob.* **gipsować**.

zaglądać *ipf.* **1.** (= *patrzeć w głąb czegoś*) look (*do czegoś l. w coś* into sth); **zaglądać do kieliszka** *pot.* booze it up; **śmierć zajrzała mi w oczy** I faced death, I almost died. **2.** (= *odwiedzać*) call (*do kogoś* on sb).

zaglądnąć *pf.* -**ij** *pot.* = **zajrzeć**.

zagłada *f.* extermination, annihilation; **broń masowej zagłady** weapons of mass destruction; **ulec zagładzie** be exterminated, be annihilated.

zagładzać *ipf.* starve. ~ **się** *ipf.* starve o.s.

zagłaskać *pf.* -**głaszczę** *l.* -**głaskam** -**głaszczesz** *l.* -**głaskasz**, **zagłaskiwać** *ipf. pot.* (= *zadręczyć nadmierną czułością*) kill with kindness.

zagłębiać *ipf.*, **zagłębić** *pf.* (= *zanurzyć*) immerse; (*np. ręce w kieszeniach*) sink; (*np. wiosło w wodzie*) dip. ~ **się** *ipf.*, **zagłębić się** *pf.* **1.** (= *zanurzać się*) immerse; (*np. o wiertle w ścianie*) sink; **zagłębić się w fotelu** sink into an armchair. **2.** (= *wjeżdżać, zapuszczać się*) go deep, go far out; **zagłębiać się w las** go deep into a forest. **3.** *lit.* (= *zajmować się intensywnie*) become absorbed, become engrossed; **zagłębiać się w książce** become absorbed *l.* engrossed in a book; **zagłębiać się w myślach** be deep *l.* lost in thought.

zagłębie *n. Gen.pl.* -**i** *geol., górn.* basin; **zagłębie węglowe** coal field.

zagłębienie *n.* **1.** (*od uderzenia, np. w stole, desce*) nitch, notch. **2.** (*np. terenu*) hollow, depression.

zagłodzić *pf. zob.* **zagładzać się**. ~ **się** *pf. zob.* **zagładzać się**.

zagłosować *pf. zob.* **głosować**.

zagłówek *mi* -**wk**- *Gen.* -**a** bolster; *zwł. mot.* headrest.

zagłuszać *ipf.*, **zagłuszyć** *pf.* **1.** (= *tłumić dźwięki*) drown, drown out; (*stację radiową*) jam; **zagłuszać wyrzuty sumienia** deaden one's pangs of conscience. **2.** (*o roślinach*) (= *blokować rozrost*) choke; **chwasty zagłuszają moje rośliny** the weeds are choking my plants. ~ **się** *ipf.*, **zagłuszyć się** *pf.* drown each other out, drown one another out.

zagmatwać *pf. zob.* **gmatwać**. ~ **się** *pf. zob.* **gmatwać się**.

zagmatwanie *n.* (= *gmatwanina*) tangle; (= *zawiłość*) complexity.

zagmatwany *a.* tangled, confused.

zagnać *pf. zob.* **zaganiać**.

zagniatać *ipf.* 1. (= *wyrabiać ciasto*) knead. 2. (= *gniotąc, niszczyć np. ubranie*) crumple, crease. 3. (*np. papierosa*) stamp out; (*np. kogoś w tłumie*) trample. ~ **się** *ipf.* crumple, crease.

zagniazdownik *ma orn.* nidifugous bird.

zagnić *pf.* **-gniję -gnijesz, -gnij** become partly rotten.

zagniecenie *n.* crease.

zagnieść *pf.* **-gniotę -gnieciesz -gniótł -gniotła -gnietli** *zob.* **zagniatać**. ~ **się** *pf. zob.* **zagniatać się**.

zagniewany *a.* angry, cross (*na kogoś* with sb).

zagnieździć się *pf.* **-gnieżdżę -gnieździsz, zagnieżdżać się** *ipf.* 1. (= *założyć gniazdo*) nest. 2. (= *zapanować*) prevail; (= *zakorzenić się*) take root.

zagoić *pf.* **-goję -goisz, -gój** *zob.* **goić**. ~ **się** *pf. zob.* **goić się**.

zagon *mi* 1. *roln.* bed. 2. *hist., wojsk.* (= *oddział dokonujący wypadu*) advanced detachment; (= *wypad*) incursion.

zagonek *mi* **-nk-** *Gen.* **-a** (= *grządka*) bed.

zagonić *pf. zob.* **zaganiać**.

zagonik *mi Gen.* **-a** *l.* **-u** = **zagonek**.

zagoniony *a.* **-eni** *pot.* on the go; (= *przepracowany*) overworked.

zagorzale *adv.* 1. (*popierać, bronić*) ardently, staunchly; (*walczyć*) fiercely. 2. (*dyskutować*) heatedly.

zagorzały *a.* 1. (*o kibicu, fanie*) ardent, staunch; (*o wrogu, przeciwniku*) fierce. 2. (= *ożywiony, żarliwy*) (*o rozmowie, dyskusji*) heated.

zagospodarować *pf. zob.* **zagospodarowywać**. ~ **się** *pf. zob.* **zagospodarowywać się**.

zagospodarowany *a.* (*np. o terenie*) developed.

zagospodarowywać *ipf.* (*teren*) develop; (*zasoby, środki*) put to (appropriate) use; (*maszyny, urządzenia*) make *l.* render operational; (= *uczynić dochodowym*) make profitable. ~ **się** *ipf.* settle in.

zagościć *pf.* **-goszczę -gościsz** (= *pojawić się*) (*o radości, spokoju*) settle, occur; **zagościć u kogoś** honor sb with a visit, *Br.* honour sb with a visit; **w jego sercu zagościł ból** a pain settled in his heart; **uśmiech nigdy już nie zagościł na jej twarzy** a smile never brightened her face again.

zagotować *pf.* boil. ~ **się** *pf.* 1. (= *zacząć wrzeć*) boil, start boiling. 2. (= *wzburzyć się*) flare up, boil with rage; **w tłumie się zagotowało** the crowd stirred.

zagrabiać *ipf.*, **zagrabić** *pf.* 1. (= *zgarniać grabiami*) rake up. 2. (= *przywłaszczać*) seize, capture; (*ziemie, tereny*) carve out.

zagrabki *pl. Gen.* **-ów** *roln.* raked-up hay.

zagracać *ipf.*, **zagracić** *pf. pot.* clutter.

zagrać *pf. zob.* **grać**, **zagrywać**.

zagradzać *ipf.* 1. (= *stawiać przeszkodę*) obstruct, bar; **zagrodzić komuś drogę** bar sb's way; *przen.* stand in sb's way (*do czegoś* to sth). 2. (= *otaczać płotem*) fence.

zagranica *f.* foreign countries; **stosunki z zagranicą** foreign relations; **wrócić z zagranicy** return from abroad.

zagraniczniak, zagranicznik *mp pot.* (= *cudzoziemiec*) foreigner, outlander.

zagraniczny *a.* foreign; **goście zagraniczni** foreign visitors, visitors from abroad; **handel zagraniczny** foreign trade; **inwestycje zagraniczne** foreign investment; **kapitał zagraniczny** foreign capital; **podróże zagraniczne** travel abroad, foreign travel; **Ministerstwo Spraw Zagranicznych** *polit.* the Ministry of Foreign Affairs; *US* the State Department; *Br.* the Foreign and Commonwealth Office.

zagranie *n.* 1. *sport* move, play. 2. *pot.* (= *sposób postępowania*) move.

zagrażać *ipf.* threaten (*komuś / czemuś* sb/ sth); **zagraża ci niebezpieczeństwo** you are in danger; **zagraża nam głód** we are in danger of starvation; **miastu zagraża epidemia** the city is in danger of an epidemic.

zagroda *f. Gen.pl.* **-ód** 1. (= *dom wiejski z zabudowaniami*) farmstead. 2. (= *odgrodzone miejsce dla zwierząt*) pen, enclosure.

zagrodowy *a.* farmstead; **szlachcic zagrodowy** *hist.* yeoman.

zagrodzić *pf.* **-grodzę -grodzisz, -grodź** *l.* **-gródź** *zob.* **zagradzać**.

zagrozić *pf.* **-grożę -grozisz, -groź** *l.* **-gróź** 1. *zob.* **zagrażać**. 2. (= *postraszyć*) threaten, menace (*komuś / czemuś* sb/sth).

zagrożenie *n.* (*stan*) threat, menace; (*czynnik*) hazard, risk; **zagrożenie dla demokracji** threat to democracy; **zagrożenie dla zdrowia** health risk, health hazard; **zagrożenie ekologiczne** environmental risk, environmental hazard; threat to the environment; **zagrożenie pożarowe** fire hazard, fire risk; **zagrożenie społeczne** public menace; **stanowić zagrożenie dla kogoś/czegoś** pose a threat to sb/sth, be a threat *l.* danger to sb/sth.

zagródka *f. Gen.pl.* **-ek** *zob.* **zagroda**.

zagruntować *pf.*, **zagruntowywać** *ipf.* ground.

zagruzować *pf.* (= *pokryć gruzem*) cover with rubble; (= *zasypać gruzem*) lumber with rubble.

zagrycha *f. pot.* snack, food (*eaten to chase a drink of liquor*).

zagrypiony *a.* **-eni** *pot.* suffering from (the) flu.

zagrywać *ipf.* **-am -asz** *sport* serve.

zagrywka *f. Gen.pl.* **-ek** 1. *sport* serve. 2. *pot.* (= *niespodziewane zachowanie*) gambit, ploy; **pokerowa zagrywka** clever move.

zagryzać *ipf.* 1. (= *zakąszać*) chase a drink of liquor (*with food l. a snack*). 2. (= *przygryzać*) bite; **zagryzać wargi** bite one's lips. 3. (*o zwierzętach*) (= *pozbawiać życia, gryząc*) bite to death. ~ **się** *ipf.* 1. (*o zwierzętach*) (= *pozbawiać się wzajemnie życia*) bite each other to death, bite one another to death. 2. (*o ludziach*) (= *zadręczać się nawzajem*) torture each other, torment each other. 3. (= *zamartwiać się*) worry.

zagryźć (się) *pf.* **-gryzę -gryziesz, -gryzł -gryźli** *zob.* **zagryzać (się)**.

zagrzać *pf.* **-grzeję -grzejesz -grzali** *l.* **-grzeli** *zob.* **zagrzewać**. ~ **się** *pf. zob.* **zagrzewać się**.

Zagrzeb *mi* -**bi**- *Gen.* -**a** *geogr.* Zagreb.

zagrzebać (się) *pf.* -**bię -biesz** *zob.* **zagrzebywać (się)**.

zagrzebywać *ipf.* bury. ~ **się** *ipf.* bury o.s., burrow; **zagrzebać się na wsi/na odludziu** bury o.s. in the country/somewhere off the beaten track.

zagrzewać *ipf.* **1.** (= *podgrzewać*) warm up, heat up; **nie zagrzać gdzieś miejsca** not stay somewhere long; **nie zagrzała nigdzie miejsca** she never stayed anywhere long. **2.** (= *pobudzać*) animate, spur on; **zagrzewać kogoś do (zrobienia) czegoś** spur sb on to (do) sth. ~ **się** *ipf.* **1.** (= *podgrzewać się*) warm up, heat up; get warm. **2.** (= *rozgrzewać się*) warm up, get warm. **3.** (= *rozgrzewać się nadmiernie*) (*np. o silniku*) overheat. **4.** (= *zachęcać się wzajemnie*) animate each other, animate one another; **zagrzewać się do (zrobienia) czegoś** spur each other *l.* one another on to (do) sth.

zagrzmieć *pf.* -**grzmię -grzmisz, -grzmij 1.** *zob.* **grzmieć. 2. zagrzmiało** there was a clap of thunder.

zagrzybić *pf.* mold; *Br.* mould. ~ **się** *pf.* mold; *Br.* mould.

zagrzybiony *a.* -**eni** moldy; *Br.* mouldy.

zagubić *pf.* lose. ~ **się** *pf.* **1.** (= *zostać zagubionym*) get lost; **zagubiły mu się ważne dokumenty** he lost some important documents. **2.** (= *zabłądzić*) get lost. **3.** (= *zaplątać się*) get confused.

zagubienie *n.* loss.

zagubiony *a.* -**eni 1.** (= *trudny do zlokalizowania*) (*np. o wyspie*) remote; (*o osadzie, wyspie*) remote, secluded. **2.** (= *bezradny, niepewny*) lost; **być/czuć się zagubionym** be/feel lost, be at a loss.

zagulgotać *pf.* (*o wodzie, małym dziecku*) gurgle; (*o indyku*) gobble.

zagustować *pf.* get to like, come to enjoy (*w czymś* sth).

zagwarantować *pf. zob.* **gwarantować**.

zagważdżać *ipf. zob.* **zagwoździć**.

zagwizdać *pf.* -**gwiżdżę -gwiżdżesz** *zob.* **gwizdać**.

zagwozdka *f. Gen.pl.* -**ek** *pot.* (= *problem*) problem, difficulty; (= *przeszkoda*) obstacle.

zagwoździć *pf.* -**gwożdżę -gwoździsz** (*drzwi*) nail up; **zagwoździć działo** spike a gun.

zahaczać *ipf.* **1.** (= *wieszać*) hook (*coś o coś* sth on *l.* onto sth); (= *zaczepiać*) catch (*coś o coś* sth on sth). **2.** *pot.* (= *zwracać się z pytaniem*) ask (*kogoś o coś* sb about sth); accost (*kogoś* sb). **3.** *pot.* (= *odwiedzać, wstępować*) stop off (*o kogoś / coś* at sb's place/somewhere). **4.** *pot.* (= *wynajdywać błędy*) find fault (*coś* with sth); question (*coś* sth). ~ **się** *ipf.* **1.** (= *zaczepiać się*) catch (*o coś* on sth). **2.** *pot.* (= *zatrzymywać się tymczasowo*) stay temporarily; (= *znaleźć tymczasową pracę*) find a temporary job; **zahaczyć się w szkole** land a teaching job.

zahaczyć (się) *pf. zob.* **zahaczać (się)**.

zahamować *pf. zob.* **hamować**.

zahamowanie *n. psych.* inhibition.

zaharować się *pf.,* **zaharowywać się** *ipf. pot.*

overwork, work one's hands to the bone; **zaharować się na śmierć** work o.s. to death.

zahartować *pf. zob.* **hartować**. ~ **się** *pf. zob.* **hartować się**.

zahartowany *a.* **1.** (= *uodporniony*) hardened, inured. **2.** *techn.* hardened.

zahipnotyzować *pf. zob.* **hipnotyzować**.

zaholować *pf. zob.* **holować**.

zahuczeć *pf.* -**ę -ysz** (*o ludziach*) roar (*na kogoś* at sb); (*o burzy*) rumble; (*o działach*) boom; (*o sowie*) hoot; **sala zahuczała od oklasków** there was a thunder of applause.

zahukany *a. pot.* cowed.

zahulać *pf.* party, carouse.

ZAIKS *abbr.* (= *Związek Autorów i Kompozytorów Scenicznych*) Association of Stage Writers and Composers (*in Poland*).

zaimek *mi* -**mk**- *Gen.* -**a** *gram.* pronoun; **zaimek dzierżawczy** possessive pronoun; **zaimek osobowy** personal pronoun; **zaimek zwrotny** reflexive pronoun.

zaimkowy *a. gram.* pronominal.

zaimponować *pf. zob.* **imponować**.

zaimpregnować *pf. zob.* **impregnować**.

zaimprowizować *pf. zob.* **improwizować**.

zaimprowizowany *a.* improvised, impromptu; extemporaneous, extempore.

zainaugurować *pf. zob.* **inaugurować**.

zainfekować *pf. zob.* **infekować**.

zainicjować *pf. zob.* **inicjować**.

zainkasować *pf. zob.* **inkasować**.

zainscenizować *pf. zob.* **inscenizować**.

zainspirować *pf. zob.* **inspirować**.

zainstalować *pf. zob.* **instalować**. ~ **się** *pf. zob.* **instalować się**.

zainteresować *pf.* arouse interest; **zainteresować kogoś czymś** arouse sb's interest in sth. ~ **się** *pf.* **1.** (= *okazać ciekawość*) take interest (*czymś* in sth). **2.** (= *okazać troskę*) express *l.* show concern (*kimś / czymś* about sb/sth); **zainteresować się kimś** (= *poczuć sympatię do kogoś*) feel attracted to sb.

zainteresowania *pl. Gen.* -**ń** interests; **zainteresowania artystyczne/językowe** interest in art/ languages.

zainteresowanie *n.* interest; **z zainteresowaniem** with interest; **okazywać zainteresowanie czymś** show interest in sth; **wzbudzać czyjeś zainteresowanie** arouse sb's interest.

zainteresowany *a.* interested; **być zainteresowanym czymś** be interested in sth; **być czymś żywotnie zainteresowanym** have a vested interest in sth. – *mp* interested party.

zaintonować *pf. zob.* **intonować**.

zaintrygować *pf. zob.* **intrygować**.

zainwestować *pf. zob.* **inwestować**.

Zair *mi geogr.* Zaire, Zaïre.

Zairczyk *mp,* **Zairka** *f. Gen.pl.* -**ek** Zairian, Zairean, Zairese.

zairski *a.* Zairian, Zairean, Zairese.

zaiskrzyć *pf.* **1.** = **zaiskrzyć się**. **2.** *pot.* (= *pojąć, zrozumieć*) get the hang of it. ~ **się** *pf.* **1.** (= *wydać iskrę*) spark. **2.** (= *zalśnić*) sparkle.

zaiste *adv. przest.* indeed.

zaistnieć *pf.* **1.** *lit.* (= *pojawić się*) come into being, come into existence; (*o trudnościach*) arise. **2.** *lit.* (= *stać się znanym*) become known, become popular (*jako ktoś* as sb).

zaiwaniać *ipf. pot.* **1.** (*iść*) scurry; (*biec*) dart. **2.** (*pracować*) apply o.s. (*przy czymś* to sth).

zaiwanić *pf. pot.* (= *ukraść*) snitch, pinch.

zajad *mi zob.* **zajady.**

zajadać *ipf. pot.* chow down; *Br.* tuck in; **zajadać z apetytem** chow down, eat heartily. **~ się** *ipf.* gorge o.s. (*czymś* on sth).

zajadle *adv.* (*ujadać*) fiercely.

zajadłość *f.* (= *zaciekłość*) virulence; (*walki*) fierceness.

zajadły *a.* (= *zaciekły*) virulent; (*walka, dyskusja*) fierce; (*wróg*) bitter.

zajady *pl. zwł. pat.* perlèche; *pot.* sore lip.

zajarzyć *pf. pot.* get; *Br. t.* twig; **chyba nie zajarzył** I think he didn't get it. **~ się** *pf.* light up, become bright.

zajaśnieć *pf.* **1.** (= *rozbłysnąć*) flash, shine; (*o latarni*) light up; (*o słońcu*) come out. **2.** *przen.* brighten; **jej twarz zajaśniała radością** her face brightened with joy.

zajazd *mi Loc.* **-eździe** **1.** (*hotel*) inn. **2.** *hist.* (= *wypad, najazd*) foray; (= *zajęcie majątku*) seizure.

zajazgotać *pf.* **-oczę -oczesz** *l.* **-ocę -ocesz, -ocz** (*o dzwonku*) blare; (*o psie, człowieku*) yap.

zając *ma Gen.pl.* **-ęcy** *zool.* hare (*Lepus*); **robota nie zając, nie ucieknie** don't rush it, you can do it later, take it easy.

zajączek *ma* **-czk-** **1.** (= *mały zając*) leveret; (*pieszczotliwie*) bunny; **zajączek wielkanocny** Easter bunny. **2.** *bot.* downy bolete (*Xerocomus subtomentosus*). **3.** *pot.* (= *ruchoma plamka światła*) glint; **puszczać zajączki** play at catching sunbeams in a mirror.

zająć *pf.* **zajmę zajmiesz, zajmij** *zob.* **zajmować.** **~ się** *pf.* **1.** *zob.* **zajmować się.** **2.** *lit.* (= *zacząć się palić*) catch fire. **3.** (= *zacząć coś robić*) take up; **zająć się malarstwem** take up painting.

zająkiwać się *ipf.,* **zająknąć się** *pf.* **-ij** stammer; **nie zająknąć się o czymś** not utter *l.* breathe a word about sth; **ani się nie zająknął, gdy się o tym dowiedział** he never batted an eyelid when he learned about it.

zajebisty *a. wulg.* (= *niezwykły*) out-fucking-standing, fucking great.

zajechać *pf.* **-jadę -jedziesz** *zob.* **zajeżdżać.**

zajezdnia *f. Gen.pl.* **-i** depot; **zajezdnia autobusowa** bus depot; **zajezdnia tramwajowa** streetcar depot; *Br.* tram depot.

zajeździć *pf.* **-jeżdżę -jeździsz** *zob.* **zajeżdżać** 6.

zajeżdżać *ipf.* **1.** (= *dojeżdżać do celu*) arrive, reach. **2.** (= *podjeżdżać*) pull up outside, drive up. **3.** (= *wstępować*) stop by (*do kogoś/czegoś* sb's place/sth). **4.** (= *zablokować*) bar; **zajechać komuś drogę** cut in on sb. **5.** *pot.* (= *śmierdzieć*) stink, reek. **6.** (= *zamęczać konia*) override.

zajęcia *pl. Gen.* **-ć** *szkoln., uniw.* classes; **plan zajęć** timetable; **być na zajęciach** be in class.

zajęcie *n.* **1.** (= *wykonywana czynność*) occu-

pation, pursuit; **mieć dużo zajęć** have a lot (of things) to do. **2.** (= *praca zarobkowa*) occupation, job. **3.** *prawn.* attachment; distraint, distress. **4.** *przest.* (= *zaciekawienie*) interest; **z zajęciem** with interest, attentively.

zajęczeć *pf.* **-ę -ysz** moan, groan.

zajęczy *a.* **1.** (*dotyczący zająca*) hare, hare's; (*w języku fachowym*) leporine; **zajęcza warga** *pat.* harelip. **2.** (*zrobiony ze skóry zająca*) hare.

zajęczyca *f.* doe-hare.

zajęty *a.* (*o człowieku*) busy; (*o miejscu*) taken, occupied; (*o taksówce*) on duty; (*o telefonie*) busy, engaged; **zajęte!** occupied!; **być zajętym czymś** be busy with sth, be busy doing sth; be occupied with sth; **on jest bardzo zajęty** he is very busy.

zajmować *ipf.* **1.** (= *wypełniać przestrzeń*) occupy, take up; **zajmować miejsce** take a *l.* one's seat; **zajmować miejsce komuś/sobie** reserve *l.* keep a seat for sb/o.s.; **zająć pierwsze/ostatnie miejsce** come *l.* finish *l.* be first/last; **zajmować stanowisko** (= *obejmować posadę*) take a post; **zająć stanowisko wobec kogoś/czegoś** take a stand on sb/sth; **zająć stolik** take a table, sit at a table. **2.** (= *wypełniać czas*) occupy; **zajmować komuś czas** take up sb's time; **ta praca domowa zajęła mi dwie godziny** it took me two hours to do this homework; **to mi zajmie chwilkę** it will take me a second *l.* moment. **3.** (= *brać w użytkowanie*) take, occupy; **zajmować dwa pokoje** occupy two rooms. **4.** (= *brać w posiadanie, zagrabiać*) seize, capture. **5.** (= *dać coś do roboty*) occupy; **zajmować kogoś** employ sb's time; **zajmij go czymś** give him sth to do; **zajmować dzieci zabawą** occupy children with play. **6.** *lit.* (= *zaciekawiać*) interest, absorb. **7.** *form.* (= *rekwirować*) seize, distrain. **8.** (*o chorobach*) (= *rozprzestrzeniać się*) affect, spread; **choroba zajęła mu oba płuca** the disease affected both his lungs. **~ się** *ipf.* **1.** (= *wykonywać, robić*) do (*czymś* sth); be busy doing (*czymś* sth); **czym się zajmujesz?** what do you do?, what do you do for a living?; **zajmować się czymś** *l.* **robieniem czegoś** busy o.s. with sth *l.* doing sth. **2.** (= *opiekować się*) look after (*kimś* sb); take care (*kimś* of sb); **zajmować się swoimi sprawami** go about one's (own) business; **zajmij się gośćmi** why don't you take care of our guests.

zajmująco *adv.* (= *interesująco*) interestingly; (= *wciągająco*) engrossingly, absorbingly.

zajmujący *a.* (*o człowieku, wykładzie*) interesting; (*o książce, opowieści*) engrossing, absorbing; (*o pracy*) absorbing.

zajob *mi pot.* quirk; **mieć zajoba** be a bit lacking upstairs; **mieć zajoba na punkcie czegoś** be mad about sth; **zajoba można dostać od tej roboty!** this work is driving (freaking) me nuts!

zajodynować *pf. zob.* **jodynować.**

zajrzeć *pf.* **-ę -ysz, -yj** *zob.* **zaglądać.**

zajście *n.* incident, occurrence; **zajścia uliczne** street riots.

zajść *pf.* **zajdę zajdziesz zaszedł zaszła zaszli** *zob.* **zachodzić.**

zajzajer *mi pot.* pungent drink.

zakalcowaty *a. kulin.* slack-baked; soggy, sodden.

zakalec *mi* **-lc-** *Gen.* **-a** *kulin.* **ciasto/chleb z zakalcem** slack-baked cake/bread.

zakała *f. l. mp decl. like f. Gen.pl.* **-ł** *l.* **-ów** *pot.* disgrace; **zakała rodziny** disgrace to one's family.

zakałapućkać się *pf.* be lost for words.

zakamarek *mi* **-rk-** *Gen.* **-a** corner, recess.

zakamuflować *pf. zob.* **kamuflować.** **~ się** *pf. zob.* **kamuflować się.**

zakańczać *ipf.* = **zakończyć.**

zakapior *mp pot.* thug.

zakapować *pf. zob.* **kapować.**

zakapslować *pf. zob.* **kapslować.**

zakapturzyć *pf.* hood.

zakasać *pf.* **-szę -szesz** *zob.* **zakasywać.**

zakasłać *pf.* = **zakaszleć.**

zakasować *pf. pot.* (= *przewyższyć*) go one better (*kogoś* than sb); outdo (*kogoś* sb).

zakasywać *ipf.* roll up; **zakasać rękawy** *t. przen.* roll one's sleeves up.

zakaszleć *pf.* **kaszleć** cough.

zakaszlnąć *pf.* **-ij** = **zakaszleć.**

zakatalogować *pf. zob.* **katalogować.**

zakatarzenie *n.* runny nose.

zakatarzony *a.* **-eni** having a runny nose.

zakatarzyć się *pf.* catch a cold.

zakatować *pf.* torture to death.

zakatrupić *pf. pot.* do in, bump off.

zakaz *mi* ban; **zakaz palenia** no smoking; **zakaz postoju** no waiting; **zakaz skrętu w lewo/prawo** no left/right turn; **zakaz wjazdu** no entry; **zakaz wstępu** no entry; **zakaz zatrzymywania się** no parking; **przestrzegać zakazu** observe a ban; **uchylić zakaz** lift a ban; **wydać zakaz** impose a ban, place a ban; **złamać zakaz** break a ban, breach a ban.

zakazać *pf.* **-każę -każesz** *zob.* **zakazywać.**

zakazany *a.* **1.** (= *zabroniony*) forbidden, prohibited, banned; **zakazany owoc** forbidden fruit. **2.** *pot.* (= *odrażający*) seedy.

zakazić *pf.* **-żę -zisz** *zob.* **zakażać.**

zakazywać *ipf.* forbid, prohibit; **zakazywać komuś (zrobienia) czegoś** forbid sb (to do) sth.

zakaźny *a. pat.* infectious, communicable, contagious; **choroba zakaźna** infectious disease, communicable disease, contagious disease; **oddział zakaźny** isolation ward, infectious diseases ward; **szpital zakaźny** infectious diseases hospital; (*zwł. dla trędowatych*) lazaretto, lazaret.

zakażać *pf.* infect.

zakażenie *n.* **1.** (= *infekcja*) infection. **2.** (*czynność*) infecting.

zakażony *a.* **-eni** *zwł. pat.* infected.

zakąsić *pf.* **-szę -sisz** *zob.* **zakąszać.**

zakąska *f. Gen.pl.* **-ek** (*zimna*) appetizer, hors d'oeuvre; (*ciepła*) appetizer; (**podać coś**) **na zakąskę** (serve sth) as an appetizer.

zakąszać *ipf.* chase a drink of liquor (*with food l. a snack*).

zakątek *mi* **-tk-** *Gen.* **-a** (*pokoju*) nook; (*kraju*) remote part.

zakichany *a. pot.* (= *marny*) damned.

zakiełkować *pf. zob.* **kiełkować.**

zakipieć *pf.* **-pię -pisz** **1.** (= *zagotować się*) boil, start boiling. **2.** (= *rozzłościć się*) flare up, boil with anger.

zakiszać *pf.* **-szę -sisz** *zob.* **zakiszać.** **~ się** *pf. zob.* **zakiszać się.**

zakisnąć *pf.* **-kisnę -kiśniesz, -kiśnij, -kisnął** *l.* **-kisł -kisła -kisnęli** *l.* **-kiśli** sour.

zakiszać *ipf.* (*ogórki, kapustę*) pickle; *roln.* (*paszę*) ensile; **zakisić ogóra** *wulg.* hide the salami. **~ się** *ipf.* become pickled; *roln.* become ensiled.

zaklajstrować *pf. zob.* **klajstrować.**

zaklaskać *pf.* **-klaszczę -klaszczesz** *l.* **-klaskam klaskasz, -klaszcz 1.** (= *klasnąć*) clap one's hands. **2.** (= *zacząć klaskać*) start clapping, start applauding. **3.** (= *wydać dźwięk przypominający klaskanie*) smack.

zaklasyfikować *pf. zob.* **klasyfikować.** **~ się** *pf. zob.* **klasyfikować się.**

zakląć *pf.* **-klnę -klniesz, -klnij 1.** *zob.* **zaklinać.** **2.** (= *powiedzieć przekleństwo*) swear, curse; **zakląć pod nosem** swear under one's breath.

zakleić *pf.* **-kleję -kleisz, zaklejać** *ipf.* (= *skleić*) glue *l.* stick together; (*kopertę*) seal; (*dziurę w dętce*) repair.

zaklekotać *pf.* **-oczę -oczesz** *l.* **-ocę -ocesz** *l.* **-otam -otasz 1.** (*o bocianie*) clatter. **2.** (= *zaturkotać*) rattle, start rattling; clatter, start clattering.

zaklepać *pf.* **-pię -piesz, zaklepywać** *ipf.* **1.** (= *rozpłaszczyć, klepiąc*) hammer down. **2.** *pot.* (*sprawę*) clinch, fix; (= *załatwić*) land (*coś komuś* sb sth).

zakleszczać *ipf.*, **zakleszczyć** *pf.* jam. **~ się** *ipf.*, **zakleszczyć się** *pf.* jam, get jammed.

zaklęcie *n.* **1.** (= *magiczna formułka*) charm, magic spell, incantation. **2.** *lit.* (= *prośba*) entreaty, plea.

zaklęsłość *f.* = **zaklęśnięcie.**

zaklęsnąć *pf.* **-klęśnie -klęsnął** *l.* **-kląsł -klęsła -klęśli** sink, fall in.

zaklęśnięcie *n.* **1.** (= *zapadlina*) hollow. **2.** (= *zapadnięcie się*) sinking, falling in.

zaklęty *a.* enchanted; **milczeć jak zaklęty** be struck dumb, be dumbstruck.

zaklinacz *mp* charmer; **zaklinacz węży** snake charmer.

zaklinać *ipf.* **1.** *lit.* (= *błagać*) entreat, plea. **2.** (= *rzucać czary*) put a spell on (*kogoś/coś* on sb/ sth); cast a spell (*kogoś/coś* on sb/sth); ... **i zaklął księcia w bryłę lodu**... and turned the prince into a block of ice. **~ się** *ipf.* swear; **zaklinać się na wszystkie świętości** swear to God.

zaklinować *pf.*, **zaklinowywać** *ipf.* **1.** (= *wbić klin, zabezpieczyć klinem*) wedge. **2.** (= *zakleszczyć*) jam; (= *zablokować*) block. **~ się** *pf.*, **zaklinowywać się** *ipf.* get stuck.

zakład *mi* **1.** (= *przedsiębiorstwo*) company, enterprise; (*produkcyjny*) plant, factory; (*usługowy*) shop, parlor, *Br.* parlour; **zakład fryzjerski** (*zwł. damski*) hairdresser's; (*męski*) barbershop; **zakład naprawczy** repair shop; **zakład pogrzebowy** funeral parlor; **zakład produkcyjny** manufacturing plant; **zakład przemysłowy** industrial plant. **2.** (= *placówka*) institution, establishment; **zakład badawczy/naukowy** research/scientific institute; **zakład studiów nad przekładem** department of translation studies; **zakład karny** penitentiary, correctional facility; **zakład poprawczy** reformatory, reform school. **3.** (*rodzaj umowy*) bet; **zakład o sto dolarów** hundred-dollar bet; **przegrać/wygrać zakład** lose/win a bet; **robić zakłady** bet, make bets; **trzymam zakład, że...** I bet you that...; **o co zakład?** what's the *l.* your bet?, how much you wanna bet? **4.** (= *podwinięty materiał, zakładka*) tuck.

zakładać *ipf.* **1.** (= *zapoczątkowywać, powoływać*) (*towarzystwo, spółkę*) establish; (*firmę*) set up; (*spółkę, miasto*) found; **zakładać gniazdo** build *l.* make a nest; **zakładać komuś kartotekę** *l.* **teczkę** make up *l.* open sb's file; **zakładać rodzinę** start a family. **2.** (= *nakładać*) (*ubranie, okulary*) put on; **zakładać nogę na nogę** cross one's legs. **3.** (= *umieszczać, montować*) (*gaz, elektryczność, ładunki wybuchowe*) install. **4.** (= *podwijać*) turn up; **zakładać stronę w książce** mark a page in a book. **5.** (= *przyjmować jakąś tezę*) assume, suppose; **załóżmy, że...** let's assume that... **6.** (= *planować, projektować*) anticipate, foresee, forecast; **zakładamy duży wzrost sprzedaży** we anticipate a significant increase in sales. **7.** (= *płacić*) pay (*za kogoś* for sb). **8.** (= *pokrywać powierzchnię, zapełniać*) (*np. biurko papierami*) cover, heap. **9.** *prawn.* lodge, file; **zakładać apelację** lodge an appeal; **zakładać protest** file a protest; **zakładać rewizję (od wyroku)** lodge an appeal (against a sentence). **~ się** *ipf.* **1.** (= *robić zakład*) bet; **chcesz się założyć?** (do you) want to bet?, wanna bet?; **zakładać się z kimś o coś** bet sb sth. **2.** (= *krzyżować się*) overlap.

zakładka *f. Gen.pl.* **-ek 1.** (= *pliska*) tuck. **2.** (*do książki*) bookmark.

zakładniczka *f. Gen.pl.* **-ek, zakładnik** *mp* hostage.

zakładowy *a.* factory, plant; **fundusz zakładowy** company fund; **kapitał zakładowy** *ekon.* initial capital.

zakładzik *mi* parlor, *Br.* parlour.

zakłamanie *n.* hypocrisy.

zakłamany *a.* hypocritical.

zakłopotać *pf.* **-oczę -oczesz** *l.* **-ocę -ocesz, -ocz** embarrass. **~ się** *pf.* **1.** (= *zmartwić się*) become concerned (*o kogoś/coś* about sb/sth). **2.** (= *zmieszać się*) become embarrassed.

zakłopotanie *n.* embarrassment; **z zakłopotaniem** in embarrassment; **wprawić kogoś w zakłopotanie** embarrass sb.

zakłopotany *a.* embarrassed.

zakłócać *ipf.* **1.** (= *naruszać*) disturb. **2.** (= *powodować zakłócenia*) disrupt; (*odbioru*) cause interference (*coś* to sth).

zakłócenie *n.* **1.** (= *naruszenie*) disruption, disturbance; **zakłócenie porządku publicznego** breach *l.* disturbance of the peace. **2.** *radio, telew.* interference; **zakłócenia atmosferyczne** atmospherics.

zakłócić *pf. zob.* **zakłócać.**

zakłuć *pf.*, **zakłuwać** *ipf.* **1.** (= *zabić czymś ostrym*) stab to death. **2.** (= *ukłuć*) prick. **3.** (= *zaboleć przenikliwie*) cause a sharp *l.* stabbing pain; **zakłuło mnie w boku** I felt a stabbing pain in my side. **~ się** *pf.*, **zakłuwać się** *ipf.* (= *ukłuć się*) prick.

zakneblować *pf. zob.* **kneblować.**

zakochać się *pf. zob.* **zakochiwać się.**

zakochany *a.* **1.** (= *kochający*) in love (*w kimś* with sb). **2.** (= *zafascynowany*) fascinated (*w czymś* by *l.* about *l.* with sth). – *mp* lover.

zakochiwać się *ipf.* **1.** (= *obdarzać miłością*) fall in love (*w kimś* with sb); **zakochać się po uszy** fall head over heels in love. **2.** (= *bardzo lubić*) fall in love (*w czymś* with sth); become a lover (*w czymś* of sth).

zakodować *pf. zob.* **kodować.**

zakodowany *a.* encoded, coded.

zakole *n. Gen.pl.* **-i 1.** (= *łuk rzeki, drogi*) bend. **2.** (= *półkolista łysina*) receding hairline.

zakołatać *pf.* **-aczę** *l.* **-atam -aczesz** *l.* **-atasz** *zob.* **kołatać.**

zakołysać *pf.* **-yszę -yszesz** swing, rock. **~ się** *pf.* swing, rock.

zakomenderować *pf. zob.* **komenderować.**

zakompleksiony *a.* **-eni** *pot.* having a lot of hang-ups.

zakomunikować *pf. zob.* **komunikować.**

zakon *mi zw. rel.* order; **zakon kontemplacyjny** contemplative order; **zakon rycerski** order of knights; **Trzeci Zakon** *rz.-kat.* the Third Order.

zakonnica *f. rel.* nun, religious.

zakonnik *mp rel.* monk, friar; religious.

zakonny *a. rel.* (*o ślubach, regule*) monastic; **brat zakonny** monk, friar; **siostra zakonna** nun.

zakonotować *pf. przest., żart.* remember.

zakonserwować *pf. zob.* **konserwować.** **~ się** *pf. zob.* **konserwować się.**

zakonserwowany *a.* preserved; (*w puszce*) canned.

zakonspirować *pf.* conceal. **~ się** *pf.* **1.** (= *stworzyć tajną organizację*) form a secret *l.* underground organization. **2.** (= *ukryć się*) hide.

zakontraktować *pf. zob.* **kontraktować.**

zakończenie *n.* **1.** (= *koniec*) (*powieści, opowiadania*) ending. **2.** (*pracy*) end; (*wypracowania, referatu*) conclusion; **szczęśliwe zakończenie** happy ending; **zakończenie nerwowe** *anat.* nerve ending, end-foot; **na zakończenie** in conclusion, in closing.

zakończyć *pf.* **1.** (= *skończyć*) end, finish; (= *doprowadzić do końca*) bring to an end; (= *zamknąć*) (*np. prace nad czymś*) conclude; (= *ukończyć*) (*prace, badania*) complete; **zakończyć życie** end one's life. **2.** (= *być ostatnią fazą*) conclude. **~ się** *pf.* end, finish.

zakopać *pf.* **-pię -piesz** *zob.* **zakopywać.** **~ się** *pf. zob.* **zakopywać się.**

zakopcić *pf.* **1.** (= *okopcić*) soot. **2.** *pot.* (= *nadymić*) fill with smoke. **3.** *pot.* (= *zapalić papierosa*) have a fag, have a smoke. **~ się** *pf.* **1.** (= *pokryć się sadzą*) be *l.* become sooted. **2.** (= *wypełnić się dymem*) be *l.* become filled with smoke.

zakopcować *pf. zob.* **kopcować**.

zakopiański *a.* Zakopane; **w stylu zakopiańskim** Zakopane (folk) style (*house etc.*).

zakopiańszczyzna *f.* Zakopane folk style art.

zakopywać *ipf.* **1.** (= *przykrywać ziemią*) bury; **zakopać topór wojenny** bury the hatchet. **2.** (= *grzebać*) bury, inter. ~ **się** *ipf.* **1.** (= *zagrzebywać się*) bury o.s. **2.** *pot.* (= *osiedlać się na odludziu*) bury o.s.; **zakopać się na wsi/na odludziu** bury o.s. in the country/somewhere off the beaten track.

zakorkować *pf. zob.* **korkować**. ~ **się** *pf. zob.* **korkować się**.

zakorzeniać *ipf.,* **zakorzenić** *pf.* instil, inculcate. ~ **się** *ipf.,* **zakorzenić się** *pf.* **1.** (= *zapuszczać korzenie*) take root, root. **2.** (= *wchodzić w zwyczaj*) take root.

zakorzeniony *a.* **1.** (*o roślinie*) rooted. **2.** (= *ustalony*) established, rooted; **głęboko zakorzeniony** (*o nienawiści*) deeply ingrained, deep-rooted; (*o obawach*) deeply ingrained, deep-seated.

zakos *mi* hairpin bend; **wić się zakosami** zigzag.

zakosić *pf.* **-oszę -osisz** *pot.* **1.** (= *ukraść*) pinch. **2.** (= *zebrać, dostać np. wszystkie nagrody*) bag.

zakosztować *pf. zob.* **kosztować**.

zakotłować się *pf.* seethe, whirl; **w tłumie zakotłowało się** the crowd stirred; **w kraju zakotłowało się** *przen.* there was unrest throughout the country.

zakotwiczać *ipf.,* **zakotwiczyć** *pf. żegl.* **1.** (= *mocować na kotwicy*) anchor, moor. **2.** (= *stawać na kotwicy*) lie at anchor. ~ **się** *ipf.,* **zakotwiczyć się** *pf. żegl.* **1.** (= *mocować na kotwicy*) anchor, moor. **2.** (= *stawać na kotwicy*) lie at anchor.

zakpić *pf.* **-ij** *zob.* **kpić**.

zakradać się *pf.* **1.** (= *podchodzić niepostrzeżenie*) sneak in, creep up. **2.** *lit.* (= *wkradać się*) (*o błędzie*) slip (*do czegoś* into sth); (*o niepokoju*) creep; **do serca zakradł się jej strach/niepokój** fear/doubt crept into her heart.

zakrakać *pf.* **-kraczę -kraczesz 1.** (*o krukach, wronach itp.*) caw. **2.** *pot.* (= *zakrzyczeć*) shout down.

zakrapiać *ipf.* **1.** (= *zakraplać*) put drops in. **2.** *pot.* (= *zapijać posiłek alkoholem*) wash food down with alcohol. ~ **się** *ipf. pot.* (= *upijać się*) get sloshed.

zakraplacz *mi Gen.* **-a** dropper.

zakraplać *pf.* put (eye- *l.* nose-) drops in.

zakraść się *pf.* **-kradnę kradniesz, -kradnij, -kradł** *zob.* **zakradać się**.

zakratować *pf. zob.* **kratować**.

zakrawać *pf.* be like; **to zakrawa na kpiny** *l.* żarty this must be a joke, this sounds ridiculous.

zakres *mi* **1.** (= *granica zasięgu*) (*środków, obowiązków, działania*) range; (*tematyczny*) scope; (*uprawnień*) extent; **badania z zakresu geologii** geological research, research in the field of geology; **(robić coś) we własnym zakresie** (do sth) on sb's own, (do sth) using one's own

means; **wchodzić w zakres czegoś** be within the scope of sth. **2.** *radio* (wave) band. **3.** *log.* (= *denotacja*) extension, denotation.

zakresowy *a.* range.

zakreślać *ipf.,* **zakreślić** *pf.* **1.** (= *oznaczać*) mark, highlight. **2.** *przen.* (= *wyznaczać*) determine, specify; (*granice*) mark off. **3.** (= *rysować okrąg, półkole*) draw (*usu. a circle l. semicircle*).

zakręcać *ipf.,* **zakręcić** *pf.* **1.** (= *zamykać, kręcąc*) (*kurek, gaz*) turn off; (*słoik*) twist on. **2.** (= *zawijać*) bend; (*włosy*) curl. **3.** (= *wykonywać zakręt*) turn. **4.** (*o drodze itp.*) (= *wyginać się*) take a turn, turn. **5.** (= *obracać w koło*) turn; **zakręcić korbą** turn a crank; **zakręciło mi się w nosie** I felt like sneezing. ~ **się** *pf. zob.* **kręcić się**.

zakręt *mi* bend, turn; **zakręt śmierci** sharp and dangerous bend, dogleg; **zakręt historii** *przen.* a turning point (in history); **brać zakręt** take a turn; **ściąć zakręt** cut the bend, cut into the oncoming lane.

zakrętas *mi Gen.* **-a** *pot.* flourish.

zakrętka *f. Gen.pl.* **-ek** (bottle) cap.

zakroczny *a. sport* hind, posterior.

zakrojony *a.* **zakrojony na wielką skalę** full-scale; **zakrojony na szeroką skalę** far-flung.

zakropić *pf. zob.* **zakrapiać**. ~ **się** *pf. zob.* **zakrapiać się**.

zakroplić *pf. zob.* **zakraplać**.

zakrwawić *pf.* blood, bloody. ~ **się** *pf.* **1.** (= *zaplamić się krwią*) be stainded with blood, become blooded. **2.** (= *zranić się*) *rzad.* bloody.

zakrwawiony *a.* bloody, bloodstained.

zakryć *pf.* **-kryję -kryjesz, -kryj** *zob.* **zakrywać**. ~ **się** *pf. zob.* **zakrywać się**.

zakrystia *f. Gen.* **-ii** *kośc.* sacristy, vestry.

zakrystian *mp pl.* **-anie** *l.* **-ani** *Gen.* **-an** *l.* **-anów** *kośc.* (= *opiekujący się zakrystią*) sacristan, sacrist; (= *kościelny*) sexton.

zakrywać *ipf.* **-am -asz** (*np. dłonie ręką*) cover; (= *zasłaniać*) (*np. widok*) obscure; (= *osłaniać*) (*np. od wiatru*) shelter (*od czegoś* from sth). ~ **się** *ipf.* cover o.s.; **niebo zakryło się chmurami** the sky clouded over.

zakrzątnąć się *pf.* **-ij** bustle; **zakrzątnąć się koło czegoś** *t. przen.* take care of sth; **zakrzątnąć się koło kogoś** (= *zająć się kimś*) take care of sb; (= *starać się o czyjeś względy*) (try to) win favor with sb, *Br.* (try to) win favour with sb.

zakrzep *mi pat.* thrombus, intravascular clot.

zakrzepły *a.* clotted, congealed.

zakrzepnąć *pf.* **-pnij, -pł** *l.* **-pnął -pła -pli** *zob.* **krzepnąć**.

zakrzepowy *a. pat.* thrombotic, thrombosed.

zakrztusić się *pf.* **-szę -sisz** *zob.* **krztusić się**.

zakrzyczeć *pf.* **-ę -ysz, zakrzykiwać** *ipf.* **1.** (= *krzyknąć*) shout, cry. **2.** (= *zagłuszyć*) shout down.

zakrzyknąć *pf.* **-ij** = **zakrzyczeć**.

zakrzywiać *ipf.,* **zakrzywić** *pf.* bend, crook, curve. ~ **się** *ipf.,* **zakrzywić się** *pf.* bend, curve.

zakrzywienie *n.* bend, curve.

zakrzywiony *a.* (= *zgięty*) bent; (= *powykrzywiany*) curved; (= *krzywy, skrzywiony*) crooked; **zakrzywiony nos** crooked nose.

zaksięgować *pf. zob.* **księgować**.

zaktualizować *pf. zob.* **aktualizować**. ~ **się** *pf. zob.* **aktualizować się**.

zaktywizować *pf. zob.* **aktywizować**. ~ **się** *pf. zob.* **aktywizować się**.

zakuć *pf. zob.* **zakuwać**.

zakulisowy *a.* **1.** (= *mieszczący się za kulisami*) backstage. **2.** (= *potajemny*) backstage, behind-the-scenes.

zakumulować *pf. zob.* **akumulować**. ~ **się** *pf. zob.* **akumulować się**.

zakup *mi* **1.** (= *kupowanie*) purchase; **cena zakupu** purchase price. **2.** (= *sprawunek*) purchase; **dobry/zły zakup** good/bad buy.

zakupić *pf.*, **zakupywać** *ipf.* purchase.

zakupy *pl. Gen.* **-ów** (= *robienie sprawunków*) shopping; **iść na zakupy** go shopping, go to the shops; **robić zakupy** shop, do shopping; **siatka** *l.* **torba na zakupy** shopping bag.

zakurzony *a.* dusty.

zakurzyć *pf.* **1.** (= *pokryć kurzem*) dust, cover with dust. **2.** *pot.* (= *zapalić papierosa, fajkę*) have a smoke. ~ **się** *pf.* **1.** (= *pokryć się kurzem*) dust, become dusty. **2.** (= *zakłębić się*) rise in clouds; **zakurzyło się za samochodem** the car raised a cloud of dust; **zakurzyło się z komina** smoke started spilling from the chimney.

zakusy *pl. Gen.* **-ów** designs; **mieć** *l.* **robić zakusy na coś** have designs on sth.

zakutać *pf. pot.* (= *owinąć*) wrap up, muffle up.

zakutany *a. pot.* wrapped up, muffled up.

zakuty *a.* **1.** (*np. w kajdany*) chained. **2.** (= *tępy, ograniczony*) blunt, dull; **zakuty łeb** *pot.* blockhead.

zakuwać *ipf.* **1.** (= *łączyć, mocować*) close up, clench; **zakuwać kogoś w kajdany** chain sb. **2.** *pot.* (= *uczyć się intensywnie*) cram; *Br.* swot.

zakwakać *pf.* quack.

zakwalifikować *pf. zob.* **kwalifikować**. ~ **się** *pf. zob.* **kwalifikować się**.

zakwas *mi kulin.* starter; **zakwas chlebowy** leaven.

zakwasić *pf.* **-szę -sisz**, **zakwaszać** *ipf.* **1.** (*kapustę, ogórki*) pickle; (*mleko*) (let go) sour. **2.** (= *czynić kwaśnym*) (*glebę*) acidify; (*zupę*) sour. ~ **się** *pf.*, **zakwaszać się** *ipf.* **1.** (*o kapuście, ogórkach*) be pickled; (*o mleku*) turn sour. **2.** (*o glebie*) acidify.

zakwaszenie *n. roln.* acidification.

zakwaterować *pf. zob.* **zakwaterowywać**.

zakwaterować się *pf.* (= *zająć kwaterę*) take lodgings, take quarters.

zakwaterowanie *n.* accommodation, lodging.

zakwaterowywać *ipf.* accommodate, quarter.

zakwefiony *a.* wearing a yashmak *l.* yashmac.

zakwestionować *pf. zob.* **kwestionować**.

zakwiczeć *pf.* **1.** (*o świni*) squeak. **2.** (*np. z bólu*) squeal.

zakwilić *pf.* **1.** (*o ptakach*) (= *zaśpiewać*) chirp, chirrup. **2.** (= *zapłakać*) (*o dziecku*) wail, whimper; (*o psie*) yelp, whimper.

zakwitać *ipf.*, **zakwitnąć** *pf.* **-tnij**, **-tł** *l.* **-tnął -tła -tli 1.** (= *pokrywać się kwiatami*) bloom, blos-

som. **2.** (= *pokrywać się planktonem*) bloom. **3.** (= *pokrywać się pleśnią*) mold over, mould over.

zalać *pf.* **-leję -lejesz -lali** *l.* **-leli** *zob.* **zalewać**. ~ **się** *pf. zob.* **zalewać się**.

zalakować *pf. zob.* **lakować**.

zalany *a. pot.* (= *pijany*) drunk, sloshed.

zalatany *a. pot.* (= *zagoniony*) on the go, run off one's feet; (= *przepracowany*) overworked.

zalatywać *ipf.* **1.** (*o zapachu*) (= *docierać*) waft. **2.** (= *śmierdzieć*) stink, reek (*czymś* of sth).

zaląc się *pf.* **-lęgnie -lągł -lęgła** *zob.* **zalęgnąć się**.

zalążek *mi* **-żk-** *Gen.* **-a 1.** *bot.* ovule. **2.** *lit.* (= *początek*) germ.

zalążnia *f. Gen.pl.* **-i** *bot.* ovary.

zalec *pf.* **-legnę -legniesz, -legnij, -legł = zalegnąć**.

zalecać *ipf. lit.* (= *doradzać*) recommend (*coś komuś* sth to sb); advise (*coś komuś* sb to do sth); **zaleca się ostrożność** you are *l.* one is advised to be careful. ~ **się** *ipf.* woo, court (*do kogoś* sb).

zalecenie *n.* **1.** (*rada*) recommendation, advice. **2.** (*coś zaleconego*) recommendation; **godny zalecenia** highly recommended.

zalecić *pf. zob.* **zalecać**.

zalecieć *pf.* **-cę -cisz 1.** *zob.* **zalatywać**. **2.** (= *dolecieć*) reach destination (*by flying*). **3.** *pot.* (= *biegnąc, dotrzeć*) reach destination (*by running*).

zaleczony *a.* partly healed.

zaleczyć *pf.* (= *wyleczyć*) cure (*temporarily or superficially*).

zaledwie *particle* only; merely, scarcely; **zaledwie wczoraj** only yesterday; **to zaledwie początek** it is a mere beginning, it's just a beginning; **ona ma zaledwie czternaście lat** she is only fourteen, she is scarcely fourteen; **spałem zaledwie parę godzin** I only slept for a couple of hours. — *conj.* no sooner, as soon as; **zaledwie przyjechał, a już...** no sooner had he arrived than...; *por.* **ledwie**.

zalegać *ipf.* **1.** (*o kurzu, śniegu*) linger; **zalegać na rynku** be a drug on the market; **tłumy zalegały ulice** crowds were filling the streets; **zaległa cisza** silence settled. **2.** (= *spóźniać się*) be late (*z czymś* with sth); **zalegać z pracą** be behind with one's work; **zalegać z czynszem** be in arrears with one's rent. **3.** *geol.* occur.

zalegalizować *pf. zob.* **legalizować**.

zaległość *f.* (*w nauce, w pracy*) backlog; (*w płatnościach*) arrears; **zaległość podatkowa** outstanding tax; **mieć zaległości w czymś** be behind with sth; **miec zaległości w płaceniu czynszu** be in arrears with one's rent; **odrabiać zaległości w pracy** catch up with one's work.

zaległy *a.* outstanding, overdue; **spłacić zaległe płatności** settle oustanding payments.

zalegnąć *pf.* **-legnę -legniesz, -legnij, -legł** *zob.* **zalegać 1.**

zalepiać *ipf.*, **zalepić** *pf.* (*np. dziurę w ścianie*) fill; (*kopertę*) seal.

zalesiać *ipf.*, **zalesić** *pf.* afforest, wood.

zalesienie *n.* forestation, afforestation.

zaleszczotki *pl. zool.* book scorpions (*Pseudo-scorpiones*).

zaleta *f.* (*duchowa, moralna*) virtue; (= *pozytyw*) advantage; **zalety mieszkania na wsi/w mieście** the advanteges of living in the country/in the city; **on ma swoje zalety** he has some good points.

zalew *mi* **1.** (= *zalewanie*) flooding, flood. **2.** (= *sztuczne jezioro*) reservoir, artificial lake. **3.** (*zatoka*) lagoon. **4.** (= *napływ*) flood (*kogoś/czegoś* of sb/sth).

zalewa *f.* (*octowa*) marinade; (*do ogórków*) pickle; (*słona*) brine.

zalewać *ipf.* **1.** (= *moczyć*) drench. **2.** (= *zatapiać*) (*o cieczy*) flood; **zalać coś wodą/mlekiem** pour water/milk over sth; **zalać palę** *pot.* booze it up; **zalewać robaka** *pot.* drown one's sorrow in drink. **3.** (= *plamić*) (*o płynie*) stain; **zalać obrus winem** spill wine on the tablecloth; **krew mnie zalewa!** *pot.* my blood is up!; **niech cię nagła krew zaleje!** to hell with you! **4.** (*otwór*) fill; (*szparę*) stop up (*czymś* with sth); **zalać komuś sadła za skórę** make things hot *l.* lively for sb. **5.** *zw. ipf. pot.* (= *blagować*) tell fibs. ~ **się** *ipf.* **1.** (= *oblewać się*) spill (*czymś* sth over o.s.); **zalewać się łzami** dissolve in tears. **2.** *pot.* (= *upijać się*) get stoned.

zalewajka *f. Gen.pl.* **-ek** *pot., kulin.* potato soup.

zalewowy *a.* **1.** (*dotyczący zalewania*) flood; **teren zalewowy** floodland. **2.** (*dotyczący zalewu morskiego*) lagoon.

zaleźć *pf.* **-lezę -leziesz -lazł -leźli** **1.** *pot.* (= *docierać*) shuffle along, shamble along. **2.** *pot.* (= *wbijać się pod coś*) stick (*gdzieś* under sth); **zaleźć komuś za skórę** *przen.* get under sb's skin.

zależeć *ipf.* **-ę -ysz** depend (*od kogoś/czegoś* on sb/sth); **to zależy** it depends; **bardzo mi na tym zależy** it is very important for me; **to zależy od ciebie** it's up to you, it depends on you; **zależy mi na tobie** I care about you; **zależy mi na pośpiechu** *l.* **czasie** (= *muszę to szybko zrobić*) I am in a hurry, I am pressed for time; (= *chciałbym, aby to szybko zrobiono*) this is rather urgent; **nie zależy mi!** I don't care!

zależnie *adv.* depending (*od kogoś/czegoś* on sb/sth).

zależność *f.* **1.** (= *relacja*) interrelation (*czegoś od czegoś* between sth and sth); **w zależności od czegoś** depending on sth. **2.** (= *niesamodzielność*) dependence (*od kogoś* on sb).

zależny *a.* dependent (*od kogoś/czegoś* on sb/sth); **mowa zależna** *gram.* reported speech; **przypadek zależny** *jęz.* oblique case; **wszystko to jest zależne od...** it all depends on...

zalęgać się *ipf.*, **zalęgnąć się** *pf.* **-lągł -lęgła** (*o zwierzętach, robactwie*) (= *rozmnożyć się*) breed; (= *zagnieździć się*) infest (*gdzieś* sth); **w szafie zalęgły się mole** the wardrobe was infested by moths; **zalęgła się w nim myśl, by...** it entered his mind to...

zalękniony *a.* **-eni** frightened, apprehensive, anxious.

zalicytować *pf. zob.* **licytować**.

zaliczać *ipf.* **1.** (= *klasyfikować*) class, classify

(*kogoś/coś do czegoś* sb/sth as sth). **2.** (= *uznawać, wliczać*) recognize (*coś jako coś* sth as sth); (*próbę, skok*) *sport* declare valid. **3.** *uniw.* (*egzamin*) pass; (*semestr, rok*) complete; (*zajęcia*) get a credit for; **zaliczać komuś coś** give sb a credit for sth. **4.** *pot.* (= *odfajkowywać, odbyć*) do. **5.** *wulg.* (= *odbywać stosunek płciowy*) score (*kogoś* sb). ~ **się** *ipf.* be numbered (*do* among) rank.

zaliczenie *n.* **1.** *uniw.* credit. **2.** (= *uznanie*) recognition; **za zaliczeniem pocztowym** COD (*US = collect on delivery*) (*Br. = cash on delivery*).

zaliczeniowy *a. uniw.* credit; **kolokwium zaliczeniowe** final test, final.

zaliczka *f. Gen.pl.* **-ek** advance, advance payment; **dawać komuś zaliczkę** advance money to sb.

zaliczkowo *adv.* in advance.

zaliczkowy *a.* advance; **wpłata zaliczkowa** advance payment.

zaliczyć *pf. zob.* **zaliczać**. ~ **się** *pf. zob.* **zaliczać się**.

zalotnie *adv.* coquettishly, flirtatiously.

zalotnik *mp przest.* suitor.

zalotność *f.* coquetry, coquettishness; flirtatiousness.

zalotny *a.* coquettish, flirtatious.

zaloty *pl. Gen.* **-ów** *lit.* courtship, advances; (*u zwierząt*) mating ritual.

zalśnić *pf.* (*o oczach, tafli jeziora*) glisten; (= *zaświecić, zabłysnąć*) glitter; (= *zamigotać*) sparkle.

zaludniać *ipf.*, **zaludnić** *pf.* **-ij** populate, people. ~ **się** *ipf.*, **zaludnić się** *pf.* (= *zostać zasiedlonym*) become populated; (= *stać się pełnym ludzi*) (*np. o plażach, kurortach w czasie wakacji*) come alive with people.

zaludnienie *n.* population; **gęstość zaludnienia** population density.

zaludniony *a.* populated, peopled; **gęsto/słabo zaludniony** densely/sparsely populated.

zalutować *pf.* solder up.

zał. *abbr.* **1.** (= *załącznik*) encl. (= *enclosure*). **2.** (= *założony*) est., estab. (= *established*).

załadować *pf.*, **załadowywać** *ipf.* **1.** (= *umieścić ładunek*) load; (*do pociągu t.*) entrain; (*do samolotu t.*) emplane; **załadować komuś** deal sb a blow. **2.** (= *nabić broń*) load, charge. ~ **się** *pf.*, **załadowywać się** *ipf. pot.* (*do pociągu, samochodu, samolotu*) board (*do czegoś* sth); (*na statek*) embark (*do czegoś* sth).

załadunek *mi* **-nk-** loading; (*na statek*) embarkation, embarkment.

załadunkowy *a.* loading; embarkation, embarkment.

załagodzić *pf.* **-godzę -godzisz, -godź** *l.* **-gódź** *zob.* **łagodzić**.

załamać *pf.* **-mię -miesz** *zob.* **załamywać**. ~ **się** *pf. zob.* **załamywać się**.

załamanie *n.* **1.** (= *zagięcie*) bend; (*materiału*) fold. **2.** (= *depresja*) breakdown, crack-up; **załamanie nerwowe** nervous breakdown. **3.** *fiz.* refraction. **4.** *ekon.* slump. ~ **się** *n.* (*dachu, mostu, lodu*) collapse.

załamek *mi* -mk- *Gen.* -a (= *fałda*) fold; (= *zmarszczka*) crease.

załamywać *ipf.* **1.** (= *zaginać*) bend; (= *tkaninę*) fold; **załamywać ręce** wring one's hands. **2.** (*np. most*) cause to collapse; (*np. dach*) cave in. **3.** (= *wpędzać w depresję*) depress. **4.** *fiz.* refract. **~ się** *ipf.* **1.** (= *zaginać się*) bend; (*o głosie*) break; (*o tkaninie*) fold; (= *marszczyć się*) crease; **głos załamał mu się ze wzruszenia** his voice broke with emotion; **kolana** *l.* **nogi się pod nim załamały** *l.* **ugięły** his legs sank under him. **2.** (*np. o moście, lodzie*) collapse; (*np. o dachu*) cave in. **3.** (*o człowieku*) break down, crack up. **4.** (= *ustępować*) (*np. o oporze, ataku*) collapse, break down. **5.** *fiz.* be refracted.

załapać *pf.* -pię -piesz, **załapywać** *ipf.* **1.** *pot.* (= *chwycić*) catch (*coś czymś* sth with sth). **2.** *pot.* (= *dostać*) land (*coś* sth); **załapać dobrą pracę/rolę w filmie** land a good job/role in a film. **3.** *pot.* (= *zrozumieć*) latch on (*coś* to sth). **4.** (= *zarabiać sprute oczka*) mend a ladder, mend a run. **~ się** *pf.*, **załapywać się** *ipf.* *pot.* (= *dostać*) luck (*na coś* into sth); land o.s. (*na coś* sth); **załapać się na fajną imprezę** luck into a cool party; **załapać się do dobrej pracy** land o.s. a good job.

załaskotać *pf.* -oczę -oczesz *l.* -ocę -ocesz, -ocz tickle; **coś mnie załaskotało w nogę/policzek** I felt a tickle on my leg/cheek.

załatać *pf.* patch up.

załatwiać *ipf.*, **załatwić** *pf.* **1.** *pot.* (= *doprowadzać do skutku*) take care (*coś* of sth); **załatwiać coś od ręki** make short work of sth, rush sth through; **załatwić coś komuś** fix sb up with sth; **załatwić potrzebę** relieve o.s.; **ja to załatwię** let me handle that; **załatwcie to między sobą** settle this among yourselves. **2.** *pot.* (= *obsługiwać*) serve; **załatwiać coś odmownie** (*np. podanie o coś*) turn sth down. **3.** *zw. pf. pot.* (= *rozprawiać się*) fix (*kogoś* sb). **4.** *tylko pf.* (= *zabijać*) take care (*kogoś* sb); fix (*kogoś* sb). **~ się** *ipf.*, **załatwić się** *pf.* *pot.* **1.** (= *wypróżniać się*) relieve o.s. **2.** *tylko pf.* (= *przeziębić się*) catch a cold.

załatwienie *n.* settlement; **mieć coś do załatwienia** have a business to attend to; **to jest do załatwienia** (= *to można załatwić*) it can be done; (= *to trzeba załatwić*) it is to be taken care of.

załatwiony *a.* (= *doprowadzony do skutku*) taken care of; **załatwione!** (= *zrobiłem to*) done!; (= *na pewno to zrobię*) consider it done!; **jestem załatwiony** *pot.* I'm dead now!

załazić *ipf.* -łażę -łazisz *zob.* **zaleźć.**

załączać *ipf.* (*w liście*) enclose (*coś do czegoś* sth with sth); (*w poczcie elektronicznej*) attach (*coś do czegoś* sth to sth); **załączam serdeczne pozdrowienia** with kind regards.

załączenie *n.* enclosure; attachment; **w załączeniu...** (*w liście*) please find enclosed...; (*w poczcie elektronicznej*) please find attached...

załącznik *mi* *Gen.* -a (*do listu*) enclosure; (*do umowy, książki*) addendum, appendix; (*do poczty elektronicznej*) attachment (*do czegoś* to sth).

załączyć *pf. zob.* **załączać.**

załganie *n.* hypocrisy.

załgany *a.* hypocritical.

załkać *pf.* sob.

załoga *f. Gen.pl.* -óg **1.** (*statku, samolotu, pociągu*) crew. **2.** (*zakładu, fabryki*) staff. **3.** (*twierdzy*) garrison; (*czołgu, samolotu bojowego*) crew. **4.** *przest., pot.* (= *towarzystwo, grupa*) crew.

załogant *mp* *żegl.* crew member.

załogowy *a.* (*pomieszczenia, pokoje*) crew; **lot załogowy** manned flight.

załom *mi* **1.** (= *zakręt*) bend; (= *wygięcie*) twist. **2.** (= *wnęka*) recess. **3.** (= *róg*) corner.

załomek *mi* -mk- *Gen.* -a *l.* -u = **załom.**

załomotać *pf.* -oczę -oczesz *l.* -ocę -ocesz, -ocz **1.** (*o sercu*) thud; **serce mu załomotało** (*ze strachu, zdenerwowania*) his heart thudded. **2.** (= *zastukać*) knock; **załomotać do drzwi** bang on the door; **ktoś załomotał do drzwi** there was a bang on the door.

załopotać *pf.* -oczę -oczesz *l.* -ocę -ocesz, -ocz (*skrzydłami*) flap; (*np. o fladze na wietrze*) flutter; **załopotać skrzydłami** (*o ptaku*) flap its wings.

założenia *pl. Gen.* -ń (= *wytyczne*) guidelines, principles.

założenie *n.* **1.** (= *przesłanka*) assumption, premise; **w założeniu** originally; **wychodzić z założenia, że...** assume that... **2.** *bud.* (= *układ, projekt*) layout. **3.** (*miasta*) foundation; (*firmy*) establishment.

założyciel *mp*, **założycielka** *f. Gen.pl.* -ek founder.

założycielski *a.* founder's; **komitet założycielski** founding committee.

założyć *pf. zob.* **zakładać. ~ się** *pf. zob.* **zakładać się.**

załzawiony *a.* **1.** (= *przesiąknięty łzami*) watery. **2.** (*o oczach*) tearful, teary.

zamach *mi* **1.** (= *atak*) attack (*na kogoś/coś* on sb/sth); (= *zamordowanie*) assassination (*kogoś* of sb); (= *próba zamordowania*) assassination attempt (*na kogoś* on sb); **zamach bombowy** bomb attack; **zamach stanu** coup d'état, coup; **zamach terrorystyczny** terrorist attack; **dokonać zamachu na kogoś** *l.* **czyjeś życie** (*nieudanego*) make an attempt on sb *l.* on sb's life, try to assassinate sb; (*udanego*) assassinate sb; **knuć zamach** plot an assassination attempt; **paść ofiarą zamachu** fall victim to an assassination; **udaremnić zamach** foil *l.* prevent an assassination attempt; **uniknąć zamachu** escape an assassination attempt. **2.** (= *zamachnięcie się*) sweep, swing; **za jednym zamachem** *pot.* at one go.

zamachać *pf.* (*ręką, chusteczką*) wave; (*ogonem*) wag; **zamachać komuś na pożegnanie** wave goodbye to sb, wave sb goodbye; **pies zamachał ogonem** the dog wagged its tail.

zamachnąć się *pf.* -ij (= *machnąć ręką*) swing one's arm; (= *wziąć rozmach*) take a swing (*na kogoś/coś* at sb/sth).

zamachowiec *mp* -wc- *pl.* -y assassin; (*podkładający l. rzucający bomby*) bomber.

zamachowy *a.* **1.** (*związany z zamachem*) assassination; **akcja zamachowa** assassination attempt. **2.** *sport* swing. **3. koło zamachowe** *techn.* flywheel.

zamaczać *ipf.* (*przypadkowo*) get wet, wet; (*celowo*) soak (*coś w czymś* sth in sth); **zamoczyłem sobie koszulę** I got my shirt wet. **~ się** *ipf.* get wet.

zamajaczyć *pf.* **1.** (= *zarysować się mgliście*) loom; **zamajaczyć na horyzoncie** loom on the horizon. **2.** (*np. w gorączce*) rave.

zamakać *ipf.* soak, get wet.

zamalować *pf.*, **zamalowywać** *ipf.* **1.** (= *pokryć farbą*) paint (*czymś* with sth). **2.** (= *pokryć malowidłami*) cover with paintings. **3.** *pot.* (= *uderzyć*) plug (*komuś* sb).

zamanifestować *pf. zob.* **manifestować**.

zamarkować *pf. zob.* **markować**.

zamartwiać się *ipf.* worry (*czymś* about sth); **zamartwiać się na śmierć** worry o.s. to death.

zamartwica *f. pat.* asphyxia.

zamartwić się *pf. zob.* **zamartwiać się**.

zamarudzić *pf. pot.* dally, loiter.

zamarynować *pf. zob.* **marynować**.

zamarzać *ipf.*, **zamarznąć** *pf.* -znij, -zł *l.* -znął -zła -zli **1.** (= *zmieniać się w lód*) freeze. **2.** (= *ginąć od mrozu*) freeze to death.

zamarzać *ipf.*, **zamorzyć** *pf.* **zamorzyć kogoś głodem** starve sb to death.

zamarznięty *a.* **1.** (= *pokryty lodem*) frozen. **2.** (= *zmarły wskutek mrozu*) frozen to death.

zamarzyć *pf.* dream (*o czymś* of sth). **~ się** *pf.* **1.** (= *oddać się marzeniom*) abandon o.s. to one's dreams. **2.** (= *przyjść do głowy*) enter sb's head; **zamarzyła jej się podróż dookoła świata** she fantasized about a travel around the world.

zamaskować *pf. zob.* **maskować**. **~ się** *pf. zob.* **maskować się**.

zamaskowany *a.* (*drzwi, wejście*) concealed; (*twarz, bandyta*) masked.

zamaszystość *f.* **1.** (= *rozmach*) przest. vigor, *Br.* vigour. **2.** (= *zawadiackość*) bluster, swagger.

zamaszysty *a.* **1.** (= *energiczny*) (*ruch, gest*) sweeping; (*krok*) vigorous. **2.** (*pismo, podpis*) sweeping. **3.** (= *zawadiacki*) blustering, swaggering.

zamaszyście *adv.* **1.** (*iść*) vigorously. **2.** (*pisać, podpisywać się*) in a sweeping hand.

zamawiać *ipf.* **1.** (= *rezerwować*) (*bilety, stolik*) book, reserve; (*meble u stolarza, ubranie u krawca*) order; (*rozmowę telefoniczną*) place; **zamawiać wizytę u kogoś** make an appointment with sb. **2.** (*obiad, pizzę do domu, książkę z wydawnictwa*) order. **3.** (= *najmować*) hire. **4.** (= *wykonywać praktyki magiczne*) charm, bewitch; **zamawiać chorobę** perform a healing spell. **~ się** *ipf.* announce one's visit.

zamazać *pf.* -mażę -mażesz *zob.* **zamazywać**. **~ się** *pf. zob.* **zamazywać się**.

zamazany *a.* **1.** (= *niewyraźny*) blurred, bleary. **2.** (= *umazany*) smeared, dirtied. **3.** (= *załzawiony*) tearful.

zamazywać *ipf.* **1.** (= *zamalowywać, pokrywać*) (*np. farbą*) smear, daub (*czymś* with sth). **2.** (= *wymazać*) black out, blot out (*czymś* with

sth). **3.** *lit.* (= *czynić niewyraźnym*) blur; **zamazywać różnice** blur distinctions. **~ się** *ipf.* **1.** (= *być zamazanym*) become effaced, become obliterated. **2.** (= *brudzić się*) get smeared, get dirty. **3.** *lit.* (= *stawać się niewyraźnym*) blur, become blurred.

zamącić *pf. zob.* **mącić**. **~ się** *pf. zob.* **mącić się**.

zamążpójście *n.* marriage.

Zambia *f. Gen.* **-ii** *geogr.* Zambia.

Zambijczyk *mp*, **Zambijka** *f.* Zambian.

zambijski *a.* Zambian.

zamczysko *n.* (large and stately) castle.

zameczek *mi* -czk- *Gen.* **-a** *l.* **-u** (small) castle.

zamek *mi* -mk- *Gen.* **-a 1.** (*mechanizm do zamykania*) lock; **zamek błyskawiczny** zipper; *Br.* zip, zip-fastener. **2.** *wojsk.* (*część broni*) lock. **3.** *Gen.* **-u** (*budowla warowna*) castle; **budować zamki na lodzie** *l.* **piasku** build castles in the air.

zameldować *pf.* register (*sb as a tenant*). **~ się** *pf.* register (*as a tenant*).

zameldowany *a.* registered.

zamelinować *pf. pot.* hide. **~ się** *pf. pot.* (= *ukryć się*) go into hiding; (= *znaleźć sobie kryjówkę*) (*zwł. o przestępcy*) find o.s. a hideout.

zamerdać *pf.* wag; **pies zamerdał ogonem** the dog wagged its tail.

zamerykanizować *pf. zob.* **amerykanizować**. **~ się** *pf. zob.* **amerykanizować się**.

zamęczać *ipf.*, **zamęczyć** *pf.* **1.** (= *torturować*) torture. **2.** *tylko pf.* (= *torturując, pozbawić życia*) torture to death. **3.** (= *dręczyć*) pester, plague (*czymś* with sth). **~ się** *ipf.*, **zamęczyć się** *pf.* (*fizycznie*) slave away, wear o.s. out; (*psychicznie*) torment o.s.

zamęt *mi* confusion; **mieć zamęt w głowie** be confused, be muddleheaded; **siać zamęt** spread confusion.

zamętnica *f. bot.* horned pondweed (*Zannichellia*).

zamężna *a.* married. **–** *f. Gen.* **-ej** married woman.

zamglenie *n.* mist, haze.

zamglić *pf.* mist, haze over. **~ się** *pf.* mist, haze over.

zamglony *a.* misty, hazy; (*o oczach*) bleary.

zamgławiać *ipf. roln.* spray (*an insecticide on plants*).

zamian *mi* **w zamian za coś** in exchange for sth, in return for sth.

zamiana *f.* **1.** (= *wymiana*) exchange. **2.** (= *przekształcenie*) conversion (*czegoś w coś* of sth into sth).

zamiar *mi* intention; **mieć zamiar coś zrobić** intend to do sth; **mieć dobre/złe zamiary** have good/evil *l.* bad intentions; **nosić się z zamiarem zrobienia czegoś** have the intention of doing sth; **przejrzeć czyjeś zamiary** see through sb's game; **kupiłem ten dom z zamiarem sprzedania go dla zysku** I bought this house with a view to selling it at a profit; **nie mam najmniejszego zamiaru z nim rozmawiać** I don't have the slightest intention of talking to him; **miałem właśnie zamiar... ** I was about to...

zamiast *prep.* **+** *Gen.* instead of; **pij mleko za-**

miast kawy drink milk instead of coffee; **zamiast pójść z nami...** instead of joining us..., rather than join us... – *conj.* instead of; **pomógłbyś, zamiast się śmiać** you could help instead of laughing.

zamiatacz *mp*, **zamiataczka** *f.* sweeper; **zamiatacz ulic** streetsweeper; *Br. t.* roadsweeper.

zamiatać *ipf.* **1.** (*śmieci*) sweep up; (*miotłą t.*) broom. **2.** (*np. o wietrze*) sweep; **zamiatała suknią po podłodze** her dress was trailing behind her.

zamiatarka *f. Gen.pl.* **-ek** sweeper.

zamieć *f. pl.* **-e** snowstorm, blizzard.

zamiejscowy *a.* **1.** (*np. pracownik*) (= *dojeżdżający*) commuting; (= *niemiejscowy*) out-of-town. **2.** (*rozmowa*) long-distance; *Br. t.* trunk. – *mp* non-local, stranger.

zamieniać *ipf.*, **zamienić** *pf.* **1.** (= *wymieniać*) exchange (*coś na coś* sth for sth); **zamienić parę słów z kimś** have a word or two with sb; **zamienił stryjek siekierkę na kijek** sb made a losing bargain. **2.** (= *przekształcać*) turn (*coś w coś* into to sth) (*kogoś w coś* sb into sth); **zamieniać słowa w czyn** turn words into action. **~ się** *ipf.*, **zamienić się** *pf.* **1.** (= *wymieniać się*) swap (*czymś l. na coś* sth). **2.** (= *przeobrażać się*) turn (*w kogoś/coś* into sb/sth); **zamieniać się w słuch** be all ears; **zamieniać się w słup soli** be dumbfounded; **zamienić się z kimś miejscami** *l.* **na miejsca** change places with sb.

zamiennia *f. Gen.pl.* **-i** *teor.lit.* (= *metonimia*) metonymy.

zamiennie *adv.* interchangeably.

zamiennik *mi Gen.* **-a** substitute.

zamienny *a.* exchangeable, interchangeable; **części zamienne** spare parts, replacement parts; **handel zamienny** barter trade, barter; **lokal zamienny** temporary accommodation.

zamierać *ipf.* **1.** (= *przestawać żyć*) decay, die; (*o roślinie*) wither; **serce we mnie zamarło** *przen.* my heart sank. **2.** (*o dźwiękach, głosie*) die away, fade away; **głos zamarł mi w gardle** the words stuck in my throat. **3.** (= *nieruchomieć*) (*o człowieku*) freeze; (*o ruchu ulicznym*) die down; (*o życiu gospodarczym*) come to a standstill; **zamierać z przerażenia** be petrified.

zamierzać *ipf.* intend (*coś zrobić* to do sth). **~ się** *ipf.* aim a blow (*na kogoś/coś* at sb/sth).

zamierzchły *a. lit.* immemorial, distant; **w zamierzchłych czasach** in the dim and distant past.

zamierzenie *n.* intention (*zrobienia czegoś* of doing sth).

zamierzony *a.* (*skutek, efekt*) intended; (= *celowy*) deliberate; (= *zaplanowany*) planned.

zamierzyć *pf. zob.* **zamierzać. ~ się** *pf. zob.* **zamierzyć się.**

zamieszać *pf. zob.* **mieszać.**

zamieszanie *n.* **1.** (= *chaos*) confusion, chaos; **robić zamieszanie** cause confusion, create confusion; **wprowadzać zamieszanie** spread confusion. **2.** (= *wzburzenie*) commotion.

zamieszany *a.* implicated, mixed up (*w coś* in sth).

zamieszczać *ipf.* (*ogłoszenie w gazecie*) place; (*artykuł, wzmiankę w gazecie*) run.

zamieszkać *pf.* (= *osiedlić się*) take up residence.

zamieszkały *a.* **1.** (= *mieszkający*) residing, resident; **zamieszkały przy...** residing at...; *zwł. prawn. l. form.* domiciled at...; **zamieszkały w...** resident in...; *zwł. prawn. l. form.* domiciled in... **2.** (= *zamieszkany*) inhabited.

zamieszkanie *n.* **miejsce zamieszkania** place of residence.

zamieszki *pl. Gen.* **-szek** riots; **tłumić zamieszki** put down riots, suppress riots; **wywoływać zamieszki** (*o jakimś wydarzeniu*) spark riots.

zamieszkiwać *ipf.* **1.** (*o zwierzętach*) inhabit. **2.** (*o ludziach*) (= *mieszkać na stałe w jakiejś miejscowości*) reside; (= *zajmować jakiś teren*) (*o plemionach, ludach*) inhabit.

zamieścić *pf.* **-mieszczę -mieścisz** *zob.* **zamieszczać.**

zamieść *pf.* **-miotę -mieciesz -miótł -miotła -mietli** *zob.* **zamiatać.**

zamigotać *pf.* **-oczę -oczesz** *l.* **-ocę -ocesz, -ocz** (*np. o płomieniu świecy*) flicker; (*np. o tafli jeziora*) glitter; (*np. o gwiazdach*) twinkle; (*np. o oczach*) sparkle.

zamilczeć *pf.* **-ę -ysz** **1.** (= *zataić*) keep secret, pass over in silence. **2.** = **zamilknąć.**

zamilknąć *pf.* **-knij, -kł** *l.* **-knął -kła -kli** *zob.* **milknąć.**

zamiłowanie *n.* passion (*do czegoś* for sth); fondness (*do czegoś* of sth); **mieć zamiłowanie do (robienia) czegoś** have a passion for (doing) sth, be fond of (doing) sth; **robić coś z zamiłowaniem** put one's heart into (doing) sth; **ogrodnik/wędkarz z zamiłowania** keen gardener/angler.

zamiłowany *a.* fond (*w czymś* of sth); keen (*w czymś* on sth).

zaminować *pf. zob.* **minować.**

zamknąć *pf.* **-ij** *zob.* **zamykać. ~ się** *pf. zob.* **zamykać się.**

zamknięcie *n.* **1.** (= *zamek*) lock, latch, fastening, fastener, shut, clasp, hasp, snap, catch, bolt. **2.** (= *miejsce zamknięte*) closing, close, closure, restraint, seclusion; **trzymać kogoś w zamknięciu** restrain sb, coop sb up.

zamknięty *a.* **1.** (= *ograniczony w przestrzeni*) close, closed, boxed, confined, no-go area, shut; (*o dziedzińcu*) confined yard. **2.** (= *nieudostępniony, elitarny*) closed, private, exclusive; (*o pokazie*) private show, exclusive show; (*o obradach*) closed session; **konkurs zamknięty** restricted competition; **przy drzwiach zamkniętych** behind closed doors, in closed session, in camera. **3.** (= *skryty*) pent-up, reserved; **zamknięty w sobie** indrawn, introvert, self-contained, withdrawn, remote, inward-looking.

zamkowy *a.* **1.** (*dotyczący zamknięcia*) of a lock, of a fastener. **2.** (*dotyczący budowli*) of a castle.

zamocować *pf.*, **zamocowywać** *ipf.* fasten, fix, secure.

zamoczyć *pf. zob.* **zamaczać. ~ się** *pf. zob.* **zamaczać się.**

zamoknąć *pf.* **-ij** *zob.* **zamakać**.
zamontować *pf.*, **zamontowywać** *ipf.* set up, fit up, install.
zamordować *pf. zob.* **mordować**.
zamordowana *f. Gen.* **-ej**, **zamordowany** *mp* murdered *l.* killed person.
zamordysta *mp pot.* despot, tyrant, dictator, autocrat, oppressor, bully.
zamordyzm *mi pot.* despotism, bullying, tyranny.
zamorski *a.* transmarine, ultramarine, overseas, from beyond the sea.
zamortyzować *pf. zob.* **amortyzować**. ~ **się** *pf. zob.* **amortyzować się**.
zamorzyć *pf. zob.* **morzyć**. ~ **się** *pf. zob.* **morzyć się**.
zamotać *pf.* (= *owinąć*) wrap up, muffle up.
zamotać się *pf.* **1.** (= *owinąć się*) wrap oneself up, muffle oneself up. **2.** *przen.* (= *zaplątać się*) get tangled, get entangled (*w coś* in *l.* with sth).
zamożnie *adv.* affluently, richly, wealthily.
zamożność *f.* wealth, affluence, riches.
zamożny *a.* wealthy, affluent, rich, substantial, well-off, well-to-do, moneyed, prosperous.
zamówić *pf. zob.* **zamawiać**. ~ **się** *pf. zob.* **zamawiać się**.
zamówienie *n.* order (*na coś* for sth) commission (*np. dzieło sztuki*) (*na coś* for sth) requisition, indent; **jak na zamówienie** custom-made; **zrobić coś na zamówienie** make sth to order.
zamówieniowy *a.* **blankiet zamówieniowy** order form.
zamózgowie *n. Gen.pl.* **-i** *anat.* rhomben cephalon.
zamrażać *ipf.* **1.** (= *ochładzać*) freeze, chill, refrigerate, ice, congeal. **2.** *ekon.* lock up, tie up, freeze; (*ceny, płace, inwestycje, kapitał*) freeze prices, wages, investments, capital. ~ **się** *ipf.* freeze, ice.
zamrażalnia *f. Gen.pl.* **-i** sharp freezer, sharp freezer room.
zamrażalnictwo *n.* refrigerating engineering.
zamrażalnik *mi Gen.* **-a** freezer, freezing compartment.
zamrażarka *f. Gen.pl.* **-ek** freezer, deep freezer.
zamroczenie *n.* blackout, obfuscation, stupor, fuddle; **zamroczenie alkoholowe** drunken stupor.
zamroczony *a.* **-eni** fuddled, obfuscated, light-headed, blacked out.
zamroczyć *pf.* darken, dim, obfuscate, gloom, black out. ~ **się** *pf.* **1.** (= *odurzyć się*) get besotted *l.* befuddled. **2.** (= *zasępić się*) cloud (over).
zamrozić (się) *pf.* **-mrożę** **-mrozisz**, **-mroź** *l.* **-mróż** *zob.* **zamrażać (się)**.
zamróz *mi* **-o-** hoarfrost, frost, rime; *geol.* frost action.
zamruczeć *pf.* **-ę** **-ysz** **1.** (*o zwierzętach*) (= *zacząć mruczeć*) start purring, start growling. **2.** (= *odezwać się niewyraźnie*) mutter.
zamrugać *pf.* **1.** (= *mrugnąć kilkakrotnie*) blink, wink. **2.** (= *zamigotać*) wink, flicker, twinkle.

zamrzeć *pf.* **-mrę** **-mrzesz**, **-mrzyj**, **-marł** *zob.* **zamierać**.
zamsz *mi Gen.pl.* **-ów** **1.** (*skóra*) chamois leather, shammy. **2.** (*materiał*) suede cloth.
zamszak *mi* **-a** (= *but zamszowy*) suede shoe.
zamszowy *a.* chamois, suede, shammy.
zamulać *ipf.*, **zamulić** *pf.* silt up.
zamurować *pf.*, **zamurowywać** *ipf.* brick sth up *l.* in, brick sth off, wall sth up, immure; **zamurowało mnie** *pot.* I was struck dumb.
zamustrować (się) *pf. żegl.* ship, embark, sign on.
zamydlać *ipf.*, **zamydlić** *pf.* soap; **zamydlać komuś oczy** *pot.* throw dust in sb's eyes, pull the wool over sb's eyes, hoodwink sb.
zamykać *ipf.* **1.** (= *zasłaniać wylot, ryglować*) close, shut, lock, bar, bolt, latch, hasp; **zamykać na cztery spusty** lock sth away, lock sth up, lock and bar; **zamknąć komuś usta** shut sb's mouth, button sb's mouth, silence sb. **2.** (= *tarasować*) enclose, block, obstruct, close (*sth*) off; **zamykać komuś drogę do czegoś** *przen.* exclude sb from sth; **zamykać granicę** close the border; **zamykać ruch** stop the traffic; **zamykać coś dla ruchu kołowego** cone sth off. **3.** (= *kończyć, podsumowywać*) close, wind up, put an end to sth, adjourn; **zamykać listę** close the list; **zamykać cudzysłów** unquote, close a quotation; **zamykać nawias** close a bracket; **zamykać pochód** bring up the rear. **4.** (= *pozbawiać wolności*) lock (*sb*) up, imprison. **5.** (= *likwidować*) close down. **6.** (= *umieszczać pod kluczem*) keep (*sth*) locked up, put (*sth*) under lock and key. **7.** (= *składać*) shut. **8.** *lit.* (= *wyrażać, ujmować*) express, comprise; **zamykać coś w kilku zdaniach** express sth in a few words. **9.** *pot.* (= *odcinać, wstrzymywać*) shut off, turn off. ~ **się** *ipf.* **1.** (= *odgradzać się*) bar o.s. in sth, shut oneself, close, shut, be closed, cloister o.s. (away); **zamykać się w sobie** clam up, retire into o.s., retreat into o.s., turn in on o.s., shrink into o.s. **2.** (= *zatrzaskiwać się*) latch, snap; **drzwi się u nas nie zamykają** there is an endless procession of visitors coming and going out of our house; **oczy mi się zamykają** my eyes are closing; **usta jej się nie zamykają** she could talk a donkey's head off; **zamknij się!** *pot.* shut up! **3.** (= *składać się*) close, shut. **4.** (= *kończyć się*) come to an end, come to a close.
zamysł *mi lit.* design, purpose, intention.
zamyślać *ipf. przest.* intend, plan, contemplate, think of doing sth. ~ **się** *ipf.* ponder (*nad kimś / czymś* on *l.* over *l.* about sb/sth) muse (*nad kimś / czymś* on *l.* over sb/sth) meditate (*nad kimś / czymś* on *l.* upon sb/sth) be lost in thought, retreat into one's thought, fall into a reverie.
zamyślenie *n.* abstraction, pensiveness, thoughtfulness, reverie, musings, meditation, pondering, brown study, cogitation.
zamyślić *pf. zob.* **zamyślać**. ~ **się** *pf. zob.* **zamyślać (się)**.
zamyślony *a.* abstracted, broody, cogitative, meditative, pensive, preoccupied, lost in reverie, thoughtful, contemplative.

zanadrze *n.* bosom, lap; **mieć** *l.* **chować coś w zanadrzu** have sth up one's sleeve, have sth in store.

zanadto *adv.* too, overmuch, beyond measure.

zanalizować *pf. zob.* **analizować**.

zanegować *pf. zob.* **negować**.

zaniechać *pf. form.* abort, give up, relinquish, renounce, forsake, desist, forbear, waive, drop.

zaniechanie *n. prawn.* abandonment, desistance, omission, relinquishment, renunciation, forbearance.

zanieczyszczać *ipf.* dirty, soil, litter, pollute, contaminate, defile, foul, vitiate.

zanieczyszczenie *n.* **1.** (= *zabrudzenie*) impurity, dirt, litter, refuse, rubbish. **2.** (= *brud, domieszka*) dross, contamination, pollution, defilement, vitiation.

zanieczyścić *pf.* -szczę -ścisz *zob.* **zanieczyszczać**.

zaniedbać *pf. zob.* **zaniedbywać**. ~ **się** *pf. zob.* **zaniedbywać się**.

zaniedbanie *n.* **1.** (= *brak staranności*) negligence, neglect, carelessness, default, failure, remissness, slackness. **2.** (= *niechlujstwo*) sloppiness, untidiness.

zaniedbany *a.* neglected, uncared-for, untidy, unkempt, sloppy, disheveled, down-at-heel.

zaniedbywać *ipf.* neglect, be negligent, omit, fail. ~ **się** *ipf.* slack off, become remiss, be negligent (*w czymś* of sth).

zaniemóc *pf.* -mogę -możesz -mógł -mogła -mogli *lit.* fall ill.

zaniemówić *pf.* dummy up, be struck dumb, be at a loss for words, be lost for words, be speechless (*z czegoś* with sth).

zaniepokoić *pf.* -koję -koisz, -kój disconcert, upset, worry, disquiet, disturb, perturb, alarm, make sb uneasy, put in a flutter. ~ **się** *pf.* take warning, take alarm, grow uneasy, be upset, be disquieted, be disturbed, be perturbed, be concerned, be in a flutter.

zaniepokojenie *n.* alarm, disquiet, concern, anxiety, uneasiness.

zanieść *pf.* -niosę -niesiesz -niósł -niosła -nieśli *zob.* **zanosić**. ~ **się** *pf. zob.* **zanosić się**.

zaniewidzieć *pf.* -dzę -dzisz -dzą go blind, become blind, be struck blind, lose one's eyesight.

zanik *mi* **1.** (= *zanikanie*) decay, decline, demise, disappearance, wane, dissolution, (*fal radiowych*) fading. **2.** *pat.* atrophy, obliteration, involution; **zanik mięśni** muscular dystrophy; **zanik pamięci** memory failure, amnesia.

zanikać *ipf.*, **zaniknąć** *pf.* -nął *l.* -kł -knęła *l.* -kła **1.** (= *ginąć z oczu*) disappear, vanish, fade away, evanesce. **2.** (= *przestawać istnieć*) decay, decline, deteriorate, die out, sink, dwindle, wither, atrophy.

zanim *conj.* before, by the time, prior to; **skończę, zanim wrócisz** I will finish before you come back.

zaniżać *ipf.*, **zaniżyć** *pf.* lower, understate; **zaniżyć cenę czegoś** lower the price of sth, underprice sth.

zanocować *pf.* put up (at a hotel), spend the night, stay overnight.

zanokcica *f.* **1.** *pat.* whitlow, agnail, hangnail. **2.** *wet.* fouls. **3.** *bot.* spleenwort, fingerfern (*Asplenium*); walking fern (*Camptosorus rhizophyllus*).

zanosić *ipf.* -szę -sisz **1.** (= *dostarczać*) carry, take; **zanosić modły, prośby** *lit.* offer prayers, requests. **2.** (= *unosić*) convey, carry, bear, bring; **gdzie cię zaniosło?** *pot.* where did you go? **3.** (= *zawiewać, zasypywać*) cover, drift. ~ **się** *ipf.* **1.** (= *nie móc opanować*) choke (*czymś l. od czegoś* with sth); **zanosić się śmiechem** roar with laughter, hoot with laughter. **2. zanosi się na deszcz** it looks like rain, it is going to rain; **zanosi się na to, że...** it looks as if, it looks as though; **nie zanosi się na to** that is not likely.

zanotować *pf. zob.* **notować**.

zantagonizować *pf. zob.* **antagonizować**.

zanucić *pf.* -cę -cisz hum, sing.

zanudzać *ipf.* bore, ram sth down sb's throat, badger (*prośbami*). ~ **się** *ipf.* be bored stiff.

zanudzić (się) *pf. zob.* **zanudzać (się)**.

zanurzać *ipf.* immerse, dip, submerge, douse. ~ **się** *ipf.* **1.** (= *pogrążać się*) sink, immerse o.s. (*w czymś* in sth) plunge, dip. **2.** (= *być zanurzanym*) dive, be submerged.

zanurzenie *n.* immersion, submergence, dive, plunge, dip.

zanurzyć *pf. zob.* **zanurzać**. ~ **się** *pf. zob.* **zanurzać się**.

Zanzibar *mi geogr.* Zanzibar.

zań *lit.* (= *za niego*) *zob.* **za**.

zaobrączkować *pf. zob.* **obrączkować**.

zaobrączkowany *a.* ringed.

zaobserwować *pf. lit.* (= *dostrzec*) observe, notice, perceive.

zaoceaniczny *a.* transoceanic.

zaocznie *adv.* **1.** (= *pod czyjąś nieobecność*) in absence, by default. **2.** *uniw.* extramurally.

zaoczny *a.* **1.** (= *odbywający się bez udziału osoby zainteresowanej*) by default. **2.** *uniw.* extramural, external, non-resident.

zaoferować *pf. zob.* **oferować**.

zaofiarować *pf.* **1.** (= *zadeklarować, zapewnić*) offer, bid, make an offer. **2.** *lit.* (= *podarować*) give sb a present. ~ **się** *pf.* offer, volunteer (*z czymś* sth).

zaogniać *ipf.* **1.** (= *powodować stan zapalny*) irritate, inflame, fester. **2.** *lit.* (= *zaostrzać*) embitter, envenom; (*sytuację, spór*) envenom the situation, the dispute. **3.** *lit.* (= *wywoływać rumieńce*) flush. ~ **się** *ipf.* **1.** (*o ranie*) (= *jątrzyć się*) become inflamed, become irritated, fester. **2.** *lit.* (= *zaostrzać się*) aggravate. **3.** *lit.* (= *rumienić się*) flush.

zaognić (się) *pf.* -ij *zob.* **zaogniać (się)**.

zaognienie *n.* **1.** (= *stan zapalny*) inflamation, irritation. **2.** *lit.* (= *wzrost napięcia*) inflammation, embitterment.

zaokrąglać *ipf.* **1.** (= *czynić okrągłym*) round, round off. **2.** (= *wyrównywać*) make even, round down (*w dół*), round up (*w górę*). ~ **się** *ipf.* **1.** (=

nabierać okrągłych kształtów) round out. **2.** (= *wyrównywać się*) become rounded off.

zaokrąglenie *n.* curve, curvaceousness, rounding, roundness.

zaokrąglić *pf.* **-ij** *zob.* **zaokrąglać**. **~ się** *pf. zob.* **zaokrąglać się.**

zaokrętować *pf.* **1.** *żegl.* (= *umieścić na statku*) embark. **2.** *żegl.* (= *przyjąć do załogi*) enlist. **zaokrętować się** *pf.* **1.** (= *wejść na statek jako pasażer*) board ship, take ship, embark. **2.** (= *przyjąć pracę na statku*) enlist.

zaoleić *pf.* **-eję -eisz** grease, smear with grease, oil (*napuścić oleju*).

zaopatrywać *ipf.* **1.** *form.* (= *dostarczać*) provide, supply, equip, furnish (*w coś* with sth). **2.** (= *wyposażać*) fit out, equip, furnish, stock (*w coś* with sth); **zaopatrywać książkę we wstęp** preface a book; **zaopatrywać pismo w pieczęć** affix a seal to a document. **~ się** *ipf.* provide o.s., equip o.s. (*w coś* with sth).

zaopatrzenie *n.* **1.** (= *środki do życia, sprzęt*) supply, maintenance, provision, victualling, equipment. **2.** *pot.* (= *dział w zakładzie pracy*) commissariat, delivery department.

zaopatrzeniowiec *mp* **-wc-** *pl.* **-y** *pot.* buyer, provider.

zaopatrzeniowy *a.* supply.

zaopatrzony *a.* furnished, supplied, provided; **dobrze, słabo zaopatrzony** well-off, badly-off, well, badly stocked, well, badly provided.

zaopatrzyć *pf. zob.* **zaopatrywać**. **~ się** *pf. zob.* **zaopatrywać się.**

zaopiekować się *pf. zob.* **opiekować się.**

zaopiniować *pf. zob.* **opiniować.**

zaoponować *pf. zob.* **oponować.**

zaorać *pf.* **-orzę -orzesz** *zob.* **zaorywać**. **~ się** *pf. zob.* **zaorywać się.**

zaorany *a.* ploughed, fallow.

zaorywać *ipf.* plow, fallow, break up (earth), harrow. **~ się** *ipf.* (= *wkopywać się*) sink, plow (*w coś* into sth).

zaostrzać *ipf.* **1.** (= *czynić ostrym*) sharpen. **2.** (= *czynić wyrazistszym*) sharpen; **zaostrzyć rysy** sharpen outlines. **3.** (= *czynić bardziej rygorystycznym*) sharpen, tighten; **zaostrzać przepisy** sharpen regulations. **4.** (= *potęgować*) sharpen, whet, stimulate, heighten, intensify; **zaostrzać apetyt** whet sb's appetite. **~ się** *ipf.* **1.** (= *nabierać wyrazistości*) sharpen, become sharper. **2.** (= *nabierać intensywności*) sharpen, be whetted, be intensified, be stimulated, be heightened. **3.** (= *wzmagać się*) intensify, be heightened, flare up, rise.

zaostrzyć (się) *pf. zob.* **zaostrzać (się).**

zaoszczędzać *ipf.*, **zaoszczędzić** *pf.* **1.** (= *odkładać*) save, put sth by; **zaoszczędzić na czymś** economize on sth. **2.** (= *nie narażać*) spare (*komuś czegoś* sb sth); save (*komuś czegoś* sb sth *l.* sth for sb).

zaowocować *pf. zob.* **owocować.**

zapach *mi* **1.** (= *woń*) odour, smell, tang; (*przyjemna*) aroma, fragrance, perfume, scent;

(*nieprzyjemna*) whiff, reek, stench. **2.** *pot.* (= *olejek do ciast*) flavour.

zapachnieć *pf.* **-nie** scent, emit a smell, emit a fragrance.

zapachowy *a.* aromatic.

zapaćkać *pf.* **1.** (= *pobrudzić*) besmear, splotch, beslobber. **2.** *pot.* (= *pomalować niedbale*) daub, bedaub.

zapadać *ipf.* **1.** (= *osuwać się*) drop, sink, subside; **kurtyna zapada** the curtain falls; **zapadać w sen** fall asleep, fall into a sleep, lapse into a sleep, drop off; **klamka zapadła** *pot.* there is no return, it's all over. **2.** (= *następować*) fall, set in; (*o nocy, ciemnościach*) descend; **noc zapada** night is falling; (*o milczeniu*) lapse into silence; (*o wyroku*) be pronounced; (*o decyzji*) be taken; (*o uchwale*) be passed. **3.** (= *wpadać w chorobę*) fall ill *l.* sick, be taken ill (*na coś* with sth); **ktoś zapada na zdrowiu** sb's health deteriorates. **4.** (= *zaszywać się, kryć się*) hide; (*o ptakach*) settle. **~ się** *ipf.* sink, cave in (*w czymś l. coś* on sth), collapse; **zapadać się pod ziemię** *przen.* vanish off the face of the earth, sink through the floor.

zapadalność *f. med.* incidence (*na coś* of sth).

zapadka *f. Gen.pl.* **-ek** catch, click, detent, dog, latch, pawl, ratchet.

zapadkowy *a. techn.* ratchet, tumbler.

zapadlisko *n.* cave-in, hollow, cavity, depression, swallow hole.

zapadły *a.* (*o oczach, policzkach*) sunken, hollow; **zapadła dziura** hole, the sticks, tumbledown place.

zapadnia *f. Gen.pl.* **-i** *teatr* trapdoor.

zapadnięty *a.* hollow, sunken, cavernous.

zapakować *pf. zob.* **pakować**. **~ się** *pf. zob.* **pakować się.**

zapalać *ipf.* **1.** (= *wzniecać ogień*) kindle, set on fire, set fire, light; **zapalać zapałkę** strike a match; **zapalać papierosa/fajkę** light a cigarette/ a pipe; **mogę zapalić?** can I have a smoke?; **zapali pan?** would you like to smoke? **2.** (= *włączać*) light, switch on, ignite. **3.** (= *rozbudzać entuzjazm*) animate, inflame, rouse (*kogoś* sb, *do czegoś* into sth), excite. **4.** *pot.* (= *uruchamiać silnik*) kick over, ignite, start. **~ się** *ipf.* **1.** (= *zajmować się ogniem*) catch fire. **2.** (= *zaczynać się świecić*) be lit, shine. **3.** (= *nabierać entuzjazmu*) become enthusiastic (*do czegoś* over sth). **4.** (= *podniecać się*) be fired up, be excited (*do czegoś* about sth).

zapalający *a. wojsk.* incendiary.

zapalarka *f. Gen.pl.* **-ek 1.** (*urządzenie do zapalania gazu*) lighter. **2.** *techn.* (= *urządzenie uruchamiające zapalnik*) exploder, shot lighter.

zapalczywie *adv.* hotheadedly, passionately, impetuously, vehemently.

zapalczywość *f.* hotheadedness, impetuosity, vehemence, passionateness.

zapalczywy *a.* hotheaded, passionate, hotblooded, quick-tempered, short-tempered, impetuous, vehement.

zapalenie *n. pat.* inflammation; **zapalenie płuc** pneumonia; **zapalenie wyrostka robaczkowego** appendicitis.

zapaleniec *mp* -ńc- *Voc.* -ńcze *l.* -u *pl.* -y enthusiast, hot head.

zapalić *pf. zob.* **zapalać**. ~ **się** *pf. zob.* **zapalać się**.

zapalniczka *f. Gen.pl.* -ek lighter.

zapalnik *mi Gen.* -a fuse, detonator, firing; **zapalnik czasowy** time fuse.

zapalny *a.* **1.** (= *łatwo palny*) inflammable, ignitable, combustible; **punkt zapalny** *przen.* trouble spot, sore point. **2.** *med.* inflammatory.

zapalony *a.* -eni keen, enthusiastic, fervent, zealous.

zapał *mi* enthusiasm, fervor, zeal, eagerness, keenness, mettle; **słomiany zapał** short-lived zeal *l.* enthusiasm, transient ardour; **z zapałem** with keenness; **mieć zapał do czegoś** be full of enthusiasm for sth.

zapałać *pf. lit.* be inflamed (*czymś* with sth).

zapałczany *a.* match- (box etc.), match-making (industry).

zapałka *f. Gen.pl.* -ek match.

zapamiętać *pf. zob.* **zapamiętywać**. ~ **się** *pf. zob.* **zapamiętywać się**.

zapamiętale *adv.* passionately, with abandon, frantically, frenziedly, fanatically, rabidly.

zapamiętały *a.* abandoned, passionate, frantic, frenzied, fanatic, rabid.

zapamiętanie *n.* **1.** passion, intensity, zeal, fervor; **(robić coś) z zapamiętaniem** (do sth) with (great) passion; **w zapamiętaniu** like there were no tomorrow; **kochać do zapamiętania** love to distraction. **2. wart zapamiętania** recordable, memorable; **niewart zapamiętania** forgettable; **zdolność zapamiętania** retention.

zapamiętywać *ipf.* remember, memorize, keep in mind, retain; **zapamiętaj to sobie** mark my words, keep this in mind; **zapamiętać coś komuś** score sth against sb. ~ **się** *ipf. lit.* lose oneself, be engrossed *l.* engaged *l.* lost (*w czymś* in sth); be beside oneself (*w czymś* with sth); **zapamiętać się w pracy** lose oneself in work, be absorbed in work.

zapanować *pf. zob.* **panować**.

zapaprać *pf.* -przę -przesz *pot.* (*dywan, buty*) mess up, soil, smear, smudge. ~ **się** *pf. pot.* smear/soil one's hands/face; get smeared all over.

zaparafować *pf. zob.* **parafować**.

zaparcie *n.* **1.** (= *poświęcenie*) determination, self-denial, sacrifice, dedication, devotion; **z zaparciem** with all one's might, with might and main; **robić coś z zaparciem** be determined to do sth, do sth with determination; **pracować z całym zaparciem nad czymś** be working devotedly/with all determination on sth. **2.** (= *zatwardzenie*) constipation, astriction; **cierpiący na zaparcia** constipated, costive; **wywoływać zaparcia** constipate.

zaparkować *pf. zob.* **parkować**.

zaparować *pf.* (*o szybie, okularach*) steam up; (*o oknach*) mist up/over, fog up.

zaparowany *a.* steamy; (*o oknie*) fogged; (*o szybie, okularach*) steamed-up.

zaparty *a.* **z zapartym tchem** with bated breath, breathlessly; **czekać z zapartym tchem** hold one's breath; **patrzeć z zapartym tchem** be all eyes.

zaparzaczka *f. Gen.pl.* -ek (*do herbaty*) tea infuser, tea ball.

zaparzać *ipf.* (*kawę w zaparzaczu*) percolate; (*herbatę, zioła*) infuse, brew; (*pasze*) scald, heat. ~ **się** *ipf.* (*o herbacie, kawie*) brew; (*o kawie*) percolate.

zaparzyć (się) *pf. zob.* **zaparzać (się)**.

zapas *mi* **1.** (= *zasób, rezerwa*) reserve, stock, store, pileup; (*czasu*) margin; (*towaru*) inventory, stock-in-trade; (*żywności*) provisions; **żelazny zapas** iron ration, stockpile; **duży zapas** wide margin; **cieszyć się na zapas** look forward to sth; **mieć coś w zapasie** store up, have in stock; *przen.* have another string/two strings to one bow, have a shot in the locker; **w zapasie** in store, to spare; **z zapasem czasu** with time to spare; **zapas wyczerpany** out of stock; **zakup na zapas** forward buying; **uzupełnić zapas paliwa** refuel; **martwić się na zapas** borrow trouble. **2.** (= *element wymienny*) refill (*do czegoś* for sth). **3.** (*pasek materiału*) surplus, extra scrap/fold.

zapasik *mi* = **zapas** 1.

zapaska *f. Gen.pl.* -ek apron, pinafore.

zapaskudzać *ipf.*, **zapaskudzić** *pf. pot.* (*dywan, podwórze*) muck up, louse up, mess up.

zapasowy *a.* (*o kole, pokoju, części*) spare; (in) reserve; (*o urządzeniu, wyposażeniu*) auxiliary; (*o baterii, żarówce*) replacement; (*wyjściu, schodach*) emergency; (*o kluczu*) duplicate; **koło zapasowe** spare wheel/tire, fifth wheel; **zapasowy plan** fallback; **część zapasowa** spare (part); **kopia zapasowa** *komp.* backup copy/file; **drużyna zapasowa** scrub team.

zapastować *pf.* (*podłogę*) wax.

zapasy *pl. Gen.* -ów **1.** (*rezerwa żywności*) stock, store, supply, hoard; (*paliwa*) refuel; **robić zapasy (na zimę)** build a stock of sth, stock/stoke up on sth, hoard up; **zapasy żywności** hoard provisions; **uzupełniać zapasy** restock; **wyczerpywać zapasy czegoś** be running low on sth; **do wyczerpania zapasów** while stock lasts. **2.** (= *mocowanie się*) wrestling; **iść w zapasy z kimś** measure oneself against sb, contend with sb, measure swords with sb. **3.** *sport* (= *zapaśnictwo*) wrestling; **zapasy drużynowe** tag wrestling; **zapasy w stylu wolnym** all-in wrestling.

zapaszek *mi* -szk- faint smell, odor.

zapaść¹ *pf.* -pasę -pasiesz, -paś, -pasł -paśli (= *utuczyć*) overfeed, fatten.

zapaść² *f. pat.* collapse; **zapaść sercowa** circulatory collapse.

zapaść się¹ *pf.* -padnę -padniesz, -padnij, -padł *zob.* **zapadać się**.

zapaść się² *pf.* (= *zostać przekarmionym*) overfeed, fatten, grow fat.

zapaśnictwo *n. sport* wrestling.

zapaśniczy *a. sport* wrestling, grapple.

zapaśnik *mp sport* wrestler, fighter, athlete; **zapaśnik sumo** sumo wrestler.

zapatrywać się *ipf.* (= *mieć pogląd*) **1.** think

(*na coś* of sth); view, be of the opinion; **jak się zapatrujesz na...?** what do you think of...?, what is your opinion on...?; **zapatrywać się na coś przychylnie** be agreeable to sth, take a favorable view of sth; **zapatrywać się na coś cynicznie/ entuzjastycznie** be cynical/enthusiastic about sth; **zapatrywać się na coś pesymistycznie/optymistycznie** have *l.* take a pessimistic/optimistic view of sth; **zapatrywać się jednakowo na coś** be of one mind about sth. **2.** (= *wzorować się*) take the example (*na kogoś* of sb); follow (*sb's*) example, take after.

zapatrywanie *n.* opinion, view, outlook (*na coś* on sth); standpoint, belief; **zapatrywania rasistowskie** racist sentiments; **mieć skrajne zapatrywania** hold extreme views; **podzielać czyjeś zapatrywania** share sb's views.

zapatrzony *a.* **-eni** with one's eyes fixed (*w coś* on sth); **zapatrzony w siebie** full of oneself, selfish, self-concentrated; **być zapatrzonym w kogoś** be infatuated with sb, be under the spell of sb.

zapatrzyć się *pf.* **1.** fasten one's look, fix one's gaze (*w kogoś/coś* on sb/sth); *przen.* set one's mind (*w kogoś* on sb); get infatuated (*w kogoś* with sb/sth). **2.** (=*brać z kogoś wzór*) take after, follow the example of; look up (*w kogoś* to sb).

zapchać *pf. zob.* **zapychać**. **~ się** *pf. zob.* **zapychać się**.

zapchajdziura *f.* *pot.* jerk town, rathole, hicksville, dump.

zapchany *a.* packed, jam-packed; (*o pokoju*) crowded, packed, crammed, full; (*o porze, rurze*) clogged, blocked; (*o nosie*) stuffed-up, congested; (*o półkach w sklepie*) well-stocked, loaded; **zapchany po brzegi** solid packed, filled to the brim, brimming.

zapchlony (*o zwierzęciu*) *a.* flea-bitten, flea-infested, infested with fleas.

zapełniać *ipf.* **1.** (= *umieszczać*) stock (up), fill (*czymś* with sth). **2.** (= *wypełniać przestrzeń*) saturate, fill (up); (*o tłumie*) crowd, throng, cram. **3.** *lit.* (= *wypełniać*) fill (up), pack; (*czas, lukę*) fill (*czymś* with sth). **~ się** *ipf.* fill up, become full, get crowded/crammed; **sala powoli się zapełniała** the hall was slowly getting crowded.

zapełnić (się) *pf.* **-ij** *l.* **-ń** *zob.* **zapełniać (się)**.

zaperzać się *ipf.*, **zaperzyć się** *pf.* flare up, fly out, get on one's high horse, get irritated.

zaperzony *a.* **-eni** irritated, tetchy, with his/her hackles up, hot under the collar.

zapeszać *ipf.*, **zapeszyć** *pf.* put a jinx (*coś* on sth); jinx, bewitch with the evil eye; **nie mówmy o tym, żeby nie zapeszyć** let's not talk about it or we'll jinx it.

zapewne *particle* **1.** *lit.* (= *przypuszczalnie*) presumably. **2.** *lit.* (= *niewątpliwie*) surely, to be sure, doubtless; **zapewne...** I dare say...

zapewniać *ipf.* **1.** (= *upewniać*) assure, ensure (*kogoś o czymś* sb of sth); assert; **zapewnić o swojej niewinności** protest *l.* maintain *l.* assert one's innocence; **zapewnić, że...** assert that..., give an assurance that..., affirm that... **2.** (= *gwarantować*) provide (*coś* for sth); secure, ensure (*coś komuś* sth for/to sb); administer (*coś komuś* sth to

sb); (*wyżywienie, transport*) lay on; **zapewnić komuś przewagę** give sb a head start; **zapewnić komuś byt** make provision for sb; **zapewnić komuś mieszkanie** house sb, provide sb with a place to live; **zapewnić komuś alibi** alibi sb; **zapewnić komuś bezpieczeństwo** assure/guarantee sb's safety; **zapewnić czemuś powodzenie** be the making of sth, make sth a success; **zapewnić sobie zwycięstwo** secure victory; **zapewnić komuś czołową pozycję** vault sb into prominence. **~ się** *ipf.* assure (*o czymś* of sth); declare; **wzajemnie zapewniali się o swojej przyjaźni** they assured each other of their friendship, they declared friendship to each other.

zapewnić (się) *pf.* **-ij** *zob.* **zapewniać (się)**.

zapewnienie *n.* affirmation, assertion, reassurance, declaration, statement; (*świadczeń, opieki*) provision; **solenne zapewnienie** protestation; **zapewnienie jakości** quality assurance; **zapewnienie bezpieczeństwa** risk management.

zapędy *pl. Gen.* **-ów** **1.** *pot.* (= *ambicje*) aspirations, ambitions. **2.** (= *zapały, porywy*) attempts, endeavors, efforts; **pohamować czyjeś zapędy** stamp on sb, curb/bridle sb's endeavors.

zapędzać *ipf.* **1.** (= *zaganiać*) drive, bustle, hurry; (*do zagrody*) yard, corral, drive in; **zapędzić do nory** run to earth *l.* ground; **zapędzić kogoś w kozi róg** drive sb into a corner, bring sb to bay, knock sb into a cocked hat; **zapędzać kogoś do pracy** drive sb to work. **2.** (= *nakłaniać*) compel, urge (*kogoś do (zrobienia) czegoś* sb to (do) sth); make (*kogoś do zrobienia czegoś* sb do sth). **~ się** *ipf.* **1.** (= *zapuszczać się*) (*np. w głąb lasu*) venture, advance, plunge. **2.** *pot.* (= *dawać się ponieść emocjom*) go too far, get carried away, let oneself go.

zapędzić (się) *pf. zob.* **zapędzać (się)**.

zapędzony *a.* (*zalatany*) busy, in a rush/hurry, bustling, as busy as a bee; **zapędzony w kozi róg** behind the eight ball.

zapiać *pf.* **-pieję -piejesz -piali** *l.* **-pieli** *zob.* **piać**.

zapiaszczyć *pf.* (*np. port, przystań*) sand up, cover with sand.

zapiąć *pf.* **-pnę -pniesz, -pnij** *zob.* **zapinać**. **~ się** *pf. zob.* **zapinać się**.

zapić *pf.* **-piję -pijesz, -pij** *zob.* **zapijać**. **~ się** *pf. zob.* **zapijać się**.

zapiec *pf.* **-piekę -pieczesz -piekł** **1.** *zob.* **zapiekać**. **2.** (= *wywołać piekący ból*) sting, chafe, smart, rub; **oczy zapiekły go od dymu** his eyes smarted from the smoke. **~ się** *pf. zob.* **zapiekać się**.

zapiecek *mi* **-ck-** *Gen.* **-a** chimney corner.

zapieczętować *pf. zob.* **pieczętować**.

zapiekać *ipf.* *kulin.* bake, roast, gratinate; (*w naczyniu*) casserole. **~ się** *ipf.* **1.** *kulin.* bake, roast. **2.** (= *nie dawać się poruszyć, zasychać*) clot, coagulate; (*o wargach*) chap; (*o śrubie*) block. **3.** (= *umacniać się, zacinać się*) (*o człowieku*) grow obstinate (*w czymś* in sth); **zapiekł się w złości** he was uncompromising in his anger, he grew obstinate in his anger; (*o gniewie, złości, wściekłości*) become ingrained/rooted; (*w kimś*) in sb.

zapiekanka *f. Gen.pl.* **-ek** *kulin.* casserole, timbale; (*w cieście, z nadzieniem mięsnym lub warzywnym*) pie; (*z sera, jajek i tartej bułki*) ramekin; (*z grubego makaronu*) lasagna.

zapiekany *a. kulin.* roast, au gratin; **jabłka zapiekane w cieście** apple fritters.

zapieklić się *pf. pot.* (= *zacietrzewić się*) flare up, lose one's cool, fly off the handle, work oneself into a frenzy, fly into a temper/passion.

zapiekły *a.* **1.** (= *spiekły, zeschnięty*) clotted, coagulated; (*o ranie, krwi*) incrusted. **2.** (= *tkwiący w czyjejś pamięci*) rankling, festering.

zapienić się *pf. zob.* **pienić się**.

zapieprzać *ipf.* **1.** *pot.* (= *iść szybko*) tear along. **2.** *pot.* (= *pracować intensywnie*) sweat, work like a horse; **zapieprzać jak mały samochodzik** work one's rear end off, work one's butt *l.* tail off.

zapieprzyć *pf. pot.* (= *ukraść*) hook, snatch, stick up.

zapierać[1] *ipf.* (= *prać wstępnie*) pre-wash; (*plamę*) wash away.

zapierać[2] *ipf.* **1.** (= *tamować*) obstruct, hinder, bolt; (*oddech*) hold; **dech mi zaparło** *przen.* it took my breath away; **zapierający dech w piersiach** breathtaking, stunning. **2.** (= *mocno opierać*) ram, dig into the ground. ~ **się** *ipf.* **1.** (= *opierać się mocno*) jib (*o coś* at sth); brace (*czemuś* against sth). **2.** *lit.* (= *wypierać się*) (*kogoś, czegoś*) deny, renounce, repudiate, forsake.

zapierdalać *ipf.* **1.** *wulg.* (= *iść szybko*), go full blast. **2.** *wulg.* (= *pracować intensywnie*) work one's ass off, break one's balls.

zapierdolić *pf. wulg.* (= *ukraść*) rip off, rustle, snatch.

zapierniczać *ipf. pot.* = **zapieprzać**.

zapierniczyć *pf. pot.* = **zapieprzyć**.

zapiewajło *mp decl. like f. in sing. pl.* **-y** *l.* **-owie** *pot.* leading singer.

zapięcie *n.* **1.** (*urządzenie do zapinania*) clasp, buckle, hook; (*do koszuli, kołnierzyka*) stud; (*u buta*) strap; (*w ubraniu*) fastener, fastening. **2.** (*miejsce zapięcia*) fastening; **bez zapięcia** (*o sukience*) step-in.

zapijaczony *a.* **-eni** **1.** *pot.* (= *pijany*) sottish, drink-sodden, blind drunk, wiped. **2.** *pot.* (= *właściwy pijakowi*) (*wzrok, głos*) drunken; **zapijaczone oczy** beer-goggles.

zapijać *ipf.* **1.** (= *popijać*) wash down, sip; **zapijać kanapki herbatą** wash down sandwiches with a cup of tea. **2.** (= *pić, żeby zapomnieć o czymś*) (*smutki, żale*) drink away, drown; **zapijał smutki w butelce whisky** he was drowning his sorrows in a bottle of whiskey. ~ **się** *ipf. pot.* soak up, tank up, gargle, drink till all is blue; **zapijać się na śmierć** drink oneself into one's grave.

zapinać *ipf.* (*koszulę, guzik, pasy*) do up, fasten; (*buty, zegarek*) strap; (*na sprzączkę*) buckle; (*na haftkę*) hook up; (*na guzik*) button up; (*na zamek*) zip; (*na zatrzask*) clip; **zapiąć pas bezpieczeństwa** fasten one's seatbelt, belt up; **zapinać coś na ostatni guzik** *przen.* get sth shipshape/in perfect trim. ~ **się** *ipf.* **1.** (= *zapinać ubranie na*

sobie samym) do up, button up. **2.** (= *mieć zapięcie jakiegoś rodzaju*) fasten, close; (*na guziki*) button; (*na zamek*) zip; **suknia zapina się z tyłu** the dress fastens behind *l.* at the back.

zapinka *f. Gen.pl.* **-ek** buckle, clasp, clip, fastener; (*hełmu, kasku*) chinstrap.

zapis *mi* **1.** (= *rejestrowanie*) record, recording. **2.** (= *to, co zapisane*) record, notation, entry; **zapis nagrania** tapescript; **zapis cyfrowy** *komp.* digital recording; **ścieżka zapisu** *komp.* band; **zapis drgań** oscillogram; **zapis fonetyczny** phonography; **zapis stenograficzny** stenographic record; **zapis przebiegu służby wojskowej** service record; **brak zapisów o czymś** sth went unrecorded. **3.** *prawn.* bequest, legacy, devise; **dokonywać zapisu na rzecz kogoś** endow. **4.** *muz.* notation, score; **zapis dźwięku** sound record.

zapisać *pf.* **-piszę** **-piszesz** *zob.* **zapisywać**. ~ **się** *pf. zob.* **zapisywać się**.

zapiski *pl. Gen.* **-ów** notes, jottings; (*z zebrania*) minutes.

zapisy *pl. Gen.* **-ów** enrollment, registration, signing up, recruitment (*na coś* for sth, *dó czegoś* for sth).

zapisywać *ipf.* **1.** (= *notować*) put down, write down, note down, get down, jot down; keep a record/tally (*coś* of sth); (*punkty w grze*) score; **zapisywać coś na czyjś rachunek** chalk sth up to sb, put sth down to sb's account; **zapisać coś na swoim koncie** (*np. osiągnięcie*) ring sth up, chalk sth up; **zapisywać coś w pamięci** engrave sth in the memory; **zapisać na czyjąś niekorzyść** score up against sb; **zapisać złotymi zgłoskami** mark with a white stone; **zapisać w testamencie** bequeath; **zapisać w dzienniku** journalize. **2.** (= *zapełniać pismem*) commit to paper/writing, fill with writing. **3.** (= *wciągać, zgłaszać*) put down, enroll (*do czegoś* for sth, *na coś* for sth). **4.** (= *ofiarowywać w testamencie*) (*dobra rzeczowe*) devise; (*dobra osobiste*) bequeath; endow. **5.** (*o lekarzu, zalecać*) (*leki*) prescribe. **6.** (= *utrwalać*) save; (*dane, dźwięk*) record; **zapisać na dysku** save; **zapisać nutami** note. ~ **się** *ipf.* **1.** (= *wpisywać się*) enter one's name; **zapisać się do lekarza** register with a doctor. **2.** (= *zgłaszać uczestnictwo*) enroll, register, sign up (*do czegoś* for sth, *na coś* for sth); join; **zapisać się w czyjejś pamięci** have one's name engraved in sb's memory, stand out in sb's memory; **dobrze/źle zapisał się w mojej pamięci** I keep him in my good/black books; **zapisać się w historii** go down in history; **zapisać się złotymi zgłoskami** distinguish oneself, make oneself famous, make one's name.

zapiszczeć *pf.* **-ę** **-ysz** **1.** (= *wydać pisk*) squeak, squeal, shriek, peep. **2.** (*o przedmiotach*) (= *zaskrzypieć*) creak, squeak, scrape.

zapity *a.* **1.** *pot.* (= *pijany*) sodden, sozzled, tanked up. **2.** *pot.* (*właściwy pijakowi*) (*głos, wzrok*) drunken; **zapite oczy** beer-goggles.

zaplamić *pf. zob.* **plamić**. ~ **się** *pf. zob.* **plamić się**.

zaplanować *pf. zob.* **planować**.

zaplanowany *a.* planned, lined up, scheduled; (*małżeństwo*) arranged; (*wydatki, rezultat*) intended; **precyzyjnie zaplanowany** tight-knit; **dobrze zaplanowany** well-thought-out.

zaplatać *ipf.* plait, tress, braid, interlace; (*w warkoczyki*) cornrow; **zaplatać dłonie** lace one's fingers, clasp one's hands.

zaplatać (się) *pf.* -czę -czesz *zob.* **zaplątywać (się)**.

zaplątywać *ipf.* (*nici, sznurek*) entangle, tangle up, foul; **zaplątać kogoś w zbrodnię** involve/implicate sb in crime. ~ **się. 1.** (= *zasupłać się*) foul, get tangled, tangle up; (*w wodorosty, sieci*) entangle; (*w sieci*) enmesh; (*wełnę*) knot, ravel; **język mu się zaplątał** his tongue faltered. **2.** (= *zostać unieruchomionym*) catch, snare, entrap. **3.** *pot.* (= *zgubić wątek*) lose the thread; **zaplątać się w zeznaniach** get lost in one's testimony. **4.** *pot.* (= *uwikłać się*) get in a tangle, become entangled/implicated/involved, get mixed up (*w coś w sth*). **5.** *pot.* (= *znaleźć się gdzieś przypadkiem*) happen to be somewhere; **dziecko zaplątało się w tłumie** the baby got lost in the crowd.

zaplecze *n. Gen.pl.* -y (*sklepu*) back, back-up facilities; (*techniczne*) equipment; (*intelektualne*) potential; (*dużego miasta*) hinterland; *wojsk.* parados; **zaplecze materiałowe** resource base; **zaplecze konferencyjne** conference facilities.

zapleść *pf.* -plotę -pleciesz -plótł -plotła -pletli *zob.* **zaplatać**.

zapleśnieć *pf. zob.* **pleśnieć**.

zaplombować *pf. zob.* **plombować**.

zapluć *pf. zob.* **zapluwać**. ~ **się** *pf. zob.* **zapluwać się**.

zapluskwić *pf.* -ij **1.** bug, infest with (bed)-bugs. **2.** (= *założyć podsłuch*) bug, tap, wire-tap.

zapluty *a.* **1.** (= *odrażający*) disgusting, filthy, mucky. **2.** *obelż.* spiteful, mean.

zapluwać *ipf.* spit all over (*coś* sth). ~ **się** *ipf.* foam, froth at the mouth; **zapluł się ze złości** he was foaming at the mouth.

zapłacenie *n.* payment; (*długu*) repayment, liquidation; (*rachunku*) reckoning, settlement, clearance; **do zapłacenia** due.

zapłacić *pf.* -cę -cisz *zob.* **płacić**.

zapładniać *ipf.* **1.** (= *powodować zapłodnienie*) inseminate, fertilize, fecundate; (*ikrę*) milt; *bot.* impregnate. **2.** (= *działać inspirująco*) inspire; **obraz zapłodnił jego wyobraźnię** the painting inspired his imagination.

zapłakać *pf.* -aczę -aczesz burst into tears, weep, wail; **zapłakać z radości/ze szczęścia** cry from joy/happiness; **zapłakał jak dziecko** he wept like a child; **zapłakać nad swoim losem** cry over one's fate.

zapłakany *a.* (*o twarzy, oczach*) in tears, tearful, teary; (*o człowieku*) crying, weeping, sobbing, in tears.

zapłakiwać się *ipf.* keep crying/weeping, lament, abandon oneself to tears, pipe one's eyes, weep one's heart out; **zapłakiwać się z żalu** wail with grief.

zapłata *f.* **1.** (= *zapłacenie*) payment, settlement, clearance; **zapłata gotówką** (net) cash; **zapłata z góry** payment in advance; **zapłata w natu-**rze payment in kind; **zapłata w towarze** truck, barter; **zapłata w ratach** payment by installments; **stopniowa zapłata** progress payment; **zapłata za grzech** the wages of sin; **zapłata za milczenie** hush money; **potwierdzenie zapłaty** voucher; **tytułem zapłaty za coś** in payment of sth; **wezwanie do zapłaty** notice to pay, summons for payment; **marna zapłata** chicken feed. **2.** (= *należność*) pay, retribution, remuneration.

zapłodnić *pf.* -ij *zob.* **zapładniać**.

zapłodnienie *n.* insemination, fecundation, fertilization; *bot.* impregnation; **sztuczne zapłodnienie** artificial insemination; **zapłodnienie in vitro** in vitro fertilization; **zapłodnienie międzyosobnicze** cross-fertilization.

zapłon *mi* ignition, spark plug; **mieć źle ustawiony zapłon** misfire; **przedwczesny zapłon** pre-ignition, premature ignition; **zapłon samoczynny** spontaneous ignition/combustion; **zapłon przyspieszony** advanced ignition; **temperatura zapłonu** flash point; *fizyka jądrowa* ignition temperature; **mieć spóźniony zapłon** *żart.* be slow off the mark.

zapłonąć *pf.* **1.** (= *zacząć płonąć*) burn up, flare up, blaze up, kindle up. **2.** (= *zaświecić się*) flash, gleam; **jego oczy zapłonęły z radości** his eyes sparkled with joy. **3.** (= *nabrać czerwonego koloru*) redden, turn red/rosy/crimson. **4.** (= *zarumienić się*) flush, blush, flame, crimson. **5.** *lit.* (= *zostać ogarniętym uczuciem*) be overwhelmed, be overcome (*czymś* with sth); **zapłonąć gniewem** flame out with anger, flash with anger; (*o uczuciach*) (= *opanować*) flame up/out; (*o gniewie*) flare up; **radość zapłonęła w jej sercu** her heart filled with joy; **zapłonęła w niej nadzieja** hope flamed in her.

zapłonić się *pf. lit.* flush, blush, turn crimson, go red/rosy.

zapłoniony *a.* -eni *lit.* (*np. o dziewczynie*) flushed, blushed, crimson.

zapłonowy *a.* ignition, flashing; **świeca zapłonowa** *mot.* spark *l.* sparking plug; **cewka zapłonowa** spark coil; **przewód zapłonowy** ignition lead; **urządzenie zapłonowe** igniter.

zapobiec *pf.* -biegnę -biegniesz, -biegnij, -biegł, **zapobiegać** *ipf.* (*agresji, wojnie, wypadkom*) prevent (*czemuś* sth (from happening)); avert (*czemuś* sth); (*niebezpieczeństwu*) head off, deter, stave off; take precautions; **lepiej zapobiegać niż leczyć** an ounce of prevention is worth a pound of cure; **zapobiegać dalszym stratom** cut one's losses; **zapobiegać (niechcianej) ciąży** prevent (an) unwanted pregnancy.

zapobieganie *n.* prevention (*czemuś* of sth); *med.* prophylaxis; **zapobieganie ciąży** contraception; **zapobieganie przestępstwom** crime prevention.

zapobiegawczo *adv.* by way of precaution, preventively; *med.* prophylactically; **działać zapobiegawczo przeciw czemuś** prevent sth.

zapobiegawczy *a.* precautionary, preventive, protective; (*o działaniu*) remedial; **areszt zapobiegawczy** protective custody; *med.* prophylactic; **leczenie zapobiegawcze** preventive treatment; **środki zapobiegawcze** preventive/remedial/precautionary measures, precautions.

zapobiegliwie *adv.* providently, with foresight, thriftily.

zapobiegliwość *f.* precaution, providence, provident care, foresight, forethought, prudence.

zapobiegliwy *a.* (*o człowieku*) foreseeing, forehanded, foresighted; (*o działalności, staraniach*) provident, thrifty.

zapocić *pf.* (*buty, bieliznę*) impregnate with sweat, get soaked with sweat; **zapociłeś koszulę** your shirt is soaking with sweat. **~ się** *pf.* (*o człowieku*) sweat, break out in a sweat; (*o szybach*) mist over, steam up.

zapoczątkować *pf.*, **zapoczątkowywać** *ipf.* (*dać początek*) originate, initiate, trigger off, spark off, pioneer; (*tradycję*) lay down; (*kampanię wyborczą*) launch; **zapoczątkować modę na coś** set the trend for sth; **zapoczątkować nową epokę w dziejach czegoś** usher in a new era of sth.

zapodać *pf.*, **zapodawać** *ipf.* -aję -ajesz, -awaj **1.** *pot.* (= *poinformować*) inform, brief, tip off, clue up. **2.** (*muzykę*) get on the air, get out.

zapodziać *pf.* -dzieję -dziejesz -dziali *l.* -dzieli, **zapodziewać** *ipf. pot.* mislay, misplace, lose; **zapodziałam gdzieś okulary** I forgot where I put my glasses. **~ się** *pf.*, **zapodziewać się** *ipf. pot.* disappear, vanish, get/be lost, be lost to view/sight.

zapolować *pf.* (*na dzika, kuropatwy*) go on a hunt, go hunting.

zapominać *ipf.* **1.** (= *przestawać pamiętać*) forget (*o kimś, czymś* about sb/sth); (*np. kluczy*) leave behind; (*o czymś przykrym*) push sth to the back of one's mind, put sth behind; **zapominać o czymś na chwilę** set sth by; **zapomnieć o dawnych urazach** wipe the slate clean; **nie zapomnieć komuś dobroci** remember sb's kindness; **nie zapomnij o obietnicy** don't fail to keep your promise; **nie zapominać komuś krzywdy** harbor resentment at sb, bear sb a grudge; **zapomnieć komuś krzywdy** forgive sb a wrong; **zapominać o bożym** *l.* **całym świecie** be lost to the world; **nie mogę o niej zapomnieć** I can't get her off my mind; **nie zapominaj, że...** don't forget that...; **czy przypadkiem o czymś nie zapomniałeś?** aren't you forgetting sth?; **nie zapomnieć coś zrobić** be sure to do sth, keep sth in mind; **nie zapomnij zamknąć drzwi** be sure to lock the door; **zapomnijmy o tym, co nas dzieli** let's bury our differences; **zapomnieć swojej kwestii** *teatr* forget one's lines; **nigdy ci tego nie zapomnę!** (*wyraz wdzięczności*) I will never forget what you did for me; (*groźba*) you will never live that down, you shall smart from this. **2.** (= *zostawiać przez nieuwagę*) forget, leave, leave behind. **3.** (= *nie zrobić przez roztargnienie*) forget; **na śmierć zapomniałam** I clean *l.* plumb forgot. **4.** (= *tracić umiejętność*) forget; **zapomniałeś języka w gębie?** *pot.* (has the) cat got your tongue?, are you tongue-tied?; **dużo już zapomniał z francuskiego** his French is a little rusty. **5.** (= *zaniedbywać*) neglect (*coś zrobić* to do sth); (*celowo*) omit (*coś*

zrobić to do sth); **zapomniany przez Boga** Godforsaken. **~ się** *ipf.* forget oneself, misbehave.

zapominalski *a. pot.* forgetful, oblivious, absent-minded. – *mp pot.* forgetter, scatter-brain.

zapomnieć *pf.* -nę -nisz, -nij *zob.* zapominać. **~ się** *pf. zob.* zapominać się.

zapomnienie *n.* **1.** (= *niepamięć*) oblivion, obscurity, neglect, eclipse; **pójść** *l.* **odejść w zapomnienie** fall/fade/sink into oblivion, be thrown on the scrap heap, be lost in the mists of time; **ocalić coś od zapomnienia** save from sinking into oblivion; **wydobyć kogoś/coś z zapomnienia** bring sb/sth back from oblivion; **skazywać coś na zapomnienie** consign sth to oblivion; **pozostawać w zapomnieniu** remain in eclipse/oblivion; **chwilowe zapomnienie** memory lapse. **2.** (= *roztargnienie*) absent-mindedness, forgetfulness; **(zostawić coś) przez zapomnienie** through a lapse of memory. **3.** (= *oderwanie od rzeczywistości*) oblivion, abstraction; **szukać zapomnienia w czymś** seek oblivion in sth; **napój zapomnienia** *lit.* nepenthe; **rzeka zapomnienia** waters of forgetfulness; **dający zapomnienie** oblivious.

zapomoga *f. Gen.pl.* -óg relief, benefit, handout, grant, subsistence allowance; **korzystać z zapomogi** be on the dole.

zapomogowy *a.* relief; **fundusz zapomogowy** relief fund; **lokalny fundusz zapomogowy** community chest; **kasa zapomogowo-pożyczkowa** provident society.

zapora *f. Gen.pl.* -ór **1.** (= *przegroda*) hedge, dam, wall, fence; **zapora wodna** barrage, water dam; **zapora drogowa** roadblock; **wznosić zapory społeczne** erect social barriers. **2.** *wojsk.* (*przeciwczołgowa*) caltrop, anti-tank barrier; **zapora ogniowa** fire curtain.

zaporowy *a.* **1.** (*dotyczący przegrody*) bar, barrier; (*o jeziorze*) barrier. **2.** (= *restrykcyjny, ograniczający*) restrictive; (*o cłach, cenie*) protective; **cło zaporowe** protective custom duty. **3.** *wojsk.* barrage; (*o balonie*) barrage; (*o ogniu*) barrage, defensive, curtain.

Zaporoże *n. hist.* Zaporizhya.

zapotnieć *pf.* (*o człowieku*) get sweaty, be in a sweat; (*o szkle*) mist over, steam up.

zapotrzebować *pf. form.* (*pracowników*) staff; (*towaru, sprzętu*) order, provide for.

zapotrzebowanie *n.* **1.** *form.* (= *popyt*) call, demand, need (*na coś* for sth); **istnieje duże zapotrzebowanie na coś** sth is in great demand; **zapotrzebowanie pokarmowe** nutritional requirements; **zaspokajać zapotrzebowanie** meet *l.* satisfy demand. **2.** *form.* (= *zamówienie*) requisition; **złożyć zapotrzebowanie na coś** make a requisition for sth.

zapowiadacz *mp pot.* announcer, presenter, broadcaster, anchorman.

zapowiadać *ipf.* **1.** (= *oznajmiać, ogłaszać*) announce, advertise, make known; (*o symptomach*) prognosticate, signal, indicate. **2.** (= *uprzedzać kategorycznie*) warn; **zapowiedział, że nikt nie może się spóźnić** he made it clear that nobody should be late. **3.** (= *być oznaką, wróżyć*) forebode, forecast, foreshadow, portend; **to nie**

zapowiada nic dobrego nothing good will come of this. **~ się** *ipf.* **1.** (= *ogłaszać zamiar przybycia*) announce one's arrival. **2.** (= *rokować*) promise, shape up, show signs of; **dobrze się zapowiadać** be shaping up well, show promise; **zapowiadać się ciekawie** promise to be interesting; **zapowiada się dobra zabawa** this sounds like fun; **zapowiada się na świetnego chirurga** he is a promising surgeon; **zapowiada się upalne lato** it's going to be a hot summer, it looks like the summer will be hot.

zapowiadający się *a.* promising, of great promise; **dobrze zapowiadający się pisarz** a writer in the bud, budding/promising/up-and-coming/talented writer.

zapowiedzieć (się) *pf.* -wiem -wiesz, -wiedz *zob.* **zapowiadać (się).**

zapowiedź *n.* **1.** (= *oznajmienie*) (*wizyty, reform*) announcement; (*programu*) advertisement; (*oficjalna*) statement; **zgodnie z zapowiedzią** as was announced; (*zjawić się*) **bez zapowiedzi** (appear *l.* arrive) unannounced. **2.** (= *oznaka, wróżba*) foreboding, omen, earnest, prognostication, foretoken (*czegoś* of sth); (*nowego filmu*) preview, trailer; **zapowiedź niebezpieczeństwa** a scent of danger. **3.** *kośc.* banns; **dać na zapowiedzi** *pot.* ask the banns, have one's banns called; **ogłaszać zapowiedzi** call *l.* publish *l.* put up *l.* read the banns.

zapowietrzać *ipf.* *przest.* (*zakażać*) infect, cause infection, spread to. **~ się** *ipf.* get air-locked.

zapowietrzony *a.* (*o grzejniku, hamulcach*) **1.** air-locked. **2.** (*chory na chorobę zakaźną*) *przest.* plague-stricken, infected.

zapowietrzyć (się) *pf.* *zob.* **zapowietrzać (się).**

zapoznać (się) *pf.* *zob.* **zapoznawać (się).**

zapoznany *a.* *przest.* (= *niedoceniony*) obscure, unrecognized, unappreciated, unhonored.

zapoznawać *ipf.* -aję -ajesz, -awaj **1.** (= *zaznajomić*) introduce (*kogoś z czymś* sb to sth); acquaint (*kogoś z czymś* sb with sth); instruct (*kogoś z czymś* sb of sth); initiate (*kogoś z czymś* sb in/into sth). **2.** (= *przedstawić*) acquaint (*kogoś z kimś* sb with sb); introduce (*kogoś z kimś* sb to sb); **chciałbym cię zapoznać z moją matką** I'd like to introduce you to my mother, I'd like you to meet my mother **~ się** *ipf.* **1.** (= *zaznajomić się*) acquaint oneself, familiarize, become familiar (*z czymś* with sth); take cognizance (*z czymś* of sth); **zapoznać kogoś z najnowszymi informacjami** bring sb up to date; **zapoznać się bliżej ze sprawą** go into the matter. **2.** (= *zawierać znajomość*) make acquaintance (*z kimś* with sb).

zapoznawczy *a.* (*o kursie*) orientation; (*o wieczorku*) get-together; **spotkanie zapoznawcze** mixer.

zapożyczać *ipf.* (*pomysł, wyraz*) borrow (*od kogoś* from sb); (*obyczaj*) adopt, appropriate, take in. **~ się** *ipf.* go/get/run into debt, run up a debt/debts (*u kogoś* with sb).

zapożyczenie *n.* *jęz.* borrowing, loanword; (*zwyczaj, sposób zachowania*) foreignism.

zapożyczyć (się) *pf.* *zob.* **zapożyczać (się).**

zapóźnienie *n.* (*np. gospodarcze*) backwardness, underdevelopment.

zapóźniony *a.* -eni (*o gościach, o wiośnie*) belated, late; (*o samolocie*) delayed; (*o liście*) tardy; (*w rozwoju*) backward.

zapracować (się) *pf.* *zob.* **zapracowywać (się).**

zapracowany *a.* earned, deserved; (*o osobie*) up to the eye in work, busy; **ciężko zapracowane pieniądze** hard-earned money.

zapracowywać *ipf.* earn, work for, deserve; **zapracować sobie na sukces** pay one's dues, sing for one's supper; **zapracować na utrzymanie** make/earn one's living, be the bread-winner; **uczeń zapracował na pochwałę** the student deserved a praise. **~ się** *ipf.* be up to the eye in work, work one's guts out *l.* one's head off, slave away.

zaprać *pf.* -piorę -pierzesz *zob.* **zapierać**[1].

zapragnąć *pf.* -ij *lit.* long, wish, yearn (*czegoś* for sth); crave (*czegoś* sth); **zapragnąć czegoś z całej siły** set one's heart on sth; **czego dusza zapragnie** you name it, everything one's heart could desire; **ile dusza zapragnie** at will, to one's heart content.

zaprasować *pf.*, **zaprasowywać** *ipf.* iron a crease; **zaprasować kant na czymś** iron a crease into sth; **starannie zaprasowane spodnie** well-creased trousers.

zapraszać *ipf.* **1.** (= *prosić o przybycie*) invite (*na coś* for/to sth); request sb's presence; **zapraszać kogoś do domu** have sb down/in; **zaprosić kogoś do tańca** ask sb to dance; **zapraszać kogoś do siebie** ask sb to come over/round. **2.** (= *zachęcać, nakłaniać*) invite, encourage (*do (zrobienia) czegoś* to do sth); lead sb on (*do czegoś* to sth). **~ się** *ipf.* **1.** (= *zapraszać się nawzajem*) invite each other. **2.** (= *wpraszać się*) come uninvited; force one's presence (*do kogoś* upon sb).

zaprawa *f.* **1.** *bud.* (= *spoiwo murarskie*) mortar, grout; **impregnować zaprawą** mordant, treat with a mordant. **2.** *sport* exercise, training, workout; **sucha zaprawa** cold-storage training. **3.** (= *przyprawa*) seasoning, condiment. **4.** *sztuka* (= *grunt*) dope, ground, undercoat. **5.** *roln.* (*do nasion*) (seed) dressing. **6.** *chem.* mordant.

zaprawdę *adv.* *przest.* in truth, forsooth, indeed, in good sooth, verily.

zaprawiać *ipf.* **1.** (= *dodawać*) leaven; season, spice (*czymś* with sth); (*słodem*) malt; (*chmielem*) hop; **słowa zaprawione goryczą** *przen.* words tainted with bitterness. **2.** (= *wprawiać*) school, coach (*kogoś do czegoś* sb in sth); train (*kogoś do czegoś* sb for/in sth); **zaprawiać w rzemiośle** bring up in a craft. **3.** *zw. pf. pot.* (= *uderzyć*) hit, give (*sb*) a blow, whack, give (*sb*) a biff. **~ się** *ipf.* **1.** (= *wprawiać się*) train (*w czymś* in sth); accustom oneself, inure (*w czymś* to sth). **2.** *pot.* (= *upijać się*) hit the bottle, jazz up, tank up, booze up.

zaprawić (się) *pf.* *zob.* **zaprawiać (się).**

zaprawiony *a.* -eni **1.** (= *wprawiony*) seasoned; inured (*w czymś* to sth); experienced, skilled (*w czymś* in sth); practiced (*w czymś* at sth); **zapra-**

wiony w bojach (*o polityku, dziennikarzu*) hard-bitten, battle-scarred. **2.** *pot.* (= *pijany*) plastered, pie-eyed, jazzed up, tuned.

zaprawowy *a.* **1.** *sport* training, body-building, drilling. **2.** *chem.* (*o barwnikach*) mordant.

zaprażka *f. Gen.pl.* **-ek** soup thickener made of browned butter and flour.

zapreliminować *pf. zob.* **preliminować**.

zaprenumerować *pf. zob.* **prenumerować**.

zaprezentować *pf. zob.* **prezentować**. **~ się** *pf. zob.* **prezentować się**.

zaprogramować *pf. zob.* **programować**.

zaprojektować *pf. zob.* **projektować**.

zaproponować *pf. zob.* **proponować**.

zaprosić *pf.* **-szę -sisz** *zob.* **zapraszać**. **~ się** *pf. zob.* **zapraszać się**.

zaprosiny *pl. Gen.* **-n** *pot.* invitation, invite.

zaproszenie *n.* **1.** (= *prośba o przyjście*) invitation (*na coś* to sth); call (*na coś* for sth); (*np. do dyskusji*) encouragement; **na czyjeś zaproszenie** at sb's invitation; **bez zaproszenia** without invitation, uninvited, unbidden, unasked; **przyjąć/ nie przyjąć zaproszenia** accept/decline an invitation; **skorzystać z czyjegoś zaproszenia** take sb up on an invitation; **dostać zaproszenie** be invited; **wystosować zaproszenie do kogoś** extend an invitation to sb. **2.** (*kartka*) invitation.

zaprotegować *pf. zob.* **protegować**.

zaprotestować *pf. zob.* **protestować**.

zaprotokołować *pf. zob.* **protokołować**.

zaprowadzać *ipf.*, **zaprowadzić** *pf.* **1.** (= *prowadzić dokądś*) show (*kogoś dokądś* sb to sth); (*dzieci, wycieczkę*) land, guide; (*o drodze*) lead, take; **ta ulica zaprowadzi cię do centrum** this road will take you downtown; **kłótnia zaprowadziła ich do sądu** the quarrel landed them in court. **2.** (= *wprowadzać*) initiate, bring into existence, introduce; **zaprowadzić gdzieś porządek/ ład** set sth in order; **zaprowadzić modę** set the fashion. **3.** *pot.* (= *zakładać*) establish; (*zeszyt*) set up; (*światło*) install.

zaprószyć *pf.* dust, cover with dust; (*np. podłogę mąką*) scatter, spread; **zaprószyłem sobie oko** something got into my eye; **zaprószyć ogień** start a fire.

zapruć się *pf. pot.* (= *upić się*) get tipsy, booze up, soak up.

zapruty *a. pot.* (= *pijany*) pie-eyed, jazzed up, sauced, tuned up.

zapryskać *ipf.*, **zapryskiwać** *pf.* (*ubranie, szybę*) splash, spatter, spray.

zaprzaniec *mp* **-ńc-** *pl.* **-y** *lit.* recreant, renegade.

zaprząc *pf.* **-przęgę -przężesz -prząż** *l.* **-przeż, -przągł -przęgła -przęgli** *zob.* **zaprzęgać**.

zaprzątać *ipf.*, **zaprzątnąć** *pf.* **-ij** (= *absorbować*) preoccupy, occupy, engage, absorb; **zaprzątać sobie głowę kimś/czymś** trouble one's head about sb/sth; **zaprzątać czyjąś uwagę** absorb/take/occupy up sb's attention.

zaprzeczać *ipf.* **1.** (= *nie zgadzać się*) deny, refute; (*twierdzeniu, wiedzy*) disclaim. **2.** (= *nie*

uznawać) deny, reject, refuse; (*oskarżeniu*) repudiate; **nie da się zaprzeczyć, że...** there's no denying the fact that...; **trudno temu zaprzeczyć** it stands to reason; **zaprzeczyć czyimś zeznaniom** refute sb's testimony; **zaprzeczyć oskarżeniu** deny *l.* counter a charge; **kategorycznie zaprzeczyć oskarżeniu** meet a charge with a flat denial. **3.** (= *być w sprzeczności*) contradict, negate; **zaprzeczać faktom** fly in the face of facts.

zaprzeczenie *n.* **1.** (*wypowiedź, pismo zaprzeczające*) disaffirmation, denial; **zaprzeczenie oskarżeniu** denial of the charge. **2.** (= *negacja*) negation, contradiction; (*twierdzenia*) repudiation, rejection; **kategoryczne zaprzeczenie** flat denial; **jest zaprzeczeniem ojca** he is the opposite of his father.

zaprzeczony *a.* (*np. o twierdzeniu*) negated, rejected; **zdanie zaprzeczone** negative sentence.

zaprzeczyć *pf. zob.* **zaprzeczać**.

zaprzeć *pf.* **-prę -przesz, -przyj, -parł** *zob.* **zapierać**. **~ się** *pf. zob.* **zapierać się**.

zaprzedać *pf.*, **zaprzedawać** *ipf.* **-aję -ajesz, -awaj** *lit.* (*ojczyznę*) betray, sell; **zaprzedać duszę (diabłu)** sell one's soul (to the devil). **~ się** *pf.*, **zaprzedawać się** *ipf. lit.* sell one's soul, betray one's cause/ideals; (*wrogom*) sell oneself (*komuś* to sb).

zaprzepaszczać *ipf.*, **zaprzepaścić** *pf.* **-szczę -ścisz** (*talent, zdolności*) waste, ruin; (*majątek, pieniądze*) squander; (*okazję, szansę*) miss; (*wysiłek, pracę*) negate; **zaprzepaścić okazję** let it/ sth slip through one's fingers; **zaprzepaścić swoje szanse** compromise one's chances.

zaprzestać *pf.* **-anę -aniesz** *zob.* **zaprzestawać**.

zaprzestanie *n.* cessation (*czegoś* of sth); desistance (*czegoś* from sth); (*starań*) giving up (*czegoś* of sth); resigning (*czegoś* from sth); **zaprzestanie działań wojennych** cessation of hostilities.

zaprzestawać *ipf.* **-aję -ajesz, -awaj** *lit.* stop, cease, give up, quit, drop (*czegoś* doing sth); desist (*czegoś* from sth); **nie zaprzestawać czegoś** press on/forward/ahead with sth.

zaprzeszły *a.* pluperfect; **czas zaprzeszły** *gram.* pluperfect, past perfect.

zaprzęg *mi* (*konny*) team, span, yoke; **psi zaprzęg** dog-team; **w zaprzęgu** in the traces; **zaprzęg czterokonny** four-in-hand, coach-and-four; **sanie z psim zaprzęgiem** dog-sled; **wóz z zaprzęgiem** rig; **powozić zaprzęgiem** team; **jazda psim zaprzęgiem** mush.

zaprzęgać *ipf.* harness (*do czegoś* to sth); (*konia, wóz*) hitch up; (*zwierzę pociągowe*) yoke, gear up; **zaprzęgać kogoś do pracy** put sb at work, set *l.* get sb to work.

zaprzęgnąć *pf.* **-ij** = **zaprząc**.

zaprzęgowy *a.* **koń zaprzęgowy** drayhorse, dobbin, carriage horse, hackney; **wóz zaprzęgowy** wagon.

zaprzychodować *pf. handl.* enter in the books, book.

zaprzyjaźnić się *pf.* **-jaźnij** *l.* **jaźń** be/make friends, strike up a friendship, chum up (*z kimś* with sb); cotton up (*z kimś* to sb).

zaprzyjaźniony *a.* **-eni** befriended, friendly, familiar, chummy, clubby, thick (*z kimś* with sb).

zaprzysiąc *pf.* **-sięgnę -sięgniesz, -sięgnij, -siągł -sięgła -sięgli, zaprzysięgać** *ipf.* **1.** (= *złożyć przysięgę*) attest/promise under oath, swear. **2.** (= *odebrać przysięgę*) swear (sb) in (*kogoś na coś* sb to sth); administer an oath (*kogoś* to sb); **zaprzysięgać świadka** swear a witness. ~ **się** *pf.*, **zaprzysięgać się** *ipf.* swear (*że się coś zrobi/czegoś nie zrobi* to do sth/not to do sth); **zaprzysięgła się, że nie wyjdzie za mąż** she promised herself that she'd never get married.

zaprzysięgły *a.* sworn; (*o abstynencie, wegetarianinie, miłośniku czegoś*) confirmed; (*o zwolenniku lub wrogu jakiejś idei*) avowed, staunch, ardent, professed.

zaprzysięgnąć *pf.* **-sięgnę -sięgniesz, -sięgnij, -siągł -sięgła -sięgli** = **zaprzysiąc**. ~ **się** *pf.* = **zaprzysiąc się**.

zaprzysiężenie *n.* (*odebranie przysięgi*) swearing in, administration of an oath; (*przysięga*) oath, pledge, vow, attestation.

zaprzysiężony *a.* **-eni** (*o świadku, zeznaniu*) sworn; **być zaprzysiężonym** be under/upon/on oath; **zaprzysiężone zeznanie** sworn testimony; **zaprzysiężony biegły/świadek** sworn expert/witness.

zapstrzyć *pf.* **-yj** *pot.* (*o muchach*) spot, stain; **muchy zapstrzyły firankę** the net-curtain got fly-blown.

zapuchnąć *pf.* **-puchnij, -puchł** *l.* **-puchnął -puchła -puchli** swell, puff up; **oczy zapuchłe od płaczu** eyes swollen from weeping.

zapuchnięty *a.* (*o oczach, twarzy*) swollen, puffed-up.

zapudrować *pf.* (*twarz*) powder, dust/sprinkle with powder.

zapukać *pf.* knock, rap, tap (*do drzwi/okna* at/on the door/window).

zapusty *pl. Gen.* **-ów** Shrovetide, Shrove Tuesday.

zapuszczać *ipf.* **1.** (= *wprowadzać*) sink, thrust, plunge; (*sondę*) cast; (*krople*) put; **zapuszczać korzenie** *dosł.* root, strike roots; *przen.* take root, put down roots; **zapuszczać żurawia** *żart.* crane forward, steal a glance. **2.** *zw. pf.* (= *zaniedbywać*) (*mieszkanie, ogródek*) neglect; **zapuszczać włosy, brodę** grow hair/a beard. **3.** *pot.* (= *uruchamiać silnik*) kick-start, start up, crank up. **4.** (= *zasuwać*) (*żaluzje, zasłony*) let down, draw. ~ **się** *ipf.* venture, plunge (*dokąd* into sth); (*o krowie*) stray; **zapuszczać się w nieznane** enter the unknown; **zapuszczać się w rozmowę, dyskusję** plunge/drift into conversation/discussion.

zapuszczony *a.* neglected, tacky; (*o mieszkaniu, pokoju*) messy, trashed, muddled; (*o budynku, dzielnicy*) run-down, unsound; (*o wyglądzie, osobie*) down-at-heel, sluttish, seedy; (*o ogrodzie*) overgrown.

zapuścić *pf.* **-puszczę -puścisz** *zob.* **zapuszczać**. ~ **się** *pf. zob.* **zapuszczać się**.

zapychać *ipf.* **1.** (= *zatykać*) (*rurę, szparę*) jam, clog, block (*coś czymś* sth with sth); (*nos*) congest, stuff. **2.** (= *zajmować przestrzeń*) stuff (*sth*) full, fill, crowd, cram, stock. ~ **się** *ipf.* **1.** (= *zatykać się*) get choked/clogged/blocked (*czymś* with sth); (*o nosie*) bung up, stuff up. **2.** (*poczuć dławiący ucisk w przełyku*) choke. **3.** *pot.* (= *objadać się*) cram, binge, munch up, muck out.

zapylać *ipf.* **1.** (= *kurzyć*) dust; (*powietrze*) pollute, contaminate. **2.** *bot.* pollinate; **zapylać krzyżowo** cross-pollinate; **naturalnie zapylony** open-pollinated.

zapylenie *n.* **1.** *bot.* pollination; **zapylenie krzyżowe** cross-pollination. **2.** (*zanieczyszczenie pyłami*) dustiness; (*powietrza*) pollution.

zapylić *pf. zob.* **zapylać**.

zapytać *pf. zob.* **zapytywać**. ~ **się** *pf. zob.* **zapytywać się**.

zapytanie *n.* inquiry, query, question; *komp.* interrogation; **znak zapytania** question/interrogation mark; **być pod znakiem zapytania** (*o losach, przyszłości*) be on a knife-edge, be called in question; **stawiać pod znakiem zapytania** cast doubt(s) on sth, put sth in jeopardy, call sth in question; (*wnioski, argumenty*) vitiate; **coś stoi pod znakiem zapytania** a question mark hangs over sth.

zapytywać *ipf.* ask (*kogoś o coś* sb about sth) (*o kogoś* after/for sb); inquire (*o kogoś* after sb); question, query; **zapytać o godzinę/drogę** inquire the time/way; **zapytać o opinię** ask sb's opinion; **zapytać o pozwolenie** ask permission; **dziękuję, że zapytałeś** thanks for asking; **spróbować zapytać kogoś** try sb. ~ **się** *ipf.* ask, inquire (*o coś/kogoś* after/for sb); **zapytać się o cenę** ask for the price.

zapyziały *a. pot.* sluggish, trashed, seedy; **zapyziała dziura** shithole, mudhole; **w zapyziałej dziurze** out in the sticks.

zarabiać *ipf.* **1.** (= *pracować zarobkowo*) earn; **zarabiać na życie** earn one's living/daily bread, make a living, win one's bread (*robiąc coś* doing sth); **zarabiać piórem** earn one's living by writing; **zarabiać na kogoś** maintain sb; **zarabiać na utrzymanie rodziny** bring home the bacon; **zarabiać na chleb** earn a crust. **2.** (= *uzyskiwać dochody*) earn, gain, make money; (*o filmie, książce*) be a moneymaker; **uczciwie zarabiać na życie** earn an honest living, turn *l.* make an honest penny; **zarabiać w nieuczciwy sposób** live by *l.* on one's wits; **zarobić kupę forsy** make a packet, make a fast *l.* quick *l.* an easy buck; **zarobić na czysto** take home, clear, make a clear profit of sth; **zarabiać średnio 30 tys. dolarów rocznie** average $30,000 a year; **ile tam zarabiasz?** how much are you making there?; **zarobić na czymś** make a profit of sth, make money on sth; **dobrze zarabiać** make good money; **zarabiać na siebie** (*o narzędziu pracy*) earn one's keep; **osoba mało/średnio/dużo zarabiająca** low/average/high earner. **3.** (= *zagniatać ciasto*) knead. **4.** *pot.* (= *dostawać*) (*złe stopnie*) get, earn. **5.** *pot.* (= *łapać uszkodzenia w dzianiniu*) knit up, darn, mend.

zarachować *pf. zob.* **zarachowywać**.

zarachowanie *n. handl.* calculation; **druk ścisłego zarachowania** calculation form.

zarachowywać *ipf. handl.* calculate, enter in the books.

zaradczy *a.* remedial; **środek zaradczy** countermeasure, remedy; **podejmować kroki/działania zaradcze** take precautionary/remedial measures.

zaradność *f.* resource, ingenuity, initiative, inventiveness; **cenił sobie zaradność żony** he appreciated his wife's resourcefulness.

zaradny *a.* resourceful, ingenious, inventive, creative.

zaradzić *pf. lit.* (*problemowi*) remedy, solve, find a way out; (*złu, brakom*) redress; (*niebezpieczeństwu*) obviate; **zaradzić brakowi** make up a deficiency; **czy można temu zaradzić?** can this be helped?; **nie mogę temu zaradzić** there's nothing I can do about it.

zaranie *n. lit.* (*świata, życia*) dawn, daybreak, morning; **od zarania dziejów** since the dawn of time.

zarastać *ipf.* **1.** (*o roślinach*) (= *rozprzestrzeniać się*) overgrow, cover with weeds. **2.** (= *pokrywać się*) (*roślinami, włosami*) grow, get overgrown (*czymś* with sth). **3.** (= *zabliźniać się*) skin over, close, cicatrize.

zaraz *adv.* **1.** (= *niezwłocznie*) directly, promptly, right now, straightaway; **od zaraz** *pot.* right away; **zaraz wracam** I won't be long *l.* a minute, I'll be right back; **zaraz będę gotowy** I won't be a minute *l.* jiffy. **2.** (= *tuż po, wkrótce*) straight after, right after; (*nastąpić, wydarzyć się, zwł. o nieszczęściu*) in the wake of sth; **zaraz po tym, jak...** immediately after..., once, directly; **zaraz po pracy** straight after work; **zaraz potem** the next minute; **zaraz następnego dnia** the very next day. **3.** *pot.* (= *niedaleko*) just; **zaraz za rogiem** just round the corner. – *int.* **zaraz, zaraz!** (= *nie tak prędko*) wait a second *l.* minute *l.* moment!; (= *niech się zastanowię*) let me think *l.* see...

zaraza *f.* **1.** (*epidemia*) plague; (*zwł. roślinna, zwierzęca*) blast, pest, pestilence, murrain; **zaraza bydlęca** rinderpest; **zaraza ziemniaczana** potato blight; **zaraza ogniowa** (*choroba bakteryjna jabłoni i grusz*) fireblight; **dotykać zarazą** plague; **powodujący zarazę** pestiferous; **siedlisko zarazy** pesthole; **strzec się jak zarazy** *pot.* avoid sb/sth like the plague; (*plaga społeczna*) epidemic. **2.** *pot.* (*wyzwisko*) plague; **być jak zaraza** turn up like a bad penny.

zarazek *mi* **-zk-** *Gen.* **-a** germ, contagium, bug; **rozsiewać zarazki** (*o chorym*) be infectious/contagious.

zarazem *adv.* just *l.* all the same, at the same time, as well; **aktor i zarazem reżyser** actor and director rolled into one.

zarazić *pf.* **-ażę -azisz** *zob.* **zarażać.** ~ **się** *pf. zob.* **zarażać się.**

zaraźliwie *adv.* **1.** (= *zakaźnie*) contagiously, infectiously. **2.** (= *w sposób udzielający się innym*) (*np. śmiać się*) infectiously.

zaraźliwy *a.* **1.** (= *zakaźny*) infectious, communicable, pestilent; **choroba zaraźliwa** contagion. **2.** (= *udzielający się innym*) catching, taking; (*o śmiechu, entuzjazmie, akcencie*) contagious, infectious.

zarażać *ipf.* **1.** (= *wywoływać chorobę zakaźną*) infect (*czymś* with sth); pass on, give, spread (*kogoś czymś* sth to sb); **zaraziła mnie odrą** she gave me her measles. **2.** (= *wywoływać taki sam stan psychiczny*) (*zapałem*) infect; (*kogoś czymś*) sb with sth; imbue (*kogoś czymś* sb with sth); stimulate; **zarażać kogoś entuzjazmem do czegoś** enthuse sb with sth. ~ **się** *ipf.* **1.** (= *nabawiać się choroby zakaźnej*) catch, get (*czymś od kogoś* sth from/off sb); become infected (*czymś* with sth); **zaraziłem się od niej odrą** she gave me her measles. **2.** (= *przyjmować czyjś nastrój*) be bitten, be influenced, be affected (*czymś* by sth); **zarazić się bakcylem żeglarstwa** be bitten by the sailing bug, catch *l.* get the sailing bug.

zarąbać *pf.* **-bię -biesz** hack (to pieces), chop; **zarąbać na śmierć** hack to death.

zardzewiały *a.* rust-eaten, rust-covered, rusty.

zardzewieć *pf. zob.* **rdzewieć.**

zareagować *pf. zob.* **reagować.**

zarechotać *pf.* **-oczę -oczesz** *l.* **-ocę -ocesz, -ocz** (*o żabie*) croak; (*o człowieku*) chortle, chuckle, gurgle.

zarejestrować *pf. zob.* **rejestrować.** ~ **się** *pf. zob.* **rejestrować się.**

zarejestrowany *a.* registered; (*o broni*) licensed; (*o towarzystwie*) incorporated; **zarejestrowany znak handlowy** registered trademark; **być zarejestrowanym jako bezrobotny** be registered as unemployed.

zareklamować *pf. zob.* **reklamować.**

zarekomendować *a. zob.* **rekomendować.**

zarekwirować *pf. zob.* **rekwirować.**

zarepetować *pf. zob.* **repetować.**

zarezerwować *pf. zob.* **rezerwować.**

zarezerwowany *a.* reserved (*dla kogoś / na coś* for sb/sth); (*o pokoju, stoliku*) booked; (*o miejscu*) taken; **cały zarezerwowany** (*o hotelu*) booked solid.

zaręczać *ipf.* **1.** (= *gwarantować*) guarantee, warrant, ensure, secure; **zaręczam ci, że niewiele osób o tym wie** not many people know that, I warrant it; **zaręczam ci** (*ostrzegam*) I promise *l.* assure you; **zaręczyć bezpieczeństwo** ensure safety. **2.** (= *zapewniać usilnie*) affirm that..., assure; **zaręczał, że się nie spóźni** he assured that he'd be on time; **zaręczać o swojej lojalności** affirm one's loyalty. **3.** *zw. pf.* (= *doprowadzać do zaręczyn*) betroth, handfast. ~ **się** *ipf.* get engaged *l.* espoused; betroth *l.* get betrothed (*z kimś* to sb).

zaręczyć (się) *pf. zob.* **zaręczać (się).**

zaręczynowy *a.* engagement; **pierścionek zaręczynowy** engagement ring.

zaręczyny *pl. Gen.* **-n** engagement, betrothal, handfasting; **zerwać zaręczyny** break off one's engagement.

zarękawek *mi* **-wk-** *Gen.* **-a** (*ochraniacz na rękaw*) oversleeve.

zarobaczony *a.* verminous, infested.

zarobek *mi* **-bk-** **1.** (= *wynagrodzenie*) makings, screw, earnings, wages; **miesięczny zaro-**

bek salary. **2.** (= *praca*) work, means of livelihood, job; **szukać zarobku** look for a job; **dla zarobku** for a living. **3.** (= *zysk*) gain, profit; **łatwy zarobek** gravy; **zarobek na czarno** black money; **nieuczciwe zarobki** ill-gotten gains.

zarobić *pf.* **-rób 1.** *zob.* **zarabiać. 2.** *pot.* (= *dostać cios*) score a blow.

zarobkować *ipf. przest.* earn a living, win one's bread; **od młodych lat musiał zarobkować** he had to earn his living when he was a young boy.

zarobkowo *adv.* for money; **pracujący zarobkowo** gainfully employed; **traktować sztukę zarobkowo** treat art as a source of income.

zarobkowy *a.* (*o pracy*) paid, gainful; **dla celów zarobkowych** for economic/financial purposes; **pracownik zarobkowy** wage earner; **możliwości zarobkowe** earning capacity; **praca zarobkowa** gainful employment/work.

zarodek *mi* **-dk-** *Gen.* **-a 1.** *biol.* embryo, fetus, germ; *med.* conceptus; **komórka zarodka** germ cell; **w zarodku** *przen.* in the bud; **zdusić w zarodku** (*np. inicjatywę*) throttle sth, nip *l.* crush sth in the bud; **bohater w zarodku** a hero in the making; **zarodek niezgody** the seeds of dissent. **2.** *bot.* bud, plumule, embryonic plant. **3. zarodek krystalizacji** *chem.* crystal nucleus.

zarodkowy *a.* **1.** *biol.* embryonic, germinal; **plazma zarodkowa** plasm; **płód w stadium zarodkowym** embryonic fetus; **ząb zarodkowy** (*u płazów, gadów, ptaków*) egg tooth. **2.** *bot.* embryonic.

zarodnia *f. Gen.pl.* **-i** *bot.* spore case, sporangium; (*u paproci i mchów*) fructification; **komora zarodni** loculus.

zarodnik *mi Gen.* **-a** *bot.* gemma, spore, sporule; **zarodnik podstawkowy** basidiospore; **wytwarzać zarodniki** spore.

zarodnikowy *a. bot.* cryptogamous, cryptogamic.

zarodowy *a. roln.* brood, pedigree; **bydło zarodowe** cattle for breeding; **kwoka/klacz zarodowa** brood hen/mare.

zaroić się *pf.* **-roi -roił 1.** (= *zacząć się gromadzić*) swarm, teem, crowd; **na ulicy zaroił się tłum ludzi** the street swarmed with people. **2.** (= *wypełnić się*) swarm, be crowded *l.* thronged *l.* teeming *l.* bristling (*od kogoś / czegoś* with sb/sth); **hotel zaroił się od policjantów** the hotel was teeming with policemen.

zaropieć *pf.* (*o ranie*) suppurate, fester, matter; **zaropiałe oczy** festered eyes.

zarosnąć *pf.* **-rośnie -rósł -rosła -rośli** *zob.* **zarastać.**

zarost *mi* beard, facial hair, growth; **niegolony zarost** unshaven growth; **lekki/kilkudniowy zarost** stubble; **modny zarost** designer stubble; **popołudniowy zarost** five o'clock shadow; **ze zgolonym zarostem** barefaced, smooth-chinned.

zarośla *pl. Gen.* **-i** bush, overgrowth, scrub, brushwood; **zarośla paproci** bracken; **pokryty zaroślami** scrubby.

zarośnięty *a.* (*o ogrodzie*) overgrown (*czymś* with sth); bushy; (*o stawie*) weedy; (*o człowieku*) shaggy, unshaven; **zarośnięty brudem** filthy, muddy, slimy; **zarośnięty palmami** palmy.

zarozumiale *adv.* (*spoglądać, zachowywać się*) arrogantly, presumptuously, conceitedly, priggishly.

zarozumialec *mp* **-lc-** *pl.* **-y** bighead, prig, jackanapes, gascon.

zarozumialstwo *n.* bigheadedness, arrogance, cocksureness.

zarozumiałość *f.* conceit, self-importance, self-opinion, superciliousness.

zarozumiały *a.* **1.** (= *mający wysokie mniemanie o sobie*) (*o człowieku*) conceited, chesty, above oneself, cocky, self-opinionated, self-important, too big for one's breeches. **2.** (*świadczący o zarozumialstwie*) (*o minie, zachowaniu*) conceited, arrogant, haughty.

zarówno *conj.* **zarówno..., jak...** alike; **zarówno dziewczęta, jak i chłopcy** girls and boys alike, girls as well as boys, both girls and boys.

zaróżowić się *pf.* **-ij** go rosy/red, flush, color up, crimson; **jej policzki zaróżowiły się od zimna** her cheeks got red from cold; **zaróżowić się z zakłopotania** flush/blush in embarrassment.

zaróżowienie *n.* (*różowa plama*) pink spot; (*na policzkach*) blush.

zaróżowiony *a.* **-eni** (*o cerze, policzkach*) rosy, red, pinkish, glowing.

zarumienić *pf. zob.* **rumienić. ~ się** *pf. zob.* **rumienić się.**

zarumienienie *n.* red spot, redness, floridity; **zarumienienie skóry wkrótce zeszło** the redness soon disappeared from the skin; (*policzków*) blush.

zarumieniony *a.* **-eni** (*o policzkach, twarzy*) florid, flushed, red, glowing; (*o cieście*) browned.

zarwać *pf.* **-rwę -rwiesz, -rwij** *zob.* **zarywać.**

zarybiać *ipf.*, **zarybić** *pf.* stock (with fry); **zarybiać rzekę, staw pstrągiem** stock a river/pond with trout.

zarybienie *n.* fry-stocking.

zaryczeć *pf.* **-ę -ysz 1.** (*o zwierzętach*) (= *wydać ryk*) roar out, howl. **2.** (= *zahuczeć*) (*o silniku*) whir, purr. **3.** (= *wrzasnąć*) yell, roar, shriek.

zaryć *pf.* **-ryję -ryjesz, -ryj** (*kopytami, o koniu*) balk (*przed czymś* at sth); burrow; (*o samochodzie*) plow, *Br.* plough, smash (*w coś* into sth); **zaryć głową w ziemię** hit one's head on the ground, hit ground head first. **~ się** *pf.* burrow, plow (*w coś* into sth); **wóz zarył się w błocie** the carriage got stuck in the mud.

zaryglować *ipf.*, **zaryglowywać** *pf.* (*drzwi, wyjście*) bar, bolt, latch.

zarykiwać się *ipf. pot.* cry one's eyes out, blubber; **zarykiwać się ze śmiechu** split one's sides with laughter, roar/shake with laughter.

zarys *mi* **1.** (= *kontur*) (*szczytów, budynku*) line, silhouette, contour; (*twarzy*) profile. **2.** (= *plan, szkic*) outline, (rough) draft, sketch, layout; (*umowy, porozumienia, planu*) framework; **w ogólnych zarysach** in broad *l.* rough outline, in outline *l.* rough; **omówić coś w ogólnym zarysie** give an overview of sth; **przedstawić w zary-**

sie outline, adumbrate, paint sth with a broad brush; **zarys sytuacji** background. **3.** (= *zbiór podstawowych wiadomości*) outline, synopsis; **historia Polski w zarysie** an outline history of Poland.

zarysować (się) *pf. zob.* **zarysowywać (się).**

zarysowywać *ipf.* **1.** (= *pokryć rysunkami*) cover with drawings, draw all over. **2.** (= *zrobić rysę*) scratch, scrape, graze. **3.** (= *przedstawić ogólnie*) draw out, outline, sketch, adumbrate. **~ się** *ipf.* **1.** (= *pokryć się rysami*) (*o podłodze, szybie, filiżance*) break, crack, get scratched. **2.** (= *stać się widocznym*) (*o kształcie, konturze, sylwetce*) emerge, loom, be outlined; **czyjś kształt zarysował się w ciemności** sb's figure loomed out in the darkness. **3.** (= *uwydatnić się*) stand out; **wyraźnie zarysowany** clear-cut; (*o twarzy*) rugged; (*o nosie*) prominent; (*o sylwetce, konturach, śladach*) sharply/clearly defined (*na tle czegoś* against sth).

zarywać *ipf.* **-am -asz 1.** (= *powodować załamanie, obsunięcie*) (*podłogę, łóżko*) break. **2.** (= *zużywać czas kosztem czegoś*) **zarywać noce** sit up all night, burn the midnight oil, pull an all-nighter; **zarywać egzamin** bust, strike out, flag. **3. zarywać laski** *pot.* (= *podrywać dziewczyny*) pull the birds, score. **~ się** *ipf.* break down, collapse, give in; **zarywać się ze śmiechu** split one's sides with laughter, choke with laughter.

zaryzykować *pf. zob.* **ryzykować.**

zarząd *mi* **1.** (*jednostka organizacyjna*) board, governing body; (*towarzystwa*) directory; (*instytucji, organizacji*) trustee; *uniw.* regent; **zarząd spółki** management of a company, company management; **zarząd majątkiem** land agency; **zarząd masy upadłościowej** receivership; **zarząd powierniczy** trusteeship, trust; **zarząd miejski** municipal government. **2.** (*zespół ludzi*) board (of directors); **członek zarządu** (executive) officer, governor, director; **prezes zarządu** chief executive officer. **3.** (= *zarządzanie*) management, administration, stewardship; **zarząd komisaryczny** executive committee board; **zarząd państwowy** state control; **pod czyimś zarządem** in the charge of sb, under the stewardship of sb; **sprawować zarząd nad czymś** be in charge of sth, have control over sth.

zarządca *mp* (*instytucji*) governor, administrator, manager; (*majątku*) trustee; (*posiadłości, domu, majątku*) steward; *prawn.* administrator; **zarządca majątku** land agent; **zarządca posiłkowy** administrator ancillary; **zarządca masy upadłościowej** *ekon.* receiver, administrator of a bankrupt's estate.

zarządzać *ipf.* **1.** (= *nakazywać*) (*głosowanie, zbiórkę*) ordain, arrange, order. **2.** (= *kierować*) administer; (*instytucją*) govern; (*firmą*) run; (*majątkiem*) steward; **przedsiębiorstwem, państwem** manage; **zarządzający firmą** executive secretary.

zarządzanie *n.* management, administration, conduct (*czymś* of sth); (*firmą*) running; (*majątkiem*) stewardship; **zarządzanie bazą danych** database management; **zarządzanie finansami**

finance management; **zarządzanie zasobami naturalnymi** conservation; **złe/niewłaściwe zarządzanie** mismanagement; **zarządzanie i administracja** *uniw.* business studies; **konsultant/ka ds. zarządzania** management consultant; **licencjat z zarządzania** Bachelor of Business Administration; **mgr zarządzania** Master of Business Administration; **szczebel zarządzania** echelon.

zarządzenie *n.* order, ordinance, disposition, ruling, prescription; *admin.* decree; **wydać zarządzenie** issue a disposition/an order; **według zarządzenia** *prawn.* by precept; **odgórne zarządzenie** directive; **lokalne zarządzenie** by-law.

zarządzić *pf. zob.* **zarządzać.**

zarzec się *pf.* **-rzeknę -rzekniesz, -rzeknij, -rzekł, zarzekać się** *ipf.* (*palenia, picia wódki*) renounce, give up; **zarzekł się, że nigdy tam nie pójdzie** he promised himself never to go there.

zarzewie *n. Gen.pl.* **-i 1.** *lit.* (= *żar*) firebrand, embers, glow. **2.** *lit.* (= *zaczątek*) (*konfliktu, wojny*) source, seeds, germs.

zarzucać *ipf.*, **zarzucić** *pf.* **1.** (= *rzucając, zaczepiać, przewieszać*) (*linę, lasso*) dab, noose (*na coś* around sth); (*plecak, koc, sznur*) throw; (*wędkę, sieć*) cast; (*płaszcz*) hang; **zarzucać komuś ręce na szyję** fling one's arms round sb's neck. **2.** (= *wkładać na siebie w pośpiechu*) throw, fling; **zarzucać coś na ramiona** throw sth about one's shoulders. **3.** (= *rzucając, pokrywać*) scatter, strew; (*obowiązkami*) swamp (*kogoś czymś* sb with sth); (*towarem*) saturate; **zarzucać kogoś pytaniami** bombard sb with questions, fire/shower questions at sb; **zarzucać rynek towarami** flood/saturate the market with goods. **4.** (= *wytykać*) (*kłamstwo, zdradę*) accuse (*coś komuś* sb of sth); taunt, reproach (*coś komuś* sb with sth); lay sth at sb's door; **trudno komuś/czemuś cokolwiek zarzucić** sb/sth is hard *l.* difficult to fault; **nie móc nic sobie zarzucić** walk tall; **nie mogę mu nic zarzucić** I have no fault to find with him. **5.** (= *porzucać*) drop, call a halt (*coś to sth*); lay aside; (*naukę, palenie, obyczaj*) give up; (*plan, przekonania, zwyczaj*) relinquish; (*pomysł, plan*) ditch, throw/toss/chuck overboard. **6.** (*o pojeździe*) (= *wpadać w boczny poślizg*) skid, side-slip.

zarzut *mi* **1.** *prawn.* accusation, charge, demurrer; (*nie poparty dowodami*) allegation; **bez zarzutu** flawless, faultless, irreproachable, beyond/above reproach; **pod zarzutem morderstwa/oszustwa** on suspicion of murder/fraud; **stanąć przed sądem pod zarzutem czegoś** be charged with sth, be accused of sth; **przedstawić komuś zarzut popełnienia przestępstwa** charge sb with an offence, press/prefer charges against sb; **aresztować kogoś pod zarzutem czegoś** arrest sb on a charge of sth; **zarzut morderstwa** murder rap; **uwolnić kogoś od zarzutu czegoś** vindicate, clear sb's name; **odpierać zarzuty** rejoin; **odparcie zarzutu** rejoinder; **odpowiadać na zarzuty** answer charges. **2.** (= *pretensja, obiekcja*) blame, reproof, complaint, objection, rap; **błahy zarzut** cavil; **fałszywy zarzut** bum rap; **ostry zarzut** brickbat; **zarzut obciążający** damning indictment; **wysuwać błahe zarzuty** cavil (*przeciwko komuś/czemuś* at sb/sth); **robić komuś zarzuty** blame sb for sth, find fault with sb; **postawić komuś zarzut** bring/lay/make an accusation against sb, raise objections to sb.

zarzygać *pf. pot.* puke (all over), chuck up, throw up; **zarzygał sobie buty** he chucked all over his shoes.

zarzynać *ipf.* **1.** (= *zabijać ostrym narzędziem*) butcher, stick, cut throat; **zarzynać zwierzę** slaughter an animal. **2.** *pot.* (= *niszczyć*) (*gospodarkę*) bring to ruin, ruin; (*samochód*) run *l.* drive sth into the ground. **~ się** *ipf.* **1.** (= *kaleczyć się*) (*żyletką, szkłem*) cut; **zarżnąć się w palec** cut one's finger. **2.** *pot.* (= *doprowadzać się do stanu wyczerpania*) push oneself; **zarzynać się pracą** work one's butt/nuts off, break one's tail off; **zarzynać się (finansowo)** go broke/bankrupt, cut one's throat financially.

zarzynany *a.* slaughtered; **kwiczeć jak zarzynane prosię** *pot.* make the welkin ring, cry blue murder.

zarżeć *pf.* **-rżę -rżysz, -rżyj 1.** (*o koniu*) (= *wydać rżenie*) neigh, whinny. **2.** *pot.* (*o człowieku*) (= *zaśmiać się nieprzyjemnie*) guffaw, chortle, gurgle.

zarżnąć *pf.* **-ij** *zob.* **zarzynać**. **~ się** *pf. zob.* **zarzynać się**.

zasada *f.* **1.** (= *reguła*) rule, principle, tenet, precept; **na jakiej zasadzie?** by what right?; **na równych zasadach** on equal terms; **zgodnie z zasadą, że...** on the principle that...; **praktyczna zasada** rule of thumb; **pierwsza/druga/trzecia zasada dynamiki** first/second/third law of motion; **zasada nieoznaczoności (Heisenberga)** indeterminacy principle; **zasada przyjemności** *psych.* (*u Freuda*) pleasure principle; **zasada względności** principle of relativity; **zasada zachowania energii** principle of conservation of energy; **zasady prawdopodobieństwa** laws of average; **zasada przedawnienia** *prawn.* statute of limitations. **2.** (= *norma*) law, rule; **w zasadzie** in principle; **człowiek bez zasad** unprincipled; **człowiek z zasadami** a man *l.* woman of principle; **o wzniosłych zasadach** high-minded, high-principled; **być pozbawionym zasad** have no backbone/principles; **być niezgodnym z zasadami** be against principles, unprincipled; **grać zgodnie z zasadami** play by rules; **kłócić się z zasadami** go against the grain; **dla zasady** on principle, as a matter of principle; **łamać zasady** break the rules; **naginać zasady** bend *l.* stretch the rules, stretch a point; **mieć swoje zasady** be set in one's habits *l.* ways; **stosować się do zasad** follow *l.* obey *l.* observe the rules; **zasady przyzwoitości** the decencies, the properties; **z zasady** (= *zgodnie z przekonaniami*) in principle; (= *zazwyczaj*) as a rule. **3.** *chem.* alkali, base; **przechodzić w zasadę** alkalify.

zasadniczo *adv.* **1.** (= *całkowicie*) fundamentally, substantially, in substance/principle. **2.** (= *na ogół*) as a rule, basically, essentially.

zasadniczy *a.* **1.** (= *podstawowy*) (*o różnicach, argumentach, cechach*) basic, primary, essen-

tial, fundamental, vital (*dla czegoś* to sth); **zasadnicza część czegoś** the body of sth; **zasadnicza przyczyna czegoś** the underlying/root cause of sth; **warunek zasadniczy** prerequisite (*czegoś* for *l.* to *l.* of sth); **postawa zasadnicza** *wojsk.* position of attention; **ustawa zasadnicza** *prawn.* constitution; **zasadnicza służba wojskowa** *wojsk.* mandatory military service; **zasadnicza kwestia** vital point; **w kwestiach zasadniczych** in substance; **odgrywać zasadniczą rolę** play a vital part/role; **barwy zasadnicze** primary colors; **mieć zasadnicze znaczenie** be crucially important; **wynagrodzenie zasadnicze** basic/primary salary. **2.** (= *pryncypialny*) principled.

zasadnie *adv. lit.* legitimately, justifiably, soundly.

zasadność *f. lit.* justness; (*argumentu, krytyki, decyzji*) validity, plausibility; (*roszczenia*) legitimacy; (*zażalenia*) justice; **potwierdzać zasadność** validate.

zasadny *a. lit.* legitimate, just; (*o argumencie, krytyce*) valid, sound; (*o postępowaniu*) justifiable; **logicznie zasadny** self-justifying.

zasadowość *f. chem.* alkalescence, alkalinity, basicity.

zasadowy *a. chem.* alkaline, alkalescent, basic; **skały zasadowe** alkaline rocks.

zasadzać *ipf.* **1.** *lit.* (= *opierać, brać za podstawę*) base, ground (*na czymś* on/upon sth); (*teorię*) found (*na czymś* on/upon sth). **2.** *przest.* (= *sadzać za stołem*) seat sb somewhere. **~ się** *ipf.* **1.** *lit.* (= *opierać się*) (*o teorii*) be founded, be grounded (*na czymś* on sth); (*o rozumowaniu*) repose on sth (*na czymś* on/upon sth). **2.** (= *zaczaić się*) lie in ambush *l.* wait, lay a trap (*na kogoś/coś* for sth); waylay.

zasadzić *pf. zob.* **sadzić, zasadzać**.

zasadzka *f.* Gen.pl. **-ek** trap, ambush, setup, booby trap; (*zwł. policyjna*) stake-out; **wpaść w zasadzkę** fall into a trap; **zaatakować z zasadzki** ambush; **zasadzki losu** the toils of fortune.

zasalutować *pf. zob.* **salutować**.

zasapać *pf.* **-pię -piesz** (*o lokomotywie*) puff; (*o chorym człowieku*) breathe heavily. **~ się** *pf.* pant, lose one's breath, huff and puff.

zasapany *a.* out of breath, puffing, puffy, breathless.

zasądzać *ipf.*, **zasądzić** *pf.* **-dzę -dzisz 1.** (= *przyznawać*) adjudge, grant, concede (*coś na rzecz kogoś* sth to sb); (*odszkodowanie*) award. **2.** (= *skazywać*) sentence (*na coś* to sth); **zasądzać na śmierć** sentence to death.

zaschnąć *pf.* **-schnij, -schnął** *l.* **-sechł -schła -schli** *zob.* **zasychać**.

zaschnięty *a.* (*o kwiecie, liściu*) withered; (*o błocie*) dry, dried up.

zaserwować *pf. zob.* **serwować**.

zasępiać *ipf.* deject, depress, cast down; **ta wiadomość zasępiła go** the news made him sad/depressed him. **~ się** *ipf.* gloom, become gloomy/dejected/despondent, get depressed, cloud up.

zasępić (się) *pf. zob.* **zasępiać (się)**.

zasępiony *a.* **-eni** morose.

zasiać *pf.* **-sieję -siejesz -siali** *l.* **-sieli** *zob.* **zasie-**

wać; **cicho jak makiem zasiał** you could hear a pin drop.

zasiadać *ipf.*, **zasiąść** *pf.* **-siądę -siądziesz, -siądź, -siadł -siedli 1.** (= *sadowić się*) sit down; **zasiąść na ławie oskarżonych** *prawn.* be in dock; **zasiadać w ławie przysięgłych** *prawn.* serve on a jury; **zasiąść na tronie** be on/take the throne; **zasiadać w komisji** sit on a committee. **2.** (= *przystępować*) settle (down) (*do czegoś* to sth).

zasiec *pf.* **-siekę -sieczesz -siekł** slash to pieces.

zasiedlać *ipf.*, **zasiedlić** *pf.* (= *zaludniać*) people, settle, populate.

zasiedzenie *n.* *prawn.* prescription; **nabyć przez zasiedzenie** acquire by prescription.

zasiedziały *a.* resident; **zasiedziały lokator** sitting tenant.

zasiedzieć się *pf.* **-dzę -dzisz 1.** (= *długo zabawić*) stay too long, wear out one's welcome. **2.** (= *przebywać gdzieś stale*) linger, tarry. **3.** (= *poświęcać dużo czasu czemuś*) linger over sth.

zasiekać *pf.* = zasiec.

zasieki *pl.* *Gen.* **-ów** *wojsk.* wire entanglement; *hist.* (*z gałęzi*) abatis.

zasiew *mi* **1.** (= *siew*) seed, sowing. **2.** (= *łan roślin*) crops.

zasiewać *ipf.* **1.** (= *siać*) sow. **2.** (= *zajmować pod siew*) put a field under corn. **3.** (= *wywoływać*) spark off, trigger.

zasięg *mi* range, coverage, extent, reach; **zasięg samolotu** *lotn.* range; **zasięg nadajnika** broadcast coverage; **bliskiego, dalekiego zasięgu** *wojsk.* short/long-range; **o krótkim zasięgu** (*o broni*) close-range; **o szerokim zasięgu** (*o częstotliwości*) broadband; **pocisk lotniczy dalekiego zasięgu** *wojsk.* standoff missile; **w zasięgu ręki** within arm's reach; **w zasięgu wzroku** within eyeshot; **w zasięgu** within reach; **w zasięgu/poza zasięgiem strzału/głosu** within/out of gunshot/hail; **znajdować się poza zasięgiem** be beyond reach.

zasięgać *ipf.*, **zasięgnąć** *pf.* **-ij** derive, get, obtain; (*czyjejś rady*) consult sb, seek sb's advice; **zasięgnąć języka** obtain information, reconnoiter.

zasilacz *mi Gen.* **-a** *el.* feed, feeder, power supply unit.

zasilać *ipf.* **1.** feed, supply, replenish; (*glebę*) enrich. **2.** *techn.* (= *zaopatrywać*) feed; (*w energię, wodę*) supply.

zasilający *a.* *techn.* (*o kablu, pompie*) supply, feeding.

zasilanie *n.* *techn.* power, feed, supply; **zasilanie awaryjne** emergency power supply; **włączać, wyłączać zasilanie** turn the power on/off.

zasilić *pf. zob.* zasilać.

zasiłek *mi* **-łk-** (*świadczenie*) benefit, allowance; **zasiłek chorobowy** sick benefit; **zasiłek dla bezrobotnych** unemployment compensation; **zasiłek rodzinny** baby bonus, child allowance/benefit; **być na zasiłku** *pot.* be on the dole, be on welfare.

zaskakiwać *ipf.* **1.** (= *atakować nieoczekiwanie*) surprise, make a surprise attack. **2.** (= *na-*

stępować nieoczekiwanie) amaze, baffle; **zaskoczyła nas ulewa** we were caught in the rain. **3.** (= *zadziwiać*) take sb aback, surprise, take sb by surprise. **4.** *zw. pf.* (*o mechanizmach*) (= *zacząć działać*) snap, click; **silnik zaskoczył** the engine cranked.

zaskakująco *adv.* amazingly, surprisingly.

zaskakujący *a.* amazing, baffling, surprising.

zaskamlać *pf.* **-lam** *l.* **-lę -lasz** *l.* **-lesz, -laj** *l.* **-l** whine.

zaskarbiać *ipf.*, **zaskarbić** *pf.* **zaskarbiać sobie czyjeś względy** *lit.* find *l.* gain *l.* win favor with sb; **zaskarbić sobie serca widzów** steal the show/scene/limelight.

zaskarżać *ipf.*, **zaskarżyć** *pf.* implead, prosecute, sue (*kogoś za coś* sb for sth); **zaskarżyć wyrok** appeal against a sentence.

zasklepiać *ipf.* coffin. **~ się** *ipf.* **1.** (= *pokrywać się skorupą*) encrust; (*o ranie*) skin over. **2.** (*o człowieku*) (= *zamykać się w sobie*) seclude o.s., retire into one's shell.

zasklepić (się) *pf. zob.* **zasklepiać (się)**.

zaskoczenie *n.* amazement, bafflement, surprise; **ku mojemu zaskoczeniu** to my amazement; **działanie przez zaskoczenie** shock tactics; **zdobyć coś przez zaskoczenie** *wojsk.* take sth by surprise; **z zaskoczenia** (*o ataku*) hit-and-run.

zaskoczony *a.* **-eni** taken aback, baffled, startled, surprised.

zaskoczyć *pf. zob.* **zaskakiwać**.

zaskowyczeć *pf.* **-ę -ysz** yelp.

zaskórniak *mi Gen.* **-a** *pot.* pin money.

zaskórnik *mi Gen.* **-a** *med.* blackhead.

zaskórny *a.* *geol.* subsoil.

zaskroniec *ma* **-ńc-** *zool.* grass snake (*Natrix*).

zaskrzeczeć *pf.* **-ę -ysz** screech.

zaskrzypieć *pf.* **-pię -pisz** creak.

zaskwierczeć *pf.* sizzle.

zasłabnąć *pf.* **-bnij, -bł** *l.* **-bnął -bła -bli** collapse.

zasłać *pf.* **-ścielę -ścielesz** *zob.* **zaścielać**.

zasłaniać *ipf.* **1.** (= *zakrywać*) conceal, overcast, screen, shade, shadow, veil; **zasłaniać komuś widok** block sb's view. **2.** (= *osłaniać*) screen, shield; (*twarz*) mask. **~ się** *ipf.* **1.** (= *zakrywać się*) cover, shade. **2.** (= *osłaniać się*) protect *l.* shelter o.s. (*przed czymś* from sth). **3.** (= *usprawiedliwiać się*) excuse o.s.

zasłona *f.* **1.** (= *to, co zasłania*) blind, screen, veil; **zasłona dymna** *wojsk.* smoke screen; **zasłona ogniowa** *wojsk.* fire curtain; **zasłona prysznicowa** shower curtain; **spuszczać zasłonę na coś** *przen.* draw the curtains on/upon sth; **zasłona spadła mi z oczu** the scales fell from my eyes. **2.** *sport* guard.

zasłonka *f. Gen.pl.* **-ek** small curtain.

zasłonić *pf. zob.* **zasłaniać**. **~ się** *pf. zob.* **zasłaniać się**.

zasłonowy *a.* curtain.

zasłuchać się *pf.* listen with all ears.

zasłuchany *a.* listening with rapt attention.

zasługa *f.* merit, service, contribution; **krzyż zasługi** cross of merit; **położył wiele zasług w...** *lit.* he had a share in the attainment of...; **przy-**

pisać sobie zasługę za coś take the credit for sth.

zasługiwać *ipf.* deserve (*na coś* sth); **propozycja zasługuje na uwagę** the proposal is worthy of notice; **zasługiwać na naganę** be worthy of reproach; **zasługiwać na uznanie** deserve credit; **zasługiwać na coś lepszego** deserve better.

zasłużenie *adv.* deservedly, justly.

zasłużony *a.* -eni **1.** (= *mający dużo zasług*) deserving, meritorious. **2.** (= *należący się*) deserved, well-earned. – *mp* veteran; (*na cmentarzu*) **aleja zasłużonych** Heroes' Hill.

zasłużyć *pf. zob.* **zasługiwać.** ~ **się** *pf.* make a contribution.

zasłynąć *pf.* earn a name (*jako* as).

zasłyszany *a.* heard.

zasłyszeć *pf.* -ę -ysz hear.

zasmakować *pf.* **1.** (= *polubić*) acquire a taste (*w czymś* for sth). **2.** (= *spodobać się*) develop a taste; **zasmakowała mi węgierska kuchnia** I developed a taste for Hungarian cuisine; **zasmakowała nam swoboda** we tasted freedom.

zasmarkać *pf.* **1.** *pot.* (= *ubrudzić wydzieliną z nosa*) smear with snots. **2.** *pot.* (= *wydmuchać nos*) blow one's nose.

zasmarkany *a. pot.* (= *ubrudzony wydzieliną z nosa l. marny*) snotty.

zasmarować *pf.*, **zasmarowywać** *ipf.* **1.** (= *zamazać*) smear. **2.** (= *zabrudzić*) soil, grease. **3.** *pot.* (= *zabazgrać*) scrawl, daub.

zasmażać *ipf. kulin.* brown.

zasmażka *f. Gen.pl.* -ek *kulin.* roux.

zasmażyć *pf. zob.* **zasmażać.**

zasmradzać *ipf.*, **zasmrodzić** *pf. pot.* fill with stench, stink sth up.

zasmucać *ipf.*, **zasmucić** *pf.* sadden, get down. ~ **się** *ipf.*, **zasmucić się** *pf.* be down, be saddened.

zasnąć *pf.* -snę -śniesz, -śnij *zob.* **zasypiać; zasnąć na wieki** *l.* **snem wiecznym** *euf.* take one's last sleep.

zasnuć *pf.*, **zasnuwać** *ipf. lit.* cover, cloud over, envelop. ~ **się** *pf.*, **zasnuwać się** *ipf. lit.* be enveloped.

zasobnie *adv. lit.* richly, wealthily.

zasobnik *mi Gen.* -a *lotn.* capsule; *wojsk.* connex.

zasobność *f.* **1.** *lit.* (= *obfitość*) abundance. **2.** *lit.* (= *zamożność*) wealth, affluence.

zasobny *a.* **1.** *lit.* (= *obfitujący*) abundant (*w coś* in sth). **2.** *lit.* (= *bogaty*) affluent.

zasoby *pl. Gen.* -ów (= *złoża*) reserves, resources; **zasoby naturalne** natural reserves; **zasoby mieszkalne** housing stock; **zasoby ludzkie** human resources.

zasolenie *n.* salinity.

zasolić *pf.* cure.

zasób *mi* -o- (= *rezerwa*) fund, stock, hoard; (*wody, pieniędzy*) stock; (*słów*) lexicon.

ZASP *abbr.* (= *Związek Artystów Scen Polskich*) the Association of Polish Stage Artists.

zaspa *f.* bank, drift.

zaspać *pf.* -śpię -śpisz, -śpij **1.** *zob.* **zasypiać. 2.** (= *przespać oznaczony czas*) oversleep.

zaspany *a.* sleepy, heavy with sleep.

zaspokajać *ipf.*, **zaspokoić** *pf.* -koję -koisz, -kój satisfy, fullfil; (*potrzeby*) meet; **zaspokajać czyjąś dumę/próżność** feed sb's pride/vanity; (*głód*) satisfy, sate; (*pragnienie*) quench.

zasrać *pf. zob.* **zasrywać.**

zasraniec *mp* -ńc- *pl.* -y *wulg.* piss-ant, shit-face.

zasrany *a. wulg.* shitty; **nie twój zasrany interes!** it's not your shitty business!

zasrywać *ipf.* -am -asz *wulg.* shit (all over sth).

zassać *pf.* -ssę -ssiesz, -ssij *zob.* **zasysać.**

zastać *pf.* -stanę -staniesz *zob.* **zastawać.**

zastanawiać *ipf.* puzzle; **to mnie zastanowiło** it made me think. ~ **się** *ipf.* debate, consider (*nad czymś* sth); reflect (*nad czymś* on sth); **jeszcze się zastanów** think it over, think twice.

zastanawiający *a.* curious, puzzling.

zastanowić *pf.* -ów *zob.* **zastanawiać.** ~ **się** *pf. zob.* **zastanawiać się.**

zastanowienie *n.* reflection, thought; **czas do zastanowienia** time to make one's choice; **bez zastanowienia** off the top of one's head, right off the bat; **po (głębszym) zastanowieniu** on second thoughts.

zastany *a.* existing.

zastarzały *a.* (*np. o urazie*) inveterate.

zastaw *mi* **1.** caution money, deposit; *fin.* security; *ekon.* pledge; *prawn.* guarantee. **2. pożyczanie pod zastaw** pawnbroking; **dać coś w zastaw** gage, pop, hock, pawn.

zastawa *f.* service; (*stołowa*) dinner set, tableware.

zastawać *ipf.* -aję -ajesz, -awaj **1.** (= *przychodząc, spotykać*) find, meet, come across; **nie zastałem go w domu** I didn't catch him in. **2.** (*nieoczekiwanie*) walk in on sb; **zastać kogoś przy życiu** find sb alive.

zastawca *mp prawn.* pledger.

zastawiać *ipf.* **1.** (= *stawiając, zapełniać*) cram, spread; **zastawiać stół** lay the table. **2.** (= *tarasować*) block, obstruct. **3.** (= *dawać w zastaw*) pledge, pawn, gage. **4.** (= *umieszczać*) (*sidła, sieć, pułapkę*) set. **5.** (= *osłaniać*) shield. ~ **się** *ipf.* (= *zasłaniać się*) shield o.s., protect o.s.

zastawić (się) *pf. zob.* **zastawiać (się).**

zastawka *f. Gen.pl.* -ek **1.** *anat.* valve. **2.** *techn.* gate.

zastawny *a.* **list zastawny** *handl.* pawnticket.

zastąpić *pf. zob.* **zastępować.**

zastąpienie *n.* replacement, substitution; **nie do zastąpienia** irreplaceable.

zastękać *pf.* groan, moan.

zastęp *mi* **1.** (*jednostka organizacyjna w harcerstwie*) patrol, pack. **2.** *lit.* (= *grupa ludzi*) host. **3. Pan Zastępów** *rel.* the Lord of Hosts. **4.** *lit.* (= *wojsko*) army.

zastępca *mp* secondary, assistant, deputy; **zastępca dowódcy** *wojsk.* executive officer; **zastępca dyrektora** associate director, assistant manager.

zastępczo *adv.* in the place of sb, in lieu of sb.

zastępczy *a.* supplementary, replacement; (*o matce*) surrogate; (*o rodzinie*) foster.

zastępczyni *f.* deputy, fill-in, replacement, substitute.

zastępować *ipf.* 1. (= *wyręczać*) stand in for sb; **zastępować komuś matkę, ojca** be a mother/father to sb. 2. (= *zamieniać*) replace (*kogoś / coś* sb/sth, *kimś / czymś* with sb/sth). 3. **zastępować komuś drogę** bar/block sb's way.

zastępowy *mp* scout master, patrol leader.

zastępstwo *n.* replacement, fill-in; **w zastępstwie kogoś** standing in for sb; **robić coś w zastępstwie kogoś** do sth in sb's stead; **mieć zastępstwo** (*w szkole*) sub.

zastoina *f. med.* stasis.

zastoinowy *a.* **torbiel zastoinowa** *pat.* retention cyst; **zastoinowa niewydolność serca** congestive heart failure.

zastopować *pf.* 1. *pot.* (= *zatrzymać*) stop. 2. *sport* (*piłkę*) kill.

zastosować *ipf. zob.* **zastosowywać.** ~ **się** *ipf. zob.* **zastosowywać się.**

zastosowanie *n.* application, deployment, use; **mieć, znaleźć zastosowanie w czymś** hold, be applicable.

zastosowywać *ipf.* apply, deploy. ~ **się** *ipf.* comply (*do czegoś* with sth).

zastój *mi* -o- *Gen.pl.* -ów 1. (= *stagnacja*) stagnancy, stagnation, standstill. 2. *med.* stasis. 3. *ekon.* downturn.

zastrachany *a. pot.* intimidated, shy.

zastrajkować *pf. zob.* **strajkować.**

zastraszać *ipf.* intimidate, terrify.

zastraszająco *adv.* **w zastraszająco szybkim tempie** at an alarming rate.

zastraszający *a.* alarming, appaling.

zastraszyć *pf. zob.* **zastraszać.**

zastrugać *pf.* sharpen, taper.

zastrzał *mi* 1. *med.* felon. 2. *techn.* strut, brace.

zastrzec (się) *pf.* -egę -eżesz -egł *zob.* **zastrzegać (się).**

zastrzegać *ipf.* condition; **zastrzegać sobie prawo do czegoś** reserve the right to sth; **zastrzec czek** *fin.* stop a check, put a stop on a check. ~ **się** *ipf.* warn, caution; **zastrzegł się, że...** he made it clear that...

zastrzelić *pf.* 1. (= *zabić*) gun down, shoot. 2. *pot.* (= *zaskoczyć*) nonplus, stump; **zastrzelił mnie tym pytaniem** he stumped me with that question. ~ **się** *pf.* shoot o.s.

zastrzeżenie *n.* 1. (= *wątpliwość*) reservation, objection; **z tym zastrzeżeniem, że...** with the reservation that...; **bez zastrzeżeń** without reservation(s); **mieć zastrzeżenia do kogoś/czegoś** have reservations about sb/sth; **nie mam żadnych zastrzeżeń** I have no objections. 2. (= *klauzula*) reservation, stipulation, condition; **z zastrzeżeniem praw** *prawn.* without prejudice.

zastrzeżony *a.* patent, reserved, restricted; **prawnie zastrzeżony** proprietary; **wszelkie prawa zastrzeżone** all rights reserved; **zastrzeżony telefon** unlisted telephone number; **znak towarowy zastrzeżony** registered trademark.

zastrzyk *mi* 1. (= *iniekcja*) injection, hypodermic; **zastrzyk domięśniowy** intramuscular injec-

tion; **zastrzyk dożylny** intravenous injection; **zastrzyk z trucizną** (*metoda egzekucji*) lethal injection; **dostać zastrzyk** get an injection; **zrobić komuś zastrzyk** give sb an injection, inject sb. 2. (*jednorazowe wsparcie*) infusion; **zastrzyk energii** tonic, shot in the arm; **zastrzyk adrenaliny** a rush of adrenaline; **niespodziewany zastrzyk finansowy** melon.

zastrzykiwać *ipf.*, **zastrzyknąć** *pf.* -nij inject.

zastukać *pf.* knock, tap.

zastygać *ipf.*, **zastygnąć** *pf.* -gnij, -gł *l.* -gnął -gła-gli 1. (= *krzepnąć*) congeal, freeze, set; **krew komuś zastyga na myśl o czymś** sth makes sb's blood run cold. 2. (= *nieruchomieć*) freeze.

zasugerować *pf. zob.* **sugerować.** ~ **się** *pf. zob.* **sugerować się.**

zasunąć *pf.* 1. *zob.* **zasuwać.** 2. *pot.* (= *uderzyć*) whack. 3. **zasunąć gadkę** *pot.* blow hot air, talk a mile a minute.

zasuszać *ipf.* desiccate, dry. ~ **się** *ipf.* get dried.

zasuszony *a.* -eni *pot.* (*o człowieku*) (= *pomarszczony*) desiccated, wizened.

zasuszyć *pf. zob.* **zasuszać.** ~ **się** *pf. zob.* **zasuszać się.**

zasuwa *f.* 1. (*zamek*) latch. 2. *techn.* (= *urządzenie do regulacji*) register, damper.

zasuwać *ipf.* 1. (= *zakrywać*) bar, cover up, draw; (*za pomocą zasuwki*) bolt. 2. (= *wsuwać*) push, slide; (*szufladę*) push in. 3. *pot.* (= *pędzić*) tank, nip along; **zasuwać jak mały motorek** *pot.* work *l.* run *l.* go like stink; **zasuwać na piechotę** hoof it, shank.

zasuwka *f. Gen.pl.* -ek = **zasuwa.**

zasuwowy *a.* bolt.

zaswędzić *pf.* -dził, **zaswędzieć** *pf.* -dział itch.

zasychać *ipf.* dry up; **zaschło mi w ustach/gardle** my mouth/throat went dry.

zasyczeć *pf.* -ę -ysz 1. (= *syknąć*) hiss. 2. (= *odezwać się drwiąco*) hiss.

zasygnalizować *pf. zob.* **sygnalizować.**

zasyłać *ipf. przest.* send; **zasyłać pozdrowienia** send one's greetings.

zasymilować *pf. zob.* **asymilować.** ~ **się** *pf. zob.* **asymilować się.**

zasypać *pf.* -pię -piesz 1. *zob.* **zasypywać.** 2. (= *przygnieść*) cover in, bestrew; **kogoś zasypało śniegiem** sb's snow-bound. 3. *pot.* (= *zdradzić*) spill one's guts, squeal, nark on. ~ **się** *pf. zob.* **zasypywać się.**

zasypiać *ipf.* 1. (= *zapadać w sen*) fall asleep; (*mimowolnie*) drop off. 2. **nie zasypiać gruszek w popiele** not let the grass grow under one's feet.

zasypka *f. Gen.pl.* -ek dusting-powder; **zasypka dla dzieci** baby powder.

zasypywać *ipf.* 1. (= *zapełniać otwór*) fill up, cover up, bury. 2. (= *sypiąc, pokrywać*) pour, cover up; **zasypywać kogoś/coś pociskami** pelt sb/sth. 3. (= *obdarzać obficie*) swamp, overwhelm, shower, ply (*kogoś czymś* sb with sth); **zasypywać kogoś pytaniami** besiege sb with questions; **zasypywać rynek towarami** flood *l.* inundate the market with goods; **zasypywać ko-**

goś gradem przekleństw hail curses on sb. ~ się *ipf.* get covered up *l.* swamped.

   zasysać *ipf.* aspirate, draw; *techn.* suck in.

   zaszachować *pf. zob.* **szachować.**

   zaszaleć *pf. pot.* splurge, cut loose.

   zaszantażować *pf. zob.* **szantażować.**

   zaszargać *pf. zob.* **szargać.**

   zaszczebiotać *pf.* **-oczę -oczesz** *l.* **-ocę -ocesz** *l.* **-otam -otasz, -ocz** *l.* **-otaj** twitter, chatter, chirp.

   zaszczekać *pf.* bark.

   zaszczepiać *ipf.,* **zaszczepić** *pf.* **1.** (= *uszlachetniać drzewa*) engraft. **2.** *med.* inoculate, vaccinate (*przeciwko czemuś* against sth). **3.** *lit.* (= *wpajać*) implant; **zaszczepić komuś zasady** instill principles into sb. **~ się** *ipf.,* **zaszczepić się** *pf.* be inoculated, be vaccinated (*przeciwko czemuś* against sth).

   zaszczękać *pf.* clang, clatter; **zaszczękał zębami** his teeth started chattering.

   zaszczuć *pf.* **1.** (= *zagonić na śmierć*) hunt down, hound to death. **2.** (= *doprowadzić do depresji*) bait.

   zaszczycać *ipf.,* **zaszczycić** *pf.* grace, favor (*kogoś czymś* sb with sth); **zaszczycić kogoś swoją obecnością** honor sb with one's presence.

   zaszczycony *a.* **-eni** privileged; **czuję się zaszczycony** I'm honored.

   zaszczyt *mi* **1.** (= *wyróżnienie*) distinction; honor; *Br.* honour; privilege; **ktoś ma zaszczyt zaprosić kogoś na...** sb requests the presence of sb at...; **mam zaszczyt powiadomić Pana/Panią** I have the honor to inform you; **mam zaszczyt przedstawić/zaprosić...** I have the privilege of introducing/inviting...; **mieć zaszczyt coś zrobić** have the honor of doing sth, be proud to do sth; **poczytujemy to sobie za zaszczyt** we esteem it an honor; **przynosić komuś/czemuś zaszczyt** be an honor to sb/sth, do honor to sb/sth, grace sb/sth; **przypadł jej w udziale zaszczyt wygłoszenia wykładu inauguracyjnego** she had the distinction of delivering the opening lecture. **2.** *lit.* (= *dostojeństwo, honory*) distinctions; **dojść do zaszczytów** rise to eminence.

   zaszczytnie *adv.* creditably, highly.

   zaszczytny *a.* creditable, honorable, honorific; **zaszczytne miejsce** place of honor; **zaszczytne stanowisko** post of eminence.

   zaszeleścić *pf.* **-eszczę -eścisz** rustle.

   zaszemrać *pf.* **-mrzę -mrzesz** *zob.* **szemrać.**

   zaszeptać *pf.* **-pczę -pczesz** *l.* **-pcę -pcesz, -pcz** whisper.

   zaszeregować *pf. zob.* **zaszeregowywać.**

   zaszeregowanie *n.* classification; (*filmu*) rating.

   zaszeregowywać *ipf.* classify; **zaszeregować do niższej kategorii** downgrade; **zaszeregować do wyższej kategorii** upgrade.

   zaszewka *f. Gen.pl.* **-ek** dart, tuck.

   zaszklić się *pf.* glaze over, become glazed.

   zaszkodzić *pf.* cripple, hurt, disserve; **nie zaszkodzi coś zrobić** there's no harm in doing sth; **coś mi zaszkodziło** sth upset my stomach.

   zaszlachtować *pf.* slaughter.

   zaszlochać *pf.* burst out sobbing.

   zaszłość *f.* **1.** *fin.* item, entry. **2.** *prawn.* event, occurrence.

   zasznurować *pf. zob.* **sznurować.**

   zaszokować *pf.* shock.

   zaszpachlować *pf.* putty.

   zaszpuntować *pf.* bung up, cork up.

   zasztyletować *pf.* stab, dagger.

   zaszufladkować *pf. pot.* pigeonhole, pin a label on sb.

   zaszumieć *pf.* **-mi -miał** *zob.* **szumieć.**

   zaszurać *pf.* **1.** (= *spowodować szelest*) shuffle. **2.** *pot.* (= *wywołać awanturę*) spark off an argument.

   zaszyć *pf.* **-szyję -szyjesz, -szyj** *zob.* **zaszywać.** **~ się** *pf. zob.* **zaszywać się.**

   zaszyfrować *pf.,* **zaszyfrowywać** *ipf.* encipher; (*wiadomość, telegram*) code.

   zaszywać *ipf.* **-am -asz** (= *szyjąc, usuwać rozdarcie*) stitch (*sth*) up, sew (*sth*) up; **zaszyj dziurkę, póki mała** a stitch in time saves nine. **~ się** *ipf.* (= *ukrywać się*) hide o.s.; **zaszywać się w bibliotece** sequester o.s. in a library.

   zaś *conj.* while, whereas, on the other hand; **niektórzy są gotowi do współpracy, inni zaś nie** some are ready to cooperate while some are not. **– particle** particularly; **lubił czytać wszystkie książki, najbardziej zaś kryminały** he liked reading all books and whodunnits particularly.

   zaścianek *mi* **-nk-** *Gen.* **-a** *l.* **-u** **1.** hamlet. **2.** *hist.* yeomen's settlement. **3.** *przen.* (= *miejsce zacofane*) backwater.

   zaściankowość *f.* insularity, localeism, provincialism.

   zaściankowy *a.* **1.** **szlachcic zaściankowy** *hist.* duniwassal. **2.** (= *ograniczony, zacofany*) insular, parochial, suburban.

   zaścielać *ipf.,* **zaścielić** *ipf.,* **zaściełać** *ipf.* (= *ścieląc, rozpościerać*) cover; **zasłać łóżko** make the bed.

   zaślepiać *ipf.,* **zaślepić** *pf.* blindfold, blind (*na coś* to sth).

   zaślepienie *n.* blindness; (*miłosne*) infatuation.

   zaślepiony *a.* **-eni** blind, infatuated.

   zaślinić *pf.* slaver, slobber. **~ się** *pf.* slaver.

   zaślubiać *ipf.,* **zaślubić** *pf. lit.* wed.

   zaślubiny *pl. Gen.* **-n** *lit.* espousal, nuptials.

   zaśmiać się *pf.* **-śmieję -śmiejesz -śmiali** *l.* **-śmieli** give a laugh.

   zaśmiardnąć *pf.* **-dł** *l.* **-dnął -dła -dli** = **zaśmierdnąć.**

   zaśmiecać *ipf.,* **zaśmiecić** *pf.* (= *zarzucać śmieciami*) litter up; **zaśmiecać sobie umysł** clutter up one's mind.

   zaśmiecony *a.* littered with sth, messy.

   zaśmierdnąć *pf.* **-dł** *l.* **-dnął -dła -dli** stink.

   zaśmierdzieć *pf.* **-dzi** stink. **~ się** *pf.* go smelly.

   zaśmiewać się *ipf.* split one's sides with laughter, laugh one's head off.

   zaśniedziały *a. pot.* rusty; (*o sztućcach*) tarnished.

   zaśniedzieć *pf. pot.* grow rusty.

   zaśnieżony *a.* snowy; (*o górze*) snow-capped.

   zaśnięcie *n.* **1.** (= *pogrążenie się we śnie*)

falling asleep; **tuż przed zaśnięciem** last thing at night. **2. zaśnięcie Matki Boskiej** *rel.* dormition of the Blessed Mother.

zaśpiewać *pf.* **1.** (= *wykonać utwór muzyczny, śpiewając*) sing; **zaśpiewać dla kogoś** give sb a song. **2.** (*o ptakach*) sing. **3.** *pot.* (= *zażądać wygórowanej ceny*) demand.

zaśpię *itp. pf. zob.* **zaspać.**

zaświadczać *ipf.* attest, certify, testify.

zaświadczenie *n.* certificate, testimonial; **zaświadczenie lekarskie** medical certificate; **zaświadczenie o dobrym stanie zdrowia** a clean bill of health; **wydać zaświadczenie** issue a certificate.

zaświadczyć *pf. zob.* **zaświadczać.**

zaświaty *pl. Gen.* **-ów** the other world, the underworld; **gość z zaświatów** visitant.

zaświecić *pf.* **1.** (= *zapalić*) (*lampę, świecę*) light; (*zapałkę*) strike. **2.** (= *poświecić*) shine, give light. **3.** (= *zabłysnąć*) sparkle; **zaświeciło słońce** the sun started shining; **oczy zaświeciły mu gniewem** fury glinted in his eyes. **~ się** *ipf.* (= *rozbłysnąć*) shine, flash; **oczy jej się zaświeciły** her eyes twinkled.

zaświergotać *ipf.* **-oczę -oczesz** *l.* **-ocę -ocesz** *l.* otam -otasz, -ocz *l.* -otaj chirrup, chirp, twitter.

zaświerzbieć *pf.* **-bi** itch; **zaświerzbiała mnie ręka** my hand itched; **zaświerzbiał mnie język** I itched to say something.

zaświnić *pf. pot.* muck up. **~ się** *pf. pot.* muck up.

zaświtać *pf.* dawn; **zaświtało mi, że...** it dawned on me that...

zataczać *ipf.* **1.** (= *tocząc, przesuwać*) roll, wheel. **2. zataczać łuk** describe a curve; (*o krajobrazie*) sweep; **zataczać coraz szersze kręgi** expand in ever-widening circles. **~ się** *ipf.* **1.** (= *przesuwać się bezwładnie*) bumble, lurch along/on, stagger, sway. **2.** (= *tocząc, przesuwać się gdzieś*) roll.

zataić *pf.* **-aję -aisz, zatajać** *ipf.* keep/hold back; **zataić grzechy** *rel.* hold back one's sins.

zatamować *pf.* dam; **zatamować krew** stop a wound, staunch the flow of blood.

zatankować *pf.* **1.** *mot.* tank up; **zatankować do pełna** fill up. **2.** *pot.* (= *upić się*) booze up, hit the booze.

zatańczyć *pf.* have a dance.

zatapiać *ipf.* **1.** (= *topić*) drown, flood; (*statek*) scupper, sink; **zatopić nóż w ciele ofiary** sheathe a knife in the victim's body; **zatopić w czymś kły** sink one's teeth into sth. **2.** (*o powodzi*) (= *zalewać*) flood, deluge, drown. **3.** *techn.* seal. **~ się** *ipf.* **1.** (= *pogrążać się w wodzie*) sink, plunge. **2.** (= *oddawać się czemuś*) lose o.s. (*w czymś* in sth).

zatarasować *pf.* barricade, bar. **~ się** *pf.* barricade o.s.

zatarcie *n.* **1.** obliteration, effacement. **2.** *techn.* seizure.

zatarg *mi* clash, dispute, quarrel.

zatargać *pf.* **1.** *pot.* (= *zanieść*) drag. **2.** *pot.* (= *poszarpać*) tug.

zataszczyć *pf. pot.* (= *zanieść*) lug.

zatelefonować *pf.* make a phone call.

zatelegrafować *pf.* send a wire.

zateleksować *pf.* telex.

zatelepać *pf.* **-pię -piesz** *pot.* shake.

zatem *conj. lit.* then, therefore, so; **a zatem** now then; **wszystko zostało już powiedziane, można zatem przejść do podsumowania** all has been said so we can recap now; **a zatem nie zna pani podejrzanego?** so you don't know the suspect?

zatemperować *pf.* sharpen.

zaterkotać *pf.* **-oczę -oczesz** *l.* **-ocę -ocesz** *l.* -otam -otasz, -ocz *l.* -otaj clatter, rattle.

zatęchły *a.* **1.** (= *spleśniały*) moldy; (*o powietrzu, piwnicy, słomie*) stuffy, moldy, frousy, stale. **2.** *przen.* (= *staroświecki*) (*o środowisku*) stale.

zatęchnąć *pf.* **-chł** go moldy.

zatęsknić *pf.* **-ij** *zob.* **tęsknić.**

zatętnić *pf.* **-ij** *zob.* **tętnić.**

zatkać *pf. zob.* **zatykać.** **~ się** *pf.* **1.** *zob.* **zatykać się.** **2.** *pot.* (= *milknąć*) shut up; **zatkaj się!** shut up!

zatknąć *pf.* **-ij** *zob.* **zatykać.**

zatłoczony *a.* congested, crowded, mobbed; (*o autobusie*) packed; (*o pubie*) busy.

zatłoczyć *pf.* crowd, mob.

zatłuc *pf.* **-ukę -uczesz -ukł** *pot.* (= *zabić*) frag; **zatłuc kogoś na śmierć** drub sb to death. **~ się** *pf. pot.* (= *zabić się wzajemnie*) blast one another.

zatłuszczenie *n.* greasiness.

zatłuszczony *a.* greasy, oily.

zatłuścić *pf.* **-uszczę -uścisz** stain with grease, leave greasy stains. **~ się** *pf.* stain o.s.

zatnę *itp. pf. zob.* **zaciąć.**

zatoczka *f. Gen.pl.* **-ek** *geogr.* cove, inlet; *mot.* lay-by; (*do zawracania*) turnaround.

zatoczyć *pf. zob.* **zataczać.** **~ się** *pf. zob.* **zataczać się.**

zatoka *f.* **1.** *geogr.* gulf, bay, firth; **Zatoka Perska** the Persian Gulf; **Zatoka Biskajska** the Bay of Biscay. **2.** (*na jezdni*) lay-by. **3.** *anat., biol.* sinus, lacuna. **4.** (*łysina*) receding hairline, bald patch.

zatokowy *a. biol.* sinuate; **Prąd Zatokowy** *geogr.* the Gulf Stream.

zatonąć *pf.* **1.** (*utonąć*) go under, drown. **2.** *przen.* (= *pogrążyć się w czymś*) lose o.s.; (*w zapomnieniu*) sink into oblivion.

zatopić *pf. zob.* **zatapiać.** **~ się** *pf. zob.* **zatapiać się.**

zatopiony *a.* **1.** (= *pod wodą*) sunken, under water; (*o polach*) flooded. **2.** *przen.* (= *pogrążony*) deep; **zatopiony w myślach** deep in thought; **zatopiony w pracy** knee-deep in work.

zator *mi* **1.** (*na drodze*) block, congestion. **2.** (*na rzece*) jam; **zator uliczny** holdup, bottleneck. **3.** *pat.* embolus; **zator mózgu** cerebral embolism.

zatracać *ipf.* lose; **zatracać poczucie czasu** lose count of time. **~ się** *ipf.* lose o.s. (*w czymś* in sth).

zatracenie *n. lit.* (= *zagłada*) doom, destruction.

zatracić *pf. zob.* **zatracać.** ~ **się** *pf. zob.* **zatracać się.**

zatrajkotać *pf.* -oczę -oczesz *l.* -ocę -ocesz *l.* -otam -otasz, -ocz *l.* -otaj **1.** *pot.* (= *powiedzieć coś szybko*) jabber. **2.** *pot.* (= *zagadać*) out-talk everybody else. **3.** *pot.* (= *zagrzechotać*) rattle.

zatrajlować *pf. pot.* (= *powiedzieć zbyt dużo*) talk a mile a minute.

zatratować *pf.* trample to death.

zatrąbić *pf.* toot one's horn.

zatrącać *ipf.*, **zatrącić** *pf.* **1.** (= *napomykać*) allude, hint. **2.** *tylko ipf.* (= *być podobnym do czegoś*) be reminiscent of sth; **zatrącać z francuska** speak with a French accent.

zatriumfować *pf. zob.* **triumfować.**

zatroskać się *pf.* show concern.

zatroskanie *n.* anxiety, concern.

zatroskany *a.* careful, solicitous; **wielce zatroskany kimś/czymś** greatly exercised about sb/sth.

zatroszczyć się *pf.* take care (*o kogoś / coś* of sb/sth).

zatrucie *n. med.* poisoning, intoxication; **zatrucie pokarmowe** food poisoning; **zatrucie ciążowe** gestosis.

zatruć *pf. zob.* **zatruwać.** ~ **się** *pf. zob.* **zatruwać się.**

zatrudniać *ipf.* employ, engage, hire. ~ **się** *ipf.* become employed.

zatrudnić (się) *pf.* -ij *zob.* **zatrudniać (się).**

zatrudnienie *n.* **1.** (= *praca zawodowa*) occupation. **2.** *ekon.* employment, placement; (*zwł. na czas określony*) engagement.

zatrudniona *f. Gen.* -ej, **zatrudniony** *mp* employed, employee, staff member.

zatruwać *ipf.* empoison; **zatruwać komuś życie** *pot.* make things warm for sb. ~ **się** *ipf.* poison o.s.

zatrważać *ipf.* = **zatrwożyć.**

zatrważający *a.* staggering, alarming, disquieting.

zatrwożony *a.* -eni upset, alarmed.

zatrwożyć *pf.* -trwóż *zob.* **zatrważać.**

zatryumfować *pf. zob.* **triumfować.**

zatrzask *mi* **1.** catch, clasp, click; (*przy odzieży*) press stud. **2.** (*przy drzwiach, oknie*) latch; **zatrzask sprężynowy** lock spring. **3. zatrzask magazynka** *wojsk.* safety catch.

zatrzaskiwać *ipf.* **1.** (= *zamykać drzwi*) latch; (= *zamykać gwałtownie*) bang shut, slam. **2.** (= *zamykać kogoś w jakimś miejscu*) trap. ~ **się** *ipf.* **1.** (= *zamykać się gwałtownie*) bang down; **drzwi się zatrzasnęły** the door slammed shut. **2.** (= *zamykać siebie w jakimś miejscu*) get trapped; **zatrzasnął się w windzie** he got trapped in an elevator.

zatrzasnąć (się) *pf.* -ij *zob.* **zatrzaskiwać (się).**

zatrząść *pf.* -trzęsę -trzęsiesz, -trząś *l.* -trzęś, -trząsł -trzęsła -trzęśli shake; **zatrząść czymś w posadach** shake *l.* rock sth to its foundations. ~ **się** *pf.* shake, rock; **ściany zatrzęsły się od braw** applause shook the walls; **miasto zatrzęsło się od plotek** the town was agog *l.* abuzz with gossip; **zatrząść się z gniewu** shake with rage.

zatrzeć *pf.* -trę -trzesz, -trzyj, -tarł *zob.* **zacierać.** ~ **się** *pf. zob.* **zacierać się.**

zatrzepotać *pf.* -oczę -oczesz *l.* -ocę -ocesz, -ocz flutter; **zatrzepotać powiekami** bat one's eyelashes.

zatrzeszczeć *pf.* -ę -ysz crackle, crack.

zatrzęsienie *n. pot.* lots, oodles; **zatrzęsienie ludzi** hoards of people.

zatrzymać *pf. zob.* **zatrzymywać.** ~ **się** *pf. zob.* **zatrzymywać się.**

zatrzymana *f. Gen.* -ej, **zatrzymany** *mp prawn.* detainee.

zatrzymanie *n. prawn.* apprehension, arrest, arrestment, detention.

zatrzymywać *ipf.* **1.** (= *nie pozwalać iść, biec, jechać*) stop, bring to a standstill, hold; **zatrzymać na kimś wzrok** settle/fix one's gaze on sb; **zatrzymać bieg wypadków** stay the course of events. **2.** (= *unieruchamiać*) stop; (*samochód, przemytników*) intercept; (*wodę, ciepło, prowizję*) retain. **3.** (= *nie pozwalać komuś odejść*) hold, keep; **zatrzymać gości na kolacji** keep the guests to dinner; **zatrzymywać coś w pamięci** keep sth in mind. **4.** *prawn.* (*podejrzanego*) apprehend. **5.** (= *nie oddawać*) retain, keep; **zatrzymam sobie twoją fotografię** I'll keep your picture; **zatrzymaj to dla siebie** keep it to yourself. ~ **się** *ipf.* (= *przystawać*) **1.** stop; (*po drodze*) stop over; (*o wzroku*) settle (*na kimś / czymś* on sb/sth); (*w hotelu*) stay; (*o pojeździe*) pull up; **czy ten ekspres zatrzymuje się w Kutnie?** does this express train call at Kutno?; **zatrzymywać się na jakimś temacie** dwell on a subject; **zatrzymać się w pół drogi** stop half-way; **czas zatrzymał się w miejscu** the time came to a standstill. **2.** (= *przestawać funkcjonować*) stop. **3.** (= *mieszkać gdzieś chwilowo*) stay.

zatupać *pf.* -pię -piesz patter, stamp one's feet.

zatuszować *pf.*, **zatuszowywać** *ipf.* cover up, squelch, hush up.

zatwardzenie *n. pat.* constipation.

zatwardziałość *f. lit.* impenitence, obduracy.

zatwardziały *a. lit.* die-hard, impenitent, obdurate; (*o przestępcy*) hardened.

zatwierdzać *ipf.*, **zatwierdzić** *pf.* approve, authorize, confirm, endorse; (*decyzję, umowę*) validate.

zatyczka *f. Gen.pl.* -ek plug, obturator, spigot, spile, spill; **zatyczka do uszu** earplug.

zatykać *ipf.* **1.** (= *zamykać otwór*) close; (*dziurę, otwór*) plug, chock up; (*butelkę*) cork; (*uszy*) wad; **aż go zatkało** he was flabbergasted/stumped; **zatyka mi dech w piersiach** I'm breathless; **zatkać komuś czymś gębę** *pot.* squelch sb. **2.** (= *umocowywać*) stick, shove, insert; (*flagę*) hoist. ~ **się** *ipf.* get clogged/blocked/choked; **umywalka się zatkała** the basin got clogged.

zatytułować *pf.* entitle; (*ustawę*) intitule.

zatytułowany *a.* entitled, titled; **książka zatytułowana...** the book entitled...

zaufać *pf.* confide in, trust, rely on.

zaufanie *n.* confidence, trust, faith; **mąż zaufania** intermediary; **wotum zaufania** vote of confidence; **nadużycie zaufania** breach of trust; **tele-**

fon zaufania helpline, hotline; **pokładać zaufanie w kimś** place confidence in sb; **darzyć kogoś zaufaniem** trust in sb; **nadużyć czyjegoś zaufania** abuse sb's trust, take advantage of sb.

zaufany a. confidential, trusted.

zaułek mi **-łk-** Gen. **-a** alley, backstreet; **ślepy zaułek** cul-de-sac, dead end.

zauroczenie n. spell, infatuation.

zauroczyć pf. besot, charm.

zausznik mp przest. talebearer.

zautomatyzować pf. zob. **automatyzować**.

zauważać ipf. **1.** (= dostrzegać) notice, perceive; **dać się zauważyć** become visible. **2.** (= robić uwagę) remark; **pozwolę sobie zauważyć, że...** I'll take the liberty to point out that...

zauważalny a. appreciable, noted, noticeable, observable; (o poprawie, wpływie) marked.

zauważyć pf. zob. **zauważać**.

zawada f. cumbrance, encumbrance, hindrance, stumbling block; **stać komuś na zawadzie** stand in sb's way.

zawadiacki a. rakish, saucy, swashbuckling; (np. o kapelusiku) pert.

zawadiacko adv. pertly, rakishly; (uśmiechać się) boisterously.

zawadiaka mp pl. **-ki** l. **-cy** bucko, fire-eater, hell-raiser, swashbuckler.

zawadzać ipf., **zawadzić** pf. **1.** (= zaczepiać) graze, scrape, knock; (o kant stołu, o krzesło) strike. **2. nie zawadzi spróbować** it won't harm to try, there's no harm in having a try; **złej baletnicy zawadza rąbek u spódnicy** a bad workman blames his tools. **3.** (= być komuś ciężarem) hinder, hamper, impede; **nie chcę nikomu zawadzać** I don't want to be in anybody's way. **4.** pot. (= wstępować gdzieś) stop on one's way; **zawadzić o czyjś dom** drop in on sb.

zawahać się pf. hesitate, waver, pause.

zawalać¹ pf. (= zabrudzić) smear.

zawalać² ipf. **1.** (= zasypywać) cover up, bury, crush, lumber up. **2.** (= spowodować runięcie) bring sth down, cause to collapse. **3.** pot. (= nie wywiązywać się z obowiązków) bungle; **zawalić egzamin** fluff, flub; **zawalić robotę** foul up, gum up. **~ się** ipf. **1.** come down, collapse, founder. **2.** pot. (o planach) come unglued.

zawalczyć pf. pot. fight.

zawalić pf. zob. **zawalać**. **~ się** pf. zob. **zawalać się**.

zawalidroga f. Gen.pl. **-óg** idler, loafer.

zawalony a. (o domu, murze) collapsed; **zawalony pracą** swamped with work; **być zawalonym czymś** be up to one's neck in sth.

zawał mi **1.** pat. (serca) heart attack, infarct. **2.** górn. cave-in.

zawałowiec mp **-wc-** pl. **-y** heart attack patient.

zawałowy a. **1.** pat. infarctional. **2.** górn. (o odcinku) cave-in.

zawarcie n. conclusion, transaction.

zawarczeć pf. **-ę -ysz 1.** (o psie) growl. **2.** (o silniku) hum, whirr.

zawarować pf., **zawarowywać** ipf. stipulate, guarantee.

zawartość f. (torebki, kieszeni) contents; (książki, tłuszczu, alkoholu) content; **o niskiej zawartości tłuszczu** low-fat.

zaważyć pf. (= wywrzeć wpływ) influence (na czymś sth); **wypadek zaważył na jego karierze** the accident had a powerful impact on his career.

zawczasu adv. in advance; beforehand; **bilety zawczasu zarezerwowane** tickets booked in advance; **ostrzeżenie zawczasu** early warning.

zawdzięczać ipf. **zawdzięczać coś komuś** owe sth to sb; **wszystko zawdzięczam tylko sobie** I owe everything to myself.

zawekować pf. preserve (in a preserving jar).

zawezwać pf. **-wę -wiesz, -wij** form. summon.

zawędrować pf. reach.

zawęzić pf. **-żę -zisz**, **zawężać** ipf. narrow down.

zawiać pf. **-wieje** zob. **zawiewać**.

zawiadamiać ipf., **zawiadomić** pf. notify; inform; **zawiadomić kogoś o czymś** notify sb of sth; **z żalem/przyjemnością zawiadamiamy...** we regret/are pleased to inform you...

zawiadomienie n. notification, notice; **zawiadomienie o ślubie/pogrzebie** wedding/funeral card.

zawiadowca mp kol. **zawiadowca stacji** kol. stationmaster; **zawiadowca stacji rozrządowej** kol. yardmaster.

zawiadywać ipf. lit. handle.

zawiany a. pot. (śniegiem) snowswept; (facet) tipsy.

zawias mi hinge; **wyrwać drzwi z zawiasów** tear the door from its hinges; **zdejmować z zawiasów** unhinge.

zawiązać pf. **-wiążę -wiążesz** zob. **zawiązywać**. **~ się** pf. zob. **zawiązywać się**.

zawiązany a. tied up; **z zawiązanymi oczami** blindfolded.

zawiązek mi **-zk-** Gen. **-a** l. **-u** biol. blastema; **zawiązek zęba** dent. tooth bud.

zawiązywać ipf. **1.** (= wiążąc, łączyć końce) (sznurowadło, węzeł) tie. **2.** (= obwiązywać) do up; **zawiązać w tobół** rope a bundle; **zawiązywać komuś oczy** blindfold sb. **3.** (= organizować) set up; organize. **4.** bot. (owoce, nasiona) set. **~ się** ipf. **1.** (= być organizowanym) form. **2.** bot. (o owocu) set.

zawiedziony a. **-dzeni** disappointed; disillusioned; (nadzieje) dashed; **zawiedziony w miłości** deceived in love.

zawieja f. Gen. **-ei** snowstorm; blizzard.

zawierać ipf. **1.** (= mieścić w sobie) contain. **2.** (= obejmować treścią) include. **3.** (= ustanawiać coś) (zgodę) reach; (układ, umowę) conclude; (pokój) make; **zawrzeć z kimś przyjaźń** strike friendship with sb; **zawrzeć z kimś znajomość** make sb's acquaintance; **zawrzeć związek małżeński** enter into marriage. **~ się** ipf. be contained (w czymś in sth).

zawierucha f. **1.** (= wichura) blustery l. stormy weather. **2.** przen. (= burzliwe czasy) turmoil; **zawierucha wojenna** turmoil of war.

zawieruszać ipf. mislay. **~ się** ipf. get mislaid;

(*o przesyłce*) go astray; (*o kluczach, książce*) disappear.

zawieruszyć (się) *pf. zob.* **zawieruszać (się)**.

zawierzać *ipf.*, **zawierzyć** *pf.* trust (*komuś coś* sb with sth).

zawiesić *pf.* -szę -sisz 1. *zob.* **zawieszać**. 2. **zawiesić ścianę obrazkami** (= *zapełnić*) cover the wall with pictures. ~ **się** *pf. zob.* **zawieszać się**.

zawiesina *f. chem., fiz.* suspension.

zawiesistość *f.* thickness.

zawiesisty *a.* thick.

zawieszać *ipf.* 1. (= *wieszając, umocowywać*) (*lampę, obraz, zasłonę*) hang; **zawiesić głos** pause; **zawiesić coś na kołku** *pot.* put on the backburner. 2. (*wstrzymywać*) (*działalność, karę, pracownika, ucznia*) suspend. ~ **się** *ipf.* crash, hang up.

zawieszenie *n.* 1. (= *napięcie emocjonalne*) suspense; **trzymać kogoś w zawieszeniu** keep sb in suspense. 2. **zostawić coś w zawieszeniu** leave sth hanging in the air. 3. **zawieszenie broni** truce. 4. *prawn.* suspension; **wyrok w zawieszeniu** suspended sentence; **zawieszenie wykonania wyroku** stay of execution. 5. *mot.* suspension. 6. *komp.* crash, hung-up.

zawieszka *f. Gen.pl.* -ek *techn.* **zawieszka wahadła** suspension spring.

zawieść *pf.* -wiodę -wiedziesz -wiódł -wiodła -wiedli *zob.* **zawodzić**. ~ **się** *pf. zob.* **zawodzić się**.

zawietrzna *f. Gen.* -ej *żegl.* leeward; **na l. od zawietrznej** leeward.

zawietrzny *a.* leeward; **brzeg zawietrzny** lee shore.

zawiewać *ipf.* 1. (*o wietrze*) blow; **chyba mnie zawiało** *pot.* I think I caught a bit of a chill. 2. (*o śniegu*) cover. 3. (= *dochodzić z wiatrem*) drift; (*o zapachu*) waft; **z ogrodu zawiewał zapach kwiatów** fragrance of flowers wafted from the garden.

zawieźć *pf.* -wiozę -wieziesz -wiózł -wiozła -wieźli *zob.* **zawozić**.

zawijać *ipf.* 1. (= *owijać*) (*w bandaż, chustę*) swathe; (*paczkę w papier, kanapkę*) wrap (up); (*prezent*) do up. 2. (= *podwijać*) (*rękawy*) roll up. 3. **zawinąć do portu** (*o statku*) call at a port. ~ **się** *ipf.* 1. (= *otulać się*) (*kocem, kołdrą l. w koc, w kołdrę*) wrap o.s. (*w coś* in sth). 2. (= *zaginać się*) (*o kołnierzu*) curl up.

zawijany *a. kulin.* rolled; -roll; **wołowe zrazy zawijane** beef roulades; beef roll-ups.

zawijas *mi Gen.* -a flourish.

zawikłać *pf.* complicate. ~ **się** *pf.* tangle up; entangle.

zawikłany *a.* convoluted; (*o wątku, problemie*) involved.

zawile *adv.* (*tłumaczyć*) convolutedly.

zawilec *mi* -lc- *Gen.* -a anemone (*Anemone*).

zawilgnąć *pf.* -gł -gła get damp.

zawilgocenie *n.* dampness; (*budynku, ścian*) rising damp.

zawilgocić *pf.* moisten.

zawilgocony *a.* moist; damp; (*o mieszkaniu*) dank.

zawiłości *pl. Gen.* -i intricacies (*czegoś* of sth); complexities.

zawiłość *f.* (= *kunszt*) 1. complexity; (*stylu*) convolution. 2. (= *brak przejrzystości*) (*wywodu*) cloudiness.

zawiły *a.* complex; (*o kwestii*) intricate; (*o akcji, stylu*) convoluted.

zawinąć *pf. zob.* **zawijać**. ~ **się** *pf. zob.* **zawijać się**.

zawiniątko *n. Gen.pl.* -tek bundle.

zawinić *pf.* be at fault; **kto zawinił?** who is to blame?

zawirować *pf.* whirl; **zawirowało mi w oczach** my head whirled.

zawisać *ipf.*, **zawisnąć** *pf.* -snę -śniesz, -śnij, -sł *l.* -snął -sła -śli *l.* -snęli 1. (= *być zawieszonym*) hang; **zawisnąć na linie** hang from a rope; **zawisnąć nad przepaścią** be on the brink of a precipice; **zawisnąć na włosku** *przen.* hang by a thread; **zawisnąć na szubienicy** *l.* **na suchej gałęzi** swing. 2. (= *nieruchomieć w locie*) hover. 3. *lit.* (= *zależeć*) be contingent (*od czegoś* on sth).

zawistnie *adv.* enviously.

zawistny *a.* envious; jealous; **patrzeć na coś zawistnym wzrokiem** cast an envious eye on *l.* at sth.

zawiść *f.* envy; jealousy; **budzić zawiść** stir up *l.* arouse envy.

zawitać *pf.* come; **kiedy pan do nas zawita?** when will you grace us with a visit?

zawity *a. prawn.* **termin** *l.* **okres zawity** final date.

zawlec *pf.* -wlokę *l.* -wlekę -wleczesz -wlókł *l.* -wlekł -wlokła *l.* -wlekła -wlekli 1. (= *wlekąc, zaciągnąć*) drag. 2. (= *przenieść coś bezwolnie*) (*ospę, dżumę*) carry. ~ **się** *pf. pot.* (= *dotrzeć*) drag o.s.; **zawlókł się do samochodu** he dragged himself to his car.

zawleczka *f. Gen.pl.* -ek 1. (*przy puszce z napojem*) pull-tab; *techn.* pin; cotter (pin). 2. *wojsk.* safety pin.

zawładnąć *pf.* -ij capture; seize; (*o uczuciach, myślach*) take possession (*kimś* of sb).

zawłaszczać *ipf.*, **zawłaszczyć** *pf.* appropriate.

zawoalowany *a.* veiled.

zawodniczka *f. Gen.pl.* -ek, **zawodnik** *mp* 1. *sport* competitor. 2. (*w teleturnieju*) contestant.

zawodność *f.* fallibility; unreliability.

zawodny *a.* (*pamięć*) fallible; (*urządzenie*) unreliable.

zawodowiec *mp* -wc- *pl.* -y professional.

zawodowo *adv.* professionally; (*pracować*) work professionally.

zawodowstwo *n.* professionalism; **przejść na zawodowstwo** turn professional.

zawodowy *a.* professional; (*o szkole*) vocational; trade; (*o chorobie*) occupational; (*o dyplomacie, polityku*) career; **tajemnica zawodowa** trade secret; **zawodowy sportowiec** pro; **związek zawodowy** labor union; **żołnierz zawodowy** regular.

zawodówka *f. Gen.pl.* -ek *pot.* vocational *l.* trade school.

zawody *pl. Gen.* -ów *sport* competition; contest.

zawodzić *ipf.* -wodzę -wodzisz, -wódź **1.** (= *sprawiać zawód*) disappoint; let down; (*o urzędzeniu, pamięci*) fail; **przyjaciele go zawiedli** friends let him down; **nadzieje nas zawiodły** we were disappointed in our hopes; **pamięć mnie zawodzi** my memory fails me; **czułam, że zawodzą mnie nerwy** I felt my temper fray; **zawodzić oczekiwania** fall short of expectations. **2.** *lit.* (= *prowadzić gdzieś*) lead; **droga nas zawiodła do lasu** the road lead us to the forest; **dokąd cię zawiedzie nienawiść?** where will hate lead you? **3.** *tylko ipf.* (= *płacząc, ubolewać*) wail; **zawodzić wniebogłosy** wail loudly. ~ **się** *ipf.* (= *doznawać zawodu*) be disappointed (*na kimś/czymś* with sb/sth); **zawiodła się w miłości** she was disappointed in love.

zawojować *pf.*, **zawojowywać** *ipf.* conquer.

zawołać *pf.* **1.** (= *krzyknąć*) cry out. **2.** (= *przywołać*) call.

zawołanie *n.* **1.** (= *przywołanie*) call; **być na każde zawołanie** be at sb's beck and call. **2.** *hist.* cry; **zawołanie bojowe** battle cry.

zawołany *a.* (*lekarz, nauczyciel*) born.

zaworowy *a.* *techn.* **luz zaworowy** valve clearance.

zawozić *ipf.* -wożę -wozisz, -woź *l.* -wóź transport, take, carry.

zawód *mi* -o- **1.** (= *kwalifikacje*) profession; occupation; **kim on jest z zawodu?** what's his profession?; **zawód aktora/lekarza/nauczyciela** acting/medical/teaching profession; **zawód wyuczony** learned profession; **zawód wykonywany** practiced profession; **pracować w swoim zawodzie** practice one's profession; **z zawodu** by profession. **2.** (= *rozczarowanie*) letdown; disappointment; **zawód miłosny** disappointment in love; **sprawić komuś zawód** be a disappointment to sb.

zawój *mi* -o- turban.

zawór *mi* -o- *techn.* valve; **zawór bezpieczeństwa** safety valve; **zawór odcinający** shut-off valve.

zawracać *ipf.* **1.** (= *zmieniać kierunek*) turn back *l.* round. **2.** (= *kierować kogoś z powrotem*) turn back; (*samochód*) swing around; **zawrócić komuś w głowie** turn sb's head; **nie zawracać komuś głowy czymś** *przen.* not to bother sb about sth. ~ **się** *ipf.* turn back.

zawracanie *n.* turning back; *mot.* U-turn; **zawracanie głowy** hassle, nuisance.

zawrotnie *adv.* dizzyingly; **w zawrotnie szybkim tempie** at a dizzying pace.

zawrotny *a.* (*o cenach, karierze*) staggering; (*o tempie, prędkości*) dizzy(ing).

zawrócić *pf.* *zob.* **zawracać.** ~ **się** *pf.* *zob.* **zawracać się.**

zawrót *mi* -o- **zawroty głowy** *med.* dizziness; vertigo.

zawrzeć[1] *pf.* -wrę -wrzesz, -wrzyj, -warł *zob.* **zawierać.** ~ **się** *zob.* **zawierać się.**

zawrzeć[2] *pf.* (= *zagotować się*) **1.** come to a boil; **w pokoju zawrzało jak w ulu** room buzzed like a beehive; **krew mi zawrzała w żyłach** my blood boiled in my veins. **2.** *przen.* (= *wybuch-*

nąć) break out; **dyskusja zawrzała** discussion erupted. **3.** *przen.* (= *wzburzyć się*) seethe; boil; **zawrzeć oburzeniem** seethe *l.* boil with anger. **4.** *przen.* (= *zatętnić*) buzz; **ulica zawrzała plotkami** street buzzed with rumor.

zawstydzać *ipf.*, **zawstydzić** *pf.* (put to) shame. ~ **się** *pf.* be ashamed.

zawstydzenie *n.* abashment; shame.

zawstydzony *a.* ashamed; abashed.

zawsze *adv.* always; **dla mnie to, co zawsze** I'll have the same as usual; **zawsze ci powtarzałem, żeby...** I always told you to...; **raz na zawsze** once and for all; **na zawsze** for ever. – *particle* **ale zawsze** but still; **to zawsze coś** that's always sth; **zawsze gdy** whenever.

zawszony *a.* -eni lousy; louse-infested.

zawtórować *pf.* (*o instrumencie*) back; accompany; (*o osobie*) back up.

zawyć *pf.* -wyję -wyjesz, -wyj (*o psie, człowieku*) howl; **o silniku, syrenie** scream.

zawyrokować *pf.* **1.** (= *wydać wyrok*) judge. **2.** (= *wyrazić opinię*) decide.

zawyżać *ipf.*, **zawyżyć** *pf.* overestimate; (*ceny, koszty*) inflate; (*dane*) overstate.

zawziąć się *pf.* -wezmę -weźmiesz, -weźmij take the bit between one's teeth; **zawziąć się na kogoś** have it in for sb.

zawzięcie *adv.* stubbornly; (*pracować*) relentlessly; (*dyskutować, kłócić się*) vehemently.

zawziętość *f.* (= *zapamiętanie*) vehemence; (= *upór*) doggedness; **z zawziętością** (= *zapamiętale*) vehemently; (= *z uporem*) doggedly.

zawzięty *a.* (*opór*) dogged; (*mina*) determined; (*przeciwnik*) sworn; (*rywalizacja*) hot.

zazdrosny *a.* (= *świadczący o zazdrości*) (*t. o osobę*) jealous (*o kogoś/coś* of sb/sth); (*o majątek, pochodzenie*) envious.

zazdrościć *ipf.* -szczę -ścisz envy (*komuś czegoś* sb sth).

zazdrość *f.* **1.** (= *żal z powodu czyjegoś powodzenia*) envy; jealousy; **patrzeć z zazdrością** look with envy; **żółknąć z zazdrości** be green with envy. **2.** (= *niepokój o wierność partnera*) jealousy; **ukłucie zazdrości** pang of jealousy; **zżerany przez zazdrość** devoured by jealousy.

zazdrośnica *f.* jealous woman.

zazdrośnie *adv.* with jealousy; (*strzec*) jealously.

zazdrośnik *mp* jealous man.

zazębiać się *ipf.*, **zazębić się** *pf.* **1.** *techn.* mesh; (*o kołach zębatych*) tooth. **2.** *przen.* (= *splatać się*) be inteconnected.

zazgrzytać *pf.* grate.

zazieleniać *ipf.*, **zazielenić** *pf.* **1.** (= *pokrywać roślinnością*) cover with greenery. **2.** (= *brudzić na zielono*) green. ~ **się** *ipf.*, **zazielenić się** *pf.* turn green; *bot.* come into leaf.

zaziębiać *ipf.* **zaziębiać kogoś** give sb a cold. ~**się** *ipf.* catch a cold.

zaziębić (się) *pf.* *zob.* **zaziębiać (się).**

zaziębienie *n.* *med.* cold.

zaziębiony *a.* -eni **jestem zaziębiony** I've got a cold.

zaznaczać *ipf.* **1.** (= *oznaczać*) mark; (*na ma-*

pie, planie) designate; **zaznaczać kółkiem** circle. **2.** (= *uwydatniać*) emphasize. **3.** (= *stwierdzać z naciskiem*) stress; emphasize; **zaznaczyła, że nie ma z tym nic wpólnego** she stressed that she had nothing to do with it. ~**się** *ipf.* (= *uwydatniać się*) be evident.

zaznaczyć (się) *pf. zob.* **zaznaczać (się)**.

zaznać *pf. zob.* **zaznawać**.

zaznajamiać *ipf.* acquaint (*kogoś z kimś / czymś* sb with sb/sth). ~ **się** *ipf.* familiarize o.s. (*z czymś* with sth).

zaznajomić (się) *pf. zob.* **zaznajamiać (się)**.

zaznawać *ipf.* experience; **nie zaznasz spokoju** you will know no peace.

zazwyczaj *adv.* usually; **zazwyczaj nie jadam tak późno** I usually don't eat so late.

zażalenie *n.* complaint; **złożyć zażalenie (na kogoś)** lodge a complaint (against sb).

zażarcie *adv.* fiercely; **pies ujada zażarcie na kogoś** dog is yapping fiercely at sb.

zażartować *pf.* joke.

zażarty *a.* (*o walce, dyskusji*) fierce; (*o wrogu*) sworn.

zażądać *ipf. zob.* **żądać**.

zażegnać *pf.*, **zażegnywać** *ipf.* prevent; head off; (*konflikt*) resolve; **zażegnać niebezpieczeństwo konfliktu na tle etnicznym** head off a danger of ethnic conflict.

zażenowanie *n.* embarrassment.

zażenowany *a.* embarrassed; **czuję się zażenowany** I feel embarrassed.

zażerać *pf. pot.* gobble up. ~ **się** *pf. pot.* gobble up.

zażgać *pf. pot.* cut.

zażółcić *pf.* yellow. ~ **się** *pf.* turn yellow.

zażyczyć *pf.* demand; **ma wszystko, czego sobie zażyczy** he's got everything he can wish for; **zażyczył sobie rozmowy z dyrektorem** he demanded to talk to the manager.

zażyć *pf.* **-żyję -żyjesz, -żyj** *zob.* **zażywać**.

zażyłość *f.* intimacy.

zażyły *a.* familiar; intimate; **być z kimś w zażyłych stosunkach** be on intimate *l.* familiar terms with sb.

zażywać *ipf.* **-am -asz 1.** (= *przyjmować lekarstwo*) take. **2.** (= *doświadczać*) enjoy; **zażywać kąpieli** bathe; **zażywać ruchu** get exercise.

zażywny *a.* (*o kobiecie, mężczyźnie*) portly.

ząb *mi* **-ę-** *Gen.* **-a 1.** (*do gryzienia*) tooth; **boli mnie ząb** I have (a) tootache; **coś na ząb** *pot.* a bit; **dać komuś w zęby** *pot.* punch sb on the jaw; **darowanemu koniowi w zęby się nie zagląda** don't look a gift horse in the mouth; **nie rozumiem ani w ząb** I can't understand a thing; **oko za oko, ząb za ząb** an eye for an eye, a tooth for a tooth; **pasta do zębów** toothpaste; **płacz i zgrzytanie zębów** wailing and gnashing of teeth; **uzbrojony po zęby** armed to the teeth; **zacisnąć zęby** clench one's teeth; **ząb czasu** tooth of time; **ząb mądrości** wisdom tooth; **ząb mleczny** milk tooth; **ząb stały** permanent tooth; **ząb trzonowy** molar; **połamać sobie zęby na czymś** break one's teeth on sth; **rwać zęby** pull teeth; **szczękał zębami** his teeth were chattering; **szczerzyć zęby** grin; **sztu-**

czne zęby false teeth; **trzymać język za zębami** hold one's tongue; **zgrzytać zębami** gnash one's teeth. **2.** (= *coś przypominającego ząb*) (*widelca, wideł*) prong; (*grzebienia, piły*) tooth; (*koła zębatego*) cog.

ząbek *mi* **-bk-** *Gen.* **-a 1.** *emf. zob.* **ząb**; **dziecku wyrzyna się pierwszy ząbek** the baby's first tooth is coming through. **2.** (= *cząstka główki czosnku*) clove. **3.** **wycięty w ząbki** serrated.

ząbkować *ipf.* teethe.

ząbkowanie *n.* (= *wychodzenie nowych zębów*) **1.** teething. **2.** (= *wycięcie w ząbki*) serration.

zbabieć *pf. żart.* become unmanly.

zbaczać *ipf.* deviate; stray; **zbaczać z kursu** veer off course.

zbadać *pf. zob.* **badać**.

zbagatelizować *pf. zob.* **bagatelizować**.

zbałamucić *pf.* **1.** (= *pozyskać czyjeś względy*) seduce. **2.** (= *wprowadzić kogoś w błąd*) deceive. **3.** (= *zmarnować czas*) while away.

zbankrutować *pf.* go bankrupt.

zbankrutowany *a.* bankrupt.

zbaranieć *pf.* be stunned *l.* dumbfounded; **zbaranieć ze zdumienia** stare in amazement.

zbawca *mp* rescuer; *t. rel.* savior.

zbawczy *a.* (= *dobroczynny*) beneficial, salutary.

zbawczyni *f. zob.* **zbawca**.

zbawiać *ipf.* (= *wybawiać z trudnej sytuacji*) save, rescue, deliver, redeem (*sb*) (*od czegoś* from sth); *rel.* save.

Zbawiciel *mp rel.* Savior; Redeemer.

zbawić *pf. zob.* **zbawiać**.

zbawienie *n. t. rel.* redemption; salvation.

zbawiennie *adv.* beneficially.

zbawienny *a.* beneficial; salutary.

zbeletryzować *pf.* fictionalize.

zbełtać *pf.* stir (*sth*) up.

zbereźnik *mp pl.* **-icy** *l.* **-iki** lecher, debaucher; **stary zbereźnik** *pog. l. żart.* dirty old man.

zbesztać *pf. pot.* scold, tell (*sb*) off (*za coś* for sth).

zbezczeszczać *ipf.*, **zbezcześcić** *pf.* **-szczę -ścisz** desecrate, defile.

zbędny *a.* useless, needless, redundant, superfluous.

zbić *pf.* **zbiję zbijesz, zbij 1.** *zob.* **zbijać**. **2.** (= *sprawić lanie*) give (*sb*) a thrashing; **zbić kogoś do nieprzytomności** beat sb unconscious; **zbić kogoś na kwaśne jabłko** beat sb to a jelly; beat sb black and blue. **3.** (= *stłuc*) break. **4.** (= *skaleczyć*) hurt, cut. ~ **się** *pf.* **1.** *zob.* **zbijać się**. **2.** (= *stłuc się*) break, get broken *l.* smashed; **wazon się zbił** the vase got broken.

zbiec (się) *pf.* **zbiegnę zbiegniesz, zbiegnij, zbiegł** *zob.* **zbiegać (się)**.

zbiednieć *pf.* get poorer, grow poor, become impoverished.

zbiedzony *a.* emaciated, lank, worn to a shadow, haggard, drawn.

zbieg¹ *mp pl.* **-owie** (= *uciekinier*) fugitive, runaway.

zbieg² *mi pl.* **-i** (= *zetknięcie się*) junction, confluence; **zbieg ulic** confluence (of streets), street junction; **zbieg okoliczności** coincidence.

zbiegać *ipf.* **1.** (= *biec w dół*) run downhill; **zbiec po schodach** run downstairs. **2.** (= *uciekać*) run away; **zbiec z więzienia** escape from prison. **3.** (= *upływać*) pass, go by. – *pf.* (= *przewędrować*) run all over. ~ **się** *ipf.* **1.** (*gromadzić się*) gather, crowd, flock. **2.** (= *łączyć się w jednym punkcie*) converge. **3.** (= *mieć miejsce w tym samym czasie*) coincide. **4.** (= *kurczyć się*) shrink.

zbiegnąć *pf.* **-gnij, -gł** *zob.* **zbiegać.**

zbiegowisko *n.* gathering, crowd.

zbieleć *pf.* whiten; **oko mu zbielało na ten widok** *żart.* the sight knocked him.

zbieracki *a.* collecting; **pasja zbieracka** passion for collecting.

zbieractwo *n.* **1.** (= *kolekcjonowanie*) collecting. **2.** *antrop.* gathering.

zbieracz *mp,* **zbieraczka** *f. Gen.pl.* **-ek 1.** (= *kolekcjoner*) collector. **2.** *ogr.* picker, gatherer. **3.** *antrop.* gatherer.

zbierać *ipf.* **1.** (= *gromadzić*) collect, gather; **zebrać myśli** collect *l.* gather one's thoughts; **zebrać siły** gather (up) one's strength, brace up; **zebrać odwagę** pluck *l.* muster up one's courage; **zbierać same piątki** *szkoln.* get straight As. **2.** (= *zwoływać*) gather, assemble. **3.** (= *uprzątać*) clear, pick up. **4.** *roln.* (*zboże*) harvest; (*owoce*) pick, gather; **kto wiatr sieje, burzę zbiera** he who sows the wind shall reap the whirlwind. **5.** (*układać*) style; **zebrać włosy w kok** put the hair in a bun. **6.** *krawiectwo* gather, take in; **zebrać z boków** take in the sides; **zebrać fałdy** take in folds. ~ **się** *ipf.* **1.** (= *gromadzić się*) gather; meet, convene; **Izba Reprezentantów zbierze się jutro** the House of Representatives will convene tomorrow; **zebrać się w kupę** *pot.* pull o.s. together. **2.** (= *łącząc się, tworzyć skupisko*) gather, accumulate; **chmury zebrały się na horyzoncie** clouds gathered on the horizon. **3.** (= *być gromadzonym*) be collected, be assembled; **ziarnko do ziarnka, a zbierze się miarka** take care of the cents and the dollars will take care of themselves. **4.** (= *przygotowywać się*) prepare, get ready (*do czegoś* for sth) (*do zrobienia czegoś* to do sth); **zbierać się w drogę** prepare to leave; **powinniśmy się zbierać** we ought to get ready to leave; **zebrać się na odwagę** summon up one's courage; **zebrać się w sobie** brace up; **zbiera się na deszcz** it's going to rain; **zbiera mi się na wymioty** I feel sick.

zbieranina *f.* mixed lot.

zbiesić *pf.* **-szę -sisz** drive (*sb*) wild, infuriate. ~ **się** *pf.* run wild.

zbieżność *f.* convergence, concurrence; **zbieżność kół** *mot.* toe-in.

zbieżny *a.* convergent, concurrent; **zez zbieżny** *med.* convergent *l.* internal squint.

zbijać *ipf.* **1.** (= *łączyć za pomocą gwoździ*) nail down. **2.** (= *zrzucać*) throw off; **jej cios zbił go z nóg** her blow knocked him down; **zbić kogoś z tropu** stop sb in his *l.* her tracks; confuse sb; diconcert sb; **zbijać bąki** goof around *l.* off, fool

away time, loiter away. ~ **się** *ipf.* (= *skupiać się*) concentrate.

zbilansować *pf. zob.* **bilansować.**

zbiorczy *a.* collective, comprehensive; **konto zbiorcze** *fin.* joint account.

zbiorek *mi* **-rk-** (= *tomik*) collection.

zbiorę *itd. pf. zob.* **zebrać.**

zbiornica *f.* collecting center.

zbiornik *mi Gen.* **-a 1.** (*naczynie*) container, tank. **2.** *hydrol.* reservoir; **zbiornik retencyjny** storage reservoir.

zbiornikowiec *mi* **-wc-** *Gen.* **-a** *żegl.* (oil) tanker.

zbiorowisko *n.* **1.** (= *nagromadzenie*) accumulation, gathering, collection. **2.** *bot.* (plant) community.

zbiorowo *adv.* collectively, together.

zbiorowość *f.* community.

zbiorowy *a.* **1.** collective; **odpowiedzialność zbiorowa** collective responsibility; **umowa zbiorowa** *ekon.* collective agreement; **rzeczownik/liczebnik zbiorowy** *gram.* collective noun/numeral; **rezerwacja zbiorowa** block booking. **2.** (= *plony*) crop.

zbiór *mi* **-o- 1.** (= *zestawienie, nagromadzenie*) collection, set; **zbiór wierszy/opowiadań** collection of poems/short stories. **2.** *pl.* (= *kolekcja*) collection; **zbiory muzealne** museum collection. **3.** *mat.* set, class; **zbiór pusty** empty *l.* nullset; **zbiór skończony/nieskończony** finite/infinite set; **zbiór przeliczalny/nieprzeliczalny** denumerable/non-denumerable set; **teoria zbiorów** set theory; **suma/iloczyn zbiorów** the union/intersection of sets. **4.** *roln.* (= *sprzęt zboża*) harvest. **5.** *zw. pl. roln.* (= *zebrane zboże*) crop; **obfite zbiory** abundant crops; **zbiór na pniu** standing crop.

zbiórka *f. Gen.pl.* **-ek 1.** (= *zebranie*) gathering, meeting. **2.** (= *zbieranie, gromadzenie*) collection, gathering.

zbir *mp pl.* **-y** thug, cutthroat.

zbitka *f. Gen.pl.* **-ek** cluster; **zbitka spółgłosek** *l.* **spółgłoskowa** *fon.* consonantal cluster.

zbity *a.* **1.** (= *pobity*) beaten up. **2.** (= *zraniony wskutek uderzenia*) injured; **wyrzucić kogoś na zbity pysk** throw sb out head first. **3.** (= *twardo ubity*) packed. **4.** (= *rozbity na kawałki*) broken.

zbiurokratyzować *pf. zob.* **biurokratyzować.**

zblaknąć *pf.* **-knie -kł** *l.* **-knął -kła** fade, pale.

zblamować się *pf. pot.* make a fool of o.s., lose face, put one's foot in it.

zblazowany *a.* blasé, bored, jaded.

zblednąć *pf.* **zblednij, zbladł** *l.* **zbladnął zbladła** *l.* **zbledła zbledli 1.** (= *stać się bladym*) pale, turn white. **2.** (= *wypłowieć*) fade, lose color.

zbliznowacenie *n. med.* cicatrization.

zbliznowacieć *pf. med.* cicatrize, heal over.

zbliżać *ipf.* **1.** (= *przybliżać*) bring nearer *l.* closer; **zbliżać coś do oka** bring sth close to the eye. **2.** (= *zaprzyjaźniać*) become close, make friends with; **zbliżać ludzi** bring (*people*) together *l.* closer to one another. **3.** (= *czynić lepiej znanym*) make (*sth*) familiar. **4.** (= *czynić podobnym*) liken, assimilate. ~ **się** *ipf.* **1.** (= *przysu-*

wać się, podchodzić) approach (*do kogoś/czegoś* sb/sth); come up (*do kogoś/czegoś* to sb/sth). **2.** (= *zaprzyjaźniać się*) become close, make friends (*z kimś* with sb). **3.** *tylko ipf.* (= *być podobnym*) approximate. **4.** *tylko ipf.* (= *następować*) be coming *l.* approaching; draw up; **zbliża się czas czegoś** the time for sth is coming.

zbliżenie *n.* **1.** (= *kontakt*) close *l.* friendly relations; **zbliżenie z ludźmi** close relations with people; **zbliżenie fizyczne** sexual intercourse. **2.** *fot., film* close-up.

zbliżony *a.* similar, approximate; **kręgi zbliżone do kogoś** sb's close associates.

zbliżyć (się) *pf. zob.* **zbliżać (się).**

zblokować *pf.* **1.** (*łączyć*) form a block, unite in a block, connect. **2.** *techn.* clutch.

zbluzgać *pf. pot.* give (*sb*) hell, jump all over (*sb*).

zbłaźnić się *pf.* **-ij** make a fool of o.s.

zbłądzić *pf.* **1.** (= *zgubić drogę*) stray, go astray, lose one's way, get lost. **2.** *lit.* (= *popełnić błąd*) err.

zbłąkany *a.* stray; **zbłąkana kula** *przen.* stray bullet.

zbocze *n. Gen.pl.* **-y** slope, incline.

zboczenie *n.* **1.** *psych.* perversion, aberration, deviation; **zboczenie seksualne** sexual deviation. **2.** (= *zejście z kursu*) deviation; **zboczenie z drogi** detour.

zboczeniec *mp* **-ńc-** *pl.* **-y** *pog.* pervert.

zboczony *a.* **-eni** perverted; **ty chyba jesteś zboczony** you must be crazy *l.* nuts.

zboczyć *pf. zob.* **zbaczać.**

zbojkotować *pf. zob.* **bojkotować.**

zbolały *a.* **1.** (= *obolały*) aching, sore, painful. **2.** (= *smutny, bolesciwy*) sorrowful; *lit.* dolorous.

zbombardować *pf.* bomb.

zborny *a.* **punkt zborny** rallying point.

zboru *mi zob.* **zbór.**

zboże *n. Gen.pl.* **zbóż 1.** (*roślina*) crop (plant). **2.** (*ziarno*) cereal. **3.** *przen.* **zapłacić jak za zboże** pay through the nose.

zbożny *a. lit.* worthy, godly.

zbożowy *a.* grain, cereal; **rośliny zbożowe** cereals; **kawa zbożowa** chicory coffee; **wołek zbożowy** grain weevil (*Calandra granaria*).

zbój *mp Gen.pl.* **-ów** robber, highwayman; *pog.* (= *bandzior*) thug.

zbójca *mp lit.* robber, bandit, highwayman.

zbójecki *a.* robbers'; **banda zbójecka** band of robbers; *pog.* (= *zbrodniczy*) criminal.

zbójnicki *a.* highland robbers'.

zbójnik *mp* highland robber.

zbór *mi* **-o- 1.** *rel.* (= *gmina*) (Protestant) community. **2.** *rel.* (= *świątynia*) Protestant church *l.* chapel.

zbraknąć *pf.* **-knie -kło** *zob.* **zabraknąć.**

zbratać (się) *pf. zob.* **bratać (się).**

zbrązowieć *pf. zob.* **brązowieć.**

zbroczyć *pf.* **zbroczyć coś krwią** stain sth with blood.

zbrodnia *f. Gen.pl.* **-i 1.** (= *przestępstwo*) crime; **zbrodnia doskonała** perfect crime; **zbrodnia ludobójstwa** genocide; **zbrodnia przeciwko**

ludzkości crime against humanity; **zbrodnie wojenne** war crimes. **2.** *prawn.* (= *czyn naganny*) felony.

zbrodniarka *f. Gen.pl.* **-ek, zbrodniarz** *mp* criminal; **zbrodniarz wojenny** war criminal.

zbrodniczy *a.* criminal.

zbroić[1] *pf.* **zbroję zbroisz, zbrój, zbroić coś** (= *spłatać figla*) do mischief, play a prank.

zbroić[2] *ipf.* **zbroję zbroisz, zbrój 1.** (= *wyposażać w broń*) arm. **2.** *techn.* reinforce. **3.** *bud.* develop, furnish (*sth*) with utilities. **~ się** *ipf.* (= *wyposażać się w broń*) arm o.s.

zbroja *f. Gen.* **-oi** *broń, hist.* armor, *Br.* armour.

zbrojarz *mp bud.* steel fixer.

zbrojenie *n.* **1.** *bud.* reinforcement. **2.** *pl. wojsk.* armament; **wyścig zbrojeń** armament race.

zbrojeniowy *a.* **1.** *wojsk.* arms; **przemysł zbrojeniowy** arms industry, military sector. **2.** *techn.* reinforcing; **drut/pręt zbrojeniowy** reinforcing wire/rod.

zbrojmistrz *mp Gen.pl.* **-ów** armorer.

zbrojnie *adv.* militarily, by force of arms.

zbrojny *a.* armed, military; **siły zbrojne** armed forces; **interwencja zbrojna** military intervention.

zbrojownia *f. Gen.pl.* **-i** armory.

zbrukać *pf. lit.* soil, besmirch (*sth*) (*czymś* with sth). **~ się** *pf. lit.* soil one's hands (*czymś* with sth).

zbrutalizować *pf.* brutalize.

zbryzgać *pf.* spatter, splash, splatter (*sb l. sth*) (*czymś* with sth); **zbryzgać kogoś/coś wodą** splash water over sb/sth.

zbrzydnąć *pf.* **-dnij, -dł** *l.* **-dnął -dła -dli 1.** (= *stać się brzydkim*) grow *l.* become ugly, lose one's beauty. **2.** (= *sprzykrzyć się*) pall (*komuś* on sb); **zbrzydło mi to** I'm sick of it.

zbrzydzić *pf.* **zbrzydzić coś komuś** make sb loathe sth; **zbrzydzić sobie coś** be sick of sth.

zbudować *pf.* **1.** (*wznieść*) build, raise, erect, construct; **nie od razu Kraków zbudowano** Rome wasn't built in a day. **2.** (*stworzyć*) create; **zbudować coś od podstaw** create sth from scratch. **3.** (= *sporządzić*) construct. **4.** (= *ułożyć*) arrange, compose.

zbudowany *a.* **1.** (= *wzniesiony*) built, raised, constructed, erected. **2.** (= *ułożony*) composed, constructed; **zdanie niepoprawnie zbudowane** incorrectly composed sentence. **3.** *lit.* (= *podniesiony na duchu*) elevated (*czymś* by sth).

zbudzić *pf.* **1.** wake (*sb*) (up), awaken, arouse, waken; **zbudzić kogoś ze snu** arouse sb from sleep; **ten hałas zbudziłby umarłego** this noise could wake *l.* awaken the dead. **2.** (= *wywołać*) arouse, raise, awaken, wake; **zbudzić w czyimś umyśle wątpliwość/podejrzenie** raise doubt/suspicion in sb's mind; **zbudzić miłość w czyimś sercu** wake love in sb's heart. **~ się** *pf.* **1.** (= *przebudzić się*) wake (up), awaken, waken. **2.** (= *dać się odczuć*) rise, stir; **w jej sercu zbudziła się litość** pity stirred in her heart.

zbujać *pf. pot.* fool, hoax.

zbuk *mi Gen.* **-a** *pot.* addled egg, rotten egg.

zbulwersować *pf. zob.* **bulwersować.**

zbuntować (się) *pf. zob.* **buntować (się).**

zbuntowany *a.* rebellious, insurgent; **zbuntowana młodzież** rebellious youth; **zbuntowane oddziały** rebel *l.* insurgent troops.

zburzyć *pf.* **1.** (= *rozwalić*) ruin, demolish, pull (*sth*) down. **2.** (= *zmącić, przerwać*) break, interrupt. **3.** (= *zwichrzyć*) ruffle. ~ **się** *pf.* **1.** (*o wodzie*) seethe, boil. **2.** *pot.* (= *rozgniewać się*) blow one's stack.

zbutwiały *a.* decayed, rotten.

zbutwieć *pf. zob.* **butwieć.**

zbycie *n.* **na zbyciu** *handl.* in stock.

zbyć *pf.* **zbędę zbędziesz, zbądź** *zob.* **zbywać.**

zbyt[1] *mi handl.* sale, sales; **rynek zbytu** outlet, ready market.

zbyt[2] *adv.* too; (= *zbytnio, nad miarę*) excessively, unduly, overly; **zbyt mało czasu/pieniędzy** too little time/money; **zbyt ambitny** too *l.* overly ambitious; overambitious.

zbytecznie *adv.* unnecessarily, needlessly.

zbyteczny *a.* unnecessary, needless, superfluous.

zbytek *mi* -tk- **1.** (= *przepych*) luxury. **2.** *iron.* (= *nadmiar*) excess; **to zbytek łaski z twojej strony** that's too kind of you.

zbytki *pl. Gen.* -ów (= *figle*) pranks, tricks.

zbytkowny *a. lit.* luxurious, sumptuous.

zbytni *a.* excessive, undue; **nie cieszył się zbytnią popularnością** *iron.* he wasn't too popular.

zbytnio *adv.* excessively, overly, unduly, too; **nie bierz sobie tego zbytnio do serca** don't take it too seriously; don't take it to heart; **ona zbytnio mu ufała** she trusted him too much.

zbywać *pf.* -am -asz **1.** (= *sprzedawać*) sell (off). **2.** (= *ignorować*) ignore, get rid of, dismiss. **3.** (= *wystąpić w nadmiarze*) be in excess, be left over. **4.** *gt. ipf. z przeczeniem* **nie zbywa komuś na czymś** sb doesn't lack sth; **na czelności mu nie zbywa** he has a lot of cheek; **nie zbędzie ci na niczym** *przest.* you shall want for nothing.

zbywalność *f. prawn.* transferability.

zbywalny *a. prawn.* transferable.

zbzikować *pf. pot.* go nuts (*na punkcie kogoś/ czegoś* about *l.* on sb/sth).

zbzikowany *a. pot.* crazy, kooky, cranky.

z-ca *abbr.* (= *zastępca*) deputy.

zdać *pf.* **zdadzą 1.** *zob.* **zdawać. 2.** (= *pomyślnie złożyć egzamin*) pass; **zdać egzamin** pass an exam *l.* examination. ~ **się** *pf.* **1.** *zob.* **zdawać się. 2.** (= *przydać się*) prove useful, come in handy; **nie zdać się na nic** be no use; **to się (nie) zda psu na budę** it's completely useless.

zdalny *a. techn.* remote; **zdalne sterowanie** remote control.

zdanie *n.* **1.** (*wypowiedzenie*) sentence; **w kilku zdaniach** in a couple of sentences; **nie umie dwóch zdań sklecić** he doesn't know how to put two sentences together; **urwać w pół zdania** stop in the middle of a sentence *l.* in mid-sentence. **2.** (= *opinia*) opinion; **wyrobić sobie zdanie** form an opinion (*o kimś/czymś* about sb/sth); **moim zdaniem** in my opinion; to my mind; as far as I am concerned; **bez dwóch zdań** (there are) no

two ways about it; **nie mam zdania** I have no opinion; **jestem zdania, że...** I'm of the opinion that...; **zdania są podzielone** opinions are divided, opinions vary. **3.** *gram.* sentence; (= *część zdania złożonego*) clause; **zdanie proste/złożone** simple/complex sentence; **zdanie rozwinięte** compound sentence; **zdanie nadrzędne/podrzędne/współrzędne** main/subordinate/coordinate clause; **zdanie dopełnieniowe/przydawkowe/okolicznikowe** complementary/attributive/adverbial clause; **równoważnik zdania** verbless sentence, sentence fragment. **4.** *log.* proposition. **5.** *muz.* phrase.

zdaniowy *a. gram.* sentence; **akcent zdaniowy** sentence stress.

zdany *a.* dependent (*na kogoś/coś* on sb/sth); **być zdanym na własne siły** be left on one's own resources.

zdarcie *n.* **nie do zdarcia** hardy, tough, durable.

zdarł *itd. pf. zob.* **zedrzeć.**

zdarzać *ipf.* put sth in sb's way; **brać, co los zdarzy** take what fortune puts in one's way; **przypadek zdarzył, że...** chance would have it that... ~ **się** *ipf.* happen, occur; **tak się zdarzyło, że...** it so happened that...; **zdarzył się dziwny wypadek** a strange incident occurred *l.* took place; **nieczęsto się zdarza, żeby...** it seldom *l.* rarely happens that...; **gdyby ci się zdarzyło go zobaczyć** should you happen to see him.

zdarzenie *n.* **1.** event, occurrence, incident; **przebieg zdarzeń** the course of events. **2.** **z prawdziwego zdarzenia** real, genuine; **specjalista z prawdziwego zdarzenia** genuine expert.

zdarzyć (się) *pf. zob.* **zdarzać (się).**

zdatny *a.* fit, suitable; **woda zdatna do picia** drinkable water; **zdatny do użytku** fit for use; **zdatny do służby (wojskowej)** fit for service.

zdawać *ipf.* -aję -ajesz, -awaj **1.** (= *przekazywać*) turn over; **zdać z czegoś sprawę** *l.* **relację** deliver *l.* render an account of sth, give an account of, relate sth; **zdać sobie sprawę z czegoś** realize sth, be aware of sth. **2.** *tylko ipf.* **zdawać (egzamin)** take an exam *l.* examination; **zdawać na studia** take an entrance exam (to university). ~ **się** *ipf.* **1.** (= *polegać*) rely, fall back (*na kogoś/ coś* on sb/sth); **zdać się na los** be resigned to one's fate; **zdaj się na mnie** you can count on me; trust me. **2.** (*o czymś pozornym*) appear, seem; **chwila zdaje się wiecznością** a moment seems to last forever; **chyba ci się zdaje** you must be imagining things. **3.** (*wyraża przypuszczenie l. niepewność*) **zdaje mi się, że...** it seems (to me) that...; **zdaje się, że to radio jest zepsute** this radio seems to be out of order.

zdawczo-odbiorczy, zdawczy *a.* **protokół zdawczo-odbiorczy** delivery acceptance certificate.

zdawkowo *adv.* casually, offhand.

zdawkowy *a.* **1.** (= *dokonany od niechcenia*) casual, brusque, offhand; **zdawkowa uwaga** casual remark. **2.** **moneta zdawkowa** *lit.* small currency.

zdążać *ipf.*, **zdążyć** *pf.* **1.** (= *nadążać*) keep pace, keep up (*za kimś/czymś* with sb/sth). **2.**

(= *być na czas*) be in time (*na coś* for sth). **3.** (= *zrobić coś w wyznaczonym czasie*) finish on time, meet the deadline; **zdążymy przed zmierzchem** we'll make it before dusk. **4.** *tylko ipf. lit.* (= *podążać*) head (*ku czemuś* for *l.* toward sth); **zdążać donikąd** be getting nowhere.

zdecentralizować *pf. zob.* **decentralizować**.

zdechlak *mp pl.* **-ki** *l.* **-cy** *pot.* weakling, softy.

zdechły *a.* **1.** (*o zwierzęciu*) (= *martwy*) dead. **2.** *pot.* (= *skrajnie zmęczony*) used up, dead tired, exhausted; **jestem zupełnie zdechły** I'm exhausted.

zdechnąć *pf.* **-chnij, -chł** *zob.* **zdychać**.

zdecydować *pf.* **1.** (= *postanowić*) decide (*o czymś* on sth); make *l.* take *l.* give a decision (*o czymś* on sth). **2.** (= *mieć zasadnicze znaczenie*) be decisive, decide; **okoliczności zdecydowały inaczej** circumstances decided otherwise; **zdecydował o tym przypadek** chance decided it. **~ się** *pf.* **1.** (= *postanowić*) make up one's mind, reach a decision; decide, resolve (*na coś* on sth) (*zrobić coś* to do sth); (= *dokonać wyboru*) make a choice; **musisz zdecydować** you have to choose. **2.** (= *zostać rozstrzygniętym*) be decided, be settled, be resolved.

zdecydowanie[1] *n.* resolution, resolve, determination, firmness.

zdecydowanie[2] *adv.* **1.** (= *stanowczo*) firmly, strongly, resolutely. **2.** (= *niewątpliwie*) definitely, undoubtedly.

zdecydowany *a.* **1.** (= *stanowczy*) firm, determined, resolute; **zdecydowany na coś** bent on sth; **zdecydowany zrobić coś** determined to do sth; **on jest zdecydowany na wszystko** he will stick *l.* stop at nothing. **2.** (= *niewątpliwy*) unquestionable; **zdecydowane zwycięstwo** sweeping victory.

zdefasonować *pf.* put (*sth*) out of shape.

zdefiniować *pf. zob.* **definiować**.

zdeformować *pf. zob.* **deformować**.

zdefraudować *pf. zob.* **defraudować**.

zdegenerować się *pf. zob.* **degenerować się**.

zdegenerowany *a.* degenerated, degraded.

zdegradować *pf.* **1.** (= *ukarać obniżeniem stopnia*) demote (*z czegoś* from sth, *do czegoś* to sth); (= *pomniejszyć rangę l. znaczenie*) reduce (*do czegoś* to sth); degrade, belittle. **2.** *chem.* degrade. **~ się** *pf.* **1.** undergo demotion *l.* reduction (*do czegoś* to sth). **2.** *chem.* undergo degradation.

zdegustowany *a.* disgusted, dismayed.

zdejmę *itd. pf. zob.* **zdjąć**.

zdejmować *pf.* **1.** (= *ściągać*) take (*sth*) down *l.* off, remove; (*ubranie*) take (*sth*) off; (*zwł. kapelusz*) *form.* doff; **zdjąć pokrywkę z pudełka** take the lid off a box; **zdjąć książkę z półki** take a book down from the shelf; **zdjąć płaszcz/buty/kapelusz** take off one's coat/shoes/hat. **2.** *przen.* **zdjąć komuś kamień z serca** *przen.* take a weight *l.* load off sb's mind; **zdjąć przedstawienie (z afisza)** take off a performance; **wyglądasz jak zdjęty z krzyża** you look more dead than alive. **3.** (= *usunąć*) remove, take (*sb l.* sth) off; **zdjąć kogoś (ze stanowiska)** *pot.* take sb off (his *l.* her position); **zdjąć**

straże *l.* **posterunki** *wojsk.* withdraw the guard. **4.** (*o emocjach*) (= *ogarniać*) seize (*sb*); **zdjął ją strach/lęk/niepokój** she was seized with fear/anxiety/concern. **5.** (= *uchylać, odwoływać*) lift, cancel, take (*sth*) back; **zdejmować embargo** lift an embargo; **zdjąć z kogoś zaklęcie** free sb from a spell; **zdjąć z kogoś odpowiedzialność za coś** relieve sb of responsibility for sth. **6.** *pot.* (= *fotografować*) take a shot of (*sb l.* sth). **~ się** *ipf. pot.* (= *fotografować się*) get photographed.

zdekapitalizować się *pf. zob.* **dekapitalizować się**.

zdeklarować się *pf.* state one's position (*w sprawie czegoś* on sth); declare (*za czymś* / *przeciwko czemuś* for/against sth).

zdeklarowany *a.* avowed, professed.

zdeklasować (się) *pf. zob.* **deklasować (się)**.

zdeklasowany *a.* degraded, declassed.

zdekompletować *pf. zob.* **dekompletować**.

zdekompletowany *a.* incomplete.

zdekomunizować *pf. zob.* **dekomunizować**.

zdekoncentrować (się) *pf. zob.* **dekoncentrować (się)**.

zdekonspirować (się) *pf. zob.* **dekonspirować (się)**.

zdelegalizować *pf. zob.* **delegalizować**.

zdelegalizowany *a.* outlawed, officially banned.

zdemaskować (się) *pf. zob.* **demaskować (się)**.

zdematerializować (się) *pf. zob.* **dematerializować (się)**.

zdementować *pf. zob.* **dementować**.

zdemilitaryzować *pf. zob.* **demilitaryzować**.

zdemilitaryzowany *a. polit.* demilitarized; **strefa zdemilitaryzowana** demilitarized zone.

zdemobilizować *pf. zob.* **demobilizować**.

zdemolować *pf. zob.* **demolować**.

zdemontować *pf. zob.* **demontować**.

zdemoralizować (się) *pf. zob.* **demoralizować (się)**.

zdemoralizowany *a.* **1.** (= *o osłabionym morale*) demoralized. **2.** (= *pozbawiony zasad*) corrupt, depraved.

zdenerwować *pf.* irritate, annoy, upset, exasperate. **~ się** *pf.* get upset, get irritated.

zdenerwowanie *n.* irritation, annoyance, exasperation.

zdenerwowany *a.* upset, irritated, annoyed, exasperated.

zdeponować *pf. zob.* **deponować**.

zdeprawować (się) *pf. zob.* **deprawować (się)**.

zdeprawowany *a.* depraved, corrupt.

zdeprecjonować *pf. zob.* **deprecjonować**.

zdeprymować *pf. zob.* **deprymować**.

zdeptać *pf.* **-pczę -pczesz** *l.* **-pcę -pcesz, -pcz** **1.** (= *depcząc, zniszczyć; t. przen.*) trample (*sth*) (down), crush (*sth*) (with the feet), stamp (*sth*) out. **2.** (= *potraktować z pogardą*) trample on (*sth*); **zdeptać czyjeś prawa/uczucia** trample on sb's rights/feelings. **3.** (= *przemierzyć*) walk about all over (*sth*).

zderzać się *ipf.* collide, crash.

zderzak *mi Gen.* **-a** **1.** *mot.* bumper. **2.** *kol.* buffer.

zderzenie *n.* **1.** (= *wzajemne uderzenie*) collision (*z czymś* with sth); crash, impact; **zderzenie samolotów/samochodów** air/car crash; **zderzenie czołowe/boczne** head-on/side collision; **zderzenie sprężyste** *fiz.* elastic collision; **w chwili zderzenia** *fiz.* on impact. **2.** (= *konfrontacja*) clash.

zderzyć się *pf. zob.* **zderzać się**.

zdesperowany *a.* desperate.

zdeterminowany *a.* determined, resolute.

zdetonować *pf. zob.* **detonować**.

zdetronizować *pf. zob.* **detronizować**.

zdewaluować *pf. zob.* **dewaluować**.

zdewastować *pf. zob.* **dewastować**.

zdezaktualizować się *pf. zob.* **dezaktualizować się**.

zdezawuować (się) *pf. zob.* **dezawuować (się)**.

zdezelowany *a.* (*o meblu, sprzęcie domowym*) dilapidated, rickety; (*o pojeździe*) battered, wrecked; *pred.* falling to pieces; (*o części odzieży*) worn; *pred.* the worse for wear.

zdezerterować *pf. zob.* **dezerterować**.

zdezintegrować *pf. zob.* **dezintegrować**.

zdezorganizować *pf. zob.* **dezorganizować**.

zdezorientować *pf. zob.* **dezorientować**.

zdezorientowany *a.* confused, confounded, disoriented; *pred.* at a loss.

zdezynfekować *pf. zob.* **dezynfekować**.

zdębieć *pf. zob.* **dębieć**.

zdiagnozować *pf. zob.* **diagnozować**.

zdjąć *pf.* **zdejmę zdejmiesz, zdejmij** *zob.* **zdejmować**.

zdjęcie *n.* **1.** (= *zdejmowanie*) removal, taking down; **zdjęcie z krzyża** *rel.* (*t. jako motyw w sztuce*) the Deposition (from the Cross). **2. zdjęcie kar kościelnych** *rz.-kat.* absolution from ecclesiastic penalties. **3.** (= *fotografia*) photograph, picture; *pot.* photo, pic; shot, snap, snapshot; **na zdjęciu** in the photograph; **zrobić komuś/czemuś zdjęcie** take a picture of sb/sth; photograph sb/sth; **zdjęcie rentgenowskie** X-ray, radiograph.

zdjęciowy *a.* photographic, pictorial; **sesja/ekipa zdjęciowa** photographic session/team; **dokumentacja zdjęciowa** pictorial record.

zdjęty *a.* removed; *pot.* (= *zwolniony*) fired; **jak z krzyża zdjęty** more dead than alive.

zdławić *pf.* **1.** *lit.* (= *zadusić*) strangle, choke, throttle. **2.** (= *stłumić siłą*) suppress, quell. **3.** (= *powstrzymać*) hold back, check, restrain.

zdmuchiwać *ipf.*, **zdmuchnąć** *pf.* **-ij 1.** (= *dmuchając, gasić*) blow (*sth*) out. **2.** (= *dmuchając, usuwać*) blow (*sth*) off; **zdmuchnąć komuś coś sprzed nosa** snatch sth (away) from under sb's nose. **3.** *tylko pf. pot.* (= *zjeść łapczywie*) gobble (*sth*) up *l.* down.

zdobić *pf.* **zdób 1.** (= *dekorować*) decorate, adorn. **2.** (= *być ozdobą*) grace; **nie suknia zdobi człowieka** it is not the cowl that makes the monk.

zdobnictwo *n.* **1.** decorative art. **2.** (*ozdoby*) ornamentation.

zdobniczy *a.* decorative; **sztuka zdobnicza** decorative art; **motyw zdobniczy** decorative *l.* ornamental motif.

zdobny *a.* **zdobny w coś** *l.* **czymś** *lit.* decorated *l.* ornamented with sth.

zdobycz *f. pl.* **-e 1.** (= *coś uzyskanego*) acquisition; **zdobycze terytorialne** *polit.* territorial acquisitions. **2.** (= *łup wojenny*) booty, loot. **3.** (= *ofiara drapieżnika*) prey. **4.** (= *obiekt polowania*) quarry. **5.** (= *trofeum*) trophy. **6.** *pl.* (= *osiągnięcia*) achievements, accomplishments.

zdobyczny *a.* trophy; **broń zdobyczna** trophy weapons.

zdobyć *pf.* **-będę -będziesz, -bądź, zdobywać** *ipf.* **-am -asz 1.** (= *zagarnąć*) capture, conquer, seize, take. **2.** (= *uzyskać*) get, acquire, find. **3.** (= *osiągnąć*) win, achieve, gain, obtain; **zdobyć bramkę** score a goal; **zdobyć ostrogi** *przen.* win one's spurs; **zdobyć szczyt** climb a summit. **4.** (= *zjednać sobie kogoś*) win (*sb*) over; **zdobyć czyjeś serce** win sb's heart; **zdobyć męża/żonę** win a husband/wife. **~ się** *pf.*, **zdobywać się na coś** (= *wykrzesać z siebie*) summon sth (up); **zdobywać się na odwagę/energię** summon up one's courage/energy; **zdobywać się na szczerość** dare to speak frankly; **zdobywać się na zrobienie czegoś** bring o.s. to do sth.

zdobywca *mp* **1.** (= *ktoś, kto dokonał podboju; t. przen.*) conqueror; **zdobywcy bieguna południowego** conquerors of the South Pole; **zdobywca serc** conqueror of hearts; **Wilhelm Zdobywca** *hist.* William the Conqueror. **2.** (= *ktoś, kto odniósł sukces we współzawodnictwie*) winner; **zdobywca pierwszej nagrody** winner of the first prize; **zdobywca Oskara/nagrody Nobla** Academy Award/Nobel Prize winner. **3.** *sport* (= *ktoś, kto zdobywa bramki, punkty itp.*) scorer.

zdobywczy *a.* conquering; **wyprawa zdobywcza** conquest.

zdobywczyni *f. zob.* **zdobywca**.

zdolność *f.* **1.** (= *sprawność, umiejętność*) skill, ability; *pl.* (= *uzdolnienia*) talent, gift; **zdolność logicznego myślenia** ability of logical thinking; **zdolności organizacyjne** organizational skills; **on ma wielkie zdolności** he's very talented. **2.** (= *możność działania*) capacity, capability; **zdolność prawna** legal capacity; **zdolność produkcyjna** economic capacity.

zdolny *a.* **1.** (= *bystry*) bright, smart; (= *utalentowany*) gifted, talented. **2.** (= *posiadający warunki l. kwalifikacje*) **zdolny do czegoś** fit for sth; **zdolny do (zrobienia) czegoś** (= *mający siłę, śmiałość l. możliwość*) capable of (doing) sth; **mężczyźni zdolni do noszenia broni** men capable of carrying arms; **on jest zdolny do wszystkiego** he's capable of anything.

zdołać *pf.* **zdołać coś zrobić** be able to do sth, manage to do sth.

zdołować *pf. zob.* **dołować**.

zdominować *pf.* dominate.

zdopingować *pf.* motivate, encourage (*sb*) (*do (zrobienia) czegoś* to (do) sth).

zdrabniać *ipf.* use the pet *l.* diminutive form of (*sth*).

zdrada *f.* **1.** (= *wiarołomstwo*) treachery, breach of faith; **zdrada stanu** high treason. **2.** (=

niewierność) infidelity, unfaithfulness; **zdrada małżeńska** adultery, marital infidelity.

zdradliwy *a.* **1.** (= *podstępny*) treacherous, insidious. **2.** (= *zwodniczy*) deceptive; (= *niebezpieczny*) dangerous.

zdradzać *ipf.* **1.** (= *przechodzić na stronę nieprzyjaciela*) betray, be a traitor; **zdradzić ojczyznę** betray one's country; **zdradzić czyjeś zaufanie** betray sb's trust *l.* confidence. **2.** (= *sprzeniewierzać się*) betray (*sb l. sth*); fail (*sb*). **3.** (= *być niewiernym w małżeństwie, uczuciach*) be unfaithful to sb. **4.** (= *ujawniać*) give away, reveal, disclose; **nieład w pokoju zdradzał czyjąś obecność** mess in the room gave away sb's presence. **5. zdradzać objawy czegoś** (= *przejawiać*) show signs *l.* symptoms of sth. **~ się** *ipf.* **1.** (= *być wobec siebie niewiernymi*) be unfaithful to each other. **2.** (= *ujawniać się*) give o.s. away; **nie zdradzał się ze swoimi zamiarami** he didn't give away his intentions.

zdradzić (się) *pf. zob.* **zdradzać (się)**.

zdradziecki *a.* treacherous, traitorous, insidious.

zdrajca *mp*, **zdrajczyni** *f.* **1.** (= *ktoś, kto przeszedł na stronę nieprzyjaciela*) traitor; (*o kobiecie t.*) traitress. **2.** (= *sprzeniewierca*) betrayer.

zdrapać *pf.* **-pię -piesz** *zob.* **zdrapywać**.

zdrapka *f. Gen.pl.* **-ek** scratch card.

zdrapywać *ipf.* scratch (*sth*) off *l.* away, scrape (*sth*) off *l.* away (*z czegoś* from sth).

zdrewniały *a.* woody, lignified.

zdrewnieć *pf.* grow woody, lignify.

zdrętwiały *a.* numb, stiff.

zdrętwieć *pf.* grow numb, stiffen.

zdrobniale *adv.* diminutively; **zwracać się do kogoś zdrobniale** nickname sb.

zdrobniały *a.* diminutive; **imię zdrobniałe** pet name.

zdrobnić *pf.* **-ij** *zob.* **zdrabniać**.

zdrobnienie *n. jęz.* diminutive.

zdrojowy *a.* spring, spa.

zdrowie *n.* health; **ministerstwo zdrowia** ministry of health; **świadectwo zdrowia** health certificate, certificate of health; **ośrodek zdrowia** health center, clinic; **służba zdrowia** health service, health care; **końskie zdrowie** the health of an ox, robust health; **być okazem zdrowia** be the picture of health; **tryskać zdrowiem** radiate health; **jak pana zdrowie?** how are you doing?; **na zdrowie!** (*toast*) cheers!; (*po kichnięciu*) (God) bless you!; **zapaść na zdrowiu** lose one's health; **to kosztuje mnie dużo zdrowia** it's causing me a lot of worry, it stresses me out a lot, it takes a heavy toll of me; **wracać, powrócić do zdrowia** recover, recuperate, regain one's health; **jak pragnę zdrowia** *pot.* as I'm sitting *l.* standing.

zdrowieć *pf.* get better.

zdrowo *adv.* **1.** healthily. **2.** (= *będąc zdrowym*) in good health; **wyglądać/trzymać się zdrowo** look/stay well. **3.** (= *korzystnie dla zdrowia*) healthily. **4.** *pot.* (= *mocno*) soundly, hard; **zdrowo oberwać** be hit hard.

zdroworozsądkowy *a.* commonsense, practical.

zdrowotność *f.* state of health.

zdrowotny *a.* **urlop zdrowotny** sick leave; **warunki zdrowotne** sanitary conditions.

zdrowy *a.* **1.** (= *odznaczający się zdrowiem*) healthy, sound; *pred.* well. **2.** *pot.* (= *tryskający zdrowiem*) robust; (*zwł. o kobiecie*) buxom; **bądź zdrów** keep well; **cały i zdrowy** safe and sound; **być przy zdrowych zmysłach** be mentally sound, be of sound mind; **zdrowy jak ryba** *l.* **rydz** as right as rain; as fit as a fiddle; in perfect health; **gadaj zdrów** *pot.* whatever you say; **w zdrowym ciele zdrowy duch** sound mind in a sound body. **3.** (= *rozsądny*) sound, sensible, reasonable; **zdrowy rozsądek** common sense; **zdrowy osąd** sound judgment; **na zdrowy rozum...** common sense tells us that... **4.** (= *moralny*) wholesome. **5.** (= *służący zdrowiu*) healthy, wholesome. **6.** (= *będący objawem zdrowia*) healthy, sound; **zdrowy sen** sound sleep. **7.** (= *niezepsuty, nierobaczywy*) sound. **8.** *pot.* (= *duży, silny*) mighty, sound, hard; **zdrowe lanie** sound beating *l.* thrashing.

zdrożeć *pf.* go up (in price).

zdrożny *a.* wrong, sinful, immoral.

zdrożony *a.* tired (by travel), fatigued, wayworn.

zdrój *mi* **-o-** *Gen.pl.* **-ów 1.** *lit.* (= *źródło*) spring. **2.** (= *kurort*) resort, spa.

zdrów *a. indecl. zob.* **zdrowy**.

zdrówko *n. Gen.pl.* **-ek** *żart.* health; **jak zdrówko?** how are you doing?

zdruzgotać *pf.* **-oczę -oczesz** *l.* **-ocę -ocesz**, **-ocz** crush, shatter.

zdruzgotany *a.* crushed; **była zdruzgotana tą wiadomością** she was devastated by this message.

zdrzemnąć się *pf.* **-ij** take a nap, doze off.

zdublować *pf.* **1.** double, repeat. **2.** *teatr* understudy sb *l.* sth. **3.** *sport* (= *wyprzedzić o okrążenie*) lap. **~ się** *pf.* (= *pojawić się w dwóch egzemplarzach*) occur twice.

zdumieć (się) *pf. zob.* **zdumiewać (się)**.

zdumienie *n.* astonishment; **wprawić kogoś w zdumienie** astonish sb, amaze sb; **ku memu zdumieniu** to my astonishment.

zdumiewać *ipf.* astonish, amaze. **~ się** *ipf.* be amazed.

zdumiewający *a.* astounding, astonishing, amazing, stupendous.

zdumiony *a.* **-eni** astounded, astonished, amazed (*czymś* at sth) (*słysząc/widząc coś* to hear/see sth).

zdun *mp pl.* **-i** *l.* **-owie** stove fitter.

zdurnieć *pf. pot.* lose one's head, take leave of one's senses.

zdusić *pf.* **-szę -sisz 1.** (= *zgnieść*) squeeze, squash. **2.** (= *zgasić*) smother, extinguish. **3.** (= *stłumić*) supress; (*bunt, powstanie*) crush, quell.

zduszony *a.* supressed, stifled; **zduszony szept** low whisper.

zdwajać *ipf.*, **zdwoić** *pf.* **-wój 1.** (= *podwajać*) double. **2.** (= *potęgować*) heighten.

zdybać *pf.* **-bię -biesz** *pot.* catch sb doing sth.

zdychać *ipf.* **1.** (*o zwierzęciu*) die; **pogoda pod zdechłym psem** lousy weather. **2.** *pog.* (*o czło-*

wieku) be damned, go to devil; **zdychać z głodu** be starving *l.* starved.

zdymisjonować *pf.* depose.

zdynamizować *pf.* make more dynamic.

zdyscyplinowanie *n.* discipline.

zdyscyplinowany *a.* disciplined.

zdyskontować *pf.* **1.** *handl.* discount. **2.** (= *wyciągnąć korzyść*) take advantage of.

zdyskredytować *pf. zob.* **dyskredytować**.

zdyskwalifikować *pf. zob.* **dyskwalifikować**.

zdystansować się *pf. zob.* **dystansować się**.

zdyszany *a.* breathless, winded; *pred.* out of breath, short of breath.

zdziadzieć *pf.* **1.** *pot.* (= *zestarzeć się*) grow old. **2.** *pot.* (= *zbiednieć*) get poorer.

zdziałać *pf. lit.* accomplish, achieve.

zdziczały *a.* **1.** (semi-)wild; *biol.* feral. **2.** (= *nieokrzesany, barbarzyński*) savage, brutal, barbarous.

zdziczeć *pf.* **1.** (= *stać się dzikim*) run wild; *biol.* become feral. **2.** (= *ulec zdziczeniu*) become brutal.

zdziczenie *n.* brutality, barbarousness.

zdziecinnieć *pf.* grow childish *l.* infantile.

zdziecinnienie *n.* dotage, second childhood.

zdzielić *pf. pot.* (= *uderzyć*) clout, knock, bump.

zdzierać *ipf.* **1.** (= *szarpiąc, usuwać*) tear (*sth*) off; **zedrzeć komuś zasłonę z oczu** *przen.* open sb's eyes. **2.** (= *niszczyć wskutek noszenia*) wear (*sth*) out *l.* down. **3. zdzierać z kogoś (skórę)** *pot.* (= *żądać zbyt wysokiej zapłaty*) rip sb off. **~ się** *ipf.* **1.** (= *niszczyć się*) wear out. **2.** *pot.* (= *niszczyć zdrowie*) ruin one's health; **nerwy mi się zdarły** my nerves are frayed *l.* frazzled.

zdzierca *mp Gen.pl.* **-ów** extortioner.

zdzierstwo *n. pot.* extortion, rip-off.

zdzierżyć *pf.* hold; suffer, bear, stand (*sth*); **już dłużej (tego) nie zdzierżę** I can't stand it any more.

zdziesiątkować *pf. zob.* **dziesiątkować**.

zdziesiątkowany *a.* decimated.

zdzira *f. pot., obelż.* whore, hooker, bitch.

zdziwaczeć *pf.* go queer (in the head).

zdziwić *pf.* surprise; **nic mnie już nie zdziwi** nothing will surprise me any more. **~ się** *pf.* be surprised; **nie zdziwiłbym się, gdyby...** I wouldn't be surprised if...

zdziwienie *n.* surprise.

zdziwiony *a.* **-eni** surprised.

zdzwonić się *pf. pot.* get in touch by phone.

zdźwigać się *pf.* strain o.s.

ze *prep. zob.* **z**.

zebra *f.* **1.** *zool.* zebra; **zebra górska** mountain zebra (*Equus zebra*); **zebra Grévy'ego** Grévy's zebra (*E. grevyi*). **2.** (*przejście dla pieszych*) crosswalk; *Br.* zebra crossing.

zebrać (się) *pf.* **zbiorę zbierzesz** *zob.* **zbierać (się)**.

zebranie *n.* meeting, gathering, assembly; **zebranie sprawozdawczo-wyborcze** general election meeting; **zebranie otwarte** open meeting; **walne zebranie** general meeting; **zebranie towarzyskie** social gathering, get-together.

zebu *n. indecl. zool.* zebu (*Bos indicus*).

zecer *mp druk.* typesetter, compositor.

zecernia *f. Gen.pl.* **-i** *l.* **-ń** composing room *l.* department.

zecerski *a.* typesetting, composing; **błąd zecerski** misprint.

zechcieć *pf.* **-chcę -chcesz, -chciej** be willing to do sth; **czy zechce** *l.* **nie zechciałaby pani usiąść** would you like to take a seat.

zedrzeć (się) *pf.* **zedrę zedrzesz, zedrzyj, zdarł** *zob.* **zdzierać (się)**.

Zefir *mp mitol.* Zephyr.

zefir *mi poet.* zephyr.

zefirek *mi* **-rk-** *Gen.* **-a** *l.* **-u** breeze.

zegar *mi Gen.* **-a** **1.** (*do mierzenia czasu*) clock; **zegar z kukułką** cuckoo clock; **zegar wiszący** wall clock; **zegar stojący** grandfather clock; **zegar słoneczny** sundial; **zegar kwarcowy** *el.* quartz clock; **zegar atomowy** *fiz.* atomic clock; **zgodnie ze wskazówkami zegara** clockwise; **w kierunku przeciwnym do wskazówek zegara** counterclockwise; **zegar się spóźnia/śpieszy** the clock is slow/fast. **2.** (*licznik*) meter.

zegarek *mi* **-rk-** *Gen.* **-a** watch; **jak w zegarku** like clockwork; **zajmie mi to dosłownie pięć minut z zegarkiem w ręku** it will take me exactly five minutes, it will take me just five minutes by the clock; **na moim zegarku jest już trzecia** it's three by my watch.

zegarmistrz *mp pl.* **-owie** *Gen.pl.* **-ów** watchmaker.

zegarmistrzowski *a.* watchmaker; **zegarmistrzowska precyzja** surgical precision.

zegarowy *a.* time, clock; **bomba zegarowa** time bomb; **mechanizm zegarowy** clockwork.

zegarynka *f. Gen.pl.* **-ek** speaking clock, telephone time service.

zegnać *pf.* **1.** *zob.* **zganiać**. **2.** (= *zmęczyć gonieniem*) jade. **3.** (= *przemierzyć*) run in search for sth.

zegnę *itd. pf. zob.* **zgiąć**.

zegzemplifikować *pf. zob.* **egzemplifikować**.

zejście *n.* **1.** (= *droga w dół*) descent. **2.** *med.* (= *zgon*) decease.

zejść *pf.* **zejdę zejdziesz zszedł** *l.* **zeszedł zeszła zeszli** **1.** *zob.* **schodzić**. **2.** (= *przejść wielokrotnie*) walk (*a way*) many times. **~ się** *pf. zob.* **schodzić się**.

zekranizować *pf. zob.* **ekranizować**.

zelektryfikować *pf.* electrify.

zelektryzować *pf.* electrify.

zelota *mp* fanatic, zealot, enthusiast.

zelować *ipf.* sole.

zelówka *f. Gen.pl.* **-ek** sole.

zelżeć *pf.* ease, subside.

zelżyć *pf.* **-yj** insult, revile, disparage, villify.

zełgać *pf. pot.* lie, tell a lie.

zemdleć *pf.* faint.

zemdlenie *n.* fainting.

zemdlić *pf.* make sb feel sick, sicken; **zemdliło mnie** I felt sick.

zemdlony *a.* **-eni** in a faint; **upadła zemdlona** she fainted and fell down.

zemleć *pf.* **zmielę zmielesz, zmełł zmełła zmełli** *l.* **zmielił zmieliła zmielili** grind; (*mięso*) mince.

zemrzeć *pf.* **zemrę zemrzesz, zemrzyj, zmarł** die, pass away.

zemsta *f.* revenge, vengeance, retaliation; **pragnienie zemsty** desire of revenge; **pałać chęcią zemsty** be filled with the thoughts of vengeance; **poprzysiąc komuś zemstę** swear revenge on sb; **zemsta jest rozkoszą bogów** revenge is mine.

zemścić się *pf.* **-mszczę -mścisz** **1.** (= *dokonać zemsty*) revenge o.s. (on sb), take it out on sb. **2.** (= *wywołać złe następstwa*) come back to haunt you.

zen *mi rel.* Zen.

zendra *f. metal.* scale.

zenit *mi* **1.** *astron.* zenith; **słońce w zenicie** the Sun at its zenith. **2.** (= *najwyższy poziom*) zenith; **podniecenie sięgało zenitu** excitement reached the zenith.

zenza *f. żegl.* = **zęza**.

zepchnąć (się) *pf.* **-ij** *zob.* **spychać (się)**.

zepnę *itd. pf. zob.* **spinać**.

zeppelin *mi Gen.* **-a** *lotn.* zeppelin, airship.

zeprać *pf.* **spiorę spierzesz** = **sprać**; *zob.* **spierać**.

zepsucie *n.* depravity, corruption, spoiling.

zepsuć *pf.* **1.** (= *uszkodzić*) break, damage; **zepsuć sobie oczy** ruin one's eyes; **zepsuć powietrze** pollute the air. **2.** (= *pogorszyć*) get worse, aggravate. **3.** (= *odebrać przyjemność*) spoil, ruin; **zepsuć komuś humor** spoil sb's good mood; **zepsuć nastrój** spoil the atmosphere *l.* mood; **zepsuć przyjęcie** ruin a party. **4.** (= *rozpieścić*) spoil, pamper. **5.** (= *zdemoralizować*) corrupt, deprave, demoralize. **~ się** *pf.* **1.** (= *przestać działać*) break down, get damaged, stop working. **2.** (*o jedzeniu*) go bad. **3.** (= *pogorszyć się*) deteriorate, get worse; (*o obyczajach*) go corrupt; **nasze relacje się zepsuły** our relations have deteriorated.

zepsuty *a.* **1.** (= *uszkodzony*) broken, out of order. **2.** (= *dotknięty rozkładem*) (*o jedzeniu*) spoiled; (*o zębach*) decayed. **3.** (= *niemoralny*) corrupt, depraved; **zepsuty do szpiku kości** thoroughly corrupt.

zerkać *ipf.*, **zerknąć** *pf.* **-ij** peep, peek.

zero *n.* **1.** (*cyfra*) zero. **2.** *techn.* zero; **zero absolutne** *l.* **bezwzględne** absolute zero. **3.** (= *nic*) zero, nothing, zilch, nought; **zainteresowanie spadło do zera** the interest has reached the zero mark; **sprzedaż sprowadza się do zera** the sale reaches the vanishing point; **ostrzyc się na zero** shave off one's hair; **mniej niż zero** the lowest of the low. **4.** *pog.* (= *człowiek przeciętny*) nobody, cipher; **jesteś zwykłym zerem** you're a mere cipher.

zerować *ipf.* reset.

zerowy *a.* zero; **południk zerowy** *geogr.* prime meridian; **punkt/stan zerowy** *fiz.* zero point/state; **zabytek klasy zerowej** national historical landmark; *Br.* Grade I listed building.

zerówka *f. Gen.pl.* **-ek 1.** *pot.* (*cyfra*) zero. **2.** *pot., szkoln.* pre-elementary school (*in Poland*).

zerwać (się) *pf.* **-rwę -rwiesz, -rwij** *zob.* **zrywać (się)**.

zeżrzeć *pf.* **-ij 1.** *zob.* **zrzynać. 2.** *pot.* (= *sprawić lanie*) give (*sb*) a thrashing. **3.** *wulg.* (= *odbyć stosunek z kobietą*) fuck. **~ się** *pf. wulg.* have a crap; **zeżrzeć się w gacie** *t. przen.* shit o.s.

zeschły *a.* = **zeschnięty**.

zeschnąć (się) *pf.* **-nij, zeschnął** *l.* **zesechł** *l.* **zsechł, zeschła zeschli** *zob.* **zsychać (się)**.

zeschnięty *a.* dry, dried, withered; (*o ziemi, skórze, wargach*) parched.

zeskakiwać *ipf.*, **zeskoczyć** *pf.* (= *skakać w dół*) jump down (*skądś* from sth); jump off (*skądś* of sth).

zeskanować *pf. zob.* **skanować**.

zeskok *mi sport* landing.

zeskrobać *pf.* **-bię -biesz, zeskrobywać** *ipf.* scrape off.

zesłać *pf.* **-ślę -ślesz, -ślij** *zob.* **zsyłać**.

zesłanie *n.* (*kara*) exile; **na zesłaniu** in exile; **udać się na zesłanie** go into exile.

zesłaniec *mp* **-ńc- Voc. -cze** *pl.* **-y** exile, exiled person.

zesłańczy *a.* exile.

zesmrodzić się *pf. pot.* let out a fart; pollute the air.

zespalać *ipf.* join, link together, unite. **~ się** *ipf.* join, unite, team.

zespawać *pf.* weld (*sth*) together.

zespolić (się) *pf. zob.* **zespalać (się)**.

zespołowo *adv.* in a team.

zespołowy *a.* team, common, collective; **praca zespołowa** teamwork; **klasyfikacja zespołowa** *sport* team classification.

zespół *mi* **-o- 1.** (*grupa profesjonalistów*) group, team. **2.** (*grupa muzyczna*) band, group. **3.** (*zbiór*) set, group. **4.** *bud.* complex. **5.** (= *drużyna sportowa*) team; **kapitan zespołu** captain. **6.** *techn.* aggregate, unit.

zesrać się *pf.*, **zesrywać się** *ipf.* **-am -asz** *wulg.* shit; **choćbyś się zesrał** no chance.

zestalać *ipf.*, **zestalić** *pf. chem.* solidify.

zestarzeć się *pf.* age, grow old.

zestaw *mi* **1.** (= *komplet*) set; (*mebli*) suite; (*narzędzi*) kit. **2.** (= *zbiór*) set, collection; (*kolorów*) combination; (*pytań*) set. **3.** *techn.* (= *zespół, bateria*) aggregate, unit.

zestawiać *ipf.*, **zestawić** *pf.* **1.** (= *zdjąwszy, odstawiać*) put away. **2.** (= *zdjąwszy, przestawiać niżej*) take down. **3.** (= *składać w całość*) put together; **zestawić złamaną kość** set a broken leg. **4.** (= *porównywać*) compare, confront; **zestawiać coś z czymś** set sth against sth, juxtapose sth with sth; **zestawiać tłumaczenie z oryginałem** juxtapose the translation with the original. **5.** (= *sporządzać spis, zestawienie*) draw up, compile.

zestawienie *n.* **1.** (= *porównanie*) comparison, juxtaposition; **w zestawieniu z czymś** in comparison with. **2.** (= *kompozycja*) composition, arrangement, combination. **3.** (= *wykaz, spis*) register, breakdown.

zestrajać *ipf.* put in tune, tune (up). **~ się** *ipf.* tune up.

zestroić (się) *pf.* -ój *zob.* **zestrajać (się)**.

zestrój *mi* -o- *Gen.pl.* -ów harmony, concord, consonance; **zestrój akcentowy** *fon.* consonance.

zestrugać *pf.*, **zestrugiwać** *ipf.* whittle down *l.* away.

zestrzelać *ipf.*, **zestrzelić** *pf.*, **zestrzeliwać** *ipf.* shoot (*sb l. sth*) down.

zestrzyc *pf.* -strzygę -strzyżesz -strzygł, zestrzygać *ipf.* clip off.

ze szczętem *adv.* completely, utterly, thoroughly.

zeszczupleć *pf.* grow slim, lose weight.

zeszkapieć *pf.* **1.** (*o koniu*) grow thin. **2.** *pot.* (*o człowieku*) go to the dogs.

zeszlifować *pf.*, **zeszlifowywać** *ipf.* grind down.

zeszłoroczny *a.* last year's; **obchodzi mnie to tyle, co zeszłoroczny śnieg** I don't care a damn *l.* a fig (about it).

zeszłowieczny *a.* **1.** of the last century. **2.** *przen.* (= *staroświecki, niedzisiejszy*) old-worldly; *pred.* passé, out of date.

zeszły *a.* last, past; **w zeszłym roku** last year; **zeszłej niedzieli** last Sunday; **za zeszły miesiąc** for the last month; **z zeszłego tygodnia** from the last week.

zeszmacić *pf. pot.* **1.** (*odzież*) wear (*sth*) out (into rags). **2.** *przen.* (*człowieka*) deprave, corrupt. **~ się** *pf. pot.* get depraved *l.* corrupted.

zeszpecić *pf.* make (*sb l. sth*) look ugly, deface, disfigure, mar (*sb's*) looks. **~ się** *pf.* turn ugly.

zesztukować *pf.* piece together, eke out.

zesztywnieć *pf.* **1.** (= *stać się sztywnym*) stiffen. **2.** (= *stać się oschłym*) become cold *l.* standoffish.

zeszycik *mi* notebook.

zeszyć *pf.* -szyję -szyjesz, -szyj *zob.* **zszywać**.

zeszyt *mi* **1.** (*do notatek*) notebook; **zeszyt w kratkę/w szerokie linie/w wąskie linie/gładki** checked/big-lined/narrow-lined/plain notebook. **2.** (= *numer czasopisma*) issue, number.

zeszytowy *a.* notebook.

zeszywać *ipf.* -am -asz *zob.* **zszywać**.

ześlę *itp. pf. zob.* **zesłać**.

ześlizg *mi* **1.** *techn.* chute. **2.** *sport* slide.

ześlizgiwać się *ipf.*, **ześlizgnąć się** *pf.* -ij, **ześliznąć się** *pf.* -znę -źniesz, -źnij slide down, slip; **noga mi się ześliznęła z krawężnika** my foot slipped off the curb.

ześrodkować *pf.* concentrate, focus. **~ się** *pf.* concentrate, focus (*na czymś* on sth).

ześrodkowywać (się) *ipf. zob.* **ześrodkować (się)**.

ześrubować *pf.*, **ześrubowywać** *ipf.* screw together.

zeświecczać *ipf.* secularize.

zeświecczeć *pf.* -eję -ejesz become secularized.

zeświecczyć *pf. zob.* **zeświecczać**.

ześwinić się *pf. pot.* behave like a swine.

zet *mi Gen.* -a **1.** (*litera*) the letter z; **od a do zet** from start to finish. **2.** (= *coś nieokreślonego*) z; **pociąg wyrusza z miejscowości igrek do miejscowości zet** the train goes from the place Y to the place Z.

zetknąć (się) *pf.* -ij *zob.* **stykać (się)**.

zetleć *pf.* **1.** (= *spalić się*) smoulder (away), burn away without a flame. **2.** (= *rozpaść się*) rot, decay.

zetrzeć (się) *pf.* zetrę zetrzesz, zetrzyj, starł *zob.* **ścierać (się)**.

zeuropeizować (się) *pf. zob.* **europeizować (się)**.

Zeus *mp mit.* Zeus.

zeus *ma icht.* John Dory (*Zeus faber*).

zew *mi lit.* call, appeal; **zew krwi** the call of the wild; **zew natury** the call of nature.

zewidencjonować *pf. zob.* **ewidencjonować**.

zewnątrz *adv.* **z zewnątrz** from (the) outside; **na zewnątrz** outside, outdoors, out there; **od zewnątrz** from (the) outside. – *prep.* + *Gen.* **na zewnątrz budynku** outside the building.

zewnętrznie *adv.* **1.** (= *od zewnątrz*) externally, on the outside; **stosować zewnętrznie** *med.* apply externally. **2.** (= *powierzchownie*) superficially; **ona jest zewnętrznie podobna do matki** she looks like her mother; she resembles her mother in appearance.

zewnętrzny *a.* external, outside, exterior, outer; **świat zewnętrzny** outer world; **wpływy zewnętrzne** external influence; **wygląd zewnętrzny** external appearance; **do użytku zewnętrznego** *med.* for external use; not to be applied internally; **objawy zewnętrzne** *med.* external symptoms; **obrażenia zewnętrzne** *med.* external injuries; **ucho zewnętrzne** *anat.* outer *l.* external ear; **kąt zewnętrzny** *geom.* exterior angle.

zewrzeć (się) *pf.* zewrę zewrzesz, zewrzyj, zwarł *zob.* **zwierać (się)**.

zewsząd *adv.* from everywhere, from far and wide; (= *z każdej strony*) all around, all about, on every side; **miasto otoczone zewsząd lasami** the city was completely surrounded with woods.

zez *mi Gen.* -a squint; **zrobić zeza** cross one's eyes; **zez zbieżny/rozbieżny** *pat.* convergent/divergent squint; **patrzeć na kogoś, na coś zezem** squint, frown on sb/sth, look at sb/sth from the corner of the eye.

zezłościć *pf.* -oszczę -ościsz anger, exasperate, irritate. **~ się** *pf.* be irritated *l.* exasperated.

zeznać *pf. zob.* **zeznawać**.

zeznanie *n. prawn.* testimony; **złożyć zeznanie** testify, give evidence; **odwołać zeznanie** recant *l.* repudiate *l.* retract one's testimony.

zeznawać *ipf.* -aję -ajesz, -awaj *prawn.* testify, give evidence; **zeznawać pod przysięgą** testify under oath.

zezować *ipf.* **1.** (= *mieć zeza*) squint, be cross-eyed. **2.** *pot.* (= *patrzeć ukradkiem*) squint, look obliquely (*na kogoś/coś* at sb/sth).

zezowaty *a.* cross-eyed, squint-eyed; **zezowate szczęście** bad *l.* tough luck.

zezwalać *ipf.* allow, permit (*na coś* sth); approve (*na coś* of sth).

zezwierzęcenie *n.* bestiality, barbarity.

zezwolenie *n.* permission, permit; **oficjalne zezwolenie na wyjazd** official leave permit; **wydać zezwolenie** issue a permit.

zezwolić *pf.* -ól *zob.* **zezwalać**.

zeźlić *pf.* **-ij** raise sb's dander. ~ **się** *pf.* get one's dander up.

zeżreć *pf.* **zeżrę zeżresz, zeżryj, zżarł** *l.* **zeżarł** *zob.* **zżerać.**

zęba *itd. mi zob.* **ząb.**

zębatka *f. Gen.pl.* **-ek** *techn.* rack, gear (toothed) rack.

zębatkowy *a. techn.* cogged.

zębaty *a.* **1.** (= *uzębiony*) toothed. **2.** (= *powycinany w ząbki*) serrated; (*o murze*) crenelated; *Br.* crenellated. **3.** *techn.* cogged.

zębina *f. anat.* dentine.

zębodół *mi* **-do-** *anat.* alveolus.

zębowość *f. fon.* dentality.

zębowy *a. fon.* dental; **spółgłoski zębowe** dental consonants; dentals.

zęza *f. żegl.* bilge.

ZG *abbr.* (= *Zarząd Główny*) General Headquarters.

zgadać się *pf.* find a common topic (*z kimś* with sb); **zgadaliśmy się, że...** we found in the course of the conversation that...; **zgadało się o was** we happened to start talking about you.

zgadnąć *pf.* **-ij, zgadł** *zob.* **zgadywać.**

zgaduj-zgadula *f. Gen.pl.* **-i** guessing game (*played by children*). – *int. dziec.* you guess!

zgadywać *ipf.* guess; *form.* conjecture; **zgadywać czyjeś myśli** read sb's mind.

zgadywanka *f. Gen.pl.* **-ek** quiz; guessing game.

zgadzać się *ipf.* **1.** (= *przyzwalać*) agree, give one's consent (*na coś* to sth); **zgadzać się na ustępstwa** make concessions; **zgadzam się z tobą bez zastrzeżeń** I couldn't agree more; I fully agree with you. **2.** (= *podzielać czyjąś opinię*) agree (*z kimś* with sb); **nie mogę się z wami zgodzić** I can't agree with you; **zgadzać się z samym sobą** rest easy with o.s. **3.** *tylko ipf.* (= *być w zgodzie ze stanem faktycznym*) be correct; (= *nie być w sprzeczności*) tally (*z czymś* with sth); **coś tu się nie zgadza** something's wrong here; **te dwie listy nie zgadzają się (ze sobą)** these two lists don't tally (with each other); **rachunek się zgadza** the check *l.* (*Br.*) cheque is correct; **tak, zgadza się** yes, it's correct *l.* true.

zgaga *f.* **1.** *pat.* heartburn. **2.** *pot.* (= *ktoś dokuczliwy*) nuisance, pest, pain in the neck.

zganiać *ipf.* **1.** (= *spędzać w jedno miejsce*) round up, gather together. **2.** (= *przeganiać*) drive away.

zganić *pf.* rebuke, reprimand, scold (*sb*) (*za coś* for sth).

zgapić się *pf. pot.* miss one's opportunity.

zgarbić się *pf.* stoop, bow *l.* bend one's back.

zgarnąć *pf.* **-ij, zgarniać** *ipf.* **1.** rake up *l.* together. **2. zgarniać forsę** *pot.* make money like hay.

zgasić *pf.* **-szę -sisz 1.** (= *spowodować zgaśnięcie*) put out, extinguish. **2.** (= *wyłączyć*) switch off, turn off; **zgasić silnik** switch off the engine. **3.** (= *stłumić*) kill, suppress, damp (*sth*) down; (*pozbawić chęci l. energii*) *pot.* take the pep out of (*sb*); **zgasić czyjś zapał/czyjąś energię**

damp down sb's enthusiasm/energy; **zgasić czyjeś pomysły** pour *l.* throw cold water on sb's ideas.

zgasnąć *pf.* **-snę -śniesz, -śnij, -sł -śli 1.** (= *przestać się palić*) go out. **2.** (*o silniku*) stall; *pot.* die; **silnik zgasł** the engine died. **3.** *przen.* (= *stracić blask*) darken, become dim; **słońce zgasło** the sun went down. **4.** (= *zaniknąć*) disappear, fade (away); **nadzieja zgasła** the hope faded. **5.** *emf.* (= *umrzeć*) expire.

zgaszony *a.* **-eni** subdued, downcast, depressed; **siedział smutny i zgaszony** he sat there (looking) sad and downcast.

zgermanizować (się) *pf. zob.* **germanizować (się).**

zgęstnieć *pf.* thicken.

zgęszczać *ipf.* thicken, condense, compress (air). ~ **się** *ipf.* thicken.

zgęszczenie *n.* condensation.

zgęścić (się) *pf. zob.* **zgęszczać (się).**

zgiąć (się) *pf.* **zegnę zegniesz, zegnij** *zob.* **zginać (się).**

zgiełk *mi* tumult, turmoil, uproar, noise.

zgiełkliwy *a.* tumultuous, noisy.

zgięcie *n.* bend.

zgilotynować *pf. zob.* **gilotynować.**

zginacz *mi Gen.* **-a** *anat.* flexor.

zginać *ipf.* **1.** (= *pochylać*) bend, bow down; **zginać przed kimś kark** bow and scrape to sb, bow down to sb; **zginać przed kimś kolana** kneel down in front of sb. **2.** (= *wyginać*) curve, inflect. ~ **się** *ipf.* **1.** (= *pochylać się*) bend, bow, stoop. **2.** (= *wyginać się*) bend.

zginarka *f. Gen.pl.* **-ek** *techn.* bender, bending machine *l.* press.

zginąć *pf.* **1.** (= *stracić życie*) perish, die, be killed; **zginąć na polu chwały** lose one's life on the field of honor. **2.** (= *przepaść*) disappear, fade away; **oby nie zginęła polska gościnność** may the Polish hospitality never disappear. **3.** (= *zapodziać się*) get lost; **zginęły moje okulary** my glasses are missing; **czy coś pani zginęło?** have you lost anything?

zgliszcza *pl. Gen.* **-szcz** *l.* **-szczy** ashes, smoldering ruins.

zgliwieć *pf.* ferment into slimy substance.

zgładzić *pf. lit.* (= *zabić*) put (*sb*) to death, kill.

zgłaszać *ipf.* propose, submit, put (*sth*) forward *l.* forth; **zgłaszać pytania/zastrzeżenia** raise questions/objections; **zgłaszać czyjąś kandydaturę** propose sb as a candidate (*do czegoś* for sth); **zgłosić poprawkę** propose an amendment. ~ **się** *ipf.* **1.** (= *zwracać się dokądś*) report; **zgłosił się do lekarza** he reported to the doctor. **2.** (= *okazywać chęć uczestnictwa*) apply, sign up; **zgłosić się do konkursu** enter a contest; **zgłosić się do odpowiedzi** raise one's hand. **3.** (= *odpowiadać na dzwoniący telefon*) answer; **nikt się nie zgłasza** nobody's answering.

zgłębiać *ipf.,* **zgłębić** *pf.* **1.** (= *poznawać dogłębnie*) explore, study thoroughly; **zgłębić zagadkę/tajemnicę** fathom a mystery/secret. **2.** (= *pogłębiać*) deepen.

zgłębnik *mi Gen.* **-a** *med.* probe, bougie.

zgłębnikować *ipf. med.* probe.

zgłębnikowanie *n. med.* probing, sounding.

zgłodnieć *pf.* get hungry.

zgłosić (się) *pf.* **-szę -sisz** *zob.* **zgłaszać (się).**

zgłoska *f. Gen.pl.* **-ek 1.** *fon.* syllable. **2.** *przen.* **zapisać się złotymi zgłoskami** engrave one's name in letters of gold (*w czymś* in sth).

zgłoskotwórczy *a. fon.* syllabic.

zgłoskowiec *mi* **-wc-** *Gen.* **-a** *jęz.* abbreviation.

zgłoszenie *n.* **1.** (= *powiadomienie*) notification. **2.** (= *oferta*) application.

zgłoszeniowy *a.* (*o formularzu*) application.

zgłupieć *pf.* **1.** *pot.* (= *stać się głupim*) become *l.* get silly. **2.** *pot.* (= *stracić pewność siebie*) lose one's head *l.* confidence.

zgnębić *pf.* **1.** (= *przygnębić*) worry, bother, depress, deject. **2.** (= *pognębić*) oppress, persecute.

zgniatacz *mi Gen.* **-a** *hutn.* slabbing *l.* blooming mill.

zgniatać *ipf.* **1.** (= *gnieść*) crumple. **2.** (= *miażdżyć*) squash, crush. **3.** *tylko ipf. techn.* crush.

zgnić *pf.* **zgniję zgnijesz, zgnij 1.** (*zepsuć się*) rot, decay, go off. **2.** *pot.* (= *umrzeć*) rot.

zgnieść *pf.* **zgniotę zgnieciesz zgniótł zgniotła zgnietli** *zob.* **zgniatać.**

zgnilizna *f.* **1.** (*zapach*) foul smell. **2.** (= *demoralizacja*) depravity, corruption. **3.** *ogr.* canker. **4.** *leśn.* decompost.

zgniłek *mi* **-łk-** *Gen.* **-a** (*owoc, warzywo*) spoiled *l.* damaged fruit *l.* vegetable. – *mp* **-łk-** *pl.* **-i** *pot.* (*człowiek*) rouge, scoundrel.

zgniłozielony *a.* brownish green.

zgniły *a.* rotten, putrid; (*o kolorze*) brownish.

zgnoić *pf.* **-ój** *pot.* **1.** (= *zniszczyć, poniżyć*) destroy. **2.** (= *ostro skrytykować*) slam, pan.

zgnuśniały *a.* listless, sluggish.

zgnuśnieć *pf.* become slack, grow sluggish.

zgoda *f.* **1.** (= *pojednanie*) harmony, concord; **być w zgodzie ze swoim sumieniem** be square with one's conscience; **zgoda buduje, niezgoda rujnuje** united we stand divided we fall. **2.** (= *aprobata*) permission, approval, assent, consent; **wyrazić zgodę na coś** give one's assent *l.* consent to sth; **uzyskać czyjąś zgodę** get *l.* secure sb's consent *l.* permission; **bez czyjejś zgody** without sb's consent. **3.** *gram.* agreement, concord. – *int.* (very) good, all right.

zgodnie *adv.* **1.** (= *w zgodzie*) in harmony, in concord. **2.** (= *jednomyślnie, jednogłośnie*) unanimously, in unison. **3.** **zgodnie z czymś** according to sth, in accordance with sth; **wszystko poszło zgodnie z planem** everything went according to plan.

zgodność *f.* harmony, conformity, unanimity.

zgodny *a.* **1.** (= *skłonny do zgody*) agreeable, accommodating, peaceful. **2.** (= *jednomyślny*) unanimous, concordant; **zgodne działanie** concerted action. **3.** (= *dostosowany, dający się pogodzić*) compatible (*z czymś* with sth). **4.** (= *niesprzeczny*) consistent (*z czymś* with sth); **zgodny z prawem** legal.

zgodzić się *pf.* **zgódź** *zob.* **zgadzać się.**

zgolić *pf.* **zgol** *l.* **zgól** shave off.

zgoła *adv. lit.* quite, completely. – *particle* (*z przeczeniem*) at all; **nie powiedział nic zgoła** he didn't say anything at all.

zgon *mi form.* decease, demise; **akt zgonu** death certificate; **stwierdzić zgon** state a death.

zgonić *pf. zob.* **zganiać.**

zgorszenie *n.* scandal, outrage; **siać zgorszenie** cause scandals.

zgorszony *a.* **-eni** scandalized, shocked, outraged, disgusted.

zgorszyć *pf.* scandalize, shock. **~ się** *pf.* be scandalized/shocked.

zgorzel *f. pl.* **-e 1.** *med.* gangrene; **zgorzel gazowa** gas gangrene. **2.** *ogr.* gangrene. **3.** *leśn.* gangrene.

zgorzelina *f.* **1.** *leśn.* gangrene. **2.** *techn.* scale.

zgorzelinowy *a.* gangrenous.

zgorzkniałość *f.* bitterness.

zgorzkniały *a.* bitter.

zgorzknieć *pf.* grow *l.* become embittered.

zgotować *pf. lit.* give, prepare.

zgrabiać *ipf.* **1.** (*zgarniać*) rake up. **2.** (*usuwać*) rake away.

zgrabiały *a.* numb; **zgrabiały z zimna** numb with cold.

zgrabić *pf. zob.* **zgrabiać.**

zgrabieć *pf.* go numb.

zgrabnie *adv.* **1.** (= *zwinnie*) nimbly, deftly, adroitly. **2.** (= *ładnie, foremnie*) nicely, smartly; **bardzo ci zgrabnie w tej sukience** you look very smart in this dress. **3.** (= *gładko, bez trudu*) smoothly, easily, neatly.

zgrabny *a.* **1.** (= *zwinny*) deft, agile, nimble, adroit. **2.** (= *ładny, foremny*) shapely, nice, neat.

zgrać (się) *pf. zob.* **zgrywać (się).**

zgraja *f. Gen.* **-ai 1.** (= *banda*) band, gang. **2.** (= *sfora psów*) pack.

zgramolić się *pf. pot.* **zgramolić się z czegoś** crawl down from sth.

zgranie *n.* harmony; **zgranie w czasie** timing.

zgrany *a.* harmonious; (*o grupie, zespole*) well-integrated.

zgred *mp pl.* **-y** *l.* **-dzi** *pog.* **1.** (= *człowiek starszy*) old fogy *l.* fogey. **2.** (= *ojciec*) (one') old man.

zgromadzać *ipf.* = **gromadzić.**

zgromadzenie *n.* **1.** (*sesja*) meeting, gathering, session; **walne zgromadzenie** general assembly; **zgromadzenie ustawodawcze** legislative assembly; **Zgromadzenie Konstytucyjne** Constitutional Assembly. **2.** *rel.* (= *zakon*) congregation.

zgromadzić (się) *pf. zob.* **gromadzić (się).**

zgromić *pf.* scold, reprimand, rebuke; **zgromić kogoś wzrokiem** wither sb with a glance.

zgroza *f.* horror; **patrzeć ze zgrozą** look horrified; **o zgrozo!** how awful!, horrors!

zgrubiały *a. jęz.* augmentative.

zgrubieć *pf.* **1.** (= *stać się grubym*) grow thicker. **2.** (= *przybrać na wadze*) fatten up, put on *l.* gain weight. **3.** (= *stracić delikatność*) become gruff *l.* callous; (*o głosie*) break.

zgrubienie *n.* **1.** (= *wypukłość*) swelling. **2.** *jęz.* augmentative form.

zgrubny *a. techn.* rough, coarse.

zgrupować *pf.* **1.** (*zebrać*) group. **2.** (*ułożyć*) classify, arrange.

zgrupowanie *n.* **1.** *wojsk.* concentration. **2.** *sport* climatization session.

zgrywa *f. pot.* act.

zgrywać *ipf.* **-am -asz 1.** (= *harmonizować*) harmonize. **2.** (= *synchronizować*) synchronize. **3. zgrywać kolor** *karty* play a suit. **~ się** *ipf.* **1.** *pot.* (= *wygłupiać się*) fool about *l.* around. **2.** *pot.* (= *pozować*) act, play (*na kogoś* sb). **3.** *teatr* (= *przesadzać w grze aktorskiej*) ham it up. **4.** (= *przegrywać w grze hazardowej*) gamble away one's money.

zgrywus *mp pl.* **-y** *pot.* prankster, joker.

zgryz *mi* **1.** *med.* bite, occlusion; **prawidłowy zgryz** correct occlusion; **wada zgryzu** occlusion defect. **2.** *pot.* (= *zmartwienie*) worry.

zgryzać *ipf.* crack, crunch, chew.

zgryzota *f.* grief, heartbreak.

zgryźć *pf.* **zgryzę zgryziesz zgryzł zgryźli** *zob.* **zgryzać.**

zgryźliwie *adv.* harshly, snappishly; **mówić o kimś zgryźliwie** talk harshly about sb.

zgryźliwiec *mp* **-wc-** *pl.* **-y** *pot.* snappy person.

zgryźliwość *f.* **1.** harshness. **2.** (= *kąśliwa uwaga*) cutting *l.* caustic remark.

zgryźliwy *a.* harsh, caustic.

zgrzać *pf.* **zgrzeję zgrzejesz zgrzali** *l.* **zgrzeli** sweat. **~ się** *pf.* become hot.

zgrzany *a.* hot; **nie pij zimnego, bo jesteś zgrzany** you're sweating so don't drink anything cold.

zgrzeblarka *f. Gen.pl.* **-ek** *tk.* carding machine.

zgrzeblić *pf. tk.* card, comb.

zgrzebło *n. Gen.pl.* **-eł 1.** (*do czyszczenia koni*) currycomb. **2.** *tk.* card. **3.** *myśl.* legs of birds of terrestrial habits.

zgrzebny *a.* sackcloth; *tk.* carded; *t. przen.* coarse, rough; **zgrzebne maniery** rough manners.

zgrzeszyć *pf.* **1.** *rel.* sin, commit a sin; **zgrzeszyć przeciwko czemuś** offend against; **zgrzeszyć czymś** sin by doing sth. **2.** (= *uchybić czemuś*) infringe sth.

zgrzewać *ipf. techn.* seal (by heating).

zgrzewarka *f. Gen.pl.* **-ek** welder.

zgrzybiały *a.* doddering, decrepit.

zgrzyt *mi* **1.** (= *odgłos zgrzytania*) grate, grind, jar; **zgrzyty i trzaski** noise interference, blasting; **bez najmniejszego zgrzytu** without the slightest hitch. **2.** *pot.* (= *sprzeczka*) argument. **3.** *pot.* (= *niemiłe wrażenie*) embarrassment; **ale zgrzyt!** what an embarrassment!

zgrzytać *ipf.* **1.** (= *wydawać zgrzyty*) grate, screech, grind; **zawiasy zgrzytają** the hinges are grating. **2. zgrzytać zębami** grind *l.* gnash one's teeth.

zgrzytanie *n.* grating (sounds); **płacz i zgrzytanie zębów** weeping and gnashing of teeth.

zgrzytliwy *a.* grating, rasping.

zgrzytnąć *pf.* **-ij** *zob.* **zgrzytać.**

zguba *f.* **1.** (= *rzecz zgubiona*) lost property. **2.**

(= *klęska*) ruin, destruction, undoing; **ocalić kogoś od zguby** save sb's bacon; **to było jego zgubą** that was his undoing; **skazany na zgubę** doomed, fated.

zgubić *pf.* **1.** (= *stracić*) lose; **zgubić oczko** *dzierganie* miss a stich; **zgubić drogę** get lost, lose one's way; **zgubić wątek** lose the thread; **zgubić takt** miss the bar; **zgubić rytm** miss the rythm; **lepiej z mądrym zgubić, niż z głupim znaleźć** it's better to lose sth with the wise than to find sth with the stupid. **2.** (= *doprowadzić kogoś do klęski*) bring sb to ruin, bring about sb's destruction; **zgubiła ją zazdrość** jealousy brought her to ruin. **~ się** *pf.* **1.** (= *zabłądzić*) get lost, lose one's way; **zgubił się w plątaninie ulic** he got lost in the web of the streets. **2.** (= *stracić orientację w czymś*) get mixed up *l.* confused; **zgubić się w szczegółach** get bogged down in details. **3.** (= *wzajemnie stracić się z oczu*) lose the sight of each other; **zgubić się w tłumie** get lost in a crowd. **4.** (= *zostać zgubionym*) get lost, be mislaid; **gdzieś zgubiły się moje okulary** my glasses are missing somewhere. **5.** (= *doprowadzić się do klęski*) bring about *l.* engineer one's own destruction; **zgubiła się przez swoją zazdrość** jealousy caused her own destruction, jealousy lost her.

zgubny *a.* pernicious, destructive.

zgwałcić *pf.* **1.** (=) rape. **2.** (= *naruszyć*) violate.

zhańbić *pf.* disgrace, dishonor. **~ się** *pf.* disgrace o.s.

zhardzieć *pf.* become haughty, grow arrogant.

zharmonizować *pf. zob.* **harmonizować.**

zheblować *pf.* plane away *l.* down.

zhierarchizować *pf. zob.* **hierarchizować.**

ZHP *abbr.* (= *Związek Harcerstwa Polskiego*) the Polish Scouting Association.

ZHR *abbr.* (= *Związek Harcerstwa Rzeczypospolitej*) the Scouting Association of the Polish Republic.

zhumanizować *pf.* humanize.

ziać *ipf.* **zieję ziejesz ziali** *l.* **zieli 1.** (= *oddychać z trudem*) pant, gasp (for breath). **2.** (= *buchać*) belch (out); **ziać ogniem** belch fire. **3.** (= *wydzielać*) give off; **ziać stęchlizną** reek of stench; **ziać pustką** be empty. **4.** (= *uzewnętrzniać uczucia*) emanate; **ziać nienawiścią/gniewem** breathe hatred/anger. **5.** (= *rozwierać się*) gape; **pod stopami ziała przepaść** there was an abyss under the feet.

ziarenko *n. Gen.pl.* **-ek** *zob.* **ziarnko.**

ziarniak *mi Gen.* **-a** *pat.* granuloma.

ziarnina *f. med.* granulation.

ziarninowy *a. med.* granulate.

ziarnistość *f.* granulation.

ziarnisty *a.* **1.** (= *mający postać ziarna*) granular. **2.** (= *złożony z ziaren*) grainy.

ziarnko *n. Gen.pl.* **-nek 1.** (= *nasionko*) seed; **ziarnko ryżu/żyta/pszenicy** grain of rice/rye/wheat; **ziarnko maku/gorczycy/pieprzu** poppy/mustard/pepper seed; **ziarnko kawy** coffee bean; **ziarnko grochu** pea; **ziarnko do ziarnka, zbierze się miarka** take care of the pennies and the dollars will take care of themselves; **coś trafiło się (komuś), jak ślepej kurze ziarnko** sb got sth by a fluke. **2.** (= *drobina*) grain, particle; **ziarnko piasku/soli** grain of sand/salt. **3.** *przen.* (= *odrobina*) (little) bit; **ziarnko prawdy** grain of truth.

ziarno *n. Gen.pl.* -**ren 1.** (= *nasiono*) seed; **ziarno siewne/kwalifikowane** *roln.* sowable/certified seed; **ziarno na mąkę** flour seed; **ziarno pszenicy/ żyta/owsa/jęczmienia** grain of wheat/rye/oats/ barley; **ziarno kawy/kakaowe** coffee/cocoa bean; **oddzielać ziarno od plew** separate the wheat from the chaff. **2.** (= *drobina*) grain, particle; **ziarno piasku/złota** grain of sand/gold; **ziarno prawdy** *przen.* grain of truth.

ziąb *mi* chill, cold; **ziąb przeszedł mi po plecach** a chill ran down my spine.

zidentyfikować *pf. zob.* **identyfikować**.

zidiocieć *pf.* become idiotic.

zielarski *a.* herbal.

zielarstwo *n.* herbal medicine.

zielarz *mp* herbalist.

ziele *n. pl.* **zioła** *Gen.* **ziół** herb; **zioła lecznicze/ przyprawowe** medicinal/seasoning herbs; **jaskólcze ziele** *bot.* (greater) celandine (*Chelidonium maius*); **kurze ziele** *bot.* tormentil, bloodroot (*Potentilla erecta*).

zieleniak *mi Gen.* -**a** *pot.* (*stragan warzywny*) **1.** greengrocer's stall. **2.** (*wino*) young wine.

zielenica *f. bot.* (= *glon z klasy Chlorophyceae*) green alga.

zielenić się *ipf.* **1.** (= *stawać się zielonym*) turn green. **2.** (= *być zielonym*) show green.

zieleniec *mi* -**ńc**- *Gen.* -**a** lawn.

zielenieć *ipf.* **1.** (= *stawać się zielonym*) turn green. **2.** (= *blednąć*) turn pale; **zielenieć z zazdrości** be green with envy. **3.** (= *być zielonym*) show green.

zielenina *f.* greens.

zieleń *f. pl.* -**e 1.** (*kolor*) green. **2.** (*barwnik*) green; **zieleń chromowa** chrome green; **zieleń malachitowa** malachite green; **zieleń miedziana** green verdigris. **3.** (*roślinność*) greenery; **pas zieleni** green belt. **4.** (= *zielone gałązki do ozdoby*) green.

zielistka *f. Gen.pl.* -**ek** *bot.* spider plant (*Chlorophytum*).

zielnik *mi Gen.* -**a** herbarium.

zielny *a.* herbal; **rośliny zielne** *bot.* herbaceous plants.

zielonawy *a.* = **zielonkawy**.

zielone *n. Gen.* -**ego** *pot.* (= *zielone gałązki do ozdoby*) green; **grać w zielone** play green (*children's game in which a green object must be shown on request*).

zielonka *f. Gen.pl.* -**ek 1.** *roln.* (*pasza*) green fodder. **2.** *bot.* (*grzyb*) man-on-horseback (*Tricholoma equestre*).

zielonkawy *a.* greenish.

zielono *adv.* green; **pomalować coś na zielono** paint sth green; **mieć zielono w głowie** *pot.* (= *być niedojrzałym i naiwnym*) be wet behind the ears.

zielony *a.* -**eńszy**, -**eni** *l.* -**oni 1.** *koloru zielonego* green; **herbata zielona** green tea; **tereny zielo-**ne green areas (*in a city*); **pasza/mieszanka zielona** *roln.* green fodder/mixture; **nawozy zielone** green manure; **Zielone Świątki** *rel.* Pentecost; Whit Sunday, Whitsunday, Whitsun; **zielone światło dla czegoś** *przen.* green light to sth, go-ahead for sth; **pójść na zieloną trawkę** be fired. **2.** (= *blady*) pale. **3.** (*o owocu*) (= *niedojrzały*) green, unripe; **nie mam zielonego pojęcia** I haven't the foggiest *l.* faintest idea.

zielsko *n.* weed.

ziemia *f.* **1.** (= *kula l. skorupa ziemska*) (the) earth; **Ziemia** *astron.* the Earth; **na ziemi** on earth; **trzęsienie ziemi** earthquake. **2.** (*w różnych wyrażeniach przenośnych*) **zetrzeć coś z powierzchni ziemi** wipe sth off the face of the earth; **poruszyć niebo i ziemię** move heaven and earth; **nie z tej ziemi** out of this world. **3.** (= *gleba*) soil, earth; **żyzna ziemia** fertile soil; **pójść do ziemi** go to one's grave; **gryźć ziemię** *przen.* bite the dust. **4.** (= *podłoże, grunt; t. przen.*) ground; **na ziemi** on the ground; **pod ziemią** underground; **nad ziemią** above ground; **na ziemię** *l.* ku ziemi to the ground; **w ziemi** in the ground; **podnieść coś z ziemi** pick sth up off the ground; **suknia do samej ziemi** full-length dress; **spać na gołej ziemi** sleep on the ground; **kłaniać się do samej ziemi** bow to the ground; **stąpać** *l.* chodzić po ziemi have one's both feet on the ground; **zrównać coś z ziemią** raze sth to the ground; **nogi mi wrosły w ziemię** I stood rooted to the ground *l.* to the spot; **zapaść się pod ziemię** disappear without a trace; **ziemia pali się komuś pod nogami** things are getting hot for sb; **wydobyć coś spod ziemi** conjure sth up; **wyrosnąć jakby spod ziemi** spring up; **niech mu ziemia lekką będzie** may he rest in peace. **5.** (= *rola, grunt uprawny*) land, ground; **ziemia orna/jałowa** arable/barren land. **6.** (= *kraina*) land, region; **ziemia mlekiem i miodem płynąca** fertile land; **ziemia niczyja** no-man's land; **Ziemia Święta** the Holy Land; **Ziemia Baffina** *geogr.* Baffin's Land. **7.** *hist.* (*jednostka administracyjna*) land, district. **8.** *geol., techn.* (*rodzaj skały*) earth; **ziemia fulerska/okrzemkowa** filler's/diatomaceous earth. **9.** *pl. chem.* **ziemie alkaliczne/rzadkie** alkaline/rare earths.

Ziemianin *mp pl.* -**anie** *Gen.* -**an** (= *mieszkaniec Ziemi*) terrestrial; (*zwł. w literaturze fantastycznonaukowej*) earthling.

ziemianin *mp pl.* -**anie** *Gen.* -**an** (*dziedzic*) landowner.

Ziemianka *f. Gen.pl.* -**ek** *zob.* **Ziemianin**.

ziemianka *f. Gen.pl.* -**ek 1.** *zob.* **ziemianin**. **2.** (*rodzaj schronienia l. domostwa*) *t. wojsk.* dugout.

ziemiański *a.* landowning.

ziemiaństwo *n.* (= *dziedzice*) landed gentry.

ziemiopłód *mi* -**płod**- agricultural product.

ziemisty *a.* earthy; (*o cerze*) sallow.

ziemniaczany *a. kulin.* potato; **stonka ziemniaczana** *ent.* Colorado beetle (*Leptinotarsa decimlineata*).

ziemniak *mi Gen.* -**a** *kulin., bot.* potato (*Solanum tuberosum*); **ziemniaki w mundurkach** jacket potatoes.

ziemny *a.* earth; **nasyp ziemny** earthworks; **prace ziemne** excavations; **umocnienia ziemne** earthworks; **gaz ziemny** natural gas; **orzech ziemny** *bot.* peanut (plant) (*Arachis hypogaea*); **orzeszek ziemny** *zw. pl. kulin.* peanut.

ziemski *a.* **1.** (= *dotyczący planety*) terrestrial, the earth's; **kula ziemska** the globe; **skorupa ziemska** the earth's crust; **oś ziemska** the earth's axis. **2.** (= *powszedni*) earthly, worldly; **ziemskie troski** worldly concerns. **3.** (= *dotyczący roli*) land; **dobra ziemskie** landed property; **obywatel ziemski** *hist.* landowner.

ziewać *ipf.*, **ziewnąć -ij** yawn; **ziewać od ucha do ucha** let out a gigantic yawn.

ziewnięcie *n.* yawn.

zięba *f. orn.* chaffinch (*Fringilla coelebs*).

ziębić *ipf.* chill, cool; **to mnie ani ziębi, ani grzeje** I don't care about it either way, it leaves me cold.

ziębnąć *ipf.* **ziębnij, ziębnął** *l.* **ziąbł ziębła ziębli** freeze, be cold, feel chilly.

zięć *mp pl.* **-owie** *Gen.* **-ów** son-in-law.

zignorować *pf. zob.* **ignorować**.

zilustrować *pf. zob.* **ilustrować**.

zima *f.* winter; **w zimie** *l.* **zimą** *l.* **zimą** in winter; **płaszcz/buty na zimę** winter coat/boots; **pod zimę** *l.* **ku zimie** *przest.* it's getting on toward winter; **zima za pasem** winter is almost here.

zimnawy *a.* tepid, coldish.

zimne *n. Gen.* **-ego** cold; **dmuchać na zimne** burnt child dreads the fire.

zimnica *f. pot.* the cold.

zimno[1] *n.* (= *niska temperatura*) cold; **podmuch zimna** gust of cold air; **fala zimna z północy** cold wave; **zimno ciągnie od podłogi** cold is creeping up from the floor.

zimno[2] *adv.* **1.** (= *nieciepło*) cold; **jest mi zimno** I am *l.* feel cold; **robi się zimno** it's getting cold; **zimno dzisiaj** it's cold today; **zimno jak w psiarni** *pot.* icy cold; **(potrawa) na zimno** dish served cold; **kalkulować na zimno** calculate calmly. **2.** (= *obojętnie*) indifferently; **patrzeć na kogoś zimno** look at sb indifferently; **przywitać kogoś zimno** give sb an icy welcome.

zimnokrwisty *a. biol. l. przen.* cold-blooded; **koń zimnokrwisty** *hodowla* cold-blooded horse.

zimnolubny *a. biol.* cryophilic.

zimnowalcowany *a. hutn.* cold-rolled.

zimnowojenny *a. polit.* cold-war.

zimny *a.* **1.** (= *nieciepły*) cold; **masz zimne ręce/nogi** your hands/feet are cold; **zimny klimat** cold climate; **zimny posiłek** cold supper; **zimny tusz/prysznic** cold douche/shower; **zimne ognie** sparklers. **2.** *przen.* **zimna wojna** *polit.* cold war; **zimne barwy** *sztuka* cool *l.* cold colors; **z zimną krwią** in cold blood; **zachować zimną krew** stay calm; *pot.* keep one's cool; **oblać kogoś zimną wodą** *przen.* disillusion sb; **zimny jak głaz** stonecold. **3.** (= *beznamiętny*) cold-hearted, dispassionate, cold; **zimne wyrachowanie** cold calculation; **zimny drań** cold-hearted rascal; **spotkać się z zimnym powitaniem** meet with an icy welcome.

zimorodek *ma* **-dk-** *orn.* (= *ptak z rodziny Alce-*

dinae) kingfisher; **zimorodek olbrzymi** kookaburra, laughing jackass (*Daceo novaeguineae*).

zimotrwały *a. bot.* hardy, cold-resistant.

zimować *ipf.* **1.** (= *spędzać zimę*) winter; spend the winter; (= *zapadać w sen zimowy*) hibernate; **pokażę ci, gdzie raki zimują** I'll teach you a lesson. **2.** *szkoln.* repeat a year *l.* course.

zimowisko *n.* **1.** (*obóz*) winter camp. **2.** (*kurort*) winter resort. **3.** *biol.* (= *sen zimowy*) hibernation, winter sleep.

zimowit *mi bot.* colchicum (*Colchicum*); **zimowit jesienny** meadow saffron, autumn crocus (*C. autumnale*).

zimowy *a.* winter; **miesiące zimowe** winter months; **wakacje zimowe** winter vacation; **płaszcz zimowy** winter coat; **sen zimowy** *biol.* winter sleep, hibernation.

zimozielony *a. bot.* evergreen.

zindustrializować *pf. zob.* **industrializować**.

zindywidualizować *pf. zob.* **indywidualizować**.

zinstrumentować *pf. muz.* arrange (a musical composition) for several instruments.

zinstytucjonalizować *pf. zob.* **instytucjonalizować**.

zintegrować *pf. zob.* **integrować**.

zintensyfikować *pf. zob.* **intensyfikować**.

zinterpretować *pf. zob.* **interpretować**.

zioła *pl. Gen.* **ziół** (= *lekarstwo*) herbs.

zioło *n. Gen.pl.* **-ół** *zob.* **ziele**.

ziołolecznictwo *n.* herbalism, treatment by the use of herbs.

ziołowy *a.* herbal; **herbata ziołowa** herbal *l.* herb tea.

ziomek *mp* **-mk-** *pl.* **-owie** compatriot, fellow countryman.

ziomkostwo *n. polit.* compatriot status.

zionąć *ipf. l. pf.* **1.** (= *chwytać oddech*) pant, gasp for breath. **2.** (= *wyrzucać ustami l. wylotem*) belch (out), spew (out), breathe; **zionąć ogniem/dymem** belch *l.* breathe fire/smoke; **zionąć przekleństwami** *przen.* hurl curses (*na kogoś* at sb). **3.** *przen.* (= *wyrażać uczucia*) breathe; **zionąć nienawiścią/gniewem** breathe hatred/anger. **4.** *przen.* (= *rozwierać się*) gape.

ziółko *n. Gen.pl.* **-ek** *l. pot.* (= *zioło*) herb. **2.** *pot.* (= *gagatek*) scallywag.

zipać *ipf.* **zipię zipiesz, zipnąć** *pf.* **zipnij** take a breath!; **ledwie zipie** he's more dead than alive, be on one's last legs; **ani zipnął** he did not breathe a word.

zirytować (się) *pf. zob.* **irytować (się)**.

zirytowany *a.* irritated, annoyed.

ziszczać *ipf.*, **ziścić** *pf.* **-szczę -ścisz** *lit.* realize, fulfill. **~ się** *ipf.*, **ziścić się** *pf. lit.* come true, be fulfilled; **ziszczone marzenia** dreams come true.

zjadacz *ma zool.* devourer. *– mp* (*człowiek*) eater; **zwykły zjadacz chleba** the man in the street.

zjadać *ipf.* **1.** (= *spożywać*) eat; (*o regularnym posiłku*) have; **zjadać śniadanie** have breakfast; **co zjesz na śniadanie?** what would you like for breakfast?; **lubić dobrze zjeść** have a healthy appetite; **wydaje się mu, że zjadł wszystkie rozumy** he thinks he knows everything; **mógłbym zjeść**

konia z kopytami I'm so hungry I could eat a horse; **zjeść na czymś zęby** know sth out-and-out; **nie bój się, przecież cię nie zjem** don't be scared, I won't eat you. **2.** *przen.* (= *zużywać*) use up, consume; **zjadać paliwo/prąd/energię** use up fuel/electricity/energy. **3.** *przen.* (= *niszczyć*) consume, eat up; **rak zjada czyjąś wątrobę** cancer consumes sb's liver; **rdza zjada karoserię samochodu** rust eats away at the body of the car.

zjadę *itd. pf. zob.* **zjechać.**

zjadliwie *adv.* **1.** (= *szyderczo*) sarcastically, scornfully; **uśmiechać się zjadliwie** smirk. **2.** *żart.* (= *apetycznie*) **ryba wygląda całkiem zjadliwie** the fish looks quite eatable.

zjadliwość *f.* scorn, sarcasm.

zjadliwy *a.* **1.** (= *szyderczy*) scorning, scornful, sarcastic; **zjadliwa satyra** stinging *l.* pungent *l.* biting satire; **zjadliwa uwaga** scathing remark; **zjadliwy uśmieszek** smirk. **2.** (= *trujący*) poisonous, toxic. **3.** *żart.* (= *apetyczny*) eatable.

zjadł *itd. pf. zob.* **zjeść.**

zjarać *pf. pot.* (= *spalić*) burn down.

zjaśnieć *pf.* -**eje** get lighter.

zjawa *f.* apparition, phantom, ghost.

zjawiać się *ipf.*, **zjawić się** *pf.* **1.** (= *ukazywać się*) appear. **2.** (= *pojawiać się, przychodzić*) show up, turn up; **zjawiać się gdzieś/u kogoś** show up somewhere/at sb's place; **zjawił się punktualnie** he turned up on time.

zjawisko *n.* **1.** *nauk.* phenomenon; **zjawisko chemiczne/fizyczne/meteorologiczne/naturalne/społeczne** chemical/physical/meterological/natural/social phenomenon. **2.** (= *coś rzadkiego l. nadzwyczajnego*) (rare) phenomenon. **3.** *lit.* (= *zjawa*) apparition, vision.

zjawiskowy *a.* **1.** (= *nadzwyczajny, nieziemski*) phenomenal. **2.** *lit.* (= *dotyczący zjawy*) visional, apparitional.

zjazd *mi Loc.* **zjeździe 1.** (= *zjeżdżanie*) downhill ride *l.* drive *l.* run; **trasa zjazdu** downhill route; **zjazd do kopalni** lift down to a mine; **zjazd narciarski** *sport* downhill run. **2.** *mot.* (*z drogi, autostrady*) exit; (*na postój*) pull-off; *Br.* pull-up. **3.** *mot.* (= *powrót do bazy*) return to the depot. **4.** *narciarstwo* (= *stok*) slope; **stromy/łagodny zjazd** steep/gentle slope. **5.** *polit.* (= *zgromadzenie*) convention, congress; **zjazd partii** party congress *l.* convention; **delegat na zjazd** party convention delegate. **6.** (= *spotkanie osób przybyłych z daleka*) reunion; **zjazd rodzinny** family reunion. **7.** *pot.* (*osoby zgromadzone*) assembly, conference.

zjazdowiec *mp* -**wc-** *pl.* -**y** *sport* contestant, downhill racer.

zjazdowy *a.* **1.** (= *związany z obradami*) congress, congressional. **2.** *sport* downhill; **bieg zjazdowy** *narciarstwo* downhill race.

zjazdówka *f. Gen.pl.* -**ek** *sport* (= *narta*) downhill-run ski.

zjechać (się) *pf.* **zjadę zjedziesz** *zob.* **zjeżdżać (się).**

zjednać *pf. zob.* **zjednywać.**

zjednoczenie *n.* **1.** (= *łączenie się w całość*) unification. **2.** (*organizacja*) union.

zjednoczeniowy *a.* unificatory.

zjednoczony *a.* -**eni 1.** *polit.* united; **Stany Zjednoczone Ameryki Północnej** the United States of America; **Zjednoczone Królestwo Wielkiej Brytanii i Irlandii Północnej** the United Kingdom of Great Britain and Northern Ireland; **Organizacja Narodów Zjednoczonych** United Nations; **Polska Zjednoczona Partia Robotnicza** *hist.* Polish United Workers' Party. **2.** (= *wspólny, zespołowy*) unified; **zjednoczonym wysiłkiem** by unified effort.

zjednoczyć *pf.* unite. ~ **się** *pf.* unite.

zjednywać *ipf.* propitiate, conciliate; **zjednywać kogoś czymś** win sb over with sth; **zjednać sobie sympatię** win.

zjełczały *a.* rancid, rank.

zjełczeć *pf.* grow rancid.

zjeść *pf.* **zjem zjesz zjedzą, zjedz, zjadł zjedli** *zob.* **zjadać.**

zjeździć *pf.* **zjeżdżę zjeździsz** visit, travel.

zjeździe *mi zob.* **zjazd.**

zjeżdżać *ipf.* **1.** (*z góry w dół*) go down *l.* downhill; **zjeżdżać samochodem** drive downhill; **zjeżdżać na rowerze** ride *l.* pedal downhill; **zjeżdżać na sankach/nartach** go sledding/skiing; **zjechać z góry na sankach/nartach** sledge/ski down. **2.** (= *zbaczać z drogi*) go out of the way, turn; **zjeżdżać na bok** *l.* **na pobocze** pull over; **zjeżdżać w prawo przed nadjeżdżającym samochodem** swerve right. **3.** (= *wracać do bazy*) return; **zjeżdżać do zajezdni** return to the depot. **4.** *lit.* (= *przybyć z wizytą*) visit. **5.** *pot.* (= *obsuwać się*) slip off; **okulary zjechały mi z nosa** the glasses slipped off my nose. **6.** *tylko pf. pot.* (= *krytykować*) slate. **7.** *tylko ipf. pot.* (= *uciekać*) run away; **zjeżdżaj stąd** get lost, beat it. ~ **się** *ipf.* (= *gromadzić się*) arrive, assemble, meet; **zjeżdżać się na konferencję z wszystkich stron Polski** arrive for a conference from all over Poland.

zjeżdżalnia *f. Gen.pl.* -**i** *l.* -**ń** slide.

zjeżyć *pf.* bristle, ruffle; **zjeżyć komuś włosy na głowie** make sb's hair stand on end; make sb's hair curl. ~ **się** *pf.* **1.** (= *nastroszyć się*) bristle (up); (*o włosach*) rise, stand on end. **2.** *pot.* (= *zdenerwować się*) bristle (with rage).

zjonizować (się) *pf. zob.* **jonizować (się).**

zlać *pf.* **zleję zlejesz zlali** *l.* **zleli 1.** *zob.* **zlewać. 2.** *pot.* (= *zbić*) beat up, give sb a thrashing. ~ **się** *pf.* **1.** *zob.* **zlewać się. 2.** *pot.* (= *oddać mocz pod siebie*) wet one's pants.

zlaicyzować *pf.* secularize, laicize.

zlany *a.* wet; **zlany potem** sweating wet, wet *l.* drenched with sweat.

zlasować (się) *pf. zob.* **lasować (się).**

zlatać *pf. pot.* run all over. ~ **się** *pf. pot.* rush till one is tired.

zlatynizować (się) *pf. zob.* **latynizować (się).**

zlatywać *pf.* **1.** (= *spadać*) fall off *l.* down; **zlecieć z półki** fall off (of) the shelf; **zlecieć w przepaść** fall into a precipice; **zlecieć na podłogę/ziemię** fall down on the floor/ground; **czapka zlatuje mi na czoło** the cap is falling *l.* coming down on my forehead; **spodnie z niego zlatują** the pants are too loose for him. **2.** (= *sfruwać*) fly off

l. down. **3.** *pot.* (= *zbiegać szybko*) run down, race down, storm down; **zleciał po schodach** he raced down the stairs. ~ **się** *ipf.* **1.** *pot.* (= *szybko przychodzić w jedno miejsce*) come running *l.* rushing up. **2.** (= *sfruwać w jedno miejsce*) flock.
zlazł *itp.* *pf. zob.* **zleźć**.
ząc się *pf.* **zlęknę zlękniesz, zlęknij, ząkł zlękła zlękli** *zob.* **zlęknąć się.**
zlecać *ipf.* **1.** (= *polecać*) order. **2.** (= *zamawiać wykonanie zadania*) commission, contract; **zlecać komuś zrobienie czegoś** commission sb to do sth.
zlecenie *n.* **1.** (= *polecenie*) order; **zlecenie wypłaty** money order. **2.** (= *umowa dotycząca jakiegoś zadania*) commission, contract.
zleceniobiorca *mp* firm accepting an order.
zleceniodawca *mp* client, customer.
zlecić *pf. zob.* **zlecać.**
zlecieć *pf.* **-cę -cisz 1.** *zob.* **zlatywać. 2.** *tylko pf.* (= *upłynąć*) fly by, pass (quickly), slip away; **jakoś nam zleciało do wieczora** the time has flown by till the evening; **podróż szybko zleciała** the journey took a little while. ~ **się** *pf. zob.* **zlatywać się.**
zleję *itd. pf. zob.* **zlać.**
zlekceważyć *pf.* scorn, disregard, ignore.
zleksykalizować się *pf. jęz.* become lexicalized.
zleksykalizowany *a. jęz.* lexicalized.
zleniwieć *ipf.* grow lazy, become sluggish *l.* idle.
zlepek *mi* **-pk- 1.** (= *masa sklejonych cząstek*) conglutination, conglomerate. **2.** (= *mieszanka*) mélange, mixture, medley.
zlepiać *ipf.* glue together, stick together. ~ **się** *ipf.* stick together, conglutinate.
zlepić (się) *pf. zob.* **zlepiać (się).**
zlew *mi* sink; **zlew kuchenny** kitchen sink.
zlewać *ipf.* **1.** (= *odlewać*) pour out; **zlać z wierzchu** decant. **2.** (= *przelewać*) pour off; **zlać do jednego naczynia** pour together. **3.** (= *lejąc, moczyć*) drench. ~ **się** *ipf.* **1.** (= *lejąc się, łączyć się*) merge, mix, blend; (*o rzekach*) meet, form a confluence. **2.** (= *oblewać się czymś*) sprinkle o.s. with sth; **zlewać się perfumami** pour lots of perfume on o.s.; **zlać się potem** be drenched with sweat. **3.** (= *oblewać się nawzajem*) drench one another with water.
zlewisko *n. hydrol.* catchment area.
zlewka *f. Gen.pl.* **-ek** *chem.* beaker.
zlewki *pl. Gen.* **-wek** (*resztki*) slops.
zlewnia *f. Gen.pl.* **-i 1.** (*mleczarnia*) dairy, creamery. **2.** *geogr.* reception basin.
zlewozmywak *mi Gen.* **-a** sink (unit).
zleźć (się) *pf.* **zlezę zleziesz zlazł zleźli** *zob.* **złazić (się).**
zleżały *a.* stale, fusty, musty.
zlęknąć się *pf.* **zlęknij, ząkł zlękła zlękli** take fright, balk (*czegoś* at sth); **zlęknąć się kary** fear punishment; **ząkł się na widok ojca** the sight of his father frightened him.
zliberalizować *pf. zob.* **liberalizować.**
zlicytować *pf. zob.* **licytować.**
zliczać *ipf.,* **zliczyć** *pf.* count (up); **nie umieć zliczyć do trzech** not know what two and two is;

not know how many beans make five; **można ich zliczyć na palcach jednej ręki** there are just a few of them; **przyszło ich tyle, że nie zliczę** so many have arrived that I've lost count of them.
zlikwidować *pf. zob.* **likwidować.**
zlinczować *pf. zob.* **linczować.**
zlitować się *pf.* **zlitować się nad kimś** (= *poczuć wobec kogoś litość*) have pity on sb; (= *pomóc komuś z litości*) take pity on sb; **zlituj się!** have mercy!, have a heart!
zlizać *pf.* **zliżę zliżesz, zlizywać** *ipf.* lick up/off.
zlodowacenie *n. geol.* glaciation.
zlodowacieć *pf.* **1.** (= *pokryć się lodem*) freeze sth over. **2.** (= *zmarznąć*) freeze, get frozen.
zlokalizować *pf. zob.* **lokalizować.**
zlot *mi* **1.** (= *zgromadzenie*) rally, gathering. **2.** *myśl.* flocking together birds before migration.
zlustrować *pf. zob.* **lustrować.**
zlutować *pf. zob.* **lutować.**
zluzować (się) *pf. zob.* **zluzowywać (się).**
zluzowywać *ipf.* **1.** (= *zmienić kogoś*) relieve, take over from sb. **2.** (= *rozluźnić*) loosen, slacken. ~ **się** *ipf.* **1.** (= *zastąpić jeden drugiego*) relieve/replace one another. **2.** (= *obluzować się*) loosen, ease off.
zł *abbr.* (= *złoty*) zloty.
złagodnieć *pf.* **1.** (= *stać się łagodnym*) soften, grow milder/more gentle. **2.** (= *stać się mniej intensywnym*) relent, abate, subside.
złagodzenie *n. prawn.* commutation; **złagodzenie kary** commutation of a sentence.
złagodzić *pf.* **-godzę -godzisz, -godź** *l.* **-gódź 1.** (= *uczynić łagodnym*) soften, lessen/diminish severity, mitigate; **złagodzić karę/zakaz/wyrok** mitigate a punishment/ban/verdict. **2.** (= *uczynić mniej intensywnym*) alleviate; **złagodzić ból/napięcie/rozdrażnienie** alleviate pain/tension/exasperation.
złajać *pf.* **-ję -jesz** *pot.* scold, rebuke.
złakniony *a.* **-eni 1.** (= *głodny*) hungry; (*jedzenia*) hungry, starving. **2.** (= *pragnący*) avid/eager/dying for; **złakniony wypoczynku/wiadomości** eager for relax/the news, dying for some rest/news.
złakomić *pf.* tempt; **złakomić kogoś możliwością wyjazdu** be tempted by a chance of trip. ~**się** *pf.* **1.** be tempted by, yield to the temptation. **2.** (= *połakomić się*) yield to the temptation; **złakomić się na drugi kawałek tortu** yield to the temptation and have another slice of cake. **3.** (= *połaszczyć się*) be attracted/tempted by; **złakomił się na łatwy zarobek** he was attracted/tempted by an easy profit.
złamać *pf.* **-mię -miesz 1.** (= *przełamać*) break; **złamać pieczęć** break a seal; **złamać kark** break one's neck; **złamać szyfr** break a code; **żeby kózka nie skakała, toby nóżki nie złamała** play with fire and you are going to get burnt. **2.** *med.* break, fracture. **3.** (= *pokonać*) break (down); crush; overcome; **złamać komuś serce** break sb's heart; **złamać komuś życie** make sb unhappy. **4.** *prawn.* break, breach, violate, transgress; **złamać słowo** break one's word *l.* promise, go back

on one's word. **5.** *druk.* make up; impose. ~ **się**
pf. **1.** (= *przełamać się*) break. **2.** *pot.* (= *ulec namowom*) yield, give in.
złamanie *n.* **1.** (= *przełamanie*) breaking; **na
złamanie karku** at breakneck speed. **2.** *med.*
fracture; **złamanie otwarte** open *l.* penetrating
fracture; **złamanie zamknięte** closed *l.* non-pene-
trating fracture. **3.** *prawn.* breach, violation,
infraction; **złamanie prawa** breach of law; **złamanie obietnicy małżeństwa** breach of promise.
złamany *a.* **1.** (= *przełamany*) broken. **2.** *med.*
broken, fractured. **3.** (= *przygnębiony*) depressed, dejected.
złapać *pf.* **-pię -piesz 1.** (= *pozbawić wolności*)
catch; seize; apprehend. **2.** *pot.* (= *zatrzymać kogoś*) catch, get hold of sb; **nie udało mi się go złapać w biurze** I didn't manage to get hold of him
in the office; **złapać kogoś na kłamstwie** catch sb
out (lying); **złapał mnie na gorącym uczynku** he
caught me red-handed. **3.** (= *schwytać coś*)
catch; **złapać oddech** catch one's breath; **złapać
pociąg, autobus, samolot itp.** *pot.* catch a train,
bus, plane, etc.; **złapać gumę** *pot.* have a flat tire.
4. (= *uchwycić*) grab, catch, get *l.* take hold of (sb
l. sth); **złapać kogoś za kołnierz** grab sb by the
collar; **złapać kogoś za rękę** take sb by the hand;
przen. catch sb stealing, catch sb red-handed;
złapać kogoś za słowo catch sb out, turn sb's
words against them; **uważaj, bo prąd cię złapie**
watch out or you'll get an electric shock. **5.** (*o
odczuciach*) (= *wystąpić nagle*) come over; **złapa-
łem grypę** I caught flu; I got the flu; **złapał mnie
kurcz** I was seized with a cramp. **6.** (*o zjawiskach przyrody*) (= *zaskoczyć kogoś*) catch; **zła-
pała mnie burza** I was caught in a storm. ~ **się**
pf. **1.** (= *chwycić się za coś*) clutch, grasp; **złapać
się za głowę** clutch one's head; **złapać się za kolano** grasp one's knee; **złapać się na czymś** catch
o.s. doing sth; **złapać się za coś** *pot.* start doing
sth, get down to sth. **2.** (= *chwycić siebie nawzajem*) catch each other *l.* one another; grab each
other *l.* one another. **3.** (= *być schwytanym*) get
caught. **4.** *przen.* (= *być oszukanym*) be taken
in, be deceived.
złazić *ipf.* **-żę -zisz 1.** *pot.* (= *schodzić w dół*)
climb down; **złazić po drabinie** climb down the
ladder; **złazić z konia** dismount. **2.** *pot.* (= *łuszczyć się*) come off, peel (off); **skóra ci zlezie** your
skin will peel; **cała farba zlazła z okien** all the
paint came off the window frames. – *pf.* **-żę -zisz**
pot. (= *przemierzyć*) roam; **zlaziłem cały Nowy
Jork** I've seen all of New York. ~ **się** *ipf.* (= *gromadzić się*) crowd, gather. – *pf. pot.* (= *nachodzić się*) exhaust o.s. walking.
złącze *n. Gen.pl.* **-y** *techn.* joint; connection;
coupling; bond; **złącze kolankowe** U-bend, elbow
joint; **złącze kulkowe** ball-and-socket joint, ball
joint.
złączka *f. Gen.pl.* **-ek** *techn.* connector, junction; **złączka instalacyjna** connection block; **złączka rurowa** joint, coupler, coupling; **złączka
gwintowa** thread.
złączyć *pf.* zob. **łączyć.** ~ **się** *pf.* zob. **łączyć się.**
złe *n. Gen.* **-ego 1.** (= *coś niemoralnego*) evil; **z**

dwojga złego of the two evils; **nie miej mi za złe**
don't hold it against me. **2.** (= *coś, co szkodzi komuś*) harm; **doznać wiele złego** suffer a lot of
harm; **na domiar złego** to make matters worse;
nie ma tego złego, co by na dobre nie wyszło every cloud has a silver lining; **siła złego na jednego** when it rains it pours. **3.** (= *diabeł*) the evil
one, devil, Satan; **złe nie śpi** accidents will happen.
zło *n. Loc.* **-u** evil; **zło moralne** moral evil; **przyczyna** *l.* **źródło zła** the root of (all) evil; **wykorzenić** *l.* **wytępić zło** root out evil; **zniszczyć zło w
zarodku** destroy evil at its source *l.* root; **walczyć
ze złem** fight evil; **wyrządzić komuś wiele zła** do
a lot of harm to sb; **wybrać mniejsze zło** choose
the lesser evil; **zło konieczne** necessary evil; **naprawić zło** right a wrong, redress a wrong.
złocenie *n.* (*powłoka*) gilt, plating; (*ozdoba*)
gilt ornament.
złocić *ipf.* **1.** (= *pokrywać złotem*) gild,
overgild. **2.** *przen.* (= *nadawać kolor złoty*)
overgild, make gold(en) *l.* gold yellow. ~ **się** *ipf.*
become gold(en) *l.* gold yellow; glitter, sparkle.
złocień *mi Gen.* **-a** *bot.* chrysanthemum (*Chrysanthemum*).
złocisty *a.* golden; **gronkowiec złocisty** *biol.*
Staphylococcus aureus (*Staphylococcus aure-
us*).
złociście *adv.* in golden color.
złociutki *a.* golden; **mój złociutki** *przest.* my
dear.
złocony *a.* gilded, gold-plated.
złoczyńca *mp lit.* villain.
złodziej *mp Gen.pl.* **-ei** thief; **złodziej kieszonkowy** pickpocket; **na złodzieju czapka gore** a
guilty conscience needs an accuser; **okazja czyni
złodzieja** opportunity makes a thief, the hole
calls the thief.
złodziejaszek *mp* **-szk-** *pl.* **-i** *żart. l. iron.* petty
thief.
złodziejka *f. Gen.pl.* **-ek 1.** (= *kobieta złodziej*)
zob. **złodziej. 2.** *pot.* (*kontakt*) adapter.
złodziejski *a.* thievish; thieves'; **złodziejskie
nasienie** a born thief.
złodziejstwo *n. pot.* thieving.
złoić *pf.* **złój** zob. **łoić.**
złom *mi* **1.** (= *odpadki metalowe*) scrap (metal); **oddawać coś na złom** scrap sth; **skup złomu**
scrap yard; **złom metali kolorowych** non-ferrous
metal(s) scrap. **2.** (= *odłamany blok*) detached
block. **3.** *leśn., ogr.* broken *l.* fallen branches;
deadfall.
złomować *ipf.* scrap.
złomowisko *n.* scrap heap, scrap yard.
złomowy *a.* scrap; **materiały złomowe** scrap.
złorzeczenie *n.* abuse, curses; cursing.
złorzeczyć *ipf.* curse.
złościć *ipf.* **-szczę -ścisz** anger, irritate. ~ **się**
ipf. be angry, be cross; anger, become angry; **złościć się o byle co** *l.* **bez powodu** get all bent out
of shape over nothing; **złościć się na kogoś** be
angry *l.* cross with sb.
złość *f.* anger, wrath; **atak** *l.* **paroksyzm złości**
fit of anger; **napady złości** outbursts of anger;

wpaść w złość lose one's temper; **dusić w sobie złość** repress *l.* suppress one's anger; **trząść się ze złości** be seething with anger; **wyładować swoją złość** give vent to *l.* vent one's anger; **złość mnie bierze, kiedy widzę, że...** it angers me when I see that...; **na złość komuś** to spite sb; **jak na złość** as if out of spite; **pękać ze złości** be bursting with anger; **złość piękności szkodzi** anger detracts from one's beauty.

złośliwie *adv.* maliciously.

złośliwiec *mp* -wc- *pl.* -y malicious person; tease.

złośliwości *pl. Gen.* -i (*docinki*) caustic remarks.

złośliwość *f.* **1.** (*usposobienie*) malice; **złośliwość rzeczy martwych** (I guess) things have a mind of their own; **złośliwość losu** that's fate, that's life. **2.** *pat.* malignancy, malignance; **złośliwość nowotworu** malignancy of a neoplasm *l.* tumor.

złośliwy *a.* **1.** (= *uszczypliwy*) malicious; **człowiek złośliwy z natury** person malicious by nature. **2.** *pat.* malignant; pernicious; **nowotwór złośliwy** malignant neoplasm *l.* tumor; **anemia złośliwa** pernicious an(a)emia.

złośnica *f.* shrew.

złośnik *mp* spitfire.

złotawy *a.* gold(-like), golden; **związki złotawe** *chem.* aurous compounds.

złotko *n. Gen.pl.* -tek **1.** *emf.* dear, honey; **moje złotko!** my dear! **2.** *pot.* (= *folia aluminiowa*) tinfoil.

złotnictwo *n.* goldsmithery.

złotniczy *a.* goldsmith's; goldsmithing.

złotnik *mp* goldsmith.

złoto[1] *n.* **1.** (*metal*) gold; **czyste** *l.* **szczere złoto** pure gold; **sztaba złota** bar of gold; **stop złota** gold alloy; **gorączka złota** *t. hist.* gold rush; **poszukiwacze złota** gold diggers; **pierścionek ze złota** gold ring; **złoto dukatowe** *przest.* fine gold; **sztuczne złoto** tombac; **parytet złota** *ekon.* gold parity; **czarne złoto** *przen.* coal; **żyła** *l.* **kopalnia złota** *przen.* gold mine; **być na wagę złota** be worth one's weight in gold; **nie wszystko złoto, co się świeci** all is not gold that glitters; **mowa jest srebrem, milczenie złotem** speech is silver but silence is golden. **2.** (*wyrób*) goldwork; **ornat haftowany złotem** vestment embroidered with gold; **coś kapie złotem** sth is gaudily ornate with gold. **3.** *przest.* (*pieniądze*) gold; **sypać złotem** spend lavishly; **zgarniać złoto** make a lot of money.

złoto[2] *adv.* in gold color; **coś się mieni złoto** sth sparkles in gold color(s).

złotodajny *a. zwł. górn.* auriferous, gold-bearing.

złotogłów *mi* -ow- *l.* -owi- *Gen.* -wiu *l.* -wia *l.* -wu *Loc.* -wiu *l.* -wie *pl.* -wia *l.* -wy *Gen.* -wi *l.* -wiów *l.* -wów **1.** *tk.* samite, cloth of gold. **2.** *bot.* Turk's cap lily (*Lilium martagon*).

złotonośny *a. zwł. górn.* auriferous, gold-bearing.

złotousty *a. lit.* eloquent.

złotowłosy *a.* golden-haired.

złotowy *a.* **1.** *chem.* auric; **związek złotowy** auric compound. **2.** *ekon.* zloty, PLN; **złotowy system monetarny** zloty monetary system.

złotówka *f. Gen.pl.* -ek one zloty; one zloty coin; **za symboliczną złotówkę** for a token sum.

złotówkowy *a.* zloty.

złoty *a.* **1.** (= *ze złota*) gold, golden; **złoty medal** gold medal; **złoty medalista** gold medalist; **złote runo** *mit., t. przen.* the Golden Fleece; **złoty cielec** *Bibl., t. przen.* golden calf; **złota księga** golden book; **złota młodzież** gilded youth; **złote wesele** *l.* **gody** golden wedding (anniversary); **złote jabłko** *l.* **złoty interes** *l.* **złota żyła** gold mine; **obiecywać komuś złote góry** promise the earth to sb; **zapisać się złotymi zgłoskami** engrave one's name in letters of gold; **zabić kurę, która znosi złote jajka** kill the goose that lays the golden eggs. **2.** (= *złocisty*) golden; **złota kula** *bot.* coneflower, golden glow (*Rudbeckia laciniata*); **złota reneta** *ogr.* golden russet; **złota rybka** *icht.* goldfish; **złota jesień** Indian summer. **3.** (= *doskonały*) golden; **to złoty człowiek** he has a heart of gold, he is an extremely obliging person; **złota wolność** *hist.* privileges enjoyed by the Polish nobility in the 16th and 17th centuries; **złoty wiek** golden age; **złota myśl** maxim, adage; **złota seria** winning streak; **mieć złote serce** have a heart of gold; **złota rączka** handyman; **złoty środek** golden mean, happy medium; **mój złoty!** *emf.* my dear! – **mi** zloty, PLN; **zarabiam około dwóch tysięcy złotych** I earn about two thousand zlotys.

złowić *pf.* **złów** catch.

złowieszczo *adv.* ominously, sinisterly.

złowieszczy *a.* ominous, sinister.

złowrogi *a.* ominous, sinister.

złowrogo *adv.* ominously, sinisterly.

złowróżbny *a. lit.* ominous, sinister.

złoże *n. Gen.pl.* złóż *zwł. górn.* deposit; bed.

złożenie *n.* **1.** *jęz.* compound. **2.** *szermierka* engagement.

złożoność *f.* complexity.

złożony *a.* **1.** (*z kilku części*) complex, compound, composite; **cukier złożony** *chem.* polysaccharide, polysaccharose; **węglowodan złożony** *chem.* complex carbohydrate; **orzeczenie złożone** *gram.* complete predicate, predicate (complex), verb and complement; **wyraz złożony** *jęz.* compound (word); **zdanie złożone** *gram.* compound *l.* multiple sentence; **liczba złożona** *mat.* composite number; **być złożonym z** be composed of. **2.** (= *zawiły*) complex, complicated; **złożony problem** complex problem.

złożyć *pf.* -óż *zob.* **składać.** ~ **się** *pf. zob.* **składać się.**

złóg *mi* -o- *pat.* concrement, deposit, concretion.

złóż[1] *n. zob.* **złoże.**

złóż[2] *pf. zob.* **złożyć.**

złuda *f. lit.* illusion; fallacy.

złudny *a.* illusory; fallacious.

złudzenia *pl. Gen.* -eń (= *mrzonki*) illusions; (day)dreams; **nie mam złudzeń co do kogoś** *l.* **czegoś** I have no illusions about sb *l.* sth; **pozbawić kogoś złudzeń** disillusion sb.

złudzenie *n.* illusion; **nie mogę się oprzeć złudzeniu, że...** I can't resist the feeling that...; **złudzenie optyczne** optical illusion; **być do złudzenia podobnym do kogoś** be the spitting image of sb.

złupić *pf. lit.* (= *obrabować*) loot, plunder; **złupić skórę z kogoś** rip sb off.

złuszczać *ipf.*, **złuszczyć** *pf.* flake, peel. **~ się** *ipf.*, **złuszczyć się** *pf.* flake, peel (off).

zły *a.* **gorszy; źli 1.** (= *nieetyczny*) evil, wicked; bad; ill; **zły duch** the evil one, devil, Satan; evil spirit; **złe towarzystwo** bad *l.* fast company; **zła wola** ill will; **zła wiara** *prawn.* bad faith, mala fides; **działać w złej wierze** *zwł. prawn.* act in bad faith; **zły to ptak, co własne gniazdo kala** it is a foolish bird that defiles *l.* soils its own nest, it is an ill bird that fouls its own nest. **2.** (= *rozgniewany*) angry, cross; **jestem zły na ciebie** I am angry *l.* cross with you; **uwaga! zły pies** beware of the dog!; **zły humor** bad mood; **patrzeć na kogoś** *l.* **coś złym okiem** disapprove of sb *l.* sth. **3.** (= *niesumienny*) poor; bad; **zły ojciec** bad father; **zły robotnik** poor worker; **obym był złym prorokiem** may I be wrong, I hope I am wrong; **złej tanecznicy przeszkadza rąbek u spódnicy** a bad workman (always) blames his tools, a bad writer blames his pen. **4.** (= *niekorzystny*) unfavorable, bad; **przedstawiać coś w złym świetle** put *l.* present sth in an unfavorable light. **5.** (= *niepomyślny*) bad, inauspicious; **mam zły dzień** I am having a bad day; **mam dla ciebie złe wiadomości** I have bad news for you; **robić dobrą minę do złej gry** put on a brave face; **wymówić coś w złą godzinę** jinx sth; **urodzić się pod złą gwiazdą** be born under a bad sign; **tylko nie zrób sobie czegoś złego** don't hurt yourself; **mieć zły sen** have a bad dream. **6.** (= *niewłaściwy*) wrong, improper; bad; poor; **mieć zły wzrok** have poor eyesight; **zły przewodnik** *fiz.* bad conductor; **zła pogoda** bad weather; **być w złej formie** be in bad shape; **znam cię jak zły szeląg** *l.* **grosz** I know you very well; **dobre wino nie jest złe** *żart.* drinking good wine won't do you any harm; **w złym guście** in bad taste; **złe traktowanie** ill-treatment. **7.** (= *niezgodny z intencjami*) wrong; **idziesz w złym kierunku** you're heading in a wrong direction; **sprowadzić kogoś na złą drogę** lead sb astray. – *mp* **1.** (= *zły człowiek*) bad person; **złego diabli nie porwą** the devil protects *l.* looks after his own, the devil's children have the devil's luck, naught is never in danger. **2.** (= *diabeł*) the evil one, devil, Satan.

zm. *abbr.* (= *zmarły*) d. (*died*).

zmacerować *pf. zob.* **macerować**.

zmachać *pf. pot.* tire, fag (out). **~ się** *pf. pot.* tire.

zmachany *a. pot.* dog-tired; (*o koniu*) overridden; **jestem zmachany** I am exhausted, I am done in.

zmagać się *ipf.* struggle; **zmagać się z kimś** struggle with sb; **zmagać się z chorobą** struggle with an illness.

zmaganie *n.* struggle; strife; **zmagania z chorobą** struggle against an illness.

zmagazynować *pf.* store; gather.

zmaglować *pf. zob.* **maglować**.

zmajoryzować *pf. form.* outvote; outnumber.

zmajstrować *pf.* **1.** *pot.* (= *skonstruować*) put together, make. **2.** *pot.* (= *zrobić coś złego*) do (sth wrong).

zmaleć *pf. zob.* **maleć**.

zmalować *pf. pot.* do (sth wrong).

zmaltretować *pf. zob.* **maltretować**.

zmałpować *pf. pot.* parrot.

zmanierować *pf. zob.* **manierować**. **~ się** *pf. zob.* **manierować się**.

zmanierowanie *n.* affected behavior, mannerism.

zmanierowany *a.* mannered.

zmarkotnieć *pf.* sadden, become sad, become sullen.

zmarła *f. Gen.* **-ej** the deceased, the late.

zmarły *a.* deceased, dead; **mój zmarły mąż** my late husband; **ostatnio zmarły biskup** the late bishop. – *mp* the deceased, the late; **Dzień Zmarłych** All Saints' Day, Allhallows.

zmarniały *a.* (*o człowieku*) pined away; (*o kapuście, burakach, kwiatach*) withered.

zmarnieć *pf. zob.* **marnieć**.

zmarnotrawić *pf.* waste; squander.

zmarnować *pf. zob.* **marnować**. **~ się** *pf. zob.* **marnować się**.

zmarszczenie *n.* **1.** wrinkling; knitting. **2.** gathering.

zmarszczka *f. Gen.pl.* **-ek 1.** (*na twarzy*) wrinkle, crease. **2.** (*w kąciku oka*) wrinkle. **3.** (*na wodzie*) ripple. **4.** (*na materiale*) wrinkle, crease. **5.** (*na papierze*) crease.

zmarszczyć *pf. zob.* **marszczyć**. **~ się** *pf. zob.* **marszczyć się**.

zmartwić *pf. zob.* **martwić**. **~ się** *pf. zob.* **martwić się**.

zmartwieć *pf. biol.* necrotize; *przen.* freeze; **zmartwieć w bezruchu** freeze, be motionless; **zmartwieć z przerażenia** *l.* **ze strachu** be petrified.

zmartwienie *n.* worry; trouble; problem; **ktoś ma zmartwienie z kimś** sb causes trouble to sb; **mieć zmartwienie z kimś** *l.* **czymś** have trouble with sb *l.* sth.

zmartwiony *a.* **-eni** worried; troubled; **mama jest bardzo zmartwiona** mom is very worried; **zmartwiony czymś** *l.* **z jakiegoś powodu** worried about sth *l.* because of sth.

zmartwychwstać *pf.* **-wstanę -wstaniesz** *zob.* **zmartwychwstawać**.

zmartwychwstanie *n. rel.* Resurrection.

zmartwychwstaniec *mp* **-ńc-** *pl.* **-y** *rz.-kat.* member of the Community of the Resurrection; **kościół zmartwychwstańców** Community of the Resurrection; **ojciec zmartwychwstaniec** friar of the Order of Resurrection.

zmartwychwstanka *f. Gen.pl.* **-ek** *rz.-kat.* member of the Community of Resurrection; **siostra zmartwychwstanka** sister of the Order of Resurrection.

zmartwychwstawać *ipf.* **-aję -ajesz, -awaj** *rel.* resurrect.

zmarzlak *mp pl.* **-i** *żart.* chilly person.

zmarzlina *f. geogr.* permafrost.

zmarzluch *mp pl.* **-y** *żart.* chilly person.

zmarznąć *pf.* **-znij, -zł** *l.* **-znął -zła -zli** 1. (= *odczuć zimno*) freeze; **zmarznąć do szpiku kości** freeze to the bone. 2. (*o roślinach*) freeze.

zmarznięty *a.* 1. (= *stwardniały*) frozen. 2. (= *przemarznięty*) cold.

zmasakrować *pf. zob.* **masakrować**.

zmasować *pf. zob.* **zmasowywać**.

zmasowany *a. wojsk.* concentrated.

zmasowywać *ipf. wojsk.* concentrate.

zmaterializować *pf.* 1. materialize, realize. 2. *pot.* materialize. **~ się** *pf.* 1. (= *stać się realnym*) materialize, come true. 2. *pot.* (= *stać się dbającym wyłącznie o pieniądze*) become materialistic.

zmaterializowany *a.* 1. (= *wprowadzony w życie*) materialized, realized; implemented. 2. (= *owładnięty materializmem*) materialized, materialistic.

zmatowieć *pf.* tarnish, become tarnished.

zmawiać *ipf.* say; **zmówić modlitwę** say a prayer.

zmaza *f.* 1. *przest.* (= *brud, plama*) stain, blot; **zmaza nocna** *med.* nocturnal pollution *l.* emission. 2. *lit.* (= *skaza moralna*) blemish, flaw.

zmazać *pf.* **zmażę zmażesz**, zmazywać *ipf.* 1. (= *zetrzeć*) (*napis*) rub out, erase; (*tablicę*) wipe off, erase. 2. (= *wynagrodzić*) wipe away, expiate.

zmącić *pf.* 1. (= *uczynić mętnym*) muddy; stir. 2. (= *zakłócić*) disturb; break; interrupt; **zmącić czyjś spokój** disturb sb's peace; **dzwonek zmącił ciszę** bell *l.* ring(ing) broke the silence. **~ się** *pf.* 1. (= *stracić przezroczystość*) become muddy. 2. *przen.* (= *pomieszać się*) get confused; **myśli mi się zmąciły w głowie** I got confused.

zmącony *a.* 1. (= *mętny*) muddy; **zmącone oczy** *l.* **źrenice** muddy eyes; **zmącona świadomość** confused mind. 2. (= *zakłócony*) disturbed; broken; interrupted.

zmądrzeć *pf.* grow wise *l.* wiser.

zmechacić *pf.* nap; teasel.

zmechanizować *pf. zob.* **mechanizować**. **~ się** *pf. zob.* **mechanizować się**.

zmechanizowany *a.* mechanized; automated.

zmeliorować *pf. zob.* **meliorować**.

zmęczenie *n.* tiredness, fatigue; **czuć zmęczenie w nogach** be dead on one's feet; **powłóczyć nogami ze zmęczenia** be down at the heel; **zmęczenie materiału** *techn.* fatigue.

zmęczeniowy *a. techn.* fatigue.

zmęczony *a.* tired, fatigued, weary; **jestem zmęczony** I am tired; **zmęczony czekaniem** tired of waiting.

zmęczyć *pf.* 1. (= *znużyć*) tire, fatigue, weary; **zmęczył mnie spacer** the walk tired me; **zmęczyć kogoś rozmową** tire *l.* bore sb with a conversation. 2. *pot.* (= *ukończyć z trudem*) wade (through); **zmęczyć książkę** wade through a book. **~ się** *pf.* get tired, tire, fatigue.

zmętnieć *pf.* become turbid.

zmętnienie *n.* turbidity; opacity.

zmężnieć *pf.* grow into a man, grow up; grow strong(er).

zmiana *f.* 1. (= *zmienienie*) change; **zmiana pogody** change of weather; **zmiana trybu życia** change in one's way of life; **zmiana na lepsze** *l.* **na gorsze** change for better *l.* for worse. 2. (= *wymiana czegoś na coś*) exchange; change; **zmiana warty** changing the guard; **zmiana świateł na skrzyżowaniu** change of traffic lights; **zmiana frontu** veer, change of position; **robić coś na zmianę z kimś** take turns with sb in doing sth; **zmiana dekoracji** *pot.* change of situation, new circumstances. 3. (*czas pracy*) shift; **pracować na pierwszą** *l.* **drugą zmianę** work the first *l.* the second shift; **praca na trzy zmiany** three-shift work (system); **zmiana dzienna** *l.* **nocna** day *l.* night shift. 4. (*pracownicy*) shift; **strajkuje druga zmiana** the second shift is on strike. 5. (*bielizna*) change. 6. *pat.* change, alteration, transformation; lesion; **zmiany gruźlicze** phthisic *l.* tuberculotic lesions; **zmiana nowotworowa** cancerous *l.* neoplastic lesion.

zmianowanie *n. roln.* crop rotation.

zmianowość *f.* shift work.

zmianowy *a.* shift; **zmianowy system pracy** shift system, shift work (system). **– mp** shift manager.

zmiatać *ipf.* 1. (= *usuwać miotłą*) sweep. 2. *pot.* (= *znikać*) leave, disappear; **zmiataj stąd!** clear off!, go away!

zmiażdżyć *pf.* 1. (= *rozgnieść*) crush. 2. *przen.* (= *pokonać*) crush, defeat, overcome.

zmiąć *pf.* **zemnę zemniesz, zemnij** crumple.

zmieniać *ipf.*, zmienić *pf.* 1. (= *przeobrażać*) change; **zmieniać sens czyjejś wypowiedzi** distort sb's words; **zmieniać zdanie** change one's mind. 2. (= *wymieniać*) exchange; **zmieniać bieg** *mot.* change gear; **zmieniać pas** *mot.* change lanes; **zmienić nazwisko** change one's surname; **zmienić front** veer, change one's position; **zmienić wiarę** *l.* **religię** convert, become converted; **zmieniać coś w coś innego** change *l.* turn sth into sth else. **~ się** *ipf.*, **zmienić się** *pf.* 1. (= *przeobrażać się*) change; **zmienić się na lepsze** *l.* **na gorsze** change for (the) better *l.* for worse; **zmienić się nie do poznania** change beyond recognition; **poczwarka zmieniła się w motyla** the chrysalis turned into a butterfly. 2. (= *wymieniać się*) change; **czekam, aż się zmieni światło na zielone** I am waiting for the lights to change into green; **sytuacja zmienia się jak w kalejdoskopie** things are changing quickly, situation is changing quickly.

zmienna *f. Gen.* **-ej** *mat.* variable; variate; **zmienna niezależna** independent variable; **zmienna zależna** dependent variable; response variable *l.* variate.

zmienniczka *f. Gen.pl.* **-ek** *zob.* **zmiennik¹**.

zmiennik¹ *mp pl.* **-cy** (= *ten, kto zmienia kogoś*) alternate, worker alternating with another at the same job.

zmiennik² *mi Gen.* **-a** *pl.* **-i** *techn.* changer; **zmiennik indukcyjności** adjustable *l.* variable inductor.

zmiennocieplny *a. zool.* heterothermic, ectothermic, poikilothermic, cold-blooded.

zmienność *f.* **1.** (= *zmienianie się*) changeability, variability; **zmienność pogody** weather unsteadiness; **zmienność losu** twists of fate. **2.** (= *niestałość*) changeability, changeableness; **zmienność kobiety** fickleness of a woman, a woman turns hot and cold.

zmienny *a.* **1.** (= *niestały*) changeable, variable; **gwiazda zmienna** *astron.* variable star; **ruch jednostajnie zmienny** *fiz.* uniformly variable motion; **ruch zmienny** *fiz.* variable *l.* nonuniform motion; **prąd zmienny** *fiz.* alternating current; **zmienne koleje losu** vicissitudes, ups and downs. **2.** (*o człowieku*) (= *chwiejny*) volatile, changeable; **zmienny w uczuciach** unsteady in one's feelings.

zmierzać *ipf. lit.* head; **zmierzać na południe** *l.* **północ** head south *l.* north; **zmierzać w stronę** head for *l.* towards; **zmierzać do celu** *przen.* pursue an aim; **do czego zmierzasz?** what are you driving at?

zmierzch *mi* **1.** (*pora dnia*) dusk, twilight; **o zmierzchu** at dusk; **przed zmierzchem** before dusk; **zmierzch zapada** it's getting dark. **2.** *przen.* (= *kres*) twilight; **u zmierzchu kariery** in the twilight of one's career; **zmierzch cywilizacji** twilight of civilization.

zmierzchać się *ipf.* dusk, get dark.

zmierzchowy *a.* dusk, twilight; **ślepota zmierzchowa** *pat.* twilight blindness, aknephascopia.

zmierzić *pf.* -rżę -rzisz disgust, sicken.

zmierznąć *pf.* -znę -zniesz *l.* -źniesz, -znij *l.* -źnij, -zł -zli *l.* -źli *rzad.* pall.

zmierzwiać *ipf.* ruffle, tousle, dishevel. ~ **się** *ipf.* become ruffled, become tousled, become dishevel(l)ed.

zmierzwić (się) *pf. zob.* **zmierzwiać (się)**.

zmierzyć *pf.* **1.** (= *wymierzyć*) measure, gauge; **zmierzyć ciśnienie** take (sb's) blood pressure; **zmierzyć temperaturę** take (sb's) temperature; **zmierzyć tętno** take (sb's) pulse; **zmierzyć linijką** measure with a ruler; **zmierzyć kogoś spojrzeniem** *l.* **wzrokiem** eye sb, size sb up. **2.** (= *przymierzyć*) try on. ~ **się** *pf.* **1.** (= *określić swoje wymiary*) take one's own measurements. **2.** (= *określić wymiary sobie nawzajem*) take each other's measurements. **3.** (= *spróbować swoich sił w walce*) pit o.s. against; **zmierzyć się z kimś** *l.* **z czymś** pit o.s. against sb *l.* sth.

zmieszać *ipf.* **1.** (= *mieszając, łączyć*) blend, mix; stir; **zmieszać kogoś z błotem** sling mud at sb. **2.** (= *speszyć kogoś*) confuse; **zmieszać kogoś swoim zachowaniem** confuse sb with one's behavior. ~ **się** *pf.* **1.** (= *połączyć się*) blend, mix; **zmieszać się z czymś** blend *l.* combine with sth. **2.** (= *speszyć się*) get confused; **zmieszać się na czyjś widok** get confused at the sight of sb.

zmieszanie *n.* **1.** blending, mixing; stirring. **2.** confusion; embarrassment.

zmieszany *a.* (= *speszony*) confused; **czułem się zmieszany** I felt confused.

zmieścić *pf.* -szczę -ścisz **1.** manage to fit, manage to put; **zmieścić coś w czymś** find

enough room for sth somewhere, manage to fit *l.* put sth somewhere. **2.** admit, receive, accomodate; house; hold; seat. ~ **się** *pf.* fit; **plecak nie zmieścił się do bagażnika** there was not enough room for the backpack in the trunk.

zmieść *pf.* **zmiotę zmieciesz zmiótł zmiotła zmietli** **1.** *zob.* **zmiatać**. **2.** *pot.* (= *zjeść szybko*) polish off.

zmiędlić *pf.* -dl *l.* -dlij **1.** swingle, scutch. **2.** *pot.* crumple.

zmiękczać *ipf.* **1.** (= *czynić miękkim*) soften; **zmiękczyć wodę** soften water; **zmiękczyć spółgłoskę** *fon.* palatalize a consonant. **2.** *przen.* (= *rozczulić*) soften; **zmiękczyć czyjeś serce** soften sb's heart; **zmiękczyć kogoś łzami** soften sb's with sb's tears. ~ **się** *ipf.* **1.** (= *stać się miękkim*) soften. **2.** *jęz.* become palatalized. **3.** *przen.* (= *stać się skłonnym do ustępstw*) soften.

zmiękczyć (się) *pf. zob.* **zmiękczać (się)**.

zmięknąć *pf.* -knij, -kł *l.* -knął -kła -kli **1.** (= *stać się miękkim*) soften; **rura mu zmiękła** *pot.* he has come down a peg. **2.** *przen.* (= *stać się skłonnym do ustępstw*) soften. **3.** (= *stać się łagodnym*) soften; **serce mu zmiękło** his heart softened.

zmiętosić *pf.* -szę -sisz crumple. ~ **się** *pf.* crumple.

zmiętoszony *a.* crumpled.

zmięty *a.* crumpled.

zmiksować *pf. zob.* **miksować**.

zmilczeć *pf.* -ę -ysz *przest.* pass over in silence; make no mention of; disregard, ignore; **zmilczeć zniewagę** ignore an insult.

zmilitaryzować *pf. zob.* **militaryzować**.

zmiłować się *pf.* show mercy, have mercy; **zmiłować się nad kimś** have mercy on sb; **zmiłuj się!** have mercy!

zminiaturyzować *pf. zob.* **miniaturyzować**.

zminimalizować *pf. zob.* **minimalizować**.

zmiotka *f. Gen.pl.* -ek brush.

zmitologizować *pf. zob.* **mitologizować**.

zmitrężyć *pf. przest.* waste.

zmitygować *pf.* moderate; restrain, check. ~ **się** *pf.* control o.s.

zmizernieć *pf.* become sickly, waste; pine away.

zmniejszać *ipf.* reduce, lessen, diminish, decrease; (*zużycie paliwa, energii*) reduce; (*prędkość*) reduce; (*koszty*) reduce; (*racje żywnościowe*) diminish, decrease. ~ **się** *ipf.* decrease, lessen; **odległość się zmniejsza** the distance decreases; **upał się zmniejszył** the heat decreased; **ból ciągle się nie zmniejsza** the pain won't recede.

zmniejszyć (się) *pf. zob.* **zmniejszać (się)**.

zmobilizować *pf. zob.* **mobilizować**. ~ **się** *pf. zob.* **mobilizować się**.

zmoczyć *pf.* wet; moisten; soak; **zmoczyłem sobie buty** I got my shoes wet; **zmoczyłem nogi** I got wet feet; **deszcz mnie zmoczył** I got wet in the rain. ~ **się** *pf.* get wet.

zmodernizować *pf. zob.* **modernizować**.

zmodyfikować *pf. zob.* **modyfikować**.

zmogę *itd. pf. zob.* **zmóc**.

zmokły *a.* (soaking) wet, soaked; **wyglądać jak**

zmokła kura look like a drowned rat, look like a wet hen.

zmoknąć *pf.* **zmoknij, zmoknął** *l.* **zmókł zmokła zmokli** get wet (in the rain); **zmoknąć do suchej nitki** get soaking wet.

zmonopolizować *pf. zob.* **monopolizować**.

zmontować *pf.* **1.** (= *połączyć*) assemble, put together, set up. **2.** *pot.* (= *zorganizować*) organize; muster; **zmontować imprezę** throw a party.

zmora *f. Gen.pl.* **-or** *l.* **-ór 1.** (*sen*) nightmare. **2.** (= *upiór*) ghost, phantom, apparition. **3.** (= *udręka*) specter; **zmora głodu** specter of famine.

zmordować *pf.* **1.** (= *utrudzić*) tire, fatigue, exhaust, do in; (*konia*) override; **zmordować kogoś forsownym marszem** tire sb with a strenuous march *l.* hike. **2.** *pot.* (= *zrobić coś z trudem*) toil (through), wade through, plow through. ~ **się** *pf.* tire, become extremely fatigued, exhaust o.s., be done in.

zmotoryzowany *a.* motorized; **turysta zmotoryzowany** motorized tourist.

zmowa *f. Gen.pl.* **-ów** conspiracy; **zmowa milczenia** conspiracy of silence; **być z kimś w zmowie** be in league with sb.

zmóc *pf.* **zmogę zmożesz zmógł zmogła zmogli** get the better of; overcome, overpower; **choroba go zmogła** illness got the better of him; **sen mnie zmógł** I fell asleep; **coś mnie zmogło** *pot.* I'm not feeling OK.

zmór *f. zob.* **zmora**.

zmów *f. zob.* **zmowa**.

zmówić *pf. zob.* **zmawiać**. ~ **się** *pf. zob.* **zmawiać się**.

zmrok *mi* dusk, nightfall; **przed zmrokiem** before dark; **po zmroku** after dark.

zmrozić *pf.* **zmrożę zmrozisz, zmróź** *l.* **zmroź** freeze, chill; **coś komuś zmroziło krew w żyłach** sth made sb's blood run cold.

zmrużać *ipf.*, **zmrużyć** *pf.* squint, blink; **całą noc nie zmrużyłem oka** I didn't sleep a wink all night.

zmrużenie *n.* wink; **bez zmrużenia oczu** *l.* **powiek** (= *bez namysłu*) without batting an eyelid.

zmumifikować *pf. zob.* **mumifikować**.

zmumifikowany *a.* mummified.

zmurszały *a.* rotten.

zmurszeć *pf.* rot.

zmusić (się) *pf.* **-szę -sisz** *zob.* **zmuszać (się)**.

zmuszać *ipf.* force, make; **zmusić kogoś do zrobienia czegoś** *l.* **żeby coś zrobił** force sb to do sth, make sb do sth. ~ **się** *ipf.* bring o.s., force o.s.; **zmuszać się do czegoś** force o.s. into sth.

zmyć *pf.* **zmyję zmyjesz, zmyj** *zob.* **zmywać**. ~ **się** *pf. zob.* **zmywać się**.

zmydlać *ipf.* use up (*soap*). ~ **się** *ipf* run out.

zmydlić (się) *pf. zob.* **zmydlać (się)**.

zmykać *ipf.* scamper away, make o.s. scarce; **zmykać przed kimś/czymś** run away from sb/sth; **zmykaj (stąd)!** hop it!, get out of here!

zmylić *pf.* **1.** (= *wprowadzić w błąd*) mislead, deceive; **zmylić czyjąś czujność** deceive sb despite his vigilance. **2.** (= *pomylić, pomieszać*) confuse; **zmylić ślad** cover one's tracks.

zmyłka *f. Gen.pl.* **-ek** *pot.* slipup, bloomer.

zmysł *mi* **1.** (*zdolność organizmu*) sense; **zmysł słuchu/wzroku/dotyku/węchu/równowagi/smaku** sense of hearing/sight/touch/smell/balance/taste; **szósty zmysł** sixth sense. **2.** (*predyspozycja*) sense, flair; **zmysł praktyczny/artystyczny/estetyczny** practical/artistic/aesthetic sense; *zob. t.* **zmysły**.

zmysłowo *adv.* **1.** (= *seksownie*) sensually, sensously; **zmysłowo wyglądać** look sexy. **2.** (= *za pomocą zmysłów*) sensorily; (*postrzegać*) through one's senses, by means of one's senses.

zmysłowość *f.* sensuality.

zmysłowy *a.* **1.** (= *seksowny*) sensual, sensuous. **2.** (= *postrzegany zmysłami*) sensory, sensorial; **narządy zmysłowe** sense organs.

zmysły *pl. Gen.pl.* **-łów 1.** (= *świadomość*) senses; **pomieszanie zmysłów** madness, lunacy; **być przy zdrowych zmysłach** be of sound mind; **odchodzić od zmysłów (ze zmartwienia)** be out of one's mind *l.* senses (with worry); **postradać zmysły** take leave of one's senses; **nikt przy zdrowych zmysłach by...** nobody in his right mind would... **2.** (= *popęd płciowy*) libido, sexuality.

zmyślać *ipf.*, **zmyślić** *pf.* make up, fib; **przestań zmyślać!** stop telling tales!

zmyślnie *adv.* ingeniously, cleverly.

zmyślny *a.* **1.** (*o człowieku*) (= *sprytny*) clever; (= *przebiegły*) cunning. **2.** (*o urządzeniu*) (= *pomysłowy*) ingenious.

zmyślony *a.* (= *fikcyjny*) fictitious; (= *kłamliwy*) bogus.

zmyty *a.* washed down, washed off; (*o napisie*) effaced; **poszedł jak zmyty** he went away with a flea in his ear.

zmywacz *mi Gen.* **-a 1.** (*rozpuszczalnik*) solvent; **zmywacz do farb** paint-stripper; **zmywacz do paznokci** nail polish remover. **2.** (*urządzenie*) washer.

zmywać *ipf.* **-am -asz 1.** (*czyścić*) (*podłogę*) wash; (*plamy, brud*) wash off; **zmywać naczynia** wash up, wash the dishes; **zmyć komuś głowę** take sb to task, give sb a dressing down. **2.** *przen.* (= *naprawiać*) wipe away. **3.** (*drogę, most*) wash away. ~ **się** *ipf.* **1.** (= *dawać się usunąć*) wash off. **2.** *pot.* (= *znikać*) clear off; **no to się zmywam** I gotta be going.

zmywak *mi Gen.* **-a 1.** (*naczynie*) sink. **2.** (*szmatka*) dishcloth; (*na rączce*) mop.

zmywalny *a.* washable.

zmywarka *f. Gen.pl.* **-ek** washer; **zmywarka do naczyń** dishwasher.

znachor *mp*, **znachorka** *f. Gen.pl.* **-ek** quack, charlatan.

znachorski *a.* quackish; (*o terapii, leku*) quack.

znachorstwo *n.* quackery.

znacjonalizować *pf. zob.* **nacjonalizować**.

znacząco *adv.* meaningfully, significantly; (= *wymownie*) tellingly.

znaczący *a.* **1.** (= *wymowny*) meaningful, telling; **nic nieznaczący gest** insignificant gesture. **2.** (= *ważny, istotny*) significant.

znaczek *mi* **-czk-** *Gen.* **-a 1.** (*oznaczenie*) mark; (*np. na liście*) tick. **2.** (*nalepka*) stamp; **znaczek**

pocztowy stamp, postage stamp; **znaczek skarbowy** stamp, duty stamp; **naklejać znaczek na list** stamp a letter. **3.** (*odznaka*) badge.

znaczenie *n.* **1.** (= *treść*) meaning, sense; **w pełnym tego słowa znaczeniu** in the full sense of the word. **2.** (= *ważność czegoś*) significance, importance; **mieć duże/małe znaczenie** be of great/little importance; **nabierać znaczenia** acquire importance, come into prominence; **tracić na znaczeniu** diminish in importance; **zyskiwać na znaczeniu** gain in importance; **to nie ma (najmniejszego) znaczenia** it doesn't matter (in the slightest); **to jest bez znaczenia** it is of no importance, it is of no significance; **to jest dla mnie bez znaczenia** it doesn't matter to me; **jak gdyby to miało (jakiekolwiek) znaczenie** as if that mattered (at all); **twoje pochodzenie nie ma tu żadnego znaczenia** your (social) background is of no importance here.

znaczeniowy *a. jęz.* semantic, significative; **treść znaczeniowa wyrazu** semantic content of a word; **zakres znaczeniowy wyrazu** semantic range of a word.

znacznie *adv.* considerably, significantly; **poczuła się znacznie lepiej** she felt much better; **pogoda znacznie się poprawiła** the weather improved significantly.

znacznik *mi Gen.* **-a** *roln.* marker.

znaczny *a.* **1.** (= *duży*) considerable, substantial, significant. **2.** *przest.* (= *wyróżniający się*) conspicuous.

znaczyć *ipf.* **1.** (= *wyrażać sens*) mean, signify; **to nic nie znaczy** it doesn't mean anything; **nie rozumiem, co to znaczy** I don't understand what it means; **co to ma znaczyć!?** what is that supposed to mean!?; **co to wszystko znaczy!?** what does all this mean!?; **był z kolegą, to znaczy z Jurkiem** he was with a friend, I mean with Jurek; **to znaczy...** that is... **2.** (= *mieć znaczenie*) matter, be of importance; mean; **to dla mnie wiele znaczy** it means a lot to me; **czy rodzina dla ciebie nic nie znaczy?** isn't the family of any importance to you? **3.** (= *znakować*) mark.

znać *ipf.* **1.** (= *mieć wiedzę o czymś*) know; **znać życie** know all about life; **znać coś na pamięć** know sth by heart; **dać komuś znać (o czymś)** let sb know (of sth); **dać znać na policję** inform the police; **znam to miejsce** I know this place; **nie znam tego modelu** I don't know this model; **nie dał znać o sobie** I haven't heard from him; **znam ten ból** *pot.* I know how it feels; **daj znać** let me know. **2.** (= *być komuś przedstawionym*) know (*kogoś* sb); be acquainted (*kogoś* with sb); **znać kogoś jak zły szeląg** know sb like a bad penny; **nie znam jej** I don't know her; **znam ją od kilku lat** I have known her for a few years; **znam go osobiście** I know him personally; **znam go tylko z widzenia** I know him only by sight; **nie chcę cię znać** I don't want to have anything to do with you; **niech cię nie znam!** go on with you! **3.** (= *umieć coś*) know, can; **nie znam francuskiego** I can't speak French; **nie znam tej historii** I don't know this story. **4.** (= *wiedzieć o istnieniu*) know; **nie znać lęku** *l.* **strachu** know no fear, be a

stranger to fear; **nie znać litości** know no pity, be a stranger to pity; **wtedy nie znali telefonu** there were no telephones at that time; **jego chciwość nie zna granic** his greed knows no bounds. **5.** (= *widać*) show, be visible; **znać, że potrzebujesz wypoczynku** I can see that you need a rest; **znać na niej zmęczenie** I can see that she is tired. **~ się** *ipf.* **1.** (*siebie samego*) know o.s.; **znam się** I know myself. **2.** (= *być sobie przedstawionym*) know each other; **znamy się od dziecka** we have known each other since we were children. **3.** (= *mieć wiedzę*) know; **znać się na czymś** be knowledgeable about sth; **znać się na żartach** know how to take a joke; **znać się na czymś jak kura na pieprzu** not know the first thing about sth; **znać się na rzeczy** know a thing or two about...; **nie znasz się na tym** you know nothing about it, that's not in your line.

znad *prep.* + *Gen.* from above; **znad morza/rzeki** from the seaside/river; **podnieść wzrok znad biurka** look up from behind one's desk.

znajda *f. l. mp decl. like f. Gen.pl.* **-d** *l.* **-ów** foundling.

znajdować *ipf.* **1.** (= *odnajdować, odszukiwać*) find; **być jak znalazł** come in handy. **2.** (= *wynajdować*) find; **znaleźć pracę/męża** find a job/husband; **znajdować w czymś upust** find expression in sth; **znajdować w czymś przyjemność** find pleasure in sth; **nie znajduję słów podziwu** I can't find words to express my admiration; **znajdziesz dla mnie chwilę czasu?** could you find a moment for me?; **znaleźć wspólny język** find a common ground. **3.** (= *natrafiać*) (*poparcie, zrozumienie*) meet (*coś* with sth); **znaleźć u kogoś zrozumienie** meet with sb's understanding; **znaleźć śmierć od kuli/pod kołami samochodu** meet one's death from a bullet/in a car accident. **4.** (= *uzyskiwać*) gain, find; **znaleźć uznanie** win approval; **coś znajduje zastosowanie w czymś** sth is useful for *l.* in sth, sth is applicable to sth. **5.** *przest.* (= *osądzać*) find; **znajduję cię w dobrym zdrowiu** I find that you are in good health. **~ się** *ipf.* **1.** (= *mieścić się*) be located, be situated. **2.** (= *dawać się odszukać*) be found. **3.** (= *być wyszukiwanym*) be discovered; **znajdzie się na to rada** *l.* **sposób** that can be solved; **znajdzie się na niego rada** *l.* **sposób** he will be brought to reason. **4.** (= *ukazywać się*) appear, come out; be published; **powieść znajdzie się w sprzedaży w maju** the novel will appear in May; **notatka znalazła się w prasie** the notice was published in the press. **5.** (= *przebywać gdzieś*) be, find o.s.; **znaleźć się na bruku** land on the street; **znaleźć się na liście** be listed; **znajdować się w dobrych rękach** be in good hands; **coś znajduje się w czyichś rękach** sth is in sb's hand; **ktoś znajduje się w czyichś rękach** sb is in sb's power; **po dziesięciu minutach znalazł się na rynku** after 10 minutes he found himself at the market square; **czy ktoś wie, gdzie się znajdujemy?** does anybody know where we are? **6.** *tylko ipf.* (= *występować*) occur, be found; **w wodzie znajduje się tlen i wodór** water is made of oxygen and hydrogen. **7.** (= *doznawać czegoś*) experience; **znaleźć się w trudnej**

sytuacji, **w kłopotach** be in trouble. **8.** (= *być w jakimś stanie*) be, find o.s.; **zamek znajduje się w ruinie** the castle is ruined.

znajoma *f. Gen.* **-ej** acquaintance; **pewna moja znajoma** a woman I know.

znajomość *f.* **1.** (*stosunki towarzyskie*) acquaintance; **mieć znajomości** have connections, have contacts; **nawiązać** *l.* **zawrzeć z kimś znajomość** make sb's acquaintance, become acquainted with sb; **odnowić z kimś znajomość** renew one's acquaintance with sb; **po znajomości** as between friends. **2.** (*wiedza*) knowledge; **znajomość angielskiego/psychiki ludzkiej** knowledge of English/human psyche.

znajomy *a.* **1.** (= *taki, którego się zna*) known, of one's acquaintance; **znajomy lekarz powiedział mi, że...** A doctor I know told me that... **2.** (= *nieobcy*) familiar. – *mp* acquaintance; **pewien mój znajomy** a man I know.

znak *mi* **1.** (= *symbol informujący*) sign; **znak diakrytyczny** diacritic; **znak dodawania/odejmowania/mnożenia/dzielenia** plus/minus/multiplication/division sign; **znak drogowy** road sign, traffic sign; **znak fabryczny** *l.* **towarowy** trademark; **znak interpunkcyjny** punctuation mark; **znak jakości** quality symbol, mark of quality; **znak korektorski** proof-readers' mark; **znak krzyża** sign of the cross; **znak wodny** watermark; **znak zapytania** question mark; **znak zodiaku** sign of the zodiac; **znaki szczególne** distinguishing marks; **pod znakiem czegoś** under the banner of sth; **dać znak** signal; **dać komuś znak ręką** gesture for sb; **dawać znaki życia** show signs of life; **dawać się komuś we znaki** (*o osobie*) give sb a hard time; (*o sytuacji*) get on top of sb; (*o pracy, trudach*) take its toll on sb; **być pod znakiem zapytania** be open to doubt; **stawiać coś pod znakiem zapytania** call sth into question; **jego przyszłość stoi pod znakiem zapytania** there is a question mark over his future; **stawiać między czymś a czymś znak równości** equate sth and sth, make the equation between sth and sth. **2.** (= *dowód*) sign, token; **znak przyjaźni/miłości** sign of friendship/love; **na znak wdzięczności** as a token of gratitude. **3.** (= *omen*) sign, omen; **to dobry/zły znak** this is a good/bad sign, this is a good/bad omen; **wszystkie znaki na niebie i na ziemi wskazują, że...** all the signs are that... **4.** (*ślad*) trace; **ani znaku życia** no trace of life.

znakomicie *adv.* **1.** (= *wyśmienicie*) superbly, brilliantly; **wyglądać/czuć się znakomicie** look/feel great; **znakomicie znać niemiecki** speak brilliant German. **2.** *lit.* (= *znacznie*) remarkably, significantly; **znakomicie przyczynić się do czegoś** contribute to sth remarkably.

znakomitość *f.* **1.** (= *osoba wybitna*) celebrity. **2.** (*to, co wybitne*) brilliance, excellence.

znakomity *a.* **1.** (= *wybitny*) distinguished, superb. **2.** (= *wyśmienity*) excellent, superb. **3.** *lit.* (= *znaczny*) remarkable; **znakomita większość** the vast majority.

znakować *ipf.* (*pisemnie*) mark; (*naklejką*) label; (*pieczątką*) stamp; (*zwierzęta*) brand.

znalazca *mp*, **znalazczyni** *f.* finder.

znalezisko *n.* find, finding.

znaleźć *pf.* **znajdę znajdziesz znalazł znaleźli** *zob.* **znajdować.** ~ **się** *pf.* **1.** *zob.* **znajdować się. 2.** (= *odpowiednio się zachować*) know how to behave; **umieć się znaleźć w każdej sytuacji** be able to do the right thing at the right moment.

znaleźne *n. Gen.* **-ego** finder's reward.

znamienity *a.* (= *znakomity*) eminent, illustrious; (= *wybitny*) outstanding; **znamienita osoba** person of rank; **być znamienitego rodu** be of noble stock.

znamienny *a.* characteristic (*dla kogoś / czegoś* of sb/sth).

znamię *n.* **-mieni-** *pl.* **-mion- 1.** (*na skórze*) birthmark. **2.** (= *właściwość*) trait, stamp. **3.** *bot.* stigma.

znamionować *ipf.* indicate.

znamionowy *a. techn.* nominal.

znany *a.* (*otoczenie, środowisko*) well-known, familiar; (*aktor, piosenkarka*) well-known, famous; (*oszust, przestępca*) notorious; **mało znany** little-known; **być znanym z czegoś** (*w sensie pozytywnym*) be famous for sth, have a reputation for sth; (*w sensie negatywnym*) be notorious for sth, have a reputation for sth.

znarowić *pf.* **-ów** make skittish. ~ **się** *pf.* get skittish.

znaturalizować *pf.* naturalize.

znawca *mp*, **znawczyni** *f.* expert (*czegoś* in *l.* on sth); **znawca szachów/literatury rosyjskiej** chess/Russian literature expert.

znawstwo *n.* competence, expertness (*czegoś* in sth); **ze znawstwem** expertly.

znerwicowany *a.* (= *neurotyczny*) neurotic; (*w wyniku ciężkich przejść, doświadczeń*) traumatized.

zneutralizować *ipf. t. chem.* neutralize.

znęcać się *ipf.* abuse (*nad kimś* sb); **znęcać się nad zwierzętami** torment animals; **przestań się nade mną znęcać!** stop tormenting me!

znęcanie się *n.* abuse.

znęcić *pf.* (*łatwym zyskiem, dobrą pracą*) tempt, seduce; (= *zwabić*) (*np. zwierzę nagrodą*) lure.

znękany *a.* harried; (*o wyrazie twarzy, spojrzeniu*) worn out, tormented.

znicz *mi Gen.* **-a** *Gen.pl.* **-y** *l.* **-ów** candle; **znicz olimpijski** the Olympic torch.

zniechęcać *ipf.* discourage (*kogoś do czegoś* sb from (doing) sth); **zniechęcić kogoś do siebie** disaffect sb; **zniechęcać kogoś trudnościami** discourage sb with difficulties. ~ **się** *ipf.* become discouraged (*do czegoś* from (doing) sth); **zniechęcić się trudnościami** get discouraged by difficulties.

zniechęcenie *n.* discouragement.

zniechęcić *pf. zob.* **zniechęcać.** ~ **się** *pf. zob.* **zniechęcać się.**

zniecierpliwić *pf.* make impatient; **zniecierpliwić kogoś czymś** make sb impatient with sth. ~ **się** *pf.* become impatient (*czymś* with sth).

zniecierpliwienie *n.* (= *niecierpliwość*) impatience; (= *niepokój*) restlessness.

zniecierpliwiony *a.* **-eni** (= *niecierpliwy*) impatient; (= *niespokojny*) restless.

znieczulać *ipf.* **1.** *med.* anesthetize; *Br.*anaesthetize. **2.** (= *uczynić niewrażliwym*) desensitize (*na coś* to sth).

znieczulający *a.* *med.* **środek znieczulający** anesthetic; *Br.* anaesthetic.

znieczulenie *n.* *med.* anesthesia; *Br.* anaesthesia; **znieczulenie ogólne/miejscowe** general/local anesthesia; **w znieczuleniu** under anesthetic; *Br.* under anaesthetic.

znieczulica *f.* *lit.* callousness; **znieczulica społeczna** social callousness.

znieczulić *pf.* *zob.* **znieczulać**.

zniedołężniały *a.* decrepit.

zniedołężnieć *pf.* become decrepit.

zniedołężnienie *n.* decrepitude; **zniedołężnienie starcze** senility.

zniekształcać *ipf.* **1.** (= *deformować*) deform, disfigure, distort. **2.** (*czyjeś słowa, rzeczywistość*) distort, twist. **~ się** *ipf.* become deformed, become disfigured.

zniekształcenie *n.* (*obrazu, informacji*) distortion; *pat.* (*twarzy, organu*) deformity.

zniekształcić *pf.* *zob.* **zniekształcać**. **~ się** *pf.* *zob.* **zniekształcać się**.

zniekształcony *a.* **1.** (= *zdeformowany*) deformed, misshapen; (*o obrazie, głosie*) distorted. **2.** (= *wypaczony*) (*o czyichś słowach, rzeczywistości*) distorted, twisted.

znielubić *pf.* *pot.* start to dislike.

zniemczeć *pf.* become Germanized, Germanize.

zniemczyć *pf.* Germanize.

znienacka *adv.* (= *niespodziewanie*) unexpectedly; (= *nagle*) suddenly; **zaskoczyć kogoś znienacka** take sb unawares.

znienawidzić *pf.* come to hate, get to hate (*kogoś/coś* sb/sth). **~ się** *pf.* **1.** (*nawzajem*) come to hate one another. **2.** (*siebie samego*) come to hate o.s.

znieprawiać *ipf.*, **znieprawić** *pf.* deprave.

znieruchomieć *pf.* be transfixed, become motionless.

zniesienie *n.* **1.** (= *ścierpienie*) tolerance, endurance; **(ból) nie do zniesienia** unbearable (pain). **2.** (*niewolnictwa, cenzury*) abolition; (*sankcji, embarga*) lifting.

zniesławiać *ipf.*, **zniesławić** *pf.* *lit.* (*pisemnie*) libel; (*ustnie*) slander.

zniesławienie *n.* *prawn.* (*pisemne*) libel; (*ustne*) slander.

znieść *pf.* **zniosę zniesiesz zniósł zniosła znieśli** *zob.* **znosić**. **~ się** *pf.* *zob.* **znosić się**.

zniewaga *f.* insult, affront; **ta zniewaga krwi wymaga** *żart.* this insult calls for vengeance, this calls for blood to be shed.

zniewalać *ipf.* **1.** (= *zjednywać sobie*) captivate; **zniewalać publiczność** captivate the audience. **2.** *lit.* (= *zmuszać*) constrain (*kogoś do czegoś* sb to do sth); **zniewolić kobietę** *przest.* violate a woman.

zniewalający *a.* (*głos, uśmiech, spojrzenie*) captivating; (*uroda*) magnetic.

znieważać *ipf.*, **znieważyć** *pf.* insult, affront; **znieważyć kogoś czynnie** *prawn.* slap sb in the face. **~ się** *ipf.* insult one another.

zniewieściałość *f.* effeminacy.

zniewieściały *a.* effeminate.

zniewolić *pf.* *zob.* **zniewalać**.

znikać *ipf.* **1.** (= *stawać się niewidocznym*) disappear, vanish; **zniknąć w tłumie** vanish in the crowd; **słońce znikło za chmurami** the sun disappeared behind the clouds. **2.** (= *wychodzić skądś*) disappear, slip away; **zniknąć bez śladu** disappear without a trace; (*o osobie t.*) leave no forwarding address; **zniknąć z czyjegoś życia** disappear from sb's life; **zniknąć z pola widzenia** get out of sight, recede from view. **3.** (= *ginąć*) vanish, disappear; **znikła biżuteria** the jewels disappeared. **4.** (= *zanikać*) disappear, vanish; **jedzenie znikało z talerzy** the food was disappearing from the plates; **zniknąć z powierzchni ziemi** be wiped off the face of the earth, disappear *l.* vanish from the face of the earth.

znikąd *adv.* from nowhere, out of nowhere; **człowiek znikąd** man from nowhere.

zniknąć *pf.* **-ij** *zob.* **znikać**.

znikomo *adv.* in a minimal degree, minutely; **znikomo się do czegoś przyczynić** make a minute contribution to sth.

znikomość *f.* minuteness.

znikomy *a.* minute, slight.

zniszczalność *f.* destructibility.

zniszczalny *a.* destructible.

zniszczeć *pf.* be destroyed (*od czegoś* by sth); (*o budynkach*) be ruined, fall into ruin.

zniszczenie *n.* destruction; (= *dewastacja*) devastation; **odbudować miasto ze zniszczeń** rebuild a destroyed town.

zniszczony *a.* destroyed; (= *zdewastowany*) devastated; (*o człowieku*) worn out; (*o organizmie*) wasted; **zniszczone zdrowie** ruined health; **ręce zniszczone pracą** toil-worn hands.

zniszczyć *pf.* **1.** (= *zepsuć*) destroy; (= *zdewastować*) devastate; (= *zrujnować*) ruin. **2.** (= *zużyć*) (*np. buty, ubranie*) wear out; **zniszczyć komuś karierę** wreck sb's career; **zniszczę go!** I will destroy him! **3.** (= *usunąć, unicestwić*) destroy. **4.** *pot.* (= *pozbawić kogoś majątku*) ruin; **zniszczyć kogoś finansowo** bring sb to ruin. **~ się** *pf.* (*o ubraniu, obuwiu*) be worn out.

znitować *pf.* *zob.* **nitować**.

zniweczyć *pf.* *lit.* (*plany*) thwart, frustrate; (*nadzieje*) destroy, shatter.

zniwelować *pf.* *zob.* **niwelować**.

zniżać *ipf.* **1.** (= *obniżać*) lower; **zniżyć głos** lower one's voice; **zniżyć lot** descend. **2.** (= *zmniejszać wartość*) reduce, lower. **~ się** *ipf.* **1.** (= *opadać*) (= *mieć coraz mniejszą wysokość*) descend. **2.** (= *dostosowywać się*) condescend (*do czegoś* to sth). **3.** (= *poniżać się, upokorzyć się*) stoop (*do czegoś* to sth).

zniżka *f.* *Gen.pl.* **-ek** reduction, discount; (*np. studencka, inwalidzka*) concession; **ze zniżką** (*kupić, sprzedać*) at a discount; **3% zniżki** 3% discount; **bilet ze zniżką** (*np. dla studentów, inwali-*

dów) concession ticket; (*np. wycieczkowy, kupiony w promocji*) saver ticket.

zniżkować *ipf.* (*o cenach*) sag; (*o walutach, cenach na giełdzie*) be falling.

zniżkowy *a.* reduced, discount; **bilet zniżkowy** concession ticket; **cena zniżkowa** reduced price, discount price; **tendencja zniżkowa** *fin.* downward trend.

zniżyć *pf. zob.* **zniżać**. ~ **się** *pf. zob.* **zniżać się**.

znoić się *ipf. lit.* toil (*przy l. nad czymś* at sth).

znojny *a. lit.* exhausting; **znojny dzień** toilsome day.

znokautować *pf. zob.* **nokautować**.

znormalizować *pf. zob.* **normalizować**.

znormalnieć *pf. zob.* **normalnieć**.

znos *mi żegl.* drift; (*boczny*) leeway.

znosić *ipf.* **-szę -sisz** **1.** (= *niosąc, przemieścić w dół*) carry down, take down. **2.** (= *nosząc, gromadzić*) gather; **znieść jajko** lay an egg. **3.** (*o prądzie wody, powietrzu*) (= *zmieniać kurs*) drift, carry; **znieść statek z kursu** carry a ship out of its course. **4.** (= *niszczyć*) wipe off; (*o powodzi*) sweep away; **znieść miasto z powierzchni ziemi** raze a city to the ground; **znieść wroga z powierzchni ziemi** wipe the enemy off the face of the earth. **5.** (= *unieważniać*) (*prawo, dekret*) abolish; (*sankcje, embargo*) lift; **znieść zakaz** lift a ban; **znieść poddaństwo** abolish serfdom. **6.** (= *poddawać się czemuś bez protestu*) bear, endure, tolerate; **nie znosić brudu/hałasu** can't stand *l.* bear dirt/noise, hate dirt/noise; **pomarańcze źle znoszą transport** oranges travel badly; **ta roślina nie znosi słońca** this plant doesn't tolerate sunshine; **nie znoszę jej!** I can't stand *l.* bear her! — *pf.* **-szę -sisz** (= *zniszczyć odzież*) wear out. ~ **się** *ipf.* **1.** (= *tolerować się*) tolerate each other; **oni się nie znoszą** they hate each other, there is no love lost between them. **2.** *zw. ipf. fiz.* cancel each other, neutralize each other. – *pf.* (*np. o obuwiu*) wear out.

znoszony *a.* worn out, shabby.

znośnie *adv.* bearably, tolerably; **mieszkać znośnie** live in tolerable conditions.

znośny *a.* bearable, tolerable.

znowelizować *pf. zob.* **nowelizować**.

znowu *adv.* again, once again; **znowu się spóźniłeś** you are late again. – *particle* (= *właściwie*) after all; **nie taki znowu tani** not that cheap; **to nie jest znowu taki zły pomysł** it's not such a bad idea after all; **o co mu znowu chodzi?** what is his problem now?; **co znowu?!** what is it now?!

znój *mi* **-o-** *Gen.pl.* **-ów** *lit.* toil.

znów *adv. zob.* **znowu**. – *particle zob.* **znowu**.

znudzenie *n.* boredom; **do znudzenia** ad nauseam; **ziewać ze znudzenia** yawn of boredom, yawn one's head off.

znudzić *pf.* bore (*kogoś czymś* sb with sth). ~ **się** *pf.* **1.** (= *odczuć nudę*) be bored (*czymś* with sth). **2.** (= *stać się nudnym*) become boring; **znudziło mi się to** I'm fed up with it.

znudzony *a.* **-eni** bored, fed up; **znudzony życiem** bored with life, jaded with life.

znużenie *n.* weariness, fatigue; **ze znużeniem**

(*np. powiedzieć coś*) wearily; **padać ze znużenia** drop with fatigue.

znużony *a.* **-eni** weary; **być znużonym czymś** be tired of sth.

znużyć *pf.* tire, weary; (*o nadmiarze uczuć, słodyczy*) cloy. ~ **się** *pf.* get *l.* grow weary, weary (*czymś* of sth).

zob. *abbr.* (= *zobacz*) s. (= *see*), qv (= *quod vide*).

zobaczenie *n.* **do zobaczenia!** see you!; **do zobaczenia wkrótce** see you soon; **do zobaczenia wieczorem** I'll see you tonight.

zobaczyć *pf.* **1.** (= *spostrzec*) see, catch sight of; **zobaczyć kawał świata** see a bit of the world, travel around the world; **co ona w nim zobaczyła?** what did she see in him? **2.** (= *przekonać się*) see, find; **zobaczymy, jak to będzie** we will see how it's gonna be; **zobaczysz!** you'll see! **3.** (= *spotkać kogoś*) meet; **zobaczyć matkę po pięciu latach** meet one's mother after 5 years. ~ **się** *pf.* **1.** (= *ujrzeć się*) see o.s.; **zobaczyć się w lustrze** see o.s. in the mirror, see one's reflection in the mirror. **2.** (= *spotkać się z kimś*) see (*z kimś* sb).

zobaczysko *n. pot.* **do zobaczyska** I'll see you later.

zobiektywizować *pf. zob.* **obiektywizować**.

zobligować *pf. zob.* **obligować**.

zobojętniać *ipf.*, **zobojętnić** *pf.* **-ij** **1.** (= *czynić kogoś nieczułym*) render indifferent, desensitize. **2.** *chem.* (= *zneutralizować*) neutralize.

zobojętnieć *pf.* become indifferent, grow indifferent (*na coś* to sth); **praca mi zobojętniała** I have lost interest in my work.

zobojętnienie *n.* **1.** (= *brak zainteresowania*) indifference (*na coś* to sth). **2.** *chem.* neutralization.

zobowiązać *pf.* **-wiążę -wiążesz** *zob.* **zobowiązywać**. ~ **się** *pf. zob.* **zobowiązywać się**.

zobowiązanie *n.* **1.** (= *obowiązek*) obligation; (= *obietnica*) committment; **zobowiązania bieżące** *fin.* current liabilities; **zobowiązanie finansowe** financial obligation; **złożyć zobowiązanie** make a committment; **wywiązywać się ze zobowiązań** meet one's obligations, fulfil one's obligations. **2.** *prawn.* obligation, liability.

zobowiązany *a.* obliged; **być zobowiązanym do czegoś** be obliged to do sth; **jestem Panu bardzo zobowiązany** I'm much obliged to you.

zobowiązywać *ipf.* oblige (*kogoś do czegoś* sb to do sth); **zobowiązać kogoś do zachowania tajemnicy** pledge sb to secrecy. ~ **się** *ipf.* commit o.s. (*do czegoś* to doing sth); **zobowiązać się do dotrzymania tajemnicy** pledge o.s. to keep secret.

zobrazować *pf.* (= *opisać*) depict, picture; (= *przedstawić*) represent.

zodiak *mi* zodiac; **znak zodiaku** sign of the zodiac, zodiac sign.

zodiakalny *a. astron.* zodiacal; **światło zodiakalne** zodiacal light.

zogniskować *pf. lit.* focus; **zogniskować na sobie zainteresowanie** focus attention on o.s. ~ **się** *pf. lit.* focus (*na czymś* on sth).

zohydzać *ipf.*, **zohydzić** *pf.* make repugnant; **zohydzić coś komuś** make sth repugnant to sb;

zohydzić kogoś w czyichś oczach make sb hateful to sb.

zoidiogamia *f. bot.* zoidogamy.

zoil *mp lit.* Zoilus.

zol *mi Gen.pl.* **-i** *l.* **-ów** *chem.* sol.

zołza *f. uj.* (*kobieta*) shrew.

zołzy *pl. pat., wet.* strangles.

zombi, zombie *mp* zombie.

ZOMO *abbr.* (= *Zmotoryzowane Odwody Milicji Obywatelskiej*) *hist.* Motorized Detachments of the Citizens' Militia (*in Poland*).

zomowiec *mp* **-wc-** *pot., hist.* member of the Motorized Detachments of the Citizens' Militia.

zona *f.* zone.

zoo *n. indecl.* zoo.

z o.o. *abbr.* (= *z ograniczoną odpowiedzialnością*) Ltd (= *limited liability*).

zoobentos *mi ekol.* zoobenthos.

zoocenoza *f. zool.* zoocenosis.

zoochoria *f. biol.* zoochory.

zoofag *ma zool.* zoophagan.

zoofil *mp* zoophiliac.

zoofilia *f. Gen.* **-ii** *pat.* zoophilia, zoophilism; bestiality.

zoogeografia *f. Gen.* **-ii** zoogeography.

zoogeograficzny *a.* zoogeographic.

zoohigiena *f.* animal hygiene.

zoohigieniczny *a.* animal hygiene.

zoolatria *f. Gen.* **-ii** *rel.* zoolatry.

zoolog *mp pl.* **-dzy** *l.* **-owie** zoologist.

zoologia *f. Gen.* **-ii** zoology.

zoologiczny *a.* zoological; **ogród zoologiczny** zoological gardens.

zoomorficzny *a.* zoomorphic.

zoomorfizm *mi* zoomorphism.

zoonoza *f. med., wet.* zoonosis.

zoopatologia *f.* animal pathology.

zooplankton *f.* zooplankton.

zoopsychologia *f. Gen.* **-ii** animal psychology.

zoosfera *f. ekol.* zoosphere.

zoosocjologia *f. Gen.* **-ii** animal sociology.

zoospora *f. bot.* zoospore.

zoosporangium *f. bot.* zoosporangium.

zootechniczny *a.* zootechnical.

zootechnik *mp* zootechnician.

zootechnika *f.* animals husbandry, zootechnics.

zoperować *pf. med.* operate (*kogoś* on sb).

zoptymalizować *pf. zob.* **optymalizować**.

zorać *pf.* **zorzę zorzesz** **1.** *roln.* plow, *Br.* plough. **2.** *przen.* (= *porobić bruzdy*) furrow.

zorany *a.* plowed, *Br.* ploughed; **ściana zorana kulami** wall pockmarked with bullets.

zorganizować *pf.* **1.** (= *urządzić*) organize, arrange. **2.** (= *zrzeszyć*) associate. **3.** *pot.* (= *załatwić*) fix up. ~ **się** *pf.* **1.** (= *zrzeszyć się*) organize, associate. **2.** (= *ukonstytuować się*) be set up, be formed.

zorganizowany *a.* (*grupa, osoba*) organized; (*wycieczka*) guided.

zorientować *pf.* **1.** (*poinformować*) inform, brief (*w czymś l. co do czegoś* on sth); **zorientować kogoś w sytuacji** inform sb about the situation; **zorientować kogoś co do warunków uczest-**

nictwa inform sb about the conditions of participation. **2.** (*usytuować*) direct; **zorientować katedrę na północ** direct the cathedral towards the north; **zorientować mapę** orient a map. ~ **się** *pf.* (*w terenie*) orientate o.s.; (= *zdać sobie sprawę*) realize; **zorientowałem się, że...** I realized that...

zorientowany *a.* well-informed, well-versed; **partia zorientowana lewicowo/prawicowo** left-/ right-wing party; **być dobrze zorientowanym w czymś** be well-versed in sth; **katedra jest zorientowana na północ** the cathedral is directed towards the north.

zoroastryzm *mi rel.* Zoroastrianism, Zoroastrism; Mazdaism.

zorza *f. Gen.pl.* **zórz** (*poranna*) dawn, daybreak; (*wieczorna*) afterglow; **zorza polarna** aurora; (*na biegunie północnym*) aurora borealis, northern lights; (*na biegunie południowym*) aurora australis, southern lights.

zostać *pf.* **-stanę** **-staniesz**, **zostawać** *ipf.* **-aję** *-ajesz*, **-awaj** **1.** (= *pozostawać*) stay, remain; **zostać w domu/w łóżku** stay at home/in bed; **zostać na noc** stay overnight, stay for the night; **zostać u kogoś na obiedzie** stay for dinner at sb's; **zostać w tej samej klasie** repeat a grade; **zostać w tyle** lag behind; **niech to zostanie między nami** let this remain between me and you, let's keep it between us. **2.** (= *być resztą*) be left, remain; **z całej klasy zostały tylko dwie dziewczyny** only two girls out of the whole class were left *l.* remained; **została z niego skóra i kości** he is mere skin and bones; **czy zostało jeszcze trochę czasu?** is there any time left?; **kamień na kamieniu nie zostanie** not a stone will be left standing. **3.** (= *być spuścizną*) be left; **został mi po wujku dom** I inherited a house from my uncle. **4.** (= *być w sytuacji*) be left; **zostałem bez grosza przy duszy** I was left penniless; **zostać przy swoim** stick to one's opinion; **zostać przy życiu** stay alive, survive. **5.** *tylko pf.* (= *stać się kimś*) become; **zostać ojcem/matką** become a father/mother; **zostać lekarzem/inżynierem** become a doctor/an engineer; **zostać protestantem/katolikiem** become a protestant/catholic; **zostać samotnym** be left alone. **6.** *tylko pf.* (= *doznać czegoś*) get; **zostać zrozumianym** be understood; **budynek został zniszczony** the building got destroyed; **samochód został uszkodzony** the car got damaged.

zostawiać *ipf.*, **zostawić** *pf.* **1.** (= *nie zabierać czegoś*) leave, leave behind; **zostawić coś komuś na pamiątkę** leave sth (behind) to sb; **nie zostawić na kimś suchej nitki** pick sb to pieces. **2.** (= *opuszczać kogoś*) leave; **zostaw mnie w spokoju** leave me alone; **zostaw nas samych** leave us alone; **zostawić coś własnemu biegowi** leave sth to its own course; **zostawić coś na pastwę losu** leave sth to its fate; **zostaw go!** leave him alone!, let him go!; **zostaw to!** leave it! **3.** (= *przekazywać w spadku*) leave, bequeath (*komuś coś* sth to sb); **zostawić komuś spadek** leave sb a legacy. **4.** (= *wywoływać*) evoke; **zostawić po sobie dobre wrażenie** leave a good impression. **5.** (= *nie reagować*) leave; **zostawić zarzuty bez komentarza** leave allegations with no comment; **zostawić list**

bez odpowiedzi leave a letter without an answer, leave a letter unanswered. **6.** (= *dawać do dyspozycji*) leave; **zostawić coś komuś do dyspozycji** leave sth at sb's disposal; **zostawić coś pod czyjąś opieką** leave sth in sb's care; **zostawić komuś czas do namysłu** leave *l.* give sb some time to think sth over; **zostawić komuś decyzję** let sb decide; **zostaw to mnie** leave it to me; **zostawiam to tobie** I'll leave it to you. **7.** (= *odkładać*) put aside, keep; **zostawić coś sobie** keep sth; **zostawiłem ci w kuchni parę kanapek** I left you some sandwiches in the kitchen; **zostawiłem sobie parę złotych** I put a few pennies aside.

zowąd *adv.* from there; **ni stąd, ni zowąd** out of the blue.

ZOZ *abbr.* (= *Zakład Opieki Zdrowotnej*) area health service administration.

zórz *f. zob.* **zorza**.

zrabować *pf. zob.* **rabować**.

zracjonalizować *pf. zob.* **racjonalizować**.

zradiofonizować *pf. zob.* **radiofonizować**.

zradykalizować *pf. zob.* **radykalizować**.

zrakowacieć *pf. med.* cancerate.

zramolały *a.* soft-witted; **zramolały starzec** old crock.

zramoleć *pf. pot.* get soft-witted.

zranić *pf.* **1.** (= *skaleczyć*) wound, injure; **zranić kogoś nożem** wound sb with a knife; **zranić sobie rękę szkłem** cut one's hand with a bit of glass. **2.** (= *sprawić przykrość*) hurt sb; **zranić czyjeś uczucia** hurt sb's feelings. **~ się** *pf.* (= *skaleczyć się*) cut o.s.

zranienie *n.* wound, injury.

zrastać się *ipf.* **1.** (*o kościach*) knit, knit together. **2.** (*o ranie*) heal up. **3.** (= *łączyć się w całość*) fuse, blend (*w coś* into sth). **4.** (= *zespalać się*) grow into one (*z czymś* with sth); **jego nazwisko zrosło się z wynalazkiem** his name is identified with the invention.

zraszacz *mi Gen.* **-a** *ogr.* sprinkler.

zraszać *ipf.* sprinkle; **zrosić ziemię krwią** *lit.* stain the ground with blood.

zraz *mi Gen.* **-a 1.** *kulin.* beef roulade. **2.** *ogr.* scion.

zrazić *pf.* **-żę -zisz** *zob.* **zrażać**. **~ się** *pf. zob.* **zrażać się**.

zrazik *mi Gen.* **-a 1.** *kulin.* beef roulade. **2.** *anat.* lobule.

zrazu *adv. przest.* initially, at the beginning.

zrażać *ipf.* alienate, antagonize; **zrażać kogoś do siebie** antagonize sb; **zrażać kogoś opryskliwością** discourage sb with being surly. **~ się** *ipf.* (= *rozczarowywać się*) become discouraged; (*w obliczu trudności*) lose heart; **zrażać się do kogoś/czegoś** take a dislike to sb/sth.

zrąb *mi* **-ę- 1.** *bud.* framework. **2.** (= *podstawa*) foundation; (= *zarys*) outline; **zręby kultury/literatury** foundations of culture/literature. **3.** (*krawędź*) edge. **4.** *leśn.* (*wyrąb*) felling; (*obszar po wyrębie*) clearing.

zrąbać *pf.* **-bię -biesz**, **zrąbywać** *ipf.* **1.** (*drzewo*) cut down, fell. **2.** *tylko pf. pot.* (= *skrytykować*) slam, slate.

zrealizować *pf.* realize; **zrealizować swoje ma-**

rzenia realize one's dreams; **zrealizować czyjeś marzenia** make sb's dreams come true.

zreasumować *pf.* summarize, recapitulate.

zrecenzować *pf.* review.

zredagować *pf.* (*list, odpowiedź*) draw up.

zredukować *pf.* reduce.

zreferować *pf.* report (*coś* on sth).

zrefinansować *pf. zob.* **refinansować**.

zreflektować *pf. zob.* **reflektować**. **~ się** *pf.* (= *pohamować się*) check o.s.; **w porę się zreflektować** think twice of sth.

zreformować *pf. zob.* **reformować**.

zrefundować *pf. zob.* **reimburse**.

zregenerować *pf. zob.* **regenerować**.

zrehabilitować *pf. zob.* **rehabilitować**. **~ się** *pf. zob.* **rehabilitować się**.

zrejonizować *pf. zob.* **rejonizować**.

zrejterować *pf.* chicken out (*przed czymś* from sth).

zrekapitulować *pf.* recapitulate.

zrekompensować *pf. zob.* **rekompensować**.

zrekonstruować *pf. zob.* **rekonstruować**.

zrekultywować *pf. zob.* **rekultywować**.

zrelacjonować *pf. zob.* **relacjonować**.

zrelaksować *pf. zob.* **relaksować**. **~ się** *pf. zob.* **relaksować się**.

zrelaksowany *a.* relaxed; **poczułem się zrelaksowany** I felt relaxed.

zrelatywizować *pf. zob.* **relatywizować**.

zremisować *pf.* draw (*z kimś* with sb).

zreorganizować *pf.* reorganize.

zreperować *pf. zob.* **reperować**.

zresztą *adv.* (= *w końcu*) after all; (= *poza tym*) in any case; **co to mnie zresztą obchodzi** why would I care, anyway; **przyznam się zresztą, że...** I admit nevertheless that...; **było bardzo miło, zresztą jak zawsze** it was very nice as usual.

zreumatyzowany *a. pat.* rheumatic.

zrewaloryzować *pf. zob.* **rewaloryzować**.

zrewaluować *pf. zob.* **rewaluować**.

zrewanżować się *pf. zob.* **rewanżować się**.

zrewidować *pf. zob.* **rewidować**.

zrewolucjonizować *pf. zob.* **rewolucjonizować**.

zrezygnować *pf. zob.* **rezygnować**.

zrezygnowany *a.* resigned.

zrębowy *a.* **1.** *bud.* framework. **2.** *leśn.* felling.

zręcznie *adv.* **1.** (= *zwinnie*) adroitly. **2.** (= *sprytnie*) cleverly. **3.** (= *umiejętnie*) skillfully; *Br.* skilfully.

zręcznościowy *a.* developing dexterity; **gra zręcznościowa** dexterity game.

zręczność *f.* **1.** (= *zwinność*) agility; (*manualna*) dexterity. **2.** (= *spryt*) cleverness.

zręczny *a.* **1.** (= *zwinny*) adroit. **2.** (= *sprytny*) clever. **3.** (= *umiejętny*) skillful, *Br.* skilful.

zripostować *pf. zob.* **ripostować**.

zrobaczywieć *pf. zob.* **robaczywieć**.

zrobić *pf.* **zrób 1.** (= *wytworzyć, wyprodukować*) make; **zrobić śniadanie/kawę** make breakfast/some coffee; **zrobić coś na drutach** knit sth; **zrobić coś szydełkiem** crochet sth; **zrobić coś z niczego** make sth out of nothing; **zrobić coś od ręki** do sth while you wait; **zrobić z igły widły**

make a mountain out of a molehill; **i w Paryżu nie zrobią z owsa ryżu** you can't make a silk purse from a sow's ear. **2.** (= *dokonać czegoś*) make, do; **zrobić ruch/krok** make a move/step; **zrobić pranie/porządki** do the laundry/cleaning; **zrobić komuś zastrzyk** give sb an injection; **zrobić interes na czymś** make money out of sth; **zrobić karierę** make a career; **zrobić komuś grzeczność** do sb a favor, *Br.* do sb a favour; **zrobić komuś wstyd** bring shame on sb; **zrobić z kogoś człowieka** make a person out of sb; **zrobić z kimś/z czymś koniec** do away with sb/sth; **zrobić z czymś porządek** put sth in order; **zrobić oko do kogoś** wink at sb; **zrobić pierwszy krok/wielki krok naprzód** make the first step/a giant step forward; **zrobić dobry początek** make a good start; **zrobić zakupy** do shopping; **zrobić z czegoś użytek** make use of sth; **zrobić wyjątek** make an exception; **zrobić zdjęcie** take a picture; **zrobić pieniądze** *l.* **majątek na czymś** make a fortune on sth; **zrobić kasę na czymś** *pot.* make money on sth; **zrobić komuś kawał** play a joke on sb; **zrobić komuś na złość** spite sb; **zrobić z kogoś durnia** *l.* **wariata** make a fool out of sb; **zrobić skok na bank** *sl.* raid a bank; **zrobił wiele/wszystko, aby...** he did a lot/everything to...; **nie wiem, co z tym zrobiłem** I have no idea what I did with it; **uważaj, bo coś sobie zrobisz** be careful or you'll hurt yourself; **to ci dobrze zrobi** it will do you good; **co mogę dla ciebie zrobić?** what can I do for you?, is there anything I can do for you?; **co mi możecie zrobić?** *pot.* what can you do to me?; **co z tym fantem zrobić?** what to do with it? **3.** (= *zachować się*) do; act, behave; **zrobić dobrze/źle** do the right/wrong thing; **co ja zrobię bez ciebie?** what will I do without you?; **co ja zrobię, że...** I can't help it that... **4.** (= *zorganizować*) make, organize; **zrobić zebranie** organize a meeting; **zrobić przyjęcie** throw a party; **zrobić sobie święto** take a day off. **~ się** *pf.* **1.** (= *stać się*) become, turn out; **zrobiło się komuś żal kogoś/czegoś** sb felt sorry for sb/sth; **zrobiło się głośno koło kogoś/czegoś** sb/sth received a lot of attention; **zrobiło mi się niedobrze** I felt faint; **zrobiło mi się smutno/radośnie** I felt sad/happy; **co się z niego zrobiło?!** look what became of him! **2.** (= *nastać*) get; **zrobiła się noc** the night fell; **zrobił się dzień** the day began; **zrobiło się późno/zimno** it got late/cold; **zrobiła się zima/wiosna** winter/spring came; **zrobiło się zamieszanie** there was some commotion; **zrobił się tłok/bałagan** there was a crowd/mess. **3.** *pot.* (= *wykreować się*) dress up, spruce up; **zrobić się na bóstwo** doll o.s. up.

    zrobi *int. pot.* consider it done.

    zrodzić *pf.* **zrodzę zrodzisz, zródź** *l.* **zródź** give rise (*coś* to sth); **coś zrodziło w kimś podejrzenia** sth gave rise to sb's suspicions. **~ się** *pf.* be born, arise; **zrodziło się podejrzenie, że...** a suspicion arose that...; **zrodził się plan, by...** there arose a plan to...

    zrogowacenie *n.* callus, callosity.
    zrogowaciały *a.* callous, corneous.
    zrogowacieć *pf.* become horny, become corneous.

    zrolować *pf.* roll up.
    zrolowany *a.* rolled up.
    zrosić *pf.* -szę -sisz *zob.* **zraszać.**
    zrosnąć się *pf.* **zrosnę zrośniesz, zrośnij, zrósł zrosła zrośli** *zob.* **zrastać się.**
    zrost *mi* **1.** (= *połączenie*) fusion; (*np. dwóch miast*) amalgamation. **2.** *pat.* adhesion. **3.** *jęz.* phrasal compound.
    zrostowy *a.* **1.** *pat.* adhesional. **2.** *jęz.* phrasal compound.
    zrośnięty *a.* grown together; (*o roślinach, organach*) accrete; **zrośnięte brwi** meeting eyebrows.
    zrozpaczony *a.* (*człowiek, spojrzenie*) desperate; **być zrozpaczonym** be in despair; **powiedzieć coś zrozpaczonym głosem** say sth in a desperate voice.
    zrozumiale *adv.* intelligibly, comprehensibly.
    zrozumiałość *f.* comprehensibility, intelligibility.
    zrozumiały *a.* **1.** (= *wyraźny*) comprehensible, intelligible. **2.** (= *uzasadniony*) understandable.
    zrozumieć *pf.* -miem -miesz **1.** (= *pojąć*) understand, comprehend. **2.** (= *zdać sobie sprawę z czegoś*) realize; **zrozumiałem swój błąd** I realized my mistake; **zrozumiałem, że powinienem wyjść** I realized that I should leave. **~ się** *pf.* understand each other.
    zrozumienie *n.* **1.** (= *pojmowanie*) understanding, comprehension; **dać komuś do zrozumienia, że...** give sb to understand that... **2.** (= *uświadomienie sobie*) realization. **3.** (= *wyrozumiałość*) understanding; **ze zrozumieniem** with understanding; **mieć zrozumienie dla kogoś/czegoś** have understanding for sb/sth.
    zrób *pf. zob.* **zrobić.**
    zróść się *pf.* **zrosnę zrośniesz, zrośnij, zrósł zrosła zrośli** *zob.* **zrastać się.**
    zrównać *pf. zob.* **zrównywać. ~ się** *pf. zob.* **zrównywać się.**
    zrównanie *n.* *astron.* equinox; **zrównanie jesienne/wiosenne** autumnal/vernal equinox.
    zrównoważony *a.* (*człowiek*) even-tempered, level-headed; (*charakter*) equable; (*budżet*) balanced.
    zrównoważyć *pf.* (= *doprowadzić do równowagi*) *fin.* balance.
    zrównywać *ipf.* **1.** (= *czynić równym*) level, flatten; **zrównać coś z ziemią** level sth with the ground, raze sth to the ground. **2.** (= *czynić równym wobec prawa*) make equal; **zrównać wobec prawa** make equal in the eyes of the law. **~ się** *ipf.* **1.** (= *osiągnąć jednakowy poziom*) come level, draw level (*z kimś / czymś* with sb/sth). **2.** (= *jadąc, idąc, doganiać*) catch up (*z kimś / czymś* with sb/sth). **3.** (= *być niwelowanym*) get levelled.
    zróżnicować *pf.* differentiate. **~ się** *pf.* differentiate.
    zróżnicowanie *n.* diversity.
    zróżnicowany *a.* diverse; **kraj zróżnicowany pod względem etnicznym** country of diverse ethnicities.

zrudzieć *pf.* -eję -ejesz *zob.* **rudzieć**.
zrugać *pf. pot.* (= *zwymyślać*) scold.
zrujnować *pf.* **1.** (= *zniszczyć*) ruin; **zrujnować sobie zdrowie** ruin one's health; **zrujnować szczęście** ruin one's happiness. **2.** (= *doprowadzić do bankructwa*) ruin, bring to ruin. ~ **się** *pf.* (= *doprowadzić się do bankructwa*) ruin o.s.
zrumienić *pf. kulin.* brown. ~ **się** *pf. kulin.* brown.
zrusyfikować *pf.* Russify.
zruszać *ipf. ogr.* loosen (*the soil*).
zruszczyć *pf.* become Russianized, Russianize.
zruszyć *pf. zob.* **zruszać**.
zrutynizować *pf.* (= *uczynić rutynowym*) make routine; (*np. określone procedury w firmie*) routinize.
zryczałtowany *a.* flat-rate.
zryć *pf.* zryję zryjesz, zryj burrow.
zrymować *pf. zob.* **rymować**.
zryw *mi* spurt; **zryw rewolucyjny** revolutionary impulse; **pracować zrywami** work in *l.* by fits and starts.
zrywać *ipf.* -am -asz **1.** (= *odrywać*) (*kwiaty, owoce*) pick; (*owoce*) pluck; (*o wietrze*) (*dach*) blow off, tear off; (*o rzece*) (*most*) wash away. **2.** (= *zdzierać*) (*plakat, bandaż*) tear off. **3.** (= *rozrywać*) (*strunę, sznurek, więzy*) break; (*o rzece*) (*tamę*) burst; (*linię energetyczną, połączenie*) cut off; **zerwać więzy przyjaźni** *przen.* break up a friendship. **4.** (= *tracić z kimś kontakt*) break up, split up (*z kimś* with sb); **zerwać z przyjaciółmi** break one's ties with friends; **zerwać z przeszłością/przesądami** do away with one's past/superstitions; **zerwać z nałogiem** quit *l.* kick a habit, break o.s. of a habit. **5.** (= *unieważniać*) (*umowę, zaręczyny*) (*stosunki, związki*) break off, sever; **zerwać stosunki dyplomatyczne** break off diplomatic relations. **6.** *pot.* (= *narażać na szwank*) strain, sprain; **zerwać sobie głos/nogi** strain one's voice/legs; **śmieszne, że boki zrywać** it's side-splitting. ~ **się** *ipf.* **1.** (= *odrywać się*) break; **nić się zerwała** the thread broke; **pies zerwał się z łańcucha** the dog slipped its chain. **2.** (= *podrywać się*) jump, leap up; **zrywać się na równe nogi** jump to one's feet. **3.** (= *nagle się pojawiać*) (*o burzy, wietrze*) break out. **4.** *pot.* (= *wstawać z łóżka*) get up.
zrywność *f.* pick-up.
zrywny *a.* (*o pojeździe*) with good pick-up.
zrządzać *ipf.* cause, bring about; **los tak zrządził, że...** it was fated *l.* ordained that...
zrządzenie *n.* decree; **zrządzenie losu** stroke of fate.
zrządzić *pf. zob.* **zrządzać**.
zrzec się *pf.* zrzeknę zrzekniesz, zrzeknij, zrzekł *zob.* **zrzekać się**.
zrzednąć *pf.* -dnął *l.* -dł -dła, zrzednieć *pf.* thin; **zrzedła mu mina** his face fell.
zrzekać się *ipf.* relinquish (*czegoś* sth).
zrzeszać *ipf.* associate. ~ **się** *ipf.* associate.
zrzeszenie *n.* association.
zrzeszyć *pf. zob.* **zrzeszać**. ~ **się** *pf. zob.* **zrzeszać się**.

zrzęda *f. l. mp decl. like f. Gen.pl.* -d *l.* -ów *pot.* grouch.
zrzędliwy *a. pot.* grouchy.
zrzędność *f. pot.* grouchiness.
zrzędny *a.* grouchy.
zrzędzić *ipf. pot.* grouch.
zrzucać *ipf.* **1.** (= *rzucać w dół*) throw down, cast down; (*np. śnieg z dachu*) throw off; (*o koniu*) (*jeźdźca*) throw; **zrzucić żagle** *żegl.* let out the sails; **zrzucić pięć kilogramów** lose five kilograms; **zrzucić parę kilo** lose a few stone; **zrzucić kogoś ze schodów** throw sb down the stairs. **2.** (= *wyzwolić się*) throw off; **zrzucić mundur/sutannę** take of the uniform/cassock; **zrzucić jarzmo** throw *l.* shake off the yoke; **zrzucić na kogoś winę** pin the blame on sb; **zrzucić kamień z serca** unburden one's soul; **zrzucić z siebie odpowiedzialność** shift off the responsibility; **zrzucić swoje obowiązki na czyjeś barki** devolve one's duties on *l.* upon sb. **3.** (= *rozebrać się*) take off; **zrzucić ubranie** take off one's clothes; **zrzucić maskę obłudy** throw off the mask of hypocrisy. **4.** (*o roślinach, zwierzętach*) (*liście, skórę*) shed. **5.** (*karty*) discard. ~ **się** *ipf. pot.* (= *składać się na coś*) chip in (*na coś* for sth).
zrzucić (się) *pf. zob.* **zrzucać (się)**.
zrzut *mi wojsk.* (*czynność*) (*ładunek*) airdrop.
zrzutka *f. Gen.pl.* -ek **1.** *pot.* (= *składka*) whip-round; **robić zrzutkę** have a whip-round. **2.** *jeźdz.* fault. **3.** *karty* discard.
zrzynać *ipf.* **1.** (= *tnąc, rozdzielić*) cut off. **2.** (= *kosić*) mow; (= *siekać*) shred. **3.** *szkoln.* (= *przepisywać*) crib, copy.
zrzynek *mi* shred.
zsadzać *ipf.*, zsadzić *pf.* help down (*z czegoś* off sth).
zsechł *pf. zob.* **zsychać**.
zserowacieć *pf. pat.* caseate.
zsiadać *ipf.* get off, dismount. ~ **się** *ipf.* (*o mleku*) curdle.
zsiadły *a.* curdy; **zsiadłe mleko** curds.
zsiąść *pf.* zsiądę zsiądziesz zsiadł zsiedli *zob.* **zsiadać**. ~ **się** *pf. zob.* **zsiadać się**.
zsikać się *pf. pot.* pee in one's pants.
zsinieć *pf.* turn blue; **zsinieć z zimna** turn blue with cold.
zsiusiać się *pf. dziec.* wet o.s.
ZSP *abbr.* (= *Zrzeszenie Studentów Polskich*) the Polish Students Association.
ZSRR *abbr.* (= *Związek Socjalistycznych Republik Radzieckich*) *hist.* USSR (= *Union of Soviet Socialist Republics*).
zstąpić *pf.*, zstępować *ipf.* descend; **zstąpić na ziemię** come down to earth; **zstąpić z niebios** descend from heaven.
zstępny *a. prawn.* **linia zstępna** descending line.
zstępujący *a. meteor.* downward, descending; **prądy zstępujące** downward currents.
zsumować *pf.*, zsumowywać *ipf.* sum up, total up.
zsunąć (się) *pf. zob.* **zsuwać (się)**.
zsuwać *ipf.* **1.** (= *ciągnąć, zdjąć*) slide down. **2.** (= *przesuwając, połączyć*) (*stoły, krzesła*) put

together; (*zasłony, firanki*) pull together. ~ **się** *ipf.* (= *spaść*) (*np. z półki*) slide off; (*o bucie*) slip off.

zsuwnia *f. Gen.pl.* -**i** *techn.* chute.

zsychać *ipf.* **1.** (*o roślinach*) dry up, wither. **2.** (*o skórze, ziemi*) dry, parch. ~ **się** *ipf.* = **zsychać**.

zsyłać *ipf.* **1.** *lit.* (*karę*) send (*coś na kogoś* sth on sb). **2.** (= *wywozić*) send; **zesłać na wygnanie** send into exile.

zsyłka *f. Gen.pl.* -**ek** *hist.* exile.

zsynchronizować *pf. zob.* **synchronizować**.

zsyntetyzować *pf. zob.* **syntetyzować**.

zsyp *mi* **1.** (= *zsypywanie*) pouring. **2.** (*na śmieci*) garbage chute; *Br.* rubbish chute.

zsypać *pf.* -**pię** -**piesz**, **zsypywać** *ipf.* pour, dump (*coś do czegoś* sth into sth).

zsypisko *n.* **1.** (*teren*) dumping area. **2.** (= *rumowisko*) rubble.

zszargać *pf.* **1.** (= *zniszczyć*) (*ubranie*) wear out; (= *poszarpać, wystrzępić*) fray. **2.** *przen.* (= *nadwątlić*) undermine; **zszargać komuś/sobie zdrowie/opinię** ruin sb's/one's health/reputation; **zszargać komuś/sobie nerwy** fray sb's/one's nerves.

zszarpać (się) *pf.* -**pię** -**piesz** *zob.* **zszarpywać (się)**.

zszarpywać *ipf.* **1.** (= *zerwać szarpnięciem*) tear off. **2.** *tylko pf.* (= *postrzępić*) fray. **3.** *tylko pf. przen.* (= *nadwątlić*) undermine; **zszarpać komuś/sobie zdrowie** ruin sb's/one's health; **zszarpać komuś/sobie nerwy** fray sb's/one's nerves. ~ **się** *ipf.* (= *podrzeć się*) fray.

zszarzeć *pf.* turn gray; *Br.* turn grey.

zszedł *itd. pf. zob.* **zejść**.

zszokować *pf. zob.* **szokować**.

zszumować *pf.* scum, skim.

zszyć *pf.* **zszyję zszyjesz**, **zszyj** *zob.* **zszywać**.

zszywacz *mi Gen.* -**a** stapler.

zszywać *ipf.* -**am** -**asz** **1.** (*materiał*) sew (together); (*rane*) stitch, suture. **2.** (*kartki*) staple.

zszywka *f. Gen.pl.* -**ek** staple.

zubażać *ipf.* impoverish.

zubożeć *pf.* become impoverished.

zubożyć *pf. zob.* **zubażać**.

zuch *mp pl.* -**y** **1.** (= *młodszy harcerz*) Cub Scout, Cub. **2.** (= *śmiałek*) daredevil; **zuch z ciebie!** well done!

zuchowaty *a.* plucky.

zuchowy *a.* Cub Scout.

zuchwale *adv.* **1.** (= *bezczelnie*) impertinently. **2.** (= *odważnie*) daringly.

zuchwalstwo *n.* **1.** (= *arogancja*) impudence, impertinence. **2.** (= *odwaga*) bravery.

zuchwałość *f.* impudence, impertinence.

zuchwały *a.* **1.** (= *bezczelny*) impertinent. **2.** (= *odważny*) daring; **kradzież zuchwała** *prawn.* aggravated larceny.

zunifikować *pf. zob.* **unifikować**.

zuniformizować *pf. zob.* **uniformizować**.

zupa *f.* soup; **zupa w proszku/błyskawiczna** powdered/instant soup; **zupa z puszki** *l.* **w puszce** canned soup.

zupełnie *adv.* completely; **jest zupełnie jasne,**

że... it is very clear that...; **zupełnie poważnie** quite seriously; **wyglądać zupełnie jak...** look just like...; **zupełnie taki sam jak...** exactly the same as...; **mieć zupełnie ten sam kolor** be identical in color; **być zupełnie bez ambicji** have no ambition whatsoever.

zupełność *f.* **w zupełności** completely.

zupełny *a.* complete; **masz zupełną rację** you are quite right; **przeobrażenie zupełne** *biol.* complete metamorphosis.

zupka *f. Gen.pl.* -**ek** soup.

zurbanizować *pf. zob.* **urbanizować**.

Zurych *mi geogr.* Zurich.

ZUS *abbr.* (= *Zakład Ubezpieczeń Społecznych*) the Social Insurance Institution.

zużycie *n.* **1.** (*paliwa, energii*) consumption. **2.** (*urządzeń, rzeczy*) wear.

zużyć *pf.* -**żyję** -**żyjesz**, -**żyj** *zob.* **zużywać**. ~ **się** *pf. zob.* **zużywać się**.

zużytkować *pf.*, **zużytkowywać** *ipf. form.* **1.** (*energię, paliwo*) consume, use up. **2.** (*dane, informacje, wiedzę*) utilize, use.

zużyty *a.* **1.** (= *podniszczony*) worn out. **2.** (= *wyczerpany, wykorzystany*) used.

zużywać *ipf.* -**am** -**asz** **1.** (*zasoby, czas, energię*) use, consume; (*zapasy*) use up, consume. **2.** (= *niszczyć*) wear. **3.** (= *marnować*) waste. ~ **się** *ipf.* **1.** (= *niszczyć się, kończyć się*) wear out *l.* away. **2.** (= *zaczynać brakować*) be running short.

zw. *abbr.* **1.** (= *zwany*) aka, a.k.a. (= *also known as*). **2.** (= *zwykle*) usu. (= *usually*).

zwabiać *ipf.*, **zwabić** *pf.* (*psa, kury*) drive; **zwabić kogoś dokądś** wile sb into/to sth.

zwać *ipf.* **zwę zwiesz, zwij** call; **jak go zwą?** what do you call him?; **tak zwany** so-called. ~ **się** *ipf.* call o.s.; **obiad/lekarz itd. co się zowie** *lit.* some *l.* real dinner/doctor etc.; **to jest obiad/lekarz itd. co się zowie** *lit.* now that's what I call a dinner/doctor etc.

zwada *f. arch.* fray; **szukać zwady (z kimś)** pick a quarrel (with sb).

zwalać *ipf.* **1.** (= *strącać, przewracać, burzyć*) knock down; **zwalić kogoś na ziemię** *l.* **z nóg** knock sb off sb's feet. **2.** (= *wyładowywać*) dump; **zwalać (na kupę)** (= *ładować*) heap (up), pile (up). **3.** **zwalać coś na kogoś** (= *obarczać*) *pot.* (*winę*) pin sth on sb; (*obowiązki*) load sb down with sth. **4.** *pot., szkoln.* (= *odpisywać*) crib (*od kogoś* off (of) sb). ~ **się** *ipf.* **1.** (= *spadać*) fall *l.* come down; (= *przewracać się*) fall; **zwalić się na łóżko** *pot.* hit the sack; **drzewo zwaliło się na samochód** the tree crushed the car; **zwalić się z nóg** *pot.* take a spill. **2.** *pot.* (= *przybywać*) descend; **zwalić się komuś na kark** *l.* **na głowę** *pot.* descend on sb.

zwalczać *ipf.* combat, fight (against). ~ **się** *ipf.* combat *l.* fight each other.

zwalczyć *pf. zob.* **zwalczać**.

zwalić *pf.* **1.** *zob.* **zwalać**. **2.** **zwalić (sobie) konia** *l.* **gruchę** *wulg.* (= *onanizować się*) jack off, whack off. ~ **się** *pf. zob.* **zwalać się**.

zwalisko *n. geol.* rockfall, rockslide.

zwalisty *a.* hefty, strapping.

zwalniacz *mi Gen.* **-a** *techn.* **1.** (= *wyłącznik blokady*) release. **2.** (= *spowalniacz*) retardant.

zwalniać *ipf.* **1.** (= *opóźniać*) delay, slow down. **2.** (= *zmniejszać prędkość*) slow down; **zwalniać przed zakrętem** *mot.* slow down to make a turn. **3.** (= *uwalniać*) *blokadę, więźnia* release; **zwolnić kogoś za kaucją** release sb on bail. **4.** (= *rozluźniać*) (*uścisk*) relax; (*więzy*) loosen. **5.** (*z obowiązku*) free, let off, exempt; (*z obecności*) excuse; **zwolnić kogoś z/od opłaty** waive a fee for sb. **6.** (*z pracy*) dismiss, fire; **zwolnić kogoś z pracy** dismiss sb (from a job). **7.** (= *oddawać do dyspozycji*) (*mieszkanie, lokal, posadę*) vacate, free. **~ się** *ipf.* **1.** (*uzyskiwać pozwolenie*) be excused (*z czegoś* from sth). **2. zwalniać się (z pracy)** (= *składać rezygnację*) quit (one's job), leave (one's job); (= *urywać się*) leave work early; (= *wychodzić na chwilę*) leave one's workplace. **3.** (= *stawać się niezajętym*) become free *l.* available.

zwał *mi* **1.** (= *hałda, pryzma*) bank, heap; **zwały śniegu** snow banks. **2.** *górn.* dump.

zwałować[1] *ipf.* (= *składować*) (*śmieci, złom, odpadki*) dump.

zwałować[2] *pf.* (= *ugnieść wałem*) roll.

zwałowarka *f. Gen.pl.* **-ek** *zwł. górn.* dumping conveyer.

zwałowisko *n.* dump, dumping ground.

zwany *a.* **tak zwany** so-called.

zwapnieć *pf. pat.* calcify.

zwapnienie *n. pat.* calcification; **zwapnienie naczyń krwionośnych** atherosclerosis.

zwarcie[1] *n.* **1.** *el.* short (circuit). **2.** (= *zetknięcie się*) contact. **3.** *fon.* occlusion, stop; **zwarcie krtaniowe** glottal stop. **4.** *boks* clinch. **5.** *wojsk.* clash.

zwarcie[2] *adv.* (= *ciasno*) densely.

zwariować *pf. pot.* (= *oszaleć, stracić rozsądek*) lose one's mind, go mad; **nie dać się zwariować** keep one's senses.

zwariowany *a. pot.* (= *nieobliczalny, szalony*) crazy (*na jakimś punkcie* about sth).

zwarł *itd. pf. zob.* **zewrzeć**.

zwartość *f.* density.

zwarty *a.* **1.** (= *gęsty*) dense; (= *ciasny*) tight. **2.** (*o społeczności*) close-knit. **3.** (= *jednomyślny*) (*o froncie, rodzinie*) united. **4.** (= *spójny*) (*o kompozycji, opowiadaniu*) pithy. **5.** *fon.* stop; **spółgłoska zwarta** stop (consonant). **6. szyk zwarty** *wojsk.* close formation.

zwarzony *a.* sour; **zwarzona mina** sour face; **zwarzony mrozem** frost-bitten.

zwarzyć *pf.* curd. **~ się** *pf.* (*o mleku*) go *l.* turn sour.

zważać *ipf.* **zważać na coś** (= *zwracać uwagę*) pay attention to sth; **nie zważać na coś/kogoś** ignore sth/sb.

zważyć *pf.* **1.** *zob.* **zważać**. **2.** (= *zmierzyć wagę*) weight. **~ się** *pf.* weight o.s.

zważywszy *prep.* **zważywszy na coś/że...** considering sth/that...

zwąchać *pf. pot.* nose out, ferret out, scent out; **zwąchać pismo nosem** smell a rat. **~ się** *pf. pot.* (= *skumać się*) club together.

zwątpić *pf.* **zwątpić (w coś/kogoś)** have doubts (about sth/sb), doubt (in sth/sb).

zwątpienie *n.* doubts; **ogarnęło kogoś zwątpienie** sb has doubts.

zwekslować *pf. zob.* **wekslować**.

zwerbalizować *pf. zob.* **werbalizować**.

zwerbować *pf. zob.* **werbować**.

zweryfikować *pf. zob.* **weryfikować**.

zwę *itd. ipf. zob.* **zwać**.

zwędzić *pf. pot.* (= *ukraść*) swipe, filch.

zwęglać *ipf.* **1.** (= *spalić na węgiel*) char. **2.** *chem., techn.* carbonize. **~ się** *ipf.* **1.** (= *spalić się na węgiel*) char, become charred. **2.** *chem., techn.* carbonize.

zwęglić (się) *pf. zob.* **zwęglać (się)**.

zwęglony *a.* charred.

zwęszyć *pf.* (*o zwierzęciu, człowieku*) scent.

zwęzić *pf.* **-żę -zisz, zwężać** *ipf.* narrow; *krawiectwo* take in. **~ się** *pf.*, **zwężać się** *ipf.* (*ku końcowi*) taper (off); (*z czasem*) narrow.

zwężenie *n.* narrowing; *pat.* stenosis; „**zwężenie drogi**" *mot.* "road narrows"; **zwężenie aorty** *pat.* aortic stenosis.

zwężka *f. Gen.pl.* **-ek** *techn.* reducer.

zwiać *pf.* **zwieję zwiejesz 1.** *zob.* **zwiewać. 2.** *roln.* (*zboże*) winnow.

zwiad *mi wojsk.* **1.** (= *rozpoznanie*) reconnaissance. **2.** (*pododdział*) advance guard *l.* party, point.

zwiadowca *mp wojsk.* scout, reconnoiterer.

zwiadowczy *a. wojsk.* reconnaissance, scouting.

zwiady *pl. Gen.* **-ów** (= *przeszpiegi*) scouting; **iść na zwiady** scout.

zwiastować *ipf.* **1.** *lit.* (= *zapowiadać*) foreshadow, augur; (*coś dobrego*) herald; (*coś złego*) portend. **2.** *rel.* (= *oznajmiać*) annunciate.

zwiastun *mi Gen.* **-a** *pl.* **-y 1.** *film* trailer. **2.** (= *zapowiedź*) sign, harbinger; **zwiastun wiosny** harbinger of spring. **3.** *med.* symptom. – *mp pl.* **-i** *lit.* herald.

związać *pf.* **związę związesz** *zob.* **związywać. ~ się** *pf. zob.* **związywać się**; *zob.* **wiązać się**.

związany *a.* **1.** (= *skrępowany linami*) tied up. **2.** (= *zawiązany*) tied; **mam związane ręce** *gł. przen.* my hands are tied. **3.** (= *zobligowany*) bound; **związany obietnicą/umową** bound by a promise/contract. **4. związany z czymś** (= *wiążący się*) related to sth, relating to sth; **to nie jest związane z tematem dyskusji** it has nothing to do with the matter at hand.

związek *mi* **-zk- 1.** (= *powiązanie*) connection, relationship, association (*między czymś a czymś* between sth and sth); **w związku z czymś** in connection to *l.* with sth; **w związku z tym** therefore, accordingly; **mieć związek z czymś** be related to sth; **nie mieć związku z czymś** be unrelated to sth; **mówić bez związku** speak incoherently; **związek z przyrodą** relationship with nature; **zerwać związki z czymś/kimś** break ties with sth/sb; **jaki to ma związek z tematem?** what's the relevance of this?; **nawiązać związki z kimś/czymś** establish relationships with sb/sth; **związek przyczynowy** *fil.* causal relationship; **związek**

frazeologiczny *jęz.* phrase; (*zrzeszenie*) union; **związek zawodowy** trade union; **Związek Radziecki** *hist.* the Soviet Union; **Związek Socjalistycznych Republik Radzieckich** *hist.* the Union of Soviet Socialist Republics. **2.** (*partnerstwo*) relationship; **żyć w wolnym związku** live together, cohabit; **związek małżeński** marriage; **związek homoseksualny** homosexual relationship. **3.** *chem.* compound; **związek organiczny/nieorganiczny** organic/inorganic compound. **4.** *gram.* **związek rządu** government; **związek zgody** concord, agreement.

związkowiec *mp* -wc- *pl.* -y (trade) unionist.

związkowy *a.* (trade) union; **ruch związkowy** labor movement, (trade) unionism.

związywać *ipf.* **1.** (*sznurowadła, chustkę, sznurek*) tie; **osobę** tie up; **związać coś w kokardkę** tie sth in a bow; **nie móc związać końca z końcem** cannot make ends meet; **związać paczkę sznurkiem** tie a string around a box; **związać włosy wstążką** tie one's hair with a ribbon. **2.** (*o betonie*) set. ~ **się** *ipf.* tie o.s.

zwichnąć *pf.* -ij **1.** *pat.* (*rękę, palec*) dislocate. **2.** (= *zniszczyć*) (*karierę, życie*) ruin.

zwichnięcie *n. med.* dislocation.

zwichrować *pf.* warp, twist. ~ **się** *pf.* warp, twist.

zwichrowanie *n.* warp, twist.

zwichrowany *a.* (*o drzwiach*) warped; (*o człowieku, sposobie myślenia*) twisted.

zwichrzyć *pf.* (*włosy, czuprynę*) ruffle. ~ **się** *pf.* ruffle.

zwid *mi* apparition; **chyba masz zwidy** you must be seeing things.

zwidzieć się *pf. 3 os. sing.* -i, **coś ci się zwidziało** you must be seeing things.

zwiedzać *ipf.*, **zwiedzić** *pf.* (= *odwiedzać*) visit; (= *oglądać*) see.

zwiedzieć się *pf.* **zwiem zwiesz zwiedzą, zwiedz, zwiedzieć się o czymś** find out about sth.

zwielokrotniać *ipf.* multiply; *tel.* (*kanał*) multiplex. ~ **się** *ipf.* multiply.

zwielokrotnić (się) *pf.* -ij *zob.* **zwielokrotniać (się)**.

zwielokrotnieć *pf.* multiply.

zwieńczać *ipf.* (*budowlę*) top, crown; (*dzieło*) crown.

zwieńczenie *n.* **1.** (*budowli*) top. **2.** (*kariery*) height.

zwieńczyć *pf. zob.* **zwieńczać**.

zwieracz *mi Gen.* -a *anat.* sphincter.

zwierać *ipf.* **1.** *el.* short-circuit, short. **2.** *lit.* (= *łączyć*) join (together); **zwierać szeregi** join forces, close up. ~ **się** *ipf.* **1.** *el.* short-circuit, short. **2.** (= *dotykać się*) touch. **3.** (= *skupiać się*) (*o tłumie, grupie*) converge. **4.** *boks, zapasy* (= *obejmować się*) clinch.

zwierciadlany *a.* *opt.* mirror; **teleskop zwierciadlany** reflecting telescope, reflector.

zwierciadło *n. Gen.pl.* -deł **1.** (= *lustro*) looking glass, mirror. **2.** **zwierciadło wody** water surface; **zwierciadło płaskie/sferyczne/wklęsłe/wypukłe** *opt.* plane/spherical/concave/convex mir-

ror; **przedstawiać coś w krzywym zwierciadle** lampoon sth.

zwierz *ma Gen.pl.* -ów **1.** *lit.* (= *zwierzę*) beast. **2.** *lit., myśl.* (= *zwierzyna*) game; **gruby zwierz** big game.

zwierzać *ipf. arch. l. lit.* reveal; **zwierzać komuś sekret** confide in sb. ~ **się** *ipf.* confide; **zwierzać się komuś z czegoś** tell sb sth in confidence, reveal sth to sb; **zwierzać się komuś z sekretów** confide in sb.

zwierzak *ma pot.* critter; **domowe zwierzaki** pets.

zwierzątko *n. Gen.pl.* -tek **1.** *dimin.* (= *zwierzę*) animal; (*domowe*) pet. **2.** (*zabawka*) toy animal; **pluszowe zwierzątko** furry toy.

zwierzchni *a.* superior; **władze zwierzchnie** authorities.

zwierzchnictwo *n.* (= *władza*) authority (*nad kimś / czymś* over sb/sth); (= *dominacja*) domination (*nad kimś / czymś* over sb/sth).

zwierzchniczka *f. Gen.pl.* -ek, **zwierzchnik** *mp* superior.

zwierzenie *n.* confession.

zwierzę *n.* -rzęci- *pl.* -rzęt- *Gen.* -ąt **1.** animal; **zwierzę domowe** pet; **zwierzę mięsożerne** carnivore; **zwierzę futerkowe** furry animal. **2.** *pot., uj.* (= *łajdak*) animal.

zwierzęcy *a.* animal; **tłuszcz/produkty pochodzenia zwierzęcego** animal fat/produce *l.* products.

zwierzostan *mi tylko sing. ekol.* animal population; *myśl.* game stock.

zwierzyć *pf. zob.* **zwierzać**. ~ **się** *pf. zob.* **zwierzać się**.

zwierzyna *f. myśl.* game; **gruba zwierzyna** big game; **zwierzyna płowa** deer; **zwierzyna drobna** small game.

zwierzyniec *mi* -ńc- *Gen.* -a game park *l.* preserve; *lit.* paradise.

zwiesić (się) *pf. zob.* **zwieszać (się)**.

zwieszać *ipf.* hang (down); (= *dyndać*) dangle; **zwiesić głowę** hang (down) one's head; **zwiesić nos na kwintę** make a long face. ~ **się** *ipf.* hang; (= *dyndać*) dangle.

zwieść *pf.* **zwiodę zwiedziesz zwiódł zwiodła zwiedli** *zob.* **zwodzić**.

zwietrzały *a.* **1.** (*o żywności*) stale; (*o napoju gazowanym*) flat. **2.** (*o skale*) weathered.

zwietrzeć *pf.* **1.** (= *zestarzeć się*) go stale. **2.** *geol.* weather.

zwietrzelina *f. geol.* (rock) waste.

zwietrzyć *pf.* scent (out); **zwietrzyć niebezpieczeństwo** scent danger; **zwietrzyć interes** smell money.

zwiewać *ipf.* -am -asz **1.** *pot.* (= *uciekać*) split, beat it. **2.** (= *zdmuchiwać*) blow (down).

zwiewnie *adv.* (*poruszać się*) airily, gracefully.

zwiewny *a.* airy; (*o sukience*) filmy.

zwieźć *pf.* **zwiozę zwieziesz zwiózł zwiozła zwieźli** *zob.* **zwozić**.

zwiędły *a.* withered, wilted.

zwiędnąć *pf.* **zwiędnę zwiędniesz, zwiędnij, zwiądł** *l.* **zwiędnął zwiędła zwiędli** wither, wilt.

zwiędnięty *a.* withered, wilted.

zwiększać *ipf.* increase, augment. ~ **się** increase, grow.

zwiększyć (się) *pf. zob.* **zwiększać (się)**.

zwięzłość *f.* succinctness, conciseness.

zwięzły *a.* **1.** (= *lakoniczny*) succinct, concise. **2.** (= *zwarty*) (*o glebie, skale, drewnie*) solid, firm.

zwięźle *adv.* succinctly, concisely.

zwijać *ipf.* roll (up); (*na szpulę*) wind, coil; **zwijać żagle** *żegl.* take in sails; *przen.* get out; (= *likwidować*) pack up; **zwijać obóz** break camp; **zwijać manatki** *pot.* up sticks; **zwijać interes** *pot.* pack (it) up. ~ **się** *ipf.* **1.** (= *zawijać się*) curl (up); (= *skręcać się*) roll (up); (*na szpulę*) coil; **zwinąć się w kłębek** curl up; **zwijać się z bólu** writhe in pain. **2.** *pot.* (= *uwijać się*) get cracking, look sharp. **3.** *pot.* (= *wynosić się*) pack (it) up.

zwilgotnieć *ipf.* dampen, moisten.

zwilżacz *mi Gen.* **-a** *techn.* (= *urządzenie*) humidifier; (= *substancja*) wetting agent.

zwilżać *ipf.,* **zwilżyć** *pf.* wet, moisten, dampen; **zwilżyć sobie gardło** *żart.* wet one's whistle.

zwinąć *pf. zob.* **zwijać**. ~ **się** *pf. zob.* **zwijać się**.

zwinka *f. Gen.pl.* **-ek** *t.* **jaszczurka zwinka** *zool.* sand lizard (*Lacerta agilis*).

zwinnie *adv.* nimbly, agilely, deftly.

zwinność *f.* nimbness, agileness, deftness.

zwinny *a.* nimb, agile, deft.

zwiotczały *a.* flabby, limp.

zwiotczeć *pf.* go flabby, go limp.

zwis *mi* **1.** (*skalny, śnieżny*) overhang. **2.** (*na drążku*) hang. **3.** *el.* dip. **4.** *lotn.* bank.

zwisać *ipf.,* **zwisnąć** *pf.* **zwisnę zwiśniesz, zwiśnij, zwisnął** *l.* **zwisł zwisła zwisnęli** *l.* **zwiśli** (= *wisieć*) hang (down); (= *obwisać*) droop.

zwitek *mi* **-tk-** *Gen.* **-a** roll; (*banknotów*) wad.

zwlec *pf.* **zwlokę** *l.* **zwlekę zwleczesz zwlókł** *l.* **zwlekł zwlokła** *l.* **zwlekła zwlekli** (= *zaciągnąć*) drag. ~ **się** *pf.* (= *zejść*) drag o.s.; **zwlec się z łóżka** drag o.s. out of bed.

zwlekać *ipf.* **1.** **zwlekać (z czymś)** (= *odwlekać*) delay (sth), drag one's feet (on sth). **2.** (= *ściągać, ciągnąć*) *zob.* **zwlec**.

zwłaszcza *adv.* especially, particularly, in particular; **a zwłaszcza nie...** least of all...; **lubię literaturę, zwłaszcza francuską** I like literature, especially French literature; **mrozy są dokuczliwe zwłaszcza w styczniu** frosts are particularly troublesome in January; **zwłaszcza że...** especially that...; **zwłaszcza z tego powodu** especially for that reason.

zwłoka *f.* (= *opóźnienie*) delay; **bez (chwili) zwłoki** without (any) delay; **sprawa niecierpiąca zwłoki** urgent matter; **grać na zwłokę** play *l.* stall for time; **kara za zwłokę** *prawn.* late fee.

zwłoki *pl. Gen.* **-k** corpse.

zwłóczyć *pf. roln.* harrow.

zwłóknieć *pf. pat.* fibrose.

zwłóknienie *n. pat.* fibrosis.

zwodniczo *adv.* deceptively.

zwodniczy *a.* deceptive.

zwodować *pf. żegl.* (*statek*) launch.

zwodu *itd. mi zob.* **zwód**.

zwodzić *ipf.* **zwódź** (= *oszukiwać*) deceive; (= *łudzić*) delude.

zwodzony *a.* **most zwodzony** *bud.* drawbridge.

zwojować *pf.* win, get; **(z nim) wiele nie zwojujesz** you won't get very far (with him).

zwoju *itd. mi zob.* **zwój**.

zwolenniczka *f. Gen.pl.* **-ek, zwolennik** *mp* supporter, follower, advocate (*czegoś / kogoś* of sth/ sb).

zwolnić *pf.* **-ij** *zob.* **zwalniać**. ~ **się** *pf.* **-ij** *zob.* **zwalniać się**.

zwolnienie *n.* **1.** (= *usprawiedliwienie, nieobecność*) leave; **(być) na zwolnieniu** (be) on leave; **zwolnienie lekarskie** doctor's leave. **2.** (= *usunięcie*) (*z pracy*) dismissal; (*z wojska*) discharge. **3.** (= *ulga*) exemption; **zwolnienie od podatków** tax exemption.

zwolniony *a.* **1.** (= *spowolniony*) delayed, slow; **w zwolnionym tempie** in slow motion; **zdjęcia zwolnione** *film* time-lapse photography; **pracować na zwolnionych obrotach** go slow. **2.** (= *wyrzucony*) (*z pracy*) dismissed; (*z wojska*) discharged. **3.** (= *wypuszczony*) released, discharge; **zwolniony z więzienia** released *l.* discharged from prison. **4.** (= *niepodlegający obowiązkowi*) exempt (*od / z czegoś* from sth); **kwota zwolniona (od podatku)** tax deduction.

zwołać *pf.,* **zwoływać** *ipf.* **1.** (*spotkanie, zebranie, posiedzenie*) call, summon. **2.** (*ludzi*) summon, call together.

zwornik *mi Gen.* **-a** *bud.* keystone.

zwozić *ipf.* **zwożę zwozisz, zwoź** *l.* **zwóź 1.** (= *dostarczać w jedno miejsce*) bring (in). **2.** (*w dół*) take down.

zwód *mi* **-o-** *sport* feint.

zwój *mi* **-o-** *Gen.pl.* **-ów** (= *rolka, zwitek*) roll; (*drutu*) coil; (*papieru*) scroll; **zwoje nerwowe** *anat.* ganglia.

zwózka *f. Gen.pl.* **-ek** transport, haulage.

zwracać *ipf.* **1.** (= *kierować*) (*wzrok, oczy*) turn. **2.** (= *oddawać*) (*pożyczkę, książkę*) return, give back. **3.** *fin.* (*zaległość*) repay; (*koszty*) reimburse, cover. **4.** (= *wymiotować*) vomit. **5.** **zwrócić uwagę (na coś/kogoś)** pay attention (to sth/sb), take note (of sth/sb); **zwracać (komuś) uwagę** make comments; **zwrócić komuś uwagę na coś** draw sb's attention to sth; **ktoś/coś zwraca (czymś) uwagę** sb/sth attracts *l.* draws attention (with sth). ~ **się** *ipf.* **1.** (= *kierować się*) turn; **zwrócić się do kogoś o pomoc** turn to sb for help; **zwrócić się z prośbą/propozycją** make a request/suggestion; **zwrócić się (do kogoś) z pytaniem** put *l.* address *l.* pose a question (to sb); **zwracać się do kogoś po imieniu** first-name sb; **zwrócić się ku naturze** turn to nature. **2.** *ekon.* pay off.

zwrot *mi* **1.** (= *skręt*) turn; **wykonać zwrot w prawo/w lewo** make *l.* take a right/left turn. **2.** (*nowy kierunek*) turn; *polit.* swing, turnabout; **zwrot w badaniach** new direction in research. **3.** (= *zainteresowanie się*) turn; **zwrot ku fizyce jądrowej** turn to atomic physics. **4.** (= *oddanie*) return; **zwrot butelek** bottle return; *prawn.* restitution, restoration. **5.** *fin.* (= *spłata*) return, repayment; **zwrot kosztów** reimbursement. **6.** *handl.* refund; **gwarancja zwrotu pieniędzy** money-back guarantee. **7.** *jęz.* phrase, expression; **zwrot grzecznościowy** polite expression. – *int.* **w tył/w lewo/w prawo zwrot!** *wojsk.* about/left/right face!

zwrotka *f. Gen.pl.* **-ek** *wers.* stanza; *muz.* verse.

zwrotnica *f.* **1.** *kol.* switch. **2.** *el., telew.* branching filter.

zwrotnicowy *a. kol.* switch.

zwrotniczy *a. kol.* switch. – *mp kol.* switchman.

zwrotnik *mi Gen.* **-a** *geogr.* tropic; **Zwrotnik Koziorożca/Raka** Tropic of Capricorn/Cancer.

zwrotnikowy *a.* (*o obszarach, klimacie*) tropical.

zwrotność *f.* **1.** (= *sterowność*) maneuverability; *Br.* manoeuvrability, manageability; (= *szybkie reagowanie np. na ruch kierownicą*) responsiveness. **2.** (= *zwinność*) agility, nimbleness.

zwrotny *a.* **1.** (= *sterowny*) maneuverable; *Br.* manoeuvrable, manageable; (= *szybko reagujący np. na ruch kierownicą*) responsive. **2.** (= *zmieniający kierunek na wsteczny*) reversing; **sprzężenie zwrotne** *komp.* feedback; **punkt zwrotny** turning point; (*zwł. w nauce*) (= *przełom*) breakthrough; **punkt zwrotny** *l.* **martwy** (*tłoka*) dead center; *Br.* dead centre. **3.** (= *przeznaczony do oddania*) returnable; **adres zwrotny** return address; **butelka zwrotna** returnable bottle; **pożyczka zwrotna** returnable *l.* repayable loan. **4.** *jęz.* reflexive; **czasownik zwrotny** reflexive verb; **strona zwrotna** reflexive voice, the reflexive.

zwroty *pl. Gen.* **-ów** (= *produkty niesprzedane*) returns, returned merchandise.

zwrócić *pf. zob.* **zwracać.** ~ **się** *pf. zob.* **zwracać się.**

zwulgaryzować *pf. zob.* **wulgaryzować.**

zwycięski *a.* (= *ten, który odniósł zwycięstwo*) victorious; (= *tryumfalny*) triumphant; *sport* winning; **zwycięska drużyna** winning team.

zwycięsko *adv.* triumphantly; **wyjść zwycięsko z opresji** emerge victorious from trouble.

zwycięstwo *n.* victory; *sport* win; **łatwe zwycięstwo** runaway victory; *sport* easy win; **miażdżące zwycięstwo** sweeping *l.* thumping victory; **zasłużone zwycięstwo** well-deserved victory; **zdecydowane zwycięstwo** unquestionable victory; **zwycięstwo na całej linii** overwhelming victory; **odnieść zwycięstwo** win *l.* gain a victory (*nad kimś / czymś* over sb/sth); **Pyrrusowe zwycięstwo** Cadmean *l.* Pyrrhic victory; **przechylić szalę zwycięstwa na czyjąś stronę** tip the scales in favor of sb; *Br.* tip the scales in favour of sb; **Dzień Zwycięstwa** Victory Day, V-Day; (*w II wojnie światowej, 08.05.1945*) Victory-in-Europe Day, V-E Day.

zwycięzca *mp* winner; (*zwł. w wojnie, bitwie*) victor; **murowany zwycięzca** (*zwł. w wyścigu*) (dead) cert; **stanąć po stronie zwycięzcy** climb *l.* jump *l.* get on the bandwagon.

zwyciężać *ipf.*, **zwyciężyć** *pf.* **1.** (= *pokonać*) conquer; **zwyciężyć nieprzyjaciela/rywala/przeciwnika** conquer one's enemy/rival/opponent. **2.** (= *odnosić zwycięstwo*) prevail (*kogoś / coś* of sb/sth); (*sport*) win; **zwyciężył głos rozsądku** the voice of reason prevailed; **prawda zwyciężi** truth will prevail. **3.** (= *zawładnąć*) take the upper hand; **zwyciężyła w nim ciekawość** curiosity took the upper hand of him. **4.** (= *przezwyciężać*) overcome; **zwyciężyć nałóg** overcome an addiction, break o.s. of an addiction.

zwyciężczyni *f.* (= *ta, która zwyciężyła*) victress; *sport, przen.* winner.

zwyczaj *mi Gen.pl.* **-ów 1.** (= *obyczaj*) custom; **starodawny zwyczaj** time-honored custom; **zrobić coś zgodnie z panującym zwyczajem** do sth according to the prevailing custom; **coś uświęcone zwyczajem** sth sanctified by tradition; **jak zwyczaj każe** as the custom has it, by custom *l.* convention; **jest w zwyczaju...** it is customary to...; **okulary, zwyczajem wszystkich okularów, przepadły** the glasses, as glasses have a habit of doing, disappeared. **2.** (= *przyzwyczajenie*) habit; **mam zwyczaj pić kawę rano** I usually drink coffee in the morning; **nie mam zwyczaju...** it is not my usual practice to...; **ma zwyczaj się powtarzać** he has the trick of repeating himself; **swoim zwyczajem nic nie powiedział** as was his wont, he said nothing; **weszło w zwyczaj, że...** it has become customary to..., it has become a habit to...; **weszło u niego w zwyczaj...** he has fallen into the habit of...; **to wyszło ze zwyczaju** it's no longer customary; **dobry zwyczaj, nie pożyczaj** lend your money and lose your friend.

zwyczajnie *adv.* **1.** (= *normalnie*) ordinarily, as usual; **wyglądać zwyczajnie** look ordinary; **zachowywać się zwyczajnie** behave as usual. **2.** (= *po prostu*) simply; **nie jest głupi, jest zwyczajnie leniwy** he's not stupid, but simply lazy.

zwyczajny *a.* **1.** (= *zwykły*) ordinary, regular, usual; **członek zwyczajny** ordinary member; **kiełbasa zwyczajna** pork sausage (*of coarsely ground pork meat*); **profesor zwyczajny** full professor; (*zwł. w odniesieniu do uczelni nieanglojęzycznych*) professor ordinarius; **zwyczajna kolej rzeczy** the usual course of events. **2.** (= *przeciętny*) (*o człowieku*) ordinary; (*o rzeczy*) everyday, common(place); (*o jedzeniu*) plain. **3.** *biol.* (= *pospolity*) common. **4.** (= *oczywisty*) downright, sheer, mere; **zwyczajny tchórz** downright *l.* mere coward; **zwyczajna bezmyślność** sheer thoughlessness.

zwyczajowo *adv.* customarily, according to custom; **zwyczajowo przyjęty sposób postępowania** the usual *l.* customary procedure.

zwyczajowy *a.* customary; **prawo zwyczajowe** (*niepisana norma prawna*) custom; (*ogół niepisanych norm prawnych*) custom law.

zwykle *adv.* usually, typically, for the most part; **jak zwykle** as usual; (**więcej/szybciej/cieplej**) **niż zwykle** (more/faster/warmer) than usual; **jak zwykle jesteś nieprzygotowany!** that's typical! you are unprepared!; **jak zwykle w takich wypadkach** as is usual in such cases; **obiad zwy-**

kle jadam o piątej I usually have dinner at five; było więcej ludzi niż zwykle there were more people than usual; poproszę to, co zwykle (w barze, pubie) I'll have my usual l. regular.

zwykły a. **1.** (= pospolity) ordinary, common; (= zgodny ze zwyczajem) usual, habitual; **zwykła kolej rzeczy** the usual course of events; **o zwykłej porze** at the usual time; **zwykła większość** prawn. simple majority. **2.** (= przeciętny) common, simple; (o jedzeniu) plain; **rok zwykły** common year; **ułamek zwykły** mat. simple l. common l. vulgar fraction; **zwykły dzień** weekday; **zwykli ludzie** common people. **3.** (= oczywisty) downright, sheer, mere; **zwykły tchórz** downright l. mere coward; **zwykła bezmyślność** sheer thoughlessness.

zwymiotować pf. vomit.

zwymyślać pf. berate, bawl out; **zwymyślać kogoś od ostatnich** give sb a dressing down.

zwyrodnialec mp -lc- Voc. -cze l. -cu pl. -y degenerate.

zwyrodniały a. degenerate.

zwyrodnieć pf. degenerate.

zwyrodnienie n. degeneration.

zwyrodnieniowy a. med. degenerative.

zwyżka f. Gen.pl. -ek rise; (gwałtowna) surge; **grać na zwyżkę** fin. bull; **zwyżka temperatury/ciśnienia** meteor. temperature/pressure rise; **zwyżka formy** sport improvement in form, upsurge in form.

zwyżkować ipf. rise.

zwyżkowy a. rising, upward; **giełda** bullish; **tendencja zwyżkowa** rising l. upward trend l. tendency; **wykazywać tendencję zwyżkową** show a rising tendency.

zwyżkujący a. rising, bouyant; **giełda** bullish; **zwyżkujący rynek** giełda bull market.

zydel mi -dl- Gen. -a Gen.pl. -i l. -ów stool.

zydwestka f. Gen.pl. -ek żegl. sou'wester.

zygospora f. biol. zygospore.

zygota f. biol. zygote.

zygzak mi Gen. -a zigzag.

zygzakowaty a. zigzag; **żmija zygzakowata** adder (Vipera berus).

zymaza f. biochem. zymase.

zymogen mi zymogen.

zymologia f. biol. zymology.

zys ma orn. golden eagle (Aquila chrysaetos).

zysk mi **1.** (nadwyżka) profit, gain; **zysk brutto/netto** gross/net profit; **brudny zysk** filthy lucre; **czysty zysk** clear profit; **łatwy l. szybki zysk** (zwł. nielegalny) pickings; **zyski kapitałowe** capital gains; **zysk z akcji** fin. earnings per share; **rachunek zysków i strat** profit and loss account; **stopa zysku** rate of profit, profit rate; **nieobliczony na zysk** (o organizacji) nonprofit; **dziesięcioprocentowy zysk** a yield of 10 per cent; **pogoń za zyskiem** greed, cupidity; **udział w zyskach** ekon. profit sharing; **mieć udział w zyskach** have one's share in the profits; **osiągnąć l. wypracować zysk** fin. make (a) profit; **przynosić zysk** bring l. yield profit; (o firmie) make money; **sprzedać coś z zyskiem** sell sth at a profit. **2.** (= korzyść) gain.

zyskać pf., **zyskiwać** ipf. **1.** (= osiągać korzyść) profit, benefit; **zyskać na czymś** profit from l. by sth; **zyskać na czasie** gain time; **próbować zyskać na czasie** (np. odwlekając jakąś decyzję) play for time; **zyskać na czyjejś naiwności** benefit from sb's naivity. **2.** (= uzyskiwać) gain, earn, win; **zyskać doświadczenie** gain experience; **zyskać pewność, że...** become certain that...; **zyskać umiejętność** acquire a skill; **zyskać wiedzę** gain l. acquire knowledge; **zyskać czyjś aplauz** win sb's appreciation; **zyskać czyjąś przyjaźń** win l. gain sb's friendship; **zyskać nowych przyjaciół** make new friends; **zyskać czyjeś uznanie** win sb's recognition; **zyskać czyjąś sympatię** win l. gain sb's liking l. affinity; **zyskać czyjąś wdzięczność** earn sb's gratitude; **zyskać czyjeś względy** l. **względy u kogoś** win favor with sb; **zyskać czyjeś zaufanie** gain l. win sb's trust l. confidence; **zyskać rozgłos** gain publicity; **zyskać sławę** vault to fame. **3.** (= pozyskiwać kogoś) gain, win (sb) over; **zyskać w kimś przyjaciela** win sb over as a friend; **idea zyskała nowych zwolenników** the idea gained new supporters. **4.** (= nabierać waloru) improve, gain; **on bardzo zyskuje przy bliższym poznaniu** he's a really nice guy once you get to know him; **zyskała w moich oczach** she gained in my view, she gained in my opinion, she rose in my esteem; **zyskać na wartości** increase l. gain in value.

zyskowność f. profitability.

zyskowny a. profitable.

zyzania f. bot. wild l. Indian l. water rice (Zizania aquatica).

zza prep. + Gen. **1.** (= spoza) from behind; **zza grobu** from beyond the grave; **zza rogu ulicy wyskoczył samochód** a car pulled out from behind the corner; **zza pazuchy** out of one's breast pocket; **wyciągnął zza pazuchy pomiętą kartkę papieru** he produced a badly crumpled piece of paper out of his breast pocket. **2.** (= poprzez) through; **zza chmur wyszło słońce** the sun started shining through the clouds.

zziajać się pf. get out of breath.

zziajany a. breathless, panting.

zzielenieć pf. **1.** (= stać się zielonym) become green. **2.** (= zblednąć) l. turn green; **zzielenieć z zazdrości** be l. go green with envy.

zziębnąć pf. -ij be cold; **zziębnąć l. zmarznąć do szpiku kości** be chilled to the bone.

zziębnięty a. bitter cold; **stałem na przystanku zziębnięty** I was standing on the bus stop freezing.

zzuć pf., **zzuwać** ipf. take off (one's shoes).

zżarł itd. pf. zob. **zeżreć**.

zżąć pf. zeżnę zeżniesz, zeżnij zob. **zżynać**.

zżerać ipf. **1.** (o zwierzętach) devour. **2.** pot. (o człowieku) gobble, wolf down. **3.** (o chorobie, czynnikach szkodliwych) (niszczyć) corrode, gnaw (coś at l. upon sth) eat away (kogoś / coś at sb/sth).

zżęty a. reaped, mown; **świeżo zżęte siano** freshly reaped hay.

zżółknąć pf. -ij become l. turn yellow.

zżyć się *pf.* **zżyję zżyjesz, zżyj** *zob.* **zżywać się.**

zżymać się *ipf.* **1.** (= *obruszać się*) bridle (*na kogoś/coś* at sb/sth). **2.** (= *reagować gniewnie*) fret and fume. **3.** (= *wzdrygać się*) flinch, shudder, writhe; **zżymać się na samą myśl o czymś** shudder to think about sth.

zżynać *ipf.* **1.** *roln.* reap. **2.** *szkoln.* (= *odpisywać*) crib.

zżyty *a.* (*o grupie, społeczności*) close-knit; **jesteśmy ze sobą bardzo zżyci** we are very close to one another.

zżywać się *ipf.* **-am -asz 1.** (= *przyzwyczajać się do kogoś*) become intimate (*z kimś* with sb). **2.** (= *przyzwyczajać się do czegoś*) get accustomed (*z czymś* to sth).

Ź

Ź, ź *n. indecl.* (*litera*) Z with an accent, z with an accent; Z acute, z acute.

ździebełko *n. Gen.pl.* **-ek** **1.** (= *trawka, łodyżka*) blade, stalk. **2.** (= *odrobinka*) a (little) bit, a pinch (*czegoś* of sth); **ani ździebełka** not a whit.

ździebko *adv. Gen.pl.* **-bek** (= *trochę*) a little, a bit, a pinch.

ździerstwo *n. zob.* **zdzierstwo.**

źdźbło *n. Gen.pl.* **-beł** **1.** (*łodyga*) stalk, stem; **źdźbło trawy** blade of grass. **2.** (= *odrobina*) grain, particle, speck; **ani źdźbła prawdy w tym nie ma** there is not a speck *l.* grain of truth in it.

źdźbłowy *a.* **rdza źdźbłowa** *bot.* stem rust (*Puccinia graminium*).

żgać *ipf.*, **żgnąć** *pf.* **-ij** = **żgać.**

źle *adv.* **gorzej** **1.** (= *niedobrze*) badly, wrongly, improperly, ill; **być źle wychowanym** be bad *l.* ill mannered; be mannerless; have no manners; **źle się zachowywać** misbehave/misconduct; be rude; **bardzo źle o czymś świadczyć** be an indictment of sth; **mieć źle w głowie** *pot.* be nuts; be crazy; be out of one's mind; **źle się sprzedawać** sell badly; **źle się zacząć** get off to a bad start; **źle zacząć** (*znajomość*) get off the wrong foot; **źle coś zrozumieć** misunderstand *l.* misinterpret *l.* misapprehend sth; take sth in ill part; **nie zrozum mnie źle** don't get me wrong; **źle dobrany** (*o osobach, rzeczach*) ill-assorted, mismatched; **źle skrywany** (*o żalu, pogardzie*) ill-disguised; **źle wymawiać** mispronounce; **źle stosować** misapply; **źle ocenić** (*sytuację, odległość, osobę*) misjudge; **źle rozegrać** (*sytuację*) mishandle; **źle coś widzieć** (*np. scenę z góry*) have a bad view of sth; **być źle ubranym** be badly dressed; look dowdy; **źle działać** (*o urządzeniu*) perform badly; **źle zaprojektowany** badly designed. **2.** (= *słabo, mizernie*) poorly, badly; **źle się czuć** feel bad *l.* awful *l.* unwell; **źle wyglądać** look bad *l.* awful; **z kimś jest źle** sb is in a serious condition; **źle odżywiony** ill nourished, malnourished; **źle sytuowany** badly off. **3.** (= *mało*) badly, insufficiently; **źle zarabiać** be badly paid; **źle opłacany** (*o pracowniku*) underpaid. **4.** (= *nieuczciwie*) **źle się prowadzić** have a bad reputation; **źle mu z oczu patrzy** *pot.* (= *nie budzi zaufania*) he doesn't inspire confidence. **5.** (= *negatywnie, niekorzystnie*) badly, poorly; **mówić o kimś źle** evil of sb; **źle kogoś nastrajać** put sb in a bad mood; **źle na czymś wyjść** lose out on sth. **6.** (= *nieżyczliwie*) **źle traktować** maltreat, ill-treat, mistreat, abuse (*sb*); treat sb badly; **źle komuś życzyć** wish sb ill; bear malice to sb; **nie życzyć komuś źle** bear sb no malice; **źle wróżyć** augur badly. **7.** (= *nieprzyjemnie, ciężko, smutno*) hard, sadly; **źle mi bez ciebie** I feel so bad *l.* sad without you; **czuję się źle w jego towarzystwie** I don't feel comfortable in his company; I don't feel at ease when he is around. **8.** (= *niepomyślnie*) badly; **komuś źle poszło na egzaminie** sb did badly in an exam; **źle się komuś powodzi** sb is doing badly; **źle trafiłeś** it's not the right time *l.* moment; **on źle skończy** he will come to no good; he will come to a bad *l.* sticky end; **źle się skończyć** come to grief *l.* a bad end *l.* no good; **źle na tym wyjdziesz** you will lose on it; **źle się komuś przysłużyć** do sb a bad service. **9.** (*o niepomyślnej sytuacji*) badly, bad; **źle z nami** we're done for; **oj, źle!** too bad!; **gorzej niż źle** worse than bad; **nie tak źle** not too bad; **gorzej już być nie może** it can't be worse than that; things have gone from bad to worse; **i tak źle, i tak niedobrze** we are in a cleft stick.

źrebak *ma* colt, pony.

źrebaki *pl. Gen.* **-ów** *pot.* (*futro*) pony-skins, colt skins.

źrebiątko *n. Gen.pl.* **-ek** baby foal.

źrebić się *ipf.* (*o klaczy konia*) foal.

źrebię *n.* **-bięci-** *pl.* **-bięt-** *Gen.* **-ąt** **1.** foal; (*płci męskiej*) colt. **2. Źrebię** *astron.* (*gwiazdozbiór*) Equuleus.

źrebięcy *a.* colt's, foal's; **skóra źrebięca** colt-skin.

źrebna *a.* (*o klaczy*) in foal.

źrenica *f.* **1.** (*oka*) pupil; **zwężenie źrenicy** *pat.* miosis; **strzec kogoś/czegoś jak źrenicy oka** guard sb/sth like the apple of one's eye. **2.** *pl. lit.* (= *oczy, tęczówki*) eyes; **błękitne źrenice** blue eyes.

źródełko *n. Gen.pl.* **-łek** springlet; fount, fountain.

źródlany *a.* spring; **woda źródlana** spring water.

źródło *n. Gen.pl.* **-deł** **1.** (*o wodzie*) spring, source, fountain-head, well; **źródło rzeki** source; **źródło artezyjskie** artesian well; **gorące źródła** hot springs; **źródło naftowe** oil well; **źródło gazowe** natural gas well; **słone źródło** salina; **źródło krasowe** limestone spring; **źródło siarkowe** sulfur spring; **rzeka ma źródło w górach** the river rises *l.* takes its source in the mountains. **2.** (= *geneza, początek*) source, origin; **źródło energii** source of energy; **źródło światła** illuminator; **źródło życia** source of life; **źródło radości** source of joy; **źródło kłopotów** the source of the trouble;

niewyczerpane źródło wellspring; **pewne/miarodajne źródło** reliable/good source; **anonimowe źródło informacji** nameless source of information; **podać/zacytować komuś dokładne źródło informacji** give/quote sb chapter and verse; **to ma swoje źródło w...** it stems from...; it has its roots in...; it springs from...; **źródło wszelkiego zła** the source *l.* root of all evil; **źródło wszelkiej mądrości** the fount of all wisdom; **źródło napędu** *techn.* prime mover; **źródło promieniowania alfa** *fiz.* alpha emitter. **3.** (= *materiały do badań*) sources, materials; **źródła archiwalne** archives; **źródła historyczne** historical records; **źródła rękopiśmienne** *l.* **pisane** written sources; **sięgać do źródeł** go back to sources; **bez powoływania się na źródło** without an acknowledgment.

źródłosłów *mi* -o- (= *etymologia*) **1.** etymology, derivation. **2.** (= *część wyrazu*) root, radical.

źródłowo *adv.* according to the sources.

źródłowy *a.* **materiały źródłowe** source materials; **badania źródłowe** source research; **tekst źródłowy** source text; **praca źródłowa** source-based work; **kod źródłowy** *komp.* source code.

źródłoznawczy *a.* *nauk.* **publikacje źródłoznawcze** source-books.

źródłoznawstwo *n.* *nauk.* study of source texts.

Ż

Ż, ż *n. indecl.* (*litera*) Z with a dot (above), z with a dot (above); dotted Z, dotted z.

żaba *f. zool.* (= *płaz z rodziny Raninae; pot.* = *jakikolwiek płaz bezogonowy*) frog; **żaba rycząca/ byk** bullfrog (*Rana catesbeiana*); **rechot żab** croaking of the frogs.

żabi *a.* frog's, batrachian, froggy; **żabi skrzek** *zool.* frogspawn; **mieć żabie oczy** have frog eyes; **żabi skok** (= *krótka podróż*) hop.

żabieniec *mi* -ńc- *Gen.* -a *bot.* water plantain (*Alisma*).

żabiściek *mi bot.* (= *roślina z rodziny Hydrocharitaceae*) frogbit; **żabiściek pływający** American frogbit (*Limnobium spongia*).

żabka *f. Gen.pl.* -ek **1.** *emf. zob.* **żaba**; **żabka drzewna** *l.* **żabka zielona** *zool.* tree toad, tree frog (*Hyla arborea*). **2.** (*do butów*) metal plate. **3.** (*do firanek, zasłon*) curtain hook; (*klamerka*) clip. **4.** *bud.* crocket. **5.** *muz.* (*u smyczka*) frog. **6.** *sport* (*w pływaniu*) breaststroke; **pływać żabką** swim breaststroke. **7.** *sport* (= *podskoki w przysiadzie*) knee bend jump. **8.** *techn.* (*klucz ślusarski*) wrench. **9.** *wet.* frog.

żabojad *mp pl.* -y *pot., żart. l. pog.* (= *Francuz*) froggy, frog.

żabot *mi strój* jabot, frill, ruffle.

żachnąć się *pf.* -ij bridle, bristle, snort angrily (*na coś/kogoś* at sth/sb).

żaden[1] *a.* **1.** (= *ani jeden*) any, no, none; (*z dwóch*) neither; **nie mam żadnych marzeń** I have no dreams, I don't have any dreams; **nie ma tam żadnego hotelu** there's no hotel (down) there; **nie przyszedł żaden list** there haven't been any letters; **pod żadnym pozorem** on no account, on no consideration; **bez żadnego skutku** to no purpose; **bez żadnego znaczenia** of no importance; **nie mieć żadnego wyboru** have no choice; **żadną miarą** by no means; **w żaden (inny) sposób** in any other way, otherwise; **żadnych oznak życia** no signs of life; **żadnych ale!** no ifs, ands, or buts!; **za żadną cenę** *l.* **za żadne pieniądze** not for the world; **w żadnym razie** *l.* **pod żadnym pozorem** under no circumstances, in no case, by no means; **w żadnym wypadku!** absolutely not!, certainly not! **2.** (= *w małym stopniu, o małej wartości*) no; **żaden ze mnie bohater** I am no hero; **to żadna pociecha** *pot.* that's no consolation.

żaden[2] *pron.* none; (*z dwóch*) neither; **żaden z tych dwóch mi się nie podoba** I like neither; I don't like either.

żagiel *mi* -gl- *Gen.* -a *żegl.* sail; **żagiel gniezdny** topsail; **żagiel pomocniczy** studding sail; **żagiel statyczny** sky-sail; **żagiel rozprzowy** spritsail; **żagiel balonowy** balloon sail; **żagiel dziobowy** headsail; **żagiel gaflowy** gaff, spencer; **żagiel lugrowy** lugsail; **głowa żagla** headboard; **ucho żagla** cringle; **pod pełnymi żaglami** full sail; **ze zwiniętymi żaglami** under bare poles; **z postawionymi żaglami** in *l.* under sail; **postawić wszystkie żagle** crowd on sail; **stawiać żagle** make *l.* set sail; **pod żaglami** under canvas; **zwinąć żagle** take in the sails, take in a reef; **wybierać żagiel** fill away; **dryfować bez żagli** hull; **złapać wiatr w żagle** *przen.* get a good start.

żagielek *mi* -lk- *Gen.* -a *żegl.* **1.** small sail. **2.** *bud.* pendentive; squinch, scoinson, panache. **3.** *bot.* (*w kwiecie roślin motylkowych*) vexillum; (*w kwiecie roślin strączkowych*) standard.

żagiew *f.* -gwi- *Gen., Dat. i Loc.* -gwi *pl.* -e **1.** (= *głownia*) fire-brand, torch. **2.** *bot.* (*grzyb*) bracket fungus, shelf fungus (*Polyporus*).

żaglowiec *mi* -wc- *Gen.* -a **1.** (*statek*) sailing ship, sailer. **2.** *icht.* (*ryba*) sail-fish (*Istiophorus platypterus*); (= *skalar*) angelfish (*Pterophyllum scalare*).

żaglowy *a.* sailing; **płótno żaglowe** sailcloth; **łódź żaglowa** sailing boat; **statek żaglowy** sailing ship; **lot żaglowy** soaring flight.

żaglówka *f. Gen.pl.* -ek (*łódź*) sailer, sail boat; *Brit.* sailing boat.

żak[1] *mp pl.* **żacy** *hist.* (= *student*) student, schoolboy.

żak[2] *mi Gen.* -a *pl.* -i (*sieć rybacka*) fishing net (*used to catch eels*).

żakard *mi tk.* **1.** (*tkanina*) Jacquard. **2.** (*maszyna*) Jacquard loom. **3.** (*część maszyny*) Jacquard.

żakardowy *a.* **1.** (= *żakardowa tkanina*) Jacquard. **2.** *tk.* (= *wyposażony w żakard*) Jacquard.

żakiet *mi* (*damski*) jacket; (*męski*) jacket (coat).

żakinada *f.* (= *juwenalia*) Students' Festival.

żako *n. indecl. orn.* (= *papuga szara*) grey parrot (*Psittacus erithacus*).

żakowski *a.* (= *uczniowski*) student, schoolboy; **żakowski figiel** schoolboy trick.

żal[1] *mi* **1.** (= *smutek*) sorrow; (*zwł. po stracie bliskiej osoby*) grief (*z jakiegoś powodu* over *l.* at sth); **pogrążyć się w żalu** grieve, mourn, be sorrowful, be grief-stricken; **usychać z żalu** be dying from sorrow; **serce mi pęka z żalu** my heart bleeds; **mam nadzieję, że nie masz do mnie żalu?** I hope you have no hard feelings toward me; **nie**

pomogą spóźnione żale it's no use crying over spilt milk; **z żalem zawiadamiamy, że...** we regret to inform that...; **z żalem** with deep regret; **zrobił to bez żalu** he did it without regret. **2.** (= *skrucha*) regret, remorse, contrition; **żal za grzechy** *rel.* penitence, repentance; **żal niedoskonały** (*z obawy przed karą*) attrition. **3.** (= *rozgoryczenie, uraza*) grivance (*do kogoś* against sb); **mieć do kogoś żal** bear sb a grudge.

żal² *adv.* (= *smutno*) **zrobiło mi się żal** I felt sorry; **czego oczy nie widzą, tego sercu nie żal** what the eye sees not, the heart craves not; **strasznie mi jej żal** I feel sorry for her, I pity her.

żale *pl. Gen.* **-ów 1.** (= *narzekanie, skargi*) grievances, lamentations, laments; **daremne żale** futile lamentations; **wylewać swoje żale** pour out one's troubles, air one's grievances. **2.** *teor.lit.* (*utwór liryczny*) lament; **gorzkie żale** *rel.* Lenten psalms.

żalić się *ipf.* complain, moan, air ones grievances (*na kogoś/coś* about sb/sth) (*przed kimś* to sb); lament (*na coś* sth); pour o.s. out, pour ones troubles out.

żaluzja *f.* **1.** blind, sunblind; **żaluzja pozioma** Venetian blind; **żaluzja zwijana** roller blind; (*listwowa*) jalousie; **podnosić/spuszczać żaluzje** roll the blinds up/down. **2.** (*zwijana krata w sklepach*) shutter. **3.** *muz.* (*w organach*) swell blind.

żałoba *f.* **1.** (= *rozpacz po czyjejś śmierci*) mourning, mournfulness, bereavement; **być pogrążonym w żałobie** be grief stricken/bereaved; **żałoba narodowa** national mourning. **2.** (= *okres po śmierci bliskich*) mourning; **głęboka żałoba** close mourning; **być w żałobie po kimś** mourn sb's death. **3.** (*strój*) mourning; **chodzić w żałobie** *l.* nosić żałobę wear mourning; **okryć się żałobą** go into mourning (*po kimś* for *l.* over sb).

żałobnie *adv.* mournfully, lugubriously, as a sign of mourning.

żałobnik¹ *mp pl.* **-cy 1.** (= *osoba w żałobie*) mourner. **2.** (= *pracownik zakładu pogrzebowego*) pallbearer.

żałobnik² *ma pl.* **-i** *ent.* (*motyl*) mourning cloak; *Br.* Camberwell beauty (*Nymphalis antiopa*).

żałobny *a.* mournful, lugubrious, plangent; **msza żałobna** requiem (mass); **nabożeństwo żałobne** funeral service, memorial service (*za kogoś* for sb); **pieśń żałobna** dirge, lament; **uroczystość żałobna** memorial ceremony; **żałobny strój wdowy** (widow's) weeds; **wstążka żałobna** mourning ribbon; **kondukt żałobny** funeral procession; **marsz żałobny** funeral march.

żałosny *a.* **1.** (= *przepełniony żalem, smutny*) doleful, sad, woeful; (*o głosie, spojrzeniu, wyglądzie*) miserable, plaintive, forlorn; **żałosne zawodzenia** lamentations; **żałosny płacz** lament; **żałosna mina** miserable look. **2.** (= *nędzny, wzbudzający litość*) pathetic, abject, piteous, pitiable, pitiful; (*o sumie, rozmiarach*) measly; (*o kondycji czegoś*) lamentable; **żałosny wygląd** pathetic look; **żałosny poziom sztuki** poor *l.* pa-

thetic condition of art; **w żałosny sposób** deplorably.

żałość *f. lit.* grief, sorrow, dolefulness.

żałośnie *adv.* **1.** (= *smutno, z żalem*) plaintively, dolefully, sadly, woefully, abjectly, miserably, lamentably; **żałośnie się skarżyć** complain dolefully; **żałośnie skomleć** whine piteously. **2.** (= *wzbudzając współczucie*) pathetically, abjectly, pitiful, dolefully; **żałośnie wyglądać** look miserable.

żałować *ipf.* **1.** (= *odczuwać żal*) regret (*czegoś* sth), be sorry (*czegoś* for sth); (*kogoś, czyjegoś odejścia*) moan, mourn (*kogoś* for sb); **żałuję, że nie wiedziałam** I regret *l.* I am sorry that I didn't know; **żałować, że się coś zrobiło** regret doing sth; **nie czas żałować róż, gdy płoną lasy** it's no use crying over spilt milk; **będziesz (tego) żałować** you'll be sorry (for that); **gorzko żałować** regret bitterly; **nie żałować** have *l.* feel no regrets. **2.** (= *odczuwać skruchę*) (*czynów, grzechów*) repent (*czegoś* (doing) sth/of sth) rue, regret (*czegoś* sth); **żałować za grzechy** repent of one's sins; **żałować swojej wypowiedzi** regret saying *l.* having said sth. **3.** (= *litować się, współczuć*) pity (*kogoś* sb) feel sorry (*kogoś* for sb). **4.** (= *skąpić*) stint, pinch (*czegoś* on sth); grudge, begrudge (*komuś czegoś* sb sth); **żałować na coś pieniędzy** stint money on sth; **wszystkiego sobie żałować** stint o.s. on everything; **nie żałować sobie** spoil o.s., indulge o.s.; **nie żałować wysiłków** spare no efforts. **5.** (*przy odmowie*) regret, be sorry; **żałuję, ale...** I regret but...; I'm sorry but...; **żałuję, że nie mogę ci pomóc** I wish I could help you, if only I could help you.

żandarm *mp wojsk.* **1.** military policeman. **2.** (*we Francji i krajach francuskojęzycznych*) gendarme.

żandarmeria *f. Gen.* **-ii** *hist.* gendarmerie; **żandarmeria wojskowa** military police, MP; **oddział żandarmerii wojskowej** provost guard; **komendant żandarmerii wojskowej** provost marshall.

żar *mi* **1.** (= *coś dającego ciepło*) heat, glow; (*w kominku*) glowing embers; **biały żar** white heat; **żar bucha z czegoś** sth glows with heat. **2.** (= *upał, gorąco*) heat, swelter, fever; **żar się z nieba leje** it's scorching. **3.** (= *żarliwość, zapał*) ardor, fervor, fire; **żar namiętności** flame of passion.

żarcie *n.* **1.** (= *pokarm dla zwierząt*) fodder, feeding stuff; **żarcie dla psów** dog food. **2.** (= *liche jedzenie*) chow, eats, grub, scoff. **3.** *pot.* (= *jedzenie, zwł. obfite*) **chińskie żarcie** chinky; **wielkie żarcie** big chow-down.

żarcik *mi* joke, trick; **niewinny żarcik** innocent little joke.

żargon *mi jęz.* jargon, argot; (*specjalistyczny*) lingo; (*zawodowy, klasowy*) patter; **żargon urzędowy** gobbledygook; **mówić żargonem** jargon, jargonize, use jargon/slang; **żargon przestępczy/studencki** criminal/student slang; **żargon prawniczy** legalese, legal jargon; **żargon dziennikarski** journalese; **żargon techniczny** technobabble.

żargonowy *a.* jargony, slangy; **żargonowe słowo/opis** jargony word/description.

żarliwie *adv.* earnestly, passionately, fervently; **modlić się żarliwie** pray passionately; **żarliwie kogoś bronić** support sb wholeheartedly.

żarliwość *f.* ardor, fervency, zeal, earnestness; **mówił z wielką żarliwością** he spoke with great earnestness.

żarliwy *a.* **1.** (= *gorliwy, fanatyczny, zapalony*) ardent, fervent, earnest, zealous, passionate; **żarliwy obrońca** staunch supporter. **2.** (= *pełen żarliwości*) passionate; (*o mowie, obronie*) spirited, impassioned; (*o romansie, scenie miłosnej*) torrid; **żarliwa modlitwa** impassioned prayer.

żarłacz *ma icht.* shark; **żarłacz biały (ludojad)** great white shark (*Carcharodon carcharias*); **żarłacz błękitny** blue shark (*Prionace glauca*); **żarłacz szary** tope (*Galeorhinus galeus*); **żarłacz tygrysi** tiger shark (*Galeocerdo cuvieri*).

żarło *n.* *Gen.pl.* **-reł** *pot.* (= *jedzenie*) grub, chow-down, chow, bite.

żarłocznie *adv.* gluttonously, greedily, voraciously, ravenously; **jeść żarłocznie** wolf down one's food.

żarłoczność *f.* voraciousness, gluttony, greed; *pat.* polyphagia; **napad żarłoczności** (*zwł. u osoby dotkniętej bulimią*) binge.

żarłoczny *a.* voracious, ravenous, gluttonous, greedy; *pat.* polyphagous.

żarłok *mp pl.* **-i** glutton, gourmandizer.

żarna *pl.* *Gen.* **żaren** *l.* **żarn** quern, hand-mill; **kamień do żaren** quern-stone; **mleć zboże w (na) żarnach** grind corn in the quern.

żarnowiec *mi* **-wc-** *Gen.* **-a** *bot.* **żarnowiec miotlasty** broom (*Sarothamnus scoparius*).

żaroodporność *f.* heat resistance.

żaroodporny *a.* heat-resistant, ovenproof, heat-proof; **szkło żaroodporne** flameproof glass, Pyrex; **naczynia żaroodporne** ovenware; **żaroodporne naczynie do zapiekanek** casserole.

żarowy *a.* incandescent; **lampa żarowa** incandescent lamp; **żarowe oświetlenie** incandescent light.

żarówka *f.* *Gen.pl.* **-ek** (light) bulb; **mleczna, matowa żarówka** milky bulb; **żarówka halogenowa** halogen bulb; **żarówka błyskowa** flashbulb; **przepalona żarówka** burnt bulb.

żart *mi* joke; **żart słowny** jest; (= *gra słów*) pun; **stroić sobie żarty z kogoś** pull sb's leg, play a joke *l.* prank *l.* trick *l.* hoax on sb; **zrobić coś dla żartu** do sth for fun *l.* for a joke *l.* for sport *l.* for banter; **głupie żarty** silly jokes; **niesmaczny, nieprzyzwoity żart** dirty joke; **złośliwy żart** vicious joke; **powiedzieć coś żartem** say sth tongue-in-cheek; **obrócić coś w żart** make sth into a joke, make a joke of sth, treat sth as a joke; **zakrawać na żart** verge on the ridiculous; **znać się na żartach** know how to take a joke; **zrozumieć żart** see the joke; **żarty się kogoś trzymają** sb is full of jest *l.* a joker; **żarty na bok** joking apart *l.* aside, all kidding aside; **nie na żarty** seriously; **to nie żarty** that's no laughing matter, it's no joke; **wolne żarty** you are joking, I suppose; **być przedmiotem żartów** be a jest *l.* a figure of fun *l.* the laughing stock; **skory do żartów** jocose, jocular; **pół żartem, pół serio** half in jest half serious; **z przeziębieniem nie ma żartów** you shouldn't take chances

with a chill; **w żartach** in fun, in play, jestingly, jokingly; **dobry żart tynfa wart** there's nothing like a good joke.

żartobliwie *adv.* facetiously, jocosely, jocularly, playfully, joshingly; **żartobliwie komuś dokuczać** josh sb.

żartobliwy *a.* humorous, playful, facetious, tongue-in-cheek; (*o uwadze*) jocular, sportive; **żartobliwe powiedzonko** a funny saying; **żartobliwa propozycja** a tongue-in-cheek proposal.

żartować *ipf.* **1.** (= *dowcipkować*) joke, jest, banter, fool (around), kid; **żartować z kogoś/czegoś** make fun of sb/sth, poke fun at sb, triffle with sb/sth, tease sb, jest about sb/sth; **żartować sobie z kogoś** tease sb, poke fun at sb; **nie żartujesz?** no kidding?; **nie należy z tego żartować** these things aren't to be trifled with; **chyba żartujesz** you must be joking *l.* kidding, you're kidding *l.* joking, you don't mean it; **ja tylko żartowałem** I was only kidding *l.* joking. **2.** *zawsze z przeczeniem* (= *być surowym, mówić poważnie*) **on nie żartuje** he means business; he is serious.

żartowniś *mp Gen.pl.* **-ów** jester, josher, kidder, wag, joker; **niezły z ciebie żartowniś** you are such a joker.

żarzyć się *ipf.* **1.** (= *tlić się, palić się bez płomienia*) incandesce, glow. **2.** (= *błyszczeć, jarzyć się*) glow, shine.

żąć *ipf.* **żnę żniesz, żnij** cut, reap, mow.

żądać *ipf.* demand, require (*czegoś od kogoś* sth from *l.* of sb); claim; insist (*czegoś* on sth); **żądać, żeby ktoś coś zrobił** demand *l.* insist that sb do sth; **żądać satysfakcji** demand satisfaction from sb; **żądać od kogoś odpowiedzi** press sb for an answer; **żądać wyjaśnień od kogoś** call *l.* bring sb into account; **żądać odszkodowania** claim damages; **żądać zwrotu** (*pieniędzy, podadków*) reclaim, claim.

żądanie *n.* demand, claim (*czegoś* for sth) requirement; **stawiać, spełniać żądania** make, satisfy demands; **wygórowane żądania** toll order; **pożyczka na żądanie** *bank* callable loan; **żądanie odszkodowania** claim for damages; **żądania płacowe** wage claims; **na własne żądanie** at one's own will *l.* request; **przystanek na żądanie** request stop.

żądlić *ipf.* sting.

żądło *n.* *Gen.pl.* **-deł 1.** (*u owada*) sting; **żądło osy/pszczoły** wasp/bee sting; *pot.* (*u węża*) fang. **2.** (= *dotkliwe doznanie uczucia*) sting, pain, anguish; **żądło nienawiści/zazdrości/gniewu** sting of hatred/envy/rage.

żądłówka *f.* *Gen.pl.* **-ek** *ent.* aculeate insect.

żądny *a.* desirous (*czegoś* of sth) greedy, eager (*czegoś* for sth); **żądny sławy** eager for recognition; **żądny władzy, pieniędzy** greedy for power, money; **żądny przygód** adventurous; **żądny krwi** bloodthirsty.

żądza *f.* **1.** (= *pragnienie*) *uj.* craving, greed, lust (*czegoś* for sth) hankering (*czegoś* after sth); **żądza bogactwa, władzy** greed *l.* lust for wealth, power; **żądza krwi** blood lust; avidity, eagerness; **żądza wiedzy** eagerness to learn; **żądza przygód** adventurousness. **2.** (= *pożądanie fizyczne*) lust, (sexual) desire; **patrzeć na kogoś z pożądaniem** look at sb with lust.

żbik *ma zool.* wildcat (*Felis silvestris*).

że[1] *conj.* **1.** (*wprowadza zdanie podrzędne rozwijające treść*) that; **ona mówi, że on nie przyjdzie** she says (that) he won't come; **wiem, że to niemożliwe** I know (that) it's impossible. **2.** (*wprowadza zdanie podrzędne wyrażające przyczynę, uzasadnienie*) as, because, for; **nie zrobię tego dlatego, że już ci nie wierzę** I won't do it because I don't trust you anymore. **3.** (*wprowadza zdanie podrzędne wyrażające skutek*) so... that; **był tak zmęczony, że ledwie szedł** he was so tired that he could hardly walk. **4.** (*w związkach wyrazowych*) **mimo że** *l.* **tyle że** despite the fact that, in spite of the fact that; **nadal był zdrów, tyle że się postarzał** he was still in good health, except (for the fact) that he grew old.

że[2] *particle* **1.** (*rozpoczyna zdanie*) **że też o tym nie wiedziałam!** I wish I had known; **że już nie wspomnę...** let alone...; **że tak powiem** so to say, so to speak; **że już nie wspomnę o X** never mind X, not to mention X. **2.** (*w składzie wyrażeń o charakterze spójnikowym lub modalnym*) although, nevertheless; **mimo że był chory, poszedł do szkoły** although he was sick he went to school, he was sick, nevertheless he went to school; **omalże** almost; **tylko że** only. **3.** (*wyraża zniecierpliwienie, zdziwienie*) **wejdźże** do come in; **przestańże** I wish you would stop.

żeberka *pl. Gen.* **-rek** *kulin.* spare ribs; **żeberka pieczone/duszone** roast/stewed ribs; **żeberka z kapustą** ribs with sauerkraut.

żeberko *n. Gen.pl.* **-rek 1.** (*kość*) rib; *kulin.* rib. **2.** *bud.* (*w sklepieniach*) lierne. **3.** *techn.* rib, fin; **żeberko kaloryfera** radiator fin. **4.** *bot.* (*np. liścia*) rib.

żeberkowy *a. techn.* finned, gilled; **chłodnica żeberkowa** ribbed *l.* gilled cooler; **żeberkowy kaloryfer** fin radiators; **cylinder żeberkowy** gilled cylinder.

żebractwo *n.* **1.** (= *żebranie*) begging, beggary. **2.** (= *żebracy*) beggars, vagrancy, mendicants.

żebraczka *f. Gen.pl.* **-ek** zob. **żebrak.**

żebraczy *a.* beggar's, beggarly, mendicant; **żebraczy kij** *przen.* beggary; **żebracza pensja** beggar's pay; **zakon żebraczy** *rel.* mendicant order.

żebrać *ipf.* **-brzę -brzesz 1.** (= *prosić o jałmużnę*) beg (one's bread), go begging, seek charity *l.* alms, ask for money. **2.** (= *błagać*) beg, ask (*o coś* for sth); **żebrać o życie, o przebaczenie** beg for life, forgiveness.

żebrak *mp pl.* **-cy** *l.* **-ki** beggar, pauper, medincant.

żebranina *f.* **1.** (= *proszenie o jałmużnę*) begging (one's bread), seeking charity *l.* alms. **2.** (= *błaganie*) asking, begging (*o coś* for sth).

żebro *n. Gen.pl.* **żeber 1.** (*kość*) rib; **żebro prawdziwe** *anat.* true rib; **żebro wolne** *l.* **rzekome** *anat.* false rib; **można komuś policzyć żebra** sb is all skin and bone, sb is a bag of bones; **porachować, policzyć komuś żebra** beat the living daylights out of sb; **zajechać komuś pod (piąte) żebro**

cut sb to the quick. **2.** *bud.* rib, fillet, groin. **3.** *techn.* rib, fin. **4.** *geol.* mullion.

żebrować *ipf. techn., bud.* rib, groin; **żebrowane sklepienie** groined vault.

żebrowanie *n.* **1.** *bud.* ribbing; (*sklepienia*) groin. **2.** *techn.* ribbing; **żebrowanie kadłuba statku** ribbing *l.* gilling of a ship hull.

żebrowy *a.* **1.** *anat.* rib; **kość żebrowa** rib cage. **2.** *bud.* ribbed, finned, groined; **sklepienie żebrowe** groined *l.* ribbed vault. **3.** *techn.* finned, ribbed.

żebry *pl. Gen.* **-ów** *przest.* beggary; **chodzić na żebry** go (a-)begging, seek alms, beg one's bread.

żeby[1] *conj.* **1.** (*wprowadza zdanie podrzędne wyrażające cel*) to, so as to, in order to; **żeby nie...** (so as) not to...; **spotkali się, żeby porozmawiać** they met to talk; **usunięto wszystkich, żeby zapobiec panice** everyone was removed *l.* so as to *l.* in order to prevent panic. **2.** (*wyraża konsekwencję, warunek*) to; **on jest zbyt taktowny, żeby to zrobić** he is too polite to do it; **zrobiliby wszystko, żeby tylko być razem** they would do everything to be together. **3.** (*rozwijające, dopełniające treść*) **chciał, żebyśmy już sobie poszli** he wanted us to leave; **trzeba, żeby się wziął do pracy** he ought to get down to work; **zażądał/nalegał, żebyśmy zostali** he demanded/insisted that we (should) stay. **4.** (= *gdyby*) if; **żebyś wiedziała, co ludzie mówią** if only you knew what they say; **żeby nie on/ona...** if it weren't for him/her...; **nie, żebym miał coś przeciwko temu** not that I mind. **5.** (= *choćby*) if; **chyba żeby** unless; **żeby się świat walił** (even) if the world fell apart; **żebym miał paść trupem** if it killed me, if I were to fall dead.

żeby[2] *particle* **1.** (= *oby*) may; **żeby go diabli wzięli** may he go to hell, let him go to hell; **żebyśmy tylko zdrowi byli** let us all stay in good health; **żeby go pokręciło** bad luck to him. **2.** (*wyraża nacisk l. żądanie*) **a żebyś wiedział** (you) bet your life; **żeby mi tu było cicho**! I demand silence!

żegadło *n. Gen.pl.* **-deł 1.** pig-sticker. **2.** *chir.* cautery.

żeglarski *a.* nautical, yachting; (= *odbywający podróże morskie*) seafaring, seaman's; **żeglarskie regaty** yacht race, regatta; **klub żeglarski** yachting club; **naród żeglarski** seafaring nation.

żeglarstwo *n.* sailing, seafaring; **uprawiać żeglarstwo** sail; **żeglarstwo jachtowe** yachting.

żeglarz *mp* sailor, seaman, seafarer, yachtsman. *– ma ent.* (*motyl*) scarce swallowtail (*Iphiclides podalirius*).

żeglować *ipf.* **1.** (= *prowadzić statek*) sail, navigate; (= *pływać na statku*) sail, voyage; **żeglować po morzu** sail across the sea; **żeglować po Internecie** *pot.* surf the Internet. **2.** (*o statku, łodzi*) sail. **3.** (= *przemieszczać się w powietrzu*) sail.

żeglowność *f.* (*drogi wodnej*) navigability.

żeglowny *a.* navigable; **żeglowna rzeka** a navigable river; **kanał żeglowny** shipway, waterway, ship canal.

żegluga *f.* **1.** (= *żeglowanie*) navigation, sailing, seafaring; (= *transport wodny*) shipping (trade); **żegluga śródlądowa** inland navigation; **żegluga morska** sea navigation; **żegluga rzeczna** river navigation; **żegluga przybrzeżna** coasting; **żegluga kabotażowa** cabotage; **żegluga towarowa** *l.* handlowa shipping industry; **żegluga pasażerska** passenger navigation; **żegluga powietrzna** aerial navigation; **nadający się do żeglugi** (*o drodze wodnej*) navigable; (*o statku*) seaworthy. **2.** (= *praca na statku*) seafaring.

żeglugowy *a.* shipping, navigation; **przepisy żeglugowe** navigation laws.

żegnać *ipf.* **1.** (*przu pożegnaniu*) say goodbye (*kogoś/coś* to sb/sth); **żegnać kogoś** bid sb farewell *l.* goodbye; **żegnać jakieś miejsce** say goodbye to a place, quit a place; **żegnajcie!** goodbye!, farewell!; **żegnam pana** *iron.* I won't keep you any longer. **2.** (= *błogosławić*) bless (*kogoś* sb) make a sign of the cross (*kogoś* over sb). ~ **się** *ipf.* **1.** (*przy pożegnaniu*) say goodbye (*z kimś* to sb); **żegnać się z kimś** bid sb farewell *l.* goodbye; **żegnać się z życiem** say goodbye to one's life. **2.** (= *robić znak krzyża*) cross onself, make the sign *l.* a sign of the cross.

żel *mi chem.* gel, jelly; **żel do układania włosów** styling gel; **żel pod prysznic** shower gel; **przechodzić w żel** gelatinize.

żelastwo *n.* scrap-iron.

żelatyna *f.* gelatin; **żelatyna w proszku** powdered gelatin; **żelatyna wybuchowa** blasting gelatin.

żelazawy *a. chem.* ferrous.

żelazica *f. pat.* siderosis.

żelazisty *a.* irony; *chem.* ferruginous, chalybeate; **meteoryt żelazisty** iron meteorite, siderite.

żelazko *n. Gen.pl.* -zek iron; **żelazko na duszę** flat iron, box iron; **żelazko z nawilżaczem** steam iron; **żelazko bezprzewodowe** cordless iron; *techn.* (*do spoinowania*) jointer.

żelazny *a.* **1.** (= *zawierający żelazo*) iron; **ruda żelazna** iron ore. **2.** (= *zrobiony z żelaza*) iron; **wyroby żelazne** ironware, ironmongery, hardware; **żelazna kurtyna** *techn.* fire-proof curtain; *polit., hist.* the Iron Curtain; **sklep żelazny** hardware store, ironmonger's. **3.** *przen.* (= *stały*) iron; (*o regule*) hard and fast; (*o woli, determinacji*) steely; (*o wymówce, alibi*) cast-iron; **żelazny rygor** iron discipline; **żelazna logika** iron logic; **żelazna porcja** iron ration; **żelazny kapitał** reserve fund; **żelazny repertuar (teatru)** stock (of a theater); **żelazna zasada** iron-clad principle; **żelazny zapas** stockpile; **żelazne płuco** *med.* iron lung; **list żelazny** *hist.* safe conduct; **za żelazną kurtyną** *przen.* behind the iron curtain. **4.** (= *mocny*) iron; **żelazne mięśnie** muscles made of steel; **żelazne nerwy** nerves made of steel; **rządzić żelazną ręką** rule with a rod of iron, rule with a heave *l.* iron hand; **żelazna wola** iron will.

żelazo *n.* **1.** *chem.* (*pierwiastek*) iron; **ruda żelaza** *geol.* iron ore; **tlenek żelaza** iron oxide. **2.** (*stop*) iron; **hartować żelazo** harden the steel; **żelazo lane** cast iron; **żelazo krzyżowe** X-iron; **żelazo kute** wrought iron; **stop żelaza** ferrous alloy;

epoka żelaza *archeol.* the Iron Age; **ktoś jest jak z żelaza** sb is iron-cast; **człowiek z żelaza** iron man, man of iron; **huta żelaza** steel mill; **kuć żelazo, póki gorące** strike while the iron is hot. **3.** *lit.* (= *zbroja*) armour, steel. **4.** (= *narzędzia żelazne*) iron; **żelaza włazowe** climbing-irons.

żelazobeton *mi techn.* ferroconcrete, reinforced concrete.

żelazobetonowy *a. techn.* ferroconcrete, made of reinforced concrete.

żelazochrom *mi techn.* ferrochromium.

żelazocyjanek *mi* -nk- *chem.* ferrocyanide; **żelazocyjanek potasu** potassium ferrocyanide.

żelazodajny *a.* ferruginous.

żelazofosfor *mi techn.* ferro-phosphorus.

żelazokoks *mi techn.* ferrocoke.

żelazokrzem *mi techn.* ferro-silicon.

żelazomangan *mi techn.* ferro-manganese.

żelazomolibden *mi techn.* ferro-molybdenum.

żelazonośny *a.* ferriferous.

żelazopodobny *a.* ironlike.

żelazoryt *mi techn.* iron engraving.

żelazorytnictwo *n. sztuka* iron engraving.

żelazostop *mi techn.* ferro-alloy.

żelazowanad *mi techn.* ferro-vanadium.

żelazowiec *mi* -wc- *Gen.* -a *chem.* **żelazowce** iron group.

żalazowolfram *mi techn.* ferro-tungsten.

żelazowy *a. chem.* ferric; **związki żelazowe** ferric compounds; **błękit żelazowy** iron blue.

żelbet *mi techn.* reinforced concrete.

żelbetowy *a. techn.* (made of) reinforced concrete.

żeleźniak *mi Gen.* -a (= *piecyk*) cast iron stove.

żeliwny *a.* cast-iron; **żeliwna patelnia** cast-iron (frying) pan.

żeliwo *n. techn.* cast-iron; **białe żeliwo** white cast-iron.

żenada *f.* embarrassment; **bez żenady** unceremoniously.

żeneta *f. zool.* genet (*Genetta*).

żeniaczka *f. Gen.pl.* -ek *pot.* marriage, matrimony; **nie w głowie mu żeniaczka** he's not the marrying kind.

żenić *ipf.* marry (*kogoś z kimś* sb to sb). ~ **się** *ipf.* marry (*z kimś* sb); **żenić się ponownie** remarry; **nie żenić się** stay single.

żenować *ipf.* (= *krępować*) embarrass, mortify (*kogoś* sb), make sb uncomfortable *l.* self-conscious.

żenująco *adv.* embarrassingly, painfully.

żenujący *a.* embarrassing, disconcerting, mortifying; **żenująca uwaga** discomfiting remark.

żeński *a.* **1.** (*dotyczący kobiet*) female; **żeńska szkoła** girl's school; **rodzaj żeński** *jęz.* feminine; **rym żeński** *teor.lit.* feminine rhyme. **2.** *biol.* female; **osobniki żeńskie** females; **żeńskie komórki płciowe** female reproductive cells; **kwiat żeński** *bot.* female flower.

żeńszeniowy *a.* ginseng; **kosmetyki żeńszeniowe** ginseng cosmetics.

żeń-szeń *mi Gen.* -a *bot.* ginseng (*Panax ginseng*); **korzeń żeń-szenia** ginseng (root).

żer *mi* **1.** (= *pożeranie*) feeding. **2.** (= *pożywie-nie zwierząt*) food, fodder. **3.** (= *łup, pastwa*) prey; **być wydanym na żer czegoś** fall prey to sth.

żerdka *f. Gen.pl.* **-ek** (= *drążek*) pole; (*kanarka, papugi*) perch.

żerdź *f. pl.* **-dzie** (*dla kur*) perch; (*drąg*) pole; **żerdź wiertnicza** *techn.* drill stem, adjusting rod.

żeremie *n. Gen.pl.* **-i** beaver lodge.

żerny *a.* **komórka żerna** *biol.* phagocyte.

żerować *ipf.* **1.** (*o dzikich zwierzętach*) feed, raven. **2.** (*o ludziach*) (= *wykorzystywać*) prey, batten (*na czymś* on *l.* upon sth); **żerować na czyjejś naiwności, na ludzkim nieszczęściu** prey upon *l.* take advantage of sb's naivety, misfortune.

żerowisko *n.* feeding ground; (*dzikich zwierząt*) haunt.

żeton *mi* **1.** (= *szton*) counter; (*do automatu*) token; (*w ruletce*) jetton; (*w grach hazardowych*) chip. **2.** (= *odznaka*) badge.

żętyca *f.* (= *serwatka*) whey of ewe's milk.

żgać *ipf.*, **żgnąć** *pf.* **-ij** prod, poke (*kogoś/coś czymś* sb/sth with sth); jab (*kogoś czymś* sth at sb); **żgać kogoś nożem** stab sb with a knife.

żigolak *mp pl.* **-cy** *l.* **-ki** *pog.* = **żigolo** 2.

żigolo *mp pl.* **-owie** *Gen.* **-ów** **1.** (= *fordanser*) gigolo. **2.** *pog.* gigolo, lady's man, lady killer, toy boy.

żleb *mi* couloir, gully.

żłobek *mi* **-bk-** *Gen.* **-a** **1.** (*dla dzieci*) day care center; *Br.* (day) nursery, crèche. **2.** (= *rowek*) groove; *geol.* rill, rillet; *techn.* furrow; (*pionowy*) flute. **3.** (= *mały żłób*) trough.

żłobić *ipf.* **żłób** **1.** (= *drążyć*) furrow, gouge, flute, channel; *geol.* erode, chatter. **2.** (= *wycinać rowki*) groove, rout, furrow; (*drewno*) trench.

żłobienie *n.* (= *rowek*) groove, furrow, gouge; *geol.* erosion.

żłobkować *ipf.* groove, rabbet, gouge; *bud.* (*kolumnę*) flute.

żłobkowanie *n.* grooving, rabbeting, gouging, fluting, channeling.

żłopać *ipf.* **-pię -piesz** (= *łapczywie pić*) guzzle, swig, lap; (*piwo*) swill.

żłób *mi* **-o-** *Gen.* **-u** **1.** (= *koryto*) trough, manger, crib. **2.** *pot.* (= *źródło korzyści*) trough; **dorwać się do żłobu** get one's snout in the trough; **odsunąć kogoś od żłobu** kick sb out of power. **3.** (= *zagłębienie, jar*) gully, trough. – *mp* **-o-** *Gen.* **-a** *pl.* **-y** *pot.* (= *głupi, nieokrzesany człowiek*) blockhead.

żłóbek *mi* **-bk-** *Gen.* **-a** **1.** (= *mały żłób*) trough, manger, crib. **2.** (*Chrystusa*) *rel.* crèche; *Br.* crib. **3.** *przest.* = **żłobek** 1.

żmija *f. Gen.* **żmii** **1.** *zool.* viper, adder (*rodzina* **Viperidea**); **żmija zygzakowata** adder (*Vipera berus*); **żmija sykliwa** puff adder (*Bitis arietans*); **żmija żebrowana** asp (*Vipera aspis*); **jad żmii** viper's venom. **2.** (= *człowiek podstępny*) viper, serpent; **wyhodować żmiję na własnym łonie** nourish a viper in one's bossom.

żmijka *f. Gen.pl.* **-ek** **1.** *emf. zob.* **żmija**. **2.** *zool.* lesser weever (*Trachinus vipera*). **3.** (*do przetykania kanalizacji*) go-devil.

żmijowato *adv.* in a snake-like fashion, like a serpent.

żmijowaty *a.* viperish, viperine, viperous, snake-like.

żmijowy *a. zool.* viper's, viperine; **żmijowy jad** viper's venom; **maść żmijowa** viper ointment.

żmudnie *adv.* arduously, laboriously, strenuously, painfully.

żmudny *a.* (= *uciążliwy, trudny*) arduous, laborious, strenuous; **żmudna dłubanina** sweaty *l.* uphill job.

Żmudzin *mp*, **Żmudzinka** *f. Gen.pl.* **-ek** Samogitian.

żmudzki, żmudziński *a.* Samogitian.

Żmudź *f. hist., geogr.* Samogitia (*part of Lithuania*).

żniwa *pl. Gen.* **-w** harvest; **czas żniw** harvesting; **małe żniwa** small harvest.

żniwiarka *f. Gen.pl.* **-ek** **1.** *techn.* harvester, reaper, reaping machine. **2.** (*pracownica*) harvester, reaper.

żniwiarkomłocarnia *f. Gen.pl.* **-i** *techn.* reaper-thresher.

żniwiarz *mp* reaper, harvester.

żniwny *a.* harvest, harvesting.

żniwo *n.* **1.** *roln.* harvest. **2.** *przen.* toll, harvest; **śmierć zbierała swoje żniwo** death took its toll; **zebrać gorzkie żniwo** reap a bitter harvest.

żołądek *mi* **-dk-** *Gen.* **-a** *anat.* stomach; **ból żołądka** stomach ache; **strusi żołądek** digestion of an ostrich; **rozstrój żołądka** *pat.* upset stomach; **z pustym żołądkiem** on an empty stomach; **mieć wrażliwy żołądek** have a delicate stomach; **żołądek podchodzi komuś do gardła** sb's stomach is churning; **przez żołądek do serca mężczyzny** the way to a man's heart is through his stomach; **mieć płukanie żołądka** have one's stomach pumped; **wrzód żołądka** *pat.* gastric *l.* stomach ulcer; **nieżyt żołądka** *pat.* gastritis.

żołądkować się *ipf. pot.* be ratty/snapish, fret, fume.

żołądkowiec *mp* **-wc-** *pl.* **-y** *pot.* weak-stomached person.

żołądkowy *a.* stomach, stomachic, gastric; **sok żołądkowy** gastric juice; **pompa żołądkowa** stomach pomp; **naczynia żołądkowe** stomachic vessels.

żołądź *f.* **-ę-** *pl.* **-e** **1.** *bot.* acorn. **2.** *anat.* glans (penis). **3.** *karty* (= *trefl*) clubs.

żołd *mi* pay; **być na czyimś żołdzie** be in the pay of sb.

żołdacki *a.* crude military; **żołdacka samowola** soldier's lawlessness.

żołdactwo *n. pog.* the soldiery.

żołdak *mp pl.* **-cy** *l.* **-ki** *pog.* brutal *l.* marauding soldier.

żołędny *a. karty* (= *treflowy*) of clubs.

żołędziowy *a.* acorn; **lampa żołędziowa** *radio* acorn tube.

żołna *f. orn.* bee-eater (*Merops*).

żołnierski *a.* military, soldier's, soldierly, martial; **żołnierski mundur** soldiers uniform; **po żoł-niersku** soldier-fashion.

żołnierz *mp* soldier, serviceman; *poet.* war-rior; **żołnierz zawodowy/najemny** regular/merce-nary soldier; **zginąć śmiercią żołnierza** die a sol-dier's death; **Grób Nieznanego Żołnierza** the Tomb of the Unknown Warrior *l.* Soldier; (*szere-gowy*) man; **żołnierz kawalerii** trooper; **żołnierz ciężkozbrojny** man-at-arms; **żołnierz piechoty morskiej** marine; **żołnierz piechoty** foot soldier, infantryman; **żołnierze** (*wojsko*) the troops, the military; **żołnierze szeregowi** the ranks.

żołnierzyk *mp pl.* **-i** young soldier. – *mi Gen.* **-a** (*figurka*) (**ołowiany**) **żołnierzyk** toy soldier.

żona *f.* wife; **pojął ją za żonę** he took her to be his (wedded) wife; **rodzina żony** in-laws.

żonaty[1] *a.* married; **żonaty mężczyzna** mar-ried man; **ponownie żonaty** remarried.

żonaty[2] *mp* married man.

żongler *mp* (*artysta cyrkowy*) juggler.

żonglerka *f.* 1. (*sztuka żonglowania*) juggling, jugglery. 2. *Gen.pl.* **-ek** (*o kobiecie*) *zob.* **żongler**.

żonglować *ipf.* 1. (*w cyrku*) juggle. 2. (*posłu-giwać się czymś z wprawą*) juggle; **żonglować słowami** juggle with words.

żonkil *mi Gen.* **-a** *bot.* jonquil (*Narcissus jon-quilla*); daffodil (*Narcissus pseudonarcissus*).

żonkoś *mp Gen.pl.* **-siów** *żart. l. iron.* **młody żonkoś** young husband.

żonobójca *mp* uxoricide, murderer of one's wife.

żonobójstwo *n.* uxoricide, murder of one's wife.

żorżeta *f. tk.* georgette.

żółcić *ipf.* yellow, make *l.* paint *l.* stain (*sth*) yellow.

żółcień *mi Gen.* **-a** *bot.* curcuma (*Curcuma*). – *f. Gen.* **-i** *pl.* **-e** *chem.* (*pigment*) yellow pigment; **żółcień kadmowa/chromowa/neapolitańska** cad-mium/chrome/antimony yellow; **żółcień kanar-kowa** canary.

żółciopędny *a. med.* cholagogue; **zioła żółcio-pędne** cholagogue herbs.

żółciotwórczy *a.* biligenic.

żółciowy *a.* biliary; *pat.* bilious; **przewody żół-ciowe** *anat.* bile ducts; **woreczek** *l.* **pęcherzyk żółciowy** *anat.* gall bladder; **kamienie żółciowe** *med.* gallstones; **kamica żółciowa** *med.* cholelithiasis, development of gallstones; **kolka żółciowa** *med.* biliary colic.

żółć *f.* 1. *fizj.* bile, gall. 2. *przen.* (= *gniew, iry-tacja*) bitterness, gall, anger; **wylać całą żółć na kogoś** vent one's spleen on sb; **człowiek bez żółci** person of temperate disposition; **żółć się w nim burzyła** *l.* **żółć go zalewała** *pot.* his blood was boil-ing. 3. *pl.* **-e** (*kolor*) yellow.

żółknąć *ipf.* **-knij, -kł** *l.* **-knął -kła -kli** turn yel-low; **żółknąć z zazdrości** go green with envy.

żółtaczka *f. Gen.pl.* **-ek** *med.* jaundice; **żółtacz-ka wszczepienna** hepatitis B.

żółtaczkowy *a.* icteric.

żółtawoblady *a.* yellowish pale.

żółtawobrązowy *a.* yellowish brown.

żółtawobrunatny *a.* yellowish tawny.

żółtawoczerwony *a.* yellowish red.

żółtawoszary *a.* yellowish grey.

żółtawozielony *a.* yellowish green.

żółtawy *a.* yellowish, yellowy.

żółtek *mp* **-tk-** *pl.* **-i** *pog.* (*Chińczyk*) Chink, Chinky; (*Japończyk*) Jap; (*osoba z Dalekiego Wschodu*) gook.

żółtko *n. Gen.pl.* **-ek** yolk (of an egg).

żółtkowy *a.* yolky; *zool.* vitelline; **pęcherzyk żółtkowy** *zool.* yolk sac.

żółtlica *f. bot.* Frenchweed (*Galinsoga parvi-flora*).

żółtnica *f. bot.* **żółtnica pomarańczowa** osage orange (*Maclura pomifera*).

żółto *adv.* yellow; **pomalować coś na żółto** paint sth yellow; **ubrany na żółto** dressed in yel-low.

żółtobiały *a.* yellow white.

żółtobrzeżek *ma* **-żk-** *zool.* **pływak żółtobrzeżek** great diving beetle, predaceous diving beetle (*Dytiscus marginalis*).

żółtoczerwony *a.* yellow red.

żółtodziób *mp* **-o-** *l.* **-ó-** *pl.* **-y** *iron.* rookie, greenhorn.

żółtooki *a.* yellow-eyed.

żółtopióry *a.* yellow-feathered.

żółtoróżowy *a.* yellow pink.

żółtosiwy *a.* yellow grey.

żółtoskóry *a.* yellow-skinned.

żółtoszary *a.* yellow grey.

żółtość *f.* yellowness, yellow color.

żółtowłosy *a.* yellow-haired.

żółtozielony *a.* yellow green.

żółtoziem *mi roln.* loess.

żółty *a.* yellow; (*w sygnalizacji świetlnej*) am-ber; **ciałko żółte** *anat.* yellow body; **plamka żółta** *anat.* yellow spot, macula lutea; **żółta febra** *med.* yellow fever; **żółta rasa** *antrop.* yellow race; **żółte światło** *mot.* amber.

żółw *ma* **-wi-** *zool.* (*lądowy*) tortoise; (*morski, pot. t. jakikolwiek*) turtle; **iść jak żółw** walk at a snail's *l.* tortoise's pace.

żółwi *a.* tortoise's, turtle's; *zool., form.* testudi-nal, testudinary; (*o żółwiach morskich*) chen-ian; **iść żółwim krokiem** walk at a snail's *l.* tor-toise's pace; **żółwie tempo** snail's pace.

żółwiak *ma zool.* (= *żółw z rodziny Trionychi-dae*) softshell turtle.

żółwik *ma* small tortoise *l.* turtle.

żółwiowaty *a.* tortoise-like *l.* turtle-like.

żółwiowy *a.* tortoise, turtle; **zupa żółwiowa** *ku-lin.* turtle soup.

żrąco *adv.* caustically, mordantly, corrosively.

żrący *a.* 1. (*o substancjach chemicznych*) (= *gryzący, palący*) caustic, mordant, corrosive; **żrący kwas** caustic *l.* corrosive acid. 2. *przen.* (= *zjadliwy, złośliwy*) caustic, vitriolic.

żreć *ipf.* **żrę żresz, żryj, żarł** 1. (*o zwierzętach*) (= *jeść*) eat, feed. 2. (*o człowieku*) (= *pożerać*) gobble, wolf down. 3. (= *przeżerać, niszczyć*) eat away (*coś* at sth) eat (*coś* into sth). 4. (*o uczu-ciach, doznaniach*) consume, eat into; **żarła ją tę-sknota** she was being consumed by longing, longing was eating into her. **~ się** *ipf. pot.* (= *kłó-*

cić się) lead a cat-and-dog life (*z kimś* with sb), bicker *l.* haggle constantly (*z kimś o coś* with sb over sth).

żuaw *mp hist., wojsk.* Zouave.

żubr *ma zool.* European bison, wisent (*Bison bonasus*).

żubroń *ma hodowla* cross between wisent and domestic cow.

żubrowisko *n.* forest reserve allocated for the European bison (*a protected species*).

żubrówka *f. Gen.pl.* **-ek 1.** *bot.* (*trawa*) vanilla grass (*Hierochloe odorata*). **2.** (*wódka*) bison vodka (*scented with vanilla grass*).

żubrzątko *n. Gen.pl.* **-tek** (European) bison calf.

żubrzy *a.* (European) bison's; *form.* bisontine.

żubrzyca *f.* (European) bison cow.

żuchwa *f. anat.* (*zwł. u człowieka*) lower jaw; (*u innych kręgowców*) mandible, jawbone; *pot.* (*każda szczęka*) jaw.

żuchwowy *a.* mandibular.

żucie *n.* chewing, mastication; **guma do żucia** chewing gum.

żuć *ipf.* chew, masticate; **żuć w ustach przekleństwa** mutter curses.

żuk *ma* **1.** *zool.* (*chrząszcz*) dung beetle (*Geotrupes*). **2.** *pot.* (= *każdy chrząszcz*) beetle.

żul *mp Gen.pl.* **-i** *l.* **-ów** *pot.* (= *pijak, menel*) wino, drunk.

żulia *f. Gen.* **-ii** *pot.* winos, drunks.

żulik *mp pl.* **-i** *pot. zob.* **żul**.

żuławy *pl. Gen.* **-w** *geogr.* marshland.

żupa *f.* **1.** (*kopalnia*) mine; **żupa solna** salt mine. **2.** (*terytorium*) territory occupied by a clan (*under the leadership of a zupan*).

żupan *mi Gen.* **-a 1.** *strój, hist.* national dress of Polish nobility. **2.** (*naczelnik*) chieftain, zupan.

żur *mi* (*zupa*) traditional Polish soup made from fermented bread or rye flour.

żuraw *ma* **-wi-** *zool.* (*ptak*) crane (*Gruidae*). − *mi* **-wi-** *Gen.* **-a 1.** (*przy studni*) well sweep. **2.** (*dźwig*) crane, derrick; **żuraw portowy** harbor *l.* wharf crane. **3. zapuszczać żurawia** *żart.* crane (forward).

żurawi *a.* (*dotyczący ptaka*) crane's; (*w języku fachowym*) alectoridine.

żurawina *f. bot., kulin.* cranberry (*Vaccinium oxycoccus*).

żurawinowy *a.* cranberry.

żurek *mi* **-rk-** (*zupa*) *zob.* **żur**.

żurnal *mi Gen.* **-a** *l.* **-u** *Gen.pl.* **-i** *l.* **-ów** (*czasopismo*) fashion magazine.

żurnalista *mp*, **żurnalistka** *f. Gen.pl.* **-ek** journalist.

żurnalistyka *f.* journalism.

żużel *mi* **-żl-** *Gen.* **-a** *l.* **-u 1.** (*produkt procesów hutniczych*) cinders, clinker. **2.** (*tor wyścigowy*) cinder track, speedway track. **3.** *pot., sport* speedway.

żużlobeton *mi techn.* slag cement.

żużlobetonowy *a. techn.* slag cement; **cegła żużlobetonowa** cinder block; *Br.* breeze block.

żużlowiec *mp* **-wc-** *pl.* **-y** *sport* speedway racer.

żużlowy *a.* **1.** (= *z żużlu*) (of) cinder, (of) clinker, slag. **2.** *sport* speedway; **sport żużlowy** speedway; **tor żużlowy** cinder track, speedway track; **zawody żużlowe** speedway competition.

żwacz *mi Gen.* **-a 1.** *anat.* (*mięsień*) masseter. **2.** *anat.* (*komora żołądka przeżuwaczy*) rumen, paunch.

żwawo *adv.* (= *szybko*) briskly; (= *z werwą*) vigorously.

żwawość *f.* (= *szybkość*) briskness; (= *werwa*) vigorousness.

żwawy *a.* (= *szybki*) brisk; (= *pełen werwy*) vigorous.

żwir *mi* gravel.

żwirek *mi* grit.

żwirować *ipf.* gravel (*a path etc.*).

żwirowaty *a.* gravelly, gritty; **żwirowate dno** gritty bottom.

żwirowisko *n.* gravel heap.

żwirownia *f. Gen.pl.* **-i** (*kopalnia*) gravel pit.

żwirowy *a.* gravel; **żwirowa alejka** gravel path.

żwirówka *f. Gen.pl.* **-ek** gravelled road.

życica *f. bot.* darnel (*Lolium*).

życie *n.* **1.** (*stan organizmu*) life; **życie zwierząt/roślin/człowieka** animal/plant/human life; **życie płodowe** fetal life; **budzić się do życia** (*np. o roślinach, opowiadaniu*) come to life; **życie ledwie się w nim kołacze** *l.* nie pozostało mu wiele życia he is not long for this world. **2.** (= *istnienie, egzystencja*) life; **ciężkie/łatwe** *l.* **lekkie życie** hard/easy life; **warunki życia** living conditions; **dawać komuś miesiąc życia** (= *rokować*) give sb a month to live; **narażać życie** risk one's life; **z narażeniem życia** at the risk of one's life; **uratować komuś życie** save sb's life; **pierwszy raz w życiu** for the first time in one's life; **życie intymne** love life; **życie osobiste** *l.* **prywatne** private life; **życie naukowe** scientific life; **życie kulturalne** cultural life; **życie seksualne** sexual life; **jedwabne życie** charmed life *l.* existence, the good life; **kawał życia** plenty of time (*of one's life*); **wstępować na nową drogę życia** embark on a new career; **jesień życia** the autumn of one's life; **wiosna życia** the spring of one's life; **ubezpieczenie na życie** life insurance; **życie wieczne** *rel.* eternal life; **życie pozagrobowe** *rel.* afterlife; **życie po śmierci** life after death; **życie na pełnych obrotach** life in the fast lane; **życie nocne** nightlife; **życie to nie bajka** life is not a bed of roses; **sprawa życia i śmierci** a matter of life and death; **pan życia i śmierci** master of life and death; **szkoła życia** school of life; **walka na śmierć i życie** life-and-death struggle, mortal combat; **historia wzięta z życia** true-life story; **do końca życia** as long as I live; **póki życia** as long as life endures; **zbliżać się do kresu życia** be nearing one's end; **za życia** in *l.* during one's lifetime; **patrzeć serio na życie** treat one's life seriously; **być nie do życia** be lifeless, be dog-tired; **dać znak życia** give signs of life; **nie dawać znaku życia** give no signs of life; **darować komuś życie** spare sb *l.* sb's life; **kochać kogoś/coś nad życie** love sb/sth more than life itself; **odebrać komuś życie** take sb's life; **targnąć się na swoje życie** *l.* **odebrać sobie życie** take one's life; **powołać do życia** call into existence; **pozostać przy życiu** remain alive; **pożegnać się z życiem** meet one's death *l.* end; **mieć własne życie** have a life of one's own; **ujść z życiem** escape with one's life; **utrzymać przy życiu** keep alive; **usunąć się z czyjegoś życia** withdraw from sb's life; **używać życia** live it up; **wchodzić w życie** come into force *l.* effect; **wcielać coś w życie** put sth into effect; **rozpoczynać nowe życie** start *l.* get a new life; turn over a new leaf; get a new lease of life; **zakończyć życie** end one's life; **zatruwać komuś życie** be the bane of sb's life; **zrobić komuś z życia piekło** make sb's life hell; **złamać komuś życie** ruin sb's life; **czyjeś życie wisi na włosku** sb's life is hanging by a hair's breadth; **dać komuś życie** give birth to sb; **towarzysz/-ka życia** life's companion; **składać życie w ofierze** sacrifice one's life; **poświęcić** *l.* **oddać za kogoś/ coś życie** lay down *l.* give one's life for sb/sth; **poświęcić (swoje) życie komuś/czemuś** dedicate one's life to sb/sth; **cudem ujść z życiem** have a close shave; **prowadzić podwójne/cnotliwe/normalne życie** live a double/virtuous/normal life; **pieskie życie** dog's life; **rajskie życie** the life of Riley; **samo życie!** that's life!; **uciekaj, jeśli ci życie miłe!** run for your life!; run for dear life!; **życie jak w Madrycie** *żart.* the life of Riley; **drogo sprzedać życie** sell one's life dearly; **miłość czyjegoś życia** (= *ukochana osoba; t. przen. = pasja*) the love of sb's life *l.* of a lifetime; **o mało (co) nie stracić życia** come near losing one's life; **przez resztę życia** for the rest of one's life; **człowiek uczy się przez całe życie** you *l.* we live and learn; **ustawić kogoś na całe życie** set sb up for life; **i to ma być życie!** *przen.* what a life!; **życie ci ucieka** life is passing you by; **życie musi toczyć się dalej** the show must go on. **3.** (= *energia życiowa, temperament*) life, vigor; *Br.* vigour; **on jest bez życia** he's lifeless; **z życiem** with vigour; **nabierać życia** (*o opowieści, filmie*) come to life; **tchnąć w coś nowe życie** breathe new life into sth; **żyć pełnią życia** live one's life to the full; **nigdy w życiu!** not on my *l.* your life!; **wystraszyłem się jak nigdy w życiu** I was scared half to death. **4.** (= *ruch*) activity; **tętnić życiem** teem with activity. **5.** *pot.* (= *utrzymanie, wyżywienie*) living; **środki do życia** means of subsistence; **brak środków do życia** destitution; **być bez środków do życia** be down at heel; **życie ponad stan** life beyond one's means; **zarabiać na życie** earn one's living *l.* keep; **jak on zarabia na życie?** what does he do for a living?

życiodajny *a.* life-giving.

życiorys *mi* **1.** (*dokument*) curriculum vitae, CV; (*zwł. do podania o pracę*) résumé; **napisać życiorys** write one's CV *l.* résumé. **2.** (= *koleje życia*) biography; **mieć nieciekawy życiorys** (= *nieinteresujący*) have an uninteresting biography; (= *wstydliwy, haniebny*) have a blot *l.* blots on one's reputation; **przerwa w życiorysie** *euf.* drunken spell; **miałem wczoraj ostrą przerwę w życiorysie** I got absolutely drunk last night.

życiowo *adv.* practically, realistically.

życiowość *f.* realistic attitude.

życiowy *a.* **1.** (*dotyczący życia biologicznego*) vital; **funkcje/procesy życiowe** vital functions/ processes. **2.** (*dotyczący życia w sensie społecznym itp.*) life; (**czyjaś**) **filozofia życiowa** (sb's) philosophy of life; **mądrość życiowa** life wisdom; (*u osób starszych*) wisdom of old age; **życiowa tragedia** life tragedy; **poziom życiowy** living standard, standard of living; **przestrzeń życiowa** living space; **życiowy rekord** *sport* personal best, PB; **start życiowy** new beginning; **kaleka życiowy** *l.* **oferma życiowa** born loser; **życiowy rozbitek** outcast, derelict; **życiowa szansa** the chance of a lifetime. **3.** *pot.* (= *doświadczony, praktyczny*) realistic, practical, experienced; **życiowy człowiek** (*o kimś doświadczonym*) man *l.* woman of experience; (*o kimś wyrozumiałym*) realistic and understanding person.

życzenia *pl. Gen.* **-ń** (= *gratulacje, powinszowania*) wishes; **życzenia urodzinowe** birthday wishes; **życzenia świąteczne** (*bożonarodzeniowe*) Christmas wishes; (*wielkanocne*) Easter wishes; **składać komuś życzenia** wish sb all the best (*for their birthday etc.*); **z najlepszymi życzeniami** (*w liście, na kartce*) (my) best regards.

życzenie *n.* wish; (= *pragnienie*) desire; **pozostawiać wiele do życzenia** leave a lot *l.* much to be desired; **wyrazić życzenie** make a wish; **zastosować się do czyichś życzeń** defer to sb's wishes; **zrobić coś na czyjeś życzenie** do sth on sb's request; **zgodnie z życzeniami** according to one's wishes; **pobożne życzenia** wishful thinking; **ostatnie życzenie** dying wish; **utwór na życzenie** *radio, telew.* request.

życzliwie *adv.* kindly, sympathetically.

życzliwość *f.* kindness, sympathy; **okazać komuś życzliwość** show good will toward sb; **spotkać się z życzliwością** *l.* **doznać życzliwości** *l.* cieszyć się życzliwością enjoy sb's favor; **zjednać sobie czyjąś życzliwość** gain sb's favor; **atmosfera wzajemnej życzliwości** atmosphere of mutual sympathy.

życzliwy[1] *a.* kind (*w stosunku do kogoś / czegoś* to/toward sb/sth), sympathetic (*w stosunku do kogoś / czegoś* to/toward sb/sth); **patrzeć na kogoś życzliwym okiem** look at sb with favor.

życzliwy[2] *mp* **1.** (= *osoba życzliwa*) well-wisher. **2.** *iron.* (*w podpisie listu*) in good faith.

życzyć *ipf.* **1.** (= *pragnąć czegoś*) wish; **życzyć komuś czegoś** wish sb sth; **życzyć sobie czegoś** wish (for) sth; **czego sobie Pan/i życzy?** (*w sklepie*) (how) can I help you?; (*w urzędzie*) what can I do for you?; **czy życzy Pan/i sobie coś jeszcze?** (*w restauracji*) would you like anything else?; **życzyć komuś dobrej nocy** wish *l.* bid sb good night, say good night to sb; **dobrze/źle komuś życzyć** wish sb well/ill; **on ma wszystko, czego człowiek może sobie życzyć** he's got everything a human being can wish for; **nie życzę sobie tego/żeby ktokolwiek wchodził do mojego pokoju** I won't have *l.* am not having it/anybody come into my room; **jak sobie życzysz** as you wish. **2.** (= *winszować*) wish; **życzyć komuś szczęścia/ szczęśliwego Nowego Roku/wszystkiego najlepszego** wish sb luck/a happy New Year/all the best; **życzę ci wszystkiego najlepszego** all the best to you, I wish you all the best; **życzyć komuś szybkiego** *l.* **rychłego powrotu do zdrowia** wish sb a speedy recovery; **życzyć komuś miłej podróży** wish sb a nice journey; **życzę ci miłej podróży** enjoy your trip.

żyć *ipf.* **żyję żyjesz, żyj** **1.** (= *być żywym*) live, be alive; **długo/krótko żyć** live long/briefly, live a long/short life; **niech żyje...! long live...!; jak długo żyję** never in my life, in all my born days; **ledwie żyć** (= *być zmęczonym*) be dead on one's feet; **nie dawać komuś żyć** plague sb, make sb's life difficult; **żyć nie umierać!** that's what you call life!, heaven on earth!; **(on/ona) nie żyje!** (*okrzyk przerażenia*) he's/she's dead! **2.** (= *egzystować w jakichś warunkach*) live; **żyć w ciągłym strachu** live in *l.* under constant fear; **żyć w biedzie** live in poverty; **żyć o chlebie i wodzie** live on bread and water; **żyć powietrzem** *przen.* live on air; **żyć dla kogoś** live (one's life) for sb; **żyć czymś** be totally absorbed by sth; **on żyje robieniem słowników** making dictionaries is the very breath of his life; **żyć marzeniami** live in a dream world; **żyć nadzieją** live sustained by hope; **żyć nerwami** live on one's nerves; **żyć samotnie** live alone; (*z wyboru*) keep to oneself; **żyć (sobie) jak król** *l.* **po królewsku** live like a king; **żyć swoim życiem** be living one's own life; **żyć w grzechu** live in sin; **żyć cudzym kosztem** *l.* **na czyjś koszt** live off sb, live at sb else's cost; **komuś się dobrze/źle żyje** sb is well off/badly off; **żyć jak u Pana Boga za piecem** be as snug as a bug in a rug; **żyć z dnia na dzień** live from hand to mouth, live from day to day; **żyć dniem dzisiejszym** live for the day; **żyć pełną piersią** live one's life to the full; **żyć wspomnieniami** live sustained by one's memories; **teraz wiem, że żyję** now I know that I'm alive *l.* living; **nie samym chlebem człowiek żyje** man doth not live by bread alone; **jak żyjesz?** how's life?, how's life treating you? **3.** (= *obcować z kimś*) get along (*z kimś* with sb); **żyć z kimś dobrze/źle** get along well/badly with sb, be on good/bad terms with sb; **żyć z kimś** (*cieleśnie*) live with sb; **żyć z kimś jak pies z kotem** lead a cat-and-dog-life with sb; **żyć z kimś na kocią łapę** *pot.* shack up with sb; **żyć z kimś na wiarę** cohabit with sb; **oni nie mogą bez siebie żyć** they can't live without each other. **4.** (= *mieszkać, znajdować się*) live; **żyć w mieście/na wsi** live in the city/in the country; **żyć pod jednym dachem** live under the same roof. **5.** (= *trwać*) live, survive, be alive; **żyć w czyjejś pamięci** live *l.* survive in sb's memory; **żyć w czyichś wspomnieniach** be alive in sb's memories. **6.** (= *utrzymywać się*) live, make one's living; **żyć z pensji** live on one's salary; **żyć z zasiłków** live on the dole; **żyć z procentów** live on the interest of one's savings; **żyć z pracy rąk** live by the labor of one's hands; **żyć na wysokiej stopie** butter both sides of one's bread; live in the lap of luxury; **żyć ponad stan** live beyond one's means; **żyć z ołówkiem w ręku** scrimp and scrape, economize; **mieć z czego żyć** have enough to live on; keep the pot boiling; **z czego ona żyje?** what does she do for a living?

Żyd *mp* Jew.

żyd *mp* (= *wyznawca judaizmu*) Jew.

żydek *mp* *pog.* kike, sheeny.

żydłaczyć *ipf. przest.* speak Polish with a Jewish accent.

żydłak *mp pog.* yid.

żydokomuna *f. pog.* (= *komuniści pochodzenia żydowskiego*) communists of Jewish descent.

żydostwo *n.* **1.** *pog.* (= *Żydzi*) Jewry. **2.** (= *cechy żydowskie*) Jewishness.

żydowski *a.* Jewish; **język żydowski** Yiddish; **naród żydowski** the Jewish nation; **ryba po żydowsku** *kulin.* sweet-boiled fish.

Żydówka *f. Gen.pl.* **-ek** Jewess, Jewish woman.

żydówka *f. Gen.pl.* **-ek** (= *wyznawczyni judaizmu*) Jewess.

żyjący *pl.* the living.

żyjątko *n. Gen.pl.* **-ek** small creature; *przest. zool.* animalcule, animalculum.

żylak *mi Gen.* **-a** *pat.* varix.

żylaki *pl. pat.* varicose veins.

żylasty *a.* (*o człowieku*) sinewy, wiry; (*o mięsie*) stringy.

żyleta *f.* (= *osoba o nieprzyjemnym charakterze*) rasper.

żyletka *f. Gen.pl.* **-ek** razor blade; **golić się żyletką** shave with a razor.

żylistek *mi* deutzia (*Deutzia*).

żylny *a.* venous; **krew żylna** venous blood; **krwotok żylny** venous hemorrhage; **ciśnienie żylne** venous pressure.

żyła *f.* **1.** (*naczynie krwionośne*) vein; **dawać sobie w żyłę** *sl.* (= *używać narkotyków dożylnie*) shoot up, crank up, fix; **ścinać** *l.* **mrozić krew w żyłach** curdle sb's blood; **wypruwać sobie żyły** work one's fingers to the bone; **w jej żyłach płynie polska/niemiecka krew** there's Polish/German blood running in her veins. **2.** *geol.* vein; (*cienka*) thread; (*np. w płycie marmurowej*) vein; **żyła złota** gold vein; **żyła wodna** water vain; **złota żyła** *przen.* gold mine; **trafić na żyłę złota** *przen.* strike oil. **3.** *techn.* (= *część przewodu*) strand. **4.** (= *skąpiec*) stiff; **nie bądź żyła!** *pot.* (*w prośbach*) be a sport!

żyłka *f. Gen.pl.* **-ek** **1.** (*naczynie krwionośne*) veinlet, venule. **2.** (*nić*) (*z jelit, włosia*) catgut, gimp; **żyłka wędkarska** *l.* **nylonowa** fishing line. **3.** *pot.* (= *zamiłowanie, talent*) bent; **mieć żyłkę do czegoś** have a bent for sth; **żyłka podróżnicza/do interesów** bent for travelling/business. **4.** *bot., ent.* (= *nerw*) vein, nervure, nerve. **5.** *min.* vein.

żyłkowanie *n.* **1.** (*u owadów*) venation. **2.** (*w skale*) the grain.

żyłkowany *a.* **1.** (*o liściach, skrzydłach owadów*) venose. **2.** (*o skale*) venous, veined.

żyłować *ipf.* **1.** (= *usuwać żyły*) trim (*meat before cooking*), remove veins (*from meat before cooking*). **2.** *pot.* (= *przemęczać pracą*) sweat (*with labor*). **~ się** *ipf.* (= *wysilać się*) drudge, exert oneself.

żyrafa *f.* **1.** *zool.* giraffe (*Giraffa*). **2.** (= *osoba o długich i chudych nogach*) spindlelegs.

żyrandol *mi Gen.* **-a** chandelier.

żyrant *mp* (= *poręczyciel*) guarantor, surety.

żyro *n. handl.* guarantee, guaranty.

żyrobusola *f. Gen.pl.* **-i** *żegl., lotn.* gyrocompass.

żyroklinometr *mi Gen.* **-a** *lotn.* gyroclinometer.

żyrokompas *mi żegl., lotn.* gyrocompass.

żyromagnetyczny *a.* gyromagnetic.

żyrondysta *mp hist.* Girondist.

żyropilot *mi Gen.* **-a** *lotn., żegl.* gyropilot.

żyroskop *mi techn.* gyroscope.

żyroskopowy *a. techn.* gyroscopic.

żyrostat *mi techn.* gyrostat.

żyrotron *mi techn.* gyrotron.

żyrować *ipf. handl.* guarantee, stand surety (*komuś* for sb).

żytni *a.* rye; **żytni chleb** rye bread; **mąka żytnia** rye flour; **wódka żytnia** rye vodka; **whisky żytnia** rye (whiskey).

żytniówka *f. Gen.pl.* **-ek** (*wódka*) rye vodka.

żytnisko *n. roln.* rye field.

żyto *n.* **1.** *bot., roln.* rye (*Secale cereale*). **2.** (*ziarno*) rye.

żyw *a. indecl. arch.* (= *żywy*) alive; **kto żyw** one and all; **pókim żyw** as long as I live.

żywcem *adv.* alive; **pogrzebać/spalić kogoś żywcem** bury/burn sb alive; **żywcem mnie nie wezmą** they won't take me alive.

żywica *f.* resin; **żywica akrylowa** acrylic resin; **żywica epoksydowa** epoxy (resin); **żywica syntetyczna** synthetic resin.

żywiciel[1] *mp* bread-winner, provider.

żywiciel[2] *ma biol.* host; **żywiciel główny** definitive host; **żywiciel pośredni** intermediate host.

żywicielka *f. Gen.pl.* **-ek** *zob.* **żywiciel**[1].

żywicielski *a.* **organizm żywicielski** *biol.* host organism.

żywicować *ipf.* draw resin (*from a tree by cutting its bark*).

żywicowy *a.* resinous.

żywiczność *f.* resinousness.

żywiczny *a.* resinous (*smell etc.*).

żywić *ipf.* **1.** (= *karmić*) feed, nourish. **2.** *lit.* (= *odczuwać*) (*miłość, nienawiść*) feel; (*pogardę*) nurse, foster; **żywić do kogoś urazę** bear *l.* harbor a grudge *l.* grievance against sb; **nie żywić do kogoś urazy** bear no animosity toward sb, bear sb no malice; **nie żywić do kogoś wrogich uczuć** bear sb no ill will; **żywić nadzieję** cherish hope. **~ się** *ipf.* feed (*czymś* on sth).

żywiec *ma* **-wc- 1.** (= *zwierzęta na rzeź*) slaughter livestock, livestock for slaughter. **2.** (*w wędkarstwie*) (= *przynęta*) live-bait; **operować na żywca** operate without an anaesthetic.

żywienie *n.* (= *karmienie*) nutrition, feeding; **żywienie człowieka** human nutrition; **żywienie zwierząt** animal nutrition; **zakład zbiorowego żywienia** (= *stołówka*) cafeteria; (= *restauracja*) restaurant.

żywieniowiec *mp* **-wc-** *pl.* **-y** nutritionist.

żywieniowy *a.* (of) nutrition, nutritional, nutritive.

żywik *mi zool.* zoea.

żywioł *mi* **1.** (= *siła przyrody*) element; **cztery żywioły** the four elements; **żywioł ognia/wody** fire/water; **groźne żywioły** dangerous elements; **puścić coś na żywioł** let sth take its course; **walczyć z żywiołem** fight with an element (*e.g. a flood, fire*); **wydać na pastwę żywiołów** expose to the fury of the elements. **2.** (= *dziedzina zainteresowań*) element; **być** *l.* **poczuć się** *l.* **znaleźć się w swoim żywiole** be in one's element. **3.** (= *zbiorowisko ludzkie*) element; **żywioł obcy** foreign element. **4.** (*element treści utworu literackiego*) element.

żywiołowo *adv.* **1.** (= *gwałtownie*) impulsively. **2.** (= *spontanicznie*) spontaneously.

żywiołowość *f.* **1.** (= *gwałtowność*) impulsiveness. **2.** (= *spontaniczność*) spontaneity, spontaneousness.

żywiołowy *a.* **1.** (= *powstały w wyniku działania żywiołu*) elemental; **klęska żywiołowa** natural disaster; **obszar klęski żywiołowej** disaster zone. **2.** (= *gwałtowny*) impulsive. **3.** (= *spontaniczny*) spontaneous.

żywnie *adv.* **co/jak ci się żywnie podoba** whatever/however you please; **wolno mu robić, co mu się żywnie podoba** he's free to do whatever he likes *l.* pleases.

żywnościowy *a.* food; **artykuły żywnościowe** foodstuffs, victuals; **kartka żywnościowa** food stamp.

żywność *f.* (= *pożywienie*) food; **zdrowa żywność** health foods *l.* foodstuffs; **przetwórstwo żywności** food processing.

żywo *adv.* **1.** (= *energicznie, szybko*) (*iść, poruszać się*) briskly; (*dyskutować*) animatedly; (*reagować*) strongly; **żywo się czymś interesować** take a keen interest in sth; **co żywo** *arch. l. żart.* fortwith, tout de suite; **jako żywo** *arch. l. żart.* upon my life. **2.** (= *będąc żywym*) alive; **żywo urodzony** born alive; **nadawać na żywo** broadcast live.

żywokost *mi bot.* comfrey (*Symphytum*).

żywopłot *mi* hedge, hedgerow.

żyworodność *f. bot., zool.* viviparity, vivipary, viviparism, viviparousness.

żyworodny *a. bot., zool.* viviparous.

żyworódka *f. Gen.pl.* **-ek 1.** *zool.* (*jaszczurka*) (European) common lizard (*Lacerta vivipara*). **2.** *zool.* (*ślimak*) river snail (*Viviparus viviparus*). **3.** *icht.* viviparous fish. **4.** *bot.* mother-of-thousands (*Bryophyllum / Kalanchoe*).

żywostan *mi* biocenosis.

żywość *f.* (*ruchów*) liveliness; (*kolorów, opisu*) vividness; (*dyskusji*) animation, animatedness.

żywot *mi Gen.* **-a 1.** *lit.* (= *życie*) life; **barwny żywot** life full of adventure; **dokonać żywota** end one's days, go the way of all flesh; **mieć krótki żywot** have but a short life; **prowadzić skromny i cichy żywot** live in a small way; **wieść samotny żywot** lead a lonely life *l.* existence; **żywot wieczny** *rel.* eternal life. **2.** (= *życiorys*) life; **żywoty świętych** the lives of the saints.

żywotnie *adv.* vitally; **żywotnie zainteresowany czymś** having a vested interest in sth.

W
Z
Ż

żywotnik *mi Gen.* **-a** *bot.* thuja, thuya (*Thuja*); **żywotnik wschodni** arbor vitae (*T. orientalis*).

żywotność *f.* **1.** (= *witalność*) vitality. **2.** (= *czas działania*) life, life span.

żywotny *a.* **1.** (= *energiczny*) lively, vital; **rzeczownik żywotny** *jęz.* animate noun. **2.** (= *życiodajny*) vital. **3.** (= *aktualny*) vital; **żywotny interes** vested interest; **mieć w czymś żywotny interes** have a vested interest in sth.

żywy *a.* **1.** (= *żyjący*) living, live, alive; **żywa istota** live being; **żywy inwentarz** livestock; **przyroda żywa** living nature; **handel żywym towarem** (*niewolnikami*) slave trade; **sto kilogramów żywej wagi** (*o kimś*) he *l.* she weighs one hundred kilos; **żywa pagina** *druk.* running head; **żywy język** *jęz.* living *l.* modern language; **żywa mowa** living *l.* colloquial speech; **żywa torpeda** *wojsk.* human *l.* manned torpedo; **żywy obraz** *przest.* living picture, tableau vivant; **żywe srebro** (= *rtęć*) mercury; (= *ktoś ruchliwy, energiczny*) live wire; **nie ma tu żywego ducha** *l.* żywej duszy not a living soul here; **żywa kronika** (*ekspert*) living chronicle; (*świadek*) eye-witness to history; **żywy trup** living dead; **to on jak żywy!** it's him to the life!; it's the living *l.* spitting image of him!; **być ledwie żywym** be dead on one's feet; **wszystko, co żywe** one and all; **żywe ciało** *l.* mięso *pot.* live *l.* living flesh; **kłamać w żywe oczy** lie through one's teeth, tell a brazen lie; **śmiać się komuś w żywe oczy** laugh sb in the face; **zapierać się w żywe oczy** deny with impudence; **dotknąć kogoś do żywego** cut sb to the quick; **żywi i umarli** the quick and the dead; **poszukiwany żywy lub martwy** wanted dead or alive; **niech żywi nie tracą nadziei** while there's life there's hope. **2.** (= *energiczny, ruchliwy*) lively, animated; **żywa gestykulacja** animated *l.* lively gesticulation. **3.** (= *intensywny, wyrazisty*) vivid; **żywe kolory** vivid *l.* bright colors; **żywe wspomnienia** vivid memories. **4.** (*o stylu, fabule, akcji*) (= *wartki*) vivid, swift; **żywy dialog** swift dialog. **5.** (= *prawdziwy, autentyczny, naturalny*) keen; **żywe zainteresowanie** keen interest (*kimś* / *czymś* in sb/sth); **żywa gotówka** hard *l.* ready cash; **kląć w żywy kamień** turn the air blue, curse a blue streak.

żyzność *f.* (= *urodzajność*) fertility.

żyzny *a.* **żyźniejszy** **1.** (*o glebie*) (= *urodzajny*) fertile, fecund; **żyzna ziemia** fertile soil. **2.** (= *mający urodzajne gleby*) fertile; **żyzny kraj** fertile land.

Kraje świata / Countries of the world

Afganistan	Afghanistan	Grecja	Greece
Albania	Albania	Grenada	Grenada
Algieria	Algeria	Gruzja	Georgia
Andora	Andorra	Gujana	Guyana
Angola	Angola	Gwatemala	Guatemala
Antigua i Barbuda	Antigua and Barbuda	Gwinea	Guinea
Arabia Saudyjska	Saudi Arabia	Gwinea Równikowa	Equatorial Guinea
Argentyna	Argentina	Gwinea-Bisau	Guinea-Bissau
Armenia	Armenia	Haiti	Haiti
Australia	Australia	Hiszpania	Spain
Austria	Austria	Holandia	Netherlands
Azerbejdżan	Azerbaijan	Honduras	Honduras
Bahamy	Bahamas	Indie	India
Bahrajn	Bahrain	Indonezja	Indonesia
Bangladesz	Bangladesh	Irak	Iraq
Barbados	Barbados	Iran	Islamic Republic of Iran
Belgia	Belgium	Irlandia	Ireland
Belize	Belize	Islandia	Iceland
Benin	Benin	Izrael	Israel
Bhutan	Bhutan	Jamajka	Jamaica
Białoruś	Belarus	Japonia	Japan
Boliwia	Bolivia	Jemen	Yemen
Bośnia-Hercegowina	Bosnia and Herzegovina	Jordania	Jordan
		Kambodża	Cambodia
Botswana	Botswana	Kamerun	Cameroon
Brazylia	Brazil	Kanada	Canada
Brunei	Brunei Darussalam	Katar	Qatar
Bułgaria	Bulgaria	Kazachstan	Kazakhstan
Burkina Faso	Burkina Faso	Kenia	Kenya
Burundi	Burundi	Kirgistan	Kyrgyzstan
Chile	Chile	Kiribati	Kiribati
Chiny	China	Kolumbia	Colombia
Chorwacja	Croatia	Komory	Comoros
Cypr	Cyprus	Kongo	Congo
Czad	Chad	Korea Płd.	Republic of Korea
Czechy	Czech Republic	Korea Płn.	Democratic People's Republic of Korea
Dania	Denmark		
Dominika	Dominica	Kostaryka	Costa Rica
Dominikana	Dominican Republic	Kuba	Cuba
Dżibuti	Djibouti	Kuwejt	Kuwait
Egipt	Egypt	Laos	Lao People's Democratic Republic
Ekwador	Ecuador		
Erytrea	Eritrea	Lesotho	Lesotho
Estonia	Estonia	Liban	Lebanon
Etiopia	Ethiopia	Liberia	Liberia
Fidżi	Fiji	Libia	Libyan Arab Jamahiriya
Filipiny	Philippines	Lichtenstein	Liechtenstein
Finlandia	Finland	Litwa	Lithuania
Francja	France	Luksemburg	Luxembourg
Gabon	Gabon	Łotwa	Latvia
Gambia	Gambia	Macedonia	Macedonia
Ghana	Ghana	Madagaskar	Madagascar